ABBREVIATIONS AND SPECIAL SYMBOLS

autres abréviations / other abbreviations

abréviation	abrév, abbr	abbreviated, abbreviation
adjectif	ADJ	adjective
adverbe	ADV	adverb
approximativement	approx	approximately
argot	arg	slang
article	ART	article
attribut	attrib	predicative
australien, Australie	Austral	Australian, Australia
auxiliaire	aux	auxiliary
belgicisme	Belg	Belgian idiom
britannique, Grande-Bretagne	Brit	British, Great Britain
canadien, Canada	Can	Canadian, Canada
mot composé	COMP	compound, in compounds
comparatif	compar	comparative
conditionnel	cond	conditional
conjonction	conj	conjunction
conjugaison	conjug	conjugation
défini	déf, def	definite
démonstratif	dém, dem	demonstrative
dialectal, régional	dial	dialect
diminutif	dim	diminutive
direct	dir	direct
écossais, Écosse	Écos	Scottish, Scotland
par exemple	eg	for example
épithète	épith	before noun
surtout	esp	especially
et cætera, et cetera	etc	et cetera
euphémisme	euph	euphemism
par exemple	ex	for example
exclamation	excl	exclamation
féminin	f, fem	feminine
au figuré	fig	figuratively
féminin pluriel	fpl	feminine plural
langue soignée	frm	formal language
futur	fut	future
en général, généralement	gén, gen	in general, generally
helvétisme	Helv	Swiss idiom
humoristique	hum	humorous
impératif	impér, imper	imperative
impersonnel	impers	impersonal
indéfini	indéf, indef	indefinite
indicatif	indic	indicative
indirect	indir	indirect
infinitif	infin	infinitive
inséparable	insep	inseparable
interrogatif	interrog	interrogative
invariable	inv	invariable
irlandais, Irlande	Ir	Irish, Ireland
ironique	iro	ironic
irrégulier	irrég, irreg	irregular
littéral, au sens propre	lit	literally
littéraire	littér, liter	literary
locution	LOC	locution
masculin	m, masc	masculine
masculin et féminin	mf	masculine and feminine
masculin pluriel	mpl	masculine plural
nom	N	noun
nord de l'Angleterre	N Angl	North of England
négatif	nég, neg	negative
nord de l'Angleterre	N Engl	North of England
nom féminin	NF	feminine noun
nom masculin	NM	masculine noun
nom masculin et féminin	NMF	masculine and feminine noun
nom masculin, féminin	NM,F	masculine, feminine noun
non comptable	NonC	uncountable
nom pluriel	NPL	plural noun
numéral	num	numeral
néo-zélandais, Nouvelle-Zélande	NZ	New Zealand
objet	obj	object
opposé	opp	opposite
emploi réfléchi	o.s.	oneself
passif	pass	passive
péjoratif	péj, pej	pejorative
personnel	pers	personal
particule de verbe	phr vb elem	phrasal verb element
pluriel	pl	plural
possessif	poss	possessive
préfixe	préf, pref	prefix
préposition	PRÉP, PREP	preposition
prétérit	prét, pret	preterite
pronom	PRON	pronoun
proverbe	Prov	proverb
participe présent	prp	present participle
participe passé	ptp	past participle
quelque chose	qch	something
quelqu'un	qn	somebody, someone
relatif	rel	relative
quelqu'un	sb	somebody, someone
écossais, Écosse	Scot	Scottish, Scotland
séparable	SEP	separable
singulier	sg	singular
argot	sl	slang
terme de spécialiste	SPÉC, SPEC	specialist term
quelque chose	sth	something
subjonctif	subj	subjunctive
suffixe	suf	suffix
superlatif	superl	superlative
américain, États-Unis	US	American, United States
généralement	usu	usually
verbe	VB	verb
verbe intransitif	VI	intransitive verb
verbe pronominal	VPR	pronominal verb
verbe transitif	VT	transitive verb
verbe à particule inséparable	VT FUS	phrasal verb with inseparable particle
verbe transitif et intransitif	VTI	transitive and intransitive verb
verbe transitif indirect	VT INDIR	indirect transitive verb

DICTIONNAIRE
FRANÇAIS-ANGLAIS
ANGLAIS-FRANÇAIS

FRENCH-ENGLISH
ENGLISH-FRENCH
DICTIONARY

Collins ROBERT French Dictionary

le Robert & Collins

Dictionnaire

FRANÇAIS-ANGLAIS ANGLAIS-FRANÇAIS

EIGHTH EDITION/HUITIÈME ÉDITION
2006

HarperCollins Publishers
Westerhill Road, Bishopbriggs
Glasgow G64 2QT
Great Britain

ISBN-13
978-0-00-722108-0
ISBN-10
0-00-722108-8

www.collins.co.uk

Dictionnaires Le Robert-SEJER
25, avenue Pierre de Coubertin
75013 Paris
France

ISBN
2-84-902117-2

www.lerobert.com

A catalogue record for this book is available from the British Library

Service Marketing Commercial France
25, avenue Pierre de Coubertin
75013 Paris
France

computer typeset by/photocomposition par

MCP Jouve, Saran, France

Printed and bound by/imprimé par
Maury-Imprimeur SA - Malesherbes, France
relié à la NRI à Auxerre - Dépôt légal Avril 2006
N° d'éditeur 10121117 - N° d'impression 120196

Principaux collaborateurs/Main Contributors

HUITIÈME ÉDITION/EIGHTH EDITION

Direction éditoriale
société DICTIONNAIRES LE ROBERT
représentée par
Marianne Durand

Publishing Management
HARPERCOLLINS
Lorna Knight
Michela Clari

Chef de projet/Project Manager
Martyn Back

Coordination éditoriale
Dominique Le Fur

Editorial Management
Maree Airlie

avec/with
Silke Zimmermann
Joyce Littlejohn

Rédaction/Editors
Jean-François Allain
Laurence Larroche
Janet Gough

Lecture-correction/Editorial Staff
Annick Valade
Nathalie Kristy, Anne-Marie Lentaigne
Brigitte Orcel, Méryem Puill-Chatillon, Laure-Anne Voisin
Gaëlle Amiot-Cadey, Laurent Jouet

Conception technique et maquette/Design Manager
Gonzague Raynaud - Maud Laheurte

Principaux collaborateurs/Main Contributors

SIXIÈME ET SEPTIÈME ÉDITIONS/SIXTH AND SEVENTH EDITIONS

Direction éditoriale
société DICTIONNAIRES LE ROBERT
représentée par
Pierre Varrod

Publishing Management
HARPERCOLLINS
Lorna Sinclair Knight
Michela Clari

Chef de projet/Project Manager
Martyn Back

Coordination éditoriale
Dominique Le Fur

Editorial Management
Sabine Citron

avec/with
Silke Zimmermann

Rédaction/Editors
Daphne Day - Phyllis Gautier
Jean-François Allain - Laurence Larroche - Harry Campbell
Frances Illingworth - Janet Gough

Lecture-correction/Editorial Staff
Brigitte Orcel, Anne-Marie Lentaigne
Muriel Richard, Marie-Odile Martin, Charlotte Testa
Gaëlle Amiot-Cadey, Maggie Seaton

Informatique éditoriale
Kamal Loudiyi

Data Management
Stewart Russell
Robert Scovell

Conception technique et maquette/Design Manager
Gonzague Raynaud
Couverture/Cover : Caumon

Principaux collaborateurs/Main Contributors

CINQUIÈME ÉDITION/FIFTH EDITION

Direction éditoriale
société DICTIONNAIRES LE ROBERT
représentée par
Pierre Varrod

Publishing Director
HARPERCOLLINS
Lorna Sinclair Knight

Direction de l'ouvrage
Alain Duval
chef de projet
Martyn Back

Projet Management
Michela Clari
with
Carol MacLeod

Responsable de la rédaction
Dominique Le Fur
avec/with
Brigitte Vienne

Senior Editors
Janet Gough
Sabine Citron

Rédaction/Editors
Jean-François Allain, Claire Bigot, Harry Campbell, Gearóid Cronin,
Daphne Day, Christèle Éon, Hélène Fabre, Phyllis Gautier, Bob Grossmith,
Frances Illingworth, Jacques Lesca, Christine Penman,
Christian Salzedo, Donald Watt

Anglais américain/American English
Kathleen Micham, John Wright

Coordination éditoriale/Editorial Management
Vivian Marr
with
Isobel Gordon, Silke Zimmermann

Secrétariat de rédaction et correction/Editorial Staff
Elspeth Anderson, Cécile Aubinière-Robb, Anne-Marie Banks, Anne Convery,
Sylvie Fontaine, Sandra Harper, Angela Jack, Irene Lakhani, Anne Lindsay
Caitlin McMahon, Maggie Seaton, Jill Williams

Informatique éditoriale/Data Management
Ray Carrick, Kamal Loudiyi, Jane Creevy, Paul Hasset,
André Gautier

remerciements à/thanks to: Geoffrey Bremner, Jeremy Butterfield, Gonzague Raynaud, Keith Foley, Hélène Bernaert, Chantal Testa, Duncan Marshal, Hazel Mills, Gerry McIntyre, Brigitte Orcel, Anne-Marie Lentaigne

Principaux collaborateurs/Main Contributors

TROISIÈME ET QUATRIÈME ÉDITIONS/ THIRD AND FOURTH EDITIONS

direction rédactionnelle/general editors
Alain Duval, Lorna Sinclair Knight

rédacteurs/editors
Diana Feri, Stephen Clarke, Dominique Le Fur
Laurence Hautekeur, Françoise Morcellet, Jill Campbell

chef de projet/editorial management
Vivian Marr

autres collaborateurs/other contributors: Christine Penman, Jean-Benoit Ormal-Grenon, Cécile Aubinière-Robb

administration, secrétariat et correction/editorial staff: Elspeth Anderson, Luc Audrain, Anne Baudrillard, Linda Chestnutt, Chantal Combes, Elizabeth Cunningham, Annick Dehais, Anne Dickinson, Susan Dunsmore, Sylvie Fontaine, Élisabeth Huault, Lesley Johnston, Irene Lakhani, Joyce Littlejohn, Dominique Lopin, Kamal Loudiyi, Fiona MacGregor, Carol MacLeod, Maimie McGadie, Janice McNeillie, Val McNulty, Hellen Ranson, Gonzague Raynaud, Diane Robinson, Megan Thomson, Lydia Vigné, Silke Zimmermann

DEUXIÈME ÉDITION/SECOND EDITION

dirigée par/by
Alain Duval, Rosemary C. Milne, Hélène M. A. Lewis,
Lorna Sinclair, Renée Birks

autres collaborateurs/other contributors
Guy Jean Forgue (américanismes/American language)
Charles Lynn Clark, Susan Lochrie, Geneviève Lebaut, Joëlle Sampy,
Ann Goodman, Renée Gillot-Gautier, Florence Millar

administration, secrétariat et correction/administrative staff
William T. McLeod, Richard Thomas, Barbara Christie, Carol Purdon,
Elspeth Anderson, Catherine E. Love, Anne Marie Banks

PREMIÈRE ÉDITION/FIRST EDITION

par/by
Beryl T. Atkins, Alain Duval, Rosemary C. Milne

et/and
Pierre-Henri Cousin, Hélène M. A. Lewis, Lorna A. Sinclair,
Renée O. Birks, Marie-Noëlle Lamy

autres collaborateurs/other contributors
John Scullard, Edwin Carpenter, Margaret Curtin, Kenneth Gibson, Gerry Kilroy,
Michael Janes, Anthony Linforth, Trevor Peach, Elise Thomson

avec/with
comité de lecture/readers' panel
Paul Robert
Martine Bercot, Gilberte Gagnon, Maryline Hira, Lucette Jourdan, Denis Keen,
Jean Mambrino, Jacques Mengin, Robert Mengin, Marie Christine de Montoussé,
Alain Rey, Josette Rey-Debove, Colette Thompson, Elaine Williamson

CONTENTS / SOMMAIRE

We would like to acknowledge the help and cooperation of all those who have kindly given permission for their material to be incorporated in the Bank of English and the Banque de français moderne.

Nous tenons à remercier pour leur aide et pour leur coopération tous ceux qui nous ont aimablement autorisés à incorporer leurs textes dans la « Bank of English » et dans la « Banque de français moderne ».

INTRODUCTION

Since Collins and Le Robert first joined forces in the 1970s, both have used a combination of proven know-how and cutting-edge technology to stay at the forefront of language developments. Using both the Collins Word Web — an unparalleled 2.5 billion-word analytical database — and the vast treasurehouse of French language resources developed at Dictionnaires Le Robert, we can recognise when new words and phrases emerge, the precise contexts in which they are used, and even subtle changes in meaning. All of this ensures that when you use a Collins-Robert dictionary, you are one of the best-informed language users in the world.

Several refinements have been introduced for the present edition. Hundreds of new words and meanings have been added, taking into account developments in such rapidly evolving fields as technology, communications and medicine. New examples from colloquial language have also been included to reflect the ever-changing nature of everyday French and English. New typography gives the text a modern, contemporary feel, and the layout of the dictionary entries has been improved, with each compound word presented on a new line for ease of reference. Signposting of meanings has been made even clearer, with more explicit information on context and usage. Finally, and most noticeably, the introduction of colour headwords has further enhanced the general clarity and user-friendliness of the text.

A good bilingual dictionary must not only provide a complete general picture of two living languages, it must also reflect the changes that take place as these languages evolve. Constantly revised and augmented using some of the largest lexical databases in the world, the Collins-Robert remains the richest resource for lovers of the French language everywhere.

INTRODUCTION

Les Dictionnaires Le Robert et Collins, depuis le début de leur collaboration dans les années 1970, allient un savoir-faire reconnu à des technologies de pointe, afin de se maintenir aux avant-postes des évolutions linguistiques. Grâce au Collins Word Web, base de données analytique de 2,5 milliards de mots, unique au monde, grâce à l'immense trésor que constituent les ressources en langue française des dictionnaires Le Robert, nous pouvons déterminer le moment où émergent de nouveaux mots ou de nouvelles expressions, préciser le contexte de leur usage et en souligner les subtils glissements de sens. Ainsi, en consultant un *Robert et Collins*, vous êtes assuré de compter parmi les utilisateurs de dictionnaires bilingues les mieux informés du monde.

La présente édition a fait l'objet de plusieurs enrichissements. Des centaines de nouveaux mots et de nouveaux sens ont été ajoutés, en tenant compte des développements dans les domaines qui connaissent une rapide progression, tels la technologie, les communications, la médecine. De nouveaux exemples tirés du langage familier ont été par ailleurs intégrés pour refléter l'évolution permanente qui caractérise le français et l'anglais de tous les jours. Une nouvelle typographie confère au texte un aspect moderne, plus actuel, et l'organisation des entrées a été améliorée, chaque mot composé apparaissant sur une ligne séparée pour une consultation aisée. La signalisation des sens a encore gagné en clarté grâce à des informations plus explicites sur le contexte et l'usage. Enfin, et c'est la nouveauté la plus visible, l'adoption de la couleur pour les entrées contribue à accroître encore la facilité d'utilisation du dictionnaire.

Un bon dictionnaire bilingue n'a pas pour seule mission de fournir une image complète de deux langues vivantes, il doit aussi être le reflet des changements qui s'opèrent au cours de l'évolution de ces langues. Constamment revu et augmenté à l'aide de certaines des plus grandes bases de données lexicales du monde, *Le Robert et Collins* demeure la plus riche des ressources pour tous les amoureux de la langue anglaise.

USING THE DICTIONARY

WORD ORDER

caldron /ˈkɔːldrən/ N ⇒ **cauldron**

Alphabetical order is followed throughout. If two variant spellings are not alphabetically adjacent, each is treated as a separate headword; where the information is not duplicated, there is a cross-reference to the form treated in depth. For the alphabetical order of compounds in French, see **COMPOUNDS**. Phrasal verbs are grouped together at the end of the main verb (eg **fall through** at the end of **fall**).

honor /ˈɒnəʳ/ N (US) ⇒ **honour**

honour, honor (US) /ˈɒnəʳ/ N 1

American variations in spelling are treated in the same fashion.

Icarus /ˈɪkərəs/ N Icare *m*

ICAO /ˌaɪsiːeɪˈəʊ/ N (abbrev of **International Civil Aviation Organization**) OACI *f*

Proper names, as well as abbreviations and acronyms, will be found in their alphabetical place in the word list.

blow[1] /bləʊ/ (vb : pret **blew**, ptp **blown**) N 1 **to give a ~** *(through mouth)* souffler ; *(through nose)* se moucher

blow[2] /bləʊ/ N 1 *(lit) (= impact)* coup *m* ; *(with fist)* coup *m* de poing ◆ **to come to ~s** en venir aux mains ◆ **at one ~**

Superior numbers are used to separate words of like spelling: **blow[1]**, **blow[2]**.

COMPOUNDS

body /ˈbɒdɪ/ N *[...]*

COMP *[...]*

body search N fouille *f* corporelle ◆ **to carry out a ~ search on sb** fouiller qn ◆ **to submit to** *or* **undergo a ~ search** se faire fouiller

body shop N *(for cars)* atelier *m* de carrosserie

body snatcher N *(Hist)* déterreur *m*, -euse *f* de cadavres

body stocking N combinaison *f* de danse

body-surf VI faire du body(-surf)

body-surfing N *(NonC)* body(-surf) *m*

body swerve N *(Sport)* écart *m*

body warmer N gilet *m* matelassé

Entries may include sections headed COMP (compounds). In these will be found English hyphenated words, such as **body-surf** (under **body**), and **point-to-point** (under **point**), and unhyphenated combinations of two or more elements, such as **hazardous waste** (under **hazardous**), **air traffic control** (under **air**).

Compounds are presented in alphabetical order.

Single words such as **blackbird** and **partygoer**, which are made up of two elements, but are not hyphenated, appear as headwords in the main alphabetical list.

English spelling is variable in this area, and there are possible alternatives: **backhander/back-hander, paintbrush/paint brush/paint-brush** etc. If the single word form is the most common, this will be treated as a headword; **paintbrush** therefore does not appear in the entry **paint**. When looking for a word of this type, users should bear in mind that it may be found either in a compound section, or as a headword.

On the French side, only unhyphenated combinations, such as **gaz naturel** and **modèle déposé**, appear in compound sections. Alphabetical order is not affected by linking prepositions, thus **Casque bleu** precedes **casque à pointe**. The part of speech is given where it could be ambiguous or where there is more than one. Hyphenated words, such as **arrière-pensée** and **lave-glace**, are treated as headwords. If a word can appear both with or without a hyphen, both spellings are given.

GUIDE D'UTILISATION

ORDRE DES MOTS

Le principe général est l'ordre alphabétique. Les variantes orthographiques qui ne suivent pas immédiatement la forme traitée dans l'ordre alphabétique figurent à leur place dans la nomenclature avec un renvoi à la forme qui est traitée. Pour l'ordre d'apparition des composés, voir ci-dessous **LES COMPOSÉS**. Les verbes à particule anglais sont regroupés à la fin de l'entrée contenant le verbe souche (par exemple **fall through** sous **fall**).

kabbalistique /kabalistik/ ADJ ⇒ **cabalistique**

Les variantes orthographiques américaines sont traitées de la même manière.

honor /ˈɒnəʳ/ N (US) ⇒ **honour**
honour, honor (US) /ˈɒnəʳ/ N 1

Les noms propres, ainsi que les sigles et acronymes, figurent à leur place dans l'ordre alphabétique général.

ICAO /ˌaɪsiːeɪˈəʊ/ N (abbrev of **International Civil Aviation Organization**) OACI *f*
Icarus /ˈɪkərəs/ N Icare *m*

Les homographes sont suivis d'un chiffre qui permet de les distinguer.

raie¹ /RE/ NF 1 *(= trait)* line; *(Agr = sillon)* furrow; *(= éraflure)* mark, scratch
raie² /RE/ NF *(= poisson)* skate, ray; *(Culin)* skate

LES COMPOSÉS

Certains articles comportent une section COMP (composés). En anglais, y figurent des groupes de mots avec trait d'union tels que **body-surf** (sous **body**) et **point-to-point** (sous **point**) ainsi que des groupes de mots sans trait d'union tels que **hazardous waste** (sous **hazardous**) et **air traffic control** (sous **air**).

Les composés sont présentés par ordre alphabétique.

Les mots soudés tels que **blackbird** et **partygoer** apparaissent comme des entrées normales à leur place dans l'ordre alphabétique.

L'orthographe anglaise est assez variable dans ce domaine et il existe souvent plusieurs variantes : **backhander/back-hander, paintbrush/paint brush/paint-brush**, etc. Si la forme en un seul mot est la plus fréquente, le composé est présenté comme entrée à part entière. Ainsi **paintbrush** n'apparaît pas sous **paint**. Lors de sa recherche, l'utilisateur doit donc garder à l'esprit qu'un mot de ce type peut se trouver soit dans un groupe de composés, soit dans l'ordre alphabétique général.

En français, les composés sans trait d'union comme **gaz naturel** ou **modèle déposé** apparaissent sous le premier mot, dans la catégorie COMP. La présence de prépositions n'influe pas sur l'ordre alphabétique : ainsi, **Casque bleu** précède **casque à pointe**. Les catégories grammaticales sont indiquées lorsqu'il y a un risque d'erreur ou que le composé traité comporte plusieurs catégories grammaticales. Les composés à trait d'union comme **arrière-pensée** ou **lave-glace** sont traités comme des entrées à part entière et donnés à leur place dans l'ordre alphabétique général. Lorsque les deux orthographes, avec et sans trait d'union, sont possibles, elles sont toutes deux signalées à l'utilisateur.

casque /kask/ NM *[...]*
COMP **Casque bleu** blue helmet *ou* beret ◆ **les ~s bleus** the UN peacekeeping force, the blue helmets *ou* berets
casque de chantier hard hat
casque colonial pith helmet, topee
casque intégral full-face helmet
casque à pointe spiked helmet

PLURALS

Irregular plural forms of English words are given in the English-French part, those of French words and compounds in the French-English part.

cheval (pl **-aux**) /ʃ(ə)val, o/ NM 1
abat-son (pl **abat-sons**) /abasɔ̃/ NM louvre *(Brit) ou* louver *(US)* (boards)

In French, all plurals which do not consist of *headword + s* are shown, eg: **cheval, -aux**.

In English, a knowledge of the basic rules is assumed:

1 Most English nouns take *-s* in the plural: **bed-s, site-s.**
2 Nouns that end in *-s, -x, -z, -sh* and some in *-ch* /tʃ/ take *-es* in the plural: **boss-es, box-es, dish-es, patch-es.**
3 Nouns that end in *-y* not preceded by a vowel change the *-y* to *-ies* in the plural: **lady-ladies, berry-berries** (but **tray-s, key-s**).

child /tʃaɪld/ (pl **children**) N 1 enfant
children /ˈtʃɪldrən/ NPL of **child**

Plural forms of the headword which differ substantially from the singular form are listed in their alphabetical place in the word list with a cross-reference, and repeated under the singular form.

chic /ʃiːk/ ADJ chic *inv*, élégant

French invariable plurals are marked *inv* on the English-French side for ease of reference.

GENDERS

belle /bɛl/ ADJ, NF → **beau**

Feminine forms in French which are separated alphabetically from the masculine form in the word list are shown as separate headwords with a cross-reference to the masculine form.

blanchisseur /blɑ̃ʃisœʀ/ NM *(lit)* launderer; *[d'argent sale]* money launderer
blanchisseuse /blɑ̃ʃisøz/ NF laundress
baladeur, -euse /baladœʀ, øz/ ADJ wandering, roving ◆ **avoir la main baladeuse** *ou* **les mains baladeuses** to have wandering *ou* groping* hands ◆ **un micro ~ circulait dans le public** a microphone circulated round the audience NM *(= magnétophone)* Walkman ®, personal stereo NF **baladeuse** *(= lampe)* inspection lamp

A feminine headword requiring a different translation from its masculine form is given either a separate entry or a separate category.

In the English-French part the feminine forms of French adjectives are given only where these are not regular. The following are considered regular adjective inflections:

-, e; -ef, -ève; -eil, -eille; -er, -ère; -et, -ette; -eur, -euse; -eux, -euse; -ien, -ienne; -ier, -ière; -if, -ive; -il, -ille; -on, -onne; -ot, -otte

gardener /ˈgɑːdnəʳ/ N jardinier *m*, -ière *f*

When the translation of an English noun could be either masculine or feminine, according to sex, the feminine form of the French noun translation is always given.

PLURIEL

Les formes plurielles qui présentent des difficultés sont données dans la langue de départ.

En français, les pluriels autres que ceux qui se forment par le simple ajout du *-s* sont indiqués ; celui des composés avec trait d'union est également donné.

cheval (pl **-aux**) /ʃ(ə)val, o/ NM 1

abat-son (pl **abat-sons**) /abasɔ̃/ NM louvre (*Brit*) *ou* louver (*US*) (boards)

En anglais, les pluriels formés régulièrement ne sont pas donnés :

1. La plupart des noms prennent *-s* au pluriel : **bed-s, site-s.**
2. Les noms se terminant par *-s, -x, -z, -sh* et *-ch* /tʃ/ prennent *-es* au pluriel : **boss-es, box-es, dish-es, patch-es.**
3. Les noms se terminant par *-y* non précédé d'une voyelle changent au pluriel le *-y* en *-ies* : **lady-ladies, berry-berries** (mais **tray-s, key-s**).

Quand le pluriel d'un mot est très différent du singulier, il figure à sa place dans la nomenclature générale avec un renvoi ; il est répété sous le singulier.

ail (pl **ails** *ou* **aulx**) /aj, o/ NM garlic

aulx /o/ NMPL → **ail**

Dans la partie anglais-français, les mots français invariables au pluriel sont suivis de l'indication *inv*.

chic /ʃiːk/ ADJ chic *inv*, élégant

GENRE

Les formes féminines des mots français qui ne suivent pas directement le masculin dans l'ordre alphabétique sont données à leur place normale dans la nomenclature, avec un renvoi au masculin ; elles sont répétées sous celui-ci.

belle /bel/ ADJ, NF → **beau**

Un mot féminin exigeant une traduction différente du masculin fait l'objet soit d'un article séparé soit d'une catégorie bien individualisée dans le cas d'articles complexes.

blanchisseur /blɑ̃ʃisœʀ/ NM (*lit*) launderer; [*d'argent sale*] money launderer

blanchisseuse /blɑ̃ʃisøz/ NF laundress

baladeur, -euse /baladœʀ, øz/ ADJ wandering, roving ◆ **avoir la main baladeuse** *ou* **les mains baladeuses** to have wandering *ou* groping * hands ◆ **un micro ~ circulait dans le public** a microphone circulated round the audience NM (*= magnétophone*) Walkman ®, personal stereo NF **baladeuse** (*= lampe*) inspection lamp

Dans la partie anglais-français, le féminin des adjectifs français se construisant régulièrement n'est pas indiqué. Sont considérées comme régulières les formes suivantes :

-, e ; -ef, -ève ; -eil, -eille ; -er, -ère ; -et, -ette ; -eur, -euse ; -eux, -euse ; -ien, -ienne ; -ier, -ière ; -if, -ive ; -il, -ille ; -on, -onne ; -ot, -otte.

Quand un nom anglais peut recevoir une traduction au masculin ou au féminin, selon le sexe, la forme féminine est toujours mentionnée.

gardener /ˈgɑːdnəʳ/ N jardinier *m*, -ière *f*

REPETITION OF THE HEADWORD WITHIN THE ENTRY

wax¹ /wæks/ N (NonC) cire *f* ; *(for skis)* fart *m* ; *(in ear)* cérumen *m*, (bouchon *m* de) cire *f* ; → **beeswax, sealing²** VT *[+ floor, furniture]* cirer, encaustiquer ; *[+ skis]* farter ; *[+ shoes, moustache]* cirer ; *[+ thread]* poisser ; *[+ car]* lustrer ◆ **to ~ one's legs** s'épiler les jambes à la cire
COMP *[candle, doll, seal, record]* de *or* en cire
wax bean N *(US)* haricot *m* beurre *inv*
waxed cotton N coton *m* huilé
waxed jacket N veste *f* de *or* en coton huilé
waxed paper N papier *m* paraffiné
wax museum N *(esp US)* musée *m* de cire
wax paper N ⇒ **waxed paper**

To save space, where the headword occurs in its full form within the entry it is replaced by ~.
Compounds and phrasal verbs are shown in full.

PHRASES AND IDIOMS

break /breɪk/ ... VT 1 [...]
◆ **to ~ one's back** *(lit)* se casser la colonne vertébrale ◆ **he almost broke his back trying to lift the stone** il s'est donné un tour de reins en essayant de soulever la pierre ◆ **he's ~ing his back to get the job finished in time** il s'échine à finir le travail à temps ◆ **to ~ the back of a task** *(Brit)* faire le plus dur *or* le plus gros d'une tâche ◆ **to ~ sb's heart** briser le cœur de qn ◆ **to ~ one's heart over sth** avoir le cœur brisé par qch ◆ **it ~s my heart to think that** ... cela me brise le cœur de penser que ... ; → **ball¹, barrier, bone, bread, code, ice, path¹, record, surface, wind¹**

Phrases and idiomatic expressions are preceded by a black lozenge. They are generally placed under the first element or the first word in the phrase. For example **to break somebody's heart** and **to break the back of a task** are both included under **break**. However **to lend somebody a hand** is under **hand** because it is equally possible to say **to give somebody a hand.**

Where required as cross-reference directs the user to the location of a phrase. At **break**, cross-references to **ice and record** indicate that **to break the ice** and **to break a record** are treated at these entries.

◆ **aller et venir** *(entre deux endroits)* to come and go; *(dans une pièce)* to pace up and down ◆ **tu sais, la chance, ça va ça vient** luck comes and goes, you know, you win some, you lose some ◆ **avec lui l'argent, ça va, ça vient** when it comes to money, it's easy come, easy go with him;

Some important phrases are made prominent by a blue lozenge in the margin.

INDICATING MATERIAL

General indicating material takes the following forms:

In parentheses ( )

climber /ˈklaɪməʳ/ N *(= person)* grimpeur *m*, -euse *f* ; *(= mountaineer)* alpiniste *mf*, ascensionniste *mf* ; *(fig pej: also* **social climber***)* arriviste *mf (pej)* ; *(= plant)* plante *f*

1 Synonyms preceded by =.

employment /ɪmˈplɔɪmənt/ N *(NonC = jobs collectively)* emploi *m (NonC)* ; *(= a job)* emploi *m*, travail *m* ; *(modest)* place *f* ; *(important)* situation

2 Partial definitions and other information which guide the user.

ordain /ɔːˈdeɪn/ VT 1 *[God, fate]* décréter *(that* que) ; *[law]* décréter *(that* que), prescrire *(that* que + *subj)* ; *[judge]* ordonner *(that* que + *subj)*

3 Syntactical information to allow the non-native speaker to use the translation correctly. This information is given after the translation.

In square brackets [ ]

fade /feɪd/ VI 1 *[colour]* passer, perdre son éclat ; *[material]* passer, se décolorer ; *[light]* baisser, diminuer ; *[flower]* se faner, se flétrir

1 Within verb entries, typical noun subjects of the headword.

branch /brɑːntʃ/ N 1 *[of tree, candelabra]* branche *f* ; *[of river]* bras *m*, branche *f* ; *[of mountain chain]* ramification *f* ;

2 Within noun entries, typical noun complements of the headword.

RÉPÉTITION DU MOT DANS L'ARTICLE

Par souci d'économie de place, le mot est remplacé par le signe ~ lorsqu'il est répété dans le corps de l'article sans subir de modification orthographique.
Les composés ainsi que les verbes anglais à particule sont donnés en toutes lettres.

cire /siʀ/ NF *(gén)* wax; *(pour meubles, parquets)* polish; *[d'oreille]* (ear)wax ◆ **~ d'abeille** beeswax ◆ **~ à cacheter/à épiler** sealing/depilatory wax ◆ **~ liquide** liquid wax ◆ **s'épiler les jambes à la ~** to wax one's legs ◆ **personnage en ~** waxwork dummy; → **musée**
COMP **cire anatomique** wax anatomical model
cire perdue cire perdue, lost wax

LES LOCUTIONS ET EXEMPLES

Les phrases et les expressions idiomatiques sont précédées d'un losange noir. Elles figurent généralement sous le premier élément fixe de la phrase, par exemple **chercher la petite bête** se trouve sous **chercher**. Le cas échéant, un renvoi prévient l'utilisateur de l'emplacement d'une phrase, par exemple sous **chercher**, les renvois à **histoire** et **noise** indiquent que les expressions **chercher des histoires à quelqu'un** et **chercher noise à quelqu'un** sont traitées dans les entrées **histoire** et **noise**.

chercher /ʃɛʀʃe/ ► conjug 1 ◄ VT [...]
6 *(locutions)* **~ midi à quatorze heures** to complicate the issue ◆ **~ la petite bête** to split hairs ◆ **~ une aiguille dans une botte** ou **meule de foin** to look for a needle in a haystack ◆ **~ des poux dans la tête de qn** * to try to make trouble for sb ◆ **~ querelle à qn** to try to pick a quarrel with sb ◆ **cherchez la femme !** cherchez la femme!; → **crosse, fortune, histoire, noise, salut**

Certaines phrases importantes sont précédées d'un losange bleu en marge qui permet de les repérer plus facilement.

◆ **aller et venir** *(entre deux endroits)* to come and go; *(dans une pièce)* to pace up and down ◆ **tu sais, la chance, ça va ça vient** luck comes and goes, you know, you win some, you lose some ◆ **avec lui l'argent, ça va, ça vient** when it comes to money, it's easy come, easy go with him;

INDICATIONS D'EMPLOI

Les indications guidant le lecteur prennent les formes suivantes :

Entre parenthèses ( )

1 Les synonymes précédés du signe =.

décent, e /desɑ̃, ɑ̃t/ ADJ *(= bienséant)* decent, proper; *(= discret, digne)* proper; *(= acceptable) [logement, salaire]* decent; *[prix]*

2 Les précisions susceptibles de guider l'usager.

décaper /dekape/ ► conjug 1 ◄ VT *(gén)* to clean, to cleanse; *(à l'abrasif)* to scour; *(à l'acide)* to pickle; *(à la brosse)* to scrub;

3 Les indications d'ordre grammatical permettant au lecteur étranger d'utiliser le mot correctement. Elles sont données après la traduction.

accessible /aksesibl/ ADJ *[lieu]* accessible *(à* to) ; *[personne]* approachable; *[œuvre]* accessible; *[but]* attainable;

Entre crochets [ ]

1 Les noms sujets précisant le sens d'une entrée verbe.

décroître /dekʀwatʀ/ ► conjug 55 ◄ VI *[nombre, population, intensité, pouvoir]* to decrease, to diminish, to decline; *[eaux, fièvre]* to subside, to go down; *[popularité]* to decline, to drop;

2 Les noms compléments d'une entrée nom.

bajoues /baʒu/ NFPL *[d'animal]* cheeks, pouches; *[de personne]* jowls, heavy cheeks

impair /ɪm'pɛəʳ/ VT [+ abilities, faculties] détériorer, diminuer ; [+ relations] porter atteinte à ; [+ negotiations] entraver ; [+ health] abîmer, détériorer ; [+ sight, hearing] abîmer, affaiblir ; [+ mind, strength] diminuer

3 Typical objects of verbs, preceded by +.

distinct /dɪs'tɪŋkt/ ADJ 1 (= definite) [impression, preference, likeness, advantage, disadvantage] net before n ; [increase, progress] sensible, net before n ; [possibility] réel

4 Typical noun complements of adjectives.

briskly /'brɪsklɪ/ ADV [move] vivement ; [walk] d'un bon pas ; [speak] brusquement ; [act] sans tarder

5 Typical verb or adjective complements of adverbs.

Other indicators

aerodynamics /'ɛərəudaɪ'næmɪks/ N (NonC) aérodynamique f

implement /'ɪmplɪmənt/ N outil m, instrument m ◆ ~s équipement m NonC, matériel m NonC ;

(NonC) stands for "uncountable" and serves to mark nouns which are not normally used in the plural or with the indefinite article or with numerals. (NonC) occurs only as a warning device in cases where a non-native speaker might otherwise use the word wrongly. There has been no attempt to give an exhaustive account of "uncountability" in English. (NonC) is also used as an indicator to distinguish meanings in the source language.

tympan /tɛ̃pɑ̃/ NM 1 (Anat) eardrum, tympanum (SPÉC)

(SPÉC) stands for "technical term". In this example, it indicates that the common English word is "eardrum" and that "tympanum" is restricted to the vocabulary of specialists.

AEA /,eɪiː'eɪ/ N (Brit) (abbrev of **Atomic Energy Authority**) ≃ CEA m

≃ is used when the source language headword or phrase has no equivalent in the target language and is therefore untranslatable. In such cases the nearest cultural equivalent is given.

Yorkshire /'jɔːkʃəʳ/ N Yorkshire m
COMP **Yorkshire pudding** N (Brit Culin) pâte à *crêpe cuite qui accompagne un rôti de bœuf*

An explanatory gloss (in italics) may be given in cases where there is no cultural equivalent in the target language.

her /hɜːʳ/ PERS PRON 1 [...] ◆ **I know HIM but I have never seen HER** lui je le connais, mais elle je ne l'ai jamais vue

Small capitals are used to indicate the spoken stress in certain English expressions.

Field labels

cell /sel/ N 1 (gen, Bot, Phot, Telec) cellule f ; (Elec) élément m (de pile) ◆ **to form a** ~ (Pol) créer une cellule
2 (Police etc) cellule f ◆ **he spent the night in the ~s** il a passé la nuit au poste or en cellule ; → **condemn**

parabola /pə'ræbələ/ N parabole f (Math)

Labels indicating subject fields occur in the following cases:

1 To differentiate various meanings of the headword.

2 When the meaning is clear in the source language but may be ambiguous in the target language.

A full list of the abbreviated field labels is given on inside covers.

[3] Les compléments d'objet d'une entrée verbe, précédés du signe +.

défaire /defɛʀ/ ▸ conjug 60 ◂ **VT** [1] *[+ échafaudage]* to take down, to dismantle; *[+ installation électrique]* to dismantle; *[+ sapin de Noël]* to take down
[2] *(= découdre, dénouer) [+ couture, tricot]* to undo, to unpick (Brit); *[+ écheveau]* to undo, to unravel, to unwind; *[+ corde, nœud, ruban]* to undo, to untie; *[+ cheveux, nattes]* to undo

[4] Les noms que peut qualifier une entrée adjectif.

élancé, e /elɑ̃se/ (ptp de **élancer**) **ADJ** *[clocher, colonne, taille, personne]* slender

[5] Les verbes ou adjectifs modifiés par une entrée adverbe.

joliment /ʒɔlimɑ̃/ **ADV** [1] *(= élégamment) [décoré, habillé]* nicely

Autres indicateurs

(NonC) signifie "non comptable". Il est utilisé pour indiquer qu'un nom ne s'emploie pas normalement au pluriel et ne se construit pas, en règle générale, avec l'article indéfini ou avec un numéral. *(NonC)* a pour but d'avertir le lecteur étranger lorsque celui-ci risquerait d'employer le mot de manière incorrecte ; mais notre propos n'est nullement de donner une liste exhaustive de ces mots en anglais. *(NonC)* est parfois utilisé comme indication dans la langue de départ, lorsque c'est le seul moyen de distinguer emplois "non comptables" et "comptables".

aboiement /abwamɑ̃/ **NM** [1] *[de chien]* bark
◆ **~s** barking *(NonC)*

clignement /kliɲ(ə)mɑ̃/ **NM** blinking *(NonC)*

(SPÉC) signifie "terme de spécialiste". Dans l'exemple ci-contre le mot anglais d'usage courant est "eardrum" alors que "tympanum" ne se rencontre que dans le vocabulaire des spécialistes.

tympan /tɛ̃pɑ̃/ **NM** [1] *(Anat)* eardrum, tympanum *(SPÉC)*

≃ introduit une équivalence culturelle, lorsque le terme de la langue de départ n'a pas d'équivalent exact dans la langue d'arrivée, et n'est donc pas à proprement parler traduisible.

bêtise /betiz/ **NF** *[...]*
~ **de Cambrai** ≃ mint humbug *(Brit)*, ≃ piece of hard mint candy *(US)*

Une glose explicative peut être donnée lorsqu'il n'existe pas d'équivalent dans la langue d'arrivée.

achards /aʃaʀ/ **NMPL** *spicy relish made with finely chopped fruit and vegetables*

On a eu recours aux petites capitales pour indiquer, dans certaines expressions, l'accent d'insistance qui rend ou requiert une nuance particulière du français.

toi /twa/ **PRON PERS** [1] *(sujet, objet)* you *[...]*
◆ **qui l'a vu ? ~ ?** who saw him? did you? ◆ **~ mentir ? ce n'est pas possible** YOU tell a lie? I can't believe it

Domaines

Les indications de domaine figurent dans les cas suivants :

[1] Pour indiquer les différents sens d'un mot et introduire les traductions appropriées.

cuirasse /kɥiʀas/ **NF** *(Hist) [de chevalier]* breastplate; *(Naut)* armour(-plate *ou* -plating) *(Brit)*, armor(-plate *ou* -plating)

[2] Quand la langue de départ n'est pas ambiguë, mais que la traduction peut l'être.

comprimé /kɔ̃pʀime/ **NM** *(= pilule)* tablet

La liste des indications de domaine apparaissant sous forme abrégée figure en pages de garde.

STYLE LABELS

A dozen or so indicators of register are used to mark non-neutral words and expressions. These indicators are given for both source and target languages and serve mainly as a warning to the user using the foreign language. The following paragraphs explain the meaning of the most common style labels.

heretofore /ˌhɪətʊˈfɔː^{r}/ ADV *(frm)* *(= up to specified point)* jusque-là ; *(= up to now)* jusqu'ici

(frm) denotes formal language such as that used on official forms, in pronouncements and other formal communications.

kidology * /kɪˈdɒlədʒɪ/ N *(Brit)* bluff *m*

* indicates that the expression, while not forming part of standard language, is used by all educated speakers in a relaxed situation but would not be used in a formal essay or letter.

kisser ⁑ /ˈkɪsə^{r}/ N gueule⁑ *f*

⁑ indicates that the expression is used by some but not all educated speakers in a very relaxed situation. Such words should be handled with extreme care by non-native speakers unless they are very fluent in the language and are very sure of their company.

arse *** /ɑːs/ *(esp Brit)* N cul*** *m*

*** means "Danger!" Such words are liable to offend in any situation, and are therefore to be avoided by the non-native speaker.

botheration † * /ˌbɒðəˈreɪʃən/ EXCL flûte ! *, la barbe ! *

† denotes old-fashioned terms which are no longer in wide current use but which the foreign user is likely to find in reading.

gageure /gaʒyʀ/ NF [...] (†† = *pari)* wager

†† denotes obsolete words which the user will normally find only in classical literature.

ordalie /ɔʀdali/ NF *(Hist)* ordeal

The use of † and †† should not be confused with the label *(Hist)*. *(Hist)* does not apply to the expression itself but denotes the historical context of the object it refers to.

ostentatoire /ɔstɑ̃tatwaʀ/ ADJ *(littér)* ostentatious

(liter), *(littér)* denote an expression which belongs to literary or poetic language.

beseech /bɪˈsiːtʃ/ (pret, ptp **besought** *or* **beseeched**) VT *(liter)* [1] *(= ask for)* *[+ permission]* demander instamment, solliciter ; *[+ pardon]* implorer

The user should not confuse these style labels with the field labels *(Literat)*, *(Littérat)* which indicate that the expression belongs to the field of literature. Similarly the user should note that the abbreviation *(lit)* indicates the literal, as opposed to the figurative *(fig)*, meaning of a word.

camer (se) /kame/ ► conjug 1 ◄ VPR *(arg Drogue)* to be on drugs

sorted * /ˈsɔːtɪd/ ADJ [1] *(= arranged)* arrangé ◆ **in a few months everything should be ~** dans quelques mois tout devrait être arrangé [2] *(Drugs sl)* **are you ~?** tu as ce qu'il te faut ?

For the purpose of this dictionary the indicators *(sl)* for slang and *(arg)* for argot mark specific areas of vocabulary restricted to clearly defined groups of speakers (eg schoolchildren, soldiers, etc) and for this reason a field label is added to the label *(sl)* or *(arg)* marking the departure language expression.

All the labels and symbols above are used to mark either an individual word or phrase, or a whole category, or even a complete entry. Where a headword is marked with asterisks, any phrases in the entry will only have asterisks if they are of a different register from the headword.

NIVEAUX DE LANGUE

Une quinzaine d'indications de registre accompagnent les mots et expressions qui présentent un écart par rapport à la langue courante. Ces indications sont données aussi bien dans la langue de départ que dans la langue d'arrivée et constituent avant tout un avertissement au lecteur utilisant la langue étrangère. Les paragraphes suivants précisent le sens des principaux niveaux de langue :

frm indique le style administratif, les formules officielles, la langue soignée.

agréer /agʀee/ ▸ conjug 1 ◂ *(frm)* VT *(= accepter)* *[+ demande, excuses]* to accept;

* marque la majeure partie des expressions familières et les incorrections de langage employées dans la langue de tous les jours. Ce signe conseille au lecteur d'être prudent.

accro* /akʀo/ (abrév de **accroché**) ADJ 1 *(Drogue)* **être ~** to have a habit, to be hooked* ◆ **être ~ à l'héroïne** to be hooked on heroin*

⁑ marque les expressions très familières qui sont à employer avec la plus grande prudence par le lecteur étranger, qui devra posséder une grande maîtrise de la langue et savoir dans quel contexte elles peuvent être utilisées.

taulard, -arde⁑ /tolaʀ, aʀd/ NM,F convict, con⁑

⁂ marque le petit nombre d'expressions courantes que le lecteur étranger doit pouvoir reconnaître, mais dont l'emploi risque d'être ressenti comme fortement indécent ou injurieux.

baiser² /beze/ ▸ conjug 1 ◂ VT 1 *(frm)* *[+ main, visage, sol]* to kiss
2 *(⁂: sexuellement)* to screw⁂, to lay⁂, to fuck⁂

† marque les termes ou expressions démodés, qui ont quitté l'usage courant mais que l'étranger peut encore rencontrer au cours de ses lectures.

indéfrisable † /ɛ̃defʀizabl/ NF perm, permanent (US)

†† marque les termes ou expressions archaïques, que le lecteur ne rencontrera en principe que dans les œuvres classiques.

gageure /gaʒyʀ/ NF *[...]* (*†† = pari)* wager

On évitera de confondre ces signes avec l'indication *(Hist)*, qui ne marque pas le niveau de langue du mot lui-même mais souligne que l'objet désigné ne se rencontre que dans un contexte historiquement daté.

ordalie /ɔʀdali/ NF (Hist) ordeal

(littér), *(liter)* marquent les expressions de style poétique ou littéraire.

ostentatoire /ɔstɑ̃tatwaʀ/ ADJ *(littér)* ostentatious

beseech /bɪ'siːtʃ/ (pret, ptp **besought** *or* **beseeched**) VT *(liter)* 1 *(= ask for)* *[+ permission]* demander instamment, solliciter ; *[+ pardon]* implorer

Le lecteur veillera à ne pas confondre ces indications avec *lit* d'une part (sens propre, emploi littéral) et *Littérat*, *Literat* de l'autre (domaine de la littérature).

Les indications *arg* (argot) et *sl* (slang) désignent les termes appartenant au vocabulaire de groupes restreints (tels que les écoliers, les militaires) et l'indication du domaine approprié leur est adjointe dans la langue de départ.

camer (se) /kame/ ▸ conjug 1 ◂ VPR *(arg Drogue)* to be on drugs

sorted* /'sɔːtɪd/ ADJ 1 *(= arranged)* arrangé ◆ **in a few months everything should be ~** dans quelques mois tout devrait être arrangé
2 *(Drugs sl)* **are you ~?** tu as ce qu'il te faut ?

Les indications de niveau de langue peuvent soit s'attacher à un mot ou à une expression isolés, soit marquer une catégorie entière ou même un article complet. Lorsqu'un mot est suivi d'astérisques, les locutions et exemples de l'article correspondant ne prendront à leur tour l'astérisque que s'ils appartiennent à un niveau de langue différent.

PUNCTUATION

alluring /əˈljʊərɪŋ/ ADJ séduisant, charmant

A comma is used to separate translations which have the same or very similar meanings.

melting /ˈmeltɪŋ/ ADJ *[snow]* fondant ; *(fig) [voice, look]* attendri ; *[words]* attendrissant

A semi-colon separates translations which are not interchangeable. As a general rule, indicators are given to differentiate between non-interchangeable translations.

sailboarding /ˈseɪlˌbɔːdɪŋ/ N planche *f* à voile ◆ **to go ~** faire de la planche à voile

A black lozenge precedes every new phrase.

freshly /ˈfreʃlɪ/ ADV *[ground, grated, dug]* fraîchement ◆ **~ baked bread** du pain qui sort *or* frais sorti du four

In the translation of phrases, an alternative translation of only part of the phrase is preceded by either *or* or *ou*.

eyetooth /ˈaɪtuːθ/ N (pl **eyeteeth** /ˈaɪtiːθ/) canine *f* supérieure ◆ **I'd give my eyeteeth * for a car like that/to go to China** qu'est-ce que je ne donnerais pas pour avoir une voiture comme ça/pour aller en Chine

An oblique / indicates alternatives in the source language, which are reflected exactly in the target language.

bromide /ˈbrəʊmaɪd/ N 1 *(Chem, Typ)* bromure *m* ; *(Med *)* bromure *m* (de potassium)

esteem /ɪsˈtiːm/ VT 1 *(= think highly of) [+ person]* avoir de l'estime pour, estimer ; *[+ quality]* apprécier ◆ **our (highly) ~ed colleague** notre (très) estimé collègue *or* confrère

Parentheses within illustrative phrases or their translations indicate that the material they contain is optional. Such parentheses may be given for phrases in both source and target language.

CROSS-REFERENCES

sainteté /sɛ̃tte/ NF 1 *[de personne]* saintliness, godliness; *[d'Évangile, Vierge]* holiness; *[de lieu]* holiness, sanctity; *[de mariage]* sanctity; → **odeur**

These are used to refer the user to the headword under which a certain compound or idiom has been treated (see **PHRASES AND IDIOMS** p. XVIII).

vendredi /vɑ̃dʀədi/ NM Friday ◆ **Vendredi** *(= personnage de Robinson Crusoé)* Man Friday ◆ **c'était un ~ treize** it was Friday the thirteenth; *pour autres loc voir* **samedi**

Friday /ˈfraɪdɪ/ N vendredi *m* ◆ **~ the thirteenth** vendredi treize ; → **good** ; *for other phrases see* **Saturday**

They are also used to draw the user's attention to the full treatment of such words as numerals, days of the week and months of the year under certain key words. The key words which have been treated in depth are:

(French) **six, sixième, soixante, samedi, septembre.**
(English) **six; sixth, sixty, Saturday, September.**

CROSS-REFERENCES TO LANGUAGE IN USE

refuse[1] /rɪˈfjuːz/ LANGUAGE IN USE 8.3, 9.3, 12

Words which are also covered in Language in Use have a shaded cross-reference at the top of the entry. In this example, the user is referred to topics on **Disagreement** (chapter 12), **Intentions and Desires** (chapter 8, § 3), and **Permission** (chapter 9, § 3).

PONCTUATION

Une virgule sépare les traductions considérées comme équivalentes ou pratiquement équivalentes.

légitime /leʒitim/ ADJ 1 *(= légal) [droits, gouvernement]* legitimate, lawful;

Un point-virgule sépare les traductions qui ne sont pas interchangeables. En règle générale, le point-virgule est accompagné d'une indication qui précise la différence de sens.

direct, e /diʀɛkt/ ADJ 1 *(= sans détour) [route, personne, reproche, regard]* direct; *[question]* direct, straight; *[allusion]* direct, pointed

Un losange noir précède chaque phrase.

danger /dɑ̃ʒe/ NM danger ◆ **un grave ~ nous menace** we are in serious *ou* grave danger ◆ **courir un ~** to run a risk ◆ **en cas de ~** in case of emergency

Les traductions offrant plusieurs variantes interchangeables à partir d'un tronc commun sont séparées par *ou* ou par *or*.

ravi, e /ʀavi/ (ptp de **ravir**) ADJ *(= enchanté)* delighted ... ◆ **~ de vous connaître** delighted *ou* pleased to meet you

Le trait oblique / permet de regrouper des expressions de sens différent ayant un élément en commun ; cette structure est reflétée dans la langue d'arrivée.

académie /akademi/ NF [...] 2 *(= école)* academy ◆ **~ de dessin/danse** art/dancing school, academy of art/dancing

abouter /abute/ ► conjug 1 ◄ VT to join (up) (end to end)

Les parenthèses figurant à l'intérieur des expressions ou de leur traduction indiquent que les mots qu'elles contiennent sont facultatifs.

Ces parenthèses peuvent figurer en corrélation.

esteem /ɪs'tiːm/ VT 1 *(= think highly of) [+ person]* avoir de l'estime pour, estimer ; *[+ quality]* apprécier ◆ **our (highly) ~ed colleague** notre (très) estimé collègue *or* confrère

RENVOIS

Ils renvoient le lecteur à l'article dans lequel est traitée une certaine expression, où figure un certain composé (voir **LOCUTIONS ET EXEMPLES** p. XIX).

Ils attirent également l'attention de l'usager sur certains mots-clés qui ont été traités en profondeur ; pour les numéraux, **six, sixième** et **soixante** ; pour les jours de la semaine, **samedi** ; pour les mois de l'année **septembre**. Dans la nomenclature anglaise, ce sont les mots **six, sixth, sixty, Saturday, September**.

sainteté /sɛ̃tte/ NF 1 *[de personne]* saintliness, godliness; *[d'Évangile, Vierge]* holiness; *[lieu]* holiness, sanctity; *[de mariage]* sanctity; → **odeur**

vendredi /vɑ̃dʀədi/ NM Friday ◆ **Vendredi** *(= personnage de Robinson Crusoé)* Man Friday ◆ **c'était un ~ treize** it was Friday the thirteenth; *pour autres loc voir* **samedi**

Friday /'fraɪdɪ/ N vendredi *m* ◆ **~ the thirteenth** vendredi treize ; → **good** ; *for other phrases see* **Saturday**

RENVOIS À LA GRAMMAIRE ACTIVE

Les mots qui font l'objet d'un développement dans la Grammaire active sont accompagnés de l'indication **GRAMMAIRE ACTIVE** suivie d'un ou de plusieurs numéros. Ces numéros renvoient à la rubrique correspondante.

Dans l'exemple ci-contre, l'usager est renvoyé aux rubriques **la Suggestion** (chapitre 1, § 1), **Propositions** (chapitre 3), **la Permission** (chapitre 9, § 1) et **l'Obligation** (chapitre 10, § 4).

permettre /pɛʀmɛtʀ/ GRAMMAIRE ACTIVE 1.1, 3, 9.1, 10.4

VERBS

baisser /bese/ ▸ conjug 1 ◂ VT

arise /əˈraɪz/ (pret **arose**, ptp **arisen** /əˈrɪzn/) VI
1 *[difficulty]* survenir, surgir

Tables of French and English verbs are included in the supplements (page 2249 for French verbs and page 2270 for English verbs).
At each verb headword in the French-English part of the dictionary, a number refers the user to these tables.
The preterite and past participle of English strong verbs are given at the main verb entry.

VPR **se baisser** *(pour ramasser)* to bend down, to stoop; *(pour éviter)* to duck ◆ **il n'y a qu'à se ~ (pour les ramasser)** *(lit)* they're lying thick on the ground; *(fig)* they're there for the taking

In the French-English part of the dictionary, verbs which are true pronominals are treated in a separate grammatical category.

grandir /gʀɑ̃diʀ/ ▸ conjug 2 ◂ VI *[...]*
VT 1 *(= faire paraître grand) [microscope]* to magnify ◆ **~ les dangers/difficultés** to exaggerate the dangers/difficulties ◆ **ces chaussures te grandissent** those shoes make you (look) taller ◆ **il se grandit en se mettant sur la pointe des pieds** he made himself taller by standing on tiptoe

Pronominal uses which indicate a reciprocal, reflexive or passive sense are shown only if the translation requires it. In such cases they may be given within the transitive category of the verb as an illustrative phrase.

étendu, e¹ /etɑ̃dy/ (ptp de **étendre**) ADJ

broken /ˈbrəʊkən/ VB ptp of **break**
ADJ 1 *(= cracked, smashed) [cup, window, branch, biscuits etc]* cassé ; *(= uneven, rugged)*

If the translation of a past participle cannot be reached directly from the verb entry or if the past participle has adjectival value then the past participle is treated as a headword.

CULTURAL NOTES

AOC /aose/ NF (abrév de **appellation d'origine contrôlée**) ◆ **fromage/vin ~** AOC cheese/wine *(with a guarantee of origin)*

AOC

AOC is the highest French wine classification. It indicates that the wine meets strict requirements concerning the vineyard of origin, the type of vine grown, the method of production, and the volume of alcohol present. → **VDQS**

Extra information on culturally significant events, institutions, traditions and customs that cannot be given in an ordinary translation or gloss is given in the form of notes following the relevant entry.

VERBES

Les tables de conjugaison des verbes français et anglais sont données en annexe (page 2249 pour les verbes français et page 2270 pour les verbes anglais).
Dans la nomenclature française, chaque verbe est suivi d'un numéro qui renvoie le lecteur à ces tables.
Le prétérit et le participe passé des verbes forts anglais sont donnés après le verbe dans le corps de l'article. Une liste des principaux verbes forts figure également en annexe p. 2350.

baisser /bese/ ▸ conjug 1 ◂ VT
arise /əˈraɪz/ pret **arose,** ptp **arisen** /əˈrɪzn/ VI
1 *[difficulty]* survenir, surgir

Dans la partie français-anglais, les emplois véritablement pronominaux des verbes sont traités dans une catégorie à part.

VPR **se baisser** *(pour ramasser)* to bend down, to stoop; *(pour éviter)* to duck ◆ **il n'y a qu'à se ~ (pour les ramasser)** *(lit)* they're lying thick on the ground; *(fig)* they're there for the taking

Les emplois pronominaux à valeur réciproque, réfléchie ou passive ne figurent dans le dictionnaire que lorsque la traduction l'exige. En pareil cas, ils peuvent être simplement donnés dans la catégorie appropriée du verbe transitif, à titre d'exemple.

grandir /gʀɑ̃diʀ/ ▸ conjug 2 ◂ VI *[...]*
VT 1 *(= faire paraître grand) [microscope]* to magnify ◆ **~ les dangers/difficultés** to exaggerate the dangers/difficulties ◆ **ces chaussures te grandissent** those shoes make you (look) taller ◆ **il se grandit en se mettant sur la pointe des pieds** he made himself taller by standing on tiptoe

Si la traduction d'un participe passé ne peut se déduire directement du verbe, ou si le participe a pris une valeur adjective, il est traité comme mot à part entière et figure à sa place alphabétique dans la nomenclature.

étendu, e[1] /etɑ̃dy/ (ptp de **étendre**) ADJ
broken /ˈbrəʊkən/ VB (ptp of **break**)
ADJ 1 *(= cracked, smashed) [cup, window, branch, biscuits etc]* cassé ; *(= uneven, rugged)*

NOTES CULTURELLES

Des informations concernant des événements culturellement importants, des traditions et coutumes ou des institutions, qui ne pouvaient être données dans le corps même des articles sous forme de traductions ou de gloses, sont présentées juste en-dessous de l'entrée sous forme de notices.

A LEVELS

Diplôme britannique préparé en deux ans, qui sanctionne la fin des études secondaires et permet l'accès à l'enseignement supérieur. Contrairement au baccalauréat français, dont le résultat est global, les **A levels** sont obtenus séparément dans un nombre limité de matières (trois en moyenne) choisies par le candidat. Le système d'inscription dans l'enseignement supérieur étant sélectif, les élèves cherchent à obtenir les meilleures mentions possibles afin de pouvoir choisir plus facilement leur université.
En Écosse, l'équivalent des **A levels** est le "Higher", ou "Higher Grade", qui se prépare en un an et porte sur cinq matières au maximum. → **GCSE**

NOTES ON TRANSLATION

Special notes alert the reader when the translation of a word is not the one that might be expected.

> ⚠ **globally** is not translated by **globalement**, which means 'as a whole'.

> ⚠ The French word **pédant** refers not to a person obsessed with detail but to someone who shows off their knowledge.

LONG ENTRIES

Entries that are very long because they cover function words (**to, do, à, faire** etc) or words that are used in a large number of set structures (**time, head, affaire, heure** etc) are given special treatment in this dictionary.

Long entries with more than one part of speech begin with a special "menu" that shows how they are structured.

Special notes inside the entry either explain important points of grammar and usage or refer the user to another part of the dictionary. The word BUT (or MAIS) introduces exceptions to any general point that has been made in such a note.

The beginning of each semantic category is clearly signposted with indicators in boxes.

aller /ale/

▸ conjug 9 ◂

1 VERBE INTRANSITIF	4 VERBE PRONOMINAL
2 VERBE IMPERSONNEL	5 LOC EXCLAMATIVES
3 VERBE AUXILIAIRE	6 NOM MASCULIN

1 - VERBE INTRANSITIF

1 = se déplacer, partir to go ◆ **où vas-tu ?** where are you going? ◆ **il t'attend, va!** he's waiting for you, go on!

> **aller** se traduit régulièrement par un verbe spécifique en anglais :

◆ **j'allais par les rues désertes** I walked ou wandered through the empty streets ◆ **il allait trop vite quand il a eu son accident** he was driving *ou* going too fast when he had his accident ◆ **en ville, on va plus vite à pied qu'en voiture** in town it is quicker to walk than to go by car ◆ ~ **à Paris en voiture/en avion** to drive/fly to Paris ◆ **il y est allé à** *ou* **en vélo** he cycled there, he went there on his bike ◆ **j'irai à pied** I'll walk, I'll go on foot

♦ **aller et venir** *(entre deux endroits)* to come and go; *(dans une pièce)* to pace up and down

♦ **ça va, ça vient** ◆ **tu sais, la chance, ça va ça vient** luck comes and goes, you know, you win some, you lose some ◆ **avec lui l'argent, ça va, ça vient** when it comes to money, it's easy come, easy go with him

♦ **aller** + *préposition (= se rendre)* ◆ ~ **à** to go to ◆ ~ **à Caen/à la campagne** to go to Caen/to the country ◆ ~ **au lit/à l'église/à l'école** to go to bed/to church/to school ◆ ~ **en Allemagne** to go to Germany ◆ ~ **chez le boucher/chez un ami** to go to the butcher's/to a friend's (place)

NOTES SUR LA TRADUCTION

Lorsque la traduction d'un mot n'est pas celle que l'on pourrait attendre, nous attirons l'attention du lecteur sur ce fait au moyen d'un encadré.

⚠ Au sens de 'maintenant', **actuellement** ne se traduit pas par **actually**.

 **éventuel** ne se traduit pas par le mot anglais **eventual**, qui a le sens de 'final'.

ARTICLES LONGS

Les articles qui sont particulièrement longs, soit parce qu'ils traitent de mots-outils (**à, faire, to, do** etc.), soit parce qu'ils couvrent beaucoup d'expressions lexicales (**affaire, heure, head, time** etc.), bénéficient d'un traitement spécifique dans notre dictionnaire.

Les articles longs comprenant plus d'une catégorie grammaticale s'ouvrent par un "menu" qui présente leur structure.

Des notes à l'intérieur des articles expliquent certains points de grammaire et d'usage importants. Le mot MAIS (ou BUT) attire l'attention de l'usager sur des exceptions aux règles énoncées.

Chaque catégorie sémantique est clairement signalée par un indicateur mis en relief.

get /get/

vb : pret, ptp **got**, ptp (US) **gotten**

1 TRANSITIVE VERB	3 COMPOUNDS
2 INTRANSITIVE VERB	4 PHRASAL VERBS

1 – TRANSITIVE VERB

1 = have, receive, obtain avoir

avoir covers a wide range of meanings, and like **get** is unspecific.

◆ **I go whenever I ~ the chance** j'y vais dès que j'en ai l'occasion ◆ **he's got a cut on his finger** il a une coupure au doigt ◆ **he got a fine** il a eu une amende ◆ **she ~s a good salary** elle a un bon salaire ◆ **not everyone ~s a pension** tout le monde n'a pas la retraite ◆ **you need to ~ permission from the owner** il faut avoir la permission du propriétaire ◆ **I got a lot of presents** j'ai eu beaucoup de cadeaux ◆ **he got first prize** il a eu le premier prix ◆ **you may ~ a surprise** tu pourrais avoir une surprise

Some **get** + noun combinations may take a more specific French verb.

◆ **we can ~ sixteen channels** nous pouvons recevoir seize chaînes ◆ **it was impossible to ~ help** il était impossible d'obtenir de l'aide ◆ **he got help from the others** il s'est fait aider par les autres ◆ **first I need to ~ a better idea of the situation** je dois d'abord me faire une meilleure idée de la situation ◆ **I think he got the wrong impression** je pense qu'il s'est fait des idées ◆ **they ~ lunch at school** ils déjeunent *or* ils mangent à l'école ◆ **he got his money by exploiting others** il s'est enrichi en exploitant les autres ◆ **if I'm not working I ~ no pay** si je ne travaille pas je ne suis pas payé

PRONUNCIATION OF FRENCH

Transcription

The symbols used to record the pronunciation of French are those of the International Phonetic Association. The variety of French transcribed is that shown in *Le Nouveau Petit Robert,* ie standard Parisian speech. Within this variety of French, variant pronunciations are to be observed. In particular, there is a marked tendency among speakers today to make no appreciable distinction between: /a/ and /ɑ/, **patte** /pat/ and **pâte** /pɑt/ both tending towards the pronunciation /pat/; /ɛ̃/ and /œ̃/, **brin** /bʀɛ̃/ and **brun** /bʀœ̃/ both tending towards the pronunciation /bʀɛ̃/. The distinction between these sounds is maintained in the transcription.

Headwords

Each headword has its pronunciation transcribed between obliques. In the case of words having a variant pronunciation (eg **tandis** /tɑ̃di/, /tɑ̃dis/), the one pronunciation given is that regarded by the editorial team as preferable, often on grounds of frequency.

Morphological variations

Morphological variations of headwords are shown phonetically where necessary, without repetition of the root (eg **journal** (pl **-aux**) /ʒuʀnal, o/).

Compound words

Compound words derived from headwords and shown within an entry are given without phonetic transcription (eg **brosse** /bʀɔs/, but **brosse à cheveux**). The pronunciation of compounds is usually predictable, being that of the citation form of each element, associated with the final syllable stress characteristic of the language (see following paragraph).

Syllable stress

In normal, unemphatic speech, the final syllable of a word, or the final syllable of a sense group, carries a moderate degree of stress. The syllable stressed is given extra prominence by greater length and intensity. The exception to this rule is a final syllable containing a mute *e*, which is never stressed. In view of this simple rule, it has not been considered necessary to indicate the position of a stressed syllable of a word by a stress mark in the phonetic transcription.

Closing of /ɛ/

Under the influence of stressed /y/, /i/, or /e/ vowels, an /ɛ/ in an open syllable tends towards a closer /e/ sound, even in careful speech. In such cases, the change has been indicated: **aimant** /ɛmɑ̃/, but **aimer** /eme/; **bête** /bɛt/, but **bêtise** /betiz/.

Mute e /ə/

Within isolated words, a mute *e* /ə/ preceded by a single pronounced consonant is regularly dropped (eg **follement** /fɔlmɑ̃/; **samedi** /samdi/).

Opening of /e/

As the result of the dropping of an /ə/ within a word, an /e/ occurring in a closed syllable tends towards /ɛ/, as the transcription shows (eg **événement** /evɛnmɑ̃/; **élevage** /ɛlvaʒ/).

Aspirate h

Initial *h* in the spelling of a French word does not imply strong expulsion of breath, except in the case of certain interjections. Initial *h* is called 'aspirate' when it is incompatible with liaison (**des haricots** /de'aʀiko/) or elision (**le haricot** /lə'aʀiko/). Aspirate *h* is shown in transcriptions by an apostrophe placed at the beginning of the word (eg **hibou** /'ibu/).

Consonants and assimilation

Within a word and in normal speech, a voiceless consonant may be voiced when followed by a voiced consonant (eg **exemple** /ɛgzɑ̃pl/), and a voiced consonant may be devoiced when followed by a voiceless consonant (eg **absolument** /apsɔlymɑ̃/). When this phenomenon is regular in a word, it is shown in transcription (eg **abside** /apsid/). In speech, its frequency varies from speaker to speaker. Thus, while the citation form of **tasse** is /tɑs/, the group **une tasse de thé** may be heard pronounced /yntɑsdəte/ or /yntɑzdəte/.

Sentence stress

Unlike the stress pattern of English associated with meaning, sentence stress in French is associated with rhythm. The stress falls on the final syllable of the sense groups of which the sentence is formed (see **Syllable stress**). In the following example : *quand il m'a vu, il a traversé la rue en courant pour me dire un mot*, composed of three sense groups, the syllables **vu, -rant** and **mot** carry the stress, being slightly lengthened.

Intonation French intonation is less mobile than English and is closely associated with sentence stress. The most marked rises and falls occur normally on the final syllable of sense groups. Thus, in the sentence given above, the syllables **vu** and **-rant** are spoken with a slight rise (indicating continuity), while the syllable **mot** is accompanied by a fall in the voice (indicating finality). In the case of a question, the final syllable will normally also be spoken with rising voice.

PHONETIC TRANSCRIPTION OF FRENCH
TRANSCRIPTION PHONÉTIQUE DU FRANÇAIS

VOWELS		CONSONANTS	
[i]	**il**, v**ie**, l**y**re	[p]	**p**ère, sou**p**e
[e]	bl**é**, jou**er**	[t]	**t**erre, vi**t**e
[ɛ]	**lai**t, jou**et**, m**e**rci	[k]	**c**ou, **qu**i, sa**c**, **k**épi
[a]	pl**a**t, p**a**tte	[b]	**b**on, ro**b**e
[ɑ]	b**as**, p**â**te	[d]	**d**ans, ai**d**e
[ɔ]	m**o**rt, d**o**nner	[g]	**g**are, ba**gue**
[o]	m**o**t, d**ô**me, **eau**, g**au**che	[f]	**f**eu, neu**f**, **ph**oto
[u]	gen**ou**, r**ou**e	[s]	**s**ale, **c**elui, **ç**a, de**ss**ous, ta**ss**e, na**t**ion
[y]	r**u**e, vêt**u**	[ʃ]	**ch**at, ta**ch**e
[ø]	p**eu**, d**eu**x	[v]	**v**ous, rê**v**e
[œ]	p**eu**r, m**eu**ble	[z]	**z**éro, mai**s**on, ro**s**e
[ə]	l**e**, pr**e**mier	[ʒ]	**j**e, **g**ilet, **g**eôle
[ɛ̃]	mat**in**, pl**ein**	[l]	**l**ent, so**l**
[ɑ̃]	s**an**s, v**en**t	[ʀ]	**r**ue, veni**r**
[ɔ̃]	b**on**, **om**bre	[m]	**m**ain, fe**mm**e
[œ̃]	l**un**di, br**un**	[n]	**n**ous, to**nn**e, a**n**imal
		[ɲ]	a**gn**eau, vi**gn**e
SEMI-CONSONANTS		[h]	**h**op ! (exclamative)
		[']	**h**aricot (no liaison)
[j]	**y**eux, pa**ill**e, p**i**ed	[ŋ]	words borrowed from English: campi**ng**
[w]	**ou**i, n**ou**er	[x]	words borrowed from Spanish or Arabic: **j**ota
[ɥ]	h**u**ile, l**u**i		

PRONONCIATION DE L'ANGLAIS

La notation phonétique La notation adoptée est celle de l'Association phonétique internationale. L'ouvrage de base qui nous a constamment servi d'outil de référence est l'*English Pronouncing Dictionary* de Daniel Jones, qui, mis à jour par le Professeur A.C. Gimson, continue de faire autorité en France et partout ailleurs où l'on apprend l'anglais britannique.

La transcription correspond à la *received pronunciation (RP)*, variété de l'anglais britannique la plus généralement étudiée dans le monde d'aujourd'hui. Elle correspond également, à quelques exceptions près, à celle de la 14e édition de l'*English Pronouncing Dictionary (EPD)* (Cambridge University Press). Ce système de transcription présente l'avantage d'utiliser des signes qui indiquent clairement la distinction à la fois quantitative et qualitative qui existe entre les voyelles tendues et relâchées (par exemple : [iː], [ɪ] ; [ɜː], [ə]).

TRANSCRIPTION PHONÉTIQUE DE L'ANGLAIS
PHONETIC TRANSCRIPTION OF ENGLISH

CONSONNES

[p]	**p**at, pope
[b]	**b**at, **b**a**b**y
[t]	**t**ab, s**t**ru**t**
[d]	**d**ab, men**d**e**d**
[k]	**c**ot, **k**iss, **ch**ord
[g]	**g**ot, a**g**o**g**
[f]	**f**ine, ra**ff**e
[v]	**v**ine, ri**v**er
[s]	pot**s**, **s**it, ri**ce**
[z]	pod**s**, bu**zz**
[θ]	**th**in, ma**th**s
[ð]	**th**is, o**th**er
[ʃ]	**sh**ip, **s**ugar
[ʒ]	mea**s**ure
[tʃ]	**ch**ance
[dʒ]	**j**ust, e**dg**e
[l]	**l**ittle, p**l**ace
[r]	**r**an, sti**rr**ing
[m]	ra**m**, **mumm**y
[n]	ra**n**, **n**ut
[ŋ]	ra**ng**, ba**n**k
[h]	**h**at, re**h**eat
[j]	**y**et, mill**i**on
[w]	**w**et, be**w**ail
[x]	lo**ch**

VOYELLES ET DIPHTONGUES

[iː]	b**ea**d, s**ee**
[ɑː]	b**ar**d, c**al**m
[ɔː]	b**or**n, c**or**k
[uː]	b**oo**n, f**oo**l
[ɜː]	b**ur**n, f**er**n, w**or**k
[ɪ]	s**i**t, p**i**ty
[e]	s**e**t, l**e**ss
[æ]	s**a**t, **a**pple
[ʌ]	f**u**n, c**o**me
[ɒ]	f**o**nd, w**a**sh
[ʊ]	f**u**ll, s**oo**t
[ə]	compos**er**, **a**bove
[eɪ]	b**ay**, f**a**te
[aɪ]	b**uy**, l**ie**
[ɔɪ]	b**oy**, v**oi**ce
[əʊ]	n**o**, ag**o**
[aʊ]	n**ow**, pl**ough**
[ɪə]	t**ier**, b**eer**
[ɛə]	t**ar**e, f**air**
[ʊə]	t**our**

DIVERS

Un caractère en italique représente un son qui peut ne pas être prononcé

[ʳ]	représente un [r] entendu s'il forme une liaison avec la voyelle du mot suivant
[ˈ]	accent tonique
[ˌ]	accent secondaire

Pour des raisons d'économie de place, une seule prononciation est donnée pour chaque mot, à l'exclusion des variantes communes. La prononciation ainsi transcrite est celle la plus fréquemment entendue selon l'*EPD*, ou, dans le cas de néologismes et de mots nouveaux, selon les membres de l'équipe Collins-Le Robert.

Il a été jugé inutile de compliquer la tâche de l'utilisateur en indiquant la prononciation de mots sortant du cadre du vocabulaire britannique. Ainsi, **aluminium, aluminum** sont transcrits : /ˌæljʊˈmɪnɪəm/, /əˈluːmɪnəm/, bien que la seconde forme, exclusivement américaine, ne s'entende normalement qu'avec un accent américain. Il s'agit, dans de tels cas, d'une approximation qui ne met pas en cause la compréhension du mot employé.

Les formes réduites

Certains mots monosyllabiques, en nombre limité, ayant une fonction plus structurale que lexicale, sont sujets, surtout à l'intérieur d'un énoncé, à une réduction vocalique plus ou moins importante. Le mot **and**, isolé, se prononce /ænd/ ; mais, dans la chaîne parlée, il se prononcera, à moins d'être accentué, /ənd, ən, n/ selon le débit du locuteur et selon le contexte. Les mots qui sont le plus souvent touchés par cette réduction vocalique sont les suivants : *a, an, and, as, at, but, for, from, of, some, than, that, the, them, to, us, am, is, are, was, were, must, will, would, shall, should, have, has, had, do, does, can, could*

L'accent tonique

Voir tableau page suivante.

L'accent secondaire

Dans un mot, toute syllabe accentuée en plus de celle qui porte l'accent tonique porte un accent secondaire, c'est-à-dire un accent ayant moins d'intensité que l'accent tonique. L'accent secondaire est noté au moyen du signe (ˌ) devant la syllabe intéressée. Par exemple : **composition** /ˌkɒmpəˈzɪʃən/ (accent secondaire sur /ˌkɒm/ ; accent tonique sur /ˈzɪʃ/).

Les composés

La prononciation des mots ou groupes de mots rassemblés dans la catégorie **COMP** d'un article n'est pas indiquée, car elle correspond à celle du mot-souche suivie de celle du mot ou des mots formant le reste du composé mais avec une restriction importante : pour des raisons pratiques, on considérera que la grande majorité des composés à deux éléments ne sont accentués que sur le premier élément, cette accentuation s'accompagnant d'une chute de la voix. Exemple : **'foodstuffs, 'food prices'.**

L'accent de phrase

À la différence du français dont l'accent de phrase (syllabe allongée) tombe normalement sur la dernière syllabe des groupes de souffle, l'anglais met en relief la syllabe accentuée de chaque mot apportant un nouvel élément d'information. Dans la pratique cela veut dire que les mots lexicaux reçoivent un accent de phrase, tandis que les mots grammaticaux n'en reçoivent pas (voir ci-dessus **Les formes réduites**). Il est logique, dans un tel système, que même les mots lexicaux ne soient pas accentués s'ils n'apportent pas de nouveaux éléments d'information ; c'est le cas, notamment, de mots ou de concepts répétés dans une même séquence ; ils sont accentués une première fois, mais ils perdent leur accent par la suite. De même, lorsqu'une idée est répétée dans une même séquence, les mots qui l'expriment ne sont plus mis en relief lors de sa réapparition. Par contre, les éléments contrastifs de la phrase anglaise sont toujours fortement accentués.

Exemple : *John's recently bought himself a car, and Peter's got a new one too.*

Accents sur : John, recently, bought, car, Peter, too.

Accents contrastifs sur : **John** (facultatif) et **Peter**. Absence d'accent sur : **'s got a new one**, qui n'apporte aucun nouvel élément d'information et pourrait être supprimé : (**and Peter, too**).

L'intonation

L'intonation en anglais, beaucoup plus qu'en français, révèle le sentiment du locuteur vis-à-vis des propos qu'il tient. Dans les deux langues, l'intonation est liée à l'accent de phrase. L'intonation française, tout comme l'accent de phrase, se manifeste sur la dernière syllabe des groupes de souffle : légère montée de la voix à l'intérieur de la phrase, avec une chute ou une montée sur la syllabe finale, selon qu'il s'agit d'une déclarative ou d'une interrogative. En anglais, l'intonation est liée au sens, et se manifeste sur toutes les syllabes accentuées de la phrase (voir ci-dessus **L'accent de phrase**). La phrase anglaise type présente une intonation commençant relativement haut, et descendant progressivement vers le grave sur les syllabes accentuées. Sur la dernière syllabe accentuée de la phrase, la voix marque soit une chute, soit une montée, plus importante qu'en français, selon le type de phrase : une chute, s'il s'agit d'une indication de finalité (déclaratives, impératives, etc) ; une montée s'il s'agit d'une invitation au dialogue (interrogatives, requêtes polies, etc). Plus le discours est animé et plus l'écart entre l'aigu et le grave se creuse. Des mots ayant un sens affectif intense tendent à faire monter la voix beaucoup plus haut que n'exigent les habitudes du discours français.

L'ACCENT TONIQUE

Tout mot anglais isolé, de deux syllabes ou plus, porte un accent tonique. Cet accent est noté au moyen du signe (') placé devant la syllabe intéressée ; par exemple : **composer** /kəm'pəʊzə'/. Le francophone doit veiller à bien placer l'accent tonique sous peine de poser de sérieux problèmes de compréhension à ses interlocuteurs. Le tableau suivant indique un certain nombre de suffixes qui permettent de prévoir la place de l'accent tonique sur de nombreux mots. Ce tableau est donné à titre indicatif et ne prétend pas être exhaustif.

TABLEAU DES SUFFIXES DÉTERMINANT LA POSITION DE L'ACCENT TONIQUE

	SUFFIXE	EXEMPLE	EXCEPTIONS	REMARQUES
ACCENT SUR SYLLABE FINALE	**-ee**	refu'gee	'coffee, 'toffee, com'mittee, 'pedigree	
	-eer	engi'neer		
	-ese	Japa'nese		
	-esque	pictu'resque		
	-ette	quar'tette	'etiquette, 'omelette	
	-ate	cre'ate		verbes de 2 syllabes
	-fy	de'fy		verbes de 2 syllabes
	-ise, -ize	ad'vise		verbes de 2 syllabes
ACCENT SUR PÉNULTIÈME	**-ial**	com'mercial		
	-ian	I'talian		
	-ic, -ics	eco'nomics	'Arabic, a'rithmetic, 'Catholic, 'heretic, 'lunatic, 'politics	les suffixes **-ical, -ically** ne modifient pas la place de l'accent tonique, et n'admettent pas d'exceptions, par exemple : po'litical, po'litically, arith'metical
	-ion	infor'mation	'dandelion, ('televison)*	
	-ish	di'minish	im'poverish	verbes en **-ish**
	-itis	appendi'citis		
	-osis	diag'nosis	(meta'morphosis)*	* **NB : Les mots placés entre parenthèses ont aussi une accentuation conforme au modèle**
ACCENT SUR ANTÉPÉNULTIÈME	**-ety**	so'ciety		
	-ity	sin'cerity		
	-itive	com'petitive		
	-itude	'attitude		
	-grapher	pho'tographer		
	-graphy	pho'tography		
	-logy	bi'ology		
	-ate	ap'preciate		pour les verbes de 2 syllabes, voir plus haut
	-fy	'pacify		
	-ise, -ize	'advertise	'characterize, 'regularize, 'liberalize, 'nationalize	pour les verbes de 2 syllabes, voir plus haut

DICTIONNAIRE FRANÇAIS-ANGLAIS

FRENCH-ENGLISH DICTIONARY

Aa

A¹, a¹ /a/ NM (= *lettre*) A, a ◆ **de A à Z** from A to Z ◆ **feuille A3/A4** sheet of A3/A4 paper ◆ **c'est du format A4** it's A4 (paper) ◆ **prouver** *ou* **démontrer qch par A + B** to prove sth conclusively
COMP **a commercial** at sign

A² (abrév de **ampère**) amp

A³ /a/ NF (abrév de **autoroute**) ≈ M (*Brit*) ◆ **l'A10** the A10 motorway (*Brit*) *ou* highway (*US*)

A⁴ (abrév de **apprenti conducteur**) P plate (*on car of newly qualified driver*)

a² (abrév de **are**) a

à /a/
PRÉPOSITION

contraction **à** + **le** = **au** ; **à** - **les** = **aux**.

Lorsque **à** se trouve dans des locutions du type **obéir à**, **apprendre qch à qn**, **lent à s'habiller**, **l'admission au club**, reportez-vous à l'autre mot.

1 [lieu : position] in ◆ **habiter à Paris/au Canada/à Bali** to live in Paris/in Canada/in Bali ◆ **on s'est arrêté à Toulouse** we stopped in Toulouse ◆ **je suis à la cuisine** I'm in the kitchen ◆ **il faisait chaud au théâtre** it was hot in the theatre

Notez qu'avec certains édifices l'anglais n'utilisera pas l'article si l'accent est mis sur leur fonction plutôt que sur leur localisation.

◆ **être à l'hôpital** (*en visite*) to be at the hospital; [*malade*] to be in hospital ◆ **être à l'école** (*de passage*) to be at the school; [*élève*] to be at school ◆ **il faisait chaud à l'église** it was hot in church

Lorsque **à**, indiquant la position plutôt que le mouvement, est suivi d'un nom d'île, il se traduit le plus souvent par **on**.

◆ **vivre à Paros/l'île de Wight** to live on Paros/the Isle of Wight

2 [lieu : direction] (= *vers*) to; (= *dans*) into ◆ **aller à Lille/au Canada** to go to Lille/Canada ◆ **aller à Paros/aux Açores** to go to Paros/the Azores ◆ **aller au marché/au théâtre** to go to the market/the theatre ◆ **entrez au salon** come into the lounge ◆ **au lit, les enfants !** off to bed children!, time for bed children!

Notez qu'avec certains édifices l'anglais n'utilisera pas l'article si l'accent est mis sur leur fonction plutôt que sur leur localisation.

◆ **aller à l'hôpital** (*en visite*) to go to the hospital; [*malade*] to go into hospital ◆ **elle va à l'église tous les dimanches** she goes to church every Sunday ◆ **je suis allé à l'église pour photographier les vitraux** I went to the church to photograph the windows ◆ **il n'aime pas aller à l'école** he doesn't like going to school ◆ **elle s'est précipitée à l'école mais ils étaient déjà partis** she dashed to the school but they had already gone

3 [lieu : étape de voyage, adresse] at ◆ **l'avion a atterri à Luton** the plane landed at Luton ◆ **le train ne s'est pas arrêté à Montélimar** the train didn't stop at Montélimar ◆ **j'habite au (numéro) 26 (de la rue Pasteur)** I live at number 26 (rue Pasteur) ◆ **habiter au 4ᵉ étage** to live on the 4th floor

4 [lieu : provenance] from ◆ **je l'ai eu à la bibliothèque** I got it from the library ◆ **prendre de l'eau au puits/à la rivière** to get water from the well/the river

5 [distance] **Paris est à 400 km de Londres** Paris is 400 km from London ◆ **c'est à 3 km/5 minutes (d'ici)** it's 3 km/5 minutes away (from here) ◆ **c'est à 4 heures de route** it's a 4-hour drive

6 [= jusqu'à] **de Paris à Londres** from Paris to London ◆ **du lundi au vendredi** from Monday to Friday ◆ **il leur faut 4 à 5 heures** they need 4 to 5 hours ◆ **on a fait 8 à 9 kilomètres** we did 8 or 9 kilometres ◆ **à lundi/la semaine prochaine !** see you on Monday/next week!

7 [temps, moment précis, occasion] at ◆ **à 6 heures** at 6 (o'clock) ◆ **je vous verrai à Noël** I'll see you at Christmas ◆ **on se reverra à sa réception** we'll see each other again at his party ◆ **je vous verrai aux vacances** I'll see you in the holidays

Lorsque **à** signifie **lors de**, l'anglais emploie souvent une proposition temporelle introduite par **when**.

◆ **je n'étais pas là à leur arrivée** I wasn't there when they arrived ◆ **à sa naissance, il pesait 3 kg** he weighed 3 kilos when he was born ◆ **vous serez payé à l'achèvement des travaux** you'll be paid when the work is finished

8 [temps, époque] in ◆ **la poésie au 19ᵉ siècle** poetry in the 19th century

9 [appartenance, possession] **c'est à moi/à eux** it's mine/theirs, it belongs to me/to them ◆ **ce livre est à Luc** this book belongs to Luc *ou* is Luc's ◆ **à qui est ce stylo ?** whose pen is this? ◆ **c'est une amie à lui/à eux** she is a friend of his/theirs ◆ **ils n'ont pas de maison à eux** they haven't got a house of their own ◆ **la voiture à Paul** * Paul's car ◆ **on avait la plage à nous (tous seuls)** we had the beach to ourselves ◆ **à moi le Canada/Paris !** Canada/Paris here I come! ◆ **à nous la belle vie !** it's the good life for us from now on! ◆ **je suis à toi pour toujours** I'm yours forever ◆ **je suis à vous dans deux minutes** I'll be with you in a couple of minutes

10 [responsabilité] **c'était à toi d'y aller** it was up to you to go ◆ **ce n'est pas à moi de le dire/de décider** it's not for me to say/to decide, it's not up to me to say/to decide

11 [ordre de passage] **à toi !** (*dans un jeu*) your turn (to play)!; (*échecs, dames*) your move!; (*en lançant une balle*) to you! ◆ **c'est à qui (le tour) ?** (*dans un jeu*) whose turn is it?; (*dans une file d'attente*) who's next, please? ◆ **à vous les studios/Paris** (TV, *Rad*) over to you in the studio/in Paris

12 [dédicace] for, to; (*dans les souhaits*) to ◆ **à mon fils, pour ses 20 ans** to *ou* for my son, on his 20th birthday ◆ **à Julie !** (*dans un toast*) to Julie! ◆ **à ta nouvelle maison !** to your new house! ◆ **à tes 30 ans !** happy 30th birthday! ◆ **à mon épouse regrettée** in memory of my dear wife

13 [= au nombre de] **nous y sommes allés à cinq** five of us went ◆ **ils l'ont soulevé à (eux) deux** the two of them lifted it up together ◆ **ils ont fait le travail à trois/à eux tous** they did the work between the three of them/between them ◆ **ils couchent à trois dans la même chambre** they sleep three to a room ◆ **à trois, nous irons plus vite** it'll be quicker if three of us do it ◆ **nous n'entrerons jamais à six dans sa voiture** the six of us will never get into his car ◆ **on peut rentrer à six dans la voiture** the car can hold six people

14 [= par, chaque] **faire du 90 à l'heure** to do 90 km an *ou* per hour ◆ **c'est à 5 € le kilo** it's €5 a kilo ◆ **être payé à la semaine/au mois** to be paid weekly/monthly, to be paid by the week/the month ◆ **gagner (par) 2 à 1** to win (by) 2 goals to 1, to win 2-1 ◆ **il mène (par) 3 jeux à 2** he's leading (by) 3 games to 2, he's leading 3-2

15 [= avec] with

Lorsque **à** est utilisé dans une description, il est rendu soit par **with** soit par une locution adjectivale.

◆ **robe à manches** dress with sleeves ◆ **robe à manches courtes** short-sleeved dress ◆ **enfant aux yeux bleus/aux cheveux longs** child with blue eyes/long hair, blue-eyed/long-haired child ◆ **la dame au chapeau vert** the lady in *ou* with the green hat ◆ **l'homme à la pipe** the man with the pipe, the man smoking a pipe; (*titre de tableau*) Man with Pipe

16 [= au moyen de] with; (*avec instrument de musique*) on ◆ **couper qch au couteau** to cut sth with a knife ◆ **faire la cuisine à l'huile/au**

beurre to cook with oil/butter ◆ **canard aux petits pois/aux pruneaux** duck with peas/ prunes ◆ **il l'a joué au piano/violon** he played it on the piano/violin ◆ **sardines à l'huile** sardines in oil ◆ **regarder qch à la jumelle** to look at sth through binoculars ◆ **le générateur marche au gazole** the generator runs on diesel ◆ **j'y suis allé à pied** I went on foot

17 [= d'après, au vu de] according to, from ◆ **à ce qu'il prétend** according to what he says ◆ **à ce que j'ai compris** from what I understood ◆ **à son expression, je dirais qu'il est content** judging from his expression I'd say he is pleased ◆ **c'est aux résultats qu'on le jugera** he will be judged on his results

18 [= provoquant] to ◆ **à sa consternation** to his dismay ◆ **à ma grande surprise** to my great surprise, much to my surprise

19 [imminence] **le temps est à la pluie/neige** it looks like rain/snow, there's rain/snow on the way

20 [suivi d'une activité] **quand elle est à son tricot/à sa peinture*** when she's doing her knitting/painting ◆ **allez Paul, à la vaisselle !** come on Paul, get cracking* with that washing-up! ◆ **le livre est à la reliure** the book is (away) being bound ◆ **au travail tout le monde!** come on everybody, let's get to work! ◆ **elle est au tennis** *(gén)* she's playing tennis; *(à son cours)* she's at her tennis lesson

21 [locutions]

◆ **à la ...** *(= à la manière de)* ◆ **cuisiné à la japonaise** cooked Japanese-style ◆ **le socialisme à la française** French-style socialism ◆ **une histoire à la Tolstoï** a story in the style of Tolstoy *ou* à la Tolstoy ◆ **vivre à l'américaine** to live like an American

◆ **à** + *infinitif (= pour)* ◆ **c'est une machine à polir les pierres** it's a machine (designed) for polishing stones ◆ **je n'ai rien à lire/faire** I have nothing to read/do ◆ **j'ai quelque chose à te montrer** I've got something to show you ◆ **il a été le premier à le dire, mais ils sont plusieurs à le penser** he was the first one to say it, but there are quite a few people who think the same ◆ **ils sont deux à l'avoir fait** two of them did it ◆ **elle est toujours à le taquiner** she keeps teasing him, she's forever teasing him

◆ **à** + *infinitif (nécessité, devoir)* ◆ **c'est à faire aujourd'hui** it has to be done *ou* it must be done today ◆ **ce sont des choses à prévoir** these things have to be *ou* need to be thought about ◆ **il est à ménager** he should be *ou* needs to be handled carefully ◆ **le poisson est à manger tout de suite** the fish needs to be *ou* must be eaten at once ◆ **tout est à refaire** it's all got to be done again ◆ **ces journaux sont à jeter** these papers can be thrown out

◆ **à** + *infinitif (cause)*

> Lorsque **à** + *infinitif* a une valeur causale, il se traduit généralement par un gérondif ou une proposition temporelle.

◆ **à le voir si maigre, j'ai eu pitié** when I saw how thin he was I felt sorry for him ◆ **à le fréquenter, on se rend compte que ...** when you've been with him for a while, you realize that ... ◆ **il nous fait peur à conduire si vite** he frightens us driving so fast [MAIS] **à l'entendre/le voir, on dirait qu'il est ivre** to hear him/look at him you'd think he was drunk, he sounds/looks drunk ◆ **vous le buterez à le punir ainsi** you'll antagonize him if you punish him like that

◆ **à** + *infinitif (conséquence)* ◆ **c'est à vous rendre fou** it's enough to drive you crazy ◆ **c'est à se demander si** it makes you wonder if ◆ **c'est à croire qu'ils nous prennent pour des idiots** you'd think that they took us for complete idiots

Å (abrév de **angström**) Å

Aaron /aʀɔ̃/ **NM** Aaron

AB (abrév de **assez bien**) quite good, ≃ C+

abaissable /abɛsabl/ **ADJ** *[siège]* reclining *(épith)*

abaissant, e /abɛsɑ̃, ɑt/ **ADJ** degrading

abaisse /abɛs/ **NF** rolled-out pastry ◆ **faites une ~ de 3 mm** roll out the pastry to a thickness of 3 mm

abaisse-langue /abɛslɑ̃g/ **NM INV** tongue depressor, spatula *(Brit)*

abaissement /abɛsmɑ̃/ **NM** 1 *(= action d'abaisser) [de levier] (en tirant)* pulling down; *(en poussant)* pushing down; *[de température, valeur, taux]* lowering, bringing down ◆ **l'~ de l'âge de la retraite/des barrières douanières** lowering the retirement age/customs barriers 2 *(= fait de s'abaisser) [de température, valeur, taux]* fall, drop *(de* in); *[de terrain]* downward slope ◆ **l'~ de la moralité** the decline in moral standards 3 *(= conduite obséquieuse)* subservience, self-abasement; *(= conduite choquante)* degradation 4 † *(= humiliation)* humiliation; *(= déchéance)* debasing; *(Rel)* humbling

abaisser /abese/ ▸ conjug 1 ◂ **VT** 1 *[+ levier] (= tirer)* to pull down; *(= pousser)* to push down; *[+ store]* to lower, to pull down; *[+ siège]* to put down ◆ **cette vitre s'abaisse-t-elle ?** does this window go down? ◆ **~ le drapeau** *(course automobile)* to lower the flag

2 *[+ température, valeur, taux]* to lower, to reduce; *[+ niveau, mur]* to lower ◆ **~ le coût de la main d'œuvre** to lower *ou* reduce labour costs ◆ **~ l'âge de la retraite** to bring down *ou* lower the retirement age

3 *(Math) [+ chiffre]* to bring down, to carry; *[+ perpendiculaire]* to drop

4 *(= rabaisser) [personne]* to humiliate; *[vice]* to debase; *(Rel)* to humble ◆ **~ la puissance des nobles** to reduce the power of the nobles

5 *(Culin) [+ pâte]* to roll out

VPR s'abaisser 1 *(= diminuer) [température, valeur, taux]* to fall, to drop; *[terrain]* to slope down; *(Théât) [rideau]* to fall *(sur* on)

2 *(= s'humilier)* to humble o.s. ◆ **je ne m'abaisserai pas à présenter des excuses** I won't stoop so low as to apologize

abaisseur /abɛsœʀ/ **ADJ M, NM** ◆ **(muscle) ~** depressor

abalone /abalɔn/ **NM** abalone

abandon /abɑ̃dɔ̃/ **NM** 1 *(= délaissement) [de personne, lieu]* desertion, abandonment ◆ **~ de poste** desertion of one's post ◆ **~ du domicile conjugal** *(Jur)* desertion

2 *(= renonciation) [d'idée, privilège, fonction, recherches]* giving up; *[de droit]* giving up, relinquishment; *[de course, championnat]* withdrawal *(de* from); ◆ **après l'~ de notre équipe** *(Sport)* after our team was forced to retire *ou* withdraw ◆ **gagner par ~** to win by default ◆ **faire ~ de ses biens à qn** to make over one's property to sb ◆ **faire ~ de ses droits sur** to relinquish *ou* renounce one's right(s) to ◆ **~ de soi-même** self-abnegation

3 *(= manque de soin)* neglected state ◆ **l'(état d')~ où se trouvait la ferme** the neglected state (that) the farm was in

◆ **à l'abandon** ◆ **jardin à l'~** neglected garden, garden run wild *ou* in a state of neglect ◆ **laisser qch à l'~** to neglect sth

4 *(= confiance)* lack of constraint ◆ **parler avec ~** to talk freely *ou* without constraint ◆ **dans ses moments d'~** in his moments of abandon, in his more expansive moments

5 *(= nonchalance)* **étendu sur le sofa avec ~** sprawled out on the sofa ◆ **l'~ de son attitude/ses manières** his relaxed *ou* easy-going attitude/manners

6 *(Ordin)* abort

abandonné, e /abɑ̃dɔne/ (ptp de **abandonner**) **ADJ** 1 *[attitude, position]* relaxed; *(avec volupté)* abandoned 2 *[jardin]* neglected; *[route, usine]* disused ◆ **vieille maison ~e** deserted old house 3 *(= délaissé) [conjoint]* abandoned ◆ **enfants ~s à eux-mêmes** children left to their own devices ◆ **tout colis ~ sera détruit** any luggage left unattended will be destroyed

abandonner /abɑ̃dɔne/ ▸ conjug 1 ◂ **VT** 1 *(= délaisser) [+ lieu]* to desert, to abandon; *[+ personne] (gén)* to leave, to abandon; *(intentionnellement)* to desert, to abandon; *[+ voiture, animal]* to abandon ◆ **il a été abandonné à la naissance** he was abandoned at birth ◆ **son courage l'abandonna** his courage failed *ou* deserted him ◆ **ses forces l'abandonnèrent** his strength failed him ◆ **l'ennemi a abandonné ses positions** the enemy abandoned their positions ◆ **~ son poste** *(Mil)* to desert one's post ◆ **~ le terrain** *(Mil)* to take flight; *(fig)* to give up ◆ **~ le domicile conjugal** *(Jur)* to desert *ou* abandon the family home ◆ **il a été abandonné des médecins** † the doctors have given up on him

2 *(= renoncer à) [+ fonction]* to give up, to relinquish; *[+ études, projet, recherches]* to give up, to abandon; *[+ matière scolaire]* to drop, to give up; *[+ technique]* to abandon, to give up; *[+ hypothèse]* to abandon, to drop; *[+ droit, privilèges]* to give up, to relinquish; *[+ course]* to withdraw *ou* retire from, to abandon ◆ **~ tout espoir (de faire qch)** to give up *ou* abandon all hope (of doing sth) ◆ **le joueur a dû ~** the player had to retire *ou* withdraw ◆ **~ le pouvoir** to give up power ◆ **~ la lutte** *ou* **la partie** *(lit, fig)* to give up the fight *ou* the struggle ◆ **~ les poursuites** *(Jur)* to drop the charges ◆ **j'abandonne !** I give up!

3 *(Ordin)* to abort

4 *(Bourse)* ◆ **le napoléon abandonne 1,5 € à 49,2 €** napoleons lost *ou* shed €1.5 at €49.2

5 ◆ **~ à** *(gén)* to give *ou* leave to ◆ **elle lui abandonna sa main** she let him take her hand ◆ **~ à qn le soin de faire qch** to leave it up to sb to do sth ◆ **~ qn à son (triste) sort** to leave *ou* abandon *(littér)* sb to their fate ◆ **~ qch au pillage/à la destruction** to leave sth to be pillaged/to be destroyed ◆ **le verger a été abandonné aux herbes folles** the orchard has become overrun with weeds ◆ **abandonnez votre corps aux délices d'un bain chaud** luxuriate in a hot bath

VPR s'abandonner 1 *(= se relâcher)* to let o.s. go; *(= se confier)* to open up ◆ **elle s'abandonna dans mes bras** she sank into my arms

◆ **s'abandonner à** *(= se laisser aller à) [+ passion, joie, débauche]* to give o.s. up to; *[+ paresse, désespoir]* to give way to ◆ **s'~ à la rêverie** to indulge in *ou* give o.s. up to daydreaming ◆ **s'~ au bien-être** to luxuriate in a sense of well-being ◆ **il s'abandonna au sommeil** he let himself drift off to sleep

2 *(† = se donner sexuellement)* to give o.s. *(à* to)

abaque /abak/ **NM** *(= boulier)* abacus; *(= graphique)* graph; *(Archit)* abacus

abasourdi, e /abazuʀdi/ **ADJ** stunned

abasourdir /abazuʀdiʀ/ ▸ conjug 2 ◂ **VT** 1 *(= étonner)* to stun, to dumbfound 2 *(= étourdir) [bruit]* to stun, to daze

abasourdissement /abazuʀdismɑ̃/ **NM** bewilderment, stupefaction

abâtardir /abɑtaʀdiʀ/ ▸ conjug 2 ◂ **VT** *[+ race, vertu]* to cause to degenerate; *[+ qualité]* to debase **VPR s'abâtardir** *[race, vertu]* to degenerate; *[qualité]* to become debased ◆ **langue abâtardie** bastardized *ou* debased language

abâtardissement /abɑtaʀdismɑ̃/ **NM** *[de race, vertu]* degeneration; *[de qualité]* debasement; *[de langue, style]* bastardization, debasement

abat-jour /abaʒuʀ/ **NM INV** *[de lampe]* lampshade; *(Archit)* splay

abats /aba/ NMPL *[de volaille]* giblets; *[de bœuf, porc]* offal

abat-son (pl **abat-sons**) /abasɔ̃/ NM louvre *(Brit) ou* louver *(US)* (boards)

abattage /abataʒ/ NM 1 *[d'animal]* slaughter, slaughtering; *[d'arbre]* felling, cutting (down); 2 *[de minerai]* extracting 3 **(vente à l')~** selling in bulk at knock-down prices 4 **avoir de l'~** * (= *entrain*) to be dynamic, to have plenty of go* ◆ **il a de l'~** (= *force*) he's a strapping fellow 5 *[de prostituée]* **faire de l'~**** to get through dozens of punters* (Brit) a day (*ou* night), to turn dozens of tricks** (US) a day (*ou* night)

abattant /abatɑ̃/ NM *[de table]* flap, leaf; *[de siège de W-C]* lid

abattement /abatmɑ̃/ NM 1 (= *dépression*) dejection, despondency ◆ **être dans un extrême ~** to be in very low spirits 2 (= *fatigue*) exhaustion 3 (*Fin* = *rabais*) reduction; *(fiscal)* (tax) allowance ◆ **~ forfaitaire** standard deduction *ou* allowance

abattis /abati/ NMPL *[de volaille]* giblets; (* = *bras et jambes*) limbs; → **numéroter** NM (*Can* = *terrain déboisé*) brushwood ◆ **faire un ~** to clear fell *(Brit) ou* clear cut *(US)* land

abattoir /abatwaʀ/ NM slaughterhouse, abattoir ◆ **envoyer des hommes à l'~** * to send men to the slaughter

abattre /abatʀ/ ▸ conjug 41 ◂ VT 1 (= *faire tomber*) *[+ maison, mur]* to pull *ou* knock down; *[+ arbre]* to cut down, to fell; *[+ roche, minerai]* to break away, to hew; *[+ quilles]* to knock down; *[+ avion]* to bring *ou* shoot down; *(fig) [+ adversaire, rival]* to bring down ◆ **le vent a abattu la cheminée** the wind blew the chimney down ◆ **la pluie abattait la poussière** the rain settled the dust

2 (= *tuer*) *[+ personne, oiseau]* to shoot down; *[+ fauve]* to shoot, to kill; *[+ animal domestique]* to destroy, to put down; *[+ animal de boucherie]* to slaughter ◆ **c'est l'homme à ~** *(fig)* he's the one you've (*ou* we've *etc*) got to get rid of

3 (= *ébranler*) *[fièvre]* to weaken, to drain (of energy); *[mauvaise nouvelle, échec]* to demoralize, to shatter*; *[efforts]* to tire out, to wear out ◆ **la maladie l'a abattu** the illness left him very weak, the illness drained him of energy ◆ **être abattu par la fatigue/la chaleur** to be overcome by tiredness/the heat

◆ **se laisser abattre** to get discouraged ◆ **Mme Martin, qui n'est pas femme à se laisser ~, est allée voir le maire** Mme Martin, who's not one to get discouraged, went to see the mayor ◆ **ne te laisse pas ~ !** don't get discouraged!, don't let things get you down! ◆ **se laisser ~ par des échecs** to be demoralized by failures

4 (= *affaiblir*) *[+ courage]* to weaken; *[+ fierté]* to humble

5 *[+ carte]* to lay down ◆ **~ son jeu** *ou* **ses cartes** *(lit, fig)* to lay *ou* put one's cards on the table, to show one's hand

6 (= *faire*) ◆ **~ du travail** to get through a lot of work

VPR **s'abattre** 1 (= *tomber*) *[personne]* to fall (down), to collapse; *[cheminée]* to fall *ou* crash down ◆ **le mât s'est abattu** the mast came *ou* went crashing down

2 ◆ **s'~ sur** *[pluie]* to beat down on; *[ennemi]* to swoop down on, to fall on; *[ciseau de proie]* to swoop down on; *[moineaux]* to sweep down on(to); *[coups, injures]* to rain on

abattu, e /abaty/ (ptp de **abattre**) ADJ (= *fatigué*) worn out, exhausted; (= *faible*) *[malade]* very weak, feeble; (= *déprimé*) downcast, demoralized; → **bride**

abat-vent (pl **abat-vent(s)**) /abavɑ̃/ NM *[de cheminée]* chimney cowl; *[de fenêtre, ouverture]* louvre *(Brit) ou* louver *(US)* (boards)

abbatial, e (mpl **-iaux**) /abasjal, jo/ ADJ abbey *(épith)* NF **abbatiale** abbey-church

abbaye /abei/ NF abbey

abbé /abe/ NM *[d'abbaye]* abbot; (= *prêtre*) priest ◆ **~ mitré** mitred abbot; → **monsieur**

abbesse /abɛs/ NF abbess

abc /abese/ NM (= *livre*) ABC *ou* alphabet book; (= *rudiments*) ABC, fundamentals ◆ **c'est l'~ du métier** it's basic to this job

abcès /apsɛ/ NM *(Méd)* abscess; *[de gencive]* gumboil, abscess ◆ **vider** *ou* **crever l'~** *(dans un conflit)* to clear the air ◆ **il faut crever l'~ au sein du parti** it's time to sort out the party's problems once and for all ◆ **~ de fixation** *(fig)* focal point for grievances

Abdias /abdjas/ NM Obadiah

abdication /abdikasjɔ̃/ NF *(lit, fig)* abdication ◆ **l'~ des parents devant leurs enfants** parents' abdication of authority over their children

abdiquer /abdike/ ▸ conjug 1 ◂ VI *[roi]* to abdicate ◆ **la justice abdique devant le terrorisme** justice gives way in the face of *ou* before terrorism ◆ **dans ces conditions j'abdique*** in that case I give up VT *[+ ambition, droits, valeurs, rôle, responsabilités]* to give up ◆ **~ la couronne** to abdicate the throne ◆ **~ ses croyances/son autorité** to give up *ou* renounce one's beliefs/one's authority

abdomen /abdɔmɛn/ NM abdomen

abdominal, e (mpl **-aux**) /abdɔminal, o/ ADJ abdominal NMPL **abdominaux** abdominals, stomach muscles ◆ **faire des abdominaux** to do *ou* work one's abdominals

abdos* /abdo/ NMPL (abrév de **abdominaux**) abs*

abducteur /abdyktœʀ/ ADJ M, NM ◆ **(muscle) ~** abductor (muscle)

abduction /abdyksjɔ̃/ NF *(Anat)* abduction

abécédaire /abesedɛʀ/ NM alphabet primer

abeille /abɛj/ NF bee ◆ **~ maçonne** mason bee ◆ **~ tueuse** killer bee; → **nid, reine**

Abel /abɛl/ NM Abel

aber /abɛʀ/ NM *(Géog)* aber

aberrant, e /abeʀɑ̃, ɑ̃t/ ADJ 1 (= *insensé*) absurd ◆ **c'est ~ !** it's absurd *ou* ridiculous! ◆ **il est ~ qu'il parte** it's absurd for him to leave 2 *(Bio)* aberrant; *(Ling)* irregular

> ⚠ Attention à ne pas traduire automatiquement **aberrant** par le mot anglais **aberrant**, qui a des emplois spécifiques et est d'un registre plus soutenu.

aberration /abeʀasjɔ̃/ NF 1 (= *absurdité*) **c'est une ~ !** it's absurd! ◆ **la cohabitation de ces deux peuples est une ~** it's absurd that these two peoples should live alongside one another ◆ **cette politique tarifaire est une ~** this pricing policy is absurd 2 (= *égarement*) **dans un moment** *ou* **instant d'~** in a moment of madness ◆ **dans un moment d'~, j'ai invité mon patron à dîner** in a moment of madness I invited my boss to dinner ◆ **par quelle ~ a-t-il accepté ?** whatever possessed him to accept? 3 *(Astron, Phys)* aberration COMP **aberration chromosomique** chromosomal abnormality

> ⚠ Attention à ne pas traduire automatiquement **aberration** par le mot anglais **aberration**, qui a des emplois spécifiques et est d'un registre plus soutenu.

abêtir VT, **s'abêtir** VPR /abetiʀ/ ▸ conjug 2 ◂ ◆ **ça va vous ~, vous allez vous ~** it'll addle your brain

abêtissant, e /abetisɑ̃, ɑ̃t/ ADJ *[travail]* mind-numbing

abêtissement /abetismɑ̃/ NM (= *état*) mindlessness ◆ **l'~ des masses par la télévision** (= *action*) the stupefying effect of television on the masses

abhorrer /abɔʀe/ ▸ conjug 1 ◂ VT *(littér)* to abhor, to loathe

Abidjan /abidʒɑ̃/ N Abidjan

abîme /abim/ NM 1 (= *gouffre*) abyss, gulf ◆ **l'~ qui nous sépare** *(fig)* the gulf *ou* chasm between us 2 *(locutions)* **au bord de l'~** *[pays, banquier]* on the brink *ou* verge of ruin; *[personne]* on the brink *ou* verge of despair ◆ **être au fond de l'~** *[personne]* to be in the depths of despair *ou* at one's lowest ebb; *[pays]* to have reached rock-bottom ◆ **les ~s de l'enfer/de la nuit/du temps** *(littér)* the depths of hell/night/time ◆ **être plongé dans un ~ de perplexité** *(frm)* to be utterly *ou* deeply perplexed ◆ **c'est un ~ de bêtise** *(frm)* he's abysmally *ou* incredibly stupid

abîmé, e /abime/ (ptp de **abîmer**) ADJ (= *détérioré*) damaged, spoiled ◆ **il était plutôt ~ * après le match** he was a bit battered and bruised after the match

abîmer /abime/ ▸ conjug 1 ◂ VT 1 (= *endommager*) to damage, to spoil ◆ **la pluie a complètement abîmé mon chapeau** the rain has ruined my hat 2 (** = *frapper*) **~ qn** to beat sb up ◆ **je vais t'~ le portrait** I'll smash your face in* VPR **s'abîmer** 1 *[objet]* to get damaged; *[fruits]* to go bad, to spoil ◆ **s'~ les yeux** to ruin *ou* strain one's eyes, to spoil one's eyesight 2 *(littér) [navire]* to sink, to founder; *[avion]* to crash ◆ **l'avion s'est abîmé dans la mer** the plane crash-landed in the sea ◆ **elle s'abîmait dans ses réflexions** she was lost in thought ◆ **s'~ dans la douleur** to lose o.s. in pain

abject, e /abʒɛkt/ ADJ despicable

abjectement /abʒɛktəmɑ̃/ ADV abjectly

abjection /abʒɛksjɔ̃/ NF abjection, abjectness

abjuration /abʒyʀasjɔ̃/ NF abjuration, recantation (*de* of); ◆ **faire ~ de** to abjure

abjurer /abʒyʀe/ ▸ conjug 1 ◂ VT to abjure, to recant

Abkhazie /abkazi/ NF Abkhazia

ablatif /ablatif/ NM ablative ◆ **à l'~** in the ablative ◆ **~ absolu** ablative absolute

ablation /ablasjɔ̃/ NF *(Méd)* removal, ablation (SPÉC); *(Géol)* ablation

ablette /ablɛt/ NF bleak

ablutions /ablysjɔ̃/ NFPL *(gén)* ablutions ◆ **faire ses ~** to perform one's ablutions

abnégation /abnegasjɔ̃/ NF (self-)abnegation, self-denial ◆ **avec ~** selflessly

aboiement /abwamɑ̃/ NM 1 *[de chien]* bark ◆ **~s** barking (NonC) 2 *(péj)* (= *cri*) shout, bark ◆ **~s** (= *critiques, exhortations*) rantings

abois /abwa/ NMPL baying ◆ **aux ~** *[animal]* at bay; *[personne]* in desperate straits; *(financièrement)* hard-pressed

abolir /abɔliʀ/ ▸ conjug 2 ◂ VT *[+ coutume, loi]* to abolish, to do away with

abolition /abɔlisjɔ̃/ NF abolition ◆ **l'~ de l'esclavage** the abolition of slavery

abolitionnisme /abɔlisjɔnism/ NM abolitionism

abolitionniste /abɔlisjɔnist/ ADJ, NMF abolitionist

abominable /abɔminabl/ ADJ 1 (= *monstrueux*) appalling 2 (= *exécrable*) *(sens affaibli) [repas, temps]* awful COMP **l'abominable homme des neiges** the abominable snowman

abominablement /abɔminabləmɑ̃/ ADV *[se conduire, s'habiller]* abominably ◆ **~ cher** terribly *ou* dreadfully expensive ◆ **~ laid** horribly *ou* dreadfully ugly

abomination /abɔminasjɔ̃/ NF (= *horreur, crime*) ◆ **c'est une ~ !** it's awful *ou* appalling! ◆ **dire des ~s** to say awful *ou* appalling things

abominer /abɔmine/ ► conjug 1 ◄ VT (*littér* = *exécrer*) to loathe, to abominate

abondamment /abɔ̃damɑ̃/ ADV (*gén*) abundantly, plentifully; [*écrire*] prolifically; [*manger, boire*] copiously; [*pleuvoir*] heavily; [*rincer*] thoroughly; [*illustré*] lavishly ◆ **prouver ~ qch** to provide ample proof *ou* evidence of sth ◆ **ce problème a été ~ commenté** much has been said about this issue

abondance /abɔ̃dɑ̃s/ NF 1 (= *profusion*) abundance ◆ **des fruits en ~** plenty of *ou* an abundance of fruit, fruit in abundance *ou* in plenty ◆ **ses larmes coulaient en ~** he wept profusely ◆ **il y a (une) ~ de** [+ *nourriture, gibier*] there is plenty of; [+ *détails, dossiers*] there are plenty of ◆ **année d'~** year of plenty ◆ **~ de biens ne nuit pas** (*Prov*) an abundance of goods does no harm; → **corne** 2 (= *richesses*) affluence ◆ **vivre dans l'~** to live in affluence ◆ **~ d'idées** wealth of ideas 3 ◆ **parler d'~** (= *improviser*) to improvise, to extemporize; (= *parler beaucoup*) to speak at length

abondant, e /abɔ̃dɑ̃, ɑ̃t/ ADJ [*documentation, bibliographie*] extensive; [*récolte*] fine (*épith*), abundant; [*réserves*] plentiful; [*végétation*] lush, luxuriant; [*chevelure*] thick; [*pluies*] heavy; [*larmes*] profuse, copious; (*Méd*) [*règles*] heavy ◆ **une ~e production littéraire** an extensive *ou* prolific literary output ◆ **recevoir un courrier ~** to receive a great deal of mail *ou* a large quantity of mail ◆ **il y a une ~e littérature sur ce sujet** a great deal has been written on the subject ◆ **cela requiert une main-d'œuvre ~e** it requires a plentiful *ou* an abundant supply of labour ◆ **il me fit d'~es recommandations** he gave me copious advice ◆ **illustré d'~es photographies** illustrated with numerous photographs, lavishly illustrated with photographs ◆ **les pêches sont ~es sur le marché** peaches are in plentiful *ou* generous supply ◆ **il lui faut une nourriture ~e** he must have plenty to eat *ou* plenty of food

abonder /abɔ̃de/ ► conjug 1 ◄ VI 1 (= *être nombreux*) [*exemples, projets, témoignages*] to abound ◆ **les erreurs abondent dans ce devoir** this essay is full of *ou* riddled with mistakes ◆ **les légumes abondent cette année** there are plenty of vegetables this year, vegetables are plentiful *ou* in plentiful supply this year ◆ **les rumeurs abondent sur le sujet** there are lots of rumours flying around about this

2 ◆ **~ en** (= *être plein de*) to be full of, to abound with *ou* in ◆ **les forêts abondent en gibier** the forests are teeming with *ou* abound with game ◆ **son œuvre abonde en images** his work is rich in *ou* is full of imagery ◆ **le marché abonde en nouveautés** the market is full of new products

3 (= *être d'accord*) **je ne peux qu'~ en ce sens** I fully agree *ou* I agree wholeheartedly (with that) ◆ **il a abondé dans notre sens** he was in complete *ou* full agreement with us

abonné, e /abɔne/ GRAMMAIRE ACTIVE 54.5 (ptp de **abonner**)

ADJ 1 (= *inscrit*) **être ~ à un journal** to subscribe to a paper ◆ **être ~ au téléphone** to have a phone ◆ **être ~ au gaz** to have gas, to be a gas consumer ◆ **être ~ au câble** to have cable (television) ◆ **être ~ à une messagerie électronique** to have *ou* to be on e-mail ◆ **être ~ à Internet** to be on the Internet

2 (* = *habitué*) **il y est ~ !** he makes (quite) a habit of it! ◆ **il est ~ à la première/dernière place** he always comes first/last ◆ **il semblait ~ au succès/à l'échec** he seemed to be on a winning/losing streak ◆ **nos entreprises publiques sont ~es aux déficits** our state-owned companies have quite a talent for losing money

NM,F (*Presse, Téléc, TV*) subscriber; [*de messagerie électronique, radiotéléphone*] user; [*d'électricité, gaz*] consumer; (*Rail, Sport, Théât*) season-ticket holder ◆ **il n'y a plus d'~ au numéro que vous avez demandé** the number you have dialled has been disconnected ◆ **se mettre** *ou* **s'inscrire aux ~s absents** (*Téléc*) to put one's phone on to the answering service ◆ **une fois encore, la commission est aux ~s absents** (*fig*) once again, there is no response from the commission

abonnement /abɔnmɑ̃/ NM (*Presse*) subscription; (*Rail, Sport, Théât*) season ticket ◆ **magazine vendu uniquement par** *ou* **sur ~** magazine available only on *ou* by subscription ◆ **prendre** *ou* **souscrire un ~ à un journal** to subscribe to *ou* take out a subscription to a paper ◆ **service (des) ~s** [*de journal, magazine*] subscriptions sales office ◆ **spectacle hors ~s** show not included on a season ticket ◆ **l'~ pour 10 séances d'UV coûte 100 €** a course of 10 sunbed sessions costs €100 ◆ **~ jeunes/familles** (*pour club, musée*) special (membership) rates for young people/families ◆ **(coût de l')~** (*Téléc*) rental; (*Gaz, Élec*) standing charge ◆ **tarif ~** [*de journal, magazine*] special subscription rate; → **carte**

abonner /abɔne/ ► conjug 1 ◄ VT ◆ **~ qn (à qch)** (*Presse*) to take out a subscription (to sth) for sb; (*Sport, Théât*) to buy sb a season ticket (for sth) VPR **s'abonner** (*Presse*) to subscribe, to take out a subscription (*à* to); (*Rail, Sport, Théât*) to buy a season ticket (*à* for); ◆ **s'~ au câble** to subscribe to cable (television) ◆ **s'~ à Internet** to get connected to *ou* get onto the Internet

abord /abɔʀ/ GRAMMAIRE ACTIVE 53.2, 53.5

NM 1 (= *manière d'accueillir*) manner ◆ **être d'un ~ rude/rébarbatif** to have a rough/an off-putting manner ◆ **être d'un ~ facile/difficile** to be approachable/not very approachable

2 (= *accès*) access, approach ◆ **lieu d'un ~ difficile** place with difficult means of access, place that is difficult to get to ◆ **lecture d'un ~ difficile** reading matter which is difficult to get into *ou* difficult to get to grips with

3 (*locutions*)

◆ **d'abord** (= *en premier lieu*) first; (= *au commencement*) at first; (= *essentiellement*) primarily; (*introduisant une restriction*) for a start, for one thing ◆ **allons d'~ chez le boucher** let's go to the butcher's first ◆ **il fut (tout) d'~ poli, puis il devint grossier** he was polite at first *ou* initially, and then became rude ◆ **cette ville est d'~ un centre touristique** this town is primarily *ou* first and foremost a tourist centre ◆ **d'~, il n'a même pas 18 ans** for a start *ou* in the first place, he's not even 18

◆ **dès l'abord** from the outset, from the very beginning

◆ **au premier abord** at first sight, initially

NMPL **abords** (= *environs*) (*gén*) surroundings; [*de ville, village*] outskirts ◆ **dans ce quartier et aux ~s** in this neighbourhood and the surrounding area

◆ **aux abords de** [*de ville, bâtiment*] in the area around *ou* surrounding; [*d'âge*] around, about; [*de date*] around ◆ **aux ~s de la soixantaine, il prit sa retraite** he retired when he was about sixty

abordable /abɔʀdabl/ ADJ [*prix*] reasonable; [*marchandise, menu*] affordable, reasonably priced; [*personne*] approachable; [*lieu*] accessible; [*auteur, texte*] accessible ◆ **livre peu ~** rather inaccessible book

abordage /abɔʀdaʒ/ NM 1 (= *assaut*) attacking ◆ **à l'~ !** up lads and at 'em! * ◆ **ils sont allés à l'~** they boarded the ship; → **sabre** 2 (= *accident*) collision

aborder /abɔʀde/ GRAMMAIRE ACTIVE 53.2, 53.3 ► conjug 1 ◄

VT 1 (= *arriver à*) [+ *rivage, tournant, montée*] to reach ◆ **les coureurs abordent la ligne droite** the runners are entering the home straight ◆ **il aborde la vieillesse avec inquiétude** he's worried about getting old ◆ **nous abordons une période difficile** we're about to enter a difficult phase

2 (= *approcher*) [+ *personne*] to approach, to go *ou* come up to ◆ **il m'a abordé avec un sourire** he came up to me *ou* approached me with a smile

3 [+ *sujet*] to broach; [+ *activité*] to take up, to tackle; [+ *problème*] to tackle ◆ **il n'a abordé le roman que vers la quarantaine** he didn't take up writing novels until he was nearly forty ◆ **j'aborde maintenant le second point** I'll now move on to the second point

4 [+ *navire*] (= *attaquer*) to board; (= *heurter*) to collide with

VI [*navire*] to land, to touch *ou* reach land ◆ **ils ont abordé à Carnac** they landed at Carnac

aborigène /abɔʀiʒɛn/ ADJ (*gén*) aboriginal; (*relatif aux peuplades australiennes*) Aboriginal NMF aborigine ◆ **~ d'Australie** (Australian) Aborigine

abortif, -ive /abɔʀtif, iv/ (*Méd*) ADJ abortive; → **pilule** NM abortifacient (*SPÉC*)

abouchement /abuʃmɑ̃/ NM (*Tech*) joining up end to end; (*Méd*) anastomosis

aboucher /abuʃe/ ► conjug 1 ◄ VT (*Tech*) to join up (end to end); (*Méd*) to join up, to anastomose (*SPÉC*) ◆ **~ qn avec** (*fig*) to put sb in contact *ou* in touch with VPR **s'aboucher** ◆ **s'~ avec qn** to get in touch with sb, to make contact with sb

Abou Dhabi /abudabi/ N Abu Dhabi

abouler* /abule/ ► conjug 1 ◄ VT (= *donner*) to hand over ◆ **aboule !** hand it over! *, give it here! * ◆ **aboule le fric !** come on, hand it over! * VPR **s'abouler** (= *venir*) to come ◆ **aboule-toi !** come (over) here!

aboulie /abuli/ NF ab(o)ulia

aboulique /abulik/ ADJ ab(o)ulic (*SPÉC*) NMF (*Méd*) person suffering from ab(o)ulia ◆ **son mari est un ~** (*fig*) her husband is utterly apathetic *ou* (totally) lacking in willpower

Abou Simbel /abusimbɛl/ N Abu Simbel

about /abu/ NM (*Tech*) butt

aboutement /abutmɑ̃/ NM (= *action*) joining (end to end); (= *état*) join

abouter /abute/ ► conjug 1 ◄ VT to join (up) (end to end)

abouti, e /abuti/ ADJ [*projet*] successfully completed; [*œuvre*] accomplished ◆ **très ~** [*produit*] very well-designed; [*spectacle, mise en scène*] highly polished ◆ **ce n'est pas très ~** it's far from perfect

aboutir /abutiʀ/ GRAMMAIRE ACTIVE 53.4 ► conjug 2 ◄ VI 1 (= *réussir*) [*démarche, personne*] to succeed ◆ **ses efforts/tentatives n'ont pas abouti** his efforts/attempts have come to nothing *ou* have failed ◆ **faire ~ des négociations/un projet** to bring negotiations/a project to a successful conclusion

2 (= *arriver à, déboucher sur*) **~ à** *ou* **dans** to end (up) in *ou* at ◆ **la route aboutit à un cul-de-sac** the road ends in a cul-de-sac ◆ **une telle philosophie aboutit au désespoir** such a philosophy results in *ou* leads to despair ◆ **~ en prison** to end up in prison ◆ **les négociations n'ont abouti à rien** the negotiations have come to nothing, nothing has come of the negotiations ◆ **il n'aboutira jamais à rien dans la vie** he'll never get anywhere in life ◆ **en additionnant le tout, j'aboutis à 12 €** adding it all up I get €12

aboutissants /abutisɑ̃/ NMPL → **tenant**

aboutissement /abutismɑ̃/ NM (= *résultat*) [*d'efforts, opération*] outcome, result; (= *succès*) [*de plan*] success

aboyer /abwaje/ ► conjug 8 ◄ VI to bark; (*péj* = *crier*) to shout, to yell ♦ ~ **après** *ou* **contre qn** to bark *ou* yell at sb; → **chien**

aboyeur † /abwajœʀ/ NM (*Théât.*) barker †; (*dans une réception*) usher (*who announces guests at a reception*)

abracadabra /abʀakadabʀa/ EXCL abracadabra

abracadabrant, e /abʀakadabʀɑ̃, ɑ̃t/ ADJ fantastic, preposterous ♦ **histoire** ~**e** cock-and-bull story

Abraham /abʀaam/ NM Abraham

abraser /abʀɑze/ ► conjug 1 ◄ VT to abrade

abrasif, -ive /abʀɑzif, iv/ ADJ, NM abrasive

abrasion /abʀɑzjɔ̃/ NF (*gén, Géog*) abrasion

abréaction /abʀeaksjɔ̃/ NF abreaction

abrégé /abʀeʒe/ NM [*de livre, discours*] summary, synopsis; [*de texte*] summary, précis; (= *manuel, guide*) short guide ♦ **faire un** ~ **de** to summarize, to précis ♦ ~ **d'histoire** concise guide to history

♦ **en abrégé** (= *en miniature*) in miniature; (= *en bref*) in brief, in a nutshell ♦ **répéter qch en** ~ to repeat sth in a few words ♦ **mot/phrase en** ~ word/sentence in a shortened *ou* an abbreviated form ♦ **voilà, en** ~**, de quoi il s'agissait** to cut (*Brit*) *ou* make (*US*) a long story short, this is what it was all about

abrègement /abʀɛʒmɑ̃/ NM [*ce durée*] cutting short, shortening; [*de texte*] abridgement

abréger /abʀeʒe/ ► conjug 3 et 6 ◄ VT [+ *vie*] to shorten; [+ *durée, visite*] to cut short, to shorten; [+ *conversation, vacances*] to cut short; [+ *texte*] to shorten, to abridge; [+ *mot*] to abbreviate, to shorten ♦ ~ **les souffrances de qn** to put an end to sb's suffering ♦ **pour** ~ **les longues soirées d'hiver** to while away the long winter evenings, to make the long winter evenings pass more quickly ♦ **version abrégée** [*de livre*] abridged version ♦ **forme abrégée** shortened *ou* abbreviated form ♦ **docteur s'abrège souvent en Dr** doctor is often shortened *ou* abbreviated to Dr ♦ **abrège !*** come *ou* get to the point!

abreuver /abʀœve/ ► conjug 1 ◄ VT [1] [+ *animal*] to water [2] (= *saturer*) ~ **qn de** to overwhelm *ou* shower sb with ♦ ~ **qn d'injures** to heap *ou* shower insults on sb ♦ **le public est abreuvé de films d'horreur** (*inondé*) the public is swamped with horror films; (*saturé*) the public has had its fill of *ou* has had enough of horror films [3] (= *imbiber*) (*gén*) to soak, to drench (*de* with); [+ *matière, surface*] to prime ♦ **terre abreuvée d'eau** sodden *ou* waterlogged ground VPR **s'abreuver** [*animal*] to drink; * [*personne*] to quench one's thirst ♦ **s'**~ **de télévision** (*péj*) to be addicted to television, to be a television addict

abreuvoir /abʀœvwaʀ/ NM (= *mare*) watering place; (= *récipient*) drinking trough

abréviation /abʀevjasjɔ̃/ NF abbreviation

abri /abʀi/ NM [1] (= *refuge, cabane*) shelter ♦ ~ **à vélos** bicycle shed ♦ ~ **souterrain/antiatomique** (*Mil*) air-raid/(atomic) fallout shelter ♦ **tous aux** ~**s !** (*hum*) take cover!, run for cover! ♦ **construire un** ~ **pour sa voiture** to build a carport ♦ **température sous** ~ shade temperature

[2] (= *protection*) refuge (*contre* from) protection (*contre* against); ♦ ~ **fiscal** tax shelter

♦ **à l'abri** ♦ **être/mettre à l'**~ (*des intempéries*) to be/put under cover; (*du vol, de la curiosité*) to be/put in a safe place ♦ **se mettre à l'**~ to shelter, to take cover ♦ **être à l'**~ **de** (= *protégé de*) [+ *pluie, vent, soleil*] to be sheltered from; [+ *danger, soupçons*] to be safe *ou* shielded from; (= *protégé par*) [+ *mur, feuillage*] to be sheltered *ou* shielded by ♦ **à l'**~ **des regards** hidden from view ♦ **personne n'est à l'**~ **d'une erreur** we all make mistakes ♦ **elle est à l'**~ **du besoin** she is free from financial worries ♦ **la solution retenue n'est pas à l'**~ **de la critique** the solution opted for is open to criticism *ou* is not above criticism ♦ **leur entreprise s'est développée à l'**~ **de toute concurrence** their company has grown because it has been shielded *ou* protected from competition ♦ **mettre qch à l'**~ **de** [+ *intempéries*] to shelter sth from; [+ *regards*] to hide sth from ♦ **mettre qch à l'**~ **d'un mur** to put sth in the shelter of a wall ♦ **conserver à l'**~ **de la lumière/de l'humidité** (*sur étiquette*) store *ou* keep in a dark/dry place ♦ **se mettre à l'**~ **de** [+ *pluie, vent, soleil*] to take shelter from; [+ *soupçons*] to place o.s. above ♦ **se mettre à l'**~ **du mur/du feuillage** to take cover *ou* shelter by the wall/under the trees; → **indiscret**

Abribus ® /abʀibys/ NM bus shelter

abricot /abʀiko/ NM (= *fruit*) apricot; → **pêche¹** ADJ INV apricot(-coloured)

abricoté, e /abʀikɔte/ ADJ [*gâteau*] apricot (*épith*); → **pêche¹**

abricotier /abʀikɔtje/ NM apricot tree

abriter /abʀite/ ► conjug 1 ◄ VT [1] (= *protéger*) (*de la pluie, du vent*) to shelter (*de* from); (*du soleil*) to shelter, to shade (*de* from); (*de radiations*) to screen (*de* from); ♦ **abritant ses yeux de sa main** shading his eyes with his hand ♦ **le côté abrité** (*de la pluie*) the sheltered side; (*du soleil*) the shady side ♦ **maison abritée** house in a sheltered spot

[2] (= *héberger*) [+ *réfugié*] to shelter, to give shelter to; [+ *criminel*] to harbour (*Brit*), to harbor (*US*) ♦ **ce bâtiment abrite 100 personnes/nos bureaux** the building accommodates 100 people/houses our offices ♦ **le musée abrite de superbes collections** the museum houses some very fine collections ♦ **la réserve abritait des espèces végétales uniques** the nature reserve provided a habitat for some unique plant species ♦ **le parti abrite différents courants** different political tendencies are represented in the party ♦ **l'écurie n'abrite plus que trois chevaux** only three horses are now kept in the stables

VPR **s'abriter** to (take) shelter (*de* from), to take cover (*de* from); ♦ **s'**~ **derrière la tradition/un alibi** to hide behind tradition/an alibi ♦ **s'**~ **derrière son chef/le règlement** to hide behind one's boss/the rules ♦ **s'**~ **des regards indiscrets** to avoid prying eyes

abrogatif, -ive /abʀɔgatif, iv/ ADJ rescissory

abrogation /abʀɔgasjɔ̃/ NF repeal, abrogation

abrogeable /abʀɔʒabl/ ADJ repealable

abroger /abʀɔʒe/ ► conjug 3 ◄ VT to repeal, to abrogate

abrupt, e /abʀypt/ ADJ [1] (= *escarpé*) [*pente*] abrupt, steep; [*falaise*] sheer [2] [*personne, ton*] abrupt, brusque; [*manières*] abrupt; [*jugement*] rash ♦ **de façon** ~**e** abruptly NM steep slope

abruptement /abʀyptəmɑ̃/ ADV [*descendre*] steeply, abruptly; [*annoncer*] abruptly

abruti, e /abʀyti/ (ptp de **abrutir**) ADJ [1] (= *hébété*) stunned, dazed (*de* with); ♦ ~ **par l'alcool** befuddled *ou* stupefied with drink [2] (* = *bête*) idiotic *, moronic * NM,F * idiot *

abrutir /abʀytiʀ/ ► conjug 2 ◄ VT [1] (= *fatiguer*) to exhaust ♦ **la chaleur m'abrutit** the heat makes me dopey * *ou* knocks me out ♦ ~ **qn de travail** to work sb silly *ou* stupid ♦ **ces discussions m'ont abruti** these discussions have left me quite dazed ♦ **s'**~ **à travailler** to work o.s. silly ♦ **leur professeur les abrutit de travail** their teacher drives them stupid with work ♦ **tu vas t'**~ **à force de lire** you'll overtax *ou* exhaust yourself reading so much [2] (= *abêtir*) ~ **qn** to deaden sb's mind ♦ **l'alcool l'avait abruti** he was stupefied with drink ♦ **s'**~ **à regarder la télévision** to become mindless through watching (too much) television

abrutissant, e /abʀytisɑ̃, ɑ̃t/ ADJ [*travail*] mind-destroying ♦ **ce bruit est** ~ this noise drives you mad *ou* wears you down

abrutissement /abʀytismɑ̃/ NM (= *fatigue extrême*) (mental) exhaustion; (= *abêtissement*) mindless state ♦ **l'**~ **des masses par la télévision** the stupefying effect of television on the masses

ABS /abeɛs/ NM (abrév de **Antiblockiersystem**) ABS

abscisse /apsis/ NF abscissa ♦ **en** ~ on the abscissa

abscons, e /apskɔ̃, ɔ̃s/ ADJ abstruse, recondite

absence /apsɑ̃s/ NF [1] [*de personne*] absence ♦ **qui avait remarqué son** ~ **à la réunion ?** who noticed his absence from the meeting *ou* the fact that he was not at the meeting? ♦ **cet employé accumule les** ~**s** this employee is frequently absent; → **briller**

[2] [*de chose*] (*positive*) absence; (*négative*) lack ♦ **l'**~ **de symptômes** the absence of symptoms ♦ **l'**~ **de concertation entre le gouvernement et les entrepreneurs** the lack of dialogue between government and business leaders ♦ ~ **de goût** lack of taste ♦ **l'**~ **de rideaux** the fact that there are (*ou* were) no curtains ♦ **il constata l'**~ **de sa valise** he noticed that his suitcase was missing

[3] (= *défaillance*) ~ **(de mémoire)** mental blank ♦ **il a des** ~**s** at times his mind goes blank

[4] (*locutions*)

♦ **en l'absence de** in the absence of ♦ **en l'**~ **de preuves** in the absence of proof ♦ **en l'**~ **de sa mère, c'est Anne qui fait la cuisine** Anne's doing the cooking while her mother's away *ou* in her mother's absence

absent, e /apsɑ̃, ɑ̃t/ ADJ [1] [*personne*] (*gén*) away (*de* from); (*pour maladie*) absent (*de* from), off * ♦ **être** ~ **de son travail** to be absent from work, to be off work * ♦ **il est** ~ **de Paris/de son bureau en ce moment** he's out of *ou* away from Paris/his office at the moment ♦ **conférence internationale dont la France était** ~**e** international conference from which France was absent

[2] [*sentiment*] lacking, absent; [*objet*] missing ♦ **discours d'où toute émotion était** ~**e** speech in which there was no trace of emotion ♦ **il constata que sa valise était** ~**e** he noticed that his suitcase was missing

[3] (= *distrait*) [*air*] vacant

[4] (*Jur*) missing

NM,F (*Scol*) absentee; (*littér* = *mort, en voyage*) absent one (*littér*); (= *disparu*) missing person ♦ **le ministre/le champion a été le grand** ~ **de la réunion** the minister/the champion was the most notable absentee at the meeting ♦ **les** ~**s ont toujours tort** (*Prov*) it's always the people who aren't there that get the blame

absentéisme /apsɑ̃teism/ NM (*gén*) absenteeism; (= *école buissonnière*) truancy

absentéiste /apsɑ̃teist/ NMF absentee ♦ **c'est un** ~**, il est du genre** ~ he is always *ou* frequently absent ♦ **propriétaire** ~ absentee landlord ♦ **élève** ~ truant

absenter (s') /apsɑ̃te/ ► conjug 1 ◄ VPR (*gén*) to go out, to leave; (*Mil*) to go absent ♦ **s'**~ **de** [+ *pièce*] to go out of, to leave; [+ *ville*] to leave ♦ **s'**~ **quelques instants** to go out for a few moments ♦ **je m'étais absenté de Paris** I was away from *ou* out of Paris ♦ **elle s'absente souvent de son travail** she is frequently off work * *ou* away from work ♦ **cet élève s'ab-**

sente trop souvent this pupil is too often absent (from school)

abside /apsid/ NF apse

absidial, e (mpl **-iaux**) /apsidjal, jo/ ADJ apsidal

absidiole /apsidjɔl/ NF apsidiole

absinthe /apsɛ̃t/ NF (= *liqueur*) absinth(e); (= *plante*) wormwood, absinth(e)

absolu, e /apsɔly/ ADJ 1 (= *total*) absolute ◆ **en cas d'~e nécessité** if absolutely necessary ◆ **être dans l'impossibilité ~e de faire qch** to find it absolutely impossible to do sth ◆ **c'est une règle ~e** it's a hard-and-fast rule, it's an unbreakable rule ◆ **j'ai la preuve ~e de sa trahison** I have absolute *ou* positive proof of his betrayal; → **alcool**

2 (= *entier*) [*ton*] peremptory; [*jugement, caractère*] rigid, uncompromising

3 (*opposé à relatif*) [*valeur, température*] absolute ◆ **considérer qch de manière ~e** to consider sth absolutely *ou* in absolute terms

4 [*majorité, roi, pouvoir*] absolute

5 (*Ling*) [*construction*] absolute ◆ **verbe employé de manière ~e** verb used absolutely *ou* in the absolute ◆ **génitif/ablatif ~** genitive/ablative absolute; → **superlatif**

NM ◆ **l'~** the absolute ◆ **juger dans l'~** to judge out of context *ou* in the absolute

absolument /apsɔlymɑ̃/ ADV 1 (= *entièrement*) absolutely ◆ **avoir ~ raison** to be completely right ◆ **s'opposer ~ à qch** to be entirely *ou* absolutely opposed to sth, to be completely *ou* dead* against sth ◆ **~ pas !** certainly not! ◆ **~ rien** absolutely nothing, nothing whatever 2 (= *à tout prix*) absolutely ◆ **vous devez ~ ...** you really must ... ◆ **il veut ~ revenir** he's determined to come back 3 (= *oui*) absolutely ◆ **vous êtes sûr ? – ~ !** are you sure? – definitely *ou* absolutely! 4 (*Ling*) absolutely

absolution /apsɔlysjɔ̃/ NF 1 (*Rel*) absolution (*de* from); ◆ **donner l'~ à qn** to give sb absolution 2 (*Jur*) dismissal (*of case, when defendant is considered to have no case to answer*)

absolutisme /apsɔlytism/ NM absolutism

absolutiste /apsɔlytist/ ADJ absolutistic NMF absolutist

absolutoire /apsɔlytwaʀ/ ADJ (*Rel, Jur*) absolutory

absorbable /apsɔʀbabl/ ADJ absorbable

absorbant, e /apsɔʀbɑ̃, ɑ̃t/ ADJ [*matière, papier*] absorbent; [*tâche*] absorbing, engrossing; (*Bot, Zool*) [*fonction, racines*] absorptive ◆ **société ~e** surviving company NM absorbent

absorber /apsɔʀbe/ ► conjug 1 ◄ VT 1 (= *avaler*) [*+ médicament*] to take; [*+ aliment, boisson*] to swallow; [*+ parti*] to absorb; [*+ firme*] to take over, to absorb

2 (= *résorber*) (*gén*) to absorb; [*+ liquide*] to absorb, to soak up; [*+ tache*] to remove, to lift; [*+ dette*] to absorb; [*+ bruit*] to absorb ◆ **crème vite absorbée par la peau** cream that is absorbed rapidly by the skin ◆ **le noir absorbe la lumière** black absorbs light ◆ **cet achat a absorbé presque toutes mes économies** I used up *ou* spent nearly all my savings when I bought that ◆ **ces dépenses absorbent 39% du budget** this expenditure accounts for 39% of the budget

3 (= *accaparer*) [*+ attention, temps*] to occupy, to take up ◆ **mon travail m'absorbe beaucoup, je suis très absorbé par mon travail** my work takes up *ou* claims a lot of my time ◆ **absorbé par son travail/dans sa lecture, il ne m'entendit pas** he was engrossed in *ou* absorbed in his work/in his book and he didn't hear me ◆ **cette pensée absorbait mon esprit, j'avais l'esprit absorbé par cette pensée** my mind was completely taken up with this thought

VPR **s'absorber** ◆ **s'~ dans une lecture/une tâche** (= *se plonger*) to become absorbed *ou* engrossed in a book/a task

absorbeur /apsɔʀbœʀ/ NM absorber ◆ **volant à ~ d'énergie** energy-absorbing steering wheel ◆ **~ d'odeur(s)** air freshener ◆ **~ d'humidité** dehumidifier

absorption /apsɔʀpsjɔ̃/ NF 1 [*de médicament*] taking; [*d'aliment*] swallowing ◆ **l'~ d'alcool est fortement déconseillée** you are strongly advised not to drink alcohol 2 [*de parti*] absorption; [*de firme*] takeover, absorption 3 (= *résorption*) (*gén*) absorption; [*de tache*] removal ◆ **les qualités d'~ des bruits du matériau** the ability of this material to absorb sound ◆ **l'~ des rayons ultraviolets par l'ozone** the absorption of ultra-violet rays by the ozone layer

absoudre /apsudʀ/ ► conjug 51 ◄ VT (*Rel, littér*) to absolve (*de* from); (*Jur*) to dismiss; → **absolution**

absoute /apsut/ NF [*d'office des morts*] absolution; [*de jeudi saint*] general absolution

abstenir (s') /apstəniʀ/ ► conjug 22 ◄ VPR 1 ◆ **s'~ de qch** to refrain *ou* abstain from sth ◆ **s'~ de faire** to refrain from doing ◆ **s'~ de vin** to abstain from wine ◆ **s'~ de boire du vin** to refrain from drinking wine ◆ **s'~ de tout commentaire, s'~ de faire des commentaires** to refrain from comment *ou* commenting ◆ **dans ces conditions je préfère m'~** in that case I'd rather not ◆ **"agences s'abstenir"** (*dans petites annonces*) "no agencies"; → **doute** 2 (*Pol*) to abstain (*de voter* from voting)

abstention /apstɑ̃sjɔ̃/ NF (*dans un vote*) abstention; (= *non-intervention*) non-participation

abstentionnisme /apstɑ̃sjɔnism/ NM abstaining, non-voting

abstentionniste /apstɑ̃sjɔnist/ NMF non-voter, abstainer

abstinence /apstinɑ̃s/ NF abstinence ◆ **faire ~** (*Rel*) to refrain from eating meat

abstinent, e /apstinɑ̃, ɑ̃t/ ADJ abstemious, abstinent

abstract /abstʀakt/ NM abstract

abstraction /apstʀaksjɔ̃/ NF (= *fait d'abstraire*) abstraction; (= *idée abstraite*) abstraction, abstract idea ◆ **faire ~ de** to leave aside, to disregard ◆ **en faisant ~** *ou* **~ faite des difficultés** leaving aside *ou* disregarding the difficulties

abstraire /apstʀɛʀ/ ► conjug 50 ◄ VT (= *isoler*) to abstract (*de* from) to isolate (*de* from); (= *conceptualiser*) to abstract VPR **s'abstraire** to cut o.s. off (*de* from)

abstrait, e /apstʀɛ, ɛt/ ADJ abstract NM 1 (= *artiste*) abstract painter ◆ **l'~** (= *genre*) abstract art 2 (*Philos*) **l'~** the abstract ◆ **dans l'~** in the abstract

abstraitement /apstʀɛtmɑ̃/ ADV abstractly, in the abstract

abstrus, e /apstʀy, yz/ ADJ abstruse, recondite

absurde /apsyʀd/ ADJ (*Philos*) absurd; (= *illogique*) absurd, preposterous; (= *ridicule*) absurd, ridiculous ◆ **ne sois pas ~ !** don't be ridiculous *ou* absurd! NM ◆ **l'~** the absurd ◆ **l'~ de la situation** the absurdity of the situation ◆ **raisonnement** *ou* **démonstration par l'~** reductio ad absurdum

absurdement /apsyʀdəmɑ̃/ ADV absurdly

absurdité /apsyʀdite/ NF absurdity ◆ **dire une ~** to say something absurd *ou* ridiculous ◆ **dire des ~s** to talk nonsense

Abû Dhabî /abudabi/ N ⇒ **Abou Dhabi**

Abuja /abuʒa/ N Abuja

abus /aby/ NM 1 (= *excès*) [*de médicaments, alcool, drogues*] abuse ◆ **20% des accidents sont dus à l'abus d'alcool** 20% of accidents are drink-related ◆ **l'incidence de l'~ d'alcool sur les comportements violents** the involvement of drink *ou* problem drinking in violent behaviour ◆ **l'~ d'aspirine** excessive use *ou* overuse of aspirin ◆ **nous avons fait des** *ou* **quelques ~ hier soir** we overdid it *ou* we overindulged last night ◆ **il y a de l'~ !*** that's going a bit too far!*, that's a bit much!

2 (= *injustice*) injustice ◆ **il n'a cessé de dénoncer les ~ dont sont victimes les Indiens** he has consistently drawn attention to the injustices suffered by the Indians

3 (= *mauvais usage*) abuse ◆ **le développement du travail indépendant autorise tous les ~** the growth in freelance work opens the way to all kinds of abuses

COMP **abus d'autorité** abuse *ou* misuse of authority

abus de biens sociaux (*Jur*) misuse of company property

abus de confiance (*Jur*) breach of trust; (= *escroquerie*) confidence trick

abus de langage misuse of language

abus de pouvoir abuse *ou* misuse of power

abus sexuels sexual abuse

abuser /abyze/ ► conjug 1 ◄ VT INDIR **abuser de** 1 (= *exploiter*) [*+ situation, crédulité*] to exploit, to take advantage of; [*+ autorité, puissance*] to abuse, to misuse; [*+ hospitalité, amabilité, confiance*] to abuse; [*+ ami*] to take advantage of ◆ **~ de sa force** to misuse one's strength ◆ **je ne veux pas ~ de votre temps** I don't want to take up *ou* waste your time ◆ **je ne voudrais pas ~ (de votre gentillesse)** I don't want to impose (upon your kindness) ◆ **~ d'une femme** (*gén*) to abuse a woman (sexually); (*euph*) to take advantage of a woman ◆ **alors là, tu abuses !** now you're going too far! *ou* overstepping the mark! ◆ **je suis compréhensif, mais il ne faudrait pas ~** I'm an understanding sort of person but don't try taking advantage *ou* don't push me too far ◆ **elle abuse de la situation** she's taking advantage*

2 (= *user avec excès*) **~ de l'alcool** to drink excessively *ou* to excess ◆ **~ de ses forces** to overexert o.s., to overtax one's strength ◆ **il ne faut pas ~ des médicaments/des citations** you shouldn't take too many medicines/use too many quotes ◆ **il ne faut pas ~ des bonnes choses** you can have too much of a good thing, enough is as good as a feast ◆ **il use et (il) abuse de métaphores** he uses too many metaphors

VT [*escroc*] to deceive; [*ressemblance*] to mislead ◆ **se laisser ~ par de belles paroles** to be taken in *ou* misled by fine words

VPR **s'abuser** (*frm*) (= *se tromper*) to be mistaken; (= *se faire des illusions*) to delude o.s. ◆ **si je ne m'abuse** if I'm not mistaken

abusif, -ive /abyzif, iv/ ADJ [*pratique*] improper; [*mère, père*] over-possessive; [*prix*] exorbitant, excessive; [*punition*] excessive ◆ **usage ~ de son autorité** improper use *ou* misuse of one's authority ◆ **usage ~ d'un mot** misuse *ou* wrong use of a word ◆ **c'est peut-être ~ de dire cela** it's perhaps putting it a bit strongly to say that

Abû Simbel /abusimbɛl/ N ⇒ **Abou Simbel**

abusivement /abyzivmɑ̃/ ADV (*Ling* = *improprement*) wrongly, improperly; (= *excessivement*) excessively, to excess ◆ **il s'est servi ~ de lui** he took advantage of him

abyme /abim/ NM ◆ **mise en ~** (*Littérat*) mise en abyme

abyssal, e (mpl **-aux**) /abisal, o/ ADJ (*Géog*) abyssal; (*fig*) unfathomable

abysse /abis/ NM (*Géog*) abyssal zone

abyssin, e /abisɛ̃, in/ ADJ ⇒ **abyssinien**

Abyssinie /abisini/ NF Abyssinia

abyssinien, -ienne /abisinjɛ̃, jɛn/ ADJ Abyssinian NM,F **Abyssinien(ne)** Abyssinian

AC /ase/ NF (abrév de **appellation contrôlée**) appellation contrôlée *(label guaranteeing district of origin of a wine)*

acabit /akabi/ NM *(péj)* ◆ **être du même** ~ to be cast in the same mould ◆ **ils sont tous du même** ~ they're all the same *ou* all much of a muchness ◆ **fréquenter des gens de cet** ~ to mix with people of that type *ou* like that

acacia /akasja/ NM (= *faux acacia*) locust tree, false acacia; (= *mimosacée*) acacia

académicien, -ienne /akademisjɛ̃, jɛn/ NM,F *(gén)* academician; *[de l'Académie française]* member of the Académie française, Academician; *(Antiq)* academic

académie /akademi/ NF 1 (= *société savante*) learned society; *(Antiq)* academy ◆ **l'Académie royale de** the Royal Academy of ◆ **l'Académie des sciences** the Academy of Science ◆ **l'Académie de médecine** the Academy of Medicine ◆ **l'Académie de chirurgie** the College of Surgeons ◆ **l'Académie (française)** the Académie française, the French Academy

2 (= *école*) academy ◆ ~ **de dessin/danse** art/dancing school, academy of art/dancing ◆ ~ **de cinéma** film school ◆ ~ **militaire** military academy ◆ ~ **de billard** billiard hall *(where lessons are given)*

3 *(Scol, Univ = région)* regional education authority

4 *(Art = nu)* nude; *(hum = anatomie)* anatomy *(hum)*

ACADÉMIE

France is divided into areas known as **académies** for educational administration purposes. Each **académie** is administered by a government representative, the « recteur d'académie ». Allocation of teaching posts is centralized in France, and newly qualified teachers often begin their careers in **académies** other than the one in which they originally lived.

Another significant feature of the **académies** is that their school holidays begin on different dates, partly to avoid congestion on popular holiday routes.

ACADÉMIE FRANÇAISE

Founded by Cardinal Richelieu in 1634, this prestigious learned society has forty elected life members, commonly known as « les Quarante » or « les Immortels ». They meet in a building on the quai Conti in Paris, and are sometimes referred to as « les hôtes du quai Conti ». The building's ornate dome has given rise to the expression « être reçu sous la coupole », meaning to be admitted as a member of the « Académie ». The main aim of the **Académie française** is to produce a definitive dictionary of the French language. This dictionary, which is not on sale to the general public, is often used to arbitrate on what is to be considered correct usage.

académique /akademik/ ADJ *(péj, littér, Art)* academic; *(de l'Académie française)* of the Académie Française, of the French Academy; *(Scol)* of the regional education authority ◆ **année** ~ *(Belg, Can, Helv)* academic year; → **inspection, palme**

académisme /akademism/ NM *(péj)* academicism

Acadie /akadi/ NF *(Hist)* Acadia ◆ **l'**~ *(Géog)* the Maritime Provinces

ACADIE

This area of eastern Canada was under French rule until the early eighteenth century, when it passed into the hands of the British. Most French-speaking **Acadiens** were deported, those who went to Louisiana becoming known as « Cajuns ». Many later returned to the Maritime Provinces of Canada, however, and formed a French-speaking community with a strong cultural identity that present-day **Acadiens** are eager to preserve.

acadien, -ienne /akadjɛ̃, jɛn/ ADJ Acadian NM *(Ling)* Acadian NM,F **Acadien(ne)** Acadian

acajou /akaʒu/ NM *(à bois rouge)* mahogany; (= *anacardier*) cashew ADJ INV mahogany *(épith)*

acalorique /akalɔʀik/ ADJ calorie-free

acanthe /akɑ̃t/ NF (= *plante*) acanthus ◆ **(feuille d')**~ *(Archit)* acanthus

a cap(p)ella /akapela/ LOC ADJ, LOC ADV a capella ◆ **chanter a cap(p)ella** to sing a capella

acariâtre /akaʀjɑtʀ/ ADJ *[caractère]* sour, cantankerous; *[personne]* cantankerous ◆ **d'humeur** ~ sour-tempered

acaricide /akaʀisid/ ADJ mite-killing, acaricidal *(SPEC)* NM mite-killer, acaricide *(SPEC)*

acarien /akaʀjɛ̃/ NM mite, acarid *(SPEC)*; *(dans la poussière)* dust mite

accablant, e /akablɑ̃, ɑ̃t/ ADJ *[chaleur]* oppressive; *[témoignage]* overwhelming, damning; *[responsabilité]* overwhelming; *[douleur]* excruciating; *[travail]* exhausting

accablement /akabləmɑ̃/ NM (= *abattement*) despondency, dejection; (= *oppression*) exhaustion

accabler /akable/ ► conjug 1 ◄ VT 1 *[chaleur, fatigue]* to overwhelm, to overcome; *(littér) [fardeau]* to weigh down ◆ **accablé de chagrin** prostrate *ou* overwhelmed with grief ◆ **les troupes, accablées sous le nombre** the troops, overwhelmed *ou* overpowered by numbers 2 *[témoignage]* to condemn, to damn ◆ **sa déposition m'accable** his evidence is overwhelmingly against me 3 (= *faire subir*) ~ **qn d'injures** to heap abuse on sb ◆ ~ **qn de reproches/critiques** to heap reproaches/criticism on sb ◆ **il m'accabla de son mépris** he poured scorn on me ◆ ~ **qn d'impôts** to overburden sb with taxes ◆ ~ **qn de travail** to overburden sb with work, to pile work on sb ◆ ~ **qn de questions** to bombard sb with questions ◆ **il nous accablait de conseils** *(iro)* he overwhelmed us with advice

accalmie /akalmi/ NF *(gén)* lull; *[de vent, tempête]* lull *(de* in); *[de fièvre]* respite *(dans* in) remission *(dans* of); *[d'affaires, transactions]* slack period; *[de combat]* lull, break; *[de crise politique ou morale]* period of calm, lull *(de* in); ◆ **profiter d'une** ~ **pour sortir** to take advantage of a calm spell to go out ◆ **nous n'avons pas eu un seul moment d'**~ **pendant la journée** we didn't have a single quiet moment during the whole day

accaparant, e /akapaʀɑ̃, ɑ̃t/ ADJ *[métier, enfant]* demanding

accaparement /akapaʀmɑ̃/ NM *[de pouvoir, production]* monopolizing; *[de marché]* cornering, capturing

accaparer /akapaʀe/ ► conjug 1 ◄ VT 1 (= *monopoliser) [+ production, pouvoir, conversation, attention, hôte]* to monopolize; *[+ marché, vente]* to corner, to capture ◆ **les enfants l'ont tout de suite accaparée** the children claimed all her attention straight away ◆ **ces élèves brillants qui accaparent les prix** those bright pupils who carry off all the prizes ◆ **il accapare la salle de bains pendant des heures** he hogs* the bathroom for hours 2 (= *absorber) [travail]* to take up the time and energy of ◆ **il est complètement accaparé par sa profession** his job takes up all his time and energy ◆ **les enfants l'accaparent** the children take up all her time (and energy)

accapareur, -euse /akapaʀœʀ, øz/ ADJ monopolistic NM,F *(péj)* monopolizer, grabber*

accédant, e /aksedɑ̃, ɑ̃t/ NM,F ◆ ~ **(à la propriété)** first-time property owner *ou* homeowner

accéder /aksede/ GRAMMAIRE ACTIVE 39.3 ► conjug 6 ◄ VT INDIR **accéder à** 1 (= *atteindre) [+ lieu, sommet]* to reach, to get to; *[+ honneur, indépendance]* to attain; *[+ grade]* to rise to; *[+ responsabilité]* to accede to ◆ ~ **directement à** to have direct access to ◆ **on accède au château par le jardin** you can get to the castle through the garden, access to the castle is through the garden ◆ ~ **au trône** to accede to the throne ◆ ~ **à la propriété** to become a property owner *ou* homeowner, to buy property for the first time 2 *(Ordin)* to access 3 (= *exaucer) [+ requête, prière]* to grant, to accede to *(frm)*; *[+ vœux]* to meet, to comply with; *[+ demande]* to accommodate, to comply with

accélérateur, -trice /akseleʀatœʀ, tʀis/ ADJ accelerating NM accelerator ◆ ~ **de particules** particle accelerator ◆ **donner un coup d'**~ *(lit)* to accelerate, to step on it*; (= *se dépêcher*) to step on it*, to get a move on* ◆ **donner un coup d'**~ **à l'économie** to give the economy a boost ◆ **donner un coup d'**~ **aux réformes** to speed up the reforms

accélération /akseleʀasjɔ̃/ NF *[de véhicule, machine]* acceleration; *[de travail]* speeding up; *[de pouls]* quickening ◆ **l'**~ **de l'histoire** the speeding-up of the historical process

accéléré, e /akseleʀe/ ADJ accelerated ◆ **à un rythme** ~ quickly ◆ **procédure** ~**e** *(Jur)* expeditious procedure NM *(Ciné)* speeded-up motion

◆ **en accéléré** ◆ **film en** ~ speeded-up film ◆ **faire défiler une vidéo en** ~ to fast-forward a video

accélérer /akseleʀe/ ► conjug 6 ◄ VT *[+ rythme]* to speed up, to accelerate; *[+ processus, travail]* to speed up ◆ ~ **le pas** to quicken one's pace *ou* step ◆ **il faut** ~ **la baisse des taux d'intérêt** interest rates must be lowered more quickly ◆ ~ **le mouvement** to get things moving, to hurry *ou* speed things up; → **cours, formation, vitesse** VI to accelerate, to speed up ◆ **accélère !*** hurry up!, get a move on!* VPR **s'accélérer** *[rythme]* to speed up, to accelerate; *[pouls]* to quicken; *[événements]* to gather pace

accéléromètre /akseleʀɔmɛtʀ/ NM accelerometer

accent /aksɑ̃/ NM 1 (= *prononciation*) accent ◆ **avoir l'**~ **paysan/du Midi** to have a country/southern (French) accent ◆ **parler sans** ~ to speak without an accent

2 *(Orthographe)* accent ◆ **y a-t-il un** ~ **sur le e ?** is there an accent on the e?

3 *(Phon)* accent, stress; *(fig)* stress ◆ **mettre l'**~ **sur** *(lit)* to stress, to put the stress *ou* accent on; *(fig)* to stress, to emphasize ◆ **l'**~ **est mis sur la production** the emphasis is on production

4 (= *inflexion*) tone (of voice) ◆ ~ **suppliant/plaintif** beseeching/plaintive tone ◆ ~ **de sincérité/de détresse** note of sincerity/of distress ◆ **récit qui a l'**~ **de la sincérité** story which has a ring of sincerity ◆ **avec des** ~**s de rage** in accents of rage ◆ **les** ~**s de cette musique** the strains of this music ◆ **les** ~**s de l'espoir/de l'amour** the accents of hope/love ◆ **un discours aux** ~**s nationalistes** a speech with nationalist undertones

COMP **accent aigu** acute accent ◆ **e** ~ **aigu** e acute

accent circonflexe circumflex (accent)

◆ **sourcils en ~ circonflexe** arched eyebrows
accent grave grave accent ◆ **e ~ grave** e grave
accent de hauteur pitch
accent d'intensité tonic *ou* main stress
accent de mot word stress
accent nasillard nasal twang
accent de phrase sentence stress
accent tonique ⇒ **accent d'intensité**
accent traînant drawl

accenteur /aksɑ̃tœʀ/ NM ◆ **~ mouchet** dunnock, hedge sparrow

accentuation /aksɑ̃tɥasjɔ̃/ NF [1] *[de lettre]* accentuation; *[de syllabe]* stressing, accentuation ◆ **les règles de l'~** *(Phon)* the rules of stress ◆ **faire des fautes d'~** to get the stress wrong [2] *[de silhouette, contraste, inégalités]* accentuation; *[d'effort, poussée]* intensification *(de* in); ◆ **une ~ de la récession** a deepening of the recession

accentué, e /aksɑ̃tɥe/ (ptp de **accentuer**) ADJ *(= marqué)* marked, pronounced; *(= croissant)* increased; *[lettre, caractère]* accented

accentuel, -elle /aksɑ̃tɥɛl/ ADJ *[syllabe]* stressed, accented ◆ **système ~ d'une langue** stress *ou* accentual system of a language

accentuer /aksɑ̃tɥe/ ▸ conjug 1 ◂ VT [1] *[+ lettre]* to accent; *[+ syllabe]* to stress, to accent ◆ **syllabe (non) accentuée** (un)stressed *ou* (un)accented syllable [2] *[+ silhouette, contraste, inégalités]* to accentuate; *[+ goût]* to bring out; *[+ effort, poussée]* to increase, to intensify ◆ **les cours du pétrole ont accentué leur repli** oil prices are sinking further VPR **s'accentuer** *[tendance, hausse, contraste, traits]* to become more marked *ou* pronounced ◆ **l'inflation s'accentue** inflation is becoming more pronounced *ou* acute ◆ **le froid s'accentue** it's becoming colder

acceptabilité /aksɛptabilite/ NF *(Ling)* acceptability

acceptable /aksɛptabl/ GRAMMAIRE ACTIVE 38.2 ADJ [1] *(= passable)* satisfactory, fair ◆ **ce café/vin est ~** this coffee/wine is reasonable *ou* okay* [2] *(= recevable) [condition]* acceptable [3] *(Ling)* acceptable

acceptation /aksɛptasjɔ̃/ NF *(gén)* acceptance ◆ **~ bancaire** bank acceptance

accepter /aksɛpte/ GRAMMAIRE ACTIVE 39.1, 46.5, 52.1, 52.5 ▸ conjug 1 ◂ VT [1] *(= recevoir volontiers)* to accept; *[+ proposition, condition]* to agree to, to accept; *[+ pari]* to take on, to accept ◆ **acceptez-vous les chèques ?** do you take cheques? ◆ **acceptez-vous Jean Leblanc pour époux ?** do you take Jean Leblanc to be your husband? ◆ **elle accepte tout de sa fille** she puts up with *ou* takes anything from her daughter ◆ **j'en accepte l'augure** *(littér, hum)* I'd like to believe it ◆ **~ le combat** *ou* **le défi** to take up *ou* accept the challenge ◆ **elle a été bien acceptée dans le club** she's been well received at the club ◆ **il n'accepte pas que la vie soit une routine** he won't accept that life should be a routine ◆ **~ la compétence des tribunaux californiens** to defer to California jurisdiction [2] *(= être d'accord)* to agree *(de faire* to do); ◆ **je n'accepterai pas que tu partes** I won't let you leave ◆ **je n'accepte pas de partir** I refuse to leave, I will not leave ◆ **je ne crois pas qu'il acceptera** I don't think he'll agree

acception /aksɛpsjɔ̃/ NF *(Ling)* meaning, sense ◆ **dans toute l'~ du mot** *ou* **terme** in every sense *ou* in the full meaning of the word, using the word in its fullest sense ◆ **sans ~ de** without distinction of

accès /aksɛ/ NM [1] *(= possibilité d'approche)* access *(NonC)* ◆ **une grande porte interdisait l'~ du jardin** a big gate prevented access to the garden ◆ **"accès interdit à toute personne étrangère aux travaux"** "no entry *ou* no admittance to unauthorized persons" ◆ **l'~ aux soins/au logement** access to health care/to housing ◆ **"accès aux quais"** "to the trains"
◆ **d'accès facile** *[lieu, port]* (easily) accessible; *[personne]* approachable; *[traité, manuel]* easily understood; *[style]* accessible
◆ **d'accès difficile** *[lieu]* hard to get to, not very accessible; *[personne]* not very approachable; *[traité, manuel]* hard to understand
◆ **avoir accès à qch** to have access to sth
◆ **avoir accès auprès de qn** to have access to sb
◆ **donner accès à** *[+ lieu]* to give access to; *(en montant)* to lead up to; *[+ carrière]* to open the door *ou* way to
[2] *(= voie)* **les ~ de la ville** the approaches to the town ◆ **les ~ de l'immeuble** the entrances to the building
[3] *(Ordin)* access ◆ **port/temps/point d'~** access port/time/point ◆ **~ protégé** restricted access ◆ **~ aux données** access to data
[4] *(= crise) [de colère, folie]* fit; *[de fièvre]* attack, bout; *[d'enthousiasme]* burst ◆ **~ de toux** fit *ou* bout of coughing ◆ **être pris d'un ~ de mélancolie/de tristesse** to be overcome by melancholy/sadness ◆ **la Bourse de Paris a eu un ~ de faiblesse** the Paris Bourse dipped slightly ◆ **par ~** on and off

accessibilité /aksesibilite/ NF accessibility *(à* to)

accessible /aksesibl/ ADJ *[lieu]* accessible *(à* to); *[personne]* approachable; *[œuvre]* accessible; *[but]* attainable; *(Ordin)* accessible ◆ **parc ~ au public** gardens open to the public ◆ **elle n'est ~ qu'à ses amies** only her friends are able *ou* allowed to see her ◆ **ces études sont ~s à tous** the course is open to everyone; *(financièrement)* the course is within everyone's pocket; *(intellectuellement)* the course is within the reach of everyone ◆ **être ~ à la pitié** to be capable of pity

accession /aksesjɔ̃/ NF ◆ **~ à** *[+ pouvoir, fonction]* accession to; *[+ indépendance]* attainment of; *[+ rang]* rise to; *(frm) [+ requête, désir]* granting of, compliance with ◆ **pour faciliter l'~ à la propriété** to facilitate home ownership

accessit /aksesit/ NM *(Scol)* ≈ certificate of merit

accessoire /akseswaʀ/ ADJ *[idée]* of secondary importance; *[clause]* secondary ◆ **l'un des avantages ~s de ce projet** one of the added *ou* incidental advantages of this plan ◆ **c'est d'un intérêt tout ~** this is only of minor *ou* incidental interest ◆ **frais ~s** *(gén)* incidental expenses; *(Fin, Comm)* ancillary costs ◆ **dommages-intérêts ~s** *(Jur)* incidental damages NM [1] *(gén)* accessory; *(Théât)* prop ◆ **~s de toilette** toilet accessories; → **magasin** [2] *(Philos)* **l'~** the unessential ◆ **distinguer l'essentiel de l'~** to distinguish essentials from non-essentials

accessoirement /akseswaʀmɑ̃/ ADV incidentally; *(= en conséquence)* consequently, ultimately ◆ **~, son nom complet est William Jefferson Clinton** incidentally, his full name is William Jefferson Clinton

accessoiriser /akseswaʀize/ ▸ conjug 1 ◂ VT *[+ tailleur, costume]* to accessorize

accessoiriste /akseswaʀist/ NM prop(s) man NF prop(s) woman

accident /aksidɑ̃/ NM [1] *(gén)* accident; *[de voiture, train]* accident, crash; *[d'avion]* crash ◆ **il n'y a pas eu d'~ de personnes** there were no casualties, no one was injured ◆ **il y a eu plusieurs ~s mortels sur la route** there have been several road deaths *ou* several fatalities on the roads ◆ **avoir un ~** to have an accident, to meet with an accident
[2] *(= mésaventure)* **les ~s de sa carrière** the setbacks in his career ◆ **les ~s de la vie** life's ups and downs, life's trials ◆ **les ~s qui ont entravé la réalisation du projet** the setbacks *ou* hitches which held up the project ◆ **c'est un simple ~, il ne l'a pas fait exprès** it was just an accident, he didn't do it on purpose
[3] *(Méd)* illness, trouble ◆ **elle a eu un petit ~ de santé** she's had a little trouble with her health ◆ **un ~ secondaire** a complication
[4] *(Philos)* accident
[5] *(littér) (= hasard)* (pure) accident; *(= fait mineur)* minor event ◆ **par ~** by chance, by accident ◆ **si par ~ tu ...** if by chance you ..., if you happen to ...
[6] *(Mus)* accidental
COMP **accident d'avion** air *ou* plane crash
accident cardiaque heart attack
accident de la circulation road accident
accident corporel personal accident, accident involving bodily injury
accidents domestiques accidents in the home
accident de montagne mountaineering *ou* climbing accident
accident de parcours hiccup *(fig)*
accident de la route ⇒ **accident de la circulation**
accident de terrain accident *(SPÉC)*, undulation ◆ **les ~s de terrain** the unevenness of the ground
accident du travail accident at work, industrial accident
accident vasculaire cérébral stroke, cerebro-vascular accident *(SPEC)*
accident de voiture car accident *ou* crash

accidenté, e /aksidɑ̃te/ (ptp de **accidenter**) ADJ [1] *[région]* undulating, hilly; *[terrain]* uneven; *[carrière]* chequered *(Brit)*, checkered *(US)* [2] *[véhicule]* damaged; *[avion]* crippled NM,F casualty, injured person ◆ **~ de la route** road accident victim ◆ **~ du travail** victim of an accident at work *ou* of an industrial accident

accidentel, -elle /aksidɑ̃tɛl/ ADJ *(= fortuit) [événement]* accidental, fortuitous; *(= par accident) [mort]* accidental; → **signe**

accidentellement /aksidɑ̃tɛlmɑ̃/ ADV [1] *(= par hasard)* accidentally, by accident *ou* chance ◆ **il était là ~** he just happened to be there [2] *[mourir]* in an accident

accidenter /aksidɑ̃te/ ▸ conjug 1 ◂ VT *[+ personne]* to injure, to hurt; *[+ véhicule]* to damage

accidentogène /aksidɑ̃tɔʒɛn/ ADJ ◆ **risque ~** accident risk ◆ **zone ~** accident risk area

accise /aksiz/ NF *(Belg, Can)* excise ◆ **droits d'~** excise duties

acclamation /aklamasjɔ̃/ NF ◆ **élire qn par ~** to elect sb by acclamation ◆ **~s** cheers, cheering ◆ **il est sorti sous les ~s du public** he left to great cheering from the audience

acclamer /aklame/ ▸ conjug 1 ◂ VT to cheer, to acclaim ◆ **on l'acclama roi** they acclaimed him king

acclimatable /aklimatabl/ ADJ acclimatizable, acclimatable *(US)*

acclimatation /aklimatasjɔ̃/ NF acclimatization, acclimation *(US)*; → **jardin**

acclimatement /aklimatmɑ̃/ NM acclimatization, acclimation *(US)*

acclimater /aklimate/ ▸ conjug 1 ◂ VT *[+ plante, animal]* to acclimatize, to acclimate *(US)*; *[+ idée, usage]* to introduce VPR **s'acclimater** *[personne, animal, plante]* to become acclimatized, to adapt (o.s. *ou* itself) *(à* to); *[usage, idée]* to become established *ou* accepted

accointances /akwɛ̃tɑ̃s/ NFPL *(péj)* contacts, links ◆ **avoir des ~** to have contacts *(avec* with; *dans* in, among)

accolade /akɔlad/ NF [1] *(= embrassade)* embrace *(on formal occasion)*; *(Hist = coup d'épée)* accolade ◆ **donner/recevoir l'~** to embrace/be embraced [2] *(Typo)* brace ◆ **mots (mis) en ~** words bracketed together [3] *(Archit, Mus)* accolade

accoler /akɔle/ ► conjug 1 ◄ VT *(gén)* to place side by side; *(Typo)* to bracket together ◆ **~ une chose à une autre** to place one thing beside *ou* next to another ◆ **il avait accolé à son nom celui de sa mère** he had joined *ou* added his mother's maiden name to his surname

accommodant, e /akɔmɔdɑ̃, ɑ̃t/ ADJ accommodating

accommodation /akɔmɔdasjɔ̃/ NF *(Opt)* accommodation; *(= adaptation)* adaptation

accommodement /akɔmɔdmɑ̃/ NM [1] *(littér = arrangement)* compromise, accommodation *(littér)* ◆ **trouver des ~s avec le ciel/avec sa conscience** to come to an arrangement with the powers above/with one's conscience [2] *(Culin)* preparation

accommoder /akɔmɔde/ ► conjug 1 ◄ VT [1] *[+ plat]* to prepare *(à* in, with); ◆ **~ les restes** to use up the left-overs

[2] *(= concilier)* **~ le travail avec le plaisir** to combine business with pleasure ◆ **~ ses principes aux circonstances** to adapt *ou* alter one's principles to suit the circumstances

[3] †† *(= arranger) [+ affaire]* to arrange; *[+ querelle]* to put right; *(= réconcilier) [+ ennemis]* to reconcile, to bring together; *(= malmener)* to treat harshly ◆ **~ qn** *(= installer confortablement)* to make sb comfortable

VI *(Opt)* to focus *(sur* on)

VPR **s'accommoder** [1] **s'~ à** † *(= s'adapter à)* to adapt to

[2] *(= supporter)* **s'~ de** *[+ personne]* to put up with ◆ **il lui a bien fallu s'en ~** he just had to put up with it *ou* accept it ◆ **je m'accommode de peu** I'm content *ou* I can make do with little ◆ **elle s'accommode de tout** she'll put up with anything ◆ **il s'accommode mal de la vérité** he's uncomfortable *ou* doesn't feel at home with the truth

[3] *(= s'arranger avec)* **s'~ avec** † *[+ personne]* to come to an agreement *ou* arrangement with *(sur* about); ◆ **son allure s'accommode mal avec sa vie d'ascète** his appearance is hard to reconcile with his ascetic lifestyle

[4] *(Culin)* **le riz peut s'~ de plusieurs façons** rice can be served in several ways

accompagnateur, -trice /akɔ̃paɲatœʀ, tʀis/ NM,F *(Mus)* accompanist; *(= guide)* guide; *(Scol)* accompanying adult; *[de voyage organisé]* courier

accompagnement /akɔ̃paɲmɑ̃/ NM [1] *(Mus)* accompaniment ◆ **sans ~** unaccompanied ◆ **musique d'~** accompanying music [2] *(Culin)* accompaniment ◆ **(servi) en ~ de** served with [3] *(= escorte)* escort; *(fig)* accompaniment ◆ **l'~ d'un malade** giving (psychological) support to a terminally-ill patient ◆ **mesures/plan d'~** *[de loi, réforme]* accompanying measures/programme ◆ **livret d'~** *[de vidéo]* accompanying booklet

accompagner /akɔ̃paɲe/ ► conjug 1 ◄ VT [1] *(= escorter)* to go with, to accompany; *[+ malade]* to give (psychological) support to ◆ **~ un enfant à l'école** to take a child to school ◆ **~ qn à la gare** to go to the station with sb ◆ **il s'était fait ~ de sa mère** he had got his mother to go with him *ou* to accompany him ◆ **Mark est-il ici ? – oui, il m'a accompagnée** is Mark here? – yes, he came with me ◆ **être accompagné de *ou* par qn** to have sb with one, to be with sb ◆ **est-ce que vous êtes accompagné ?** have you got somebody with you? is there somebody with you? ◆ **tous nos vœux vous accompagnent** all our good wishes go with you ◆ **mes pensées t'accompagnent** my thoughts are with you ◆ **~ qn du regard** to follow sb with one's eyes

[2] *(= assortir)* to accompany, to go with ◆ **il accompagna ce mot d'une mimique expressive** he gestured expressively as he said the word ◆ **une lettre accompagnait les fleurs** a letter came with the flowers ◆ **l'agitation qui accompagna son arrivée** the fuss surrounding his arrival

[3] *(Mus)* to accompany *(à* on)

[4] *(Culin)* **du chou accompagnait le rôti** the roast was served with cabbage ◆ **le beaujolais est ce qui accompagne le mieux cette viande** a Beaujolais goes best with this meat, Beaujolais is the best wine to serve with this meat

VPR **s'accompagner** [1] ◆ **s'~ de** *(= s'assortir de)* to be accompanied by ◆ **leurs discours doivent s'~ de mesures concrètes** their speeches must be backed up with concrete measures, they need to follow their speeches up with concrete measures ◆ **la guerre s'accompagne toujours de privations** war is always accompanied by hardship ◆ **le poisson s'accompagne d'un vin blanc sec** fish is served with a dry white wine

[2] *(Mus)* ◆ **s'~ à** to accompany o.s. on ◆ **il s'accompagna (lui-même) à la guitare** he accompanied himself on the guitar

> ⚠ Attention à ne pas traduire automatiquement **accompagner** par **to accompany**, qui est d'un registre plus soutenu.

accompli, e /akɔ̃pli/ (ptp de **accomplir**) ADJ [1] *(= parfait, expérimenté)* accomplished; *(Ling) [+ aspect]* perfective [2] *(= révolu)* **avoir 60 ans ~s** to be over 60, to have turned 60; → **fait¹**

accomplir /akɔ̃pliʀ/ ► conjug 2 ◄ VT [1] *[+ devoir, tâche]* to carry out; *[+ exploit]* to achieve; *[+ mission]* to accomplish; *[+ promesse]* to fulfil; *[+ rite]* to perform ◆ **~ des merveilles** to work wonders ◆ **les progrès accomplis dans ce domaine** advances (made) in this field ◆ **il a enfin pu ~ ce qu'il avait décidé de faire** at last he managed to achieve what he had decided to do ◆ **la satisfaction du devoir accompli** the satisfaction of having done one's duty

[2] *[+ apprentissage, service militaire] (= faire)* to do; *(= terminer)* to complete

VPR **s'accomplir** [1] *(= se réaliser) [souhait]* to come true ◆ **la volonté de Dieu s'est accomplie** God's will was done

[2] *(= s'épanouir)* **elle s'accomplit dans son travail** she finds her work very fulfilling

> ⚠ Attention à ne pas traduire automatiquement **accomplir** par **to accomplish**, qui est d'un registre plus soutenu.

accomplissement /akɔ̃plismɑ̃/ NM [1] *[de devoir, promesse]* fulfilment; *[de mauvaise action]* committing; *[de tâche, mission]* accomplishment; *[d'exploit]* achievement [2] *(= fin) [d'apprentissage, service militaire]* completion

accord /akɔʀ/ GRAMMAIRE ACTIVE 38.1, 38.2, 39.1, 53.6

NM [1] *(= entente)* agreement; *(= concorde)* harmony ◆ **l'~ fut général** there was general agreement ◆ **le bon ~ régna pendant 10 ans** harmony reigned for 10 years; → **commun**

[2] *(= traité)* agreement ◆ **passer un ~ avec qn** to make an agreement with sb ◆ **~ à l'amiable** informal *ou* amicable agreement ◆ **~ bilatéral** bilateral agreement ◆ **les ~s d'Helsinki/de Camp David** the Helsinki/Camp David agreement

[3] *(= permission)* consent, agreement ◆ **il veut signer le contrat – elle ne donnera jamais son ~** he wants to sign the contract – she'll never agree ◆ **l'agence a donné son ~ pour la commercialisation du produit** the agency has given permission for the product to be put on sale ◆ **nous avons son ~ de principe** he has agreed in principle

[4] *(= harmonie) [de couleurs]* harmony

[5] *(Gram) [d'adjectif, participe]* agreement ◆ **~ en genre et en nombre** agreement in gender and number

[6] *(Mus) (= notes)* chord, concord; *(= réglage)* tuning ◆ **~ parfait** triad ◆ **~ de tierce** third ◆ **~ de quarte** fourth

[7] *(locutions)*

◆ **d'accord** ◆ **d'~ !** OK! *, (all) right! ◆ **être d'~** to agree, to be in agreement ◆ **être d'~ avec qn** to agree with sb ◆ **nous sommes d'~ pour dire que ...** we agree that ... ◆ **se mettre *ou* tomber d'~ avec qn** to agree *ou* come to an agreement with sb ◆ **être d'~ pour faire** to agree to do ◆ **il est d'~ pour nous aider** he's willing to help us ◆ **je ne suis pas d'~ pour le laisser en liberté** I don't agree that he should be left at large ◆ **je ne suis pas d'~ avec toi** I disagree *ou* don't agree with you ◆ **essayer de mettre deux personnes d'~** to try to get two people to come to *ou* to reach an agreement, to try to get two people to see eye to eye ◆ **je les ai mis d'~ en leur donnant tort à tous les deux** I ended their disagreement by pointing out that they were both wrong ◆ **c'est d'~, nous sommes d'~** (we're) agreed, all right ◆ **c'est d'~ pour demain** it's agreed for tomorrow, OK for tomorrow * ◆ **alors là, (je ne suis) pas d'~ !** * I don't agree!, no way! *

◆ **en accord avec** ◆ **en ~ avec le directeur** in agreement with the director ◆ **en ~ avec le paysage** in harmony *ou* in keeping with the landscape ◆ **en ~ avec vos instructions** in accordance *ou* in line with your instructions

COMP **accord complémentaire** *(Jur)* additional agreement

Accord général sur les tarifs douaniers et le commerce General Agreement on Tariffs and Trade

Accord de libre-échange nord-américain North American Free Trade Agreement

accord de modération salariale pay restraints agreement

Accord sur la réduction du temps de travail *agreement on the reduction of working hours*

accord salarial wage settlement

accord transactionnel transactional agreement

accordable /akɔʀdabl/ ADJ *(Mus)* tunable; *[faveur]* which can be granted

accordage /akɔʀdaʒ/ NM tuning

accord-cadre (pl **accords-cadres**) /akɔʀkɑdʀ/ NM outline *ou* framework agreement

accordement /akɔʀdəmɑ̃/ NM ⇒ **accordage**

accordéon /akɔʀdeɔ̃/ NM accordion ◆ **~ à clavier** piano-accordion ◆ **en ~** * *[voiture]* crumpled up; *[pantalon, chaussette]* wrinkled (up) ◆ **on a eu une circulation en ~** the traffic was moving in fits and starts ◆ **l'entreprise a procédé à un coup d'~ sur son capital** the company has gone from increasing to dramatically reducing its capital

accordéoniste /akɔʀdeɔnist/ NMF accordionist

accorder /akɔʀde/ GRAMMAIRE ACTIVE 53.1

► conjug 1 ◄

VT [1] *(= donner) [+ faveur, permission]* to grant; *[+ allocation, pension]* to give, to award *(à* to); ◆ **on lui a accordé un congé exceptionnel** he's been given *ou* granted special leave ◆ **elle accorde à ses enfants tout ce qu'ils demandent** she lets her children have *ou* she gives her children anything they ask for ◆ **pouvez-vous m'~ quelques minutes ?** can you spare me a few minutes?; → **main**

[2] *(= admettre)* **~ à qn que ...** to admit (to sb) that ... ◆ **vous m'accorderez que j'avais raison** you'll admit *ou* concede I was right ◆ **je vous l'accorde, j'avais tort** I'll admit it, I was wrong

3 (= attribuer) ~ **de l'importance à qch** to attach importance to sth ◆ ~ **de la valeur à qch** to attach value to sth, to value sth

4 [+ instrument] to tune ◆ **ils devraient ~ leurs violons** * (sur un récit, un témoignage) they ought to get their story straight *

5 (Gram) **(faire)** ~ **un verbe/un adjectif** to make a verb/an adjective agree (avec with)

6 (= mettre en harmonie) [+ personnes] to bring together ◆ ~ **ses actions avec ses opinions** to act in accordance with one's opinions ◆ ~ **la couleur du tapis avec celle des rideaux** to match the colour of the carpet with (that of) the curtains

VPR **s'accorder** 1 (= être d'accord) to agree, to be agreed; (= se mettre d'accord) to agree ◆ **ils s'accordent pour ou à dire que le film est mauvais** they agree that it's not a very good film ◆ **ils se sont accordés pour le faire élire** they agreed to get him elected

2 (= s'entendre) [personnes] to get on together ◆ **(bien/mal) s'~ avec qn** to get on (well/badly) with sb

3 (= être en harmonie) [couleurs] to match, to go together; [opinions] to agree; [sentiments, caractères] to be in harmony ◆ **s'~ avec** [opinion] to agree with; [sentiments] to be in harmony ou in keeping with; [couleur] to match, to go with ◆ **il faut que nos actions s'accordent avec nos opinions** we must act in accordance with our opinions

4 (Ling) to agree (avec with); ◆ **s'~ en nombre/genre** to agree in number/gender

5 (= se donner) **il ne s'accorde jamais de répit** he never gives himself a rest, he never lets up * ◆ **je m'accorde 2 jours pour finir** I'm giving myself 2 days to finish

accordeur /akɔʀdœʀ/ NM (Mus) tuner

accordoir /akɔʀdwaʀ/ NM tuning hammer ou wrench

accorte /akɔʀt/ ADJ F (hum) winsome, comely

accostage /akɔstaʒ/ NM (Naut) coming alongside; [de personne] accosting

accoster /akɔste/ ▸ conjug 1 ◂ VT 1 (gén, péj) [+ personne] to accost 2 (Naut) [+ quai, navire] to come ou draw alongside; (emploi absolu) to berth

accotement /akɔtmɑ̃/ NM [de route] shoulder, verge (Brit), berm (US); [de chemin de fer] shoulder ◆ ~ **non stabilisé**, ~ **meuble** soft shoulder ou verge (Brit) ◆ ~ **stabilisé** hard shoulder

accoter /akɔte/ ▸ conjug 1 ◂ VT to lean, to rest (contre against; sur on) VPR **s'accoter** ◆ **s'~ à ou contre** to lean against

accotoir /akɔtwaʀ/ NM [de bras] armrest; [de tête] headrest

accouchée /akuʃe/ NF (new) mother

accouchement /akuʃmɑ̃/ NM (= naissance) (child)birth, delivery; (= travail) labour (Brit), labor (US) ◆ ~ **provoqué** induced labour ◆ ~ **à terme** delivery at full term, full-term delivery ◆ ~ **avant terme** early delivery, delivery before full term ◆ ~ **naturel** natural childbirth ◆ ~ **prématuré** premature birth ◆ ~ **sans douleur** painless childbirth ◆ **pendant l'~** during the delivery

accoucher /akuʃe/ ▸ conjug 1 ◂ VT ◆ ~ **qn** to deliver sb's baby, to deliver sb VI 1 (= être en travail) to be in labour (Brit) ou labor (US); (= donner naissance) to have a baby, to give birth ◆ **où avez-vous accouché ?** where did you have your baby? ◆ **elle accouchera en octobre** her baby is due in October ◆ ~ **avant terme** to give birth prematurely ◆ ~ **d'un garçon** to give birth to a boy, to have a (baby) boy 2 (hum) ~ **de** [+ roman] to produce (with difficulty) ◆ **accouche !** * spit it out! *, out with it! *; → **montagne**

accoucheur, -euse /akuʃœʀ, øz/ NM,F ◆ **(médecin)** ~ obstetrician NF **accoucheuse** (= sage-femme) midwife

accouder (s') /akude/ ▸ conjug 1 ◂ VPR to lean (on one's elbows) ◆ **s'~ sur ou à** to lean (one's elbows) on, to rest one's elbows on ◆ **accoudé à la fenêtre** leaning on one's elbows at the window

accoudoir /akudwaʀ/ NM armrest

accouplement /akupləmɑ̃/ NM 1 [de roues] coupling (up); [de wagons] coupling (up), hitching (up); [de générateurs] connecting (up); [de tuyaux] joining (up), connecting (up); [de moteurs] coupling, connecting (up); (fig) [de mots, images] linking 2 (= copulation) mating, coupling

accoupler /akuple/ ▸ conjug 1 ◂ VT 1 (ensemble) [+ animaux de trait] to yoke; [+ roues] to couple (up); [+ wagons] to couple (up), to hitch (up); [+ générateurs] to connect (up); [+ tuyaux] to join (up), to connect (up); [+ moteurs] to couple, to connect (up); [+ mots, images] to link ◆ **ils sont bizarrement accouplés** * they make a strange couple, they're an odd pair 2 ◆ ~ **une remorque/un cheval à** to hitch a trailer/horse (up) to ◆ ~ **un moteur/un tuyau à** to connect an engine/a pipe to 3 (= faire copuler) to mate (à, avec, et with) VPR **s'accoupler** to mate, to couple

accourir /akuʀiʀ/ ▸ conjug 11 ◂ VI (lit) to rush up, to run up (à, vers to); (fig) to hurry, to hasten, to rush (à, vers to); ◆ **à mon appel il accourut immédiatement** he came as soon as I called ◆ **ils sont accourus (pour) le féliciter** they rushed up ou hurried to congratulate him

accoutrement /akutʀəmɑ̃/ NM (péj) getup *, rig-out * (Brit)

accoutrer /akutʀe/ ▸ conjug 1 ◂ (péj) VT (= habiller) to get up *, to rig out * (Brit) (de in) VPR **s'accoutrer** to get o.s. up *, to rig o.s. out * (Brit) (de in); ◆ **il était bizarrement accoutré** he was wearing the strangest getup *

accoutumance /akutymɑ̃s/ NF (= habitude) habituation (à to); (= besoin) addiction (à to)

accoutumé, e /akutyme/ (ptp de **accoutumer**) ADJ usual ◆ **comme à l'~e** as usual ◆ **plus/moins/mieux qu'à l'~e** more/less/better than usual

accoutumer /akutyme/ ▸ conjug 1 ◂ VT ◆ ~ **qn à qch/à faire qch** to accustom sb ou get sb used to sth/to doing sth ◆ **on l'a accoutumé à ou il a été accoutumé à se lever tôt** he has been used ou accustomed to getting up early VPR **s'accoutumer** ◆ **s'~ à qch/à faire qch** to get used ou accustomed to sth/to doing sth ◆ **il s'est lentement accoutumé** he gradually got used ou accustomed to it

Accra /akʀa/ N Accra

accra /akʀa/ NM fritter (in Creole cooking)

accréditation /akʀeditasjɔ̃/ NF accreditation ◆ **badge ou carte d'~** official pass ◆ **accorder ou donner une ~ à** to accredit

accréditer /akʀedite/ ▸ conjug 1 ◂ VT [+ rumeur] to substantiate, to give substance to; [+ idée, thèse] to substantiate, to back up; [+ personne] to accredit (auprès de to); ◆ **banque accréditée** accredited bank VPR **s'accréditer** [rumeur] to gain ground

accréditif, -ive /akʀeditif, iv/ ADJ accreditive ◆ **carte accréditive** credit card NM (Fin) letter of credit; (Presse) press card

accrétion /akʀesjɔ̃/ NF (Géol) accretion ◆ **disque d'~** (Astron) accretion disk

accro * /akʀo/ (abrév de **accroché**) ADJ 1 (Drogue) **être** ~ to have a habit, to be hooked * ◆ **être ~ à l'héroïne** to be hooked on heroin * 2 (= fanatique) **être** ~ to be hooked * NMF addict ◆ **les ~s du deltaplane** hang-gliding addicts

accroc /akʀo/ NM 1 (= déchirure) tear ◆ **faire un ~ à** to make a tear in, to tear 2 [de réputation] blot (à on); [de règle] breach, infringement (à of); ◆ **faire un ~ à** [+ règle] to bend; [+ réputation] to tarnish 3 (= anicroche) hitch, snag ◆ **sans ~(s)** [se dérouler] without a hitch, smoothly ◆ **quinze ans d'une passion sans ~(s)** fifteen years of unbroken passion

accrochage /akʀɔʃaʒ/ NM 1 (= collision en voiture) collision, bump *, fender-bender * (US); (Mil = combat) skirmish; (Boxe) clinch 2 (= dispute) brush; (plus sérieux) clash 3 [de tableau] hanging; [de wagons] coupling, hitching (up) (à to)

accroche /akʀɔʃ/ NF (Publicité) lead-in, catcher, catch line ou phrase ◆ ~ **de une** (Presse) splash headline

accroché, e * /akʀɔʃe/ (ptp de **accrocher**) ADJ 1 (= amoureux) **être** ~ to be hooked * 2 (Drogue) **être** ~ to have a habit (arg), to be hooked * ◆ ~ **à l'héroïne** hooked on heroin *

accroche-cœur (pl **accroche-cœurs**) /akʀɔʃkœʀ/ NM kiss (Brit) ou spit (US) curl

accrocher /akʀɔʃe/ ▸ conjug 1 ◂ VT 1 (= suspendre) [+ chapeau, tableau] to hang (up) (à on); (= attacher) [+ wagons] to couple, to hitch together ◆ ~ **un wagon à** to hitch ou couple a carriage (up) to ◆ ~ **un ver à l'hameçon** to fasten ou put a worm on the hook ◆ **maison accrochée à la montagne** house perched on the mountainside; → **cœur**

2 (accidentellement) [+ jupe, collant] to catch (à on); [+ aile de voiture] to catch (à on) to bump (à against); [+ voiture] to bump into; [+ piéton] to hit; [+ pile de livres, meuble] to catch (on) ◆ **rester accroché aux barbelés** to be caught on the barbed wire

3 (= attirer) [+ attention, lumière] to catch ◆ ~ **le regard** to catch the eye ◆ **la vitrine doit ~ le client** the window display should attract customers

4 (* = saisir) [+ occasion] to get; [+ personne] to get hold of; [+ mots, fragments de conversation] to catch

5 (Boxe) to clinch ◆ **il s'est fait ~ au troisième set** (Tennis) he got into difficulties in the third set

VI 1 [fermeture éclair] to stick, to jam; [pourparlers] to come up against a hitch ou snag ◆ **cette traduction accroche par endroits** this translation is a bit rough in places ◆ **cette planche accroche quand on l'essuie** the cloth catches on this board when you wipe it

2 (* = plaire) [disque, slogan] to catch on ◆ **ça accroche entre eux** they hit it off *

3 (* = s'intéresser) **elle n'accroche pas en physique** she can't get into physics * ◆ **l'art abstrait, j'ai du mal à ~** abstract art does nothing for me *

VPR **s'accrocher** 1 (= se cramponner) to hang on ◆ **s'~ à** [+ branche, pouvoir] to cling to, to hang on to; [+ espoir, personne] to cling to ◆ **accroche-toi bien !** hold on tight!

2 (* = être tenace) [malade] to cling on, to hang on; [étudiant] to stick at it; [importun] to cling ◆ **pour enlever la tache, tiens, accroche-toi !** you'll have a hell of a job getting the stain out! *

3 (= entrer en collision) [voitures] to bump into each other, to clip each other; (Boxe) to go ou get into a clinch; (Mil) to skirmish

4 (= se disputer) to have a brush; (plus sérieux) to have a clash (avec with); ◆ **ils s'accrochent tout le temps** they're always at loggerheads ou always quarrelling

5 (= en faire son deuil) **tu peux te l'~** you can kiss it goodbye *, you've got a hope * (Brit) (iro)

accrocheur, -euse /akʀɔʃœʀ, øz/ ADJ [1] *[personne, sportif]* resolute [2] *[mélodie, refrain]* catchy; *[slogan, titre]* attention-grabbing; *[effet, utilisation]* striking

accroire /akʀwaʀ/ VT *(utilisé uniquement à l'infinitif) (frm ou hum)* ◆ **faire** *ou* **laisser ~ qch à qn** to delude sb into believing sth ◆ **et tu veux me faire ~ que ...** and you expect me to believe that ... ◆ **il veut nous en faire ~** he's trying to deceive us *ou* take us in ◆ **il ne s'en est pas laissé ~** he wouldn't be taken in

accroissement /akʀwasmɑ̃/ NM increase (*de* in); *[de nombre, production]* growth (*de* in) increase (*de* in); ◆ **~ démographique nul** zero population growth

accroître /akʀwatʀ/ ► conjug 55 ◄ VT *[+ somme, plaisir, confusion]* to increase, to add to; *[+ réputation]* to enhance, to add to; *[+ gloire]* to increase, to heighten; *[+ production]* to increase (*de* by); ◆ **~ son avance sur qn** to increase one's lead over sb VPR **s'accroître** to increase, to grow ◆ **sa part s'est accrue de celle de son frère** his share was increased by that of his brother

accroupi, e /akʀupi/ (ptp de **s'accroupir**) ADJ squatting *ou* crouching (down) ◆ **en position ~e** in a squatting *ou* crouching position

accroupir (s') /akʀupiʀ/ ► conjug 2 ◄ VPR to squat *ou* crouch (down)

accroupissement /akʀupismɑ̃/ NM squatting, crouching

accu * /aky/ NM (abrév de **accumulateur**) battery

accueil /akœj/ NM [1] *(= réception)* welcome, reception; *[de sinistrés, film, idée]* reception ◆ **rien n'a été prévu pour l'~ des touristes** no provision has been made to accommodate tourists, no tourist facilities have been provided ◆ **quel ~ a-t-on fait à ses idées ?** what sort of reception did his ideas get?, how were his ideas received? ◆ **merci de votre ~** *(chez des amis)* thanks for having me (*ou* us); *(contexte professionnel, conférence)* thank you for making me (*ou* us) feel so welcome ◆ **faire bon ~ à** *[+ idée, proposition]* to welcome ◆ **faire bon ~ à qn** to welcome sb, to make sb welcome ◆ **faire mauvais ~ à** *[+ idée, suggestion]* to receive badly ◆ **faire mauvais ~ à qn** to make sb feel unwelcome, to give sb a bad reception ◆ **faire bon/mauvais ~ à un film** to give a film a good/bad reception ◆ **le projet a reçu un ~ favorable** the plan was favourably *ou* well received ◆ **d'~** *[centre, organisation]* reception *(épith)*; *[paroles, cérémonie]* welcoming, of welcome ◆ **page d'~** *(Internet)* homepage; → **famille, hôtesse, pays¹, structure, terre**

[2] *(= bureau)* reception ◆ **adressez-vous à l'~** ask at reception

accueillant, e /akœjɑ̃, ɑ̃t/ ADJ welcoming, friendly

accueillir /akœjiʀ/ ► conjug 12 ◄ VT [1] *(= aller chercher)* to meet, to collect; *(= recevoir, donner l'hospitalité à)* to welcome ◆ **je suis allé l'~ à la gare** *(à pied)* I went to meet him at the station; *(en voiture)* I went to collect him *ou* pick him up at the station ◆ **il m'a bien accueilli** he made me very welcome, he gave me a warm welcome ◆ **il m'a mal accueilli** he made me feel very unwelcome ◆ **il m'a accueilli sous son toit/dans sa famille** he welcomed me into his house/his family ◆ **cet hôtel peut ~ 80 touristes** this hotel can accommodate 80 tourists ◆ **ils se sont fait ~ par des coups de feu/des huées** they were greeted with shots/boos *ou* catcalls

[2] *[+ idée, demande, film, nouvelle]* to receive ◆ **être bien/mal accueilli** to be well/badly received ◆ **il accueillit ma suggestion avec un sourire** he greeted *ou* received my suggestion with a smile ◆ **comment les consommateurs ont-ils accueilli ce nouveau produit ?** how did consumers react *ou* respond to this new product?

acculer /akyle/ ► conjug 1 ◄ VT ◆ **~ qn à** *[+ mur]* to drive sb back against; *[+ ruine, désespoir]* to drive sb to the brink of; *[+ choix, aveu]* to force sb into ◆ **acculé à la mer** driven back to the edge of the sea ◆ **~ qn contre** to drive sb back to *ou* against ◆ **~ qn dans** *[+ impasse, pièce]* to corner sb in ◆ **nous sommes acculés, nous devons céder** we're cornered, we must give in

acculturation /akyltyʀasjɔ̃/ NF acculturation *(frm)*

acculturer /akyltyʀe/ ► conjug 1 ◄ VT *[+ groupe]* to help adapt *ou* adjust to a new culture, to acculturate *(frm)*

accumulateur /akymylatœʀ/ NM accumulator, (storage) battery; *(Ordin)* accumulator ◆ **~ de chaleur** storage heater

accumulation /akymylasjɔ̃/ NF *[de documents, richesses, preuves, marchandises]* accumulation; *[d'irrégularités, erreurs]* series ◆ **une ~ de stocks** a build-up in stock ◆ **radiateur à ~ (nocturne)** *(Élec)* (night-)storage heater

accumuler /akymyle/ ► conjug 1 ◄ VT *[+ documents, richesses, preuves, erreurs]* to accumulate, to amass; *[+ marchandises]* to accumulate, to stockpile; *[+ énergie]* to store ◆ **les intérêts accumulés pendant un an** the interest accrued over a year ◆ **il accumule les gaffes** he makes one blunder after another ◆ **le retard accumulé depuis un an** the delay that has built up over the past year ◆ **j'accumule les ennuis en ce moment** it's just one problem after another at the moment VPR **s'accumuler** *[objets, problèmes, travail]* to accumulate, to pile up ◆ **les dossiers s'accumulent sur mon bureau** I've got files piling up on my desk

accusateur, -trice /akyzatœʀ, tʀis/ ADJ *[doigt, regard]* accusing; *[documents, preuves]* accusatory, incriminating NM,F accuser ◆ **~ public** *(Hist)* public prosecutor *(during the French Revolution)*

accusatif, -ive /akyzatif, iv/ NM accusative case ◆ **à l'~** in the accusative ADJ accusative

accusation /akyzasjɔ̃/ NF [1] *(gén)* accusation; *(Jur)* charge, indictment ◆ **porter** *ou* **lancer une ~ contre** to make *ou* level an accusation against ◆ **il a lancé des ~s de corruption/de fraude contre eux** he accused them of bribery/of fraud, he levelled accusations of bribery/of fraud against them ◆ **mettre en ~** † to indict ◆ **mise en ~** † indictment ◆ **c'est une terrible ~ contre notre société** it's a terrible indictment of our society ◆ **abandonner l'~** *(Jur)* to drop the charge; → **acte, chambre, chef²** [2] *(= ministère public)* **l'~** the prosecution

accusatoire /akyzatwaʀ/ ADJ *(Jur)* accusatory

accusé, e /akyze/ (ptp de **accuser**) ADJ *(= marqué)* marked, pronounced NM,F accused; *[de procès]* defendant ◆ **~, levez-vous !** ≈ the defendant will rise!; → **banc** COMP **accusé de réception** acknowledgement of receipt

accuser /akyze/ GRAMMAIRE ACTIVE 47.2 ► conjug 1 ◄

VT [1] *[+ personne]* to accuse ◆ **~ de** to accuse of; *(Jur)* to charge with, to indict for ◆ **~ qn d'ingratitude** to accuse sb of ingratitude ◆ **~ qn d'avoir volé de l'argent** to accuse sb of stealing *ou* having stolen money ◆ **tout l'accuse** everything points to his guilt *ou* his being guilty

[2] *(= rendre responsable) [+ pratique, malchance, personne]* to blame (*de* for); ◆ **accusant son mari de ne pas s'être réveillé à temps** blaming her husband for not waking up in time ◆ **accusant le médecin d'incompétence pour avoir causé la mort de l'enfant** blaming the doctor's incompetence for having caused the child's death, blaming the child's death on the doctor's incompetence

[3] *(= souligner) [+ effet, contraste]* to emphasize, to accentuate ◆ **cette robe accuse sa maigreur** this dress makes her look even thinner

[4] *(= montrer)* to show ◆ **la balance accusait 80 kg** the scales registered *ou* read 80 kg ◆ **~ la quarantaine** to look forty ◆ **~ le coup** *(lit, fig)* to stagger under the blow, to show that the blow has struck home ◆ **elle accuse la fatigue de ces derniers mois** she's showing the strain of these last few months ◆ **la Bourse accuse une baisse de 3 points/un léger mieux** the stock exchange is showing a 3-point fall/a slight improvement ◆ **~ réception de** to acknowledge receipt of

VPR **s'accuser** [1] ◆ **s'~ de qch/d'avoir fait qch** *(= se déclarer coupable)* to admit to sth/to having done sth; *(= se rendre responsable)* to blame o.s. for sth/for having done sth ◆ **mon père, je m'accuse (d'avoir péché)** *(Rel)* bless me, Father, for I have sinned ◆ **en protestant, il s'accuse** by objecting, he is admitting his guilt

[2] *(= s'accentuer) [tendance]* to become more marked *ou* pronounced

ace /ɛs/ NM *(Tennis)* ace ◆ **faire un ~** to serve an ace

acerbe /asɛʀb/ ADJ caustic, acid ◆ **d'une manière ~** caustically, acidly

acéré, e /aseʀe/ ADJ *[griffe, pointe]* sharp; *[lame]* sharp, keen; *[raillerie, réplique]* scathing, biting ◆ **critique à la plume ~e** critic with a scathing pen

acétate /asetat/ NM acetate

acétique /asetik/ ADJ acetic

acétone /asetɔn/ NF acetone

acétylène /asetilɛn/ NM acetylene; → **lampe**

acétylsalicylique /asetilsalisilik/ ADJ ◆ **acide ~** acetylsalicylic acid

achalandé, e /aʃalɑ̃de/ **bien achalandé** LOC ADJ *(= bien fourni)* well-stocked; *(† = très fréquenté)* well-patronized

achards /aʃaʀ/ NMPL *spicy relish made with finely chopped fruit and vegetables*

acharné, e /aʃaʀne/ (ptp de **s'acharner**) ADJ *[combat, concurrence, adversaire]* fierce, bitter; *[discussion]* heated; *[volonté]* dogged; *[campagne]* fierce; *[travail, efforts]* unremitting, strenuous; *[poursuivant, poursuite]* relentless; *[travailleur]* relentless, determined; *[défenseur, partisan]* staunch, fervent; *[joueur]* hardened ◆ **~ contre** dead (set) against ◆ **~ à faire** set on doing, determined to do ◆ **c'est l'un des plus ~s à combattre la pauvreté** he is one of the most active campaigners in the fight against poverty ◆ **~ à leur perte** intent on bringing about their downfall ◆ **quelques ~s restaient encore** a dedicated few stayed on

acharnement /aʃaʀnəmɑ̃/ NM *[de combattant, résistant]* fierceness, fury; *[de poursuivant]* relentlessness; *[de travailleur]* determination, unremitting effort ◆ **son ~ au travail** the determination with which he tackles his work ◆ **avec ~** *[poursuivre]* relentlessly; *[travailler]* relentlessly, furiously; *[combattre]* bitterly, fiercely; *[résister]* fiercely; *[défendre]* staunchly ◆ **se battant avec ~** fighting tooth and nail ◆ **cet ~ contre les fumeurs m'agace** it gets on my nerves the way smokers are being hounded like this COMP **acharnement thérapeutique** prolonging life by technological means

acharner (s') /aʃaʀne/ ► conjug 1 ◄ VPR [1] *(= tourmenter)* ◆ **s'~ sur** *[+ victime, proie]* to go at fiercely and unrelentingly ◆ **s'~ contre qn** *[malchance]* to dog sb; *[adversaire]* to set o.s. against sb, to have got one's knife into sb ◆ **elle s'acharne après cet enfant** she's always hounding that child [2] *(= s'obstiner sur)* ◆ **s'~ sur** *[+ calculs, texte]* to work away furiously at ◆ **je m'acharne à le leur faire comprendre** I'm desperately trying to get them to understand it ◆ **il s'acharne inutilement** he's wasting his efforts

achat /aʃa/ NM 1 (= *chose achetée*) purchase ◆ **faire un ~** to make a purchase ◆ **il a fait un ~ judicieux** he made a wise buy *ou* purchase ◆ **faire des ~s** to shop, to go shopping ◆ **il est allé faire quelques ~s** he has gone out to buy a few things *ou* to do some shopping ◆ **faire ses ~s (de Noël)** to do one's (Christmas) shopping ◆ **montre-moi tes ~s** show me what you've bought ◆ **je ferai mes derniers ~s à l'aéroport** I'll buy the last few things I need at the airport

2 (*action*) **faire l'~ de qch** to purchase *ou* buy sth ◆ **faire un ~ groupé** to buy several items at once ◆ **c'est cher à l'~ mais c'est de bonne qualité** it's expensive (to buy) but it's good quality ◆ **la livre vaut 11 F à l'~** the buying rate for sterling is 11 francs ◆ **ces titres ont fait l'objet d'~s massifs** these securities have been bought up in great numbers; → **central, offre, ordre², pouvoir²** *etc*

COMP **achat d'espace** (*Publicité*) space buying
achat d'impulsion (= *action*) impulse buying; (= *chose*) impulse buy *ou* purchase
achat en ligne on-line purchase
achat de précaution (= *action*) hedge buying

acheminement /aʃ(ə)minmɑ̃/ NM [*de courrier, colis*] delivery (*vers* to); [*de troupes*] transporting ◆ **~ de marchandises** carriage of goods ◆ **l'~ des secours aux civils** getting help to civilians

acheminer /aʃ(ə)mine/ ▸ conjug 1 ◂ VT [+ *courrier, colis*] to forward, to dispatch (*vers* to); [+ *troupes*] to transport (*vers* to); [+ *train*] to route (*sur, vers* to); ◆ **~ un train supplémentaire sur Dijon** to put on an extra train to Dijon ◆ **le pont aérien qui acheminera l'aide humanitaire dans la région** the airlift that will bring humanitarian aid to the region VPR **s'acheminer** ◆ **s'~ vers** [+ *endroit*] to make one's way towards, to head for; [+ *conclusion, solution*] to move towards; [+ *guerre, destruction, ruine*] to head for

acheter /aʃ(ə)te/ ▸ conjug 5 ◂ VT 1 (*gén*) to buy, to purchase ◆ **~ qch à qn** (*à un vendeur*) to buy *ou* purchase sth from sb; (*pour qn*) to buy sth for sb, to buy sb sth ◆ **~ en grosses quantités** to buy in bulk, to bulk-buy (*Brit*) ◆ **j'achète mon fromage au détail** I buy my cheese loose ◆ **~ à la hausse/à la baisse** (*Bourse*) to buy for a rise/for a fall ◆ **ça s'achète dans les quincailleries** you can buy it *ou* it can be bought in hardware stores, it's on sale in hardware stores ◆ **je me suis acheté une montre** I bought myself a watch ◆ **(s')~ une conduite** to turn over a new leaf, to mend one's ways; → **comptant, crédit** 2 (*en corrompant*) [+ *vote, appui*] to buy; [+ *électeur, juge*] to bribe, to buy ◆ **se laisser ~** to let o.s. be bribed *ou* bought ◆ **on peut ~ n'importe qui** every man has his price, everyone has their price

acheteur, -euse /aʃ(ə)tœʀ, øz/ NM,F buyer ◆ **il est ~** he wants to buy it ◆ **il n'a pas encore trouvé d'~ pour sa voiture** he hasn't yet found anyone to buy his car *ou* a buyer for his car ◆ **article qui ne trouve pas d'~** item which does not sell *ou* which finds no takers ◆ **la foule des ~s** the crowd of shoppers

achevé, e /aʃ(ə)ve/ (ptp de **achever**) ADJ [*canaille*] out-and-out, thorough; [*artiste*] accomplished; [*art, grâce*] perfect ◆ **d'un ridicule ~** perfectly ridiculous ◆ **tableau d'un mauvais goût ~** picture in thoroughly bad taste NM ◆ **~ d'imprimer** colophon

achèvement /aʃɛvmɑ̃/ NM [*de travaux*] completion; (*littér* = *perfection*) culmination; → **voie**

achever /aʃ(ə)ve/ ▸ conjug 5 ◂ VT 1 (= *terminer*) [+ *discours, repas*] to finish, to end; [+ *livre*] to finish, to reach the end of; (= *parachever*) [+ *tâche, tableau*] to complete, to finish ◆ **~ ses jours à la campagne** to end one's days in the country ◆ **le soleil achève sa course** (*littér*) the sun completes its course ◆ **~ (de parler)** to finish (speaking) ◆ **il partit sans ~ (sa phrase)** he left in mid sentence *ou* without finishing his sentence ◆ **~ de se raser/de se préparer** to finish shaving/getting ready ◆ **le pays achevait de se reconstruire** the country was just finishing rebuilding itself

2 (= *porter à son comble*) **cette remarque acheva de l'exaspérer** the remark really brought his irritation to a head ◆ **cette révélation acheva de nous plonger dans la confusion** this revelation was all we needed to confuse us completely

3 (= *tuer*) [+ *blessé*] to finish off; [+ *cheval*] to destroy; (= *fatiguer, décourager*) to finish (off); (* = *vaincre*) to finish off ◆ **cette mauvaise nouvelle va ~ son père** this bad news will finish his father off ◆ **cette longue promenade m'a achevé !** that long walk finished me (off)!

VPR **s'achever** (= *se terminer*) to end (*par, sur* with); (*littér*) [*jour, vie*] to come to an end, to draw to a close ◆ **ainsi s'achèvent nos émissions de la journée** (TV) that brings to an end our programmes for today

Achgabat /aʃgabat/ N Ashkhabad

achigan /aʃigɑ̃/ NM (*Can*) (black) bass ◆ **~ à grande bouche** large-mouth bass ◆ **~ à petite bouche** small-mouth bass ◆ **~ de roche** rock bass

Achille /aʃil/ NM Achilles; → **talon**

achillée /akile/ NF achillea

achoppement /aʃɔpmɑ̃/ NM ◆ **pierre** *ou* **point d'~** stumbling block

achopper /aʃɔpe/ ▸ conjug 1 ◂ VT INDIR ◆ **~ sur** [+ *difficulté*] to come up against; (*littér*) [+ *pierre*] to stumble against *ou* over ◆ **les pourparlers ont achoppé** the talks came up against a stumbling block

achromatique /akʀɔmatik/ ADJ achromatic

acide /asid/ ADJ (*lit, fig*) acid, sharp; (*Chim*) acid; → **pluie** NM acid

COMP **acide aminé** amino-acid
acide gras fatty acid ◆ **~ gras saturé/insaturé** saturated/unsaturated fatty acid

acidifiant, e /asidifjɑ̃, jɑ̃t/ ADJ acidifying NM acidifier

acidificateur /asidifikatœʀ/ NM acidifying agent, acidifier

acidification /asidifikasjɔ̃/ NF acidification

acidifier VT, **s'acidifier** VPR /asidifje/ ▸ conjug 7 ◂ to acidify

acidité /asidite/ NF (*lit, fig*) acidity, sharpness; (*Chim*) acidity

acidose /asidoz/ NF acidosis

acidulé, e /asidyle/ ADJ [*goût*] slightly acid; [*voix*] shrill; [*couleur*] acid; → **bonbon**

acier /asje/ NM steel ◆ **~ inoxydable/trempé** stainless/tempered steel ◆ **~ rapide** high-speed steel ◆ **d'~** [*poutre, colonne*] steel (*épith*), of steel; [*regard*] steely ◆ **muscles d'~** muscles of steel; → **gris, moral, nerf**

aciérie /asjeʀi/ NF steelworks

aciériste /asjeʀist/ NM steelmaker

acmé /akme/ NF (*littér* = *apogée*) acme, summit; (*Méd*) crisis

acné /akne/ NF acne ◆ **avoir de l'~** to have acne, to suffer from acne ◆ **~ juvénile** teenage acne

acnéique /akneik/ ADJ prone to acne (*attrib*) NMF acne sufferer

acolyte /akɔlit/ NM (*péj* = *associé*) confederate, associate; (*Rel*) acolyte, server

acompte /akɔ̃t/ NM (= *arrhes*) deposit; (*sur somme due*) down payment; (= *versement régulier*) instalment; (*sur salaire*) advance; (*à un entrepreneur*) progress payment ◆ **recevoir un ~** (*sur somme due*) to receive something on account, to receive a down payment ◆ **verser un ~** to make a deposit ◆ **ce week-end à la mer, c'était un petit ~ sur nos vacances** that weekend at the seaside was like a little foretaste of our holidays; → **provisionnel**

> ⚠ **acompte** ne se traduit pas par **account**, qui a le sens de 'compte'.

aconier /akɔnje/ NM lighterman

aconit /akɔnit/ NM aconite, aconitum

a contrario /akɔ̃tʀaʀjo/ ADV, ADJ a contrario

acoquiner (s') /akɔkine/ ▸ conjug 1 ◂ VPR (*péj*) to get together, to team up (*avec* with)

Açores /asɔʀ/ NFPL ◆ **les ~** the Azores

à-côté (pl **à-côtés**) /akote/ NM [*de problème*] side issue; [*de situation*] side aspect; (= *gain, dépense secondaire*) extra ◆ **avec ce boulot, il se fait des petits ~s** * with this job, he makes a bit extra *ou* on the side *

à-coup (pl **à-coups**) /aku/ NM [*de moteur*] cough; [*de machine*] jolt, jerk; [*d'économie, organisation*] jolt ◆ **travailler par ~s** to work by *ou* in fits and starts ◆ **avancer par ~s** to jerk forward *ou* along ◆ **sans ~s** smoothly ◆ **le moteur eut quelques ~s** the engine coughed (and spluttered)

acousticien, -ienne /akustisjɛ̃, jɛn/ NM,F acoustician

acoustique /akustik/ ADJ acoustic ◆ **trait distinctif ~** (*Phon*) acoustic feature; → **cornet** NF (= *science*) acoustics (*sg*); (= *sonorité*) acoustics ◆ **il y a une mauvaise ~** the acoustics are bad

acquéreur /akeʀœʀ/ NM buyer ◆ **j'ai trouvé/je n'ai pas trouvé ~ pour mon appartement** I have/I haven't found a buyer for my apartment, I've found someone/I haven't found anyone to buy my apartment ◆ **se porter ~ (de qch)** to announce one's intention to buy *ou* purchase (sth) ◆ **se rendre ~ de qch** to purchase *ou* buy sth

acquérir /akeʀiʀ/ ▸ conjug 21 ◂ VT 1 [+ *propriété, meuble*] to acquire; (*en achetant*) to purchase, to buy; (*Bourse*) [+ *titre*] to acquire, to purchase; [+ *société*] to acquire; → **bien** 2 (= *obtenir*) [+ *faveur, célébrité*] to win, to gain; [+ *habileté, autorité, nationalité, habitude*] to acquire; [+ *importance, valeur, statut*] to acquire, to gain ◆ **~ la certitude de qch** to become certain of sth ◆ **~ la preuve de qch** to gain *ou* obtain (the) proof of sth ◆ **leur entreprise a acquis une dimension européenne** their company has acquired *ou* taken on a European dimension ◆ **l'expérience s'acquiert avec le temps** experience is something you acquire with time ◆ **il s'est acquis une solide réputation** he has built up a solid reputation ◆ **il s'est acquis l'estime/l'appui de ses chefs** he won *ou* gained his superiors' esteem/support

acquêt /akɛ/ NM acquest; → **communauté**

acquiescement /akjesmɑ̃/ NM 1 (= *approbation*) approval, agreement ◆ **il leva la main en signe d'~** he raised his hand in approval *ou* agreement 2 (= *consentement*) acquiescence, assent ◆ **donner son ~ à qch** to give one's assent to sth

acquiescer /akjese/ ▸ conjug 3 ◂ VI 1 (= *approuver*) to approve, to agree ◆ **il acquiesça d'un signe de tête** he nodded in agreement, he nodded his approval 2 (= *consentir*) to acquiesce, to assent ◆ **~ à une demande** to acquiesce to *ou* in a request, to assent to a request

acquis, e /aki, iz/ (ptp de **acquérir**) ADJ 1 [*fortune, qualité, droit*] acquired ◆ **caractères ~** acquired characteristics; → **vitesse**

2 *[fait]* established, accepted ◆ **il est maintenant ~ que ...** it has now been established that ..., it is now accepted that ... ◆ **rien n'est jamais ~** you can't take anything for granted

◆ **tenir qch pour acquis** *(comme allant de soi)* to take sth for granted; *(comme décidé)* to take sth as settled *ou* agreed

3 *(locutions)*

◆ **être acquis à** ◆ **ce droit nous est ~** we have now established this right as ours ◆ **ses faveurs nous sont ~es** we can count on *ou* be sure of his favour ◆ **être ~ à un projet** to be in complete support of *ou* completely behind a plan ◆ **cette région est ~e à la gauche** this region is a left-wing strong-hold *ou* is solidly left-wing ◆ **il est (tout) ~ à notre cause** we have his complete support

NM 1 *(= avantage)* asset ◆ **sa connaissance de l'anglais est un ~ précieux** his knowledge of English is a valuable asset ◆ **~ sociaux** social benefits ◆ **~ territoriaux** territorial acquisitions

2 *(= connaissance)* **cet élève vit sur ses ~** this pupil gets by on what he already knows

3 *(opposé à inné)* ◆ **l'inné et l'~** nature and nurture

acquisition /akizisjɔ̃/ NF 1 *(= action, processus)* acquisition, acquiring ◆ **faire l'~ de qch** to acquire sth; *(par achat)* to purchase sth ◆ **l'~ du langage** language acquisition ◆ **l'~ de la nationalité française** the acquisition of French nationality ◆ **l'~ de données** *(Ordin)* data acquisition 2 *(= objet)* acquisition; *(par achat)* purchase ◆ **nouvelle ~** *[de bibliothèque]* accession

acquit /aki/ NM *(Comm = décharge)* receipt ◆ **"pour acquit"** "received"

◆ **par acquit de conscience** just to be sure ◆ **par ~ de conscience, il a revérifié** just to be sure, he double-checked

acquittement /akitmɑ̃/ NM 1 *[d'accusé]* acquittal ◆ **verdict d'~** verdict of not guilty 2 *[de facture]* payment, settlement *[de droit, impôt]* payment; *[de dette]* discharge, settlement

acquitter /akite/ ► conjug 1 ◄ VT 1 *[+ accusé]* to acquit 2 *[+ droit, impôt]* to pay; *[+ dette]* to pay (off), to settle, to discharge; *[+ facture]* *(gén)* to pay, to settle; *(Comm)* to receipt 3 ◆ **~ qn de** *[+ dette, obligation]* to release sb from VPR **s'acquitter** ◆ **s'~ de** *[+ dette]* to pay (off), to settle; *[+ dette morale, devoir]* to discharge; *[+ promesse]* to fulfil, to carry out; *[+ obligation]* to fulfil, to discharge; *[+ fonction, tâche]* to fulfil, to carry out ◆ **comment m'~ (envers vous) ?** how can I ever repay you? *(de* for)

acre /akʀ/ NF *(Hist)* ≃ acre NM *(Can)* acre (4,046.86 m²)

âcre /ɑkʀ/ ADJ *[odeur, saveur]* acrid, pungent; *(littér)* acrid

âcreté /ɑkʀəte/ NF acridity

acrimonie /akʀimɔni/ NF acrimony

acrimonieux, -ieuse /akʀimɔnjø, jøz/ ADJ acrimonious

acrobate /akʀɔbat/ NMF acrobat

acrobatie /akʀɔbasi/ NF *(= tour)* acrobatic feat; *(= art)* acrobatics *(sg)* ◆ **~s aériennes** aerobatics ◆ **faire des ~s** to perform acrobatics ◆ **il a fallu se livrer à des ~s comptables/budgétaires** we had to juggle the accounts/the budget ◆ **à force d'~s financières, il a sauvé son entreprise** he managed to save his company with some financial sleight of hand *ou* thanks to some financial gymnastics ◆ **mon emploi du temps tient de l'~** * I have to tie myself in knots * to cope with my timetable

acrobatique /akʀɔbatik/ ADJ acrobatic

acronyme /akʀɔnim/ NM acronym

Acropole /akʀɔpɔl/ NF ◆ **l'~** the Acropolis

acrostiche /akʀɔstiʃ/ NM acrostic

acrylique /akʀilik/ ADJ, NM acrylic; → **peinture**

actant /aktɑ̃/ NM *(Ling)* agent

acte /akt/ NM 1 *(= action)* action ◆ **~ instinctif/réflexe** instinctive/reflex action ◆ **moins de paroles, des ~s !** let's have less talk and more action! ◆ **ce crime est l'~ d'un fou** this crime is the work of a madman ◆ **passer à l'~** *(Psych)* to act; *(après menace)* to put one's threats into action ◆ **en ~** *(Philos)* in actuality

◆ **acte de** act of ◆ **un ~ de bravoure/de lâcheté/de cruauté** an act of bravery/cowardice/cruelty, a brave/cowardly/cruel act ◆ **plusieurs ~s de terrorisme ont été commis** several acts of terrorism have been committed ◆ **ce crime est un ~ de folie** this crime is an act of madness

2 *(Jur) [de notaire]* deed; *[d'état civil]* certificate ◆ **dont ~** *(Jur)* duly noted *ou* acknowledged

3 *(Théât, fig)* act ◆ **pièce en un ~** one-act play ◆ **le dernier ~ du conflit se joua en Orient** the final act of the struggle was played out in the East

4 *[de congrès]* **~s** proceedings

5 *(locutions)*

◆ **demander acte** ◆ **demander ~ que/de qch** to ask for formal acknowledgement that/of sth

◆ **prendre acte** ◆ **prendre ~ de qch** to note sth ◆ **prendre ~ que ...** to record formally that ... ◆ **nous prenons ~ de votre promesse** we have noted *ou* taken note of your promise

◆ **donner acte** ◆ **donner ~ que** to acknowledge formally that ◆ **donner ~ de qch** to acknowledge sth formally

◆ **faire acte de** ◆ **faire ~ de citoyen** to act *ou* behave as a citizen ◆ **faire ~ d'autorité** to make a show of authority ◆ **faire ~ de candidature** to apply, to submit an application ◆ **faire ~ de présence** to put in a token appearance ◆ **il a au moins fait ~ de bonne volonté** he has at least shown some goodwill

COMP **acte d'accusation** bill of indictment, charge *(Brit)*
acte d'amnistie amnesty
les Actes des Apôtres the Acts of the Apostles
acte d'association partnership agreement *ou* deed, articles of partnership
acte authentique ⇒ **acte notarié**
acte de banditisme criminal act
acte de baptême baptismal certificate
acte de charité act of charity
acte de commerce commercial act *ou* deed
acte constitutif *[de société]* charter
acte de contrition act of contrition
acte de décès death certificate
acte d'espérance act of hope
acte de l'état civil *birth, marriage or death certificate*
acte de foi act of faith
acte gratuit gratuitous act, acte gratuit
acte de guerre act of war
acte judiciaire judicial document ◆ **signifier *ou* notifier un ~ judiciaire** to serve legal process *(à* on)
acte manqué *(Psych)* revealing blunder
acte de mariage marriage certificate
acte médical medical treatment *(NonC)*
acte de naissance birth certificate
acte notarié notarial deed, deed executed by notary
acte de notoriété affidavit
acte officiel *(Jur)* instrument
acte sexuel sex act
acte de succession attestation of inheritance
l'Acte unique (européen) the Single European Act
acte de vente bill of sale; → **seing**

acteur /aktœʀ/ NM *(Théât, Ciné)* actor; *(fig)* player ◆ **~ de cinéma** film *ou* movie *(US)* actor ◆ **~ de théâtre** stage *ou* theatre actor ◆ **tous les ~s du film sont excellents** the entire cast in this film are *ou* is excellent ◆ **les principaux ~s économiques** the key economic players ◆ **les ~s de la politique mondiale** the actors *ou* players on the world political stage ◆ **les ~s sociaux** the main organized forces in society ◆ **les trois ~s de ce drame** *(fig)* the three people involved in *ou* the three protagonists in the tragedy; → **actrice**

actif, -ive /aktif, iv/ ADJ *[personne, participation]* active; *[poison, médicament]* active, potent; *(au travail) [population]* working; *(Bourse) [marché]* buoyant; *(Phys) [substance]* activated, active; *(Élec) [circuit, élément]* active; *(Ling)* active ◆ **les principes ~s du médicament** the active principles of the drug ◆ **prendre une part active à qch** to take an active part in sth ◆ **dans la vie active** in his (*ou* one's *etc*) working life ◆ **entrer dans la vie active** to begin one's working life; → **armée², charbon, corruption** *etc*

NM 1 *(Ling)* active (voice) ◆ **à l'~** in the active voice

2 *(Fin)* assets; *[de succession]* credits ◆ **~ circulant** current *ou* floating assets ◆ **~ réalisable et disponible** current assets ◆ **porter une somme à l'~** to put a sum on the assets side ◆ **sa gentillesse est à mettre à son ~** his kindness is a point in his favour, on the credit *ou* plus * side there is his kindness (to consider) ◆ **il a plusieurs crimes à son ~** he has several crimes to his name ◆ **il a plusieurs records à son ~** he has several records to his credit *ou* name

3 *(= qui travaille)* working person ◆ **les ~s** people who work, the working population

NF **active** *(Mil)* **l'active** the regular army ◆ **officier d'active** regular officer

actinide /aktinid/ NM actinide, actinon

actinium /aktinjɔm/ NM actinium

action¹ /aksjɔ̃/ NF 1 *(= acte)* action, act ◆ **~ audacieuse** act of daring, bold action ◆ **faire une bonne ~** to do a good deed ◆ **j'ai fait ma bonne ~ de la journée** I've done my good deed for the day ◆ **commettre une mauvaise ~** to do something (very) wrong, to behave badly ◆ **~ d'éclat** brilliant feat ◆ **~ de grâce(s)** *(Rel)* thanksgiving

2 *(= activité)* action ◆ **passer à l'~** *(gén, fig)* to take action; *(Mil)* to go into battle *ou* action ◆ **le moment est venu de passer à l'~** the time has come for action ◆ **être en ~** *[forces]* to be at work ◆ **entrer en ~** *[troupes, canon]* to go into action; *[usine]* to go into operation; *[mécanisme]* to start ◆ **mettre en ~** *[+ mécanisme]* to set going; *[+ plan]* to put into action ◆ **le dispositif de sécurité se mit en ~** the security device went off *ou* was set off; → **champ¹, feu¹, homme**

3 *(= effet) [de machine]* action; *[d'éléments naturels, médicament]* effect ◆ **ce médicament est sans ~** this medicine is ineffective *ou* has no effect ◆ **la pierre s'est fendue sous l'~ du gel** the frost caused the stone to crack ◆ **la transformation s'opère sous l'~ des bactéries** the transformation is caused by the action of bacteria

4 *(= initiative)* action ◆ **engager une ~ commune** to take concerted action ◆ **recourir à l'~ directe** to resort to *ou* have recourse to direct action ◆ **~ revendicative** *[d'ouvriers]* industrial action *(NonC)*; *[d'étudiants]* protest *(NonC)*; → **journée**

5 *(= politique, mesures)* policies ◆ **l'~ gouvernementale** the government's policies ◆ **l'~ économique et sociale** economic and social policy ◆ **l'~ humanitaire** humanitarian aid ◆ **pour financer notre ~ en faveur des réfugiés** in order to finance our aid programme for refugees ◆ **le développement de l'~ culturelle à l'étranger** the development of cultural initiatives abroad ◆ **son ~ à la tête du minis-**

tère a été critiquée he was criticized for what he did as head of the ministry; → **programme**
6 *[de pièce, film]* (= *mouvement, péripéties*) action; (= *intrigue*) plot ◆ ~ ! action! ◆ **l'~ se passe en Grèce** the action takes place in Greece ◆ **film d'~** action film ◆ **roman (plein) d'~** action-packed novel
7 *(Jur)* action (at law), lawsuit ◆ ~ **collective** class action ◆ ~ **juridique/civile** legal/civil action ◆ ~ **en diffamation** libel action; → **intenter**
8 *(Sport)* **il a été blessé au cours de cette** ~ he was injured during that bit of play ◆ **il y a eu deux ~s dangereuses devant nos buts** there were two dangerous attacking moves right in front of our goal ◆ **il y a eu de belles ~s au cours de ce match** there was some fine play during the match ◆ **revoyons l'~** let's have an action replay
9 *(Helv = vente promotionnelle)* special offer ◆ **robes en ~** dresses on special offer

action² /aksjɔ̃/ NF *(Fin)* share ◆ **~s** shares, stock(s) ◆ ~ **cotée** listed *ou* quoted share ◆ ~ **gratuite/ordinaire/nominative/au porteur** free/ordinary/registered/bearer share ◆ ~ **préférentielle** *ou* **à dividende prioritaire** preference share *(Brit)*, preferred share *(US)* ◆ ~ **de chasse** hunting rights ◆ **ses ~s sont en hausse/baisse** *(fig)* his stock is rising/falling; → **société**

actionnaire /aksjɔnɛʀ/ NMF shareholder

actionnarial, e /aksjɔnaʀjal, o/ (mpl **actionnariaux**) ADJ stock *(épith)*, share *(épith)* ◆ **la structure ~e de l'entreprise** the company's share structure

actionnariat /aksjɔnaʀja/ NM (= *détention d'actions*) shareholding; (= *personnes*) shareholders

actionnement /aksjɔnmɑ̃/ NM activating, activation

actionner /aksjɔne/ ▸ conjug 1 ◂ VT 1 *[+ levier, manette]* to operate; *[+ mécanisme]* to activate; *[+ machine]* to drive, to work ◆ **moteur actionné par la vapeur** steam-powered *ou* -driven engine ◆ ~ **la sonnette** to ring the bell 2 *(Jur)* to sue, to bring an action against ◆ ~ **qn en dommages et intérêts** to sue sb for damages

activateur, -trice /aktivatœʀ, tʀis/ ADJ activating *(épith)* NM activator

activation /aktivasjɔ̃/ NF *(Chim, Phys)* activation; *(Bio)* initiation of development

activé, e /aktive/ (ptp de **activer**) ADJ *(Sci)* activated; → **charbon**

activement /aktivmɑ̃/ ADV actively ◆ **participer ~ à qch** to take an active part *ou* be actively involved in sth ◆ **le suspect est ~ recherché par la police** a major police search for the suspect is under way

activer /aktive/ ▸ conjug 1 ◂ VT 1 (= *accélérer*) *[+ processus, travaux]* to speed up; (= *aviver*) *[+ feu]* to stoke 2 *(Chim)* to activate 3 (= *actionner*) *[+ dispositif]* to set going; *(Ordin)* to activate VI (* = *se dépêcher*) to get a move on*, to get moving* VPR **s'activer** (= *s'affairer*) to bustle about ◆ **s'~ à faire** to be busy doing ◆ **active-toi !*** get a move on!*

activisme /aktivism/ NM activism

activiste /aktivist/ ADJ, NMF activist

activité /aktivite/ NF 1 (= *fonctionnement*) activity ◆ **l'~ économique** economic activity ◆ **cesser ses ~s** *[entreprise]* to cease trading *ou* operations ◆ **la concurrence nous a forcé à cesser nos ~s** our competitors have put us out of business ◆ **pratiquer une ~ physique régulière** to take regular exercise, to exercise regularly ◆ **elle déborde d'~** *[personne]* she's incredibly active
2 (= *occupation non rémunérée, passe-temps*) activity ◆ **le club propose de multiples ~s culturelles** the club provides a wide range of cultural activities
3 (= *emploi*) job ◆ ~ **professionnelle** occupation ◆ **avoir une ~ salariée** to be in paid *ou* gainful *(frm)* employment ◆ **le passage de l'~ à la retraite** the transition from working life to retirement; *(Mil)* the transfer from the active to the retired list ◆ **cesser son ~** *[salarié]* to stop working; *[médecin]* to stop practising
4 (= *domaine d'intervention*) *[d'entreprise]* (line of) business ◆ **notre ~ principale est l'informatique** our main line of business is computing ◆ **ils ont étendu leurs ~s à la distribution** they have branched out into distribution
5 (= *animation*) *[de rue, ville]* bustle ◆ **les rues sont pleines d'~** the streets are bustling with activity *ou* are very busy
6 *(locution)*
◆ **en activité** ◆ **être en ~** *[volcan]* to be active; *[entreprise]* to be trading, to be in business; *[centrale nucléaire, usine]* to function, to be in operation; *[salarié]* to be working ◆ **le nombre des médecins en ~** the number of practising doctors ◆ **être en pleine ~** *[usine]* to be operating at full strength, to be in full operation; *[personne]* to be very busy; *(hum)* to be hard at it*

actrice /aktʀis/ NF *(Théât, Ciné, fig)* actress ◆ ~ **de cinéma** film *ou* movie *(US)* actress ◆ ~ **de théâtre** stage *ou* theatre actress

actuaire /aktɥɛʀ/ NMF actuary

actualisation /aktɥalizasjɔ̃/ NF 1 (= *mise à jour*) *[d'ouvrage, règlement]* updating ◆ **ils réclament l'~ du salaire minimum** they are calling for a review of the minimum wage 2 *(Fin) [de coûts]* updated forecast; *[de somme due]* discounting 3 *(Ling, Philos)* actualization

actualiser /aktɥalize/ ▸ conjug 1 ◂ VT 1 (= *mettre à jour*) *[+ ouvrage, règlement]* to update, to bring up to date; *[+ salaires]* to review 2 *(Fin) [+ coûts]* to give an updated forecast of; *[+ somme due]* to discount ◆ **cash-flow actualisé** discounted cash flow 3 *(Ling, Philos)* to actualize

actualité /aktɥalite/ NF 1 *[de livre, sujet]* topicality ◆ **livre d'~** topical book 2 (= *événements*) **l'~** current affairs ◆ **l'~ sportive** the sports news 3 *(Ciné, Presse)* **les ~s** the news ◆ **il est passé aux ~s*** he was on the news ◆ **~s télévisées/régionales** television/local *ou* regional news 4 *(Philos)* actuality

> ⚠ **actualité** se traduit par **actuality** uniquement au sens philosophique.

actuariel, -elle /aktɥaʀjɛl/ ADJ actuarial ◆ **taux** *ou* **rendement ~ brut** gross annual interest yield *ou* return

actuel, -elle /aktɥɛl/ ADJ 1 (= *présent*) present, current ◆ **à l'heure ~le** at the present time ◆ **à l'époque ~le** nowadays, in this day and age ◆ **le monde ~** the world today, the present-day world ◆ **l'~ Premier ministre** the current Prime Minister 2 (= *d'actualité*) *[livre, problème]* topical 3 *(Philos, Rel, Fin)* actual

> ⚠ **actuel** se traduit rarement par le mot anglais **actual**, qui a le sens de 'réel'.

actuellement /aktɥɛlmɑ̃/ ADV 1 (= *maintenant*) currently, at present ◆ **ce pays assure ~ la présidence de l'Union européenne** this country currently holds the presidency of the European Union ◆ **avez-vous un emploi ? – pas ~** have you got a job? – not at the moment 2 *(Philos)* actually

> ⚠ Au sens de 'maintenant', **actuellement** ne se traduit pas par **actually**.

acuité /akɥite/ NF *[de son]* shrillness; *[de douleur, problème, crise]* acuteness; *[de sens]* sharpness, acuteness ◆ ~ **visuelle** visual acuity

acuponcteur, acupuncteur /akypɔ̃ktœʀ/ NM acupuncturist

acuponcture, acupuncture /akypɔ̃ktyʀ/ NF acupuncture

acyclique /asiklik/ ADJ *(gén)* non-cyclical; *(Chim)* acyclic

a/d (abrév de **à dater, à la date de**) as from

ADAC /adak/ NM (abrév de **avion à décollage et atterrissage courts**) STOL

adage¹ /adaʒ/ NM (= *maxime*) adage, saying

adage² /adaʒ/ NM *(Danse)* adagio

adagio /ada(d)ʒjo/ NM adagio

Adam /adɑ̃/ NM Adam ◆ **en costume** *ou* **tenue d'~** *(hum)* in one's birthday suit; → **pomme**

adamantin, e /adamɑ̃tɛ̃, in/ ADJ *(littér)* adamantine

adaptabilité /adaptabilite/ NF adaptability

adaptable /adaptabl/ ADJ adaptable

adaptateur, -trice /adaptatœʀ, tʀis/ NM,F (= *personne*) adapter NM (= *dispositif*) adapter

adaptatif, -ive /adaptatif, iv/ ADJ adaptive ◆ **système d'optique adaptative** adaptive optics system

adaptation /adaptasjɔ̃/ NF 1 *(gén)* adaptation (*à* to); ◆ **faire un effort d'~** to try to adapt ◆ **capacité** *ou* **faculté d'~** adaptability (*à* to); ◆ **il lui a fallu un certain temps d'~** it took him some time to adapt 2 *(Ciné, Théât)* adaptation; *(Mus)* arrangement ◆ ~ **cinématographique** film *ou* screen adaptation ◆ ~ **télévisée** television adaptation

adapter /adapte/ ▸ conjug 1 ◂ VT 1 (= *rattacher, joindre*) to attach ◆ ~ **une prise à** to fit a plug to 2 (= *approprier*) **le traitement semble bien adapté (à la maladie)** the treatment seems to be appropriate (to the illness) ◆ **ces mesures sont-elles bien adaptées à la situation ?** are these measures really appropriate to the situation? ◆ ~ **la musique aux paroles** to fit the music to the words 3 (= *modifier*) *[+ conduite, méthode, organisation]* to adapt (*à* to); *[+ roman, pièce]* to adapt (*pour* for) VPR **s'adapter** 1 (= *s'habituer*) to adapt (o.s.) (*à* to) 2 (= *s'appliquer*) **s'~ à** *ou* **sur qch** *[objet, prise]* to fit sth

ADAV /adav/ NM (abrév de **avion à décollage et atterrissage verticaux**) VTOL

addenda /adɛ̃da/ NM INV addenda

Addis Abeba /adisabeba/ N Addis Ababa

additif, -ive /aditif, iv/ ADJ *(Math)* additive NM (= *note, clause*) additional clause, rider; (= *substance*) additive ◆ ~ **budgétaire** supplemental budget ◆ ~ **alimentaire** food additive

addition /adisjɔ̃/ NF 1 *(Math) (gén)* addition; (= *problème*) addition, sum ◆ **faire une ~** to do a sum ◆ **par ~ de** by adding, by the addition of 2 (= *facture*) bill, check *(US)* ◆ **payer** *ou* **régler l'~** *(lit)* to pay *ou* settle the bill; *(fig)* to pick up the tab ◆ **l'~ va être lourde** the cost will be high

additionnel, -elle /adisjɔnɛl/ ADJ additional; → **centime**

additionner /adisjɔne/ ▸ conjug 1 ◂ VT *(lit, fig)* to add up ◆ ~ **qch à** to add sth to ◆ ~ **le vin de sucre** to add sugar to the wine, to mix sugar with the wine ◆ **additionné d'alcool** *(sur étiquette)* with alcohol added VPR **s'additionner** to add up

additionneur /adisjɔnœʀ/ NM *(Ordin)* adder

adducteur /adyktœʀ/ ADJ M, NM ◆ **(canal)** ~ feeder (canal) ◆ **(muscle)** ~ adductor

adduction /adyksjɔ̃/ NF *(Anat)* adduction ◆ ~ **d'eau** water conveyance ◆ **travaux d'~ d'eau** laying on water

Adélaïde /adelaid/ NF Adelaide

ADEME / adɛm / NF (abrév de **Agence de l'environnement et de la maîtrise de l'énergie**) → **agence**

Aden / adɛn / N Aden

adénine / adenin / NF adenine

adénome / adenom / NM adenoma

adénosine / adenozin / NF adenosine

adénovirus / adenoviʀys / NM adenovirus

adepte / adɛpt / NMF *[de doctrine, mouvement]* follower; *[d'activité]* enthusiast ◆ **faire des ~s** to gain followers ◆ **les ~s du deltaplane** hang-gliding enthusiasts

> ⚠ **adepte** ne se traduit pas par le mot anglais **adept**, qui a le sens de 'expert'.

adéquat, e / adekwa(t), at / ADJ *(gén)* appropriate, suitable; *(Gram)* adequate ◆ **utiliser le vocabulaire ~** to use the appropriate vocabulary ◆ **ces installations ne sont pas ~es** these facilities are not suitable

adéquation / adekwasjɔ̃ / NF adequacy ◆ **la question de l'~ du mode de scrutin européen est posée** the question of the adequacy of the European voting system has arisen ◆ **~ entre ... et ...** balance between ... and ... ◆ **un rapport sur l'~ entre besoins et effectifs** a report on the balance between requirements and available staff

◆ **être en adéquation avec qch** to match sth ◆ **son discours n'est pas tout à fait en ~ avec son comportement** his behaviour *ou* what he does does not exactly match what he says ◆ **cette crème agit en ~ parfaite avec la peau** this cream works in perfect harmony with one's skin

adhérence / adeʀɑ̃s / NF *(gén)* adhesion *(à* to); *[de pneus, semelles]* grip *(à* on) adhesion *(à* to); ◆ **~ (à la route)** *[de voiture]* roadholding

adhérent, e / adeʀɑ̃, ɑ̃t / ADJ *[pays]* member *(épith)* ◆ **les pays ~s** the member nations ◆ **les personnes non ~es à l'association** non-members of the association NM,F member ◆ **carte d'~** membership card

adhérer / adeʀe / ▸ conjug 6 ◂ **adhérer à** VT INDIR
1 *(= coller)* to stick to, to adhere to ◆ **~ à la route** *[pneu]* to grip the road; *[voiture]* to hold the road ◆ **ça adhère bien** it sticks *ou* adheres well, it holds the road well 2 *(= se rallier à)* *[+ plan, projet]* to subscribe to; *[+ traité]* to adhere to; *[+ point de vue]* to support, to subscribe to; *[+ idéal, philosophie]* to adhere to 3 *(= devenir membre de)* to join; *(= être membre de)* to be a member of, to belong to

adhésif, -ive / adezif, iv / ADJ adhesive, sticky ◆ **pansement ~** sticking plaster *(Brit)*, Band-Aid ® *(US)* ◆ **papier ~** sticky(-backed) paper NM adhesive

adhésion / adezjɔ̃ / NF 1 *(= inscription)* joining; *(= fait d'être membre)* membership *(à* of); ◆ **son ~ au club** his joining the club ◆ **ils ont demandé leur ~ à l'UE** they've applied to join the EU, they've applied for EU membership ◆ **bulletin/campagne d'~** membership form/drive ◆ **il y a 3 nouvelles ~s cette semaine** 3 new members joined this week, there have been 3 new memberships this week 2 *(= accord)* adherence *(à* to); ◆ **leur ~ au traité** their adherence to the treaty 3 *(Phys) (= force)* adhesion

> ⚠ Attention à ne pas traduire automatiquement **adhésion** par le mot anglais **adhesion**, qui a des emplois spécifiques et est d'un registre plus soutenu.

ad hoc / adɔk / ADJ INV 1 *(= approprié) [formation, méthode, solution]* appropriate ◆ **c'est l'homme ~** he's just the man we need ◆ **j'ai trouvé le lieu ~ pour la réception** I've found the ideal *ou* the perfect place for the reception 2 *[organisme, mission]* ad hoc ◆ **commission ~** ad hoc committee

adieu (pl **adieux**) / adjø / NM 1 *(= salut)* goodbye, farewell *(littér)* ◆ **dire ~ à** *(lit, fig)* to say goodbye to ◆ **d'~** *[repas, visite]* farewell *(épith)* ◆ **baiser d'~** parting *ou* farewell kiss ◆ **tu peux dire ~ à ta sieste !** you can forget about your nap! ◆ **tu peux dire ~ à ton argent !** you can kiss your money goodbye! * 2 *(= séparation)* **~x** farewells ◆ **faire ses ~x (à qn)** to say one's farewells (to sb) ◆ **il a fait ses ~x à la scène/au journalisme** he bade farewell to the stage/to journalism EXCL *(définitif) (littér)* farewell; *(dial = au revoir)* bye *; *(dial = bonjour)* hi * ◆ **~ la tranquillité/les vacances** goodbye to (our) peace and quiet/our holidays

adipeux, -euse / adipø, øz / ADJ fat, adipose *(Spéc)*; *[visage]* fleshy

adiposité / adipozite / NF adiposity

adjacent, e / adʒasɑ̃, ɑ̃t / ADJ adjacent, adjoining ◆ **~ à** adjacent to, adjoining; → **angle**

adjectif, -ive / adʒɛktif, iv / ADJ adjectival, adjective *(épith)* NM adjective ◆ **~ substantivé/qualificatif** nominalized/qualifying adjective ◆ **~ attribut/épithète** predicative/attributive adjective ◆ **~ verbal** verbal adjective

adjectival, e (mpl **-aux**) / adʒɛktival, o / ADJ adjectival ◆ **locution ~e** adjectival phrase

adjectivé, e / adʒɛktive / ADJ used as an adjective

adjectivement / adʒɛktivmɑ̃ / ADV adjectivally, as an adjective

adjoindre / adʒwɛ̃dʀ / ▸ conjug 49 ◂ VT 1 *(= associer)* ◆ **un collaborateur à qn** to appoint sb as an assistant to sb ◆ **~ qn à une équipe** to give sb a place in a team ◆ **s'~ un collaborateur** to take on *ou* appoint an assistant 2 *(= ajouter)* ~ **une pièce/un dispositif à qch** to attach *ou* affix a part/device to sth ◆ **~ un chapitre à un ouvrage** to add a chapter to a book; *(à la fin)* to append a chapter to a book ◆ **à ces difficultés est venu s'~ un nouveau problème** in addition to all these difficulties there was now a new problem

adjoint, e / adʒwɛ̃, wɛ̃t / (ptp de **adjoindre**) ADJ assistant ◆ **commissaire/directeur ~** assistant commissioner/manager NM,F deputy, assistant ◆ **~ au maire** deputy mayor ◆ **~ d'enseignement** non-certificated teacher *(with tenure)* NM *(Ling)* adjunct

adjonction / adʒɔ̃ksjɔ̃ / NF 1 *(gén)* addition *(à* to); ◆ **produits sans ~ de colorant/sel** products with no added colouring/salt 2 *(Math, Ling)* adjunction

adjudant / adʒydɑ̃ / NM *(gén)* warrant officer; *(dans l'armée de l'air américaine)* senior master sergeant ◆ **~ chef** warrant officer 1st class *(Brit)*, chief warrant officer *(US)*

adjudicataire / adʒydikatɛʀ / NMF *(aux enchères)* purchaser; *(= soumissionnaire)* successful bidder

adjudicateur, -trice / adʒydikatœʀ, tʀis / NM,F *[d'enchères]* seller; *[de contrat]* awarder

adjudication / adʒydikasjɔ̃ / NF 1 *(= vente aux enchères)* sale by auction; *(= marché administratif)* invitation to tender, putting up for tender; *(= contrat)* contract ◆ **par (voie d')~** by auction, by tender ◆ **mettre en vente par ~** to put up for sale by auction ◆ **offrir par ~** to put up for tender ◆ **~ forcée** compulsory sale 2 *(= attribution) [de contrat]* awarding *(à* to); *[de meuble, tableau]* auctioning *(à* to)

adjuger / adʒyʒe / ▸ conjug 3 ◂ VT 1 *(aux enchères)* to knock down, to auction *(à* to); ◆ **une fois, deux fois, trois fois, adjugé(, vendu) !** going, going, gone! ◆ **le document a été adjugé pour 3 000 €** the document went for *ou* was sold for €3,000 2 *(= attribuer) [+ contrat, avantage, récompense]* to award; *(* = donner) [+ place, objet]* to give VPR **s'adjuger** *(= obtenir) [+ contrat, récompense]* to win; *(Sport) [+ place, titre]* to win; *(= s'approprier)* to take for o.s. ◆ **il s'est adjugé la meilleure place** he has taken the best seat for himself, he has given himself the best seat ◆ **ils se sont adjugé 24% du marché** they have taken over *ou* cornered 24% of the market ◆ **leur parti s'est adjugé 60% des sièges** their party have won *ou* carried off 60% of the seats

adjuration / adʒyʀasjɔ̃ / NF entreaty, plea

adjurer / adʒyʀe / ▸ conjug 1 ◂ VT ◆ **~ qn de faire** to implore *ou* beg sb to do

adjuvant / adʒyvɑ̃ / NM *(= médicament)* adjuvant; *(= additif)* additive; *(= stimulant)* stimulant; *(Ling)* adjunct

ad lib(itum) / adlib(itɔm) / ADV ad lib

admettre / admɛtʀ / ▸ conjug 56 ◂ VT 1 *(= laisser entrer) [+ visiteur, démarcheur]* to let in ◆ **la salle ne pouvait ~ que 50 personnes** the room could only accommodate *ou* hold 50 people ◆ **les chiens ne sont pas admis dans le magasin** dogs are not allowed in the shop; *(sur écriteau)* no dogs (allowed) ◆ **il fut admis dans le bureau du directeur** he was ushered *ou* shown into the director's office ◆ **l'air/le liquide est admis dans le cylindre** the air/the liquid is allowed to pass into the cylinder

2 *(= recevoir) [+ hôte]* to receive; *[+ nouveau membre]* to admit; *(à l'hôpital)* to admit ◆ **~ qn à sa table** to receive sb at one's table ◆ **il a été admis chez le ministre** he was received by the minister, he was allowed to see the minister ◆ **se faire ~ dans un club** to be admitted to a club

3 *(Scol, Univ) (à un examen)* to pass; *(dans une classe)* to admit, to accept ◆ **ils ont admis 30 candidats** they passed 30 of the candidates ◆ **il a été admis au concours** he passed *ou* got through the exam ◆ **il a été admis en classe supérieure** he will move up into the next class ◆ **lire la liste des admis au concours** to read the list of successful candidates in the exam

4 *(= convenir de) [+ défaite, erreur]* to admit, to acknowledge ◆ **il n'admet jamais ses torts** he never accepts *ou* admits he's in the wrong ◆ **je suis prêt à ~ que vous aviez raison** I'll admit that you were right ◆ **il est admis que, c'est chose admise que** it's an accepted *ou* acknowledged fact that, it's generally admitted that ◆ **admettons !** *(pour concéder)* if you say so! ◆ **admettons qu'il ne l'ait pas fait exprès** let's say he didn't do it on purpose

5 *(= accepter) [+ excuses, raisons, thèse]* to accept; *(Jur) [+ pourvoi]* to accept

6 *(= supposer)* to suppose, to assume ◆ **en admettant que** supposing *ou* assuming that ◆ **admettons qu'elle soit venue** let's suppose *ou* assume that she came

7 *(= tolérer) [+ ton, attitude, indiscipline]* to allow, to accept ◆ **je n'admets pas qu'il se conduise ainsi** I won't allow *ou* permit him to behave like that, I won't stand for *ou* accept such behaviour (from him) ◆ **~ qn à siéger** *(Admin)* to admit sb *(as a new member)* ◆ **admis à faire valoir ses droits à la retraite** *(Admin)* entitled to retire

8 *(= laisser place à)* to admit of ◆ **ton qui n'admet pas de réplique** tone (of voice) which brooks no reply ◆ **règle qui n'admet aucune exception** rule which allows of *ou* admits of no exception ◆ **règle qui admet plusieurs exceptions** rule which allows for several exceptions

administrateur, -trice / administʀatœʀ, tʀis / NM,F *(gén)* administrator; *[de banque, entreprise]* director; *[de fondation]* trustee ◆ **~ de biens** property manager ◆ **~ judiciaire** receiver ◆ **~ civil** *high-ranking civil servant acting as aide to a minister*

administratif, -ive / administʀatif, iv / ADJ administrative

administration /administʀasjɔ̃/ **NF** 1 *(= gestion) [d'affaires, entreprise]* management, running; *[de fondation]* administration; *[de pays]* running, government; *[de commune]* running ◆ **je laisse l'~ de mes affaires à mon notaire** I leave my lawyer to deal with my affairs, I leave my affairs in the hands of my lawyer ◆ **~ légale** guardianship ◆ **être placé sous ~ judiciaire** *[de société]* to go into receivership ◆ **la ville a été mise sous ~ de l'ONU** the town has been placed under UN administration; → **conseil**

2 *[de médicament, sacrement]* administering, administration

3 *(= service public)* (sector of the) public services ◆ **l'Administration** ≃ the Civil Service ◆ **l'~ locale** local government ◆ **être** *ou* **travailler dans l'~** to work in the public services ◆ **l'~ des Douanes** the Customs Service ◆ **l'~ des Eaux et Forêts** ≃ the Forestry Commission *(Brit)*, the Forestry Service *(US)* ◆ **l'~ fiscale, l'~ des Impôts** the tax department, ≃ the Inland Revenue *(Brit)*, the Internal Revenue *(US)* ◆ **l'~ centrale** *(Police)* police headquarters ◆ **l'~ pénitentiaire** the prison authorities

4 *(= gouvernement)* administration ◆ **l'~ Carter** the Carter administration

administrativement /administʀativmɑ̃/ **ADV** administratively ◆ **interné ~** formally committed (to a psychiatric hospital), sectioned *(Brit)*

administré, e /administʀe/ **NM,F** ◆ **le maire et ses ~s** the mayor and the citizens of his town, the mayor and the citizens he is responsible to

administrer /administʀe/ ▸ **conjug 1** ◂ **VT** 1 *(= gérer) [+ affaires, entreprise]* to manage, to run; *[+ fondation]* to administer; *[+ pays]* to run, to govern; *[+ commune]* to run 2 *(= dispenser) [+ justice, remède, sacrement]* to administer; *[+ coup, gifle]* to deal, to administer; *(Jur) [+ preuve]* to produce

admirable /admiʀabl/ **ADJ** admirable, wonderful ◆ **être ~ de courage** to show admirable *ou* wonderful courage ◆ **portrait ~ de vérité** portrait showing a wonderful likeness

admirablement /admiʀabləmɑ̃/ **ADV** admirably, wonderfully

admirateur, -trice /admiʀatœʀ, tʀis/ **NM,F** admirer

admiratif, -ive /admiʀatif, iv/ **ADJ** admiring ◆ **d'un air ~** admiringly

admiration /admiʀasjɔ̃/ **NF** admiration ◆ **faire l'~ de qn, remplir qn d'~** to fill sb with admiration ◆ **tomber/être en ~ devant qch/qn** to be filled with/lost in admiration for sth/sb

admirativement /admiʀativmɑ̃/ **ADV** admiringly, in admiration

admirer /admiʀe/ GRAMMAIRE ACTIVE 40.4 ▸ **conjug 1** ◂ **VT** to admire; *(iro)* to marvel at

admissibilité /admisibilite/ **NF** *[de postulant]* eligibility *(à* for); *(à un examen) eligibility to sit the oral part of an exam*

admissible /admisibl/ **ADJ** 1 *[procédé]* admissible, acceptable; *[excuse]* acceptable ◆ **ce comportement n'est pas ~** this behaviour is quite inadmissible *ou* unacceptable 2 *[postulant]* eligible *(à* for); *(Scol, Univ) eligible to sit the oral part of an exam* **NMF** eligible candidate

admission /admisjɔ̃/ **NF** 1 *(dans un lieu, club)* admission, admittance, entry *(à* to); ◆ **il a appris son ~ au concours** *(Univ)* he found out that he had passed the exam ◆ **son ~ (au club) a été obtenue non sans mal** he had some difficulty in gaining admission *ou* entry (to the club) ◆ **faire une demande d'~ à un club** to apply to join *ou* make an application to join a club, to apply for membership of a club ◆ **~ temporaire d'un véhicule** *(Douane)* temporary importation of a vehicle ◆ **le nombre des ~s au concours** the number of successful candidates in the exam 2 *(Tech = introduction)* intake; *(dans moteur de voiture)* induction; → **soupape**

admonestation /admɔnɛstasjɔ̃/ **NF** *(littér)* admonition, admonishment

admonester /admɔnɛste/ ▸ **conjug 1** ◂ **VT** *(gén, Jur)* to admonish

admonition /admɔnisjɔ̃/ **NF** *(littér, Jur)* admonition, admonishment

ADN /adeɛn/ **NM** (abrév de **acide désoxyribonucléique**) DNA

adnominal, e (mpl **-aux**) /adnɔminal, o/ **ADJ** *(Ling)* adnominal

ado * /ado/ **NMF** (abrév de **adolescent, e**) teenager, teen * *(US)*

adobe /adɔb/ **NM** adobe

adolescence /adɔlesɑ̃s/ **NF** adolescence ◆ **ses années d'~** his adolescent *ou* teenage years

adolescent, e /adɔlesɑ̃, ɑ̃t/ **ADJ** adolescent *(épith)* **NM,F** adolescent, teenager; *(Méd, Psych)* adolescent

Adonis /adɔnis/ **NM** *(Myth, fig)* Adonis

adonner (s') /adɔne/ ▸ **conjug 1** ◂ **s'adonner à VPR** *[+ art]* to devote o.s. to; *[+ études]* to give o.s. over to, to devote o.s. to; *[+ sport, passe-temps]* to devote o.s. to, to go in for; *[+ pratiques]* to indulge in ◆ **il s'adonnait à la boisson/au jeu** he was a confirmed drinker/gambler ◆ **venez vous ~ aux joies du ski** come and experience the joys of skiing

adoptable /adɔptabl/ **ADJ** *[enfant]* eligible for adoption; *[mesure]* that can be adopted

adoptant, e /adɔptɑ̃, ɑ̃t/ **NM,F** person wishing to adopt

adopter /adɔpte/ ▸ **conjug 1** ◂ **VT** 1 *(Jur) [+ enfant]* to adopt 2 *(= accueillir, accepter) [+ personne, animal]* to adopt ◆ **elle a su se faire ~ par ses nouveaux collègues** she's managed to gain acceptance with her new colleagues 3 *[+ attitude, religion, nom, mesure]* to adopt; *[+ cause]* to take up, to adopt ◆ **"l'essayer c'est l'adopter !"** "try it - you'll love it!" 4 *[+ loi]* to pass; *[+ motion]* to pass, to adopt ◆ **cette proposition a été adoptée à l'unanimité** the proposal was carried unanimously

adoptif, -ive /adɔptif, iv/ **ADJ** ◆ **enfant ~** *(gén)* adoptive child; *(dans une famille d'accueil)* ≃ foster child ◆ **parent ~** *(gén)* adoptive parent; *(= nourricier)* ≃ foster parent

adoption /adɔpsjɔ̃/ **NF** 1 *[d'enfant]* adoption ◆ **~ plénière** adoption ◆ **~ simple** ≃ fostering ◆ **pays d'~** country of adoption ◆ **un Londonien d'~** a Londoner by adoption 2 *[d'attitude, religion, nom, mesure, cause]* adoption 3 *[de loi]* passing; *[de motion]* passing, adoption

adorable /adɔʀabl/ **ADJ** *[personne, bébé, animal]* *(= charmant, mignon)* sweet; *[maison, village]* lovely ◆ **il a été absolument ~** he was really sweet

> ⚠ **adorable** se traduit rarement par le mot anglais **adorable**, qui est d'un registre plus soutenu.

adorablement /adɔʀabləmɑ̃/ **ADV** delightfully, adorably

adorateur, -trice /adɔʀatœʀ, tʀis/ **NM,F** *(Rel, fig)* worshipper

adoration /adɔʀasjɔ̃/ **NF** adoration, worship ◆ **être en ~ devant** to worship, to idolize; *[+ enfant]* to dote on

adorer /adɔʀe/ GRAMMAIRE ACTIVE 34.2 ▸ **conjug 1** ◂ **VT** 1 *(= rendre un culte à)* to worship ◆ **adorez l'Éternel** worship the Lord 2 *(= aimer passionnément)* to adore ◆ **il adore ses enfants** he adores his children 3 *(= raffoler de)* to love ◆ **j'adore le chocolat** I love chocolate ◆ **j'adore tremper mes tartines dans du chocolat chaud** I love dunking my bread in hot chocolate; → **brûler**

adosser /adose/ ▸ **conjug 1** ◂ **VT** ◆ **~ à** *ou* **contre qch** *[+ meuble]* to stand against sth; *[+ échelle]* to stand *ou* lean against sth; *[+ bâtiment]* to build against *ou* onto sth, to build against *ou* onto sth ◆ **~ un crédit à une hypothèque/un contrat d'assurance-vie** to secure a loan with a mortgage/a life-insurance policy **VPR** **s'adosser** ◆ **s'~ à** *ou* **contre qch** *[personne]* to lean back against sth; *[bâtiment]* to be built against *ou* onto sth, to back onto sth ◆ **il était adossé au pilier** he was leaning back against the pillar ◆ **le village est adossé à la montagne** the village is built right up against the mountain

adoubement /adubmɑ̃/ **NM** *(Hist)* dubbing

adouber /adube/ ▸ **conjug 1** ◂ **VT** *(Hist)* to dub; *(Dames, Échecs)* to adjust

adoucir /adusiʀ/ ▸ **conjug 2** ◂ **VT** 1 *[+ saveur]* to make milder *ou* smoother; *[+ acidité]* to reduce; *[+ rudesse, voix, peau]* to soften; *[+ couleur, contraste]* to soften, to tone down; *[+ caractère, personne]* to mellow; *[+ chagrin, conditions pénibles, épreuve, solitude]* to ease; *[+ dureté, remarque]* to mitigate, to soften ◆ **cette coiffure lui adoucit le visage** that hairstyle softens her features ◆ **pour ~ ses vieux jours** to comfort him in his old age ◆ **le vent du sud a adouci la température** the south wind has made the weather milder ◆ **~ la condamnation de qn** to reduce sb's sentence; → **musique** 2 *[+ eau, métal]* to soften **VPR** **s'adoucir** *[voix, couleur, peau]* to soften; *[caractère, personne]* to mellow ◆ **la température s'est adoucie** the weather has got milder

adoucissant, e /adusisɑ̃, ɑ̃t/ **ADJ** *[crème, lotion]* for smoother skin; *[sirop]* soothing **NM** fabric softener, fabric conditioner

adoucissement /adusismɑ̃/ **NM** 1 *[de peau, mœurs]* softening; *[de climat]* improvement ◆ **on espère un ~ de la température** we are hoping for milder weather ◆ **apporter des ~s aux conditions de vie des prisonniers** to make the living conditions of the prisoners easier *ou* less harsh 2 *[d'eau, métal]* softening

adoucisseur /adusisœʀ/ **NM** ◆ **~ (d'eau)** water softener

ad patres * /adpatʀɛs/ **ADV** ◆ **expédier** *ou* **envoyer qn ~** *(hum)* to send sb to kingdom come *

adrénaline /adʀenalin/ **NF** adrenalin

adressage /adʀesaʒ/ **NM** *[de courrier]* mailing; *(Ordin)* addressing ◆ **mode d'~** addressing mode

adresse[1] /adʀɛs/ GRAMMAIRE ACTIVE 51.5 **NF** 1 *(= domicile)* address ◆ **partir sans laisser d'~** to leave without giving a forwarding address ◆ **je connais quelques bonnes ~s de restaurants** I know some good restaurants to go to ◆ **c'est une/la bonne ~ pour les chaussures** it's a good place/the place to go for shoes; → **carnet, tromper** 2 *(frm = message)* address 3 *(Ling)* address ◆ **(mot) ~** *[de dictionnaire]* headword 4 ◆ **à l'~ de** *(= à l'intention de)* for the benefit of **COMP** **adresse électronique** e-mail address

adresse[2] /adʀɛs/ **NF** *(= habileté)* deftness, dexterity; *(= subtilité, finesse)* cleverness; *(= tact)* adroitness ◆ **jeu/exercice d'~** game/exercise of skill ◆ **il eut l'~ de ne rien révéler** he cannily gave nothing away; → **tour²**

adresser /adʀese/ GRAMMAIRE ACTIVE 48.2, 48.3, 50.3 ▸ **conjug 1** ◂ **VT** 1 ◆ **~ une lettre/un colis à** *(= envoyer)* to send a letter/parcel to; *(= écrire l'adresse)* to address a letter/parcel to ◆ **la lettre m'était personnellement adressée** the letter was addressed to me personally ◆ **mon médecin m'a adressé à un spécialiste** my doctor sent *ou* referred me to a specialist

2 ◆ ~ **une remarque/une requête à** to address a remark/a request to ◆ ~ **une accusation/un reproche à** to level an accusation/a reproach at *ou* against ◆ ~ **une allusion/un coup à** to aim a remark/a blow at ◆ ~ **un compliment/ses respects à** to pay a compliment/one's respects to ◆ ~ **une prière à** to address a prayer to; *(à Dieu)* to offer (up) a prayer to ◆ ~ **un regard furieux à qn** to direct an angry look at sb ◆ **il m'adressa un signe de tête/un geste de la main** he nodded/waved at me ◆ ~ **un sourire à qn** to give sb a smile, to smile at sb ◆ ~ **la parole à qn** to speak to *ou* address sb ◆ **il m'adressa une critique acerbe** he criticized me harshly ◆ **je vous adresse mes meilleurs vœux** *(sur lettre)* please accept my best wishes

3 *(Ordin)* to address

VPR **s'adresser** 1 *(= parler à)* **s'~ à qn** *[personne]* to speak to sb, to address sb; *[remarque]* to be aimed at sb ◆ **il s'adresse à un public féminin** *[discours, magazine]* it is intended for *ou* aimed at a female audience; *[auteur]* he writes for *ou* is addressing a female readership ◆ **ce livre s'adresse à notre générosité** this book appeals to our generosity ◆ **et cela s'adresse aussi à vous !** and that goes for you too!

2 *(= aller trouver)* **s'~ à** *[+ personne]* to go and see; *(Admin) [+ personne, bureau]* to apply to ◆ **adressez-vous au concierge** go and see (*ou* ask, tell *etc*) the concierge ◆ **adressez-vous au secrétariat** enquire at the office, go and ask at the office ◆ **il vaut mieux s'~ à Dieu qu'à ses saints** *(hum)* it's best to go straight to the top

adret /adʀɛ/ NM south-facing slope

Adriatique /adʀijatik/ ADJ F, NF ◆ **(mer)** ~ Adriatic (Sea)

adroit, e /adʀwa, wat/ ADJ *(= habile)* skilful, deft; *(= subtil)* clever, shrewd; *(= plein de tact)* adroit ◆ ~ **de ses mains** clever with one's hands ◆ **c'était très ~ de sa part** it was very clever *ou* shrewd of him

adroitement /adʀwatmɑ̃/ ADV *(= habilement)* skilfully, deftly; *(= subtilement)* cleverly, shrewdly; *(= avec tact)* adroitly

ADSL /adeɛsɛl/ N (abrév de **Asynchronous Digital Subscriber Line**) ADSL

adsorber /atsɔʀbe/ ▸ conjug 1 ◂ VT to adsorb

adsorption /atsɔʀpsjɔ̃/ NF adsorption

adulateur, -trice /adylatœʀ, tʀis/ NM,F *(littér)* *(= admirateur)* adulator; *(= flatteur)* sycophant

adulation /adylasjɔ̃/ NF *(littér)* *(= admiration)* adulation; *(= flatterie)* sycophancy

aduler /adyle/ ▸ conjug 1 ◂ VT *(littér)* *(= admirer)* to adulate; *(= flatter)* to flatter

adulte /adylt/ ADJ *[personne]* adult *(épith)*; *[animal, plante]* fully-grown, mature; *(= mûr)* *[attitude, comportement]* adult, mature; → **âge** NMF adult, grown-up

adultère /adyltɛʀ/ ADJ *[relations, désir]* adulterous ◆ **femme** ~ adulteress ◆ **homme** ~ adulterer NM *(acte)* adultery; → **constat**

adultérin, e /adylteʀɛ̃, in/ ADJ *(Jur)* *[enfant]* born of adultery

ad valorem /advalɔʀɛm/ LOC ADJ ad valorem

advenir /advəniʀ/ ▸ conjug 22 ◂ VB IMPERS 1 *(= survenir)* ~ **que ...** to happen that ..., to come to pass that ... *(littér)* ◆ ~ **à** to happen to, to befall *(littér)* ◆ **qu'est-il advenu au prisonnier ?** what has happened to the prisoner? ◆ **il m'advient de faire** I sometimes happen to do ◆ **advienne que pourra** come what may ◆ **quoi qu'il advienne** whatever happens *ou* may happen 2 *(= devenir, résulter de)* ~ **de** to become of ◆ **qu'est-il advenu du prisonnier/du projet ?** what has become of the prisoner/the project? ◆ **on ne sait pas ce qu'il en adviendra** nobody knows what will come of it *ou* how it will turn out VI *(= arriver)* to happen

adventice /advɑ̃tis/ ADJ 1 *(Bot)* self-propagating ◆ **plante** ~ weed 2 *(Philos, littér = accessoire)* adventitious

adventif, -ive /advɑ̃tif, iv/ ADJ *(Bot)* *[bourgeon, racine]* adventitious

adventiste /advɑ̃tist/ ADJ, NMF Adventist

adverbe /advɛʀb/ NM adverb

adverbial, e (mpl **-iaux**) /advɛʀbjal, jo/ ADJ adverbial

adverbialement /advɛʀbjalmɑ̃/ ADV adverbially

adversaire /advɛʀsɛʀ/ NMF *(gén)* opponent; *(Mil)* enemy; *[de théorie, traité]* opponent ◆ **il ne faut pas sous-estimer l'~** you shouldn't underestimate your opponent; *(Mil)* you shouldn't underestimate the enemy

> ⚠ **adversaire** se traduit rarement par le mot anglais **adversary**, qui est d'un registre plus soutenu.

adversatif, -ive /advɛʀsatif, iv/ ADJ, NM adversative

adverse /advɛʀs/ ADJ *[partie, forces, bloc]* opposing ◆ **la fortune** ~ *(littér)* adverse fortune ◆ **la partie** ~ *(Jur)* the other side

adversité /advɛʀsite/ NF adversity

ad vitam æternam * /advitametɛʀnam/ LOC ADV for ever

AE /aə/ NM (abrév de **adjoint d'enseignement**) → **adjoint** NFPL (abrév de **affaires étrangères**) → **affaire**

aède /aɛd/ NM (Greek) bard

AELE /aəelə/ NF (abrév de **Association européenne de libre-échange**) EFTA

aérage /aeʀaʒ/ NM ventilation

aérateur /aeʀatœʀ/ NM ventilator

aération /aeʀasjɔ̃/ NF *[de pièce, literie]* airing; *[de terre, racine]* aeration; *(= circulation d'air)* ventilation; → **conduit**

aéré, e /aeʀe/ (ptp de **aérer**) ADJ *[pièce]* airy, well-ventilated; *[page]* well spaced out; → **centre**

aérer /aeʀe/ ▸ conjug 6 ◂ VT *[+ pièce, literie]* to air; *[+ terre, racine]* to aerate; *(= alléger)* *[+ exposé, présentation]* to lighten VPR **s'aérer (la tête)** *[personne]* to get some fresh air

aérien, -ienne /aeʀjɛ̃, jɛn/ ADJ 1 *[espace, droit]* air *(épith)*; *[navigation, photographie]* aerial *(épith)*; *[attaque]* aerial *(épith)*, air *(épith)* ◆ **base aérienne** air base; → **compagnie, ligne**[1], **métro** 2 *(= léger)* *[silhouette]* sylphlike; *[démarche]* light; *[étoffe, vêtement]* floaty; *[musique, poésie, architecture]* ethereal 3 *(Bot)* *[racine]* aerial; *(Téléc)* *[circuit, câble]* overhead *(épith)*; *(Géog)* *[courant, mouvement]* air *(épith)* NM *(Radio = antenne)* aerial

aérobic /aeʀɔbik/ NF aerobics *(sg)*

aérobie /aeʀɔbi/ ADJ aerobic

aérobiologie /aeʀobjɔlɔʒi/ NF aerobiology

aéro-club (pl **aéro-clubs**) /aeʀoklœb/ NM flying club

aérodrome /aeʀodʀom/ NM airfield, aerodrome *(Brit)*, airdrome *(US)*

aérodynamique /aeʀodinamik/ ADJ *[expérience]* aerodynamics *(épith)*; *[ligne, véhicule]* streamlined, aerodynamic ◆ **soufflerie** ~ wind tunnel NF aerodynamics *(sg)*

aérodynamisme /aeʀodinamism/ NM aerodynamic shape

aérofrein /aeʀofʀɛ̃/ NM air brake

aérogare /aeʀogaʀ/ NF (air) terminal

aéroglisseur /aeʀoglisœʀ/ NM hovercraft

aérogramme /aeʀɔgʀam/ NM airmail letter

aérographe /aeʀɔgʀaf/ NM airbrush

aérolit(h)e /aeʀɔlit/ NM aerolite, aerolith

aéromobile /aeʀɔmɔbil/ ADJ airborne

aéromodèle /aeʀɔmɔdɛl/ NM model plane

aéromodélisme /aeʀɔmɔdelism/ NM model aircraft making

aéromodéliste /aeʀomɔdelist/ NMF model plane enthusiast

aéronaute /aeʀonot/ NMF aeronaut

aéronautique /aeʀonotik/ ADJ *[équipement, ingénieur]* aeronautical ◆ **construction/constructeur** ~ aircraft construction/constructor ◆ **l'industrie** ~ the aviation *ou* aeronautics industry ◆ **entreprise** *ou* **société** ~ aviation company, aeronautics firm NF aeronautics *(sg)*

aéronaval, e (pl **aéronavals**) /aeʀonaval/ ADJ ◆ **forces ~es** air and sea forces, naval aviation forces ◆ **groupe** ~ naval aviation unit ◆ **base ~e** naval airbase NF **aéronavale** ◆ **l'aéronavale** ≃ the Fleet Air Arm *(Brit)*, ≃ Naval Aviation *(US)*

aéronef /aeʀɔnɛf/ NM *(Admin)* aircraft

aérophagie /aeʀɔfaʒi/ NF ◆ **il a** *ou* **fait de l'~** he suffers from abdominal wind

aéroplane † /aeʀɔplan/ NM aeroplane *(Brit)*, airplane *(US)*

aéroport /aeʀɔpɔʀ/ NM airport

aéroporté, e /aeʀopɔʀte/ ADJ *[opération, division, troupes]* airborne; *[matériel]* airlifted, brought *ou* ferried by air *(attrib)*; *[missile]* air-launched

aéroportuaire /aeʀopɔʀtɥɛʀ/ ADJ *[installations, autorités]* airport *(épith)*

aéropostal, e (mpl **-aux**) /aeʀopɔstal, o/ ADJ airmail *(épith)* NF **Aéropostale** ◆ **l'Aéropostale** *(Hist)* the (French) airmail service

aérosol /aeʀɔsɔl/ NM aerosol ◆ **bombe** ~ spray *ou* aerosol can ◆ **déodorant/peinture en** ~ spray deodorant/paint

aérospatial, e (mpl **-iaux**) /aeʀospasjal, jo/ ADJ aerospace *(épith)* NF **aérospatiale** aerospace science

aérostat /aeʀɔsta/ NM aerostat

aérostatique /aeʀɔstatik/ ADJ aerostatic NF aerostatics *(sg)*

aérotrain ® /aeʀotʀɛ̃/ NM hovertrain

AF /aɛf/ NF (abrév de **allocations familiales**) → **allocation**

AFAT /afat/ NF (abrév de **auxiliaire féminin de l'armée de terre**) *member of the women's army*

affabilité /afabilite/ NF affability

affable /afabl/ ADJ affable

affablement /afabləmɑ̃/ ADV affably

affabulateur, -trice /afabylatœʀ, tʀis/ NM,F inveterate liar, storyteller

affabulation /afabylasjɔ̃/ NF 1 *(= mensonges)* **c'est de l'~, ce sont des ~s** it's all made up, it's pure fabrication 2 *[de roman]* (construction of the) plot

affabuler /afabyle/ ▸ conjug 1 ◂ VI to invent *ou* make up stories

affacturage /afaktyʀaʒ/ NM *(Jur)* factoring

affactureur /afaktyʀœʀ/ NM *(Jur)* factor

affadir /afadiʀ/ ▸ conjug 2 ◂ VT *[+ aliment]* to make tasteless *ou* insipid; *[+ couleur]* to make dull; *[+ style]* to make dull *ou* uninteresting VPR **s'affadir** *[couleur]* to become dull; *[style]* to become dull, to pall; *[aliment]* to lose its flavour *(Brit)* *ou* flavor *(US)*, to become tasteless *ou* insipid

affadissement /afadismɑ̃/ NM *[d'aliment]* loss of flavour *(Brit)* ou flavor *(US)* (*de* in, from); *[de saveur, style]* weakening (*de* of); *[de couleurs, sensations]* dulling (*de* of)

affaiblir /afebliʀ/ ▸ conjug 2 ◂ VT *(gén)* to weaken VPR **s'affaiblir** *[personne, autorité, résolution]* to weaken, to grow ou become weaker; *[facultés]* to deteriorate; *[vue]* to grow dim ou weaker; *[son]* to fade (away), to grow fainter; *[intérêt]* to wane; *[vent]* to abate, to die down; *[monnaie]* to weaken ◆ **le sens de ce mot s'est affaibli** the word has lost much of its meaning ◆ **utiliser un mot dans son sens affaibli** to use the weaker meaning of a word

affaiblissement /afeblismɑ̃/ NM *[de personne, autorité, résolution]* weakening; *[de facultés]* deterioration; *[de bruit]* fading (away); *[de monnaie]* weakening; *[d'intérêt]* waning ◆ **l'~ de notre pays au plan international** our country's waning influence on the international scene ◆ **on note un ~ progressif des syndicats** the power of the unions is gradually weakening ◆ **l'~ des valeurs morales** the sharp decline in ou deterioration of moral values

affaire /afɛʀ/

1 NOM FÉMININ 3 COMPOSÉS
2 NOM FÉMININ PLURIEL

1 - NOM FÉMININ

1 = problème, question matter, business ◆ **j'ai une ~ urgente à régler** I've got (some) urgent business to deal with, I've got an urgent matter to settle ◆ **ce n'est pas une petite** ou **une mince ~** it's no small matter ◆ **ce n'est pas une petite ~ de le faire obéir** getting him to obey is no easy matter ou no mean task ◆ **l'amour, c'est la grande ~ de sa vie** love is the most important thing in his life ◆ **j'en fais une ~ de principe** it's a matter of principle (for me) ◆ **c'est une ~ de goût/de mode** it's a matter of taste/fashion ◆ **le sport ne devrait pas être une ~ d'argent** sport shouldn't be about money ◆ **c'est une ~ d'hommes** it's men's business ◆ **c'est l'~ d'un spécialiste** it's a job for a specialist ◆ **c'est mon ~, pas la tienne** it's my business ou affair, not yours ◆ **ce n'est pas ton ~** it's none of your business ◆ **comment je fais ? – c'est ton ~ !** what do I do? – that's YOUR problem! ◆ **j'en fais mon ~** I'll deal with it, leave it to me ◆ **il en a fait une ~ personnelle** he took it personally ◆ **avec les ordinateurs, il est à son ~** when it comes to computers, he knows what he's about ou he knows his stuff* ◆ **dans les soirées, il est à son ~** he's in his element at parties ◆ **il en a fait toute une ~** he made a dreadful fuss about it, he made a great song and dance about it ◆ **(aller à Glasgow,) c'est toute une ~** it's quite a business (getting to Glasgow) ◆ **c'est une autre ~** that's quite another matter ou a different kettle of fish ◆ **c'est l'~ de quelques minutes/quelques clous** it's a matter of a few minutes/a few nails, it'll only take a few minutes/a few nails ◆ **le temps/l'âge ne fait rien à l'~** time/age has got nothing to do with it ◆ **en voilà une ~ !** what a (complicated) business! ◆ **ce n'est pas une ~ !** it's no big deal!, it's nothing to get worked up about!* ◆ **quelle ~ !** what a carry-on!* ◆ **la belle ~ !** big deal!, so what? ◆ **tirer** ou **sortir qn d'~** to help sb out, to get sb out of a tight spot* ◆ **ce médecin m'a tiré d'~** this doctor pulled me through ◆ **il est tiré** ou **sorti d'~** *(après une maladie)* he's pulled through; *(après des ennuis)* he's got over it ◆ **il est assez grand pour se tirer d'~ tout seul** he's big enough to manage on his own ou to sort it out by himself

2 = ce qui convient **j'ai ton ~** I've got (just) what you want ◆ **cet employé fera/ne fait pas l'~** this employee will do nicely/won't do (for the job) ◆ **ça fait mon ~** that's (just) what I want ou need ◆ **cela fera bien l'~ de quelqu'un** that will (certainly) come in handy ou do nicely for somebody ◆ **faire son ~ à qn*** (= *le malmener*) to give sb a beating*; (= *le tuer*) to do sb in*; → **connaître**

3 = ensemble de faits connus du public affair; (= *scandale*) scandal; (= *crise*) crisis ◆ **l'~ Dreyfus** the Dreyfus affair ◆ **l'~ des otages** the hostage crisis ◆ **l'~ du sang contaminé** the contaminated blood scandal ou affair ◆ **la population est révoltée par les ~s** the country is up in arms over the scandals ◆ **une grave ~ de corruption/d'espionnage** a serious corruption/spy scandal ◆ **c'est une sale ~** it's a nasty business; → **suivre**

4 Jur, Police case ◆ **l'~ Dufeu** the Dufeu case ◆ **être sur une ~** to be on a case ◆ **une ~ de vol** a case of theft ◆ **son ~ est claire** it's an open and shut case; → **entendu**

5 = transaction deal; (= *achat avantageux*) bargain ◆ **une (bonne) ~** a good deal, a (good) bargain ◆ **une mauvaise ~** a bad deal ou bargain ◆ **faire ~ avec qn** to conclude ou clinch a deal with sb ◆ **il est sur une grosse ~ avec la Russie** he's onto a big (business) deal with Russia ◆ **l'~ est faite !** ou **conclue !** that's the deal settled! ◆ **l'~ est dans le sac*** it's in the bag*

6 = entreprise business, concern ◆ **il a monté/il dirige une ~ d'import-export** he set up/he runs an import-export business ◆ **c'est une ~ qui marche/en or** it's a going concern/a gold mine

7 locutions

◆ **avoir affaire à** [+ *cas, problème*] to be faced with, to have to deal with; [+ *personne*] (= *s'occuper de*) to be dealing with; (= *être reçu ou examiné par*) to be dealt with by ◆ **nous avons ~ à un dangereux criminel** we are dealing with a dangerous criminal ◆ **tu auras ~ à moi/lui** *(menace)* you'll be hearing from me/him

2 - NOM FÉMININ PLURIEL

affaires

1 = intérêts publics et privés affairs ◆ **les ~s culturelles/de la municipalité/publiques** cultural/municipal/public affairs ◆ **les Affaires étrangères** Foreign Affairs ◆ **Affaires extérieures** *(au Canada)* External Affairs *(Can)* ◆ **être aux ~s** *(Pol)* to be in office ◆ **se mêler des ~s des autres** to interfere in other people's business ◆ **occupe-toi** ou **mêle-toi de tes ~s !** mind your own business!

2 = activités commerciales business *(sg)* ◆ **être dans les ~s** to be in business ◆ **parler (d')~s** to talk ou discuss business ◆ **ils font beaucoup d'~s ensemble** they do a lot of business together ◆ **les ~s reprennent** business is picking up ◆ **il est dur en ~s** he's a tough businessman ◆ **être en ~s avec qn** to be doing business with sb ◆ **il est venu pour ~s** he came on business ◆ **les ~s sont les ~s** business is business ◆ **d'~(s)** *[repas, voyage, relations]* business *(épith)* ◆ **les milieux d'~s sont optimistes** the business community is optimistic; → **chiffre**

3 = objets personnels things, belongings; (= *habits*) clothes, things ◆ **mes ~s de tennis** my tennis kit ou things ◆ **range tes ~s !** put your things away!

4 locution

◆ **toutes affaires cessantes** immediately, forthwith *(frm)*

3 - COMPOSÉS

affaire de cœur love affair

affaire d'État *(Pol)* affair of state ◆ **il en a fait une ~ d'État*** he made a great song and dance about it ou a great issue of it

affaire de famille (= *entreprise*) family business ou concern; (= *problème*) family problem ou matter

affaire d'honneur matter ou affair of honour

affaire de mœurs *(gén)* sex scandal; *(Jur)* sex case

---

affairé, e /afeʀe/ (ptp de **s'affairer**) ADJ busy

affairement /afɛʀmɑ̃/ NM bustling activity

affairer (s') /afeʀe/ ▸ conjug 1 ◂ VPR to busy o.s., to bustle about ◆ **s'~ auprès** ou **autour de qn** to fuss around sb ◆ **s'~ à faire qch** to busy o.s. doing sth, to bustle about doing sth

affairisme /afeʀism/ NM (political) racketeering

affairiste /afeʀist/ NM *(péj)* huckster, wheeler-dealer* ◆ **sous ce régime il n'y a pas de place pour l'~** there is no place under this government for political racketeering ou for those who want to use politics to line their own pockets

affaissement /afɛsmɑ̃/ NM *[de route, sol]* subsidence, sinking; *[de corps, muscles, poutre]* sagging; *[de forces]* ebbing; *[de volonté]* weakening ◆ **~ de terrain** subsidence *(NonC)*

affaisser /afese/ ▸ conjug 1 ◂ VT [+ *route, sol*] to cause to subside VPR **s'affaisser** 1 (= *fléchir*) *[route, sol]* to subside, to sink; *[corps, poutre]* to sag; *[plancher]* to cave in, to give way; *[forces]* to ebb ◆ **le sol était affaissé par endroits** the ground had subsided ou sunk in places 2 (= *s'écrouler*) *[personne]* to collapse ◆ **il s'était affaissé sur le sol** he had collapsed ou crumpled in a heap on the ground ◆ **il était affaissé dans un fauteuil/sur le sol** he was slumped in an armchair/on the ground

affaler /afale/ ▸ conjug 1 ◂ VT [+ *voile*] to lower, to haul down VPR **s'affaler** 1 (= *tomber*) to collapse, to fall; (= *se laisser tomber*) to collapse, to slump ◆ **affalé dans un fauteuil** slumped ou slouched in an armchair ◆ **au lieu de rester là affalé à ne rien faire, viens m'aider** don't just sit there doing nothing, come and give me a hand 2 *(Naut)* **s'~ le long d'un cordage** to slide down a rope

affamé, e /afame/ (ptp de **affamer**) ADJ starving, famished ◆ **~ de gloire** hungry ou greedy for fame; → **ventre**

affamer /afame/ ▸ conjug 1 ◂ VT [+ *personne, ville*] to starve

affameur, -euse /afamœʀ, øz/ NM,F *(péj)* tight-fisted employer *(who pays starvation wages)*

affect /afɛkt/ NM affect

affectation /afɛktasjɔ̃/ NF 1 *[d'immeuble, somme]* allocation, allotment (*à* to, for); ◆ **l'~ du signe + à un nombre** the addition of the plus sign to a number, the modification of a number by the plus sign 2 (= *nomination*) (*à un poste*) appointment; (*à une région, un pays*) posting ◆ **rejoindre son ~** to take up one's posting 3 (= *manque de naturel*) affectation, affectedness ◆ **avec ~** affectedly

affecté, e /afɛkte/ (ptp de **affecter**) ADJ (= *feint*) affected, feigned; (= *maniéré*) affected

affecter /afɛkte/ ▸ conjug 1 ◂ VT 1 (= *feindre*) to affect, to feign ◆ **~ de faire qch** to pretend to do sth ◆ **~ un grand chagrin** to affect ou feign great sorrow, to put on a show of great sorrow ◆ **~ un langage poétique** *(littér)* to affect ou favour a poetic style of language ◆ **il affecta de ne pas s'y intéresser** he pretended not to be interested in it

2 (= *destiner*) to allocate, to allot (*à* to, for); ◆ **~ des crédits à la recherche** to allocate funds for research

3 (= *nommer*) (*à une fonction, un bureau*) to appoint; (*à une région, un pays*) to post (*à* to)

④ *(= émouvoir)* to affect, to move; *(= concerner)* to affect ◆ **il a été très affecté par leur mort** he was deeply affected by their deaths
⑤ *(Math)* to modify ◆ **nombre affecté du coefficient 2/du signe plus** number modified by *ou* bearing the coefficient 2/a plus sign
⑥ *(Méd)* to affect ◆ **les oreillons affectent surtout les jeunes enfants** mumps mostly affects young children
⑦ *(= prendre)* **ce muscle affecte la forme d'un triangle** this muscle is triangle-shaped *ou* is in the form of a triangle

affectif, -ive /afɛktif, iv/ ADJ emotional; *(Psych)* affective

affection /afɛksjɔ̃/ NF ① *(= tendresse)* affection, fondness ◆ **avoir de l'~ pour qn** to feel affection for sb, to be fond of sb ◆ **prendre qn en ~, se prendre d'~ pour qn** to become fond of *ou* attached to sb ② *(Méd)* ailment, affection ③ *(Psych)* affection

affectionné, e /afɛksjɔne/ (ptp de **affectionner**) ADJ *(frm)* ◆ **votre fils ~** your loving *ou* devoted son ◆ **votre ~** yours affectionately

affectionner /afɛksjɔne/ ► conjug 1 ◄ VT *[+ chose]* to have a liking for, to be fond of; *[+ personne]* to be fond of

affectivité /afɛktivite/ NF affectivity

affectueusement /afɛktɥøzmɑ̃/ ADV affectionately, fondly ◆ **~ vôtre** yours affectionately

affectueux, -euse /afɛktɥø, øz/ ADJ *[personne]* affectionate; *[pensée, regard]* affectionate, fond

afférent, e /afeʀɑ̃, ɑ̃t/ ADJ ① *(Admin)* **~ à** *[fonction]* pertaining to, relating to ◆ **questions y ~es** related questions ◆ **part ~e à** *(Jur)* portion accruing to ② *(Méd)* afferent

affermage /afɛʀmaʒ/ NM *(par le propriétaire)* leasing; *(par le fermier)* renting ◆ **contrat d'~** lease

affermer /afɛʀme/ ► conjug 1 ◄ VT *[propriétaire]* to lease; *[fermier]* to rent

affermir /afɛʀmiʀ/ ► conjug 2 ◄ VT *[+ pouvoir, position]* to consolidate, to strengthen; *[+ principes]* to strengthen; *[+ contrôle]* to tighten up; *[+ tendance]* to reinforce; *[+ autorité]* to reinforce, to strengthen; *[+ muscles]* to tone up ◆ **~ sa prise** *(Sport)* to tighten one's grip ◆ **cela l'a affermi dans sa résolution** that strengthened his resolve ◆ **d'autres preuves ont affermi ma certitude** new evidence convinced me even more VPR **s'affermir** *[pouvoir]* to consolidate itself, to be reinforced; *[détermination, principe]* to be strengthened; *[autorité, tendance]* to be reinforced; *[monnaie]* to strengthen; *[muscles]* to become firmer, to firm up ◆ **la reprise économique devrait s'~** the economic recovery should consolidate itself

affermissement /afɛʀmismɑ̃/ NM *[de pouvoir, position]* consolidation, strengthening; *[de tendance]* reinforcement; *[de monnaie]* strengthening

affété, e /afete/ ADJ *(littér)* affected

afféterie /afetʀi/ NF *(littér)* affectation *(NonC)*, preciosity

affichage /afiʃaʒ/ NM ① *[d'affiche, résultats]* putting *ou* sticking up, posting; *(Théât)* billing ◆ **l'~** billsticking, billposting ◆ **"affichage interdit"** "stick no bills", "post no bills" ◆ **interdit à l'~** *[magazine]* not for public display ◆ **campagne d'~** poster campaign; → **panneau, tableau** ② *(sur écran)* display ◆ **montre à ~ numérique** digital watch ◆ **~ du numéro** *(sur téléphone)* caller display

affiche /afiʃ/ NF ① *(officielle)* public notice; *(Admin)* bill; *(électorale)* poster ◆ **la vente a été annoncée par voie d'~** the sale was advertised on public noticeboards ② *(Théât)* (play)bill ◆ **quitter l'~** to come off, to close ◆ **tenir longtemps l'~** to have a long run ◆ **il y a une belle ~ pour cette pièce** this play has an excellent cast; → **tête**

◆ **à l'affiche** ◆ **mettre à l'~** to bill ◆ **ce spectacle est resté à l'~ plus d'un an** the show ran for over a year ◆ **le film n'est plus à l'~ à Paris** the film is no longer being shown in Paris

afficher /afiʃe/ ► conjug 1 ◄ VT ① *[+ résultats]* to put *ou* stick up, to post; *(Théât)* to bill; *(Ordin)* to display ◆ **"défense d'afficher"** "stick no bills", "post no bills" ◆ **~ complet** to be sold out ② *[+ émotion, mépris, qualité]* to exhibit, to display; *[+ vice]* to flaunt ◆ **~ ses opinions politiques** to make no secret of one's political views ◆ **le ministre a affiché sa volonté d'aider les petites entreprises** the minister has made it clear that he wishes to help small businesses VPR **s'afficher** ① *(= apparaître)* to be displayed ◆ **un menu s'affiche à l'écran** a menu is displayed on the screen ◆ **l'hypocrisie qui s'affiche sur tous les visages** the hypocrisy which is plain to see on everybody's face ② *(= se montrer)* to flaunt o.s. ◆ **s'~ avec son amant** to carry on openly in public with one's lover

affichette /afiʃɛt/ NF *(officielle)* small public notice; *(Admin, Théât)* small bill *ou* poster; *(publicitaire, électorale)* small poster

afficheur, -euse /afiʃœʀ, øz/ NM,F billsticker, billposter NM *(= dispositif)* display

affichiste /afiʃist/ NMF poster designer *ou* artist

affidé, e /afide/ NM,F *(péj)* accomplice, henchman

affilage /afilaʒ/ NM *[de couteau, outil]* sharpening, whetting; *[de rasoir]* sharpening, honing

affilé, e[1] /afile/ (ptp de **affiler**) ADJ *[outil, couteau]* sharp; *[intelligence]* keen; → **langue**

affilée[2] /afile/ **d'affilée** LOC ADV in a row ◆ **8 heures d'~** 8 hours at a stretch *ou* solid ◆ **boire plusieurs verres d'~** to drink several glasses in a row *ou* in succession

affiler /afile/ ► conjug 1 ◄ VT *[+ couteau, outil]* to sharpen, to whet; *[+ rasoir]* to sharpen, to hone

affiliation /afiljasjɔ̃/ NF affiliation

affilié, e /afilje/ (ptp de **affilier**) NM,F affiliated member

affilier /afilje/ ► conjug 7 ◄ VT to affiliate *(à* to) VPR **s'affilier** to become affiliated, to affiliate o.s. *(ou* itself) *(à* to)

affiloir /afilwaʀ/ NM *(= outil)* sharpener; *(= pierre)* whetstone; *(pour couteau)* steel

affinage /afinaʒ/ NM *[de métal]* refining; *[de verre]* fining; *[de fromage]* maturing

affinement /afinmɑ̃/ NM *[d'analyse]* refinement, honing; *[de concept]* refinement; *[de goût, manières, style]* refinement

affiner /afine/ ► conjug 1 ◄ VT ① *[+ métal]* to refine; *[+ verre]* to fine; *[+ fromage]* to complete the maturing (process) of ◆ **fromage affiné en cave** cheese matured in a cellar ② *[+ analyse, image, style, stratégie]* to hone, to refine; *[+ concept]* to refine; *[+ esprit, mœurs]* to refine; *[+ sens]* to make keener, to sharpen ③ *[+ taille, hanches]* to slim (down); *[+ chevilles]* to make slender ◆ **ce maquillage vous affinera le visage** this make-up will make your face look thinner VPR **s'affiner** ① *[analyse, concept]* to become (more) refined; *[style]* to become (more) refined *ou* polished; *[odorat, goût]* to become sharper *ou* keener ② *[personne]* to slim (down); *[taille]* to become slimmer; *[chevilles]* to become (more) slender; *[visage]* to get thinner; *[grain de la peau]* to become finer

affineur, -euse /afinœʀ, øz/ NM,F *[de métal]* refiner; *[de verre]* finer

affinité /afinite/ NF *(entre personnes)* affinity; *(entre œuvres)* similarity ◆ **les deux auteurs ont des ~s** the two writers have affinities, there are similarities between the two writers ◆ **l'actrice s'identifie au personnage de Daphné, elle a des ~s avec elle** the actress identifies with the character of Daphné, she has an affinity with her ◆ **nous avions des ~s littéraires** we felt the same way about books ◆ **"plus si affinités"** *(petite annonce)* "possibly more"

affirmatif, -ive /afiʀmatif, iv/ ADJ *[réponse, proposition]* affirmative; *[personne, ton]* assertive, affirmative; *(Ling)* affirmative, positive ◆ **il a été ~ à ce sujet** he was quite positive on that score *ou* about that ◆ **~ !** *(Mil, hum)* affirmative!; → **signe** NM *(Ling)* affirmative, positive ◆ **à l'~** in the affirmative, in the positive NF **affirmative** affirmative ◆ **répondre par l'affirmative** to answer yes *ou* in the affirmative ◆ **dans l'affirmative** in the event of the answer being yes *ou* of an affirmative reply *(frm)* ◆ **nous espérons que vous viendrez : dans l'affirmative, faites-le-nous savoir** we hope you'll come and if you can (come) please let us know

affirmation /afiʀmasjɔ̃/ NF ① *(= allégation)* claim ◆ **l'~ selon laquelle ce pays aurait immergé des déchets nucléaires** the claim that this country has dumped nuclear waste at sea ② *(Ling)* assertion ③ *(= fait d'affirmer, expression)* assertion ◆ **l'~ de la liberté et de la dignité de la personne humaine** the assertion *ou* affirmation of the freedom and dignity of human beings ◆ **pour lui, toute ~ de sa propre personnalité est jugée suspecte** for him any assertion of one's own personality is regarded as suspect ◆ **une fraction de la population est tentée par l'~ intolérante de son identité** part of the population is tempted to assert its identity in an intolerant way

affirmativement /afiʀmativmɑ̃/ ADV in the affirmative, affirmatively

affirmer /afiʀme/ GRAMMAIRE ACTIVE 53.3, 53.5
► conjug 1 ◄ VT ① *(= soutenir)* to claim, to say ◆ **il affirme l'avoir vu s'enfuir** he claims *ou* says that he saw him run off ◆ **il affirme que c'est de votre faute** he claims *ou* says that it is your fault ◆ **tu affirmes toujours tout sans savoir** you're always very sure about things you know nothing about ◆ **pouvez-vous l'~ ?** can you be positive about it?, can you say that for sure? ◆ **on ne peut rien ~ encore** we can't say anything positive yet ◆ **'c'est lui' affirma-t-elle** 'it's him', she said ◆ **~ sur l'honneur que ...** to give one's word of honour that ...
② *(= manifester) [+ originalité, autorité, position]* to assert ◆ **talent/personnalité qui s'affirme** talent/personality which is asserting itself ◆ **il s'affirme comme l'un de nos meilleurs romanciers** he is establishing himself as one of our best novelists
③ *(= proclamer)* to affirm, to assert ◆ **le président a affirmé sa volonté de régler cette affaire** the president affirmed *ou* asserted his wish to settle the matter

> ⚠ Attention à ne pas traduire automatiquement **affirmer** par **to affirm**, qui a des emplois spécifiques et est d'un registre plus soutenu.

affixe /afiks/ NM *(Ling)* affix

affleurement /aflœʀmɑ̃/ NM *(Géol)* outcrop; *(fig)* emergence; *(Tech)* flushing

affleurer /aflœʀe/ ► conjug 1 ◄ VI *[rocs, récifs]* to show on the surface; *[filon, couche]* to show on the surface, to outcrop *(SPÉC)*; *[sentiment, sensualité]* to come *ou* rise to the surface ◆ **quelques récifs affleuraient (à la surface de l'eau)** a few reefs showed on the surface (of the water) VT *(Tech)* to make flush, to flush

afflictif, -ive /afliktif, iv/ ADJ *(Jur)* corporal

affliction /afliksjɔ̃/ NF *(littér)* affliction ◆ **être dans l'~** to be in a state of affliction

affligé, e /afliʒe/ (ptp de **affliger**) ADJ ◆ **être ~ de** *[maladie]* to be afflicted with ◆ **il était ~ d'une femme acariâtre** he was afflicted *ou* cursed with a cantankerous wife ◆ **les ~s** *(littér)* the afflicted

affligeant, e /afliʒɑ̃, ɑ̃t/ ADJ distressing; *(iro)* pathetic

affliger /afliʒe/ ▸ conjug 3 ◂ VT (= *attrister*) to distress, to grieve; *(littér = accabler)* to smite *(littér)* *(de* with); ◆ **s'~ de qch** to be distressed *ou* grieved about sth ◆ **la nature l'avait affligé d'un nez crochu** *(hum)* nature had afflicted *ou* cursed him with a hooked nose

affluence /aflyɑ̃s/ NF *[de gens]* crowds, throng *(littér)* ◆ **les heures d'~** *[de trains, circulation]* the rush hour; *[de magasin]* the peak shopping period, the busy period

affluent /aflyɑ̃/ NM tributary, affluent *(SPÉC)*

affluer /aflye/ ▸ conjug 1 ◂ VI *[fluide, sang]* to rush, to flow *(à, vers* to); *[foule]* to flock ◆ **les dons affluaient de partout** donations came flooding in from all over ◆ **l'argent afflue dans les caisses de la banque** money is flowing *ou* flooding into the coffers of the bank

afflux /afly/ NM [1] *[de fluide]* inrush; *(Élec)* flow [2] *[d'argent]* inflow; *[de réfugiés, touristes]* influx ◆ **~ de capitaux** capital inflow ◆ **~ de main-d'œuvre** inflow *ou* influx of labour

affolant, e /afɔlɑ̃, ɑ̃t/ ADJ (= *effrayant*) frightening; (= *troublant*) *[situation, nouvelle]* distressing, disturbing ◆ **c'est ~ !*** it's alarming! ◆ **à une vitesse ~e** at an alarming rate

affolé, e /afɔle/ (ptp de **affoler**) ADJ [1] (= *effrayé*) panic- *ou* terror-stricken ◆ **je suis ~ de voir ça*** I'm appalled *ou* horrified at that ◆ **air ~** look of panic [2] *[boussole]* wildly fluctuating

affolement /afɔlmɑ̃/ NM [1] (= *effroi*) panic ◆ **pas d'~ !*** don't panic! [2] *[de boussole]* wild fluctuations

affoler /afɔle/ ▸ conjug 1 ◂ VT (= *effrayer*) to throw into a panic, to terrify; *(littér = troubler)* to drive wild, to throw into a turmoil VPR **s'affoler** *[personne]* to lose one's head; *[gouvernement]* to panic, to lose one's nerve ◆ **la Bourse s'est affolée** there was panic on the Stock Exchange ◆ **ne nous affolons pas*** let's not panic *ou* get in a panic*, let's keep our heads

affouillement /afujmɑ̃/ NM undermining

affouiller /afuje/ ▸ conjug 1 ◂ VT to undermine

affranchi, e /afʀɑ̃ʃi/ (ptp de **affranchir**) NM,F (= *esclave*) emancipated *ou* freed slave; (= *libertin*) emancipated man *(ou* woman)

affranchir /afʀɑ̃ʃiʀ/ ▸ conjug 2 ◂ VT [1] *(avec des timbres)* to put a stamp *ou* stamps on, to stamp; *(à la machine)* to frank ◆ **lettre affranchie/non affranchie** stamped/unstamped letter, franked/unfranked letter ◆ **j'ai reçu une lettre insuffisamment affranchie** I received a letter with insufficient postage on it ◆ **machine à ~** franking machine [2] *[+ esclave]* to enfranchise, to emancipate; *[+ peuple, pays]* to free; *(fig) [+ esprit, personne]* to free, to emancipate ◆ **~ qn de** *[+ contrainte, influence]* to free sb from [3] ◆ **~ qn** *(arg Crime = mettre au courant)* to give sb the low-down*, to put sb in the picture* [4] *(Cartes)* to clear VPR **s'affranchir** ◆ **s'~ de** *[+ domination, convenances]* to free o.s. from

affranchissement /afʀɑ̃ʃismɑ̃/ NM [1] *(avec des timbres)* stamping; *(à la machine)* franking; (= *prix payé*) postage [2] *[d'esclave]* emancipation, freeing; *[de peuple, pays]* freeing; *(fig) [d'esprit, personne]* freeing, emancipation

affres /afʀ/ NFPL *(littér)* ◆ **être dans les ~ de la mort** to be in the throes of death ◆ **le pays s'enfonce dans les ~ d'une crise financière** the country is in the throes of a financial crisis ◆ **dans ce film, il évoque les ~ de la création** in this film, he portrays the trials and tribulations of the creative process

affrètement /afʀɛtmɑ̃/ NM chartering

affréter /afʀete/ ▸ conjug 6 ◂ VT to charter

affréteur /afʀetœʀ/ NM *[de bateau, avion]* charterer; *[de véhicule]* hirer

affreusement /afʀøzmɑ̃/ ADV *[souffrir, blesser]* horribly; *[difficile, vulgaire]* terribly ◆ **~ laid** hideously ugly ◆ **ce plat est ~ mauvais** this food is terrible *ou* awful ◆ **on est ~ mal assis** these seats are terribly uncomfortable ◆ **~ en retard** dreadfully late

affreux, -euse /afʀø, øz/ ADJ (= *très laid*) hideous, ghastly; (= *effroyable, abominable*) dreadful, awful ◆ **quel temps ~ !** what dreadful *ou* awful weather! ◆ **j'ai un mal de tête ~** I've got a terrible headache; → **jojo** NM *(arg Mil)* (white) mercenary

affriander /afʀijɑ̃de/ ▸ conjug 1 ◂ VT *(littér)* to allure, to entice

affriolant, e /afʀijɔlɑ̃, ɑ̃t/ ADJ *[perspective, programme]* appealing, exciting; *[femme]* alluring; *[vêtement]* alluring

affrioler /afʀijɔle/ ▸ conjug 1 ◂ VT to tempt

affriquée /afʀike/ ADJ F affricative NF affricate

affront /afʀɔ̃/ NM (= *insulte*) affront ◆ **faire (un) ~ à qn** to affront sb

affrontement /afʀɔ̃tmɑ̃/ NM *(Mil, Pol)* confrontation

affronter /afʀɔ̃te/ ▸ conjug 1 ◂ VT *[+ adversaire, danger]* to confront, to face ◆ **~ la mort** to face *ou* brave death ◆ **~ le mauvais temps** to brave the bad weather VPR **s'affronter** *[adversaires]* to confront each other ◆ **ces deux théories s'affrontent** these two theories clash *ou* are in direct opposition

affublement /afybləmɑ̃/ NM *(péj)* attire

affubler /afyble/ ▸ conjug 1 ◂ VT ◆ **~ qn de** *[+ vêtement]* to deck *ou* rig* *(Brit)* sb out in ◆ **~ qn d'un sobriquet** to attach a nickname to sb ◆ **il s'affubla d'un vieux manteau** he donned an old coat ◆ **affublé d'un vieux chapeau** wearing an old hat

affût /afy/ NM [1] ◆ **~ (de canon)** (gun) carriage [2] *(Chasse)* hide *(Brit)*, blind *(US)*
◆ **à l'affût** ◆ **chasser à l'~** to hunt game from a hide *(Brit)* *ou* blind *(US)* ◆ **être à l'~** to be lying in wait ◆ **être à l'~ de qch** *(fig)* to be on the look-out for sth ◆ **se mettre à l'~** to lie in wait

affûtage /afytaʒ/ NM sharpening, grinding

affûter /afyte/ ▸ conjug 1 ◂ VT *[+ lame]* to sharpen, to grind; *[+ arguments, stratégie]* to hone ◆ **oreilles affûtées** sharp ears

affûteur /afytœʀ/ NM (= *personne*) grinder

affûteuse /afytøz/ NF (= *machine*) grinder, sharpener

afghan, e /afgɑ̃, an/ ADJ Afghan; → **lévrier** NM (= *langue*) Afghan NM,F **Afghan(e)** Afghan

Afghanistan /afganistɑ̃/ NM Afghanistan

aficionado /afisjɔnado/ NM aficionado

afin /afɛ̃/ GRAMMAIRE ACTIVE 35.2 PRÉP ◆ **~ de** to, in order to ◆ **~ que nous le sachions** so that *ou* in order that we should know

AFNOR /afnɔʀ/ NF (abrév de **Association française de normalisation**) *French Industrial Standards Authority*, ≃ BSI *(Brit)*, ANSI *(US)*

afocal, e (mpl **-aux**) /afɔkal, o/ ADJ afocal

a fortiori /afɔʀsjɔʀi/ LOC ADV all the more, a fortiori *(frm)*

AFP /aɛfpe/ NF (abrév de **Agence France-Presse**) French Press Agency

AFPA /afpa/ NF (abrév de **Association pour la formation professionnelle des adultes**) *adult professional education association*

africain, e /afʀikɛ̃, ɛn/ ADJ African NM,F **Africain(e)** African

africanisation /afʀikanizasjɔ̃/ NF Africanization

africanisme /afʀikanism/ NM Africanism

africaniste /afʀikanist/ NMF Africanist

afrikaans /afʀikɑ̃s/ NM, ADJ INV Afrikaans

afrikander /afʀikɑ̃dɛʀ/, **afrikaner** /afʀikanɛʀ/ ADJ, NMF Afrikaner

Afrique /afʀik/ NF Africa ◆ **l'~ australe/du Nord** Southern/North Africa ◆ **l'~ du Sud** South Africa ◆ **l'~ noire** black Africa

afro* /afʀo/ ADJ INV Afro ◆ **coiffure ~** Afro (hairstyle *ou* hairdo*)

afro-américain, e /afʀoamerikɛ̃, ɛn/ ADJ Afro-American, African-American NM,F **Afro-Américain(e)** Afro-American, African-American

afro-asiatique (pl **afro-asiatiques**) /afʀoazjatik/ ADJ Afro-Asian NMF **Afro-Asiatique** Afro-Asian

afro-brésilien, -ienne /afʀobʀeziljɛ̃, jɛn/ ADJ Afro-Brazilian NM,F **Afro-Brésilien(ne)** Afro-Brazilian

AG* /aʒe/ NF (abrév de **assemblée générale**) *(Écon)* AGM; *[d'étudiants]* EGM

agaçant, e /agasɑ̃, ɑ̃t/ ADJ irritating, annoying

agacement /agasmɑ̃/ NM irritation, annoyance

agacer /agase/ ▸ conjug 3 ◂ VT [1] ◆ **~ qn** (= *énerver*) to get on sb's nerves, to irritate sb; (= *taquiner*) to pester *ou* tease sb ◆ **~ les dents de qn** to set sb's teeth on edge ◆ **~ les nerfs de qn** to get on sb's nerves ◆ **ça m'agace !** it's getting on my nerves! ◆ **agacé par le bruit** irritated *ou* annoyed by the noise ◆ **agacé de l'entendre** irritated by what he said [2] *(littér = aguicher)* to excite, to lead on

agaceries /agasʀi/ NFPL coquetries, provocative gestures

Agamemnon /agamɛmnɔ̃/ NM Agamemnon

agapanthe /agapɑ̃t/ NF agapanthus

agapes /agap/ NFPL *(hum)* banquet, feast

agar-agar (pl **agars-agars**) /agaʀagaʀ/ NM agar(-agar)

agate /agat/ NF agate

agave /agav/ NM agave

AGE /aʒea/ NF (abrév de **assemblée générale extraordinaire**) EGM

âge /ɑʒ/ NM [1] *(gén)* age ◆ **quel ~ avez-vous ?** how old are you?, what age are you? ◆ **à l'~ de 8 ans** at the age of 8 ◆ **j'ai votre ~** I'm your age, I'm the same age as you ◆ **ils sont du même ~** they're the same age ◆ **il est d'un ~ canonique** *(hum)* he's a venerable age ◆ **elle est d'un ~ avancé** she's getting on in years, she's quite elderly ◆ **d'~ moyen, entre deux ~s** middle-aged ◆ **il ne paraît** *ou* **fait pas son ~** he doesn't look his age ◆ **elle porte bien son ~** she looks good for her age ◆ **il fait plus vieux que son ~** he looks older than he is ◆ **sans ~, qui n'a pas d'~** ageless ◆ **on a l'~ de ses artères** you're as old as you feel ◆ **il a vieilli avant l'~** he's got *ou* he's old before his time ◆ **il a pris de l'~** he's aged ◆ **amusez-vous, c'est de votre ~** enjoy yourself, you should (do) at your age ◆ **à son ~** at his age ◆ **j'ai passé l'~ de le faire** I'm too old for that ◆ **avec l'~ il se calmera** he'll settle down as he gets older ◆ **des gens de tout ~** people of all ages ◆ **être en ~ de se marier** to be of marriageable age, to be old enough to get married ◆ **porto de 15 ans d'~** 15-year-old port ◆ **le premier ~** the first three months; → **bas[1], quatrième, troisième**
[2] (= *ère*) age ◆ **ça existait déjà à l'~ des cavernes !** *(hum)* that dates back to the Stone Age!

COMP **l'âge adulte** *(gén)* adulthood; *(pour un homme)* manhood; *(pour une femme)* womanhood ◆ **à l'~ adulte** in adulthood
l'âge bête ◆ **c'est l'~ bête** it's an awkward *ou* difficult age
l'âge du bronze the Bronze Age
l'âge critique the change of life
l'âge du fer the Iron Age
l'âge d'homme manhood
l'âge ingrat ⇒ **l'âge bête**
l'âge légal the legal age ◆ **avoir l'~ légal** to be legally old enough
âge mental mental age
l'âge mûr maturity
l'âge d'or the golden age
l'âge de (la) pierre the Stone Age
l'âge de la pierre polie the Neolithic age
l'âge de la pierre taillée the Palaeolithic age
l'âge de raison the age of reason
l'âge de la retraite retirement age
l'âge tendre (= *petite enfance*) childhood; (= *adolescence*) youth ◆ **à l'~ tendre de quatorze ans** at the tender age of fourteen ◆ **d'~ tendre** young
l'âge viril ⇒ **l'âge d'homme**

âgé, e /ɑʒe/ ADJ ◆ **être ~** to be old, to be elderly ◆ **être ~ de 9 ans** to be 9 years old, to be 9 years of age ◆ **enfant ~ de 4 ans** 4-year-old child ◆ **dame ~e** elderly lady ◆ **les personnes ~es** the elderly

agence /aʒɑ̃s/ NF (= *succursale*) branch (office); (= *bureaux*) offices; (= *organisme*) agency, bureau
COMP **agence commerciale** sales office *ou* agency
Agence pour l'énergie nucléaire Atomic Energy Authority
Agence de l'environnement et de la maîtrise de l'énergie *French energy conservation agency,* ≃ Energy Efficiency Office *(Brit)*
agence immobilière estate agency *(Brit)*, estate agent's (office) *(Brit)*, real estate agency *(US)*
agence d'intérim temping agency
Agence internationale de l'énergie atomique International Atomic Energy Agency
agence matrimoniale marriage bureau
Agence nationale pour l'emploi *French national employment office,* ≃ Jobcentre *(Brit)*
agence de placement employment agency *ou* bureau
agence de presse news *ou* press agency, news service *(US)*
agence de publicité advertising *ou* publicity agency
agence de renseignements information bureau *ou* office
Agence spatiale européenne European Space Agency
agence de tourisme tourist agency
agence de voyages travel agency

agencé, e /aʒɑ̃se/ (ptp de **agencer**) ADJ ◆ **bien ~** *(gén)* well-organized; *[phrase]* well-constructed; *[local] (en meubles)* well-equipped; *(en espace)* well-arranged, well laid-out ◆ **mal ~** *[local] (en meubles)* poorly-equipped; *(en espace)* badly laid-out

agencement /aʒɑ̃smɑ̃/ NM *[d'éléments]* organization; *[de phrase, roman]* construction; *[de couleurs]* combination; *[de local]* (= *disposition*) arrangement, layout; (= *équipement*) equipment ◆ **~s modernes** modern fittings *ou* equipment

agencer /aʒɑ̃se/ ► conjug 3 ◄ VT *[+ éléments]* to put together, to combine; *[+ couleurs]* to combine; *[+ phrase, roman]* to construct, to put together; *[+ local]* (= *disposer*) to lay out, to arrange; (= *équiper*) to equip VPR **s'agencer** *[éléments]* to combine

agenda /aʒɛ̃da/ NM ① (= *carnet*) diary *(Brit)*, datebook *(US)*, calendar *(US)* ② (= *activités*) schedule ◆ **~ très chargé** very busy schedule
COMP **agenda de bureau** desk diary *(Brit) ou* calendar *(US)*
agenda électronique electronic organizer *ou* diary *(Brit)*

> ⚠ **agenda** ne se traduit pas par le mot anglais **agenda**, qui a le sens de 'ordre du jour'.

agenouillement /aʒ(ə)nujmɑ̃/ NM *(littér)* kneeling

agenouiller (s') /aʒ(ə)nuje/ ► conjug 1 ◄ VPR to kneel (down) ◆ **être agenouillé** to be kneeling ◆ **s'~ devant l'autorité** to bow before authority

agenouilloir /aʒ(ə)nujwaʀ/ NM (= *escabeau*) hassock, kneeling stool; (= *planche*) kneeling plank

agent /aʒɑ̃/ NM ① *(Police)* policeman ◆ **pardon, monsieur l'~** excuse me, officer *ou* constable *(Brit)* ◆ **elle est ~** she's a police-woman
② (= *représentant*) agent; *(Admin)* officer, official ◆ **arrêter un ~ ennemi** to arrest an enemy agent ◆ **~ exclusif** sole agent ◆ **~ en franchise** franchised dealer
③ *(Chim, Gram, Sci)* agent; → **complément**
COMP **agent d'accueil** greeter
agent administratif administrative officer
agent d'ambiance *person whose job it is to liaise informally with customers, passengers etc*
agent artistique (artistic) agent
agent d'assurances insurance agent
agent de change † stockbroker
agent de la circulation policeman on traffic duty, ≃ traffic policeman
agent commercial (sales) representative
agent comptable accountant
agent consulaire consular official *ou* officer
agent double double agent
agent électoral campaign organizer *ou* aide
agent d'entretien cleaning operative, maintenance person
agent de l'État public sector employee
agent du fisc tax official *ou* officer
agent de la force publique member of the police force
agent du gouvernement government official
agent immobilier estate agent *(Brit)*, real estate agent *(US)*
agent de liaison *(Mil)* liaison officer
agent littéraire literary agent
agent de maîtrise supervisor
agent maritime shipping agent
agent de médiation ⇒ **agent d'ambiance**
agent de police policeman ◆ **elle est ~** she's a policewoman
agent provocateur agent provocateur
agent public ⇒ **agent de l'État**
agent de publicité advertising agent
agent de renseignements intelligence agent
agent de sapidité flavour enhancer
agent secret secret agent
agent de surface ⇒ **agent d'entretien**
agent technique technician
agent de transmission *(Mil)* despatch rider, messenger
agent voyer ≃ borough surveyor

agentif /aʒɑ̃tif/ NM *(Ling)* agentive

aggiornamento /a(d)ʒjɔʀnamento/ NM ① *(Rel)* aggiornamento ② *(fig)* **il a entrepris un ~ du Parti travailliste** he set about modernizing the Labour Party

agglo * /aglo/ NM abrév de **aggloméré**

agglomérat /aglɔmeʀa/ NM *(Géol)* agglomerate; *[de personnes]* mixture; *[d'objets]* cluster

agglomération /aglɔmeʀasjɔ̃/ NF ① (= *ville*) town ◆ **l'~ parisienne** Paris and its suburbs, the urban area of Paris ◆ **limitation de vitesse en ~** speed limit in built-up areas ② *[de nations, idées]* conglomeration; *[de matériaux]* conglomeration, agglomeration

aggloméré, e /aglɔmeʀe/ NM (= *bois*) chipboard, Masonite ® *(US)*; (= *pierre*) conglomerate; (= *charbon*) briquette

agglomérer /aglɔmeʀe/ ► conjug 6 ◄ VT (= *amonceler*) to pile up; *[+ bois, pierre]* to compress VPR **s'agglomérer** *(Tech)* to agglomerate; (= *s'amonceler*) to pile up; (= *se rassembler*) to conglomerate, to gather ◆ **population agglomérée** dense population

agglutinant, e /aglytinɑ̃, ɑt/ ADJ *(gén)* agglutinating; *[langue]* agglutinative NM agglutinant

agglutination /aglytinasjɔ̃/ NF *(Bio, Ling)* agglutination

agglutiner /aglytine/ ► conjug 1 ◄ VT to stick together; *(Bio)* to agglutinate ◆ **les passants s'agglutinaient devant la vitrine** passers-by gathered in front of the window

agglutinogène /aglytinɔʒɛn/ NM agglutinogen

aggravant, e /agʀavɑ̃, ɑt/ ADJ *[facteur]* aggravating; → **circonstance**

aggravation /agʀavasjɔ̃/ NF *[de mal, situation]* worsening, aggravation; *[d'impôt, chômage]* increase

aggraver /agʀave/ ► conjug 1 ◄ VT (= *faire empirer*) to make worse, to aggravate; (= *renforcer*) to increase ◆ **~ la récession** to deepen the recession ◆ **~ le déficit budgétaire** to increase the budget deficit ◆ **~ la situation** to make matters worse ◆ **ça ne fera qu'~ nos problèmes** it will only make our problems worse ◆ **la répression n'a fait qu'~ la crise** repression has deepened *ou* aggravated the crisis ◆ **tu aggraves ton cas** you're making things worse for yourself ◆ **il a aggravé la marque** *ou* **le score à la 35ᵉ minute** he increased their lead in the 35th minute
VPR **s'aggraver** (= *empirer*) to get worse, to worsen; (= *se renforcer*) to increase ◆ **le chômage s'est fortement aggravé** unemployment has increased sharply, there has been a sharp increase in unemployment

> ⚠ Attention à ne pas traduire automatiquement **aggraver** par **to aggravate**, qui est d'un registre plus soutenu.

agile /aʒil/ ADJ agile ◆ **~ de ses mains** nimble with one's fingers ◆ **d'un geste ~** with a quick gesture ◆ **~ comme un singe** as agile as a goat

agilement /aʒilmɑ̃/ ADV nimbly, with agility

agilité /aʒilite/ NF agility, nimbleness

agio /aʒjo/ NM ① (= *différence de cours*) Exchange premium ② (= *frais*) **~s** (bank) charges

agiotage /aʒjɔtaʒ/ NM speculation

agioter /aʒjɔte/ ► conjug 1 ◄ VI to speculate

agioteur, -euse /aʒjɔtœʀ, øz/ NM,F speculator

agir /aʒiʀ/ GRAMMAIRE ACTIVE 53.2 ► conjug 2 ◄
VI ① *(gén)* to act; (= *se comporter*) to behave, to act ◆ **il faut ~ tout de suite** we must act *ou* do something at once, we must take action at once ◆ **il a agi de son plein gré/en toute liberté** he acted quite willingly/freely ◆ **il agit comme un enfant** he acts *ou* behaves like a child ◆ **il a bien/mal agi envers sa mère** he behaved well/badly towards his mother ◆ **il a sagement agi** he did the right thing, he acted wisely ◆ **le syndicat a décidé d'~** the union has decided to take action *ou* to act ◆ **~ en ami** to behave *ou* act like a friend ◆ **~ au nom de qn** to act on behalf of sb; → **façon, manière**
② (= *exercer une influence*) **~ sur qch** to act on sth ◆ **~ sur qn** to bring pressure to bear on sb ◆ **~ sur le marché** *(Bourse)* to influence the market ◆ **~ auprès de qn** to use one's influence with sb

3 *(locution)*
♦ **faire agir** ♦ **faire ~ la loi** to put *ou* set the law in motion ♦ **il a fait ~ son syndicat/ses amis** he got his union/friends to act *ou* take action ♦ **je ne sais pas ce qui le fait ~ ainsi** I don't know what prompts him to *ou* makes him act like that
4 *(= opérer) [médicament]* to act, to work; *[influence]* to have an effect *(sur* on); ♦ **le remède agit lentement** the medicine is slow to take effect, the medicine acts *ou* works slowly ♦ **laisser ~ la nature** to let nature take its course ♦ **la lumière agit sur les plantes** light acts on *ou* has an effect on plants
VB IMPERS **s'agir** 1 ♦ **il s'agit de ...** *(= il est question de)* it is a matter *ou* question of ... ♦ **dans ce film il s'agit de 3 bandits** this film is about 3 gangsters ♦ **décide-toi, il s'agit de ton avenir** make up your mind, it's your future that's at stake ♦ **les livres dont il s'agit** the books in question ♦ **quand il s'agit de manger, il est toujours là** when it comes to food, he's never far away ♦ **quand il s'agit de travailler, il n'est jamais là** when there's any work to be done, he's never there *ou* around ♦ **on a trouvé des colonnes : il s'agirait/il s'agit d'un temple grec** some columns have been found: it would appear to be/it is a Greek temple ♦ **de quoi s'agit-il ?** what is it?, what's it (all) about? ♦ **voilà ce dont il s'agit** that's what it's (all) about ♦ **il ne s'agit pas d'argent** it's not a question of money ♦ **il ne s'agit pas de ça !** that's not it! *ou* the point! ♦ **il s'agit bien de ça !** *(iro)* that's hardly the problem! ♦ **il s'agissait bien de son frère** it was (about) his brother after all
2 *(= il est nécessaire de faire)* **il s'agit de faire vite** we must act quickly, the thing (to do) is to act quickly ♦ **il s'agit pour lui de réussir** what he has to do is succeed ♦ **maintenant, il ne s'agit pas de plaisanter** this is no time for jokes ♦ **avec ça, il ne s'agit pas de plaisanter** that's no joking matter ♦ **maintenant il s'agit de garder notre avance** now it's a matter *ou* question of maintaining our lead, now what we have to do *ou* must do is maintain our lead ♦ **il s'agit** *ou* **s'agirait de s'entendre : tu viens ou tu ne viens pas ?** let's get one thing clear *ou* straight – are you coming or aren't you? ♦ **il s'agit de savoir ce qu'il va faire** it's a question of knowing what he's going to do, what we have to establish is what he's going to do
3 *(loc)* **s'agissant de qn/qch** as regards sb/sth ♦ **s'agissant de sommes aussi importantes, il faut être prudent** when such large amounts are involved, one must be careful

AGIRC /aʒiʀk/ **NF** (abrév de **Association générale des institutions de retraite des cadres**) *confederation of executive pension funds*

âgisme /ɑʒism/ **NM** ageism

agissant, e /aʒisɑ̃, ɑ̃t/ **ADJ** *(= actif)* active; *(= efficace)* efficacious, effective ♦ **minorité ~e** active *ou* influential minority

agissements /aʒismɑ̃/ **NMPL** *(péj)* schemes, intrigues ♦ **surveiller les ~ de qn** to keep an eye on what sb is up to *

agitateur, -trice /aʒitatœʀ, tʀis/ **NM,F** *(Pol)* agitator **NM** *(Chim)* stirring rod

agitation /aʒitasjɔ̃/ **NF** 1 *[de personne] (ayant la bougeotte)* restlessness, fidgetiness; *(affairé)* bustle; *(troublé)* agitation 2 *[de mer]* roughness, choppiness; *[d'air]* turbulence; *[de lieu, rue]* hustle and bustle 3 *(Pol)* unrest, agitation

agité, e /aʒite/ (ptp de **agiter**) **ADJ** 1 *[personne] (= ayant la bougeotte)* restless, fidgety; *(= affairé)* bustling *(épith)*; *(= troublé)* agitated 2 *[mer]* rough, choppy; *(Naut)* moderate; *[vie]* hectic; *[époque]* troubled; *[nuit]* restless ♦ **mer peu ~e** slight sea *ou* swell ♦ **avoir le sommeil ~** to toss about in one's sleep **NM,F** *(Psych)* manic person ♦ **c'est un ~** he's manic

agiter /aʒite/ ▸ conjug 1 ◂ **VT** 1 *(= secouer) [+ bras, mouchoir]* to wave; *[+ ailes]* to flap, to flutter; *[+ queue]* to wag; *[+ bouteille, liquide]* to shake; *[+ menace]* to brandish ♦ **~ avant l'emploi** shake (well) before use ♦ **~ l'air de ses bras** to wave one's arms about ♦ **le vent agite doucement les branches** the wind gently stirs the branches ♦ **le vent agite violemment les branches** the wind shakes the branches ♦ **les feuilles, agitées par le vent** the leaves, fluttering in the wind ♦ **bateau agité par les vagues** boat tossed about *ou* rocked by the waves ♦ **~ le spectre** *ou* **l'épouvantail de qch** to raise the spectre of sth
2 *(= inquiéter)* to trouble, to perturb
3 *(= débattre) [+ question, problème]* to discuss, to debate
VPR **s'agiter** 1 *[employé, serveur]* to bustle about; *[malade]* to move about *ou* toss restlessly; *[enfant, élève]* to fidget; *[foule, mer]* to stir ♦ **s'~ dans son sommeil** to toss and turn in one's sleep ♦ **les pensées qui s'agitent dans ma tête** the thoughts going round and round about in my head ♦ **le peuple s'agite** the masses are getting restless ♦ **s'~ sur sa chaise** to wriggle about on one's chair
2 *(* = se dépêcher)* to get a move on *

> ⚠ Attention à ne pas traduire automatiquement **agiter** par **to agitate**, qui est d'un registre plus soutenu.

agit-prop /aʒitpʀɔp/ **NF INV** agitprop

agneau (pl **agneaux**) /aɲo/ **NM** lamb; *(= fourrure)* lambskin ♦ **son mari est un véritable ~** her husband is as meek as a lamb ♦ **mes ~x** *(iro)* my dears *(iro)* ♦ **l'Agneau de Dieu** the Lamb of God ♦ **l'Agneau pascal** the Paschal Lamb ♦ **l'~ sans tache** *(Rel)* the lamb without stain ♦ **l'~ du sacrifice** the sacrificial lamb; → **doux, innocent**

agnelage /aɲ(ə)laʒ/ **NM** *(= mise bas)* lambing; *(= époque)* lambing season

agneler /aɲ(ə)le/ ▸ conjug 5 ◂ **VI** to lamb

agnelet /aɲ(ə)lɛ/ **NM** small lamb, lambkin †

agneline /aɲ(ə)lin/ **NF** lamb's wool

agnelle /aɲɛl/ **NF** (female) lamb

agnosticisme /agnɔstisism/ **NM** agnosticism

agnostique /agnɔstik/ **ADJ, NMF** agnostic

agonie /agɔni/ **NF** *(avant la mort)* death pangs ♦ **entrer en ~** to be on the point of death ♦ **être à l'~** to be close to death ♦ **longue ~** slow death ♦ **son ~ fut longue** he died a slow death ♦ **l'~ d'un régime** the death throes of a régime

> ⚠ **agonie** se traduit rarement par **agony**, qui a le sens de 'angoisse'.

agonir /agɔniʀ/ ▸ conjug 2 ◂ **VT** to revile ♦ **~ qn d'injures** to hurl insults *ou* abuse at sb, to heap insults *ou* abuse on sb

agonisant, e /agɔnizɑ̃, ɑ̃t/ **ADJ** *(littér ou fig)* dying ♦ **la prière des ~s** prayers for the dying, last rites

agoniser /agɔnize/ ▸ conjug 1 ◂ **VI** to be dying ♦ **un blessé agonisait dans un fossé** a wounded man lay dying in a ditch

> ⚠ **agoniser** ne se traduit pas par **to agonize**, qui a le sens de 'se tourmenter'.

agora /agɔʀa/ **NF** *(Antiq)* agora; *(= espace piétonnier)* concourse

agoraphobe /agɔʀafɔb/ **ADJ, NMF** agoraphobic

agoraphobie /agɔʀafɔbi/ **NF** agoraphobia

agouti /aguti/ **NM** agouti

agrafage /agʀafaʒ/ **NM** *[de vêtement]* hooking (up), fastening (up); *[de papiers]* stapling; *(Méd)* putting in of clips

agrafe /agʀaf/ **NF** *[de vêtement]* hook (and eye) fastener; *[de papiers]* staple; *(Méd)* clip

agrafer /agʀafe/ ▸ conjug 1 ◂ **VT** 1 *[+ vêtement]* to hook (up), to fasten (up); *[+ papiers]* to staple 2 *(* = arrêter)* to bust *, to nab *

agrafeuse /agʀaføz/ **NF** stapler

agraire /agʀɛʀ/ **ADJ** *[politique, loi]* agrarian; *[mesure, surface]* land *(épith)*; → **réforme**

agrammatical, e (mpl **-aux**) /agʀamatikal, o/ **ADJ** agrammatical

agrandir /agʀɑ̃diʀ/ ▸ conjug 2 ◂ **VT** 1 *(= rendre plus grand) [+ passage]* to widen; *[+ trou]* to make bigger, to enlarge; *[+ usine, domaine]* to enlarge, to extend; *[+ écart]* to increase; *[+ photographie]* to enlarge, to blow up *; *(à la loupe)* to magnify; *(en photocopiant)* to enlarge ♦ **ce miroir agrandit la pièce** this mirror makes the room look bigger *ou* larger ♦ **(faire) ~ sa maison** to extend one's house
2 *(= développer)* to extend, to expand ♦ **pour ~ le cercle de ses activités** to widen *ou* extend the scope of one's activities
3 *(= ennoblir) [+ âme]* to uplift, to elevate
VPR **s'agrandir** *[ville, famille]* to grow, to expand; *[écart]* to widen, to grow; *[passage]* to get wider; *[trou]* to get bigger ♦ **il nous a fallu nous ~** we had to expand, we had to find a bigger place ♦ **ses yeux s'agrandirent sous le coup de la surprise** his eyes widened *ou* grew wide with surprise

agrandissement /agʀɑ̃dismɑ̃/ **NM** *[de local]* extension; *[de puissance, ville]* expansion; *(Photo) (= action)* enlargement; *(= photo)* enlargement, blow-up *

agrandisseur /agʀɑ̃disœʀ/ **NM** enlarger

agraphie /agʀafi/ **NF** agraphia

agrarien, -ienne /agʀaʀjɛ̃, jɛn/ **ADJ, NM** *(Hist, Pol)* agrarian

agréable /agʀeabl/ **ADJ** pleasant ♦ **~ à voir** nice to see ♦ **~ à l'œil** pleasing to the eye ♦ **~ à vivre** *[personne]* easy *ou* pleasant to live with; *[lieu]* pleasant to live in ♦ **il est toujours ~ de ...** it is always pleasant *ou* nice to ... ♦ **ce que j'ai à dire n'est pas ~** what I have to say isn't (very) pleasant ♦ **si ça peut lui être ~** if that will please him ♦ **il me serait ~ de ...** it would be a pleasure for me to ..., I should be pleased to ... ♦ **être ~ de sa personne** † to be pleasant-looking *ou* personable **NM** ♦ **l'~ de la chose** the pleasant *ou* nice thing about it; → **joindre**

> ⚠ Attention à ne pas traduire automatiquement **agréable** par le mot anglais **agreeable**, qui est d'un registre plus soutenu et a d'autres sens.

agréablement /agʀeabləmɑ̃/ **ADV** pleasantly ♦ **je suis très ~ surpris** I'm very pleasantly surprised ♦ **nous avons ~ passé la soirée** we had a pleasant *ou* nice evening

agréé, e /agʀee/ (ptp de **agréer**) **ADJ** *[bureau, infirmière, nourrice]* registered ♦ **fournisseur ~** authorized *ou* registered dealer; → **comptable** **NM** († : *Jur)* counsel, attorney *(US) (appearing for parties before a commercial court)*

agréer /agʀee/ ▸ conjug 1 ◂ *(frm)* **VT** *(= accepter) [+ demande, excuses]* to accept; *[+ fournisseur, matériel]* to approve ♦ **veuillez ~, Monsieur** *ou* **je vous prie d'~, Monsieur, l'expression de mes sentiments distingués** *ou* **les meilleurs** *ou* **l'assurance de ma considération distinguée** *(formule épistolaire)* yours sincerely, sincerely yours *(US)*; *(plus impersonnel)* yours faithfully **VT INDIR** **agréer à** *[+ personne]* to please, to suit ♦ **si cela vous agrée** if it suits *ou* pleases you, if you are agreeable

agrég * /agʀɛg/ **NF** abrév de **agrégation**

agrégat /agʀega/ NM *(Constr, Écon, Géol)* aggregate; *(péj)* *[d'idées]* mishmash

agrégatif, -ive /agʀegatif, iv/ NM,F *candidate for the agrégation*

agrégation /agʀegasjɔ̃/ NF [1] *(Univ) high-level competitive examination for recruiting teachers in France* [2] *[de particules]* aggregation

agrégé, e /agʀeʒe/ (ptp de **agréger**) NM,F *qualified teacher (holder of the agrégation);* → **professeur**

agréger /agʀeʒe/ ▸ conjug 3 et 6 ◂ VT *[+ particules]* to aggregate ◆ **~ qn à un groupe** to incorporate sb into a group ◆ **s'~ à un groupe** to incorporate o.s. into a group

agrément /agʀemɑ̃/ NM [1] *(littér = charme)* *[de personne, conversation]* charm; *[de visage]* attractiveness, charm; *[de lieu, climat]* pleasantness, agreeableness, amenity *(littér)* ◆ **sa compagnie est pleine d'~** he is very pleasant company ◆ **ville/maison sans ~** unattractive town/house, town/house with no agreeable *ou* attractive features ◆ **les ~s de la vie** the pleasures of life, the pleasant things in life ◆ **faire un voyage d'~** to go on *ou* make a pleasure trip; → **art, jardin, plante**[1] [2] *(frm = consentement)* consent, approval; *(Jur)* assent ◆ **donner son ~ à qch** to give one's consent *ou* assent to sth [3] *(Mus)* **(note d')~** grace note

agrémenter /agʀemɑ̃te/ ▸ conjug 1 ◂ VT ◆ **~ qch de** *(= décorer)* to embellish *ou* adorn sth with; *(= relever)* to accompany sth with ◆ **agrémenté de broderies** trimmed *ou* embellished with embroidery ◆ **conférence agrémentée de projections** lecture accompanied by slides ◆ **~ un récit d'anecdotes** to pepper *ou* enliven a story with anecdotes ◆ **dispute agrémentée de coups** *(iro)* argument enlivened with blows

agrès /agʀɛ/ NMPL [1] *(Sport)* apparatus *(sg)* [2] † *[de bateau, avion]* tackle ◆ **exercices aux ~** exercises on the apparatus, apparatus work

agresser /agʀese/ ▸ conjug 1 ◂ VT to attack ◆ **il s'est senti agressé** *(physiquement)* he felt they *(ou you etc)* were being aggressive towards him; *(psychologiquement)* he felt they *(ou you etc)* were hostile towards him ◆ **il l'a agressée verbalement et physiquement** he subjected her to verbal and physical abuse ◆ **agressé par la vie moderne** feeling the strains *ou* stresses of modern life

agresseur, euse /agʀesœʀ, øz/ NM, F attacker, assailant ◆ **(pays) ~** aggressor

agressif, -ive /agʀesif, iv/ ADJ *(gén)* aggressive *(envers* towards, with); ◆ **d'un ton ~** aggressively ◆ **campagne publicitaire agressive** aggressive advertising campaign

agression /agʀesjɔ̃/ NF *(contre une personne)* attack; *(contre un pays)* aggression; *(dans la rue)* mugging; *(Psych)* aggression ◆ **~ nocturne** attack *ou* assault at night ◆ **être victime d'une ~** to be mugged ◆ **les ~s de la vie moderne** the stresses of modern life

agressivement /agʀesivmɑ̃/ ADV aggressively

agressivité /agʀesivite/ NF aggression, aggressiveness

agreste /agʀɛst/ ADJ *(littér)* rustic

agricole /agʀikɔl/ ADJ *[accord, machine, ressources, enseignement]* agricultural; *[produits, travaux]* farm *(épith)*, agricultural; *[population]* farming *(épith)*, agricultural ◆ **syndicat ~** farmers' union ◆ **lycée ~** ≃ secondary school *(Brit)* *ou* high school *(US)* which trains farmers ◆ **le monde ~** the agricultural *ou* farming world; → **comice, exploitation**

agriculteur, -trice /agʀikyltœʀ, tʀis/ NM,F farmer

agriculture /agʀikyltyʀ/ NF agriculture, farming ◆ **~ raisonnée** sustainable agriculture

agripper /agʀipe/ ▸ conjug 1 ◂ VT *(= se retenir à)* to grab *ou* clutch (hold of), to grasp; *(= arracher)* to snatch, to grab VPR **s'agripper** ◆ **s'~ à qch** to cling on to sth, to clutch *ou* grip sth ◆ **ne t'agrippe pas à moi** don't cling on to *ou* hang on to me

agritourisme /agʀituʀizm/ NM agri(-)tourism

agroalimentaire /agʀoalimɑ̃tɛʀ/ ADJ *[industrie]* food-processing ◆ **produits ~s** processed foodstuffs NM ◆ **l'~** the food-processing industry

agrochimie /agʀoʃimi/ NF agrochemistry

agrochimique /agʀoʃimik/ ADJ agrochemical

agroforesterie /agʀɔfɔʀɛstʀi/ NF agro(-)forestry

agro-industrie (pl **agro-industries**) /agʀoɛ̃dystʀi/ NF agribusiness

agro-industriel, -elle /agʀoɛ̃dystʀijɛl/ ADJ agro-industrial

agronome /agʀɔnɔm/ NMF agronomist ◆ **ingénieur ~** agricultural engineer

agronomie /agʀɔnɔmi/ NF agronomy, agronomics *(sg)*

agronomique /agʀɔnɔmik/ ADJ agronomic(al)

agrume /agʀym/ NM citrus fruit

aguerrir /ageʀiʀ/ ▸ conjug 2 ◂ VT to harden ◆ **~ qn contre qch** to harden sb to *ou* against sth, to inure sb to sth ◆ **des troupes aguerries** *(au combat)* seasoned troops; *(à l'effort)* trained troops ◆ **s'~** to become hardened ◆ **s'~ contre** to become hardened to *ou* against, to inure o.s. to

aguets /agɛ/ **aux aguets** LOC ADV on the look-out, on the watch

aguichant, e /agiʃɑ̃, ɑ̃t/ ADJ enticing, tantalizing

aguiche /agiʃ/ NF teaser

aguicher /agiʃe/ ▸ conjug 1 ◂ VT to entice, to lead on

aguicheur, -euse /agiʃœʀ, øz/ ADJ enticing, tantalizing NM *(= enjôleur)* seducer NF **aguicheuse** *(= allumeuse)* tease, vamp

ah /ɑ/ EXCL [1] *(réponse, réaction exclamative)* ah!, oh! ◆ **~ ?, ~ bon ?, ~ oui ?** *(question)* really?, is that so? ◆ **~ bon** *(résignation)* oh *ou* ah well ◆ **~ oui** *(insistance)* oh yes, yes indeed ◆ **~ non** *(insistance)* oh no, certainly *ou* definitely not ◆ **~ bien (ça) alors !** *(surprise)* well, well!, just fancy! *(Brit)*; *(indignation)* well really! ◆ **~ bien oui** well of course [2] *(intensif)* ah!, oh! ◆ **~ ! j'allais oublier** oh! *ou* ah! I nearly forgot ◆ **~, ~ ! je t'y prends** aha! *ou* oho! I've caught you at it ◆ **~, qu'il est lent !** oh, he's so slow! NM ◆ **pousser un ~ de soulagement** to sigh with relief, to give a sigh of relief ◆ **des ~ d'allégresse** oohs and ahs of joy

ahan †† /aɑ̃/ NM ◆ **à grand ~** with much striving

ahaner /aane/ ▸ conjug 1 ◂ VI *(†† ou littér)* *(= peiner)* to labour *(Brit)*, to labor *(US)*; *(= respirer)* to breathe heavily ◆ **ahanant sous le fardeau** labouring under the burden

ahuri, e /ayʀi/ (ptp de **ahurir**) ADJ *(= stupéfait)* stunned, flabbergasted; *(= hébété, stupide)* stupefied ◆ **avoir l'air ~** to look stunned *ou* stupefied ◆ **ne prends pas cet air ~** don't look so flabbergasted NM,F *(péj)* blockhead*, nitwit*

ahurir /ayʀiʀ/ ▸ conjug 2 ◂ VT to dumbfound, to astound

ahurissant, e /ayʀisɑ̃, ɑ̃t/ ADJ stupefying, astounding; *(sens affaibli)* staggering

ahurissement /ayʀismɑ̃/ NM stupefaction

aï /ai/ NM *(= animal)* three-toed sloth, ai

aiche /ɛʃ/ NF ⇒ **èche**

aide[1] /ɛd/ NF [1] *(= assistance)* help, assistance ◆ **apporter son ~ à qn** to help *ou* assist sb ◆ **son ~ nous a été précieuse** he was a great help to us, his help was invaluable to us ◆ **appeler/crier à l'~** to call/shout for help ◆ **appeler qn à son ~** to call to sb for help ◆ **venir en ~ à qn** to help sb, to come to sb's assistance *ou* aid ◆ **à l'~ !** help! ◆ **sans l'~ de personne** without any help (from anyone), completely unassisted *ou* unaided

[2] *(locution)*

◆ **à l'aide de** with the help *ou* aid of ◆ **ouvrir qch à l'~ d'un couteau** to open sth with a knife

[3] *(en équipement, en argent etc)* aid ◆ **l'~ humanitaire/alimentaire** humanitarian/food aid *ou* relief ◆ **~ de l'État** government *ou* state aid

[4] *(Équitation)* **~s** aids

[5] *(Ordin)* help ◆ **~ en ligne (contextuelle)** (context-sensitive) on-line help

COMP **aide au développement** development aid
aide à l'embauche employment incentive
aide judiciaire legal aid
aide médicale (gratuite) (free) medical aid
aide personnalisée au logement ≃ housing benefit *(Brit)* *ou* subsidy *(US)*
aide au retour repatriation grant *(for immigrants returning to their country of origin)*
aide sociale social security *(Brit)*, welfare *(US)*

aide[2] /ɛd/ NMF *(= personne)* assistant ◆ **~-chimiste/-chirurgien** assistant chemist/surgeon ◆ **~-maçon** builder's mate *(Brit)* *ou* labourer

COMP **aide de camp** aide-de-camp
aide de cuisine kitchen hand
aide électricien electrician's mate *(Brit)* *ou* helper *(US)*
aide familiale *(= personne)* mother's help *(Brit)* *ou* helper *(US)*, home help
aide jardinier gardener's helper *ou* mate *(Brit)*, under-gardener *(Brit)*
aide de laboratoire laboratory assistant
aide maternelle ⇒ **aide familiale**

aide-comptable (pl **aides-comptables**) /ɛdkɔ̃tabl/ NMF accountant's assistant

aide-mémoire /ɛdmemwaʀ/ NM INV *(gén)* aide-mémoire; *(Scol)* crib

aide-ménagère (pl **aides-ménagères**) /ɛdmenaʒɛʀ/ NF home help *(Brit)*, home helper *(US)*

aider /ede/ ▸ conjug 1 ◂ VT to help ◆ **~ qn (à faire qch)** to help sb (to do sth) ◆ **~ qn à monter/à descendre/à traverser** to help sb up/down/across *ou* over ◆ **il l'a aidé à sortir de la voiture** he helped him out of the car ◆ **il m'a aidé de ses conseils** he gave me some helpful advice ◆ **~ qn financièrement** to help sb (out) *ou* assist sb financially, to give sb financial help ◆ **il m'aide beaucoup** he helps me a lot, he's a great help to me ◆ **je me suis fait ~ par ou de mon frère** I got my brother to help *ou* to give me a hand ◆ **elle ne se déplace qu'aidée de sa canne** she can only get about with (the aid *ou* help of) her walking stick ◆ **il n'est pas aidé !*** *(hum)* nature hasn't been kind to him! ◆ **on n'est pas aidé avec un chef comme lui !** having him for a boss doesn't exactly make things easy!

VI to help ◆ **elle est venue pour ~** she came to help *ou* to give a hand ◆ **~ à la cuisine** to help (out) in *ou* give a hand in the kitchen ◆ **le débat aiderait à la compréhension du problème** discussion would contribute towards an understanding of the problem, discussion would help us to understand the problem ◆ **ça aide à passer le temps** it helps (to) pass the time ◆ **l'alcool aidant, il se mit à parler** helped on by the alcohol *ou* with the help of alcohol, he began to speak; → **dieu**

VPR **s'aider** 1 *(réfléchi)* ◆ **s'~ de** to use, to make use of ◆ **atteindre le placard en s'aidant d'un escabeau** to reach the cupboard by using a stool *ou* with the aid of a stool ◆ **en s'aidant de ses bras** using his arms to help him

2 *(réciproque)* **entre voisins il faut s'~** neighbours should help each other (out) ◆ **aide-toi, le ciel t'aidera** *(Prov)* God helps those who help themselves *(Prov)*

aide-soignant, e (mpl **aides-soignants**) /ɛdswanjɑ̃, ɑ̃t/ NM,F nursing auxiliary *(Brit)*, nurse's aide *(US)*

aïe /aj/ EXCL *(douleur)* ouch!, ow! ◆ **aïe aïe aïe !, ça se présente mal** dear oh dear, things don't look too good!

AIEA /aiəa/ NF (abrév de **Agence internationale de l'énergie atomique**) IAEA

aïeul /ajœl/ NM *(littér)* grandfather ◆ **les ~s** the grandparents

aïeule /ajœl/ NF *(littér)* grandmother

aïeux /ajø/ NMPL *(littér)* forefathers, forebears *(littér)* ◆ **mes ~ !** (*, † *ou hum*) my godfathers! * †, by jingo! * †

aigle /ɛgl/ NM (= *oiseau, lutrin*) eagle ◆ **il a un regard d'~** he has eyes like a hawk, he's eagle-eyed ◆ **ce n'est pas un ~** * he's no genius

COMP **aigle d'Amérique** American eagle
aigle chauve bald eagle
aigle de mer (= *oiseau*) sea eagle; (= *poisson*) eagle ray
aigle royal golden eagle

NF (= *oiseau, insigne*) eagle

aiglefin /ɛgləfɛ̃/ NM haddock

aiglon, -onne /ɛglɔ̃, ɔn/ NM,F eaglet ◆ **l'Aiglon** *(Hist)* Napoleon II

aigre /ɛgʀ/ ADJ 1 *[fruit]* sour, sharp; *[vin]* vinegary, sour; *[goût, odeur, lait]* sour ◆ **tourner à l'~** *(fig)* to turn sour; → **crème** 2 *[son, voix]* sharp, shrill 3 *[froid]* bitter; *[vent]* keen, cutting *(épith)* 4 *[propos, critique]* cutting *(épith)*, harsh

aigre-doux, aigre-douce (mpl **aigres-doux**, fpl **aigres-douces**) /ɛgʀədu, dus/ ADJ *[sauce]* sweet and sour; *[fruit]* bitter-sweet; *[propos]* bitter-sweet

aigrefin /ɛgʀəfɛ̃/ NM swindler, crook

aigrelet, -ette /ɛgʀəlɛ, ɛt/ ADJ *[petit-lait, pomme]* sourish; *[vin]* vinegarish; *[voix, son]* shrill

aigrement /ɛgʀəmɑ̃/ ADV *[répondre, dire]* sourly

aigrette /ɛgʀɛt/ NF (= *plume*) feather; (= *oiseau*) egret; (= *bijou*) aigret(te); *(Bot)* pappus

aigreur /ɛgʀœʀ/ NF 1 (= *acidité*) *[de petit-lait]* sourness; *[de vin]* sourness, acidity; *[de pomme]* sourness, sharpness 2 (= *acrimonie*) sharpness, harshness NFPL **aigreurs** ◆ **avoir des ~s (d'estomac)** to have heartburn

aigri, e /egʀi/ (ptp de **aigrir**) ADJ embittered, bitter

aigrir /egʀiʀ/ ► conjug 2 ◄ VT *[+ personne]* to embitter; *[+ caractère]* to sour VPR **s'aigrir** *[aliment]* to turn sour; *[caractère]* to sour ◆ **il s'est aigri** he has become embittered

aigu, -uë /egy/ ADJ 1 *[son, voix]* high-pitched, shrill; *[note]* high-pitched, high 2 *[crise, problème]* acute; *[douleur]* acute, sharp; *[intelligence]* keen, acute 3 (= *pointu*) sharp, pointed; → **accent, angle** NM *(Mus) (sur bouton de réglage)* treble ◆ **les ~s** the high notes ◆ **passer du grave à l'~** to go from low to high pitch

aigue-marine (pl **aigues-marines**) /ɛgmaʀin/ NF aquamarine

aiguière /egjɛʀ/ NF ewer

aiguillage /egɥijaʒ/ NM *(Rail)* (= *action*) shunting *(Brit)*, switching *(US)*; (= *instrument*) points *(Brit)*, switch *(US)* ◆ **le déraillement est dû à une erreur d'~** the derailment was due to faulty shunting *(Brit) ou* switching *(US)* ◆ **il y a eu une erreur d'~** *(fig) (gén)* it (*ou* he *etc*) was sent to the wrong place; *(orientation scolaire)* he was (*ou* they were *etc*) pointed *ou* steered in the wrong direction; → **cabine, poste²**

aiguille /egɥij/ NF 1 *(Bot, Couture, Méd)* needle ◆ **travail à l'~** needlework; → **chercher, fil, tirer** 2 *[de compteur, boussole, gramophone]* needle; *[d'horloge]* hand; *[de balance]* pointer, needle; *[de cadran solaire]* pointer, index; *[de clocher]* spire; *(Rail)* point *(Brit)*, switch *(US)*; *(Géog)* (= *pointe*) needle; (= *cime*) peak ◆ **en forme d'~** needle-shaped ◆ **la petite/grande ~** *[d'horloge]* the hour/minute hand, the little/big hand

COMP **aiguille à coudre** sewing needle
aiguille de glace icicle
aiguille hypodermique hypodermic (needle)
aiguille de pin pine needle
aiguille à repriser darning needle
aiguille à tricoter knitting needle

aiguillée /egɥije/ NF length of thread *(for use with needle at any one time)*

aiguiller /egɥije/ ► conjug 1 ◄ VT 1 (= *orienter*) to direct ◆ **~ un enfant vers des études techniques** to direct *ou* steer a child towards technical studies ◆ **on l'a mal aiguillé** *(Scol)* he was steered in the wrong direction ◆ **~ la conversation sur un autre sujet** to steer the conversation onto another subject ◆ **~ la police sur une mauvaise piste** to put the police onto the wrong track 2 *(Rail)* to shunt *(Brit)*, to switch *(US)*

aiguillette /egɥijɛt/ NF *[de pourpoint]* aglet; *(Culin, Mil)* aiguillette

aiguilleur /egɥijœʀ/ NM *(Rail)* pointsman *(Brit)*, switchman *(US)* ◆ **~ du ciel** *(Aviat)* air-traffic controller

aiguillon /egɥijɔ̃/ NM *[d'insecte]* sting; *[de bouvier]* goad; *[de plante]* thorn; *(fig)* spur, stimulus

aiguillonner /egɥijɔne/ ► conjug 1 ◄ VT *[+ bœuf]* to goad; *(fig)* to spur *ou* goad on

aiguisage /egizaʒ/ NM *[de couteau, outil]* sharpening

aiguiser /egize/ ► conjug 1 ◄ VT 1 *[+ couteau, outil]* to sharpen 2 *[+ appétit]* to whet, to stimulate; *[+ sens]* to excite, to stimulate; *[+ esprit]* to sharpen; *[+ style]* to polish

aiguiseur, -euse /egizœʀ, øz/ NM,F sharpener, grinder

aiguisoir /egizwaʀ/ NM sharpener, sharpening tool

aïkido /aikido/ NM aikido

ail (pl **ails** *ou* **aulx**) /aj, o/ NM garlic; → **gousse, saucisson, tête**

ailante /ɛlɑ̃t/ NM tree of heaven, ailanthus *(SPÉC)*

aile /ɛl/ NF 1 *[d'oiseau, château]* wing; *[de moulin]* sail; *[d'hélice, ventilateur]* blade, vane; *[de nez]* wing; *[de voiture]* wing *(Brit)*, fender *(US)*; *[de pont]* abutment

2 *(Sport)* wing ◆ **il joue à l'~ gauche** he plays left wing

3 *(Mil, Pol)* wing ◆ **l'~ dure du parti** the hardline wing of the party, the hardliners in the party ◆ **~ marchante** *(Mil)* wheeling flank

4 *(locutions)* **l'oiseau disparut d'un coup d'~** the bird disappeared with a flap of its wings ◆ **d'un coup d'~ nous avons gagné Orly** we reached Orly in no time (at all) ◆ **avoir des ~s** *(fig)* to have wings ◆ **il s'est senti pousser des ~s** he felt as if he'd grown wings ◆ **l'espoir lui donnait des ~s** hope lent *ou* gave him wings ◆ **prendre sous son ~ (protectrice)** to take under one's wing ◆ **sous l'~ maternelle** under one's mother's *ou* the maternal wing ◆ **avoir un coup dans l'~** * (= *être ivre*) to have had one too many *; (= *être en mauvaise posture*) to be in a very bad way *; → **peur, plomb, tire-d'aile** *etc*

COMP **aile de corbeau** (= *couleur*) inky black, jet-black
aile delta (= *aile*) delta wing; (= *deltaplane*) hang-glider ◆ **faire de l'~ delta** to go hang-gliding
aile libre (= *Sport*) hang-gliding; (= *appareil*) hangglider

ailé, e /ele/ ADJ *(littér)* winged

aileron /ɛlʀɔ̃/ NM *[de poisson]* fin; *[d'oiseau]* pinion; *[d'avion]* aileron; *[de voiture]* aerofoil; *(Archit)* console

ailette /ɛlɛt/ NF *[de missile, radiateur]* fin; *[de turbine, ventilateur]* blade ◆ **~ de refroidissement** cooling fan

ailier /elje/ NM *(gén)* winger; *(Rugby)* flanker, wing-forward

aillade /ajad/ NF (= *sauce*) garlic dressing *ou* sauce; (= *croûton*) garlic crouton

ailler /aje/ ► conjug 1 ◄ VT to flavour with garlic

ailleurs /ajœʀ/ GRAMMAIRE ACTIVE 53.5 ADV (= *autre part*) somewhere else, elsewhere ◆ **nulle part ~** nowhere else ◆ **partout ~** everywhere else ◆ **il est ~, il a l'esprit ~** his thoughts are *ou* his mind is elsewhere, he's miles away ◆ **ils viennent d'~** they come from somewhere else ◆ **nous sommes passés (par) ~** we went another way ◆ **je l'ai su par ~** I heard of it from another source

♦ **d'ailleurs** (= *en plus*) besides, moreover ◆ **d'~ il faut avouer que ...** anyway *ou* besides we have to admit that ... ◆ **ce vin, d'~ très bon, n'est pas ...** this wine, which I may add is very good *ou* which is very good by the way, is not ... ◆ **lui non plus d'~** neither does (*ou* is, has *etc*) he, for that matter

♦ **par ailleurs** (= *autrement*) otherwise, in other respects; (= *en outre*) moreover, furthermore

ailloli /ajɔli/ NM aioli, garlic mayonnaise

aimable /ɛmabl/ ADJ 1 (= *gentil*) *[parole]* kind, nice; *[personne]* kind, nice, amiable *(frm)* ◆ **c'est un homme ~** he's a (very) nice man ◆ **tu es bien ~ de m'avoir attendu** it was very nice *ou* kind of you to wait for me ◆ **c'est très ~ à vous** *ou* **de votre part** it's most kind of you ◆ **soyez assez ~ pour ...** *(frm)* would you be so kind *ou* good as to ... ◆ **~ comme une porte de prison** like a bear with a sore head 2 († = *agréable*) *[endroit, moment]* pleasant 3 († † = *digne d'amour*) lovable, amiable †

aimablement /ɛmabləmɑ̃/ ADV *[agir]* kindly, nicely; *[répondre, recevoir]* amiably, nicely; *[refuser]* politely ◆ **il m'a offert ~ à boire** he kindly offered me a drink

aimant¹ /ɛmɑ̃/ NM magnet ◆ **~ (naturel)** magnetite *(NonC)*, lodestone

aimant², e /ɛmɑ̃, ɑ̃t/ ADJ loving, affectionate

aimantation /ɛmɑ̃tasjɔ̃/ NF magnetization

aimanté, e /ɛmɑ̃te/ (ptp de **aimanter**) ADJ *[aiguille, champ]* magnetic

aimanter /ɛmɑ̃te/ ► conjug 1 ◄ VT to magnetize

aimer /eme/ GRAMMAIRE ACTIVE 28.1, 34.1, 34.2, 34.3, 34.4, 35.4, 35.5, 39.2 ► conjug 1 ◄

VT 1 *(d'amour)* to love; *(d'amitié, attachement, goût)* to like, to be fond of ◆ **~ beaucoup** *[+ personne]* to like very much, to be very fond of; *[+ animaux, choses]* to like very much, to love ◆ **il l'aime d'amour** he really loves her ◆ **il l'aime à la folie** he adores her, he's crazy about her * ◆ **elle a réussi à se faire ~ de lui** she managed to win his love *ou* heart ◆ **essayer de se faire ~ de qn** to try to win sb's affection ◆ **j'aime une bonne tasse de café après déjeuner** I like *ou* love a nice cup of coffee after lunch ◆ **les hortensias aiment l'ombre** hydrangeas like shade ◆ **tous ces trucs-là, tu aimes, toi ?** * do you go in for all that kind of stuff?* ◆ **un enfant mal aimé** a child who doesn't get enough love ◆ **il est mal aimé du public** the public don't like him ◆ **je n'aime pas beaucoup cet acteur** I don't like that actor very much, I'm not very keen on *(Brit)* that actor ◆ **elle n'aime pas le tennis** she doesn't like tennis, she's not keen on *(Brit)* tennis ◆ **elle aime assez bavarder avec les voisins** she quite *ou* rather likes chatting with the neighbours ◆ **les enfants aiment qu'on s'occupe d'eux** children like *ou* love attention ◆ **elle n'aime pas qu'il sorte le soir** she doesn't like him going out *ou* him to go out at night ◆ **~ faire, ~ à faire** *(littér)* to like doing *ou* to do ◆ **j'aime à penser** *ou* **à croire que ...** *(frm ou hum)* I like to think that ... ◆ **qui m'aime me suive !** *(hum)* anyone who wants to come with me is welcome! ◆ **qui m'aime aime mon chien** *(Prov)* love me love my dog

◆ **aimer bien** to like, to be fond of ◆ **elle aime bien bavarder avec les voisins** she quite *ou* rather likes chatting with the neighbours ◆ **les enfants aiment bien qu'on s'occupe d'eux** children like *ou* love attention ◆ **qui aime bien châtie bien** *(Prov)* spare the rod and spoil the child *(Prov)*

◆ **aimer mieux** to prefer ◆ **on lui apporte des fleurs, elle aimerait mieux des livres** they bring her flowers but she'd rather have *ou* she'd prefer books ◆ **il aurait mieux aimé se reposer que d'aller au cinéma** he'd rather have rested *ou* he'd have preferred to rest than go to the cinema ◆ **j'aime mieux te dire qu'il va m'entendre !*** I'm going to give him a piece of my mind, I can tell you!

◆ **aimer autant** ◆ **j'aimerais autant que ce soit elle qui m'écrive** I'd rather it was she who wrote to me ◆ **il aime** *ou* **aimerait autant ne pas sortir aujourd'hui** he'd just as soon not go out today, he'd be just as happy not going out today ◆ **j'aime autant vous dire que je n'irai pas !** I may as well tell you that I won't go! ◆ **j'aime autant qu'elle ne soit pas venue** I'm just as happy *ou* it's (probably) just as well she didn't come ◆ **j'aime autant ça !*** *(ton menaçant)* I'm pleased to hear it!, that sounds more like it! *; *(soulagement)* what a relief!

2 *(au conditionnel = vouloir)* **aimeriez-vous une tasse de thé ?** would you like a cup of tea? ◆ **elle aimerait aller se promener** she'd like to go for a walk ◆ **j'aimerais vraiment venir** I'd really like to come, I'd love to come ◆ **je n'aimerais pas être dehors par ce temps** I wouldn't want *ou* like to be out in this (sort of) weather ◆ **j'aimerais assez/je n'aimerais pas ce genre de manteau** I'd rather *ou* quite like/wouldn't like a coat like that

VPR s'aimer 1 *(= s'apprécier soi-même)* to like o.s. ◆ **je ne m'aime pas avec ce chapeau** I don't like myself in this hat

2 *(= s'apprécier réciproquement)* **ils s'aiment** they're in love, they love each other ◆ **aimez-vous les uns les autres** love one another ◆ **ces deux-là ne s'aiment guère** there's no love lost between those two

3 *(= faire l'amour)* to make love

aine /ɛn/ **NF** *(Anat)* groin

aîné, e /ene/ **ADJ** *(= plus âgé)* elder, older; *(= le plus âgé)* eldest, oldest **NM** 1 *[de famille]* **l'~ (des garçons)** the eldest boy ◆ **mon (frère) ~** *(plus âgé)* my older *ou* elder brother; *(le plus âgé)* my oldest *ou* eldest brother ◆ **mon ~** my oldest *ou* eldest son 2 *(relation d'âge)* **il est mon ~** he's older than me ◆ **il est mon ~ de 2 ans** he's 2 years older than me, he's 2 years my senior ◆ **respectez vos ~s** *(littér)* respect your elders

NF aînée 1 *[de famille]* **l'~e (des filles)** the oldest *ou* eldest daughter ◆ **ma sœur ~e, mon ~e** *(plus âgée)* my older *ou* elder sister; *(la plus âgée)* my oldest *ou* eldest sister 2 *(relation d'âge)* **elle est mon ~e** she's older than me ◆ **elle est mon ~e de 2 ans** she's 2 years older than me, she's 2 years my senior

aînesse /ɛnɛs/ **NF** → **droit³**

ainsi /ɛ̃si/ GRAMMAIRE ACTIVE 53.5 **ADV** 1 *(= de cette façon)* in this way *ou* manner ◆ **je préfère agir ~** I prefer to do it this way ◆ **il faut procéder ~** this is what you have to do ◆ **c'est ~ que ça s'est passé** that's the way *ou* how it happened ◆ **pourquoi me traites-tu ~ ?** why do you treat me like this *ou* this way? ◆ **~ finit son grand amour** thus ended his great love ◆ **il n'en est pas ~ pour tout le monde** it's not so *ou* the case for everyone ◆ **s'il en est ~** *ou* **puisque c'est ~, je m'en vais** if *ou* since that's the way it is, I'm leaving, if *ou* since that's how it is, I'm leaving ◆ **s'il en était ~** if this were the case ◆ **il en sera ~ et pas autrement** that's the way it's going to be and that's that ◆ **~ va le monde** that's the way of the world

2 *(littér = en conséquence)* thus; *(= donc)* so ◆ **ils ont perdu le procès, ~ ils sont ruinés** they lost the case and so they are ruined ◆ **~ tu vas partir !** so, you're going to leave!

3 *(littér = de même)* so, in the same way ◆ **comme le berger mène ses moutons, ~ le pasteur guide ses ouailles** as the shepherd leads his sheep, so the minister guides his flock

4 *(locutions)*

◆ **ainsi que** (just) as ◆ **~ qu'il vous plaira** *(littér)* (just) as it pleases you ◆ **~ que nous avons dit hier** just as we said yesterday ◆ **la jalousie, ~ qu'un poison subtil, s'insinuait en lui** like a subtle poison, jealousy was slowly taking hold of him ◆ **sa beauté ~ que sa candeur me frappèrent** I was struck by her beauty as well as her innocence

◆ **pour ainsi dire** so to speak, as it were ◆ **ils sont pour ~ dire ruinés** they are ruined, so to speak *ou* as it were, you might say they are ruined

◆ **ainsi soit-il** *(Rel)* amen; *(fig)* so be it

◆ **et ainsi de suite** and so on

aïoli /ajɔli/ **NM** ⇒ **ailloli**

air¹ /ɛʀ/ **NM** 1 *(= gaz)* air; *(= brise)* (light) breeze; *(= courant d'air)* draught *(Brit)*, draft *(US)* ◆ **l'~ de la campagne/de la mer** the country/sea air ◆ **l'~ de la ville ne lui convient pas** town air *ou* the air of the town doesn't suit him ◆ **on manque d'~ ici** there's no air in here, it's stuffy in here ◆ **donnez-nous un peu d'~** give us some (fresh) air ◆ **sortir à l'~ libre** to go out into the open air ◆ **mettre la literie à l'~** to put the bedclothes (out) to air *ou* out for an airing, to air the bedclothes ◆ **se promener les fesses à l'~** to walk around bare-bottomed ◆ **sortir prendre l'~** to go out for some *ou* a breath of (fresh) air ◆ **il y a des ~s** *(Naut)* there's a wind (up) ◆ **il y a un peu d'~ aujourd'hui** there's a light *ou* slight breeze today ◆ **on sent de l'~ qui vient de la porte** you can feel a draught *(Brit)* *ou* draft *(US)* from the door; → **bol, chambre, courant** *etc*

◆ **plein air** open air ◆ **les enfants ont plein ~ le mercredi** *(Scol)* the children have games *ou* sport on Wednesdays

◆ **en plein air** *[piscine]* outdoor *(épith)*, open-air *(épith)*; *[spectacle, cirque]* open-air *(épith)*; *[jouer]* outdoors; *[s'asseoir]* outdoors, (out) in the open (air)

◆ **de plein air** *[activité, jeux]* outdoor *(épith)*

2 *(= espace)* air ◆ **s'élever dans l'~** *ou* **dans les ~s** to rise (up) into the skies *ou* the air ◆ **transports par ~** air transport, transport by air ◆ **l'avion a pris l'~** the plane has taken off ◆ **de l'~** *[hôtesse, ministère]* air *(épith)*; → **armée², école, mal²**

3 *(= atmosphère, ambiance)* atmosphere ◆ **il est allé prendre l'~ du bureau** he has gone to see how things look *ou* what things look like at the office ◆ **tout le monde se dispute, l'~ de la maison est irrespirable** everyone's quarrelling and the atmosphere in the house is unbearable ◆ **il a besoin de l'~ de la ville** he needs the atmosphere of the town ◆ **vivre** *ou* **se nourrir de l'~ du temps** to live on air *ou* on nothing at all ◆ **c'est dans l'~ du temps** it's part of the current climate ◆ **ces idées étaient dans l'~ à cette époque** those ideas were in the air at that time ◆ **il y a de la bagarre/de l'orage dans l'~** there's a fight/storm brewing ◆ **la grippe est dans l'~** there's a lot of flu about

4 *(locutions)*

◆ **en l'air** *[paroles, promesses]* idle, empty; *[dire]* rashly ◆ **regarder en l'~** to look up ◆ **avoir le nez en l'~** to gaze vacantly into space ◆ **jeter qch en l'~** to throw sth (up) into the air ◆ **ce ne sont encore que des projets en l'~** the plans are still very much up in the air ◆ **tout était en l'~ dans la pièce** *(désordre)* the room was in a total mess ◆ **flanquer*** *ou* **ficher*** *ou* **foutre**‡ **tout en l'~** *(= jeter)* to chuck* *ou* sling* *(Brit)* it all away *ou* out; *(= abandonner)* to chuck it all in‡ *ou* up‡ *(Brit)* ◆ **ce contretemps a fichu en l'~ mon week-end*** this hitch has completely messed up my weekend* ◆ **en courant, il a flanqué le vase en l'~*** he knocked the vase over as he ran past ◆ **se ficher*** *ou* **se foutre**‡ **en l'~** *(accidentellement)* to smash o.s. up*; *(= se suicider)* to do o.s. in*; → **parler**

COMP air comprimé compressed air

air conditionné *(système)* air conditioning; *(atmosphère)* conditioned air ◆ **le bureau a l'~ conditionné** the office has air conditioning *ou* is air-conditioned

air liquide liquid air

air² /ɛʀ/ **NM** 1 *(= apparence, manière)* air ◆ **d'un ~ décidé** in a resolute manner ◆ **sous son ~ calme c'est un homme énergique** beneath his calm appearance he is a forceful man ◆ **un garçon à l'~ éveillé** a lively-looking boy ◆ **ils ont un ~ de famille** there's a family likeness between them ◆ **ça lui donne l'~ d'un clochard** it makes him look like a tramp ◆ **avoir grand ~** to look very impressive ◆ **ça m'a tout de même coûté 750 €, l'~ de rien** even so, it still cost me €750; → **faux²**

2 *(= expression)* look, air ◆ **d'un ~ perplexe** with a look *ou* an air of perplexity, with a perplexed air *ou* look ◆ **je lui trouve un drôle d'~** I think he looks funny *ou* very odd ◆ **prendre un ~ éploré** to put on *ou* adopt a tearful expression ◆ **elle a pris son petit ~ futé pour me dire** she told me in her sly little way, she put on that sly look she has *ou* of hers to tell me ◆ **prendre un ~ entendu** to put on a knowing air ◆ **prendre un ~ pincé** to put on a prim expression ◆ **avec un ~ de ne pas y toucher** looking as if butter wouldn't melt in his *(ou* her) mouth ◆ **il a dit ça avec son ~ de ne pas y toucher** he said it with the most innocent expression on his face

3 *(locutions)*

◆ **avoir l'air** ◆ **avoir l'~ de** to look like ◆ **elle a l'~ d'une enfant** she looks like a child ◆ **ça m'a l'~ d'un mensonge** it looks to me *ou* sounds to me like a lie ◆ **ça m'a l'~ d'être assez facile** it strikes me as being fairly easy, it looks fairly easy to me ◆ **elle a l'~ intelligent(e)** she looks *ou* seems intelligent ◆ **il a l'~ stupide – il en a l'~ et la chanson*** he looks idiotic – he doesn't just look it either* ◆ **il a eu l'~ de ne pas comprendre** he looked as if *ou* as though he didn't understand, he didn't seem to understand; *(faire semblant)* he pretended not to understand ◆ **elle n'avait pas l'~ de vouloir travailler** she didn't look as if *ou* as though she wanted to work ◆ **il est très ambitieux sans en avoir l'~** he might not look it but he's very ambitious, he's very ambitious although he might not *ou* doesn't really look it ◆ **ça (m')a tout l'~ d'être une fausse alerte** it looks (to me) as if it's a false alarm ◆ **il a l'~ de vouloir**

neiger it looks like snow ◆ **de quoi j'ai l'~ maintenant !***, **j'ai l'~ fin maintenant !*** I look like a real idiot *ou* a right fool now* ◆ **sans avoir l'~ d'y toucher** looking as if butter wouldn't melt in his (*ou* her) mouth

◆ **l'air de rien** ◆ **il a pris l'argent dans la caisse, l'~ de rien** he took the money from the cash register without batting an eyelid ◆ **il n'a l'~ de rien, mais il sait ce qu'il fait** you wouldn't think it to look at him but he knows what he's doing ◆ **cette plante n'a l'~ de rien, pourtant elle donne de très jolies fleurs** this plant doesn't look much but it has very pretty flowers ◆ **sans avoir l'~ de rien, filons discrètement** let's just behave naturally and slip away unnoticed

air[3] /ɛʀ/ NM *[d'opéra]* aria; (= *mélodie*) tune, air ◆ **l'~ d'une chanson** the tune of a song ◆ **~ d'opéra** operatic aria ◆ **~ de danse** dance tune ◆ **~ connu** (*lit, fig*) familiar tune ◆ **chanter des slogans sur l'~ des lampions** to chant slogans

airain /ɛʀɛ̃/ NM (*littér*) bronze

air-air /ɛʀɛʀ/ ADJ INV (*Mil*) air-to-air

airbag ® /ɛʀbag/ NM (*Aut*) air bag

Airbus ® /ɛʀbys/ NM Airbus ®

aire /ɛʀ/ NF (= *zone*) area, zone; (*Math*) area; *[d'aigle]* eyrie

COMP **aire d'atterrissage** landing strip; (*pour hélicoptère*) landing pad
aire de battage (*Agr*) threshing floor
aires continentales (*Géol*) continental shields
aire d'embarquement boarding area
aire de jeux (adventure) playground
aire de lancement launch site
aire linguistique linguistic region
aire de repos (*sur autoroute*) rest area (*on motorway* etc)
aire de service service station, motorway services (*Brit*), service plaza (*US*)
aire de stationnement (*pour véhicules*) parking area; (*pour avions*) apron
aire de vent (*Naut*) rhumb ◆ **suivant l'~ de vent** following the rhumb-line route, taking a rhumb-line course

airelle /ɛʀɛl/ NF (= *myrtille*) blueberry, bilberry ◆ **~ des marais** cranberry

air-sol /ɛʀsɔl/ ADJ INV (*Mil*) air-to-ground

air-terre /ɛʀtɛʀ/ ADJ INV (*Mil*) air-to-ground

aisance /ɛzɑ̃s/ NF [1] (= *facilité*) ease ◆ **s'exprimer avec une rare** *ou* **parfaite ~** to express o.s. with great ease ◆ **il patinait avec une rare** *ou* **parfaite ~** he skated with the greatest of ease *ou* with great ease ◆ **il y a beaucoup d'~ dans son style** he has an easy *ou* a very fluent style [2] (= *richesse*) affluence ◆ **vivre dans l'~** to be comfortably off *ou* well-off, to live comfortably [3] (*Couture*) **redonner de l'~ sous les bras** to give more freedom of movement under the arms; → **pli** [4] → **cabinet, fosse, lieu**[1]

aise /ɛz/ NF [1] (*littér*) joy, pleasure ◆ **j'ai tant d'~ à vous voir** I'm so pleased to see you ◆ **sourire d'~** to smile with pleasure ◆ **tous ces compliments la comblaient d'~** she was overjoyed at all these compliments

[2] (*locutions*)

◆ **à l'aise** ◆ **être à l'~** (*dans une situation*) to be *ou* feel at ease; (*dans un vêtement, fauteuil*) to be *ou* feel comfortable; (= *être riche*) to be comfortably off *ou* comfortable ◆ **être mal à l'~** (*dans une situation*) to be *ou* feel ill at ease; (*dans un vêtement, fauteuil*) to be *ou* feel uncomfortable ◆ **mettez-vous à l'~** make yourself comfortable, make yourself at home ◆ **leur hôtesse les mit tout de suite à l'~** their hostess immediately put them at (their) ease *ou* made them feel immediately at home ◆ **faire qch à l'~*** to do sth easily ◆ **tu comptes faire ça en deux heures ? – à l'~ !*** do you think you can do that in two hours? – easily! *ou* no problem!* ◆ **on tient à quatre à l'~ dans cette voiture** this car holds four (quite) comfortably, four can get in this car (quite) comfortably

◆ **à son/votre** *etc* **aise** ◆ **être à son ~** (*dans une situation*) to be *ou* feel at ease; (= *être riche*) to be comfortably off *ou* comfortable ◆ **être mal à son ~** (*dans une situation*) to be *ou* feel ill at ease ◆ **mettez-vous à votre ~** make yourself comfortable, make yourself at home ◆ **en prendre à son ~ avec qch** to make free with sth, to do exactly as one likes with sth ◆ **vous en prenez à votre ~ !** you're taking things nice and easy! ◆ **tu en parles à ton ~ !** it's easy (enough) *ou* it's all right for you to talk! ◆ **à votre ~ !** please yourself!, just as you like!

NFPL **aises** ◆ **aimer ses ~s** to like *ou* be fond of one's (creature) comforts ◆ **tu prends tes ~s !** (*iro*) make yourself at home, why don't you! (*iro*)

ADJ (*littér*) ◆ **bien ~** delighted, most pleased (*de* to); ◆ **j'ai terminé – j'en suis fort ~** I've finished – I'm so glad *ou* I am most pleased

aisé, e /eze/ ADJ [1] (= *facile*) easy (*à faire* to do) [2] (= *dégagé*) *[démarche]* easy, graceful; *[style]* flowing, fluent [3] (= *riche*) well-to-do, comfortably off (*attrib*), well-off

aisément /ezemɑ̃/ ADV (= *sans peine*) easily; (= *sans réserves*) readily; (= *dans la richesse*) comfortably

aisselle /ɛsɛl/ NF (*Anat*) armpit; (*Bot*) axil

AIT /aite/ NF (abrév de **Association internationale du tourisme**) → **association**

Aix-la-Chapelle /ɛkslaʃapɛl/ N Aachen

Ajax /aʒaks/ NM Ajax

ajonc /aʒɔ̃/ NM gorse bush ◆ **des ~s** gorse (*NonC*), furze (*NonC*)

ajour /aʒuʀ/ NM (*gén pl*) *[de broderie, sculpture]* openwork (*NonC*)

ajouré, e /aʒuʀe/ (ptp de **ajourer**) ADJ *[mouchoir]* openwork (*épith*), hemstitched; *[bijou, sculpture]* which has an openwork design

ajourer /aʒuʀe/ ▸ conjug 1 ◂ VT *[+ sculpture]* to ornament with openwork; *[+ mouchoir]* to hemstitch

ajournement /aʒuʀnəmɑ̃/ NM *[d'assemblée]* adjournment; *[de réunion, élection, décision, rendez-vous]* postponement; *[de candidat]* referral; *[de conscrit]* deferment

ajourner /aʒuʀne/ ▸ conjug 1 ◂ VT *[+ assemblée]* to adjourn; *[+ réunion, élection, décision, rendez-vous]* to postpone, to put off; *[+ candidat]* to refer; *[+ conscrit]* to defer ◆ **réunion ajournée d'une semaine/au lundi suivant** meeting adjourned *ou* delayed for a week/until the following Monday

ajout /aʒu/ NM *[de texte]* addition

ajouter /aʒute/ GRAMMAIRE ACTIVE 53.5 ▸ conjug 1 ◂

VT [1] (= *mettre, faire ou dire en plus*) to add ◆ **ajoute un peu de sel** put a bit more salt in, add a bit of salt ◆ **je dois ~ que ...** I should add that ... ◆ **sans ~ un mot** without (saying *ou* adding) another word ◆ **ajoutez à cela qu'il pleuvait** on top of that *ou* what's more, it was raining ◆ **ajoutez à cela sa maladresse naturelle** add to that his natural clumsiness

[2] ◆ **~ foi aux dires de qn** to give credence to sb's statements, to believe sb's statements

VT INDIR **ajouter à** (*littér*) to add to ◆ **ton arrivée ajoute à mon bonheur** I am even happier now you are here, your arrival adds to my happiness

VPR **s'ajouter** ◆ **s'~ à** to add to ◆ **ces malheurs venant s'~ à leur pauvreté** these misfortunes adding further to their poverty ◆ **ceci, venant s'~ à ses difficultés** this coming on top of *ou* to add further to his difficulties ◆ **à ces dépenses viennent s'~ les impôts** on top of *ou* in addition to these expenses there are taxes

ajustage /aʒystaʒ/ NM fitting

ajusté, e /aʒyste/ (ptp de **ajuster**) ADJ *[vêtement]* tailored ◆ **robe étroitement ~e** tight-fitting dress

ajustement /aʒystəmɑ̃/ NM *[de statistique, prix]* adjustment; *[de pièces assemblées]* fitting ◆ **~ monétaire** currency adjustment *ou* realignment ◆ **le projet est finalisé, à quelques ~s près** the project is completed, give or take a few finishing touches

ajuster /aʒyste/ ▸ conjug 1 ◂ VT [1] (= *régler*) *[+ ceinture, prix, politique]* to adjust; *[+ vêtement]* to alter ◆ **il leur est difficile d'~ leurs vues** it's difficult for them to reconcile their views [2] (= *adapter*) *[+ tuyau]* to fit (*à* into); ◆ **~ l'offre à la demande** to adjust *ou* adapt supply to demand, to match supply to *ou* and demand [3] (= *viser*) **~ qn** to aim at sb, to take aim at sb ◆ **~ son tir** *ou* **son coup** to adjust one's aim; → **tir** [4] † *[+ coiffure]* to tidy, to arrange; *[+ tenue]* to arrange; *[+ cravate]* to straighten

VPR **s'ajuster** [1] (*pièces assemblées*) to fit (together) [2] († = *se rhabiller*) to adjust *ou* tidy one's dress †

ajusteur /aʒystœʀ/ NM metal worker

Alabama /alabama/ NM Alabama

alacrité /alakʀite/ NF (*littér*) alacrity

Aladin /aladɛ̃/ NM Aladdin

alaise /alɛz/ NF undersheet, drawsheet

alambic /alɑ̃bik/ NM (*Chim*) still

alambiqué, e /alɑ̃bike/ ADJ (*péj*) *[style, discours]* convoluted, involved; *[personne, esprit]* over-subtle

alangui, e /alɑ̃gi/ (ptp de **alanguir**) ADJ *[attitude, geste]* languid; *[rythme, style]* languid, lifeless

alanguir /alɑ̃giʀ/ ▸ conjug 2 ◂ VT [1] *[fièvre]* to make feeble *ou* languid, to enfeeble; *[chaleur]* to make listless *ou* languid; *[plaisirs, vie paresseuse]* to make indolent *ou* languid ◆ **être tout alangui par la chaleur** to feel listless *ou* languid with the heat [2] *[+ récit]* to make nerveless *ou* lifeless VPR **s'alanguir** to grow languid *ou* weak, to languish

alanguissement /alɑ̃gismɑ̃/ NM languidness, languor

alarmant, e /alaʀmɑ̃, ɑ̃t/ ADJ alarming

alarme /alaʀm/ NF [1] (= *signal de danger*) alarm ◆ **donner** *ou* **sonner l'~** to sound *ou* raise the alarm ◆ **(système d')~** alarm system; → **pistolet, signal, sirène, sonnette** [2] (= *inquiétude*) alarm ◆ **jeter l'~** to cause alarm ◆ **à la première ~** at the first sign of danger

alarmer /alaʀme/ ▸ conjug 1 ◂ VT to alarm VPR **s'alarmer** to become alarmed (*de, pour* about, at); ◆ **il n'a aucune raison de s'~** he has *ou* there is no cause for alarm

alarmisme /alaʀmism/ NM alarmism

alarmiste /alaʀmist/ ADJ, NMF alarmist

Alaska /alaska/ NM Alaska ◆ **la route de l'~** the Alaska Highway ◆ **la chaîne de l'~** the Alaska Range

albacore /albakɔʀ/ NM albacore

albanais, e /albanɛ, ɛz/ ADJ Albanian NM (= *langue*) Albanian NM,F **Albanais(e)** Albanian

Albanie /albani/ NF Albania

albâtre /albɑtʀ/ NM alabaster ◆ **d'~, en ~** alabaster (*épith*)

albatros /albatʀos/ NM (= *oiseau*) albatross; (*Golf*) albatross (*Brit*), double eagle (*US*)

Alberta /albɛʀta/ NF Alberta

albigeois, e /albiʒwa, waz/ ADJ [1] (*Géog*) of *ou* from Albi [2] (*Hist*) Albigensian NM,F **Albigeois(e)** inhabitant *ou* native of Albi NMPL

(*Hist*) ◆ **les Albigeois** the Albigenses, the Albigensians; → **croisade**

albinisme /albinism/ NM albinism

albinos /albinos/ NMF, ADJ INV albino

Albion /albjɔ̃/ NF ◆ **(la perfide)** ~ (perfidious) Albion

album /albɔm/ NM 1 (= *livre*) album ◆ ~ **(de) photos/de timbres** photo/stamp album ◆ ~ **à colorier** *ou* **de coloriages** colouring (*Brit*) *ou* coloring (*US*) book ◆ ~ **de presse** scrapbook ◆ ~ **de bandes dessinées** cartoon book 2 (= *disque*) album ◆ ~ **de 2 CD** double CD

albumen /albymɛn/ NM albumen

albumine /albymin/ NF albumin

albumineux, -euse /albyminø, øz/ ADJ albuminous

albuminurie /albyminyʀi/ NF albuminuria

albuminurique /albyminyʀik/ ADJ albuminuric

alcade /alkad/ NM alcalde

alcaïque /alkaik/ ADJ Alcaic ◆ **vers ~s** Alcaics

alcali /alkali/ NM alkali ◆ ~ **volatil** ammonia

alcalin, e /alkalɛ̃, in/ ADJ alkaline

alcalinité /alkalinite/ NF alkalinity

alcaloïde /alkalɔid/ NM alkaloid

alcalose /alkaloz/ NF alkalosis

Alceste /alsɛst/ NM Alcestis

alchémille /alkemij/ NF lady's mantle

alchimie /alʃimi/ NF (*lit, fig*) alchemy

alchimique /alʃimik/ ADJ alchemical, of alchemy

alchimiste /alʃimist/ NMF alchemist

alcool /alkɔl/ NM 1 (*Chim*) alcohol ◆ ~ **absolu éthylique** pure ethyl alcohol ◆ ~ **à brûler** methylated spirit(s), meths (*Brit*) ◆ ~ **camphré** camphorated alcohol ◆ ~ **rectifié** rectified spirit ◆ ~ **à 90°** surgical spirit ◆ **lampe à** ~ spirit lamp
2 (= *boisson*) alcohol (*NonC*) ◆ **l'~ au volant** drinking and driving, drink-driving (*Brit*), drunk-driving (*US*) ◆ **boire de l'~** (*gén*) to drink alcohol; (*eau-de-vie*) to drink spirits (*Brit*) *ou* (hard) liquor (*US*) ◆ **il ne tient pas l'~** he can't take his drink ◆ **il ne prend jamais d'~** he never drinks *ou* touches alcohol ◆ **le cognac est un** ~ cognac is a brandy *ou* spirit (*Brit*) ◆ **vous prendrez bien un petit** ~ you won't say no to a little brandy ◆ ~ **de prune/poire** plum/pear brandy ◆ ~ **de menthe** medicinal mint spirit ◆ ~ **blanc** colourless spirit ◆ ~ **de grain** grain alcohol ◆ **bière/boisson sans** ~ non-alcoholic *ou* alcohol-free beer/drink

alcoolémie /alkɔlemi/ NF ◆ **taux d'~** alcohol level (in the blood)

alcoolier /alkɔlje/ NM distiller

alcoolique /alkɔlik/ ADJ, NMF alcoholic ◆ **les Alcooliques anonymes** Alcoholics Anonymous

alcooliser /alkɔlize/ ► conjug 1 ◄ VT to alcoholize ◆ **boissons alcoolisées/non alcoolisées** alcoholic/soft drinks ◆ **très peu alcoolisé** very low in alcohol ◆ **déodorant alcoolisé** alcohol-based deodorant

alcoolisme /alkɔlism/ NM alcoholism ◆ ~ **aigu/chronique/mondain** acute/chronic/social alcoholism

alcoolo* /alkɔlo/ ADJ alcoholic NMF alcoholic, lush*

alcoolo-dépendant, e (mpl **alcoolo-dépendants**) /alkɔlodepɑ̃dɑ̃, ɑ̃t/ NMF, ADJ alcohol-dependent

alcoologue /alkɔlɔg/ NMF ◆ **médecin** ~ *doctor specializing in the treatment of alcoholism*

alcoomètre /alkɔmɛtʀ/ NM alcoholometer

alcootest ® /alkɔtɛst/ NM (= *objet*) Breathalyser ® (*Brit*), Breathalyzer ® (*US*); (= *épreuve*) breath-test ◆ **faire subir un ~ à qn** to give sb a breath test, to breath-test sb, to breathalyse (*Brit*) *ou* breathalyze (*US*) sb

alcôve /alkov/ NF alcove, recess (*in a bedroom*) ◆ **d'~** (*fig*) bedroom (*épith*), intimate; → **secret**

alcyon /alsjɔ̃/ NM (*Myth*) Halcyon

al dente /aldɛnte/ LOC ADV, LOC ADJ al dente

ALE /aələ/ NF (abrév de **Association de libre-échange**) FTA

aléa /alea/ NM unknown quantity ◆ **en comptant avec tous les ~s** taking all the unknown factors into account ◆ **les ~s de l'existence** the vagaries of life ◆ **les ~s de l'examen** the uncertainties of the exam ◆ **après bien des ~s** after many ups and downs ◆ **ce sont les ~s du show-business** these things happen in show business ◆ **~s thérapeutiques** unforeseeable medical complications

aléatoire /aleatwaʀ/ ADJ 1 (= *risqué*) [*gains, succès*] uncertain; [*marché*] risky, uncertain 2 (*Math*) [*grandeur*] random; (*Ordin*) [*nombre, accès*] random; (*Mus*) aleatoric, aleatory; → **contrat**

aléatoirement /aleatwaʀmɑ̃/ ADV randomly

alémanique /alemanik/ ADJ, NM Alemannic; → **suisse**

ALENA, Alena /alena/ NM (abrév de **Accord de libre-échange nord-américain**) NAFTA

alène, alêne /alɛn/ NF awl

alentour /alɑ̃tuʀ/ ADV around ◆ **tout ~** *ou* **à l'entour** †† all around ◆ ~ **de qch** around sth ◆ **les villages d'~** the neighbouring *ou* surrounding villages

alentours /alɑ̃tuʀ/ NMPL 1 (= *environs*) [*de ville*] surroundings, neighbourhood (*Brit*), neighborhood (*US*) ◆ **les ~ sont très pittoresques** the surroundings *ou* environs are very picturesque ◆ **dans les ~** in the vicinity *ou* neighbourhood ◆ **aux ~ de Dijon** in the Dijon area ◆ **il gagne aux ~ de 1 500 €** he earns (something) in the region of €1,500, he earns around *ou* about €1,500 ◆ **aux ~ de 8 heures** some time around 8 (o'clock), round about 8 (o'clock) (*Brit*) 2 (*Art*) [*de tapisserie*] border

Aléoutiennes /aleusjɛn/ ADJ FPL, NFPL ◆ **les (îles)** ~ the Aleutian Islands, the Aleutians

Alep /alɛp/ N Aleppo

alerte /alɛʀt/ ADJ [*personne, geste*] agile, nimble; [*esprit*] alert, agile; [*vieillard*] spry, agile; [*style*] brisk, lively NF 1 (= *signal de danger, durée du danger*) alert, alarm ◆ **donner l'~** to give the alert *ou* alarm ◆ **donner l'~ à qn** to alert sb ◆ ~ **aérienne** air raid warning ◆ ~ **à la bombe** bomb scare ◆ ~ **à la pollution** pollution alert ◆ **en cas d'~** if there is an alert ◆ **système d'~** alarm system ◆ **les nuits d'~** nights on alert; → **cote, état, faux²** 2 (= *avertissement*) warning sign; (= *inquiétude*) alarm ◆ **à la première** ~ at the first warning sign ◆ **l'~ a été chaude** *ou* **vive** there was intense *ou* considerable alarm ◆ ~ **cardiaque** heart flutter EXCL watch out!

alerter /alɛʀte/ ► conjug 1 ◄ VT (= *donner l'alarme à*) to alert; (= *informer*) to inform, to notify; (= *prévenir*) to warn ◆ ~ **l'opinion publique** to alert public opinion ◆ **les pouvoirs publics ont été alertés** the authorities have been informed *ou* notified, it has been brought to the attention of the authorities

alésage /alezaʒ/ NM (= *action*) reaming; (= *diamètre*) bore

alèse /alɛz/ NF ⇒ **alaise**

aléser /aleze/ ► conjug 6 ◄ VT to ream

alevin /alvɛ̃/ NM alevin, young fish (*bred artificially*)

alevinage /alvinaʒ/ NM (= *action*) stocking with alevins *ou* young fish; (= *pisciculture*) fish farming

aleviner /alvine/ ► conjug 1 ◄ VT (= *empoissonner*) to stock with alevins *ou* young fish VI (= *pondre*) to spawn

Alexandre /alɛksɑ̃dʀ/ NM Alexander ◆ ~ **le Grand** Alexander the Great

Alexandrie /alɛksɑ̃dʀi/ N Alexandria

alexandrin, e /alɛksɑ̃dʀɛ̃, in/ ADJ [*art, poésie*] (*Hist*) Alexandrian; [*prosodie*] alexandrine NM alexandrine

alezan, e /alzɑ̃, an/ ADJ, NM,F (= *cheval*) chestnut ◆ ~ **clair** sorrel

alfa /alfa/ NM (= *herbe*) Esparto (grass); (= *papier*) Esparto paper

algarade /algaʀad/ NF (*littér*) (= *gronderie*) angry outburst; (= *dispute*) quarrel

algèbre /alʒɛbʀ/ NF (*Math*) algebra ◆ **par l'~** algebraically ◆ **c'est de l'~ pour moi*** it's (all) Greek to me*

algébrique /alʒebʀik/ ADJ algebraic

algébriquement /alʒebʀikmɑ̃/ ADV algebraically

algébriste /alʒebʀist/ NMF algebraist

Alger /alʒe/ N Algiers

Algérie /alʒeʀi/ NF Algeria

algérien, -ienne /alʒeʀjɛ̃, jɛn/ ADJ Algerian NM,F **Algérien(ne)** Algerian

algérois, e /alʒeʀwa, waz/ ADJ of *ou* from Algiers NM,F **Algérois(e)** inhabitant *ou* native of Algiers NM (= *région*) ◆ **l'Algérois** the Algiers region

algie /alʒi/ NF algia

ALGOL /algɔl/ NM ALGOL

algonkin, e, algonquin, e /algɔ̃kɛ̃, in/ ADJ Algonqui(a)n NM (= *langue*) Algonqui(a)n NM,F **Algonkin(e)** Algonqui(a)n

algorithme /algɔʀitm/ NM algorithm

algorithmique /algɔʀitmik/ ADJ algorithmic NF study of algorithms

algothérapie /algoteʀapi/ NF algotherapy, seaweed baths

algue /alg/ NF (*de mer*) seaweed (*NonC*); (*d'eau douce*) alga ◆ **~s** (*de mer*) seaweed; (*d'eau douce*) algae ◆ **~s séchées** (*Culin*) dried seaweed ◆ **~s brunes/vertes/marines** brown/green/marine algae ◆ **bain d'~s** seaweed bath

Alhambra /alɑ̃bʀa/ NM ◆ **l'~** the Alhambra

alias /aljas/ ADV alias, also known as NM (*Ordin*) alias

Ali Baba /alibaba/ NM Ali Baba ◆ **"Ali Baba et les quarante voleurs"** "Ali Baba and the Forty Thieves"; → **caverne**

alibi /alibi/ NM alibi

Alice /alis/ NF Alice ◆ **"Alice au pays des merveilles"** "Alice in Wonderland"

aliénabilité /aljenabilite/ NF alienability

aliénable /aljenabl/ ADJ alienable

aliénant, e /aljenɑ̃, ɑ̃t/ ADJ alienating

aliénataire /aljenatɛʀ/ NMF alienee

aliénateur, -trice /aljenatœʀ, tʀis/ NM,F (*Jur*) alienator

aliénation /aljenasjɔ̃/ NF (*gén*) alienation ◆ ~ **(mentale)** (*Méd*) (mental) derangement, insanity

aliéné, e /aljene/ (ptp de **aliéner**) NM,F insane person, lunatic (*péj*); → **asile**

aliéner /aljene/ ► conjug 6 ◄ VT 1 (*Jur* = *céder*) to alienate; [+ *droits*] to give up ◆ ~ **un bien** (*Jur*) to dispose of property ◆ ~ **sa liberté entre les mains de qn** to relinquish one's freedom to sb

◆ **un traité qui aliène leur liberté** a treaty which alienates their freedom ② *(= rendre hostile)* *[+ partisans, opinion publique]* to alienate *(à qn* from sb); ◆ **s'~ ses partisans/l'opinion publique** to alienate one's supporters/public opinion ◆ **s'~ un ami** to alienate *ou* estrange a friend ◆ **s'~ l'affection de qn** to alienate sb's affections, to estrange sb ③ *(Philos, Sociol)* ~ **qn** to alienate sb

aliéniste † /aljenist/ NMF psychiatrist

Aliénor /aljenɔʀ/ NF Eleanor ◆ ~ **d'Aquitaine** Eleanor of Aquitaine

alignement /aliɲ(ə)mɑ̃/ NM ① *(= action)* aligning, lining up; *(= rangée)* alignment, line ◆ **les ~s de Carnac** the Carnac menhirs *ou* alignments *(SPÉC)* ② *(Mil)* **être à l'~** to be in line ◆ **se mettre à l'~** to fall into line, to line up ◆ **sortir de l'~** to step out of line *(lit)* ◆ **à droite/gauche, ~ !** right/left, dress! ③ *[de rue]* building line ◆ **maison frappée d'~** house affected by a road widening scheme ④ *(Pol, Fin)* alignment ◆ ~ **monétaire** monetary alignment *ou* adjustment

aligner /aliɲe/ ▸ conjug 1 ◂ VT ① *[+ objets]* to align, to line up *(sur* with); *[+ chiffres]* to string together, to string up a line of; *[+ arguments]* to reel off; *(Mil)* to form into lines, to draw up in lines ◆ **il alignait des allumettes sur la table** he was lining up *ou* making lines of matches on the table ◆ **il n'arrivait pas à ~ deux mots de suite** he couldn't string a sentence *ou* two words together ◆ **les enfants étaient alignés le long de la route** the children were lined up along the roadside ◆ **pour acheter cette voiture, il va falloir les ~*** *(= payer)* that car will set you back a bit*

② *[+ rue]* to modify the (statutory) building line of

③ *(Fin, Pol)* to bring into alignment *(sur* with); ◆ ~ **sa conduite sur** to bring one's behaviour into line with, to modify one's behaviour to conform with

④ (* *= punir*) ~ **qn** to do sb* ◆ **il s'est fait ~** he got done* ◆ **il a aligné son adversaire en trois sets** *(Tennis)* he smashed* his opponent in three sets

VPR **s'aligner** *[soldats]* to fall into line, to line up ◆ **s'~ sur** *[+ politique]* to conform to the line of; *[+ pays, parti]* to align o.s. with ◆ **tu peux toujours t'~ !*** just try and match that!, beat that!*

aligoté /aligɔte/ ADJ M, NM aligoté

aliment /alimɑ̃/ NM ① *(= nourriture)* food ◆ **bien mâcher les ~s** to chew one's food well ◆ **le pain est un ~** bread is (a) food *ou* a type of food ◆ **comment conserver vos ~s** how to keep food fresh ◆ ~ **riche/complet/liquide** rich/whole/liquid food ◆ **~s pour chiens/chats** dog/cat food ◆ **~s pour bétail** cattle feed ② *(Jur)* ~s maintenance

alimentaire /alimɑ̃tɛʀ/ ADJ ① *[aide, hygiène]* food *(épith)*; *[besoins]* dietary *(épith)*; *[habitudes]* eating *(épith)*, dietary *(épith)* ◆ **notre comportement ~** our eating patterns ② *(péj)* *[activité]* done to earn a living *ou* some cash ◆ **c'est de la littérature/peinture ~** these kinds of books/paintings are just potboilers ◆ **pour lui ce n'est qu'un travail ~** to him it's just a job that pays the rent

alimentation /alimɑ̃tasjɔ̃/ NF ① *(= régime)* diet ◆ ~ **de base** staple diet ◆ ~ **équilibrée/mal équilibrée** balanced/unbalanced diet ◆ ~ **lactée** milk diet ◆ **bon** *ou* **ticket d'~** food voucher ② *(= secteur commercial)* food trade ◆ **il travaille dans l'~** he works in the food trade; *(= industrie)* he works in the food industry ◆ **magasin d'~** food shop, grocery store *(US)* ◆ **rayon ~** food *ou* grocery section ③ *(= action)* *[de personne, chaudière]* feeding; *[de moteur, circuit]* supplying, feeding ◆ **l'~ en eau des grandes villes** supplying water to *ou* the supply of water to large towns ◆ **d'~** *[pompe, ligne]* feed *(épith)*; → **tuyau**

alimenter /alimɑ̃te/ ▸ conjug 1 ◂ VT ① *[+ personne, animal]* to feed

② *[+ chaudière]* to feed; *[+ moteur, circuit]* to supply, to feed; *[+ caisse, compte bancaire, fonds]* to put money into; *[+ marché]* to supply *(en* with); ◆ **le tuyau alimente le moteur en essence** the pipe feeds *ou* supplies petrol *(Brit)* *ou* gasoline *(US)* to the engine ◆ ~ **une ville en gaz/électricité** to supply a town with gas/electricity

③ *[+ conversation]* *[personne]* to keep going, to sustain; *[+ curiosité]* to feed; *[+ inflation, polémique, rumeurs, soupçons]* to fuel ◆ **cela a alimenté la conversation** it gave us (*ou* them etc) something to talk about ◆ **ces faits vont ~ notre réflexion** these facts will provide food for thought

VPR **s'alimenter** *[personne]* to eat ◆ **s'~ seul** to feed o.s. ◆ **le malade recommence à s'~** the patient is starting to eat again *ou* to take food again

alinéa /alinea/ NM *(= passage)* paragraph; *(= ligne)* indented line *(at the beginning of a paragraph)* ◆ **nouvel ~** new line

alisier /alizje/ NM sorb, service tree

alitement /alitmɑ̃/ NM confinement to (one's) bed

aliter /alite/ ▸ conjug 1 ◂ VT to confine to (one's) bed ◆ **rester alité** to remain confined to (one's) bed, to remain bedridden ◆ **infirme alité** bedridden invalid VPR **s'aliter** to take to one's bed

alizé /alize/ ADJ M, NM ◆ **(vent) ~** trade wind

alkékenge /alkekɑ̃ʒ/ NM Chinese lantern, winter *ou* ground cherry

Allah /ala/ NM Allah

allaitante /alɛtɑ̃t/ ADJ F ◆ **femme ~** nursing mother ◆ **vache ~** brood cow

allaitement /alɛtmɑ̃/ NM *[de bébé]* feeding; *[d'animal]* suckling ◆ ~ **maternel** breast-feeding ◆ ~ **mixte** mixed feeding ◆ ~ **au biberon** bottle-feeding ◆ **pendant l'~** while breast-feeding

allaiter /alete/ ▸ conjug 1 ◂ VT *[femme]* to (breast-)feed; *[animal]* to suckle ◆ ~ **au biberon** to bottle-feed ◆ **elle allaite encore** she's still breast-feeding (the baby)

allant, e /alɑ̃, ɑt/ ADJ *(littér = alerte)* *[personne]* sprightly, active; *[musique]* lively NM *(= dynamisme)* drive, energy ◆ **avoir de l'~** to have plenty of drive *ou* energy ◆ **avec ~** energetically

alléchant, e /aleʃɑ̃, ɑt/ ADJ *[odeur]* mouth-watering, tempting; *[proposition]* tempting, enticing; *[prix]* attractive

allécher /aleʃe/ ▸ conjug 6 ◂ VT *[odeur]* to make one's mouth water, to tempt; *[proposition]* to tempt, to entice ◆ **alléché par l'odeur** tempted by the smell ◆ **alléché par des promesses fallacieuses** lured by false promises

allée /ale/ NF ① *[de ville]* avenue; *[de jardin]* path; *[de parc]* path, walk; *(plus large)* avenue; *[de forêt]* wide path; *(menant à une maison)* drive, driveway; *[de cinéma, autobus]* aisle ◆ ~ **cavalière** bridle path ◆ **les ~s du pouvoir** the corridors of power

② *(locution)*

♦ **allées et venues** comings and goings ◆ **que signifient ces ~s et venues dans le couloir ?** why all this to-ing and fro-ing in the corridor? ◆ **ceci l'oblige à de constantes ~s et venues (entre Paris et la province)** this means he has to keep shuttling back and forth (between Paris and the provinces) ◆ **j'ai perdu mon temps en ~s et venues** I've wasted my time going back and forth *ou* to-ing and fro-ing ◆ **le malade l'obligeait à de constantes ~s et venues** the patient kept him constantly on the run *ou* running about (for him)

allégation /a(l)legasjɔ̃/ NF *(= affirmation)* allegation; *(= citation)* citation

allégé, e /aleʒe/ (ptp de **alléger**) ADJ low-fat ◆ **(produits) ~s** low-fat products

allégeance /aleʒɑ̃s/ NF allegiance ◆ **faire ~ à qn** to swear allegiance to sb

allégement, allègement /alɛʒmɑ̃/ NM ① *[de fardeau, véhicule]* lightening ② *[de personnel]* reduction *(de* in) ③ *[de coûts, impôts, charges sociales]* reduction *(de* in); ◆ ~ **fiscal** tax relief ◆ ~ **de la dette** debt relief ◆ **notre objectif demeure l'~ de nos dettes** our aim remains to reduce our debts ④ *[de contrôles]* easing; *[de formalités]* simplification ⑤ *[de douleur]* alleviation

alléger /aleʒe/ ▸ conjug 6 et 3 ◂ VT ① *(en poids)* *[+ fardeau]* to lighten; *[+ véhicule]* to make lighter; *[+ skis]* to unweight ◆ ~ **qn de son portefeuille*** *(hum)* to relieve sb of their wallet ② *(en nombre)* *[+ personnel]* to streamline, to reduce ◆ ~ **les effectifs** *(Scol)* to reduce numbers in the classroom ◆ **pour ~ notre dispositif militaire** to reduce our military presence ③ *(Fin)* *[+ coûts, impôts, charges sociales, dette]* to reduce ④ *(= simplifier)* *[+ contrôles]* to ease; *[+ formalités]* to simplify ◆ ~ **les programmes scolaires** to cut the number of subjects on the school syllabus ⑤ *(= rendre moins pénible)* *[+ douleur]* to alleviate, to relieve; *[+ conditions de détention]* to ease

allégorie /a(l)legɔʀi/ NF allegory

allégorique /a(l)legɔʀik/ ADJ allegorical

allégoriquement /a(l)legɔʀikmɑ̃/ ADV allegorically

allègre /a(l)lɛgʀ/ ADJ *[personne, humeur]* cheerful, light-hearted; *[démarche]* lively, jaunty; *[musique]* lively, merry ◆ **il descendait la rue d'un pas ~** he was walking gaily *ou* cheerfully down the street

allégrement, allègrement /a(l)lɛgʀəmɑ̃/ ADV ① *(= gaiement)* gaily, cheerfully ② *(hum)* **le coût de l'opération dépasse ~ les 50 millions** the cost of the operation is well over 50 million ◆ **le virus voyage ~ d'un ordinateur à l'autre** the virus merrily travels from one computer to another

allégresse /a(l)legʀɛs/ NF elation ◆ **ce fut l'~ générale** there was general rejoicing *ou* jubilation

alléguer /a(l)lege/ ▸ conjug 6 ◂ VT ① *[+ fait]* to use as an excuse; *[+ excuse, raison, preuve]* to put forward ◆ **ils refusèrent de m'écouter, alléguant que ...** they refused to listen, claiming that ... ② *(littér = citer)* to cite, to quote

allèle /alɛl/ NM allele

alléluia /a(l)leluja/ NM, EXCL *(Rel)* alleluia, hallelujah

Allemagne /almaɲ/ NF Germany ◆ **l'~ fédérale** the Federal German Republic ◆ ~ **de l'Ouest/de l'Est** West/East Germany; → **république**

allemand, e /almɑ̃, ɑd/ ADJ German; → **république** NM *(Ling)* German; → **bas¹, haut** NM,F **Allemand(e)** German ◆ **bon ~** *(Helv)* German *(as opposed to Swiss German)* NF **allemande** *(Mus)* allemande

aller /ale/

► conjug 9 ◄

1 VERBE INTRANSITIF	4 VERBE PRONOMINAL
2 VERBE IMPERSONNEL	5 LOC EXCLAMATIVES
3 VERBE AUXILIAIRE	6 NOM MASCULIN

1 - VERBE INTRANSITIF

1 [= se déplacer, partir] to go ◆ **où vas-tu ?** where are you going? ◆ **il t'attend, va !** he's waiting for you, go on!

aller se traduit souvent par un verbe spécifique en anglais.

◆ **j'allais par les rues désertes** I walked *ou* wandered through the empty streets ◆ **il allait trop vite quand il a eu son accident** he was driving *ou* going too fast when he had his accident ◆ **en ville, on va plus vite à pied qu'en voiture** in town it is quicker to walk than to go by car ◆ ~ **à Paris en voiture/en avion** to drive/fly to Paris ◆ **il y est allé à** *ou* **en vélo** he cycled there, he went there on his bike ◆ **j'irai à pied** I'll walk, I'll go on foot ◆ **où sont allés les 300 € ?** *(= qu'a-t-on acheté avec ?)* what did the €300 go on?; *(= où l'argent est-il passé ?)* where did that €300 go?

◆ **aller et venir** *(entre deux endroits)* to come and go; *(dans une pièce)* to pace up and down

◆ **ça va, ça vient** ◆ **tu sais, la chance, ça va ça vient** luck comes and goes, you know, you win some, you lose some ◆ **avec lui l'argent, ça va, ça vient** when it comes to money, it's easy come, easy go with him

◆ **aller** + *préposition (= se rendre)* ◆ ~ **à** to go to ◆ ~ **à Caen/à la campagne** to go to Caen/to the country ◆ ~ **au lit/à l'église/à l'école** to go to bed/to church/to school ◆ ~ **en Allemagne** to go to Germany ◆ ~ **chez le boucher/chez un ami** to go to the butcher's/to a friend's (place) ◆ **je vais sur** *ou* **vers Lille** *(en direction de)* I'm going towards Lille; *(but du voyage)* I'm heading for Lille ◆ ~ **aux renseignements/aux nouvelles** to go and inquire/and find out the news

Notez l'utilisation du perfect et du pluperfect **have/had been** ; **have/had gone** implique que le sujet n'est pas encore revenu.

◆ **je ne suis jamais allé à New York/en Corse** I've never been to New York/Corsica ◆ **étiez-vous déjà allés en Sicile ?** had you been to Sicily before? ◆ **il n'est pas là ? – non il est allé au tennis** he's not there? – no, he's gone to play tennis

2 [euph] *(aux toilettes)* to go to the toilet ◆ **tu es allé ce matin ?** have you been (to the toilet) this morning? ◆ **ça fait** ~ * it makes you go *

3 [dans le temps, une évolution] **on va à la catastrophe/la ruine** we're heading for disaster/ruin ◆ ~ **sur ses 30 ans** to be getting on for *(Brit) ou* going on *(US)* 30 ◆ **on va vers une guerre civile** we're heading for civil war ◆ **où allons-nous ?** what are things coming to? ◆ **j'irai (jusqu')à la Commission européenne s'il le faut** I'll take it to the European Commission if necessary

4 [= mener, s'étendre] to go *(à* to); ◆ **cette route doit** ~ **quelque part** this road must go somewhere ◆ **ses champs vont jusqu'à la forêt** his fields go *ou* stretch as far as the forest

5 [= durer] **l'abonnement va jusqu'en juin** the subscription lasts *ou* runs till June ◆ **le contrat allait jusqu'en mai** the contract ran until May ◆ **la période qui va du 22 mai au 15 juillet** from 22 May to 15 July

6 [= se porter] **comment allez-vous ?** how are you? ◆ **comment va ton frère ? – il va bien/mal** *(physiquement)* how's your brother? – he's fine/he's not very well; *(moralement)* how's your brother? – he's fine/not too happy ◆ **cela fait des années qu'il va mal** he hasn't been well for years ◆ **(comment) ça va ? – ça va** how's things? * *ou* how are you doing? – fine *ou* not so bad * ◆ **ça va mieux maintenant** I'm feeling better now ◆ **ça va ? – faudra bien que ça aille** * how's things * *ou* how are you doing? – fine *ou* not so bad ◆ **ça va ? – on fait** ~ * you all right? * – so-so * ◆ **non mais ça va pas (la tête) !** * you're crazy! *, you must be crazy! * ◆ **non mais ça va, te gêne pas !** * don't mind me!

7 [= se passer, fonctionner] **(comment) ça va au bureau ? – ça va** how's it going at the office? – fine *ou* not so bad * ◆ **ça va comme ça ? – faudra bien que ça aille** * is it all right like that? – it'll have to be * ◆ **comment vont les affaires ? – elles vont bien/mal** how's business? – fine/not too good ◆ **ça va mal en Asie/à la maison** things aren't going too well *ou* things aren't looking so good in Asia/at home ◆ **ça va mal** ~ **si tu continues** there's going to be trouble if you carry on like that ◆ **notre économie va mieux** the economy is doing better *ou* is looking up ◆ **ça va mieux pour lui maintenant** things are going better for him now ◆ **ça ne va pas mieux ! il veut une voiture pour son anniversaire !** whatever next! he wants a car for his birthday! ◆ **ça ne va pas sans difficulté** it's no easy job ◆ **ça va tout seul** *(= c'est facile)* it's a cinch *, it's a doddle * *(Brit)* ◆ **ça ne va pas tout seul** it's not exactly easy

◆ **plus ça va** ◆ **plus ça va, plus l'inquiétude grandit** people are getting more and more worried ◆ **plus ça va, plus je me dis que j'ai eu tort** the more I think about it, the more I realize how wrong I was ◆ **plus ça va, plus nous produisons des déchets** we just keep producing more and more waste ◆ **plus ça va, moins ça va** things are going from bad to worse

8 [= convenir] ~ **(bien) avec** to go (well) with ◆ ~ **bien ensemble** *[couleurs, styles]* to go well together ◆ **ils vont bien ensemble** *[personnes]* they make a nice couple ◆ **ce tableau va bien/mal sur ce mur** the picture looks right/doesn't look right on that wall ◆ **ici, cette couleur n'ira pas** that colour just won't work *ou* go here ◆ **la clé ne va pas dans la serrure** the key won't go in *ou* doesn't fit the lock ◆ **les ciseaux ne vont pas pour couper du carton** scissors won't do *ou* are no good for cutting cardboard ◆ **votre plan ne va pas** your plan won't work

9 [locutions]

◆ **aller à** *(= être attribué à) [prix, récompense, part d'héritage]* to go to; *(= aller bien) [forme, mesure]* to fit; *[style, genre]* to suit ◆ **le maison ira à la cadette** the house will go to the youngest daughter ◆ **l'argent ira à la restauration du clocher** the money will go towards restoring the bell tower ◆ **cette robe te va très bien** *(couleur, style)* that dress really suits you; *(taille)* that dress fits you perfectly ◆ **vos projets me vont parfaitement** your plans suit me fine ◆ **rendez-vous demain 4 heures ? – ça me va** * tomorrow at 4? – OK, fine * ◆ **ça lui va mal** *ou* **bien** *(hum)* **de critiquer les autres** he's got a nerve * criticizing other people, he's a fine one * to criticize

◆ **aller** + *participe présent*

Lorsque **aller** sert à exprimer la progression, il est souvent rendu par un comparatif.

◆ ~ **en empirant** to get worse and worse ◆ **le bruit va croissant** the noise is getting louder and louder ◆ **notre rythme de travail ira en s'accélérant** we'll have to work more and more quickly [MAIS] ~ **en augmentant** to keep increasing

◆ **y aller** ◆ **on y va ?** *(avant un départ)* shall we go?; *(avant d'agir)* shall we start? ◆ **allons-y (Alonzo *) !** let's go! ◆ **allez-y, c'est votre tour** go on, it's your turn ◆ **allez-y, vous ne risquez rien** go ahead *ou* go on, you've nothing to lose ◆ **comme vous y allez !, vous y allez un peu fort !** that's going a bit far! ◆ **non mais vas-y, insulte-moi !** * go on, insult me, why don't you! ◆ **vas-y doucement** *ou* **mollo** * gently does it ◆ **27 divisé par 7, il y va 3 (et il reste 6)** *(Math)* 27 divided by 7 is *ou* goes 3 (remainder 6)

◆ **y aller de** *(= contribuer)* ◆ **chacun y est allé de son commentaire** everyone had their say, everyone put in their two cents * *(US)* ◆ **il y est allé de sa petite chanson** * he gave us a little song ◆ **il y est allé de sa petite larme** * he had a little cry

2 - VERBE IMPERSONNEL

◆ **il y va/allait de** *(= ce qui est/était en jeu)* ◆ **il y va de votre vie/de votre santé** your life/your health is at stake *ou* depends on it ◆ **il y allait de notre honneur !** our honour was at stake!

◆ **il en va de** *(= c'est la même chose pour)* ◆ **il en va de même pour tous les autres** the same applies to *ou* goes for all the others ◆ **il en va de l'édition comme des autres secteurs** it's the same in publishing as in other sectors, the same goes for publishing as for other sectors

◆ **ça y va/y allait** * *(valeur intensive)* ◆ **ça y va le whisky chez eux !** they certainly get through a lot of whisky! ◆ **ça y va les billets de 100 euros avec lui !** he certainly gets through those 100 euro notes! ◆ **ça y allait les insultes !** you should have heard the abuse!

3 - VERBE AUXILIAIRE

◆ **aller** + *infinitif*

Notez l'utilisation de **and** et de **to** entre les deux verbes en anglais ; **to** exprime généralement une idée d'intention alors que **and** met l'accent sur l'accomplissement de l'action.

◆ **il est allé se renseigner** *(gén)* he went to get some information; *(a obtenu les informations)* he went and got some information ◆ ~ **voir qn à l'hôpital** to go and visit sb in hospital ◆ **va te laver les mains** go and wash your hands

Lorsque **aller** exprime le futur immédiat, il est parfois traduit par le futur simple ; la forme **be going to** s'utilise plutôt lorsque le locuteur met quelqu'un en garde ou exprime une intention.

◆ **tu vas être en retard** you're going to be late, you'll be late ◆ **il va descendre dans une minute** he'll be (coming) down in a minute ◆ **ça va prendre un quart d'heure** that'll take *ou* it's going to take a quarter of an hour ◆ **je vais lui dire** I'm going to tell him ◆ **je vais le faire tout de suite** I'll do it right away ◆ **ils allaient commencer** they were going to start, they were about to start [MAIS] **je vais te dire une chose** let me tell you something *(valeur intensive)* ◆ **ne va pas te faire du souci inutilement** don't go and get *ou* don't go getting all worried for no reason ◆ **allez donc voir si c'est vrai !** who knows if it's true! ◆ **n'allez pas vous imaginer que ...** don't you go imagining that ... ◆ **pourvu qu'il n'aille pas penser que ...** as long as he doesn't get the idea that ... ◆ **va** *ou* **allez savoir** * **!** who knows? ◆ **va lui expliquer ça, toi !** you try explaining that to him! ◆ **va me dire pourquoi j'ai fait ça/il s'est mis en colère ?** I have no idea why I did that/why he got angry

4 - VERBE PRONOMINAL

s'en aller

1 [= partir] to go (away); *(= déménager)* to move, to leave ◆ **bon, je m'en vais** right, I'm off *ou* I'm going ◆ **elle s'en va en vacances demain** she goes *ou* is going away on holiday tomorrow ◆ **ils s'en vont à Paris** they are going *ou* off to Paris ◆ **il s'en est allé** *ou* **s'est en allé** * **sans rien dire** he went away *ou* he left without saying anything ◆ **va-t'en !, allez-vous-en !** go away! ◆ **va-t-en de là !** get out of here!

◆ **ils s'en vont du quartier** they are leaving the area, they are moving away from the area

Notez que lorsque **aller** est suivi d'un adverbe de manière, l'anglais utilise généralement un verbe spécifique ; reportez-vous à l'adverbe.

◆ **s'en ~ subrepticement** to steal *ou* sneak away ◆ **elle s'est en allée sur la pointe des pieds** she tiptoed away

2 euph = mourir to go ◆ **il s'en va** he's going *ou* fading ◆ **quand je m'en irai** when I'm gone MAIS **il s'en est allé paisiblement** he passed away peacefully

3 = quitter un emploi to leave; *(= prendre sa retraite)* to retire, to leave

4 = disparaître *[tache] (gén)* to come off; *(sur tissu)* to come out; *[temps, années]* to pass, to go by ◆ **ça s'en ira au lavage** *[boue]* it'll wash off, it'll come off in the wash; *[tache]* it'll wash out ◆ **tout son argent s'en va en CD** all his money goes on CDs, he spends all his money on CDs

5 valeur intensive **je m'en vais leur montrer de quoi je suis capable** I'll show them what I'm made of! ◆ **va-t'en voir si c'est vrai !*** who knows if it's true!

5 - LOC EXCLAMATIVES

♦ **allons !, allez !, va !** *(pour stimuler)* ◆ **allons !, allez !** go on!, come on! ◆ **allez (la) France !** *(Sport)* come on France! ◆ **allez, allez** *ou* **allons, allons, circulez** come on now, move along ◆ **allons, cesse de m'ennuyer !** *(impatience)* will you just stop bothering me!; *(pour encourager, réconforter)* ◆ **allons, allons, il ne faut pas pleurer** come on now *ou* come, come, you mustn't cry ◆ **tu t'en remettras, va** don't worry, you'll get over it ◆ **ce n'est pas grave, allez !** come on, it's not so bad *ou* serious! ◆ **allez, au revoir !** 'bye then! *

♦ **allons bon!** ◆ **allons bon ! qu'est-ce qui t'est encore arrivé ?** *(agacement)* NOW what's happened? ◆ **il est tombé – allons bon !** *(ennui)* he's fallen over – oh dear! ◆ **allons bon, j'ai oublié mon sac !** oh dear, I've left my bag behind!

♦ **allons donc!** *(incrédulité)* come on!, come off it! * ◆ **notre planète est menacée – allons donc !** the planet is in danger – oh come on! ◆ **lui paresseux ? allons donc ! c'est lui qui fait tout** lazy, him? you've got to be kidding *, he's the one who does all the work ◆ **lui m'aider ? allons donc !** help me, him? that'll be the day! *

♦ **va donc!** ⁑ ◆ **va donc, eh crétin !** *(insulte)* you stupid idiot! *

♦ **ça va!** * *(= assez)* that's enough!; *(= d'accord)* OK, OK * ◆ **tes remarques désobligeantes, ça va comme ça !** I've had just about enough of your nasty comments! ◆ **alors, tu viens ? – ça va(, ça va) j'arrive !** are you coming then? – OK, OK, I'm coming! ◆ **ça fait dix fois que je te le dis – ça va, je vais le faire !** I've told you ten times – look, I'll do it, OK?

♦ **va pour ...** * ◆ **va pour une nouvelle voiture !** all right we'll GET a new car! ◆ **va pour 5 € !** *(dans un marchandage)* OK, €5 then! ◆ **j'aimerais ~ à Tokyo – alors va pour Tokyo !** I'd like to go to Tokyo – Tokyo it is then!

6 - NOM MASCULIN

1 = trajet outward journey ◆ **l'~ s'est bien passé** the (outward) journey *ou* the journey there went off well ◆ **j'irai vous voir à l'~** I'll come and see you on the way there ◆ **je ne fais que l'~ et retour** *ou* **l'~-retour** I'm just going there and back ◆ **j'ai fait plusieurs ~s et retours entre chez moi et la pharmacie** I made several trips to the chemist's ◆ **le dossier a fait plusieurs ~s et retours entre nos services** the file has been shuttled between departments; → **match**

2 = billet single (ticket) *(Brit)*, one-way ticket *(US)* ◆ **trois ~s (simples) pour Tours** three singles *(Brit) ou* one-way tickets *(US)* to Tours

♦ **aller-retour, aller et retour** return (ticket) *(Brit)*, round-trip ticket *(US)* ◆ **l'~-retour Paris-New York coûte 500 €** Paris-New York is €500 return *(Brit) ou* round-trip *(US)* ◆ **donner un ~-retour à qn** * *(= le gifler)* to give sb a box round the ears

allergène /alɛʀʒɛn/ ADJ allergenic NM allergen

allergénique /alɛʀʒenik/ ADJ allergenic

allergie /alɛʀʒi/ NF allergy ◆ **faire une ~** *(lit, fig)* to be allergic *(à* to); ◆ **~ respiratoire/cutanée** respiratory/skin allergy

allergique /alɛʀʒik/ ADJ *(lit, fig)* allergic *(à* to)

allergisant, e /alɛʀʒizɑ̃, ɑ̃t/ ADJ *[substance]* allergenic NM allergen

allergologie /alɛʀgɔlɔʒi/ NF study of allergies

allergologiste /alɛʀgɔlɔʒist/, **allergologue** /alɛʀgɔlɔg/ NMF allergist

alliacé, e /aljase/ ADJ alliaceous

alliage /aljaʒ/ NM alloy ◆ **un ~ disparate de doctrines** *(péj)* a hotchpotch of doctrines ◆ **roues en ~ léger** alloy wheels

alliance /aljɑ̃s/ NF 1 *(entre gouvernements, pays)* alliance; *(Bible)* covenant ◆ **faire** *ou* **conclure une ~ avec un pays** to enter into an alliance with a country ◆ **faire ~ avec qn** to ally oneself with sb; → **saint, triple** 2 *(frm = mariage)* union, marriage ◆ **neveu/oncle par ~** nephew/uncle by marriage ◆ **entrer par ~ dans une famille** to marry into a family, to become united by marriage with a family 3 *(= bague)* (wedding) ring 4 *(= mélange)* combination ◆ **l'~ de la musique et de la poésie** the union of music and poetry COMP **alliance de mots** *(Littérat)* bold juxtaposition (of words), oxymoron

allié, e /alje/ (ptp de **allier**) ADJ *[pays, forces]* allied ◆ **famille ~e** family *ou* relations by marriage NM,F *(= pays)* ally; *(= ami, soutien)* ally; *(= parent)* relative by marriage ◆ **les Alliés** *(Pol)* the Allies

allier /alje/ ▸ conjug 7 ◂ VT *[+ efforts]* to combine, to unite; *[+ couleurs]* to match; *[+ gouvernements, pays]* to ally; *[+ métaux]* to alloy ◆ **elle allie l'élégance à la simplicité** she combines elegance with simplicity ◆ **ils sont alliés à une puissante famille** they are related by marriage to a powerful family VPR **s'allier** *[efforts]* to combine, to unite; *[couleurs]* to match; *[familles]* to become united by marriage, to become allied *(à* to, with); *[gouvernements, pays]* to become allies *ou* allied; *[métaux]* to alloy ◆ **la France s'allia à l'Angleterre** France allied itself with England

alligator /aligatɔʀ/ NM alligator

allitération /a(l)liteʀasjɔ̃/ NF alliteration

allô /alo/ EXCL *(Téléc)* hello!, hullo! *(Brit)*

allocataire /alɔkatɛʀ/ NMF recipient

allocation /alɔkasjɔ̃/ NF 1 *[d'argent]* allocation; *[d'indemnité]* granting; *(Fin) [d'actions]* allotment; *[de temps]* allotment, allocation

2 *(= somme)* allowance ◆ **toucher les ~s** * to draw *ou* get family allowance

COMP **allocation (de) chômage** jobseeker's allowance *(NonC) (Brit)*, unemployment insurance *(NonC) (US)*

allocations familiales *(= argent) state allowance paid to families with dependent children*, ≃ family allowance *(Brit)*, child benefit *(Brit)*, welfare *(US)*; *(= bureau)* ≃ family allowance department *(Brit)*, child benefit office *(Brit)*, welfare center *(US)*

allocation (de) logement rent allowance *ou* subsidy

allocation de maternité maternity allowance *ou* benefit

allocation parentale (d'éducation) *allowance paid to a parent who has stopped work to bring up a young child*

allocation de parent isolé *allowance for one-parent families*

allocation de rentrée scolaire *allowance for children going back to school*

allocs * /alɔk/ NFPL (abrév de **allocations familiales**) → **allocation**

allocutaire /a(l)lɔkytɛʀ/ NMF addressee

allocution /a(l)lɔkysjɔ̃/ NF (short) speech ◆ **~ télévisée** (short) televised speech

allogène /alɔʒɛn/ ADJ *[population]* non-native; *(fig) [éléments]* foreign

allonge /alɔ̃ʒ/ NF 1 *(= pièce)* extension; *[de table]* leaf; 2 *(= crochet)* (butcher's) hook 3 *(Boxe)* reach ◆ **avoir une bonne ~** to have a long reach

allongé, e /alɔ̃ʒe/ (ptp de **allonger**) ADJ 1 *(= étendu)* **être ~** to be stretched out, to be lying *(sur* on); ◆ **rester ~** to stay lying down ◆ **~ sur le dos** lying on one's back, supine *(frm)* 2 *(= long)* long; *(= étiré)* elongated; *(= oblong)* oblong ◆ **faire une mine ~e** to pull *ou* make a long face

allongement /alɔ̃ʒmɑ̃/ NM 1 *[de distance, vêtement]* lengthening; *[de route, voie ferrée]* lengthening, extension 2 *[de durée]* extension ◆ **avec l'~ des jours** with the days getting *ou* growing longer ◆ **contribuer à l'~ de la durée de vie** *ou* **de l'espérance de vie** to contribute to greater *ou* increased life expectancy ◆ **pour éviter l'~ des listes d'attente** to prevent waiting lists (from) getting any longer 3 *[de métal]* elongation; *(Ling) [de phonème]* lengthening; *(Tech) [d'aile d'avion]* aspect ratio

allonger /alɔ̃ʒe/ ▸ conjug 3 ◂ VT 1 *(= rendre plus long) [+ vêtement]* to lengthen, to make longer *(de* by); *(en défaisant l'ourlet)* to let down; *[+ délai, durée]* to extend ◆ **~ le pas** to quicken one's pace ◆ **cette coiffure lui allonge le visage** that hair style makes her face look longer

2 *(= étendre) [+ bras, jambe]* to stretch (out); *[+ malade]* to lay *ou* stretch out ◆ **~ le cou (pour apercevoir qch)** to crane *ou* stretch one's neck (to see sth) ◆ **la jambe allongée sur une chaise** with one leg up on *ou* stretched out on a chair

3 ⁑ *[+ somme]* to fork out *; *[+ coup]* to deal, to land * ◆ **~ qn** to knock sb flat ◆ **il va falloir les ~** we'll *(ou* you'll *etc)* have to cough up *

4 *[+ sauce]* to thin (down) ◆ **~ la sauce** * *(fig)* to spin it out

VI *[jours]* to get *ou* grow longer, to lengthen

VPR **s'allonger** 1 *(= devenir ou paraître plus long) [ombres, jours]* to get *ou* grow longer, to lengthen; *[enfant]* to grow taller; *[discours, visite]* to drag on; *[durée]* to get longer; *[file, liste d'attente]* to get longer, to grow ◆ **son visage s'allongea à ces mots** his face fell when he heard this ◆ **la route s'allongeait devant eux** the road stretched away before them

2 *(= s'étendre)* to lie down, to stretch (o.s.) out; *(pour dormir)* to lie down ◆ **s'~ dans l'herbe** to lie down *ou* stretch (o.s.) out on the grass

allopathe /alɔpat/ ADJ allopathic NMF allopath, allopathist

allopathie /alɔpati/ NF allopathy

allopathique /alɔpatik/ ADJ allopathic

allophone /alɔfɔn/ ADJ *(= non natif)* ◆ **étudiants ~s** students who are non-native speakers NMF *(= locuteur non natif)* non-native speaker NM *(Ling)* allophone

allosaure /alozɔʀ/ NM allosaurus

allotropie /alɔtʀɔpi/ NF allotropy

allotropique /alɔtʀɔpik/ ADJ allotropic

allouer /alwe/ ▸ conjug 1 ◂ VT *[+ argent]* to allocate; *[+ indemnité]* to grant; *(Fin) [+ actions]* to allot; *[+ temps]* to allot, to allow ◆ **pendant le temps alloué** during the allotted time, during the time allowed

allumage /alymaʒ/ NM 1 *(= action) [de feu]* lighting, kindling; *[de poêle]* lighting; *[d'électricité]* switching *ou* turning on; *[de gaz]* lighting, putting *ou* turning on 2 *[de moteur]* ignition ◆ **avance à l'~** ignition *ou* spark advance ◆ **régler l'~** to adjust the timing; → **autoallumage**

allumé, e* /alyme/ ADJ *(= fou)* crazy*, nuts*; *(= ivre)* smashed*, pissed* *(Brit)*, trashed* *(US)*

allume-cigare (pl **allume-cigares**) /alymsigaʀ/ NM cigar lighter

allume-feu (pl **allume-feu(x)**) /alymfø/ NM firelighter

allume-gaz /alymgɑz/ NM INV gas lighter *(for cooker)*

allumer /alyme/ ▸ conjug 1 ◂ VT 1 *[+ feu]* to light, to kindle; *[+ bougie, poêle]* to light; *[+ cigare, pipe]* to light (up); *[+ incendie]* to start, to light ◆ **il alluma sa cigarette à celle de son voisin** he lit (up) his cigarette from his neighbour's, he got a light from his neighbour's cigarette ◆ **le feu était allumé** the fire was lit, the fire was going ◆ **laisse le poêle allumé** leave the stove on *ou* lit

2 *[+ électricité, lampe, radio]* to put *ou* switch *ou* turn on; *[+ gaz]* to light, to put *ou* turn on ◆ **laisse la lumière allumée** leave the light on ◆ **allume dans la cuisine** put the light(s) on in the kitchen ◆ **le bouton n'allume pas, ça n'allume pas** the light doesn't come on *ou* work ◆ **où est-ce qu'on allume ?** where is the switch?

3 *(= éclairer)* to put the light(s) on ◆ **une pièce** to put the light(s) on in a room ◆ **sa fenêtre était allumée** there was a light (on) at his window ◆ **laisse le salon allumé** leave the light(s) on in the sitting-room

4 *[+ colère, envie, haine]* to arouse, to stir up; *[+ amour]* to kindle

5 *(* = aguicher)* to turn on, to tease

6 *(* = tuer)* to burn*

VPR **s'allumer** *[incendie]* to blaze, to flare up; *[lumière]* to come *ou* go on; *[radiateur]* to switch (itself) on; *[sentiment]* to be aroused ◆ **ça s'allume comment ?** how do you switch it on? ◆ **le désir s'alluma dans ses yeux** his eyes lit up with desire ◆ **ses yeux s'allumèrent** his eyes lit up ◆ **ce bois s'allume bien** this wood is easy to light *ou* burns easily ◆ **sa fenêtre s'alluma** a light came *ou* went on at his window

allumette /alymɛt/ NF 1 *(pour allumer)* match; *(= morceau de bois)* match(stick) ◆ **~ de sûreté** *ou* **suédoise** safety match ◆ **~ tison** fuse ◆ **il a les jambes comme des ~s** he's got legs like matchsticks 2 *(Culin)* flaky pastry finger ◆ **~ au fromage** cheese straw *(Brit)* *ou* stick *(US)*; → **pomme**

allumeur /alymœʀ/ NM *[de voiture]* distributor; *[de fusée, appareil à gaz]* igniter ◆ **~ de réverbères** *(Hist)* lamplighter

allumeuse /alymøz/ NF *(péj)* teaser, tease

allure /alyʀ/ NF 1 *(= vitesse) [de véhicule]* speed; *[de piéton]* pace ◆ **rouler** *ou* **aller à vive** *ou* **grande/faible** *ou* **petite ~** to drive *ou* go at high *ou* great/low *ou* slow speed ◆ **à toute ~** *[rouler]* at top *ou* full speed, at full tilt; *[réciter, dîner]* as fast as one can ◆ **à cette ~, nous n'aurons jamais fini à temps** at this rate we'll never be finished in time

2 *(= démarche)* walk, gait *(littér)*; *(= prestance)* bearing; *(= attitude)* air, look; *(* = aspect) [d'objet, individu]* look, appearance ◆ **avoir de l'~, ne pas manquer d'~** to have style, to have a certain elegance ◆ **avoir fière** *ou* **grande** *ou* **belle/piètre ~** to cut a fine/a shabby figure ◆ **avoir une drôle d'~/bonne ~** to look odd *ou* funny/fine ◆ **d'~ sportive** sporty-looking ◆ **d'~ louche/bizarre** fishy-/odd-looking ◆ **les choses prennent une drôle d'~** things are taking a funny *ou* an odd turn ◆ **la ville prend des ~s de fête foraine** the town is beginning to look like *ou* resemble a funfair

3 *(= comportement)* **~s** ways ◆ **choquer par sa liberté d'~s** to shock people with one's unconventional behaviour ◆ **il a des ~s de voyou** he behaves *ou* carries on* like a hooligan

4 *(Équitation)* gait; *(Naut)* trim

allusif, -ive /a(l)lyzif, iv/ ADJ allusive

allusion /a(l)lyzjɔ̃/ NF *(= référence)* allusion *(à* to); *(avec sous-entendu)* hint *(à* at); ◆ **~ malveillante** innuendo ◆ **faire ~ à** to allude to, to hint at ◆ **par ~** allusively

alluvial, e (mpl **-iaux**) /a(l)lyvjal, jo/ ADJ alluvial

alluvionnement /a(l)lyvjɔnmɑ̃/ NM alluviation

alluvions /a(l)lyvjɔ̃/ NFPL alluvial deposits, alluvium *(sg)*

almanach /almana/ NM almanac

Almaty /almati/ N Almaty

almée /alme/ NF Egyptian dancing girl, almah

aloès /alɔɛs/ NM aloe

aloi /alwa/ NM ◆ **de bon ~** *[plaisanterie, gaieté]* honest, respectable; *[individu]* worthy, of sterling *ou* genuine worth; *[produit]* good quality ◆ **de mauvais ~** *[plaisanterie, gaieté]* unsavoury, unwholesome; *[individu]* dubious; *[produit]* of doubtful quality

alopécie /alɔpesi/ NF alopecia

alors /alɔʀ/ ADV 1 *(= à cette époque)* then, at that time ◆ **il était ~ étudiant** he was a student then *ou* at that time ◆ **les femmes d'~ portaient la crinoline** women in those days *ou* at that time wore crinolines ◆ **le ministre d'~ M. Dupont** the then minister Mr Dupont, the minister at that time, Mr Dupont; → **jusque**

2 *(= dans ce cas)* then; *(= en conséquence)* so ◆ **vous ne voulez pas de mon aide ? ~ je vous laisse** you don't want my help? I'll leave you to it then ◆ **il ne comprenait pas, ~ on l'a mis au courant** he didn't understand so they put him in the picture ◆ **~ qu'est-ce qu'on va faire ?** *(= dans ce cas)* what are we going to do then?; *(= donc)* so what are we going to do?

3 *(locution)*

◆ **alors + que** *(simultanéité)* while, when; *(opposition)* whereas ◆ **~ même que** *(= même si)* even if, even though; *(= au moment où)* while, just when ◆ **on a sonné ~ que j'étais dans mon bain** the bell rang while *ou* when I was in the bath ◆ **elle est sortie ~ que le médecin le lui avait interdit** she went out although *ou* even though the doctor had told her not to ◆ **il est parti travailler à Paris ~ que son frère est resté au village** he went to work in Paris whereas *ou* while his brother stayed behind in the village ◆ **~ même qu'il me supplierait** even if he begged me, even if *ou* though he were to beg me

4 * **~ tu viens (oui ou non) ?** well (then), are you coming (or not)?, are you coming then (or not)? ◆ **~ ça, ça m'étonne** now that really does surprise me ◆ **~ là je ne peux pas vous répondre** well that I really can't tell you ◆ **~ là je vous arrête** well I must stop you there ◆ **et (puis) ~ ?** and then what (happened)? ◆ **il pleut – et ~ ?** it's raining – so (what)? ◆ **alors alors !, ~ quoi !** come on!; → **non**

alose /aloz/ NF shad

alouette /alwɛt/ NF lark ◆ **~ (des champs)** skylark ◆ **attendre que les ~s vous tombent toutes rôties dans la bouche** to wait for things to fall into one's lap; → **miroir**

alourdir /aluʀdiʀ/ ▸ conjug 2 ◂ VT 1 *[+ véhicule]* to weigh *ou* load down, to make heavy; *[+ phrase]* to make heavy *ou* cumbersome; *[+ démarche, traits]* to make heavy; *[+ esprit]* to dull; *[+ atmosphère, climat]* to make more tense ◆ **il avait la tête alourdie par le sommeil** his head was heavy with sleep ◆ **vêtements alourdis par la pluie** heavy, rain-soaked clothes ◆ **les odeurs d'essence alourdissaient l'air** petrol fumes hung heavy on the air, the air was heavy with petrol fumes 2 *(= augmenter) [+ dette, facture, comptes]* to increase VPR **s'alourdir** *[personne, paupières]* to become *ou* grow heavy ◆ **sa taille/elle s'est alourdie** her waist/she has thickened out ◆ **le bilan s'est encore alourdi** the death toll has risen again

alourdissement /aluʀdismɑ̃/ NM 1 *[de véhicule, objet]* increased weight, heaviness; *[de phrase, style, pas]* heaviness; *[d'esprit]* dullness, dulling; *[de taille]* thickening ◆ **pour éviter l'~ de la procédure** to prevent the procedure from becoming more lengthy and cumbersome 2 *[de dette, facture]* increase *(de* in)

aloyau /alwajo/ NM sirloin

alpaga /alpaga/ NM *(= animal, lainage)* alpaca

alpage /alpaʒ/ NM *(= pré)* high mountain pasture; *(= époque) season spent by sheep etc in mountain pasture*

alpaguer* /alpage/ ▸ conjug 1 ◂ VT *(gén)* to collar*; *(Police)* to collar*, to nab* *(Brit)* ◆ **se faire ~** to get collared*

alpe /alp/ NF *(= pré)* alpine pasture NFPL **Alpes** ◆ **les Alpes** the Alps

alpestre /alpɛstʀ/ ADJ alpine

alpha /alfa/ NM alpha ◆ **l'~ et l'oméga** *(Rel, fig)* the alpha and omega ◆ **particule ~** *(Phys)* alpha particle

alphabet /alfabɛ/ NM *(= système)* alphabet; *(= livre)* alphabet *ou* ABC book ◆ **~ morse** Morse code

alphabétique /alfabetik/ ADJ alphabetical ◆ **par ordre ~** in alphabetical order

alphabétiquement /alfabetikmɑ̃/ ADV alphabetically

alphabétisation /alfabetizasjɔ̃/ NF elimination of illiteracy *(de* in); ◆ **l'~ d'une population** teaching a population to read and write ◆ **campagne d'~** literacy campaign ◆ **taux d'~** literacy rate

alphabétisé, e /alfabetize/ (ptp de **alphabétiser**) ADJ literate ◆ **population faiblement ~e** population with a low level of literacy

alphabétiser /alfabetize/ ▸ conjug 1 ◂ VT *[+ pays]* to eliminate illiteracy in; *[+ population]* to teach how to read and write

alphanumérique /alfanymeʀik/ ADJ alphanumeric

alphapage ® /alfapaʒ/ NM radiopager *(which displays messages)* ◆ **envoyer qch par ~** to send sth via a radiopager

alpin, e /alpɛ̃, in/ ADJ alpine; → **chasseur, ski**

alpinisme /alpinism/ NM mountaineering, mountain climbing

alpiniste /alpinist/ NMF mountaineer, climber

alsacien, -ienne /alzasjɛ̃, jɛn/ ADJ Alsatian NM *(= langue)* Alsatian NM,F **Alsacien(ne)** Alsatian

altérabilité /alteʀabilite/ NF *[de denrée, aliment]* perishability

altérable /alteʀabl/ ADJ *[denrée, aliment]* perishable

altération /alteʀasjɔ̃/ NF 1 *(= falsification) [de fait, texte, vérité]* distortion, falsification; *[de monnaie]* falsification; *[de vin, aliment, qualité]* adulteration 2 *(= détérioration) [de vin, aliment, qualité, matière, santé]* deterioration ◆ **l'~ de**

leurs relations the deterioration of their relationship ◆ **l'~ de son visage/de sa voix** his distorted features/broken voice 3 *(= modification)* change, modification 4 *(Mus)* accidental; *(Géol)* weathering

altercation / altɛʀkasjɔ̃ / NF altercation

alter ego / altɛʀego / NM INV alter ego ◆ **il est mon ~** he is my alter ego

altérer / alteʀe / ▸ conjug 6 ◂ VT 1 *(= falsifier)* *[+ texte, faits, vérité]* to distort, to falsify; *[+ monnaie]* to falsify; *[+ vin, aliments, qualité]* to adulterate

2 *(= abîmer)* *[+ vin, aliments, qualité]* to spoil; *[+ matière]* to alter, to debase; *[+ sentiments]* to alter, to spoil; *[+ couleur]* to alter; *[+ visage, voix]* to distort; *[+ santé, relations]* to impair, to affect ◆ **d'une voix altérée** in a broken voice ◆ **la chaleur a altéré la viande** the heat made the meat go bad *ou* go off *(Brit)*

3 *(= modifier)* to alter, to change ◆ **ceci n'a pas altéré mon amour pour elle** this has not altered my love for her

4 *(= assoiffer)* to make thirsty ◆ **altéré d'honneurs** *(littér)* thirsty *ou* thirsting for honours ◆ **fauve altéré de sang** wild animal thirsting for blood ◆ **il était altéré** his throat was parched

VPR **s'altérer** *[vin]* to become spoiled; *[viande]* to go bad, to go off *(Brit)*, to spoil *(US)*; *[matière, couleur]* to undergo a change; *[visage]* to change, to become distorted; *[sentiments]* to alter, to be spoilt; *[relations]* to deteriorate ◆ **sa santé s'altère de plus en plus** his health is deteriorating further *ou* is getting progressively worse ◆ **sa voix s'altéra sous le coup de la douleur** grief made his voice break, grief distorted his voice

altérité / alteʀite / NF otherness

altermondialisation / altɛʀmɔ̃djalizasjɔ̃ / NF alterglobalization

altermondialisme / altɛʀmɔ̃djalism / NM alter-globalism

alternance / altɛʀnɑ̃s / NF alternation; *(Pol)* *changeover of political power between parties* ◆ **l'~ chaud/froid** the alternation of hot and cold ◆ **les soldats ont commencé la sale besogne, ~ de violence et d'intimidation** the soldiers began their dirty work, alternating between violence and intimidation

◆ **en alternance** ◆ **faire qch en ~** *(= se relayer)* to take it in turns to do sth ◆ **les deux pièces sont jouées en ~** the two plays are performed alternately ◆ **cette émission reprendra en ~ avec d'autres programmes** this broadcast will alternate with other programmes; → **formation**

alternant, e / altɛʀnɑ̃, ɑ̃t / ADJ alternating

alternateur / altɛʀnatœʀ / NM alternator

alternatif, -ive¹ / altɛʀnatif, iv / ADJ *(= périodique)* alternate; *(Philos)* alternative; *(Élec)* alternating; *[médecine]* alternative

alternative² / altɛʀnativ / NF *(= dilemme)* alternative; (* *= possibilité)* alternative, option; *(Philos)* alternative ◆ **être dans une ~** to have to choose between two alternatives

alternativement / altɛʀnativmɑ̃ / ADV alternately, in turn

alterne / altɛʀn / ADJ *(Bot, Math)* alternate

alterné, e / altɛʀne / (ptp de **alterner**) ADJ *[rimes]* alternate; *(Math)* *[série]* alternating ◆ **circulation ~e** *(pour travaux)* contraflow (system); *(pour pollution) selective ban on vehicle use (based on registration numbers) during periods of heavy pollution* ◆ **la prise ~e de deux médicaments** taking two medicines in alternation; → **stationnement**

alterner / altɛʀne / ▸ conjug 1 ◂ VT *[+ choses]* to alternate; *[+ cultures]* to rotate, to alternate VI to alternate *(avec* with); ◆ **ils alternèrent à la présidence** they took (it in) turns to be chairman

altesse / altɛs / NF *(= prince)* prince; *(= princesse)* princess ◆ **votre Altesse** *(= titre)* your Highness ◆ **Son Altesse sérénissime/royale** His *ou* Her Serene/Royal Highness

altier, -ière / altje, jɛʀ / ADJ *[caractère]* haughty ◆ **cimes altières** *(littér)* lofty peaks *(littér)*

altimètre / altimɛtʀ / NM altimeter

altimétrie / altimetʀi / NF altimetry

altiport / altipɔʀ / NM altiport *(SPÉC)*, mountain airfield

altiste / altist / NMF viola player, violist

altitude / altityd / NF 1 *(par rapport à la mer)* altitude, height above sea level; *(par rapport au sol)* height ◆ **~s** *(fig)* heights ◆ **être à 500 mètres d'~** to be at a height *ou* an altitude of 500 metres, to be 500 metres above sea level ◆ **en ~** at high altitude, high up ◆ **les régions de basse ~** low-lying areas 2 *(en avion)* **perdre de l'~** to lose altitude *ou* height ◆ **prendre de l'~** to gain altitude ◆ **voler à basse/haute ~** to fly at low/high altitude

alto / alto / NM *(= instrument)* viola NF contralto ADJ ◆ **saxo(phone)/flûte ~** alto sax(ophone)/flute

altruisme / altʀɥism / NM altruism

altruiste / altʀɥist / ADJ altruistic NMF altruist

altuglas ® / altyglas / NM *thick form of Perspex* ®

alu * / aly / NM abrév de **aluminium**

aluminate / alyminat / NM aluminate

alumine / alymin / NF alumina

aluminium / alyminjɔm / NM aluminium *(Brit)*, aluminum *(US)*

alun / alœ̃ / NM alum

alunir / alyniʀ / ▸ conjug 2 ◂ VI to land on the moon

alunissage / alynisaʒ / NM (moon) landing

alvéolaire / alveolɛʀ / ADJ alveolar

alvéole / alveɔl / NF *ou* M *[de ruche]* alveolus, cell; *(Géol)* cavity ◆ **~ dentaire** tooth socket, alveolus *(SPÉC)* ◆ **~s dentaires** alveolar ridge, teeth ridge, alveoli *(SPÉC)* ◆ **~ pulmonaire** air cell, alveolus *(SPÉC)*

alvéolé, e / alveɔle / ADJ honeycombed, alveolate *(SPÉC)*

Alzheimer / alzajmœʀ / NM ◆ **maladie d'~** Alzheimer's disease ◆ **il a un ~** * he has got Alzheimer's (disease)

AM / aɛm / (abrév de **assurance maladie**) → **assurance**

amabilité / amabilite / NF kindness ◆ **ayez l'~ de** (would you) be so kind *ou* good as to ◆ **plein d'~ envers moi** extremely kind to me ◆ **faire des ~s à qn** to show politeness *ou* courtesy to sb ◆ **échanger des ~s** *(iro = des insultes)* to hurl abuse at one another

amadou / amadu / NM touchwood, tinder

amadouer / amadwe / ▸ conjug 1 ◂ VT *(= enjôler)* to coax, to cajole; *(= adoucir)* to mollify, to soothe ◆ **~ qn pour qu'il fasse qch** to wheedle *ou* cajole sb into doing sth

amaigrir / amegʀiʀ / ▸ conjug 2 ◂ VT 1 *(= rendre plus maigre)* to make thin *ou* thinner ◆ **joues amaigries par l'âge** cheeks wasted with age ◆ **je l'ai trouvé très amaigri** I found him much thinner, I thought he looked much thinner ◆ **10 années de prison l'ont beaucoup amaigri** 10 years in prison have left him very much thinner 2 *[+ pâte]* to thin down; *[+ poutre]* to reduce the thickness of VPR **s'amaigrir** to get thin *ou* thinner

amaigrissant, e / amegʀisɑ̃, ɑ̃t / ADJ *[produit, régime]* slimming *(Brit)*, reducing *(US)*

amaigrissement / amegʀismɑ̃ / NM 1 *(pathologique)* *[de corps]* loss of weight; *[de visage, membres]* thinness 2 *(volontaire)* slimming ◆ **un ~ de 3 kg** a loss (in weight) of 3 kg; → **cure¹**

amalgamation / amalgamasjɔ̃ / NF *(Métal)* amalgamation

amalgame / amalgam / NM 1 *(Métal, Dentisterie)* amalgam 2 *(péj = mélange)* (strange) mixture *ou* blend ◆ **un ~ d'idées** a hotchpotch of ideas ◆ **faire l'~ entre deux idées** to confuse two ideas ◆ **il ne faut pas faire l'~ entre parti de droite et parti fasciste** you shouldn't lump the right-wing and fascist parties together

amalgamer / amalgame / ▸ conjug 1 ◂ VT *(Métal)* to amalgamate; *(= mélanger)* to combine *(à, avec* with); *(= confondre)* *[+ idées, réalités]* to confuse VPR **s'amalgamer** *(Métal)* to be amalgamated; *(= s'unir)* to combine

amande / amɑ̃d / NF 1 *(= fruit)* almond ◆ **~s amères/douces** bitter/sweet almonds ◆ **~s pilées** ground almonds ◆ **en ~** almond-shaped, almond *(épith)*; → **pâte** 2 *(= noyau)* kernel 3 *(= mollusque)* queen scallop

amandier / amɑ̃dje / NM almond (tree)

amandine / amɑ̃din / NF *(= gâteau)* almond tart

amanite / amanit / NF Amanita COMP **amanite phalloïde** death cap **amanite tue-mouches** fly agaric

amant / amɑ̃ / NM lover ◆ **~ de passage** casual lover ◆ **les deux ~s** the two lovers ◆ **prendre un ~** to take a lover

amante †† / amɑ̃t / NF *(= fiancée)* betrothed †, mistress †

amarante / amaʀɑ̃t / NF amaranth ADJ INV amaranthine

amariner / amaʀine / ▸ conjug 1 ◂ VT 1 *[+ navire ennemi]* to take over and man 2 *[+ matelot]* to accustom to life at sea ◆ **elle n'est pas** *ou* **ne s'est pas encore amarinée** she hasn't got used to being at sea yet, she hasn't found her sea legs yet

amarrage / amaʀaʒ / NM *(Naut)* mooring ◆ **être à l'~** to be moored

amarre / amaʀ / NF *(Naut = cordage)* rope *ou* cable ◆ **les ~s** the moorings; → **larguer, rompre**

amarrer / amaʀe / ▸ conjug 1 ◂ VT *[+ navire]* to moor, to make fast; *[+ cordage]* to make fast, to belay; *(hum)* *[+ paquet, valise]* to tie down ◆ **la navette s'est amarrée à la station orbitale** the shuttle has docked with the space station

amaryllis / amaʀilis / NF amaryllis

amas / amɑ / NM 1 *(lit = tas)* heap, pile; *[de souvenirs, idées]* mass ◆ **tout un ~ de qch** a whole heap *ou* pile of sth 2 *(Astron)* star cluster 3 *(Min)* mass

amasser / amɑse / ▸ conjug 1 ◂ VT 1 *(= amonceler)* *[+ choses]* to pile up, to accumulate; *[+ fortune]* to amass, to accumulate ◆ **il ne pense qu'à ~ (de l'argent)** all he thinks of is amassing *ou* accumulating wealth 2 *(= rassembler)* *[+ preuves, données]* to amass, to gather (together); → **pierre** VPR **s'amasser** *[choses, preuves]* to pile up, to accumulate; *[foule]* to gather, to mass ◆ **les preuves s'amassent contre lui** the evidence is building up *ou* piling up against him

amateur / amatœʀ / NM 1 *(= non-professionnel)* amateur ◆ **équipe ~** amateur team ◆ **talent d'~** amateur talent ◆ **peintre/musicien/photographe ~** amateur painter/musician/photographer ◆ **faire de la peinture en ~** to do a bit of painting (as a hobby)

2 *(péj)* dilettante, mere amateur ◆ **travail d'~** amateurish work ◆ **faire qch en ~** to do sth amateurishly

[3] *(= connaisseur)* ~ **de** lover of ◆ ~ **d'art/de musique** art/music lover ◆ **être ~ de films/de concerts** to be an avid *ou* a keen *(Brit)* film-/concert-goer, to be keen on *(Brit)* films/concerts ◆ **elle est très ~ de framboises** she is very fond of *ou* she loves raspberries ◆ **le jazz, je ne suis pas ~** I'm not really a jazz fan, I'm not all that keen on jazz *(Brit)*

[4] * *(= acheteur)* taker; *(= volontaire)* volunteer ◆ **il reste des carottes, il y a des ~s ?** *ou* **avis aux ~s !** there are some carrots left, are there any takers?; → **trouver**

amateurisme /amatœʀism/ **NM** *(Sport)* amateurism; *(péj)* amateurism, amateurishness ◆ **c'est de l'~ !** it's so amateurish!

amazone /amazon/ **NF** [1] *(= écuyère)* horsewoman ◆ **tenue d'~** woman's riding habit ◆ **monter en ~** to ride sidesaddle [2] *(= jupe)* long riding skirt [3] *(* = prostituée)* prostitute *(who picks up her clients in a car)* [4] ◆ **Amazone** *(Géog, Myth)* Amazon

Amazonie /amazɔni/ **NF** Amazonia

amazonien, -ienne /amazɔnjɛ̃, jɛn/ **ADJ** Amazonian

ambages /ɑ̃baʒ/ **sans ambages LOC ADV** without beating about the bush, in plain language

ambassade /ɑ̃basad/ **NF** [1] *(= institution, bâtiment)* embassy; *(= charge)* ambassadorship, embassy; *(= personnel)* embassy staff *(pl) ou* officials, embassy ◆ **l'~ de France** the French Embassy [2] *(= mission)* mission ◆ **être envoyé en ~ auprès de qn** to be sent on a mission to sb

ambassadeur /ɑ̃basadœʀ/ **NM** *(Pol, fig)* ambassador ◆ ~ **extraordinaire** ambassador extraordinary *(auprès de* to); ◆ **l'~ de la pensée française** the representative *ou* ambassador of French thought

ambassadrice /ɑ̃basadʀis/ **NF** *(= diplomate)* ambassador, ambassadress *(auprès de* to); *(= épouse)* ambassador's wife, ambassadress; *(fig)* representative, ambassador

ambiance /ɑ̃bjɑ̃s/ **NF** *(= atmosphère)* atmosphere; *(= environnement)* surroundings; *[de famille, équipe]* atmosphere ◆ **l'~ de la salle** the atmosphere in the house, the mood of the audience ◆ **il vit dans une ~ calme** he lives in calm *ou* peaceful surroundings ◆ **il y a de l'~ !*** there's a great atmosphere here!* ◆ **il va y avoir de l'~ quand tu vas lui dire ça !*** things are going to get ugly* when you tell him that! ◆ **mettre de l'~** to liven things up* ◆ **mettre qn dans l'~** to put sb in the mood ◆ **l'~ est à la fête** there's a party atmosphere; → **éclairage, musique**

ambiant, e /ɑ̃bjɑ̃, jɑ̃t/ **ADJ** *[air]* surrounding, ambient; *[température]* ambient; *[idéologie, scepticisme]* prevailing, pervading

ambidextre /ɑ̃bidɛkstʀ/ **ADJ** ambidextrous

ambigu, -uë /ɑ̃bigy/ **ADJ** ambiguous

ambiguïté /ɑ̃bigɥite/ **NF** [1] *(caractère)* ambiguousness, ambiguity ◆ **une réponse sans ~** an unequivocal *ou* unambiguous reply ◆ **parler/répondre sans ~** to speak/reply unambiguously *ou* without ambiguity [2] *(Ling)* ambiguity [3] *(terme)* ambiguity

ambitieusement /ɑ̃bisjøzmɑ̃/ **ADV** ambitiously

ambitieux, -ieuse /ɑ̃bisjø, jøz/ **ADJ** ambitious ◆ ~ **de plaire** *(littér)* anxious to please, desirous to please *(littér)* **NM,F** ambitious person

ambition /ɑ̃bisjɔ̃/ GRAMMAIRE ACTIVE 35.2, 35.4 **NF** ambition ◆ **il met toute son ~ à faire** his only *ou* sole ambition is to do ◆ **elle a l'~ de réussir** her ambition is to succeed ◆ **il a de grandes ~s** he has great *ou* big ambitions

ambitionner /ɑ̃bisjɔne/ ▸ conjug 1 ◂ **VT** to seek *ou* strive after ◆ **il ambitionne d'escalader l'Everest** it's his ambition to *ou* his ambition is to climb Everest

ambivalence /ɑ̃bivalɑ̃s/ **NF** ambivalence

ambivalent, e /ɑ̃bivalɑ̃, ɑ̃t/ **ADJ** ambivalent

amble /ɑ̃bl/ **NM** *[de cheval]* amble ◆ **aller l'~** to amble

ambler /ɑ̃ble/ ▸ conjug 1 ◂ **VI** *[cheval]* to amble

amblyope /ɑ̃bljɔp/ **ADJ** ◆ **il est ~** he has a lazy eye, he is amblyopic *(SPÉC)* **NMF** person with a lazy eye *ou* amblyopia *(SPÉC)*

amblyopie /ɑ̃bljɔpi/ **NF** lazy eye, amblyopia *(SPÉC)*

ambre /ɑ̃bʀ/ **NM** ◆ ~ **(jaune)** amber ◆ ~ **gris** ambergris ◆ **couleur d'~** amber(-coloured)

ambré, e /ɑ̃bʀe/ **ADJ** *[couleur]* amber; *[parfum]* amber-based

ambroisie /ɑ̃bʀwazi/ **NF** *(Myth)* ambrosia; *(= plante)* ambrosia, ragweed ◆ **c'est de l'~ !** *(fig)* this is food fit for the gods!

ambrosiaque /ɑ̃bʀozjak/ **ADJ** ambrosial

ambulance /ɑ̃bylɑ̃s/ **NF** ambulance ◆ **on ne tire pas sur une ~** *(fig)* you don't kick somebody when they're down

ambulancier, -ière /ɑ̃bylɑ̃sje, jɛʀ/ **NM,F** *(= conducteur)* ambulance driver; *(= infirmier)* ambulance man *(ou* woman)

ambulant, e /ɑ̃bylɑ̃, ɑ̃t/ **ADJ** *[comédien, musicien]* itinerant, strolling; *[cirque, théâtre]* travelling ◆ **c'est un squelette/dictionnaire ~*** he's a walking skeleton/dictionary; → **marchand, vendeur** *etc*

ambulatoire /ɑ̃bylatwaʀ/ **ADJ** *(Méd)* *[soins, consultation]* outpatient *(épith)*, ambulatory *(SPÉC)* ◆ **médecine/chirurgie ~** outpatient care/surgery

AME /aɛmə/ **NM** (abrév de **accord monétaire européen**) EMA

âme /ɑm/ **NF** [1] *(gén, Philos, Rel)* soul ◆ **(que) Dieu ait son ~** (may) God rest his soul ◆ **sur mon ~** †† upon my soul †; → **recommander, rendre**

[2] *(= centre de qualités intellectuelles et morales)* soul, mind ◆ **avoir** *ou* **être une ~ généreuse** to have great generosity of spirit ◆ **avoir** *ou* **être une ~ basse** *ou* **vile** be evil-hearted *ou* evil-minded ◆ **avoir** *ou* **être une ~ sensible** to be a sensitive soul, to be very sensitive ◆ **ce film n'est pas pour les ~s sensibles** *(frm)* this film is not for the squeamish *ou* the faint-hearted ◆ **grandeur** *ou* **noblesse d'~** high- *ou* noble-mindedness ◆ **en mon ~ et conscience** in all conscience *ou* honesty ◆ **de toute mon ~** *(littér)* with all my soul ◆ **il y a mis toute son ~** he put his heart and soul into it

[3] *(= centre psychique et émotif)* soul ◆ **faire qch avec ~** to do sth with feeling ◆ **ému jusqu'au fond de l'~** profoundly moved ◆ **c'est un corps sans ~** he has no soul ◆ **il est musicien dans l'~** he's a musician through and through ◆ **il a la technique mais son jeu est sans ~** his technique is good but he plays without feeling *ou* his playing is soulless

[4] *(= personne)* soul ◆ **un village de 600 ~s** *(frm)* a village of 600 souls ◆ **on ne voyait ~ qui vive** you couldn't see a (living) soul, there wasn't a (living) soul to be seen ◆ **bonne ~*** kind soul ◆ **est-ce qu'il n'y aura pas une bonne ~ pour m'aider ?** won't some kind soul give me a hand? ◆ **il y a toujours de bonnes ~s pour critiquer** *(iro)* there's always some kind soul ready to criticize *(iro)* ◆ ~ **charitable** *(péj)* well-meaning soul *(iro)* ◆ **il est là/il erre comme une ~ en peine** he looks like/he is wandering about like a lost soul ◆ **être l'~ damnée de qn** to be sb's henchman *ou* tool ◆ **il a trouvé l'~ sœur** he has found a soul mate

[5] *(= principe qui anime)* soul, spirit ◆ **l'~ d'un peuple** the soul *ou* spirit of a nation ◆ **l'~ d'un complot** the moving spirit in a plot ◆ **être l'~ d'un parti** to be the soul *ou* leading light of a party ◆ **elle a une ~ de sœur de charité** she is the very soul *ou* spirit of charity ◆ **elle a une ~ de chef** she has the soul of a leader

[6] *(Tech) [de canon]* bore; *[d'aimant]* core; *[de violon]* soundpost; → **charge, état, fendre** *etc*

améliorable /ameljɔʀabl/ **ADJ** improvable

amélioration /ameljɔʀasjɔ̃/ **NF** [1] *(= fait de s'améliorer)* improvement ◆ **l'~ de son état de santé** the improvement in his health, the change for the better in his health ◆ **on assiste à une ~ des conditions de travail** working conditions are improving ◆ **une ~ de la conjoncture** an economic upturn, an improvement in the state of the economy [2] *(= changement)* improvement ◆ **apporter des ~s à** to make improvements to ◆ **faire des ~s dans une maison** *(= travaux)* to make improvements to a house

améliorer /ameljɔʀe/ ▸ conjug 1 ◂ **VT** to improve ◆ ~ **sa situation** to improve one's situation ◆ **pour ~ l'ordinaire** *(argent)* to top up one's basic income; *(repas)* to make things a bit more interesting **VPR s'améliorer** to improve ◆ **tu ne t'améliores pas avec l'âge !** you're not getting any better with age!, you don't improve with age, do you?

amen /amɛn/ **NM INV** *(Rel)* amen ◆ **dire ~ à qch/à tout** to say amen to sth/everything, to agree religiously to sth/everything

aménageable /amenaʒabl/ **ADJ** *[horaire]* flexible; *[grenier]* suitable for conversion *(en* into)

aménagement /amenaʒmɑ̃/ **NM** [1] *(= agencement) [de local]* fitting-out; *[de parc]* laying-out ◆ **l'~ d'une chambre en bureau** converting a bedroom into an office ◆ **plan d'~** development plan

[2] *(= équipements)* ~**s** facilities ◆ **les nouveaux ~s de l'hôpital** the new hospital facilities

[3] *(= ajustement)* adjustment ◆ **demander des ~s financiers/d'horaire** to request certain financial adjustments/adjustments to one's timetable

[4] *(= création) [de route]* making, building; *[de gradins, placard]* putting in

COMP l'aménagement de l'espace *(Admin)* environmental planning

aménagement de peine *(Jur)* reduced sentencing

aménagement régional regional development

aménagement rural rural development

aménagement du temps de travail *(= réforme)* reform of working hours; *(= gestion)* flexible time management

l'aménagement du territoire ≃ town and country planning *(Brit)*

aménagement urbain urban development

aménager /amenaʒe/ ▸ conjug 3 ◂ **VT** [1] *(= équiper) [+ local]* to fit out; *[+ parc]* to lay out; *[+ territoire]* to develop; *[+ horaire] (gén)* to plan, to work out; *(= modifier)* to adjust ◆ **horaire aménagé** *(travail)* flexible working hours; *(Scol)* flexible timetable ◆ ~ **une chambre en bureau** to convert a bedroom into a study ◆ **s'~ des plages de repos** to take a rest from time to time [2] *(= créer) [+ route]* to make, to build; *[+ gradins, placard]* to put in ◆ ~ **un bureau dans une chambre** to fix up a study in a bedroom

aménageur, -euse /amenaʒœʀ, øz/ **NM,F** *specialist in national and regional development*, ≃ town and country planner *(Brit)*, city planner *(US)*

amendable /amɑ̃dabl/ **ADJ** *(Pol)* amendable; *(Agr)* which can be enriched

amende /amɑ̃d/ **NF** fine ◆ **mettre à l'~** to fine; *(fig)* to take to task ◆ **il a eu 100 € d'~** he got a €100 fine, he was fined €100 ◆ **"défense d'entrer sous peine d'amende"** "trespassers will be prosecuted *ou* fined" ◆ **faire ~ honorable** to make amends

amendement /amɑ̃dmɑ̃/ **NM** *(Pol)* amendment; *(Agr)* (= *opération*) enrichment; (= *substance*) enriching agent

amender /amɑ̃de/ ▸ conjug 1 ◂ **VT** *(Pol)* to amend; *(Agr)* to enrich; *[+ conduite]* to improve, to amend **VPR** **s'amender** to mend one's ways

amène /amɛn/ **ADJ** *(littér = aimable) [propos, visage]* affable; *[personne, caractère]* amiable, affable ◆ **des propos peu ~s** unkind words

amener /am(ə)ne/ ▸ conjug 5 ◂ **VT** 1 (= *faire venir*) *[+ personne, objet]* to bring (along); (= *acheminer*) *[+ cargaison]* to bring, to convey ◆ **on nous amène les enfants tous les matins** they bring the children to us every morning, the children are brought to us every morning ◆ **amène-la à la maison** bring her round *(Brit) ou* around *(US)* (to the house), bring her home ◆ **le sable est amené à Paris par péniche** sand is brought *ou* conveyed to Paris by barge ◆ **qu'est-ce qui vous amène ici ?** what brings you here? ◆ **vous nous avez amené le beau temps !** you've brought the nice weather with you!; → **mandat**

2 (= *provoquer*) to bring about, to cause ◆ **~ la disette** to bring about *ou* cause a shortage ◆ **~ le typhus** to cause typhus

3 (= *inciter*) **~ qn à faire qch** *[circonstances]* to lead sb to do sth; *[personne]* to bring sb round to doing sth, to get sb to do sth; *(par un discours persuasif)* to talk sb into doing sth ◆ **la crise pourrait ~ le gouvernement à agir** the crisis might induce *ou* lead the government to take action ◆ **elle a été finalement amenée à renoncer à son voyage** she was finally induced *ou* driven to give up her trip ◆ **je suis amené à croire que ...** I am led to believe *ou* think that ... ◆ **c'est ce qui m'a amené à cette conclusion** that is what led *ou* brought me to that conclusion

4 (= *diriger*) to bring ◆ **~ qn à ses propres idées/à une autre opinion** to bring sb round *(Brit) ou* around *(US)* to one's own ideas/to another way of thinking ◆ **~ la conversation sur un sujet** to bring the conversation round *(Brit) ou* around *(US)* to a subject, to lead the conversation on to a subject ◆ **système amené à un haut degré de complexité** system brought to a high degree of complexity

5 *[+ transition, conclusion, dénouement]* to present, to introduce ◆ **exemple bien amené** well-introduced example

6 *(Pêche) [+ poisson]* to draw in; *(Naut) [+ voile, pavillon]* to strike ◆ **~ les couleurs** *(Mil)* to strike colours

7 *(Dés) [+ paire, brelan]* to throw

VPR **s'amener** * (= *venir*) to come along ◆ **amène-toi ici !** get over here! * ◆ **tu t'amènes ?** are you going to get a move on? *, come on! * ◆ **il s'est amené avec toute sa bande** he turned up *ou* showed up * with the whole gang

aménité /amenite/ **NF** (= *amabilité*) *[de propos]* affability; *[de personne, caractère]* amiability, affability ◆ **sans ~** unkindly ◆ **se dire des ~s** *(iro)* to exchange uncomplimentary remarks

aménorrhée /amenɔʀe/ **NF** amenorrhoea

amenuisement /amənɥizmɑ̃/ **NM** *[de valeur, avance, espoir]* dwindling; *[de chances]* lessening; *[de ressources]* diminishing, dwindling

amenuiser /amənɥize/ ▸ conjug 1 ◂ **VPR** **s'amenuiser** *[valeur, avance, espoir]* to dwindle; *[chances]* to grow slimmer, to lessen; *[risque]* to diminish, to lessen; *[différences]* to become less marked; *[provisions, ressources]* to run low; *[temps]* to run out **VT** *[+ objet]* to thin down; *(fig)* to reduce

amer[1] /amɛʀ/ **NM** *(Naut)* seamark

amer[2], **-ère** /amɛʀ/ **ADJ** *(lit, fig)* bitter ◆ **~ comme chicotin** * as bitter as anything ◆ **avoir la bouche amère** to have a bitter taste in one's mouth

amérasien, -ienne /ameʀazjɛ̃, jɛn/ **ADJ** Amerasian **NM,F** **Amérasien(ne)** Amerasian

amèrement /amɛʀmɑ̃/ **ADV** bitterly

américain, e /ameʀikɛ̃, ɛn/ **ADJ** American; → **œil** **NM** (= *anglais américain*) American (English) **NM,F** **Américain(e)** American **NF** **américaine** *(automobile)* American car ◆ **à l'~e** *(gén)* in the American style; *(Culin)* à l'Américaine ◆ **course à l'~e** (bicycle) relay race

américanisation /ameʀikanizasjɔ̃/ **NF** americanization

américaniser /ameʀikanize/ ▸ conjug 1 ◂ **VT** to Americanize **VPR** **s'américaniser** to become Americanized

américanisme /ameʀikanism/ **NM** Americanism

américaniste /ameʀikanist/ **NMF** Americanist, American specialist

américium /ameʀisjɔm/ **NM** americium

amérindien, -ienne /ameʀɛ̃djɛ̃, jɛn/ **ADJ** Amerindian, American Indian **NM,F** **Amérindien(ne)** Amerindian, American Indian

Amérique /ameʀik/ **NF** America ◆ **~ centrale/latine/du Nord/du Sud** Central/Latin/North/South America

Amerloque * /amɛʀlɔk/ **NMF**, **Amerlo(t)** /amɛʀlo/ **NM** Yankee *, Yank *

amerrir /ameʀiʀ/ ▸ conjug 2 ◂ **VI** *[avion]* to land (on the sea), to make a sea-landing; *[engin spatial]* to splash down

amerrissage /ameʀisaʒ/ **NM** *[d'avion]* (sea) landing; *[d'engin spatial]* splashdown

amertume /amɛʀtym/ **NF** *(lit, fig)* bitterness ◆ **plein d'~** full of bitterness, very bitter

améthyste /ametist/ **NF, ADJ INV** amethyst

ameublement /amœbləmɑ̃/ **NM** (= *meubles*) furniture; *(action)* furnishing ◆ **articles d'~** furnishings ◆ **commerce d'~** furniture trade

ameublir /amœbliʀ/ ▸ conjug 2 ◂ **VT** *(Agr)* to loosen, to break down

ameuter /amøte/ ▸ conjug 1 ◂ **VT** 1 (= *attrouper*) *[+ curieux, passants]* to draw a crowd of; *[+ voisins]* to bring out; (= *soulever*) *[+ foule]* to rouse, to stir up, to incite *(contre* against); ◆ **ses cris ameutèrent les passants** his shouts drew a crowd of passers-by ◆ **elle a ameuté l'opinion internationale contre les pollueurs** she mobilized international opinion against the polluters ◆ **tais-toi, tu vas ~ toute la rue !** * be quiet, you'll have the whole street out! ◆ **tu n'as pas besoin d'~ tout le quartier !** * you don't have to tell the whole neighbourhood!, you don't have to shout it from the rooftops! 2 *[+ chiens]* to form into a pack **VPR** **s'ameuter** (= *s'attrouper*) *[passants]* to gather, to mass together; *[voisins]* to come out; (= *se soulever*) to band together, to gather into a mob ◆ **des passants s'ameutèrent** an angry crowd gathered

AMF /aɛmɛf/ **NF** (abrév de **Autorité des Marchés Financiers**) FSA *(Brit)* ; ≈ SEC *(US)*

ami, e /ami/ **NM,F** 1 (= *personne proche*) friend ◆ **un vieil ~ de la famille** *ou* **de la maison** an old friend of the family, an old family friend ◆ **~ d'enfance** childhood friend ◆ **~ intime** (very) close *ou* intimate friend, bosom friend ◆ **il m'a présenté son ~e** he introduced his girlfriend to me ◆ **elle est sortie avec ses ~es** she's out with her (girl) friends ◆ **c'était signé "un ami qui vous veut du bien"** it was signed "a well-wisher *ou* a friend" ◆ **se faire un ~ de qn** to make *ou* become friends with sb ◆ **faire ~-~ avec qn** * to be buddy-buddy with sb * ◆ **nous sommes entre ~s** *(deux personnes)* we're friends; *(plus de deux)* we're all friends ◆ **je vous dis ça en ~** I'm telling you this as a friend ◆ **nous sommes des ~s de vingt ans** we've been friends for twenty years ◆ **~s des bêtes/de la nature** animal/nature lovers ◆ **société** *ou* **club des ~s de Balzac** Balzac club *ou* society ◆ **un célibataire/professeur de mes ~s** a bachelor/teacher friend of mine ◆ **être sans ~s** to be friendless, to have no friends ◆ **parents et ~s** friends and relations *ou* relatives ◆ **~ des arts** patron of the arts ◆ **le meilleur ~ de l'homme** man's best friend ◆ **nos ~s à quatre pattes** our four-legged friends

2 *(euph = amant)* boyfriend; (= *maîtresse*) girlfriend ◆ **l'~e de l'assassin** the murderer's lady-friend; → **bon**[1], **petit**

3 *(interpellation)* **mes chers ~s** gentlemen; *(auditoire mixte)* ladies and gentlemen ◆ **mon cher ~** my dear fellow *ou* chap *(Brit)* ◆ **ça, mon (petit) ~** now look here ◆ **ben mon ~ !** * **si j'avais su** gosh! * *ou* blimey! * *(Brit)* if I had known that! ◆ **oui mon ~ !** *(entre époux)* yes my dear!

ADJ *[visage, pays]* friendly; *[regard]* kindly, friendly ◆ **tendre à qn une main ~e** to lend *ou* give sb a helping hand ◆ **être très ~ avec qn** to be very friendly *ou* very good friends with sb ◆ **nous sommes très ~s** we're very close *ou* good friends ◆ **être ~ de l'ordre** to be a lover of order

amiable /amjabl/ **ADJ** *(Jur)* amicable ◆ **~ compositeur** conciliator

◆ **à l'amiable** *[divorce, solution]* amicable ◆ **vente à l'~** private sale, sale by private agreement ◆ **partage à l'~** amicable partition ◆ **accord** *ou* **règlement à l'~** amicable agreement, out-of-court settlement ◆ **régler une affaire à l'~** to settle a difference out of court

amiante /amjɑ̃t/ **NM** asbestos ◆ **plaque/fil d'~** asbestos sheet *ou* plate/thread

amibe /amib/ **NF** amoeba

amibiase /amibjɑz/ **NF** amoebiasis

amibien, -ienne /amibjɛ̃, jɛn/ **ADJ** *[maladie]* amoebic **NMPL** **amibiens** Amoebae

amical, e (mpl **-aux**) /amikal, o/ **ADJ** *[personne, relations]* friendly ◆ **match ~, rencontre ~e** friendly (match) ◆ **peu ~** unfriendly **NF** **amicale** association, club *(of people having the same interest)* ◆ **~e des anciens élèves** old boys' association *(Brit)*, alumni association *(US)*

amicalement /amikalmɑ̃/ **ADV** in a friendly way ◆ **il m'a salué ~** he gave me a friendly wave ◆ **(bien) ~** *(formule épistolaire)* best wishes, yours

amidon /amidɔ̃/ **NM** starch

amidonner /amidɔne/ ▸ conjug 1 ◂ **VT** to starch

amincir /amɛ̃siʀ/ ▸ conjug 2 ◂ **VT** to thin (down) ◆ **cette robe l'amincit** this dress makes her look slim(mer) *ou* thin(ner) ◆ **visage aminci par la tension** face drawn with tension *ou* hollow with anxiety **VPR** **s'amincir** *[couche de glace, épaisseur de tissu]* to get thinner

amincissant, e /amɛ̃sisɑ̃, ɑ̃t/ **ADJ** *[crème, régime]* slimming *(Brit)*, reducing *(US)*

amincissement /amɛ̃sismɑ̃/ **NM** thinning (down) ◆ **l'~ de la couche de glace a causé l'accident** the ice had got thinner and that was what caused the accident

amine /amin/ **NF** amine

aminé, e /amine/ **ADJ** → **acide**

amiral, e (mpl **-aux**) /amiʀal, o/ **ADJ** ◆ **vaisseau** *ou* **bateau ~** flagship **NM** admiral **NF** **amirale** admiral's wife

amirauté /amiʀote/ **NF** *(gén)* admiralty; (= *fonction*) admiralty, admiralship

amitié /amitje/ GRAMMAIRE ACTIVE 48.2 **NF** 1 (= *sentiment*) friendship ◆ **prendre qn en ~, se**

prendre d'~ pour qn to befriend sb ◆ **se lier d'~ avec qn** to make friends with sb ◆ **nouer une ~ avec qn** *(littér)* to strike up a friendship with sb ◆ **avoir de l'~ pour qn** to be fond of sb, to have a liking for sb ◆ **faites-moi l'~ de venir** do me the kindness *ou* favour of coming ◆ **l'~ franco-britannique** Anglo-French *ou* Franco-British friendship ◆ **~ particulière** *(euph)* homosexual relationship 2 *(formule épistolaire)* **~s** all the very best, very best wishes *ou* regards ◆ **~s, Paul** kind regards, Paul, yours, Paul ◆ **elle vous fait** *ou* **transmet toutes ses ~s** she sends her best wishes *ou* regards 3 *(† = civilités)* **faire mille ~s à qn** to give sb a warm and friendly welcome

Amman /aman/ **N** Amman

ammoniac, -aque /amɔnjak/ **ADJ** ammoniac ◆ **sel ~** sal ammoniac **NM** *(= gaz)* ammonia **NF** **ammoniaque** ammonia (water)

ammoniacal, e (mpl **-aux**) /amɔnjakal, o/ **ADJ** ammoniacal

ammoniaqué, e /amɔnjake/ **ADJ** ammoniated

ammonite /amɔnit/ **NF** ammonite

ammonium /amɔnjɔm/ **NM** ammonium

amnésie /amnezi/ **NF** amnesia ◆ **~ collective** collective amnesia

amnésique /amnezik/ **ADJ** amnesic **NMF** amnesiac, amnesic

amniocentèse /amnjosɛtɛz/ **NF** amniocentesis

amnios /amnjos/ **NM** amnion

amnioscopie /amnjɔskɔpi/ **NF** fetoscopy

amniotique /amnjɔtik/ **ADJ** amniotic ◆ **cavité/liquide ~** amniotic cavity/liquid

amnistiable /amnistjabl/ **ADJ** who may be amnestied

amnistie /amnisti/ **NF** amnesty ◆ **loi d'~** law of amnesty ◆ **bénéficier d'une ~ générale/partielle/totale** to be granted a general/partial/complete amnesty

amnistié, e /amnistje/ (ptp de **amnistier**) **ADJ** *[personne, fait]* amnestied **NM,F** amnestied prisoner

amnistier /amnistje/ ▸ conjug 7 ◂ **VT** *[+ personne]* to grant an amnesty to, to amnesty; *[+ délit]* to grant an amnesty for

amocher * /amɔʃe/ ▸ conjug 1 ◂ **VT** to mess up *, to make a mess of * ◆ **tu l'as drôlement amoché** you've made a terrible mess of him * ◆ **se faire ~ dans un accident/une bagarre** to get messed up * in an accident/a fight ◆ **elle/la voiture était drôlement amochée** she/the car was a terrible mess * ◆ **il s'est drôlement amoché en tombant** he smashed himself up pretty badly when he fell

amoindrir /amwɛ̃dʀiʀ/ ▸ conjug 2 ◂ **VT** *[+ autorité]* to weaken, to diminish; *[+ forces]* to weaken; *[+ fortune, quantité]* to diminish, to reduce; *[+ personne] (physiquement)* to make weaker, to weaken; *(moralement, mentalement)* to diminish ◆ **~ qn (aux yeux des autres)** to diminish *ou* belittle sb (in the eyes of others) **VPR** **s'amoindrir** *[autorité, facultés]* to weaken, to diminish; *[forces]* to weaken, to grow weaker; *[quantité, fortune]* to diminish

amoindrissement /amwɛ̃dʀismɑ̃/ **NM** *[d'autorité]* lessening, weakening; *[de forces]* weakening; *[de fortune, quantité]* reduction; *[de personne] (physique)* weakening; *(moral, mental)* diminishing

amollir /amɔliʀ/ ▸ conjug 2 ◂ **VT** *[+ chose]* to soften, to make soft; *[+ personne] (moralement)* to soften; *(physiquement)* to weaken, to make weak; *[+ volonté, forces, résolution]* to weaken ◆ **cette chaleur vous amollit** this heat makes you feel (quite) limp *ou* weak **VPR** **s'amollir** *[chose]* to go soft; *[courage, énergie]* to weaken; *[jambes]* to go weak; *[personne] (= perdre courage)* to grow soft, to weaken; *(= s'attendrir)* to soften, to relent

amollissant, e /amɔlisɑ̃, ɑ̃t/ **ADJ** *[climat, plaisirs]* enervating

amollissement /amɔlismɑ̃/ **NM** *[de chose]* softening; *[de personne] (moral)* softening; *(physique)* weakening; *[de volonté, forces, résolution]* weakening ◆ **l'~ général est dû à ...** the general weakening of purpose is due to ...

amonceler /amɔ̃s(ə)le/ ▸ conjug 4 ◂ **VT** *[+ choses]* to pile *ou* heap up; *[+ richesses]* to amass, to accumulate; *[+ documents, preuves]* to accumulate, to amass **VPR** **s'amonceler** *[choses]* to pile *ou* heap up; *[courrier, demandes]* to pile up, to accumulate; *[nuages]* to bank up; *[neige]* to drift into banks; *[difficultés]* to pile up ◆ **les preuves s'amoncellent contre lui** the evidence is building up *ou* piling up against him

amoncellement /amɔ̃sɛlmɑ̃/ **NM** 1 *(= tas) [d'objets]* pile, mass; *[de problèmes]* series ◆ **~ de nuages** cloudbank 2 *(= accumulation)* **devant l'~ des demandes** faced with a growing number of requests ◆ **~ de preuves** accumulation of evidence

amont /amɔ̃/ **ADJ INV** *[ski, skieur]* uphill *(épith)* **NM** *[de cours d'eau]* upstream water; *[de pente]* uphill slope ◆ **les rapides/l'écluse d'~** the upstream rapids/lock ◆ **l'~ était coupé de rapides** the river upstream was a succession of rapids

◆ **en amont** *(rivière)* upstream, upriver; *(pente)* uphill; *(dans l'industrie pétrolière)* upstream ◆ **les contrôles en ~** the checks carried out beforehand ◆ **en ~ de** *[+ rivière]* upstream *ou* upriver from; *[+ pente]* uphill from, above; *(fig)* before ◆ **en ~ de cette opération** prior to this operation ◆ **intervenir en ~ d'une tâche** to intervene before a task is carried out

amoral, e (mpl **-aux**) /amɔʀal, o/ **ADJ** amoral

amoralisme /amɔʀalism/ **NM** amorality

amoralité /amɔʀalite/ **NF** amorality

amorçage /amɔʀsaʒ/ **NM** 1 *(= action) [d'hameçon, ligne]* baiting; *[d'emplacement]* ground baiting 2 *[de dynamo]* energizing; *[de siphon, obus, pompe]* priming 3 *(= dispositif)* priming cap, primer

amorce /amɔʀs/ **NF** 1 *(Pêche) [d'hameçon]* bait; *[d'emplacement]* ground bait 2 *(= explosif) [de cartouche]* primer, priming; *[d'obus]* percussion cap; *[de mine]* priming; *[de pistolet d'enfant]* cap 3 *(= début) [de route]* initial section; *[de trou]* start; *[de pellicule, film]* trailer; *[de conversations, négociations]* starting up, beginning; *[d'idée, projet]* beginning, germ ◆ **l'~ d'une réforme/d'un changement** the beginnings of a reform/change 4 *(Ordin)* **(programme) ~** bootstrap

amorcer /amɔʀse/ ▸ conjug 3 ◂ **VT** 1 *[+ hameçon, ligne]* to bait ◆ **il amorce au ver de vase** *[+ ligne]* he baits his line with worms; *[+ emplacement]* he uses worms as ground bait

2 *[+ dynamo]* to energize; *[+ siphon, obus, pompe]* to prime

3 *[+ route, tunnel]* to start *ou* begin building, to make a start on; *[+ travaux]* to begin, to make a start on; *[+ trou]* to begin *ou* start to bore ◆ **la construction est amorcée depuis deux mois** work has been in progress *ou* been under way for two months

4 *[+ réformes, évolution]* to initiate, to begin; *[+ virage]* to take ◆ **il amorça un geste pour prendre la tasse** he made as if to take the cup ◆ **~ la rentrée dans l'atmosphère** *[fusée]* to initiate re-entry into the earth's atmosphere ◆ **une descente s'amorce après le virage** after the bend the road starts to go down

5 *(Pol = entamer) [+ dialogue]* to start (up); *[+ négociations]* to start, to begin ◆ **une détente est amorcée** *ou* **s'amorce** there are signs of (the beginnings of) a détente

amorphe /amɔʀf/ **ADJ** 1 *(= apathique) [personne, esprit, caractère, attitude]* passive; *[marché]* dull 2 *(Minér)* amorphous

amorti, e /amɔʀti/ (ptp de **amortir**) **NM** *(Tennis)* drop shot ◆ **faire un ~** *(Ftbl)* to trap the ball ◆ **faire un ~ de la poitrine** to chest the ball down **NF** **amortie** *(Tennis)* drop shot

amortir /amɔʀtiʀ/ ▸ conjug 2 ◂ **VT** 1 *(= diminuer) [+ choc]* to absorb, to cushion; *[+ coup, chute]* to cushion, to soften; *[+ bruit]* to deaden, to muffle; *[+ passions, douleur]* to deaden, to dull 2 *(Fin) [+ dette]* to pay off, to amortize *(SPÉC)*; *[+ titre]* to redeem; *[+ matériel]* to write off the cost of, to depreciate *(SPÉC)* ◆ **il utilise beaucoup sa voiture pour l'~** *(gén)* he uses his car a lot to make it pay *ou* to recoup the cost to himself ◆ **maintenant, notre équipement est amorti** we have now written off the (capital) cost of the equipment 3 *(Archit)* to put an amortizement *ou* amortization on

amortissable /amɔʀtisabl/ **ADJ** *(Fin)* redeemable

amortissement /amɔʀtismɑ̃/ **NM** 1 *(Fin) [de dette]* paying off; *[de titre]* redemption; *(= provision comptable)* reserve *ou* provision for depreciation ◆ **l'~ de ce matériel se fait en trois ans** it takes three years to recoup *ou* to write off the cost of this equipment ◆ **~s admis par le fisc** capital allowances 2 *(= diminution) [de choc]* absorption 3 *(Archit)* amortizement, amortization

amortisseur /amɔʀtisœʀ/ **NM** shock absorber

amour /amuʀ/ **NM** 1 *(= sentiment)* love ◆ **parler d'~** to speak of love ◆ **se nourrir** *ou* **vivre d'~ et d'eau fraîche** * to live on love alone ◆ **j'ai rencontré le grand ~** I have met the love of my life ◆ **vivre un grand ~** to be passionately *ou* deeply in love ◆ **entre eux, ce n'est pas le grand ~** there's no love lost between them ◆ **~ platonique** platonic love ◆ **lettre/mariage/roman d'~** love letter/match/story ◆ **fou d'~** madly *ou* wildly in love ◆ **~ fou** wild love *ou* passion, mad love ◆ **ce n'est plus de l'~, c'est de la rage!** * it's not love, it's raving madness! *; → **filer, saison**

2 *(= acte)* love-making *(NonC)* ◆ **pendant l'~, elle murmurait des mots tendres** while they were making love *ou* during their love-making, she murmured tender words ◆ **l'~ libre** free love ◆ **l'~ physique** physical love ◆ **faire l'~** to make love *(avec* to, with)

3 *(= personne)* love; *(= aventure)* love affair ◆ **premier ~** *(= personne)* first love; *(= aventure)* first love (affair) ◆ **ses ~s de jeunesse** *(= aventures)* the love affairs *ou* loves of his youth; *(= personnes)* the loves *ou* lovers of his youth ◆ **c'est un ~ de jeunesse** she's one of his old loves *ou* flames * ◆ **des ~s de rencontre** casual love affairs ◆ **à tes ~s !** * *(hum) (quand on trinque)* here's to you!; *(quand on éternue)* bless you! ◆ **comment vont tes ~s ?** * *(hum)* how's your love life? *

4 *(= terme d'affection)* **mon ~** my love, my sweet ◆ **cet enfant est un ~** that child's a real darling ◆ **passe-moi l'eau, tu seras un ~** be a darling *ou* dear and pass me the water, pass me the water, there's a darling *ou* a dear *(Brit)* ◆ **un ~ de bébé/de petite robe** a lovely *ou* sweet little baby/dress

5 *(Art)* cupid ◆ **(le dieu) Amour** *(Myth)* Eros, Cupid

6 **~ en cage** *(= plante)* Chinese lantern, winter *ou* ground cherry

7 *(locutions)* **pour l'~ de Dieu** for God's sake, for the love of God ◆ **pour l'~ de votre mère** for your mother's sake ◆ **faire qch pour l'~ de l'art** * to do sth for the love of it ◆ **avoir l'~ du travail bien fait** to love to see a job well done ◆ **faire qch avec ~** to do sth with loving care

NFPL amours *(littér) (= personnes)* loves; *(= aventures)* love affairs; → **ancillaire**

amouracher (s') /amuʀaʃe/ ► conjug 1 ◄ **VPR** *(péj)* **s'amouracher de** to become infatuated with

amourette /amuʀɛt/ **NF** *(= relation)* passing fancy, passing love affair

amoureusement /amuʀøzmɑ̃/ **ADV** lovingly, amorously

amoureux, -euse /amuʀø, øz/ **ADJ** 1 *(= épris) [personne]* in love *(de* with); ◆ **tomber** ~ to fall in love *(de* with); ◆ **être** ~ **de la musique/la nature** to be a music-/nature-lover, to be passionately fond of music/nature ◆ **il est** ~ **de sa voiture** *(hum)* he's in love with his car *(hum)* 2 *(= d'amour) [aventures]* love *(épith)*, amorous ◆ **déboires** ~ disappointments in love ◆ **vie amoureuse** love life 3 *(= ardent) [tempérament, personne]* amorous; *[regard] (= tendre)* loving; *(= voluptueux)* amorous **NM,F** *(gén)* lover; († = *soupirant)* love, sweetheart ◆ **un** ~ **de la nature** a nature-lover, a lover of nature ◆ ~ **transi** bashful lover ◆ **partir en vacances en** ~ to go off on a romantic holiday

amour-propre (pl **amours-propres**) /amuʀpʀɔpʀ/ **NM** self-esteem, pride

amovibilité /amɔvibilite/ **NF** *(Jur)* removability

amovible /amɔvibl/ **ADJ** *[doublure, housse, panneau]* removable, detachable; *(Jur)* removable

ampélopsis /ɑ̃pelɔpsis/ **NM** ampelopsis

ampérage /ɑ̃peʀaʒ/ **NM** amperage

ampère /ɑ̃pɛʀ/ **NM** ampere, amp

ampèremètre /ɑ̃pɛʀmɛtʀ/ **NM** ammeter

amphétamine /ɑ̃fetamin/ **NF** amphetamine ◆ **être sous ~s** to be on amphetamines

amphi * /ɑ̃fi/ **NM** abrév de **amphithéâtre**

amphibie /ɑ̃fibi/ **ADJ** amphibious, amphibian **NM** amphibian

amphibiens /ɑ̃fibjɛ̃/ **NMPL** amphibia, amphibians

amphigouri /ɑ̃figuʀi/ **NM** amphigory

amphigourique /ɑ̃figuʀik/ **ADJ** amphigoric

amphithéâtre /ɑ̃fiteɑtʀ/ **NM** *(Archit)* amphitheatre *(Brit)*, amphitheater *(US)*; *(Univ)* lecture theatre *(Brit) ou* theater *(US)*; *(Théât)* (upper) gallery ◆ ~ **morainique** *(Géol)* morainic cirque *ou* amphitheatre

amphitryon /ɑ̃fitʀijɔ̃/ **NM** *(hum ou littér = hôte)* host

amphore /ɑ̃fɔʀ/ **NF** amphora

ample /ɑ̃pl/ **ADJ** *[manteau]* roomy; *[jupe, manche]* full; *[geste]* wide, sweeping; *[voix]* sonorous; *[style]* rich, grand; *[projet]* vast; *[vues, sujet]* wide-ranging, extensive ◆ **faire ~(s) provision(s) de qch** to get in an ample *ou* a plentiful supply of sth ◆ **donner** ~ **matériel à discussion** to provide plenty to talk about ◆ **pour plus** ~ **informé je tenais à vous dire** ... for your further information I should tell you ... ◆ **veuillez m'envoyer de plus ~s renseignements sur** ... please send me further details of ... *ou* further information about ...; → **jusque**

amplement /ɑ̃pləmɑ̃/ **ADV** *[expliquer, mériter]* fully, amply ◆ **gagner** ~ **sa vie** to earn a very good living ◆ **ça suffit** ~, **c'est** ~ **suffisant** that's more than enough, that's ample ◆ **les récents événements ont** ~ **démontré que** ... recent events have been ample proof that ... ◆ **son attitude justifie** ~ **ma décision** his attitude is ample justification for my decision, his attitude fully *ou* amply justifies my decision

ampleur /ɑ̃plœʀ/ **NF** 1 *[de vêtement]* fullness; *[de voix]* sonorousness; *[de geste]* liberalness; *[de style, récit]* opulence ◆ **donner de l'~ à une robe** to give fullness to a dress 2 *(= importance) [de crise, problème, dégâts]* scale, extent; *[de déficit]* size, extent; *[de sujet, projet]* scope; *[de vues]* range ◆ **vu l'~ des dégâts** ... in view of the extent *ou* the scale of the damage ... ◆ **l'~ des moyens mis en œuvre** the sheer size *ou* the massive scale of the measures implemented ◆ **sans grande** ~ of limited scope, small-scale *(épith)* ◆ **de grande/faible** ~ large-/small-scale *(épith)* ◆ **des inondations d'une** ~ **sans précédent** flooding on an unprecedented scale ◆ **ces manifestations prennent de l'~** the demonstrations are increasing in scale

ampli * /ɑ̃pli/ **NM** (abrév de **amplificateur**) amp * ◆ **~-tuner** tuner amplifier

ampliation /ɑ̃plijasjɔ̃/ **NF** *(= duplicata)* certified copy; *(= développement)* amplification ◆ ~ **des offres de preuves** amplification of previous evidence

amplificateur /ɑ̃plifikatœʀ/ **NM** *(Phys, Radio)* amplifier; *(Photo)* enlarger *(permitting only fixed enlarging)*

amplification /ɑ̃plifikasjɔ̃/ **NF** 1 *(= développement) [de tendance, mouvement, échanges, coopération]* development; *(= augmentation)* increase ◆ **une** ~ **de l'agitation sociale** an increase in social unrest 2 *(= exagération) [d'incident]* exaggeration 3 *(Photo)* enlarging; *(Opt)* magnifying

amplifier /ɑ̃plifje/ ► conjug 7 ◄ **VT** 1 *[+ tendance]* to accentuate; *[+ mouvement, échanges, coopération]* to cause to develop 2 *(= exagérer) [+ incident]* to magnify, to exaggerate 3 *[+ son, courant]* to amplify; *[+ image] (Photo)* to enlarge; *(Opt)* to magnify **VPR s'amplifier** *(= se développer) [mouvement, tendance, échange, pensée]* to develop; *(= s'aggraver)* to get worse ◆ **les affrontements s'amplifient** the clashes are getting worse

amplitude /ɑ̃plityd/ **NF** 1 *(Astron, Phys)* amplitude 2 *[de températures]* range 3 *(= importance)* **l'~ de la catastrophe** the magnitude of the catastrophe

ampoule /ɑ̃pul/ **NF** 1 *(Élec)* bulb 2 *(Pharm)* phial, vial; *(pour seringue)* ampoule, ampule 3 *(Méd : à la main, au pied)* blister, ampulla *(SPÉC)*

COMP ampoule autocassable phial *(with a snap-off top)*

ampoule à baïonnette bayonet bulb

ampoule à vis screw-fitting bulb

ampoulé, e /ɑ̃pule/ **ADJ** *[style]* pompous

amputation /ɑ̃pytasjɔ̃/ **NF** *[de membre]* amputation; *[de texte, roman, fortune]* drastic cut *ou* reduction *(de* in); *[de budget]* drastic cutback *ou* reduction *(de* in)

amputé, e /ɑ̃pyte/ (ptp de **amputer**) **ADJ** *[membre]* amputated; *[personne]* who has had a limb amputated **NM,F** amputee ◆ **c'est un** ~ he has lost an arm *(ou* a leg), he has had an arm *(ou* a leg) off * *(Brit)* ◆ **c'est un** ~ **des deux jambes** he's lost both his legs

amputer /ɑ̃pyte/ ► conjug 1 ◄ **VT** 1 *[+ membre]* to amputate ◆ **il a été amputé** he had an amputation ◆ **il a été amputé d'une jambe** he had his leg amputated 2 *[+ texte, fortune]* to cut *ou* reduce drastically; *[+ budget]* to cut back *ou* reduce drastically *(de* by); ◆ ~ **un pays d'une partie de son territoire** to sever a country of a part of its territory

Amsterdam /amstɛʀdam/ **N** Amsterdam

amuïr (s') /amɥiʀ/ ► conjug 2 ◄ **VPR** *(Phon)* to become mute, to be dropped *(in pronunciation)*

amuïssement /amɥismɑ̃/ **NM** *(Phon) dropping of a phoneme in pronunciation*

amulette /amylɛt/ **NF** amulet

amure /amyʀ/ **NF** *(Naut)* tack ◆ **aller bâbord/tribord ~s** to go on the port/starboard tack

amurer /amyʀe/ ► conjug 1 ◄ **VT** *[+ voile]* to haul aboard the tack of, to tack

amusant, e /amyzɑ̃, ɑ̃t/ **ADJ** *(= distrayant) [jeu]* amusing, entertaining; *(= drôle) [film, remarque, convive]* amusing, funny ◆ **c'est (très)** ~ *[jeu]* it's (great) fun ◆ **c'était** ~ **à voir** it was amusing *ou* funny to see ◆ **l'~ de l'histoire c'est que** ... the funny *ou* amusing thing about it all is that ...

amuse-bouche (pl **amuse-bouche(s)**) /amyzbuʃ/ **NM** appetizer, snack

amuse-gueule (pl **amuse-gueule(s)**) /amyzgœl/ **NM** appetizer, snack

amusement /amyzmɑ̃/ **NM** 1 *(= divertissement)* amusement *(NonC)* ◆ **pour l'~ des enfants** for the children's amusement *ou* entertainment, to amuse *ou* entertain the children 2 *(= jeu)* game; *(= activité)* diversion, pastime 3 *(= hilarité)* amusement *(NonC)*

amuser /amyze/ ► conjug 1 ◄ **VT** 1 *(= divertir)* to amuse, to entertain; *(involontairement)* to amuse

2 *(= faire rire) [histoire drôle]* to amuse ◆ **ces remarques ne m'amusent pas du tout** I don't find those remarks at all amusing, I'm not in the least amused by such remarks ◆ **tu m'amuses avec tes grandes théories** you make me laugh with your great theories ◆ **faire le pitre pour** ~ **la galerie** to clown around to amuse the crowd

3 *(= plaire)* **ça ne m'amuse pas de devoir aller leur rendre visite** I don't enjoy having to go and visit them ◆ **si vous croyez que ces réunions m'amusent** if you think I enjoy these meetings

4 *(= détourner l'attention de) [+ ennemi, caissier]* to distract ◆ **pendant que tu l'amuses, je prends l'argent** while you keep him busy *ou* distract him, I'll take the money

5 *(= tromper)* to delude, to beguile

VPR s'amuser 1 *(= jouer) [enfants]* to play ◆ **s'~ avec** *[+ jouet, personne, chien]* to play with; *[+ stylo, ficelle]* to play *ou* fiddle with ◆ **s'~ à un jeu** to play a game ◆ **ils se sont amusés tout l'après-midi à faire des châteaux de sable** they had fun *ou* they played all afternoon building sandcastles ◆ **ils se sont amusés à arroser les passants** they were messing around * spraying passers-by with water ◆ **pour s'~ ils ont allumé un grand feu de joie** they lit a big bonfire for fun ◆ **ne t'amuse pas à recommencer, sinon !** don't you do *ou* start that again, or else!

2 *(= se divertir)* to have fun, to enjoy o.s.; *(= rire)* to have a good laugh ◆ **s'~ à faire qch** to have fun doing sth, to enjoy o.s. doing sth ◆ **nous nous sommes bien amusés** we had great fun *ou* a great time * ◆ **qu'est-ce qu'on s'amuse !** this is great fun! ◆ **j'aime autant te dire qu'on ne s'est pas amusés** it wasn't much fun, I can tell you ◆ **on ne va pas s'~ à cette réunion** we're not going to have much fun at this meeting ◆ **on ne faisait rien de mal, c'était juste pour s'~** we weren't doing any harm, it was just for fun *ou* for a laugh

3 *(= batifoler)* to mess about * *ou* around * ◆ **on n'a pas le temps de s'~** there's no time to mess around *

4 *(littér = se jouer de)* **s'~ de qn** to make a fool of sb

amusette /amyzɛt/ **NF** diversion ◆ **elle n'a été pour lui qu'une** ~ she was mere sport to him, she was just a passing fancy for him ◆ **au lieu de perdre ton temps à des ~s tu ferais mieux de travailler** instead of frittering your time away on idle pleasures you should do some work

amuseur, -euse /amyzœʀ, øz/ **NM,F** entertainer ◆ **ce n'est qu'un** ~ *(péj)* he's just a clown

amygdale /amidal/ NF tonsil ◆ **se faire opérer des ~s** to have one's tonsils removed *ou* out

amygdalite /amidalit/ NF tonsillitis

amylacé, e /amilase/ ADJ starchy

amylase /amilɑz/ NF amylase

amyle /amil/ NM amyl ◆ **nitrite d'~** amyl nitrite

amylique /amilik/ ADJ ◆ **alcool ~** amyl alcohol

AN /aɛn/ NF (abrév de **Assemblée nationale**) → **assemblée**

an /ɑ̃/ NM 1 (= *durée*) year ◆ **après 5 ~s de prison** after 5 years in prison ◆ **dans 3 ~s** in 3 years, in 3 years' time (*Brit*) ◆ **une amitié de 20 ~s** a friendship of 20 years' standing
2 (= *âge*) year ◆ **un enfant de six ~s** a six-year-old child, a six-year-old ◆ **porto de 10 ~s d'âge** 10-year-old port ◆ **il a 22 ~s** he's 22 (years old) ◆ **il n'a pas encore 10 ~s** he's not yet 10
3 (= *point dans le temps*) year ◆ **4 fois par ~** 4 times a year ◆ **il reçoit tant par ~** he gets so much a year *ou* per annum ◆ **le jour** *ou* **le premier de l'~, le nouvel ~** New Year's Day ◆ **bon ~ mal ~** taking one year with another, on average ◆ **en l'~ 300 de Rome** in the Roman year 300 ◆ **en l'~ 300 de notre ère/avant Jésus-Christ** in (the year) 300 AD/BC ◆ **en l'~ de grâce ...** (*frm ou hum*) in the year of grace ... ◆ **l'~ II de la république** (*Hist*) the second year of the French Republic ◆ **je m'en moque** *ou* **je m'en soucie comme de l'~ quarante** I couldn't care less (about it), I don't give a damn* (about it)
4 (*littér*) **les ~s l'ont courbé** he is bent with age ◆ **l'outrage des ~s** the ravages of time ◆ **courbé sous le poids des ~s** bent under the weight of years *ou* age

ana (pl **ana(s)**) /ana/ NM ana

anabaptisme /anabatism/ NM anabaptism

anabaptiste /anabatist/ ADJ, NMF anabaptist

anabolisant, e /anabɔlizɑ̃, ɑt/ ADJ anabolic NM anabolic steroid

anabolisme /anabɔlism/ NM anabolism

anacarde /anakaʀd/ NM cashew (nut)

anacardier /anakaʀdje/ NM cashew (tree)

anachorète /anakɔʀɛt/ NM anchorite

anachronique /anakʀɔnik/ ADJ anachronistic, anachronous

anachronisme /anakʀɔnism/ NM anachronism

anacoluthe /anakɔlyt/ NF anacoluthon

anaconda /anakɔ̃da/ NM anaconda

Anacréon /anakʀeɔ̃/ NM Anacreon

anacréontique /anakʀeɔ̃tik/ ADJ anacreontic

anaérobie /anaeʀɔbi/ ADJ anaerobic

anaglyphe /anaglif/ NM anaglyph

anagrammatique /anagʀamatik/ ADJ anagrammatical

anagramme /anagʀam/ NF anagram

anal, e (mpl **-aux**) /anal, o/ ADJ anal

analeptique /analɛptik/ ADJ analeptic

analgésie /analʒezi/ NF analgesia

analgésique /analʒezik/ ADJ, NM analgesic

anallergique /analɛʀʒik/ ADJ hypoallergenic

analogie /analɔʒi/ NF analogy ◆ **par ~ avec** by analogy with

analogique /analɔʒik/ ADJ analogical

analogiquement /analɔʒikmɑ̃/ ADV analogically

analogue /analɔg/ ADJ 1 (= *semblable*) analogous, similar (*à* to) 2 (*Bio*) analogous NM (*Chim, Bio*) analogue; (*fig*) ◆ **sans ~** without comparison

analphabète /analfabɛt/ ADJ, NMF illiterate

analphabétisme /analfabetism/ NM illiteracy

analysable /analizabl/ ADJ analysable, analyzable (*US*)

analysant, e /analizɑ̃, ɑt/ NM,F analysand

analyse /analiz/ NF 1 (= *examen*) analysis ◆ **faire l'~ de** to analyze ◆ **ça ne résiste pas à l'~** it doesn't stand up to analysis ◆ **avoir l'esprit d'~** to have an analytic(al) mind ◆ **en dernière ~** in the final *ou* last analysis
2 (*Méd*) test ◆ **~ de sang/d'urine** blood/urine test ◆ **(se) faire faire des ~s** to have some tests (done); → **laboratoire**
3 (*Psych*) analysis, psychoanalysis ◆ **il est en ~, il fait une ~** he's undergoing *ou* having analysis
4 (*Math*) (= *discipline*) calculus; (= *exercice*) analysis
COMP **analyse combinatoire** combinatorial analysis
analyse en constituants immédiats constituent analysis
analyse factorielle factor *ou* factorial analysis
analyse financière financial analysis
analyse fonctionnelle functional job analysis
analyse grammaticale parsing ◆ **faire l'~ grammaticale de** to parse
analyse logique sentence analysis (*Brit*), diagramming (*US*)
analyse de marché market analysis *ou* survey
analyse sectorielle cross-section analysis
analyse spectrale spectrum analysis
analyse de système systems analysis
analyse transactionnelle transactional analysis
analyse du travail job analysis

analysé, e /analize/ NM,F (*Psych*) *person who has undergone analysis*

analyser /analize/ ► conjug 1 ◄ VT (*gén*) to analyze; (*Psych*) to (psycho)analyze; (*Méd*) [+ *sang, urine*] to test; (*analyse grammaticale*) to parse

analyseur /analizœʀ/ NM (*Phys*) analyser ◆ **~ syntaxique** (*Ordin*) parser

analyste /analist/ NMF (*gén, Math*) analyst; (= *psychanalyste*) analyst, psychoanalyst ◆ **~-programmeur** programme analyst ◆ **~ financier/de marché** financial/market analyst ◆ **~ de systèmes** systems analyst

analytique /analitik/ ADJ analytic(al) NF analytics (*sg*)

analytiquement /analitikmɑ̃/ ADV analytically

anamorphose /anamɔʀfoz/ NF anamorphosis

ananas /anana(s)/ NM (= *fruit, plante*) pineapple

anapeste /anapɛst/ NM anapaest

anaphore /anafɔʀ/ NF anaphora

anaphorique /anafɔʀik/ ADJ anaphoric

anaphylactique /anafilaktik/ ADJ anaphylactic ◆ **choc ~** anaphylactic shock

anar * /anaʀ/ NMF abrév de **anarchiste**

anarchie /anaʀʃi/ NF (*Pol, fig*) anarchy

anarchique /anaʀʃik/ ADJ anarchic(al) ◆ **de façon** *ou* **manière ~** anarchically

anarchiquement /anaʀʃikmɑ̃/ ADV anarchically

anarchisant, e /anaʀʃizɑ̃, ɑt/ ADJ anarchistic

anarchisme /anaʀʃism/ NM anarchism

anarchiste /anaʀʃist/ ADJ anarchistic NMF anarchist

anarchosyndicalisme /anaʀkosɛ̃dikalism/ NM anarcho-syndicalism

anarchosyndicaliste /anaʀkosɛ̃dikalist/ NMF anarcho-syndicalist

anastigmat /anastigma(t)/ ADJ M, NM ◆ **(objectif) ~** anastigmat, anastigmatic lens

anastigmatique /anastigmatik/ ADJ anastigmatic

anastrophe /anastʀɔf/ NF anastrophe

anathématiser /anatematize/ ► conjug 1 ◄ VT (*lit, fig*) to anathematize

anathème /anatɛm/ NM (= *excommunication, excommunié*) anathema ◆ **prononcer un ~ contre qn, frapper qn d'~** (*Rel*) to excommunicate sb, to anathematize sb ◆ **jeter l'~ sur** (*fig*) to curse, to anathematize (*frm*)

Anatolie /anatɔli/ NF Anatolia

anatomie /anatɔmi/ NF 1 (= *science*) anatomy 2 (= *corps*) anatomy ◆ **dans ce film, elle montre beaucoup de son ~** (*hum*) she shows a lot of bare flesh in this film 3 († = *dissection*) (*Méd*) anatomy; (*fig*) analysis ◆ **faire l'~ de** (*fig*) to dissect (*fig*), to analyse ◆ **pièce d'~** anatomical subject

anatomique /anatɔmik/ ADJ (*gén*) anatomic(al); [*fauteuil, oreiller*] contour (*épith*); → **cire, planche**

anatomiquement /anatɔmikmɑ̃/ ADV anatomically

anatomiste /anatɔmist/ NMF anatomist

ANC /aɛnse/ NM (abrév de **African National Congress**) ANC

ancestral, e (mpl **-aux**) /ɑ̃sɛstʀal, o/ ADJ ancestral

ancêtre /ɑ̃sɛtʀ/ NMF 1 (= *aïeul*) ancestor; (* = *vieillard*) old man (*ou* woman) ◆ **nos ~s les Gaulois** our ancestors *ou* forefathers the Gauls 2 (= *précurseur*) [*de personne, objet*] forerunner, precursor ◆ **c'est l'~ de la littérature moderne** he's the father of modern literature

anche /ɑ̃ʃ/ NF (*Mus*) reed

anchoïade /ɑ̃ʃɔjad/ NF anchovy paste

anchois /ɑ̃ʃwa/ NM anchovy

ancien, -ienne /ɑ̃sjɛ̃, jɛn/ ADJ 1 (= *vieux*) (*gén*) old; [*coutume, château, loi*] ancient; [*objet d'art*] antique ◆ **dans l'~ temps** in the olden days, in times gone by ◆ **il est plus ~ que moi dans la maison** he has been with *ou* in the firm longer than me ◆ **une ancienne amitié** an old *ou* long-standing friendship ◆ **~s francs** old francs ◆ **cela lui a coûté 10 millions d'~s francs** it cost him 10 million old francs; → **testament**
2 (*avant nom* = *précédent*) former ◆ **son ancienne femme** his ex-wife, his former *ou* previous wife ◆ **c'est mon ~ quartier/ancienne école** it's my old neighbourhood/school, that's where I used to live/go to school
3 (= *antique*) [*langue, civilisation, histoire*] ancient ◆ **dans les temps ~s** in ancient times ◆ **la Grèce/l'Égypte ancienne** ancient Greece/ Egypt
NM (= *mobilier ancien*) ◆ **l'~** antiques
NM,F 1 (= *personne âgée*) elder, old man (*ou* woman) ◆ **et le respect pour les ~s ?** (*hum*) have some respect for your elders! ◆ **les ~s du village** the village elders
2 (= *personne expérimentée*) senior *ou* experienced person; (*Mil*) old soldier ◆ **c'est un ~ dans la maison** he has been with *ou* in the firm a long time
3 (*Hist*) **les ~s** the Ancients ◆ **les ~s et les modernes** (*Littérat*) the Ancients and the Moderns
4 (*Scol*) **~ (élève)** former pupil, old boy (*Brit*), alumnus (*US*) ◆ **ancienne (élève)** former pupil, old girl (*Brit*), alumna (*US*)

LOC ADJ **à l'ancienne** LOC ADV *[meuble]* old-style, traditional(-style); *[confiture]* made in the traditional way ◆ **faire qch à l'ancienne** to do sth in the traditional way ◆ **cuisiner à l'~ne** to use traditional cooking methods

COMP **ancien combattant** war veteran, ex-serviceman

l'Ancien Régime the Ancien Régime

> ⚠ **ancien** se traduit par le mot anglais **ancient** uniquement au sens de 'très ancien', 'antique'.

anciennement /ɑ̃sjɛnmɑ̃/ ADV (= *autrefois*) formerly

ancienneté /ɑ̃sjɛnte/ NF 1 (= *durée de service*) length of service; (= *privilèges obtenus*) seniority ◆ **il a 10 ans d'~ dans la maison** he has been with *ou* in the firm (for) 10 years ◆ **à l'~** by seniority 2 *[de maison]* age; *[d'objet d'art]* age, antiquity; *[d'amitié, relation]* length ◆ **compte tenu de l'~ de cette pratique/loi** considering how long this practice/law has been in existence

ancillaire /ɑ̃silɛʀ/ ADJ ◆ **devoirs ~s** duties as a servant ◆ **relations/amours ~s** *(hum)* relations/amorous adventures with the servants

ancolie /ɑ̃kɔli/ NF columbine

ancrage /ɑ̃kʀaʒ/ NM 1 *(Naut)* anchorage 2 (= *attache*) *[de poteau, câble]* anchoring; *[de mur]* cramping 3 (= *incrustation*) **l'~ de nos valeurs dans la culture** the way our values are rooted in culture ◆ **le vote confirme l'~ à gauche de la région** the polls confirm that the region is a left-wing stronghold ◆ **pour faciliter l'~ d'entreprises dans la région** to help companies gain a foothold in the region ◆ **point d'~** *[de véhicule]* anchorage point; *(fig) [de politique]* foundation stone ◆ **la monnaie d'~ du SME** the anchor currency of the EMS

ancre /ɑ̃kʀ/ NF 1 *(Naut)* ~ **(de marine)** anchor ◆ ~ **de miséricorde** *ou* **de salut** sheet anchor ◆ **être à l'~** to be *ou* lie at anchor ◆ **jeter l'~** to cast *ou* drop anchor; → **lever¹** 2 *(Constr)* cramp(-iron), anchor; *(Horlogerie)* anchor escapement, recoil escapement

ancré, e /ɑ̃kʀe/ (ptp de **ancrer**) ADJ (= *enraciné*) ◆ **la région reste profondément ~e à gauche** the region is still firmly left-wing *ou* remains a left-wing stronghold ◆ **le sentiment monarchiste est très ~ dans ce pays** monarchist sentiment is deeply rooted in this country ◆ **un musicien très ~ dans l'Asie centrale** a musician with strong central Asian roots ◆ **une conviction très ~e** a deeply-held conviction ◆ **dans cette région, la chasse demeure très ~e** this region has a long tradition of hunting

ancrer /ɑ̃kʀe/ ► conjug 1 ◄ VT 1 *[+ bateau]* to anchor 2 *[+ poteau, câble]* to anchor; *[+ mur]* to cramp 3 (= *incruster*) ~ **qch dans la tête de qn** to fix sth firmly in sb's mind ◆ **il a cette idée ancrée dans la tête** he's got this idea firmly fixed in his mind VPR **s'ancrer** 1 *[bateau]* to anchor, to cast *ou* drop anchor 2 (= *s'incruster*) **quand une idée s'ancre dans l'esprit des gens** when an idea takes root *ou* becomes fixed in people's minds ◆ **il s'est ancré dans la tête que ...** he got it into *ou* fixed in his head that ... ◆ **le groupe cherche à s'~ économiquement dans la région** the group is trying to gain an economic foothold in the region

andain /ɑ̃dɛ̃/ NM swath

andalou, -ouse /ɑ̃dalu, uz/ ADJ Andalusian NM,F **Andalou(se)** Andalusian

Andalousie /ɑ̃daluzi/ NF Andalusia, Andalucia

andante /ɑ̃dɑ̃t/ ADV, NM andante

Andes /ɑ̃d/ NFPL ◆ **les ~** the Andes

andin, e /ɑ̃dɛ̃, in/ ADJ Andean NM,F **Andin(e)** Andean

andorran, e /ɑ̃dɔʀɑ̃, an/ ADJ Andorran NM,F **Andorran(e)** Andorran

Andorre /ɑ̃dɔʀ/ NF Andorra ◆ **~-la-Vieille** Andorra la Vella

andouille /ɑ̃duj/ NF 1 *(Culin)* andouille *(sausage made of chitterlings, eaten cold)* 2 (* = *imbécile*) dummy*, twit* *(Brit)*, prat* *(Brit)* ◆ **faire l'~** to act the fool ◆ **espèce d'~ !, triple ~ !** you dummy!*, you (stupid) prat!* *(Brit)*

andouiller /ɑ̃duje/ NM tine, (branch of) antler

andouillette /ɑ̃dujɛt/ NF andouillette *(sausage made of chitterlings, eaten hot)*

androcéphale /ɑ̃dʀosefal/ ADJ with a human head

androgène /ɑ̃dʀɔʒɛn/ ADJ *[hormone]* androgen; *[effet]* androgenic NM androgen

androgyne /ɑ̃dʀɔʒin/ ADJ androgynous NM androgyne

androgynie /ɑ̃dʀɔʒini/ NF androgyny

androïde /ɑ̃dʀɔid/ NM android

andrologie /ɑ̃dʀɔlɔʒi/ NF andrology

andrologue /ɑ̃dʀɔlɔg/ NMF andrologist

Andromaque /ɑ̃dʀɔmak/ NF Andromache

Andromède /ɑ̃dʀɔmɛd/ NF Andromeda

andropause /ɑ̃dʀopoz/ NF male menopause

androstérone /ɑ̃dʀosteʀɔn/ NF androsterone

âne /ɑn/ NM 1 (= *animal*) donkey ◆ **être comme l'~ de Buridan** to be unable to decide between two alternatives ◆ **il y a plus d'un ~ (à la foire) qui s'appelle Martin** *(hum)* a lot of people are called that, that's a very common name; → **dos** 2 (* = *personne*) ass*, fool ◆ **faire l'~ pour avoir du son** to act *ou* play dumb to find out what one wants to know ◆ ~ **bâté** † stupid ass*; → **bonnet, pont**

> **ÂNE DE BURIDAN**
>
> The origin of this expression is a philosophical text, supposedly written by Buridan in the 14th century, about an ass that starves to death because he cannot choose between two identical heaps of oats. The term has come to refer to any person who finds it impossible to make up their mind.

anéantir /aneɑ̃tiʀ/ ► conjug 2 ◄ VT 1 (= *détruire*) *[+ ville, armée, peuple]* to annihilate, to wipe out; *[+ efforts]* to wreck, to destroy; *[+ espoirs]* to dash, to destroy; *[+ sentiment]* to destroy 2 (= *déprimer : gén pass*) *[chaleur]* to overwhelm, to overcome; *[fatigue]* to exhaust, to wear out; *[chagrin]* to crush ◆ **la nouvelle l'a anéanti** the news completely broke him VPR **s'anéantir** *[espoir]* to be dashed

anéantissement /aneɑ̃tismɑ̃/ NM 1 (= *destruction*) *[de ville, armée, peuple]* annihilation, wiping out; *[d'efforts, sentiment]* destruction ◆ **c'est l'~ de tous mes espoirs** that's the end of *ou* that has dashed all my hopes ◆ **ce régime vise à l'~ de l'individu** this régime aims at the complete suppression *ou* annihilation of the individual 2 (= *fatigue*) exhaustion; (= *abattement*) dejection

anecdote /anɛkdɔt/ NF *(gén)* anecdote ◆ **l'~** (= *détails*) trivial detail ◆ **pour l'~** as a matter of interest ◆ **cet historien ne s'élève pas au-dessus de l'~** *(péj)* this historian doesn't rise above the anecdotal

anecdotique /anɛkdɔtik/ ADJ *[caractère, aspect]* trivial ◆ **le caractère ~ de cet incident** the trivial nature of the incident ◆ **ce sujet n'a qu'un intérêt ~** this subject is only of passing *ou* minor interest ◆ **cette histoire est ~** this story relates to an isolated incident ◆ **une histoire ~ de la télévision** a collection of TV trivia NM ◆ **l'~** the details ◆ **on nous a reproché de faire dans l'~ et le superficiel** we've been taken to task for concerning ourselves with superficial details ◆ **ne tombons pas dans l'~** let's not get too concerned with minor details

> ⚠ Attention à ne pas traduire automatiquement **anecdotique** par **anecdotal**, qui a le sens de 'isolé', 'non généralisable'.

anecdotiquement /anɛkdɔtikmɑ̃/ ADV incidentally ◆ **~, je vous avoue que j'ai toujours trouvé cela ridicule** incidentally, I must admit I've always found this ridiculous

anémiant, e /anemjɑ̃, ɑ̃t/ ADJ *(Méd)* causing anaemia *(Brit) ou* anemia *(US)*; *(fig)* debilitating

anémie /anemi/ NF *(Méd)* anaemia *(Brit)*, anemia *(US)*; *(fig) [d'économie]* weakness ◆ ~ **pernicieuse** pernicious anaemia ◆ ~ **falciforme** sickle cell anaemia

anémié, e /anemje/ (ptp de **anémier**) ADJ *(Méd)* anaemic *(Brit)*, anemic *(US)*; *(fig)* weakened, enfeebled

anémier /anemje/ ► conjug 7 ◄ VT *(Méd)* to make anaemic *(Brit) ou* anemic *(US)*; *(fig)* to weaken VPR **s'anémier** *(Méd)* to become anaemic *(Brit) ou* anemic *(US)*

anémique /anemik/ ADJ *(Méd, fig)* anaemic *(Brit)*, anemic *(US)*

anémomètre /anemɔmɛtʀ/ NM *(pour un fluide)* anemometer; *(pour le vent)* anemometer, wind gauge

anémone /anemɔn/ NF anemone ◆ ~ **sylvie** wood anemone ◆ ~ **de mer** sea anemone

ânerie /ɑnʀi/ NF 1 *(caractère)* stupidity ◆ **il est d'une ~ !** he's a real ass!* 2 (= *parole*) stupid *ou* idiotic remark; *(action)* stupid mistake, blunder ◆ **arrête de dire des ~s !** stop talking nonsense! *ou* rubbish *(Brit)*! ◆ **faire une ~** to make a blunder, to do something silly

anéroïde /aneʀɔid/ ADJ → **baromètre**

ânesse /ɑnɛs/ NF she-ass, jenny

anesthésiant, e /anɛstezjɑ̃, ɑ̃t/ ADJ, NM anaesthetic *(Brit)*, anesthetic *(US)* ◆ ~ **local** local anaesthetic

anesthésie /anɛstezi/ NF (= *état d'insensibilité, technique*) anaesthesia *(Brit)*, anesthesia *(US)*; (= *opération*) anaesthetic *(Brit)*, anesthetic *(US)* ◆ **sous ~** under anaesthetic *ou* anaesthesia ◆ ~ **générale/locale** general/local anaesthetic ◆ **je vais vous faire une ~** I'm going to give you an anaesthetic

anesthésier /anɛstezje/ ► conjug 7 ◄ VT *(Méd) [+ organe]* to anaesthetize *(Brit)*, to anesthetize *(US)*; *[+ personne]* to give an anaesthetic *(Brit) ou* anesthetic *(US)* to, to anaesthetize *(Brit)*, to anesthetize *(US)*; *(fig)* to deaden, to benumb, to anaesthetize *(Brit)*, to anesthetize *(US)* ◆ **j'étais comme anesthésié** *(fig)* I felt completely numb

anesthésique /anɛstezik/ ADJ *[substance]* anaesthetic *(Brit)*, anesthetic *(US)* NM anaesthetic *(Brit)*, anesthetic *(US)*

anesthésiste /anɛstezist/ NMF anaesthetist *(Brit)*, anesthesiologist *(US)*

aneth /anɛt/ NM dill

anévrisme /anevʀism/ NM aneurism; → **rupture**

anfractuosité /ɑ̃fʀaktɥozite/ NF crevice

ange /ɑ̃ʒ/ NM 1 *(Rel)* angel ◆ **bon/mauvais ~** good/bad angel ◆ **être le bon ~ de qn** to be sb's good *ou* guardian angel ◆ **être le mauvais ~ de qn** to be an evil influence on sb

2 (= *personne*) angel ◆ **oui mon ~** yes, darling ◆ **va me chercher mes lunettes tu seras un ~**

be an angel *ou* a darling and get me my glasses ◆ **il est sage comme un ~** he's an absolute angel, he's as good as gold ◆ **il est beau comme un ~** he's absolutely gorgeous ◆ **avoir une patience d'~** to have the patience of a saint ◆ **c'est un ~ de douceur/de bonté** he's sweetness/kindness itself

3 *(= poisson)* angel fish

4 *(locutions)* **un ~ passa** there was an awkward pause *ou* silence ◆ **être aux ~s** to be in seventh heaven; → **discuter**

COMP **ange déchu** *(Rel)* fallen angel
l'ange exterminateur *(Rel)* the exterminating angel
ange gardien *(Rel, fig)* guardian angel; *(= garde du corps)* bodyguard; → **cheveu, faiseur**

Angelino /ɑ̃ʒlino/ NMF Angelino

angélique[1] /ɑ̃ʒelik/ ADJ *(Rel, fig)* angelic(al)

angélique[2] /ɑ̃ʒelik/ NF *(= plante)* angelica

angéliquement /ɑ̃ʒelikmɑ̃/ ADV angelically, like an angel

angélisme /ɑ̃ʒelism/ NM *(Rel)* angelism ◆ **l'~ du gouvernement** the government's naïve optimism

angelot /ɑ̃ʒ(ə)lo/ NM *(Art)* cherub

angélus /ɑ̃ʒelys/ NM angelus

angine /ɑ̃ʒin/ NF *(= amygdalite)* tonsillitis; *(= pharyngite)* pharyngitis ◆ **avoir une ~** to have a sore throat ◆ **~ de poitrine** angina (pectoris)

> ⚠ **angine** se traduit par le mot anglais **angina** uniquement au sens de 'angine de poitrine'.

angineux, -euse /ɑ̃ʒinø, øz/ ADJ anginal

angiome /ɑ̃ʒjom/ NM angioma

angioplastie /ɑ̃ʒjoplasti/ NF angioplasty

angiosperme /ɑ̃ʒjospɛʀm/ ADJ angiospermous NFPL **les angiospermes** angiosperms, the Angiospermae *(SPÉC)*

anglais, e /ɑ̃glɛ, ɛz/ ADJ English; → **assiette, broderie, crème** *etc* NM 1 ◆ **Anglais** Englishman ◆ **les Anglais** *(en général)* English people, the English; *(abusivement = Britanniques)* British people, the British; *(= hommes)* Englishmen ◆ **les Anglais ont débarqué** * *(= j'ai mes règles)* I've got the curse *, I've got my period 2 *(= langue)* English ◆ **~ canadien/britannique/américain** Canadian/British/American English ◆ **parler ~** to speak English NF **anglaise** 1 ◆ **Anglaise** Englishwoman 2 *(Coiffure)* **~es** ringlets 3 *(Écriture)* = modern English handwriting LOC ADJ, LOC ADV **à l'anglaise** *[légumes]* boiled; *[parc, jardin]* landscaped ◆ **cuit à l'~e** boiled; → **filer**

angle /ɑ̃gl/ GRAMMAIRE ACTIVE 53.3
NM 1 *[de meuble, rue]* corner ◆ **à l'~ de ces deux rues** at *ou* on the corner of these two streets ◆ **le magasin qui fait l'~** the shop on the corner ◆ **la maison est en ~** the house stands directly *ou* is right on the corner ◆ **meuble d'~** corner unit

2 *(Math)* angle

3 *(= aspect)* angle, point of view ◆ **vu sous cet ~** seen from *ou* looked at from that point of view

4 *[de caractère, personne]* rough edge; → **arrondir**

COMP **angles adjacents** adjacent angles
angle aigu acute angle
angles alternes alternate angles ◆ **~s alternes externes/internes** exterior/interior alternate angles
angle de braquage lock
angle de chasse *[de voiture]* castor angle
angle de couverture *(Photo)* lens field
angle dièdre dihedral angle
angle droit right angle ◆ **faire un ~ droit** to be at right angles *(avec* to)
angle facial facial angle
angle d'incidence angle of incidence
angle d'inclinaison angle of inclination
angle inscrit (à un cercle) inscribed angle (of a circle)
angle de marche ⇒ **angle de route**
angle mort dead angle, blind spot
angle obtus obtuse angle
angle optique optic angle
angle de réfraction angle of refraction
angle rentrant re-entrant angle
angle de route *(Mil)* bearing, direction of march
angle saillant salient angle
angle de tir firing angle
angle visuel visual angle

Angleterre /ɑ̃glətɛʀ/ NF England; *(abusivement = Grande Bretagne)* (Great) Britain

anglican, e /ɑ̃glikɑ̃, an/ ADJ, NM,F Anglican

anglicanisme /ɑ̃glikanism/ NM Anglicanism

angliche * /ɑ̃gliʃ/ *(hum ou péj)* ADJ English, British NMF **Angliche** Brit *, Britisher * ◆ **les Angliches** the Brits *

angliciser /ɑ̃glisize/ ▸ conjug 1 ◂ VT to anglicize VPR **s'angliciser** to become anglicized

anglicisme /ɑ̃glisism/ NM anglicism

angliciste /ɑ̃glisist/ NMF *(= étudiant)* student of English *(language and civilization)*; *(= spécialiste)* anglicist, English specialist

anglo- /ɑ̃glɔ/ PRÉF anglo- ◆ **~irlandais** Anglo-Irish

anglo-américain (pl **anglo-américains**) /ɑ̃gloameʀikɛ̃/ ADJ Anglo-American NM *(= variété de l'anglais)* American English NM,F **Anglo-Américain(e)** Anglo-American

anglo-arabe (pl **anglo-arabes**) /ɑ̃gloaʀab/ ADJ, NM *(= cheval)* Anglo-Arab

anglo-canadien, -ienne (mpl **anglo-canadiens**) /ɑ̃glokanadjɛ̃, jɛn/ ADJ Anglo-Canadian NM *(= variété de l'anglais)* Canadian English NM,F **Anglo-Canadien(ne)** English Canadian

anglomane /ɑ̃glɔman/ NMF anglomaniac

anglomanie /ɑ̃glɔmani/ NF anglomania

anglo-normand, e (mpl **anglo-normands**) /ɑ̃glonɔʀmɑ̃, ɑ̃d/ ADJ Anglo-Norman; → **île** NM 1 *(= dialecte)* Anglo-Norman, Norman French 2 *(= cheval)* Anglo-Norman (horse)

anglophile /ɑ̃glɔfil/ ADJ, NMF anglophile

anglophilie /ɑ̃glɔfili/ NF anglophilia

anglophobe /ɑ̃glɔfɔb/ ADJ anglophobic NMF anglophobe

anglophobie /ɑ̃glɔfɔbi/ NF anglophobia

anglophone /ɑ̃glɔfɔn/ ADJ *[personne]* English-speaking, Anglophone; *[littérature]* English-language *(épith)*, in English *(attrib)* NMF English speaker, Anglophone

anglo-saxon, -onne (mpl **anglo-saxons**) /ɑ̃glosaksɔ̃, ɔn/ ADJ Anglo-Saxon ◆ **les pays ~s** Anglo-Saxon countries NM *(= langue)* Anglo-Saxon NM,F **Anglo-Saxon(ne)** Anglo-Saxon

angoissant, e /ɑ̃gwasɑ̃, ɑ̃t/ ADJ *[situation, silence]* harrowing, agonizing ◆ **nous avons vécu des jours ~s** we suffered days of anguish

angoisse /ɑ̃gwas/ NF 1 *(NonC, gén, Psych)* anxiety; *(plus forte)* fear ◆ **crises d'~** anxiety attacks ◆ **l'~ métaphysique** *(Philos)* angst ◆ **l'~ le saisit** he was overwhelmed by a feeling of anxiety ◆ **plus les examens approchent, plus l'~ monte** the closer the exams get the more acute the anxiety becomes ◆ **l'~ de la mort** fear of death ◆ **il vivait dans l'~** he lived in fear ◆ **il vivait dans l'~ d'un accident** he lived in dread of an accident, he dreaded an accident ◆ **vivre des jours d'~** to go through *ou* suffer days of anguish ◆ **c'est l'~** * it's nerve-racking ◆ **quelle ~, ces factures à payer !** * these bills are a terrible worry! 2 *(= peur)* dread *(NonC)*, fear ◆ **avoir des ~s** *(= sensation d'étouffement)* to feel one is suffocating

angoissé, e /ɑ̃gwase/ (ptp de **angoisser**) ADJ anxious; *(plus fort)* acutely anxious; *[question, silence]* agonized NM,F anxious person

angoisser /ɑ̃gwase/ ▸ conjug 1 ◂ VT *(= inquiéter)* to distress, to cause distress to; *(= oppresser)* to choke VI (* = *être angoissé)* to be worried sick *

Angola /ɑ̃gɔla/ NM Angola

angolais, e /ɑ̃gɔlɛ, ɛz/ ADJ Angolan NM,F **Angolais(e)** Angolan

angor /ɑ̃gɔʀ/ NM angina ◆ **crise d'~** attack of angina

angora /ɑ̃gɔʀa/ ADJ, NM angora

angstrœm, angström /aŋstʀœm/ NM angstrom (unit)

anguille /ɑ̃gij/ NF eel ◆ **~ de mer** conger eel ◆ **il m'a filé entre les doigts comme une ~** he slipped right through my fingers, he wriggled out of my clutches ◆ **il y a ~ sous roche** there's something in the wind

angulaire /ɑ̃gylɛʀ/ ADJ angular; → **pierre**

anguleux, -euse /ɑ̃gylø, øz/ ADJ *[menton, visage]* angular; *[coude]* bony

anharmonique /anaʀmɔnik/ ADJ anharmonic

anhydre /anidʀ/ ADJ anhydrous

anhydride /anidʀid/ NM anhydride

anicroche * /anikʀɔʃ/ NF hitch, snag ◆ **sans ~s** *[se passer]* smoothly, without a hitch

ânier, -ière /ɑnje, jɛʀ/ NM,F donkey-driver

aniline /anilin/ NF aniline

animal, e (mpl **-aux**) /animal, o/ ADJ 1 *[espèce, règne, graisse, vie]* animal *(épith)* ◆ **protéine (d'origine) ~e** animal protein 2 *[force, réaction]* animal *(épith)*; *[sensualité]* raw, animal *(épith)*; → **esprit** NM 1 *(= gén)* animal ◆ **~ familier** *ou* **de compagnie** pet ◆ **~ de laboratoire** laboratory animal ◆ **animaux de boucherie** animals for slaughter 2 *(* ou péj) (= personne brutale)* animal; *(= personne stupide)* silly devil * ◆ **où est parti cet ~ ?** where did that devil * go?

animalcule /animalkyl/ NM micro-organism, animalcule *(SPEC)*

animalerie /animalʀi/ NF *[de laboratoire]* animal house; *(= magasin)* pet shop

animalier, -ière /animalje, jɛʀ/ ADJ *[peintre, sculpteur]* animal *(épith)*, wildlife *(épith)*; *[film, photographie]* wildlife *(épith)* ◆ **cinéaste ~** maker of wildlife films; → **parc** NM 1 *(Art)* painter *(ou* sculptor) of animals, animal painter *(ou* sculptor) 2 *[de laboratoire]* animal keeper

animalité /animalite/ NF animality

animateur, -trice /animatœʀ, tʀis/ NM,F 1 *(= professionnel) [de spectacle, émission de jeux]* host, compere *(Brit)*, emcee *(US)*; *[d'émission culturelle]* presenter; *[de music-hall]* compere *(Brit)*, emcee *(US)*; *[de discothèque]* disc jockey, DJ; *[de club]* leader, sponsor *(US)*; *[de camp de vacances]* activity leader, camp counselor *(US)* ◆ **~ (de) radio** radio presenter 2 *(= personne dynamique)* **c'est un ~ né** he's a born organizer ◆ **l'~ de cette entreprise** the driving force behind *ou* the prime mover in this undertaking ◆ **ce poste requiert des qualités d'~ d'équipe** this post requires leadership qualities 3 *(Ciné = technicien)* animator

>  **animateur** se traduit par le mot anglais **animator** uniquement au sens de 'auteur de dessins animés'.

animation /animasjɔ̃/ NF 1 *(= vie) [de quartier, regard, personne]* life, liveliness; *[de discussion]* animation, liveliness; (= *affairement*) *[de rue, quartier, bureau]* (hustle and) bustle ◆ **son arrivée provoqua une grande** ~ his arrival caused a great deal of excitement ◆ **parler avec** ~ to talk animatedly ◆ **mettre de l'**~ to liven things up ◆ **mettre de l'**~ **dans une soirée** to liven up a party

2 (= *activités*) activities ◆ **chargé de l'**~ **culturelle/sportive** in charge of cultural/sports activities; → **centre**

3 *[d'équipe, groupe de travail]* leadership ◆ **l'**~ **d'une équipe** the leadership of a team ◆ **il veut un métier en relation avec l'**~ **des jeunes** he wants a job involving youth leadership ◆ **les cadres ont un rôle d'**~ a manager's role is to lead

4 (*Ciné*) animation ◆ **comme on le voit sur l'**~ **satellite** (*Météo*) as we can see from the satellite picture ◆ **l'**~ **en 3D** 3D animation ◆ **une** ~ **montée à partir d'une série d'images fixes** a film made from a series of stills; → **cinéma, film**

animé, e /anime/ (ptp de **animer**) ADJ 1 *[rue, quartier]* (= *affairé*) busy; (= *plein de vie*) lively; *[regard, visage]* lively; *[discussion]* animated, lively; *[enchères]* brisk ◆ **la Bourse est ~e** the Stock Market is lively, trading is brisk 2 (*Ling, Philos*) animate

animer /anime/ ▸ conjug 1 ◂ VT 1 (= *mener*) *[+ spectacle, émission de jeux]* to host, to compere (*Brit*), to emcee (*US*); *[+ émission culturelle]* to present; *[+ discussion]* to lead; *[+ réunion]* to run, to lead

2 (= *dynamiser, motiver*) *[+ parti]* to be the driving force in; *[+ équipe]* to lead

3 (= *donner de la vie à*) *[+ ville, soirée, conversation]* to liven up; *[+ visage]* to animate, to light up; *[+ peinture, statue]* to bring to life; (*Philos*) *[+ nature, matière]* to animate ◆ **l'enthousiasme qui animait son regard** the enthusiasm which shone in his eyes ◆ **les meilleurs joueurs seront présents, ce qui va** ~ **le tournoi** the top players will be there, which will make for an exciting tournament

4 (= *stimuler*) *[haine, désir]* to drive (on); *[foi]* to sustain; *[espoir]* to nourish, to sustain ◆ **animé par** *ou* **de** *[+ volonté]* driven (on) by; *[+ désir]* prompted by ◆ **animé des meilleures intentions** motivated by the best intentions ◆ ~ **le marché** (*Bourse*) to stimulate the market ◆ **le patriotisme qui animait les soldats** the sense of patriotism that spurred the soldiers on

5 (*surtout au passif* = *mouvoir*) **l'objet est animé d'un mouvement de rotation** the object rotates ◆ **le balancier était animé d'un mouvement régulier** the pendulum was moving in a steady rhythm *ou* swinging steadily

VPR **s'animer** *[personne, rue]* to come to life, to liven up; *[statue]* to come to life; *[conversation]* to become animated, to liven up; *[foule, objet inanimé]* to come to life; *[match]* to liven up; *[yeux, traits]* to light up ◆ **les machines semblaient s'**~ **d'une vie propre** the machines seemed to have a life of their own

animisme /animism/ NM animism

animiste /animist/ ADJ *[théorie]* animist(ic); *[société, population]* animist NMF animist

animosité /animozite/ NF (= *hostilité*) animosity (*contre* towards, against)

anion /anjɔ̃/ NM anion

anis /ani(s)/ NM (= *plante*) anise; (*Culin*) aniseed; (= *bonbon*) aniseed ball ◆ ~ **étoilé** star anise ◆ **à l'**~ aniseed (*épith*)

aniser /anize/ ▸ conjug 1 ◂ VT to flavour with aniseed ◆ **goût anisé** taste of aniseed

anisette /anizɛt/ NF anisette

Ankara /ɑ̃kaʀa/ N Ankara

ankylose /ɑ̃kiloz/ NF ankylosis

ankyloser /ɑ̃kiloze/ ▸ conjug 1 ◂ VT to stiffen, to ankylose (*SPÉC*) ◆ **être tout ankylosé** to be stiff all over ◆ **mon bras ankylosé** my stiff arm ◆ **cette routine qui nous ankylose** this mind-numbing routine VPR **s'ankyloser** *[membre]* to stiffen up, to ankylose (*SPÉC*); *[institution]* to be stagnating; *[esprit]* to become stultified *ou* dulled

annales /anal/ NFPL annals ◆ **ça restera dans les** ~* that'll go down in history (*hum*) ◆ **un cas unique dans les** ~ **du crime** a case that is unique in the history of crime

annamite † /anamit/ ADJ Annamese, Annamite NMF **Annamite** Annamese, Annamite

Annapurna /anapuʀna/ NM (*Géog*) Annapurna

Anne /an/ NF Ann, Anne ◆ ~ **d'Autriche** Anne of Austria ◆ ~ **Boleyn** Anne Boleyn ◆ ~ **de Bretagne** Anne of Brittany

anneau (pl **anneaux**) /ano/ NM 1 (= *cercle, bague*) ring; (= *partie d'une bague*) hoop; (= *boucle d'oreille*) hoop (earring); *[de chaîne]* link; *[de préservatif]* rim ◆ ~ **de rideau** curtain ring 2 (*Algèbre*) ring; (*Géom*) ring, annulus 3 *[de colonne]* annulet; *[de champignon]* annulus; *[de ver]* segment, metamere (*SPÉC*); *[de serpent]* coil 4 (*Sport*) **les ~x** the rings ◆ **exercices aux ~x** ring exercises

COMP **anneaux colorés** (*Opt*) Newton's rings
anneau de croissance *[d'arbre]* annual *ou* growth ring
anneau épiscopal bishop's ring
anneau nuptial wedding ring
anneau oculaire (*Opt*) eye ring
anneaux olympiques Olympic rings
anneaux de Saturne Saturn's rings
anneau sphérique (*Géom*) (spherical) annulus *ou* ring
anneau de vitesse (*Sport*) race track

année /ane/ GRAMMAIRE ACTIVE 50.2

NF 1 (= *durée*) year ◆ **il y a bien des ~s qu'il est parti** he's been gone for many years, it's many years since he left ◆ **la récolte d'une** ~ a *ou* one year's harvest ◆ **tout au long de l'**~ the whole year (round), throughout the year ◆ **payé à l'**~ paid annually ◆ **en** ~ **pleine** (*Fin*) in a full year ◆ **les bénéfices en** ~ **pleine** the full-year profits ◆ ~ **de base** (*Fin*) base year

2 (= *âge, Scol, Univ*) year ◆ **il est dans sa vingtième** ~ he is in his twentieth year ◆ **l'**~ **universitaire** the academic year ◆ **de première/deuxième** ~ (*Scol, Univ*) first-/second-year (*épith*)

3 (= *point dans le temps*) year ◆ **les ~s de guerre** the war years ◆ ~ **de naissance** year of birth ◆ **les ~s 60** the sixties, the 60s ◆ **en l'**~ **700 de notre ère/avant Jésus-Christ** (*littér*) in (the year) 700 AD/BC; → **bon¹, souhaiter**

COMP **année bissextile** leap year
année budgétaire financial year
année calendaire, **année civile** calendar year
les années folles the Roaring Twenties
année de référence (*Fin, Jur*) base year ◆ **l'**~ **de référence 1984** (*Stat*) the 1984 benchmark
année sainte Holy Year

année-lumière (pl **années-lumière**) /anelymjɛʀ/ NF light year ◆ **à des années-lumière de** (*lit, fig*) light years away from ◆ **c'est à des années-lumière de mes préoccupations** it's the last thing on my mind ◆ **ma sœur et moi sommes à des années-lumière** there's a world of difference between my sister and me

annelé, e /an(ə)le/ ADJ ringed; *[plante, animal]* annulate; *[colonne]* annulated

annexe /anɛks/ GRAMMAIRE ACTIVE 53.2 ADJ 1 (= *secondaire*) *[activités, produits, services]* ancillary; *[tâches]* subsidiary; *[considérations]* secondary; *[budget, revenu]* supplementary ◆ **avantages ~s** fringe benefits ◆ **frais ~s** incidental expenses ◆ **effets ~s** side effects ◆ **il fait des travaux ~s** (*pour compléter son salaire*) he does other jobs on the side 2 (= *attaché*) *[document]* annexed, appended ◆ **les bâtiments ~s** the annexes NF 1 *[de document]* (= *pièces complémentaires*) appendix; (= *pièces additives*) annex(e); *[de contrat]* (*gén*) rider; (= *liste*) schedule (*de, à* to); ◆ **en** ~ in the appendix 2 (*Constr*) annex(e) 3 (= *embarcation*) tender, dinghy

annexer /anɛkse/ ▸ conjug 1 ◂ VT *[+ territoire]* to annex; *[+ document]* to append, to annex (*à* to) VPR **s'annexer** * (= *s'attribuer*) *[+ bureau, personne]* to commandeer (*hum*)

annexion /anɛksjɔ̃/ NF (*Pol*) annexation

annexionnisme /anɛksjɔnism/ NM annexationism

annexionniste /anɛksjɔnist/ ADJ, NMF annexationist

Annibal /anibal/ NM Hannibal

annihilation /aniilasjɔ̃/ NF 1 *[d'efforts, espoirs, résistance]* destruction; *[de peuple]* annihilation 2 (*Phys*) annihilation

annihiler /aniile/ ▸ conjug 1 ◂ VT *[+ efforts]* to wreck, to destroy; *[+ espoirs]* to dash, to wreck; *[+ résistance]* to wipe out, to destroy; *[+ personne, esprit]* to crush; *[+ peuple]* to annihilate, to wipe out

anniversaire /anivɛʀsɛʀ/ GRAMMAIRE ACTIVE 50.3 NM *[de personne]* birthday; *[d'événement, mariage, mort]* anniversary ◆ **bon** *ou* **joyeux** ~ ! happy birthday! ◆ **c'est l'**~ **de leur mariage** it's their (wedding) anniversary ◆ **cadeau/carte d'**~ birthday present/card ADJ ◆ **la date** *ou* **le jour** ~ **de la victoire** the anniversary of the victory

> ⚠ **anniversaire** se traduit par **anniversary** uniquement au sens de 'commémoration'.

annonce /anɔ̃s/ GRAMMAIRE ACTIVE 46.1 NF 1 *[d'accord, décision, résultat]* announcement ◆ **l'**~ **officielle des fiançailles** the official announcement of the engagement ◆ **faire une** ~ to make an announcement ◆ **à l'**~ **de cet événement** when the event was announced ◆ **il cherche l'effet d'**~ he wants to make an impact ◆ **"annonce personnelle"** "personal message" ◆ ~ **judiciaire** *ou* **légale** legal notice

2 (*Cartes*) declaration; (*Bridge*) (*gén*) bid; (*finale*) declaration

3 (= *publicité*) (newspaper) advertisement; (*pour emploi*) job advertisement ◆ **petites ~s, ~s classées** classified advertisements *ou* ads*, classifieds, small ads* (*Brit*) ◆ **mettre** *ou* **passer une** ~ **(dans un journal)** to put *ou* place an advertisement in a paper ◆ **journal d'~s** free sheet ◆ **page des petites ~s** (*dans un journal*) classifieds page, small-ads page (*Brit*)

annoncer /anɔ̃se/ GRAMMAIRE ACTIVE 51.1 ▸ conjug 3 ◂

VT 1 (= *informer de*) *[+ fait, décision, nouvelle]* to announce (*à* to); ◆ ~ **à qn que ...** to tell sb that ..., to announce to sb that ... ◆ **on m'a annoncé par lettre que ...** I was informed *ou* advised by letter that ... ◆ **je lui ai annoncé la nouvelle** (*gén*) I told her the news, I announced the news to her; (*mauvaise nouvelle*) I broke the news to her ◆ **on annonce l'ouverture d'un nouveau magasin** they're advertising the opening of a new shop ◆ **on annonce la sortie prochaine de ce film** the forthcoming release of this film has been announced ◆ **les journaux ont annoncé leur mariage** their marriage has been announced in the papers ◆ **on annonce un grave incendie** a serious fire is reported to have broken out

2 (= *prédire*) *[+ pluie, détérioration]* to forecast ◆ **on annonce un ralentissement économique dans les mois à venir** a slowdown in the economy is forecast *ou* predicted for the co-

ming months ◆ **la défaite annoncée du parti** the predicted defeat of the party

3 *(= signaler) [présage]* to foreshadow, to foretell; *[signe avant-coureur]* to herald; *[sonnerie, pas]* to announce, to herald ◆ **les nuages qui annoncent une tempête** clouds that herald a storm ◆ **ça n'annonce rien de bon** it bodes ill ◆ **ce radoucissement annonce la pluie/le printemps** this warmer weather is a sign that rain/spring is on the way ◆ **la cloche qui annonce la fin des cours** the bell announcing *ou* signalling the end of classes

4 *(= introduire) [+ personne]* to announce ◆ **il entra sans se faire ~** he went in without being announced *ou* without announcing himself ◆ **qui dois-je ~ ?** what name shall I say?, whom shall I announce?

5 *(Cartes)* to declare; *(Bridge) (gén)* to bid; *(= demander un contrat)* to declare ◆ **~ la couleur** *(lit)* to declare trumps; *(fig)* to lay one's cards on the table

VPR **s'annoncer** 1 *(= se présenter)* **comment est-ce que ça s'annonce ?** *[situation]* how is it shaping up? *ou* looking? ◆ **le temps s'annonce orageux** the weather looks stormy ◆ **l'année s'annonce excellente** it promises to be an excellent year ◆ **ça s'annonce bien** that looks promising ◆ **le projet s'annonce bien/mal** the project has got off to a good/bad start

2 *(= arriver) [événement, crise]* to approach ◆ **la révolution qui s'annonçait** the signs of the coming revolution ◆ **l'hiver s'annonçait** winter was on the way

3 *[personne] (= donner son nom)* to announce o.s. ◆ **annoncez-vous au concierge en arrivant** make yourself known *ou* say who you are to the concierge when you arrive ◆ **il s'annonçait toujours en frappant 3 fois** he always announced himself by knocking 3 times ◆ **tu viens ici quand tu veux, tu n'as pas besoin de t'~** you can come here whenever you like, you don't have to let me know in advance

annonceur, -euse /anɔ̃sœʀ, øz/ NM,F *(Radio, TV)* announcer NM *(= publicité)* advertiser

annonciateur, -trice /anɔ̃sjatœʀ, tʀis/ ADJ ◆ **signe ~** *[de maladie, crise]* warning sign; *[de catastrophe]* portent; *[d'amélioration, reprise économique]* indication, sign ◆ **~ de** *[+ événement favorable]* heralding; *[+ événement défavorable]* heralding, forewarning ◆ **vent ~ de pluie** wind that heralds rain NM,F herald, harbinger *(littér)*

Annonciation /anɔ̃sjasjɔ̃/ NF ◆ **l'~** *(= événement)* the Annunciation; *(= fête)* Annunciation Day, Lady Day

annotateur, -trice /anɔtatœʀ, tʀis/ NM,F annotator

annotation /anɔtasjɔ̃/ NF annotation

annoter /anɔte/ ► conjug 1 ◄ VT to annotate

annuaire /anɥɛʀ/ GRAMMAIRE ACTIVE 54.1 NM *[d'organisme]* yearbook, annual; *[de téléphone]* (telephone) directory, phone book ◆ **~ électronique** electronic directory ◆ **je ne suis pas dans l'~** I'm ex-directory, I'm not in the phone book

annualisation /anɥalizasjɔ̃/ NF *[de comptes]* annualization ◆ **l'~ du temps de travail** the calculation of working hours on a yearly basis

annualiser /anɥalize/ ► conjug 1 ◄ VT *(gén)* to make annual; *[+ comptes]* to annualize ◆ **taux annualisé** annualized rate ◆ **travail à temps partiel annualisé** *part-time work where the hours worked are calculated on a yearly basis*

annualité /anɥalite/ NF *(gén)* yearly recurrence ◆ **l'~ du budget/de l'impôt** yearly budgeting/taxation

annuel, -elle /anɥɛl/ ADJ annual, yearly; → **plante**[1]

annuellement /anɥɛlmɑ̃/ ADV annually ◆ **les 50 000 tonnes de métal que l'usine produit ~** the 50,000 tonnes of metal the factory produces annually ◆ **les chiffres publiés ~ par l'institut** the figures which the institute publishes annually *ou* once a year ◆ **les 100 millions d'euros alloués ~ au ministère** the 100 million euros that are allocated to the ministry every year *ou* annually

annuité /anɥite/ NF *(gén)* annual instalment *(Brit) ou* installment *(US)*, annual payment; *[de dette]* annual repayment ◆ **avoir toutes ses ~s** *[de pension]* to have (made) all one's years' contributions

annulable /anylabl/ ADJ annullable, liable to annulment *(attrib)*

annulaire /anylɛʀ/ ADJ annular, ring-shaped NM ring finger, third finger

annulation /anylasjɔ̃/ NF *[de contrat]* invalidation, nullification; *[de jugement, décision]* quashing; *[d'engagement, réservation, commande]* cancellation; *[d'élection, acte, examen]* nullification; *[de mariage]* annulment ◆ **ils demandent l'~ de leur dette** they are asking for their debt to be cancelled

annuler /anyle/ GRAMMAIRE ACTIVE 47.4, 48.3 ► conjug 1 ◄ VT *[+ contrat]* to invalidate, to void; *[+ jugement, décision]* to quash; *[+ engagement]* to cancel, to call off; *[+ élection, acte, examen]* to nullify, to declare void; *[+ mariage]* to annul; *[+ réservation]* to cancel; *[+ commande]* to cancel, to withdraw; *[+ dette]* to cancel ◆ **le fax annule les distances** fax machines make distance irrelevant VPR **s'annuler** *[poussées, efforts]* to cancel each other out

anoblir /anɔbliʀ/ ► conjug 2 ◄ VT to ennoble, to confer a title of nobility on

anoblissement /anɔblismɑ̃/ NM ennoblement

anode /anɔd/ NF anode

anodin, e /anɔdɛ̃, in/ ADJ *[personne]* insignificant; *[détail]* trivial, insignificant; *[propos, remarque]* innocuous, harmless ◆ **ce n'est pas un acte ~** it's not a trivial matter ◆ **dire qch de façon ~e** to say sth blandly ◆ **s'il a dit cela, ce n'est pas ~** if he said that, he meant something by it

anodique /anɔdik/ ADJ anodic

anodiser /anɔdize/ ► conjug 1 ◄ VT to anodize

anomal, e (mpl **-aux**) /anɔmal, o/ ADJ *(Gram)* anomalous

anomalie /anɔmali/ NF *(gén, Astron, Gram)* anomaly; *(Bio)* abnormality; *(= défaut technique)* (technical) fault ◆ **~ chromosomique/génétique** chromosomal/genetic abnormality *ou* defect

anomie /anɔmi/ NF anomie

ânon /ɑnɔ̃/ NM *(= petit de l'âne)* ass's foal; *(= petit âne)* little ass *ou* donkey

anone /anɔn/ NF sugar apple, annona

ânonnement /ɑnɔnmɑ̃/ NM *(inexpressif)* drone; *(hésitant)* faltering *ou* mumbling (speech)

ânonner /ɑnɔne/ ► conjug 1 ◄ VTI *(de manière inexpressive)* to drone on; *(en hésitant)* to mumble away ◆ **~ sa leçon** to mumble one's way through one's lesson

anonymat /anɔnima/ NM anonymity ◆ **sous (le) couvert de l'~, sous couvert d'~** anonymously ◆ **garder** *ou* **conserver l'~** to remain anonymous, to preserve one's anonymity ◆ **dans un total ~** in total anonymity ◆ **respecter l'~ de qn** to respect sb's desire for anonymity *ou* desire to remain anonymous

anonyme /anɔnim/ ADJ *(= sans nom) [auteur, interlocuteur, appel, lettre]* anonymous; *[main, voix]* unknown; *(= impersonnel) [décor, meubles]* impersonal; → **alcoolique, société**

anonymement /anɔnimmɑ̃/ ADV anonymously

anonymiser /anɔnimize/ VT to anonymize

anophèle /anɔfɛl/ NM anopheles

anorak /anɔʀak/ NM anorak

anorexie /anɔʀɛksi/ NF anorexia ◆ **~ mentale** anorexia nervosa

anorexigène /anɔʀɛksiʒɛn/ ADJ *[substance, effet]* appetite-suppressing ◆ **médicament ~** appetite suppressant (drug) NM appetite suppressant

anorexique /anɔʀɛksik/ ADJ, NMF anorexic

anormal, e (mpl **-aux**) /anɔʀmal, o/ ADJ 1 *(Sci, Méd)* abnormal; *(= insolite) [situation]* unusual; *[comportement]* abnormal, unusual ◆ **si vous voyez quelque chose d'~, signalez-le** if you notice anything unusual *ou* irregular, report it 2 *(= injuste)* unfair ◆ **il est ~ que ...** it isn't right *ou* it's unfair that ... NM,F († , *Méd)* abnormal person

anormalement /anɔʀmalmɑ̃/ ADV *[se développer]* abnormally; *[se conduire, agir]* unusually, abnormally; *[chaud, grand]* unusually, abnormally

anormalité /anɔʀmalite/ NF abnormality

anoxie /anɔksi/ NF anoxia

anoxique /anɔksik/ ADJ anoxic

ANPE /aɛnpe/ NF (abrév de **Agence nationale pour l'emploi**) → **agence**

anse /ɑ̃s/ NF *[de panier, tasse]* handle; *(Géog)* cove; *(Anat)* loop, flexura *(SPÉC)* ◆ **~ (de panier)** *(Archit)* basket-handle arch ◆ **faire danser** *ou* **valser l'~ du panier** *(hum)* to make a bit out of the shopping money *

antagonique /ɑ̃tagɔnik/ ADJ antagonistic

antagonisme /ɑ̃tagɔnism/ NM antagonism

antagoniste /ɑ̃tagɔnist/ ADJ *[forces, propositions]* antagonistic; *(Anat) [muscles]* antagonist NMF antagonist

antalgique /ɑ̃talʒik/ ADJ, NM analgesic

antan /ɑ̃tɑ̃/ NM *(littér)* ◆ **d'~** of yesteryear, of long ago ◆ **ma jeunesse d'~** my long-lost youth ◆ **ma force d'~** my strength of former days ◆ **mes plaisirs d'~** my erstwhile pleasures

Antananarivo /ɑ̃tananaʀivo/ N Antananarivo

Antarctide /ɑ̃taʀktid/ NF ◆ **l'~** Antarctica

antarctique /ɑ̃taʀktik/ ADJ *[région]* Antarctic ◆ **l'océan Antarctique** the Antarctic Ocean NM **Antarctique** ◆ **l'Antarctique** *(= océan)* the Antarctic; *(= continent)* Antarctica

antécédence /ɑ̃tesedɑ̃s/ NF antecedence

antécédent, e /ɑ̃tesedɑ̃, ɑt/ NM 1 *(Gram, Math, Philos)* antecedent 2 *(Méd : surtout pl)* medical *ou* case history ◆ **elle a des ~s d'hypertension artérielle** she has a past *ou* previous history of high blood pressure ◆ **avez-vous des ~s familiaux de maladies cardiaques ?** is there any history of heart disease in your family? NMPL **antécédents** *[de personne]* past *ou* previous history; *[d'affaire]* past *ou* previous history, antecedents ◆ **avoir de bons/mauvais ~s** to have a good/bad previous history ◆ **~s judiciaires** criminal record ◆ **ses ~s politiques** his political background

antéchrist /ɑ̃tekʀist/ NM Antichrist

antécime /ɑ̃tesim/ NF *[de montagne]* foresummit, subsidiary summit

antédiluvien, -ienne /ɑ̃tedilyvjɛ̃, jɛn/ ADJ *(lit, fig)* antediluvian

anténatal, e (mpl **s**) /ɑ̃tenatal/ ADJ *[diagnostic, examen, dépistage]* antenatal *(épith)*, prenatal *(épith)*

antenne /ɑ̃tɛn/ NF 1 *(= dispositif) (Radio, TV)* aerial *(Brit)*, antenna *(US)*; *[de radar]* antenna 2 *(= diffusion) (Radio, TV)* **je donne l'~ à Paris** (we'll go) over to Paris now ◆ **garder l'~** to stay on the air ◆ **quitter l'~** to go off the air ◆ **nous devons bientôt rendre l'~** we have to go back to the studio soon ◆ **je rends l'~ au studio** and now back to the studio ◆ **être à l'~** to be on the air ◆ **passer à l'~** to be on the air ◆ **sur notre ~** on our station ◆ **le concert sera diffusé sur l'~ de France-Musique** the concert will be broadcast on France-Musique ◆ **temps d'~** airtime ◆ **vous avez droit à 2 heures d'~** you are entitled to 2 hours' broadcasting time *ou* airtime ◆ **leur parti est interdit d'~** their party is banned from radio and television, there is a broadcasting ban on their party ◆ **hors ~, le ministre a déclaré que …** off the air, the minister declared that …
3 *[d'insecte]* antenna, feeler ◆ **avoir des ~s** *(fig)* to have a sixth sense ◆ **avoir des ~s dans un ministère** *(fig)* to have contacts in a ministry
4 *(= unité)* branch; *(Mil = poste avancé)* outpost ◆ **~ médicale** medical unit
5 *(Naut = vergue)* lateen yard
COMP **antenne parabolique** *ou* **satellite** satellite dish, dish antenna *(US)*
antenne relais relay antenne

> ⚠ Au sens de 'antenne de radio ou de télévision', **antenne** se traduit par **antenna** uniquement en anglais américain.

antépénultième /ɑ̃tepenyltjɛm/ ADJ antepenultimate NF antepenultimate syllable, antepenult

antéposer /ɑ̃tepoze/ ▸ conjug 1 ◂ VT to place *ou* put in front of the word ◆ **sujet antéposé** subject placed *ou* put in front of the verb

antéposition /ɑ̃tepozisjɔ̃/ NF *(Ling)* anteposition

antérieur, e /ɑ̃teʀjœʀ/ ADJ 1 *(dans le temps) [époque, situation]* previous, earlier ◆ **c'est ~ à la guerre** it was prior to the war ◆ **cette décision était ~e à son départ** that decision was taken prior to his departure ◆ **dans une vie ~e** in a former life 2 *(dans l'espace) [partie]* front *(épith)* ◆ **membre ~** forelimb ◆ **patte ~e** *[de cheval, vache]* forefoot; *[de chien, chat]* forepaw 3 *(Ling) [voyelle]* front *(épith)*; → **futur, passé**

antérieurement /ɑ̃teʀjœʀmɑ̃/ ADV earlier ◆ **~ à** prior *ou* previous to

antériorité /ɑ̃teʀjɔʀite/ NF *[d'événement, phénomène]* precedence; *(Gram)* anteriority

anthologie /ɑ̃tɔlɔʒi/ NF anthology; → **morceau**

anthozoaires /ɑ̃tozɔɛʀ/ NMPL ◆ **les ~** the Anthozoa

anthracite /ɑ̃tʀasit/ NM anthracite ADJ INV dark grey *(Brit) ou* gray *(US)*, charcoal grey *(Brit) ou* gray *(US)*

anthrax /ɑ̃tʀaks/ NM *(= tumeur)* carbuncle

anthropique /ɑ̃tʀɔpik/ ADJ anthropic

anthropocentrique /ɑ̃tʀɔposɑ̃tʀik/ ADJ anthropocentric

anthropocentrisme /ɑ̃tʀɔposɑ̃tʀism/ NM anthropocentrism

anthropoïde /ɑ̃tʀɔpɔid/ ADJ anthropoid NM anthropoid (ape)

anthropologie /ɑ̃tʀɔpɔlɔʒi/ NF anthropology

anthropologique /ɑ̃tʀɔpɔlɔʒik/ ADJ anthropological

anthropologiste /ɑ̃tʀɔpɔlɔʒist/, **anthropologue** /ɑ̃tʀɔpɔlɔg/ NMF anthropologist

anthropométrie /ɑ̃tʀɔpɔmetʀi/ NF anthropometry

anthropométrique /ɑ̃tʀɔpɔmetʀik/ ADJ anthropometric(al) ◆ **fiche ~** mugshot

anthropomorphe /ɑ̃tʀɔpɔmɔʀf/ ADJ anthropomorphous

anthropomorphique /ɑ̃tʀɔpɔmɔʀfik/ ADJ anthropomorphic

anthropomorphisme /ɑ̃tʀɔpɔmɔʀfism/ NM anthropomorphism

anthropomorphiste /ɑ̃tʀɔpɔmɔʀfist/ ADJ anthropomorphist, anthropomorphic NMF anthropomorphist

anthroponymie /ɑ̃tʀɔpɔnimi/ NF *(Ling)* anthroponomy

anthropophage /ɑ̃tʀɔpɔfaʒ/ ADJ cannibalistic, cannibal *(épith)* NMF cannibal

anthropophagie /ɑ̃tʀɔpɔfaʒi/ NF cannibalism

anthropopithèque /ɑ̃tʀɔpɔpitɛk/ NM anthropopithecus

anthume /ɑ̃tym/ ADJ *[œuvre]* published during the author's lifetime

anti /ɑ̃ti/ PRÉF ◆ **anti(-)** anti- ◆ **~-impérialisme** anti-imperialism ◆ **l'~-art/-théâtre** anti-art/-theatre ◆ **flash ~-yeux rouges** flash with red-eye reduction feature ◆ **loi ~casseur(s)** *law against looting* NM *(hum)* ◆ **le parti des ~s** those who are anti *ou* against, the anti crowd *

anti-acnéique /ɑ̃tiakneik/ ADJ *[traitement, préparation]* anti-acne *(épith)*

antiacridien, -ienne /ɑ̃tiakʀidjɛ̃, jɛn/ ADJ locust control *(épith)* ◆ **la lutte antiacridienne** the fight to control locusts

antiadhésif, -ive /ɑ̃tiadezif, iv/ ADJ *[poêle, revêtement]* non-stick *(épith)*

antiaérien, -ienne /ɑ̃tiaeʀjɛ̃, jɛn/ ADJ *[batterie, canon, missile]* anti-aircraft; *[abri]* air-raid *(épith)*

anti-âge /ɑ̃tiaʒ/ ADJ INV anti-ageing

antialcoolique /ɑ̃tialkɔlik/ ADJ ◆ **campagne ~** campaign against alcohol ◆ **ligue ~** temperance league

antiallergique /ɑ̃tialɛʀʒik/ ADJ anti-allergic NM anti-allergic drug

antiatomique /ɑ̃tiatɔmik/ ADJ anti-radiation ◆ **abri ~** fallout shelter

anti-aveuglant, e /ɑ̃tiavœglɑ̃, ɑ̃t/ ADJ anti-dazzle

anti-avortement /ɑ̃tiavɔʀtəmɑ̃/ ADJ INV anti-abortion, pro-life

antibalistique /ɑ̃tibalistik/ ADJ *[missile]* anti-ballistic

antibiothérapie /ɑ̃tibjoteʀapi/ NF antibiotic therapy

antibiotique /ɑ̃tibjɔtik/ ADJ, NM antibiotic ◆ **être/mettre sous ~s** to be/put on antibiotics

antiblocage /ɑ̃tiblɔkaʒ/ ADJ INV ◆ **système ~ des roues** antilock braking system, ABS

antibogue /ɑ̃tibɔg/ ADJ debugging NM debugging tool

antibois /ɑ̃tibwa/ NM chair-rail

antibrouillard /ɑ̃tibʀujaʀ/ ADJ, NM ◆ **(phare) ~** fog lamp *(Brit)*, fog light *(US)*

antibruit /ɑ̃tibʀɥi/ ADJ INV ◆ **mur ~** *(= qui empêche le bruit)* soundproof wall; *(= qui diminue le bruit)* noise-reducing wall ◆ **campagne ~** campaign against noise pollution

antibuée /ɑ̃tibɥe/ ADJ INV ◆ **dispositif ~** demister ◆ **bombe/liquide ~** anti-mist spray/liquid

anticalcaire /ɑ̃tikalkɛʀ/ ADJ ◆ **poudre ~** water softener NM water softener

anticancéreux, -euse /ɑ̃tikɑ̃seʀø, øz/ ADJ cancer *(épith)* ◆ **centre ~** *(= laboratoire)* cancer research centre; *(= hôpital)* cancer hospital ◆ **médicament ~** anti-cancer drug

anticellulite /ɑ̃tiselylit/ ADJ INV anti-cellulite *(épith)*

anticerne /ɑ̃tisɛʀn/ NM concealer *(to cover shadows under the eyes)*

antichambre /ɑ̃tiʃɑ̃bʀ/ NF antechamber, anteroom ◆ **faire ~** † to wait humbly *ou* patiently (for an audience with sb)

antichar /ɑ̃tiʃaʀ/ ADJ anti-tank

antichoc /ɑ̃tiʃɔk/ ADJ *[montre]* shockproof

antichute /ɑ̃tiʃyt/ ADJ INV ◆ **lotion ~** hair restorer

anticipation /ɑ̃tisipasjɔ̃/ NF 1 *(gén, Sport, Fin, Mus)* anticipation ◆ **par ~** *[rembourser]* in advance ◆ **paiement par ~** payment in advance *ou* anticipation, advance payment ◆ **était-ce une réponse par ~ ?** was he anticipating the question by giving that reply? 2 *(Écon)* **~s** expectations ◆ **~s inflationnistes** inflationary expectations 3 *(futuriste)* **littérature d'~** science fiction ◆ **roman/film d'~** science-fiction *ou* futuristic novel/film 4 *(Ordin)* look-ahead

anticipé, e /ɑ̃tisipe/ (ptp de **anticiper**) ADJ *[élections, retour]* early *(épith)* ◆ **remboursement ~** repayment before due date ◆ **élections ~es** early elections ◆ **retraite ~e** early retirement ◆ **avec mes remerciements ~s** thanking you in advance *ou* in anticipation

anticiper /ɑ̃tisipe/ ▸ conjug 1 ◂ VI *(= prévoir, calculer)* to anticipate; *(en imaginant)* to look *ou* think ahead, to anticipate what will happen; *(en racontant)* to jump ahead ◆ **n'anticipons pas** let's not look *ou* think too far ahead, let's not anticipate ◆ **mais j'anticipe !** but I'm getting ahead of myself! VT INDIR **anticiper sur** *[+ récit, rapport]* to anticipate ◆ **~ sur l'avenir** to anticipate the future ◆ **sans vouloir ~ sur ce que je dirai tout à l'heure** without wishing to go into what I shall say later ◆ **il anticipe bien (sur les balles)** *(Sport)* he's got good anticipation VT *(Comm) [+ paiement]* to pay before due, to anticipate; *(Sport)* to anticipate; *[+ avenir, événement, reprise économique]* to anticipate

anticlérical, e (mpl **-aux**) /ɑ̃tikleʀikal, o/ ADJ anticlerical NM,F anticleric(al)

anticléricalisme /ɑ̃tikleʀikalism/ NM anticlericalism

anticlinal, e (mpl **-aux**) /ɑ̃tiklinal, o/ ADJ, NM anticlinal

anticoagulant, e /ɑ̃tikɔagylɑ̃, ɑ̃t/ ADJ, NM anticoagulant

anticollision /ɑ̃tikɔlizjɔ̃/ ADJ INV ◆ **système ~** collision avoidance system, anti-collision system

anticolonialisme /ɑ̃tikɔlɔnjalism/ NM anticolonialism

anticolonialiste /ɑ̃tikɔlɔnjalist/ ADJ, NMF anticolonialist

anticommunisme /ɑ̃tikɔmynism/ NM anticommunism

anticommuniste /ɑ̃tikɔmynist/ ADJ, NMF anticommunist

anticonceptionnel, -elle /ɑ̃tikɔ̃sɛpsjɔnɛl/ ADJ contraceptive ◆ **moyens ~s** contraceptive methods, methods of birth control

anticonformisme /ɑ̃tikɔ̃fɔʀmism/ NM nonconformism

anticonformiste /ɑ̃tikɔ̃fɔʀmist/ ADJ, NMF nonconformist

anticonstitutionnel, -elle /ɑ̃tikɔ̃stitysjɔnɛl/ ADJ unconstitutional

anticonstitutionnellement /ɑ̃tikɔ̃stitysjɔnɛlmɑ̃/ ADV unconstitutionally

anticorps /ɑ̃tikɔʀ/ NM antibody

anticyclone /ɑ̃tisiklon/ NM anticyclone

anticyclonique /ɑ̃tisiklonik/ ADJ anticyclonic

antidater /ɑ̃tidate/ ▸ conjug 1 ◂ VT to put a false date on ◆ **ces documents ont été antidatés** these documents have been given earlier dates

antidéflagration /ɑ̃tideflagʀasjɔ̃/ ADJ INV ◆ **porte** ~ blast-proof door

antidémarrage /ɑ̃tidemaʀaʒ/ ADJ INV ◆ **dispositif** ~ (engine) immobiliser

antidémocratique /ɑ̃tidemɔkʀatik/ ADJ (= *opposé à la démocratie*) antidemocratic; (= *peu démocratique*) undemocratic

antidépresseur /ɑ̃tidepʀesœʀ/ ADJ M, NM antidepressant

antidérapant, e /ɑ̃tideʀapɑ̃, ɑ̃t/ ADJ *[tapis, sol, surface]* non-slip; *[pneu]* non-skid

antidétonant, e /ɑ̃tidetɔnɑ̃, ɑ̃t/ ADJ, NM antiknock

antidiphtérique /ɑ̃tidifteʀik/ ADJ *[sérum]* diphtheria *(épith)*

antidiurétique /ɑ̃tidjyʀetik/ ADJ, NM antidiuretic

antidopage /ɑ̃tidɔpaʒ/ ADJ *[loi, contrôle]* doping *(épith)*, anti-doping *(épith)* ◆ **subir un contrôle** ~ to be dope-tested

antidote /ɑ̃tidɔt/ NM *(lit, fig)* antidote *(contre, de* for, against)

antidouleur /ɑ̃tidulœʀ/ ADJ INV *[médicament, traitement]* painkilling *(épith)* ◆ **centre** ~ pain control unit NM painkiller

antidrogue /ɑ̃tidʀɔg/ ADJ INV *[lutte]* against drug abuse; *[campagne]* anti-drug(s) ◆ **brigade** ~ drug squad

antidumping /ɑ̃tidœmpiŋ/ ADJ INV antidumping

antiéconomique /ɑ̃tiekɔnɔmik/ ADJ uneconomical

antieffraction /ɑ̃tiefʀaksjɔ̃/ ADJ *[vitres]* burglar-proof

antiémétique /ɑ̃tiemetik/ ADJ, NM antiemetic

anti-émeute(s) /ɑ̃tiemøt/ ADJ *[police, brigade, unité]* riot *(épith)*

antienne /ɑ̃tjɛn/ NF *(Rel)* antiphony; *(fig littér)* chant, refrain

antiépileptique /ɑ̃tiepilɛptik/ ADJ antiepileptic NM antiepileptic drug

antiesclavagisme /ɑ̃tiɛsklavaʒism/ NM opposition to slavery; *(Hist US)* abolitionism

antiesclavagiste /ɑ̃tiɛsklavaʒist/ ADJ antislavery, opposed to slavery *(attrib)*; *(Hist US)* abolitionist NMF opponent of slavery; *(Hist US)* abolitionist

anti-européen, -enne /ɑ̃tiøʀɔpeɛ̃, ɛn/ ADJ anti-European NM,F anti-European ◆ **les ~s du parti** the anti-European wing of the party

antifasciste /ɑ̃tifaʃist/ ADJ, NMF antifascist

antifongique /ɑ̃tifɔ̃ʒik/ ADJ, NM antifungal

anti-g /ɑ̃tiʒe/ ADJ INV ◆ **combinaison** ~ G-suit

antigang /ɑ̃tigɑ̃g/ ADJ INV, NM ◆ **la brigade ~, l'~** the (police) commando squad

antigel /ɑ̃tiʒɛl/ ADJ INV, NM antifreeze

antigène /ɑ̃tiʒɛn/ NM antigen

antigivrant, e /ɑ̃tiʒivʀɑ̃, ɑ̃t/ ADJ anti-icing *(épith)* NM anti-icer

Antigone /ɑ̃tigɔn/ NF Antigone

antigouvernemental, e (mpl **-aux**) /ɑ̃tiguvɛʀnəmɑ̃tal, o/ ADJ antigovernment(al)

antigravitationnel, -elle /ɑ̃tigʀavitasjɔnɛl/ ADJ antigravity *(épith)*

antigrippe /ɑ̃tigʀip/ ADJ INV ◆ **vaccin** ~ flu vaccine

antigros /ɑ̃tigʀo/ ADJ ◆ **racisme** ~ fattism

Antigua-et-Barbuda /ɑ̃tigwaebaʀbyda/ NPL Antigua and Barbuda

antiguais, e /ɑ̃tigwɛ, ɛz/ ADJ Antiguan NM,F **Antiguais(e)** Antiguan

antiguerre /ɑ̃tigɛʀ/ ADJ INV antiwar

antihausse /ɑ̃tios/ ADJ INV *[mesures]* aimed at curbing price rises, anti-inflation *(épith)*

antihéros /ɑ̃tieʀo/ NM anti-hero

antihistaminique /ɑ̃tiistaminik/ ADJ, NM antihistamine

antihygiénique /ɑ̃tiiʒjenik/ ADJ unhygienic

anti-inflammatoire /ɑ̃tiɛ̃flamatwaʀ/ ADJ, NM anti-inflammatory

anti-inflationniste /ɑ̃tiɛ̃flasjɔnist/ ADJ *[mesure]* anti-inflationary, counter-inflationary

anti-IVG /ɑ̃tiiveʒe/ ADJ INV *[commando, mouvement]* pro-life

antijeu /ɑ̃tiʒø/ NM ◆ **faire de l'**~ to be unsporting *ou* unsportsmanlike

antillais, e /ɑ̃tijɛ, ɛz/ ADJ West Indian NM,F **Antillais(e)** West Indian

Antilles /ɑ̃tij/ NFPL ◆ **les** ~ the West Indies ◆ **les Grandes/Petites** ~ the Greater/Lesser Antilles ◆ **les ~ françaises** the French West Indies ◆ **la mer des** ~ the Caribbean Sea

antilope /ɑ̃tilɔp/ NF antelope

antimatière /ɑ̃timatjɛʀ/ NF antimatter

antimilitarisme /ɑ̃timilitaʀism/ NM antimilitarism

antimilitariste /ɑ̃timilitaʀist/ ADJ, NMF antimilitarist

antimissile /ɑ̃timisil/ ADJ antimissile

antimite /ɑ̃timit/ ADJ (anti-)moth *(épith)* NM mothproofing agent, moth repellent; (= *boules de naphtaline*) mothballs

antimoine /ɑ̃timwan/ NM antimony

antimonarchique /ɑ̃timɔnaʀʃik/ ADJ antimonarchist, antimonarchic(al)

antimonarchiste /ɑ̃timɔnaʀʃist/ NMF antimonarchist

antimondialisation /ɑ̃timɔ̃djalizasjɔ̃/ NF antiglobalization

antimondialiste /ɑ̃timɔ̃djalist/ ADJ, NMF antiglobalist

antimoustiques /ɑ̃timustik/ NM INV ◆ **crème** ~ mosquito repellent cream

antimycosique /ɑ̃timikozik/ ADJ, NM antimycotic

antinational, e (mpl **-aux**) /ɑ̃tinasjɔnal, o/ ADJ antinational

antinazi, e /ɑ̃tinazi/ ADJ, NM,F anti-Nazi

antinomie /ɑ̃tinɔmi/ NF antinomy

antinomique /ɑ̃tinɔmik/ ADJ antinomic(al)

antinucléaire /ɑ̃tinykleɛʀ/ ADJ antinuclear ◆ **les (militants) ~s** anti-nuclear campaigners, the anti-nuclear lobby

Antioche /ɑ̃tjɔʃ/ N Antioch

Antiope /ɑ̃tjɔp/ NF (abrév de **acquisition numérique et télévisualisation d'images organisées en pages d'écriture**) ≈ Videotex ®, Teletext ® *(Brit)*, Ceefax ® *(Brit)*

antioxydant, e /ɑ̃tiɔksidɑ̃, ɑ̃t/ ADJ, NM antioxidant

antipaludéen, -enne /ɑ̃tipalydeɛ̃, ɛn/ ADJ anti-malarial NM anti-malarial drug

antipaludique /ɑ̃tipalydik/ ADJ *[vaccin]* antimalarial ◆ **la lutte** ~ the fight against malaria NM anti-malarial drug

antipape /ɑ̃tipap/ NM antipope

antiparasite /ɑ̃tipaʀazit/ ADJ anti-interference *(épith)* ◆ **dispositif** ~ suppressor

antiparasiter /ɑ̃tipaʀazite/ ▸ conjug 1 ◂ VT to fit a suppressor to

antiparlementaire /ɑ̃tipaʀləmɑ̃tɛʀ/ ADJ antiparliamentary

antiparlementarisme /ɑ̃tipaʀləmɑ̃taʀism/ NM antiparliamentarianism

antiparticule /ɑ̃tipaʀtikyl/ NF 1 *(Phys)* antiparticle 2 ◆ **filtre ~s** dust filter

antipasti /ɑ̃tipasti/ NMPL *(Culin)* antipasti

antipathie /ɑ̃tipati/ NF antipathy ◆ **l'~ entre ces deux communautés** the hostility *ou* antipathy between the two communities ◆ **avoir de l'~ pour qn** to dislike sb

antipathique /ɑ̃tipatik/ ADJ *[personne]* disagreeable, unpleasant; *[endroit]* unpleasant ◆ **il m'est** ~ I don't like him, I find him most disagreeable

antipatriotique /ɑ̃tipatʀijɔtik/ ADJ antipatriotic; (= *peu patriote*) unpatriotic

antipatriotisme /ɑ̃tipatʀijɔtism/ NM antipatriotism

antipelliculaire /ɑ̃tipelikylɛʀ/ ADJ antidandruff *(épith)*

antipersonnel /ɑ̃tipɛʀsɔnɛl/ ADJ INV antipersonnel

antiphrase /ɑ̃tifʀɑz/ NF antiphrasis ◆ **par** ~ ironically

antipode /ɑ̃tipɔd/ NM ◆ **les ~s** *(Géog)* the antipodes ◆ **être aux ~s** to be on the other side of the world ◆ **votre théorie est aux ~s de la mienne** our theories are poles apart, your theory and mine are at opposite extremes

antipoétique /ɑ̃tipɔetik/ ADJ unpoetic

antipoison /ɑ̃tipwazɔ̃/ ADJ INV ◆ **centre** ~ treatment centre for poisoning cases

antipoliomyélitique /ɑ̃tipɔljɔmjelitik/ ADJ ◆ **vaccin** ~ polio vaccine

antipollution /ɑ̃tipɔlysjɔ̃/ ADJ INV antipollution *(épith)*

antiprotéase /ɑ̃tipʀɔteɑz/ ADJ, NF ◆ **(molécule)** ~ protease inhibitor

antiprotectionniste /ɑ̃tipʀɔtɛksjɔnist/ ADJ free-trade *(épith)* NMF free trader

antiprurigineux, -euse /ɑ̃tipʀyʀiʒinø, øz/ ADJ, NM antipruritic

antipsychiatrie /ɑ̃tipsikjatʀi/ NF antipsychiatry

antipyrétique /ɑ̃tipiʀetik/ ADJ antipyretic

antipyrine /ɑ̃tipiʀin/ NF antipyrine

antiquaille /ɑ̃tikaj/ NF *(péj)* piece of old junk

antiquaire /ɑ̃tikɛʀ/ NMF antique dealer

antique /ɑ̃tik/ ADJ 1 (= *de l'Antiquité*) *[vase, objet]* antique, ancient; *[style]* ancient ◆ **objets d'art ~s** antiquities 2 *(littér* = *très ancien) [coutume, objet]* ancient; *(péj) [véhicule, chapeau]* antiquated, ancient NM ◆ **l'~** *(de l'Antiquité)* classical art *ou* style

antiquité /ɑ̃tikite/ NF 1 (= *période*) **l'Antiquité** antiquity ◆ **l'Antiquité grecque/romaine** Greek/Roman antiquity ◆ **dès la plus haute Antiquité** since earliest antiquity, from very ancient times 2 (= *ancienneté*) antiquity, (great) age ◆ **de toute** ~ from the beginning of time, from time immemorial 3 (= *objet de l'Antiquité*) piece of classical art; (= *objet ancien*) antique ◆ **~s** (= *œuvres de l'Antiquité*) antiquities; *(= meubles anciens)* antiques ◆ **marchand/magasin d'~s** antique dealer/shop

antirabique /ɑ̃tiʀabik/ ADJ ◆ **vaccin** ~ rabies vaccine

antirachitique /ɑ̃tiʀaʃitik/ ADJ antirachitic

antiracisme /ɑ̃tiʀasism/ NM antiracism

antiraciste /ɑ̃tiʀasist/ ADJ, NMF antiracist, antiracialist *(Brit)*

antiradar /ɑ̃tiʀadaʀ/ ADJ *[missile]* anti-radar *(épith)* NM anti-radar missile

antireflet /ɑ̃tiʀəflɛ/ ADJ INV *[surface]* non-reflecting; *(Photo)* bloomed

antireligieux, -ieuse /ɑ̃tiʀ(ə)liʒjø, jøz/ ADJ antireligious

antirépublicain, e /ɑ̃tiʀepyblikɛ̃, ɛn/ ADJ antirepublican

antirétroviral, e (mpl **-aux**) /ɑ̃tiʀetʀoviʀal, o/ ADJ antiretroviral NM antiretroviral drug

antirévolutionnaire /ɑ̃tiʀevɔlysjɔnɛʀ/ ADJ antirevolutionary

antirides /ɑ̃tiʀid/ ADJ anti-wrinkle *(épith)*

antiroman /ɑ̃tiʀɔmɑ̃/ NM ◆ **l'**~ the antinovel, the anti-roman

antirouille /ɑ̃tiʀuj/ ADJ INV anti-rust *(épith)* NM INV rust inhibitor, anti-rust (paint *ou* primer)

antiroulis /ɑ̃tiʀuli/ ADJ anti-roll *(épith)*

antiscorbutique /ɑ̃tiskɔʀbytik/ ADJ antiscorbutic

antisèche /ɑ̃tisɛʃ/ NF *(arg Scol)* crib, cheat sheet* *(US)*

antiségrégationniste /ɑ̃tisegʀegasjɔnist/ ADJ antisegregationist

antisémite /ɑ̃tisemit/ ADJ anti-Semitic NMF anti-Semite

antisémitisme /ɑ̃tisemitism/ NM anti-Semitism

antisepsie /ɑ̃tisɛpsi/ NF antisepsis

antiseptique /ɑ̃tisɛptik/ ADJ, NM antiseptic

antisida /ɑ̃tisida/ ADJ INV *[campagne, vaccin]* against AIDS, AIDS *(épith)*; *[traitement]* for AIDS, AIDS *(épith)*

antisismique /ɑ̃tisismik/ ADJ earthquake-proof *(épith)*

antislash /ɑ̃tislaʃ/ NM backslash

antisocial, e (mpl **-iaux**) /ɑ̃tisɔsjal, jo/ ADJ *(Pol)* antisocial

anti-sous-marin, e /ɑ̃tisumaʀɛ̃, in/ ADJ anti-submarine

antispasmodique /ɑ̃tispasmɔdik/ ADJ, NM antispasmodic

antisportif, -ive /ɑ̃tispɔʀtif, iv/ ADJ *(opposé au sport)* anti-sport; *(peu élégant)* unsporting, unsportsmanlike

antistatique /ɑ̃tistatik/ ADJ, NM antistatic

antistrophe /ɑ̃tistʀɔf/ NF antistrophe

antisubversif, -ive /ɑ̃tisybvɛʀsif, iv/ ADJ counter-subversive

antitabac /ɑ̃titaba/ ADJ INV ◆ **campagne** ~ anti-smoking campaign ◆ **loi** ~ *law prohibiting smoking in public places*

antitache(s) /ɑ̃titaʃ/ ADJ *[traitement]* stain-repellent

antiterroriste /ɑ̃titeʀɔʀist/ ADJ antiterrorist

antitétanique /ɑ̃titetanik/ ADJ *[sérum]* (anti-)tetanus *(épith)*

antithèse /ɑ̃titɛz/ NF *(gén)* antithesis ◆ **c'est l'~ de** *(= le contraire)* it is the opposite of

antithétique /ɑ̃titetik/ ADJ antithetic(al)

antitout* /ɑ̃titu/ ADJ INV *[personne]* systematically opposed to everything NMF INV person who is systematically opposed to everything

antitoxine /ɑ̃titɔksin/ NF antitoxin

antitoxique /ɑ̃titɔksik/ ADJ antitoxic

antitrust /ɑ̃titʀœst/ ADJ INV *[loi, mesures]* anti-monopoly *(Brit)*, anti-trust *(US)*

antituberculeux, -euse /ɑ̃titybɛʀkylø, øz/ ADJ *[sérum]* tuberculosis *(épith)*

antitumoral, e (pl **-aux**) /ɑ̃titymɔʀal, o/ ADJ *(Méd)* *[substance, action]* anti-tumour *(épith)* *(Brit)*, anti-tumor *(épith)* *(US)*

antitussif, -ive /ɑ̃titysif, iv/ ADJ *[comprimé]* cough *(épith)*, antitussive *(SPÉC)* NM cough mixture, antitussive *(SPÉC)*

antivariolique /ɑ̃tivaʀjɔlik/ ADJ ◆ **vaccin** ~ smallpox vaccine

antivénéneux, -euse /ɑ̃tivenenø, øz/ ADJ antidotal

antivenimeux, -euse /ɑ̃tivənimø, øz/ ADJ ◆ **sérum** ~, **substance antivenimeuse** antivenin, antivenene

antiviral, e (mpl **-aux**) /ɑ̃tiviʀal, o/ ADJ, NM antiviral

antivirus /ɑ̃tiviʀys/ NM *(Méd)* antiviral drug; *(Ordin)* antivirus

antivol /ɑ̃tivɔl/ NM, ADJ INV ◆ **(dispositif)** ~ anti-theft device; *[de cycle]* lock; *(sur volant de voiture)* (steering) lock ◆ **mettre un** ~ **sur son vélo** to put a lock on *ou* to lock one's bike

antonomase /ɑ̃tɔnɔmaz/ NF antonomasia

antonyme /ɑ̃tɔnim/ NM antonym

antonymie /ɑ̃tɔnimi/ NF antonymy

antre /ɑ̃tʀ/ NM *(littér = caverne)* cave; *[d'animal]* den, lair; *(fig)* den; *(Anat)* antrum

anurie /anyʀi/ NF anuria

anus /anys/ NM anus ◆ ~ **artificiel** colostomy

Anvers /ɑ̃vɛʀ/ N Antwerp

anxiété /ɑ̃ksjete/ NF anxiety ◆ **avec** ~ anxiously ◆ **être dans l'**~ to be very anxious *ou* worried

anxieusement /ɑ̃ksjøzmɑ̃/ ADV anxiously

anxieux, -ieuse /ɑ̃ksjø, jøz/ ADJ *[personne, regard]* anxious, worried; *[attente]* anxious ◆ **crises anxieuses** anxiety attacks ◆ ~ **de** anxious to NM,F worrier

anxiogène /ɑ̃ksjɔʒɛn/ ADJ *[situation, effet]* stressful, anxiety-provoking *(SPÉC)*

anxiolytique /ɑ̃ksjɔlitik/ ADJ tranquillizing NM tranquillizer

AOC /aose/ NF (abrév de **appellation d'origine contrôlée**) ◆ **fromage/vin** ~ AOC cheese/wine *(with a guarantee of origin)*

> **AOC**
>
> **AOC** is the highest French wine classification. It indicates that the wine meets strict requirements concerning the vineyard of origin, the type of vine grown, the method of production, and the volume of alcohol present. → **VDQS**

aoriste /aɔʀist/ NM aorist

aorte /aɔʀt/ NF aorta

aortique /aɔʀtik/ ADJ aortic

août /u(t)/ NM August; *pour loc voir* **septembre** *et* **quinze**

aoûtat /auta/ NM harvest tick *ou* mite *(Brit)*, chigger *(US)*

aoûtien, -ienne* /ausjɛ̃, jɛn/ NM,F August holiday-maker *(Brit)* *ou* vacationer *(US)*

AP /ape/ NF (abrév de **Assistance publique**) → **assistance**

ap. (abrév de **après**) after ◆ **en 300** ~ **J.-C.** in 300 AD

apache /apaʃ/ ADJ 1 *(= indien)* Apache 2 († = *canaille*) **il a une allure** ~ he has a tough *ou* vicious look (about him) NMF **Apache** Apache ◆ **les Apaches** the Apaches NM († = *voyou*) ruffian, tough

apaisant, e /apɛzɑ̃, ɑ̃t/ ADJ 1 *(= qui soulage)* *[musique, silence, crème]* soothing 2 *(= pacificateur)* *[discours]* conciliatory

apaisement /apɛzmɑ̃/ NM 1 *[de passion, désir, soif, faim]* appeasement ◆ **après l'~ de la tempête** once the storm had died down 2 *(= soulagement)* relief; *(= assurance)* reassurance ◆ **cela lui procura un certain** ~ this brought him some relief ◆ **donner des ~s à qn** to reassure sb 3 *(Pol)* appeasement ◆ **une politique d'**~ a policy of appeasement

apaiser /apeze/ ▸ conjug 1 ◂ VT 1 *[+ personne, foule]* to calm down, to pacify; *[+ animal]* to calm down 2 *[+ faim]* to appease; *[+ soif]* to slake, to appease; *[+ conscience]* to salve, to soothe; *[+ scrupules]* to allay; *[+ douleur]* to soothe ◆ **pour** ~ **les esprits** to calm people down VPR **s'apaiser** 1 *[personne, malade, animal]* to calm *ou* quieten down 2 *[vacarme, excitation, tempête]* to die down, to subside; *[vagues, douleur]* to die down; *[passion, désir]* to cool; *[soif, faim]* to be assuaged *ou* appeased; *[scrupules]* to be allayed ◆ **sa colère s'est un peu apaisée** he's calmed down a bit

apanage /apanaʒ/ NM *(= privilège)* privilege ◆ **être l'~ de qn/qch** to be the privilege *ou* prerogative of sb/sth ◆ **avoir l'~ de qch** to have the sole *ou* exclusive right to sth, to possess sth exclusively ◆ **il croit avoir l'~ du bon sens** he thinks he's the only one with any common sense

aparté /apaʀte/ NM *(= entretien)* private conversation *(in a group)*; *(Théât, gén = remarque)* aside ◆ **en** ~ in an aside

apartheid /apaʀted/ NM apartheid ◆ **politique d'**~ apartheid policy

apathie /apati/ NF apathy

apathique /apatik/ ADJ apathetic

apathiquement /apatikmɑ̃/ ADV apathetically

apatride /apatʀid/ ADJ stateless NMF stateless person

APE /apeə/ NF (abrév de **Assemblée parlementaire européenne**) EP

APEC /apɛk/ NF (abrév de **Association pour l'emploi des cadres**) executive employment agency

Apennin(s) /apenɛ̃/ NM(PL) ◆ **l'**~, **les ~s** the Apennines

aperception /apɛʀsɛpsjɔ̃/ NF apperception

apercevoir /apɛʀsəvwaʀ/ ▸ conjug 28 ◂ VT 1 *(= voir)* to see; *(brièvement)* to catch sight of, to catch a glimpse of; *(= remarquer)* to notice ◆ **on apercevait au loin un clocher** a church tower could be seen in the distance 2 *(= se rendre compte de)* *[+ danger, contradictions]* to see, to perceive; *[+ difficultés]* to see, to foresee ◆ **si on fait cela, j'aperçois des problèmes** if we do that, I (can) see problems ahead *ou* I (can) foresee problems VPR **s'apercevoir** 1 *(réfléchi)* *[personnes]* to see *ou* notice each other ◆ **elle s'aperçut dans le miroir** she caught a glimpse *ou* caught sight of herself in the mirror 2 *(= se rendre compte)* **s'~ de** to notice ◆ **s'~ que** ... to notice *ou* realize that ... ◆ **sans s'en** ~ without realizing, inadvertently ◆ **ça s'aperçoit à peine** it's hardly noticeable, you can hardly see it

aperçu /apɛʀsy/ NM 1 *(= idée générale)* general survey ◆ ~ **sommaire** brief survey ◆ **cela vous donnera un bon** ~ **de ce que vous allez visiter** that will give you a good idea *ou* a general idea of what you are about to visit 2 *(= point de vue personnel)* insight *(sur* into) 3 *(Ordin)* ~ **avant impression** print preview

apéritif, -ive /apeʀitif, iv/ NM 1 *(= boisson, moment)* apéritif, drink *(taken before lunch or dinner)* ◆ **prendre l'~** to have an apéritif ◆ **venez prendre l'~** come for drinks ◆ **ils sont arrivés à l'~** they came when we were having drinks ◆ **un bon porto ne se boit jamais à l'~** a good port is never drunk as an apéritif ◆ **servir des canapés à l'~** to serve canapés as an appetizer 2 *(fig)* **en guise d'~** as a starter ◆ **en guise d'~, la chaîne a présenté un court métrage de Fellini** as a starter the channel showed a short film by Fellini ADJ *(littér)* ◆ **une boisson apéritive** a drink that stimulates the appetite ◆ **ils firent une promenade apéritive** they went for a walk to work up an appetite

apéro * /apeʀo/ NM abrév de **apéritif**

aperture /apɛʀtyʀ/ NF *(Ling)* aperture

apesanteur /apəzɑ̃tœʀ/ NF weightlessness ◆ **être en (état d') ~** to be weightless

à-peu-près /apøpʀɛ/ NM INV vague approximation ◆ **il est resté dans l'~** he was very vague; → **près**

apeuré, e /apœʀe/ ADJ frightened, scared

apex /apɛks/ NM *(Astron, Bot, Sci)* apex; *(Ling) [de langue]* apex, tip; *(= accent latin)* macron

aphasie /afazi/ NF aphasia

aphasique /afazik/ ADJ, NMF aphasic

aphérèse /afeʀɛz/ NF aphaeresis

aphone /afɔn/ ADJ voiceless, aphonic *(SPÉC)* ◆ **je suis presque ~ d'avoir trop crié** I've nearly lost my voice *ou* I'm hoarse from shouting so much

aphonie /afɔni/ NF aphonia

aphorisme /afɔʀism/ NM aphorism

aphrodisiaque /afʀɔdizjak/ ADJ, NM aphrodisiac

Aphrodite /afʀɔdit/ NF Aphrodite

aphte /aft/ NM ulcer, aphtha *(SPÉC)* ◆ **~ buccal** mouth ulcer

aphteux, -euse /aftø, øz/ ADJ aphthous; → **fièvre**

api /api/ → **pomme**

à-pic /apik/ NM cliff

apical, e (mpl **-aux**) /apikal, o/ ADJ apical ◆ **r ~** trilled r NF **apicale** apical consonant

apico-alvéolaire /apikoalveolɛʀ/ ADJ, NF apico-alveolar

apico-dental, e (mpl **-aux**) /apikodɑ̃tal, o/ ADJ apico-dental NF **apico-dentale** apico-dental

apicole /apikɔl/ ADJ beekeeping *(épith)*, apiarian *(SPÉC)*, apicultural *(SPÉC)*

apiculteur, -trice /apikyltœʀ, tʀis/ NM,F beekeeper, apiarist *(SPÉC)*, apiculturist *(SPÉC)*

apiculture /apikyltyʀ/ NF beekeeping, apiculture *(SPÉC)*

apitoiement /apitwamɑ̃/ NM *(= pitié)* pity, compassion

apitoyer /apitwaje/ ▸ conjug 8 ◂ VT to move to pity ◆ **~ qn sur le sort de qn** to make sb feel sorry for sb ◆ **regard/sourire apitoyé** pitying look/smile VPR **s'apitoyer** ◆ **s'~ sur qn** *ou* **le sort de qn** to feel pity for sb, to feel sorry for sb ◆ **s'~ sur son propre sort** to feel sorry for o.s.

ap. J.-C. (abrév de **après Jésus-Christ**) AD

APL /apeɛl/ NF (abrév de **aide personnalisée au logement**) → **aide**[1]

aplanir /aplaniʀ/ ▸ conjug 2 ◂ VT *[+ terrain, surface]* to level; *[+ difficultés]* to smooth away *ou* out, to iron out; *[+ obstacles]* to smooth away VPR **s'aplanir** *[terrain]* to become level ◆ **les difficultés se sont aplanies** the difficulties smoothed themselves out

aplanissement /aplanismɑ̃/ NM *[de terrain]* levelling; *[de difficultés]* smoothing away, ironing out; *[d'obstacles]* smoothing away

aplat /apla/ NM *(= teinte)* flat tint; *(= surface)* flat, solid (plate)

aplati, e /aplati/ (ptp de **aplatir**) ADJ *[forme, objet, nez]* flat ◆ **c'est ~ sur le dessus/à son extrémité** it's flat on top/at one end

aplatir /aplatiʀ/ ▸ conjug 2 ◂ VT *[+ objet]* to flatten; *[+ couture]* to press flat; *[+ cheveux]* to smooth down, to flatten; *[+ pli]* to smooth (out); *[+ surface]* to flatten (out) ◆ **~ qch à coups de marteau** to hammer sth flat ◆ **~ qn** * to flatten sb * ◆ **~ (le ballon** *ou* **un essai)** *(Rugby)* to score a try, to touch down VPR **s'aplatir** 1 *[personne]* **s'~ contre un mur** to flatten o.s. against a wall ◆ **s'~ par terre** *(= s'étendre)* to lie flat on the ground; *(* = tomber)* to fall flat on one's face ◆ **s'~ devant qn** *(= s'humilier)* to crawl to sb, to grovel before sb 2 *[choses] (= devenir plus plat)* to become flatter; *(= être écrasé)* to be flattened *ou* squashed ◆ **s'~ contre** * *(= s'écraser)* to smash against

aplatissement /aplatismɑ̃/ NM *(gén)* flattening; *(fig = humiliation)* grovelling ◆ **l'~ de la terre aux pôles** the flattening-out *ou* -off of the earth at the poles

aplomb /aplɔ̃/ NM 1 *(= assurance)* composure, (self-)assurance; *(péj = insolence)* nerve *, cheek * *(Brit)* ◆ **garder son ~** to keep one's composure, to remain composed ◆ **perdre son ~** to lose one's composure, to get flustered ◆ **tu ne manques pas d'~ !** you've got a nerve * *ou* a cheek * *(Brit)*!
2 *(= équilibre)* balance, equilibrium; *(= verticalité)* perpendicularity ◆ **perdre l'~** *ou* **son ~** *[personne]* to lose one's balance ◆ **à l'~ du mur** at the base of the wall
◆ **d'aplomb** *[corps]* steady, balanced; *[bâtiment, mur]* plumb ◆ **se tenir d'~ (sur ses jambes)** to be steady on one's feet ◆ **être d'~** *[objet]* to be balanced *ou* level; *[mur]* to be plumb ◆ **ne pas être d'~** *[mur]* to be out of *ou* off plumb ◆ **mettre** *ou* **poser qch d'~** to straighten sth (up) ◆ **le vase n'est pas (posé) d'~** the vase isn't level ◆ **tu n'as pas l'air d'~** * you look under the weather, you look off-colour * *(Brit)* ◆ **remettre d'~** *[+ bateau]* to right; *[+ entreprise]* to put back on its feet ◆ **ça va te remettre d'~** * that'll put you right *ou* on your feet again ◆ **se remettre d'~** *(après une maladie)* to pick up, to get back on one's feet again ◆ **le soleil tombait d'~** the sun was beating down
3 *(Équitation)* **~s** stand

apnée /apne/ NF apnoea *(Brit)*, apnea *(US)* ◆ **être en ~** to be holding one's breath ◆ **plonger en ~** to dive without any breathing apparatus ◆ **~ du sommeil** sleep apnoea *(Brit) ou* apnea *(US)*

apnéiste /apneist/ NMF *diver who dives without breathing apparatus*

apocalypse /apɔkalips/ NF *(Rel)* apocalypse ◆ **l'Apocalypse** *(= livre)* (the Book of) Revelation, the Apocalypse ◆ **atmosphère d'~** doom-laden *ou* end-of-the-world atmosphere ◆ **paysage/vision d'~** apocalyptic landscape/vision

apocalyptique /apɔkaliptik/ ADJ *(Rel)* apocalyptic; *(fig) [paysage, vision]* apocalyptic

apocope /apɔkɔp/ NF apocope

apocryphe /apɔkʀif/ ADJ apocryphal, of doubtful authenticity; *(Rel)* Apocryphal NM apocryphal book ◆ **les ~s** the Apocrypha

apode /apɔd/ ADJ apodal, apodous NM apodal *ou* apodous amphibian ◆ **les ~s** apodal *ou* apodous amphibians, the Apoda *(SPÉC)*

apodictique /apɔdiktik/ ADJ apodictic

apogée /apɔʒe/ NM 1 *(Astron)* apogee 2 *(fig) [de carrière]* peak, height; *[d'art, mouvement]* peak, zenith ◆ **être à son ~** *[carrière]* to reach its peak; *[art, mouvement]* to reach its peak ◆ **artiste à son ~** artist at his *(ou* her) peak ◆ **à l'~ de sa gloire/carrière** at the height of his *(ou* her) fame/career

apolitique /apɔlitik/ ADJ *(= indifférent)* apolitical, unpolitical; *(= indépendant)* non-political

apolitisme /apɔlitism/ NM *(= indifférence)* apolitical *ou* unpolitical attitude; *(= indépendance)* non-political stand; *[d'organisme]* non-political character

apollon /apɔlɔ̃/ NM 1 *(Myth)* **Apollon** Apollo 2 *(= homme)* Apollo, Greek god 3 *(= papillon)* apollo

apologétique /apɔlɔʒetik/ ADJ *(Philos, Rel)* apologetic NF apologetics *(sg)*

apologie /apɔlɔʒi/ NF 1 *(= défense)* apology, apologia ◆ **faire l'~ de** *(gén)* to try and justify; *(Jur)* to vindicate 2 *(= éloge)* praise ◆ **faire l'~ de** to praise, to speak (very) highly of

apologiste /apɔlɔʒist/ NMF apologist

apologue /apɔlɔg/ NM apologue

apophyse /apɔfiz/ NF apophysis

apoplectique /apɔplɛktik/ ADJ apoplectic

apoplexie /apɔplɛksi/ NF apoplexy ◆ **attaque d'~** stroke, apoplectic fit

apoptose /apɔptoz/ NF apoptosis

aporie /apɔʀi/ NF aporia

apostasie /apɔstazi/ NF apostasy

apostasier /apɔstazje/ ▸ conjug 7 ◂ VI to apostatize, to renounce the faith

apostat, e /apɔsta, at/ ADJ, NM,F apostate, renegade

a posteriori /apɔsteʀjɔʀi/ LOC ADV, LOC ADJ *(Philos)* a posteriori; *(gén)* after the event ◆ **il est facile, ~, de dire que …** it is easy enough, after the event *ou* with hindsight, to say that …

apostille /apɔstij/ NF apostil

apostiller /apɔstije/ ▸ conjug 1 ◂ VT to add an apostil to

apostolat /apɔstɔla/ NM *(Bible)* apostolate, discipleship; *(= prosélytisme)* ministry ◆ **il est chargé de l'~ des laïcs** he is responsible for the lay ministry ◆ **c'est une nouvelle forme d'~** it is a new type of ministry ◆ **ce métier est un ~** this job has to be a vocation

apostolique /apɔstɔlik/ ADJ apostolic; → **nonce**

apostrophe[1] /apɔstʀɔf/ NF *(Rhétorique)* apostrophe; *(= interpellation)* rude remark *(shouted at sb)* ◆ **mot mis en ~** word used in apostrophe ◆ **lancer des ~s à qn** to shout rude remarks at sb

apostrophe[2] /apɔstʀɔf/ NF *(Gram)* apostrophe

apostropher /apɔstʀɔfe/ ▸ conjug 1 ◂ VT *(= interpeller)* to shout at, to address sharply VPR **s'apostropher** to shout at each other ◆ **les deux automobilistes s'apostrophèrent violemment** the two motorists hurled abuse at each other

apothème /apɔtɛm/ NM apothem

apothéose /apɔteoz/ NF 1 *(= consécration)* apotheosis ◆ **cette nomination est pour lui une ~** this appointment is a supreme honour for him ◆ **les tragédies de Racine sont l'~ de l'art classique** Racine's tragedies are the apotheosis *ou* pinnacle of classical art ◆ **ça a été l'~ !** *(iro)* that was the last straw! 2 *(gén, Théât = bouquet)* grand finale ◆ **finir dans une ~** to end in a blaze of glory 3 *(Antiq = déification)* apotheosis

apothicaire †† /apɔtikɛʀ/ NM apothecary † ◆ **des comptes d'~** complicated calculations

apôtre /apotʀ/ NM 1 *(Rel)* apostle ◆ **faire le bon ~** to take a holier-than-thou attitude * 2 *(= porte-parole)* advocate, apostle ◆ **se faire l'~ de** to make o.s. the advocate *ou* apostle of

Appalaches /apalaʃ/ NMPL ♦ **les (monts)** ~ the Appalachian Mountains, the Appalachians

appalachien, -ienne /apalaʃjɛ̃, jɛn/ ADJ Appalachian

apparaître /apaʀɛtʀ/ ► conjug 57 ◄ VI 1 (*= se montrer*) *[jour, personne, fantôme]* to appear (*à* to); *[difficulté, vérité]* to appear, to come to light; *[signes, obstacles]* to appear; *[fièvre, boutons]* to break out ♦ **la vérité lui apparut soudain** the truth suddenly dawned on him ♦ **la silhouette qui apparaît/les problèmes qui apparaissent à l'horizon** the figure/the problems looming on the horizon 2 (*= sembler*) to seem, to appear (*à* to); ♦ **ces remarques m'apparaissent fort judicieuses** these comments seem *ou* sound very wise to me ♦ **je dois t'~ comme un monstre** I must seem like a monster to you VB IMPERS ♦ **il apparaît que ...** it appears *ou* turns out that ...

apparat /apaʀa/ NM 1 (*= pompe*) pomp ♦ **d'~** *[dîner, habit, discours]* ceremonial ♦ **en grand ~** (*pompe*) with great pomp and ceremony; (*habits*) in full regalia ♦ **sans ~** *[réception]* unpretentious 2 (*Littérat*) ~ **critique** critical apparatus, apparatus criticus

apparatchik /apaʀatʃik/ NM apparatchik

appareil /apaʀɛj/ GRAMMAIRE ACTIVE 54.2, 54.3, 54.4

NM 1 (*= machine, instrument*) (*gén*) piece of apparatus, device; (*électrique, ménager*) appliance; (*Radio, TV = poste*) set; (*Photo*) camera

2 (*= téléphone*) (tele)phone ♦ **qui est à l'~ ?** who's speaking? ♦ **Paul à l'~** Paul speaking

3 (*= avion*) aircraft (*inv*)

4 (*Méd*) appliance; (*pour fracture*) splint; (*auditif*) hearing aid; (*de contention dentaire*) brace; (* *= dentier*) dentures, plate

5 (*Anat*) apparatus, system ♦ ~ **digestif/respiratoire/urogénital** digestive/respiratory/urogenital apparatus *ou* system ♦ ~ **phonatoire** vocal apparatus *ou* organs

6 (*= structures*) apparatus, machinery ♦ **l'~ policier/du parti** the police/the party apparatus *ou* machinery ♦ **l'~ législatif** *ou* **des lois** the legal apparatus *ou* machinery ♦ **l'~ industriel/militaire/productif** the industrial/military/production apparatus

7 (*littér*) (*= dehors fastueux*) air of pomp; (*= cérémonie fastueuse*) ceremony ♦ **l'~ magnifique de la royauté** the opulent trappings of royalty; → **simple**

8 (*Archit = agencement*) bond

9 (*Gym*) ~**s** apparatus (*sg*) ♦ **exercices aux ~s** exercises on the apparatus, apparatus work

10 (*Culin = préparation*) mixture

COMP **appareil critique** (*Littérat*) critical apparatus, apparatus criticus
appareil électroménager household *ou* domestic appliance
appareil de levage lifting appliance, hoist
appareil de mesure measuring device
appareil orthopédique orthopaedic (*Brit*) *ou* orthopedic (*US*) appliance
appareil photo, appareil photographique camera
appareil à sous † (*= distributeur*) vending machine; (*= jeu*) slot machine, fruit machine (*Brit*)

appareillage /apaʀɛjaʒ/ NM 1 (*Naut*) (*= départ*) casting off, getting under way; (*= manœuvres*) preparations for casting off *ou* getting under way 2 (*= équipement*) equipment ♦ ~ **électrique** electrical equipment 3 *[d'handicapé]* fitting with a prosthesis; *[de sourd]* fitting with a hearing aid 4 (*Archit*) (*= agencement*) bonding; (*= taille*) dressing

appareiller /apaʀeje/ ► conjug 1 ◄ VI (*Naut*) to cast off, to get under way VT 1 (*Naut*) *[+ navire]* to rig, to fit out 2 (*Archit*) (*= agencer*) to bond; (*= tailler*) to dress 3 *[+ handicapé]* to fit with a prosthesis; *[+ sourd]* to fit with a hearing aid 4 (*= coupler*) to pair; (*= assortir*) to match up; (*= accoupler*) to mate (*avec* with)

apparemment /apaʀamɑ̃/ ADV (*= de toute évidence*) apparently; (*= en surface*) seemingly ♦ **théories ~ contradictoires** seemingly contradictory theories ♦ **remarques ~ insignifiantes** seemingly trivial remarks ♦ **il va mieux ?** – ~ is he any better? – apparently

apparence /apaʀɑ̃s/ NF 1 (*= aspect*) *[de maison, personne]* appearance, aspect ♦ ~ **physique** physical appearance ♦ **bâtiment de belle ~** fine-looking building ♦ **il a une ~ négligée** he looks shabby ♦ **homme d'~** *ou* **à l'~ sévère** severe-looking man ♦ **quelques fermes d'~ prospère** some farms that appeared prosperous, some prosperous-looking farms

2 (*= déguisement*) appearance ♦ **sous cette ~ souriante** beneath that smiling exterior ♦ **sous l'~ de la générosité** under the guise of generosity ♦ **ce n'est qu'une (fausse) ~** it's a mere façade

3 ♦ **les ~s** appearances ♦ **les ~s sont contre lui** appearances are against him ♦ **il ne faut pas se fier aux ~s** don't be fooled *ou* deceived by appearances ♦ **tu te fies trop aux ~s** you rely too much on appearances ♦ **sauver les ~s** to keep up appearances ♦ **comme ça, les ~s sont sauves** that way, nobody loses face

4 (*= semblant, vestige*) semblance ♦ **une ~ de liberté** a semblance of freedom

5 (*Philos*) appearance

6 (*locutions*) **malgré l'~** *ou* **les ~s** in spite of appearances ♦ **contre toute ~** against all expectations ♦ **selon toute ~, il s'agit d'un suicide** it would appear *ou* seem that it was suicide, there is every indication that it was suicide

♦ **en apparence** ♦ **en ~, leurs critiques semblent justifiées** on the face of it, their criticism seems justified ♦ **une remarque en ~ pertinente** an apparently *ou* a seemingly relevant remark ♦ **les gens sont rassurés, au moins en ~** people are reassured, at least they seem to be *ou* at least on the face of it ♦ **ce problème n'est facile qu'en ~** this problem only appears to be easy ♦ **ce n'est qu'en ~ qu'il est heureux** it's only on the surface *ou* outwardly that he's happy

apparent, e /apaʀɑ̃, ɑt/ ADJ 1 (*= visible*) *[appréhension, gêne]* obvious, noticeable; *[ruse]* obvious ♦ **de façon ~e** visibly, conspicuously ♦ **sans raison/cause ~e** without apparent *ou* obvious reason/cause ♦ **plafond avec poutres ~es** ceiling with exposed beams ♦ **coutures ~es** topstitched seams 2 (*= superficiel*) *[solidité, causes]* apparent (*épith*) ♦ **ces contradictions ne sont qu'~es** these are only outward *ou* surface discrepancies 3 (*= trompeur*) *[bonhomie, naïveté]* seeming, apparent ♦ **sous son ~e gentillesse** beneath his kind-hearted façade

apparenté, e /apaʀɑ̃te/ (ptp de **apparenter**) ADJ (*= de la même famille*) related; (*= semblable*) similar (*à* to); ♦ ~ **(au parti) socialiste** (*Pol*) in alliance with the Socialists ♦ **les libéraux et ~s** the Liberals and their electoral allies

apparentement /apaʀɑ̃tmɑ̃/ NM (*Pol*) grouping of electoral lists (*in proportional representation system*)

apparenter (s') /apaʀɑ̃te/ ► conjug 1 ◄ VPR **s'apparenter à** (*Pol*) to ally o.s. with (*in elections*); (*par mariage*) to marry into; (*= ressembler à*) to be similar to, to have certain similarities to

appariement /apaʀimɑ̃/ NM (*littér*) (*= assortiment*) matching; (*= assemblage*) pairing; (*= accouplement*) mating

apparier /apaʀje/ ► conjug 7 ◄ VT (*littér*) (*= assortir*) to match; (*= coupler*) to pair; (*= accoupler*) to mate

appariteur /apaʀitœʀ/ NM (*Univ*) ≈ porter (*Brit*), campus policeman (*US*) ♦ ~ **musclé** (*hum*) strong-arm attendant (*hired at times of student unrest*)

apparition /apaʀisjɔ̃/ NF 1 (*= manifestation*) *[d'étoile, symptôme, signe]* appearance; *[de personne]* appearance, arrival; *[de boutons, fièvre]* outbreak ♦ **faire son ~** *[personne]* to make one's appearance, to appear; *[symptômes]* to appear; *[fièvre]* to break out ♦ **il n'a fait qu'une (courte ou brève) ~** (*à une réunion*) he only put in *ou* made a brief appearance; (*dans un film*) he only made a brief appearance, he made a cameo appearance ♦ **par ordre d'~ à l'écran** (*dans générique de film*) in order of appearance 2 (*= vision*) apparition; (*= fantôme*) apparition, spectre (*Brit*), specter (*US*) ♦ **avoir des ~s** to see *ou* have visions

apparoir /apaʀwaʀ/ VB IMPERS (*frm ou hum*) ♦ **il appert (de ces résultats) que ...** it appears (from these results) that ...

appartement /apaʀtəmɑ̃/ NM 1 *[de maison, immeuble]* flat (*Brit*), apartment (*surtout US*); *[d'hôtel]* suite ♦ **vivre dans un** *ou* **en ~** to live in a flat (*Brit*) *ou* apartment (*surtout US*); → **chien, plante**[1] 2 ♦ ~**s** *[de château]* apartments ♦ **elle s'est retirée dans ses ~s** *[reine]* she retired to her apartments; (*hum*) she retired to her room *ou* chamber 3 (* *Can = pièce*) room

appartenance /apaʀtənɑ̃s/ NF (*à une race, une famille, un ensemble*) membership (*à* of); (*à un parti*) adherence (*à* to) membership (*à* of); ♦ **leur sentiment d'~ à cette nation** their sense of belonging to the nation

appartenir /apaʀtəniʀ/ ► conjug 22 ◄ VT INDIR **appartenir à** 1 (*= être la possession de*) to belong to ♦ **ceci m'appartient** this is mine, this belongs to me ♦ **la maison m'appartient en propre** I'm the sole owner of the house ♦ **pour des raisons qui m'appartiennent** for reasons of my own *ou* which concern me (alone) ♦ **le choix ne m'appartient pas** it isn't for me to choose ♦ **un médecin ne s'appartient pas** a doctor's time *ou* life is not his own 2 (*= faire partie de*) *[+ famille, race, parti]* to belong to, to be a member of VB IMPERS ♦ **il appartient/n'appartient pas au comité de décider si ...** it is up to/not up to the committee to decide if ...

appas /apɑ/ NMPL (*littér*) charms

appât /apɑ/ NM (*Pêche*) bait; (*fig*) lure, bait ♦ **mettre un ~ à l'hameçon** to bait one's hook ♦ **l'~ du gain/d'une récompense** the lure of gain/a reward; → **mordre**

appâter /apɑte/ ► conjug 1 ◄ VT *[+ poissons, gibier, personne]* to lure, to entice; *[+ piège, hameçon]* to bait

appauvrir /apovʀiʀ/ ► conjug 2 ◄ VT *[+ personne, sol, langue]* to impoverish; *[+ sang]* to make thin, to weaken VPR **s'appauvrir** *[personne, sol, pays]* to grow poorer, to become (more) impoverished; *[langue]* to become impoverished; *[sang]* to become thin *ou* weak; *[race]* to degenerate

appauvrissement /apovʀismɑ̃/ NM *[de personne, sol, langue, pays]* impoverishment; *[de sang]* thinning; *[de race]* degeneration ♦ **l'~ de la couche d'ozone** the depletion of the ozone layer ♦ **l'~ culturel et intellectuel** cultural and intellectual decline

appeau (pl **appeaux**) /apo/ NM (*= instrument*) bird call; (*= oiseau, fig*) decoy ♦ **servir d'~ à qn** to act as a decoy for sb

appel /apɛl/ NM 1 (*= cri*) call ♦ **accourir à l'~ de qn** to come running in answer to sb's call ♦ ~ **à l'aide** *ou* **au secours** call for help ♦ **elle a entendu des ~s** *ou* **des cris d'~** she heard someone calling out, she heard cries ♦ **à son ~, elle se retourna** she turned round when he called ♦ **l'Appel du 18 juin** (*Hist*) *General de*

Gaulle's radio appeal to the French people to resist the Nazi occupation

2 *(= sollicitation)* call ◆ **dernier ~ pour le vol AF 850** *(dans aéroport)* last call for flight AF 850 ◆ ◆ **à l'insurrection/aux armes/aux urnes** call to insurrection/to arms/to vote ◆ **lancer un ~ au calme** to appeal *ou* call for calm, to issue an appeal for calm ◆ **à l'~ des syndicats ...** in response to the call of the trade unions ... ◆ **manifestation à l'~ d'une organisation** demonstration called by an organization ◆ **il me fit un ~ du regard** he gave me a meaningful glance ◆ **c'était un ~ du pied** it was an indirect *ou* a veiled appeal ◆ **il a fait un ~ du pied au chef de l'autre parti** he made covert advances to the leader of the other party ◆ **faire un ~ de phares** to flash one's headlights *ou* one's high beams *(US)* ◆ **offre/prix d'~** introductory offer/price ◆ **article** *ou* **produit d'~** loss leader

3 *(Jur = recours)* appeal *(contre* against, from*)*; ◆ **faire ~ d'un jugement** to appeal against a judgment ◆ **juger en ~/sans ~** to judge on appeal/without appeal; → **cour**

◆ **sans appel** *(fig) [décision]* final; *[décider]* irrevocably

◆ **faire appel** to appeal, to lodge an appeal

◆ **faire appel à** *(= invoquer)* to appeal to; *(= avoir recours à)* to call on, to resort to *(fig = nécessiter)* to require ◆ **faire ~ au bon sens/à la générosité de qn** to appeal to sb's common sense/generosity ◆ **faire ~ à ses souvenirs** to call up one's memories ◆ **il a dû faire ~ à tout son courage** he had to summon up *ou* muster all his courage ◆ **faire ~ à l'armée** to call in the army ◆ **on a dû faire ~ aux pompiers** they had to call the firemen ◆ **ils ont fait ~ au président pour que ...** they appealed to *ou* called on the president to ... ◆ **ce problème fait ~ à des connaissances qu'il n'a pas** this problem calls for *ou* requires knowledge he hasn't got

4 *(= voix)* call ◆ **l'~ du devoir/de la religion** the call of duty/of religion ◆ **l'~ de la raison/de sa conscience** the voice of reason/of one's conscience ◆ **l'~ du large** the call of the sea

5 *(= vérification de présence) (Scol)* register, registration; *(Mil)* roll call ◆ **absent/présent à l'~** *(Scol)* absent/present (for the register *ou* at registration); *(Mil)* absent/present at roll call ◆ **manquer à l'~** *[élève, militaire]* to be absent at roll call; *[chose, personne]* to be missing ◆ **l'~ des causes** *(Jur)* the reading of the roll of cases *(to be heard)*; → **cahier, manquer, numéro**

◆ **faire l'appel** *(Scol)* to take the register *(Brit)*, to take attendance *(US)*; *(Mil)* to call the roll ◆ **faire l'~ nominal des candidats** to call out the candidates' names

6 *(Mil = mobilisation)* call-up ◆ ◆ **de la classe 1995** 1995 call-up, call-up of the class of 1995; → **devancer**

7 *(Téléc)* ~ **(téléphonique)** (telephone *ou* phone) call ◆ **un poste avec signal d'~** a phone with call waiting function; → **numéro**

8 *(Cartes)* signal *(à* for*)*; ◆ **faire un ~ à pique** to signal for a spade

9 *(Athlétisme = élan)* take-off ◆ **pied d'~** take-off foot

10 *(Ordin)* call

COMP **appel d'air** in-draught *(Brit)*, in-draft *(US)* ◆ **ça fait ~ d'air** there's a draught *(Brit) ou* draft *(US)*

appel en couverture *(Bourse)* request for cover

appel de fonds call for capital ◆ **faire un ~ de fonds** to call up capital

appel à maxima *appeal by prosecution against the harshness of a sentence*

appel à minima *appeal by prosecution against the leniency of a sentence*

appel de note *(Typo)* footnote reference, reference mark

appel d'offres invitation to tender *ou* bid *(US)*

appel au peuple appeal *ou* call to the people

appel à témoins call for witnesses

appel (en) visio *(Téléc)* video call

appelant, e /ap(ə)lɑ̃, ɑ̃t/ *(Jur)* ADJ ◆ **partie ~e** appellant NM,F appellant

appelé /ap(ə)le/ NM *(Mil)* conscript, draftee *(US)*, selectee *(US)* ◆ **il y a beaucoup d'~s et peu d'élus** *(Rel, fig)* many are called but few are chosen

appeler /ap(ə)le/ GRAMMAIRE ACTIVE 54 ▸ conjug 4 ◂

VT 1 *(= interpeller) [+ personne, chien]* to call ◆ ~ **le nom de qn** to call out sb's name ◆ ~ **qn à l'aide** *ou* **au secours** to call to sb for help ◆ ~ **qn (d'un geste) de la main** to beckon (to) sb

2 *(Téléc) [+ personne]* to phone, to call; *[+ numéro]* to dial

3 *(= faire venir) (gén)* to call, to summon; *[+ médecin, taxi, police]* to call, to send for; *[+ pompiers]* to call out; *[+ ascenseur]* to call ◆ ~ **les fidèles à la prière** to summon *ou* call the faithful to prayer ◆ ~ **une classe (sous les drapeaux)** *(Mil)* to call up a class (of recruits) ◆ **Dieu/la République vous appelle** *(frm ou hum)* God/the Republic is calling you ◆ **le devoir m'appelle** *(hum)* duty calls ◆ **le patron l'a fait ~** the boss sent for him ◆ **il a été appelé auprès de sa mère malade** he was called *ou* summoned to his sick mother's side ◆ ~ **la colère du ciel sur qn** to call down the wrath of heaven upon sb ◆ **j'appelle la bénédiction de Dieu sur vous** may God bless you

4 *(Jur)* ~ **une cause** to call (out) a case ◆ **en attendant que notre cause soit appelée** waiting for our case to come up *ou* be called ◆ ~ **qn en justice** *ou* **à comparaître** to summon sb before the court

5 *(= nommer)* to call ◆ ~ **qn par son prénom** to call *ou* address sb by their first name ◆ ~ **qn Monsieur/Madame** to call sb Sir/Madam ◆ ~ **les choses par leur nom** to call things by their rightful name ◆ ~ **un chat un chat** to call a spade a spade ◆ **voilà ce que j'appelle écrire !** now that's what I call writing! ◆ **il va se faire ~ Arthur !*** he's going to get a dressing down* *ou* a rollicking* *(Brit)*

6 *(= désigner)* ~ **qn à** *[+ poste]* to appoint *ou* assign sb to ◆ **être appelé à de hautes/nouvelles fonctions** to be assigned important/new duties ◆ **sa nouvelle fonction l'appelle à jouer un rôle important** his new duties will require him to play an important role ◆ **être appelé à un brillant avenir** to be destined for a brilliant future ◆ **la méthode est appelée à se généraliser** the method looks likely *ou* set to become widely used

7 *(= réclamer) [situation, conduite]* to call for, to demand ◆ **j'appelle votre attention sur ce problème** I call your attention to this problem ◆ **ses affaires l'appellent à Lyon** he has to go to Lyons on business ◆ ~ **qch de ses vœux** to wish for sth

8 *(= entraîner)* **une lâcheté en appelle une autre** one act of cowardice leads to *ou* begets *(frm)* another ◆ **ceci appelle une réflexion** *ou* **une remarque** this calls for comment

9 *(Cartes) [+ carte]* to call for

10 *(Ordin) [+ fichier]* to call (up)

VI 1 *(= crier)* ~ **à l'aide** *ou* **au secours** to call for help ◆ **elle appelait, personne ne venait** she called (out) but nobody came

2 ◆ **en ~ à** to appeal to ◆ **en ~ de** to appeal against ◆ **j'en appelle à votre bon sens** I appeal to your common sense

VPR **s'appeler** 1 *(= être nommé)* to be called ◆ **il s'appelle Paul** his name is Paul, he's called Paul ◆ **comment s'appelle cet oiseau ?** what's the name of this bird?, what's this bird called? ◆ **comment ça s'appelle en français ?** what's that (called) in French?, what do you call that in French? ◆ **voilà ce qui s'appelle une gaffe/être à l'heure !** now that's what's called a blunder/being on time! ◆ **je te prête ce livre, mais il s'appelle Reviens !*** I'll lend you this book but I want it back! ◆ **elle ne sait plus comment elle s'appelle*** *(= désorientée)* she's totally confused, she doesn't know what day it is*

2 *[personnes]* to call to each other ◆ **on s'appelle ce soir (au téléphone)** you ring me or I'll ring you this evening ◆ **nous nous appelons par nos prénoms** we're on first-name terms, we call each other by our first names

appellatif /apelatif/ ADJ M, NM *(Ling)* ◆ **(nom) ~** appellative

appellation /apelasjɔ̃/ NF designation, appellation; *(littér = mot)* term, name ◆ ~ **d'origine** label of origin ◆ ~ **(d'origine) contrôlée** appellation (d'origine) contrôlée *(label guaranteeing the origin of wine and cheese)* ◆ **vin d'~** appellation contrôlée wine, wine carrying a guarantee of origin

appendice /apɛ̃dis/ NM *[de livre]* appendix; *(Anat) (gén)* appendage, appendix ◆ **l'~** *[d'intestin]* the appendix ◆ ~ **nasal** *(hum)* nose

appendicectomie /apɛ̃disɛktɔmi/ NF appendectomy

appendicite /apɛ̃disit/ NF appendicitis ◆ **faire de l'~ chronique** to have a grumbling appendix ◆ **avoir une crise d'~** to have appendicitis ◆ **se faire opérer de l'~** to have one's appendix removed

appendiculaire /apɛ̃dikylɛʀ/ ADJ appendicular NMPL **appendiculaires** ◆ **les ~s** appendicularians, the Appendicularia *(SPÉC)*

appentis /apɑ̃ti/ NM *(= bâtiment)* lean-to; *(= auvent)* penthouse (roof), sloping roof

appert /apɛʀ/ → **apparoir**

appertisé, e /apɛʀtize/ ADJ *[denrée]* sterilized (in a hermetic container)

appesantir /apəzɑ̃tiʀ/ ▸ conjug 2 ◂ VT *[+ tête, paupières]* to weigh down; *[+ objet]* to make heavier; *[+ gestes, pas]* to slow (down); *[+ esprit]* to dull ◆ ~ **son bras** *ou* **autorité sur** *(littér)* to strengthen one's authority over VPR **s'appesantir** *[tête]* to grow heavier; *[gestes, pas]* to become slower; *[esprit]* to grow duller; *[autorité]* to grow stronger ◆ **s'~ sur un sujet/des détails** to dwell at length on a subject/on details ◆ **inutile de s'~** no need to dwell on that

appesantissement /apəzɑ̃tismɑ̃/ NM *[de démarche]* heaviness; *[d'esprit]* dullness; *[d'autorité]* strengthening

appétence /apetɑ̃s/ NF appetence ◆ **avoir de l'~ pour** to have a partiality for, to be partial to

appétissant, e /apetisɑ̃, ɑ̃t/ ADJ *[nourriture]* appetizing, mouth-watering; *[personne]* delectable ◆ **peu ~** unappetizing

appétit /apeti/ NM 1 *(pour la nourriture)* appetite ◆ **avoir de l'~, avoir bon ~, avoir un solide ~** to have a good *ou* hearty appetite ◆ **bon ~ !** *(hôte)* bon appétit!; *(serveur)* enjoy your meal!, enjoy! *(US)* ◆ **perdre l'~** to lose one's appetite ◆ **il n'a pas d'~** he's got no appetite ◆ **ouvrir l'~ de qn, donner de l'~ à qn, mettre qn en ~** to give sb an appetite ◆ **ce premier essai m'a mis en ~** *(fig)* this first attempt has given me a taste for it *ou* has whetted my appetite ◆ **avoir un ~ d'oiseau/d'ogre** to eat like a bird/horse ◆ **manger avec ~** *ou* **de bon ~** to eat heartily *ou* with appetite ◆ **manger sans ~** to eat without appetite ◆ **l'~ vient en mangeant** *(lit)* appetite comes with eating; *(fig)* you get a taste for it

2 *(= désir)* appetite *(de* for*)*; ◆ ~ **sexuel** sexual appetite

applaudimètre /aplodimɛtʀ/ NM applause meter, clapometer* *(Brit)* ◆ **elle a gagné à l'~** she got the loudest *ou* warmest applause

applaudir /aplodiʀ/ ▸ conjug 2 ◂ VT to applaud, to clap; (= *approuver*) to applaud, to commend ◆ **applaudissons notre sympathique gagnant** let's give the winner a big hand VI to applaud, to clap ◆ ~ **à tout rompre** to bring the house down VT INDIR **applaudir à** (*littér* = *approuver*) [+ *initiative*] to applaud, to commend ◆ ~ **des deux mains à qch** to approve heartily of sth, to commend sth warmly VPR **s'applaudir** (= *se réjouir*) **je m'applaudis de n'y être pas allé !** I'm congratulating myself *ou* patting myself on the back for not having gone!

applaudissement /aplodismɑ̃/ NM 1 (= *acclamations*) ~**s** applause (NonC), clapping (NonC) ◆ **des ~s nourris éclatèrent** loud applause *ou* clapping broke out ◆ **sortir sous les ~s** to go off to great applause ◆ **un tonnerre d'~s** thunderous applause 2 (*littér* = *approbation*) approbation, commendation (*à* of)

applicabilité /aplikabilite/ NF applicability

applicable /aplikabl/ ADJ applicable ◆ **être ~ à** [*loi*] to apply to, to be applicable to ◆ **ce règlement est difficilement ~** this rule is difficult to apply

applicateur /aplikatœʀ/ ADJ M applicator (*épith*) NM (= *dispositif*) applicator

applicatif, -ive /aplikatif, iv/ ADJ ◆ **logiciel ~** application

application /aplikasjɔ̃/ NF 1 (= *pose*) [*d'enduit, peinture, pommade*] application ◆ **renouveler l'~ tous les jours** apply every day

2 (= *mise en pratique*) (*gén*) application; [*de peine*] enforcement; [*de règlement, décision*] implementation; [*de loi*] enforcement, application; [*de remède*] administration; [*de recette*] use ◆ **mettre en ~** [+ *décision*] to put into practice, to implement; [+ *loi*] to enforce, to apply; [+ *théorie*] to put into practice, to apply ◆ **mise en ~** [*de décision*] implementation; [*de loi*] enforcement, application; [*de théorie*] application ◆ **mesures prises en ~ de la loi** measures taken to enforce *ou* apply the law ◆ **entrer en ~** to come into force ◆ **champ d'~** area of application

3 ◆ ~**s** [*de théorie, méthode*] applications ◆ **les ~s de cette théorie** the (possible) applications of the theory

4 (= *attention*) application ◆ ~ **à qch** application to sth ◆ **travailler avec ~** to work diligently, to apply o.s. ◆ **son ~ à faire qch** the zeal with which he does sth

5 (*Couture*) appliqué (work) ◆ ~ **de dentelles** appliqué lace ◆ ~ **de velours** velvet appliqué

6 (*Math*) mapping

7 (*Ordin*) application (program)

applique /aplik/ NF (= *lampe*) wall light; (*Couture*) appliqué

appliqué, e /aplike/ (ptp de **appliquer**) ADJ 1 [*personne*] industrious, assiduous; [*écriture*] careful ◆ **bien ~** [*baiser*] firm; [*coup*] well-aimed 2 [*linguistique, mathématiques*] applied

appliquer /aplike/ ▸ conjug 1 ◂ VT 1 (= *poser*) [+ *peinture, revêtement, cataplasme*] to apply (*sur* to); ◆ ~ **une échelle sur** *ou* **contre un mur** to put *ou* lean a ladder against a wall ◆ ~ **son oreille sur** *ou* **à une porte** to put one's ear to a door

2 (= *mettre en pratique*) (*gén*) to apply; [+ *peine*] to enforce; [+ *règlement, décision*] to implement, to put into practice; [+ *loi*] to enforce, to apply; [+ *remède*] to administer; [+ *recette*] to use ◆ ~ **un traitement à une maladie** to apply a treatment to an illness

3 (= *consacrer*) ~ **son esprit à l'étude** to apply one's mind to study ◆ ~ **tous ses soins à faire qch** to put all one's effort into doing sth

4 (= *donner*) [+ *gifle, châtiment*] to give; [+ *qualificatif*] to use ◆ ~ **un baiser/sobriquet à qn** to give sb a kiss/nickname ◆ **je lui ai appliqué ma main sur la figure** I struck *ou* slapped him across the face, I struck *ou* slapped his face

VPR **s'appliquer** 1 (= *coïncider*) **s'~ sur** to fit over ◆ **le calque s'applique exactement sur son modèle** the tracing fits exactly over its model

2 (= *correspondre*) **s'~ à** to apply to ◆ **cette remarque ne s'applique pas à vous** this remark doesn't apply to you

3 (= *s'acharner*) **s'~ à faire qch** to make every effort to do sth ◆ **s'~ à l'étude de** to apply o.s. to the study of ◆ **élève qui s'applique** pupil who applies himself

appog(g)iature /apɔ(d)ʒjatyʀ/ NF appoggiatura

appoint /apwɛ̃/ NM 1 (= *monnaie*) **l'~** the right *ou* exact change ◆ **faire l'~** to give the right *ou* exact change ◆ **"prière de faire l'appoint"** (*sur pancarte*) "exact change only please" 2 (= *complément*) (extra) contribution, (extra) help ◆ **salaire d'~** secondary *ou* extra income ◆ **travail d'~** second job ◆ **radiateur d'~** back-up *ou* extra heater

appointements /apwɛ̃tmɑ̃/ NMPL salary

appointer /apwɛ̃te/ ▸ conjug 1 ◂ VT to pay a salary to ◆ **être appointé à l'année/au mois** to be paid yearly/monthly

appontage /apɔ̃taʒ/ NM landing (*on an aircraft carrier*)

appontement /apɔ̃tmɑ̃/ NM landing stage, wharf

apponter /apɔ̃te/ ▸ conjug 1 ◂ VI to land (*on an aircraft carrier*)

apport /apɔʀ/ NM 1 (= *approvisionnement*) [*de capitaux*] contribution, supply; [*de chaleur, air frais, eau potable*] supply ◆ **l'~ de devises par le tourisme** the currency that tourism brings in ◆ **leur ~ financier** their financial contribution ◆ ~ **personnel** (*Fin*) personal capital contribution, ≃ deposit (*when buying a house*) ◆ **l'~ d'alluvions d'une rivière** the alluvia brought *ou* carried down by a river ◆ **l'~ de** *ou* **en vitamines d'un aliment** the vitamins provided by *ou* the vitamin content of a food ◆ ~ **calorique** [*d'aliment*] calorie content ◆ **l'~ calorique quotidien** the daily calorie intake

2 (= *contribution*) contribution ◆ **l'~ de notre civilisation à l'humanité** our civilization's contribution to humanity

3 (*Jur*) ~**s** property ◆ ~**s en communauté** *goods contributed by man and wife to the joint estate* ◆ ~**s en société** (*Fin*) capital invested

apporter /apɔʀte/ ▸ conjug 1 ◂ VT 1 [+ *objet*] to bring ◆ **apporte-le-moi** bring it to me ◆ **apporte-le-lui** take it to him ◆ **apporte-le en montant** bring it up with you ◆ **apporte-le en venant** bring it with you (when you come), bring it along ◆ **qui a apporté toute cette boue ?** who brought in all this mud? ◆ **le vent d'ouest nous apporte toutes les fumées d'usine** the west wind blows *ou* carries all the factory fumes our way ◆ **vent qui apporte la pluie** wind that brings rain

2 [+ *satisfaction, repos, soulagement*] to bring, to give; [+ *ennuis, argent, nouvelles*] to bring; [+ *preuve, solution*] to supply, to provide ◆ ~ **sa contribution à qch** to make one's contribution to sth ◆ ~ **des modifications à qch** [*ingénieur*] to make *ou* introduce changes in sth; [*progrès*] to bring about changes in sth ◆ ~ **du soin à qch/à faire qch** to exercise care in sth/in doing sth ◆ ~ **de l'attention à qch/à faire qch** to bring one's attention to bear on sth/on doing sth ◆ **elle y a apporté toute son énergie** she put all her energy into it ◆ **son livre n'apporte rien de nouveau** his book contributes *ou* says nothing new ◆ **leur enseignement m'a beaucoup apporté** I got a lot out of their teaching ◆ **s'~ beaucoup** (*couple*) to get a lot out of being together

apposer /apoze/ ▸ conjug 1 ◂ VT (*frm*) [+ *sceau, timbre, plaque*] to affix; [+ *signature*] to append (*frm*); (*Jur*) [+ *clause*] to insert ◆ ~ **les scellés** (*Jur*) to affix the seals (*to prevent unlawful entry*) ◆ ~ **une mention sur un produit** to display consumer information on a product

apposition /apozisjɔ̃/ NF 1 (*Gram*) apposition ◆ **en ~** in apposition 2 [*de sceau, timbre, plaque, scellés*] affixing; [*de signature*] appending (*frm*); (*Jur*) [*de clause*] insertion

appréciable /apʀesjabl/ ADJ 1 (= *évaluable*) noticeable ◆ **la différence était ~** the difference was noticeable 2 (= *assez important*) appreciable ◆ **un nombre ~ de gens** a good many *ou* a good few people 3 (= *agréable*) [*qualité, situation*] nice, pleasant ◆ **c'est ~ de pouvoir se lever tard** it's nice to be able to get up late

appréciateur, -trice /apʀesjatœʀ, tʀis/ NM,F judge, appreciator

appréciatif, -ive /apʀesjatif, iv/ ADJ (= *estimatif*) appraising, evaluative; (= *admiratif*) appreciative; → **état**

appréciation /apʀesjasjɔ̃/ NF 1 (= *évaluation*) [*de distance, importance*] estimation, assessment; (= *expertise*) [*d'objet*] valuation ◆ ~ **des risques** (*Assurances*) estimation of risks, risk assessment 2 (= *jugement*) **soumettre qch à l'~ de qn** to ask for sb's assessment of sth ◆ **je laisse cela à votre ~** I leave you to judge for yourself ◆ **commettre une erreur d'~** to be mistaken in one's assessment ◆ **les ~s du professeur sur un élève** the teacher's assessment of a pupil ◆ **"appréciation du professeur"** (*sur livret*) "teacher's comments *ou* remarks" 3 (= *augmentation*) [*de monnaie*] appreciation

apprécier /apʀesje/ GRAMMAIRE ACTIVE 34.2, 34.3 ▸ conjug 7 ◂

VT 1 (= *aimer*) [+ *qualité*] to value; [+ *repas*] to enjoy ◆ ~ **qn** (= *le trouver sympathique*) to like sb; (= *l'estimer*) to value sb ◆ **un plat très apprécié en Chine** a very popular dish in China ◆ **son discours n'a pas été apprécié par la droite** his speech did not go down well with the right ◆ **je n'apprécie guère votre attitude** I don't like your attitude ◆ **il n'a pas apprécié !** he wasn't too happy!

2 (= *évaluer*) [+ *distance, importance*] to estimate, to assess; (= *expertiser*) [+ *objet*] to value, to assess the value of ◆ **ils ont visité le site pour ~ la qualité des installations** they visited the site to assess the quality of the facilities

3 (= *discerner*) [+ *nuance*] to perceive

VPR **s'apprécier** 1 (= *s'estimer*) to like each other ◆ **ils s'apprécient beaucoup** they really like each other

2 (*Fin*) to rise, to appreciate ◆ **le franc s'est nettement apprécié par rapport au mark** the franc has risen *ou* appreciated sharply against the mark

appréhender /apʀeɑ̃de/ ▸ conjug 1 ◂ VT 1 (= *arrêter*) to apprehend 2 (= *redouter*) to dread ◆ ~ **(de faire) qch** to dread (doing) sth ◆ ~ **que ...** to fear that ... 3 (= *comprendre*) [+ *situation*] to apprehend, to grasp

appréhensif, -ive /apʀeɑ̃sif, iv/ ADJ apprehensive, fearful (*de* of)

appréhension /apʀeɑ̃sjɔ̃/ NF 1 (= *crainte*) apprehension, anxiety ◆ **envisager qch avec ~** to be apprehensive *ou* anxious about sth ◆ **avoir de l'~** to be apprehensive ◆ **son ~ de l'examen/de l'avenir** his anxiety *ou* fears about the exam/the future 2 (= *compréhension*) [*de situation, réalité*] apprehension

apprenant, e /apʀənɑ̃, ɑ̃t/ NM,F learner

apprendre /apʀɑ̃dʀ/ ▸ conjug 58 ◂ VT 1 [+ *leçon, métier*] to learn ◆ ~ **que/à lire/à nager** to learn that/(how) to read/(how) to swim ◆ ~ **à se servir de qch** to learn (how) to use sth ◆ ~ **à connaître qn** to get to know sb ◆ **il apprend**

vite he's a quick learner, he learns quickly ◆ **l'espagnol s'apprend vite** *ou* **facilement** Spanish is easy to learn; → **cœur**

2 *[+ nouvelle]* to hear, to learn; *[+ événement, fait]* to hear of, to learn of; *[+ secret]* to be told *(de qn* by sb); ◆ **j'ai appris hier que ...** I heard *ou* learnt yesterday that ... ◆ **j'ai appris son arrivée par des amis/par la radio** I heard of *ou* learnt of his arrival through friends/on the radio ◆ **apprenez que je ne me laisserai pas faire !** be warned that *ou* let me make it quite clear that I won't be trifled with!

3 *(= annoncer)* ~ **qch à qn** to tell sb (of) sth ◆ **il m'a appris la nouvelle** he told me the news ◆ **il m'apprend à l'instant sa démission/qu'il va partir** he has just told me of his resignation/that he's going to leave ◆ **vous ne m'apprenez rien !** you haven't told me anything new! *ou* anything I don't know already!, that's no news to me!

4 *(= enseigner)* ~ **qch à qn** to teach sb sth, to teach sth to sb ◆ ~ **à qn à faire** to teach sb (how) to do ◆ **il a appris à son chien à obéir/qu'il doit obéir** he taught his dog to obey/that he must obey ◆ **je vais lui ~ à vivre** I'll teach him a thing or two, I'll straighten *ou* sort *(Brit)* him out ◆ **ça lui apprendra (à vivre) !** that'll teach him (a lesson)! ◆ **on n'apprend pas à un vieux singe à faire des grimaces** don't teach your grandmother to suck eggs *(Brit)*

apprenti, e /apʀɑ̃ti/ **NM,F** *[de métier]* apprentice; *(= débutant)* novice, beginner ◆ ~ **conducteur** learner driver *(Brit)*, student driver *(US)* ◆ ~ **mécanicien** apprentice *ou* trainee mechanic, mechanic's apprentice ◆ ~ **philosophe** *(péj)* novice philosopher ◆ ~ **sorcier** sorcerer's apprentice ◆ **jouer à l'~ sorcier** *ou* **aux ~s sorciers** to play God

apprentissage /apʀɑ̃tisaʒ/ **NM** 1 *(= formation)* apprenticeship ◆ **mettre qn en ~** to apprentice sb *(chez* to); ◆ **être en ~** to be apprenticed *ou* an apprentice *(chez* to); ◆ **faire son ~** to serve one's apprenticeship, to do one's training *(chez* with); ◆ **faire son ~ de mécanicien** to serve one's apprenticeship as a mechanic ◆ **école** *ou* **centre d'~** training school

2 *(= initiation)* **l'~ de l'anglais/ de la lecture/de l'amour** learning English/(how) to read/about love ◆ **l'~ de la patience** learning to be patient, learning patience

◆ **faire l'apprentissage de** *[+ douleur, vie active]* to have one's first experience of, to be initiated into ◆ **le pays fait le difficile ~ de la démocratie** the country is taking its first difficult steps in democracy; → **contrat, taxe**

apprêt /apʀɛ/ **NM** 1 *(= opération) [de cuir, tissu]* dressing; *[de papier]* finishing; *(Peinture)* sizing, priming 2 *(= substance) [de cuir, tissu]* dressing; *(= peinture)* size, primer ◆ **couche d'~** coat of primer 3 *(= affectation)* **sans ~** unaffected ◆ **elle est d'une beauté sans ~** she has a kind of natural beauty

apprêtage /apʀɛtaʒ/ **NM** *[de cuir, tissu]* dressing; *[de papier]* finishing; *[de peinture]* sizing, priming

apprêté, e /apʀete/ (ptp de **apprêter**) **ADJ** *(= affecté) [manière, style]* affected

apprêter /apʀete/ ► conjug 1 ◄ **VT** 1 *[+ nourriture]* to prepare, to get ready ◆ ~ **un enfant/une mariée** *(= habiller)* to get a child/bride ready, to dress a child/bride 2 *[+ peau, papier, tissu]* to dress, to finish; *[+ surface à peindre]* to size, to prime **VPR s'apprêter** 1 ◆ **s'~ à qch/à faire qch** *(= se préparer)* to get ready for sth/to do sth, to prepare (o.s.) for sth/to do sth ◆ **nous nous apprêtions à partir** we were getting ready *ou* preparing to leave ◆ **je m'apprêtais à le dire** I was just about to say so 2 *(= faire sa toilette)* to dress o.s., to prepare o.s.

apprivoisable /apʀivwazabl/ **ADJ** tameable ◆ **difficilement ~** difficult to tame

apprivoisé, e /apʀivwaze/ (ptp de **apprivoiser**) **ADJ** tame, tamed

apprivoisement /apʀivwazmɑ̃/ **NM** *(= action)* taming; *(= état)* tameness

apprivoiser /apʀivwaze/ ► conjug 1 ◄ **VT** *[+ animal, personne difficile]* to tame; *[+ personne timide]* to bring out of his *(ou* her) shell ◆ **je commence tout juste à ~ l'ordinateur** I'm just beginning to get to grips with the computer **VPR s'apprivoiser** *[animal]* to become tame; *[personne difficile]* to become easier to get on with; *[personne timide]* to come out of one's shell

approbateur, -trice /apʀɔbatœʀ, tʀis/ **ADJ** approving ◆ **signe de tête ~** nod of approval, approving nod **NM,F** *(littér)* approver

approbatif, -ive /apʀɔbatif, iv/ **ADJ** ⇒ **approbateur, -trice**

approbation /apʀɔbasjɔ̃/ GRAMMAIRE ACTIVE 40.2 **NF** *(= jugement favorable)* approval, approbation; *(= acceptation)* approval ◆ **donner son ~ à un projet** to give one's approval to a project ◆ **ce livre a rencontré l'~ du grand public** this book has been well received by the public ◆ **conduite/travail digne d'~** commendable behaviour/work ◆ ~ **des comptes** *(Fin)* approval of the accounts

> ⚠ Attention à ne pas traduire automatiquement **approbation** par le mot anglais **approbation**, qui est d'un registre plus soutenu.

approchable /apʀɔʃabl/ **ADJ** *[chose]* accessible; *[personne]* approachable ◆ **le ministre est difficilement ~** the minister is rather inaccessible *ou* is not very accessible

approchant, e /apʀɔʃɑ̃, ɑ̃t/ **ADJ** *[style, genre]* similar *(de* to); *[résultat]* close *(de* to); ◆ **quelque chose d'~** something like that, something similar ◆ **rien d'~** nothing like that

approche /apʀɔʃ/ **NF** 1 *(= arrivée) [de personne, véhicule, événement]* approach ◆ **à mon ~ il sourit** he smiled as I came up to him ◆ **à l'~ de l'hiver** at the approach of winter, as winter approached ◆ **"(train) à l'approche"** *(dans une gare)* "train now approaching" ◆ **s'enfuir à l'~ du danger** to flee at the first sign of danger ◆ **à l'~** *ou* **aux ~s de la cinquantaine, il ...** as he neared *ou* approached fifty, he ...; → **lunette, travail**[1]

2 *(= abord)* **être d'~ difficile** *[personne]* to be unapproachable, to be difficult to approach; *[lieu]* to be inaccessible, to be difficult of access; *[musique, auteur]* to be difficult to understand ◆ **être d'~ aisée** *[personne]* to be approachable, to be easy to approach; *[lieu]* to be (easily) accessible; *[musique, auteur]* to be easy to understand ◆ **manœuvres** *ou* **travaux d'~** *(Mil)* approaches; *(fig)* manoeuvres, manoeuvrings

3 *(= parages)* **les ~s de la ville** the area (immediately) surrounding the town ◆ **aux ~s de la ville elle pensa ...** as she neared *ou* approached the town she thought ... ◆ **les ~s de l'île sont dangereuses** the waters around the island are dangerous

4 *(= façon d'envisager)* approach ◆ **l'~ de ce problème** the approach to this problem ◆ **ce n'est qu'une ~ sommaire de la question** this is only a brief introduction to the question

5 *(Typo) (= espace)* spacing; *(= faute)* spacing error; *(= signe)* close-up mark

6 *(en avion)* **nous sommes en ~ finale** we are on our final approach

7 *(Golf)* approach ◆ **coup d'~** approach shot

approché, e /apʀɔʃe/ (ptp de **approcher**) **ADJ** *[résultat, idée]* approximate

approcher /apʀɔʃe/ ► conjug 1 ◄ **VT** 1 *[+ objet]* to put nearer, to move nearer ◆ ~ **une table d'une fenêtre** to move a table nearer to a window ◆ **approche ta chaise** bring your chair nearer *ou* closer ◆ **il approcha les deux chaises l'une de l'autre** he moved the two chairs closer together ◆ **il approcha le verre de ses lèvres** he lifted *ou* raised the glass to his lips ◆ **elle approcha son visage du sien** she brought her face close to his

2 *[+ personne] (= aller)* to go near, to approach; *(= venir)* to come near, to approach ◆ **ne l'approchez pas !** don't go near him!, keep away from him!

3 *(= côtoyer)* to be in contact with; *(= entrer en contact avec)* to approach

VI *[date, saison]* to approach, to draw near; *[personne, orage]* to approach, to come nearer; *[nuit, jour]* to approach, to draw on ◆ **le jour approche où ...** the day is approaching when ... ◆ **approchez, approchez !** come closer! ◆ **approche que je t'examine** come here and let me look at you

VT INDIR approcher de *[+ lieu]* to approach, to get closer to ◆ **nous approchons du but** we're getting there ◆ ~ **de la perfection** to come close to perfection ◆ **il approche de la cinquantaine** he's approaching *ou* he's getting on for fifty ◆ **l'aiguille du compteur approchait du 80** the needle on the speedometer was approaching *ou* nearing 80

VPR s'approcher *(= venir)* to come near, to approach; *(= aller)* to go near, to approach ◆ **il s'est approché pour me parler** he came up to speak to me ◆ **l'enfant s'approcha de moi** the child came up to me ◆ **ne t'approche pas de moi** don't come near me ◆ **s'~ du micro** *(venir)* to come up to the mike; *(se rapprocher)* to get closer *ou* nearer to the mike ◆ **approche-toi !** come here! ◆ **approchez-vous du feu** go and sit *(ou* stand) near the fire ◆ **s'~ de la réalité** to come near to reality

approfondi, e /apʀɔfɔ̃di/ (ptp de **approfondir**) **ADJ** *[connaissances, étude]* thorough, detailed; *[débat]* in-depth

approfondir /apʀɔfɔ̃diʀ/ ► conjug 2 ◄ **VT** 1 *[+ canal, puits]* to deepen, to make deeper 2 *[+ question, étude]* to go (deeper) into; *[+ connaissances]* to deepen, to increase ◆ **il vaut mieux ne pas ~ le sujet** it's better not to go into the matter too closely ◆ **sans ~** superficially

approfondissement /apʀɔfɔ̃dismɑ̃/ **NM** *[de canal, puits]* deepening (NonC); *[de connaissances]* deepening (NonC), increasing (NonC) ◆ **l'~ de cette étude serait souhaitable** it would be a good idea to take this study further

appropriation /apʀɔpʀijasjɔ̃/ **NF** 1 *(Jur)* appropriation 2 *(= adaptation)* suitability, appropriateness *(à* to)

approprié, e /apʀɔpʀije/ (ptp de **approprier**) **ADJ** appropriate ◆ **la recherche d'une solution ~e à la crise** the effort to find an appropriate solution to the crisis ◆ **il n'est pas toujours facile de trouver le traitement ~** it's not always easy to find the appropriate *ou* right treatment ◆ **"tout le monde" semble une réponse ~e à cette question** "everybody" seems to be the answer to this question

approprier /apʀɔpʀije/ ► conjug 7 ◄ **VT** *(= adapter)* to suit, to adapt *(à* to); ◆ ~ **son style à l'auditoire** to suit one's style to one's audience, to adapt one's style to (suit) one's audience **VPR s'approprier** 1 *(= s'adjuger) [+ bien]* to appropriate; *[+ pouvoir, droit, propriété, découverte]* to take over, to appropriate 2 *(= s'adapter à)* **s'~ à** to be appropriate to, to suit

approuver /apʀuve/ GRAMMAIRE ACTIVE 38.1, 38.2, 40.3, 40.4 ► conjug 1 ◄ **VT** 1 *(= être d'accord avec) [+ attitude]* to approve of ◆ **il a démissionné et je l'approuve** he resigned, and I agree with him *ou* approve (of his doing so) ◆ **on a besoin**

de se sentir approuvé one needs to feel the approval of others ◆ **je n'approuve pas qu'il parte maintenant** I don't approve of his leaving now [2] *(= avaliser) [+ comptes, médicament, procès-verbal, nomination]* to approve; *[+ projet de loi]* to approve, to pass; *[+ contrat]* to ratify; → **lu**

approvisionnement /apʀɔvizjɔnmɑ̃/ **NM** [1] *(= action)* supplying *(en, de* of); ◆ **l'~ en légumes de la ville** supplying the town with vegetables ◆ **~s sauvages** panic buying [2] *(= réserves)* supplies, stock ◆ **il avait tout un ~ de cigarettes** he was well stocked with cigarettes, he had a large stock of cigarettes

approvisionner /apʀɔvizjɔne/ ► conjug 1 ◄ **VT** *[+ magasin, commerçant]* to supply *(en, de* with); *[+ compte bancaire]* to pay *ou* put money into; *[+ fusil]* to load ◆ **ils sont bien approvisionnés en fruits** they are well supplied *ou* stocked with fruit **VPR s'approvisionner** to stock up *(en* with) to lay in supplies *(en* of); ◆ **s'~ en bois** to stock up with wood, to get supplies of wood ◆ **je m'approvisionne au supermarché** I shop at the supermarket

approvisionneur, -euse /apʀɔvizjɔnœʀ, øz/ **NM,F** supplier

approximatif, -ive /apʀɔksimatif, iv/ **ADJ** *[calcul, évaluation, traduction]* rough; *[nombre, prix]* approximate; *[termes]* vague ◆ **parler un français ~** to speak broken French

approximation /apʀɔksimasjɔ̃/ **NF** *(gén)* approximation, (rough) estimate; *(Math)* approximation ◆ **par ~s successives** by trial and error

approximativement /apʀɔksimativmɑ̃/ **ADV** *[calculer, évaluer]* roughly; *[compter]* approximately

appt (abrév de **appartement**) apt

appui /apɥi/ **NM** [1] *(lit, fig)* support; *(Alpinisme)* press hold ◆ **prendre ~ sur** *[personne]* to lean on; *(du pied)* to stand on; *[objet]* to rest on ◆ **son pied trouva un ~** he found a foothold ◆ **avoir besoin d'~** to need (some) support ◆ **trouver un ~ chez qn** to receive support from sb ◆ **j'ai cherché un ~ auprès de lui** I turned to him for support ◆ **avoir l'~ de qn** to have sb's support *ou* backing ◆ **il a des ~s au ministère** he has connections in the ministry

◆ **à l'appui** in support of this, to back this up ◆ **avec preuves à l'~** with evidence to prove it ◆ **il m'a expliqué comment faire avec démonstration à l'~** he told me how to do it and backed this up with a demonstration ◆ **à l'~ de son témoignage** in support of his evidence, to back up his evidence; → **barre, point¹**

[2] *(Mus) [de voix]* placing ◆ **consonne d'~** *(Poésie)* supporting consonant ◆ **voyelle d'~** support vowel

COMP appui aérien air support
appui de fenêtre window ledge
appui financier financial support *ou* backing
appui logistique logistic backup *ou* support
appui tactique tactical support

appuie-bras /apɥibʀa/ **NM INV** armrest

appuie-main (pl **appuie-main(s)**) /apɥimɛ̃/ **NM** maulstick

appuie-tête (pl **appuie-tête(s)**) /apɥitɛt/ **NM** *[de voiture, fauteuil de dentiste]* headrest, head restraint; *[de fauteuil]* antimacassar

appuyé, e /apɥije/ (ptp de **appuyer**) **ADJ** *(= insistant) [regard]* fixed, intent; *[geste]* emphatic; *(= excessif) [politesse]* overdone ◆ **il a rendu un hommage ~ à son collègue** he paid a glowing tribute to his colleague

appuyer /apɥije/ GRAMMAIRE ACTIVE 53.2, 53.6 ► conjug 8 ◄

VT [1] *(= poser) [+ objet, coudes, front]* to lean *(contre* against; *sur* on); ◆ **~ une échelle contre un mur** to lean *ou* stand a ladder against a wall ◆ **~ sa main sur l'épaule de qn** to rest one's hand on sb's shoulder

[2] *(= presser)* to press ◆ **il dut ~ son genou sur la valise pour la fermer** he had to press *ou* push the suitcase down with his knee to close it ◆ **appuie ton doigt sur le pansement** put *ou* press your finger on the dressing

[3] *(= étayer)* **~ un mur par qch** to support *ou* prop up a wall with sth

[4] *(= soutenir) [+ personne, candidature, politique]* to support, to back ◆ **il a appuyé sa thèse de documents convaincants** his thesis was well documented ◆ **~ la demande de qn** to support sb's request

[5] *(Mil) [+ attaque]* to back up ◆ **l'offensive sera appuyée par l'aviation** the offensive will be backed up from the air *ou* given air support

VI [1] *(= presser sur)* **~ sur** *[+ bouton]* to press, to push; *[+ frein]* to apply, to put one's foot on; *[+ pédales]* to press down on; *[+ levier]* to press (down); *[+ gâchette]* to pull ◆ **~ sur le champignon*** to step on the gas*, to put one's foot down *(Brit)*

[2] *(= reposer sur)* **~ sur** to rest on ◆ **la voûte appuie sur des colonnes** the vault rests on columns *ou* is supported by columns

[3] *(= insister sur)* **~ sur** *[+ mot, argument, syllabe]* to stress, to emphasize; *(Mus) [+ note]* to accentuate, to accent ◆ **n'appuyez pas trop** don't press the point ◆ **~ sur la chanterelle** to harp on

[4] *(= se diriger)* **~ sur la droite** *ou* **à droite** to bear (to the) right

VPR s'appuyer [1] *(= s'accoter)* **s'~ sur/contre** to lean on/against ◆ **appuie-toi à mon bras** lean on my arm

[2] *(fig = compter)* **s'~ sur** *[+ personne, autorité]* to lean on ◆ **s'~ sur un parti** *(Pol)* to rely on the support of a party ◆ **s'~ sur l'amitié de qn** to rely *ou* depend on sb's friendship ◆ **s'~ sur des découvertes récentes pour démontrer ...** to use recent discoveries to demonstrate ... ◆ **sur quoi vous appuyez-vous pour avancer cela ?** what evidence do you have to support what you're saying?

[3] *(* = subir) [+ importun, discours ennuyeux]* to put up with*; *[+ corvée]* to take on ◆ **qui va s'~ le ménage ?** who'll get landed* with the housework? ◆ **chaque fois c'est nous qui nous appuyons toutes les corvées** it's always us who get stuck* *ou* landed* with all the chores ◆ **il s'est appuyé le voyage de nuit** he ended up having to travel at night

âpre /ɑpʀ/ **ADJ** [1] *[goût, vin]* pungent, acrid; *[hiver, vent, temps]* bitter, harsh; *[son, voix, ton]* harsh [2] *[vie]* harsh; *[combat, discussion]* bitter; *[détermination, résolution]* grim; *[concurrence, critique]* fierce ◆ **après d'~s marchandages** after some intense haggling [3] ◆ **~ au gain** grasping, greedy

âprement /ɑpʀəmɑ̃/ **ADV** *[lutter]* bitterly, grimly; *[critiquer]* fiercely

après /apʀɛ/

GRAMMAIRE ACTIVE 33.2

1 PRÉPOSITION	2 ADVERBE

1 - PRÉPOSITION

[1] temps after ◆ **il est entré ~ elle** he came in after her ◆ **venez ~ 8 heures** come after 8 ◆ **~ beaucoup d'hésitations il a accepté** after much hesitation he accepted ◆ **~ tout ce que j'ai fait pour lui** after everything I've done for him ◆ **tu l'injuries, et ~ ça tu t'étonnes qu'il se vexe** you insult him and then you're surprised that he takes offence ◆ **jour ~ jour** day after day, day in day out ◆ **page ~ page** page after page, page upon page

◆ **après** + *infinitif* ◆ **~ avoir lu ta lettre, je ...** after I read *ou* after reading your letter, I ... ◆ **elle s'est décidée ~ avoir longtemps hésité** she made up her mind after much hesitation ◆ **~ être rentré chez lui, il ...** after he got home, he ... ◆ **~ manger** when you've *(ou* I've *etc)* eaten ◆ **ce sont des propos d'~ boire** it's the drink talking

◆ **après coup** after the event, afterwards ◆ **il n'a compris/réagi qu'~ coup** he didn't understand/react until afterwards

◆ **après que** + *indicatif* after ◆ **~ que je l'ai quittée** after I left her ◆ **venez me voir ~ que vous lui aurez parlé** come and see me after *ou* when you've spoken to him

◆ **après quoi** ◆ **elle l'a grondé, ~ quoi il a été sage** she told him off and after that he behaved himself

◆ **et (puis) après?** *(pour savoir la suite)* and then what?; *(pour marquer l'indifférence)* so what?*, what of it?

[2] ordre d'importance, hiérarchie **sa famille passe ~ ses malades** his family comes after *ou* second to his patients ◆ **~ le capitaine vient le lieutenant** after captain comes lieutenant ◆ **~ vous, je vous en prie** after you

◆ **après tout** after all ◆ **~ tout, ce n'est qu'un enfant** after all he is only a child ◆ **et pourquoi pas, ~ tout ?** after all, why not?

[3] espace *(= plus loin que)* after, past; *(= derrière)* behind, after ◆ **~ le pont, la route rétrécit** the road narrows after the bridge ◆ **sa maison est (juste) ~ la mairie** his house is (just) past the town hall ◆ **j'étais ~ elle dans la queue** I was behind *ou* after her in the queue ◆ **le chien court ~ sa balle** the dog's running after his ball ◆ **elle traîne toujours ~ elle 2 petits chiens** she's always got 2 little dogs in tow

[4] en s'accrochant **grimper ~ un poteau** to climb (up) a pole ◆ **sa jupe s'accrochait ~ les ronces** her skirt kept catching on the brambles

[5] *: agressivité at ◆ **le chien aboyait ~ eux** the dog was barking at them ◆ **il est furieux ~ eux** he's mad* at them ◆ **~ qui en a-t-il ?** who has he got it in for?* ◆ **elle est toujours ~ lui** *(surveillance)* she's always breathing down his neck*; *(harcèlement)* she's always (going) on at him* *(Brit) ou* nagging (at) him, she keeps on at him all the time*

[6] locutions

◆ **d'après**

(= en suivant un modèle, un auteur etc) ◆ **portrait peint d'~ nature** portrait painted from life ◆ **dessin d'~ Ingres** drawing after Ingres, drawing in the style *ou* manner of Ingres ◆ **scénario d'~ un roman de Balzac** screenplay adapted from a novel by Balzac

(= selon) ◆ **d'~ lui/elle** according to him/her, in his/her opinion ◆ **d'~ moi** in my opinion ◆ **(à en juger) d'~ son regard/ce qu'il a dit** from the look he gave/what he said ◆ **ne jugez pas d'~ les apparences** don't go *ou* judge by appearances ◆ **ne jugez pas d'~ ce qu'il dit** don't go by what he says ◆ **d'~ la météo/les sondages** according to the weather forecast/the polls ◆ **d'~ ma montre** by my watch

2 - ADVERBE

[1] dans le temps *(= ensuite)* afterwards, next; *(= plus tard)* later ◆ **venez me voir ~** come and see me afterwards ◆ **aussitôt ~** immediately *ou* straight after(wards) ◆ **longtemps ~** long *ou* a long time after(wards) ◆ **qu'allons-nous faire ~ ?** what are we going to do next? *ou* afterwards? ◆ **~, c'est ton tour** it's your turn next ◆ **deux jours/semaines ~** two days/weeks later ◆ **les réformes, ce sera pour ~** reforms will come later ◆ **~ tu iras dire que ...** next you'll be saying that ... ◆ **il est resté**

deux jours, et ~ il est parti he stayed two days and afterwards *ou* and then he left

2 dans l'espace **tu vois la poste ? sa maison est juste** ~ do you see the post office? his house is just a bit further on ◆ **ce crochet là-bas, ton manteau est pendu** ~ your coat's (hanging) on that peg over there

3 dans un ordre **qu'est-ce qui vient ~ ?** what comes next?, what's to follow? ◆ **il pense surtout à ses malades, sa famille passe ~** he thinks of his patients first, his family comes second ◆ **~, nous avons des articles moins chers** otherwise we have cheaper things

4 locutions

◆ **d'après** (= *suivant*) ◆ **la semaine/le mois d'~** (*dans le temps*) the following *ou* next week/month, the week/month after ◆ **le train d'~ est plus rapide** the next train is faster ◆ **tu vois le cinéma ? c'est la rue d'~** (*dans l'espace*) do you see the cinema? it's the next street along (from there)

---

après-demain /apʀɛd(ə)mɛ̃/ ADV the day after tomorrow

après-dîner † (pl **après-dîners**) /apʀɛdine/ NM evening ◆ **conversations d'~** after-dinner conversations

après-guerre (pl **après-guerres**) /apʀɛgɛʀ/ NM post-war years ◆ **d'~** post-war (*épith*)

après-midi /apʀɛmidi/ NM *ou* NF INV afternoon ◆ **dans l'~** in the afternoon

après-rasage (pl **après-rasages**) /apʀɛʀɑzaʒ/ ADJ INV [*lotion, mousse*] aftershave (*épith*) NM aftershave

après-shampo(o)ing (pl **après-shampo(o)ings**) /apʀɛʃɑ̃pwɛ̃/ NM (hair) conditioner

après-ski (pl **après-ski(s)**) /apʀɛski/ NM 1 (= *chaussure*) snow boot 2 (= *loisirs*) **l'~** après-ski ◆ **tenue d'~** après-ski outfit

après-soleil /apʀɛsɔlɛj/ ADJ INV after-sun (*épith*) NM INV after-sun cream (*ou* lotion)

après-vente /apʀɛvɑ̃t/ ADJ INV ◆ **(service) ~** after-sales service

âpreté /ɑpʀəte/ NF 1 [*de goût, vin*] pungency; [*d'hiver, vent, temps*] bitterness, harshness; [*de son, voix, ton*] harshness 2 [*de vie*] harshness; [*de discussion*] bitterness; [*de détermination, résolution*] grimness; [*de concurrence, critique*] fierceness

a priori /apʀijɔʀi/ LOC ADV (*Philos*) a priori; (*gén*) [*intéressant, surprenant*] at first sight ◆ **refuser qch ~** to refuse sth out of hand ◆ **~, la date ne devrait pas changer** in principle, the date shouldn't change ◆ **tu es libre samedi ? – ~ oui** are you free on Saturday? – I should be LOC ADJ (*Philos*) a priori NM INV (*Philos*) apriorism; (*gén*) prejudice ◆ **avoir des ~** to be biased *ou* prejudiced (*envers* towards; *contre* against); ◆ **j'ai abordé le problème sans ~** I approached the problem with an open mind

apriorisme /apʀijɔʀism/ NM apriorism

aprioriste /apʀijɔʀist/ ADJ aprioristic, apriorist (*épith*) NMF a priori reasoner, apriorist

à-propos /apʀɔpo/ NM (= *présence d'esprit*) presence of mind; [*de remarque, acte*] aptness ◆ **avec beaucoup d'~ le gouvernement a annoncé ...** with consummate timing the government has announced ... ◆ **répondre avec ~** to make an apt *ou* a suitable reply ◆ **avoir beaucoup d'~** (*dans ses réponses*) to have the knack of saying the right thing; (*dans ses actes*) to have the knack of doing the right thing ◆ **son manque d'~ lui nuit** his inability to say *ou* do the right thing does him a lot of harm ◆ **avoir l'esprit d'~** to be quick off the mark

APS /apeɛs/ NM (abrév de **Advanced Photo System**) APS

apte /apt/ ADJ 1 ◆ **~ à qch** capable of sth ◆ **~ à faire** capable of doing, able to do ◆ **~ à exercer une profession** (*intellectuellement*) (suitably) qualified for a job; (*physiquement*) capable of doing a job ◆ **je ne suis pas ~ à juger** I'm not able *ou* not in a position to judge ◆ **~ (au service)** (*Mil*) fit for service 2 (*Jur*) **~ à** fit to *ou* for

aptère /aptɛʀ/ ADJ [*animal*] apterous; [*temple*] apteral ◆ **la Victoire ~** the apteral Victory

aptéryx /apteʀiks/ NM (= *oiseau*) kiwi

aptitude /aptityd/ NF 1 (= *faculté*) aptitude, ability; (= *don*) gift, talent ◆ **test d'~** aptitude test ◆ **son ~ à étudier** *ou* **à** *ou* **pour l'étude** his aptitude for study *ou* studying ◆ **avoir de grandes ~s** to be very gifted *ou* talented 2 (*Jur*) fitness (*à* to)

apurement /apyʀmɑ̃/ NM [*de comptes*] auditing; [*de dette*] discharging, wiping off

apurer /apyʀe/ ▸ conjug 1 ◂ VT [+ *comptes*] to audit; [+ *dette*] to discharge, to wipe off

aquacole /akwakɔl/ ADJ ◆ **élevage ~** (= *activité*) aquaculture, fish farming; (= *entreprise*) fish farm

aquaculteur, -trice /akwakyltœʀ, tʀis/ NM,F (*gén*) aquaculturalist; [*de poissons*] fish farmer

aquaculture /akwakyltyʀ/ NF (*gén*) aquiculture, aquaculture; [*de poissons*] fish farming

aquafortiste /akwafɔʀtist/ NMF aquafortist, etcher

aquagym /akwaʒim/ NF aquaerobics (*sg*)

aquaplanage /akwaplanaʒ/ NM aquaplaning

aquaplane /akwaplan/ NM aquaplane

aquaplaning /akwaplaniŋ/ NM ⇒ **aquaplanage**

aquarelle /akwaʀɛl/ NF (= *technique*) watercolours (*Brit*), watercolors (*US*); (= *tableau*) watercolour (*Brit*), watercolor (*US*) ◆ **faire de l'~** to paint in watercolours

aquarellé, e /akwaʀele/ ADJ [*dessin*] done in watercolour(s) (*Brit*) *ou* watercolor(s) (*US*)

aquarelliste /akwaʀelist/ NMF watercolourist (*Brit*), watercolorist (*US*)

aquariophile /akwaʀjɔfil/ NMF tropical fish enthusiast, aquarist

aquariophilie /akwaʀjɔfili/ NF keeping tropical fish

aquarium /akwaʀjɔm/ NM aquarium, fish tank ◆ **~ d'eau de mer** marine aquarium

aquatique /akwatik/ ADJ 1 (= *qui vit dans l'eau*) [*plante*] aquatic, water (*épith*) ◆ **animal ~** aquatic animal ◆ **oiseau ~** aquatic bird, water-bird 2 **paysage ~** (*sous l'eau*) underwater landscape; (*marécageux*) watery landscape ◆ **parc ~** aqua park

aquavit /akwavit/ NM aquavit

aqueduc /ak(ə)dyk/ NM (*Tech, Anat*) aqueduct

aqueux, -euse /akø, øz/ ADJ aqueous; → **humeur**

à quia /akɥija/ LOC ADV (*littér*) ◆ **mettre qn ~** to nonplus sb ◆ **être ~** to be at a loss for a reply

aquifère /akɥifɛʀ/ ADJ ◆ **nappe ~** aquifer, water-bearing layer *ou* stratum NM aquifer

aquilin, e /akilɛ̃, in/ ADJ aquiline

aquilon /akilɔ̃/ NM (*littér*) north wind

A.R. 1 (abrév de **Altesse royale**) → **altesse** 2 (abrév de **aller (et) retour**) → **aller**

ara /aʀa/ NM macaw

arabe /aʀab/ ADJ [*désert*] Arabian; [*nation, peuple*] Arab; [*art, langue, littérature*] Arabic, Arab ◆ **(cheval) ~** Arab (horse); → **république, téléphone** NM (= *langue*) Arabic ◆ **l'~ littéral** written Arabic NM **Arabe** Arab NF **Arabe** Arab woman (*ou* girl)

arabesque /aʀabɛsk/ NF arabesque ◆ **~ de style** stylistic ornament, ornament of style

arabica /aʀabika/ NM arabica

Arabie /aʀabi/ NF Arabia ◆ **le désert d'~** the Arabian desert COMP **Arabie Saoudite** Saudi Arabia

arabique /aʀabik/ ADJ Arabian; → **gomme**

arabisant, e /aʀabizɑ̃, ɑt/ NM,F Arabist, Arabic scholar

arabisation /aʀabizasjɔ̃/ NF arabization

arabiser /aʀabize/ ▸ conjug 1 ◂ VT to arabize

arabisme /aʀabism/ NM Arabism

arable /aʀabl/ ADJ arable

arabo-islamique (pl **arabo-islamiques**) /aʀaboislamik/ ADJ Arab-Islamic

arabophone /aʀabɔfɔn/ ADJ Arabic-speaking (*épith*) NMF Arabic speaker

arachide /aʀaʃid/ NF (= *plante*) groundnut (plant); (= *graine*) peanut, groundnut, monkey nut (*Brit*)

arachnéen, -enne /aʀakneɛ̃, ɛn/ ADJ (*littér* = *léger*) gossamer (*épith*), of gossamer; (= *propre à l'araignée*) arachnidan

arachnide /aʀaknid/ NM arachnid ◆ **les ~s** the Arachnida (*SPÉC*)

arachnoïde /aʀaknɔid/ NF arachnoid (membrane)

arachnoïdien, -ienne /aʀaknɔidjɛ̃, jɛn/ ADJ arachnoid

arack /aʀak/ NM arrack

araignée /aʀeɲe/ NF 1 (= *animal*) spider (= *araignée de mer*) spider crab ◆ **il a une ~ au plafond** * he's got a screw loose *, he's got bats in the belfry * (*Brit*) ◆ **~ du matin, chagrin, ~ du soir, espoir** (*Prov*) seeing a spider in the morning brings bad luck, seeing a spider in the evening brings good luck; → **toile** 2 (= *crochet*) grapnel 3 (*Boucherie*) *cut of beef used to make steaks* 4 (*Pêche*) square net

COMP **araignée d'eau** water strider, pondskater

araignée de mer spider crab

araire /aʀɛʀ/ NM swing plough (*Brit*) *ou* plow (*US*)

arak /aʀak/ NM ⇒ **arack**

araméen, -enne /aʀameɛ̃, ɛn/ ADJ Aram(a)ean, Aramaic NM (= *langue*) Aramaic, Aram(a)ean NM,F **Araméen(ne)** Aram(a)ean

Ararat /aʀaʀa(t)/ N ◆ **le mont ~** Mount Ararat

arasement /aʀɑzmɑ̃/ NM 1 (= *mise à niveau*) [*de mur*] levelling; [*de bois*] (*en rabotant*) planing (-down); (*en sciant*) sawing 2 (*Géol*) [*de relief*] erosion

araser /aʀɑze/ ▸ conjug 1 ◂ VT 1 (= *mettre de niveau*) to level; (*en rabotant*) to plane (down); (*en sciant*) to saw; (= *diminuer*) to reduce 2 (*Géol*) [+ *relief*] to erode

aratoire /aʀatwaʀ/ ADJ ploughing (*Brit*), plowing (*US*) ◆ **travaux ~s** ploughing ◆ **instrument ~** ploughing implement

araucaria /aʀokaʀja/ NM monkey puzzle (tree), araucaria

arbalète /aʀbalɛt/ NF crossbow

arbalétrier /aʀbaletʀije/ NM 1 (= *personne*) crossbowman 2 (= *poutre*) rafter

arbitrage /aʀbitʀaʒ/ NM 1 (*Comm, Pol* = *action*) arbitration; (*Bourse*) arbitrage; (= *sentence*) arbitrament ◆ **~ obligatoire** compulsory arbitration ◆ **recourir à l'~** to go to arbitration 2 (*Boxe, Ftbl, Rugby*) refereeing; (*Cricket, Hockey, Tennis*) umpiring ◆ **erreur d'~** refereeing error; (*Cricket, Hockey, Tennis*) umpiring error

arbitragiste /aʀbitʀaʒist/ NMF (Bourse) arbitrager, arbitrageur

arbitraire /aʀbitʀɛʀ/ ADJ (= despotique, contingent) arbitrary NM ♦ **le règne de l'~** the reign of the arbitrary ♦ **l'~ du signe linguistique/d'une décision** the arbitrary nature ou the arbitrariness of the linguistic sign/of a decision

arbitrairement /aʀbitʀɛʀmɑ̃/ ADV arbitrarily

arbitral, e (mpl -aux) /aʀbitʀal, o/ ADJ 1 (Jur) arbitral 2 (Boxe, Ftbl, Rugby) referee's (épith); (Cricket, Hockey, Tennis) umpire's (épith) ♦ **décision ~e** referee's ou umpire's decision

arbitre /aʀbitʀ/ NM 1 (Boxe, Ftbl, Rugby) referee, ref*; (Cricket, Hockey, Tennis) umpire ♦ **faire l'~** to (be the) referee ou umpire ♦ **~ de chaise** (Tennis) umpire; → **libre** 2 (= conciliateur) arbiter; (Jur) arbitrator ♦ **servir d'~ dans un conflit social** to act as an arbiter ou arbitrate in an industrial dispute ♦ **~ du bon goût** arbiter of (good) taste

arbitrer /aʀbitʀe/ ▸ conjug 1 ◂ VT 1 [+ conflit] to arbitrate; [+ personnes] to arbitrate between; (Fin) to carry out an arbitrage operation on 2 (Boxe, Ftbl, Rugby) to referee; (Cricket, Hockey, Tennis) to umpire

arboré, e /aʀbɔʀe/ ADJ [région] wooded; [jardin] planted with trees

arborer /aʀbɔʀe/ ▸ conjug 1 ◂ VT [+ vêtement] to sport; [+ sourire] to wear; [+ air] to display; [+ décoration] to sport, to display; [+ drapeau] to bear, to display ♦ **le journal arbore un gros titre** the paper is carrying a big headline ♦ **~ l'étendard de la révolte** to bear the standard of revolt

arborescence /aʀbɔʀesɑ̃s/ NF (Agr) arborescence; (Ling, Math) tree (diagram); (Ordin) tree (structure)

arborescent, e /aʀbɔʀesɑ̃, ɑ̃t/ ADJ [plante] arborescent ♦ **fougère ~e** tree fern ♦ **réseau ~** tree network ♦ **menu ~** (Ordin) menu tree, tree-structured menu

arboretum /aʀbɔʀetɔm/ NM arboretum

arboricole /aʀbɔʀikɔl/ ADJ [technique] arboricultural; [animal] arboreal

arboriculteur, -trice /aʀbɔʀikyltœʀ, tʀis/ NM,F tree grower, arboriculturist (SPÉC)

arboriculture /aʀbɔʀikyltyʀ/ NF tree cultivation, arboriculture (SPÉC)

arborisé, e /aʀbɔʀize/ ADJ planted with trees, arborized (SPEC)

arbouse /aʀbuz/ NF arbutus berry

arbousier /aʀbuzje/ NM arbutus, strawberry tree

arbre /aʀbʀ/ NM 1 (Bot, Ling) tree ♦ **faire l'~ fourchu/droit** to do a handstand (with one's legs apart/together) ♦ **les ~s vous cachent la forêt** (fig) you can't see the wood (Brit) ou forest (US) for the trees ♦ **c'est abattre** ou **couper l'~ pour avoir le fruit** that's sacrificing long-term gains for short-term profits ♦ **faire grimper** ou **faire monter qn à l'~*** to have sb on*, to pull sb's leg* ♦ **entre l'~ et l'écorce il ne faut pas mettre le doigt** (Prov) do not meddle in other people's affairs

2 [de moteur] shaft

COMP **arbre d'agrément** ou **d'ornement** ornamental tree
arbre à cames camshaft ♦ **avec ~ à cames en tête** with overhead camshaft
arbre d'entraînement drive shaft
arbre fruitier fruit tree
arbre généalogique family tree ♦ **faire son ~ généalogique** to draw up one's family tree
arbre d'hélice propeller shaft
arbre de Judée Judas tree
arbre de mai May tree
arbre-manivelle NM (pl **arbres-manivelles**) crankshaft
arbre moteur driving shaft
arbre de Noël (= sapin) Christmas tree; (= fête d'entreprise) Christmas party
arbre à pain breadfruit tree
arbre de transmission propeller shaft
arbre de vie (Anat) arbor vitae, tree of life; (Bible) tree of life

arbrisseau (pl **arbrisseaux**) /aʀbʀiso/ NM shrub

arbuste /aʀbyst/ NM small shrub, bush

arbustif, -ive /aʀbystif, iv/ ADJ [végétation] shrubby ♦ **culture arbustive** cultivation of shrubs ou bushes

ARC /aʀk/ NM (abrév de **AIDS-related complex**) ARC

arc /aʀk/ NM (= arme) bow; (Géom) arc; (Anat, Archit) arch ♦ **l'~ de ses sourcils** the arch ou curve of her eyebrows ♦ **la côte formait un ~** the coastline formed an arc; → **corde, lampe, soudure, tir**

COMP **arc brisé** Gothic arch
arc de cercle (Géom) arc of a circle ♦ **ça forme un ~ de cercle** (gén) it forms an arc ♦ **en ~ de cercle** in an arc
arc électrique electric arc
arc outrepassé Moorish arch
arc en plein cintre Roman arch
arc réflexe reflex arc
arc de triomphe triumphal arch ♦ **l'Arc de Triomphe** the Arc de Triomphe
arc voltaïque ⇒ **arc électrique**

arcade /aʀkad/ NF (Archit) arch, archway ♦ **~s** arcade, arches ♦ **les ~s d'un cloître/d'un pont** the arches ou arcade of a cloister/of a bridge ♦ **se promener sous les ~s** to walk through the arcade ou underneath the arches; → **jeu**

COMP **arcade dentaire** dental arch
arcade sourcilière arch of the eyebrows ♦ **il a été touché à l'~ sourcilière** he got a cut above his eye

Arcadie /aʀkadi/ NF Arcadia

arcane /aʀkan/ NM 1 (fig : gén pl = mystère) mystery 2 (Alchimie) arcanum

arcature /aʀkatyʀ/ NF arcature

arc-boutant (pl **arcs-boutants**) /aʀkbutɑ̃/ NM flying buttress

arc-bouter /aʀkbute/ ▸ conjug 1 ◂ VT (Archit) to buttress VPR **s'arc-bouter** to lean, to press (à, contre (up) against; sur on); ♦ **arc-bouté contre le mur, il essayait de pousser la table** pressing (up) ou bracing himself against the wall, he tried to push the table

arceau (pl **arceaux**) /aʀso/ NM (Archit) arch; (Croquet) hoop; (Méd) cradle ♦ **~ (de sécurité)** [de voiture] roll bar

arc-en-ciel (pl **arcs-en-ciel**) /aʀkɑ̃sjɛl/ NM rainbow

archaïque /aʀkaik/ ADJ 1 (Art, Ling) archaic 2 (péj) outdated

archaïsant, e /aʀkaizɑ̃, ɑ̃t/ ADJ archaistic NM,F archaist

archaïsme /aʀkaism/ NM archaism

archange /aʀkɑ̃ʒ/ NM archangel ♦ **l'~ (Saint) Michel/Gabriel** the Archangel Michael/Gabriel

arche /aʀʃ/ NF 1 (Archit) arch 2 (Rel) ark ♦ **l'~ de Noé** Noah's Ark ♦ **l'~ d'alliance** the Ark of the Covenant

archéologie /aʀkeɔlɔʒi/ NF archaeology (Brit), archeology (US)

archéologique /aʀkeɔlɔʒik/ ADJ archaeological (Brit), archeological (US)

archéologue /aʀkeɔlɔg/ NMF archaeologist (Brit), archeologist (US)

archer /aʀʃe/ NM archer, bowman

archet /aʀʃɛ/ NM (Mus, gén) bow ♦ **donner des coups d'~** to bow ♦ **coup d'~** bow-stroke

archétypal, e (mpl **-aux**) /aʀketipal, o/ ADJ archetypal

archétype /aʀketip/ NM (gén) archetype; (Bio) prototype ADJ (gén) archetypal; (Bio) prototypal, prototypic

archétypique /aʀketipik/ ADJ archetypical

archevêché /aʀʃəveʃe/ NM (= territoire) archdiocese, archbishopric; (= charge) archbishopric; (= palais) archbishop's palace

archevêque /aʀʃəvɛk/ NM archbishop

archi... /aʀʃi/ PRÉF 1 (* = extrêmement) tremendously, enormously ♦ **archibondé, archicomble, archiplein** chock-a-block*, jam-packed ♦ **archiconnu** extremely ou very well-known ♦ **archidifficile** incredibly difficult ♦ **archimillionnaire** millionaire several times over 2 (dans les titres) (= premier) arch...; → **archidiacre, archiduc** etc

archidiaconat /aʀʃidjakɔna/ NM (= dignité) archdeaconry

archidiaconé /aʀʃidjakɔne/ NM (= territoire) archdeaconry

archidiacre /aʀʃidjakʀ/ NM archdeacon

archidiocèse /aʀʃidjɔsɛz/ NM archdiocese

archiduc /aʀʃidyk/ NM archduke

archiduchesse /aʀʃidyʃɛs/ NF archduchess

archiépiscopal, e (mpl **-aux**) /aʀʃiepiskɔpal, o/ ADJ archiepiscopal

archiépiscopat /aʀʃiepiskɔpa/ NM archbishopric (office), archiepiscopate

archimandrite /aʀʃimɑ̃dʀit/ NM archimandrite

Archimède /aʀʃimɛd/ NM Archimedes; → **vis**

archimédien, -ienne /aʀʃimedjɛ̃, jɛn/ ADJ Archimedean

archipel /aʀʃipɛl/ NM archipelago ♦ **l'~ malais** the Malay Archipelago ♦ **l'~ des Kouriles** the Kuril Islands

archiphonème /aʀʃifɔnɛm/ NM archiphoneme

archiprêtre /aʀʃipʀɛtʀ/ NM archpriest

architecte /aʀʃitɛkt/ NMF (lit, fig) architect

COMP **architecte d'intérieur** interior designer
architecte naval naval architect
architecte de réseaux (Ordin) network architect

architectonique /aʀʃitɛktɔnik/ ADJ architectonic NF architectonics (sg)

architectural, e (mpl **-aux**) /aʀʃitɛktyʀal, o/ ADJ architectural

architecturalement /aʀʃitɛktyʀalmɑ̃/ ADV architecturally

architecture /aʀʃitɛktyʀ/ NF (lit, Ordin) architecture; (fig) structure ♦ **~ civile/militaire/religieuse** civil/military/religious architecture ♦ **merveille d'~** marvellous piece of architecture

architecturé, e /aʀʃitɛktyʀe/ ▸ conjug 1 ◂ ADJ ♦ **bien ~** [œuvre musicale, roman] well-structured ♦ **des phrases savamment ~es** carefully crafted sentences ♦ **~ autour de...** structured around...

architrave /aʀʃitʀav/ NF architrave

archivage /aʀʃivaʒ/ NM (gén) filing; (Ordin) filing, archival storage ♦ **~ électronique** electronic filing ou storage

archiver /aʀʃive/ ▸ conjug 1 ◂ VT to archive, to file

archives /aʀʃiv/ NFPL archives, records ♦ **les Archives nationales** the National Archives, ≃ the Public Records Office (Brit) ♦ **ça restera**

dans les ~ ! * that will go down in history! ◆ **je vais chercher dans mes ~** I'll look through my files ou records

archiviste /aʀʃivist/ NMF archivist

archivolte /aʀʃivɔlt/ NF archivolt

arçon /aʀsɔ̃/ NM *(Équitation)* tree; → **cheval, pistolet, vider**

arc-rampant (pl **arcs-rampants**) /aʀkʀɑ̃pɑ̃/ NM rampant arch

arctique /aʀktik/ ADJ *[région]* Arctic ◆ **l'océan (glacial) Arctique** the Arctic ocean NM **Arctique** ◆ **l'Arctique** the Arctic

ardemment /aʀdamɑ̃/ ADV ardently, fervently

Ardenne /aʀdɛn/ NF *(= région de France, Belgique et Luxembourg)* ◆ **l'~** the Ardennes

Ardennes /aʀdɛn/ NFPL *(= département français)* ◆ **les ~** the Ardennes ◆ **la bataille des ~** the Battle of the Bulge

ardent, e /aʀdɑ̃, ɑ̃t/ ADJ 1 *(= brûlant) (gén)* burning; *[tison]* glowing; *[feu]* blazing; *[yeux]* fiery *(de* with*)*; *[couleur]* flaming, fiery; *[chaleur, soleil]* scorching, blazing; *[fièvre, soif]* raging; → **buisson, chapelle, charbon** 2 *(= vif) [foi]* fervent, passionate; *[colère]* burning, raging; *[passion, désir]* burning, ardent; *[piété, haine, prière]* fervent, ardent; *[lutte]* ardent, passionate; *[discours]* impassioned 3 *(= bouillant) [amant]* ardent, hot-blooded; *[jeunesse, caractère]* fiery, passionate; *[joueur]* keen; *[partisan]* ardent, keen; *[cheval]* mettlesome, fiery ◆ **être ~ au travail/ au combat** to be a zealous worker/an ardent fighter

ardeur /aʀdœʀ/ NF *[de foi, prière]* fervour *(Brit)*, fervor *(US)*; *[de partisan, joueur]* enthusiasm; *[de caractère]* fieriness ◆ **l'~ du soleil** the heat of the sun ◆ **les ~s de l'été** *(littér)* the heat of summer ◆ **les ~s de l'amour** *(littér)* the ardour of love ◆ **modérez vos ~s !** *(littér ou hum)* control yourself! ◆ **l'~ réformatrice du gouvernement** the government's reforming zeal ◆ **son ~ au travail ou à travailler** his zeal ou enthusiasm for work ◆ **défendre une cause avec ~** to champion a cause passionately

ardillon /aʀdijɔ̃/ NM *[de boucle]* tongue

ardoise /aʀdwaz/ NF 1 *(= matière)* slate ◆ **toit d'~s** slate roof ◆ **couvrir un toit d'~(s)** to slate a roof 2 *(* = dette)* unpaid bill ◆ **avoir une ~ de 50 € chez l'épicier** *(fig)* to owe €50 at the grocer's ADJ INV *(couleur)* slate-grey *(Brit)* ou -gray *(US)*

ardoisé, e /aʀdwaze/ ADJ slate-grey *(Brit)* ou -gray *(US)*

ardoisier, -ière /aʀdwazje, jɛʀ/ ADJ *[gisement]* slaty; *[industrie]* slate *(épith)* NM *(= ouvrier)* slate-quarry worker; *(= propriétaire)* slate-quarry owner NF **ardoisière** slate quarry

ardu, e /aʀdy/ ADJ *[travail]* arduous, laborious; *[problème]* difficult; *[pente]* steep

are /aʀ/ NM are, one hundred square metres

areligieux, -ieuse /aʀ(ə)liʒjø, jøz/ ADJ areligious

aréna /aʀena/ NF *(Can Sport)* arena, (skating) rink

arène /aʀɛn/ NF 1 *(= piste)* arena ◆ **l'~ politique** the political arena ◆ **descendre dans l'~** *(fig)* to enter the arena 2 ◆ **~s** *(Archit)* amphitheatre *(Brit)*, amphitheater *(US)*; *[de courses de taureaux]* bullring ◆ **les ~s de Nîmes** the amphitheatre of Nîmes 3 *(Géol)* sand, arenite *(SPÉC)* ◆ **~ granitique** *(Géol)* granitic sand

arénicole /aʀenikɔl/ NF sandworm

aréole /aʀeɔl/ NF areola

aréomètre /aʀeɔmɛtʀ/ NM hydrometer

aréométrie /aʀeɔmetʀi/ NF hydrometry

aréopage /aʀeɔpaʒ/ NM *(fig, hum)* learned assembly ◆ **l'Aréopage** *(Antiq)* the Areopagus

arête /aʀɛt/ NF 1 *[de poisson]* (fish)bone ◆ **~ centrale** backbone, spine ◆ **c'est plein d'~s** it's full of bones, it's very bony ◆ **enlever les ~s d'un poisson** to bone a fish ◆ **sans ~s** boneless 2 *(= bord) [de cube, pierre, ski]* edge; *[de toit]* ridge; *[de voûte]* groin; *[de montagne]* ridge, crest; *[de nez]* bridge 3 *[de seigle, orge]* beard ◆ **~s** beard

areu /aʀø/ EXCL *(langage de bébé)* ◆ **areu areu** goo-goo ◆ **faire areu areu** to gurgle

argent /aʀʒɑ̃/ NM 1 *(= métal)* silver ◆ **en ~, d'~** silver; → **noce, parole**

2 *(= couleur)* silver ◆ **cheveux/reflets (d') ~** silvery hair/glints

3 *(Fin)* money *(NonC)* ◆ **il a de l'~** he's got money, he's well off ◆ **il l'a fait pour (de) l'~** he did it for money ◆ **il se fait un ~ fou** * he makes pots * ou loads * of money ◆ **c'est un homme/une femme d'~** he/she loves money ◆ **politique de l'~ cher** tight ou dear *(Brit)* money policy; → **couleur, manger, puissance**

4 *(locutions)* **l'~ de la drogue** drug(s) money ◆ **j'en ai/j'en veux pour mon ~** I've got/I want (to get) my money's worth ◆ **on en a pour son ~** it's good value (for money), it's worth every penny ◆ **on n'en a jamais que pour son ~** you get what you pay for ◆ **faire ~ de tout** to turn everything into cash, to make money out of anything ◆ **jeter l'~ par les fenêtres** to throw money away ou down the drain ◆ **avoir de l'~ plein les poches** * to have plenty of money, to be rolling in money * ◆ **l'~ n'a pas d'odeur** *(Prov)* money has no smell ◆ **l'~ ne fait pas le bonheur** *(Prov)* money can't buy happiness ◆ **l'~ va à l'~** *(Prov)* money attracts money ◆ **point ou pas d'~, point ou pas de Suisse** *(Prov)* nothing for nothing

COMP **argent comptant** ◆ **payer ~ comptant** to pay cash ◆ **prendre qch/les paroles de qn pour ~ comptant** to take sth/what sb says at (its) face value

argent liquide ready money, (ready) cash

argent noir ou sale dirty money

argent de poche pocket money ◆ **ils lui donnent 15 € par semaine d'~ de poche** they give him €15 a week pocket money

argenté, e /aʀʒɑ̃te/ (ptp de **argenter**) ADJ *[couleur, cheveux]* silver, silvery ◆ **en métal ~** *[couverts]* silver-plated ◆ **je ne suis pas très ~ en ce moment** * I'm pretty broke at the moment *, I'm not too well-off just now; → **renard**

argenter /aʀʒɑ̃te/ ► conjug 1 ◄ VT *[+ miroir]* to silver; *[+ couverts]* to silver(-plate); *(fig littér)* to give a silvery sheen to, to silver *(littér)*

argenterie /aʀʒɑ̃tʀi/ NF silver, silverware; *(de métal argenté)* silver plate ◆ **faire l'~** to polish ou clean the silver

argenteur /aʀʒɑ̃tœʀ/ NM silverer

argentier /aʀʒɑ̃tje/ NM 1 *(Hist)* Superintendent of Finance ◆ **le grand ~** *(hum)* the Minister of Finance 2 *(= meuble)* silver cabinet

argentifère /aʀʒɑ̃tifɛʀ/ ADJ silver-bearing, argentiferous *(SPÉC)*

argentin[1]**, e** /aʀʒɑ̃tɛ̃, in/ ADJ *[son, voix]* silvery

argentin[2]**, e** /aʀʒɑ̃tɛ̃, in/ ADJ Argentinian *(Brit)*, Argentinean *(US)*, Argentine *(épith)* NM,F **Argentin(e)** Argentinian *(Brit)*, Argentinean *(US)*, Argentine

Argentine /aʀʒɑ̃tin/ NF ◆ **l'~** Argentina, the Argentine

argentique /aʀʒɑ̃tik/ ADJ ◆ **photo ~** traditional photography ◆ **appareil photo ~** traditional camera

argenture /aʀʒɑ̃tyʀ/ NF *[de miroir]* silvering; *[de couverts]* silver-plating, silvering

argile /aʀʒil/ NF clay ◆ **~ à silex** clay-with-flints; → **colosse**

argileux, -euse /aʀʒilø, øz/ ADJ clayey

argon /aʀgɔ̃/ NM argon

argonaute /aʀgonot/ NM *(Myth)* Argonaut; *(= animal marin)* argonaut, paper nautilus

Argos /aʀgɔs/ N Argos

argot /aʀgo/ NM slang ◆ **~ de métier** trade slang ◆ **parler ~** to use slang ◆ **mot d'~** slang word

argotique /aʀgɔtik/ ADJ *(= de l'argot)* slang; *(= très familier)* slangy

argotisme /aʀgɔtism/ NM slang term

argousin †† /aʀguzɛ̃/ NM *(péj ou hum)* rozzer † *(péj)*, bluebottle † *(péj)*

arguer /aʀgɥe/ ► conjug 1 ◄ *(littér)* VT 1 *(= déduire)* to deduce ◆ **il ne peut rien ~ de ces faits** he can draw no conclusion from these facts 2 *(= prétexter)* **~ que ...** to argue that ..., to claim that ... ◆ **il est toujours possible d'~ que le mauvais temps a empêché le tournage** one can always claim that bad weather made filming impossible ◆ **la société peut ~ qu'elle n'est pas la seule à connaître des difficultés** the company can argue that it isn't the only one to be experiencing difficulties VT INDIR **arguer de** ◆ **il refusa, arguant de leur manque de ressources** he refused, on the grounds that they lacked resources

> ⚠ Au sens de 'déduire', **arguer** ne se traduit pas par **to argue**.

argument /aʀgymɑ̃/ GRAMMAIRE ACTIVE 53.2, 53.3 NM *(gén)* argument ◆ **tirer ~ de qch** to use sth as an argument ou excuse ◆ **~ frappant** strong ou convincing argument; *(hum = coup)* blow ◆ **~ massue** sledgehammer argument ◆ **~ publicitaire** advertising claim ◆ **~ de vente** selling proposition ou point

argumentaire /aʀgymɑ̃tɛʀ/ NM *(gén)* argument; *(= document commercial)* sales leaflet ou blurb

argumentation /aʀgymɑ̃tasjɔ̃/ NF argumentation

argumenter /aʀgymɑ̃te/ ► conjug 1 ◄ VI to argue *(sur* about*)*; ◆ **~ de qch** to use sth as an argument ◆ **discours bien argumenté** well-argued speech

argus /aʀgys/ NM 1 ◆ **l'~ (de l'automobile)** *guide to secondhand car prices*, ≃ Glass's directory *(Brit)*, the Blue Book *(US)* ◆ **~ de la photo** *guide to secondhand photographic equipment prices*; → **coter** 2 *(= oiseau)* argus pheasant

argutie /aʀgysi/ NF *(littér : gén péj)* quibble ◆ **~s** quibbling

aria /aʀja/ NF *(Mus)* aria

Ariane /aʀjan/ NF Ariadne; → **fil**

arianisme /aʀjanism/ NM Arianism

aride /aʀid/ ADJ 1 *(= sec) [vent, climat]* dry 2 *(= stérile) [sol]* arid 3 *(fig) [sujet, matière]* dry; *[tâche]* thankless ◆ **cœur ~** heart of stone

aridité /aʀidite/ NF *(= sécheresse) [de vent, climat]* dryness; *(= stérilité) [de sol]* aridity; *[de sujet, matière]* dryness; *[de tâche]* thanklessness ◆ **l'~ de son cœur** his hard-heartedness

arien, -ienne /aʀjɛ̃, jɛn/ ADJ, NM,F Arian

ariette /aʀjɛt/ NF arietta, ariette

Arioste /aʀjɔst/ NM ◆ **l'~** Ariosto

aristo * /aʀisto/ NMF *(péj)* (abrév de **aristocrate**) aristocrat, nob * † *(Brit)*, toff * † *(Brit)*

aristocrate /aʀistɔkʀat/ NMF aristocrat

aristocratie /aʀistɔkʀasi/ NF aristocracy

aristocratique /aʀistɔkʀatik/ ADJ aristocratic

aristocratiquement /aʀistɔkʀatikmɑ̃/ ADV aristocratically

Aristophane /aʀistɔfan/ NM Aristophanes

Aristote /aʀistɔt/ NM Aristotle

aristotélicien, -ienne /aʀistɔtelisjɛ̃, jɛn/ ADJ, NM,F Aristotelian

aristotélisme /aʀistɔtelism/ NM Aristotelianism

arithméticien, -ienne /aʀitmetisjɛ̃, jɛn/ NM,F arithmetician

arithmétique /aʀitmetik/ NF (= *science*) arithmetic; (= *livre*) arithmetic book ADJ arithmetical

arithmétiquement /aʀitmetikmɑ̃/ ADV arithmetically

Arizona /aʀizɔna/ NM ♦ **l'~** Arizona

Arkansas /aʀkɑ̃sas/ NM ♦ **l'~** Arkansas

arlequin /aʀləkɛ̃/ NM (*Théât*) Harlequin ♦ **bas (d')~** harlequin stockings; → **habit**

arlequinade /aʀləkinad/ NF (*fig*) buffoonery; (*Théât*) harlequinade

arlésien, -ienne /aʀlezjɛ̃, jɛn/ ADJ of *ou* from Arles NM,F **Arlésien(ne)** inhabitant *ou* native of Arles NF **arlésienne** ♦ **jouer l'arlésienne** *ou* **les arlésiennes** [*personne*] to keep well out of sight, to never show up ♦ **le dialogue, cette arlésienne de la vie politique** dialogue, that elusive phenomenon in politics

L'Arlésienne

The origin of the expression « jouer l'arlésienne » is Georges Bizet's opera of the same name, adapted from a book by Alphonse Daudet, in which the main character never actually appears. It has come to refer to any person or thing which, although much talked about, never materializes.

armada /aʀmada/ NF (*péj*) ♦ **une ~ de** [*de personnes*] a whole army *ou* mob of; [*de voitures*] a fleet of ♦ **l'Invincible Armada** the Spanish Armada

armagnac /aʀmaɲak/ NM armagnac

armateur /aʀmatœʀ/ NM (= *propriétaire*) shipowner; (= *exploitant*) ship's manager ♦ **~-affréteur** owner-charterer

armature /aʀmatyʀ/ NF 1 (*gén* = *carcasse*) [*de tente, montage, parapluie*] frame; (*Constr*) framework, armature (*SPÉC*); (*fig* = *infrastructure*) framework ♦ **~ de corset** corset bones *ou* stays ♦ **soutien-gorge à/sans ~** underwired/unwired bra 2 (*Mus*) key signature 3 (*Phys*) [*de condensateur*] electrode; [*d'aimant*] armature

arme /aʀm/ NF 1 (= *instrument*) (*gén*) weapon; (= *fusil, revolver*) gun ♦ **~s** weapons, arms ♦ **fabrique d'~s** arms factory ♦ **l'~ du crime** the murder weapon ♦ **des policiers sans ~(s)** unarmed police; → **bretelle, maniement, port²**

♦ **en armes** ♦ **soldats en ~s** (*avec des armes*) armed soldiers; (*prêts à se battre*) soldiers under arms ♦ **un peuple en ~s** a nation in arms ♦ **ils sont entrés en ~s dans la ville** they came into the town under arms

2 (= *élément d'une armée*) arm ♦ **les trois ~s** the three services *ou* arms ♦ **l'~ de l'infanterie** the infantry ♦ **dans quelle ~ sert-il ?** which service is he in?, which branch (of the army) does he serve in?

3 (*Mil*) **la carrière** *ou* **le métier des ~s** soldiering ♦ **le succès de nos ~s** (*littér*) the success of our armies ♦ **aux ~s !** to arms! ♦ **compagnon** *ou* **frère d'~s** comrade-in-arms ♦ **appeler un régiment sous les ~s** to call up a regiment; → **homme, place, prise²**

4 (= *moyen d'action*) weapon ♦ **~ à double tranchant** double-edged weapon *ou* sword ♦ **il est sans ~** he's defenceless (*Brit*) *ou* defenseless (*US*) (*contre* against); ♦ **donner** *ou* **fournir des ~s à qn** to give sb weapons (*contre* against); ♦ **tu leur donnes des ~s contre toi-même** you're giving them a stick to beat you with

5 (*Escrime*) **les ~s** fencing ♦ **faire des ~s** to fence; → **maître, passe¹, salle**

6 (*Héraldique*) **~s** arms, coat of arms ♦ **aux ~s de** bearing the arms of; → **héraut**

7 (*locutions*) **porter les ~s** to be a soldier ♦ **prendre les ~s** (= *se soulever*) to rise up in arms; (*pour défendre son pays*) to take up arms ♦ **avoir l'~ au bras** to have one's weapon in (one's) hand ♦ **~ à la bretelle !** ≃ slope arms! ♦ **~ sur l'épaule !** shoulder arms! ♦ **~ au pied !** attention! (*with rifle on ground*) ♦ **rester** *ou* **demeurer l'~ au pied** (*fig*) to hold fire ♦ **portez ~ !** shoulder arms! ♦ **présentez ~ !** present arms! ♦ **reposez ~ !** order arms! ♦ **déposer** *ou* **mettre bas les ~s** to lay down (one's) arms ♦ **rendre les ~s** to lay down one's arms, to surrender ♦ **faire ses premières ~s** to start out, to begin one's career (*dans* in); ♦ **il a fait ses (premières) ~s en Afrique** he started his military career in Africa, he first saw service in Africa ♦ **partir avec ~s et bagages** to pack up and go ♦ **passer l'~ à gauche*** to kick the bucket* ♦ **à ~s égales** on equal terms ♦ **passer qn par les ~s** to shoot sb by firing squad ♦ **prendre le pouvoir/régler un différend par les ~s** to take power/settle a dispute by force ♦ **mourir les ~s à la main** to die fighting ♦ **ils ont défendu la ville les ~s à la main** they took up arms to defend the town; → **appel, fait¹, gens¹, pris, suspension**

COMP **l'arme absolue** the ultimate weapon
arme d'assaut assault weapon
arme atomique atomic weapon
arme biologique biological weapon
arme blanche knife ♦ **se battre à l'~ blanche** to fight with knives
arme de chasse hunting weapon
arme chimique chemical weapon
armes de destruction massive weapons of mass destruction
arme d'épaule rifle
arme à feu firearm
arme de guerre weapon of war
arme de jet projectile
arme légère light weapon
arme lourde heavy weapon
arme nucléaire nuclear weapon ♦ **avoir l'~ nucléaire** to have nuclear weapons
arme de poing handgun
arme de service [*de policier*] service revolver *ou* gun

⚠ Au singulier, **arme** ne se traduit pas par le mot anglais **arm.**

armé, e¹ /aʀme/ (ptp de **armer**) ADJ [*personne, forces, conflit*] armed ♦ **~ jusqu'aux dents** *ou* **de pied en cap** armed to the teeth ♦ **attention, il est ~ !** careful, he's armed! ♦ **~ de** armed with ♦ **être bien ~ pour passer un examen** to be well-equipped to take an examination ♦ **bien ~ contre le froid** well-equipped against the cold ♦ **canne ~e d'un bout ferré** stick fitted with a steel tip, stick tipped with steel; → **béton, ciment, force, vol²** NM (= *position*) cock

armée² /aʀme/ NF 1 (*Mil*) army ♦ **~ de mercenaires** mercenary army ♦ **l'~ d'occupation/de libération** the occupying/liberating army *ou* forces ♦ **la Grande Armée** (*Hist*) the Grande Armée (*army of Napoleon*) ♦ **être à l'~** to be doing one's military service ♦ **être dans l'~** to be in the army ♦ **c'est un peu l'~ mexicaine*** (*péj*) it's a case of too many generals and not enough soldiers

2 (*péj*) army ♦ **une ~ de domestiques/rats** an army of servants/rats ♦ **regardez-moi cette ~ d'incapables** just look at this hopeless bunch* *ou* crew*; → **corps, zone**

COMP **armée active** regular army
l'armée de l'air the Air Force
armée de conscription conscript army
armée de métier professional army
l'armée des Ombres (*Hist*) *the French Resistance*
armée permanente standing army
armée régulière regular army
l'Armée républicaine irlandaise the Irish Republican Army
armée de réserve reserve
l'Armée rouge the Red Army
l'Armée du Salut the Salvation Army
l'armée de terre the Army

armement /aʀməmɑ̃/ NM 1 (= *action*) [*de pays, armée*] armament; [*de personne*] arming; [*de fusil*] cocking; [*d'appareil-photo*] winding-on 2 (= *armes*) [*de soldat*] arms, weapons; [*de pays, troupe, avion*] arms, armament(s) ♦ **usine d'~** arms factory ♦ **la limitation des ~s** arms limitation ♦ **les dépenses d'~s de la France** France's expenditure on arms *ou* weapons; → **course** 3 (*Naut* = *équipement*) fitting-out, equipping

Arménie /aʀmeni/ NF Armenia; → **papier**

arménien, -ienne /aʀmenjɛ̃, jɛn/ ADJ Armenian NM (= *langue*) Armenian NM,F **Arménien(ne)** Armenian

armer /aʀme/ ► conjug 1 ◄ VT 1 (*lit*) to arm (*de* with; *contre* against); ♦ **~ qn contre les difficultés de la vie** to equip sb to deal with life's difficulties, to arm sb against life's difficulties 2 (*Hist*) **~ qn chevalier** to dub sb knight 3 [+ *navire*] to fit out, to equip 4 [+ *fusil*] to cock; [+ *appareil-photo*] to wind on 5 (= *renforcer*) [+ *béton, poutre*] to reinforce (*de* with); ♦ **~ un bâton d'une pointe d'acier** to fit a stick with a steel tip, to fit a steel tip on(to) a stick

VPR **s'armer** (= *s'équiper*) to arm o.s. (*de* with; *contre* against); ♦ **s'~ de courage** to summon up one's courage, to steel o.s. ♦ **il faut s'~ de patience** you have to be patient

armistice /aʀmistis/ NM armistice ♦ **l'Armistice** (= *fête*) Armistice Day

armoire /aʀmwaʀ/ NF (*gén*) cupboard, closet (*US*); (= *penderie*) wardrobe

COMP **armoire frigorifique** cold room *ou* store
armoire à glace (*lit*) wardrobe with a mirror; (* *fig* = *costaud*) great hulking brute*
armoire à linge linen cupboard (*Brit*) *ou* closet (*US*)
armoire normande large wardrobe
armoire à pharmacie medicine chest *ou* cabinet
armoire de toilette bathroom cabinet (with a mirror)

armoiries /aʀmwaʀi/ NFPL coat of arms, armorial bearings

armoise /aʀmwaz/ NF artemisia, wormwood

armorial, e (mpl **-iaux**) /aʀmɔʀjal, jo/ ADJ, NM armorial

armoricain, e /aʀmɔʀikɛ̃, ɛn/ ADJ Armorican; → **homard**

armorier /aʀmɔʀje/ ► conjug 7 ◄ VT to emblazon

armure /aʀmyʀ/ NF 1 (*Mil*) armour (*NonC*) (*Brit*), armor (*NonC*) (*US*) ♦ **une ~** a suit of armour ♦ **chevalier en ~** knight in armour 2 (= *tissage*) weave 3 [*de câble*] (metal) sheath 4 (*Mus*) key signature 5 (*Phys*) armature

armurerie /aʀmyʀʀi/ NF (= *fabrique*) arms factory; (= *magasin*) [*d'armes à feu*] gunsmith's; [*d'armes blanches*] armourer's (*Brit*), armorer's (*US*); (= *profession*) arms manufacture

armurier /aʀmyʀje/ NM (= *fabricant, marchand*) [*d'armes à feu*] gunsmith; [*d'armes blanches*] armourer (*Brit*), armorer (*US*); (*Mil*) armourer (*Brit*), armorer (*US*)

ARN /aɛʀɛn/ NM (abrév de **acide ribonucléique**) RNA ♦ **~ messager/de transfert** messenger/transfer RNA

arnaque* /aʀnak/ NF con (trick)* ♦ **il a monté plusieurs ~s immobilières** he organized several property frauds ♦ **ce régime amaigrissant, c'est une belle ~** this diet is a real con*

◆ **c'est (de) l'~** *(= c'est trop cher)* it's a rip-off*, it's daylight robbery

arnaquer* /aʀnake/ ► conjug 1 ◄ VT 1 *(= escroquer)* to swindle, to do* *(Brit)* ◆ **je me suis fait ~ de 30 €** I was cheated *ou* done* *(Brit)* out of €30 2 *(= arrêter)* to nab* ◆ **se faire ~** to get nabbed*

arnaqueur, -euse* /aʀnakœʀ, øz/ NM,F swindler, cheat, con artist*

arnica /aʀnika/ NF arnica

arobase /aʀɔbaz/ NF at *(sign)*

arolle /aʀɔl/ NM *(Helv) (= arbre)* Arolla pine

aromate /aʀɔmat/ NM *(= herbe)* herb; *(= épice)* spice ◆ **~s** seasoning (NonC) ◆ **ajoutez quelques ~s** add seasoning

aromathérapie /aʀɔmateʀapi/ NF aromathe

aromathérapeute /aʀɔmateʀapøt/ NMF aromatherapist

aromatique /aʀɔmatik/ ADJ *(gén, Chim)* aromatic

aromatiser /aʀɔmatize/ ► conjug 1 ◄ VT to flavour *(Brit)*, to flavor *(US)* ◆ **aromatisé à la vanille** vanilla-flavoured

arôme, arome /aʀom/ NM *[de plat]* aroma; *[de café, vin]* aroma, fragrance; *[de fleur]* fragrance; *(= goût)* flavour *(Brit)*, flavor *(US)*; *(ajouté à un aliment)* flavouring *(Brit)*, flavoring *(US)* ◆ **crème ~ chocolat** chocolate-flavoured cream dessert

aronde †† /aʀɔ̃d/ NF swallow; → **queue**

arpège /aʀpɛʒ/ NM arpeggio ◆ **faire des ~s** to play arpeggios

arpéger /aʀpeʒe/ ► conjug 6 et 3 ◄ VT *[+ passage]* to play in arpeggios; *[+ accord]* to play as an arpeggio, to spread

arpent /aʀpɑ̃/ NM *(Hist)* arpent *(about an acre)* ◆ **il a quelques ~s de terre** *(fig)* he's got a few acres

arpentage /aʀpɑ̃taʒ/ NM *(= technique)* (land) surveying; *(= mesure)* measuring, surveying

arpenter /aʀpɑ̃te/ ► conjug 1 ◄ VT *[+ pièce, couloir]* to pace (up and down); *(= mesurer) [+ terrain]* to measure, to survey

arpenteur /aʀpɑ̃tœʀ/ NM (land) surveyor; → **chaîne**

arpète*, **arpette*** /aʀpɛt/ NMF apprentice

arpion⁑ /aʀpjɔ̃/ NM hoof⁑, foot

arqué, e /aʀke/ (ptp de **arquer**) ADJ *[objet, sourcils]* arched, curved ◆ **avoir le dos ~** to be hunchbacked ◆ **le dos ~ sous l'effort** his back bowed under the strain ◆ **il a les jambes ~es** he's bandy-legged *ou* bowlegged ◆ **nez ~** hooknose, hooked nose

arquebuse /aʀkəbyz/ NF (h)arquebus

arquebusier /aʀkəbyzje/ NM *(= soldat)* (h)arquebusier

arquer /aʀke/ ► conjug 1 ◄ VT *[+ objet, tige]* to curve; *[+ dos]* to arch VI *[objet]* to bend, to curve; *[poutre]* to sag ◆ **il ne peut plus ~*** he can't walk any more VPR **s'arquer** to curve

arrachage /aʀaʃaʒ/ NM *[de légume]* lifting; *[de plante, arbre]* uprooting; *[de dent]* extracting, pulling *(US)*; *[de sac]* snatching ◆ **l'~ des mauvaises herbes** weeding

arraché /aʀaʃe/ NM *(Sport)* snatch

◆ **à l'arraché** ◆ **il soulève 130 kg à l'~** he can do a snatch using 130 kg ◆ **obtenir la victoire à l'~** to snatch victory ◆ **ils ont eu le contrat à l'~** they just managed to snatch the contract

arrache-clou (pl **arrache-clous**) /aʀaʃklu/ NM nail wrench

arrachement /aʀaʃmɑ̃/ NM 1 *(= chagrin)* wrench ◆ **ce fut un véritable ~ pour elle de partir** it was a real wrench for her to leave 2 *(= déchirement)* tearing

arrache-pied /aʀaʃpje/ **d'arrache-pied** LOC ADV relentlessly

arracher /aʀaʃe/ ► conjug 1 ◄ VT 1 *(= déraciner) [+ légume]* to lift; *[+ souche, plante]* to pull up, to uproot; *[+ mauvaises herbes]* to pull up; *[+ cheveux]* to tear *ou* pull out; *[+ dent]* to take out, to extract, to pull *(US)*; *[+ poil, clou]* to pull out ◆ **j'ai passé la matinée à ~ des mauvaises herbes** I've been weeding all morning ◆ **je vais me faire ~ une dent** I'm going to have a tooth out *ou* extracted *ou* pulled *(US)*

2 *(= enlever) [+ chemise, membre]* to tear off; *[+ affiche]* to tear down; *[+ feuille, page]* to tear out *(de* of); ◆ **je vais lui ~ les yeux** I'll scratch his eyes out ◆ **cette séparation lui a arraché le cœur** he was heartbroken by this separation ◆ **ce spectacle lui arracha le cœur** the sight of it broke his heart, it was a heartrending sight for him ◆ **ça arrache (la gorge)**⁑ *[plat]* it'll blow your head off*; *[boisson]* it's really rough!

3 *(= prendre)* **~ à qn** *[+ portefeuille, arme]* to snatch *ou* grab from sb; *[+ argent]* to get out of sb ◆ **~ des larmes/un cri à qn** to make sb cry/cry out ◆ **ils ont arraché la victoire à la dernière minute** they snatched victory at the last minute ◆ **il lui arracha son sac à main** he snatched *ou* grabbed her handbag from her ◆ **je lui ai arraché cette promesse/ces aveux/la vérité** I dragged this promise/this confession/the truth out of him

4 *(= soustraire)* **~ qn à** *[+ famille, pays]* to tear *ou* drag sb away from; *[+ passion, vice, soucis]* to rescue sb from; *[+ sommeil, rêve]* to drag sb out of *ou* from; *[+ sort, mort]* to snatch sb from; *[+ habitudes, méditation]* to force sb out of ◆ **~ qn des mains d'un ennemi** to snatch sb from the hands of an enemy ◆ **la mort nous l'a arraché** death has snatched *ou* torn him from us ◆ **il m'a arraché du lit à 6 heures** he got *ou* dragged me out of bed at 6 o'clock

VPR **s'arracher** 1 *(= se déchirer)* **tu t'es arraché les vêtements sur le grillage** you've torn your clothes on the fence ◆ **s'~ les cheveux** *(lit)* to tear *ou* pull out one's hair; *(fig)* to tear one's hair out ◆ **s'~ les yeux** *(fig)* to scratch each other's eyes out

2 *(= se battre pour avoir)* ◆ **s'~ qn/qch** to fight over sb/sth ◆ **on s'arrache leur dernier CD** everybody is desperate to get hold of their latest CD ◆ **les cinéastes se l'arrachent** film directors are falling over themselves *ou* are fighting to get him to act in their films

3 *(= partir)* ◆ **s'~ de** *ou* **à** *[+ pays, famille]* to tear o.s. away from; *[+ habitude, méditation, passion]* to force o.s. out of; *[+ lit]* to drag o.s. from, to force o.s. out of ◆ **on s'arrache ?**⁑ let's split!⁑

arracheur /aʀaʃœʀ/ NM → **mentir**

arracheuse /aʀaʃøz/ NF *(Agr)* lifter, grubber

arraisonnement /aʀɛzɔnmɑ̃/ NM *(Naut)* inspection

arraisonner /aʀɛzɔne/ ► conjug 1 ◄ VT *(Naut)* to inspect

arrangeant, e /aʀɑ̃ʒɑ̃, ɑ̃t/ ADJ accommodating, obliging

arrangement /aʀɑ̃ʒmɑ̃/ NM 1 *(= action) [de fleurs, coiffure, voyage]* arranging 2 *(= agencement) [de mobilier, maison]* layout, arrangement; *[de fiches]* order, arrangement; *[de mots]* order ◆ **l'~ de sa coiffure** the way her hair is done *ou* arranged ◆ **l'~ de sa toilette** the way she is dressed 3 *(= accord)* agreement, arrangement ◆ **arriver** *ou* **parvenir à un ~** to come to an agreement *ou* an arrangement ◆ **sauf ~ contraire** unless other arrangements are made ◆ **~ de famille** *(Jur)* family settlement *(in financial matters)* 4 *(Mus)* arrangement ◆ **~ pour guitare** arrangement for guitar 5 *(Math)* arrangement 6 *(= préparatifs)* **~s** arrangements

arranger /aʀɑ̃ʒe/ ► conjug 3 ◄ VT 1 *(= disposer) (gén)* to arrange; *[+ coiffure]* to tidy ◆ **~ sa cravate/sa jupe** to straighten one's tie/skirt

2 *(= organiser) [+ voyage, réunion]* to arrange, to organize; *[+ rencontre, entrevue]* to arrange ◆ **~ sa vie/ses affaires** to organize one's life/one's affairs ◆ **il a tout arrangé pour ce soir** he has seen to *ou* he has arranged everything for tonight ◆ **ce combat de catch était arrangé à l'avance** this wrestling match was fixed *ou* was a put-up job*

3 *(= régler) [+ différend]* to settle ◆ **il a essayé d'~ les choses** *ou* **l'affaire** *ou* **le coup*** he tried to sort *ou* straighten the matter out ◆ **tout est arrangé** everything is settled *ou* sorted out ◆ **et ce qui n'arrange rien, il est en retard !** and he's late, which doesn't help matters! ◆ **ce contretemps n'arrange pas nos affaires** this setback doesn't help matters

4 *(= convenir)* to suit, to be convenient for ◆ **ça ne m'arrange pas tellement** it doesn't really suit me ◆ **cela m'arrange bien** that suits me nicely *ou* fine ◆ **à 6 heures si ça vous arrange** at 6 o'clock if that suits you *ou* if that's convenient ◆ **tu le crois parce que ça t'arrange** you believe him because it suits you (to do so)

5 *(= réparer) [+ voiture, montre]* to fix, to put right; *[+ robe] (= recoudre)* to fix, to mend; *(= modifier)* to alter ◆ **il faudrait ~ votre texte, il est confus** you need to sort out this piece - it's a mess

6 *(* = malmener)* to work over*, to sort out* *(Brit)* ◆ **il s'est drôlement fait ~** he got a real working over*, they really sorted him out* *(Brit)* ◆ **te voilà bien arrangé !** what a state *ou* mess you've got yourself in!* ◆ **il s'est fait ~ le portrait** he got his face bashed in* *ou* smashed in*

7 *(Mus)* to arrange

VPR **s'arranger** 1 *(= se mettre d'accord)* to come to an agreement *ou* an arrangement ◆ **arrangez-vous avec le patron** you'll have to sort it out with the boss ◆ **s'~ à l'amiable** to come to a friendly *ou* an amicable agreement

2 *(= s'améliorer) [querelle]* to be settled; *[situation]* to work out, to sort itself out *(Brit)*; *[santé]* to get better ◆ **le temps n'a pas l'air de s'~** it doesn't look as though the weather is improving *ou* getting any better ◆ **tout va s'~** everything will work out (all right) *ou* sort itself out *(Brit)* ◆ **les choses s'arrangèrent d'elles-mêmes** things worked *ou* sorted *(Brit)* themselves out ◆ **ça ne s'arrange pas*, il est plus têtu que jamais** he's not getting any better, he's more stubborn than ever ◆ **il ne fait rien pour s'~** he doesn't do himself any favours ◆ **alors, ça s'arrange entre eux ?** are things getting (any) better between them?

3 *(= se débrouiller)* to manage ◆ **arrangez-vous comme vous voudrez mais je les veux demain** I don't mind how you do it but I want them for tomorrow ◆ **tu t'arranges toujours pour avoir des taches !** you always manage to dirty your clothes! ◆ **il va s'~ pour finir le travail avant demain** he'll see to it that *ou* he'll make sure (that) he finishes the job before tomorrow ◆ **il s'est arrangé pour avoir des places gratuites** he has managed to get some free seats ◆ **arrangez-vous pour venir me chercher à la gare** arrange it so that you can come and meet me at the station ◆ **c'est ton problème, arrange-toi !** it's your problem, you deal with it *ou* sort it out!

4 *(= se contenter)* ◆ **s'~ de** to make do with, to put up with ◆ **il s'est arrangé du fauteuil pour dormir** he made do with the armchair to sleep in ◆ **il faudra bien s'en ~** we'll just have to put up with it

5 *(= se classer)* to be arranged ◆ **ses arguments s'arrangent logiquement** his arguments are logically arranged

6 (= *se rajuster*) to tidy o.s. up ◆ **elle s'arrange les cheveux** she's fixing her hair

7 (* = *se faire mal*) **tu t'es bien arrangé !** you've got yourself in a fine state!, you do look a mess! *

⚠ Au sens de 'convenir', **arranger** ne se traduit pas par **to arrange**.

arrangeur, -euse /aʀɑ̃ʒœʀ, øz/ **NM,F** *(Mus)* arranger

arrérages /aʀeʀaʒ/ **NMPL** arrears

arrestation /aʀɛstasjɔ̃/ **NF** arrest ◆ **procéder à l'~ de qn** to arrest sb ◆ **être/mettre en état d'~** to be/place *ou* put under arrest ◆ **se mettre en état d'~** to give o.s. up to the police ◆ **ils ont procédé à une douzaine d'~s** they made a dozen arrests

COMP **arrestation préventive** ≃ arrest
arrestation provisoire taking into preventive custody

arrêt /aʀɛ/ **NM** 1 (= *lieu*) stop ◆ ~ **d'autobus** bus stop ◆ ~ **fixe** compulsory stop ◆ ~ **facultatif** request stop

2 *[de machine, véhicule]* stopping; *[de développement, croissance]* stopping, checking; *[d'hémorragie]* stopping, arrest ◆ **attendez l'~ complet (du train/de l'avion)** wait until the train/aircraft has come to a complete stop *ou* standstill ◆ **cinq minutes d'~** *[de trajet]* a 5-minute stop; *[de cours]* a 5-minute break ◆ **"arrêts fréquents"** *(sur véhicule)* "frequent stops" ◆ **véhicule à l'~** stationary vehicle ◆ **être à l'~** *[véhicule, conducteur]* to be stationary ◆ **faire un ~** *[train]* to stop, to make a stop; *[gardien de but]* to make a save ◆ **le train fit un ~ brusque** the train came to a sudden stop *ou* standstill ◆ **nous avons fait plusieurs ~s** we made several stops *ou* halts ◆ **marquer un ~ avant de continuer à parler** to pause *ou* make a pause before speaking again ◆ ~ **buffet** * snack break, pit stop * *(US)* ◆ ~ **pipi** * loo stop * *(Brit)*, bathroom break *(US)* ◆ **donner un coup d'~ à** to check, to put a brake on

3 *(Mil)* **~s** arrest ◆ **~s simples/de rigueur** open/close arrest ◆ **~s de forteresse** confinement *(in military prison)* ◆ **mettre qn aux ~s** to put sb under arrest; → **maison, mandat**

4 *(Jur = décision)* judgement, decision ◆ **faire ~ sur les appointements de qn** to issue a writ of attachment (on sb's salary) ◆ **les ~s du destin** *(littér)* the decrees of destiny *(littér)*

5 *(Couture)* **faire un ~** to fasten off the thread; → **point²**

6 (= *dispositif*) *[de machine]* stop mechanism; *[de serrure]* ward; *[de fusil]* safety catch ◆ **appuyez sur l'~** press the stop button ◆ ~ **sur image** *(Audiov = dispositif)* freeze frame ◆ **faire un ~ sur image** to freeze on a frame

7 *(Ski)* stop; *(Boxe)* stoppage ◆ **il a perdu/gagné par ~ de l'arbitre** he won/lost on a stoppage

8 *(Chasse)* **rester** *ou* **tomber en ~** *(lit)* to point; *(fig)* to stop short ◆ **être en ~** *(lit)* to be pointing *(devant* at); *(fig)* to stand transfixed *(devant* before) → **chien**

LOC ADV **sans arrêt** (= *sans interruption*) *[travailler, pleuvoir]* without stopping, non-stop; (= *très fréquemment*) *[se produire, se détraquer]* continually, constantly ◆ **ce train est sans ~ jusqu'à Lyon** this train is non-stop to Lyon

COMP **arrêt du cœur** cardiac arrest, heart failure
l'arrêt des hostilités the cessation of hostilities
arrêt de jeu *(Sport)* stoppage ◆ **jouer les ~s de jeu** to play injury time
arrêt (de) maladie sick leave ◆ **être en ~ (de) maladie** to be on sick leave ◆ **se mettre en ~ (de) maladie** to go sick
arrêt de mort death warrant ◆ **il avait signé son ~ de mort** *(fig)* he had signed his own death warrant
arrêt de travail (= *grève*) stoppage (of work); (= *congé de maladie*) sick leave; (= *certificat*) doctor's *ou* medical certificate
arrêt de volée *(Rugby)* **faire un ~ de volée** to make a mark

arrêté, e /aʀete/ (ptp de **arrêter**) **ADJ** *[décision, volonté]* firm, immutable; *[idée, opinion]* fixed, firm ◆ **c'est une chose ~e** the matter *ou* it is settled **NM** 1 (= *décision administrative*) order, decree *(frm)* ◆ ~ **ministériel** departmental *ou* ministerial order ◆ ~ **municipal** ≃ by(e)-law ◆ ~ **préfectoral** order of the prefect 2 *(Fin)* ~ **de compte** *(fermeture)* settlement of account; *(relevé)* statement of account *(to date)*

arrêter /aʀete/ ▸ conjug 1 ◂ **VT** 1 (= *immobiliser*) *[+ personne, machine, montre]* to stop; *[+ cheval]* to stop, to pull up; *[+ moteur]* to switch off, to stop ◆ **arrêtez-moi près de la poste** drop me off by the post office ◆ **il m'a arrêté dans le couloir pour me parler** he stopped me in the corridor to speak to me ◆ **ici, je vous arrête !** *(dans la conversation)* I must stop *ou* interrupt you there!

2 (= *entraver*) *[+ développement, croissance]* to stop, to check; *[+ foule, ennemi]* to stop, to halt; *[+ hémorragie]* to stop, to arrest ◆ **le trafic ferroviaire est arrêté à cause de la grève** trains have been brought to a standstill *ou* a halt because of the strike ◆ **rien n'arrête la marche de l'histoire** nothing can stop *ou* check the march of history ◆ **on n'arrête pas le progrès !** *(hum)* the wonders of modern science! *(hum)* ◆ **nous avons été arrêtés par un embouteillage** we were held up *ou* stopped by a traffic jam ◆ **seul le prix l'arrête** it's only the price that stops him ◆ **rien ne l'arrête** there's nothing to stop him ◆ **arrête les frais !** * drop it! * ◆ **bon, on arrête les frais** * OK, let's stop this before it gets any worse

3 (= *abandonner*) *[+ études, compétition, sport]* to give up; *[+ représentations]* to cancel ◆ ~ **la fabrication d'un produit** to discontinue (the manufacture of) a product ◆ **on a dû ~ les travaux à cause de la neige** we had to stop work *ou* call a halt to the work because of the snow

4 (= *faire prisonnier*) to arrest ◆ **il s'est fait ~ hier** he got himself arrested yesterday ◆ **je vous arrête !** you're under arrest!

5 *(Fin)* *[+ compte]* (= *fermer*) to settle; (= *relever*) to make up ◆ **les comptes sont arrêtés chaque fin de mois** statements (of account) are made up at the end of every month

6 *(Couture)* *[+ point]* to fasten off

7 (= *fixer*) *[+ jour, lieu]* to appoint, to decide on; *[+ plan]* to decide on; *[+ derniers détails]* to finalize ◆ ~ **son attention/ses regards sur** to fix one's attention/gaze on ◆ ~ **un marché** to make a deal ◆ **il a arrêté son choix** he's made his choice ◆ **ma décision est arrêtée** my mind is made up ◆ ~ **que ...** *(Admin)* to rule that ...

8 *(Méd)* ~ **qn** to give sb sick leave ◆ **elle est arrêtée depuis 3 semaines** she's been on sick leave for 3 weeks

VI to stop ◆ ~ **de fumer** to give up *ou* stop smoking ◆ **il n'arrête pas** he just never stops, he's always on the go ◆ **il n'arrête pas de critiquer tout le monde** he never stops criticizing people, he's always criticizing people ◆ **arrête de parler !** stop talking! ◆ **arrête !** stop it!, stop that! ◆ **ça n'arrête pas !** * it never stops!

VPR **s'arrêter** 1 (= *s'immobiliser*) *[personne, machine, montre]* to stop; *[train, voiture]* *(gén)* to stop; *(en se garant)* to pull up ◆ **nous nous sommes arrêtés sur le bas-côté** we pulled up *ou* stopped by the roadside ◆ **s'~ court** *ou* **net** *[personne]* to stop dead *ou* short; *[cheval]* to pull up; *[bruit]* to stop suddenly ◆ **le train ne s'arrête pas à toutes les gares** the train doesn't stop *ou* call at every station ◆ **nous nous sommes arrêtés 10 jours à Lyon** we stayed *ou* stopped * 10 days in Lyons

2 (= *s'interrompre*) to stop, to break off ◆ **la route s'arrête ici** the road ends *ou* stops here ◆ **s'~ pour se reposer/pour manger** to break off *ou* stop for a rest/to eat ◆ **arrête-toi un peu, tu vas t'épuiser** stop for a while *ou* take a break or you'll wear yourself out ◆ **les ouvriers se sont arrêtés à 17 heures** *(grève)* the workmen stopped work *ou* downed tools *(Brit)* at 5 o'clock; *(heure de fermeture)* the workmen finished (work) *ou* stopped work at 5 o'clock ◆ **sans s'~** without stopping, without a break ◆ **ce serait dommage de s'~ en si bon chemin** it would be a shame to stop *ou* give up while things are going so well

3 (= *cesser*) *[développement, croissance]* to stop, to come to a standstill; *[hémorragie]* to stop ◆ **le travail s'est arrêté dans l'usine en grève** work has stopped in the striking factory, the striking factory is at a standstill ◆ **s'~ de manger/marcher** to stop eating/walking ◆ **s'~ de fumer/boire** to give up *ou* stop smoking/drinking ◆ **l'affaire ne s'arrêtera pas là !** you *(ou* they *etc)* haven't heard the last of this!

4 ◆ **s'~ sur** *[choix, regard]* to fall on ◆ **il ne faut pas s'~ aux apparences** you should always look beyond appearances ◆ **s'~ à des détails** to waste time worrying about details ◆ **s'~ à un projet** to settle on *ou* fix on a plan ◆ **arrêtons-nous un instant sur ce tableau** let us turn our attention to this picture for a moment

arrhes /aʀ/ **NFPL** deposit ◆ **verser des ~** to pay *ou* leave a deposit

arriération /aʀjeʀasjɔ̃/ **NF** 1 *(Psych)* retardation ◆ ~ **affective** emotional retardation 2 ◆ ~ **économique** *[de pays]* economic backwardness ◆ **certains villages sont en voie d'~** some villages are slipping into economic decline

arriéré, e /aʀjeʀe/ **ADJ** 1 *[paiement]* overdue, in arrears *(attrib)*; *[dette]* out-standing 2 *(Psych)* *[enfant, personne]* backward, retarded; *(Scol)* educationally subnormal; *[région, pays]* backward, behind the times *(attrib)*; *[croyances, méthodes, personne]* out-of-date, behind the times *(attrib)* **NM** 1 (= *choses à faire, travail*) backlog 2 (= *paiement*) arrears ◆ **il voulait régler l'~ de sa dette** he wanted to settle his arrears ◆ **il refuse de lui payer un ~ de salaire d'un mois** he's refusing to pay her a month's back salary

arrière /aʀjɛʀ/ **NM** 1 *[de voiture]* back; *[de bateau]* stern; *[de train]* rear ◆ **à l'~** *(Naut)* aft, at the stern ◆ **à l'~ de** *(Naut)* at the stern of, abaft ◆ **se balancer d'avant en ~** to rock backwards and forwards ◆ **avec le moteur à l'~** with the engine at the back, with a rear-mounted engine ◆ **l'~ (du pays)** *(en temps de guerre)* the home front, the civilian zone ◆ **l'~ tient bon** morale on the home front *ou* behind the lines is high

◆ **en arrière** (= *derrière*) behind; (= *vers l'arrière*) backwards ◆ **être/rester en ~** to be/lag *ou* drop behind ◆ **regarder en ~** *(lit)* to look back *ou* behind; *(fig)* to look back ◆ **faire un pas en ~** to step back(wards), to take a step back ◆ **aller/marcher en ~** to go/walk backwards ◆ **se pencher en ~** to lean back (wards) ◆ **en ~ toute !** *(Naut)* full astern! ◆ **100 ans en ~** 100 years ago *ou* back ◆ **il faut remonter loin en ~ pour trouver une telle sécheresse** we have to go a long way back (in time) to find a similar drought ◆ **revenir en ~** *[marcheur]* to go back, to retrace one's steps; *[orateur]* to go back over what has been said; *[civilisation]* to regress; *(avec magnétophone)* to rewind; *(dans ses pensées)* to look back ◆ **renverser la tête en ~** to tilt one's head back(wards) ◆ **le chapeau en ~** his hat tilted back(wards) ◆ **être peigné** *ou* **avoir**

les cheveux en ~ to have one's hair brushed *ou* combed back

♦ **en arrière de** behind ♦ **rester** *ou* **se tenir en ~ de qch** to stay behind sth ♦ **il est très en ~ des autres élèves** he's a long way behind the other pupils

2 *(Sport = joueur) (gén)* fullback; *(Volley)* backline player ♦ **~ gauche/droit** *(Ftbl)* left/right back; *(Basket)* left/right guard ♦ **~ central** *(Ftbl)* centre back ♦ **~ volant** sweeper

3 *(Mil)* **les ~s** the rear ♦ **attaquer les ~s de l'ennemi** to attack the enemy in the rear ♦ **assurer** *ou* **protéger ses ~s** *(lit)* to protect the rear; *(fig)* to leave o.s. a way out

ADJ INV ♦ **roue/feu ~** rear wheel/light ♦ **siège ~** *[de voiture]* back seat; *[de moto]* pillion; → **machine, marche**[1], **vent**

EXCL ♦ **en ~ ! vous gênez** stand *ou* get back! you're in the way ♦ **~, misérable !** † behind me, wretch! †

arrière-ban (pl **arrière-bans**) /aʀjɛʀbɑ̃/ NM → **ban**

arrière-bouche (pl **arrière-bouches**) /aʀjɛʀbuʃ/ NF back of the mouth

arrière-boutique (pl **arrière-boutiques**) /aʀjɛʀbutik/ NF back shop

arrière-chœur (pl **arrière-chœurs**) /aʀjɛʀkœʀ/ NM retrochoir

arrière-cour (pl **arrière-cours**) /aʀjɛʀkuʀ/ NF backyard

arrière-cuisine (pl **arrière-cuisines**) /aʀjɛʀkɥizin/ NF scullery

arrière-fond (pl **arrière-fonds**) /aʀjɛʀfɔ̃/ NM *[de tableau, scène]* background ♦ **en ~** in the background

arrière-garde (pl **arrière-gardes**) /aʀjɛʀgaʀd/ NF rearguard ♦ **livrer un combat** *ou* **une bataille d'~** *(lit, fig)* to fight a rearguard action *ou* battle

arrière-gorge (pl **arrière-gorges**) /aʀjɛʀgɔʀʒ/ NF back of the throat

arrière-goût (pl **arrière-goûts**) /aʀjɛʀgu/ NM *(lit, fig)* aftertaste ♦ **ses propos ont un ~ de racisme** his comments smack of racism

arrière-grand-mère (pl **arrière-grands-mères**) /aʀjɛʀgʀɑ̃mɛʀ/ NF great-grandmother

arrière-grand-oncle (pl **arrière-grands-oncles**) /aʀjɛʀgʀɑ̃tɔ̃kl/ NM great-great-uncle

arrière-grand-père (pl **arrière-grands-pères**) /aʀjɛʀgʀɑ̃pɛʀ/ NM great-grandfather

arrière-grands-parents /aʀjɛʀgʀɑ̃paʀɑ̃/ NMPL great-grandparents

arrière-grand-tante (pl **arrière-grands-tantes**) /aʀjɛʀgʀɑ̃tɑ̃t/ NF great-great-aunt

arrière-pays /aʀjɛʀpei/ NM INV hinterland ♦ **dans l'~ niçois** in the countryside just inland from Nice

arrière-pensée (pl **arrière-pensées**) /aʀjɛʀpɑ̃se/ NF *(= motif inavoué)* ulterior motive; *(= réserves, doute)* reservation ♦ **je l'ai dit/fait sans ~** I had no ulterior motive when I said/did it ♦ **cette mesure n'est pas dénuée d'~s politiques** there's a political agenda behind this measure

arrière-petit-cousin (pl **arrière-petits-cousins**) /aʀjɛʀpətikuzɛ̃/ NM cousin three times removed

arrière-petite-cousine (pl **arrière-petites-cousines**) /aʀjɛʀpətitkuzin/ NF cousin three times removed

arrière-petite-fille (pl **arrière-petites-filles**) /aʀjɛʀpətitfij/ NF great-granddaughter

arrière-petite-nièce (pl **arrière-petites-nièces**) /aʀjɛʀpətitnjɛs/ NF great-grandniece, great-great-niece

arrière-petit-fils (pl **arrière-petits-fils**) /aʀjɛʀpətifis/ NM great-grandson

arrière-petit-neveu (pl **arrière-petits-neveux**) /aʀjɛʀpətin(ə)vø/ NM great-grandnephew, great-great-nephew

arrière-petits-enfants /aʀjɛʀpətizɑ̃fɑ̃/ NMPL great-grandchildren

arrière-plan (pl **arrière-plans**) /aʀjɛʀplɑ̃/ NM background ♦ **à l'~** in the background ♦ **ces préoccupations ont été reléguées à l'~** these concerns were put on the back burner *ou* relegated to the background

arrière-port (pl **arrière-ports**) /aʀjɛʀpɔʀ/ NM inner harbour

arriérer /aʀjeʀe/ ▸ conjug 6 ◂ *(Fin)* VT *[+ paiement]* to defer VPR **s'arriérer** to fall into arrears, to fall behind with one's *ou* the payments

arrière-saison (pl **arrière-saisons**) /aʀjɛʀsɛzɔ̃/ NF end of autumn, late autumn, late fall *(US)* ♦ **un soleil d'~** late-autumn *ou* late-fall *(US)* sunshine

arrière-salle (pl **arrière-salles**) /aʀjɛʀsal/ NF back room; *[de café, restaurant]* inner room

arrière-train (pl **arrière-trains**) /aʀjɛʀtʀɛ̃/ NM *[d'animal]* hindquarters; *(hum) [de personne]* behind*, hindquarters

arrimage /aʀimaʒ/ NM *(Naut)* stowage, stowing

arrimer /aʀime/ ▸ conjug 1 ◂ VT *(Naut) [+ cargaison]* to stow; *(gén) [+ colis]* to lash down, to secure

arrimeur /aʀimœʀ/ NM stevedore

arrivage /aʀivaʒ/ NM *[de marchandises]* consignment, delivery; *[de personnes]* batch ♦ **un nouvel ~ de volontaires** a new batch of volunteers ♦ **fruits frais, selon ~** fresh fruit, as available

arrivant, e /aʀivɑ̃, ɑ̃t/ NM,F newcomer ♦ **nouvel ~** newcomer, new arrival ♦ **combien d'~s y avait-il hier ?** how many new arrivals were there yesterday?, how many people arrived yesterday? ♦ **les premiers ~s de la saison** the first arrivals of the season

arrivée /aʀive/ NF 1 *(gén)* arrival; *[de course, coureur]* finish ♦ **l'~ de ce produit sur le marché** the appearance of this product on the market ♦ **c'est l'~ des abricots sur les marchés** apricots are beginning to arrive in *ou* are coming into the shops ♦ **j'attends l'~ du courrier** I'm waiting for the post *ou* mail to come *ou* arrive ♦ **"arrivées"** *(dans une gare, un aéroport)* "arrivals" ♦ **contactez-nous à votre ~ à l'aéroport** contact us (up)on your arrival at the airport ♦ **il m'a téléphoné dès son ~ à Megève** he phoned me as soon as he arrived in Megève ♦ **à l'~** *[de course]* at the finish; *(* = au bout du compte)* at the end of the day ♦ **j'irai l'attendre à l'~ (du train)** I'll go and get him at the station, I'll go and meet him off the train *(Brit)* ♦ **à leur ~ au pouvoir** when they came *(ou* come) to power; → **gare**[1], **juge, ligne**[1]

2 *(Tech)* **~ d'air/d'eau/de gaz** *(= robinet)* air/water/gas inlet; *(= processus)* inflow of air/water/gas

arriver /aʀive/ ▸ conjug 1 ◂ VI 1 *(au terme d'un voyage) [train, personne]* to arrive ♦ **~ à** *[+ ville]* to arrive at, to get to ♦ **~ de** *[+ ville, pays]* to arrive from ♦ **~ en France** to arrive in *ou* reach France ♦ **~ chez des amis** to arrive at friends' ♦ **~ chez soi** to arrive *ou* get home ♦ **nous sommes arrivés** we've arrived, we're there ♦ **le train doit ~ à 6 heures** the train is due to arrive *ou* is due in at 6 o'clock ♦ **il est arrivé par le train/en voiture** he arrived by train/by car *ou* in a car ♦ **réveille-toi, on arrive !** wake up, we're almost there! ♦ **cette lettre m'est arrivée hier** this letter reached me yesterday ♦ **~ le premier** *(à une course)* to come in first; *(à une soirée, une réception)* to be the first to arrive, to arrive first ♦ **les premiers arrivés** the first to arrive, the first arrivals; → **destination, mars, port**[1]

2 *(= approcher) [saison, nuit, personne, véhicule]* to come ♦ **~ à grands pas/en courant** to stride up/run up ♦ **j'arrive !** (I'm) coming!, just coming! ♦ **le train arrive en gare** the train is pulling *ou* coming into the station ♦ **la voici qui arrive** here she comes (now) ♦ **allez, arrive*, je suis pressé !** hurry up *ou* come on, I'm in a hurry! ♦ **ton tour arrivera bientôt** it'll soon be your turn ♦ **on va commencer à manger, ça va peut-être faire ~ ton père** we'll start eating, perhaps that will make your father come ♦ **pour faire ~ l'eau jusqu'à la maison ...** to lay the water on for *(Brit) ou* to bring the water (up) to the house ... ♦ **l'air/l'eau arrive par ce trou** the air/water comes in through this hole ♦ **pour qu'arrive plus vite le moment où il la reverrait** to bring the moment closer when he would see her again; → **chien**

3 *(= atteindre)* **~ à** *[+ niveau, lieu]* to reach, to get to; *[+ personne, âge]* to reach, to get to; *[+ poste, rang]* to attain, to reach; *[+ résultat, but, conclusion]* to reach, to arrive at ♦ **la nouvelle est arrivée jusqu'à nous** the news has reached us *ou* got to us ♦ **le bruit arrivait jusqu'à nous** the noise reached us ♦ **je n'ai pas pu ~ jusqu'au chef** I wasn't able to get as far as the boss ♦ **comment arrive-t-on chez eux ?** how do you get to their house? ♦ **le lierre arrive jusqu'au 1er étage** the ivy goes up to *ou* goes up as far as the 1st floor ♦ **l'eau lui arrivait (jusqu')aux genoux** the water came up to his knees, he was knee-deep in water ♦ **et le problème des salaires ? – j'y arrive** and what about the wages problem? – I'm just coming to that ♦ **il ne t'arrive pas à la cheville** *(fig)* he can't hold a candle to you, he's not a patch on you *(Brit)* ♦ **~ au pouvoir** to come to power

4 *(= réussir)* **~ à** *(+ infinitif)* to manage to do sth, to succeed in doing sth ♦ **pour ~ à lui faire comprendre qu'il a tort** to get him to understand he's wrong ♦ **il n'arrive pas à le comprendre** he just doesn't understand it ♦ **je n'arrive pas à comprendre son attitude** I just don't *ou* can't understand his attitude ♦ **je n'arrive pas à faire ce devoir** I can't do this exercise ♦ **tu y arrives ?** how are you getting on? ♦ **je n'y arrive pas** I can't do *ou* manage it ♦ **~ à ses fins** to get one's way, to achieve one's ends ♦ **il n'arrivera jamais à rien** he'll never get anywhere, he'll never achieve anything ♦ **on n'arrivera jamais à rien avec lui** we'll never get anywhere with him

5 *(= atteindre une réussite sociale)* to succeed (in life), to get on (in life) ♦ **il veut ~** he wants to get on *ou* succeed (in life) ♦ **il se croit arrivé** he thinks he's made it* *ou* he's arrived

6 *(= se produire)* to happen ♦ **c'est arrivé hier** it happened *ou* occurred yesterday ♦ **ce genre d'accident n'arrive qu'à lui !** that sort of accident only (ever) happens to him! ♦ **ce sont des choses qui arrivent** these things (will) happen ♦ **cela peut ~ à n'importe qui** it could *ou* can happen to anyone ♦ **tu n'oublies jamais ? – ça m'arrive** don't you ever forget? – yes, sometimes ♦ **cela ne m'arrivera plus !** I won't let it happen again! ♦ **tu ne sais pas ce qui m'arrive !** you'll never guess what happened (to me)! ♦ **il croit que c'est arrivé*** he thinks he's made it* ♦ **ça devait lui ~** he had it coming to him* ♦ **tu vas nous faire ~ des ennuis*** you'll get us into trouble

7 *(locutions)*

♦ **en arriver à** *(= finir par)* to come to ♦ **on n'en est pas encore arrivé là !** *(résultat négatif)* we've not come to *ou* reached that (stage) yet!; *(résultat positif)* we've not got that far yet! ♦ **on en arrive à se demander si ...** it makes you wonder whether ... ♦ **il faudra bien en ~ là** it'll have to come to that (eventually) ◆ **c'est triste d'en ~ là** it's sad to be reduced to that

VB IMPERS (= *survenir*) **il est arrivé un télégramme** a telegram has come *ou* arrived ◆ **il est arrivé un accident** there's been an accident ◆ **il lui est arrivé un accident** he's had an accident, he has met with an accident ◆ **il (lui) est arrivé un malheur** something dreadful has happened (to him) ◆ **il lui arrivera des ennuis** he'll get (himself) into trouble ◆ **il m'arrive toujours des aventures incroyables** incredible things are always happening to me ◆ **quoi qu'il arrive** whatever happens ◆ **comme il arrive souvent** as often happens, as is often the case

◆ **il arrive** *etc* **que** *ou* **de** ◆ **il arrive que j'oublie** ◆ **il m'arrive d'oublier** I sometimes forget ◆ **il peut ~ qu'elle se trompe, il peut lui ~ de se tromper** she does occasionally make a mistake, it occasionally happens that she makes a mistake ◆ **il peut ~ qu'elle se trompe mais ce n'est pas une raison pour la critiquer** she may make mistakes but that's no reason to criticize her ◆ **il pourrait ~ qu'ils soient sortis** it could be that they've gone out, they might have gone out ◆ **s'il lui arrive** *ou* **arrivait de faire une erreur, prévenez-moi** if he should happen *ou* if he happens to make a mistake, let me know ◆ **il m'est arrivé plusieurs fois de le voir/faire** I have seen him/done it several times ◆ **il ne lui arrive pas souvent de mentir** it isn't often that he lies, he doesn't often lie

arrivisme /aʀivism/ NM (*péj*) (ruthless) ambition, pushiness; (*social*) social climbing

arriviste /aʀivist/ NMF (*péj*) go-getter*, careerist; (*social*) social climber

arrobase /aʀɔbaz/ NF, **arrobas** /aʀɔbas/ NM (*en informatique*) at symbol

arroche /aʀɔʃ/ NF orache, orach (*US*)

arrogance /aʀɔgɑ̃s/ NF arrogance; **avec ~** arrogantly

arrogant, e /aʀɔgɑ̃, ɑ̃t/ ADJ arrogant

arroger (s') /aʀɔʒe/ ▸ conjug 3 ◂ VPR [*+ pouvoirs, privilèges*] to assume (without right); [*+ titre*] to claim (falsely *ou* without right) ◆ **s'~ le droit de ...** to assume the right to ..., to take it upon o.s. to ...

arrondi, e /aʀɔ̃di/ (ptp de **arrondir**) ADJ [*objet, forme, relief*] round, rounded; [*visage*] round; [*voyelle*] rounded NM (*gén* = *contour*) roundness; (= *atterrissage*) flare-out, flared landing; (= *couture*) hemline (*of skirt*)

arrondir /aʀɔ̃diʀ/ ▸ conjug 2 ◂ VT 1 [*+ objet, contour*] to round, to make round; [*+ rebord, angle*] to round off; [*+ phrases*] to polish, to round out; [*+ gestes*] to make smoother; [*+ caractère*] to make more agreeable, to smooth the rough edges off; [*+ voyelle*] to round, to make rounded; [*+ jupe*] to level; [*+ visage, taille, ventre*] to fill out, to round out ◆ **~ les angles** (*fig*) to smooth things over 2 (= *accroître*) [*+ fortune*] to swell; [*+ domaine*] to increase, to enlarge ◆ **~ ses fins de mois** to supplement one's income 3 (= *simplifier*) [*+ somme, nombre*] to round off ◆ **~ au franc inférieur/supérieur** to round down/up to the nearest franc VPR **s'arrondir** [*relief*] to become round(ed); [*taille, joues, ventre, personne*] to fill out; [*fortune*] to swell

arrondissement /aʀɔ̃dismɑ̃/ NM 1 (*Admin*) district

2 [*de voyelle*] rounding; [*de fortune*] swelling; [*de taille, ventre*] rounding, filling out

ARRONDISSEMENT

The French metropolitan and overseas départements are divided into over 300 smaller administrative areas known as **arrondissements**, which in turn are divided into « cantons » and « communes ». There are usually three or four **arrondissements** in a « département ». The main town in an **arrondissement** (the « chef-lieu d'arrondissement ») is the home of the « sous-préfecture ». The « sous-préfet d'arrondissement » reports to the « préfet » and deals with local administration, development and public order.

Marseilles, Lyons and Paris are divided into city districts known as **arrondissements**, each with its own local council (the « conseil d'arrondissement ») and mayor. The number of the **arrondissement** appears in addresses at the end of the post code. → **COMMUNE, CONSEIL, DÉPARTEMENT**

arrosage /aʀozaʒ/ NM [*de pelouse*] watering; [*de voie publique*] spraying ◆ **cette plante nécessite des ~s fréquents** this plant needs frequent watering; → **lance, tuyau**

arroser /aʀoze/ ▸ conjug 1 ◂ VT 1 [*personne*] [*+ plante, terre*] to water; (*avec un tuyau*) to water, to hose; (*légèrement*) to sprinkle; [*+ champ*] to spray; [*+ rôti*] to baste ◆ **~ qch d'essence** to pour petrol (*Brit*) *ou* gasoline (*US*) over sth ◆ **arrosez d'huile d'olive** drizzle with olive oil

2 [*pluie*] [*+ terre*] to water; [*+ personne*] (*légèrement*) to make wet; (*fortement*) to drench, to soak ◆ **c'est la ville la plus arrosée de France** it is the wettest city *ou* the city with the highest rainfall in France ◆ **se faire ~*** to get drenched *ou* soaked

3 (*Géog*) [*fleuve*] to water

4 (*Mil*) (*avec fusil, balles*) to spray (*de* with); (*avec canon*) to bombard (*de* with)

5 (*TV, Radio*) [*+ territoire*] to cover

6 (* = *fêter*) [*+ événement, succès*] to drink to

7 (* = *accompagner d'alcool*) [*+ repas*] to wash down (with wine)*; [*+ café*] to lace (with a spirit) ◆ **après un repas bien arrosé** after a meal washed down with plenty of wine, after a pretty boozy* meal ◆ **... le tout arrosé de champagne** ... all washed down with champagne

8 (* = *soudoyer*) [*+ personne*] to grease *ou* oil the palm of

9 (*littér*) [*sang*] to soak ◆ **~ une photographie de ses larmes** to let one's tears fall upon a photograph ◆ **terre arrosée de sang** blood-soaked earth

VPR **s'arroser** ◆ **tu as gagné, ça s'arrose !*** you've won - that calls for a drink *ou* let's drink to that!

arroseur /aʀozœʀ/ NM 1 [*de jardin*] waterer; [*de rue*] water cartman ◆ **c'est l'~ arrosé** it's a case of the biter (being) bit 2 (= *tourniquet*) sprinkler

arroseuse /aʀozøz/ NF [*de rue*] water cart

arrosoir /aʀozwaʀ/ NM watering can

arrt abrév de **arrondissement**

arsenal (pl **-aux**) /aʀsənal, o/ NM (*Mil*) arsenal; [*de mesures, lois*] arsenal; (* = *attirail*) gear* (*NonC*), paraphernalia (*NonC*) ◆ **l'~ du pêcheur/du photographe** the fisherman's/photographer's gear *ou* paraphernalia ◆ **tout un ~ de vieux outils** a huge collection *ou* assortment of old tools ◆ **~ (de la marine** *ou* **maritime)** (*Naut*) naval dockyard ◆ **~ juridique** judicial arsenal

arsenic /aʀsənik/ NM arsenic ◆ **empoisonnement à l'~** arsenic poisoning

arsenical, e (mpl **-aux**) /aʀsənikal, o/ ADJ [*substance*] arsenical

arsénieux /aʀsenjø/ ADJ M arsenic (*épith*) ◆ **oxyde** *ou* **anhydride ~** arsenic trioxide, arsenic

arsouille † /aʀsuj/ NM *ou* NF (= *voyou*) ruffian ◆ **il a un air ~** (= *voyou*) he looks like a ruffian; (= *malin*) he looks crafty

art /aʀ/ NM 1 (= *esthétique*) art ◆ **l'~ espagnol/populaire** Spanish/popular art ◆ **l'~ pour l'~** art for art's sake ◆ **livre/critique d'~** art book/critic ◆ **c'est du grand ~ !** (*activité*) it's poetry in motion!; (*travail excellent*) it's an excellent piece of work!; (*iro : tableau exécrable*) call that art?! ◆ **le septième ~** cinema ◆ **le huitième ~** television ◆ **le neuvième ~** comic strips, strip cartoons (*Brit*), comics (*US*); → **amateur**

2 (= *technique*) art ◆ **~ culinaire/militaire/oratoire** the art of cooking/of warfare/of public speaking ◆ **l'~ de la conversation** the art of conversation ◆ **il est passé maître dans l'~ de** he's a past master in the art of ◆ **un homme/les gens de l'~** a man/the people in the profession ◆ **demandons à un homme de l'~ !** let's ask a professional!; → **règle**

3 (= *adresse*) [*d'artisan*] skill, artistry; [*de poète*] skill, art ◆ **faire qch avec un ~ consommé** to do sth with consummate skill ◆ **c'est tout un ~** it's quite an art ◆ **il a l'~ et la manière** he's got the know-how *ou* he knows what he's doing and he does it in style

◆ **l'art de** + *infinitif* ◆ **l'~ de faire qch** the art of doing sth, a talent *ou* flair for doing sth, the knack of doing sth* ◆ **il a l'~ de me mettre en colère** he has a talent *ou* a knack* for making me angry ◆ **ce style a l'~ de me plaire** this style appeals to me ◆ **ça a l'~ de m'endormir** (*hum*) it sends me to sleep every time ◆ **réapprendre l'~ de marcher** to re-learn the art of walking

COMP **arts d'agrément** accomplishments
arts appliqués ⇒ **arts décoratifs**
art déco art deco
arts décoratifs decorative arts
l'art dramatique dramatic art, drama
les arts du feu ceramics (*sg*)
arts graphiques graphic arts
les arts libéraux the liberal arts
arts martiaux martial arts
arts ménagers (= *technique*) home economics, homecraft (*NonC*), domestic science ◆ **les Arts ménagers** (*salon*) ≃ the Ideal Home Exhibition
les Arts et Métiers *higher education institute for industrial art and design*
l'art nègre African art
art nouveau Art Nouveau
les arts plastiques the visual arts, the fine arts
art poétique (= *technique*) poetic art; (= *doctrine*) ars poetica, poetics (*sg*)
les arts de la rue street performance
les arts de la scène *ou* **du spectacle** the performing arts
les arts de la table the art of entertaining (*preparing and presenting food*)
art de vivre way of life

art. (abrév de **article**) art

Arte /aʀte/ N (*TV*) *Franco-German cultural television channel*

artefact /aʀtefakt/ NM artefact

Artémis /aʀtemis/ NF Artemis

artère /aʀtɛʀ/ NF 1 (*Anat*) artery 2 (= *route*) **(grande) ~** (*en ville*) main road, thoroughfare; (*entre villes*) main (trunk) road

artériel, -ielle /aʀteʀjɛl/ ADJ (*Anat*) arterial; → **tension**

artériographie /aʀteʀjɔgʀafi/ NF arteriography

artériole /aʀteʀjɔl/ NF arteriole

artériosclérose /aʀteʀjoskleʀoz/ NF arteriosclerosis

artérite /aʀteʀit/ NF arteritis

artésien, -ienne /aʀtezjɛ̃, jɛn/ ADJ Artois (*épith*), of ou from Artois; → **puits**

arthrite /aʀtʀit/ NF arthritis ◆ **avoir de l'~** to have arthritis

arthritique /aʀtʀitik/ ADJ, NMF arthritic

arthritisme /aʀtʀitism/ NM arthritism

arthropode /aʀtʀɔpɔd/ NM arthropod

arthrose /aʀtʀoz/ NF (degenerative) osteoarthritis

arthrosique /aʀtʀozik/ ADJ osteoarthritic NMF osteoarthritis sufferer

Arthur /aʀtyʀ/ NM Arthur ◆ **le roi ~** King Arthur; → **appeler**

arthurien, -ienne /aʀtyʀjɛ̃, jɛn/ ADJ [*cycle, mythe*] Arthurian

artichaut /aʀtiʃo/ NM artichoke; → **cœur, fond**

article /aʀtikl/ NM 1 (= *objet en vente*) item, article ◆ **baisse sur tous nos ~s** all (our) stock ou all items reduced, reduction on all items ◆ **~ d'importation** imported product ◆ **nous ne faisons plus cet ~** we don't stock that item ou product any more ◆ **faire l'~** (*pour vendre qch*) to give the sales pitch; (*fig*) to sing sth's ou sb's praises

2 [*de journal*] article; [*de dictionnaire*] entry

3 (= *chapitre*) point; [*de loi, traité*] article ◆ **les 2 derniers ~s de cette lettre** the last 2 points in this letter ◆ **sur cet ~** on this point ◆ **sur l'~ de** in the matter of, in matters of

4 (*Gram*) article ◆ **~ contracté/défini/élidé/indéfini/partitif** contracted/definite/elided/indefinite/partitive article

5 (*Ordin*) record, item

6 ◆ **à l'~ de la mort** at death's door, at the point of death

COMP **articles de bureau** office accessories
articles de consommation courante convenience goods
article de foi (*lit, fig*) article of faith
article de fond (*Presse*) feature article
articles de luxe luxury goods
articles de mode fashion accessories
articles de Paris † fancy goods
articles de sport (*vêtements*) sportswear; (*objets*) sports equipment
articles de toilette toiletries
articles de voyage travel goods

articulaire /aʀtikylɛʀ/ ADJ articular; → **rhumatisme**

articulation /aʀtikylasjɔ̃/ NF 1 (*Anat*) joint; (*Tech*) articulation ◆ **~s des doigts** knuckles, finger joints ◆ **~ du genou/de la hanche/de l'épaule** knee/hip/shoulder joint ◆ **~ en selle** saddle joint 2 [*de discours, raisonnement*] linking sentence ◆ **la bonne ~ des parties de son discours** the sound structuring of his speech 3 (*Ling*) articulation ◆ **point d'~** point of articulation 4 (*Jur*) enumeration, setting forth

articulatoire /aʀtikylatwaʀ/ ADJ articulatory

articulé, e /aʀtikyle/ (ptp de **articuler**) ADJ 1 (= *avec des articulations*) [*membre*] jointed, articulated; [*objet*] jointed; [*poupée*] with movable joints (*épith*) ◆ **autobus ~** articulated bus 2 [*langage*] articulate NM ◆ **~ dentaire** bite

articuler /aʀtikyle/ ► conjug 1 ◄ VT 1 [+ *mot*] (= *prononcer clairement*) to articulate, to pronounce clearly; (= *dire*) to pronounce, to utter ◆ **il articule bien/mal ses phrases** he articulates ou speaks/doesn't articulate ou speak clearly ◆ **il articule mal** he doesn't articulate ou speak clearly ◆ **articule !** speak clearly!

2 (= *joindre*) [+ *mécanismes, os*] to articulate, to joint; [+ *idées*] to link (up ou together) ◆ **élément/os qui s'articule sur un autre** element/bone that is articulated with ou is jointed to another ◆ **~ un discours sur deux thèmes principaux** to structure a speech around ou on two main themes ◆ **toute sa défense s'articule autour de cet élément** his entire defence hinges ou turns on this factor ◆ **les parties de son discours s'articulent bien** the different sections of his speech are well linked ou hang together well ◆ **une grande salle autour de laquelle s'articulent une multitude de locaux** a large room surrounded by a multitude of offices

3 (*Jur*) [+ *faits, griefs*] to enumerate, to set out

artifice /aʀtifis/ NM (clever ou ingenious) device, trick; (*péj*) trick ◆ **~ de calcul** (clever) trick of arithmetic ◆ **~ comptable** accounting device ◆ **~ de style** stylistic device ◆ **user d'~s pour paraître belle** to resort to tricks ou artifice to make oneself look beautiful ◆ **l'~ est une nécessité de l'art** art cannot exist without (some) artifice ◆ **sans ~(s)** [*présentation*] simple; [*s'exprimer*] straightforwardly, unpretentiously; → **feu**[1]

artificiel, -ielle /aʀtifisjɛl/ ADJ 1 (= *fabriqué*) artificial; [*fibre*] man-made; [*colorant*] artificial, synthetic; [*dent*] false; [*île*] artificial, man-made; → **insémination, intelligence** *etc* 2 (*péj*) [*raisonnement, style*] artificial, contrived; [*vie, besoins*] artificial; [*gaieté*] forced, artificial

artificiellement /aʀtifisjɛlmɑ̃/ ADV artificially ◆ **fabriqué ~** man-made, synthetically made

artificier /aʀtifisje/ NM (= *fabricant*) firework(s) manufacturer ou maker; (= *pyrotechnicien*) pyrotechnician; (*pour désamorçage*) bomb disposal expert

artificieux, -ieuse /aʀtifisjø, jøz/ ADJ (*littér*) guileful, deceitful

artillerie /aʀtijʀi/ NF artillery, ordnance ◆ **~ de campagne** field artillery ◆ **~ de marine** naval guns ◆ **grosse ~, ~ lourde** (*lit, fig*) heavy artillery ◆ **pièce d'~** piece of artillery, gun ◆ **tir d'~** artillery fire

artilleur /aʀtijœʀ/ NM artilleryman, gunner

artimon /aʀtimɔ̃/ NM (= *voile*) mizzen; (= *mât*) mizzen(mast); → **mât**

artisan /aʀtizɑ̃/ NM 1 (= *patron*) self-employed craftsman, craft worker ◆ **les petits ~s** small craftsmen ◆ **il a été ~ avant de travailler pour moi** he ran his own business ou he was self-employed before coming to work for me ◆ **~ boulanger** master baker ◆ **~ boucher** (*sur vitrine*) ≈ quality butcher 2 (= *auteur, cause*) [*d'accord, politique, victoire*] architect ◆ **~ de la paix** peacemaker ◆ **il est l'~ de sa propre ruine** he has brought about ou he is the author of his own ruin

artisanal, e (mpl **-aux**) /aʀtizanal, o/ ADJ [*production*] (= *limitée*) small-scale (*épith*), on a small scale (*attrib*); (= *traditionnelle*) traditional ◆ **entreprise ~e** small company ◆ **foire ~e** arts and crafts fair, craft fair ◆ **pêche ~e** local ou small-scale fishing ◆ **la production ~e de ce médicament** the production of this medicine on a small scale ◆ **il exerce une activité ~e** he's a self-employed craftsman ◆ **la fabrication se fait de manière très ~e** (*traditionnellement*) the style of production is very traditional; (*à petite échelle*) the style of production is very much that of a cottage industry ◆ **bombe de fabrication ~e** home-made bomb ◆ **produits artisanaux** crafts, handicrafts

artisanalement /aʀtizanalmɑ̃/ ADV ◆ **fabriqué ~** [*pain, fromage*] made using traditional methods; [*objet*] hand-crafted

artisanat /aʀtizana/ NM (= *métier*) craft industry ◆ **l'~ local** (= *industrie*) local crafts ou handicrafts ◆ **l'~ d'art** arts and crafts

artiste /aʀtist/ NMF 1 (*gén*) artist; (= *interprète*) performer; [*de music-hall, cirque*] artiste, entertainer ◆ **~ dramatique/de cinéma** stage/film actor ou actress ◆ **~ invité** guest artist ◆ **~ peintre** artist, painter; → **entrée, travail**[1] 2 (*péj* = *bohème*) bohemian ADJ [*personne, style*] artistic ◆ **il est du genre ~** (*péj*) he's the artistic ou bohemian type

artiste-interprète (pl **artistes-interprètes**) /aʀtistɛtɛʀpʀɛt/ NMF [*de musique*] composer and performer; [*de chanson, pièce*] writer and performer

artistement /aʀtistəmɑ̃/ ADV artistically

artistique /aʀtistik/ ADJ artistic

artistiquement /aʀtistikmɑ̃/ ADV artistically

ARTT /aɛʀtete/ NM (abrév de **accord sur la réduction du temps de travail**) agreement on the reduction of working hours

arum /aʀɔm/ NM arum lily

aryen, -yenne /aʀjɛ̃, jɛn/ ADJ Aryan NM,F **Aryen(ne)** Aryan

arythmie /aʀitmi/ NF arrhythmia

AS /aɛs/ NFPL (abrév de **assurances sociales**) → **assurance** NF (abrév de **association sportive**) → **association**

as /ɑs/ NM 1 (= *carte, dé*) ace ◆ **l'~** (*Hippisme, au loto*) number one 2 (* = *champion*) ace* ◆ **un ~ de la route/du ciel** a crack driver/pilot ◆ **l'~ de l'école** the school's star pupil 3 (*Tennis*) ace ◆ **réussir** ou **servir un ~** to serve an ace 4 (*locutions*) **être ficelé** ou **fagoté comme l'~ de pique*** to be dressed any old how* ◆ **être (plein) aux ~**‡ to be loaded*, to be rolling in it*

◆ **passer à l'as** ◆ **les apéritifs sont passés à l'~*** (= *on ne les a pas payés*) we got away without paying for the drinks, we got the drinks for free* ◆ **mes vacances sont passées à l'~*** my holidays went by the board (*Brit*), my vacation went down the drain ◆ **il n'y avait pas assez de place, mon texte est passé à l'~** there wasn't enough room so my article was ditched*

ASA /aza/ NM INV (abrév de **American Standards Association**) (*Photo*) ASA

asbeste /asbɛst/ NM asbestos

asbestose /asbɛstoz/ NF asbestosis

ascendance /asɑ̃dɑ̃s/ NF 1 (*généalogique*) ancestry ◆ **son ~ paternelle** his paternal ancestry ◆ **être d'~ bourgeoise** to be of middle-class descent 2 (*Astron*) rising, ascent ◆ **~ thermique** (*Météo*) thermal

ascendant, e /asɑ̃dɑ̃, ɑt/ ADJ [*astre*] rising, ascending; [*mouvement, direction*] upward; [*courant*] rising; [*progression*] ascending; [*trait*] rising; (*Généalogie*) [*ligne*] ancestral ◆ **mouvement ~ du piston** upstroke of the piston NM 1 (= *influence*) (powerful) influence, ascendancy (*sur* over); ◆ **subir l'~ de qn** to be under sb's influence 2 (*Admin*) **~s** ascendants 3 (*Astron*) rising star; (*Astrol*) ascendant

ascenseur /asɑ̃sœʀ/ NM lift (*Brit*), elevator (*US*); (*Ordin*) scroll bar ◆ **l'~ social** the social ladder; → **renvoyer**

ascension /asɑ̃sjɔ̃/ NF 1 (= *montée*) [*de ballon*] ascent, rising; [*de fusée*] ascent 2 (= *escalade*) [*de montagne*] ascent ◆ **faire l'~ d'une montagne** to climb a mountain, to make the ascent of a mountain ◆ **la première ~ de l'Everest** the first ascent of Everest ◆ **c'est une ~ difficile** it's a difficult climb ◆ **faire des ~s** to go (mountain) climbing 3 [*d'homme politique*] (*sociale*) rise ◆ **~ professionnelle** career ou professional advancement 4 (*Rel*) **l'Ascension** the Ascension; (*jour férié*) Ascension (Day) ◆ **l'île de l'Ascension** Ascension Island 5 (*Astron*) **~ droite** right ascension

ascensionnel, -elle /asɑ̃sjɔnɛl/ ADJ *[mouvement]* upward; *[force]* upward, elevatory ◆ **vitesse ~le** climbing speed; → **parachute**

ascensionniste /asɑ̃sjɔnist/ NMF ascensionist

ascèse /asɛz/ NF asceticism

ascète /asɛt/ NMF ascetic

ascétique /asetik/ ADJ ascetic

ascétisme /asetism/ NM asceticism

ASCII /aski/ NM (abrév de **American Standard Code for Information Interchange**) ASCII ◆ **code ~** ASCII code

ascorbique /askɔʀbik/ ADJ *[acide]* ascorbic

ASE /aɛsə/ NF (abrév de **Agence spatiale européenne**) ESA

asémantique /asemɑ̃tik/ ADJ asemantic

asepsie /asɛpsi/ NF asepsis

aseptique /asɛptik/ ADJ aseptic

aseptisation /asɛptizasjɔ̃/ NF *[de pièce]* fumigation; *[de pansement, ustensile]* sterilization; *[de plaie]* disinfection

aseptisé, e /asɛptize/ (ptp de **aseptiser**) ADJ [1] *(Méd)* sterilized [2] *(fig)* *[univers, images]* sanitized; *[document, discours]* impersonal; *[relation entre personnes]* sterile; *[film, roman]* anodyne, bland

aseptiser /asɛptize/ ▸ conjug 1 ◂ VT *[+ pièce]* to fumigate; *[+ pansement, ustensile]* to sterilize; *[+ plaie]* to disinfect

asexué, e /asɛksɥe/ ADJ *(Bio)* asexual; *[personne]* sexless, asexual

ashkénaze /aʃkenɑz/ ADJ, NMF Ashkenazi

ashram /aʃʀam/ NM ashram

asiate** /azjat/ NMF *(injurieux)* Asian

asiatique /azjatik/ ADJ Asian ◆ **la grippe ~** Asian flu ◆ **le Sud-Est ~** South-East Asia ◆ **la communauté ~ de Paris** the far eastern community in Paris NMF **Asiatique** Asian

Asie /azi/ NF Asia ◆ **~ Mineure** Asia Minor ◆ **~ centrale** Central Asia ◆ **~ du Sud-Est** South-east Asia

asile /azil/ NM [1] *(= institution)* **~ (de vieillards)** † old people's home, retirement home ◆ **~ psychiatrique** mental home ◆ **~ (d'aliénés)** † (lunatic) asylum † ◆ **~ de nuit** night shelter, hostel [2] *(= refuge)* refuge; *(dans une église)* sanctuary ◆ **demander ~ à qn** to ask sb for refuge ◆ **demander l'~ politique** to seek political asylum ◆ **il a trouvé ~ chez un ami** he found refuge at the home of a friend ◆ **droit d'~** *(Rel)* right of sanctuary; *(politique)* right of asylum ◆ **sans ~** homeless

Asmara /asmaʀa/ N Asmara

asocial, e (mpl **-iaux**) /asɔsjal, jo/ ADJ *[comportement]* antisocial NM,F social misfit, socially maladjusted person

asparagus /aspaʀagys/ NM *(= plante d'ornement)* asparagus fern

aspartam(e) /aspaʀtam/ NM aspartame

aspect /aspɛ/ GRAMMAIRE ACTIVE 53.1, 53.2 NM [1] *(= allure)* *[de personne, objet, paysage]* appearance, look ◆ **homme d'~ sinistre** sinister-looking man, man of sinister appearance ◆ **l'intérieur de cette grotte a l'~ d'une église** the inside of the cave resembles *ou* looks like a church ◆ **les nuages prenaient l'~ de montagnes** the clouds took on the appearance of mountains ◆ **ce château a un ~ mystérieux** the castle has an air of mystery (about it) [2] *(= angle)* *[de question]* aspect, side ◆ **vu sous cet ~** seen from that angle ◆ **j'ai examiné le problème sous tous ses ~s** I considered all aspects *ou* sides of the problem [3] *(Astrol, Ling)* aspect [4] *(littér = vue)* sight ◆ **à l'~ de** at the sight of

> ⚠ Au sens de 'allure' ou 'vue', **aspect** ne se traduit pas par le mot anglais **aspect**.

asperge /aspɛʀʒ/ NF [1] *(= plante)* asparagus; → **pointe** [2] *(* = personne)* **(grande) ~** beanpole*, string bean* *(US)*

asperger /aspɛʀʒe/ ▸ conjug 3 ◂ VT *[+ surface]* to spray; *(légèrement)* to sprinkle; *(Rel)* to sprinkle; *[+ personne]* to splash *(de* with); ◆ **s'~ le visage** to splash one's face with water ◆ **le bus nous a aspergés au passage*** the bus splashed us *ou* sprayed water over us as it went past ◆ **se faire ~*** *(par une voiture)* to get splashed; *(par un arroseur)* to get wet

aspérité /aspeʀite/ NF [1] *(= partie saillante)* bump ◆ **les ~s de la table** the bumps on the table, the rough patches on the surface of the table ◆ **sans ~s** *[chemin, surface]* smooth [2] *(littér)* *[de caractère, remarques, voix]* harshness ◆ **sans ~s** *[caractère]* mild; *[remarques]* uncontroversial; *[voix]* smooth ◆ **gommer les ~s de qch** to smooth the rough edges off sth

aspersion /aspɛʀsjɔ̃/ NF spraying, sprinkling; *(Rel)* sprinkling of holy water, aspersion

asphalte /asfalt/ NM asphalt

asphalter /asfalte/ ▸ conjug 1 ◂ VT to asphalt

asphérique /asfeʀik/ ADJ *(Photo)* *[lentille]* aspherical

asphodèle /asfɔdɛl/ NM asphodel

asphyxiant, e /asfiksjɑ̃, jɑt/ ADJ *[fumée]* suffocating, asphyxiating; *[atmosphère]* stifling, suffocating; → **gaz**

asphyxie /asfiksi/ NF *(gén)* suffocation, asphyxiation; *(Méd)* asphyxia; *[de plante]* asphyxiation; *(fig)* *[de personne]* suffocation; *[d'industrie]* stifling

asphyxier /asfiksje/ ▸ conjug 7 ◂ VT *(lit)* to suffocate, to asphyxiate; *(fig)* *[+ industrie, esprit]* to stifle ◆ **mourir asphyxié** to die of suffocation *ou* asphyxiation VPR **s'asphyxier** *(accident)* to suffocate, to be asphyxiated; *(suicide)* to suffocate o.s.; *(fig)* to suffocate ◆ **il s'est asphyxié au gaz** he gassed himself

aspic /aspik/ NM *(= serpent)* asp; *(= plante)* aspic ◆ **~ de volaille/de foie gras** *(Culin)* chicken/foie gras in aspic

aspirant, e /aspiʀɑ̃, ɑt/ ADJ suction *(épith)*, vacuum *(épith)*; → **pompe**[1] NM,F *(= candidat)* candidate *(à* for) NM *(Mil)* officer cadet; *(Naut)* midshipman, middie* *(US)*

aspirateur, -trice /aspiʀatœʀ, tʀis/ ADJ aspiratory NM *(domestique)* vacuum (cleaner), Hoover ® *(Brit)*; *(Constr, Méd)* aspirator ◆ **passer les tapis à l'~** to vacuum *ou* hoover the carpets, to run the vacuum cleaner *ou* Hoover over the carpets ◆ **passer l'~** to vacuum, to hoover ◆ **passer** *ou* **donner un coup d'~ dans la voiture** to give the car a quick going-over with the vacuum cleaner *ou* Hoover

COMP **aspirateur(-)balai** upright vacuum cleaner *ou* Hoover ®

aspirateur de site site capture software package

aspirateur(-)traîneau *(horizontal)* cylinder vacuum cleaner *ou* Hoover ®

aspiration /aspiʀasjɔ̃/ NF [1] *(en inspirant)* inhaling *(NonC)*, inhalation; *(Ling)* aspiration ◆ **de longues ~s** long deep breaths [2] *[de liquide]* *(avec une paille)* sucking (up); *(avec une pompe)* sucking up, drawing up; *(= technique d'avortement)* vacuum extraction [3] *(= ambition)* aspiration *(vers, à* for, after); *(= souhait)* desire, longing *(vers, à* for)

aspiré, e /aspiʀe/ (ptp de **aspirer**) ADJ *(Ling)* aspirated ◆ **h ~** aspirate h NF **aspirée** aspirate

aspirer /aspiʀe/ ▸ conjug 1 ◂ VT [1] *[+ air, odeur]* to inhale, to breathe in; *[+ liquide]* *(avec une paille)* to suck (up); *(avec une pompe)* to suck *ou* draw up ◆ **~ et refouler** to pump in and out [2] *(Ling)* to aspirate VT INDIR **aspirer à** *[+ honneur, titre]* to aspire to; *[+ genre de vie, tranquillité]* to desire, to long for ◆ **aspirant à quitter cette vie surexcitée** longing to leave this hectic life ◆ **~ à la main de qn** † to be sb's suitor †, to aspire to sb's hand †

aspirine /aspiʀin/ NF aspirin ◆ **(comprimé** *ou* **cachet d')~** aspirin ◆ **prenez 2 ~s** take 2 aspirins; → **blanc**

aspiro-batteur (pl **aspiro-batteurs**) /aspiʀobatœʀ/ NM vacuum cleaner, Hoover ® *(Brit)* *(which beats as it sweeps)*

ASS /as/ NF (abrév de **allocation de solidarité spécifique**) *minimum Social Security benefit*

assagir /asaʒiʀ/ ▸ conjug 2 ◂ VT [1] *(= calmer)* *[+ personne]* to quieten *(Brit)* *ou* quiet *(US)* down, to settle down; *[+ passion]* to subdue, to temper, to quieten *(Brit)*, to quiet *(US)* ◆ **elle n'arrivait pas à ~ ses cheveux rebelles** she couldn't do anything with her hair [2] *(littér = rendre plus sage)* to make wiser VPR **s'assagir** *[personne]* to quieten *(Brit)* *ou* quiet *(US)* down, to settle down; *[style, passions]* to become subdued

assagissement /asaʒismɑ̃/ NM *[de personne]* quietening *(Brit)* *ou* quieting *(US)* down, settling down; *[de passions]* subduing

assaillant, e /asajɑ̃, ɑt/ NM,F assailant, attacker

assaillir /asajiʀ/ ▸ conjug 13 ◂ VT *(lit)* to assail, to attack; *(fig)* to assail *(de* with); ◆ **assailli de questions** assailed *ou* bombarded with questions

assainir /aseniʀ/ ▸ conjug 2 ◂ VT *[+ quartier, logement]* to clean up, to improve the living conditions in; *[+ marécage]* to drain; *[+ air, eau]* to purify, to decontaminate; *[+ finances, marché]* to stabilize; *[+ monnaie]* to rehabilitate, to re-establish ◆ **la situation s'est assainie** the situation has become healthier ◆ **~ l'atmosphère** *(fig)* to clear the air

assainissement /asenismɑ̃/ NM *[de quartier, logement]* cleaning up; *[de marécage]* draining; *[d'air, eau]* purification, decontamination; *[de finances, marché]* stabilization ◆ **~ monétaire** rehabilitation *ou* re-establishment of a currency ◆ **~ budgétaire** stabilization of the budget ◆ **des travaux d'~** drainage work

assaisonnement /asɛzɔnmɑ̃/ NM *(= méthode)* *[de salade]* dressing, seasoning; *[de plat]* seasoning; *(= ingrédient)* seasoning

assaisonner /asɛzɔne/ ▸ conjug 1 ◂ VT [1] *(Culin)* *(avec sel, poivre, épices)* to season *(de, avec* with) to add seasoning to; *(avec huile, citron)* to dress *(de, avec* with); *(fig)* *[+ discours]* to spice (up) ◆ **j'ai trop assaisonné la salade** I've put too much dressing on the salad [2] (* †) *[+ personne]* *(verbalement)* to tell off*; *(financièrement)* to clobber*, to sting*

assassin, e /asasɛ̃, in/ NM *(gén)* murderer; *(Pol)* assassin ◆ **l'~ court toujours** the killer *ou* murderer is still at large ◆ **à l'~ !** murder! ADJ *[œillade]* provocative ◆ **lancer un regard ~ à qn** to look daggers at sb ◆ **une (petite) phrase ~e** a jibe

assassinat /asasina/ NM murder; *(Pol)* assassination

assassiner /asasine/ ▸ conjug 1 ◂ VT to murder; *(Pol)* to assassinate ◆ **mes créanciers m'assassinent !*** my creditors are bleeding me white!*

assaut /aso/ NM *(Mil)* assault, attack *(de* on); *(Boxe, Escrime)* bout; *(Alpinisme)* assault; *(fig)* *[de temps]* onslaught ◆ **donner l'~ à, monter à l'~ de** to storm, to attack ◆ **ils donnent l'~** they're attacking ◆ **à l'~ !** charge! ◆ **résister aux ~s de l'ennemi** to resist the enemy's attacks *ou* onslaughts ◆ **partir à l'~ de** *(lit)* to attack ◆ **de petites firmes sont parties à l'~ d'un marché international** small firms are seeking to capture the international market • **prendre d'~** *(lit)* to take by storm, to assault • **prendre une place d'~** *(fig)* to grab a seat • **les librairies étaient prises d'~** people flocked to the bookshops • **ils faisaient ~ de politesse** they were falling over each other to be polite; → char

assèchement /asɛʃmɑ̃/ NM 1 *(par l'homme) [de terrain]* draining; *[de réservoir]* draining, emptying 2 *(= processus naturel) [de terrain]* drying (out); *[de réservoir]* drying (up) 3 *(Fin) [de marché, crédits]* drying up

assécher /aseʃe/ ▸ conjug 6 ◂ VT 1 *[+ terrain] [homme]* to drain; *[vent, évaporation]* to dry (out); *[+ réservoir] [homme]* to drain, to empty; *[vent, évaporation]* to dry (up) 2 *[+ marché, crédits]* to dry up VPR **s'assécher** *[cours d'eau, réservoir]* to dry up

ASSEDIC /asedik/ NFPL (abrév de **Association pour l'emploi dans l'industrie et le commerce**) *organization managing unemployment insurance payments*

assemblage /asɑ̃blaʒ/ NM 1 *(= action) [d'éléments, parties]* assembling, putting together; *(Menuiserie)* assembling, jointing; *[de meuble, maquette, machine]* assembling, assembly; *(Ordin)* assembly; *(Typo) [de feuilles]* gathering; *(Couture) [de pièces]* sewing together; *[de robe, pull-over]* sewing together *ou* up, making up • ~ **de pièces par soudure/collage** soldering/glueing together of parts 2 *(Menuiserie = jointure)* joint • ~ **à vis/par rivets/à onglet** screwed/rivet(ed)/mitre joint 3 *(= structure)* **une charpente est un ~ de poutres** the framework of a roof is an assembly of beams • **toit fait d'~s métalliques** roof made of metal structures 4 *(= réunion) [de couleurs, choses, personnes]* collection 5 *(Art = tableau)* assemblage

assemblé /asɑ̃ble/ NM *(Danse)* assemblé

assemblée /asɑ̃ble/ NF *(gén = réunion, foule)* gathering; *(= réunion convoquée)* meeting; *(Pol)* assembly • **l'~ des fidèles** *(Rel)* the congregation • ~ **mensuelle/extraordinaire/plénière** monthly/extraordinary/plenary meeting • ~ **générale** *(Écon)* annual general meeting *(Brit)*, general meeting *(US)*; *[d'étudiants]* (extraordinary) general meeting • ~ **générale extraordinaire** extraordinary general meeting • **réunis en ~** gathered *ou* assembled for a meeting • **à la grande joie de l'~** to the great joy of the assembled company *ou* of those present • **l'Assemblée (nationale)** the French National Assembly • **l'Assemblée parlementaire européenne** the European Parliament • ~ **délibérante** *(Pol)* deliberating assembly

ASSEMBLÉE NATIONALE

The term **Assemblée nationale** has been used to refer to the lower house of the French parliament since 1946, though the old term « la Chambre des députés » is sometimes still used. Its members are elected in the « élections législatives » for a five-year term. It has similar legislative powers to the House of Commons in Britain and the House of Representatives in the United States. Sittings of the **Assemblée nationale** are public, and take place in a semicircular amphitheatre (« l'Hémicycle ») in the Palais Bourbon. → DÉPUTÉ, ÉLECTIONS

assembler /asɑ̃ble/ ▸ conjug 1 ◂ VT 1 *(= réunir) [+ données, matériaux]* to gather, to collect; *(Pol) [+ comité]* to convene, to assemble; † *[+ personnes]* to assemble, to gather; *(Typo) [+ feuilles]* to gather • ~ **les pieds** *(Danse)* to take up third position 2 *(= joindre) [+ meuble, machine]* to assemble; *[+ pull, robe]* to sew together, to make up; *(Menuiserie)* to joint; *[+ couleurs, sons]* to put together • ~ **par soudure/collage** to solder/glue together VPR **s'assembler** *[foule]* to gather, to collect; *[participants, conseil, groupe]* to assemble, to gather; *[nuages]* to gather; → **ressembler**

assembleur, -euse /asɑ̃blœʀ, øz/ NM,F *(= ouvrier) (gén)* assembler, fitter; *(Typo)* gatherer NM *(Ordin)* assembler NF **assembleuse** *(Typo = machine)* gathering machine

assener, asséner /asene/ ▸ conjug 5 ◂ VT *[+ coup]* to strike; *[+ argument]* to thrust forward; *[+ propagande]* to deal out; *[+ réplique]* to thrust *ou* fling back • ~ **un coup à qn** to deal sb a blow

assentiment /asɑ̃timɑ̃/ GRAMMAIRE ACTIVE 38.3 NM *(= consentement)* assent, consent; *(= approbation)* approval • **sans mon ~** without my consent • **donner son ~ à** to give one's assent *ou* consent to

asseoir /aswaʀ/ ▸ conjug 26 ◂ VT 1 • ~ **qn** *(personne debout)* to sit sb down; *(personne couchée)* to sit sb up • ~ **qn sur une chaise/dans un fauteuil** to sit *ou* seat sb on a chair/in an armchair • ~ **un enfant sur ses genoux** to sit a child on one's knee • ~ **un prince sur le trône** *(fig)* to put *ou* set a prince on the throne; → aussi **assis**

2 • **faire ~ qn** to ask sb to sit down • **faire ~ ses invités** to ask one's guests to sit down *ou* to take a seat • **je leur ai parlé après les avoir fait ~** I talked to them after asking them to sit down • **fais-la ~, elle est fatiguée** get her to sit down, she's tired

3 *(frm = affermir) [+ réputation]* to establish, to assure; *[+ autorité, théorie]* to establish • ~ **une maison sur du granit** to build a house on granite • ~ **les fondations sur** to lay *ou* build the foundations on • ~ **sa réputation sur qch** to build one's reputation on sth • ~ **une théorie sur des faits** to base a theory on facts • ~ **son jugement sur des témoignages dignes de foi** to base one's judgment on reliable evidence

4 *(* = stupéfier)* to stagger, to stun • **son inconscience m'assoit** his foolishness staggers me, I'm stunned by his foolishness • **j'en suis** *ou* **reste assis de voir que ...** I'm staggered *ou* flabbergasted * to see that ...

5 *(Fin)* ~ **un impôt** to base a tax, to fix a tax *(sur on)*

VPR **s'asseoir** *[personne debout]* to sit (o.s.) down; *[personne couchée]* to sit up • **asseyez-vous donc** do sit down, do have *ou* take a seat • **asseyez-vous par terre** sit (down) on the floor • **il n'y a rien pour s'~** there's nothing to sit on • **le règlement, je m'assieds dessus !** * you know what you can do with the rules! ‡ • **s'~ à califourchon (sur qch)** to sit (down) astride (sth) • **s'~ en tailleur** to sit (down) cross-legged

assermenté, e /asɛʀmɑ̃te/ ADJ *[témoin, expert]* on oath *(attrib)*

assertif, -ive /asɛʀtif, iv/ ADJ *[phrase]* declarative

assertion /asɛʀsjɔ̃/ NF assertion

asservi, e /asɛʀvi/ (ptp de **asservir**) ADJ *[peuple]* enslaved; *[presse]* subservient • **moteur ~** servomotor

asservir /asɛʀviʀ/ ▸ conjug 2 ◂ VT *(= assujettir) [+ personne]* to enslave; *[+ pays]* to reduce to slavery, to subjugate; *(littér = maîtriser) [+ passions, nature]* to overcome, to master • **être asservi** *[moteur]* to have servo-control • **être asservi à** to be a slave to

asservissant, e /asɛʀvisɑ̃, ɑ̃t/ ADJ *[règles]* oppressive • **avoir un travail ~** to have a very demanding job

asservissement /asɛʀvismɑ̃/ NM *(= action)* enslavement; *(lit, fig = état)* slavery, subservience *(à to)*; *(Élec)* servo-control *(NonC)* *(à by)*

assesseur /asesœʀ/ NM assessor

assez /ase/ GRAMMAIRE ACTIVE 41 ADV 1 *(= suffisamment) (avec vb)* enough; *(devant adj, adv)* enough, sufficiently • **bien ~** quite enough, plenty • **tu as (bien) ~ mangé** you've had *ou* eaten (quite) enough, you've had (quite) enough to eat • **c'est bien ~ grand** it's quite big enough • **plus qu'~** more than enough • **je n'ai pas ~ travaillé** I haven't done enough work, I haven't worked enough • **il ne vérifie pas ~ souvent** he doesn't check often enough • **tu travailles depuis ~ longtemps** you've been working (for) long enough • **ça a ~ duré !** this has gone on long enough! • **combien voulez-vous ? est-ce que 10 € c'est ~ ? – c'est bien ~** how much do you want? is €10 enough? – that will be plenty *ou* ample • **il a juste ~** he has just enough; → **peu**

♦ **assez de** *(quantité, nombre)* enough • **avez-vous acheté ~ de pain/d'oranges ?** have you bought enough *ou* sufficient bread/enough oranges? • **il n'y a pas ~ de viande** there's not enough meat • **ils sont ~ de deux pour ce travail** the two of them are enough *ou* will do * for this job • **j'en ai ~ de 3** 3 will be enough for me *ou* will do (for) me * • **n'apportez pas de verres, il y en a ~** don't bring any glasses, there are enough *ou* we have enough

♦ **assez + pour** enough • **as-tu trouvé une boîte ~ grande pour tout mettre ?** have you found a big enough box *ou* a box big enough to put it all in? • **le village est ~ près pour qu'elle puisse y aller à pied** the village is near enough for her to walk there • **je n'ai pas ~ d'argent pour m'offrir cette voiture** I can't afford (to buy myself) this car, I haven't got enough money to buy myself this car • **il est ~ idiot pour refuser !** he's stupid enough to refuse! • **il n'est pas ~ sot pour le croire** he's not so stupid as to believe it

2 *(intensif)* rather, quite • **la situation est ~ inquiétante** the situation is rather *ou* somewhat worrying • **ce serait ~ agréable d'avoir un jour de congé** it would be rather *ou* quite nice to have a day off • **il était ~ tard quand ils sont partis** it was quite *ou* pretty * late when they left • **j'ai oublié son adresse, est-ce ~ bête !** how stupid (of me), I've forgotten his address! • **je l'ai ~ vu !** I've seen (more than) enough of him! • **elle était déjà ~ malade il y a 2 ans** she was already quite ill 2 years ago • **je suis ~ de ton avis** I'm inclined to agree with you

3 *(locutions)* **en voilà ~ !, c'est ~ !, c'en est ~ !** I've had enough!, enough is enough! • ~ **!** that will do!, that's (quite) enough! • ~ **parlé** *ou* **de discours, des actes !** that's enough talk, let's have some action!

♦ **en avoir assez** *(= ne plus supporter)* to have had enough • **j'en ai (plus qu')~ de toi et de tes jérémiades** * I've had (more than) enough of you and your moaning

assidu, e /asidy/ ADJ 1 *(= régulier) [présence, client, lecteur]* regular • **élève/employé ~** pupil/employee with a good attendance record 2 *(= appliqué) [soins, effort]* constant, unremitting; *[travail]* diligent; *[relations]* sustained; *[personne]* diligent, assiduous 3 *(= empressé) [personne]* attentive *(auprès de* to) • **faire une cour ~e à qn** to be assiduous in one's attentions to sb, to woo sb assiduously

assiduité /asidɥite/ NF *(= ponctualité)* regularity; *(= empressement)* attentiveness, assiduity *(à to)* • **son ~ aux cours** his regular attendance at classes • **fréquenter un bistrot avec ~** to be a regular at a bar • **poursuivre une femme de ses ~s** *(frm ou hum)* to woo a woman assiduously

assidûment /asidymɑ̃/ ADV *[fréquenter]* faithfully, assiduously; *[travailler, s'entraîner]* assiduously

assiégé, e /asjeʒe/ (ptp de **assiéger**) ADJ *[garnison, ville]* besieged, under siege *(attrib)* NM,F ◆ **les ~s** the besieged

assiégeant, e /asjeʒɑ̃, ɑ̃t/ NM,F besieger ADJ ◆ **les troupes ~es** the besieging troops

assiéger /asjeʒe/ ► conjug 3 et 6 ◄ VT *[+ ville]* to besiege, to lay siege to; *[+ armée]* to besiege; *(fig) [+ guichet, porte, personne]* to mob, to besiege; *(= harceler)* to beset ◆ **assiégé par l'eau/les flammes** hemmed in by water/flames ◆ **à Noël les magasins étaient assiégés** the shops were taken by storm *ou* mobbed at Christmas ◆ **ces pensées/tentations qui m'assiègent** these thoughts/temptations that beset *ou* assail me

assiette /asjɛt/ NF 1 *(= vaisselle)* plate; *(= contenu)* plate(ful)

2 *(= équilibre) [de cavalier]* seat; *[de navire]* trim; *[de colonne]* seating ◆ **perdre son ~** *(Équitation)* to lose one's seat, to be unseated ◆ **avoir une bonne ~** *(Équitation)* to have a good seat, to sit one's horse well ◆ **il n'est pas dans son ~ aujourd'hui** * he's not feeling (quite) himself today, he's (feeling) a bit off-colour *(Brit)* today

3 *[d'hypothèque] property or estate on which a mortgage is secured* ◆ **~ fiscale** *ou* **de l'impôt/de la TVA** tax/VAT base ◆ **l'~ des cotisations sociales** *the basis on which social security contributions are assessed*

COMP **assiette anglaise** *ou* **de charcuterie** assorted cold meats
assiette composée mixed salad *(of cold meats and vegetables)*
assiette creuse soup dish *ou* plate
assiette à dessert dessert plate
assiette nordique *ou* **scandinave** plate of assorted smoked fish
assiette à pain side plate
assiette plate (dinner) plate
assiette à potage *ou* **à soupe** ⇒ **assiette creuse**
assiette scandinave ⇒ **assiette nordique**

assiettée /asjete/ NF *(gén)* plate(ful); *[de soupe]* plate(ful), dish

assignable /asiɲabl/ ADJ *(= attribuable) [cause, origine]* ascribable, attributable *(à* to)

assignat /asiɲa/ NM *(Hist) banknote used during the French Revolution*

assignation /asiɲasjɔ̃/ NF *(Jur) [de parts]* assignation, allocation ◆ **~ (en justice)** writ ◆ **~ (à comparaître)** *[de prévenu]* summons; *[de témoin]* subpoena ◆ **~ à résidence** house arrest

assigner /asiɲe/ ► conjug 1 ◄ VT 1 *(= attribuer) [+ part, place, rôle]* to assign, to allot; *[+ valeur, importance]* to attach, to ascribe; *[+ cause, origine]* to ascribe, to attribute *(à* to) 2 *(= affecter) [+ somme, crédit]* to allot, to allocate *(à* to) to earmark *(à* for) 3 *(= fixer) [+ limite, terme]* to set, to fix *(à* to); ◆ **~ un objectif à qn** to set sb a goal 4 *(Jur)* **~ (à comparaître)** *[+ prévenu]* to summons; *[+ témoin]* to subpoena, to summons ◆ **~ qn (en justice)** to issue a writ against sb, to serve a writ on sb ◆ **~ qn à résidence** to put sb under house arrest

assimilable /asimilabl/ ADJ 1 *[connaissances]* which can be assimilated *ou* absorbed; *[nourriture]* assimilable; *[immigrant]* who can be assimilated 2 ◆ **~ à** *(= comparable à)* comparable to

assimilation /asimilasjɔ̃/ NF 1 *[d'aliments, immigrants, connaissances]* assimilation ◆ **~ chlorophyllienne** photosynthesis ◆ **~ culturelle** cultural assimilation 2 *(= comparaison)* **l'~ de ce bandit à un héros/à Napoléon est un scandale** it's a scandal making this criminal out to be a hero/to liken *ou* compare this criminal to Napoleon ◆ **l'~ des techniciens aux ingénieurs** the classification of technicians as engineers, the inclusion of technicians in the same category as engineers

assimilé, e /asimile/ (ptp de **assimiler**) ADJ *(= similaire)* comparable, similar ◆ **ce procédé et les méthodes ~es** this process and other comparable *ou* similar methods ◆ **farines et produits ~s** flour and related products NM *(Mil) non-combatant ranking with the combatants* ◆ **les cadres et ~s** management and employees of similar status ◆ **les fonctionnaires et ~s** civil servants and those in a similar category

assimiler /asimile/ ► conjug 1 ◄ VT 1 *[+ connaissances]* to assimilate, to take in; *[+ aliments, immigrants]* to assimilate ◆ **un élève qui assimile bien** a pupil who assimilates things easily *ou* takes things in easily ◆ **ses idées sont du Nietzsche mal assimilé** his ideas are just a few ill-digested notions (taken) from Nietzsche

2 ◆ **~ qn/qch à** *(= comparer à)* to liken *ou* compare sb/sth to; *(= classer comme)* to put sb/sth into the same category as ◆ **ils demandent à être assimilés à des fonctionnaires** they are asking to be put in the same category as civil servants

VPR **s'assimiler** 1 *[aliments, immigrants]* to assimilate, to be assimilated; *[connaissances]* to be assimilated

2 ◆ **s'~ à** *(= se comparer à) [personne]* to liken o.s. *ou* compare o.s. to ◆ **cet acte s'assimile à un règlement de compte(s)** this act can be seen *ou* considered as a settling of (old) scores

assis, e[1] /asi, iz/ (ptp de **asseoir**) ADJ 1 *[personne]* sitting (down), seated ◆ **position** *ou* **station ~e** sitting position ◆ **la position** *ou* **station ~e lui est douloureuse** he finds sitting painful ◆ **être ~** to be sitting (down) *ou* seated ◆ **demeurer ~** *(frm)* to remain seated ◆ **nous étions très bien/mal ~** *(sur des chaises)* we had very comfortable/uncomfortable seats; *(par terre)* we were very comfortably/uncomfortably seated ◆ **~ en tailleur** sitting cross-legged ◆ **~ à califourchon sur** sitting astride, straddling ◆ **~ !** *(à un chien)* sit!; *(à un enfant)* sit down! ◆ **rester ~** to remain seated ◆ **restez ~ !** *(= ne bougez pas)* sit still!; *(= ne vous levez pas)* don't get up! ◆ **nous sommes restés ~ pendant des heures** we sat for hours; → **entre, magistrature, place, position;** → aussi **asseoir**

2 *(= assuré) [fortune]* secure; *[personne]* stable; *[autorité]* (well-)established ◆ **maintenant que son fils a une situation bien ~e** now that his son is well-established

Assise /asiz/ N Assisi ◆ **Saint François d'~** Saint Francis of Assisi

assise[2] /asiz/ NF *(Constr)* course; *(Bio, Géol)* stratum; *[de raisonnement]* basis, foundation ◆ **leur ~ politique** their political base

assises /asiz/ NFPL *(Jur)* assizes; *[d'association, parti politique]* conference ◆ **~ nationales** national conference ◆ **tenir ses ~** to hold its conference ◆ **procès d'~** trial; → **cour**

assistanat /asistana/ NM 1 *(Scol)* assistantship 2 *(Sociol) (= soutien)* (state) support; *(péj)* mollycoddling *(péj)*, nannying *(péj) (Brit)*; *(= aide financière)* (state) aid; *(péj)* handouts *(péj)*, charity *(péj)*

assistance /asistɑ̃s/ NF 1 *(= public) [de conférence]* audience; *[de débat, meeting]* participants; *[de messe]* congregation

2 *(= aide)* assistance ◆ **donner/prêter ~ à qn** to give/lend sb assistance ◆ **~ aux anciens détenus** prisoner after-care

3 *(= présence)* attendance *(à* at)

COMP **assistance éducative** educational support *(for children with particular needs)*
assistance judiciaire legal aid
assistance médicale (gratuite) (free) medical care
Assistance publique ◆ **les services de l'Assistance publique** ≃ the health and social security services ◆ **être à l'Assistance publique** to be in (state *ou* public) care ◆ **enfant de l'Assistance (publique)** child in care *(Brit) ou* in state custody *(US)* ◆ **les hôpitaux de l'Assistance publique** state- *ou* publicly-owned hospitals
assistance respiratoire artificial respiration
assistance sociale *(= aide)* social aid; *(= métier)* social work
assistance technique technical aid

> ⚠ Au sens de 'public', **assistance** ne se traduit pas par le mot anglais **assistance**.

assistant, e /asistɑ̃, ɑ̃t/ NM,F 1 *(gén, Scol)* assistant; *(Univ)* ≃ assistant lecturer *(Brit)*, teaching assistant *(US)* ◆ **~e de direction** management secretary ◆ **~ d'éducation** classroom assistant ◆ **~ (de langue)** language assistant ◆ **~e maternelle** child minder *(Brit)*, child caregiver *(US)* ◆ **~e sociale** *(gén)* social worker; *(Scol)* school counsellor, school social worker ◆ **le directeur et son ~e** the manager and his personal assistant *ou* his PA; → **maître** 2 *[d'assemblée]* **les ~s** those present NM *(= ordinateur)* assistant

assisté, e /asiste/ (ptp de **assister**) ADJ 1 *(Jur, Méd, Sociol)* supported by *ou* cared for by the state; *(financièrement)* receiving (state) aid ◆ **enfant ~** child in care *(Brit) ou* state custody *(US)* 2 *[freins]* servo-assisted ◆ **~ par ordinateur** computer-aided, computer-assisted; → **direction, procréation, publication, traduction** NM,F ◆ **les ~s** *(recevant une aide financière)* people receiving (state) aid; *(péj)* people receiving handouts *(péj)*, welfare scroungers *(péj)* ◆ **il a une mentalité d'~** he can't do anything for himself

assister /asiste/ ► conjug 1 ◄ VT INDIR **assister à** *[+ cérémonie, conférence, messe]* to be (present) at, to attend; *[+ match, spectacle]* to be at; *[+ dispute]* to witness ◆ **il a assisté à l'accouchement de sa femme** he was there when his wife gave birth, he was at the birth of his child ◆ **vous pourrez ~ en direct à cet événement** *(TV)* you'll be able to see the event live (on television) ◆ **on assiste à une montée du chômage** unemployment is on the increase ◆ **nous assistons actuellement en Europe à des changements fondamentaux** there are fundamental changes taking place in Europe, Europe is witnessing fundamental changes ◆ **depuis le début de l'année, on assiste à une reprise de l'économie** the economy has picked up since the beginning of the year, there has been an upturn in the economy since the beginning of the year ◆ **il a assisté à l'effondrement de son parti** he saw the collapse of his party

VT *(= aider)* to assist; *(financièrement)* to give aid to ◆ **~ qn dans ses derniers moments** *(frm)* to comfort sb in their last hour ◆ **~ les pauvres** † to minister to the poor *(frm)*

> ⚠ **assister** se traduit par **to assist** uniquement au sens de 'aider'.

associatif, -ive /asɔsjatif, iv/ ADJ 1 *(Sociol) [réseau]* of associations ◆ **le mouvement ~** associations ◆ **des représentants du milieu ~** representatives of associations ◆ **la vie associative** community life ◆ **il a de nombreuses activités associatives** he's involved in several associations 2 *(Math)* associative

association /asɔsjasjɔ̃/ NF 1 *(gén = société)* association; *(Comm, Écon)* partnership ◆ **~ de malfaiteurs** *(Jur)* criminal conspiracy ◆ **~ de consommateurs** consumer association ◆ **~ sportive** sports association ◆ **~ loi (de) 1901** (non-profit-making) association ◆ **Association internationale du tourisme** International Tourism Association ◆ **Association européenne de libre-échange** European Free Trade Association

2 *[d'idées, images]* association; *[de couleurs, intérêts]* combination
3 (= *participation*) association, partnership ◆ **l'~ de ces deux écrivains a été fructueuse** the two writers have had a very fruitful partnership ◆ **son ~ à nos travaux dépendra de ...** whether or not he joins us in our work will depend on ... ◆ **travailler en ~** to work in partnership (*avec* with)

associationnisme /asɔsjasjɔnism/ NM (*Philos*) associationism

associationniste /asɔsjasjɔnist/ ADJ, NMF associationist

associativité /asɔsjativite/ NF (*Math*) associativity

associé, e /asɔsje/ (ptp de **associer**) ADJ (*Univ*) *[assistant, professeur]* visiting ◆ **membre ~** associate member NM,F (*gén*) associate; (*Comm, Fin*) partner, associate ◆ **~ principal** senior partner

associer /asɔsje/ ▸ conjug 7 ◂ VT 1 ◆ **~ qn à** (= *faire participer à*) *[+ profits]* to give sb a share of; *[+ affaire]* to make sb a partner in ◆ **~ qn à son triomphe** to let sb share in one's triumph
2 ◆ **~ qch à** (= *rendre solidaire de*) to associate *ou* link sth with; (= *allier à*) to combine sth with ◆ **il associe la paresse à la malhonnêteté** he combines laziness with dishonesty
3 (= *grouper*) *[+ idées, images, mots]* to associate; *[+ couleurs, intérêts]* to combine (*à* with)
VPR **s'associer** 1 (= *s'unir*) *[firmes]* to join together, to form an association; *[personnes]* (*gén*) to join forces, to join together; (*pour créer une entreprise*) to form a partnership ◆ **s'~ à** *ou* **avec** *[firme]* to join with, to form an association with; *[personne]* (*gén*) to join (forces) with; (*pour créer une entreprise*) to go into partnership with; *[bandits]* to fall in with ◆ **on va lui faire un cadeau, tu t'associes à nous ?** we're going to get him a present, do you want to come in with us?
2 (= *participer à*) **s'~ à** *[+ projet]* to join in; *[+ douleur]* to share in ◆ **je m'associe aux compliments que l'on vous fait** I would like to join with those who have complimented you
3 (= *s'allier*) *[couleurs, qualités]* to be combined (*à* with); ◆ **ces couleurs s'associent à merveille** these colours go together beautifully
4 (= *s'adjoindre*) **s'~ qn** to take sb on as a partner

assoiffé, e /aswafe/ ADJ (*lit*) thirsty ◆ **~ de** (*fig*) thirsting for *ou* after (*littér*) ◆ **monstre ~ de sang** (*littér ou hum*) bloodthirsty monster

assoiffer /aswafe/ ▸ conjug 1 ◂ VT *[temps, course]* to make thirsty

assolement /asɔlmɑ̃/ NM (systematic) rotation (of crops)

assoler /asɔle/ ▸ conjug 1 ◂ VT *[+ champ]* to rotate crops on

assombri, e /asɔ̃bʀi/ (ptp de **assombrir**) ADJ *[ciel]* dark; *[visage, regard]* gloomy, sombre (*Brit*), somber (*US*)

assombrir /asɔ̃bʀiʀ/ ▸ conjug 2 ◂ VT 1 (= *obscurcir*) (*gén*) to darken; *[+ pièce]* to make dark *ou* gloomy; *[+ couleur]* to make dark 2 (= *attrister*) *[+ personne]* to fill with gloom; *[+ assistance]* to cast a gloom over; *[+ visage, avenir, voyage]* to cast a shadow over VPR **s'assombrir** 1 *[ciel, pièce]* to darken, to grow dark; *[couleur]* to grow sombre (*Brit*) *ou* somber (*US*), to darken 2 *[personne, caractère]* to become gloomy *ou* morose; *[visage, regard]* to cloud over ◆ **la situation politique s'est assombrie** the political situation has become gloomier

assombrissement /asɔ̃bʀismɑ̃/ NM *[de ciel, pièce]* darkening ◆ **l'~ des perspectives économiques** the increasingly gloomy economic prospects

assommant, e* /asɔmɑ̃, ɑ̃t/ ADJ (= *ennuyeux*) deadly* boring *ou* dull ◆ **il est ~** he's a deadly* bore, he's deadly* dull *ou* boring

assommer /asɔme/ ▸ conjug 1 ◂ VT (*lit*) (= *tuer*) to batter to death; (= *étourdir*) *[+ animal]* to knock out, to stun; *[+ personne]* to knock out, to knock senseless; (*fig*) (*moralement*) to crush; (* = *ennuyer*) to bore stiff*, to bore to tears* *ou* to death* ◆ **être assommé par le bruit/la chaleur** to be overwhelmed by the noise/overcome by the heat ◆ **si je lui mets la main dessus je l'assomme*** if I can lay my hands on him I'll beat his brains out*

assommoir †† /asɔmwaʀ/ NM (= *massue*) club; (= *café*) café, grogshop † (*Brit*) ◆ **c'est le coup d'~ !** (*prix*) it's extortionate!

Assomption /asɔ̃psjɔ̃/ NF (*Rel*) ◆ **(la fête de) l'~** (the feast of) the Assumption; (= *jour férié*) Assumption Day

assonance /asɔnɑ̃s/ NF assonance

assonant, e /asɔnɑ̃, ɑ̃t/ ADJ assonant, assonantal

assorti, e /asɔʀti/ (ptp de **assortir**) ADJ 1 (= *en harmonie*) **des époux bien/mal ~s** a well-/badly-matched couple ◆ **être ~ à** *[+ couleur]* to match ◆ **chemise avec cravate ~e** shirt with matching tie 2 (= *varié*) *[bonbons]* assorted ◆ **"hors-d'œuvre/fromages assortis"** "assortment of hors d'œuvres/cheeses" 3 (= *achalandé*) **magasin bien/mal ~** well-/poorly-stocked shop 4 (= *accompagné*) **être ~ de** *[+ conditions, conseils]* to be accompanied with

> ⚠ **assorti** se traduit par **assorted** uniquement au sens de 'varié'.

assortiment /asɔʀtimɑ̃/ NM 1 *[de bonbons, fromages, fruits, hors-d'œuvre]* assortment; *[de livres]* collection; *[de vaisselle, outils]* set ◆ **je vous fais un ~ ?** shall I give you an assortment? 2 (= *harmonie*) *[de couleurs, formes]* arrangement, ensemble 3 (*Comm* = *lot, stock*) stock, selection

assortir /asɔʀtiʀ/ ▸ conjug 2 ◂ VT 1 (= *accorder*) *[+ couleurs, motifs]* to match (*à* to; *avec* with); ◆ **elle assortit la couleur de son écharpe à celle de ses yeux** she chose the colour of her scarf to match her eyes ◆ **elle avait su ~ ses invités** she had mixed *ou* matched her guests cleverly 2 (= *accompagner de*) ◆ **~ qch de** *[+ conseils, commentaires]* to accompany sth with 3 (= *approvisionner*) *[+ commerçant]* to supply; *[+ magasin]* to stock (*de* with) VPR **s'assortir** 1 *[couleurs, motifs]* to match, to go (well) together; *[caractères]* to go together, to be well matched ◆ **le papier s'assortit aux rideaux** the wallpaper matches *ou* goes (well) with the curtains 2 (= *s'accompagner de*) **ce livre s'assortit de notes** this book has accompanying notes *ou* has notes with it

assoupi, e /asupi/ (ptp de **assoupir**) ADJ *[personne]* dozing; *[sens, intérêt, douleur]* dulled; *[haine]* lulled

assoupir /asupiʀ/ ▸ conjug 2 ◂ VT *[+ personne]* to make drowsy; *[+ sens, intérêt, douleur]* to dull; *[+ passion]* to lull VPR **s'assoupir** *[personne]* to doze off; *[intérêt]* to be dulled

assoupissement /asupismɑ̃/ NM 1 (= *sommeil*) doze; (= *somnolence*) drowsiness 2 (= *action*) *[de sens]* numbing; *[de facultés, intérêt]* dulling; *[de douleur]* deadening

assouplir /asupliʀ/ ▸ conjug 2 ◂ VT *[+ cuir]* to soften, to make supple; *[+ membres, corps]* to make supple; *[+ règlements, mesures]* to relax; *[+ principes]* to make more flexible, to relax ◆ **~ le caractère de qn** to make sb more manageable ◆ **~ les horaires** to produce a more flexible timetable VPR **s'assouplir** *[cuir]* to soften, to become supple; *[membres, corps]* to become supple; *[règlements, mesures]* to relax; *[principes]* to become more flexible, to relax ◆ **il faut que je m'assouplisse** I must loosen up ◆ **son caractère s'est assoupli** he has become more manageable

assouplissant, e /asuplisɑ̃, ɑ̃t/ ADJ *[produit, formule]* softening NM ◆ **~ (textile)** (fabric) softener

assouplissement /asuplismɑ̃/ NM *[de cuir]* softening; *[de membres, corps]* suppling up; *[de règlements, mesures, principes]* relaxing ◆ **faire des exercices d'~** to limber up, to do (some) limbering up exercises ◆ **mesures d'~ du crédit** (*Écon*) easing of credit restrictions ◆ **mesures d'~ des formalités administratives** measures to relax administrative regulations ◆ **l'~ de la politique monétaire** the relaxing of monetary policy

assouplisseur /asuplisœʀ/ NM (fabric) softener

assourdir /asuʀdiʀ/ ▸ conjug 2 ◂ VT 1 (= *rendre sourd*) *[+ personne]* to deafen 2 (= *amortir*) *[+ bruit]* to deaden, to muffle VPR **s'assourdir** (*Ling*) to become voiceless, to become unvoiced

assourdissant, e /asuʀdisɑ̃, ɑ̃t/ ADJ deafening

assourdissement /asuʀdismɑ̃/ NM 1 *[de personne]* (= *état*) (temporary) deafness; (= *action*) deafening 2 *[de bruit]* deadening, muffling 3 (*Ling*) devoicing

assouvir /asuviʀ/ ▸ conjug 2 ◂ VT *[+ faim]* to satisfy, to assuage (*frm*); *[+ passion]* to assuage (*frm*)

assouvissement /asuvismɑ̃/ NM *[de faim]* satisfaction, satisfying; *[de passion]* assuaging (*frm*)

ASSU /asy/ NF (abrév de **Association du sport scolaire et universitaire**) *university and school sports association*

assujetti, e /asyʒeti/ (ptp de **assujettir**) ADJ *[peuple]* subject, subjugated ◆ **~ à** *[norme, loi]* subject to; *[taxe]* liable *ou* subject to ◆ **les personnes ~es à l'impôt** (*Admin*) persons liable to *ou* for tax

assujettir /asyʒetiʀ/ ▸ conjug 2 ◂ VT (= *contraindre*) *[+ peuple]* to subjugate, to bring into subjection; (= *fixer*) *[+ planches, tableau]* to secure, to make fast ◆ **~ qn à une règle** to subject sb to a rule VPR **s'assujettir** (*à une règle*) to submit (*à* to)

assujettissant, e /asyʒetisɑ̃, ɑ̃t/ ADJ *[travail]* demanding, exacting

assujettissement /asyʒetismɑ̃/ NM (= *contrainte*) constraint; (= *dépendance*) subjection ◆ **~ à l'impôt** tax liability

assumer /asyme/ ▸ conjug 1 ◂ VT 1 (= *prendre*) (*gén*) to assume; *[+ responsabilité, tâche, rôle]* to take on, to assume; *[+ commandement]* to take over; *[+ poste]* to take up ◆ **~ la responsabilité de faire qch** to take it upon oneself to do sth ◆ **~ les frais de qch** to meet the cost *ou* expense of sth 2 (= *remplir*) *[+ poste]* to hold; *[+ rôle]* to fulfil ◆ **après avoir assumé ce poste pendant 2 ans** having held the post for 2 years 3 (= *accepter*) *[+ conséquence, situation, douleur, condition]* to accept ◆ **tu as voulu te marier, alors assume !** you wanted to get married, so you'll just have to take *ou* accept the consequences! VPR **s'assumer** to be at ease with o.s. ◆ **être incapable de s'~** to be unable to come to terms with o.s. ◆ **elle s'assume financièrement** she is financially self-sufficient

assurable /asyʀabl/ ADJ insurable

assurage /asyʀaʒ/ NM (*Alpinisme*) belay

assurance /asyʀɑ̃s/ NF 1 (= *confiance en soi*) self-confidence, (self-)assurance ◆ **avoir de l'~** to be self-confident *ou* (self-)assured ◆ **prendre de l'~** to gain (self-)confidence *ou* (self-)

assurance ◆ **parler avec** ~ to speak confidently *ou* with assurance *ou* with confidence

2 *(= garantie)* assurance, undertaking *(Brit)* ◆ **donner à qn l'~ formelle que ...** to give sb a formal assurance *ou* undertaking that ... ◆ **il veut avoir l'~ que tout se passera bien** he wants to be sure that everything goes well ◆ **veuillez agréer l'~ de ma considération distinguée** *ou* **de mes sentiments dévoués** *(formule épistolaire)* yours faithfully *ou* sincerely, sincerely yours *(US)*

3 *(= contrat)* insurance (policy) ◆ **contrat d'~** insurance policy ◆ **compagnie** *ou* **société/groupe d'~s** insurance company/group ◆ **produits d'~** insurance products ◆ **contracter** *ou* **prendre une ~ contre qch** to take out insurance *ou* an insurance policy against sth ◆ **il est dans les ~s** he's in insurance, he's in the insurance business; → **police², prime¹**

4 *(Alpinisme)* belay

COMP **assurance automobile** car *ou* automobile *(US)* insurance
assurance bagages luggage insurance
assurance chômage unemployment insurance ◆ **le régime d'~ chômage** the state unemployment insurance scheme ◆ **caisse d'~ chômage** *(= fonds)* unemployment insurance fund; *(= bureau)* unemployment insurance office
assurance décès whole-life insurance
assurance incendie fire insurance
assurance invalidité-vieillesse disablement insurance
assurance maladie health insurance ◆ **régime d'~ maladie** health insurance scheme
assurance maritime marine insurance
assurance multirisques comprehensive insurance
assurance personnelle personal insurance
assurance responsabilité-civile ⇒ **assurance au tiers**
assurances sociales ≃ social security, welfare *(US)* ◆ **il est (inscrit) aux ~s sociales** he's on the state health scheme *(Brit) ou* plan *(US)*, he pays National Insurance *(Brit)*
assurance au tiers third-party insurance
assurance tous risques *(Aut)* comprehensive insurance
assurance vie life assurance *ou* insurance *(Brit)* ◆ **contrat d'~ vie** life assurance *ou* insurance *(Brit)* policy
assurance vieillesse pension scheme ◆ **le régime d'~ vieillesse** the state pension scheme ◆ **caisse d'~ vieillesse** *(fonds)* retirement fund; *(bureau)* pensions office
assurance contre le vol insurance against theft
assurance voyage travel insurance

assurance-crédit (pl **assurances-crédits**) /asyʀɑ̃skʀedi/ NF credit insurance

assuré, e /asyʀe/ (ptp de **assurer**) ADJ 1 *[réussite, échec]* certain, sure; *[situation, fortune]* assured ◆ **son avenir est ~ maintenant** his future is certain *ou* assured now ◆ **une entreprise ~e du succès** an undertaking which is sure to succeed *ou* whose success is assured

2 *[air, démarche]* assured, (self-)confident; *[voix]* assured, steady; *[main, pas]* steady ◆ **mal ~** *[voix, pas]* uncertain, unsteady, shaky ◆ **il est mal ~ sur ses jambes** he's unsteady on his legs

3 *(locutions)* **tenir pour ~ que ...** to be confident that ..., to take it as certain that ... ◆ **tenez pour ~ que ...** rest assured that ... ◆ **il se dit ~ de cela** he says he is confident of that

NM,F *(Assurances) (assurance-vie)* assured *ou* insured person; *(autres assurances)* insured person, policyholder ◆ **l'~** the assured, the policyholder ◆ **~ social** *person paying social security contributions*

assurément /asyʀemɑ̃/ ADV *(frm)* most certainly, assuredly ◆ **~, ceci présente des difficultés** this does indeed present difficulties ◆ **(oui) ~** yes indeed, yes most certainly ◆ **~ il viendra** he will most certainly come

assurer /asyʀe/ GRAMMAIRE ACTIVE 42.1
▸ conjug 1 ◂

VT 1 *(= certifier)* **~ à qn que ...** to assure sb that ... ◆ **~ que ...** to affirm that ... ◆ **cela vaut la peine, je vous assure** it's worth it, I assure you ◆ **je t'assure !** *(ton exaspéré)* really!

2 *(= confirmer)* **~ qn de** *[+ amitié, bonne foi]* to assure sb of ◆ **sa participation nous est assurée** we have been assured of his participation *ou* that he'll take part

3 *(par contrat)* to insure (*contre* against); ◆ **~ qn sur la vie** to give sb (a) life assurance *ou* insurance *(Brit)*, to assure sb's life ◆ **faire ~ qch** to insure sth, to have *ou* get sth insured ◆ **être assuré** to be insured

4 *(= exécuter, fournir) [+ fonctionnement, permanence]* to maintain; *[+ travaux]* to carry out, to undertake; *[+ surveillance]* to provide, to maintain; *[+ service]* to operate, to provide; *[+ financement]* to provide ◆ **~ la surveillance des locaux** to guard the premises ◆ **l'avion qui assure la liaison entre Genève et Aberdeen** the plane that operates between Geneva and Aberdeen ◆ **l'armée a dû ~ le ravitaillement des sinistrés** the army had to provide supplies for the victims ◆ **~ sa propre défense** *(Jur)* to conduct one's own defence ◆ **~ la direction d'un service** to head up a department, to be in charge of a department ◆ **~ le remplacement de pièces défectueuses** to replace faulty parts ◆ **~ le suivi d'une commande** to follow up an order

5 *(= garantir) [+ bonheur, protection, stabilité]* to ensure; *[+ succès, paix]* to ensure, to secure; *[+ avenir, fortune]* to secure; *[+ revenu]* to provide ◆ **~ à ses enfants la meilleure éducation possible** to provide one's children with the best possible education ◆ **cela devrait leur ~ une vie aisée** that should ensure that they lead a comfortable life ◆ **ce but leur a assuré la victoire** this goal ensured their victory ◆ **~ ses arrières** to ensure *ou* make sure one has something to fall back on ◆ **cela m'assure un toit pour quelques jours** that means I'll have somewhere to stay for a few days

6 *(= affermir) [+ pas, prise, échelle]* to steady; *(= fixer) [+ échelle, volet]* to secure; *(Alpinisme)* to belay ◆ **il assura ses lunettes sur son nez** he fixed his glasses firmly on his nose

7 *(= protéger) [+ frontières]* to protect (*contre* against)

VI *(* = être à la hauteur)* to be very good ◆ **ne pas ~** to be useless* *ou* no good* ◆ **je n'assure pas du tout en allemand** I'm absolutely useless* *ou* no good at German

VPR **s'assurer** 1 *(= vérifier)* **s'~ que/de qch** to make sure that/of sth, to ascertain that/sth ◆ **assure-toi qu'on n'a rien volé** make sure *ou* check that nothing has been stolen ◆ **assure-toi si les volets sont fermés** make sure the shutters are closed ◆ **je vais m'en ~** I'll make sure, I'll check

2 *(= contracter une assurance)* to insure o.s. (*contre* against); ◆ **s'~ contre** *(= se prémunir) [+ attaque, éventualité]* to insure (o.s.) against ◆ **s'~ sur la vie** to insure one's life, to take out (a) life assurance *ou* insurance *(Brit)*

3 *(= se procurer) [+ aide, victoire]* to secure, to ensure ◆ **il s'est assuré un revenu** he made sure of an income for himself, he ensured *ou* secured himself an income ◆ **s'~ l'accès de** to secure access to ◆ **s'~ le contrôle de** *[+ banque, ville]* to take control of

4 *(= s'affermir)* to steady o.s. (*sur* on); *(Alpinisme)* to belay o.s. ◆ **s'~ sur sa selle** to steady o.s. in one's saddle

5 *(frm = arrêter)* **s'~ de la personne de qn** to apprehend sb

assureur /asyʀœʀ/ NM *(= agent)* insurance agent; *(= société)* insurance company; *(Jur = partie)* insurers; *[d'entreprise]* underwriters ◆ **~-conseil** insurance consultant ◆ **~-vie** life insurer

Assyrie /asiʀi/ NF Assyria

assyrien, -ienne /asiʀjɛ̃, jɛn/ ADJ Assyrian
NM,F **Assyrien(ne)** Assyrian

aster /asteʀ/ NM aster

astérie /asteʀi/ NF starfish

astérisque /asteʀisk/ NM asterisk ◆ **marqué d'un ~** asterisked

astéroïde /asteʀɔid/ NM asteroid

asthénie /asteni/ NF asthenia

asthénique /astenik/ ADJ, NMF asthenic

asthmatique /asmatik/ ADJ, NMF asthmatic

asthme /asm/ NM asthma

asticot /astiko/ NM *(gén)* maggot; *(pour la pêche)* maggot, gentle

asticoter* /astikɔte/ ▸ conjug 1 ◂ VT to needle, to get at* *(Brit)* ◆ **cesse donc d'~ ta sœur !** stop needling *ou* getting at* *(Brit) ou* plaguing *(Brit)* your sister!

astigmate /astigmat/ ADJ astigmatic NMF astigmat(ic)

astigmatisme /astigmatism/ NM astigmatism

astiquer /astike/ ▸ conjug 1 ◂ VT *[+ arme, meuble, parquet]* to polish; *[+ bottes, métal]* to polish, to shine

astragale /astʀagal/ NM 1 *(= os)* talus, astragalus; 2 *(= plante)* astragalus; 3 *(= moulure)* astragal

astrakan /astʀakɑ̃/ NM astrakhan

astral, e (mpl **-aux**) /astʀal, o/ ADJ astral

astre /astʀ/ NM star ◆ **l'~ du jour/de la nuit** *(littér)* the day/night star *(littér)*

astreignant, e /astʀeɲɑ̃, ɑ̃t/ ADJ *[travail]* exacting, demanding

astreindre /astʀɛ̃dʀ/ ▸ conjug 49 ◂ VT ◆ **~ qn à faire** to compel *ou* oblige *ou* force sb to do ◆ **~ qn à un travail pénible/une discipline sévère** to force a trying task/a strict code of discipline (up)on sb VPR **s'astreindre** ◆ **s'~ à faire** to force *ou* compel o.s. to do ◆ **elle s'astreignait à un régime sévère** she forced herself to keep to a strict diet ◆ **astreignez-vous à une vérification rigoureuse** make yourself carry out a thorough check

astreinte /astʀɛ̃t/ NF *(= obligation)* constraint, obligation; *(Jur)* penalty *(imposed on daily basis for non-completion of contract)* ◆ **être d'~** *[médecin, technicien]* to be on call

astringence /astʀɛ̃ʒɑ̃s/ NF astringency

astringent, e /astʀɛ̃ʒɑ̃, ɑ̃t/ ADJ, NM astringent

astrolabe /astʀɔlab/ NM astrolabe

astrologie /astʀɔlɔʒi/ NF astrology

astrologique /astʀɔlɔʒik/ ADJ astrological

astrologue /astʀɔlɔg/ NMF astrologer

astronaute /astʀonot/ NMF astronaut

astronautique /astʀonotik/ NF astronautics *(sg)*

astronef † /astʀɔnɛf/ NM spaceship, spacecraft

astronome /astʀɔnɔm/ NMF astronomer

astronomie /astʀɔnɔmi/ NF astronomy

astronomique /astʀɔnɔmik/ ADJ *(lit, fig)* astronomical, astronomic

astronomiquement /astʀɔnɔmikmɑ̃/ ADV astronomically

astrophysicien, -ienne /astʀofizisjɛ̃, jɛn/ NM,F astrophysicist

astrophysique /astʀofizik/ ADJ astrophysical NF astrophysics *(sg)*

astuce /astys/ NF 1 *(= caractère)* shrewdness, astuteness ◆ **il a beaucoup d'~** he is very shrewd *ou* astute 2 *(= truc)* (clever) way, trick ◆ **l'~ c'est d'utiliser de l'eau au lieu de pétrole** the trick *ou* the clever bit *(Brit)* here is to use water instead of oil ◆ **les ~s du métier** the tricks of the trade ◆ **c'est ça l'~ !** that's the trick! *ou* the clever bit! *(Brit)* 3 * *(= jeu de mots)* pun; *(= plaisanterie)* wisecrack* ◆ **faire des ~s** to make wisecracks* ◆ **~ vaseuse** lousy* pun

astucieusement /astysjøzmɑ̃/ ADV cleverly

astucieux, -ieuse /astysjø, jøz/ ADJ clever ◆ **l'idée astucieuse de cours d'informatique à domicile** the clever idea of home computing courses ◆ **grâce à un système ~** thanks to an ingenious *ou* a clever system ◆ **on peut employer le four à micro-ondes de façon astucieuse** there are clever ways of using a microwave

Asturies /astyʀi/ NFPL ◆ **les ~** the Asturias

Asunción /asunsjɔn/ N Asuncion

asymétrie /asimetʀi/ NF asymmetry

asymétrique /asimetʀik/ ADJ asymmetric(al)

asymptomatique /asɛ̃ptɔmatik/ ADJ *[infection, personne]* asymptomatic ◆ **porteur ~** asymptomatic carrier

asymptote /asɛ̃ptɔt/ ADJ asymptotic NF asymptote

asymptotique /asɛ̃ptɔtik/ ADJ asymptotic

asynchrone /asɛ̃kʀon/ ADJ asynchronous

asyndète /asɛ̃dɛt/ NF asyndeton

asyntaxique /asɛ̃taksik/ ADJ asyntactic(al)

ataraxie /ataʀaksi/ NF ataraxia, ataraxy

atavique /atavik/ ADJ atavistic

atavisme /atavism/ NM atavism ◆ **c'est de l'~ !** it's heredity coming out!

ataxie /ataksi/ NF ataxia

ataxique /ataksik/ ADJ ataxic NMF ataxia sufferer

atchoum /atʃum/ EXCL atishoo

atèle /atɛl/ NM spider monkey

atelier /atəlje/ NM 1 *(= local) [d'artisan]* workshop; *[d'artiste]* studio; *[de couturières]* workroom; *[de haute couture]* atelier ◆ **~ de fabrication** workshop 2 *(= groupe) (Art)* studio; *(Scol)* work-group; *(dans un colloque)* discussion group, workshop ◆ **les enfants travaillent en ~s** *(Scol)* the children work in small groups ◆ **~ de production** *(TV)* production unit 3 *[d'usine]* shop, workshop ◆ **~ protégé** sheltered workshop 4 *[de franc-maçonnerie]* lodge; → **chef**[1]

atemporel, -elle /atɑ̃pɔʀɛl/ ADJ *[vérité]* timeless

atermoiement /atɛʀmwamɑ̃/ NM prevarication, procrastination *(NonC)*

atermoyer /atɛʀmwaje/ ► conjug 8 ◄ VI *(= tergiverser)* to procrastinate, to temporize

athée /ate/ ADJ atheistic NMF atheist

athéisme /ateism/ NM atheism

Athéna /atena/ NF Athena, (Pallas) Athene

athénée /atene/ NM *(Belg = lycée)* ≈ secondary school, high school *(US)*

Athènes /atɛn/ N Athens

athénien, -ienne /atenjɛ̃, jɛn/ ADJ Athenian NM,F **Athénien(ne)** Athenian ◆ **c'est là que les Athéniens s'atteignirent** *ou* **s'éteignirent** *(hum)* that's when all hell broke loose*

athérome /ateʀom/ NM atheroma

athérosclérose /ateʀoskleʀoz/ NF atherosclerosis

athlète /atlɛt/ NMF athlete ◆ **corps d'~** athletic body ◆ **regarde l'~ !, quel ~ !** *(hum)* just look at muscleman! *(hum)*

athlétique /atletik/ ADJ athletic

athlétisme /atletism/ NM athletics *(Brit) (NonC)*, track and field events *(US)* ◆ **~ sur piste** track athletics

Atlantide /atlɑ̃tid/ NF ◆ **l'~** Atlantis

atlantique /atlɑ̃tik/ ADJ Atlantic ◆ **les Provinces ~s** *(Can)* the Atlantic Provinces NM **Atlantique** ◆ **l'Atlantique** the Atlantic (Ocean)

atlantisme /atlɑ̃tism/ NM Atlanticism

atlantiste /atlɑ̃tist/ ADJ *[politique]* Atlanticist, which promotes the Atlantic Alliance NMF Atlanticist

atlas /atlɑs/ NM 1 *(= livre, vertèbre)* atlas 2 ◆ **Atlas** *(Myth)* Atlas ◆ **l'Atlas** *(Géog)* the Atlas Mountains

atmosphère /atmɔsfɛʀ/ NF atmosphere ◆ **haute/basse ~** upper/lower atmosphere ◆ **essai nucléaire en ~** nuclear test in the atmosphere ◆ **j'ai besoin de changer d'~** I need a change of air *ou* scenery ◆ **en ~ normale/contrôlée/stérile** in a normal/controlled/sterile atmosphere *ou* environment ◆ **~ de fête** festive atmosphere

atmosphérique /atmɔsfeʀik/ ADJ atmospheric; → **courant, perturbation**

atoca /atɔka/ NM *(Can = fruit)* cranberry

atoll /atɔl/ NM atoll

atome /atom/ NM atom ◆ **~-gramme** gram atom ◆ **il n'a pas un ~ de bon sens** he hasn't a grain *ou* an ounce of common sense ◆ **avoir des ~s crochus avec qn** to have a lot in common with sb, to hit it off with sb*

atomique /atɔmik/ ADJ atomic → **bombe**

atomisation /atɔmizasjɔ̃/ NF atomization

atomisé, e /atɔmize/ (ptp de **atomiser**) ADJ *[savoir, marché]* fragmented; *[mouvement politique]* fragmented, splintered ◆ **parti politique ~** *(fig)* atomized *ou* fragmented political party NM,F victim of an atomic bomb explosion ◆ **les ~s d'Hiroshima** the victims of the Hiroshima atom bomb

atomiser /atɔmize/ ► conjug 1 ◄ VT *(Phys)* to atomize; *(Mil)* to destroy with atomic *ou* nuclear weapons; *[+ marché]* to fragment; *[+ société]* to atomize, to fragment; *[+ parti]* to break up

atomiseur /atɔmizœʀ/ NM *(gén)* spray; *[de parfum]* atomizer

atomiste /atɔmist/ ADJ, NMF ◆ **(savant) ~** atomic scientist

atomistique /atɔmistik/ ADJ, NF ◆ **(théorie) ~** atomic theory

atonal, e (mpl **atonals**) /atɔnal/ ADJ atonal

atonalité /atɔnalite/ NF atonality

atone /atɔn/ ADJ 1 *(= sans vitalité) [être]* lifeless; *(= sans expression) [regard]* expressionless; *(Méd)* atonic 2 *(Ling)* unstressed, unaccented, atonic

atonie /atɔni/ NF *(Ling, Méd)* atony; *(= manque de vitalité)* lifelessness

atours /atuʀ/ NMPL *(† ou hum)* attire, finery ◆ **dans ses plus beaux ~** in her loveliest attire † *(hum)*, in all her finery *(hum)*

atout /atu/ NM 1 *(Cartes)* trump ◆ **jouer ~** to play a trump; *(en commençant)* to lead (with) a trump ◆ **on jouait ~ cœur** hearts were trumps ◆ **~ maître** master trump ◆ **roi/reine d'~** king/queen of trumps ◆ **3 sans ~** 3 no trumps 2 *(fig) (= avantage)* asset; *(= carte maîtresse)* trump card ◆ **l'avoir dans l'équipe est un ~** he's an asset to our team ◆ **avoir tous les ~s (dans son jeu)** to hold all the cards *ou* aces ◆ **avoir plus d'un ~ dans sa manche** to have more than one ace up one's sleeve

atoxique /atɔksik/ ADJ non-poisonous

ATP /atepe/ NF (abrév de **Association des tennismen professionnels**) ATP

atrabilaire /atʀabilɛʀ/ ADJ *(†† ou hum)* bilious, atrabilious *(frm)*

âtre /ɑtʀ/ NM hearth

Atrée /atʀe/ NM Atreus

Atrides /atʀid/ NMPL ◆ **les ~** the Atridae

atrium /atʀijɔm/ NM *(Archit, Anat)* atrium

atroce /atʀɔs/ ADJ 1 *(= abominable)* dreadful; *[crime, conditions]* atrocious, dreadful; *[torture]* appalling; *[faim, événement]* terrible 2 *(= très mauvais)* atrocious

> ⚠ Attention à ne pas traduire automatiquement **atroce** par **atrocious**.

atrocement /atʀɔsmɑ̃/ ADV 1 *[souffrir]* terribly; *[torturer]* brutally ◆ **il s'est vengé ~** he wreaked a terrible *ou* dreadful revenge ◆ **elle avait ~ peur** she was terribly *ou* dreadfully frightened 2 *(= très)* dreadfully

atrocité /atʀɔsite/ NF 1 *(= qualité) [de crime, action]* atrocity, atrociousness; *[de spectacle]* ghastliness 2 *(= acte)* atrocity, outrage ◆ **dire des ~s sur qn** to say wicked *ou* atrocious things about sb ◆ **cette nouvelle tour est une ~** that new tower is an atrocity *ou* a real eyesore

atrophie /atʀɔfi/ NF *(Méd)* atrophy ◆ **une ~ du désir** an atrophy of desire ◆ **l'~ industrielle dont souffre ce pays** the country's industrial decline

atrophié, e /atʀɔfje/ (ptp de **atrophier**) ADJ *(lit, fig)* atrophied

atrophier /atʀɔfje/ ► conjug 7 ◄ VT *(Méd)* to atrophy; *(fig)* to starve VPR **s'atrophier** *[membres, muscle]* to waste away, to atrophy; *(fig)* to atrophy

atropine /atʀɔpin/ NF atropine, atropin

attabler (s') /atable/ ► conjug 1 ◄ VPR *(pour manger)* to sit down at (the) table ◆ **s'~ autour d'une bonne bouteille** to sit (down) at the table for a drink ◆ **s'~ à la terrasse d'un café** to sit at a table outside a café ◆ **il vint s'~ avec eux** he came to sit at their table ◆ **les clients attablés** the seated customers

attachant, e /ataʃɑ̃, ɑ̃t/ ADJ *[film, roman]* captivating; *[enfant]* endearing

attache /ataʃ/ NF 1 *(en ficelle)* (piece of) string; *(en métal)* clip, fastener; *(= courroie)* strap 2 *(Anat)* **~s** *[d'épaules]* shoulder joints; *[de bassin]* hip joints; *(= poignets et chevilles)* wrists and ankles 3 *(fig) (= lien)* tie ◆ **~s** *(= famille)* ties, connections ◆ **avoir des ~s dans une région** to have family ties *ou* connections in a region 4 *(Bot)* tendril 5 *(locutions)* **être à l'~** *[animal]* to be tied up; *[bateau]* to be moored ◆ **point d'~** *[de bateau]* mooring (post); *(fig)* base; → **port**[1]

attaché, e /ataʃe/ (ptp de **attacher**) ADJ 1 ◆ **~ à** *[+ personne, animal, lieu, idée]* attached to; *[+ habitude]* tied to ◆ **~ à la vie** attached to life ◆ **pays très ~ à son indépendance** country that sets great store by its independence 2 ◆ **~ à** *(= affecté à)* **être ~ au service de qn** to be in sb's personal service ◆ **les avantages ~s à ce poste** the benefits attached to *ou* that go with the position ◆ **son nom restera ~ à cette découverte** his name will always be linked *ou* connected with this discovery NM,F attaché ◆ **~ d'ambassade/de presse/militaire** embassy/

press/military attaché ◆ ~ **d'administration** administrative assistant ◆ ~ **commercial/culturel** commercial/cultural attaché ◆ ~ **de clientèle** *(Banque)* account manager

attaché-case (pl **attachés-cases**) /ataʃekɛz/ **NM** attaché case

attachement /ataʃmɑ̃/ **NM** 1 *(à une personne, à un animal)* affection (à for) attachment (à to); *(à un lieu, à une idée, à la vie)* attachment (à to); *(à une politique, à une cause)* commitment (à to); ◆ **vouer un ~ viscéral à** to be strongly *ou* deeply attached to ◆ **leur ~ à lutter contre le chômage** their commitment to fighting unemployment 2 *(Constr)* daily statement *(of work done and expenses incurred)*

attacher /ataʃe/ ▸ conjug 1 ◂ **VT** 1 *[+ animal, plante, paquet]* to tie up; *[+ prisonnier]* to tie up, to bind; *(avec une chaîne)* to chain up; *[+ volets]* to fasten, to secure; *(plusieurs choses ensemble)* to tie together, to bind together ◆ ~ **une étiquette à une valise** to tie a label on(to) a case ◆ **il attacha sa victime sur une chaise** he tied his victim to a chair ◆ ~ **les mains d'un prisonnier** to tie a prisoner's hands together, to bind a prisoner's hands (together) ◆ **la ficelle qui attachait le paquet** the string that was tied round the parcel ◆ **est-ce bien attaché ?** is it well *ou* securely tied (up)? ◆ **il ne les attache pas avec des saucisses** * he's a bit tight-fisted
2 *[+ ceinture]* to do up, to fasten; *[+ robe]* *(à boutons)* to do up, to button up, to fasten; *(à fermeture éclair)* to do up, to zip up; *[+ lacets, chaussures]* to do up, to tie up; *[+ fermeture, bouton]* to do up ◆ **veuillez ~ votre ceinture** *(en avion)* (please) fasten your seatbelts ◆ **attachez vos ceintures !** * *(hum)* hold on to your hats! *
3 *[+ papiers]* *(= épingler)* to pin together, to attach; *(= agrafer)* to staple together, to attach ◆ ~ **à** *(= épingler)* to pin to; *(= agrafer)* to staple onto
4 *(fig = lier à)* **il a attaché son nom à cette découverte** he has linked *ou* put his name to this discovery ◆ **des souvenirs l'attachent à ce village** *(qu'il a quitté)* he still feels attached to the village because of his memories; *(qu'il habite)* his memories keep him here in this village ◆ **il a su s'~ ses étudiants** he has won the loyalty of his students ◆ **plus rien ne l'attachait à la vie** nothing held her to life any more
5 *(= attribuer)* to attach ◆ ~ **de la valeur** *ou* **du prix à qch** to attach great value to sth, to set great store by sth
6 *(frm = adjoindre)* ~ **des gardes à qn** to give sb a personal guard ◆ ~ **qn à son service** to engage sb, to take sb into one's service
7 *(= fixer)* ~ **son regard** *ou* **ses yeux sur** to fix one's eyes upon
VI *(Culin)* to stick ◆ **le riz a attaché** the rice has stuck ◆ **poêle qui n'attache pas** non-stick frying pan
VPR s'attacher 1 *(gén)* to do up, to fasten (up) (avec, par with); *[robe]* *(à boutons)* to button up, to do up; *(à fermeture éclair)* to zip up, to do up; *[fermeture, bouton]* to do up ◆ **ça s'attache derrière** it does up at the back, it fastens (up) at the back ◆ **s'~ à** *[+ corde]* to attach o.s. to; *[+ siège]* to fasten o.s. to
2 *(= se prendre d'affection pour)* **s'~ à** to become attached to ◆ **cet enfant s'attache vite** this child soon becomes attached to people
3 *(= accompagner)* **s'~ aux pas de qn** to follow sb closely, to dog sb's footsteps ◆ **les souvenirs qui s'attachent à cette maison** the memories attached to *ou* associated with that house
4 *(= prendre à cœur)* **s'~ à faire qch** to endeavour *(Brit)* *(frm)* *ou* endeavor *(US)* *(frm)* *ou* attempt to do sth

attaquable /atakabl/ **ADJ** *(Mil)* open to attack; *[testament]* contestable

attaquant, e /atakɑ̃, ɑ̃t/ **NM,F** *(Mil, Sport)* attacker; *(Fin)* raider ◆ **l'avantage est à l'~** the advantage is on the attacking side

attaque /atak/ **NF** 1 *(Mil, Police)* attack *(contre* on); ◆ **lancer** *ou* **mener une ~ contre** to launch *ou* make an attack on ◆ **aller** *ou* **monter à l'~** to go into the attack ◆ **à l'~ !** attack! ◆ **passer à l'~** to move into the attack ◆ ~ **d'artillerie/nucléaire** artillery/nuclear attack ◆ ~ **à la bombe** bomb attack, bombing
2 *(= agression) [de banque, train]* raid; *[de personne]* attack *(de* on)
3 *(Sport)* attack; *[de coureur]* spurt; *(Alpinisme)* start; *(Escrime)* attack ◆ **il a lancé une ~ à 15 km de l'arrivée** he put on a spurt 15 km from the finishing line ◆ **jeu/coup d'~** attacking game/shot ◆ **repartir à l'~** to go back on the attack
4 *(= critique)* attack *(contre* on); ◆ **ce n'était pas une ~ personnelle** it wasn't a personal attack, it was nothing personal ◆ **elle a été l'objet de violentes ~s dans la presse** she came in for severe criticism from the press ◆ **une ~ en règle** a virulent attack
5 *(Méd)* attack *(de* of); ◆ **avoir une ~** *(cardiaque)* to have a heart attack; *(hémorragie cérébrale)* to have a stroke; *(d'épilepsie)* to have a seizure *ou* fit
6 *(Mus)* attack
7 *(Cartes)* lead
8 *(loc)*
◆ **d'attaque** * *(= en forme)* on *ou* in (top) form ◆ **il n'est pas d'~ ce matin** he's not on form this morning ◆ **se sentir** *ou* **être assez d'~ pour faire qch** to feel up to doing sth
COMP attaque aérienne air raid *ou* attack
attaque d'apoplexie apoplectic attack *ou* fit
attaque cardiaque heart attack
attaque à main armée hold-up, armed robbery ◆ **commettre une ~ à main armée contre une banque** to hold up a bank
attaque de nerfs † fit of hysteria

attaquer /atake/ ▸ conjug 1 ◂ **VT** 1 *(= assaillir)* *[+ pays]* to attack, to launch an attack (up)on; *[+ personne]* to attack, to assault ◆ **l'armée prussienne attaqua** the Prussian army attacked ◆ ~ **de front/par derrière** to attack from the front/from behind *ou* from the rear ◆ ~ **(qn) par surprise** to make a surprise attack (on sb) ◆ **allez, Rex attaque !** *(à un chien)* kill, Rex, kill! ◆ **on a été attaqués par les moustiques** we were attacked by mosquitoes
2 *(= critiquer) [+ abus, réputation, personne]* to attack
3 *(= endommager) [rouille, infection]* to attack; *[+ humidité]* to damage ◆ **la pollution attaque notre environnement** pollution is having a damaging effect on *ou* is damaging our environment ◆ **l'acide attaque le fer** acid attacks *ou* eats into iron
4 *(= aborder) [+ difficulté, obstacle]* to tackle; *[+ chapitre]* to make a start on; *[+ discours]* to launch into; *[+ travail]* to set about, to get down to; *(Alpinisme)* to start ◆ **il attaqua les hors-d'œuvre** * he got going on * *ou* tucked into * *(Brit)* the hors d'œuvres
5 *(Mus) [+ morceau]* to strike up, to launch into; *[+ note]* to attack
6 *(Jur) [+ jugement, testament]* to contest; *[+ mesure]* to challenge ◆ ~ **qn en justice** to take sb to court, to sue sb
7 *(Cartes)* ~ **trèfle/de la reine** to lead a club/the queen
VI *(Sport)* to attack; *[coureur]* to put on a spurt
VPR s'attaquer ◆ **s'~ à** *[+ personne, abus, mal]* to attack; *[+ problème]* to tackle, to attack, to take on ◆ **s'~ à plus fort que soi** to take on more than one's match

attardé, e /ataʀde/ **ADJ** 1 † *[enfant]* retarded 2 *(= en retard) [promeneur]* late, belated *(littér)* 3 *(= démodé) [personne, goût]* old-fashioned, behind the times *(attrib)* **NM,F** 1 ◆ ~ **(mental)** † (mentally) retarded child 2 *(Sport)* **les ~s** the stragglers

attarder /ataʀde/ ▸ conjug 1 ◂ **VT** to make late
VPR s'attarder 1 *(= se mettre en retard)* to linger (behind) ◆ **s'~ chez des amis** to stay on at friends' ◆ **s'~ à boire** to linger over drinks *ou* a drink ◆ **il s'est attardé au bureau pour finir un rapport** he's stayed late *ou* on at the office to finish a report ◆ **s'~ au café** to linger at a café ◆ **s'~ pour cueillir des fleurs** to stay behind to pick flowers ◆ **elle s'est attardée en route** she dawdled *ou* lingered *ou* tarried *(littér)* on the way ◆ **ne nous attardons pas ici** let's not stay any longer 2 *(fig)* **s'~ sur une description** to linger over a description ◆ **s'~ à des détails** to dwell on details

atteindre /atɛ̃dʀ/ ▸ conjug 49 ◂ **VT** 1 *(= parvenir à) [+ lieu, limite]* to reach; *[+ objet haut placé]* to reach, to get at; *[+ objectif]* to reach, to arrive at, to attain; *[+ prix, valeur]* to reach ◆ ~ **son but** *[personne]* to reach one's goal, to achieve one's aim; *[mesure]* to be effective, to fulfil its purpose; *[missile]* to hit its target, to reach its objective ◆ **il n'atteint pas mon épaule** he doesn't come up to *ou* reach my shoulder ◆ **la Seine a atteint la cote d'alerte** the Seine has risen to *ou* reached danger level ◆ **il a atteint (l'âge de) 90 ans** he's reached his 90th birthday ◆ **cette tour atteint 30 mètres** the tower is 30 metres high ◆ **les peupliers peuvent ~ une très grande hauteur** poplars can grow to *ou* reach a very great height ◆ **la corruption y atteint des proportions incroyables** corruption there has reached incredible proportions; → **bave**
2 *(= contacter) [+ personne]* to get in touch with, to contact, to reach
3 *(= toucher) [pierre, balle, tireur]* to hit (à in); *[événement, maladie, reproches]* to affect ◆ **il a atteint la cible** he hit the target ◆ **il a eu l'œil atteint par un éclat d'obus** he was hit in the eye by a bit of shrapnel ◆ **la maladie a atteint ses facultés mentales** the illness has affected *ou* impaired his mental faculties ◆ **les reproches ne l'atteignent pas** criticism doesn't affect him, he is unaffected by criticism ◆ **le malheur qui vient de l'~** the misfortune which has just struck him ◆ **il a été atteint dans son amour-propre** his pride has been hurt *ou* wounded
VT INDIR atteindre à *(littér = parvenir à) [+ but]* to reach, to achieve ◆ ~ **à la perfection** to attain (to) *ou* achieve perfection

atteint, e[1] /atɛ̃, ɛt/ **ADJ** 1 *(= malade)* **être ~ de** *[+ maladie]* to be suffering from ◆ **il a été ~ de surdité** he became *ou* went deaf ◆ **le poumon est gravement/légèrement ~** the lung is badly/slightly affected ◆ **il est gravement/légèrement ~** he is seriously/only slightly ill ◆ **les malades les plus ~s** the worst cases, the worst affected 2 *(* = fou)* touched *, cracked * 3 *(Admin)* **être ~ par la limite d'âge** to have to retire *(because one has reached the official retirement age)*

atteinte[2] /atɛ̃t/ **NF** 1 *(= préjudice)* attack (à on); ◆ ~ **à l'ordre public** breach of the peace ◆ ~ **à la sûreté de l'État** offence against national security ◆ ~ **à la vie privée** invasion of privacy
◆ **porter atteinte à** *[+ droits]* to infringe; *[+ intérêts]* to be damaging to; *[+ liberté, dignité, honneur, principe]* to strike a blow at; *[+ image, intégrité]* to undermine; *[+ réputation]* to damage
◆ **hors d'atteinte** *(lit)* out of reach; *(fig)* beyond reach, out of reach ◆ **un pays où une voiture reste souvent un rêve hors d'~** a country in which a car is often an unattainable dream ◆ **hors d'~ de** *[+ projectile]* out of range *ou* reach of ◆ **hors d'~ de la justice** beyond the reach of *ou* out of reach of justice

2 *(Méd = crise)* attack *(de* of); ◆ **les premières ~s du mal** the first effects of the illness

attelage /at(ə)laʒ/ NM 1 *[de cheval]* harnessing, hitching up; *[de bœuf]* yoking, hitching up; *[de charrette, remorque]* hitching up; *(Rail) [de wagons]* coupling 2 *(= harnachement, chaînes) [de chevaux]* harness; *[de bœuf]* yoke; *[de remorque]* coupling, attachment; *(Rail)* coupling 3 *(= équipage) [de chevaux]* team; *[de bœufs]* team; *[de deux bœufs]* yoke

atteler /at(ə)le/ ► conjug 4 ◄ VT *[+ cheval]* to harness, to hitch up; *[+ bœuf]* to yoke, to hitch up; *[+ charrette, remorque]* to hitch up; *(Rail) [+ wagons] (à un convoi)* to couple on; *(l'un à l'autre)* to couple ◆ **le cocher était en train d'~** the coachman was getting the horses harnessed ◆ **~ qn à un travail** *(fig)* to put sb on a job ◆ **il est attelé à ce travail depuis ce matin** he has been working away at this job since this morning VPR **s'atteler** ◆ **s'~ à** *[+ travail, tâche, problème]* to get down to

attelle /atɛl/ NF *[de cheval]* hame; *(Méd)* splint

attenant, e /at(ə)nɑ̃, ɑ̃t/ ADJ *(= contigu)* adjoining ◆ **jardin ~ à la maison** garden adjoining the house ◆ **la maison ~e à la mienne** *(ou* **la sienne** *etc)* the house next door

attendre /atɑ̃dʀ/ ► conjug 41 ◄ VT 1 *[personne] [+ personne, événement]* to wait for, to await *(littér)* ◆ **maintenant, nous attendons qu'il vienne/de savoir** we are now waiting for him to come/waiting to find out ◆ **attendez qu'il vienne/de savoir pour partir** wait until he comes/you know before you leave, wait for him to come/wait and find out before you leave ◆ **attends la fin du film** wait until the film is over *ou* until the end of the film ◆ **aller ~ un train/qn au train** to (go and) meet a train/sb off the train ◆ **il est venu m'~ à la gare** he came to meet me *ou* he met me at the station ◆ **j'attends le** *ou* **mon train** I'm waiting for the *ou* my train ◆ **~ le moment favorable** to bide one's time, to wait for the right moment ◆ **j'attends le week-end avec impatience** I'm looking forward to the weekend, I can't wait for the weekend ◆ **~ qn comme le Messie** to wait eagerly for sb ◆ **nous n'attendons plus que lui pour commencer** we're just waiting for him to arrive, then we can start ◆ **qu'est-ce qu'on attend pour partir ?** what are we waiting for? let's go! ◆ **il faut ~ un autre jour/moment pour lui parler** we'll have to wait till another day/time to speak to him ◆ **on ne t'attendait plus** we had given up on you ◆ **êtes-vous attendu ?** are you expected?, is anyone expecting you? ◆ **il attend son heure** he's biding his time ◆ **je n'attends qu'une chose, c'est qu'elle s'en aille** I (just) can't wait for her to go ◆ **il n'attendait que ça !, c'est tout ce qu'il attendait !** that's just what he was waiting for! ◆ **l'argent qu'il me doit, je l'attends toujours** he still hasn't given me the money he owes me, I'm still waiting for the money he owes me

♦ **en attendant** *(= pendant ce temps)* meanwhile, in the meantime; *(= en dépit de cela)* all the same be that as it may ◆ **en attendant, j'ai le temps de finir mon travail** meanwhile *ou* in the meantime I've time to finish my work ◆ **en attendant l'heure de partir, il jouait aux cartes** he played cards until it was time to go *ou* while he was waiting to go ◆ **on ne peut rien faire en attendant de recevoir sa lettre** we can't do anything until we get his letter ◆ **en attendant qu'il revienne, je vais vite faire une course** while I'm waiting for him to come back I'm going to pop down* to the shop ◆ **en attendant, c'est moi qui fais tout !** all the same, it's me that does everything!; → **dégel**

2 *[voiture]* to be waiting for; *[maison]* to be ready for; *[mauvaise surprise]* to be in store for, to await, to wait for; *[gloire]* to be in store for, to await ◆ **il ne sait pas encore le sort qui l'attend !** he doesn't know yet what's in store for him! *ou* awaiting him! ◆ **je sais ce qui m'attend si je lui dis ça !** I know what'll happen to me if I tell him that! ◆ **une brillante carrière l'attend** he has a brilliant career in store (for him) *ou* ahead of him ◆ **le dîner vous attend** dinner's ready (when you are)

3 *(sans complément d'objet) [personne, chose]* to wait; *[chose] (= se conserver)* to keep ◆ **j'ai attendu 2 heures** I waited (for) 2 hours ◆ **j'ai failli ~ !** *(iro)* you took your time! ◆ **attendez un instant** wait a moment, hang on a minute* ◆ **attends, je vais t'expliquer** wait, let me explain ◆ **attendez voir*** let me *ou* let's see *ou* think* ◆ **attendez un peu** let's see, wait a second; *(menace)* just (you) wait! ◆ **vous attendez ou vous voulez rappeler plus tard ?** *(Téléc)* will you hold on or do you want to call back later? ◆ **tu peux toujours ~ !, tu peux ~ longtemps !** *(iro)* you'll be lucky!, you've got a hope! *(Brit)*, you haven't a prayer! *(US)* ◆ **le train n'attendra pas** the train won't wait ◆ **ce travail attendra/peut ~** this work will wait/can wait ◆ **ces fruits ne peuvent pas ~ (demain)** this fruit won't keep (until tomorrow) ◆ **un soufflé n'attend pas** a soufflé has to be eaten straight away ◆ **sans (plus) ~** *(= immédiatement)* straight away ◆ **faites-le sans ~** do it straight away *ou* without delay ◆ **il faut agir sans plus ~** we must act without further delay *ou* straight away

♦ **faire attendre** ◆ **faire ~ qn** to keep sb waiting ◆ **se faire ~** to keep people waiting, to be a long time coming ◆ **le conférencier se fait ~** the speaker is late ◆ **il aime se faire ~** he likes to keep you *ou* people waiting ◆ **excusez-moi de m'être fait ~** sorry to have kept you (waiting) ◆ **la paix se fait ~** peace is a long time coming ◆ **leur riposte ne se fit pas ~** they didn't take long to retaliate

4 *(= escompter, prévoir) [+ personne, chose]* to expect ◆ **~ qch de qn/qch** to expect sth from sb/sth ◆ **il n'attendait pas un tel accueil** he wasn't expecting such a welcome ◆ **on attendait beaucoup de ces pourparlers** they had great hopes *ou* they expected great things of the talks ◆ **elle est arrivée alors qu'on ne l'attendait plus** she came when she was no longer expected *ou* when they'd given up on her ◆ **j'attendais mieux de cet élève** I expected better of this pupil, I expected this pupil to do better ◆ **je n'en attendais pas moins de vous** I expected no *ou* nothing less of you

5 ◆ **~ un enfant** *ou* **un bébé**, ◆ **~ famille** *(Belg)* to be expecting a baby, to be expecting ◆ **ils attendent la naissance pour le 10 mai** the baby is due on 10 May

VT INDIR **attendre après*** *[+ chose]* to be in a hurry for, to be anxious for; *[+ personne]* to be waiting for ◆ **l'argent que je t'ai prêté, je n'attends pas après** I'm not desperate for the money I lent you ◆ **je n'attends pas après lui/son aide !** I can get along without him/his help!

VPR **s'attendre** 1 *[personnes]* to wait for each other

2 ◆ **s'~ à qch** *(= escompter, prévoir)* to expect sth *(de, de la part de* from); ◆ **il ne s'attendait pas à gagner** he wasn't expecting to win ◆ **est-ce que tu t'attends vraiment à ce qu'il écrive ?** do you really expect him to write? ◆ **on ne s'attendait pas à ça de sa part** we didn't expect that of him ◆ **avec lui on peut s'~ à tout** you never know what to expect with him ◆ **tu t'attendais à quoi ?** what did you expect? ◆ **Lionel ! si je m'attendais (à te voir ici) !*** Lionel, fancy meeting you here! ◆ **elle s'y attendait** she expected as much ◆ **il fallait** *ou* **on pouvait s'y ~** it was to be expected ◆ **comme il fallait s'y ~ ...** as one would expect ..., predictably enough ...

attendri, e /atɑ̃dʀi/ (ptp de **attendrir**) ADJ *[air, regard]* melting *(épith)*, tender

attendrir /atɑ̃dʀiʀ/ ► conjug 2 ◄ VT *[+ viande]* to tenderize; *(fig) [+ personne]* to move (to pity); *[+ cœur]* to soften, to melt ◆ **il se laissa ~ par ses prières** her pleadings made him relent *ou* yield VPR **s'attendrir** to be moved *ou* touched *(sur* by); ◆ **s'~ sur (le sort de) qn** to feel (sorry) for sb ◆ **s'~ sur soi-même** to feel sorry for o.s.

attendrissant, e /atɑ̃dʀisɑ̃, ɑ̃t/ ADJ moving, touching

attendrissement /atɑ̃dʀismɑ̃/ NM *(tendre)* emotion, tender feelings; *(apitoyé)* pity ◆ **ce fut l'~ général** everybody got emotional ◆ **pas d'~ !** let's not be emotional!

attendrisseur /atɑ̃dʀisœʀ/ NM *(Boucherie)* tenderizer ◆ **viande passée à l'~** tenderized meat

attendu, e /atɑ̃dy/ (ptp de **attendre**) ADJ *[personne, événement, jour]* long-awaited; *(= prévu)* expected ◆ **être très ~** to be eagerly expected PRÉP *(= étant donné)* given, considering ◆ **~ que** seeing that, since, given *ou* considering that; *(Jur)* whereas NMPL *(Jur)* ◆ **~s du jugement** grounds for the decision

attentat /atɑ̃ta/ NM 1 *(= attaque, agression) (gén : contre une personne)* murder attempt; *(Pol)* assassination attempt; *(contre un bâtiment)* attack *(contre* on); ◆ **un ~ a été perpétré contre le président** an attempt has been made on the life of the president, there has been an assassination attempt on the president 2 *(= atteinte)* **c'est un ~ contre la vie d'une personne** it is an attempt on someone's life

COMP **attentat à la bombe** bomb attack, (terrorist) bombing
attentat à la liberté violation of liberty
attentat aux mœurs offence against public decency
attentat à la pudeur indecent assault
attentat suicide suicide bombing
attentat contre la sûreté de l'État conspiracy against the security of the state
attentat à la voiture piégée car-bombing

attentatoire /atɑ̃tatwaʀ/ ADJ prejudicial *(à* to) detrimental *(à* to)

attente /atɑ̃t/ NF 1 *(= expectative)* wait, waiting *(NonC)* ◆ **cette ~ fut très pénible** the wait was unbearable ◆ **l'~ est ce qu'il y a de plus pénible** it's the waiting which is hardest to bear ◆ **l'~ se prolongeait** the wait was growing longer and longer ◆ **délai** *ou* **temps d'~** waiting time ◆ **il y a 10 minutes d'~** there's a 10-minute wait ◆ **position d'~** wait-and-see attitude ◆ **solution d'~** temporary solution

♦ **en attente** ◆ **demande en ~** request pending ◆ **le projet est en ~** the project is on hold ◆ **laisser un dossier en ~** to leave a file pending ◆ **mettre qn en ~** *(Téléc)* to put sb on hold ◆ **pour écouter les messages en ~, appuyez ...** *(sur répondeur)* to listen to messages, press ...

♦ **en attente de** ◆ **malade en ~ de greffe** patient waiting for a transplant ◆ **détenu en ~ de jugement** prisoner awaiting trial

♦ **dans l'attente de** ◆ **vivre dans l'~ d'une nouvelle** to spend one's time waiting for (a piece of) news ◆ **dans l'~ de vos nouvelles** looking forward to hearing from you; → **salle**

2 *(= espoir)* expectation ◆ **répondre à l'~** *ou* **aux ~s de qn** to come *ou* live up to sb's expectations ◆ **contre toute ~** contrary to (all) expectation(s)

attenter /atɑ̃te/ ► conjug 1 ◄ VT 1 ◆ **~ à la vie de qn** to make an attempt on sb's life ◆ **~ à ses jours** to attempt suicide ◆ **~ à la sûreté de l'État** to conspire against the security of the state 2 *(fig = violer)* **~ à** *[+ liberté, droits]* to violate

attentif, -ive /atɑ̃tif, iv/ ADJ [1] (= vigilant) [personne, air] attentive ◆ **regarder qn d'un œil ~** to look at sb attentively ◆ **écouter d'une oreille attentive** to listen attentively ◆ **être ~ à tout ce qui se passe** to pay attention to everything that's going on ◆ **sois donc ~ !** pay attention! [2] (= scrupuleux) [examen] careful, close, searching; [travail] careful; [soin] scrupulous ◆ **~ à son travail** careful ou painstaking in one's work ◆ **~ à ses devoirs** heedful ou mindful of one's duties ◆ **~ à ne blesser personne** careful not to hurt anyone [3] (= prévenant) [soins] thoughtful; [prévenance] watchful ◆ **~ à plaire** anxious to please ◆ **~ à ce que tout se passe bien** keeping a close watch to see that all goes well

attention /atɑ̃sjɔ̃/ GRAMMAIRE ACTIVE 29.2, 29.3, 53.6 NF [1] (= concentration) attention; (= soin) care ◆ **avec ~** [écouter] carefully, attentively; [examiner] carefully, closely ◆ **attirer/détourner l'~ de qn** to attract/divert ou distract sb's attention ◆ **fixer son ~ sur** to focus one's attention on ◆ **faire un effort d'~** to make an effort to concentrate ◆ **demander un effort d'~** to require careful attention ◆ **je demande toute votre ~** can I have your full attention? ◆ **ce cas/projet mérite toute notre ~** this case/project deserves our undivided attention ◆ **"à l'attention de M. Dupont"** "for the attention of Mr Dupont" ◆ **votre candidature a retenu notre ~** we considered your application carefully; → **signaler**

[2] (locutions) **~ ! tu vas tomber !** watch out ou mind (out) (Brit) ou careful! you're going to fall! ◆ **"attention chien méchant"** "beware of the dog" ◆ **"attention travaux"** "caution, work in progress" ◆ **"attention à la marche"** "be careful of the step", "mind the step" (Brit) ◆ **~ ! je n'ai pas dit cela** careful! I didn't say that ◆ **~ au départ !** the train is now leaving! ◆ **"attention, peinture fraîche"** "(caution) wet paint" ◆ **"attention, fragile"** (sur colis) "fragile, handle with care" ◆ **~ les yeux !*** watch out!*

◆ **faire attention** (= prendre garde) to be careful, to take care ◆ **faire bien ou très ~** to pay careful attention ◆ **(fais) ~ à ta ligne** you'd better watch your waistline ◆ **fais ~ à ne pas trop manger** mind ou be careful you don't eat too much ◆ **fais ~ (à ce) que la porte soit fermée** make sure ou mind the door's shut ◆ **fais bien ~ à toi** (= prends soin de toi) take good care of yourself; (= sois vigilant) be careful

◆ **faire ou prêter attention à** (= remarquer) to pay attention ou heed to ◆ **as-tu fait ~ à ce qu'il a dit ?** did you pay attention to ou listen carefully to what he said? ◆ **il n'a même pas fait ~ à moi/à ce changement** he didn't (even) take any notice of me/the change ◆ **tu vas faire ~ quand il entrera et tu verras** look carefully ou have a good look when he comes in and you'll see what I mean ◆ **ne faites pas ~ à lui** pay no attention to him, take no notice of him, never mind him

[3] (= prévenance) attention, thoughtfulness (NonC) ◆ **être plein d'~s pour qn** to be very attentive towards sb ◆ **ses ~s me touchaient** I was touched by his attentions ou thoughtfulness ◆ **quelle charmante ~ !** how very thoughtful!, what a lovely thought!

attentionné, e /atɑ̃sjɔne/ ADJ (= prévenant) thoughtful, considerate (pour, auprès de towards)

attentisme /atɑ̃tism/ NM wait-and-see policy, waiting-game

attentiste /atɑ̃tist/ NMF partisan of a wait-and-see policy ADJ [politique] wait-and-see (épith)

attentivement /atɑ̃tivmɑ̃/ ADV [lire, écouter] attentively, carefully; [examiner] carefully, closely

atténuantes /atenɥɑ̃t/ ADJ FPL → **circonstance**

atténuation /atenɥasjɔ̃/ NF [1] (= fait d'atténuer) [de douleur] alleviation, easing; [faute] mitigation; [de responsabilité] lightening; [de coup, effet] softening; (Jur) [de punition, peine] mitigation ◆ **~ d'un virus** (Méd) attenuation of a virus ◆ **cette crème permet l'~ des rides** this cream smooths out wrinkles [2] (= fait de s'atténuer) [de douleur] dying down, easing; [de sensation, bruit] dying down; [de violence, crise] subsiding, abatement; [de couleur] softening [3] (= adoucissement) [de lumière] subduing, dimming; [de couleur, son] softening, toning down

atténuer /atenɥe/ ► conjug 1 ◄ VT [1] [+ douleur] to alleviate, to ease; [+ rancœur] to mollify, to appease; [+ propos, reproches] to tone down; [+ rides] to smooth out [2] [+ faute] to mitigate; [+ responsabilité] to lighten; [+ punition] to mitigate; [+ coup, effets] to soften; [+ faits] to water down; (Fin) [+ pertes] to cushion; [+ risques] to limit [3] [+ lumière] to subdue, to dim; [+ couleur, son] to soften, to tone down VPR **s'atténuer** [1] [douleur] to ease, to die down; [sensation] to die down; [violence, crise] to subside, to abate [2] [bruit] to die down; [couleur] to soften ◆ **leurs cris s'atténuèrent** their cries grew quieter ou died down

atterrant, e /ateʀɑ̃, ɑ̃t/ ADJ appalling

atterrer /ateʀe/ ► conjug 1 ◄ VT to dismay, to appal (Brit), to appall (US) ◆ **il était atterré par cette nouvelle** he was aghast ou shattered (Brit) at the news ◆ **sa bêtise m'atterre** his stupidity appals me, I am appalled by ou aghast at his stupidity ◆ **air atterré** look of utter dismay

atterrir /ateʀiʀ/ ► conjug 2 ◄ VI (en avion) to land, to touch down; (dans un bateau) to land ◆ **~ sur le ventre** [personne] to land flat on one's face; [avion] to make a belly landing ◆ **~ en prison/dans un village perdu*** to land up* (Brit) ou land* (US) in prison/in a village in the middle of nowhere ◆ **le travail a finalement atterri sur mon bureau*** the work finally landed on my desk ◆ **atterris !*** come back down to earth!

atterrissage /ateʀisaʒ/ NM (Aviat, Naut) landing ◆ **à l'~** at the moment of landing, at touchdown ◆ **~ en catastrophe/sur le ventre/sans visibilité** crash/belly/blind landing ◆ **~ forcé** emergency ou forced landing ◆ **~ en douceur** (Aviat, Écon) soft landing; → **piste, terrain, train**

attestation /atɛstasjɔ̃/ NF [1] [de fait] attestation [2] (= document) certificate; [de diplôme] certificate of accreditation ou of attestation ◆ **~ médicale** doctor's certificate ◆ **~ sur l'honneur** affidavit ◆ **~ de nationalité française/domiciliation** proof of French citizenship/residence ◆ **~ de conformité** safety certificate

attester /atɛste/ ► conjug 1 ◄ VT [1] (= certifier) [+ fait] to testify to, to vouch for ◆ **~ que ...** to testify that ..., to vouch for the fact that ..., to attest that ...; [témoin] to testify that ... ◆ **ce fait est attesté par tous les témoins** this fact is confirmed by all the witnesses ◆ **comme en attestent les procès-verbaux** as the minutes show ◆ **~ (de) l'innocence de qn** to prove sb's innocence ◆ **certains documents attestent de l'ancienneté de ce vase** there are documents which attest to the antiquity of this vase

[2] (= démontrer) [chose, preuve] to attest to, to testify to ◆ **comme en attestent les sondages** as the polls show ◆ **cette attitude atteste son intelligence ou atteste qu'il est intelligent** this attitude testifies to his intelligence ◆ **les fissures attestent de la violence de cette collision** the cracks attest to the force of the collision ◆ **forme attestée** (Ling) attested form ◆ **mot non attesté dans ou par les dictionnaires** word not attested by dictionaries

[3] (littér = prendre à témoin) **j'atteste les dieux que ...** I call the gods to witness that ...

attiédir † /atjediʀ/ ► conjug 2 ◄ VT (littér) [+ eau] to make lukewarm; [+ climat] to make more temperate, to temper; [+ désir, ardeur] to temper, to cool VPR **s'attiédir** [eau] (plus chaud) to get warmer; (plus frais) to get cooler; [climat] to become more temperate; (littér) [désir, ardeur] to cool down, to wane

attifer* /atife/ ► conjug 1 ◄ VT (= habiller) to get up* (de in); ◆ **regardez comme elle est attifée !** look at her get-up!* ◆ **attifée d'une robe à volants** dolled up* in a flounced dress VPR **s'attifer** to get o.s. up* (de in)

attiger‡ /atiʒe/ ► conjug 3 ◄ VI to go a bit far*, to overstep the mark

Attila /atila/ NM Attila

attique[1] /atik/ ADJ (Antiq) Attic ◆ **finesse/sel ~** Attic wit/salt NF **Attique** ◆ **l'Attique** Attica

attique[2] /atik/ NM (Constr) attic (storey (Brit) ou story (US))

attirail* /atiʀaj/ NM gear*, paraphernalia ◆ **~ de pêche** fishing tackle ◆ **~ de bricoleur/cambrioleur** handyman's/burglar's tools ou tool kit

attirance /atiʀɑ̃s/ NF attraction (pour, envers for); ◆ **éprouver de l'~ pour qch/qn** to be ou feel drawn towards sth/sb, to be attracted to sth/sb ◆ **l'~ du vide** the lure of the abyss

attirant, e /atiʀɑ̃, ɑ̃t/ ADJ attractive, appealing ◆ **femme très ~e** alluring ou very attractive woman

attirer /atiʀe/ GRAMMAIRE ACTIVE 53.6 ► conjug 1 ◄ VT [1] (gén, Phys) to attract; (en appâtant) to lure, to entice ◆ **il m'attira dans un coin** he drew me into a corner ◆ **~ qn dans un piège/par des promesses** to lure ou entice sb into a trap/with promises ◆ **ce spectacle va ~ la foule** this show will really draw ou attract the crowds ou will be a real crowd-puller ◆ **~ l'attention de qn sur qch** to draw sb's attention to sth ◆ **il essaya d'~ son attention** he tried to attract ou catch his attention

[2] (= plaire à) [pays, projet] to appeal to; [personne] to attract, to appeal to ◆ **être attiré par une doctrine/qn** to be attracted ou drawn to a doctrine/sb ◆ **affiche/robe qui attire les regards** eye-catching poster/dress ◆ **il est très attiré par elle** he finds her very attractive

[3] (= causer) [+ ennuis] to cause, to bring ◆ **tu vas t'~ des ennuis** you're going to cause trouble for yourself ou bring trouble upon yourself ◆ **ses discours lui ont attiré des sympathies** his speeches won ou gained ou earned him sympathy ◆ **s'~ des critiques/la colère de qn** to incur criticism/sb's anger, to bring criticism on/sb's anger down on o.s. ◆ **s'~ des ennemis** to make enemies for o.s. ◆ **je me suis attiré sa gratitude** I won ou earned his gratitude

attiser /atize/ ► conjug 1 ◄ VT [+ feu] (avec tisonnier) to poke (up), to stir up; (en éventant) to fan; [+ curiosité, haine] to stir, to arouse; [+ convoitise] to arouse; [+ désir] to stir, to kindle; [+ querelle] to stir up ◆ **j'ai soufflé pour ~ la flamme** I blew on the fire to make it burn

attitré, e /atitʀe/ ADJ (= habituel) [marchand, place] regular, usual; (= agréé) [marchand] accredited, appointed, registered; [journaliste] accredited ◆ **fournisseur ~ d'un chef d'État** purveyors by appointment to a head of state

attitude /atityd/ GRAMMAIRE ACTIVE 33.1 NF (= maintien) bearing; (= comportement) attitude; (= point de vue) standpoint, attitude; (= affectation) façade ◆ **prendre des ~s gracieuses** to adopt graceful poses ◆ **avoir une ~ décidée** to have a determined air ◆ **prendre une ~ ferme** to adopt a firm standpoint ou attitude ◆ **le**

socialisme chez lui n'est qu'une ~ his socialism is only a façade

attouchement /atuʃmɑ̃/ **NM** touch, touching *(NonC)*; *(Méd)* palpation ◆ **se livrer à des ~s sur qn** *(gén)* to fondle *ou* stroke sb; *(Jur)* to interfere with sb

attracteur /atʀaktœʀ/ **NM** *(Sci)* attractor

attractif, -ive /atʀaktif, iv/ **ADJ** *(Phys) [phénomène]* attractive; *(= attrayant) [offre, prix, taux]* attractive

attraction /atʀaksjɔ̃/ **NF** [1] *(gén = attirance, Ling, Phys)* attraction ◆ **~ universelle** gravitation ◆ **~ moléculaire** molecular attraction [2] *(= centre d'intérêt)* attraction; *(= partie d'un spectacle)* attraction; *(= numéro d'un artiste)* number ◆ **l'~ vedette** the star attraction ◆ **quand passent les ~s ?** *(boîte de nuit)* when is the cabaret *ou* floorshow on? ◆ **ils ont renouvelé leurs ~s** *(cirque)* they have changed their programme (of attractions *ou* entertainments), they have taken on some new acts; → **parc**

attractivité /atʀaktivite/ **NF** *[de région]* attractiveness, appeal; *[de programme, émission]* appeal

attrait /atʀɛ/ **NM** [1] *(= séduction) [de paysage, doctrine, plaisirs]* appeal, attraction; *[de danger, aventure]* appeal ◆ **ses romans ont pour moi beaucoup d'~** I find his novels very appealing, his novels appeal to me very much ◆ **éprouver un ~** *ou* **de l'~ pour qch** to be attracted to sth, to find sth attractive *ou* appealing [2] *(= charmes)* **~s** attractions

attrapade * /atʀapad/ **NF** row *, telling off *

attrape /atʀap/ **NF** *(= farce)* trick; → **farce¹**

attrape-couillon ⁑ (pl **attrape-couillons**) /atʀapkujɔ̃/ **NM** con *, con game *

attrape-mouche (pl **attrape-mouches**) /atʀapmuʃ/ **NM** *(= plante, piège)* flytrap; *(= oiseau)* flycatcher; *(= papier collant)* fly-paper

attrape-nigaud * (pl **attrape-nigauds**) /atʀapnigo/ **NM** con *, con game *

attraper /atʀape/ ▸ **conjug 1** ◂ **VT** [1] *[+ ballon]* to catch; *[+ journal, crayon]* to pick up

[2] * *[+ train]* to catch, to get, to hop * *(US)*; *[+ contravention, gifle]* to get

[3] *[+ personne, voleur, animal]* to catch ◆ **toi, si je t'attrape !** if I catch you! ◆ **que je t'y attrape !** * don't let me catch you doing that!, if I catch you doing that!

[4] *[+ maladie]* to catch, to get ◆ **tu vas ~ froid** *ou* **du mal** you'll catch cold ◆ **j'ai attrapé un rhume/son rhume** I've caught a cold/a cold from him *ou* his cold ◆ **j'ai attrapé mal à la gorge** I've got a sore throat ◆ **tu vas ~ la mort** you'll catch your death (of cold) ◆ **il a attrapé un coup de soleil** he got sunburnt ◆ **la grippe s'attrape facilement** flu is very catching

[5] *(= intercepter) [+ mots]* to pick up

[6] *(= acquérir) [+ style, accent]* to pick up ◆ **il faut ~ le coup** *ou* **le tour de main** you have to get *ou* learn the knack

[7] *(* = gronder)* to tell off * ◆ **se faire ~ (par qn)** to be told off (by sb) *, to get a telling off (from sb) * ◆ **mes parents vont m'~** I'm really going to get it ⁑ from my parents, my parents are going to give me a real telling off * ◆ **ils se sont attrapés pendant une heure** they went at each other for a whole hour *

[8] *(= tromper)* to take in ◆ **se laisser ~** to be had * *ou* taken in ◆ **tu as été bien attrapé** *(trompé)* you were had all right *; *(surpris)* you were caught out there all right

attrape-touristes /atʀapturist/ **NM INV** tourist trap

attrape-tout /atʀaptu/ **ADJ INV** *[parti politique]* catch-all *(épith)*

attrayant, e /atʀɛjɑ̃, ɑ̃t/ **ADJ** *[spectacle, taux]* attractive; *[idée]* appealing, attractive; *[projet]* appealing ◆ **c'est une lecture ~e** it makes *ou* it's pleasant reading ◆ **peu ~** *[travail]* unappealing; *[paysage]* unattractive; *[proposition]* unattractive, unappealing

attribuable /atʀibɥabl/ **ADJ** attributable *(à* to); ◆ **les décès directement ~s au tabagisme** deaths which are directly attributable to smoking ◆ **la crise est ~ tout d'abord aux chefs politiques** primary responsibility for the crisis belongs to the political leaders, the political leaders have primary responsibility for the crisis

attribuer /atʀibɥe/ GRAMMAIRE ACTIVE 44.2 ▸ **conjug 1** ◂ **VT** [1] *(= allouer) [+ prix]* to award; *[+ avantages, privilèges]* to grant, to accord; *[+ place, rôle]* to allocate, to assign; *[+ biens, part]* to allocate *(à* to); ◆ **le numéro que vous avez demandé n'est plus attribué** *(Téléc)* the number you have dialled is no longer available ◆ **s'~ le meilleur rôle/la meilleure part** to give o.s. the best role/the biggest share, to claim the best role/the biggest share for o.s.

[2] *(= imputer) [+ faute]* to attribute, to impute; *[+ pensée, intention]* to attribute, to ascribe *(à* to); ◆ **à quoi attribuez-vous cet échec/accident ?** what do you put this failure/accident down to?, what do you attribute *ou* ascribe this failure/accident to?

[3] *(= accorder) [+ invention, mérite]* to attribute *(à* to); ◆ **on lui attribue l'invention de l'imprimerie** the invention of printing has been attributed to him, he has been credited with the invention of printing ◆ **la critique n'attribue que peu d'intérêt à son livre** the critics find little of interest in his book *ou* consider his book of little interest ◆ **~ de l'importance à qch** to attach importance to sth ◆ **s'~ tout le mérite** to claim all the merit for o.s.

attribut /atʀiby/ **NM** *(= caractéristique, symbole)* attribute; *(Gram)* complement ◆ **adjectif ~** predicative adjective ◆ **nom ~** noun complement

attributaire /atʀibytɛʀ/ **NMF** *[de prestations]* beneficiary; *[d'actions]* allotee; *[de prix]* prizewinner

attributif, -ive /atʀibytif, iv/ **ADJ** [1] *(Jur)* **acte ~** act of assignment [2] *(Ling)* **fonction attributive** complement function ◆ **syntagme ~** complement ◆ **verbe ~** link verb, copula

attribution /atʀibysjɔ̃/ **NF** [1] *[de prix]* awarding; *[d'avantages]* granting; *[de place, rôle, part]* allocation; *[d'œuvre, invention]* attribution [2] *(= prérogatives, pouvoirs)* **~s** remit, attributions ◆ **cela n'entre pas dans mes ~s** that's not part of my remit

attristant, e /atʀistɑ̃, ɑ̃t/ **ADJ** *[nouvelle, spectacle]* saddening

attrister /atʀiste/ ▸ **conjug 1** ◂ **VT** to sadden ◆ **cette nouvelle nous a profondément attristés** we were greatly saddened by *ou* grieved at the news **VPR s'attrister** to be saddened *(de* by) to become sad *(de qch* at sth; *de voir que* at seeing that)

attroupement /atʀupmɑ̃/ **NM** *[de foule]* gathering; *(= groupe)* crowd, mob *(péj)*

attrouper (s') /atʀupe/ ▸ **conjug 1** ◂ **VPR** to gather (together), to flock together, to form a crowd

atypique /atipik/ **ADJ** atypical

au /o/ → **à**

aubade /obad/ **NF** dawn serenade ◆ **donner une ~ à qn** to serenade sb at dawn

aubaine /obɛn/ **NF** godsend; *(financière)* windfall ◆ **profiter de l'~** to make the most of one's good fortune *ou* of the opportunity ◆ **quelle (bonne) ~ !** what a godsend! *ou* stroke of luck!

aube¹ /ob/ **NF** [1] *(= lever du jour)* dawn, daybreak, first light ◆ **à l'~** at dawn *ou* daybreak *ou* first light ◆ **avant l'~** before dawn *ou* daybreak [2] *(= début)* dawn, beginning ◆ **à l'~ de** at the dawn of

aube² /ob/ **NF** *(Rel)* alb

aube³ /ob/ **NF** *(Tech) [de bateau]* paddle, blade; *[de moulin]* vane; *[de ventilateur]* blade, vane ◆ **roue à ~s** paddle wheel

aubépine /obepin/ **NF** hawthorn ◆ **fleurs d'~** may (blossom), hawthorn blossom

auberge /obɛʀʒ/ **NF** inn ◆ **il prend la maison pour une ~ !** * he treats this place like a hotel! ◆ **~ de (la) jeunesse** youth hostel ◆ **c'est l'~ espagnole** *(repas)* everyone's bringing some food along, it's potluck *(US)*; *(situation chaotique)* it's a madhouse *; → **sortir¹**

aubergine /obɛʀʒin/ **NF** [1] *(= légume)* aubergine *(Brit)*, eggplant *(US)* ◆ **caviar d'~** ≈ aubergine *(Brit) ou* eggplant *(US)* dip [2] *(† * = contractuelle)* traffic warden *(Brit)*, meter maid * *(US)* **ADJ INV** aubergine(-coloured)

aubergiste /obɛʀʒist/ **NMF** *[d'hôtel]* hotel-keeper; *[d'auberge]* innkeeper, landlord ◆ **père** *ou* **mère ~** *[d'auberge de jeunesse]* (youth-hostel) warden

aubette /obɛt/ **NF** *(Belg)* bus shelter

aubier /obje/ **NM** sapwood

auburn /obœʀn/ **ADJ INV** auburn

aucun, e /okœ̃, yn/ **ADJ** [1] *(négatif)* no, not any ◆ **~ historien n'en a parlé** no historian spoke of it ◆ **il n'a ~e preuve** he has no proof, he doesn't have any proof ◆ **sans faire ~ bruit** without making a noise *ou* any noise ◆ **ils ne prennent ~ soin de leurs vêtements** they don't take care of their clothes (at all) ◆ **ils n'ont eu ~ mal à trouver le chemin** they had no trouble finding the way, they found the way without any trouble

[2] *(interrogatif, positif)* any ◆ **il lit plus qu'~ autre enfant** he reads more than any other child ◆ **croyez-vous qu'~ auditeur aurait osé le contredire ?** do you think that any listener would have dared to contradict him?

PRON [1] *(négatif)* none ◆ **il n'aime ~ de ces films** he doesn't like any of these films ◆ **~ de ses enfants ne lui ressemble** none of his children are like him ◆ **je ne pense pas qu'~ d'entre nous puisse y aller** I don't think any of us can go ◆ **combien de réponses avez-vous eues ? – ~e** how many answers did you get? – not one *ou* none

[2] *(interrogatif, positif)* any, any one ◆ **il aime ses chiens plus qu'~ de ses enfants** he is fonder of his dogs than of any (one) of his children ◆ **pensez-vous qu'~ ait compris ?** do you think anyone *ou* anybody understood?

[3] *(littér)* **d'~s** some ◆ **d'~s aiment raconter que ...** there are some who like to say that ...

aucunement /okynmɑ̃/ **ADV** in no way, not in the least, not in the slightest ◆ **il n'est ~ à blâmer** he's not in the least to blame, he's in no way *ou* not in any way to blame ◆ **acceptez-vous ? – ~** will you agree? – certainly not

audace /odas/ **NF** [1] *(= témérité)* daring, boldness, audacity; *(Art : = originalité)* daring; *(= effronterie)* audacity, effrontery ◆ **avoir l'~ de** to have the audacity to, to dare to [2] *(= geste osé)* daring gesture; *(= innovation)* daring idea *ou* touch ◆ **elle lui en voulait de ses ~s** she held his boldness *ou* his bold behaviour against him ◆ **une ~ de génie** a daring touch of genius ◆ **~s de style** daring innovations of style ◆ **les ~s de la mode** the daring creations of high fashion

audacieusement /odasjøzmɑ̃/ **ADV** boldly ◆ **robe ~ décolletée** daringly low-cut dress

audacieux, -ieuse /odasjø, jøz/ **ADJ** *[soldat, action, architecture]* daring, bold; *[artiste, projet]* daring ♦ **un geste** ~ a bold gesture ♦ **les plus** ~ the boldest among them; → **fortune**

au-delà /od(ə)la/ LOC ADV → **delà** NM ♦ **l'**~ the beyond

au-dessous /odəsu/, **au-dessus** /odəsy/ → **dessous, dessus**

au-devant /od(ə)vɑ̃/ LOC PRÉP **au-devant de** ahead of ♦ **aller** ~ **de qn** to go and meet sb ♦ **aller** ~ **des désirs de qn** to anticipate sb's wishes LOC ADV ahead

audibilité /odibilite/ NF audibility

audible /odibl/ ADJ audible

audience /odjɑ̃s/ NF [1] *(frm = entretien)* interview, audience ♦ **donner** ~ **à qn** to grant sb an audience

[2] *(Jur = séance)* hearing ♦ **l'**~ **reprendra à 14 heures** the court will reconvene at 2 o'clock

[3] *(= attention)* interest ♦ **ce projet eut beaucoup d'**~ the project aroused much interest ♦ **cet écrivain a trouvé** ~ **auprès des étudiants** this author has had a favourable reception from students *ou* is popular with students ♦ **ce parti bénéficie de la plus large** ~ this party has the largest following

[4] *(= spectateurs, auditeurs)* audience ♦ **faire de l'**~ *(Radio, TV)* to attract a large audience ♦ **gagner des points d'**~ to go up in the ratings ♦ **taux d'**~ *(TV)* viewing figures; *(Radio)* listening figures ♦ **part d'**~ audience share ♦ **9,4 points d'**~ 9.4 points in the ratings, 9.4 rating points *(US)* ♦ **cette série a battu tous les records d'**~ the series has broken all viewing *ou* listening records ♦ **heure de grande** ~ *(TV)* peak viewing time; *(Radio)* peak listening time

audimat ® /odimat/ NM INV *(= appareil)* audience research device; *(= taux d'écoute)* ratings ♦ **avoir un bon** ~**, faire de l'**~ to have good ratings

audimètre /odimɛtʀ/ NM audience research device

audio /odjo/ ADJ INV *[fréquence, matériel, cassette]* audio

audioconférence /odjokɔ̃ferɑ̃s/ NF conference call

audio-électronique (pl **audio-électroniques**) /odjoelɛktʀɔnik/ ADJ audiotronic

audiofréquence /odjofʀekɑ̃s/ NF audio frequency

audiogramme /odjogʀam/ NM audiogram

audioguidage /odjogidaʒ/ NM ♦ **système d'**~ audio-guide, audio-guiding system

audioguide /odjogid/ NM tape guide

audiomètre /odjomɛtʀ/ NM audiometer

audiométrie /odjometʀi/ NF audiometry

audionumérique /odjonymeʀik/ ADJ digital

audio-oral, e (mpl **audio-oraux**) /odjooʀal, o/ ADJ *[exercices, méthode]* audio *(épith)*

audiophone /odjofɔn/ NM hearing aid

audioprothésiste /odjopʀɔtezist/ NMF hearing aid specialist

audiotexte /odjotɛkst/ NM audiotext

audiotypie /odjotipi/ NF audiotyping

audiotypiste /odjotipist/ NMF audiotypist

audiovisuel, -elle /odjovizɥɛl/ ADJ audiovisual NM ♦ **l'**~ *(= équipement)* audiovisual aids; *(= méthodes)* audiovisual techniques *ou* methods; *(= radio et télévision)* radio and television

audit /odit/ NM [1] *(= contrôle)* audit ♦ **faire l'**~ **de** to audit [2] *(= personne)* auditor

auditer /odite/ ► conjug 1 ◄ VT to audit

auditeur, -trice /oditœʀ, tʀis/ NM,F *(gén, Radio)* listener; *(Ling)* hearer; *(Fin)* auditor ♦ **le conférencier avait charmé ses** ~**s** the lecturer had captivated his audience ♦ ~ **libre** *(Univ)* *person who registers to sit in on lectures,* auditor *(US)* ♦ ~ **à la Cour des comptes** junior official *(at the Cour des Comptes)*

auditif, -ive /oditif, iv/ ADJ auditory ♦ **troubles** ~**s** hearing problems *ou* difficulties ♦ **aide** *ou* **prothèse auditive** hearing aid

audition /odisjɔ̃/ NF [1] *(Mus, Théât) (= essai)* audition; *(= récital)* recital; *(= concert d'élèves)* concert *(de* by); ♦ **passer une** ~ to audition, to have an audition [2] *(Jur)* hearing ♦ **après une heure d'**~ **par le juge** after a one-hour hearing before the judge ♦ **procéder à l'**~ **d'un témoin** to hear a witness [3] *(= écoute)* listening *(de* to); ♦ **salle conçue pour l'**~ **de la musique** room designed for listening to music [4] *(= ouïe)* hearing

auditionner /odisjɔne/ ► conjug 1 ◄ VT to audition, to give an audition to VI to be auditioned, to audition

auditoire /oditwaʀ/ NM audience ADJ *(Ling)* auditory

auditorium /oditɔʀjɔm/ NM auditorium

auge /oʒ/ NF *(Agr, Constr)* trough ♦ **vallée en** ~**,** ~ **glaciaire** *(Géog)* U-shaped valley, trough ♦ **passe ton** ~ **!** * *(hum)* give us your plate! *

Augias /oʒjas/ NM Augeas; → **écurie**

augmentatif, -ive /ɔgmɑ̃tatif, iv/ ADJ *(Gram)* augmentative

augmentation /ɔgmɑ̃tasjɔ̃/ NF *(= accroissement) (gén)* increase; *[de prix, population, production]* increase, rise *(de* in); ♦ ~ **de capital** increase in capital ♦ ~ **de salaire** pay rise *(Brit)*, (pay) raise *(US)* ♦ **réclamer une** ~ **(de salaire)** *(collectivement)* to make a wage claim; *(individuellement)* to put in for a pay rise *(Brit) ou* raise *(US)* ♦ **l'**~ **des salaires par la direction** the management's raising of salaries ♦ **l'**~ **des prix par les commerçants** the raising *ou* putting up of prices by shopkeepers

augmenter /ɔgmɑ̃te/ ► conjug 1 ◄ VT [1] *[+ salaire, prix, impôts]* to increase, to raise, to put up; *[+ nombre]* to increase, to raise, to augment; *[+ production, quantité, dose]* to increase, to step up, to raise; *[+ durée]* to increase; *[+ difficulté, inquiétude]* to add to, to increase; *[+ intérêt]* to heighten ♦ ~ **les prix de 10%** to increase *ou* raise *ou* put up prices by 10% ♦ **il augmente ses revenus en faisant des heures supplémentaires** he augments *ou* supplements his income by working overtime ♦ **sa collection s'est augmentée d'un nouveau tableau** he has extended *ou* enlarged his collection with a new painting, he has added a new painting to his collection ♦ ~ **(de 5 mailles)** *(Tricot)* to increase (5 stitches) ♦ **tierce augmentée** *(Mus)* augmented third ♦ **ceci ne fit qu'**~ **sa colère** this only added to his anger; → **édition**

[2] ♦ ~ **qn (de 75 €)** to increase sb's salary (by €75), to give sb a (€75) rise *(Brit) ou* raise *(US)* ♦ **il n'a pas été augmenté depuis 2 ans** he has not had *ou* has not been given a rise *(Brit) ou* raise *(US) ou* a salary increase for 2 years

VI *(= grandir) [salaire, prix, impôts]* to increase, to rise, to go up; *[marchandises]* to go up; *[poids, quantité]* to increase; *[population, production]* to grow, to increase, to rise; *[douleur]* to grow *ou* get worse, to increase; *[difficulté, inquiétude]* to grow, to increase ♦ ~ **de poids/volume** to increase in weight/volume; → **vie**

augure /ogyʀ/ NM [1] *(= devin) (Hist)* augur; *(hum)* soothsayer, oracle ♦ **consulter les** ~**s** to consult the oracle [2] *(= présage)* omen; *(Hist)* augury ♦ **être de bon** ~ to be of good omen, to augur well ♦ **résultat de bon** ~ promising *ou* encouraging result ♦ **être de mauvais** ~ to be ominous *ou* of ill omen, to augur ill ♦ **cela me paraît de bon/mauvais** ~ that's a good/bad sign, that augurs well/badly *ou* ill; → **accepter, oiseau**

augurer /ogyʀe/ ► conjug 1 ◄ VT ♦ **que faut-il** ~ **de son silence?** what must we gather *ou* understand from his silence? ♦ **je n'augure rien de bon de cela** I don't foresee *ou* see any good coming from *ou* out of it ♦ **cela augure bien/mal de la suite** that augurs well/ill (for what is to follow)

Auguste /ogyst/ NM Augustus ♦ **le siècle d'**~ *(Antiq)* the Augustan age

auguste /ogyst/ ADJ *[personnage, assemblée]* august; *[geste]* noble, majestic NM ♦ **l'**~ ≈ Coco the clown

augustin, e /ogystɛ̃, in/ NM,F *(Rel)* Augustinian

augustinien, -ienne /ogystinjɛ̃, jɛn/ ADJ Augustinian

aujourd'hui /oʒuʀdɥi/ ADV [1] *(= ce jour-ci)* today ♦ ~ **en huit** a week from today, a week today *(Brit)*, today week *(Brit)* ♦ **il y a** ~ **10 jours que** ... it's 10 days ago today that ... ♦ **c'est tout pour** ~ that's all *ou* that's it for today ♦ **à dater** *ou* **à partir d'**~ (as) from today, from today onwards ♦ **je le ferai dès** ~ I'll do it this very day ♦ **alors cette bière, c'est pour** ~ **ou pour demain ?** *(hum)* any chance of getting that beer sometime today? ♦ **ça ne date pas d'**~ *[objet]* it's not exactly new; *[situation, attitude]* it's nothing new; → **jour** [2] *(= de nos jours)* today, nowadays, these days ♦ **les jeunes d'**~ young people nowadays, (the) young people of today

aulne /o(l)n/ NM alder

aulx /o/ NMPL → **ail**

aumône /omon/ NF *(= don)* charity *(NonC)*, alms; *(= action de donner)* almsgiving ♦ **vivre d'**~**(s)** to live on charity ♦ **demander l'**~ *(lit)* to ask *ou* beg for charity *ou* alms; *(fig)* to beg ♦ **faire l'**~ to give alms *(à* to); ♦ **dix euros ! c'est une** ~ ten euros, that's a beggarly sum! ♦ **je ne vous demande pas l'**~ I'm not asking for charity ♦ **faire** *ou* **accorder l'**~ **d'un sourire à qn** to favour sb with a smile

aumônerie /omonʀi/ NF chaplaincy

aumônier /omonje/ NM chaplain

aumônière /omonjɛʀ/ NF *(Hist, Rel)* purse

aune[1] /on/ NM ⇒ **aulne**

aune[2] /on/ NF ≈ ell ♦ **il fit un nez long d'une** ~**, son visage s'allongea d'une** ~ he pulled a long face *ou* a face as long as a fiddle *(Brit)* ♦ **notre succès se mesure à l'**~ **de la satisfaction de nos clients** our success is measured in terms of customer satisfaction

auparavant /opaʀavɑ̃/ ADV *(= d'abord)* before(hand), first; *(= avant)* before(hand), previously

auprès /opʀɛ/ ADV *(littér)* nearby

LOC PRÉP **auprès de** [1] *(= à côté de)* next to, close to, by; *(= au chevet de, aux côtés de)* with ♦ **rester** ~ **d'un malade** to stay with an invalid ♦ **s'asseoir** ~ **de la fenêtre/de qn** to sit down by *ou* close to the window/by *ou* next to *ou* close to sb

[2] *(= comparé à)* compared with, in comparison with, next to ♦ **notre revenu est élevé** ~ **du leur** our income is high compared with *ou* in comparison with *ou* next to theirs

[3] *(= s'adressant à)* **faire une demande** ~ **des autorités** to apply to the authorities, to lodge a request with the authorities ♦ **faire une démarche** ~ **du ministre** to approach the minister, to apply to the minister ♦ **ambassadeur** ~ **du Vatican** ambassador to the Vatican

[4] *(= dans l'opinion de)* in the opinion of ♦ **il passe pour un incompétent** ~ **de ses collègues** his colleagues regard him as incompetent, he is incompetent in the opinion of his colleagues

auquel /okɛl/ → **lequel**

aura /ɔʀa/ NF aura

auréole /ɔʀeɔl/ NF 1 (Art, Astron) halo, aureole ◆ ~ **de cheveux blonds** halo of blond hair ◆ **entouré de l'~ du succès** flushed with success ◆ **paré de l'~ du martyre** wearing a martyr's crown ou the crown of martyrdom ◆ **parer qn d'une** ~ to glorify sb 2 (= tache) ring

auréoler /ɔʀeɔle/ ▸ conjug 1 ◂ VT (gén ptp) (= glorifier) to glorify; (Art) to encircle with a halo ◆ **tête auréolée de cheveux blancs** head with a halo of white hair ◆ **auréolé de gloire** wreathed in ou crowned with glory ◆ **être auréolé de prestige** to have an aura of prestige VPR **s'auréoler** ◆ **s'~ de** to take on an aura of

auréomycine /ɔʀeɔmisin/ NF aureomycin (Brit), Aureomycin ® (US)

auriculaire /ɔʀikyleʀ/ NM little finger ADJ auricular; → **témoin**

auriculothérapie /ɔʀikyloteʀapi/ NF aural acupuncture

aurifère /ɔʀifeʀ/ ADJ gold-bearing

aurification /ɔʀifikasjɔ̃/ NF [de dent] filling with gold

aurifier /ɔʀifje/ ▸ conjug 7 ◂ VT [+ dent] to fill with gold

aurige /ɔʀiʒ/ NM charioteer ◆ **l'Aurige de Delphes** (Art) the Charioteer of Delphi

Aurigny /ɔʀiɲi/ NF Alderney

aurochs /ɔʀɔk/ NM aurochs

aurore /ɔʀɔʀ/ NF 1 (= lever du jour) dawn, daybreak, first light ◆ **à l'~** at dawn ou first light ou daybreak ◆ **avant l'~** before dawn ou daybreak ◆ **se lever/partir aux ~s** to get up/leave at the crack of dawn 2 (littér = début) dawn, beginning ◆ **à l'~ de** at the dawn of

COMP **aurore australe** southern lights, aurora australis

aurore boréale northern lights, aurora borealis

aurore polaire polar lights

auscultation /ɔskyltasjɔ̃/ NF auscultation

ausculter /ɔskylte/ ▸ conjug 1 ◂ VT to sound (the chest of), to auscultate (SPÉC)

auspices /ɔspis/ NMPL 1 (Antiq) auspices 2 ◆ **sous de bons/mauvais** ~ under favourable/unfavourable auspices ◆ **sous les ~ de qn** under the patronage ou auspices of sb ◆ **la réunion a commencé sous les meilleurs** ~ the meeting got off to a most auspicious start

aussi /osi/ GRAMMAIRE ACTIVE 32.3, 53.5

ADV 1 (= également) too, also ◆ **je suis fatigué et eux** ~ I'm tired and so are they ou and they are too ◆ **il travaille bien et moi** ~ he works well and so do I ◆ **il parle ~ l'anglais** he also speaks English, he speaks English as well ou too ◆ **lui ~ parle l'anglais** he speaks English too ou as well, he too speaks English ◆ **il parle l'italien et ~ l'anglais** he speaks Italian and English too ou as well, he speaks Italian and also English ◆ **il a la grippe – lui ~ ?** he's got the flu – him too? * ou him as well? ◆ **c'est ~ mon avis** I think so too ou as well, that's my view too ou as well ◆ **faites bon voyage – vous** ~ have a good journey – you too ou (the) same to you ◆ **il ne suffit pas d'être doué, il faut ~ travailler** it's not enough to be talented, you also have to work ◆ **toi ~, tu as peur ?** so you are afraid too? ou as well?

2 (comparaison)

◆ **aussi ... que** as ... as ◆ **il est ~ bête que méchant** ou **qu'il est méchant** he's as stupid as he is ill-natured ◆ **viens ~ souvent que tu voudras** come as often as you like ◆ **s'il pleut ~ peu que l'an dernier** if it rains as little as last year ◆ **il devint ~ riche qu'il l'avait rêvé** he became as rich as he had dreamt he would ◆ **pas ~ riche qu'on le dit** not as rich as he is said to be ◆ **la piqûre m'a fait tout ~ mal que la blessure** the injection hurt me just as much as the injury (did) ◆ ~ **vite que possible** as quickly as possible ◆ **d'~ loin qu'il nous vit il cria** far away though he was he shouted as soon as he saw us

3 (= si, tellement) so ◆ **je ne te savais pas ~ bête** I didn't think you were so ou that* stupid ◆ **comment peut-on laisser passer une ~ bonne occasion ?** how can one let slip such a good opportunity? ou so good an opportunity? ◆ **je ne savais pas que cela se faisait ~ facilement (que ça)** I didn't know that could be done as easily (as that) ou so easily ou that easily* ◆ ~ **léger qu'il fût** light though he was ◆ ~ **idiot que ça puisse paraître** silly though ou as it may seem

4 (= tout autant) ~ **bien** just as well, just as easily ◆ **tu peux ~ bien dire non** you can just as easily ou well say no ◆ **puisqu'~ bien tout est fini** (littér) since everything is finished ◆ **ça peut ~ bien représenter une montagne qu'un animal** it could just as well ou easily represent a mountain as an animal ◆ ~ **sec*** straight away, there and then

CONJ (= en conséquence) therefore, consequently ◆ **je suis faible, ~ ai-je besoin d'aide** I'm weak, therefore ou consequently I need help ◆ **tu n'as pas compris, ~ c'est ta faute : tu n'écoutais pas** you haven't understood, well, it's your own fault – you weren't listening

aussitôt /osito/ ADV straight away, immediately ◆ ~ **arrivé/descendu il s'attabla** as soon as he arrived/came down he sat down at table ◆ ~ **le train arrêté, elle descendit** as soon as ou immediately (Brit) the train stopped she got out ◆ ~ **dit, ~ fait** no sooner said than done ◆ ~ **après son retour** straight ou directly ou immediately after his return ◆ **il est parti ~ après** he left straight ou directly ou immediately after ◆ ~ **que** as soon as ◆ ~ **que je le vis** as soon as ou the moment I saw him

austère /ɔsteʀ/ ADJ [personne, vie, style, monument] austere; [livre, lecture] dry ◆ **coupe ~ d'un manteau** severe cut of a coat

austérité /ɔsteʀite/ NF [de personne, vie, style, monument] austerity; [de livre, lecture] dryness ◆ **~s** (Rel) austerities ◆ **mesures/politique d'~** (Pol) austerity measures/policy

austral, e (mpl **australs**) /ɔstʀal/ ADJ southern, austral (SPÉC) ◆ **pôle ~** South Pole; → **aurore**

Australasie /ɔstʀalazi/ NF Australasia ◆ **d'~** [produit, habitant] Australasian

Australie /ɔstʀali/ NF ◆ **l'~** (the Commonwealth of) Australia ◆ **~-Méridionale/-Occidentale** South/Western Australia

australien, -ienne /ɔstʀaljɛ̃, jɛn/ ADJ Australian NM,F **Australien(ne)** Australian

australopithèque /ɔstʀalɔpitɛk/ NM Australopithecus

autan /otɑ̃/ NM ◆ **(vent d')~** (strong and hot) southerly wind

autant /otɑ̃/ ADV 1 (quantité) **j'en voudrais encore** ~ I'd like as much again ◆ **ils sont ~ à plaindre l'un que l'autre** you have to feel just as sorry for both of them

◆ **autant de** (quantité) as much (que as); (nombre) as many (que as); ◆ **il y a (tout) ~ de place ici (que là-bas)** there's (just) as much room here (as over there) ◆ **il n'y a pas ~ de neige que l'année dernière** there isn't as much ou there's not so much snow as last year ◆ **nous avons ~ de voitures qu'eux** we have as many cars as they have ◆ **il nous prêtera ~ de livres qu'il pourra** he'll lend us as many books as he can ◆ **ils ont ~ de mérite l'un que l'autre** they have equal merit ◆ **ils ont ~ de talent l'un que l'autre** they are both equally talented ◆ **tous ces enfants sont ~ de petits menteurs** all these children are so many little liars ◆ **toutes ces photos sont ~ de preuves** these photos all constitute proof

◆ **comme autant de** (= pareils à) ◆ **les gens tout en bas, comme ~ de fourmis** the people far below, like so many ants

◆ **autant que** ◆ **tous ~ que vous êtes** every single one of you, the whole lot of you (Brit) ◆ **nous sommes ~ qu'eux** we are as many as they are ou as them, there are as many of us as of them

2 (intensité) as much (que as); ◆ **il travaille toujours** ~ he works as hard as ever, he's still working as hard ◆ **pourquoi travaille-t-il ~ ?** why does he work so much? ou so hard? ◆ **rien ne lui plaît ~ que de regarder les autres travailler** there is nothing he likes so much as ou likes better than watching others work ◆ **intelligent, il l'est ~ que vous** he's just as intelligent as you are ◆ **il peut crier ~ qu'il veut** he can scream as much as he likes ◆ **cet avertissement vaut pour vous ~ que pour lui** this warning applies to you as much as to him ◆ **courageux ~ que compétent** courageous as well as competent, as courageous as he is competent ◆ ~ **prévenir la police** it would be as well to tell the police; → **aimer**

3 (= tellement) (quantité) so much, such; (nombre) so many, such a lot of ◆ **elle ne pensait pas qu'il aurait ~ de succès/qu'il mangerait ~** she never thought that he would have so much ou such success ou be so successful/that he would eat so much ou such a lot ◆ **vous invitez toujours ~ de gens ?** do you always invite so many people ou such a lot of people? ◆ **j'ai rarement vu ~ de monde** I've seldom seen such a crowd ou so many people

4 (locutions) ~ **dire qu'il ne sait rien/qu'il est fou** you ou one might as well say that he doesn't know anything/that he's mad ◆ ~ **pour moi !** my mistake! ◆ **il ne le fera qu'~ qu'il saura que vous êtes d'accord** he'll only do it in so far as he knows you agree ◆ ~ **d'hommes, ~ d'avis** (Prov) every man to his own opinion

◆ **autant ... autant** ◆ ~ **il est généreux, ~ elle est avare** he is as generous as she is miserly ◆ ~ **il aime les chiens, ~ il déteste les chats** he likes dogs as much as he hates cats

◆ **autant que possible** as much ou as far as possible ◆ **il voudrait, ~ que possible, éviter les grandes routes** he would like to avoid the major roads as much ou as far as possible

◆ **c'est autant de** ◆ **c'est ~ de gagné** ou **de pris** that's something at least ◆ **c'est ~ de fait** that's that done at least

◆ **pour autant** for all that ◆ **vous l'avez aidé mais il ne vous remerciera pas pour ~** you helped him but you won't get any thanks from him for all that ◆ **il a gagné, cela ne signifie pas pour ~ qu'il est le meilleur** he won, but that doesn't mean that he's the best

◆ **(pour) autant que** ◆ **(pour) ~ que je** (ou **qu'il** etc) **sache** as far as I know (ou he etc knows), to the best of my (ou his etc) knowledge

◆ **d'autant** ◆ **ce sera augmenté d'~** it will be increased accordingly ou in proportion

◆ **d'autant (plus) ... que** ◆ **d'~ (plus) que** all the more so since ou because ou as ◆ **c'est d'~ plus dangereux qu'il n'y a pas de parapet** it's all the more dangerous since ou because there is no parapet ◆ **écrivez-lui, d'~ (plus) que je ne suis pas sûr qu'il vienne demain** you'd better write to him especially as ou since I'm not sure if he's coming tomorrow

◆ **d'autant plus !** all the more reason!

◆ **d'autant mieux** ◆ **cela se gardera d'~ mieux (que ...)** it will keep even better ou all the better (since ...)

◆ **d'autant moins** ◆ **nous le voyons d'~ moins qu'il habite très loin maintenant** we

see him even less now *ou* we see even less of him now that he lives a long way away
◆ **en ... autant** (= *la même chose*) the same ◆ **je ne peux pas en dire** ~ I can't say the same (for myself) ◆ **je peux en faire** ~ I can do as much *ou* the same

autarcie /otaʀsi/ **NF** autarchy, self-sufficiency ◆ **vivre en** ~ to be self-sufficient

autarcique /otaʀsik/ **ADJ** autarchic, self-sufficient

autel /otɛl/ **NM** 1 (*Rel*) altar ◆ ~ **portatif** portable altar ◆ **conduire qn à l'~** (= *l'épouser*) to lead sb to the altar ◆ **conduire** *ou* **mener sa fille à l'~** to take one's daughter down the aisle; → **trône** 2 (*littér*) altar ◆ **dresser un** ~ *ou* **des ~s à qn** to worship sb, to put sb on a pedestal ◆ **sacrifier qch sur l'~ de** to sacrifice sth on the altar of

auteur, e /otœʀ/ **NM, F** 1 [*de texte, roman*] author, writer; [*d'opéra*] composer; [*de procédé*] originator, author; [*de crime, coup d'état*] perpetrator ◆ **l'~ de l'invention** the inventor ◆ **il en est l'~** (*invention*) he invented it; (*texte*) he wrote it, he's the author ◆ **l'~ de ce canular** the hoaxer ◆ **l'~ de l'accident** the person who caused the accident ◆ **l'~ de ce tableau** the painter ◆ **qui est l'~ de cette affiche ?** who designed this poster? ◆ **"auteur inconnu"** (*dans un musée*) "anonymous", "artist unknown" ◆ **il fut l'~ de sa propre ruine** he was the author of his own ruin ◆ **Prévert est l'~ des paroles, Kosma de la musique** Prévert wrote the words *ou* lyrics and Kosma composed the music ◆ **l'~ de mes jours** († *ou hum*) my noble progenitor † (*hum*) ◆ **~-compositeur(-interprète)** singer-songwriter ◆ **film d'~** arthouse film *ou* movie ◆ **cinéma d'~** arthouse films *ou* movies; → **droit**³
2 (= *écrivain*) author ◆ **lire tout un** ~ to read all of an author's works ◆ **c'est un ~ connu** (*femme*) she is a well-known author; → **femme**

authenticité /otɑ̃tisite/ **NF** [*d'œuvre d'art, récit, document, signature*] authenticity

authentification /otɑ̃tifikasjɔ̃/ **NF** authentication

authentifier /otɑ̃tifje/ ▸ **conjug 7** ◂ **VT** to authenticate

authentique /otɑ̃tik/ **ADJ** [*œuvre d'art, récit*] authentic, genuine; [*signature, document*] authentic; [*sentiment*] genuine ◆ **un ~ Van Gogh** a genuine Van Gogh ◆ **c'est vrai ?** – ~ **!** really? – really!; → **acte**

authentiquement /otɑ̃tikmɑ̃/ **ADV** genuinely, authentically; [*rapporter*] faithfully

autisme /otism/ **NM** autism

autiste /otist/ **ADJ, NMF** autistic

autistique /otistik/ **ADJ** autistic

auto /oto/ **NF** (= *voiture*) car, automobile (*US*) ◆ **~s tamponneuses** bumper cars, dodgems (*Brit*); → **salon, train** **ADJ INV** ◆ **assurance** ~ car *ou* motor (*Brit*) *ou* automobile (*US*) insurance ◆ **frais** ~ running costs (*of a car*)

auto... /oto/ **PRÉF** self- ◆ **auto(-)adhésif** self-adhesive

autoallumage /otoalymaʒ/ **NM** pre-ignition

autoberge /otobɛʀʒ/ **NM** riverside *ou* embankment expressway

autobiographie /otobjɔgʀafi/ **NF** autobiography

autobiographique /otobjɔgʀafik/ **ADJ** autobiographic(al)

autobronzant, e /otobʀɔ̃zɑ̃, ɑt/ **ADJ** self-tanning (*épith*), instant tanning (*épith*) **NM** **autobronzant** self-tanning cream

autobus /ɔtɔbys/ **NM** bus ◆ ~ **à impériale** (*Hist*) double decker (bus) ◆ ~ **scolaire** (*Can*) school bus

autocar /ɔtɔkaʀ/ **NM** coach (*Brit*), bus (*US*); (*de campagne*) country bus

autocaravane /otokaʀavan/ **NF** motor caravan (*Brit*), motorhome (*US*), camper (*US*)

autocariste /otokaʀist/ **NM** coach *ou* bus operator

autocassable /otokɑsabl/ **ADJ** [*ampoule*] with a snap-off top

autocélébration /otoselebʀasjɔ̃/ **NF** (*péj*) self-congratulation ◆ **l'heure est à l'~ chez les élus** the newly-elected representatives are in a self-congratulatory mood *ou* are busy patting themselves on the back

autocensure /otosɑ̃syʀ/ **NF** self-censorship

autocensurer (s') /otosɑ̃syʀe/ ▸ **conjug 1** ◂ **VPR** to practise self-censorship, to censor o.s.

autocéphale /otosefal/ **ADJ** (*Rel*) autocephalous

autochenille /otoʃ(ə)nij/ **NF** half-track

autochrome /otokʀom/ **ADJ** [*film, plaque*] autochrome **NF** (= *plaque*) autochrome (*early colour photograph*)

autochtone /ɔtɔktɔn/ **ADJ** native, autochthonous (*SPÉC*); (*Géol*) autochthonous **NMF** native, autochthon (*SPÉC*)

autoclave /otoklav/ **ADJ, NM** (*Méd, Tech*) ◆ (**appareil** *ou* **marmite**) ~ autoclave

autocollant, e /otokɔlɑ̃, ɑt/ **ADJ** [*étiquette*] self-adhesive, self-sticking; [*papier*] self-adhesive; [*enveloppe*] self-seal, self-adhesive **NM** sticker

autocopiant, e /otokɔpjɑ̃, ɑt/ **ADJ** [*papier*] self-copy

autocorrection /otokɔʀɛksjɔ̃/ **NF** autocorrection

autocrate /otokʀat/ **NM** autocrat

autocratie /otokʀasi/ **NF** autocracy

autocratique /otokʀatik/ **ADJ** autocratic

autocratiquement /otokʀatikmɑ̃/ **ADV** autocratically

autocritique /otokʀitik/ **NF** self-criticism ◆ **faire son** ~ to criticize o.s.

autocuiseur /otokɥizœʀ/ **NM** pressure cooker

autodafé /otodafe/ **NM** auto-da-fé

autodéfense /otodefɑ̃s/ **NF** self-defence ◆ **groupe d'~** vigilante group *ou* committee

autodénigrement /otodenigʀəmɑ̃/ **NM** self-denigration

autodérision /otodeʀizjɔ̃/ **NF** self-mockery, self-derision ◆ **pratiquer l'~** to mock o.s.

autodésigner (s') /otodeziɲe/ ▸ **conjug 1** ◂ **VPR** to designate o.s.

autodestructeur, -trice /otodɛstʀyktœʀ, tʀis/ **ADJ** self-destructive

autodestruction /otodɛstʀyksjɔ̃/ **NF** self-destruction

autodétermination /otodetɛʀminasjɔ̃/ **NF** self-determination

autodétruire (s') /otodetʀɥiʀ/ ▸ **conjug 38** ◂ **VPR** [*bande*] to self-destruct; [*entreprise, pays, civilisation*] to destroy itself; [*personne*] to destroy o.s.

autodidacte /otodidakt/ **ADJ** self-taught **NMF** self-taught person, autodidact (*frm*)

autodiscipline /otodisiplin/ **NF** self-discipline

autodissolution /otodisɔlysjɔ̃/ **NF** [*d'assemblée, association, parti*] self-dissolution

autodissoudre (s') /otodisudʀ/ ▸ **conjug 51** ◂ **VPR** [*assemblée, parti*] to dissolve itself

autodrome /otodʀom/ **NM** motor-racing track, autodrome

auto-école (pl **auto-écoles**) /otoekɔl/ **NF** driving school ◆ **moniteur d'~** driving instructor

autoérotique /otoeʀɔtik/ **ADJ** auto-erotic

autoérotisme /otoeʀɔtism/ **NM** auto-eroticism, auto-erotism

autoévaluation /otoevalɥasjɔ̃/ **NF** self-assessment

autoévaluer (s') /otoevalɥe/ ▸ **conjug 1** ◂ **VPR** to assess oneself

autofécondation /otofekɔ̃dasjɔ̃/ **NF** self-fertilization

autofinancement /otofinɑ̃smɑ̃/ **NM** self-financing

autofinancer (s') /otofinɑ̃se/ ▸ **conjug 3** ◂ **VPR** [*entreprise*] to be *ou* become self-financing ◆ **programme de recherches autofinancé** self-supporting *ou* self-financed research programme

autoflagellation /otoflaʒelasjɔ̃/ **NF** self-flagellation

autofocus /otofɔkys/ **ADJ, NM** autofocus

autoformation /otofɔʀmasjɔ̃/ **NF** self-training

autogène /otoʒɛn/ **ADJ** → **soudure**

autogérer (s') /otoʒeʀe/ ▸ **conjug 1** ◂ **VPR** to be self-managing ◆ **organisme autogéré** self-managed *ou* -run body

autogestion /otoʒɛstjɔ̃/ **NF** (*gén*) self-management; (*avec les ouvriers*) joint worker-management control

autogestionnaire /otoʒɛstjɔnɛʀ/ **ADJ** self-managing (*épith*)

autogire /otoʒiʀ/ **NM** autogiro, autogyro

autographe /ɔtɔgʀaf/ **ADJ, NM** autograph

autogreffe /otogʀɛf/ **NF** autograft

autoguidage /otogidaʒ/ **NM** self-steering, self-guiding ◆ **système d'~** (*Mil*) homing system

autoguidé, e /otogide/ **ADJ** self-guided

auto-immune /otoi(m)myn/ **ADJ F** autoimmune

auto-immunisation /otoimynizasjɔ̃/ **NF** autoimmunization

auto-induction /otoɛ̃dyksjɔ̃/ **NF** (*Phys*) self-induction

auto-intoxication /otoɛ̃tɔksikasjɔ̃/ **NF** auto-intoxication

autolimitation /otolimitasjɔ̃/ **NF** [*d'importations*] voluntary restraint ◆ **accords d'~** voluntary restraint agreements

autolubrifiant, e /otolybʀifjɑ̃, jɑt/ **ADJ** self-lubricating

autolyse /otoliz/ **NF** autolysis

automate /ɔtɔmat/ **NM** 1 (= *robot, personne*) automaton ◆ **marcher comme un** ~ to walk like a robot 2 [*de tickets de transport*] (automatic) ticket machine

automaticité /ɔtɔmatisite/ **NF** automaticity

automation /ɔtɔmasjɔ̃/ **NF** automation

automatique /ɔtɔmatik/ **GRAMMAIRE ACTIVE 54.3**
ADJ automatic; → **distributeur** **NM** (*Téléc*) ≈ subscriber trunk dialling (*Brit*), STD (*Brit*), direct distance dialing (*US*); (= *revolver*) automatic

automatiquement /ɔtɔmatikmɑ̃/ **ADV** automatically

automatisation /ɔtɔmatizasjɔ̃/ **NF** automation

automatiser /ɔtɔmatize/ ▸ **conjug 1** ◂ **VT** to automate

automatisme /ɔtɔmatism/ NM *[de machine]* automatic functioning; *[de personne]* automatic reflex ◆ **~ mental** mental reflex ◆ **s'entraîner pour acquérir des ~s** to practice in order to develop automatic reflexes ◆ **il essuie les verres avec l'~ de l'habitude** he dries the glasses as if he's on automatic pilot ◆ **l'Institut national de recherche en informatique et ~** the National Research Institute for Computing and Automation

automédication /otomedikasjɔ̃/ NF self-medication ◆ **faire de l'~** to medicate o.s.

automédon /ɔtɔmedɔ̃/ NM († *ou hum*) coachman

automitrailleuse /otomitʀajøz/ NF armoured *(Brit) ou* armored *(US)* car

automnal, e (mpl **-aux**) /ɔtɔnal, o/ ADJ autumnal

automne /ɔtɔn/ NM autumn, fall *(US)* ◆ **en ~** in (the) autumn, in the fall *(US)* ◆ **il est à l'~ de ses jours** *(fig)* he's in the autumn *ou* fall *(US)* of his life

automobile /ɔtɔmɔbil/ ADJ *[véhicule]* self-propelled, motor *(épith)*, automotive; *[course, sport]* motor *(épith)*; *[assurance, industrie]* motor *(épith)*, car *(épith)*, automobile *(épith) (US)*; → **canot** NF *(= voiture)* motor car *(Brit)*, automobile *(US)* ◆ **l'~** *(= industrie)* the car *ou* motor *ou* automobile *(US)* industry; *(Sport, = conduite)* driving, motoring *(Brit)* ◆ **termes d'~** motoring terms ◆ **être passionné d'~** to be a car fanatic ◆ **aimer les courses d'~s** to like motor *(Brit) ou* car *(US)* racing

automobilisme /ɔtɔmɔbilism/ NM driving, motoring *(Brit)*

automobiliste /ɔtɔmɔbilist/ NMF driver, motorist *(Brit)*

automoteur, -trice /otomɔtœʀ, tʀis/ ADJ self-propelled, motorized, motor *(épith)*, automotive NF **automotrice** electric railcar

automutilation /otomytilasjɔ̃/ NF self-mutilation

automutiler (s') /otomytile/ ► conjug 1 ◄ VPR *[personne, animal]* to mutilate o.s.

autoneige /otonɛʒ/ NF *(Can)* snowmobile *(US, Can)*, snowcat

autonettoyant, e /otonetwajɑ̃, ɑ̃t/ ADJ self-cleaning *(épith)*

autonome /ɔtɔnɔm/ ADJ 1 *[territoire]* autonomous, self-governing ◆ **groupuscule ~** group of political extremists; → **port¹** 2 *[personne]* self-sufficient; *(Philos) [volonté]* autonomous; *(Ordin)* off-line; → **scaphandre**

autonomie /ɔtɔnɔmi/ NF 1 *(gén)* autonomy ◆ **certains Corses veulent l'~** some Corsicans want home rule *ou* autonomy *ou* self-government 2 *[de voiture, avion]* range ◆ **cette voiture a une ~ de 100 kilomètres** the car has a range of 100 kilometres ◆ **ce baladeur a une ~ de trois heures** this personal stereo gives three hours of listening from each charge ◆ **~ en communication** *[de téléphone]* talk time ◆ **~ en veille** *[d'appareil, téléphone]* standby time

autonomiste /ɔtɔnɔmist/ ADJ, NMF *(Pol)* separatist

autonyme /otonim/ ADJ autonymous

autoparodie /otopaʀɔdi/ NF self-parody

autopont /otopɔ̃/ NM flyover *(Brit)*, overpass *(US)*

autoportrait /otopɔʀtʀɛ/ NM self-portrait

autoproclamé, e /otopʀɔklame/ (ptp de **s'autoproclamer**) ADJ *(péj)* self-proclaimed

autoproclamer (s') /otopʀɔklame/ ► conjug 1 ◄ VPR *(péj) [personne]* to proclaim o.s. ◆ **il s'est autoproclamé expert** he has set himself up as an expert, he has proclaimed himself (to be) an expert

autopromotion /otopʀɔmosjɔ̃/ NF self-promotion

autopropulsé, e /otopʀɔpylse/ ADJ self-propelled

autopropulsion /otopʀɔpylsjɔ̃/ NF self-propulsion

autopsie /ɔtɔpsi/ NF autopsy, post-mortem (examination); *(fig)* post-mortem ◆ **faire** *ou* **pratiquer une ~** to carry out an autopsy *ou* a post-mortem (examination) *(sur* on)

autopsier /ɔtɔpsje/ ► conjug 7 ◄ VT *[+ corps]* to carry out an autopsy *ou* a post-mortem (examination) on

autopunition /otopynisjɔ̃/ NF self-punishment

autoradio /otoʀadjo/ NM car radio

autoradiographie /otoʀadjɔgʀafi/ NF autoradiograph

autorail /otoʀaj/ NM railcar

autorégulateur, -trice /otoʀegylatœʀ, tʀis/ ADJ self-regulating

autorégulation /otoʀegylasjɔ̃/ NF self-regulation

autorisation /ɔtɔʀizasjɔ̃/ NF *(= permission)* permission, authorization *(de qch* for sth; *de faire* to do); *(= permis)* permit ◆ **nous avions l'~ du professeur** we had the teacher's permission ◆ **avoir l'~ de faire qch** to have permission *ou* be allowed to do sth; *(Admin)* to be authorized to do sth ◆ **le projet doit recevoir l'~ du comité** the project must be authorized *ou* passed by the committee ◆ **~ d'absence** leave of absence ◆ **~ d'accès** *(Ordin)* access permission ◆ **~ de crédit** credit line, line of credit ◆ **~ de mise sur le marché** *permit to market a product* ◆ **~ de vol** flight clearance ◆ **~ parentale** parental consent

autorisé, e /ɔtɔʀize/ (ptp de **autoriser**) ADJ *[agent, version]* authorized; *[opinion]* authoritative ◆ **dans les milieux ~s** in official circles ◆ **nous apprenons de source ~e que ...** we have learnt from official sources that ...

autoriser /ɔtɔʀize/ GRAMMAIRE ACTIVE 36.2 ► conjug 1 ◄

VT 1 ◆ **~ qn à faire** *(= donner la permission de)* to give *ou* grant sb permission to do, to authorize sb to do; *(= habiliter à) [personne, décret]* to give sb authority to do, to authorize sb to do ◆ **il nous a autorisés à sortir** he has given *ou* granted us permission to go out, we have his permission to go out ◆ **sa faute ne t'autorise pas à le condamner** the fact that he made a mistake doesn't give you the right to pass judgment on him ◆ **tout nous autorise à croire que ...** everything leads us to believe that ... ◆ **se croire autorisé à dire que ...** to feel one is entitled *ou* think one has the right to say that ...

2 *(= permettre) [personne] [+ manifestation, sortie]* to authorize, to give permission for; *[+ projet]* to pass, to authorize ◆ **le sel ne m'est pas autorisé** I'm not allowed to eat salt ◆ **"stationnement autorisé sauf le mardi"** "car parking every day except Tuesdays"

3 *(= rendre possible) [chose]* to make possible ◆ **l'imprécision de cette loi autorise les abus** loopholes in this law make abuses possible *ou* open the way to abuses ◆ **expression autorisée par l'usage** expression sanctioned *ou* made acceptable by use

4 *(littér = justifier)* to justify

VPR **s'autoriser** 1 *(= invoquer)* **s'~ de qch pour faire** to use sth as an excuse to do ◆ **je m'autorise de notre amitié pour ...** in view of our friendship I permit myself to ...

2 *(= se permettre)* **on s'autorise à penser que ...** one is justified in thinking that ... ◆ **s'~ un cigare de temps en temps** to allow o.s. a cigar from time to time

> ⚠ Attention à ne pas traduire automatiquement **autoriser** par **to authorize**, qui est d'un registre plus soutenu.

autoritaire /ɔtɔʀitɛʀ/ ADJ *[personne]* domineering; *[ton, manière]* overbearing; *[régime, mesures]* authoritarian

autoritairement /ɔtɔʀitɛʀmɑ̃/ ADV in an authoritarian way

autoritarisme /ɔtɔʀitaʀism/ NM authoritarianism

autorité /ɔtɔʀite/ NF 1 *(= pouvoir)* authority *(sur* over); ◆ **l'~ que lui confère son expérience/âge** the authority conferred upon him by experience/age ◆ **avoir de l'~ sur qn** to have authority over sb ◆ **être sous l'~ de qn** to be under sb's authority ◆ **avoir ~ pour faire** to have authority to do ◆ **air d'~** authoritative air, air of authority ◆ **il n'a aucune ~ sur ses élèves** he has no control over his pupils

2 *(= expert, ouvrage)* authority ◆ **l'une des grandes ~s en la matière** one of the great authorities on the subject

3 *(Admin)* **l'~, les ~s** the authorities ◆ **l'~ militaire/législative** the military/legislative authorities ◆ **les ~s civiles et religieuses/locales** the civil and religious/local authorities ◆ **agent** *ou* **représentant de l'~** representative of authority ◆ **adressez-vous à l'~** *ou* **aux ~s compétente(s)** apply to the proper authorities ◆ **l'Autorité palestinienne** the Palestinian Authority

4 *(Jur)* **l'~ de la loi** the authority *ou* power of the law ◆ **l'~ de la chose jugée** res judicata ◆ **être déchu de l'~ parentale** to lose one's parental rights ◆ **vendu par ~ de justice** sold by order of the court

5 *(locutions)* **d'~** *(= de façon impérative)* on one's own authority; *(= sans réflexion)* out of hand, straight off, unhesitatingly ◆ **de sa propre ~** on one's own authority ◆ **faire ~** *[livre, expert]* to be accepted as an authority, to be authoritative

autoroute /otoʀut/ NF motorway *(Brit)*, highway *(US)*, freeway *(US)* ◆ **l'~ du soleil** *the A6 and A7 motorways to the south of France*

COMP **autoroute de dégagement** *toll-free stretch of motorway leading out of a big city*

autoroutes électroniques electronic highways

autoroutes de l'information information highways

autoroute à péage toll motorway *(Brit)*, turnpike *(US)*

autoroute urbaine urban *ou* inner-city motorway *(Brit)*, throughway *(US)*, expressway *(US)*

autoroutier, -ière /otoʀutje, jɛʀ/ ADJ motorway *(épith) (Brit)*, freeway *(épith) (US)*, highway *(épith) (US)*

autosatisfaction /otosatisfaksjɔ̃/ NF self-satisfaction

auto-stop /otostɔp/ NM hitch-hiking, hitching* ◆ **pour rentrer, il a fait de l'~** *(long voyage)* he hitched* *ou* hitch-hiked home; *(courte distance)* he thumbed *ou* hitched* a lift home ◆ **il a fait le tour du monde en ~** he hitch-hiked around the world, he hitched* his way round the world ◆ **j'ai pris quelqu'un en ~** I picked up a *ou* gave a lift to a hitch-hiker *ou* hitcher* ◆ **il nous a pris en ~** he picked us up, he gave us a lift

auto-stoppeur, -euse (mpl **auto-stoppeurs**) /otostɔpœʀ, øz/ NM,F hitch-hiker, hitcher* ◆ **prendre un ~** to pick up a hitch-hiker *ou* hitcher*

autostrade † /otostʀad/ NF motorway *(Brit)*, freeway *(US)*, highway *(US)*

autosubsistance /otosybzistɑ̃s/ NF self-sufficiency ◆ **agriculture d'~** subsistence farming

autosuffisance /otosyfizɑ̃s/ NF self-sufficiency

autosuffisant, e /otosyfizɑ̃, ɑ̃t/ ADJ self-sufficient

autosuggestion /otosygʒɛstjɔ̃/ NF auto-suggestion

autotracté, e /ototʀakte/ ADJ self-propelled

autotransfusion /ototʀɑ̃sfyzjɔ̃/ NF autologous transfusion

autour[1] /otuʀ/ ADV around ◆ **tout ~** all around ◆ **maison avec un jardin ~** house surrounded by a garden, house with a garden around *ou* round *(Brit)* it

◆ **autour de** *(lieu)* around, round *(Brit)*; *(temps, somme)* about, around, round about *(Brit)* ◆ **il regarda ~ de lui** he looked around (him) *ou* about (him) ◆ **discussion ~ d'un projet** discussion on *ou* about a project ◆ ~ **d'un bon café** over a nice cup of coffee; → **tourner**

autour[2] /otuʀ/ NM *(= oiseau)* goshawk

autovaccin /otovaksɛ̃/ NM autogenous vaccine, autovaccine

autre /otʀ/ GRAMMAIRE ACTIVE 53.5

ADJ INDÉF 1 *(= différent)* other, different ◆ **je préfère l'~ robe/les ~s chaussures** I prefer the other dress/the other shoes ◆ **revenez une ~ fois** come back another *ou* some other time ◆ **revenez un ~ jour** come back another *ou* some other day ◆ **il n'y a pas d'~ moyen d'entrer** there's no other way *ou* there isn't any other way of getting in ◆ **c'est une ~ question/un ~ problème** that's another *ou* a different question/problem ◆ **la réalité est tout ~** the reality is quite *ou* altogether different ◆ **je fais ça d'une ~ façon** I do it a different way *ou* another way *ou* differently ◆ **ils ont un (tout) ~ mode de vie/point de vue** they have a (completely) different way of life/point of view ◆ **vous ne le reconnaîtrez pas, c'est un (tout) ~ homme** you won't know him, he's completely different *ou* he's a changed man ◆ **après ce bain je me sens un ~ homme** I feel (like) a new man after that swim ◆ **en d'~s lieux** elsewhere ◆ **~s temps ~s mœurs** *(Prov)* customs change with the times, autres temps autres mœurs; → **côté, part**

◆ **autre chose** ◆ **c'est (tout) ~ chose** that's a different *ou* another matter (altogether) ◆ **parlons d'~ chose** let's talk about something else *ou* different ◆ **c'est ça et pas ~ chose** it's that or nothing ◆ **ce n'est pas ~ chose que de la jalousie** that's just jealousy, that's nothing but jealousy ◆ **ah ~ chose ! j'ai oublié de vous dire que ...** oh, one more thing! I forgot to tell you that ... ◆ **une chose est de rédiger un rapport, ~ chose est d'écrire un livre** it's one thing to draw up a report, but quite another thing *ou* but another thing altogether to write a book ◆ **c'est quand même ~ chose !** *(admiratif)* it's really something else!, it's in a different league! ◆ **voilà ~ chose !*** *(incident)* that's all I (*ou* we) need!; *(impertinence)* what a nerve*! *ou* cheek!, the cheek of it!

2 *(= supplémentaire)* other ◆ **elle a 2 ~s enfants** she has 2 other *ou* 2 more children ◆ **donnez-moi un ~ livre/une ~ tasse de thé** give me another book/cup of tea ◆ **donne-lui une ~ chance** give him another *ou* one more chance ◆ **il y a beaucoup d'~s solutions** there are many other *ou* many more solutions ◆ **bien *ou* beaucoup d'~s choses encore** many *ou* plenty more besides ◆ **c'est un ~ Versailles** it's another Versailles ◆ **c'est un ~ moi-même** he's my alter ego ◆ **des couteaux, des verres et ~s objets indispensables** knives, glasses and other necessary items ◆ **il m'a dit ça sans ~ précision** he didn't go into any more detail than that ◆ **~ chose, Madame ?** anything else, madam?

3 *(de deux : marque une opposition)* other ◆ **de l'~ côté de la rue** on the other *ou* opposite side of the street ◆ **dans l'~ sens** in the other *ou* opposite direction ◆ **mets ton ~ manteau** put your other coat on ◆ **ses premiers films étaient d'une ~ qualité** his first films were of an altogether different quality *ou* in a different league; → **monde**

4 *(dans le temps)* **l'~ jour, l'~ fois** the other day ◆ **l'~ lundi*** *(= lundi dernier)* last Monday; *(dans un passé récent)* one Monday recently ◆ **l'~ semaine*** the other week ◆ **tu me le diras une ~ fois** tell me another time

5 *(avec pron pers)* **faut pas nous raconter des histoires, à nous ~s !*** there's no point telling fibs to US! ◆ **nous ~s, on est prudents*** WE are *ou* WE'RE cautious ◆ **taisez-vous, vous ~s*** be quiet, you people *ou* the rest of you *ou* you lot* *(Brit)* ◆ **et vous ~s qu'en pensez-vous ?** what do you people *ou* you lot* *(Brit)* think? ◆ **nous ~s Français, nous aimons la bonne cuisine** we French like good food

PRON INDÉF 1 *(= qui est différent)* another (one) ◆ **il en aime une ~** he's in love with another woman, he loves another ◆ **d'~s** others ◆ **aucun ~, nul ~, personne d'~** no one else, nobody else ◆ **les deux ~s** the other two, the two others ◆ **prendre qn pour un ~/une ~ chose pour une ~** to take *ou* mistake sb for sb else/sth for sth else ◆ **envoyez-moi bien ce livre, je n'en veux pas d'~** make sure you send me that book, I don't want any other ◆ **un ~ que moi/lui aurait refusé** anyone else (but me/him) would have refused ◆ **elle n'est pas plus bête qu'une ~** she's no more stupid than anyone else ◆ **X, Y, Z, et ~s** X, Y, Z and others *ou* etc ◆ **il en a vu d'~s !** he's seen worse! ◆ **il n'en fait jamais d'~s !** that's just typical of him!, that's just what he always does! ◆ **et l'~ (là)*, il vient avec nous ?** what about him, is he coming with us? ◆ **et l'~ qui n'arrête pas de klaxonner !*** and then there's that idiot who keeps blowing his horn! ◆ **vous en êtes un ~ !** †* you're a fool! ◆ **à d'~s !*** (that's) a likely story!, go tell it to the marines!*; → **entre, rien**

2 *(= qui vient en plus)* **donnez m'en un ~** give me another (one) *ou* one more ◆ **qui/quoi d'~ ?** who/what else? ◆ **quelqu'un/quelque chose d'~** somebody *ou* someone/something else ◆ **rien/personne d'~** nothing/nobody *ou* no one else ◆ **deux enfants, c'est assez, je n'en veux pas d'~/d'~s** two children are enough, I don't want another (one)/any more

3 *(marque une opposition)* **l'~** the other (one) ◆ **les ~s** *(= choses)* the others, the other ones; *(= personnes)* the others ◆ **les ~s ne veulent pas venir** the others don't want to come ◆ **il se moque de l'opinion des ~s** he doesn't care what other people think ◆ **il va facilement vers les ~** he's very sociable ◆ **avec toi, c'est toujours les ~s qui ont tort** you always think that other people are in the wrong *ou* that it's the other person who's in the wrong; → **côté, ni**

4 *(dans le temps)* **d'une minute/semaine à l'~** *(= bientôt)* any minute/week (now) ◆ **d'un instant à l'~** *(= n'importe quand)* any time; *(= soudain)* from one moment to the next; *(= bientôt)* very soon

NM *(Philos)* ◆ **l'~** the other

autrefois /otʀəfwa/ ADV in the past, once, formerly ◆ **d'~** of the past, of old, past *(épith)* ◆ ~ **ils s'éclairaient à la bougie** in the past *ou* in bygone days they used candles for lighting ◆ ~ **je préférais le vin** (in the past) I used to prefer wine

autrement /otʀəmɑ̃/ ADV 1 *(= différemment)* differently ◆ **il faut s'y prendre (tout) ~** we'll have to go about it in (quite) another way *ou* (quite) differently ◆ **avec ce climat il ne peut en être ~** with the climate the way it is, it can't be any other way *ou* how else could it be! ◆ **cela ne peut s'être passé ~** it can't have happened any other way ◆ **agir ~ que d'habitude** to act differently from usual ◆ **comment aller à Londres ~ que par le train ?** how can we get to London other than by train? ◆ ~ **appelé** otherwise known as ◆ **tu pourrais me parler ~ !** don't you talk to me like that! ◆ **pour eux il en va ~** things are different for them

2 *(avec faire)* **il n'y a pas moyen de faire ~, on ne peut pas faire ~** it's impossible to do otherwise *ou* to do anything else ◆ **il n'a pas pu faire ~ que de me voir** he couldn't help seeing me *ou* help but see me

3 *(= sinon)* otherwise; *(idée de menace)* otherwise, or else ◆ **travaille bien, ~ tu auras de mes nouvelles !** work hard, otherwise *ou* or else you'll be hearing a few things from me!

4 *(* = à part cela)* otherwise, apart *ou* aside from that ◆ **la viande était bonne, ~ le repas était quelconque** the meat was good but apart from that *ou* but otherwise the meal was pretty nondescript

5 *(* comparatif)* far (more) ◆ **il est ~ intelligent** he is far more intelligent, he is more intelligent by far ◆ **c'est ~ meilleur** it's far better, it's better by far (*que* than)

6 ◆ **pas ~** *(* = pas spécialement)* not particularly *ou* especially ◆ **cela ne m'a pas ~ surpris** that didn't particularly surprise me

7 ◆ ~ **dit** *(= en d'autres mots)* in other words

Autriche /otʀiʃ/ NF Austria

autrichien, -ienne /otʀiʃjɛ̃, jɛn/ ADJ Austrian NM,F **Autrichien(ne)** Austrian

autruche /otʀyʃ/ NF ostrich ◆ **faire l'~** *(fig)* to bury one's head in the sand; → **estomac, politique**

autrui /otʀɥi/ PRON others ◆ **respecter le bien d'~** to respect other people's property *ou* the property of others ◆ **ne fais pas à ~ ce que tu ne voudrais pas qu'on te fît** do unto others as you would have them do unto you, do as you would be done by

auvent /ovɑ̃/ NM *[de maison]* canopy; *[de tente]* awning, canopy

auvergnat, e /ovɛʀɲa, at/ ADJ of *ou* from (the) Auvergne NM *(= dialecte)* Auvergne dialect NM,F **Auvergnat(e)** inhabitant *ou* native of (the) Auvergne

aux /o/ → **à**

auxiliaire /ɔksiljɛʀ/ ADJ *(Ling, Mil, gén)* auxiliary *(épith)*; *[cause, raison]* secondary, subsidiary ◆ **bureau ~** sub-office ◆ **mémoire ~** *(Ordin)* additional *ou* extra memory ◆ **programme ~** *(Ordin)* auxiliary routine; → **maître** NMF *(= assistant)* assistant, helper ◆ ~ **de justice** representative of the law ◆ ~ **médical** medical auxiliary NM *(Gram, Mil)* auxiliary

auxiliairement /ɔksiljɛʀmɑ̃/ ADV *(Ling)* as an auxiliary; *(fig = secondairement)* secondarily, less importantly

auxiliariat /ɔksiljaʀja/ NM *(Scol)* ◆ **pendant mon ~** during my time as a supply *(Brit)* *ou* substitute *(US)* teacher

auxquels, auxquelles /okɛl/ → **auquel**

AV /ave/ (abrév de **avis de virement**) → **avis**

av.[1] abrév de **avenue**

av.[2] (abrév de **avant**) before ◆ **en 300 ~ J.-C.** in 300 BC

avachi, e /avaʃi/ (ptp de **avachir**) ADJ 1 *[cuir, feutre]* limp; *[chaussure, vêtement]* misshapen, out of shape ◆ **pantalon ~** baggy trousers 2 *[personne]* *(= fatigué)* drained; *(péj = indolent)* sloppy ◆ ~ **sur son bureau** slumped over his desk ◆ ~ **sur la plage** lounging *ou* stretched out lazily on the beach

avachir /avaʃiʀ/ ▸ conjug 2 ◂ VT 1 *[+ cuir, feutre]* to make limp; *[+ chaussure, vêtement]* to make shapeless, to put out of shape 2 *[+ personne] (physiquement)* to drain; *(péj : moralement)* to make sloppy VPR **s'avachir** 1 *[cuir]* to become limp; *[vêtement]* to go out of shape, to become shapeless 2 *[personne] (physiquement)* to become flabby; *(péj : moralement)* to become sloppy

avachissement /avaʃismɑ̃/ NM 1 *[de vêtement, cuir]* loss of shape 2 *[de personne] (physique)* flabbiness; *(péj : moral)* sloppiness

aval[1] /aval/ NM *[de cours d'eau]* downstream water; *[de pente]* downhill slope ◆ **l'~ était coupé de rapides** the river downstream was a succession of rapids ◆ **les rapides/l'écluse d'~** the downstream rapids/lock ◆ **skieur/ski ~** downhill skier/ski

◆ **en aval** *(cours d'eau)* downstream, downriver; *(pente)* downhill; *(dans une hiérarchie)* lower down ◆ **les opérations en ~** operations further down the line

◆ **en aval de** *[+ cours d'eau]* downstream *ou* down-river from; *[+ pente]* downhill from ◆ **les opérations en ~ de la production** the operations coming after *ou* following production

aval[2] (pl **avals**) /aval/ NM (= *soutien*) backing, support; *(Comm, Jur)* guarantee (de for); ◆ **donner son ~ à qn** to give sb one's support, to back sb ◆ **donner son ~ à qch** to give consent to sth ◆ **obtenir l'~ de qn** to get the consent of sb ◆ **donner son ~ à une traite** to guarantee *ou* endorse a draft

avalanche /avalɑ̃ʃ/ NF 1 *(Géog)* avalanche ◆ **~ poudreuse/de fond** dry/wet avalanche ◆ **cône d'~** avalanche cone; → **couloir** 2 *(fig) [de coups]* hail, shower; *[de compliments]* flood, torrent; *[de réclamations, prospectus]* avalanche

avalancheux, -euse /avalɑ̃ʃø, øz/ ADJ *[zone, pente]* avalanche-prone

avaler /avale/ ▸ conjug 1 ◂ VT 1 *[+ nourriture]* to swallow (down); *[+ boisson]* to swallow (down), to drink (down); *[+ roman]* to devour; *(Alpinisme) [+ corde]* to take in ◆ ~ **la fumée** *[fumeur]* to inhale (the smoke) ◆ ~ **qch d'un trait** *ou* **d'un seul coup** to swallow sth in one gulp, down sth in one* ◆ ~ **son café à petites gorgées** to sip one's coffee ◆ ~ **sa salive** to swallow ◆ **j'ai eu du mal à ~ ma salive** *(fig)* I gulped ◆ **il a avalé de travers** it went down the wrong way ◆ **il n'a rien avalé depuis 2 jours** he hasn't eaten a thing *ou* had a thing to eat for 2 days ◆ **la machine a avalé ma carte de crédit** the machine ate *ou* swallowed my credit card

2 (* = *accepter*) *[+ mensonge, histoire]* to swallow; *[+ affront]* to swallow, to take; *[+ mauvaise nouvelle]* to accept ◆ **on lui ferait ~ n'importe quoi** he would swallow anything ◆ **il a eu du mal à ~ la pilule** *(fig)* it was a hard *ou* bitter pill for him to swallow ◆ **c'est dur** *ou* **difficile à ~** it's hard *ou* difficult to swallow ◆ ~ **des couleuvres** *ou* **des boas (constrictors)*** *(affront)* to swallow an affront; *(mensonge)* to swallow a lie, to be taken in ◆ ~ **ses mots** to mumble ◆ ~ **les kilomètres** to eat up the miles ◆ ~ **l'obstacle** *[cheval]* to take the jump in its stride

3 *(locutions)* **on dirait qu'il a avalé son parapluie** *ou* **sa canne** he's so (stiff and) starchy ◆ ~ **son bulletin de naissance** *(hum)* to kick the bucket*, to snuff it‡ ◆ **j'avalerais la mer et les poissons !** I could drink gallons (and gallons)! ◆ **il veut tout ~** *[ambitieux]* he thinks he can take anything on

avaleur, -euse /avalœʀ, øz/ NM,F ◆ ~ **de sabres** sword swallower

avaliser /avalize/ ▸ conjug 1 ◂ VT *[+ plan, entreprise]* to back, to support; *(Comm, Jur)* to endorse, to guarantee

à-valoir /avalwaʀ/ NM INV advance (*sur* on); ◆ **j'ai un ~ de 13 € dans ce grand magasin** I've €13 credit at this store

avance /avɑ̃s/ NF 1 (= *marche, progression*) advance ◆ **accélérer/ralentir son ~** to speed up/slow down one's advance

2 *(sur un concurrent)* lead ◆ **avoir/prendre de l'~ sur qn** to have/take the lead over sb ◆ **10 minutes/3 kilomètres d'~** a 10-minute/3-kilometre lead ◆ **avoir une longueur d'~** to be a length ahead ◆ **il a un an d'~** *(Scol)* he's a year ahead ◆ **leur ~ dans le domaine scientifique** their lead in the field of science ◆ **perdre son ~** to lose one's *ou* the lead ◆ **cet élève est tombé malade et a perdu son ~** this pupil fell ill and lost the lead he had (on the rest of the class) ◆ **je t'accompagnerai – la belle ~ !** *(iro)* I'll go with you – that'll really help! *(iro)*

3 *(sur un horaire)* **avoir/prendre de l'~** to be/get ahead of schedule; *(dans son travail)* to be/get ahead in *ou* with one's work ◆ **le train a dix minutes d'~** the train is 10 minutes early ◆ **le train a pris de l'~/dix minutes d'~** the train has got ahead/has got 10 minutes ahead of schedule ◆ **arriver avec 5 minutes d'~** *[train]* to arrive 5 minutes early *ou* 5 minutes ahead of time; *[personne]* to arrive 5 minutes early ◆ **avec cinq minutes d'~ sur les autres** 5 minutes earlier than the others ◆ **le train a perdu son ~** the train has lost the time it had gained ◆ **ma montre a 10 minutes d'~** my watch is 10 minutes fast ◆ **ma montre prend de l'~/beaucoup d'~** my watch is gaining *ou* gains/gains a lot ◆ ~ **à l'allumage** *[de voiture]* ignition advance

4 (= *acompte*) advance ◆ ~ **de fonds** advance ◆ **faire une ~ de 15 € à qn** to advance sb €15, to make sb an advance of €15 ◆ ~ **(sur salaire)** advance (on one's salary) ◆ ~ **sur marché/sur recettes** advance on contract/against takings

5 ◆ **~s** (= *ouvertures*) overtures; *(galantes)* advances ◆ **faire des ~s à qn** to make overtures *ou* advances to sb

6 *(locutions)*

◆ **en avance** *(sur l'heure fixée)* early; *(sur l'horaire)* ahead of schedule ◆ **être en ~ sur qn** to be ahead of sb ◆ **être en ~ d'une heure** *(sur l'heure fixée)* to be an hour early; *(sur l'horaire)* to be an hour ahead of schedule ◆ **dépêche-toi, tu n'es pas en ~ !** hurry up, you haven't got much time *ou* you're running out of time! ◆ **tous ces problèmes ne m'ont pas mis en ~** all these problems haven't helped ◆ **les crocus sont en ~ cette année** the crocuses are early this year ◆ **leur fils est très en ~ dans ses études/sur les autres enfants** their son is well ahead in his studies/ahead of the other children ◆ **il est en ~ pour son âge** he's advanced for his age, he's ahead of his age group ◆ **leur pays est en ~ dans le domaine scientifique** their country leads *ou* is ahead in the field of science ◆ **il était très en ~ sur son temps** *ou* **son époque** he was well ahead of *ou* in advance of his time ◆ **nous sommes en ~ sur le programme** we're ahead of schedule

◆ **à l'avance, d'avance, par avance** in advance ◆ **réserver une place un mois à l'~** to book a seat one month ahead *ou* in advance ◆ **prévenir qn 2 heures à l'~** to give sb 2 hours' notice, to notify *ou* warn sb 2 hours beforehand *ou* in advance ◆ **payable à l'~** *ou* **d'~** payable in advance ◆ **en vous remerciant à l'~** *ou* **d'~** thanking you in advance *ou* in anticipation ◆ **merci d'~** thanks (in advance) ◆ **d'~ je peux vous dire que ...** I can tell you in advance *ou* right now that ... ◆ **d'~ il pouvait deviner** already *ou* even then he could guess ◆ **je m'en réjouis d'~** I'm already looking forward to it ◆ **ça a été arrangé d'~** it was prearranged, it was arranged beforehand *ou* in advance

avancé, e[1] /avɑ̃se/ (ptp de **avancer**) ADJ 1 *[élève, civilisation, technique]* advanced ◆ **la saison/journée était ~e** it was late in the season/day ◆ **la nuit était ~e** it was well into the night ◆ **il est très ~ dans son travail** he's well ahead with his work ◆ **il est rentré à une heure ~e de la nuit** he got home late at night ◆ **elle a travaillé jusqu'à une heure ~e de la nuit** she worked late into the night ◆ **son roman est déjà assez ~** he's already quite a long way on *ou* quite far ahead with his novel ◆ **je suis peu/très ~ dans mon roman** I haven't got very far into/I'm well into my novel ◆ **les pays les moins ~s** the least developed countries ◆ **cet enfant n'est vraiment pas ~ pour son âge** this child is not at all advanced for his age ◆ **être d'un âge ~** to be getting on *ou* be advanced in years ◆ **dans un état ~ de ...** in an advanced state of ... ◆ **sa maladie est à un stade très ~** his illness is at a very advanced stage ◆ **après toutes ses démarches, il n'en est pas plus ~** after all the steps he has taken, he's no further on than he was before ◆ **nous voilà bien ~s !*** *(iro)* a long way that's got us! *(iro)*, a (fat) lot of good that's done us! * *(iro)*

2 (= *d'avant-garde*) *[opinion, idée]* progressive, advanced

3 (= *qui se gâte*) *[fruit, fromage]* overripe ◆ **ce poisson est ~** this fish is bad *ou* is going off *(Brit)*

4 *(Mil) [poste]* advanced

5 *(Sport) [match]* early

avancée[2] /avɑ̃se/ NF 1 (= *progrès*) advance 2 (= *surplomb*) overhang

avancement /avɑ̃smɑ̃/ NM 1 (= *promotion*) promotion ◆ **avoir** *ou* **prendre de l'~** to be promoted, to get promotion ◆ ~ **à l'ancienneté** promotion according to length of service ◆ **possibilités d'~** prospects *ou* chances of promotion 2 (= *progrès*) *[de travaux]* progress; *[de sciences, techniques]* advancement 3 (= *mouvement*) forward movement 4 *(Jur)* ~ **d'hoirie** advancement

avancer /avɑ̃se/ ▸ conjug 3 ◂ VT 1 *[+ objet]* to move *ou* bring forward; *[+ tête]* to move forward; *[+ main]* to hold out, to put out (*vers* to); *[+ pion]* to move forward ◆ ~ **le cou** to crane one's neck ◆ ~ **un siège à qn** to draw up *ou* bring forward a seat for sb ◆ **le blessé avança les lèvres pour boire** the injured man put his lips forward to drink ◆ **la voiture de Madame est avancée** († *ou hum*) your carriage awaits, Madam † *(hum)* ◆ ~ **(les aiguilles d') une pendule** to put (the hands of) a clock forward *ou* on *(Brit)*

2 *[+ opinion, hypothèse]* to put forward, to advance ◆ **ce qu'il avance paraît vraisemblable** what he is putting forward *ou* suggesting seems quite plausible

3 *[+ date, départ]* to bring forward ◆ **il a dû ~ son retour** he had to bring forward the date of his return

4 (= *faire progresser*) *[+ travail]* to speed up ◆ **est-ce que cela vous avancera si je vous aide ?** will it speed things up (for you) *ou* will you get on more quickly if I lend you a hand? ◆ **ça n'avance pas nos affaires** that doesn't improve matters for us ◆ **cela t'avancera à quoi de courir ?** what good will it do you to run? ◆ **cela ne t'avancera à rien de crier*** shouting won't get you anywhere, you won't get anywhere by shouting

5 *[+ argent]* to advance; (= *prêter*) to lend

VI 1 (= *progresser*) to advance, to move forward; *[bateau]* to make headway ◆ **l'armée avance sur Paris** the army is advancing on Paris ◆ **il avança d'un pas** he took *ou* moved a step forward ◆ **il avança d'un mètre** he moved one metre forward, he came one metre nearer ◆ **mais avance donc !** move on *ou* forward *ou* up, will you! ◆ **il essayait de faire ~ son âne** he tried to get his donkey to move (on) *ou* to make his donkey move (on) ◆ **ça n'avançait pas sur la route** the traffic was almost at a standstill *ou* was crawling along

2 *(dans le temps, dans une évolution)* to make progress ◆ **la nuit avance** night is wearing on ◆ **faire** ~ *[+ travail]* to speed up; *[+ élève]* to bring on, to help to make progress; *[+ science, recherche]* to further ◆ ~ **vite/lentement dans son travail** to make good/slow progress in one's work ◆ ~ **péniblement dans son travail** to plod on slowly with *ou* make halting progress in one's work ◆ ~ **en âge** to be getting on (in years) ◆ ~ **en grade** to be promoted, to get promotion ◆ **et les travaux, ça avance ?*** how's the work coming on?* ◆ **son livre n'avance guère** he's not making much headway *ou* progress with his book ◆ **tout cela n'avance à rien** that doesn't get us any further *ou* anywhere ◆ **je travaille mais il me semble que je n'avance pas** I'm working but I don't seem to be getting anywhere

3 *[montre, horloge]* to gain ◆ ~ **de dix minutes par jour** to gain 10 minutes a day ◆ **ma montre avance, j'avance** my watch is fast ◆ **ma montre avance** *ou* **j'avance de dix minutes** my watch is *ou* I'm 10 minutes fast

4 *[cap, promontoire]* to project, to jut out *(dans* into); *[lèvre, menton]* to protrude ◆ **un balcon qui avance (de 3 mètres) sur la rue** a balcony that juts out *ou* projects (3 metres) over the street

VPR **s'avancer** 1 *(= aller en avant)* to move forward; *(= progresser)* to advance ◆ **il s'avança vers nous** he came towards us ◆ **la procession s'avançait lentement** the procession advanced slowly *ou* moved slowly forward ◆ **il s'est avancé dans son travail** he made some progress with his work ◆ **je profite de cette heure libre pour m'**~ I'm making the most of this free hour to get ahead with my work

2 *(= s'engager)* to commit o.s., to stick one's neck out* ◆ **je ne peux pas m'**~ **sans connaître la question** I don't know enough about it to venture *ou* hazard an opinion, I can't commit myself without knowing more about it ◆ **je ne crois pas trop m'**~ **en disant que** ... I don't think I'm going too far if I say that ...

avanie /avani/ **NF** *(littér)* snub ◆ **subir une** ~ to be snubbed ◆ **faire** *ou* **infliger des ~s à qn** to snub sb

avant /avɑ̃/

GRAMMAIRE ACTIVE 53.1

1 PRÉPOSITION	3 NOM MASCULIN
2 ADVERBE	4 ADJECTIF INVARIABLE

1 - PRÉPOSITION

1 dans le temps before ◆ **il est parti** ~ **nous/la fin** he left before us/the end ◆ ~ **son accident il était très gai** he was very cheerful before his accident ◆ **peu** ~ **mon mariage** shortly *ou* a short time before I got married ◆ **il n'est pas arrivé** ~ **9 heures** he didn't arrive until 9

◆ **avant de** + *infinitif* before ◆ **à prendre** ~ **de manger** to be taken before food *ou* meals ◆ **dînez donc** ~ **de partir** do have a meal before you go ◆ **consultez-moi** ~ **de prendre une décision** consult me before making your decision *ou* before you decide

◆ **avant que** + *subjonctif* before ◆ **je veux lire sa lettre** ~ **qu'elle (ne) l'envoie** I want to read her letter before she sends it (off) ◆ **n'envoyez pas cette lettre** ~ **que je (ne) l'aie lue** don't send this letter before *ou* until I have read it

2 précédant une durée for ◆ **il n'arrivera pas** ~ **une demi-heure** he won't be here for another half hour yet *ou* for half an hour yet ◆ **ça ne pourra pas débuter** ~ **plusieurs jours** it can't start for another few days (yet) *ou* for a few days yet ◆ ~ **peu** shortly ◆ **on ne le reverra pas** ~ **longtemps** we won't see him again for a while *ou* for some time

3 = au plus tard by ◆ **il me le faut** ~ **demain** I must have it by tomorrow

4 = en moins de within ◆ **ça doit être terminé** ~ **une semaine/un mois** it has to be finished within a week/a month

5 dans l'espace before ◆ **sa maison est (juste)** ~ **la poste** his house is just before the post office ◆ **j'étais** ~ **lui dans la queue** I was in front of him *ou* before him in the queue *(Brit) ou* in the line *(US)* ◆ **on s'est arrêté juste** ~ **Paris** we stopped just outside *ou* before Paris ◆ **la poste est juste** ~ **d'arriver à la gare** the post office is just before you come to the station

6 indiquant une priorité before; *(dans une liste, un classement)* ahead of ◆ **il met sa santé** ~ **sa carrière** he puts his health before *ou* above his career, he values his health above his career ◆ **le capitaine est** ~ **le lieutenant** captain comes before *ou* is above lieutenant ◆ **en classe, elle est** ~ **sa sœur** she is ahead of her sister at school

◆ **avant tout, avant toute chose** *(= ce qui est le plus important)* above all; *(= tout d'abord, en premier)* first and foremost ◆ ~ **tout, il faut éviter la guerre** above all (things) war must be avoided ◆ **il faut** ~ **tout vérifier l'état du toit** first and foremost we must see what state the roof is in

2 - ADVERBE

1 = auparavant before, beforehand, first ◆ **venez me parler** ~ come and talk to me first *ou* beforehand ◆ **le voyage sera long, mangez** ~ it's going to be a long journey so have something to eat beforehand *ou* before you go *ou* first

◆ **d'avant** *(= précédent)* before, previous ◆ **la semaine/le mois d'**~ the week/the month before, the previous week/month ◆ **les gens d'**~ **étaient plus aimables** the previous people were nicer, the people who were there before were nicer ◆ **le train d'**~ **était plein** the earlier *ou* previous train was full

2 = autrefois *(suivi de l'imparfait)* ~, **je mangeais plus de viande** I used to eat more meat ◆ ~, **je n'aimais pas la physique** I didn't use *ou* used to like physics, I never used to like physics ◆ ~, **c'était très beau ici** it used to be very beautiful here

3 précédé d'une durée before(hand), previously, earlier ◆ **quelques semaines** ~ a few *ou* some weeks before(hand) *ou* previously *ou* earlier ◆ **bien** *ou* **longtemps** ~ long before (that) ◆ **peu (de temps)** ~ not long before (that), shortly before that *ou* beforehand

4 dans l'espace before ◆ **tu vois la boulangerie ? le fleuriste est juste** ~ you see the baker's? the florist's is just this side of it ◆ **n'avancez pas plus** ~, **c'est dangereux** don't go any further (forward), it's dangerous ◆ **il s'était engagé trop** ~ **dans le bois** he had gone too far *ou* too deep into the wood

◆ **en avant** *[+ mouvement]* forward; *[+ position]* in front, ahead *(de* of); ◆ **en** ~, **marche !** forward march! ◆ **en** ~ **toute !** *(Naut)* full steam ahead! ◆ **la voiture fit un bond en** ~ the car lurched forward ◆ **être en** ~ *(d'un groupe de personnes)* to be (out) in front ◆ **marcher en** ~ **de la procession** to walk in front of the procession ◆ **les enfants sont partis en** ~ the children have gone on ahead ◆ **partez en** ~, **on vous rejoindra** you go on (ahead), we'll catch up with you ◆ **regarder en** ~ *(fig)* to look ahead *(fig)* ◆ **mettre qch en** ~ to put sth forward, to advance sth ◆ **mettre qn en** ~ *(pour se couvrir)* to use sb as a front, to hide behind sb; *(pour aider qn)* to push sb forward *ou* to the front ◆ **il aime se mettre en** ~ he likes to push himself forward, he likes to be in the forefront

5 progression **ils sont assez** ~ **dans leurs recherches** they have come a long way in their research ◆ **n'hésitez pas à aller plus** ~ don't hesitate to go further *ou* on ◆ **il s'est engagé trop** ~ he has got *ou* become too involved, he has committed himself too deeply ◆ **fort** ~ **dans la nuit** far *ou* well into the night

3 - NOM MASCULIN

1 = partie antérieure *[d'avion, voiture, train]* front; *[de navire]* bow(s)

◆ **à l'avant** ◆ **voyager à l'**~ **du train** to travel in the front of the train ◆ **dans cette voiture on est mieux à l'**~ it's more comfortable in the front of this car

◆ **aller de l'avant** to forge ahead

2 Sport = joueur *(gén)* forward; *(Volley)* frontline player ◆ **la ligne des ~s** the forward line

3 Mil **l'**~ the front

4 - ADJECTIF INVARIABLE

= antérieur *[roue, siège]* front ◆ **la partie** ~ the front part; → **traction**

avantage /avɑ̃taʒ/ **GRAMMAIRE ACTIVE 28.1, 53.4 NM**

1 *(= intérêt)* advantage ◆ **cette solution a l'**~ **de ne léser personne** this solution has the advantage of not hurting anyone ◆ **tirer** ~ **de la situation, tourner une situation à son** ~ to take advantage of the situation, to turn the situation to one's advantage

◆ **avoir avantage à** + *infinitif* ◆ **il a** ~ **à y aller** it will be to his advantage to go, it will be worth his while to go ◆ **j'ai** ~ **à acheter en gros** it's worth my while to *ou* it's worth it for me to buy in bulk ◆ **tu aurais** ~ **à te tenir tranquille*** you'd do better to keep quiet, you'd do well to keep quiet ◆ **il aurait grand** ~ **à** it would be very much to his advantage to, he would be well advised to

2 *(= supériorité)* advantage ◆ **avoir un** ~ **sur qn** to have an advantage over sb ◆ **j'ai sur vous l'**~ **de l'expérience** I have the advantage of experience over you ◆ **ils ont l'**~ **du nombre** they have the advantage of numbers *(sur* over)

3 *(Fin = gain)* benefit ◆ **~s accessoires** additional benefits ◆ **~s en nature** fringe benefits, benefits in kind ◆ ~ **pécuniaire** financial benefit ◆ **~s sociaux** welfare benefits ◆ ~ **fiscal** tax break

4 *(Mil, Sport, fig)* advantage; *(Tennis)* advantage, vantage *(Brit)* ◆ **avoir l'**~ to have the advantage *(sur* over) to have the upper hand, to be one up* *(sur* on); ◆ ~ **service/dehors** *(Tennis)* advantage in/out, van(tage) in/out *(Brit)*, ad in/out* *(US)*

5 *(frm = plaisir)* pleasure ◆ **j'ai (l'honneur et) l'**~ **de vous présenter M. Leblanc** it is my (honour and) privilege to introduce Mr Leblanc ◆ **que me vaut l'**~ **de votre visite ?** to what do I owe the pleasure *ou* honour of your visit? *(frm)*

6 *(locution)*

◆ **à son/ton** *etc* **avantage** ◆ **être à son** ~ *(sur une photo)* to look one's best; *(dans une conversation)* to be at one's best ◆ **elle est à son** ~ **avec cette coiffure** that hair style really flatters her ◆ **il s'est montré à son** ~ he was seen in a favourable light *ou* to advantage ◆ **c'est (tout) à ton** ~ it's (entirely) to your advantage ◆ **changer à son** ~ to change for the better

avantager /avɑ̃taʒe/ ► conjug 3 ◄ **VT** 1 *(= donner un avantage à)* to favour *(Brit)*, to favor *(US)*, to give an advantage to ◆ **elle a été avantagée par la nature** she's blessed with natural beauty ◆ **il a été avantagé par rapport à ses frères** he has been given an advantage over his brothers ◆ **être avantagé dès le départ** *(dans la vie)* to have a head start *(par rapport à* on) 2 *(= mettre en valeur)* to flatter ◆ **ce chapeau l'avantage** that hat's very flattering on her, she looks good in that hat

avantageusement /avɑ̃taʒøzmɑ̃/ ADV *[vendre]* at a good price; *[décrire]* favourably (Brit), favorably (US), flatteringly • **la situation se présente ~** the situation looks favourable

avantageux, -euse /avɑ̃taʒø, øz/ ADJ 1 (= *profitable) [affaire]* worthwhile, profitable; *[prix]* attractive • **ce serait plus ~ de ...** it would be more profitable *ou* worthwhile to ... • **en grands paquets, c'est plus ~** large packets are better value *ou* more economical 2 (= *présomptueux) [air, personne]* conceited • **il a une idée assez avantageuse de lui-même** he has a very high opinion of himself, he thinks a lot of himself 3 (= *flatteur) [portrait, chapeau]* flattering • **prendre des poses avantageuses** to show o.s. off to one's best advantage

avant-bras /avɑ̃bʀɑ/ NM INV forearm

avant-centre (pl **avants-centres**) /avɑ̃sɑ̃tʀ/ NM centre-forward (Brit), center-forward (US) • **il est** *ou* **joue ~** he plays centre-forward

avant-coureur (pl **avant-coureurs**) /avɑ̃kuʀœʀ/ ADJ M precursory, premonitory • **signe ~** forerunner, harbinger *(littér)*

avant-dernier, -ière (mpl **avant-derniers**) /avɑ̃dɛʀnje, jɛʀ/ ADJ, NM,F next to last, last but one *(Brit) (sg seulement)*, penultimate

avant-garde (pl **avant-gardes**) /avɑ̃gaʀd/ NF *(Mil)* vanguard; *(Art, Pol)* avant-garde • **art/poésie/idées d'~** avant-garde art/poetry/ideas • **être à l'~ de** to be in the vanguard of

avant-gardisme /avɑ̃gaʀdism/ NM avant-gardism

avant-gardiste (pl **avant-gardistes**) /avɑ̃gaʀdist/ ADJ, NMF avant-gardist

avant-goût (pl **avant-goûts**) /avɑ̃gu/ NM foretaste

avant-guerre (pl **avant-guerres**) /avɑ̃gɛʀ/ NM *ou* NF pre-war years • **d'~** pre-war *(épith)* ADV before the war

avant-hier /avɑ̃tjɛʀ/ ADV the day before yesterday

avant-main (pl **avant-mains**) /avɑ̃mɛ̃/ NF forequarters

avant-midi * /avɑ̃midi/ NM *ou* NF INV *(Belg, Can)* morning

avant-mont (pl **avant-monts**) /avɑ̃mɔ̃/ NM foothills

avant-port (pl **avant-ports**) /avɑ̃pɔʀ/ NM outer harbour

avant-poste (pl **avant-postes**) /avɑ̃pɔst/ NM outpost • **aux ~s du combat pour la liberté** in the vanguard of the struggle for freedom • **aux ~s des technologies nouvelles** on the cutting edge of new technology

avant-première (pl **avant-premières**) /avɑ̃pʀəmjɛʀ/ NF preview • **j'ai vu le film en ~** I saw a preview of the film • **ce film sera projeté en ~ au Rex** the film will be previewing at the Rex

avant-projet (pl **avant-projets**) /avɑ̃pʀɔʒɛ/ NM pilot study

avant-propos /avɑ̃pʀɔpo/ NM INV foreword

avant-scène (pl **avant-scènes**) /avɑ̃sɛn/ NF *(Théât)* (= *partie de la scène)* apron, proscenium; (= *loge)* box *(at the front of the house)*

avant-soirée (pl **avant-soirées**) /avɑ̃swaʀe/ NF • **l'~** the early evening

avant-toit (pl **avant-toits**) /avɑ̃twa/ NM eaves

avant-train (pl **avant-trains**) /avɑ̃tʀɛ̃/ NM *[d'animal]* foreparts, forequarters; *[de véhicule]* front axle assembly *ou* unit

avant-veille (pl **avant-veilles**) /avɑ̃vɛj/ NF • **l'~** two days before *ou* previously • **c'était l'~ de Noël** it was the day before Christmas Eve *ou* two days before Christmas

avare /avaʀ/ ADJ 1 *[personne]* miserly • **~ de paroles/compliments** sparing of *ou* with words/compliments • **elle n'est pas ~ de discours/de promesses** she's full of talk/promises • **il n'est pas ~ de confidences** he's quite happy to confide in people 2 *(littér = peu abondant) [terre]* meagre (Brit), meager (US); *[lumière]* dim, weak NMF miser

avarice /avaʀis/ NF miserliness

avaricieux, -ieuse /avaʀisjø, jøz/ *(littér)* ADJ miserly, niggardly, stingy NM miser, niggard, skinflint

avarie /avaʀi/ NF *[de navire, véhicule]* damage (NonC); *[de cargaison, chargement]* damage (NonC) (in transit), average (SPÉC)

avarié, e /avaʀje/ (ptp de **avarier**) ADJ *[aliment]* rotting; *[navire]* damaged • **cette viande est ~e** this meat has gone bad *ou* off (Brit)

avarier /avaʀje/ ► conjug 7 ◄ VT to spoil, to damage VPR **s'avarier** *[fruits, viande]* to go bad, to rot

avatar /avataʀ/ NM 1 *(Rel)* avatar 2 *(fig)* (= *incarnation)* manifestation • **un nouvel ~ de** a new *ou* the latest manifestation of 3 (= *mésaventure)* reverse • **~s** misadventures

à vau-l'eau /avolo/ ADV → **vau-l'eau**

AVC /avese/ (abrév de **accident vasculaire cérébral**) CVA, stroke

Ave /ave/ NM INV • **~ (Maria)** Hail Mary, Ave Maria

avec /avɛk/ PRÉP 1 *(accompagnement, accord)* with • **elle est sortie ~ les enfants** she's gone out with the children • **son mariage ~ Marc a duré 8 ans** her marriage to Marc lasted (for) 8 years • **ils ont les syndicats ~ eux** they've got the unions on their side *ou* behind them • **je pense ~ cet auteur que ...** I agree with this writer that ... • **elle est ~ Robert** (= *elle le fréquente)* she's going out with Robert; (= *ils vivent ensemble)* she's living with Robert • **séparer/distinguer qch d'~ qch d'autre** to separate/distinguish sth from sth else • **divorcer d'~ qn** to divorce sb • **se séparer d'~ qn** to leave sb, to part from sb • **elle s'est séparée d'~ X** she has separated from X

2 *(comportement = envers)* to, towards, with • **comment se comportent-ils ~ vous ?** how do they behave towards *ou* with you? • **il est très doux/gentil ~ moi** he's very gentle with/kind to me

3 *(moyen, manière)* with; *(ingrédient)* with, from, out of • **vous prenez votre thé ~ du lait ?** do you have *ou* take your tea with milk?, do you have *ou* take milk in your tea? • **boire ~ une paille** to drink through a straw • **maison ~ jardin** house with a garden • **faire qch ~ (grande) facilité** to do sth with (great) ease *ou* (very) easily • **parler ~ colère/bonté/lenteur** to speak angrily *ou* with anger/kindly/slowly • **chambre ~ salle de bain** room with a bathroom *ou* its own bathroom • **couteau ~ (un) manche en bois** knife with a wooden handle, wooden-handled knife • **gâteau fait ~ du beurre** cake made with butter • **ragoût fait ~ des restes** stew made out of *ou* from (the) left-overs • **c'est fait (entièrement) ~ du plomb** it's made (entirely) of lead • **voyageant ~ un passeport qui ...** travelling on a passport which ...

4 *(cause, simultanéité, contraste)* with • **on oublie tout ~ le temps** one forgets everything in time *ou* in the course of time *ou* with (the passing of) time • **~ les élections, on ne parle plus que politique** with the elections (on) no one talks anything but politics • **~ l'inflation et le prix de l'essence, les voitures se vendent mal** what with inflation and the price of petrol, cars aren't selling very well • **il est difficile de marcher ~ ce vent** it's difficult to walk in *ou* with this wind • **~ un peu de travail, il aurait gagné le prix** with a little work *ou* if (only) he had done a little work he would have won the prize • **~ toute ma bonne volonté, je ne suis pas parvenu à l'aider** with the best will in the world *ou* for all my goodwill I couldn't help him • **se lever ~ le jour** to get up *ou* rise with the sun *ou* dawn, to get up at daybreak • **ils sont partis ~ la pluie** they left in the rain

5 *(opposition)* with • **rivaliser/combattre ~ qn** to vie/fight with sb • **elle s'est fâchée ~ tous leurs amis** she has fallen out with all their friends

6 *(locutions)*

◆ **avec cela, avec ça** * • **et ~ ça, madame ?** *(dans un magasin)* anything else? • **il conduit mal et ~ ça il conduit trop vite** he drives badly and what's more *ou* on top of that he drives too fast • **~ cela que tu ne le savais pas !** what do you mean you didn't know!, as if you didn't know! • **et ~ ça qu'il est complaisant !** *(iro)* and it's not as if he were helpful either!, and he's not exactly *ou* even helpful either! • **~ tout ça j'ai oublié le pain** in the midst of all this I forgot about the bread

ADV * • **tiens mes gants, je ne peux pas conduire ~** hold my gloves, I can't drive with them on • **rends-moi mon stylo, tu allais partir ~ !** give me back my pen, you were going to walk off with it! • **(il) faudra bien faire ~** he (*ou* we *etc*) will have to make do

aveline /av(ə)lin/ NF (= *noix)* filbert

avelinier /av(ə)linje/ NM (= *arbre)* filbert

aven /avɛn/ NM sinkhole, pothole, swallow hole (Brit)

avenant, e /av(ə)nɑ̃, ɑ̃t/ ADJ *[personne, sourire]* pleasant, welcoming; *[manières]* pleasant, pleasing; *[maison]* attractive NM 1 *[de police d'assurance]* endorsement; *[de contrat]* amendment (*à* to); • **faire un ~ à** *[+ police d'assurance]* to endorse; *[+ contrat]* to amend

2 *(locution)*

◆ **à l'avenant** in keeping (*de* with); • **la maison était luxueuse, et le mobilier était à l'~** the house was luxurious, and the furniture was equally so *ou* was in keeping with it • **la table coûtait 1 000 €, et tout était à l'~** the table cost €1,000 and everything else was just as expensive

avènement /avɛnmɑ̃/ NM *[de roi]* accession (*à* to); *[de régime, politique, idée]* advent; *[de Messie]* Advent, Coming

avenir[1] /av(ə)niʀ/ NM 1 (= *futur)* future; (= *postérité)* future generations • **avoir des projets d'~** to have plans for the future, to have future plans • **dans un proche ~** in the near future • **elle m'a prédit mon ~** she told my fortune • **l'~ le dira** only time will tell • **l'~ appartient à ceux qui se lèvent tôt** *(Prov)* the early bird catches the worm *(Prov)*

2 (= *bien-être)* future (well-being) • **assurer l'~ de ses enfants** to secure one's children's future

3 (= *carrière)* future, prospects • **il a de l'~** he has a good future *ou* good prospects • **artiste/entreprise pleine d'~** up-and-coming artist/company • **son ~ est derrière lui** his future is behind him, he's got no future • **métier d'~** job with a future *ou* with prospects • **il n'y a aucun ~ dans ce métier** there's no future *ou* there are no prospects in this job, this is a dead-end job • **projet sans ~** project without prospects of success *ou* without a future

4 • **à l'~** (= *dorénavant)* from now on, in future

avenir[2] /av(ə)niʀ/ NM *(Jur)* writ of summons *(from one counsel to another)*

Avent /avɑ̃/ NM • **l'~** Advent

aventure /avɑ̃tyʀ/ NF 1 (= *péripétie, incident)* adventure; (= *entreprise)* venture; (= *liaison amoureuse)* affair • **fâcheuse ~** unfortunate experience ◆ ~ **effrayante** terrifying experience ◆ **film/roman d'~s** adventure film/story ◆ ~ **amoureuse** *ou* **sentimentale** love affair ◆ **avoir une ~ (galante) avec qn** to have an affair with sb

[2] ◆ **l'~** adventure ◆ **esprit d'~** spirit of adventure ◆ **sortir la nuit dans ce quartier, c'est l'~ !** going out at night in this area is a risky business! ◆ **j'ai du travail pour 6 mois, après c'est l'~** I've got work for 6 months, but after that, who knows?

[3] ◆ **dire la bonne ~** to tell fortunes ◆ **dire la bonne ~ à qn** to tell sb's fortune; → **diseur**

[4] *(locutions)* **marcher à l'~** to walk aimlessly ◆ **si, d'~** *ou* **par ~** *(littér)* if by any chance

aventuré, e /avɑ̃tyʀe/ (ptp de **aventurer**) ADJ *[entreprise]* risky, chancy; *[hypothèse]* risky, venturesome

aventurer /avɑ̃tyʀe/ ▸ conjug 1 ◂ VT *[+ somme, réputation, vie]* to risk, to put at stake, to chance; *[+ remarque, opinion]* to venture VPR **s'aventurer** to venture (*dans* into; *sur* onto); ◆ **s'~ à faire qch** to venture to do sth ◆ **s'~ sur un terrain glissant** *(fig)* to tread on dangerous ground, to skate on thin ice

aventureux, -euse /avɑ̃tyʀø, øz/ ADJ *[personne, esprit]* adventurous, enterprising, venturesome; *[imagination]* bold; *[projet, entreprise]* risky, rash, chancy; *[vie]* adventurous

aventurier /avɑ̃tyʀje/ NM adventurer

aventurière /avɑ̃tyʀjɛʀ/ NF adventuress

aventurisme /avɑ̃tyʀism/ NM *(Pol)* adventurism

aventuriste /avɑ̃tyʀist/ ADJ *(Pol)* adventurist

avenu, e[1] /av(ə)ny/ ADJ → **nul**

avenue[2] /av(ə)ny/ NF *[de ville]* (= *boulevard*) avenue; *[de parc]* (= *allée*) drive, avenue ◆ **les ~s du pouvoir** *(littér)* the roads to power

avéré, e /aveʀe/ (ptp de **s'avérer**) ADJ *[fait]* established, known; *[terroriste, criminel]* known ◆ **il est ~ que ...** it is a known *ou* recognized fact that ...

avérer (s') /aveʀe/ ▸ conjug 6 ◂ VPR ◆ **il s'avère que ...** it turns out that ... ◆ **ce remède s'avéra inefficace** this remedy proved (to be) *ou* turned out to be ineffective ◆ **il s'est avéré un employé consciencieux** he proved (to be) *ou* turned out to be a conscientious employee

avers /avɛʀ/ NM obverse *(of coin, medal)*

averse /avɛʀs/ NF (= *pluie*) shower (of rain); *[d'insultes, pierres]* shower ◆ **forte ~** heavy shower, downpour ◆ ~ **orageuse** thundery shower ◆ **être pris par** *ou* **recevoir une ~** to be caught in a shower ◆ **il n'est pas né** *ou* **tombé de la dernière ~*** *(fig)* he wasn't born yesterday

aversion /avɛʀsjɔ̃/ GRAMMAIRE ACTIVE 34.3 NF aversion (*pour* to) loathing (*pour* for); ◆ **avoir en ~, avoir de l'~ pour** to have an aversion to, to loathe ◆ **prendre en ~** to take a (strong) dislike to

averti, e /avɛʀti/ (ptp de **avertir**) ADJ *[public]* informed; *[connaisseur, expert]* well-informed ◆ **c'est un film réservé à des spectateurs ~s** this film is only suitable for an informed audience ◆ **~ de** *[+ problèmes etc]* aware of ◆ **être très ~ des travaux cinématographiques contemporains** to be very well up on *ou* well informed about the contemporary film scene; → **homme**

avertir /avɛʀtiʀ/ ▸ conjug 2 ◂ VT (= *prévenir*) to tell, to inform (*de qch* of sth); (= *mettre en garde*) to warn (*de qch* of sth); ◆ **avertissez-le de ne pas recommencer** tell *ou* warn him not to do it again ◆ **tenez-vous pour averti** be warned, don't say you haven't been warned ◆ **avertissez-moi dès que possible** let me know as soon as possible

avertissement /avɛʀtismɑ̃/ NM (= *avis*) warning (*à* to); (= *présage*) warning, warning sign; (= *réprimande*) *(Sport)* caution; *(Scol)* warning ◆ **recevoir un ~** to receive a warning ◆ **les syndicats ont adressé un sévère ~ au gouvernement** the unions have issued a stern warning to the government ◆ **~ (au lecteur)** (= *préface*) foreword ◆ **~ sans frais** *(Jur)* notice of assessment; *(fig)* clear warning (*à* to)

avertisseur, -euse /avɛʀtisœʀ, øz/ ADJ warning NM *[de voiture]* horn, hooter *(Brit)* ◆ **~ (d'incendie)** (fire) alarm

aveu (pl **aveux**) /avø/ NM [1] *[de crime]* confession; *[d'amour]* confession, avowal *(littér)*; *[de fait, faiblesse]* admission ◆ **c'est l'~ d'un échec de la part du gouvernement** it's an admission of defeat on the part of the government ◆ **un ~ d'impuissance** an admission of helplessness *ou* powerlessness ◆ **faire l'~ d'un crime** to confess to a crime ◆ **faire des ~x complets** to make a full confession ◆ **passer aux ~x** to make a confession ◆ **revenir sur ses ~x** to retract one's confession ◆ **je dois vous faire un ~, je ne les aime pas non plus** I have a confession to make, I don't like them either

[2] *(frm : selon)* **de l'~ de qn** according to sb ◆ **de l'~ même du témoin** on the witness's own testimony

[3] *(frm)* **sans ~** *[homme, politicien]* disreputable

[4] *(littér* = *assentiment)* consent ◆ **sans l'~ de qn** without sb's authorization *ou* consent

aveuglant, e /avœglɑ̃, ɑ̃t/ ADJ *[lumière]* blinding, dazzling; *[vérité]* glaring *(épith)*

aveugle /avœgl/ ADJ *[personne]* blind; *[passion, dévouement, obéissance]* blind; *[attentat, violence]* indiscriminate, random; *[terrorisme]* indiscriminate; *[fenêtre, façade, mur, couloir]* blind ◆ **point ~** *(Anat)* blind spot ◆ **devenir ~** to go blind ◆ **~ d'un œil** blind in one eye ◆ **je ne suis pas ~ !** I'm not blind! ◆ **son amour le rend ~** he's blinded by love ◆ **l'amour est ~** love is blind ◆ **avoir une confiance ~ en qn** to trust sb blindly, to have blind faith in sb ◆ **être ~ aux défauts de qn** to be blind to sb's faults ◆ **l'instrument ~ du destin** the blind *ou* unwitting instrument of fate; → **naissance** NM blind man ◆ **les ~s** the blind ◆ **faire qch en ~** to do sth blindly ◆ **c'est un ~-né** he was born blind, he has been blind from birth; → **double, royaume** NF blind woman

aveuglement /avœgləmɑ̃/ NM *(littér* = *égarement)* blindness

aveuglément /avœglemɑ̃/ ADV blindly

aveugler /avœgle/ ▸ conjug 1 ◂ VT [1] *(lit, fig)* (= *rendre aveugle*) to blind; (= *éblouir*) to dazzle, to blind [2] *[+ fenêtre]* to block *ou* brick up; *[+ voie d'eau]* to stop up VPR **s'aveugler** ◆ **s'~ sur qn/qch** to be blind to *ou* shut one's eyes to sb's defects/sth

aveuglette /avœglɛt/ **à l'aveuglette** LOC ADV ◆ **avancer à l'~** to grope (one's way) along, to feel one's way along ◆ **descendre à l'~** to grope one's way down ◆ **prendre des décisions à l'~** to take decisions in the dark *ou* blindly

aveulir /avøliʀ/ ▸ conjug 2 ◂ *(littér)* VT to enfeeble, to enervate VPR **s'aveulir** to weaken

aveulissement /avølismɑ̃/ NM *(littér)* enfeeblement, enervation

aviaire /avjɛʀ/ ADJ avian

aviateur /avjatœʀ/ NM airman, aviator

aviation /avjasjɔ̃/ NF [1] *(Mil)* (= *corps d'armée*) air force; (= *avions*) aircraft, air force [2] ◆ **l'~** (= *sport, métier de pilote*) flying; (= *secteur commercial*) aviation; (= *moyen de transport*) air travel ◆ **coupe/meeting d'~** flying cup/meeting ◆ **usine d'~** aircraft factory ◆ **compagnie d'~** airline company; → **champ**[1], **terrain**

COMP **aviation de chasse** fighter force
aviation navale fleet air arm *(Brit)*, naval air force *(US)*

aviatrice /avjatʀis/ NF airwoman, aviator, aviatrix

avicole /avikɔl/ ADJ poultry *(épith)* ◆ **établissement ~** poultry farm

aviculteur, -trice /avikyltœʀ, tʀis/ NM,F poultry farmer

aviculture /avikyltyʀ/ NF poultry farming

avide /avid/ ADJ (= *cupide*) *[personne]* greedy, grasping; *[regard, yeux]* greedy; (= *passionné*) *[lecteur]* avid ◆ **~ de** *[plaisir, sensation]* eager *ou* avid for; *[+ argent, nourriture]* greedy for; *[+ pouvoir, honneurs, succès, connaissances]* hungry for ◆ **~ de faire qch** eager to do sth ◆ **~ de sang** *ou* **de carnage** bloodthirsty

avidement /avidmɑ̃/ ADV *[écouter]* eagerly; *[lire]* avidly; *[regarder]* intently, eagerly; *[compter, manger]* greedily

avidité /avidite/ NF (= *passion*) eagerness; (= *cupidité, voracité*) greed ◆ **lire avec ~** to read avidly ◆ **manger avec ~** to eat greedily

avifaune /avifon/ NF avifauna

Avignon

Created by the actor-director Jean Vilar in 1947, the **Festival d'Avignon** is one of the most important events in the French cultural calendar. The town is taken over by theatregoers in late July and early August, and many of its historic buildings are transformed into performance spaces. The most prestigious shows of the festival take place in the courtyard of the Palais des Papes, the old Papal palace in the town centre.

Note that when translating the phrase « in Avignon » the preposition « en » can be used instead of the usual « à », especially in formal speech or writing (for example, « ce spectacle a été créé en Avignon »).

avilir /aviliʀ/ ▸ conjug 2 ◂ VT *[+ personne]* to degrade, to debase, to demean; *[+ monnaie]* to debase; *[+ marchandise]* to cause to depreciate VPR **s'avilir** *[personne]* to degrade o.s., to debase o.s., to demean o.s.; *[monnaie, marchandise]* to depreciate

avilissant, e /avilisɑ̃, ɑ̃t/ ADJ *[spectacle]* degrading, shameful, shaming *(épith)*; *[conduite, situation, travail]* degrading, demeaning

avilissement /avilismɑ̃/ NM *[de personne]* degradation, debasement; *[de monnaie]* debasement; *[de marchandise]* depreciation

aviné, e /avine/ ADJ *(littér)* *[personne]* inebriated, intoxicated; *[voix]* drunken ◆ **il a l'haleine ~e** his breath smells of alcohol

avion /avjɔ̃/ NM (= *appareil*) plane, aircraft *(pl inv)*, aeroplane *(Brit)*, airplane *(US)* ◆ **l'~** *(Sport)* flying ◆ **défense/batterie contre ~s** anti-aircraft defence/battery ◆ **ils sont venus en ~** they came by air *ou* by plane, they flew (here) ◆ **par ~** *(sur lettre)* by air(mail)

COMP **avion de bombardement** bomber
avion de chasse fighter (plane), interceptor
avion commercial commercial aircraft
avion à décollage et atterrissage courts short takeoff and landing aircraft, STOL aircraft
avion à décollage et atterrissage verticaux vertical takeoff and landing aircraft, VTOL aircraft
avion furtif stealth bomber *ou* plane
avion de ligne airliner
avion en papier paper aeroplane
avion postal mail plane
avion à réaction jet (plane)
avion de reconnaissance reconnaissance

aircraft *ou* plane
avion renifleur sniffer plane
avion sanitaire air ambulance
avion spatial space plane
avion de tourisme private aircraft *ou* plane
avion de transport transport aircraft

avion-cargo (pl **avions-cargos**) /avjɔ̃kaʀgo/ **NM** (air) freighter, cargo aircraft

avion-cible (pl **avions-cibles**) /avjɔ̃sibl/ **NM** target aircraft

avion-citerne (pl **avions-citernes**) /avjɔ̃sitɛʀn/ **NM** air tanker

avion-école (pl **avions-écoles**) /avjɔ̃ekɔl/ **NM** training plane

avionique /avjɔnik/ **NF** avionics *(sg)*

avionneur /avjɔnœʀ/ **NM** aircraft manufacturer

avion-radar (pl **avions-radars**) /avjɔ̃ʀadaʀ/ **NM** radar plane

avion-suicide (pl **avions-suicide**) /avjɔ̃sɥisid/ **NM** suicide plane

avion-taxi (pl **avions-taxis**) /avjɔ̃taksi/ **NM** taxiplane

aviron /aviʀɔ̃/ **NM** [1] *(= rame)* oar; *(= sport)* rowing ◆ **faire de l'~** to row [2] *(Can)* paddle

avironner /aviʀɔne/ ► conjug 1 ◄ **VT** *(Can)* to paddle

avis /avi/ **GRAMMAIRE ACTIVE 28.1, 29.1, 29.2, 33.1, 33.2, 38.1, 40.1, 53.5**

NM [1] *(= opinion)* opinion ◆ **donner son ~** to give one's opinion *ou* views *(sur* on, about); ◆ **les ~ sont partagés** opinion is divided ◆ **être du même ~ que qn, être de l'~ de qn** to be of the same opinion as sb, to share sb's view ◆ **on ne te demande pas ton ~ !** who asked you? ◆ **je ne suis pas de votre ~** I don't agree (with you) ◆ **à mon ~ c'est ...** in my opinion *ou* to my mind it is ... ◆ **si tu veux mon ~, il est ...** if you ask me *ou* if you want my opinion, he's ... ◆ **c'est bien mon ~** I quite agree ◆ **à mon humble ~** *(iro)* in my humble opinion ◆ **de l'~ de tous, il ne sera pas élu** the unanimous view *ou* the general opinion is that he won't be elected; → **changer, deux**

[2] *(= conseil)* advice *(NonC)* ◆ **un ~ amical** a friendly piece of advice, a piece of friendly advice, some friendly advice ◆ **suivre l'~ *ou* les ~ de qn** to take *ou* follow sb's advice ◆ **sur l'~ de qn** on sb's advice

[3] *(= notification)* notice; *(Fin)* advice ◆ **lettre d'~** letter of advice ◆ **~ de crédit/de débit** credit/debit advice ◆ **~ d'appel d'offres** invitation to tender *ou* to bid ◆ **jusqu'à nouvel ~** until further notice ◆ **sauf ~ contraire** unless otherwise informed, unless one hears to the contrary; *(sur étiquette)* unless otherwise indicated ◆ **~ de coup de vent** *(en mer)* gale warning ◆ **~ de tempête** storm warning ◆ **~ aux amateurs !*** any takers?* ◆ **donner ~ de/que ...** † to give notice of/that ...; → **préalable**

[4] *(Admin = recommandation)* opinion ◆ **les membres ont émis un ~** the members put forward an opinion ◆ **on a pris l'~ du conseil** they took the opinion of the council ◆ **~ favorable/défavorable** *(Admin)* accepted/rejected ◆ **la commission a émis un ~ favorable** the commission gave its approval

[5] *(locutions)* **il était d'~ de partir *ou* qu'on parte immédiatement** he thought *ou* he was of the opinion that we should leave at once ◆ **m'est ~ que ...** († *ou hum*) methinks † *(hum)* ...

COMP **avis de décès** death notice
avis d'expédition *(Comm)* advice of dispatch
avis d'imposition tax notice
avis au lecteur foreword
avis de mise en recouvrement *(Fin)* notice of assessment
avis de mobilisation mobilization notice
avis au public public notice; *(= en-tête)* notice to the public
avis de réception acknowledgement of receipt
avis de recherche *(= affiche) [de criminel]* wanted poster; *[de disparu]* missing person poster ◆ **lancer un ~ de recherche** *(pour criminel)* to issue a description of a wanted person; *(pour disparu)* to issue a description of a missing person
avis de virement advice of bank transfer

avisé, e /avize/ (ptp de **aviser**) **ADJ** sensible, wise ◆ **être bien/mal ~ de faire** to be well-/ill-advised to do

aviser /avize/ ► conjug 1 ◄ **VT** [1] *(frm = avertir)* to advise, to inform *(de* of) to notify *(de* of, about); ◆ **il ne m'en a pas avisé** he didn't notify me of *ou* about it [2] *(littér = apercevoir)* to catch sight of, to notice **VI** ◆ **cela fait, nous aviserons** once that's done, we'll see where we stand ◆ **sur place, nous aviserons** we'll see once we're there ◆ **~ à qch** to see to sth **VPR** **s'aviser** [1] *(= remarquer)* **s'~ de qch** to realize *ou* become aware of sth suddenly ◆ **il s'avisa que ...** he suddenly realized that ... [2] *(= s'aventurer à)* **s'~ de faire qch** to dare (to) do sth, to take it into one's head to do sth ◆ **et ne t'avise pas d'aller lui dire** and don't you dare go and tell him

aviso /avizo/ **NM** advice-boat

avitaminose /avitaminoz/ **NF** vitamin deficiency, avitaminosis *(SPÉC)*

aviver /avive/ ► conjug 1 ◄ **VT** [1] *[+ douleur physique, appétit]* to sharpen; *[+ regrets, chagrin]* to deepen; *[+ intérêt, désir]* to kindle, to arouse; *[+ colère]* to stir up; *[+ souvenirs]* to stir up, to revive; *[+ querelle]* to stir up, to add fuel to; *[+ passion]* to arouse, to excite, to stir up; *[+ regard]* to brighten; *[+ couleur]* to brighten (up); *[+ feu]* to revive, to stir up ◆ **l'air frais leur avait avivé le teint** the fresh air had given them some colour *ou* had put some colour into their cheeks [2] *(Méd) [+ plaie]* to open up [5] *(Tech) [+ bronze]* to burnish; *[+ poutre]* to square off **VPR** **s'aviver** *[douleur]* to sharpen; *[regrets]* to deepen; *[regard]* to brighten

av. J.-C. (abrév de **avant Jésus-Christ**) BC

avocaillon /avɔkajɔ̃/ **NM** *(péj)* pettifogger, small-town lawyer

avocasserie /avɔkasʀi/ **NF** *(péj)* pettifoggery, chicanery

avocassier, -ière /avɔkasje, jɛʀ/ **ADJ** *(péj)* pettifogging

avocat[1], e /avɔka, at/ **NM,F** [1] *(Jur)* lawyer, attorney(-at-law) *(US)*, advocate *(Écos)*; *(d'assises)* ≈ barrister *(Brit)* ◆ **consulter son ~** to consult one's lawyer ◆ **l'accusé et son ~** the accused and his counsel

[2] *(fig = défenseur)* advocate, champion ◆ **se faire l'~ d'une cause** to advocate *ou* champion *ou* plead a cause ◆ **fais-toi mon ~ auprès de lui** plead with him on my behalf

COMP **avocat d'affaires** business lawyer
avocat de la défense counsel for the defence *ou* defendant, defending counsel *(Brit)*, defense counsel *(US)*
l'avocat du diable *(Rel, fig)* the devil's advocate ◆ **se faire l'~ du diable** *(fig)* to be *ou* play devil's advocate
avocat d'entreprise company *ou* corporate lawyer
avocat général counsel for the prosecution, prosecuting attorney *(US)*, assistant procurator fiscal *(Écos)*
l'avocat de la partie civile the counsel for the plaintiff
avocat plaidant court lawyer *(Brit)*, trial lawyer *(US)*
avocat sans cause briefless barrister *(Brit)* *ou* attorney *(US)*

avocat[2] /avɔka/ **NM** *(= fruit)* avocado (pear)

avocatier /avɔkatje/ **NM** avocado (tree), avocado pear tree

avocette /avɔsɛt/ **NF** avocet

avoine /avwan/ **NF** oats; → **farine, flocon, fou**

avoir /avwaʀ/
► conjug 34 ◄

1 VERBE TRANSITIF	4 NOM MASCULIN
2 VERBE AUXILIAIRE	5 NOM MASCULIN PLURIEL
3 VERBE IMPERSONNEL	

Lorsque **avoir** fait partie d'une expression figée comme **avoir raison, avoir peur, avoir faim**, reportez-vous au nom.

1 - VERBE TRANSITIF

[1] possession

Lorsque **avoir** signifie **posséder, disposer de**, il se traduit généralement par **have** ou plus familièrement par **have got**, mais uniquement au présent ; cette dernière forme est moins courante en anglais américain.

◆ **j'ai la réponse/trois frères** I have *ou* I've got the answer/three brothers ◆ **il n'a pas d'argent** he has *ou* he's got no money, he hasn't got any money, he doesn't have any money ◆ **il n'avait pas d'argent** he had no money *ou* didn't have any money ◆ **on ne peut pas tout ~** you can't have everything ◆ **as-tu son adresse ?** have you got his address?, do you have his address?

[2] localisation

Lorsque **avoir** est utilisé pour localiser un bâtiment, un objet etc, il peut se traduire par **have (got)** mais l'anglais préférera souvent une tournure avec **be**.

◆ **vous avez la gare tout près** the station is nearby ◆ **vous avez un parc au bout de la rue** you've got *ou* there's a park down the road ◆ **vous tournez à droite et vous aurez la poste juste en face de vous** you turn right and you'll see the post office just opposite *ou* and the post office is just opposite ◆ **tu as les verres sur la dernière étagère** the glasses are on the top shelf, you'll find the glasses on the top shelf

[3]

La tournure familière dans laquelle **avoir** est suivi d'un adjectif possessif en corrélation avec un participe passé ou une relative n'est pas traduite ou est rendue par **have** et un possessif.

◆ **j'ai eu mon appareil photo volé** I had my camera stolen ◆ **ils ont leur fille qui part au Québec** they've got their daughter going to Quebec ◆ **j'ai mes rhumatismes qui me font souffrir** my rheumatism's playing me up*

[4] *= obtenir* *[+ produit, renseignement, train]* to get ◆ **nous avons très bien la BBC** we (can) get the BBC very clearly ◆ **pouvez-vous nous ~ ce livre ?** can you get this book for us?, can you get us this book? ◆ **essayez de m'~ Paris (au téléphone)** could you put me through to Paris *ou* get me Paris? ◆ **je n'ai pas pu ~ Luc (au téléphone)** I couldn't get through to Luc, I didn't manage to get Luc on the phone ◆ **je n'arrive pas à ~ Paris** I can't get through to Paris

[5] *= porter* *[+ vêtements]* to wear, to have on ◆ **il avait un pantalon beige** he was wearing beige trousers ◆ **qu'est-ce qu'il avait sur lui ?** what was he wearing?, what did he have on? ◆ **elle a toujours des gants/un foulard** she always wears gloves/a scarf ◆ **la femme qui a le chapeau/le corsage bleu** the woman with *ou* in the blue hat/blouse

6 | caractérisation |

> Lorsque **avoir** introduit une caractéristique physique ou morale, il est rendu soit par **have** soit par **be + adjectif**.

◆ **il a les yeux bleus** he has (got) blue eyes ◆ **son regard a quelque chose de méchant, il a quelque chose de méchant dans le regard** he's got a nasty look in his eye ◆ **il a du courage/de l'ambition/du toupet** he has (got) courage/ambition/cheek, he is courageous/ambitious/cheeky | MAIS | **il avait les mains qui tremblaient** his hands were shaking

7 | avec forme, dimension | to be ◆ ~ **3 mètres de haut/4 mètres de long** to be 3 metres high/4 metres long ◆ **cette chaise a une jolie ligne** this chair is a nice shape ◆ **je veux une chaise qui ait cette forme** I want a chair (that's) this shape ◆ **je voudrais un pull qui ait cette couleur** I'd like a jumper (in) this colour

8 | avec un âge | to be ◆ **il a dix ans** he is ten (years old) ◆ **j'ai l'impression d'~ 20 ans** I feel as if I were 20 ◆ **il a dans les cinquante ans** he's about *ou* around 50 ◆ **il a dans les** *ou* **environ 45 ans** he's in his mid-forties ◆ **elle a entre 50 et 60 ans** she's between 50 and 60, she's in her fifties ◆ **elle venait d'~ 38 ans** she had just turned 38

> Lorsque l'on a une proposition relative, l'anglais peut employer une tournure adjectivale.

◆ **les étudiants qui ont 18 ans** 18-year-old students, students who are 18 (years old) ◆ **des enfants qui ont entre 10 et 15 ans** children (who are) between 10 and 15, 10 to 15 year-olds ◆ **des bâtiments qui ont plus de 250 ans** buildings (that are) more than 250 years old

9 | = souffrir de | *[+ rhume, maladie]* to have ◆ **il a la rougeole** he's got measles ◆ **il a eu la rougeole à 10 ans** he had measles when he was 10 | MAIS | **il ne veut pas dire ce qu'il a** he won't say what's wrong (with him)

10 | = éprouver | ~ **le sentiment/l'impression que** to have the feeling/the impression that ◆ **qu'est-ce que tu as ?** what's the matter (with you)?, what's wrong (with you)? ◆ **il a sûrement quelque chose** I'm sure there's something the matter with him *ou* something wrong with him ◆ **qu'est-ce que tu as ? – j'ai que je suis exténué** what's the matter? – I'll tell you what the matter is, I'm worn out ◆ **il a qu'il est jaloux** he's jealous, that's what's wrong *ou* the matter with him ◆ **qu'est-ce qu'il a à pleurer ?** what's he crying for?

11 | = faire |

> Lorsque **avoir** signifie **exprimer** ou **faire**, il se traduit généralement par un verbe spécifique en anglais ; cherchez sous le substantif.

◆ **il eut un geste d'énervement** he made an irritated gesture ◆ **elle eut un sourire malin** she gave a knowing smile, she smiled knowingly ◆ **il eut une grimace de douleur** he winced ◆ **elle a eu un regard haineux** she gave us a spiteful look ◆ **ils ont eu des remarques malheureuses** they made *ou* passed *(Brit)* some unfortunate remarks

12 | = recevoir | ~ **des amis à dîner** to have friends to dinner ◆ **j'ai eu mon frère à déjeuner** I had my brother round for lunch ◆ **il aime ~ des amis** he likes to have friends over *ou* round *(Brit)*, he likes to entertain friends

13 | suivi d'une activité | to have ◆ **ils ont des soirées deux ou trois fois par semaine** they have parties two or three times a week ◆ **je n'ai rien ce soir** I've nothing on this evening, I'm not doing anything this evening ◆ **j'ai français à 10 heures** *(Scol)* I've got French at 10

14 | = toucher, attraper, vaincre | to get ◆ **je l'ai eu !** *(cible)* got it! ◆ **ils ont fini par ~ le coupable** they got the culprit in the end ◆ **dans la fusillade, ils ont eu le chef de la bande** in the shoot-out they got the gang leader ◆ **on les aura !** we'll have *ou* get them! * ◆ **je t'aurai !** I'll get you! * ◆ **elle m'a eu au sentiment** she took advantage of my better nature

15 | * = duper | *[escroc]* to have*, to take in*, to con**; *[plaisantin]* to take in* ◆ **ils m'ont eu, j'ai été eu**** I've been had* ◆ **je t'ai bien eu !** got you there!* ◆ **se faire ~** *(par escroc)* to be had*, to be taken in*; *(par un plaisantin)* to be taken in* ◆ **je me suis fait ~ de 5 €** I was conned out of €5** ◆ **il s'est laissé ~** he let himself be taken in*

16 | locutions |

◆ **avoir à** + *infinitif (= devoir)* ◆ **j'ai à travailler** I've got some work to do ◆ **il a un bouton à recoudre** he's got a button that needs sewing on

◆ **n'avoir qu'à** ◆ **tu n'as qu'à me téléphoner demain** just give me a ring tomorrow ◆ **tu n'as qu'à appuyer sur le bouton, et ça se met en marche** (you) just press the knob, and it starts working ◆ **c'est simple, vous n'avez qu'à lui écrire** it's simple, all you have to do is write to him ◆ **tu n'avais qu'à ne pas y aller** you shouldn't have gone (in the first place) ◆ **s'il n'est pas content, il n'a qu'à partir** if he doesn't like it, he can always leave

◆ **en avoir**** *(= être courageux)* to have guts* *ou* balls**

2 - VERBE AUXILIAIRE

> En tant qu'auxiliaire, **avoir** se traduit par **have** sauf dans certains emplois du passé qui sont rendus par des prétérits.

◆ **j'ai déjà couru 10 km** I've already run 10 km ◆ **il a été renvoyé deux fois** he has been dismissed twice ◆ **quand il eut** *ou* **a eu parlé** when he had spoken ◆ **il n'est pas bien, il a dû trop manger** he is not well, he must have eaten too much ◆ **nous aurons terminé demain** we'll have finished tomorrow ◆ **si je l'avais vu** if I had seen him ◆ **j'étais pressé, j'ai couru** I was in a hurry so I ran ◆ **il a fini hier** he finished yesterday

3 - VERBE IMPERSONNEL

il y a

1 | réalité, existence, suivi d'un nom singulier | there is; *(suivi d'un nom pluriel)* there are ◆ **il y a un chien à la porte** there's a dog at the door ◆ **il n'y avait que moi** there was only me, I was the only one ◆ **il y a eu trois blessés** three people were injured, there were three injured ◆ **il y a voiture et voiture !** there are cars and cars!

◆ **il y en a, y en a** * *(avec antécédent au singulier)* there is some; *(avec antécédent au pluriel)* there are some ◆ **j'achète du pain ? – non, il y en a (encore)** shall I buy some bread? – no, there's some left ◆ **quand y en a pour deux, y en a pour trois** * *(nourriture)* there's plenty for everyone; *(place)* there's plenty of room for everyone ◆ **il y en a pour dire** *ou* **qui disent ...** there are some *ou* those who say ..., some say ... ◆ **quand il n'y en a plus, il y en a encore !** * there's plenty more where that came from! * ◆ **il y en a qui feraient mieux de se taire!** some people would do better to keep quiet! ◆ **il y en a, je vous jure!** * some people, honestly! *, really, some people! *

◆ **il n'y en a que pour** ◆ **il n'y en a que pour mon petit frère, à la maison** my little brother gets all the attention at home ◆ **il n'y en a eu que pour lui pendant l'émission** the whole programme revolved around him

◆ **qu'y a-t-il?, qu'est-ce qu'il y a?** *(= que se passe-t-il)* what is it?, what's the matter?, what's up?*; *(= qu'est-ce qui ne va pas)* what's wrong?, what's the matter?, what's up?*

◆ **il y a que** * ◆ **il y a que nous sommes mécontents !** we're annoyed, that's what! *

◆ **il n'y a (pas) que** ◆ **il n'y a pas que toi** you're not the only one! ◆ **il n'y a que lui pour faire cela !** only HE would do that!, trust him to do that! ◆ **il n'y a pas que nous à le dire** we're not the only ones who say *ou* to say that

◆ **(il n')y a pas** * ◆ **il n'y a pas, (il) faut que je parte** it's no good, I've got to go ◆ **y a pas, il faut qu'il désobéisse** he just won't do as he's told ◆ **il n'y a pas à dire, il est très intelligent** there's no denying he's very intelligent

◆ **il n'y a qu'à** + *infinitif*, **y a qu'à** + *infinitif** ◆ **il n'y a qu'à les laisser partir** just let them go ◆ **il n'y a qu'à protester** we'll just have to protest, why don't we protest ◆ **y a qu'à lui dire** * why don't we just tell him ◆ **y avait qu'à le prendre, alors !** * why didn't you take it then!

2 | = il se passe | **il y a eu des émeutes dans la capitale** there have been riots in the capital ◆ **il y a eu un accident/une inondation** there has been an accident/flooding ◆ **qu'est-ce qu'il y a eu ?** what's happened? ◆ **il y a eu quelque chose de grave** something serious has happened

◆ **il y avait une fois ...** once upon a time, there was ...

3 | avec une durée |

> Dans le cas d'une action non révolue, **for** s'emploie avec le present perfect lorsque le verbe français est au présent, et avec le pluperfect lorsque le verbe français est à l'imparfait.

◆ **il y a 10 ans que je le connais** I've known him (for) 10 years ◆ **il y avait longtemps qu'elle désirait ce livre** she had wanted *ou* been wanting this book for a long time

> Dans le cas d'une action révolue, on emploie **ago** et le prétérit.

◆ **il y a 10 ans, nous étions à Paris** 10 years ago we were in Paris ◆ **il est né il y a tout juste un an** he was born just one year ago ◆ **il y a 10 jours/10 minutes que nous sommes rentrés, nous sommes rentrés il y a 10 jours/10 minutes** we got back 10 days/10 minutes ago, we have been back 10 days/10 minutes ◆ **il n'y a pas un quart d'heure qu'il est parti** he left not a quarter of an hour ago | MAIS | **il y aura 10 ans demain que je ne l'ai vu** it will be 10 years tomorrow since I last saw him

4 | suivi d'une distance | **il y a 10 km d'ici à Paris** it is 10 km from here to Paris ◆ **combien y a-t-il d'ici à Lille ?** how far is it from here to Lille?

4 - NOM MASCULIN

1 | = bien | assets ◆ **il a investi tout son ~ dans l'entreprise** he invested all his assets in the firm ◆ **son ~ était bien peu de chose** what he had wasn't much

2 | Comm | *(= actif)* credit (side); *(= billet de crédit)* credit note ◆ ~ **fiscal** *(Fin)* tax credit ◆ **vous pouvez me faire un ~ ?** can you give me a credit note?

5 - NOM MASCULIN PLURIEL

avoirs holdings, assets ◆ **~s à l'étranger** foreign assets *ou* holdings ◆ **~s en caisse** *ou* **en numéraire** cash holdings ◆ **~s financiers** financial resources

avoirdupoids /avwaʀdypwa/ **NM** avoirdupois

avoisinant, e /avwazinɑ̃, ɑ̃t/ **ADJ** *[région, pays]* neighbouring *(Brit)*, neighboring *(US)*; *[rue, ferme]* nearby, neighbouring *(Brit)*, neighboring *(US)* ◆ **dans les rues ~es** in the nearby streets, in the streets close by *ou* nearby

avoisiner /avwazine/ ► conjug 1 ◄ **VT** *[+ lieu]* *(= être proche de)* to be near *ou* close to; *(= être contigu à)* to border on; *[prix, température, taux]* to be close to ◆ **son indifférence avoisine le mé-**

pris his indifference borders on *ou* verges on contempt

avortement /avɔʀtəmɑ̃/ NM 1 *(Méd)* abortion ◆ **campagne contre l'~** anti-abortion campaign ◆ **~ thérapeutique** termination (of pregnancy) *(for medical reasons)* 2 **l' ~ de** *(fig)* the failure of

avorter /avɔʀte/ ▸ conjug 1 ◂ VI 1 *(Méd)* to have an abortion, to abort ◆ **faire ~ qn** *[personne]* to give sb an abortion, to abort sb; *[remède]* to make sb abort ◆ **se faire ~** to have an abortion 2 *(fig)* to fail, to come to nothing ◆ **faire ~ un projet** to frustrate *ou* wreck a plan ◆ **projet avorté** abortive plan VT *(Méd)* to abort, to perform an abortion on

avorteur, -euse /avɔʀtœʀ, øz/ NM,F abortionist

avorton /avɔʀtɔ̃/ NM *(péj = personne)* little runt *(péj)*; *(= arbre, plante)* puny *ou* stunted specimen; *(= animal)* puny specimen

avouable /avwabl/ ADJ acceptable ◆ **procédés peu ~s** fairly disreputable methods

avoué, e /avwe/ (ptp de **avouer**) NM ≈ solicitor *(Brit)*, attorney-at-law *(US)* ADJ *[ennemi, revenu, but]* avowed

avouer /avwe/ ▸ conjug 1 ◂ VT *[+ amour]* to confess, to avow *(littér)*; *[+ crime]* to confess (to), to own up to; *[+ fait]* to acknowledge, to admit; *[+ faiblesse, vice]* to admit to, to confess to ◆ **~ avoir menti** to admit *ou* confess that one has lied, to admit *ou* own up to lying ◆ **~ que ...** to admit *ou* confess that ... ◆ **elle est douée, je l'avoue** she is gifted, I (must) admit; → **faute** VI 1 *(= se confesser) [coupable]* to confess, to own up 2 *(= admettre)* to admit, to confess ◆ **tu avoueras, c'est un peu fort !** you must admit *ou* confess, it is a bit much! VPR **s'avouer** ◆ **s'~ coupable** to admit *ou* confess one's guilt ◆ **s'~ vaincu** to admit *ou* acknowledge defeat ◆ **s'~ déçu** to admit to being disappointed

avril /avʀil/ NM April ◆ **en ~ ne te découvre pas d'un fil** *(Prov)* ≈ ne'er cast a clout till May be out; → **poisson, premier**; *pour autres loc voir* **septembre**

avunculaire /avɔ̃kylɛʀ/ ADJ avuncular

AWACS /awaks/ NM (abrév de **Airborne Warning And Control System**) AWACS ◆ **(avion) ~** AWACS (plane) ◆ **avion-radar ~** AWACS early-warning (radar) plane

axe /aks/ NM 1 *(= ligne)* axis 2 *(= essieu)* axle
◆ **dans l'axe** *(= dans le prolongement)* ◆ **cette rue est dans l'~ de l'église** this street is directly in line with the church ◆ **mets-toi bien dans l'~ (de la cible)** line up on the target, get directly in line with the target
3 *(= route)* trunk road *(Brit)*, main highway *(US)* ◆ **les grands ~s (routiers)** the main roads, the major trunk roads *(Brit)*, the main highways *(US)* ◆ **les vols réguliers sur l'~ Paris-Marseille** the regular flights on the Paris-Marseilles route ◆ **~ rouge** *(à Paris)* no stopping zone, clearway *(Brit)* 4 *(fig) [de débat, théorie, politique]* main line 5 *(Hist, Pol)* **l'Axe** the Axis ◆ **l'~ Paris-Bonn dans la construction européenne** the Paris-Bonn axis in the construction of Europe

axel /aksɛl/ NM axel

axer /akse/ ▸ conjug 1 ◂ VT ◆ **~ qch sur/autour de** to centre *(Brit)* *ou* center *(US)* sth on/around ◆ **il est très axé sur la politique** he's very interested in politics ◆ **leur rapport est axé sur l'environnement** their report focuses on the environment

> ⚠ **axer** ne se traduit pas par **to axe**, qui a le sens de 'couper à la hache'.

axial, e (mpl **-iaux**) /aksjal, jo/ ADJ axial ◆ **éclairage ~** central overhead lighting

axillaire /aksilɛʀ/ ADJ axillary

axiomatique /aksjɔmatik/ ADJ axiomatic NF axiomatics *(sg)*

axiome /aksjom/ NM axiom

axis /aksis/ NM axis (vertebra)

axone /akson/ NM axon(e)

ayant cause (pl **ayants cause**) /ɛjɑ̃koz/ NM *(Jur)* legal successor, successor in title ◆ **les ayants cause du défunt** the beneficiaries of the deceased

ayant droit (pl **ayants droit**) /ɛjɑ̃dʀwa/ NM 1 *(Jur)* ⇒ **ayant cause** 2 *[de prestation, pension]* eligible party ◆ **~ à** party entitled to *ou* eligible for

ayatollah /ajatɔla/ NM ayatollah ◆ **les ~s de la morale** moral zealots

ayurvédique /ajyʀvedik/ ADJ Ayurvedic

azalée /azale/ NF azalea

Azerbaïdjan /azɛʀbaidʒɑ̃/ NM Azerbaijan

azerbaïdjanais, e /azɛʀbaidʒanɛ, ɛz/ ADJ Azerbaijani NM *(Ling)* Azerbaijani NM,F **Azerbaïdjanais(e)** Azerbaijani

azéri, e /azeʀi/ ADJ Azeri, Azerbaijani NM *(= langue)* Azerbaijani NM,F **Azéri(e)** Azeri, Azerbaijani

AZERTY /azɛʀti/ ADJ INV ◆ **clavier ~** AZERTY keyboard

azimut /azimyt/ NM *(Astron)* azimuth; *(fig)* ◆ **chercher qn dans tous les ~s** to look everywhere *ou* all over the place for sb, to search high and low for sb
◆ **tous azimuts** * *(= dans toutes les directions)* everywhere, all over the place; *[offensive, campagne]* all-out *(épith)*; *[négociation]* wide-ranging *(épith)*; *[réformes]* wholesale ◆ **la banque a connu une expansion tous ~s** the bank has undergone a dramatic expansion ◆ **il attaque tous ~s** he lashes out in all directions ◆ **elle téléphonait tous ~s** she phoned around everywhere

azimutal, e (mpl **-aux**) /azimytal, o/ ADJ azimuthal

azimuté, e * /azimyte/ ADJ crazy *, nuts *, mad

Azincourt /azɛ̃kuʀ/ N Agincourt

azote /azɔt/ NM nitrogen

azoté, e /azɔte/ ADJ *[substance, base]* nitrogenous; → **engrais**

AZT /azedte/ NM (abrév de **azidothymidine**) AZT

aztèque /astɛk/ ADJ Aztec NMF **Aztèque** Aztec

azur /azyʀ/ NM *(littér)* *(= couleur)* azure, sky blue; *(= ciel)* skies, sky; → **côte**

azuré, e /azyʀe/ (ptp de **azurer**) ADJ azure

azuréen, -enne /azyʀeɛ̃, ɛn/ ADJ 1 *(= de la côte d'Azur)* of the French Riviera 2 *(littér) [yeux, bleu, ciel]* azure

azurer /azyʀe/ ▸ conjug 1 ◂ VT *[+ linge]* to blue; *(littér)* to azure, to tinge with blue

azyme /azim/ ADJ unleavened; → **pain** NM unleavened bread ◆ **fête des Azymes** Passover

Bb

B, b[1] /be/ NM (= *lettre*) B, b

b[2] (abrév de **bien**) *(Scol)* g, good

b2b /bitubi/ ADJ (abrév de **business to business**) B2B

b2c /bitusi/ ADJ (abrév de **business to consumer**) B2C

B. A. /bea/ NF (abrév de **bonne action**) good deed ◆ **faire sa ~ (quotidienne)** to do one's good deed for the day

B.A.-BA /beaba/ NM SG ◆ **le ~** the ABC (*de* of); ◆ **il n'en est qu'au ~** he's just starting off, he's just a beginner

baba[1] * /baba/ NM *(Culin)* baba ◆ **~ au rhum** rum baba

baba[2] /baba/ NM ◆ **il l'a eu dans le ~** *‡* it was one in the eye for him * ADJ ◆ **j'en suis resté ~** * I was flabbergasted *ou* dumbfounded, I was gobsmacked * *(Brit)*

baba[3] * /baba/, **baba cool** * (pl **babas cool** /babakul/) NMF, ADJ hippy

Babel /babɛl/ N Babel; → **tour**[1]

babeurre /babœʀ/ NM buttermilk

babil /babil/ NM *(littér)* *[de bébé]* babble; *[d'enfant]* prattle; *[d'adulte]* chatter; *[d'oiseau]* twittering; *[de ruisseau]* babbling

babillage /babijaʒ/ NM *[d'enfant]* prattle; *[d'adulte]* chatter

babillard, e /babijaʀ, aʀd/ ADJ *(littér)* *[adulte]* chattering; *[bébé]* babbling; *[oiseau]* twittering; *[ruisseau]* babbling, chattering NM,F *(personne)* chatterbox NM *(Can)* notice *ou* bulletin board ◆ **~ électronique** electronic bulletin board NF **babillarde** * (= *lettre*) letter, note

babiller /babije/ ► conjug 1 ◄ VI *[personne]* to chatter; *[bébé]* to babble; *[enfant]* to prattle; *[oiseau]* to twitter; *[ruisseau]* to babble, to chatter

babines /babin/ NFPL *[d'animal]* chops; * *[de personne]* chops *, lips; → **lécher**

babiole /babjɔl/ NF (= *bibelot*) trinket, knick-knack; (= *vétille*) trifle, triviality ◆ **offrir une ~** (= *cadeau*) to give a small token *ou* a little something

bâbord /babɔʀ/ NM port (side) ◆ **par** *ou* **à ~** on the port side, to port ◆ **par ~ arrière** aft on the port side

babouche /babuʃ/ NF babouche, slipper *(worn in North African countries and the Middle East)*

babouin /babwɛ̃/ NM baboon

baboune * /babun/ NF *(Can)* lip ◆ **faire la ~** *(de déception, de dédain)* to pout; *(de dégoût)* to grimace ◆ **elle m'a fait la ~ toute la journée** she was sulky *ou* huffy * with me all day

baby /babi/ ADJ INV ◆ **taille ~** baby size NM (= *whisky*) shot of scotch

baby-blues /babibluz/ NM INV baby blues *, postnatal depression ◆ **avoir le ~** to have the baby blues *, to be suffering from postnatal depression

baby-boom (pl **baby-booms**) /babibum/ NM baby boom ◆ **les enfants du ~** the baby-boomers

baby-foot (pl **baby-foots**) /babifut/ NM INV (= *jeu*) table football; (= *appareil*) football table

Babylone /babilɔn/ N Babylon

babylonien, -ienne /babilɔnjɛ̃, jɛn/ ADJ Babylonian NM,F **Babylonien(ne)** Babylonian

baby-sitter (pl **baby-sitters**) /babisitœʀ/ NMF baby-sitter

baby-sitting (pl **baby-sittings**) /babisitiŋ/ NM baby-sitting ◆ **faire du ~** to baby-sit, to do baby-sitting

bac[1] /bak/ NM 1 (= *bateau*) *(gén)* ferry, ferryboat; *(pour voitures)* car-ferry ◆ **~ aérien** air ferry 2 (= *récipient*) tub; *(dans une usine)* tank, vat; *(Peinture, Photo)* tray; *[d'évier]* sink; *[de courrier, imprimante]* tray ◆ **~ à douche** shower tray ◆ **~ (à fleurs)** planter, tub ◆ **~ à glace** ice-tray ◆ **~ à laver** washtub, (deep) sink ◆ **~ à légumes** vegetable compartment *ou* tray ◆ **~ à réserve d'eau** self-watering planter ◆ **~ à sable** sandpit ◆ **évier (à) deux ~s** double sink unit ◆ **glace vendue en ~s de deux litres** ice-cream sold in two-litre tubs 3 (= *présentoir*) display stand ◆ **dans les ~s à partir de septembre** available from September

bac[2] * /bak/ NM (abrév de **baccalauréat**) 1 *(en France)* **formation ~ + 3** ≈ 3 years' higher education; *pour autres loc voir* **baccalauréat** 2 *(au Canada = licence)* ≈ BA

baccalauréat /bakalɔʀea/ NM 1 *(en France)* baccalauréat, school leaving certificate, ≈ A-levels *(Brit)*, high school diploma *(US)*

2 *(au Canada = licence)* ≈ BA ◆ **~ en droit** law degree, LLB *(Brit)*

> **BACCALAURÉAT**
>
> The « bac », as it is popularly known, is the school leaving examination all French schoolchildren take in their final year at the « lycée ». Before beginning their **baccalauréat** studies, pupils choose a specialization known as a « série », represented by an initial letter: a « bac » with a scientific bias is known as a « bac S » (for « scientifique ») while an arts-oriented « bac » is referred to as a « bac L » (for « littéraire »), for example. When the word « bac » is followed by a plus sign and a number, this refers to the number of years of formal study completed since obtaining the baccalauréat qualification: « bac » + 3 refers to the « licence » or equivalent, « bac » + 4 to the « maîtrise », etc. These abbreviations are often used in job advertisements to indicate the level of qualification required.

baccara /bakaʀa/ NM *(Casino)* baccara(t)

baccarat /bakaʀa/ NM ◆ **(cristal de) ~** Baccarat crystal

bacchanale /bakanal/ NF 1 (= *danse*) bacchanalian *ou* drunken dance; († = *orgie*) orgy, drunken revel 2 *(Antiq)* **~s** Bacchanalia

bacchante /bakɑ̃t/ NF *(Antiq)* bacchante NFPL **bacchantes** * moustache, whiskers *(hum)*

Bacchus /bakys/ NM Bacchus

Bach /bak/ NM Bach

bâchage /bɑʃaʒ/ NM covering

bâche /bɑʃ/ NF 1 (= *toile*) canvas cover *ou* sheet; *[de camion]* tarpaulin, tarp *(US)*; *[de piscine]* (plastic *ou* canvas) cover ◆ **~ goudronnée** tarpaulin, tarp *(US)* 2 *(Tech)* (= *réservoir*) tank, cistern; (= *carter*) housing; (= *serre*) forcing frame

bachelier, -ière /baʃəlje, jɛʀ/ NM,F *person who has passed the baccalauréat*

bâcher /bɑʃe/ ► conjug 1 ◄ VT to cover with a canvas sheet, to put a canvas sheet over ◆ **camion bâché** covered truck *ou* lorry *(Brit)*

bachique /baʃik/ ADJ *(Antiq, fig)* Bacchic ◆ **fêtes ~s** bacchanalian revels ◆ **chanson ~** drinking song

bachot[1] † * /baʃo/ NM ⇒ **baccalauréat**; → **boîte**

bachot[2] /baʃo/ NM (small) boat, skiff

bachotage /baʃɔtaʒ/ NM (*Scol*) cramming, swotting (*Brit*) ◆ **faire du** ~ to cram *ou* swot (*Brit*) (for an exam)

bachoter /baʃɔte/ ▸ conjug 1 ◂ VI (*Scol*) to cram *ou* swot (*Brit*) (for an exam)

bacillaire /basilɛʀ/ ADJ [*maladie*] bacillary; [*malade*] tubercular

bacille /basil/ NM (*gén*) germ, bacillus (*SPÉC*) ◆ **le ~ virgule** the comma bacillus ◆ **le ~ de Koch/de Hansen** Koch's/Hansen('s) bacillus

bacillose /basiloz/ NF (*gén*) bacillus infection; (= *tuberculose*) tuberculosis

backgammon /bakgamɔn/ NM backgammon

bâclage /bɑklaʒ/ NM botching

bâcler /bɑkle/ ▸ conjug 1 ◂ VT [+ *travail, devoir*] to botch (up); [+ *cérémonie*] to skip through, to hurry over ◆ **~ sa toilette** to have a quick wash ◆ **la fin du film est bâclée** the ending of the film is a bit of a mess ◆ **c'est du travail bâclé** it's slapdash work

bacon /bekɔn/ NM (= *lard*) bacon; (= *jambon fumé*) smoked loin of pork ◆ **œufs au ~** bacon and eggs

bactéricide /bakteʀisid/ ADJ bactericidal NM bactericide

bactérie /bakteʀi/ NF bacterium ◆ **~s** bacteria ◆ **on a découvert une nouvelle ~** a new strain of bacteria *ou* a new bacterium has been discovered ◆ **~ multi-résistante** multiresistant bacterium, superbug*

bactérien, -ienne /bakteʀjɛ̃, jɛn/ ADJ [*contamination, pollution*] bacterial

bactériologie /bakteʀjɔlɔʒi/ NF bacteriology

bactériologique /bakteʀjɔlɔʒik/ ADJ [*arme, examen*] bacteriological

bactériologiste /bakteʀjɔlɔʒist/ NMF bacteriologist

bactériophage /bakteʀjɔfaʒ/ NM bacteriophage

badaboum* /badabum/ EXCL crash, bang, wallop!

badaud, e /bado, od/ NM,F (*qui regarde*) onlooker; (*qui se promène*) passer-by ADJ ◆ **les Parisiens sont très ~s** Parisians are full of idle curiosity

badauder † /badode/ ▸ conjug 1 ◂ VI (= *se promener*) to stroll (*dans* about); (= *regarder*) to gawk, to gawp

badauderie † /badodʀi/ NF (idle) curiosity

baderne /badɛʀn/ NF (*péj*) ◆ **(vieille) ~** old fogey*

badge /badʒ/ NM (*gén*) badge, button (*US*); (*d'identité*) name badge *ou* tag; (*pour visiteur*) visitor's badge, (visitor's) pass; (= *carte électronique*) swipe card

badgé, e /badʒe/ ADJ [*personne*] wearing a badge

badgeage /badʒaʒ/ NM badging

badger /badʒe/ ▸ conjug 1 ◂ VI to badge

badgeuse /badʒøz/ NF badge reader

badiane /badjan/ NF star anis, badian

badigeon /badiʒɔ̃/ NM [*de mur intérieur*] distemper; [*de mur extérieur*] (*lait de chaux*) whitewash; (*coloré*) coloured distemper, colourwash (*Brit*) ◆ **un coup de ~** a coat of distemper *ou* whitewash

badigeonnage /badiʒɔnaʒ/ NM 1 [*de mur intérieur*] distempering; [*de mur extérieur*] (*au lait de chaux*) whitewashing; (*coloré*) colourwashing 2 [*de plaie*] painting

badigeonner /badiʒɔne/ ▸ conjug 1 ◂ VT 1 [+ *mur intérieur*] to distemper; [+ *mur extérieur*] (*au lait de chaux*) to whitewash; (*en couleur*) to colourwash (*Brit*) 2 (= *barbouiller*) [+ *visage, surface*] to smear, to daub, to cover (*de* with); ◆ **se ~ de crème** to smear o.s. with cream 3 [+ *plaie*] to paint (*à, avec* with); ◆ **se ~ la gorge** to paint one's throat (*à* with); ◆ **~ une plaie de qch** to swab a wound with sth 4 (*Culin*) to brush (*de* with)

badin[1], **e**[1] † /badɛ̃, in/ ADJ [*personne*] jocular; [*humeur*] light-hearted, playful; [*propos*] bantering, playful ◆ **sur un** *ou* **d'un ton ~** playfully, in a bantering *ou* jesting tone

badin[2] /badɛ̃/ NM (= *anémomètre*) airspeed indicator

badinage /badinaʒ/ NM (= *propos légers*) banter (*NonC*) ◆ **sur un ton de ~** in a bantering *ou* jesting tone, playfully

badine[2] /badin/ NF switch, rod

badiner /badine/ ▸ conjug 1 ◂ VI 1 († = *plaisanter*) to (exchange) banter, to jest † ◆ **pour ~** for a jest †, in jest 2 (*en négation*) **c'est quelqu'un qui ne badine pas** he doesn't stand for any nonsense ◆ **il ne badine pas sur la discipline** he's a stickler for discipline, he has strict ideas about discipline ◆ **il ne faut pas ~ avec ce genre de maladie** this sort of illness is not to be treated lightly ◆ **et je ne badine pas !** and I'm not joking!

badinerie † /badinʀi/ NF jest †

badminton /badmintɔn/ NM badminton

bâdrant, e* /bɑdʀɑ̃, ɑ̃t/ ADJ (*Can*) bothersome ◆ **t'es vraiment ~ avec tes questions** you're being a real nuisance *ou* a real pain in the neck* with your questions

bâdrer* /bɑdʀe/ ▸ conjug 1 ◂ VT (*Can*) to bother ◆ **tu commences à me ~ avec tes questions** you're beginning to get on my nerves with your questions

BAFA /bafa/ NM (abrév de **brevet d'aptitude à la fonction d'animateur**) → **brevet**

baffe* /baf/ NF slap, clout* (*Brit*) ◆ **donner une paire de ~s à qn** to slap sb across the face ◆ **recevoir une ~** to get slapped, to get a clip on *ou* round the ear* (*Brit*)

Baffin /bafin/ NM ◆ **mer** *ou* **baie de ~** Baffin Bay ◆ **terre de ~** Baffin Island

baffle /bafl/ NM (= *panneau*) baffle (board *ou* plate); (= *enceinte*) speaker

bafouer /bafwe/ ▸ conjug 1 ◂ VT [+ *autorité*] to flout, to scorn; [+ *droit, valeurs*] to scorn, to scoff at ◆ **mari bafoué** † cuckold †

bafouillage /bafujaʒ/ NM (= *bredouillage*) spluttering, stammering; (= *propos incohérents*) gibberish (*NonC*), babble (*NonC*)

bafouille* /bafuj/ NF (= *lettre*) letter, note

bafouiller /bafuje/ ▸ conjug 1 ◂ VI (= *bredouiller*) to splutter, to stammer; (= *divaguer*) to talk gibberish, to babble VT to splutter (out), to stammer (out) ◆ **qu'est-ce qu'il bafouille ?** what's he babbling *ou* jabbering on about?*

bafouilleur, -euse /bafujœʀ, øz/ NM,F splutterer, stammerer

bâfrer** /bɑfʀe/ ▸ conjug 1 ◂ VI to guzzle*, to stuff one's face* VT to guzzle (down)*, to gobble (down), to wolf (down)*

bâfreur, -euse** /bɑfʀœʀ, øz/ NM,F guzzler*, greedy guts* (*Brit*)

bagage /bagaʒ/ NM 1 (= *valises*) **~s** luggage (*NonC*), baggage (*NonC*) ◆ **faire/défaire ses ~s** to pack/unpack (one's luggage *ou* bags), to do one's packing/unpacking ◆ **envoyer qch en ~s accompagnés** to send sth as registered luggage ◆ **"livraison des bagages", "bagages"** (*dans un aéroport*) "baggage claim", "baggage reclaim" (*Brit*) 2 (= *valise*) bag, piece of luggage; (*Mil*) kit ◆ **~ à main** piece of hand luggage (*Brit*), carry-on bag (*US*) ◆ **il avait pour tout ~ une serviette** his only luggage was a briefcase 3 (= *connaissances*) stock of knowledge; (= *diplômes*) qualifications ◆ **son ~ intellectuel/littéraire** his stock *ou* store of general/literary knowledge ◆ **ce métier exige un bon ~ technique** you need a good technical background for this profession

bagagerie /bagagʀi/ NF luggage shop

bagagiste /bagaʒist/ NM (= *manutentionnaire*) baggage *ou* luggage handler; (= *porteur*) porter

bagarre* /bagaʀ/ NF 1 ◆ **la ~** fighting ◆ **il cherche/veut la ~** he's looking for/wants a fight ◆ **il va y avoir de la ~ pour la première place** there's going to be a tough fight for first place ◆ **dès qu'ils sont ensemble, c'est la ~** as soon as they're together, they're at each other's throats 2 (= *rixe*) fight, scuffle; (*entre ivrognes*) brawl; (*fig : entre deux orateurs*) set-to, barney* (*Brit*) ◆ **~ générale** free-for-all ◆ **de violentes ~s ont éclaté** violent scuffles broke out

bagarrer* /bagaʀe/ ▸ conjug 1 ◂ VI (*en paroles*) to argue, to wrangle; (*physiquement*) to fight ◆ **ça bagarrait dur à l'Assemblée** things got very rowdy *ou* heated in Parliament VPR **se bagarrer** (= *se battre*) to fight, to scuffle, to scrap*; (= *se disputer*) to have a set-to ◆ **on s'est bagarré dur dans les rues** there was violent fighting in the streets

bagarreur, -euse* /bagaʀœʀ, øz/ ADJ [*caractère*] aggressive, fighting (*épith*) ◆ **il est ~** (= *batailleur*) he's always getting into fights; (= *ambitieux*) he's a fighter NM,F (= *ambitieux*) fighter; (*Sport*) battler

bagasse /bagas/ NF bagasse

bagatelle /bagatɛl/ NF 1 (= *objet*) small thing, trinket; († = *bibelot*) knick-knack, trinket 2 (= *somme*) trifling *ou* paltry sum, trifle ◆ **ça m'a coûté la ~ de 500 €** it cost me the trifling sum of €500 *ou* a mere €500 3 (= *vétille*) trifle ◆ **perdre son temps à des ~s** to fritter away one's time, to waste time on trifles ◆ **~s !** † fiddlesticks! † 4 (= *sexe*) († *ou hum*) **être porté sur la ~** [*homme*] to be a bit of a philanderer, to be fond of the women; [*femme*] to be fond of the men

Bagdad /bagdad/ N Baghdad

bagnard /baɲaʀ/ NM convict ◆ **une vie de ~** (*fig*) a slave's existence

bagne /baɲ/ NM (*Hist*) (= *prison*) penal colony; (= *peine*) penal servitude, hard labour ◆ **être condamné au ~** to be sentenced to hard labour ◆ **quel ~ !*, c'est le ~ !*** (*fig*) it's sheer slavery!

bagnole* /baɲɔl/ NF car ◆ **il aime faire de la ~** he likes driving ◆ **ça, c'est de la ~ !** now that's what I call a car!

bagou(t)* /bagu/ NM volubility, glibness (*péj*) ◆ **avoir du ~(t)** to have the gift of the gab, to have a glib tongue (*péj*) ◆ **quel ~t il a !** he'd talk the hind leg(s) off a donkey!*

bagouse** /baguz/ NF (= *bijou*) ring

baguage /bagaʒ/ NM [*d'oiseau, arbre*] ringing

bague /bag/ NF 1 (= *bijou*) ring; [*de cigare*] band; [*d'oiseau*] ring; [*de canette de boisson*] ring-pull, pull-tab ◆ **~ de fiançailles** engagement ring ◆ **il a la ~ au doigt** (*hum*) he's married *ou* hitched* (*hum*) 2 (*Tech*) (= *pièce métallique*) collar ◆ **~ allonge** extension tube ◆ **~ d'assemblage** bushing ◆ **~ intermédiaire/de réglage** (*Photo*) adapter/setting ring ◆ **~ de serrage** jubilee clip

bagué, e /bage/ (ptp de **baguer**) ADJ [*oiseau*] ringed, banded (*US*); [*main, doigt*] beringed; [*homard*] with its pincers tied together ◆ **cigare ~ (d'or)** cigar with a (gold) band

baguenaude* /bagnod/ NF ◆ **être en ~** to be gallivanting about

baguenauder VI, **se baguenauder*** VPR /bagnode/ ▸ conjug 1 ◂ (= *faire un tour*) to go for a stroll; (= *traîner*) to trail around, to mooch about* (*Brit*)

baguer /bage/ ► conjug 1 ◄ VT 1 *[+ oiseau, arbre]* to ring; *(Tech) [+ pièce métallique]* to collar 2 *(Couture)* to baste, to tack

baguette /bagɛt/ NF 1 *(= bâton)* stick, switch ◆ **~s** *(pour manger)* chopsticks ◆ **~ de chef d'orchestre** (conductor's) baton ◆ **sous la ~ de Luc Petit** under the baton of Luc Petit, conducted by Luc Petit, with Luc Petit conducting ◆ **mener** *ou* **faire marcher qn à la ~** to rule sb with a rod of iron *ou* an iron hand
2 *(= pain)* baguette, French stick
3 *(Constr)* beading, strip of wood; *(= cache-fils)* (plastic *ou* wood) casing
4 *(= motif sur chaussette, bas)* clock
COMP **baguette de coudrier** hazel stick *ou* switch
baguette de fée magic wand
baguette de fusil ramrod
baguette magique magic wand ◆ **résoudre qch d'un coup de ~ magique** to solve sth by waving a magic wand
baguette de protection latérale *[de voiture]* side trim
baguette de sourcier divining rod
baguette de tambour *(lit)* drumstick ◆ **cheveux raides comme des ~s de tambour** dead straight *ou* really straight hair
baguette viennoise stick of Vienna bread

bah /bɑ/ EXCL *(indifférence)* pooh!; *(doute)* well!, really!

Bahamas /baamas/ NFPL ◆ **les (îles) ~** the Bahamas

bahamien, -ienne /baamjɛ̃, ɛn/ ADJ Bahamian NM,F **Bahamien(ne)** Bahamian

Bahreïn /barɛn/ NM Bahrain ◆ **à ~** in Bahrain

bahreïni, e /barɛ(j)ni/ ADJ Bahraini, Bahreini NM,F **Bahreïni(e)** Bahraini, Bahreini

baht /bat/ NM baht

bahut /bay/ NM 1 *(= coffre)* chest; *(= buffet)* sideboard 2 *(arg Scol)* school 3 * *(= camion)* lorry *(Brit)*, truck *(surtout US)*; *(= voiture)* car; *(= taxi)* cab

bai, e[1] /bɛ/ ADJ *[cheval]* bay

baie[2] /bɛ/ NF 1 *(Géog)* bay ◆ **la ~ d'Hudson** Hudson Bay ◆ **la ~ de Somme** the Baie de Somme ◆ **la ~ des Anges** the Baie des Anges *(in Nice)* ◆ **la Grande Baie australienne** the Great Australian Bight ◆ **la ~ James** James Bay ◆ **la ~ des Cochons** the Bay of Pigs 2 *(Archit)* opening ◆ **~ vitrée** *(= fenêtre) (gén)* plate glass window; *(panoramique)* picture window

baie[3] /bɛ/ NF *(= fruit)* berry ◆ **~s rouges** red berries ◆ **~s roses** pink peppercorns

baignade /bɛɲad/ NF *(= action)* swimming; *(= lieu)* swimming place ◆ **"baignade interdite"** "no swimming", "swimming prohibited" ◆ **c'est l'heure de la ~** it's time for a swim

baigner /beɲe/ ► conjug 1 ◄ VT 1 *[+ bébé, chien]* to bath *(Brit)*, to bathe *(US)*; *[+ pieds, visage, yeux]* to bathe ◆ **visage baigné de larmes/sueur** face bathed in tears/sweat
2 *[mer, rivière]* to wash, to bathe; *[lumière]* to bathe ◆ **baigné de soleil** bathed in sunlight
VI 1 *(= tremper dans l'eau) [linge]* to soak, to lie soaking *(dans in)*; *(= tremper dans l'alcool) [fruits]* to steep, to soak *(dans in)*; ◆ **la viande baignait dans la graisse** the meat was swimming in grease ◆ **la victime baignait dans son sang** the victim was lying in a pool of blood ◆ **la ville baigne dans la brume** the town is shrouded *ou* wrapped in mist ◆ **tout baigne (dans l'huile)** * everything's hunky-dory *, everything's looking great * ◆ **ça baigne !** * great! *, couldn't be better! *
2 *(fig)* **il baigne dans la joie** his joy knows no bounds, he is bursting with joy ◆ **~ dans le mystère** *[affaire]* to be shrouded *ou* wrapped in mystery; *[personne]* to be completely mystified *ou* baffled ◆ **~ dans la culture** to be immersed in culture *ou* surrounded by culture
VPR **se baigner** *(dans la mer, une piscine)* to go swimming, to have a swim; *(dans une baignoire)* to have a bath

baigneur, -euse /bɛɲœr, øz/ NM,F swimmer, bather *(Brit)* NM *(= jouet)* baby doll

baignoire /bɛɲwar/ NF 1 *[de salle de bains]* bath(tub), tub *(US)* ◆ **~ sabot** ≈ hip-bath ◆ **~ à remous** whirlpool *ou* spa bath ◆ **faire subir à qn le supplice de la ~** to torture sb by ducking 2 *(Théât)* ground floor box, baignoire 3 *[de sous-marin]* conning tower

Baïkal /bajkal/ NM ◆ **le (lac) ~** Lake Baikal

bail (pl **baux**) /baj, bo/ NM lease ◆ **prendre à ~** to lease, to take out a lease on ◆ **donner à ~** to lease (out) ◆ **faire/passer un ~** to draw up/enter into a lease ◆ **ça fait un ~ que je ne l'ai pas vu !** * it's ages since I (last) saw him!, I haven't seen him for ages!
COMP **bail commercial** commercial lease
bail à ferme farming lease
bail à loyer (house-)letting lease *(Brit)*, rental lease *(US)*

baille /bɑj/ NF 1 *(Naut = baquet)* (wooden) bucket 2 (* *= eau*) **la ~** *(gén)* the water; *(= mer)* the drink * ◆ **tomber à la ~** to fall into the water *ou* the drink * ◆ **à la ~ !** *(= tous dans l'eau !)* everybody in!

bâillement /bɑjmɑ̃/ NM 1 *[de personne]* yawn 2 *[de col]* gaping *ou* loose fit

bailler /baje/ ► conjug 1 ◄ VT († † *ou hum*) to give ◆ **vous me la baillez belle** *ou* **bonne !** that's a tall tale!

bâiller /bɑje/ ► conjug 1 ◄ VI 1 *[personne]* to yawn ◆ **~ à s'en décrocher la mâchoire** *ou* **comme une carpe** to yawn one's head off ◆ **~ d'ennui** to yawn with *ou* from boredom 2 *(= être trop large) [col]* to gape; *[chaussure]* to be too loose 3 *(= être entrouvert) [couture, boutonnage]* to gape; *[porte]* to be ajar *ou* half-open; *(= être décousu) [chaussure]* to be split open, to gape

bailleur, bailleresse /bajœr, bajrɛs/ NM,F *[de local]* lessor ◆ **~ de fonds** backer, sponsor ◆ **~ de licence** licensor, licenser

bailli /baji/ NM bailiff

bailliage /bajaʒ/ NM bailiwick

bâillon /bɑjɔ̃/ NM *(lit, fig)* gag ◆ **mettre un ~ à qn** to gag sb

bâillonner /bɑjɔne/ ► conjug 1 ◄ VT *[+ personne]* to gag; *[+ presse, opposition, opinion]* to gag, to muzzle

bain /bɛ̃/ NM 1 *(dans une baignoire)* bath; *(dans une piscine, la mer)* swim ◆ **prendre un ~** *(dans une baignoire)* to have a bath; *(dans la mer, une piscine)* to have a swim, to take a dip ◆ **~ d'algues/de boue** seaweed/mud bath ◆ **~ de sang** blood bath ◆ **ce séjour à la campagne fut pour elle un ~ de fraîcheur** *ou* **de jouvence** that stay in the country put new life into her *ou* revitalized her
2 *(= liquide)* bath(water); *(Chim, Photo)* bath ◆ **~ (de teinture)** dye bath ◆ **~ de fixateur/de révélateur** *(Photo)* fixing/developing bath
3 *(= récipient, baignoire)* bath(tub), tub *(US)*; *[de teinturier]* vat
4 *(= piscine)* **petit/grand ~** shallow/deep end ◆ **~s** *(= lieu)* baths
5 *(locutions)*
◆ **dans le + bain** * ◆ **nous sommes tous dans le même ~** we're all in the same boat ◆ **tu seras vite dans le ~** you'll soon pick it up *ou* get the hang of it * *ou* find your feet *(Brit)* ◆ **mettre qn dans le ~** *(= informer)* to put sb in the picture; *(= compromettre)* to incriminate sb, to implicate sb ◆ **en avouant, il nous a tous mis dans le ~** by owning up, he's involved us all (in it) *ou* mixed us all up in it ◆ **se (re)mettre dans le ~** to get (back) into the swing of things
COMP **bain de bouche** *(= liquide)* mouthwash, oral rinse ◆ **faire des ~s de bouche** to use a mouthwash *ou* an oral rinse
bain de foule walkabout ◆ **prendre un ~ de foule** to mingle with the crowd, to go on a walkabout
bain linguistique *ou* **de langue** ◆ **il n'y a rien de tel que le ~ linguistique** *ou* **de langue pour apprendre l'anglais** there's nothing like total immersion as a way of learning English
bains de mer sea bathing *(Brit) ou* swimming
bain moussant bubble *ou* foam bath
bain d'œil *ou* **oculaire** *(= soin)* eye bath; *(= liquide)* eyewash
bain de pieds foot-bath
bains publics (public) baths
bain à remous whirlpool *ou* spa bath
bains romains Roman baths
bain de siège sitz bath ◆ **prendre un ~ de siège** to have a sitz bath
bain de soleil *(= corsage)* sun top, halter ◆ **robe ~ de soleil** sun dress ◆ **prendre un ~ de soleil** to sunbathe ◆ **les ~s de soleil lui sont déconseillés** he has been advised against sunbathing
bain turc Turkish bath
bain de vapeur steam bath

bain-marie (pl **bains-maries**) /bɛ̃mari/ NM (hot water in) double boiler, bain-marie ◆ **faire chauffer au ~** *[+ sauce]* to heat in a bain-marie *ou* a double boiler; *[+ boîte de conserve]* to immerse in boiling water

bains-douches /bɛ̃duʃ/ NMPL ◆ **~ municipaux** public baths (with showers)

baïonnette /bajɔnɛt/ NF *(Élec, Mil)* bayonet ◆ **charger ~ au canon** to charge with fixed bayonets; → **ampoule, douille**

baisable ** /bɛzabl/ ADJ fuckable ** ◆ **elle est tout à fait ~** I'd like to give her one **

baise ** /bɛz/ NF screwing ** ◆ **il ne pense qu'à la ~** all he ever thinks about is sex ◆ **une bonne ~** a good screw ** *ou* fuck **

baise-en-ville * /bɛzɑ̃vil/ NM INV overnight bag

baisemain /bɛzmɛ̃/ NM ◆ **il lui fit le ~** he kissed her hand ◆ **le ~ ne se pratique plus** it is no longer the custom to kiss a woman's hand

baisement /bɛzmɑ̃/ NM kissing ◆ **~ de main** kissing of hands

baiser[1] /beze/ NM kiss ◆ **gros ~** big kiss ◆ **un ~ rapide (sur la joue)** a quick peck (on the cheek) ◆ **~ d'adieu** parting kiss ◆ **bons ~s** *(en fin de lettre)* love ◆ **~ de paix** kiss of peace ◆ **~ de Judas** *(Bible)* kiss of Judas; *(= trahison)* Judas kiss ◆ **donner** *ou* **faire un ~ à qn** to give sb a kiss ◆ **envoyer un ~ à qn** to blow a kiss to sb

baiser[2] /beze/ ► conjug 1 ◄ VT 1 *(frm) [+ main, visage, sol]* to kiss 2 (** *: sexuellement*) to screw **, to lay **, to fuck ** ◆ **c'est une mal(-)baisée** *(péj)* she could do with a good lay ** 3 (** *= tromper, vaincre*) to have *, to screw ** ◆ **il a été baisé, il s'est fait ~** he was really had *, he really got screwed ** 4 (** *= comprendre*) **ses histoires, on y baise rien** you can't understand a fucking ** *ou* bloody ** *(Brit)* thing of what he says VI (** *: sexuellement*) to screw **, to fuck ** ◆ **il/elle baise bien** he's/she's a good fuck ** *ou* lay **

baiseur, -euse ** /bɛzœr, øz/ NM,F ◆ **c'est un sacré ~** *(actif)* he's always at it **; *(doué)* he's a really good screw **, he's really good in bed

baisse /bɛs/ NF *[de température, prix, niveau, pouvoir d'achat]* fall, drop *(de in)*; *[de baromètre, pression]* fall; *(Bourse)* fall; *[de popularité]* decline, drop *(de in)*; ◆ **~ de l'activité économique** downturn *ou* downswing in the economy ◆ **"baisse sur les légumes"** *(par surproduction)* "vegetables down in price"; *(en réclame)* "special offer on vegetables" ◆ **sans ~ de salaire** without salary cuts, without lowering salaries

◆ **à la baisse** ◆ **être à la ~** *(Bourse)* to be falling ◆ **jouer à la ~** *(Bourse)* to play for a fall, to go a bear ◆ **réviser** *ou* **revoir les chiffres à la ~** to revise figures downwards

◆ **être en baisse** *[prix, chômage, actions]* to be going down, to be dropping; *[niveau]* to be dropping; *[demande]* to be slackening; *[natalité]* to be falling; *[popularité]* to be declining *ou* on the wane ◆ **les affaires sont en ~** there's a slump in business, business is on a downturn ◆ **son moral est en ~** his morale is getting lower and lower ◆ **la production est en ~ de 8% par rapport à l'année dernière** production is 8% down on last year

baisser /bese/ ▸ conjug 1 ◂ **VT** 1 *[+ objet]* to lower; *[+ store]* to lower, to pull down; *[+ vitre]* to lower, to let down; *(à la manivelle)* to wind down; *[+ col]* to turn down; *(Théât)* *[+ rideau]* to lower, to ring down ◆ **baisse la branche pour que je puisse l'attraper** pull the branch down so (that) I can reach it ◆ **~ pavillon** *(Naut)* to lower *ou* strike the flag; *(fig)* to show the white flag, to give in ◆ **une fois le rideau baissé** *(Théât)* once the curtain was down

2 *[+ main, bras]* to lower ◆ **~ la tête** to lower *ou* bend one's head; *(de chagrin, honte)* to hang *ou* bow one's head; *[plantes]* to wilt, to droop ◆ **baisse la tête, il y a une poutre** watch *ou* mind your head, there's a beam in the way ◆ **~ les yeux** to look down, to lower one's eyes ◆ **elle entra, les yeux baissés** she came in with downcast eyes ◆ **faire ~ les yeux à qn** to outstare sb, to stare sb out ◆ **~ le nez** * *(de honte)* to hang one's head ◆ **~ le nez dans son livre** * to bury one's nose in one's book ◆ **~ le nez dans son assiette** * to bend over one's plate ◆ **~ les bras** *(fig)* to give up, to throw in the towel * *ou* sponge *

3 *[+ chauffage, éclairage, radio, son]* to turn down; *[+ voix]* to lower ◆ **~ le feu** *(Culin)* turn down *ou* lower the heat; → **ton²**

4 *[+ prix]* to lower, to bring down, to reduce ◆ **faire ~ la tension/le chômage** to reduce tension/unemployment

5 *[+ mur]* to lower

VI 1 *[température, prix]* to fall, to drop, to go down; *[baromètre]* to fall; *[pression]* *(Bourse)* to drop, to fall; *[marée]* to go out, to ebb; *[eaux]* to subside, to go down; *[réserves, provisions]* to run *ou* get low; *[popularité]* to decline; *[soleil]* to go down, to sink; → **estime**

2 *[vue, mémoire, forces, santé]* to fail, to dwindle; *[talent]* to decline, to wane ◆ **le jour baisse** the light is failing *ou* dwindling ◆ **il a beaucoup baissé ces derniers temps** he has really gone downhill recently

VPR se baisser *(pour ramasser)* to bend down, to stoop; *(pour éviter)* to duck ◆ **il n'y a qu'à se ~ (pour les ramasser)** *(lit)* they're lying thick on the ground; *(fig)* they're there for the taking

baissier, -ière /besje, jɛʀ/ *(Bourse)* **ADJ** *[marché, tendance]* bear *(épith)*, bearish *(épith)* **NM** bear

bajoues /baʒu/ **NFPL** *[d'animal]* cheeks, pouches; *[de personne]* jowls, heavy cheeks

bakchich /bakʃiʃ/ **NM** baksheesh

bakélite ® /bakelit/ **NF** Bakelite ®

bakongo /bakɔ̃go/ **ADJ** Bakongo **NMF Bakongo** Bakongo ◆ **les Bakongos** the Bakongo (people)

Bakou /baku/ **N** Baku

BAL /bal/ (abrév de **boîte aux lettres**) **NF** mailbox

bal (pl **bals**) /bal/ **NM** *(= réunion)* dance; *(habillé)* ball; *(= lieu)* dance hall ◆ **aller au ~** to go dancing ◆ **ouvrir le ~** *(lit)* to lead *ou* open the dancing; *(fig)* to make the first move ◆ **mener** *ou* **conduire le ~** *(fig)* to call the tune *ou* the shots *, to say what goes *

COMP bal champêtre open-air dance
bal costumé fancy dress ball *(Brit)*, costume ball *(US)*
bal des débutantes *ou* **des débs** * coming-out ball
bal masqué masked ball
bal musette popular dance *(to the accordion)*
bal populaire *ou* **public** ≃ local dance *ou* hop * †
bal du 14 juillet Bastille Day dance *(free and open to all)*; → LE QUATORZE JUILLET

balade * /balad/ **NF** *(à pied)* walk, stroll; *(en voiture)* drive, ride; *(à vélo, moto)* ride; *(en bateau)* ride, trip ◆ **être en ~** to be out for a walk *(ou* a drive *etc)* ◆ **faire une ~, aller en ~** to go for a walk *(ou* a drive *etc)* ◆ **j'ai fait une ~ à ski** I went skiing *ou* for a ski

balader * /balade/ ▸ conjug 1 ◂ **VT** 1 *(= traîner)* *[+ chose]* to trail around, to carry about; *[+ personne]* to trail around

2 *(= promener)* *[+ personne]* to take for a walk; *[+ animal]* to walk, to take for a walk; *(en voiture)* to take for a drive *ou* a ride

3 *(= malmener)* **elle s'est fait ~ pendant le premier set** *(Tennis)* her opponent had her running all over the place in the first set ◆ **ils nous ont baladés pendant la première mi-temps** *(Rugby, Ftbl)* they walked all over us * in the first half

VPR se balader 1 *(à pied)* to go for a walk *ou* a stroll; *(en voiture)* to go for a drive *ou* ride *ou* run; *(à vélo, moto)* to go for a ride; *(en bateau)* to go for a ride; *(= traîner)* to traipse round ◆ **pendant qu'ils se baladaient** while they were out for a walk *(ou* drive *etc)* ◆ **aller se ~ en Afrique** to go touring round Africa ◆ **la lettre s'est baladée de bureau en bureau** the letter was sent *ou* shuttled around from one office to another

2 *(= être en désordre)* **des câbles se baladent partout** there are cables trailing all over the place ◆ **mes cassettes se sont baladées dans la valise** my tapes got knocked around my suitcase

3 *(* = être très à l'aise)* **il s'est baladé en chimie** he sailed through his chemistry exam

baladeur, -euse /baladœʀ, øz/ **ADJ** wandering, roving ◆ **avoir la main baladeuse** *ou* **les mains baladeuses** to have wandering *ou* groping * hands ◆ **un micro ~ circulait dans le public** a microphone circulated round the audience **NM** *(= magnétophone)* Walkman ®, personal stereo **NF baladeuse** *(= lampe)* inspection lamp

baladin † /baladɛ̃/ **NM** wandering entertainer *ou* actor, strolling player †

balafon /balafɔ̃/ **NM** balafon, African xylophone

balafre /balɑfʀ/ **NF** *(= blessure au visage)* gash; *(intentionnelle)* slash; *(= cicatrice)* scar

balafrer /balɑfʀe/ ▸ conjug 1 ◂ **VT** 1 *(= blesser au visage)* to gash; *(intentionnellement)* to slash, to scar ◆ **il s'est balafré** he gashed his face ◆ **une cicatrice lui balafrait la joue** he had a scar running down his cheek 2 *(= enlaidir)* *[+ ville, paysage]* to scar; *[+ vitrine, bâtiment]* to deface ◆ **de grandes lézardes balafrent les édifices** the buildings are scarred *ou* disfigured by huge cracks

balai /balɛ/ **NM** 1 *(gén)* broom, brush; *[de bruyère, genêt]* broom; *(Élec)* brush; *[d'essuie-glace]* blade ◆ **passer le ~** to sweep the floor, to give the floor a sweep ◆ **du ~!** * beat it! *, clear off! *

◆ **coup de balai** ◆ **donner un coup de ~** *(lit)* to give the floor a (quick) sweep, to sweep the floor; *(fig)* to make a clean sweep ◆ **il y a eu un coup de ~ dans la société** they've made a clean sweep in the company, there have been across-the-board redundancies in the company 2 *(‡ = an)* **il a 80 ~s** he's 80 (years old) 3 *(Mus)* (wire) brush

COMP balai de crin horsehair brush
balai éponge squeezy *(Brit)* *ou* sponge *(US)* mop
balai mécanique carpet sweeper

balai-brosse (pl **balais-brosses**) /balɛbʀɔs/ **NM** (long-handled) scrubbing brush

balaise ‡ /balɛz/ **ADJ** ⇒ **balèze**

balalaïka /balalaika/ **NF** balalaika

balance¹ /balɑ̃s/ **NF** 1 *(gén)* scales; *(à deux plateaux)* pair of scales; *(à bascule)* weighing machine; *(pour salle de bains)* (bathroom) scales; *(pour cuisine)* (kitchen) scales; *(Chim, Phys)* balance ◆ **monter sur la ~** to get on the scales

2 *(locutions)* **tenir la ~ égale entre deux rivaux** to hold the scales even between two rivals ◆ **être en ~** *[proposition, sort]* to hang in the balance; *[candidat]* to be under consideration ◆ **mettre dans la** *ou* **en ~ le pour et le contre** to weigh up the pros and cons ◆ **mettre tout son poids dans la ~** to use one's power to tip the scales ◆ **si on met dans la ~ son ancienneté** if you take his seniority into account

3 *(Écon, Pol, Élec)* balance ◆ **~ de l'actif et du passif** balance of assets and liabilities

4 *(Astron)* **la Balance** Libra, the Balance ◆ **être (de la) Balance** to be (a) Libra *ou* a Libran

5 *(Pêche)* drop-net

COMP balance automatique electronic scales
balance commerciale *ou* **du commerce** balance of trade
balance des comptes balance of payments
balance électronique electronic scales
balance des forces balance of power
balance de ménage kitchen scales
balance des paiements ⇒ **balance des comptes**
balance des pouvoirs balance of power
balance de précision precision balance
balance (de) Roberval (Roberval's) balance
balance romaine steelyard

balance² /balɑ̃s/ **NF** *(arg Crime)* stool pigeon *, grass ‡ *(Brit)*, fink ‡ *(US)*

balancé, e /balɑ̃se/ (ptp de **balancer**) **ADJ** ◆ **phrase bien/harmonieusement ~e** well-turned/nicely balanced phrase ◆ **elle est bien ~e** * she's well put together *, she's got a good chassis * *(US)*

balancelle /balɑ̃sɛl/ **NF** couch hammock *(Brit)*, glider (US)

balancement /balɑ̃smɑ̃/ **NM** 1 *(= mouvement)* *[de corps]* sway(ing); *[de bras]* swing(ing); *[de bateau]* rocking, motion; *[de hanches, branches]* swaying 2 *(Littérat, Mus)* balance

balancer /balɑ̃se/ ▸ conjug 3 ◂ **VT** 1 *[+ chose, bras, jambe]* to swing; *[+ bateau, bébé]* to rock; *(sur une balançoire)* to swing, to push ◆ **veux-tu que je te balance ?** do you want me to push you *ou* give you a push? ◆ **le vent balançait les branches** the wind rocked the branches *ou* set the branches swaying

2 *(* = lancer)* to fling, to chuck * ◆ **balance-moi mon crayon** throw *ou* chuck * me over my pencil *(Brit)*, toss me my pencil ◆ **~ qch à la tête de qn** to fling *ou* chuck * sth at sb's head

3 *(* = dire)* *[+ méchanceté, insanités]* to hurl ◆ **il m'a balancé ça en pleine figure** he just came out with it * straight to my face ◆ **qu'est-ce qu'il leur a balancé !** he really let them have it! *

4 *(* = se débarrasser de)* *[+ vieux meubles]* to chuck out * *ou* away *, to toss out ◆ **balance ça à la poubelle** chuck it * in the bin *(Brit)* *ou* the trash *(US)* ◆ **j'ai envie de tout ~** *(travail)* I feel like throwing *ou* chucking * it all in ◆ **~ qn** *(= renvoyer)* to give sb the boot ‡ *ou* the push ‡ *(Brit)*, to chuck sb out * ◆ **il s'est fait ~ de son club** he got kicked out * *ou* chucked out * of his club

5 *(= équilibrer)* *[+ compte, phrases, paquets]* to balance ◆ **~ le pour et le contre** † to weigh (up) the pros and cons ◆ **tout bien balancé** *(frm)* all things considered

⑥ *(arg Crime = dénoncer)* to finger‡, to grass on‡

VI ① *(† = hésiter)* to waver, to hesitate, to dither ◆ **entre les deux mon cœur balance** *(hum)* I'm torn between the two

② *(= osciller) [objet]* to swing

③ *(* = être rythmé)* **ça balance !** it's rocking! *ou* swinging!

VPR **se balancer** ① *(= osciller) [bras, jambes]* to swing; *[bateau]* to rock; *[branches]* to sway; *[personne] (sur une balançoire)* to swing, to have a swing; *(sur une bascule)* to seesaw, to play on a seesaw ◆ **se ~ sur ses jambes** to sway about, to sway from side to side ◆ **ne te balance pas sur ta chaise !** don't tip back on your chair! ◆ **se ~ sur ses ancres** to ride at anchor

② *(* = se jeter)* to throw o.s. ◆ **il s'est balancé du 10e étage** he threw himself from the 10th floor

③ ◆ **s'en ~** *(* = s'en ficher)* **je m'en balance** I don't give a damn* *ou* darn* *(US)* (about it), I couldn't care less (about it)

balancier /balɑ̃sje/ **NM** *[de pendule]* pendulum; *[de montre]* balance wheel; *[d'équilibriste]* (balancing) pole; *[de bateau]* outrigger

balançoire /balɑ̃swaʀ/ **NF** *(suspendue)* swing; *(sur pivot)* seesaw, teeter-totter *(US)* ◆ **faire de la ~** to have a go on a *(ou* the) swing

balayage /balɛjaʒ/ **NM** *(= nettoyage)* sweeping; *(Élec, Radio)* scanning; *[d'essuie-glace]* wipe; *[de cheveux]* highlighting ◆ **se faire faire un ~** to have highlights (put in one's hair), to have one's hair highlighted

balayer /baleje/ ▸ conjug 8 ◂ **VT** ① *(= ramasser) [+ poussière, feuilles mortes]* to sweep up, to brush up ② *(= nettoyer) [+ pièce]* to sweep (out); *[+ trottoir]* to sweep; *[+ pare-brise]* to wipe ◆ **le vent balayait la plaine** the wind swept across *ou* scoured the plain ◆ **ils feraient mieux de ~ devant leur porte** *(fig)* they should clean up their own back yard ③ *(= chasser) [+ feuilles mortes]* to sweep away; *[+ soucis, obstacles]* to brush aside, to sweep away; *[+ objections]* to brush aside ◆ **l'armée balayait tout sur son passage** the army swept aside all that lay in its path ◆ **le gouvernement a été balayé** the government was swept out of office ④ *(= parcourir) [phares]* to sweep (across); *[vague, regard]* to sweep over; *(Élec, Radio) [radar]* to scan; *[tir]* to sweep (across)

balayette /balɛjɛt/ **NF** small (hand)brush

balayeur, -euse /balɛjœʀ, øz/ **NM,F** roadsweeper *(Brit)*, streetsweeper *(US)* **NF** **balayeuse** *(= machine)* roadsweeping *(Brit) ou* streetsweeping *(US)* machine, roadsweeper *(Brit)*, streetsweeper *(US)*

balayures /balejyʀ/ **NFPL** sweepings

balbutiant, e /balbysjɑ̃, ɑ̃t/ **ADJ** *[voix]* stammering; *[discours]* hesitant; *[science]* in its infancy *(attrib)* ◆ **une démocratie ~e** a fledgling democracy

balbutiement /balbysimɑ̃/ **NM** *(= paroles confuses)* stammering, mumbling; *[de bébé]* babbling ◆ **les premiers ~s de l'enfant** the child's first faltering attempts at speech ◆ **~s** *(= débuts)* beginnings ◆ **cette science en est à ses premiers ~s** this science is still in its infancy

balbutier /balbysje/ ▸ conjug 7 ◂ **VI** *[bègue, personne ivre]* to stammer; *[bébé]* to babble **VT** to stammer (out), to falter out

balbuzard /balbyzaʀ/ **NM** ◆ **~ (pêcheur)** osprey

balcon /balkɔ̃/ **NM** *(Constr)* balcony ◆ **(premier) ~** *(Théât)* dress *ou* lower circle, mezzanine *(US)* ◆ **deuxième ~** upper circle, balcony *(Brit)* ◆ **loge/fauteuil de ~** box/seat in the dress circle; → **monde**

balconnet /balkɔnɛ/ **NM** ◆ **(soutien-gorge à) ~** half-cup bra

baldaquin /baldakɛ̃/ **NM** *(= dais)* baldaquin, canopy; *[de lit]* tester, canopy; → **lit**

Bâle /bɑl/ **N** Basle, Basel

Baléares /baleaʀ/ **NFPL** ◆ **les (îles) ~** the Balearic Islands, the Balearics ◆ **en vacances aux ~** ≃ on holiday in Majorca *(ou Minorca ou Ibiza)*

baleine /balɛn/ **NF** ① *(= animal)* whale ◆ **~ blanche/bleue/franche** white/blue/right whale ◆ **~ à bosse** humpback whale ◆ **rire** *ou* **se marrer comme une ~*** to laugh like a drain* ② *(= fanon)* (piece of) whalebone, baleen ◆ **soutien-gorge à/sans ~s** underwired/unwired bra ◆ **~ de corset** (corset-)stay ◆ **~ de parapluie** umbrella rib

baleiné, e /balene/ **ADJ** *[col]* stiffened; *[corset]* boned; *[soutien-gorge] (gén)* boned; *(sous les bonnets)* underwired

baleineau (pl **baleineaux**) /baleno/ **NM** whale calf

baleinier, -ière /balenje, jɛʀ/ **ADJ** whaling **NM** *(= pêcheur, bateau)* whaler **NF** **baleinière** whaler, whale *ou* whaling boat

balèze‡ /balɛz/ **ADJ** *(= musclé)* brawny, strapping *(épith)*; *(= excellent)* terrific*, great* *(en* at) **NMF** strapping fellow *(ou woman etc)*

Bali /bali/ **N** Bali

balinais, e /balinɛ, ɛz/ **ADJ** Balinese **NM,F** **Balinais(e)** Balinese

balisage /balizaʒ/ **NM** ① *(= balises) (en mer)* beacons, buoys; *(sur piste d'atterrissage)* beacons, runway lights; *(sur route)* (road) signs; *(sur piste de ski)* markers ② *(= pose de balises) (en mer)* marking with buoys; *[de chemin de randonnée, piste de ski]* marking out ③ *(Ordin) [de texte]* tagging, marking up

balise[1] /baliz/ **NF** ① *(Naut)* beacon, (marker) buoy; *(Aviat)* beacon, runway light; *(Aut)* (road) marker; *(Ski)* marker ◆ **~ radio** radio beacon ◆ **~ de détresse** distress beacon ② *(Ordin)* tag

balise[2] /baliz/ **NF** *(= fruit)* canna fruit

baliser /balize/ ▸ conjug 1 ◂ **VT** ① *(Naut)* to mark out with beacons *ou* buoys; *(Aviat)* to mark out with beacons *ou* lights; *[+ sentier, piste de ski]* to mark out ◆ **sentier balisé** waymarked footpath ② *(fig)* ◆ **~ son avenir** to map out one's future ◆ **~ le terrain** to prepare the ground ◆ **~ le chemin** to pave the way ◆ **nos chercheurs avancent sur un terrain déjà bien balisé** our researchers are exploring well-charted territory ◆ **un marché bien balisé** *(Écon)* a well-defined market ③ *(Ordin) [+ texte]* to tag, to mark up **VI** *(‡ = avoir peur)* to have the jitters* ◆ **il balise pour son examen** he's freaking out‡ *ou* he's really worked up about his exam

baliseur /balizœʀ/ **NM** *(= personne)* ≃ (Trinity House) buoy-keeper; *(= bateau)* ≃ Trinity House boat

balistique /balistik/ **ADJ** ballistic ◆ **expertise ~** ballistic test **NF** ballistics *(sg)*

baliveau (pl **baliveaux**) /balivo/ **NM** *(= arbre)* sapling; *(Constr)* scaffold(ing) pole

baliverne /balivɛʀn/ **NF** *(= propos)* fatuous remark ◆ **dire des ~s** to talk nonsense *ou* twaddle ◆ **s'amuser à des ~s** to fool around ◆ **~(s) !** † balderdash! †, fiddlesticks! †

balkanique /balkanik/ **ADJ** Balkan ◆ **les États ~s** the Balkan States

balkanisation /balkanizasjɔ̃/ **NF** *(Pol)* Balkanization; *(fig)* balkanization

balkaniser /balkanize/ ▸ conjug 1 ◂ **VT** *(Pol)* to Balkanize; *(fig)* to balkanize

Balkans /balkɑ̃/ **NMPL** ◆ **les ~** the Balkans

ballade /balad/ **NF** *(= poème court, Mus)* ballade; *(= poème long)* ballad

ballant, e /balɑ̃, ɑ̃t/ **ADJ** ◆ **les bras ~s** with arms dangling, with swinging arms ◆ **ne reste pas là, les bras ~s*** don't just stand there looking helpless ◆ **les jambes ~es** with legs dangling **NM** *(= mou) [de câble]* slack, play; *[de chargement]* sway, roll ◆ **avoir du ~** *[câble]* to be slack; *[chargement]* to be slack *ou* loose ◆ **donner du ~ à une corde** to give some slack *ou* play to a rope

ballast /balast/ **NM** *(Rail)* ballast, roadbed *(US)*; *(Naut)* ballast tank

balle[1] /bal/ **NF** ① *(= projectile)* bullet ◆ **~ dum-dum/explosive/traçante** dum-dum/explosive/tracer bullet ◆ **~ en caoutchouc/de plastique** rubber/plastic bullet ◆ **~ à blanc** blank ◆ **~ perdue** stray bullet ◆ **tirer à ~s réelles** to fire live bullets ◆ **finir avec douze ~s dans la peau*** to end up in front of a firing squad ◆ **prendre une ~ dans la peau*** to get shot *ou* plugged‡ ◆ **tué par ~s** shot dead ◆ **se tirer une ~ dans le pied** *(fig)* to shoot o.s. in the foot

② *(Sport)* ball ◆ **~ de ping-pong/de golf** table tennis/golf ball ◆ **jouer à la ~** to play (with a) ball ◆ **à toi la ~ !** catch! ◆ **la ~ est dans leur camp** *(fig)* the ball is in their court; → **saisir**

③ *(Sport = coup)* shot, ball ◆ **c'est une belle ~** that's a nice ball *ou* a good shot ◆ **faire des** *ou* **quelques ~s** *(Tennis, Ping-Pong)* to knock the ball around a bit, to have a knock-up *(Brit)* ◆ **~ de jeu/match/set** *(Tennis)* game/match/set point ◆ **~ de service** service ball ◆ **deuxième ~** second serve *ou* service ◆ **c'est une ~ de 3 jeux à 2** it's game point at 2 games all

④ *(* = franc)* franc

balle[2] /bal/ **NF** *[de graine]* husk, chaff

balle[3] /bal/ **NF** *[de coton, laine]* bale

balle[4]* /bal/ **NF** chubby face ◆ **il a une bonne ~** he's got a jolly face

baller /bale/ ▸ conjug 1 ◂ **VI** *[bras, jambes]* to dangle, to hang loosely; *[tête]* to hang; *[chargement]* to be slack *ou* loose

ballerine /bal(ə)ʀin/ **NF** *(= danseuse)* ballerina, ballet dancer; *(= chaussure)* ballet shoe

ballet /balɛ/ **NM** ① *(= spectacle)* ballet; *(= musique)* ballet music ◆ **les Ballets russes** *(= compagnie)* the Russian Ballet ◆ **~ aquatique** water ballet ◆ **~s roses/bleus** *(fig) sexual orgies organized by paedophiles* ② ◆ **~ diplomatique** flurry of diplomatic activity

ballon[1] /balɔ̃/ **NM** ① *(gén)* ball ◆ **~ de football** football *(Brit)*, soccer ball *(US)* ◆ **~ de rugby** rugby ball ◆ **~ de basket** basketball ◆ **~ de volley** volleyball ◆ **jouer au ~** to play (with a) ball ◆ **le ~ rond** *(= football)* soccer ◆ **le ~ ovale** *(= rugby)* rugby, rugger* *(Brit)* ◆ **~ en** *ou* **de baudruche** balloon ◆ **avoir le ~**‡ *(= être enceinte)* to have a bun in the oven*, to be up the spout* *(Brit)*

② *(= aérostat)* balloon ◆ **monter en ~** to go up in a balloon ◆ **voyager en ~** to travel by balloon

③ *(= verre) (à vin)* round wineglass; *(à cognac)* balloon *ou* brandy glass ◆ **un ~ de rouge*** a glass of red wine

④ *(* = Alcootest)* **souffler dans le ~** to take a breath test *ou* Breathalyzer test ® ◆ **soufflez dans le ~, s'il vous plaît** blow in(to) the bag, please

⑤ *(Chim)* balloon

COMP **ballon de barrage** barrage balloon

ballon captif captive balloon

ballon dirigeable airship

ballon d'eau chaude hot-water tank

ballon d'essai *(Météo)* pilot balloon; *(= test)* experiment *(to test reaction)*, trial balloon *(US)* ◆ **lancer un ~ d'essai** *(fig)* to put out feelers, to fly a kite *(Brit)*, to send out a trial balloon *(US)*

ballon d'oxygène *(lit)* oxygen bottle; *(fig)* lifesaver ◆ **cet argent a apporté un ~ d'oxygène à l'entreprise** the money has given the company a much-needed shot in the arm

ballon² /balɔ̃/ NM *(Géog)* rounded mountain in the *Vosges* ◆ **le Ballon d'Alsace** the Ballon d'Alsace

ballonné, e /balɔne/ (ptp de **ballonner**) ADJ *[ventre]* bloated, distended ◆ **je suis** *ou* **je me sens ~, j'ai le ventre ~** I feel bloated

ballonnements /balɔnmɑ̃/ NMPL ◆ **avoir des ~s** *[personne]* to feel bloated; *[animal]* to have bloat

ballonner /balɔne/ ▸ conjug 1 ◂ VT *[+ ventre]* to distend; *[+ personne]* to blow out; *(Vét) [+ animal]* to cause bloat in

ballonnet /balɔnɛ/ NM *(= petit ballon)* (small) balloon; *(en chirurgie)* balloon

ballon-panier /balɔ̃panje/ NM INV *(Can)* basketball

ballon-sonde (pl **ballons-sondes**) /balɔ̃sɔ̃d/ NM meteorological *ou* weather *ou* pilot balloon

ballon-volant /balɔ̃vɔlɑ̃/ NM INV *(Can)* volleyball

ballot /balo/ NM 1 *(= paquet)* bundle, package 2 *(* = nigaud)* nitwit*, dumdum* ADJ silly ◆ **tu es/c'est ~ de l'avoir oublié** you're/it's a bit silly *ou* daft *(Brit)* to have forgotten it

ballotin /balɔtɛ̃/ NM ◆ **~ de chocolats** (small punnet-shaped) box of chocolates

ballottage /balɔtaʒ/ NM *(Pol)* ◆ **il y a ~** there will have to be a second ballot, people will have to vote again ◆ **M. Dupont est en ~** Mr Dupont has to stand again at *(Brit) ou* run again on *(US)* the second ballot ◆ **être en ~ favorable** to stand a very good chance of winning at the second ballot

ballottement /balɔtmɑ̃/ NM *[d'objet]* banging about, rolling around; *[de tête, membres]* lolling; *[de train]* jolting; *[de poitrine]* bouncing; *[de bateau]* tossing, bobbing; *[de personne]* shaking

ballotter /balɔte/ ▸ conjug 1 ◂ VI *[objet]* to roll around, to bang about; *[tête, membres]* to loll; *[poitrine]* to bounce; *[bateau]* to toss, to bob about; *[train]* to jolt along VT *(gén pass)* 1 *(= secouer) [+ personne]* to shake about, to jolt; *[+ bateau]* to toss (about) ◆ **on est ballotté dans ce train** you get shaken about *ou* thrown about in this train 2 *(= tirailler)* **ballotté par des choix difficiles** torn between difficult choices 3 *(= déplacer sans ménagement)* to shunt (around) ◆ **cet enfant a été ballotté entre plusieurs écoles** this child has been shifted around *ou* shunted around from school to school

ballottine /balɔtin/ NF ≃ meat loaf *(made with poultry)*

ball-trap (pl **ball-traps**) /baltʀap/ NM *(= lieu)* shooting ground; *(= sport)* clay-pigeon shooting, trap-shooting; *(avec 2 cibles)* skeet-shooting; *(= machine)* trap

balluchon /balyʃɔ̃/ NM † bundle (of clothes), belongings ◆ **faire son ~*** to pack up one's bags

balnéaire /balneɛʀ/ ADJ swimming, bathing *(Brit)*; → **station**

balnéothérapie /balneoteʀapi/ NF balneotherapy

balourd, e /baluʀ, uʀd/ ADJ *(= maladroit)* clumsy, oafish NM,F *(= lourdaud)* dolt, oaf NM *(Tech) (= déséquilibre)* unbalance

balourdise /baluʀdiz/ NF 1 *(= maladresse)* clumsiness, oafishness; *(= manque de finesse)* oafishness, doltishness 2 *(= gaffe)* blunder, boob* *(Brit)*

balsa /balza/ NM balsa (wood)

balsamier /balzamje/ NM balsam tree

balsamine /balzamin/ NF balsam

balsamique /balzamik/ ADJ balsamic

balte /balt/ ADJ *[pays, peuple]* Baltic ◆ **les pays ~s** the Baltic States

balthazar /baltazaʀ/ NM 1 *(† = banquet)* feast, banquet 2 *(= bouteille)* balthazar

baltique /baltik/ ADJ *[mer, région]* Baltic NF **Baltique** ◆ **la Baltique** the Baltic (Sea)

baluchon /balyʃɔ̃/ NM ⇒ **balluchon**

balustrade /balystʀad/ NF *(Archit)* balustrade; *(= garde-fou)* railing, handrail

balustre /balystʀ/ NM 1 *(Archit)* baluster; *[de siège]* spoke 2 ◆ **(compas à) ~** bow(-spring) compass

balzacien, -ienne /balzasjɛ̃, jɛn/ ADJ *(= qui appartient à Balzac)* of Balzac; *(= qui rappelle Balzac)* typical of Balzac

balzan, e /balzɑ̃, an/ ADJ *[cheval]* with white stockings NF **balzane** *(= tache)* white stocking

Bamako /bamako/ N Bamako

bambara /bɑ̃baʀa/ ADJ Bambara NM *(= langue)* Bambara NMF **Bambara** Bambara ◆ **les Bambaras** the Bambara (people)

bambin /bɑ̃bɛ̃/ NM small child, little kid*

bambochard, e †* /bɑ̃bɔʃaʀ, aʀd/ ADJ, NM,F ⇒ **bambocheur, -euse**

bambocher †* /bɑ̃bɔʃe/ ▸ conjug 1 ◂ VI *(= faire la noce)* to live it up*, to have a wild time

bambocheur, -euse †* /bɑ̃bɔʃœʀ, øz/ ADJ *[tempérament]* revelling NM,F *(= noceur)* reveller

bambou /bɑ̃bu/ NM *(= plante)* bamboo; *(= canne)* bamboo (walking) stick ◆ **attraper un coup de ~** † to get a touch of sunstroke* ◆ **avoir le coup de ~*** *(= être fatigué)* to be bushed* *ou* shattered* *(Brit)* ◆ **dans ce restaurant, c'est le coup de ~*** *(= prix exorbitant)* they really fleece* you in that restaurant; → **pousse**

bamboula* /bɑ̃bula/ NF ◆ **faire la ~** to live it up*, to have a wild time

bambouseraie /bɑ̃buzʀɛ/ NF bamboo plantation

ban /bɑ̃/ NM 1 *[de mariage]* **~s** banns 2 *[d'applaudissements]* round of applause; *[de tambour]* drum roll; *[de clairon]* bugle call, fanfare ◆ **faire un ~** to applaud *ou* cheer ◆ **un ~ pour Marc Durand !** *(applaudissements)* (let's have) a big hand for* *ou* a round of applause for Marc Durand!; *(acclamations)* ≃ three cheers for Marc Durand! 3 *(Hist)* proclamation 4 *(locutions)* **être/mettre au ~ de l'Empire** *(Hist)* to be banished/banish from the Empire ◆ **être/mettre au ~ de la société** to be outlawed/outlaw from society

◆ **le ban et l'arrière-ban** *(Hist)* the barons and vassals ◆ **le ~ et l'arrière-~ de sa famille/de ses amis** all of *ou* every last one of his relatives/his friends

banal¹, e¹ (mpl **banals**) /banal/ ADJ 1 *(= sans originalité) [roman, conversation, idée]* banal, trite; *[vie]* humdrum, banal; *[personne]* run-of-the-mill, ordinary ◆ **un personnage peu ~** an unusual character ◆ **ça, ce n'est pas ~ !** that's rather out of the ordinary! 2 *(= courant) [nom]* commonplace; *[incident]* everyday *(épith)*, commonplace ◆ **il n'y a rien là que de très ~** there is nothing at all unusual *ou* out of the ordinary about that ◆ **une grippe ~e** a common-or-garden case of flu ◆ **quoi de plus ~ qu'un mariage ?** what could be more mundane *ou* ordinary than a wedding? 3 *(Ordin)* general-purpose ◆ **mémoire ~e** general-purpose storage NM ◆ **haïr le ~** to hate what is banal *ou* what is trite

banal², e² (mpl **-aux**) /banal, o/ ADJ *(Hist)* ◆ **four/moulin ~** communal *ou* village oven/mill

banalement /banalmɑ̃/ ADV *[commencer, arriver]* in the most ordinary way

banalisation /banalizasjɔ̃/ NF 1 ◆ **la ~ de la violence** the way in which violence has become a feature of everyday life ◆ **la ~ des greffes** the fact that organ transplants are now quite commonplace *ou* widely practised 2 *[de campus]* opening to the police

banaliser /banalize/ ▸ conjug 1 ◂ VT 1 *[+ pratique] (= rendre courant)* to make commonplace; *(= minimiser)* to trivialize ◆ **ce qui banalise la vie quotidienne** what makes life humdrum *ou* robs life of its excitement ◆ **~ la violence** to make violence seem ordinary *ou* part of everyday life 2 *[+ campus]* to open to the police ◆ **voiture banalisée** *(Police)* unmarked police car 3 *(Rail) [+ locomotive]* to man with several crews; *[+ voie]* to make two-way VPR **se banaliser** *[pratiques]* to become commonplace; *[violence]* to become part of everyday life

banalité /banalite/ NF 1 *(= caractère) [de roman, conversation, idée]* banality, triteness; *[de vie]* banality; *[de personne]* ordinariness; *[d'incident]* triviality ◆ **d'une ~ affligeante** appallingly trite 2 *(= propos)* truism, platitude, trite remark ◆ **on a échangé des ~s** we made small talk, we talked about this and that

banane /banan/ NF 1 *(= fruit)* banana ◆ **~ plantain** plantain 2 *[de moteur]* overrider 3 *(Coiffure)* quiff *(Brit)*, pompadour *(US)*; → **chignon** 4 *(arg Mil)* medal, gong* *(Brit)* 5 *(arg Aviat)* twin-rotor helicopter, chopper* 6 *(= sac)* hip bag, waist-bag *(Brit)*, bumbag* *(Brit)*, fanny pack* *(US)* 7 *(Élec)* **(fiche-)~** banana plug 8 *(* = idiot)* **~ !** you silly twit!*, you dork!* *(US)* 9 ◆ **avoir la ~*** to be on top form

bananer* /banane/ ▸ conjug 1 ◂ VT ◆ **il s'est fait ~** *(= disputer)* he got told off*; *(= battre)* he got thrashed*

bananeraie /bananʀɛ/ NF banana plantation

bananier, -ière /bananje, jɛʀ/ NM 1 *(= arbre)* banana tree 2 *(= bateau)* banana boat ADJ banana *(épith)*

banc /bɑ̃/ NM 1 *(= siège)* seat, bench ◆ **~ public** park bench ◆ **~ (d'école)** (school) bench ◆ **nous sommes connus sur les ~s de l'école** we've known each other since we were at school together ◆ **les ~s de l'opposition** *(Pol)* the opposition benches

2 *(Géol, Géog) (= couche)* layer, bed; *[de coraux]* reef ◆ **~ de vase** mudbank ◆ **~ de brouillard** *(gén)* fog patch; *(en mer)* fog bank ◆ **~ de brume** bank of mist ◆ **~ de glace** ice floe ◆ **les ~s de Terre-Neuve** the Grand Banks of Newfoundland

3 *[de poissons]* school, shoal *(Brit)*

4 *(= établi)* (work) bench

COMP **banc des accusés** dock, bar ◆ **être au ~ des accusés** to be in the dock

banc des avocats bar

banc d'église pew

banc d'essai *(Tech)* test bed; *(fig)* testing ground, test bed ◆ **mettre qch au ~ d'essai** to test sth out

banc d'huîtres *(= huîtrière)* oyster bed; *(de restaurant)* oyster display

banc des ministres ≃ government front bench

banc de musculation weight *ou* exercise bench

banc de nage thwart

banc de neige *(Can)* snowdrift, snowbank

banc de sable sandbank, sandbar

banc des témoins *(Jur)* witness box *(Brit)*, witness stand *(US)*

banc de touche (substitutes') bench

bancable /bɑ̃kabl/ ADJ bankable

bancaire /bɑ̃kɛʀ/ ADJ bank; *[réseau, groupe]* banking, bank; *[système, commission]* banking ◆ **chèque ~** bank cheque *(Brit) ou* check *(US)*

bancal, e (mpl **bancals**) /bɑ̃kal/ ADJ 1 *[table, chaise]* wobbly, rickety 2 *[idée, raisonnement]* shaky, unsound 3 *[personne] (= boiteux)* lame; *(= aux jambes arquées)* bandy-legged

bancarisé, e /bɑ̃kaʀize/ ADJ *(Fin) [population, pays]* with banking facilities ◆ **pays peu/fortement ~** country with few/extensive banking facilities

bancassurance /bɑ̃kasyʀɑ̃s/ NF banking and insurance

banco /bɑ̃ko/ NM *(Jeux)* banco ◆ **faire ~** to go banco ◆ **~ !** * *(fig)* you're on! *

banc-titre (pl **bancs-titres**) /bɑ̃titʀ/ NM *(Audiov)* rostrum camera, animation stand

bandage /bɑ̃daʒ/ NM 1 *(= objet) [de blessé]* bandage ◆ **~ herniaire** surgical appliance, truss 2 *(= objet) [de roue] (en métal)* band, hoop; *(en caoutchouc)* tyre *(Brit)*, tire *(US)* 3 *(= action) [de blessé]* bandaging; *[de ressort]* stretching; *[d'arc]* bending

bandana /bɑ̃dana/ NM banda(n)na

bandant, e‡ /bɑ̃dɑ̃, ɑ̃t/ ADJ *[film, livre]* sexy* ◆ **elle est vachement ~e** she's a real turn-on‡ ◆ **ce n'est pas très ~** it's not exactly thrilling

bande¹ /bɑ̃d/ NF 1 *(= ruban) (en tissu, métal)* band, strip; *(en papier)* strip; *(de sable)* strip, tongue; *(Ciné)* film; *[de magnétophone]* tape; *(Presse)* wrapper; *(Méd)* bandage ◆ **~ (de mitrailleuse)** (ammunition) belt ◆ **~ de terre** strip *ou* tongue of land ◆ **la ~ de Gaza** the Gaza strip

2 *(= dessin, motif)* stripe; *[de chaussée]* line; *[d'assiette]* band

3 *(Billard)* cushion ◆ **jouer la ~** to play (the ball) off the cushion ◆ **faire/obtenir qch par la ~** to do/get sth by devious means *ou* in a roundabout way ◆ **apprendre qch par la ~** to hear of sth indirectly *ou* through the grapevine*

4 *(Naut)* list ◆ **donner de la ~** to list

5 *(Élec, Phys, Radio)* band ◆ **~ (de fréquence)** waveband, frequency band ◆ **sur la ~ AM/FM** on AM/FM

COMP **bande d'absorption** *(Phys)* absorption band
bande amorce *[de pellicule, cassette]* leader
bande d'arrêt d'urgence hard shoulder, berm *(US)*
bande chromosomique chromosome band
bande dessinée comic strip, strip cartoon *(Brit)*; *(= livre)* comic book
bande d'émission emission band
bande d'essai *(Photo)* test strip
bande étalon *(Photo)* reference strip, test gauge
bande gaufrée *(Photo)* apron
bande magnétique magnetic tape
bande de manœuvre *(Ordin)* scratch tape
bande molletière puttee
bande originale (original) soundtrack
bande passante pass band
bande perforée punched *ou* perforated *ou* paper tape
bande protectrice *(Photo)* duplex paper
bande de roulement *[de pneu]* tread
bandes rugueuses rumble strips
bande sonore *[de film]* soundtrack; *(sur route)* rumble strip
bande Velpeau ® crêpe bandage *(Brit)*, Ace ® bandage *(US)*
bande vidéo videotape

BANDE DESSINÉE

The **bande dessinée** or **BD** enjoys a huge following in France and Belgium amongst adults as well as children. The strip cartoon is accorded both literary and artistic status, and is known as « le neuvième art ». An international strip cartoon festival takes place in the French town of Angoulême at the end of January each year.

bande² /bɑ̃d/ NF 1 *(= groupe)* band, group ◆ **une ~ d'amis** a group of friends ◆ **ils sont partis en ~** they set off in a group, they all went off together 2 *(= gang) [de pirates]* band; *[de voleurs]* gang, band ◆ **~ armée** armed gang *ou* band ◆ **il ne fait pas partie de leur ~** he's not in their crowd *ou* gang ◆ **la ~ des Quatre** *(Pol)* the Gang of Four ◆ **faire ~ à part** to go off on one's own 3 *(* : péj)* **~ de** bunch of *, pack of * ◆ **~ d'imbéciles !** pack of idiots! *, bunch of fools! * ◆ **c'est une ~ de paresseux** they're a lazy bunch * *ou* crowd * *ou* lot *(Brit)* 4 *[d'oiseaux]* flock; *[de loups, chiens]* pack; *[de lions, singes]* troop

bande-annonce (pl **bandes-annonces**) /bɑ̃danɔ̃s/ NF *(Ciné)* trailer

bandeau (pl **bandeaux**) /bɑ̃do/ NM 1 *(= ruban)* headband, bandeau; *(= pansement)* head bandage; *(pour les yeux)* blindfold ◆ **mettre un ~ à qn** to blindfold sb ◆ **avoir un ~ sur l'œil** to wear an eye patch ◆ **avoir un ~ sur les yeux** *(fig)* to be blind 2 *(Coiffure)* **porter les cheveux en ~x** to wear one's hair parted down the middle and looped back at the sides 3 *(Archit)* string course 4 *[de livre]* publicity strip 5 *(Ordin)* banner ◆ **~ publicitaire** banner ad

bandelette /bɑ̃dlɛt/ NF strip of cloth, (narrow) bandage; *[de momie]* wrapping, bandage

bander /bɑ̃de/ ▸ conjug 1 ◂ VT 1 *(= entourer) [+ genou, plaie]* to bandage ◆ **~ les yeux à qn** to blindfold sb ◆ **les yeux bandés** blindfold(ed) 2 *(= tendre) [+ corde]* to strain, to tauten; *[+ arc]* to bend; *[+ ressort]* to stretch, to tauten; *[+ muscles]* to tense VI **‡ to have a hard-on**‡

banderille /bɑ̃dʀij/ NF banderilla

banderole /bɑ̃dʀɔl/ NF *(= drapeau)* banderole ◆ **~ publicitaire** advertising streamer

bande-son (pl **bandes-son**) /bɑ̃dsɔ̃/ NF *(Ciné)* soundtrack

bandit /bɑ̃di/ NM *(= brigand)* bandit; *(= voleur)* thief; *(= assassin)* murderer; *(= escroc)* crook, shark *; (* *= enfant)* rascal ◆ **~ armé** gunman, armed gangster ◆ **~ de grand chemin** highwayman ◆ **~ manchot** † one-armed bandit

banditisme /bɑ̃ditism/ NM crime *(NonC)* ◆ **le grand ~** organized crime ◆ **500 € pour cette réparation, c'est du ~ !** €500 for this repair job – it's daylight robbery!

bandonéon /bɑ̃dɔneɔ̃/ NM bandoneon

bandoulière /bɑ̃duljɛʀ/ NF *(gén)* shoulder strap; *(Mil)* bandoleer, bandolier ◆ **en ~** slung across the shoulder

bang /bɑ̃g/ NM INV *[d'avion supersonique]* supersonic bang, sonic boom EXCL bang!, crash!

Bangkok /bɑ̃nkɔk/ N Bangkok

bangladais, e /bɑ̃gladɛ, ɛz/ ADJ Bangladeshi NM,F **Bangladais(e)** Bangladeshi

Bangladesh /bɑ̃gladɛʃ/ NM Bangladesh

Bangui /bɑ̃gi/ N Bangui

banian /banjɑ̃/ ADJ banyan, banian ◆ **figuier ~** banyan tree

banjo /bɑ̃(d)ʒo/ NM banjo

Banjul /bɑ̃ʒul/ N Banjul

banlieue /bɑ̃ljø/ NF suburbs, outskirts ◆ **proche ~** inner suburbs ◆ **moyenne ~** intermediate suburbs ◆ **grande ~** outer suburbs ◆ **Paris et sa ~** Greater Paris ◆ **la grande ~ de Paris** the outer suburbs of Paris, the commuter belt of Paris ◆ **la ~ rouge** the Communist-controlled suburbs of Paris ◆ **une ~ ouvrière** a working-class suburb ◆ **habiter en ~** to live in the suburbs
♦ **de banlieue** suburban; *[train, liaison]* commuter, suburban; *[jeunes]* from the suburbs

BANLIEUE

The connotations of suburbia in France are quite different from those that prevail in many English-speaking countries. For historical, economic and social reasons, many suburbs of large French towns have become severely depressed in recent years; the word **banlieue** thus tends to conjure up images of violence and urban decay, and has similar connotations to the English term « inner city ». Young people in many such suburbs have developed a strong cultural identity that includes rap music and « verlan ».
→ VERLAN

banlieusard, e /bɑ̃ljøzaʀ, aʀd/ NM,F (suburban) commuter, suburbanite *(hum)*

banne /ban/ NF 1 *(= toile)* canopy 2 *(= panier)* wicker basket

bannette /banɛt/ NF 1 *(Naut = couchette)* bunk 2 *(= corbeille)* small wicker basket

banni, e /bani/ (ptp de **bannir**) NM,F exile

bannière /banjɛʀ/ NF 1 *(= drapeau)* banner ◆ **la ~ étoilée** the Star-Spangled Banner ◆ **se battre** *ou* **se ranger sous la ~ de qn** to fight on sb's side *ou* under sb's banner 2 *(* = pan de chemise)* **se promener en ~** to be walking round with one's shirt-tail hanging out 3 *(Ordin)* banner ◆ **~ publicitaire** banner ad

bannir /baniʀ/ ▸ conjug 2 ◂ VT *[+ citoyen]* to banish; *[+ pensée]* to banish, to dismiss; *[+ mot, sujet, aliment]* to banish, to exclude *(de* from); *[+ usage]* to prohibit, to put a ban on

bannissement /banismɑ̃/ NM banishment

banque /bɑ̃k/ NF 1 *(= établissement)* bank ◆ **il a 3 millions en** *ou* **à la ~** he's got 3 million in the bank ◆ **mettre des chèques en ~** to bank cheques ◆ **la grande ~ appuie sa candidature** the big banks are backing his candidature ◆ **la Banque de France/d'Angleterre** the Bank of France/of England

2 *(= activité, métier)* **la ~** banking

3 *(Jeux)* bank ◆ **tenir la ~** to be (the) banker

4 *(Méd)* **~ des yeux/du sang/du sperme/d'organes** eye/blood/sperm/organ bank

COMP **banque d'affaires** merchant bank
banque alimentaire food bank
banque(-)assurance banking and insurance
banque centrale central bank
Banque centrale européenne European Central Bank
banque de dépôt deposit bank
banque directe *(= activité)* direct banking
banque de données data bank
banque d'émission bank of issue
banque d'escompte discount bank
Banque européenne d'investissement European Investment Bank
Banque européenne pour la reconstruction et le développement European Bank for Reconstruction and Development
banque d'images picture library
Banque internationale pour la reconstruction et le développement International Bank for Reconstruction and Development
Banque mondiale World Bank
Banque des règlements internationaux Bank for International Settlements

banquer † * /bɑ̃ke/ ▸ conjug 1 ◂ VI to cough up *, to stump up * *(Brit)*

banqueroute /bɑ̃kʀut/ NF *(Fin)* (fraudulent) bankruptcy; *(Pol)* bankruptcy; *(littér)* failure ◆ **faire ~** to go bankrupt

banqueroutier, -ière /bɑ̃kʀutje, jɛʀ/ NM,F (fraudulent) bankrupt

banquet /bɑ̃kɛ/ NM dinner; *(d'apparat)* banquet

banqueter /bɑ̃k(ə)te/ ▸ conjug 4 ◂ VI (lit) to banquet; (= festoyer) to feast

banquette /bɑ̃kɛt/ NF 1 [de train] seat; [de voiture] (bench) seat; [de restaurant] (wall) seat; [de piano] (duet) stool ◆ **jouer devant les ~s** (Théât) to play to an empty house ◆ **faire ~** (dans un bal) to be a wallflower 2 (Archit) window seat 3 (Mil) ~ **de tir** banquette, firestep 4 (= talus) berm(e); (= chemin) path

banquier /bɑ̃kje/ NM (Fin, Jeux) banker

banquise /bɑ̃kiz/ NF ice field; (flottante) ice floe

bantou, e /bɑ̃tu/ ADJ Bantu NM (= langue) Bantu NM,F **Bantou(e)** Bantu

bantoustan /bɑ̃tustɑ̃/ NM Bantustan

banyuls /banjuls, banjyls/ NM Banyuls (sweet fortified wine drunk as an apéritif)

banzaï * /bɑ̃(d)zaj/ EXCL bingo!

baobab /baɔbab/ NM baobab

baoulé, e /baule/ ADJ Baoule NM,F **Baoulé(e)** Baoule ◆ **les Baoulés** the Baoule people

baptême /batɛm/ NM 1 (= sacrement) baptism; (= cérémonie) christening, baptism ◆ **donner le ~ à** to baptize, to christen ◆ **recevoir le ~** to be baptized ou christened 2 [de cloche] blessing, dedication; [de navire] naming, christening

COMP **baptême de l'air** first flight
baptême du feu baptism of fire
baptême de la ligne (Naut) (first) crossing of the line
baptême du sang (littér) baptism of blood

baptiser /batize/ ▸ conjug 1 ◂ VT 1 (Rel) to baptize, to christen ◆ **faire ~ un enfant** to have a child baptized ou christened 2 [+ cloche] to bless, to dedicate; [+ navire] to name, to christen 3 (= appeler) to call, to christen, to name ◆ **on le baptisa Paul** he was christened Paul ◆ **on baptisa la rue du nom du maire** the street was named after the mayor 4 (= surnommer) to christen, to dub ◆ **la pièce qu'il baptisait pompeusement salon** the room which he pompously dubbed the drawing room 5 * [+ vin, lait] to water down

baptismal, e (mpl **-aux**) /batismal, o/ ADJ baptismal

baptisme /batism/ NM baptism

baptiste /batist/ ADJ, NMF Baptist

baptistère /batistɛʀ/ NM baptistry

baquet /bakɛ/ NM tub; → **siège**[1]

bar[1] /baʀ/ NM (= établissement, comptoir) bar ◆ ~ **américain** cocktail bar ◆ ~ **à vin(s)/à huîtres** wine/oyster bar ◆ ~ **à bière(s)** bar specializing in a wide variety of beers

bar[2] /baʀ/ NM (= poisson) bass

bar[3] /baʀ/ NM (Phys) bar

Barabbas /baʀabas/ NM Barabbas

barachois /baʀaʃwa/ NM (Can) lagoon

baragouin * /baʀagwɛ̃/ NM gibberish, double Dutch

baragouinage * /baʀagwinaʒ/ NM (= façon de parler) gibbering; (= propos) gibberish, double Dutch

baragouiner * /baʀagwine/ ▸ conjug 1 ◂ VI to gibber, to talk gibberish ou double Dutch VT [+ langue] to speak badly; [+ discours, paroles] to jabber out, to gabble ◆ **il baragouine un peu l'espagnol** he can speak a bit of Spanish ◆ **qu'est-ce qu'il baragouine ?** what's he jabbering on about? *

baragouineur, -euse * /baʀagwinœʀ, øz/ NM,F jabberer

baraka ⁑ /baʀaka/ NF luck ◆ **avoir la ~** to be lucky

baraque /baʀak/ NF 1 (= cabane) shed, hut; (= boutique) stand, stall ◆ ~ **foraine** fairground stall 2 * (= maison) place *, shack *; (= appartement) place *; (péj = entreprise) dump *, hole * ◆ **une belle ~** a smart place * ◆ **quand je suis rentré à la ~** when I got back to my place * ◆ **quelle (sale) ~ !** what a lousy dump! ⁑, what a hole! *; → **casser** 3 (⁑ = homme) burly ou beefy * guy

baraqué, e * /baʀake/ ADJ hefty, well-built

baraquement /baʀakmɑ̃/ NM ◆ **~(s)** group of huts; (Mil) camp

baratin * /baʀatɛ̃/ NM (= boniment) sweet talk *, smooth talk *; (= verbiage) chatter, hot air ⁑; [de vendeur] patter *, sales talk, sales pitch ◆ **assez de ~ !** cut the cackle! * ou the chat! * (Brit) ◆ **faire son ou du ~ à qn** (gén) to sweet-talk sb *, to chat sb up * (Brit), to feed sb some lines * (US) ◆ **faire son ou le ~ à un client** to give a customer the sales talk ou pitch * ou patter * ◆ **avoir du ~** to have all the patter *, to be a smooth talker

baratiner * /baʀatine/ ▸ conjug 1 ◂ VT ◆ ~ **qn** (= amadouer) to sweet-talk sb *, to chat sb up * (Brit); (= draguer) to chat sb up * (Brit), to feed sb some lines * (US) ◆ ~ **le client** to give a customer the sales talk ou pitch * ou patter * VI (= bavarder) to chatter, to natter * (Brit)

baratineur, -euse * /baʀatinœʀ, øz/ NM,F (= beau parleur, menteur) smooth talker; (= bavard) gasbag *, windbag * NM (= dragueur) smooth talker

baratte /baʀat/ NF [de beurre] churn

baratter /baʀate/ ▸ conjug 1 ◂ VT to churn

barbacane /baʀbakan/ NF (= bastion) barbican; (= meurtrière) loophole; (= drain) weeper

Barbade /baʀbad/ NF ◆ **la ~** Barbados

barbadien, -ienne /baʀbadjɛ̃, ɛn/ ADJ Barbadian NM,F **Barbadien(ne)** Barbadian

barbant, e * /baʀbɑ̃, ɑ̃t/ ADJ boring, dull ◆ **ce qu'il est ~ !** isn't he a bore! * ◆ **ce que c'est ~ !** isn't it a drag! *

barbaque ⁑ /baʀbak/ NF (péj) meat

barbare /baʀbaʀ/ ADJ 1 [invasion, peuple] barbarian, barbaric 2 (péj) [mœurs, musique, crime] barbaric, barbarous NM (Hist, fig) barbarian

barbarement /baʀbaʀmɑ̃/ ADV barbarously, barbarically

barbaresque /baʀbaʀɛsk/ ADJ (Hist = d'Afrique du Nord) Barbary Coast (épith) ◆ **les États ~s** the Barbary Coast

Barbarie /baʀbaʀi/ NF (Hist) ◆ **la ~** the Barbary Coast

barbarie /baʀbaʀi/ NF (= manque de civilisation) barbarism; (= cruauté) barbarity

barbarisme /baʀbaʀism/ NM (Gram) barbarism

barbe[1] /baʀb/ NF 1 [de personne] beard ◆ **une ~ de 3 mois** 3 months' (growth of) beard ◆ **il a une ~ de 3 jours** he's got 3 days' stubble on his chin ◆ **sans ~** [adulte] clean-shaven, beardless; [adolescent] (= imberbe) beardless ◆ **il a de la ~ (au menton)** (adulte) he needs a shave; (adolescent) he already has a few hairs on his chin ◆ **avoir une ~, porter la ou une ~** to have a beard ◆ **faire la ~ à qn** to trim sb's beard ◆ **il n'a pas encore de ~ au menton et il croit tout savoir** (hum) he's still in short pants ou he's still wet behind the ears * and he thinks he knows it all

2 [de chèvre, singe, oiseau] beard

3 [de plume] barb; [de poisson] barbel; [d'orge] beard (NonC) ◆ **~s** whiskers

4 (= aspérité) **~s** [de papier] ragged edge; [de métal] jagged edge

5 (locutions) **à la ~ de qn** under sb's nose ◆ **dérober qch à la ~ de qn** to take * sth from under sb's nose ◆ **vieille ~** * old stick-in-the-mud *, old fogey * ◆ **marmonner dans sa ~** to mumble ou mutter into one's beard ◆ **rire dans sa ~** to laugh up one's sleeve ◆ **la ~ !** * damn (it)! ⁑, blast! * (Brit) ◆ **il faut que j'y retourne, quelle ~ !** * I've got to go back – what a drag! * ◆ **oh toi, la ~ !** * oh shut up, you! *

COMP **barbe de capucin** wild chicory
barbe à papa candy-floss (Brit), cotton candy (US)

barbe[2] /baʀb/ NM ◆ **(cheval) ~** barb

barbeau (pl **barbeaux**) /baʀbo/ NM 1 (= poisson) barbel 2 (= plante) cornflower 3 (⁑ = souteneur) pimp, ponce

Barbe-Bleue /baʀbəblø/ NM Bluebeard

barbecue /baʀbəkju/ NM 1 (= repas, cuisine) barbecue ◆ **faire un ~** to have a barbecue 2 (= matériel) barbecue set ◆ **faire cuire qch au ~** to barbecue sth

barbelé, e /baʀbəle/ NM barbed wire (NonC) ◆ **les ~s** the barbed wire fence ou fencing ◆ **s'égratigner après les ~s** to get scratched on the barbed wire ◆ **derrière les ~s** (fig) [prisonnier] in a prison camp ADJ ◆ **fil de fer ~** barbed wire (NonC)

barber * /baʀbe/ ▸ conjug 1 ◂ VT to bore stiff *, to bore to tears * VPR **se barber** to be bored stiff *, to be bored to tears * (à faire doing)

Barberousse /baʀbəʀus/ NM Barbarossa

barbet[1] /baʀbɛ/ NM ◆ **(rouget) ~** red mullet, goatfish (US)

barbet[2] /baʀbɛ/ NM ◆ **(chien) ~** water spaniel

barbiche /baʀbiʃ/ NF goatee (beard)

barbichette * /baʀbiʃɛt/ NF (small) goatee (beard)

barbichu, e /baʀbiʃy/ ADJ [personne] with a goatee (beard) NM man with a goatee (beard)

barbier /baʀbje/ NM †† barber; (Can) (men's) hairdresser

barbillon /baʀbijɔ̃/ NM 1 [de plume, hameçon] barb; [de poisson] barbel ◆ **~s** [de bœuf, cheval] barbs 2 (= poisson) (small) barbel

barbiturique /baʀbityʀik/ ADJ barbituric NM barbiturate

barbon /baʀbɔ̃/ NM († ou péj) ◆ **(vieux) ~** greybeard, old fogey *

barbotage /baʀbɔtaʒ/ NM 1 (* = vol) filching *, pinching * (Brit) 2 (dans l'eau) paddling; (en éclaboussant) splashing about; [de canard] dabbling 3 (dans la boue) paddling ou squelching (Brit) around 4 [de gaz] bubbling

barboter /baʀbɔte/ ▸ conjug 1 ◂ VT (* = voler) to pinch * (Brit), to whip * (à from, off); ◆ **elle lui a barboté son briquet** she's filched * his lighter VI 1 (dans l'eau) to paddle; (en éclaboussant) to splash about; [canard] to dabble; (dans la boue) to paddle ou squelch (Brit) around 2 [gaz] to bubble

barboteur, -euse[1] /baʀbɔtœʀ, øz/ ADJ ◆ **il est (du genre) ~** * ◆ **c'est un ~** he's a bit light-fingered (Brit) ou sticky-fingered (US) NM (Chim) bubble chamber

barboteuse[2] /baʀbɔtøz/ NF (= vêtement) rompers

barbouillage /baʀbujaʒ/ NM 1 (= peinture) daub; (= écriture) scribble, scrawl ◆ **feuille couverte de ~s** sheet of paper covered with scrawls ou scribblings 2 (= action de peindre) daubing; (= action d'écrire) scribbling, scrawling

barbouille * /baʀbuj/ NF (péj) painting ◆ **il fait de la ~** (hum) he does a bit of painting

barbouiller /baʀbuje/ ▸ conjug 1 ◂ VT 1 (= couvrir, salir) to smear, to daub (de with) to cover (de with, in); ◆ **il a le visage tout barbouillé de chocolat** he's got chocolate (smeared) all over his face, he's got his face all covered in chocolate

2 *(péj = peindre)* *[+ mur]* to daub *ou* slap paint on ◆ **il barbouille (des toiles) de temps en temps** he does a bit of painting from time to time
3 *(péj = écrire, dessiner)* to scribble *(sur* on); ◆ **~ une feuille de dessins** to scribble *ou* scrawl drawings on a piece of paper ◆ **~ du papier** to cover a piece of paper with scrawls, to scrawl all over a piece of paper ◆ **~ un slogan sur un mur** to daub a slogan on a wall
4 *(* = rendre malade)* **~ l'estomac** to upset the stomach ◆ **être barbouillé, avoir l'estomac barbouillé** to feel queasy *ou* sick
VPR **se barbouiller** ◆ **se ~ de qch** to smear o.s. with sth ◆ **il s'est barbouillé de confiture** he's smeared jam all over his face

barbouilleur, -euse /baʀbujœʀ, øz/ NM,F *(péj)* *(= artiste)* dauber; *(= peintre en bâtiment)* bad *ou* slapdash painter ◆ **~ de papier** hack (writer)

barbouillis /baʀbuji/ NM *(= écriture)* scribble, scrawl; *(= peinture)* daub

barbouze* /baʀbuz/ NF *ou* NM 1 *(= barbe)* beard 2 *(= policier)* secret (government) police agent; *(= garde du corps)* bodyguard

barbu, e /baʀby/ ADJ *[personne]* bearded; *(Bio)* barbate NM bearded man, man with a beard; *(hum ou péj = islamiste)* Islamic fundamentalist NF **barbue** *(= poisson)* brill

barcarolle /baʀkaʀɔl/ NF barcarolle

barcasse /baʀkas/ NF boat

Barcelone /baʀsəlɔn/ N Barcelona

barda* /baʀda/ NM gear*; *(Mil)* kit ◆ **il a tout un ~ dans la voiture** he's got a whole load* of stuff in the car

bardage /baʀdaʒ/ NM *(Constr)* weatherboarding, cladding *(Brit)*, siding *(US)*

bardane /baʀdan/ NF burdock

barde[1] /baʀd/ NM *(= poète)* bard

barde[2] /baʀd/ NF *(Culin, Mil)* bard

bardeau[1] (pl **bardeaux**) /baʀdo/ NM *[de toit]* shingle

bardeau[2] (pl **bardeaux**) /baʀdo/ NM ⇒ **bardot**

barder /baʀde/ ► conjug 1 ◄ VT 1 *(Culin)* to bard 2 *(= couvrir)* *[+ cheval]* to bard
◆ **bardé de** ◆ **bardé de fer** *[cheval]* barded; *[soldat]* armour-clad; *[porte]* with iron bars ◆ **poitrine bardée de décorations** chest bedecked with medals ◆ **bardé de diplômes** with a whole string *ou* array of qualifications
3 *(fig)* **être bardé** to be immune *(contre* to)
VB IMPERS * ◆ **ça va ~** things are going to get hot, all hell is going to break loose ◆ **ça a bardé !** *(dans une réunion)* the sparks really flew!; *(dans les rues)* things got pretty hot!

bardot /baʀdo/ NM hinny

barème /baʀɛm/ NM *(= table de référence)* table, list; *(= tarif)* scale of charges, price list; *(Rail)* fare schedule ◆ **~ de l'impôt** tax scale ◆ **~ de correction** *(Scol)* marking *(Brit)* *ou* grading *(US)* scheme ◆ **hors ~** off the (salary) scale *(attrib)*

barge[1] /baʀʒ/ NF *(= bateau)* barge; *(= meule)* (rectangular) haystack

barge[2]* /baʀʒ/ ADJ ⇒ **barjo(t)**

barguigner /baʀgiɲe/ ► conjug 1 ◄ VI *(littér ou hum)* ◆ **sans ~** without shilly-shallying

baril /baʀi(l)/ NM *[de pétrole]* barrel; *[de vin]* barrel, cask; *[de poudre]* keg, cask; *[de harengs]* barrel; *[de lessive]* drum

barillet /baʀijɛ/ NM 1 *[de serrure, revolver]* cylinder; *[de pendule]* barrel ◆ **serrure à ~** cylinder *ou* Yale ® lock 2 *(= petit baril)* small barrel *ou* cask

bariolage /baʀjɔlaʒ/ NM *(= résultat)* riot *ou* medley of colours; *(= action)* daubing

bariolé, e /baʀjɔle/ (ptp de **barioler**) ADJ *[vêtement]* many-coloured, rainbow-coloured, gaudy *(péj)*; *[groupe]* colourfully dressed, gaily coloured

barioler /baʀjɔle/ ► conjug 1 ◄ VT to splash *ou* daub bright colours on, to streak with bright colours

barjo(t)* /baʀʒo/ ADJ nuts*, crazy*, barmy* *(Brit)* ◆ **bande de ~ts !** bunch of nutcases*!

barmaid /baʀmɛd/ NF barmaid

barman /baʀman/ (pl **barmans** *ou* **barmen** /baʀmɛn/) NM barman, bartender *(surtout US)*

bar-mitsva, Bar-Mitzva /baʀmitsva/ NF INV Bar Mitzvah

barnache /baʀnaʃ/, **barnacle** /baʀnakl/ NF ⇒ **bernache**

baromètre /baʀɔmɛtʀ/ NM *(lit, fig)* barometer ◆ **le ~ baisse** the glass *ou* barometer is falling ◆ **le ~ est au beau fixe/à la pluie** the barometer is set (at) fair/is pointing to rain ◆ **le ~ est au beau (fixe)** *(fig)* things are looking good* ◆ **~ enregistreur/anéroïde** recording/aneroid barometer

barométrique /baʀɔmetʀik/ ADJ barometric(al)

baron[1] /baʀɔ̃/ NM 1 *(= titre)* baron; → **Monsieur** 2 *(fig = magnat)* baron, lord ◆ **les ~s de la presse** the press barons *ou* lords

baron[2] /baʀɔ̃/ NM ◆ **~ d'agneau** baron of lamb

baronnage /baʀɔnaʒ/ NM *(= titre)* barony; *(= corps des barons)* baronage

baronne /baʀɔn/ NF baroness

baronnet /baʀɔnɛ/ NM baronet

baronnie /baʀɔni/ NF barony

baroque /baʀɔk/ ADJ 1 *(Archit, Art, Mus)* baroque ◆ **perle ~** baroque pearl 2 *[idée]* weird, strange, wild NM baroque

barotraumatisme /baʀotʀomatism/ NM barotrauma

baroud /baʀud/ NM *(arg Mil)* fighting ◆ **~ d'honneur** last-ditch struggle, gallant last stand

baroudeur, -euse /baʀudœʀ, øz/ NM,F *(Mil)* firebrand, fighter ◆ **c'est un ~** he knocks about* *ou* travels around a lot

barouf* /baʀuf(lə)/ NM *(= vacarme)* row*, din*, racket* ◆ **faire du ~** to create a racket*, to make a row*; *(= protester)* to kick up a fuss* *ou* stink*

barque /baʀk/ NF small boat, small craft ◆ **~ à moteur** (small) motorboat ◆ **~ de pêche** small fishing boat ◆ **il mène bien sa ~** he's doing alright for himself, he manages his affairs very well
◆ **charger la barque** *(= exagérer)* to overdo it

barquette /baʀkɛt/ NF 1 *(= tarte)* pastry boat, small tart 2 *(= récipient)* container; *(pour fruits)* punnet, carton

barracuda /baʀakyda/ NM barracuda

barrage /baʀaʒ/ NM 1 *[de rivière, lac]* dam, barrage; *(à fleur d'eau)* weir ◆ **~ de retenue** flood barrier ◆ **~ flottant** floating boom *ou* barrier 2 *(= barrière)* barrier; *(d'artillerie, de questions)* barrage ◆ **~ de police** *(gén)* (police) roadblock; *(= cordon d'agents)* police cordon; *(= chevaux de frise)* (police) barricade ◆ **établir un ~ (routier)** *[manifestants]* to set up a roadblock ◆ **match de ~** *(Sport)* relegation match 3 *(fig)* **faire ~ à** to hinder, to stand in the way of ◆ **il y a eu un ~ de la direction** the management has put up a barrier 4 *(Cartes)* pre-emptive bid, pre-empt

barre /baʀ/ NF 1 *(gén = tige, morceau)* bar; *(de fer)* rod, bar; *(de bois)* piece, rod; *(d'or)* bar ◆ **~ (transversale)** *(Ftbl, Rugby)* crossbar ◆ **~s de fixation ou de toit** *(sur une voiture)* roof bars ◆ **~ de savon** † cake *ou* bar of soap ◆ **c'est le coup de ~ dans ce restaurant*** you pay through the nose* in that restaurant ◆ **j'ai un coup de ~*** *(fatigue)* I feel drained *ou* shattered*
2 *(Danse)* barre ◆ **exercices à la ~** exercises at the barre, barre exercises
3 *(Naut)* helm; *[de petit bateau]* tiller ◆ **être à la ou tenir la ~** *(lit, fig)* to be at the helm ◆ **prendre la ~** *(lit, fig)* to take the helm ◆ **redresser la ~** *(lit)* to right the helm; *(fig)* to get things back on an even keel
4 *(Jur)* **~ du tribunal** bar ◆ **~ (des témoins)** witness box *(Brit)*, witness stand *(US)* ◆ **être appelé à la ~** to be called as a witness ◆ **comparaître à la ~** to appear as a witness
5 *(Géog)* *(= houle)* *(gén)* race; *(à l'estuaire)* bore; *(= banc de sable)* (sand) bar; *(= crête de montagne)* ridge
6 *(= trait)* line, dash, stroke; *(du t, f)* stroke ◆ **faire des ~s** to draw lines (on a page) ◆ **mets une ~ à ton t** cross your t ◆ **~ de fraction** *line separating top and bottom figures of a fraction* ◆ **~ d'addition** *line ruled above total of a sum* ◆ **~ oblique** *(Typo)* slash, oblique (stroke), solidus *(SPÉC)*
7 *(= niveau)* mark ◆ **franchir la ~ des 10%** to pass the 10% mark ◆ **placer la ~ à 10** *(Scol)* to set the pass mark *ou* the passing grade *(US)* at 10 ◆ **mettre** *ou* **placer la ~ plus haut** to raise the stakes ◆ **vous placez la ~ trop haut** you set your standards too high
8 ◆ **~s** *(† = jeu)* ≃ prisoners' base ◆ **avoir ~(s) sur qn** *(frm)* *(avantage)* to have an advantage over sb; *(pouvoir)* to have power over *ou* a hold on sb
9 *[de cheval]* bar
10 *(= douleur)* pain ◆ **j'ai une ~ sur la poitrine** my chest feels tight
COMP **barre d'accouplement** tie-rod
barre antiroulis anti-roll bar
barre d'appui (window) rail
barres asymétriques asymmetric bars
barre de céréales muesli *(Brit)* *ou* granola *(US)* bar
barre chocolatée chocolate bar, bar of chocolate, candy bar *(US)*
barre de défilement *(Ordin)* scroll bar
barre à disques *(Sport)* barbell
barre d'espacement space bar
barre fixe horizontal *ou* chinning bar
barre de menu *(Ordin)* menu bar
barre de mesure *(Mus)* bar line
barre à mine crowbar
barre omnibus *(Élec)* busbar
barre d'outils *(Ordin)* tool bar
barres parallèles parallel bars
barre de remorquage tow bar
barre de reprise *(Mus)* repeat mark(s) *ou* sign
barre de titre *(Ordin)* title bar
barre de torsion torsion bar

barré, e /baʀe/ (ptp de **barrer**) ADJ 1 *[dent]* impacted 2 *(* = engagé, parti)* **il/c'est mal ~** he's/it's off to a bad start ◆ **il est mal ~ pour avoir son examen** his chances of passing the exam are pretty slim ◆ **on est bien ~ avec un chef comme lui !** *(iro)* we won't get very far with a boss like him! 3 * *(= fou)* crazy NM *(Mus)* barré

barreau (pl **barreaux**) /baʀo/ NM 1 *[d'échelle]* rung; *[de cage, fenêtre]* bar ◆ **être derrière les ~x** *[prisonnier]* to be behind bars ◆ **~ de chaise** *(lit)* (chair) rung *ou* crossbar; *(* = cigare)* fat cigar 2 *(Jur)* bar ◆ **entrer** *ou* **être admis** *ou* **reçu au ~** to be called to the bar

barrement /baʀmɑ̃/ NM *[de chèque]* crossing

barrer /baʀe/ ► conjug 1 ◄ VT 1 *(= obstruer)* *[+ porte]* to bar; *[+ fenêtre]* to bar up; *[+ chemin, route]* to bar; *(par accident)* to block; *(pour travaux, par la police)* to close (off), to seal *ou* shut off; *(par barricades)* to barricade ◆ **~ le passage** *ou* **la route à qn** *(lit)* to stand in sb's way, to block *ou* bar sb's way; *(fig)* to stand in sb's way ◆ **il est**

barré par son supérieur his boss is standing in his way ◆ **des rochers nous barraient la route** rocks blocked *ou* barred our way ◆ **"rue barrée"** "road closed"

2 *(= rayer) [+ mot, phrase]* to cross out, to score out; *[+ surface, feuille]* to cross; *[+ chèque]* to cross ◆ **chèque barré** crossed cheque (Brit), check for deposit only (US) ◆ **chèque non barré** open *ou* uncrossed cheque (Brit) ◆ **barre ton t** cross your t ◆ **les rides qui barraient son front** the wrinkles which lined his forehead

3 *(Naut)* to steer ◆ **quatre/deux barré** *(Sport)* coxed four/pair

VI *(Naut)* to steer, to take the helm

VPR se barrer * *[personne]* to clear off*; *[fixations]* to come out ◆ **barre-toi !** clear off! *, beat it! *, scram! * ◆ **le tuyau se barre** the pipe is falling off ◆ **il s'est barré de chez lui** he walked out on his family *

barrette /baʀɛt/ **NF** 1 *(pour cheveux)* (hair) slide (Brit), barrette (US); *(= bijou)* brooch; *(= médaille)* bar 2 *(Ordin)* ~ **(de mémoire)** memory module 3 *(arg Drogue)* ~ **(de cannabis)** (one gram) bar of cannabis 4 *(Rel)* biretta ◆ **recevoir la ~** to receive the red hat

barreur, -euse /baʀœʀ, øz/ **NM,F** *(gén, homme)* helmsman; *(femme)* helmswoman; *(Aviron)* cox(swain) ◆ **quatre avec/sans ~** coxed/coxless four

barricade /baʀikad/ **NF** barricade; → **côté**

barricader /baʀikade/ ▸ conjug 1 ◂ **VT** *[+ porte, fenêtre, rue]* to barricade **VPR se barricader** ◆ **se ~ dans/derrière** to barricade o.s. in/behind ◆ **se ~ chez soi** to lock *ou* shut o.s. in

barrière /baʀjɛʀ/ **NF** *(= clôture)* fence; *(= porte)* gate; *(lit, fig = obstacle)* barrier; *(Hist = octroi)* tollgate ◆ **dresser une ~** to put up a barrier *(entre* between); ◆ **franchir la ~ de la langue** to break through the language barrier

COMP barrière de corail coral reef ◆ **la Grande Barrière (de corail)** the Great Barrier Reef

barrière de dégel *roadsign warning of dangerous road conditions during a thaw*

barrière douanière trade *ou* tariff barrier

barrière naturelle natural barrier

barrière (de passage à niveau) level (Brit) *ou* grade (US) crossing gate

barrière de sécurité *(dans les rues)* crowd barrier; *(pour un bébé)* safety gate

barrique /baʀik/ **NF** barrel, cask; → **plein**

barrir /baʀiʀ/ ▸ conjug 2 ◂ **VI** *[éléphant]* to trumpet

barrissement /baʀismɑ̃/ **NM** trumpeting

bartavelle /baʀtavɛl/ **NF** rock partridge

barycentre /baʀisɑ̃tʀ/ **NM** barycentre (Brit), barycenter (US)

baryton /baʀitɔ̃/ **ADJ, NM** baritone ◆ **~-basse** base-baritone

baryum /baʀjɔm/ **NM** barium

bas[1], basse[1] /bɑ, bɑs/

1 ADJECTIF	3 NOM MASCULIN
2 ADVERBE	4 COMPOSÉS

1 - ADJECTIF

1 [= de faible hauteur] *[siège, porte, colline, nuages]* low; *[ciel]* low, overcast; *[maison]* low-roofed; *[terrain]* low(-lying) ◆ **le soleil est ~ sur l'horizon** the sun is low on the horizon ◆ **les basses branches** *ou* **les branches basses d'un arbre** the lower *ou* bottom branches of a tree ◆ **les branches de cet arbre sont basses** the branches of this tree hang low ◆ **il a le front ~** he has a low brow *ou* forehead ◆ **~ sur pattes** *[animal]* short-legged; * *[personne]* short-legged, stumpy-legged; * *[meuble]* with short legs; → **main, oreille, plafond, profil, table** *etc*

2 [= peu élevé] *[prix, chiffre, température, niveau, rendement]* low; *(Élec) [fréquence]* low ◆ **les ~ salaires** low salaries ◆ **la Seine est très basse en ce moment** the Seine is very low at the moment ◆ **c'est (la) marée basse, c'est la basse mer** the tide is low *ou* out, it's low tide ◆ **à marée basse** at low tide *ou* water ◆ **un enfant en ~ âge** a young *ou* small child

3 [= peu audible] *[son]* low; → **messe, voix**

4 [= grave] *[note]* low; *[voix]* deep, low

5 [= humble] *[naissance]* low, lowly ◆ **personnes de basse condition** people from humble backgrounds ◆ **basses besognes** menial tasks; *(péj)* dirty work ◆ **les ~ quartiers de la ville** the seedy *ou* poor parts of the town ◆ **les ~ morceaux** *(Boucherie)* the cheap cuts

6 [= mesquin] *[jalousie, vengeance]* base, petty; *[action]* base, mean ◆ **c'était ~ de sa part** it was a mean *ou* despicable thing for him to do ◆ **c'est encore un exemple de basses manœuvres politiciennes** this is yet another example of base political manoeuvring ◆ **elle n'a pas agi pour de basses raisons (commerciales)** she didn't act out of base (commercial) motives; → **coup**

7 [Ling] **le ~ latin** low Latin ◆ **le ~ allemand** Low German, plattdeutsch *(SPÉC)*

8 [Géog] **la Basse Seine** the Lower Seine ◆ **le Bas Languedoc** Lower Languedoc ◆ **les Bas Bretons** the inhabitants of Lower Brittany ◆ **le Bas Canada** *(Hist Can)* Lower Canada

2 - ADVERBE

1 [dans l'espace] *[voler, viser]* low ◆ **mets tes livres/le tableau plus ~** put your books/the picture lower down ◆ **ma maison est plus ~ dans la rue** my house is further down the street ◆ **comme l'auteur le dit plus ~** as the author says further on ◆ **voir plus ~** see below ◆ **mettre** *ou* **traiter qn plus ~ que terre** to treat sb like dirt

2 [dans une hiérarchie] **il est assez ~ dans la hiérarchie** he's quite low down in the hierarchy ◆ **être au plus ~** *[prix]* to be at their lowest, to have reached rock bottom; *[cote de popularité, inflation]* to be at its lowest ◆ **le dollar n'a jamais été aussi ~** the dollar has reached a new *ou* an all-time low

3 [= mal en point, en mauvaise posture] **le malade est bien ~** the patient is very low ◆ **être au plus ~** *[personne]* to be very low, to be at a very low ebb; *[secteur économique]* to be at a very low ebb ◆ **la Bourse est au plus ~ depuis 1988** the stock exchange is at its lowest since 1988 ◆ **son image est au plus ~ dans l'opinion** his public image is at an all-time low

4 [= doucement] *[parler]* softly, in a low voice ◆ **dire qch/parler tout ~** to say sth/speak in a whisper *ou* in a very low voice ◆ **mets la télé tout ~** put the TV on very low ◆ **mettez la radio/le chauffage plus ~** turn the radio/heating down

5 [Mus = dans les graves] *[chanter]* low

6 [locutions figées]

◆ **à bas** ◆ **à ~ le fascisme/les tyrans !** down with fascism/tyrants!

◆ **bas les** *+ nom* ◆ **~ les masques !** drop the pretence! ◆ **~ les pattes !** *(à un chien)* down!; (* *: à une personne)* (keep your) hands off! *, (keep your) paws off! *

◆ **mettre bas** *[animal]* to give birth, to drop *(SPÉC)* ◆ **mettre ~ les armes** *(Mil)* to lay down one's arms; *(fig)* to throw in the sponge ◆ **mettre ~ les masques** to stop pretending, to drop one's mask

◆ **mise bas** *[d'animal]* birth, dropping

3 - NOM MASCULIN

[de page, escalier, colline] foot, bottom; *[de visage]* lower part; *[de mur]* foot; *[de jupe, pantalon]* bottom ◆ **le ~ du ventre** the lower abdomen ◆ **une maison du ~ de la rue Blanche** a house at the bottom (end) of rue Blanche ◆ **il a une malformation du ~ de la colonne vertébrale** he has a malformation of the lower spine ◆ **faire les ~ d'un pantalon** to hem a pair of trousers

◆ **au bas, dans le bas** at the bottom ◆ **son nom est inscrit au ~** his name is written at the bottom ◆ **la colonne est évasée dans le ~** the pillar widens out at the bottom

◆ **au bas de, dans le bas de** *[de page, escalier, colline, côte]* at the bottom *ou* foot of; *[d'armoire, immeuble, écran]* at the bottom of; *[de vêtement] (gén)* at the bottom of; *(tout autour)* round the bottom of ◆ **au ~ de l'échelle sociale** at the bottom of the social ladder ◆ **dans le ~ du corps** in the lower part of the body ◆ **j'ai mal au** *ou* **dans le ~ du dos** my lower back is aching, I've got a pain in my lower back ◆ **dans le ~ de la ville** at the lower end of the town ◆ **l'équipe se retrouve au** *ou* **dans le ~ du classement** the team is at the bottom of the league

◆ **de bas en haut** *[s'ouvrir]* from the bottom up(wards); *[compter, lire]* from the bottom up ◆ **il la contempla de ~ en haut** he looked her up and down

◆ **d'en bas** ◆ **les dents/la mâchoire d'en ~** the lower teeth/jaw ◆ **les chambres d'en ~** the downstairs rooms ◆ **le supermarché d'en ~ vend du pain** the supermarket below sells bread ◆ **ceux d'en ~** *(= voisins)* the people (who live) below; *(= personnes humbles)* the lower orders ◆ **le bruit vient d'en ~** the noise is coming from downstairs *ou* from down below ◆ **vu d'en ~, cela ressemble à ...** seen from below, it looks like ...

◆ **du bas** *[dents, mâchoire]* lower ◆ **l'étagère/le tiroir du ~** the bottom shelf/drawer ◆ **les appartements du ~** the downstairs flats (Brit) *ou* apartments (US), the flats (Brit) *ou* apartments (US) downstairs *ou* down below

◆ **en bas** *(dans une maison)* downstairs ◆ **il habite en ~** he lives downstairs *ou* down below ◆ **les voleurs sont passés par en ~** the thieves got in downstairs ◆ **je ne peux pas rester la tête en ~ trop longtemps** I can't stay upside down for too long ◆ **il se tenait à la branche, la tête en ~** he was hanging upside down from the branch ◆ **le tableau est posé la tête en ~** * the picture is upside down

◆ **en bas de** *(dans l'espace)* ◆ **en ~ de la côte/de l'escalier** at the bottom *ou* foot of the hill/of the stairs ◆ **il m'attend en ~ de l'immeuble** he's waiting for me outside the building ◆ **signez en ~ de cette page** sign at the bottom of this page ◆ **ils sont en ~ du classement** they're at the bottom of the league ◆ **en ~ de 100 dollars** *(Can)* under 100 dollars

4 - COMPOSÉS

bas de casse *(Typo)* **NM** lower case

bas[2] /bɑ/ **NM** stocking; *(de footballeur)* sock; *(de bandit masqué)* stocking mask ◆ **~ de contention** *ou* **à varices** * support stockings *ou* hose ◆ **~ fins** sheer stockings ◆ **~ (de) nylon** nylon stockings, nylons ◆ **~ sans couture** seamless stockings ◆ **~ résille** fishnet stockings ◆ **~ de soie** silk stockings ◆ **~ de laine** *(lit)* woollen stockings; *(fig)* savings, nest egg

basal, e (mpl **-aux**) /bɑzal, o/ **ADJ** basal

basalte /bazalt/ **NM** basalt

basaltique /bazaltik/ **ADJ** basalt(ic)

basane /bazan/ **NF** *(= peau)* basan, bazan; *[de pantalon de cavalier]* leather padding

basané, e /bazane/ **ADJ** *[teint, visage] [de vacancier]* (sun-)tanned, sunburnt (Brit); *[de marin]* tanned, weather-beaten; *(= foncé)* swarthy ◆ **individu au teint ~** dark-skinned individual **NM,F** *(injurieux)* ≃ darky *(injurieux)*

bas-côté (pl **bas-côtés**) /bakote/ NM 1 *[de route]* verge, shoulder *(US)* 2 *[d'église]* (side) aisle 3 *(Can = appentis)* lean-to (shed), penthouse

basculant, e /baskylɑ̃, ɑ̃t/ ADJ *[siège]* tip-up *(épith)*; → **benne**

bascule /baskyl/ NF 1 *(= balance) [de marchandises]* weighing machine ◆ **~ (automatique)** *[de personne]* scales 2 *(= balançoire)* seesaw, teeter-totter *(US)* ◆ **cheval/fauteuil à ~** rocking horse/chair ◆ **mouvement de ~** *(lit)* rocking motion; *(fig)* turnaround ◆ **le mouvement de ~ de l'électorat** the swing in the mood of the electorate ◆ **pratiquer une politique de ~** to run with the hare and hunt with the hounds 3 *(= mécanisme)* bascule ◆ **~ (bistable)** *(Ordin)* flip-flop ◆ **interrupteur à ~** *(Élec)* toggle switch 4 *(Lutte)* lift-over

basculer /baskyle/ ► conjug 1 ◄ VI 1 *[personne]* to topple *ou* fall over, to overbalance; *[objet]* to fall *ou* tip over; *[benne, planche, wagon]* to tip up; *[tas]* to topple (over) ◆ **il bascula dans le vide** he toppled over the edge

2 *(= changer)* to change dramatically ◆ **ma vie a basculé** my life was turned upside down ◆ **~ dans l'opposition** to swing *ou* go over to the opposition ◆ **~ dans le chaos** to be plunged into chaos ◆ **~ dans le cauchemar** to plunge into a nightmare ◆ **~ à gauche** *(Pol)* to swing to the left ◆ **tout a basculé quand le Pérou a été touché par la crise** things changed dramatically *ou* took a very different turn when Peru was affected by the crisis ◆ **le match a basculé à la 37e minute** the match changed course *ou* turned dramatically in the 37th minute

3 *(Ordin)* to toggle; *(Élec)* to switch *(sur* to*)*

4 *(locutions)*

◆ **faire basculer** *[+ benne]* to tip up; *[+ contenu]* to tip out; *[+ appel téléphonique]* to divert; *[+ personne]* to knock off balance, to topple over ◆ **la gauche européenne peut faire ~ la majorité au Parlement** the European left may tilt the balance of power in the parliament ◆ **faire ~ l'opinion du côté des étudiants** to swing opinion in favour of the students ◆ **son mariage avec un Espagnol a fait ~ son destin** her marriage with a Spaniard changed the course of her life ◆ **la guerre a fait ~ sa vie** the war changed the course of her life ◆ **l'homme qui peut faire ~ son pays dans le troisième millénaire** the man who can propel his country into the third millennium ◆ **l'essai qui a fait ~ le match en faveur de Castres** the try which turned *ou* swung the match in favour of Castres ◆ **les trois témoins qui peuvent encore faire ~ le procès** the three witnesses who could still change the course of the trial

VT to tilt; *[+ charges]* to move

basculeur /baskylœʀ/ NM 1 *(Élec)* rocker switch 2 *[de benne]* tipper

base /bɑz/ NF 1 *[de bâtiment, colonne, triangle, montagne]* base; *[de gâteau, maquillage]* base; *(Anat, Chim, Math, Ordin)* base; *(Ling = racine)* root ◆ **calculer en ~ 2/10** to calculate in base 2/10 ◆ **~ (de vernis à ongles)** (nail varnish) base coat

2 *(= lieu, Mil)* base ◆ **~ navale/aérienne** naval/air base ◆ **rentrer à sa** *ou* **la ~** to return to base

3 *(Pol)* **la ~** the rank and file, the grass roots ◆ **militant de ~** grassroots activist

4 *(= fondement)* basis ◆ **~s** basis *(sg)*, foundations ◆ **~s d'un traité/d'un accord** basis of a treaty/of an agreement ◆ **raisonnement fondé sur des ~s solides** solidly-based argument ◆ **il a des ~s solides en anglais** he has a good grounding in English *ou* a sound basic knowledge of English ◆ **jeter/saper les ~s de ...** to lay/undermine the foundations of ...

5 *(locutions)*

◆ **à base de** ◆ **produit à ~ de soude** soda-based product ◆ **cocktail à ~ de gin** gin-based cocktail

◆ **à la base** *(= fondamentalement)* basically, fundamentally

◆ **à la base de** *(= au cœur de)* ◆ **être à la ~ de** to be at the root of

◆ **de base** *(gén)* basic; *[employé]* low-ranking; *[vocabulaire]* basic, core ◆ **les métiers de ~ d'une entreprise** a company's core activities ◆ **forme de ~** base form

◆ **sur la base de** ◆ **sur la ~ de ces renseignements** on the basis of this information ◆ **ces départs s'effectuent sur la ~ du volontariat** the redundancies will take place on a voluntary basis

COMP **base de départ** *(fig)* starting point *(fig)*
base de données database
base d'imposition taxable amount
base de lancement launching site
base de loisirs sports and recreation park
base d'opérations base of operations, operations base
base de ravitaillement supply base
base de temps *(Ordin)* clock

base(-)ball (pl **base(-)balls**) /bɛzbol/ NM baseball

Bas-Empire /bazɑ̃piʀ/ NM ◆ **le ~** the late Roman Empire

baser /bɑze/ ► conjug 1 ◄ VT 1 *(= fonder)* to base *(sur* on*)*; ◆ **une économie basée sur le pétrole** an oil-based economy 2 **être basé quelque part** *(gén, Mil)* to be based somewhere VPR **se baser** *(= se fonder)* ◆ **se ~ sur** to base one's judgement on ◆ **sur quoi vous basez-vous ?** what is the basis of your argument?

bas-fond (pl **bas-fonds**) /bafɔ̃/ NM 1 *(Naut) (= haut-fond)* shallow, shoal; *(= dépression)* depression 2 *(péj)* **les ~s de la société** the lowest depths *ou* the dregs of society ◆ **les ~s de la ville** the seediest *ou* slummiest parts of the town

BASIC /bazik/ NM BASIC

basilic /bazilik/ NM *(= plante)* basil; *(= animal)* basilisk

basilique /bazilik/ NF *(Rel)* basilica

basique /bazik/ ADJ *(gén, Chim)* basic NM *(= vêtement)* basic item, basic

basket /baskɛt/ NM *(Sport)* basketball NF *(= chaussure)* **~s** *(gén)* sneakers, trainers *(Brit)*, ≈ tennis shoes *(US)*; *(pour joueur)* basketball boots *(Brit)*, high-tops *(US)* ◆ **être à l'aise dans ses ~s*** to be at ease with o.s. ◆ **des adolescents mal dans leurs ~s** unhappy teenagers, teenagers with problems; → **lâcher**

basket-ball (pl **basket-balls**) /basketbol/ NM basketball

basketteur, -euse /basketœʀ, øz/ NM,F basketball player

basmati /basmati/ ADJ ◆ **riz ~** basmati rice

basquaise /baskɛz/ ADJ F *(Culin)* ◆ **poulet ~** basquaise chicken NF **Basquaise** Basque (woman)

basque[1] /bask/ ADJ Basque ◆ **le Pays ~** the Basque Country NM *(= langue)* Basque NMF **Basque** Basque

basque[2] /bask/ NF *[d'habit]* skirt(s); *[de robe]* basque; → **pendu**

bas-relief (pl **bas-reliefs**) /baʀəljɛf/ NM bas relief, low relief ◆ **en ~** bas-relief *(épith)*, low-relief *(épith)*, in bas *ou* low relief

basse[2] /bɑs/ NF 1 *(= chanteur)* bass; *(= voix)* bass (voice); *(= contrebasse)* (double) bass; *(= guitare)* bass ◆ **flûte/trombone ~** bass flute/trombone ◆ **~ de viole** bass viol, viola da gamba; → **doucement** 2 *(= partie)* **~ chiffrée** figured bass ◆ **~ continue** (basso) continuo, thorough bass ◆ **~ contrainte** *ou* **obstinée** ground bass

basse-cour (pl **basses-cours**) /baskuʀ/ NF *(= lieu)* farmyard; *(= animaux)* farmyard animals ◆ **c'est une vraie ~ ce bureau !** *(péj)* this office is like a henhouse!

basse-fosse (pl **basses-fosses**) /bɑsfos/ NF *(littér)* dungeon

bassement /bɑsmɑ̃/ ADV basely, meanly, despicably

bassesse /bɑsɛs/ NF 1 *(= servilité)* servility; *(= mesquinerie)* meanness, baseness, lowness 2 *(= acte servile)* servile act; *(= acte mesquin)* low *ou* mean *ou* base *ou* despicable act ◆ **il ferait des ~s pour avoir de l'avancement** he'd stoop to anything to get promoted

basset /basɛ/ NM *(= chien)* basset (hound)

basse-taille (pl **basses-tailles**) /bɑstaj/ NF *(Mus)* bass baritone

bassin /basɛ̃/ NM 1 *(Anat)* pelvis 2 *(= pièce d'eau)* ornamental lake; *(plus petit)* pond; *[de piscine]* pool; *[de fontaine]* basin ◆ **petit/grand ~** *[de piscine]* small/main pool ◆ **~ de décantation** settling basin *ou* tank 3 *(Naut)* dock ◆ **~ de radoub/de marée** dry *ou* graving/tidal dock 4 *(= cuvette)* bowl; *(Méd)* bedpan 5 *(Géog, Géol)* basin ◆ **~ houiller/minier** coal/mineral field *ou* basin ◆ **~ hydrographique** catchment basin *ou* area ◆ **le Bassin parisien** the Paris Basin ◆ **~ de retenue (d'un barrage)** (dam) reservoir ◆ **~ industriel/sidérurgique** industrial/steel-producing area 6 *(Écon)* area ◆ **~ d'emploi(s)** labour market area

bassine /basin/ NF 1 *(= cuvette)* bowl, basin ◆ **~ à confiture** preserving pan 2 *(= contenu)* bowl(ful)

bassiner /basine/ ► conjug 1 ◄ VT 1 *[+ plaie]* to bathe; *(Agr)* to sprinkle *ou* spray (water on) 2 *[+ lit]* to warm (with a warming pan) 3 *(* = ennuyer)* to bore ◆ **elle nous bassine** she's a pain in the neck*

bassinet /basinɛ/ NM *(Anat)* renal pelvis; → **cracher**

bassinoire /basinwaʀ/ NF *(Hist)* warming pan

bassiste /basist/ NMF *(= contrebassiste)* double bass player; *(= guitariste)* bass guitarist

basson /basɔ̃/ NM *(= instrument)* bassoon; *(= musicien)* bassoonist

bassoniste /basɔnist/ NMF bassoonist

basta* /basta/ EXCL that's enough!

baste †† /bast/ EXCL *(= indifférence)* never mind!, who cares?; *(= dédain)* pooh!

bastide /bastid/ NF 1 *(= maison)* (country) house *(in Provence)* 2 *(Hist = village)* walled town *(in S.W. France)*

bastille /bastij/ NF fortress, castle ◆ **la Bastille** *(Hist)* the Bastille

bastingage /bastɛ̃gaʒ/ NM *(Naut)* (ship's) rail; *(Hist)* bulwark

bastion /bastjɔ̃/ NM *(= fortification)* bastion; *(fig)* bastion, stronghold

baston** /bastɔ̃/ NM *ou* NF fight, punch-up* *(Brit)* ◆ **il va y avoir du ~** things are going to get nasty

bastonnade /bastɔnad/ NF drubbing, beating

bastonner (se)** /bastɔne/ ► conjug 1 ◄ VPR to fight

bastos /bastos/ NF *(arg Crime = balle)* slug*

bastringue* /bastʀɛ̃g/ NM 1 *(= objets)* junk*, clobber** *(Brit)* ◆ **et tout le ~** the whole caboodle* *(Brit) ou* kit and caboodle* *(US)* 2 *(= bruit)* racket*, din* 3 *(= bal)* (local) dance hall; *(= orchestre)* band

Basutoland /basytɔlɑ̃d/ NM Basutoland

bas-ventre (pl **bas-ventres**) /bavɑ̃tʀ/ NM *(= région génitale)* groin (area); *(= abdomen)* lower abdomen ◆ **il a reçu un coup de genou dans le ~** he was kneed in the groin

BAT /beate/ NM (abrév de **bon à tirer**) → **bon¹**

bat. abrév de **bâtiment**

bât /bɑ/ NM *[d'âne, mule]* packsaddle ◆ **c'est là où le ~ blesse** *(fig)* there's the rub

bataclan * /batakla/ NM junk*, clobber* *(Brit)* ◆ **et tout le ~** the whole caboodle* *(Brit) ou* kit and caboodle* *(US)*

bataille /bataj/ NF 1 *(Mil)* battle; (= *rixe, querelle*) fight; (= *controverse*) fight, dispute ◆ ~ **de rue** street fight *ou* battle ◆ ~ **juridique** legal battle ◆ **la vie est une dure ~** life is a hard fight *ou* struggle ◆ **il arrive toujours après la ~** *(fig)* he always turns up when it's too late
◆ **en bataille** *(Mil, Naut)* in battle order *ou* formation ◆ **il a les cheveux en ~** his hair's a mess ◆ **le chapeau en ~** with his hat on askew ◆ **être garé en ~** to be parked at an angle (to the kerb)
2 *(Cartes)* beggar-my-neighbour
COMP **bataille aérienne** air battle
bataille aéronavale sea and air battle
bataille de boules de neige snowball fight
bataille électorale electoral battle
bataille navale *(Mil)* naval battle; (= *jeu*) battleships ◆ **faire une ~ navale** to play battleships
bataille rangée pitched battle
bataille terrestre land battle

batailler /bataje/ ▸ conjug 1 ◂ VI (= *lutter*) to fight, to battle ◆ ~ **dur ou ferme** to fight hard

batailleur, -euse /batajœʀ, øz/ ADJ pugnacious, aggressive ◆ **il est ~** he loves a fight NM,F (= *arriviste*) fighter

bataillon /batajɔ̃/ NM *(Mil)* battalion; *(fig)* crowd, herd

bâtard, e /bataʀ, aʀd/ ADJ 1 *[enfant]* † illegitimate, bastard † *(péj)* *(épith)* 2 *[œuvre, solution]* hybrid *(épith)* ◆ **chien ~** mongrel 3 *[écriture]* slanting round-hand NM,F *(péj)* (= *personne*) illegitimate child, bastard † *(péj)*; (= *chien*) mongrel NM *(Boulangerie)* (short) loaf of bread NF **bâtarde** (= *écriture*) slanting round-hand

bâtardise /bataʀdiz/ NF bastardy † *(péj)*, illegitimacy

batave /batav/ ADJ *(Hist)* Batavian; *(hum)* Dutch ◆ **la République ~** the Batavian Republic NMF **Batave** *(Hist)* Batavian; *(hum)* Dutch person

batavia /batavja/ NF Webb lettuce

bateau (pl **bateaux**) /bato/ NM 1 *(gén)* boat; *(grand)* ship ◆ ~ **à moteur/à rames/à voiles** motor/rowing/sailing boat ◆ **prendre le ~** (= *embarquer*) to embark, to take the boat *(à* at); (= *voyager*) to go by boat, to sail ◆ **faire du ~** *(à voiles)* to go sailing; *(à rames)* to go boating; *(à moteur)* to go out on a motorboat ◆ **mener qn en ~** *(fig)* to take sb for a ride*, to lead sb up the garden path*
2 *[de trottoir]* dip (in front of a driveway entrance) ◆ **il s'est garé devant le ~** he parked in front of the driveway entrance
3 *(Couture)* **encolure** *ou* **décolleté ~** boat neck
4 (* = *mystification*) hoax, joke ◆ **monter un ~ (à qn)** to play a practical joke (on sb)
ADJ INV (* = *banal*) hackneyed ◆ **c'est (un sujet** *ou* **thème) ~** it's the same old theme* *ou* the favourite topic (that crops up every time)
COMP **bateau amiral** flagship
bateau de commerce merchant ship *ou* vessel
bateau de guerre warship, battleship
bateau de pêche fishing boat
bateau de plaisance yacht
bateau pneumatique inflatable boat
bateau de sauvetage lifeboat
bateau à vapeur steamer, steamship

bateau-citerne (pl **bateaux-citernes**) /batositeʀn/ NM tanker

bateau-école (pl **bateaux-écoles**) /batoekɔl/ NM training ship

bateau-feu (pl **bateaux-feux**) /batofø/ NM lightship

bateau-lavoir (pl **bateaux-lavoirs**) /batolavwaʀ/ NM wash-shed (on river) ◆ **capitaine** *ou* **amiral de ~** *(péj ou hum)* freshwater sailor

bateau-mouche (pl **bateaux-mouches**) /batomuʃ/ NM river boat *(for sightseeing, especially in Paris)*

bateau-phare (pl **bateaux-phares**) /batofaʀ/ NM lightship

bateau-pilote (pl **bateaux-pilotes**) /batopilɔt/ NM pilot boat

bateau-pompe (pl **bateaux-pompes**) /batopɔ̃p/ NM fireboat

bateleur, -euse /batlœʀ, øz/ NM,F † tumbler; *(péj)* buffoon

batelier /batəlje/ NM *(gén)* boatman, waterman; *[de bac]* ferryman

batelière /batəljeʀ/ NF *(gén)* boatwoman; *[de bac]* ferrywoman

batellerie /batɛlʀi/ NF 1 (= *transport*) inland water transport *ou* navigation, canal transport 2 (= *bateaux*) river and canal craft

bâter /bate/ ▸ conjug 1 ◂ VT to put a packsaddle on; → **âne**

bat-flanc /baflɑ/ NM INV *[de lit]* boards

bath †* /bat/ ADJ INV *[personne, chose]* super*, great*, smashing* *(surtout Brit)*

bathymètre /batimɛtʀ/ NM bathometer, bathymeter

bathymétrie /batimetʀi/ NF bathometry, bathymetry

bathymétrique /batimetʀik/ ADJ bathymetric

bathyscaphe /batiskaf/ NM bathyscaphe

bathysphère /batisfɛʀ/ NF bathysphere

bâti, e /bati/ (ptp de **bâtir**) ADJ 1 *(Constr)* **terrain ~** developed site ◆ **terrain non ~** undeveloped site 2 *(fig)* **cette dissertation est bien/mal ~e** this essay is/is not well constructed ◆ **Robert est bien ~** Robert is well-built NM 1 *(Couture)* tacking *(NonC)* ◆ **point de ~** tacking stitch 2 *(Constr)* *[de porte]* frame; *[de machine]* stand, support, frame

batifolage /batifɔlaʒ/ NM 1 (= *folâtrerie*) frolicking *ou* larking *(Brit)* about 2 (= *flirt*) dallying, flirting 3 (= *perte de temps*) messing *ou* larking *(Brit)* about

batifoler * /batifɔle/ ▸ conjug 1 ◂ VI 1 (= *folâtrer*) to frolic *ou* lark *(Brit)* about 2 (= *flirter*) to dally, to flirt *(avec* with) 3 *(péj* = *perdre son temps)* to mess *ou* lark *(Brit)* about

batik /batik/ NM batik

bâtiment /batimɑ/ NM 1 (= *édifice*) building ◆ **~s d'habitation** living quarters ◆ **~s d'exploitation** farm buildings *ou* sheds 2 (= *industrie*) **le ~** the building industry *ou* trade ◆ **être dans le ~** to be in the building trade, to be a builder 3 *(Naut)* ship, vessel ◆ ~ **de guerre** warship

bâtir /batiʀ/ ▸ conjug 2 ◂ VT 1 *(Constr)* to build ◆ **(se) faire ~ une maison** to have a house built ◆ **se ~ une maison** to build o.s. a house ◆ ~ **sur le roc/sable** *(lit, fig)* to build on rock/sand ◆ **terrain/pierre à ~** building land/stone 2 *[+ hypothèse]* to build (up); *[+ phrase]* to construct, to build; *[+ fortune]* to amass, to build up; *[+ réputation]* to build (up), to make *(sur* on); *[+ plan]* to draw up 3 *(Couture)* to tack, to baste ◆ **fil/coton à ~** tacking *ou* basting thread/cotton VPR **se bâtir** ◆ **la maison s'est bâtie en 3 jours** the house was built *ou* put up in 3 days

bâtisse /batis/ NF 1 (= *maison*) building; *(péj)* great pile *ou* edifice 2 (= *maçonnerie*) masonry

bâtisseur, -euse /batisœʀ, øz/ NM,F builder ◆ ~ **d'empire** empire builder

batiste /batist/ NF batiste, cambric, lawn

Batobus ® /batobys/ NM river bus

bâton /batɔ̃/ NM 1 (= *morceau de bois*) stick; (= *canne*) stick, staff *(littér)*; *(Rel* = *insigne)* staff; (= *trique*) club, cudgel; *(à deux mains)* staff; *[d'agent de police]* baton ◆ **il est mon ~ de vieillesse** *(hum)* he is the prop *ou* staff of my old age *(hum)*
2 *[de craie, encens, réglisse]* stick ◆ ~ **de rouge (à lèvres)** lipstick
3 (= *trait*) vertical line *ou* stroke ◆ **faire des ~s** *(Scol)* to draw vertical lines *(when learning to write)* ◆ **caractères ~(s)** *(Typo)* sans-serif characters
4 (* = *million de centimes*) ten thousand francs
5 *(locutions)* **il m'a mis des ~s dans les roues** he put a spoke in my wheel, he put a spanner *(Brit) ou* wrench *(US)* in the works (for me) ◆ **parler à ~s rompus** to talk about this and that ◆ **conversation à ~s rompus** desultory conversation
COMP **bâton de berger** shepherd's crook
bâton blanc † *[d'agent de police]* policeman's baton
bâton de chaise chair rung
bâton de maréchal *(lit)* marshal's baton ◆ **ce poste, c'est son ~ de maréchal** *(fig)* that's the highest post he'll ever hold
bâton de pèlerin *(Rel)* pilgrim's staff ◆ **prendre son ~ de pèlerin** to set out on a mission
bâton de pluie rainstick
bâton de ski ski stick *ou* pole

bâtonner †† /batɔne/ ▸ conjug 1 ◂ VT to beat with a stick, to cudgel

bâtonnet /batɔnɛ/ NM short stick *ou* rod; *(Anat)* rod; *(pour nettoyer les oreilles)* cotton bud ◆ ~ **glacé** ice pop ◆ **~s de poisson pané** fish fingers *(Brit)*, fish sticks *(US)*

bâtonnier, -ière /batɔnje, jɛʀ/ NM,F ≈ president of the Bar

batracien /batʀasjɛ̃/ NM batrachian

battage /bataʒ/ NM 1 *[de tapis, or]* beating; *[de céréales]* threshing 2 (* = *publicité*) hype* ◆ ~ **médiatique** media hype ◆ **faire du ~ autour de qch/qn** to give sth/sb a plug*, to hype sth/sb*

battant, e /batɑ, ɑt/ NM *[de cloche]* clapper, tongue; *[de volet]* shutter, flap ◆ ~ **(de porte)** (left-hand *ou* right-hand) door *(of a double door)* ◆ ~ **(de fenêtre)** (left-hand *ou* right-hand) window ◆ **porte à double ~** *ou* **à deux ~s** double door(s) NM,F (= *personne*) fighter *(fig)*, go-getter* ADJ → **battre, pluie, tambour**

batte /bat/ NF *(à beurre)* dasher; *[de blanchisseuse]* washboard; *(Sport)* bat

battement /batmɑ/ NM 1 (= *claquement*) *[de porte, volet]* banging *(NonC)*; *[de pluie]* beating *(NonC)*, (pitter-)patter *(NonC)*; *[de tambour]* beating *(NonC)*, rattle *(NonC)*; *[de voile, toile]* flapping *(NonC)*
2 (= *mouvement*) *[d'ailes]* flapping *(NonC)*, fluttering *(NonC)*, beating *(NonC)*; *[de cils]* fluttering *(NonC)*; *[de rames]* plash *(NonC)*, splash *(NonC)* ◆ ~ **de paupières** blinking *(NonC)* ◆ **~s de jambes** leg movements
3 *(Méd)* *[de cœur]* beat, beating *(NonC)*; *[de pouls]* beat, throbbing *(NonC)*, beating *(NonC)*; *(irrégulier)* fluttering *(NonC)*; *[de tempes]* throbbing *(NonC)* ◆ **avoir/donner des ~s de cœur** to get *ou* have/give palpitations
4 (= *intervalle*) interval ◆ **deux minutes de ~** (= *pause*) a two-minute break; (= *attente*) two minutes' wait; (= *temps libre*) two minutes to spare ◆ **j'ai une heure de ~ de 10 à 11** I'm free

for an hour *ou* I've got an hour to spare between 10 and 11
5 *(Radio)* beat; *(Phon)* flap

batterie /batʀi/ NF 1 *(électrique)* battery; → **recharger**
2 *(Mus = percussion)* percussion (instruments); *(Jazz = instruments)* drum kit ◆ **Luc Cohen à la ~** Luc Cohen on drums *ou* percussion
3 *(Mil)* battery ◆ **~ de missiles/antichars/côtière** missile/anti-tank/ coastal battery ◆ **mettre des canons en ~** to unlimber guns ◆ **les journalistes attendaient, caméras en ~** the journalists were waiting with their cameras at the ready ◆ **changer/dresser ses ~s** *(fig)* to change/lay *ou* make one's plans ◆ **dévoiler ses ~s** *(fig)* to unmask one's guns
4 *(= groupe) [de tests, radars, mesures]* battery ◆ **~ de projecteurs** bank of spotlights
5 ◆ **~ de cuisine** pots and pans, kitchen utensils; *(* = décorations)* gongs*, ironmongery*
6 *(Agr)* battery ◆ **élevage en ~** battery farming *ou* rearing ◆ **poulets de ~** battery chickens
7 *(Danse)* batterie

batteur /batœʀ/ NM 1 *(Culin)* whisk, beater 2 *(= métier) (Mus)* drummer, percussionist; *(Agr)* thresher; *(Métal)* beater; *(Cricket)* batsman; *(Base-ball)* batter

batteuse /batøz/ NF 1 *(Agr)* threshing machine 2 *(Métal)* beater

battle-dress /batœldʀɛs/ NM INV battle-dress

battoir /batwaʀ/ NM 1 *[de laveuse]* beetle, battledore; *(à tapis)* (carpet) beater 2 *(= grandes mains)* **~s*** huge hands, enormous mitts‡

battre /batʀ/ ► conjug 41 ◄ VT 1 *(= vaincre) [+ adversaire, équipe]* to beat, to defeat ◆ **se faire ~** to be beaten *ou* defeated ◆ **il ne se tient pas pour battu** he doesn't consider himself beaten *ou* defeated ◆ **~ qn (par) 6 à 3** *(Sport)* to beat sb 6-3 ◆ **~ qn à plate(s) couture(s)** to thrash sb, to beat sb hands down; → **record**
2 *[+ personne] (= frapper)* to beat, to strike, to hit ◆ **elle ne bat jamais ses enfants** she never hits *ou* smacks her children ◆ **~ qn comme plâtre*** to beat the living daylights out of sb*, to thrash *ou* beat sb soundly ◆ **~ qn à mort** to batter *ou* beat sb to death ◆ **regard de chien battu** hangdog *ou* cowering look ◆ **femmes battues** battered women
3 *[+ tapis, linge, fer, or]* to beat; *[+ blé]* to thresh ◆ **il faut ~ le fer pendant qu'il est chaud** *(Prov)* we (*ou* you *etc*) should strike while the iron is hot *(Prov)* ◆ **il battit l'air/l'eau des bras** his arms thrashed the air/water ◆ **~ le fer à froid** to cold hammer iron ◆ **son manteau lui bat les talons** his coat is flapping round his ankles ◆ **~ le briquet** † to strike a light
4 *(= agiter) [+ beurre]* to churn; *[+ blanc d'œuf]* to beat (up), to whip, to whisk; *[+ crème]* to whip; *[+ cartes]* to shuffle; → **neige**
5 *(= parcourir) [+ région]* to scour, to comb ◆ **~ le pays** to scour the countryside ◆ **~ les buissons** *(Chasse)* to beat the bushes (for game) ◆ **hors des sentiers battus** off the beaten track ◆ **~ la campagne** *(fig)* to let one's mind wander ◆ **~ le pavé** to wander aimlessly about *ou* around
6 *(= heurter) [pluie]* to beat *ou* lash against; *[mer]* to beat *ou* dash against; *(Mil) [+ positions, ennemis]* to batter ◆ **littoral battu par les tempêtes** storm-lashed coast
7 *(Mus)* **~ la mesure** to beat time ◆ **~ le tambour** *(lit)* to beat the drum; *(fig)* to shout from the rooftops ◆ **~ le rappel** to call to arms ◆ **~ le rappel de ses souvenirs** to summon up one's old memories ◆ **~ le rappel de ses amis** to rally one's friends ◆ **~ la retraite** to sound the retreat
8 *(locutions)* **~ la breloque** † *[appareil]* to be erratic ◆ **son cœur bat la breloque** his heart is none too good, he has a bad *ou* dicky* *(Brit)* heart ◆ **son cœur battait la chamade** his heart was pounding *ou* beating wildly ◆ **~ en brèche une théorie** to demolish a theory ◆ **~ froid à qn** to cold-shoulder sb, to give sb the cold shoulder ◆ **~ son plein** *[saison touristique]* to be at its height; *[fête]* to be going full swing ◆ **~ la semelle** to stamp one's feet (to keep warm) ◆ **~ pavillon britannique** to fly the British flag, to sail under the British flag ◆ **~ monnaie** to strike *ou* mint coins ◆ **~ sa coulpe** to beat one's breast *(fig)* ◆ **j'en ai rien à ~**‡ I don't give a damn‡
VI *[cœur, pouls]* to beat; *[montre, métronome]* to tick; *[pluie]* to beat, to lash *(contre* against); *[porte, volets]* to bang, to rattle; *[voile, drapeau]* to flap; *[tambour]* to beat ◆ **son cœur bat pour lui** *(hum)* he's her heart-throb ◆ **son cœur battait d'émotion** his heart was beating wildly *ou* pounding with emotion ◆ **le cœur battant** with beating *ou* pounding heart; → **retraite**
VT INDIR **battre de** ◆ **~ des mains** to clap one's hands; *(fig)* to dance for joy, to exult ◆ **~ du tambour** to beat the drum ◆ **l'oiseau bat des ailes** the bird is beating *ou* flapping its wings ◆ **~ de l'aile** *(fig)* to be in a bad way
VPR **se battre** 1 *(dans une guerre, un combat)* to fight *(avec* with; *contre* against); *(= se disputer)* to quarrel; *(fig)* to fight, to battle, to struggle *(contre* against); ◆ **se ~ comme des chiffonniers** to fight like cat and dog ◆ **se ~ au couteau/à la baïonnette** to fight with knives/bayonets ◆ **nos troupes se sont bien battues** our troops fought well *ou* put up a good fight ◆ **se ~ en duel** to fight a duel ◆ **se ~ contre des moulins à vent** to tilt at windmills ◆ **il faut se ~ pour arriver à obtenir quelque chose** you have to fight to get what you want ◆ **se ~ avec un problème** to struggle *ou* battle with a problem
2 *(fig)* **se ~ les flancs** to rack one's brains ◆ **je m'en bats l'œil**‡ I don't care a fig* *ou* a damn‡

battu, e[1] /baty/ (ptp de **battre**) ADJ → **battre, jeté, œil, pas**[1]**, terre**

battue[2] /baty/ NF *(Chasse)* battue, beat; *(pour retrouver qn)* search

batture /batyʀ/ NF *(Can)* sand bar, strand

bau (pl **baux**) /bo/ NM *(Naut)* beam

baud /bo/ NM *(Ordin)* baud

baudelairien, -ienne /bodlɛʀjɛ̃, jɛn/ ADJ of Baudelaire, Baudelairean

baudet /bodɛ/ NM 1 *(= âne)* donkey, ass 2 *(Menuiserie)* trestle, sawhorse

baudrier /bodʀije/ NM *[d'épée]* baldric; *[de drapeau]* shoulder-belt; *(Alpinisme)* harness; *(pour matériel)* gear sling; → **Orion**

baudroie /bodʀwa/ NF angler (fish)

baudruche /bodʀyʃ/ NF *(= caoutchouc)* rubber; *(péj) (= personne)* wimp*, spineless character; *(= théorie)* empty theory, humbug* ◆ **ça s'est dégonflé comme une ~** it came to nothing *ou* vanished into thin air; → **ballon**[1]

bauge /boʒ/ NF *[de sanglier, porc]* wallow

baume /bom/ NM *(lit)* balm, balsam; *(fig)* balm ◆ **~ après-rasage/pour les lèvres** aftershave/lip balm ◆ **ça lui a mis du ~ au cœur** *(consolé)* it was a great comfort to him; *(rassuré)* it heartened him

Baumé /bome/ N → **degré**

baux /bo/ pl de **bail, bau**

bauxite /boksit/ NF bauxite

bavard, e /bavaʀ, aʀd/ ADJ *[personne]* talkative; *[discours, récit]* long-winded, wordy ◆ **il est ~ comme une pie** he's a real chatterbox NM,F chatterbox, prattler; *(péj)* gossip, blabbermouth*

bavardage /bavaʀdaʒ/ NM *(= papotage)* chatting, talking; *(= jacasserie)* chattering, prattling; *(= commérage)* gossiping ◆ **j'entendais leur(s) ~(s)** I could hear them talking *ou* chattering

bavarder /bavaʀde/ ► conjug 1 ◄ VI 1 *(= papoter)* to chat, to talk; *(= jacasser)* to chatter, to prattle; *(= commérer)* to gossip ◆ **arrêtez de ~ !** stop that chattering! 2 *(= divulguer un secret)* to blab*, to give the game away, to talk

bavarois, e /bavaʀwa, waz/ ADJ Bavarian NM,F 1 *(= personne)* **Bavarois(e)** Bavarian 2 *(Culin)* bavarois ◆ **~(e) aux fraises** strawberry bavarois

bavasser* /bavase/ ► conjug 1 ◄ VI *(= bavarder)* to blather (on)*, to natter* *(Brit)*

bave /bav/ NF *[de personne]* dribble; *[d'animal]* slaver, slobber; *[de chien enragé]* foam, froth; *[d'escargot]* slime; *[de crapaud]* spittle; *(fig)* venom, malicious words ◆ **la ~ du crapaud n'atteint pas la blanche colombe** *(Prov)* sticks and stones might break my bones but names will never hurt me *(Prov)*

baver /bave/ ► conjug 1 ◄ VI 1 *[personne]* to dribble; *(beaucoup)* to slobber, to drool; *[animal]* to slaver, to slobber; *[chien enragé]* to foam *ou* froth at the mouth; *[stylo]* to leak; *[pinceau]* to drip; *[liquide]* to run
♦ **en baver*** ◆ **en ~ d'admiration** to gasp in admiration ◆ **en ~ d'envie** to be green with envy ◆ **en ~** *(= souffrir)* to have a rough *ou* hard time of it* ◆ **il m'en a fait ~** he really gave me a rough *ou* hard time* ◆ **elle n'a pas fini d'en ~ avec son fils** she hasn't seen the last of her troubles with her son yet
2 *(littér)* **~ sur la réputation de qn** to besmear *ou* besmirch sb's reputation
VT ◆ **il en a bavé des ronds de chapeau** ‡ his eyes nearly popped out of his head*

bavette /bavɛt/ NF 1 *[de tablier, enfant]* bib; *(= garde-boue)* mudguard, mud flap 2 *(= viande)* undercut; → **tailler**

baveux, -euse /bavø, øz/ ADJ *[bouche]* dribbling, slobbery; *[enfant]* dribbling ◆ **omelette baveuse** runny omelette ◆ **lettre baveuse** *(Typo)* blurred *ou* smeared letter

Bavière /bavjɛʀ/ NF Bavaria

bavoir /bavwaʀ/ NM bib

bavolet /bavɔlɛ/ NM *[de manteau]* (gun) flap

bavure /bavyʀ/ NF 1 *(= tache)* smudge, smear; *(Tech) [de moule]* burr 2 *(= erreur)* blunder ◆ **~ policière** police blunder ◆ **sans ~(s)** *[travail]* flawless, faultless

bayadère /bajadɛʀ/ NF bayadère ADJ *[tissu]* colourfully striped

bayer /baje/ ► conjug 1 ◄ VI ◆ **~ aux corneilles** to stand gaping, to stand and gape

bayou /baju/ NM bayou

bazar /bazaʀ/ NM 1 *(= magasin)* general store; *(oriental)* bazaar ◆ **psychologie de ~** pop psychology 2 *(* = effets)* junk* *(NonC)*, gear‡ *(NonC)*, things* 3 *(* = désordre)* clutter, jumble, shambles *(NonC)* ◆ **quel ~ !** what a shambles!* ◆ **il a mis le ~ dans mes photos** he jumbled all my photos up ◆ **et tout le ~** and all the rest, and what have you*

bazarder* /bazaʀde/ ► conjug 1 ◄ VT *(= jeter)* to get rid of, to chuck out*; *(= vendre)* to get rid of, to sell off, to flog‡ *(Brit)*

bazooka /bazuka/ NM bazooka

BCBG /besebeʒe/ ADJ (abrév de **bon chic bon genre**) → **bon**[1]

BCBG

The adjective « bon chic bon genre » or **BCBG** refers to a particular stereotype of the French upper middle class. To be **BCBG** is to be quite well-off (though not necessarily wealthy), to be conservative in both outlook and dress, and to attach importance to social standing and outward signs of respectability.

BCE /beseə/ NF (abrév de **Banque centrale européenne**) ECB

BCG ® /beseʒe/ NM (abrév de **bacille Bilié Calmette et Guérin**) BCG ®

BD /bede/ NF [1] (abrév de **bande dessinée**) **la** ~ comic strips, strip cartoons (*Brit*), comics (*US*) ◆ **une** ~ (*dans un journal*) a comic strip, a strip cartoon (*Brit*); (*= livre*) a comic book ◆ **auteur de** ~ comic strip writer, strip cartoonist (*Brit*) ◆ **l'histoire romaine en** ~ a comic-strip book of Roman history; → BANDE DESSINÉE [2] (abrév de **base de données**) DB

bd abrév de **boulevard**

bê /bɛ/ EXCL baa!

beach-volley /bitʃvɔlɛ/ NM beach volleyball

beagle /bigl/ NM beagle

béant, e /beɑ̃, ɑ̃t/ ADJ [*blessure*] gaping, open; [*bouche*] gaping, wide open; [*yeux*] wide open; [*gouffre*] gaping, yawning

béarnais, e /bearnɛ, ɛz/ ADJ [*personne*] from the Béarn ◆ **(sauce)** ~**e** Béarnaise sauce NM,F **Béarnais(e)** inhabitant *ou* native of the Béarn

béat, e /bea, at/ ADJ [1] (*hum*) (*= heureux*) [*personne*] blissfully happy; (*= content de soi*) smug [2] (*= niais*) [*sourire, air*] beatific, blissful ◆ **optimisme** ~ blind optimism ◆ **admiration** ~**e** blind *ou* dumb admiration ◆ **être** ~ **d'admiration** to be struck dumb with admiration ◆ **regarder qn d'un air** ~ to look at sb in open-eyed wonder

béatement /beatmɑ̃/ ADV [*sourire*] beatifically ◆ **il contemplait** ~ **son assiette** he was looking at his plate with an expression of blissful contentment ◆ **on s'endormit** ~ **jusqu'à l'heure du dîner** we slept blissfully until dinner time

béatification /beatifikasjɔ̃/ NF beatification

béatifier /beatifje/ ► conjug 7 ◄ VT to beatify

béatitude /beatityd/ NF (*Rel*) beatitude; (*= bonheur*) bliss ◆ **les Béatitudes** the Beatitudes

beatnik /bitnik/ NMF beatnik ◆ **la génération** ~ the beat generation

Béatrice /beatris/ NF Beatrice

beau, belle /bo, bɛl/

Devant nom masculin commençant par voyelle ou **h** muet = **bel**; masculin pluriel = **beaux**

1 ADJECTIF	3 NOM FÉMININ
2 NOM MASCULIN	

1 - ADJECTIF

[1] (*= qui plaît au regard, à l'oreille*) [*objet, paysage, jambes*] beautiful, lovely; [*femme*] beautiful, good-looking; [*homme*] handsome, good-looking ◆ **il m'a fait un très** ~ **cadeau** he gave me a really nice *ou* a lovely present ◆ **il a une belle tête** he's got a nice face ◆ **les** ~**x quartiers** the smart *ou* posh* districts ◆ **le** ~ **Serge était là** (*hum*) the gorgeous Serge was there ◆ **il est** ~ **comme le jour** *ou* **comme un dieu** he's like a Greek god ◆ **tu es** ~ **comme un camion tout neuf !*** (*hum*) don't you look smart! ◆ **il est** ~ **garçon** he's good-looking ◆ **se faire** ~ to get dressed up *ou* spruced up ◆ **se faire belle** (*= s'habiller, se maquiller*) to do o.s. up ◆ **avec lui, c'est sois belle et tais-toi** he expects you to just sit there and look pretty ◆ **porter** ~ (*littér*) to look dapper ◆ **mettre ses** ~**x habits** to put on one's best clothes

[2] (*= qui plaît à l'esprit, digne d'admiration*) [*discours, match*] fine; [*film, poème, roman*] beautiful, fine; [*nom*] beautiful ◆ **il a fait du** ~ **travail** he did a really good job ◆ **il y a quelques** ~**x moments dans cette pièce** there are some fine moments in the play ◆ **elle a fait une belle carrière** she had a successful career ◆ **c'est une belle mort** it's a good way to go ◆ **une belle âme** a fine *ou* noble nature ◆ **un** ~ **geste** a noble act, a fine gesture ◆ **ce n'est pas** ~ **de mentir** it isn't nice to tell lies ◆ **il ferait** ~ **voir que ...** it would be a fine thing if ... ◆ **il ferait** ~ **voir qu'il mente !** he'd better not be lying!; → **joueur** *etc*

[3] (*= agréable*) [*voyage*] lovely; [*journée*] beautiful, fine ◆ **par une belle soirée d'été** on a beautiful *ou* fine summer's evening ◆ **il fait** ~ the weather's fine *ou* nice ◆ **il fait très** ~ the weather's beautiful ◆ **la mer était belle** (*sans vagues*) the sea was calm ◆ **c'est le bel âge** those are the best years of your life ◆ **c'est le plus** ~ **jour de ma vie !** this is the best day of my life! ◆ **c'est trop** ~ **pour être vrai** it's too good to be true ◆ **ce serait trop** ~ **!** that would be too much to hope for!; → **jeu, rôle** *etc*

[4] (*intensif*) [*revenu, profit*] handsome; [*résultat, occasion*] excellent, fine; [*brûlure, peur*] nasty ◆ **ça fait une belle somme !** that's a tidy* sum (of money)! ◆ **il en reste un** ~ **morceau** there's still a good bit (of it) left ◆ **le film a remporté un** ~ **succès** the film was a big *ou* great success ◆ **ça a fait un** ~ **scandale** it caused quite a scandal, it caused a big scandal ◆ **95 ans, c'est un bel âge** 95 is a good age *ou* a fine old age ◆ **il est arrivé un** ~ **matin/jour** he turned up one fine morning/day ◆ **il a attrapé une belle bronchite** he's got a nasty attack *ou* a bad bout of bronchitis ◆ **c'est un** ~ **menteur** he's a terrible *ou* the most awful liar ◆ **c'est un** ~ **salaud**‡ he's a real bastard*‡

[5] (*locutions*) **tout** ~**(, tout** ~**) !** † steady on!, easy does it!

◆ **avoir beau** + *infinitif* ◆ **on a** ~ **faire/dire, ils n'apprennent rien** whatever you do/say *ou* no matter what you do/say, they don't learn anything ◆ **on a** ~ **protester, personne n'écoute** however much *ou* no matter how much you protest, no one listens ◆ **il a eu** ~ **essayer, il ...** however much *ou* whatever he tried, he ..., try as he might, he ... ◆ **on a** ~ **dire, il n'est pas bête** say what you like, he is not stupid

◆ **l'avoir belle de** * ◆ **il l'avait belle de s'échapper/de lui dire ce qu'il pensait** it would have been easy for him to escape/to say what he thought

◆ **bel et bien** well and truly ◆ **il s'est bel et bien trompé** he got it well and truly wrong ◆ **cet homme a bel et bien existé** the man really did exist ◆ **il est bel et bien mort** he's well and truly dead, he's dead all right* ◆ **ils sont bel et bien entrés par la fenêtre** they got in through the window, there's no doubt about that, they got in through the window all right*

◆ **de plus belle** even more ◆ **crier de plus belle** to shout even louder ◆ **rire de plus belle** to laugh even louder *ou* harder ◆ **reprendre de plus belle** [*combat, polémique, violence*] to start up again with renewed vigour ◆ **continuer de plus belle** [*discrimination, répression*] to be worse than ever

2 - NOM MASCULIN

[1] (*esthétiquement*) **le** ~ the beautiful ◆ **le culte du** ~ the cult of beauty ◆ **elle n'aime que le** ~ she only likes what is beautiful ◆ **elle n'achète que du** ~ she only buys the best quality

[2] (*Helv = beau temps*) nice weather ◆ **ils ont annoncé du** ~ they've forecast nice weather ◆ **il fait grand** ~ it's lovely weather

[3] (*locutions*) **c'est du** ~ **!** (*iro*) lovely! (*iro*); (*reproche*) that was a fine thing to do! (*iro*); (*consternation*) this is a fine business! *ou* a fine mess! ◆ **le plus** ~ **de l'histoire, c'est que ...** the best part is that ...

◆ **au beau** ◆ **être au** ~ [*temps*] to be fine, to be set fair ◆ **être au** ~ **(fixe)** [*baromètre*] to be set fair; [*relations*] to be as good as ever ◆ **nos rapports ne sont pas au** ~ **fixe** things are a bit strained between us ◆ **son moral n'est pas au** ~ **fixe** he's in low spirits ◆ **la situation n'est pas au** ~ **fixe** things aren't looking too good

◆ **faire le beau** [*chien*] to sit up and beg; (*péj*) [*personne*] to curry favour (*devant* with)

3 - NOM FÉMININ

belle

[1] (*= femme*) beautiful woman ◆ **sa belle** (*= compagne*) his lady friend ◆ **ma belle !*** sweetie!*, sweetheart! ◆ **"la Belle au bois dormant"** (*Littérat*) "Sleeping Beauty" ◆ **"la Belle et la Bête"** (*Littérat*) "Beauty and the Beast"

[2] (*Jeux, Sport*) decider, deciding match ◆ **on fait la belle ?** shall we play a decider?

[3] (**: iro = action, parole*) **en faire de belles** to get up to mischief ◆ **il en a fait de belles quand il était jeune** he was a bit wild when he was young ◆ **en apprendre/dire de belles sur qn** to hear/say things about sb (*euph*) ◆ **j'en ai entendu de belles sur son compte** I've heard some stories about him

[4] [*prisonnier*] **se faire la belle*** to break out of jail, to go over the wall*

beaucoup /boku/ ADV [1] (*modifiant verbe*) a lot, (very) much, a great deal ◆ **il mange** ~ he eats a lot ◆ **elle lit** ~ she reads a great deal *ou* a lot ◆ **elle ne lit pas** ~ she doesn't read much *ou* a great deal *ou* a lot ◆ **la pièce ne m'a pas** ~ **plu** I didn't like the play very much ◆ **il s'intéresse** ~ **à la peinture** he's very interested in painting, he takes a lot *ou* a great deal of interest in painting ◆ **il y a** ~ **à faire/voir** there's a lot to do/see ◆ **il a** ~ **voyagé/lu** he has travelled/read a lot *ou* extensively *ou* a great deal

◆ **beaucoup de** (*quantité*) a great deal of, a lot of, much; (*nombre*) many, a lot of, a good many ◆ ~ **de monde** a lot of people, a great *ou* good many people ◆ **avec** ~ **de soin/plaisir** with great care/pleasure ◆ **il ne reste pas** ~ **de pain** there isn't a lot of *ou* isn't (very) much bread left ◆ **j'ai** ~ **(de choses) à faire** I have a lot (of things) to do ◆ **pour ce qui est de l'argent/du lait, il en reste** ~**/il n'en reste pas** ~ as for money/milk, there is a lot left/there isn't a lot *ou* much left ◆ **vous attendiez des touristes, y en a-t-il eu** ~ **? – oui (il y en a eu)** ~ you were expecting tourists and were there many *ou* a lot (of them)? – yes there were (a good many *ou* a lot of them) ◆ **j'en connais** ~ **qui pensent que ...** I know a great many (people) *ou* a lot of people who think that ... ◆ **il a** ~ **d'influence** he has a great deal *ou* a lot of influence, he is very influential ◆ **il a eu** ~ **de chance** he's been very lucky

◆ **de beaucoup** by far, by a long way ◆ **elle est de** ~ **la meilleure élève** she's by far *ou* she's far and away the best pupil, she's the best pupil by far ◆ **il l'a battu de** ~ he beat him by miles* *ou* by a long way ◆ **il est de** ~ **ton aîné** he's very much *ou* a great deal older than you ◆ **il est de** ~ **supérieur** he is greatly *ou* far superior ◆ **il préférerait de** ~ **s'en aller** he'd much rather leave ◆ **il s'en faut de** ~ **qu'il soit au niveau** he is far from being up to standard, he's nowhere near up to standard

[2] (*modifiant adv*) much, far, a good deal, a lot ◆ ~ **plus rapide** much *ou* a good deal *ou* a lot

quicker ◆ **elle travaille ~ trop** she works far too much ◆ **elle travaille ~ trop lentement** she works much *ou* far too slowly ◆ **se sentir ~ mieux** to feel much *ou* miles* better ◆ **~ plus d'eau** much *ou* a lot *ou* far more water ◆ **~ moins de gens** many *ou* a lot *ou* far fewer people ◆ **il est susceptible, il l'est même ~** he's touchy, in fact he's very touchy indeed

3 *(employé seul = personnes)* many ◆ **ils sont ~ à croire que ..., ~ croient que ...** many *ou* a lot of people think that ... ◆ **~ d'entre eux** a lot *ou* many of them

4 *(locutions)* **c'est déjà ~ de l'avoir fait** *ou* **qu'il l'ait fait** it was quite something *ou* quite an achievement to have done it at all ◆ **à ~ près** far from it ◆ **c'est ~ dire** that's an exaggeration *ou* an overstatement, that's saying a lot ◆ **être pour ~ dans une décision/une nomination** to be largely responsible for a decision/an appointment, to have a big hand in making a decision/an appointment ◆ **il y est pour ~** he's largely responsible for it, he had a lot to do with it

beauf* /bof/ **ADJ** *[goûts, tenue]* tacky* **NM** 1 *(= beau-frère)* brother-in-law 2 *(péj)* narrow-minded Frenchman with conservative attitudes and tastes

> **BEAUF**
>
> The word **beauf** is an abbreviation of « beau-frère » (brother-in-law). It is a pejorative and humorous term used to refer to stereotypical ordinary Frenchmen who are perceived as being somewhat vulgar, narrow-minded and chauvinistic.

beau-fils (pl **beaux-fils**) /bofis/ **NM** *(= gendre)* son-in-law; *(d'un remariage)* stepson

beaufort /bofɔʀ/ **NM** 1 *(= fromage) type of gruyère cheese* 2 ◆ **Beaufort** → **échelle**

beau-frère (pl **beaux-frères**) /bofʀɛʀ/ **NM** brother-in-law

beaujolais /boʒɔlɛ/ **NM** 1 *(= région)* **le Beaujolais** the Beaujolais region 2 *(= vin)* beaujolais, Beaujolais ◆ **le ~ nouveau** (the) beaujolais *ou* Beaujolais nouveau, (the) new beaujolais *ou* Beaujolais

beau-papa* (pl **beaux-papas**) /bopapa/ **NM** father-in-law, dad-in-law* *(Brit)*

beau-père (pl **beaux-pères**) /bopɛʀ/ **NM** *(= père du conjoint)* father-in-law; *(= nouveau mari de la mère)* stepfather

beaupré /bopʀe/ **NM** bowsprit

beauté /bote/ **NF** 1 *(gén)* beauty; *[d'homme]* handsomeness ◆ **les ~s de Rome** *(= belles choses)* the beauties of Rome ◆ **de toute ~** very beautiful, magnificent ◆ **c'est ça la ~ de la chose** that's the beauty of it ◆ **se (re)faire une ~** to powder one's nose, to do one's face* ◆ **faire qch pour la ~ du geste** to do sth for the sake of it ◆ **la ~ du diable** youthful beauty *ou* bloom; → **concours, produit, reine, soin**

◆ **en beauté** ◆ **vous êtes en ~ ce soir** you look radiant this evening ◆ **finir** *ou* **terminer qch en ~** to complete sth brilliantly, to finish sth with a flourish ◆ **finir en ~** to end with a flourish, to finish brilliantly

2 *(= belle femme)* beauty

beaux /bo/ **ADJ MPL** → **beau**

beaux-arts /bozaʀ/ **NMPL** 1 *(= arts)* ◆ **les ~** fine arts 2 *(= école) (à Paris)* the (École des) Beaux-Arts *(the French national college of art and architecture)*; *(en province)* art college

beaux-parents /bopaʀɑ̃/ **NMPL** *[d'homme]* wife's parents, in-laws*; *[de femme]* husband's parents, in-laws*

bébé /bebe/ **NM** *(= enfant, animal)* baby; *(= poupée)* dolly* ◆ **~ éléphant/girafe** baby elephant/giraffe ◆ **elle attend un ~** she's expecting a baby ◆ **avoir** *ou* **faire un ~** to have a baby ◆ **faire le ~** to behave *ou* act like a baby ◆ **il est resté très ~** he's stayed very babyish ◆ **jeter le ~ avec l'eau du bain** to throw out the baby with the bathwater ◆ **on lui a repassé** *ou* **refilé le ~*** he was left holding the baby ◆ **(syndrome du) ~ secoué** shaken baby syndrome

COMP **bébé-bulle** bubble baby *(baby who has to live in a sterile environment because of an immune deficiency)*

bébé-éprouvette test-tube baby

bébé-nageur *baby that swims*

bebelle /bəbɛl/, **bébelle** /bebɛl/ **NF** *(Can = bibelot)* knick-knack ◆ **range tes bébelles** tidy away your things

bébête* /bebɛt/ **ADJ** silly **NF** bug ◆ **une petite ~** a creepy crawly*, a bug

be-bop (pl **be-bops**) /bibɔp/ **NM** (be)bop

bec /bɛk/ **NM** 1 *[d'oiseau]* beak, bill ◆ **oiseau qui se fait le ~** bird that sharpens its beak *(contre* on); ◆ **(nez en) ~ d'aigle** aquiline *ou* hook nose ◆ **coup de ~** *(lit)* peck; *(fig)* dig, cutting remark

2 *(= pointe) [de plume]* nib; *[de carafe, casserole]* lip; *[de théière]* spout; *[de flûte, trompette]* mouthpiece; *(Géog)* bill, headland; *(sur vêtement)* pucker ◆ **ça fait un ~ dans le dos** it puckers in the back

3 *(* = bouche)* mouth ◆ **ouvre ton ~ !** open your mouth!, mouth open!* ◆ **ferme ton ~ !** just shut up!* ◆ **il n'a pas ouvert le ~** he never opened his mouth, he didn't say a word ◆ **la pipe au ~** with his pipe stuck* in his mouth ◆ **clore** *ou* **clouer le ~ à qn** to reduce sb to silence, to shut sb up*; → **prise²**

4 *(locutions)* **tomber sur un ~*** *(obstacle temporaire)* to hit a snag; *(impasse)* to be stymied*; *(échec)* to come unstuck* ◆ **être** *ou* **rester le ~ dans l'eau*** to be left in the lurch, to be left high and dry ◆ **défendre qch ~ et ongles** to fight tooth and nail for sth

5 *(* : Can, Belg, Helv = baiser)* kiss, peck

COMP **bec Auer** Welsbach burner

bec Bunsen Bunsen burner

bec fin* gourmet

bec de gaz lamppost, gaslamp

bec verseur pourer

bécane* /bekan/ **NF** *(= moto)* bike*; *(= machine)* machine; *(= ordinateur)* computer

bécarre /bekaʀ/ **NM** *(Mus)* natural ◆ **sol ~** G natural

bécasse /bekas/ **NF** *(= oiseau)* woodcock; *(* = sotte)* (silly) goose*

bécasseau (pl **bécasseaux**) /bekaso/ **NM** sandpiper; *(= petit de la bécasse)* young woodcock

bécassine /bekasin/ **NF** *(= oiseau)* snipe; *(* = sotte)* (silly) goose*

bec-croisé (pl **becs-croisés**) /bɛkkʀwaze/ **NM** crossbill

bec-de-cane (pl **becs-de-cane**) /bɛkdəkan/ **NM** *(= poignée)* doorhandle; *(= serrure)* catch

bec-de-lièvre (pl **becs-de-lièvre**) /bɛkdəljɛvʀ/ **NM** harelip

bec-de-perroquet (pl **becs-de-perroquet**) /bɛkdəpeʀɔkɛ/ **NM** *(Méd)* osteophyte

bêchage /bɛʃaʒ/ **NM** digging, turning over

béchamel /beʃamɛl/ **NF** ◆ **(sauce) ~** béchamel (sauce), white sauce

bêche /bɛʃ/ **NF** spade

bêcher /beʃe/ ► conjug 1 ◄ **VT** *(Agr)* to dig, to turn over **VI** *(* = crâner)* to be stuck-up *ou* toffee-nosed* *(Brit)*

bêcheur, -euse* /bɛʃœʀ, øz/ **ADJ** stuck-up*, toffee-nosed* *(Brit)* **NM,F** stuck-up* *ou* toffee-nosed* *(Brit)* person

bécot* /beko/ **NM** kiss, peck ◆ **gros ~** smacker*

bécoter* /bekɔte/ ► conjug 1 ◄ **VT** to kiss **VPR** **se bécoter*** to smooch

becquée /beke/ **NF** beakful ◆ **donner la ~ à** to feed

becquerel /bɛkʀɛl/ **NM** becquerel

becquet /bekɛ/ **NM** 1 *(Internet)* bookmark 2 *(= adhésif)* (removable) self-stick note, Post-it (note) ® 3 *[de voiture]* **~ (arrière)** spoiler 4 *(Alpinisme)* (rocky) spike

becquetance* /bɛktɑ̃s/ **NF** grub*, chow* *(US)*

becqueter /bɛkte/ ► conjug 4 ◄ **VT** *(oiseau)* to peck (at); *(* = manger)* to eat ◆ **qu'y a-t-il à ~ ce soir ?** what's for dinner tonight?

bectance* /bɛktɑ̃s/ **NF** ⇒ **becquetance**

becter* /bɛkte/ ► conjug 1 ◄ **VT** ⇒ **becqueter**

bedaine* /bədɛn/ **NF** paunch, potbelly*

bédé* /bede/ **NF** ⇒ **BD 1**

bedeau (pl **bedeaux**) /bədo/ **NM** verger, beadle †

bédéphile /bedefil/ **NMF** comic strip *ou* strip cartoon fan*

bedon* /bədɔ̃/ **NM** paunch, potbelly*

bedonnant, e* /bədɔnɑ̃, ɑt/ **ADJ** potbellied*, paunchy, portly

bedonner* /bədɔne/ ► conjug 1 ◄ **VI** to get a paunch, to get potbellied*

bédouin, -ouine /bedwɛ̃, win/ **ADJ** Bedouin **NM,F** **Bédouin(e)** Bedouin

BEE /beøø/ **NM** (abrév de **Bureau européen de l'environnement**) → **bureau**

bée /be/ **ADJ F** ◆ **être** *ou* **rester bouche ~** *(lit)* to stand open-mouthed *ou* gaping *(de* with); *(d'admiration)* to be lost in wonder; *(de surprise)* to be flabbergasted *(devant* at); ◆ **il en est resté bouche ~** his jaw dropped, he was flabbergasted*

béer /bee/ ► conjug 1 ◄ **VI** *(littér)* 1 *[ouverture, bouche]* to be (wide) open 2 *[personne]* **~ d'admiration/d'étonnement** to gape *ou* stand gaping in admiration/amazement

beffroi /befʀwa/ **NM** belfry

bégaiement /begɛmɑ̃/ **NM** *(lit)* stammering, stuttering ◆ **~s** *(fig = débuts)* faltering *ou* hesitant beginnings

bégayant, e /begɛjɑ̃, ɑt/ **ADJ** stammering, stuttering

bégayement /begɛmɑ̃/ **NM** ⇒ **bégaiement**

bégayer /begeje/ ► conjug 8 ◄ **VI** to stammer, to stutter, to have a stammer **VT** to stammer (out), to falter (out)

bégonia /begɔnja/ **NM** begonia

bègue /bɛg/ **NMF** stammerer, stutterer **ADJ** ◆ **être ~** to stammer, to have a stammer

bégueule /begœl/ **ADJ** prudish **NF** fastidious person ◆ **faire sa ~** to be a spoilsport

bégueulerie † /begœlʀi/ **NF** prudishness, prudery

béguin /begɛ̃/ **NM** 1 *(* toquade)* **avoir le ~ pour qn** to have a crush on sb*, to be sweet on sb* ◆ **elle a eu le ~ pour cette petite ferme** she took quite a fancy to that little farmhouse 2 *(= bonnet)* bonnet

béguinage /beginaʒ/ **NM** *(Rel)* Beguine convent

béguine /begin/ **NF** *(Rel)* Beguine

bégum /begɔm/ **NF** begum

behaviorisme /bievjɔʀism/ **NM** behaviourism

behavioriste /bievjɔʀist/ **ADJ, NMF** behaviourist

Behring /beʀiŋ/ **N** ⇒ **Béring**

BEI /beəi/ **NF** (abrév de **Banque européenne d'investissement**) EIB

beige /bɛʒ/ **ADJ, NM** beige

beigeasse /bɛʒas/, **beigeâtre** /bɛʒɑtʀ/ ADJ *(péj)* dirty beige *(péj)*, oatmeal *(épith)*

beigne[1]‡ /bɛɲ/ NF slap, clout* *(Brit)* ◆ **donner une ~ à qn** to slap sb, to clout sb* *(Brit)*, to give sb a clout* *(Brit)*

beigne[2] /bɛɲ/ NM *(Can)* doughnut

beignet /bɛɲɛ/ NM *[de fruits, légumes]* fritter; *(= pâte frite)* doughnut ◆ **~ aux pommes** apple doughnut *ou* fritter

Beijing /beidʒin/ N Beijing

béké /beke/ NMF *(terme des Antilles françaises)* white Creole *(in the French West Indies)*

bel /bɛl/ ADJ → **beau**

Belarus /belaʀys/ NM Belarus

bêlement /bɛlmɑ̃/ NM bleat(ing)

bêler /bele/ ▸ conjug 1 ◂ VI to bleat

belette /bəlɛt/ NF weasel

belge /bɛlʒ/ ADJ Belgian ◆ **histoires ~s** *jokes told against Belgians by the French* NMF **Belge** Belgian

belgicisme /bɛlʒisism/ NM Belgian-French word (*ou* phrase)

Belgique /bɛlʒik/ NF Belgium

belgitude /bɛlʒityd/ NF Belgian identity

Belgrade /bɛlgʀad/ N Belgrade

bélier /belje/ NM 1 *(= mouton)* ram 2 *(= machine)* ram, pile driver; *(Mil)* (battering) ram ◆ **coup de ~** waterhammer ◆ **~ hydraulique** hydraulic ram; → **voiture** 3 *(Astron)* **le Bélier** Aries, the Ram ◆ **être (du) Bélier** to be (an) Aries *ou* an Arian

bélître †† /belitʀ/ NM rascal, knave †

Belize /beliz/ NM Belize

belizien, -ienne /belizjɛ̃, jɛn/ ADJ Belizean NM,F **Belizien(ne)** Belizean

belladone /beladɔn/ NF *(= plante)* deadly nightshade, belladonna; *(= substance)* belladonna

bellâtre /bɛlatʀ/ NM buck, swell*

belle /bɛl/ ADJ, NF → **beau**

belle-de-jour (pl **belles-de-jour**) /bɛldəʒuʀ/ NF 1 *(= plante)* convolvulus, morning glory 2 *(euph = prostituée)* prostitute, lady of the night *(euph)*

belle-de-nuit (pl **belles-de-nuit**) /bɛldənɥi/ NF 1 *(= plante)* marvel of Peru 2 *(euph = prostituée)* prostitute, lady of the night *(euph)*

belle-doche‡ (pl **belles-doches**) /bɛldɔʃ/ NF *(péj)* mother-in-law

belle-famille (pl **belles-familles**) /bɛlfamij/ NF *[d'homme]* wife's family, in-laws*; *[de femme]* husband's family, in-laws*

belle-fille (pl **belles-filles**) /bɛlfij/ NF *(= bru)* daughter-in-law; *(d'un remariage)* stepdaughter

belle-maman* (pl **belles-mamans**) /bɛlmamɑ̃/ NF mother-in-law, mum-in-law* *(Brit)*

bellement /bɛlmɑ̃/ ADV *(= bel et bien)* well and truly; († *avec art*) nicely, gently

belle-mère (pl **belles-mères**) /bɛlmɛʀ/ NF *(= mère du conjoint)* mother-in-law; *(= nouvelle épouse du père)* stepmother

belles-lettres /bɛllɛtʀ/ NFPL ◆ **les ~** great literature, belles-lettres

belle-sœur (pl **belles-sœurs**) /bɛlsœʀ/ NF sister-in-law

bellicisme /belisism/ NM bellicosity, warmongering

belliciste /belisist/ ADJ warmongering, bellicose NMF warmonger

belligérance /beliʒeʀɑ̃s/ NF belligerence, belligerency

belligérant, e /beliʒeʀɑ̃, ɑ̃t/ ADJ, NM,F belligerent

belliqueux, -euse /belikø, øz/ ADJ *[humeur, personne]* quarrelsome, aggressive; *[politique, peuple]* warlike, bellicose, hawkish ◆ **multiplier les déclarations belliqueuses** to do a lot of sabre-rattling

bellot, -otte †* /belo, ɔt/ ADJ *[enfant]* pretty, bonny *(Brit)*

Belmopan /bɛlmɔpan/ N Belmopan

belon /bəlɔ̃/ NF *ou* m Belon oyster

belote /bəlɔt/ NF *(= jeu)* belote; *(= partie)* game of belote

bélouga, béluga /beluga/ NM beluga

belvédère /belvedɛʀ/ NM *(= terrasse)* panoramic viewpoint, belvedere; *(= édifice)* belvedere

bémol /bemɔl/ NM 1 *(Mus)* flat ◆ **en si ~** in B flat 2 *(fig)* reservation ◆ **mettre un ~** *ou* **des ~s à*** to tone down ◆ **ils ont mis un ~ à leurs revendications** they have toned down their demands ◆ **mettre un ~ à ses ambitions** to scale down one's ambitions ◆ **c'est un excellent produit, seul ~ : l'ajout de colorant alimentaire** it's an excellent product, my only reservation concerns the addition of food colouring ◆ **seul ~, le coût** the only drawback is the cost

ben* /bɛ̃/ ADV well, er* ◆ **~ oui/non** well, yes/no ◆ **~ quoi ?** so (what)? ◆ **eh ~** well, er*

bénard‡ /benaʀ/ NM trousers, pants *(US)*

bénédicité /benedisite/ NM grace, blessing ◆ **dire le ~** to say grace *ou* the blessing

bénédictin, e /benediktɛ̃, in/ ADJ, NM,F Benedictine; → **travail**[1]

bénédiction /benediksjɔ̃/ NF 1 *(Rel = consécration)* benediction, blessing; *[d'église]* consecration; *[de drapeau, bateau]* blessing ◆ **donner la ~ à** to bless ◆ **~ nuptiale** marriage ceremony; *(partie de la cérémonie)* marriage blessing 2 *(= assentiment, faveur)* blessing ◆ **donner sa ~ à** to give one's blessing to 3 (* = *aubaine*) ◆ **(du ciel)** blessing, godsend

bénef* /benɛf/ NM (abrév de **bénéfice**) profit ◆ **c'est tout ~** it's a great deal*

bénéfice /benefis/ NM 1 *(= profit)* profit ◆ **réaliser de gros ~s** to make a big profit *ou* big profits ◆ **faire du ~** to make a profit ◆ **prise de ~(s)** profit-taking

2 *(= avantage)* advantage, benefit ◆ **c'est tout ~** it's to your *(ou* our *etc)* advantage ◆ **il a obtenu un divorce à son ~** *(Jur)* he ob-tained a divorce in his favour ◆ **il perd tout le ~ de sa bonne conduite** he loses all the benefits he has gained from his good behaviour ◆ **concert donné au ~ des aveugles** concert given to raise funds for *ou* in aid of the blind ◆ **conclure une affaire à son ~** to complete a deal to one's advantage ◆ **pourquoi nier, quel ~ peux-tu en tirer ?** what's the point of (your) denying it?, what good is there in (your) denying it? ◆ **le ~ du doute** the benefit of the doubt ◆ **au ~ de l'âge** *(Jur)* by virtue of age

3 *(Rel)* benefice, living

COMP **bénéfice d'exploitation** operating profit

bénéfice d'inventaire ◆ **sous ~ d'inventaire** *(Fin)* without liability to debts beyond assets descended ◆ **je n'accepte leur théorie que sous ~ d'inventaire** it's only with certain reservations that I accept their theory

bénéfice net par action *(Fin)* price earning ratio

bénéfices non distribués *(Fin)* (accumulated) retained earnings

> ⚠ Au sens commercial et religieux, **bénéfice** ne se traduit pas par **benefit**.

bénéficiaire /benefisjɛʀ/ ADJ *[opération]* profit-making, profitable ◆ **solde ~** credit balance; → **marge** NMF *(gén)* beneficiary; *[de testament]* beneficiary; *[de chèque]* payee ◆ **être le ~ de qch** to benefit by sth

bénéficier /benefisje/ ▸ conjug 7 ◂ VT INDIR 1 ◆ **~ de** *(= jouir de)* *[+ avantage]* to have, to enjoy; *(= obtenir)* *[+ remise]* to get, to have; *(= tirer profit de)* *[+ situation, mesure]* to benefit by *ou* from, to gain by ◆ **~ d'un préjugé favorable** to be favourably considered ◆ **~ d'un non-lieu** to be (unconditionally) discharged ◆ **~ de circonstances atténuantes** to be granted mitigating circumstances ◆ **faire ~ qn de certains avantages** to enable sb to enjoy certain advantages ◆ **faire ~ qn d'une remise** to give *ou* allow sb a discount 2 ◆ **~ à** *(= profiter à)* to benefit ◆ **ces mesures doivent ~ aux plus démunis** these measures should benefit the poorest in society

bénéfique /benefik/ ADJ *[effet, aspect]* beneficial ◆ **l'influence ~ de Vénus** *(Astrol)* the benign *ou* favourable influence of Venus

Benelux /benelyks/ NM ◆ **le ~** Benelux, the Benelux countries

benêt /bənɛ/ NM simpleton ◆ **grand ~** big ninny*, stupid lump‡ ◆ **faire le ~** to act stupid *ou* daft* *(Brit)* ADJ M simple(-minded), silly

bénévolat /benevɔla/ NM voluntary work

bénévole /benevɔl/ ADJ *[aide]* voluntary; *[travail]* voluntary, unpaid ◆ **à titre ~** on a voluntary basis NMF volunteer, voluntary helper *ou* worker

bénévolement /benevɔlmɑ̃/ ADV voluntarily; *[travailler]* voluntarily, for nothing

Bengale /bɛ̃gal/ NM Bengal; → **feu**[1]

bengali /bɛ̃gali/ ADJ Bengali, Bengalese NM *(= langue)* Bengali; *(= oiseau)* waxbill NMF **Bengali** Bengali, Bengalese

Bénichon /beniʃɔ̃/ NF *(Helv = fête)* ◆ **la ~** *Autumn festival celebrated in the canton of Fribourg*

bénigne /beniɲ/ ADJ F → **bénin**

bénignité /beniɲite/ NF 1 *[de maladie]* **pour distinguer malignité et ~** to distinguish between benign and malignant conditions ◆ **la ~ de ces accès** the mildness of these attacks 2 *(littér)* *[de personne]* benignancy, kindness

Bénin /benɛ̃/ NM Benin ◆ **République populaire du ~** People's Republic of Benin

bénin, -igne /benɛ̃, iɲ/ ADJ 1 *[maladie, remède]* mild, harmless; *[tumeur]* benign; *[accident]* slight, minor; *[punition]* mild 2 *(littér)* *[humeur, critique]* benign, kindly

béninois, e /beninwa, waz/ ADJ Beninese NM,F **Béninois(e)** Beninese

béni-oui-oui* /beniwiwi/ NM INV *(péj)* yes man* *(péj)*

bénir /beniʀ/ ▸ conjug 2 ◂ VT 1 *(Rel)* *[+ fidèle, objet]* to bless; *[+ mariage]* to bless, to solemnize; → **dieu** 2 *(= remercier)* to be eternally grateful to, to thank God for ◆ **soyez béni !** bless you! ◆ **ah, toi, je te bénis !** *(iro)* oh curse you *ou* damn you!‡ ◆ **~ le ciel de qch** to thank God for sth ◆ **béni soit le jour où ...** thank God for the day (when) ... ◆ **je bénis cette coïncidence** (I) thank God for this coincidence

bénit, e /beni, it/ ADJ *[pain, cierge]* consecrated; *[eau]* holy

bénitier /benitje/ NM *(Rel)* stoup, font; → **diable, grenouille**

benjamin, e /bɛ̃ʒamɛ̃, in/ NM,F *[de famille]* youngest child; *(Sport)* ≃ junior *(12-13 years old)*

benjoin /bɛ̃ʒwɛ̃/ NM benzoin

benne /bɛn/ NF 1 *(Min)* truck, skip *(Brit)*, tub *(US)* 2 *[de camion]* *(basculante)* tipper; *(amovible)* skip; *[de grue]* scoop, bucket; *[de téléphérique]* (cable-)car ◆ **~ à ordures** dustcart *(Brit)*, garbage truck *(US)* ◆ **camion à ~ basculante** dump truck, tipper lorry *(Brit)*

benoît, e /bənwa, wat/ ADJ *(littér)* complacent ◆ **les écueils du militantisme** ~ the pitfalls of uncritical militancy

benoîtement /bənwatmɑ̃/ ADV *(littér)* uncritically ◆ **ils ne veulent pas avaliser ~ les décisions de leurs dirigeants** they don't intend to support uncritically the decisions of their leaders ◆ **nous sommes tombés ~ dans le panneau** we gullibly fell into the trap

benzène /bɛ̃zɛn/ NM benzene

benzine /bɛ̃zin/ NF 1 benzine 2 *(Helv = essence)* petrol

benzol /bɛ̃zɔl/ NM benzol

Béotie /beɔsi/ NF Boeotia

béotien, -ienne /beɔsjɛ̃, jɛn/ ADJ Boeotian NM,F *(péj)* philistine NM,F **Béotien(ne)** Boeotian

BEP /beøpe/ NM (abrév de **brevet d'études professionnelles**) → **brevet**

BEPC /beøpese/ NM (abrév de **brevet d'études du premier cycle**) → **brevet**

béquée /beke/ NF ⇒ **becquée**

béquet /bekɛ/ NM ⇒ **becquet**

béqueter /bekte/ VT ⇒ **becqueter**

béquille /bekij/ NF 1 *[d'infirme]* crutch ◆ **marcher avec des ~s** to walk *ou* be on crutches 2 *[de motocyclette, mitrailleuse]* stand; *[d'avion]* tail skid; *[de bateau]* shore, prop ◆ **mettre une ~ sous qch** to prop *ou* shore sth up 3 *(fig) (= aide)* crutch 4 *[de serrure]* handle

béquiller /bekije/ ▸ conjug 1 ◂ VT *(Naut)* to shore up VI * to walk with *ou* on crutches

ber /bɛʀ/ NM *(Can = berceau)* cradle

berbère /bɛʀbɛʀ/ ADJ Berber NM *(= langue)* Berber NMF **Berbère** Berber

bercail /bɛʀkaj/ NM *(Rel, fig)* fold ◆ **rentrer au ~** *(hum)* to return to the fold

berçante * /bɛʀsɑ̃t/ NF *(Can)* ◆ **(chaise) ~** rocking chair

berce[1] /bɛʀs/ NF *(= plante)* hogweed

berce[2] /bɛʀs/ NF *(Belg = berceau)* cradle, crib

berceau (pl **berceaux**) /bɛʀso/ NM 1 *(= lit)* cradle, crib; *(= lieu d'origine)* birthplace; *[de civilisation]* cradle ◆ **dès le ~** from birth, from the cradle ◆ **il les prend au ~ !*** he snatches them straight from the cradle!, he's a baby *ou* cradle snatcher! 2 *(Archit)* barrel vault; *(= charmille)* bower, arbour; *(Naut)* cradle; → **voûte**

bercelonnette /bɛʀsəlɔnɛt/ NF rocking cradle, cradle on rockers

bercement /bɛʀsəmɑ̃/ NM rocking (movement)

bercer /bɛʀse/ ▸ conjug 3 ◂ VT 1 *[+ bébé]* to rock; *(dans ses bras)* to rock, to cradle; *[+ navire]* to rock ◆ **les chansons qui ont bercé notre enfance** the songs that we grew up with ◆ **je me suis laissé ~ par sa voix** his voice lulled me ◆ **il a été bercé trop près du mur** ⁑ *(hum)* he's a bit soft in the head* 2 *(= apaiser) [+ douleur]* to lull, to soothe 3 *(= tromper)* ~ **de** to delude with VPR **se bercer** ◆ **se ~ de** to delude o.s. with ◆ **se ~ d'illusions** to harbour illusions, to delude o.s.

berceur, -euse /bɛʀsœʀ, øz/ ADJ *[rythme]* lulling, soothing NF **berceuse** 1 *(= chanson)* lullaby, cradlesong; *(Mus)* berceuse 2 *(= fauteuil)* rocking chair

BERD /bɛʀd/ NF (abrév de **Banque européenne pour la reconstruction et le développement**) EBRD

béret /beʀɛ/ NM beret ◆ ~ **basque** Basque beret ◆ **les ~s bleus/verts** *(Mil)* the Blue/Green Berets

Bérézina /beʀezina/ NF *(Géog)* ◆ **la ~** the Berezina river; *(fig)* ◆ **c'est la ~ !** it's a complete disaster!

bergamasque /bɛʀgamask/ NF bergamask

bergamote /bɛʀgamɔt/ NF bergamot orange

bergamotier /bɛʀgamɔtje/ NM bergamot

berge /bɛʀʒ/ NF 1 *[de rivière]* bank ◆ **route** *ou* **voie sur ~** riverside *ou* embankment expressway 2 (⁑ *= année*) **il a 50 ~s** he's 50 (years old)

berger /bɛʀʒe/ NM 1 *(lit, Rel)* shepherd ◆ **chien de ~** sheepdog; → **étoile, réponse** 2 *(= chien)* sheepdog ◆ ~ **allemand** German shepherd, alsatian *(Brit)* ◆ ~ **des Pyrénées** Pyrenean mountain dog

bergère /bɛʀʒɛʀ/ NF 1 *(= personne)* shepherdess 2 *(= fauteuil)* wing chair

bergerie /bɛʀʒəʀi/ NF 1 *(= abri)* sheepfold; → **loup** 2 *(Littérat = pièce, poème)* pastoral 3 *(Comm = comptoir)* counter

bergeronnette /bɛʀʒəʀɔnɛt/ NF wagtail ◆ ~ **flavéole/des ruisseaux** yellow/grey wagtail

béribéri /beʀibeʀi/ NM beriberi

Béring /beʀiŋ/ N ◆ **le détroit de ~** the Bering Strait ◆ **mer de ~** Bering Sea

berk * /bɛʀk/ EXCL yuk! *

berkélium /bɛʀkeljɔm/ NM berkelium

berlander * /bɛʀlɑ̃de/ ▸ conjug 1 ◂ VI *(Can)* to prevaricate, to equivocate

Berlin /bɛʀlɛ̃/ N Berlin ◆ **~-Est/-Ouest** *(Hist)* East/West Berlin

berline /bɛʀlin/ NF 1 *(= voiture)* saloon (car) *(Brit)*, sedan *(US)*; (†† *: à chevaux*) berlin 2 *(Min)* truck

berlingot /bɛʀlɛ̃go/ NM 1 *(= bonbon)* ≈ boiled sweet *(Brit)*, piece of hard candy *(US)* 2 *(= emballage)* (pyramid-shaped) carton; *(pour shampooing)* sachet

berlinois, e /bɛʀlinwa, waz/ ADJ of *ou* from Berlin NM,F **Berlinois(e)** Berliner

berlot /bɛʀlo/ NM *(Can)* sleigh

berlue /bɛʀly/ NF ◆ **j'ai la ~** I must be seeing things

berme /bɛʀm/ NF *[de canal]* path; *[de fossé]* verge

bermuda /bɛʀmyda/ NM Bermuda shorts, Bermudas

Bermudes /bɛʀmyd/ NFPL Bermuda; → **triangle**

bermudien, -ienne /bɛʀmydjɛ̃, jɛn/ ADJ Bermudan, Bermudian NM,F **Bermudien(ne)** Bermudan, Bermudian

bernache /bɛʀnaʃ/ NF *(= crustacé)* barnacle ◆ ~ **(nonnette)** *(= oie)* barnacle goose ◆ ~ **cravant** brent goose

bernacle /bɛʀnakl/ NF barnacle goose

bernardin, e /bɛʀnaʀdɛ̃, in/ NM,F Bernardine, Cistercian

bernard-l'(h)ermite /bɛʀnaʀlɛʀmit/ NM INV hermit crab

Berne /bɛʀn/ N Bern

berne /bɛʀn/ NF ◆ **en ~** ≈ at half-mast ◆ **mettre en ~** ≈ to half-mast ◆ **avoir le moral en ~** to feel dispirited

berner /bɛʀne/ ▸ conjug 1 ◂ VT *(= tromper)* to fool, to hoax; *(Hist) [+ personne]* to toss in a blanket ◆ **il s'est laissé ~ par leurs promesses** he was taken in by their promises

bernicle /bɛʀnikl/ NF ⇒ **bernique**[1]

Bernin /bɛʀnɛ̃/ NM ◆ **le ~** Bernini

bernique[1] /bɛʀnik/ NF *(= coquillage)* limpet

bernique[2] * /bɛʀnik/ EXCL *(= rien à faire)* nothing doing! *, not a chance! *ou* hope!

béryl /beʀil/ NM beryl

béryllium /beʀiljɔm/ NM beryllium

berzingue ⁑ /bɛʀzɛ̃g/ ADV ◆ **à tout(e) ~** flat out *

besace /bəzas/ NF beggar's bag *ou* pouch

bésef ⁑ /bezɛf/ ADV ◆ **il n'y en a pas ~** *(quantité)* there's not much (of it) *ou* a lot (of it); *(nombre)* there aren't many (of them) *ou* a lot (of them)

besicles /bezikl/ NFPL *(Hist)* spectacles; *(hum)* glasses, specs *

bésigue /bezig/ NM bezique

besogne /bəzɔɲ/ NF *(= travail)* work (NonC), job ◆ **se mettre à la ~** to set to work ◆ **c'est de la belle ~** *(lit)* this is nice work; *(iro)* this is a nice mess ◆ **une sale ~** a nasty job ◆ **les basses ~s** the dirty work

◆ **aller vite en besogne** to jump the gun ◆ **ce serait aller (un peu) vite en ~** it would be jumping the gun, it would be a bit premature

besogner /bəzɔɲe/ ▸ conjug 1 ◂ VI to toil (away), to drudge

besogneux, -euse /bəzɔɲø, øz/ ADJ († *= miséreux*) needy, poor; *(= travailleur)* industrious, hard-working

besoin /bəzwɛ̃/ NM 1 *(= exigence)* need (**de** for); ◆ **~s (d'argent)** financial needs ◆ **~s essentiels** basic needs ◆ **nos ~s en énergie** our energy needs *ou* requirements ◆ **subvenir** *ou* **pourvoir aux ~s de qn** to provide for sb's needs ◆ **éprouver le ~ de faire qch** to feel the need to do sth ◆ **mentir est devenu un ~ chez lui** lying has become compulsive *ou* a need with him

2 *(= pauvreté)* **le ~** need, want ◆ **être dans le ~** to be in need *ou* want ◆ **une famille dans le ~** a needy family ◆ **pour ceux qui sont dans le ~** for the needy ◆ **cela les met à l'abri du ~** that will keep the wolf from their door ◆ **c'est dans le ~ qu'on reconnaît ses vrais amis** in times of trouble you find out who your true friends are, a friend in need is a friend indeed *(Prov)*

3 *(euph)* **~s naturels** nature's needs ◆ **faire ses ~s** *[personne]* to relieve o.s. *(Brit)*; *[animal domestique]* to do its business ◆ **satisfaire un ~ pressant** to answer an urgent call of nature

4 *(locutions)* **si le ~ s'en fait sentir, en cas de ~** if the need arises, in case of necessity ◆ **pour les ~s de la cause** for the purpose in hand ◆ **pas ~ de dire qu'il ne m'a pas cru** it goes without saying *ou* needless to say he didn't believe me ◆ **il n'est pas ~ de mentionner que ...** there is no need to mention that ...

◆ **avoir besoin** ◆ **avoir ~ de qn** to need sb ◆ **avoir ~ de qch** to need sth, to be in need of sth, to want sth ◆ **avoir ~ de faire qch** to need to do sth ◆ **il n'a pas ~ de venir** he doesn't need *ou* have to come, there's no need for him to come ◆ **il a ~ que vous l'aidiez** he needs your help *ou* you to help him ◆ **je n'ai pas ~ de vous rappeler que ...** there's no need (for me) to remind you that ... ◆ **ce tapis a ~ d'être nettoyé** this carpet needs *ou* wants *(Brit)* cleaning ◆ **il a grand ~ d'aide** he needs help badly, he's badly in need of help ◆ **il avait bien ~ de ça !** *(iro)* that's just what he needed! *(iro)* ◆ **est-ce que tu avais ~ d'y aller ?*** did you really have to go?, what did you want to go for anyway! *

◆ **au besoin** if necessary, if need(s) be

◆ **si besoin est, s'il en est besoin** if need(s) be, if necessary

Bessarabie /besaʀabi/ NF Bessarabia

bestiaire /bɛstjɛʀ/ NM 1 *(= livre)* bestiary 2 *(= gladiateur)* gladiator

bestial, e (mpl **-iaux**) /bɛstjal, jo/ ADJ *[meurtre, violence]* brutal; *[personne, plaisir]* bestial ◆ **sa force ~e** his brute strength

bestialement /bɛstjalmɑ̃/ ADV bestially, brutishly

bestialité /bɛstjalite/ NF (= *sauvagerie*) bestiality, brutishness; (= *perversion*) bestiality

bestiaux /bɛstjo/ NMPL (*gén*) livestock; (= *bovins*) cattle ◆ **ils ont été parqués comme des ~ dans des camps** they were herded *ou* corralled into camps

bestiole /bɛstjɔl/ NF (*gén*) creature; (= *insecte*) insect, bug*; (*rampant*) creepy crawly*

best of* /bɛstɔf/ NM INV ◆ **un ~ des Beatles** a compilation of the greatest hits of the Beatles ◆ **un ~ de leurs émissions** a selection of highlights of their programmes

best-seller (pl **best-sellers**) /bɛstsɛlœʀ/ NM best seller

bêta¹, -asse* /beta, as/ ADJ silly, stupid NM,F goose*, silly billy* ◆ **gros ~ !** big ninny!*, silly goose!*

bêta² /beta/ NM (*Ling, Phys, Méd*) beta

bêtabloquant /betablɔkɑ̃/ NM beta-blocker

bêtacarotène /betakaʀɔtɛn/ NM betacarotene

bétail /betaj/ NM (*gén*) livestock; (= *bovins, fig*) cattle ◆ **gros ~** cattle ◆ **petit ~** small livestock ◆ **le ~ humain qu'on entasse dans les camps** the people who are crammed like cattle into the camps

bétaillère /betajɛʀ/ NF livestock truck

bêta-test (pl **bêta-tests**) /betatɛst/ NM (*Ordin*) beta-test

bêta-version (pl **bêta-versions**) /betavɛʀsjɔ̃/ NM (*Ordin*) beta version

bête /bɛt/ NF ⓵ (= *animal*) animal; (= *insecte*) insect, creature ◆ **~ sauvage** (wild) beast ◆ **nos amies les ~s** our four-legged friends ◆ **aller soigner les ~s** to go and see to the animals ◆ **gladiateur livré aux ~s** gladiator flung to the beasts ◆ **pauvre petite ~** poor little thing* *ou* creature ◆ **ce chien est une belle ~** this dog is a fine animal *ou* beast ◆ **c'est une belle ~ !*** (*hum* = *homme*) what a hunk!* ◆ **tu as une petite ~ sur ta manche** there's an insect *ou* a creepy crawly* on your sleeve ◆ **ces sales ~s ont mangé mes carottes** those wretched creatures have been eating my carrots

◆ **comme + bête(s)*** ◆ **travailler comme une ~** to work like a dog ◆ **malade comme une ~** sick as a dog ◆ **on s'est éclatés comme des ~s** we had a whale of a time*

⓶ (= *personne*) (*bestial*) beast; († : *stupide*) fool ◆ **c'est une méchante ~** he is a wicked creature ◆ **quelle sale ~ !** (*enfant*) what a wretched pest!; (*adulte*) what a horrible creature!, what a beast! ◆ **faire la ~** to act stupid *ou* daft*, to play the fool ◆ **c'est une brave** *ou* **une bonne ~ !** (*hum*) he is a good-natured sort *ou* soul ◆ **grande** *ou* **grosse ~ !*** (*terme d'affection*) you big silly!* ◆ **en maths, c'est la ~ !*** (*admiratif*) he's a wizard *ou* he's an ace* at maths!

ADJ ⓵ (= *stupide*) [*personne, idée, sourire*] stupid, silly, foolish, idiotic ◆ **ce qu'il peut être ~ !** what a fool he is! ◆ **il est plus ~ que méchant** he may be stupid but he's not malicious, he's stupid rather than really nasty ◆ **il est loin d'être ~, il a oublié d'être ~** he's far from *ou* anything but stupid, he's no fool ◆ **et moi, ~ et discipliné, j'ai obéi** and I did exactly what I was told, without asking myself any questions ◆ **être ~ comme ses pieds*** *ou* **à manger du foin*** to be too stupid for words, to be as thick as a brick* ◆ **lui, pas si ~, est parti à temps** knowing better *ou* being no fool, he left in time ◆ **ce film est ~ à pleurer** this film is too stupid for words ◆ **c'est ~, on n'a pas ce qu'il faut pour faire des crêpes** it's a shame *ou* it's too bad we haven't got what we need for making pancakes ◆ **que je suis ~ !** how silly *ou* stupid of me!, what a fool I am! ◆ **ce n'est pas ~** that's not a bad idea

⓶ (* = *très simple*) **c'est tout ~** it's quite *ou* dead* simple ◆ **~ comme chou** simplicity itself, as easy as pie* *ou* as winking*

COMP **bête à bon dieu** ladybird, ladybug (*US*)
bête à concours swot* (*Brit*), grind* (*US*)
bête à cornes horned animal; (*hum*) snail
bête curieuse (*iro*) queer *ou* strange animal ◆ **ils nous ont regardés comme des ~s curieuses** they looked at us as if we had just landed from Mars *ou* as if we had two heads
bête fauve big cat; (*fig*) wild animal *ou* beast
bête féroce wild animal *ou* beast
bête noire ◆ **c'est ma ~ noire** (*chose*) that's my pet hate *ou* my bête noire *ou* my pet peeve* (*US*); (*personne*) I just can't stand him
bête de race pedigree animal
bête sauvage ⇒ **bête féroce**
bête de scène great performer
bête de sexe* sex machine*
bête de somme beast of burden
bête de trait draught animal

bétel /betɛl/ NM betel

bêtement /bɛtmɑ̃/ ADV stupidly, foolishly; [*sourire*] stupidly ◆ **tout ~** quite simply

Bethléem /betleɛm/ N Bethlehem

Bethsabée /betsabe/ NF Bathsheba

bêtifiant, e /betifjɑ̃, jɑ̃t/ ADJ inane, asinine

bêtifier /betifje/ ▸ conjug 7 ◂ VI to prattle stupidly, to talk twaddle ◆ **en parlant aux enfants, elle bêtifie toujours** she always tends to talk down to children

bêtise /betiz/ NF ⓵ (*NonC* = *stupidité*) stupidity, foolishness, folly ◆ **être d'une ~ crasse** to be incredibly stupid ◆ **j'ai eu la ~ d'accepter** I was foolish enough to accept ◆ **c'était de la ~ d'accepter** it was folly to accept

⓶ (= *action stupide*) silly *ou* stupid thing; (= *erreur*) blunder ◆ **faire une ~** (= *action stupide, tentative de suicide*) to do something stupid *ou* silly; (= *erreur*) to make a blunder, to boob* ◆ **ne faites pas de ~s, les enfants** don't get into *ou* up to mischief, children ◆ **ne dis pas de ~s** don't talk nonsense *ou* rubbish (*Brit*)

⓷ (= *bagatelle*) trifle, triviality ◆ **dépenser son argent en ~s** to spend *ou* squander one's money on rubbish (*Brit*) *ou* garbage ◆ **ils se disputent sans arrêt pour des ~s** they're forever arguing over trifles

⓸ (= *bonbon*) **~ de Cambrai** ≈ mint humbug (*Brit*), piece of hard mint candy (*US*)

⓹ (*Can*) **~s*** insults, rude remarks

bêtisier /betizje/ NM (= *livre*) collection of howlers; (*Radio, TV*) collection of out-takes

béton /betɔ̃/ NM concrete ◆ **~ armé** reinforced concrete ◆ **~ cellulaire** air-entrained concrete ◆ **en ~** (*lit*) concrete (*épith*) ◆ **(en) ~*** [*alibi, argument, contrat*] cast-iron; [*garantie, certitude*] cast-iron, ironclad; [*organisation*] ultra-efficient ◆ **un dossier en ~** (*en justice*) a water-tight case ◆ **faire** *ou* **jouer le ~** (*Ftbl*) to play defensively ◆ **laisse ~ !*** forget it!*

bétonnage /betɔnaʒ/ NM ⓵ (*Constr*) concreting ◆ **pour éviter le ~ du littoral** to prevent the coast from becoming a sprawl of concrete ⓶ (*Ftbl*) defensive play

bétonner /betɔne/ ▸ conjug 1 ◂ VT ⓵ (*Constr*) to concrete ◆ **surface bétonnée** concrete surface ◆ **ils bétonnent nos côtes** our coastline is being covered in concrete ⓶ (= *consolider*) [+ *position, résultat*] to consolidate ◆ **elle bétonne ses positions** she is consolidating her position ◆ **~ un dossier** to make a case watertight VI ⓵ (*Constr*) to build using concrete ⓶ (*Ftbl*) to play defensively

bétonneur /betɔnœʀ/ NM (*péj*) (building) developer

bétonneuse /betɔnøz/, **bétonnière** /betɔnjɛʀ/ NF cement mixer

bette /bɛt/ NF ◆ **~s** (Swiss) chard ◆ **une ~** a piece of chard

betterave /bɛtʀav/ NF ◆ **~ fourragère** mangel-wurzel, beet ◆ **~ (rouge)** beetroot (*Brit*), beet (*US*) ◆ **~ sucrière** sugar beet

betteravier, -ière /bɛtʀavje, jɛʀ/ ADJ [*culture, exploitation*] (sugar) beet (*épith*) NM beet grower

beuglant* /bøglɑ̃/ NM honky-tonk*

beuglante* /bøglɑ̃t/ NF (= *cri*) yell, holler*; (= *chanson*) song ◆ **pousser une ~** to yell, to give a yell *ou* holler*

beuglement /bøgləmɑ̃/ NM ⓵ [*de vache*] lowing (*NonC*), mooing (*NonC*); [*de taureau*] bellowing (*NonC*) ⓶ [*de personne*] bawling (*NonC*), bellowing, hollering* (*NonC*) ◆ **pousser des ~s** to bawl, to bellow ⓷ [*de radio, télévision*] blaring (*NonC*)

beugler /bøgle/ ▸ conjug 1 ◂ VI ⓵ [*vache*] to low, to moo; [*taureau*] to bellow ⓶ * [*personne*] to bawl, to bellow, to holler* ⓷ [*radio, TV*] to blare ◆ **faire ~ sa télé** to have one's TV on (at) full blast* VT [+ *chanson*] to bellow out, to belt out*

beur /bœʀ/ NMF *second-generation North African living in France* ADJ [*culture, musique*] *of second-generation North Africans living in France*

> **BEUR**
>
> **Beur** is the term used to refer to a person born in France of North African immigrant parents. It is not a racist term and is often used by the media, anti-racist groups and second-generation North Africans themselves. The word itself originally came from the « verlan » rendering of the word « arabe ». → **VERLAN**

beurk* /bœʀk/ EXCL ⇒ **berk**

beurre /bœʀ/ NM ⓵ (*laitier*) butter ◆ **~ salé/demi-sel** salted/slightly salted butter ◆ **~ doux** unsalted butter ◆ **au ~** [*plat*] (cooked) in butter; [*pâtisserie*] made with butter ◆ **faire la cuisine au ~** to cook with butter ◆ **~ fondu** melted butter; → **inventer, motte, œil**

⓶ (*végétal*) **~ de cacao/de cacahuètes** cocoa/peanut butter

⓷ (= *purée*) paste ◆ **~ d'anchois/d'écrevisses** anchovy/shrimp paste

⓸ (*locutions*) **le couteau entre dans cette viande comme dans du ~** this meat is like butter to cut ◆ **c'est entré comme dans du ~** it went like a (hot) knife through butter ◆ **cette viande, c'est du ~ !** this is very tender meat ◆ **ça va mettre du ~ dans les épinards** that'll be some handy extra money for you (*ou* him *etc*), that'll help you (*ou* him *etc*) make ends meet ◆ **faire son ~ (sur le dos de qn)** to make a packet* *ou* a pile* (off sb) ◆ **il n'y en a pas plus que de ~ en broche** there is (*ou* are) none at all ◆ **on ne peut pas avoir le ~ et l'argent du ~** you can't have your cake and eat it; → **compter**

COMP **beurre d'escargot** ⇒ **beurre persillé**
beurre laitier dairy butter
beurre noir (*Culin*) brown (butter) sauce
beurre persillé garlic and parsley butter

beurré, e /bœʀe/ (ptp de **beurrer**) ADJ (* = *ivre*) plastered* NM butter-pear, beurré NF **beurrée** † (*Can*) slice of bread and peanut butter

beurre-frais /bœʀfʀɛ/ ADJ INV (= *couleur*) buttercup yellow

beurrer /bœʀe/ ▸ conjug 1 ◂ VT to butter ◆ **tartine beurrée** slice of bread and butter VPR **se beurrer*** to get plastered*

beurrier, -ière /bœʀje, jɛʀ/ ADJ [*industrie, production*] butter (*épith*) ◆ **région beurrière** butter-producing region NM butter dish

beuverie /bøvʀi/ NF drinking bout *ou* session, binge *

bévue /bevy/ NF blunder ◆ **commettre une** ~ to make a blunder

bey /bɛ/ NM bey

Beyrouth /beʀut/ N Beirut

bézef ⁑ /bezɛf/ ADV ⇒ **bésef**

Bhoutan, Bhutân /butɑ̃/ NM Bhutan

bhoutanais, e /butanɛ, ɛz/ ADJ Bhutanese NM,F **Bhoutanais(e)** Bhutanese

bi[1] * /bi/ ADJ, NMF (abrév de **bisexuel, -elle**) bi *

bi[2] * /bi/ NM (*Can* = *baiser*) kiss ◆ **fais-moi un** ~ kiss me, give me a kiss

bi... /bi/ PRÉF bi... ◆ **bidimensionnel** two-dimensional

biacide /biasid/ ADJ, NM diacid

Biafra /bjafʀa/ NM Biafra

biafrais, e /bjafʀɛ, ɛz/ ADJ Biafran NM,F **Biafrais(e)** Biafran

biais, e /bjɛ, jez/ ADJ *[arc]* skew

NM 1 *(= moyen)* way, means; *(= détour, artifice)* expedient, dodge * ◆ **chercher un ~ pour obtenir qch** to find some means of getting sth *ou* some expedient for getting sth ◆ **il a trouvé le** *ou* **un ~ (pour se faire exempter)** he found a dodge * *ou* he managed to find a way (to get himself exempted) ◆ **par quel ~ a-t-il réussi à s'introduire dans le pays ?** by what roundabout means did he manage to get into the country?

◆ **par le biais de** *(= par l'intermédiaire de)* through; *(= au moyen de)* by means of ◆ **réserver par le ~ d'une agence** to book through an agency ◆ **communiquer par le ~ du fax** to communicate by *ou* via fax

2 *(= aspect)* angle, way ◆ **c'est par ce ~ qu'il faut aborder le problème** the problem should be approached from this angle *ou* in this way

3 *[de tissu] (= sens)* bias; *(= bande)* bias binding ◆ **coupé** *ou* **taillé dans le** ~ cut on the bias *ou* the cross ◆ **jupe en** ~ skirt cut on the bias

4 *(= ligne oblique)* slant

◆ **en biais, de biais** *[poser]* slantwise, at an angle; *[aborder un sujet]* indirectly, in a roundabout way ◆ **une allée traverse le jardin en** ~ a path cuts diagonally across the garden ◆ **regarder qn de** ~ to give sb a sidelong glance

5 *(Sociol)* bias

biaisé, e /bjeze/ (ptp de **biaiser**) ADJ 1 *(= faussé) [échantillon, données]* biased; *[vision]* distorted ◆ **une perception ~e de la réalité** a distorted *ou* skewed view of reality ◆ **depuis cet incident, les relations entre les deux pays sont un peu ~es** since this incident the two countries have had a somewhat skewed relationship ◆ **leurs questions sont toujours ~es** their questions always have a certain slant to them 2 *(= avec un parti pris) [reportage, conclusion, raisonnement, analyse]* biased ◆ **la composition du jury était ~e** the jury was made up of an unrepresentative sample of people

biaiser /bjeze/ ▸ conjug 1 ◂ VI 1 *(= louvoyer)* to sidestep the issue, to prevaricate 2 *(= obliquer)* to change direction VT *(Stat) [+ résultat]* to bias

biathlète /biatlɛt/ NMF biathlete

biathlon /biatlɔ̃/ NM biathlon

bi-bande /bibɑ̃d/ ADJ *[téléphone mobile]* dual band

bibelot /biblo/ NM *(sans valeur)* trinket, knick-knack; *(de valeur)* bibelot, curio

biberon /bibʀɔ̃/ NM feeding bottle, baby's bottle ◆ **élevé au** ~ bottle-fed ◆ **l'heure du** ~ (baby's) feeding time ◆ **élever** *ou* **nourrir au** ~ to bottle-feed ◆ **il est à 6 ~s (par jour)** he's on 6 feeds (a day)

biberonner ⁑ /bibʀɔne/ ▸ conjug 1 ◂ VI to tipple *, to booze *

bibi[1] * /bibi/ NM pillbox hat

bibi[2] ⁑ /bibi/ PRON me, yours truly *(hum)*

bibine * /bibin/ NF (weak) beer, dishwater *(hum)* ◆ **une infâme** ~ a foul *ou* loathsome brew

bibi(t)te /bibit/ NF *(Can)* insect, bug *

bible /bibl/ NF *(= livre, fig)* bible ◆ **la Bible** the Bible

bibli * /bibli/ NF abrév de **bibliothèque**

bibliobus /biblijobys/ NM mobile library, bookmobile (US)

bibliographe /biblijɔgʀaf/ NMF bibliographer

bibliographie /biblijɔgʀafi/ NF bibliography

bibliographique /biblijɔgʀafik/ ADJ bibliographic(al)

bibliomane /biblijɔman/ NMF booklover

bibliomanie /biblijɔmani/ NF bibliomania

bibliophile /biblijɔfil/ NMF bibliophile *(frm)*, booklover

bibliophilie /biblijɔfili/ NF love of books

bibliothécaire /biblijɔtekɛʀ/ NMF librarian

bibliothéconomie /biblijɔtekɔnɔmi/ NF library science

bibliothèque /biblijɔtɛk/ NF *(= édifice, pièce)* library; *(= meuble)* bookcase; *(= collection)* library, collection (of books) ◆ **~ de gare** station bookstall *(Brit) ou* newsstand *(US)* ◆ **~ municipale/universitaire** public/university library ◆ **~ de prêt** lending library

Bibliothèque nationale

The « BN », as it is popularly known, was founded in 1537 by Francis I. Situated in the rue de Richelieu in Paris, it is a copyright deposit library holding important historic collections of printed and manuscript material. The building has become too small to house the collections adequately, and most of its material has been transferred to the Bibliothèque François Mitterrand in the south-east of the city.

biblique /biblik/ ADJ biblical

bibliquement /biblikmɑ̃/ ADV biblically ◆ **connaître ~ qn** *(hum ou frm)* to know sb in the biblical sense *(hum)*, to have carnal knowledge of sb *(frm)*

bic ® /bik/ NM ◆ **(pointe)** ~ ≈ Biro ®, ball-point pen, Bic ® (pen) *(US)*

bicaméral, e (mpl **-aux**) /bikameʀal, o/ ADJ bicameral, two-chamber *(épith)*

bicaméralisme /bikameʀalism/, **bicamérisme** /bikameʀism/ NM bicameral *ou* two-chamber system

bicarbonate /bikaʀbɔnat/ NM bicarbonate ◆ **~ de soude** bicarbonate of soda, sodium bicarbonate, baking soda

bicarburation /bikaʀbyʀasjɔ̃/ NF ◆ **voiture fonctionnant en** ~ dual-fuel car

bicarré, e /bikaʀe/ ADJ *(Math)* biquadratic

bicentenaire /bisɑ̃t(ə)nɛʀ/ NM bicentenary, bicentennial

bicéphale /bisefal/ ADJ two-headed, bicephalous *(SPÉC)*

biceps /bisɛps/ NM biceps ◆ **avoir des** *ou* **du** ~ * to have a strong *ou* good pair of arms

biche /biʃ/ NF hind, doe ◆ **un regard** *ou* **des yeux de** ~ doe-like eyes ◆ **ma** ~ *(terme d'affection)* darling, pet *

bicher * /biʃe/ ▸ conjug 1 ◂ VI 1 *[personne]* to be pleased with o.s. 2 *(= aller)* **ça biche ?** how's things? *, things OK with you? *

bichette /biʃɛt/ NF *(terme d'affection)* ◆ **(ma)** ~ darling, pet *

Bichkek /biʃkɛk/ N Pishpek

bichlorure /biklɔʀyʀ/ NM bichloride

bichon, -onne /biʃɔ̃, ɔn/ NM,F *(= chien)* bichon frise ◆ **mon** ~ * pet *, love *

bichonner /biʃɔne/ ▸ conjug 1 ◂ VT *[+ personne]* to pamper, to cosset ◆ **il bichonne sa moto/la pelouse** he lavishes care on his motorbike/the lawn VPR **se bichonner** to dress up, to spruce o.s. up ◆ **elle est en train de se ~ dans sa chambre** *(péj)* she's getting dolled up * in her room

bichromate /bikʀɔmat/ NM bichromate

bichromie /bikʀɔmi/ NF two-colour process ◆ **en** ~ in two colours

biclou * /biklu/ NM *(= bicyclette)* bike

bicolore /bikɔlɔʀ/ ADJ bicolour(ed) *(Brit)*, bicolor(ed) *(US)*, two-colour(ed) *(Brit)*, two-color(ed) *(US)*, two-tone; *(Cartes)* two-suited

biconcave /bikɔ̃kav/ ADJ biconcave

biconvexe /bikɔ̃vɛks/ ADJ biconvex

bicoque * /bikɔk/ NF house, place * ◆ **ils ont une petite ~ au bord de la mer** * they've got a little place by the sea

bicorne /bikɔʀn/ NM cocked hat ADJ two-horned

bicot ⁑* /biko/ NM *(injurieux)* (North African) Arab

bicross /bikʀɔs/ NM *(= vélo)* ≈ mountain bike; *(= sport)* ≈ mountain biking

biculturel, -elle /bikyltyʀɛl/ ADJ bicultural

bicycle /bisikl/ NM *(Hist : à grande et petite roues)* penny farthing (bicycle) *(Brit)*, ordinary *(US)*; *(Can)* bicycle

bicyclette /bisiklɛt/ NF 1 *(= véhicule)* bicycle, bike * ◆ **aller à la ville à** *ou* **en** ~ to go to town by bicycle, to cycle to town ◆ **faire de la** ~ to go cycling, to cycle ◆ **sais-tu faire de la ~ ?** can you cycle?, can you ride a bike? * 2 *(Sport)* cycling

bicylindre /bisilɛ̃dʀ/ ADJ *[moteur]* twin-cylinder NM *(= moto)* twin-cylinder motorbike

bidasse * /bidas/ NM *(= conscrit)* soldier, squaddy *(arg Mil) (Brit)*

bide /bid/ NM 1 (⁑ = *ventre*) belly * ◆ **avoir du** ~ to have a potbelly 2 (* = *échec*) *(gén)* flop *, fiasco ◆ **il a essayé de la draguer, mais ça a été le** ~ he tried to pick her up but failed miserably ◆ **être** *ou* **faire un** ~ *(Théât, Ciné)* to be a flop * *ou* a washout *ou* a bomb * *(US)*

bidet /bidɛ/ NM 1 *(= cuvette)* bidet 2 *(= cheval)* (old) nag

bidirectionnel, -elle /bidiʀɛksjɔnɛl/ ADJ bidirectional

bidoche ⁑ /bidɔʃ/ NF meat

bidon /bidɔ̃/ NM 1 *(gén)* can, tin; *(à huile, à essence)* can; *(à peinture)* tin; *[de cycliste, soldat]* water bottle, flask ◆ **~ à lait** milk-churn ◆ **huile en** ~ oil in a can 2 (⁑ = *ventre*) belly * 3 (⁑ = *bluff*) **c'est du** ~ that's a load of hot air *ou* bull ⁑ *ou* codswallop ⁑ *(Brit)* ◆ **ce n'est pas du ~!** I'm (*ou* he's *etc*) not kidding! ⁑ ADJ INV (* = *simulé*) phoney *, phony * *(US)*; *[élection]* rigged ◆ **une démocratie** ~ a sham *ou* phoney * democracy ◆ **il est** ~ he's a phoney * *ou* phony * *(US)*

bidonnage * /bidɔnaʒ/ NM *[de reportage, CV]* faking ◆ **cette interview, c'était du** ~ that interview was faked *ou* was a put-up * job

bidonnant, e ⁑ /bidɔnɑ̃, ɑt/ ADJ hilarious ◆ **c'était** ~ it was a scream *

bidonner /bidɔne/ ▸ conjug 1 ◂ VPR **se bidonner** ⁑ to split one's sides (laughing) *, to be doubled up (with laughter), to crease up * **VT** (* = *truquer) [+ reportage, CV]* to fake

bidonville /bidɔ̃vil/ **NM** shanty town

bidouillage * /bidujaʒ/ **NM**, **bidouille** * /biduj/ **NF** ◆ **c'est du ~** it's just been cobbled together

bidouiller * /biduje/ ▸ **conjug 1** ◂ **VT** 1 *(gén = réparer)* to (have a) tinker with; *(Ordin) [+ programme]* to hack up ◆ **j'ai réussi à le ~** I've managed to fix it for the time being 2 *(péj = truquer) [+ compteur]* to fiddle with, to fix; *[+ élection]* to rig

bidouilleur, -euse * /bidujœʀ, øz/ **NM,F** ◆ **c'est un ~** *(habile)* he's quite good with his hands; *(péj)* he's a bit of a botcher *

bidous * /bidu/ **NMPL** *(Can)* money, dough *

bidule * /bidyl/ **NM** *(= machin)* thing, thingy * *(Brit)*; *(= personne)* what's-his-name * *(ou* what's-her-name *) ◆ **eh ~ !** hey (you) what's-your-name! *

bief /bjɛf/ **NM** 1 *[de canal]* reach 2 *[de moulin]* ~ **d'amont** headrace ◆ ~ **d'aval** tail race *ou* water

bielle /bjɛl/ **NF** *[de locomotive]* connecting rod; *[de voiture]* track rod

biellette /bjɛlɛt/ **NF** stub axle

biélorusse /bjelɔʀys/ **ADJ** Byelorussian **NMF** **Biélorusse** Byelorussian

Biélorussie /bjelɔʀysi/ **NF** Byelorussia

bien /bjɛ̃/

1 ADVERBE	3 NOM MASCULIN
2 ADJECTIF INVARIABLE	4 COMPOSÉS

1 - ADVERBE

1 = de façon satisfaisante *[jouer, dormir, travailler]* well; *[conseiller, choisir]* well, wisely; *[fonctionner]* properly, well ◆ **aller** *ou* **se porter ~, être ~ portant** to be well, to be in good health ◆ **comment vas-tu ? – ~/très ~ merci** how are you? – fine/very well, thanks ◆ **nous avons ~ travaillé aujourd'hui** we've done some good work today ◆ **il a ~ réussi** he's done well (for himself) ◆ **cette porte ne ferme pas ~** this door doesn't shut properly ◆ **la télé ne marche pas ~** the TV isn't working properly *ou* right ◆ **il s'habille ~** he dresses well *ou* smartly ◆ **il parle ~ l'anglais** he speaks good English, he speaks English well ◆ **elle est ~ coiffée aujourd'hui** her hair looks nice today ◆ **on est ~ nourri dans cet hôtel** the food's good in that hotel ◆ **il a ~ pris ce que je lui ai dit** he took what I said in good part *ou* quite well ◆ **il s'y est ~ pris (pour le faire)** he went about it the right way ◆ **si je me rappelle ~** if I remember right(ly) *ou* correctly ◆ **ni ~ ni mal** so-so * ◆ **il n'écrit ni ~ ni mal** *(auteur)* he's so-so as an author

2 = selon les convenances, la morale, la raison *[se conduire, agir]* well, decently ◆ **il pensait ~ faire** he thought he was doing the right thing ◆ **vous avez ~ fait** you did the right thing, you did right ◆ **il a ~ fait de partir** he was quite right *ou* he did right to go ◆ **faire ~ les choses** to do things properly *ou* in style ◆ **vous faites ~ de me le dire !** you did well to tell me!, it's a good thing you've told me! ◆ **vous feriez ~ de partir tôt** you'd do well *ou* you'd be well advised to leave early ◆ **ça commence à ~ faire * !** this has gone on quite long enough!, this is getting beyond a joke! ◆ ~ **lui en a pris** it was just as well he did it

3 = sans difficulté *[supporter]* well; *[se rappeler]* well, clearly ◆ **on comprend très ~ pourquoi** you can certainly understand *ou* see why ◆ **il peut très ~ le faire** he's perfectly capable of doing it

4 exprimant le degré *(= très)* very, really; *(= beaucoup)* very much, thoroughly; *(= trop)* rather ◆ ~ **mieux** much better ◆ ~ **souvent** quite often ◆ **nous sommes ~ contents de vous voir** we're very *ou* awfully glad to see you ◆ ~ **plus heureux/cher** far *ou* much happier/more expensive ◆ **c'est un ~ beau pays** it's a really *ou* truly beautiful country ◆ **nous avons ~ ri** we had a good laugh ◆ **les enfants se sont ~ amusés** the children thoroughly enjoyed themselves *ou* had great fun ◆ **vos œufs sont ~ frais ?** are your eggs really fresh? ◆ **question ~ délicate** highly sensitive question ◆ ~ **trop bête** far too stupid ◆ **elle est ~ jeune (pour se marier)** she is very *ou* rather young (to be getting married) ◆ **c'est ~ moderne pour mes goûts** it's rather too modern for my taste ◆ **il me paraît ~ sûr de lui** he seems to be rather *ou* pretty * sure of himself to me

5 = effectivement indeed, definitely; *(interrog = réellement)* really ◆ **nous savons ~ où il se cache** we know perfectly well *ou* quite well where he's hiding ◆ **j'avais ~ dit que je ne viendrais pas** I (certainly) did say that I wouldn't come ◆ **je trouve ~ que c'est un peu cher mais tant pis** I do think it's rather expensive *ou* I agree it's rather expensive but never mind ◆ **c'est ~ une erreur** it's definitely *ou* certainly a mistake ◆ **était-ce ~ une erreur ?** was it really *ou* in fact a mistake? ◆ **c'est ~ à ton frère que je pensais** it was indeed your brother I was thinking of ◆ **ce n'est pas lui mais ~ son frère qui est docteur** it's his brother not him who is a doctor ◆ **dis-lui ~ que ...** be sure to *ou* and tell him that ..., make sure you tell him that ... ◆ **je vous avais ~ averti** I gave you ample warning, I did warn you ◆ **c'est ~ mon manteau ?** that is my coat, isn't it?

6 dans une exclamative **il s'agit ~ de ça !** *(= vraiment, justement)* as if that's the point! ◆ **voilà ~ les femmes !** that's women for you! ◆ **c'est ~ ça, on t'invite et tu te décommandes !** that's you all over *ou* that's just like you! – we invite you over and then you say you can't come!

7 avec valeur intensive **ferme ~ la porte** shut the door properly, make sure you shut the door ◆ **tourne ~ ton volant à droite** turn your wheel hard to the right ◆ **écoute-moi ~** listen to me carefully ◆ **regardez ~ ce qu'il va faire** watch what he does carefully ◆ **mets-toi ~ en face** stand right *ou* straight opposite ◆ **percez un trou ~ au milieu** drill a hole right in the centre ◆ **tiens-toi ~ droit** stand quite straight ◆ **il est mort et ~ mort** he's dead and gone ◆ **c'est ~ compris ?** is that quite clear *ou* understood? ◆ **c'est ~ promis ?** is that a firm promise? ◆ **il arrivera ~ à se débrouiller** he'll manage to cope all right ◆ **j'espère ~ !** I should hope so (too)! ◆ **où peut-il ~ être ?** where on earth can he be? ◆ ~ **à vous** *(dans une lettre)* yours

8 = malgré tout **il fallait ~ que ça se fasse** it just had to be done ◆ **il faut ~ le supporter** you've just got to put up with it ◆ **il pourrait ~ venir nous voir de temps en temps !** he could at least come and see us now and then!

9 = volontiers *(précédé d'un verbe au conditionnel)* **je mangerais ~ un morceau** I could do with a bite to eat, I wouldn't mind something to eat ◆ **je l'aiderais ~, mais ...** I wish I could help him, but ... ◆ **j'irais ~ mais ...** I'd love to go but ... ◆ **je voudrais ~ t'y voir !** I'd like *ou* love to see you try!, I'd sure like * *(US)* to see you try! ◆ **je te verrais ~ en jaune** I think you'd look good in yellow

10 = au moins at least ◆ **il y a ~ 3 jours que je ne l'ai vu** I haven't seen him for at least 3 days ◆ **cela vaut ~ ce prix là** it's worth at least that

11 locutions

◆ **bien du, bien de la** a great deal of ◆ **elle a eu ~ du mal** *ou* **de la peine à le trouver** she had a good *ou* great deal of difficulty in *ou* no end of trouble * in finding it ◆ **ça fait ~ du monde** that's an awful lot of people ◆ **ils ont eu ~ de la chance** they were really very lucky

◆ **bien des** a good many ◆ **je connais ~ des gens qui auraient protesté** I know a good many *ou* quite a few people who would have protested

◆ **bien que** although, though ◆ ~ **que je ne puisse pas venir** although *ou* though I can't come

◆ **bien sûr** of course ◆ ~ **sûr qu'il viendra !** of course he'll come!

◆ **pour bien faire** ◆ **pour ~ faire il faudrait partir maintenant** the best thing would be to leave now ◆ **pour ~ faire, il aurait fallu terminer hier** it would have been better if we had finished yesterday

2 - ADJECTIF INVARIABLE

1 = satisfaisant *[film, tableau, livre]* good ◆ **elle est très ~ comme secrétaire** she's a very good *ou* competent secretary ◆ **donnez-lui quelque chose de ~** give him something really good ◆ **ce serait ~ s'il venait** it would be good if he were to come

◆ **bien!** *(approbation)* good!, fine!; *(pour changer de sujet)* OK!, all right! ◆ **bien ! bien !, c'est ~ !** *(exaspération)* all right! all right!, OK! OK!

2 Scol, sur copie good ◆ **assez ~** quite good ◆ **très ~** very good

3 = en bonne forme well, in good form *ou* health ◆ **je ne suis pas ~** I don't feel very well ◆ **tu n'es pas ~ ?** are you feeling OK? ◆ **il n'était pas très ~ ce matin** he was out of sorts *ou* off colour * *(Brit)* this morning ◆ **t'es pas ~, non ?** * are you crazy ?

4 = beau *[personne]* good-looking, nice-looking; *[chose]* nice ◆ **elle était très ~ quand elle était jeune** she was very attractive *ou* good-looking when she was young ◆ **il est ~ de sa personne** he's a good-looking man *ou* a fine figure of a man ◆ **ils ont une maison tout ce qu'il y a de ~** * they've got a really lovely *ou* nice house ◆ **ce bouquet fait ~ sur la cheminée** those flowers look nice on the mantelpiece

5 = à l'aise **il est ~ partout** he is *ou* feels at home anywhere ◆ **on est ~ à l'ombre** it's pleasant *ou* nice in the shade ◆ **on est ~ ici** it's nice here, we like it here ◆ **je suis ~ dans ce fauteuil** I'm very comfortable in this chair ◆ **elle se trouve ~ dans son nouveau poste** she's very happy in her new job ◆ **laisse-le, il est ~ où il est** leave him alone – he's quite all right where he is *ou* he's fine where he is ◆ **vous voilà ~ !** *(iro)* now you've done it!, you're in a fine mess now!

6 = acceptable *(socialement)* nice; *(moralement)* right ◆ **c'est pas ~ de dire ça** it's not nice to say that ◆ **ce n'est pas ~ de faire ça** it's not nice *ou* right to do that ◆ **c'est ~ ce qu'il a fait là** it was very good *ou* decent *ou* nice of him to do that ◆ **c'est ~ à vous de les aider** it's good *ou* nice of you to help them ◆ **c'est un type ~** * he's a nice guy * *ou* bloke * *(Brit)* ◆ **c'est une femme ~** she's a very nice woman ◆ **des gens ~** very nice *ou* decent people

7 = en bons termes **être ~ avec qn** to be on good terms *ou* get on well with sb ◆ **ils sont ~ ensemble** they're on the best of terms ◆ **se mettre ~ avec qn** to get on the good *ou* right side of sb, to get into sb's good books *

3 - NOM MASCULIN

1 NonC = ce qui est avantageux, agréable good ◆ **le ~ public** the public good ◆ **c'est pour ton ~ !** it's for your own good! ◆ **pour le (plus grand) ~ de l'humanité** for the (greater) good of humanity ◆ **grand ~ vous fasse !** *(iro)* much good may it do you!, you're welcome to it! ◆ **être du dernier ~ avec qn** *(littér)* to be on the closest possible terms *ou* on intimate terms with sb

◆ **faire du bien** ◆ **faire du ~ à qn/qch** to do sb/sth good ◆ **ça ne va pas faire de ~ à sa réputation** that's not going to do his reputation any good ◆ **ses paroles m'ont fait du ~** what he said did me good ◆ **ça fait du ~ de se confier** it's good to talk ◆ **je me suis cogné la tête, ça ne fait pas de** *ou* **du ~ !** I bumped my head and it really hurt *ou* it didn't half * *(Brit)* hurt ◆ **ça fait du ~ par où ça passe** * **!** that hits the spot!

◆ **dire du bien de** ◆ **dire du ~ de qn** to speak well of sb ◆ **on a dit le plus grand ~ de ce livre/de cet acteur** this book/this actor has been highly praised, people have spoken very highly *ou* favourably of this book/this actor ◆ **on dit beaucoup de ~ de ce restaurant** this restaurant has got a very good name, people speak very highly of this restaurant

◆ **vouloir du bien à qn** to wish sb well ◆ **un ami qui vous veut du ~** *(iro)* a well-wisher *(iro)*

◆ **en bien** ◆ **je trouve qu'il a changé en ~** I find he has changed for the better *ou* he has improved ◆ **parler en ~ de qn** to speak favourably *ou* well of sb

2 = avantage **finalement cet échec temporaire a été un ~** in the end this setback was a good thing ◆ **son départ a été un ~ pour l'entreprise** it was a good thing for the firm that he left

3 = ce qui a une valeur morale ◆ **le ~** good ◆ **savoir discerner le ~ du mal** to be able to tell good from evil *ou* right from wrong ◆ **faire le ~** to do good ◆ **rendre le ~ pour le mal** to return good for evil

4 = possession possession, property *(NonC)*; *(= argent)* fortune; *(= terre)* estate ◆ **~s** goods ◆ **cet ordinateur est son ~ le plus cher** this computer is his most treasured possession ◆ **la tranquillité est le seul ~ qu'il désire** peace of mind is all he asks for ◆ **il considère tout comme son ~** he regards everything as being his property *ou* his own ◆ **il a dépensé tout son ~** he has gone through his entire fortune ◆ **avoir du ~ (au soleil)** to have property ◆ **laisser tous ses ~s à qn** to leave all one's (worldly) goods *ou* possessions to sb ◆ **il est très attaché aux ~s de ce monde** he lays great store by worldly goods *ou* possessions ◆ **~ mal acquis ne profite jamais** *(Prov)* ill-gotten gains seldom prosper *(Prov)* ill gotten ill spent

4 - COMPOSÉS

biens de consommation consumer goods
biens durables consumer durables
biens d'équipement capital equipment *ou* goods; *(industriels)* plant
biens d'équipement ménager household goods
bien de famille family estate
biens fonciers real estate, property *(Brit)*, landed property
biens immédiatement disponibles off-the-shelf goods
biens immeubles, biens immobiliers ⇒ **biens fonciers**
biens indirects capital goods
biens intermédiaires *(Admin)* intermediate goods
bien marchand commodity
biens meubles, biens mobiliers personal property *ou* estate, movables
biens privés private property
biens publics public property
biens successoraux hereditaments
biens en viager life estate

bien-aimé, e (mpl **bien-aimés**) /bjɛ̃neme/ ADJ, NM,F beloved

bien-être /bjɛ̃nɛtʀ/ NM INV *(physique, psychologique)* well-being; *(matériel)* comfort, material well-being

bienfaisance /bjɛ̃fəzɑ̃s/ NF charity ◆ **association** *ou* **œuvre de ~** charitable organization, charity ◆ **l'argent sera donné à des œuvres de ~** the money will be given to charity

bienfaisant, e /bjɛ̃fəzɑ̃, ɑ̃t/ ADJ 1 *[effets]* salutary, beneficial; *[pluie]* life-giving ◆ **eaux aux vertus ~es** health-giving waters ◆ **l'influence ~e de Vénus** *(Astrol)* the favourable *ou* benign influence of Venus 2 † *[personne]* beneficent *(frm)*, kindly

bienfait /bjɛ̃fɛ/ NM 1 *(= faveur)* kindness, kind deed ◆ **c'est un ~ du ciel !** it's a godsend! *ou* a blessing! ◆ **un ~ n'est jamais perdu** *(Prov)* a good turn *ou* deed never goes amiss 2 *(surtout pl = avantage)* benefit ◆ **les ~s du progrès** the benefits of progress ◆ **les ~s d'un traitement** the beneficial effects of a course of treatment ◆ **il commence à ressentir les ~s de son séjour à la campagne** he is beginning to feel the benefit of his stay in the country

bienfaiteur /bjɛ̃fɛtœʀ/ NM benefactor

bienfaitrice /bjɛ̃fɛtʀis/ NF benefactress

bien-fondé (pl **bien-fondés**) /bjɛ̃fɔ̃de/ NM *[d'opinion, assertion]* validity; *(Jur) [de plainte]* cogency

bien-fonds (pl **biens-fonds**) /bjɛ̃fɔ̃/ NM real estate, landed property

bienheureux, -euse /bjɛ̃nœʀø, øz/ ADJ 1 *(Rel)* blessed, blest *(littér)* 2 *(littér)* happy ◆ **~ ceux qui …** lucky are those who … NMPL ◆ **les ~** the blessed, the blest

biennal, e (mpl **-aux**) /bjenal, o/ ADJ biennial NF **biennale** biennial event

bien-pensant, e (mpl **bien-pensants**) /bjɛ̃pɑ̃sɑ̃, ɑ̃t/ ADJ *(Rel)* God-fearing; *(péj = conformiste)* right-thinking NM,F ◆ **les ~s** *(Rel)* God-fearing people; *(péj = conformistes)* right-thinking people

bienséance /bjɛ̃seɑ̃s/ NF propriety, decorum ◆ **les ~s** the proprieties

bienséant, e /bjɛ̃seɑ̃, ɑ̃t/ ADJ *[action, conduite]* proper, seemly, becoming ◆ **il n'est pas ~ de bâiller** it is unbecoming *ou* unseemly to yawn

bientôt /bjɛ̃to/ ADV soon ◆ **à ~ !** see you soon!, bye for now! * ◆ **c'est ~ dit** it's easier said than done, it's easy to say ◆ **on est ~ arrivé** we'll soon be there, we'll be there shortly ◆ **on ne pourra ~ plus circuler dans Paris** before long it will be impossible to drive in Paris ◆ **c'est pour ~ ?** is it due soon?, any chance of its being ready soon?; *(naissance)* is the baby expected *ou* due soon? ◆ **il est ~ minuit** it's nearly midnight ◆ **il aura ~ 30 ans** he'll soon be 30 ◆ **il eut ~ fait de finir son travail** † he finished his work in no time, he lost no time in finishing his work

bienveillance /bjɛ̃vɛjɑ̃s/ NF benevolence, kindness *(envers* to); ◆ **avec ~** *[dire, regarder]* benevolently, kindly; *[parler]* kindly ◆ **examiner un cas avec ~** to give favourable consideration to a case ◆ **je sollicite de votre haute ~ …** *(Admin)* I beg (leave) to request …

bienveillant, e /bjɛ̃vɛjɑ̃, ɑ̃t/ ADJ benevolent, kindly

bienvenu, e /bjɛ̃v(ə)ny/ ADJ ◆ **remarque ~e** apposite *ou* well-chosen remark NM,F ◆ **vous êtes le ~, soyez le ~** you're very welcome, pleased to see you * ◆ **une tasse de café serait la ~e** a cup of coffee would be (most) welcome NF **bienvenue** welcome ◆ **souhaiter la ~e à qn** to welcome sb ◆ **~e à vous !** welcome (to you)!, you are most welcome! ◆ **allocution de ~e** welcoming speech ◆ **~e à Paris/en Italie !** welcome to Paris/to Italy! ◆ **~e parmi nous !** welcome (to the department *ou* company *ou* neighbourhood *etc*)! ◆ **~e !** *(Can = je vous en prie)* you're welcome!

bière[1] /bjɛʀ/ NF beer ◆ **garçon, deux ~s !** waiter, two beers!
COMP **bière blanche** wheat beer
bière blonde ≈ lager, light ale *(Brit)*, light beer *(US)*
bière brune ≈ brown ale *(Brit)*, dark beer *(US)*; → **petit, pression**

bière[2] /bjɛʀ/ NF coffin, casket *(US)* ◆ **mettre qn en ~** to put *ou* place sb in their coffin ◆ **la mise en ~ a eu lieu ce matin** the body was placed in the coffin this morning

biface /bifas/ NM *(Archéol)* flint, biface

biffage /bifaʒ/ NM crossing out

biffer /bife/ ► conjug 1 ◄ VT to cross out, to strike out ◆ **~ à l'encre/au crayon** to ink/pencil out

biffeton * /biftɔ̃/ NM (bank)note, bill *(US)*

biffin /bifɛ̃/ NM *(arg Mil)* foot soldier, infantryman; († * = *chiffonnier)* rag-and-bone man

biffure /bifyʀ/ NF crossing out

bifide /bifid/ ADJ bifid

bifidus /bifidys/ NM bifidus ◆ **yaourt au ~** yogurt containing bifidus, bio yogurt

bifocal, e (mpl **-aux**) /bifɔkal, o/ ADJ bifocal ◆ **lunettes ~es** bifocals

bifteck /biftɛk/ NM steak ◆ **~ de cheval** horsemeat steak ◆ **deux ~s** two steaks, two pieces of steak; → **défendre, gagner, haché**

bifurcation /bifyʀkasjɔ̃/ NF *[de route]* fork, junction; *(Rail)* fork; *[d'artère, tige]* branching; *(fig = changement)* change

bifurquer /bifyʀke/ ► conjug 1 ◄ VI 1 *[route, voie ferrée]* to fork, to branch off 2 *[véhicule]* to turn off *(vers, sur* for, towards); *(fig) [personne]* to branch off *(vers* into); ◆ **~ sur la droite** to turn *ou* bear right

bigame /bigam/ ADJ bigamous NMF bigamist

bigamie /bigami/ NF bigamy

bigarade /bigaʀad/ NF Seville *ou* bitter orange

bigarré, e /bigaʀe/ (ptp de **bigarrer**) ADJ 1 *(= bariolé) [vêtement]* many-coloured, rainbow-coloured; *[groupe]* colourfully dressed, gaily coloured 2 *(fig) [foule]* motley *(épith)*; *[société, peuple]* heterogeneous, mixed

bigarreau (pl **bigarreaux**) /bigaʀo/ NM bigarreau, bigaroon (cherry) ◆ **yaourt aux ~x** cherry yogurt

bigarrer /bigaʀe/ ► conjug 1 ◄ VT to colour in many hues

bigarrure /bigaʀyʀ/ NF coloured pattern ◆ **la ~** *ou* **les ~s d'un tissu** the medley of colours in a piece of cloth, the gaily-coloured pattern of a piece of cloth

Big Bang, big bang /bigbɑ̃g/ NM INV *(Astron)* big bang; *(fig = réorganisation)* shake-up

bigle † /bigl/ ADJ → **bigleux**

bigler † * /bigle/ ► conjug 1 ◄ VT *[+ personne]* to look at VI *(= loucher)* to squint, to have a squint ◆ **arrête de ~ sur** *ou* **dans mon jeu** stop peeping at my cards *, take your beady eyes off my cards *

bigleux, -euse * /biglø, øz/ ADJ 1 *(= myope)* short-sighted ◆ **quel ~ tu fais !** you need glasses! 2 *(= qui louche)* squint(-eyed), cross-eyed

bigophone * /bigɔfɔn/ NM phone, blower * *(Brit)*, horn * *(US)* ◆ **passer un coup de ~ à qn** to get on the blower * *(Brit)* *ou* horn * *(US)* to sb, to give sb a buzz * *ou* ring

bigophoner * /bigɔfɔne/ ► conjug 1 ◄ VI to be on the blower * *(Brit)* *ou* horn * *(US)* ◆ **~ à qn** to give sb a buzz * *ou* a ring

bigorneau (pl **bigorneaux**) /bigɔʀno/ NM winkle

bigorner † * /bigɔʀne/ ► conjug 1 ◄ VT *[+ voiture]* to smash up VPR **se bigorner** *(= se battre)* to come to blows, to scrap * *(avec* with)

bigot, e /bigo, ɔt/ *(péj)* ADJ sanctimonious, holier-than-thou NM,F sanctimonious *ou* holier-than-thou person

⚠ **bigot** ne se traduit pas par le mot anglais **bigot**, qui a le sens de 'sectaire'.

bigoterie /bigɔtʀi/ NF *(péj)* sanctimoniousness

bigouden, -ène /bigudɛ̃, ɛn/ ADJ of *ou* from the Pont-l'Abbé region *(in Brittany)* NM,F **Bigouden (-ène)** native *ou* inhabitant of the Pont-l'Abbé region NF **bigoudène** *(= coiffe) woman's headdress worn in the Pont-l'Abbé region*

bigoudi /bigudi/ NM (hair-)curler, roller ◆ **elle était en ~s** her hair was in curlers *ou* rollers

bigre * /bigʀ/ EXCL *(hum)* gosh! *, holy smoke! *

bigrement * /bigʀəmɑ̃/ ADV *[bon, chaud, cher]* darned *, jolly * *(Brit)*; *[changer, ressembler]* a heck of a lot * ◆ **on a ~ bien mangé** we had a jolly good meal * *(Brit)*, we had one dandy meal * *(US)*

biguine /bigin/ NF beguine

Bihar /biaʀ/ NM ◆ **le ~** Bihar

bihebdomadaire /biɛbdɔmadɛʀ/ ADJ twice-weekly

bijection /biʒɛksjɔ̃/ NF bijection

bijou (pl **bijoux**) /biʒu/ NM 1 jewel ◆ **les ~x d'une femme** a woman's jewels *ou* jewellery ◆ **~x (de) fantaisie** costume jewellery ◆ **~x de famille** *(lit)* family jewels; *(* : hum)* wedding tackle * *(Brit)*, family jewels * *(US)* ◆ **mon ~** *(terme d'affection)* my love, pet 2 *(= chef-d'œuvre)* gem ◆ **un ~ de précision** a marvel of precision

bijouterie /biʒutʀi/ NF *(= boutique)* jeweller's (shop); *(= commerce)* jewellery business *ou* trade; *(= art)* jewellery-making; *(= bijoux)* jewellery

bijoutier, -ière /biʒutje, jɛʀ/ NM,F jeweller

bikini ® /bikini/ NM bikini

bilabial, e (mpl **-iaux**) /bilabjal, jo/ ADJ bilabial NF **bilabiale** bilabial

bilame /bilam/ NM *(Phys)* bimetallic strip

bilan /bilɑ̃/ NM 1 *(Fin)* balance sheet, statement of accounts ◆ **dresser** *ou* **établir son ~** to draw up the balance sheet ◆ **~ de liquidation** statement of affairs *(in a bankruptcy petition)*
2 *(= évaluation)* appraisal, assessment; *(= résultats)* results; *(= conséquences)* consequences ◆ **le ~ du gouvernement** the government's track record ◆ **quel a été le ~ de ces négociations ?** what was the upshot *ou* the end result of the negotiations? ◆ **faire le ~ d'une situation** to take stock of *ou* assess a situation ◆ **quand on arrive à 50 ans on fait le ~** when you reach 50 you take stock (of your life) ◆ **~ de compétences** skills assessment
3 *[de catastrophe] (= nombre de morts)* (death) toll ◆ **d'après un premier ~** *ou* **un ~ provisoire** according to the first reports coming in ◆ **"émeute dans la capitale, bilan : 3 morts"** "riots in the capital: 3 dead" ◆ **~ provisoire : 300 blessés** so far, 300 people are known to have been injured
4 *(Méd)* **~ de santé** (medical) checkup ◆ **se faire faire un ~ de santé** to go for *ou* have a checkup ◆ **faire le ~ de santé de l'économie** to assess the current state of the economy

bilatéral, e (mpl **-aux**) /bilateʀal, o/ ADJ bilateral ◆ **stationnement ~** parking on both sides (of the road)

bilatéralement /bilateʀalmɑ̃/ ADV bilaterally

bilboquet /bilbɔkɛ/ NM ≈ cup-and-ball (toy)

bile /bil/ NF *(Anat, fig = amertume)* bile ◆ **se faire de la ~ * (pour)** to get worried (about), to worry o.s. sick (about) *; → **échauffer**

biler (se) * /bile/ ► conjug 1 ◄ VPR *(gén nég)* to worry o.s. sick * (*pour* about); ◆ **ne vous bilez pas !** don't get all worked up! * *ou* het up! *, don't get yourself all worried! ◆ **il ne se bile pas** he's not one to worry, he doesn't let things bother him

bileux, -euse * /bilø, øz/ ADJ easily upset *ou* worried ◆ **il n'est pas ~, ce n'est pas un ~** he's not one to worry, he doesn't let things bother him ◆ **quel ~ tu fais !** what a fretter * *ou* worrier you are!

bilharziose /bilaʀzjoz/ NF bilharziasis, schistosomiasis

biliaire /biljɛʀ/ ADJ biliary; → **calcul, vésicule**

bilieux, -euse /biljø, øz/ ADJ *[teint]* bilious, yellowish; *[personne, tempérament]* irritable, testy

bilingue /bilɛ̃g/ ADJ bilingual

bilinguisme /bilɛ̃gɥism/ NM bilingualism

billard /bijaʀ/ NM 1 *(= jeu)* billiards *(sg)*; *(= table)* billiard table; *(= salle)* billiard room ◆ **faire un ~** *ou* **une partie de ~** to play (a game of) billiards 2 *(* : locutions)* **passer sur le ~** to go under the surgeon's knife, to have an operation ◆ **c'est du ~** it's quite *ou* dead easy *, it's a piece of cake * *ou* a cinch ◆ **cette route est un vrai ~** this road is incredibly smooth *ou* as smooth as a billiard table
COMP **billard américain** pool
billard électrique pinball machine
billard français French billiards
billard japonais *(= partie)* (game of) pinball; *(= table)* pinball machine
billard russe bar billiards

bille /bij/ NF 1 *(= boule) [d'enfant]* marble; *[de billard]* (billiard) ball ◆ **jouer aux ~s** to play marbles, to have a game of marbles ◆ **déodorant à ~** roll-on deodorant ◆ **il a attaqué** *ou* **foncé ~ en tête** * *(fig)* he didn't beat about the bush * ◆ **reprendre** *ou* **récupérer** *ou* **retirer ses ~s** *(fig)* to pull out ◆ **il a su placer ses ~s** * *(fig)* he made all the right moves ◆ **toucher sa ~ au tennis/en histoire** * to know a thing or two about tennis/history; → **roulement, stylo** 2 ◆ **~ de bois** billet, block of wood 3 *(* = visage)* mug *, face ◆ **il a fait une drôle de ~ !** you should have seen his face! ◆ **~ de clown** funny face ◆ **il a une bonne ~** he's got a jolly face 4 *(* = yeux)* **~s** round eyes

billet /bijɛ/ NM 1 *(= ticket)* ticket ◆ **~ de quai/train/loterie** platform/train/lottery ticket ◆ **~ collectif** group ticket; → **aller**
2 *(= argent)* note, bill *(US)* ◆ **~ de 20 €** €20 note ◆ **ça coûte 500 ~s** * it costs 5,000 francs; ◆ **je te fiche** *ou* **flanque mon ~ qu'il ne viendra pas !** * I bet my bottom dollar * *ou* I bet you anything he won't come!; → **faux²**
3 *(littér ou † = lettre)* note, short letter ◆ **~ d'humeur** *(Presse)* column
COMP **billet de banque** banknote
billet de commerce promissory note, bill of exchange
billet doux billet doux *(hum)*, love letter
billet de faveur complimentary ticket
billet de logement *(Mil)* billet
billet à ordre promissory note, bill of exchange
billet de parterre † * ◆ **prendre** *ou* **ramasser un ~ de parterre** to fall flat on one's face, to come a cropper * *(Brit)*
billet au porteur bearer order
billet de retard *(Scol)* late slip, tardy slip *(US)*; *(Admin) note from public transport authorities attesting late running of train etc*
billet de trésorerie commercial paper
le billet vert *(Écon)* the dollar

billetterie /bijɛtʀi/ NF *[d'argent]* cash dispenser, cash point, ATM; *[de tickets]* (automatic) ticket machine

billevesées /bijvəze/ NFPL *(littér = sornettes)* nonsense *(NonC)*

billion /biljɔ̃/ NM million million, trillion *(surtout US)*

billot /bijo/ NM *[de boucher, bourreau, cordonnier]* block; *(Can)* log (of wood) ◆ **j'en mettrais ma tête sur le ~** *(fig)* I'd stake my life on it

bilobé, e /bilɔbe/ ADJ bilobate, bilobed

bimbeloterie /bɛ̃blɔtʀi/ NF *(= objets)* knick-knacks, fancy goods *(Brit)*; *(= commerce)* knick-knack *ou* fancy goods *(Brit)* business

bimensuel, -elle /bimɑ̃sɥɛl/ ADJ twice monthly, bimonthly, fortnightly *(Brit)*, semimonthly *(US)* NM *(= revue)* fortnightly review *(Brit)*, semimonthly *(US)*

bimensuellement /bimɑ̃sɥɛlmɑ̃/ ADV twice a month, fortnightly *(Brit)*, semimonthly *(US)*

bimestriel, -elle /bimɛstʀijɛl/ ADJ bimonthly

bimétallique /bimetalik/ ADJ bimetallic

bimétallisme /bimetalism/ NM bimetallism

bimoteur /bimɔtœʀ/ ADJ twin-engined NM twin-engined plane

binage /binaʒ/ NM hoeing, harrowing

binaire /binɛʀ/ ADJ binary NM *(Ordin)* binary code ◆ **codé en ~** binary coded

binational, e (mpl **-aux**) /binasjɔnal, o/ ADJ *[personne]* having dual nationality NM,F person with dual nationality

biner /bine/ ► conjug 1 ◄ VT to hoe, to harrow

binette /binɛt/ NF 1 *(Agr)* hoe 2 *(* = visage)* face, mug *

bing /biŋ/ EXCL smack!, thwack!

bingo /biŋgo/ NM *(Can) (= jeu)* ≈ bingo *(using letters as well as numbers)*; *(= partie)* ≈ game of bingo ◆ **~ !** bingo!

biniou /binju/ NM *(Mus)* (Breton) bagpipes ◆ **donner un coup de ~ à qn** * *(= téléphone)* to give sb a buzz * *ou* a ring

binoclard, e * /binɔklaʀ, aʀd/ ADJ, NM,F ◆ **il est** *ou* **c'est un ~** he wears specs *, he's a four-eyes *

binocle /binɔkl/ NM pince-nez

binoculaire /binɔkylɛʀ/ ADJ binocular

binôme /binom/ NM *(Math, Bio)* binomial; *(= deux personnes)* two-person team ◆ **travailler en ~** to work in pairs *ou* in twos NMF ◆ **mon ~** *(= personne)* my partner

bio * /bjo/ NF 1 (abrév de **biographie**) bio * 2 abrév de **biologie** ADJ (abrév de **biologique**) *[agriculture, engrais, nourriture]* organic ◆ **produits ~(s)** *(= aliments)* organic food; *(= non-polluants)* eco-friendly products

biocarburant /bjokaʀbyʀɑ̃/ NM biofuel

biochimie /bjoʃimi/ NF biochemistry

biochimique /bjoʃimik/ ADJ biochemical

biochimiste /bjoʃimist/ NMF biochemist

biocompatible /bjokɔ̃patibl/ ADJ biocompatible

biodégradabilité /bjodegʀadabilite/ NF biodegradability

biodégradable /bjodegʀadabl/ ADJ biodegradable

biodégradation /bjodegʀadasjɔ̃/ NF biodegradation

biodiversité /bjodivɛʀsite/ NF biodiversity

biodynamique /bjodinamik/ ADJ *[agriculture, méthode]* biodynamic

bioénergétique /bjoenɛʀʒetik/ ADJ bioenergetic NF bioenergetics *(sg)*

bioénergie /bjoenɛʀʒi/ NF bioenergy

bioéthique /bjoetik/ NF bioethics *(sg)*

biogaz /bjogaz/ NM biogas

biogenèse /bjoʒənɛz/ NF biogenesis

biogénétique /bjoʒenetik/ NF biogenetics

biogéographe /bjoʒeɔgʀaf/ NMF biogeographer

biogéographie /bjoʒeɔgʀafi/ NF biogeography

biogéographique /bjoʒeɔgʀafik/ ADJ biogeographical

biographe /bjɔgʀaf/ NMF biographer

biographie /bjɔgʀafi/ NF biography ◆ ~ **romancée** biographical novel

biographique /bjɔgʀafik/ ADJ biographical

bio-industrie (pl **bio-industries**) /bjoɛ̃dystʀi/ NF bioindustry

biologie /bjɔlɔʒi/ NF biology ◆ ~ **animale/végétale** animal/plant biology ◆ ~ **cellulaire/médicale/moléculaire** cellular/medical/molecular biology

biologique /bjɔlɔʒik/ ADJ 1 *(gén)* biological 2 *[produits, aliments]* organic ◆ **agriculture** ~ organic farming

> ⚠ Au sens de 'écologique', **biologique** ne se traduit pas par **biological**.

biologiquement /bjɔlɔʒikmɑ̃/ ADV biologically ◆ **produit** ~ **cultivé** organically grown product

biologiste /bjɔlɔʒist/ NMF biologist

biomasse /bjomas/ NF biomass

biomatériau (pl **biomatériaux**) /bjomateʀjo/ NM biomaterial

biomédecine /bjomedsin/ NF biomedicine

biométrie /bjometʀi/ NF biometrics ◆ ~ **faciale** facial biometrics

bionique /bjɔnik/ NF bionics *(sg)* ADJ bionic

biophysicien, -ienne /bjofizisjɛ̃, jɛn/ NM,F biophysicist

biophysique /bjofizik/ NF biophysics *(sg)*

biopsie /bjɔpsi/ NF biopsy

biorythme /bjoʀitm/ NM biorhythm

biosphère /bjosfɛʀ/ NF biosphere

biostatistique /bjostatistik/ NF biostatistics *(sg)*

biosynthèse /bjosɛ̃tez/ NF biosynthesis

biotechnique /bjotɛknik/, **biotechnologie** /bjotɛknɔlɔʒi/ NF biotechnology

biotechnologique /bjotɛknɔlɔʒik/ ADJ biotechnological

bioterrorisme /bjotɛʀɔʀism/ NM bioterrorism

bioterroriste /bjotɛʀɔʀist/ NMF bioterrorist

biotope /bjɔtɔp/ NM biotope

biovigilance /bjoviʒilɑ̃s/ NF biotech monitoring

bioxyde /bijɔksid/ NM dioxide

bip /bip/ GRAMMAIRE ACTIVE 54.3 NM 1 *(= son) (court)* b(l)eep; *(continu)* b(l)eeping ◆ **faire** ~ to b(l)eep ◆ **parlez après le** ~ **sonore** speak after the tone *ou* beep 2 *(= appareil)* bleep(er), beeper

bipale /bipal/ ADJ twin-bladed

biparti, e /bipaʀti/, **bipartite** /bipaʀtit/ ADJ *(Bot)* bipartite; *(Pol)* two-party, bipartite, bipartisan

bipartisme /bipaʀtism/ NM *(Pol)* bipartisanship

bipasse /bipas/ NM ⇒ **by-pass**

bip-bip (pl **bips-bips**) /bipbip/ NM ⇒ **bip**

bipède /bipɛd/ ADJ, NM biped

biper[1] /bipe/ ▸ conjug 1 ◂ VT to page

biper[2] /bipœʀ/ NM *(Téléc)* beeper, bleeper

biphasé, e /bifɑze/ ADJ diphase, two-phase

biplace /biplas/ ADJ, NM two-seater

biplan /biplɑ̃/ ADJ ◆ **avion** ~ biplane NM biplane

bipolaire /bipɔlɛʀ/ ADJ bipolar

bipolarisation /bipɔlaʀizasjɔ̃/ NF *(Pol)* polarization *(entre* of, between); ◆ **la** ~ **Est-Ouest de l'Europe** the way Europe is polarized between East and West

bipolarité /bipɔlaʀite/ NF bipolarity

bique /bik/ NF nanny-goat ◆ **vieille** ~* *(péj)* old hag, old bag* ◆ **grande** ~* beanpole

biquet, -ette /bikɛ, ɛt/ NM,F *(= chevreau)* kid ◆ **mon** ~ *(terme d'affection)* love

biquotidien, -ienne /bikɔtidjɛ̃, jɛn/ ADJ twice-daily

birbe † /biʀb/ NM *(péj)* ◆ **vieux** ~ old fuddy-duddy*, old fogey*

bircher /biʀʃɛʀ/ NM *(Helv = muesli)* muesli

BIRD /biʀd/ NF (abrév de **Banque internationale pour la reconstruction et le développement**) IBRD

biréacteur /biʀeaktœʀ/ NM twin-engined jet

biréfringence /biʀefʀɛ̃ʒɑ̃s/ NF birefringence

biréfringent, e /biʀefʀɛ̃ʒɑ̃, ɑ̃t/ ADJ birefringent

birème /biʀɛm/ NF *(Antiq)* bireme

birman, e /biʀmɑ̃, an/ ADJ Burmese NM *(= langue)* Burmese NM,F **Birman(e)** Burmese

Birmanie /biʀmani/ NF Burma

biroute /biʀut/ NF 1 *(* = pénis)* dick**, cock**, prick** 2 *(arg Mil = manche à air)* wind sock

bis[1] /bis/ ADV *(Mus : sur partition)* repeat, twice ◆ ~ **!** *(Théât)* encore! ◆ **12** ~ *(numéro)* 12a ◆ ~ **repetita** it's the same story (all over) again; → **itinéraire** NM *(Théât)* encore

bis[2]**, e**[1] /bi, biz/ ADJ greyish-brown, brownish-grey; → **pain**

bisaïeul /bizajœl/ NM great-grandfather

bisaïeule /bizajœl/ NF great-grandmother

bisannuel, -elle /bizanɥɛl/ ADJ biennial

bisbille* /bizbij/ NF squabble, tiff ◆ **être en** ~ **avec qn** to be at loggerheads with sb

bisbrouille /bizbʀuj/ NF *(Belg = fâcherie)* tiff ◆ **ils sont en** ~ they've had a tiff *ou* falling-out

biscornu, e /biskɔʀny/ ADJ *[forme]* irregular, crooked; *[maison]* crooked, oddly shaped; *[idée, esprit]* quirky, peculiar; *[raisonnement]* tortuous, quirky ◆ **un chapeau** ~ a shapeless hat

biscoteaux* /biskɔto/ NMPL biceps ◆ **avoir des** ~ to have a good pair of biceps

biscotte /biskɔt/ NF *type of thick biscuit which looks like rounds of toast*, melba toast *(US)*

biscuit /biskɥi/ NM 1 *(Culin) (= gâteau sec)* biscuit *(Brit)*, cookie *(US)*; *(= pâte)* sponge cake ◆ ~ **salé** cracker, cheese biscuit *(Brit)* ◆ **ne t'embarque pas** *ou* **ne pars pas sans** ~**s** *(fig)* make sure you're well prepared 2 *(= céramique)* biscuit, bisque

COMP **biscuit (à) apéritif** cracker, cocktail snack

biscuit pour chien dog biscuit

biscuit à la cuiller sponge finger *(Brit)*, lady finger *(US)*

biscuit de Savoie sponge cake

biscuiterie /biskɥitʀi/ NF *(= usine)* biscuit *(Brit) ou* cookie *(US)* factory; *(= commerce)* biscuit *(Brit) ou* cookie *(US)* trade

bise[2] /biz/ NF *(= vent)* North wind

bise[3] /biz/ NF *(= baiser)* kiss ◆ **faire une** *ou* **la** ~ **à qn** to kiss sb, to give sb a kiss ◆ **faire une grosse** ~ **à qn** to give sb a big kiss ◆ **il lui a fait une petite** ~ he gave her a quick peck* *ou* kiss ◆ **grosses** ~**s** *(sur lettre)* lots of love *(de* from) much love *(de* from)

biseau (pl **biseaux**) /bizo/ NM 1 *(= bord) (gén)* bevel, bevelled edge; *(à 45°)* chamfer, chamfered edge ◆ **en** ~ *(gén)* bevelled, with a bevelled edge; *(à 45°)* chamfered, with a chamfered edge ◆ **tailler en** ~ *(gén)* to bevel; *(à 45°)* to chamfer 2 *(= outil)* bevel

biseautage /bizotaʒ/ NM *(gén)* bevelling; *(à 45°)* chamfering

biseauter /bizote/ ▸ conjug 1 ◂ VT *(gén)* to bevel; *(à 45°)* to chamfer; *[+ cartes]* to mark

bisexualité /bisɛksɥalite/ NF bisexuality, bisexualism

bisexué, e /bisɛksɥe/ ADJ bisexual

bisexuel, -elle /bisɛksɥɛl/ ADJ bisexual NM,F bisexual

bismuth /bismyt/ NM bismuth

bison /bizɔ̃/ NM *(d'Amérique)* (American) bison, buffalo (US); *(d'Europe)* European bison, wisent ◆ **Bison futé** *traffic monitoring service that informs drivers about congestion on French roads and suggests alternative routes*

bisou* /bizu/ NM kiss ◆ **faire un** ~ **à qn** to give sb a kiss ◆ **faire un petit** ~ **à qn** to give sb a peck* *ou* kiss ◆ **gros** ~**s** *(sur lettre)* lots of love *(de* from)

bisque /bisk/ NF *(Culin)* bisque ◆ ~ **de homard** lobster soup, bisque of lobster

bisquer* /biske/ ▸ conjug 1 ◂ VI to be riled* *ou* nettled ◆ **faire** ~ **qn** to rile* *ou* nettle sb

Bissau /bisao/ N Bissau

bisse /bis/ NM *(Helv = canal) irrigation channel in the mountains*

bissecteur, -trice /bisɛktœʀ, tʀis/ ADJ bisecting NF **bissectrice** bisector, bisecting line

bissection /bisɛksjɔ̃/ NF bisection

bisser /bise/ ▸ conjug 1 ◂ VT *(= faire rejouer) [+ acteur, chanson]* to encore; *(= rejouer) [+ morceau]* to play again, to sing again

bissextile /bisɛkstil/ ADJ F → **année**

bissexué, e /bisɛksɥe/ ADJ ⇒ **bisexué, e**

bissexuel, -elle /bisɛksɥɛl/ ADJ, NM,F ⇒ **bisexuel, -elle**

bistable /bistabl/ ADJ *(Élec)* bistable

bistouri /bistuʀi/ NM bistoury *(SPÉC)*, surgical knife ◆ **enlever qch au** ~ to remove sth surgically ◆ **donner un coup de** ~ *(fig)* to take drastic action *ou* measures

bistre /bistʀ/ ADJ *[couleur]* blackish-brown, bistre; *[objet]* bistre-coloured, blackish-brown; *[peau, teint]* swarthy NM bistre

bistré, e /bistʀe/ (ptp de **bistrer**) ADJ *[teint]* tanned, swarthy

bistrer /bistʀe/ ▸ conjug 1 ◂ VT *[+ objet]* to colour with bistre; *[+ peau]* to tan

bistro(t) /bistʀo/ NM 1 *(* = café)* ≈ pub, bar *(US)*, café ◆ **faire les** ~**s** to go on a bar-crawl 2 *(† = cafetier)* ≈ café owner

bistrotier, -ière /bistʀɔtje, jɛʀ/ NM,F ≈ publican *(Brit)*, bar manager *(US)*

BIT /beite/ NM (abrév de **Bureau international du travail**) ILO

bit /bit/ NM *(Ordin)* bit

bite, bitte[1]** /bit/ NF *(= pénis)* prick**, cock**, dick**

biter, bitter** /bite/ ▸ conjug 1 ◂ VT ◆ **j'y bitte rien** I can't understand a fucking thing**

bithérapie /biteʀapi/ NF double therapy

bitoniau* /bitɔnjo/ NM whatsit*

bitos* /bitos/ NM hat, headgear* *(NonC)*

bitte[2] /bit/ NF 1 *[de navire]* bitt ◆ ~ **(d'amarrage)** *[de quai]* mooring post, bollard 2 ⇒ **bite**

bitture* /bityʀ/ NF ⇒ **biture**

bitumage /bitymaʒ/ NM asphalting

bitume /bitym/ NM *(Chim, Min)* bitumen; *(= revêtement)* asphalt, Tarmac ®, blacktop *(US)*; *(fig = route)* road ◆ **arpenter le** ~ to walk the streets

bitumé, e /bityme/ (ptp de **bitumer**) ADJ *[route]* asphalted, asphalt *(épith)*, tarmac *(épith)*; *[carton]* bitumized

bitum(in)er /bitym(in)e/ ▸ conjug 1 ◂ VT *[+ route]* to asphalt, to tarmac

bitum(in)eux, -euse /bitym(in)ø, øz/ ADJ bituminous

biture‡ /bityʀ/ NF ◆ **prendre une ~** to get drunk *ou* plastered‡ ◆ **il tient une de ces ~s** he's plastered‡, he's blind drunk*

biturer (se)‡ /bityʀe/ ▸ conjug 1 ◂ VPR to get drunk *ou* plastered‡

biunivoque /biynivɔk/ ADJ *(fig)* one-to-one; *(Math)* → **correspondance**

bivalent, e /bivalɑ̃, ɑ̃t/ ADJ *(Chim)* bivalent; *[professeur]* teaching two subjects

bivalve /bivalv/ ADJ, NM bivalve

bivouac /bivwak/ NM bivouac

bivouaquer /bivwake/ ▸ conjug 1 ◂ VI to bivouac

bizarre /bizaʀ/ ADJ *[personne, conduite]* strange, odd, peculiar; *[idée, raisonnement, temps]* odd, strange, funny*; *[vêtement]* strange *ou* funny (-looking) ◆ **tiens, c'est ~** that's odd *ou* funny* NM ◆ **le ~** the bizarre ◆ **le ~ dans tout cela ...** what's strange *ou* peculiar about all that ...

bizarrement /bizaʀmɑ̃/ ADV strangely, oddly

bizarrerie /bizaʀʀi/ NF *[de personne]* odd *ou* strange *ou* peculiar ways; *[d'idée]* strangeness, oddness; *[de situation, humeur]* strange *ou* odd nature ◆ **~s** *[de langue, règlement]* peculiarities, oddities, quirks ◆ **ce sont les ~s du système** these are the quirks *ou* the vagaries of the system

bizarroïde* /bizaʀɔid/ ADJ weird

bizness* /biznes/ NM ⇒ **business**

bizut /bizy/ NM *(arg Scol)* freshman, first-year student, fresher *(Brit)*

bizutage /bizytaʒ/ NM *(arg Scol)* ragging *(Brit)*, hazing *(US) (of new student etc)*

> **BIZUTAGE**
>
> New arrivals at certain « grandes écoles » and other educational institutions are called « bizuts » or « bizuths », and when they arrive at school in September, they are often subjected to an initiation ceremony known as **bizutage**. This usually involves being subjected to light-hearted ordeals by one's new classmates, but can sometimes degenerate into humiliating and cruel pranks. For this reason, the tradition has become more controversial in recent years, and many schools have outlawed it.

bizuter /bizyte/ ▸ conjug 1 ◂ VT *(arg Scol)* to rag *(Brit)*, to haze *(US) (new student etc)*

bizuth /bizy/ NM ⇒ **bizut**

BK /beka/ NM (abrév de **bacille de Koch**) Koch's bacillus

blabla(bla)* /blabla(bla)/ NM twaddle*, claptrap* ◆ **il y a beaucoup de ~ dans sa dissertation** there's a lot of waffle* *(Brit)* in his paper

blablater* /blablate/ ▸ conjug 1 ◂ VI to blabber on*, to waffle on* *(Brit)*

black* /blak/ ADJ *[personne, culture, musique]* black NMF black person ◆ **les ~s** black people, blacks NM ◆ **travailler** *ou* **bosser au ~*** to work on the side; *(deuxième emploi)* to moonlight; *[clandestin]* to work illegally

blackboulage /blakbulaʒ/ NM blackballing

blackbouler /blakbule/ ▸ conjug 1 ◂ VT *(à une élection)* to blackball; *(* : à un examen)* to fail

black-jack (pl **black-jacks**) /blak(d)ʒak/ NM blackjack

black-out /blakaut/ NM *(Élec, Mil, fig)* blackout ◆ **faire le ~ sur qch** *(fig)* to impose a (news) blackout on sth

blafard, e /blafaʀ, aʀd/ ADJ *[teint]* pale, pallid, wan; *[couleur, lumière, soleil]* pale ◆ **l'aube ~e** the pale light of dawn

blague /blag/ NF [1] *(* = histoire, plaisanterie)* joke; *(= farce)* practical joke, trick ◆ **faire une ~ à qn** to play a trick *ou* a joke on sb ◆ **sans ~ ?** really?, you're kidding!‡ ◆ **sans ~, ~ à part** seriously, joking apart, kidding aside* *(US)* ◆ **non mais sans ~, tu me prends pour qui ?** no really *ou* come on, what do you take me for? ◆ **il prend tout à la ~** he can never take anything seriously ◆ **ne me raconte pas de ~s !** you're having *(Brit) ou* putting *(US)* me on!*, pull the other one!* *(Brit)* ◆ **c'est de la ~ tout ça !** it's all talk !, it's all bull !‡
[2] *(* = erreur)* silly thing, blunder, stupid mistake ◆ **faire une ~** to make a blunder *ou* a stupid mistake ◆ **faire des ~s** to do silly *ou* stupid things ◆ **attention, pas de ~s !** be careful!, no messing about!*
[3] ◆ **~ (à tabac)** (tobacco) pouch

blaguer* /blage/ ▸ conjug 1 ◂ VI to be joking *ou* kidding* *(sur* about); ◆ **j'ai dit cela pour ~** I said it for a joke *ou* lark* *(Brit)* ◆ **on ne blague pas avec ça** you shouldn't joke about that, that's not something to joke about VT to tease, to make fun of, to kid*, to take the mickey out of‡ *(Brit)*

blagueur, -euse /blagœʀ, øz/ ADJ *[sourire, air]* ironical, teasing; *[ton, manière]* jokey* ◆ **il est (très) ~** he's (really) good fun NM,F *(gén)* joker; *(= farceur)* practical joker

blair‡ /blɛʀ/ NM nose, beak‡, hooter‡ *(Brit)*

blaireau (pl **blaireaux**) /blɛʀo/ NM [1] *(= animal)* badger [2] *(pour barbe)* shaving brush [3] *(‡ péj)* nerd* *(péj)*

blairer‡ /bleʀe/ ▸ conjug 1 ◂ VT ◆ **je ne peux pas le ~** I can't stand *ou* bear him

blâmable /blɑmabl/ ADJ blameful

blâme /blɑm/ NM [1] *(= désapprobation)* blame; *(= réprimande)* reprimand, rebuke ◆ **encourir le ~ de qn** *[personne, action]* to incur sb's condemnation *ou* censure ◆ **rejeter le ~ sur qn** to put the blame on sb [2] *(Admin, Sport = punition)* reprimand ◆ **donner un ~ à qn** to reprimand sb ◆ **recevoir un ~** to be reprimanded, to incur a reprimand

blâmer /blɑme/ ▸ conjug 1 ◂ VT *(= désavouer)* to blame; *(= réprimander)* to reprimand, to rebuke ◆ **je ne te blâme pas de** *ou* **pour l'avoir fait** I don't blame you for having done it

blanc, blanche /blɑ̃, blɑ̃ʃ/ ADJ [1] *(= sans couleur)* white; *(= pâle)* white, pale ◆ **~ de colère/de peur** white with anger/fear ◆ **~ comme neige** (as) white as snow, snow-white ◆ **~ comme un cachet d'aspirine** white as a sheet ◆ **il devint ~ comme un linge** he went *ou* turned as white as a sheet; → **arme, bois, bonnet**
[2] *[page, bulletin de vote]* blank; *[papier non quadrillé]* unlined, plain ◆ **il a rendu copie blanche** *ou* **sa feuille blanche** *(Scol)* he handed in a blank paper ◆ **prenez une feuille blanche** take a clean *ou* blank piece of paper ◆ **voter ~** to return a blank vote; → **carte, examen**
[3] *(= innocent)* pure, innocent ◆ **~ comme neige** *ou* **comme la blanche hermine** as pure as the driven snow
[4] *[domination, justice, pouvoir]* white ◆ **la race blanche** the white *ou* Caucasian race ◆ **de race blanche** white, Caucasian ◆ **l'Afrique blanche** white Africa
[5] *(Sci) [bruit]* white
[6] *(Fin)* **ça a été une opération blanche** we *(ou* they *etc)* broke even, we *(ou* they *etc)* didn't lose or gain by it ◆ **cette privatisation sera une opération blanche pour l'État** the government will neither gain nor lose from this privatization
[7] *(Tennis)* **jeu ~** love game
NM [1] *(= couleur)* white ◆ **peindre qch en ~** to paint sth white ◆ **le ~ de sa robe tranchait sur sa peau brune** her white dress *ou* the white of her dress contrasted sharply with her dark skin; → **but**
[2] *(= linge)* **laver séparément le ~ et la couleur** to wash whites and coloureds separately ◆ **vente de ~** white sale, sale of household linen ◆ **magasin de ~** linen shop ◆ **la quinzaine du ~** (annual) sale of household linen, (annual) white sale
[3] *(Cosmétique)* white (face-)powder
[4] *(= espace non écrit)* blank, space; *[de bande magnétique]* blank; *[de domino]* blank ◆ **il y a eu un ~ (dans la conversation)** there was a break *ou* a lull in the conversation; *(dû à la gêne)* there was an embarrassed silence ◆ **laisser un ~** to leave a blank *ou* space ◆ **il faut laisser le nom en ~** the name must be left blank *ou* must not be filled in; → **chèque, signer**
[5] *(= vin)* white wine
[6] *(Culin)* **~ (d'œuf)** (egg) white ◆ **~ (de poulet)** white (meat), breast of chicken ◆ **elle n'aime pas le ~** she doesn't like the white (meat) *ou* the breast
[7] ◆ **le ~ (de l'œil)** the white (of the eye); → **regarder, rougir**
[8] *(= personne)* **un Blanc** a White, a white man ◆ **les Blancs** white people
[9] ◆ **à ~** *[charger]* with blanks ◆ **tirer à ~** to fire blanks ◆ **balle à ~** blank ◆ **cartouche à ~** blank (cartridge); → **chauffer, saigner**
NF **blanche** [1] *(= femme)* **une Blanche** a white woman
[2] *(Mus)* minim *(Brit)*, half-note *(US)*
[3] *(Billard)* white (ball)
[4] *(arg Drogue)* horse *(arg)*, smack *(arg)*
COMP **blanc de baleine** spermaceti
blanc de blanc(s) blanc de blanc(s)
blanc cassé off-white
blanc de céruse white lead
blanc de chaux whitewash
blanc d'Espagne whiting, whitening
blanc de zinc zinc oxide

blanc-bec (pl **blancs-becs**) /blɑ̃bɛk/ NM greenhorn*, tenderfoot*

blanc-bleu‡ /blɑ̃blø/ ADJ INV ◆ **il n'est pas ~ dans cette affaire** he's not entirely blameless *ou* innocent in this affair

blanc-cassis (pl **blancs-cassis**) /blɑ̃kasi(s)/ NM kir *(apéritif made with white wine and blackcurrant liqueur)*

blanchâtre /blɑ̃ʃɑtʀ/ ADJ whitish, off-white

blanche /blɑ̃ʃ/ ADJ, NF → **blanc**

Blanche-Neige /blɑ̃ʃnɛʒ/ NF Snow White

blancheur /blɑ̃ʃœʀ/ NF whiteness

blanchiment /blɑ̃ʃimɑ̃/ NM *(= décoloration)* bleaching; *(= badigeonnage)* whitewashing; *[d'argent]* laundering ◆ **~ dentaire** tooth whitening

blanchir /blɑ̃ʃiʀ/ ▸ conjug 2 ◂ VT [1] *(gén)* to whiten, to lighten; *[+ mur]* to whitewash; *[+ cheveux]* to turn grey *ou* white; *[+ toile]* to bleach ◆ **le soleil blanchit l'horizon** the sun is lighting up the horizon ◆ **la neige blanchit les collines** the snow is turning the hills white ◆ **~ à la chaux** to whitewash
[2] *(= nettoyer) [+ linge] (fig) [+ argent]* to launder ◆ **il est logé, nourri et blanchi** he gets bed and board and his laundry is done for him
[3] *(= disculper) [+ personne]* to exonerate, to absolve, to clear; *[+ réputation]* to clear ◆ **il en est sorti blanchi** he cleared his name
[4] *(Culin, Agr)* **(faire) ~** to blanch

5 *(Typo)* *[+ page]* to white out, to blank
VI *[personne, cheveux]* to turn *ou* go grey *ou* white; *[couleur, horizon]* to become lighter ◆ **son teint a blanchi** he is looking *ou* has got paler, he has lost colour ◆ **~ de peur** to blanch *ou* blench *ou* go white with fear ◆ **blanchi sous le harnais** *ou* **harnois** *(littér)* worn down by hard work
VPR **se blanchir** to exonerate o.s. *(de* from) to clear one's name

blanchissage /blɑ̃ʃisaʒ/ NM *[de linge]* laundering; *[de sucre]* refining ◆ **donner du linge au ~** to send linen to the laundry ◆ **note de ~** laundry bill

blanchissant, e /blɑ̃ʃisɑ̃, ɑ̃t/ ADJ *[agent, produit]* whitening

blanchissement /blɑ̃ʃismɑ̃/ NM whitening ◆ **ce shampooing retarde le ~ des cheveux** this shampoo stops your hair (from) going grey *ou* white

blanchisserie /blɑ̃ʃisʀi/ NF laundry

blanchisseur /blɑ̃ʃisœʀ/ NM *(lit)* launderer; *[d'argent sale]* money launderer

blanchisseuse /blɑ̃ʃisøz/ NF laundress

blanc-manger (pl **blancs-mangers**) /blɑ̃mɑ̃ʒe/ NM *(Culin)* blancmange

blanc-seing (pl **blancs-seings**) /blɑ̃sɛ̃/ NM *(lit)* signature to a blank document ◆ **donner un ~ à qn** *(fig)* to give sb a blank cheque

blanquette /blɑ̃kɛt/ NF 1 *(Culin)* **~ de veau/d'agneau** blanquette of veal/of lamb, veal/lamb in white sauce 2 *(= vin)* sparkling white wine

blase* /blaz/ NM ⇒ **blaze**

blasé, e /blɑze/ (ptp de **blaser**) ADJ blasé ◆ **il pourrait être ~, mais il continue à s'émerveiller** you might think he would have lost his enthusiasm, but he goes on getting excited ◆ **une information à émouvoir le plus ~ des marchands de tableaux** a piece of information calculated to excite the most phlegmatic picture dealer NM,F ◆ **faire le ~** to affect indifference

blaser /blɑze/ ► conjug 1 ◄ VT to make blasé *ou* indifferent ◆ **être blasé de** to be bored with *ou* tired of VPR **se blaser** to become bored *(de* with) to become tired *(de* of) to become blasé *(de* about)

blason /blazɔ̃/ NM 1 *(= armoiries)* coat of arms, blazon; → **redorer** 2 *(= science)* heraldry 3 *(Littérat = poème)* blazon

blasonner /blazɔne/ ► conjug 1 ◄ VT *(= orner d'armoiries)* to blazon, to emblazon

blasphémateur, -trice /blasfematœʀ, tʀis/ ADJ *[personne]* blaspheming, blasphemous NM,F blasphemer

blasphématoire /blasfematwaʀ/ ADJ *[parole]* blasphemous

blasphème /blasfɛm/ NM blasphemy

blasphémer /blasfeme/ ► conjug 6 ◄ VTI to blaspheme

blatérer /blateʀe/ ► conjug 6 ◄ VI *[chameau]* to bray

blatte /blat/ NF cockroach

blaze* /blaz/ NM *(= nez)* beak*, hooter* *(Brit)*; *(= nom)* name

blazer /blazɛʀ/ NM blazer

blé /ble/ NM 1 *(= céréale)* wheat, corn *(Brit)* ◆ **le ~ en herbe** *(Agr)* wheat on the blade ◆ **~ dur** hard wheat, durum wheat ◆ **~ noir** buckwheat ◆ **~ d'Inde*** *(Can)* maize, (Indian) corn *(US, Can)* ◆ **les ~s** the corn *(Brit)*, the wheat; → **blond, fauché** 2 *(* = argent)* dough*, lolly* *(Brit)*

bled /blɛd/ NM 1 * village; *(péj)* hole*, godforsaken place* ◆ **c'est un ~ perdu** *ou* **paumé** it's a godforsaken place* *ou* hole* (in the middle of nowhere) 2 *(en Afrique du Nord)* **le ~** the interior (of North Africa) ◆ **habiter dans le ~*** *(fig)* to live in the middle of nowhere *ou* at the back of beyond

blême /blɛm/ ADJ *[teint]* pallid, deathly pale; *[lumière]* pale, wan ◆ **~ de rage/de colère** livid *ou* white with rage/anger

blêmir /blemiʀ/ ► conjug 2 ◄ VI *[personne]* to turn *ou* go pale, to pale; *[lumière]* to grow pale ◆ **de colère** to go livid *ou* white with anger

blêmissement /blemismɑ̃/ NM *[de teint, lumière]* paling

blende /blɛ̃d/ NF blende

blennie /bleni/ NF *(= poisson)* blenny

blennorragie /blenɔʀaʒi/ NF gonorrhoea *(Brit)*, gonorrhea *(US)*

blèsement /blɛzmɑ̃/ NM lisping

bléser /bleze/ ► conjug 6 ◄ VI to lisp

blessant, e /blesɑ̃, ɑ̃t/ ADJ *(= offensant)* cutting, biting, hurtful

blessé, e /blese/ (ptp de **blesser**) ADJ *(= meurtri)* hurt, injured; *(dans une agression)* wounded; *(= offensé)* hurt, upset ◆ **être ~ à la tête/au bras** to have a head/an arm injury *ou* wound ◆ **il était ~ dans son amour-propre** his pride was hurt
NM wounded *ou* injured man, casualty; *(Mil)* wounded soldier, casualty ◆ **les ~s** *(dans un accident)* the injured; *(Mil)* the wounded ◆ **l'accident a fait 10 ~s** 10 people were injured *ou* hurt in the accident ◆ **grand ~** seriously injured person
NF **blessée** wounded *ou* injured woman, casualty
COMP **blessé grave** seriously *ou* severely injured *ou* wounded person
blessé de guerre person who was wounded in the war ◆ **les ~s de guerre** the war wounded
blessé léger slightly injured person ◆ **l'attentat a fait 30 ~s légers** 30 people were slightly injured *ou* suffered minor *ou* slight injuries in the bomb attack
blessés de la route road casualties, people *ou* persons injured in road accidents

blesser /blese/ ► conjug 1 ◄ VT 1 *(= meurtrir, dans un accident)* to hurt, to injure; *(Mil, dans une agression)* to wound; *[ceinture, chaussure]* to hurt ◆ **il a été blessé d'un coup de couteau** he received a knife wound, he was stabbed (with a knife) ◆ **être blessé dans un accident de voiture** to be injured in a car accident ◆ **ses chaussures lui blessent le talon** his shoes are making his heels sore; → **bât**
2 *(= agresser)* **sons qui blessent l'oreille** sounds which offend the ear *ou* grate on the ear ◆ **couleurs qui blessent la vue** colours which offend *ou* shock the eye
3 *(= offenser)* to hurt (the feelings of), to upset, to wound ◆ **~ qn au vif** to cut sb to the quick ◆ **il s'est senti blessé dans son orgueil** *ou* **son amour-propre** his pride was hurt ◆ **des paroles qui blessent** cutting words, wounding *ou* cutting remarks
4 *(littér = porter préjudice à)* *[+ règles, convenances]* to offend against; *[+ intérêts]* to go against, to harm ◆ **cela blesse son sens de la justice** that offends his sense of justice
VPR **se blesser** 1 *(= se faire mal)* to hurt o.s. ◆ **il s'est blessé en tombant** he fell and injured himself ◆ **il s'est blessé (à) la jambe** he injured *ou* hurt his leg
2 *(= se vexer)* to take offence ◆ **il se blesse pour un rien** he's easily hurt *ou* offended, he's quick to take offence

blessure /blesyʀ/ NF *(accidentelle)* injury; *(intentionnelle, morale)* wound ◆ **quelle ~ d'amour-propre pour lui !** what a blow to his pride *ou* self-esteem!; → **coup**

blet, blette[1] /blɛ, blɛt/ ADJ *[fruit]* overripe

blette[2] /blɛt/ NF ⇒ **bette**

blettir /bletiʀ/ ► conjug 2 ◄ VI to become overripe

blettissement /bletismɑ̃/ NM overripeness

bleu, e /blø/ ADJ 1 *[couleur]* blue ◆ **~ de froid** blue with cold ◆ **être ~ de colère** to be livid *ou* purple with rage ◆ **il avait le menton ~** he had a five-o'clock shadow; → **enfant, fleur, maladie, peur**
2 *(= meurtri)* bruised ◆ **avoir les jambes toutes ~es** *(= marbré)* to have mottled legs *(due to bad circulation)*
3 *[steak]* very rare, underdone
NM 1 *(= couleur)* blue ◆ **regarde le ~ de ce ciel** look how blue the sky is ◆ **le ~ des mers du Sud** the blue of the South Seas ◆ **le grand ~** the sunlit ocean ◆ **il n'y a vu que du ~*** *(fig)* he didn't notice a thing, he didn't catch on*
2 *(= marque sur la peau)* bruise ◆ **être couvert de ~s** to be covered in bruises, to be black and blue* ◆ **se faire un ~ au genou/bras** to bruise one's knee/arm ◆ **des ~s à l'âme** emotional scars
3 *(= vêtement)* **~(s) (de travail)** overalls ◆ **~ (de chauffe)** overalls, boiler suit *(Brit)*
4 *(arg Mil = recrue)* rookie *(arg)*, new *ou* raw recruit; *(gén = débutant)* beginner, greenhorn* ◆ **tu me prends pour un ~ ?** do you take me for a novice?
5 *(= fromage)* blue(-veined) cheese
6 *(Culin)* **truite au ~** trout au bleu
7 ◆ **~ (de lessive)** (dolly) blue ◆ **passer le linge au ~** to blue the laundry
8 *(Can)* **les Bleus** the Conservatives
9 *(Sport)* ◆ **les Bleus** the French team
COMP **bleu acier** steel blue
bleu ardoise slaty *ou* slate blue
bleu canard peacock blue
bleu ciel sky blue
bleu de cobalt cobalt blue
bleu glacier ice blue
bleu horizon sky blue
bleu indigo indigo blue
bleu lavande lavender blue
bleu marine navy blue
bleu de méthylène methylene blue
bleu noir blue-black
bleu nuit midnight blue
bleu outremer ultramarine
bleu pervenche periwinkle blue
bleu pétrole petrol blue
bleu de Prusse Prussian blue
bleu roi royal blue
bleu turquoise turquoise blue
bleu vert blue-green

bleuâtre /bløɑtʀ/ ADJ bluish

bleuet /bløɛ/ NM cornflower; *(Can)* blueberry

bleuetière /bløetjɛʀ/, **bleuetterie** /bløɛtʀi/ NF *(Can)* blueberry grove

bleuir /bløiʀ/ ► conjug 2 ◄ VTI to turn blue

bleuissement /bløismɑ̃/ NM turning blue

bleusaille /bløzaj/ NF *(arg Mil = recrue)* rookie *(arg)*, new *ou* raw recruit ◆ **la ~** *(collectivement)* the rookies *(arg)*

bleuté, e /bløte/ ADJ *[reflet]* bluish; *[verre]* blue-tinted

blindage /blɛ̃daʒ/ NM 1 *(= action)* *[de porte]* reinforcing; *(Mil)* fitting of armour plating; *(Élec)* screening; *(Constr)* timbering, shoring up 2 *(= résultat)* *[de porte]* reinforcement; *(Mil)* armour plating; *(Élec)* screening; *(Constr)* shoring up, timbering

blinde /blɛ̃d/ **à tout(e) blinde*** LOC ADV *[rouler]* flat out*; *[partir]* like a shot* ◆ **il est arrivé à toute ~** *(en voiture)* he drove up at top *ou* breakneck speed; *(à pied)* he arrived like a shot*

blindé, e /blɛ̃de/ (ptp de **blinder**) ADJ ① *(Mil)* *[division]* armoured; *[engin, train]* armoured, armour-plated; *[abri]* bombproof; *[porte]* reinforced ② (* = *endurci)* immune, hardened *(contre* to); ◆ **il a essayé de me faire peur mais je suis** ~ he tried to frighten me but I'm immune to his threats ③ (⁑ = *ivre)* plastered⁑, sloshed⁑ ④ * (= *riche)* ◆ ~ **(de fric** *ou* **de thunes)** rolling in it* NM *(Mil)* tank ◆ ~ **léger de campagne** combat car ◆ ~ **de transport de troupes** armoured personnel carrier ◆ **les ~s** the armour

blinder /blɛ̃de/ ▸ conjug 1 ◂ VT ① *[+ porte]* to reinforce ② *(Mil)* to armour, to put armour plating on ③ *(Élec)* to screen ④ *(Constr)* to shore up, to timber ⑤ (* = *endurcir)* to harden, to make immune *(contre* to) ⑥ (⁑ = *soûler)* ~ **qn** to get sb plastered* *ou* sloshed* VPR **se blinder** ① (* = *s'endurcir)* to harden o.s., to become immune *(contre* to) ② (⁑ = *se soûler)* to get plastered* *ou* sloshed*

blinis /blinis/ NM blini ◆ **des** ~ blinis

blister /blistɛʀ/ NM blister pack ◆ **mettre sous** ~ to blisterpack

blizzard /blizaʀ/ NM blizzard

bloc /blɔk/ NM ① *[de pierre, marbre, bois]* block ◆ **fait d'un seul** ~ made in one piece ◆ **ça forme un seul** ~ it forms a single block ◆ **ça s'est détaché d'un seul** ~ it came off all in one piece ◆ ~ **erratique** *(Géol)* erratic block

② *(Papeterie)* pad ◆ ~ **de bureau** office notepad, desk pad ◆ ~ **de papier à lettres** writing pad

③ (= *système d'éléments)* unit; *(Ordin)* block ◆ **ces éléments forment (un)** ~ these elements make up a unit ◆ ~ **de mémoire** *(Ordin)* storage *ou* memory block

④ (= *groupe, union)* group; *(Pol)* bloc ◆ ~ **économique/monétaire/régional** economic/monetary/regional bloc ◆ **le** ~ **communiste/capitaliste** *(Pol)* the communist/capitalist bloc ◆ **pays divisé en deux ~s adverses** *(Pol)* country split into two opposing blocs *ou* factions

⑤ *(Bourse)* *[d'actions]* block ◆ **achat/vente en** ~ block purchase/sale

⑥ *(Méd)* ~ **(opératoire)** (operating) theatre *(Brit)*, operating room *(US)* ◆ **il est au** ~ he's in (the) theatre *(US)*, he's in the operating room *(US)*

⑦ (⁑ = *prison)* **mettre qn au** ~ to clap sb in clink⁑ *ou* in the nick⁑ *(Brit)* ◆ **j'ai eu 10 jours de** ~ I got 10 days in clink⁑ *ou* in the nick⁑ *(Brit)*

⑧ *(locutions)* **se retourner tout d'un** ~ to swivel round

◆ **faire bloc** to join forces, to unite *(avec* with; *contre* against)

◆ **à bloc** ◆ **serrer** *ou* **visser qch à** ~ to screw sth up as tight as possible *ou* as far as it will go ◆ **fermer un robinet à** ~ to turn a tap right off *ou* off hard

◆ **en bloc** *[acheter, vendre]* as a whole; *[refuser, nier]* out of hand, outright ◆ **ils ont condamné en** ~ **l'attitude des USA** they were united *ou* unanimous in their condemnation of the US attitude

COMP **bloc à appartements** *(Can)* block of flats *(Brit)*, apartment building *ou* house *(US)*
bloc de culasse breech-block
bloc de départ *(Sport)* starting-block
bloc optique *[de voiture]* headlamp assembly
bloc sonore *(Ciné)* sound unit

blocage /blɔkaʒ/ NM ① *[de prix, salaires]* freeze, freezing; *[de compte bancaire]* freezing ② *(Constr)* rubble ③ *(Psych)* block ◆ **avoir** *ou* **faire un** ~ to have a mental block ④ *[de frein, roues]* locking; *[d'écrou]* overtightening ◆ ~ **de mémoire** *(Ordin)* memory block

bloc-cuisine (pl **blocs-cuisines**) /blɔkkɥizin/ NM compact kitchen unit *(incorporating a sink, fridge and hob)*

bloc-cylindres (pl **blocs-cylindres**) /blɔksilɛ̃dʀ/ NM cylinder block

bloc-diagramme (pl **blocs-diagrammes**) /blɔkdjagʀam/ NM block diagram

bloc-évier (pl **blocs-éviers**) /blɔkevje/ NM sink unit

blockhaus /blɔkos/ NM *(Mil)* blockhouse, pillbox

bloc-moteur (pl **blocs-moteurs**) /blɔkmɔtœʀ/ NM engine block

bloc-notes (pl **blocs-notes**) /blɔknɔt/ NM (= *cahier)* desk pad, scratch pad; *(avec pince)* clipboard; *(Ordin)* notepad

bloc-système (pl **blocs-systèmes**) /blɔksistɛm/ NM *(Rail)* block system

blocus /blɔkys/ NM blockade ◆ **le** ~ **continental** *(Hist)* the Continental System ◆ ~ **économique** economic blockade ◆ **lever/forcer le** ~ to raise/run the blockade ◆ **faire le** ~ **de** to blockade

blog /blɔg/ NM blog

bloggeur, euse /blɔgœʀ, øz/ NM, F blogger

blogging /blɔgiŋ/ NM blogging

bloguer /blɔge/ VI to blog

blond, blonde[1] /blɔ̃, blɔ̃d/ ADJ *[cheveux]* fair, blond(e); *[personne]* fair, fair-haired, blond(e); *[blé, sable]* golden ◆ ~ **cendré** ash-blond ◆ ~ **roux** sandy, light auburn ◆ ~ **vénitien** strawberry blonde, titian *(littér)* ◆ **tabac** ~ mild *ou* light *ou* Virginia tobacco ◆ **bière ~e** ≈ lager ◆ **il est** ~ **comme les blés** his hair is golden blond(e), he has golden blond(e) hair NM (= *couleur)* blond, light gold; (= *homme)* fair-haired man NF **blonde** ① (= *femme)* blonde; (* : *Can* = *compagne)* girlfriend ◆ **~e incendiaire** blonde bombshell *(hum)* ◆ **~e oxygénée/platinée** *ou* **platine** peroxide/platinum blonde ◆ **une vraie ~e** a natural blonde ◆ **c'est une fausse ~e** she's not a real blonde ② (= *bière)* ≈ lager, light ale *(Brit)* ③ (= *cigarette)* Virginia cigarette

blondasse /blɔ̃das/ ADJ *(péj)* dull blond(e)

blondeur /blɔ̃dœʀ/ NF *(littér)* *[de cheveux]* fairness; *[de blés]* gold

blondin /blɔ̃dɛ̃/ NM fair-haired child *ou* young man; (†† = *élégant)* dandy

blondine /blɔ̃din/ NF fair-haired child *ou* young girl

blondinet /blɔ̃dinɛ/ NM fair-haired boy

blondinette /blɔ̃dinɛt/ NF fair-haired girl

blondir /blɔ̃diʀ/ ▸ conjug 2 ◂ VI *[cheveux]* to go fairer; *(littér)* *[blés]* to turn golden; *[oignons]* to become transparent ◆ **faire** ~ **des oignons** to fry onions lightly (until they are transparent) VT *[+ cheveux, poils]* to bleach

bloquer /blɔke/ ▸ conjug 1 ◂ VT ① (= *immobiliser accidentellement)* *[+ freins, machine, porte]* to jam; *[+ écrou]* to overtighten; *[+ roue]* to lock ◆ **le mécanisme est bloqué** the mechanism is jammed *ou* stuck ◆ **être bloqué par les glaces** to be stuck in the ice, to be icebound ◆ **être bloqué par un accident/la foule** to be held up by an accident/the crowd ◆ **je suis bloqué chez moi** I'm stuck at home ◆ **je suis bloqué** *(physiquement)* I can't move, I'm stuck ◆ **j'ai les reins bloqués** my back has seized up

② (= *immobiliser volontairement)* *[+ objet en mouvement]* to stop; *[+ roue]* *(avec une cale)* to put a block under; *(avec une pierre)* to wedge; *[+ écrou]* to tighten; *[+ porte]* *(avec une cale)* to wedge ◆ **j'ai bloqué la porte avec une chaise** *(ouverte)* I propped the door open with a chair; *(fermée)* I propped a chair against the door to keep it shut ◆ ~ **qn contre un mur** to pin sb against a wall ◆ **bloque la roue pendant que je la regonfle** hold the wheel still while I pump it up

③ (= *obstruer)* to block (up); *(Mil)* to blockade ◆ **route bloquée par la glace/la neige** icebound/snowbound road ◆ **un camion bloque la route** a truck is blocking the road, the road is blocked by a truck ◆ **des travaux bloquent la route** there are road works in *ou* blocking the way ◆ **les enfants bloquent le passage** the children are standing in *ou* blocking the way, the children are stopping me *(ou* us *etc)* getting past ◆ **des manifestants bloquent la circulation** demonstrators are holding up the traffic

④ *[+ processus]* to bring to a standstill ◆ **les négociations sont bloquées** the talks are deadlocked *ou* are at a standstill ◆ **la situation est complètement bloquée** the situation is at a complete standstill ◆ **ça bloque au niveau de la direction** management are holding things up

⑤ (= *grouper)* to lump together, to put *ou* group together ◆ **les cours sont bloqués sur six semaines** *(Scol)* the classes are spread over six weeks

⑥ *(Sport)* *[+ ballon]* to block; *(Billard)* *[+ bille]* to jam, to wedge

⑦ *[+ marchandises]* to stop, to hold up; *[+ crédit, salaires]* to freeze; *[+ compte en banque]* to stop, to freeze

⑧ *(psychologiquement)* **ça me bloque d'être devant un auditoire** I freeze (up) if I have to speak in public ◆ **quand on le critique, ça le bloque** whenever people criticize him he tenses up *ou* gets all tensed up ◆ **il est bloqué** *(dans sa réflexion)* he has a mental block (about things)

⑨ (* = *réserver)* *[+ jour]* to reserve, to put aside

⑩ (* : *Belg)* *[+ examen]* to cram for, to swot for* *(Brit)*

VPR **se bloquer** *[porte]* to jam, to get stuck, to stick; *[machine]* to jam; *[roue]* to lock; *[frein]* to jam, to lock on; *[clé]* to get stuck; *[genou]* to lock; *(Psych)* to have a mental block ◆ **devant un auditoire, il se bloque** in front of an audience he just freezes (up)

> ⚠ Attention à ne pas traduire automatiquement **bloquer** par **to block**, qui a des emplois spécifiques.

bloqueur * /blɔkœʀ/ NM *(Belg)* swot* *(Brit)*

blottir (se) /blɔtiʀ/ ▸ conjug 2 ◂ VPR to curl up, to huddle up ◆ **se** ~ **contre qn** to snuggle up to sb ◆ **se** ~ **dans les bras de qn** to snuggle up in sb's arms ◆ **blottis les uns contre les autres** curled up *ou* huddled up (close) against one another ◆ **blotti parmi les arbres** nestling *ou* huddling among the trees

blousant, e /bluzɑ̃, ɑt/ ADJ *[robe, chemisier]* loose-fitting *(and gathered at the waist)*

blouse /bluz/ NF (= *tablier)* overall; (= *chemisier)* blouse, smock; *[de médecin]* (white) coat; *[de paysan]* smock; *(Billard)* pocket ◆ **les ~s blanches** (= *médecins)* hospital doctors

blouser[1] /bluze/ ▸ conjug 1 ◂ VI *[robe, chemisier]* to be loose-fitting *(and gathered at the waist)*

blouser[2] ⁑ /bluze/ ▸ conjug 1 ◂ VT to con⁑, to trick, to pull a fast one on⁑ ◆ **se faire** ~ to be had* *ou* conned⁑ VPR **se blouser** † (= *se tromper)* to make a mistake *ou* a blunder

blouser[3] /bluze/ ▸ conjug 1 ◂ VT *(Billard)* to pot, to pocket

blouson /bluzɔ̃/ NM blouson ◆ ~ **de cuir** leather jacket ◆ ~ **d'aviateur** flying jacket ◆ ~ **noir** † ≈ hell's angel, teddy-boy *(Brit)*

blue-jean (pl **blue-jeans**) /bludʒin/ NM (pair of) jeans

blues /bluz/ NM INV 1 *(= music)* blues music; *(= chanson)* blues song ◆ **aimer le** ~ to like the blues ◆ **écouter du** ~ to listen to the blues *ou* to blues music 2 *(* = mélancolie)* **le** ~ the blues* ◆ **avoir le** ~**, avoir un coup de** ~ to have the blues*, to feel blue*

bluette † /blyɛt/ NF 1 *(= étincelle)* spark, sparkle 2 *(= livre)* witty little piece (of writing); *(= film)* sentimental film

bluff * /blœf/ NM bluff ◆ **c'est du** ~ *ou* **un coup de** ~ **!** he's *(ou* they're *etc)* just bluffing !

bluffer * /blœfe/ ▸ conjug 1 ◂ VI to bluff, to try it on* *(Brit)*; *(Cartes)* to bluff VT 1 *(= tromper)* to fool, to put on*, to have on *(Brit)*; *(Cartes)* to bluff 2 *(= impressionner)* to impress ◆ **j'ai été bluffé** I was really impressed ◆ **elle m'a totalement bluffé** she really took my breath away, she really bowled me over

bluffeur, -euse * /blœfœʀ, øz/ NM,F bluffer

blush /blœʃ/ NM blusher

blutage /blytaʒ/ NM *[de farine]* bo(u)lting

bluter /blyte/ ▸ conjug 1 ◂ VT *[+ farine]* to bo(u)lt

BN /beɛn/ NF (abrév de **Bibliothèque nationale**) → **bibliothèque**

BO /beo/ NF (abrév de **bande originale**) → **bande**[1]

boa /bɔa/ NM *(= serpent, accessoire)* boa ◆ ~ **constricteur** boa constrictor ◆ **elle portait un** ~ she was wearing a (feather) boa

Boadicée /bɔadise/ NF Boadicea

boat people /botpipœl/ NMPL boat people

bob[1] /bɔb/ NM *(Sport)* bob(sleigh)

bob[2] /bɔb/ NM *(= chapeau)* cotton sunhat

bobard * /bɔbaʀ/ NM *(= mensonge)* lie, fib*; *(= histoire)* tall story, yarn

bobèche /bɔbɛʃ/ NF candle-ring

bobet, -ette /bɔbɛ, ɛt/ ADJ *(Helv = sot)* stupid, foolish

bobinage /bɔbinaʒ/ NM *(gén = action)* winding; *(Élec)* coil(s)

bobine /bɔbin/ NF 1 *[de fil]* reel, bobbin; *[de métier à tisser]* bobbin, spool; *[de machine à écrire, à coudre]* spool; *(Photo)* spool, reel; *(Élec)* coil ◆ ~ **d'induction** induction coil ◆ ~ **(d'allumage)** coil ◆ ~ **de pellicule** roll of film 2 *(* = visage)* face, mug* ◆ **il a fait une drôle de** ~ **!** what a face he made! ◆ **tu en fais une drôle de** ~ **!** you look a bit put out!*

bobineau (pl **bobineaux**) /bɔbino/ NM ⇒ **bobinot**

bobiner /bɔbine/ ▸ conjug 1 ◂ VT to wind

bobinette †† /bɔbinɛt/ NF (wooden) latch

bobineur, -euse /bɔbinœʀ, øz/ NM,F *(= personne)* winder NM *(= appareil)* coiler NF **bobineuse** winding machine

bobinoir /bɔbinwaʀ/ NM winding machine

bobinot /bɔbino/ NM reel, bobbin

bobo[1] /bobo/ NM *(langage enfantin) (= plaie)* sore; *(= coupure)* cut ◆ **avoir** ~ to be hurt, to have a pain ◆ **avoir** ~ **à la gorge** to have a sore throat ◆ **ça (te) fait** ~ **?** does it hurt?, is it sore? ◆ **il n'y a pas eu de** ~ there was no harm done

bobo *[2] /bobo/ (abrév de **bourgeois bohème**) NMF bobo* *(middle-class person who leads a Bohemian lifestyle)*

bobonne †* /bɔbɔn/ NF ◆ **(sa)** ~ his old woman*, his missus* *(Brit)*, his old lady* *(US)* ◆ **oui** ~ *(hum)* yes love* *ou* dearie*

bobsleigh /bɔbslɛg/ NM bobsleigh

bocage /bɔkaʒ/ NM 1 *(Géog)* bocage *(farmland criss-crossed by hedges and trees)* 2 *(littér = bois)* grove, copse

bocager, -ère /bɔkaʒe, ɛʀ/ ADJ *(littér = boisé)* wooded ◆ **paysage** ~ *(Géog)* bocage landscape

bocal (pl **-aux**) /bɔkal, o/ NM jar ◆ ~ **à poissons rouges** goldfish bowl ◆ **mettre en bocaux** *[+ fruits, légumes]* to preserve, to bottle

Boccace /bɔkas/ NM Boccaccio

boche *‡/bɔʃ/ *(péj)* ADJ Boche NM **Boche** Jerry*, Kraut*

Bochimans /bɔʃiman/ NMPL Bushmen

bock /bɔk/ NM *(= verre)* beer glass; *(= bière)* glass of beer

body /bɔdi/ NM *(gén)* body(suit); *(Sport)* leotard

body(-)board /bɔdibɔʀd/ NM *(= planche)* bodyboard; *(= sport)* bodyboarding ◆ **faire du body(-)board** to go bodyboarding

Boers /buʀ/ NMPL ◆ **les** ~ the Boers ◆ **la guerre des** ~ the Boer war

bœuf (pl **bœufs**) /bœf, bø/ NM 1 *(= bête)* ox; *(de boucherie)* bullock, steer *(US)*; *(= viande)* beef ◆ ~**s de boucherie** beef cattle ◆ ~ **mode** stewed beef with carrots ◆ ~ **en daube** bœuf en daube, beef stew ◆ **il a un** ~ **sur la langue** he has been paid to keep his mouth shut* ◆ **on n'est pas des** ~**s !*** we're not galley slaves!*; → **charrue, fort**[1]**, qui** 2 *(arg Mus)* jam session ◆ **faire un** ~ to jam ADJ INV ◆ **effet/succès** ~ * tremendous* *ou* fantastic* effect/success

> ⚠ **bœuf** se traduit par **beef** uniquement au sens de 'viande de bœuf'.

bof /bɔf/ EXCL ◆ **il est beau!** – ~ he's good-looking! – do you really think so? *ou* d'you reckon?* ◆ **qu'en penses-tu ?** – ~ what do you think of it? – not a lot ◆ **ça t'a plu ?** – ~ did you like it? – not really ◆ ~**, si tu y tiens vraiment** oh, alright, if you really want to ◆ **la** ~ **génération, la génération** ~ the couldn't-care-less generation

bogee, bogey /bɔgi/ NM *(Golf)* bogy, bogey, bogie

bogomile /bɔgɔmil/ ADJ, NM Bogomil

Bogota /bɔgɔta/ N Bogota

bogue[1] /bɔg/ NF *[de châtaigne, marron]* bur

bogue[2] /bɔg/ NM *(Ordin)* bug ◆ **le** ~ **de l'an 2000** the millennium bug

bogué, e /bɔge/ ADJ *(Ordin)* bug-ridden

boguer /bɔge/ VI *[logiciel] (= dysfonctionner)* to malfunction

boguet /bɔgɛ/ NM *(* Helv = cyclomoteur)* moped

Bohême /bɔɛm/ NF Bohemia

bohème /bɔɛm/ ADJ Bohemian NMF bohemian ◆ **mener une vie de** ~ to lead a Bohemian life NF *(= milieu)* ◆ **la** ~ Bohemia NM *(= verre)* Bohemian glass ◆ **un vase en** ~ a Bohemian glass vase

bohémien, -ienne /bɔemjɛ̃, jɛn/ ADJ Bohemian NM *(= langue)* Bohemian NM,F *(= gitan)* gipsy ◆ **Bohémien(ne)** *(= de Bohême)* Bohemian

boire /bwaʀ/ ▸ conjug 53 ◂ VT 1 *(= ingurgiter)* to drink ◆ **offrir/donner à** ~ **à qn** to get sb/give sb something to drink *ou* a drink ◆ ~ **à la santé/au succès de qn** to drink sb's health/to sb's success ◆ **on a bu une bouteille à nous deux** we drank a (whole) bottle between the two of us ◆ ~ **jusqu'à plus soif** to drink one's fill, to drink until one's thirst is quenched ◆ **il boit l'argent du ménage** he drinks away the housekeeping money, he spends all the housekeeping money on drink ◆ ~ **une** *ou* **la tasse*** *(fig) (en nageant)* to swallow *ou* get a mouthful of water ◆ **ce vin se boit bien** *ou* **se laisse** ~ this wine goes down nicely*, this wine is very drinkable ◆ **donner à** ~ **à un enfant** to give a child something to drink ◆ **faire** ~ **un malade** to help a sick person to drink ◆ **faire** ~ **un cheval** to water a horse; → **coup, verre**

2 *(gén emploi absolu = boire trop)* to drink ◆ **il s'est mis à** ~ he has taken to drink, he has started drinking ◆ **il a bu, c'est évident** he has obviously been drinking ◆ ~ **comme un trou*** *ou* **comme une éponge*** to drink like a fish ◆ **il boit sec** he's a heavy drinker

3 *(= absorber)* to soak up, to absorb ◆ **ce papier boit l'encre** the ink soaks into this paper ◆ **ce buvard boit bien l'encre** this blotter soaks up the ink well ◆ **la plante a déjà tout bu** the plant has already soaked up all the water ◆ **cette plante boit beaucoup*** this is a very thirsty plant*

4 *(locutions)* ~ **les paroles de qn** to drink in sb's words, to lap up what sb says* ◆ ~ **le calice jusqu'à la lie** to drain one's cup to the (last) dregs *ou* last drop ◆ **il y a à** ~ **et à manger là-dedans** *(dans une boisson)* there are bits floating about in it; *(fig) (= qualités et défauts)* it's got its good points and its bad; *(= vérités et mensonges)* you have to pick and choose what to believe ◆ **qui a bu boira** *(Prov)* a leopard never changes its spots *(Prov)* once a thief always a thief *(Prov)* → **lait**

NM ◆ **le** ~ **et le manger** food and drink ◆ **il en perd le** ~ **et le manger** *(fig)* he's losing sleep over it *(ou* her *etc)*, he can't eat or sleep because of it *(ou* her *etc)*

bois /bwɑ/ NM 1 *(= forêt, matériau)* wood ◆ **c'est en** ~ it's made of wood ◆ **chaise de** *ou* **en** ~ wooden chair ◆ **ramasser du petit** ~ to collect sticks *ou* kindling ◆ **son visage était de** ~ his face was impassive, he was poker-faced ◆ **je ne suis pas de** ~ I'm only human, I'm only flesh and blood; → **chèque**

2 *(= objet en bois) (gravure)* woodcut; *(manche)* shaft, handle

3 *[de cerf]* antler

4 *(Mus)* woodwind instrument ◆ **les** ~ the woodwind (instruments *ou* section)

5 *(Golf)* wood

6 *(locutions)* **sortir du** ~ *(= déclarer ses intentions)* to make one's intentions clear ◆ **on n'est pas sorti du** ~ *(= tiré d'affaire)* we're not out of the woods yet ◆ **faire un** ~ *(Tennis)* to hit the ball off the wood ◆ **je ne suis pas du** ~ **dont on fait les flûtes** † I'm not going to let myself be pushed around, I'm not just anyone's fool ◆ **touchons du** ~ **!*** touch wood!* *(Brit)*, knock on wood!* *(US)* ◆ **il va voir de quel** ~ **je me chauffe !** I'll show him (what I'm made of)!, just let me get my hands on him! ◆ **il fait feu** *ou* **flèche de tout** ~ he'll use any means available to him

COMP **bois blanc** deal ◆ **table en** ~ **blanc** deal table
bois à brûler firewood
bois de charpente timber, lumber *(US)*
bois de chauffage *ou* **de chauffe** firewood
bois de construction timber, lumber *(US)*
bois debout *(Can)* standing timber
bois d'ébène *(Hist péj = esclaves)* black gold
bois exotique tropical hardwood
les bois de justice the guillotine
bois de lit bedstead
bois de menuiserie timber, lumber *(US)*
bois mort deadwood
bois d'œuvre timber, lumber *(US)*
bois rond *(Can)* unhewn timber
bois de rose rosewood
bois tropical ⇒ **bois exotique**
bois vert green wood; *(Menuiserie)* unseasoned *ou* green timber

boisage /bwazaʒ/ NM *(= action)* timbering; *(= matière)* timber work

bois-brûlé, e † (mpl **bois-brûlés**) /bwabʀyle/ NM,F *(Can)* half-breed Indian, bois-brûlé *(Can)*

boisé, e /bwaze/ (ptp de **boiser**) ADJ *[région, parc]* wooded; *[vin]* woody, boisé ◆ **région très/peu** ~**e** densely *ou* thickly/sparsely wooded area

boisement /bwazmɑ̃/ NM afforestation

boiser /bwaze/ ► conjug 1 ◄ VT [+ région] to afforest, to plant with trees; [+ galerie] to timber

boiserie /bwazʀi/ NF ◆ ~(s) (= lambris) panelling (Brit), paneling (US); (= éléments de menuiserie) woodwork ◆ **on va peindre les ~s** we're going to paint the woodwork

boisseau (pl **boisseaux**) /bwaso/ NM ① (†† = mesure) ≈ bushel; (Can) bushel (36,36 litres) ◆ **c'est un vrai ~ de puces !*** he's a menace!* ou a pest!* ◆ **garder** ou **mettre sous le ~** [+ projet] to keep secret; [+ problème embarrassant] to brush ou sweep under the carpet ② (= tuyau) flue

boisson /bwasɔ̃/ NF drink; (*: Can) hard liquor, spirits ◆ **ils apportent la ~** they're bringing the drinks ◆ **être pris de ~** (littér) to be drunk, to be under the influence (hum) ◆ **il est porté sur la ~** he likes his drink, he's a bit of a boozer* ◆ **~ alcoolisée** alcoholic drink ou beverage (frm) ◆ **~ non alcoolisée** soft drink ◆ **~ fraîche/chaude** cold/hot drink

boîte /bwat/ NF ① (= récipient) (en carton, bois) box; (en métal) box, tin; [de conserves] tin (Brit), can ◆ **mettre des haricots en ~** to can beans ◆ **des tomates en ~** tinned (Brit) ou canned (US) tomatoes ◆ **il a mangé toute la ~ de caramels** he ate the whole box of toffees ◆ **mettre qn en ~*** (fig) to pull sb's leg*, to take the mickey out of sb‡ (Brit) ◆ **la mise en ~* du gouvernement par les journaux satiriques** the ridiculing of the government by the satirical press ◆ **il ne supporte pas la mise en ~*** he can't stand having his leg pulled, he can't stand being made a joke of ◆ **c'est dans la ~*** (Ciné) it's in the can*

② (* = cabaret) nightclub ◆ **aller** ou **sortir en ~** to go (out) to a nightclub, to go (night-)clubbing*

③ * (= lieu de travail, firme) company; (= école) school ◆ **quelle (sale) ~ !** what a dump!‡, what a crummy hole!‡ ◆ **je veux changer de ~** (= entreprise) I want to work for another company; (= école) I want to change schools ◆ **j'en ai marre de cette ~ !** I'm fed up with this place! ◆ **il s'est fait renvoyer de la ~** (= entreprise) he got fired*; (= école) he got thrown out ou expelled ◆ **elle travaille pour une ~ de pub*** she works for an advertising company

COMP **boîte d'allumettes** box of matches
boîte à archives box file
boîte à bachot (péj) crammer('s), cramming school
boîte à bijoux jewellery (Brit) ou jewelry (US) box
boîte de camembert camembert box ◆ **ferme ta ~ à camembert !*** shut up!*, shut your face !‡
boîte de conserve tin (Brit) ou can (US) of food
boîte de couleurs box of paints, paintbox
boîte à couture ⇒ **boîte à ouvrage**
boîte crânienne (Anat) cranium, brainpan*
boîte de dialogue (Ordin) dialogue box
boîte d'essieu axle box
boîte expressive (Orgue) swell (box)
boîte à gants [de voiture] glove compartment
boîte à idées suggestion box
boîte à images TV
boîte à ou **aux lettres** (publique) post box, mailbox (US); (privée) letterbox (Brit), mailbox (US) ◆ **mettre une lettre à la ~ (aux lettres)** to post (Brit) ou mail a letter ◆ **je leur sers de ~ à lettres** I'm their go-between
boîte à lettres électronique electronic mailbox
boîte à malice bag of tricks
boîte à musique musical box
boîte noire [d'avion] black box
boîte de nuit nightclub ◆ **faire les ~s de nuit** to go (night)clubbing*
boîte à ordures dustbin (Brit), garbage ou trash can (US)
boîte à outils toolbox
boîte à ouvrage sewing box, workbox
boîte de Pandore Pandora's box
boîte de Pétri Petri dish
boîte postale PO Box
boîte à rythmes beatbox
boîte à thé tea caddy
boîte de vitesses gearbox
boîte vocale (Téléc) voice mail (NonC)

boitement /bwatmɑ̃/ NM limping

boiter /bwate/ ► conjug 1 ◄ VI [personne] to limp, to walk with a limp; [meuble] to wobble; [raisonnement] to be unsound ou shaky ◆ **~ bas** to limp badly ◆ **~ de la jambe gauche** to limp with one's left leg

boiteux, -euse /bwatø, øz/ ADJ [personne] lame, who limps (attrib); [meuble] wobbly, rickety; [paix, projet, compromis] shaky; [union] ill-assorted; [raisonnement] unsound, shaky; [explication] lame, weak; [vers] lame; [phrase] (incorrecte) grammatically wrong; (mal équilibrée) cumbersome, clumsy ◆ **c'était un mariage ~** the(ir) marriage was shaky NM,F lame person, gimp‡

boîtier /bwatje/ NM (gén) case; (pour appareil photo) body ◆ **~ de différentiel** (dans moteur) differential housing ◆ **~ électrique** electric torch (Brit), flashlight (US) ◆ **~ de montre** watchcase

boitillement /bwatijmɑ̃/ NM slight limp

boitiller /bwatije/ ► conjug 1 ◄ VI to limp slightly, to have a slight limp

boit-sans-soif* /bwasɑ̃swaf/ NMF INV drunkard, lush*, piss artist‡ (Brit)

bol /bɔl/ NM ① (= récipient) bowl; (= contenu) bowl, bowlful ◆ **prendre un (bon) ~ d'air** (fig) to get a breath of fresh air ◆ **cheveux coupés au ~** pudding-basin haircut (Brit), bowl cut (US) ② (Pharm) bolus ◆ **~ alimentaire** bolus ③ (‡ : loc) **avoir du ~** to be lucky ou jammy‡ (Brit) ◆ **ne pas avoir de ~** to be unlucky ◆ **pas de ~ !** hard ou bad luck! ◆ **pas de ~, il est déjà parti** no luck, he's already left ④ (* Can) ⇒ **bolle**

bolchevik, bolchevique /bɔlʃəvik/ ADJ, NMF Bolshevik, Bolshevist

bolchevisme /bɔlʃəvism/ NM Bolchevism

bolcheviste /bɔlʃəvist/ ADJ, NMF ⇒ **bolchevik**

bolduc /bɔldyk/ NM curling ribbon, gift-wrap ribbon, bolduc (SPÉC)

bolée /bɔle/ NF bowl(ful)

boléro /bɔleʀo/ NM (Habillement, Mus) bolero

bolet /bɔlɛ/ NM boletus

bolide /bɔlid/ NM (Astron) meteor, bolide (SPÉC); (= voiture) (high-powered) racing car ◆ **comme un ~** [arriver, passer] at top speed ◆ **il fonce comme un ~, c'est un vrai ~** he really whizzes along

Bolivie /bɔlivi/ NF Bolivia

bolivien, -ienne /bɔlivjɛ̃, jɛn/ ADJ Bolivian NM,F **Bolivien(ne)** Bolivian

bollard /bɔlaʀ/ NM (Naut) bollard

bolle* /bɔl/ NF (Can) head, bonce* (Brit) ◆ **j'ai mal à la ~** I've got a headache

bolognais, e /bɔlɔɲɛ, ɛz/ ADJ Bolognese; (Culin) bolognese NM,F **Bolognais(e)** Bolognese

bombance †* /bɔ̃bɑ̃s/ NF feast, beanfeast* (Brit) ◆ **faire ~** to revel, to have a beanfeast* (Brit)

bombarde /bɔ̃baʀd/ NF (Mil, Mus) bombard

bombardement /bɔ̃baʀdəmɑ̃/ NM ① (= pilonnage) bombardment; (avec bombes) bombing; (avec obus) shelling ◆ **~ aérien** air raid, aerial bombing (NonC) ② (avec des cailloux, des tomates) pelting ③ (Phys) bombardment ◆ **~ atomique** atomic bombardment

bombarder /bɔ̃baʀde/ ► conjug 1 ◄ VT ① (Mil) to bombard; (avec bombes) to bomb; (avec obus) to shell ② ◆ **~ de** [+ cailloux, tomates] to pelt with; [+ questions, critiques, appels] to bombard with ③ (Phys) to bombard ④ (* = catapulter) **on l'a bombardé directeur** he was thrust into ou pitchforked into the position of manager

bombardier /bɔ̃baʀdje/ NM (= avion) bomber; (= aviateur) bombardier ◆ **~ d'eau** fire-fighting aircraft, tanker plane (US)

Bombay /bɔ̃bɛ/ N Bombay

bombe /bɔ̃b/ NF ① (Mil, Ordin) bomb ◆ **attentat à la ~** bombing, bomb attack ◆ **comme une ~** (= de façon inattendue) unexpectedly, out of the blue ◆ **il est arrivé comme une ~ dans mon bureau** he burst into my office ◆ **la nouvelle a éclaté comme une ~** ou **a fait l'effet d'une ~** the news came as a bombshell ou was a bolt from the blue

② (= atomiseur) spray ◆ **en ~** (gén) in an aerosol (attrib) ◆ **peinture/chantilly en ~** aerosol paint/cream ◆ **déodorant/insecticide en ~** deodorant/insect spray

③ (Équitation) riding cap ou hat

④ **faire la ~*** to have a wild time

⑤ * (= belle femme) ◆ **c'est une ~** she's gorgeous

COMP **bombe aérosol** aerosol can ou spray
bombe anti-crevaison instant puncture sealant
bombe antigel de-icing spray
bombe atomique atom(ic) bomb ◆ **la ~ atomique** the Bomb
bombe à billes ⇒ **bombe à fragmentation**
bombe au cobalt (Méd) cobalt therapy unit, telecobalt machine
bombe déodorante deodorant spray
bombe à eau water bomb
bombe à fragmentation cluster bomb
bombe glacée (Culin) bombe glacée, ice-cream pudding (Brit)
bombe H H-bomb
bombe à hydrogène hydrogen bomb
bombe incendiaire incendiary ou fire bomb
bombe insecticide insect spray, fly spray
bombe lacrymogène teargas grenade
bombe de laque hair spray
bombe logique (Ordin) logic bomb
bombe au napalm napalm bomb
bombe à neutrons neutron bomb
bombe de peinture paint spray, can of aerosol paint
bombe radiologique dirty bomb
bombe à retardement time bomb
bombe sexuelle* sex bomb*
bombe volcanique (Géol) volcanic bomb

⚠ Au sens de 'aérosol', **bombe** ne se traduit pas par le mot anglais **bomb**.

bombé, e /bɔ̃be/ (ptp de **bomber**) ADJ [forme] rounded, convex; [cuiller] rounded; [poitrine] thrown out; [front] domed; [mur] bulging; [dos] humped, hunched; [route] cambered ◆ **verre ~** balloon-shaped glass

bombement /bɔ̃bmɑ̃/ NM [de forme] convexity; [de route] camber; [de front] bulge

bomber¹ /bɔ̃be/ ► conjug 1 ◄ VT ① ◆ **~ le torse** ou **la poitrine** (lit) to stick out ou throw out one's chest; (fig) to puff out one's chest, to swagger about ② (Peinture) to spray (-paint) VI ① [route] to camber; [mur] to bulge; (Menuiserie) to warp ② (* = rouler vite) to belt along*

bomber² /bɔ̃bœʀ/ NM (= blouson) bomber jacket

bombonne /bɔ̃bɔn/ NF ⇒ **bonbonne**

bombyx /bɔ̃biks/ NM silk moth, bombyx

bôme /bom/ NF (Naut) boom

bon[1], bonne[1] /bɔ̃, bɔn/

GRAMMAIRE ACTIVE 50.2

1 ADJECTIF	4 NOM MASCULIN
2 ADVERBE	5 NOM FÉMININ
3 EXCLAMATION	6 COMPOSÉS

1 - ADJECTIF

1 [= de qualité] *(gén)* good; *[fauteuil, lit]* good, comfortable ◆ **il a de bonnes jambes** he has a good *ou* strong pair of legs ◆ **une bonne paire de chaussures** a good (strong) pair of shoes ◆ **il a fait du ~ travail** he's done a good job ◆ **marchandises/outils de bonne qualité** good quality goods/tools

2 [= adéquat, compétent, sûr] *[docteur, élève, employé]* good; *[instrument, système, remède]* good, reliable; *[conseil]* good, sound; *[excuse, raison]* good, valid; *[placement, monnaie, entreprise]* sound ◆ **être ~ en anglais** to be good at English ◆ **pour le ~ fonctionnement du moteur** for the motor to work efficiently *ou* properly ◆ **tout lui est ~ pour me discréditer** he'll stop at nothing to discredit me ◆ **~ pour le service** *(Mil)* fit for service

3 [= agréable] *[odeur, vacances, repas]* good, pleasant, nice; *[surprise]* pleasant, nice ◆ **un ~ petit vin** a nice (little) wine ◆ **un ~ vin** a good wine ◆ **une bonne tasse de thé** a nice (hot) cup of tea ◆ **un ~ bain chaud** a nice hot bath ◆ **elle aime les bonnes choses** she likes good food and drink ◆ **nous avons passé une bonne soirée** we had a pleasant *ou* nice evening ◆ **c'était vraiment ~** *(à manger, à boire)* it was *ou* tasted really good *ou* nice ◆ **l'eau est bonne** *(à la mer, à la piscine)* the water's warm *ou* nice ◆ **elle est bien bonne celle-là !** *(iro)* that's a good one!

4 [= moralement ou socialement irréprochable] *[lectures, fréquentations, pensées, famille]* good ◆ **les bonnes gens** good *ou* honest people ◆ **il est ~ père et ~ fils** he's a good father and a good son ◆ **d'un ~ milieu social** from a good social background

5 [= charitable] *[personne]* good, kind(-hearted); *[action]* good, kind; *[parole]* kind, comforting ◆ **une bonne dame m'a fait entrer** some good woman let me in ◆ **être ~ pour les animaux** to be kind to animals ◆ **vous êtes bien** *ou* **trop ~** you are really too kind, it's really too kind *ou* good of you ◆ **il est ~ comme du ~ pain** he has a heart of gold ◆ **elle est bonne fille** she's a nice *ou* good-hearted girl, she's a good sort* ◆ **vous êtes ~ vous (avec vos idées impossibles) !*** *(iro)* you're a great help (with your wild ideas)! ◆ **vas-y demain – tu es ~ toi !* je n'ai pas que ça à faire !** *(iro)* go tomorrow – you've got a nerve!* I've got things to do!

6 [= valable, utilisable] *[billet, passeport, timbre]* valid ◆ **médicament/yaourt ~ jusqu'au 5 mai** medicine/yoghurt to be consumed *ou* used before 5 May ◆ **est-ce que la soupe va être encore bonne avec cette chaleur ?** will the soup have kept *ou* will the soup still be all right in this heat? ◆ **ce joint de caoutchouc n'est plus ~** this rubber washer is no longer any good ◆ **est-ce que ce pneu/ce vernis est encore ~ ?** is this tyre/varnish still fit to be used *ou* still usable? ◆ **la balle est/n'est pas bonne** *(Tennis)* the ball was in/was out

7 [= favorable] *[opinion, rapport]* good, favourable; *(Scol) [bulletin, note]* good ◆ **le diagnostic du médecin n'est pas très ~** the doctor's diagnosis isn't very good

8 [= recommandé] *[alimentation]* good ◆ **ce n'est pas un ~ champignon** it's not an edible mushroom ◆ **cette eau est-elle bonne (à boire) ?** is this water fit *ou* all right to drink?, is this water drinkable? ◆ **est-ce bien ~ de fumer tant ?** is it a good thing *ou* is it wise to smoke so much? ◆ **ce serait une bonne chose s'il restait là-bas** it would be a good thing if he stayed there ◆ **il serait ~ que vous les préveniez** it would be a good idea *ou* thing to let them know ◆ **il est ~ de louer tôt** it's as well *ou* it's advisable to book early ◆ **croire** *ou* **juger** *ou* **trouver ~ de faire qch** to think *ou* see fit to do sth ◆ **il semblerait ~ de ...** it would seem sensible *ou* a good idea to ... ◆ **trouvez-vous ~ qu'il y aille ?** do you think it's a good thing for him to go? ◆ **quand/comme vous le jugerez ~** when/as you see fit ◆ **quand/comme ~ vous semble** when/as you think best ◆ **allez-y si ~ vous semble** go ahead if you think it best ◆ **~ pour la santé/pour le mal de tête** good for your health/for headaches ◆ **c'est ~ pour ce que tu as !** it'll do you good! ◆ **la baisse des taux, c'est ~ pour l'économie** the reduction in interest rates is good for the economy ◆ **la télévision, c'est ~ pour ceux qui n'ont rien à faire** television is all right *ou* fine for people who have nothing to do ◆ **cette solution, c'est ~ pour toi, mais pas pour moi** that solution's OK for you but not for me

9 [* = attrapé, condamné] **je suis ~ !** I've had it!* ◆ **le voilà ~ pour une contravention** he's in for a fine now* ◆ **le voilà ~ pour recommencer** now he'll have to start all over again

10 [sur imprimé] **~ pour pouvoir** procuration given by ◆ **~ pour un lot de 6 bouteilles** *(sur coupon)* this voucher *ou* coupon may be exchanged for a pack of 6 bottles ◆ **~ pour une réduction de 2 €** €2 off next purchase

11 [= utile]

◆ **bon à** ◆ **c'est ~ à savoir** that's useful to know, that's worth knowing ◆ **c'est toujours ~ à prendre** there's no reason to turn it down, it's better than nothing ◆ **tout n'est pas ~ à dire** some things are better left unsaid ◆ **puis-je vous être ~ à quelque chose ?** can I be of any use *ou* help to you?, can I do anything for you? ◆ **ce drap est (tout juste) ~ à faire des torchons** this sheet is (just) about good enough for *ou* is only fit for dusters *(Brit) ou* dustcloths *(US)* ◆ **c'est (tout juste) ~ à nous créer des ennuis** it will only create problems for us, all it will do is create problems for us ◆ **c'est ~ à jeter** it's fit for the dustbin, it might as well be thrown out

12 [= correct] *[solution, méthode, réponse, calcul]* right, correct ◆ **au ~ moment** at the right *ou* proper time ◆ **sur le ~ côté de la route** on the right *ou* proper side of the road ◆ **le ~ côté du couteau** the cutting *ou* sharp edge of the knife ◆ **le ~ usage** correct usage (of language) ◆ **je suis ~ là ?*** *(en positionnant qch)* is this OK?, how's that? ◆ **les ~s comptes font les ~s amis** *(Prov)* bad debts make bad friends

13 [intensif de quantité] good ◆ **un ~ kilomètre** a good kilometre ◆ **une bonne livre/semaine/heure** a good pound/week/hour ◆ **il a reçu une bonne fessée** he got a good spanking ◆ **la voiture en a pris un ~ coup*** the car got pretty smashed up* ◆ **ça fait un ~ bout de chemin !** that's quite a distance *ou* a good way! ◆ **il est tombé une bonne averse/couche de neige** there has been a heavy shower/fall of snow ◆ **après un ~ moment** after quite some time *ou* a good while ◆ **laissez une bonne marge** leave a good *ou* wide margin ◆ **il faudrait une bonne gelée pour tuer la vermine** what's needed is a hard frost to kill off the vermin ◆ **ça aurait besoin d'une bonne couche de peinture/d'un ~ coup de balai** it needs *ou* would need a good coat of paint/a good sweep-out ◆ **ça fait un ~ poids à traîner !** that's quite a *ou* some load to drag round! ◆ **une bonne moitié** at least half

14 [en apostrophe] **mon ~ monsieur** my good man ◆ **ma bonne dame** my good woman ◆ **mon ~ ami** my dear *ou* good friend

15 [dans des souhaits] **bonne (et heureuse) année !** happy New Year! ◆ **bonne chance !** good luck!, all the best! ◆ **~ courage !** all the best! ◆ **~ dimanche !** have a nice Sunday! ◆ **bonne fin de semaine !** enjoy the rest of the week!, have a good weekend! ◆ **~ match !** *(à un spectateur)* enjoy the game!; *(à un joueur)* have a good game! ◆ **bonne promenade !** have a nice walk! ◆ **bonne rentrée !** *(Scol)* I hope the new term starts well! ◆ **~ retour !** safe journey back!, safe return! ◆ **bonne route !** safe journey! ◆ **bonne santé !** (I) hope you keep well! ◆ **bonnes vacances !** have a good holiday! *(Brit) ou* vacation! *(US)* ◆ **~ voyage !** safe journey!, have a good journey! ◆ **au revoir et bonne continuation** goodbye and I hope all goes well (for you) *ou* and all the best!; → **anniversaire, appétit, souhaiter** *etc*

16 [= amical] *[ambiance]* good, pleasant, nice; *[regard, sourire]* warm, pleasant ◆ **relations de ~ voisinage** good neighbourly relations ◆ **un ~ (gros) rire** a hearty *ou* cheery laugh ◆ **c'est un ~ camarade** he's a good friend

2 - ADVERBE

◆ **faire bon** ◆ **il fait ~ ici** it's nice *ou* pleasant here ◆ **il fait ~ au soleil** it's nice and warm in the sun ◆ **il fait ~ chaud** *(Helv)* it's nice and warm ◆ **il fait ~ vivre à la campagne** it's a nice life in the country ◆ **une ville où il fait ~ vivre** a town that's really nice to live in ◆ **il ne ferait pas ~ le contredire** we (*ou* you *etc*) would be ill-advised to contradict him

◆ **pour de bon** (= *définitivement*) for good; (= *vraiment*) really ◆ **si tu continues, je vais me fâcher pour de ~** if you keep that up, I'm really going to get angry

3 - EXCLAMATION

[= d'accord] all right!, OK!*; *(énervement)* (all) right!, OK!* ◆ **~ ! ça suffit maintenant !** (all) right! *ou* OK! that's enough! ◆ **bon ! bon !** all right! all right! ◆ **~ ! je le ferai moi-même** (all) right then I'll do it myself

4 - NOM MASCULIN

1 [= personne] good *ou* upright person ◆ **les ~s et les méchants** good people and bad people; *(dans un western)* the goodies and the baddies *(Brit)*, the good guys and the bad guys

2 [= morceau, partie] **mange le ~ et laisse le mauvais** eat the good part and leave the bad part ◆ **avoir du ~** *[solution, principe]* to have its advantages *ou* its good points ◆ **il y a du ~ dans ce qu'il dit** there is some merit *ou* there are some good points in what he says ◆ **il y a du ~ et du mauvais** it has its good and its bad points ◆ **il y a du ~ et du moins ~** parts of it are good and parts of it are not so good, some bits are better than others

5 - NOM FÉMININ

bonne

1 [= histoire] **en voilà une bonne !** that's a good one! ◆ **tu en as de bonnes, toi !*** *(iro)* you're kidding!*, you must be joking!*

2 [locutions]

◆ **avoir qn à la bonne*** to like sb, to be in* *ou* in solid* *(US)* with sb ◆ **il m'a à la bonne** I'm in his good books*

6 - COMPOSÉS

bonne amie († *ou hum*) girlfriend, sweetheart

bon chic bon genre *[personne]* chic but conservative, Sloaney* *(Brit)*, preppy* *(US)*; *[bar, soirée]* chic but conservative, Sloaney* *(Brit)* ◆ **le style ~ chic ~ genre des villes bourgeoises** the conservative chic of middle-class towns → **BCBG**

bon enfant LOC ADJ *[personne, sourire]* good-natured; *[atmosphère]* friendly

bonne femme *(péj = femme)* woman ◆ **sa**

bonne femme *(péj = épouse)* his old woman*, his missus* ◆ **pauvre petite bonne femme** *(= enfant)* poor little thing
une bonne pâte an easy-going fellow, a good sort
bon à rien, bonne à rien ADJ **cet enfant n'est ~ à rien** this child is no good *ou* use at anything ◆ **cet appareil n'est ~ à rien** this instrument is useless *ou* isn't much good *ou* use for anything NM,F good-for-nothing, ne'er-do-well
bon Samaritain *(Bible, fig)* good Samaritan
bonne sœur* nun
bon teint ADJ *[couleur]* fast; *(fig) [syndicaliste]* staunch, dyed-in-the-wool
bon à tirer ADJ passed for press NM final corrected proof ◆ **donner le ~ à tirer** to pass for press
bon vivant NM bon viveur *ou* vivant ◆ **c'est un ~ vivant** he's a bon viveur *ou* vivant, he likes the good things in life

bon[2] /bɔ̃/ NM *(= formulaire)* slip, form; *(= coupon d'échange)* coupon, voucher; *(Fin = titre)* bond
COMP **bon de caisse** cash voucher
bon de commande order form
bon d'épargne savings certificate
bon d'essence petrol *(Brit) ou* gas *(US)* coupon
bon de garantie guarantee (slip)
bon de livraison delivery slip
bon de réduction reduction coupon *ou* voucher
bon du Trésor (Government) Treasury bill
bon à vue demand note

Bonaparte /bɔnapaʀt/ NM Bonaparte

bonapartisme /bɔnapaʀtism/ NM Bonapartism

bonapartiste /bɔnapaʀtist/ ADJ, NMF Bonapartist

bonard, e* /bɔnaʀ, aʀd/ ADJ ◆ **c'est ~** *(= facile)* it's no sweat*; *(= bien)* it's great*

bonasse /bɔnas/ ADJ *(gén)* easy-going; *(péj)* meek ◆ **accepter qch d'un air ~** *(gén)* to accept sth good-naturedly; *(péj)* to accept sth meekly

bonbec* /bɔ̃bɛk/ NM *(= bonbon)* sweetie* *(Brit)*, candy *(US)*

bonbon /bɔ̃bɔ̃/ NM sweet *(Brit)*, sweetie* *(Brit)*, piece of candy *(US)* ◆ **j'en ai ras le ~*** I'm fed up to the back teeth*; → **casser**
COMP **bonbon acidulé** acid drop
bonbon anglais fruit drop
bonbon au chocolat chocolate
bonbon fourré sweet *(Brit) ou* piece of candy *(US)* with soft centre
bonbon à la menthe mint, humbug *(Brit)*
bonbon au miel honey drop

bonbonne /bɔ̃bɔn/ NF *(recouverte d'osier)* demijohn; *(à usage industriel)* carboy ◆ **~ de gaz** gas bottle

bonbonnière /bɔ̃bɔnjɛʀ/ NF *(= boîte)* sweet *(Brit) ou* candy *(US)* box, bonbonnière; *(fig = appartement)* bijou flat *(Brit)*, exquisite apartment *(US)*, bijou residence *(hum)*

bond /bɔ̃/ NM 1 *[de personne, animal] (gén)* leap, bound, jump; *(de la position accroupie)* spring; *[de balle]* bounce ◆ **faire des ~s** *(= sauter)* to leap *ou* spring up *ou* into the air; *(= gambader)* to leap *ou* jump about ◆ **faire un ~ d'indignation** to leap *ou* jump up indignantly ◆ **faire un ~ de surprise** to start with surprise ◆ **franchir qch d'un ~** to clear sth with one jump *ou* bound ◆ **se lever d'un ~** to leap *ou* jump *ou* spring up ◆ **d'un ~ il fut près d'elle** in a single leap *ou* bound he was at her side ◆ **il ne fit qu'un ~ jusqu'à l'hôpital** he rushed *ou* dashed off to the hospital → **saisir, faux[2]**
◆ **au bond** ◆ **j'ai pris *ou* saisi l'occasion au ~** I jumped at *ou* I seized the opportunity ◆ **saisir une remarque au ~** to pounce *ou* jump on a remark
2 *(= progression)* **les prix ont fait un ~** prices have shot up *ou* soared ◆ **la science a fait un grand ~ en avant** science has taken a great leap forward ◆ **l'économie nationale a fait un ~ (en avant)** the country's economy has leapt forward *ou* taken a leap forward ◆ **progresser par ~s** to progress by leaps and bounds; *(Mil)* to advance by successive dashes

bonde /bɔ̃d/ NF 1 *(= bouchon) [de tonneau]* bung, stopper; *[d'évier, baignoire]* plug; *[d'étang]* sluice gate 2 *(= trou) [de tonneau]* bunghole; *[d'évier, baignoire]* plughole

bondé, e /bɔ̃de/ ADJ packed, jam-packed*

bondieusard, e* /bɔ̃djøzaʀ, aʀd/ *(péj)* ADJ sanctimonious, churchy* NM,F sanctimonious *ou* churchy* person, Holy Joe* *(péj) (Brit)*

bondieuserie /bɔ̃djøzʀi/ NF *(péj) (= piété)* religiosity, devoutness; *(= bibelot)* religious trinket *ou* bric-à-brac *(NonC)*

bondir /bɔ̃diʀ/ ▸ conjug 2 ◂ VI 1 *(= sauter) [homme, animal]* to jump *ou* leap *ou* spring up; *[balle]* to bounce (up) ◆ **~ de joie** to jump *ou* leap for joy ◆ **~ de colère** to fume with anger ◆ **il bondit d'indignation** he leapt up indignantly ◆ **cela me fait ~*** *(fig)* it makes my blood boil*, it makes me hopping mad* *(Brit)* 2 *(= gambader)* to jump *ou* leap about 3 *(= sursauter)* to start ◆ **~ de surprise/de frayeur** to start with surprise/fright 4 *(= se précipiter)* **~ vers *ou* jusqu'à** to dash *ou* rush to ◆ **~ sur sa proie** to pounce on one's prey 5 *(= augmenter) [valeur boursière, prix]* to shoot up

bondissant, e /bɔ̃disɑ̃, ɑ̃t/ ADJ leaping, jumping

bondissement /bɔ̃dismɑ̃/ NM *[d'animal]* leaping *(NonC)*

bongo /bɔ̃go/ NM *(Mus)* bongo (drum)

bonheur /bɔnœʀ/ GRAMMAIRE ACTIVE 50.3 NM 1 *(= félicité)* happiness; *(= joie)* joy ◆ **trouver le ~** to find true happiness ◆ **le ~ de vivre/d'aimer** the joy of living/of loving ◆ **avoir le ~ de voir son enfant réussir** to have the joy of seeing one's child succeed ◆ **faire le ~ de qn** to make sb happy, to bring happiness to sb ◆ **si ce ruban peut faire ton ~, prends-le** if this ribbon is what you're looking for *ou* can be any use to you, take it ◆ **alors, tu as trouvé ton ~ ?** so, did you find what you wanted *ou* what you were looking for? ◆ **des vacances ! quel ~ !** holidays! what bliss! *ou* what a delight! ◆ **quel ~ de vous revoir !** what a pleasure it is to see you again!
2 *(= chance)* (good) luck, good fortune ◆ **il ne connaît pas son ~ !** he doesn't know *ou* realize (just) how lucky he is!, he doesn't know *ou* realize his luck!* ◆ **avoir le ~ de faire** to be lucky enough *ou* have the good fortune to do ◆ **il eut le rare ~ de gagner 3 fois** he had the unusual good fortune of winning *ou* to win 3 times ◆ **porter ~ à qn** to bring sb luck ◆ **ça porte ~ de ...** it's lucky to ...
◆ **par bonheur** fortunately, luckily ◆ **par un ~ inespéré** by an unhoped-for stroke of luck *ou* good fortune
3 *(locutions)* **avec ~** *(littér)* felicitously ◆ **mêler avec ~ le tragique et le comique** to blend the tragic and the comic skilfully ◆ **le ~ des uns fait le malheur des autres** *(Prov)* one man's meat is another man's poison *(Prov)*
◆ **au petit bonheur (la chance)*** *[répondre]* off the top of one's head*; *[faire]* haphazardly, any old how* ◆ **il n'y a pas de véritable sélection, c'est au petit ~ la chance** there's no real selection (process), it's just pot luck *ou* the luck of the draw

bonheur-du-jour (pl **bonheurs-du-jour**) /bɔnœʀdyʒuʀ/ NM escritoire, writing desk

bonhomie /bɔnɔmi/ NF affability, bonhomie

bonhomme /bɔnɔm/ NM (pl **bonshommes** /bɔ̃zɔm/) 1 * *(= homme)* guy*, chap* *(Brit)*, fellow*, bloke* *(Brit)*; *(= mari)* old man* ◆ **dessiner des bonshommes** to draw little men ◆ **un petit ~ de 4 ans** a little chap* *ou* lad* *ou* fellow* of 4 ◆ **dis-moi, mon ~** tell me, sonny* *ou* little fellow* ◆ **c'était un grand ~** he was a great man* ◆ **aller *ou* suivre son petit ~ de chemin** to carry on *ou* go on in one's own sweet way 2 (* *Can = père*) old man*, father
ADJ (pl **bonhommes**) *[air, regard]* good-natured
COMP **bonhomme de neige** snowman
bonhomme de pain d'épice gingerbread man

boni † /bɔni/ NM *(= bénéfice)* profit ◆ **50 € de ~** a 50-euro profit

boniche* /bɔnij/ NF *(péj)* maid, skivvy* *(Brit)* ◆ **je ne suis pas ta ~** I'm not your skivvy *(Brit) ou* slave ◆ **faire la ~ pour qn** to be sb's slave, to skivvy for sb* *(Brit)*

bonification[1] /bɔnifikasjɔ̃/ NF 1 *(= amélioration) [de terre, vins]* improvement 2 *(Sport) (= points)* bonus (points); *(= avantage)* advantage, start

bonification[2] /bɔnifikasjɔ̃/ NF *(Fin = remise)* discount, rebate ◆ **~s d'intérêt** interest rate subsidies, preferential interest rates

bonifier[1] VT, **se bonifier** VPR /bɔnifje/ ▸ conjug 7 ◂ to improve

bonifier[2] /bɔnifje/ ▸ conjug 7 ◂ VT *(Fin)* to give as a bonus ◆ **prêt *ou* crédit (à taux) bonifié** government subsidized *ou* low-interest loan

boniment /bɔnimɑ̃/ NM *(= baratin)* sales talk *(NonC)*, patter* *(NonC)*; (* *= mensonge)* tall story, humbug *(NonC)* ◆ **faire le *ou* du ~ à qn** to give sb the sales talk *ou* patter* ◆ **faire du ~ à une femme** to try and pick up a woman*, to chat a woman up* *(Brit)* ◆ **raconter des ~s*** to spin yarns *ou* tall stories

bonimenter /bɔnimɑ̃te/ ▸ conjug 1 ◂ VI to give the sales talk *ou* patter*

bonimenteur, -euse /bɔnimɑ̃tœʀ, øz/ NM,F smooth talker; *[de foire]* barker

bonite /bɔnit/ NF bonito

bonjour /bɔ̃ʒuʀ/ GRAMMAIRE ACTIVE 48.2 NM 1 *(gén)* hello; *(matin)* (good) morning; *(après-midi)* (good) afternoon; *(Can = au revoir)* good day *(frm)*, good morning, good afternoon ◆ **~ chez vous !** hello to everybody at home! ◆ **avec lui, c'est ~ bonsoir** I only ever say hello to him ◆ **donnez-lui le ~ de ma part** give him my regards, remember me to him ◆ **dire ~ à qn** to say hello to sb ◆ **est-ce que je peux passer te dire un petit ~ ?** can I drop in (to say hello)?
2 (* *: locutions)* **le bus aux heures de pointe, ~ (les dégâts) !*** taking the bus in the rush hour is absolute hell!* ◆ **tu aurais vu sa moto après l'accident ! ~ (les dégâts) !*** you should've seen his bike after the accident! what a mess! ◆ **si son père l'apprend, ~ (les dégâts) !** if his father finds out about it, sparks will fly *ou* all hell will be let loose!* ◆ **si tu l'invites, ~ l'ambiance !** if you invite him, it'll ruin the atmosphere! ◆ **pour l'ouvrir, ~ !** there's no way to get it open

Bonn /bɔn/ N Bonn

bonne[2] /bɔn/ NF maid, domestic ◆ **~ d'enfants** nanny, child's nurse *(US)* ◆ **~ à tout faire** maid of all work, skivvy *(Brit)*; *(hum)* general dogsbody *ou* factotum ◆ **je ne suis pas ta ~** I'm not your skivvy *ou* slave; → **bon[1]**

bonne-maman (pl **bonnes-mamans**) /bɔnmamɑ̃/ NF granny*, grandma

bonnement /bɔnmɑ̃/ ADV **tout bonnement** just, quite simply ◆ **sa performance est tout ~ hallucinante** his performance is just *ou* quite simply staggering ◆ **c'est tout ~ magnifique** it's just wonderful ◆ **dire tout ~ que ...** to say quite simply that ...

bonnet /bɔnɛ/ NM 1 *(= coiffure)* bonnet, hat; *[de bébé]* bonnet 2 *[de soutien-gorge]* cup 3 *(= es-*

tomac de ruminant) reticulum 4 *(locutions)* **prendre qch sous son ~** to make sth one's concern *ou* responsibility, to take it upon o.s. to do sth ◆ **c'est ~ blanc et blanc ~** it amounts to the same thing ◆ **jeter son ~ par-dessus les moulins** to kick over the traces, to have one's fling; → **gros, tête**

COMP **bonnet d'âne** dunce's cap
bonnet de bain bathing cap
bonnet de nuit *(Habillement)* nightcap; (**fig)* wet blanket*, killjoy, spoilsport
bonnet phrygien Phrygian cap
bonnet à poils bearskin
bonnet de police forage cap, garrison *ou* overseas cap *(US)*; → MARIANNE

bonneteau /bɔnto/ **NM** three card trick *ou* monte *(US)*

bonneterie /bɔnɛtʀi/ **NF** *(= objets)* hosiery; *(= magasin)* hosier's shop, hosiery; *(= commerce)* hosiery trade

bonnetier, -ière /bɔntje, jɛʀ/ **NM,F** hosier

bonnette /bɔnɛt/ **NF** *(Photo)* supplementary lens; *(Naut)* studding sail, stuns'l; *(Mil) [de fortification]* bonnet

bonniche /bɔniʃ/ **NF** ⇒ **boniche**

bonobo /bɔnɔbo/ **NM** pygmy chimpanzee, bonobo

bon-papa (pl **bons-papas**) /bɔ̃papa/ **NM** grandad*, grandpa

bonsaï /bɔ̃(d)zaj/ **NM** bonsai

bonsoir /bɔ̃swaʀ/ **NM** 1 *(en arrivant)* hello, good evening; *(en partant)* good evening, good night; *(en se couchant)* good night ◆ **souhaiter le ~ à qn** to say good night to sb, to wish sb goodnight 2 (* *: locution = rien à faire)* **~ !** nothing doing!*, not a chance!*, not on your life!* ◆ **pour s'en débarrasser ~ !** it's going to be sheer *ou* absolute hell* getting rid of it

bonté /bɔ̃te/ **NF** 1 *(= caractère)* kindness, goodness ◆ **ayez la ~ de faire** would you be so kind *ou* good as to do? ◆ **faire qch par pure ~ d'âme** to do sth out of the goodness of one's heart ◆ **avec ~** kindly ◆ **~ divine !** *ou* **du ciel !** good heavens!* 2 *(= acte)* (act of) kindness ◆ **merci de toutes vos ~s** thank you for all your kindness *ou* for all the kindness you've shown me ◆ **avoir des ~s pour qn** to be very kind to sb

bonus /bɔnys/ **NM** 1*(Assurances)* no-claims bonus 2 *[de DVD]* bonus footage *(NonC)*

bonze /bɔ̃z/ **NM** 1 *(Rel)* bonze *(Buddhist monk)* 2 (* *= personnage important)* bigwig* ◆ **vieux ~**‡ old fossil‡

bonzerie /bɔ̃zʀi/ **NF** Buddhist monastery

bonzesse /bɔ̃zɛs/ **NF** bonze *(Buddhist nun)*

boogie-woogie (pl **boogie-woogies**) /bugiwugi/ **NM** boogie-woogie

book /buk/ **NM** ⇒ **press-book**

booké, e * /buke/ **ADJ** *(= occupé)* busy ◆ **ce n'est pas possible mardi, je suis déjà ~** Tuesday's out, I've already got something on

bookmaker /bukmɛkœʀ/ **NM** bookmaker

booléen, -enne /buleɛ̃, ɛn/ **ADJ** *(Math, Ordin)* boolean

boom /bum/ **NM** *(= expansion)* boom ◆ **être en plein ~** *[secteur]* to be booming; (* *= en plein travail)* to be really busy

boomer /bumœʀ/ **NM** *(Hi-Fi)* woofer

boomerang /bumʀɑ̃g/ **NM** *(lit, fig)* boomerang ◆ **faire ~, avoir un effet ~** *(fig)* to backfire

booster[1] /bustœʀ/ **NM** *[de fusée]* booster, launching vehicle; *[d'autoradio]* booster

booster[2] /buste/ ► conjug 1 ◄ **VT** *[+ économie, ventes]* to boost; *[+ moteur]* to soup up*

boots /buts/ **NMPL** boots

boqueteau (pl **boqueteaux**) /bɔkto/ **NM** copse

borax /bɔʀaks/ **NM** borax

borborygme /bɔʀbɔʀigm/ **NM** rumble, rumbling noise (in one's stomach), borborygmus *(SPÉC)*

bord /bɔʀ/ **NM** 1 *[de route]* side, edge; *[de rivière]* side, bank; *[de lac]* edge, side, shore; *[de cratère]* edge, rim, lip; *[de forêt, table]* edge; *[de précipice]* edge, brink; *[de verre, tasse]* brim, rim; *[d'assiette]* edge, rim; *[de plaie]* edge ◆ **le ~ des paupières** the rim of the eye ◆ **le ~ de la mer** the seashore ◆ **~ du trottoir** edge of the pavement, kerb *(Brit)*, curb *(US)* ◆ **une maison au ~ du lac** a house by the lake *ou* at the lakeside, a lakeside house ◆ **se promener au ~ de la rivière** to go for a walk along the riverside *ou* the river bank *ou* by the river ◆ **passer ses vacances au ~ de la mer** to spend one's holidays at the seaside *ou* by the sea, to go to the seaside for one's holidays ◆ **pique-niquer au ~** *ou* **sur le ~ de la route** to (have a) picnic at *ou* by the roadside ◆ **laisser** *ou* **abandonner qn sur le ~ de la route** *(fig)* to leave sb by the wayside ◆ **au ~ de l'eau** at the water's edge ◆ **se promener au ~ de l'eau** to go for a walk along the water's edge ◆ **en été les ~s du lac sont envahis de touristes** in summer the shores of the lake are overrun by tourists ◆ **il a regagné le ~ à la nage** *(dans la mer)* he swam ashore *ou* to the shore; *(dans une rivière)* he swam to the bank ◆ **verre rempli jusqu'au ~** *ou* **à ras ~** glass full *ou* filled to the brim

2 *[de vêtement, mouchoir]* edge, border; *[de chapeau]* brim ◆ **chapeau à large(s) ~(s)** wide-brimmed *ou* broad-brimmed hat ◆ **le ~ ourlé d'un mouchoir** the rolled hem of a handkerchief ◆ **~ à ~** *[coudre, coller]* edge to edge ◆ **veste ~ à ~** edge-to-edge jacket

3 *(= navire)* **les hommes du ~** the crew ◆ **jeter par-dessus ~** to throw overboard ◆ **journal** *ou* **livre de ~** log(book), ship's log

◆ **à bord** on board, aboard ◆ **monter à ~** to go on board *ou* aboard ◆ **prendre qn à son ~** to take sb aboard *ou* on board ◆ **monter à ~ d'un navire** to board a ship, to go on board *ou* aboard ship ◆ **la marchandise a été expédiée à ~ du SS Wallisdown** the goods were shipped on SS Wallisdown ◆ **M. Morand, à ~ d'une voiture bleue** Mr Morand, driving *ou* in a blue car

4 *(Naut = bordée)* tack ◆ **tirer des ~s** to tack, to make tacks ◆ **tirer un ~** to tack, to make a tack

5 (* *Can)* side ◆ **de mon ~** on my side ◆ **prendre le ~** to make off

6 *(locutions)* **être au ~ de la ruine/du désespoir** to be on the verge *ou* brink of ruin/despair ◆ **au ~ de la tombe** on the brink of death ◆ **au ~ des larmes** on the verge of tears ◆ **nous sommes du même ~** we are on the same side, we are of the same opinion; *(socialement)* we are all of a kind ◆ **de tout ~** of all kinds ◆ **à pleins ~s** abundantly, freely ◆ **il est un peu fantaisiste/sadique sur les ~s*** he's a bit of an eccentric/a sadist

bordage /bɔʀdaʒ/ **NM** *(Couture)* edging, trimming **NMPL** **bordages** 1 *[d'un bateau] (en bois)* planks, planking; *(en fer)* plates, plating 2 *(Can)* inshore ice

bordé /bɔʀde/ **NM** 1 *(Couture)* braid, trimming 2 *(Naut) (en bois)* planking; *(en fer)* plating

bordeaux /bɔʀdo/ **NM** *(= vin)* Bordeaux (wine) ◆ **~ rouge** red Bordeaux, claret *(Brit)* **ADJ INV** maroon, burgundy

bordée /bɔʀde/ **NF** 1 *(= salve)* broadside ◆ **~ d'injures** *(fig)* torrent *ou* volley of abuse 2 *(Naut = quart)* watch 3 *(= parcours)* tack ◆ **tirer des ~s** to tack, to make tacks ◆ **tirer une ~** *(fig)* to go on a spree* *ou* binge* 4 (* *Can)* **une ~ de neige** a heavy snowfall

bordel‡ /bɔʀdɛl/ **NM** 1 *(= hôtel)* brothel, whorehouse* 2 *(= chaos)* mess, shambles *(sg)* ◆ **quel ~ !** what a bloody** *(Brit) ou* goddamned‡ *(US)* shambles! ◆ **si tout le monde a accès aux dossiers, ça va être le ~** if everyone has access to the files it'll be bloody** *(Brit) ou* goddamned‡ *(US)* chaos ◆ **mettre** *ou* **foutre**‡ **le ~** to create havoc, to cause bloody** *(Brit) ou* goddamned‡ *(US)* chaos ◆ **mettre** *ou* **foutre**‡ **le ~ dans qch** to screw‡ *ou* bugger** *(Brit)* sth up ◆ **~ !** hell!*, bloody hell!‡ *(Brit)*, shit!** ◆ **arrête de gueuler, ~ (de merde) !** stop shouting for Christ's sake!** *ou* for fuck's sake!** ◆ **... et tout le ~** ... and God knows what else*

bordelais, e /bɔʀdəlɛ, ɛz/ **ADJ** of *ou* from Bordeaux, Bordeaux *(épith)* **NM,F** **Bordelais(e)** inhabitant *ou* native of Bordeaux **NM** *(= région)* ◆ **le Bordelais** the Bordeaux region **NF** **bordelaise** *(Culin)* **entrecôte (à la) ~e** Bordelaise entrecôte steak

bordélique‡ /bɔʀdelik/ **ADJ** chaotic, shambolic* *(Brit)*

border /bɔʀde/ ► conjug 1 ◄ **VT** 1 *(Couture) (= entourer)* to edge, to trim *(de* with); *(= ourler)* to hem, to put a hem on 2 *(= longer) [arbres, immeubles, maisons]* to line; *[sentier]* to run alongside ◆ **allée bordée de fleurs** path edged *ou* bordered with flowers ◆ **rue bordée de maisons** road lined with houses ◆ **rue bordée d'arbres** tree-lined road 3 *[+ personne, couverture]* to tuck in ◆ **~ un lit** to tuck the blankets in 4 *(Naut) (en bois)* to plank; *(en fer)* to plate 5 *(Naut) [+ voile]* to haul on, to pull on; *[+ avirons]* to ship

bordereau (pl **bordereaux**) /bɔʀdəʀo/ **NM** *(= formulaire)* note, slip; *(= relevé)* statement, summary; *(= facture)* invoice

COMP **bordereau d'achat** purchase note
bordereau d'envoi dispatch note
bordereau de livraison delivery slip *ou* note
bordereau de versement pay(ing)-in slip

bordure /bɔʀdyʀ/ **NF** *(= bord)* edge; *(= cadre)* surround, frame; *[de gazon, fleurs]* border; *[d'arbres]* line; *(Couture)* border, edging, edge; *[de voile]* foot ◆ **~ de trottoir** kerb *(Brit)*, curb *(US)*, kerbstones *(Brit)*, curbstones *(US)* ◆ **en ~ de** *(= le long de)* running along, alongside, along the edge of; *(= à côté de)* next to, by; *(= près de)* near (to) ◆ **en ~ de route** *[maison, champ]* by the roadside *(attrib)*; *[restaurant, arbre]* roadside *(épith)* ◆ **papier à ~ noire** black-edged paper, paper with a black edge

bore /bɔʀ/ **NM** boron

boréal, e (mpl **-aux**) /bɔʀeal, o/ **ADJ** boreal; → **aurore**

borgne /bɔʀɲ/ **ADJ** 1 *[personne]* one-eyed, blind in one eye ◆ **fenêtre ~** obstructed window 2 *(fig = louche) [hôtel, rue]* shady

borique /bɔʀik/ **ADJ** boric

Boris /bɔʀis/ **NM** Boris ◆ **"Boris Godounov"** *(Littérat)* "Boris Godunov"

bornage /bɔʀnaʒ/ **NM** *[de terrain]* boundary marking, demarcation

borne /bɔʀn/ **NF** 1 *(kilométrique)* kilometre-marker, ≃ milestone; *[de terrain]* boundary stone *ou* marker; *(autour d'un monument)* bollard *(Brit)*, post ◆ **~ d'incendie** fire hydrant ◆ **ne reste pas là planté comme une ~ !*** don't just stand there like a statue!

2 *(fig)* **~s** limit(s), bounds ◆ **il n'y a pas de ~s à la bêtise humaine** human folly knows no bounds ◆ **franchir** *ou* **dépasser les ~s** to go too far ◆ **mettre des ~s à** to limit

◆ **sans borne(s)** boundless, unbounded ◆ **il lui vouait une admiration sans ~(s)** he felt boundless *ou* unbounded admiration for her

3 (* *= kilomètre)* kilometre

4 *(Élec)* terminal

5 *(Téléc)* **~ téléphonique** *ou* **d'appel** *(pour taxi)* taxi rank *(Brit) ou* stand *(US)* telephone; *(pour secours)* emergency telephone ◆ **~ de paiement** pay point

6 (Ordin) ~ **interactive/Minitel** interactive/ Minitel terminal

7 (Math) bound ◆ ~ **inférieure/supérieure** lower/upper bound

borné, e /bɔʀne/ (ptp de **borner**) ADJ 1 *[personne]* narrow-minded, short-sighted; *[esprit, vie]* narrow; *[intelligence]* limited 2 (Math) bounded

borne-fontaine (pl **bornes-fontaines**) /bɔʀn(ə)fɔ̃tɛn/ NF 1 *[d'eau potable]* public drinking fountain 2 (Can = bouche d'incendie) fire hydrant

Bornéo /bɔʀneo/ N Borneo

borner /bɔʀne/ ► conjug 1 ◄ VT 1 *[+ ambitions, besoins, enquête]* to limit, to restrict (à faire to doing; à qch to sth) 2 *[+ terrain]* to mark out *ou* off, to mark the boundary of ◆ **arbres qui bornent un champ** trees which border a field ◆ **immeubles qui bornent la vue** buildings which limit *ou* restrict one's view VPR **se borner** (= se contenter de) **se ~ à faire** to content o.s. with doing, to be content to do ◆ **se ~ à qch** to content o.s. with sth ◆ **se ~ à faire/à qch** (= se limiter à) *[personne]* to restrict *ou* confine o.s. to doing/to sth; *[visite, exposé]* to be limited *ou* restricted to doing/to sth ◆ **je me borne à vous faire remarquer que ...** I would just *ou* merely like to point out to you that ... ◆ **il s'est borné à resserrer les vis** he just *ou* merely tightened up the screws

bort(s)ch /bɔʀtʃ/ NM bors(c)h

bosco /bɔsko/ NM (Naut) quartermaster

bosniaque /bɔsnjak/ ADJ Bosnian NMF **Bosniaque** Bosnian

Bosnie /bɔsni/ NF Bosnia

Bosnie-Herzégovine /bɔsniɛʀzegɔvin/ NF Bosnia-Herzegovina

bosnien, -ienne /bɔsnjɛ̃, jɛn/ ADJ, NM,F ⇒ **bosniaque**

boson /bozɔ̃/ NM boson

Bosphore /bɔsfɔʀ/ NM ◆ **le ~** the Bosphorus ◆ **le détroit du ~** the Bosphorus Strait(s)

bosquet /bɔskɛ/ NM copse, grove

bossage /bɔsaʒ/ NM (Archit) boss ◆ **~s** bosses, bossage

bossa-nova (pl **bossas-novas**) /bɔsanɔva/ NF bossa nova

bosse /bɔs/ NF 1 *[de chameau, bossu]* hump; *(en se cognant)* bump, lump; (= éminence) bump; (Ski) mogul, bump ◆ **se faire une ~ au front** to get a bump on one's forehead ◆ **route pleine de ~s** (very) bumpy road ◆ **ski sur ~s** mogul skiing; → **rouler**

◆ **avoir la bosse de** * to be good at, to have a gift for ◆ **avoir la ~ des maths** to be good at maths, to have a gift for maths ◆ **avoir la ~ du commerce** to be a born businessman (*ou* businesswoman)

2 (Naut) ~ **d'amarrage** pointer

bosselage /bɔslaʒ/ NM embossment

bosseler /bɔsle/ ► conjug 4 ◄ VT (= déformer) to dent; (= marteler) to emboss ◆ **tout bosselé** battered, badly dented; *[+ front]* bruised, covered in bumps *(attrib)*; *[+ sol]* bumpy

bossellement /bɔsɛlmɑ̃/ NM embossing

bosselure /bɔslyʀ/ NF (= défaut) dent; (= relief) embossment

bosser * /bɔse/ ► conjug 1 ◄ VI (= travailler) to work (*dans* in); (= travailler dur) (intellectuellement) to work hard, to slog away * (Brit); (physiquement) to slave away, to work one's guts out ‡ VT *[+ examen]* to slog away for * (Brit), to swot for (Brit) ◆ ~ **son anglais** to slog away at *ou* swot for * one's English

bosseur, -euse * /bɔsœʀ, øz/ ADJ hard-working NM,F slogger * (Brit), hard worker

bossoir /bɔswaʀ/ NM *[de bateau]* davit; *[d'ancre]* cathead

bossu, e /bɔsy/ ADJ *[personne]* hunchbacked ◆ **dos ~** hunch(ed) back ◆ **redresse-toi, tu es tout ~** sit up, you're getting round-shouldered NM,F hunchback; → **rire**

boston /bɔstɔ̃/ NM (= danse, jeu) boston

bot, bote /bo, bɔt/ ADJ ◆ **main ~e** club-hand ◆ **pied ~** club-foot

botanique /bɔtanik/ ADJ botanical NF botany

botaniste /bɔtanist/ NMF botanist

Botnie /bɔtni/ NF ◆ **le golfe de ~** the Gulf of Bothnia

Botox ® /bɔtɔks/ NM Botox ®

botrytis /bɔtʀitis/ NM (Agr) botrytis

Botswana /bɔtswana/ NM Botswana

botswanais, e /bɔtswanɛ, ɛz/ ADJ of *ou* from Botswana NM,F **Botswanais(e)** inhabitant *ou* native of Botswana

botte[1] /bɔt/ NF 1 (high) boot ◆ **~ de caoutchouc** wellington (boot) (Brit), gumboot (Brit), rubber boot (US) ◆ **~ de cheval** *ou* **de cavalier** riding boot ◆ **~ d'égoutier** wader ◆ **les ~s de sept lieues** the seven-league boots ◆ **la ~ (de l'Italie)** the boot (of Italy) 2 (locutions) **être à la ~ de qn** to be under sb's heel *ou* thumb, to be sb's puppet ◆ **avoir qn à sa ~** to have sb under one's heel *ou* thumb ◆ **cirer** *ou* **lécher les ~s de qn** * to lick sb's boots ◆ **être sous la ~ de l'ennemi** to be under the enemy's heel

botte[2] /bɔt/ NF *[de fleurs, légumes]* bunch; *[de foin]* (en gerbe) bundle, sheaf; (au carré) bale

botte[3] /bɔt/ NF (Escrime) thrust ◆ **porter une ~ à** (lit) to make a thrust at; (fig) to hit out at ◆ ~ **secrète** (fig) secret weapon

botter /bɔte/ ► conjug 1 ◄ VT 1 (= mettre des bottes à) to put boots on; (= vendre des bottes à) to sell boots to ◆ **se ~** to put one's boots on ◆ **botté de cuir** with leather boots on, wearing leather boots 2 ◆ **~ les fesses** *ou* **le derrière de qn** ‡ to kick *ou* boot ‡ sb in the behind *, to give sb a kick up the backside ‡ *ou* in the pants ‡ 3 (* = plaire) **ça me botte** ‡ I fancy * (Brit) *ou* like *ou* dig ‡ that ◆ **ce film m'a botté** I really liked that film 4 (Ftbl) to kick VI (Ftbl) to kick the ball; (Ski) to ball up ◆ ~ **en touche** (lit, fig) to kick the ball into touch

botteur /bɔtœʀ/ NM (Rugby) kicker

bottier /bɔtje/ NM *[de bottes]* bootmaker; *[de chaussures]* shoemaker

bottillon /bɔtijɔ̃/ NM ankle boot; *[de bébé]* bootee

bottin ® /bɔtɛ̃/ NM telephone directory, phonebook ◆ **Bottin mondain** ≈ Who's Who

bottine /bɔtin/ NF (ankle) boot ◆ ~ **à boutons** button-boot

botulique /bɔtylik/ ADJ ◆ **bacille ~** botulinus ◆ **toxine ~** botulism toxin, botox

botulisme /bɔtylism/ NM botulism

boubou /bubu/ NM boubou, bubu (traditional African dress)

bouc /buk/ NM 1 (= animal) (billy) goat ◆ **sentir** *ou* **puer le ~** ‡ to stink *, to pong ‡ (Brit) ◆ ~ **émissaire** scapegoat 2 (= barbe) goatee (beard)

boucan * /bukɑ̃/ NM din *, racket * ◆ **faire du ~** (= bruit) to kick up * a din * *ou* a racket *; (= protestation) to kick up * a fuss

boucane ‡ /bukan/ NF (Can) smoke

boucaner /bukane/ ► conjug 1 ◄ VT *[+ viande]* to smoke, to cure; *[+ peau]* to tan

boucanier /bukanje/ NM (= pirate) buccaneer

bouchage /buʃaʒ/ NM 1 *[de bouteille]* corking 2 *[de trou, fente]* filling up *ou* in; *[de fuite]* plugging, stopping 3 *[de fenêtre, porte]* blocking (up) 4 *[de lavabo]* blocking (up), choking up

bouche /buʃ/ NF 1 (Anat) mouth; *[de volcan, fleuve, four]* mouth; *[de canon]* muzzle ◆ **embrasser à pleine ~** to kiss full on the lips *ou* mouth ◆ **parler la ~ pleine** to talk with one's mouth full ◆ **avoir la ~ amère** to have a bitter taste in one's mouth ◆ **j'ai la ~ sèche** my mouth feels *ou* is dry ◆ **j'ai la ~ pâteuse** my tongue feels thick *ou* coated ◆ **il a 5 ~s à nourrir** he has 5 mouths to feed ◆ **les ~s inutiles** (dans une population) the non-active *ou* unproductive population ◆ **provisions de ~** provisions ◆ **dépenses de ~** food bills ◆ **vin court/long en ~** wine with a short/long finish; → **garder**

2 (= organe de la communication) mouth ◆ **fermer la ~ à qn** to shut sb up ◆ **garder la ~ close** to keep one's mouth shut ◆ **il n'a pas ouvert la ~ de la soirée** he didn't open his mouth *ou* he didn't say a word all evening ◆ **dans sa ~, ce mot surprend** when he says *ou* uses it, that word sounds odd ◆ **il a toujours l'injure à la ~** he's always ready with an insult ◆ **il n'a que ce mot-là à la ~** that's all he ever talks about ◆ **de ~ à oreille** by word of mouth, confidentially ◆ **~ cousue !** * don't breathe a word!, mum's the word! * ◆ **son nom est dans toutes les ~s** his name is a household word *ou* is on everyone's lips ◆ **aller** *ou* **passer de ~ en ~** to be rumoured about ◆ **il en a plein la ~** he can talk of nothing else ◆ **nos sentiments s'expriment par sa ~** our feelings are expressed through his words

3 (loc) **s'embrasser à ~ que veux-tu** to kiss eagerly ◆ **faire la fine** *ou* **petite ~** to turn one's nose up ◆ **avoir la ~ en cœur** to simper ◆ **et pour la bonne ~, le dernier roman de Legrand** and last but by no means least, Legrand's latest novel ◆ **nous avons gardé** *ou* **réservé pour la bonne ~ un enregistrement inédit de Bechet** we have saved the best till last *ou* and last but not least – a previously unreleased Bechet recording; → **bée**

COMP **bouche d'aération** air vent *ou* inlet

bouche de chaleur hot-air vent *ou* inlet

bouche d'égout manhole

bouche à feu (Hist) piece (of ordnance), gun

bouche d'incendie fire hydrant

bouche de métro metro entrance

bouché, e[1] /buʃe/ (ptp de **boucher**[1]) ADJ 1 *[temps, ciel]* cloudy, overcast 2 (= obstrué) *[passage]* blocked ◆ **j'ai les oreilles ~es** my ears are blocked (up) ◆ **j'ai le nez ~** my nose is blocked (up) *ou* stuffed up 3 (* = stupide) *[personne]* stupid, thick ‡ ◆ **~ à l'émeri** dead from the neck up *, as thick as a brick ‡ (Brit) 4 (= sans avenir) **le secteur de la publicité est ~** there are absolutely no openings in the advertising industry ◆ **il n'a devant lui qu'un horizon ~** his prospects don't look very bright

bouche-à-bouche /buʃabuʃ/ NM INV kiss of life (Brit), mouth-to-mouth resuscitation (Brit) *ou* respiration (US) ◆ **faire du ~ à qn** to give sb the kiss of life, to give sb mouth-to-mouth resuscitation (Brit) *ou* respiration (US)

bouchée[2] /buʃe/ NF 1 (= quantité) mouthful ◆ **pour une ~ de pain** for a song, for next to nothing ◆ **mettre les ~s doubles** to put on a spurt, to work twice as hard ◆ **ne faire qu'une ~ d'un plat** to gobble up *ou* polish off a dish in next to no time ◆ **ne faire qu'une ~ d'un adversaire** to make short work of an opponent 2 (Culin) ~ **(au chocolat)** chocolate ◆ ~ **à la reine** *vol-au-vent filled with chopped sweetbreads in a rich sauce*

boucher[1] /buʃe/ ► conjug 1 ◄ VT 1 (= fermer) *[+ bouteille]* to cork, to put the *ou* a cork in 2 (= colmater) *[+ trou, fente]* to fill up *ou* in; *[+ fuite]* to plug, to stop ◆ **ça (ou elle etc) lui en a bouché un coin** * he was staggered * *ou* flabbergasted * *ou* gobsmacked ‡ (Brit)

3 (= condamner) *[+ fenêtre, porte]* to block (up)

4 (= engorger) [+ lavabo] to block (up), to choke (up) ◆ **sécrétions qui bouchent les pores** secretions which block up *ou* clog up the pores ◆ **j'ai les oreilles bouchées** my ears are blocked (up) ◆ **j'ai le nez bouché** my nose is blocked (up) *ou* stuffed up *ou* bunged up* ◆ **~ le passage** to be *ou* stand in the way ◆ **~ le passage à qn** to be *ou* stand in sb's way, to block sb's way ◆ **~ la vue** to block the view ◆ **on l'a employé pour ~ les trous** we used him as a stopgap

VPR **se boucher** *[évier]* to get blocked *ou* choked *ou* clogged up; *[temps]* to get cloudy, to become overcast ◆ **se ~ le nez** to hold one's nose ◆ **se ~ les oreilles** to put one's fingers in one's ears *ou* one's hands over one's ears; *(= refuser d'entendre)* to turn a deaf ear ◆ **se ~ les yeux** to put one's hands over one's eyes, to hide one's eyes; *(= refuser de voir)* to turn a blind eye

boucher[2] /buʃe/ NM *(lit, fig)* butcher

bouchère /buʃɛʀ/ NF (woman) butcher; *(= épouse)* butcher's wife

boucherie /buʃʀi/ NF *(= magasin)* butcher's (shop); *(= métier)* butchery (trade); *(fig)* slaughter ◆ **animaux de ~** animals for slaughter ◆ **~ chevaline** *ou* **hippophagique** horse(meat) butcher's ◆ **~ charcuterie** butcher's (shop) with delicatessen

bouche-trou (pl **bouche-trous**) /buʃtʀu/ NM *(= personne)* fill-in, stopgap, stand-in; *(= chose)* stopgap, pinch-hitter* *(NonC)*

bouchon /buʃɔ̃/ NM 1 *(en liège)* cork; *(en verre)* stopper; *(en plastique)* stopper, top; *(en chiffon, papier)* plug, bung *(Brit)*; *[de bidon, réservoir]* cap; *[de tube]* top; *[d'évier]* plug ◆ **~ d'objectif** *(Photo)* lens cap ◆ **~ antivol** locking petrol *(Brit)* *ou* gas *(US)* cap ◆ **~ de vidange** drain plug ◆ **vin qui sent le ~** corked *ou* corky wine ◆ **~ de cérumen** earwax *ou* cerumen plug; → **pousser** 2 *(Pêche)* float 3 *(pour un cheval)* **~ (de paille)** wisp 4 *(Aut = embouteillage)* holdup, traffic jam ◆ **un ~ de 12 km** a 12-km tailback

bouchonnage /buʃɔnaʒ/ NM *[de cheval]* rubbing-down, wisping-down *(Brit)*

bouchonné, e /buʃɔne/ ADJ *[vin]* corked, corky

bouchonner /buʃɔne/ ▸ conjug 1 ◂ VT *[+ cheval]* to rub down, to wisp down *(Brit)* VI *(Aut)* ◆ **ça bouchonne en ville** there's heavy congestion in town

bouchot /buʃo/ NM mussel bed ◆ **moules de ~** farmed mussels

bouclage /buklaʒ/ NM *(* = mise sous clés)* locking up *ou* away, imprisonment; *(= encerclement)* surrounding, sealing off; *(Presse) [de journal]* closing, putting to bed

boucle /bukl/ NF *[de ceinture, soulier]* buckle; *[de cheveux]* curl; *[de ruban, voie ferrée, rivière]* loop; *(Sport)* lap; *(en avion)* loop; *(Ordin)* loop ◆ **fais une ~ à ton j** put a loop on your j ◆ **fais une ~ à ton lacet** tie your shoelace in a bow

◆ **en boucle** constantly ◆ **ce disque est passé en ~ dans le hall de l'hôtel** this record plays constantly in the hotel lobby ◆ **des appels à l'aide sont diffusés en ~ à la radio** appeals for aid are constantly broadcast on the radio COMP **boucle d'oreille** earring ◆ **~ d'oreille à vis** *(ou* **à crochets)** pierced earring, earring for pierced ear ◆ **~ d'oreille à clip** *ou* **à pince** clip-on (earring)

bouclé, e /bukle/ (ptp de **boucler**) ADJ *[cheveux, fourrure]* curly; *[personne]* curly-haired ◆ **il avait la tête ~e** his hair was curly *ou* all curls

boucler /bukle/ ▸ conjug 1 ◂ VT 1 *(= fermer) [+ ceinture]* to buckle, to fasten (up); * *[+ porte]* to lock ◆ **~ sa valise** *(lit)* to fasten one's suitcase; *(fig)* to pack one's bags ◆ **tu vas la ~ !**‡ will you shut your trap!‡, will you belt up!‡ *(Brit)*

2 *(= terminer) [+ affaire]* to finish off, to settle; *[+ circuit]* to complete, to go round; *[+ budget]* to balance; *[+ article]* to finish ◆ **il faut ~** *(Presse)* we've got to put the paper to bed ◆ **le dossier est bouclé** the file is closed ◆ **arriver à ~ ses fins de mois** to manage to stay in the black *ou* to make ends meet at the end of the month ◆ **~ la boucle** *(en avion)* to loop the loop ◆ **on est revenu par l'Espagne pour ~ la boucle** we came back through Spain to make (it) a round trip ◆ **la boucle est bouclée** we've *(ou* they've) come full circle ◆ **dans le cycle de production la boucle est bouclée** the cycle of production is now completed

3 *(* = enfermer)* to lock up, to put under lock and key ◆ **ils ont bouclé le coupable** they've locked up the criminal *ou* put the criminal under lock and key ◆ **être bouclé chez soi** to be cooped up *ou* stuck* at home

4 *(Mil, Police = encercler)* to seal off, to cordon off

VI 1 *[cheveux]* to curl, to be curly ◆ **elle commence à ~** her hair is getting curly

2 *(Ordin)* to get stuck in a loop

bouclette /buklɛt/ NF small curl

bouclier /buklije/ NM *(Mil, fig)* shield; *(Police)* riot shield ◆ **faire un ~ de son corps à qn** to shield sb with one's body ◆ **~ thermique** *(Espace)* heat shield ◆ **~ atomique** *ou* **nucléaire** nuclear defences ◆ **~ humain** human shield

Bouddha /buda/ NM Buddha ◆ **bouddha** *(= statuette)* Buddha

bouddhique /budik/ ADJ Buddhist

bouddhisme /budism/ NM Buddhism ◆ **~ zen** zen Buddhism

bouddhiste /budist/ ADJ, NMF Buddhist ◆ **~ zen** zen Buddhist

bouder /bude/ ▸ conjug 1 ◂ VI to sulk VT *[+ personne]* to cold-shoulder; *[+ produit]* to be reluctant to buy; *[+ conférence, exposition]* to stay away from ◆ **~ la nourriture** to have no appetite ◆ **~ son plaisir** to deny o.s. a good thing ◆ **ils ont boudé mon gâteau** they hardly touched my cake ◆ **le public a boudé sa pièce** hardly anybody went to see his play ◆ **les électeurs ont boudé les urnes** many voters stayed away from the polls ◆ **cet événement a été boudé par les médias** the event received hardly any media coverage ◆ **le soleil va ~ le nord du pays** the north of the country won't see much of the sun ◆ **ils se boudent** they're not on speaking terms, they're not speaking

bouderie /budʀi/ NF *(= état)* sulkiness *(NonC)*; *(= action)* sulk

boudeur, -euse /budœʀ, øz/ ADJ sulky, sullen NF **boudeuse** *(= siège)* dos-à-dos

boudin /budɛ̃/ NM 1 *(Culin)* **~ (noir)** ≃ black pudding *(Brit)*, blood sausage *(US)* ◆ **~ blanc** ≃ white pudding *(Brit)* *ou* sausage *(US)* ◆ **~ antillais** *small, spicy black pudding* ◆ **faire du ~*** *(= bouder)* to sulk; → **eau** 2 *(gonflable)* ring, tube 3 *(* = doigt)* podgy *ou* fat finger 4 *(* = fille)* fat lump (of a girl)‡ *(péj)*, fatty‡ *(péj)*

boudiné, e /budine/ (ptp de **boudiner**) ADJ 1 *[doigt]* podgy 2 *(= serré)* **~ dans** squeezed into, bursting out of ◆ **~ dans un corset** strapped into *ou* bulging out of a tight-fitting corset ◆ **je me sens ~e dans cette robe** I feel like I can't breathe in this dress

boudiner /budine/ ▸ conjug 1 ◂ VT 1 *[+ fil, soie]* to rove; *[+ fil métallique]* to coil 2 *(* = serrer)* **sa robe la boudine** her dress is much too tight for her

boudoir /budwaʀ/ NM *(= salon)* boudoir; *(= biscuit)* sponge *(Brit)* *ou* lady *(US)* finger

boue /bu/ NF *(gén)* mud; *[de mer, canal]* sludge; *(= dépôt)* sediment ◆ **~s thermales** heated mud ◆ **~s d'épuration** sewage sludge *(NonC)*, silt ◆ **~s activées** *(Méd)* activated sludge *(NonC)* ◆ **traîner qn dans la ~** *(fig)* to drag sb's name through the mud ◆ **couvrir qn de ~** *(fig)* to throw *ou* sling mud at sb

bouée /bwe/ NF *(de signalisation)* buoy; *(d'enfant)* rubber ring ◆ **~ de corps-mort** mooring buoy ◆ **~ de sauvetage** *(lit)* lifebelt; *(fig)* lifeline ◆ **~ sonore** radio buoy

boueux, -euse /bwø, øz/ ADJ muddy; *(Typo)* blurred, smudged NM *(* = éboueur)* dustman *(Brit)*, bin man* *(Brit)*, garbage man *(US)*

bouffant, e /bufɑ̃, ɑ̃t/ ADJ *[manche]* puff(ed) *(épith)*, full; *[cheveux]* bouffant; *[pantalon]* baggy NM *[de jupe, manche]* fullness; *[de cheveux]* fullness, volume; *[de pantalon]* bagginess

bouffarde* /bufaʀd/ NF pipe

bouffe[1] /buf/ ADJ → **opéra**

bouffe[2]‡ /buf/ NF food, grub‡, nosh‡ *(Brit)* ◆ **il ne pense qu'à la ~** he only ever thinks of his stomach, all he ever thinks about is food ◆ **faire la ~** to do the cooking, to get the grub ready‡ ◆ **ils font de la bonne ~ dans ce resto** they do good food in that restaurant ◆ **on se téléphone et on se fait une ~** I'll give you a ring and we'll meet up for a bite* (to eat)

bouffée /bufe/ NF *[de parfum]* whiff; *[de pipe, cigarette]* puff, draw, drag*; *[de colère]* outburst; *[d'orgueil]* fit ◆ **~ d'air** *ou* **de vent** puff *ou* breath *ou* gust of wind ◆ **une ~ d'air frais** *ou* **pur** *(lit, fig)* a breath of fresh air ◆ **~ de chaleur** *(Méd)* hot flush *(Brit)* *ou* flash *(US)*; *(gén)* gust *ou* blast of hot air ◆ **~ délirante** *(Psych)* delirious episode ◆ **par ~s** in gusts; → **oxygène**

bouffer[1] /bufe/ ▸ conjug 1 ◂ VI *[cheveux]* to be full, to have volume ◆ **faire ~ une jupe/une manche** to make a skirt fuller/a sleeve puff out ◆ **faire ~ ses cheveux** to add volume *ou* fullness to one's hair

bouffer[2]‡ /bufe/ ▸ conjug 1 ◂ VT 1 *(gén)* to eat; *(= engloutir)* to gobble up*, to wolf down ◆ **cette voiture bouffe de l'essence** this car really drinks petrol *(Brit)* *ou* guzzles gas *(US)* ◆ **se ~ le nez** *(constamment)* to be always at each other's throat(s); *(ponctuellement)* to have a go at one another*, to scratch each other's eyes out* ◆ **~ du curé** to be violently anticlerical ◆ **je l'aurais bouffé !** I could have murdered him! ◆ **j'ai cru qu'elle allait le ~** I thought she was going to eat him alive ◆ **on s'est fait ~**‡ *(= vaincre)* we got a real hammering* ◆ **j'en ai bouffé des polars cet été*** I read loads* of detective novels over the summer

2 *(emploi absolu)* to eat ◆ **on bouffe mal ici** the food *ou* grub* *(Brit)* here isn't up to much ◆ **on a bien bouffé ici** the food was great* here

3 *(* = accaparer)* **il ne faut pas se laisser ~ par ses enfants/son travail** you shouldn't let your children/work eat up *ou* take up all your time (and energy) ◆ **ça me bouffe tout mon temps** it eats up *ou* takes up all my time

bouffetance‡ /buftɑ̃s/ NF ⇒ **bouffe**[2]

bouffeur, -euse‡ /bufœʀ, øz/ NM,F (greedy) pig*, greedy guts* *(Brit)*

bouffi, e /bufi/ (ptp de **bouffir**) ADJ *[visage]* puffed up, bloated; *[yeux]* swollen, puffy; *(fig)* swollen, puffed up *(de* with); ◆ **(hareng) ~** bloater ◆ **tu l'as dit ~ !*** *(hum)* you said it!

bouffir /bufiʀ/ ▸ conjug 2 ◂ VT to puff up VI to become bloated, to puff up

bouffissure /bufisyʀ/ NF puffiness *(NonC)*, bloatedness *(NonC)*, puffy swelling

bouffon, -onne /bufɔ̃, ɔn/ ADJ farcical, comical NM *(= pitre)* buffoon, clown; *(Hist)* jester; *(* = imbécile)* fool ◆ **le ~ du roi** the court jester

bouffonnerie /bufɔnʀi/ NF 1 *[de personne]* clownishness; *[de situation]* drollery 2 ◆ **~s** *(= comportement)* antics, buffoonery; *(= paroles)* jesting ◆ **faire des ~s** to clown around, to play the fool

bougainvillée /bugɛ̃vile/ NF, **bougainvillier** /bugɛ̃vilje/ NM bougainvillea

bouge /buʒ/ NM (= *taudis*) hovel, dump*; (= *bar louche*) low dive*

bougé /buʒe/ NM (*Photo*) (*dû au photographe*) camera shake; (*dû au sujet*) blur

bougeoir /buʒwaʀ/ NM (*bas*) candle-holder; (*haut*) candlestick

bougeotte* /buʒɔt/ NF ◆ **avoir la ~** (= *voyager*) to be always on the move; (= *remuer*) to fidget, to have the fidgets*, to have ants in one's pants*

bouger /buʒe/ ▸ conjug 3 ◂ VI 1 (= *remuer*) to move; (= *se révolter*) to be restless ◆ **ne bouge pas** keep still, don't move *ou* budge ◆ **il n'a pas bougé (de chez lui)** he stayed in *ou* at home ◆ **la terre a bougé** (*tremblement de terre*) the ground shook ◆ **un métier où l'on bouge** an active job, a job where you are always on the move ◆ **quand la police l'a arrêté, personne n'a bougé** (*fig*) when the police arrested him no-one lifted a finger (to help)
2 (= *changer*) to change ◆ **les prix n'ont pas bougé** prices have stayed put* *ou* the same ◆ **ça ne bouge pas beaucoup dans ce service** nothing much ever changes in this department ◆ **ce tissu ne bouge pas** (*gén*) this material wears *ou* will wear well; (*en dimensions*) this material neither shrinks nor goes out of shape ◆ **les couleurs ne bougeront pas** the colours won't fade ◆ **ses idées n'ont pas bougé** his ideas haven't altered, he hasn't changed his ideas
3 (* = *être actif*) [*personne*] to get out and about ◆ **secteur qui bouge** fast-moving sector ◆ **c'est une ville qui bouge** it's a very lively town, there's a lot happening in this town
VT * [+ *objet*] to move, to shift* ◆ **il n'a pas bougé le petit doigt** he didn't lift a finger (to help)
VPR **se bouger** * 1 (= *se déplacer*) to move ◆ **bouge-toi de là !** shift over!*, shift out of the way!*, scoot over!* (*US*)
2 (= *faire un effort*) to do something ◆ **je m'ennuie – alors bouge-toi un peu !** I'm bored – then do something about it! ◆ **si tu veux le contrat, il faut que tu te bouges** if you want the contract, you'd better get moving *ou* get a move on* ◆ **elle ne s'est pas beaucoup bougée pour m'aider** she didn't go out of her way to help me

bougie /buʒi/ NF 1 (= *chandelle*) candle ◆ **~ chauffe-plats** tea light 2 [*de moteur*] spark(ing) plug, plug ◆ **ampoule de 40 ~s** † 40 candle-power bulb 3 († * = *visage*) face, dial* ◆ **faire une drôle de ~** to make *ou* pull (*Brit*) a face

bougna(t) †* /buɲa/ NM (= *charbonnier*) coalman; (= *marchand de charbon*) coal merchant (*who also runs a small café*)

bougnoul(e) ** /buɲul/ NMF (*injurieux*) (= *Arabe*) Arab

bougon, -onne /bugɔ̃, ɔn/ ADJ grumpy, grouchy* NM,F grumbler, grouch*

bougonnement /bugɔnmɑ̃/ NM grumbling, grouching*

bougonner /bugɔne/ ▸ conjug 1 ◂ VI to grouch* (to o.s.), to grumble VT to mutter, to mumble

bougre* /bugʀ/ NM (= *type*) guy*, fellow*, chap* (*Brit*); (= *enfant*) (little) rascal ◆ **bon ~** good sort* *ou* chap* ◆ **pauvre ~** poor devil* *ou* blighter* ◆ **ce ~ d'homme** that confounded man ◆ **~ d'idiot !** *ou* **d'animal !** stupid *ou* confounded idiot!*, silly blighter!* (*Brit*) ◆ **ce n'est pas un mauvais ~** he's not a bad guy* ◆ **il le savait, le ~ !** the so-and-so knew it! EXCL good Lord!*, strewth!* (*Brit*), I'll be darned!* (*US*)

bougrement* /bugʀəmɑ̃/ ADV (*hum*) terribly ◆ **nous en avons ~ besoin** we need it terribly

bougresse* /bugʀɛs/ NF woman; (*péj*) hussy, bitch**

bouiboui*, boui-boui* (pl **bouis-bouis**) /bwibwi/ NM (*gén*) unpretentious (little) restaurant; (*péj*) greasy spoon*

bouif †* /bwif/ NM cobbler

bouillabaisse /bujabɛs/ NF bouillabaisse, fish soup

bouillant, e /bujɑ̃, ɑ̃t/ ADJ (= *brûlant*) [*boisson*] boiling (hot), scalding; (= *qui bout*) [*eau, huile*] boiling; [*tempérament*] fiery; [*personne*] (= *emporté*) fiery-natured, hotheaded; (= *fiévreux*) boiling (hot)* ◆ **~ de colère** seething *ou* boiling with anger

bouillasse* /bujas/ NF (= *gadoue*) muck

bouille* /buj/ NF (= *visage*) face, mug* (*péj*) ◆ **avoir une bonne ~** to have a cheerful friendly face

bouilleur /bujœʀ/ NM (= *distillateur*) distiller ◆ **~ de cru** home distiller ◆ **~ de cru clandestin** moonshiner

bouilli, e[1] /buji/ (ptp de **bouillir**) ADJ boiled NM boiled meat ◆ **~ de bœuf** *beef stew*

bouillie[2] /buji/ NF [*de bébé*] baby's cereal; [*de vieillard*] gruel, porridge ◆ **réduire en ~** [+ *légumes, fruits*] to reduce to a pulp; [+ *adversaire*] to beat to a pulp ◆ **~ bordelaise** Bordeaux mixture ◆ **c'est de la ~ pour les chats** (*fig*) it's gibberish* ◆ **il a été réduit en ~** [*adversaire*] he was beaten to a pulp ◆ **sa voiture a été réduite en ~** his car was smashed to pieces

bouillir /bujiʀ/ ▸ conjug 15 ◂ VI 1 (*lit*) to boil, to be boiling ◆ **commencer à ~** to reach boiling point, to be nearly boiling ◆ **l'eau bout** the water is boiling ◆ **l'eau ne bout plus** the water has stopped boiling, the water has gone *ou* is off the boil (*Brit*) ◆ **~ à gros bouillons** to boil fast
◆ **faire bouillir** ◆ **faire ~ de l'eau** to boil water, to bring water to the boil ◆ **faire ~ du linge/des poireaux** to boil clothes/leeks ◆ **faire ~ un biberon** to sterilize a (baby's) bottle by boiling ◆ **avoir de quoi faire ~ la marmite** (*fig*) to have enough to keep the pot boiling ◆ **c'est elle qui fait ~ la marmite** she's the breadwinner, she's the one who brings home the bacon
2 (*fig*) to boil ◆ **à voir ça, je bous !** seeing that makes my blood boil! ◆ **~ d'impatience** to seethe with impatience ◆ **~ de rage/de haine** to seethe *ou* boil with anger/hatred ◆ **faire ~ qn** to make sb's blood boil
VT [+ *eau, linge*] to boil

bouilloire /bujwaʀ/ NF kettle ◆ **~ électrique** electric kettle; (*haute*) jug kettle

bouillon /bujɔ̃/ NM 1 (= *soupe*) stock, bouillon ◆ **~ de légumes/poulet** vegetable/chicken stock ◆ **prendre** *ou* **boire un ~*** (*en nageant*) to swallow *ou* get a mouthful; (*Fin*) to take a tumble*, to come a cropper* (*Brit*) 2 (= *bouillonnement*) bubble (in boiling liquid) ◆ **au premier ~** as soon as it starts to boil ◆ **couler à gros ~s** to gush out, to come gushing out 3 (*arg Presse*) **~s** unsold copies 4 (*Couture*) puff ◆ **rideau à ~s** Austrian blind
COMP **bouillon cube** stock *ou* bouillon cube
bouillon de culture culture fluid
bouillon gras meat stock
bouillon maigre clear stock
bouillon d'onze heures* poisoned drink, lethal potion

bouillonnant, e /bujɔnɑ̃, ɑ̃t/ ADJ [*liquide chaud*] bubbling; [*torrent*] foaming, frothing ◆ **bain ~** whirlpool bath

bouillonné /bujɔne/ NM (*Couture*) ruffle

bouillonnement /bujɔnmɑ̃/ NM [*de liquide chaud*] bubbling; [*de torrent*] foaming, frothing ◆ **~ d'idées** ferment of ideas

bouillonner /bujɔne/ ▸ conjug 1 ◂ VI [*liquide chaud*] to bubble; [*torrent*] to foam, to froth; [*idées*] to bubble up ◆ **~ de colère** to seethe *ou* boil with anger ◆ **il bouillonne d'idées** his mind is teeming with ideas, he's bubbling with ideas

bouillotte /bujɔt/ NF hot-water bottle

boulange* /bulɑ̃ʒ/ NF bakery trade ◆ **être dans la ~** to be a baker (by trade)

boulanger /bulɑ̃ʒe/ NM baker

boulangère /bulɑ̃ʒɛʀ/ NF (woman) baker; (= *épouse*) baker's wife; → **pomme**

boulangerie /bulɑ̃ʒʀi/ NF (= *magasin*) baker's (shop), bakery; (= *commerce*) bakery trade ◆ **~-pâtisserie** bread and pastry shop

boulangisme /bulɑ̃ʒism/ NM *right-wing movement led by General Boulanger, who staged an abortive coup d'État in 1889*

boulangiste /bulɑ̃ʒist/ ADJ, NMF Boulangist; → **boulangisme**

boule /bul/ NF 1 (*Billard, Croquet*) ball; (*Boules*) bowl; (*Géol*) tor ◆ **jouer aux ~s** to play bowls ◆ **jouer à la ~** (*Casino*) to play (at) boule ◆ **roulé en ~** [*animal*] curled up in a ball; [*paquet*] rolled up in a ball ◆ **petite ~ de poil** (= *animal*) little ball of fluff ◆ **être en ~*** (*fig*) to be in a temper, to be hopping mad* (*Brit*) ◆ **se mettre en ~** [*hérisson*] to roll up into a ball; * [*personne*] to fly off the handle* ◆ **ça me met en ~*** it drives me mad *ou* really gets my goat*
2 (* = *grosseur*) lump ◆ **avoir une ~ dans la gorge** (*fig*) to have a lump in one's throat ◆ **j'ai les ~s*** (= *anxieux*) I've got butterflies* (in my stomach); (= *furieux*) I'm really *ou* hopping mad* (*Brit*) ◆ **ça fout les ~s*** (= *ça angoisse*) it's really scary*, it gives you the creeps*; (= *ça énerve*) it's damn annoying*
3 (* = *tête*) head, nut* ◆ **perdre la ~** to go bonkers* *ou* nuts*, to go off one's rocker* ◆ **coup de ~*** headbutt ◆ **avoir la ~ à zéro** to have a shaven head
COMP **boule de billard** billiard ball ◆ **avoir une ~ de billard** (*fig*) to be as bald as a coot* *ou* an egg*
boule de commande (*Ordin*) trackball
boule de cristal crystal ball ◆ **je ne lis pas dans les ~s de cristal !** I haven't got a crystal ball!, I'm not a clairvoyant!
boule de feu fireball
boule de gomme (*Pharm*) throat pastille; (= *bonbon*) fruit pastille *ou* gum, gumdrop
boules de gui mistletoe berries
boule de loto lotto *ou* lottery ball ◆ **yeux en ~s de loto** big round eyes
boule de neige snowball ◆ **faire ~ de neige** (*fig*) to snowball
boule de pain round loaf
boule puante stink bomb
boule Quiès ® (wax) earplug, (wax) ear stopper

BOULES

This popular French game takes several forms, including « pétanque », which originated in the South of France, and « boule lyonnaise » from Lyons. The idea of the game is to throw steel balls towards a small wooden ball called the « cochonnet », if necessary knocking one's opponent's **boules** out of the way in the process. The winner is the player who finishes closest to the « cochonnet ».

bouleau (pl **bouleaux**) /bulo/ NM (silver) birch

boule-de-neige (pl **boules-de-neige**) /buldənɛʒ/ NF (= *fleur*) guelder-rose; (= *arbre*) snowball tree

bouledogue /buldɔg/ NM bulldog

bouler /bule/ ▸ conjug 1 ◂ VI to roll along ◆ **elle a boulé dans l'escalier** she fell head over heels down the stairs ◆ **envoyer ~ qn*** to send sb packing*

boulet /bulɛ/ NM 1 [*de forçat*] ball and chain ◆ **~ (de canon)** cannonball ◆ **traîner un ~** (*fig*) to have a millstone around *ou* round (*Brit*) one's neck ◆ **c'est un (véritable) ~ pour ses parents** he's a millstone around *ou* round (*Brit*) his parents' neck ◆ **arriver comme un ~ de canon** to come bursting in *ou* crashing in ◆ **tirer à ~s rouges sur qn** to lay into sb tooth and nail 2 [*de charbon*] (coal) nut 3 [*d'animal*] fetlock

boulette /bulɛt/ NF 1 [*de papier*] pellet; (*Culin*) meatball ◆ **~ empoisonnée** lump of poisoned meat 2 (* = *bévue*) blunder ◆ **faire une ~** to make a blunder; (*paroles*) to drop a brick*

boulevard /bulvaʀ/ NM boulevard ◆ **les ~s extérieurs** the outer boulevards of Paris ◆ **les grands ~s** the grand boulevards ◆ **pièce** *ou* **comédie de ~** light comedy; → **périphérique, théâtre**

boulevardier, -ière /bulvaʀdje, jɛʀ/ ADJ ◆ **le comique ~** light comedy (*typical of the théâtre de Boulevard*) NM,F *writer of light comedy for the theatre*

bouleversant, e /bulvɛʀsɑ̃, ɑ̃t/ ADJ very moving

bouleversement /bulvɛʀsəmɑ̃/ NM [*d'habitudes, vie politique*] disruption ◆ **le ~ de son visage** the utter distress on his face, his distraught face ◆ **ce fut un vrai ~** it was a real upheaval

bouleverser /bulvɛʀse/ ▸ conjug 1 ◂ VT 1 (= *émouvoir*) to move deeply; (= *causer un choc à*) to shatter ◆ **bouleversé par l'angoisse/la peur** distraught with anxiety/fear ◆ **la nouvelle les a bouleversés** they were deeply distressed *ou* upset by the news, they were shattered by the news 2 (= *modifier*) [*+ plan, habitude*] to disrupt, to change completely *ou* drastically 3 (= *déranger*) to turn upside down

boulgour /bulguʀ/ NM (*Culin*) bulg(h)ur (wheat)

boulier /bulje/ NM (= *abaque*) abacus; (*Billard*) scoring board

boulimie /bulimi/ NF bulimia, binge-eating syndrome (*US*) ◆ **il fait de la ~*** he's a compulsive eater ◆ **être saisi d'une ~ de lecture/de cinéma** to be seized by a compulsive desire to read/to go the cinema

boulimique /bulimik/ ADJ (*Méd*) bulimic ◆ **une lectrice ~** a voracious reader, a woman with a huge appetite for books NMF (*Méd*) bulimic ◆ **pour les ~s de jazz** for jazz fanatics ◆ **un ~ de** [*+ culture, idées, musique etc*] a person with a huge appetite ford ◆ **un ~ de travail** a workaholic

boulingrin /bulɛ̃gʀɛ̃/ NM lawn

bouliste /bulist/ NMF bowls player

Boulle /bul/ NM INV ◆ **style/commode ~** boul(l)e *ou* buhl style/chest of drawers

boulocher /bulɔʃe/ ▸ conjug 1 ◂ VI [*pull, tissu*] to pill

boulodrome /bulodʀom/ NM area for playing boules

boulon /bulɔ̃/ NM bolt; (*avec son écrou*) nut and bolt ◆ **(res)serrer les ~s** (*fig*) to tighten a few screws

boulonnage /bulɔnaʒ/ NM (= *assemblage*) bolting (on); (= *serrage*) bolting (down)

boulonnais, e /bulɔnɛ, ɛz/ ADJ of *ou* from Boulogne NM,F **Boulonnais(e)** inhabitant *ou* native of Boulogne NM (= *cheval*) *type of draught horse bred in the Boulogne region*

boulonner /bulɔne/ ▸ conjug 1 ◂ VT (= *serrer*) to bolt (down); (= *assembler*) to bolt (on) VI * to work ◆ **~ (dur)** to slog* *ou* slave* away

boulot[1], **-otte** /bulo, ɔt/ ADJ (= *trapu*) plump, tubby*

boulot[2]* /bulo/ NM 1 (= *travail*) work (*NonC*) ◆ **on a du ~** (*gén*) we've got work to do; (= *tâche difficile*) we've got our work cut out for us ◆ **j'ai un ~ fou en ce moment** I'm up to my eyes in work *ou* I'm snowed under with work at the moment* ◆ **ce n'est pas du ~ !** that's not work!, (do you) call that work! ◆ **elle a 4 enfants à élever, quel ~ !** she has 4 children to bring up, that's quite a job! *ou* that's a lot of work! ◆ **il est ~ ~** with him it's just work, work, work* ◆ **faire le ~** to do the work ◆ **ça/elle a fait du bon ~** it's/she's done a good job ◆ **il a repeint la cuisine, t'aurais vu le ~ !** he repainted the kitchen and it was an absolute disaster! ◆ **allez, au ~ !** let's get cracking!*, let's get this show on the road!* ◆ **je suis au ~ depuis 7 heures du matin** I've been at work since 7 o'clock this morning ◆ **aller au ~** to go to work ◆ **se mettre au ~** to get down *ou* knuckle* down to work ◆ **allez, faut retourner au ~ !** come on, back to the grind!*; → **métro, sale**

2 (= *emploi*) job, work (*NonC*) ◆ **il a trouvé du ~** *ou* **un ~** he's found work *ou* a job ◆ **petit ~** casual job ◆ **j'ai fait des petits ~s** I did odd jobs *ou* casual work ◆ **être sans ~** to be out of work *ou* unemployed ◆ **gardien de musée, c'est le bon ~** a job as a museum attendant is a cushy number* ◆ **ils ont fait un super ~** they've done a great job

3 (= *lieu de travail*) work (*NonC*), place of work ◆ **je sors du ~ à 18 h** I finish work at 6 o'clock

boulotter* /bulɔte/ ▸ conjug 1 ◂ VI to eat ◆ **on a bien boulotté** we had a good meal ◆ **qu'est-ce qu'elle boulotte !** you should see what she can put away! VT to eat, to gobble up

boum /bum/ EXCL (*chute*) bang!; (*explosion*) boom!, bang! ◆ **faire ~** (*langage enfantin*) to go bang* ◆ **~ par terre !** whoops a daisy! NM (= *explosion*) bang ◆ **on entendit un grand ~** there was an enormous bang; ◆ **être en plein ~*** to be in full swing, to be going full blast* NF (* = *fête*) party

boumer* /bume/ ▸ conjug 1 ◂ VI ◆ **ça boume** everything's going fine *ou* dandy* (*US*) ◆ **ça boume ?** how's things?* *ou* tricks?*

boumerang /bumʀɑ̃g/ NM ⇒ **boomerang**

bounioul /bunjul/ NM ⇒ **bougnoul(e)**

bouquet[1] /bukɛ/ NM 1 [*de fleurs*] bunch (of flowers); (*soigneusement composé*) bouquet; (*petit*) posy; (* : *Can* = *plante d'ornement*) (house) plant ◆ **~ d'arbres** clump of trees ◆ **faire un ~** to make up a bouquet ◆ **le ~ de la mariée** the bride's bouquet ◆ **~ de persil/thym** bunch of parsley/thyme ◆ **~ garni** (*Culin*) bouquet garni (*bunch of mixed herbs*) 2 [*de feu d'artifice*] finishing *ou* crowning piece (*in a firework display*) ◆ **c'est le ~ !*** (*fig*) that takes the cake* (*Brit*) *ou* the biscuit!* (*US*) 3 [*de vin*] bouquet, nose ◆ **vin qui a du ~** wine which has a good bouquet *ou* nose 4 (*Jur*) [*de viager*] initial payment 5 (*TV*) multichannel package

bouquet[2] /bukɛ/ NM (= *crevette*) prawn

bouquetière /buk(ə)tjɛʀ/ NF flower seller, flower girl

bouquetin /buk(ə)tɛ̃/ NM ibex

bouquin* /bukɛ̃/ NM book

bouquiner* /bukine/ ▸ conjug 1 ◂ VTI to read ◆ **il passe son temps à ~** he always has his nose in a book

bouquiniste /bukinist/ NMF secondhand bookseller (*esp along the Seine in Paris*)

bourbe /buʀb/ NF mire, mud

bourbeux, -euse /buʀbø, øz/ ADJ miry, muddy

bourbier /buʀbje/ NM (quag)mire; (*fig*) (= *situation*) mess; (= *entreprise*) unsavoury *ou* nasty business, quagmire

bourbon /buʀbɔ̃/ NM (= *whisky*) bourbon

bourbonien, -ienne /buʀbɔnjɛ̃, jɛn/ ADJ Bourbon (*épith*) ◆ **nez ~** long aquiline nose

bourdaine /buʀdɛn/ NF alder buckthorn

bourde* /buʀd/ NF (= *gaffe*) blunder, boob*; (= *faute*) slip, mistake ◆ **faire une ~** (= *gaffe*) to boob* (*Brit*), to blunder, to drop a clanger* (*Brit*); (= *faute*) to make a (silly) mistake, to goof up* (*US*)

bourdon[1] /buʀdɔ̃/ NM 1 (= *abeille*) bumblebee ◆ **avoir le ~*** to have the blues*; → **faux**[2] 2 (*Mus*) (= *cloche*) great bell; [*de cornemuse*] bourdon, drone; [*d'orgue*] bourdon

bourdon[2] /buʀdɔ̃/ NM (*Typo*) omission, out

bourdon[3] /buʀdɔ̃/ NM (= *bâton*) pilgrim's staff

bourdonnant, e /buʀdɔnɑ̃, ɑ̃t/ ADJ [*insecte*] buzzing, humming, droning; [*ville*] buzzing with activity ◆ **il avait la tête ~e** *ou* **les oreilles ~es** his ears were buzzing *ou* ringing

bourdonnement /buʀdɔnmɑ̃/ NM [*d'insecte*] buzz(ing) (*NonC*); [*d'abeille*] buzz(ing) (*NonC*), drone (*NonC*); [*de voix*] buzz (*NonC*), hum (*NonC*); [*de moteur*] hum(ming) (*NonC*), drone (*NonC*); [*d'avion*] drone (*NonC*) ◆ **j'ai un ~ dans les oreilles** *ou* **des ~s d'oreilles** my ears are buzzing *ou* ringing

bourdonner /buʀdɔne/ ▸ conjug 1 ◂ VI [*insecte*] to buzz; [*abeille*] to buzz, to drone; [*moteur*] to hum, to drone ◆ **ça bourdonne dans mes oreilles** my ears are buzzing *ou* ringing

bourg /buʀ/ NM (*gén*) market town; (*petit*) village ◆ **au ~, dans le ~** in town, in the village

bourgade /buʀgad/ NF village, (small) town

bourge* /buʀʒ/ ADJ, NMF (abrév de **bourgeois**) (*péj*) bourgeois (*péj*)

bourgeois, e /buʀʒwa, waz/ ADJ 1 (*Sociol*) middle-class 2 (*gén péj* = *conventionnel*) [*culture, préjugé, goûts*] bourgeois, middle-class ◆ **avoir l'esprit ~** to have a conventional outlook ◆ **mener une petite vie ~e** to lead a comfortable middle-class existence 3 (= *cossu*) [*quartier*] middle-class; [*appartement*] plush NM,F 1 (*Sociol*) bourgeois, middle-class person ◆ **grand ~** upper middle-class person ◆ **les ~** (*péj*) the wealthy (classes); → **épater** 2 (*Hist*) (= *citoyen*) burgher; (= *riche roturier*) bourgeois NM (*Can*) head of household, master NF **bourgeoise** ◆ **la** *ou* **ma ~e*** (*hum*) (= *épouse*) the wife*, the missus*

bourgeoisement /buʀʒwazmɑ̃/ ADV [*penser, réagir*] conventionally; [*vivre*] comfortably

bourgeoisie /buʀʒwazi/ NF 1 (*Sociol*) middle class(es), bourgeoisie ◆ **petite ~** lower middle class ◆ **moyenne ~** middle class ◆ **grande ~** upper middle class 2 (*Hist* = *citoyenneté*) bourgeoisie, burgesses

bourgeon /buʀʒɔ̃/ NM (*Bot*) bud; († = *bouton*) pimple, spot (*Brit*) ◆ **~ gustatif** (*Anat*) taste bud

bourgeonnement /buʀʒɔnmɑ̃/ NM (*Bot*) budding; (*Méd*) granulation (*SPÉC*)

bourgeonner /buʀʒɔne/ ▸ conjug 1 ◂ VI (*Bot*) to (come into) bud; (*Méd*) [*plaie*] to granulate (*SPÉC*) ◆ **son visage bourgeonne** (*fig*) he's getting pimples *ou* spots (*Brit*)

bourgmestre /buʀgmɛstʀ/ NM burgomaster

bourgogne /buʀgɔɲ/ NM (= *vin*) burgundy NF **Bourgogne** (= *région*) **la Bourgogne** Burgundy

bourguignon, -onne /buʀgiɲɔ̃, ɔn/ ADJ Burgundian ◆ **un (bœuf) ~** (*Culin*) bœuf bourguignon, beef stewed in red wine NM,F **Bourguignon(ne)** Burgundian

bourlinguer /buʀlɛ̃ge/ ► conjug 1 ◄ VI [1] (= *naviguer*) to sail; (* = *voyager*) to travel around a lot*, to knock about a lot* ◆ **il a bourlingué dans tout l'hémisphère sud** he has travelled all over the southern hemisphere [2] (*Naut = avancer péniblement*) to labour

bourlingueur, -euse* /buʀlɛ̃gœʀ, øz/ NM,F ◆ **c'est un ~** he's a globe-trotter

bourrache /buʀaʃ/ NF borage

bourrade /buʀad/ NF (*du poing*) thump; (*du coude*) dig, prod

bourrage /buʀaʒ/ NM [*de coussin*] stuffing; [*de poêle, pipe*] filling; [*de fusil*] wadding; [*d'imprimante, photocopieur*] paper jam ◆ **il y a un ~ (de papier)** the paper has got stuck *ou* jammed in the machine ◆ **~ de crâne*** (= *propagande*) brainwashing; (= *récits exagérés*) eyewash*, hot air*; (*Scol*) cramming

bourrasque /buʀask/ NF gust of wind, squall ◆ **~ de neige** flurry of snow ◆ **le vent souffle en ~s** the wind is blowing in gusts

bourrasser* /buʀase/ ► conjug 1 ◄ VT (*Can*) to browbeat, to bully

bourratif, -ive /buʀatif, iv/ ADJ (*gén*) filling; (*péj*) stodgy

bourre[1] /buʀ/ NF [1] [*de coussin*] stuffing; (*en poils*) hair; (*en laine, coton*) wadding, flock; [*de bourgeon*] down; [*de fusil*] wad [2] (*locutions*) **se tirer la ~**⁑ to jostle for first place ◆ **de première ~*** great*, brilliant* (*Brit*)

◆ **à la bourre**⁑ (= *en retard*) late; (= *pressé*) pushed for time* ◆ **être à la ~ dans son travail**⁑ to be behind with one's work

bourre[2] †⁑ /buʀ/ NM (= *policier*) cop* ◆ **les ~s** the fuzz⁑, the cops*

bourré, e[1] /buʀe/ (ptp de **bourrer**) ADJ [1] (= *plein à craquer*) [*salle, compartiment*] packed, jam-packed*, crammed (*de* with); [*sac*] crammed, stuffed (*de* with); ◆ **portefeuille ~ de billets** wallet stuffed with notes ◆ **devoir ~ de fautes** exercise riddled with mistakes ◆ **il est ~ de tics** he's always twitching ◆ **il est ~ de complexes** he's got loads of hang-ups*, he's really hung-up* ◆ **il est /le film est ~ d'idées** he's/the film is bursting with ideas ◆ **c'est ~ de vitamines** it's packed with vitamins [2] (⁑ = *ivre*) ◆ **~ (comme un coing)** sloshed⁑, plastered⁑

bourreau (pl **bourreaux**) /buʀo/ NM [1] (= *tortionnaire*) torturer [2] (*Hist*) [*de guillotine*] executioner, headsman; [*de pendaison*] executioner, hangman

COMP **bourreau des cœurs** ladykiller

bourreau d'enfants child-batterer, baby-batterer

bourreau de travail glutton for work*, workaholic*

bourrée[2] /buʀe/ NF (*Mus*) bourrée

bourrelé, e /buʀ(ə)le/ ADJ (*littér*) ◆ **~ de remords** stricken with *ou* racked by remorse ◆ **~ de soupçons** racked by suspicion

bourrelet /buʀlɛ/ NM [1] (*gén*) roll; [*de porte, fenêtre*] draught excluder (*Brit*), weather strip (*US*) [2] ◆ **~ (de chair)** fold *ou* roll of flesh ◆ **~ (de graisse)** (*gén*) roll of fat; (*à la taille*) spare tyre* (*Brit*) *ou* tire* (*US*)

bourrelier /buʀəlje/ NM saddler

bourrellerie /buʀɛlʀi/ NF saddlery

bourrer /buʀe/ ► conjug 1 ◄ VT [1] (= *remplir*) [*+ coussin*] to stuff; [*+ pipe, poêle*] to fill; [*+ valise*] to stuff *ou* cram full ◆ **~ une dissertation de citations** to cram an essay with quotations ◆ **~ un sac de papiers** to stuff *ou* cram papers into a bag ◆ **~ les urnes** (*Pol*) to rig the ballot

[2] ◆ **~ qn de nourriture** to stuff sb with food ◆ **ne te bourre pas de gâteaux** don't stuff* yourself *ou* fill yourself up* with cakes ◆ **les frites, ça bourre !** chips really fill you up!

[3] (*locutions*) **~ le crâne à qn*** (= *endoctriner*) to stuff* sb's head full of ideas, to brainwash sb; (= *en faire accroire*) to feed sb a lot of eyewash*; (*Scol*) to cram sb ◆ **~ qn de coups** to beat sb up ◆ **se faire ~ la gueule**⁑ to get one's head bashed in⁑ ◆ **se ~ la gueule**⁑ (= *se battre*) to beat one another up⁑; (= *se soûler*) to get sloshed⁑ *ou* plastered⁑ *ou* pissed⁑ (*Brit*)

VI [1] (⁑ = *se dépêcher*) (*en voiture, en moto*) to go flat out*, to tear along*, to belt along*; (*au travail*) to go *ou* work flat out*

[2] [*papier*] to jam

bourriche /buʀiʃ/ NF [*d'huîtres*] hamper, basket; (*Pêche*) keep-net

bourrichon* /buʀiʃɔ̃/ NM ◆ **se monter le ~** to get ideas ◆ **monter le ~ à qn** to put ideas into sb's head (*contre* against)

bourricot /buʀiko/ NM (small) donkey

bourrin* /buʀɛ̃/ NM horse, nag*

bourrique /buʀik/ NF [1] (= *âne*) donkey, ass; (= *ânesse*) she-ass [2] * (= *imbécile*) ass, blockhead*; (= *têtu*) pigheaded* person ◆ **faire tourner qn en ~** to drive sb to distraction *ou* up the wall*; → **soûl, têtu**

bourriquet /buʀikɛ/ NM ⇒ **bourricot**

bourru, e /buʀy/ ADJ [*personne, air*] surly; [*voix*] gruff

bourrure /buʀyʀ/ NF (*Can*) stuffing (*in saddle etc*)

bourse /buʀs/ NF [1] (= *porte-monnaie*) purse ◆ **la ~ ou la vie !** your money or your life!, stand and deliver! ◆ **sans ~ délier** without spending a penny ◆ **avoir la ~ dégarnie** to be hard-up* ◆ **avoir la ~ bien garnie** (*ponctuellement*) to be flush*; (*en permanence*) to have well-lined pockets, to have a well-lined purse ◆ **ils font ~ commune** they share expenses ◆ **il nous a ouvert sa ~** he lent us some money ◆ **c'est trop cher pour ma ~** I can't afford it, it's more than I can afford; → **cordon, portée**[2]

[2] (= *marché boursier*) **la Bourse** the Stock Exchange ◆ **la Bourse de Paris** the Bourse, the Paris Stock Exchange ◆ **la Bourse de Londres/de New York** the London/New York Stock Exchange ◆ **la Bourse monte/descend** the market is going up/down ◆ **valoir tant en Bourse** to be worth so much on the Stock Exchange *ou* Market ◆ **jouer à la Bourse** to speculate *ou* gamble on the Stock Exchange *ou* Market; → **coter**

[3] [*d'objets d'occasion*] sale ◆ **~ aux livres** second-hand book sale

[4] ◆ **~ (d'études)** (*Scol*) grant; (*obtenue par concours*) scholarship

[5] (*Anat*) **~ séreuse** bursa ◆ **~s** scrotum

COMP **Bourse du** *ou* **de commerce** produce exchange, commodity market

Bourse de l'emploi ≃ Jobcentre

Bourse des marchandises ⇒ **Bourse du commerce**

Bourse du travail *trades union centre*, ≃ trades council (*Brit*)

Bourse des valeurs Stock Market, Stock *ou* Securities Exchange

boursicotage /buʀsikɔtaʒ/ NM dabbling on the stock exchange

boursicoter /buʀsikɔte/ ► conjug 1 ◄ VI to dabble on the stock exchange

boursicoteur, -euse /buʀsikɔtœʀ, øz/, **boursicotier, -ière** /buʀsikɔtje, jɛʀ/ NM,F small-time speculator, small investor

boursier, -ière /buʀsje, jɛʀ/ ADJ [1] (*Scol, Univ*) **étudiant ~** grant holder; (*par concours*) scholarship holder [2] (*Bourse*) stock-market (*épith*), stock-exchange (*épith*) ◆ **marché ~** stock market ◆ **indice ~** stock market index ◆ **valeurs boursières** stocks and shares NM,F [1] (= *étudiant*) grant holder; (*par concours*) scholarship holder [2] (= *agent de change*) stockbroker; (= *opérateur*) stock exchange operator

boursouflage /buʀsuflaʒ/ NM [*de visage*] swelling, puffing-up; [*de style*] turgidity

boursouflé, e /buʀsufle/ (ptp de **boursoufler**) ADJ [*visage*] puffy, swollen, bloated; [*main*] swollen; [*surface peinte*] blistered; (*fig*) [*style, discours*] bombastic, turgid

boursouflement /buʀsufləmɑ̃/ NM ⇒ **boursouflage**

boursoufler /buʀsufle/ ► conjug 1 ◄ VT to puff up, to bloat VPR **se boursoufler** [*peinture*] to blister; [*visage, main*] to swell (up)

boursouflure /buʀsuflyʀ/ NF [*de visage*] puffiness; [*de style*] turgidity, pomposity; (= *cloque*) blister; (= *enflure*) swelling

bouscaud, e /busko, od/ ADJ (*Can*) thickset

bouscueil /buskœj/ NM (*Can*) break-up of ice (in rivers and lakes)

bousculade /buskylad/ NF (= *remous*) hustle, jostle, crush; (= *hâte*) rush, scramble ◆ **dans la ~** in the rush *ou* crush ◆ **pas de ~ !** don't push! ◆ **ça a été la ~ ce week-end** it was a real rush *ou* scramble this weekend

bousculer /buskyle/ ► conjug 1 ◄ VT [1] [*+ personne*] (= *pousser*) to jostle, to shove; (= *heurter*) to bump into *ou* against, to knock into *ou* against; (= *presser*) to rush, to hurry (up); (*Mil*) to drive from the field ◆ **je n'aime pas qu'on me bouscule** (*fig*) I don't like to be pressured *ou* rushed ◆ **être (très) bousculé** (*fig*) to be rushed off one's feet

[2] [*+ objet*] (= *heurter*) to knock *ou* bump into; (= *faire tomber*) to knock over; (= *déranger*) to knock about

[3] [*+ idées*] to shake up, to liven up; [*+ traditions*] to shake up; [*+ habitudes*] to upset; [*+ emploi du temps, calendrier*] to upset, to disrupt

VPR **se bousculer** (= *se heurter*) to jostle each other; (* = *se dépêcher*) to get a move on* ◆ **les souvenirs/idées se bousculaient dans sa tête** his head was buzzing with memories/ideas ◆ **on se bouscule pour aller voir ce film** there's a mad rush on* to see the film ◆ **ça se bouscule au portillon*** (= *bégayer*) he can't get his words out fast enough ◆ **les gens ne se bousculent pas (au portillon)*** (= *s'enthousiasmer*) people aren't exactly queuing up* (*Brit*) *ou* lining up (*US*)

bouse /buz/ NF ◆ **de la ~ (de vache)** (cow *ou* cattle) dung (*NonC*) ◆ **une ~ (de vache)** a cow pat

bouseux⁑ /buzø/ NM (*péj*) bumpkin, yokel

bousier /buzje/ NM dung-beetle

bousillage* /buzijaʒ/ NM [1] [*de travail*] botching, bungling [2] [*d'appareil, moteur*] wrecking, busting up⁑; [*de voiture, avion*] smashing up*

bousiller* /buzije/ ► conjug 1 ◄ VT [1] (= *bâcler*) [*+ travail*] to botch, to bungle, to louse up⁑ [2] (= *détériorer*) [*+ appareil, moteur*] to bust up⁑, to wreck; [*+ voiture, avion*] to smash up*, to total* (*US*) ◆ **ça a bousillé sa vie/carrière** it wrecked his life/career ◆ **se ~ la santé** to ruin one's health ◆ **on est en train de ~ les forêts** we're trashing* the forests [3] (= *tuer*) [*+ personne*] to bump off⁑, to do in⁑ ◆ **se faire ~** to get done in⁑ *ou* bumped off⁑

bousilleur, -euse* /buzijœʀ, øz/ NM,F bungler, botcher

boussole /busɔl/ NF compass ◆ **perdre la ~*** (*fig*) to go off one's head, to go bonkers*

boustifaille⁑ /bustifaj/ NF grub⁑, nosh⁑ (*Brit*)

bout /bu/

1 NOM MASCULIN 2 COMPOSÉS

1 - NOM MASCULIN

1 = extrémité, fin [de ficelle, planche, rue, table] end; [de nez, langue, oreille] tip; [de canne] end, tip ◆ ~ **du doigt** fingertip ◆ ~ **du sein** nipple ◆ **à ~ rond/carré** round-/square-ended ◆ **cigarette à ~ de liège** cork-tipped cigarette ◆ **à l'autre ~ du couloir** at the other *ou* far end of the corridor ◆ **commençons par un ~ et nous verrons** let's get started *ou* make a start and then we'll see ◆ **cette vieille voiture s'en va par tous les ~s*** this old car is falling apart ◆ **on ne sait pas par quel ~ le prendre** you just don't know how to tackle *ou* handle him ◆ **prendre qch par le bon ~** to approach *ou* handle sth the right way ◆ **tenir le bon ~*** *(fig) (= être sur la bonne voie)* to be on the right track; *(= avoir fait le plus gros du travail)* to be getting near the end of one's work, to be past the worst *(hum)* ◆ **on n'en voit pas le ~** there doesn't seem to be any end to it; → **monde, nez, tunnel**

2 = morceau [de ficelle, pain, papier] piece, bit ◆ **un ~ de terrain** a patch *ou* plot of land ◆ **un ~ de pelouse/de ciel bleu** a patch of lawn/of blue sky ◆ **un petit ~ d'homme*** a (mere) scrap of a man ◆ **un petit ~ de femme** a slip of a woman ◆ **un (petit) ~ de chou*** *ou* **de zan*** a little kid* *ou* nipper* *(Brit)* ◆ **bonjour, ~ de chou** hello, poppet* *(Brit) ou* my little love ◆ **on a fait un ~ de chemin ensemble** *(lit)* we walked part of the way together; *(fig) (en couple)* we were together for a while; *(au travail)* we worked together for a while ◆ **jusqu'à Paris, cela fait un (bon) ~ de chemin** *ou* **un ~*** it's some distance *ou* quite a long way to Paris ◆ **il m'a fait un ~ de conduite** he went part of the way with me ◆ **il est resté un bon ~ de temps** he stayed a while *ou* quite some time ◆ **avoir un ~ de rôle dans une pièce** to have a small *ou* bit part *ou* walk-on part in a play ◆ **mettre les ~s*** to hop it* *(Brit)*, to skedaddle*, to scarper* *(Brit)*; → **connaître**

3 Naut = cordage /but/ (length of) rope

4 expressions figées

◆ **à bout** ◆ **être à ~** *(= fatigué)* to be exhausted, to be all in*; *(= en colère)* to have had enough, to be at the end of one's patience ◆ **ma patience est à ~** I'm at the end of my patience ◆ **pousser qn à ~** to push sb to the limit (of his patience)

◆ **à bout de** ◆ **à ~ de bras** *[tenir, porter] (lit)* at arm's length ◆ **nous avons porté le club à ~ de bras pendant 2 ans** *(fig)* we struggled to keep the club going for 2 years ◆ **être à ~ d'arguments** to have run out of arguments ◆ **être à ~ de force(s)** to have no strength left ◆ **à ~ de forces, il s'écroula** worn out *ou* exhausted, he collapsed ◆ **être à ~ de nerfs** to be at the end of one's tether, to be just about at breaking point ◆ **à ~ de souffle** *(lit)* breathless, out of breath *(attrib)*; *(fig) [machine, gouvernement]* on its last legs* ◆ **le moteur est à ~ de souffle** the engine is about to give up the ghost ◆ **venir à ~ de** *[+ travail]* to get through, to get to the end of; *[+ adversaire]* to get the better of, to overcome; *[+ repas, gâteau]* to get through ◆ **je n'en viendrai jamais à ~** I'll never manage it, I'll never get through it; → **course**

◆ **à bout portant, à bout touchant** † *[tirer, tuer]* point-blank, at point-blank range

◆ **à tout bout de champ** all the time ◆ **il m'interrompait à tout ~ de champ** he interrupted me at every opportunity, he kept on interrupting me ◆ **elle se regarde dans la glace à tout ~ de champ** she's forever looking at herself in the mirror

◆ **au bout de** *(dans l'espace)* ◆ **au ~ de la rue** at the end of the street ◆ **au ~ du jardin** at the bottom *ou* end of the garden ◆ **la poste est tout au ~ du village** the post office is at the far end of the village; *(dans le temps)* after ◆ **au ~ d'un mois** after a month, a month later ◆ **au ~ d'un moment** after a while ◆ **il est parti au ~ de trois minutes** he left after three minutes ◆ **au ~ du compte** in the last analysis, all things considered ◆ **il n'est pas au ~ de ses peines** he's not out of the wood *(Brit) ou* woods *(US)* yet, his troubles still aren't over ◆ **être au ~ du rouleau*** *(= être épuisé)* to be exhausted; *(= être sans ressources)* to be running short (of money); *(= être près de la mort)* to have come to the end of the road

◆ **bout à bout** end to end ◆ **mettre des planches/tuyaux ~ à ~** to lay planks/pipes end to end ◆ **il a reconstitué l'histoire en mettant ~ à ~ tous les indices** he reconstructed what had happened by piecing all the clues *ou* evidence together

◆ **de bout en bout** ◆ **lire un livre de ~ en ~** to read a book from cover to cover *ou* right through *ou* from start to finish ◆ **parcourir une rue de ~ en ~** to go from one end of a street to the other

◆ **du bout de** ◆ **manger du ~ des dents** to pick *ou* nibble at one's food ◆ **du ~ des doigts** *[effleurer, pianoter]* with one's fingertips ◆ **le public a applaudi du ~ des doigts** *(fig)* the audience clapped half-heartedly ◆ **du ~ des lèvres** *[accepter, approuver]* reluctantly, half-heartedly ◆ **il écarta les feuilles mortes du ~ du pied** he pushed aside the dead leaves with his toe

◆ **d'un bout à l'autre** ◆ **il a traversé le pays/continent d'un ~ à l'autre** he travelled the length and breadth of the country/continent ◆ **je l'ai lu d'un ~ à l'autre sans m'arrêter** I read it right through *ou* from cover to cover without stopping ◆ **ce film est passionnant d'un ~ à l'autre** the film is compelling from start to finish *ou* right through ◆ **d'un ~ à l'autre de la ville** from one end of the town to the other ◆ **d'un ~ à l'autre de ses œuvres** throughout *ou* all through his works ◆ **d'un ~ à l'autre de l'année** all year round ◆ **d'un ~ à l'autre du voyage** from the beginning of the journey to the end, throughout *ou* right through the journey

◆ **en bout de** at the end *ou* bottom of ◆ **assis en ~ de table** sitting at the end *ou* bottom *ou* foot of the table; → **chaîne, course**

◆ **jusqu'au bout** ◆ **nous sommes restés jusqu'au ~** we stayed right to the end ◆ **ce travail lui déplaît mais il ira jusqu'au ~** he doesn't like this job but he'll see it through ◆ **ils ont combattu jusqu'au ~** they fought to the bitter end ◆ **rebelle jusqu'au ~** rebellious to the end *ou* the last

◆ **jusqu'au bout de** ◆ **il faut aller jusqu'au ~ de ce qu'on entreprend** if you take something on you must see it through (to the end) ◆ **aller jusqu'au ~ de ses idées** to follow (one's ideas) through ◆ **il est aristocrate/russe jusqu'au ~ des ongles** he's an aristocrat/he's Russian through and through ◆ **elle est professionnelle jusqu'au ~ des ongles** she's a professional to her fingertips

◆ **sur le bout de** ◆ **j'ai son nom sur le ~ de la langue** his name is on the tip of my tongue ◆ **il sait sa leçon sur le ~ du doigt** *ou* **des doigts** he knows his lesson backwards *ou* off pat* *(Brit)* ◆ **elle connaît la question sur le ~ des doigts** she knows the subject inside out

2 - COMPOSÉS

bout de l'an *(Rel)* memorial service *(held on the first anniversary of a person's death)*
bout d'essai *(Ciné)* screen test, test film ◆ **tourner un ~ d'essai** to do a screen test
bout filtre filter tip ◆ **cigarettes (à) ~ filtre** filter tip cigarettes, tipped cigarettes

boutade /butad/ NF 1 *(= trait d'esprit)* witticism; *(= plaisanterie)* joke ◆ **il a répondu par une ~** he made a witty reply ◆ **il s'en est sorti par une ~** he joked his way out of it ◆ **elle l'a dit par ~** she said it in jest ◆ **ce n'est pas une ~** it's not a joke, I'm not joking ◆ **c'était une ~ !** it was a joke! 2 *(† = caprice)* whim ◆ **par ~** as the whim takes him *(ou her etc)*, fits and starts

bout-dehors (pl **bouts-dehors**) /budəɔʀ/ NM *(Naut)* boom

boute-en-train /butɑ̃tʀɛ̃/ NM INV *(= personne)* live wire* ◆ **c'était le ~ de la soirée** he was the life and soul of the party ◆ **on ne peut pas dire que c'est un ~** he's not exactly the life and soul of the party

boutefeu /butfø/ NM *(Hist)* linstock; *(† = personne)* firebrand

bouteille /butɛj/ NF 1 *(= récipient)* bottle; *(= contenu)* bottle(ful) ◆ **boire à la ~** to drink (straight) from the bottle ◆ **~ d'air comprimé/de butane/de gaz** cylinder of compressed air/of butane gas/of gas ◆ **~ de Leyde** Leyden jar ◆ **~ d'un litre/de 2 litres** litre/2-litre bottle ◆ **~ de vin** *(= récipient)* wine bottle; *(= contenu)* bottle of wine ◆ **bière en ~** bottled beer ◆ **mettre du vin en ~s** to bottle wine ◆ **mise en ~** bottling ◆ **vin qui a 10 ans de ~** wine that has been in (the) bottle for 10 years ◆ **boire une (bonne) ~** to drink *ou* have a bottle of (good) wine ◆ **aimer la ~** to be fond of the bottle, to like one's tipple*
2 *(locutions)* **prendre de la ~*** to be getting on in years, to be getting long in the tooth* ◆ **il a de la ~*** *(dans son métier)* he's been around a long time ◆ **c'est la ~ à l'encre** you can't make head nor tail of it ◆ **jeter une ~ à la mer** *(lit)* to throw a bottle (with a message) in the sea; *(fig)* send out an SOS

bouter /bute/ ► conjug 1 ◄ VT *(littér ou †)* to drive, to push *(hors de* out of)

bouteur /butœʀ/ NM bulldozer ◆ **~ biais** angledozer

boutique /butik/ NF 1 *(= magasin)* shop, store; *[de grand couturier]* boutique ◆ **~ en plein vent** open-air stall ◆ **robe/tailleur ~** designer dress/suit; → **fermer, parler** 2 *(* = lieu de travail)* place*, hole* ◆ **quelle sale ~ !** what a dump!*

boutiquier, -ière /butikje, jɛʀ/ NM,F shopkeeper *(Brit)*, storekeeper *(US)*

boutoir /butwaʀ/ NM *[de sanglier]* snout ◆ **coup de ~** *(Mil, Sport, gén)* thrust; *[de vent, vagues]* battering *(NonC)*

bouton /butɔ̃/ NM 1 *(Couture)* button 2 *(= mécanisme) (Élec)* switch; *[de porte, radio]* knob; *[de sonnette]* (push-)button 3 *(Bot)* bud ◆ **en ~** in bud ◆ **~ de rose** rosebud 4 *(Méd)* pimple, spot *(Brit)*, zit* *(surtout US)* ◆ **~ d'acné** pimple, spot *(Brit) (caused by acne)* ◆ **avoir des ~s** to have pimples *ou* spots *(Brit)*, to have a pimply face ◆ **ça me donne des ~s*** *(fig)* it makes my skin crawl

COMP **bouton de chemise** shirt button
bouton de col collar stud
bouton de culotte trouser *ou* pant *(US)* button
bouton de fièvre cold sore, fever blister *ou* sore
bouton de guêtre gaiter button ◆ **il ne manque pas un ~ de guêtre** *(fig)* everything is in apple-pie order
bouton de manchette cufflink

bouton-d'or (pl **boutons-d'or**) /butɔ̃dɔʀ/ NM *(= fleur)* buttercup; *(= couleur)* buttercup yellow

boutonnage /butɔnaʒ/ NM buttoning(-up) ◆ **avec ~ à droite/à gauche** right/left buttoning *(épith)*, which buttons on the right/left ◆ **manteau à double ~** double-buttoning coat

boutonner /butɔne/ ► conjug 1 ◄ VT 1 *[+ vêtement]* to button *ou* fasten (up) 2 *(Escrime)* to button VPR **se boutonner** *[vêtement]* to button (up); *[personne]* to button (up) one's coat (*ou* trousers *etc*)

boutonneux, -euse /butɔnø, øz/ ADJ pimply, spotty *(Brit)*

boutonnière /butɔnjɛʀ/ NF *(Couture)* buttonhole; (= *bouquet*) buttonhole *(Brit)*, boutonniere *(US)* ◆ **avoir une fleur à la ~** to wear a flower in one's buttonhole, to wear a buttonhole *(Brit)* *ou* boutonniere *(US)* ◆ **porter une décoration à la ~** to wear a decoration on one's lapel ◆ **faire une ~ (à qn)** (= *incision*) to make a small incision (in sb's abdomen)

bouton-poussoir (pl **boutons-poussoirs**) /butɔ̃puswaʀ/ NM push button

bouton-pression (pl **boutons-pression**) /butɔ̃pʀesjɔ̃/ NM snap fastener, press stud *(Brit)*

boutre /butʀ/ NM dhow

bout-rimé (pl **bouts-rimés**) /buʀime/ NM *(Littérat)* (= *poème*) poem in set rhymes ◆ **bouts-rimés** (= *fins de vers*) rhyme endings, bouts rimés

bouturage /butyʀaʒ/ NM taking (of) cuttings, propagation (by cuttings)

bouture /butyʀ/ NF cutting ◆ **faire des ~s** to take cuttings

bouturer /butyʀe/ ► conjug 1 ◄ VT to take a cutting from, to propagate (by cuttings) VI to put out suckers

bouvet /buvɛ/ NM *(Menuiserie)* rabbet plane

bouvier /buvje/ NM (= *personne*) herdsman, cattleman; (= *chien*) sheep dog

bouvillon /buvijɔ̃/ NM bullock, steer *(US)*

bouvreuil /buvʀœj/ NM bullfinch

bouzouki /buzuki/ NM bouzouki

bovarysme /bɔvaʀism/ NM bovarism

bovidé /bɔvide/ ADJ M bovid NM bovid ◆ **~s** bovids

bovin, e /bɔvɛ̃, in/ ADJ *(lit, fig)* bovine ◆ **viande ~e** beef NM bovine ◆ **~s** cattle

bowling /buliŋ/ NM (= *jeu*) (tenpin) bowling; (= *salle*) bowling alley

box /bɔks/ NM *[d'hôpital, dortoir]* cubicle; *[d'écurie]* loose box; *[de porcherie]* stall, pen; (= *garage*) lock-up (garage) ◆ **~ des accusés** *(Jur)* dock ◆ **dans le ~ des accusés** *(lit, fig)* in the dock

box(-calf) /bɔks(kalf)/ NM box calf ◆ **sac en ~(-calf)** calfskin bag

boxe /bɔks/ NF boxing ◆ **match de ~** boxing match ◆ **~ anglaise** boxing ◆ **~ américaine** full contact ◆ **~ française** ≈ kick boxing ◆ **~ thaï** Thai boxing ◆ **faire de la ~** to box

boxer[1] /bɔkse/ ► conjug 1 ◄ VI to box, to be a boxer ◆ **~ contre** to box against, to fight VT *(Sport)* to box against, to fight; (* = *frapper*) to thump*, to punch

boxer[2] /bɔksɛʀ/ NM boxer (dog)

boxer[3] /bɔksœʀ/ NM, **boxer-short** (pl **boxer-shorts**) /bɔksœʀʃɔʀt/ NM boxer shorts, boxers

boxeur, -euse /bɔksœʀ, øz/ NM,F boxer

box-office (pl **box-offices**) /bɔksɔfis/ NM box office ◆ **film en tête du ~** box-office success *ou* hit

boxon‡ /bɔksɔ̃/ NM 1 (= *maison close*) brothel, whorehouse* † 2 (= *désordre*) **c'est le ~ !** it's a shambles!

boy /bɔj/ NM (= *serviteur*) (native) servant boy, (house)boy; *(Music-hall)* ≈ male dancer

boyard /bɔjaʀ/ NM *(Hist)* boyar(d)

boyau (pl **boyaux**) /bwajo/ NM 1 (= *intestins*) **~x** *[d'animal]* guts, entrails; * *[de personne]* insides*, guts* ◆ **elle a le ~ de la rigolade*** she's always giggling* ◆ **il a toujours un ~ de vide*** he's always hungry; → **tripe** 2 (= *corde*) **~ (de chat)** (cat)gut 3 (= *passage*) (narrow) passageway; (= *tuyau*) narrow pipe; *(Mil)* communication trench, sap; *(Min)* (narrow) gallery 4 *[de bicyclette]* (racing) tyre, tubeless tyre 5 *(pour saucisse)* casing

boycott /bɔjkɔt/, **boycottage** /bɔjkɔtaʒ/ NM boycotting *(NonC)*, boycott

boycotter /bɔjkɔte/ ► conjug 1 ◄ VT to boycott

boy-scout † (pl **boy(s)-scouts**) /bɔjskut/ NM (boy) scout ◆ **avoir une mentalité de ~*** to have a (rather) naïve *ou* ingenuous outlook

BP /bepe/ (abrév de **boîte postale**) PO Box

BPF (abrév de **bon pour francs**) *amount payable on a cheque*

brabançon, -onne /bʀabɑ̃sɔ̃, ɔn/ ADJ of *ou* from Brabant NM,F **Brabançon(ne)** inhabitant *ou* native of Brabant NM ◆ **(cheval) ~** *type of draught horse bred in the Brabant region* NF **Brabançonne** ◆ **la Brabançonne** the Belgian national anthem

brabant /bʀabɑ̃/ NM 1 *(Agr)* **double ~** swivel plough *(Brit)* *ou* plow *(US)* 2 *(Géog)* **le Brabant** Brabant

bracelet /bʀaslɛ/ NM 1 *[de poignet]* bracelet; *[de bras]* bangle; *[de cheville]* ankle bracelet, bangle; *[de montre]* strap, bracelet; *(d'identité)* identity bracelet, name tag 2 (= *élastique*) rubber band 3 *(arg Police)* **~s** (= *menottes*) handcuffs ◆ **on lui a passé les ~s** they handcuffed him COMP **bracelet de force** (leather) wristband

bracelet-montre (pl **bracelets-montres**) /bʀaslɛmɔ̃tʀ/ NM wristwatch

brachial, e (mpl **-iaux**) /bʀakjal, jo/ ADJ brachial

brachiopode /bʀakjɔpɔd/ NM brachiopod

brachycéphale /bʀakisefal/ ADJ brachycephalic NMF brachycephalic person

brachycéphalie /bʀakisefali/ NF brachycephaly

braconnage /bʀakɔnaʒ/ NM poaching

braconner /bʀakɔne/ ► conjug 1 ◄ VI to poach

braconnier, -ière /bʀakɔnje, jɛʀ/ NM,F poacher

bradage /bʀadaʒ/ NM selling off

brader /bʀade/ ► conjug 1 ◄ VT (= *vendre à prix réduit*) to sell cut-price *(Brit)* *ou* cut-rate *(US)*; (= *vendre en solde*) to have a clearance sale of; (= *vendre bon marché*) to sell off; (= *sacrifier*) to sacrifice ◆ **à ce prix-là, c'est bradé** at that price, they're giving it away ◆ **le gouvernement de l'époque fut accusé de ~ le patrimoine de l'État** the government of the time was accused of sacrificing the country's heritage

braderie /bʀadʀi/ NF (= *magasin*) discount centre; (= *marché*) market *(held once or twice a year, where goods are sold at reduced prices)* ◆ **la grande ~ des entreprises publiques** *(péj)* the massive *ou* wholesale sell-off of state-owned companies

bradeur, -euse /bʀadœʀ, øz/ NM,F discounter

bradycardie /bʀadikaʀdi/ NF abnormally low rate of heartbeat, bradycardia *(SPÉC)*

braguette /bʀagɛt/ NF *[de pantalon]* fly, flies; *(Hist)* codpiece

brahmane /bʀɑman/ NM Brahmin, Brahman

brahmanique /bʀɑmanik/ ADJ Brahminical

brahmanisme /bʀɑmanism/ NM Brahminism, Brahmanism

Brahmapoutre /bʀamaputʀ/, **Brahmaputra** /bʀamaputʀa/ NM Brahmaputra

brahmine /bʀɑmin/ NF Brahmani, Brahmanee

brai /bʀɛ/ NM pitch, tar

braies /bʀɛ/ NFPL *(Hist)* breeches *(worn by Gauls)*

braillard, e* /bʀɑjaʀ, aʀd/ ADJ 1 (= *criard*) bawling *(épith)*, yelling *(épith)* ◆ **des haut-parleurs ~s** blaring loudspeakers ◆ **des mouettes ~es** screeching gulls 2 (= *pleurard*) *[enfant]* bawling *(épith)*, howling *(épith)*, squalling *(épith)* NM,F ◆ **c'est un ~** he's always bawling

braille /bʀɑj/ NM Braille

braillement* /bʀɑjmɑ̃/ NM 1 (= *cris*) bawling *(NonC)*, yelling *(NonC)* 2 (= *pleurs*) bawling *(NonC)*, howling *(NonC)*, squalling *(NonC)* ◆ **les ~s de l'enfant** the bawling of the child

brailler* /bʀɑje/ ► conjug 1 ◄ VI (= *crier*) to bawl, to yell; (= *pleurer*) to bawl, to howl ◆ **il faisait ~ sa radio** his radio was blaring, he had his radio blaring *ou* on full blast VT *[+ chanson, slogan]* to bawl out

brailleur, -euse /bʀɑjœʀ, øz/ ADJ, NM,F ⇒ **braillard**

braiment /bʀɛmɑ̃/ NM bray(ing)

brain-trust (pl **brain-trusts**) /bʀɛntʀœst/ NM brain trust, brains trust

braire /bʀɛʀ/ ► conjug 50 ◄ VI *(lit, fig)* to bray ◆ **faire ~ qn**‡ to get on sb's nerves *ou* wick‡ *(Brit)*

braise /bʀɛz/ NF 1 *[de feu]* **la ~, les ~s** the (glowing) embers; (= *charbon de bois*) live charcoal ◆ **être sur la ~** *(fig)* to be on tenterhooks ◆ **yeux de ~** fiery eyes, eyes like coals 2 †‡ (= *argent*) cash*, dough‡, bread‡

braiser /bʀeze/ ► conjug 1 ◄ VT to braise ◆ **bœuf/chou braisé** braised beef/cabbage

bramement /bʀɑmmɑ̃/ NM 1 *[de cerf]* bell, troat 2 (= *hurlement*) wailing

bramer /bʀɑme/ ► conjug 1 ◄ VI 1 *[cerf]* to bell, to troat 2 * (= *brailler*) to bawl; (= *se lamenter*) to wail

bran /bʀɑ̃/ NM bran ◆ **~ de scie** sawdust

brancard /bʀɑ̃kaʀ/ NM 1 (= *bras*) *[de charrette]* shaft; *[de civière]* shaft, pole; → **ruer** 2 (= *civière*) stretcher

brancarder /bʀɑ̃kaʀde/ ► conjug 1 ◄ VT *[+ personne]* to carry on a stretcher

brancardier, -ière /bʀɑ̃kaʀdje, jɛʀ/ NM,F stretcher-bearer

branchage /bʀɑ̃ʃaʒ/ NM branches, boughs ◆ **~s** fallen *ou* lopped-off branches, lops

branche /bʀɑ̃ʃ/ NF 1 *(Bot)* branch, bough ◆ **~ mère** main branch ◆ **sauter de ~ en ~** to leap from branch to branch ◆ **céleri en ~s** (sticks of) celery ◆ **n'essaie pas de te raccrocher** *ou* **de te rattraper aux ~s*** *(fig)* don't try to make up for what you've said; → **vieux**
2 (= *ramification*) *[de nerfs, veines]* branch, ramification; *[de rivière, canalisation, bois de cerf]* branch; *[de lunettes]* side-piece; *[de compas]* leg; *[de ciseaux]* blade; *[de fer à cheval]* half; *[de famille]* branch ◆ **la ~ aînée** the elder *ou* eldest branch of the family ◆ **la ~ maternelle** the maternal branch of the family, the mother's side of the family ◆ **avoir de la ~** †* to be of good stock
3 (= *secteur*) branch; *(Helv Scol = sujet)* subject ◆ **les ~s de la science moderne** the different branches of modern science ◆ **notre fils s'orientera vers une ~ technique** our son will specialize in technical subjects ◆ **la ~ politique/militaire de cette organisation** the political/military wing *ou* arm of the organization
4 *(Helv)* **~ de chocolat** narrow bar of chocolate

branché, e* /bʀɑ̃ʃe/ (ptp de **brancher**) ADJ 1 (= *dans le vent*) *[personne, café]* trendy, hip* ◆ **en langage ~** in trendy slang 2 (= *enthousiasmé*) **elle est très ~e jazz/informatique** she's really into jazz/computers ◆ **il est ~ sur Anne** he's really keen on Anne

branchement /bʀɑ̃ʃmɑ̃/ NM 1 (= *fils connectés*) connection ◆ **vérifiez les ~s** check the connections 2 (= *action*) *[d'appareil à gaz, tuyau]* connecting (up); *[d'eau, gaz, électricité, réseau]* linking up 3 *(Rail)* branch line 4 *(Ordin)* branch

brancher /bʀɑ̃ʃe/ ▸ conjug 1 ◂ VT 1 *[+ appareil électrique] (à une prise)* to plug in ◆ ~ **qch sur qch** to plug sth into sth, to connect sth up with sth 2 *[+ appareil à gaz, tuyau, eau, gaz, électricité]* to connect (up) ◆ **être branché sur un réseau** to be linked *ou* connected to a network

3 *(= allumer) [+ télévision]* to turn on

4 *(* = mettre en relation)* ~ **qn avec qn** to put sb in contact with sb

5 *(= orienter)* ~ **qn sur un sujet** to start sb off on a subject ◆ **quand on l'a branché** *ou* **quand il est branché là-dessus il est intarissable** when he's launched on that *ou* when somebody gets him started on that he can go on forever

6 *(* = intéresser)* **ce qui me branche** what grabs me* *ou* gives me a buzz* ◆ **ça ne me branche pas** *[idée]* it doesn't grab me*; *[musique, activité]* it doesn't do anything for me ◆ **ça te brancherait d'aller au ciné ?** (do you) fancy going to see a film?* ◆ **il ne me branche pas trop son frère** I'm not too gone* on *ou* too keen on his brother

VPR **se brancher** 1 *(= se connecter)* **où est-ce que ça se branche ?** where does that plug in? ◆ **où est-ce que je peux me ~ ?** where can I plug it in? ◆ **se ~ sur un réseau/Internet** to get onto *ou* connect to a network/the Internet

2 *(* = entrer en relation)* **se ~ avec qn** to get in contact with sb

branchette /bʀɑ̃ʃɛt/ NF small branch, twig

branchial, e (mpl **-iaux**) /bʀɑ̃ʃjal, jo/ ADJ branchial

branchies /bʀɑ̃ʃi/ NFPL gills

branchiopode /bʀɑ̃ʃjɔpɔd/ NM branchiopod

branchu, e /bʀɑ̃ʃy/ ADJ branchy

brandade /bʀɑ̃dad/ NF ◆ ~ **(de morue)** brandade *(dish made with cod)*

brande /bʀɑ̃d/ NF *(= lande)* heath(land); *(= plantes)* heath, heather, brush

brandebourg /bʀɑ̃dbuʀ/ NM *(Habillement)* frog ◆ **à ~(s)** frogged N **Brandebourg** Brandenburg ◆ **la porte de Brandebourg** the Brandenburg Gate

brandebourgeois, e /bʀɑ̃dbuʀʒwa, waz/ ADJ Brandenburg *(épith)* ◆ **"les concertos brandebourgeois"** *(Mus)* "the Brandenburg Concertos" NM,F **Brandebourgeois(e)** inhabitant *ou* native of Brandenburg

brandir /bʀɑ̃diʀ/ ▸ conjug 2 ◂ VT *[+ arme]* to brandish; *[+ document]* to brandish, to flourish

brandon /bʀɑ̃dɔ̃/ NM firebrand *(lit)* ◆ ~ **de discorde** bone of contention

brandy /bʀɑ̃di/ NM brandy

branlant, e /bʀɑ̃lɑ̃, ɑ̃t/ ADJ *[dent]* loose; *[mur]* shaky; *[escalier, meuble]* rickety, shaky; *[pas]* unsteady, tottering, shaky; *(fig) [régime]* tottering, shaky; *[raison]* shaky

branle /bʀɑ̃l/ NM *[de cloche]* swing ◆ **donner le ~ à** to set in motion, to set rolling

◆ **mettre en branle** *[+ cloche]* to swing; *(fig)* to set in motion ◆ **se mettre en ~** to go into action ◆ **toute une panoplie répressive est mise en ~ pour faire taire les dissidents** a whole apparatus of repression has gone into action to silence the dissidents

branle-bas /bʀɑ̃lba/ NM INV bustle, commotion ◆ **dans le ~ du départ** in the confusion *ou* bustle of departure ◆ **être en ~** to be in a state of commotion ◆ **mettre qch en ~** to turn sth upside down, to cause commotion in sth

◆ **branle-bas de combat** *(Naut) (= manœuvre)* preparations for action ◆ **"branle-bas de combat !"** *(ordre)* "action stations!" ◆ **sonner le ~ de combat** to sound action stations ◆ **mettre en ~ de combat** to clear the decks (for action) ◆ **ça a été le ~ de combat** *(fig)* it was action stations

branlée /bʀɑ̃le/ NF 1 *(‡ = coups)* hammering* ◆ **recevoir une ~** to get hammered*, to get a hammering* 2 *(** = masturbation) [d'homme]* hand job‡, wank** *(Brit)* ◆ **il n'en fout pas une ~** he doesn't do a stroke of work

branlement /bʀɑ̃lmɑ̃/ NM *[de tête]* wagging, shaking

branler /bʀɑ̃le/ ▸ conjug 1 ◂ VT 1 ◆ ~ **la tête** *ou* *(hum)* **du chef** to shake *ou* wag one's head 2 *(** = faire)* **qu'est-ce qu'ils branlent ?** what the hell are they up to?‡ ◆ **il n'en branle pas une** he does fuck all** *ou* bugger all** *(Brit)* ◆ **j'en ai rien à ~** I don't give a fuck** VI *[échafaudage]* to be shaky *ou* unsteady; *[meuble]* to be shaky *ou* rickety; *[dent]* to be loose ◆ **ça branle dans le manche** things are a bit shaky VPR **se branler** ** *[homme]* to jerk off**, to have a wank** *(Brit)*; *[femme]* to masturbate ◆ **je m'en branle** I don't give a (flying) fuck**

branlette ** /bʀɑ̃lɛt/ NF ◆ **la ~** wanking** *(Brit)*, jerking off** ◆ **se faire une ~** ** to (have a) wank** *(Brit)*, to jerk (o.s.) off**

branleur, -euse ‡ /bʀɑ̃lœʀ, øz/ NM,F *(= paresseux)* lazy swine *ou* bugger** *(Brit)*

branleux, -euse ‡ /bʀɑ̃lø, øz/ ADJ *(Can)* shilly-shallying*

branque * /bʀɑ̃k/, **branquignol** * /bʀɑ̃kiɲɔl/ ADJ crazy*, barmy* *(Brit)* NM crackpot*, nutter‡ *(Brit)*

braquage /bʀakaʒ/ NM 1 *[de voiture]* (steering) lock; → **angle, rayon** 2 *(arg Crime)* stickup

braque /bʀak/ ADJ * crazy*, barmy* *(Brit)* NM *(= chien)* pointer

braquemart /bʀakmaʀ/ NM 1 *(Hist = épée)* brackmard (††), (double-bladed) sword 2 *(**= pénis)* dick**, cock**

braquer /bʀake/ ▸ conjug 1 ◂ VT 1 *(= diriger)* ~ **une arme sur** to point *ou* aim a weapon at ◆ ~ **un télescope/un projecteur sur** to train a telescope/a spotlight on ◆ ~ **son regard/attention sur** to turn one's gaze/attention towards, to fix one's gaze/attention on ◆ **tous les regards étaient braqués sur eux** all eyes were upon them ◆ **les (feux des) projecteurs sont braqués sur la famille royale** the royal family are in the spotlight

2 *[+ roue]* to swing

3 ‡ *(= attaquer) [+ banque, personne]* to hold up; *(= menacer) [+ personne]* to pull one's gun on, to hold up

4 ~ **qn** *(= buter)* to put sb's back up*, to make sb dig in his heels ◆ ~ **qn contre qch** to turn sb against sth ◆ **il est braqué** he won't budge, he's dug his heels in

VI *[automobiliste]* to turn the (steering) wheel ◆ ~ **bien/mal** *[voiture]* to have a good/bad lock ◆ ~ **à fond** to put on the full lock ◆ **braquez vers la gauche/la droite** turn left/right

VPR **se braquer** to dig one's heels in ◆ **se ~ contre qch** to set one's face against sth

braquet /bʀakɛ/ NM *[de bicyclette]* gear ratio ◆ **changer de ~** *(lit)* to change gear; *(fig)* to take a different approach ◆ **le gouvernement a changé de ~ après cet attentat** the government has taken a different approach since this attack ◆ **mettre le petit ~** to change into lower gear ◆ **mettre le grand ~** *(lit)* to change into higher gear; *(fig)* to get a move-on*, to shift into high gear* *(US)*

braqueur ‡ /bʀakœʀ/ NM *(= gangster)* hold-up man*

bras /bʀa/ NM 1 *(Anat)* arm ◆ **une serviette sous le ~** with a briefcase under one's arm ◆ **un panier au ~** with a basket on one's arm ◆ **donner le ~ à qn** to give sb one's arm ◆ **prendre le ~ de qn** to take sb's arm ◆ **être au ~ de qn** to be on sb's arm ◆ **se donner le ~** to link arms ◆ **~ dessus, ~ dessous** arm in arm ◆ **on a dû transporter tout cela à ~** we had to carry all that ◆ **les ~ en croix** with one's arms spread ◆ **les ~ croisés** *(lit)* with one's arms folded ◆ **rester les ~ croisés** *(fig)* to sit idly by ◆ **tendre** *ou* **allonger le ~ vers qch** to reach out for sth, to stretch out one's hand *ou* arm for sth ◆ **tomber dans les ~ de qn** to fall into sb's arms ◆ **il est mort dans mes ~** he died in my arms ◆ **(viens) dans mes ~ mon fils !** come and let me kiss *ou* hug you, my son!; → **arme, force, plein** *etc*

2 *(= travailleur)* hand, worker ◆ **manquer de ~** to be short-handed, to be short of manpower *ou* labour

3 *(= pouvoir)* **le ~ de la justice** the arm of the law ◆ **le ~ séculier** *(Rel)* the secular arm ◆ **le ~ armé du parti** the military wing *ou* arm of the party

4 *[de manivelle, outil, pompe]* handle; *[de fauteuil]* arm(rest); *[de grue]* jib; *[de sémaphore, ancre, électrophone, moulin, essuie-glace]* arm; *[de croix]* limb; *[d'aviron, brancard]* shaft; *(Naut) [de vergue]* brace

5 *[de fleuve]* branch

6 *[de cheval]* shoulder; *[de mollusque]* tentacle

7 *(Ordin)* ~ **d'accès** *ou* **de lecture-écriture** access *ou* positioning arm

8 *(locutions)* **en ~ de chemise** in (one's) shirt sleeves ◆ **saisir qn à ~-le-corps** to seize sb round the waist, to seize sb bodily ◆ **avoir le ~ long** *(fig)* to have a long arm ◆ **à ~ ouverts, les ~ ouverts** with open arms *(lit, fig)* ◆ **les ~ tendus** with outstretched arms ◆ **tomber sur qn à ~ raccourcis*** to set (up)on sb, to pitch into sb* ◆ **lever les ~ au ciel** to throw up one's arms ◆ **les ~ m'en tombent** I'm flabbergasted* *ou* stunned ◆ **avoir** *ou* **se retrouver avec qch/qn sur les ~*** to have sth/sb on one's hands, to be stuck* *ou* landed* with sth/sb ◆ **il a une nombreuse famille sur les ~*** he's got a large family to look after ◆ **avoir une sale histoire sur les ~*** to have a nasty business on one's hands ◆ **partir avec qch sous le ~** to make off with sth ◆ **(être) dans les ~ de Morphée** *(hum)* (to be) in the arms of Morpheus ◆ **faire un ~ d'honneur à qn** ≃ to put two fingers up at sb*, to give sb the V-sign *(Brit)* *ou* the finger** *(US)*; → **bout, couper, gros** *etc*

COMP **bras cassé** *(= personne)* no-hoper*

bras droit *(fig)* right-hand man

bras de fer *(Sport)* Indian wrestling *(NonC)*, arm-wrestling *(NonC)* ◆ **faire une partie de ~ de fer avec qn** to arm-wrestle with sb ◆ **la partie de ~ de fer entre patronat et syndicats** the trial of strength between the bosses and the unions

bras de levier lever arm ◆ **faire ~ de levier** to act as a lever

bras de mer arm *ou* stretch of the sea, sound

bras mort *(gén)* backwater; *(= lac)* oxbow lake, cutoff

brasage /bʀazaʒ/ NM brazing

braser /bʀaze/ ▸ conjug 1 ◂ VT to braze

braserade /bʀazeʀad/ NF portable barbecue

brasero /bʀazeʀo/ NM brazier

brasier /bʀazje/ NM *(= incendie)* (blazing) inferno, furnace; *(fig = foyer de guerre)* inferno ◆ **son cœur/esprit était un ~** his heart/mind was on fire *ou* ablaze

Brasilia /bʀazilja/ N Brasilia

brasiller /bʀazije/ ▸ conjug 1 ◂ VI *[mer]* to glimmer; *[bougie]* to glow red

brassage /bʀasaʒ/ NM 1 *[de bière]* brewing 2 *(= mélange)* mixing ◆ ~ **des gaz** *(dans moteur)* mixing ◆ **notre pays est celui qui a connu le plus grand ~ de population** our country is the one in which there is the greatest intermixture of nationalities ◆ **le service militaire**

était un outil de ~ social et régional military service brought about a mixing of social and regional groups ◆ **un lieu de ~ culturel** a cultural melting pot [3] *(Naut)* bracing

brassard /bʀasaʀ/ NM armband ◆ **~ de deuil** black armband ◆ **~ de capitaine** *(Sport)* captain's armband

brasse /bʀas/ NF [1] *(= sport)* breast-stroke; *(= mouvement)* stroke ◆ **~ coulée** breast-stroke ◆ **~ papillon** butterfly(-stroke) ◆ **nager la ~** to swim breast-stroke ◆ **faire quelques ~s** to do a few strokes [2] (†† *= mesure)* ≃ 6 feet; *(Naut)* fathom

brassée /bʀase/ NF armful; (* : *Can) [de machine à laver]* load ◆ **par ~s** in armfuls

brasser /bʀase/ ▸ conjug 1 ◂ VT [1] *(= remuer)* to stir (up); *(= mélanger)* to mix; *[+ pâte]* to knead; *[+ salade]* to toss; *[+ cartes]* to shuffle; *[+ argent]* to handle a lot of ◆ **~ des affaires** to be in big business ◆ **~ du vent** *(fig)* to blow hot air* [2] *[+ bière]* to brew [3] *(Naut)* to brace

brasserie /bʀasʀi/ NF [1] *(= café)* brasserie [2] *(= fabrique de bière)* brewery; *(= industrie)* brewing industry

brasseur, -euse /bʀasœʀ, øz/ NM,F [1] *[de bière]* brewer [2] **~ d'affaires** big businessman [3] *(Sport)* breast-stroke swimmer

brassière /bʀasjɛʀ/ NF [1] *[de bébé]* (baby's) vest *(Brit) ou* undershirt *(US)* ◆ **~ (de sauvetage)** life jacket [2] *(= soutien-gorge)* cropped bra; *(Can)* bra

brasure /bʀazyʀ/ NF *(= procédé)* brazing; *(= résultat)* brazed joint, braze; *(= métal)* brazing metal

Bratislava /bʀatislava/ N Bratislava

bravache /bʀavaʃ/ NM braggart, blusterer ◆ **faire le ~** to swagger about ADJ swaggering, blustering

bravade /bʀavad/ NF act of bravado ◆ **par ~** out of bravado

brave /bʀav/ ADJ [1] *(= courageux) [personne, action]* brave, courageous, gallant *(littér)* ◆ **faire le ~** to act brave, to put on a bold front [2] *(avant n) (= bon)* good, nice, fine; *(= honnête)* decent, honest ◆ **c'est une ~ fille** she's a nice girl ◆ **c'est un ~ garçon** he's a good *ou* nice fellow *ou* lad *(Brit)* ◆ **ce sont de ~s gens** they're good *ou* decent people *ou* souls ◆ **il est bien ~** he's not a bad chap* *(Brit) ou* guy* *(US)*, he's a nice enough fellow ◆ **mon ~ (homme)** my good man *ou* fellow ◆ **ma ~ dame** my good woman NM *(gén)* brave man; *(= Indien)* brave ◆ **~ entre les ~s** † bravest of the brave †

⚠ **brave** se traduit par le mot anglais **brave** uniquement au sens de 'courageux'.

bravement /bʀavmɑ̃/ ADV *(= courageusement)* bravely, courageously, gallantly *(littér)*; *(= résolument)* boldly

braver /bʀave/ ▸ conjug 1 ◂ VT *(= défier) [+ personne]* to stand up to; *[+ autorité, tabou]* to defy; *[+ règle]* to defy; *[+ danger, mort]* to brave ◆ **~ l'opinion** to fly in the face of (public) opinion ◆ **~ les océans** to brave the seas

bravo /bʀavo/ GRAMMAIRE ACTIVE 40.1, 50.6 EXCL *(= félicitations)* well done!, bravo!; *(= approbation)* hear! hear!; *(iro)* well done! NM cheer ◆ **un grand ~ pour ...!** a big cheer for ...!, let's hear it for ...!

bravoure /bʀavuʀ/ NF bravery, braveness, gallantry *(littér)*; → **morceau**

Brazzaville /bʀazavil/ N Brazzaville

break /bʀɛk/ NM [1] *(= voiture)* estate (car) *(Brit)*, station wagon *(US)* [2] *(= pause)* break ◆ **(se) faire un ~** to take a break [3] *(Boxe, Tennis)* break ◆ **balle de ~** break point ◆ **faire le ~** to break

brebis /bʀəbi/ NF *(= mouton)* ewe ◆ **les ~** *(Rel)* the flock ◆ **~ égarée** stray *ou* lost sheep ◆ **~ galeuse** black sheep ◆ **à ~ tondue Dieu mesure le vent** *(Prov)* the Lord tempers the wind to the shorn lamb *(Prov)*

brèche /bʀɛʃ/ NF *[de mur]* breach, opening, gap; *(Mil)* breach; *[de lame]* notch, nick ◆ **faire** *ou* **ouvrir une ~ dans le front ennemi** *(Mil)* to make a breach in *ou* to breach the enemy line ◆ **s'engouffrer dans la ~** *(fig)* to leap *ou* step into the breach ◆ **faire une ~ à sa fortune** to make a hole in one's fortune ◆ **il est toujours sur la ~** *(fig)* he's always beavering away*; → **battre**

bréchet /bʀeʃɛ/ NM wishbone

brechtien, -ienne /bʀɛʃtjɛ̃, jɛn/ ADJ Brechtian

bredouillage /bʀədujaʒ/ NM mumbling

bredouille /bʀəduj/ ADJ *(gén)* empty-handed ◆ **rentrer ~** *(Chasse, Pêche)* to go *ou* come home empty-handed *ou* with an empty bag

bredouillement /bʀədujmɑ̃/ NM ⇒ **bredouillage**

bredouiller /bʀəduje/ ▸ conjug 1 ◂ VI *(= bégayer)* to stammer; *(= marmonner)* to mumble VT *(= bégayer)* to stammer (out); *(= marmonner)* to mumble

bref, brève /bʀɛf, ɛv/ GRAMMAIRE ACTIVE 53.4 ADJ *[rencontre, discours, lettre]* brief, short; *[voyelle, syllabe]* short ◆ **d'un ton ~** sharply, curtly ◆ **soyez ~ et précis** be brief and to the point ◆ **à ~ délai** shortly ADV ◆ **(enfin) ~** *(= pour résumer)* to make *ou* cut *(Brit)* a long story short, in short, in brief; *(= passons)* let's not waste any more time; *(= donc)* anyway ◆ **en ~** in short, in brief NM *(Rel)* (papal) brief NF **brève** *(= syllabe)* short syllable; *(= voyelle)* short vowel; *(Journalisme)* news *(sg)* in brief ◆ **brèves de comptoir** bar-room philosophising *(NonC)*

brelan /bʀəlɑ̃/ NM *(Cartes)* three of a kind ◆ **~ d'as** three aces

brêle * /bʀɛl/ NF loser* ◆ **quelle ~ ce gardien de but !** that goalie's a wanker**!

breloque /bʀəlɔk/ NF (bracelet) charm; → **battre**

brème /bʀɛm/ NF [1] *(= poisson)* bream [2] *(arg Cartes)* card

Brésil /bʀezil/ NM Brazil

brésil /bʀezil/ NM *(= bois)* brazil (wood)

brésilien, -ienne /bʀeziljɛ̃, jɛn/ ADJ Brazilian NM *(= langue)* Brazilian Portuguese NM,F **Brésilien(ne)** Brazilian

Bretagne /bʀətaɲ/ NF Brittany

bretèche /bʀətɛʃ/ NF gatehouse, bartizan

bretelle /bʀətɛl/ NF [1] *[de sac]* (shoulder) strap; *[de vêtement]* strap; *[de fusil]* sling ◆ **~s** *[de pantalon]* braces *(Brit)*, suspenders *(US)* ◆ **robe à ~s** strappy dress ◆ **porter l'arme** *ou* **le fusil à la ~** to carry one's weapon slung over one's shoulder; → **remonter** [2] *[de voie ferrée]* crossover; *[de route]* slip road *(Brit)*, entrance (*ou* exit) ramp, on (*ou* off) ramp *(US)* ◆ **~ de raccordement** access road ◆ **~ de contournement** bypass

breton, -onne /bʀətɔ̃, ɔn/ ADJ Breton NM *(= langue)* Breton NM,F **Breton(ne)** Breton

bretonnant, e /bʀətɔnɑ̃, ɑ̃t/ ADJ *(Ling)* Breton-speaking; *(attaché aux traditions)* preserving Breton culture

bretteur /bʀɛtœʀ/ NM †† swashbuckler; *(= duelliste)* duellist

bretzel /bʀɛtzɛl/ NM pretzel

breuvage /bʀœvaʒ/ NM beverage; *(= mélange)* concoction; *(magique)* potion

brève /bʀɛv/ ADJ, NF → **bref**

brevet /bʀəvɛ/ NM [1] *(= diplôme)* diploma, certificate; *(Hist = note royale)* royal warrant; *(Scol) exam taken at the age of 15,* ≃ GCSE *(Brit)* ◆ **avoir son ~** *(Scol)* ≃ to have (passed) one's GCSEs *(Brit)*

[2] *(Naut)* certificate, ticket ◆ **~ de capitaine** master's certificate *ou* ticket ◆ **~ de commandant** *(Mil)* major's brevet

[3] *(Jur)* **~ (d'invention)** letters patent, patent ◆ **~ en cours d'homologation** patent pending

[4] *(fig = garantie)* guarantee ◆ **donner à qn un ~ d'honnêteté** to testify to *ou* guarantee sb's honesty ◆ **on peut lui décerner un ~ de persévérance** he deserves a medal for perseverance

COMP **brevet d'apprentissage** ≃ certificate of apprenticeship

brevet d'aptitude à la fonction d'animateur *certificate for activity leaders in children's holiday centres*

brevet des collèges, **brevet d'études du premier cycle** † *exam taken at the age of 15,* ≃ GCSE *(Brit)*

brevet d'études professionnelles *technical school certificate*

brevet de pilote pilot's licence

brevet de secourisme first aid certificate

brevet de technicien *vocational training certificate taken at age 16*

brevet de technicien supérieur *vocational training certificate taken after the age of 18*

brevetable /bʀəv(ə)tabl/ ADJ patentable

breveté, e /bʀəv(ə)te/ (ptp de **breveter**) ADJ [1] *[invention]* patented ◆ **~ sans garantie du gouvernement** patented *(without official government approval)* [2] *(= diplômé) [technicien]* qualified, certificated; *(Mil) [officier]* commissioned NM,F *(Admin, Jur)* patentee

breveter /bʀəv(ə)te/ ▸ conjug 4 ◂ VT *[+ invention]* to patent ◆ **faire ~ qch** to take out a patent for sth

bréviaire /bʀevjɛʀ/ NM *(Rel)* breviary; *(fig)* bible

BRI /beɛʀi/ NF (abrév de **Banque des règlements internationaux**) BIS

briard, e /bʀijaʀ, aʀd/ ADJ of *ou* from Brie NM,F **Briard(e)** inhabitant *ou* native of Brie NM *(= chien)* Briard (sheepdog)

bribe /bʀib/ NF *(= fragment)* bit, scrap ◆ **~s de conversation** snatches of conversation ◆ **~s de nourriture** scraps of food ◆ **les ~s de sa fortune** the remnants of his fortune ◆ **par ~s** in snatches, piecemeal

bric /bʀik/ **de bric et de broc** LOC ADV *(= de manière disparate)* any old way*, any old how* ◆ **meublé de ~ et de broc** furnished with bits and pieces *ou* with odds and ends ◆ **une équipe faite de ~ et de broc** a randomly assembled team

bric-à-brac /bʀikabʀak/ NM INV [1] *(= objets)* bric-a-brac, odds and ends; *(fig)* bric-a-brac, trimmings [2] *(= magasin)* junk shop

bricelet /bʀislɛ/ NM *(Helv) waffle type biscuit*

brick /bʀik/ NM [1] *(Naut)* brig [2] *(Culin)* brik *(pastry parcel)*

bricolage /bʀikɔlaʒ/ NM [1] *(= passe-temps)* do-it-yourself, DIY* *(Brit)*; *(= travaux)* odd jobs ◆ **j'ai du ~ à faire** I've got a few (odd) jobs to do ◆ **rayon ~** do-it-yourself department ◆ **magasin de ~** DIY store *(Brit)* [2] *(= réparation)* makeshift repair *ou* job ◆ **c'est du ~ !** *(péj)* it's a rush job!*

bricole /bʀikɔl/ NF [1] * *(= babiole)* trifle; *(= cadeau)* something small, token; *(= menu travail)* easy job, small matter ◆ **il ne reste que des ~s** there are only a few bits and pieces *ou* a few odds and ends left ◆ **il ne me reste que quelques ~s à faire** I only have a few odd things left to do ◆ **ça coûte 10 € et des ~s** it costs €10 or so ◆ **il va lui arriver des ~s*** he's going to run into trouble [2] *[de cheval]* breast harness [3] *(Can)* **~s*** *(= bretelles)* braces *(Brit)*, suspenders *(US)*

bricoler /bʀikɔle/ ▸ conjug 1 ◂ **VI** *(menus travaux)* to do little jobs; *(réparations)* to do odd jobs; *(passe-temps)* to tinker about *ou* around ◆ **elle aime** ~ she likes DIY ◆ **j'aime bien** ~ **dans la maison** I like doing little jobs around the house **VT** *(= réparer)* to fix (up), to mend; *(= mal réparer)* to tinker *ou* mess (about) with; *(= fabriquer)* to cobble up *ou* together, to knock up* *(Brit)*

bricoleur /bʀikɔlœʀ/ **NM** handyman, do-it-yourselfer*, DIY man* *(Brit)* ◆ **il est** ~ he's good with his hands, he's very handy* ◆ **je ne suis pas très** ~ I'm not much of a handyman

bricoleuse /bʀikɔløz/ **NF** handywoman, do-it-yourselfer*, DIY woman* *(Brit)*

bride /bʀid/ **NF** 1 *(Équitation)* bridle ◆ **tenir un cheval en** ~ to curb a horse ◆ **tenir ses passions/une personne en** ~ to keep one's passions/a person in check, to keep a tight rein on one's passions/a person ◆ **jeter** *ou* **laisser** *ou* **mettre la** ~ **sur le cou** *ou* **col à un cheval** to give a horse the reins, to give a horse his head ◆ **laisser la** ~ **sur le cou à qn** to give *ou* leave sb a free hand ◆ **les jeunes ont maintenant la** ~ **sur le cou** young people can just do as they like nowadays ◆ **tu lui laisses trop la** ~ **sur le cou** you don't keep a tight enough rein on him ◆ **tenir la** ~ **haute à un cheval** to rein in a horse ◆ **tenir la** ~ **haute à qn** *(fig)* to keep a tight rein on sb ◆ **aller à** ~ **abattue** *ou* **à toute** ~ to ride flat out*, to ride hell for leather* ◆ **tourner** ~ *(lit)* to turn back; *(fig)* to do an about-turn; → **lâcher**

2 *[de vêtement] (en cuir)* strap; *[de bonnet]* string

3 *(Couture) [de boutonnière]* bar; *[de bouton]* loop; *[de dentelle]* bride

4 *(Tech) [de bielle]* strap; *[de tuyau]* flange

5 *(Méd)* adhesion

bridé, e /bʀide/ (ptp de **brider**) **ADJ** ◆ **avoir les yeux** ~**s** to have slanting eyes

brider /bʀide/ ▸ conjug 1 ◂ **VT** 1 *[+ cheval]* to bridle; *[+ moteur]* to restrain; *[+ impulsion]* to curb, to restrain; *[+ croissance, consommation, investissement, liberté]* to curb; *[+ création, imagination]* to curb, to keep in check; *[+ personne]* to keep in check ◆ ~ **sa colère** to restrain one's anger ◆ **logiciel bridé** restricted-access software, crippleware* ◆ **il est bridé dans son costume, son costume le bride** his suit is too tight for him 2 *(Culin)* to truss 3 *[+ boutonnière]* to bind; *[+ tuyau]* to clamp, to flange; *(Naut)* to lash together

bridge[1] /bʀidʒ/ **NM** *(Cartes)* bridge ◆ ~ **contrat** contract bridge ◆ ~ **aux enchères** auction bridge ◆ **faire un** ~ to play *ou* have a game of bridge

bridge[2] /bʀidʒ/ **NM** *(= prothèse)* bridge

bridger /bʀidʒe/ ▸ conjug 3 ◂ **VI** to play bridge

bridgeur, -euse /bʀidʒœʀ, øz/ **NM,F** bridge player

bridon /bʀidɔ̃/ **NM** snaffle

brie /bʀi/ **NM** Brie (cheese)

briefer /bʀife/ ▸ conjug 1 ◂ **VT** to brief

briefing /bʀifiŋ/ **NM** briefing ◆ **faire un** ~ **à l'intention de l'équipe de vente** to brief the sales force

brièvement /bʀijɛvmɑ̃/ **ADV** briefly ◆ **l'euro était tombé** ~ **en dessous de ce niveau** the euro briefly fell below this level

brièveté /bʀijɛvte/ **NF** brevity, briefness

brigade /bʀigad/ **NF** *(Mil)* brigade; *(Police)* squad; *(gén = équipe)* gang, team

COMP **brigade anti-émeute** riot police *(NonC) ou* squad
brigade antigang anti-terrorist squad
brigade canine police dog unit
brigade criminelle Crime *ou* Murder Squad
brigade financière financial police, ≃ Fraud Squad
brigade de gendarmerie *(corps)* gendarmerie squad; *(bâtiment)* gendarmerie
Brigades internationales International Brigades
brigade des mineurs *police department dealing with young offenders and young victims of crime*
brigade des mœurs, brigade mondaine† Vice Squad
brigade de recherche dans l'intérêt des familles ≃ missing persons bureau
brigade de répression et d'intervention ⇒ **brigade antigang**
les Brigades rouges the Red Brigades
brigade de sapeurs-pompiers fire brigade
brigade des stupéfiants *ou* **des stups*** drug(s) squad
brigade volante flying squad

brigadier /bʀigadje/ **NM** *(Police)* ≃ sergeant; *(Mil) [d'artillerie]* bombardier; *[de blindés, cavalerie, train]* corporal ◆ ~**-chef** ≃ lance sergeant

brigand /bʀigɑ̃/ **NM** († = *bandit)* brigand, bandit; *(péj = filou)* twister *(Brit)*, sharpie* *(US)*, crook; *(hum = enfant)* rascal, imp

brigandage /bʀigɑ̃daʒ/ **NM** (armed) robbery, banditry †, brigandage ◆ **commettre des actes de** ~ to engage in robbery with violence ◆ **c'est du** ~ **!** *(fig)* it's daylight robbery!

brigantin /bʀigɑ̃tɛ̃/ **NM** *(Naut)* brig

brigantine /bʀigɑ̃tin/ **NF** *(Naut)* spanker

brigue /bʀig/ **NF** *(littér)* intrigue ◆ **obtenir qch par** ~ to get sth by intrigue

briguer /bʀige/ ▸ conjug 1 ◂ **VT** *[+ poste, honneur, faveur]* to strive to get; *[+ amitié]* to strive to win; *[+ suffrages]* to solicit, to canvass (for) ◆ **il brigue la succession du président** he has his eye on the presidency ◆ **il brigue un second mandat de président** he is seeking a second term of office as president

brillamment /bʀijamɑ̃/ **ADV** brilliantly ◆ **réussir** ~ **un examen** to pass an exam with flying colours ◆ **il a** ~ **remporté les élections** he won the election hands down

brillance /bʀijɑ̃s/ **NF** *(Astron)* brilliance; *(= éclat)* sheen; *[de cheveux]* sheen, lustre; *[de peau]* shininess; *[de tissu]* sheen

brillant, e /bʀijɑ̃, ɑt/ **ADJ** 1 *(= luisant)* shiny; *(= étincelant)* sparkling, bright; *[chaussures]* well-polished, shiny; *[cheveux]* glossy; *[couleur]* bright, brilliant ◆ **elle avait les yeux** ~**s de fièvre/d'impatience** her eyes were bright with fever/impatience ◆ **il avait les yeux** ~**s de convoitise/colère** his eyes glittered with envy/anger; → **peinture, sou**

2 *(= remarquable)* brilliant, outstanding; *[situation]* excellent; *[carrière]* brilliant; *[succès]* brilliant, dazzling, outstanding; *[avenir]* brilliant, bright; *[conversation]* brilliant, sparkling ◆ **avoir une intelligence** ~**e** to be outstandingly intelligent, to be brilliant ◆ **c'est un** ~ **orateur** he is a brilliant speaker ◆ **elle a été** ~**e à l'examen** she did brilliantly in her exam ◆ **sa santé n'est pas** ~**e** his health isn't too good ◆ **ce n'est pas** ~ *[travail]* it's not too good, it's not up to much *(Brit)*; *[situation]* it's far from satisfactory

NM 1 *(= éclat) (étincelant)* sparkle, brightness; *(luisant)* shine; *[de cheveux]* glossiness; *[de couleur]* brightness, brilliance; *[d'étoffe]* sheen; *(par usure)* shine ◆ **le** ~ **de son esprit/style** the brilliance of his mind/style ◆ **donner du** ~ **à un cuir** to polish up a piece of leather

2 *(= diamant)* brilliant ◆ **taillé/monté en** ~ cut/mounted as a brilliant

3 *(= cosmétique)* ~ **à lèvres** lip gloss

brillantine /bʀijɑ̃tin/ **NF** brilliantine

briller /bʀije/ ▸ conjug 1 ◂ **VI** 1 *(gén) [lumière, soleil]* to shine; *[diamant, eau]* to sparkle, to glitter; *[étoile]* to twinkle, to shine (brightly); *[métal]* to glint, to shine; *[feu, braises]* to glow (brightly); *[flammes]* to blaze; *[éclair]* to flash; *[chaussures]* to shine; *[surface polie, humide]* to shine, to glisten ◆ **frotte fort, il faut que ça brille** *(cuivre)* rub hard, we want a nice shine; *(salle de bains)* give it all a good scrub, we want it sparkling clean ◆ **faire** ~ **les meubles/l'argenterie** to polish the furniture/the silver ◆ **faire** ~ **ses chaussures** to shine *ou* polish one's shoes ◆ **tout brille dans sa salle de bains** everything is spick and span in his bathroom ◆ **faire** ~ **les avantages de qch à qn** to paint a glowing picture of sth to sb; → **tout**

2 *[yeux]* to shine, to sparkle; *[nez, peau]* to be shiny; *[larmes]* to glisten ◆ **ses yeux brillaient de joie** his eyes sparkled with joy ◆ **ses yeux brillaient de convoitise** his eyes glinted greedily

3 *[personne]* to shine, to stand out ◆ ~ **en société** to shine in company ◆ ~ **à un examen** to do brilliantly in an exam, to come through an exam with flying colours ◆ **le désir de** ~ the longing to stand out (from the crowd), the desire to be the centre of attention

◆ **briller par** ◆ ~ **par son talent/éloquence** to be outstandingly talented/eloquent ◆ **il ne brille pas par le courage/la modestie** courage/modesty is not his strong point *ou* his forte ◆ ~ **par son absence** to be conspicuous by one's absence

brimade /bʀimad/ **NF** *(= vexation)* vexation; *(Mil, Scol : d'initiation)* ragging *(NonC) (Brit)*, hazing *(NonC) (US)* ◆ **faire subir des** ~**s à qn** to harry sb, to harass sb; *(Mil, Scol)* to rag sb *(Brit)*, to haze sb *(US)*

brimbalement* /bʀɛ̃balmɑ̃/ **NM** ⇒ **bringuebalement**

brimbaler* /bʀɛ̃bale/ ▸ conjug 1 ◂ **VI, VT** ⇒ **bringuebaler**

brimborion /bʀɛ̃bɔʀjɔ̃/ **NM** *(= colifichet)* bauble, trinket

brimer /bʀime/ ▸ conjug 1 ◂ **VT** *(= soumettre à des vexations)* to aggravate, to bully; *[+ élève, recrue]* to rag *(Brit)*, to haze *(US)* ◆ **il se sent brimé** he feels he's being got at* *(Brit) ou* gotten at* *(US)* ◆ **je suis brimé*** I'm being got* at *(Brit) ou* gotten at* *(US)*

brin /bʀɛ̃/ **NM** 1 *[de blé, herbe]* blade; *[de bruyère, mimosa, muguet]* sprig; *[d'osier]* twig; *[de paille]* wisp ◆ **un beau** ~ **de fille** *(fig)* a fine-looking girl

2 *[de chanvre, lin]* yarn, fibre; *[de corde, fil, laine]* strand

3 *(locutions)*

◆ **un brin*** ◆ **un** ~ **plus grand/haut** a bit *ou* a little *ou* a fraction *ou* a shade bigger/higher ◆ **je suis un** ~ **embêté** I'm a trifle *ou* a shade worried ◆ **s'amuser un** ~ to have a bit of fun ◆ **un** ~ **de** a touch *ou* grain *ou* bit of ◆ **il n'a pas un** ~ **de bon sens** he hasn't got an ounce *ou* a grain of common sense ◆ **avec un** ~ **de nostalgie** with a touch *ou* hint of nostalgia ◆ **il y a en lui un** ~ **de folie/méchanceté** there's a touch of madness/malice in him ◆ **faire un** ~ **de causette** to have a bit of a chat*, to have a little chat ◆ **faire un** ~ **de cour à une femme** to flirt a little with a woman ◆ **faire un** ~ **de toilette** to have a quick wash ◆ **il n'y a pas un** ~ **de vent** there isn't a breath of wind

4 *(Radio) [d'antenne]* wire

brindezingue* /bʀɛ̃dzɛ̃g/ **ADJ** nutty*, crazy*

brindille /bʀɛ̃dij/ **NF** twig

bringue[1]* /bʀɛ̃g/ **NF** ◆ **grande** ~ beanpole*

bringue[2]* /bʀɛ̃g/ **NF** ◆ **faire la** ~ to have a wild time ◆ ~ **à tout casser** wild party

bringuebalement* /bʀɛ̃g(ə)balmɑ̃/, **brinquebalement*** /bʀɛ̃kbalmɑ̃/ **NM** *(= mouvement)* shaking (about); *(= bruit)* rattle

bringuebaler* /bʀɛ̃g(ə)bale/, **brinquebaler*** /bʀɛ̃kbale/ ▸ conjug 1 ◂ VI *[tête]* to shake about, to joggle; *[voiture]* to shake *ou* jolt about, to joggle; *(avec bruit)* to rattle ◆ **une vieille auto toute bringuebalante** a ram shackle *ou* broken-down old car ◆ **il y a quelque chose qui bringuebale dans ce paquet** something is rattling in this packet VT to cart (about)

brio /bʀijo/ NM (= *virtuosité)* brilliance; *(Mus)* brio ◆ **avec** ~ *(Mus)* with *ou* con brio; *(réussir un examen)* with flying colours ◆ **faire qch avec** ~ to do sth brilliantly ◆ **il raconte avec** ~ **la conquête du Far West** he gives a brilliant description of the conquest of the Far West

brioche /bʀijɔʃ/ NF brioche ◆ **jambon en** ~ *ham in a pastry case* ◆ **prendre de la** ~ * (= *embonpoint)* to develop a paunch, to get a bit of a tummy * ◆ **« Qu'ils mangent de la** ~**! »** *(Hist)* "Let them eat cake!"

brioché, e /bʀijɔʃe/ ADJ (baked) like a brioche; → **pain**

brique /bʀik/ NF 1 *(Constr)* brick; *[de savon]* bar, cake; *[de tourbe]* block, slab; *[de lait]* carton ◆ **mur de** *ou* **en** ~**(s)** brick wall ◆ ~ **pleine/creuse** solid/hollow brick ◆ **bouffer des** ~**s**⁎ to have nothing to eat 2 (* = *dix mille francs)* **une** ~ ten thousand francs 3 *(Naut)* ~ **à pont** holystone ADJ INV brick red

briquer /bʀike/ ▸ conjug 1 ◂ VT * to polish up; *(Naut)* to holystone, to scrub down

briquet[1] /bʀikɛ/ NM (cigarette) lighter ◆ ~**-tempête** windproof lighter; → **battre**

briquet[2] /bʀikɛ/ NM (= *chien)* beagle

briquetage /bʀik(ə)taʒ/ NM (= *mur)* brickwork; (= *enduit)* imitation brickwork

briqueter /bʀik(ə)te/ ▸ conjug 4 ◂ VT 1 (= *bâtir)* to brick, to build with bricks 2 (= *peindre)* to face with imitation brickwork

briqueterie /bʀik(ə)tʀi/ NF brickyard, brickfield

briqueteur /bʀik(ə)tœʀ/ NM bricklayer

briquetier /bʀik(ə)tje/ NM (= *ouvrier)* brickyard worker, brickmaker; (= *entrepreneur)* brick merchant

briquette /bʀikɛt/ NF briquette ◆ **c'est de la** ~ * it's not up to much *(Brit)*

bris /bʀi/ NM breaking ◆ ~ **de clôture** *(Jur)* trespass, breaking-in ◆ ~ **de glaces** *(dans voiture)* broken windows ◆ ~ **de scellés** *(Jur)* breaking of seals

brisant, e /bʀizɑ̃, ɑt/ ADJ high-explosive *(épith)* ◆ **obus** ~ high-explosive shell NM 1 (= *vague)* breaker 2 (= *écueil)* shoal, reef 3 (= *brise-lames)* groyne, breakwater

briscard /bʀiskaʀ/ NM *(Hist Mil)* veteran, old soldier ◆ **c'est un vieux** ~ * **de la politique** he's a veteran of *ou* an old hand in politics

brise /bʀiz/ NF breeze ◆ ~ **de mer/terre** sea/land breeze

brisé, e /bʀize/ (ptp de **briser**) ADJ ◆ ~ **(de fatigue)** worn out, exhausted ◆ ~ **(de chagrin)** overcome by sorrow, brokenhearted; → **arc, ligne**[1]**, pâte**

brise-bise /bʀizbiz/ NM INV half-curtain

brisées /bʀize/ NFPL ◆ **marcher sur les** ~ **de qn** to poach *ou* intrude on sb's preserve *ou* territory ◆ **suivre les** ~ **de qn** to follow in sb's footsteps

brise-fer /bʀizfɛʀ/ NMF INV ◆ **cet enfant est un vrai** ~**!** that child is a real little vandal!

brise-glace (pl **brise-glaces**) /bʀizglas/ NM (= *navire)* icebreaker; *[de pont]* icebreaker, ice apron

brise-jet (pl **brise-jets**) /bʀizʒɛ/ NM tap swirl *(Brit)*, anti-splash faucet nozzle *(US)*

brise-lame(s) (pl **brise-lames**) /bʀizlam/ NM breakwater, mole

brise-motte(s) (pl **brise-mottes**) /bʀizmɔt/ NM harrow

briser /bʀize/ ▸ conjug 1 ◂ VT 1 (= *casser)* [+ *objet]* to break, to smash; [+ *mottes de terre]* to break up; [+ *chaîne, fers]* to break ◆ ~ **qch en mille morceaux** to smash sth to smithereens, to break sth into little pieces *ou* bits, to shatter sth (into little pieces) ◆ ~ **la glace** *(lit, fig)* to break the ice

2 (= *saper, détruire)* [+ *carrière, vie]* to ruin, to wreck; [+ *personne]* (= *épuiser)* to tire out, to exhaust; (= *abattre la volonté de)* to break, to crush; [+ *espérance]* to smash, to shatter, to crush; [+ *cœur, courage]* to break; [+ *traité, accord]* to break; [+ *amitié]* to break up, to bring to an end ◆ ~ **l'élan de qn** to kill sb's enthusiasm ◆ **d'une voix brisée par l'émotion** in a voice choked with emotion ◆ **ces épreuves l'ont brisé** these trials and tribulations have left him a broken man ◆ **il en a eu le cœur brisé** it broke his heart, he was heartbroken about it ◆ **chagrin qui brise le cœur** heartbreaking grief *ou* sorrow ◆ **tu me les brises !**⁎⁎ you're really pissing me off !⁎⁎, you're really getting on my tits!⁎⁎ *(Brit)*

3 (= *avoir raison de)* [+ *volonté]* to break, to crush; [+ *rebelle]* to crush, to subdue; [+ *opposition, résistance]* to crush, to break down; [+ *grève]* to break (up); [+ *révolte]* to crush, to quell ◆ **il était décidé à** ~ **les menées de ces conspirateurs** he was determined to put a stop to *ou* to put paid to *(Brit)* the schemings of these conspirators

4 (= *mettre fin à)* [+ *silence, rythme]* to break; *(frm)* [+ *entretien]* to break off

VI *(littér)* 1 (= *rompre)* ~ **avec qn** to break with sb ◆ **brisons là !** † enough said!

2 (= *déferler)* *[vagues]* to break

VPR **se briser** 1 *[vitre, verre]* to break, to shatter, to smash; *[bâton, canne]* to break, to snap

2 *[vagues]* to break *(contre* against)

3 *[cœur]* to break, to be broken; *[voix]* to falter, to break

4 *[résistance]* to break down, to snap; *[assaut]* to break up *(sur* on; *contre* against); *[espoir]* to be dashed ◆ **nos efforts se sont brisés sur cette difficulté** our efforts were frustrated *ou* thwarted by this difficulty

brise-soleil /bʀizsɔlɛj/ NM INV (slatted) canopy *ou* awning

brise-tout /bʀiztu/ NMF INV (= *maladroit)* butterfingers * ◆ **cet enfant est un vrai** ~ **!** that child is a real little vandal!

briseur, -euse /bʀizœʀ, øz/ NM,F breaker, wrecker ◆ ~ **de grève** strikebreaker

brise-vent (pl **brise-vent(s)**) /bʀizvɑ̃/ NM windbreak

brisquard /bʀiskaʀ/ NM ⇒ **briscard**

bristol /bʀistɔl/ NM (= *papier)* Bristol board; (= *carte de visite)* visiting card

brisure /bʀizyʀ/ NF (= *cassure)* break, crack; *[de charnière]* joint, break ◆ ~**s de riz** broken rice

britannique /bʀitanik/ ADJ British NMF **Britannique** British person, Britisher *(US)*, Briton ◆ **c'est un Britannique** he's British *ou* a Britisher *(US)* ◆ **les Britanniques** the British

brittonique /bʀitɔnik/ ADJ, NM Brythonic, Brittonic

broc /bʀo/ NM pitcher, jug; *(de table de toilette)* ewer

brocante /bʀɔkɑ̃t/ NF (= *commerce)* secondhand trade, secondhand market; (= *marché)* secondhand market; (= *objets)* secondhand goods ◆ **il est dans la** ~ he deals in secondhand goods ◆ **acheter qch à la** ~ to buy sth at the flea market

brocanter /bʀɔkɑ̃te/ ▸ conjug 1 ◂ VI to deal in secondhand goods

brocanteur, -euse /bʀɔkɑ̃tœʀ, øz/ NM,F secondhand goods dealer

brocard[1] /bʀɔkaʀ/ NM (= *chevreuil)* brocket

brocard[2] /bʀɔkaʀ/ NM *(littér ou* † = *moquerie)* gibe, taunt

brocarder /bʀɔkaʀde/ ▸ conjug 1 ◂ VT *(littér ou* †*)* to gibe at, to taunt

brocart /bʀɔkaʀ/ NM brocade

brochage /bʀɔʃaʒ/ NM 1 *[de feuilles imprimées]* binding *(with paper)* 2 *[de tissu]* brocading 3 *[de pièces métalliques]* broaching

broche /bʀɔʃ/ NF 1 (= *bijou)* brooch 2 (= *objet pointu)* *(Culin)* spit; *(Tex)* spindle; *(Tech)* drift, pin, broach; *(Élec)* pin; *(Méd)* pin ◆ ~ **(à glace)** *(Alpinisme)* ice piton ◆ **faire cuire à la** ~ to spit-roast ◆ **poulet/agneau à la** ~ spit-roasted chicken/lamb

broché, e /bʀɔʃe/ (ptp de **brocher**) NM *(Tex)* (= *procédé)* brocading; (= *tissu)* brocade ADJ ◆ **livre** ~ paperback ◆ **édition** ~**e** paperback edition

brocher /bʀɔʃe/ ▸ conjug 1 ◂ VT 1 *(Imprim)* to bind *(with paper)*, to put a paperback cover on 2 [+ *tissu]* to brocade ◆ **tissu broché d'or** gold brocade 3 [+ *pièces métalliques]* to broach

brochet /bʀɔʃɛ/ NM (= *poisson)* pike

brochette /bʀɔʃɛt/ NF 1 *(Culin)* (= *ustensile)* skewer; (= *plat)* kebab, brochette ◆ **rognons en** ~ kidney kebab 2 *(fig)* ~ **de décorations** row of medals ◆ ~ **de personnalités/de criminels** bunch of VIPs/criminals

brocheur, -euse /bʀɔʃœʀ, øz/ NM,F (= *personne)* *[de livres]* book binder; *[de tissus]* brocade weaver NM (= *machine à brocher les tissus)* brocade loom NF **brocheuse** (= *machine à brocher les livres)* binder, binding machine

brochure /bʀɔʃyʀ/ NF 1 (= *magazine)* brochure, booklet, pamphlet ◆ ~ **touristique** tourist brochure 2 *[de livre]* (paper) binding 3 *[de tissu]* brocaded pattern *ou* figures

brocoli /bʀɔkɔli/ NM broccoli

brodequin /bʀɔd(ə)kɛ̃/ NM (laced) boot; *(Hist Théât)* buskin, sock ◆ **les** ~**s** *(Hist* = *supplice)* the boot

broder /bʀɔde/ ▸ conjug 1 ◂ VT [+ *tissu]* to embroider *(de* with); [+ *récit]* to embroider VI (= *exagérer)* to embroider, to embellish; (= *trop développer)* to elaborate ◆ ~ **sur un sujet** to elaborate on a subject

broderie /bʀɔdʀi/ NF (= *art)* embroidery; (= *objet)* piece of embroidery, embroidery *(NonC)*; (= *industrie)* embroidery trade ◆ **faire de la** ~ to embroider, to do embroidery ◆ ~ **anglaise** broderie anglaise

brodeur /bʀɔdœʀ/ NM embroiderer

brodeuse /bʀɔdøz/ NF (= *ouvrière)* embroideress; (= *machine)* embroidery machine

broiement /bʀwamɑ̃/ NM ⇒ **broyage**

bromate /bʀɔmat/ NM bromate

brome /bʀom/ NM *(Chim)* bromine

bromique /bʀɔmik/ ADJ bromic

bromure /bʀɔmyʀ/ NM 1 *(Chim)* bromide ◆ ~ **d'argent/de potassium** silver/potassium bromide 2 (= *papier)* bromide paper; (= *épreuve)* bromide (proof)

bronca /bʀɔ̃ka/ NF *(dans une arène)* cheering; (= *huées de mécontentement)* booing

bronche /bʀɔ̃ʃ/ NF bronchus *(SPÉC)* ◆ **les** ~**s** the bronchial tubes ◆ **cela dégage les** ~**s** this clears the bronchial tubes ◆ **j'ai les** ~**s prises** my chest is congested

broncher /bʀɔ̃ʃe/ ▸ conjug 1 ◂ VI *[cheval]* to stumble ◆ **personne n'osait** ~ * no one dared move a muscle *ou* say a word ◆ **le premier qui bronche ... !*** the first person to budge* *ou* make a move ...!

◆ **sans broncher*** (*= sans protester*) uncomplainingly, meekly; (*= sans se tromper*) faultlessly, without faltering; (*= sans peur*) without turning a hair, without flinching

bronchiole /bʀɔ̃ʃjɔl/ **NF** (*Anat*) bronchiole

bronchique /bʀɔ̃ʃik/ **ADJ** bronchial

bronchite /bʀɔ̃ʃit/ **NF** bronchitis (*NonC*) ◆ **avoir une bonne** ~ to have (got) a bad bout *ou* attack of bronchitis

bronchiteux, -euse /bʀɔ̃ʃitø, øz/ **ADJ** [*personne*] suffering from bronchitis, bronchitic (*SPÉC*) **NM,F** person suffering from bronchitis, bronchitic (*SPÉC*)

bronchitique /bʀɔ̃ʃitik/ **ADJ** bronchitic (*SPÉC*) ◆ **il est** ~ he suffers from bronchitis

bronchopneumonie (pl **bronchopneumonies**) /bʀɔ̃kopnømɔni/ **NF** bronchopneumonia (*NonC*)

brontosaure /bʀɔ̃tozɔʀ/ **NM** brontosaurus

bronzage /bʀɔ̃zaʒ/ **NM** 1 [*de peau*] (sun) tan ◆ ~ **intégral** allover tan ◆ **séance de** ~ **artificiel** tanning session ◆ **je vais parfaire mon** ~ I'm going to work on my tan 2 [*de métal*] bronzing

bronzant, e /bʀɔ̃zɑ̃, ɑ̃t/ **ADJ** [*lait, lotion*] tanning (*épith*), suntan (*épith*)

bronze /bʀɔ̃z/ **NM** (*= métal, objet*) bronze

bronzé, e /bʀɔ̃ze/ (ptp de **bronzer**) **ADJ** (sun-)tanned

bronzer /bʀɔ̃ze/ ▸ **conjug 1** ◂ **VT** [*+ peau*] to tan; [*+ métal*] to bronze **VI** [*peau, personne*] to get a tan ◆ **les gens qui (se) bronzent** *ou* **se font** ~ **sur la plage** people who sunbathe on the beach ◆ **je bronze vite** I tan easily

bronzette* /bʀɔ̃zɛt/ **NF** ◆ **faire de la** ~ to sunbathe

bronzeur /bʀɔ̃zœʀ/ **NM** (*= fondeur*) bronze-smelter; (*= fabricant*) bronze-smith

broquette /bʀɔkɛt/ **NF** (*= clou*) tack

brossage /bʀɔsaʒ/ **NM** brushing

brosse /bʀɔs/ **NF** 1 (*= ustensile*) brush; [*de peintre*] (paint)brush ◆ **donne un coup de** ~ **à ta veste** give your jacket a brush ◆ **passer le tapis à la** ~ to give the carpet a brush, to brush the carpet ◆ **passer le carrelage à la** ~ to give the tiled floor a scrub ◆ **il sait manier la** ~ **à reluire** he really knows how to suck up to people* *ou* butter people up 2 (*Coiffure*) crew cut ◆ **avoir les cheveux en** ~ to have a crew cut 3 (*Can*) **prendre une** ~⁑ to get drunk *ou* smashed⁑

COMP **brosse à chaussures** shoebrush

brosse à cheveux hairbrush

brosse en chiendent scrubbing brush

brosse à dents toothbrush

brosse à habits clothesbrush

brosse métallique wire brush

brosse à ongles nailbrush

brosser /bʀɔse/ ▸ **conjug 1** ◂ **VT** 1 (*= nettoyer*) to brush; [*+ cheval*] to brush down; [*+ plancher, carrelage*] to scrub ◆ **viens ici que je te brosse** come here and let me give you a brush ◆ ~ **des miettes sur une table** to brush crumbs off a table 2 (*Art, fig = peindre*) to paint ◆ ~ **un vaste tableau de la situation** to paint a broad picture of the situation 3 (*Sport*) [*+ balle*] to put spin on 4 (** : Belg*) [*+ cours*] to skip **VPR** **se brosser** 1 (*= frotter*) to brush one's clothes, to give one's clothes a brush ◆ **se** ~ **les dents** to brush *ou* clean one's teeth ◆ **se** ~ **les cheveux** to brush one's hair 2 (⁑ *: locutions*) **se** ~ **le ventre** to go without food ◆ **tu peux (toujours) te** ~ ! you'll have to do without!, nothing doing!⁑, you can whistle for it!⁑

brosserie /bʀɔsʀi/ **NF** (*= usine*) brush factory; (*= commerce*) brush trade

brossier, -ière /bʀɔsje, jɛʀ/ **NM,F** (*= ouvrier*) brush maker; (*= commerçant*) brush dealer

brou /bʀu/ **NM** (*= écorce*) husk, shuck (*US*) ◆ ~ **de noix** (*Menuiserie*) walnut stain; (*= liqueur*) walnut liqueur

broue⁑ /bʀu/ **NF** (*Can*) [*de bière*] froth; [*de mer*] foam

brouet /bʀuɛ/ **NM** († † *= potage*) gruel; (*péj ou hum*) brew

brouette /bʀuɛt/ **NF** wheelbarrow

brouettée /bʀuete/ **NF** (wheel)barrowful

brouetter /bʀuete/ ▸ **conjug 1** ◂ **VT** to (carry in a) wheelbarrow

brouhaha /bʀuaa/ **NM** (*= tintamarre*) hubbub

brouillage /bʀujaʒ/ **NM** (*Radio*) (*intentionnel*) jamming; (*accidentel*) interference; (*TV*) scrambling; (*fig*) [*de points de repère*] blurring ◆ ~ **des pistes** confusion

brouillard /bʀujaʀ/ **NM** 1 (*dense*) fog; (*léger*) mist; (*mêlé de fumée*) smog ◆ ~ **de chaleur** heat haze ◆ ~ **givrant** freezing fog ◆ ~ **à couper au couteau** thick *ou* dense fog, peasouper* ◆ **il fait** *ou* **il y a du** ~ it's foggy ◆ **être dans le** ~ (*fig*) to be in the dark; → **foncer**[1] 2 (*= livre de commerce*) daybook

brouillasser /bʀujase/ ▸ **conjug 1** ◂ **VB IMPERS** to drizzle

brouille /bʀuj/ **NF** disagreement, breach, quarrel ◆ ~ **légère** tiff ◆ **être en** ~ **avec qn** to have fallen out with sb, to be on bad terms with sb

brouillé, e /bʀuje/ (ptp de **brouiller**) **ADJ** 1 (*= fâché*) **être** ~ **avec qn** to have fallen out with sb, to be on bad terms with sb ◆ **être** ~ **avec les dates/l'orthographe*** to be hopeless *ou* useless* at dates/spelling 2 (*= altéré*) **avoir le teint** ~ to have a muddy complexion; → **œuf**

brouiller /bʀuje/ ▸ **conjug 1** ◂ **VT** 1 (*= troubler*) [*+ contour, vue, yeux*] to blur; [*+ papiers, idées*] to mix up, to muddle up; [*+ combinaison de coffre*] to scramble; [*+ message*] (*lit*) to scramble; (*fig*) to confuse; [*+ frontières, repères*] to blur ◆ **la buée brouille les verres de mes lunettes** my glasses are misting up ◆ **la pluie a brouillé l'adresse** the rain has smudged *ou* blurred the address ◆ ~ **les pistes** *ou* **cartes** to confuse *ou* cloud the issue ◆ **cette déclaration a brouillé l'image du président** the statement has tarnished the president's image

2 (*= fâcher*) to set at odds, to put on bad terms ◆ **cet incident l'a brouillé avec sa famille** the incident set him at odds with *ou* put him on bad terms with his family ◆ **elle m'a brouillé avec l'informatique** she really put me off computers

3 (*Radio*) [*+ émission*] (*volontairement*) to jam; (*par accident*) to cause interference to; (*TV*) to scramble

VPR **se brouiller** 1 (*= se troubler*) [*vue*] to become blurred; [*souvenirs, idées*] to get mixed up *ou* muddled up, to become confused ◆ **tout se brouilla dans sa tête** everything became confused *ou* muddled in his mind

2 (*= se fâcher*) **se** ~ **avec qn** to fall out *ou* quarrel with sb ◆ **depuis qu'ils se sont brouillés** since they fell out (with each other)

3 [*ciel*] to cloud over ◆ **le temps se brouille** it's going *ou* turning cloudy, the weather is breaking

brouillerie /bʀujʀi/ **NF** ⇒ **brouille**

brouilleur /bʀujœʀ/ **NM** jammer

brouillon, -onne /bʀujɔ̃, ɔn/ **ADJ** (*= qui manque de soin*) untidy; (*= qui manque d'organisation*) unmethodical, unsystematic, muddle-headed ◆ **élève** ~ careless pupil ◆ **avoir l'esprit** ~ to be muddle-headed **NM,F** (*= personne*) muddler, muddlehead **NM** [*de lettre, devoir*] rough copy; (*= ébauche*) (rough) draft; [*de calculs, notes*] rough work ◆ **(papier)** ~ rough paper ◆ **prendre qch au** ~ to make a rough copy of sth; → **cahier**

broum /bʀum/ **EXCL** brum

broussaille /bʀusɑj/ **NF** ◆ ~**s** undergrowth, brushwood, scrub ◆ **avoir les cheveux en** ~ to have tousled hair ◆ **sourcils en** ~ bushy eyebrows

broussailleux, -euse /bʀusɑjø, øz/ **ADJ** [*terrain, sous-bois*] bushy, scrubby; [*ronces*] brambly; [*jardin*] overgrown; [*sourcils, barbe*] bushy; [*cheveux*] bushy, tousled

broussard* /bʀusaʀ/ **NM** bushman

brousse /bʀus/ **NF** ◆ **la** ~ the bush ◆ **c'est en pleine** ~* (*fig*) it's at the back of beyond*, it's in the middle of nowhere

broutage /bʀutaʒ/ **NM** ⇒ **broutement**

broutard /bʀutaʀ/ **NM** grass-fed calf

broutement /bʀutmɑ̃/ **NM** 1 [*de mouton*] grazing; [*de lapin*] nibbling; [*de vache, cerf*] browsing 2 [*de rabot*] chattering

brouter /bʀute/ ▸ **conjug 1** ◂ **VT** 1 [*+ herbe*] to graze on, to browse on 2 ⁑ [*+ sexe féminin*] to go down on*⁑ ◆ **il nous les broute !** he's a fucking pain in the neck!*⁑ **VI** 1 [*mouton, vache, cerf*] to graze, to browse 2 (*Tech*) [*rabot*] to chatter 3 [*freins*] to grab; [*embrayage, voiture*] to judder

broutille /bʀutij/ **NF** (*= bagatelle*) trifle ◆ **c'est de la** ~* (*de mauvaise qualité*) it's just junk, it's cheap rubbish (*Brit*); (*sans importance*) it's not worth mentioning, it's nothing of any consequence ◆ **perdre son temps à des** ~**s** to lose one's time over trifles *ou* trivial matters

brownie /bʀɔni/ **NM** (*Culin*) brownie

brownien, -ienne /bʀonjɛ̃, jɛn/ **ADJ** [*mouvement, particules*] Brownian ◆ **agité de mouvements** ~**s** (*fig*) rushing about in all directions

broyage /bʀwajaʒ/ **NM** 1 [*de pierre, sucre, os*] grinding, crushing; [*de poivre, blé, couleurs*] grinding 2 [*de chanvre, lin*] braking

broyer /bʀwaje/ ▸ **conjug 8** ◂ **VT** 1 (*= concasser*) [*+ pierre, sucre, os*] to grind (to a powder), to crush; [*+ poivre, blé, couleurs*] to grind 2 (*= écraser*) [*+ chanvre, lin*] to brake; [*+ doigt, main*] to crush ◆ **il a été broyé par une machine** he was crushed to death in a machine 3 (*= mastiquer*) [*+ aliments*] to grind, to break up

◆ **broyer du noir** to brood ◆ **dès qu'elle est seule, elle broie du noir** when she's alone, she starts brooding ◆ **nos industriels broient du noir** our industrialists are despondent

broyeur, -euse /bʀwajœʀ, øz/ **ADJ** crushing, grinding **NM** (*= ouvrier*) grinder, crusher; (*= machine*) grinder, crusher; [*de chanvre, lin*] brake ◆ ~ **(de cailloux)** pebble grinder

brrr /bʀʀ/ **EXCL** brr!

bru /bʀy/ **NF** daughter-in-law

bruant /bʀyɑ̃/ **NM** bunting (*bird*) ◆ ~ **jaune** yellowhammer ◆ ~ **des roseaux** reed bunting

brucelles /bʀysɛl/ **NFPL** tweezers

brucellose /bʀyseloz/ **NF** brucellosis

brugnon /bʀyɲɔ̃/ **NM** nectarine

brugnonier /bʀyɲɔnje/ **NM** nectarine tree

bruine /bʀɥin/ **NF** (fine) drizzle, Scotch mist

bruiner /bʀɥine/ ▸ **conjug 1** ◂ **VB IMPERS** to drizzle

bruineux, -euse /bʀɥinø, øz/ **ADJ** drizzly

bruire /bʀɥiʀ/ ▸ **conjug 2** ◂ **VI** [*feuilles, tissu, vent*] to rustle; [*ruisseau*] to murmur; [*insecte*] to buzz, to hum ◆ **le marché financier s'est mis à** ~ **des rumeurs les plus bizarres** the money market has started buzzing with the strangest rumours

bruissement /bʀɥismɑ̃/ NM *[de feuilles, tissu, vent]* rustle, rustling; *[de ruisseau]* murmur; *[d'insecte]* buzz(ing), humming

bruit /bʀɥi/ NM 1 *(gén)* sound, noise; *(désagréable)* noise ◆ **j'ai entendu un ~** I heard a noise ◆ **un ~ de vaisselle** the clatter of dishes ◆ **un ~** *ou* **des ~s de moteur/voix** the sound of an engine/of voices ◆ **un ~** *ou* **des ~s de marteau** (the sound of) hammering ◆ **un ~ de verre brisé** the tinkle *ou* sound of broken glass ◆ **un ~ de pas** (the sound of) footsteps ◆ **le ~ d'un plongeon** a splash ◆ **le ~ de la pluie contre les vitres** the sound *ou* patter of the rain against the windows ◆ **le ~ des radios** the noise *ou* blare of radios ◆ **les ~s de la rue** street noises ◆ **~ de fond** background noise ◆ **le ~ familier des camions** the familiar rumble of the lorries ◆ **~ sourd** thud ◆ **~ strident** screech, shriek ◆ **on n'entend aucun ~ d'ici** you can't hear a sound from here ◆ **passer dans un ~ de tonnerre** to thunder past

2 *(opposé à silence)* **le ~** noise ◆ **j'ai entendu du ~** I heard a noise ◆ **il y a trop de ~** there's too much noise, it's too noisy ◆ **je ne peux pas travailler dans le ~** I can't work in a noisy environment ◆ **le ~ est insupportable ici** the noise is unbearable here ◆ **sans ~** noiselessly, without a sound, silently ◆ **faire du ~** *[objet, machine]* to make a *ou* some noise ◆ **les enfants font du ~, c'est normal** it's natural for children to be noisy ◆ **arrêtez de faire du ~** stop being so noisy ◆ **cette machine fait un ~ infernal** this machine makes a dreadful noise *ou* racket*

3 *(= perturbation)* **beaucoup de ~ pour rien** much ado about nothing, a lot of fuss about nothing ◆ **faire grand ~** *[affaire, déclaration, film, nouvelle]* to cause quite a stir ◆ **faire grand ~** *ou* **beaucoup de ~ autour de qch** to make a great fuss *ou* to-do about sth ◆ **cette nouvelle a été annoncée à grand ~** the news was announced amid much publicity *ou* fanfare ◆ **il fait plus de ~ que de mal** his bark is worse than his bite

4 *(= nouvelle)* rumour ◆ **le ~ de son départ ...** the rumour of his departure ... ◆ **le ~ court qu'il doit partir** there's a rumour going about that he is to leave ◆ **c'est un ~ qui court** it's a rumour that's going around ◆ **se faire l'écho d'un ~** to repeat a rumour ◆ **répandre de faux ~s (sur)** to spread false rumours *ou* tales (about) ◆ **les ~s de couloir à l'Assemblée nationale** parliamentary rumours ◆ **~s de guerre** rumours of war ◆ **~ de bottes** sabre-rattling ◆ **il n'est ~ †† dans la ville que de son arrivée** his arrival is the talk of the town

5 *(Téléc)* noise ◆ **~ de souffle** *(Méd)* murmur ◆ **~ de galop** *(Méd)* galop rhythm

bruitage /bʀɥitaʒ/ NM sound effects

bruiter /bʀɥite/ ▸ conjug 1 ◂ VT to add the sound effects to

bruiteur, -euse /bʀɥitœʀ, øz/ NM,F sound-effects engineer

brûlage /bʀylaʒ/ NM *[de cheveux]* singeing; *[de café]* roasting; *[d'herbes]* burning ◆ **faire un ~ à qn** to singe sb's hair

brûlant, e /bʀylɑ̃, ɑ̃t/ ADJ 1 *(= chaud)* *[objet]* burning (hot), red-hot; *[plat]* piping hot; *[liquide]* boiling (hot), scalding; *[soleil]* scorching, blazing; *[air]* burning ◆ **il a le front ~ (de fièvre)** his forehead is burning (with fever) 2 *(= passionné)* *[regard, pages]* fiery, impassioned 3 *(= controversé)* *[sujet]* highly topical ◆ **être sur un terrain ~** to touch on a hotly debated issue ◆ **c'est d'une actualité ~e** it's the burning question *ou* issue of the hour

brûlé, e /bʀyle/ (ptp de **brûler**) ADJ ◆ **il est ~*** *(gén)* he's had* *ou* blown* it; *[espion]* his cover is blown*; → **crème, terre, tête** NM,F *(= personne)* burnt person ◆ **grand ~** victim of third-degree burns, badly burnt person NM ◆ **ça sent le ~** *(lit)* there's a smell of burning; *(fig)* there's trouble brewing ◆ **cela a un goût de ~** it tastes burnt *ou* has a burnt taste

brûle-gueule (pl **brûle-gueules**) /bʀylgœl/ NM short (clay) pipe

brûle-parfum (pl **brûle-parfums**) /bʀylpaʀfœ̃/ NM perfume burner

brûle-pourpoint /bʀylpuʀpwɛ̃/ **à brûle-pourpoint** LOC ADV 1 *(= brusquement)* point-blank 2 († † *= à bout portant)* at point-blank range

brûler /bʀyle/ ▸ conjug 1 ◂ VT 1 *(= détruire)* *[+ objet, ordures, corps]* to burn; *[+ maison, village]* to burn down ◆ **être brûlé vif** *(accident)* to be burnt alive *ou* burnt to death; *(supplice)* to be burnt at the stake ◆ **il a brûlé ses dernières cartouches** *(fig)* he's shot his bolt ◆ **~ ses vaisseaux** *(fig)* to burn one's bridges *ou* one's boats *(Brit)* ◆ **~ le pavé** † to ride *ou* run hell for leather* ◆ **~ les planches** *(Théât)* to give a spirited performance ◆ **~ ce que l'on a adoré** to burn one's old idols

2 *(= endommager)* *[flamme]* to burn; *[eau bouillante]* to scald; *[fer à repasser]* to singe, to scorch; *[soleil]* *[+ herbe]* to scorch; *[+ peau]* to burn; *[gel]* *[+ bourgeon]* to nip, to damage; *[acide]* *[+ peau]* to burn, to sear; *[+ métal]* to burn, to attack, to corrode ◆ **il a la peau brûlée par le soleil** his skin is sunburnt ◆ **le soleil nous brûle** the sun is scorching *ou* burning

3 *(= donner une sensation de brûlure à)* to burn ◆ **le radiateur me brûlait le dos** the radiator was burning *ou* scorching my back ◆ **j'ai les yeux qui me brûlent, les yeux me brûlent** my eyes are smarting *ou* stinging ◆ **j'ai la figure qui (me) brûle** my face is burning ◆ **la gorge lui brûle** he's got a burning sensation in his throat ◆ **l'argent lui brûle les doigts** money burns a hole in his pocket ◆ **cette question me brûlait les lèvres** I was dying to ask that question

4 *(= traiter)* *[+ café]* to roast; *[+ pointes de cheveux]* to singe; *(Méd)* to cauterize

5 *(= consommer)* *[+ électricité, charbon]* to burn, to use; *[+ cierge, encens, calories]* to burn ◆ **ils ont brûlé tout leur bois** they've burnt up *ou* used up all their wood ◆ **~ la chandelle par les deux bouts** to burn the candle at both ends ◆ **j'irai ~ un cierge pour toi** *(hum)* I'll go and light a candle for you, I'll cross my fingers for you

6 *(= ignorer)* **~ un stop** to ignore a stop sign ◆ **~ un feu rouge** to go through a red light, to run a red light *(US)* ◆ **~ un signal/une station** *[train]* to go through *ou* past a signal/a station (without stopping) ◆ **~ une étape** to cut out a stop ◆ **~ les étapes** *(= réussir rapidement)* to shoot ahead; *(= trop se précipiter)* to cut corners, to take short cuts ◆ **~ la politesse à qn** to leave sb abruptly (without saying goodbye)

VI 1 *[charbon, feu]* to burn; *[maison, forêt]* to be on fire; *(Culin)* to burn ◆ **ce bois brûle très vite** this wood burns (up) very quickly ◆ **j'ai laissé ~ le rôti** I burnt the roast ◆ **on a laissé ~ l'électricité** *ou* **l'électricité a brûlé toute la journée** the lights have been left on *ou* have been burning away all day; → **torchon**

2 *(= être très chaud)* to be burning (hot) *ou* scalding ◆ **son front brûle de fièvre** his forehead is burning ◆ **ne touche pas, ça brûle** don't touch that, you'll burn yourself *ou* you'll get burnt ◆ **tu brûles !** *(jeu, devinette)* you're getting hot!

3 ◆ **~ de faire qch** *(= être impatient)* to be burning *ou* be dying to do sth ◆ **~ d'impatience** to seethe with impatience ◆ **~ (d'amour) pour qn** († *ou hum)* to be infatuated *ou* madly in love with sb ◆ **~ d'envie** *ou* **du désir de faire qch** to be dying *ou* longing to do sth

VPR **se brûler** 1 *(gén)* to burn o.s.; *(= s'ébouillanter)* to scald o.s. ◆ **je me suis brûlé la langue** I burnt my tongue ◆ **se ~ les doigts** *(lit)* to burn one's fingers; *(fig)* to get one's fingers burnt ◆ **le papillon s'est brûlé les ailes à la flamme** the moth burnt *ou* singed its wings in the flame ◆ **se ~ la cervelle** to blow one's brains out

2 (* : *Can)* to exhaust o.s., to wear o.s. out

brûlerie /bʀylʀi/ NF *[de café]* *(= usine)* coffee-roasting plant; *(= magasin)* coffee-roasting shop; *[d'alcool]* (brandy) distillery

brûleur /bʀylœʀ/ NM *(= dispositif)* burner

brûlis /bʀyli/ NM *(= technique)* slash-and-burn technique; *(= terrain)* field *(where vegetation has been slashed and burnt)* ◆ **culture sur ~** slash-and-burn agriculture *ou* farming

brûloir /bʀylwaʀ/ NM *(= machine)* coffee roaster

brûlot /bʀylo/ NM 1 *(Hist Naut)* fire ship; *(= personne)* firebrand ◆ **lancer un ~ contre** *(fig)* to launch a scathing *ou* blistering attack on 2 *(Can)* midge, gnat

brûlure /bʀylyʀ/ NF *(= lésion)* burn; *(= sensation)* burning sensation ◆ **~ (d'eau bouillante)** scald ◆ **~ de cigarette** cigarette burn ◆ **~ du premier degré** first-degree burn ◆ **~s d'estomac** heartburn *(NonC)*

brumaire /bʀymɛʀ/ NM Brumaire *(second month of French Republican calendar)*

brume /bʀym/ NF *(= brouillard)* *(léger)* mist; *(de chaleur)* haze; *(dense)* fog; *(Naut)* fog ◆ **être dans les ~s du sommeil/de l'alcool** to be half asleep/in a drunken stupor; → **banc, corne**

brumeux, -euse /bʀymø, øz/ ADJ 1 *[temps]* misty, foggy; *[ciel]* hazy 2 *[poésie, philosophie, raisonnement]* obscure, hazy; *[idée, souvenir]* vague, hazy

brumisateur ® /bʀymizatœʀ/ NM spray, atomiser

brun, brune /bʀœ̃, bʀyn/ ADJ *[yeux, couleur]* brown; *[cheveux]* brown, dark; *[peau]* dusky, swarthy, dark; *(= bronzé)* tanned, brown; *[tabac]* dark; *[bière]* brown ◆ **il est ~** *(cheveux)* he's dark-haired; *(bronzé)* he's tanned ◆ **il est ~ (de peau)** he's dark-skinned ◆ **~ roux** (dark) auburn NM *(= couleur)* brown; *(= homme)* dark-haired man NF **brune** 1 *(= bière)* ≈ brown ale 2 *(= cigarette) cigarette made of dark tobacco* 3 *(= femme)* brunette 4 *(littér)* **à la ~e** at twilight, at dusk

brunante /bʀynɑ̃t/ NF *(Can)* ◆ **à la ~** at twilight, at dusk

brunâtre /bʀynɑtʀ/ ADJ brownish

brunch /bʀœ(t)ʃ/ NM brunch

Brunéi /bʀynei/ NM Brunei

brunéien, -ienne /bʀyneјɛ̃, jɛn/ ADJ of *ou* from Brunei NM,F **Brunéien(ne)** inhabitant *ou* native of Brunei

brunette /bʀynɛt/ NF brunette

brunir /bʀyniʀ/ ▸ conjug 2 ◂ VI *[personne, peau]* to get a tan; *[cheveux]* to go darker; *[caramel]* to brown VT 1 *[+ peau]* to tan; *[+ cheveux]* to darken 2 *[+ métal]* to burnish, to polish

brunissage /bʀynisaʒ/ NM *(Tech)* burnishing; *(Culin)* browning

brunissement /bʀynismɑ̃/ NM *[de peau]* tanning

brunissoir /bʀyniswaʀ/ NM burnisher

brunissure /bʀynisyʀ/ NF *[de métal]* burnish; *(Agr)* potato rot; *[de vigne]* brown rust

brunoise /bʀynwaz/ NF *(Culin)* diced vegetable ◆ **fine ~ de carottes** finely diced carrots ◆ **taillez la courgette en ~** dice the courgette

bruschetta /bʀuskɛta/ NF bruschetta

brushing /bʀœʃiŋ/ NM blow-dry ◆ **faire un ~ à qn** to blow-dry sb's hair

⚠ **brushing** ne se traduit pas par le mot anglais **brushing**, qui n'est pas un terme de coiffure.

brusque /bʀysk/ ADJ [1] (= rude, sec) *[personne, manières]* brusque, abrupt, blunt; *[geste]* brusque, abrupt, rough; *[ton]* curt, abrupt, blunt • **être ~ avec qn** to be curt *ou* abrupt with sb [2] (= soudain) *[départ, changement]* abrupt, sudden; *[virage]* sharp; *[envie]* sudden • **la ~ aggravation de la crise économique** the sudden worsening of the economic crisis

brusquement /bʀyskəmɑ̃/ ADV [1] (= sèchement) brusquely, abruptly, bluntly [2] (= subitement) suddenly

brusquer /bʀyske/ ▸ conjug 1 ◂ VT [1] (= précipiter) to rush, to hasten • **attaque brusquée** surprise attack • **il ne faut rien ~** we mustn't rush things [2] *[+ personne]* to rush, to chivvy*

brusquerie /bʀyskəʀi/ NF brusqueness, abruptness

brut, e[1] /bʀyt/ ADJ [1] *[diamant]* uncut, rough; *[pétrole]* crude; *[minerai]* crude, raw; *[sucre]* unrefined; *[soie, métal]* raw; *[toile]* unbleached; *[laine]* untreated; *[idée]* crude, raw; *[art]* primitive; *[donnée]* raw • **les faits ~s** the hard facts • **à l'état ~** *[diamant]* in the rough; *[matière]* untreated, unprocessed • **informations à l'état ~** raw data • **~ de béton** *ou* **de décoffrage** *[pilier, mur]* raw concrete; *(fig)* rough and ready • **~ de fonderie** *[pièce]* unpolished; *(fig)* rough and ready • **force ~e** brute force *ou* physical violence

[2] *[champagne]* brut, dry; *[cidre]* dry

[3] *(Comm, Fin) [bénéfice, poids, salaire]* gross • **il touche 5 000 € ~s par mois** he earns €5,000 gross per month, he grosses €5,000 per month • **ils ont fait un bénéfice ~ de 5 millions** they made a gross profit of *ou* they grossed 5 million • **ça fait 100 €/100 kg ~, ça fait ~ 100 €/100 kg** that makes €100/100 kg gross; → **marge, produit, résultat**

NM [1] (= pétrole) crude (oil) • **~ lourd/léger** heavy/light crude

[2] (= champagne) brut *ou* dry champagne; (= cidre) dry cider

[3] (= salaire) gross salary

brutal, e (mpl **-aux**) /bʀytal, o/ ADJ [1] (= violent) *[personne, caractère]* rough, brutal, violent; *[instinct]* savage; *[jeu]* rough • **être ~ avec qn** to be rough with sb • **force ~e** brute force [2] (= abrupt, cru) *[langage, franchise]* blunt; *[vérité]* plain, unvarnished; *[réalité]* stark • **il a été très ~ dans sa réponse** he gave a very blunt answer [3] (= soudain) *[mort, changement]* sudden; *[choc, coup]* brutal

brutalement /bʀytalmɑ̃/ ADV [1] (= violemment) *[pousser, saisir, attaquer]* brutally [2] (= sèchement) *[dire, répondre, déclarer]* bluntly [3] (= subitement) *[chuter, mourir, changer]* suddenly

brutaliser /bʀytalize/ ▸ conjug 1 ◂ VT *[+ personne]* *(gén)* to ill-treat; *(physiquement)* to knock about*, to manhandle; *[+ enfant]* *(à l'école)* to bully; *[+ machine]* to treat roughly • **femme brutalisée par son mari** battered wife

brutalité /bʀytalite/ NF [1] (= violence) roughness; *(plus cruelle)* brutality; *(Sport)* rough play *(NonC)* • **avec ~** brutally • **il l'a dit fermement mais sans ~** he was firm about it without being brutal [2] (= acte) brutality • **~s policières** police brutality [3] (= soudaineté) suddenness, abruptness

brute[2] /bʀyt/ NF (= homme brutal) brute, animal; (= homme grossier) lout; *(littér = animal)* brute, beast • **taper sur qch comme une ~*** to bash* away at sth (savagely) • **frapper qn comme une ~** to hit out at sb brutishly • **travailler comme une ~*** to work like a dog • **~ épaisse*** lout • **c'est une sale ~ !*** he's a real brute!* • **tu es une grosse ~ !*** you're a big bully!

Brutus /bʀytys/ NM Brutus

Bruxelles /bʀysɛl/ N Brussels; → **chou**[1]

bruxellois, e /bʀykselwa, waz/ ADJ of *ou* from Brussels NM,F **Bruxellois(e)** inhabitant *ou* native of Brussels

bruyamment /bʀɥijamɑ̃/ ADV *[rire, parler]* noisily, loudly; *[protester]* loudly

bruyant, e /bʀɥijɑ̃, ɑ̃t/ ADJ *[personne, réunion]* noisy, boisterous; *[rue]* noisy; *[rire]* loud; *[succès]* resounding *(épith)* • **ils ont accueilli la nouvelle avec une joie ~e** they greeted the news with whoops* *ou* with loud cries of joy

bruyère /bʀyjɛʀ/ NF (= plante) heather; (= terrain) heath(land) • **pipe en (racine de) ~** briar pipe; → **coq**[1]**, terre**

bryophytes /bʀijɔfit/ NFPL bryophytes

BT /bete/ NM (abrév de **brevet de technicien**) → **brevet**

BTP /betepe/ NMPL (abrév de **bâtiments et travaux publics**) *public buildings and works sector*

BTS /betees/ NM (abrév de **brevet de technicien supérieur**) → **brevet**

BU /bey/ NF (abrév de **bibliothèque universitaire**) → **bibliothèque**

bu, e /by/ ptp de **boire**

buanderette /bɥɑ̃dʀɛt/ NF *(Can)* launderette *(Brit)*, Laundromat ® *(US)*

buanderie /bɥɑ̃dʀi/ NF wash house, laundry; *(Can = blanchisserie)* laundry

Buba* /buba/ NF (abrév de **Bundesbank**) • **la ~** the Bundesbank

bubale /bybal/ NM bubal

bubon /bybɔ̃/ NM bubo

bubonique /bybɔnik/ ADJ bubonic; → **peste**

Bucarest /bykaʀɛst/ N Bucharest

buccal, e (mpl **-aux**) /bykal, o/ ADJ oral; → **cavité, voie**

buccin /byksɛ̃/ NM whelk

buccodentaire /bykodɑ̃tɛʀ/ ADJ *[hygiène]* oral

bûche /byʃ/ NF [1] *[de bois]* log • **~ de Noël** Yule log • **~ glacée** ice-cream Yule log [2] (* = lourdaud) blockhead*, clot* *(Brit)*, clod* *(US)*, lump* • **rester (là) comme une ~** to sit there like a (great) lump* [3] (* = chute) fall, spill • **ramasser une ~** to come a cropper* *(Brit)*, to take a (headlong) spill *(US)*

bûcher[1] /byʃe/ NM [1] (= remise) woodshed [2] *(funéraire)* (funeral) pyre; (= supplice) stake • **être condamné au ~** to be condemned to (be burnt at) the stake

bûcher[2]* /byʃe/ ▸ conjug 1 ◂ VT *[étudiant]* to bone up on*, to swot up* *(Brit)* VI to swot* *(Brit)*, to cram* *(US)*

bûcher[3] /byʃe/ ▸ conjug 1 ◂ *(Can)* VT *[+ arbres]* to fell, to cut down, to chop down VI to fell trees

bûcheron, -onne /byʃʀɔ̃, ɔn/ NM,F woodcutter, lumberjack *(esp in Canada)*

bûchette /byʃɛt/ NF (dry) twig, stick (of wood); *(pour compter)* rod, stick

bûcheur, -euse* /byʃœʀ, øz/ ADJ hard-working NM,F slogger*, swot* *(Brit)*, grind* *(US)*

bucolique /bykɔlik/ ADJ bucolic, pastoral NF bucolic, pastoral (poem)

Budapest /bydapɛst/ N Budapest

budget /bydʒɛ/ NM budget • **~ annexe** supplementary budget • **~ d'exploitation** working *ou* operating budget • **~ de fonctionnement** operating budget • **~ d'investissement** capital budget • **~ prévisionnel** provisional budget • **~ publicitaire** *[d'annonceur]* advertising budget; *[d'agence de publicité]* advertising account • **~ social** welfare budget • **le client au ~ modeste** the customer on a tight budget • **vacances pour petits ~s** *ou* **~s modestes** low-cost *ou* -budget holidays • **film à gros ~** big-budget film; → **boucler**

budgétaire /bydʒetɛʀ/ ADJ *[dépenses, crise, politique]* budget *(épith)*; *[déficit]* budgetary • **débat ~** budget debate, debate on the budget

budgéter /bydʒete/ ▸ conjug 6 ◂ VT ⇒ **budgétiser**

budgétisation /bydʒetizasjɔ̃/ NF inclusion in the budget

budgétiser /bydʒetize/ ▸ conjug 1 ◂ VT to include in the budget, to budget for

budgétivore /bydʒetivɔʀ/ ADJ high-spending *(épith)*

buée /bɥe/ NF *[d'haleine]* condensation, steam; *[d'eau chaude]* steam; *(sur vitre)* mist, steam, condensation; *(sur miroir)* mist • **couvert de ~** misted up, steamed up • **faire de la ~** to make steam

Buenos Aires /bwenɔzɛʀ/ N Buenos Aires

buffet /byfɛ/ NM [1] (= meuble) sideboard • **~ de cuisine** dresser *(Brit)*, kitchen cabinet *(US)*; → **danser** [2] *[de réception]* (= table) buffet; (= repas) buffet (meal) • **~ campagnard** ≈ cold table • **~ froid** cold buffet • **~ (de gare)** station buffet • **~ roulant** refreshment trolley *(Brit)* *ou* cart *(US)* [3] (* = ventre) stomach, belly* • **il n'a rien dans le ~** *(à jeun)* he hasn't had anything to eat; *(peureux)* he has no guts* [4] • **~ (d'orgue)** (organ) case

buffle /byfl/ NM buffalo

bug /bœg/ NM *(Ordin)* bug • **le ~ de l'an 2000** the millennium bug

buggy /bygi/ NM buggy

bugle[1] /bygl/ NM (= instrument) bugle

bugle[2] /bygl/ NF (= plante) bugle

bugne /byɲ/ NF sweet fritter

building /bildiŋ/ NM high-rise building, tower block

buire /bɥiʀ/ NF ewer

buis /bɥi/ NM (= arbre) box(wood) *(NonC)*, box tree; (= bois) box(wood)

buisson /bɥisɔ̃/ NM bush • **~ ardent** *(Bible)* burning bush • **~ de langoustines** *langoustine arranged in a pyramid shape*

buissonnant, e /bɥisɔnɑ̃, ɑ̃t/ ADJ *[plante]* bush-like; *[favoris]* bushy, luxuriant

buissonneux, -euse /bɥisɔnø, øz/ ADJ *[terrain]* bushy, full of bushes; *[végétation]* scrubby

buissonnière /bɥisɔnjɛʀ/ ADJ F → **école**

Bujumbura /buʒumbuʀa/ N Bujumbura

bulbe /bylb/ NM *(Bot)* bulb, corm; *(Archit)* onion-shaped dome • **~ pileux** *(Anat)* hair bulb • **~ rachidien** medulla (oblongata)

bulbeux, -euse /bylbø, øz/ ADJ *(Bot)* bulbous; *[forme]* bulbous, onion-shaped

bulgare /bylgaʀ/ ADJ Bulgarian NM (= langue) Bulgarian NMF **Bulgare** Bulgarian, Bulgar

Bulgarie /bylgaʀi/ NF Bulgaria

bulldog /buldɔg/ NM ⇒ **bouledogue**

bulldozer /buldozɛʀ/ NM bulldozer • **c'est un vrai ~** *(fig)* he steamrollers (his way) through everything

bulle[1] /byl/ NF [1] *[d'air, boisson, savon, verre]* bubble; *(sur la peau)* blister, bulla *(SPÉC)* • **faire des ~s** *[liquide]* to bubble; *[personne]* to blow bubbles • **~ d'air** air bubble; *(Tech)* airlock; → **coincer, chambre, chier** [2] (= enceinte stérile) bubble [3] (= espace protégé) cocoon • **la ~ familiale** the family cocoon • **~ financière/spéculative** *(Écon)* financial/speculative bubble • **vivre dans une ~** to live in a bubble [4] *[de bande dessinée]* balloon • **~ d'aide** *(Ordin)* help bubble [5] *[d'emballage]* **film à ~s, emballage-~**

bubble-wrap ◆ **enveloppe à ~s** padded envelope [6](Rel) bull [7](arg Scol = zéro) nought, zero

bulle² /byl/ NM ◆ **(papier)** ~ Manilla paper

bullé, e /byle/ ADJ bubble (épith) ◆ **verre ~** bubble glass

buller* /byle/ ► conjug 1 ◄ VI (= paresser) to laze around

bulletin /byltɛ̃/ NM [1] (= reportage, communiqué) bulletin, report; (= magazine) bulletin; (= formulaire) form; (= certificat) certificate; (= billet) ticket; (Scol) report

[2] (Pol) ballot paper ◆ **voter à ~ secret** to vote by secret ballot

COMP **bulletin de bagage** luggage ticket, baggage check (surtout US)
bulletin blanc (Pol) blank vote
bulletin de commande order form
bulletin de consigne left-luggage (Brit) ou checkroom (US) ticket
bulletin des cours (Bourse) official list, stock-exchange list
bulletin d'information news bulletin
bulletin météorologique weather forecast
bulletin de naissance birth certificate
bulletin de notes ⇒ **bulletin scolaire**
bulletin nul (Pol) spoiled ou spoilt (Brit) ballot paper
bulletin de paie ⇒ **bulletin de salaire**
bulletin de participation (dans un concours) entry form
bulletin de salaire pay-slip, wage slip, salary advice (Brit)
bulletin de santé medical bulletin
bulletin scolaire school report (Brit), report (card) (US)
bulletin trimestriel end-of-term report
bulletin de versement (Helv) slip to accompany payments made through the post office
bulletin de vote (Pol) ballot paper

bulletin-réponse (pl **bulletins-réponses**) /byltɛ̃ʀepɔ̃s/ NM (dans un concours) entry form, reply slip

bulleur*, -euse /bylœʀ, øz/ NM,F lazybones

bull-terrier (pl **bull-terriers**) /bultɛʀje/ NM bull terrier

bulot /bylo/ NM whelk

bungalow /bœ̃galo/ NM (en Inde) bungalow; [de motel] chalet

bunker¹ /bœnkœʀ/ NM (Golf) bunker, sand trap (US)

bunker² /bunkœʀ, bunkɛʀ/ NM bunker

Bunsen /bœnsɛn/ N → **bec**

buraliste /byʀalist/ NMF [de bureau de tabac] shopkeeper selling tobacco products, stamps and sometimes newspapers; [de poste] clerk

bure /byʀ/ NF (= étoffe) frieze, homespun; (= vêtement) [de moine] frock, cowl ◆ **porter la ~** to be a monk

bureau (pl **bureaux**) /byʀo/ NM [1] (= meuble) desk; (sur écran d'ordinateur) desktop

[2] (= cabinet de travail) study

[3] (= lieu de travail, pièce, édifice) office ◆ **le ~ du directeur** the manager's office ◆ **pendant les heures de ~** during office hours ◆ **nos ~x seront fermés** our premises ou the office will be closed ◆ **il travaille dans les ~x*** he has a desk ou an office job ◆ **le ~ des pleurs est fermé** (hum) moaning (about it) will get you nowhere ◆ **emploi de ~** desk ou office job ◆ **équipement/mobilier de ~** office equipment/furniture; → **chef¹, deuxième**

[4] (= section) department; (Mil) branch, department

[5] (= comité) committee; (exécutif) board ◆ **aller à une réunion du ~** to go to a committee meeting ◆ **élire le ~** [syndicats] to elect the officers (of the committee)

COMP **bureau d'accueil** reception
bureau d'aide sociale welfare office
bureau de bienfaisance welfare office
bureau de change bureau de change (Brit), foreign exchange office (US)
bureau des contributions tax office
bureau à cylindre roll-top desk
bureau de douane customs house
bureau d'études [d'entreprise] research department; (= cabinet) research consultancy
Bureau européen de l'environnement European Environment Office
bureau exécutif executive committee
Bureau international du travail International Labour Office
bureau de location booking ou box office
bureau ministre pedestal desk
bureau des objets trouvés lost and found (office), lost property office (Brit)
bureau de placement employment agency
bureau politique [de parti] party executives; [de parti communiste] politburo
bureau de poste post office
bureau de renseignements information service
bureau de tabac shop selling tobacco products, stamps and sometimes newspapers
bureau de tri sorting office
Bureau de vérification de la publicité independent body which regulates the advertising industry
bureau de vote polling station

bureaucrate /byʀokʀat/ NMF bureaucrat

bureaucratie /byʀokʀasi/ NF (péj, gén) bureaucracy; (= employés) officials, officialdom (NonC) ◆ **toute cette ~ m'agace** all this red tape gets on my nerves

bureaucratique /byʀokʀatik/ ADJ bureaucratic

bureaucratisation /byʀokʀatizasjɔ̃/ NF bureaucratization

bureaucratiser /byʀokʀatize/ ► conjug 1 ◄ VT to bureaucratize

bureautique /byʀotik/ NF office automation ◆ **application ~** office automation application

burette /byʀɛt/ NF [1] (Chim) burette; (Culin, Rel) cruet; [de mécanicien] oilcan [2] (** = testicules) **~s** balls**

burgrave /byʀgʀav/ NM (Hist) burgrave

burin /byʀɛ̃/ NM chisel; (Art) (= outil) burin, graver; (= gravure) engraving, print

buriné, e /byʀine/ (ptp de **buriner**) ADJ [visage] (deeply) lined, craggy

buriner /byʀine/ ► conjug 1 ◄ VT (Art) to engrave; (Tech) to chisel, to chip

Burkina(-Faso) /byʀkina(faso)/ NM Burkina-Faso

burkinabé /byʀkinabe/ ADJ of ou from Burkina-Faso NMF **Burkinabé** inhabitant ou native of Burkina-Faso

burlat /byʀla/ NF type of cherry

burlesque /byʀlɛsk/ ADJ (Théât) burlesque; (= comique) comical, funny; (= ridicule) ludicrous, ridiculous ◆ **le ~** the burlesque

burnes** /byʀn/ NFPL (= testicules) balls** ◆ **tu me casses les ~ !** you're getting on my wick!* (Brit), you're really pissing me off!**

burnous /byʀnu(s)/ NM [d'Arabe] burnous(e); [de bébé] baby's cape; → **suer**

burqa /byʀka/ NF burqa

burundais, e /buʀundɛ, ɛz/ ADJ Burundian NM,F **Burundais(e)** Burundian

Burundi /buʀundi/ NM Burundi

bus /bys/ NM (= véhicule, dispositif informatique) bus

busard /byzaʀ/ NM harrier ◆ **~ Saint-Martin** hen harrier

buse¹ /byz/ NF (= oiseau) buzzard; (* = imbécile) dolt*

buse² /byz/ NF (= tuyau) (gén) pipe; (Tech) duct ◆ **~ d'aération** ventilation duct ◆ **~ de carburateur** carburettor choke tube ◆ **~ de haut fourneau** blast nozzle ◆ **~ d'injection** injector (nozzle)

business* /biznɛs/ NM [1] (= affaires) business ◆ **qu'est-ce que c'est que ce ~ ?** what's all this mess about?* [2] (= truc, machin) thingumajig*, thingummy* (Brit)

busqué, e /byske/ ADJ ◆ **avoir le nez ~** to have a hooked ou a hook nose

buste /byst/ NM (= torse) chest; (= seins) bust; (= sculpture) bust ◆ **photographier qn en ~** to take a head-and-shoulder photograph of sb

bustier /bystje/ NM (= sous-vêtement) long-line (strapless) bra; (= corsage) off-the-shoulder top; → **robe**

but /by(t)/ GRAMMAIRE ACTIVE 35.2 NM [1] (= objectif) aim, goal, objective ◆ **il n'a aucun ~ dans la vie** he has no aim in life ◆ **il a pour ~ ou il s'est donné pour ~ de faire** his aim is to do, he is aiming to do ◆ **aller droit au ~** to come ou go straight to the point ◆ **nous touchons au ~** the end ou our goal is in sight ◆ **être encore loin du ~** to have a long way to go ◆ **prenons comme ~ (de promenade) le château** let's go ou walk as far as the castle ◆ **leur ~ de promenade favori** their favourite walk ◆ **aller ou errer sans ~** to wander aimlessly about ou around ◆ **à ~ lucratif** profit-making, profit-seeking ◆ **à ~ non lucratif, sans ~ lucratif** non-profit-making (Brit), non-profit (US), not-for-profit (US)

[2] (= intention) aim, purpose, object; (= raison) reason; (Gram) purpose ◆ **dans le ~ de faire** with the intention ou aim of doing, in order to do ◆ **je lui écris dans le ~ de ...** my aim in writing to him is to ... ◆ **je fais ceci dans le seul ~ de ...** my sole aim in doing this is to ... ◆ **c'est dans ce ~ que nous partons** it's with this aim in view that we're leaving ◆ **faire qch dans un ~ déterminé** to do sth for a definite reason, to do sth with one aim ou object in view ◆ **c'était le ~ de l'opération ou de la manœuvre** that was the object ou point of the operation, this was the object of the exercise ◆ **aller à l'encontre du ~ recherché** to defeat the object ◆ **fermer toutes les routes forestières irait à l'encontre du ~ visé** closing all the forest tracks would defeat the object ou would be counterproductive ◆ **complément de ~** (Gram) purpose clause

[3] (Sport, Ftbl etc) goal; (Tir) target, mark; (Pétanque = cochonnet) jack ◆ **gagner/perdre (par) 3 ~s à 2** to win/lose by 3 goals to 2 ◆ **marquer ou rentrer* un ~** to score a goal ◆ **~ en argent/en or** silver/golden goal

[4] (locution)

◆ **de but en blanc** suddenly, point-blank, just like that* ◆ **il me demanda de ~ en blanc si ...** he asked me point-blank ou straight out if ...

butane /bytan/ NM ◆ **(gaz) ~** (pour camping, industrie) butane; (à usage domestique) calor gas ®

butanier /bytanje/ NM butane tanker

buté, e¹ /byte/ (ptp de **buter**) ADJ [personne, air] stubborn, obstinate, mulish

butée² /byte/ NF [1] (Archit) abutment [2] (de mécanisme, tiroir) stop; [de piscine] end wall; (Ski) toe-piece

buter /byte/ ► conjug 1 ◄ VI [1] (= achopper) to stumble, to trip ◆ **~ contre qch** (= trébucher) to stumble over sth, to catch one's foot on sth; (= cogner) to bump ou bang into ou against sth; (= s'appuyer) to be supported by sth, to rest against sth ◆ **~ contre une difficulté** to come up against a difficulty, to hit a snag* ◆ **nous**

butons sur ce problème depuis le début this problem has been a stumbling block right from the start ◆ ~ **sur un mot** to stumble over *ou* trip over a word

2 *(Ftbl)* to score a goal

VT 1 *[+ personne]* to antagonize ◆ **cela l'a buté** it made him dig his heels in

2 *(= renforcer) [+ mur, colonne]* to prop up

3 (* = *tuer*) to bump off *, to do in *

VPR se buter 1 *(= s'entêter)* to dig one's heels in, to get obstinate *ou* mulish

2 *(= se heurter)* **se ~ à une personne** to bump into a person ◆ **se ~ à une difficulté** to come up against a difficulty, to hit a snag *

buteur /bytœʀ/ **NM** *(Ftbl)* striker

butin /bytɛ̃/ **NM** *[d'armée]* spoils, booty, plunder; *[de voleur]* loot; *(fig)* booty ◆ ~ **de guerre** spoils of war

butiner /bytine/ ▸ **conjug 1** ◂ **VI** *[abeilles]* to gather pollen (and nectar) **VT** *[abeilles] [+ fleurs]* to gather pollen (and nectar) from; *[+ nectar, pollen]* to gather; *(fig)* to gather, to glean, to pick up

butineur, -euse /bytinœʀ, øz/ **ADJ** pollen-gathering *(épith)* **NF butineuse** pollen-gathering bee

butoir /bytwaʀ/ **NM** *(Rail)* buffer; *(Tech)* stop ◆ ~ **de porte** doorstop, door stopper; → **date**

butor /bytɔʀ/ **NM** 1 (* : *péj = malotru*) boor 2 *(= oiseau)* bittern

buttage /bytaʒ/ **NM** earthing-up

butte /byt/ **NF** *(= tertre)* mound, hillock ◆ ~ **de tir** butt ◆ **~-témoin** outlier

◆ **être en butte à** *[+ difficultés]* to be exposed to ◆ **il est en ~ à l'hostilité de ses collègues** he is facing hostility from his colleagues

butter /byte/ ▸ **conjug 1** ◂ **VT** 1 *(Agr) [+ plante]* to earth up; *[+ terre]* to ridge 2 (* = *tuer*) to bump off *, to do in *

buvable /byvabl/ **ADJ** drinkable, fit to drink ◆ **ampoule** ~ phial to be taken orally ◆ **c'est ~ !** * it's not too bad! ◆ **ce type n'est pas ~** * the guy's unbearable *ou* insufferable

buvard /byvaʀ/ **NM** *(= papier)* blotting paper *(NonC)*; *(= sous-main)* blotter

buvette /byvɛt/ **NF** 1 *(= café)* refreshment room; *(en plein air)* refreshment stall 2 *[de ville d'eaux]* pump room

buveur, -euse /byvœʀ, øz/ **NM,F** 1 *(= ivrogne)* drinker 2 *(= consommateur)* drinker; *[de café]* customer ◆ ~ **de bière** beer drinker ◆ **c'est une grande buveuse de café** she drinks a lot of coffee

BVP /bevepe/ **NM** (abrév de **Bureau de vérification de la publicité**) ≈ ASA *(Brit)*

by-pass /bajpas/ **NM** *(= dispositif)* by-pass; *(= intervention chirurgicale)* by-pass operation

byssus /bisys/ **NM** byssus

Byzance /bizɑ̃s/ **N** Byzantium ◆ **c'est ~ !** * *(fig)* what luxury!

byzantin, e /bizɑ̃tɛ̃, in/ **ADJ** *(Hist)* Byzantine; *(péj) [débat]* protracted and trivial ◆ **des querelles ~es** protracted wrangling

byzantinisme /bizɑ̃tinism/ **NM** logic-chopping, (love of) hair-splitting

byzantiniste /bizɑ̃tinist/, **byzantinologue** /bizɑ̃tinɔlɔg/ **NMF** Byzantinist, specialist in Byzantine art

BZH (abrév de **Breizh**) Brittany

Cc

C¹, c¹ /se/ NM (= lettre) C, c ♦ **(langage) C** (Ordin) C (language) ♦ **c cédille** c cedilla

C² (abrév de **Celsius, centigrade**) C

c² abrév de **centime**

c', ç' /s/ abrév de **ce²**

CA /sea/ NM [1] (abrév de **chiffre d'affaires**) → **chiffre** [2] (abrév de **conseil d'administration**) → **conseil**

ça¹ /sa/ PRON DÉM [1] (gén) that, it; (* : pour désigner, près) this; (plus loin) that ♦ **je veux ~, non pas ~, ~ là-bas** I want that one, not this one, that one over there ♦ **qu'est-ce que ~ veut dire ?** what does that *ou* it *ou* this mean? ♦ **~ m'agace de l'entendre se plaindre** it gets on my nerves hearing him complain ♦ **faire des études, ~ ne le tentait guère** studying didn't really appeal to him

[2] (péj : désignant qn) he, she, they ♦ **et ~ va à l'église !** and to think he (*ou* she *etc*) goes to church!

[3] (insistance) **il ne veut pas venir – pourquoi ~ ?** he won't come – why not? *ou* why's that? *ou* why won't he? ♦ **j'ai vu Pierre Borel – qui ~ ?/quand ~ ?/où ~ ?** I saw Pierre Borel – who?/when was that?/where was that?

[4] (locutions) **tu crois ~ !** that's what YOU think! ♦ **~ ne fait rien** it doesn't matter ♦ **on dit ~ !** that's what they (*ou* you *etc*) say! ♦ **voyez-vous ~ !** how do you like that!, did you ever hear of such a thing! ♦ **(ah) ~ non !** most certainly not! ♦ **(ah) ~ oui !** absolutely!, (yes) definitely! ♦ **c'est ~, continue !** (iro) that's right, just you carry on! * (iro) ♦ **~ par exemple !** (indignation) well!, well really!; (surprise) well I never! ♦ **~ alors !** (my) goodness! * ♦ **me faire ~ à moi !** fancy doing that to me (of all people)! ♦ **on dirait un Picasso/du champagne – il y a de ~ *** it looks like a Picasso/tastes like champagne – yes, (I suppose) it does a bit ♦ **tu pars à cause du salaire ? – il y a de ~ *** are you leaving because of the salary? – it is partly that ♦ **j'ai 5 jours de congé, c'est déjà ~ ou toujours ~ (de pris)** I've got 5 days off, that's something at least; → **faire, pas²**

ça² /sa/ NM (Psych = inconscient) id

çà /sa/ ADV [1] ♦ **~ et là** here and there [2] († † = ici) hither † (aussi hum)

cabale /kabal/ NF [1] (= complot) cabal, conspiracy ♦ **monter une ~ contre qn** to mount a conspiracy against sb [2] (Hist) cab(b)ala, kab(b)ala

cabaliste /kabalist/ NMF cab(b)alist

cabalistique /kabalistik/ ADJ (= mystérieux) [signe] cabalistic, arcane; (Hist) cabalistic

caban /kabɑ̃/ NM (= veste longue) car coat, three-quarter (length) coat; [de marin] reefer *ou* pea jacket

cabane /kaban/ NF [1] (en bois) hut, cabin; (en terre) hut; (pour rangements, animaux) shed; (Helv = refuge de montagne) mountain refuge [2] (* : péj = bicoque) shack ♦ **qui commande dans cette ~ ?** (= domicile) who's the boss in this damn place ? [3] (* = prison) **en ~** in (the) clink*, in the nick* (Brit) ♦ **3 ans de ~** 3 years in (the) clink* *ou* in the nick* (Brit) *ou* inside*

COMP **cabane à lapins** (lit) rabbit hutch; (fig) rabbit hutch, box
cabane à outils toolshed
cabane de rondins log cabin
cabane à sucre * (Can) sap house (Can)

cabanon /kabanɔ̃/ NM [1] (en Provence = maisonnette) [de campagne] (country) cottage; [de littoral] cabin, chalet [2] (= remise) shed, hut [3] (= cellule) [d'aliénés] padded cell

cabaret /kabaʀɛ/ NM (= boîte de nuit) night club, cabaret; († = café) tavern, inn; → **danseur**

cabaretier, -ière † /kabaʀ(ə)tje, jɛʀ/ NM,F innkeeper

cabas /kabɑ/ NM (= sac) shopping bag

cabestan /kabɛstɑ̃/ NM capstan; → **virer**

cabillaud /kabijo/ NM (fresh) cod (pl inv)

cabine /kabin/ GRAMMAIRE ACTIVE 54.2 NF [de navire, véhicule spatial] cabin; [d'avion] cockpit; [de train, grue] cab; [de piscine] cubicle; [de laboratoire de langues] booth; (Can) motel room, cabin (US, Can) ♦ **entraînement en ~s** (Scol) language lab training *ou* practice

COMP **cabine d'aiguillage** signal box
cabine (d'ascenseur) lift (cage) (Brit), (elevator) car (US)
cabine de bain (gén) beach *ou* bathing hut; (sur roulettes) bathing machine
cabine de douche shower cubicle *ou* stall (US)
cabine d'essayage fitting room
cabine de pilotage (gén) cockpit; (dans avion de ligne) flight deck
cabine de plage beach *ou* bathing hut
cabine de projection projection room
cabine spatiale cabin (of a spaceship)
cabine de téléphérique cablecar
cabine téléphonique telephone booth *ou* kiosk, pay-phone, call *ou* (tele)phone box (Brit)

cabinet /kabinɛ/ NM [1] (= local professionnel) [de dentiste] surgery (Brit), office (US); [de médecin] consulting-room, surgery (Brit), office (US); [de notaire, huissier] office; [d'avocat, juge] chambers; [d'agent immobilier] agency

[2] (= clientèle) [d'avocat, médecin] practice

[3] (Pol) (= gouvernement) cabinet; (= collaborateurs) staff ♦ **le ~ du ministre** the minister's (personal *ou* private) staff; → **chef¹**

[4] [d'exposition] exhibition room

[5] (= meuble) cabinet

[6] † (= bureau) study; (= réduit) closet †

NMPL **cabinets** (= toilettes) toilet, lavatory, loo * (Brit), bathroom (US) ♦ **aller aux ~s** to go to the toilet (Brit) *ou* the bathroom (US) ♦ **il est aux ~s** he's in the toilet *ou* loo * (Brit) *ou* bathroom (US) ♦ **~s extérieurs** outdoor lavatory, outhouse (US)

COMP **cabinet d'affaires** business consultancy
cabinet d'aisances † water closet †, lavatory
cabinet d'architectes firm of architects
cabinet d'assurances insurance firm *ou* agency
cabinet d'avocats law firm
cabinet-conseil, cabinet de consultants consulting firm
cabinet de consultation consulting-room, surgery (Brit), doctor's office (US)
cabinet dentaire dental surgery (Brit), dentist's office (US)
cabinet d'études consultancy
cabinet d'experts comptables *ou* **d'expertise comptable** chartered accountant's (Brit), certified public accountant's (US)
cabinet juridique law consultancy
cabinet de lecture † reading room
cabinet médical (sur une plaque) medical practice, surgery (Brit); (= bureau) surgery (Brit), doctor's office (US)
cabinet particulier private dining room
cabinet de recrutement recruitment agency *ou* consultancy
cabinet de toilette bathroom
cabinet de travail study

câblage /kɑblaʒ/ NM [1] (Élec = fils) wiring [2] (TV) [de quartier, rue] cabling ♦ **nous attendons le ~ du quartier** we're waiting for the area to be cabled [3] [de dépêche, message] cabling [4] (Tech) [de torons] twisting together

câble /kɑbl/ NM [1] (= filin) cable ♦ **~ métallique** wire cable [2] (TV) cable ♦ **la télévision par ~, le ~** cable (television), cablevision ♦ **vous avez le ~ ?** have you got cable? ♦ **transmettre par ~** to broadcast on cable, to cablecast (US) [3] († = dépêche) cable

COMP **câble d'accélérateur** accelerator cable
câble d'amarrage mooring line
câble coaxial coaxial cable
câble de démarreur *ou* **de démarrage** (pour voiture) jump lead (Brit), jumper cable (US)
câble électrique (electric) cable

câble de frein brake cable
câble de halage towrope, towline
câble hertzien radio link *(by hertzian waves)*
câble de remorquage ⇒ **câble de halage**
câble de transmission transmission cable

câblé, e /kɑble/ (ptp de **câbler**) ADJ [1] *(TV)* *[chaîne, réseau]* cable *(épith)* ◆ **la ville est ~e** the town has cable television ◆ **les personnes ~es** people with cable [2] *(Ordin)* wired [3] *(* = à la mode) [personne]* trendy*, hip* ◆ **il est ~ informatique/jazz** he's really into computers/jazz

câbler /kɑble/ ▸ conjug 1 ◂ VT [1] *[+ dépêche, message]* to cable [2] *(Tech)* *[+ torons]* to twist together (into a cable) [3] *(TV)* *[+ quartier, rue]* to install cable television in, to cable

câblerie /kɑbləʀi/ NF cable-manufacturing plant

câblier /kɑblije/ NM *(= navire)* cable ship

câblo-distributeur (pl **câblo-distributeurs**) /kɑblodistʀibytœʀ/ NM cable company

câblo-distribution (pl **câblo-distributions**) /kablodistʀibysjɔ̃/ NF cable television, cablevision

câblo-opérateur (pl **câblo-opérateurs**) /kɑblooperatœʀ/ NM cable (television) operator

cabochard, e* /kabɔʃaʀ, aʀd/ ADJ *(= têtu)* pigheaded*, mulish ◆ **c'est un ~** he's pigheaded*

caboche /kabɔʃ/ NF [1] *(* = tête)* head ◆ **mets-toi ça dans la ~** get that into your thick head *ou* skull* ◆ **quand il a quelque chose dans la ~** when he's got something into his head [2] *(= clou)* hobnail

cabochon /kabɔʃɔ̃/ NM *(= bouchon)* stopper; *(= brillant)* cabochon; *(= clou)* stud

cabossé, e /kabɔse/ (ptp de **cabosser**) ADJ *[chapeau, instrument, voiture]* battered ◆ **une casserole toute ~e** a battered *ou* badly dented saucepan

cabosser /kabɔse/ ▸ conjug 1 ◂ VT *(= bosseler)* to dent

cabot* /kabo/ NM [1] *(péj = chien)* dog, mutt* [2] *(arg Mil = caporal)* ≈ corporal, corp *(arg)* *(Brit)* ADJ, NM ⇒ **cabotin**

cabotage /kabɔtaʒ/ NM *(Naut)* coastal navigation ◆ **petit/grand ~** inshore/seagoing navigation ◆ **faire du ~** to sail along the coast

caboter /kabɔte/ ▸ conjug 1 ◂ VI *(Naut)* to sail along the coast ◆ **~ le long des côtes d'Afrique** to sail along the African coast

caboteur /kabɔtœʀ/ NM *(= bateau)* tramp, coaster

cabotin, e /kabɔtɛ̃, in/ *(péj)* ADJ theatrical ◆ **il est très ~** he likes to show off *ou* hold the centre of the stage NM,F *(gén)* show-off; *(= acteur)* ham (actor)*

cabotinage /kabɔtinaʒ/ NM *[de personne, enfant]* showing off; *[d'acteur]* ham* *ou* third-rate acting

cabotiner /kabɔtine/ ▸ conjug 1 ◂ VI *[acteur]* to ham it up*

cabrer /kɑbʀe/ ▸ conjug 1 ◂ VT *[+ cheval]* to rear (up); *[+ avion]* to nose up ◆ **faire ~ son cheval** to make one's horse rear (up) ◆ **~ qn** to put sb's back up ◆ **~ qn contre qn** to turn *ou* set sb against sb VPR **se cabrer** [1] *[cheval]* to rear (up); *[avion]* to nose up [2] *(fig)* *[personne]* to get on one's high horse

cabri /kabʀi/ NM kid *(young goat)*

cabriole /kabʀijɔl/ NF *(= bond)* *[d'enfant, chevreau]* caper; *(= culbute)* *[de clown, gymnaste]* somersault; *(Danse)* cabriole; *(Équitation)* capriole, spring ◆ **les ~s de certains politiciens** *(péj)* the antics of some politicians ◆ **faire des ~s** *[chevreau, enfant]* to caper *ou* cavort (about); *[cheval]* to cavort

cabrioler /kabʀijɔle/ ▸ conjug 1 ◂ VI *(= gambader)* to caper *ou* cavort (about)

cabriolet /kabʀijɔlɛ/ NM *(Hist)* cabriolet; *(= voiture décapotable)* convertible

cabus /kaby/ NM → **chou¹**

CAC /kak/ NM (abrév de **compagnie des agents de change**) *institute of stockbrokers* ◆ **l'indice ~ 40** the CAC(-40) index

caca /kaka/ NM * poo* *(Brit)*, poop* *(US)* ◆ **faire ~** to do a poo* *(Brit)* *ou* a poop* *(US)* ◆ **il a marché dans du ~ de chien** he stepped in some dog dirt ◆ **son travail, c'est (du) ~** his work is absolute garbage ◆ **on est dans le ~** we're in a (bit of a) mess* ◆ **c'est ~ boudin** it's yucky* *ou* yukky* ◆ **faire un ~ nerveux*** to go off the deep end* COMP **caca d'oie** *(= couleur)* greenish-yellow

cacah(o)uète, cacahouette /kakawɛt/ NF [1] *(= arachide)* peanut; *(Agr)* groundnut; ◆ **il est payé des ~s *ou* trois ~s*** he earns peanuts* → **beurre, pesant** [2] *(* = tir puissant)* bullet-like shot, belter* ◆ **il m'a envoyé une ~** he blasted the ball to me

cacao /kakao/ NM *(= poudre)* cocoa (powder); *(= boisson)* cocoa; *(= graine)* cocoa bean

cacaoté, e /kakaɔte/ ADJ chocolate-flavoured

cacaotier /kakaɔtje/, **cacaoyer** /kakaɔje/ NM cacao (tree)

cacarder /kakaʀde/ ▸ conjug 1 ◂ VI *[oie]* to honk

cacatoès /kakatɔɛs/ NM cockatoo

cacatois /kakatwa/ NM *(= voile)* royal ◆ **mât de ~** royal mast ◆ **grand/petit ~** main/fore royal

cachalot /kaʃalo/ NM sperm whale

cache¹ /kaʃ/ NM *(Ciné, Photo)* mask; *(gén)* card *(for covering one eye, masking out a section of text)*; *(Ordin)* cache

cache² /kaʃ/ NF *(= cachette)* hiding place; *(pour butin)* cache ◆ **~ d'armes** arms cache

caché, e /kaʃe/ (ptp de **cacher**) ADJ *(gén)* hidden; *[sentiments]* inner(most), secret ◆ **vie ~e** *(= secrète)* secret *ou* hidden life; *(retirée)* secluded life; → **face**

cache-cache /kaʃkaʃ/ NM INV *(lit, fig)* hide-and-seek ◆ **jouer à ~, faire une partie de ~** to play hide-and-seek *(avec* with)

cache-cœur (pl **cache-cœurs**) /kaʃkœʀ/ NM crossover top *(ou sweater etc)*

cache-col (pl **cache-col(s)**) /kaʃkɔl/ NM scarf, muffler

Cachemire /kaʃmiʀ/ NM Kashmir

cachemire /kaʃmiʀ/ NM *(= laine)* cashmere ◆ **motif *ou* impression *ou* dessin ~** paisley pattern ◆ **écharpe en ~** cashmere scarf ◆ **écharpe (à motif) ~** paisley(-pattern) scarf

cachemirien, -ienne /kaʃmiʀjɛ̃, ɛn/ ADJ Kashmiri NM,F **Cachemirien(ne)** Kashmiri

cache-misère* /kaʃmizɛʀ/ NM INV *(= vêtement)* *wrap or coat worn to hide old or dirty clothes* ◆ **le rideau servait de ~** the curtain was there to hide unsightly things

cache-nez /kaʃne/ NM INV scarf, muffler

cache-plaque (pl **cache-plaque(s)**) /kaʃplak/ NM hob cover

cache-pot (pl **cache-pot(s)**) /kaʃpo/ NM flowerpot holder

cache-prise (pl **cache-prise(s)**) /kaʃpʀiz/ NM socket cover

cacher /kaʃe/ ▸ conjug 1 ◂ VT [1] *(= dissimuler volontairement)* *[+ objet]* to hide, to conceal; *[+ malfaiteur]* to hide ◆ **le chien est allé ~ son os** the dog's gone to bury its bone ◆ **~ ses cartes *ou* son jeu** *(lit)* to keep one's cards *ou* hand up; *(fig)* to keep *ou* play one's cards close to one's chest

[2] *(= masquer)* *[+ accident de terrain, trait de caractère]* to hide, to conceal ◆ **les arbres nous cachent le fleuve** we can't see the river because of the trees ◆ **tu me caches la lumière** you're in my light ◆ **son silence cache quelque chose** he's hiding something by not saying anything ◆ **qu'est-ce que ça cache ?** what's behind all this? ◆ **les mauvaises herbes cachent les fleurs** you can't see the flowers for the weeds; → **arbre**

[3] *(= garder secret)* *[+ fait, sentiment]* to hide, to conceal *(à qn* from sb); ◆ **~ son âge** to keep one's age a secret ◆ **on ne peut plus lui ~ la nouvelle** you can't keep *ou* hide the news from him *(ou* her) any longer ◆ **pour ne rien vous ~** to be perfectly honest (with you) ◆ **il ne m'a pas caché qu'il désire partir** he's been quite open with me about wanting to leave ◆ **il n'a pas caché que cela lui déplaisait** he made no secret of the fact that he didn't like it

VPR **se cacher** [1] *(= se dissimuler)* *[personne, soleil]* to hide ◆ **va te ~ !** get out of my sight!, be gone! † *(aussi hum)* ◆ **se ~ de qn** to hide from sb ◆ **il se cache pour fumer** he smokes in secret ◆ **il se cache d'elle pour boire** he drinks behind her back ◆ **je ne m'en cache pas** I'm quite open about it, I make no secret of it ◆ **faire qch sans se ~ *ou* s'en ~** to do sth openly, to do sth without hiding *ou* concealing the fact ◆ **il l'a fait sans se ~ de nous** he did it without hiding *ou* concealing it from us ◆ **inutile de se ~ derrière son petit doigt** it's no use trying to hide from the facts

[2] *(= être caché)* *[personne]* to be hiding; *[malfaiteur, évadé]* to be in hiding; *[chose]* to be hidden ◆ **il se cache de peur d'être puni** he's keeping out of sight *ou* he's hiding in case he gets punished

[3] *(= être masqué)* *[accident de terrain, trait de caractère]* to be concealed ◆ **la maison se cache derrière des arbres** the house is concealed *ou* hidden behind some trees

cache-radiateur (pl **cache-radiateur(s)**) /kaʃʀadjatœʀ/ NM radiator cover

cachère /kaʃɛʀ/ ADJ INV ⇒ **kascher**

cache-sexe (pl **cache-sexe(s)**) /kaʃsɛks/ NM G-string

cache-sommier (pl **cache-sommiers**) /kaʃsɔmje/ NM valance

cachet /kaʃɛ/ NM [1] *(= comprimé)* tablet ◆ **un ~ d'aspirine** an aspirin (tablet); → **blanc** [2] *(= timbre)* stamp; *(= sceau)* seal ◆ **~ (de la poste)** postmark ◆ **sa lettre porte le ~ de Paris** his letter is postmarked Paris *ou* has a Paris postmark ◆ **à envoyer le 15 septembre au plus tard, le ~ de la poste faisant foi** to be postmarked 15 September at the latest ◆ **le ~ de l'originalité/du génie** the stamp of originality/genius; → **lettre** [3] *(= style, caractère)* style, character ◆ **cette petite église avait du ~** there was something very characterful about that little church, that little church had (great) character ◆ **c'est le toit qui donne son ~ à *ou* fait le ~ de la maison** it's the roof that gives character to the house [4] *[d'acteur]* fee ◆ **courir le ~** to chase after any sort of work

cachetage /kaʃtaʒ/ NM sealing

cache-tampon /kaʃtɑ̃pɔ̃/ NM INV hunt the thimble

cacheter /kaʃte/ ▸ conjug 4 ◂ VT to seal ◆ **envoyer qch sous pli cacheté** to send sth in a sealed envelope ◆ **vin cacheté** wine in a sealed bottle; → **cire**

cacheton* /kaʃtɔ̃/ NM *[d'acteur]* fee ◆ **courir le ~** to be prepared to do anything

cachetonner* /kaʃtɔne/ ▸ conjug 1 ◂ VI *[acteur]* to play bit parts

cachette /kaʃɛt/ NF *(gén)* hiding-place; *[de fugitif]* hideout

◆ **en cachette** *[agir, fumer]* on the sly, secretly; *[économiser, voir qn]* secretly ◆ **il boit en ~** he's a secret drinker, he drinks secretly ◆ **en ~ de qn** *(action répréhensible)* behind sb's back; *(action non répréhensible)* unknown to sb

cachexie † /kaʃɛksi/ **NF** cachexia, cachexy

cachot /kaʃo/ **NM** *(= cellule)* dungeon; *(= punition)* solitary confinement

cachotterie /kaʃɔtʀi/ **NF** *(= secret)* mystery ◆ **c'est une nouvelle ~ de sa part** it's another of his (little) mysteries ◆ **faire des ~s** to be secretive, to act secretively ◆ **faire des ~s à qn** to keep secrets *ou* things from sb

cachottier, -ière /kaʃɔtje, jɛʀ/ **ADJ** secretive ◆ **cet enfant est (un) ~** he's a secretive child

cachou /kaʃu/ **NM** *(= bonbon)* cachou

cacique /kasik/ **NM** *(= Indien)* cacique ◆ **les ~s du parti** the party bosses ◆ **c'était le ~** *(arg Scol)* he came first, he got first place

cacochyme /kakɔʃim/ **ADJ** († *ou hum)* ◆ **vieillard ~** doddery old man

cacophonie /kakɔfɔni/ **NF** cacophony ◆ **quelle ~ !** *(péj)* what a racket! *

cacophonique /kakɔfɔnik/ **ADJ** cacophonous

cactée /kakte/, **cactacée** /kaktase/ **NF** cactus ◆ **les ~s** *ou* **cactacées** cacti, Cactaceae *(SPÉC)*

cactus /kaktys/ **NM INV** cactus

c.-à-d. (abrév de **c'est-à-dire**) i.e.

cadastral, e (mpl **-aux**) /kadastʀal, o/ **ADJ** cadastral ◆ **plan ~** cadastral map

cadastre /kadastʀ/ **NM** land registry

cadastrer /kadastʀe/ ► conjug 1 ◄ **VT** to survey and register *(at the land registry)*

cadavéreux, -euse /kadaveʀø, øz/ **ADJ** ⇒ **cadavérique**

cadavérique /kadaveʀik/ **ADJ** *[teint]* deathly pale; *[pâleur]* deathly; *[visage]* cadaverous ◆ **un homme au teint ~** a man with a deathly pale face; → **rigidité**

cadavre /kadavʀ/ **NM** 1 *(humain)* body, corpse; *(animal)* carcass, body ◆ **~ ambulant** walking *ou* living corpse ◆ **il y a un ~ entre eux** they've got someone's blood on their hands ◆ **il y a un ~ dans le placard** there's a skeleton in the cupboard *(Brit) ou* closet *(US)* 2 *(* = bouteille vide, de vin etc)* empty (bottle), dead soldier *, dead man * *(Brit)*

caddie /kadi/ **NM** 1 *(Golf)* caddie ◆ **être le ~ de qn** to caddie for sb, to be sb's caddie 2 ® *(= chariot)* (supermarket *ou* shopping) trolley *(Brit)*, caddy *(US)*, (grocery) cart *(US)*

cade /kad/ **NM** cade ◆ **huile de ~** oil of cade

cadeau (pl **cadeaux**) /kado/ **NM** 1 *(= présent)* present, gift *(de qn* from sb); ◆ **faire un ~ à qn** to give sb a present *ou* gift ◆ **~ de mariage/de Noël** wedding/Christmas present ◆ **~ publicitaire** free gift, freebie *, giveaway * *(US)*

2 *(locutions)* **faire ~ de qch à qn** *(offrir)* to make sb a present of sth, to give sb sth as a present; *(laisser)* to let sb keep sth, to give sb sth ◆ **il a décidé d'en faire ~ (à quelqu'un)** he decided to give it away (to somebody) ◆ **je vous fais ~ des détails** I'll spare you the details ◆ **ils ne font pas de ~x** *[examinateurs, police]* they don't let you off lightly ◆ **ils ne nous ont pas fait de ~** *[équipe adverse]* they really gave us a run for our money ◆ **garde la monnaie, je t'en fais ~** you can keep the change ◆ **en ~** *[offrir, recevoir]* as a present ◆ **les petits ~x entretiennent l'amitié** there's nothing like a little present between friends ◆ **c'était un ~ empoisonné** it was more of a curse than a blessing, it was a poisoned chalice ◆ **c'est pas un ~ !*** it's *(ou* he's *etc)* a real pain! *

cadenas /kadnɑ/ **NM** padlock ◆ **fermer au ~** to padlock

cadenasser /kadnɑse/ ► conjug 1 ◄ **VT** to padlock **VPR** **se cadenasser** to lock o.s. in

cadence /kadɑ̃s/ **NF** 1 *(= rythme) [de vers, chant, danse]* rhythm ◆ **marquer la ~** to beat out the rhythm 2 *(= vitesse, taux)* rate, pace ◆ **~ de tir/de production** rate of fire/of production ◆ **à la ~ de 10 par jour** at the rate of 10 a day ◆ **à une bonne ~** at a good pace *ou* rate ◆ **ils nous font travailler à une ~ infernale** we have to work at a furious pace ◆ **forcer la ~** to force the pace 3 *(Mus) [de succession d'accords]* cadence; *[de concerto]* cadenza

◆ **en cadence** *(= régulièrement)* rhythmically; *(= ensemble, en mesure)* in time

cadencé, e /kadɑ̃se/ (ptp de **cadencer**) **ADJ** 1 *(= rythmé)* rhythmic(al); → **pas¹** 2 *(Ordin)* **processeur ~ à 1 GHz** processor with a clock speed of 1 GHz, 1 GHz processor 3 *(Transport)* **liaison ~e, service ~** regular service

cadencer /kadɑ̃se/ ► conjug 3 ◄ **VT** *[+ débit, phrases, allure, marche]* to put rhythm into, to give rhythm to

cadet, -ette /kadɛ, ɛt/ **ADJ** *(de deux)* younger; *(de plusieurs)* youngest

NM 1 *[de famille]* **le ~** the youngest child *ou* boy *ou* one ◆ **le ~ des garçons** the youngest boy *ou* son ◆ **mon (frère) ~** my younger brother ◆ **le ~ de mes frères** my youngest brother ◆ **le père avait un faible pour son ~** the father had a soft spot for his youngest boy

2 *(relation d'âge)* **il est mon ~** he's younger than me ◆ **il est mon ~ de 2 ans** he's 2 years younger than me, he's 2 years my junior ◆ **c'est le ~ de mes soucis** that's the least of my worries

3 *(Tennis, Ping-Pong, Ftbl etc) 15-17 year-old player; (Athlétisme) 15-17 year-old athlete; (Hist)* cadet *(gentleman who entered the army to acquire military skill and eventually a commission)*

NF **cadette** 1 *[de famille]* **la cadette** the youngest child *ou* girl *ou* one ◆ **la cadette des filles** the youngest girl *ou* daughter ◆ **ma (sœur) cadette** my younger sister

2 *(relation d'âge)* **elle est ma cadette** she's younger than me

3 *(Tennis, Ping-Pong, Ftbl etc) 15-17 year-old player; (Athlétisme) 15-17 year-old athlete*

cadmium /kadmjɔm/ **NM** cadmium ◆ **jaune de ~** cadmium yellow

cador * /kadɔʀ/ **NM** *(= chien)* dog, mutt *, pooch * *(US)*; *(péj = personne importante)* heavyweight * ◆ **c'est pas un ~** *(péj)* he's no bright spark *

cadrage /kadʀaʒ/ **NM** 1 *(Photo, Ciné) (= action)* framing; *(= résultat)* composition 2 *[de budget, projet]* guidelines ◆ **lettre de ~ (budgétaire) du Premier ministre** budget guidelines *(sent by the Prime Minister to ministers and the managers of state-controlled companies)* ◆ **le ~ de leur politique économique** their economic policy guidelines

cadran /kadʀɑ̃/ **NM** *[de téléphone, boussole, compteur]* dial; *[de montre, horloge]* dial, face; *[de baromètre]* face; → **tour²** **COMP** **cadran solaire** sundial

cadrat /kadʀa/ **NM** *(Typo)* quad

cadratin /kadʀatɛ̃/ **NM** *(Typo)* em quad

cadre /kadʀ/ **NM** 1 *[de tableau, porte, bicyclette]* frame ◆ **il roulait à bicyclette avec son copain sur le ~** he was riding his bicycle with his friend on the crossbar

2 *(= tableau)* picture

3 *(= caisse)* **~ (d'emballage** *ou* **de déménagement)** crate, packing case ◆ **~-conteneur** container

4 *(sur formulaire)* space, box ◆ **ne rien écrire dans ce ~** do not write in this space, leave this space blank

5 *(= décor)* setting; *(= entourage)* surroundings ◆ **vivre dans un ~ luxueux/austère** to live in luxurious/austere surroundings ◆ **maison située dans un ~ de verdure** house in a leafy setting ◆ **quel ~ magnifique !** what a magnificent setting! ◆ **le ~ est très beau mais la nourriture mauvaise** the setting is beautiful but the food is bad ◆ **~ de vie** (living) environment

6 *(= limites)* scope ◆ **rester/être dans le ~ de** to remain/be *ou* fall within the scope of ◆ **cette décision sort du ~ de notre accord** this decision is outside *ou* beyond the scope of our agreement ◆ **il est sorti du ~ de ses fonctions** he went beyond the scope of *ou* overstepped the limits of his responsibilities ◆ **respecter le ~ de la légalité** to remain within (the bounds of) the law ◆ **sortir du ~ étroit de la vie quotidienne** to get out of the straitjacket *ou* the narrow confines of everyday life

7 *(= contexte)* context, framework ◆ **dans le ~ de** *[de réformes, recherches, festival]* within the context *ou* framework of

8 *(= structure)* structure, framework ◆ **le ~ juridique/institutionnel** the legal/institutional framework; → **loi-cadre**

9 *(= chef, responsable)* executive, manager; *(Mil)* officer ◆ **les ~s** management, the managerial staff ◆ **elle est passée ~** she has been upgraded to a managerial position *ou* to the rank of manager, she's been made an executive ◆ **~ subalterne** junior executive *ou* manager ◆ **~ supérieur** *ou* **de direction** senior executive *ou* manager ◆ **~ moyen** middle executive *ou* manager ◆ **les ~s moyens** middle management, middle-grade managers *(US)* ◆ **jeune ~ dynamique** *(hum)* upwardly mobile young executive

10 *(Admin = liste du personnel)* **entrer dans/figurer sur les ~s (d'une compagnie)** to be (placed) on/be on the books (of a company) ◆ **être rayé des ~s** *(= licencié)* to be dismissed; *(= libéré)* to be discharged ◆ **hors ~** detached, seconded *(Brit)*

11 *[de radio]* frame antenna

12 *(Photo)* **~ de développement** processing rack ◆ **viseur à ~ lumineux** collimator viewfinder

cadrer /kadʀe/ ► conjug 1 ◄ **VI** *(= coïncider)* to tally *(avec* with) to conform *(avec* to, with); ◆ **ce qu'il a fait ne cadre pas du tout avec sa personnalité** what he did was completely out of character **VT** 1 *(Photo)* to centre *(Brit)*, to center *(US)* ◆ **~ un plan** to frame a shot ◆ **l'image était mal cadrée** the picture wasn't properly centred 2 *(= définir) [+ politique]* to establish guidelines for; *[+ projet]* to define the parameters of ◆ **ce projet était mal cadré** the project had not been properly thought through 3 *(Ftbl) [+ tir]* to line up ◆ **c'était une frappe parfaitement cadrée** he lined up *ou* centered the shot beautifully

cadreur /kadʀœʀ/ **NM** *(Ciné)* cameraman

caduc, caduque /kadyk/ **ADJ** 1 *(Jur) (= nul)* null and void; *(= périmé)* lapsed ◆ **devenir ~** *[legs]* to become null and void; *[loi]* to lapse ◆ **rendre qch ~** to render sth null and void, to invalidate sth 2 *(= périmé) [théorie]* outmoded, obsolete ◆ **rendre ~** *[+ revendication, méthode, distinction]* to make obsolete 3 *(Bot)* **à feuilles caduques** deciduous 4 *(Ling)* **e ~** mute e

caducée /kadyse/ **NM** caduceus

cæcum /sekɔm/ **NM** caecum

cæsium /sezjɔm/ **NM** caesium

CAF¹ /kaf/ (abrév de **coût, assurance, fret**) CIF

CAF² /kaf/ **NF** (abrév de **caisse d'allocations familiales**) → **caisse**

cafard¹ /kafaʀ/ **NM** 1 *(= insecte)* cockroach 2 *(* = mélancolie)* **un coup de ~** a fit of depression *ou* of the blues * ◆ **avoir le ~** to be feeling down * *ou* low *, to be down in the dumps * ◆ **ça lui donne le ~** it depresses him, it gets him down *

cafard², e /kafaʀ, aʀd/ NM,F *(péj)* [1] *(* = rapporteur)* sneak, telltale, tattletale *(US)* [2] *(† = hypocrite)* hypocrite

cafardage* /kafaʀdaʒ/ NM *(= rapportage)* sneaking, taletelling, tattling *(US)*

cafarder* /kafaʀde/ ▸ conjug 1 ◂ VT *(= dénoncer)* to tell tales on, to sneak on* *(Brit)*, to tattle on *(US)* VI [1] *(= rapporter)* to tell tales, to sneak* *(Brit)*, to tattle *(US)* [2] *(= être déprimé)* to be feeling down* *ou* low*, to be down in the dumps*

cafardeur, -euse¹ /kafaʀdœʀ, øz/ NM,F *(péj)* sneak, telltale, tattletale *(US)*

cafardeux, -euse² /kafaʀdø, øz/ ADJ [1] *(= déprimé)* *[personne]* feeling down *ou* low* *(attrib)*, down in the dumps* *(attrib)* [2] *(= déprimant)* depressing

caf'conc'* /kafkɔ̃s/ NM abrév de **café-concert**

café /kafe/ NM [1] *(= plante, boisson, produit, moment)* coffee ◆ **au ~, on parlait politique** we talked politics over coffee ◆ **il est arrivé au ~** he came in when we were having coffee; → **cuiller, service**
[2] *(= lieu)* café ◆ **le ~ du coin** the local café, ≃ the local* *(Brit)* ◆ **ce ne sont que des propos de ~ du Commerce** *(gén)* it's just bar-room philosophizing; *(politique)* it's just bar-room politics
COMP **café complet** ≃ continental breakfast
café crème *coffee with hot, frothy milk*
café décaféiné decaffeinated coffee
café express espresso coffee
café filtre filter(ed) coffee
café en grains coffee beans
café instantané instant coffee
café au lait coffee with milk, white coffee *(Brit)* ◆ **robe ~ au lait** coffee-coloured dress
café liégeois coffee ice cream *(with whipped cream)*
café lyophilisé (freeze-dried) instant coffee
café noir *ou* **nature** black coffee
café en poudre instant coffee
café soluble instant coffee

café-bar (pl **cafés-bars**) /kafebaʀ/ NM café bar

café-concert (pl **cafés-concerts**) /kafekɔ̃sɛʀ/ NM *café where singers entertain customers*

caféiculture /kafeikyltyʀ/ NF coffee growing

caféier /kafeje/ NM coffee tree

caféière /kafejɛʀ/ NF coffee plantation

caféine /kafein/ NF caffeine

café-restaurant (pl **cafés-restaurants**) /kafeʀɛstɔʀɑ̃/ NM café restaurant

cafet'*, **cafét'*** /kafɛt/ NF abrév de **cafétéria**

café-tabac (pl **cafés-tabacs**) /kafetaba/ NM café *(where cigarettes may be purchased)*

cafetan /kaftɑ̃/ NM caftan

cafeter* /kafte/ VTI ⇒ **cafter**

cafétéria /kafeteʀja/ NF cafeteria

cafeteur, -euse* /kaftœʀ, øz/ NM,F ⇒ **cafteur, -euse**

café-théâtre (pl **cafés-théâtres**) /kafeteɑtʀ/ NM *(= genre) light entertainment performed in small theatres; (= endroit)* small theatre *(Brit) ou* theater *(US)* ◆ **il a fait trois ans de ~** ≃ he did three years as a stand-up comedian

cafetier, -ière /kaftje, jɛʀ/ NM,F café-owner NF **cafetière** [1] *(= pot)* coffeepot; *(= machine)* coffee-maker ◆ **cafetière électrique** electric coffee-maker ◆ **cafetière à l'italienne** espresso maker ◆ **cafetière à piston** cafetiere [2] *(‡ = tête)* head, nut*, noodle*

cafouillage* /kafujaʒ/ NM muddle, shambles *(sg)* ◆ **un ~ technique** a technical hitch ◆ **un ~ informatique** a glitch ◆ **il y a eu un ~ devant les buts** there was some confusion in front of the goal ◆ **après des semaines de ~ le gouvernement a finalement pris une décision** after weeks of confusion the government has at last made a decision

cafouiller* /kafuje/ ▸ conjug 1 ◂ VI *[organisation, administration]* to be in a shambles *ou* mess; *[candidat]* to get into a muddle ◆ **ça cafouille** *[moteur, appareil, télévision]* it's playing up, it isn't working properly ◆ **dans cette affaire, le gouvernement cafouille** the government's in a real shambles over this affair, the government is floundering over this affair ◆ **la défense parisienne a cafouillé et les Nantais ont marqué** the Paris defence fell apart and Nantes scored

cafouilleur, -euse* /kafujœʀ, øz/, **cafouilleux, -euse*** /kafujø, øz/ ADJ *[organisation, discussion]* chaotic ◆ **les passes étaient souvent cafouilleuses** the passes were often bungled* NM,F muddler, bungler

cafouillis /kafuji/ NM ⇒ **cafouillage**

cafter* /kafte/ ▸ conjug 1 ◂ VT *(= dénoncer)* to tell tales on, to sneak on* *(Brit)*, to tattle on *(US)* VI to tell tales, to sneak* *(Brit)*, to tattle *(US)*

cafteur, -euse* /kaftœʀ, øz/ NM,F sneak, telltale, tattletale *(US)*

cage /kaʒ/ NF [1] *[d'animaux]* cage ◆ **mettre en ~** *[+ animal]* to put in a cage; *[+ voleur]* to lock up ◆ **dans ce bureau, je me sens comme un animal en ~** I feel cooped up in this office [2] *[de roulement à billes, pendule]* casing; *[de maison]* shell [3] *(* : Sport = but)* goal
COMP **cage d'ascenseur** lift *(Brit) ou* elevator *(US)* shaft
cage d'escalier (stair)well
cage d'extraction *(Min)* cage
cage de Faraday Faraday cage
cage à lapins *(lit)* (rabbit) hutch; *(fig)* rabbit hutch, box
cage à oiseaux birdcage
cage à poules *(lit)* hen-coop; *(pour enfants)* jungle-gym, climbing frame; *(péj = immeuble)* rabbit hutch, box
cage thoracique ribcage

cageot /kaʒo/ NM [1] *[de légumes, fruits]* crate [2] *(‡ = femme laide)* dog‡

cagette /kaʒɛt/ NF *[de légumes, fruits]* crate

cagibi /kaʒibi/ NM *(= débarras)* boxroom *(Brit)*, storage room *(US)*; *(= remise)* shed

cagna /kaɲa/ NM *(arg Mil = abri)* dugout

cagnard /kaɲaʀ/ NM *(dans le Midi)* [1] *(= lieu) sunny spot sheltered from the wind* [2] *(= soleil)* blazing sun ◆ **en plein ~** in the blazing sun

cagne /kaɲ/ NF → **khâgne**

cagneux¹, -euse /kaɲø, øz/ ADJ *[cheval, personne]* knock-kneed; *[jambes]* crooked ◆ **genoux ~** knock knees

cagneux², -euse /kaɲø, øz/ NM,F → **khâgneux, -euse**

cagnotte /kaɲɔt/ NF *(= caisse commune)* kitty; *[de jeu]* pool, kitty; *(* = économies)* nest egg

cagot, e /kago, ɔt/ *(†† ou péj)* ADJ *[allure, air]* sanctimonious NM,F sanctimonious hypocrite

cagoule /kagul/ NF *[de moine]* cowl; *[de pénitent]* hood, cowl; *[de bandit]* hood, mask; *(= passe-montagne)* balaclava

cagoulé, e /kagule/ ADJ *[bandit]* masked, wearing a balaclava

cahier /kaje/ NM [1] *(Scol)* notebook, exercise book [2] *(= revue)* journal; *(= partie détachable)* pull-out supplement [3] *(Typo)* signature, gathering
COMP **cahier d'appel** *(Scol)* register *(Brit)*, attendance sheet *(US)*
cahier de brouillon roughbook *(Brit)*, notebook (for rough drafts) *(US)*
cahier des charges *[de production]* specifications, requirements *(US)*; *[de contrat]* terms of reference, terms and conditions; *[d'entreprise]* mission statement
cahier de cours notebook, exercise book
cahier de devoirs homework book
cahier de doléances *(Hist)* register of grievances
cahier d'exercices exercise book
cahier à spirale spiral notebook
cahier de textes homework notebook *ou* diary
cahier de travaux pratiques lab book

cahin-caha* /kaɛ̃kaa/ ADV ◆ **aller ~** *[troupe, marcheur]* to hobble along; *[affaires]* to struggle along ◆ **la vie continue ~** life trundles on ◆ **alors ça va ? – ~** *(santé)* how are you? – (I'm) so-so

cahors /kaɔʀ/ NM *(= vin)* cahors *(red wine made in the south west of France)*

cahot /kao/ NM *(= secousse)* jolt, bump ◆ **~s** *(fig)* ups and downs

cahotant, e /kaɔtɑ̃, ɑ̃t/ ADJ ⇒ **cahoteux**

cahotement /kaɔtmɑ̃/ NM bumping, jolting

cahoter /kaɔte/ ▸ conjug 1 ◂ VT *[+ véhicule]* to jolt; *[+ voyageurs]* to jolt *ou* bump about; *[vicissitudes]* to buffet about ◆ **une famille cahotée par la guerre** a family buffeted *ou* tossed about by the war VI *[véhicule]* to trundle along ◆ **le petit train cahotait le long du canal** the little train trundled along by the canal

cahoteux, -euse /kaɔtø, øz/ ADJ *[route]* bumpy, rough ◆ **il a eu un parcours un peu ~** he had a rather chequered career

cahute /kayt/ NF *(= cabane)* shack, hut; *(péj)* shack

caïd /kaid/ NM [1] * *(= meneur) [de pègre]* boss, big chief*; *[de classe, bureau]* big shot*; *(= as, crack)* ace* ◆ **le ~ de l'équipe** the star of the team, the team's top man ◆ **en mécanique, c'est un ~** he's an ace* at mechanics ◆ **jouer les ~s** *ou* **au ~** to swagger about [2] *(en Afrique du Nord = fonctionnaire)* kaid

caillasse /kajas/ NF loose stones ◆ **pente couverte de ~** scree-covered slope, slope covered with loose stones ◆ **ce n'est que de la ~** *(péj)* it's just like gravel, it's just loose stones

caille /kaj/ NF *(= oiseau)* quail ◆ **chaud comme une ~** warm as toast ◆ **rond comme une ~** plump as a partridge ◆ **oui ma ~** * *(affectueusement)* yes poppet* *(Brit) ou* honey* *(US)*

caillé /kaje/ NM curds

caillebotis /kajbɔti/ NM *(= treillis)* grating; *(= plancher)* duckboards

caillement /kɑjmɑ̃/ NM *[de lait]* curdling; *[de sang]* coagulating, clotting

cailler /kaje/ ▸ conjug 1 ◂ VI [1] *[lait]* to curdle ◆ **faire ~ du lait** to curdle milk [2] *(‡ = avoir froid)* to be freezing ◆ **ça caille dehors** it's freezing outside, it's brass monkey weather‡ ◆ **ça caille ici !** it's freezing in here! VPR **se cailler** [1] *[lait]* to curdle; *[sang]* to coagulate, to clot; → **lait** [2] *(‡ = avoir froid)* to be freezing ◆ **on se (les) caille !, on se caille les miches** *ou* **les meules** it's freezing cold!, it's bloody freezing!*‡ *(Brit)*

caillera‡ /kajʀa/ chav‡ *(Brit)*, punk‡ *(US)*

caillot /kajo/ NM (blood) clot

caillou (pl **cailloux**) /kaju/ NM [1] *(gén)* stone; *(= petit galet)* pebble; *(= grosse pierre)* boulder; *(* = diamant)* stone ◆ **des tas de ~x d'empierrement** heaps of road metal ◆ **c'est du ~** *(= mauvaise terre)* it's nothing but stones ◆ **il a un ~ à la place du cœur** he has a heart of stone [2] *(= îlot)* rock ◆ **le Caillou*** New Caledonia [3] *(arg Drogue)* rock [4] *(* = tête)* head, nut* ◆ **il n'a pas un poil** *ou* **cheveu sur le ~** * he's as bald as a coot *ou* an egg

cailloutage /kajutaʒ/ NM *(= action)* metalling; *(= cailloux)* (road) metal, ballast

caillouter /kajute/ ▸ conjug 1 ◂ VT *(= empierrer)* to metal

caillouteux, -euse /kajutø, øz/ ADJ *[route, terrain]* stony; *[plage]* pebbly, shingly

cailloutis /kajuti/ NM *(gén)* gravel; *[de route]* (road) metal, ballast

caïman /kaimɑ̃/ NM cayman, caiman

Caïmans /kaimɑ̃/ NFPL ◆ **les (îles)** ~ the Cayman Islands

Caïn /kaɛ̃/ NM Cain

Caire /kɛʀ/ NM ◆ **Le** ~ Cairo

cairn /kɛʀn/ NM 1 *(Alpinisme)* cairn 2 *(= chien)* cairn (terrier)

caisse /kɛs/ NF 1 *(pour emballage)* box; *[de fruits, légumes]* crate; *[de bouteilles]* case; *[de plantes]* tub; *(= litière de chat)* litter tray

2 *(= boîte, carcasse) [d'horloge]* casing; *[d'orgue]* case; *[de véhicule]* bodywork; *[de tambour]* cylinder

3 *(Fin) (= tiroir)* till; *(= machine)* cash register, till; *(portable)* cashbox ◆ **petite** ~ *(= somme d'argent)* petty cash, float* *(US)* ◆ **avoir de l'argent en** ~ to have ready cash ◆ **ils n'ont plus un sou en** ~ they haven't got a penny *ou* a cent *(US)* left in the bank ◆ **faire la** ~ to count up the money in the till, to do the till ◆ **être à la** ~ *(temporairement)* to be at *ou* on the cashdesk; *(= être caissier)* to be the cashier ◆ **tenir la** ~ to be the cashier; *(hum)* to hold the purse strings ◆ **les ~s de l'État** the state coffers ◆ **se servir** *ou* **piquer* dans la** ~ to have one's fingers *ou* hand in the till ◆ **partir avec la** ~ to make off with the contents of the till *ou* the takings; → **bon[2], livre[1]**

4 *(= guichet) [de boutique]* cashdesk; *[de banque]* cashier's desk; *[de supermarché]* check-out ◆ **passer à la** ~ *(lit)* to go to the cashdesk *ou* cashier; *(= être payé)* to collect one's money; *(= être licencié)* to get paid off ◆ **on l'a prié de passer à la** ~ he was asked to collect his last wages and go

5 *(= établissement, bureau)* office; *(= organisme)* fund ◆ ~ **d'entraide** mutual aid fund

6 *(Mus = tambour)* drum; → **gros**

7 *(‡ = poitrine)* chest ◆ **il s'en va ou part de la** ~ his lungs are giving out

8 *(* = voiture)* motor* *(Brit)*, auto* *(US)* ◆ **vieille** ~ old heap*, old banger* *(Brit)*, jalopy *(US)*

COMP **caisse d'allocations familiales** family allowance office *(Brit)*, ≃ welfare center *(US)*

caisse claire *(Mus)* side *ou* snare drum

caisse comptable ⇒ **caisse enregistreuse**

caisse des dépôts et consignations deposit and consignment office

caisse à eau *(Naut, Rail)* water tank

caisse d'emballage packing case

caisse des écoles *state body that finances extra-curricular activities, school meals, etc.*

caisse enregistreuse cash register

caisse d'épargne savings bank

Caisse nationale d'assurance maladie *national state health insurance office*

caisse noire secret funds

caisse à outils toolbox

caisse de prévoyance contingency *ou* reserve fund

caisse primaire d'assurance maladie *state health insurance office*, ≃ Department of Health office *(Brit)*, Medicaid office *(US)*

caisse de résonance resonance chamber

caisse de retraite superannuation *ou* pension fund

caisse à savon *(lit)* soapbox; *(péj = meuble)* old box

caisse de secours relief *ou* emergency fund

caisse de sécurité sociale *Social Security office*

caisse de solidarité *(Scol)* school fund

caisse du tympan middle ear, tympanic cavity *(SPÉC)*

caissette /kɛsɛt/ NF (small) box

caissier, -ière /kesje, jɛʀ/ NM,F *[de banque]* cashier; *[de magasin]* cashier, assistant at the cash-desk; *[de supermarché]* check-out assistant *(Brit) ou* clerk *(US)*, checker *(US)*; *[de cinéma]* cashier, box-office assistant

caisson /kɛsɔ̃/ NM 1 *(= caisse)* box, case; *[de bouteilles]* crate; *(= coffrage)* casing; *(Mil = chariot)* caisson 2 *(Tech : immergé)* caisson ◆ ~ **hyperbare** hyperbaric chamber ◆ **le mal** *ou* **la maladie des ~s** caisson disease, decompression sickness, the bends* 3 *[de plafond]* caisson, coffer; → **plafond, sauter** 4 *(= haut-parleur)* ~ **de graves** *ou* **de basses** woofer

cajoler /kaʒɔle/ ► conjug 1 ◄ VT *(= câliner)* to cuddle, to make a fuss of; *(† = amadouer)* to coax, to cajole ◆ ~ **qn pour qu'il donne qch** *ou* **pour obtenir qch** to try to wheedle sth out of sb

cajolerie /kaʒɔlʀi/ NF 1 *(= caresses)* **~s** cuddling ◆ **faire des ~s à qn** to make a fuss of sb, to give sb a cuddle 2 *(† = flatterie)* cajoling *(NonC)*, cajolery ◆ **arracher une promesse à qn à force de ~s** to wheedle a promise out of sb

cajoleur, -euse /kaʒɔlœʀ, øz/ ADJ 1 *(= câlin)* loving, affectionate 2 *(= flatteur)* flattering NM,F *(= flatteur)* charmer

cajou /kaʒu/ NM ◆ **(noix de)** ~ cashew nut

cajun /kaʒœ̃/ ADJ INV Cajun NM *(= langue)* Cajun NMF **Cajun** Cajun

cake /kɛk/ NM fruit cake

cal /kal/ NM *(Bot, Méd)* callus

cal. (abrév de **calorie**) cal

calabrais, e /kalabʀɛ, ɛz/ ADJ Calabrian NM,F **Calabrais(e)** Calabrian

Calabre /kalabʀ/ NF Calabria

calage /kalaʒ/ NM 1 *(avec une cale, un coin) [de meuble, fenêtre, porte]* wedging; *[de roue]* chocking, wedging; *(avec une vis, une goupille) [de poulie]* keying; *[de cheville, objet pivotant]* wedging, locking 2 *[de moteur]* stalling ◆ **après deux ~s successifs** having stalled twice

calamar /kalamaʀ/ NM squid

calamine /kalamin/ NF 1 *(Minér)* calamine 2 *(= résidu dans moteur)* carbon deposits

calaminer (se) /kalamine/ ► conjug 1 ◄ VPR *[cylindre etc]* to be caked with soot, to coke up *(Brit)*, to get coked up *(Brit)*

calamistré, e /kalamistʀe/ ADJ *[cheveux]* waved and brilliantined

calamité /kalamite/ NF *(= malheur)* calamity; *(* : hum)* disaster ◆ **ce type est une** ~* that guy is a (walking) disaster*

calamiteux, -euse /kalamitø, øz/ ADJ calamitous

calancher‡ /kalɑ̃ʃe/ ► conjug 1 ◄ VI to croak‡, to kick the bucket‡, to snuff it‡ *(Brit)*

calandre /kalɑ̃dʀ/ NF *[d'automobile]* radiator grill; *(= machine)* calender

calanque /kalɑ̃k/ NF *(= crique)* rocky inlet *(in the Mediterranean)*

calao /kalao/ NM hornbill

calcaire /kalkɛʀ/ ADJ 1 *(= qui contient de la chaux) [sol, terrain]* chalky, calcareous *(SPÉC)*; *[eau]* hard 2 *(Géol) [roche, plateau, relief]* limestone *(épith)* 3 *(Méd) [dégénérescence]* calcareous; *(Chim) [sels]* calcium *(épith)* NM *(Géol)* limestone; *[de bouilloire]* fur *(Brit)*, sediment *(US)* ◆ **faire un coup de** ~‡ *(déprimé)* to have a touch of the blues*; *(en colère)* to fly off the handle

calcanéum /kalkaneɔm/ NM calcaneum

calcédoine /kalsedwan/ NF chalcedony

calcémie /kalsemi/ NF plasma calcium level

calcif‡ /kalsif/ NM ⇒ **calecif**

calcification /kalsifikasjɔ̃/ NF *(Méd)* calcification

calcifié, e /kalsifje/ (ptp de **calcifier**) ADJ calcified

calcifier VT, **se calcifier** VPR /kalsifje/ ► conjug 7 ◄ to calcify

calcination /kalsinasjɔ̃/ NF calcination

calciné, e /kalsine/ (ptp de **calciner**) ADJ *[débris, os]* charred, burned to ashes *(attrib)*; *[rôti]* charred, burned to a cinder *(attrib)*

calciner /kalsine/ ► conjug 1 ◄ VT 1 *[+ rôti]* to burn to a cinder ◆ **la plaine calcinée par le soleil** *(littér)* the sun-scorched *ou* sun-baked plain 2 *(Tech = brûler) [+ pierre, bois, métal]* to calcine *(SPÉC)* VPR **se calciner** *[rôti]* to burn to a cinder; *[débris]* to burn to ashes

calcique /kalsik/ ADJ calcic ◆ **déficit** ~ calcium deficiency

calcite /kalsit/ NF calcite

calcium /kalsjɔm/ NM calcium

calcul /kalkyl/ NM 1 *(= opération)* calculation; *(= exercice scolaire)* sum ◆ ~ **des retraites** *(Admin)* pension calculation ◆ ~ **de l'impôt (sur le revenu)** tax assessment ◆ **se tromper dans ses ~s, faire une erreur de** ~ to miscalculate, to make a mistake in one's calculations ◆ **si on fait le** ~ when you add it all up; → **règle**

2 *(= discipline)* **le** ~ arithmetic ◆ **fort en** ~ good at arithmetic *ou* sums ◆ **le** ~ **différentiel/intégral/des prédicats** differential/integral/predicate calculus

3 *(= estimation)* **~s** reckoning(s), calculations ◆ **d'après mes ~s** by my reckoning, according to my calculations

4 *(= plan)* calculation *(NonC)*; *(= arrière-pensée)* ulterior motive ◆ **~s intéressés** self-interested motives ◆ **par** ~ with an ulterior motive, out of (calculated) self-interest ◆ **faire un bon** ~ to calculate correctly *ou* right ◆ **faire un mauvais** ~ to miscalculate, to make a miscalculation

5 *(Méd)* stone, calculus *(SPÉC)*

COMP **calcul algébrique** calculus

calcul biliaire gallstone

calcul mental *(= discipline)* mental arithmetic; *(= opération)* mental calculation

calcul des probabilités probability theory ◆ **un simple** ~ **des probabilités vous indiquera que ...** calculating the probability will show you that ...

calcul rénal kidney stone, renal calculus *(SPÉC)*

calculable /kalkylabl/ ADJ calculable, which can be calculated *ou* worked out

calculateur, -trice /kalkylatœʀ, tʀis/ ADJ *(= intéressé)* calculating NM *(= machine)* computer ◆ ~ **numérique/analogique** digital/analog computer NF **calculatrice** *(= machine)* calculator NM,F *(= personne)* calculator

calculer /kalkyle/ ► conjug 1 ◄ VT 1 *[+ prix, quantité, surface]* to work out, to calculate ◆ **il calcule vite** he calculates quickly, he's quick at figures *ou* at calculating ◆ **il calcula mentalement la distance** he worked out *ou* calculated the distance in his head; → **machine, règle**

2 *(= évaluer) [+ chances, conséquences]* to calculate, to work out, to weigh up ◆ ~ **son élan** *(Sport)* to judge one's run-up ◆ ~ **que ...** to work out *ou* calculate that ... ◆ **tout bien calculé** everything *ou* all things considered; → **risque**

3 *(= préméditer) [+ geste, effets]* to plan, to calculate; *[+ plan, action]* to plan ◆ **elle calcule continuellement** she's always calculating ◆ ~ **son coup** to plan one's move (carefully) ◆ **ils avaient calculé leur coup** they had it all figured out* ◆ **avec une gentillesse calculée** with calculated kindness

VI (= *économiser*) to budget carefully, to count the pennies ♦ **ces gens qui calculent** (*péj*) people who are always counting their pennies *ou* who work out every penny

calculette /kalkylɛt/ NF calculator ♦ **~ de poche** pocket calculator

caldoche /kaldɔʃ/ ADJ white New Caledonian (*épith*) NMF **Caldoche** white New Caledonian

cale[1] /kal/ NF 1 (= *soute*) hold; → **fond** 2 (= *chantier, plan incliné*) slipway ♦ **~ de chargement** slipway ♦ **~ sèche** *ou* **de radoub** dry *ou* graving dock

cale[2] /kal/ NF (= *coin*) [*de meuble, caisse*] wedge; (*Golf*) wedge; [*de roue*] chock, wedge ♦ **mettre une voiture sur ~s** to put a car on blocks

calé, e* /kale/ (ptp de **caler**) ADJ 1 (= *savant*) [*personne*] bright ♦ **être ~ en chimie/en histoire** to be really good at chemistry/at history ♦ **je ne suis pas très ~ en la matière** I don't know much about it ♦ **c'est drôlement ~ ce qu'il a fait** what he did was terribly clever 2 (= *ardu*) [*problème*] tough

calebasse /kalbɑs/ NF (= *récipient*) calabash, gourd

calèche /kalɛʃ/ NF barouche (*horse-drawn carriage*)

calecif‡ /kalsif/ NM pants (*Brit*), shorts (*US*)

caleçon /kalsɔ̃/ NM 1 [*d'homme*] boxer shorts, shorts (*US*) ♦ **3 ~s** 3 pairs of boxer shorts *ou* shorts (*US*) ♦ **~ de bain** swimming *ou* bathing trunks ♦ **~(s) long(s)** long johns* 2 [*de femme*] leggings

Calédonie /kaledɔni/ NF Caledonia

calédonien, -ienne /kaledɔnjɛ̃, jɛn/ ADJ Caledonian NM,F **Calédonien(ne)** Caledonian

calembour /kalɑ̃buʀ/ NM pun, play on words (*NonC*)

calembredaine /kalɑ̃bʀədɛn/ NF (= *plaisanterie*) silly joke ♦ **~s** (= *balivernes*) balderdash (*NonC*), nonsense (*NonC*)

calendaire /kalɑ̃dɛʀ/ ADJ calendar (*épith*)

calendes /kalɑ̃d/ NFPL (*Antiq*) calends; → **renvoyer**

calendos‡ /kalɑ̃dos/ NM Camembert (cheese)

calendrier /kalɑ̃dʀije/ NM (= *jours et mois*) calendar; (= *programme*) schedule ♦ **~ d'amortissement** repayment schedule ♦ **~ à effeuiller/perpétuel** tear-off/everlasting calendar ♦ **~ électoral** electoral calendar ♦ **le ~ républicain** the French Revolutionary Calendar ♦ **~ des examens** exam timetable ♦ **~ des rencontres** (*Ftbl*) fixture(s) timetable *ou* list ♦ **~ de travail** work schedule *ou* programme ♦ **~ scolaire** school schedule

cale-pied /kalpje/ NM INV [*de vélo*] toe clip

calepin /kalpɛ̃/ NM notebook

caler /kale/ ► conjug 1 ◄ VT 1 (*avec une cale, un coin*) [+ *meuble*] to put a wedge under, to wedge; [+ *fenêtre, porte*] (*pour la maintenir ouverte*) to wedge open; (*pour la maintenir fermée*) to wedge shut; [+ *roue*] to chock, to wedge

2 (*avec une vis, une goupille*) [+ *poulie*] to key; [+ *cheville, objet pivotant*] to wedge, to lock

3 (*avec des coussins etc*) [+ *malade*] to prop up ♦ **~ sa tête sur l'oreiller** to prop *ou* rest one's head on the pillow ♦ **des coussins lui calaient la tête, il avait la tête (bien) calée par des coussins** his head was propped up on *ou* supported by cushions

4 (= *appuyer*) [+ *pile de livres, de linge*] to prop up ♦ **~ qch dans un coin/contre qch** to prop sth up in a corner/against sth

5 [+ *moteur, véhicule*] to stall

6 (*Naut*) [+ *mât*] to house

7 (* = *bourrer*) **ça cale (l'estomac)** it fills you up ♦ **non merci, je suis calé** no thanks, I'm full up * *ou* I've eaten more than my fill

8 (*Imprim*) to lock up

VI 1 [*véhicule, moteur, conducteur*] to stall

2 * (= *être bloqué*) to be stuck; (= *abandonner*) to give up ♦ **~ sur un exercice difficile** to be stuck on a difficult exercise ♦ **il a calé avant le dessert** he gave up before the dessert ♦ **il a calé sur le dessert** he couldn't finish his dessert

3 (*Naut*) **~ trop** to have too great a draught ♦ **~ 8 mètres** to draw 8 metres of water

VPR **se caler** 1 ♦ **se ~ dans un fauteuil** to settle o.s. comfortably in an armchair ♦ **se ~ les joues*** to stuff o.s., to have a good feed* (*Brit*)

2 ♦ **se ~ sur** (= *s'aligner sur*) **le rythme des recrutements a dû se ~ sur l'augmentation de la demande** recruitment has had to keep pace with the increase in demand ♦ **on fait en sorte que nos prévisions se calent sur les leurs** we make sure our forecasts are in line with theirs

caleter‡ VI, **se caleter** VPR /kalte/ ► conjug 1 ◄ ⇒ **calter**

calfatage /kalfataʒ/ NM (*Naut*) ca(u)lking

calfater /kalfate/ ► conjug 1 ◄ VT (*Naut*) to ca(u)lk

calfeutrage /kalføtʀaʒ/, **calfeutrement** /kalføtʀəmɑ̃/ NM [*de pièce, porte*] draughtproofing (*Brit*), draftproofing (*US*); [*de fissure*] filling, stopping up

calfeutrer /kalføtʀe/ ► conjug 1 ◄ VT [+ *pièce, porte*] to (make) draughtproof (*Brit*) *ou* draftproof (*US*); [+ *fissure*] to fill, to stop up ♦ **calfeutré** [*pièce, porte*] draughtproof (*Brit*) (*épith*), draftproof (*US*) (*épith*) ♦ **~ une fenêtre avec un bourrelet** to put (a) weather-strip round a window VPR **se calfeutrer** (= *s'enfermer*) to shut o.s. up *ou* away; (*pour être au chaud*) to get cosy

calibrage /kalibʀaʒ/ NM [*d'œufs, fruits, charbon*] grading; [*de conduit, cylindre, fusil*] calibration; [*de pièce travaillée*] gauging; (*Imprim*) [*de texte*] castoff

calibre /kalibʀ/ NM 1 (= *diamètre*) [*de fusil, canon*] calibre (*Brit*), caliber (*US*), bore; [*de tuyau*] bore, diameter; [*d'obus, balle*] calibre (*Brit*), caliber (*US*); [*de cylindre, instrument de musique*] bore; [*de câble*] diameter; [*d'œufs, fruits*] grade; [*de boule*] size ♦ **de gros ~** [*pistolet*] large-bore (*épith*); [*obus*] large-calibre (*épith*) ♦ **pistolet de ~ 7,35** 7.35 mm (calibre) pistol 2 (*arg Crime* = *pistolet*) rod (*arg*), gat (*arg*) 3 (= *instrument*) (*pour mesurer*) gauge; (*pour reproduire*) template 4 (= *envergure*) calibre (*Brit*), caliber (*US*) ♦ **son frère est d'un autre ~** his brother is of another calibre altogether ♦ **c'est rare un égoïsme de ce ~** you don't often see selfishness on such a scale

calibrer /kalibʀe/ ► conjug 1 ◄ VT 1 (= *mesurer*) [+ *œufs, fruits, charbon*] to grade; [+ *conduit, cylindre, fusil*] to calibrate; (*Imprim*) [*texte*] to cast off 2 (= *finir*) [+ *pièce travaillée*] to gauge

calice /kalis/ NM (*Rel*) chalice; (*Bot, Physiol*) calyx; → **boire**

calicot /kaliko/ NM (= *tissu*) calico; (= *banderole*) banner

califat /kalifa/ NM caliphate

calife /kalif/ NM caliph ♦ **il veut être ~ à la place du ~** he wants to be top dog*

Californie /kalifɔʀni/ NF California

californien, -ienne /kalifɔʀnjɛ̃, jɛn/ ADJ Californian NM,F **Californien(ne)** Californian

californium /kalifɔʀnjɔm/ NM californium

califourchon /kalifuʀʃɔ̃/ **à califourchon** LOC ADV astride ♦ **s'asseoir à ~ sur qch** to straddle sth, to sit astride sth ♦ **être à ~ sur qch** to be astride sth ♦ **monter à ~** (*Équitation*) to ride astride

câlin, e /kɑlɛ̃, in/ ADJ (= *qui aime les caresses*) [*enfant, chat*] cuddly, cuddlesome; (= *qui câline*) [*personne, ton, regard*] tender, loving NM cuddle ♦ **faire un (petit) ~** *ou* **des ~s à qn** to make a fuss of sb, to give sb a cuddle

câliner /kɑline/ ► conjug 1 ◄ VT to cuddle, to make a fuss of

câlinerie /kɑlinʀi/ NF (= *tendresse*) tenderness ♦ **~s** (= *caresses*) caresses ♦ **faire des ~s à qn** to cuddle sb, to make a fuss of sb

calisson /kalisɔ̃/ NM calisson (*lozenge-shaped sweet made of ground almonds*)

calleux, -euse /kalø, øz/ ADJ [*peau*] horny, callous ♦ **corps ~** (*Anat*) corpus callosum

calligramme /ka(l)ligʀam/ NM (= *poème*) calligramme

calligraphe /ka(l)ligʀaf/ NMF calligrapher, calligraphist

calligraphie /ka(l)ligʀafi/ NF (= *technique*) calligraphy, art of handwriting ♦ **c'est de la ~** it's lovely handwriting, the handwriting is beautiful

calligraphier /ka(l)ligʀafje/ ► conjug 7 ◄ VT [+ *titre, phrase*] to write artistically, to calligraph (*SPÉC*)

calligraphique /ka(l)ligʀafik/ ADJ calligraphic

callipyge /ka(l)lipiʒ/ ADJ (*hum*) callipygian, big-bottomed ♦ **la Vénus ~** Callipygian Venus

callosité /kalozite/ NF callosity

calmant, e /kalmɑ̃, ɑ̃t/ ADJ 1 (*Pharm*) (= *tranquillisant*) tranquillizing (*épith*); (*contre la douleur*) painkilling (*épith*) 2 (= *apaisant*) [*paroles*] soothing NM (= *tranquillisant*) tranquillizer, sedative; (= *antidouleur*) painkiller

calmar /kalmaʀ/ NM squid

calme /kalm/ ADJ (*gén*) quiet, calm; (= *paisible*) peaceful; [*mer*] calm; [*nuit, air*] still; [*chambre*] quiet; [*marché financier, affaires*] quiet ♦ **malgré leurs provocations il restait très ~** he remained quite calm *ou* cool *ou* unruffled in spite of their taunts ♦ **le malade a eu une nuit ~** the patient has had a quiet *ou* peaceful night

NM 1 (= *sang-froid*) coolness, composure ♦ **garder son ~** to keep cool *ou* calm, to keep one's composure *ou* one's cool* ♦ **perdre son ~** to lose one's composure *ou* one's cool* ♦ **avec un ~ incroyable** with incredible composure ♦ **recouvrant son ~** recovering *ou* regaining his composure

2 (= *tranquillité*) (*gén*) peace (and quiet), calm; [*de nuit*] stillness; [*d'endroit*] peacefulness ♦ **il me faut du ~ pour travailler** I need peace and quiet to work ♦ **du ~ !** (= *restez tranquille*) keep quiet!; (= *pas de panique*) keep calm! *ou* cool! ♦ **le malade doit rester au ~** the patient needs quiet ♦ **ramener le ~** (= *arranger les choses*) to calm things down; (= *rétablir l'ordre*) to restore calm ♦ **le ~ avant la tempête** the calm *ou* lull before the storm

3 **(zones des) ~s équatoriaux** (*Naut*) doldrums (*lit*) ♦ **~ plat** dead *ou* flat calm ♦ **c'est le ~ plat dans les affaires** business is dead quiet *ou* practically at a standstill ♦ **depuis que je lui ai envoyé cette lettre c'est le ~ plat** I haven't heard a thing since I sent him that letter

calmement /kalməmɑ̃/ ADV [*agir*] calmly ♦ **la journée s'est passée ~** the day passed quietly

calmer /kalme/ ► conjug 1 ◄ VT 1 (= *apaiser*) [+ *personne*] to calm (down), to pacify; [+ *querelle, discussion*] to quieten down (*Brit*), to quiet down (*US*); [+ *révolte*] to subdue; (*littér*) [+ *tempête, flots*] to calm ♦ **~ les esprits** to calm people down, to pacify people ♦ **attends un peu, je vais te ~ !*** just you wait, I'll (soon)

quieten (Brit) ou quiet (US) you down! ◆ ~ **le jeu** (lit, fig) to calm things down
2 (= réduire) [+ douleur, inquiétude] to soothe, to ease; [+ nerfs, agitation, crainte, colère] to calm, to soothe; [+ fièvre] to bring down; [+ impatience] to curb; [+ faim] to appease; [+ soif] to quench; [+ ardeur] to cool, to subdue
VPR **se calmer** 1 [personne] (= s'apaiser) to calm down, to cool down; (= faire moins de bruit) to quieten down (Brit), to quiet down (US); (= se tranquilliser) to calm down; [discussion, querelle] to quieten down (Brit), to quiet down (US); [tempête] to die down; [mer] to become calm ◆ **on se calme !** * (= taisez-vous) be quiet!; (= pas de panique) calm down!
2 (= diminuer) [douleur] to ease, to subside; [faim, soif, inquiétude] to ease; [crainte, impatience, fièvre] to subside; [colère, ardeur] to cool, to subside

calmos * / kalmos / EXCL calm down!

calomel / kalɔmɛl / NM calomel

calomniateur, -trice / kalɔmnjatœʀ, tʀis / ADJ (= diffamateur) slanderous; (par écrit) libellous NM,F (= diffamateur) slanderer; (par écrit) libeller

calomnie / kalɔmni / NF slander (NonC), calumny; (écrite) libel; (sens affaibli) maligning (NonC) ◆ **cette ~ l'avait profondément blessé** he'd been deeply hurt by this slander ou calumny ◆ **écrire des ~s** to write libellous things ◆ **dire une ~/des ~s** to say something slanderous/slanderous things

calomnier / kalɔmnje / ► conjug 7 ◄ VT (= diffamer) to slander; (par écrit) to libel; (sens affaibli = vilipender) to malign

calomnieux, -ieuse / kalɔmnjø, jøz / ADJ [propos] slanderous; (par écrit) libellous ◆ **dénonciation calomnieuse** (Jur) false accusation

caloporteur / kalopɔʀtœʀ / ADJ, NM ⇒ **caloriporteur**

calorie / kalɔʀi / NF calorie ◆ **aliment riche/pauvre en ~s** food with a high/low calorie content, high-/low-calorie food ◆ **menu basses ~s** low-calorie meal ◆ **ça donne des ~s** * it warms you up ◆ **tu aurais besoin de ~s !** * you need building up!

calorifère / kalɔʀifɛʀ / ADJ heat-giving NM † stove

calorifique / kalɔʀifik / ADJ calorific

calorifuge / kalɔʀifyʒ / ADJ (heat-)insulating, heat-retaining NM insulating material

calorifugeage / kalɔʀifyʒaʒ / NM lagging, insulation

calorifuger / kalɔʀifyʒe / ► conjug 3 ◄ VT to lag, to insulate (against loss of heat)

caloriporteur / kalɔʀipɔʀtœʀ / ADJ, NM ◆ **(fluide)** ~ coolant

calorique / kalɔʀik / ADJ 1 (Diététique) calorie (épith) ◆ **apport** ~ calorie content ◆ **ration** ~ calorie requirements ◆ **c'est très** ~ it's very calorific, it has a lot of calories 2 (= calorifique) calorific ◆ **valeur** ~ calorific value

calot / kalo / NM 1 (Mil = casquette) forage cap, overseas cap (US) 2 (= bille) (large) marble, alley

calotin, e / kalɔtɛ̃, in / (péj) ADJ sanctimonious, churchy * NM,F sanctimonious churchgoer, Holy Joe *

calotte / kalɔt / NF 1 (= bonnet) skullcap 2 (péj) **la** ~ (= le clergé) the priests, the cloth; (= le parti dévot) the church party 3 (= partie supérieure) [de chapeau] crown; [de voûte] calotte 4 (* = gifle) slap ◆ **il m'a donné une** ~ he gave me a slap in the face
COMP **la calotte des cieux** the dome ou vault of heaven
calotte crânienne top of the skull
calotte glaciaire icecap
calotte sphérique segment of a sphere

calotter * / kalɔte / ► conjug 1 ◄ VT (= gifler) to slap

calquage / kalkaʒ / NM tracing

calque / kalk / NM 1 (= dessin) tracing ◆ **prendre un ~ d'un plan** to trace a plan 2 (= papier transparent) tracing paper 3 (= reproduction) [d'œuvre d'art] exact copy; [d'événement] carbon copy; [de personne] spitting image 4 (Ling) calque, loan translation

calquer / kalke / ► conjug 1 ◄ VT (= copier) [+ plan, dessin] to trace; (fig) to copy exactly ◆ **calqué de l'anglais** (Ling) translated literally from English ◆ ~ **son comportement sur celui de son voisin** to model one's behaviour on that of one's neighbour, to copy one's neighbour's behaviour exactly

calter‡ VI, **se calter**‡ VPR / kalte / ► conjug 1 ◄ (= décamper) to make o.s. scarce *, to scarper * (Brit), to buzz off * (Brit)

calumet / kalymɛ / NM peace pipe ◆ **fumer le ~ de la paix** (lit) to smoke the pipe of peace; (fig) to bury the hatchet

calva * / kalva / NM abrév de **calvados**

calvados / kalvados / NM 1 (= eau-de-vie) Calvados 2 (= département) ◆ **le Calvados** Calvados

calvaire / kalvɛʀ / NM 1 (= épreuve) ordeal ◆ **le ~ du Christ** Christ's martyrdom ou suffering on the cross ◆ **après 10 ans de ~ en prison** after a 10-year ordeal in prison ◆ **sa vie fut un long** ~ his life was one long martyrdom ou tale of suffering ◆ **un enfant comme ça, c'est un ~ pour la mère** a child like that must be a real burden to his mother ◆ **quel ~ pour elle !** how awful for her! 2 (= croix) (au bord de la route) roadside cross ou crucifix, calvary; (= peinture) Calvary 3 (Rel) **le Calvaire** Calvary

Calvin / kalvɛ̃ / NM Calvin

calvinisme / kalvinism / NM Calvinism

calviniste / kalvinist / ADJ Calvinist, Calvinistic NMF Calvinist

calvitie / kalvisi / NF baldness (NonC) ◆ ~ **précoce** premature baldness (NonC)

calypso / kalipso / NM calypso

camaïeu / kamajø / NM (= peinture) monochrome ◆ **en** ~ [paysage, motif] monochrome (épith) ◆ **en ~ bleu** in blue monochrome ◆ **un ~ de roses** various shades of pink

camail / kamaj / NM (Rel) cappa magna

camarade / kamaʀad / NMF friend ◆ **le ~ Durand** (Pol) comrade Durand ◆ **elle voyait en lui un bon** ~ she saw him as a good friend
COMP **camarade d'atelier** workmate (Brit), shop buddy * (US)
camarade de chambre roommate
camarade de classe classmate
camarade d'étude fellow student
camarade de jeu playmate
camarade de promotion fellow student (from a grande école)
camarade de régiment old army friend, friend from one's army days

camaraderie / kamaʀadʀi / NF (entre deux personnes) friendship; (dans un groupe) camaraderie ◆ **je l'ai aidé par esprit de** ~ I helped him out of a spirit of friendship

camard, e / kamaʀ, aʀd / ADJ [nez] pug (épith); [personne] pug-nosed NF **Camarde** (littér) **la Camarde** the (Grim) Reaper

camarguais, e / kamaʀgɛ, ɛz / ADJ of ou from the Camargue ◆ **(bottes) ~es** suede cowboy boots NM,F **Camarguais(e)** inhabitant ou native of the Camargue

Camargue / kamaʀg / NF ◆ **la** ~ the Camargue

cambiste / kɑ̃bist / NM foreign exchange broker ou dealer; [de devises des touristes] moneychanger

Cambodge / kɑ̃bɔdʒ / NM Cambodia

cambodgien, -ienne / kɑ̃bɔdʒjɛ̃, jɛn / ADJ Cambodian NM,F **Cambodgien(ne)** Cambodian

cambouis / kɑ̃bwi / NM dirty oil ou grease ◆ **mettre les mains dans le** ~ to get one's hands dirty

cambré, e / kɑ̃bʀe / (ptp de **cambrer**) ADJ ◆ **être ~, avoir les reins ~s** to have an arched back ◆ **avoir le pied très** ~ to have very high insteps ou arches

cambrer / kɑ̃bʀe / ► conjug 1 ◄ VT 1 [+ pied] to arch ◆ ~ **la taille ou le dos ou les reins** to throw back one's shoulders, to arch one's back 2 (Tech) [+ pièce de bois] to bend; [+ métal] to curve; [+ tige, semelle] to arch VPR **se cambrer** (= se redresser) to throw back one's shoulders, to arch one's back

cambrien, -ienne / kɑ̃bʀijɛ̃, ijɛn / ADJ, NM Cambrian

cambriolage / kɑ̃bʀijɔlaʒ / NM (= activité, méthode) burglary, housebreaking, breaking and entering (Jur); (= coup) break-in, burglary

cambrioler / kɑ̃bʀijɔle / ► conjug 1 ◄ VT to break into, to burgle, to burglarize (US)

cambrioleur, -euse / kɑ̃bʀijɔlœʀ, øz / NM,F burglar, housebreaker

cambrousse * / kɑ̃bʀus / NF (= campagne) country ◆ **en pleine** ~ out in the sticks *, in the back of beyond ◆ **frais arrivé de sa** ~ (péj) fresh from the backwoods ou the sticks *

cambrure / kɑ̃bʀyʀ / NF 1 (= courbe, forme) [de poutre, taille, reins] curve; [de semelle, pied] arch; [de route] camber ◆ **sa ~ de militaire** his military bearing 2 (= partie) ~ **du pied** instep ◆ ~ **des reins** small ou hollow of the back ◆ **pieds qui ont une forte** ~ feet with high insteps ◆ **reins qui ont une forte** ~ back which is very arched

cambuse / kɑ̃byz / NF 1 * (= pièce) pad *; (= maison) shack *, place; (= taudis) hovel 2 (Naut) storeroom

came[1] / kam / NF (Tech) cam; → **arbre**

came[2] / kam / NF (arg Drogue) (gén) dope *; (= héroïne) junk *; (= cocaïne) snow *; (‡ = marchandise) stuff *; (péj = pacotille) junk *, trash *

camé, e[1] * / kame / (ptp de **se camer**) ADJ high *, spaced out * ◆ **complètement** ~ completely spaced out *, high as a kite * NM,F druggy *; (à l'héroïne) junkie *

camée[2] / kame / NM cameo

caméléon / kameleɔ̃ / NM (= lézard) chameleon; (fig) chameleon; (péj) turncoat

camélia / kamelja / NM camellia

camélidé / kamelide / NM member of the camel family ◆ **les ~s** members of the camel family, the Camelidae (SPÉC)

camelot / kamlo / NM street pedlar ou vendor ◆ **les Camelots du roi** (Hist) militant royalist group in 1930s

camelote * / kamlɔt / NF 1 (= pacotille) **c'est de la** ~ it's junk * ou rubbish * (Brit) ou schlock‡ (US) 2 (= marchandise) stuff * ◆ **il vend de la belle** ~ he sells nice stuff *

camembert / kamɑ̃bɛʀ / NM (= fromage) Camembert (cheese); (* = graphique) pie chart

camer (se) / kame / ► conjug 1 ◄ VPR (arg Drogue) to be on drugs

caméra / kameʀa / NF (Ciné, TV) camera; [d'amateur] cine-camera, movie camera (US) ◆ ~ **sonore** sound camera ◆ ~ **vidéo** video camera, camcorder ◆ **devant les ~s de (la) télévision** in front of the television cameras, on TV ◆ **être derrière la** ~ [réalisateur] to be behind the camera ◆ **la ~ invisible** ou **cachée** (= émission) candid camera

cameraman /kameʀaman/ (pl **cameramen** /kameʀamɛn/) **NM** cameraman

caméraphone /kameʀafɔn/ **NM** camera phone, camphone

camériste /kameʀist/ **NF** (= *femme de chambre*) chambermaid; *(Hist)* lady-in-waiting

Cameroun /kamʀun/ **NM** Cameroon; *(Hist)* Cameroons ◆ **République unie du ~** United Republic of Cameroon

camerounais, e /kamʀunɛ, ɛz/ **ADJ** Cameroonian **NM,F** **Camerounais(e)** Cameroonian

caméscope /kameskɔp/ **NM** camcorder, video camera

camion /kamjɔ̃/ **NM** 1 (= *poids lourd*) lorry *(Brit)*, truck *(surtout US)*; *(dont l'arrière fait corps avec la cabine)* van *(Brit)*, truck *(surtout US)* 2 (= *chariot*) wag(g)on, dray 3 *[de peintre]* (= *seau*) (paint-)pail

COMP **camion (à) benne** tipper (truck)
camion de déménagement removal *(Brit)* *ou* moving *(US)* van
camion militaire army lorry *(Brit)* *ou* truck
camion (à) remorque lorry *(Brit)* *ou* truck *(US)* with a trailer, tractor-trailer *(US)*
camion (à) semi-remorque articulated lorry *(Brit)*, trailer truck *(US)*

camion-citerne (pl **camions-citernes**) /kamjɔ̃sitɛʀn/ **NM** tanker (lorry) *(Brit)*, tank truck *(US)*

camion-grue (pl **camions-grues**) /kamjɔ̃gʀy/ **NM** crane-truck

camionnage /kamjɔnaʒ/ **NM** haulage *(Brit)*, trucking *(US)*

camionnette /kamjɔnɛt/ **NF** (small) van; *(ouverte)* pick-up (truck) ◆ **~ de livraison** delivery van

camionneur /kamjɔnœʀ/ **NM** (= *chauffeur*) lorry *(Brit)* *ou* truck *(US)* driver, trucker *(US)*; (= *entrepreneur*) haulage contractor *(Brit)*, road haulier *(Brit)*, trucking contractor *(US)* ◆ **pull (à) col ~** sweater with a zip-up collar

camionneuse /kamjɔnøz/ **NF** 1 (= *conductrice*) lorry *(Brit)* *ou* truck *(US)* driver, trucker *(US)* 2 (* = *lesbienne*) bull dyke*

camisard /kamizaʀ/ **NM** Camisard *(French Protestant insurgent after the revocation of the Edict of Nantes)*

camisole /kamizɔl/ **NF** †† (= *blouse*) camisole †; (= *chemise de nuit*) nightshirt

COMP **camisole chimique** suppressants
camisole de force straitjacket

camomille /kamɔmij/ **NF** (= *plante*) camomile; (= *tisane*) camomile tea

Camorra /kamɔʀa/ **NF** ◆ **la ~** the Camorra

camorriste /kamɔʀist/ **NM** camorrista

camouflage /kamuflaʒ/ **NM** 1 *(Mil)* (= *action*) camouflaging; (= *résultat*) camouflage 2 *[d'argent]* concealing, hiding; *[d'erreur]* camouflaging, covering-up ◆ **le ~ d'un crime en accident** disguising a crime as an accident

camoufler /kamufle/ ▸ conjug 1 ◂ **VT** *(Mil)* to camouflage; (= *cacher*) *[+ argent]* to conceal, to hide; *[+ erreur, embarras]* to conceal, to cover up; (= *déguiser*) *[+ défaite, intentions]* to disguise ◆ **~ un crime en accident** to disguise a crime as an accident, to make a crime look like an accident **VPR** **se camoufler** to camouflage o.s.

camouflet /kamuflɛ/ **NM** *(littér)* snub ◆ **infliger un ~ à qn** to snub sb

camp /kɑ̃/ **NM** 1 *(Alpinisme, Mil, Sport* = *emplacement)* camp ◆ **~ de prisonniers/de réfugiés** prison/refugee camp ◆ **rentrer au ~** to come *ou* go back to camp ◆ **le Camp du drap d'or** the Field of the Cloth of Gold; → **aide², feu¹**

2 (= *séjour*) **faire un ~ d'une semaine** to go camping for a week, to go for a week's camping holiday *(Brit)* *ou* vacation *(US)* ◆ **le ~ vous fait découvrir beaucoup de choses** you discover lots of things when you go camping

3 (= *parti, faction*) *(Jeux, Sport)* side; *(Pol)* camp ◆ **changer de ~** *[joueur]* to change sides; *[soldat]* to go over to the other side ◆ **à cette nouvelle la consternation/l'espoir changea de ~** on hearing this, it was the other side which began to feel dismay/hopeful ◆ **dans le ~ opposé/victorieux** in the opposite/winning camp ◆ **passer dans le ~ adverse** to go over to the opposite *ou* enemy camp; → **balle¹**

COMP **camp de base** base camp
camp de camping campsite, camping site
camp de concentration concentration camp
camp d'entraînement training camp
camp d'extermination extermination camp
camp fortifié fortified camp
camp de la mort death camp
camp de nudistes nudist camp
camp retranché ⇒ **camp fortifié**
camp de toile campsite, camping site
camp de travail labour *(Brit)* *ou* labor *(US)* camp
camp de vacances ≃ children's holiday camp *(Brit)*, summer camp *(US)*
camp volant camping tour *ou* trip; *(Mil)* temporary camp ◆ **vivre** *ou* **être en ~ volant** † to live out of a suitcase

campagnard, e /kɑ̃paɲaʀ, aʀd/ **ADJ** *[vie, manières, village, meubles, style, cuisine]* country *(épith)*; *[paysage]* rural ◆ **un repas ~** a cold spread ◆ **demeure** *ou* **résidence** *ou* **propriété ~e** country house, house in the country; → **buffet, gentilhomme** **NM** countryman, country fellow; *(péj)* rustic *(péj)*, hick *(péj)* ◆ **~s** country-folk, country people; *(péj)* rustics *(péj)* **NF** **campagnarde** country-woman

campagne /kɑ̃paɲ/ **NF** 1 (= *habitat*) country; (= *paysage*) countryside; *(Agr* = *champs ouverts)* open country ◆ **la ville et la ~** town and country ◆ **la ~ anglaise** the English countryside ◆ **dans la ~ environnante** in the surrounding countryside ◆ **en pleine ~** right in the middle of the country(side) ◆ **à la ~** in the country ◆ **auberge/chemin de ~** country inn/lane ◆ **les travaux de la ~** farm *ou* agricultural work; → **battre, maison** *etc*

2 *(Mil)* campaign ◆ **faire ~** to fight (a campaign) ◆ **les troupes en ~** the troops on campaign *ou* in the field ◆ **entrer en ~** to embark on a campaign ◆ **la ~ d'Italie/de Russie** the Italian/Russian campaign ◆ **artillerie/canon de ~** field artillery/gun

3 *(Pol, Presse)* campaign *(pour* for; *contre* against); ◆ **~ électorale** election campaign ◆ **~ d'affichage** poster campaign ◆ **~ de propagande** propaganda campaign ◆ **~ publicitaire** *ou* **de publicité** advertising *ou* publicity campaign ◆ **~ de vaccination** vaccination programme ◆ **~ de vente** sales campaign *ou* drive ◆ **~ de fouilles** series of excavations ◆ **faire ~ pour un candidat** to campaign *ou* canvass for *ou* on behalf of a candidate ◆ **partir en ~** to launch a campaign *(contre* against); ◆ **mener une ~ pour/contre** to campaign for/against, to lead a campaign for/against ◆ **tout le monde se mit en ~ pour lui trouver une maison** everybody set to work *ou* got busy to find him a house

4 (= *récolte*) harvest ◆ **~ sucrière** sugar cane *(ou* sugar beet) harvest ◆ **~ de pêche** fishing season

campagnol /kɑ̃paɲɔl/ **NM** vole

campanaire /kɑ̃panɛʀ/ **ADJ** ◆ **l'art ~** campanology ◆ **inscription ~** inscription on a bell

campanile /kɑ̃panil/ **NM** *[d'église]* campanile; (= *clocheton*) bell-tower

campanule /kɑ̃panyl/ **NF** bellflower, campanula

campement /kɑ̃pmɑ̃/ **NM** (= *camp*) camp, encampment ◆ **matériel de ~** camping equipment ◆ **chercher un ~ pour la nuit** to look for somewhere to set up camp *ou* for a camping place for the night ◆ **établir son ~ sur les bords d'un fleuve** to set up (one's) camp on the bank of a river ◆ **~ de nomades/d'Indiens** camp *ou* encampment of nomads/of Indians ◆ **revenir à son ~** *(Mil)* to return to camp

camper /kɑ̃pe/ ▸ conjug 1 ◂ **VI** to camp ◆ **on campait à l'hôtel/dans le salon** *(hum)* we were camping out at *ou* in a hotel/in the lounge; → **position** **VT** 1 *[+ troupes]* to camp out ◆ **campés pour 2 semaines près du village** camped (out) for 2 weeks by the village 2 (= *esquisser*) *[+ caractère, personnage]* to portray; *[+ récit]* to construct ◆ **personnage bien campé** vividly sketched *ou* portrayed character 3 (= *poser*) **~ sa casquette sur l'oreille** to pull *ou* clap one's cap on firmly over one ear ◆ **se ~ des lunettes sur le nez** to plant* a pair of glasses on one's nose **VPR** **se camper** ◆ **se ~ devant qn** to plant o.s. in front of sb* ◆ **se ~ sur ses jambes** to stand firm

campeur, -euse /kɑ̃pœʀ, øz/ **NM,F** camper

camphre /kɑ̃fʀ/ **NM** camphor

camphré, e /kɑ̃fʀe/ **ADJ** camphorated; → **alcool**

camphrier /kɑ̃fʀije/ **NM** camphor tree

camping /kɑ̃piŋ/ **NM** 1 (= *activité*) **le ~** camping ◆ **faire du ~** to go camping; → **sauvage** 2 (= *lieu*) campsite, camping site

camping-car (pl **camping-cars**) /kɑ̃piŋkaʀ/ **NM** camper, Dormobile ® *(Brit)*, motorhome *(US)*, RV *(US)*

camping-gaz ® /kɑ̃piŋgɑz/ **NM INV** camp(ing) stove

campo(s) †* /kɑ̃po/ **NM** ◆ **demain on a ~s** tomorrow is a day off, we've got tomorrow off *ou* free ◆ **on a eu** *ou* **on nous a donné ~s à 4 heures** we were free *ou* told to go at 4 o'clock

campus /kɑ̃pys/ **NM** campus

camus, e /kamy, yz/ **ADJ** *[nez]* pug *(épith)*; *[personne]* pug-nosed

Canaan /kanaɑ̃/ **NM** Canaan

Canada /kanada/ **NM** Canada

canada /kanada/ **NF** *apple of the pippin variety*

Canada Dry ® /kanadadʀaj/ **NM** Canada Dry ® ◆ **c'est une version ~** *(fig)* it's a watered-down version

Canadair ® /kanadɛʀ/ **NM** fire-fighting plane

canadianisme /kanadjanism/ **NM** Canadianism

canadien, -ienne /kanadjɛ̃, jɛn/ **ADJ** Canadian **NM,F** **Canadien(ne)** Canadian ◆ **Canadien(ne) français(e)** French Canadian **NF** **canadienne** (= *veste*) fur-lined jacket; (= *canoë*) (Canadian) canoe; (= *tente*) (ridge) tent

canaille /kanɑj/ **ADJ** *[manières]* cheap, coarse ◆ **sous ses airs ~s, il est sérieux** he might look a bit rough and ready, but he is reliable **NF** *(péj)* (= *salaud*) bastard**; (= *escroc*) crook, shyster *(US)*, chiseler *(US)*; *(hum* = *enfant)* rascal, (little) devil ◆ **la ~** *(péj* = *populace)* the rabble *(péj)*, the riffraff *(péj)*

canaillerie /kanɑjʀi/ **NF** 1 *[d'allure, ton]* vulgarity, coarseness 2 (= *malhonnêteté*) *[de procédés, personne]* crookedness 3 (= *action malhonnête*) dirty *ou* low trick

canal (pl **-aux**) /kanal, o/ **NM** 1 *(artificiel)* canal; (= *détroit*) channel; (= *tuyau, fossé*) conduit, duct; *(Anat)* canal, duct; *(TV, Ordin)* channel ◆ **le ~ de Panama/Suez** the Panama/Suez Canal ◆ **le ~ de Mozambique** the Mozambique Channel ◆ **~ lacrymal** tear *ou* lacrimal

(SPÉC) duct ◆ **Canal Plus, Canal +** *French pay TV channel*
2 *(= intermédiaire)* **par le ~ d'un collègue** through *ou* via a colleague ◆ **par le ~ de la presse** through the medium of the press ◆ **par un ~ amical** *(littér)* through a friend
COMP **canal d'amenée** feeder canal
canal biliaire biliary canal, bile duct
canal déférent vas deferens
canal de dérivation diversion canal
canal de distribution distribution channel
canal de fuite tail-race
canal d'irrigation irrigation canal
canal maritime ship canal
canal médullaire medullary cavity *ou* canal
canal de navigation ship canal

canalisation /kanalizasjɔ̃/ NF 1 *(= tuyau)* (main) pipe ◆ **~s** *(= réseau)* pipes; *(Élec)* cables 2 *(= aménagement) [de cours d'eau]* canalization 3 *[de demandes, foule]* channelling, funnelling

canaliser /kanalize/ ▸ conjug 1 ◂ VT 1 *[+ foule, demandes, énergie]* to channel, to funnel 2 *[+ fleuve]* to canalize; *[+ région]* to provide with a network of canals

cananéen, -enne /kananeɛ̃, ɛn/ ADJ Canaanite NM *(= langue)* Canaanite NM,F **Cananéen(ne)** Canaanite

canapé /kanape/ NM 1 *(= meuble)* sofa, settee *(Brit)* ◆ **~ transformable** *ou* **convertible** sofa bed, bed settee *(Brit)* 2 *(Culin)* open sandwich; *(pour apéritif)* canapé ◆ **crevettes sur ~** shrimp canapé, canapé of shrimps

canapé-lit (pl **canapés-lits**) /kanapeli/ NM sofa bed

canaque /kanak/ ADJ Kanak NMF **Canaque** Kanak

canard /kanaʀ/ NM 1 *(= oiseau, Culin)* duck; *(mâle)* drake; → **froid, mare, vilain** 2 * *(= journal)* paper; *(péj)* rag * 3 *(= fausse note)* false note ◆ **faire un ~** to hit a false note 4 *(terme d'affection)* **mon (petit) ~** pet, poppet * *(Brit)* 5 *(* = sucre) sugar lump dipped in brandy or coffee*
COMP **canard de Barbarie** Muscovy *ou* musk duck
canard boiteux * lame duck
canard laqué Peking duck
canard mandarin mandarin duck
canard à l'orange duck in orange sauce
canard sauvage wild duck
canard siffleur wigeon
canard souchet shoveler

canardeau (pl **canardeaux**) /kanaʀdo/ NM duckling

canarder * /kanaʀde/ ▸ conjug 1 ◂ VT *(au fusil)* to snipe at, to take potshots at; *(avec pierres)* to pelt *(avec* with); ◆ **ça canardait de tous les côtés** there were bullets flying all over the place VI *(Mus)* to hit a false note

canardière /kanaʀdjɛʀ/ NF *(= mare)* duckpond; *(= fusil)* punt gun

canari /kanaʀi/ NM, ADJ INV canary ◆ **(jaune) ~** canary yellow

Canaries /kanaʀi/ NFPL ◆ **les (îles) ~** the Canary Islands, the Canaries

canasson /kanasɔ̃/ NM *(péj = cheval)* nag *(péj)*

canasta /kanasta/ NF canasta

Canberra /kɑ̃beʀa/ N Canberra

cancan /kɑ̃kɑ̃/ NM 1 *(= racontar)* piece of gossip ◆ **~s** gossip, tittle-tattle ◆ **faire courir des ~s (sur qn)** to spread gossip *ou* stories (about sb), to tittle-tattle (about sb) 2 *(= danse)* cancan

cancaner /kɑ̃kane/ ▸ conjug 1 ◂ VI 1 *(= bavarder, médire)* to gossip 2 *[canard]* to quack

cancanier, -ière /kɑ̃kanje, jɛʀ/ ADJ gossipy, scandalmongering *(épith)*, tittle-tattling *(épith)* NM,F gossip, scandalmonger, tittle-tattle

cancer /kɑ̃sɛʀ/ NM 1 *(Méd, fig)* cancer ◆ **avoir un ~ du sein/du poumon** to have breast/lung cancer, to have cancer of the breast/lung ◆ **~ du sang** leukaemia *(Brit)*, leukemia *(US)* ◆ **~ généralisé** systemic cancer 2 *(Astron)* **le Cancer** Cancer ◆ **il est (du signe) du Cancer** he's (a) Cancer; → **tropique**

cancéreux, -euse /kɑ̃seʀø, øz/ ADJ *[tumeur]* cancerous; *[personne]* with cancer NM,F person with cancer; *(à l'hôpital)* cancer patient

cancériforme /kɑ̃seʀifɔʀm/ ADJ cancer-like

cancérigène /kɑ̃seʀiʒɛn/ ADJ carcinogenic, cancer-producing

cancérisation /kɑ̃seʀizasjɔ̃/ NF ◆ **on peut craindre la ~ de l'organe** there is a risk of the organ becoming cancerous

cancériser (se) /kɑ̃seʀize/ ▸ conjug 1 ◂ VPR to become cancerous ◆ **cellules cancérisées** cancerous cells

cancérogène /kɑ̃seʀɔʒɛn/ ADJ ⇒ **cancérigène**

cancérogenèse /kɑ̃seʀɔʒənɛz/ NF carcinogenesis

cancérologie /kɑ̃seʀɔlɔʒi/ NF *(= recherche)* cancer research; *(= traitement)* cancer treatment ◆ **il est hospitalisé en ~** he's in the *(ou* a) cancer ward

cancérologique /kɑ̃seʀɔlɔʒik/ ADJ *[médecine, recherche]* cancer *(épith)*

cancérologue /kɑ̃seʀɔlɔg/ NMF cancer specialist

cancre /kɑ̃kʀ/ NM *(péj = élève)* dunce

cancrelat /kɑ̃kʀəla/ NM cockroach

candélabre /kɑ̃delabʀ/ NM *(= chandelier)* candelabra, candelabrum

candeur /kɑ̃dœʀ/ NF ingenuousness, naïvety ◆ **avec ~** naïvely

> ⚠ **candeur** ne se traduit pas par le mot anglais **candour**, qui a le sens de 'franchise'.

candi /kɑ̃di/ ADJ M → **sucre**

candida /kɑ̃dida/ NM INV candida (albicans)

candidat, e /kɑ̃dida, at/ NM,F *(à un concours, une élection)* candidate *(à* at); *(à un poste)* applicant, candidate *(à* for); ◆ **~ sortant** present *ou* outgoing incumbent ◆ **les ~s à l'examen** the examination candidates, the examinees ◆ **les ~s à l'embauche** job applicants ◆ **être ~ à la députation** to run *ou* stand *(Brit)* for the post of deputy ◆ **se porter ~ à un poste** to apply for a job, to put o.s. forward for a job ◆ **être ~ à la présidence** *(Pol)* to run *ou* stand *(Brit)* for president, to run for the presidency ◆ **les ~s à la retraite** candidates for retirement ◆ **les ~s au suicide** those contemplating suicide ◆ **je ne suis pas ~** *(fig)* I'm not interested

candidature /kɑ̃didatyʀ/ GRAMMAIRE ACTIVE 46.1 NF *(Pol)* candidacy, candidature; *(à un poste)* application *(à* for); ◆ **~ officielle** *(à un poste)* formal application; *(Pol)* official candidacy *ou* candidature ◆ **~ spontanée** *(à un poste, action)* unsolicited application; *(lettre)* unsolicited letter of application ◆ **poser sa ~ à un poste** to apply for a job, to submit one's application for a job ◆ **poser sa ~ à une élection** to stand in an election *(Brit)*, to put o.s. forward as a candidate in an election, to run for election *(US)*

candide /kɑ̃did/ ADJ ingenuous, naïve

> ⚠ **candide** ne se traduit pas par le mot anglais **candid**, qui a le sens de 'franc', 'sincère'.

candidement /kɑ̃didmɑ̃/ ADV ingenuously, naïvely

candidose /kɑ̃didoz/ NF thrush, candidiasis *(SPÉC)*

candir /kɑ̃diʀ/ ▸ conjug 2 ◂ VTI ◆ **(faire) ~** to candy

candomblé /kɑ̃dɔ̃bl/ NM candomblé

cane /kan/ NF (female) duck ◆ **œuf de ~** duck egg

caner ‡ /kane/ ▸ conjug 1 ◂ VI *(= mourir)* to kick the bucket ‡, to snuff it ‡; *(= flancher)* to chicken out *, to funk it ‡ *(Brit)*, to wimp out * *(US) (devant* in the face of)

caneton /kantɔ̃/ NM duckling

canette[1] /kanɛt/ NF *(= canard)* duckling

canette[2] /kanɛt/ NF *[de machine à coudre]* spool ◆ **~ (de bière)** *(= bouteille)* small bottle of beer; *(= boîte)* can of beer

canevas /kanvɑ/ NM 1 *[de livre, discours]* framework, basic structure 2 *(Couture) (= toile)* canvas; *(= ouvrage)* tapestry (work) 3 *(Cartographie)* network

caniche /kaniʃ/ NM poodle ◆ **~ nain** toy poodle

caniculaire /kanikylɛʀ/ ADJ *[chaleur, jour]* scorching ◆ **une journée ~** a scorcher *, a scorching (hot) day

canicule /kanikyl/ NF *(= forte chaleur)* scorching heat; *(= vague de chaleur)* heatwave ◆ **la ~** *(spécialement juillet-août)* the midsummer heat, the dog days ◆ **aujourd'hui c'est la ~** it's a scorcher today *

canidé /kanide/ NM canine ◆ **les ~s** the dog family, the Canidae *(SPÉC)*

canif /kanif/ NM penknife, pocket knife ◆ **donner un coup de ~ dans le contrat (de mariage)** * to have a bit on the side *

canin, e /kanɛ̃, in/ ADJ *[espèce]* canine; *[exposition]* dog *(épith)* ◆ **la race ~e** dogs, the dog family ◆ **une race ~e** a dog breed NF **canine** *(= dent)* canine (tooth); *(supérieure)* eyetooth; *[de chien, vampire]* fang

caninette /kaninɛt/ NF pooper-scooper motor bike * *(used to clean streets of dog mess)*

canisses /kanis/ NFPL wattle fence

caniveau (pl **caniveaux**) /kanivo/ NM gutter *(in roadway etc)* ◆ **presse de ~** *(péj)* gutter press ◆ **des procédés de ~** *(péj)* underhand methods

canna /kana/ NM *(= fleur)* canna

cannabis /kanabis/ NM cannabis

cannage /kanaʒ/ NM *(= partie cannée)* canework; *(= opération)* caning

canne /kan/ NF 1 *(= bâton)* (walking) stick, cane; *[de souffleur de verre]* blowpipe 2 (* *= jambe)* leg ◆ **il ne tient pas sur ses ~s** he's not very steady on his pins ‡ ◆ **il a des ~s de serin** * he has spindly little legs; → **sucre**
COMP **canne anglaise** crutch
canne blanche *[d'aveugle]* white stick
canne à pêche fishing rod
canne à sucre sugar cane

canné, e /kane/ (ptp de **canner**) ADJ *[siège]* cane *(épith)*

canneberge /kanbɛʀʒ/ NF cranberry

canne-épée (pl **cannes-épées**) /kanepe/ NF swordstick

cannelé, e /kanle/ (ptp de **canneler**) ADJ *[colonne]* fluted

canneler /kanle/ ▸ conjug 4 ◂ VT to flute

cannelier /kanəlje/ NM cinnamon tree

cannelle /kanɛl/ NF *(= épice)* cinnamon

cannelure /kan(ə)lyʀ/ NF *[de meuble, colonne]* flute; *[de plante]* striation ◆ **~s** *[de colonne]* fluting; *[de neige]* corrugation ◆ **~s glaciaires** striae, striations

canner /kane/ ▸ conjug 1 ◂ VT *[+ chaise]* to cane

cannette /kanɛt/ NF ⇒ **canette**[2]

canneur, -euse /kanœʀ, øz/ NM,F cane worker, caner

cannibale /kanibal/ ADJ *[tribu, animal]* cannibal *(épith)*, cannibalistic NMF cannibal

cannibalisation /kanibalizasjɔ̃/ NF *[de machine]* cannibalization ◆ **pour éviter la ~ de leurs produits** to prevent their products losing their market share *ou* the cannibalization (US) of their products

cannibaliser /kanibalize/ ▸ conjug 1 ◂ VT *[+ machine]* to cannibalize; *[+ produit]* to eat into the market share of, to cannibalize *(US)* ◆ **ce produit a été cannibalisé par ...** this product has lost (some of its) market share to ...

cannibalisme /kanibalism/ NM cannibalism

cannisses /kanis/ NFPL ⇒ **canisses**

canoë /kanɔe/ NM (= *bateau*) canoe; (= *sport*) canoeing

canoéisme /kanɔeism/ NM canoeing

canoéiste /kanɔeist/ NMF canoeist

canoë-kayak /kanɔekajak/ NM INV ◆ **faire du ~** to go canoeing ◆ **descendre une rivière en ~** to go down a river in a canoe, to canoe down a river

canon[1] /kanɔ̃/ NM 1 (= *arme*) gun, cannon; *(Hist)* cannon ◆ **~ de 75/125** 75/125mm gun *ou* cannon ◆ **coup de ~** cannon shot ◆ **des coups de ~** *(moderne)* artillery *ou* cannon fire; *(Hist)* cannon fire ◆ **service ~** * *(Tennis)* cannonball (serve) ◆ **tir ~** * *(Ftbl)* bullet-like shot; → **chair**
2 (= *tube*) *[de revolver]* barrel ◆ **fusil à ~ scié** sawn-off *(Brit) ou* sawed-off *(US)* shotgun ◆ **à deux ~s** double-barrelled; → **baïonnette**
3 *[de clé, seringue]* barrel; *[d'arrosoir]* spout
4 (= *os*) *[de bœuf, cheval]* cannonbone 5 *(Hist Habillement)* canion 6 (* = *verre*) glass (of wine)
COMP **canon antiaérien** anti-aircraft *ou* AA gun
canon antichar anti-tank gun
canon antigrêle anti-hail gun
canon à eau water cannon
canon à électrons electron gun
canon lisse smooth *ou* unrifled bore
canon de marine naval gun
canon à neige snow cannon
canon à particules particle beam weapon
canon rayé rifled bore

canon[2] /kanɔ̃/ NM 1 (= *modèle*) model, perfect example ◆ **~s** (= *normes*) canons ◆ **les ~s de la beauté** the canons of beauty ◆ **elle/il est ~** *, **c'est un ~** * *ou* **une fille/un mec ~** * she/he's gorgeous, she's/he's a bit of alright* *(Brit)* 2 *(Rel)* canon; → **droit**[3]

canon[3] /kanɔ̃/ NM *(Mus)* canon ◆ **~ à 2 voix** canon for 2 voices ◆ **chanter en ~** to sing in a round *ou* in canon

cañon /kaɲɔn/ NM canyon, cañon

canonicat /kanɔnika/ NM canonicate, canonry

canonique /kanɔnik/ ADJ canonical ◆ **forme ~** *(Ling)* base form; → **âge**

canonisation /kanɔnizasjɔ̃/ NF canonization

canoniser /kanɔnize/ ▸ conjug 1 ◂ VT to canonize

canonnade /kanɔnad/ NF cannonade ◆ **le bruit d'une ~** the noise of a cannonade *ou* of (heavy) gunfire

canonner /kanɔne/ ▸ conjug 1 ◂ VT to bombard, to shell

canonnier /kanɔnje/ NM gunner

canonnière /kanɔnjɛʀ/ NF gunboat

canope /kanɔp/ NM ◆ **(vase) ~** Canopic jar *(ou* urn *ou* vase)

canopée /kanɔpe/ NF (forest) canopy

canot /kano/ NM (= *barque*) (small *ou* open) boat, dinghy; *(Can)* Canadian canoe ◆ **~ automobile** motorboat ◆ **~ pneumatique** rubber *ou* inflatable dinghy ◆ **~ de sauvetage** lifeboat

canotage /kanɔtaʒ/ NM boating, rowing, canoeing *(Can)* ◆ **faire du ~** to go boating *ou* rowing; *(Can)* to go canoeing

canoter /kanɔte/ ▸ conjug 1 ◂ VI to go boating *ou* rowing; *(Can)* to go canoeing

canoteur, -euse /kanɔtœʀ, øz/ NM,F rower

canotier /kanɔtje/ NM (= *personne, chapeau*) boater

Canson ® /kɑ̃sɔ̃/ NM ◆ **papier ~** drawing paper

cantal /kɑ̃tal/ NM 1 (= *fromage*) Cantal (cheese) 2 (= *région*) **le Cantal** the Cantal

cantaloup /kɑ̃talu/ NM cantaloup(e), muskmelon

cantate /kɑ̃tat/ NF cantata

cantatrice /kɑ̃tatʀis/ NF *[d'opéra]* (opera) singer, prima donna; *[de chants classiques]* (professional) singer

cantharide /kɑ̃taʀid/ NF 1 (= *mouche*) cantharid 2 (= *poudre*) cantharis, cantharides, Spanish fly

cantilène /kɑ̃tilɛn/ NF song, cantilena

cantine /kɑ̃tin/ NF 1 (= *réfectoire*) *[d'entreprise]* canteen; *[d'école]* cafeteria, dining hall *(Brit)*, lunch room *(US)* ◆ **manger à la ~** *(gén)* to eat in the canteen; *(Scol)* to have school meals ◆ **ticket de ~** meal voucher *ou* ticket 2 (= *malle*) tin trunk

cantinière /kɑ̃tinjɛʀ/ NF *(Hist Mil)* canteen woman

cantique /kɑ̃tik/ NM (= *chant*) hymn; *(Bible)* canticle ◆ **le Cantique des ~s** the Song of Songs, the Song of Solomon

canton /kɑ̃tɔ̃/ NM 1 *(Pol)* *(en France)* canton, ≃ district; *(en Suisse)* canton
2 (= *section*) *[de voie ferrée, route]* section
3 († = *région*) district; *(au Canada)* township

> **CANTON**
>
> The **cantons** are electoral areas into which France's « arrondissements » are divided for administration purposes. Each **canton** usually includes several « communes », and corresponds to the constituency of a « conseiller général » who is elected in the « élections cantonales ». The main town in the **canton** has a « gendarmerie », a local tax office and sometimes a « tribunal d'instance ».
> Of the self-governing **cantons** that make up the Swiss Confederation, six are French-speaking: Jura, Vaud, Neuchâtel, Genève, Valais (also German-speaking) and Fribourg (also German-speaking). → ARRONDISSEMENT, COMMUNE, ÉLECTIONS

cantonade /kɑ̃tɔnad/ **à la cantonade** LOC ADV ◆ **parler à la ~** *(gén)* to speak to the company at large; *(Théât)* to speak (in an aside) to the audience ◆ **c'est à qui ? dit-elle à la ~** whose is this? she asked the assembled company

cantonais, e /kɑ̃tɔnɛ, ɛz/ ADJ Cantonese NM (= *langue*) Cantonese NM,F **Cantonais(e)** Cantonese

cantonal, e (mpl **-aux**) /kɑ̃tɔnal, o/ ADJ *(en France)* cantonal, ≃ district *(épith)*; *(en Suisse)* cantonal ◆ **sur le plan ~** *(en France)* at (the) local level; *(en Suisse)* at the level of the cantons ◆ **les (élections) ~es** cantonal elections; → ÉLECTIONS

cantonnement /kɑ̃tɔnmɑ̃/ NM 1 *(Mil)* (= *action*) stationing; *(chez l'habitant)* billeting, quartering; (= *lieu*) quarters, billet; (= *camp*) camp ◆ **établir un ~** to set up (a) camp ◆ **troupes en ~** billeted troops ◆ **prendre ses ~s** to take up one's quarters 2 *(Rail)* block system 3 *(Admin)* *[de forêt]* range

cantonner /kɑ̃tɔne/ ▸ conjug 1 ◂ VT 1 *(Mil)* (= *établir*) to station; *(chez l'habitant)* to quarter, to billet *(chez, dans* on) 2 (= *reléguer*) to confine ◆ **~ qn dans un travail** to confine sb to a job ◆ **~ qn à** *ou* **dans un rôle** to limit *ou* restrict sb to a role VI *(Mil)* to be stationed *(à, dans* at); *(chez l'habitant)* to be quartered *ou* billetted VPR **se cantonner** ◆ **se ~ à** *ou* **dans** to confine o.s. to

cantonnier /kɑ̃tɔnje/ NM (= *ouvrier*) roadmender, roadman

cantonnière /kɑ̃tɔnjɛʀ/ NF (= *tenture*) pelmet

canular /kanylaʀ/ NM hoax ◆ **monter un ~** to think up *ou* plan a hoax ◆ **faire un ~ à qn** to hoax sb, to play a hoax on sb

canule /kanyl/ NF cannula

canuler* /kanyle/ ▸ conjug 1 ◂ VT (= *ennuyer*) to bore; (= *agacer*) to pester

Canut /kanyt/ NM Canute, Knut

canut, -use /kany, yz/ NM,F silk worker *(in Lyon)*

canyon /kanjɔ̃, kanjɔn/ NM canyon, cañon ◆ **le Grand Canyon** the Grand Canyon

canyoning /kanjɔniŋ/ NM *(Sport)* canyoning ◆ **faire du ~** to go canyoning

CAO /seao/ NF (abrév de **conception assistée par ordinateur**) CAD

caoua * /kawa/ NM ⇒ **kawa**

caoutchouc /kautʃu/ NM 1 (= *matière*) rubber ◆ **en ~** rubber *(épith)* ◆ **~ mousse** ® foam *ou* sponge rubber ◆ **balle en ~ mousse** rubber *ou* sponge ball ◆ **~ synthétique** synthetic rubber; → **botte**[1] 2 (= *élastique*) rubber *ou* elastic band 3 † (= *imperméable*) waterproof ◆ **~s** (= *chaussures*) overshoes, galoshes 4 (= *plante verte*) rubber plant

caoutchouter /kautʃute/ ▸ conjug 1 ◂ VT to rubberize, to coat with rubber

caoutchouteux, -euse /kautʃutø, øz/ ADJ rubbery

CAP /seape/ NM (abrév de **certificat d'aptitude professionnelle**) vocational training certificate ◆ **il a un ~ de menuisier/soudeur** he's a qualified joiner/welder

cap[1] /kap/ NM 1 *(Géog)* cape; (= *promontoire*) point, headland ◆ **le ~ Canaveral** Cape Canaveral ◆ **le ~ Horn** Cape Horn ◆ **le ~ de Bonne Espérance** the Cape of Good Hope ◆ **passer** *ou* **doubler un ~** *(Naut)* to round a cape ◆ **il a passé le ~** *[malade]* he's over the worst, he's turned the corner ◆ **il a passé le ~ de l'examen** he's got over the hurdle of the exam ◆ **dépasser** *ou* **franchir** *ou* **passer le ~ des 40 ans** to turn 40 ◆ **dépasser** *ou* **franchir le ~ des 50 millions** to pass the 50-million mark 2 (= *direction*) course ◆ **changer de ~** *(lit, fig)* to change course ◆ **mettre le ~ au vent** to head into the wind ◆ **mettre le ~ au large** to stand out to sea ◆ **mettre le ~ sur** to head for ◆ **~ magnétique** magnetic course *ou* heading ◆ **tenir** *ou* **maintenir le cap** *(fig)* to steer a steady course; → **pied** 3 (= *ville*) **Le Cap** Cape Town ◆ **la province du Cap** the Cape Province

cap[2] * /kap/ ADJ (abrév de **capable**) ◆ **t'es pas ~ de le faire !** *(langage enfantin)* you couldn't do it if you tried!

capable /kapabl/ GRAMMAIRE ACTIVE 42.4, 43.4 ADJ
1 (= *compétent*) able, capable
2 (= *apte à*) **~ de faire** capable of doing ◆ **te sens-tu ~ de tout manger ?** do you feel you can eat it all?, do you feel up to eating it all? ◆ **tu n'en es pas ~** you're not up to it, you're not capable ◆ **viens te battre si tu en es ~** come and fight if you've got it in you *ou* if you dare ◆ **cette conférence est ~ d'intéresser beaucoup de gens** this lecture is likely to interest a lot of people
3 (= *qui fait preuve de*) **~ de** *[+ dévouement, courage, incartade]* capable of ◆ **il est ~ du pire comme du meilleur** he's capable of (doing)

the worst as well as the best ◆ **il est ~ de tout** he'll stop at nothing, he's capable of anything
4 * **il est ~ de l'avoir perdu/de réussir** he's quite likely to have lost it/to succeed, he's quite capable of having lost it/of succeeding ◆ **il est bien ~ d'en réchapper** he may well get over it
5 *(Jur)* competent

capacité /kapasite/ NF 1 *(= aptitude)* ability *(à* to); ◆ **~s intellectuelles** intellectual abilities *ou* capacities ◆ **~s physiques** physical abilities ◆ **en dehors de mes ~s** beyond my capabilities *ou* capacities ◆ **sa ~ d'analyse/d'analyser les faits** his capacity for analysis/for analysing facts ◆ **il a une grande ~ d'adaptation** he's very adaptable
2 *(= contenance, potentiel)* capacity; *[d'accumulateur]* capacitance, capacity ◆ **la ~ d'accueil d'une ville** the total amount of tourist accommodation in a town ◆ **de grande ~** *[avion, stade]* with a large seating capacity ◆ **~ de mémoire/de stockage** *(Ordin)* memory/disk capacity
3 *(Jur)* capacity ◆ **avoir ~ pour qch** to be (legally) entitled to sth
COMP **capacité civile** civil capacity
capacité contributive ability to pay tax
capacité en droit *basic legal qualification*
capacité électrostatique capacitance
capacité légale legal capacity
capacité thoracique *(Méd)* vital capacity

caparaçon /kapaʀasɔ̃/ NM *(Hist)* caparison

caparaçonner /kapaʀasɔne/ ► conjug 1 ◄ VT *(Hist) [+ cheval]* to caparison ◆ **caparaçonné de cuir** *(hum)* all clad in leather

cape /kap/ NF *(Habillement) (courte)* cape; *(longue)* cloak ◆ **roman (***ou* **film) de ~ et d'épée** swashbuckler; → **rire**

capé, e /kape/ ADJ *(Sport) [joueur]* capped ◆ **le joueur le plus ~ de l'équipe de France** the French team's most capped player

capeline /kaplin/ NF wide-brimmed hat

CAPES /kapes/ NM (abrév de **certificat d'aptitude au professorat de l'enseignement secondaire**) → **certificat**

> **CAPES**
>
> The **CAPES** is a competitive examination for the recruitment of French secondary school teachers. It is taken after the « licence ». Successful candidates become fully-qualified teachers (« professeurs certifiés »). → CONCOURS

capésien, -ienne * /kapesjɛ̃, jɛn/ NM,F holder of the CAPES, ≈ qualified graduate teacher

CAPET /kapɛt/ NM (abrév de **certificat d'aptitude au professorat de l'enseignement technique**) → **certificat**

capétien, -ienne /kapesjɛ̃, jɛn/ ADJ Capetian
NM,F **Capétien(ne)** Capetian

capharnaüm * /kafaʀnaɔm/ NM *(= bric-à-brac, désordre)* shambles* ◆ **quel ~ !** what a shambles! * N **Capharnaüm** Capernaum

cap-hornier (pl **cap-horniers**) /kapɔʀnje/ NM Cape Horner

capillaire /kapilɛʀ/ ADJ *(Anat, Bot, Phys)* capillary; *[soins, lotion]* hair *(épith)*; → **vaisseau** NM 1 *(Anat)* capillary 2 *(= fougère)* maidenhair fern

capillarité /kapilaʀite/ NF capillarity ◆ **par ~** by capillary action

capilliculteur, -trice /kapilikyltœʀ, tʀis/ NM,F hair designer

capilotade /kapilɔtad/ **en capilotade** LOC ADJ *[fruits, nez]* in a pulp; *[objet cassable]* in smithereens ◆ **j'ai les reins en ~** my back's killing me*

capitaine /kapitɛn/ NM 1 *(armée de terre)* captain; *(armée de l'air)* flight lieutenant *(Brit)*, captain *(US)*; *[de grand bateau]* captain, master; *[de bateau de pêche]* captain, skipper; *(Sport)* captain, skipper*; *(littér = chef militaire)* (military) leader; → **instructeur** 2 *(= poisson)* threadfin
COMP **capitaine de corvette** lieutenant commander
capitaine de frégate commander
capitaine de gendarmerie captain of the gendarmerie
capitaine d'industrie captain of industry
capitaine au long cours master mariner
capitaine de la marine marchande captain in the merchant navy *(Brit) ou* in the marine *(US)*
capitaine des pompiers fire chief, firemaster *(Brit)*, fire marshal *(US)*
capitaine de port harbour *(Brit) ou* harbor *(US)* master
capitaine de vaisseau captain

capitainerie /kapitɛnʀi/ NF harbour *(Brit) ou* harbor *(US)* master's office

capital, e (mpl **-aux**) /kapital, o/ ADJ 1 *(= principal) [erreur, question]* major *(épith)*; *[rôle]* cardinal, major *(épith)* ◆ **d'une importance ~e** of major *ou* capital importance ◆ **c'est l'œuvre ~e de Gide** it is Gide's major work ◆ **son erreur ~e** his major *ou* chief mistake; → **péché, sept**
2 *(= essentiel)* essential ◆ **il est ~ d'y aller** *ou* **que nous y allions** it is of the utmost importance *ou* it is absolutely essential that we go
3 *(Jur)* capital; → **peine**
NM 1 *(Fin = avoirs)* capital ◆ **10 millions d'euros de ~** a 10-million-euro capital, a capital of 10 million euros ◆ **au ~ de** with a capital of; → **augmentation**
2 *(= placements)* **capitaux** money, capital ◆ **la circulation/fuite des capitaux** the circulation/flight of capital
3 *(= possédants)* **le ~** capital ◆ **le ~ et le travail** capital and labour ◆ **le grand ~** big investors
4 *(= fonds, richesse)* stock, fund ◆ **le ~ de connaissances acquis à l'école** the stock *ou* fund of knowledge acquired at school ◆ **la connaissance d'une langue constitue un ~ appréciable** knowing a language is a significant *ou* major asset ◆ **le ~ artistique de la région** the artistic wealth *ou* resources of the region ◆ **accroître son ~(-)santé** to build up one's health ◆ **elle a su se bâtir un ~(-)confiance** she managed to gain *ou* win everybody's trust
NF **capitale** 1 *(Typo)* **(lettre) ~e** capital (letter) ◆ **en grandes/petites ~es** in large/small capitals ◆ **en ~es d'imprimerie** in block letters *ou* block capitals
2 *(= métropole)* capital (city) ◆ **le dimanche, les Parisiens quittent la ~e** on Sundays Parisians leave the capital ◆ **~e régionale** regional capital ◆ **la ~e du vin** the wine capital
COMP **capital circulant** working capital, circulating capital
capital constant constant capital
capital décès death benefit
capital d'exploitation working capital
capitaux fébriles hot money
capital fixe fixed (capital) assets
capitaux flottants floating capital *ou* assets
capital humain human capital
capital initial *ou* **de lancement** seed *ou* start-up money
capital social authorized capital, share capital
capitaux spéculatifs ⇒ **capitaux fébriles**
capital variable variable capital

capitalisable /kapitalizabl/ ADJ capitalizable

capitalisation /kapitalizasjɔ̃/ NF capitalization ◆ **~ boursière** market capitalization *ou* valuation

capitaliser /kapitalize/ ► conjug 1 ◄ VT 1 *(= amasser) [+ somme]* to amass; *[+ expériences, connaissances]* to build up, to accumulate ◆ **l'intérêt capitalisé pendant un an** interest accrued *ou* accumulated in a year 2 *(Fin = ajouter au capital) [+ intérêts]* to capitalize 3 *(= calculer le capital de) [+ rente]* to capitalize VI *(= amasser de l'argent)* to save, to put money by ◆ **~ sur** *[+ événement, situation, marque, savoir-faire]* to capitalize on

capitalisme /kapitalism/ NM capitalism

capitaliste /kapitalist/ ADJ, NMF capitalist

capitalistique /kapitalistik/ ADJ capital *(épith)* ◆ **intensité ~** capital intensity ◆ **industrie ~** capital-intensive industry

capital-risque /kapitalʀisk/ NM venture capital

capital-risqueur /kapitalʀiskœʀ/ NM venture capitalist

capitation /kapitasjɔ̃/ NF *(Hist)* poll tax, capitation

capiteux, -euse /kapitø, øz/ ADJ *[vin, parfum]* heady; *[femme, beauté]* intoxicating, alluring

Capitole /kapitɔl/ NM ◆ **le ~** the Capitol

capitolin, e /kapitɔlɛ̃, in/ ADJ Capitoline ◆ **le (mont) Capitolin** the Capitoline (Hill)

capiton /kapitɔ̃/ NM *(= bourre)* padding; *[de cellulite]* node of fat *(SPÉC)* ◆ **les ~s** orange-peel skin

capitonnage /kapitɔnaʒ/ NM padding

capitonner /kapitɔne/ ► conjug 1 ◄ VT *[+ siège, porte]* to pad *(de* with); ◆ **capitonné de** *(fig)* lined with ◆ **nid capitonné de plumes** nest lined with feathers ◆ **voiture capitonnée de cuir** car with padded leather trim ◆ **porte capitonnée** padded door

capitulaire /kapitylɛʀ/ ADJ *(Rel)* capitular ◆ **salle ~** chapter house

capitulard, e /kapitylaʀ, aʀd/ ADJ, NM,F defeatist

capitulation /kapitylasjɔ̃/ NF *(Mil, fig)* capitulation, surrender; *(= traité)* capitulation (treaty) ◆ **~ sans conditions** unconditional surrender

capituler /kapityle/ ► conjug 1 ◄ VI *(Mil = se rendre)* to capitulate, to surrender; *(fig = céder)* to surrender, to give in, to capitulate

capodastre /kapodastʀ/ NM *(Mus)* capo

capoeira /kapɔeiʀa/ NF capoeira

capon, -onne †† /kapɔ̃, ɔn/ ADJ cowardly NM,F coward

caporal (pl **-aux**) /kapɔʀal, o/ NM 1 *(Mil)* lance corporal *(Brit)*, private first class *(US)* ◆ **~ d'ordinaire** mess corporal ◆ **~-chef** corporal 2 *(= tabac)* caporal

caporalisme /kapɔʀalism/ NM *[de personne, régime]* petty officiousness

capot /kapo/ NM 1 *[de véhicule, moteur]* bonnet *(Brit)*, hood *(US)* 2 *(Naut) (= bâche de protection)* cover; *(= trou d'homme)* companion hatch ADJ INV *(Cartes)* ◆ **être ~** to have lost all the tricks ◆ **il nous a mis ~** he took all the tricks

capotage /kapɔtaʒ/ NM *[de véhicule]* overturning; *[de projet]* failure; *[de négociations]* breakdown

capote /kapɔt/ NF 1 *[de voiture]* top, hood *(Brit)* 2 *(gén Mil = manteau)* greatcoat 3 *(* = préservatif)* condom ◆ **~ anglaise** † French letter †

capoter /kapɔte/ ► conjug 1 ◄ VI *[véhicule]* to overturn; *[négociations]* to founder ◆ **faire ~** *[+ véhicule]* to overturn; *[+ négociations, projet]* to ruin, to scupper* *(Brit)*, to put paid to *(Brit)*

cappuccino /kaputʃino/ NM cappuccino

câpre /kɑpʀ/ NF (*Culin*) caper

Capri /kapʀi/ NF Capri

caprice /kapʀis/ NM [1] (= *lubie*) whim, caprice; (= *toquade amoureuse*) (passing) fancy ◆ **il a agi par ~** he acted on a whim ◆ **ne lui cède pas, c'est seulement un ~** don't give in to him, it's only a whim ◆ **faire un ~** to throw a tantrum ◆ **cet enfant fait des ~s** the child's being awkward *ou* temperamental [2] (= *variations*) **~s** [*de vent, marché*] vagaries, caprices ◆ **les ~s de la mode** the vagaries *ou* whims of fashion ◆ **les ~s météorologiques/climatiques** the vagaries of the weather/climate ◆ **les ~s du sort** *ou* **du hasard** the quirks of fate ◆ **une récolte exceptionnelle due à quelque ~ de la nature** an exceptional crop due to some quirk of nature [3] (*Mus*) capriccio, caprice

capricieusement /kapʀisjøzmɑ̃/ ADV capriciously, whimsically

capricieux, -ieuse /kapʀisjø, jøz/ ADJ [1] (= *fantasque*) capricious, whimsical; [*appareil*] temperamental; [*météo*] changeable, fickle; [*vent*] changeable [2] (= *difficile*) [*enfant*] awkward, temperamental ◆ **ne fais pas le ~ !** don't be awkward!

capricorne /kapʀikɔʀn/ NM [1] (*Astron*) **le Capricorne** Capricorn ◆ **il est (du signe) du Capricorne** he's (a) Capricorn; → **tropique** [2] (= *insecte*) capricorn beetle

câprier /kɑpʀije/ NM caper bush *ou* shrub

caprin, e /kapʀɛ̃, in/ ADJ (*Zool*) [*espèce*] goat (*épith*) ◆ **élevage ~** goat breeding NM member of the goat family ◆ **les ~s** members of the goat family, the Caprinae (*SPÉC*)

capriné /kapʀine/ NM ⇒ **caprin**

capsulage /kapsylaʒ/ NM [*de bouteille de vin*] capsuling; [*de bouteille de bière, d'eau*] capping

capsule /kapsyl/ NF [1] (*Anat, Bot, Pharm*) capsule [2] [*de bouteille*] cap; (*couvrant le goulot*) capsule [3] [*d'arme à feu*] (percussion) cap, primer; [*de pistolet d'enfant*] cap; → **pistolet** [4] ◆ **~ spatiale** space capsule

capsuler /kapsyle/ ► conjug 1 ◄ VT [+ *bouteille de bière, eau*] to put a cap on; [+ *bouteille de vin*] to put a capsule on

captage /kaptaʒ/ NM [*de cours d'eau*] harnessing; [*de message, émission*] picking up

capteur, -trice /kaptatœʀ, tʀis/ NM,F (*Jur*) ◆ **~ d'héritage** *ou* **de succession** legacy hunter

captation /kaptasjɔ̃/ NF [1] [*de marché, pouvoir*] capturing; [*de clientèle*] poaching ◆ **~ d'héritage** (*Jur*) captation (*SPÉC*) *ou* improper solicitation of a legacy [2] [*de cours d'eau, source*] harnessing; (*Bio*) [*de substance*] uptake

capter /kapte/ ► conjug 1 ◄ VT [1] [+ *énergie, cours d'eau*] to harness; [+ *courant*] to tap; [+ *lumière*] to catch; [+ *atmosphère*] to capture [2] [+ *attention*] to catch; [+ *confiance, bienveillance, suffrages*] to win, to gain; [+ *clientèle*] to attract ◆ **cette entreprise a capté 12% du marché** this firm has captured 12% of the market [3] (*Téléc*) [+ *message, émission, chaîne*] to pick up ◆ **on capte mal la BBC à Paris** you can't pick up *ou* get the BBC very well in Paris [4] (* = *comprendre*) to understand, to get*

capteur /kaptœʀ/ NM sensor ◆ **~ solaire** solar panel

captieux, -ieuse /kapsjø, jøz/ ADJ specious

captif, -ive /kaptif, iv/ ADJ [*personne, marché, clientèle*] captive; [*nappe d'eau*] confined; → **ballon¹** NM,F captive, prisoner

captivant, e /kaptivɑ̃, ɑ̃t/ ADJ [*film, lecture*] gripping, enthralling; [*personne*] fascinating, captivating

captiver /kaptive/ ► conjug 1 ◄ VT [+ *personne*] to fascinate, to enthrall, to captivate; [+ *attention, esprit*] to captivate

captivité /kaptivite/ NF captivity ◆ **en ~** in captivity ◆ **pendant sa ~** while he was in captivity

capture /kaptyʀ/ NF [1] (= *action*) [*de malfaiteur, animal*] catching, capture; [*d'objet*] catching; [*de navire*] capture [2] (= *objet*) **c'est une belle ~** it's a good catch [3] (*Ordin*) capture ◆ **~ d'écran** screenshot [4] (*Phys, Géog*) capture ◆ **~ électronique** electron capture

capturer /kaptyʀe/ ► conjug 1 ◄ VT [+ *malfaiteur, animal*] to catch, to capture; [+ *objet*] to catch; [+ *navire*] to capture; (*Ordin*) [+ *images*] to capture

capuche /kapyʃ/ NF hood

capuchette /kapyʃɛt/ NF rainhood

capuchon /kapyʃɔ̃/ NM [1] (*Couture*) hood; (*Rel*) cowl; (= *pèlerine*) hooded raincoat [2] [*de stylo, tube, flacon*] cap, top [3] [*de cheminée*] cowl

capucin /kapysɛ̃/ NM (*Rel*) Capuchin; (= *singe*) capuchin; → **barbe¹**

capucine /kapysin/ NF (= *plante*) nasturtium; (*Rel*) Capuchin nun

cap(-)verdien, -ienne /kapvɛʀdjɛ̃, jɛn/ ADJ Cape Verdean NM,F **Cap(-)verdien(ne)** Cape Verdean

Cap-Vert /kapvɛʀ/ NM ◆ **le ~** Cape Verde ◆ **les îles du ~** the Cape Verde Islands

caque /kak/ NF herring barrel ◆ **la ~ sent toujours le hareng** (*Prov*) what's bred in the bone will (come) out in the flesh (*Prov*)

caquelon /kaklɔ̃/ NM *earthenware or cast-iron fondue dish*

caquet* /kakɛ/ NM [*de personne*] gossip, prattle; [*de poule*] cackle, cackling ◆ **rabattre** *ou* **rabaisser le ~ de** *ou* **à qn*** to bring *ou* pull sb down a peg or two

caquetage /kaktaʒ/, **caquètement** /kakɛtmɑ̃/ NM [*de poule*] cackle, cackling; [*de personne*] prattle, prattling

caqueter /kakte/ ► conjug 4 ◄ VI [*personne*] to prattle; [*poule*] to cackle

car¹ /kaʀ/ NM coach (*Brit*), bus (*US*)
COMP **car de police** police van
car postal (*Helv*) post bus
car (de ramassage) scolaire school bus

car² /kaʀ/ CONJ because, for (*frm*)

carabin /kaʀabɛ̃/ NM (*arg Méd*) medical student

carabine /kaʀabin/ NF rifle, gun, carbine (*SPÉC*); [*de stand de tir*] rifle ◆ **~ à air comprimé** air rifle *ou* gun

carabiné, e* /kaʀabine/ ADJ [*fièvre, vent, orage*] raging, violent; [*cocktail, facture, punition*] stiff; [*amende*] heavy, stiff; [*rhume*] stinking*, shocking; [*migraine*] splitting, blinding ◆ **mal de dents ~** raging toothache

carabinier /kaʀabinje/ NM (*en Espagne*) carabinero, customs officer; (*en Italie*) carabiniere, police officer; (*Hist Mil*) carabineer ◆ **les ~s siciliens** the Sicilian carabinieri

carabosse /kaʀabɔs/ NF → **fée**

Caracas /kaʀakas/ N Caracas

caraco /kaʀako/ NM († = *chemisier*) (woman's) loose blouse; (= *sous-vêtement*) camisole

caracoler /kaʀakɔle/ ► conjug 1 ◄ VI [*cheval*] (= *évoluer*) to prance; (= *gambader*) to gambol *ou* caper about; (*Dressage*) to caracole ◆ **~ sur un cheval** to ride proud ◆ **~ en tête** [*concurrent*] to be well ahead of the others ◆ **il caracole en tête des sondages** he's riding high in the polls

caractère /kaʀaktɛʀ/ NM [1] (= *tempérament*) character, nature ◆ **être d'un** *ou* **avoir un ~ ouvert** to have an outgoing nature ◆ **être d'un** *ou* **avoir un ~ fermé** to be withdrawn ◆ **être d'un** *ou* **avoir un ~ froid/passionné** to be a cold/passionate person ◆ **avoir bon/mauvais ~** to be good-/bad-tempered, to be good-/ill-natured ◆ **il est très jeune de ~** [*adolescent*] he's very immature; [*adulte*] he has a very youthful outlook ◆ **son ~ a changé** his character has changed, he has changed ◆ **les chats ont un ~ sournois** cats have a sly nature ◆ **il a** *ou* **c'est un heureux ~** he has a happy nature ◆ **ce n'est pas dans son ~ de faire, il n'a pas un ~ à faire** it is not in his nature to do ◆ **le ~ méditerranéen/latin** the Mediterranean/Latin character ◆ **il a un sale ~*, il a un ~ de cochon*** he's a difficult *ou* an awkward so-and-so* ◆ **il a un ~ en or** he's very good-natured, he has a delightful nature

[2] (= *nature, aspect*) nature ◆ **sa présence confère à la réception un ~ officiel** his being here gives an official character *ou* flavour to the reception ◆ **la situation n'a aucun ~ de gravité** the situation shows no sign *ou* evidence of being serious ◆ **mission à ~ humanitaire** humanitarian mission, mission of a humanitarian nature

[3] (= *fermeté*) character ◆ **il a du ~** he has *ou* he's got character ◆ **il n'a pas de ~** he's got no backbone, he's spineless ◆ **style sans ~** characterless style

[4] (= *cachet, individualité*) character ◆ **la maison/cette vieille rue a du ~** the house/this old street has got character

[5] (*littér* = *personne*) character ◆ **ces ~s ne sont pas faciles à vivre** these characters *ou* people are not easy to live with; → **comique**

[6] (= *caractéristique*) characteristic ◆ **~ héréditaire/acquis** hereditary/acquired characteristic

[7] (*Écriture, Typo*) character ◆ **~ gras/maigre** heavy-/light-faced letter ◆ **~s gras** (*Typo*) bold type (*NonC*) ◆ **en gros/petits ~s** in large/small characters ◆ **en ~s d'imprimerie** in print ◆ **les ~s de ce livre** the print in this book

[8] (*Ordin*) character ◆ **~ de commande** control character ◆ **~ générique** *ou* **de remplacement** wildcard

caractériel, -elle /kaʀakteʀjɛl/ ADJ [1] [*personne*] (*Psych*) emotionally disturbed, maladjusted ◆ **il est un peu ~** (= *lunatique*) he's temperamental ◆ **un enfant ~** a problem child [2] **traits ~s** traits of character ◆ **troubles ~s** emotional problems NM,F (= *adulte*) emotionally disturbed person; (= *enfant*) problem *ou* maladjusted child

caractérisation /kaʀakteʀizasjɔ̃/ NF characterization

caractérisé, e /kaʀakteʀize/ (ptp de **caractériser**) ADJ [*erreur*] blatant ◆ **une rubéole ~e** a clear *ou* straightforward case of German measles ◆ **c'est de l'insubordination ~e** it's sheer *ou* downright insubordination

caractériser /kaʀakteʀize/ ► conjug 1 ◄ VT to characterize ◆ **avec l'enthousiasme qui le caractérise** with his characteristic enthusiasm ◆ **ça se caractérise par** it is characterized *ou* distinguished by ◆ **ce qui caractérise ce paysage** the main *ou* characteristic features of this landscape

caractéristique /kaʀakteʀistik/ GRAMMAIRE ACTIVE 53.1, 53.6 ADJ characteristic (*de* of) NF characteristic, (typical) feature ◆ **~s signalétiques** (*Admin*) particulars, personal details ◆ **~s techniques** design features

caractérologie /kaʀakteʀɔlɔʒi/ NF characterology

carafe /kaʀaf/ NF [1] (= *récipient*) decanter; [*d'eau, vin ordinaire*] carafe ◆ **une demi-~ de vin** half a carafe of wine ◆ **tomber en ~*** to break down ◆ **rester en ~*** to be left stranded, to be left high and dry ◆ **laisser qn en ~*** to leave sb high and dry [2] (* = tête) head, nut*

carafon /kaʀafɔ̃/ NM [1] (= récipient) small decanter; [d'eau, vin ordinaire] small carafe [2] (* = tête) head, nut*

caraïbe /kaʀaib/ ADJ Caribbean ◆ **les îles Caraïbes** the Caribbean islands ◆ **les Indiens ~s** the Carib Indians NMF **Caraïbe** (= personne) Carib NF(PL) **Caraïbe(s)** ◆ **la Caraïbe, les Caraïbes** the Caribbean (islands) ◆ **la mer des Caraïbes** the Caribbean (Sea)

carambolage /kaʀɑ̃bɔlaʒ/ NM [d'autos] multiple crash, pile-up; (Billard) cannon (Brit), carom (US)

carambole /kaʀɑ̃bɔl/ NF [1] (Billard) red (ball) [2] (= fruit) star fruit, carambola

caramboler /kaʀɑ̃bɔle/ ▸ conjug 1 ◂ VT to collide with, to run into ◆ **5 voitures se sont carambolées** there was a 5-car pile-up, 5 cars ran into each other ou collided VI (Billard) to cannon (Brit), to get ou make a cannon (Brit) ou carom (US)

carambouillage /kaʀɑ̃bujaʒ/ NM, **carambouille** /kaʀɑ̃buj/ NF (Jur) reselling of unlawfully owned goods

caramel /kaʀamɛl/ NM [1] (= sucre fondu) caramel; (= bonbon) (mou) caramel, fudge, chewy toffee; (dur) toffee [2] (* = tir puissant) (Ftbl) bullet-like shot, belter*; (Tennis) cannonball (serve) ADJ INV caramel (-coloured)

caramélisation /kaʀamelizasjɔ̃/ NF caramelization

caramélisé, e /kaʀamelize/ (ptp de **caraméliser**) ADJ [aliment] (= enrobé de caramel) coated with caramel, caramel-coated; [moule, plat] caramel-lined; (= très cuit, au goût de caramel) caramelized

caraméliser /kaʀamelize/ ▸ conjug 1 ◂ VT [+ sucre] to caramelize; [+ moule, pâtisserie] to coat with caramel; [+ boisson, aliment] to flavour (Brit) ou flavor (US) with caramel VI **se caraméliser** VPR [sucre] to caramelize

carapace /kaʀapas/ NF [de crabe, tortue] shell, carapace ◆ ~ **de boue** crust of mud ◆ **sommet recouvert d'une ~ de glace** summit encased in a sheath of ice ◆ **il est difficile de percer sa ~ d'égoïsme** it's difficult to penetrate the armour of his egoism ou his thickskinned self-centredness

carapater (se) * /kaʀapate/ ▸ conjug 1 ◂ VPR to skedaddle*, to run off, to hop it* (Brit)

carat /kaʀa/ NM (Bijouterie) carat ◆ **de l'or 18 ~s, du 18 ~s** 18-carat gold ◆ **il faut partir à midi, dernier ~ *** we have to leave by midday ou noon at the latest

Caravage /kaʀavaʒ/ NM ◆ **le ~** Caravaggio

caravane /kaʀavan/ NF (= convoi) caravan; (= véhicule) caravan, trailer (US) ◆ **une ~ de voitures** a procession ou stream of cars ◆ **une ~ de touristes** a stream of tourists ◆ **la ~ du Tour de France** the whole retinue of the Tour de France ◆ **la ~ publicitaire** the publicity caravan; → **chien**

caravanier, -ière /kaʀavanje, jɛʀ/ ADJ [itinéraire, chemin] caravan (épith) ◆ **tourisme ~** caravanning (Brit), RV ou camper vacationing (US) NM [1] (= conducteur de caravane) caravaneer [2] (= vacancier) caravanner (Brit), person vacationing in an RV ou a camper (US)

caravaning /kaʀavaniŋ/ NM ◆ **faire du ~** to go caravanning (Brit), to go on vacation in an RV ou a camper (US) ◆ **camp de ~** caravan site, trailer camp (US) ou court (US) ou park (US)

caravansérail /kaʀavɑ̃seʀaj/ NM (lit, fig) caravanserai

caravelle /kaʀavɛl/ NF (Hist Naut) caravel

carbochimie /kaʀbɔʃimi/ NF organic chemistry

carbonade /kaʀbɔnad/ NF (= viande) chargrilled meat ◆ ~ **flamande** beef stew

carbonate /kaʀbɔnat/ NM carbonate ◆ ~ **de soude** sodium carbonate, washing soda

carbone /kaʀbɔn/ NM (= matière, feuille) carbon ◆ **le ~ 14** carbon-14 ◆ **(papier) ~** carbon (paper); → **datation**

carboné, e /kaʀbɔne/ ADJ carbonaceous

carbonifère /kaʀbɔnifɛʀ/ ADJ (Minér) carboniferous; (Géol) Carboniferous NM Carboniferous

carbonique /kaʀbɔnik/ ADJ carbonic; → **gaz, neige** etc

carbonisation /kaʀbɔnizasjɔ̃/ NF carbonization

carbonisé, e /kaʀbɔnize/ (ptp de **carboniser**) ADJ [1] [arbre, restes] charred ◆ **il est mort ~** he was burned to death [2] (* = exténué) shattered*

carboniser /kaʀbɔnize/ ▸ conjug 1 ◂ VT [+ bois, substance] to carbonize; [+ forêt, maison] to burn to the ground, to reduce to ashes; [+ rôti] to burn to a cinder

carbonnade /kaʀbɔnad/ NF ⇒ **carbonade**

carburant /kaʀbyʀɑ̃/ ADJ M ◆ **mélange ~** mixture of petrol (Brit) ou gasoline (US) and air (in internal combustion engine) NM fuel ◆ **les ~s** fuel oils

carburateur /kaʀbyʀatœʀ/ NM carburettor (Brit), carburetor (US)

carburation /kaʀbyʀasjɔ̃/ NF [d'essence] carburation; [de fer] carburization

carbure /kaʀbyʀ/ NM carbide; → **lampe**

carburé, e /kaʀbyʀe/ (ptp de **carburer**) ADJ [air, mélange] carburetted; [métal] carburized

carburer /kaʀbyʀe/ ▸ conjug 1 ◂ VI [1] [moteur] **ça carbure bien/mal** it is well/badly tuned [2] (* = fonctionner) **il carbure au vin rouge** [personne] he drinks red wine as if it was water ◆ **elle carbure aux amphétamines/au café** she lives on amphetamines/on coffee ◆ **ça carbure sec ici !** (boisson) they're really knocking it back in here! [3] (* = travailler vite) **il va falloir ~ si on veut finir cette semaine** we'll have to work flat out if we want to finish this week VT [+ air] to carburet; [+ métal] to carburize

carburol /kaʀbyʀɔl/ NM gasohol

carcajou /kaʀkaʒu/ NM wolverine

carcan /kaʀkɑ̃/ NM (Hist) iron collar; (= contrainte) yoke, shackles ◆ **ce col est un vrai ~** this collar is like a vice ◆ **le ~ de la tradition** the straitjacket ou the fetters of tradition

carcasse /kaʀkas/ NF [1] [d'animal] carcass; [de maison] shell ◆ **je vais réchauffer ma ~ au soleil*** I'm going to toast myself in the sun* ◆ **j'ai du mal à traîner ma vieille ~*** I'm finding it difficult to drag my old bones around* ◆ **des ~s de voitures calcinées** burnt-out cars [2] (= armature) [d'abat-jour] frame; [de bateau] skeleton; [d'immeuble] shell, skeleton ◆ **pneu à ~ radiale/diagonale** radial/cross-ply tyre

carcéral, e (mpl **-aux**) /kaʀseʀal, o/ ADJ prison (épith) ◆ **régime ~** prison regime ◆ **l'univers ~** prison life

carcinogène /kaʀsinɔʒɛn/ ADJ carcinogenic

carcinogenèse /kaʀsinɔʒənɛz/ NF carcinogenesis

carcinome /kaʀsinom/ NM carcinoma

cardage /kaʀdaʒ/ NM carding

cardamine /kaʀdamin/ NF cuckooflower, lady's-smock

cardamome /kaʀdamɔm/ NF cardamom

cardan /kaʀdɑ̃/ NM universal joint; → **joint**[1]

carde /kaʀd/ NF (pour laine, tissus) card

carder /kaʀde/ ▸ conjug 1 ◂ VT to card ◆ **laine cardée** carded wool

cardeur, -euse /kaʀdœʀ, øz/ NM,F carder NF **cardeuse** (= machine) carding machine, carder

cardiaque /kaʀdjak/ ADJ (Anat) cardiac, heart (épith) ◆ **malade ~** heart case ou patient ◆ **être ~** to suffer from ou have a heart condition ◆ **chirurgie ~** heart surgery; → **crise** NMF heart case ou patient

Cardiff /kaʀdif/ N Cardiff

cardigan /kaʀdigɑ̃/ NM cardigan

cardinal, e (mpl **-aux**) /kaʀdinal, o/ ADJ [nombre] cardinal; (littér = capital) cardinal; → **point**[1] NM [1] (Rel) cardinal ◆ **~-archevêque** cardinal archbishop [2] (= nombre) cardinal number [3] (= oiseau) cardinal (bird)

cardinalat /kaʀdinala/ NM cardinalate, cardinalship

cardinalice /kaʀdinalis/ ADJ of a cardinal ◆ **conférer à qn la dignité ~** to make sb a cardinal, to raise sb to the purple; → **pourpre**

cardiogramme /kaʀdjɔgʀam/ NM cardiogram

cardiographe /kaʀdjɔgʀaf/ NM cardiograph

cardiographie /kaʀdjɔgʀafi/ NF cardiography

cardiologie /kaʀdjɔlɔʒi/ NF cardiology

cardiologique /kaʀdjɔlɔʒik/ ADJ cardiological

cardiologue /kaʀdjɔlɔg/ NMF cardiologist, heart specialist

cardio-pulmonaire (pl **cardio-pulmonaires**) /kaʀdjopylmɔnɛʀ/ ADJ cardiopulmonary

cardiotonique /kaʀdjotɔnik/ NM heart tonic

cardiovasculaire /kaʀdjovaskylɛʀ/ ADJ cardiovascular

cardite /kaʀdit/ NF carditis

cardon /kaʀdɔ̃/ NM cardoon

carême /kaʀɛm/ NM (= jeûne) fast ◆ **le Carême** (Rel = période) Lent ◆ **sermon de ~** Lent sermon ◆ **faire ~** to observe ou keep Lent, to fast during Lent ◆ **rompre le ~** to break the Lent fast ◆ **le ~ qu'il s'est imposé** the fast he has undertaken ◆ **face** ou **figure** ou **mine de ~*** long face (fig)

carême-prenant †† (pl **carêmes-prenants**) /kaʀɛmpʀənɑ̃/ NM (= période) Shrovetide (††); (= personne) Shrovetide reveller (††)

carénage /kaʀenaʒ/ NM [1] [de bateau] (= action) careening; (= lieu) careenage [2] [de véhicule] (= action) streamlining; (= partie) fairing

carence /kaʀɑ̃s/ NF [1] (Méd) deficiency ◆ ~ **alimentaire** nutritional deficiency ◆ ~ **vitaminique** ou **en vitamines** vitamin deficiency ◆ **maladie de** ou **par ~** deficiency disease [2] (= manque) shortage ◆ **une grave ~ en personnel qualifié** a serious shortage of qualified staff ◆ ~ **affective** emotional deprivation [3] (= incompétence) [de gouvernement] shortcomings, incompetence; [de parents] inadequacy [4] (= défauts) **les ~s de** [+ système, organisation] the inadequacies ou short-comings of [5] (Jur) insolvency

carencé, e /kaʀɑ̃se/ ADJ [personne] nutritionally deficient, suffering from nutritional deficiency; [régime] deficient (en in); ◆ **régime ~ en fer** diet deficient in iron, iron-deficient diet ◆ **gravement ~ en vitamine F** seriously deficient in vitamin F

carène /kaʀɛn/ NF 1 *[de bateau]* (lower part of the) hull ◆ **mettre en ~** to careen 2 *[de fleur]* carina, keel

caréner /kaʀene/ ► conjug 6 ◄ VT 1 *[+ bateau]* to careen 2 *[+ véhicule]* to streamline

caressant, e /kaʀesɑ̃, ɑ̃t/ ADJ *[enfant, animal]* affectionate; *[regard, voix]* caressing, tender; *[brise]* caressing

caresse /kaʀɛs/ NF 1 (= *câlinerie*) caress; (*à un animal*) stroke ◆ **faire des ~s à** *[+ personne]* to caress; *[+ animal]* to stroke, to pet ◆ **la ~ de la brise/des vagues** (*littér*) the caress of the breeze/of the waves 2 (†† = *flatterie*) cajolery (*NonC*), flattery (*NonC*) ◆ **endormir la méfiance de qn par des ~s** to use cajolery to allay *ou* quieten sb's suspicions

caresser /kaʀese/ ► conjug 1 ◄ VT 1 *[+ personne]* to caress; *[+ animal]* to stroke, to pet; *[+ objet]* to stroke ◆ **il lui caressait les jambes/les seins** he was stroking *ou* caressing her legs/caressing *ou* fondling her breasts ◆ **il caressait les touches du piano** he stroked *ou* caressed the keys of the piano ◆ **~ qn du regard** to gaze fondly *ou* lovingly at sb ◆ **~ qn dans le sens du poil** to stay on the right side of sb ◆ **il vaut mieux le ~ dans le sens du poil** you'd better not rub him up the wrong way ◆ **je vais lui ~ les côtes** * *ou* **l'échine** * (*hum*) I'm going to give him such a hiding 2 *[+ espoir]* to entertain, to toy with ◆ **~ le projet de faire qch** to toy with the idea of doing sth 3 (†† = *flatter*) to flatter, to fawn on

car-ferry (pl **car-ferrys** *ou* **car-ferries**) /kaʀfeʀi/ NM (car) ferry

cargaison /kaʀgɛzɔ̃/ NF cargo, freight ◆ **une ~ de bananes** a cargo of bananas ◆ **des ~s de** * *[+ lettres, demandes]* heaps *ou* piles of ◆ **des ~s de touristes** * busloads (*ou* shiploads *ou* planeloads) of tourists

cargo /kaʀgo/ NM cargo boat, freighter ◆ **~ mixte** cargo and passenger vessel

cargue /kaʀg/ NF (*Naut*) brail

carguer /kaʀge/ ► conjug 1 ◄ VT *[+ voiles]* to brail, to furl

cari /kaʀi/ NM ⇒ **curry**

cariatide /kaʀjatid/ NF caryatid

caribou /kaʀibu/ NM caribou

caricatural, e (mpl **-aux**) /kaʀikatyʀal, o/ ADJ (= *ridicule*) *[aspect, traits]* ridiculous, grotesque; (= *exagéré*) *[description, interprétation]* caricatured

caricature /kaʀikatyʀ/ NF 1 (= *dessin, description*) caricature; (*politique*) (satirical) cartoon ◆ **faire la ~ de** to make a caricature of, to caricature ◆ **une ~ de procès** a mere mockery of a trial ◆ **une ~ de la vérité** a caricature *ou* gross distortion of the truth ◆ **c'est une ~ de l'Anglais en vacances** he is a caricature of the Englishman on holiday 2 (* = *personne laide*) fright *

caricaturer /kaʀikatyʀe/ ► conjug 1 ◄ VT to caricature

caricaturiste /kaʀikatyʀist/ NMF caricaturist; (*à intention politique*) (satirical) cartoonist

carie /kaʀi/ NF 1 *[de dents, os]* caries (*NonC*) ◆ **la ~ dentaire** tooth decay, (dental) caries ◆ **j'ai une ~** I need a filling, I've got a cavity 2 *[d'arbre]* blight; *[de blé]* smut, bunt

carié, e /kaʀje/ (ptp de **carier**) ADJ *[dent]* decayed, bad

carier /kaʀje/ ► conjug 7 ◄ VT to decay, to cause to decay ◆ **dent cariée** bad *ou* decayed tooth VPR **se carier** to decay

carillon /kaʀijɔ̃/ NM 1 *[d'église]* (= *cloches*) (peal *ou* set of) bells; (= *air*) chimes ◆ **on entendait le ~ de St-Pierre/des ~s joyeux** we could hear the chimes of St Pierre/hear joyful chimes 2 *[d'horloge]* (= *système de sonnerie*) chime; (= *air*) chimes ◆ **une horloge à ~, un ~** a chiming clock 3 *[de sonnette d'entrée]* (door) chime

carillonner /kaʀijɔne/ ► conjug 1 ◄ VI 1 *[cloches]* to ring, to chime; (*à toute volée*) to peal out 2 (*à la porte*) to ring very loudly ◆ **ça ne sert à rien de ~, il n'y a personne** it's no use ringing away on the doorbell like that – there's no one in VT *[+ fête]* to announce with a peal of bells; *[+ heure]* to chime, to ring; (*fig*) *[+ nouvelle]* to broadcast

carillonneur /kaʀijɔnœʀ/ NM bell ringer

cariste /kaʀist/ NM fork-lift truck operator

caritatif, -ive /kaʀitatif, iv/ ADJ charitable ◆ **association** *ou* **organisation caritative** charity, charitable organization

carlin /kaʀlɛ̃/ NM pug(dog)

carlingue /kaʀlɛ̃g/ NF *[d'avion]* cabin; *[de bateau]* keelson

carliste /kaʀlist/ ADJ, NMF Carlist

carmagnole /kaʀmaɲɔl/ NF (= *chanson, danse*) carmagnole; (*Hist* = *veste*) short jacket (*worn during the French revolution*)

carme /kaʀm/ NM Carmelite, White Friar

carmel /kaʀmɛl/ NM (= *monastère*) *[de carmes]* Carmelite monastery; *[de carmélites]* Carmelite convent ◆ **le Carmel** (= *ordre*) the Carmelite order

carmélite /kaʀmelit/ NF Carmelite nun

carmin /kaʀmɛ̃/ NM (= *colorant*) cochineal; (= *couleur*) carmine, crimson ADJ INV carmine, crimson

carminé, e /kaʀmine/ ADJ carmine, crimson

carnage /kaʀnaʒ/ NM (*lit, fig*) carnage, slaughter ◆ **quel ~ !** what a massacre! ◆ **faire un ~** (*lit*) to cause absolute carnage ◆ **je vais faire un ~ !** (*fig*) I'm going to murder someone!

carnassier, -ière /kaʀnasje, jɛʀ/ ADJ *[animal]* carnivorous, flesh-eating; *[dent]* carnassial NM carnivore ◆ **~s** carnivores, Carnivora (*SPÉC*) NF **carnassière** (= *dent*) carnassial; (= *gibecière*) gamebag

carnation /kaʀnasjɔ̃/ NF (= *teint*) complexion; (*Peinture*) flesh tint

carnaval (pl **carnavals**) /kaʀnaval/ NM (= *fête*) carnival; (= *période*) carnival (time) ◆ **(Sa Majesté) Carnaval** (= *mannequin*) King Carnival ◆ **de ~** *[tenue, ambiance]* carnival (*épith*)

carnavalesque /kaʀnavalɛsk/ ADJ (= *grotesque*) carnivalesque

carne * /kaʀn/ NF (*péj* = *viande*) tough *ou* leathery meat; († = *cheval*) nag *, hack ◆ **quelle ~ !** (*homme*) what a swine! *ou* bastard! *; (*femme*) what a bitch! *

carné, e /kaʀne/ ADJ 1 *[alimentation]* meat (*épith*) 2 (*littér*) *[fleur, ton]* flesh-coloured

carnet /kaʀnɛ/ NM (= *calepin*) notebook; (= *liasse*) book; (*Helv Scol* = *carnet de notes*) report

COMP **carnet d'adresses** address book ◆ **avoir un ~ d'adresses bien rempli** to have a lot of (good) contacts
carnet de bal dance card
carnet de billets book of tickets
carnet de bord *[de bateau, avion]* log(book)
carnet de chèques chequebook (*Brit*), checkbook (*US*)
carnet de commandes order book ◆ **nos ~s de commandes sont pleins** we have a full order book
carnet à croquis *ou* **dessins** sketchbook
carnet de maternité *medical record of pregnancy*
carnet mondain (*Presse*) society column
carnet de notes (= *calepin*) notebook; (*Scol*) report card, school report (*Brit*) ◆ **avoir un bon ~ (de notes)** to have a good report
carnet rose (*Presse*) births column
carnet de route travel diary
carnet de santé health record
carnet à souches counterfoil book
carnet de timbres book of stamps
carnet de vol log(book)

carnier /kaʀnje/ NM gamebag

carnivore /kaʀnivɔʀ/ ADJ *[animal]* carnivorous, flesh-eating; *[insecte, plante]* carnivorous ◆ **il est très ~** (*hum*) *[personne]* he's a big meat-eater, he loves his meat NM carnivore ◆ **~s** carnivores, Carnivora (*SPÉC*)

carnotzet /kaʀnɔtzɛ/ NM (*Helv*) *part of a cellar used to entertain friends*

Caroline /kaʀɔlin/ NF ◆ **~ du Nord** North Carolina ◆ **~ du Sud** South Carolina

carolingien, -ienne /kaʀɔlɛ̃ʒjɛ̃, jɛn/ ADJ Carolingian NM,F **Carolingien(ne)** Carolingian

caroncule /kaʀɔ̃kyl/ NF (*de dindon*) wattle

carotène /kaʀɔtɛn/ NM carotene, carotin

carotide /kaʀɔtid/ ADJ, NF carotid

carottage /kaʀɔtaʒ/ NM 1 (* = *vol*) swiping *, pinching * 2 (= *extraction*) core boring

carotte /kaʀɔt/ NF 1 (= *légume*) carrot ◆ **les ~s sont cuites !** * they've (*ou* we've *etc*) had it! *, it's all up * (*Brit*) *ou* over!; → **poil** 2 (* = *récompense*) carrot ◆ **la politique de la ~ et du bâton** the carrot and stick approach *ou* policy ◆ **manier la ~ et le bâton** to use the carrot and stick approach ◆ **une ~ fiscale** a tax incentive 3 (= *échantillon*) core 4 *[de tabac]* plug; (= *enseigne*) tobacconist's (*Brit*) *ou* tobacco shop (*US*) sign ADJ INV *[cheveux]* red, carroty *; *[couleur]* carroty ◆ **objet (couleur) ~** carrot-coloured object ◆ **rouge ~** carrot red

carotter /kaʀɔte/ ► conjug 1 ◄ VT 1 (* = *voler*) to swipe *, to pinch * ◆ **~ qch à qn** to pinch * *ou* nick * sth from sb ◆ **il m'a carotté (de) 5 €, je me suis fait ~ (de) 5 €** he did * *ou* diddled * me out of €5 2 (= *forer*) to bore VI ◆ **il essaie toujours de ~** he's always trying to fiddle a bit for himself ◆ **elle carotte sur l'argent des commissions** she fiddles the housekeeping money

carotteur, -euse * /kaʀɔtœʀ, øz/, **carottier, -ière** * /kaʀɔtje, jɛʀ/ NM,F diddler *

caroube /kaʀub/ NF (= *fruit*) carob

caroubier /kaʀubje/ NM carob (tree)

carpaccio /kaʀpatʃ(j)o/ NM carpaccio

Carpates /kaʀpat/ NFPL ◆ **les ~** the Carpathians

carpe[1] /kaʀp/ NF (= *poisson*) carp; → **muet, saut**

carpe[2] /kaʀp/ NM (*Anat*) carpus

carpeau (pl **carpeaux**) /kaʀpo/ NM young carp

carpette /kaʀpɛt/ NF (= *tapis*) rug; (*péj* = *personne servile*) fawning *ou* servile person ◆ **s'aplatir comme une ~ devant qn** to fawn on sb

carpien, -ienne /kaʀpjɛ̃, jɛn/ ADJ carpal

carquois /kaʀkwa/ NM quiver

carrare /kaʀaʀ/ NM (= *marbre*) Carrara (marble)

carre /kaʀ/ NF *[de ski]* edge ◆ **prendre des ~s** to edge, to edge one's skis

Carré /kaʀe/ N ◆ **maladie de ~** canine distemper

carré, e /kaʀe/ ADJ 1 *[table, jardin, menton]* square ◆ **aux épaules ~es** square-shouldered; → **partie**[2]
2 (*Math*) square ◆ **mètre/kilomètre ~** square metre/kilometre ◆ **il n'y avait pas un centimètre ~ de place** there wasn't an inch of room, there wasn't (enough) room to swing a cat (*Brit*); → **racine**
3 (= *franc*) *[personne]* forthright, straightforward; *[réponse]* straight, straightforward

◆ **être ~ en affaires** to be aboveboard *ou* straightforward in one's (business) dealings

NM 1 *(gén)* square; *(= foulard)* scarf ◆ **découper qch en petits ~s** to cut sth up into little squares ◆ **~ de soie** silk scarf ◆ **~ de terre** patch *ou* plot (of land) ◆ **un ~ de choux/de salades** a cabbage/lettuce patch ◆ **avoir les cheveux coupés au ~, avoir une coupe au ~** to wear *ou* have one's hair in a bob ◆ **~ blanc** † *(TV) sign indicating that a film is unsuitable for children or sensitive viewers* ◆ **~ de service** *(Tennis)* service court

2 *(Mil = disposition)* square; → **former**

3 *(Naut = mess, salon)* wardroom ◆ **le ~ des officiers** the (officers') wardroom

4 *(dans un train)* group of four seats

5 *(Math)* square ◆ **le ~ de 4** 4 squared, the square of 4 ◆ **3 au ~** 3 squared ◆ **élever** *ou* **mettre** *ou* **porter un nombre au ~** to square a number

6 *(Cartes)* **un ~ d'as** four aces

7 *(Culin)* **~ de l'Est** *soft, mild, fermented cheese* ◆ **~ d'agneau** *(Boucherie)* loin of lamb

8 *(= groupe)* **le dernier ~** the last handful

9 *(arg Scol) student repeating the preparation for the grandes écoles*

carreau (pl **carreaux**) /kaʀo/ **NM** 1 *(par terre)* (floor) tile; *(au mur)* (wall) tile ◆ **~ de plâtre** plaster block

2 *(= carrelage, sol)* tiled floor ◆ **le ~ des Halles** the market at les Halles

3 *(= vitre)* (window) pane ◆ **~x*** *(= lunettes)* glasses, specs* ◆ **faire les ~x** to clean the windows ◆ **remplacer un ~** to replace a pane ◆ **regarder au ~** to look out of the window ◆ **des vandales ont cassé les ~x** vandals have smashed the windows

4 *(sur un tissu)* check; *(sur du papier)* square ◆ **à ~x** *[papier]* squared; *[mouchoir]* check *(épith)*, checked ◆ **veste à grands/petits ~x** jacket with a large/small check ◆ **laisser 3 ~x de marge** *(Scol)* leave 3 squares margin, leave a margin of 3 squares ◆ **mettre un plan au ~** *(Tech)* to square a plan

5 *(Cartes)* diamond ◆ **jouer ~** to play diamonds ◆ **le dix de ~** the ten of diamonds

6 *(Pétanque)* **faire un ~** *to hit the bowl nearest the jack and stay on its spot*

7 *[de mine]* bank

8 *(Hist = flèche)* bolt

9 *(* : locutions)* **laisser qn sur le ~** *(bagarre)* to lay *ou* knock sb out* ◆ **il est resté sur le ~** *(bagarre)* he was laid *ou* knocked out*; *(examen)* he didn't make the grade; *(chômage)* he's out of a job ◆ **se tenir à ~** to keep one's nose clean*, to watch one's step

carrefour /kaʀfuʀ/ **NM** 1 *[de routes]* crossroads *(sg)* ◆ **le ~ de l'Europe/de la drogue** the crossroads of Europe/of drug trafficking ◆ **une science au ~ de plusieurs disciplines** a science at the junction *ou* meeting point of several different disciplines ◆ **se trouver à un ~ (de sa vie/carrière)** to be at a crossroads (in one's life/career) 2 *(= rencontre, forum)* forum, symposium ◆ **~ des métiers** careers convention ◆ **~ d'idées** forum for ideas

carrelage /kaʀlaʒ/ **NM** *(= action)* tiling; *(= carreaux)* tiles, tiling *(NonC)* ◆ **poser un ~** to lay a tiled floor ◆ **laver le ~** to wash the floor

carreler /kaʀle/ ► conjug 4 ◄ **VT** *[+ mur, sol]* to tile; *[+ papier]* to draw squares on

carrelet /kaʀlɛ/ **NM** 1 *(= poisson)* plaice 2 *(= filet) square fishing net* 3 *(Tech) [de bourrelier]* half-moon needle; *[de dessinateur]* square ruler

carreleur, -euse /kaʀlœʀ, øz/ **NM,F** tiler

carrément /kaʀemɑ̃/ **ADV** 1 *(= franchement)* bluntly, straight out ◆ **je lui ai dit ~ ce que je pensais** I told him straight out what I thought 2 *(= sans hésiter)* straight ◆ **il a ~ écrit au proviseur** he wrote straight to the headmaster ◆ **vas-y ~** go right ahead ◆ **j'ai pris ~ à travers champs** I struck straight across the fields 3 *(intensif)* **il est ~ timbré*** he's definitely cracked* ◆ **cela nous fait gagner ~ 10 km/2 heures** it saves us 10 whole km *ou* a full 10 km/a whole 2 hours *ou* 2 full hours

carrer /kaʀe/ ► conjug 1 ◄ **VT** *(Math, Tech)* to square **VPR** **se carrer** ◆ **se ~ dans un fauteuil** to settle (o.s.) comfortably *ou* ensconce o.s. in an armchair ◆ **bien carré dans son fauteuil** comfortably settled *ou* ensconced in his armchair

carrier /kaʀje/ **NM** *(= ouvrier)* quarryman, quarrier; *(= propriétaire)* quarry owner ◆ **maître ~** quarry master

carrière[1] /kaʀjɛʀ/ **NF** *[de sable]* (sand)pit; *[de roches etc]* quarry

carrière[2] /kaʀjɛʀ/ **NF** 1 *(= profession)* career ◆ **en début/fin de ~** at the beginning/end of one's career ◆ **la ~** *(Pol)* the diplomatic service ◆ **embrasser la ~ des armes** † to embark on a career of arms † ◆ **faire ~ dans l'enseignement** to make one's career in teaching ◆ **il est entré dans l'industrie et y a fait (rapidement) ~** he went into industry and (quickly) made a career for himself ◆ **officier/militaire de ~** career officer/soldier 2 *(littér = cours)* course ◆ **le jour achève sa ~** the day is drawing to a close *ou* has run its course ◆ **donner (libre) ~ à** to give free rein to

carriérisme /kaʀjeʀism/ **NM** *(péj)* careerism

carriériste /kaʀjeʀist/ **NMF** *(péj)* careerist

carriole /kaʀjɔl/ **NF** 1 *(= charrette)* cart 2 *(Can)* sleigh, ca(r)riole *(US, Can)*, carryall *(US, Can)*

carrossable /kaʀɔsabl/ **ADJ** *[route etc]* suitable for (motor) vehicles

carrosse /kaʀɔs/ **NM** (horse-drawn) coach ◆ **~ d'apparat** state coach; → **cinquième, rouler**

carrosser /kaʀɔse/ ► conjug 1 ◄ **VT** *(= mettre une carrosserie à)* to fit a body to; *(= dessiner la carrosserie de)* to design a body for *ou* the body of ◆ **voiture bien carrossée** car with a well-designed body ◆ **elle est bien carrossée*** *[personne]* she's got curves in all the right places

carrosserie /kaʀɔsʀi/ **NF** *[de voiture]* *(= coque)* body(work), coachwork; *(= métier)* coachbuilding *(Brit)*, car-body making *(US)* ◆ **atelier de ~** body shop

carrossier /kaʀɔsje/ **NM** *(= constructeur)* coachbuilder *(Brit)*, car-body maker *(US)*; *(= dessinateur)* car designer ◆ **ma voiture est chez le ~** my car is in the body shop

carrousel /kaʀuzɛl/ **NM** 1 *(Équitation)* carousel; *(fig = succession rapide)* merry-go-round ◆ **le ~ des voitures officielles** the to-ing and fro-ing of official cars ◆ **un ~ d'avions dans le ciel** planes weaving patterns *ou* circling in the sky 2 *[de diapositives]* Carousel ® 3 *(Belg, Helv = manège)* merry-go-round, round-about *(Brit)*, carousel *(US)*

carrure /kaʀyʀ/ **NF** 1 *(= largeur d'épaules) [de personne]* build; *[de vêtement]* breadth across the shoulders ◆ **manteau un peu trop étroit de ~** coat which is a little tight across the shoulders ◆ **une ~ d'athlète** an athlete's build ◆ **homme de belle/forte ~** well-built/burly man 2 *[de mâchoire]* squareness; *[de bâtiment]* square shape 3 *(= envergure)* calibre *(Brit)*, caliber *(US)*, stature

carry /kaʀi/ **NM** ⇒ **curry**

cartable /kaʀtabl/ **NM** *(à poignée)* (school)bag; *(à bretelles)* satchel

carte /kaʀt/ **NF** 1 *(gén)* card ◆ **~ (postale)** (post)card ◆ **~ de visite** *(lit)* visiting card, calling card *(US)*; *(fig = expérience)* CV ◆ **ce poste au Japon, c'est une très bonne ~ de visite** having worked in Japan looks good on a CV ◆ **~ de visite professionnelle** business card

2 *(Jeux)* **~ (à jouer)** (playing) card ◆ **battre** *ou* **brasser** *ou* **mêler les ~s** to shuffle the cards ◆ **donner les ~s** to deal (the cards) ◆ **faire** *ou* **tirer les ~s à qn** to read sb's cards ◆ **avoir toutes les ~s en main** *(lit)* to have all the cards; *(fig)* to hold all the cards ◆ **jouer la ~ du charme** to turn on the charm ◆ **jouer la ~ de l'Europe** to turn towards Europe ◆ **jouer la ~ de la privatisation/la transparence** to opt for privatisation/openness ◆ **pendant sa campagne il a joué la ~ nationaliste** he played the nationalist card during his campaign ◆ **~ maîtresse** *(lit)* master (card); *(fig)* trump card ◆ **~ forcée** *(lit)* forced card ◆ **c'est la ~ forcée !** *(fig)* we have no choice!, it's Hobson's choice! ◆ **jouer ~s sur table** *(lit, fig)* to put *ou* lay one's cards on the table; → **brouiller, château**

3 *(Géog)* map; *(Astron, Météo, Naut)* chart ◆ **~ du relief/géologique** relief/geological map ◆ **~ routière** roadmap ◆ **~ du ciel** sky chart ◆ **~ de la lune** chart *ou* map of the moon ◆ **~ météorologique** *ou* **du temps** weather chart; → **rayer**

4 *(au restaurant)* menu ◆ **on prend le menu ou la ~ ?** shall we have the set menu or shall we eat à la carte? ◆ **une très bonne/très petite ~** a very good/very small menu *ou* choice of dishes

5 *(Fin)* credit card ◆ **payer par ~** to pay by credit card

6 *(Ordin)* board

7 *(locutions)*

◆ **à la carte** *[repas]* à la carte; *[retraite, plan d'investissement, voyage]* tailor-made ◆ **manger à la ~** to eat à la carte ◆ **programme à la ~** *(Scol)* free-choice curriculum, curriculum allowing pupils a choice of subjects ◆ **télévision à la ~** pay-per-view television *ou* TV ◆ **avoir un horaire à la ~** to have flexible working hours ◆ **faire du tourisme à la ~** to go on a tailor-made *ou* an à la carte holiday

◆ **en carte** ◆ **fille** *ou* **femme** *ou* **prostituée en ~** registered prostitute

COMP **carte d'abonnement** *(train)* season ticket, pass; *(Théât)* season ticket
carte d'alimentation ⇒ **carte de rationnement**
carte d'anniversaire birthday card
carte d'assuré social ≃ National Insurance card *(Brit)*, social security card *(US)*
carte bancaire banker's card
carte blanche ◆ **avoir ~ blanche** to have carte blanche *ou* a free hand ◆ **donner ~ blanche à qn** to give sb carte blanche *ou* a free hand
Carte Bleue ® debit card
carte de chemin de fer railway *(Brit) ou* train *(US)* season ticket
carte de correspondance (plain) postcard
carte de crédit credit card
carte d'électeur voting card, voter registration card *(US)*
carte d'état-major Ordnance Survey map *(Brit)*, Geological Survey map *(US)*
carte d'étudiant student card
carte d'extension de mémoire memory expansion board
carte de famille nombreuse *card issued to members of large families, allowing reduced fares etc*
carte de fidélité (regular customer's) discount card
carte du génome humain human genome map
carte graphique graphics board
carte grise ≃ (car) registration book *(Brit) ou* papers *(US)*, logbook *(Brit)*
carte d'identité identity *ou* ID card
carte d'identité scolaire pupil's identity card, student ID (card)
carte d'interface interface board
carte d'invalidité disability card
carte d'invitation invitation card

carte jeune young persons' discount card
carte journalière *(Ski)* day-pass, day-ticket
carte de lecteur library card, reader's ticket *(Brit)*, library ticket *(Brit)*
carte magnétique magnetic (strip) card ◆ **cabine téléphonique à ~ (magnétique)** cardphone
carte mécanographique ⇒ **carte perforée**
carte (à) mémoire smart card, intelligent card; *(pour téléphone)* phone card
carte mère motherboard
carte de Noël Christmas card
carte orange monthly (*ou* weekly *ou* yearly) season ticket *(for all types of transport in Paris)*
carte de paiement credit card
carte perforée punch card
carte de presse press card
carte privative charge *ou* store card
carte à puce smart card, intelligent card
carte de rationnement ration card
carte de résident residence permit
carte santé medical smart card
carte scolaire list of schools *(showing forecasts for regional requirements)*
carte de Sécurité sociale ⇒ **carte d'assuré social**
carte de séjour residence permit
carte son sound card
carte syndicale union card
carte téléphonique *ou* **de téléphone** phonecard
carte de travail work permit
carte vermeil ≃ senior citizen's rail pass
carte verte *(pour automobiliste)* green card *(Brit)*, certificate of insurance *(US)*
carte des vins wine list
carte de vœux greetings card *(Brit)*, greeting card *(US)*

CARTES

French people over the age of eighteen are required to carry a « carte d'identité » that provides proof of identity in France and can also be used instead of a passport for travel to some countries. They also have a « carte d'électeur » (voting card) and a « carte d'assuré social » bearing their social security number. Foreign nationals residing in France for more than three months must have a « carte de séjour », which is issued by their local « préfecture », and a « carte de travail » if they are employed. All car owners must have a « carte grise », which provides proof of ownership and must be shown along with one's driving licence if one is stopped by the police.

cartel /kaʀtɛl/ NM 1 *(Pol)* cartel, coalition; *(Écon)* cartel, combine ◆ **~ de la drogue** drug cartel 2 *(= pendule)* wall clock 3 *(Hist = défi)* cartel

carte-lettre (pl **cartes-lettres**) /kaʀtəlɛtʀ/ NF letter-card

cartellisation /kaʀtelizasjɔ̃/ NF *(Écon)* formation of combines

carter /kaʀtɛʀ/ NM *[de bicyclette]* chain guard; *[d'huile]* sump, oilpan *(US)*; *[de boîte de vitesses]* (gearbox) casing; *[de différentiel]* cage; *[de moteur]* crankcase

carte-réponse (pl **cartes-réponses**) /kaʀt(ə)ʀepɔ̃s/ NF *(gén)* reply card; *[de concours]* entry form

carterie /kaʀt(ə)ʀi/ NF postcard shop

cartésianisme /kaʀtezjanism/ NM Cartesianism

cartésien, -ienne /kaʀtezjɛ̃, jɛn/ ADJ, NM,F Cartesian ◆ **avoir un esprit (très) ~** to be very rational

Carthage /kaʀtaʒ/ N Carthage

carthaginois, e /kaʀtaʒinwa, waz/ ADJ Carthaginian NM,F **Carthaginois(e)** Carthaginian

cartilage /kaʀtilaʒ/ NM *(Anat)* cartilage; *[de viande]* gristle

cartilagineux, -euse /kaʀtilaʒinø, øz/ ADJ *(Anat)* cartilaginous; *[viande]* gristly

cartographe /kaʀtɔgʀaf/ NMF cartographer

cartographie /kaʀtɔgʀafi/ NF cartography, map-making ◆ **~ génique** *ou* **génétique** gene *ou* genetic mapping

cartographier /kaʀtɔgʀafje/ ▸ conjug 7 ◂ VT *[+ pays, planète]* to map, to draw a map of; *[+ génome humain]* to map

cartographique /kaʀtɔgʀafik/ ADJ cartographic(al)

cartomancie /kaʀtɔmɑ̃si/ NF fortune-telling *(with cards)*, cartomancy

cartomancien, -ienne /kaʀtɔmɑ̃sjɛ̃, jɛn/ NM,F fortune-teller *(who uses cards)*

carton /kaʀtɔ̃/ NM 1 *(= matière)* cardboard ◆ **écrit/collé sur un ~** written/pasted on (a piece of) cardboard ◆ **masque de** *ou* **en ~** cardboard mask
2 *(= boîte)* (cardboard) box, carton *(US)*; *(= contenu)* boxful; *(† = cartable)* (school)bag; *(à bretelles)* satchel ◆ **~ de lait** *(boîte)* carton of milk; *(plusieurs boîtes)* pack of milk ◆ **~-repas** pre-packaged meal ◆ **c'est quelque part dans mes ~s** *(fig)* it's somewhere in my files ◆ **le projet a dormi** *ou* **est resté dans les ~s plusieurs années** the project was shelved *ou* mothballed for several years
3 *(= cible)* target ◆ **faire un ~** *(à la fête)* to have a go on the rifle range; *(* : sur l'ennemi)* to take a potshot * *(sur* at); ◆ **faire un bon ~** to get a good score ◆ **j'ai fait un ~ en anglais** * I did really well in English, I got really good grades in English *(US)* ◆ **elle fait un ~ au hit-parade** * she's riding high *ou* she's a huge success in the charts ◆ **~ plein pour** * ... *(fig)* full marks for ... *(Brit)*, A+ for ... *(US)* ◆ **prendre un ~** * *(= subir une défaite)* to get a real hammering *
4 *(Peinture)* sketch; *(Géog)* inset map; *[de tapisserie, mosaïque]* cartoon
5 *(= carte)* card ◆ **~ d'invitation** invitation card; → **taper**
6 *(* = accident)* smash-up *
7 *(* = plaquage)* violent tackle

COMP **carton à chapeau** hatbox
carton à chaussures shoebox
carton à dessin portfolio
carton gris newsboard
carton jaune *(Sport)* yellow card; *(fig)* warning ◆ **il a reçu un ~ jaune** he got a yellow card, he was booked ◆ **les syndicats ont donné un ~ jaune au gouvernement** the unions have sent out warning signals to the government
carton ondulé corrugated cardboard
carton pâte pasteboard ◆ **de ~ pâte** *[décor]* cardboard *(épith)*
carton rouge *(Sport)* red card ◆ **recevoir un ~ rouge** *(Sport)* to get the red card; *(fig)* to be sanctioned

cartonnage /kaʀtɔnaʒ/ NM 1 *(= industrie)* cardboard industry 2 *(= emballage)* cardboard (packing) 3 *(Reliure) (= action)* boarding ◆ **~ pleine toile** *(= couverture)* cloth binding ◆ **~ souple** limp binding

cartonner /kaʀtɔne/ ▸ conjug 1 ◂ VT 1 *(= relier)* to bind in boards ◆ **livre cartonné** hardback (book) 2 *(* = heurter)* to smash into * VI * 1 *(= réussir)* to do brilliantly * *(en* in) 2 *(en voiture)* to have a smash(-up) * ◆ **ça cartonne souvent à ce carrefour** there are quite a few crashes at this crossroads

cartonnerie /kaʀtɔnʀi/ NF *(= industrie)* cardboard industry; *(= usine)* cardboard factory

cartonnier, -ière /kaʀtɔnje, jɛʀ/ NM,F *(= artiste)* tapestry *ou* mosaic designer NM *(= meuble)* filing cabinet

cartophile /kaʀtofil/ NMF postcard collector

cartouche¹ /kaʀtuʃ/ NF *(gén, Mil, Ordin)* cartridge; *[de cigarettes]* carton; → **brûler**

cartouche² /kaʀtuʃ/ NM *(Archéol, Archit)* cartouche

cartoucherie /kaʀtuʃʀi/ NF *(= fabrique)* cartridge factory; *(= dépôt)* cartridge depot

cartouchière /kaʀtuʃjɛʀ/ NF *(= ceinture)* cartridge belt; *(= sac)* cartridge pouch

caryatide /kaʀjatid/ NF ⇒ **cariatide**

caryotype /kaʀjotip/ NM karyotype

cas /kɑ/ GRAMMAIRE ACTIVE 53.5

NM 1 *(= situation)* case; *(= événement)* occurrence ◆ **~ tragique/spécial** tragic/special case ◆ **~ urgent** urgent case, emergency ◆ **comme c'est son ~** as is the case with him ◆ **un ~ très rare** a very rare occurrence ◆ **exposez-lui votre ~** state your case; *(à un médecin)* describe your symptoms ◆ **il s'est mis dans un mauvais ~** he's got himself into a tricky situation *ou* position ◆ **dans le premier ~** in the first case *ou* instance
2 *(Jur)* case ◆ **~ d'homicide/de divorce** murder/divorce case ◆ **l'adultère est un ~ de divorce** adultery is grounds for divorce ◆ **soumettre un ~ au juge** to submit a case to the judge ◆ **c'est un ~ pendable** *(hum)* he deserves to be shot *(hum)*
3 *(Méd, Sociol)* case ◆ **il y a plusieurs ~ de choléra dans le pays** there are several cases of cholera in the country ◆ **~ social** person with social problems, social misfit ◆ **c'est vraiment un ~ !** *(fig)* he's (*ou* she's) a real case! *
4 *(Ling)* case
5 *(locutions)* **dans le ~ présent** in this particular case ◆ **il accepte ou il refuse selon les ~** he accepts or refuses according to the circumstances ◆ **faire (grand) ~ de/peu de ~ de** to attach great/little importance to, to set great/little store by ◆ **il ne fait jamais aucun ~ de nos observations** he never pays any attention to *ou* takes any notice of our comments ◆ **c'est (bien) le ~ de le dire !** you said it!
◆ **au cas par cas** individually ◆ **les demandes sont examinées au ~ par ~** applications are processed individually *ou* on an individual basis
◆ **au cas** *ou* **dans le cas** *ou* **pour le cas où** ◆ **au ~** *ou* **dans le ~** *ou* **pour le ~ où il pleuvrait** in case it rains, in case it should rain ◆ **je prends un parapluie au ~ où** * I'm taking an umbrella (just) in case
◆ **dans ce cas, en ce cas** in that case ◆ **dans** *ou* **en ce ~ téléphonez-nous** in that case give us a ring
◆ **le cas échéant** if the need arises, if need be
◆ **en cas de** ◆ **en ~ d'absence** in case of *ou* in the event of absence ◆ **en ~ d'urgence** in an emergency
◆ **en aucun cas** ◆ **en aucun ~ vous ne devez vous arrêter** on no account *ou* under no circumstances are you to stop
◆ **en tout cas, en** *ou* **dans tous les cas** anyway, in any case

COMP **cas de conscience** moral dilemma ◆ **il a un ~ de conscience** he's in a moral dilemma
cas d'école textbook case, classic example
cas d'espèce individual case
cas de figure scenario ◆ **dans ce ~ de figure** in this case
cas de force majeure case of absolute necessity
cas de légitime défense case of legitimate self-defence ◆ **c'était un ~ de légitime défense** he acted in self-defence
cas limite borderline case

casanier, -ière /kazanje, jɛʀ/ ADJ *[personne, habitudes, vie]* stay-at-home* *(épith)* NM,F stay-at-home, homebody *(US)*

casaque /kazak/ NF *[de jockey]* blouse; † *[de femme]* overblouse; *(Hist) [de mousquetaire]* tabard ◆ **tourner ~** *(= fuir)* to turn tail, to flee; *(= camp)* to change sides; *(= changer d'opinion)* to do a U-turn

casbah /kazba/ NF *(en Afrique)* kasbah; *(‡ = maison)* house, place* ◆ **rentrer à la ~** to go home

cascade /kaskad/ NF 1 *[d'eau]* waterfall, cascade *(littér)*; *[de mots, chiffres]* stream; *[d'événements]* spate; *[de réformes, révélations]* series; *[d'erreurs]* string, series; *[de rires]* peal ◆ **des démissions en ~** a spate of resignations 2 *(= acrobatie)* stunt ◆ **dans ce film, c'est lui qui fait les ~s** he does the stunts in this film

cascader /kaskade/ ► conjug 1 ◄ VI *(littér)* to cascade

cascadeur /kaskadœʀ/ NM *[de film]* stuntman; *[de cirque]* acrobat

cascadeuse /kaskadøz/ NF *[de film]* stuntwoman; *[de cirque]* acrobat

case /kɑz/ NF 1 *(sur papier)* square, space; *(sur formulaire)* box; *[d'échiquier]* square ◆ **~ (à cocher)** tickbox ◆ **la ~ départ** *(Jeux)* the start ◆ **nous voilà revenus à la ~ départ, retour à la ~ départ** *(fig)* (we're) back to square one 2 *[de pupitre]* compartment, shelf; *[de courrier]* pigeonhole *(Brit)*, mail box *(US)*; *[de boîte, tiroir]* compartment ◆ **~ postale** post-office box ◆ **~ de réception** *(Ordin)* card stacker ◆ **il a une ~ vide*** *ou* **en moins*, il lui manque une ~*** he has a screw loose* 3 *(= hutte)* hut

caséine /kazein/ NF casein

casemate /kazmat/ NF blockhouse, pillbox

caser* /kɑze/ ► conjug 1 ◄ VT 1 *(= placer) [+ objets]* to shove*, to stuff; *(= loger) [+ amis]* to put up ◆ **je ne sais pas comment je vais ~ tout ce monde** I don't know how I'm going to find space for everyone *ou* fit everyone in
2 *(= trouver un moment pour) [+ activité, réunion]* to find time for ◆ **je vais voir où je peux te ~ dans mon emploi du temps** I'll see when I can fit you in
3 *(= marier) [+ fille]* to find a husband for; *(= pourvoir d'une situation)* to find a job for ◆ **ses enfants sont casés maintenant** *(emploi)* his children have got jobs now *ou* are fixed up now; *(mariage)* his children are (married and) off his hands now
VPR **se caser** *(= vivre ensemble)* to settle down; *(= trouver un emploi)* to find a (steady) job; *(= se loger)* to find a place to live ◆ **il va avoir du mal à se ~** *(célibataire)* he's going to have a job finding someone to settle down with

caserne /kazɛʀn/ NF *(Mil, fig)* barracks ◆ **~ de pompiers** fire station, fire *ou* station house *(US)* ◆ **cet immeuble est une vraie ~** this building looks like a barracks

casernement /kazɛʀnəmɑ̃/ NM *(Mil) (= action)* quartering in barracks; *(= bâtiments)* barrack buildings

caserner /kazɛʀne/ ► conjug 1 ◄ VT *(Mil)* to barrack, to quarter in barracks

cash* /kaʃ/ ADV *(= comptant)* ◆ **payer ~** to pay cash down ◆ **il m'a donné 5 000 € ~** he gave me €5,000 cash down *ou* on the nail* *(Brit) ou* on the barrel* *(US)* ◆ **il m'a tout dit comme ça, ~*** he told me everything straight out* NM cash *(NonC)*

casher /kaʃɛʀ/ ADJ INV kosher

cash-flow (pl **cash-flows**) /kaʃflo/ NM cash flow

cashmere /kaʃmiʀ/ NM ⇒ **cachemire**

casier /kazje/ NM 1 *(= compartiment)* compartment; *(= tiroir)* drawer; *(fermant à clé)* locker; *[de courrier]* pigeonhole *(Brit)*, mail box *(US)* ◆ **~ de consigne automatique** luggage locker 2 *(= meuble)* set of compartments *ou* pigeonholes *(Brit) ou* (mail)boxes *(US)*; *(à tiroirs)* filing cabinet 3 *(Police)* **~ (judiciaire)** (police *ou* criminal) record ◆ **avoir un ~ judiciaire vierge/chargé** to have a clean (police) record/a long record ◆ **son ~ fait état de cinq condamnations** he has five previous convictions 4 *(Pêche)* (lobster *etc*) pot ◆ **poser des ~s** to put out lobster pots
COMP **casier à bouteilles** bottle rack
casier fiscal tax record
casier à homards lobster pot

casino /kazino/ NM casino ◆ **économie de ~** casino economy

casoar /kazɔaʀ/ NM *(= oiseau)* cassowary; *(= plumet)* plume

Caspienne /kaspjɛn/ NF ◆ **la (mer) ~** the Caspian Sea

casque /kask/ NM 1 *[de soldat, alpiniste]* helmet; *[de motocycliste]* crash helmet; *[d'ouvrier]* hard hat ◆ **"le port du casque est obligatoire"** "this is a hard hat area", "hard hats must be worn at all times" ◆ **j'ai le ~ depuis ce matin*** I've had a headache *ou* a bit of a head* *(Brit)* since this morning 2 *(pour sécher les cheveux)* (hair-)drier 3 *(à écouteurs, gén)* headphones, earphones; *[de hi-fi]* headphones 4 *[de bec d'oiseau]* casque 5 *[de fleur]* helmet, galea
COMP **Casque bleu** blue helmet *ou* beret ◆ **les Casques bleus** the UN peacekeeping force, the blue helmets *ou* berets
casque de chantier hard hat
casque colonial pith helmet, topee
casque intégral full-face helmet
casque à pointe spiked helmet

casqué, e /kaske/ ADJ *[motocycliste, soldat]* wearing a helmet, helmeted

casquer* /kaske/ ► conjug 1 ◄ VTI *(= payer)* to cough up*, to fork out*

casquette /kaskɛt/ NF cap ◆ **~ d'officier** officer's (peaked) cap ◆ **avoir plusieurs ~s/une double ~** *(fig)* to wear several hats/two hats ◆ **il en a sous la ~*** he's really brainy*

cassable /kɑsabl/ ADJ breakable

Cassandre /kasɑ̃dʀ/ NF *(Myth)* Cassandra; *(fig)* doomsayer, doomster ◆ **les ~ de l'écologie** the ecological doomsters *ou* prophets of doom ◆ **jouer les ~** to spread doom and gloom

cassant, e /kɑsɑ̃, ɑ̃t/ ADJ 1 *[glace, substance, ongles, cheveux]* brittle; *[bois]* easily broken *ou* snapped 2 *[ton, attitude]* curt ◆ **d'une voix ~e** curtly 3 *(* = difficile)* **ce n'est pas ~** it's not exactly back-breaking *ou* tiring work

cassate /kasat/ NF cassata

cassation /kɑsasjɔ̃/ NF 1 *(Jur)* cassation; → **cour, pourvoir** 2 *(Mil)* reduction to the ranks

casse /kɑs/ NF 1 *(= action)* breaking, breakage; *(= objets cassés)* damage, breakages ◆ **il y a eu beaucoup de ~ pendant le déménagement** a lot of things were broken *ou* there were a lot of breakages during the move ◆ **payer la ~** to pay for the damage *ou* breakages ◆ **la ~ sociale** *(= réduction de prestations)* welfare cuts; *(= licenciements)* compulsory redundancies ◆ **il va y avoir de la ~*** *(fig)* there's going to be some rough stuff* ◆ **pas de ~ !** *(lit)* don't break anything!; *(* fig)* no rough stuff!*
2 *(* = endroit)* scrap yard ◆ **mettre à la ~** to scrap ◆ **vendre à la ~** to sell for scrap ◆ **bon pour la ~** fit for scrap, ready for the scrap heap ◆ **envoyer une voiture à la ~** to send a car to the breakers
3 *(Typo)* case ◆ **bas de ~** *(= caractère)* lowercase letter
4 *(= arbre, écorce)* cassia
NM *(arg Crime = cambriolage)* break-in ◆ **faire un ~ dans une bijouterie** to break into a jeweller's shop, to do a break-in at a jeweller's shop

cassé, e /kɑse/ (ptp de **casser**) ADJ 1 *[voix]* broken, cracked; *[vieillard]* bent; → **blanc, col** 2 ** (= éreinté)* (dead-)beat*, knackered‡ *(Brit)* 3 ** (= ivre, drogué)* high*

casse-burnes*‡ /kɑsbyʀn/ ADJ INV, NMF ⇒ **casse-couilles**

casse-cou* /kɑsku/ ADJ INV *[personne]* reckless; *[opération, entreprise]* risky, dangerous NMF INV *(= personne)* daredevil, reckless person; *(en affaires)* reckless person ◆ **crier ~ à qn** to warn sb

casse-couilles*‡ /kɑskuj/ ADJ INV ◆ **t'es ~ avec tes questions!** you're being a real pain in the arse*‡ *(Brit) ou* ass*‡ *(US)* with all your questions! NMF INV pain in the arse*‡ *(Brit) ou* ass*‡ *(US) ou* butt‡ *(US)*

casse-croûte /kɑskʀut/ NM INV *(= repas)* snack, lunch *(US)*; *(= sandwich)* sandwich; *(Can = restaurant)* snack bar ◆ **manger/emporter un petit ~** to have/take along a bite to eat* *ou* a snack

casse-cul*‡ /kɑsky/ ADJ INV damn *ou* bloody *(Brit)* annoying‡ ◆ **il est ~** he's a pain in the arse*‡ *(Brit) ou* ass*‡ *(US) ou* butt‡ *(US)*

casse-dalle‡ (pl **casse-dalle(s)**) /kɑsdal/ NM *(= repas)* snack, lunch *(US)*; *(= sandwich)* sandwich

casse-graine* /kɑsgʀɛn/ NM INV *(= repas)* snack, lunch *(US)*

casse-gueule‡ /kɑsgœl/ ADJ INV *[sentier]* dangerous, treacherous; *[opération, entreprise]* risky, dangerous NM INV *(= opération, entreprise)* risky *ou* dangerous business; *(= endroit)* dangerous *ou* nasty spot

casse-noisette(s) (pl **casse-noisettes**) /kɑsnwazɛt/ NM (pair of) nutcrackers *(Brit)*, nutcracker *(US)* ◆ **"Casse-Noisette"** *(Mus)* "The Nutcracker"

casse-noix /kɑsnwa/ NM INV ⇒ **casse-noisette(s)**

casse-pattes* /kɑspat/ NM INV 1 *(= escalier, côte)* **c'est un vrai ~** it's a real slog* 2 († * = alcool) rotgut*

casse-pieds* /kɑspje/ ADJ INV ◆ **ce qu'elle est ~!** *(= importune)* she's a pain in the neck!*; *(= ennuyeuse)* what a bore *ou* drag* she is! ◆ **corriger des copies, c'est ~** it's a real drag* having to correct exam papers NMF INV *(= importun)* nuisance, pain in the neck*; *(= personne ennuyeuse)* bore

casse-pipe* /kɑspip/ NM INV ◆ **aller au ~** *(= aller à la guerre)* to go to the front; *(= se faire tuer)* to go to be slaughtered ◆ **vouloir faire de la morale en politique, c'est aller au ~** if you try to preach morality in politics you're courting disaster

casser /kɑse/

► conjug 1 ◄

1 VERBE TRANSITIF	3 VERBE PRONOMINAL
2 VERBE INTRANSITIF	

1 - VERBE TRANSITIF

1 = briser *[+ objet]* to break; *[+ noix]* to crack; *[+ latte, branche]* to snap, to break ◆ **~ une dent/un bras à qn** to break sb's tooth/arm ◆ **~ qch en deux/en morceaux** to break sth in two/into pieces ◆ **~ un morceau de chocolat** to break off *ou* snap off a piece of chocolate ◆ **~ un carreau** *(volontairement)* to smash a pane; *(accidentellement)* to break a pane ◆ **il s'est mis à tout ~ autour de lui** he started smashing *ou* breaking everything in sight ◆ **je casse tout** *ou* **beaucoup en ce moment** I break every-

thing I touch at the moment ◆ **qui casse les verres les paye** *(Prov)* you pay for your mistakes

2 = endommager *[+ appareil]* to break, to bust*; *[+ volonté, moral]* to break; *[+ vin]* to spoil the flavour of ◆ **cette maladie lui a cassé la voix** this illness has ruined his voice ◆ **je veux ~ l'image qu'on a de moi** I want to change the image people have of me

3 = interrompre *[+ rythme, grève]* to break ◆ **si l'on s'arrête, ça va ~ notre moyenne horaire** if we stop, we're going to fall behind on our hourly average

4 = dégrader *[+ militaire]* to reduce to the ranks; *[+ fonctionnaire]* to demote ◆ **~ qn** *(= nuire à)* to cause sb's downfall ◆ **ça m'a cassé*** *(= ça m'a démoralisé)* I was gutted*; *(= ça m'a déconcerté)* I was gobsmacked*; *(= ça m'a fatigué)* it wore me out

5 * = attaquer **~ du facho/flic** to go fascist-/cop-bashing*

6 Admin, Jur = annuler *[+ jugement]* to quash; *[+ arrêt]* to nullify, to annul ◆ **faire ~ un jugement pour vice de forme** to have a sentence quashed on a technicality

7 Comm **~ les prix** to slash prices ◆ **~ le marché** to destroy the market

8 locutions **~ du bois** *(= s'écraser en avion)* to smash up one's plane ◆ **~ la baraque*** *(= avoir du succès)* to bring the house down ◆ **~ la baraque à qn*** *(= tout gâcher)* to mess *ou* foul* everything up (for sb) ◆ **~ la croûte*** *ou* **la graine*** to have a bite to eat* *ou* something to eat ◆ **~ la figure*** *ou* **la gueule* à qn** to smash sb's face in*, to knock sb's block off* ◆ **~ le morceau*** *(= avouer)* to spill the beans, to come clean; *(= trahir)* to give the game away*, to blow the gaff* *(Brit)* ◆ **~ les pieds à qn*** *(= fatiguer)* to bore sb stiff; *(= irriter)* to get on sb's nerves ◆ **il nous les casse !*** he's a pain (in the neck)!* ◆ **tu me casses les bonbons !*** you're a pain in the neck!*, you're getting on my nerves *ou* wick (Brit)!* ◆ **~ sa pipe*** to kick the bucket*, to snuff it* *(Brit)* ◆ **ça/il ne casse pas des briques*, ça/il ne casse rien*, ça/il ne casse pas trois pattes à un canard*** it's/he's nothing to write home about* ◆ **~ du sucre sur le dos de qn** to gossip *ou* talk about sb behind his back ◆ **il nous casse la tête** *ou* **les oreilles avec sa trompette*** he makes a terrible racket with that trumpet of his ◆ **il nous casse la tête avec ses histoires*** he bores us stiff with his stories

◆ **à tout casser*** *(= extraordinaire) [film, repas]* stupendous, fantastic; *[+ succès]* runaway *(épith)* ◆ **tu en auras pour 20 € à tout ~** *(= tout au plus)* that'll cost you €20 at the outside *ou* at the most

2 - VERBE INTRANSITIF

1 = se briser *[objet]* to break; *[baguette, corde, plaque]* to break, to snap ◆ **ça casse facilement** it breaks easily ◆ **ça casse comme du verre** it's very brittle ◆ **le pantalon doit ~ sur la chaussure** the trouser (leg) should rest on the shoe

2 * = endommager sa voiture, son bateau to break down ◆ **dans le Paris-Dakar, il a cassé au kilomètre 152** he broke down at kilometre 152 in the Paris-Dakar race ◆ **elle a cassé juste avant l'arrivée** *(Naut = démâter)* her mast broke just before the end of the race

3 = rompre *[couple]* to break *ou* split up ◆ **il était avec une actrice, mais il a cassé** he was going out with an actress but he broke up with her

3 - VERBE PRONOMINAL

se casser

1 = se briser *[d'objet]* to break ◆ **la tasse s'est cassée en tombant** the cup broke when it fell ◆ **l'anse s'est cassée** the handle came off *ou* broke (off) ◆ **se ~ net** to break *ou* snap clean off; *(en deux morceaux)* to snap in two

2 = endommager une partie de son corps **se ~ la jambe/une jambe/une dent** *[personne]* to break one's leg/a leg/a tooth ◆ **tu vas te ~ le cou !** you'll break your neck! ◆ **se ~ la figure*** *ou* **la gueule*** *(= tomber)* to fall flat on one's face, to come a cropper* *(Brit)*; *(d'une certaine hauteur)* to crash down; *(= faire faillite)* to go bankrupt, to come a cropper* *(Brit)* ◆ **se ~ la figure contre qch** to crash into sth ◆ **se ~ le nez** *(= trouver porte close)* to find no one in; *(= échouer)* to fail, to come a cropper* *(Brit)* ◆ **se ~ les dents** *(fig)* to fall flat on one's face, to come a cropper* *(Brit)*

3 * = se fatiguer **il ne s'est rien cassé** *ou* **il ne s'est pas cassé pour écrire cet article** he didn't strain himself writing this article ◆ **il ne s'est pas cassé la tête*** *ou* **la nénette*** *ou* **le tronc*** *(fig)* he didn't exactly put himself out *ou* overexert himself *ou* bust a gut* ◆ **cela fait deux jours que je me casse la tête sur ce problème** I've been racking my brains over this problem for two days

4 * = partir to split* ◆ **casse-toi !** get lost!*

casserole /kasʀɔl/ NF 1 *(= ustensile)* saucepan; *(= contenu)* saucepan(ful) ◆ **du veau à la** *ou* **en ~** braised veal ◆ **passer à la ~*** *(sexuellement)* to get screwed** *ou* laid**; *(= être tué)* to be bumped off* ◆ **ils passeront tous à la ~** *(= devront le faire)* they'll all have to go through it; *(= seront licenciés)* they're all for the chop* 2 *(péj)* **c'est une vraie ~*** *(piano)* it's a tinny piano; *(voiture)* it's a tinny car ◆ **chanter comme une ~*** to be a lousy singer* ◆ **faire un bruit de ~** to clank 3 *(* = scandale)* scandal ◆ **traîner une ~** *ou* **des ~s** to be haunted by a scandal

casse-tête (pl **casse-tête(s)**) /kastɛt/ NM *(Hist = massue)* club ◆ **~ (chinois)** *(= problème difficile)* headache *(fig)* *(= jeu)* puzzle, brain-teaser

cassette /kasɛt/ NF 1 *[de magnétophone, magnétoscope, ordinateur]* cassette ◆ **~ vidéo** video (cassette) ◆ **~ audio** audio cassette; → **magnétophone** 2 *(= coffret)* casket; *(= trésor) [de roi]* privy purse ◆ **il a pris l'argent sur sa ~ personnelle** *(hum)* he paid out of his own pocket

casseur /kasœʀ/ NM 1 *(dans une manifestation)* rioter, rioting demonstrator 2 *(* = cambrioleur)* burglar 3 *(* = bravache)* tough guy* ◆ **jouer les ~s*** to play tough* 4 *(= ferrailleur)* scrap dealer *ou* merchant *(Brit)* 5 ◆ **~ de pierres** stone breaker

Cassiopée /kasjɔpe/ NF Cassiopeia

cassis /kasis/ NM 1 *(= fruit)* blackcurrant; *(= arbuste)* blackcurrant bush; *(= liqueur)* blackcurrant liqueur, cassis 2 *(* = tête)* head, nut*, block* 3 *[de route]* bump, ridge

cassolette /kasɔlɛt/ NF *(= ustensile) earthenware dish; (= mets)* cassolette

cassonade /kasɔnad/ NF brown sugar

cassoulet /kasulɛ/ NM cassoulet *(meat and bean casserole, a specialty of SW France)*

cassure /kasyʀ/ NF 1 *(lit, fig)* break; *[de col]* fold ◆ **à la ~ du pantalon** where the trousers rest on the shoe 2 *(Géol) (gén)* break; *(= fissure)* crack; *(= faille)* fault

castagne* /kastaɲ/ NF 1 *(= action)* fighting ◆ **il aime la ~** he loves a good fight *ou* punch-up* *(Brit)* 2 *(= rixe)* fight, punch-up* *(Brit)*

castagner (se)* /kastaɲe/ ▸ conjug 1 ◂ VPR to fight, to have a punch-up* *(Brit)*

castagnettes /kastaɲɛt/ NFPL castanets ◆ **il avait les dents/les genoux qui jouaient des ~*** he could feel his teeth chattering/his knees knocking

caste /kast/ NF *(lit, péj)* caste; → **esprit**

castel /kastɛl/ NM mansion, small castle

castillan, e /kastijɑ̃, an/ ADJ Castilian NM *(= langue)* Castilian NM,F **Castillan(e)** Castilian

Castille /kastij/ NF Castile

castor /kastɔʀ/ NM *(= animal, fourrure)* beaver

castrat /kastʀa/ NM *(= chanteur)* castrato

castrateur, -trice /kastʀatœʀ, tʀis/ ADJ *(Psych)* castrating

castration /kastʀasjɔ̃/ NF *[d'homme, animal mâle]* castration; *[d'animal femelle]* spaying; *[de cheval]* gelding ◆ **complexe de ~** castration complex ◆ **~ chimique** chemical castration

castrer /kastʀe/ ▸ conjug 1 ◂ VT *(gén) [+ homme, animal mâle]* to castrate; *[+ animal femelle]* to spay; *[+ cheval]* to geld

castrisme /kastʀism/ NM Castroism

castriste /kastʀist/ ADJ Castro *(épith)*, Castroist NMF supporter *ou* follower of Castro

casuel, -elle /kɑzɥɛl/ ADJ 1 *(Ling)* **désinences ~les** case endings ◆ **système ~** case system 2 *(littér)* fortuitous NM *(† = gain variable)* commission money; *[de curé]* casual offerings

casuiste /kɑzɥist/ NM *(Rel, péj)* casuist

casuistique /kɑzɥistik/ NF *(Rel, péj)* casuistry

casus belli /kɑzysbelli/ NM INV casus belli

catabolisme /katabɔlism/ NM catabolism, katabolism

catachrèse /katakʀɛz/ NF catachresis

cataclysme /kataklism/ NM cataclysm

cataclysmique /kataklismik/ ADJ cataclysmic

catacombes /katakɔ̃b/ NFPL catacombs

catadioptre /katadjɔptʀ/ NM *(sur voiture)* reflector; *(sur chaussée)* cat's eye, Catseye ® *(Brit)*

catafalque /katafalk/ NM catafalque

catalan, e /katalɑ̃, an/ ADJ Catalan NM *(= langue)* Catalan NM,F **Catalan(e)** Catalan

catalepsie /katalɛpsi/ NF catalepsy ◆ **tomber en ~** to have a cataleptic fit

cataleptique /katalɛptik/ ADJ, NMF cataleptic

catalogage /katalɔgaʒ/ NM *[d'articles, objets]* cataloguing, cataloging *(US)*; *[de personne]* categorizing, labelling, pigeonholing *(péj)*

Catalogne /katalɔɲ/ NF Catalonia

catalogne /katalɔɲ/ NF *(Can) cloth made from woven strips of fabric*

catalogue /katalɔg/ NM *(gén)* catalogue, catalog *(US)*; *(Ordin)* directory ◆ **prix ~** list price ◆ **faire le ~ de** to catalogue, to catalog *(US)* ◆ **acheter qch sur ~** to buy sth from a catalogue ◆ **le gouvernement a annoncé un ~ de mesures sociales** the government has announced a package of social measures

cataloguer /katalɔge/ ▸ conjug 1 ◂ VT to catalogue, to catalog *(US)*, to pigeonhole; * *[+ personne]* to categorize, to label *(comme* as)

catalpa /katalpa/ NM catalpa

catalyse /kataliz/ NF catalysis

catalyser /katalize/ ▸ conjug 1 ◂ VT *(Chim, fig)* to catalyse

catalyseur /katalizœʀ/ NM *(Chim, fig)* catalyst

catalytique /katalitik/ ADJ catalytic; → **pot**

catamaran /katamaʀɑ̃/ NM *(= voilier)* catamaran; *[d'hydravion]* floats

cataphote ® /katafɔt/ NM ⇒ **catadioptre**

cataplasme /kataplasm/ NM *(Méd)* poultice, cataplasm ◆ **~ sinapisé** mustard poultice *ou* plaster ◆ **c'est un véritable ~ sur l'estomac** it lies like a lead weight on the stomach

catapultage /katapyltaʒ/ NM catapulting; *(sur porte-avions)* catapult launch

catapulte /katapylt/ NF catapult

catapulter /katapylte/ ▸ conjug 1 ◂ VT *(lit)* to catapult ◆ **il a été catapulté à ce poste** he was pitchforked *ou* catapulted into this job

cataracte /kataʀakt/ NF [1] *(= chute d'eau)* cataract ◆ **des ~s de pluie** torrents of rain [2] *(Méd)* cataract ◆ **il a été opéré de la ~** he's had a cataract operation, he's been operated on for (a) cataract

catarrhe /kataʀ/ NM catarrh

catarrheux, -euse /kataʀø, øz/ ADJ *[voix]* catarrhal, thick ◆ **vieillard ~** wheezing old man

catastase /katastaz/ NF *(Phon)* on-glide

catastrophe /katastʀɔf/ NF disaster, catastrophe ◆ **~ écologique** ecological disaster ◆ **~ aérienne/ferroviaire** air/rail crash *ou* disaster ◆ **~ naturelle** *(gén)* natural disaster; *(Assurances)* act of God ◆ **~ sanitaire** health disaster ◆ **~ ! le prof est arrivé !*** panic stations! the teacher's here! ◆ **~ ! je l'ai perdu !** Hell's bells!* I've lost it! ◆ **atterrir en ~** to make a forced *ou* an emergency landing ◆ **partir en ~** to leave in a terrible *ou* mad rush ◆ **c'est la ~ cette voiture/ces chaussures !*** this car is/these shoes are a disaster! ◆ **film ~** disaster movie *ou* film ◆ **scénario ~** *(fig)* doomsday *ou* nightmare scenario

catastrophé, e* /katastʀɔfe/ ADJ *[personne]* shattered*

catastropher* /katastʀɔfe/ ▸ conjug 1 ◂ VT to shatter*

catastrophique /katastʀɔfik/ ADJ disastrous, catastrophic

catastrophisme /katastʀɔfism/ NM [1] *(Géol)* catastrophism [2] *(= pessimisme)* gloom-mongering ◆ **faire du ~** to spread doom and gloom

catastrophiste /katastʀɔfist/ ADJ *[vision]* gloomy, (utterly) pessimistic NMF [1] *(Géol)* catastrophist [2] *(= pessimiste)* gloom-monger, (utter) pessimist

catch /katʃ/ NM (all-in) wrestling ◆ **il fait du ~** he's a wrestler

catcher /katʃe/ ▸ conjug 1 ◂ VI to wrestle

catcheur, -euse /katʃœʀ, øz/ NM,F wrestler

catéchèse /kateʃɛz/ NF catechetics *(sg)*, catechesis

catéchisation /kateʃizasjɔ̃/ NF catechization

catéchiser /kateʃize/ ▸ conjug 1 ◂ VT *(Rel)* to catechize; *(= endoctriner)* to indoctrinate, to catechize; *(= sermonner)* to lecture

catéchisme /kateʃism/ NM *(= enseignement, livre, fig)* catechism ◆ **aller au ~** to go to catechism (class), ≈ to go to Sunday school, to go to CCD* *(US)*

catéchiste /kateʃist/ NMF catechist; → **dame**

catéchumène /katekymɛn/ NMF *(Rel)* catechumen; *(fig)* novice

catégorie /kategɔʀi/ NF *(gén, Philos)* category; *(Boxe, Hôtellerie)* class; *(Admin) [de personnel]* grade ◆ **morceaux de première/deuxième ~** *(Boucherie)* prime/second cuts ◆ **hors ~** exceptional, outstanding ◆ **ranger par ~** to categorize ◆ **il est de la ~ de ceux qui ...** he comes in *ou* he belongs to the category of those who ... ◆ **~ socioprofessionnelle** socio-professional group

catégoriel, -elle /kategɔʀjɛl/ ADJ [1] *[intérêts]* sectional; *[avantages, mesures]* that apply to one or more categories of workers; *[revendications]* made by one or more categories of workers [2] *(Gram)* **indice ~** category index

catégorique /kategɔʀik/ ADJ [1] *[ton, personne]* categorical, adamant; *[démenti, refus]* flat *(épith)*, categorical ◆ **ne sois pas si ~ !** don't make such categorical statements! ◆ **il nous a opposé un refus** *ou* **un non ~** his answer was a categorical no [2] *(Philos)* categorical

catégoriquement /kategɔʀikmɑ̃/ ADV *[refuser]* point-blank, categorically; *[rejeter, condamner, démentir, nier]* categorically

catégorisation /kategɔʀizasjɔ̃/ NF categorization

catégoriser /kategɔʀize/ ▸ conjug 1 ◂ VT to categorize

catelle /katɛl/ NF *(Helv = carreau)* tile

caténaire /katenɛʀ/ ADJ, NF catenary

catgut /katgyt/ NM catgut

cathare /kataʀ/ ADJ, NMF Cathar

catharisme /kataʀism/ NM Catharism

catharsis /kataʀsis/ NF catharsis

cathartique /kataʀtik/ ADJ cathartic

Cathay /katɛ/ NM Cathay

cathédrale /katedʀal/ NF cathedral; → **verre**

Catherine /katʀin/ NF Catherine ◆ **~ la Grande** Catherine the Great; → **coiffer**

catherinette /katʀinɛt/ NF *girl of 25 still unmarried by the Feast of St Catherine*

> **CATHERINETTE**
>
> The tradition of the **catherinettes** has its origins in the dressmaking trade, where seamstresses still not married on their twenty-fifth birthday would go to a ball called « le bal des catherinettes » on Saint Catherine's Day (25 November) wearing a hat they made specially for the occasion. To wear such a hat was known as « coiffer sainte Catherine », and the expression, though a little old-fashioned, survives as a way of referring to a 25-year-old-woman who is still single.

cathéter /katetɛʀ/ NM catheter

cathétérisme /kateteʀism/ NM catheterization

catho* /kato/ ADJ, NMF abrév de **catholique**

cathode /katɔd/ NF cathode

cathodique /katɔdik/ ADJ *(Phys)* cathodic; → **écran, rayon, tube**

catholicisme /katɔlisism/ NM (Roman) Catholicism

catholicité /katɔlisite/ NF [1] *(= fidèles)* **la ~** the (Roman) Catholic Church [2] *(= orthodoxie)* catholicity

catholique /katɔlik/ ADJ [1] *[foi, dogme]* (Roman) Catholic [2] * **pas (très) ~** a bit fishy*, not very kosher* *(US)* NMF (Roman) Catholic

catimini /katimini/ **en catimini** LOC ADV on the sly *ou* quiet ◆ **sortir en ~** to steal *ou* sneak out ◆ **il me l'a dit en ~** he whispered it in my ear

catin † /katɛ̃/ NF *(= prostituée)* trollop †, harlot †

cation /katjɔ̃/ NM cation

catogan /katɔgɑ̃/ NM bow *(tying hair on the neck)*

Caton /katɔ̃/ NM Cato

cattleya /katlɛja/ NM cattleya

Catulle /katyl/ NM Catullus

Caucase /kɔkaz/ NM ◆ **le ~** the Caucasus

caucasien, -ienne /kɔkazjɛ̃, jɛn/ ADJ Caucasian NM,F **Caucasien(ne)** Caucasian

cauchemar /koʃmaʀ/ NM nightmare ◆ **faire des ~s** to have nightmares ◆ **c'est mon ~** it's a nightmare ◆ **vision de ~** nightmarish sight ◆ **ça tourne au ~** it's turning into a nightmare

cauchemarder /koʃmaʀde/ ▸ conjug 1 ◂ VI to have nightmares ◆ **faire ~ qn** to give sb nightmares

cauchemardesque /koʃmaʀdɛsk/ ADJ nightmarish

caudal, e (mpl **-aux**) /kodal, o/ ADJ caudal

caudillo /kaodijo/ NM caudillo ◆ **ses manières de ~** *(péj)* his dictatorial style

caulerpe /kolɛʀp/ NF caulerpa

cauri /kɔʀi/ NM cowrie *ou* cowry (shell)

causal, e (mpl **-aux**) /kozal, o/ ADJ causal

causalité /kozalite/ NF causality

causant, e* /kozɑ̃, ɑt/ ADJ talkative, chatty ◆ **il n'est pas très ~** he doesn't say very much, he's not very forthcoming *ou* talkative

causatif, -ive /kozatif, iv/ ADJ *(Gram) [conjonction]* causal; *[construction, verbe]* causative

cause /koz/ NF [1] *(= motif, raison)* cause ◆ **quelle est la ~ de l'accident ?** what caused the accident?, what was the cause of the accident? ◆ **on ne connaît pas la ~ de son absence** the reason for *ou* the cause of his absence is not known ◆ **être (la) ~ de qch** to be the cause of sth ◆ **la chaleur en est la ~** it is caused by the heat ◆ **la ~ en demeure inconnue** the cause remains unknown, the reason for it remains unknown ◆ **les ~s qui l'ont poussé à agir** the reasons that caused him to act ◆ **à petite ~ grands effets** *(Prov)* great oaks from little acorns grow *(Prov)* → **relation**

[2] *(Jur)* lawsuit, case; *(à plaider)* brief ◆ **~ civile** civil action ◆ **~ criminelle** criminal proceedings ◆ **la ~ est entendue** *(lit)* both sides have put their case; *(fig)* there's no doubt about it ◆ **~ célèbre** cause célèbre, famous trial *ou* case ◆ **plaider sa ~** to plead one's case ◆ **avocat sans ~(s)** briefless barrister; → **ayant cause, connaissance**

[3] *(= ensemble d'intérêts)* cause ◆ **grande/noble ~** great/noble cause ◆ **pour la bonne ~** for a good cause ◆ **il ment, mais c'est pour la bonne ~** he's lying but it's for a good reason ◆ **~ perdue** lost cause ◆ **faire ~ commune avec qn** to make common cause with sb, to side *ou* take sides with sb; → **fait[1]**

[4] *(Philos)* cause ◆ **~ première/seconde/finale** primary/secondary/final cause

[5] *(locutions)* **mettre qn hors de ~** to clear *ou* exonerate sb ◆ **fermé pour ~ d'inventaire/de maladie** closed for stocktaking *(Brit) ou* inventory *(US)*/on account of illness ◆ **et pour ~ !** and for (a very) good reason! ◆ **non sans ~ !** not without (good) cause *ou* reason!

◆ **à cause de** *(= en raison de)* because of, owing to; *(= par égard pour)* because of, for the sake of ◆ **à ~ de cet incident technique** because of *ou* owing to this technical failure ◆ **à ~ de son âge** on account of *ou* because of his age ◆ **il est venu à ~ de vous** he came for your sake *ou* because of you ◆ **ce n'est pas à ~ de lui que j'y suis arrivé !** *(iro)* it's no thanks to him I managed to do it!

◆ **en cause** ◆ **être en ~** *[personne]* to be involved *ou* concerned; *[intérêts]* to be at stake, to be involved ◆ **son honnêteté n'est pas en ~** there is no question about his honesty, his honesty is not in question ◆ **mettre en ~** *[+ innocence, nécessité, capacité]* to (call into) question; *[+ personne]* to implicate ◆ **mise en ~** *[de personne]* implication ◆ **remettre en ~** *[+ principe, tradition]* to question, to challenge ◆ **sa démission remet tout en ~** his resignation means we're back to square one ◆ **remise en ~** calling into question

causer[1] /koze/ ▸ conjug 1 ◂ VT *(= provoquer)* to cause; *(= entraîner)* to bring about ◆ **~ des ennuis à qn** to get sb into trouble, to bring sb trouble ◆ **~ de la peine à qn** to hurt sb ◆ **l'explosion a causé la mort de dix personnes** ten people died in the explosion ◆ **cette erreur a causé sa perte** this mistake brought about his downfall

causer[2] /koze/ ▸ conjug 1 ◂ VI [1] *(= s'entretenir)* to chat, to talk; *(* = discourir)* to speak, to talk ◆ **~ de qch** to talk about sth; *(propos futiles)* to chat about sth ◆ **on n'a même pas compris de quoi**

ça causait* we didn't even understand what it was all about ◆ ~ **à qn*** to talk *ou* speak to sb ◆ **assez causé !** that's enough talk! ◆ **cause toujours, tu m'intéresses !** *(iro)* oh, come off it!* ◆ **il a causé dans le poste*** *(hum)* he was on the radio ② *(= jaser)* to talk, to gossip *(sur qn* about sb); ◆ **on cause dans le village/le bureau** people are talking in the village/the office ③ *(* = avouer)* to talk ◆ **pour le faire** ~ to loosen his tongue, to make him talk VT to talk ◆ ~ **politique/travail** to talk politics/shop ◆ **elles causaient chiffons** they were talking *ou* chatting about clothes

causerie /kozʀi/ NF *(= discours)* talk; *(= conversation)* chat

causette /kozɛt/ NF chat, natter* *(Brit)* ◆ **faire la ~, faire un brin de** ~ to have a chat *ou* natter* *(Brit)* *(avec* with)

causeur, -euse /kozœʀ, øz/ ADJ talkative, chatty NM,F talker, conversationalist NF **causeuse** *(= siège)* causeuse, love seat

causse /kos/ NM causse *(limestone plateau (in south-central France))*

causticité /kostisite/ NF *(lit, fig)* causticity

caustique[1] /kostik/ ADJ *(lit, fig)* caustic ◆ **surface** ~ caustic (surface) NM *(Chim)* caustic

caustique[2] /kostik/ NF *(Opt)* caustic

cautèle /kotɛl/ NF *(littér)* cunning, guile

cauteleux, -euse /kotlø, øz/ ADJ *(littér)* cunning

cautère /kotɛʀ/ NM cautery ◆ **c'est un ~ sur une jambe de bois** it's of absolutely no use, it won't do any good at all

cautérisation /kɔteʀizasjɔ̃/ NF cauterization

cautériser /kɔteʀize/ ▸ conjug 1 ◂ VT to cauterize

caution /kosjɔ̃/ NF ① *(= somme d'argent)* *(Fin)* guarantee, security; *(Jur)* bail (bond); *(pour appartement, véhicule loué)* deposit ◆ ~ **bancaire** bank guarantee ◆ ~ **de soumission** bid bond ◆ ~ **solidaire** joint and several guarantee ◆ **il vous faut une ~ parentale** your parents have to stand guarantor *ou* surety for you ◆ **verser une ~ de 200 €** to put *ou* lay down a security *ou* a guarantee of €200 ◆ **libérer sous** ~ to release *ou* free on bail ◆ **libération** *ou* **mise en liberté sous** ~ release on bail ◆ **payer la ~ de qn** to bail sb out, to stand *(Brit)* *ou* go *(US)* bail for sb, to put up bail for sb *(US)*

② *(= appui)* backing, support ◆ **apporter** *ou* **donner sa ~ à qn/qch** to lend one's support to sb/sth

③ *(= personne)* guarantor ◆ **se porter ~ pour qn, servir de ~ à qn** *(= servir de garantie)* to stand surety *ou* security *(Brit)* for sb ◆ **servir de ~ morale à qn/qch** to give sb/sth moral support ◆ **cela ne doit pas servir de ~ à la violence aveugle** this must not be seen as an excuse for gratuitous violence; → **sujet**

> ⚠ **caution** ne se traduit pas par le mot anglais **caution**, qui a le sens de 'prudence' ou 'avertissement'.

cautionnement /kosjɔnmɑ̃/ NM *(= somme)* guarantee, security; *(= contrat)* security *ou* surety bond; *(= soutien)* support, backing ◆ ~ **électoral** deposit *(required of candidates in an election)*

cautionner /kosjɔne/ ▸ conjug 1 ◂ VT ① *(= répondre de)* *(moralement)* to answer for, to guarantee; *(financièrement)* to guarantee, to stand surety *ou* guarantor for ② *(= soutenir)* [+ *idée, décision, politique, gouvernement*] to support

cavaillon /kavajɔ̃/ NM cavaillon melon

cavalcade /kavalkad/ NF ① *(= course tumultueuse)* stampede; *(* = troupe désordonnée)* stampede, stream ② *[de cavaliers]* cavalcade ③ *(= défilé, procession)* cavalcade, procession

cavalcader /kavalkade/ ▸ conjug 1 ◂ VI *(= courir)* to stream, to stampede; *(† = chevaucher)* to cavalcade, to ride in a cavalcade

cavale /kaval/ NF ① *(littér = jument)* mare ② *(arg Prison)* **être en** ~ *(= évasion)* to be on the run ◆ **après une ~ de trois jours** after having been on the run for three days

cavaler /kavale/ ▸ conjug 1 ◂ VI ① * *(= courir)* to run; *(= se hâter)* to be on the go* ◆ **j'ai dû ~ dans tout New York pour le trouver** I had to rush all around New York to find it ② *(* = draguer)* *[homme]* to chase anything in a skirt*; *[femme]* to chase anything in trousers* ◆ ~ **après qn** to run *ou* chase after sb VT *(* = énerver)* to piss off**, to tee off* *(US)* ◆ **il commence à nous ~** we're beginning to get pissed off** *ou* cheesed off* *(Brit)* with him VPR **se cavaler** * *(= se sauver)* *[personne]* to clear off*, to leg it*, to skedaddle*; *[animal]* to run off

cavalerie /kavalʀi/ NF *(Mil)* cavalry; *[de cirque]* horses ◆ ~ **légère** *(Mil)* light cavalry *ou* horse ◆ **grosse ~, ~ lourde** *(Mil)* heavy *ou* armoured cavalry ◆ **c'est de la grosse ~** *(hum)* it's rather heavyhanded; *(nourriture)* it's really stodgy

cavaleur* /kavalœʀ/ NM wolf, womanizer ◆ **il est** ~ he chases anything in a skirt*

cavaleuse* /kavaløz/ NF ◆ **c'est une ~, elle est** ~ she chases anything in trousers*

cavalier, -ière /kavalje, jɛʀ/ ADJ ① *(= impertinent)* *[attitude, parole]* cavalier, offhand ◆ **c'est un peu ~ de sa part (de faire cela)** it's a bit cavalier of him (to do that) ② ◆ **allée** *ou* **piste cavalière** bridle path NM,F ① *(Équitation)* rider ◆ **les (quatre) ~s de l'Apocalypse** the (Four) Horsemen of the Apocalypse ◆ **faire ~ seul** to go it alone ② *[danseur]* partner ◆ **changez de ~ !** change partners! NM ① *(Mil)* trooper, cavalryman ◆ **une troupe de 20 ~s** a troop of 20 horses ② *(Échecs)* knight ③ *(= accompagnateur)* escort ④ *(= clou)* staple; *[de balance]* rider; *[de dossier]* tab; *(Ordin)* *[de carte-mère]* jumper ⑤ *(Hist Brit)* cavalier

cavalièrement /kavaljɛʀmɑ̃/ ADV off-handedly

cavatine /kavatin/ NF cavatina

cave[1] /kav/ NF ① *(= pièce)* cellar; *(voûtée)* vault; *(= cabaret)* cellar nightclub ◆ **chercher** *ou* **fouiller de la ~ au grenier** to search the house from top to bottom ② *(Œnol)* cellar ◆ **avoir une bonne** ~ to have *ou* keep a fine cellar ◆ ~ **à vin** *(= armoire)* *refrigerated wine cabinet* ③ *(= coffret à liqueurs)* liqueur cabinet; *(= coffret à cigares)* cigar box ④ *(Can)* *[de maison]* basement

> ⚠ **cave** ne se traduit pas par le mot anglais **cave**, qui a le sens de 'caverne'.

cave[2] /kav/ ADJ *(= creux)* *[yeux, joues]* hollow, sunken; → **veine**

cave[3]* /kav/ NM ① *(arg Crime)* straight *(arg)*, *someone who does not belong to the underworld* ② *(= imbécile)* sucker* ◆ **il est** ~ he's a sucker*

cave[4] /kav/ NF *(Poker)* bet

caveau (pl **caveaux**) /kavo/ NM ① *(= cave)* (small) cellar ② *(= sépulture)* vault, tomb ◆ ~ **de famille** family vault ③ *(= cabaret)* cellar club

caverne /kavɛʀn/ NF ① *(= grotte)* cave, cavern ◆ **c'est la ~ d'Ali Baba !** it's an Aladdin's cave!; → **homme** ② *(Anat)* cavity

caverneux, -euse /kavɛʀnø, øz/ ADJ ① *[voix]* hollow, cavernous ② *(Anat, Méd)* *[respiration]* cavernous; *[poumon]* with cavitations, with a cavernous lesion; → **corps** ③ *(littér)* *[montagne, tronc]* cavernous

cavernicole /kavɛʀnikɔl/ ADJ cave-dwelling *(épith)*

caviar /kavjaʀ/ NM ① *(Culin)* caviar(e) ◆ ~ **rouge** salmon roe ◆ ~ **d'aubergines** aubergine *(Brit)* *ou* eggplant *(US)* dip, *aubergine with fromage frais and olive oil* ◆ **la gauche ~** champagne socialists ② *(Presse)* **passer au ~** to blue-pencil, to censor

caviarder /kavjaʀde/ ▸ conjug 1 ◂ VT *(Presse)* to blue-pencil, to censor

caviste /kavist/ NM *(= responsable de cave)* cellarman; *(= marchand de vin)* wine merchant

cavité /kavite/ NF cavity ◆ ~ **articulaire** socket *(of bone)* ◆ ~ **pulpaire** (tooth) pulp cavity ◆ ~ **buccale** oral cavity

Cayenne /kajɛn/ N Cayenne; → **poivre**

CB[1] (abrév de **carte bancaire**) → **carte**

C.B., CB[2] /sibi/ NF (abrév de **Citizens' Band**) ◆ **la ~** CB radio

CC /sese/ NM ① (abrév de **compte courant**) C/A ② (abrév de **corps consulaire**) → **corps**

CCI /sesei/ NF (abrév de **Chambre de commerce et d'industrie**) → **chambre**

CCP /sesepe/ NM ① (abrév de **centre de chèques postaux**) → **centre** ② (abrév de **compte chèque postal**) → **compte**

CD[1] /sede/ NM INV (abrév de **compact disc**) CD ◆ ~ **audio/vidéo** audio/video CD

CD[2] /sede/ (abrév de **corps diplomatique**) CD

CDD /sedede/ NM (abrév de **contrat à durée déterminée**) → **contrat**

CDDP /sededepe/ NM (abrév de **centre départemental de documentation pédagogique**) → **centre**

CDI[1] /sedei/ NM ① (abrév de **centre de documentation et d'information**) → **centre** ② (abrév de **centre des impôts**) → **centre** ③ (abrév de **contrat à durée indéterminée**) → **contrat**

CD-I, CDI[2] /sedei/ NM INV (abrév de **compact disc interactif**) CDI ◆ **film sur** ~ CDI film

CD-R /sedeɛʀ/ NM INV (abrév de **compact disc recordable**) CD-R

CD-ROM /sedeʀɔm/ NM INV (abrév de **compact disc read only memory**) CD-ROM

CD-RW /sedeɛʀ/ NM INV (abrév de **compact disc rewritable**) CD-RW

CDS /sedeɛs/ NM (abrév de **Centre des démocrates sociaux**) *French political party*

CDV /sedeve/ NM INV (abrév de **compact disc video**) CDV

CD-vidéo /sedevideo/ NM INV (abrév de **compact disc video**) CD-video

CE /seə/ NM ① (abrév de **comité d'entreprise**) → **comité** ② (abrév de **Conseil de l'Europe**) → **conseil** ③ (abrév de **cours élémentaire**) → **cours** NF (abrév de **Communauté européenne**) EC

ce[1] /sə/

Devant voyelle ou **h** muet au masculin = **cet**, féminin = **cette**, pluriel = **ces**.

ADJECTIF DÉMONSTRATIF

①

> Lorsque **ce** est employé pour désigner quelqu'un ou quelque chose qui est proche, on le traduit par **this** ; lorsqu'il désigne quelqu'un ou quelque chose qui est éloigné, on le traduit généralement par **that** ; **ces** se traduit respectivement par **these** et **those**.

◆ ~ **chapeau** *(tout proche, que je pourrais toucher)* this hat; *(plus loin ou ailleurs)* that hat ◆ **si seulement ~ mal de tête s'en allait** if only this headache would go away ◆ **que faisais-tu avec ~ type ?*** what were you doing with that guy?* ◆ **que fais-tu avec ~ vélo dans ta chambre ?** what are you doing with that bike in your room? ◆ **je ne monterai jamais dans cette voiture !** I'm never getting into that car!

2

Lorsque **ce** se réfère à quelqu'un ou quelque chose dont le locuteur vient de parler ou qu'il a présent à l'esprit, on le traduit souvent par **this** ; si **ce** se réfère à quelqu'un ou quelque chose mentionné par un autre locuteur, on le traduit plutôt par **that** ; **ces** se traduit respectivement par **these** et **those**.

◆ **j'aime beaucoup ~ concerto** *(dont je viens de parler)* I'm very fond of this concerto; *(dont tu viens de parler)* I'm very fond of that concerto ◆ **ces questions ne m'intéressent pas** *(celles que je viens de mentionner)* these questions are of no interest to me

Notez que là où le français pourrait employer l'article défini à la place de **ce**, l'anglais l'utilise régulièrement comme substitut de **this** ou **that**.

◆ **~ petit idiot a perdu son ticket** the *ou* that little twerp* has gone and lost his ticket ◆ **il a quitté cette entreprise en 1983** he left the company in 1983 ◆ **je leur ai dit qu'il fallait le vendre mais cette idée ne leur a pas plu** I told them they should sell it but they didn't like the *ou* that idea

Notez l'emploi de **that** ou d'un possessif lorsqu'il y a reprise par un pronom.

◆ **alors, cet examen, il l'a eu ?*** so, did he pass that *ou* his exam? ◆ **alors, cette bière, elle arrive ?*** where's that *ou* my beer got to?* ◆ **et ~ rhume/cette jambe, comment ça va ?*** how's that *ou* your cold/leg?; → **ci, là**

3

Lorsque **ce** est employé pour un événement ou un moment dans le présent ou dans un avenir proche, on le traduit par **this** ; lorsqu'il désigne un événement ou un moment passé ou dans un avenir éloigné, on le traduit généralement par **that** ; **ces** se traduit respectivement par **these** et **those**.

◆ **on a bien travaillé ~ matin** we've worked well this morning ◆ **venez cet après-midi** come this afternoon ◆ **le 8 de ~ mois(-ci)** the 8th of this month ◆ **le 8 de ~ mois(-là)** the 8th of that month ◆ **il m'a semblé fatigué ces derniers jours** he's been looking tired these past few days ◆ **ces années furent les plus heureuses de ma vie** those *ou* these were the happiest years of my life MAIS **cette nuit** *(qui vient)* tonight; *(passée)* last night

4

Lorsque **ce** a une valeur intensive, il peut se traduire par un adjectif.

◆ **comment peut-il raconter ces mensonges !** how can he tell such lies! ◆ **cette générosité me semble suspecte** (all) this generosity strikes me as suspicious ◆ **aurait-il vraiment ~ courage ?** would he really have that much courage? ◆ **cette idée !** what an idea!, the idea! MAIS **ah, cette Maud!** that Maud! ◆ **~ Paul Durat est un drôle de personnage!** that Paul Durat is quite a character!

5 formules de politesse, aussi hum **si ces dames veulent bien me suivre** if you ladies will be so kind as to follow me ◆ **ces messieurs sont en réunion** the gentlemen are in a meeting

6 avec **qui, que** **cette amie chez qui elle habite est docteur** the friend she lives with is a doctor ◆ **elle n'est pas de ces femmes qui ...** she's not one of those *ou* these women who ... ◆ **il a cette manie qu'ont les enseignants de ...** he has this *ou* that habit teachers have of ...

ce² /sə/

Devant **en** et les formes du verbe **être** commençant par une voyelle = **c'** ; devant **a** = **ç'**.

Pour les locutions figées telles que **c'est, ce sont, c'est lui qui, c'est que** etc, reportez-vous à **être**.

PRONOM DÉMONSTRATIF

◆ **ce** + *pronom relatif* ◆ **~ que/qui** what; *(reprenant une proposition)* which ◆ **~ qui est important c'est ...** what really matters is ... ◆ **elle fait ~ qu'on lui dit** she does what she is told *ou* as she is told ◆ **il ne sait pas ~ que sont devenus ses amis** he doesn't know what has become of his friends ◆ **~ qui est dommage, c'est que nous n'ayons pas de jardin** we haven't got a garden, which is a pity ◆ **il faut être diplômé, ~ qu'il n'est pas** you have to have qualifications, which he hasn't ◆ **~ à quoi il pense** what he's thinking about ◆ **il a été reçu à son examen, ~ à quoi il s'attendait fort peu** he passed his exam, which he wasn't really expecting

Notez la place de la préposition en anglais.

◆ **voilà exactement ~ dont j'ai peur** that's just what I'm afraid of ◆ **c'est ~ pour quoi ils luttent** that's what they're fighting for ◆ **~ sur quoi il comptait, c'était ...** what he was counting on was ... MAIS **~ qu'entendant/que voyant, je ...** on hearing/seeing which *(frm)* I ...

Notez que **all** n'est jamais suivi de **what** et que **that** peut être omis.

◆ **tout ~ que je sais** all (that) I know ◆ **voilà tout ~ que j'ai pu savoir** that's all I managed to find out

◆ *préposition* + **ce que** + *indicatif* ◆ **à ~ qu'on dit/que j'ai appris** from what they say/what I've heard ◆ **il est resté insensible à ~ que je lui ai dit** he remained unmoved by what I said ◆ **je ne crois pas à ~ qu'il raconte** I don't believe what he says

◆ *préposition* + **ce que** + *subjonctif* ◆ **on ne s'attendait pas à ~ qu'il parle** *ou* **parlât** *(frm)* they were not expecting him *ou* he was not expected to speak ◆ **il se plaint de ~ qu'on ne l'ait pas prévenu** he is complaining that no one warned him ◆ **déçue de ~ qu'il ait oublié** disappointed that he had forgotten

◆ **ce que** *(valeur intensive)* ◆ **~ que ~ train est lent !** this train is so slow! ◆ **~ que les gens sont bêtes !** people are so stupid!, how stupid people are! ◆ **~ qu'on peut s'amuser !** isn't this fun! ◆ **~ qu'il parle bien !** he's a wonderful speaker!, isn't he a wonderful speaker! ◆ **~ qu'elle joue bien !** doesn't she play well!, what a good player she is! ◆ **~ que c'est que le destin !** that's fate for you! ◆ **~ qu'il m'agace !** he's so annoying! ◆ **~ qu'il ne faut pas entendre tout de même !** the things you hear sometimes!, the things people say! ◆ **~ qu'il ne faut pas faire pour la satisfaire !** the things you have to do to keep her happy!

◆ **ce disant** so saying, saying this

◆ **ce faisant** in so doing, in doing so ◆ **il a démissionné et, ~ faisant, il a pris un gros risque** he resigned, and by *ou* in doing so, he took a big risk

◆ **et ce** *(frm)* ◆ **j'y suis arrivé, et ~ grâce à toi** I managed it, and it was all thanks to you ◆ **elle a tout jeté, et ~ sans me le dire** she threw everything away without asking me ◆ **il a refusé, et ~ malgré notre insistance** he refused despite our urging

◆ **pour ce faire** to do this, to this end ◆ **il veut développer son entreprise, et pour ~ faire il doit emprunter** he wants to develop his company, and to do this *ou* to this end he will have to borrow money ◆ **on utilise pour ~ faire une pince minuscule** to do this you use a tiny pair of pliers

CEA /seəa/ NM (abrév de **compte d'épargne en actions**) → **compte** NF abrév de **Commissariat à l'énergie atomique** ≃ AEA *(Brit)*, AEC *(US)*

céans †† /seɑ̃/ ADV here, in this house; → **maître**

ceci /səsi/ PRON DÉM this ◆ **ce cas a ~ de surprenant que ...** this case is surprising in that ..., the surprising thing about this case is that ... ◆ **à ~ près que ...** except that ..., with the *ou* this exception that ... ◆ **~ compense cela** one thing makes up for another; → **dire**

cécité /sesite/ NF blindness ◆ **~ des neiges** snow-blindness ◆ **~ verbale** word blindness ◆ **être frappé** *ou* **atteint de ~** to go blind ◆ **la ~ politique de ce parti** the party's blinkered approach

cédant, e /sedɑ̃, ɑ̃t/ *(Jur)* ADJ assigning NM,F assignor

céder /sede/ ▸ conjug 6 ◂ VT 1 *(= donner) [+ part, place, tour]* to give up ◆ **~ qch à qn** to let sb have sth, to give sth up to sb ◆ **je m'en vais, je vous cède ma place** *ou* **je cède la place** I'm going so you can have my place *ou* I'll let you have my place ◆ **~ le pouvoir à qn** to hand over *ou* yield power to sb ◆ **et maintenant je cède l'antenne à notre correspondant à Paris** and now (I'll hand you) over to our Paris correspondent ◆ **~ ses biens** *(Jur)* to make over *ou* transfer one's property; → **parole**

2 *(= vendre) [+ commerce]* to sell, to dispose of ◆ **~ qch à qn** to let sb have sth, to sell sth to sb ◆ **le fermier m'a cédé un litre de lait** the farmer let me have a litre of milk ◆ **~ à bail** to lease ◆ **"bail à céder"** "lease for sale" ◆ **"cède maison avec jardin"** *(petite annonce)* "house with garden for sale" ◆ **il a bien voulu ~ un bout de terrain** he agreed to part with a plot of land

3 *(locutions)* **~ le pas à qn** to give way to sb ◆ **son courage ne le cède en rien à son intelligence** he's as brave as he is intelligent ◆ **il ne le cède à personne en égoïsme** he's as selfish as they come ◆ **il ne lui cède en rien** he is every bit his equal; → **terrain**

VI 1 *(= capituler)* to give in ◆ **~ par faiblesse/lassitude** to give in out of weakness/tiredness ◆ **aucun ne veut ~** no one wants to give in *ou* give way ◆ **sa mère lui cède en tout** his mother always gives in to him

2 ◆ **~ à** *(= succomber à) [+ force, tentation]* to give way to, to yield to; *(= consentir) [+ caprice, prière]* to give in to ◆ **~ à qn** *(à ses raisons, ses avances)* to give in *ou* yield to sb ◆ **il cède facilement à la colère** he loses his temper easily

3 *(= se rompre) [digue, chaise, branche]* to give way; *(= fléchir) [+ fièvre, colère]* to subside ◆ **la glace a cédé sous le poids** the ice gave (way) under the weight

cédétiste /sedetist/ ADJ CFDT *(épith)* NMF member of the CFDT

Cedex /sedɛks/ NM (abrév de **courrier d'entreprise à distribution exceptionnelle**) express postal service *(for bulk users)*

cédille /sedij/ NF cedilla

cédrat /sedʀa/ NM *(= fruit)* citron; *(= arbre)* citron (tree)

cédratier /sedʀatje/ NM citron (tree)

cèdre /sɛdʀ/ NM *(= arbre)* cedar (tree); *(Can = thuya)* cedar, arbor vitae; *(= bois)* cedar (wood) ◆ **le pays du ~** *(= Liban)* Lebanon

cédrière /sedʀijɛʀ/ NF *(Can)* cedar grove

CEE /seəə/ NF (abrév de **Communauté économique européenne**) EEC

CEEA /seəəa/ NF (abrév de **Communauté européenne de l'énergie atomique**) EAEC

CEGEP, Cegep /seʒɛp/ NM (abrév de **Collège d'enseignement général et professionnel**) *(Can)* → **collège**

cégétiste /seʒetist/ ADJ CGT *(épith)* NMF member of the CGT

CEI /seəi/ NF (abrév de **Communauté des États indépendants**) CIS

ceindre /sɛ̃dʀ/ ▸ conjug 52 ◂ VT *(littér)* 1 *(= entourer)* ~ **sa tête d'un bandeau** to put a band round one's head ◆ **la tête ceinte d'un diadème** wearing a diadem ◆ ~ **une ville de murailles** to encircle a town with walls ◆ **se ~ les reins** *(Bible)* to gird one's loins 2 *(= mettre)* *[+ armure, insigne d'autorité]* to don, to put on ◆ ~ **son épée** to buckle *ou* gird on one's sword ◆ ~ **l'écharpe municipale** ≈ to put on *ou* don the mayoral chain ◆ ~ **la couronne** to assume the crown

ceinture /sɛ̃tyʀ/ NF 1 *[de manteau, pantalon]* belt; *[de pyjama, robe de chambre]* cord; *(= écharpe)* sash; *(= gaine)* girdle ◆ **se serrer la ~*** to tighten one's belt *(fig)* ◆ **elle a tout, et nous, ~ !*** she's got everything and we've got zilch‡! *ou* sweet FA‡! *(Brit) ou* nix‡! *(US)* ◆ **faire ~*** to have to go without ◆ **personne ne lui arrive à la ~** no one can hold a candle to him*, no one can touch him*
2 *(Couture = taille)* *[de pantalon, jupe]* waistband
3 *(de sécurité)* seat belt ◆ **attacher** *ou* **mettre sa ~** *(en voiture)* to put on one's seat belt; *(en avion)* to fasten one's seat belt
4 *(= taille)* waist ◆ **nu jusqu'à la ~** stripped to the waist ◆ **l'eau lui arrivait (jusqu')à la ~** the water came up to his waist, he was waist-deep in *ou* up to his waist in water
5 *(Arts martiaux = niveau)* belt ◆ **(prise de) ~** waistlock ◆ **~ noire/blanche** black/white belt ◆ **elle est ~ bleue** she's a blue belt ◆ **coup au-dessous de la ~** *(lit, fig)* blow below the belt ◆ **il a fait des blagues très au-dessous de la ~** the jokes he told were well below the belt
6 *[de fortifications, murailles]* ring; *[d'arbres, montagnes]* belt
7 *(= métro, bus)* circle line ◆ **petite/grande ~** inner/outer circle
COMP **ceinture de chasteté** chastity belt
ceinture de flanelle flannel binder
ceinture fléchée *(Can)* arrow sash
ceinture de grossesse maternity girdle *ou* support
ceinture herniaire truss
ceinture médicale ⇒ **ceinture orthopédique**
ceinture de natation swimmer's float belt
ceinture orthopédique surgical corset
ceinture pelvienne pelvic girdle
ceinture rouge *working-class suburbs around Paris which have traditionally voted Communist*
ceinture de sauvetage lifebelt *(Brit)*, life preserver *(US)*
ceinture scapulaire pectoral girdle
ceinture de sécurité seat belt ◆ **~ de sécurité à enrouleur** inertia reel seat *ou* safety belt
ceinture verte green belt

ceinturer /sɛ̃tyʀe/ ▸ conjug 1 ◂ VT *[+ personne]* *(gén)* to grasp *ou* seize round the waist; *(Sport)* to tackle (round the waist); *[+ ville]* to surround, to encircle

ceinturon /sɛ̃tyʀɔ̃/ NM *(gén)* (wide) belt; *[d'uniforme]* belt

CEL /seəɛl/ NM (abrév de **compte d'épargne logement**) → **compte**

cela /s(ə)la/ PRON DÉM 1 *(gén, en opposition à ceci)* that ◆ **qu'est-ce que ~ veut dire ?** what does that *ou* this mean? ◆ **on ne s'attendait pas à ~** that was (quite) unexpected, we weren't expecting that ◆ **~ n'est pas très facile** that's not very easy ◆ **~ m'agace de l'entendre se plaindre** it annoys me to hear him complain ◆ **~ vaut la peine qu'il essaie** it's worth his trying ◆ **~ me donne du souci** it gives me a lot of worry ◆ **faire des études, ~ ne le tentait guère** studying did not really appeal to him
2 *(forme d'insistance)* **il ne veut pas venir – pourquoi ~ ?** he won't come – why not? *ou* why won't he? ◆ **comment ~ ?** what do you mean? ◆ **j'ai vu Marie – qui ~ ?/quand ~ ?/où ~ ?** I've seen Marie – who (do you mean)?/when was that?/where was that?
3 *(dans le temps)* **il y a deux jours de ~, il y a de ~ deux jours** two days ago ◆ **~ fait dix jours/longtemps qu'il est parti** it is ten days/a long time since he left, he has been gone ten days/a long time, he left ten days/a long time ago
4 *(locutions)* **voyez-vous ~ !** did you ever hear of such a thing! ◆ **~ ne fait rien** it *ou* that doesn't matter ◆ **et en dehors de** *ou* **à part ~ ?** apart from that? ◆ **à ~ près que ...** except that ..., with the exception that ... ◆ **avec eux, il y a ~ de bien qu'ils ...** there's one thing to their credit and that's that they ..., I'll say this for them, they ... ◆ **et moi dans tout ~, je deviens quoi ?** and what about me in all this?; → **dire**

céladon /seladɔ̃/ NM, ADJ INV ◆ **(vert) ~** celadon

Célèbes /selɛb/ NFPL Celebes, Sulawesi

célébrant /selebʀɑ̃/ *(Rel)* ADJ M officiating NM celebrant

célébration /selebʀasjɔ̃/ NF celebration

célèbre /selɛbʀ/ ADJ famous *(pour, par* for); ◆ **cette ville est ~ pour son festival** this town is famous for its festival ◆ **cet escroc, tristement ~ par ses vols** this crook, notorious for his robberies *ou* whose robberies have won him notoriety ◆ **se rendre ~ par** to achieve celebrity for *ou* on account of

célébrer /selebʀe/ GRAMMAIRE ACTIVE 51.3 ▸ conjug 6 ◂ VT 1 *[+ anniversaire, fête]* to celebrate; *[+ cérémonie]* to hold; *[+ mariage]* to celebrate, to solemnize ◆ **~ la messe** to celebrate mass 2 *(= glorifier)* *[+ exploit]* to celebrate, to extol ◆ **~ les louanges de qn** to sing sb's praises

célébrité /selebʀite/ NF *(= renommée)* fame, celebrity; *(= personne)* celebrity ◆ **parvenir à la ~** to rise to fame

celer /sәle/ ▸ conjug 5 ◂ VT *(† ou littér)* to conceal *(à qn* from sb)

céleri /sɛlʀi/ NM ◆ **~ (en branches)** celery ◆ **~(-rave)** celeriac ◆ **~ rémoulade** celeriac in remoulade (dressing); → **pied**

célérité /seleʀite/ NF promptness, swiftness ◆ **avec ~** promptly, swiftly

célesta /selɛsta/ NM celeste, celesta

céleste /selɛst/ ADJ celestial, heavenly ◆ **colère/puissance ~** celestial anger/power, anger/power of heaven ◆ **le Céleste Empire** the Celestial Empire

célibat /seliba/ NM *[d'homme]* single life, bachelorhood; *[de femme]* single life; *(par abstinence)* (period of) celibacy; *[de prêtre]* celibacy ◆ **vivre dans le ~** *[prêtre]* to be celibate

célibataire /selibatɛʀ/ ADJ *(gén)* single, unmarried; *[prêtre]* celibate; *(Admin)* single ◆ **mère ~** unmarried *ou* single mother ◆ **père ~** single father NM *(= homme)* single man, bachelor; *(Admin)* single man ◆ **la vie de ~** the life of a bachelor ◆ **club pour ~s** singles club NF *(= femme)* single woman, unmarried woman; *(Admin)* single woman ◆ **la vie de ~** the life of a single woman

> ⚠ L'adjectif **célibataire** se traduit par **celibate** uniquement quand on parle d'un prêtre.

célioscopie /seljɔskɔpi/ NF ⇒ **cœlioscopie**

celle /sɛl/ PRON DÉM → **celui**

cellier /selje/ NM storeroom *(for wine and food)*

cellophane ® /selɔfan/ NF Cellophane ® ◆ **sous ~** *[aliment]* Cellophane-wrapped, wrapped in Cellophane

cellulaire /selylɛʀ/ ADJ 1 *(Bio)* cellular ◆ **béton ~** *(Tech)* air-entrained concrete; → **téléphone** 2 *(= pénitentiaire)* **régime ~** confinement ◆ **voiture** *ou* **fourgon ~** prison van

cellule /selyl/ NF *(Bio, Bot, Jur, Mil, Photo, Pol)* cell; *(Constr = module)* unit; *[d'avion]* airframe ◆ **6 jours de ~** *(Mil)* 6 days in the cells ◆ **~ familiale** family unit ◆ **~ de réflexion** think tank ◆ **réunir une ~ de crise** to convene an emergency committee ◆ **~ photo-électrique** electric eye, photoelectric cell ◆ **~ photovoltaïque** photovoltaic cell ◆ **~ de lecture** cartridge ◆ **~ souche** *(Méd)* stem cell

cellulite /selylit/ NF *(= graisse)* cellulite; *(= inflammation)* cellulitis ◆ **avoir de la ~** to have cellulite

celluloïd /selylɔid/ NM celluloid

cellulose /selyloz/ NF cellulose ◆ **~ végétale** dietary fibre

cellulosique /selylozik/ ADJ cellulose *(épith)*

Celsius /sɛlsjys/ N ◆ **degré ~** degree Celsius

celte /sɛlt/ ADJ Celtic NMF **Celte** Celt

celtique /sɛltik/ ADJ, NM Celtic

celtitude /sɛltityd/ NF Celtic identity

celui /sәlɥi/, **celle** /sɛl/ (mpl **ceux** /sø/) (fpl **celles** /sɛl/) PRON DÉM 1 *(fonction démonstrative)* **~-ci, celle-ci** this one ◆ **ceux-ci, celles-ci** these (ones) ◆ **~-là, celle-là** that one ◆ **ceux-là, celles-là** those (ones) ◆ **vous avez le choix, celle-ci est plus élégante, mais celle-là est plus confortable** you can choose, this one's more elegant, but that one's more comfortable ◆ **une autre citation, plus littéraire celle-là** another quotation, this time a more literary one *ou* this one more literary
2 *(référence à un antécédent)* **j'ai rendu visite à mon frère et à mon oncle, ~-ci était malade** I visited my brother and my uncle and the latter was ill ◆ **elle écrivit à son frère : ~-ci ne répondit pas** she wrote to her brother, who did not answer *ou* but he did not answer ◆ **ceux-là, ils auront de mes nouvelles !** as for them *ou* that lot* *(Brit)*, I'll give them a piece of my mind! ◆ **il a vraiment de la chance, ~-là !** that guy* certainly has a lot of luck! ◆ **elle est forte** *ou* **bien bonne, celle-là !** that's a bit much! *ou* steep! * *ou* stiff! *
3 *(locutions)*
◆ **celui/celle/ceux de** ◆ **je n'aime pas cette pièce, celle de Labiche est meilleure** I don't like this play, Labiche's is better ◆ **il n'a qu'un désir, ~ de devenir ministre** he only wants one thing - (that's) to become a minister ◆ **s'il cherche un local, ~ d'en dessous est libre** if he's looking for a place, the one below is free ◆ **c'est ~ des 3 frères que je connais le mieux** of the 3 brothers he's the one I know (the) best
◆ **celui/celle/ceux d'entre** ◆ **ce livre est pour ~ d'entre vous que la peinture intéresse** this book is for whichever one of you is interested in painting ◆ **pour ceux d'entre vous qui ...** for those of *ou* among you who ...
◆ **celui/celle/ceux dont** ◆ **~ dont je t'ai parlé** the one I told you about
◆ **celui/celle/ceux que** ◆ **c'est celle que l'on accuse** she is the one who is being accused ◆ **donnez-lui le ballon jaune, c'est ~ qu'il préfère** give him the yellow ball - it's *ou* that's the one he likes best
◆ **celui/celle/ceux qui** ◆ **ses romans sont ceux qui se vendent le mieux** his novels are the ones *ou* those that sell best ◆ **il a fait ~ qui ne voyait pas** he acted as if he didn't see
4 *(avec adj, participe)* **cette marque est celle recommandée par les fabricants de machines à laver** this brand is the one recommen-

ded by washing machine manufacturers, this is the brand recommended by washing machine manufacturers ◆ ~ **proche de la fontaine** the one near the fountain ◆ **tous ceux ayant le même âge** all those of the same age

cément /semɑ̃/ NM (Métal) cement; [de dents] cementum, cement

cénacle /senakl/ NM (frm = cercle) (literary) coterie ou set; (Rel) cenacle ◆ **pénétrer dans le ~ des décideurs** to penetrate the inner sanctums of the decision-makers

cendre /sɑ̃dʀ/ NF 1 (= substance) ash, ashes ◆ **~(s)** [de charbon] ash, ashes, cinders ◆ **~ de bois** wood ash ◆ **~s volcaniques** volcanic ash ◆ **des ~s ou de la ~ (de cigarette)** (cigarette) ash ◆ **réduire en ~s** to reduce to ashes ◆ **cuire qch sous la ~** to cook sth in (the) embers ◆ **couleur de ~** ashen, ash-coloured ◆ **goût de ~** (littér) bitter taste; → **couver** 2 [de mort] ~s ashes ◆ **le jour ou le mercredi des Cendres, les Cendres** Ash Wednesday; → **renaître**

cendré, e /sɑ̃dʀe/ ADJ (= couleur) ashen ◆ **gris/blond ~** ash grey/blond ◆ **chèvre ~** goat's cheese coated in wood ash NF **cendrée** (Sport = piste) cinder track ◆ **de la ~e** (Chasse) dust shot

cendreux, -euse /sɑ̃dʀø, øz/ ADJ [terrain, substance] ashy; [couleur] ash (épith), ashy; [teint] ashen

cendrier /sɑ̃dʀije/ NM [de fumeur] ashtray; [de poêle] ash pan ◆ **~ de foyer** [de locomotive] ash box

Cendrillon /sɑ̃dʀijɔ̃/ NF Cinderella ◆ **la cendrillon de la compétition** the Cinderella of the competition

cène /sɛn/ NF 1 (Peinture, Bible) **la Cène** the Last Supper 2 (= communion protestante) (Holy) Communion, Lord's Supper, Lord's Table

cénesthésie /senɛstezi/ NF coen(a)esthesia

cénesthésique /senɛstezik/ ADJ cenesthesic, cenesthetic

cénobite /senɔbit/ NM cenobite

cénotaphe /senɔtaf/ NM cenotaph

cénozoïque /senɔzɔik/ ADJ Cenozoic NM ◆ **le ~** the Cenozoic

cens /sɑ̃s/ NM (Hist) 1 (= quotité imposable) taxable quota ou rating (as an electoral qualification) 2 (= redevance féodale) rent (paid by tenant of a piece of land to feudal superior) 3 (= recensement) census ◆ **~ électoral** ≃ poll tax

censé, e /sɑ̃se/ GRAMMAIRE ACTIVE 37.2, 37.4 ADJ ◆ **être ~ faire qch** to be supposed to do sth ◆ **je suis ~ travailler** I'm supposed to be ou I should be working ◆ **nul n'est ~ ignorer la loi** ignorance of the law is no excuse

censément /sɑ̃semɑ̃/ ADV (= en principe) supposedly; (= pratiquement) virtually; (= pour ainsi dire) to all intents and purposes

censeur /sɑ̃sœʀ/ NM 1 (Ciné, Presse) censor 2 (fig = critique) critic 3 († : Scol) ≃ deputy ou assistant head (Brit), assistant ou vice-principal (US) 4 (Hist) censor

censitaire /sɑ̃sitɛʀ/ (Hist) ADJ ◆ **suffrage ou système ~** voting system based on the poll tax NM ◆ **(électeur) ~** eligible voter (through payment of the poll tax)

censurable /sɑ̃syʀabl/ ADJ censurable

censure /sɑ̃syʀ/ NF 1 (Ciné, Presse) (= examen) censorship; (= censeurs) (board of) censors; (Psych) censor 2 († = critique) censure; (Jur, Pol = réprimande) censure ◆ **les ~s de l'Église** the censure of the Church; → **motion**

censurer /sɑ̃syʀe/ ▸ conjug 1 ◂ VT 1 (= interdire) [+ spectacle, journal, souvenirs] to censor; [+ sentiments] to suppress 2 (Jur, Pol, Rel = critiquer) to censure

> ⚠ Attention en traduisant **censurer** à bien distinguer **to censure** et **to censor**.

cent[1] /sɑ̃/ ADJ 1 (cardinal : gén) a hundred; (100 exactement) one hundred, a hundred; (multiplié par un nombre) ◆ **quatre ~s** four hundred ◆ **quatre ~ un/treize** four hundred and one/thirteen ◆ **~/deux ~s chaises** a hundred/two hundred chairs ◆ **il a eu ~ occasions de le faire** he has had hundreds of opportunities to do it ◆ **courir un ~ mètres** to run a one-hundred-metre race ou sprint ou dash (US) ◆ **piquer un ~ mètres*** (pour rattraper qn) to sprint; (pour s'enfuir) to leg it*; → **mot**

2 (ordinal) **en l'an treize ~** (inv) in the year thirteen hundred

3 (locutions) **il est aux ~ coups** he's frantic, he doesn't know which way to turn ◆ **faire les ~ pas** to pace up and down ◆ **(course de) quatre ~s mètres haies** (Sport) 400 metres hurdles ◆ **tu ne vas pas attendre ~ sept ans*** you can't wait for ever ◆ **la guerre de Cent Ans** (Hist) the Hundred Years' War ◆ **les Cent-Jours** (Hist) the Hundred Days ◆ **s'ennuyer ou s'emmerder**** **à ~ sous (de) l'heure*** to be bored to tears*, to be bored out of one's mind* ◆ **il vit à ~ à l'heure*** he leads a very hectic life; → **donner, quatre**

NM 1 (= nombre) a hundred ◆ **il y a ~ contre un à parier que ...** it's a hundred to one that ...; → **gagner**

◆ **pour cent** per cent ◆ **argent placé à cinq pour ~** money invested at five per cent ◆ **j'en suis à quatre-vingt-dix pour ~ sûr** I'm ninety per cent certain of it

◆ **cent pour cent** a hundred per cent ◆ **j'en suis sûr à ~ pour ~** I'm a hundred per cent certain ◆ **être à ~ pour ~ de ses capacités** [sportif] to be on top form ◆ **je te soutiens à ~ pour ~** I'm a ou one hundred per cent behind you

◆ **cent fois** a hundred times ◆ **je te l'ai dit ~ fois** I've told you a hundred times, I've told you once I've told you a hundred times ◆ **il a ~ fois raison** he's absolutely right ◆ **~ fois mieux/pire** a hundred times better/worse ◆ **je préférerais ~ fois faire votre travail** I'd far rather do your job, I'd rather do your job any day* ◆ **c'est ~ fois trop grand** it's far too big ◆ **une promesse ~ fois répétée** an oft-repeated promise ◆ **cette réforme ~ fois annoncée** this oft-proclaimed reform

2 (Comm) **un ~** a ou one hundred ◆ **un ~ de billes/d'œufs** a ou one hundred marbles/eggs ◆ **c'est 2 € le ~** they're €2 a hundred; pour autres loc voir **six**

cent[2] /sɛnt, (Can)/ sɛn/ NM (aux USA, au Canada = monnaie) cent; (= partie de l'euro) cent

centaine /sɑ̃tɛn/ NF 1 (= environ cent) **une ~ de** about a hundred, a hundred or so ◆ **la ~ de spectateurs qui ...** the hundred or so spectators who ... ◆ **plusieurs ~s (de)** several hundred ◆ **des ~s de personnes** hundreds of people ◆ **ils vinrent par ~s** they came in their hundreds 2 (= cent unités) hundred ◆ **10 € la ~** €10 a hundred ◆ **atteindre la ~** [collection] to reach the (one) hundred mark ◆ **la colonne des ~s** (Math) the hundreds column

centaure /sɑ̃tɔʀ/ NM (Myth) centaur

centaurée /sɑ̃tɔʀe/ NF centaury

centenaire /sɑ̃t(ə)nɛʀ/ ADJ hundred-year-old (épith) ◆ **cet arbre est ~** this tree is a hundred years old, this is a hundred-year-old tree ◆ **cette maison est plusieurs fois ~** this house is several hundred years old NMF (= personne) centenarian NM (= anniversaire) centenary

centenier /sɑ̃tənje/ NM (Hist) centurion

centésimal, e (mpl **-aux**) /sɑ̃tezimal, o/ ADJ centesimal

centiare /sɑ̃tjaʀ/ NM centiare

centième /sɑ̃tjɛm/ ADJ, NMF hundredth ◆ **je n'ai pas retenu le ~ de ce qu'il a dit** I can hardly remember a single word of what he said ◆ **je ne touche pas le ~ de ce que tu touches** I don't get a fraction of what you earn; pour autres loc voir **sixième** NF (Théât) hundredth performance

centigrade /sɑ̃tigʀad/ ADJ centigrade

centigramme /sɑ̃tigʀam/ NM centigramme (Brit), centigram (US)

centile /sɑ̃til/ NM (per)centile

centilitre /sɑ̃tilitʀ/ NM centilitre (Brit), centiliter (US)

centime /sɑ̃tim/ NM centime ◆ **je n'ai pas un ~** (fig) I haven't got a penny ou a cent (US) ◆ **~ additionnel** ≃ additional tax ◆ **ça ne m'a pas coûté un ~** it didn't cost me a thing ou a penny (Brit) ◆ **être au ~ près** (= avare) to be stingy

centimètre /sɑ̃timɛtʀ/ NM (= mesure) centimetre (Brit), centimeter (US); (= ruban) tape measure, measuring tape

centrafricain, e /sɑ̃tʀafʀikɛ̃, ɛn/ ADJ of ou from the Central African Republic ◆ **la République ~e** the Central African Republic NM,F **Centrafricain(e)** Central African

centrage /sɑ̃tʀaʒ/ NM centring (Brit), centering (US)

central, e (mpl **-aux**) /sɑ̃tʀal, o/ ADJ 1 (= du centre) [quartier] central; [partie, point] central, centre (Brit) (épith), center (US) (épith) ◆ **mon bureau occupe une position très ~e** my office is very central; → **chauffage, unité**

2 (= le plus important) [problème, idée, bureau, comité] central

3 (Jur) [pouvoir, administration] central

4 [voyelle] centre (épith) (Brit), center (épith) (US)

NM 1 (Téléc) **~ (téléphonique)** (telephone) exchange

2 (Tennis = court) centre (Brit) ou center (US) court

NF **centrale** 1 (Phys, Élec) **~e électrique** power station ou plant (US) ◆ **~e thermique au charbon/au fioul** coal-fired/oil-fired power station ou plant (US) ◆ **~e nucléaire** nuclear power station ou plant (US)

2 (= groupement) **~e syndicale ou ouvrière** group of affiliated trade unions

3 **~e d'achat(s)** central buying office

4 (= prison) prison, ≃ county jail (US), (state) penitentiary (US)

5 ◆ **Centrale** (Univ) → **école**

centralien, -ienne /sɑ̃tʀaljɛ̃, jɛn/ NM,F student (ou former student) of the École centrale

centralisateur, -trice /sɑ̃tʀalizatœʀ, tʀis/ ADJ centralizing (épith)

centralisation /sɑ̃tʀalizasjɔ̃/ NF centralization

centraliser /sɑ̃tʀalize/ ▸ conjug 1 ◂ VT to centralize ◆ **économie centralisée** centralized economy

centralisme /sɑ̃tʀalism/ NM centralism

centraliste /sɑ̃tʀalist/ ADJ centralist(ic) NMF centralist

centre /sɑ̃tʀ/ NM 1 (gén) centre (Brit), center (US) ◆ **le ~ (de la France)** central France ◆ **il habite en plein ~ (de la ville)** he lives right in the centre (of town) ◆ **il se croit le ~ du monde** he thinks the universe ou the world revolves around him ◆ **au ~ du débat** at the centre of the debate ◆ **mot ~** key word ◆ **idée ~** central idea

2 (= lieu d'activités, bâtiment, services) centre (Brit), center (US) ◆ **les grands ~s urbains/industriels/universitaires** the great urban/industrial/academic centres

[3] *(Pol)* centre *(Brit)*, center *(US)* ◆ ~ **gauche/droit** centre left/right ◆ **député du** ~ deputy of the centre

[4] *(Ftbl = joueur)* centre *(Brit)*, center *(US)*; *(= passe)* centre *(Brit)* *ou* center *(US)* pass

COMP **centre d'accueil** reception centre
centre aéré (school's) outdoor centre
centre d'animation youth centre
centre anti-douleur pain clinic
centre d'appels call centre
centre d'attraction centre of attraction
centre de chèques postaux *postal banking organization*, ≃ National Girobank *(Brit)*
centre commercial shopping centre *ou* arcade, shopping mall *(US)*
centre de contrôle *(Espace)* mission control
centre culturel arts centre
centre départemental de documentation pédagogique *local teachers' resource centre*
centre de dépression *(Mét)* depression, low pressure area
centre de détention préventive remand centre *ou* prison
centre de documentation resource centre, reference library
centre de documentation et d'information school library
centre d'éducation surveillée reformatory, reform school
centre d'études research centre
centre de formation professionnelle professional training centre
centre de gravité centre of gravity
centre de haute pression *(Météo)* high pressure area
centre d'hébergement reception centre
centre hospitalier hospital
centre hospitalier régional regional hospital
centre hospitalier spécialisé psychiatric hospital
centre hospitalier universitaire teaching *ou* university hospital
centre des impôts tax collection office *(Brit)*, Internal Revenue Service office *(US)*
centre d'influence centre of influence
centre d'information et de documentation de la jeunesse careers advisory centre
centre d'information et d'orientation careers advisory centre
centre d'intérêt centre of interest
centre de loisirs leisure centre
centre médical medical *ou* health centre
Centre national de cinématographie *French national film institute*, ≃ British Film Institute *(Brit)*, Academy of Motion Picture Arts and Sciences *(US)*
Centre national de documentation pédagogique *national teachers' resource centre*
Centre national d'enseignement à distance *national centre for distance learning*, ≃ Open University *(Brit)*
Centre national de la recherche scientifique ≃ Science and Engineering Research Council *(Brit)*, National Science Foundation *(US)*
centres nerveux *(Physiol, fig)* nerve centres
Centre régional de documentation pédagogique *regional teachers' resource centre*
Centre régional des œuvres universitaires et scolaires students' welfare office
centre de rétention (administrative) detention centre *(for illegal immigrants)*
centre de tri *(Poste)* sorting office
centres vitaux *(Physiol)* vital organs, vitals; *[d'entreprise]* vital organs; → **serveur**

centré, e /sɑ̃tʀe/ (ptp de **centrer**) ADJ ◆ ~ **sur** *[débat, texte, politique]* centered on, focused on ◆ **le reportage est trop ~ sur la politique** the report focuses *ou* concentrates too much on politics

centrer /sɑ̃tʀe/ ► conjug 1 ◄ VT to centre *(Brit)*, to center *(US)* ◆ **le sujet est mal/bien centré** *(sur photo)* the subject is off-centre *(Brit)* *ou* off-center *(US)*/right in the centre *(Brit)* *ou* center *(US)* ◆ **il n'a pas pu** ~ *(Sport)* he was unable to centre the ball ~ **une pièce/une discussion sur** to focus a play/a discussion (up)on

centre-ville (pl **centres-villes**) /sɑ̃tʀəvil/ NM town *ou* city centre *(Brit)* *ou* center *(US)*, downtown *(US)* ◆ **au** *ou* **en** ~ in the town *ou* city centre, downtown *(US)*

centrifugation /sɑ̃tʀifygasjɔ̃/ NF centrifugation

centrifuge /sɑ̃tʀifyʒ/ ADJ centrifugal

centrifuger /sɑ̃tʀifyʒe/ ► conjug 3 ◄ VT to centrifuge

centrifugeur /sɑ̃tʀifyʒœʀ/ NM, **centrifugeuse** /sɑ̃tʀifyʒøz/ NF *(Tech)* centrifuge; *(Culin)* juice extractor

centripète /sɑ̃tʀipɛt/ ADJ centripetal

centrisme /sɑ̃tʀism/ NM *(Pol)* centrism, centrist policies

centriste /sɑ̃tʀist/ ADJ, NMF centrist

centuple /sɑ̃typl/ ADJ a hundred times as large *(de* as); ◆ **mille est un nombre ~ de dix** a thousand is a hundred times ten NM ◆ **le ~ de 10** a hundred times 10 ◆ **au ~** a hundredfold ◆ **on lui a donné le ~ de ce qu'il mérite** he was given a hundred times more than he deserves

centupler /sɑ̃typle/ ► conjug 1 ◄ VTI to increase a hundred times *ou* a hundredfold ◆ ~ **un nombre** to multiply a number by a hundred

centurie /sɑ̃tyʀi/ NF *(Hist Mil)* century

centurion /sɑ̃tyʀjɔ̃/ NM centurion

CEP /seape/ NM (abrév de **certificat d'études primaires**) → **certificat**

cep /sɛp/ NM [1] ◆ ~ **(de vigne)** (vine) stock [2] *[de charrue]* stock

cépage /sepaʒ/ NM (type of) vine

cèpe /sɛp/ NM *(Culin)* cep; *(Bot)* (edible) boletus

cependant /s(ə)pɑ̃dɑ̃/ GRAMMAIRE ACTIVE 53.3 CONJ [1] *(= pourtant)* nevertheless, however, yet ◆ **ce travail est dangereux, nous allons ~ essayer de le faire** it's a dangerous job – we shall try to do it nevertheless *ou* but we'll try to do it all the same ◆ **c'est incroyable et ~ c'est vrai** it's incredible and yet it's true [2] *(littér)* *(= pendant ce temps)* meanwhile, in the meantime ◆ ~ **que** *(= tandis que)* while

céphalée /sefale/ NF cephalalgia *(SPÉC)*, headache

céphalique /sefalik/ ADJ cephalic

céphalopode /sefalɔpɔd/ NM cephalopod ◆ ~**s** cephalopods, Cephalopoda *(SPÉC)*

céphalo-rachidien, -ienne /sefaloʀaʃidjɛ̃, jɛn/ ADJ cephalo-rachidian *(SPÉC)*, cerebrospinal

céramide /seʀamid/ NM *(Cosmétique)* ceramide

céramique /seʀamik/ ADJ ceramic NF *(= matière, objet)* ceramic ◆ **la ~** *(= art)* ceramics, pottery ◆ **vase en ~** ceramic *ou* pottery vase ◆ ~ **dentaire** dental ceramics

céramiste /seʀamist/ NMF ceramic artist, ceramist

cerbère /sɛʀbɛʀ/ NM [1] *(péj)* fierce doorkeeper *ou* doorman; *(hum = concierge)* janitor [2] ◆ **Cerbère** *(Myth)* Cerberus

cerceau (pl **cerceaux**) /sɛʀso/ NM *[d'enfant, tonneau, crinoline]* hoop; *[de capote, tonnelle]* half-hoop ◆ **jouer au ~** to play with a hoop, to bowl a hoop ◆ **avoir les jambes en ~** to be bandy-legged *ou* bow-legged, to have bandy *ou* bow legs

cerclage /sɛʀklaʒ/ NM *(= action)* hooping ◆ ~ **du col de l'utérus** cervical cerclage

cercle /sɛʀkl/ NM [1] *(= forme, figure)* circle, ring; *(Géog, Géom)* circle ◆ **l'avion décrivait des ~s** the plane was circling (overhead) ◆ **itinéraire décrivant un ~** circular route ◆ **entourer d'un ~ le chiffre correct** to circle *ou* ring *ou* put a circle *ou* a ring round the correct number ◆ **faire ~ (autour de qn/qch)** to gather round (sb/sth) in a circle *ou* ring, to form a circle *ou* ring (round sb/sth) ◆ **~s imprimés sur la table par les (fonds de) verres** rings left on the table by the glasses ◆ **un ~ de badauds/de chaises** a circle *ou* ring of onlookers/chairs; → **arc, quadrature**

[2] *(= étendue) [d'activités]* scope, range ◆ **étendre le ~ de ses relations/de ses amis** to widen the circle of one's acquaintances/one's circle of friends

[3] *(= groupe)* circle ◆ **le ~ de famille** the family circle ◆ **un ~ d'amis** a circle of friends ◆ ~ **de qualité** quality circle

[4] *(= club)* society, club ◆ ~ **littéraire** literary circle *ou* society ◆ **aller dîner au ~** to go and dine at the club

[5] *(= cerceau)* hoop, band ◆ ~ **de tonneau** barrel hoop *ou* band ◆ ~ **de roue** tyre *(Brit)* *ou* tire *(US)* *(made of metal)*

[6] *(= instrument)* protractor

COMP **cercle horaire** horary circle
cercle polaire polar circle ◆ ~ **polaire arctique** Arctic Circle ◆ ~ **polaire antarctique** Antarctic Circle
cercle vertueux virtuous circle
cercle vicieux vicious circle

cercler /sɛʀkle/ ► conjug 1 ◄ VT *(gén)* to ring; *[+ tonneau]* to hoop; *[+ roue]* to tyre *(Brit)*, to tire *(US)* *(de* with); ◆ **lunettes cerclées d'écaille** horn-rimmed spectacles

cercueil /sɛʀkœj/ NM coffin, casket *(US)*

céréale /seʀeal/ NF cereal ◆ **~s** *(pour petit-déjeuner)* (breakfast) cereal

céréaliculture /seʀealikyltyʀ/ NF cereal growing

céréalier, -ière /seʀealje, jɛʀ/ ADJ cereal *(épith)* NM *(= producteur)* cereal grower ◆ **(navire)** ~ grain carrier *ou* ship

cérébelleux, -euse /seʀebelø, øz/ ADJ cerebellar

cérébral, e (mpl **-aux**) /seʀebʀal, o/ ADJ *(Méd)* *[hémisphère, lobe]* cerebral; *(= intellectuel) [travail]* mental ◆ **c'est un ~** he's quite cerebral

cérébro-spinal, e (mpl **-aux**) /seʀebʀospinal, o/ ADJ cerebrospinal

cérémonial (pl **cérémonials**) /seʀemɔnjal/ NM ceremonial

cérémonie /seʀemɔni/ NF ceremony ◆ **sans ~** *[manger]* informally; *[proposer]* without ceremony, unceremoniously; *[réception]* informal ◆ **avec ~** ceremoniously ◆ **faire des ~s** to stand on ceremony ◆ **ne fais pas tant de ~s** there's no need to stand on ceremony ◆ **tenue** *ou* **habit de ~** formal dress *(NonC)*, ceremonial dress *(NonC)* ◆ **tenue de ~** *(Mil)* dress uniform; → **maître**

cérémoniel, -ielle /seʀemɔnjɛl/ ADJ ceremonial

cérémonieusement /seʀemɔnjøzmɑ̃/ ADV ceremoniously, formally

cérémonieux, -ieuse /seʀemɔnjø, jøz/ ADJ *[ton, accueil, atmosphère]* ceremonious, formal; *[personne]* formal ◆ **il est très ~** he has a very formal manner

cerf /sɛʀ/ NM stag

cerfeuil /sɛʀfœj/ NM chervil

cerf-volant (pl **cerfs-volants**) /sɛʀvɔlɑ̃/ NM [1] *(= jouet)* kite ◆ **jouer au ~** to fly a kite [2] *(= insecte)* stag beetle

cerisaie /s(ə)ʀizɛ/ NF cherry orchard

cerise /s(ə)ʀiz/ NF cherry ◆ **la ~ sur le gâteau** *(fig)* the icing on the cake ◆ **se refaire la ~*** *(= se renflouer) (dans jeu d'argent)* to get back in the game; *(dans une entreprise)* to get back on one's feet ADJ INV cherry(-red), cerise; → **rouge**

cerisier /s(ə)ʀizje/ NM *(= arbre)* cherry (tree); *(= bois)* cherry (wood)

cérium /seʀjɔm/ NM cerium

CERN /sɛʀn/ NM (abrév de **Conseil européen pour la recherche nucléaire**) CERN

cerne /sɛʀn/ NM *[de yeux, lune]* ring; *(= tache)* ring, mark; *[d'arbre]* annual ring ◆ **les ~s de** *ou* **sous ses yeux** the (dark) rings *ou* shadows under his eyes

cerné, e /sɛʀne/ ADJ ◆ **avoir les yeux ~s** to have (dark) rings *ou* shadows under one's eyes ◆ **ses yeux ~s trahissaient sa fatigue** the (dark) rings *ou* shadows under his eyes showed how tired he was

cerneau (pl **cerneaux**) /sɛʀno/ NM unripe walnut ◆ **~x (de noix)** *(Culin)* shelled walnuts

cerner /sɛʀne/ ► conjug 1 ◄ VT 1 *(= entourer)* to encircle, to surround; *(Peinture) [+ visage, silhouette]* to outline *(de* with, in) ◆ **ils étaient cernés de toute(s) part(s)** they were surrounded on all sides, they were completely surrounded 2 *(= comprendre) [+ problème]* to define; *[+ personne]* to work out, to figure out 3 *[+ noix]* to shell *(while unripe)*; *[+ arbre]* to ring

certain, e /sɛʀtɛ̃, ɛn/ GRAMMAIRE ACTIVE 42.1, 43.1, 53.6

ADJ 1 *(après nom = incontestable) [fait, succès, événement]* certain; *[indice]* sure; *[preuve]* positive, sure; *[cause]* undoubted, sure ◆ **c'est la raison ~e de son départ** it's undoubtedly the reason he's going ◆ **ils vont à une mort ~e** they're heading for certain death ◆ **il a fait des progrès ~s** he has made definite progress ◆ **la victoire est ~e** victory is assured *ou* certain ◆ **c'est une chose ~e** it's absolutely certain ◆ **c'est ~** there's no doubt about it ◆ **c'est un crétin ! – c'est ~ !** he's a moron!* – that's for sure!* ◆ **il est maintenant ~ qu'elle ne reviendra plus** it's now (quite) certain that she won't come back, she's sure *ou* certain not to come back now ◆ **je le tiens pour ~ !** I'm certain *ou* sure of it!, I know it for a fact! ◆ **il est ~ que ce film ne convient guère à des enfants** this film is definitely unsuitable for children

2 *(= convaincu, sûr) [personne]* sure, certain ◆ **es-tu ~ de rentrer ce soir ?** are you sure *ou* certain you'll be back this evening? ◆ **il est ~ de leur honnêteté** he's convinced of their honesty, he's certain *ou* sure they are honest ◆ **on n'est jamais ~ du lendemain** you can never be sure what tomorrow will bring ◆ **elle est ~e qu'ils viendront** she's sure *ou* certain *ou* convinced they'll come; → **sûr**

3 *(Comm = déterminé) [date, prix]* definite

ADJ INDÉF *(avant nom)* 1 *(= plus ou moins défini)* **un ~** a certain, some ◆ **elle a un ~ charme** there's something quite attractive about her, she has a certain charm ◆ **dans une ~e mesure** to a certain extent, to some extent ◆ **il y a un ~ village où** there is a certain *ou* some village where ◆ **dans un ~ sens, je le comprends** in a way *ou* in a certain sense I can see his point ◆ **jusqu'à un ~ point** up to a (certain) point ◆ **il a manifesté un ~ intérêt** he showed a certain (amount of) *ou* some interest ◆ **un ~ nombre d'éléments font penser que …** a (certain) number of things lead one to think that …

2 *(parfois péj = personne)* **un ~** a (certain) ◆ **un ~ M. Leblanc vous a demandé** a Mr Leblanc asked for you ◆ **un ~ ministre disait même que …** a certain minister even said that …

3 *(intensif)* some ◆ **c'est à une ~e distance d'ici** it's quite a *ou* some distance from here ◆ **cela demande une ~e patience/un ~ courage** it takes a fair amount of patience/some *ou* a fair amount of courage ◆ **au bout d'un ~ temps** after a while *ou* some time ◆ **il a un ~ âge** he's getting on (in years) ◆ **une personne d'un ~ âge** an elderly person ◆ **il est d'un âge ~** *(hum)* he's past his prime

4 *(pl = quelques)* **~s** some, certain ◆ **dans ~s cas** in some *ou* certain cases ◆ **~es personnes ne l'aiment pas** some people don't like him ◆ **~es fois, à ~s moments** at (certain) times ◆ **sans ~es notions de base** without some *ou* certain (of the) basic notions

PRON INDÉF PL **certains** *(= personnes)* some (people); *(= choses)* some ◆ **dans ~s de ces cas** in certain *ou* some of these cases ◆ **parmi ses récits ~s sont amusants** some of his stories are amusing ◆ **pour ~s** for some (people) ◆ **~s disent que …** some (people) say that … ◆ **~s d'entre vous** some of you ◆ **il y en a ~s qui …** there are some (people) *ou* there are those who …

NM *(Fin)* fixed *ou* direct rate of exchange

certainement /sɛʀtɛnmɑ̃/ ADV *(= très probablement)* most probably, most likely; *(= sans conteste)* certainly; *(= bien sûr)* certainly, of course ◆ **il va ~ venir ce soir** he'll most probably *ou* most likely come tonight ◆ **il est ~ le plus intelligent** he's certainly *ou* without doubt the most intelligent ◆ **il y a ~ un moyen de s'en tirer** there must be some way out ◆ **puis-je emprunter votre stylo ? – ~** can I borrow your pen? – certainly *ou* of course

certes /sɛʀt/ ADV 1 *(de concession) (= sans doute)* certainly, admittedly; *(= bien sûr)* of course, certainly ◆ **il est ~ le plus fort, mais …** he is admittedly *ou* certainly the strongest, but … ◆ **~ je n'irai pas jusqu'à le renvoyer mais …** of course I wouldn't *ou* I certainly wouldn't go as far as dismissing him but … 2 *(d'affirmation)* indeed, most certainly ◆ **l'avez-vous apprécié ? – ~** did you like it? – I did indeed *ou* I most certainly did

certif* /sɛʀtif/ NM (abrév de **certificat d'études (primaires)**) → **certificat**

certifiant, e /sɛʀtifjɑ̃, ɑ̃t/ ADJ ◆ **formation ~e** training that leads to a qualification

certificat /sɛʀtifika/ NM *(= attestation)* certificate, attestation; *(= diplôme)* certificate, diploma; *(= recommandation) [de domestique]* testimonial; *(fig)* guarantee

COMP **certificat d'aptitude professionnelle** vocational training certificate

certificat d'aptitude au professorat de l'enseignement du second degré *secondary school teacher's diploma*

certificat d'aptitude au professorat de l'enseignement technique *technical teaching diploma*

certificat d'authenticité certificate of authenticity

certificat de bonne vie et mœurs character reference

certificat de concubinage *document certifying that an unmarried couple are living together as husband and wife*

certificat de décès death certificate

certificat de dépôt *(Fin)* certificate of deposit

certificat d'études primaires *certificate formerly obtained by pupils at the end of primary school*

certificat d'hébergement proof of residence

certificat d'investissement non-voting preferred share

certificat de licence † *(Univ) part of first degree*

certificat de mariage marriage certificate

certificat médical medical *ou* doctor's certificate

certificat de naissance birth certificate

certificat de navigabilité *[de bateau]* certificate of seaworthiness; *[d'avion]* certificate of airworthiness

certificat d'origine *(Comm)* certificate of origin

certificat prénuptial prenuptial medical certificate

certificat de résidence *(Admin)* certificate of residence *ou* domicile

certificat de scolarité attestation of attendance at school *ou* university

certificat de travail attestation of employment

certificateur /sɛʀtifikatœʀ/ ADJ *[personne]* who acts as a guarantor *ou* as surety ◆ **organisme ~** certification body NM *(Jur)* guarantor, certifier ◆ **~ de caution** countersurety, countersecurity

certification /sɛʀtifikasjɔ̃/ NF 1 *(Jur = assurance)* attestation, witnessing ◆ **~ de signature** attestation of signature 2 *[d'entreprise, produit]* certification ◆ **~ ISO 9000** ISO 9000 certification

certifié, e /sɛʀtifje/ (ptp de **certifier**) NM,F (qualified) secondary school *(Brit)* *ou* high-school *(US)* teacher *(holder of the CAPES)*

certifier /sɛʀtifje/ ► conjug 7 ◄ VT 1 *(= assurer)* **~ qch à qn** to assure sb of sth, to guarantee sb sth *ou* sth to sb ◆ **je te certifie qu'ils vont avoir affaire à moi !** I can assure you *ou* I'm telling you* they'll have me to reckon with! 2 *(Jur = authentifier) [+ document]* to certify, to guarantee; *[+ signature]* to attest, to witness; *[+ caution]* to counter-secure ◆ **copie certifiée conforme à l'original** certified copy of the original

certitude /sɛʀtityd/ GRAMMAIRE ACTIVE 42.1 NF certainty ◆ **c'est une ~ absolue** it's absolutely certain *ou* an absolute certainty ◆ **avoir la ~ de qch/de faire qch** to be certain *ou* sure of sth/of doing sth ◆ **j'ai la ~ d'être le plus fort** I am certain of being *ou* that I am the strongest ◆ **je peux vous dire avec ~ que …** I can tell you with certainty that …

céruléen, -enne /seʀyleɛ̃, ɛn/ ADJ *(littér)* cerulean

cérumen /seʀymɛn/ NM (ear) wax, cerumen *(SPÉC)*

cérumineux, -euse /seʀyminø, øz/ ADJ ceruminous

céruse /seʀyz/ NF ceruse; → **blanc**

cérusé, e /seʀyze/ ADJ *[bois, meuble]* white-leaded

Cervantes /sɛʀvɑ̃tɛs/ NM Cervantes

cerveau (pl **cerveaux**) /sɛʀvo/ NM 1 *(Anat)* brain; *(fig = intelligence)* brain(s), mind ◆ **le ~ humain** the human brain ◆ **avoir le ~ dérangé** *ou* *(hum)* **fêlé** to be deranged *ou* (a bit) touched* *ou* cracked* ◆ **fais travailler ton ~** use your brain; → **rhume, transport** 2 *(= personne intelligente)* brain, mind ◆ **c'est un grand ~** he has a great mind ◆ **les grands ~x de l'humanité** the great minds of history ◆ **la fuite** *ou* **l'exode des ~x** the brain drain 3 *(= organisateur)* brains ◆ **c'était le ~ de l'affaire** he was the brains behind the job, he masterminded the job ◆ **le ~ de la bande** the brains of the gang

COMP **cerveau antérieur** forebrain

cerveau électronique electronic brain

cerveau moyen midbrain

cerveau postérieur hindbrain

cervelas /sɛʀvəla/ NM saveloy

cervelet /sɛʀvəlɛ/ NM cerebellum

cervelle /sɛʀvɛl/ NF *(Anat)* brain; *(Culin)* brains ◆ **~ d'agneau** *(Culin)* lamb's brains ◆ **~ de canut** *(Culin)* *fromage blanc with chopped chives (Lyons speciality)* ◆ **se brûler** *ou* **se faire sauter la ~** to blow one's brains out ◆ **quand il a quelque chose dans la ~** when he gets something into his head ◆ **sans** ~ brainless ◆ **il n'a rien dans la** ~* he's completely brainless, he's as thick as two short planks* *(Brit)* ◆ **avoir une** ~ **d'oiseau** *ou* **de moineau** to be feather-brained *ou* bird-brained ◆ **toutes ces** ~**s folles** all these scatterbrains; → **creuser, trotter**

cervical, e (mpl **-aux**) /sɛʀvikal, o/ ADJ cervical

cervidé /sɛʀvide/ NM member of the deer family, cervid *(SPÉC)* ◆ ~**s** the deer family, Cervidae *(SPÉC)*

Cervin /sɛʀvɛ̃/ NM ◆ **le** ~ the Matterhorn

cervoise /sɛʀvwaz/ NF barley beer

CES /seəɛs/ NM 1 (abrév de **collège d'enseignement secondaire**) → **collège** 2 (abrév de **contrat emploi-solidarité**) → **contrat**

ces /se/ PRON DÉM → **ce¹**

César /sezaʀ/ NM 1 *(Hist)* Caesar ◆ **il faut rendre à** ~ **ce qui appartient à** ~ *(Prov)* render unto Caesar the things which are Caesar's *(Prov)* 2 *(Ciné)* French film award, ≃ Oscar, BAFTA award *(Brit)*

Césarée /sezaʀe/ NF Caesarea

césarien, -ienne /sezaʀjɛ̃, jɛn/ ADJ *(Hist)* Caesarean NF **césarienne** *(Méd)* Caesarean (section) ◆ **elle a eu** *ou* **on lui a fait une césarienne** she had a Caesarean (birth *ou* delivery)

césarisé, e /sezaʀize/ ADJ 1 *(Ciné)* *[comédien]* who has won a César; *[film]* that has won a César 2 *(Méd)* ◆ **les femmes** ~**es** women who have had Caesareans *ou* Caesarean births *ou* deliveries

césariser /sezaʀize/ ► conjug 1 ◄ VT *(Méd)* to perform a Caesarean (section) on

césium /sezjɔm/ NM ⇒ **cæsium**

cessant, e /sesɑ̃, ɑ̃t/ ADJ → **affaire**

cessation /sesasjɔ̃/ NF *(frm)* *[d'activité, pourparlers]* cessation; *[d'hostilités]* cessation, suspension; *[de paiements]* suspension ◆ **être en** ~ **des paiements** to be insolvent, to be unable to meet one's financial obligations

cesse /sɛs/ NF 1 ◆ **sans** ~ (= *tout le temps*) continually, constantly, incessantly; (= *sans interruption*) continuously, incessantly ◆ **elle est sans** ~ **après lui** she's continually *ou* constantly nagging (at) him, she's forever nagging (at) him ◆ **la pluie tombe sans** ~ **depuis hier** it has been raining continuously *ou* non-stop since yesterday 2 *(frm)* **il n'a de** ~ **que ...** he will not rest until ... ◆ **il n'a eu de** ~ **qu'elle ne lui cède** he gave her no peace *ou* rest until she gave in to him

cesser /sese/ ► conjug 1 ◄ VT 1 *[+ bavardage, bruit, activité]* to stop; *[+ relations]* to (bring to an) end, to break off ◆ **nous avons cessé la fabrication de cet article** we have stopped making this item, this line has been discontinued ◆ ~ **ses fonctions** to leave office ◆ ~ **ses paiements** to stop *ou* discontinue payment ◆ ~ **le combat** to stop *ou* cease fighting ◆ ~ **le travail** to stop work *ou* working

2 ◆ ~ **de faire qch** to stop doing sth ◆ **il a cessé de fumer** he's given up *ou* stopped *ou* quit* smoking ◆ **il a cessé de venir il y a un an** he stopped coming a year ago ◆ **il n'a pas cessé de pleuvoir de toute la journée** it hasn't stopped raining all day, the rain hasn't let up all day ◆ **la compagnie a cessé d'exister en 1943** the company ceased to exist *ou* ceased trading in 1943 ◆ **quand cesseras-tu** *ou* **tu vas bientôt** ~ **de faire le clown ?** when are you going to stop *ou* quit* *ou* leave off* acting the fool? ◆ **son effet n'a pas cessé de se faire sentir** its effects are still being felt

3 *(frm : répétition fastidieuse)* ◆ **ne** ~ **de il ne cesse de m'importuner** he's constantly *ou* forever bothering me ◆ **il ne cesse de dire que ...** he's constantly *ou* continually saying that ...

VI 1 *[bavardage, bruit, activités, combat]* to stop, to cease; *[relations, fonctions]* to come to an end; *[douleur]* to stop; *[fièvre]* to pass, to die down ◆ **le vent a cessé** the wind has stopped (blowing) ◆ **tout travail a cessé** all work has stopped *ou* come to a halt *ou* a standstill

2 ◆ **faire** ~ *[+ bruit]* to put a stop to, to stop; *[+ scandale]* to put an end *ou* a stop to ◆ **pour faire** ~ **les poursuites** *(Jur)* in order to have the proceedings dropped

cessez-le-feu /sesel(ə)fø/ NM INV ceasefire

cessible /sesibl/ ADJ *(Jur)* transferable, assignable

cession /sesjɔ̃/ NF *[de bail, biens, droit]* transfer ◆ **faire** ~ **de** to transfer, to assign ◆ ~**-bail** lease-back

cessionnaire /sesjɔnɛʀ/ NMF *[de bien, droit]* transferee, assignee

c'est-à-dire /setadiʀ/ CONJ 1 (= *à savoir*) that is (to say), i.e ◆ **un lexicographe,** ~ **quelqu'un qui fait un dictionnaire** a lexicographer, that is (to say), someone who compiles a dictionary 2 ◆ ~ **que** (= *en conséquence*) **l'usine a fermé,** ~ **que son frère est maintenant en chômage** the factory has shut down, which means that his brother is unemployed now ◆ **viendras-tu dimanche ? –** ~ **que j'ai du travail** *(manière d'excuse)* will you come on Sunday? – well actually *ou* well the thing is I've got some work to do ◆ **je suis fatigué –** ~ **que tu as trop bu hier** *(rectification)* I'm tired – you mean *ou* what you mean is you had too much to drink yesterday

césure /sezyʀ/ NF caesura

CET /seəte/ NM (abrév de **collège d'enseignement technique**) → **collège**

cet /sɛt/ ADJ DÉM → **ce¹**

cétacé /setase/ NM cetacean

ceux /sø/ PRON DÉM → **celui**

Ceylan /selɑ̃/ NM Ceylon

cf /seɛf/ (abrév de **confer**) cf

CFA /seɛfa/ (abrév de **Communauté financière africaine**) → **franc²**

CFAO /seɛfao/ NF (abrév de **conception et fabrication assistées par ordinateur**) CADCAM

CFC /seɛfse/ NMPL (abrév de **chlorofluorocarbures**) CFCs

CFDT /seɛfdete/ NF (abrév de **Confédération française démocratique du travail**) *French trade union*

CFF /seɛfɛf/ NMPL (abrév de **Chemins de fer fédéraux**) *(Helv)* → **chemin**

CFP /seɛfpe/ NM (abrév de **centre de formation professionnelle**) → **centre**

CFTC /seɛftese/ NF (abrév de **Confédération française des travailleurs chrétiens**) *French trade union*

cg (abrév de **centigramme**) cg

CGC /segese/ NF (abrév de **Confédération générale des cadres**) *French management union*

CGT /seʒete/ NF (abrév de **Confédération générale du travail**) *French trade union*

ch (abrév de **cheval-vapeur**) HP, h.p.

chablis /ʃabli/ NM 1 (= *vin*) Chablis *(dry white Burgundy wine)* 2 (= *bois*) windfall

chacal (pl **chacals**) /ʃakal/ NM (= *animal*) jackal; *(péj)* vulture

cha-cha(-cha) /tʃatʃa(tʃa)/ NM INV cha-cha(-cha)

chacun, e /ʃakœ̃, yn/ PRON INDÉF 1 *(d'un ensemble bien défini)* each (one) ◆ ~ **d'entre eux** each (one) of them, every one of them ◆ ~ **des deux** each *ou* both of them, each of the two ◆ **ils me donnèrent** ~ **2 €/leur chapeau** they each (of them) gave me €2/their hat, each (one) of them gave me €2/their hat ◆ **il leur donna (à)** ~ **5 €, il leur donna 5 € (à)** ~ he gave them €5 each, he gave them each €5, he gave each (one) of them €5 ◆ **il remit les livres** ~ **à sa** *ou* **leur place** he put each of the books back in its place ◆ **nous sommes entrés** ~ **à notre tour** we each went in in turn

2 *(d'un ensemble indéfini)* everyone, everybody ◆ **comme** ~ **le sait** as everyone *ou* everybody knows ◆ ~ **son tour !** wait your turn!, everyone's got to have a turn! ◆ ~ **son goût** *ou* **ses goûts** each to his own ◆ ~ **ses idées** everyone has a right to their (own) opinion, each to his own ◆ ~ **pour soi (et Dieu pour tous !)** every man for himself (and God for us all!) ◆ ~ **voit midi à sa porte** people always act in their own interests ◆ **(à)** ~ **son métier(, les vaches seront bien gardées)** *(Prov)* each man to his own trade; → **tout**

chafouin, e /ʃafwɛ̃, in/ ADJ *[visage, mine, personne]* sly

chagrin¹, e /ʃagʀɛ̃, in/ ADJ *(littér)* (= *triste*) *[air, humeur, personne]* despondent, dejected; (= *bougon*) *[personne]* ill-humoured *(Brit)* *ou* -humored *(US)*, morose ◆ **les esprits** ~**s disent que ...** disgruntled people say that ... NM 1 (= *affliction*) sorrow; *(dans le deuil)* grief ◆ **avoir du** ~ to be sad ◆ **alors, on a un gros** ~ **!** *(à un enfant)* well, you're looking sorry for yourself! ◆ **avoir un** ~ **d'amour** to have an unhappy love affair, to be disappointed in love ◆ **faire du** ~ **à qn** to upset sb ◆ **plonger qn dans un profond** ~ to plunge sb deep in grief; → **noyer²** 2 (†† = *mélancolie*) ill-humour *(Brit)* *ou* -humor *(US)*

chagrin² /ʃagʀɛ̃/ NM (= *cuir*) shagreen; → **peau**

chagrinant, e /ʃagʀinɑ̃, ɑ̃t/ ADJ distressing

chagriner /ʃagʀine/ ► conjug 1 ◄ VT (= *désoler*) to distress, to upset; (= *tracasser*) to worry, to bother

chah /ʃa/ NM ⇒ **shah**

chahut /ʃay/ NM (= *tapage*) uproar ◆ **faire du** ~ to make *ou* create an uproar

chahuter /ʃayte/ ► conjug 1 ◄ VI *(Scol)* (= *faire du bruit*) to make *ou* create an uproar; (= *faire les fous*) to mess around, to lark around* *(avec* with) VT 1 *[+ professeur]* to play up; † *[+ fille]* to tease; *[+ ministre]* to heckle ◆ **un professeur chahuté** a teacher who can't control his pupils ◆ **il se fait** ~ **par ses élèves** his pupils create mayhem in his class 2 (* = *cahoter*) *[+ objet]* to knock about 3 *(Bourse)* *[+ valeur, monnaie]* to put under pressure

chahuteur, -euse /ʃaytœʀ, øz/ ADJ rowdy, unruly NM,F rowdy

chai /ʃɛ/ NM wine and spirit store(house)

chaînage /ʃɛnaʒ/ NM 1 *(Ordin)* chaining 2 *(Constr)* clamp ◆ **poutre de** ~ (wall) tie

chaîne /ʃɛn/ NF 1 *(de métal, ornementale)* chain ◆ ~ **de bicyclette/de montre** bicycle/watch chain ◆ **attacher un chien à une** ~ to chain up a dog, to put a dog on a chain ◆ ~**s** *[de voiture]* (snow) chains

2 (= *esclavage*) ~**s** chains, bonds, fetters, shackles ◆ **briser ses** ~**s** to cast off one's chains *ou* bonds *ou* shackles

3 (= *suite*) *(gén, Anat, Chim, Méd)* chain; *[de montagnes]* chain, range ◆ **la** ~ **des Alpes** the Alpine range ◆ **faire la** ~**, former une** ~ **(humaine)** to form a (human) chain ◆ **en** ~ *[catastrophes, faillites]* a series of; → **réaction**

4 (= *méthode de production*) ~ **(de fabrication)** production line ◆ **produire qch à la** ~ to mass-produce sth, to make sth on an assembly line *ou* a production line ◆ **travailler à la** ~ to work on an assembly line *ou* a production line ◆ **il produit des romans à la** ~ he churns out one novel after another ◆ **en bout de** ~ *(fig)* at the end of the chain; → **travail¹**

5 *(TV)* channel ◆ ~ **culturelle/musicale** cultural/music channel ◆ **sur la première/deuxième** ~ on the first/second channel
6 *(Radio)* music system ◆ ~ **hi-fi/stéréo** hi-fi/stereo system ◆ ~ **compacte** mini-system, music centre *(Brit)*
7 *[de journaux]* string; *[de magasins]* chain
8 *[de tissage]* warp
9 *(= lettre)* chain letter
COMP **chaîne alimentaire** food chain
chaîne d'arpenteur (surveyor's) chain, chain measure
chaîne câblée cable channel
chaîne de caractères *(Ordin)* character string
chaîne de commandement chain of command
chaîne du froid cold chain ◆ **respecter la ~ du froid** to make sure the recommended low temperature is maintained
chaîne logistique supply chain
chaîne de montage assembly line
la chaîne parlée *(Ling)* connected speech
chaîne payante *ou* **à péage** *(TV)* pay TV channel
chaîne privée *(TV)* private channel
chaîne publique *(TV)* publicly-owned channel, public service channel *(US)*
chaîne sans fin endless chain
chaîne de solidarité support network
chaîne de sûreté *(gén)* safety chain; *[de porte]* door *ou* safety chain

chaîner /ʃene/ ► conjug 1 ◄ **VT** *(Ordin)* to chain; *(Constr)* to clamp

chaînette /ʃɛnɛt/ **NF** (small) chain ◆ **courbe** *ou* **arc en ~** *(Math)* catenary curve; → **point²**

chaînon /ʃɛnɔ̃/ **NM** *(lit, fig) [de chaîne]* link; *[de filet]* loop; *(Géog)* secondary range (of mountains) ◆ **le ~ manquant** the missing link ◆ **~ de données** *(Ordin)* data link

chair /ʃɛʀ/ **NF** 1 *[d'homme, animal, fruit]* flesh ◆ **en ~ et en os** in the flesh, as large as life *(hum)* ◆ **ce n'est qu'un être de ~ et de sang** he's only flesh and blood, he's only human ◆ **donner ~ à** *[+ personnage, pièce]* to give life to ◆ **être ni ~ ni poisson** *(indécis)* to be indecisive; *(indéfinissable)* to be neither fish nor fowl ◆ **l'ogre aime la ~ fraîche** the ogre likes a diet of warm young flesh ◆ **il aime la ~ fraîche** *(hum : des jeunes femmes)* he likes firm young flesh ◆ **entrer dans les ~s** to penetrate the flesh ◆ **~ (à saucisse)** sausage meat ◆ **je vais en faire de la ~ à pâté** *ou* **à saucisse*** I'm going to make mincemeat of him ◆ **bien en ~** well-padded *(hum)*, plump
2 *(littér, Rel : opposé à l'esprit)* flesh ◆ **souffrir dans/mortifier sa ~** to suffer in/mortify the flesh ◆ **fils/parents selon la ~** natural son/parents ◆ **sa propre ~, la ~ de sa ~** his own flesh and blood ◆ **la ~ est faible** the flesh is weak; → **péché**
3 *(Peinture)* **~s** flesh tones *ou* tints
ADJ INV ◆ **(couleur) ~** flesh-coloured *(Brit) ou* -colored *(US)*
COMP **chair à canon** cannon fodder
chair de poule avoir/donner la ~ de poule *(froid)* to have/give goosepimples *ou* gooseflesh ◆ **ça vous donne** *ou* **on en a la ~ de poule** *(chose effrayante)* it makes your flesh creep, it gives you gooseflesh

chaire /ʃɛʀ/ **NF** 1 *(= estrade) [de prédicateur]* pulpit; *[de professeur]* rostrum ◆ **monter en ~** to go up into *ou* ascend the pulpit 2 *(= poste) (Scol)* post; *(Univ)* chair ◆ **créer une ~ de français** to create a chair of French 3 ◆ **la ~ pontificale** the papal throne

chaise /ʃɛz/ **NF** chair ◆ **faire la ~** *(pour porter un blessé)* to link arms to make a seat *ou* chair ◆ **être assis** *ou* **avoir le cul‡ entre deux ~s** to be caught between two stools, to be on the horns of a dilemma; → **politique**
COMP **chaise de bébé** highchair
chaise berçante *ou* **berceuse** *(Can)* rocking chair
chaise de cuisine kitchen chair
chaise électrique electric chair
chaise haute highchair
chaise de jardin garden chair
chaise longue *(= siège pliant)* deckchair; *(= canapé)* chaise longue ◆ **faire de la ~ longue** to lie back *ou* relax in a deckchair; *(= se reposer)* to put one's feet up
chaises musicales *(= jeu, fig)* musical chairs
chaise percée commode
chaise (à porteurs) sedan(-chair)
chaise de poste poste chaise
chaise roulante wheelchair, bathchair † *(Brit)*

chaisier, -ière /ʃezje, jɛʀ/ **NM,F** 1 *(= loueur)* chair attendant 2 *(= fabricant)* chair maker

chaland¹ /ʃalɑ̃/ **NM** *(Naut)* barge

chaland², e † /ʃalɑ̃, ɑ̃d/ **NM,F** *(= client)* customer

chalandise /ʃalɑ̃diz/ **NF** ◆ **zone de ~** customer catchment area

chalazion /ʃalɑzjɔ̃/ **NM** *(Méd)* sty(e)

chalcographie /kalkɔgʀafi/ **NF** *(= gravure)* chalcography; *(= salle)* chalcography room

Chaldée /kalde/ **NF** Chaldea

chaldéen, -enne /kaldeɛ̃, ɛn/ **ADJ** Chaldean, Chaldee **NM** *(= langue)* Chaldean **NM,F** **Chaldéen(ne)** Chaldean, Chaldee

châle /ʃɑl/ **NM** shawl; → **col**

chalet /ʃalɛ/ **NM** chalet; *(Can)* summer cottage

chaleur /ʃalœʀ/ **NF** 1 *(gén, Phys)* heat; *(modérée, agréable)* warmth ◆ **quelle ~ !** it's hot!, it's boiling!* ◆ **il fait une ~ accablante** the heat's oppressive, it's oppressively hot ◆ **il faisait une ~ lourde** the air was sultry, it was very close ◆ **les grandes ~s (de l'été)** the hot (summer) days *ou* weather ◆ **"craint la chaleur"** *(sur étiquette)* "keep in a cool place" ◆ **four à ~ tournante** convection oven ◆ **~ massique** *ou* **spécifique/latente** specific/latent heat ◆ **~ animale** body heat
2 *[de discussion, passion]* heat; *[d'accueil, voix, couleur]* warmth; *[de convictions]* fervour *(Brit)*, fervor *(US)* ◆ **manquer de ~ humaine** to lack the human touch ◆ **chercher un peu de ~ humaine** to look for a bit of company ◆ **prêcher avec ~** to preach with fire *ou* fervour ◆ **défendre une cause/un ami avec ~** to put up a passionate defence of a cause/a friend
3 *[d'animal femelle]* **la période des ~s** the heat ◆ **en ~** on *(Brit) ou* in *(US)* heat
4 († *= malaise)* flush ◆ **éprouver des ~s** to have hot flushes *(Brit) ou* flashes *(US)*; → **bouffée**

chaleureusement /ʃalœʀøzmɑ̃/ **ADV** warmly

chaleureux, -euse /ʃalœʀø, øz/ **ADJ** *[personne, accueil, applaudissements, remerciements]* warm; *[félicitations]* hearty, warm ◆ **il parla de lui en termes ~** he spoke of him very warmly

châlit /ʃɑli/ **NM** bedstead

challenge /ʃalɑ̃ʒ/ **NM** *(= épreuve)* contest, tournament *(in which a trophy is at stake)*; *(= trophée)* trophy; *(= gageure, défi)* challenge

challenger /ʃalɑ̃ʒɛʀ/, **challengeur** /ʃalɑ̃ʒœʀ/ **NM** challenger

chaloir /ʃalwaʀ/ **VI** → **chaut**

chaloupe /ʃalup/ **NF** launch; (* : *Can)* rowing boat *(Brit)*, rowboat *(US, Can)* ◆ **~ de sauvetage** lifeboat

chaloupé, e /ʃalupe/ **ADJ** *[danse, rythme]* swaying; *[démarche]* rolling

chalumeau (pl **chalumeaux**) /ʃalymo/ **NM** 1 *(= outil)* blowtorch, blowlamp *(Brit)* ◆ **~ oxyacétylénique** oxyacetylene torch ◆ **ils ont découpé le coffre-fort au ~** they used a blowtorch to cut through the safe 2 *(Mus)* pipe 3 († *= paille)* (drinking) straw 4 *(Can)* spout *(fixed on the sugar maple tree for collecting maple sap)*

chalut /ʃaly/ **NM** trawl (net) ◆ **pêcher au ~** to trawl

chalutage /ʃalytaʒ/ **NM** trawling

chalutier /ʃalytje/ **NM** *(= bateau)* trawler; *(= pêcheur)* trawlerman

chamade /ʃamad/ **NF** → **battre**

chamaille /ʃamɑj/ **NF** squabble, (petty) quarrel

chamailler (se) /ʃamɑje/ ► conjug 1 ◄ **VPR** to squabble, to bicker

chamaillerie /ʃamɑjʀi/ **NF** squabble, (petty) quarrel ◆ **~s** squabbling *(NonC)*, bickering *(NonC)*

chamailleur, -euse /ʃamɑjœʀ, øz/ **ADJ** quarrelsome **NM,F** quarrelsome person

chaman /ʃaman/ **NM** shaman

chamanisme /ʃamanism/ **NM** shamanism

chamarré, e /ʃamaʀe/ (ptp de **chamarrer**) **ADJ** *[étoffe, rideaux, vêtements]* richly coloured *(Brit) ou* colored *(US)* ◆ **~ d'or/de pourpre** bedecked with gold/purple

chamarrer /ʃamaʀe/ ► conjug 1 ◄ **VT** *(littér = orner)* to bedeck, to adorn

chamarrure /ʃamaʀyʀ/ **NF** *(gén pl) [d'étoffe]* vivid *ou* loud *(péj)* combination of colours; *[d'habit, uniforme]* rich trimming

chambard* /ʃɑ̃baʀ/ **NM** *(= vacarme)* racket*, rumpus*, row* *(Brit)*; *(= protestation)* rumpus*, row* *(Brit)*; *(= bagarre)* scuffle, brawl; *(= désordre)* shambles *(sg)*, mess; *(= bouleversement)* upheaval ◆ **faire du ~** *(= protester)* to kick up a rumpus* *ou* a row* *(Brit)* ◆ **ça va faire du ~ !** it's bound to cause a rumpus* *ou* row!* *(Brit)*

chambardement* /ʃɑ̃baʀdəmɑ̃/ **NM** *(= bouleversement)* upheaval; *(= nettoyage)* clear-out ◆ **un grand ~ gouvernemental** a major government reshuffle

chambarder* /ʃɑ̃baʀde/ ► conjug 1 ◄ **VT** *(= bouleverser) [+ objets, pièce]* to turn upside down; *[+ projets, habitudes]* to turn upside down, to upset; *(= se débarrasser de)* to chuck out*, to throw out

chambellan /ʃɑ̃belɑ̃/ **NM** chamberlain

chamboulement* /ʃɑ̃bulmɑ̃/ **NM** *(= désordre)* chaos, confusion; *(= bouleversement)* upheaval

chambouler* /ʃɑ̃bule/ ► conjug 1 ◄ **VT** *(= bouleverser) [+ objets, pièce]* to turn upside down ◆ **cela a chamboulé nos projets** that messed up* our plans *ou* threw our plans right out* ◆ **il a tout chamboulé dans la maison** he has turned the (whole) house upside down

chamboule-tout /ʃɑ̃bultu/ **NM INV** *(= jeu) fairground game in which balls are thrown to knock down a pyramid of tins* ◆ **c'est une vraie partie de ~** *(fig)* it's a complete shake-up

chambranle /ʃɑ̃bʀɑ̃l/ **NM** *[de porte]* (door) frame, casing; *[de fenêtre]* (window) frame, casing; *[de cheminée]* mantelpiece ◆ **il s'appuya au ~** he leant against the doorpost

chambre /ʃɑ̃bʀ/ **NF** 1 *(pour dormir)* bedroom; (†† *= pièce)* chamber †, room ◆ **~ à un lit/à deux lits** single-/twin-bedded room ◆ **~ double** *ou* **pour deux personnes** double room ◆ **~ individuelle** single room ◆ **~ seule** *(à l'hôpital)* private room ◆ **va dans ta ~ !** go to your (bed) room! ◆ **faire ~ à part** to sleep apart *ou* in separate rooms; → **femme, musique, orchestre, robe, valet**
2 *(Pol)* House, Chamber ◆ **à la Chambre** in the House ◆ **système à deux ~s** two-house *ou* -chamber system ◆ **Chambre haute/basse** Upper/Lower House *ou* Chamber ◆ **ce n'est**

plus qu'une simple ~ d'enregistrement it simply rubber-stamps the government's decisions

3 *(Jur = section judiciaire)* division; *(Admin = assemblée, groupement)* chamber

4 *[de fusil, mine, canon]* chamber

5 *(locution)*

♦ **en chambre** ♦ **travailler en ~** to work at home, to do outwork ♦ **couturière en ~** dressmaker working at home ♦ **stratège/alpiniste en ~** *(péj)* armchair strategist/mountaineer ♦ **ces vidéos permettent de voyager en ~** with these videos, you can travel without leaving the comfort of your armchair

COMP **chambre d'accusation** court of criminal appeal

chambre à air (inner) tube ♦ **sans ~ à air** tubeless

chambre d'amis spare *ou* guest room

chambre de bonne *(lit)* maid's room; *(sous les toits)* garret

chambre à bulles bubble chamber

chambre des cartes *(Naut)* chart-house

chambre claire *(Opt)* camera lucida

chambre de combustion combustion chamber

chambre de commerce (et d'industrie) Chamber of Commerce (and Industry)

la Chambre des communes the House of Commons

chambre de compensation clearing house

chambre correctionnelle ≃ magistrates' *ou* district court

chambre à coucher *(= pièce)* bedroom; *(= mobilier)* bedroom furniture

chambre criminelle court of criminal appeal *(in the Cour de Cassation)*

la Chambre des députés the Chamber of Deputies

chambre d'enfant child's (bed)room, nursery

chambre d'étudiant student room

chambre d'explosion ⇒ **chambre de combustion**

chambre forte strongroom

chambre frigorifique, chambre froide cold room

chambre à gaz gas chamber

chambre d'hôpital hospital room

chambre d'hôte ≃ bed and breakfast

chambre d'hôtel hotel room

la Chambre des lords the House of Lords

chambre des machines engine room

chambre des métiers guild chamber, chamber of trade

chambre meublée furnished room, bed-sitter *(Brit)*

chambre noire *(Photo)* darkroom

les chambres de l'œil the aqueous chambers of the eye

la Chambre des représentants the House of Representatives

chambre des requêtes (preliminary) civil appeal court

chambre sourde anechoic chamber

chambre de sûreté *[de prison]* lockup

chambre syndicale employers' federation

chambrée /ʃɑ̃bʀe/ NF *(= pièce, occupants)* room; *[de soldats]* barrack-room ♦ **camarades** *ou* **compagnons de ~** army buddies *(quartered in the same barrack room)*

chambrer /ʃɑ̃bʀe/ ▸ conjug 1 ◂ VT 1 *[+ vin]* to bring to room temperature, to chambré; *[+ personne] (= prendre à l'écart)* to corner, to collar*; *(= tenir enfermé)* to keep in, to confine ♦ **les organisateurs ont chambré l'invité d'honneur** the organisers kept the VIP guest out of circulation *ou* to themselves 2 *(* = taquiner)* to tease ♦ **tu me chambres ?** *(canular)* are you having me on?*, are you pulling my leg?*

chambrette /ʃɑ̃bʀɛt/ NF small bedroom

chambrière /ʃɑ̃bʀijɛʀ/ NF *(= béquille de charrette)* cart-prop; *(† = servante)* chambermaid

chambriste /ʃɑ̃bʀist/ NMF chamber-music player

chameau (pl **chameaux**) /ʃamo/ NM 1 *(= animal)* camel; → **poil** 2 *(* : péj) (= enfant)* little beast*; *(= femme)* cow‡; *(= homme)* swine‡ ♦ **elle devient ~ avec l'âge** the older she gets the nastier she is ♦ **quel vieux ~ !** *(= femme)* old bag!‡; *(= homme)* nasty old man!

chamelier /ʃaməlje/ NM camel driver

chamelle /ʃamɛl/ NF female camel

chamelon /ʃam(ə)lɔ̃/ NM young camel

chamois /ʃamwa/ NM *(= animal)* chamois; *(Ski)* skiing badge *(marking degree of proficiency)*; → **peau** ADJ INV fawn, buff(-coloured *(Brit) ou* -colored *(US)*)

chamoisine /ʃamwazin/ NF shammy leather

champ[1] /ʃɑ̃/ NM 1 *(Agr)* field ♦ **~ de blé** wheatfield, field of corn *(Brit) ou* wheat ♦ **~ d'avoine/de trèfle** field of oats/clover ♦ **travailler aux ~s** to work in the fields ♦ **on s'est retrouvé en plein(s) ~(s)** we found ourselves in the middle of *ou* surrounded by fields ♦ **la vie aux ~s** life in the country, country life ♦ **fleurs des ~s** wild flowers; → **clé, travers**[2]

2 *(= domaine)* field, area ♦ **élargir le ~ de ses recherches/de ses investigations** to broaden the scope of one's research/one's investigations

3 *(Élec, Ling, Ordin, Phys)* field

4 *(Ciné, Photo)* **dans le ~** in (the) shot *ou* the picture ♦ **être dans le ~** to be in shot ♦ **sortir du ~** to go out of shot ♦ **pas assez de ~** not enough depth of focus ♦ **hors ~** off-camera *(attrib)*; → **profondeur**

5 *(locutions)* **avoir du ~** to have elbowroom *ou* room to move ♦ **laisser du ~ à qn** to leave sb room to manoeuvre ♦ **laisser le ~ libre à qn** to leave sb a clear field ♦ **vous avez le ~ libre** you're free to do as you please ♦ **prendre du ~** *(lit)* to step back, to draw back; *(fig)* to stand back ♦ **sonner aux ~s** *(Mil)* to sound the general salute

COMP **champ d'action** *ou* **d'activité** sphere of activity

champ d'aviation airfield

champ de bataille battlefield

champ clos combat area ♦ **en ~ clos** *(fig)* behind closed doors

champ de courses racecourse

champ électrique electric field

les Champs Élysées *(Myth)* the Elysian Fields; *(à Paris)* the Champs Élysées

champ de foire fairground

champ d'honneur field of honour ♦ **mourir** *ou* **tomber au ~ d'honneur** to be killed in action

champ d'investissement ils ont élargi leur ~ d'investissement they've widened their field of investment

champ lexical lexical field

champ magnétique magnetic field

champ de manœuvre parade ground

champ de Mars ≃ military esplanade

champ de mines minefield

champ de neige snowfield

champ opératoire operative field

champ optique optical field

champ ouvert *(Agr)* open field

champ sémantique semantic field

champ de tir *(= terrain)* rifle *ou* shooting range, practice ground; *(= angle de vue)* field of fire

champ visuel *ou* **de vision** field of vision *ou* view, visual field

champ[2] * /ʃɑ̃p/ NM (abrév de **champagne**) bubbly*, champers* *(Brit)*

champagne /ʃɑ̃paɲ/ ADJ INV champagne NM champagne ♦ **elle a réussi ses examens, ~ !** she passed her exams, let's get out the champagne to celebrate! ♦ **~ rosé** pink champagne NF **Champagne** ♦ **la Champagne** Champagne, the Champagne region; → **fine**[2]

champagnisation /ʃɑ̃paɲizasjɔ̃/ NF champagnization

champagniser /ʃɑ̃paɲize/ ▸ conjug 1 ◂ VT to champagnize

champenois, e /ʃɑ̃pənwa, waz/ ADJ of *ou* from Champagne ♦ **vin méthode ~e** champagne-type *ou* sparkling wine NM,F **Champenois(e)** inhabitant *ou* native of Champagne

champêtre /ʃɑ̃pɛtʀ/ ADJ *(gén)* rural; *[vie]* country *(épith)*, rural; *[odeur, route]* country *(épith)*; *[bal, fête]* village *(épith)* ♦ **fleurs ~s** wild flowers ♦ **dans un cadre** *ou* **décor ~** in a rural setting ♦ **un déjeuner ~** an al fresco lunch; → **garde**[2]

champignon /ʃɑ̃piɲɔ̃/ NM 1 *(gén)* mushroom; *(terme générique)* fungus; *(vénéneux)* toadstool, poisonous mushroom *ou* fungus; *(= mycose)* fungus ♦ **aller aux ~s** to go mushroom-picking, to go collecting mushrooms ♦ **~ comestible** (edible) mushroom, edible fungus ♦ **certains ~s sont comestibles** some fungi are edible ♦ **~ de Paris** *ou* **de couche** cultivated mushroom ♦ **~ hallucinogène** hallucinogenic mushroom, magic mushroom* ♦ **ces nouvelles industries ont proliféré comme des ~s** these new industries have sprung up *ou* sprouted like mushrooms *ou* have mushroomed; → **pousser, ville** 2 *(= nuage)* **~ (atomique)** mushroom cloud 3 *(* : = accélérateur)* accelerator; → **appuyer**

champignonnière /ʃɑ̃piɲɔnjɛʀ/ NF mushroom bed

champion, -ionne /ʃɑ̃pjɔ̃, jɔn/ ADJ * A1, first-rate ♦ **c'est ~ !** that's great!* *ou* first-rate! NM,F *(Sport = défenseur)* champion ♦ **~ du monde de boxe** world boxing champion ♦ **se faire le ~ d'une cause** to champion a cause ♦ **c'est le ~ de la gaffe** *(hum)* there's no one to beat him for tactlessness

championnat /ʃɑ̃pjɔna/ NM championship ♦ **~ du monde/d'Europe** world/European championship

chançard, e * /ʃɑ̃saʀ, aʀd/ ADJ lucky NM,F lucky devil*, lucky dog*

chance /ʃɑ̃s/ GRAMMAIRE ACTIVE 42.2, 42.3, 43.3, 50.5

NF 1 *(= bonne fortune)* (good) luck ♦ **avec un peu de ~** with a bit of luck ♦ **quelle ~ !** what a bit *ou* stroke of (good) luck!, how lucky! ♦ **c'est une ~ que ...** it's lucky *ou* fortunate that ..., it's a bit of *ou* a stroke of luck that ... ♦ **coup de ~** stroke of luck ♦ **il était là, une ~ !** *ou* **un coup de ~ !** he was there, luckily ♦ **jour de ~ !** lucky day! ♦ **ce n'est pas mon jour de ~ !** it's not my day! ♦ **la ~ a voulu qu'il y eût un médecin** by a stroke of luck *ou* luckily there was a doctor ♦ **par ~** luckily, fortunately ♦ **pas de ~ !** hard *ou* bad *ou* tough* luck!, hard lines!* *(Brit)* ♦ **c'est bien ma ~!** *(iro)* (that's) just my luck! ♦ **tu as de la ~ d'y aller** you're lucky *ou* fortunate to be going ♦ **il a la ~ d'y aller** he's lucky *ou* fortunate enough to be going, he has the good luck *ou* good fortune to be going

2 *(= hasard, fortune)* luck, chance ♦ **courir** *ou* **tenter sa ~** to try one's luck ♦ **la ~ a tourné** his *(ou her etc)* luck has changed ♦ **la ~ lui sourit** fortune smiles on him ♦ **mettre toutes les ~s de son côté** to take no chances ♦ **sa mauvaise ~ le poursuit** he is dogged by bad luck *ou* ill-luck; → **bon**[1]

3 *(= possibilité de succès)* chance ♦ **donner sa ~** *ou* **ses ~s à qn** to give sb his chance ♦ **quelles sont ses ~s (de réussir** *ou* **de succès)** ? what are his chances *ou* what chance has he got (of success *ou* of succeeding)? ♦ **il/son tir n'a laissé aucune ~ au gardien de but** he/his

shot didn't give the goalkeeper a chance ◆ **les ~s d'un accord ...** the chances of a settlement ...

◆ **avoir + chance(s)** ◆ **elle a ses** *ou* **des ~s (de gagner)** she stands a good chance (of winning) ◆ **il n'a aucune ~** he hasn't got *ou* doesn't stand a (dog's) chance ◆ **elle a une ~ sur deux de s'en sortir** she's got a fifty-fifty chance of pulling through ◆ **ils ont des ~s égales** they have equal chances *ou* an equal chance ◆ **il y a peu de ~s (pour) qu'il la voie** there's little chance (that) he'll see her, there's little chance of his seeing her, the chances of his seeing her are slim ◆ **il y a toutes les ~s que ...** there's every chance that ..., the chances *ou* odds are that ... ◆ **il y a de grandes** *ou* **fortes ~s pour qu'il vienne** there's a strong *ou* good chance he'll come, he's very likely to come ◆ **il y a des ~s*** it's very likely, I wouldn't be surprised ◆ **il y a une ~ sur cent (pour) que ...** there's one chance in a hundred *ou* a one-in-a-hundred chance that ...

chancelant, e /ʃɑ̃s(ə)lɑ̃, ɑ̃t/ ADJ *[objet]* wobbly, unsteady; *[démarche]* unsteady; *[mémoire, santé]* failing; *[autorité]* flagging; *[régime]* tottering

chanceler /ʃɑ̃s(ə)le/ ▸ conjug 4 ◂ VI *[personne]* to totter; *[ivrogne]* to reel; *[objet]* to wobble, to totter; *[autorité]* to flag; *[régime]* to totter; *[mémoire]* to fail ◆ **sa santé chancelle** he's in failing health, his health is failing ◆ **il s'avança en chancelant** he tottered forward ◆ **une société qui chancelle sur ses bases** a society which is tottering upon its foundations

chancelier /ʃɑ̃səlje/ NM *(en Allemagne, Autriche)* chancellor; *[d'ambassade]* secretary; *(Hist)* chancellor ◆ **le ~ de l'Échiquier** the Chancellor of the Exchequer ◆ **grand ~ de la Légion d'honneur** *high-ranking officer in the French Legion of Honour*; → **recteur**

chancelière /ʃɑ̃səljɛʀ/ NF footwarmer

chancellerie /ʃɑ̃sɛlʀi/ NF *[d'ambassade, consulat]* chancellery, chancery; *(Hist)* chancellery

chanceux, -euse /ʃɑ̃sø, øz/ ADJ lucky, fortunate; *(†† = hasardeux)* hazardous

chancre /ʃɑ̃kʀ/ NM *(Bot, Méd, fig)* canker ◆ **~ syphilitique** chancre ◆ **~ mou** chancroid, soft chancre ◆ **manger** *ou* **bouffer comme un ~**‡ to make a pig of oneself*

chancrelle /ʃɑ̃kʀɛl/ NF chancroid

chandail /ʃɑ̃daj/ NM (thick) sweater, (thick) jumper (Brit)

Chandeleur /ʃɑ̃dlœʀ/ NF ◆ **la ~** Candlemas

chandelier /ʃɑ̃dəlje/ NM *(à une branche)* candlestick, candleholder; *(à plusieurs branches)* candelabra

> ⚠ **chandelier** ne se traduit pas par le mot anglais **chandelier**, qui a le sens de 'lustre'.

chandelle /ʃɑ̃dɛl/ NF 1 *(= bougie)* (tallow) candle ◆ **un dîner aux ~s** a dinner by candlelight, a candlelit dinner ◆ **~ romaine** roman candle 2 *(en avion)* chandelle; *(Rugby)* up-and-under; *(Tennis)* lob; *(Gym)* shoulder stand; *(‡ = morve)* trickle of snot‡ 3 *(locutions)* **tenir la ~** *(hum)* to play gooseberry (Brit), to be a third wheel (US) ◆ **je ne tenais pas la ~ !** I wasn't there at the time! ◆ **monter en ~** *[avion]* to climb vertically ◆ **lancer en ~** *(Golf)* to loft ◆ **voir trente-six ~s** to see stars; → **brûler, économie, jeu**

chanfrein /ʃɑ̃fʀɛ̃/ NM 1 *(= surface)* bevelled edge; *(à 45°C)* chamfer 2 *[de cheval]* nose

change /ʃɑ̃ʒ/ NM 1 *(Fin) [de devises]* exchange ◆ **faire le ~** *(Banque)* to exchange money ◆ **opération de ~** (foreign) exchange transaction; → **agent, bureau** *etc* 2 *(Fin = taux d'échange)* exchange rate ◆ **le ~ est avantageux** the exchange rate is favourable ◆ **la cote des ~s** the (list of) exchange rates ◆ **au cours actuel du ~** at the current rate of exchange 3 *(Can = petite monnaie)* change 4 ◆ **~ (complet)** (disposable) nappy *(Brit) ou* diaper *(US)* 5 *(locutions)* **gagner/perdre au ~** *(Fin)* to gain/lose money on the exchange; *(fig)* to gain/lose on the exchange *ou* deal ◆ **donner le ~** to allay suspicion ◆ **donner le ~ à qn** to put sb off the scent *ou* off the track

changeable /ʃɑ̃ʒabl/ ADJ *(= transformable)* changeable, alterable

changeant, e /ʃɑ̃ʒɑ̃, ɑ̃t/ ADJ *[personne, fortune, humeur]* changeable, fickle, changing *(épith)*; *[couleur, paysage]* changing *(épith)*; *[temps]* changeable, unsettled ◆ **son humeur est ~e** he's a man of many moods *ou* of uneven temper

changement /ʃɑ̃ʒmɑ̃/ NM 1 *(= remplacement)* changing ◆ **le ~ de la roue nous a coûté 20 €** the wheel change cost us €20 ◆ **le ~ de la roue nous a pris une heure** it took us an hour to change the wheel ◆ **j'ai besoin d'un ~ d'air** I need a change of air ◆ **"changement de direction"** *(sur un écriteau)* "under new management" ◆ **il y a eu un ~ de propriétaire** it has changed hands, it has come under new ownership ◆ **~ de décor** *(paysage)* change of scene; *(Théât)* scene-change ◆ **~ à vue** *(Théât)* transformation (scene); *(fig)* (sudden) transformation

2 *(= fait de se transformer)* change *(de* in) ◆ **le ~ soudain de la température/de la direction du vent** the sudden change in temperature/wind direction

3 *(= modification)* change ◆ **~ d'adresse** change of address ◆ **~ de programme** *[de projet]* change of plan *ou* in the plan(s); *[de spectacle]* change of programme *ou* in the programme ◆ **il n'aime pas le(s) ~(s)** he doesn't like change(s) ◆ **elle a trouvé de grands ~s dans le village** she found the village greatly changed *ou* altered ◆ **il y a eu du ~** *(situation)* things have changed ◆ **il y a eu du ~ dans cette pièce** there have been a few changes (made) in this room ◆ **la situation reste sans ~** there has been no change in the situation, the situation remains unchanged ◆ **~ en bien** *ou* **en mieux** change for the better

4 *(Admin = mutation)* transfer ◆ **demander son ~** to apply for a transfer

5 **~ de vitesse** *[de voiture] (= dispositif)* gears, gear change *(Brit)*, gear stick *ou* lever *(Brit)*; *(= action)* change of gears, gear change *(Brit)*, gearshift *(US)*; *[de bicyclette]* gear(s)

6 *(Transport)* change ◆ **il y a deux ~s pour aller de Paris à Lamballe** you have to change twice *ou* make two changes to get from Paris to Lamballe

changer /ʃɑ̃ʒe/ ▸ conjug 3 ◂ VT 1 *(= modifier) [+ projets, personne]* to change ◆ **on ne le changera pas** nothing will change him *ou* make him change, you'll never change him ◆ **on ne change pas une équipe qui gagne** *(Prov)* you don't change a winning team ◆ **ce chapeau la change** that hat makes her look different ◆ **ça change tout !** that makes all the difference!, that changes everything! ◆ **une promenade lui changera les idées** a walk will take his mind off things ◆ **il n'a pas changé une virgule au rapport** he hasn't changed *ou* altered a single comma in the report ◆ **il ne veut rien ~ à ses habitudes** he doesn't want to change *ou* alter his habits in any way ◆ **je ne vois pas ce que ça change** I don't see what difference that makes ◆ **ça ne change rien (à l'affaire)** it doesn't make the slightest difference, it doesn't alter things one bit ◆ **ça ne change rien au fait que ...** it doesn't change *ou* alter the fact that ... ◆ **vous n'y changerez rien !** there's nothing you can do (about it)!

2 *(= remplacer, échanger)* to change; *(Théât) [+ décor]* to change, to shift; *[+ argent, billet]* to change; *(Can) [+ chèque]* to cash ◆ **~ 20 € contre des livres** to change 20 euros into pounds, to exchange 20 euros for pounds ◆ **~ les draps/une ampoule** to change the sheets/a bulb ◆ **il a changé sa voiture** he changed his car ◆ **ce manteau était trop petit, j'ai dû le ~** that coat was too small – I had to change *ou* exchange it ◆ **je changerais bien ma place pour la sienne** I'd like to change *ou* swap* places with him ◆ **il a changé sa montre contre celle de son ami** he exchanged his watch for his friend's, he changed *ou* swapped* watches with his friend

3 *(= déplacer)* **~ qn de poste** to move sb to a different job ◆ **~ qn/qch de place** to move sb/sth (to a different place), to shift sb/sth ◆ **ils ont changé tous les meubles de place** they've changed *ou* moved all the furniture around; → **fusil**

4 *(= transformer)* **~ qch/qn en** to change *ou* turn sth/sb into ◆ **la citrouille fut changée en carrosse** the pumpkin was changed *ou* turned into a carriage

5 *(= mettre d'autres vêtements à)* **~ un enfant/malade** to change a child/patient ◆ **~ un bébé** to change a baby's nappy *(Brit) ou* diaper *(US)*

6 *(= procurer un changement à)* **des voisins silencieux, ça nous change** it makes a change for us to have quiet neighbours, having quiet neighbours makes a change for us ◆ **ça m'a changé agréablement de ne plus entendre de bruit** it was a pleasant *ou* nice change for me not to hear any noise ◆ **ils vont en Italie, ça les changera de l'Angleterre !** they're going to Italy – it will be *ou* make a change for them after England!

VT INDIR **changer de** 1 *(= remplacer)* to change; *(= modifier)* to change, to alter ◆ **~ d'adresse/de nom/de voiture** to change one's address/name/car ◆ **~ de domicile** to move (house) ◆ **~ d'appartement** to move (into a new flat *(Brit) ou* apartment *(surtout US)*) ◆ **~ de vêtements** to change (one's clothes) ◆ **elle a changé de coiffure** she's changed her hairstyle, she's got a new hairstyle ◆ **~ de sexe** to have a sex change ◆ **~ de peau** *[animal]* to shed its skin; *[personne]* to become a different person ◆ **~ d'avis** *ou* **d'idée/de ton** to change one's mind/tune ◆ **il change d'avis comme de chemise*** he's always changing his mind ◆ **elle a changé de couleur quand elle m'a vu** *(= elle a blêmi)* she went pale *ou* she blanched when she saw me; *(= elle a rougi)* she coloured visibly when she saw me ◆ **la rivière a changé de cours** the river has altered *ou* shifted its course ◆ **elle a changé de visage** her face has changed *ou* altered; *(d'émotion)* her expression changed *ou* altered ◆ **change de disque !**‡ put another record on!‡, don't keep (harping) on *ou* don't go on about it!*

2 *(= passer dans une autre situation)* **~ de train/compartiment** to change trains/compartments ◆ **~ de vitesse** *(en conduisant, à vélo)* to change gear ◆ **changeons de crémerie**‡ *ou* **d'auberge**‡ let's take our business *ou* custom *(Brit)* elsewhere ◆ **pour mieux voir, change de place** move to another seat if you want a better view ◆ **~ de position** to alter *ou* shift *ou* change one's position ◆ **j'ai besoin de ~ d'air** I need a change of air ◆ **pour ~ d'air** for a change of air, to get a change of air ◆ **~ de côté** *(gén)* to go over *ou* across to the other side, to change sides; *(dans la rue)* to cross over (to the other side) ◆ **~ de propriétaire** *ou* **de mains** to change hands ◆ **changeons de sujet** let's change the subject ◆ **il a changé de chemin pour m'éviter** he went a different way to avoid me; → **camp, cap¹**

3 *(= échanger)* to exchange, to change, to swap* *(avec qn* with sb); ◆ **~ de place avec qn** to change *ou* exchange *ou* swap* places with sb ◆ **j'aime bien ton sac, tu changes avec moi ?*** I like your bag – will you swap* (with

me)? *ou* will you exchange *ou* do a swap * (with me)?

VI 1 (= *se transformer*) to change, to alter ◆ ~ **en bien** *ou* **en mieux/en mal** *ou* **en pire** to change for the better/the worse ◆ **il n'a pas du tout changé** he hasn't changed *ou* altered at all *ou* a bit ◆ **il a changé du tout au tout** he's transformed ◆ **les temps ont bien changé !** *ou* **sont bien changés !** (how) times have changed! ◆ **le vent a changé** the wind has changed (direction)

2 (*Transport*) to change ◆ **j'ai dû ~ à Rome** I had to change at Rome

3 (*locutions*) **pour ~ !** (*iro*) that makes a change! ◆ **et pour (pas *) ~, c'est nous qui faisons le travail** and as per usual * *ou* and just for a change (*iro*) we'll be doing the work

4 (= *procurer un changement*) **ça change des films à l'eau de rose** it makes a change from sentimental films

VPR se changer 1 (= *mettre d'autres vêtements*) to change (one's clothes) ◆ **va te ~ avant de sortir** go and change (your clothes) before you go out

2 (= *se transformer*) **se ~ en** to change *ou* turn into

changeur, -euse /ʃɑ̃ʒœʀ, øz/ **NM,F** (= *personne*) moneychanger **NM** ◆ (= *machine*) ◆ ~ **(de disques)** record changer ◆ ~ **de monnaie** change machine

chanoine /ʃanwan/ **NM** (*Rel*) canon (*person*); → **gras**

chanoinesse /ʃanwanɛs/ **NF** (*Rel*) canoness

chanson /ʃɑ̃sɔ̃/ **NF** song ◆ ~ **d'amour/à boire/de marche/populaire** love/drinking/marching/popular song ◆ ~ **enfantine/d'étudiant** children's/student song ◆ **c'est toujours la même ~** (*fig*) it's always the same old story ◆ **l'air ne fait pas la ~** do not judge by appearances, appearances are deceptive ◆ **~s que tout cela !** †† fiddle-de-dee! †, poppycock! † ◆ **ça, c'est une autre ~** that's quite a different matter *ou* quite another story; → **connaître**

COMP chanson folklorique folksong
chanson de geste chanson de geste
chanson de marins (sea) shanty
chanson de Noël (Christmas) carol
chanson de toile chanson de toile, weaving song

Chanson française

The term **la chanson française** refers to a very diverse popular musical genre. Traditional French « chansons » gained international renown in the forties thanks to stars like Édith Piaf and Charles Trenet, and in the fifties and sixties thanks to Yves Montand, Charles Aznavour and Juliette Gréco. **La chanson française** has always been characterized by the quality of its lyrics, exemplified by the work of singer-poets like Jacques Brel, Georges Brassens, Léo Ferré and Barbara.

chansonnette /ʃɑ̃sɔnɛt/ **NF** ditty, light-hearted song

chansonnier /ʃɑ̃sɔnje/ **NM** (= *artiste*) chansonnier, cabaret singer (*specializing in political satire*); (= *livre*) song-book

chant[1] /ʃɑ̃/ **NM** 1 (= *sons*) [*de personne*] singing; [*d'oiseau*] singing, warbling; (= *mélodie habituelle*) song; [*d'insecte*] chirp(ing); [*de coq*] crow(ing); [*de mer, vent, instrument*] sound, song (*littér*) ◆ **entendre des ~s mélodieux** to hear melodious singing ◆ **au ~ du coq** at cockcrow ◆ **le ~ du cygne d'un artiste** an artist's swan song ◆ **écouter le ~ des sirènes** to let o.s. be led astray

2 (= *chanson*) song ◆ ~ **patriotique/populaire** patriotic/popular song ◆ ~ **de Noël** (Christmas) carol ◆ ~ **religieux** *ou* **sacré** *ou* **d'Église** hymn ◆ ~ **de guerre** battle song

3 (= *action de chanter, art*) singing ◆ **nous allons continuer par le ~ d'un cantique** we shall continue by singing a hymn ◆ **cours/professeur de ~** singing lessons/teacher ◆ **apprendre le ~** to learn to sing ◆ **j'aime le ~ choral** I like choral *ou* choir singing ◆ ~ **grégorien** Gregorian chant ◆ ~ **à une/à plusieurs voix** song for one voice/several voices

4 (= *mélodie*) melody

5 (*Poésie*) (= *genre*) ode; (= *division*) canto ◆ ~ **funèbre** funeral lament ◆ ~ **nuptial** nuptial song *ou* poem ◆ **épopée en douze ~s** epic in twelve cantos ◆ **le ~ désespéré de ce poète** (*fig*) the despairing song of this poet

chant[2] /ʃɑ̃/ **NM** (= *côté*) edge ◆ **de** *ou* **sur ~** on edge, edgewise

chantage /ʃɑ̃taʒ/ **NM** blackmail ◆ **se livrer à un** *ou* **exercer un ~ sur qn** to blackmail sb ◆ **faire du ~** to use blackmail ◆ ~ **affectif** emotional blackmail ◆ **il (nous) a fait le ~ au suicide** he threatened suicide to blackmail us, he blackmailed us with suicide *ou* by threatening suicide

chantant, e /ʃɑ̃tɑ̃, ɑ̃t/ **ADJ** 1 (= *mélodieux*) [*accent, voix*] singsong, lilting 2 (= *qui se chante aisément*) [*air*] tuneful, catchy

chanter /ʃɑ̃te/ ▸ conjug 1 ◂ **VT** 1 [*+ chanson, opéra, messe*] to sing ◆ **l'oiseau chante ses trilles** the bird sings *ou* warbles its song ◆ **chante-nous quelque chose !** sing us a song!, sing something for us!

2 (= *célébrer*) to sing of, to sing ◆ ~ **les exploits de qn** to sing (of) sb's exploits ◆ ~ **l'amour** to sing of love ◆ ~ **les louanges de qn** to sing sb's praises; → **victoire**

3 * (= *raconter*) **qu'est-ce qu'il nous chante là ?** what's this he's telling us?, what's he (going) on about now? * ◆ **j'ai eu beau le ~ sur tous les tons** no matter how many times I've said it ◆ **il ne l'a pas chanté sur les toits** he didn't shout it from the rooftops

VI 1 [*personne*] to sing; (* : *de douleur*) to howl; [*oiseau*] to sing, to warble; [*coq*] to crow; [*poule*] to cackle; [*insecte*] to chirp; [*ruisseau*] to babble; [*bouilloire*] to sing; [*eau qui bout*] to hiss, to sing ◆ ~ **juste/faux** to sing in tune/out of tune *ou* flat ◆ ~ **pour endormir un enfant** to sing a child to sleep ◆ **chantez donc plus fort !** sing up! (*Brit*) *ou* out! (*US*) ◆ **c'est comme si on chantait** * it's like talking to a brick wall, it's a waste of breath ◆ **il chante en parlant** he's got a lilting *ou* singsong voice

2 (*par chantage*) **faire ~ qn** to blackmail sb

3 (* = *plaire*) **vas-y si le programme te chante** (you) go if the programme appeals to you *ou* if you fancy (*Brit*) the programme ◆ **cela ne me chante guère de sortir ce soir** I don't really feel like *ou* fancy (*Brit*) going out tonight ◆ **il vient quand** *ou* **si** *ou* **comme ça lui chante** he comes when *ou* if *ou* as the fancy takes him

chanterelle /ʃɑ̃tʀɛl/ **NF** 1 (= *champignon*) chanterelle 2 (*Mus*) E-string; → **appuyer** 3 (= *oiseau*) decoy (bird)

chanteur, -euse /ʃɑ̃tœʀ, øz/ **NM,F** singer ◆ ~ **de charme** crooner ◆ ~ **de(s) rues** street singer, busker (*Brit*); → **maître, oiseau**

chantier /ʃɑ̃tje/ **NM** 1 (*Constr*) building site; [*de plombier, peintre*] job; (*Can*) [*de bûcherons*] lumber camp (*US, Can*), shanty (*Can*) ◆ **le matin il est au ~** he's on (the) site in the mornings ◆ **j'ai laissé mes pinceaux sur le ~** I left my brushes at the job ◆ **"chantier interdit au public"** "no entry *ou* admittance (to the public)" ◆ **"fin de chantier"** (*sur une route*) "road clear", "end of roadworks"

◆ **en chantier** ◆ **à la maison nous sommes en ~ depuis deux mois** we've had work *ou* alterations going on in the house for two months now ◆ **il a deux livres en ~** he has two books on the go, he's working on two books ◆ **mettre en ~** [*+ projet*] to get started *ou* going

2 (= *entrepôt*) depot, yard

3 (* = *désordre*) shambles * ◆ **quel ~ dans ta chambre !** what a shambles * *ou* mess in your room!

COMP chantier de construction building site
chantier de démolition demolition site
chantier d'exploitation (*Min*) opencast working
chantier d'exploitation forestière tree-felling *ou* lumber (*US, Can*) site
chantier naval shipyard
chantier de réarmement refit yard

chantilly /ʃɑ̃tiji/ **NF** ◆ **(crème) ~** ≈ whipped cream

chantonnement /ʃɑ̃tɔnmɑ̃/ **NM** (soft) singing

chantonner /ʃɑ̃tɔne/ ▸ conjug 1 ◂ **VI** [*personne*] to sing to oneself; [*eau qui bout*] to hiss, to sing ◆ ~ **pour endormir un bébé** to sing a baby to sleep **VT** to sing, to hum ◆ ~ **une berceuse à un bébé** to sing a lullaby to a baby

chantoung /ʃɑ̃tuŋ/ **NM** Shantung (silk)

chantourner /ʃɑ̃tuʀne/ ▸ conjug 1 ◂ **VT** to jig-saw; → **scie**

chantre /ʃɑ̃tʀ/ **NM** (*Rel*) cantor; (*fig littér*) (= *poète*) bard, minstrel; (= *laudateur*) exalter, eulogist ◆ **premier ~** (*Rel*) precentor ◆ **le grand ~ de** (*fig*) the high priest of

chanvre /ʃɑ̃vʀ/ **NM** hemp ◆ **de ~** hemp (*épith*) ◆ ~ **du Bengale** jute ◆ ~ **indien** Indian hemp ◆ ~ **de Manille** Manila hemp, abaca; → **cravate**

chanvrier, -ière /ʃɑ̃vʀije, ijɛʀ/ **ADJ** hemp (*épith*) **NM,F** (= *cultivateur*) hemp grower; (= *ouvrier*) hemp dresser

chaos /kao/ **NM** (*lit, fig*) chaos ◆ **dans le ~** in (a state of) chaos

chaotique /kaɔtik/ **ADJ** chaotic

chap. (abrév de **chapitre**) chap

chapardage * /ʃapaʀdaʒ/ **NM** petty theft, pilfering (*NonC*)

chaparder * /ʃapaʀde/ ▸ conjug 1 ◂ **VTI** to pinch, to pilfer (*à* from)

chapardeur, -euse * /ʃapaʀdœʀ, øz/ **ADJ** light-fingered **NM,F** pilferer, petty thief

chape /ʃap/ **NF** 1 (*Rel*) cope 2 [*de pneu*] tread; [*de bielle*] strap; [*de poulie*] shell; [*de voûte*] coating; (*sur béton*) screed ◆ ~ **de béton** (concrete) screed ◆ **comme une ~ de plomb** like a lead weight ◆ **la ~ de plomb qui continue de peser sur l'affaire** (= *silence*) the leaden silence that continues to shroud the affair

chapeau (pl **chapeaux**) /ʃapo/ **NM** 1 (= *coiffure*) hat ◆ **saluer qn ~ bas** (*lit*) to doff one's hat to sb; (*fig*) to take one's hat off to sb ◆ **tirer son ~ à qn** * to take one's hat off to sb ◆ **il a réussi ? eh bien ~ !** * he managed it? hats off to him! *ou* well, you've got to hand it to him! ◆ **~, mon vieux !** * well done *ou* jolly good (*Brit*), old man! * ◆ **il a dû manger son ~ en public** he had to eat his words in public ◆ **je ne peux pas sortir de l'argent de mon ~** I can't just pull money out of a hat ◆ **c'est son nom qui est sorti du ~** (= *tiré au sort*) his name was first out of the hat ◆ **il est sorti du ~ des entraîneurs à la dernière minute** the trainers pulled his name out of the hat at the last minute; → **porter, travailler**

◆ **coup de chapeau** ◆ **saluer qn d'un coup de ~** to raise one's hat to sb ◆ **ça mérite un coup de ~** it's quite an achievement ◆ **coup de ~ à Paul pour sa nouvelle chanson** hats off to Paul for his new song

2 *(Tech)* *[de palier]* cap ◆ ~ **de roue** hub cap ◆ **démarrer sur les ~x de roues*** *[véhicule, personne]* to shoot off at top speed, to take off like a shot; *[affaire, soirée]* to get off to a good start ◆ **prendre un virage sur les ~x de roues** to screech round a corner
3 *(Presse)* *[d'article]* introductory paragraph
4 *[de champignon]* cap; *[de vol-au-vent]* lid, top
COMP **chapeau de brousse** safari hat
chapeau chinois *(Mus)* crescent, jingling Johnny; *(= coquillage)* limpet
chapeau cloche cloche hat
chapeau de gendarme *(en papier)* (folded) paper hat
chapeau haut-de-forme top hat
chapeau melon bowler (hat) *(Brit)*, derby *(US)*
chapeau mou trilby (hat) *(Brit)*, fedora *(US)*
chapeau de paille straw hat
chapeau de plage *ou* **de soleil** sun hat
chapeau tyrolien Tyrolean hat

chapeauté, e /ʃapote/ (ptp de **chapeauter**) ADJ with a hat on, wearing a hat

chapeauter /ʃapote/ ► conjug 1 ◄ VT *(= superviser)* to head (up), to oversee

chapelain /ʃaplɛ̃/ NM chaplain

chapelet /ʃaplɛ/ NM 1 *(= objet)* rosary, beads; *(= prières)* rosary ◆ **réciter** *ou* **dire son** ~ to say the rosary, to tell *ou* say one's beads † ◆ **le ~ a lieu à cinq heures** the rosary is at five o'clock ◆ **dévider** *ou* **défiler son** ~* to recite one's grievances 2 *(= succession)* ~ **de** *[d'oignons, injures, îles]* string of; *[d'images, conflits, déclarations]* series of ◆ ~ **de bombes** stick of bombs

chapelier, -ière /ʃapəlje, jɛʀ/ ADJ hat *(épith)* NM,F hatter

chapelle /ʃapɛl/ NF 1 *(Rel = lieu)* chapel; *(Mus = chœur)* chapel ◆ ~ **absidiale/latérale** absidial/side chapel ◆ ~ **de la Sainte Vierge** Lady Chapel ◆ ~ **ardente** *(dans une église)* chapel of rest ◆ **l'école a été transformé en ~ ardente** the school was turned into a temporary morgue; → **maître** 2 *(= coterie)* coterie, clique

chapellerie /ʃapɛlʀi/ NF *(= magasin)* hat shop, hatter('s); *(= commerce)* hat trade, hat industry

chapelure /ʃaplyʀ/ NF (dried) breadcrumbs

chaperon /ʃapʀɔ̃/ NM 1 *(= personne)* chaperon 2 *(Constr)* *[de mur]* coping 3 *(† = capuchon)* hood

chaperonner /ʃapʀɔne/ ► conjug 1 ◄ VT 1 *[+ personne]* to chaperon 2 *(Constr)* *[+ mur]* to cope

chapiteau (pl **chapiteaux**) /ʃapito/ NM 1 *[de colonne]* capital; *[de niche]* canopy 2 *[de cirque]* big top, marquee ◆ **sous le** ~ under the big top ◆ **sous le plus grand ~ du monde** in the biggest circus in the world 3 *[d'alambic]* head

chapitre /ʃapitʀ/ NM 1 *[de livre, traité]* chapter; *[de budget, statuts]* section, item ◆ **inscrire un nouveau ~ au budget** to make out a new budget head ◆ **un nouveau ~ de sa vie** a new chapter of *ou* in his life 2 *(fig = sujet)* subject, matter ◆ **il est imbattable sur ce** ~ he's unbeatable on that subject *ou* score ◆ **il est très strict sur le ~ de la discipline** he's very strict in matters of discipline *ou* about discipline ◆ **au ~ des faits divers** under the heading of news in brief 3 *(Rel = assemblée)* chapter; → **salle, voix**

chapitrer /ʃapitʀe/ ► conjug 1 ◄ VT 1 *(= réprimander)* to admonish, to reprimand; *(= faire la morale à)* to lecture *(sur* on, about); ◆ **dûment chapitré par sa mère** duly coached by his mother 2 *[+ texte]* to divide into chapters; *[+ budget]* to divide into headings, to itemize

chapka /ʃapka/ NF Russian fur hat

chapon /ʃapɔ̃/ NM capon

chaptalisation /ʃaptalizasjɔ̃/ NF *[de vin]* chaptalization

chaptaliser /ʃaptalize/ ► conjug 1 ◄ VT *[+ vin]* to chaptalize

chaque /ʃak/ ADJ 1 *(ensemble défini)* each, every ◆ ~ **élève (de la classe)** each *ou* every pupil (in the class) ◆ **ils coûtent 2 € ~*** they're €2 each *ou* apiece 2 *(ensemble indéfini)* every ◆ ~ **homme naît libre** every man is born free ◆ **il m'interrompt à ~ instant** he interrupts me every other second, he keeps interrupting me ◆ ~ **10 minutes, il éternuait*** he sneezed every 10 minutes ◆ ~ **chose à sa place/en son temps** everything in its place/in its own time; → **à**

char[1] /ʃaʀ/ NM 1 *(Mil)* tank ◆ **régiment de ~s** tank regiment 2 *[de carnaval]* (carnival) float ◆ **le défilé des ~s fleuris** the procession of flower-decked floats 3 *(† = charrette)* wagon, cart 4 *(* : Can)* car, automobile *(US)* 5 *(Antiq)* chariot ◆ **le ~ de l'Aurore** *(littér)* the chariot of the dawn ◆ **le ~ de l'État** the ship of state 6 *(locution)* **arrête ton ~!**‡ *(raconter des histoires)* shut up!*, belt up!‡ *(Brit)*; *(se vanter)* stop showing off!
COMP **char d'assaut** tank
char à banc *horse-drawn wagon with seats*
char à bœufs oxcart
char de combat ⇒ **char d'assaut**
char funèbre hearse
char à voile sand yacht, land yacht ◆ **faire du ~ à voile** to go sand-yachting *ou* land-yachting

char[2]‡ /ʃaʀ/ NM *(= bluff)* ◆ **c'est du ~ tout ça !** he's *(ou* they're *etc)* just bluffing, he's *(ou* they're *etc)* just trying it on* *(Brit)* ◆ **sans ~ !** no kidding!*

charabia* /ʃaʀabja/ NM gibberish, gobbledygook*

charade /ʃaʀad/ NF *(parlée)* riddle, word puzzle; *(mimée)* charade

charançon /ʃaʀɑ̃sɔ̃/ NM weevil

charançonné, e /ʃaʀɑ̃sɔne/ ADJ weevilly, weevilled

charbon /ʃaʀbɔ̃/ NM 1 *(= combustible)* coal (NonC); *(= escarbille)* speck of coal dust, piece of grit ◆ **être sur des ~s ardents** to be like a cat on hot bricks *ou* on a hot tin roof *(US)* ◆ **aller au ~*** *(travail)* to go to work; *(tâche ingrate, risquée)* to stick one's neck out ◆ **il faut aller au ~** *(se démener)* we've got to get out there and do what's got to be done 2 ◆ **(maladie du) ~** *[de blé]* smut, black rust; *[de bête, homme]* anthrax 3 *(Art)* *(= instrument)* piece of charcoal; *(= dessin)* charcoal drawing 4 *(Pharm)* charcoal ◆ **pastilles au ~** charcoal tablets 5 *(Élec)* *[d'arc électrique]* carbon
COMP **charbon actif** *ou* **activé** active *ou* activated carbon
charbon animal animal black
charbon de bois charcoal ◆ **cuit au ~ de bois** char-grilled, charcoal-grilled
charbon de terre †† coal

charbonnage /ʃaʀbɔnaʒ/ NM *(gén pl = houillère)* colliery, coalmine ◆ **les Charbonnages (de France)** the French Coal Board

charbonner /ʃaʀbɔne/ ► conjug 1 ◄ VT *[+ inscription]* to scrawl in charcoal ◆ ~ **un mur de dessins** to scrawl (charcoal) drawings on a wall ◆ **avoir les yeux charbonnés** to have eyes heavily rimmed with eyeliner ◆ **se ~ le visage** to blacken *ou* black one's face VI *[lampe, poêle, rôti]* to char, to go black; *(Naut)* to take on coal

charbonneux, -euse /ʃaʀbɔnø, øz/ ADJ 1 *[apparence, texture]* coal-like; *(littér = noirci, souillé)* sooty; *[yeux, regard]* dark 2 *(Méd)* **tumeur charbonneuse** anthracoid *ou* anthrasic tumour ◆ **mouche charbonneuse** anthrax-carrying fly

charbonnier, -ière /ʃaʀbɔnje, jɛʀ/ ADJ coal *(épith)* ◆ **navire ~** collier, coaler; → **mésange** NM *(= personne)* coalman; *(†† = fabriquant de charbon de bois)* charcoal burner ◆ ~ **est maître dans sa maison** *ou* **chez soi** *(Prov)* a man is master in his own home, an Englishman's home is his castle *(Brit)*, a man's home is his castle *(US)*; → **foi** NF **charbonnière** *(= four)* charcoal kiln *ou* oven

charcutage /ʃaʀkytaʒ/ NM *(péj)* ◆ ~ **électoral** gerrymandering

charcuter* /ʃaʀkyte/ ► conjug 1 ◄ VT *[+ personne]* *(dans une rixe)* to hack about*; *(= opérer)* to butcher*; *[+ rôti, volaille]* to mangle, to hack to bits; *[+ texte]* to hack ◆ **il va se faire ~** he's going to go under the (surgeon's) knife VPR **se charcuter** to cut o.s. to ribbons ◆ **ils se sont charcutés** *(bagarre)* they cut each other to ribbons, they hacked each other to bits

charcuterie /ʃaʀkytʀi/ NF *(= magasin)* pork butcher's shop and delicatessen; *(= produits)* cooked pork meats; *(= commerce)* pork meat trade; *(de traiteur)* delicatessen trade

> **CHARCUTERIE**
>
> This is a generic term referring to a wide variety of products made with pork, such as pâté, « rillettes », ham and sausages. The terms **charcuterie** or « boucherie-charcuterie » also refer to the shop where these products are sold. The « charcutier-traiteur » sells ready-prepared dishes to take away as well as **charcuterie**.

charcutier, -ière /ʃaʀkytje, jɛʀ/ NM,F pork butcher; *(= traiteur)* delicatessen dealer; *(* : péj = chirurgien)* butcher* *(fig)*

chardon /ʃaʀdɔ̃/ NM 1 *(= plante)* thistle 2 *(= pointe)* ◆ ~**s** *[de grille, mur]* spikes

chardonnay /ʃaʀdɔnɛ/ NM Chardonnay

chardonneret /ʃaʀdɔnʀɛ/ NM goldfinch

charentais, e /ʃaʀɑ̃tɛ, ɛz/ ADJ of *ou* from Charente NM,F **Charentais(e)** inhabitant *ou* native of Charente NF **charentaise** carpet slipper

charge /ʃaʀʒ/ NF 1 *(= fardeau lit)* load, burden; *(fig)* burden; *[de véhicule]* load; *[de navire]* freight, cargo; *(Archit = poussée)* load ◆ ~ **maximale** *[de camion]* maximum load ◆ **fléchir** *ou* **plier sous la ~** to bend under the load *ou* burden ◆ ~ **de travail** workload ◆ **c'est une grosse ~ de travail** it's an awful lot of work ◆ **l'éducation des enfants est une lourde ~ pour eux** educating the children is a heavy burden for them ◆ **leur mère infirme est une ~ pour eux** their invalid mother is a burden to *ou* on them
2 *(= rôle, fonction)* responsibility; *(Admin)* office; *(Jur)* practice ◆ ~ **publique/élective** public/elective office ◆ **avoir une ~ d'avocat** to have a lawyer's practice ◆ **les hautes ~s qu'il occupe** the high office that he holds ◆ **les devoirs de la ~** the duties of (the) office ◆ **on lui a confié la ~ de (faire) l'enquête** he was given the responsibility of (carrying out) the inquiry ◆ **il a la ~ de faire, il a pour ~ de faire** the onus is upon him to do, he is responsible for doing; → **femme**
3 *(envers qn)* **avoir la ~ de qn** to be responsible for sb, to have charge of sb ◆ **les enfants dont j'ai la ~** the children (who are) in my care ◆ **avoir ~ d'âmes** *[prêtre]* to be responsible for people's spiritual welfare, to have the cure of souls; *[personne]* to be responsible for people's welfare
4 *(= obligations financières)* ~**s** *[de commerçant]* expenses, costs, outgoings; *[de locataire]* maintenance *ou* service charges ◆ ~**s familiales** family expenses *ou* outgoings ◆ **la ~ fiscale** the tax burden ◆ ~**s fiscales** taxes, taxation ◆ **dans ce commerce, nous avons de lourdes ~s** we have heavy expenses *ou* costs *ou* our overheads are high in this trade ◆ **les ~s de l'État** government expenditure; → **cahier**
5 *(Jur)* charge ◆ **les ~s qui pèsent contre lui** the charges against him; → **témoin**

6 *(Mil = attaque)* charge ◆ ~ **irrégulière** *(Sport)* illegal tackle; → **pas[1], revenir, sonner**

7 *(Tech) [de fusil] (= action)* loading, charging; *(= explosifs)* charge; *(Élec) (= action)* charging; *(= quantité)* charge ◆ ~ **électrique** electric charge

8 *(= caricature)* caricature; → **portrait**

9 *(Naut = chargement)* loading

10 *(locutions)*

◆ **à + charge** ◆ **il a sa mère à (sa)** ~ he has a dependent mother, he has his mother to support ◆ **enfants à** ~ dependent children ◆ **personnes à** ~ dependents ◆ **à** ~ **pour lui de payer** on condition that he meets the costs ◆ **être à la** ~ **de qn** *[frais, réparations]* to be chargeable to sb, to be payable by sb; *[personne]* to be dependent upon sb, to be supported by sb ◆ **les frais sont à la** ~ **de l'entreprise** the costs will be borne by the firm, the firm will pay the expenses ◆ **j'accepte ton aide à** ~ **de revanche** I'll let you help me but on condition that you let me return the favour sometime

◆ **en charge** ◆ **conducteur en** ~ *(Élec)* live conductor ◆ **mettre une batterie en** ~ to charge a battery, to put a battery on charge *(Brit)* ◆ **la batterie est en** ~ the battery is being charged *ou* is on charge *(Brit)* ◆ **montée en** ~ *[d'effectifs]* increase; *[de secteur]* growth ◆ **prendre en** ~ *[+ dossier, frais, remboursement]* to take care of; *[+ passager]* to take on ◆ **prendre un enfant en** ~ *(gén)* to take charge of a child; *[Assistance publique]* to take a child into care *(Brit)*, to take a child into court custody *(US)* ◆ **l'adolescent doit se prendre en** ~ the adolescent must take responsibility for himself ◆ **prise en** ~ *(par un taxi) (= action)* picking up; *(= prix)* minimum (standard) fare; *(par la Sécurité sociale) undertaking to reimburse medical expenses* ◆ **être en** ~ **de** *(= responsable)* to be in charge of ◆ **le juge en** ~ **de ce dossier** the judge in charge of the case

COMP **charge affective** *(Psych)* emotive power

charge creuse *(Mil)* hollow-charge

charge émotionnelle ⇒ **charge affective**

charges de famille dependents

charges locatives maintenance *ou* service charges

charges patronales employers' contributions

charges sociales social security contributions

charge utile live load

charge à vide weight (when) empty, empty weight

charge virale *(Méd)* viral load

chargé, e /ʃaʀʒe/ (ptp de **charger**) ADJ 1 *(lit) [personne, véhicule]* loaded, laden (*de* with); ◆ **table ~e de mets appétissants** table laden *ou* loaded with mouth-watering dishes ◆ ~ **comme un mulet*** *ou* **un baudet*** *ou* **une mule** loaded *ou* laden (down) like a mule

2 *(= responsable de)* **être** ~ **de** *[+ travail, enfants]* to be in charge of

3 *(= rempli de)* ~ **d'honneurs** laden with honours ◆ ~ **d'ans** *ou* **d'années** *(littér)* weighed down by (the) years ◆ **c'est un lieu** ~ **d'histoire** the place is steeped in history ◆ **mot** ~ **de sens** word full of *ou* pregnant with meaning ◆ **regard** ~ **de menaces** menacing *ou* baleful look ◆ **nuage** ~ **de neige** snow-laden cloud, cloud laden *ou* heavy with snow ◆ **air** ~ **de parfums** air heavy with scent *ou* fragrance *(littér)*

4 *(= occupé) [emploi du temps]* full, heavy ◆ **notre programme est très** ~ we have a very busy schedule *ou* a very full programme

5 *(= lourd) [conscience]* troubled; *[ciel]* overcast, heavy; *[style]* overelaborate, intricate ◆ **c'est un homme qui a un passé** ~ he is a man with a past; → **hérédité**

6 *(Méd) [estomac]* overloaded; *[langue]* coated, furred ◆ **il a l'haleine ~e** his breath smells

7 *(Tech) [arme, appareil]* loaded

8 ‡ *(= ivre)* plastered‡ *(attrib)*, sloshed‡ *(attrib)*; *(= drogué)* stoned‡ *(attrib)*, spaced (out)‡ *(attrib)*

COMP **chargé d'affaires** NM chargé d'affaires

chargé de cours NM junior lecturer *ou* fellow

chargé de famille ◆ **être ~ de famille** to have family responsibilities

chargé de mission *(gén)* project leader; *(Pol)* (official) representative

chargé de recherches researcher

chargement /ʃaʀʒəmɑ̃/ NM 1 *(= action) [de camion, bagages]* loading 2 *(= marchandises)* load; *[de navire]* freight, cargo ◆ **le** ~ **a basculé** the load toppled over 3 *(Comm) (= remise)* registering; *(= paquet)* registered parcel 4 *[d'arme, caméra, logiciel]* loading; *[de chaudière]* stoking

charger /ʃaʀʒe/ ▸ conjug 3 ◂ VT 1 *[+ animal, personne, véhicule, étagère]* to load ◆ ~ **qn de paquets** to load sb up *ou* weigh sb down with parcels ◆ **je vais** ~ **la voiture** I'll go and load the car (up) ◆ **on a trop chargé cette voiture** this car has been overloaded ◆ ~ **le peuple d'impôts** to burden the people with *ou* weigh the people down with taxes ◆ ~ **sa mémoire (de faits)/un texte de citations** to overload one's memory (with facts)/a text with quotations ◆ **plat qui charge l'estomac** dish that lies heavy on the stomach

2 *(= placer, prendre) [+ objet, bagages]* to load (*dans* into); ◆ **il a chargé le sac/le cageot sur son épaule** he loaded the sack/the crate onto his shoulder, he heaved the sack over/the crate onto his shoulder ◆ ~ **un client** *[taxi]* to pick up a passenger *ou* a fare

3 *[+ fusil, caméra, logiciel]* to load; *[+ batterie]* to charge; *[+ chaudière]* to stoke, to fire; *(Couture) [+ bobine, canette]* to load *ou* fill with thread

4 *(= donner une responsabilité)* ~ **qn de qch** to put sb in charge of sth ◆ ~ **qn de faire qch** to give sb the responsibility *ou* job of doing sth, to ask sb to do sth ◆ **être chargé de faire qch** to be put in charge of doing sth, to be made responsible for doing sth ◆ **il m'a chargé d'un petit travail** he gave me a little job to do ◆ **on l'a chargé d'une mission importante** he was given an important job to do ◆ **on l'a chargé de la surveillance des enfants** *ou* **de surveiller les enfants** he was put in charge of the children, he was given the job of looking after the children ◆ **il m'a chargé de mettre une lettre à la poste** he asked me to post a letter ◆ **on m'a chargé d'appliquer le règlement** I've been instructed to apply the rule ◆ **il m'a chargé de m'occuper de la correspondance** he gave me the responsibility *ou* job of seeing to the correspondence ◆ **il m'a chargé de ses amitiés pour vous** *ou* **de vous transmettre ses amitiés** he asked me to give you his regards

5 *(= accuser) [+ personne]* to bring all possible evidence against ◆ ~ **qn de** *[+ crime]* to charge sb with

6 *(= attaquer) (Mil)* to charge (at); *(Sport)* to charge, to tackle ◆ **chargez !** charge! ◆ **il a chargé dans le tas*** he charged into them

7 *(= caricaturer) [+ portrait]* to make a caricature of; *[+ description]* to overdo, to exaggerate; *(Théât) [+ rôle]* to overact, to ham it up* ◆ **il a tendance à** ~ he has a tendency to overdo it *ou* to exaggerate

VPR **se charger** 1 ◆ **se** ~ **de** *[+ tâche]* to see to, to take care *ou* charge of, to take on; *[+ enfant, prisonnier]* to see to, to attend to, to take care of; *(iro) [+ ennemi]* to see to, to attend to ◆ **se** ~ **de faire qch** to undertake to do sth, to take it upon o.s. to do sth ◆ **il s'est chargé des enfants** he is seeing to *ou* taking care *ou* charge of the children ◆ **d'accord je m'en charge** OK, I'll see to it *ou* I'll take care of it ◆ **je me charge de le faire venir** I'll make sure *ou* I'll see to it that he comes, I'll make it my business to see that he comes

2 ‡ *(= se soûler)* to get plastered‡; *(= se droguer)* to get stoned‡

chargeur /ʃaʀʒœʀ/ NM 1 *(= personne) (gén, Mil)* loader; *(Naut) (= négociant)* shipper; *(= affréteur)* charterer 2 *(= dispositif) [d'arme à feu]* magazine, cartridge clip; *(Photo)* cartridge ◆ **il vida son ~ sur les gendarmes** he emptied his gun *ou* magazine into the police officers ◆ ~ **de batterie** (battery) charger

charia /ʃaʀja/ NF sharia, sheria

chariot /ʃaʀjo/ NM *(= charrette)* wagon, waggon *(Brit)*; *(plus petit)* truck, cart; *(= table, panier à roulettes)* trolley *(Brit)*, cart *(US)*; *(= appareil de manutention)* truck, float *(Brit)*; *[de machine à écrire, machine-outil]* carriage; *[d'hôpital]* trolley ◆ ~ **(à bagages)** (baggage *ou* luggage) trolley *(Brit) ou* cart *(US)* ◆ ~ **(de caméra)** *(Ciné)* dolly ◆ ~ **élévateur (à fourche)** fork-lift truck ◆ **le Petit/Grand Chariot** *(Astron)* the Little/Great Bear

charismatique /kaʀismatik/ ADJ charismatic

charisme /kaʀism/ NM charisma

charitable /ʃaʀitabl/ ADJ 1 *(= qui fait preuve de charité)* charitable (*envers* towards); ◆ **organisation** ~ charitable organization, charity 2 *(= gentil)* kind (*envers* to, towards); ◆ **ce n'est pas très** ~ **de votre part** that's rather uncharitable *ou* unkind of you ◆ **merci de tes conseils ~s** *(iro)* thanks for your kind advice *(iro)*; → **âme**

charitablement /ʃaʀitabləmɑ̃/ ADV *(= avec charité)* charitably; *(= gentiment)* kindly ◆ **je vous avertis** ~ **que la prochaine fois ...** *(iro)* let me give you a friendly warning that next time ...

charité /ʃaʀite/ NF 1 *(= bonté, amour)* charity; *(= gentillesse)* kindness; *(Rel)* charity, love ◆ **il a eu la** ~ **de faire** he was kind enough to do ◆ **faites-moi la** ~ **de ..., ayez la** ~ **de ...** be so kind as to ... ◆ **ce serait une** ~ **à lui faire que de ...** it would be doing him a kindness *ou* a good turn to ... ◆ **faire preuve de** ~ **chrétienne** to show Christian charity; → **dame, sœur**

2 *(= aumône)* charity ◆ **demander la** ~ *(lit)* to ask *ou* beg for charity; *(fig)* to come begging ◆ **faire la** ~ to give to charity ◆ **faire la** ~ **à** *[+ mendiants]* to give (something) to ◆ **je ne veux pas qu'on me fasse la** ~ I don't want charity ◆ **la** ~**, ma bonne dame !** could you spare me some change? ◆ **vivre de la** ~ **publique** to live on (public) charity ◆ **vivre des ~s de ses voisins** to live on the charity of one's neighbours ◆ ~ **bien ordonnée commence par soi-même** *(Prov)* charity begins at home *(Prov)* ◆ **fête de** ~ charity fête; → **vente**

charivari /ʃaʀivaʀi/ NM hullabaloo

charlatan /ʃaʀlatɑ̃/ NM *(péj) (= médecin)* quack, charlatan; *(= pharmacien, vendeur)* crook, mountebank *(littér)*; *(= plombier, maçon)* cowboy*; *(= politicien)* charlatan, phoney*

charlatanerie /ʃaʀlatanʀi/ NF ⇒ **charlatanisme**

charlatanesque /ʃaʀlatanɛsk/ ADJ *(de guérisseur) [méthodes, remède]* quack *(épith)*; *(de démagogue, d'escroc) [méthodes]* phoney*, bogus

charlatanisme /ʃaʀlatanism/ NM *[de guérisseur]* quackery, charlatanism; *[de politicien]* charlatanism, trickery

Charlemagne /ʃaʀləmaɲ/ NM Charlemagne

Charles /ʃaʀl/ NM Charles ◆ ~ **le Téméraire** Charles the Bold ◆ ~ **Quint** Charles the Fifth (of Spain) ◆ ~ **Martel** Charles Martel

charleston /ʃaʀlɛstɔn/ NM *(= danse)* charleston

charlot /ʃaʀlo/ NM 1 *(Ciné)* **Charlot** *(= personnage)* Charlie Chaplin; *(= film)* Charlie Chaplin film 2 *(péj) (= peu sérieux)* phoney*; *(= paresseux)* shirker, skiver*

charlotte /ʃaʀlɔt/ NF *(= gâteau)* charlotte; *(= coiffure)* mobcap

charmant, e /ʃaʀmɑ̃, ɑ̃t/ ADJ 1 *(= aimable)* *[hôte, jeune fille, employé]* charming; *[enfant]* sweet, delightful; *[sourire, manières]* charming, engaging ◆ **il s'est montré ~** he was charming ◆ **c'est un collaborateur ~** he is a charming *ou* delightful man to work with; → **prince** 2 *(= agréable)* *[séjour, soirée]* delightful, lovely ◆ **eh bien c'est ~ !** *(iro)* charming! *(iro)* ◆ **~e soirée !** *(iro)* great evening! *(iro)* 3 *(= ravissant)* *[robe, village, jeune fille, sourire]* lovely, charming

charme¹ /ʃaʀm/ NM *(= arbre)* hornbeam

charme² /ʃaʀm/ NM 1 *(= attrait)* *[de personne, musique, paysage]* charm ◆ **elle a beaucoup de ~** she has great charm ◆ **ça lui donne un certain ~** that gives him a certain charm *ou* appeal ◆ **cette vieille maison a son ~** this old house has its charm ◆ **c'est ce qui en fait (tout) le ~** that's where its attraction lies, that's what is so delightful about it ◆ **ça ne manque pas de ~** it's not without (a certain) charm ◆ **ça a peut-être du ~ pour vous, mais ...** it may appeal to you but ... ◆ **je suis assez peu sensible aux ~s d'une promenade sous la pluie** *(hum)* a walk in the rain holds few attractions for me

◆ **de charme** ◆ **chanteur de ~** crooner ◆ **émission/photos de ~** soft porn programme/photographs ◆ **magazine de ~** *(euph)* girlie* magazine ◆ **hôtel de ~** *attractive privately-run hotel* ◆ **il nous a fait son petit numéro de ~** he turned on the charm* ◆ **opération** *ou* **offensive de ~** charm offensive

2 *(= envoûtement)* spell ◆ **subir** *ou* **être sous le ~ de qn** to be under sb's spell ◆ **exercer un ~ sur qn** to have sb under one's spell ◆ **il est tombé sous son ~** he has fallen under her spell ◆ **tenir qn sous le ~ (de)** to captivate sb (with), to hold sb spellbound (with) ◆ **le ~ est rompu** the spell is broken ◆ **le public était sous le ~** the audience was spellbound

3 *(locutions)* **faire du ~** to turn *ou* switch on the charm ◆ **faire du ~ à qn** to try to charm sb, to use one's charm on sb ◆ **aller** *ou* **se porter comme un ~** to be *ou* feel as fit as a fiddle

NMPL **charmes** *(hum = attraits d'une femme)* charms *(hum)* ◆ **il doit avoir des ~s cachés** he must have hidden talents; → **commerce**

charmé, e /ʃaʀme/ (ptp de **charmer**) ADJ ◆ **être ~ de faire qch** to be delighted to do sth

charmer /ʃaʀme/ ▸ conjug 1 ◂ VT *[+ public]* to charm, to enchant; *[+ serpents]* to charm; *(†, littér) [+ peine, douleur]* to charm away ◆ **elle a des manières qui charment** she has charming *ou* delightful ways ◆ **spectacle qui charme l'oreille et le regard** performance that charms *ou* enchants both the ear and the eye

charmeur, -euse /ʃaʀmœʀ, øz/ ADJ *[sourire, manières]* winning, engaging; *[style]* charming NM,F *(= séducteur)* charmer ◆ **~ de serpent** snake charmer

charmille /ʃaʀmij/ NF arbour (Brit), arbor (US); *(= allée d'arbres)* tree-covered walk

charnel, -elle /ʃaʀnɛl/ ADJ *(frm)* *[amour, désir]* carnal ◆ **l'acte ~, l'union ~le** the carnal act *(frm)* ◆ **le contact ~** physical contact ◆ **enveloppe ~le** mortal coil ◆ **liens ~s** blood ties

charnellement /ʃaʀnɛlmɑ̃/ ADV *(frm, littér)* *[convoiter]* sexually ◆ **connaître ~** to have carnal knowledge of *(littér)* ◆ **pécher ~** to commit the sin of the flesh *(littér)*

charnier /ʃaʀnje/ NM *[de victimes]* mass grave; *(†† = ossuaire)* charnel house

charnière /ʃaʀnjɛʀ/ NF 1 *[de porte, fenêtre, coquille]* hinge; *[de timbre de collection]* (stamp) hinge; → **nom** 2 *(= transition)* turning point ◆ **époque/rôle ~** pivotal period/role ◆ **moment ~** turning point *(de* in*)*; ◆ **un parti ~** a party that occupies the middle ground ◆ **un roman ~** a novel that marks a turning point *ou* a transition ◆ **à la ~ de deux époques** at the cusp of two eras ◆ **la ville est située à la ~ de l'Occident et l'Orient** it's a city where East meets West 3 *(Mil)* pivot

charnu, e /ʃaʀny/ ADJ *[lèvres]* fleshy, thick; *[fruit, bras]* plump, fleshy; *[voix, timbre]* rich ◆ **les parties ~es du corps** the fleshy parts of the body ◆ **sur la partie ~e de son individu** *(hum)* on the fleshy part of his person *(hum)*

charognard /ʃaʀɔɲaʀ/ NM *(lit)* carrion eater; *(fig)* vulture

charogne /ʃaʀɔɲ/ NF *(= cadavre)* carrion *(NonC)*, decaying carcass; *(* = salaud) (femme)* bitch**; *(homme)* bastard**, sod** *(Brit)*

charolais, e /ʃaʀɔlɛ, ɛz/ ADJ of *ou* from Charolais NM **Charolais** 1 **le Charolais** *(= région)* Charolais 2 *(= viande)* ~ Charolais beef NM,F *(= bétail)* Charolais

charpente /ʃaʀpɑ̃t/ NF 1 *[de bâtiment]* frame(work), skeleton; *[de toit]* (roof) structure ◆ **~ en bois/métallique** timber/steel frame(work); → **bois** 2 *[de feuille]* skeleton; *[de roman]* structure, framework ◆ **le squelette est la ~ du corps** the skeleton is the framework of the body 3 *(= carrure)* build, frame ◆ **quelle solide ~ !** he's well-built! ◆ **~ fragile/épaisse** fragile/stocky build

charpenté, e /ʃaʀpɑ̃te/ ADJ *[vin]* robust ◆ **bien/solidement ~** *[personne]* well/solidly built; *[texte, argumentation]* well/solidly structured

charpentier /ʃaʀpɑ̃tje/ NM *(Constr)* carpenter ◆ **~ de marine** shipwright

charpie /ʃaʀpi/ NF 1 *(Hist = pansement)* shredded linen *(used to dress wounds)* 2 *(locutions)* **c'est de la ~** *[viande]* it's been cooked to shreds; *[vêtements]* they're (all) in shreds *ou* ribbons, they're falling to pieces ◆ **mettre** *ou* **réduire en ~** *[+ papier, vêtements]* *(= déchirer)* to tear to shreds; *[+ viande]* *(= hacher menu)* to mince ◆ **je vais le mettre en ~ !** I'll tear him to shreds!, I'll make mincemeat of him! ◆ **il s'est fait mettre en ~ par le train** he was mangled by the train

charre* /ʃaʀ/ NM ⇒ **char²**

charretée /ʃaʀte/ NF *(lit)* cartload *(de* of*)*; ◆ **une ~ de*, des ~s de*** *(= grande quantité de)* loads* *ou* stacks* of

charretier, -ière /ʃaʀtje, jɛʀ/ NM,F carter ◆ **de ~** *(péj)* *[langage, manières]* coarse; → **chemin, jurer**

charrette /ʃaʀɛt/ NF 1 *(lit)* cart ◆ **~ à bras** handcart, barrow ◆ **~ anglaise** dogcart ◆ **~ des condamnés** tumbril ◆ **il a fait partie de la dernière ~** *(= licenciements)* he went in the last round of redundancies *(Brit)* *ou* lay-offs 2 *(= travail urgent)* urgent job *ou* piece of work ◆ **faire une ~*** to work flat out* ◆ **être (en pleine) ~*** to be working against the clock

charriage /ʃaʀjaʒ/ NM 1 *(= transport)* carriage, cartage 2 *(Géol = déplacement)* overthrusting; → **nappe**

charrier /ʃaʀje/ ▸ conjug 7 ◂ VT 1 *(= transporter)* *(dans une brouette, sur le dos)* to cart (along); *[camion]* to carry, to cart ◆ **on a passé des heures à ~ du charbon** we spent hours heaving *ou* carting coal

2 *(= entraîner)* *[fleuve, coulée, avalanche]* to carry *ou* sweep along ◆ **le ciel** *ou* **le vent charriait de lourds nuages** *(littér)* the wind sent heavy clouds scudding across the sky ◆ **l'idéologie qu'il charrie** *(péj)* the ideology he propounds ◆ **les obscénités charriées par ses romans** the obscenities with which his novels are littered

3 **~ qn*** *(= taquiner qn)* to tease sb, to take the mickey out of sb* *(Brit)*; *(= raconter des histoires à qn)* to kid sb*, to have sb on* *(Brit)*, to put sb on* *(US)*

VI * *(= abuser)* to go too far, to overstep the mark; *(= plaisanter)* to be kidding*, to be joking* ◆ **tu charries, elle n'est pas si vieille !** come on* *ou* come off it* *(Brit)* – she's not that old! ◆ **faut pas** *ou* **faudrait pas ~ !** that's a bit much! *ou* rich!* *(Brit)*

charrieur, -euse* /ʃaʀjœʀ, øz/ NM,F ◆ **c'est un ~** *(= il abuse)* he's always going too far *ou* overstepping the mark; *(= il plaisante)* he's always having *(Brit)* *ou* putting *(US)* people on* ◆ **il est un peu ~** he's a bit of a joker*

charroi †† /ʃaʀwa/ NM *(= transport)* cartage

charron /ʃaʀɔ̃/ NM cartwright, wheelwright

charroyer /ʃaʀwaje/ ▸ conjug 8 ◂ VT *(littér)* *(par charrette)* to cart; *(laborieusement)* to cart (along), to heave (along)

charrue /ʃaʀy/ NF plough *(Brit)*, plow *(US)* ◆ **mettre la ~ devant** *ou* **avant les bœufs** *(fig)* to put the cart before the horse

charte /ʃaʀt/ NF *(Hist, Pol = convention)* charter; *(Hist = titre, contrat)* title, deed ◆ **accorder une ~ à** to grant a charter to, to charter ◆ **la Charte des Nations unies** the United Nations Charter ◆ **l'École (nationale) des ~s, les Chartes** the École des Chartes *(French national school of archival studies and palaeography)*

charter /ʃaʀtɛʀ/ NM *(= vol)* charter flight; *(= avion)* charter(ed) plane ADJ INV *[vol, billet, prix]* charter *(épith)* ◆ **avion ~** charter(ed) plane

chartisme /ʃaʀtism/ NM *(Pol Brit)* Chartism

chartiste /ʃaʀtist/ ADJ *(Pol Brit)* Chartist NMF *(= élève)* student of the École des Chartes; *(Pol Brit)* Chartist; *(= analyste)* chartist

chartreuse /ʃaʀtʀøz/ NF *(= liqueur)* chartreuse; *(= couvent)* Charterhouse, Carthusian monastery; *(= religieuse)* Carthusian nun

chartreux /ʃaʀtʀø/ NM *(= religieux)* Carthusian monk; *(= chat)* Chartreux

Charybde /kaʀibd/ NM Charybdis ◆ **tomber de ~ en Scylla** to jump out of the frying pan into the fire

chas /ʃɑ/ NM eye *(of needle)*

chasse¹ /ʃas/ NF 1 *(gén)* hunting; *(au fusil)* shooting, hunting ◆ **aller à la ~** *(gén)* to go hunting; *(avec fusil)* to go shooting *ou* hunting ◆ **aller à la ~ aux papillons** to go catching butterflies ◆ **~ au faisan** pheasant shooting ◆ **~ au lapin** rabbit shooting, rabbiting ◆ **~ au renard/au chamois/au gros gibier** fox/chamois/big game hunting ◆ **air/habits de ~** hunting tune/clothes; → **chien, cor¹, fusil** *etc*

2 *(= période)* *(gén)* hunting season; *(au fusil)* hunting season, shooting season ◆ **la ~ est ouverte/fermée** it's the open/close season *(Brit)*, it's open/closed season *(US)*

3 *(= gibier)* game ◆ **manger/partager la ~** to eat/share the game ◆ **faire (une) bonne ~** to get a good bag ◆ **bonne ~ !** *(lit)* have a good day's shooting!; *(fig)* happy hunting!

4 *(= domaine)* shoot, hunting ground ◆ **louer une ~** to rent a shoot, to rent land to shoot *ou* hunt on ◆ **une ~ giboyeuse** a well-stocked shoot

5 *(= chasseurs)* **la ~** the hunt

6 *(= avions)* **la ~** the fighters; → **avion, pilote**

7 *(= poursuite)* chase ◆ **une ~ effrénée dans les rues** a frantic chase through the streets

8 *(locutions)* **faire la ~ à** *[+ souris, moustiques]* to hunt down, to chase; *[+ abus, erreurs]* to hunt down, to track down ◆ **faire la ~ aux appartements/occasions** to go flat- *(Brit)* *ou* apartment- *(US)*/bargain-hunting ◆ **faire la ~ au**

mari to be searching *ou* looking for a husband, to be in search of a husband ◆ **prendre en ~, donner la ~ à** *[+ fuyard, voiture]* to give chase to, to chase after; *[+ avion, navire, ennemi]* to give chase to ◆ **donner la ~** to give chase ◆ **se mettre en ~ pour trouver qch** to go hunting for sth ◆ **être en ~** *[chienne]* to be on *(Brit) ou* in *(US)* heat; *[chien]* to be on the trail ◆ **qui va à la ~ perd sa place** *(Prov)* he who leaves his place loses it

COMP **chasse à l'affût** hunting (from a hide *(Brit) ou* blind *(US)*)
chasse au chevreuil deer hunting, deer-stalking
chasse à courre *(= sport)* hunting with hounds; *(= partie de chasse)* hunt
chasse au furet ferreting
chasse gardée *(lit)* private hunting (ground), private shoot; *(fig)* exclusive preserve *ou* domain ◆ **elle est mignonne – attention, c'est ~ gardée !** she's cute – hands off! she's already spoken for *ou* taken* ◆ **"chasse gardée"** *(panneau)* "private, poachers will be prosecuted"
chasse à l'homme manhunt
chasse aux sorcières witch hunt ◆ **faire la ~ aux sorcières** to conduct a witch hunt
chasse sous-marine harpooning, harpoon fishing
chasse de têtes headhunting
chasse à tir shooting
chasse au trésor treasure hunt

chasse[2] /ʃas/ **NF** [1] ◆ **~ (d'eau *ou* des cabinets)** (toilet) flush ◆ **actionner *ou* tirer la ~** to flush the toilet; *(avec chaîne)* to pull the chain [2] *(Typo)* body (width), set (width)

chassé /ʃase/ **NM** *(= danse)* chassé

châsse /ʃɑs/ **NF** *(= reliquaire)* reliquary, shrine; (** *= œil)* eye, peeper*; *(= monture) [de bague, bijou]* setting; *[de lancette]* handle

chasse-clou (pl **chasse-clous**) /ʃasklu/ **NM** nail punch

chassé-croisé (pl **chassés-croisés**) /ʃasekʀwaze/ **NM** [1] *(Danse)* chassé-croisé, set to partners [2] *(fig)* **avec tous ces chassés-croisés nous ne nous sommes pas vus depuis six mois** with all these to-ings and fro-ings we haven't seen each other for six months ◆ **une période de chassés-croisés sur les routes** a period of heavy two-way traffic ◆ **les ferries vont et viennent en un ~ régulier** the ferries ply to and fro continuously

chasselas /ʃasla/ **NM** chasselas grape

chasse-mouche (pl **chasse-mouches**) /ʃasmuʃ/ **NM** flyswatter, fly whisk *(Brit)*

chasse-neige (pl **chasse-neige(s)**) /ʃasnɛʒ/ **NM** *(= instrument)* snowplough *(Brit)*, snowplow *(US)*; *(= position du skieur)* snowplough *(Brit)*, snowplow *(US)*, wedge ◆ **~ à soufflerie** snowblower ◆ **descendre une pente en ~** to snowplough *(Brit) ou* snowplow *(US)* down a slope

chasse-pierres /ʃaspjɛʀ/ **NM INV** cowcatcher

chassepot /ʃaspo/ **NM** *(Hist)* chassepot (rifle)

chasser /ʃase/ ► conjug 1 ◄ **VT** [1] *(gén)* to hunt; *(au fusil)* to shoot, to hunt ◆ **~ à l'affût/au filet** to hunt from a hide *(Brit) ou* blind *(US)*/with a net ◆ **~ le faisan/le cerf** to go pheasant-shooting/deer hunting ◆ **il chasse le lion en Afrique** he is shooting lions *ou* lionshooting in Africa ◆ **il chasse de race** *(il est dans la lignée)* it runs in the family, he is carrying on the family tradition; → **chien**

[2] *(= faire partir) [+ importun, animal, ennemi]* to drive *ou* chase out *ou* away; *[+ domestique, fils indigne]* to turn out; *[+ immigrant]* to drive out, to expel; *[+ touristes, clients]* to drive away, to chase away ◆ **chassant de la main les insectes** brushing away *ou* driving off (the) insects with his hand ◆ **il a chassé les gamins du jardin** he chased *ou* drove the kids out of the garden ◆ **mon père m'a chassé de la maison** my father has turned *ou* thrown me out of the house ◆ **le brouillard nous a chassés de la plage** we were driven off the beach by the fog ◆ **ces touristes, ils vont finir par nous ~ de chez nous** these tourists will end up driving us away from our own homes ◆ **il a été chassé de son pays par le nazisme** he was forced to flee his country because of the Nazis, Nazism drove him from his country ◆ **chassez le naturel, il revient au galop** *(Prov)* what's bred in the bone comes out in the flesh *(Prov)* → **faim**

[3] *(= dissiper) [+ odeur]* to dispel, to drive away; *[+ idée]* to dismiss, to chase away; *[+ souci, doute]* to dispel, to drive away, to chase away; *[+ brouillard]* to dispel ◆ **essayant de ~ ces images obsédantes** trying to chase away *ou* dismiss these haunting images ◆ **il faut ~ cette idée de ta tête** you must get that idea out of your head *ou* dismiss that idea from your mind ◆ **le soleil a chassé les nuages** the sun has chased the clouds away

[4] *[+ clou]* to drive in

[5] *(= éjecter) [+ douille, eau d'un tuyau]* to drive out; → **clou**

VI [1] *(= aller à la chasse) (gén)* to go hunting; *(au fusil)* to go shooting *ou* hunting ◆ **~ sur les terres de qn** *(fig)* to poach on sb's territory

[2] *(= déraper) [véhicule, roues]* to skid; *[ancre]* to drag ◆ **~ sur ses ancres** to drag its anchors

> ⚠ **chasser** se traduit par **to chase** uniquement au sens de 'courir après'.

chasseresse /ʃasʀɛs/ **NF** *(littér)* huntress *(littér)*; → **Diane**

chasseur /ʃasœʀ/ **NM** [1] *(gén)* hunter; *(à courre)* hunter, huntsman ◆ **~-cueilleur** *(Anthropologie)* hunter-gatherer ◆ **~ de baleines** whaler ◆ **~ de phoques** sealer ◆ **~ de papillons** butterfly catcher ◆ **c'est un très bon ~** *(gén)* he's a very good hunter; *(au fusil)* he's an excellent shot ◆ **c'est un grand ~ de renards** he's a great one for foxhunting, he's a great foxhunter

[2] *(Mil) (= soldat)* chasseur; *(= avion)* fighter ◆ **le 3e ~** *(= régiment)* the 3rd (regiment of) chasseurs

[3] *(= garçon d'hôtel)* page (boy), messenger (boy), bellboy *(US)*

[4] *(Culin)* **poulet/lapin ~** chicken/rabbit chasseur *(chicken/rabbit cooked with mushrooms and white wine)*

COMP **chasseur alpin** mountain infantryman ◆ **les ~s alpins** the mountain infantry, the alpine chasseurs
chasseur d'autographes autograph hunter
chasseur à cheval *(Hist Mil)* cavalryman ◆ **les ~s à cheval** the cavalry
chasseur d'images roving amateur photographer
chasseur de mines minesweeper
chasseur à pied *(Hist Mil)* infantryman ◆ **les ~s à pied** the infantry
chasseur de primes bounty hunter
chasseur à réaction jet fighter
chasseur de sous-marins submarine chaser
chasseur de têtes *(lit, fig)* headhunter

chasseur-bombardier (pl **chasseurs-bombardiers**) /ʃasœʀbɔ̃baʀdje/ **NM** fighter-bomber

chasseuse /ʃasøz/ **NF** huntswoman, hunter, huntress *(littér)*

chassie /ʃasi/ **NF** *[de yeux]* sticky matter *(in eye)*, sleep*

chassieux, -ieuse /ʃasjø, jøz/ **ADJ** *[yeux]* sticky, gummy; *[personne, animal]* gummy- *ou* sticky-eyed ◆ **avoir les yeux ~** to have sleep* in one's eyes

châssis /ʃɑsi/ **NM** [1] *[de véhicule]* chassis; *[de machine]* sub- *ou* under-frame [2] *(= encadrement) [de fenêtre]* frame; *[de toile, tableau]* stretcher; *(Typo)* chase; *(Photo)* (printing) frame ◆ **~ mobile/dormant** opening/fixed frame [3] (** *= corps féminin)* body, figure, chassis** *(US)* ◆ **elle a un beau ~ !** she's got a hell of a figure!** [4] *(pour cultures)* cold frame

chaste /ʃast/ **ADJ** chaste; *(hum) [oreilles]* delicate ◆ **de ~s jeunes filles** chaste young girls ◆ **mener une vie ~** to lead a celibate life, to live the life of a nun *(ou* a monk)

chastement /ʃastəmɑ̃/ **ADV** chastely

chasteté /ʃastəte/ **NF** chastity; → **ceinture**

chasuble /ʃazybl/ **NF** chasuble; → **robe**

chat[1] /ʃa/ **NM** [1] *(= animal)* cat ◆ **~ persan/siamois** Persian/Siamese cat ◆ **petit ~** kitten ◆ **mon petit ~** *(terme d'affection, à un enfant)* pet*, poppet* *(Brit)*; *(à une femme)* sweetie*

[2] *(= jeu)* tag, tig *(Brit)* ◆ **jouer à ~** to play tag *ou* tig *(Brit)*, to have a game of tag *ou* tig *(Brit)* ◆ **(c'est toi le) ~ !** you're it!

[3] *(locutions)* **il n'y avait pas un ~ dehors** there wasn't a soul outside ◆ **avoir un ~ dans la gorge** to have a frog in one's throat ◆ **il a acheté cette voiture ~ en poche** he bought a pig in a poke when he got that car, he hardly even looked at the car before buying it ◆ **jouer au ~ et à la souris** to play cat and mouse ◆ **j'ai d'autres ~s à fouetter** I've other fish to fry ◆ **il n'y a pas de quoi fouetter un ~** it's nothing to make a fuss about ◆ **~ échaudé craint l'eau froide** *(Prov)* once bitten, twice shy *(Prov)* ◆ **quand le ~ n'est pas là les souris dansent** *(Prov)* when the cat's away the mice will play *(Prov)* ◆ **à bon ~ bon rat** *(Prov)* tit for tat; → **appeler, chien** *etc*

COMP **chat de gouttière** ordinary cat, alley cat
chat à neuf queues cat-o'-nine-tails
chat perché *(= jeu)* off-ground tag *ou* tig *(Brit)*
chat sauvage wildcat

chat[2] /tʃat/ **NM** *(Internet)* chat ◆ **sur le ~** on a chat line

châtaigne /ʃɑtɛɲ/ **NF** [1] *(= fruit)* (sweet) chestnut ◆ **~ d'eau** water chestnut [2] (** *= coup de poing)* punch, clout* *(Brit)* ◆ **flanquer une ~ à qn** to punch *ou* clout* *(Brit)* sb, to give sb a clout* *(Brit)* [3] *(* = décharge électrique)* (electric) shock

châtaigneraie /ʃɑtɛɲʀɛ/ **NF** chestnut grove

châtaignier /ʃɑteɲe/ **NM** *(= arbre)* (sweet) chestnut tree; *(= bois)* chestnut

châtain /ʃɑtɛ̃/ **NM** chestnut brown **ADJ M** *[cheveux]* chestnut (brown); *[personne]* brown-haired ◆ **elle est ~ clair/roux** she has light brown hair/auburn hair

château (pl **châteaux**) /ʃɑto/ **NM** [1] *(= forteresse)* castle; *(= résidence royale)* palace, castle; *(= gentilhommière)* mansion, stately home; *(en France)* château; *(= vignoble)* château ◆ **les ~x de la Loire** the châteaux of the Loire ◆ **le ~ de Versailles** the Palace of Versailles ◆ **bâtir *ou* faire des ~x en Espagne** *(fig)* to build castles in the air *ou* in Spain ◆ **il est un peu ~ branlant** he's not very steady on his legs, he's a bit wobbly on his pins* *(Brit)*; → **vie** [2] *(* : Culin)* chateaubriand

COMP **château d'arrière** *(Naut)* aftercastle
château d'avant *(Naut)* forecastle, fo'c'sle
château de cartes *(Cartes, fig)* house of cards
château d'eau water tower
château fort stronghold, fortified castle
château de sable sand castle

chateaubriand, châteaubriant /ʃatobʀijɑ̃/ **NM** *(Culin)* chateaubriand, chateaubriant

Château-la-Pompe /ʃatolapɔ̃p/ **NM INV** *(hum)* water

châtelain /ʃɑt(ə)lɛ̃/ NM 1 *(Hist = seigneur)* (feudal) lord ◆ **le ~** the lord of the manor 2 *(= propriétaire) (d'ancienne date)* squire; *(nouveau riche)* owner of a manor

châtelaine /ʃɑt(ə)lɛn/ NF 1 *(= propriétaire)* owner of a manor 2 *(= épouse)* lady (of the manor), chatelaine 3 *(= ceinture)* chatelaine, châtelaine

chat-huant (pl **chats-huants**) /ʃayɑ̃/ NM screech owl, barn owl

châtié, e /ʃɑtje/ (ptp de **châtier**) ADJ *[style]* polished, refined; *[langage]* refined

châtier /ʃɑtje/ ▸ conjug 7 ◂ VT 1 *(littér = punir) [+ coupable]* to chastise *(littér)*, to castigate *(littér)*, to punish; *[+ faute]* to punish; *(Rel) [+ corps]* to chasten, to mortify ◆ **~ l'insolence de qn** to chastise *ou* punish sb for his insolence; → **qui** 2 *(= soigner) [+ style]* to polish, to refine; *[+ langage]* to refine

chatière /ʃatjɛʀ/ NF *(= porte)* cat-flap; *(= trou d'aération)* (air-)vent, ventilation hole; *(= piège)* cat-trap

châtiment /ʃɑtimɑ̃/ NM *(littér)* chastisement *(littér)*, castigation *(littér)*, punishment ◆ **~ corporel** corporal punishment

chatoiement /ʃatwamɑ̃/ NM *[de vitraux]* glistening; *[de reflet, étoffe]* shimmer(ing); *[de bijoux, plumage]* glistening, shimmer(ing); *[de couleurs, style]* sparkle

chaton[1] /ʃatɔ̃/ NM 1 *(= petit chat)* kitten 2 *(= fleur)* catkin ◆ **~s de poussière** balls of fluff

chaton[2] /ʃatɔ̃/ NM *(= monture)* bezel, setting; *(= pierre)* stone

chatouille* /ʃatuj/ NF tickle ◆ **faire des ~s à qn** to tickle sb ◆ **craindre les ~s** *ou* **la ~** to be ticklish

chatouillement /ʃatujmɑ̃/ NM *(gén)* tickling *(NonC)*; *(dans le nez, la gorge)* tickle

chatouiller /ʃatuje/ ▸ conjug 1 ◂ VT 1 *(lit)* to tickle ◆ **arrête, ça chatouille !** don't, that tickles! *ou* you're tickling! 2 *[+ amour-propre, curiosité]* to tickle, to titillate; *[+ palais, odorat]* to titillate 3 *(† ou hum)* **~ les côtes à qn** to tan sb's hide

chatouilleux, -euse /ʃatujø, øz/ ADJ 1 *(lit)* ticklish 2 *(= susceptible) [personne, caractère]* touchy ◆ **il est un peu ~ sur le sujet** he's a bit touchy about it

chatouillis* /ʃatuji/ NM light *ou* gentle tickling ◆ **faire des ~ à qn** to tickle sb lightly *ou* gently

chatoyant, e /ʃatwajɑ̃, ɑ̃t/ ADJ *[reflet, étoffe, bijoux, plumage]* shimmering; *[couleurs, style]* sparkling ◆ **l'éclat ~ des pierreries** the way the gems sparkle in the light

chatoyer /ʃatwaje/ ▸ conjug 8 ◂ VI *[vitraux]* to glisten; *[reflet, étoffe]* to shimmer; *[bijoux, plumage]* to glisten, to shimmer; *[couleurs, style]* to sparkle

châtré* /ʃɑtʀe/ NM *(lit, fig)* eunuch ◆ **voix de ~** squeaky little voice

châtrer /ʃɑtʀe/ ▸ conjug 1 ◂ VT *[+ taureau, cheval]* to castrate, to geld; *[+ chat]* to neuter, to castrate, to fix *(US)*; *[+ homme]* to castrate, to emasculate; *(littér) [+ texte]* to mutilate, to bowdlerize

chatte /ʃat/ NF *(= animal)* (female) cat; *(**= vagin)* pussy** ◆ **elle est très ~** she's very kittenish ◆ **ma (petite) ~** *(terme d'affection)* (my) pet*, sweetie(-pie)*

chatter /tʃate/ VI to chat *(on the Net)*

chatterie /ʃatʀi/ NF *(= friandise)* titbit, dainty morsel ◆ **aimer les ~s** to love a little delicacy *ou* a dainty morsel NFPL **chatteries** † *(= caresses)* playful attentions *ou* caresses; *(= minauderies)* kittenish ways ◆ **faire des ~s à qn** to make a fuss of sb

chatterton /ʃatɛʀtɔn/ NM (adhesive) insulating tape

chatteur, -euse /tʃatœʀ, øz/ NM, F chatter

chat-tigre (pl **chats-tigres**) /ʃatigʀ/ NM tiger cat

chaud, chaude /ʃo, ʃod/ ADJ 1 *[température]* warm; *(très chaud)* hot ◆ **les climats ~s** warm climates; *(très chaud)* hot climates ◆ **l'eau du lac n'est pas assez ~e pour se baigner** the lake isn't warm enough for bathing ◆ **bois ton thé pendant qu'il est ~** drink your tea while it's hot ◆ **repas ~** hot meal ◆ **tous les plats étaient servis très ~s** all the dishes were served up piping hot ◆ **cela sort tout ~ du four** it's (piping) hot from the oven ◆ **il a des nouvelles toutes ~es** he's got some news hot from the press *ou* some hot news ◆ **sa place est encore ~e et il y en a déjà qui se pressent pour le remplacer** he's only just left and some people can't wait to step into his shoes; → **battre, main** *etc*

2 *[couverture, vêtement]* warm

3 *(= vif, passionné) [félicitations]* warm, hearty; *(littér) [amitié]* warm; *[partisan]* keen, ardent; *[admirateur]* warm, ardent; *[recommandation]* wholehearted, enthusiastic; *[discussion]* heated ◆ **la bataille a été ~e** it was a fierce battle, the battle was fast and furious ◆ **être ~ (pour faire/pour qch)*** to be enthusiastic (about doing/about sth), to be keen (on doing/on sth) *(Brit)* ◆ **il n'est pas très ~ pour conduire de nuit*** he doesn't much like driving at night, he is not very *ou* too keen *(Brit)* on driving at night

4 *(= difficile)* **les endroits ~s de la ville** the city's trouble spots ◆ **les points ~s du globe** the world's hot spots *ou* flashpoints ◆ **la rentrée sera ~e** there's going to be a lot of social unrest in the autumn ◆ **l'alerte a été ~e** it was a near *ou* close thing

5 *[voix, couleur]* warm

6 *(* = sensuel) [personne, tempérament]* hot, randy* *(Brit)* ◆ **quartier ~** red-light district ◆ **c'est un ~ lapin !** he's a bit of a skirt chaser!*, he's a randy devil!* *(Brit)*

7 *(Phys Nucl) [produits, zone]* hot

NM *(= chaleur)* ◆ **le ~** (the) heat ◆ **elle souffre autant du ~ que du froid** she suffers as much from the heat as from the cold

◆ **au chaud** ◆ **restez donc au ~** stay in the warm ◆ **garder** *ou* **tenir qch au ~** *(lit, fig)* to keep sth warm *ou* hot ◆ **garder un enfant enrhumé au ~** to keep a child with a cold (indoors) in the warmth

◆ **à chaud** ◆ **travailler à ~** *(lit)* to work under heat *(fig)* to work on the spot ◆ **réaction à ~** knee-jerk reaction ◆ **reportage à ~** on-the-spot report ◆ **il a été opéré à ~** he had an emergency operation; → **souder**

ADV ◆ **avoir ~** to be warm, to feel warm; *(très chaud)* to be hot, to feel hot ◆ **avez-vous assez ~ ?** are you warm enough? ◆ **on a trop ~ ici** it's too hot in here ◆ **j'ai eu ~ !*** *(= de la chance)* I had a lucky *ou* narrow escape, it was a close shave ◆ **il fait ~** it's hot *ou* warm ◆ **il fera ~ le jour où il voudra bien travailler*** that'll be the day when he decides to work ◆ **ça ne me fait ni ~ ni froid** I couldn't care less, it makes no difference to me ◆ **ça fait ~ au cœur** it's heart-warming ◆ **manger ~** to have a hot meal, to eat something hot ◆ **boire ~** to have *ou* take hot drinks ◆ **il a fallu tellement attendre qu'on n'a pas pu manger ~** we had to wait so long the food had gone cold ◆ **"servir chaud"** "serve hot" ◆ **~ devant !** mind your back (*ou* backs)! ◆ **une robe qui tient ~** a warm dress ◆ **tenir trop ~ à qn** to make sb too hot ◆ **ça m'a donné ~** *[course]* it made me really hot; → **souffler**

NF **chaude** *(† = flambée)* blaze

COMP **chaud et froid** *(Méd)* chill

chaudement /ʃodmɑ̃/ ADV *[s'habiller]* warmly; *[féliciter, recommander]* warmly, heartily; *[argumenter]* heatedly, hotly ◆ **~ disputé** hotly disputed ◆ **comment ça va ? – ~ !** *(hum)* how are you? – (I'm) hot!

chaude-pisse* (pl **chaudes-pisses**) /ʃodpis/ NF clap**

chaud-froid (pl **chauds-froids**) /ʃofʀwɑ/ NM *(Culin)* chaudfroid

chaudière /ʃodjɛʀ/ NF *[de locomotive, chauffage central]* boiler ◆ **~ à gaz** gas-fired boiler

chaudron /ʃodʀɔ̃/ NM cauldron

chaudronnerie /ʃodʀɔnʀi/ NF 1 *(= métier)* boilermaking, boilerwork; *(= industrie)* boilermaking industry 2 *(= boutique)* coppersmith's workshop; *(= usine)* boilerworks 3 *(= produits)* **grosse ~** industrial boilers ◆ **petite ~** pots and pans

chaudronnier, -ière /ʃodʀɔnje, jɛʀ/ NM,F *(= artisan)* coppersmith; *(= ouvrier)* boilermaker

chauffage /ʃofaʒ/ NM *(= action)* heating; *(= appareils)* heating (system) ◆ **il y a le ~ ?** is there any heating?, is it heated? ◆ **avoir un bon ~** to have a good heating system ◆ **~ au charbon/au gaz/à l'électricité** solid fuel/gas/electric heating ◆ **~ central** central heating ◆ **~ par le sol** underfloor heating ◆ **~ urbain** urban *ou* district heating system ◆ **mets le ~** *(maison)* put the heating on; *(voiture)* put the heater on; → **bois**

chauffagiste /ʃofaʒist/ NM heating engineer *ou* specialist

chauffant, e /ʃofɑ̃, ɑ̃t/ ADJ *[surface, élément]* heating *(épith)*; → **couverture, plaque**

chauffard* /ʃofaʀ/ NM *(péj)* reckless driver; *(qui s'enfuit)* hit-and-run driver ◆ **(espèce de) ~ !** roadhog!* ◆ **c'est un vrai ~** he's a real menace *ou* maniac on the roads ◆ **tué par un ~** killed by a reckless driver ◆ **on n'a pas retrouvé le ~ responsable de l'accident** the driver responsible for the accident has not yet been found

chauffe /ʃof/ NF *(= lieu)* fire-chamber; *(= processus)* stoking ◆ **surface de ~** heating-surface, fire surface ◆ **chambre de ~** *(Naut)* stokehold ◆ **tour de ~** *[de voiture de course]* warm-up lap; *[de candidat, sportif]* practice run; → **bleu**

chauffe-assiette(s) (pl **chauffe-assiettes**) /ʃofasjɛt/ NM plate-warmer

chauffe-bain (pl **chauffe-bains**) /ʃofbɛ̃/ NM water-heater

chauffe-biberon (pl **chauffe-biberons**) /ʃofbibʀɔ̃/ NM bottle-warmer

chauffe-eau /ʃofo/ NM INV *(gén)* water-heater; *(électrique)* immersion heater

chauffe-pieds /ʃofpje/ NM INV foot-warmer

chauffe-plat (pl **chauffe-plats**) /ʃofpla/ NM dish-warmer, chafing dish

chauffer /ʃofe/ ▸ conjug 1 ◂ VT 1 ◆ **(faire) ~** *[+ soupe]* to warm up, to heat up; *[+ assiette]* to warm; *[+ eau du bain]* to heat (up); *[+ eau du thé]* to boil, to heat up ◆ **~ qch au four** to heat sth up in the oven, to put sth in the oven to heat up ◆ **mets l'eau à ~** *(gén)* put the water on; *(dans une bouilloire)* put the water on to boil, put the kettle on ◆ **faites ~ la colle !** *(hum : quand on casse qch)* get the glue out! ◆ **je vais te ~ les oreilles !** I'll box your ears!, you'll get a clip round the ear!* *(Brit)*

2 *[+ appartement]* to heat ◆ **on va ~ un peu la pièce** we'll heat (up) the room a bit

3 *[soleil]* to warm, to make warm; *[soleil brûlant]* to heat, to make hot

4 *[+ métal, verre, liquide]* to heat; *[+ chaudière, locomotive]* to stoke (up), to fire ◆ **~ qch à blanc** *(lit, fig)* to make sth white-hot ◆ **~ qn à blanc** to galvanize sb into action ◆ **le public était**

chauffé à blanc excitement in the audience had reached fever pitch
5 (* = préparer) [+ candidat] to cram; [+ commando] to train up; [+ salle, public] to warm up
6 [+ muscle] to warm up
7 (* = énerver) **tu commences à me ~ sérieusement !** you're really starting to get on my nerves!
8 (* = draguer) **elle l'a chauffé toute la soirée** she spent the whole evening trying to pick him up *
9 († * = voler) to pinch *, to swipe *
VI 1 (= être sur le feu) [aliment, eau du bain] to be heating up, to be warming up; [assiette] to be warming (up); [eau du thé] to be heating up
2 (= devenir chaud) [moteur, télévision] to warm up; [four] to heat up; [chaudière, locomotive] to get up steam
3 (= devenir trop chaud) [freins, appareil, moteur] to overheat
4 (= donner de la chaleur) **le soleil chauffe** the sun's really hot ◆ **le poêle chauffe bien** the stove gives out a lot of heat ◆ **ils chauffent au charbon** they use coal for heating ◆ **le mazout chauffe bien** oil gives out a lot of heat
5 (*; locutions) **ça chauffe** (il y a de la bagarre) things are getting heated; (il y a de l'ambiance) things are livening up ◆ **ça va ~ !** sparks will fly! ◆ **le but/l'essai chauffe!** there must be a goal/try now!, they're on the brink of a goal/try! ◆ **tu chauffes !** (cache-tampon) you're getting warm(er)!
VPR **se chauffer** 1 (près du feu) to warm o.s.; (* : en faisant des exercices) to warm up ◆ **se ~ au soleil** to warm o.s. in the sun ◆ **se ~ la voix** to warm up
2 (= avoir comme chauffage) **se ~ au bois/charbon** to burn wood/coal, to use wood/coal for heating ◆ **se ~ à l'électricité** to have electric heating; → **bois**

chaufferette /ʃofʀɛt/ NF (= chauffe-pieds) foot-warmer; (= réchaud) plate warmer

chaufferie /ʃofʀi/ NF [de maison, usine] boiler room; [de navire] stokehold

chauffeur /ʃofœʀ/ NM 1 (= conducteur) (gén) driver; (privé) chauffeur ◆ **~ d'autobus** bus driver ◆ **voiture avec/sans ~** chauffeur-driven/self-drive car 2 [de chaudière] fireman, stoker
COMP **chauffeur de camion** lorry (Brit) ou truck (US) driver
chauffeur du dimanche (hum) Sunday driver
chauffeur livreur delivery driver
chauffeur de maître chauffeur
chauffeur de taxi taxi driver, cab driver

chauffeuse /ʃoføz/ NF low armless chair, unit chair

chaulage /ʃolaʒ/ NM [de sol, arbre, raisins] liming; [de mur] whitewashing

chauler /ʃole/ ▸ conjug 1 ◂ VT [+ sol, arbre, raisins] to lime; [+ mur] to whitewash

chaume /ʃom/ NM 1 (= reste des tiges) stubble ◆ **les ~s** (littér = champs) the stubble fields 2 (= toiture) thatch ◆ **couvrir de ~** to thatch; → **toit**

chaumer /ʃome/ ▸ conjug 1 ◂ VT to clear stubble from VI to clear the stubble

chaumière /ʃomjɛʀ/ NF (littér ou hum) (little) cottage; (à toit de chaume) thatched cottage ◆ **on en parlera encore longtemps dans les ~s** people will talk about it for a long time to come ◆ **ça fait pleurer dans les ~s** [feuilleton, film] it's a real tear-jerker * ◆ **il ne rêve que d'une ~ et d'un cœur** he only dreams of the simple life

chaumine /ʃomin/ NF (littér ou †) small (thatched) cottage

chaussant, e /ʃosɑ̃, ɑt/ ADJ (= confortable) well-fitting, snug-fitting ◆ **articles ~s** footwear (NonC) ◆ **ces souliers sont très ~s** these shoes are a very good fit ou fit very well

chausse /ʃos/ NF (= entonnoir) linen funnel NFPL **chausses** (Hist) hose

chaussée /ʃose/ NF 1 (= route, rue) road, roadway ◆ **traverser la ~** to cross the road ◆ **ne reste pas sur la ~** don't stay in ou on the road ou on the roadway ◆ **l'entretien de la ~** road maintenance ◆ **~ pavée** (= rue) cobbled street; (= route) cobbled ou flagged road ◆ **~ bombée** cambered road ◆ **"chaussée glissante"** "slippery road" ◆ **"chaussée déformée"** "uneven road surface"; → **pont** 2 (= chemin surélevé) causeway; (= digue) embankment ◆ **la ~ des Géants** the Giants' Causeway

chausse-pied (pl **chausse-pieds**) /ʃospje/ NM shoehorn

chausser /ʃose/ ▸ conjug 1 ◂ VT 1 (= mettre des chaussures à) [+ personne] to put shoes on; (= acheter des chaussures à) to buy shoes for ◆ **chausse les enfants pour sortir** put the children's shoes on ou help the children on with their shoes and we'll go out ◆ **chaussé de bottes/sandales** wearing boots/sandals, with boots/sandals on; → **cordonnier**
2 (= mettre) [+ chaussures, lunettes, skis] to put on ◆ **~ les étriers** (Équitation) to put one's feet into the stirrups
3 (= fournir en chaussures) **ce marchand nous chausse depuis 10 ans** this shoemaker has been supplying us with shoes for 10 years
4 (= convenir à) to fit ◆ **ces chaussures vous chaussent bien** those shoes fit you well ou are a good fit
5 [+ arbre] to earth up
6 [+ voiture] to fit tyres (Brit) ou tires (US) on ◆ **voiture bien chaussée** car with good tyres (Brit) ou tires (US)
VI ◆ **~ du 40** to take size 40 in shoes, to take a (size) 40 shoe ◆ **ces chaussures chaussent grand ou large** these shoes are wide-fitting ◆ **chaussures qui chaussent bien le pied** well-fitting shoes
VPR **se chausser** (= mettre ses chaussures) to put one's shoes on ◆ **se (faire) ~ chez ...** (= acheter des chaussures) to buy ou get one's shoes at ... ◆ **se (faire) ~ sur mesure** to have one's shoes made to measure

chausse-trap(p)e (pl **chausse-trap(p)es**) /ʃostʀap/ NF (lit, fig) trap ◆ **tomber dans/éviter une ~** to fall into/avoid a trap

chaussette /ʃosɛt/ NF sock ◆ **j'étais en ~s** I was in my socks ◆ **~s russes** foot-bindings ◆ **~s tombantes** slouch socks ◆ **elle m'a laissé tomber comme une vieille ~** * she ditched * ou jilted me

chausseur /ʃosœʀ/ NM (= fabricant) shoemaker; (= fournisseur) footwear specialist

chausson /ʃosɔ̃/ NM 1 (= pantoufle) slipper; [de bébé] bootee; [de danseur] ballet shoe ou pump ◆ **~ à pointe** blocked shoe ◆ **~s d'escalade** climbing shoes; → **point²** 2 (Culin) turnover ◆ **~ aux pommes** apple turnover

chaussure /ʃosyʀ/ NF 1 (= soulier) shoe ◆ **rayon ~s** shoe ou footwear department ◆ **trouver ~ à son pied** to find a suitable match 2 ◆ **la ~** (= industrie) the shoe industry; (= commerce) the shoe trade ou business
COMP **chaussures basses** flat shoes
chaussures cloutées ou à clous hobnailed boots
chaussures montantes ankle boots
chaussures de ski ski boots
chaussures de sport sports shoes
chaussures à talon haut high-heeled shoes, (high) heels *
chaussures vernies patent leather shoes
chaussures de ville smart shoes

chaut /ʃo/ VI (†† ou hum) ◆ **peu me ~** it matters little to me, it is of no import ou matter to me

chauve /ʃov/ ADJ [personne, crâne] bald; (littér) [colline, sommet] bare ◆ **~ comme un œuf** * ou **une bille** * ou **mon genou** * as bald as a coot

chauve-souris (pl **chauves-souris**) /ʃovsuʀi/ NF (Zool) bat

chauvin, e /ʃovɛ̃, in/ ADJ (= nationaliste) chauvinistic; (en temps de guerre) jingoistic; (en sport, dans ses goûts) biased, prejudiced NM,F (= nationaliste) chauvinist; (en temps de guerre) jingoist

chauvinisme /ʃovinism/ NM (= nationalisme) chauvinism; (en temps de guerre) jingoism; (en sport, dans ses goûts) bias, prejudice

chaux /ʃo/ NF lime ◆ **~ éteinte** slaked lime ◆ **~ vive** quicklime ◆ **blanchi ou passé à la ~** whitewashed ◆ **bâti à ~ et à sable** (littér) [maison] as solid as a rock; [personne] as strong as an ox

chavirage /ʃaviʀaʒ/ NM [de bateau] capsizing, keeling over, overturning

chavirement /ʃaviʀmɑ̃/ NM upheaval (de in)

chavirer /ʃaviʀe/ ▸ conjug 1 ◂ VI 1 [bateau] to capsize, to keel over, to overturn; [gouvernement] to founder ◆ **faire ~ un bateau** to capsize a boat 2 [pile d'objets] to keel over; [charrette] to overturn, to tip over; [yeux] to roll; [paysage, chambre] to reel, to spin; [esprit] to reel ◆ **mon cœur a chaviré** (de dégoût) my stomach heaved; (d'émotion) my heart leapt VT 1 (= renverser) [+ bateau] [vagues] to capsize, to overturn; (en cale sèche) to keel over; [+ meubles] to overturn 2 (= bouleverser) **j'en étais tout chaviré** * (ému) I was quite overcome; (affligé) I was quite shaken ◆ **musique qui chavire l'âme** music that tugs at the heartstrings

chéchia /ʃeʃja/ NF tarboosh, fez

check-list (pl **check-lists**) /(t)ʃɛklist/ NF check list

check-point (pl **check-points**) /(t)ʃɛkpɔjnt/ NM checkpoint

check-up /(t)ʃɛkœp/ NM INV check-up

chef¹ /ʃɛf/ NMF 1 (= patron, dirigeant) head, boss *; [de tribu] chief(tain), headman ◆ **~ indien** Indian chief ◆ **il a l'estime de ses ~s** he is highly thought of by his superiors ou bosses ◆ **la ~** * the boss * ◆ **grand ~** * big chief ou boss * ◆ **faire le ou jouer au petit ~** (péj) to throw one's weight around ◆ **c'est qui le ~ ici ?** who's in charge around here?
2 [d'expédition, révolte, syndicat] leader ◆ **~ spirituel** spiritual leader ◆ **avoir une âme ou un tempérament de ~** to be a born leader
3 (* = champion) **tu es un ~** you're the greatest *, you're the tops * ◆ **elle se débrouille comme un ~** she is doing a first-class job
4 (Mil) **oui, ~ !** yes, Sir!
5 (Culin) chef ◆ **spécialité du ~** chef's speciality ◆ **pâté du ~** chef's special pâté ◆ **~ de cuisine** head chef ◆ **grand ~** master chef
6 (locutions)
◆ **en chef** ◆ **commandant en ~** commander-in-chief ◆ **général en ~** general-in-chief ◆ **ingénieur/économiste en ~** chief engineer/economist ◆ **le général commandait en ~ les troupes alliées** the general was the commander-in-chief of the allied troops
ADJ INV ◆ **gardien/médecin ~** chief warden/consultant
COMP **chef d'antenne** branch manager
chef d'atelier (shop) foreman
chef de bande gang leader
chef de bataillon major (in the infantry)
chef de bureau head clerk
chef de cabinet principal private secretary (de to)
chef de campagne (Pol) campaign leader
chef de chantier (works (Brit) ou site) foreman
chef des chœurs choirmaster

chef de classe ≃ class monitor *ou* prefect *(Brit) ou* president *(US)*
chef de clinique ≃ senior registrar
chef comptable chief accountant
chef de dépôt shed *ou* yard master
chef d'école *(Art, Littérat)* leader of a school
chef d'entreprise company director
chef d'équipe foreman
chef d'escadron major (in the cavalry)
chef d'État head of state ◆ **le ~ de l'État** the Head of State
chef d'état-major chief of staff ◆ **~s d'état-major** Joint Chiefs of Staff
chef de famille head of the family *ou* householder; *(Admin)* householder
chef de file *(gén, Art)* leader; *(Pol)* party leader; *(Naut)* leading ship; *(Banque)* lead bank
chef de gare station master
chef de gouvernement head of government
chef de guerre warlord
chef mécanicien chief mechanic; *(Rail)* head driver *(Brit)*, chief engineer *(US)*
chef de musique bandmaster
chef de nage stroke (oar)
chef d'orchestre *(gén)* conductor, director *(US)*; *(jazz etc)* (band) leader
chef de parti party leader
chef de patrouille patrol leader
chef de pièce *(Mil)* captain of a gun
chef de produit product manager, brand manager
chef de projet project manager
chef de rayon department(al) supervisor, departmental manager
chef scout scout leader
chef de service section *ou* departmental head; *(Méd)* ≃ consultant
chef de train guard *(Brit)*, conductor *(US)*

chef² /ʃɛf/ NM [1] († † *ou hum = tête*) head [2] *(Jur)* ~ **d'accusation** *ou* **d'inculpation** *(= charge)* charge [3] *(locutions)* **posséder qch de son ~** *(Jur)* to own sth in one's own right ◆ **de son propre ~** *(frm)* on his own initiative, off his own bat ◆ **au premier ~** *(littér)* greatly, exceedingly ◆ **cela m'intéresse au premier ~** it's of the greatest *ou* utmost interest to me ◆ **de ce ~** *(littér)* accordingly, hence

chef-d'œuvre (pl **chefs-d'œuvre**) /ʃɛdœvʀ/ NM masterpiece, chef-d'œuvre ◆ **c'est un ~ d'hypocrisie/d'ironie** *(fig)* it is the ultimate hypocrisy/irony

chefferie /ʃɛfʀi/ NM *(Anthropologie)* chieftainship; *(Méd)* consultancy

chef-lieu (pl **chefs-lieux**) /ʃɛfljø/ NM ≃ county town

cheftaine /ʃɛftɛn/ NF *[de louveteaux]* cubmistress *(Brit)*, den mother *(US)*; *[de jeunes éclaireuses]* Brown Owl *(Brit)*, troop leader *(US)*; *[d'éclaireuses]* (guide) captain, guider

cheik /ʃɛk/ NM sheik

chelem /ʃlɛm/ NM *(Cartes)* slam ◆ **petit/grand ~** small/grand slam ◆ **faire le grand ~** *(Sport)* to do the grand slam

chemin /ʃ(ə)mɛ̃/ NM [1] *(gén)* path; *(= route)* lane; *(= piste)* track; → **croisée², voleur**
[2] *(= parcours, trajet, direction)* way *(de, pour* to); ◆ **demander/trouver le** *ou* **son ~** to ask/find the *ou* one's way ◆ **montrer le ~ à qn** to show sb the way ◆ **il y a bien une heure de ~** it takes a good hour to get there ◆ **quel ~ a-t-elle pris ?** which way did she go? ◆ **de bon matin, ils prirent le ~ de la côte** they set out *ou* off for the coast early in the morning ◆ **le ~ le plus court entre deux points** the shortest distance between two points ◆ **ils ont fait tout le ~ à pied/en bicyclette** they walked/cycled all the way *ou* the whole way ◆ **on a fait du ~ depuis une heure** we've come quite a way in an hour ◆ **se mettre en ~** to set out *ou* off ◆ **poursuivre son ~** to carry on *ou* continue on one's way ◆ **passez votre ~** *(littér)* go your way *(littér)*, be on your way ◆ **~ faisant, en ~** on the way ◆ **pour venir, nous avons pris le ~ des écoliers** we came the long way round ◆ **aller son ~** *(fig)* to go one's own sweet way ◆ **être toujours sur les ~s** to be always on the road ◆ **tous les ~s mènent à Rome** *(Prov)* all roads lead to Rome *(Prov)* → **rebrousser**
[3] *(fig)* path, way, road ◆ **le ~ de l'honneur/de la gloire** the path *ou* way of honour/to glory ◆ **le ~ de la ruine** the road to ruin ◆ **nos ~s se sont croisés** our paths crossed; → **droit²**
[4] *(locutions)* **il a encore du ~ à faire** he's still got a long way to go ◆ **faire son ~ dans la vie** to make one's way in life ◆ **il a fait du ~ !** *(arriviste, jeune cadre)* he has come up in the world; *(savant, chercheur)* he has come a long way ◆ **cette idée a fait son ~** this idea has gained ground ◆ **faire la moitié du ~** to meet sb half-way ◆ **se mettre dans** *ou* **sur le ~ de qn** to stand *ou* get in sb's way, to stand in sb's path ◆ **il est toujours sur mon ~** he turns up wherever I go; *(comme obstacle)* he always stands in my way ◆ **montrer le ~** to lead the way ◆ **l'aîné est un délinquant et le cadet suit le même ~** the eldest child is a delinquent and his younger brother is going the same way ◆ **être sur le bon ~** to be on the right track ◆ **ne t'arrête pas en si bon ~ !** don't stop now when you're doing so well *ou* after such a good start ◆ **trouver des difficultés sur son ~** to meet with difficulties ◆ **cela n'en prend pas le ~** it doesn't look very likely ◆ **est-ce qu'il va réussir ? – il n'en prend pas le ~** will he succeed? – not if he goes about it like that ◆ **le ~ de Damas** *(Rel)* the road to Damascus ◆ **trouver son ~ de Damas** to see the light

COMP **chemin d'accès** *(Ordin)* access path
chemin charretier cart track
chemin creux sunken lane
chemin critique *(Ordin)* critical path
le chemin de croix (du Christ) the Way of the Cross; *(dans une église)* the Stations of the Cross ◆ **son long ~ de croix dans les élections européennes** his long, hard battle in the European elections ◆ **la réforme de l'éducation sera le ~ de croix de ce gouvernement** it will be a long, hard road to education reform for this government
chemin de fer railway *(Brit)*, railroad *(US)*; *(= moyen de transport)* rail ◆ **par ~ de fer** by rail ◆ **employé des ~s de fer** railway *(Brit) ou* railroad *(US)* worker
Chemins de fer fédéraux Swiss Railways
chemin de halage towpath
chemin de ronde parapet *ou* rampart walk
chemin de table table runner
chemin de terre dirt track
chemin de traverse path across *ou* through the fields
chemin vicinal country road *ou* lane, minor road

chemineau (pl **chemineaux**) /ʃ(ə)mino/ NM *(littér ou † † = vagabond)* vagabond

cheminée /ʃ(ə)mine/ NF [1] *(extérieure) [de maison, usine]* chimney (stack); *[de paquebot, locomotive]* funnel, smokestack [2] *(intérieure)* fireplace; *(= foyer)* fireplace, hearth; *(= encadrement)* mantelpiece, chimney piece ◆ **un feu crépitait dans la ~** a fire was crackling in the hearth *ou* fireplace *ou* grate; → **feu¹** [3] *[de volcan]* vent; *(Alpinisme)* chimney; *[de lampe]* chimney

COMP **cheminée d'aération** ventilation shaft
cheminée des fées earth pillar
cheminée prussienne (closed) stove
cheminée d'usine factory chimney

cheminement /ʃ(ə)minmɑ̃/ NM *(= progression) [de caravane, marcheurs]* progress, advance; *[de troupes]* advance (under cover); *[de sentier, itinéraire, eau]* course, way; *[d'idées, pensée]* development, progression ◆ **il est difficile de suivre son ~ intellectuel** it is difficult to follow his reasoning *ou* line of thought

cheminer /ʃ(ə)mine/ ► conjug 1 ◄ VI *(littér)* [1] *(= marcher)* to walk (along); *(Mil = avancer à couvert)* to advance (under cover) ◆ **~ péniblement** to trudge (wearily) along ◆ **après avoir longtemps cheminé** having plodded along for ages ◆ **nous cheminions vers la ville** we wended *(littér) ou* made our way towards the town [2] *[sentier]* to make its way *(dans* along); *[eau]* to make its way, to follow its course *(dans* along); *[idées]* to follow their course ◆ **l'idée cheminait lentement dans sa tête** the idea was slowly taking root in his mind, he was slowly coming round to the idea ◆ **sa pensée cheminait de façon tortueuse** his thoughts followed a tortuous course ◆ **les eaux de la Durance cheminent entre des falaises** the waters of the Durance flow between cliffs *ou* make their way between cliffs

cheminot /ʃ(ə)mino/ NM railwayman *(Brit)*, railroad man *(US)*

chemisage /ʃ(ə)mizaʒ/ NM *(intérieur)* lining; *(extérieur)* jacketing

chemise /ʃ(ə)miz/ NF [1] *(Habillement) [d'homme]* shirt; † † *[de femme]* chemise †, shift †; *[de bébé]* vest *(Brit)*, undershirt *(US)* ◆ **~ de soirée/de sport** dress/sports shirt ◆ **être en manches** *ou* **bras de ~** to be in one's shirt sleeves ◆ **col/manchette de ~** shirt collar/cuff ◆ **je m'en moque comme de ma première ~** * I couldn't care less*, I don't care a hoot* *ou* two hoots* [2] *(= dossier)* folder; *(Tech) (= revêtement intérieur)* lining; *(= revêtement extérieur)* jacket ◆ **~ de cylindre** *(dans moteur)* cylinder liner

COMP **chemise (américaine)** (woman's) vest *(Brit) ou* undershirt *(US)*
chemises brunes *(Hist)* Brown Shirts
chemise d'homme man's shirt
chemise de maçonnerie facing
chemises noires *(Hist)* Blackshirts
chemise de nuit *[de femme]* nightdress, nightie*; *[d'homme]* nightshirt
chemises rouges *(Hist)* Redshirts

chemiser /ʃ(ə)mize/ ► conjug 1 ◄ VT *[+ intérieur]* to line; *[+ extérieur]* to jacket

chemiserie /ʃ(ə)mizʀi/ NF *(= magasin)* (men's) shirt shop; *(= rayon)* shirt department; *(= commerce)* shirt(-making) trade *ou* business

chemisette /ʃ(ə)mizɛt/ NF *[d'homme]* short-sleeved shirt; *[de femme]* short-sleeved blouse

chemisier, -ière /ʃ(ə)mizje, jɛʀ/ NM,F *(= marchand)* (gentlemen's) shirtmaker; *(= fabricant)* shirtmaker NM *(= vêtement)* blouse; → **col, robe**

chênaie /ʃɛnɛ/ NF oak grove

chenal (pl **-aux**) /ʃənal, o/ NM *(= canal)* channel, fairway; *(= rigole)* channel; *[de moulin]* millrace; *[de forge, usine]* flume

COMP **chenal de coulée** *(en fonderie)* gate, runner
chenal pro-glaciaire glaciated valley

chenapan /ʃ(ə)napɑ̃/ NM *(hum = garnement)* scallywag *(hum)*, rascal *(hum)*; *(péj = vaurien)* scoundrel, rogue

chêne /ʃɛn/ NM *(= arbre)* oak (tree); *(= bois)* oak

COMP **chêne pubescent** pubescent oak
chêne rouvre *ou* **sessile** durmast *ou* sessile oaktree
chêne vert holm oak, ilex

chéneau (pl **chéneaux**) /ʃeno/ NM *[de toit]* gutter

chêne-liège (pl **chênes-lièges**) /ʃɛnljɛʒ/ NM cork oak

chenet /ʃ(ə)nɛ/ NM firedog, andiron

chènevis /ʃɛnvi/ NM hempseed

chenil /ʃ(ə)nil/ NM [1] *(pour chiens)* kennels *(Brit)*, kennel *(US)* ◆ **mettre son chien dans un ~** to put one's dog in kennels [2] *(Helv = désordre)* mess

chenille /ʃ(ə)nij/ NF 1 (= *larve, partie d'un véhicule*) caterpillar ◆ **véhicule à ~s** tracked vehicle 2 (= *tissu*) chenille 3 (= *danse*) conga
COMP **chenille du mûrier** silkworm
chenille processionnaire processionary caterpillar

chenillé, e /ʃ(ə)nije/ ADJ [*véhicule*] with caterpillar tracks, tracked

chenillette /ʃ(ə)nijɛt/ NF (= *véhicule*) tracked vehicle

chenu, e /ʃəny/ ADJ (*littér*) [*vieillard, tête*] hoary; [*arbre*] leafless with age

cheptel /ʃɛptɛl/ NM (= *bétail*) livestock; (*Jur*) livestock (*leased*) ◆ **~ ovin d'une région** sheep population of an area
COMP **cheptel mort** farm implements
cheptel vif livestock

chèque /ʃɛk/ NM 1 (*Banque*) cheque (*Brit*), check (*US*) ◆ **faire/toucher un ~** to write *ou* make out/cash a cheque ◆ **~ de 20 €** cheque for €20; → **barrer**
2 (= *bon*) voucher ◆ **~-déjeuner** ® *ou* **-repas** *ou* **-restaurant** ® luncheon voucher (*Brit*), meal ticket (*US*) ◆ **~-cadeau** gift token ◆ **~-essence** petrol (*Brit*) *ou* gasoline (*US*) coupon *ou* voucher
COMP **chèque bancaire** cheque
chèque de banque banker's *ou* cashier's cheque
chèque en blanc (*lit, fig*) blank cheque
chèque en bois* dud cheque* (*Brit*), rubber cheque*
chèque de caution *cheque given as deposit*
chèque certifié certified cheque
chèque de dépannage loose cheque (*supplied by bank when customer does not have his own chequebook*)
chèque emploi service *automatic welfare deduction system for pay cheques for domestic help*
chèque à ordre cheque to order, order cheque
chèque au porteur bearer cheque
chèque postal *cheque drawn on a post office account* ◆ **les ~s postaux** (= *service*) the banking departments of the post office
chèque sans provision bad cheque
chèque de voyage traveller's cheque

chéquier /ʃekje/ NM chequebook (*Brit*), checkbook (*US*)

cher, chère[1] /ʃɛʀ/ ADJ 1 (*gén après nom = aimé*) [*personne, souvenir, vœu*] dear (*à* to); ◆ **ceux qui** *ou* **les êtres qui nous sont ~s** our nearest and dearest, our loved ones ◆ **des souvenirs ~s** fond memories ◆ **des souvenirs ~s à mon cœur** memories dear to my heart ◆ **c'est mon vœu le plus ~** it's my fondest *ou* dearest wish ◆ **mon désir le plus ~** *ou* **mon plus ~ désir est de ...** my greatest *ou* most cherished desire is to ... ◆ **l'honneur est le bien le plus ~** honour is one's most precious possession, one's honour is to be treasured above all else ◆ **selon une formule chère au président** as a favourite saying of the president goes, to quote a favourite expression of the president
2 (*avant nom*) dear ◆ **(mes) ~s auditeurs** dear listeners ◆ **mes bien ~s frères** (*Rel*) my dear(est) brethren ◆ **Monsieur et ~ collègue** dear colleague ◆ **ce ~ (vieux) Louis !*** dear old Louis!* ◆ **le ~ homme n'y entendait pas malice** (*hum*) the dear man didn't mean any harm by it ◆ **il était content de retrouver ses ~s livres** he was glad to be back with his beloved books ◆ **elle a retrouvé ses chères habitudes** she slipped back into the old habits she holds so dear ◆ **~s tous** (*sur lettre*) dear all
3 (*après nom = coûteux*) expensive, dear (*Brit*) ◆ **un petit restaurant pas ~** an inexpensive *ou* a reasonably priced little restaurant ◆ **c'est vraiment pas ~ !** it's really cheap! ◆ **la vie est chère à Paris** the cost of living is high in Paris, Paris is an expensive place to live ◆ **c'est moins ~ qu'en face** it's cheaper than *ou* less expensive than in the shop opposite ◆ **cet épicier est trop ~** this grocer is too expensive *ou* too dear (*Brit*) *ou* charges too much ◆ **c'est trop ~ pour ce que c'est** it's overpriced; → **vie**
NM,F (*frm ou hum*) ◆ **mon ~, ma chère** my dear ◆ **oui, très ~** yes, dearest ◆ **son ~ et tendre** her other *ou* better half (*hum*)
ADV [*valoir, coûter, payer*] a lot (of money), a great deal (of money) ◆ **article qui vaut** *ou* **coûte ~** expensive item, item that costs a lot *ou* a great deal ◆ **as-tu payé ~ ton costume ?** did you pay much *ou* a lot for your suit?, was your suit (very) expensive? ◆ **il se fait payer ~, il prend ~** he charges a lot, he's expensive ◆ **il vend ~** his prices are high, he charges high prices ◆ **ça s'est vendu ~** it went for *ou* fetched a high price *ou* a lot (of money) ◆ **je ne l'ai pas acheté ~, je l'ai eu pour pas ~*** I didn't pay much for it, I got it cheap* ◆ **je donnerais ~ pour savoir ce qu'il fait*** I'd give anything to know what he's doing ◆ **je ne donne pas ~ de sa vie/de sa réussite** I wouldn't like to bet on his chances of survival/succeeding, I wouldn't rate his chances of survival/succeeding very highly ◆ **il ne vaut pas ~** he's a good-for-nothing ◆ **tu ne vaux pas plus ~ que lui** you're no better than he is *ou* than him, you're just as bad as he is ◆ **son imprudence lui a coûté ~** his rashness cost him dear (*Brit*) *ou* a great deal (*US*) ◆ **il a payé ~ son imprudence** he paid dearly *ou* heavily for his rashness ◆ **c'est un peu ~ payé !*** that's a bit steep!*

chercher /ʃɛʀʃe/ ▸ conjug 1 ◂ VT 1 (= *essayer de trouver*) [*+ personne, chose égarée, emploi*] to look for, to search for, to try to find; [*+ solution, moyen*] to look for, to seek, to try to find; [*+ ombre, lumière, tranquillité*] to seek; [*+ citation, heure de train*] to look up; [*+ nom, terme*] to try to remember; [*+ raison, excuse*] to cast about for, to try to find, to look for ◆ **~ un mot dans un dictionnaire** to look up a word in a dictionary ◆ **~ qn du regard** *ou* **des yeux** to look *ou* glance around for sb ◆ **~ qch à tâtons** to grope *ou* fumble for sth ◆ **attends, je cherche** wait a minute, I'm trying to think ◆ **il n'a pas bien cherché** he didn't look very hard ◆ **~ partout qch/qn** to search *ou* hunt everywhere for sth/sb ◆ **~ sa voie** to look for *ou* seek a path in life ◆ **il cherchait ses mots** he was struggling to find the right words ◆ **cherche ! cherche !** (*à un chien*) fetch! ◆ **ce n'est pas la peine de ~ bien loin, c'est lui qui l'a fait** you don't have to look too far, he's the one who did it
2 (= *viser à*) [*+ gloire, succès*] to seek (after); (= *rechercher*) [*+ alliance, faveur*] to seek ◆ **il ne cherche que son intérêt** he's only out for himself
3 (= *provoquer*) [*+ danger, mort*] to court ◆ **~ la difficulté** to look for difficulties ◆ **~ la bagarre** to be looking *ou* spoiling for a fight ◆ **tu l'auras cherché !** you've been asking for it! ◆ **il l'a bien cherché** he asked for it, he had it coming to him ◆ **si on me cherche, on me trouve*** if anyone asks for it they'll get it* ◆ **tu me cherches ?*** are you looking for trouble? ◆ **~ le contact avec l'ennemi** to try to engage the enemy in combat
4 (= *prendre, acheter*) **aller ~ qch/qn** to go for sth/sb, to go and get *ou* fetch (*Brit*) sth/sb ◆ **il est venu ~ Paul** he called *ou* came for Paul, he came to get *ou* to fetch (*Brit*) Paul ◆ **il est allé me ~ de la monnaie** he's gone to get me some change ◆ **va me ~ mon sac** go and get *ou* fetch (*Brit*) my bag ◆ **qu'est-ce que tu vas ~ ? je n'ai rien dit !** what do you mean? I didn't say a thing! ◆ **où est-ce qu'il va ~ toutes ces idées idiotes !** where does he get all those stupid ideas from! ◆ **monter/descendre ~ qch** to go up/down for sth *ou* to get sth ◆ **aller ~ qch dans un tiroir** to go and get sth out of a drawer ◆ **il est allé/venu le ~ à la gare** he went/came to meet *ou* collect him at the station ◆ **aller ~ les enfants à l'école** to go to get *ou* collect *ou* fetch (*Brit*) the children from school ◆ **envoyer ~ le médecin** to send for the doctor ◆ **envoyer qn ~ le médecin** to send sb to get the doctor ◆ **ça va ~ dans les 50 €** it'll come to around €50 ◆ **ça va ~ dans les 5 ans de prison** it will mean something like 5 years in prison ◆ **ça peut aller ~ loin** (*amende*) it could mean a heavy fine
5 ◆ **~ à faire** to try to do, to attempt to do ◆ **~ à comprendre** to try to understand ◆ **faut pas ~ à comprendre*** don't even try and understand ◆ **~ à faire plaisir à qn** to try *ou* endeavour to please sb ◆ **~ à obtenir qch** to try to get *ou* obtain sth ◆ **~ à savoir qch** to try *ou* attempt to find out sth
6 (*locutions*) **~ midi à quatorze heures** to complicate the issue ◆ **~ la petite bête** to split hairs ◆ **~ une aiguille dans une botte** *ou* **meule de foin** to look for a needle in a haystack ◆ **~ des poux dans la tête de qn*** to try to make trouble for sb ◆ **~ querelle à qn** to try to pick a quarrel with sb ◆ **cherchez la femme !** cherchez la femme!; → **crosse, fortune, histoire, noise, salut**
VPR **se chercher** (= *chercher sa voie*) to search for an identity ◆ **il se cherche encore** he hasn't found himself yet

chercheur, -euse /ʃɛʀʃœʀ, øz/ ADJ [*esprit*] inquiring; → **tête** NM [*de télescope*] finder; [*de détecteur à galène*] cat's whisker ◆ **~ de fuites** gas-leak detector NM,F 1 **~ de** (*gén*) seeker of ◆ **~ d'or** gold digger ◆ **~ de trésors** treasure hunter ◆ **~ d'aventure(s)** adventure seeker, seeker after adventure 2 (= *scientifique*) researcher, research worker ◆ **~ en biologie** biology researcher

chère[2] /ʃɛʀ/ NF (†† *ou hum*) food, fare, cheer † ◆ **faire bonne ~** to eat well, to have a good meal ◆ **aimer la bonne ~** to love one's food

chèrement /ʃɛʀmɑ̃/ ADV 1 (= *durement*) dearly ◆ **~ acquis** *ou* **payé** [*avantage, victoire*] dearly bought *ou* won ◆ **~ défendu** vigorously defended ◆ **vendre** *ou* **faire payer ~ sa vie** to sell one's life dearly 2 (= *avec affection*) [*aimer*] dearly 3 († = *au prix fort*) [*vendre*] at a high price, dearly †

chéri, e /ʃeʀi/ (ptp de **chérir**) ADJ (= *bien-aimé*) beloved, dear(est) ◆ **quand il a revu son fils ~** when he saw his beloved son again ◆ **c'est l'enfant ~ du parti** he's the darling of the party ◆ **maman ~e** mother dear, mother darling ◆ **"à notre père chéri"** (*sur tombe*) "to our dearly beloved father" NM,F 1 (*terme d'affection*) darling ◆ **mon ~** (my) darling ◆ **bonjour mes ~s** (*hum*) hullo darlings (*hum*) 2 (*péj = préféré*) **c'est le ~ à sa maman*** he's mummy's (*Brit*) *ou* mommy's (*US*) little darling *ou* blue-eyed boy ◆ **c'est la ~e de ses parents** she's the apple of her parents' eye, her parents dote on her

chérif /ʃeʀif/ NM sherif

chérir /ʃeʀiʀ/ ▸ conjug 2 ◂ VT (*littér*) [*+ personne*] to cherish, to love dearly; [*+ liberté, idée*] to cherish, to hold dear; [*+ souvenir*] to cherish, to treasure

Cherokee /ʃeʀoki/ NMF Cherokee

chérot* /ʃeʀo/ ADJ M (= *coûteux*) pricey* (*Brit*), expensive

cherry /ʃeʀi/, **cherry brandy** /ʃeʀibʀɑ̃di/ NM cherry brandy

cherté /ʃɛʀte/ NF [*d'article*] high price, dearness (*Brit*); [*d'époque, région*] high prices (*de* in); ◆ **la ~ de la vie** the high cost of living, the cost of things*

chérubin /ʃeʀybɛ̃/ NM (*lit, fig*) cherub ◆ **~s** (*Art*) cherubs; (*Rel*) cherubim

chétif, -ive /ʃetif, iv/ ADJ 1 (= *malingre*) [*personne*] puny, sickly; [*plante*] scrawny, stunted; [*voix*] reedy ◆ **enfant à l'aspect ~** weedy-looking *ou* puny-looking child 2 (= *minable*) [*récolte*] meagre (*Brit*), meager (*US*), poor; [*exis-

tence] meagre *(Brit)*, meager *(US)*, mean; *[repas]* skimpy, scanty; *[raisonnement]* paltry, feeble

chétivement / ʃetivmɑ̃ / ADV *[pousser]* punily

chevaine / ʃ(ə)vɛn / NM ⇒ **chevesne**

cheval (pl **-aux**) / ʃ(ə)val, o / NM 1 *(= animal)* horse; *(= viande)* horsemeat ◆ **carrosse à deux/à six chevaux** coach and pair/and six ◆ **faire du ~** to go horse-riding ◆ **tu sais faire du ~ ?** can you ride (a horse)? ◆ **c'est un grand ~, cette fille** *(péj)* she's a strapping lass ◆ **au travail, c'est un vrai ~** he works like a Trojan ◆ **ce n'est pas le mauvais ~** he's not a bad sort *ou* soul ◆ **tu as mangé** *ou* **bouffé‡ du ~ !** you're full of beans! * ◆ **c'est changer un ~ borgne pour un aveugle** it's jumping out of the frying pan into the fire ◆ **ça ne se trouve pas sous le pas** *ou* **le sabot d'un ~** it doesn't grow on trees ◆ **on ne change pas de ~ au milieu du gué** you don't change horses in midstream; → **miser, monter[1], petit**

2 *(= unité de puissance)* horsepower *(NonC)* ◆ **elle fait combien de chevaux ?** how many cc's is it?, what horsepower is it? ◆ **c'est une 6 chevaux** it's a 6 horsepower car

3 *(arg Drogue)* horse, (big) H

4 *(locutions)* **monter sur ses grands chevaux** to get on one's high horse ◆ **de ~** * *[remède]* drastic; *[fièvre]* raging

◆ **à cheval** on horseback ◆ **se tenir bien à ~** to have a good seat, to sit well on horseback

◆ **à cheval sur** ◆ **être à ~ sur une chaise** to be (sitting) astride a chair, to be straddling a chair ◆ **village à ~ sur deux départements** village straddling two departments ◆ **à ~ sur deux mois** overlapping two (different) months, running from one month into the next ◆ **être à ~ sur deux cultures** *[ville, pays]* to be at the crossroads of two cultures; *[personne]* to have roots in two cultures; *[œuvre]* to be rooted in *ou* to span two cultures ◆ **être (très) à ~ sur le règlement/les principes** to be a (real) stickler for the rules/for principles

COMP **cheval d'arçons** pommel horse
cheval d'attelage plough *(Brit) ou* plow *(US)* horse
cheval à bascule rocking horse
cheval de bataille *(Mil)* battle horse, charger ◆ **il a ressorti son ~ de bataille** *(fig)* he's back on his hobby-horse *ou* his favourite theme again ◆ **l'opposition en a fait son ~ de bataille** the opposition have made it their key issue *ou* main concern
cheval de bois wooden horse ◆ **monter** *ou* **aller sur les chevaux de bois** to go on the merry-go-round *ou* roundabout *(Brit)*; *(† ou hum)* ◆ **manger avec les chevaux de bois** to miss a meal, to go dinnerless
cheval de chasse hunter
cheval de cirque circus horse
cheval de course racehorse
cheval de fiacre carriage horse
cheval fiscal horsepower *(for tax purposes)*
chevaux de frise chevaux-de-frise
cheval de labour carthorse, plough *(Brit) ou* plow *(US)* horse
cheval de manège school horse
cheval marin *ou* **de mer** sea horse
cheval de poste *ou* **de relais** post horse
(vieux) cheval de retour recidivist, old lag * *(Brit)*
cheval de saut vaulting horse
cheval de selle saddle horse
cheval de trait draught horse *(Brit)*, draft horse *(US)*
le cheval de Troie *(lit, fig)* the Trojan horse, the Wooden Horse of Troy

chevalement / ʃ(ə)valmɑ̃ / NM *[de mur]* shoring; *[de galerie]* (pit)head frame

chevaler / ʃ(ə)vale / ▸ conjug 1 ◂ VT *[+ mur]* to shore up

chevaleresque / ʃ(ə)valʀɛsk / ADJ *[caractère, conduite]* chivalrous, gentlemanly; *[amour]* courtly ◆ **règles ~s** rules of chivalry ◆ **l'honneur ~** the honour of a knight, knightly honour

chevalerie / ʃ(ə)valʀi / NF *(Hist = institution)* chivalry; *(= dignité, chevaliers)* knighthood; → **roman[1]**

chevalet / ʃ(ə)valɛ / NM 1 *[de peintre]* easel; *(Menuiserie)* trestle, sawhorse *(Brit)*, sawbuck *(US)*; *[de violon]* bridge; *(à feuilles mobiles)* flip chart 2 *(Hist)* **le ~** *(= torture)* the rack

chevalier / ʃ(ə)valje / NM 1 *(Hist)* knight ◆ **faire qn ~** to knight sb, to dub sb knight ◆ **"je te fais chevalier"** "I dub you knight"

2 *(= membre) [d'ordre français]* chevalier; *[d'ordre britannique]* knight ◆ **~ de la Légion d'honneur** Knight of the Legion of Honour ◆ **~ des Arts et des Lettres** *person honoured for outstanding achievement in the arts*

3 *(= oiseau)* sandpiper

COMP **chevalier aboyeur** *(= oiseau)* greenshank
chevalier blanc *(Fin)* white knight; *(= personne généreuse)* defender of good causes
chevalier du ciel pilot
chevalier errant knight-errant
chevalier gambette *(= oiseau)* redshank
chevalier gris *(Fin)* grey knight
chevalier d'industrie crook, swindler
chevalier noir *(Fin)* black knight
chevalier servant (attentive) escort
chevalier de la Table ronde Knight of the Round Table
chevaliers teutoniques Teutonic Knights
le chevalier à la Triste Figure the Knight of the Sorrowful Countenance

chevalière / ʃ(ə)valjɛʀ / NF signet ring

chevalin, e / ʃ(ə)valɛ̃, in / ADJ *[race]* of horses, equine; *[visage, œil]* horsy ◆ **la race ~e** horses; → **boucherie**

cheval-vapeur (pl **chevaux-vapeur**) / ʃ(ə)valvapœʀ / NM horsepower

chevauchée / ʃ(ə)voʃe / NF *(= course)* ride; *(= cavaliers, cavalcade)* cavalcade

chevauchement / ʃ(ə)voʃmɑ̃ / NM *(gén)* overlapping; *(Géol)* thrust fault

chevaucher / ʃ(ə)voʃe / ▸ conjug 1 ◂ VT 1 *[+ cheval, âne]* to be astride; *[+ chaise]* to sit astride, to straddle ◆ **de grosses lunettes lui chevauchaient le nez** a large pair of glasses sat on his nose ◆ **le pont chevauche l'abîme** the bridge spans the abyss 2 *[+ tuiles]* to overlap, to lap over VPR **se chevaucher** *[dents, tuiles, lettres, vacances]* to overlap (each other); *(Géol) [couches]* to overthrust, to override VI 1 *(† ou littér = aller à cheval)* to ride (on horseback) 2 ⇒ **se chevaucher**

chevau-léger (pl **chevau-légers**) / ʃ(ə)voleʒe / NM *(Hist = soldat)* member of the Household Cavalry ◆ **~s** *(= troupe)* Household Cavalry

chevêche / ʃ(ə)vɛʃ / NF little owl

chevelu, e / ʃəv(ə)ly / ADJ *[personne]* long-haired; *[tête]* hairy; *[épi]* tufted; *[racine]* bearded; → **cuir**

chevelure / ʃəv(ə)lyʀ / NF 1 *(= cheveux)* hair *(NonC)* ◆ **une ~ malade/terne** unhealthy/dull hair ◆ **elle avait une ~ abondante/une flamboyante ~ rousse** she had thick hair *ou* a thick head of hair/a shock of flaming red hair ◆ **sa ~ était magnifique** her hair was magnificent 2 *[de comète]* tail

chevesne / ʃ(ə)vɛn / NM chub

chevet / ʃ(ə)vɛ / NM 1 *[de lit]* bedhead ◆ **au ~ de qn** at sb's bedside ◆ **un nouvel entraîneur a été appelé au ~ de l'équipe** a new trainer has been brought in to sort the team out; → **lampe, livre[1], table** 2 *(Archit) [d'église]* chevet

cheveu (pl **cheveux**) / ʃ(ə)vø / NM 1 *(gén pl)* hair ◆ **~x** *(= chevelure)* hair *(NonC)* ◆ **il a le ~ rare** *(collectif)* he's balding, his hair is thinning ◆ **une femme aux ~x blonds/frisés** a fair-haired/curly-haired woman, a woman with fair/curly hair ◆ **avoir les ~x en désordre** *ou* **en bataille** *ou* **hirsutes** to have untidy *ou* dishevelled hair ◆ **(les) ~x au vent** hair streaming in the wind ◆ **elle s'est trouvé 2 ~x blancs** she has found 2 white hairs ◆ **en ~x** † hatless, bareheaded ◆ **il n'a pas un ~ sur la tête** *ou* **le caillou** * he hasn't a (single) hair on his head; → **coupe[2], brosse, épingle, filet**

2 *(locutions)* **leur survie n'a tenu qu'à un ~, il s'en est fallu d'un ~ qu'ils ne se tuent** they escaped death by a whisker ◆ **son accord n'a tenu qu'à un ~** it was touch and go whether he would agree ◆ **il s'en faut d'un ~ qu'il ne change d'avis** it's touch and go whether he'll change his mind ◆ **si vous osez toucher à un ~ de cet enfant** if you dare touch *ou* if you so much as touch a hair of this child's head ◆ **avoir mal aux ~x** * to have a hangover ◆ **avoir un ~ (sur la langue)** * to have a lisp ◆ **se faire des ~x (blancs)** * to worry o.s. sick * ◆ **arriver comme un ~ sur la soupe** * *[personne]* to turn up at the most awkward moment; *[remarque]* to be completely irrelevant ◆ **tiré par les ~x** *[histoire]* far-fetched ◆ **il y a un ~** * there's a hitch * *ou* snag * ◆ **il va y trouver un ~** * he's not going to like it one bit ◆ **se prendre aux ~x** to come to blows; → **arracher, couper**

COMP **cheveux d'ange** *(= vermicelle)* angel hair pasta; *(= décoration)* Christmas floss
cheveux de Vénus maidenhair (fern)

chevillard / ʃ(ə)vijaʀ / NM wholesale butcher

cheville / ʃ(ə)vij / NF 1 *(Anat)* ankle ◆ **l'eau lui venait** *ou* **arrivait à la ~** *ou* **aux ~s** he was ankle-deep in water, the water came up to his ankles ◆ **aucun ne lui arrive à la ~** *(fig)* he's head and shoulders above the others, there's no one to touch him ◆ **avoir les ~s qui enflent** * *(péj)* to be full of oneself, to have a swollen *ou* swelled head * *(US)* ◆ **t'as pas les ~s qui enflent ?** * *(péj)* you're very full of yourself, aren't you? ◆ **ça va les ~s ?** * *(péj)* bighead! *

2 *(= fiche) (pour joindre)* dowel, peg, pin; *(pour vis)* plug; *[d'instrument à cordes]* peg; *(Boucherie = crochet)* hook ◆ **vendre de la viande à la ~** to sell meat wholesale ◆ **~ ouvrière** *(lit)* kingpin; *(fig)* kingpin, mainspring

3 *(Littérat) [de poème]* cheville; *(péj = remplissage)* padding *(NonC)*

4 *(locution)* **être en ~ avec qn pour faire qch** to be in cahoots * with sb to do sth, to collude with sb in doing sth

cheviller / ʃ(ə)vije / ▸ conjug 1 ◂ VT *(Menuiserie)* to peg ◆ **avoir l'âme chevillée au corps** to have nine lives ◆ **avoir l'espoir chevillé au cœur** *ou* **au corps** to refuse to give up hope, to have a never-say-die attitude ◆ **avoir la méchanceté chevillée au corps** to be nasty through and through, to be downright nasty *ou* malicious

chevillette / ʃ(ə)vijɛt / NF (small) peg

chèvre / ʃɛvʀ / NF 1 *(= animal) (gén)* goat; *(femelle)* nanny-goat ◆ **devenir ~** * to go crazy ◆ **je deviens ~ moi avec tous ces formulaires/enfants !** * all these forms/these children are driving me up the wall! * ◆ **rendre** *ou* **faire devenir qn ~** * to drive sb up the wall *; → **fromage** 2 *(Tech) (= treuil)* hoist, gin; *(= chevalet)* sawhorse, sawbuck *(US)*, trestle NM *(= fromage)* goat('s) cheese, goat's-milk cheese

chevreau (pl **chevreaux**) / ʃəvʀo / NM *(= animal, peau)* kid ◆ **bondir comme un ~** to gambol like a lamb

chèvrefeuille / ʃɛvʀəfœj / NM honeysuckle

chevrette /ʃəvʀɛt/ NF 1 (= *jeune chèvre*) kid, young she-goat 2 (= *chevreuil femelle*) roe, doe; (= *fourrure*) goatskin 3 (= *trépied*) (metal) tripod

chevreuil /ʃəvʀœj/ NM roe deer; (*mâle*) roebuck; (*Can* = *cerf de Virginie*) deer; (*Culin*) venison

chevrier /ʃəvʀije/ NM (= *berger*) goatherd; (= *haricot*) (type of) kidney bean

chevrière /ʃəvʀijɛʀ/ NF goatherd

chevron /ʃəvʀɔ̃/ NM (= *poutre*) rafter; (= *galon*) stripe, chevron; (= *motif*) chevron, V(-shape) ◆ **~s** (*petits*) herringbone (pattern); (*grands*) chevron pattern ◆ **à ~s** (*petits*) herringbone; (*grands*) chevron-patterned

chevronné, e /ʃəvʀɔne/ ADJ experienced

chevrotant, e /ʃəvʀɔtɑ̃, ɑ̃t/ ADJ [*voix*] quavering, shaking; [*vieillard*] with a quavering voice

chevrotement /ʃəvʀɔtmɑ̃/ NM [*de voix*] quavering, shaking; [*de vieillard*] quavering (voice)

chevroter /ʃəvʀɔte/ ▸ conjug 1 ◂ VI [*personne*] to quaver; [*voix*] to quaver, to shake

chevrotine /ʃəvʀɔtin/ NF buckshot (*NonC*)

chewing-gum (pl **chewing-gums**) /ʃwiŋgɔm/ NM chewing gum (*NonC*) ◆ **un ~** a piece of chewing-gum

Cheyenne /ʃejɛn/ NMF Cheyenne ◆ **les ~s** the Cheyenne

chez /ʃe/ PRÉP 1 (*à la maison*) **~ soi** at home ◆ **être/rester ~ soi** to be/stay at home, to be/stay in ◆ **est-ce qu'elle sera ~ elle aujourd'hui ?** will she be at home *ou* in today? ◆ **venez ~ moi** come to my place ◆ **nous rentrons ~ nous** we are going home ◆ **j'ai des nouvelles de ~ moi** I have news from home ◆ **faites comme ~ vous** make yourself at home ◆ **on n'est plus ~ soi avec tous ces touristes !** it doesn't feel like home any more with all these tourists around! ◆ **nous l'avons trouvée ~ elle** we found her at home

2 ◆ **~ qn** (*maison*) at sb's house *ou* place; (*appartement*) at sb's place *ou* flat (*Brit*) *ou* apartment (*US*); (*famille*) in sb's family *ou* home ◆ **~ moi nous sommes 6** there are 6 of us in my *ou* our family ◆ **près de/devant/de ~ qn** near/in front of/from sb's place *ou* house ◆ **de/près de ~ nous** from/near (our) home *ou* our place *ou* our house ◆ **~ Robert/le voisin** at Robert's (house)/the neighbour's (house) ◆ **~ moi/son frère, c'est tout petit** my/his brother's place is tiny ◆ **je vais ~ lui/Robert** I'm going to his place/to Robert's (place) ◆ **il séjourne ~ moi** he is staying at my place *ou* with me ◆ **la personne ~ qui je suis allé** the person to whose house I went ◆ **passons par ~ eux/mon frère** let's drop in on them/my brother, let's drop by their place/my brother's place ◆ **~ M. Lebrun** (*sur une adresse*) c/o Mr Lebrun ◆ **~ Rosalie** (*enseigne de café*) Rosalie's, chez Rosalie ◆ **~ nous** (*pays*) in our country, at home, back home*; (*région*) at home, back home*; (*maison*) in our house, at home ◆ **~ nous au Canada/en Bretagne** (*là-bas*) back (home) in Canada/Brittany; (*ici*) here in Canada/Brittany ◆ **c'est une coutume/paysanne (bien) de ~ nous** it/she is one of our typical local customs/country girls ◆ **~ eux/vous, il n'y a pas de parlement** in their/your country there's no parliament ◆ **il a été élevé ~ les Jésuites** he was brought up in a Jesuit school *ou* by the Jesuits

3 (*avec nom de métier*) **~ l'épicier/le coiffeur** at the grocer's/the hairdresser's ◆ **je vais ~ le boucher** I'm going to the butcher's ◆ **il va ~ le dentiste/le médecin** he's going to the dentist('s)/the doctor('s)

4 (*avec groupe humain ou animal*) among ◆ **~ les Français/les Romains** among the French/the Romans ◆ **~ les fourmis/le singe** in ants/monkeys ◆ **on trouve cet instinct ~ les animaux** you find this instinct in animals ◆ **~ les politiciens** among politicians ◆ **~ les hommes/les femmes** (*Sport*) in the men's/women's

5 (*avec personne, œuvre*) **~ Balzac/Picasso on trouve de tout** in Balzac/Picasso you find a bit of everything ◆ **c'est rare ~ un enfant de cet âge** it's rare in a child of that age ◆ **~ lui, c'est une habitude** it's a habit with him ◆ **~ lui c'est le foie qui ne va pas** it's his liver that gives him trouble

6 (* : *intensif*) **c'est un abruti de ~ abruti** he's a complete fool ◆ **c'est nul de ~ nul** it's complete rubbish*

chez-soi /ʃeswa/ NM INV home (of one's own) ◆ **avoir un ~** to have a home of one's own *ou* a home to call one's own

chiadé, e‡ /ʃjade/ (ptp de **chiader**) ADJ (= *difficile*) [*problème*] tough*, stiff*; (= *approfondi*) [*exposé*] thorough; (= *perfectionné*) [*appareil*] clever, nifty*

chiader‡ /ʃjade/ ▸ conjug 1 ◂ VT [+ *leçon*] to swot up* (*Brit*), to cram; [+ *examen*] to cram for*, to swot for* (*Brit*); [+ *exposé*] to work on, to swot up* for (*Brit*) ◆ **il a chiadé sa lettre** he worked on his letter till it was perfect VI (= *travailler*) to swot* (*Brit*), to slog away* (*Brit*), to grind away (*US*)

chialer* /ʃjale/ ▸ conjug 1 ◂ VI (= *pleurer*) to blubber*

chialeur, -euse* /ʃjalœʀ, øz/ NM,F crybaby*

chiant, chiante‡ /ʃjɑ̃, ʃjɑ̃t/ ADJ [*personne, problème*] damn‡ *ou* bloody‡ (*Brit*) annoying ◆ **ce roman est ~** this novel's damn‡ *ou* bloody‡ (*Brit*) boring ◆ **c'est ~** it's a damn‡ *ou* bloody‡ (*Brit*) nuisance, it's damn‡ *ou* bloody‡ (*Brit*) annoying ◆ **~ comme la pluie** *ou* **un lundi** as boring as hell‡ ◆ **tu es ~ avec tes questions !** you're a pain in the arse** (*Brit*) *ou* ass** (*US*) with all your questions!

chiard‡ /ʃjaʀ/ NM brat

chiasme /kjasm/ NM (*Littérat*) chiasmus

chiasse /ʃjas/ NF ‡ 1 (= *colique*) **avoir/attraper la ~** (*lit*) to have/get the runs* *ou* the trots*; (*peur*) to have/get the willies*, to be/get scared witless *ou* shitless** ◆ **ça lui donne la ~** (*lit*) it gives him the runs*; (*peur*) it scares him witless *ou* shitless** 2 (= *poisse*) **c'est la ~, quelle ~** what a damn‡ *ou* bloody‡ (*Brit*) pain COMP **chiasse de mouche** fly speck

chiatique‡ /ʃjatik/ ADJ [*personne, problème*] damn‡ *ou* bloody‡ (*Brit*) annoying

chic /ʃik/ NM 1 (= *élégance*) [*de toilette, chapeau*] stylishness; [*de personne*] style ◆ **avoir du ~** [*toilette, chapeau*] to have style, to be stylish; [*personne*] to have (great) style ◆ **être habillé avec ~** to be stylishly dressed; → **bon**[1]

2 (*locutions*) **avoir le ~ pour faire qch** to have the knack of doing sth ◆ **de ~** [*peindre, dessiner*] without a model, from memory ◆ **traduire/écrire qch de ~** to translate/write sth off the cuff

ADJ INV 1 (= *élégant*) [*chapeau, toilette, personne*] stylish, smart ◆ **~ et choc** smart and stylish

2 (= *de la bonne société*) [*dîner*] smart, posh* ◆ **deux messieurs ~** two smart(-looking) gentlemen ◆ **les gens ~** the smart set, posh* people

3 (* = *gentil, généreux*) decent*, nice ◆ **c'est une ~ fille** she's a nice girl ◆ **c'est un ~ type** he's a decent sort *ou* a nice guy* *ou* a nice bloke* (*Brit*) ◆ **elle a été très ~ avec moi** she's been very nice *ou* decent to me ◆ **c'est très ~ de sa part** that's very decent *ou* nice of him

EXCL ◆ **~ (alors)!** * great!*

chicane /ʃikan/ NF 1 (= *zigzag*) [*de barrage routier*] ins and outs, twists and turns; [*de circuit automobile*] chicane; [*de gymkhana*] in and out, zigzag ◆ **des camions stationnés en ~ gênaient la circulation** lorries parked at intervals on both sides of the street held up the traffic 2 († : *Jur*) (= *objection*) quibble; (= *querelle*) squabble, petty quarrel ◆ **aimer la ~, avoir l'esprit de ~** (*disputes*) to enjoy picking quarrels with people, to enjoy bickering; (*procès*) to enjoy bickering over points of procedure ◆ **chercher ~ à qn, faire des ~s à qn** to pick petty quarrels with sb ◆ **gens de ~** pettifoggers

chicaner /ʃikane/ ▸ conjug 1 ◂ VT 1 († *ou littér*) **~ qch à qn** (= *mesurer*) to quibble with sb about *ou* over sth ◆ **nul ne lui chicane son courage** (= *contester*) no one disputes his courage *ou* calls his courage into question 2 († *ou littér* = *chercher querelle à*) **~ qn (sur *ou* au sujet de qch)** to quibble *ou* squabble with sb (over sth) ◆ **ils se chicanent continuellement** they're constantly bickering VI 1 (= *ergoter*) **~ sur** to quibble about 2 († : *Jur*) to pettifog †

chicanerie † /ʃikanʀi/ NF (= *disputes*) wrangling, petty quarrelling (*NonC*); (= *tendance à ergoter*) (constant) quibbling ◆ **toutes ces ~s** all this quibbling

chicaneur, -euse /ʃikanœʀ, øz/ ADJ argumentative, pettifogging NM,F quibbler

chicanier, -ière /ʃikanje, jɛʀ/ ADJ quibbling NM,F quibbler

chicano /ʃikano/ ADJ Chicano (*souvent injurieux*) NMF **Chicano** Chicano (*souvent injurieux*)

chiche[1] /ʃiʃ/ ADJ → **pois**

chiche[2] /ʃiʃ/ ADJ 1 (= *mesquin*) [*personne*] niggardly, mean; [*rétribution*] niggardly, paltry, mean; [*repas*] scanty, meagre (*Brit*), meager (*US*); [*existence*] meagre; [*lumière*] pale ◆ **comme cadeau, c'est un peu ~** it's not much of a gift ◆ **être ~ de paroles/compliments** to be sparing with one's words/compliments 2 (* = *capable*) **être ~ de faire qch** to be able to do sth *ou* capable of doing sth ◆ **tu n'es pas ~ (de le faire)** you couldn't (do that) ◆ **~ que je le fais !** I bet you I do it!, (I) bet you I will! ◆ **~ ?** – **~ !** are you on?* *ou* are you game?* – you're on!*

chiche-kebab (pl **chiche(s)-kebab(s)**) /ʃiʃkebab/ NM shish kebab

chichement /ʃiʃmɑ̃/ ADV [*récompenser, nourrir*] meanly, meagrely (*Brit*), meagerly (*US*); [*vivre, se nourrir*] (= *pauvrement*) poorly; (= *mesquinement*) meanly

chichi* /ʃiʃi/ NM 1 ◆ **~(s)** (= *embarras*) fuss (*NonC*), carry-on* (*NonC*); (= *manières*) fuss (*NonC*) ◆ **faire des ~s *ou* du ~** (*embarras*) to fuss, to make a fuss; (*manières*) to make a fuss ◆ **ce sont des gens à ~(s)** they're the sort of people who make a fuss ◆ **on vous invite sans ~(s)** we're inviting you informally ◆ **ce sera sans ~** it'll be quite informal 2 (= *beignet*) ≈ doughnut

chichiteux, -euse* /ʃiʃitø, øz/ ADJ (*péj*) (= *faiseur d'embarras*) troublesome; (= *maniéré*) fussy

chicon /ʃikɔ̃/ NM (= *romaine*) cos (lettuce) (*Brit*), romaine (*US*); (*Belg* = *endive*) chicory (*NonC*) (*Brit*), endive (*US*)

chicorée /ʃikɔʀe/ NF (= *salade*) endive (*Brit*), chicory (*US*); (*à café*) chicory ◆ **~ frisée** curly endive (*Brit*), escarole (*US*)

chicos* /ʃikos/ ADJ [*personne*] stylish, smart; [*quartier, restaurant*] posh* ◆ **c'est ~ chez toi !** your place is very plush!*

chicot /ʃiko/ NM [*de dent, arbre*] stump ◆ **mes ~s*** (= *mes dents*) my teeth

chicotin /ʃikɔtɛ̃/ NM → **amer**[2]

chié, e[1]‡ /ʃje/ ADJ 1 (= *bien*) damn‡ *ou* bloody‡ (*Brit*) good ◆ **elle est ~e, sa moto!** his motorbike's something else!* *ou* wicked!‡ 2 (= *difficile*) tough*, stiff* ◆ **il est ~, ce problème** it's a hell of a problem‡ 3 (= *qui exagère*) **t'es (pas) ~ d'arriver toujours en retard !** it's a bit much you always turning up late! ◆ **avoir menti comme ça, c'est** ~ what a nerve* to have lied like that

chiée[2] **/ʃje/ NF ◆ **une ~ de, des ~s de** a hell of a lot of‡

chien /ʃjɛ̃/ NM 1 (= *animal*) dog ◆ **petit** ~ (*jeune*) puppy, pup; (*de petite taille*) small dog ◆ **le ~ est le meilleur ami de l'homme** a man's best friend is his dog ◆ **"(attention) chien méchant"** "beware of the dog" ◆ **faire le ~ fou** to fool about

2 [*de fusil*] hammer, cock

3 (*injure*) **quel ~ !** (you) swine!*

4 (* = *frange*) ~**s** fringe (*Brit*), bangs (*US*)

5 (*Naut*) **coup de** ~ squall

6 (*locutions*) **coiffée à la** ~ wearing a fringe (*Brit*), wearing bangs (*US*) ◆ **oh le beau ~~ !** nice doggy!, good doggy! ◆ **c'est le ~~ à sa mémère !** (*péj*) who's mummy's (*Brit*) *ou* mommy's (*US*) little boy then! ◆ **en ~ de fusil** curled up ◆ **quel ~ de temps !** *ou* **temps de ~ !** what filthy *ou* foul weather! ◆ **c'est une vie de ~ !*** it's a dog's life! ◆ **ce métier de** ~ this rotten job* ◆ **comme un** ~ [*mourir, traiter*] like a dog ◆ **elle a du ~*** she has a certain something*, she's very attractive ◆ **c'est pas fait pour les ~s !*** it's there to be used ◆ **être** *ou* **vivre** *ou* **s'entendre comme ~ et chat** to fight like cat and dog, to always be at one another's throats ◆ **ils se sont regardés en ~s de faïence** they just stood *ou* sat glaring at each other ◆ **arriver comme un ~ dans un jeu de quilles** to turn up when least needed *ou* wanted ◆ **recevoir qn comme un ~ dans un jeu de quilles** to give sb a cold reception ◆ **faire les** *ou* **tenir la rubrique des ~s écrasés*** to write nothing but fillers ◆ **je ne suis pas ton ~ !** I'm not your slave *ou* servant! ◆ **je lui garde** *ou* **réserve un ~ de ma chienne*** I'll get even with him* ◆ **entre ~ et loup** at dusk ◆ **un ~ regarde bien un évêque** (*Prov*) a cat may look at a king (*Prov*) ◆ **les ~s aboient, la caravane passe** (*Prov*) let the world say what it will ◆ **bon ~ chasse de race** (*Prov*) like father like son (*Prov*)

ADJ INV 1 (= *avare*) mean, stingy*

2 (= *méchant*) rotten* ◆ **elle n'a pas été ~ avec toi** she was quite decent to you

COMP **chien d'appartement** house dog
chien d'arrêt pointer
chien d'attaque attack dog
chien d'avalanche mountain rescue dog
chien d'aveugle guide dog
chien de berger sheepdog
chien de chasse gun dog
chien de combat fighting dog
chien couchant setter ◆ **faire le ~ couchant** to kowtow, to toady (*auprès de* to)
chien courant hound
chien de garde guard dog, watchdog
chien de manchon lapdog
chien de mer dogfish
chien de meute hound
chien policier police dog, tracker dog
chien des Pyrénées Pyrenean mountain dog, Great Pyrenees (*US*)
chien de race pedigree dog
chien de salon ⇒ **chien de manchon**
chien savant (*lit*) performing dog; (*fig*) know-all
chien de traîneau husky

chien-assis (pl **chiens-assis**) /ʃjɛ̃asi/ NM ≈ dormer window (*Brit*), dormer (*US*)

chiendent /ʃjɛ̃dɑ̃/ NM 1 (= *plante*) couch grass, quitch (grass); → **brosse** 2 **le** ~ †* (= *l'ennui*) the trouble *ou* rub

chienlit /ʃjɑ̃li/ NF 1 (= *pagaille*) **c'est la** ~ it's havoc *ou* chaos 2 († = *mascarade*) fancy-dress (*Brit*) *ou* costume (*US*) parade

chien-loup (pl **chiens-loups**) /ʃjɛ̃lu/ NM wolfhound

chienne /ʃjɛn/ NF bitch

> Lorsque l'on ne parle pas spécifiquement du sexe de l'animal, **chienne** se traduit par **dog**.

◆ **j'ai sorti la** ~ I took the dog out ◆ **c'est un chien ou une ~ ?** is it a dog or a bitch? ◆ **~ !**‡ (= *injure*) (you) bitch!** ◆ **quelle ~ de vie !**‡ life's a bitch!‡

chier** /ʃje/ ▸ conjug 7 ◂ VI 1 (= *déféquer*) to shit**, to crap** ◆ **~ un coup** to have a crap** *ou* shit**

2 (*locutions*) **faire ~ qn** [*personne*] (= *ennuyer*) to bore the pants off sb‡; (= *tracasser, harceler*) to bug sb‡, to piss sb off**, to get up sb's nose‡ (*Brit*) ◆ **ça me fait** ~ it pisses me off**, it's a pain in the arse** (*Brit*) *ou* ass** (*US*) ◆ **envoyer ~ qn** to tell sb to piss off** *ou* bugger off** (*Brit*) ◆ **va ~ !**** fuck off!** ◆ **je me suis fait ~ pendant trois heures à réparer la voiture** I sweated my guts out‡ for three hours repairing the car ◆ **qu'est-ce qu'on se fait ~ à ses conférences !** what a fucking** *ou* bloody‡ (*Brit*) bore his lectures are! ◆ **ça va ~ (des bulles) !** there'll be one hell of a row!‡ ◆ **y a pas à ~, c'est lui le meilleur** say what you damn *ou* bloody (*Brit*) well like‡, he's the best ◆ **il faut quand même pas ~ dans la colle !** you've got a fucking nerve!** ◆ **(nul) à** ~ (= *mauvais*) [*film, livre, service*] crappy**, crap** (*attrib*); [*personne, appareil*] fucking** *ou* bloody‡ (*Brit*) useless; (= *laid*) fucking** *ou* bloody‡ (*Brit*) hideous ◆ **il a chié dans son froc**** he crapped himself**

chierie** /ʃiʀi/ NF (real) pain in the butt‡ *ou* arse** (*Brit*) *ou* ass** (*US*)

chiffe /ʃif/ NF 1 (*sans volonté*) spineless individual, drip* ◆ **je suis comme une ~ (molle)** (*fatigué*) I feel like a wet rag; → **mou**[1] 2 (= *chiffon*) rag

chiffon /ʃifɔ̃/ NM 1 (*usagé*) (piece of) rag; (*pour essuyer*) duster (*Brit*), dust cloth (*US*) ◆ **donner un coup de ~ à qch, passer un coup de ~ sur qch** to give sth a wipe *ou* go over sth with a cloth ◆ **vieux ~s** old rags ◆ **votre devoir est un vrai** ~ your homework is a dreadful mess ◆ **mettre ses vêtements en** ~ to throw down one's clothes in a crumpled heap ◆ **parler ~s*** to talk about clothes ◆ **agiter le ~** *ou* **un ~ rouge** (*fig*) to wave the *ou* a red rag; → **poupée**

2 (*Papeterie*) **le** ~ rag ◆ **fait avec du** ~ made from rags; → **papier**

COMP **chiffon à chaussures** shoe cloth *ou* rag
chiffon à meubles ⇒ **chiffon à poussière**
chiffon de papier ◆ **écrire qch sur un ~ de papier** to write sth (down) on a (crumpled) scrap of paper ◆ **ce traité n'est qu'un ~ de papier** this treaty isn't worth the paper it's written on *ou* is just a useless scrap of paper
chiffon à poussière duster (*Brit*), dust cloth (*US*)

chiffonnade /ʃifɔnad/ NF chiffonnade

chiffonné, e /ʃifɔne/ (ptp de **chiffonner**) ADJ 1 (= *fatigué*) [*visage*] worn-looking 2 (= *sympathique*) **un petit nez** ~ a pert little nose ◆ **un joli minois** ~ a funny little face

chiffonner /ʃifɔne/ ▸ conjug 1 ◂ VT 1 (*lit*) [+ *papier*] to crumple; [+ *habits*] to crease, to rumple, to crumple; [+ *étoffe*] to crease, to crumple 2 (* = *contrarier*) **ça me chiffonne** it bothers *ou* worries me ◆ **qu'est-ce qui te chiffonne ?** what's bothering *ou* worrying you? VPR **se chiffonner** ◆ **ce tissu se chiffonne facilement** this material creases easily *ou* is easily creased

chiffonnier /ʃifɔnje/ NM 1 (= *personne*) ragman, rag-and-bone man (*Brit*) ◆ **se battre** *ou* **se disputer comme des ~s** to fight like cat and dog ◆ **c'est une bataille de ~s** it's no holds barred; → EMMAÜS 2 (= *meuble*) chiffon(n)ier

chiffrable /ʃifʀabl/ ADJ ◆ **ce n'est pas** ~ it's impossible to put a figure on it

chiffrage /ʃifʀaʒ/ NM 1 [*de message*] (en)coding, ciphering; (*Ordin*) [*de données, télégramme*] ciphering 2 [*de dépenses, dommages*] assessing 3 [*de pages*] numbering 4 [*d'effets personnels, linge*] marking (with one's *ou* sb's initials) 5 (*Mus*) [*d'accord*] figuring

chiffre /ʃifʀ/ NM 1 (= *caractère*) figure, numeral, digit (*Math*); (= *nombre*) number ◆ **donne-moi un ~ entre 1 et 8** give me a number between 1 and 8 ◆ ~ **arabe/romain** Arab/Roman numeral ◆ **nombre** *ou* **numéro de 7 ~s** 7-figure *ou* 7-digit number ◆ **inflation à deux/trois ~s** double-/triple-digit inflation, two-/three-figure inflation ◆ **écrire un nombre en ~s** to write out a number in figures ◆ **science des ~s** science of numbers ◆ **aligner des ~s** to draw up columns of figures

2 (= *résultat*) figure; (= *montant*) total ◆ **15 blessés, c'est le ~ provisoire** there's a total of 15 wounded so far, at the last count there were 15 wounded ◆ **je n'ai pas les ~s en tête** I can't recall the figures ◆ **ça atteint des ~s astronomiques** it reaches an astronomical figure *ou* sum ◆ **selon les ~s officiels** according to official figures ◆ **les ~s du chômage** the unemployment *ou* jobless figures, the number of unemployed ◆ **en ~s ronds** in round figures

3 (*Comm*) ~ **(d'affaires)** turnover ◆ **il fait un ~ (d'affaires) de 3 millions** he has a turnover of 3 million ◆ **ils font du** ~ they're making money ◆ **je n'ai pas fait mon ~ cette année** I didn't get the turnover I wanted this year ◆ ~ **net/brut** net/gross figure *ou* turnover ◆ **~s de vente** sales figures ◆ **ils ont doublé leurs ~s de vente** they have doubled their sales; → **impôt**

4 (= *code*) [*de message*] code, cipher; [*de coffre-fort*] combination ◆ **écrire une lettre en ~s** to write a letter in code *ou* cipher ◆ **on a trouvé leur** ~ their code has been broken ◆ **le (service du)** ~ the cipher office

5 (= *initiales*) (set of) initials, monogram ◆ **mouchoir brodé à son** ~ handkerchief embroidered with one's initials *ou* monogram

6 (*Mus* = *indice*) figure

chiffré, e /ʃifʀe/ (ptp de **chiffrer**) ADJ 1 (= *évalué*) [*analyse, argument*] backed up by figures ◆ **données ~es** detailed facts and figures ◆ **le rapport fixe des objectifs ~s** the report sets out targets in precise figures ◆ **aucune précision ~e n'a été donnée** no figures were given ◆ **faire une proposition ~e** to propose a figure 2 (= *codé*) **langage** ~ code (language), cipher ◆ **message** ~ coded message, message in code *ou* cipher 3 (*Mus*) **basse ~e** thorough *ou* figured bass

chiffrement /ʃifʀəmɑ̃/ NM [*de texte*] (en)coding, ciphering

chiffrer /ʃifʀe/ ▸ conjug 1 ◂ VT 1 (= *coder*) [+ *message*] to (en)code, to cipher; (*Ordin*) [+ *données, télégramme*] to encode; → **message** 2 (= *évaluer*) [+ *dépenses, dommages*] to put a figure to, to assess 3 (= *numéroter*) [+ *pages*] to number 4 (= *compter*) to count 5 (= *marquer*) [+ *effets personnels, linge*] to mark (with one's *ou* sb's initials) 6 (*Mus*) [+ *accord*] to figure VI *ou* VPR **se chiffrer** ◆ **(se) ~ à** to add up to, to amount to, to come to ◆ **ça (se) chiffre à combien ?** what *ou* how much does that add up to? *ou* amount to? *ou* come to? ◆ **ça (se) chiffre par millions** it adds up to *ou* amounts to *ou* comes to millions ◆ **ça commence à ~ !** it's starting to mount up! ◆ **ça finit par ~*** it all adds up

chiffreur, -euse /ʃifʀœʀ, øz/ NM,F coder

chignole /ʃiɲɔl/ NF (= *outil*) (*à main*) (hand) drill; (*électrique*) (electric) drill; (* = *voiture*) jalopy* (*hum*)

chignon /ʃiɲɔ̃/ NM bun, chignon ◆ ~ **banane** French pleat ◆ **se faire un ~, relever ses cheveux en** ~ to put one's hair into a bun; → **crêper**

chihuahua /ʃiwawa/ NM Chihuahua

chiisme /ʃiism/ NM Shiism

chiite /ʃiit/ ADJ, NMF Shiite

Chili /ʃili/ NM Chile

chilien, -ienne /ʃiljɛ̃, jɛn/ ADJ Chilean NM,F **Chilien(ne)** Chilean

chimère /ʃimɛʀ/ NF [1] *(= illusion)* (wild) dream, pipe dream, chim(a)era *(frm)* ◆ **le bonheur est une ~** happiness is just a dream *ou* an illusion ◆ **c'est une ~ que de croire ...** it's an illusion to think that ... ◆ **tes grands projets, ~s (que tout cela) !** your grand plans are nothing but pipe dreams *ou* (idle) fancies ◆ **un monde peuplé de vagues ~s** a world filled with vague imaginings ◆ **poursuivre** *ou* **caresser des ~s** to chase rainbows [2] *(Myth)* **la Chimère** chim(a)era, Chim(a)era [3] *(Bio)* chim(a)era [4] *(= poisson)* chimaera

chimérique /ʃimeʀik/ ADJ [1] *(= utopique) [esprit, projet, idée]* fanciful; *[rêve]* wild *(épith)*, idle *(épith)* ◆ **c'est un esprit ~** he's a real dreamer [2] *(= imaginaire) [personnage]* imaginary, chimerical

chimie /ʃimi/ NF chemistry ◆ **~ organique/minérale** organic/inorganic chemistry ◆ **cours/expérience de ~** chemistry class/experiment ◆ **la merveilleuse ~ de l'amour** love's marvellous chemistry

chimio* /ʃimjo/ NF (abrév de **chimiothérapie**) chemo*

chimiothérapie /ʃimjoteʀapi/ NF chemotherapy

chimiothérapique /ʃimjoteʀapik/ ADJ chemotherapeutic

chimique /ʃimik/ ADJ chemical ◆ **ça a un goût ~** it tastes synthetic; → **produit**

chimiquement /ʃimikmɑ̃/ ADV chemically

chimiquier /ʃimikje/ NM chemical tanker

chimiste /ʃimist/ NMF chemist *(scientist)*; → **ingénieur**

chimpanzé /ʃɛ̃pɑ̃ze/ NM chimpanzee, chimp*

chinchilla /ʃɛ̃ʃila/ NM *(= animal, fourrure)* chinchilla

Chine /ʃin/ NF China ◆ **~ populaire/nationaliste** Communist *ou* Red/nationalist China ◆ **la République populaire de ~** the Chinese People's Republic, the People's Republic of China; → **crêpe[2], encre**

chine[1] /ʃin/ NM [1] *(= papier)* rice paper [2] *(= vase)* china vase; *(= porcelaine)* china

chine[2]* /ʃin/ NF [1] *(= brocante)* **faire de la ~** to hunt (around) for antiques [2] *(= porte à porte)* **vente à la ~** door-to-door selling

chiné, e /ʃine/ (ptp de **chiner**) ADJ *[étoffe]* mottled, chiné *(SPÉC)*

chiner /ʃine/ ► conjug 1 ◄ VT [1] *[+ étoffe]* to dye the warp of [2] *(* = taquiner)* to kid, to have on* *(Brit)*, to rag* ◆ **tu ne vois pas qu'il te chine** don't you see he's kidding you *ou* having you on* *(Brit)* ◆ **je n'aime pas qu'on me chine** I don't like being ragged* VI * to hunt (around) for antiques

Chinetoque** /ʃintɔk/ NMF *(injurieux = Chinois)* Chink***(injurieux)*

chineur, -euse* /ʃinœʀ, øz/ NM,F *(= brocanteur)* antique dealer; *(= amateur)* antique-hunter

chinois, e /ʃinwa, waz/ ADJ [1] *(de Chine)* Chinese; → **ombre[1]** [2] *(péj = pointilleux) [personne]* pernickety, fussy; *[règlement]* hair-splitting NM [1] *(= langue)* Chinese ◆ **c'est du ~*** *(péj)* it's all Greek to me*, it's double Dutch* *(Brit)* [2] ◆ **Chinois** Chinese, Chinese man ◆ **les Chinois** the Chinese [3] *(* : péj = maniaque)* hair-splitter [4] *(Culin = passoire)* (small conical) strainer NF **Chinoise** Chinese, Chinese woman

chinoiser /ʃinwaze/ ► conjug 1 ◄ VI to split hairs ◆ **~ sur** to quibble over

chinoiserie /ʃinwazʀi/ NF [1] *(= subtilité excessive)* hair-splitting *(NonC)* [2] *(= complications)* **~s** unnecessary complications *ou* fuss ◆ **les ~s de l'administration** red tape ◆ **tout ça, ce sont des ~s** all this is unnecessarily complicated [3] *(Art) (= décoration)* chinoiserie; *(= objet)* Chinese ornament, Chinese curio

chintz /ʃints/ NM chintz

chiot /ʃjo/ NM pup(py)

chiotte /ʃjɔt/ NF *ou* m [1] *(*‡= WC)* **~s** bog‡ *(Brit)*, can‡ *(US)*, john‡ *(US)* ◆ **aux ~s l'arbitre !** what a shitty referee!** ◆ **quelle ~ !, c'est la ~ !** what a pain in the arse!** *(Brit) ou* ass!** *(US)* ◆ **quel temps de ~ !** what shitty weather!** ◆ **c'est de la musique de ~** it's crap(py) music** ◆ **avoir un goût de ~** *[personne]* to have crap taste**; → **corvée** [2] *(‡ = voiture)* jalopy* *(hum)*

chiper* /ʃipe/ ► conjug 1 ◄ VT *(= voler) [+ portefeuille, idée]* to pinch*, to filch*; *[+ rhume]* to catch

chipeur, -euse* /ʃipœʀ, øz/ ADJ *[gamin]* thieving NM,F thief

chipie* /ʃipi/ NF vixen *(péj)* ◆ **petite ~ !** you little devil!*

chipolata /ʃipɔlata/ NF chipolata

chipotage* /ʃipɔtaʒ/ NM *(= marchandage, ergotage)* quibbling; *(pour manger)* picking *ou* nibbling (at one's food)

chipoter* /ʃipɔte/ ► conjug 1 ◄ VI *(= manger)* to be a fussy eater; *(= ergoter)* to quibble *(sur* about, over); *(= marchander)* to quibble *(sur* over); ◆ **~ sur la nourriture** to nibble *ou* pick at one's food ◆ **tu chipotes là !** now you're quibbling! ◆ **vous n'allez pas ~ pour 2 € !** you're not going to quibble about 2 euros! VPR **se chipoter** to squabble *(sur* over)

chipoteur, -euse* /ʃipɔtœʀ, øz/ ADJ *(= marchandeur)* haggling; *(= ergoteur)* quibbling; *(en mangeant)* fussy NM,F *(= marchandeur)* haggler; *(= ergoteur)* quibbler; *(en mangeant)* fussy eater

chips /ʃips/ NFPL ◆ **(pommes) ~** (potato) crisps *(Brit) ou* chips *(US)*

> ⚠ **chips** se traduit par **chips** uniquement en anglais américain.

chique /ʃik/ NF *(= tabac)* quid, chew; *(* = enflure)* (facial) swelling, lump (on the cheek); *(= puce)* chigoe, chigger; → **couper**

chiqué* /ʃike/ NM [1] *(= bluff)* pretence *(NonC)*, bluffing *(NonC)* ◆ **il a fait ça au ~** he bluffed it out ◆ **il prétend que cela le laisse froid mais c'est du ~** he claims it leaves him cold but it's all put on* [2] *(factice)* sham *(NonC)* ◆ **ces combats de catch c'est du ~** these wrestling matches are all sham *ou* all put on* *ou* are faked ◆ **combat sans ~** fight that's for real* ◆ **~ !, remboursez !** what a sham!, give us our money back! [3] *(= manières)* **faire du ~** to put on airs (and graces)

chiquement* /ʃikmɑ̃/ ADV *[s'habiller]* smartly, stylishly; *[traiter, accueillir]* kindly, decently

chiquenaude /ʃiknod/ NF *(= pichenette)* flick, flip ◆ **il l'enleva d'une ~** he flicked *ou* flipped it off ◆ **une ~ suffirait à renverser le gouvernement** it wouldn't take much to overturn the government

chiquer /ʃike/ ► conjug 1 ◄ VT *[+ tabac]* to chew; → **tabac** VI to chew tobacco

chiqueur, -euse /ʃikœʀ, øz/ NM,F tobacco-chewer

chirographaire /kiʀɔgʀafɛʀ/ ADJ unsecured

chirographie /kiʀɔgʀafi/ NF ⇒ **chiromancie**

chiromancie /kiʀɔmɑ̃si/ NF palmistry, chiromancy *(SPÉC)*

chiromancien, -ienne /kiʀɔmɑ̃sjɛ̃, jɛn/ NM,F palmist, chiromancer *(SPÉC)*

chiropracteur /kiʀɔpʀaktœʀ/ NM chiropractor

chiropracticien, -ienne /kiʀɔpʀaktisjɛ̃, jɛn/ NM,F chiropractor

chiropractie /kiʀɔpʀakti/, **chiropraxie** /kiʀɔpʀaksi/ NF chiropractic

chirurgical, e (mpl **-aux**) /ʃiʀyʀʒikal, o/ ADJ *(lit, fig)* surgical ◆ **acte ~** surgical procedure ◆ **intervention** *ou* **opération ~e** operation ◆ **frappe ~e** *(Mil)* surgical strike

chirurgie /ʃiʀyʀʒi/ NF surgery *(science)* ◆ **~ esthétique/dentaire/réparatrice** cosmetic/dental/reconstructive surgery

chirurgien, -ienne /ʃiʀyʀʒjɛ̃, jɛn/ NM,F surgeon ◆ **~-dentiste** dental surgeon ◆ **~-major** *(Mil)* army surgeon NM ◆ **(poisson) ~** surgeonfish

Chisinau /ʃizino/ N Kishinev, Chisinau

chistera /(t)ʃistera/ NF *ou* m wicker basket *(in game of pelota)*

chiure /ʃjyʀ/ NF ◆ **~ de mouche** fly speck

chlamydia (pl **chlamydiae**) /klamidja/ NF chlamydia

chlâsse‡ /ʃlas/ ADJ → **schlass**

chleuh** /ʃlø/ *(injurieux)* ADJ Kraut***(injurieux)* NMF **Chleuh** Kraut***(injurieux)*

chlinguer‡ /ʃlɛ̃ge/ VI to stink

chlorate /klɔʀat/ NM chlorate

chlore /klɔʀ/ NM chlorine

chloré, e /klɔʀe/ (ptp de **chlorer**) ADJ chlorinated

chlorer /klɔʀe/ ► conjug 1 ◄ VT to chlorinate

chlorhydrique /klɔʀidʀik/ ADJ hydrochloric

chlorique /klɔʀik/ ADJ chloric

chlorofluorocarbone /klɔʀoflyɔʀokaʀbɔn/ NM chlorofluorocarbon

chlorofluorocarbure /klɔʀoflyɔʀokaʀbyʀ/ NM chlorofluorocarbon

chloroforme /klɔʀɔfɔʀm/ NM chloroform

chloroformer /klɔʀɔfɔʀme/ ► conjug 1 ◄ VT to chloroform

chlorophylle /klɔʀɔfil/ NF chlorophyll

chlorophyllien, -ienne /klɔʀɔfiljɛ̃, jɛn/ ADJ chlorophyllous

chlorose /klɔʀoz/ NF *(Méd)* chlorosis, green-sickness *(NonC)*; *(Bot)* chlorosis

chlorure /klɔʀyʀ/ NM chloride ◆ **~ de sodium** sodium chloride ◆ **~ de chaux** chloride of lime

chlorurer /klɔʀyʀe/ ► conjug 1 ◄ VT to chlorinate

chnoque* /ʃnɔk/ NM *(péj)* ◆ **quel vieux ~ !** what an old fart!‡ ◆ **eh ! du ~ !** hey! you!

chnouf † /ʃnuf/ NF *(arg Drogue)* dope*

choc /ʃɔk/ NM [1] *(= heurt) [d'objets]* impact; *[de vagues]* crash ◆ **la carrosserie s'est déformée sous le ~** the coachwork twisted with *ou* under the impact ◆ **les barrières de sécurité absorbent les ~s** safety barriers absorb shocks ◆ **cela se brise au moindre ~** it breaks at the slightest bump *ou* knock ◆ **"résiste au(x) choc(s)"** "shock-resistant" ◆ **la résistance au ~ d'un matériau** a material's resistance to shock ◆ **la corde s'est rompue sous le ~** the sudden wrench made the rope snap *ou* snapped the rope

[2] *(= collision) [de véhicules]* crash; *[de personnes]* blow; *(plus léger)* bump ◆ **le ~ entre les véhicules fut très violent** the vehicles crashed together with tremendous force ◆ **~ meurtrier** fatal crash ◆ **il tituba sous le ~** the blow *ou* bump threw him off balance

3 (= bruit) (violent) crash, smash; (sourd) thud, thump; (métallique) clang, clash; (cristallin) clink, chink; [de gouttes, grêlons] drumming (NonC) ◆ **le ~ sourd des obus** the thud of shellfire

4 (= affrontement) [de troupes, émeutiers, équipes, intérêts, cultures, passions] clash ◆ **il y a eu un ~ sanglant entre la police et les émeutiers** there has been a violent clash between police and rioters ◆ **la petite armée ne put résister au ~** the little army could not stand up to the onslaught

5 (= émotion) shock ◆ **le ~ est rude** it comes as ou it's quite a shock ◆ **il ne s'est pas remis du ~** he hasn't got over ou recovered from the shock ◆ **ça m'a fait un drôle de ~ de le voir dans cet état** it gave me a nasty shock ou quite a turn * to see him in that state ◆ **il est encore sous le ~** (à l'annonce d'une nouvelle) he's still in a state of shock; (après un accident) he's still in shock ◆ **tenir le ~** * [personne] to cope; [machine] to hold out ◆ **après la mort de sa femme il n'a pas tenu le ~** he couldn't cope after his wife's death ◆ **encaisser le ~** * to cope; → **état**

◆ **de choc** [troupe, unité, traitement, thérapeutique, tactique] shock; [évêque, patron] high-powered ◆ **duo** ou **tandem de ~** dynamic duo

ADJ INV (= à sensation) ◆ **argument/discours/formule(-)~** shock argument/speech/formula ◆ **film/photo(-)~** shock film/photo ◆ **mesures(-)~** shock measures ◆ **"notre prix-choc : 15 €"** "our special price: €15"

COMP **choc anesthésique** shock due to anaesthetics
choc culturel culture shock
choc électrique electric shock
choc émotionnel emotional shock
choc nerveux (nervous) shock
choc opératoire post-operative shock
choc pétrolier oil crisis
choc psychologique psychological shock
choc en retour (Élec) return shock; (fig) backlash
choc septique toxic shock ◆ **faire un ~ septique** to suffer from toxic shock
choc thermique thermal shock

> ⚠ Attention à ne pas traduire automatiquement **choc** par l'anglais **shock**, qui a des emplois spécifiques.

chochotte * /ʃɔʃɔt/ NF (= femme chichiteuse) fusspot * (Brit), fussbudget (US); (= homme : mauviette) sissy *; (= homme efféminé) namby-pamby * ◆ **arrête de faire la** ou **ta ~ !** stop making such a fuss (about nothing)! * ADJ INV ◆ **elle est très ~** she fusses too much ◆ **il est très ~** (mauviette) he's a real sissy *; (efféminé) he's a real namby-pamby *

choco * /ʃɔko/ (abrév de **chocolat**) NM chocolate

chocolat /ʃɔkɔla/ NM 1 (= substance, boisson, bonbon) chocolate ◆ **mousse/crème au ~** chocolate mousse/cream ◆ **~ au lait/aux noisettes** milk/hazelnut chocolate → **barre, plaque** 2 (= couleur) chocolate (brown) 3 ◆ **être ~** † * to be thwarted ou foiled ADJ INV chocolate(-brown)

COMP **chocolat amer** bitter chocolate; (poudre) cocoa powder
chocolat blanc white chocolate
chocolat chaud hot chocolate
chocolat à croquer plain dark chocolate
chocolat à cuire cooking chocolate
chocolat fondant fondant chocolate
chocolat liégeois chocolate sundae
chocolat de ménage ⇒ **chocolat à cuire**
chocolat noir dark chocolate
chocolat à pâtisser ⇒ **chocolat à cuire**
chocolat en poudre drinking chocolate

chocolaté, e /ʃɔkɔlate/ ADJ (= additionné de chocolat) chocolate-flavoured (Brit) ou -flavored (US), chocolate (épith); (= au goût de chocolat) chocolate-flavoured (Brit) ou -flavored (US), chocolat(e)y *

chocolaterie /ʃɔkɔlatʀi/ NF (= fabrique) chocolate factory; (= magasin) chocolate shop

chocolatier, -ière /ʃɔkɔlatje, jɛʀ/ ADJ chocolate (épith) NM,F (= fabricant) chocolate maker; (= commerçant) chocolate seller

chocolatine /ʃɔkɔlatin/ NF pain au chocolat, chocolate croissant

chocottes * /ʃɔkɔt/ NFPL ◆ **avoir les ~** to have the jitters * ou the heebie-jeebies * ◆ **ça m'a filé les ~** it gave me the jitters * ou the heebie-jeebies *

chœur /kœʀ/ NM 1 (= chanteurs : gén, Rel) choir; [d'opéra, oratorio] chorus 2 (Théât = récitants) chorus 3 (fig) **un ~ de récriminations** (= concert) a chorus of recriminations ◆ **le ~ des mécontents** (= groupe) the band of malcontents 4 (Archit) choir, chancel; → **enfant** 5 (Mus) (= composition) chorus; (= hymne) chorale; (Théât = texte) chorus ◆ **~ à 4 parties** (opéra) 4-part chorus; (Rel) 4-part chorale

◆ **en chœur** (Mus) in chorus; (fig = ensemble) [chanter] in chorus; [répondre, crier] in chorus ou unison ◆ **on s'ennuyait en chœur** (hum) we were all getting bored together ◆ **tous en chœur !** all together now!

choir /ʃwaʀ/ VI (littér ou † ou hum) to fall ◆ **faire ~** to cause to fall ◆ **laisser ~ qch** to drop sth ◆ **laisser ~ ses amis** (fig) to let one's friends down ◆ **se laisser ~ dans un fauteuil** to drop into an armchair

choisi, e /ʃwazi/ (ptp de **choisir**) ADJ 1 (= sélectionné) [morceaux, passages] selected 2 (= raffiné) [langage, termes] carefully chosen; [clientèle, société] select

choisir /ʃwaziʀ/ ► conjug 2 ◄ VT 1 (gén) to choose (entre between); ◆ **des deux solutions, j'ai choisi la première** I chose ou picked the first of the two solutions, I opted ou plumped * (Brit) for the first of the two solutions ◆ **choisissez une carte/un chiffre** pick a card/a number ◆ **il faut savoir ~ ses amis** you must know how to pick ou choose your friends ◆ **dans les soldes, il faut savoir ~** in the sales, you've got to know what to choose ou how to be selective ◆ **se ~ un mari** to choose a husband ◆ **on l'a choisi parmi des douzaines de candidats** he was picked (out) ou selected ou chosen from among dozens of applicants ◆ **tu as (bien) choisi ton moment !** (iro) you really choose your moments, don't you? ◆ **tu as mal choisi ton moment si tu veux une augmentation** you picked the wrong time to ask for a rise

2 ◆ **~ de faire qch** to choose to do sth ◆ **à toi de ~ si et quand tu veux partir** it's up to you to choose if and when you want to leave

choix /ʃwa/ GRAMMAIRE ACTIVE 37.1 NM 1 (= décision) choice ◆ **je n'avais pas le ~** ou **d'autre ~** I had no choice, I had no other option ◆ **de ton ~** of your (own) choosing ◆ **le ~ d'un cadeau est souvent difficile** choosing a gift is often difficult, it's often difficult to choose a gift ◆ **avoir le ~** to have a ou the choice ◆ **faire son ~** to take ou make one's choice, to take one's pick ◆ **mon ~ est fait** I've made my choice ◆ **c'est un ~ à faire** it's a choice you have (ou he has etc) to make ◆ **faire un ~ de société** to choose the kind of society one wants to live in ◆ **~ de vie** life choice ◆ **faire ~ de qch** (frm) to select sth ◆ **laisser le ~ à qn** to leave sb (free) to choose (de faire to do); ◆ **donner le ~ à qn** to give sb the choice (de faire of doing); ◆ **arrêter** ou **fixer** ou **porter son ~ sur qch** to fix one's choice on sth, to settle on sth; → **embarras**

2 (= variété) choice, selection, variety ◆ **ce magasin offre un grand ~** this shop has a wide ou large selection (of goods) ◆ **il y a du ~** there is a choice ◆ **il n'y a pas beaucoup de ~** there isn't a great deal of ou much choice, there isn't a great selection (to choose from)

3 (= échantillonnage) **~ de** selection of ◆ **il avait apporté un ~ de livres** he had brought a selection of books

4 (locutions)

◆ **de + choix** ◆ **de ~** (= de qualité) choice (épith) ◆ **cible de ~** prime target ◆ **morceau de ~** (viande) prime cut ◆ **c'est un morceau de ~** [prestation, poème] it's first-rate ◆ **de premier ~** [fruits] class ou grade one; [agneau, bœuf] prime (épith) ◆ **il n'achète que du premier ~** he only buys top-quality products ◆ **de second ~** (gén) low-quality, low-grade; [fruits, viande] class ou grade two (Brit), market grade (US) ◆ **articles de second ~** seconds

◆ **au choix** ◆ **vous pouvez prendre, au ~, fruits ou fromages** you have a choice between ou of fruit or cheese ◆ **"dessert au choix"** "choice of desserts" ◆ **avancement au ~** (Admin) promotion on merit ou by selection ◆ **au ~ du client** as the customer chooses, according to (the customer's) preference

choke * /(t)ʃɔk/ NM (Helv = starter) choke

choléra /kɔleʀa/ NM cholera

cholérique /kɔleʀik/ ADJ (gén) choleroid; [patient] cholera (épith) NMF cholera patient ou case

cholestérol /kɔlɛsteʀɔl/ NM cholesterol

cholestérolémie /kɔlɛsteʀɔlemi/ NF cholestorolaemia (Brit), cholestorolemia (US)

chômage /ʃomaʒ/ NM unemployment ◆ **le ~ des cadres** executive unemployment, unemployment among executives ◆ **le ~ des jeunes** youth unemployment ◆ **le taux de ~** the unemployment ou jobless rate ◆ **~ saisonnier/chronique** seasonal/chronic unemployment ◆ **toucher le ~** * to get unemployment benefit (Brit), to be on the dole * (Brit), to be on welfare (US); → **allocation, indemnité**

◆ **au chômage** ◆ **être au ~** to be unemployed ou out of work ◆ **s'inscrire au ~** to apply for unemployment benefit (Brit) ou welfare (US), to sign on the dole * (Brit) ◆ **mettre qn au ~** to lay sb off, to make sb redundant (Brit) ◆ **beaucoup ont été mis au ~** there have been many layoffs ou redundancies (Brit)

COMP **chômage de longue durée** long-term unemployment
chômage partiel short-time working
chômage structurel structural unemployment
chômage technique ◆ **mettre en ~ technique** to lay off (temporarily) ◆ **le nombre de travailleurs en ~ technique** the number of workers laid off, the number of layoffs ◆ **l'ordinateur est en panne, on est en ~ technique** the computer is down so we can't do any work

chômé, e /ʃome/ (ptp de **chômer**) ADJ ◆ **jour ~** (férié) public holiday, ≃ bank holiday (Brit); (pour chômage technique) shutdown day; (de grève) strike day ◆ **fête ~e** public holiday, ≃ bank holiday (Brit)

chômedu * /ʃomdy/ NM (= inactivité) unemployment; (= indemnités) dole * (Brit), unemployment (US) ◆ **être au ~** to be on the dole * (Brit) ou on unemployment (US)

chômer /ʃome/ ► conjug 1 ◄ VI 1 (fig = être inactif) [capital, équipements] to lie idle; [esprit, imagination] to be idle, to be inactive ◆ **on n'a pas chômé** we didn't just sit around doing nothing 2 (= être sans travail) [travailleur] to be unemployed, to be out of work ou out of a job; [usine] to be ou stand idle, to be at a standstill; [industrie] to be at a standstill 3 († † = être en congé) to be on holiday (Brit) ou vacation (US) VT † † [+ jour férié] to keep

chômeur, -euse /ʃomœʀ, øz/ NM,F (gén) unemployed person ou worker; (mis au chômage) redundant worker (Brit), laid-off worker (US) ◆ **les ~s (de longue durée)** the (long-term) unemployed ◆ **le nombre des ~s** the number of unemployed ou of people out of work ◆ 3

millions de ~s 3 million unemployed *ou* people out of work

chope /ʃɔp/ NF *(= récipient)* tankard, mug; *(= contenu)* pint

choper /ʃɔpe/ ▸ conjug 1 ◂ VT [1] *(* = voler)* to pinch*, to nick* *(Brit)* [2] *(* = attraper) [+ balle, personne, maladie]* to catch ◆ **se faire ~ par la police** to get nabbed* by the police [3] *(Tennis)* to chop ◆ **balle chopée** chop

chopine /ʃɔpin/ NF *(* = bouteille)* bottle (of wine); *(†† = mesure)* half-litre *(Brit) ou* -liter *(US)*, ≃ pint; *(Can = 0,568 l)* pint ◆ **on a été boire une ~*** we went for a drink

chopper /(t)ʃɔpœʀ/ NM *(= moto)* chopper

choquant, e /ʃɔkɑ̃, ɑt/ ADJ *(= qui heurte le goût)* shocking, appalling; *(= injuste)* outrageous, scandalous; *(= indécent)* shocking, offensive

choquer /ʃɔke/ ▸ conjug 1 ◂ VT [1] *(= scandaliser)* to shock; *(plus fort)* to appal; *(= blesser)* to offend, to shock ◆ **ça m'a choqué de le voir dans cet état** I was shocked *ou* appalled to see him in that state ◆ **ce roman risque de ~** some people may find this novel offensive *ou* shocking ◆ **j'ai été vraiment choqué par son indifférence** I was really shocked *ou* appalled by his indifference ◆ **ne vous choquez pas de ma question** don't be shocked at *ou* by my question ◆ **il a été très choqué de ne pas être invité** he was most offended at not being invited ◆ **cette scène m'a beaucoup choqué** I was deeply shocked by that scene

[2] *(= aller à l'encontre de) [+ délicatesse, pudeur, goût]* to offend (against); *[+ raison]* to offend against, to go against; *[+ vue]* to offend; *[+ oreilles] [son, musique]* to jar on, to offend; *[propos]* to shock, to offend ◆ **cette question a choqué sa susceptibilité** the question offended his sensibilities

[3] *(= commotionner) [chute]* to shake (up); *[accident]* to shake (up), to shock; *[deuil, maladie]* to shake ◆ **être choqué** *(Méd)* to be in shock ◆ **il sortit du véhicule, durement choqué** he climbed out of the vehicle badly shaken *ou* shocked ◆ **la mort de sa mère l'a beaucoup choqué** the death of his mother has shaken him badly

[4] *(= heurter) (gén)* to knock (against); *[+ verres]* to clink ◆ **choquant son verre contre le mien** clinking his glass against mine

[5] *(Naut) [+ cordage, écoute]* to slacken

VPR **se choquer** *(= s'offusquer)* to be shocked ◆ **il se choque facilement** he's easily shocked

choral, e (mpl **chorals**) /kɔʀal/ ADJ choral NM choral(e) NF **chorale** choral society, choir

chorée /kɔʀe/ NF *(Méd)* ◆ **~ (de Huntington)** Huntington's chorea

chorégraphe /kɔʀegʀaf/ NMF choreographer

chorégraphie /kɔʀegʀafi/ NF choreography

chorégraphier /kɔʀegʀafje/ ▸ conjug 7 ◂ VT *(lit, fig)* to choreograph

chorégraphique /kɔʀegʀafik/ ADJ choreographic

choreute /kɔʀøt/ NM chorist *(in ancient Greece)*

choriste /kɔʀist/ NMF *[d'église]* choir member, chorister; *[d'opéra, théâtre antique]* member of the chorus ◆ **les ~s** the choir, the chorus

chorizo /ʃɔʀizo/ NM chorizo

chorus /kɔʀys/ NM ◆ **faire ~** to chorus *ou* voice one's agreement *ou* approval ◆ **faire ~ avec qn** to voice one's agreement with sb ◆ **ils ont fait ~ avec lui pour condamner ces mesures** they joined with him in voicing their condemnation of the measures

chose /ʃoz/ NF [1] *(= truc)* thing ◆ **je viens de penser à une ~** I've just thought of something ◆ **il a un tas de ~s à faire à Paris** he has a lot of things *ou* lots to do in Paris ◆ **il n'y a pas une seule ~ de vraie là-dedans** there isn't a (single) word of truth in it ◆ **critiquer est une ~, faire le travail en est une autre** criticizing is one thing, doing the work is another ◆ **ce n'est pas ~ facile *ou* aisée de …** it's not an easy thing to … ◆ **~ étrange *ou* curieuse, il a accepté** strangely *ou* curiously enough, he accepted, the strange *ou* curious thing is (that) he accepted ◆ **c'est une ~ admise que …** it's an accepted fact that …

[2] *(= événements, activités)* **les ~s** things ◆ **les ~s se sont passées ainsi** it (all) happened like this ◆ **les ~s vont mal** things are going badly ◆ **dans l'état actuel des ~s, au point où en sont les ~s** as things *ou* matters stand (at present), the way things are at the moment ◆ **ce sont des ~s qui arrivent** it's just one of those things, these things happen ◆ **regarder les ~s en face** to face up to things ◆ **prendre les ~s à cœur** to take things to heart ◆ **mettons les ~s au point** let's get things clear *ou* straight ◆ **en mettant les ~s au mieux/au pire** at best/worst ◆ **parler de ~(s) et d'autre(s)** to talk about this and that ◆ **elle a fait de grandes ~s** she has done great things; ⟶ **force, ordre**[1]

[3] *(= ce dont il s'agit)* **la ~ est d'importance** it's no trivial matter, it's a matter of some importance ◆ **la ~ dont j'ai peur, c'est que …** what *ou* the thing I'm afraid of is that … ◆ **il va vous expliquer la ~** he'll tell you all about it *ou* what it's all about ◆ **la ~ en question** the matter in hand ◆ **la ~ dont je parle** the thing I'm talking about ◆ **il a très bien pris la ~** he took it all very well ◆ **c'est la ~ à ne pas faire** that's the one thing *ou* the very thing not to do

[4] *(= réalités matérielles)* **les ~s** things ◆ **les ~s de ce monde** the things of this world ◆ **quand ils reçoivent, ils font bien les ~s** when they have guests they really do things properly ◆ **elle ne fait pas les ~s à demi *ou* à moitié** she doesn't do things by halves

[5] *(= mot)* thing ◆ **j'ai plusieurs ~s à vous dire** I've got several things to tell you ◆ **vous lui direz bien des ~s de ma part** give him my regards

[6] *(= objet)* thing ◆ **ils vendent de jolies ~s** they sell some nice things

[7] *(= personne, animal)* thing ◆ **pauvre ~ !** poor thing! ◆ **c'est une petite ~ si fragile encore** he *(ou* she) is still such a delicate little thing ◆ **être la ~ de qn** to be sb's plaything

[8] **la ~ jugée** *(Jur)* the res judicata, the final decision ◆ **la ~ publique** *(Pol)* the state *ou* nation ◆ **la ~ imprimée** *(† ou hum)* the printed word

[9] *(locutions)* **c'est ~ faite** it's done ◆ **voilà une bonne ~ de faite** that's one thing out of the way ◆ **c'est bien peu de ~** it's nothing really ◆ **(très) peu de ~** nothing much, very little ◆ **avant toute ~** above all (else) ◆ **toutes ~s égales** all (other) things being equal, all things considered ◆ **de deux ~s l'une : soit …, soit …** there are two possibilities: either …, or … ◆ **~ promise, ~ due** *(Prov)* promises are made to be kept; ⟶ **porté**

NM * [1] *(= truc, machin)* thing, thingumajig* ◆ **qu'est-ce que c'est que ce ~ ?** what's this thing here?, what's this thingumajig?*

[2] *(= personne)* what's-his-name*, thingumajig* ◆ **j'ai vu le petit ~** I saw young what's-his-name* ◆ **Monsieur Chose** Mr what's-his-name* ◆ **eh ! Chose** hey, you!

ADJ INV * ◆ **être/se sentir tout ~** *(bizarre)* to be/feel not quite oneself, to feel a bit peculiar; *(malade)* to be/feel out of sorts *ou* under the weather ◆ **ça l'a rendu tout ~ d'apprendre cette nouvelle** it made him go all funny when he heard the news

chosifier /ʃozifje/ ▸ conjug 7 ◂ VT to reify

chou[1] (pl **choux**) /ʃu/ NM [1] *(= plante)* cabbage [2] *(= ruban)* rosette [3] *(= gâteau)* choux bun; ⟶ **pâte** [4] *(* = tête)* **il n'a rien dans le ~** he's got nothing up top* ◆ **elle en a dans le ~** she's really brainy* [5] *(* locutions)* **être dans les ~x** *[projet]* to be up the spout* *(Brit)*, to be a write-off; *(Sport)* to be right out of the running; *[candidat]* to have had it ◆ **faire ~ blanc** to draw a blank ◆ **le gouvernement va faire ses ~x gras de la situation** the government will cash in on *ou* capitalize on the situation ◆ **ils vont faire leurs ~x gras de ces vieux vêtements** they'll be only too glad to make use of these old clothes; ⟶ **bout**

COMP **chou de Bruxelles** Brussels sprout

chou cabus white cabbage

chou chinois Chinese cabbage

chou chou chayote

chou à la crème cream-puff

chou frisé kale

chou palmiste cabbage tree

chou rouge red cabbage

chou vert green cabbage

chou[2]**, -te** * (mpl **choux**) /ʃu, ʃut, ʃu/ NM,F *(= amour)* darling ◆ **c'est un ~** he's a darling *ou* a dear ◆ **oui ma choute** yes, darling *ou* honey *(US) ou* poppet* *(Brit)* ADJ INV *(= ravissant)* delightful, cute* *(surtout US)* ◆ **ce qu'elle est ~** *ou* **c'est d'un ~, cette robe !** what a lovely *ou* cute* little dress! ◆ **ce qu'elle est ~ dans ce manteau !** doesn't she look just adorable in that coat?

chouan /ʃwɑ̃/ NM *18th century French counter-revolutionary in the Vendée*

Chouannerie /ʃwan(ə)ʀi/ NF *18th century French counter-revolutionary movement in the Vendée*

choucas /ʃuka/ NM jackdaw

chouchou, -te /ʃuʃu, ut/ NM,F *(* = favori)* darling, blue-eyed boy *(ou* girl) ◆ **le ~ du prof** the teacher's pet ◆ **c'est le ~ du chef** he's the boss's blue-eyed boy NM *(= élastique)* scrunchy

chouchoutage * /ʃuʃutaʒ/ NM *(= favoritisme)* pampering

chouchouter * /ʃuʃute/ ▸ conjug 1 ◂ VT to pamper, to coddle

choucroute /ʃukʀut/ NF [1] *(Culin)* sauerkraut ◆ **~ garnie** *sauerkraut with meat* ◆ **ça n'a rien à voir avec la ~*** it has nothing to do with anything* [2] *(* = coiffure)* beehive (hairstyle)

chouette[1] * /ʃwɛt/ ADJ [1] *(= beau) [objet, personne]* great* [2] *(= gentil)* nice; *(= sympathique)* great* ◆ **sois ~, prête-moi 25 €** be a dear *ou* an angel* and lend me €25 EXCL ◆ **~ (alors)!** great!*

chouette[2] /ʃwɛt/ NF *(= oiseau)* owl ◆ **chevêche** little owl ◆ **~ effraie** barn owl, screech owl ◆ **~ hulotte** tawny owl ◆ **quelle vieille ~ !** *(péj)* silly old bag!*

chou-fleur (pl **choux-fleurs**) /ʃuflœʀ/ NM cauliflower ◆ **oreilles en ~** cauliflower ears ◆ **nez en ~** swollen nose

chouïa * /ʃuja/ NM *[de sucre, bonne volonté, impatience, place]* smidgin ◆ **c'est pas ~** that's not much ◆ **un ~ trop grand/petit** (just) a shade too big/small ◆ **il manque un ~ pour que tu puisses te garer** there's not quite enough room for you to park

chouiner * /ʃwine/ ▸ conjug 1 ◂ VI *(= pleurer)* to whine

chou-navet (pl **choux-navets**) /ʃunavɛ/ NM swede *(Brit)*, rutabaga *(US)*

choupette /ʃupɛt/ NF *[de cheveux]* top-knot ◆ **ça va ~ ?*** are you alright, sweetie?*

chouquette /ʃukɛt/ NF *ball of choux pastry sprinkled with sugar*

chou-rave (pl **choux-raves**) /ʃuʀav/ NM kohlrabi

chouraver * /ʃuʀave/ ▸ conjug 1 ◂ VT ⇒ **chourer**

choure‡ /ʃuʀ/ NF (= vol) theft

chourer‡ /ʃuʀe/ ▸ conjug 1 ◂ VT to pinch*, to swipe‡, to nick‡ (*Brit*)

chow-chow (pl **chows-chows**) /ʃoʃo/ NM chow (*dog*)

choyer /ʃwaje/ ▸ conjug 8 ◂ VT (*frm = dorloter*) to cherish; (*avec excès*) to pamper; [*– idée*] to cherish

CHR /seaʃɛʀ/ NM (abrév de **centre hospitalier régional**) → **centre**

chrême /kʀɛm/ NM chrism, holy oil

chrétien, -ienne /kʀetjɛ̃, jɛn/ ADJ, NM,F Christian

chrétien-démocrate, chrétienne-démocrate (mpl **chrétiens-démocrates**) /kʀetjɛ̃demɔkʀat, kʀetjɛndemɔkʀat/ ADJ, NM,F Christian Democrat

chrétiennement /kʀetjɛnmɑ̃/ ADV [*agir*] in a Christian way; [*mourir, élever un enfant*] as a Christian ◆ **être enseveli ~** to have a Christian burial

chrétienté /kʀetjɛ̃te/ NF Christendom

christ /kʀist/ NM 1 ◆ **le Christ** Christ 2 (*Art*) crucifix, Christ (*on the cross*) ◆ **peindre un ~** to paint a figure of Christ

christiania /kʀistjanja/ NM (*Ski*) (parallel) christie, christiania

christianisation /kʀistjanizasjɔ̃/ NF conversion to Christianity

christianiser /kʀistjanize/ ▸ conjug 1 ◂ VT to convert to Christianity

christianisme /kʀistjanism/ NM Christianity

christique /kʀistik/ ADJ Christlike

Christmas /kʀistmas/ N ◆ **île ~** Christmas Island

chromage /kʀomaʒ/ NM chromium-plating

chromate /kʀɔmat/ NM chromate

chromatique /kʀɔmatik/ ADJ 1 (*Mus, Peinture, Opt*) chromatic 2 (*Bio*) chromosomal

chromatisme /kʀɔmatism/ NM (*Mus*) chromaticism; (*Opt*) (= *aberration*) chromatic aberration; (= *coloration*) colourings (*Brit*), colorings (*US*)

chromatographie /kʀɔmatɔgʀafi/ NF chromatography

chrome /kʀom/ NM (*Chim*) chromium ◆ **jaune/vert de ~** (*Peinture*) chrome yellow/green ◆ **faire les ~s*** (*d'une voiture, d'une moto*) to polish the chrome

chromé, e /kʀome/ (ptp de **chromer**) ADJ [*métal, objet*] chrome (*épith*), chromium-plated

chromer /kʀome/ ▸ conjug 1 ◂ VT to chromium-plate

chromo /kʀomo/ NM chromo

chromosome /kʀomozom/ NM chromosome ◆ **~ X/Y** X/Y chromosome

chromosomique /kʀomozomik/ ADJ [*anomalie*] chromosomal; [*analyse*] chromosome (*épith*), chromosomal

chromosphère /kʀomosfɛʀ/ NF chromosphere

chronicité /kʀɔnisite/ NF chronicity

chronique /kʀɔnik/ ADJ chronic NF (*Littérat*) chronicle; (*Presse*) column, page ◆ **~ financière** financial column *ou* page *ou* news ◆ **~ locale** local news and gossip ◆ **~ mondaine** society news ◆ **~ familiale** family saga ◆ **c'est la ~ d'une catastrophe annoncée** it's the story of an inevitable disaster

chroniquement /kʀɔnikmɑ̃/ ADV chronically

chroniqueur, -euse /kʀɔnikœʀ, øz/ NM,F (*Littérat*) chronicler; (*Presse, gén*) columnist ◆ **~ parlementaire/sportif** parliamentary/sports editor

chrono* /kʀono/ NM (abrév de **chronomètre**) stopwatch ◆ **faire du 80 (km/h) ~** *ou* **au ~** to be timed *ou* clocked at 80 ◆ **faire un bon ~** (*temps chronométré*) to do a good time

chronobiologie /kʀonobjɔlɔʒi/ NF chronobiology

chronologie /kʀɔnɔlɔʒi/ NF chronology

chronologique /kʀɔnɔlɔʒik/ ADJ chronological

chronologiquement /kʀɔnɔlɔʒikmɑ̃/ ADV chronologically

chronométrage /kʀɔnɔmetʀaʒ/ NM (*Sport*) timing

chronomètre /kʀɔnɔmɛtʀ/ NM (= *montre de précision*) chronometer; (*Sport*) stopwatch ◆ **~ de marine** marine *ou* box chronometer

chronométrer /kʀɔnɔmetʀe/ ▸ conjug 6 ◂ VT to time

chronométreur, -euse /kʀɔnɔmetʀœʀ, øz/ NM,F (*Sport*) timekeeper

chronométrique /kʀɔnɔmetʀik/ ADJ chronometric

chrysalide /kʀizalid/ NF chrysalis ◆ **sortir de sa ~** (*fig*) to blossom, to come out of one's shell

chrysanthème /kʀizɑ̃tɛm/ NM chrysanthemum

chrysolithe /kʀizɔlit/ NF chrysolite, olivine

CHS /seaʃɛs/ NM (abrév de **centre hospitalier spécialisé**) → **centre**

chtarbé, e‡ /ʃtaʀbe/ ADJ crazy

chtimi, ch'timi* /ʃtimi/ ADJ of *ou* from northern France NM (= *dialecte*) *dialect spoken in northern France* NMF native *ou* inhabitant of northern France

chtouille‡ /ʃtuj/ NF (= *blennorragie*) clap*‡; (= *syphilis*) pox*

CHU /seaʃy/ NM (abrév de **centre hospitalier universitaire**) → **centre**

chu /ʃy/ ptp de **choir**

chuchotement /ʃyʃɔtmɑ̃/ NM [*de personne, vent, feuilles*] whisper, whispering (*NonC*); [*de ruisseau*] murmur

chuchoter /ʃyʃɔte/ ▸ conjug 1 ◂ VTI [*personne, vent, feuilles*] to whisper; [*ruisseau*] to murmur ◆ **~ qch à l'oreille de qn** to whisper sth in sb's ear

chuchoterie /ʃyʃɔtʀi/ NF whisper ◆ **~s** whisperings

chuchoteur, -euse /ʃyʃɔtœʀ, øz/ ADJ whispering NM,F whisperer

chuchotis /ʃyʃɔti/ NM ⇒ **chuchotement**

chuintant, e /ʃɥɛ̃tɑ̃, ɑ̃t/ ADJ, NF (*Ling*) ◆ **(consonne) ~e** palato-alveolar fricative, hushing sound

chuintement /ʃɥɛ̃tmɑ̃/ NM (*Ling*) pronunciation of *s* sound as *sh*; (= *bruit*) soft *ou* gentle hiss

chuinter /ʃɥɛ̃te/ ▸ conjug 1 ◂ VI 1 (*Ling*) to pronounce *s* as *sh* 2 [*chouette*] to hoot, to screech 3 (= *siffler*) to hiss softly *ou* gently

chut /ʃyt/ EXCL sh!, shush!

chute /ʃyt/ NF 1 [*de pierre*] fall; (*Théât*) [*de rideau*] fall ◆ **faire une ~** [*de personne*] to (have a) fall; [*de chose*] to fall ◆ **faire une ~ de 3 mètres/mortelle** to fall 3 metres/to one's death ◆ **faire une ~ de cheval/de vélo** to fall off *ou* come off a horse/bicycle ◆ **faire une mauvaise ~** to have a bad fall ◆ **loi de la ~ des corps** law of gravity ◆ **~ libre** (*en parachutisme*) free fall ◆ **être en ~ libre** [*économie, ventes*] to plummet, to take a nose dive ◆ **de fortes ~s de pluie/neige** heavy falls of rain/snow, heavy rainfall/snowfalls ◆ **"attention, chute de pierres"** "danger, falling rocks"; → **point**

2 [*de cheveux*] loss; [*de feuilles*] fall(ing) ◆ **lotion contre la ~ des cheveux** hair restorer

3 (= *ruine*) [*d'empire*] fall, collapse; [*de commerce*] collapse; [*de roi, ministère*] (down)fall; [*de ville*] fall; [*de monnaie, cours*] fall, drop (*de* in); [*de pièce, auteur*] failure ◆ **la ~** (*Rel*) the Fall ◆ **la ~ du mur de Berlin** the fall of the Berlin Wall ◆ **il a entraîné le régime dans sa ~** he dragged the régime down with him (in his fall) ◆ **plus dure sera la ~** the harder they fall

4 ◆ **~ d'eau** waterfall ◆ **les ~s du Niagara/Zambèze** Niagara/Victoria Falls ◆ **barrage de basse/moyenne/haute ~** dam with a low/medium/high head

5 (= *baisse*) [*de température, pression*] drop, fall (*de* in) → **tension**

6 (= *déchet*) [*de papier, tissu*] offcut, scrap; [*de bois*] offcut

7 (= *fin*) [*de toit*] pitch, slope; [*de vers*] cadence; [*d'histoire drôle*] punch line ◆ **la ~ des reins** the small of the back ◆ **~ du jour** nightfall

8 (*Cartes*) **faire 3 (plis) de ~** to be 3 (tricks) down

chuter /ʃyte/ ▸ conjug 1 ◂ VI 1 (= *tomber*) [*personne*] to fall, to fall flat on one's face, to come a cropper* (*Brit*); [*prix, bourse*] to fall, to drop ◆ **faire ~ qn** (*lit, fig*) to bring sb down 2 (= *échouer*) to fail, to come a cropper* (*Brit*) ◆ **~ de deux (levées)** (*Cartes*) to go down two

chyle /ʃil/ NM (*Physiol*) chyle

chyme /ʃim/ NM (*Physiol*) chyme

Chypre /ʃipʀ/ N Cyprus ◆ **à ~** in Cyprus

chypriote /ʃipʀiɔt/ ADJ Cypriot NMF **Chypriote** Cypriot

ci /si/ ADV 1 (*dans l'espace*) **celui-~, celle-~** this one ◆ **ceux-~** these (ones) ◆ **ce livre-~** this book ◆ **cette table-~** this table ◆ **cet enfant-~** this child ◆ **ces livres-/tables-~** these books/tables 2 (*dans le temps*) **à cette heure-~** (= *à une heure déterminée*) at this time; (= *à une heure indue*) at this hour of the day, at this time of night; (= *à l'heure actuelle*) by now, at this moment ◆ **ces jours-~** (*avenir*) in the next few days; (*passé*) these past few days, in the last few days; (*présent*) these days ◆ **ce dimanche-~/cet après-midi-~ je ne suis pas libre** I'm not free this Sunday/this afternoon ◆ **non, je pars cette nuit-~** no, I'm leaving tonight 3 ◆ **de ~ de là** here and there; → **comme, par-ci par-là**

CIA /seia/ NF (abrév de **Central Intelligence Agency**) CIA

ci-après /siapʀɛ/ ADV (*gén*) below; (*Jur*) hereinafter

cibiche* /sibiʃ/ NF (= *cigarette*) ciggy*, fag* (*Brit*)

cibiste /sibist/ NMF CB user, CBer (*US*)

ciblage /siblaʒ/ NM targeting ◆ **~ des prix** target pricing

cible /sibl/ NF target ◆ **~ mouvante** moving target ◆ **être la ~ de, servir de ~ à** to be a target for, to be the target of ◆ **prendre qch pour ~** to take sth as one's target; → **langue**

cibler /sible/ ▸ conjug 1 ◂ VT [+ *catégorie d'acheteurs*] to target ◆ **produit mal ciblé** product not targeted at the right market ◆ **campagne électorale bien ciblée** welltargeted election campaign

ciboire /sibwaʀ/ NM (*Rel*) ciborium (*vessel*)

ciboule /sibul/ NF (larger) chive; (*employée en cuisine*) chives

ciboulette /sibulɛt/ NF (smaller) chive; (*employée en cuisine*) chives

ciboulot‡ /sibulo/ NM (= *tête*) head, nut*; (= *cerveau*) brain ◆ **il s'est mis dans le ~ de ...**

he got it into his head *ou* nut* to ... ◆ **il n'a rien dans le ~** he's got nothing up top*

cicatrice /sikatʀis/ NF *(lit, fig)* scar

cicatriciel, -ielle /sikatʀisjɛl/ ADJ cicatricial *(SPÉC)*, scar *(épith)*; → **tissu**

cicatrisant, e /sikatʀizɑ̃, ɑ̃t/ ADJ healing NM healing substance

cicatrisation /sikatʀizasjɔ̃/ NF *[d'égratignure]* healing; *[de plaie profonde]* closing up, healing

cicatriser /sikatʀize/ ▸ conjug 1 ◂ VT *(lit, fig)* to heal (over) ◆ **sa jambe est cicatrisée** his leg has healed VI *[plaie]* to heal (up), to form a scar; *[personne]* to heal ◆ **je cicatrise mal** I don't heal very easily VPR **se cicatriser** to heal (up), to form a scar

Cicéron /siseʀɔ̃/ NM Cicero

cicérone /siseʀɔn/ NM *(hum)* guide, cicerone ◆ **faire le ~** to act as a guide *ou* cicerone

ciclosporine /siklospɔʀin/ NF cyclosporin-A

ci-contre /sikɔ̃tʀ/ ADV opposite

CICR /seiseʀ/ NM (abrév de **Comité international de la Croix-Rouge**) → **comité**

ci-dessous /sidəsu/ ADV below

ci-dessus /sidəsy/ ADV above

ci-devant /sidəvɑ̃/ ADV († *ou hum*) formerly ◆ **mes ~ collègues** my erstwhile *ou* former colleagues NMF *(Hist)* ci-devant *(aristocrat who lost his title in the French Revolution)*

CIDEX /sidɛks/ NM (abrév de **courrier individuel à distribution exceptionnelle**) *special post office sorting service for individual clients*

CIDJ /seideʒi/ NM (abrév de **centre d'information et de documentation de la jeunesse**) → **centre**

cidre /sidʀ/ NM cider ◆ **~ bouché** *fine bottled cider* ◆ **~ doux** sweet cider

cidrerie /sidʀəʀi/ NF (= *industrie*) cider-making; (= *usine*) cider factory

cidrier /sidʀije/ NM cider producer

Cie (abrév de **compagnie**) Co

ciel /sjɛl/ NM 1 (pl littér **cieux**) (= *espace*) sky, heavens *(littér)* ◆ **les bras tendus vers le ~** with his arms stretched out heavenwards *ou* skywards ◆ **les yeux tournés vers le ~** eyes turned heavenwards *ou* skywards, gazing heavenwards *ou* skywards ◆ **haut dans le ~** *ou* **dans les cieux** *(littér)* high (up) in the sky, high in the heavens ◆ **suspendu entre ~ et terre** *[personne, objet]* suspended in mid-air; *[village]* suspended between sky and earth ◆ **tomber du ~** *(fig)* to be a godsend, to be heaven-sent ◆ **le ~ s'éclaircit** *(fig)* things are looking up ◆ **ça a été un coin de ~ bleu dans sa vie** it was a happy time in his life ◆ **sous un ~ plus clément, sous des cieux plus cléments** *(littér : climat)* beneath more clement skies *ou* a more clement sky; *(hum : endroit moins dangereux)* in healthier climes ◆ **sous d'autres cieux** in other climes ◆ **sous le ~ de Paris/de Provence** beneath the Parisian/Provençal sky ◆ **le ~ ne va pas te tomber sur la tête !** the sky isn't going to fall (in)!, it's not the end of the world!

◆ **à ciel ouvert** *[égout]* open; *[piscine, théâtre, musée]* open-air; *[mine]* opencast *(Brit)*, open cut *(US)*

2 (pl **ciels**) *(Peinture = paysage)* sky ◆ **les ~s de Grèce** the skies of Greece ◆ **les ~s de Turner** Turner's skies

3 (pl **cieux**) *(Rel)* heaven ◆ **il est au ~** he is in heaven ◆ **le royaume des cieux** the kingdom of heaven ◆ **notre Père qui es aux cieux** our Father who *ou* which art in heaven

4 (= *providence*) heaven ◆ **le ~ a écouté leurs prières** heaven heard their prayers ◆ **(juste) ~ !** good heavens! ◆ **le ~ m'est témoin que ...** heaven knows that ... ◆ **le ~ soit loué !** thank heavens! ◆ **c'est le ~ qui vous envoie !** you're heaven-sent!

COMP **ciel de carrière** quarry ceiling
ciel de lit canopy, tester

cierge /sjɛʀʒ/ NM (= *bougie*) candle → **brûler**

cieux /sjø/ pl de **ciel**

cigale /sigal/ NF cicada

cigare /sigaʀ/ NM *(lit)* cigar; (* = *tête*) head, nut* ◆ **~ (des mers)*** (= *bateau*) powerboat

cigarette /sigaʀɛt/ NF 1 *(à fumer)* cigarette ◆ **~ (à) bout filtre** filter tip, (filter-)tipped cigarette ◆ **la ~ du condamné** the condemned man's last smoke *ou* cigarette ◆ **~ russe** (= *biscuit*) *rolled sweet biscuit often served with ice cream* 2 (* = *bateau*) Cigarette ®, cigarette boat

cigarettier /sigaʀetje/ NM cigarette manufacturer, tobacco company

cigarillo /sigaʀijo/ NM cigarillo

ci-gît /siʒi/ ADV here lies

cigogne /sigɔɲ/ NF 1 (= *oiseau*) stork; 2 (= *levier*) crank brace

ciguë /sigy/ NF *(Bot = poison)* hemlock ◆ **grande ~** giant hemlock

ci-inclus, e /siɛ̃kly, yz/ ADJ enclosed ◆ **l'enveloppe ~e** the enclosed envelope ADV enclosed ◆ **~ une enveloppe** envelope enclosed

ci-joint, e (mpl **ci-joints**) /siʒwɛ̃, ɛt/ GRAMMAIRE ACTIVE 46.3, 47.1 ADJ enclosed ◆ **les papiers ~s** the enclosed papers ADV enclosed ◆ **vous trouverez ~ ...** you will find enclosed ..., please find enclosed ...

cil /sil/ NM *(Anat)* eyelash ◆ **~s vibratiles** *(Bio)* cilia

ciliaire /siljɛʀ/ ADJ *(Anat)* ciliary

cilice /silis/ NM hair shirt

cilié, e /silje/ ADJ ciliate(d) NMPL **les ciliés** ciliates, the Ciliata *(SPÉC)*

cillement /sijmɑ̃/ NM blinking

ciller /sije/ ▸ conjug 1 ◂ VI ◆ **~ (des yeux)** to blink (one's eyes) ◆ **il n'a pas cillé** *(fig)* he didn't bat an eyelid

cimaise /simɛz/ NF *(Peinture)* picture rail, picture moulding *(Brit)* *ou* molding *(US)*; *(Archit)* cyma; → **honneur**

cime /sim/ NF *[de montagne]* summit; (= *pic*) peak; *[d'arbre]* top; *(fig)* *[de gloire]* peak, height

ciment /simɑ̃/ NM cement ◆ **~ armé** reinforced concrete ◆ **~ prompt** *ou* **(à prise) rapide** quick-setting cement ◆ **~ colle** glue cement

cimenter /simɑ̃te/ ▸ conjug 1 ◂ VT 1 *(Constr)* *[+ sol]* to cement, to cover with concrete; *[+ bassin]* to cement, to line with cement; *[+ piton, anneau, pierres]* to cement 2 *(fig)* *[+ amitié, accord, paix]* to cement ◆ **l'amour qui cimente leur union** the love which binds them together

cimenterie /simɑ̃tʀi/ NF cement works

cimentier, -ière /simɑ̃tje, jɛʀ/ ADJ cement *(épith)* NM cement manufacturer

cimeterre /simtɛʀ/ NM scimitar

cimetière /simtjɛʀ/ NM *[de ville]* cemetery; *[d'église]* graveyard, churchyard ◆ **~ des chiens** pet cemetery ◆ **~ de voitures** scrapyard ◆ **~ des éléphants** elephant's graveyard ◆ **aller au ~** to visit the cemetery

cimier /simje/ NM *[de casque]* crest; *[d'arbre de Noël]* *decorative bauble for the top of the Christmas tree*

cinabre /sinabʀ/ NM cinnabar

ciné /sine/ NM (* abrév de **cinéma**) (= *art, procédé*) cinema; (= *salle*) cinema, movie theater *(US)* ◆ **aller au ~** to go to the cinema *ou* the movies *(US)*

cinéaste /sineast/ NMF *(gén)* film-maker, moviemaker *(US)*; (= *réalisateur connu*) (film) director ◆ **~-auteur** auteur

ciné-club (pl **ciné-clubs**) /sineklœb/ NM film society *ou* club

cinéma /sinema/ NM 1 (= *procédé, art, industrie*) cinema; (= *salle*) cinema, movie theater *(US)* ◆ **roman adapté pour le ~** novel adapted for the cinema *ou* the screen ◆ **faire du ~** to be a film *ou* movie *(US)* actor (*ou* actress) ◆ **de ~** *[technicien, studio]* film *(épith)*; *[projecteur, écran]* cinema *(épith)* ◆ **acteur/vedette de ~** film *ou* movie *(US)* actor/star ◆ **être dans le ~** to be in the film *ou* movie *(US)* business *ou* in films *ou* movies *(US)* ◆ **le ~ français/italien** French/Italian cinema ◆ **le ~ de Carné** Carné films ◆ **aller au ~** to go to the cinema *ou* movies *(US)* ◆ **elle se fait du ~*** she's deluding herself

2 (* = *simagrées*) **c'est du ~** it's all put on*, it's all an act ◆ **arrête ton ~ !** give it a rest! ◆ **faire tout un ~** to put on a great act*

3 (* = *complication*) fuss ◆ **c'est toujours le même ~** it's always the same old to-do* *ou* business ◆ **tu ne vas pas nous faire ton ~ !** you're not going to make a fuss *ou* a great scene *ou* a song and dance* about it!

COMP **cinéma d'animation** (= *technique*) animation; (= *films*) animated films
cinéma d'art et d'essai avant-garde *ou* experimental films *ou* cinema; (= *salle*) art house
cinéma d'auteur art-house cinema *ou* films
cinéma muet silent films *ou* movies *(US)*
cinéma parlant talking films *ou* pictures, talkies*
cinéma permanent continuous performance
cinéma de plein air open-air cinema
cinéma à salles multiples multiplex cinema

Cinémascope ® /sinemaskɔp/ NM Cinemascope ®

cinémathèque /sinematɛk/ NF film archive *ou* library; (= *salle*) film theatre *(Brit)*, movie theater *(US)*

cinématique /sinematik/ NF kinematics *(sg)*

cinématographe /sinematɔgʀaf/ NM cinematograph

cinématographie /sinematɔgʀafi/ NF film-making, movie-making *(US)*, cinematography

cinématographier /sinematɔgʀafje/ ▸ conjug 7 ◂ VT to film

cinématographique /sinematɔgʀafik/ ADJ film *(épith)*, cinema *(épith)*

cinéma-vérité /sinemaveʀite/ NM INV cinéma-vérité, ciné vérité

ciné-parc, cinéparc (pl **ciné(-)parcs**) /sineparк/ NM *(Can)* drive-in (cinema)

cinéphile /sinefil/ ADJ *[public]* cinema-going *(épith)* NMF film *ou* cinema enthusiast, film buff*, movie buff* *(US)*

cinéraire /sineʀɛʀ/ ADJ *[vase]* cinerary NF (= *plante*) cineraria

Cinérama ® /sineʀama/ NM Cinerama ®

ciné-roman (pl **ciné-romans**) /sineʀɔmɑ̃/ NM film story

cinétique /sinetik/ ADJ kinetic NF kinetics *(sg)*

cing(h)alais, e /sɛ̃galɛ, ɛz/ ADJ Sin(g)halese NM (= *langue*) Sin(g)halese NM,F **Cing(h)alais(e)** Sin(g)halese

cinglant, e /sɛ̃glɑ̃, ɑ̃t/ ADJ *[vent]* biting, bitter; *[pluie]* lashing, driving; *[propos, ironie, humour]* biting, scathing; *[échec]* bitter

cinglé, e * /sɛ̃gle/ (ptp de **cingler**) ADJ screwy*, cracked* NM,F crackpot*, nut*

cingler /sɛ̃gle/ ▸ conjug 1 ◂ VT *[personne]* to lash; *[vent, branche]* to sting, to whip (against); *[pluie]*

to lash (against); *(fig)* to lash, to sting ◆ **il cingla l'air de son fouet** he lashed the air with his whip VI *(Naut)* ◆ ~ **vers** to make for

cinoche * /sinɔʃ/ NM 1 *(= salle)* cinema, movie theater *(US)* ◆ **aller au** ~ to go to the cinema *ou* movies *(US)* 2 *(* = simagrées)* **arrête de faire du ~ !** stop making such a fuss!

cinoque * /sinɔk/ ADJ ⇒ **sinoque**

cinq /sɛ̃k/ ADJ INV, NM INV five ◆ **dire les ~ lettres** *ou* **le mot de ~ lettres** to use a rude word *ou* a four-letter word ◆ **je lui ai dit les ~ lettres** I told him where to go* ◆ **en ~ sec*** in a flash ◆ **~ à sept** *(= rendez-vous)* afternoon tryst; *pour autres loc voir* **six;** → **recevoir**

cinq-dix-quinze †* /sɛ̃diskɛ̃z/ NM *(Can)* cheap store, dime store *(US, Can)*, five-and-ten *(US, Can)*

cinquantaine /sɛ̃kɑ̃tɛn/ NF *(= âge, nombre)* about fifty

cinquante /sɛ̃kɑ̃t/ ADJ INV, NM INV fifty; *pour loc voir* **six**

cinquantenaire /sɛ̃kɑ̃tnɛʀ/ ADJ *[arbre, objet]* fifty-year-old *(épith)* ◆ **il est** ~ it *(ou* he) is fifty years old NM *(= anniversaire)* fiftieth anniversary, golden jubilee

cinquantième /sɛ̃kɑ̃tjɛm/ ADJ, NMF fiftieth; *pour loc voir* **sixième**

cinquantièmement /sɛ̃kɑ̃tjɛmmɑ̃/ ADV in the fiftieth place

cinquième /sɛ̃kjɛm/ ADJ fifth ◆ **la ~ semaine (de congés payés)** the fifth week of paid holiday *(Brit) ou* vacation *(US)* ◆ **je suis la ~ roue du carrosse*** I feel like a spare part* *(Brit)*, I feel like a fifth wheel *(US)* ◆ **~ colonne** fifth column; *pour autres loc voir* **sixième** NMF fifth NF 1 *(Scol)* ≈ second form *ou* year *(Brit)*, seventh grade *(US)* 2 *(= vitesse)* fifth gear 3 *(TV)* **la Cinquième** *French cultural TV channel broadcasting in the afternoon*

cinquièmement /sɛ̃kjɛmmɑ̃/ ADV in the fifth place

cintrage /sɛ̃tʀaʒ/ NM *[de tôle, bois]* bending

cintre /sɛ̃tʀ/ NM 1 *(Archit)* arch → **voûte** 2 *(= porte-manteau)* coathanger 3 *(Théât)* **les ~s** the flies

cintré, e /sɛ̃tʀe/ (ptp de **cintrer**) ADJ 1 *[porte, fenêtre]* arched; *[galerie]* vaulted, arched 2 *[veste]* fitted ◆ **chemise ~e** close-fitting *ou* slim-fitting shirt 3 *(* = fou)* nuts*, crackers*

cintrer /sɛ̃tʀe/ ► conjug 1 ◄ VT 1 *(Archit) [+ porte]* to arch, to make into an arch; *[+ galerie]* to vault, to give a vaulted *ou* arched roof to; 2 *[+ vêtement]* to take in at the waist 3 *[+ barre, rail, pièce en bois]* to bend, to curve

CIO /seio/ NM 1 (abrév de **centre d'information et d'orientation**) → **centre** 2 (abrév de **Comité international olympique**) IOC

cirage /siʀaʒ/ NM 1 *(= produit)* (shoe) polish 2 *(= action) [de chaussures]* polishing; *[de parquets]* polishing, waxing 3 ◆ **être dans le ~*** *(après anesthésie)* to be a bit groggy* *ou* whoozy*; *(= être mal réveillé)* to be a bit whoozy*; *(arg de pilotes)* to be flying blind ◆ **quand il est sorti du ~*** when he came to *ou* round; → **noir**

circa /siʀka/ ADV circa

circadien, -ienne /siʀkadjɛ̃, jɛn/ ADJ circadian

circoncire /siʀkɔ̃siʀ/ ► conjug 37 ◄ VT to circumcise

circoncis /siʀkɔ̃si/ (ptp de **circoncire**) ADJ circumcised

circoncision /siʀkɔ̃sizjɔ̃/ NF circumcision

circonférence /siʀkɔ̃feʀɑ̃s/ NF circumference

circonflexe /siʀkɔ̃flɛks/ ADJ ◆ **accent ~** circumflex

circonlocution /siʀkɔ̃lɔkysjɔ̃/ NF circumlocution ◆ **employer des ~s pour annoncer qch** to announce sth in a roundabout way

circonscription /siʀkɔ̃skʀipsjɔ̃/ NF *(Admin, Mil)* district, area ◆ ~ **(électorale)** *[de député]* constituency *(Brit)*, district *(US)*

circonscrire /siʀkɔ̃skʀiʀ/ ► conjug 39 ◄ VT *[+ feu, épidémie]* to contain, to confine; *[+ territoire]* to mark out; *[+ sujet]* to define, to delimit ◆ **~ un cercle/carré à** to draw a circle/square round ◆ **le débat s'est circonscrit à** *ou* **autour de cette seule question** the debate limited *ou* restricted itself to *ou* was centred round *ou* around that one question ◆ **les recherches sont circonscrites au village** the search is being limited *ou* confined to the village

circonspect, e /siʀkɔ̃spɛ(kt), ɛkt/ ADJ *[personne]* circumspect, cautious; *[silence, remarque]* prudent, cautious ◆ **observer qch d'un œil ~** to look at sth cautiously

circonspection /siʀkɔ̃spɛksjɔ̃/ NF caution, circumspection ◆ **faire preuve de ~** to be cautious

circonstance /siʀkɔ̃stɑ̃s/ NF 1 *(= occasion)* occasion ◆ **en la ~** in this case, on this occasion ◆ **en pareille ~** in such a case, in such circumstances ◆ **il a profité de la ~ pour me rencontrer** he took advantage of the occasion to meet me; → **concours**

2 *(= situation)* **~s** circumstances ◆ **~s économiques** economic circumstances ◆ **être à la hauteur des ~s** to be equal to the occasion ◆ **en raison des ~s, étant donné les ~s** in view of *ou* given the circumstances ◆ **dans ces ~s** under *ou* in these circumstances ◆ **dans les ~s présentes** *ou* **actuelles** in the present circumstances

3 *[de crime, accident]* circumstance ◆ **~s atténuantes** *(Jur)* mitigating *ou* extenuating circumstances ◆ **~ aggravante** *(Jur)* aggravating circumstance, aggravation ◆ **~s exceptionnelles** *(Jur)* exceptional circumstances ◆ **il y a une ~ troublante** there's one disturbing circumstance *ou* point ◆ **dans des ~s encore mal définies** in circumstances which are still unclear

4 *(locution)*

◆ **de circonstance** *[parole, mine, conseil]* appropriate, apt; *[œuvre, poésie]* occasional *(épith)*; *[habit]* appropriate, suitable; *[union, coalition]* of convenience

circonstancié, e /siʀkɔ̃stɑ̃sje/ ADJ *[rapport, aveux]* detailed

circonstanciel, -ielle /siʀkɔ̃stɑ̃sjɛl/ ADJ *(Gram)* adverbial ◆ **complément ~ de lieu/temps** adverbial phrase of place/time

circonvenir /siʀkɔ̃v(ə)niʀ/ ► conjug 22 ◄ VT *(frm) [+ personne, opposition]* to circumvent *(frm)*, to get round; *[+ danger]* to avoid

circonvoisin, e /siʀkɔ̃vwazɛ̃, in/ ADJ *(littér)* surrounding, neighbouring *(Brit)*, neighboring *(US)*

circonvolution /siʀkɔ̃vɔlysjɔ̃/ NF *[de rivière, itinéraire]* twist ◆ **décrire des ~s** *[rivière, route]* to twist and turn ◆ **~ cérébrale** cerebral convolution

circuit /siʀkɥi/ NM 1 *(= itinéraire touristique)* tour, (round) trip ◆ **~ d'autocar** bus trip, coach *(Brit)* tour *ou* trip ◆ **il y a un très joli ~ (à faire) à travers bois** there's a very nice trip (you can do) through the woods ◆ **faire le ~ (touristique) des volcans d'Auvergne** to tour *ou* go on a tour of the volcanoes in Auvergne

2 *(= parcours compliqué)* roundabout *ou* circuitous route ◆ **il faut emprunter un ~ assez compliqué pour y arriver** you have to take a rather circuitous *ou* roundabout route to get there ◆ **j'ai dû refaire tout le ~ en sens inverse** I had to go right back round the way I'd come *ou* make the whole journey back the way I'd come

3 *(Sport)* circuit ◆ **~ automobile** (motor-) racing circuit ◆ **course sur ~** circuit racing ◆ **~ féminin** *(Tennis)* women's circuit ◆ **sur le ~ international** on the international circuit

4 *(Élec)* circuit ◆ **couper/rétablir le ~** to break/restore the circuit ◆ **mettre qch en ~** to connect sth up ◆ **mettre hors ~** *[+ appareil]* to disconnect; *[+ personne]* to push aside ◆ **tous les ~s ont grillé** *(machine)* all the fuses have blown, there's been a burnout

5 *(Écon)* ◆ **~ des capitaux** circulation of capital

6 *(= enceinte) [de ville]* circumference

7 *(Ciné)* circuit

8 *(locutions)* **être dans le ~** to be around ◆ **est-ce qu'il est toujours dans le ~ ?** is he still around? ◆ **se remettre dans le ~** to get back into circulation ◆ **mettre qch dans le ~** to put sth into circulation, to feed sth into the system

COMP **circuit de distribution** *(Comm)* distribution network *ou* channels

circuit électrique electric(al) circuit; *[de jouet]* (electric) track

circuit fermé *(Élec, fig)* closed circuit ◆ **vivre en ~ fermé** to live in a closed world ◆ **ces publications circulent en ~ fermé** this literature has a limited *ou* restricted circulation

circuit hydraulique hydraulic circuit

circuit imprimé printed circuit

circuit intégré integrated circuit

circuit de refroidissement cooling system

circulaire /siʀkylɛʀ/ ADJ, NF circular ◆ **~ d'application** *decree specifying how a law should be enforced*

circulairement /siʀkylɛʀmɑ̃/ ADV in a circle

circulant, e /siʀkylɑ̃, ɑ̃t/ ADJ 1 *(Fin)* circulating ◆ **actif ~** current assets ◆ **capitaux ~s** circulating capital 2 *(Bio) [molécule]* circulating in the bloodstream ◆ **sang ~** circulating blood

circularité /siʀkylaʀite/ NF circularity

circulation /siʀkylasjɔ̃/ NF *[d'air, sang, argent]* circulation; *[de marchandises]* movement; *[de nouvelle]* spread; *[de trains]* running; *[de voitures]* traffic ◆ **la ~ (du sang)** the circulation ◆ **avoir une bonne/mauvaise ~** *(Méd)* to have good/bad circulation ◆ **la libre ~ des travailleurs** the free movement of labour ◆ **la ~ des idées** the free flow of ideas ◆ **pour rendre la ~ plus fluide** *(sur la route)* to improve traffic flow ◆ **route à grande ~** major road, main highway *(US)* ◆ **mettre en ~** *[+ argent]* to put into circulation; *[+ livre, produit]* to put on the market, to bring out; *[+ voiture]* to put on the road; *[+ fausse nouvelle]* to circulate, to spread (about) ◆ **mise en ~** *[d'argent]* circulation; *[de livre, produit]* putting on the market, bringing out ◆ **retirer de la ~** *[+ argent]* to take out of *ou* withdraw from circulation; *[+ médicament, produit, livre]* to take off the market, to withdraw; *(euph) [+ personne]* to get rid of ◆ **~ aérienne** air traffic ◆ **~ générale** *(Anat)* systemic circulation ◆ **~ monétaire** money *ou* currency circulation ◆ **"circulation interdite"** *(sur route)* "no vehicular traffic" ◆ **disparaître de la ~** *(fig)* to drop out of sight, to disappear from the scene; → **accident, agent**

circulatoire /siʀkylatwaʀ/ ADJ circulation *(épith)*, circulatory ◆ **troubles ~s** circulatory disorders

circuler /siʀkyle/ ► conjug 1 ◄ VI 1 *[sang, air, marchandise, argent]* to circulate; *[rumeur]* to circulate, to go around *ou* about ◆ **l'information circule mal entre les services** communication between departments is poor ◆ **il circule bien des bruits à son propos** there's a lot of gossip going around about him, there's a lot being said about him ◆ **faire ~** *[+ air, sang,*

argent, document] to circulate; *[+ marchandises]* to put into circulation; *[+ bruits]* to spread
2 *[voiture]* to go, to move; *[train]* to go, to run; *[passant]* to walk; *[foule]* to move (along) ◆ **un bus sur trois circule** one bus in three is running ◆ ~ **à droite/à gauche** to drive on the right/on the left ◆ **circulez !** move along! ◆ **faire** ~ *[+ voitures, piétons]* to move on ◆ **il est difficile de ~ à Paris** driving in Paris is difficult ◆ **on circule très bien en dehors des heures de pointe** driving is fine except during the rush hour ◆ **ça circule bien sur l'autoroute** traffic is moving freely on the motorway
3 *[plat, bonbons, lettre]* to be passed *ou* handed round; *[pétition]* to circulate ◆ **faire** ~ *[+ plat]* to hand *ou* pass round; *[+ pétition]* to circulate, to pass round

circumnavigation /siʀkɔmnavigasjɔ̃/ **NF** circumnavigation

circumpolaire /siʀkɔmpɔlɛʀ/ **ADJ** circumpolar

cire /siʀ/ **NF** *(gén)* wax; *(pour meubles, parquets)* polish; *[d'oreille]* (ear)wax ◆ ~ **d'abeille** beeswax ◆ ~ **à cacheter/à épiler** sealing/depilatory wax ◆ ~ **liquide** liquid wax ◆ **s'épiler les jambes à la** ~ to wax one's legs ◆ **personnage en** ~ waxwork dummy; → **musée** **COMP**
cire anatomique wax anatomical model
cire perdue cire perdue, lost wax

ciré /siʀe/ **NM** (= *vêtement)* oilskin

cirer /siʀe/ ► conjug 1 ◄ **VT** to polish ◆ **j'en ai rien à ~**‡ I don't give a damn‡ ◆ ~ **les bottes** *ou* **pompes de qn** * to lick sb's boots *, to suck up to sb‡; → **toile**

cireur, -euse /siʀœʀ, øz/ **NM,F** (= *personne)* *[de chaussures]* shoe-shiner, bootblack †; *[de planchers]* (floor) polisher ◆ ~ **de bottes** *ou* **pompes** * bootlicker * **NF** **cireuse** (= *appareil)* floor polisher

cireux, -euse /siʀø, øz/ **ADJ** *[matière]* waxy; *[teint]* waxen

ciron /siʀɔ̃/ **NM** *(littér)* mite

cirque /siʀk/ **NM** 1 (= *chapiteau)* big top; (= *spectacle)* circus ◆ **on est allé au** ~ we went to the circus 2 *(Antiq = arène)* circus, amphitheatre *(Brit)*, amphitheater *(US)*; → **jeu** 3 *(Géog)* cirque 4 *(* = embarras)* **quel ~ pour garer sa voiture ici !** it's such a performance * *ou* to-do * finding a place to park around here! ◆ **quel ~ il a fait quand il a appris la nouvelle !** what a scene he made when he heard the news! ◆ **arrête ton ~ !** (= *comédie)* give it a rest! * 5 *(* = désordre)* chaos ◆ **c'est le ~ ici aujourd'hui** it's absolute chaos here today, the place is a real circus today *(US)* ◆ ~ **médiatique** media circus

cirrhose /siʀoz/ **NF** cirrhosis ◆ ~ **du foie** cirrhosis of the liver

cirrocumulus /siʀokymylys/ **NM** cirrocumulus

cirrostratus /siʀostʀatys/ **NM** cirrostratus

cirrus /siʀys/ **NM** cirrus

cisaille(s) /sizɑj/ **NF(PL)** *[de pour métal]* shears; *[de pour fil métallique]* wire cutters; *[de jardinier]* (gardening) shears

cisaillement /sizɑjmɑ̃/ **NM** 1 *[de métal]* cutting; *[de branches]* clipping, pruning 2 *[de rivet, boulon]* shearing off

cisailler /sizɑje/ ► conjug 1 ◄ **VT** 1 (= *couper)* *[+ métal]* to cut; *[+ branches]* to clip, to prune; *(fig)* *[+ carrière]* to cripple 2 (= *user)* *[+ rivet, boulon]* to shear off 3 *(* = tailler maladroitement)* *[+ tissu, planche, cheveux]* to hack at **VPR** **se cisailler** (= *se couper)* to cut o.s.

cisalpin, e /sizalpɛ̃, in/ **ADJ** Cisalpine

ciseau (pl **ciseaux**) /sizo/ **NM** 1 ◆ **(paire de) ~x** *(pour tissu, papier)* (pair of) scissors; *(pour métal, laine)* shears; *(pour fil métallique)* wire cutters ◆ **~x de brodeuse** embroidery scissors ◆ **~x de couturière** dressmaking shears *ou* scissors ◆ **~x à ongles** nail scissors ◆ **en un coup de ~x** with a snip of the scissors ◆ **donner des coups de ~x dans un texte** * to make cuts in a text 2 (= *outil de maçon, de sculpteur)* chisel ◆ ~ **à froid** cold chisel 3 *(Sport = prise)* scissors (hold *ou* grip) ◆ **montée en ~x** *(Ski)* herringbone climb ◆ ~ **de jambes** *(Catch)* leg scissors ◆ **faire des ~x** to do scissor kicks; → **sauter**

ciselage /siz(ə)laʒ/ **NM** chiselling

ciseler /siz(ə)le/ ► conjug 5 ◄ **VT** *[+ pierre]* to chisel, to carve; *[+ métal]* to chase, to chisel; *[+ persil]* to chop finely; *[+ style]* to polish ◆ **les traits finement ciselés de son visage** his finely chiselled features

ciseleur, -euse /siz(ə)lœʀ, œz/ **NM, F** *[de bois, marbre]* carver; *(en orfèvrerie)* engraver

ciselure /siz(ə)lyʀ/ **NF** 1 *[de bois, marbre]* carving, chiselling; *[d'orfèvrerie]* engraving, chasing 2 (= *dessin)* *[de bois]* carving; *[d'orfèvrerie]* engraved *ou* chased pattern *ou* design, engraving

Cisjordanie /sisʒɔʀdani/ **NF** ◆ **la** ~ the West Bank

cistercien, -ienne /sistɛʀsjɛ̃, jɛn/ **ADJ, NM,F** Cistercian

citadelle /sitadɛl/ **NF** *(lit, fig)* citadel

citadin, e /sitadɛ̃, in/ **ADJ** *(gén)* town *(épith)*, urban; *[de grande ville]* city *(épith)*, urban **NM,F** city dweller, urbanite *(US)* **NF** **citadine** (= *voiture)* city car

citation /sitasjɔ̃/ **NF** 1 *[d'auteur]* quotation ◆ **"fin de citation"** "unquote", "end of quotation" 2 *(Jur)* summons ◆ ~ **à comparaître** *(à accusé)* summons to appear; *(à témoin)* subpoena 3 (= *mention)* citation ◆ ~ **à l'ordre du jour** *ou* **de l'armée** *(Mil)* mention in dispatches

cité /site/ **NF** 1 *(littér, Antiq = grande ville)* city; (= *petite ville)* town ◆ ~ **balnéaire** seaside town ◆ ~ **industrielle** industrial town ◆ **la ~ des Papes** Avignon ◆ **la Cité du Vatican** Vatican City ◆ **la ~ des Doges** Venice 2 (= *quartier)* (housing) estate *(Brit)*, project *(US)* ◆ **le problème des ~s** the problem of social unrest in deprived estates *(Brit)* *ou* projects *(US)* ◆ ~ **parlementaire** *(à Québec)* Parliament buildings; → **droit**[3]
COMP **cité ouvrière** ≃ (workers') housing estate *(Brit)* *ou* development *(US)*
cité de transit ≃ halfway house *ou* hostel, (temporary) hostel for homeless families
cité universitaire (student) hall(s) of residence

> ⚠ Le mot **cité** se traduit par **city** uniquement quand il désigne une grande ville.

cité-dortoir (pl **cités-dortoirs**) /sitedɔʀtwaʀ/ **NF** dormitory *(Brit)* *ou* bedroom *(US)* town

cité-jardin (pl **cités-jardins**) /siteʒaʀdɛ̃/ **NF** garden city

citer /site/ ► conjug 1 ◄ **VT** 1 (= *rapporter)* *[+ texte, exemples, faits]* to quote, to cite ◆ **il n'a pas pu ~ 3 pièces de Sartre** he couldn't name 3 plays by Sartre 2 ◆ ~ **(en exemple)** *[+ personne]* to hold up as an example *(pour* for); ◆ ~ **un soldat (à l'ordre du jour** *ou* **de l'armée)** to mention a soldier in dispatches 3 *(Jur)* ~ **(à comparaître)** *[+ accusé]* to summon to appear; *[+ témoin]* to subpoena

citerne /sitɛʀn/ **NF** tank; *(à eau)* water tank

cithare /sitaʀ/ **NF** zither; *(Antiq)* cithara

citoyen, -yenne /sitwajɛ̃, jɛn/ **ADJ** (= *faisant preuve de civisme)* *[entreprise, personne]* socially aware ◆ **une nation citoyenne** a nation where the notion of citizenship is central; → **rendez-vous** **NM,F** citizen ◆ **~/citoyenne d'honneur d'une ville** freeman/freewoman of a town ◆ ~ **du monde** citizen of the world

citoyenneté /sitwajɛnte/ **NF** citizenship

citrin, e /sitʀɛ̃, in/ **ADJ** citrine-coloured **NF** **citrine** (= *pierre)* citrine

citrique /sitʀik/ **ADJ** citric

citron /sitʀɔ̃/ **NM** (= *fruit)* lemon ◆ **un** *ou* **du ~ pressé** a (fresh) lemon juice ◆ ~ **vert** lime ◆ **il n'a vraiment rien dans le ~ !**‡ he's got nothing between his ears!; → **thé** **ADJ INV** lemon (-coloured *(Brit)* *ou* -colored *(US)*) ◆ **jaune ~** lemon-yellow

citronnade /sitʀɔnad/ **NF** lemon squash *(Brit)*, still lemonade *(Brit)*, lemonade *(US)*

citronné, e /sitʀɔne/ **ADJ** *[goût, odeur]* lemony; *[gâteau]* lemon(-flavoured *(Brit)* *ou* -flavored *(US)*); *[liquide]* with lemon juice added, lemon-flavoured *(Brit)* *ou* -flavored *(US)*; *[eau de toilette]* lemon-scented

citronnelle /sitʀɔnɛl/ **NF** (= *graminée)* lemon grass; (= *mélisse)* lemon balm; (= *verveine)* lemon verbena; (= *huile)* citronella (oil); (= *liqueur)* lemon liqueur

citronnier /sitʀɔnje/ **NM** lemon tree

citrouille /sitʀuj/ **NF** pumpkin ◆ **j'ai la tête comme une ~** * I feel like my head's going to explode

citrus /sitʀys/ **NM** citrus

cive /siv/ **NF** *(Culin)* spring onions

civet /sivɛ/ **NM** stew ◆ **lièvre en ~, ~ de lièvre** ≃ jugged hare

civette[1] /sivɛt/ **NF** (= *animal)* civet (cat); (= *parfum)* civet

civette[2] /sivɛt/ **NF** (= *plante)* chive; *(employée en cuisine)* chives

civière /sivjɛʀ/ **NF** stretcher

civil, e /sivil/ **ADJ** 1 (= *entre citoyens)* *[guerre, mariage]* civil ◆ **personne de la société ~e** *(Pol)* lay person; → **code, partie**[2] 2 (= *non militaire)* civilian 3 *(littér = poli)* civil, courteous **NM** 1 (= *non militaire)* civilian ◆ **se mettre en ~** *[soldat]* to dress in civilian clothes, to wear civvies *; *[policier]* to dress in plain clothes ◆ **policier en ~** plain-clothes policeman, policeman in plain clothes ◆ **soldat en ~** soldier in civvies * *ou* in mufti *ou* in civilian clothes ◆ **dans le ~** in civilian life, in civvy street * *(Brit)* 2 *(Jur)* **poursuivre qn au ~** to take civil action against sb, to sue sb in the (civil) courts

civilement /sivilmɑ̃/ **ADV** 1 *(Jur)* **poursuivre qn ~** to take civil action against sb, to sue sb in the (civil) courts ◆ **être ~ responsable** to be legally responsible ◆ **se marier ~** to have a civil wedding, ≃ to get married in a registry office *(Brit)*, to be married by a judge *(US)* 2 *(littér = poliment)* civilly

civilisable /sivilizabl/ **ADJ** civilizable

civilisateur, -trice /sivilizatœʀ, tʀis/ **ADJ** civilizing **NM,F** civilizer

civilisation /sivilizasjɔ̃/ **NF** civilization

civilisationnel, -elle /sivilizasjɔnɛl/ **ADJ** civilizational ◆ **le problème de l'identité européenne n'est pas uniquement ~** the problem of European identity is not only a matter of culture and history

civilisé, e /sivilize/ (ptp de **civiliser**) **ADJ** civilized

civiliser /sivilize/ ► conjug 1 ◄ **VT** to civilize **VPR** **se civiliser** *[peuple]* to become civilized; * *[personne]* to become more civilized

civilité /sivilite/ **NF** (= *politesse)* civility ◆ **~s** *(frm = compliments)* civilities ◆ **faire** *ou* **présenter ses ~s à** to pay one's compliments to

civique /sivik/ **ADJ** civic ◆ **avoir le sens ~** to be public-spirited; → **éducation, instruction**

civisme /sivism/ NM public-spiritedness ♦ **cours de** ~ civics *(sg)* ♦ **faire preuve de** ~ to be civic-minded ♦ **le** ~ **sanitaire** ecological *ou* environmental awareness

cl (abrév de **centilitre**) cl

clabaudage /klabodaʒ/ NM *(littér)* *[de personne]* moaning, whingeing; *[de chien]* yapping

clabauder /klabode/ ▸ conjug 1 ◂ VI *(littér)* *[personne]* to moan, to whinge *(contre* about); *[chien]* to yap ♦ ~ **contre qn** to make denigrating remarks about sb

clabauderie /klabodʀi/ NF *(littér)* ⇒ **clabaudage**

clabaudeur, -euse /klabodœʀ, øz/ *(littér)* ADJ *(= médisant)* gossiping; *(= aboyant)* yapping NM,F *(= cancanier)* gossip

clac /klak/ EXCL *[de porte]* slam!; *[d'élastique, stylo]* snap!; *[de fouet]* crack!

clafoutis /klafuti/ NM clafoutis *(tart made with fruit set in batter)*

claie /klɛ/ NF *[de fruit, fromage]* rack; *(= crible)* riddle; *(= clôture)* hurdle

clair, e[1] /klɛʀ/ GRAMMAIRE ACTIVE 42.1, 53.6

ADJ 1 *(= lumineux)* *[pièce]* bright, light; *[ciel]* clear; *[couleur, flamme]* bright ♦ **par temps** ~ on a clear day, in clear weather

2 *(= pâle)* *[teint, couleur]* light; *[tissu, robe]* light-coloured *(Brit)* *ou* -colored *(US)* ♦ **bleu/vert** ~ light blue/green

3 *(= limpide)* *[eau, son, voyelle]* clear ♦ **d'une voix ~e** in a clear voice

4 *(= peu consistant)* *[sauce, soupe]* thin; *[tissu]* thin; *[blés]* sparse

5 *(= sans ambiguïté)* *[exposé, pensée, position]* clear ♦ **cette affaire n'est pas ~e** there's something slightly suspicious about all this ♦ **avoir un esprit** ~ to be a clear thinker ♦ **je serai** ~ **avec vous** I'll be frank with you ♦ **que ce soit bien** ~ ... I want this to be perfectly clear ... ♦ **c'est** ~ **et net** it's perfectly clear ♦ **son message était** ~ **et net** his message was loud and clear ♦ **je ne ferai jamais ça, c'est** ~ **et net !** I'll never do that, there's no question *ou* no two ways* about it!

6 *(= évident)* clear, obvious ♦ **il est** ~ **qu'il se trompe** it is clear *ou* obvious that he's mistaken ♦ **son affaire est ~e, il est coupable** it's quite clear *ou* obvious that he's guilty ♦ **c'est** ~ **comme le jour** *ou* **comme de l'eau de roche** it's as clear as daylight, it's crystal-clear

♦ **le plus clair de** ♦ **il passe le plus** ~ **de son temps à rêver** he spends most of his time daydreaming ♦ **le plus** ~ **de son argent** the better part of his money

ADV ♦ **il fait** ~ it's light ♦ **il ne fait guère** ~ **dans cette pièce** it's not very light in this room ♦ **il fait aussi** ~ *ou* **on voit aussi** ~ **qu'en plein jour** it's as bright as daylight ♦ **parlons** ~ let's be frank ♦ **voir** ~ *(lit)* to see well ♦ **voir** ~ **dans un problème/une situation** to have a clear understanding of a problem/a situation, to grasp a problem/situation clearly ♦ **maintenant j'y vois plus** ~ now I've got a better idea ♦ **je vois** ~ **dans son jeu** I can see what his game is, I know exactly what he's up to*

♦ **au clair** ♦ **tirer qch au** ~ to clear sth up, to clarify sth ♦ **il faut tirer cette affaire au** ~ we must get to the bottom of this business, we must sort this business out ♦ **être au** ~ **sur qch** to be clear about *ou* on sth ♦ **mettre ses idées au** ~ to organize one's thoughts ♦ **mettre les choses au** ~ to make things clear ♦ **mettre les choses au** ~ **avec qn** to get things straight with sb

♦ **en clair** *(= c'est-à-dire)* to put it plainly; *(= non codé)* *[message]* in clear; *[émission]* unscrambled

NM 1 († = *partie usée*) **~s** worn parts, thin patches

2 ♦ **~s** *(Art)* light *(NonC)*, light areas ♦ **les ~s et les ombres** the light and shade

COMP **clair de lune** moonlight ♦ **au** ~ **de lune** in the moonlight ♦ **promenade au** ~ **de lune** stroll in the moonlight

claire[2] /klɛʀ/ NF *(= parc)* oyster bed ♦ **(huître de)** ~ fattened oyster; → **fine**[2]

clairement /klɛʀmɑ̃/ ADV clearly

clairet, -ette /klɛʀɛ, ɛt/ ADJ *[soupe]* thin; *[voix]* high-pitched ♦ **(vin)** ~ light red wine NF **clairette** light sparkling wine

claire-voie (pl **claires-voies**) /klɛʀvwa/ NF *(= clôture)* openwork fence; *[d'église]* clerestory ♦ **à** ~ openwork *(épith)*

clairière /klɛʀjɛʀ/ NF clearing, glade

clair-obscur (pl **clairs-obscurs**) /klɛʀɔpskyʀ/ NM *(Art)* chiaroscuro; *(gén)* twilight

clairon /klɛʀɔ̃/ NM *(= instrument)* bugle; *(= joueur)* bugler; *[d'orgue]* clarion (stop)

claironnant, e /klɛʀɔnɑ̃, ɑ̃t/ ADJ *[voix]* strident, resonant

claironner /klɛʀɔne/ ▸ conjug 1 ◂ VT *[+ succès, nouvelle]* to trumpet, to shout from the rooftops VI *(= parler fort)* to speak at the top of one's voice

clairsemé, e /klɛʀsəme/ ADJ *[arbres, maisons, applaudissements, auditoire]* scattered; *[blés, gazon, cheveux]* thin, sparse; *[population]* sparse, scattered

clairvoyance /klɛʀvwajɑ̃s/ NF *[de personne]* clear-sightedness, perceptiveness; *[d'esprit]* perceptiveness

clairvoyant, e /klɛʀvwajɑ̃, ɑ̃t/ ADJ 1 *(= perspicace)* *[personne]* clear-sighted, perceptive; *[œil, esprit]* perceptive; *[politique]* farsighted 2 († = *doué de vision*) sighted NM,F († : *doué de vision*) sighted person; *(= médium)* clairvoyant

clam /klam/ NM clam

clamecer‡ /klamse/ ▸ conjug 3 ◂ VI *(= mourir)* to kick the bucket‡, to snuff it‡ *(Brit)*

clamer /klame/ ▸ conjug 1 ◂ VT to shout out, to proclaim ♦ ~ **son innocence/son indignation** to proclaim one's innocence/one's indignation

clameur /klamœʀ/ NF clamour ♦ **les ~s de la foule** the clamour of the crowd ♦ **les ~s des mécontents** *(fig)* the protests of the discontented

clamser‡ /klamse/ ▸ conjug 1 ◂ VI ⇒ **clamecer**

clan /klɑ̃/ NM *(lit, fig)* clan ♦ **esprit de** ~ clannishness

clandé /klɑ̃de/ NM *(arg Crime)* *(= maison close)* brothel, knocking-shop‡ *(Brit)*; *(= maison de jeu)* gambling joint

clandestin, e /klɑ̃dɛstɛ̃, in/ ADJ *[réunion]* secret, clandestine; *[revue, organisation, imprimerie]* underground *(épith)*; *[mouvement]* underground *(épith)*, clandestine; *[commerce]* clandestine, illicit; *[travailleur, travail, immigration, avortement]* illegal NM *(= ouvrier)* illegal worker ♦ **(passager)** ~ stowaway

clandestinement /klɑ̃dɛstinmɑ̃/ ADV *(= secrètement)* secretly; *(= illégalement)* illegally ♦ **faire entrer qn** ~ **dans un pays** to smuggle sb into a country

clandestinité /klɑ̃dɛstinite/ NF 1 *[d'activité]* secret nature ♦ **dans la** ~ *(= en secret)* *[travailler]* in secret, clandestinely; *(= en se cachant)* *[vivre]* underground ♦ **entrer dans la** ~ to go underground ♦ **le journal interdit a continué de paraître dans la** ~ the banned newspaper went on being published underground *ou* clandestinely 2 **la** ~ *(Hist = la Résistance)* the Resistance

clanique /klanik/ ADJ *[rivalité, société]* clan *(épith)* ♦ **guerre** ~ clan warfare

clap /klap/ NM *(Ciné)* clapperboard

clapet /klapɛ/ NM 1 *(= soupape)* valve; *(Élec)* rectifier ♦ ~ **d'admission/d'échappement** *[de moteur]* induction/exhaust valve 2 (‡ = *bouche)* **ferme ton** ~ hold your tongue*, shut up* ♦ **quel** ~ ! what a chatterbox!*

clapier /klapje/ NM 1 *(= cabane à lapins)* hutch; *(péj = logement surpeuplé)* dump‡, hole* 2 *(= éboulis)* scree

clapotement /klapɔtmɑ̃/ NM lap(ping) *(NonC)*

clapoter /klapɔte/ ▸ conjug 1 ◂ VI *[eau]* to lap

clapotis /klapɔti/ NM lap(ping) *(NonC)*

clappement /klapmɑ̃/ NM click(ing) *(NonC)*

clapper /klape/ ▸ conjug 1 ◂ VI ♦ ~ **de la langue** to click one's tongue

claquage /klakaʒ/ NM *(= action)* pulling *ou* straining (of a muscle); *(= blessure)* pulled *ou* strained muscle ♦ **se faire un** ~ to pull *ou* strain a muscle

claquant, e* /klakɑ̃, ɑ̃t/ ADJ *(= fatigant)* killing*, exhausting

claque[1] /klak/ NF 1 *(= gifle)* slap ♦ **donner** *ou* **flanquer*** *ou* **filer*** **une** ~ **à qn** to slap sb, to give sb a slap *ou* clout* *(Brit)* ♦ **il a pris une** ~ **aux dernières élections*** *(= humiliation)* the last election was a slap in the face for him ♦ **elle a pris une** ~ **quand son mari est parti*** *(= choc)* it was a real blow to her when her husband left ♦ **mes économies ont pris une** ~ **pendant les vacances** the holidays made a hole in my savings; → **tête** 2 *(locutions)* **j'en ai ma** ~* *(excédé)* I'm fed up to the back teeth* *(Brit)* *ou* to the teeth* *(US)*; *(épuisé)* I'm dead beat* *ou* all in* 3 *(Théât)* claque ♦ **faire la** ~ to cheer 4 *(Can = protection)* galosh, overshoe

claque[2] /klak/ ADJ, NM ♦ **(chapeau)** ~ opera hat

claque[3]‡ /klak/ NM brothel, whorehouse†*, knocking-shop‡ *(Brit)*

claqué, e* /klake/ (ptp de **claquer**) ADJ *(= fatigué)* all in*, dead beat*, knackered* *(Brit)*

claquement /klakmɑ̃/ NM 1 *(= bruit répété)* *[de porte]* banging *(NonC)*, slamming *(NonC)*; *[de fouet]* cracking *(NonC)*; *[de langue]* clicking *(NonC)*; *[de doigts]* snap(ping) *(NonC)*; *[de talons]* click(ing) *(NonC)*; *[de dents]* chattering *(NonC)*; *[de drapeau]* flapping *(NonC)* 2 *(= bruit isolé)* *[de porte]* bang, slam; *[de fouet]* crack; *[de langue]* click ♦ **la corde cassa avec un** ~ **sec** the rope broke with a sharp snap

claquemurer /klakmyʀe/ ▸ conjug 1 ◂ VT to coop up ♦ **il reste claquemuré dans son bureau toute la journée** he stays cooped up *ou* shut up *ou* shut away in his office all day VPR **se claquemurer** to shut o.s. away *ou* up

claquer /klake/ ▸ conjug 1 ◂ VI 1 *[porte, volet]* to bang; *[drapeau]* to flap; *[fouet]* to crack; *[coup de feu]* to ring out ♦ **faire** ~ *[+ porte]* to bang, to slam; *[+ fouet]* to crack

2 *(= produire un bruit)* ~ **des doigts, faire** ~ **ses doigts** to click *ou* snap one's fingers ♦ ~ **des talons** to click one's heels ♦ ~ **du bec**‡ *(= avoir faim)* to be famished* ♦ **il claquait des dents** his teeth were chattering ♦ **faire** ~ **sa langue** to click one's tongue

3 *(= casser)* *[ficelle]* to snap

4 * *[télévision, moteur, lampe]* to conk out‡, to pack in*; (‡ = *mourir)* to kick the bucket‡, to snuff it‡ *(Brit)* ♦ **il a claqué d'une crise cardiaque** a heart attack finished him off ♦ ~ **dans les mains** *ou* **les doigts de qn** *[malade]* to die on sb; *[entreprise]* to go bust on sb* ♦ **le sèche-cheveux m'a claqué entre les mains** *ou* **les doigts** the hair-drier packed in on me* *ou* died on me*

VT 1 *(= gifler)* *[+ enfant]* to slap

2 *(= refermer avec bruit)* *[+ livre]* to snap shut ♦ ~ **la porte** *(lit)* to slam the door; *(fig)* to storm out ♦ **il a claqué la porte du gouvernement** he left the government in high dudgeon ♦ **il m'a**

claqué la porte au nez *(lit)* he slammed the door in my face; *(fig)* he refused to listen to me ③ *(* = fatiguer) [travail]* to exhaust, to tire out ◆ **le voyage m'a claqué** I felt dead tired* *ou* knackered‡ *(Brit)* after the journey ◆ **ne travaille pas tant, tu vas te ~** don't work so hard or you'll wear yourself out ④ *(* = casser) [+ élastique, fermeture éclair]* to bust* ⑤ *(‡ = dépenser) [+ argent]* to blow* ◆ **j'ai beaucoup claqué à Noël** I blew* a lot of cash at Christmas ⑥ *(Tennis) [+ balle, volée]* to slam ◆ **~ un but** *(Ftbl)* to drive the ball home *ou* into goal

VPR **se claquer** *(Sport)* **se ~ un muscle** to pull *ou* strain a muscle

claquette /klakɛt/ NF ① *(Danse)* **~s** tap-dancing ◆ **faire des ~s** to tap-dance; → **danseur** ② *(= claquoir)* clapper; *(Ciné)* clapperboard ③ *(= sandale) (en plastique)* beach mule; *(en bois)* exercise sandal

claquoir /klakwaʀ/ NM clapper

clarification /klaʀifikasjɔ̃/ NF clarification

clarifier /klaʀifje/ ▸ conjug 7 ◂ VT to clarify VPR **se clarifier** *[situation]* to become clearer, to be clarified

clarine /klaʀin/ NF cowbell

clarinette /klaʀinɛt/ NF clarinet

clarinettiste /klaʀinetist/ NMF clarinettist

clarisse /klaʀis/ NF (Poor) Clare

clarté /klaʀte/ NF ① *(= lumière)* light ◆ **la ~ de la lune** the light of the moon, the moonlight ◆ **à la ~ de la lampe** in the lamplight, in *ou* by the light of the lamp ② *(= luminosité) [de flamme, pièce, jour, ciel]* brightness; *[d'eau, son, verre]* clearness; *[de teint] (= pureté)* clearness; *(= pâleur)* lightness ③ *[d'explication, pensée, attitude, conférencier]* clarity ◆ **~ d'esprit** clear thinking ◆ **pour plus de ~** to be perfectly *ou* absolutely clear ④ *(= précisions)* **avoir des ~s sur une question** to have some (further *ou* bright) ideas on a subject ◆ **cela projette quelques ~s sur la question** this throws some light on the subject

clash /klaʃ/ NM clash

classable /klɑsabl/ ADJ *[document, plante]* classifiable ◆ **elle est difficilement ~** it's hard to know how to categorize her

classe /klɑs/ NF ① *(= catégorie sociale)* class ◆ **~s creuses** *(Démographie) age groups depleted by war deaths or low natality* ◆ **les ~s moyennes** the middle classes ◆ **les basses/hautes ~s (sociales)** the lower/upper (social) classes ◆ **la ~ laborieuse** *ou* **ouvrière** the working class ◆ **la ~ politique** the political community ◆ **selon sa ~ sociale** according to one's social status *ou* social class ◆ **société sans ~** classless society ② *(gén, Sci = espèce)* class; *(Admin = rang)* grade ◆ **toutes les ~s d'utilisateurs** every category of user ◆ **il est vraiment à mettre dans une ~ à part** he's really in a class of his own *ou* a class apart ◆ **hôtel de première ~** first-class hotel ◆ **~ grammaticale** *ou* **de mots** grammatical category, part of speech ◆ **~ d'âge** age group ◆ **établissement de ~** high-class establishment ◆ **de ~ internationale** world-class ◆ **hors ~** exceptional ③ *(Transport)* class ◆ **compartiment/billet de 1re/2e ~** 1st/2nd class compartment/ticket ◆ **voyager en 1re ~** to travel 1st class ◆ **~ affaires/club/économique** business/club/economy class ④ *(gén, Sport = valeur)* class ◆ **liqueur/artiste de grande ~** liqueur/artist of great distinction ◆ **c'est un acteur/joueur de première ~** he's a first-class *ou* first-rate actor/player ◆ **de ~ internationale** of international class ◆ **elle a de la ~** she's got class ◆ **ils n'ont pas la même ~** they're not in the same class ◆ **c'est une robe qui a de la ~** it's a stylish *ou* chic dress ◆ **ils sont descendus au Ritz – la ~ quoi !*** they stayed at the Ritz – classy, eh?*; → **enterrement** ⑤ *(Scol) (= ensemble d'élèves)* class, form *(Brit)*, grade *(US)*; *(= année d'études secondaires)* year ◆ **les grandes/petites ~s** the senior/junior classes ◆ **il est en ~ de 6e** ≈ he is in year 7 *(Brit)* *ou* 5th grade *(US)* ◆ **monter de ~** to go up a class ◆ **il est (le) premier/(le) dernier de la ~** he is top/bottom of the class ◆ **~ enfantine** playschool; → **préparatoire, redoubler** ⑥ *(Scol) (= cours)* class ◆ **la ~** *(= l'école)* school ◆ **la ~ d'histoire/de français** the history/French class ◆ **~ de solfège/de danse** musical theory/dancing lesson ◆ **aller en ~** to go to school ◆ **pendant/après la ~** *ou* **les heures de ~** during/after school *ou* school hours ◆ **la ~ se termine** *ou* **les élèves sortent de ~ à 16 heures** school finishes *ou* classes finish at 4 o'clock ◆ **il est en ~** *(en cours) [professeur]* he is in class, he is teaching; *[élève]* he is in class; *(à l'école) [élève]* he is at school ◆ **c'est M. Renan qui leur fait la ~** *(habituellement)* Mr Renan is their (primary school) teacher, Mr Renan takes them at (primary) school; *(en remplacement)* Mr Renan is their replacement (primary school) teacher ⑦ *(Scol = salle)* classroom; *(d'une classe particulière)* form room *(Brit)*, homeroom *(US)* ◆ **il est turbulent en ~** he's disruptive in class *ou* in the classroom ◆ **les élèves viennent d'entrer en ~** the pupils have just gone into class ⑧ *(Mil = rang)* **militaire** *ou* **soldat de 1re ~** *(armée de terre)* ≈ private *(Brit)*, private first class *(US)*; *(armée de l'air)* ≈ leading aircraftman *(Brit)*, airman first class *(US)* ◆ **militaire** *ou* **soldat de 2e ~** *(terre)* private (soldier); *(air)* aircraftman *(Brit)*, airman basic *(US)* ◆ **la ~ de 1997** *(= contingent)* the class of '97 ◆ **ils sont de la même ~** they were called up at the same time ◆ **faire ses ~s** *(lit)* to do one's recruit training; *(fig)* to learn the ropes*

ADJ INV * *[personne, vêtements, voiture]* classy* ◆ **ça fait ~** it adds a touch of class* ◆ **il a vraiment été ~ avec moi** he was really nice to me

COMP **classe de mer** ◆ **partir en ~ de mer** to go on a school study trip to the seaside

classe de nature ⇒ **classe verte**

classe de neige ◆ **partir en ~ de neige** to go on a skiing and study trip with the school

classe(-)relais *class for special needs or problem pupils*

classe de transition *transitional school year designed to help weaker pupils catch up*

classe verte ◆ **partir en ~ verte** to go on a school study trip to the countryside

classé, e /klɑse/ ADJ *[bâtiment, monument]* listed *(Brit)*, with a preservation order on it; *[vins]* classified ◆ **joueur ~** *(Tennis)* ≈ ranked player; *(Bridge)* graded *ou* master player

classement /klɑsmɑ̃/ NM ① *(= rangement) [de papiers, documents]* filing; *[de livres]* classification; *[de fruits]* grading ◆ **~ alphabétique** alphabetical classification ◆ **j'ai fait du ~ toute la journée** I've spent all day filing ◆ **j'ai fait un peu de ~ dans mes factures** I've put my bills into some kind of order ② *(= classification) [de fonctionnaire, élève]* grading; *[de joueur]* grading, ranking; *[d'hôtel]* grading, classification ③ *(= rang) [d'élève]* place *(Brit)* *ou* rank *(US)* (in class), position in class; *[de coureur]* placing ◆ **avoir un bon/mauvais ~** *[élève]* to get a high/low place in class *(Brit)*, to be ranked high/low in class *(US)*; *[coureur]* to be well/poorly placed ◆ **le ~ des coureurs à l'arrivée** the placing of the runners at the finishing line ④ *(= liste) [d'élèves]* class list (in order of merit); *[de coureurs]* finishing list; *[d'équipes]* league table ◆ **je vais vous lire le ~** I'm going to read you your (final) placings *(Brit)* (in class) *ou* rankings *(US)* ◆ **~ général** *(Cyclisme)* overall placings *(Brit)* *ou* rankings *(US)* ◆ **premier au ~ général/au ~ de l'étape** first overall/for the stage ◆ **il est second au ~ mondial** he's ranked second in the world ◆ **elle est troisième au ~ provisoire** she's third in the provisional rankings ⑤ *(= clôture) [d'affaire, dossier]* closing

classer /klɑse/ ▸ conjug 1 ◂ VT ① *(= ranger) [+ papiers]* to file; *[+ livres]* to classify; *[+ documents]* to file, to classify ◆ **~ des livres par sujet** to classify books by *ou* according to subject (matter) ◆ **~ des factures par année/client** to file invoices according to the year/the customer's name ② *(Sci = classifier) [+ animaux, plantes]* to classify ③ *(= hiérarchiser) [+ employé, élève, joueur, copie]* to grade; *[+ hôtel]* to grade, to classify ◆ **~ un édifice monument historique** to list a building *(Brit)*, to put a building on the historical register *(US)* ◆ **Jean Suchet, que l'on classe parmi les meilleurs violonistes** Jean Suchet, who ranks *ou* is rated among the top violinists ④ *(= clore) [+ affaire, dossier]* to close ◆ **c'est une affaire classée maintenant** the matter is closed now ⑤ *(péj = cataloguer) [+ personne]* to categorize ◆ **celui-là, je l'ai classé dès que je l'ai vu** I sized him up* as soon as I saw him

VPR **se classer** ◆ **se ~ premier/parmi les premiers** to come *(Brit)* *ou* come in *(US)* first/among the first ◆ **ce livre se classe au nombre des grands chefs-d'œuvre littéraires** this book ranks among the great works of literature

classeur /klɑsœʀ/ NM *(= meuble)* filing cabinet; *(= dossier)* (loose-leaf) file; *(à tirette)* binder ◆ **~ à anneaux** ring binder ◆ **~ à rideau** roll-top cabinet

classicisme /klasisism/ NM *(Art)* classicism; *(= conformisme)* conventionality

classieux, -ieuse * /klasjø, jøz/ ADJ classy*

classificateur, -trice /klasifikatœʀ, tʀis/ ADJ *[procédé, méthode]* classifying; *(= méthodique) [esprit]* methodical, orderly ◆ **obsession classificatrice** mania for categorizing *ou* classifying things NM,F classifier

classification /klasifikasjɔ̃/ NF classification

classificatoire /klasifikatwaʀ/ ADJ classificatory

classifier /klasifje/ ▸ conjug 7 ◂ VT to classify

classique /klasik/ ADJ ① *[auteur, genre, musique, langue]* classical ② *(= sobre) [coupe, vêtement, décoration]* classic, classical ③ *(= habituel) [argument, réponse, méthode, maladie]* classic, standard; *[conséquence]* usual; *[symptôme]* classic, usual; *[produit]* ordinary, regular *(US)* ◆ **c'est ~ !** it's classic! ◆ **c'est le coup ~ !*** it's the usual story ◆ **c'est la question/la plaisanterie ~** it's the classic question/joke ◆ **le cambriolage s'est déroulé suivant le plan ~** the burglary followed the standard *ou* recognized pattern ◆ **grâce à une opération maintenant ~** thanks to an operation which is now quite usual *ou* standard ④ *(Scol = littéraire)* **faire des études ~s** to study classics, to do classical studies ◆ **il est en section ~** he's in the classics stream *(Brit)*, he's in the classic program *(US)*; → **lettre**

NM ① *(= auteur) (Antiq)* classical author; *(classicisme français)* classic, classicist ◆ **(auteur) ~** *(= grand écrivain)* classic (author) ② *(= ouvrage)* classic ◆ **un ~ du cinéma** a cinema classic, a classic film ◆ **c'est un ~ du genre** it's a classic of its kind ◆ **je connais mes ~s !*** *(hum)* I know my classics!

[3] *(= genre)* **le ~** *(= musique)* classical music; *(= style)* the classic *ou* classical style

NF *(Sport)* classic; *(Cyclisme)* one-day road race

classiquement /klasikmɑ̃/ ADV classically

claudication /klodikasjɔ̃/ NF *(littér)* limp

claudiquer /klodike/ ► conjug 1 ◄ VI *(littér)* to limp

clause /kloz/ NF *(Gram, Jur)* clause ◆ **~ abusive** unfair condition ◆ **~ de conscience** conscience clause ◆ **~ dérogatoire** *ou* **échappatoire** escape clause, get-out clause ◆ **~ de la nation la plus favorisée** most-favoured-nation trading status ◆ **~ pénale** penalty clause ◆ **~ sociale** social chapter ◆ **~ de style** standard *ou* set clause ◆ **~ résolutoire** resolutive clause; → **sauvegarde**[1]

claustral, e (mpl **-aux**) /klostʀal, o/ ADJ monastic

claustration /klostʀasjɔ̃/ NF confinement

claustrer /klostʀe/ ► conjug 1 ◄ VT *(= enfermer)* to confine VPR **se claustrer** to shut o.s. up *ou* away ◆ **se ~ dans** *(fig)* to wrap *ou* enclose o.s. in

claustro * /klostʀo/ ADJ abrév de **claustrophobe**

claustrophobe /klostʀɔfɔb/ ADJ, NMF claustrophobic

claustrophobie /klostʀɔfɔbi/ NF claustrophobia

clausule /klozyl/ NF clausula

clavecin /klav(ə)sɛ̃/ NM harpsichord

claveciniste /klav(ə)sinist/ NMF harpsichordist

clavette /klavɛt/ NF *[de boulon]* key, cotter pin

clavicorde /klavikɔʀd/ NM clavichord

clavicule /klavikyl/ NF collarbone, clavicle *(SPÉC)*

clavier /klavje/ NM keyboard ◆ **à un/deux ~(s)** *[orgue, clavecin]* single-/double-manual *(épith)* ◆ **~ AZERTY/QWERTY** AZERTY/QWERTY keyboard ◆ **~ étendu** extended keyboard ◆ **au ~, Joey !** on keyboards, Joey!

claviériste /klavjeʀist/ NMF keyboard player

claviste /klavist/ NMF keyboard operator, keyboarder

clayette /klɛjɛt/ NF *(= étagère)* wicker *ou* wire rack; *(= cageot à fruits)* tray; *[de réfrigérateur]* shelf

clayon /klɛjɔ̃/ NM *(= étagère)* rack; *(= plateau)* tray

clé /kle/ NF [1] *[de serrure, pendule, boîte de conserve]* key; *[de poêle]* damper ◆ **la ~ de la porte d'entrée** the (front) door key ◆ **la ~ est sur la porte** the key is in the door ◆ **Avignon, ~ de la Provence** Avignon, the gateway to Provence ◆ **les ~s du Paradis** the keys to the Kingdom ◆ **les ~s de saint Pierre** St Peter's keys; → **fermer, tour**[2]

[2] *(= outil)* spanner *(Brit)*, wrench *(surtout US)* ◆ **un jeu de ~s** a set of spanners *ou* wrenches

[3] *[de guitare, violon]* peg; *[de clarinette]* key; *[de gamme]* clef; *[d'accordeur]* key ◆ **~ de fa/de sol/d'ut** bass *ou* F/treble *ou* G/alto *ou* C clef ◆ **il y a trois dièses à la ~** the key signature has 3 sharps ◆ **avec une altération à la ~** with a change in the key signature

[4] *[de mystère, réussite, code, rêve]* key *(de* to); ◆ **la préface nous fournit quelques ~s** the preface offers a few clues

[5] *(Lutte)* lock ◆ **il lui a fait une ~ au bras** he got him in an armlock

[6] *(locutions)* **mettre sous ~** to put under lock and key ◆ **mettre la ~ sous la porte** *ou* **le paillasson** *(= faire faillite)* to shut up shop; *(= s'enfuir)* to clear out, to do a bunk* *(Brit)* ◆ **prendre la ~ des champs** to run away *ou* off

◆ **à clés** ◆ **personnage à ~s** real-life character disguised under a fictitious name ◆ **roman à ~s** *novel in which actual persons appear as fictitious characters*

◆ **à la clé** ◆ **il y a une récompense à la ~** a reward is being offered ◆ **je vais les mettre en retenue, avec un devoir à la ~** I'll keep them behind and give them an exercise to do as well

◆ **clé(s) en main** ◆ **acheter un appartement ~s en main** to buy an apartment ready for immediate occupation *ou* with immediate entry ◆ **prix ~s en main** *[voiture]* price on the road, on-the-road price *(Brit)*, sticker price *(US)*; *[appartement]* price with immediate entry *ou* possession *ou* occupation ◆ **projet/solution/usine ~s en main** turnkey project/solution/factory

ADJ INV *[industrie, mot, position, rôle]* key *(épith)*

COMP **clé Allen** Allen wrench *ou* key *(Brit)*

clé anglaise ⇒ **clé à molette**

clé à bougie spark plug swivel

clé de contact ignition key

clé à crémaillère monkey wrench, shifting spanner *ou* wrench

clé crocodile alligator spanner *ou* wrench

clé en croix wheel brace

clé dynamométrique torque wrench

clé à ergot spanner wrench

clé à fourche ⇒ **clé plate**

clé mixte combination spanner *ou* wrench

clé à molette monkey wrench, adjustable spanner *ou* wrench

clé à pipe box *ou* socket spanner, socket wrench

clé plate open-end spanner *ou* wrench

clé polygonale ring spanner *ou* wrench

clé RIB personal code *(that appears on official slip giving bank account details)*

clé en tube hex key (wrench)

clé universelle adjustable spanner *ou* wrench

clé USB *(Ordin)* USB key

clé de voûte *(Archit, fig)* keystone

clean * /klin/ ADJ INV [1] *(= propre)* clean ◆ **c'est pas très ~ chez lui** his place isn't very clean [2] *(= soigné)* *[homme]* wholesomelooking, clean-cut; *[femme]* wholesomelooking; *[vêtements]* smart; *[décor]* stark [3] *(arg Drogue)* clean [4] *(= sympathique)* **c'était ~ de sa part** that was really nice of him

clébard * /klebaʀ/, **clebs** * /klɛps/ NM *(péj = chien)* dog, mutt *

clef /kle/ NF ⇒ **clé**

clématite /klematit/ NF clematis

clémence /klemɑ̃s/ NF *(= douceur)* *[de temps]* mildness, clemency *(frm)*; *(= indulgence)* *[de juge]* clemency, leniency

clément, e /klemɑ̃, ɑ̃t/ ADJ *(= doux)* *[temps]* mild, clement *(frm)*; *(= indulgent)* *[personne]* lenient ◆ **se montrer ~** to show clemency *(envers* towards) → **ciel**

clémentine /klemɑ̃tin/ NF clementine

clenche /klɑ̃ʃ/ NF latch

Cléopâtre /kleɔpatʀ/ NF Cleopatra

cleptomane /klɛptɔman/ NMF ⇒ **kleptomane**

cleptomanie /klɛptɔmani/ NF ⇒ **kleptomanie**

clerc /klɛʀ/ NM [1] **~ (de notaire)** clerk; → **pas**[1] [2] *(Rel)* cleric [3] *(†† = lettré)* (learned) scholar ◆ **être (grand) ~ en la matière** to be an expert on the subject ◆ **on n'a pas besoin d'être grand ~ pour deviner ce qui s'est passé !** you don't need to be a genius to guess what happened!

clergé /klɛʀʒe/ NM clergy ◆ **le bas/haut ~** the lower/higher clergy

clérical, e (mpl **-aux**) /kleʀikal, o/ ADJ *(Rel)* clerical NM,F clerical, supporter of the clergy

cléricalisme /kleʀikalism/ NM clericalism

clic /klik/ NM [1] *(= bruit, Ordin)* click ◆ **le menu s'ouvre d'un ~ de souris** the menu opens with a mouse click [2] *(TV)* **~s** sparkles, sparklies *

clic-clac /klikklak/ EXCL *[d'appareil-photo]* click!; *[de pas]* clickety-clack!; *[de sabots]* clip(pety)-clop! NM INV [1] *(= bruit)* *[de sabots]* clip(pety)-clop; *[de talons]* click [2] ◆ **(canapé** *ou* **convertible) ~** sofa bed *(with reclining back)*

cliché /kliʃe/ NM *(= lieu commun)* cliché; *(Photo)* negative; *(Typo)* plate

client, cliente /klijɑ̃, klijɑ̃t/ NM,F [1] *[de magasin, restaurant]* customer; *[de coiffeur]* client, customer; *[d'avocat]* client; *[d'hôtel]* guest, patron; *[de médecin]* patient; *[de taxi]* fare ◆ **être ~ d'un magasin** to patronize a shop, to be a regular customer at a shop ◆ **le boucher me sert bien parce que je suis (une) ~e** the butcher gives me good service because I'm a regular customer (of his) *ou* because I'm one of his regulars ◆ **le ~ est roi** the customer is always right ◆ **la France est un gros ~ de l'Allemagne** *(Écon)* France is a large trading customer of Germany ◆ **je ne suis pas ~** *(fig)* it's not my thing * *ou* my cup of tea *

[2] *(* : péj = individu)* guy *, bloke * *(Brit)* ◆ **c'est un drôle de ~** he's an odd customer *ou* bloke * *(Brit)* ◆ **pour le titre de champion du monde, Suard est un ~ sérieux** Suard is a hot contender for *ou* is making a strong bid for the world championship

[3] *(Ordin)* client

[4] *(Antiq = protégé)* client

clientèle /klijɑ̃tɛl/ NF [1] *(= ensemble des clients)* *[de restaurant, hôtel, coiffeur]* clientele; *[de magasin]* customers, clientele; *[d'avocat, médecin]* practice; *[de taxi]* fares; *[de parti politique]* supporters ◆ **le boucher a une nombreuse ~** the butcher has many customers ◆ **le candidat a conservé sa ~ électorale au deuxième tour** the candidate held on to his voters in the second round [2] *(= fait d'être client)* custom, business ◆ **accorder sa ~ à qn** to give sb one's custom *ou* business, to patronize sb ◆ **retirer sa ~ à qn** to withdraw one's custom from sb, to take one's business away from sb [3] *(Antiq = protégés)* clients

clientélisme /klijɑ̃telism/ NM *(péj)* vote-catching, clientelism ◆ **c'est du ~** it's just a vote-catching gimmick

clientéliste /klijɑ̃telist/ ADJ *[système, tradition]* based on patronage, clientelist ◆ **il y a un risque de pressions ~s** there is a danger of pressure being exerted by influential voters

clignement /kliɲ(ə)mɑ̃/ NM blinking *(NonC)* ◆ **cela l'obligeait à des ~s d'yeux continuels** it made him blink continually ◆ **un ~ d'œil** a wink

cligner /kliɲe/ ► conjug 1 ◄ VT, VT INDIR ◆ **~ les** *ou* **des yeux** *(clignoter)* to blink; *(fermer à moitié)* to screw up one's eyes ◆ **~ de l'œil** to wink *(en direction de* at)

clignotant, e /kliɲɔtɑ̃, ɑ̃t/ NM *[de voiture]* indicator; *(fig = indice de danger)* warning light *(fig)* ◆ **mettre son ~** *(Aut)* to indicate *(Brit)*, to put one's turn signal on *(US)* ◆ **tous les ~s sont allumés** *(fig)* all the warning signs *ou* danger signals are flashing ADJ *[lumière]* *(= vacillant)* flickering; *(= intermittent, pour signal)* flashing, winking

clignotement /kliɲɔtmɑ̃/ NM *[de yeux]* blinking; *[d'étoile, guirlande]* twinkling; *[de phares]* flashing; *[de lumière]* *(vacillante)* flickering; *(vue de loin)* twinkling; *(= signal)* flashing ◆ **les ~s de la lampe** the flickering of the lamplight

clignoter /kliɲɔte/ ► conjug 1 ◄ VI *[yeux]* to blink; *[étoile, guirlande]* to twinkle; *[phares]* to flash; *[lumière]* *(= vaciller)* to flicker; *(vue de loin)* to twinkle; *(= signal)* to flash, to wink ◆ **~ des yeux** to blink

clim * /klim/ NF abrév de **climatisation**

climat /klima/ NM *(lit, fig)* climate; *(littér = contrée)* clime *(littér)* ◆ **dans** *ou* **sous nos ~s** in our climate ◆ ~ **économique/politique** economic/political climate ◆ **le ~ social est très mauvais en ce moment** the public mood is very bad at the moment ◆ **pour améliorer le ~ social dans cette profession/cette usine** to improve relations between management and workers in this profession/this factory

climatique /klimatik/ **ADJ** climatic; ◆ **changement** ~ climate change → **station**

climatisation /klimatizasjɔ̃/ **NF** air conditioning

climatiser /klimatize/ ▸ **conjug 1** ◂ **VT** *[+ pièce, atmosphère]* to air-condition; *(Tech)* *[+ appareil]* to adapt for use in severe conditions ◆ **bureau climatisé** air-conditioned office

climatiseur /klimatizœʀ/ **NM** air conditioner

climatologie /klimatɔlɔʒi/ **NF** climatology

climatologique /klimatɔlɔʒik/ **ADJ** climatological

clin /klɛ̃/ **NM** ◆ ~ **d'œil** (pl **clins d'œil** *ou* **d'yeux**) *(lit)* wink; *(fig : dans un roman, un film)* allusion, veiled reference ◆ **c'est un ~ d'œil aux Marx Brothers** *(fig)* it's a nod in the direction of the Marx Brothers ◆ **c'est un ~ d'œil au lecteur** it is a veiled message to the reader ◆ **faire un ~ d'œil** *(lit)* to wink (*à* at); *(fig)* to make a veiled reference (*à* to); ◆ **en un ~ d'œil** in a flash, in the twinkling of an eye

clinfoc /klɛ̃fɔk/ **NM** flying jib

clinicien, -ienne /klinisjɛ̃, jɛn/ **NM,F** clinician

clinique /klinik/ **NF** 1 *(= établissement)* private hospital, private clinic; *(= section d'hôpital)* clinic ◆ ~ **d'accouchement** maternity hospital, maternity home *(Brit)*; → **chef**[1] 2 *(= enseignement)* clinic **ADJ** clinical; → **mort**[1]

cliniquement /klinikmɑ̃/ **ADV** clinically

clinquant, e /klɛ̃kɑ̃, ɑt/ **ADJ** *[bijoux, décor, langage]* flashy **NM** *(= lamelles brillantes)* tinsel; *(= faux bijoux)* tawdry jewellery *(Brit)* *ou* jewelery *(US)*; *[d'opéra, style]* flashiness

clip /klip/ **NM** 1 *(= broche)* brooch 2 *(= boucle d'oreille)* clip-on 3 ◆ ~ **(vidéo)** (pop) video, (music) video clip; *(promotionnel)* (promo) video 4 *(en chirurgie)* clamp

clipper /klipœʀ/ **NM** *(Naut)* clipper

cliquable /klikabl/ **ADJ** clickable

clique /klik/ **NF** 1 *(péj = bande)* clique, set 2 *(Mil = orchestre)* drum and bugle band 3 ◆ **prendre ses ~s et ses claques (et s'en aller)** * to pack up and go, to pack one's bags and leave

cliquer /klike/ ▸ **conjug 1** ◂ **VI** *(Ordin)* to click *(sur* on); ◆ ~ **deux fois** to double-click

cliquet /klikɛ/ **NM** pawl

cliqueter /klik(ə)te/ ▸ **conjug 4** ◂ **VI** *[monnaie]* to jingle, to clink, to chink; *[clés]* to rattle; *[vaisselle]* to clatter; *[verres]* to clink, to chink; *[chaînes]* to clank; *[ferraille]* to jangle; *[mécanisme]* to go clickety-clack; *[armes]* to clash; *[moteur]* to pink, to knock ◆ **j'entends quelque chose qui cliquette** I can hear something clinking

cliquetis /klik(ə)ti/, **cliquettement** /klikɛtmɑ̃/ **NM** *[de clés]* jingle *(NonC)*, clink *(NonC)*, jingling *(NonC)*; *[de vaisselle]* clatter *(NonC)*; *[de verres]* clink *(NonC)*, clinking *(NonC)*; *[de chaînes]* clank *(NonC)*, clanking *(NonC)*; *[de ferraille]* jangle *(NonC)*, jangling *(NonC)*; *[de mécanisme]* clickety-clack *(NonC)*; *[d'armes]* clash *(NonC)*; *[de moteur]* pinking *ou* knocking sound, pinking *(NonC)*; *[de machine à écrire]* rattle *(NonC)*, clicking *(NonC)* ◆ **on entendait un ~ de vaisselle** we could hear the clatter of dishes ◆ **des ~ se firent entendre** clinking noises could be heard

clisse /klis/ **NF** 1 *[de fromage]* wicker tray 2 *[de bouteille]* wicker covering

clisser /klise/ ▸ **conjug 1** ◂ **VT** *[+ bouteille]* to cover with wicker(work)

clitoridectomie /klitɔʀidɛktɔmi/ **NF** clitoridectomy

clitoridien, -ienne /klitɔʀidjɛ̃, jɛn/ **ADJ** clitoral

clitoris /klitɔʀis/ **NM** clitoris

clivage /klivaʒ/ **NM** 1 *(Géol = fissure)* cleavage 2 *(Minér)* *(= action)* cleaving; *(= résultat)* cleavage 3 *[de groupes]* split, division; *[d'idées]* distinction, split (*de* in); ◆ ~ **politique** political split ◆ **il existe un important ~ entre le nord et le sud** there is a huge divide between north and south

cliver **VT**, **se cliver** **VPR** /klive/ ▸ **conjug 1** ◂ *(Minér)* to cleave

cloaque /klɔak/ **NM** 1 *[d'animal]* cloaca 2 *(= lieu de corruption)* cesspool, cesspit; *(= endroit sale)* pigsty, dump *, tip * *(Brit)*

clochard, e /klɔʃaʀ, aʀd/ **NM,F** down-and-out, tramp, bum * *(US)*

clochardisation /klɔʃaʀdizasjɔ̃/ **NF** ◆ **les hommes sont plus touchés par la ~ que les femmes** men are more liable than women to become down-and-outs *ou* to end up living on the streets ◆ **marginaux en voie de ~** drop-outs on the road to vagrancy

clochardiser /klɔʃaʀdize/ ▸ **conjug 1** ◂ **VT** *[+ personne]* to turn into a down-and-out *ou* a tramp *ou* a bum * *(US)* ◆ **les toxicomanes clochardisés** down-and-out drug addicts **VPR** **se clochardiser** *[personne]* to become a down-and-out *ou* a tramp *ou* a bum * *(US)* ◆ **la ville se clochardise** there are more and more down-and-outs *ou* tramps *ou* bums * *(US)* in the town

cloche /klɔʃ/ **NF** 1 *[d'église]* bell ◆ **en forme de ~** bell-shaped ◆ **courbe en ~** bell curve ◆ **il a été élevé sous ~** he had a very sheltered upbringing, he was wrapped in cotton wool as a child *(Brit)* ◆ **il ne faut pas mettre nos entreprises sous ~** we shouldn't cosset our companies; → **son**[2] 2 *(= couvercle)* *[de plat]* lid; *[de plantes, légumes]* cloche 3 * *(= imbécile)* idiot, clot * *(Brit)*; *(= clochard)* down-and-out, tramp, bum * *(US)* ◆ **la ~** *(= les clochards)* down-and-outs, tramps, bums * *(US)*; *(= style de vie)* the life of a tramp 4 *(Chim)* bell jar **ADJ** 1 *(= évasé)* *[jupe]* bell-shaped; → **chapeau** 2 (* *= idiot)* idiotic, silly ◆ **qu'il est ~ ce type !** what an idiot *ou* a clot! * *(Brit)*

COMP **cloche à fromage** cheese cover

cloche à plongeur *ou* **de plongée** diving bell

Clochemerle /klɔʃmɛʀl/ **NM** *(hum)* ◆ **c'est un peu ~ ici** there's a touch of parish-pump politics about this place, a lot of petty small-town squabbling goes on here

> **CLOCHEMERLE**
>
> This term is an allusion to the title of a humorous novel, written in 1934 by Gabriel Chevallier, describing the pandemonium that erupts in a French village community following the decision to erect a public urinal next to the local church.

cloche-pied (à) /klɔʃpje/ **LOC ADV** hopping ◆ **arriver à ~** to come hopping in, to hop in ◆ **il est parti (en sautant) à ~** he hopped away *ou* off

clocher[1] /klɔʃe/ **NM** 1 *(Archit)* *(en pointe)* steeple; *(carré)* church tower 2 *(fig = village)* village ◆ **revoir son ~** to see one's home town again ◆ **de ~** *[mentalité]* parochial, small-town *(épith)*; *[querelles]* local, parochial; → **esprit**

clocher[2] * /klɔʃe/ ▸ **conjug 1** ◂ **VI** *(= être défectueux)* *[raisonnement]* to be cockeyed * ◆ **qu'est-ce qui cloche ?** what's up (with you)? * ◆ **pourvu que rien ne cloche** provided nothing goes wrong *ou* there are no hitches ◆ **il y a quelque chose qui cloche (dans ce qu'il dit)** there's something which doesn't quite fit *ou* something not quite right (in what he says) ◆ **il y a quelque chose qui cloche dans le moteur** there's something wrong *ou* there's something up * with the engine

clocheton /klɔʃtɔ̃/ **NM** *(Archit)* pinnacle

clochette /klɔʃɛt/ **NF** (small) bell; *(= partie de fleur)* bell ◆ **~s** *(= campanules)* bellflowers ◆ **~s bleues** *(= jacinthes des bois)* bluebells

clodo * /klodo/ **NM** tramp, bum * *(US)*

cloison /klwazɔ̃/ **NF** 1 *(Constr)* partition (wall) 2 *(Anat, Bot)* septum, partition ◆ ~ **nasale** nasal septum 3 *(Naut)* bulkhead ◆ ~ **étanche** watertight compartment 4 *(fig)* barrier ◆ **les ~s entre les différentes classes sociales** the barriers between the different social classes

cloisonné, e /klwazɔne/ (ptp de **cloisonner**) **ADJ** ◆ **être ~** *[sciences, services administratifs]* to be isolated *ou* cut off from one another ◆ **nous vivons dans un monde ~** we live in a compartmentalized world **NM** *(Art)* cloisonné

cloisonnement /klwazɔnmɑ̃/ **NM** *[de société, système]* compartmentalization ◆ **le ~ des services** the fact that the departments work in isolation (from one another) ◆ **à cause du ~ culturel et social** because of cultural and social barriers

cloisonner /klwazɔne/ ▸ **conjug 1** ◂ **VT** *[+ pièce]* to divide up, to partition off; *[+ tiroir]* to divide up; *[+ société]* to divide, to compartmentalize; *[+ secteurs]* to isolate

cloître /klwatʀ/ **NM** cloister

cloîtrer /klwatʀe/ ▸ **conjug 1** ◂ **VT** *(= enfermer)* to shut away (*dans* in); *(Rel)* to cloister ◆ ~ **une jeune fille** *(lit)* to put a girl in a convent; *(fig)* to keep a girl shut away (from the rest of society) ◆ **religieuse cloîtrée** nun belonging to an enclosed order **VPR** **se cloîtrer** *(= s'enfermer)* to shut o.s. up *ou* away, to cloister o.s. (*dans* in); *(Rel)* to enter a convent *ou* monastery ◆ **il est resté cloîtré dans sa chambre pendant 2 jours** he stayed shut up *ou* away in his room for 2 days ◆ **ils vivent cloîtrés chez eux sans jamais voir personne** they cut themselves off from the world *ou* they lead cloistered lives and never see anyone

clonage /klonaʒ/ **NM** *(lit, fig)* cloning ◆ ~ **thérapeutique** therapeutic cloning

clone /klon/ **NM** *(lit, fig)* clone

cloner /klone/ ▸ **conjug 1** ◂ **VT** *(lit, fig)* to clone

clope * /klɔp/ **NF** *(= cigarette)* cig *, smoke *, fag * *(Brit)* **NM** *(= mégot)* butt, dog end *

cloper * /klɔpe/ ▸ **conjug 1** ◂ **VI** to smoke ◆ **il était en train de ~** he was having a smoke, he was smoking

clopin-clopant /klɔpɛ̃klɔpɑ̃/ **ADV** *(= en boitillant)* ◆ **marcher ~** to hobble *ou* limp along ◆ **il vint vers nous ~** he hobbled towards us ◆ **sortir/entrer ~** to hobble out/in ◆ **les affaires allaient ~** business was struggling along *ou* was just ticking over ◆ **comment ça va ? – ~** how are things? – so-so *

clopiner /klɔpine/ ▸ **conjug 1** ◂ **VI** *(= boitiller)* to hobble *ou* limp along ◆ ~ **vers** to hobble *ou* limp towards

clopinettes * /klɔpinɛt/ **NFPL** ◆ **travailler pour/gagner des ~** to work for/earn peanuts *

cloporte /klɔpɔʀt/ **NM** *(= animal)* woodlouse; *(péj)* creep *

cloque /klɔk/ **NF** *[de peau, peinture]* blister; *(Bot)* leaf curl *ou* blister ◆ **être en ~** ** to be pregnant, to be in the club ** *(Brit)* ◆ **il l'a mise en ~** ** he knocked her up **, he put her in the club ** *(Brit)*

cloqué, e /klɔke/ (ptp de **cloquer**) **ADJ** *[feuilles, peinture]* blistered ◆ **étoffe ~e** seersucker *(NonC)* **NM** *(= tissu)* seersucker

cloquer /klɔke/ ► conjug 1 ◄ VI *[peau, peinture]* to blister

clore /klɔʀ/ GRAMMAIRE ACTIVE 53.4 ► conjug 45 ◄ VT
1 (= *clôturer*) *[+ liste, débat]* to close; *[+ livre, discours, spectacle]* to end, to conclude; *(Fin) [+ compte]* to close ♦ **la séance est close** the meeting is closed *ou* finished ♦ **l'incident est clos** the matter is closed ♦ **les inscriptions sont closes depuis hier** yesterday was the closing date for registration ♦ **une description clôt le chapitre** the chapter closes *ou* ends *ou* concludes with a description ♦ **le débat s'est clos sur cette remarque** the discussion ended *ou* closed with that remark 2 († *ou littér* = *conclure*) *[+ accord, marché]* to conclude 3 (*littér* = *entourer*) *[+ terrain, ville]* to enclose (*de* with) 4 (*littér* = *fermer*) *[+ porte, volets]* to close, to shut; *[+ lettre]* to seal; *[+ chemin, passage]* to close off, to seal off; → **bec**

clos, close /klo, kloz/ (ptp de **clore**) ADJ *[système, ensemble]* closed; *[espace]* enclosed ♦ **les yeux ~** *ou* **les paupières ~es, il ...** with his eyes closed *ou* shut, he ...; → **huis, maison** NM (= *pré*) (enclosed) field; (= *vignoble*) vineyard ♦ **un ~ de pommiers** an apple orchard

clôture /klotyʀ/ NF 1 (= *enceinte*) *(en planches)* fence, paling; *(en fil de fer)* (wire) fence; *(d'arbustes)* hedge; *(en ciment)* wall ♦ **mur/grille de ~** outer *ou* surrounding wall/railings; → **bris** 2 (= *fermeture*) *[de débat, liste, compte]* closing, closure; *[de bureaux, magasins]* closing; *[d'inscriptions]* closing date (de for); ♦ ~ **annuelle** *(Ciné, Théât)* annual closure ♦ **il faut y aller avant la ~** *(du festival)* we must go before it ends *ou* is over; *(d'une pièce)* we must go before it closes *ou* ends; *(du magasin)* we must go before it closes *ou* shuts ♦ **séance/date de ~** closing session/date ♦ **cours de ~** *(Bourse)* closing price ♦ **combien valait le dollar en ~ ?** what did the dollar close at? ♦ **débat de ~** adjournment debate

clôturer /klotyʀe/ ► conjug 1 ◄ VT 1 *[+ jardin, champ]* to enclose, to fence 2 *[+ débats, liste, compte]* to close; *[+ inscriptions]* to close (the list of) VI *(Bourse)* to close ♦ **la séance a clôturé en baisse** prices were down at the close (of dealing), prices closed down ♦ **le dollar a clôturé à 1 €** the dollar closed at 1 euro

clou /klu/ NM 1 *(gén)* nail; *(décoratif)* stud ♦ **fixe-le avec un ~** nail it up (*ou* down *ou* on) ♦ **pendre son chapeau à un ~** to hang one's hat on a nail
2 *[de chaussée]* stud ♦ **traverser dans les ~s, prendre les ~s (pour traverser)** to cross at the pedestrian *ou* zebra *(Brit)* crossing, to cross at the crosswalk *(US)* ♦ **être dans les ~s** *(fig)* to be on target ♦ **il a vécu sa vie dans les ~s** he led a very conventional life
3 *(Méd)* boil
4 (= *attraction principale*) *[de spectacle]* star attraction *ou* turn ♦ **le ~ de la soirée** the highlight *ou* the star turn of the evening
5 (* = *mont-de-piété*) **mettre sa montre au ~** to pawn one's watch, to put one's watch in hock*
6 (* = *instrument*) ancient machine *ou* implement ♦ **(vieux) ~** (= *voiture*) old jalopy* *ou* banger* *(Brit)*; (= *vélo*) rickety old bike, old boneshaker* *(Brit)*
7 *(locutions)* **des ~s !*** no way!*, nothing doing!* ♦ **il lui a tout expliqué mais des ~s !*** he explained everything to him but he was just wasting his breath! ♦ **je l'ai fait pour des ~s*** I did it all for nothing, I was just wasting my time ♦ **j'y suis allé pour des ~s*** it was a wild-goose chase ♦ **un ~ chasse l'autre** *(Prov)* one man goes and another steps in *ou* another takes his place; → **valoir**
COMP **clou à béton** masonry nail
clou de girofle *(Culin)* clove
clou de tapissier (upholstery) tack
clou sans tête brad
clou à tête homme veneer pin
clou à tête plate flat-headed nail

clouer /klue/ ► conjug 1 ◄ VT 1 *[+ planches, couvercle, caisse]* to nail down; *[+ tapis]* to tack *ou* nail down; *[+ tapisserie]* to nail up ♦ **il l'a cloué au sol d'un coup d'épée** he pinned him to the ground with a thrust of his sword 2 (= *immobiliser*) *[+ ennemi]* to pin down ♦ **ça l'a cloué sur place** *[étonnement, peur]* it left him rooted to the spot ♦ ~ **qn au lit** to keep sb stuck in bed* *ou* confined to bed ♦ ~ **au sol** *[+ personne]* to pin down (to the ground); *[+ avion]* to ground ♦ ~ **une pièce** *(Échecs)* to pin a piece ♦ **être** *ou* **rester cloué de stupeur** to be glued *ou* rooted to the spot with amazement; → **bec**

clouté, e /klute/ (ptp de **clouter**) ADJ *[ceinture, porte]* studded; *[chaussures]* hobnailed; → **passage**

clouterie /klutʀi/ NF nail factory

clovisse /klɔvis/ NF clam

clown /klun/ NM clown ♦ **faire le ~** to clown (about), to play the fool ♦ **c'est un vrai ~** he's a real comic ♦ ~ **blanc** whiteface clown

clownerie /klunʀi/ NF clowning *(NonC)*, silly trick ♦ **faire des ~s** to clown (about), to play the fool ♦ **arrête tes ~s** stop your (silly) antics

clownesque /klunɛsk/ ADJ *[comportement]* clownish; *[situation]* farcical

club /klœb/ NM 1 (= *association*) club ♦ **le ~ des pays riches** the club of rich nations ♦ **bienvenue au ~ !** *(hum)* welcome to the club! 2 (= *crosse de golf*) club ADJ ♦ **sandwich ~** ham salad sandwich ≃ club sandwich ♦ **cravate ~** (diagonally) striped tie; → **fauteuil**
COMP **club de gymnastique** gym
club d'investissement investment club
club de jazz jazz club
club privé exclusive night club
club de rencontre(s) singles club
club sportif sports club
club du troisième âge club for retired people, Darby and Joan club *(Brit)*
club de vacances holiday *(Brit) ou* vacation *(US)* village

cluse /klyz/ NF *(Géog)* transverse valley (in the Jura), cluse *(SPÉC)*

clystère /klistɛʀ/ NM *(Hist Méd)* clyster

Clytemnestre /klitɛmnɛstʀ/ NF Clytemnestra

CM /seem/ NM (abrév de **cours moyen**) → **cours**

cm (abrév de **centimètre**) cm ♦ ~² cm², sq. cm ♦ ~³ cm³, cu. cm

CMU NF (abrév de **couverture maladie universelle**) *free health care for people on low incomes*

CNAM /knam/ NM (abrév de **Conservatoire national des arts et métiers**) → **conservatoire** NF (abrév de **Caisse nationale d'assurance maladie**) → **caisse**

CNC /seɛnse/ NM 1 (abrév de **Centre national de cinématographie**) ≃ BFI *(Brit)*, Academy of the Movie Picture *(US)* 2 (abrév de **Comité national de la consommation**) ≃ National Consumer Council *(Brit)*, CA *(Brit)*, CPSC *(US)*

CNDP /seɛndepe/ NM (abrév de **Centre national de documentation pédagogique**) → **centre**

CNED /knɛd/ NM (abrév de **Centre national d'enseignement à distance**) → **centre**

CNIL /knil/ NF (abrév de **Commission nationale de l'informatique et des libertés**) → **commission**

CNIT /knit/ NM (abrév de **Centre national des industries et des techniques**) *exhibition centre in Paris*

CNPF /seɛnpeɛf/ NM (abrév de **Conseil national du patronat français**) *national council of French employers*, ≃ CBI *(Brit)*

CNRS /seɛnɛʀɛs/ NM (abrév de **Centre national de la recherche scientifique**) ≃ SERC *(Brit)*, NSF *(US)*

coaccusé, e /koakyze/ NM,F codefendant, coaccused

coacquéreur /koakeʀœʀ/ NM joint purchaser

coadjuteur /koadʒytœʀ/ NM coadjutor

coadjutrice /koadʒytʀis/ NF coadjutress

coadministrateur, -trice /koadministʀatœʀ, tʀis/ NM,F *(Comm)* co-director; *(Jur)* cotrustee

coagulant, e /kɔagylɑ̃, ɑ̃t/ ADJ coagulative NM coagulant

coagulateur, -trice /kɔagylatœʀ, tʀis/ ADJ coagulative

coagulation /kɔagylasjɔ̃/ NF coagulation

coaguler VTI, **se coaguler** VPR /kɔagyle/ ► conjug 1 ◄ *[sang]* to coagulate *(SPÉC)*, to clot, to congeal; *[lait]* to curdle

coalisé, e /kɔalize/ (ptp de **coaliser**) ADJ (= *allié*) *[pays]* allied; (= *conjoint*) *[efforts]* united NMPL ♦ **les ~s** the members of the coalition

coaliser /kɔalize/ ► conjug 1 ◄ VT to unite (in a coalition) VPR **se coaliser** (= *se liguer*) *(gén)* to unite; *[pays]* to form a coalition ♦ **deux des commerçants se sont coalisés contre un troisième** two of the shopkeepers joined forces *ou* united against a third

coalition /kɔalisjɔ̃/ NF coalition ♦ **gouvernement de ~** coalition government

coaltar /koltaʀ/ NM *(lit)* coal tar ♦ **être dans le ~*** *(après anesthésie)* to be a bit groggy* *ou* whoozy*; (= *être mal réveillé*) to be a bit whoozy*, to be half-asleep

coassement /kɔasmɑ̃/ NM croaking *(NonC)*

coasser /kɔase/ ► conjug 1 ◄ VI to croak

coassocié, e /koasɔsje/ NM,F copartner

coassurance /koasyʀɑ̃s/ NF mutual assurance

coati /kɔati/ NM coati

coauteur /kootœʀ/ NM 1 *(Littérat)* co-author, joint author 2 *(Jur)* accomplice

coaxial, e (mpl **-aux**) /koaksjal, jo/ ADJ coaxial

COB /kɔb/ NF (abrév de **Commission des opérations de Bourse**) *French stock exchange regulatory body*, ≃ SIB *(Brit)*, SEC *(US)*

cobalt /kɔbalt/ NM cobalt; → **bombe**

cobaye /kɔbaj/ NM *(lit, fig)* guinea-pig ♦ **servir de ~ à** to act as *ou* be used as a guinea-pig for

cobelligérant, e /kobeliʒeʀɑ̃, ɑ̃t/ ADJ cobelligerent NMPL ♦ **les ~s** the cobelligerent nations

Cobol /kɔbɔl/ NM *(Ordin)* COBOL

cobra /kɔbʀa/ NM cobra

coca /kɔka/ NM abrév de **Coca-Cola** ® Coke ® ♦ **un whisky ~** a whisky and Coke ® NF (= *substance*) coca extract NM *ou* NF (= *plante*) coca

cocagne /kɔkaɲ/ NF → **mât, pays¹**

cocaïne /kɔkain/ NF cocaine

cocaïnomane /kɔkainɔman/ NMF cocaine addict

cocard* /kɔkaʀ/ NM black eye, shiner*

cocarde /kɔkaʀd/ NF *(en tissu)* rosette; *(Hist : sur la coiffure)* cockade; *[d'avion]* roundel ♦ ~ **(tricolore)** *(sur voiture officielle)* ≃ official sticker

cocardier, -ière /kɔkaʀdje, jɛʀ/ ADJ jingoistic, chauvinistic NM,F jingoist, chauvinist

cocasse /kɔkas/ ADJ comical, funny

cocasserie /kɔkasʀi/ NF comicalness, funniness ♦ **c'était d'une ~ !** it was so funny! *ou* comical!

coccinelle /kɔksinɛl/ NF (= *insecte*) ladybird, ladybug *(US)*; (* = *voiture*) beetle *(Brit)*, bug *(US)*

coccyx /kɔksis/ NM coccyx

coche /kɔʃ/ NM (= *diligence*) (stage)coach ◆ ~ **d'eau** *(Hist)* horse-drawn barge ◆ **louper** *ou* **manquer** *ou* **rater le** ~ *(fig)* to miss the boat* *ou* one's chance; → **mouche**

cochenille /kɔʃnij/ NF *(gén)* mealybug; *(pour teinture)* cochineal insect

cocher[1] /kɔʃe/ ► conjug 1 ◄ VT *(au crayon)* to check off, to tick (off) *(Brit)*; *(d'une entaille)* to notch ◆ **cochez la bonne réponse** tick *(Brit) ou* check *(US)* the correct answer

cocher[2] /kɔʃe/ NM *(gén)* coachman, coach driver; *[de fiacre]* cabman, cabby*

cochère /kɔʃɛʀ/ ADJ F → **porte**

Cochinchine /kɔʃɛ̃ʃin/ NF Cochin China

cochlée /kɔkle/ NF cochlea

cochon, -onne /kɔʃɔ̃, ɔn/ NM 1 (= *animal*) pig, hog *(US)*; (* = *viande*) pork *(NonC)* ◆ ~ **d'Inde** guinea-pig ◆ ~ **de lait** *(gén)* piglet; *(Culin)* suck(l)ing-pig

2 (*: *péj* = *personne*) *(sale, vicieux)* dirty pig*; (= *goujat*) swine* ◆ **manger/écrire comme un** ~ to be a messy eater/writer ◆ **vieux** ~ dirty old man ◆ **petit** ~ ! you messy thing! ◆ **ce** ~ **de voisin** that swine* of a neighbour ◆ **eh bien, mon** ~ ! *(terme amical)* you old devil! *

3 *(locutions)* **quel temps de** ~ ! what lousy *ou* filthy weather! * ◆ **(et)** ~ **qui s'en dédit** * *(hum)* let's shake (hands) on it, cross my heart (and hope to die)* ◆ **un** ~ **n'y retrouverait pas ses petits** it's like a pigsty in there, it's a real mess in there ◆ **si les petits ~s ne te mangent pas** *(hum)* if the bogeyman doesn't get you ◆ **elle ira loin si les petits ~s ne la mangent pas avant** *(hum)* she'll go far if nothing gets in her way ◆ **tout homme a dans son cœur un** ~ **qui sommeille** there's a bit of the animal in every man; → **confiture, copain**

ADJ 1 (* = *obscène*) *[chanson, histoire]* dirty, smutty; *[personne]* dirty-minded

2 (* = *sale*) **il est** ~ *(sur lui)* he's filthy; *(dans son travail)* he's a messy worker ◆ **c'est pas** ~ ! it's not at all bad!

NF **cochonne** (= *personne*) *(sale)* dirty pig*; *(vicieuse)* dirty cow*

cochoncetés * /kɔʃɔ̃ste/ NFPL (= *obscénités*) filth *(NonC)*, smut *(NonC)*; (= *plaisanteries*) smutty *ou* dirty jokes ◆ **faire des** ~ *(saletés)* to make a mess ◆ **arrête de dire des** ~ stop talking dirty*

cochonnaille * /kɔʃɔnaj/ NF (= *charcuterie*) pork products ◆ **assiette de** ~ selection of cold pork *ou* ham

cochonner * /kɔʃɔne/ ► conjug 1 ◄ VT (= *mal faire*) *[+ travail]* to botch (up), to bungle; (= *salir*) *[+ vêtements]* to mess up*, to make filthy

cochonnerie * /kɔʃɔnʀi/ NF (= *nourriture*) disgusting *ou* foul food, pigswill* *(NonC)*; (= *marchandise*) rubbish *(NonC)*, trash *(NonC)*; (= *plaisanterie*) smutty *ou* dirty joke; (= *tour*) dirty *ou* low trick; (= *saleté*) filth *(NonC)* ◆ **manger des ~s** to eat junk food ◆ **faire une** ~ **à qn** to play a dirty trick on sb ◆ **le chien a fait des ~s dans la cuisine** the dog has made a mess in the kitchen ◆ **ne regarde pas ces ~s !** don't look at that filth!

cochonnet /kɔʃɔnɛ/ NM 1 (= *petit cochon*) piglet 2 *(Boules)* jack

cocker /kɔkɛʀ/ NM cocker spaniel

cockpit /kɔkpit/ NM cockpit

cocktail /kɔktɛl/ NM (= *réunion*) cocktail party; (= *boisson*) cocktail; *(fig)* mixture, potpourri ◆ ~ **de fruits/crevettes** fruit/prawn cocktail ◆ ~ **Molotov** Molotov cocktail, petrol bomb ◆ ~ **explosif** *(fig)* explosive cocktail *ou* mixture

coco[1] /koko/ NM 1 *(langage enfantin* = *œuf)* egg 2 *(terme d'affection)* pet, darling, poppet* *(Brit)* ◆ **oui, mon** ~ yes, darling 3 (*: *péj* = *type*) guy*, bloke* *(Brit)* ◆ **un drôle de** ~ an odd guy* *ou* bloke* *(Brit)*, an oddball* *ou* oddbod* *(Brit)* ◆ **toi mon ~, tu vas voir !** you've got it coming to you, buster *ou* mate!* 4 (*: *péj* = *communiste*) commie* 5 (= *réglisse*) liquorice powder; (= *boisson*) liquorice water 6 († = *noix*) coconut ◆ **beurre de** ~ coconut butter ◆ **tapis en (fibre de)** ~ coconut *ou* coir mat *ou* matting *(NonC)*; → **lait, noix** 7 (= *haricot*) *small white haricot bean*

coco[2] † /koko/ NF *(arg Drogue* = *cocaïne)* coke*, snow *(arg)*

cocon /kɔkɔ̃/ NM *(lit, fig)* cocoon ◆ **sortir du** ~ **familial** to leave the nest

cocontractant, e /kokɔ̃tʀaktɑ̃, ɑ̃t/ NM,F contracting partner

cocooner /kɔkune/ VI ► conjug 1 ◄ to stay at home ◆ **je vais** ~ **ce soir** I'm going to have a quiet night in

cocooning /kɔkuniŋ/ NM staying at home, cocooning *(US)* ◆ **j'ai envie d'une petite soirée** ~ I feel like spending a nice cosy evening at home

cocorico /kɔkɔʀiko/ NM *[de coq]* cock-a-doodle-do; *(fig)* cheer of victory ◆ **pousser un ~, faire** ~ *[coq]* to crow; *(fig)* to crow (over one's victory) ◆ **ils ont fait** ~ **un peu trop tôt** their victory celebrations were premature, they started celebrating a bit too soon EXCL *[de coq]* cock-a-doodle-do! ◆ ~ **! on a gagné !** hooray! we won!

cocoter * /kɔkɔte/ ► conjug 1 ◄ VI (= *sentir mauvais*) to stink, to pong* *(Brit)*

cocoteraie /kɔkɔtʀɛ/ NF *(naturelle)* coconut grove; *(cultivée)* coconut plantation

cocotier /kɔkɔtje/ NM coconut palm *ou* tree ◆ **sous les ~s** under the palm trees; → **secouer**

cocotte /kɔkɔt/ NF 1 *(langage enfantin* = *poule)* hen, cluck-cluck *(langage enfantin)* 2 (*: *péj* = *femme*) tart* ◆ **ça sent** *ou* **pue la** ~ it smells like a perfume factory 3 *(à un cheval)* **allez ~ !, hue ~ !** gee up! 4 (* : *terme d'affection*) **(ma)** ~ pet, sweetie* 5 (= *marmite*) casserole ◆ **faire un poulet à la** *ou* **en** ~ to casserole a chicken ◆ **poulet/veau (à la)** ~ chicken/veal casserole

COMP **Cocotte Minute** ® pressure cooker

cocotte en papier paper hen

cocotter * /kɔkɔte/ ► conjug 1 ◄ VI ⇒ **cocoter**

cocu, e * /kɔky/ ADJ deceived, cuckolded † ◆ **elle l'a fait** ~ she was unfaithful to him, she cuckolded him † NM deceived husband, cuckold †; → **veine** NF **cocue** deceived wife

cocufier * /kɔkyfje/ ► conjug 7 ◄ VT to be unfaithful to, to cuckold †

coda /kɔda/ NF *(Mus)* coda

codage /kɔdaʒ/ NM coding, encoding

code /kɔd/ NM 1 *(Jur)* code ◆ **le** ~ **civil** the civil code, ≈ common law ◆ ~ **pénal** *ou* **de procédure pénale** penal code ◆ **le** ~ **maritime/de commerce** maritime/commercial law ◆ ~ **de la nationalité** nationality law ◆ ~ **du travail** labour regulations *ou* laws ◆ ~ **de la route** highway code ◆ **il a eu le ~, mais pas la conduite** he passed on the highway code but not on the driving

2 (= *règles*) code ◆ ~ **de la politesse/de l'honneur** code of politeness/honour ◆ ~ **de bonne conduite** code of good practice ◆ ~ **vestimentaire** dress code

3 (= *écriture, message*) *(gén, Sci)* code ◆ ~ **secret** secret code ◆ **écrire qch en** ~ to write sth in code

4 *[de voiture]* **phares ~, ~s** dipped (head)lights *(Brit)*, low beams *(US)* ◆ **mettre ses ~s** *ou* **ses phares en ~(s), se mettre en ~(s)** to dip one's (head)lights *(Brit)*, to put on the low beams *(US)* ◆ **rouler en ~(s)** to drive with dipped (head)lights *(Brit) ou* on low beams *(US)*

COMP **code d'accès** *(à un immeuble)* entry code; *(à une base de données)* access code

code ASCII ASCII code

code à barres bar code

code confidentiel PIN (number)

code d'entrée entry code

code génétique genetic code

code personnel ⇒ **code confidentiel**

code postal postcode *(Brit)*, zip code *(US)*

codé, e /kɔde/ (ptp de **coder**) ADJ *(Ordin) [message]* coded; *(TV) [émission]* scrambled, coded ◆ **le langage** ~ **de certains milieux** *(fig)* the secret language used by certain social groups ◆ **c'est une société très ~e** it's a society where everything is very coded ◆ **je n'aime pas les tailleurs, c'est trop** ~ I don't like wearing suits, they're too bound up with a certain image

code-barre(s) (pl **codes-barres**) /kɔdbaʀ/ NM bar code

codébiteur, -trice /kodebitœʀ, tʀis/ NM,F joint debtor

codec /kɔdɛk/ NM *(Ordin)* codec

codécision /kodesizjɔ̃/ NF joint decision

codéine /kɔdein/ NF codeine

codemandeur, -eresse /kod(ə)mɑ̃dœʀ, dʀɛs/ NM,F joint plaintiff

coder /kɔde/ ► conjug 1 ◄ VT to code

codétenteur, -trice /kodetɑ̃tœʀ, tʀis/ NM,F *(Jur, Sport)* joint holder

codétenu, e /kodet(ə)ny/ NM,F prisoner, inmate ◆ **avec ses ~s** with his fellow prisoners *ou* inmates

CODEVI /kɔdevi/ NM (abrév de **compte pour le développement industriel**) → **compte**

codex /kɔdɛks/ NM (officially approved) pharmacopoeia

codicillaire /kɔdisilɛʀ/ ADJ *(Jur)* codicillary

codicille /kɔdisil/ NM *(Jur)* codicil

codification /kɔdifikasjɔ̃/ NF codification

codifier /kɔdifje/ ► conjug 7 ◄ VT *(Jur* = *systématiser)* to codify

codirecteur, -trice /kodiʀɛktœʀ, tʀis/ NM,F co-director, joint manager *(ou* manageress)

codirection /kodiʀɛksjɔ̃/ NF *[d'entreprise]* joint management

coéditer /koedite/ ► conjug 1 ◄ VT to co-publish

coéditeur, -trice /koeditœʀ, tʀis/ NM,F co-publisher

coédition /koedisjɔ̃/ NF co-edition

coef(f) * /kɔef/ NM abrév de **coefficient**

coefficient /kɔefisjɑ̃/ NM *(Math, Phys)* coefficient ◆ **cette matière est affectée d'un ~ trois** *(Scol)* marks *(Brit) ou* grades *(US)* in this subject are weighted by a factor of three

COMP **coefficient de dilatation** coefficient of expansion

coefficient d'élasticité modulus of elasticity

coefficient d'erreur margin of error

coefficient de marée tidal range

coefficient d'occupation des sols planning density

coefficient de pénétration dans l'air drag coefficient *ou* factor

coefficient de sécurité safety margin

cœlacanthe /selakɑ̃t/ NM coelacanth

cœlialgie /seljalʒi/ NF coeliac disease

cœliochirurgie /seljɔʃiʀyʀʒi/ NF abdominal surgery, coeliosurgery *(Brit)*, celiosurgery *(US)*

cœlioscopie /seljɔskɔpi/ NF laparoscopy

cœnesthésie /senɛstezi/ NF ⇒ **cénesthésie**

coentreprise /koɑ̃tʀəpʀiz/ NF (Écon) joint venture

coépouse /koepuz/ NF co-wife

coéquipier, -ière /koekipje, jɛʀ/ NM,F team mate

coercibilité /kɔɛʀsibilite/ NF coercibility

coercible /kɔɛʀsibl/ ADJ coercible

coercitif, -ive /kɔɛʀsitif, iv/ ADJ coercive

coercition /kɔɛʀsisjɔ̃/ NF coercion

cœur /kœʀ/

1 NOM MASCULIN 2 COMPOSÉS

1 - NOM MASCULIN

1 Anat (= organe) heart; (= poitrine) heart, breast ◆ **avoir le ~ malade** to have a weak heart ou a heart condition ◆ **heureusement que j'ai le ~ solide** (aussi hum) it's a good thing I haven't got a weak heart ◆ **serrer qn contre** ou **sur son ~** to hold ou press sb to one's heart ou breast ◆ ~ **de bœuf/de poulet** (Boucherie) ox/chicken heart ◆ **opération à ~ ouvert** open-heart surgery ◆ **on l'a opéré à ~ ouvert** he had open-heart surgery; → **battement, greffe**[1]

2 = estomac **il faut avoir le ~ bien accroché pour être ambulancier** you need a strong stomach to be an ambulance man ◆ **j'avais le ~ au bord des** ou **sur les lèvres** I thought I was going to be sick (any minute); → **mal**[2], **soulever**

3 = siège de l'amour heart ◆ **donner son ~ à qn** to lose one's heart to sb, to give sb one's heart ◆ **je ne le porte pas dans mon ~** I am not exactly ou overly fond of him ◆ **mon ~** (forme d'adresse) sweetheart ◆ **c'est un homme selon mon ~** he's a man after my own heart ◆ **c'est un film/un paysage selon mon ~** it's the kind of film/landscape I love ◆ **avoir un** ou **le ~ sensible** to be sensitive ou tender-hearted

◆ **coup de cœur** ◆ **avoir un coup de ~ pour qch** to fall in love with sth ◆ **nos coups de ~ parmi les livres du mois** our favourites among this month's new books

4 = bonté, générosité **avoir bon ~** to be kind-hearted ou good-hearted, to have one's heart in the right place ◆ **à votre bon ~ (m'sieurs-dames) !** thank you kindly! ◆ **homme/femme de ~** kind-hearted ou good-hearted man/woman ◆ **avoir le ~ sur la main** to be open-handed ◆ **manquer de ~** to be unfeeling ou heartless ◆ **il a** ou **c'est un ~ d'or** he has a heart of gold ◆ **elle a un ~ gros comme ça*** she's really big-hearted ◆ **héros au grand ~** big-hearted hero ◆ **il a un ~ de pierre, il a une pierre** ou **un caillou à la place du ~** he has a heart of stone ◆ **c'est un homme sans ~, il n'a pas de ~** he's really heartless

5 = humeur **avoir le ~ à faire qch** to feel like doing sth ◆ **je n'ai pas le ~ à rire/à sortir** I don't feel like laughing/going out, I'm not in the mood for laughing/going out ◆ **il n'a plus le ~ à rien** his heart isn't in anything any more ◆ **si le ~ vous en dit** if you feel like it, if you're in the mood ◆ **avoir le ~ joyeux** ou **gai** to feel happy ◆ **d'un ~ léger** light-heartedly ◆ **il est parti le ~ léger** he left in a light-hearted mood ◆ **il avait le ~ lourd** his heart was heavy, he was heavy-hearted ◆ **il est parti le ~ lourd** he left with a heavy heart ◆ **avoir le ~ gros** ou **serré** to have a heavy heart ◆ **mon ~ se serre à cette pensée** my heart sinks at the thought

◆ **de bon cœur** [manger, rire] heartily; [faire, accepter] willingly, readily

6 = âme, pensées intimes **c'est un ~ pur** he is a candid soul ◆ **ouvrir son ~ à qn** to open one's heart to sb ◆ **ça vient du ~ !** it comes ou is straight from the heart! ◆ **des paroles venues du ~** words from the heart, heartfelt words ◆ **je veux en avoir le ~ net** I want to be clear in my own mind (about it) ◆ **ce geste/ce discours lui est allé (droit) au ~** he was (deeply) moved ou (very) touched by this gesture/these words, this gesture/these words went straight to his heart; → **cri**

◆ **à cœur** ◆ **avoir à ~ de faire qch** to be very keen to do sth ◆ **prendre les choses à ~** to take things to heart ◆ **ce voyage me tient à ~** I've set my heart on this trip ◆ **cette cause me tient à ~** this cause is close to my heart ◆ **c'est un sujet qui me tient vraiment à ~** it's an issue I feel very strongly about

◆ **à cœur ouvert** ◆ **il m'a parlé à ~ ouvert** he opened his heart to me ◆ **nous avons eu une conversation à ~ ouvert** we had a heart-to-heart (talk)

◆ **avoir qch sur le cœur** ◆ **ce qu'il m'a dit, je l'ai sur le ~** ou **ça m'est resté sur le ~** what he said to me still rankles with me, I still feel sore about what he said to me ◆ **je vais lui dire ce que j'ai sur le ~** (gén) I'm going to tell him what's on my mind; (ce que je pense de lui) I'm going to give him a piece of my mind

◆ **cœur à cœur** ◆ **on s'est parlé ~ à ~** we had a heart-to-heart (talk)

◆ **de tout (son) cœur** [remercier, souhaiter] with all one's heart, from the bottom of one's heart ◆ **être de tout ~ avec qn dans la joie/une épreuve** to share (in) sb's happiness/sorrow ◆ **je suis de tout ~ avec vous** my thoughts are with you

7 = courage, ardeur heart, courage ◆ **comment peut-on avoir le ~ de refuser ?** how can one have ou find the heart to refuse? ◆ **le ~ lui manqua (pour ...)** his courage failed him (when it came to ...) ◆ **mettre tout son ~ dans qch/à faire qch** to put all one's heart into sth/into doing sth ◆ **avoir du ~ au ventre** * to have guts* ◆ **donner du ~ au ventre à qn** * to buck sb up* ◆ **avoir du ~ à l' ouvrage** to put one's heart into one's work ◆ **il travaille mais le ~ n'y est pas** he does the work but his heart isn't in it ◆ **redonner du ~ à qn** to give sb new heart

◆ **à cœur joie** ◆ **s'en donner à ~ joie** (= s'amuser) to have a tremendous time, to have a whale of a time*; (= critiquer) to have a field day, to go to town ◆ **les pillards s'en sont donné à ~ joie** the looters really went to town

8 = partie centrale [de chou] heart; [d'arbre, poutre] heart, core; [de fruit, pile atomique] core; [de problème, ville] heart ◆ ~ **de rumsteck/de filet** (Boucherie) prime cut of rump steak/of fillet ◆ **c'est notre ~ de cible** (Comm) it is our main ou key target group ◆ **l'édition est notre ~ d'activité** publishing is our core activity

◆ **à cœur** ◆ **fromage fait à ~** fully ripe cheese ◆ **viande cuite à ~** medium-cooked meat ◆ **viande tendre à ~** very tender meat

◆ **au cœur de** [de région, ville, forêt] in the heart of ◆ **au ~ de l'été** at the height of summer ◆ **au ~ de l'hiver** in the depths ou heart of winter ◆ **ce problème est au ~ du débat** this problem is a central issue

9 = objet heart ◆ **en (forme de) ~** heart-shaped ◆ **volets percés de ~s** shutters with heart-shaped holes; → **bouche**

10 Cartes heart ◆ **roi/as de ~** king/ace of hearts ◆ **avez-vous du ~ ?** have you got any hearts?; → **atout**

11 locutions

◆ **par cœur** [réciter, apprendre] by heart ◆ **connaître par ~** [+ poème, formule] to know (off) by heart; [+ endroit] to know like the back of one's hand ◆ **il connaît Racine par ~** he knows (the works of) Racine inside out ◆ **je te connais par ~** I know you inside out, I know you like the back of my hand ◆ **tes arguments, je les connais par ~ !** I've heard all your arguments before!, I know your arguments by heart! ◆ **savoir par ~** [+ leçon] to know (off) by heart

2 - COMPOSÉS

cœur d'artichaut (lit) artichoke heart ◆ **c'est** ou **il a un ~ d'artichaut** (fig) he falls in love with every girl he meets

cœur de céleri celery heart

cœur de palmier heart of palm

cœur-de-pigeon (pl **cœurs-de-pigeon**) /kœʀdəpiʒɔ̃/ NM variety of red cherry

coexistence /kɔɛgzistɑ̃s/ NF coexistence ◆ ~ **pacifique** peaceful coexistence

coexister /kɔɛgziste/ ▸ conjug 1 ◂ VI to coexist

coffrage /kɔfʀaʒ/ NM (pour protéger, cacher) boxing (NonC); [de galerie, tranchée] (= dispositif, action) coffering (NonC); (en béton) (= dispositif) form, formwork (NonC), shuttering (NonC); (= action) framing

coffre /kɔfʀ/ NM 1 (= meuble) chest ◆ ~ **à linge/à outils** linen/tool chest 2 [de voiture] boot (Brit), trunk (US) ◆ ~ **avant/arrière** front/rear boot (Brit) ou trunk (US) 3 (= coffrage) (gén) case; [de piano] case; [de radio] cabinet 4 [de banque, hôtel] safe; (= compartiment) safe- ou safety-deposit box; (Hist, fig = cassette) coffer ◆ **les ~s de l'État** the coffers of the state ◆ **la salle des ~s** (Banque) the strongroom, the (bank) vault 5 (* = poitrine) ◆ **le ~** the chest ◆ **il a du ~** he's got a lot of blow* ou puff* (Brit)

COMP **coffre à bagages** overhead luggage locker

coffre à bijoux jewellery (Brit) ou jewelery (US) box

coffre à jouets toybox

coffre de nuit night safe

coffre de voyage † trunk

coffre-fort (pl **coffres-forts**) /kɔfʀəfɔʀ/ NM safe

coffrer /kɔfʀe/ ▸ conjug 1 ◂ VT 1 (* = emprisonner) to throw ou put inside* ◆ **se faire ~** to get put inside* 2 (Tech) [+ béton] to place a frame ou form for; [+ tranchée, galerie] to coffer

coffret /kɔfʀɛ/ NM (gén) casket; [de disques, livres] (= contenant) box; (= contenu) boxed set ◆ ~ **à bijoux** jewel box, jewellery case ◆ **~-cadeau** presentation box

cofinancement /kofinɑ̃smɑ̃/ NM co-financing

cofinancer /kofinɑ̃se/ ▸ conjug 3 ◂ VT to finance jointly, to co-finance

cofondateur, -trice /kofɔ̃datœʀ, tʀis/ NM,F cofounder

cogérant /koʒeʀɑ̃/ NM joint manager

cogérante /koʒeʀɑ̃t/ NF joint manageress

cogérer /koʒeʀe/ ▸ conjug 6 ◂ VT to manage jointly

cogestion /koʒɛstjɔ̃/ NF co-management, joint management

cogitation /kɔʒitasjɔ̃/ NF (hum) cogitation

cogiter /kɔʒite/ ▸ conjug 1 ◂ VI (hum = réfléchir) to cogitate VT [+ histoire] to think about; [+ problème] to mull over ◆ **qu'est-ce qu'il cogite ?** what's he thinking about?

cogito /koʒito/ NM (Philos) cogito ◆ **le ~ cartésien** Descartes's cogito

cognac /kɔɲak/ NM cognac, (French) brandy ADJ INV brandy-coloured (Brit) ou -colored (US)

cognassier /kɔɲasje/ NM quince (tree), japonica

cogne †* /kɔɲ/ NM (= policier) cop* ◆ **les ~s** the cops*, the fuzz*

cognée /kɔɲe/ NF felling axe ou ax (US); → **manche**[2]

cognement /kɔɲmɑ̃/ NM (= bruit, action) banging; [de moteur] knocking

cogner /kɔɲe/ ▸ conjug 1 ◂ VT 1 (= heurter) to knock ◆ **fais attention à ne pas ~ les verres** mind you don't knock the glasses against any-

thing ♦ **quelqu'un m'a cogné en passant** somebody knocked (into) me as they went by
2 (* = *battre*) to beat up
VI 1 *[personne]* ~ **sur** *[+ clou, piquet]* to hammer on; *[+ mur]* to bang *ou* knock on; *(fort)* to hammer on ♦ ~ **du poing sur la table** to bang *ou* thump one's fist on the table ♦ ~ **à la porte/au plafond** to knock at the door/on the ceiling; *(fort)* to bang *ou* rap at the door/on the ceiling
2 *[volet, battant, branche]* to bang; *[grêle]* to hammer, to pound *(contre* against); ♦ ~ **contre** *[projectile]* to hit, to strike ♦ **un caillou est venu ~ contre le pare-brise** a stone hit the windscreen ♦ **il y a un volet qui cogne (contre le mur)** there's a shutter banging (against the wall) ♦ **le moteur cogne** the engine's knocking
3 * *[boxeur, bagarreur]* to hit out ♦ **ça va ~ à la manif** * there's going to be some rough stuff at the demo * ♦ **ce boxeur-là, il cogne dur** that boxer's a hard hitter, that boxer packs a mean punch * ♦ ~ **sur qn** to lay into sb *
4 * *[soleil]* to beat down ♦ **ça cogne !** * it's scorching! *
5 (* = *sentir mauvais*) to stink to high heaven *, to pong * *(Brit)*
VPR **se cogner** 1 ♦ **se ~ contre un mur** to bump into a wall ♦ **se ~ la tête/le genou contre un poteau** to bang one's head/knee on a post ♦ **c'est à se ~ la tête contre les murs** *(fig)* it's like banging your head against a brick wall
2 ♦ **se ~ (dessus)** * (= *se battre*) to lay into each other *

cogneur * /kɔɲœʀ/ NM (= *bagarreur, boxeur*) bruiser *

cogniticien, -ienne /kɔgnitisjɛ̃, jɛn/ NM,F cognitive scientist

cognitif, -ive /kɔgnitif, iv/ ADJ cognitive

cognition /kɔgnisjɔ̃/ NF cognition

cognitiviste /kɔgnitivist/ NMF cognitive scientist

cohabitant, e /kɔabitɑ̃, ɑt/ ADJ ♦ **couple** couple who are living together, cohabiting couple NM,F cohabitee; *(euph = concubin)* live-in lover

cohabitation /kɔabitasjɔ̃/ NF *[de couple]* living together, cohabitation; *[de plusieurs personnes]* living under the same roof; *(Pol)* cohabitation ♦ **la ~ avec mon mari était devenue impossible** it had become impossible for me and my husband to carry on living together *ou* living under the same roof

COHABITATION

The situation which occurs when, as a result of a presidential or general election, the French people find themselves with a president who represents one political party and a government which represents another. A recent example of **cohabitation** is the combination of a Socialist Prime Minister, Lionel Jospin, with a Gaullist President, Jacques Chirac.

cohabiter /kɔabite/ ► conjug 1 ◄ VI *[couple]* to live together, to cohabit; *[plusieurs personnes]* to live under the same roof; *(Pol)* to cohabit ♦ **ils cohabitent avec leurs parents** they live with their parents ♦ **faire ~ deux cultures** to reconcile two cultures

cohérence /kɔeʀɑ̃s/ NF 1 (= *logique*) *[d'arguments, politique]* coherence; *[de conduite]* consistency ♦ **le manque de ~ de sa politique** the incoherence of his policy ♦ **la ~ d'ensemble du projet** the overall coherence of the project 2 (= *homogénéité*) *[de groupe]* cohesion ♦ **pour améliorer la ~ de cette gamme** to make the range more comprehensive ♦ **la ~ de l'équipe laisse à désirer** the team is not as well-knit as it could be 3 *(Phys)* coherence

cohérent, e /kɔeʀɑ̃, ɑ̃t/ ADJ 1 (= *logique*) *[arguments]* coherent; *[politique]* coherent; *[conduite]* consistent ♦ **sois ~ (avec toi-même)** be true to yourself 2 (= *homogène*) *[équipe]* well-knit; *[groupe]* cohesive; *[gamme de produits]* comprehensive, complete 3 *(Phys)* coherent

cohéritier /koeʀitje/ NM joint heir, coheir

cohéritière /koeʀitjɛʀ/ NF joint heiress, coheiress

cohésif, -ive /kɔezif, iv/ ADJ cohesive

cohésion /kɔezjɔ̃/ NF cohesion

cohorte /kɔɔʀt/ NF (= *groupe*) troop; *(Hist Mil)* cohort

cohue /kɔy/ NF (= *foule*) crowd; (= *bousculade*) crush ♦ **c'était la ~ à l'entrée du cinéma** there was such a crush at the entrance to the cinema

coi, coite /kwa, kwat/ ADJ ♦ **se tenir ~, rester ~** to remain silent ♦ **en rester ~** to be rendered speechless

coiffage /kwafaʒ/ NM hairdressing ♦ **produit de ~** hairstyling product

coiffant, e /kwafɑ̃, ɑt/ ADJ → **gel, mousse**[1]

coiffe /kwaf/ NF 1 *[de costume régional, religieuse]* headdress 2 *[de chapeau]* lining; *(Tech)* *[de fusée]* cap; *(Anat)* *[de nouveau-né]* caul

coiffé, e /kwafe/ (ptp de **coiffer**) ADJ 1 (= *peigné*) **est-ce que tu es ~ ?** have you done your hair? ♦ **comment était-elle ~e ?** what was her hair like?, how did she have her hair? ♦ **il est toujours bien/mal ~** his hair always looks nice/a mess ♦ **être ~ en brosse** to have a crew-cut ♦ **être ~ en chien fou** to have dishevelled hair ♦ **il était ~ en arrière** he had his hair brushed *ou* combed back; → **naître** 2 (= *couvert*) **être ~ d'un béret** to be wearing a beret ♦ **le clown entra ~ d'une casserole** the clown came in with a saucepan on his head

coiffer /kwafe/ ► conjug 1 ◄ VT 1 (= *peigner*) ~ **qn** to do sb's hair ♦ **il coiffe bien** he's a good hairdresser ♦ **cheveux difficiles à ~** unmanageable hair ♦ **(aller) se faire ~** to (go and) have one's hair done
2 (= *couvrir la tête de*) ~ **(la tête d')un bébé d'un bonnet** to put a bonnet on a baby's head ♦ **ce chapeau la coiffe bien** that hat suits her *ou* looks good on her ♦ **le béret qui la coiffait** the beret she had on *ou* was wearing
3 (= *mettre*) *[+ chapeau]* to put on ♦ ~ **la mitre/la tiare** to be mitred/made Pope ♦ ~ **la couronne** to be crowned (king *ou* queen) ♦ **elle allait bientôt ~ sainte Catherine** she would soon be 25 and still unmarried; → **CATHERINETTE**
4 (= *surmonter*) **des nuages coiffaient le sommet** clouds covered the summit, the summit was topped with clouds ♦ **pic coiffé de neige** snow-capped peak
5 (= *diriger*) *[+ services]* to head up, to have overall responsibility for
6 (* = *dépasser*) ~ **qn à l'arrivée** *ou* **au poteau** to nose sb out *, to pip sb at the post * *(Brit)* ♦ **se faire ~** to be nosed out *, to be pipped at the post * *(Brit)*
VPR **se coiffer** 1 (= *se peigner*) to do one's hair ♦ **elle se coiffe toujours mal** she never manages to do anything nice with her hair ♦ **tu t'es coiffé avec un râteau** *ou* **un clou** *(hum)* you look like you've been dragged through a hedge backwards ♦ **tu t'es coiffé avec un pétard** your hair's all sticking up
2 (= *mettre comme coiffure*) **se ~ d'une casquette** to put on a cap ♦ **d'habitude, elle se coiffe d'un chapeau de paille** she usually wears a straw hat
3 (= *acheter ses chapeaux*) **se ~ chez Legrand** to buy one's hats from Legrand

coiffeur /kwafœʀ/ NM *[de dames]* hairdresser; *[d'hommes]* hairdresser, barber ♦ **les grands ~s parisiens** top Paris hairstylists

coiffeuse /kwaføz/ NF (= *personne*) hairdresser; (= *meuble*) dressing table

coiffure /kwafyʀ/ NF (= *façon d'être peigné*) hairstyle, hairdo *; (= *chapeau*) hat, headgear * *(NonC)* ♦ **la ~** *(métier)* hairdressing; → **salon**

coin /kwɛ̃/ NM 1 (= *angle*) *[d'objet, chambre]* corner ♦ **armoire/place de ~** corner cupboard/seat ♦ **va au ~ !** *(Scol)* go and stand in the corner! ♦ **envoyer** *ou* **mettre un enfant au ~** *(Scol)* to send a child to stand in the corner, to put a child in the corner ♦ **~(-)fenêtre/(-)couloir** *(Rail)* window/aisle seat, seat by the window/on the aisle
2 *[de rue]* corner ♦ **le boucher du ~** the butcher's on the corner ♦ **la blanchisserie fait le ~** the laundry is right on the corner ♦ **à tous les ~s de rue** on every street corner
3 *[de yeux, bouche]* corner ♦ **sourire en ~** half smile ♦ **regard en ~** sidelong glance ♦ **regarder/surveiller qn du ~ de l'œil** to look at/watch sb out of the corner of one's eye
4 (= *espace restreint*) *[de village, maison]* part ♦ **un ~ de terre/ciel bleu** a patch of land/blue sky ♦ **un ~ de plage** a spot on the beach ♦ **le ~ du bricoleur** *(dans un magasin)* the DIY department *(Brit)*, the home improvement department *(US)*; *(dans un journal)* DIY tips *(Brit)*, home improvement tips *(US)* ♦ **~-bureau/-repas** work/dining area ♦ **~-cuisine** kitchenette ♦ **rester dans son ~** to keep to oneself ♦ **laisser qn dans son ~** to leave sb alone ♦ **dans un ~ de ma mémoire** in the recesses of my mind *ou* memory ♦ **dans quel ~ l'as-tu mis ?** where did you put it? ♦ **je l'ai mis dans un ~** I put it somewhere ♦ **j'ai cherché dans tous les ~s (et recoins)** I looked in every nook and cranny; → **petit**
5 (= *région*) area ♦ **dans quel ~ habitez-vous ?** whereabouts do you live? ♦ **les gens du ~** the local people, the locals ♦ **vous êtes du ~ ?** do you live locally? *ou* around here? *ou* in the area? ♦ **je ne suis pas du ~** I'm not from around here, I'm a stranger here ♦ **le supermarché du ~** the local supermarket ♦ **un ~ perdu** *ou* **paumé** * a place miles from anywhere ♦ **un ~ de Paris/de la France que je connais bien** an area of Paris/of France that I know well ♦ **on a trouvé un petit ~ pas cher/tranquille pour le week-end** we found somewhere nice and cheap/nice and quiet for the weekend, we found a nice inexpensive/quiet little spot for the weekend ♦ **de tous les ~s du monde** from every corner of the world ♦ **de tous les ~s du pays** from all over the country
6 (= *objet triangulaire*) *[de reliure, cartable, sous-main]* corner (piece); *(pour coincer, écarter)* wedge; *(pour graver)* die; (= *poinçon*) hallmark ♦ **~ (de serrage)** *(Typo)* quoin ♦ **être frappé** *ou* **marqué au ~ du bon sens** to bear the stamp of commonsense
7 *(locutions)* **je n'aimerais pas le rencontrer au ~ d'un bois** I wouldn't like to meet him on a dark night ♦ **au ~ du feu** by the fireside ♦ **causerie/rêverie au ~ du feu** fireside chat/daydream; → **boucher**[1], **quatre**

coinçage /kwɛ̃saʒ/ NM wedging

coincé, e * /kwɛ̃se/ ADJ (= *complexé*) *[personne]* hung up *, uptight * ♦ **il est très ~** he has a lot of hang-ups *, he's very uptight *; → aussi **coincer**

coincement /kwɛ̃smɑ̃/ NM jamming *(NonC)*

coincer /kwɛ̃se/ ► conjug 3 ◄ VT 1 (= *bloquer*) *(intentionnellement)* to wedge; *(accidentellement)* *[+ tiroir, fermeture éclair]* to jam ♦ **le tiroir est coincé** the drawer is stuck *ou* jammed ♦ **le vélo était coincé sous le camion** the bike was wedged under the lorry ♦ **il s'est trouvé coincé contre un mur par la foule** he was pinned against a wall by the crowd ◆ **il m'a coincé entre deux portes pour me dire ...** he cornered me to tell me ... ◆ **nous étions coincés dans le couloir/dans l'ascenseur** we were stuck *ou* jammed in the corridor/in the lift ◆ **je suis coincé à la maison/au bureau** *(fig)* I'm stuck at home/at the office ◆ **ils ont coincé l'armoire en voulant la faire passer par la porte** they got the wardrobe jammed *ou* stuck trying to get it through the door ◆ ~ **la bulle**‡ to bum around*

2 (* = *attraper)* *[+ voleur]* to nab*; *[+ faussaire, fraudeur]* to catch up with

3 (* = *mettre dans une position difficile)* to put sb in a tight corner ◆ **nous sommes coincés, nous ne pouvons rien faire** we're stuck *ou* we're in a tight corner and can't do anything ◆ **je me suis fait** ~ *ou* **ils m'ont coincé sur cette question** they got me on *ou* caught me out on that question, I was caught out on that question ◆ **coincé entre son désir et la peur** caught between his desire and fear

VI *[porte]* to stick ◆ **ça coince au niveau de la direction*** there are problems at management level

VPR **se coincer** *[fermeture, tiroir]* to jam, to stick, to get jammed *ou* stuck ◆ **se** ~ **le doigt dans une porte** to catch one's finger in a door ◆ **se** ~ **un nerf*** to trap *ou* pinch a nerve ◆ **se** ~ **une vertèbre*** to trap a nerve in one's spine

coinceur /kwɛ̃sœʀ/ NM *(Alpinisme)* nut

coïncidence /kɔɛ̃sidɑ̃s/ NF *(gén, Géom)* coincidence

coïncident, e /kɔɛ̃sidɑ̃, ɑt/ ADJ *[surfaces, faits]* coincident

coïncider /kɔɛ̃side/ ▸ conjug 1 ◂ VI *[surfaces, opinions, dates]* to coincide *(avec* with); *[témoignages]* to tally ◆ **nous sommes arrivés à faire** ~ **nos dates de vacances** we've managed to get the dates of our holidays to coincide

coin-coin /kwɛ̃kwɛ̃/ NM INV *[de canard]* quack ◆ ~ **!** quack! quack!

coïnculpé, e /kɔɛ̃kylpe/ NM,F co-defendant, co-accused

coing /kwɛ̃/ NM quince

coït /kɔit/ NM coitus ◆ ~ **interrompu** coitus interruptus

coite /kwat/ ADJ F → **coi**

coke[1] /kɔk/ NM *(= combustible)* coke

coke[2] /kɔk/ NF *(arg Drogue = cocaïne)* coke*

cokéfaction /kɔkefaksjɔ̃/ NF coking

cokéfier /kɔkefje/ ▸ conjug 7 ◂ VT to coke

cokerie /kɔkʀi/ NF cokeworks, coking works

col /kɔl/ NM 1 *[de chemise, manteau]* collar ◆ **ça bâille du** ~ it gapes at the neck ◆ **pull à** ~ **rond** round-neck pullover; → **faux**[2]

2 *(Géog)* pass ◆ **le** ~ **du Simplon** the Simplon pass

3 *(= partie étroite) [de carafe, vase]* neck ◆ ~ **du fémur/de la vessie** neck of the thighbone/of the bladder ◆ **elle s'est cassé le** ~ **du fémur** she has broken her hip ◆ ~ **de l'utérus** neck of the womb, cervix

4 *(† ou littér = cou)* neck ◆ **un homme au** ~ **de taureau** a man with a bull neck, a bull-necked man

COMP **col blanc** *(= personne)* white-collar worker ◆ **la criminalité en** ~ **blanc** white-collar crime

col bleu *(= ouvrier)* blue-collar worker; *(= marin)* bluejacket

col cassé wing collar

col châle shawl collar

col cheminée high round neck, turtleneck *(Brit)*

col chemisier shirt collar

col Claudine Peter Pan collar

col dur stiff collar

col Mao Mao collar

col marin sailor's collar

col mou soft collar

col officier mandarin collar

col polo polo shirt collar

col ras du cou round neck, crew neck *(Brit)*

col roulé roll neck *(Brit)*, polo neck *(Brit)*, turtleneck

col tailleur tailored collar

col (en) V V-neck

cola /kɔla/ NM *(= arbre)* cola *ou* kola (tree) ◆ **(noix de)** ~ cola *ou* kola nut

colback‡ /kɔlbak/ NM ◆ **attraper** *ou* **prendre qn par le** ~ to grab sb by the collar

colbertisme /kɔlbɛʀtism/ NM *economic policy based on a high degree of state control (an allusion to Colbert, chief minister under Louis XIV)*

colbertiste /kɔlbɛʀtist/ ADJ *[pays, modèle]* with a policy of strong state intervention in the economy

colchique /kɔlʃik/ NM autumn crocus, meadow saffron, colchicum *(SPÉC)*

col-de-cygne (pl **cols-de-cygne**) /kɔldəsiɲ/ NM *[de plomberie, mobilier]* swan neck

colégataire /kolegatɛʀ/ NMF joint legatee

coléoptère /kɔleɔptɛʀ/ NM beetle, coleopterous insect *(SPÉC)* ◆ **~s** Coleoptera *(SPÉC)*

colère /kɔlɛʀ/ NF 1 *(= irritation)* anger ◆ **la** ~ **est mauvaise conseillère** anger is a bad counsellor ◆ **être/se mettre en** ~ to be/get angry *ou* cross ◆ **mettre qn en** ~ to make sb angry *ou* cross ◆ **passer sa** ~ **sur qn** to work off *ou* take out one's anger on sb ◆ **en** ~ **contre moi-même** angry *ou* cross with myself, mad at myself* ◆ **dit-il avec** ~ he said angrily 2 *(= accès d'irritation)* (fit of) rage ◆ **il fait des ~s terribles** he has terrible fits of anger *ou* rage ◆ **il est entré dans une** ~ **noire** he flew into a terrible rage ◆ **faire** *ou* **piquer une** ~ to throw a tantrum 3 *(littér)* wrath ◆ **la** ~ **divine** divine wrath ◆ **la** ~ **des flots** the rage *ou* wrath of the sea ADJ INV † *(= coléreux)* irascible; *(= en colère)* irate

coléreux, -euse /kɔleʀø, øz/, **colérique** /kɔleʀik/ ADJ *[caractère]* quick-tempered, irascible; *[enfant]* quick-tempered, easily angered

colibacille /kɔlibasil/ NM colon bacillus

colibacillose /kɔlibasiloz/ NF colibacillosis

colibri /kɔlibʀi/ NM hummingbird

colifichet /kɔlifiʃɛ/ NM *(= bijou)* trinket, bauble; *(= babiole)* knickknack

colimaçon /kɔlimasɔ̃/ NM † snail; → **escalier**

colin /kɔlɛ̃/ NM *(= merlu)* hake; *(= lieu noir)* coley

colineau (pl **colineaux**) /kɔlino/ NM ⇒ **colinot**

colin-maillard (pl **colin-maillards**) /kɔlɛ̃majaʀ/ NM blind man's buff

colinot /kɔlino/ NM *(= merlu)* small hake; *(= lieu noir)* small coley

colin-tampon* (pl **colin-tampons**) /kɔlɛ̃tɑ̃pɔ̃/ NM ◆ **il s'en soucie** *ou* **s'en moque comme de** ~ he doesn't give *ou* care a fig* about it

colique /kɔlik/ NF 1 *(= diarrhée)* diarrhoea ◆ **avoir la** ~ *(lit)* to have diarrhoea; *(fig = avoir peur)* to be scared stiff* 2 *(gén pl = douleur)* stomach pain, colic pain, colic *(NonC)* ◆ **être pris de violentes ~s** to have violent stomach pains ◆ ~ **hépatique/néphrétique** biliary/renal colic ◆ **quelle** ~ **!**‡ *(personne)* what a pain in the neck!*; *(chose)* what a drag!* ADJ *(Anat)* colonic

colis /kɔli/ NM parcel ◆ **envoyer/recevoir un** ~ **postal** to send/receive a parcel through the post *ou* mail ◆ **par** ~ **postal** by parcel post

Colisée /kɔlize/ NM ◆ **le** ~ the Coliseum *ou* Colosseum

colistier, -ière /kolistje, jɛʀ/ NM,F *(Pol)* fellow candidate

colite /kɔlit/ NF colitis

collabo* /kɔ(l)labo/ NMF (abrév de **collaborateur, -trice**) *(péj : Hist Pol)* collaborator, collaborationist

collaborateur, -trice /kɔ(l)labɔʀatœʀ, tʀis/ NM,F *[de collègue]* colleague; *[de journal]* contributor; *[de livre]* collaborator; *(Hist Pol) [d'ennemi]* collaborator, collaborationist

collaboration /kɔ(l)labɔʀasjɔ̃/ NF *(Pol, à un travail, un livre)* collaboration *(à* on); *(à un journal)* contribution *(à* to); ◆ **la** ~ *(Hist)* the Collaboration ◆ **s'assurer la** ~ **de qn** to enlist the services of sb ◆ **en** ~ **(étroite) avec** in (close) collaboration with

collaborationniste /kɔ(l)labɔʀasjɔnist/ ADJ *[groupe, journal, politique]* collaborationist *(épith)* NMF collaborator, collaborationist, quisling

collaborer /kɔ(l)labɔʀe/ ▸ conjug 1 ◂ VI 1 ◆ ~ **avec qn** to collaborate *ou* work with sb ◆ ~ **à** *[+ travail, livre]* to collaborate on; *[+ journal]* to contribute to 2 *(Pol)* to collaborate

collage /kɔlaʒ/ NM 1 *(à la colle forte)* sticking, gluing; *(à la colle blanche)* pasting; *[d'étiquettes]* sticking ◆ ~ **de papiers peints** paperhanging ◆ ~ **d'affiches** billposting 2 *(Art)* collage 3 *(= apprêt) [de vin]* fining; *[de papier]* sizing 4 († : *péj = concubinage)* affair ◆ **c'est un** ~ they're living together

collagène /kɔlaʒɛn/ NM collagen

collant, e /kɔlɑ̃, ɑ̃t/ ADJ *(= ajusté) [vêtement]* skintight, tight-fitting, clinging; *(= poisseux)* sticky ◆ **être** ~* *[importun]* to cling, to stick like a leech; → **papier** NM 1 *(= maillot) [de femme]* body stocking; *[de danseur, acrobate]* leotard 2 *(= bas) (gén)* tights *(Brit)*, pantyhose *(US)*; *[de danseuse]* tights NF **collante** *(arg Scol) (= convocation)* notification; *(= feuille de résultats)* results slip

collapsus /kɔlapsys/ NM *[de malade, organe]* collapse

collatéral, e (mpl **-aux**) /kɔ(l)lateʀal, o/ ADJ *[parent, artère]* collateral ◆ **(nef)** ~**e** (side) aisle ◆ **les collatéraux** *(= parents)* collaterals; *(Archit)* (side) aisles ◆ **dommages collatéraux** *(Mil)* collateral damage

collation /kɔlasjɔ̃/ NF 1 *(= repas)* light meal; *(= en-cas)* snack 2 *(= comparaison) [de manuscrit]* collation; *(= vérification) [de liste]* checking; *(Typo)* collation 3 *(frm) [de titre, grade]* conferment

collationnement /kɔlasjɔnmɑ̃/ NM *(= comparaison) [de manuscrits]* collation; *(= vérification) [de liste]* checking; *(Typo)* collation

collationner /kɔlasjɔne/ ▸ conjug 1 ◂ VT *(= comparer) [+ manuscrits]* to collate *(avec* with); *(= vérifier) [+ liste]* to check; *(Typo)* to collate

colle /kɔl/ NF 1 *(gén)* glue; *[de papiers peints]* wallpaper paste; *(= apprêt)* size ◆ ~ **(blanche** *ou* **d'écolier** *ou* **de pâte)** paste ◆ ~ **(forte)** (strong) glue, adhesive ◆ ~ **à bois** wood glue ◆ ~ **de poisson** fish glue ◆ **ce riz, c'est de la vraie** ~ **(de pâte)** this rice is like paste *ou* is a gluey *ou* sticky mass; → **chauffer, pot** 2 (* = *question)* teaser, poser* *(Brit)* ◆ **poser une** ~ **à qn** to set sb a poser* ◆ **là, vous me posez une** ~ you've stumped me there* 3 *(arg Scol) (= examen blanc)* mock oral exam; *(= retenue)* detention ◆ **mettre une** ~ **à qn** to give sb a detention ◆ **j'ai eu trois heures de** ~ I got a three-hour detention, I was kept back for three hours 4 **vivre** *ou* **être à la** ~‡ to live together, to be shacked up together‡

collecte /kɔlɛkt/ NF 1 *(= quête) [de vêtements, verre, sang]* collection; *[d'informations, données]* collection, gathering ◆ ~ **de fonds** fund-raising event 2 *(Rel = prière)* collect

collecter /kɔlɛkte/ ► conjug 1 ◄ **VT** *(gén)* to collect; *[+ informations, données]* to collect, to gather

collecteur, -trice /kɔlɛktœʀ, tʀis/ **ADJ** *[canal]* collecting ◆ **égout** ~ main sewer ◆ **organisme** ~ collection agency **NM,F** *(= personne)* collector ◆ ~ **d'impôts** tax collector ◆ ~ **de fonds** fund-raiser **NM** *[de moteur]* manifold; *(Élec)* commutator ◆ ~ **d'ondes** *(Radio)* aerial ◆ ~ **d'égouts, (grand)** ~ main sewer

collectif, -ive /kɔlɛktif, iv/ **ADJ** *[travail, responsabilité, punition]* collective; *[sport]* team *(épith)*; *[billet, réservation]* group *(épith)*; *[hystérie, licenciements]* mass *(épith)*; *[installations]* public; *(Ling)* *[terme, sens]* collective ◆ **faire une démarche collective auprès de qn** to approach sb collectively *ou* as a group ◆ **immeuble** ~ (large) block (of flats) *(Brit)*, apartment building *(US)*; → **convention, ferme²** **NM** *(= mot)* collective noun; *(= groupe de travail)* collective ◆ ~ **budgétaire** minibudget

collection /kɔlɛksjɔ̃/ **NF** 1 *[de timbres, papillons]* collection; *(Comm)* *[d'échantillons]* line; *(hum = groupe)* collection ◆ **objet/timbre de** ~ collector's item/stamp ◆ **faire (la)** ~ **de** to collect ◆ **voiture de** ~ classic car; *(de l'entre-deux-guerres)* vintage car 2 *(Mode)* collection 3 *(Édition = série)* series, collection ◆ **notre** ~ **"jeunes auteurs"** our "young authors" series *ou* collection ◆ **il a toute la** ~ **des œuvres de Larbaud** he's got the complete collection *ou* set of Larbaud's works 4 *(Méd)* ~ **de pus** gathering of pus

collectionner /kɔlɛksjɔne/ ► conjug 1 ◄ **VT** *(gén, hum)* to collect

collectionneur, -euse /kɔlɛksjɔnœʀ, øz/ **NM,F** collector

collectivement /kɔlɛktivmɑ̃/ **ADV** *(gén)* collectively; *[démissionner, protester]* in a body, collectively

collectivisation /kɔlɛktivizasjɔ̃/ **NF** collectivization

collectiviser /kɔlɛktivize/ ► conjug 1 ◄ **VT** to collectivize

collectivisme /kɔlɛktivism/ **NM** collectivism ◆ ~ **d'État** state collectivism

collectiviste /kɔlɛktivist/ **ADJ, NMF** collectivist

collectivité /kɔlɛktivite/ **NF** 1 *(= groupement)* group ◆ **la** ~ *(= le public)* the community ◆ **la** ~ **nationale** the nation (as a community) ◆ **la** ~ **des citoyens** the citizens as a whole *ou* a body ◆ **les ~s locales/publiques** the local/public authorities ◆ **~s professionnelles** professional bodies *ou* organizations 2 *(= vie en communauté)* **la** ~ community life *ou* living ◆ **vivre en** ~ to live in a community 3 *(= possession commune)* collective ownership

collector /kɔlɛktɔʀ/ **NM** *(Mus)* collector's edition

collège /kɔlɛʒ/ **NM** 1 *(= école)* school; *(privé)* private school ◆ ~ **(d'enseignement secondaire)** secondary school *(Brit)*, junior high school *(US)* ◆ ~ **(d'enseignement) technique** technical school ◆ **le Collège de France** *prestigious state-run institution of higher education which does not grant diplomas* ◆ **Collège d'enseignement général et professionnel** *(Can)* general and vocational college *(Can)*, ≈ sixth-form college *(Brit)*, junior college *(US)*

2 *(Pol, Rel = assemblée)* college ◆ ~ **électoral** electoral college; → **sacré¹**

COLLÈGE

The term **collège** refers to the type of state secondary school French children attend between the ages of 11 and 15 (ie after « école primaire » and before « lycée »). **Collège** covers the school years referred to as « sixième », « cinquième », « quatrième » and « troisième ». At the end of troisième, pupils take the examination known as the « brevet des collèges ». → **LYCÉE**

COLLÈGE DE FRANCE

The **Collège de France** in Paris is an unusual higher education establishment in that it neither organizes examinations nor confers diplomas. Professors at this prestigious place of learning are appointed by the French President and give lectures that are open to all. **Collège de France** professors in recent times have included such major intellectual figures as Roland Barthes, Michel Foucault and Claude Lévi-Strauss.

collégial, e (mpl **-iaux**) /kɔleʒjal, jo/ **ADJ** *(Rel)* collegiate; *(Pol)* collegial, collegiate ◆ **décision ~e** group *ou* collective decision **NF** **collégiale** collegiate church

collégialement /kɔleʒjalmɑ̃/ **ADV** collectively

collégialité /kɔleʒjalite/ **NF** *(Pol)* collegial administration; *(Rel)* collegiality

collégien /kɔleʒjɛ̃/ **NM** schoolboy ◆ **c'est un** ~ *(= novice)* he's an innocent, he's a bit green

collégienne /kɔleʒjɛn/ **NF** schoolgirl

collègue /kɔ(l)lɛg/ **NMF** colleague ◆ **un** ~ **de travail/bureau** a colleague from work/the office; → **Monsieur**

coller /kɔle/ ► conjug 1 ◄ **VT** 1 *(à la colle forte)* to stick, to glue; *(à la colle blanche)* to paste; *[+ étiquette, timbre]* to stick; *[+ affiche]* to stick (up) *(à, sur* on); *[+ enveloppe]* to stick down; *[+ papier peint]* to hang; *[+ film]* to splice; *(Ordin)* *[+ texte, image]* to paste ◆ ~ **deux morceaux (ensemble)** to stick *ou* glue *ou* paste two pieces together ◆ ~ **qch à** *ou* **sur qch** to stick sth on(to) sth ◆ **les cheveux collés de sang** his hair stuck together *ou* matted with blood ◆ **les yeux encore collés de sommeil** his eyes still half-shut with sleep

2 *(= appliquer)* ~ **son oreille à la porte/son nez contre la vitre** to press one's ear to *ou* against the door/one's nose against the window ◆ **il colla l'armoire contre le mur** he stood the wardrobe right against the wall ◆ **ils l'ont collé au mur** *(Mil)* they stuck him up against the wall

3 *(* = mettre)* to stick, to shove* ◆ **colle tes valises dans un coin** stick *ou* shove* *ou* dump* your bags in a corner ◆ **il en colle des pages** he writes reams* ◆ **dans ses devoirs il colle n'importe quoi** he puts *ou* sticks *ou* shoves* any old thing (down) in his homework ◆ **il se colla devant moi** he plonked* *ou* planted himself in front of me ◆ **ils se collent devant la télé dès qu'ils rentrent** they plonk themselves* in front of the TV as soon as they come in ◆ **se** ~ **un chapeau sur la tête** to stick *ou* shove a hat on one's head* ◆ **ils l'ont collé ministre** they've gone and made him a minister*; → **poing**

4 *(* = donner)* to give ◆ **il m'a collé une contravention/une punition/une gifle** he gave me a fine/a punishment/a slap ◆ **on m'a collé une fausse pièce** I've been palmed off with a false coin ◆ **on lui a collé trois ans de prison** they've stuck him in prison *ou* sent him down* for three years, they've given him three years ◆ **on lui a collé la responsabilité/la belle-mère** he's got (himself) stuck* *ou* lumbered* *(Brit)* with the responsibility/his mother-in-law

5 *(arg Scol)* *(= consigner)* to put in detention, to keep back; *(= recaler)* to fail, to flunk* *(US)* ◆ **se faire** ~ *(en retenue)* to be put in detention; *(à l'examen)* to be failed, to be flunked* *(US)*

6 *(* = embarrasser par une question)* to catch out

7 *(* = suivre)* *[+ personne]* to cling to ◆ **la voiture qui nous suit nous colle de trop près** the car behind is sitting right on our tail* ◆ **il m'a collé (après) toute la journée** he clung to me all day

8 *(= apprêter)* *[+ vin]* to fine; *[+ papier]* to size

VI 1 *(= être poisseux)* to be sticky; *(= adhérer)* to stick *(à* to)

2 *(* = bien marcher)* **ça colle ?** OK?* ◆ **ça ne colle pas entre eux** they aren't hitting it off* *ou* getting on *(Brit)* *ou* getting along (together) ◆ **il y a quelque chose qui ne colle pas** there's something wrong *ou* not right here ◆ **ça ne colle pas, je ne suis pas libre** that's no good *ou* that won't do, I'm not free ◆ **son histoire ne colle pas** his story doesn't hold together *ou* doesn't gibe *(US)*

3 *(jeux d'enfants)* **c'est à toi de** ~ it's your turn to be it, you're it now

VT INDIR ◆ ~ **à** *(= être près de)* to cling to ◆ ~ **au peloton** to stick close to the pack ◆ **robe qui colle au corps** tight-fitting *ou* clinging dress ◆ **ils nous collent au derrière*** they're right on our tail* ◆ **voiture qui colle à la route** car that grips the road ◆ **un rôle qui lui colle à la peau** a part tailor-made for him, a part which fits him like a glove ◆ **depuis, cette réputation lui colle à la peau** he's been stuck with this reputation ever since ◆ ~ **au sujet** to stick to the subject ◆ **ce roman colle à la réalité** this novel is very faithful to reality ◆ **mot qui colle à une idée** word which fits an idea closely

VPR **se coller** 1 *(= s'appuyer)* **il s'est collé contre le mur pour les laisser passer** he pressed himself against the wall to let them pass

2 *(‡ = subir)* *[+ tâche, personne]* to be *ou* get stuck* *ou* landed with* *ou* lumbered with* *(Brit)* ◆ **il va falloir se** ~ **la belle-mère pendant trois jours !** we'll have to put up with my mother-in-law for three days!

3 **se** ~ **à (faire) qch*** *(= se mettre à)* to get down to (doing) sth, to set about (doing) sth ◆ **allez, on s'y colle ?** right, shall we get down to it?

4 *(= s'accrocher)* **se** ~ **à qn** *[danseur]* to press o.s. against sb, to cling to sb; *[importun]* to stick to sb like glue *ou* like a leech ◆ **elle dansait collée à** *ou* **contre lui** she was dancing tightly pressed against him *ou* clinging tightly to him ◆ **ces deux-là sont toujours collés ensemble‡** those two *ou* that pair always go around together *ou* are never apart

5 **se** ~ **ensemble** †‡ *(= vivre ensemble)* to live together, to shack up together‡

collerette /kɔlʀɛt/ **NF** 1 *(= col)* collar; *(Hist = fraise)* ruff 2 *[de champignon]* ring, annulus; *[de tuyau]* flange

collet /kɔlɛ/ **NM** *(= piège)* snare, noose; *(= petite cape)* short cape; *[de dent]* neck; *(Boucherie, Bot)* neck; *[de pièce mécanique]* collar, flange ◆ **prendre** *ou* **saisir qn au** ~ to seize sb by the collar ◆ **mettre la main au** ~ **de qn** to get hold of sb, to collar sb* ◆ **elle est très** ~ **monté** she's very strait-laced *ou* stuffy

colleter /kɔlte/ ► conjug 4 ◄ **VT** *[+ adversaire]* to seize by the collar ◆ **il s'est fait** ~ **par la police*** he was collared* by the police **VPR** **se colleter*** *(= se battre)* to have a tussle, to tussle ◆ **se** ~ **avec** to wrestle *ou* grapple *ou* tussle with ◆ **je me suis colleté tout le travail** I had to do all the work

colleur, -euse /kɔlœʀ, øz/ **NM,F** 1 ◆ ~ **d'affiches** billsticker, billposter 2 *(arg Scol)* mock oral *examiner* NF **colleuse** *(Ciné)* splicer; *(Photo)* mounting press

colley /kɔlɛ/ NM collie

collier /kɔlje/ NM 1 *[de femme]* necklace; *[de chevalier, maire]* chain; *[de chien, cheval, chat]* (= *courroie, pelage*) collar; *(Boucherie)* neck ◆ **~ de perles** pearl necklace ◆ **~ de fleurs** garland ◆ **~ de chien** *ou* **ras du cou** (= *bijou*) choker ◆ **~ antipuces** flea collar ◆ **reprendre le ~** * to get back into harness ◆ **donner un coup de ~** to put one's back into it *; → **franc¹** 2 (= *barbe*) **~ (de barbe)** beard *(along the line of the jaw)* 3 *[de pièce mécanique]* **~ de serrage** clamp collar

collimateur /kɔlimatœʀ/ NM (= *lunette*) collimator ◆ **avoir qn/qch dans son** *ou* **le ~** *(lit)* to have sb/sth in one's sights; *(fig)* to have one's eye on sb/sth

colline /kɔlin/ NF hill

collision /kɔlizjɔ̃/ NF *[de véhicules, bateaux]* collision; *(Phys, Géog)* collision; *(fig) [d'intérêts, manifestants]* clash ◆ **entrer en ~** to collide *(avec* with); ◆ **~ en chaîne** (= *voitures*) pile-up

collisionneur /kɔlizjɔnœʀ/ NM collider

collocation /kɔlɔkasjɔ̃/ NF *(Jur) classification of creditors in order of priority; (Ling)* collocation

collodion /kɔlɔdjɔ̃/ NM collodion

colloïdal, e (mpl **-aux**) /kɔlɔidal, o/ ADJ colloidal ◆ **solution ~e** colloidal solution *ou* suspension

colloïde /kɔlɔid/ NM colloid

colloque /kɔ(l)lɔk/ NM colloquium, symposium; *(hum)* confab *

collusion /kɔlyzjɔ̃/ NF (= *complicité*) collusion *(avec* with; *entre* between)

collutoire /kɔlytwaʀ/ NM oral medication *(NonC)*; *(en bombe)* throat spray

collyre /kɔliʀ/ NM eye lotion, collyrium *(SPÉC)*

colmatage /kɔlmataʒ/ NM 1 *[de fuite]* sealing(-off), plugging; *[de fissure, trou]* filling-in, plugging; *[de déficit]* making good 2 *(Agr) [de terrain]* warping

colmater /kɔlmate/ ▸ conjug 1 ◂ VT 1 *[+ fuite]* to seal (off), to plug; *[+ fissure, trou]* to fill in, to plug; *[+ déficit, manque]* to make good, to make up ◆ **la fissure s'est colmatée toute seule** the crack has filled itself in *ou* sealed itself ◆ **~ une brèche** to close a gap 2 *(Agr) [+ terrain]* to warp

colo * /kɔlo/ NF (abrév de **colonie de vacances**) → **colonie**

coloc * /kɔlɔk/ NMF abrév de **colocataire** NF abrév de **colocation**

colocataire /kolɔkatɛʀ/ NMF *[d'immeuble]* fellow tenant, co-tenant *(Admin)*; *[d'appartement]* flatmate *(Brit)*, roommate *(US)*; *[de maison]* housemate

colocation /kolɔkasjɔ̃/ NF *(dans un appartement)* flat-sharing; *(dans une maison)* house-sharing ◆ **ils sont en ~** they rent a flat *(ou* a house) together

Cologne /kɔlɔɲ/ N Cologne; → **eau**

Colomb /kɔlɔ̃/ NM ◆ **Christophe ~** Christopher Columbus

colombage /kɔlɔ̃baʒ/ NM half-timbering ◆ **maison à ~(s)** half-timbered house

colombe /kɔlɔ̃b/ NF (= *oiseau, pacifiste*) dove

Colombie /kɔlɔ̃bi/ NF Colombia ◆ **~ britannique** British Columbia

colombien, -ienne /kɔlɔ̃bjɛ̃, jɛn/ ADJ Colombian NM,F **Colombien(ne)** Colombian

colombier /kɔlɔ̃bje/ NM dovecote

colombin¹ /kɔlɔ̃bɛ̃/ NM ◆ **(pigeon) ~** stockdove

colombin² /kɔlɔ̃bɛ̃/ NM *[d'argile]* clay coil; (*‡* = *étron*) turd *‡*

Colombine /kɔlɔ̃bin/ NF *(Théât)* Columbine

Colombo /kɔlɔ̃bo/ N Colombo

colombophile /kɔlɔ̃bɔfil/ ADJ ◆ **société ~** pigeon-fanciers' club NMF pigeon fancier

colombophilie /kɔlɔ̃bɔfili/ NF pigeon fancying

colon /kɔlɔ̃/ NM 1 (= *pionnier*) settler, colonist 2 *(en vacances)* child *(at a children's holiday camp)* 3 *(arg Mil)* colonel ◆ **eh bien, mon ~ !** * heck! *, blimey! * *(Brit)*

côlon /kolɔ̃/ NM *(Anat)* colon

colonel /kɔlɔnɛl/ NM *[d'armée de terre]* colonel; *[d'armée de l'air]* group captain *(Brit)*, colonel *(US)*

colonelle /kɔlɔnɛl/ NF 1 (= *officier*) *[d'armée de terre]* colonel; *[d'armée de l'air]* group captain *(Brit)*, colonel *(US)* 2 († = *épouse*) *[d'armée de terre]* colonel's wife; *[d'armée de l'air]* group captain's wife *(Brit)*, colonel's wife *(US)*

colonial, e (mpl **-iaux**) /kɔlɔnjal, jo/ ADJ colonial; → **casque** NM (= *soldat*) soldier of the colonial troops; (= *habitant*) colonial NF **coloniale** ◆ **la ~e** the (French) Colonial Army

colonialisme /kɔlɔnjalism/ NM colonialism ◆ **~ culturel** cultural imperialism

colonialiste /kɔlɔnjalist/ ADJ, NMF colonialist

colonie /kɔlɔni/ NF colony; (= *communauté ethnique*) community ◆ **vivre aux ~s** to live in the colonies ◆ **~ de vacances** ≈ (children's) holiday camp *(Brit)*, summer camp *(US)* ◆ **~ pénitentiaire** penal settlement *ou* colony

> **Colonie de vacances**
>
> The **colonie de vacances** or « colo » is an important part of life for many French children. **Colonies de vacances** are residential centres in the countryside, in the mountains or at the seaside where children, supervised by trained « moniteurs » and « monitrices », can participate in a range of open-air activities. The **colonie de vacances** helps break up the two-month summer holiday for parents and children alike.

colonisateur, -trice /kɔlɔnizatœʀ, tʀis/ ADJ colonizing *(épith)* NM,F colonizer

colonisation /kɔlɔnizasjɔ̃/ NF colonization

colonisé, e /kɔlɔnize/ (ptp de **coloniser**) ADJ colonized NMPL ◆ **les ~s** colonized peoples, those who have been subjected to colonization

coloniser /kɔlɔnize/ ▸ conjug 1 ◂ VT to colonize

colonnade /kɔlɔnad/ NF colonnade

colonne /kɔlɔn/ NF *(gén)* column; *(Archit)* column, pillar ◆ **en ~ par deux** *[enfants]* in twos, in a crocodile * *(Brit)*; *[soldats]* in twos ◆ **mettez-vous en ~ par quatre** line up four abreast ◆ **titre sur cinq ~s à la une** *(Presse)* headline splashed across the front page ◆ **ils ont largement ouvert leurs ~s à ce problème** *(journal)* they have given many column inches *ou* a lot of coverage to this problem ◆ **~ des unités/dizaines** *[de nombre]* unit/tens column; → **cinquième, titre, titrer**

COMP **colonne d'air** airstream
colonne barométrique barometric column
colonne blindée armoured column
colonne de direction *[de voiture]* steering column
les Colonnes d'Hercule the Pillars of Hercules
colonne montante rising main
colonne Morris (pillar-shaped) billboard
colonne de rangement *[de CD]* CD tower
colonne sèche dry riser
colonne de secours rescue party
colonne vertébrale spine, spinal *ou* vertebral column *(SPÉC)*

colonnette /kɔlɔnɛt/ NF small column

colopathie /kolopati/ NF colitis, colonitis

colophane /kɔlɔfan/ NF rosin

coloquinte /kɔlɔkɛ̃t/ NF bitter apple; *(décorative)* gourd

Colorado /kɔlɔʀado/ NM Colorado

colorant, e /kɔlɔʀɑ̃, ɑ̃t/ ADJ colouring *(Brit) ou* coloring *(US)*; → **shampooing** NM *(gén)* colouring *(Brit) ou* coloring *(US)* agent, colorant; *(pour textiles)* dye ◆ **"sans colorants artificiels"** *(sur étiquette)* "(contains) no artificial colouring" ◆ **~s vitaux** vital stains

coloration /kɔlɔʀasjɔ̃/ NF 1 (= *teinture*) *[de substance]* colouring *(Brit)*, coloring *(US)*; *[de tissu]* dyeing; *[de bois]* staining ◆ **~ naturelle** *ou* **artificielle** natural *ou* artificial colouring 2 *(pour les cheveux)* colour *(Brit)*, color *(US)* ◆ **se faire faire une ~** to have one's hair coloured *(Brit) ou* colored *(US)* 3 (= *couleur, nuance*) shade, colour(ing) *(Brit)*, color(ing) *(US)*; *[de peau]* colouring *(Brit)*, coloring *(US)* 4 *(fig) [de voix, ton]* coloration; *[de discours]* complexion ◆ **~ politique** *[de journal, mouvement]* political complexion ◆ **à** *ou* **de ~ socialiste** with socialist leanings ◆ **les éclairages donnent à ce film une ~ fantastique** the lighting gives the film an element of fantasy

colorature /kɔlɔʀatyʀ/ NF coloratura

coloré, e /kɔlɔʀe/ (ptp de **colorer**) ADJ *[teint]* florid, ruddy; *[objet]* coloured *(Brit)*, colored *(US)*; *[foule]* colourful *(Brit)*, colorful *(US)*; *[style, récit]* vivid, colourful *(Brit)*, colorful *(US)*

colorer /kɔlɔʀe/ ▸ conjug 1 ◂ VT 1 (= *teindre*) *[+ substance]* to colour *(Brit)*, to color *(US)*; *[+ tissu]* to dye; *[+ bois]* to stain ◆ **~ qch en bleu** to colour *(ou* dye *ou* stain) sth blue ◆ **le soleil colore les cimes neigeuses** *(littér)* the sun tinges the snowy peaks with colour ◆ **faire ~ la viande dans le beurre** *(Culin)* brown the meat in butter 2 *(littér* = *enjoliver) [+ récit, sentiments]* to colour *(Brit)*, to color *(US) (de* with) VPR **se colorer** 1 (= *prendre de la couleur*) *[fruit]* to turn red *(ou* yellow *ou* orange *etc)*, to colour *(Brit)*, to color *(US)* ◆ **le ciel se colore de rose** the sky takes on a rosy tinge *ou* hue ◆ **son teint se colora** her face became flushed, her colour rose 2 (= *être empreint de*) **se ~ de** to be coloured *(Brit) ou* colored *(US) ou* tinged with

coloriage /kɔlɔʀjaʒ/ NM (= *action*) colouring *(NonC) (Brit)*, coloring *(NonC) (US)*; (= *dessin*) coloured *(Brit) ou* colored *(US)* drawing

colorier /kɔlɔʀje/ ▸ conjug 7 ◂ VT *[+ carte, dessin]* to colour *(Brit) ou* color *(US)* (in) ◆ **images à ~** pictures to colour (in)

coloris /kɔlɔʀi/ NM *(gén)* colour *(Brit)*, color *(US)*, shade; *[de visage, peau]* colouring *(Brit)*, coloring *(US)* ◆ **carte de ~** *(Comm)* shade card

colorisation /kɔlɔʀizasjɔ̃/ NF colourization *(Brit)*, colorization *(US)*

coloriser /kɔlɔʀize/ ▸ conjug 1 ◂ VT to colourize *(Brit)*, to colorize *(US)*

coloriste /kɔlɔʀist/ NMF (= *peintre*) colourist *(Brit)*, colorist *(US)*; (= *enlumineur*) colourer *(Brit)*, colorer *(US)* NF (= *coiffeuse*) hairdresser *(specializing in tinting and rinsing)*

coloscopie /kɔlɔskɔpi/ NF colonoscopy

colossal, e (mpl **-aux**) /kɔlɔsal, o/ ADJ colossal, huge

colossalement /kɔlɔsalmɑ̃/ ADV colossally, hugely

colosse /kɔlɔs/ NM (= *personne*) giant *(fig)* (= *institution, État*) colossus, giant ◆ **le ~ de Rhodes** the Colossus of Rhodes ◆ **~ aux pieds d'argile** idol with feet of clay

colostrum /kɔlɔstʀɔm/ NM colostrum

colportage /kɔlpɔʀtaʒ/ NM *[de marchandises, ragots]* hawking, peddling; → **littérature**

colporter /kɔlpɔʀte/ ▸ conjug 1 ◂ VT *[+ marchandises, ragots]* to hawk, to peddle

colporteur, -euse /kɔlpɔʀtœʀ, øz/ **NM,F** (= *vendeur)* hawker, pedlar ◆ **~ de rumeurs** *ou* **ragots** * gossipmonger

colt ® /kɔlt/ **NM** (= *revolver)* gun, Colt ®

coltiner /kɔltine/ ▸ conjug 1 ◂ **VT** *[+ fardeau]* to carry, to lug * *ou* hump * *(Brit)* around **VPR se coltiner** * *[+ colis]* to lug * *ou* hump * *(Brit)* around, to carry; ⁑ *[+ travail, personne]* to be *ou* get landed * *ou* lumbered * *(Brit)* with ◆ **il va falloir se ~ ta sœur** we'll have to put up with your sister

columbarium /kɔlɔ̃baʀjɔm/ **NM** (= *cimetière)* columbarium

colvert /kɔlvɛʀ/ **NM** mallard; *(Culin)* wild duck

colza /kɔlza/ **NM** rape, colza

COM /kɔm/ **NF** (abrév de **Collectivité d'outre-mer**) *French overseas territory (formerly "Territoire d'outre-mer")*

coma /kɔma/ **NM** coma ◆ **être/tomber dans le ~** to be in/go into a coma ◆ **dans un ~ dépassé** brain-dead ◆ **~ diabétique** diabetic coma

comateux, -euse /kɔmatø, øz/ **ADJ** comatose ◆ **état ~** comatose state **NM,F** patient in a coma, comatose patient

combat /kɔ̃ba/ **NM** 1 *(Mil)* battle, fight ◆ **le ~, les ~s** the fighting *(NonC)* ◆ **~ aérien** air battle, dogfight ◆ **~ naval** naval action ◆ **ils s'entraînent au ~ aérien/naval** they're training in aerial/naval combat ◆ **~ d'arrière-garde** *(lit, fig)* rearguard action ◆ **les ~s continuent** the fighting goes on ◆ **le ~ cessa faute de combattants** the fight stopped for lack of fighters

◆ **de combat** *[avion]* combat *(épith)*; *[troupes]* combat *(épith)*, fighting; *[zone]* combat *(épith)*, battle *(épith)* ◆ **chien de ~** fighting dog; → **branle-bas, char[1], sport**

◆ **au combat** ◆ **aller au ~** to go into battle, to enter the fray *(littér)* ◆ **mort au ~** killed in action

◆ **hors de combat** ◆ **mettre hors de ~** *[+ soldat]* to put out of action; *[+ adversaire politique]* to put out of the running; *(Sport)* to put out of the fight *ou* contest

2 *(fig)* fight *(contre* against; *pour* for); ◆ **des ~s continuels entre parents et enfants** endless fighting between parents and children ◆ **le ~ contre la vie chère** the fight against the high cost of living ◆ **la vie est un ~ de tous les jours** life is a daily struggle ◆ **"étudiants, professeurs : même combat !"** "students and teachers fighting together!", "students and teachers united!" ◆ **quel ~ pour le faire manger !** it's such a struggle getting him to eat! ◆ **discours de ~** fighting speech

3 *(Sport)* match, fight ◆ **~ de boxe/de catch** boxing/wrestling match

COMP combat de coqs cockfight ◆ **les ~s de coqs ont été interdits** cockfighting has been banned

combat de gladiateurs gladiatorial combat *ou* contest

combat rapproché close combat

combat de rues street fighting *(NonC)*, street battle

combat singulier single combat

combatif, -ive /kɔ̃batif, iv/ **ADJ** *[troupes]* ready to fight; *[personne]* with a fighting spirit; *[esprit, humeur]* fighting *(épith)*

combativité /kɔ̃bativite/ **NF** *[de troupe]* readiness to fight; *[de personne]* fighting spirit

combattant, e /kɔ̃batɑ̃, ɑt/ **ADJ** *[troupe]* fighting *(épith)*, combatant *(épith)* **NM,F** *[de guerre]* combatant; *[de bagarre]* brawler; → **ancien NM** (= *oiseau) (mâle)* ruff; *(femelle)* reeve; (= *poisson)* fighting fish

combattre /kɔ̃batʀ/ ▸ conjug 41 ◂ **VT** *[+ incendie, adversaire]* to fight; *[+ théorie, politique, inflation, vice]* to combat, to fight (against); *[+ maladie] [malade]* to fight against; *[médecin]* to fight, to combat **VI** to fight *(contre* against; *pour* for)

> ⚠ Attention à ne pas traduire automatiquement **combattre** par **to combat**, qui s'utilise surtout au sens figuré.

combe /kɔ̃b/ **NF** *(Géog)* coomb, comb(e)

combien /kɔ̃bjɛ̃/ **ADV** 1 ◆ **~ de** *(quantité)* how much; *(nombre)* how many ◆ **~ de lait/de bouteilles veux-tu ?** how much milk/how many bottles do you want? ◆ **~ y en a-t-il en moins ?** *(quantité)* how much less is there (of it)?; *(nombre)* how many fewer are there (of them)? ◆ **tu en as pour ~ de temps ?** how long will you be? ◆ **depuis ~ de temps travaillez-vous ici ?** how long have you been working here? ◆ **~ de fois ?** *(nombre)* how many times?; *(fréquence)* how often?

2 ◆ **~ (d'entre eux)** how many (of them) ◆ **~ n'ouvrent jamais un livre !** just think of how many people there are who never open a book! ◆ **~ sont-ils ?** how many (of them) are there?, how many are they?

3 *(frm* = *à quel point)* **si tu savais ~/~ plus je travaille maintenant !** if you only knew how much/how much more I work now! ◆ **tu vois ~ il est paresseux** you can see how lazy he is ◆ **c'est étonnant de voir ~ il a changé** it's surprising to see how changed he is *ou* how (much) he has changed ◆ **~ vous avez raison !** how right you are!

4 (= *tellement)* **~ peu de gens/d'argent** how few people/little money ◆ **~ plus/moins de gens** how many more/fewer people ◆ **~ plus d'argent** how much more money ◆ **c'est plus long à faire mais ~ meilleur !** it takes longer to do but it's so much better! ◆ **il est bête, ô ~ !** († *ou hum)* he is stupid, (oh) so stupid! ◆ **~ d'ennui je vous cause** what a lot of trouble I'm causing you

5 (= *avec mesure)* **~ est-ce ?, ~ ça coûte ?, ça fait ~ ?** * how much is it? ◆ **~ pèse ce colis ?** how much does this parcel weigh?, how heavy is this parcel? ◆ **~ mesure-t-il ?** *(personne)* how tall is he?; *(colis)* how big is it?; *(en longueur)* how long is it?, what length is it? ◆ **vous le voulez en ~ de large ?** what width do you want (it)? ◆ **ça va augmenter de ~ ?** how much more will it go up? *ou* be? ◆ **ça va faire une différence de ~ ?** what will the difference be? ◆ **~ y a-t-il d'ici à la ville ?** how far is it from here to the town? ◆ **ça fait ~ de haut ?** how high is it?, what height is it? ◆ **il a fait ~ aux essais ?** *(Sport)* what was his time in the trials?

NM * ◆ **le ~ êtes-vous ?** *(rang)* where did you come?, where were you placed? ◆ **le ~ sommes-nous ?** *(date)* what's the date?, what date is it? ◆ **il y en a tous les ~ ?** *(fréquence) [de trains, bus]* how often do they run?

combientième * /kɔ̃bjɛtjɛm/ **ADJ** ◆ **Lincoln était le ~ président ?** what number president was Lincoln? ◆ **c'est la ~ fois que ça arrive !** how many times has that happened now! **NMF** 1 (= *rang)* **il est le ~ ?** where did he come?, where was he placed? ◆ **ce coureur est arrivé le ~ ?** where did this runner come (in)? 2 (= *énumération)* **encore un attentat, c'est le ~ ?** another attack, how many does that make *ou* is that? ◆ **donne-moi le troisième – le ~ ?** give me the third one – which one did you say?

combinaison /kɔ̃binɛzɔ̃/ **NF** 1 (= *action)* combining; *[d'éléments, sons, chiffres]* combination ◆ **~ (ministérielle)** government ◆ **~ (chimique)** *(entre plusieurs corps)* combination; (= *corps composé)* compound 2 *[de coffre-fort, loto]* combination 3 (= *vêtement) [de femme]* slip; *[d'aviateur]* flying suit; *[de motard]* leathers; *[de mécanicien]* boiler suit *(Brit)*, (one-piece) overalls *(US)*; *(Ski)* ski-suit ◆ **~ de plongée (sous-marine)** (underwater) diving suit ◆ **~ spatiale** space suit 4 (= *astuce)* device, trick; (= *manigance)* scheme ◆ **des ~s louches** shady schemes *ou* scheming *(NonC)*

combinaison-short (pl **combinaisons-shorts**) /kɔ̃binɛzɔ̃ʃɔʀt/ **NF** culotte suit

combinard, e * /kɔ̃binaʀ, aʀd/ **ADJ, NM,F** ◆ **il est ~, c'est un ~** *(péj) (astuces)* he knows all the tricks; *(manigances)* he's a schemer

combinat /kɔ̃bina/ **NM** (industrial) complex

combinatoire /kɔ̃binatwaʀ/ **ADJ** *(Ling)* combinative; *(Math)* combinatorial, combinatory **NF** (= *analyse)* combinatorial analysis, combinatorics *(sg)*

combine * /kɔ̃bin/ **NF** (= *astuce)* trick *(pour faire* to do); ◆ **la ~** *(péj* = *manigance)* scheming ◆ **il est dans la ~** he knows (all) about it, he's in on it * ◆ **entrer dans la ~** to play the game ◆ **ça sent la ~** I smell a rat, it sounds a bit fishy * ◆ **toutes leurs ~s** all their little schemes

combiné /kɔ̃bine/ **NM** *(Chim)* compound; *[de téléphone]* receiver, handset ◆ **~ (gaine-soutien-gorge)** corselette ◆ **~ (batteur-mixeur)** mixer and liquidizer *ou* blender ◆ **~ (avion-hélicoptère)** convertible helicopter, convertiplane ◆ **~ alpin/nordique** *(Ski)* alpine/nordic combination ◆ **il est 3e au ~** *(Ski)* he's 3rd overall

combiner /kɔ̃bine/ ▸ conjug 1 ◂ **VT** 1 (= *grouper) [+ éléments, sons, chiffres]* to combine *(à, avec* with); ◆ **opération combinée** joint *ou* combined operation ◆ **l'oxygène et l'hydrogène combinés** oxygen and hydrogen combined ◆ **l'inquiétude et la fatigue combinées** a combination of anxiety and tiredness 2 (= *élaborer) [+ mauvais coup, plan]* to devise, to think up; *[+ horaire, emploi du temps]* to devise, to plan ◆ **c'est eux qui ont combiné l'affaire** they thought the whole thing up ◆ **bien combiné** well thought out **VPR se combiner** *[éléments]* to combine *(avec* with)

combinette /kɔ̃binɛt/ **NF** slip

comble /kɔ̃bl/ **ADJ** *[pièce, autobus]* packed (full), jam-packed *; → **mesure, salle**

NM 1 (= *degré extrême)* height ◆ **c'est le ~ du ridicule !** that's the height of absurdity! ◆ **au ~ de la joie** overjoyed ◆ **au ~ du désespoir** in the depths of despair ◆ **être (porté) à son ~** *[joie, colère]* to be at its peak *ou* height ◆ **ceci mit le ~ à sa fureur** this brought his anger to its climax *ou* a peak

2 *(locutions)* **c'est le ~ !, c'est un ~ !** that's the last straw!, that takes the biscuit! * *(Brit) ou* cake! * *(US)* ◆ **le ~, c'est qu'il est parti sans payer** and to cap it all * he left without paying ◆ **pour ~ (de malheur) il ...** to cap *ou* crown *(Brit)* it all he ...

3 (= *charpente)* roof trussing *(SPÉC)*, roof timbers ◆ **les ~s** the attic, the loft ◆ **loger (dans une chambre) sous les ~s** to live in a garret *ou* an attic ◆ **faux ~, ~ perdu** inconvertible (part of the) attic; → **fond**

combler /kɔ̃ble/ ▸ conjug 1 ◂ **VT** 1 (= *boucher) [+ trou, fente]* to fill in ◆ **ça comblera un trou dans nos finances** that'll fill a gap in our finances 2 (= *résorber) [+ déficit]* to make good, to make up; *[+ lacune, vide]* to fill ◆ **~ son retard** to make up lost time 3 (= *satisfaire) [+ désir, espoir]* to fulfil; *[+ besoin]* to fulfil, to fill; *[+ personne]* to gratify ◆ **parents comblés par la naissance d'un enfant** parents overjoyed at the birth of a child ◆ **c'est une femme comblée** she has all that she could wish for 4 (= *couvrir)* **~ qn de** *[+ cadeaux, honneurs]* to shower sb with ◆ **il mourut comblé d'honneurs** he died laden with honours ◆ **vous me comblez d'aise** *ou* **de joie** you fill me with joy ◆ **vraiment, vous nous comblez !** really, you're too good to us!

combo /kɔ̃bo/ **NM** *(Mus)* combo

comburant, e /kɔ̃byʀɑ̃, ɑt/ **ADJ** combustive **NM** oxidizer, oxidant

combustibilité /kɔ̃bystibilite/ NF combustibility

combustible /kɔ̃bystibl/ ADJ combustible NM fuel ◆ **les ~s** fuels, kinds of fuel ◆ **~ fossile/irradié/nucléaire** fossil/spent/nuclear fuel ◆ **~ organique** biofuel, organic fuel

combustion /kɔ̃bystjɔ̃/ NF combustion ◆ **poêle à ~ lente** slow-burning stove

come-back /kɔmbak/ NM INV comeback ◆ **faire son ~** to make a comeback

COMECON /kɔmekɔn/ NM (abrév de **Council for Mutual Economic Assistance**) COMECON

comédie /kɔmedi/ NF 1 *(Théât)* comedy ◆ **jouer la ~** to act ◆ **~ de mœurs/d'intrigue** comedy of manners/of intrigue ◆ **~ de caractères** character comedy ◆ **~ de situation** situation comedy ◆ **~ dramatique** *(Théât, Ciné)* drama ◆ **de ~** *[personnage, situation] (Théât)* comedy *(épith)*; *(fig)* comical ◆ **cours de ~** acting course 2 *(fig = simulation)* playacting ◆ **c'est de la ~** it's all an act, it's all a sham ◆ **jouer la ~** to put on an act, to put it on * 3 (* *= caprice, histoires)* palaver, fuss ◆ **faire la ~** to make a fuss ou a scene ◆ **allons, pas de ~** come on, no nonsense ou fuss ◆ **c'est toujours la même ~** it's always the same palaver

COMP **comédie de boulevard** light comedy
comédie musicale musical

Comédie-Française /kɔmedifʀɑ̃sɛz/ NF ◆ **la ~** the Comédie-Française *(the French National Theatre)*

> **COMÉDIE-FRANÇAISE**
>
> This historic theatre company, also known as le « Théâtre-Français » or just « le Français », is particularly famous for its association with Molière. It was founded in 1680. It has a mainly classical repertoire, though contemporary plays are also staged. Members of the company belong to a traditional hierarchy of « sociétaires » and « pensionnaires ». The theatre itself, known as « la salle Richelieu », is part of the « Palais-Royal ».

comédien, -ienne /kɔmedjɛ̃, jɛn/ NM actor; *(= comique)* comedy actor, comedian NM,F 1 *(= hypocrite)* sham ◆ **quel ~ tu fais !** you're always putting it on! * 2 *(= pitre)* show-off NF **comédienne** *(= actrice)* actress; *(= comique)* comedy actress, comedienne

> ⚠ **comédien** se traduit par **comedian** uniquement au sens de 'acteur comique'.

comédogène /kɔmedɔʒɛn/ ADJ blackhead-forming, comedogenic *(SPEC)*

comédon /kɔmedɔ̃/ NM blackhead, comedo *(SPÉC)*

comestible /kɔmɛstibl/ ADJ edible NMPL **comestibles** (fine) foods, delicatessen ◆ **magasin de ~s** ≃ delicatessen

comète /kɔmɛt/ NF *(Astron)* comet; → **plan¹**

cométique /kɔmetik/ NM *(Can)* Eskimo sled, komatik *(US, Can)*

comice /kɔmis/ NM ◆ **~(s) agricole(s)** † agricultural show ou meeting NF **Comice pear**

coming-out* /kɔmiŋaut/ NM ◆ **faire son ~** *[homosexuel]* to come out

comique /kɔmik/ ADJ *(Théât) [acteur, film, genre]* comic; *(fig) [incident, personnage]* comical NM 1 *[de tenue, aspect physique]* comic look ou appearance ◆ **le ~ de la situation** the funny side of the situation ◆ **d'un ~ irrésistible** hilariously ou irresistibly funny ◆ **le ~ de la chose, c'est que ...** the funny ou amusing thing about it is that ... 2 *(Littérat)* **le ~** comedy ◆ **~ de caractère/de situation** character/situation comedy ◆ **~ de répétition** comedy of repetition ◆ **le ~ de boulevard** light comedy ◆ **~ troupier** coarse comedy ◆ **avoir le sens du ~** to have a sense of the comic NM,F *(= artiste)* comic; *(= dramaturge)* comedy writer ◆ **t'es un petit ~ toi !** *(iro)* quite a little joker, aren't you?

comiquement /kɔmikmɑ̃/ ADV comically

comité /kɔmite/ NM *(gén)* committee; *(permanent, élu)* board, committee ◆ **~ consultatif/exécutif/restreint** advisory/executive/select committee ◆ **~ de défense/soutien** protection/support committee ◆ **se réunir en petit ~** *(gén)* to meet in a select group; *(petite réception)* to have a small get-together

COMP **comité central** central committee
comité directeur ou **de direction** management committee
Comité économique et social *French regional commission on economic and social affairs*
comité d'entreprise workers' ou works council
comité des fêtes ≃ recreation committee
comité de gestion board of management
comité interministériel interministerial committee
Comité international de la Croix-Rouge International Committee of the Red Cross
Comité international olympique International Olympic Committee
comité de lecture reading panel ou committee
comité de liaison liaison committee
comité monétaire (européen) (European) monetary committee
Comité national de la consommation ≃ National Consumer Council *(Brit)*, Consumers' Association *(Brit)*, Consumer Product Safety Council *(US)*
Comité national d'éthique *national research ethics committee in France*
comité de pilotage steering committee

> **COMITÉ D'ENTREPRISE**
>
> All French companies with more than fifty employees must have a **comité d'entreprise**, whose members are elected by the staff and whose budget is a mandatory percentage of the wage bill. The « CE » liaises with management on issues relating to staff welfare, salaries etc, and participates in discussions concerning the general running of the company. In practice, its main function is to arrange company-subsidized benefits for the staff such as canteen lunches, cutprice cinema tickets, holidays and even Christmas presents for employees' children.

commandant /kɔmɑ̃dɑ̃/ NM *[d'armée de terre]* major; *[d'armée de l'air]* squadron leader *(Brit)*, major *(US)*; *(Aviat, Naut)* captain; *(gén : dans toute fonction de commandement)* commander, commandant ◆ **"oui mon commandant"** "yes Sir" ◆ **~ suprême** supreme commander

COMP **commandant de bord** *[d'avion]* captain
commandant en chef commander-in-chief
commandant en second second in command

commandante /kɔmɑ̃dɑ̃t/ NF major's *(ou captain's etc)* wife

commande /kɔmɑ̃d/ GRAMMAIRE ACTIVE 47.2, 47.3, 47.4 NF 1 *(Comm)* order ◆ **passer (une) ~** to put in ou place an order *(de* for); ◆ **prendre la ~** to take the order ◆ **on vous livrera vos ~s jeudi** your order will be delivered to you on Thursday ◆ **payable à la ~** cash with order ◆ **cet article est en ~** the item is on order ◆ **carnet/bulletin de ~s** order book/form ◆ **les ~s publiques** state ou government orders

2 *(Littérat, Art)* commission ◆ **passer une ~ à qn** to commission sb

3 *[d'appareil]* control *(NonC)* ◆ **les ~s** *(= dispositif)* the controls ◆ **~ à distance** remote control ◆ **~ numérique** numerical ou digital control ◆ **à ~ vocale** voice-activated ◆ **à ~ par effleurement** touch-controlled ◆ **véhicule à double ~** dual control vehicle, vehicle with dual controls ◆ **se mettre aux ~s, prendre les ~s** *(lit)* to take control, to take (over) the controls; *(fig)* to take control ◆ **passer les ~s à qn** *(lit, fig)* to hand over control ou the controls to sb ◆ **être aux ~s, tenir les ~s** *(lit)* to be in control, to be at the controls; *(fig)* to be in control; → **poste², tableau**

4 *(locutions)*

◆ **sur commande** ◆ **fait sur ~** made to order ◆ **travailler sur ~** to work to commission ◆ **ouvrage écrit/composé sur ~** commissioned work/composition ◆ **agir sur ~** to act on orders ◆ **je ne peux pas pleurer/m'amuser sur ~** I can't cry/enjoy myself to order

◆ **de commande** *[sourire]* forced, affected; *[optimisme]* fake ◆ **film/livre de ~** commissioned film/book ◆ **câble de ~** control cable ◆ **les organes** ou **leviers de ~** the controls

commandement /kɔmɑ̃dmɑ̃/ NM 1 *(= direction) [d'armée, navire]* command ◆ **avoir/prendre le ~ de** to be in ou have/take command of ◆ **sur un ton de ~** in a commanding tone ◆ **avoir l'habitude du ~** to be used to being in command; → **poste²** 2 *(= état-major)* command ◆ **le ~ a décidé que ...** it has been decided at higher command that ...; → **haut** 3 *(Rel)* commandment 4 *(= ordre)* command ◆ **à mon ~, marche !** *(Mil)* on my command, march! ◆ **avoir ~ de faire qch** † to have orders to do sth 5 *(Jur)* **~ d'huissier** court order to pay

commander /kɔmɑ̃de/ GRAMMAIRE ACTIVE 47.2
▸ conjug 1 ◂

VT 1 *(= demander) [+ marchandise, repas]* to order; *[+ œuvre d'art]* to commission ◆ **avez-vous déjà commandé ?** *(au café)* have you ordered?, has somebody taken your order? ◆ **qu'as-tu commandé pour Noël ?** what have you asked for for Christmas? ◆ **nous avons commandé le soleil !** we've ordered some sunshine!

2 *(= diriger) [+ armée, navire, expédition, attaque]* to command; *(emploi absolu)* to be in command, to be in charge ◆ **~ le feu** to give the order to shoot ou to (open) fire ◆ **c'est lui qui commande ici** he's in charge here ◆ **je n'aime pas qu'on me commande** I don't like to be ordered about ou to be given orders ◆ **à la maison, c'est elle qui commande** she's the boss at home, she's the one who gives the orders at home

3 *(= contrôler)* to control ◆ **ce bouton commande la sirène** this switch controls the siren ◆ **forteresse qui commande l'entrée du détroit** fortress which commands the entrance to the straits

4 *(= ordonner) [+ obéissance, attaque]* to order, to command ◆ **~ à qn de faire qch** to order ou command sb to do sth ◆ **il me commanda le silence** he ordered ou commanded me to keep quiet ◆ **sans vous ~, pourriez-vous taper cette lettre ?** if it's no trouble, could you type this letter?

5 *(= imposer) [+ respect, admiration]* to command

6 *(= requérir) [événements, circonstances]* to demand ◆ **la prudence commande que ...** prudence demands that ...

VT INDIR **commander à** *[+ passions, instincts]* to have command ou control over ◆ **il ne commande plus à sa jambe gauche** he no longer has any control over his left leg ◆ **il ne sait pas se ~** he can't control himself

VPR **se commander** 1 *(au négatif)* **l'amitié ne se commande pas** you can't make friends to order ◆ **l'amour ne se commande pas** you don't choose who you love ◆ **je ne peux pas le sentir, ça ne se commande pas** I can't stand him – you can't help these things

2 *(= communiquer) [pièces]* to connect, to lead into one another

commanderie /kɔmɑ̃dʀi/ **NF** *(Hist)* *(= bénéfice)* commandership; *(= maison)* commander's residence

commandeur /kɔmɑ̃dœʀ/ **NM** commander *(of an Order)* ◆ **la statue du ~** *(Littérat)* the statue of the Commendatore

commanditaire /kɔmɑ̃ditɛʀ/ **NM** *(Comm)* limited *ou* sleeping *(Brit) ou* silent *(US)* partner; *[d'exposition]* sponsor ◆ **les ~s d'un meurtre** the people behind a murder

commandite /kɔmɑ̃dit/ **NF** *(Comm = fonds)* share *(of limited partner)* ◆ **(société en) ~** limited partnership

commandité, e /kɔmɑ̃dite/ **NM,F** active *ou* acting *ou* ordinary partner

commanditer /kɔmɑ̃dite/ ▸ conjug 1 ◂ **VT** *(Comm = financer)* to finance; *[+ exposition]* to sponsor; *[+ crime]* to be behind

commando /kɔmɑdo/ **NM** commando (group) ◆ **les membres du ~** the commando members, the commandos ◆ **~(-)suicide** suicide squad

comme /kɔm/

GRAMMAIRE ACTIVE 44.1

1 CONJONCTION
2 LOCUTION ADVERBIALE
3 ADVERBE

1 - CONJONCTION

1 temps as ◆ **elle entra (juste) ~ le rideau se levait** she came in (just) as the curtain was rising

2 cause as, since ◆ **~ il pleuvait, j'ai pris la voiture** as *ou* since it was raining I took the car ◆ **~ il est lâche, il n'a pas osé parler** being a coward *ou* coward that he is, he didn't dare speak out

♦ **comme quoi**
(= disant que) to the effect that ◆ **j'ai reçu une lettre ~ quoi j'étais licencié** I got a letter to the effect that *ou* telling me I was fired
(= d'où il s'ensuit que) which goes to show that ◆ **~ quoi tout le monde peut se tromper** which (just) goes to show that anybody can make a mistake ◆ **~ quoi !** it just goes to show!

3 comparaison as, like *(devant n et pron)*; *(avec idée de manière)* as, the way* ◆ **elle a soigné son chien ~ elle aurait soigné un enfant** she nursed her dog as she would have done a child ◆ **il pense ~ nous** he thinks as we do *ou* like us ◆ **c'est un homme ~ lui qu'il nous faut** we need a man like him *ou* such as him ◆ **un homme ~ lui, on n'en fait plus** they don't make men like that any more ◆ **ce pantalon est pratique pour le travail ~ pour les loisirs** these trousers are practical for work as well as leisure ◆ **il s'ennuie en ville ~ à la campagne** he gets bored both in town and in the country, he gets bored in town as he does in the country ◆ **il écrit ~ il parle** he writes as *ou* the way he speaks ◆ **c'est une excuse ~ une autre** it's as good an excuse as any ◆ **c'est un client ~ un autre** he's just another customer ◆ **c'est une façon ~ une autre de résoudre les problèmes** that's one way of solving problems ◆ **il voudrait une moto ~ celle de son frère/la mienne** he would like a motorbike like his brother's/mine ◆ **il voudrait une moto, ~ son frère** he would like a motorbike (just) like his brother ◆ **le héros du film n'agit pas ~ dans la pièce** the hero in the film does not act as he does *ou* the way he does in the play ◆ **si, ~ nous le pensons, il a oublié** if he has forgotten, as we think he has ◆ **faites ~ vous voulez** do as you like ◆ **choisissez ~ pour vous** choose as you would for yourself, choose as if it were for yourself ◆ **~ pour faire** as if to do ◆ **il fit un geste ~ pour la frapper** he made as if to hit her *ou* as if he was going to hit her ◆ **il y a ~ un problème** there's a bit of a problem; → **dire, hasard, juste, plaire, tout** *etc*

♦ **comme ça** *ou* **cela** *(= ainsi)* like that ◆ **il est ~ ça, tu ne le changeras pas** that's the way he is, you won't change him ◆ **vous aimeriez une robe ~ ça ?** would you like a dress like that? ◆ **des choses ~ ça** things like that, that sort of thing ◆ **il a pêché un saumon ~ ça !** he caught a salmon (that was) this big!
(* : *admiratif*) great!*, fantastic!*, terrific!* ◆ **on a vu un film ~ ça !** we saw a great* *ou* fantastic* *ou* terrific* film!

2 - LOCUTION ADVERBIALE

1 intensif **alors, ~ ça, vous nous quittez ?** *(intensif)* so you're leaving us just like that? ◆ **le docteur m'a dit ~ ça*, prenez des calmants** the doctor just told me to take some tranquillizers

2 = de cette manière **je l'ai enfermé, ~ ça il ne peut pas nous suivre** I locked him in – that way he can't follow us ◆ **c'est ~ ça et pas autrement** *ou* **un point c'est tout** that's just the way it is, that's all there is to it ◆ **c'est ~ ça que je m'y prendrais** that's how I'd do it ◆ **puisque** *ou* **si c'est ~ ça, je m'en vais !** if that's how *ou* the way it is, I'm leaving!

♦ **comme ci comme ça** so-so*, fair to middling ◆ **comment ça va ? – ~ ci ~ ça** how are you? – so-so* *ou* fair to middling

♦ **comme il faut** († *ou hum = convenablement)* properly ◆ **mange/tiens-toi ~ il faut** eat/sit up properly; *(= convenable)* ◆ **une dame très ~ il faut** a fine upstanding woman

♦ **comme les autres** *(= ordinaire)* ◆ **c'est un jour/métier ~ les autres** it's just like any other day/job ◆ **il n'est pas ~ les autres** he's not like everybody else, he's different ◆ **un roman/une grève pas ~ les autres** a different kind of novel/strike ◆ **faire ~ les autres** to do as everybody else does *ou* like everybody else

♦ **comme si** as if, as though ◆ **il se conduit ~ si de rien n'était** he behaves as if *ou* as though nothing had happened ◆ **~ si nous ne savions pas !** as if we didn't know! ◆ **ce n'est pas ~ si on ne l'avait pas prévenu !** it's not as if *ou* as though he hadn't been warned! ◆ **tu n'es pas gai mais tu peux faire ~ si*** you're not happy but you can pretend (to be)

♦ *adjectif* + **comme tout** ◆ **elle est gentille ~ tout** she's so nice, she's as nice as can be ◆ **c'est facile ~ tout** it's as easy as can be ◆ **c'était amusant ~ tout** it was so *ou* terribly funny ◆ **il est menteur ~ tout** he's such a liar, he's a terrible *ou* dreadful liar

♦ **comme tout le monde** like everybody else ◆ **il a applaudi pour faire ~ tout le monde** he clapped to be like everybody else ◆ **je veux vivre ~ tout le monde** I want to lead a normal life

3 = en tant que as ◆ **nous l'avons eu ~ président** we had him as (our) president ◆ **~ étudiant, il est assez médiocre** as a student, he is rather poor

4 = tel que like, such as ◆ **les fleurs ~ la rose et l'iris sont fragiles** flowers such as *ou* like roses and irises are fragile ◆ **bête ~ il est ...** stupid as he is ... ◆ **elle n'a jamais vu de maison ~ la nôtre** she's never seen a house like ours *ou* such as ours

5
♦ **comme** + *adjectif ou participe* as though, as if ◆ **il était ~ fasciné par ces oiseaux** it was as though *ou* as if he were fascinated by these birds, he was as though *ou* as if fascinated by these birds ◆ **il était ~ fou** he was behaving like a madman ◆ **il était ~ perdu dans cette foule** it was as though *ou* as if he were lost in this crowd ◆ **~ se parlant à lui-même** as if *ou* as though talking to himself

3 - ADVERBE

how ◆ **~ ces enfants sont bruyants !** how noisy those children are!, those children are so noisy! ◆ **~ il fait beau !** what a lovely day (it is)!, what lovely weather! ◆ **tu sais ~ elle est** you know what she's like *ou* how she is ◆ **écoute ~ elle chante bien** listen (to) how beautifully she sings ◆ **~ vous y allez, vous !*** (now) hold on a minute!*, don't get carried away!; → **voir**

commémoratif, -ive /kɔmemɔʀatif, iv/ **ADJ** *[cérémonie, plaque]* commemorative *(épith)*, memorial *(épith)*; *[service]* memorial *(épith)* ◆ **discours ~** commemorative address ◆ **monument ~** memorial

commémoration /kɔmemɔʀasjɔ̃/ **NF** commemoration ◆ **en ~ de** in commemoration of

commémorer /kɔmemɔʀe/ ▸ conjug 1 ◂ **VT** to commemorate

commençant, e /kɔmɑ̃sɑ̃, ɑt/ **ADJ** beginning *(épith)* **NM,F** *(= débutant)* beginner ◆ **grand ~** absolute beginner

commencement /kɔmɑ̃smɑ̃/ **NM** 1 *(= début)* beginning, commencement *(frm)*; *(= départ)* start ◆ **il y a eu un ~ d'incendie** a small fire broke out ◆ **~ d'exécution** *(Jur) initial steps in the commission of a crime* ◆ **~ de preuve** *(Jur)* prima facie evidence ◆ **au/dès le ~** in/from the beginning, at/from the outset *ou* start ◆ **du ~ à la fin** from beginning to end, from start to finish ◆ **c'est le ~ de la fin** it's the beginning of the end ◆ **il y a un ~ à tout** you've (always) got to start somewhere 2 ◆ **~s** *[de science, métier]* *(= premiers temps)* beginnings; *(= rudiments)* basic knowledge ◆ **les ~s ont été durs** the beginning was hard

commencer /kɔmɑ̃se/ ▸ conjug 3 ◂ **VT** 1 *(= entreprendre) [+ travail, opération, repas]* to begin, to start, to commence *(frm)* ◆ **ils ont commencé les travaux de l'autoroute** they've started *ou* begun work on the motorway ◆ **j'ai commencé un nouveau chapitre** I've started *ou* begun (on) a new chapter ◆ **je vais ~ le judo/le violon** I'm going to take up judo/the violin ◆ **quelle façon de ~ l'année !** what a way to begin *ou* start the (new) year!

2 *(= entamer) [+ bouteille, produit]* to open

3 *[chose]* to begin ◆ **mot/phrase qui commence un chapitre** word/sentence which begins a chapter, opening word/sentence of a chapter ◆ **une heure de méditation commence la journée** the day begins *ou* starts with an hour of meditation

VI 1 *(= débuter)* to begin, to start, to commence *(frm)* ◆ **le concert va ~** the concert is about to begin *ou* start *ou* commence *(frm)* ◆ **tu ne vas pas ~ !*, ne commence pas !*** don't start!* ◆ **ça commence bien !** *(lit ou iro)* that's a good start!, we're off to a good start! ◆ **ça commence mal !** that's a bad start!, that's not a very good start! ◆ **pour ~** *(lit)* to begin *ou* start with; *(fig)* to begin *ou* start with, for a start ◆ **elle commence demain chez Legrand** she starts (work) tomorrow at Legrand's ◆ **c'est lui qui a commencé !** he started it! ◆ **leurs jupes commencent à 15 €** they've got skirts from €15 upwards

2 ◆ **~ à** *(ou* **de***)* **faire** to begin *ou* start to do, to begin *ou* start doing ◆ **il commençait à neiger** it was beginning *ou* starting to snow ◆ **il commençait à s'inquiéter/à s'impatienter** he was getting *ou* beginning to get nervous/impatient ◆ **je commence à en avoir assez*** I've had just about enough (of it) ◆ **ça commence à bien faire*** it's getting a bit much*

3 ◆ ~ **par qch/par faire qch** to start *ou* begin with sth/by doing sth ◆ **par quoi voulez-vous ~ ?** what would you like to begin *ou* start with? ◆ **commençons par le commencement** let's begin at the beginning ◆ **commence par faire tes devoirs, on verra après** do your homework for a start, and then we'll see ◆ **ils m'ont tous déçu, à ~ par Jean** they all let me down, especially Jean ◆ **il faut apporter du changement, à ~ par trouver de nouveaux locaux** we have to make some changes, and the first thing to do is to find new premises

commensal, e (mpl **-aux**) /kɔmɑ̃sal, o/ NM,F *(littér = personne)* companion at table, table companion; *(Bio)* commensal

commensurable /kɔmɑ̃syʀabl/ ADJ commensurable

comment /kɔmɑ̃/ ADV 1 *(= de quelle façon)* how ◆ **~ a-t-il fait ?** how did he do it?, how did he manage that? ◆ **je ne sais pas ~ il a fait cela** I don't know how he did it ◆ **~ s'appelle-t-il ?** what's his name?, what's he called? ◆ **~ appelles-tu cela ?** what do you call that? ◆ **~ allez-vous ?** *ou* **vas-tu ?** how are you? ◆ **~ est-il, ce type ?*** what sort of guy* is he?, what's he like? ◆ **~ va-t-il ?** how is he? ◆ **~ faire ?** how shall we do it? *ou* go about it? ◆ **~ se fait-il que ... ?** how is it that ...?, how come ...?* ◆ **~ se peut-il que ... ?** how can it be that ...?

2 *(excl)* **~ ?** (I beg your) pardon?, pardon me? (US), sorry?, what?* ◆ **~ ça ?** what do you mean? ◆ **~, il est mort ?** what? he's dead? ◆ **tu as assez mangé ? – et ~ !** have you had enough to eat? – I (most) certainly have! *ou* I should say so! *ou* and how!* ◆ **avez-vous bien travaillé ? – et ~ !** did you work well? – I should say so! *ou* not half!* *(Brit)* *ou* and how!* ◆ **~ donc !** by all means!, of course! ◆ **Dieu sait ~ !** goodness* *ou* God* knows how!

NM ◆ **le ~** the how ◆ **les ~(s)** the hows; → **pourquoi**

commentaire /kɔmɑ̃tɛʀ/ NM 1 *(= remarque)* comment ◆ **faire des ~s sur qch** to comment on *ou* about sth ◆ **quels ont été ses ~s sur ce qui s'est passé ?** what did he say about what happened? ◆ **~s de presse** press comments ◆ **je vous dispense de vos ~s** I can do without your comments *ou* remarks ◆ **tu feras comme je te l'ordonne, et pas de ~s !** you will do as I say and no arguments! ◆ **son attitude se passe de ~s** his attitude speaks for itself ◆ **vous avez entendu ce qu'il a dit ! – sans ~ !** did you hear him! – no comment! ◆ **sa conduite donne lieu à bien des ~s !** his behaviour has really set people talking!

2 *(= exposé)* commentary *(de* on); *(Radio, TV)* commentary ◆ **~s sportifs** sports commentary ◆ **un bref ~ de la séance** some brief comments on the meeting

3 *(Littérat = explication)* commentary ◆ **faire le ~ d'un texte** to do *ou* give a commentary on a text ◆ **édition avec ~(s)** annotated edition

4 *(Ordin, Ling)* comment

commentateur, -trice /kɔmɑ̃tatœʀ, tʀis/ NM,F *(gén, Radio, TV)* commentator

commenter /kɔmɑ̃te/ ► conjug 1 ◄ VT 1 *[+ texte, conduite, événement, actualité]* to comment on 2 *(Radio, TV)* *[+ match]* to commentate on; *[+ cérémonie officielle]* to provide the commentary for ◆ **le match sera commenté par André Leduc** André Leduc will be commentating on the match

commérage /kɔmeʀaʒ/ NM piece of gossip ◆ **~s** gossip (NonC), gossiping (NonC)

commerçant, e /kɔmɛʀsɑ̃, ɑ̃t/ ADJ 1 *[nation]* trading *(épith)*, commercial; *[quartier]* shopping *(épith)*; *[ville, activité]* commercial ◆ **rue très ~e** busy shopping street, street with many shops 2 *(= habile)* *[procédé]* commercially shrewd ◆ **il est très ~** he's got good business sense ◆ **ce n'est pas très ~** it's not a very good way to do business NM shopkeeper, tradesman, merchant (US), storekeeper (US) ◆ **~ en gros** wholesale dealer ◆ **les ~s du quartier** (the) local tradesmen *ou* shopkeepers *ou* merchants NF **commerçante** shopkeeper, storekeeper (US)

commerce /kɔmɛʀs/ NM 1 ◆ **le ~** *(= activité)* trade, commerce; *(= affaires)* business, trade ◆ **le ~ n'y est pas encore très développé** commerce *ou* trade isn't very highly developed there yet ◆ **depuis quelques mois le ~ ne marche pas très bien** business *ou* trade has been bad for a few months ◆ **opération/maison/traité de ~** commercial operation/firm/treaty ◆ **~ en** *ou* **de gros/détail** wholesale/retail trade ◆ **~ extérieur/international** foreign/international trade *ou* commerce ◆ **~ électronique** e-commerce ◆ **~ équitable** fair trade ◆ **faire du ~ (avec)** to trade (with) ◆ **être dans le ~** to be in trade ◆ **faire ~ de** † to trade in ◆ **faire ~ de ses charmes/son nom** to trade on one's charms/name; → **effet**

2 *(= circuit commercial)* **dans le ~** *[objet]* in the shops *ou* stores (US) ◆ **hors ~** for restricted sale only *(attrib)* ◆ **exemplaires hors ~** privately printed copies

3 *(= commerçants)* **le ~** shopkeepers, merchants (US) ◆ **le petit ~** small shopkeepers *ou* traders ◆ **le grand ~** large *ou* big retailers ◆ **le monde du ~** the commercial world, trading *ou* commercial circles

4 *(= boutique)* business ◆ **tenir** *ou* **avoir un ~ d'épicerie** to have a grocery business ◆ **un gros/petit ~** a big/small business; → **proximité**

5 († *ou littér)* *(= fréquentation)* (social) intercourse; *(= compagnie)* company; *(= rapport)* dealings ◆ **être d'un ~ agréable** to be pleasant company ◆ **avoir ~ avec qn** to have dealings with sb

commercer /kɔmɛʀse/ GRAMMAIRE ACTIVE 53.1, 53.2 ► conjug 3 ◄ VI to trade *(avec* with)

commercial, e (mpl **-iaux**) /kɔmɛʀsjal, jo/ ADJ *(gén)* commercial; *[activité, société, port]* commercial, trading *(épith)*; *[déficit, stratégie, guerre]* trade *(épith)* ◆ **accord ~** trade *ou* trading agreement ◆ **service ~** *[d'entreprise]* sales department ◆ **chaîne de télévision ~e** commercial television channel ◆ **anglais ~** business English ◆ **sourire ~** *(péj)* phoney professional smile NM marketing man; *(= représentant)* rep ◆ **l'un de nos commerciaux** one of our marketing people NF **commerciale** 1 *(= véhicule)* estate car (Brit), station wagon (US) 2 *(= femme)* marketing woman

commercialement /kɔmɛʀsjalmɑ̃/ ADV commercially

commercialisable /kɔmɛʀsjalizabl/ ADJ marketable

commercialisation /kɔmɛʀsjalizasjɔ̃/ NF marketing

commercialiser /kɔmɛʀsjalize/ ► conjug 1 ◄ VT to market

commère /kɔmɛʀ/ NF *(péj = bavarde)* gossip

commérer † /kɔmeʀe/ ► conjug 6 ◄ VI to gossip

commettant /kɔmetɑ̃/ NM *(Jur, Fin)* principal

commettre /kɔmɛtʀ/ ► conjug 56 ◄ VT 1 *(= perpétrer)* *[+ crime, injustice]* to commit; *[+ erreur]* to make ◆ **il a commis 2 ou 3 romans** *(hum)* he's responsible for 2 or 3 novels *(hum)*; → **faute** 2 *(littér = confier)* **~ qch à qn** to commit sth to sb, to entrust sth to sb 3 *(frm = nommer)* *[+ arbitre]* to appoint, to nominate ◆ **~ qn à une charge** to appoint *ou* nominate sb to an office ◆ **avocat commis d'office** lawyer *ou* barrister (Brit) appointed by the court VPR **se commettre** *(péj, frm)* to endanger one's reputation, to lower o.s. ◆ **se ~ avec des gens peu recommandables** to associate with rather undesirable people

comminatoire /kɔminatwaʀ/ ADJ *[ton, lettre]* threatening; *(Jur)* appointing a penalty for non-compliance

commis /kɔmi/ NM *(= vendeur)* (shop *ou* store (US)) assistant; *(= employé de bureau)* office clerk ◆ **~ aux écritures** book-keeper ◆ **~-greffier** assistant to the clerk of the court ◆ **~ de cuisine/de salle** apprentice chef/waiter ◆ **~ aux vivres** *(Naut)* ship's steward ◆ **~ voyageur** commercial traveller, travelling salesman ◆ **un grand ~ (de l'État)** a top-ranking *ou* senior civil servant

commisération /kɔmizeʀasjɔ̃/ NF commiseration

commissaire /kɔmisɛʀ/ NM 1 ◆ **~ (de police)** ≃ (police) superintendent (Brit), (police) captain (US) ◆ **~ principal, ~ divisionnaire** ≃ chief superintendent (Brit), police chief (US) ◆ **~ de police judiciaire** detective superintendent (Brit), (police) captain (US)

2 *(= responsable)* *[de rencontre sportive, fête]* steward; *[d'exposition]* organizer ◆ **~ de courses** *[de course automobile]* marshal

3 *(= envoyé)* representative

4 *[de commission]* commission member, commissioner

COMP **commissaire de l'Air** chief administrator *(in Air Force)*
commissaire du bord purser
commissaire aux comptes auditor
commissaire européen European Commissioner
commissaire du gouvernement government commissioner
Commissaire aux langues officielles *(Can)* Commissioner of Official Languages *(Can)*
commissaire de la Marine chief administrator *(in the Navy)*
commissaire au Plan planning commissioner
commissaire politique political commissioner
commissaire de la République ≃ prefect

commissaire-priseur (pl **commissaires-priseurs**) /kɔmisɛʀpʀizœʀ/ NM auctioneer

commissariat /kɔmisaʀja/ NM 1 *(= poste)* **~ (de police)** police station ◆ **~ central** police headquarters 2 *(Admin = fonction)* commissionership ◆ **~ du bord** pursership ◆ **~ aux comptes** auditorship 3 *(= commission)* commission ◆ **Commissariat à l'énergie atomique** Atomic Energy Commission ◆ **Commissariat général du Plan** State Planning Commission 4 *(= corps)* **~ de la Marine** ≃ Admiralty Board (Brit), Naval Command (US) 5 *(= service)* **~ hôtelier** catering service *(for rail companies and airlines)*

commission /kɔmisjɔ̃/ NF 1 *(= comité restreint)* committee; *(= bureau nommé)* commission ◆ **la ~ du budget** *ou* **budgétaire** *(Pol)* the Budget committee ◆ **les membres sont en ~** the members are in committee ◆ **travail en ~** work in committee ◆ **renvoi d'un texte en ~** *(Pol)* committal of a bill

2 *(= message)* message ◆ **est-ce qu'on vous a fait la ~ ?** did you get *ou* were you given the message?

3 *(= course)* errand ◆ **faire des ~s** to run errands *(pour* for); ◆ **on l'a chargé d'une ~** he was sent on an errand

4 *(= emplettes)* **~s** shopping ◆ **faire les/des ~s** to do the/some shopping ◆ **partir en ~s** to go shopping ◆ **l'argent des ~s** the shopping money

5 *(langage enfantin)* **faire la petite/grosse ~** to do number one/two *(langage enfantin)*

6 *(= pourcentage)* commission ◆ **toucher 10% de ~** *ou* **une ~ de 10%** to get 10% commission *(sur* on); ◆ **travailler à la ~** to work on commission

7 (*Comm, Jur = mandat*) commission ◆ **avoir la ~ de faire** to be empowered *ou* commissioned to do ◆ **~ d'office** court appointment of a barrister (*Brit*) *ou* counselor (*US*)

COMP **commission d'arbitrage** arbitration committee
commission d'armistice armistice council
commission bancaire national banking commission, banking watchdog
Commission de développement économique régional *French commission for regional economic development*
commission d'enquête committee *ou* commission of inquiry
Commission européenne European Commission
commission d'examen board of examiners
commission exécutive executive commission
commission des finances finance committee
commission interparlementaire ≃ joint (parliamentary) committee
commission des lois law commission
commission militaire army exemption tribunal
Commission nationale de l'informatique et des libertés *French data protection watchdog*
Commission des opérations de Bourse *French stock exchange regulatory body,* ≃ Securities and Investment Board (*Brit*), Securities and Exchange Commission (*US*)
commission paritaire joint commission (with equal representation of both sides)
commission parlementaire parliamentary commission *ou* committee
commission permanente standing committee, permanent commission
commission rogatoire letters rogatory
commission temporaire ad hoc committee

commissionnaire /kɔmisjɔnɛʀ/ NM 1 (*= livreur*) delivery boy; (*adulte*) delivery man; (*= messager*) messenger boy; (*adulte*) messenger; (*= chasseur*) page (boy); (*adulte*) commissionaire 2 (*= intermédiaire*) agent, broker ◆ **~ en douane** customs agent *ou* broker ◆ **~ de transport** forwarding agent ◆ **~ de roulage** carrier, haulage contractor (*Brit*), haulier (*Brit*)

commissionner /kɔmisjɔne/ ▸ conjug 1 ◂ VT (*Comm, Jur = mandater*) to commission

commissure /kɔmisyʀ/ NF (*Anat, Bot*) commissure ◆ **la ~ des lèvres** the corner of the mouth

commode /kɔmɔd/ ADJ 1 (*= pratique*) [*appartement, meuble*] convenient; [*outil*] handy (*pour* for; *pour faire* for doing); [*itinéraire*] handy, convenient ◆ **ce pinceau n'est pas très ~ pour les coins** this brush isn't very practical for doing corners 2 (*= facile*) easy ◆ **ce n'est pas ~** it's not easy (*à faire* to do); ◆ **ce serait trop ~ !** that would be too easy! 3 († *= souple*) [*morale, caractère*] easy-going ◆ **~ à vivre** easy to get along with *ou* get on (*Brit*) with ◆ **il n'est pas ~** (*= sévère*) he's so strict; (*= difficile*) he's really awkward *ou* difficult NF (*= meuble*) chest of drawers

commodément /kɔmɔdemɑ̃/ ADV [*porter*] conveniently; [*s'asseoir, vivre*] comfortably

commodité /kɔmɔdite/ NF 1 (*= confort*) convenience ◆ **pour plus de ~** for greater convenience ◆ **les ~s de la vie moderne** the conveniences *ou* comforts of modern life 2 (*= facilité*) **~ d'accès** ease of access 3 **~s** (†† *= toilettes*) toilet

commotion /komosjɔ̃/ NF (*= secousse*) shock ◆ **~ cérébrale** concussion ◆ **les grandes ~s sociales** the great social upheavals

commotionner /komosjɔne/ ▸ conjug 1 ◂ VT [*secousse, nouvelle*] ◆ **~ qn** to give sb a shock, to shake sb ◆ **être fortement commotionné par qch** to be badly *ou* severely shocked *ou* shaken by sth

commuable /kɔmɥabl/ ADJ [*peine*] commutable

commuer /kɔmɥe/ ▸ conjug 1 ◂ VT [*+ peine*] to commute (*en* to)

commun, e[1] /kɔmœ̃, yn/ GRAMMAIRE ACTIVE 32.5

ADJ 1 (*= collectif, de tous*) common; (*= fait ensemble*) [*décision, effort, réunion*] joint (*épith*) ◆ **pour le bien ~** for the common good ◆ **dans l'intérêt ~** in the common interest ◆ **ils ont une langue ~e qui est l'anglais** they have English as a common language ◆ **d'un ~ accord** of a common accord, of one accord; → **sens**

◆ **en commun** in common ◆ **faire la cuisine/les achats en ~** to share (in) the cooking/the shopping ◆ **vivre en ~** to live communally ◆ **faire une démarche en ~** to take joint steps ◆ **mettre ses ressources en ~** to share *ou* pool one's resources ◆ **tout mettre en ~** to share everything ◆ **lui et moi avons en ~ une passion pour les chevaux** he and I share a love of horses ◆ **ces plantes ont en ~ de pousser sur les hauteurs** a feature that these plants have in common is that they grow at high altitudes

2 (*= partagé*) [*élément*] common; [*pièce, cuisine*] communal, shared; [*dénominateur, facteur, angle*] common (*à* to); ◆ **ces deux maisons ont un jardin ~** the two houses share the same garden ◆ **le jardin est ~ aux deux maisons** the garden is shared by the two houses ◆ **les parties ~es de l'immeuble** the communal parts of the building ◆ **tout est ~ entre eux** they share everything ◆ **un ami ~** a mutual friend ◆ **la vie ~e** [*de couple*] conjugal life, life together; [*de communauté*] communal life ◆ **ils ont beaucoup de points ~s** they have a lot in common

3 (*= comparable*) [*goût, intérêt, caractère*] common (*épith*) ◆ **ils n'ont rien de ~** they have nothing in common ◆ **ce métal n'a rien de ~ avec l'argent** this metal has nothing in common with *ou* is nothing like silver ◆ **il n'y a pas de ~e mesure entre eux** there's no possible comparison between them; → **nom**

4 (*= ordinaire*) [*accident, erreur*] common; [*opinion*] commonly held, widespread; [*métal*] common ◆ **peu ~** out of the ordinary, uncommon ◆ **d'une force peu ~e** unusually *ou* uncommonly strong ◆ **il est ~ de voir ...** it is quite common *ou* quite a common thing to see ...; → **lieu**[1]

5 (*péj = vulgaire*) [*manières, voix, personne*] common

NM (*= le peuple*) ◆ **le ~ des mortels** ordinary mortals, the common run of people ◆ **le ~, les gens du ~** † (*péj*) the common people *ou* herd

◆ **hors du commun** [*personne, destin*] extraordinary

NMPL **les communs** (*= bâtiments*) the outbuildings, the outhouses

communal, e (mpl **-aux**) /kɔmynal, o/ ADJ [*dépenses*] council (*épith*) (*Brit*), community (*épith*) (*US*); [*fête, aménagements*] local (*épith*) ◆ **l'école ~e, la ~e*** (*= bâtiment*) the local (primary) school, the local grade *ou* elementary school (*US*); (*= éducation*) state education ◆ **les (terrains) communaux** common land ◆ **la maison ~e** (*Belg*) the Town Hall

communard, e /kɔmynaʀ, aʀd/ ADJ (*Hist*) of the Commune NM,F (*Hist*) communard; (*péj = communiste*) red (*péj*), commie* (*péj*)

communautaire /kɔmynotɛʀ/ ADJ community (*épith*); (*Pol*) [*droit, politique*] Community (*épith*) ◆ **le repli ~** communitarism

communautariser /kɔmynotaʀize/ ▸ conjug 1 ◂ VT [*+ politique*] to Europeanize

communautarisme /kɔmynotaʀism/ NM communitarianism

communautariste /kɔmynotaʀist/ ADJ [*modèle, politique*] communitarian

communauté /kɔmynote/ NF 1 (*= similitude*) [*d'intérêts, culture*] community ◆ **~ d'idées/de sentiments** shared ideas/feelings ◆ **~ de langue** common *ou* shared language

2 (*gén, Rel = groupe*) community ◆ **la ~ internationale/scientifique** the international/scientific community ◆ **~ urbaine** urban community ◆ **~ linguistique** speech community ◆ **vivre en ~** to live in a commune ◆ **mettre qch en ~** to pool sth

3 (*Jur : entre époux*) **biens qui appartiennent à la ~** joint estate (*of husband and wife*) ◆ **mariés sous le régime de la ~ (des biens)** married with a communal estate settlement ◆ **~ légale** communal estate ◆ **~ réduite aux acquêts** communal estate comprising only property acquired after marriage

4 (*Pol*) **la Communauté économique européenne** the European Economic Community ◆ **la Communauté européenne de l'énergie atomique** the European Atomic Energy Community ◆ **les pays de la Communauté** the members of the Community ◆ **la Communauté des États indépendants** the Commonwealth of Independent States

commune[2] /kɔmyn/ NF 1 (*= ville*) town; (*= village*) village; (*= administration*) town (*ou* village) council, municipality (*Admin*) ◆ **sur toute l'étendue de la ~** (*territoire*) throughout the entire district 2 (*Hist*) **la Commune** the Commune 3 (*Pol*) **la Chambre des ~s, les Communes** the (House of) Commons

COMMUNE

The **commune** is the smallest administrative subdivision in France. There are 38,000 **communes** in all, 90% of them having less than 2,000 inhabitants. Several small villages may make up a single **commune**. Each **commune** is administered by a « maire », who is elected by the « conseil municipal ». The inhabitants of the **commune** vote for the « conseil municipal » in the « élections municipales ». → **ARRONDISSEMENT, CANTON, DÉPARTEMENT, ÉLECTIONS, MAIRE**

communément /kɔmynemɑ̃/ ADV commonly

communiant, e /kɔmynjɑ̃, jɑ̃t/ NM,F (*Rel*) communicant ◆ **(premier) ~** young boy making his first communion ◆ **me voici en première ~e** this is me in my communion dress

communicable /kɔmynikabl/ ADJ [*expérience, sentiment*] which can be communicated; [*droit*] transferable; [*dossier*] which may be made available ◆ **ces renseignements ne sont pas ~s par téléphone** this information cannot be given over the telephone

communicant, e /kɔmynikɑ̃, ɑt/ ADJ 1 [*pièces*] communicating (*épith*); → **vase**[1] 2 [*entreprise*] that communicates effectively NM,F (*= communicateur*) communicator; (*dans un colloque*) speaker (*person giving a paper*)

communicateur, -trice /kɔmynikatœʀ, tʀis/ ADJ [*fil, pièce*] connecting (*épith*) NM,F communicator

communicatif, -ive /kɔmynikatif, iv/ ADJ [*rire, ennui*] infectious; [*personne*] communicative

communication /kɔmynikasjɔ̃/ GRAMMAIRE ACTIVE 54.3, 54.6, 54.7 NF 1 (*gén, Philos = relation*) communication ◆ **il a des problèmes de ~** he has trouble *ou* problems communicating ◆ **être en ~ avec** [*+ ami, société savante*] to be in communication *ou* contact with; [*+ esprit*] to communicate *ou* be in communication with ◆ **entrer en ~ avec** [*+ esprit, extraterrestre*] to communicate with; [*+ personne*] to get in touch *ou* contact with ◆ **mettre qn en ~ avec qn** to put sb in touch *ou* in contact with sb

[2] *(= transmission) [de fait, nouvelle]* communication; *[de dossier]* transmission ◆ **avoir ~ d'un fait** to be informed of a fact ◆ **demander ~ d'un dossier** to ask for a file ◆ **donner ~ d'une pièce** to communicate a document *(à qn* to sb); ◆ **~ interne** *(en entreprise)* internal communications

[3] *(= message)* message, communication; *(à une conférence)* paper ◆ **j'ai une ~ importante à vous faire** I have an important announcement to make ◆ **faire une ~** *[conférencier]* to read *ou* give a paper

[4] *(Téléc)* **~ (téléphonique)** (telephone *ou* phone) call ◆ **être en ~** to be on the (tele)phone *(avec qn* to sb); ◆ **entrer en ~ avec qn** to get through to sb (on the phone) ◆ **mettre qn en ~** to put sb through *(avec* to) to connect sb *(avec* with); ◆ **~ interurbaine** inter-city call, trunk call *(Brit)* ◆ **~ à longue distance** long-distance call ◆ **~ en PCV** reverse charge call *(Brit)*, collect call *(US)* ◆ **~ avec préavis** personal call *(Brit)*, person-to-person call *(US)* ◆ **vous avez la ~** you're through, I'm connecting you now ◆ **je n'ai pas pu avoir la ~** I couldn't get through

[5] *(= moyen de liaison)* communication ◆ **les grands axes de ~** the major communication routes ◆ **porte de ~** communicating door ◆ **moyens de ~** means of communication ◆ **toutes les ~s ont été coupées** all communications *ou* all lines of communication were cut off; → **voie**

[6] *(= relations publiques)* **la ~** public relations ◆ **conseil(ler) en ~** media *ou* communications consultant ◆ **action** *ou* **opération de ~** public relations exercise ◆ **agence/groupe de ~** communications firm/group ◆ **campagne de ~** publicity campaign *ou* drive ◆ **groupe de ~** communications group ◆ **le service de ~** the PR department ◆ **un homme de ~** a communicator

communier /kɔmynje/ ▸ conjug 7 ◂ VI *(Rel)* to receive communion ◆ **~ sous les deux espèces** to receive communion under both kinds ◆ **~ dans** *[+ sentiment]* to be united in ◆ **~ avec** *[+ sentiment]* to share

communion /kɔmynjɔ̃/ NF *(Rel, fig)* communion ◆ **faire sa (première) ~** *ou* **sa ~ privée** to make one's first communion ◆ **~ solennelle** † solemn communion ◆ **être en ~ avec** *[+ personne]* to be in communion with; *[+ sentiments]* to be in sympathy with ◆ **il vit en ~ avec la nature** he is at one with nature ◆ **être en ~ d'esprit avec qn** to be of the same intellectual outlook as sb ◆ **la ~ des saints** the communion of the saints

communiqué /kɔmynike/ NM communiqué ◆ **~ de presse** press release ◆ **selon un ~ officiel, …** according to an official communiqué, …

communiquer /kɔmynike/ ▸ conjug 1 ◂ VT [1] *[+ nouvelle, renseignement, demande]* to pass on *(à* to); *[+ dossier, document] (= donner)* to give *(à* to); *(= envoyer)* to send *(à* to); ◆ **~ un fait à qn** to inform sb of a fact ◆ **se ~ des renseignements** to exchange information

[2] *[+ enthousiasme, peur]* to communicate, to pass on *(à* to); *(Méd) [+ maladie]* to pass on, to give *(à qn* to sb)

[3] *[+ mouvement]* to communicate, to transmit, to impart *(à* to); *[+ lumière, chaleur]* to transmit *(à* to)

VI [1] *(= correspondre)* to communicate *(avec* with); ◆ **~ avec qn par lettre/téléphone** to communicate with sb by letter/phone ◆ **il communique bien** he's a good *ou* an effective communicator

[2] *[pièces, salles]* to communicate *(avec* with); ◆ **pièces qui communiquent** connecting rooms, rooms which communicate with one another ◆ **couloir qui fait ~ les chambres** corridor that links *ou* connects the rooms

VPR **se communiquer** *[feu, maladie]* **se ~ à** to spread to ◆ **son rire s'est communiqué aux autres** his laughter set the others off

communisant, e /kɔmynizɑ̃, ɑt/ ADJ communistic NM,F communist sympathizer

communisme /kɔmynism/ NM communism

communiste /kɔmynist/ ADJ, NMF communist

> **COMMUNISTE**
>
> The Communist Party has played a far more influential role in French politics than in most other democracies. Evidence of the French Communist Party's importance can be seen in the « banlieues rouges » (Paris suburbs with communist mayors), in the party's annual festival (la « fête de l'Humanité ») which continues to draw huge crowds, and in its newspaper, « L'Humanité », which still has a wide circulation.

commutable /kɔmytabl/ ADJ ⇒ **commuable**

commutateur /kɔmytatœʀ/ NM *(Élec)* (changeover) switch, commutator; *(Téléc)* commutation switch; *(= bouton)* (light) switch

commutatif, -ive /kɔmytatif, iv/ ADJ *(Jur, Ling, Math)* commutative

commutation /kɔmytasjɔ̃/ NF *(Jur, Math)* commutation; *(Ling)* substitution, commutation; *(Élec)* commutation, switching ◆ **~ de peine** commutation of sentence *ou* penalty ◆ **~ des messages** *(Ordin)* message switching

commutativité /kɔmytativite/ NF *[d'élément]* commutative property, commutability; *[d'addition]* commutative nature

commuter /kɔmyte/ ▸ conjug 1 ◂ VT *(Math) [+ éléments]* to commute; *(Ling) [+ termes]* to substitute, to commute

Comores /kɔmɔʀ/ NFPL ◆ **les (îles) ~** the Comoro Islands, the Comoros

comorien, -ienne /kɔmɔʀjɛ̃, jɛn/ ADJ of *ou* from the Comoros NM,F **Comorien(ne)** inhabitant *ou* native of the Comoros

compacité /kɔ̃pasite/ NF *[de foule]* density; *[de véhicule, appareil]* compactness

compact, e /kɔ̃pakt/ ADJ *(= dense) [foule, substance]* dense; *[brouillard]* dense, thick; *[quartier]* closely *ou* densely built-up; *(= de faible encombrement) [véhicule, appareil, meuble]* compact; *[poudre]* pressed ◆ **disque ~, Compact Disc** ® compact disc; → **chaîne** NM [1] *(= chaîne hi-fi)* compact music system; *(= disque)* compact disc, CD ◆ **réédition en ~** CD re-release [2] *[de poudre]* powder compact [3] *(= appareil photo)* compact camera NF **compacte** *(= voiture)* compact car

compactage /kɔ̃paktaʒ/ NM *[de sol, ordures]* compaction; *(Ordin)* compressing

compacter /kɔ̃pakte/ ▸ conjug 1 ◂ VT *(gén)* to compact; *[+ données]* to compress

compagne /kɔ̃paɲ/ NF *(= camarade)* friend; († *= épouse)* companion; *(= concubine)* partner; *[d'animal]* mate ◆ **~ de classe** classmate ◆ **~ de jeu** playmate

compagnie /kɔ̃paɲi/ NF [1] *(= présence, société)* company ◆ **il n'a pour toute ~ que sa vieille maman** he has only his old mother for company ◆ **ce n'est pas une ~ pour lui** he *(ou* she) is no company for him ◆ **en ~ de** *[+ personne]* in the company of, in company with; *[+ chose]* alongside, along with ◆ **il n'est heureux qu'en ~ de ses livres** he's only happy when (he's) surrounded by his books ◆ **en bonne/mauvaise/joyeuse ~** in good/bad/cheerful company ◆ **tenir ~ à qn** to keep sb company ◆ **être d'une ~ agréable** *ou* **de bonne ~** to be pleasant *ou* good company ◆ **voyager de ~** to travel together ◆ **aller de ~ avec** to go hand in hand with; → **fausser**

[2] *(= réunion)* gathering, party ◆ **bonsoir la ~ !** goodnight all!

[3] *(= entreprise)* company; *(= groupe de savants, écrivains)* body ◆ **~ d'assurances/théâtrale** insurance/theatrical company ◆ **~ aérienne/maritime** airline/shipping company ◆ **~ de chemin de fer** rail company ◆ **la banque X et ~** the X and company bank, the bank of X and company ◆ **tout ça, c'est voleurs et ~** * they're all a bunch * of thieves

[4] *(Mil)* company

COMP **compagnie de discipline** punishment company *(made up of convicted soldiers)*

la Compagnie des Indes *(Hist)* the East India Company

la Compagnie de Jésus the Society of Jesus

compagnie de perdreaux covey of partridges

compagnies républicaines de sécurité *state security police force in France*

compagnon /kɔ̃paɲɔ̃/ NM [1] *(= camarade, littér = époux)* companion; *(= concubin)* partner; *(= écuyer)* companion ◆ **~ d'études** fellow student ◆ **~ de travail** workmate ◆ **~ d'exil/de misère/d'infortune** companion in exile/in suffering/in misfortune [2] *(= ouvrier)* journeyman ◆ **il a deux ~s** he has two employees *ou* two people working for him [3] *(= franc-maçon)* companion

COMP **compagnon d'armes** companion- *ou* comrade-in-arms

compagnon de bord shipmate

compagnon de jeu playmate

Compagnon de la Libération French Resistance fighter

compagnon de route *(lit, Pol)* fellow traveller

compagnon de table companion at table, table companion

compagnon du Tour de France, compagnon du voyage journeyman *(touring France after his apprenticeship)*

compagnon de voyage travelling companion, fellow traveller *(lit)*

compagnonnage /kɔ̃paɲɔnaʒ/ NM *(Hist)* = (trade) guilds

comparable /kɔ̃paʀabl/ GRAMMAIRE ACTIVE 32.3 ADJ *[grandeur, élément, situation]* comparable *(à* to; *avec* with); ◆ **je n'avais jamais rien vu de ~** I'd never seen anything like it ◆ **ce n'est pas ~** there's (just) no comparison

comparaison /kɔ̃paʀɛzɔ̃/ GRAMMAIRE ACTIVE 53.5 NF [1] *(gén)* comparison *(à* to; *avec* with); ◆ **mettre qch en ~ avec** to compare sth with ◆ **faire une ~ entre X et Y** to compare X and Y, to make a comparison between X and Y ◆ **vous n'avez qu'à faire la ~** you only need to compare them ◆ **et c'est mieux ? – aucune ~ !** is it better? – (there's) no comparison! ◆ **ça ne soutient** *ou* **ne souffre pas la ~** that doesn't bear *ou* stand comparison ◆ **nous ne disposons d'aucun élément de ~** we have no point of comparison ◆ **~ n'est pas raison** *(Prov)* comparisons are odious

[2] *(Gram)* comparison ◆ **adjectif/adverbe de ~** comparative adjective/adverb

[3] *(Littérat)* simile, comparison

[4] *(locutions)*

◆ **en comparaison (de)** in comparison (with)

◆ **par comparaison** by comparison *(avec, à* with)

◆ **sans comparaison** ◆ **il est sans ~ le meilleur** he is far and away the best ◆ **c'est sans ~ avec …** it cannot be compared with …

comparaître /kɔ̃paʀɛtʀ/ ▸ conjug 57 ◂ VI *(Jur)* to appear in court ◆ **~ devant un juge** to appear before a judge; → **citation, citer**

comparant, e /kɔ̃paʀɑ̃, ɑt/ NM,F *(Jur)* party *(appearing in court)*

comparatif, -ive /kɔ̃paʀatif, iv/ ADJ *[publicité, étude]* comparative ◆ **essai** ~ comparison test NM 1 *(Gram)* comparative ◆ **au** ~ in the comparative ◆ ~ **d'infériorité/de supériorité/d'égalité** comparative of lesser/greater/similar degree 2 *(= essai)* comparison test

comparatisme /kɔ̃paʀatism/ NM comparative studies, comparat(iv)ism

comparatiste /kɔ̃paʀatist/ ADJ, NMF comparatist

comparativement /kɔ̃paʀativmɑ̃/ ADV comparatively, by comparison ◆ ~ **à** in comparison to *ou* with, compared to *ou* with

comparé, e /kɔ̃paʀe/ GRAMMAIRE ACTIVE 32.1, 53.5 (ptp de **comparer**) ADJ *[étude, littérature]* comparative

comparer /kɔ̃paʀe/ GRAMMAIRE ACTIVE 32.1, 32.4, 32.5 ▸ conjug 1 ◂ VT 1 *(= confronter)* to compare *(à, avec* with); ◆ ~ **deux choses (entre elles)** to compare two things ◆ **vous n'avez qu'à** ~ you've only to compare ◆ **comparé à** compared to *ou* with 2 *(= identifier)* to compare, to liken *(à* to); ◆ **Molière peut se** ~ *ou* **être comparé à Shakespeare** Molière can be compared *ou* likened to Shakespeare ◆ **c'est un bon écrivain mais il ne peut quand même pas se** ~ **à X** he's a good writer but he still can't compare with X ◆ **il ose se** ~ **à Picasso** he dares to compare himself with Picasso ◆ **ça ne se compare pas** there's no comparison, they can't be compared

comparse /kɔ̃paʀs/ NMF *(Théât)* supernumerary, walk-on; *(péj)* associate, stooge* ◆ **rôle de** ~ *(Théât)* walk-on part; *(péj)* minor part ◆ **nous n'avons là que les ~s, il nous faut le vrai chef** these are only the small fry, we want the real leader

compartiment /kɔ̃paʀtimɑ̃/ NM *(gén, Rail)* compartment; *[de damier]* square; *(Bourse)* section ◆ ~ **à bagages** luggage compartment ◆ ~ **à glace** freezer compartment ◆ **dans tous les ~s du jeu** in every area of the game

compartimentage /kɔ̃paʀtimɑ̃taʒ/ NM, **compartimentation** /kɔ̃paʀtimɑ̃tasjɔ̃/ NF *[d'armoire]* partitioning, compartmentation; *[d'administration, problème]* compartmentalization

compartimenter /kɔ̃paʀtimɑ̃te/ ▸ conjug 1 ◂ VT *[+ armoire]* to put compartments in; *[+ problème, administration]* to compartmentalize

comparution /kɔ̃paʀysjɔ̃/ NF *(Jur)* appearance in court ◆ **il sera jugé en** ~ **immédiate** he'll be tried immediately

compas /kɔ̃pɑ/ NM *(Géom)* (pair of) compasses; *(Naut)* compass ◆ **tracer qch au** ~ to draw sth with (a pair of) compasses ◆ **avoir le** ~ **dans l'œil** to have an accurate eye; → **naviguer**
COMP **compas à balustre** bow compass
compas d'épaisseur callipers *(Brit)*, calipers *(US)*
compas à pointes sèches dividers
compas quart de cercle wing compass
compas de réduction proportional dividers

compassé, e /kɔ̃pɑse/ ADJ *(= guindé)* formal, starchy

compassion /kɔ̃pɑsjɔ̃/ NF compassion ◆ **avec** ~ compassionately

compatibilité /kɔ̃patibilite/ NF compatibility *(entre* between); ◆ ~ **ascendante/descendante** *(Ordin)* upward/downward compatibility

compatible /kɔ̃patibl/ ADJ compatible *(avec* with); ◆ **difficilement/parfaitement** ~**s** hardly/perfectly *ou* fully compatible NM *(Ordin)* compatible (computer)

compatir /kɔ̃patiʀ/ ▸ conjug 2 ◂ VI to sympathize ◆ ~ **à la douleur de qn** to share sb's grief

compatissant, e /kɔ̃patisɑ̃, ɑ̃t/ ADJ compassionate, sympathetic

compatriote /kɔ̃patʀijɔt/ NM compatriot, fellow countryman NF compatriot, fellow countrywoman

compensable /kɔ̃pɑ̃sabl/ ADJ 1 *[perte]* that can be compensated for *(par* by) 2 *[chèque]* ~ **à Paris** to be cleared in Paris

compensateur, -trice /kɔ̃pɑ̃satœʀ, tʀis/ ADJ *[indemnité, élément, mouvement]* compensatory, compensating *(épith)* ◆ **repos** ~ time off in lieu NM compensator ◆ **(pendule)** ~ compensation pendulum

compensation /kɔ̃pɑ̃sasjɔ̃/ NF 1 *(= dédommagement)* compensation ◆ **donner qch en** ~ **d'autre chose** to give sth in compensation for sth else, to make up for sth with sth else ◆ **en** ~ **(des dégâts), à titre de** ~ **(pour les dégâts)** in compensation *ou* by way of compensation (for the damage) ◆ **c'est une piètre** *ou* **maigre** ~ **de le savoir** it's not much (of a) compensation to know that ◆ **il y en a peu mais en** ~ **c'est bon** there's not much of it but on the other hand *ou* but to make up for that it's good ◆ **avec une** ~ **salariale intégrale** pay fully made up to previous level ◆ **sans** ~ **salariale** without pay being made up to previous level
2 *(= équilibre)* balance; *(= neutralisation)* balancing; *(Phys) [de forces]* compensation; *[de maladie, infirmité]* compensation; *(Naut) [de compas]* correction; *(Psych)* compensation; *[de dette]* set-off *(Brit)*, offsetting; *[de chèques]* clearing ◆ **loi de** ~ *(Math)* law of large numbers ◆ ~ **des dépens** *(Jur)* division *ou* sharing of the costs; → **chambre**

compensatoire /kɔ̃pɑ̃satwaʀ/ ADJ compensatory, compensating ◆ **droits** ~**s** *(Fin)* countervailing duties; → **montant**

compensé, e /kɔ̃pɑ̃se/ (ptp de **compenser**) ADJ *[gouvernail]* balanced; *[horloge]* compensated ◆ **chaussures à semelles** ~**es** platform shoes, shoes with platform soles

compenser /kɔ̃pɑ̃se/ ▸ conjug 1 ◂ VT *[+ perte, dégâts, baisse, effets négatifs]* to compensate for, to make up for, to offset; *[+ absence, handicap]* to make up for, to compensate for; *(Naut) [+ compas]* to correct ◆ **ceci devrait vous permettre de** ~ **le retard accumulé** this should allow you to make up for lost time ◆ **cette perte a été largement compensée par les gains ultérieurs** this loss was largely offset by later gains ◆ **pour** ~ to compensate, to make up for it ◆ ~ **les dépens** *(Jur)* to divide *ou* share the costs, to tax each party for its own costs
VPR **se compenser** ◆ **ses qualités et ses défauts se compensent** his qualities compensate for *ou* make up for his faults ◆ **les gains et les pertes se compensent** the gains and losses cancel each other out ◆ **forces qui se compensent** *(Phys)* compensating forces; → **ceci**

⚠ Attention à ne pas traduire automatiquement **compenser** par **to compensate**, qui est d'un registre plus soutenu.

compère /kɔ̃pɛʀ/ NM 1 *(gén = complice)* accomplice; *(aux enchères)* puffer 2 † *(= ami)* crony*, comrade; *(= personne, type)* fellow

compère-loriot (pl **compères-loriots**) /kɔ̃pɛʀlɔʀjo/ NM 1 *(= orgelet)* sty(e) 2 *(= oiseau)* golden oriole

compète * /kɔ̃pɛt/ NF ⇒ **compétition**

compétence /kɔ̃petɑ̃s/ NF 1 *(= expérience)* competence *(en* in); ◆ **faire qch avec** ~ to do sth competently ◆ **avoir des** ~**s** to be competent ◆ **faire appel à la** ~ *ou* **aux** ~**s d'un spécialiste** to call (up)on the skills of a specialist ◆ **savoir utiliser les** ~**s** to know how to put people's skills *ou* abilities to the best use 2 *(= personne)* specialist, expert 3 *(= rayon d'activité)* scope of activities, domain; *(Jur)* competence ◆ ~ **territoriale** *(Jur)* jurisdiction ◆ **c'est de la** ~ **de ce tribunal** it's within the competence of this court ◆ **champ de** ~ area of competence ◆ **ce n'est pas de ma** ~**, cela n'entre pas dans mes** ~**s** that's not (in) my sphere *ou* domain

compétent, e /kɔ̃petɑ̃, ɑ̃t/ ADJ 1 *(= capable)* competent, capable ◆ ~ **en** competent in ◆ **très** ~ **en législation du travail** very well-versed in *ou* conversant with labour legislation ◆ **je ne suis pas** ~ **pour vous répondre** I'm not qualified to answer ◆ **elle est tout à fait** ~**e en la matière** she's well qualified to deal with this 2 *(= concerné) [service]* relevant, concerned *(attrib)*; *(Jur)* competent ◆ **adressez-vous à l'autorité** ~**e** apply to the authority concerned ◆ **être** ~ **pour faire qch** *[tribunal]* to have the jurisdiction to do sth

compétiteur, -trice /kɔ̃petitœʀ, tʀis/ NM,F competitor

compétitif, -ive /kɔ̃petitif, iv/ ADJ competitive

compétition /kɔ̃petisjɔ̃/ NF 1 *(Sport = activité)* **la** ~ competitive sport ◆ **faire de la** ~ to go in for competitive sports ◆ **la** ~ **automobile** motor racing ◆ **abandonner la** ~ to retire from competitive sport, to stop going in for competitions ◆ **sport de** ~ competitive sport 2 *(Sport = épreuve)* event ◆ ~ **sportive** sporting event ◆ **une** ~ **automobile** a motor-racing event ◆ **film présenté hors** ~ film presented out of competition 3 *(= rivalité)* competition *(NonC)* ◆ **entrer en** ~ **avec** to compete with ◆ **être en** ~ to be competing, to be in competition *(avec* with)

compétitivité /kɔ̃petitivite/ NF competitiveness

compil * /kɔ̃pil/ NF abrév de **compilation**

compilateur, -trice /kɔ̃pilatœʀ, tʀis/ NM,F *(souvent péj)* compiler NM *(Ordin)* compiler ◆ ~ **croisé** cross compiler

compilation /kɔ̃pilasjɔ̃/ NF 1 *(= action)* compiling, compilation; *[de textes, chansons]* compilation; *(péj = plagiat)* plagiarism ◆ **une** ~ **des meilleures chansons de Brel** the best of Brel 2 *(Ordin) [de programme]* compilation

compiler /kɔ̃pile/ ▸ conjug 1 ◂ VT 1 *[+ documents, chansons, ouvrage]* to compile 2 *(Ordin) [+ programme]* to compile

complainte /kɔ̃plɛ̃t/ NF *(Littérat, Mus)* lament

complaire /kɔ̃plɛʀ/ ▸ conjug 54 ◂ VT INDIR **complaire à** to (try to) please VPR **se complaire** ◆ **se** ~ **dans qch/à faire qch** to take pleasure in sth/in doing sth, to delight *ou* revel in sth/in doing sth

complaisamment /kɔ̃plɛzamɑ̃/ ADV *(avec obligeance)* obligingly, kindly; *(avec indulgence)* indulgently; *(avec fatuité)* complacently, smugly

complaisance /kɔ̃plɛzɑ̃s/ NF 1 *(= obligeance)* kindness *(envers* to, towards); *(= esprit accommodant)* accommodating attitude ◆ **il a eu la** ~ **de m'accompagner** *(frm)* he was kind *ou* good enough to accompany me ◆ **par** ~ out of kindness
2 *(= indulgence coupable)* indulgence, leniency; *(= connivence malhonnête)* connivance; *(= servilité)* servility, subservience; *[de conjoint trompé]* tacit consent ◆ **avoir des** ~**s pour qn** to treat sb indulgently ◆ **on a reproché à ce pays une certaine** ~ **à l'égard des terroristes** the country has been criticized for taking a soft line on terrorism ◆ **la commission d'enquête a fait son travail sans** ~ the commission of enquiry has done its job very thoroughly ◆ **sourire de** ~ polite smile ◆ **certificat** *ou* **attestation de** ~ medical *ou* doctor's certificate *(issued for non-genuine illness to oblige a patient)* ◆ **billet de** ~ *(Comm)* accommodation bill; → **pavillon**
3 *(= fatuité)* self-satisfaction, complacency ◆ **il parlait avec** ~ **de ses succès** he spoke smugly about his successes

complaisant, e /kɔ̃plɛzɑ̃, ɑ̃t/ ADJ 1 *(= obligeant)* kind, obliging; *(= arrangeant)* accommodating 2 *(= trop indulgent)* indulgent, lenient; *(= trop arrangeant)* over-obliging; *(= servile)* servile, subservient ◆ **c'est un mari ~** he turns a blind eye to his wife's goings-on ◆ **prêter une oreille ~e à qn/qch** to listen to sb/sth readily, to lend a willing ear to sb/sth 3 *(= fat)* smug, complacent

complément /kɔ̃plemɑ̃/ NM 1 *(gén, Bio, Math, Ordin)* complement; *(= reste)* rest, remainder ◆ **~ d'information** further *ou* additional information *(NonC)* ◆ **en ~ de** in addition to 2 *(Gram) (gén)* complement; *(= complément d'objet)* object ◆ **~ circonstanciel de lieu/de temps** adverbial phrase of place/time ◆ **~ (d'objet) direct/indirect** direct/indirect object ◆ **~ d'agent** agent ◆ **~ de nom** possessive phrase

complémentaire /kɔ̃plemɑ̃tɛʀ/ ADJ *(gén, Math)* complementary; *(= additionnel)* supplementary ◆ **nos caractères sont ~s** we complement each other ◆ **couleurs ~s** complementary colours ◆ **pour tout renseignement ~** for any further *ou* additional information; → **cours** NM 1 *(Math)* complement 2 *(Admin)* ◆ **~ santé** complementary health benefit

complémentarité /kɔ̃plemɑ̃taʀite/ NF complementarity, complementary nature

complet, -ète /kɔ̃plɛ, ɛt/ ADJ 1 *(= exhaustif, entier) (gén)* complete, full; *[rapport, analyse]* comprehensive, full ◆ **procéder à un examen ~ de qch** to make a full *ou* thorough examination of sth ◆ **il reste encore trois tours/jours ~s** there are still three complete *ou* full laps/three full *ou* whole days to go ◆ **pour vous donner une idée complète de la situation** to give you a fuller idea of the situation ◆ **les œuvres complètes de Voltaire** the complete works of Voltaire ◆ **le dossier est-il ~ ?** is the file complete? ◆ **une collection très complète** a very comprehensive *ou* full collection ◆ **la lecture complète de ce livre prend deux heures** it takes two hours to read this book right through *ou* from cover to cover; → **aliment, pension, riz**

2 *(= total) [échec, obscurité]* complete, total, utter; *[découragement]* complete, total ◆ **dans la misère la plus complète** in the most abject poverty ◆ **l'aviron est un sport très ~** rowing exercises your whole body ◆ **c'est ~ !*** that's all we needed!

3 *(après nom = consommé) [homme]* complete ◆ **c'est un athlète ~** he's an all-round athlete

4 *(= plein) [autobus, train]* full, full up *(attrib)* ◆ **"complet"** *(écriteau) [hôtel]* "no vacancies"; *[parking]* "full"; *[cinéma]* "sold out"; *[match]* "ground full" ◆ **le théâtre affiche ~ tous les soirs** the theatre has a full house every evening

NM *(= costume)* ◆ **~(-veston)** suit

LOC ADV **au (grand) complet** ◆ **maintenant que nous sommes au ~** now that we are all here ◆ **le groupe/bureau au grand ~** the whole *ou* entire group/office

complètement /kɔ̃plɛtmɑ̃/ ADV 1 *(= en entier) [démonter, nettoyer, repeindre]* completely; *[lire]* right through, from cover to cover; *[citer]* in full ◆ **~ nu** completely *ou* stark naked ◆ **~ trempé/terminé** completely soaked/finished ◆ **~ équipé** fully equipped ◆ **écouter ~ un CD** to listen to a CD right through, to listen to the whole of a CD 2 *(= absolument) [fou]* completely, absolutely; *[faux]* completely, absolutely, utterly; *[découragé]* completely, totally ◆ **je suis ~ d'accord avec vous** I totally agree with you 3 *(= à fond) [étudier, faire une enquête]* fully, thoroughly

compléter /kɔ̃plete/ ► conjug 6 ◄ VT 1 *(= terminer, porter au total voulu) [+ somme, effectifs]* to make up; *[+ mobilier, collection, dossier]* to complete ◆ **pour ~ votre travail/l'ensemble ...** to complete your work/the whole ... ◆ **il compléta ses études en suivant un cours d'informatique** he completed *ou* finished off his studies by taking a computing course ◆ **et pour ~ le tableau, il arriva en retard !** and to crown *ou* top it all, he arrived late! 2 *(= augmenter) [+ formation]* to complement, to supplement; *[+ connaissances, documentation, collection]* to supplement, to add to; *[+ mobilier, garde-robe]* to add to ◆ **sa collection se complète lentement** his collection is slowly building up VPR **se compléter** *[caractères, personnes, fonctions]* to complement one another

complétif, -ive /kɔ̃pletif, iv/ ADJ substantival NF **complétive** ◆ **(proposition) complétive** noun *ou* substantival clause

complétude /kɔ̃pletyd/ NF completeness

complexe /kɔ̃plɛks/ ADJ complex NM 1 *(Psych)* complex ◆ **~ d'Œdipe/d'infériorité/de supériorité** Oedipus/inferiority/superiority complex ◆ **faire des ~s, être bourré de ~s*** to have loads of hang-ups* ◆ **elle fait un ~ sur la taille de sa poitrine** she's got a complex about the size of her breasts ◆ **il est vraiment sans ~** *(hum)* he's got a nerve* ◆ **c'est une équipe de France sans ~ qui va jouer ce soir** the French team are in a very relaxed frame of mind for tonight's match 2 *(Écon : industriel, universitaire, touristique)* complex ◆ **~ routier** road network ◆ **~ hôtelier/sportif** hotel/sports complex 3 *(Chim, Math)* complex

complexer /kɔ̃plɛkse/ ► conjug 1 ◄ VT ◆ **ça le complexe terriblement** he's very hung-up* about it ◆ **être très complexé** to be very hung-up* *ou* mixed up* *(par* about)

complexification /kɔ̃plɛksifikasjɔ̃/ NF increasing complexity ◆ **cela entraîne une ~ des rapports sociaux** this makes social relationships more and more complex *ou* increasingly complex

complexifier /kɔ̃plɛksifje/ ► conjug 7 ◄ VT to make more complex, to complicate VPR **se complexifier** to become more complex *ou* complicated

complexion †† /kɔ̃plɛksjɔ̃/ NF *(= constitution)* constitution; *(= teint)* complexion; *(= humeur)* disposition, temperament

complexité /kɔ̃plɛksite/ NF complexity

complication /kɔ̃plikasjɔ̃/ NF *(= ennui)* complication; *(= complexité)* complexity ◆ **~s** *(Méd)* complications ◆ **faire des ~s** to make life difficult *ou* complicated

complice /kɔ̃plis/ ADJ 1 ◆ **être ~ de qch** to be (a) party to sth 2 *[regard, sourire]* knowing *(épith)*, of complicity *(attrib)*; *[attitude]* conniving ◆ **la nuit ~ protégeait leur fuite** *(littér)* the friendly night conspired to shelter their flight *(littér)* ◆ **on est très ~s** *[amis]* we're very close, we understand each other completely NMF 1 *(= criminel)* accomplice ◆ **être (le) ~ de qn** to be sb's accomplice, to be in collusion with sb ◆ **être ~ d'un meurtre** to be an accessory *ou* an accomplice to murder ◆ **~ par instigation/par assistance** accessory before/after the fact 2 *(dans un adultère) (Jur)* co-respondent; *(= amant)* lover; *(= maîtresse)* mistress 3 *(= compère) [de farce, projet]* partner ◆ **mon vieux ~** *(hum)* my old partner-in-crime *(hum)*

complicité /kɔ̃plisite/ NF 1 *(pour un crime, un forfait)* complicity ◆ **agir en ~ avec** to act in complicity *ou* collusion with ◆ **accusé de ~ de vol** accused of aiding and abetting a theft *ou* of being an accessory to theft 2 *(= bonne entente)* closeness, complicity ◆ **grâce à la ~ qui existe entre eux** because they're so close, because of the complicity between them

complies /kɔ̃pli/ NFPL compline

compliment /kɔ̃plimɑ̃/ NM 1 *(= louange)* compliment ◆ **elle rougit sous le ~** she blushed at the compliment ◆ **faire un ~ à qn** to pay sb a compliment ◆ **faire des ~s à qn sur sa bonne mine, faire ~ à qn de sa bonne mine** to compliment sb on how well they look ◆ **il lui fait sans cesse des ~s** he's always paying her compliments

2 *(= félicitations)* **~s** congratulations ◆ **recevoir les ~s de qn** to receive sb's congratulations, to be congratulated by sb ◆ **faire des ~s à qn** to congratulate sb *(pour* on); ◆ **(je vous fais) mes ~s !** *(lit ou iro)* congratulations!, well done!

3 *(= formule de politesse)* **~s** compliments ◆ **avec les ~s de la direction** with the compliments of the management ◆ **faites-lui mes ~s** give him my regards

4 *(= petit discours)* congratulatory speech

complimenter /kɔ̃plimɑ̃te/ ► conjug 1 ◄ VT 1 *(= louanger)* to compliment *(pour, sur, de* on) 2 *(= féliciter)* to congratulate *(pour, sur, de* on)

compliqué, e /kɔ̃plike/ (ptp de **compliquer**) ADJ 1 *(= complexe)* complicated ◆ **ne sois pas si ~ !** don't make life so difficult! ◆ **puisque tu refuses, ce n'est pas ~, moi je pars** since you refuse, that makes it easy *ou* that simplifies things– I'm leaving ◆ **il ne m'écoute jamais, c'est pas ~ !*** it's quite simple, he never listens to a word I say! ◆ **cette histoire est d'un ~ !** what a complicated story! 2 *[fracture]* compound *(épith)*

compliquer /kɔ̃plike/ ► conjug 1 ◄ VT to complicate ◆ **il nous complique l'existence** *ou* **la vie** he makes life difficult *ou* complicated for us ◆ **~ les choses** to complicate matters VPR **se compliquer** 1 *[situation, problème]* to become *ou* get complicated ◆ **ça se complique** things are getting more and more complicated 2 *[personne]* **se ~ l'existence** to make life difficult *ou* complicated for o.s.

complot /kɔ̃plo/ NM plot ◆ **~ contre la sûreté de l'État** plot to destabilize national security ◆ **mettre qn dans le ~*** to let sb in on the plot ◆ **c'est un véritable ~ contre moi !** it's a conspiracy!

comploter /kɔ̃plɔte/ ► conjug 1 ◄ VTI to plot *(de faire* to do; *contre* against); ◆ **qu'est-ce que vous complotez ?*** what are you up to?

comploteur, -euse /kɔ̃plɔtœʀ, øz/ NM,F plotter

componction /kɔ̃pɔ̃ksjɔ̃/ NF *(péj)* (affected) gravity; *(Rel)* contrition ◆ **avec ~** solemnly, with a great show of dignity

comportement /kɔ̃pɔʀtəmɑ̃/ NM behaviour *(Brit)*, behavior *(US)* *(envers, avec* towards); *[de matériel, pneus, monnaie]* performance ◆ **~ d'achat** buying patterns ◆ **~ alimentaire** eating habits ◆ **troubles du ~ alimentaire** eating disorder ◆ **~ politique** *(= habitudes de vote)* voting behaviour ◆ **~ sexuel** sexual behaviour

comportemental, e (mpl **-aux**) /kɔ̃pɔʀtəmɑ̃tal, o/ ADJ behavioural *(Brit)*, behavioral *(US)*

comportementalisme /kɔ̃pɔʀtəmɑ̃talism/ NM behaviourism *(Brit)*, behaviorism *(US)*

comportementaliste /kɔ̃pɔʀtəmɑ̃talist/ ADJ, NMF behaviourist *(Brit)*, behaviorist *(US)*

comporter /kɔ̃pɔʀte/ ► conjug 1 ◄ VT 1 *(= consister en)* to be composed of, to be made up of, to consist of, to comprise ◆ **ce roman comporte deux parties** this novel is in two parts ◆ **la maison comporte 5 pièces et une cuisine** the house comprises 5 rooms and a kitchen ◆ **l'exposition comporte 35 tableaux** the exhibition consists of 35 paintings

2 *(= être muni de)* to have, to include ◆ **son livre comporte une préface** his book has *ou* includes a preface ◆ **cette machine ne comporte aucun dispositif de sécurité** this machine has no safety mechanism ◆ **cette règle**

comporte des exceptions there are certain exceptions to this rule

3 *(= impliquer) [+ risques]* to entail, to involve ◆ **je dois accepter avec tout ce que cela comporte (de désavantages)** I must accept with all (the disadvantages) that it entails *ou* involves

VPR **se comporter** 1 *(= se conduire)* to behave ◆ **se ~ en** *ou* **comme un enfant gâté** to behave *ou* act like a spoilt child ◆ **il s'est comporté d'une façon odieuse** he behaved horribly *(avec* towards)

2 *(= réagir) [personne]* to behave; *[machine, voiture]* to perform ◆ **comment s'est-il comporté après l'accident ?** how did he behave after the accident? ◆ **notre équipe s'est très bien comportée** our team played *ou* acquitted itself very well, our team put up a good performance ◆ **comment le matériel s'est-il comporté en altitude ?** how did the equipment perform at high altitude? ◆ **ces pneus se comportent très bien sur chaussée glissante** these tyres perform very well on slippery roads ◆ **l'euro se comporte bien aujourd'hui** *(Bourse)* the euro is performing *ou* doing well today

composant, e /kɔ̃pozɑ̃, ɑ̃t/ ADJ, NM component, constituent ◆ **~s électroniques** electronic components NF **composante** *(gén, Phys)* component ◆ **les diverses ~es du parti** *(Pol)* the various elements in the party

composé, e /kɔ̃poze/ (ptp de **composer**) ADJ 1 *(Chim, Gram, Math, Mus)* compound *(épith)*; *(Bot) [fleur]* composite *(épith)*; *[feuille]* compound *(épith)*; *[bouquet, salade]* mixed; → **passé** 2 *(= guindé) [maintien, attitude]* studied NM *(Chim, Gram)* compound; *(fig)* combination, mixture NF **composée** *(Bot)* composite ◆ **~es** composites, Compositae *(SPÉC)*

composer /kɔ̃poze/ ▸ conjug 1 ◂ VT 1 *(= confectionner) [+ plat, médicament]* to make (up); *[+ équipe sportive]* to select, to put together; *[+ assemblée, équipe scientifique]* to form, to set up

2 *(= élaborer) [+ poème, lettre]* to write, to compose; *[+ musique]* to compose; *[+ tableau]* to paint; *[+ programme]* to work out, to draw up

3 *[+ numéro de téléphone]* to dial; *[+ code]* to enter

4 *(= disposer) [+ bouquet]* to arrange, to make up; *[+ vitrine]* to arrange, to lay out

5 *(= constituer) [+ ensemble, produit, groupe]* to make up; *[+ assemblée]* to form, to make up ◆ **pièces qui composent une machine** parts which (go to) make up a machine ◆ **ces objets composent un ensemble harmonieux** these objects form *ou* make a harmonious group ◆ **être composé de** to be composed of, to be made up of, to consist of ◆ **notre équipe est composée à 70% de femmes** our team is 70% women, 70% of our team are women ◆ **composé à 50% de papier recyclé** made of 50% recycled paper

6 *(Typo)* to set

7 *(frm = étudier artificiellement)* ~ **son visage** to compose one's features ◆ **~ ses gestes** to use affected gestures ◆ **il s'était composé un personnage de dandy** he had established his image as that of a dandy ◆ **se ~ un visage de circonstance** to assume a suitable expression

VI 1 *(Scol)* to do a test ◆ **~ en anglais** to take *ou* sit *(surtout Brit)* an English test

2 *(= traiter)* to compromise ◆ **~ avec** *[+ adversaire]* to come to terms with, to compromise with

VPR **se composer** *(= consister en)* ◆ **se ~ de**, **l'exposition se compose principalement de photographies** the exhibition consists mainly of photographs

composite /kɔ̃pozit/ ADJ 1 *(= hétérogène) [éléments, mobilier, matériau, groupe]* composite; *[public]* mixed; *[foule]* motley *(épith)* 2 *(Archit)* composite NM *(Archit)* composite order; *(= matériau)* composite

compositeur, -trice /kɔ̃pozitœʀ, tʀis/ NM,F *(Mus)* composer; *(Typo)* typesetter, compositor; → **amiable**

composition /kɔ̃pozisjɔ̃/ NF 1 *(= confection) [de plat, médicament]* making(-up); *[d'assemblée]* formation, setting-up; *[d'équipe sportive]* selection; *[d'équipe de chercheurs]* setting-up; *[de bouquet, vitrine]* arranging ◆ **les boissons qui entrent dans la ~ du cocktail** the drinks that go into the cocktail; → **rôle**

2 *(= élaboration) [de lettre, poème]* writing, composition; *[de symphonie]* composition; *[de tableau]* painting ◆ **une œuvre de ma ~** a work of my own composition

3 *(= œuvre) (musicale, picturale)* composition; *(architecturale)* structure ◆ **~ florale** flower arrangement

4 *(= structure) [de plan, ensemble]* structure ◆ **quelle est la ~ du passage ?** what is the structure of the passage? ◆ **la répartition des masses dans le tableau forme une ~ harmonieuse** the distribution of the masses in the picture makes for a harmonious composition

5 *(= constituants) [de mélange]* composition; *[d'équipe, assemblée]* composition, line-up ◆ **quelle est la ~ du gâteau ?** what is the cake made of?, what ingredients go into the cake? ◆ **la nouvelle ~ du Parlement européen** the new line-up in the European Parliament

6 *(Scol = examen)* test ◆ **~ de français** *(en classe)* French test *ou* exam; *(à l'examen)* French paper ◆ **~ française** *(= rédaction)* French essay *ou* composition

7 *(Typo)* typesetting, composition

8 *(locutions)* **venir à ~** to come to terms ◆ **amener qn à ~** to get sb to come to terms ◆ **être de bonne ~** to be good-natured

compost /kɔ̃pɔst/ NM compost

compostage /kɔ̃pɔstaʒ/ NM 1 *(pour mettre une date)* (date) stamping; *(= poinçonnage)* punching 2 *(Agr)* composting

composter /kɔ̃pɔste/ ▸ conjug 1 ◂ VT 1 *(= dater)* to (date) stamp; *(= poinçonner)* to punch ◆ **n'oubliez pas de ~ votre billet** don't forget to punch your ticket 2 *(Agr)* to compost

composteur /kɔ̃pɔstœʀ/ NM *(= timbre dateur)* date stamp; *(= poinçon)* ticket punching machine; *(Typo)* composing stick

compote /kɔ̃pɔt/ NF stewed fruit, compote ◆ **~ de pommes/de poires** stewed apples/pears, compote of apples/pears ◆ **j'ai les jambes en ~** * *(de fatigue)* my legs are killing me *; *(par l'émotion, la maladie)* my legs are like jelly *ou* cotton wool *(Brit)* ◆ **il a le visage en ~** * his face is black and blue *ou* is a mass of bruises

compotier /kɔ̃pɔtje/ NM fruit dish *ou* bowl

compréhensibilité /kɔ̃pʀeɑ̃sibilite/ NF *[de texte]* comprehensibility

compréhensible /kɔ̃pʀeɑ̃sibl/ ADJ *(= clair)* comprehensible, easily understood; *(= concevable)* understandable

compréhensif, -ive /kɔ̃pʀeɑ̃sif, iv/ ADJ 1 *(= tolérant)* understanding 2 *(Logique)* comprehensive

> ⚠ Au sens de 'tolérant', **compréhensif** ne se traduit pas par **comprehensive**, qui a le sens de 'complet'.

compréhension /kɔ̃pʀeɑ̃sjɔ̃/ NF 1 *(= indulgence)* understanding 2 *(= fait ou faculté de comprendre)* understanding, comprehension ◆ **pour faciliter la ~ du formulaire** to make it easier to understand the form ◆ **~ orale/écrite** *(Scol)* listening *ou* aural/reading comprehension ◆ **exercice de ~** comprehension exercise 3 *(= clarté)* understanding, intelligibility 4 *(Logique, Ling, Math)* comprehension

comprendre /kɔ̃pʀɑ̃dʀ/ GRAMMAIRE ACTIVE 53.1 ▸ conjug 58 ◂ VT 1 *[+ problème, langue]* to understand; *[+ plaisanterie]* to understand, to get *; *[+ personne] (ce qu'elle dit ou écrit)* to understand ◆ **je ne le comprends pas/je ne comprends pas ce qu'il dit, il parle trop vite** I can't understand him/I can't make out *ou* understand what he says, he speaks too quickly ◆ **vous m'avez mal compris** you've misunderstood me ◆ **il comprend mal ce qu'on lui dit** he doesn't understand what he is told ◆ **il ne comprend pas l'allemand** he doesn't understand German ◆ **~ la vie/les choses** to understand life/things ◆ **il ne comprend pas la plaisanterie** he can't take a joke ◆ **il ne comprend rien à rien** he hasn't a clue about anything, he doesn't understand a thing (about anything) ◆ **c'est à n'y rien ~** it's completely baffling, it's beyond me ◆ **tu n'as rien compris au film !** * you haven't got a clue ! * ◆ **dois-je ~ que ... ?** am I to take it *ou* understand that ...? ◆ **oui, enfin, je me comprends** well, I know what I mean ◆ **il comprend vite** he's quick, he catches on fast ◆ **tu comprends, ce que je veux c'est ...** you see, what I want is ... ◆ **il a bien su me faire ~ que je le gênais** he made it quite clear *ou* plain to me that I was annoying him

◆ **se faire comprendre** to make o.s. understood ◆ **il est difficile de bien se faire ~** it's difficult to get one's ideas across *(de qn* to sb); ◆ **j'espère que je me suis bien fait ~** I hope I've made myself quite clear

2 *(= être compréhensif envers) [+ personne]* to understand ◆ **j'espère qu'il comprendra** I hope he'll understand ◆ **~ les jeunes/les enfants** to understand young people/children ◆ **je le comprends, il en avait assez** I can understand him *ou* I know just how he felt – he'd had enough

3 *(= concevoir) [+ attitude, point de vue]* to understand ◆ **je comprends mal son attitude** I find it hard to understand his attitude ◆ **c'est comme ça que je comprends les vacances** that's what I think of as a holiday ◆ **c'est comme ça que je comprends le rôle de Hamlet** that's how I see *ou* understand the role of Hamlet ◆ **ça se comprend, il voulait partir** it's quite understandable *ou* it's perfectly natural, he wanted to go ◆ **nous comprenons vos difficultés mais nous ne pouvons rien faire** we understand *ou* appreciate your difficulties but there's nothing we can do

4 *(= se rendre compte de)* to realize, to understand *(pourquoi* why; *comment* how); ◆ **il n'a pas encore compris la gravité de son acte** he hasn't yet understood *ou* grasped the seriousness of what he did ◆ **j'ai compris ma douleur** * I realized what I'd let myself in for * ◆ **il m'a fait ~ que je devais faire attention** he made me realize that I should be careful ◆ **il a enfin compris qu'elle ne voulait pas revenir** he finally understood that she didn't want to come back

5 *(= être composé de)* to be composed of, to be made up of, to consist of, to comprise; *(= être muni de, inclure)* to include ◆ **ce manuel comprend 3 parties** this textbook is composed of *ou* is made up of *ou* comprises 3 parts ◆ **cet appareil comprend en outre un flash** this camera also has *ou* comes with a flash ◆ **le loyer ne comprend pas le chauffage** the rent doesn't include *ou* cover heating, the rent is not inclusive of heating ◆ **je n'ai pas compris là-dedans les frais de déménagement** I haven't included the removal expenses

comprenette * /kɔ̃pʀənɛt/ NF ◆ **il est dur** *ou* **lent à la ~, il a la ~ difficile** he's slow on the uptake *, he's slow to catch on *

compresse /kɔ̃pʀɛs/ NF compress

compresser /kɔ̃pʀese/ ▸ conjug 1 ◂ VT *(gén)* to squash; *[+ bois, gaz]* to compress; *[+ images, données, signaux]* to compress; *[+ coûts, dépenses]* to cut, to reduce ◆ **des vêtements compressés dans une valise** clothes squashed *ou* crammed into a suitcase

compresseur /kɔ̃pʀesœʀ/ **NM** compressor; → **rouleau**

compressibilité /kɔ̃pʀesibilite/ **NF** *(Phys)* compressibility ◆ **la ~ des dépenses** *(Fin)* the extent to which expenses can be reduced *ou* cut

compressible /kɔ̃pʀesibl/ **ADJ** *(Phys)* compressible; *[dépenses]* reducible ◆ **ces dépenses ne sont pas ~s à l'infini** these costs cannot be reduced *ou* cut down indefinitely ◆ **20 ans de prison non ~s** a 20 year jail sentence without remission

compressif, -ive /kɔ̃pʀesif, iv/ **ADJ** *[pansement]* compressive

compression /kɔ̃pʀesjɔ̃/ **NF** *[de gaz, substance, fichier, image]* compression; *[de dépenses, personnel]* reduction, cutback, cutting-down (*de* in) ◆ **~ numérique** digital compression ◆ **procéder à des ~s de crédits** to set up credit restrictions *ou* a credit squeeze ◆ **~s budgétaires** cutbacks in spending, budget restrictions *ou* cuts ◆ **~ des profits** squeeze on profits, reduction in profits ◆ **~ des coûts** cost-cutting *(NonC)* ◆ **des mesures de ~ sont nécessaires** restrictions *ou* cutbacks are needed ◆ **pompe de ~** compression pump ◆ **meurtri par ~** bruised by crushing ◆ **point de ~** *(Méd)* pressure point

comprimé /kɔ̃pʀime/ **NM** (= *pilule*) tablet ◆ **médicament en ~s** medicine in tablet form

comprimer /kɔ̃pʀime/ ► conjug 1 ◄ **VT** 1 (= *presser*) *[+ air, gaz, artère]* to compress; *[+ substance à emballer]* to press *ou* pack tightly together ◆ **sa ceinture lui comprimait l'estomac** his belt was pressing *ou* digging into his stomach ◆ **ces chaussures me compriment les pieds** these shoes pinch my feet ◆ **nous étions tous comprimés dans la voiture** we were all jammed together* *ou* packed tightly together in the car; → **air**[1] 2 (= *réduire*) *[+ dépenses, personnel]* to cut down *ou* back, to reduce; *[+ fichier]* to compress 3 (= *contenir*) *[+ larmes, colère, sentiments]* to hold back, to hold in check

compris, e /kɔ̃pʀi, iz/ (ptp de **comprendre**) **ADJ** 1 (= *inclus*) **10 € emballage ~** €10 inclusive of *ou* including packaging, €10 packaging included ◆ **10 € emballage non ~** €10 exclusive of *ou* excluding *ou* not including packaging ◆ **service ~** service included ◆ **service non ~** service not included, service extra ◆ **tout ~** all inclusive, everything included ◆ **c'est 20 € tout ~** it's €20 all inclusive *ou* all in* ◆ **il va vendre ses terres, la ferme comprise/non comprise** he's selling his land including/excluding the farm

2 ◆ **100 € y ~ l'électricité** *ou* **électricité ~e** €100 including electricity *ou* electricity included ◆ **y ~ moi** myself included, including me *ou* myself

3 (= *situé*) **être ~ entre** to be contained between *ou* by, to be bounded by ◆ **la zone ~e entre les falaises et la mer** the area (lying) between the cliffs and the sea, the area bounded by the cliffs and the sea ◆ **tous les chapitres qui sont ~ entre les pages 12 et 145** all the chapters (which are) contained *ou* included in pages 12 to 145

4 (= *d'accord*) **(c'est) ~ !** (it's) agreed! ◆ **alors c'est ~, on se voit demain** so it's agreed then, we'll see each other tomorrow ◆ **tu t'y mets tout de suite, ~ !** start right away, understand? *ou* is that understood?

compromettant, e /kɔ̃pʀɔmetɑ̃, ɑt/ **ADJ** compromising ◆ **signer cette pétition, ce n'est pas très ~** you won't commit yourself to very much by signing this petition, there's no great commitment involved in signing this petition ◆ **un homme ~** *(péj)* an undesirable associate

compromettre /kɔ̃pʀɔmɛtʀ/ ► conjug 56 ◄ **VT** *[+ personne, réputation]* to compromise; *[+ avenir, chances, santé]* to compromise, to jeopardize **VPR** **se compromettre** (= *s'avancer*) to commit o.s.; (= *se discréditer*) to compromise o.s. ◆ **se ~ dans une affaire louche** to get mixed up *ou* involved in a shady deal

compromis, e /kɔ̃pʀɔmi, iz/ (ptp de **compromettre**) **ADJ** ◆ **être ~** *[personne, réputation]* to be compromised; *[avenir, projet, chances]* to be jeopardized *ou* in jeopardy ◆ **notre sortie/collaboration me semble bien** *ou* **très ~e** our trip/continuing collaboration looks very doubtful to me ◆ **un ministre serait ~ dans cette affaire** a minister is alleged to be involved in the affair **NM** compromise ◆ **solution de ~** compromise solution ◆ **~ de vente** (provisional) sales agreement ◆ **trouver un ~ (entre)** to find *ou* reach a compromise (between)

compromission /kɔ̃pʀɔmisjɔ̃/ **NF** dishonest compromise ◆ **c'est là une ~ avec votre conscience** now you're compromising with your conscience

compta* /kɔ̃ta/ **NF** abrév de **comptabilité**

comptabilisation /kɔ̃tabilizasjɔ̃/ **NF** *(Fin)* posting

comptabiliser /kɔ̃tabilize/ ► conjug 1 ◄ **VT** (= *compter*) to count; *(Fin)* to post ◆ **tous les chômeurs ne sont pas comptabilisés dans les statistiques** not all the unemployed are included in the statistics

comptabilité /kɔ̃tabilite/ **NF** (= *science*) accountancy, accounting; *(d'une petite entreprise)* bookkeeping; (= *comptes*) accounts, books; (= *bureau, service*) accounts office *ou* department; (= *profession*) accountancy, accounting ◆ **il s'occupe de la ~ de notre entreprise** he does the accounting *ou* keeps the books for our firm ◆ **~ analytique** cost accounting ◆ **~ publique** public finance ◆ **~ à partie simple/double** single-/double-entry book-keeping

comptable /kɔ̃tabl/ **NMF** accountant ◆ **~ agréé** chartered accountant *(Brit)*, certified accountant *(Brit)*, certified public accountant *(US)* ◆ **~ du Trésor** local Treasury official ◆ **chèque adressé au ~ du Trésor** cheque addressed to the Treasury; → **chef**[1] **ADJ** 1 *(Fin) [+ règles etc]* accounting, book-keeping ◆ **il manque une pièce ~** one of the accounts is missing 2 **nom ~** *(Ling)* countable *ou* count noun 3 (= *responsable*) accountable (*de* for)

comptage /kɔ̃taʒ/ **NM** (= *action*) counting ◆ **faire un ~ rapide** to do a quick count (*de* of)

comptant /kɔ̃tɑ̃/ **ADV** *[payer]* cash, in cash; *[acheter, vendre]* for cash ◆ **verser 25 € ~** to pay €25 down, to put down €25 **NM** (= *argent*) cash ◆ **au ~** *[payer]* cash; *[acheter, vendre]* for cash ◆ **achat/vente au ~** cash purchase/sale; → **argent**

compte /kɔ̃t/

1 NOM MASCULIN 2 COMPOSÉS

1 - NOM MASCULIN

1 [= calcul] count ◆ **faire le ~ des visiteurs/erreurs** to count (up) the visitors/mistakes, to make a count of the visitors/mistakes ◆ **faire le ~ des dépenses/de sa fortune** to calculate *ou* work out the expenditure/one's wealth ◆ **comment as-tu fait ton ~ pour arriver si tard ?** *(fig)* how did you manage to arrive so late? ◆ **l'as-tu inclus dans le ~ ?** have you counted *ou* included him? ◆ **prendre qch en ~** to take sth into account ◆ **ils exigent la prise en ~ des préoccupations écologiques** they're demanding that ecological considerations be taken into account

◆ **à ce compte(-là)** (= *dans ce cas*) in that case; (= *à ce train-là*) at this *ou* that rate

◆ **tout compte fait, tous comptes faits** all things considered, when all's said and done

2 [= nombre exact] (right) number ◆ **le ~ y est** *(paiement)* that's the right amount; *(inventaire)* that's the right number, they're all there ◆ **ça ne fait pas le ~** *(paiement)* that's not enough *ou* the right amount; *(inventaire)* there's (still) something missing, they're not all there ◆ **j'ai ajouté 3 cuillerées/5 € pour faire le ~** I've added 3 spoonfuls/€5 to make up the full amount ◆ **ça devrait faire (largement) le ~** that should be (more than) enough ◆ **avez-vous le bon ~** *ou* **votre ~ de chaises ?** have you got the right number of chairs? *ou* the number of chairs you want? ◆ **je n'arrive jamais au même ~** I never get the same figure *ou* number *ou* total twice ◆ **pour faire bon ~** *(Comm)* to make up the amount; → **loin, rond**

3 [Comptabilité] account ◆ **les ~s de la nation** the national accounts ◆ **faire ses ~s** to do one's accounts *ou* books ◆ **tenir les ~s du ménage** to keep the household accounts ◆ **tenir les ~s d'une entreprise** to keep the books *ou* accounts of a firm ◆ **publier à ~ d'auteur** to publish at the author's expense ◆ **passer en ~** to place *ou* pass to account ◆ **nous sommes en ~** we have business to settle; → **apothicaire, ligne**[1]

◆ **de compte à demi** ◆ **ils sont de ~ à demi dans cette affaire** they're equal partners in this venture

◆ **être laissé pour compte** *[question, aspect]* to be neglected *ou* overlooked; *[personne]* to be left by the wayside; → **laissé-pour-compte**

4 [Banque] **~ (en banque** *ou* **bancaire)** (bank) account ◆ **~ rémunéré** interest-bearing account ◆ **~ non rémunéré** non-interest-bearing account ◆ **avoir un ~ dans une banque/à la Banque de France** to have an account with a bank/with the Banque de France ◆ **avoir de l'argent en ~** to have money in an account

5 [Ordin] account ◆ **~ utilisateur** user account

6 [= dû] **donner** *ou* **régler son ~ à un employé** *(lit)* to settle up with an employee; *(fig = renvoyer)* to give an employee his cards* *(Brit) ou* pink slip* *(US)* ◆ **demander son ~** *[employé]* to hand in one's notice ◆ **il a son ~*** *(fig) (épuisé, mort)* he's had it*, he's done for*; *(ivre)* he's had more than he can hold *ou* take ◆ **son ~ est bon** *(fig)* his number's up*, he's had it*; → **régler**

7 [= facture, addition] *(gén)* account, invoice, bill; *[d'hôtel, restaurant]* bill *(Brit)*, check *(US)* ◆ **pourriez-vous me faire mon ~ ?** would you make me out my bill? ◆ **mettez-le sur mon ~** *(au restaurant, à l'hôtel)* put it on my bill; *(dans un magasin)* charge it to *ou* put it on my account

8 [= avantage] **cela fait mon ~** that suits me ◆ **il y a trouvé son ~** he's got something out of it, he did well out of it ◆ **chacun y trouve son ~** there's something in it for everybody ◆ **si cette situation continue, c'est parce que le gouvernement y trouve son ~** if this situation continues, it's because it's to the government's advantage *ou* because it suits the government

◆ **à bon compte** *[obtenir]* (on the) cheap, for very little ◆ **s'en tirer à bon ~** to get off lightly

9 [= explications, justifications] **demander** *ou* **réclamer des ~s à qn** to ask sb for an explanation ◆ **il me doit des ~s à propos de cette perte** he owes me an explanation for this loss ◆ **rendre des ~s à qn** to explain o.s. to sb ◆ **il va bien falloir qu'il me rende des ~s** he's going to have to explain himself to me ◆ **je n'ai de ~s à rendre à personne** I'm accountable to nobody, I don't owe anybody any explanations ◆ **rendre ~ de qch à qn** to give sb an account of sth ◆ **il doit rendre ~ de tous ses déplacements** he has to account for all his move-

ments ◆ **elle rendra ~ de la réunion à ses collègues** she will brief her colleagues on the meeting

10 locutions

◆ **se rendre compte** ◆ **se rendre ~ que ...** to realize that ..., to be aware that ... ◆ **rendez-vous ~ !** just imagine! *ou* think! ◆ **il a osé me dire ça, à moi, tu te rends ~ !** he dared say that to me – can you believe it!

◆ **se rendre compte de qch** (= *réaliser*) to realize sth, to be aware of sth ◆ **je me rends très bien ~ de la situation** I am very well aware of the situation ◆ **est-ce que tu te rends vraiment ~ de ce que tu dis/fais ?** do you realize *ou* do you really know what you are saying/doing? ◆ **tu ne te rends pas ~ du travail que ça représente** you have no idea *ou* you just don't realize how much work that represents

◆ **tenir compte de qch/qn** to take sth/sb into account ◆ **il n'a pas tenu ~ de nos avertissements** he didn't take any notice of our warnings, he disregarded *ou* ignored our warnings ◆ **tenir ~ à qn de son dévouement** to take sb's devotion into account ◆ **on lui a tenu ~ de son passé** they took his past into account *ou* consideration

◆ **compte tenu de** considering

◆ **au compte de qn** *ou* **qch** ◆ **mettre qch au ~ de** (= *attribuer à*) to put sth down to, to attribute *ou* ascribe sth to ◆ **prendre qch à son ~** (*responsabilité financière*) to pay for sth; (*responsabilité morale*) to take responsibility for sth ◆ **je reprends cette maxime à mon ~** I shall make that saying my motto ◆ **il a repris la boutique à son ~** he's taken over the shop in his own name ◆ **être/s'établir** *ou* **se mettre** *ou* **s'installer à son ~** to be/set up in business for o.s., to have/set up one's own business ◆ **travailler à son ~** to be self-employed

◆ **pour le compte de qn** (= *au nom de*) on behalf of ◆ **pour mon ~ (personnel)** (= *en ce qui me concerne*) personally; (= *pour mon propre usage*) for my own use; (= *à mon profit*) for my own benefit ◆ **chacun négocie pour son propre ~** everybody negotiates for himself ◆ **la banque agit pour son propre ~** the bank is acting on its own behalf

◆ **sur le compte de qn** *ou* **qch** (= *à propos de*) about ◆ **on m'en a raconté de belles sur son ~ !** I was told a few interesting stories about him! ◆ **mettre qch sur le ~ de** (= *attribuer à*) to put sth down to, to attribute sth to ◆ **je mets son attitude sur le ~ de la fatigue** I put his attitude down to tiredness

◆ **pour le compte** ◆ **aller au tapis pour le ~** (*Boxe*) to be out for the count ◆ **tes sarcasmes l'ont envoyé au tapis pour le ~** (*hum*) your sarcastic remarks really knocked him for six *

2 - COMPOSÉS

compte bloqué escrow account
compte chèque postal post office account, ≃ National Girobank account (*Brit*)
compte(-)chèques ⇒ **compte courant**
compte commun joint account
compte courant current *ou* checking (*US*) account
compte d'épargne en actions stock market investment savings account
compte d'épargne logement *house purchase savings account giving the saver a reduced mortgage rate* ≃ building society account (*Brit*)
compte d'exploitation trading *ou* operating *ou* working account
compte joint joint account
compte numéroté *ou* **à numéro** numbered account
compte pour le développement industriel industrial development savings account
compte des profits et pertes profit and loss account
compte à rebours (*Espace, fig*) countdown
compte rendu (= *rapport*) (*gén*) account, report; [*de livre, film*] review; (*sur travaux en cours*) progress report ◆ **~ rendu d'audience** court record ◆ **faire le ~ rendu d'un match/d'une réunion** to give an account of *ou* a report on a match/meeting, to give a rundown on a match/meeting
compte sur livret deposit account

compte-fils /kɔ̃tfil/ **NM INV** (*Tech*) linen tester

compte-gouttes /kɔ̃tgut/ **NM INV** (= *pipette*) dropper ◆ **au ~** [*distribuer, dépenser*] sparingly; [*rembourser, entrer, sortir*] in dribs and drabs ◆ **injecter de l'argent au ~ dans qqch** to drip-feed money into sth

compter /kɔ̃te/

► conjug 1 ◄

GRAMMAIRE ACTIVE 35.2

1 VERBE TRANSITIF 2 VERBE INTRANSITIF

1 - VERBE TRANSITIF

1 = calculer [*+ choses, personnes, argent, jours*] to count ◆ **combien en avez-vous compté ?** how many did you count?, how many did you make it? ◆ **40 cm ? j'avais compté 30** 40 cm? I made it 30 ◆ **il a 50 ans bien comptés** he's a good 50 (years old) ◆ **on peut ~ (sur les doigts de la main) ceux qui comprennent vraiment** you can count on (the fingers of) one hand the number of people who really understand ◆ **on ne compte plus ses gaffes, ses gaffes ne se comptent plus** we've lost count of his blunders, he's made countless blunders ◆ **~ les jours/les minutes** to count the days/the minutes ◆ **~ les points** (*lit*) to count (up) the points ◆ **pendant qu'ils se disputaient moi je comptais les points** (*fig*) I just sat back and watched while they argued ◆ **pendant qu'ils se battaient je comptais les coups** I just sat back and watched while they fought ◆ **il a été compté 7** (*Boxe*) he took a count of 7; → **mouton**

2 = escompter, prévoir to reckon, to allow ◆ **combien as-tu compté qu'il nous fallait de chaises ?** how many chairs did you reckon we'd need? ◆ **j'ai compté qu'il nous en fallait 10** I reckoned we'd need 10 ◆ **combien de temps/d'argent comptez-vous pour finir les travaux ?** how much time/money do you reckon it'll take to finish the work?, how much time/money are you allowing to finish the work? ◆ **il faut (bien) ~ 10 jours/10 €** you must allow (a good) 10 days/€10, you must reckon on it taking (a good) 10 days/costing (a good) €10 ◆ **j'ai compté 90 cm pour le frigo, j'espère que ça suffira** I've allowed 90 cm for the fridge, I hope that'll do

3 = inclure to include ◆ **cela fait un mètre en comptant l'ourlet** that makes one metre counting *ou* including the hem ◆ **t'es-tu compté ?** did you count *ou* include yourself? ◆ **ne me comptez pas** don't include me

◆ **sans compter** ◆ **nous étions dix, sans ~ l'instituteur** there were ten of us, not counting the teacher ◆ **ils nous apportèrent leurs connaissances, sans ~ leur bonne volonté** they gave us their knowledge, not to mention *ou* to say nothing of their helpfulness; → aussi **verbe intransitif 2**

4 = tenir compte de to take into account ◆ **ta bonne volonté te sera comptée** your helpfulness will be taken into account

◆ **sans compter que**
(= *et de plus*) not to mention that
(= *d'autant plus que*) especially since *ou* as ◆ **il aurait dû venir, sans ~ qu'il n'avait rien à faire** he ought to have come especially since *ou* as he had nothing to do

◆ **tout bien compté** (*frm*) all things considered, all in all

5 = facturer to charge for ◆ **~ qch à qn** to charge sb for sth, to charge sth to sb ◆ **ils n'ont pas compté le café** they didn't charge for the coffee ◆ **combien vous ont-ils compté le café ?** how much did they charge you for the coffee? ◆ **ils nous l'ont compté trop cher/10 €/au prix de gros** they charged us too much/€10/the wholesale price (for it)

6 = avoir to have ◆ **la ville compte quelques très beaux monuments** the town has some very beautiful monuments ◆ **il compte 2 ans de règne/de service** he has been on the throne/in the firm for 2 years ◆ **il ne compte pas d'ennemis** he has no enemies ◆ **cette famille compte trois musiciens** there are three musicians in the family

7 = classer, ranger to consider ◆ **on compte ce livre parmi les meilleurs de l'année** this book is considered (to be) *ou* ranks among the best of the year ◆ **il le compte au nombre de ses amis** he considers him one of his friends, he numbers him among his friends

8 = verser to pay ◆ **le caissier va vous ~ 100 €** the cashier will pay you €100 ◆ **vous lui compterez 150 € pour les heures supplémentaires** you will pay him 150 euros' overtime

9 = donner avec parcimonie **il compte chaque sou qu'il nous donne** he counts every penny he gives us ◆ **les permissions leur sont comptées** their leave is rationed ◆ **il ne compte pas sa peine** he spares no trouble ◆ **ses jours sont comptés** his days are numbered ◆ **le temps m'est compté** my time is precious

10 = avoir l'intention de to intend, to plan; (= *s'attendre à*) to expect, to reckon ◆ **ils comptent partir demain** they intend *ou* plan to go tomorrow ◆ **je compte recevoir la convocation demain** I'm expecting (to receive) the summons tomorrow ◆ **je ne compte pas qu'il vienne aujourd'hui** I'm not expecting *ou* I don't expect him to come today

2 - VERBE INTRANSITIF

1 = calculer to count ◆ **il sait ~ (jusqu'à 10)** he can count (up to 10) ◆ **comment est-ce que tu as compté ?** how did you work it out? ◆ **~ sur ses doigts** to count on one's fingers ◆ **~ de tête** to count in one's head ◆ **tu as mal compté** you counted wrong, you miscounted

◆ **à compter de** (starting *ou* as) from ◆ **cette loi prendra effet à ~ du 1er mai** this law will take effect (as) from 1 May

2 = être économe to economize ◆ **avec la montée des prix, il faut ~ sans cesse** with the rise in prices you have to watch every penny (you spend) ◆ **dépenser sans ~** (= *être dépensier*) to spend extravagantly; (= *donner généreusement*) to give without counting the cost ◆ **il s'est dépensé sans ~ pour cette cause** he spared no effort in supporting the cause, he gave himself body and soul to the cause

3 = avoir de l'importance to count, to matter ◆ **c'est le résultat qui compte** it's the result that counts *ou* matters ◆ **c'est le geste qui compte** it's the thought that counts ◆ **35 ans de mariage, ça compte !** 35 years of marriage, that's quite something! ◆ **c'est un succès qui compte** it's an important success ◆ **ce qui compte c'est de savoir dès maintenant** the main thing is to find out right away ◆ **sa mère compte beaucoup pour lui** his mother is very important to him ◆ **ça ne compte pas** that doesn't count

4 = valoir to count ◆ **pour la retraite, les années de guerre comptent double** for the purposes of retirement, war service counts double ◆ **après 60 ans les années comptent double** after 60 every year counts double

5 [= figurer] ~ **parmi** to be *ou* rank among ◆ ~ **au nombre de** to be one of ◆ **il compte pour deux** he's worth two men ◆ **il compte pour quatre quand il s'agit de bagages/manger** he takes enough luggage/eats enough for four ◆ **ça compte pour beaucoup dans sa réussite/dans sa décision** that has a lot to do with his success/his decision, that is a major factor in his success/his decision ◆ **ça ne compte pour rien dans sa réussite/dans sa décision** that has nothing to do with his success/his decision ◆ **ça compte pour du beurre*** that counts for nothing, that doesn't count ◆ **et moi alors ? je compte pour du beurre ?** what am I? chopped liver? *

6 [locutions]

♦ **compter avec** (= *tenir compte de*) to take account of, to allow for ◆ **il faut ~ avec l'opinion** you've got to take account of public opinion ◆ **il faut ~ avec le temps incertain** you have to allow for changeable weather ◆ **un nouveau parti avec lequel il faut ~** a new party to be reckoned with ◆ **il faudra ~ avec lui** you'll have him to reckon with

♦ **compter sans** ◆ **on avait compté sans la grève** we hadn't reckoned on there being a strike, we hadn't allowed for the strike ◆ **c'était ~ sans son formidable courage** that was to ignore how very brave he was

♦ **compter sur** (= *se fier à*) to count on, to rely on ◆ ~ **sur la discrétion/la bonne volonté de qn** to count on *ou* rely on sb's discretion/goodwill ◆ **nous comptons sur vous (pour) demain** we're expecting you (to come) tomorrow ◆ **j'y compte bien !** I should hope so! ◆ **n'y comptez pas trop, ne comptez pas trop là-dessus** don't bank on it, don't count on it ◆ **je compte sur vous** I'm counting *ou* relying on you ◆ **vous pouvez ~ là-dessus** you can depend upon it ◆ **ne comptez pas sur moi** (you can) count me out ◆ **tu peux ~ sur lui pour le répéter partout !** you can bet (your life) he'll go and tell everyone!, you can count on him to go and tell everyone! ◆ **compte (là-)dessus et bois de l'eau (fraîche) !*** you'll be lucky!

compte-tours /kɔ̃ttuʀ/ **NM INV** rev *ou* revolution counter; *[de voiture]* rev *ou* revolution counter, tachometer

compteur /kɔ̃tœʀ/ **NM** meter ◆ ~ **d'eau/électrique/à gaz** water/electricity/gas meter ◆ ~ **Geiger** Geiger counter ◆ ~ **(kilométrique)** milometer *(Brit)*, odometer *(US)* ◆ ~ **(de vitesse)** speedometer ◆ **remettre un ~ à zéro** to reset a meter at *ou* to zero ◆ **remettre les ~s à zéro** *(fig)* to wipe the slate clean; → **relever**

comptine /kɔ̃tin/ **NF** (= *chanson*) nursery rhyme; (= *pour compter*) counting rhyme *ou* song

comptoir /kɔ̃twaʀ/ **NM** 1 *[de magasin]* counter; *[de bar]* 2 *(colonial)* trading post 3 (= *cartel*) syndicate *(for marketing)* 4 *(Fin = agence)* branch

compulsation /kɔ̃pylsasjɔ̃/ **NF** consultation

compulser /kɔ̃pylse/ ▸ conjug 1 ◂ **VT** to consult

compulsif, -ive /kɔ̃pylsif, iv/ **ADJ** compulsive

compulsion /kɔ̃pylsjɔ̃/ **NF** compulsion

comput /kɔ̃pyt/ **NM** *(Rel) reckoning of the dates of movable feasts in the religious calendar*

computation /kɔ̃pytasjɔ̃/ **NF** calculation, computation ◆ **cela échappe aux ~s** this is impossible to calculate

computationnel, -elle /kɔ̃pytasjɔnɛl/ **ADJ** computational ◆ **linguistique ~le** computational linguistics

comte /kɔ̃t/ **NM** count; *(britannique)* earl

comté /kɔ̃te/ **NM** 1 *(Hist)* earldom; *(Admin Brit, Can)* county 2 (= *fromage*) comté *(kind of gruyère cheese)*

comtesse /kɔ̃tɛs/ **NF** countess

con, conne[1] /kɔ̃, kɔn/ **ADJ** *(f aussi inv : * = stupide)* stupid ◆ **qu'il est ~ !** what a stupid bastard*,* *ou* bloody* *(Brit)* fool (he is)! ◆ **qu'elle est ~ !** *ou* **conne !** silly bitch!*,* silly cow!* *(Brit)* ◆ **il est ~ comme la lune** *ou* **comme un balai** he's a damn* *ou* bloody* *(Brit)* fool *ou* idiot ◆ **c'est pas ~ comme idée** it's not a bad idea

NM 1 (* = *crétin*) damn fool*, bloody *(Brit)* idiot*, schmuck* *(US)* ◆ **petit ~ !*** stupid little bastard!*,* ◆ **sale ~ !***bastard!*,* ◆ **bande de ~s** load of cretins* *ou* bloody idiots* *(Brit)* ◆ **faire le ~** to mess around*, to muck about* *(Brit)*, to piss about*,* ◆ **voiture/gouvernement à la ~** lousy* *ou* crummy* car/government ◆ **comme un ~** like a damn fool* *ou* bloody idiot* *(Brit)*

2 (*,*= *vagin*) cunt*,*

Conakry /kɔnakʀi/ **N** Conakry

conard* /kɔnaʀ/ **NM** ⇒ **connard**

conarde* /kɔnaʀd/ **NF** ⇒ **connarde**

conasse* /kɔnas/ **NF** ⇒ **connasse**

concassage /kɔ̃kasaʒ/ **NM** crushing

concasser /kɔ̃kase/ ▸ conjug 1 ◂ **VT** to crush ◆ **poivre concassé** crushed peppercorns

concaténation /kɔ̃katenasjɔ̃/ **NF** concatenation

concave /kɔ̃kav/ **ADJ** concave

concavité /kɔ̃kavite/ **NF** *(Opt)* concavity; *(gén = cavité)* hollow, cavity ◆ **les ~s d'un rocher** the hollows *ou* cavities in a rock

concédant /kɔ̃sedɑ̃/ **NM** *(Écon)* licensor

concéder /kɔ̃sede/ ▸ conjug 6 ◂ **VT** *[+ privilège, droit, exploitation]* to grant; *[+ point]* to concede; *[+ but, corner]* to concede, to give away ◆ **je vous concède que ...** I'll grant you that ...

concélébrant /kɔ̃selebʀɑ̃/ **NM** concelebrant

concélébrer /kɔ̃selebʀe/ ▸ conjug 6 ◂ **VT** to concelebrate

concentration /kɔ̃sɑ̃tʀasjɔ̃/ **NF** 1 *(gén, Chim)* concentration ◆ **les grandes ~s urbaines des Midlands** the great conurbations of the Midlands; → **camp** 2 (= *fusion*) **la ~ des entreprises** the merging of businesses ◆ ~ **horizontale/verticale** horizontal/vertical integration 3 ◆ ~ **(d'esprit)** concentration

concentrationnaire /kɔ̃sɑ̃tʀasjɔnɛʀ/ **ADJ** *[système]* concentration camp *(épith)*

concentré, e /kɔ̃sɑ̃tʀe/ (ptp de **concentrer**) **ADJ** 1 *[acide]* concentrated; *[lait]* condensed 2 *[candidat]* concentrating hard *(attrib)*; *[athlète]* focused ◆ **je n'étais pas assez ~** I wasn't concentrating **NM** *(chimique)* concentrated solution; (= *bouillon*) concentrate, extract ◆ ~ **de tomates** tomato purée ◆ **ce film est un ~ de sexe et de violence** the film is overloaded with sex and violence

concentrer /kɔ̃sɑ̃tʀe/ ▸ conjug 1 ◂ **VT** *(gén)* to concentrate ◆ ~ **son attention sur qch** to concentrate *ou* focus one's attention on sth

VPR se concentrer *[foule, troupes]* to concentrate ◆ **le candidat se concentra avant de répondre** the candidate gathered his thoughts *ou* thought hard before replying ◆ **je me concentre !** I'm concentrating! ◆ **se ~ sur un problème** to concentrate on a problem ◆ **les regards se concentrèrent sur moi** everybody's gaze was fixed *ou* focused on me

concentrique /kɔ̃sɑ̃tʀik/ **ADJ** *[cercle]* concentric

concept /kɔ̃sɛpt/ **NM** concept

concepteur, -trice /kɔ̃sɛptœʀ, tʀis/ **NM,F** designer ◆ ~ **graphique** graphic designer ◆ ~**-projeteur** project manager ◆ ~ **de réseaux** network designer ◆ ~**(-rédacteur) publicitaire** advertising copywriter

conception /kɔ̃sɛpsjɔ̃/ **NF** 1 *(Bio)* conception; → **immaculé** 2 *[d'objet, machine, décor]* design ◆ **"conception, réalisation : Jean Roudo"** "designed and made by Jean Roudo" ◆ **un avion d'une ~ révolutionnaire** a plane of revolutionary design ◆ ~ **assistée par ordinateur** computer-aided *ou* computer-assisted design 3 *[d'idée]* conception ◆ **notre ~ de la justice** our conception of justice ◆ **voilà quelle est ma ~ de la chose** this is how I see it ◆ **la ~ d'un tel plan est géniale** it is a brilliantly conceived plan

conceptualisation /kɔ̃sɛptɥalizasjɔ̃/ **NF** conceptualization

conceptualiser /kɔ̃sɛptɥalize/ ▸ conjug 1 ◂ **VT** to conceptualize

conceptuel, -elle /kɔ̃sɛptɥɛl/ **ADJ** conceptual

concernant /kɔ̃sɛʀnɑ̃/ **PRÉP** 1 (= *se rapportant à*) concerning, relating to, regarding ◆ **des mesures ~ ce problème seront bientôt prises** steps will soon be taken concerning *ou* regarding this problem 2 (= *quant à*) with regard to, as regards ◆ ~ **ce problème, des mesures seront bientôt prises** with regard to this problem *ou* as regards this problem *ou* as far as this problem is concerned, steps will soon be taken

concerner /kɔ̃sɛʀne/ GRAMMAIRE ACTIVE 33.2 ▸ conjug 1 ◂ **VT** to concern ◆ **cela ne vous concerne pas** (= *ce n'est pas votre affaire*) it's no concern of yours; (= *on ne parle pas de vous*) it doesn't concern you; (= *ça n'a pas d'incidence sur vous*) it doesn't affect you ◆ **en ce qui concerne cette question** with regard to this question, concerning this question, as far as this question is concerned ◆ **en ce qui me concerne** as far as I'm concerned ◆ **pour affaire vous concernant** *(Admin)* to discuss a matter which concerns you ◆ **je ne me sens pas concerné par sa remarque/son rapport** his remark/report doesn't apply to *ou* concern me

concert /kɔ̃sɛʀ/ **NM** 1 *(Mus)* concert ◆ ~ **spirituel** concert of sacred music ◆ ~ **de louanges/de lamentations/d'invectives** chorus of praise/lamentation(s)/invective ◆ **on entendit un ~ d'avertisseurs** a chorus of horns started up ◆ **en ~** in concert; → **salle** 2 *(littér)* (= *harmonie*) chorus; (= *accord*) entente, accord ◆ **un ~ de voix** a chorus of voices ◆ **le ~ des grandes puissances** the entente *ou* accord between the great powers

3 *(locutions)*

♦ **de concert** (= *ensemble*) *[partir, décider]* together; *[rire]* in unison; *[agir]* together, in concert, in unison ◆ **ils ont agi de ~ pour éviter ...** they took concerted action to avoid ... ◆ **de ~ avec** (= *en accord avec*) in cooperation *ou* conjunction with; (= *ensemble*) together with

concertant, e /kɔ̃sɛʀtɑ̃, ɑ̃t/ **ADJ** → **symphonie**

concertation /kɔ̃sɛʀtasjɔ̃/ **NF** (= *échange de vues, dialogue*) dialogue; (= *rencontre*) meeting ◆ **sans ~ préalable** without preliminary consultation(s)

concerté, e /kɔ̃sɛʀte/ (ptp de **concerter**) **ADJ** concerted

concerter /kɔ̃sɛʀte/ ▸ conjug 1 ◂ **VT** (= *organiser*) *[+ plan, entreprise, projet]* to devise **VPR se concerter** (= *délibérer*) to consult (each other)

concertina /kɔ̃sɛʀtina/ **NM** concertina

concertino /kɔ̃sɛʀtino/ **NM** concertino

concertiste /kɔ̃sɛʀtist/ **NMF** concert artiste *ou* performer

concerto /kɔ̃sɛʀto/ **NM** concerto ◆ ~ **pour piano (et orchestre)** piano concerto, concerto for piano and orchestra ◆ ~ **grosso** concerto grosso

concessif, -ive /kɔ̃sesif, iv/ *(Gram)* **ADJ** concessive **NF concessive** concessive clause

concession /kɔ̃sesjɔ̃/ NF 1 *(= faveur)* concession (*à* to); ◆ **faire des ~s** to make concessions ◆ **sans concession** *[analyse, tableau, récit, personne]* uncompromising; *[débat]* ruthless
2 *(= cession) [de terrain, exploitation]* concession ◆ **faire la ~ d'un terrain** to grant a piece of land 3 *(= exploitation, terrain, territoire)* concession; *[de cimetière]* burial plot ◆ **~ minière** mining concession ◆ **~ à perpétuité** burial plot held in perpetuity

concessionnaire /kɔ̃sesjɔnɛʀ/ NMF *(= marchand agréé)* agent, dealer; *(= bénéficiaire d'une concession)* concessionaire, concessionary ◆ **~ automobile** car dealer ◆ **disponible chez votre ~** available from your dealer ADJ *[entreprise, service]* concessionary ◆ **société ~** *(travaux publics)* contractor

concevable /kɔ̃s(ə)vabl/ ADJ conceivable ◆ **il est très ~ que ...** it's quite conceivable that ...

concevoir /kɔ̃s(ə)vwaʀ/ ▸ conjug 28 ◂ VT 1 *(= penser)* to imagine; *[+ fait, idée]* to conceive of ◆ **je n'arrive pas à ~ que c'est fini** I can't believe that it's finished ◆ **il ne conçoit pas qu'on puisse souffrir de la faim** he cannot imagine *ou* conceive that people can suffer from starvation
2 *(= élaborer, étudier) [+ voiture, maison, produit]* to design; *[+ solution, projet, moyen]* to conceive, to devise, to think up ◆ **bien/mal conçu** *[projet, livre]* well/badly thought out; *[voiture, maison]* well/badly designed
3 *(= envisager) [+ question]* to see, to view ◆ **voilà comment je conçois la chose** that's how I see it *ou* view it *ou* look at it
4 *(= comprendre)* to understand ◆ **je conçois sa déception** *ou* **qu'il soit déçu** I can understand his disappointment *ou* his being disappointed ◆ **cela se conçoit facilement** it's quite understandable, it's easy to understand ◆ **on concevrait mal qu'il puisse refuser** a refusal on his part would be difficult to understand ◆ **ce qui se conçoit bien s'énonce clairement** what is clearly understood can be clearly expressed
5 *(= rédiger) [+ lettre, réponse]* to compose ◆ **ainsi conçu, conçu en ces termes** expressed *ou* couched in these terms
6 *(littér = éprouver)* to conceive ◆ **je conçois des doutes quant à son intégrité** I have some doubts as to his integrity ◆ **il en conçut une terrible jalousie** he conceived a terrible feeling of jealousy ◆ **il conçut de l'amitié pour moi** he took a liking to me
7 *(= engendrer)* to conceive

conchylicole /kɔ̃kilikɔl/ ADJ ◆ **entreprise ~** shellfish farm ◆ **produits ~s** shellfish

conchyliculteur, -trice /kɔ̃kilikyltœʀ, tʀis/ NM,F shellfish farmer

conchyliculture /kɔ̃kilikyltyʀ/ NF shellfish farming

concierge /kɔ̃sjɛʀʒ/ NMF *[d'immeuble]* caretaker, manager (of an apartment building) (US); *[d'hôtel]* porter; *(en France)* concierge ◆ **c'est un(e) vrai(e) ~** *(fig)* he *(ou* she) is a real gossip

CONCIERGE

Many apartment buildings in French cities still have a « loge » near the entrance where the **concierge** lives with his or her family. The stereotypical image of the **concierge** is that of an amiable busybody with a tendency to spread gossip about tenants. Nowadays the term is considered slightly demeaning, and the words « gardien/gardienne d'immeuble » are often thought more acceptable.

conciergerie /kɔ̃sjɛʀʒəʀi/ NF *[de lycée, château]* caretaker's lodge; *(Can)* apartment house ◆ **la Conciergerie** *(Hist)* the Conciergerie

concile /kɔ̃sil/ NM *(Rel)* council ◆ **~ œcuménique** ecumenical council ◆ **le ~ de Trente** the Council of Trent

conciliable /kɔ̃siljabl/ ADJ *(= compatible) [opinions]* reconcilable ◆ **ce n'est pas ~ avec ...** it's not compatible with ...

conciliabule /kɔ̃siljabyl/ NM 1 *(= entretien)* consultation, confab * ◆ **tenir de grands ~s** *(iro)* to have great consultations *ou* confabs * 2 († *= réunion)* secret meeting

conciliaire /kɔ̃siljɛʀ/ ADJ conciliar ◆ **les pères ~s** the fathers of the council

conciliant, e /kɔ̃siljɑ̃, jɑ̃t/ ADJ conciliatory, conciliating

conciliateur, -trice /kɔ̃siljatœʀ, tʀis/ ADJ conciliatory, conciliating NM,F *(= médiateur)* conciliator

conciliation /kɔ̃siljasjɔ̃/ NF *(gén)* conciliation, reconciliation; *(entre époux)* reconciliation ◆ **esprit de ~** spirit of conciliation ◆ **comité de ~** arbitration committee ◆ **la ~ d'intérêts opposés** the reconciliation *ou* reconciling of conflicting interests ◆ **tentative de ~** *(gén, Pol)* attempt at (re)conciliation; *(entre époux)* attempt at reconciliation; → **procédure**

conciliatoire /kɔ̃siljatwaʀ/ ADJ *(Jur)* conciliatory

concilier /kɔ̃silje/ ▸ conjug 7 ◂ VT 1 *(= rendre compatible) [+ exigences, opinions, sentiments]* to reconcile *(avec* with) 2 *(= attirer)* to win, to gain ◆ **son charisme lui a concilié les électeurs** his charisma won him the support of the voters *ou* won over the voters 3 *(littér, Jur = réconcilier) [+ ennemis]* to reconcile, to conciliate VPR **se concilier** *(= s'attirer)* to win, to gain ◆ **se ~ les bonnes grâces de qn** to win *ou* gain sb's favour

concis, e /kɔ̃si, iz/ ADJ concise ◆ **en termes ~** concisely

concision /kɔ̃sizjɔ̃/ NF concision, conciseness ◆ **avec ~** concisely

concitoyen, -yenne /kɔ̃sitwajɛ̃, jɛn/ NM,F fellow citizen

conclave /kɔ̃klav/ NM *(Rel, Pol)* conclave ◆ **les cardinaux/ministres étaient réunis en ~** the cardinals/ministers met in conclave

concluant, e /kɔ̃klyɑ̃, ɑ̃t/ ADJ conclusive

conclure /kɔ̃klyʀ/ GRAMMAIRE ACTIVE 53.4 ▸ conjug 35 ◂
VT 1 *(= signer) [+ affaire, accord]* to conclude ◆ **~ un marché** to conclude *ou* clinch a deal ◆ **marché conclu !** it's a deal!
2 *(= terminer) [+ débat, discours, texte]* to conclude, to end ◆ **et pour ~** and to conclude ◆ **je vous demande de ~** will you please conclude ◆ **il conclut par ces mots/en disant ...** he concluded with these words/by saying ... ◆ **~ sa plaidoirie** to rest one's case
3 *(= déduire)* to conclude *(qch de qch* sth from sth); ◆ **j'en conclus que ...** I therefore conclude that ...
VI 1 *(Sport)* to score ◆ **il a conclu** * *(avec une fille)* he scored *
2 *(Jur)* **~ contre qn** *[témoignage]* to convict sb ◆ **~ contre/en faveur de qn** *[personne]* to find against/in favour (Brit) *ou* favor (US) of sb
VT INDIR **conclure à** ◆ **ils ont conclu à son innocence** they concluded that he was innocent ◆ **les juges ont conclu à l'acquittement** the judges decided on an acquittal ◆ **l'enquête a conclu à un accident** the investigation concluded that it was an accident

conclusif, -ive /kɔ̃klyzif, iv/ ADJ concluding *(épith)*

conclusion /kɔ̃klyzjɔ̃/ GRAMMAIRE ACTIVE 53.4 NF *(gén)* conclusion; *[de discours]* close ◆ **en ~** in conclusion ◆ **~, il n'est pas venu** * the net result was that he didn't come ◆ **~, on s'était trompé** * in other words, we had made a mistake NFPL **conclusions** *(Jur) [de demandeur]* pleadings, submissions; *[d'avocat]* summing-up; *[de jury]* findings, conclusions ◆ **déposer des ~s auprès d'un tribunal** to file submissions with a court

concocter * /kɔ̃kɔkte/ ▸ conjug 1 ◂ VT to concoct

concoction * /kɔ̃kɔksjɔ̃/ NF concoction

concombre /kɔ̃kɔ̃bʀ/ NM cucumber

concomitamment /kɔ̃kɔmitamɑ̃/ ADV concomitantly

concomitance /kɔ̃kɔmitɑ̃s/ NF concomitance

concomitant, e /kɔ̃kɔmitɑ̃, ɑ̃t/ ADJ *[événements, expériences]* concomitant *(à* with)

concordance /kɔ̃kɔʀdɑ̃s/ NF 1 *(gén)* agreement ◆ **la ~ de deux témoignages** the agreement of two testimonies, the fact that two testimonies tally *ou* agree ◆ **la ~ de deux résultats/situations** the similarity of *ou* between two results/situations ◆ **mettre ses actes en ~ avec ses principes** to act in accordance with one's principles 2 *(= index) (Bible)* concordance; *(Géol)* conformability ◆ **~ des temps** *(Gram)* sequence of tenses ◆ **~ de phases** *(Phys)* synchronization of phases

concordant, e /kɔ̃kɔʀdɑ̃, ɑ̃t/ ADJ *[faits]* corroborating; *(Géol)* conformable ◆ **deux témoignages ~s** two testimonies which agree *ou* which are in agreement *ou* which tally

concordat /kɔ̃kɔʀda/ NM *(Rel)* concordat; *(Comm)* composition; *[de faillite]* winding-up arrangement

concorde /kɔ̃kɔʀd/ NF *(littér = harmonie)* concord

concorder /kɔ̃kɔʀde/ ▸ conjug 1 ◂ VI *[faits, dates, témoignages]* to agree, to tally; *[idées]* to coincide, to match; *[caractères]* to match ◆ **faire ~ des chiffres** to make figures agree *ou* tally ◆ **ses actes concordent-ils avec ses idées ?** is his behaviour in accordance with his ideas?

concourant, e /kɔ̃kuʀɑ̃, ɑ̃t/ ADJ *(= convergent) [droites]* convergent; *[efforts]* concerted *(épith)*, united

concourir /kɔ̃kuʀiʀ/ ▸ conjug 11 ◂ VI 1 *[concurrent]* to compete *(pour* for); ◆ **les films qui concourent au festival** the films competing at the festival 2 *(Math = converger)* to converge *(vers* towards, on) VT INDIR **concourir à** ◆ **~ à qch/à faire qch** *[personnes]* to work towards sth/towards doing sth; *[circonstances]* to contribute to sth/to doing sth ◆ **tout concourt à notre réussite** everything is working in our favour ◆ **son intransigeance a concouru à son échec** his inflexibility contributed to *ou* was a factor in his failure

concours /kɔ̃kuʀ/ NM 1 *(= jeu, compétition)* competition; *(= examen)* competitive examination ◆ **~ agricole** agricultural show ◆ **~ hippique** *(= sport)* show-jumping ◆ **un ~ hippique** *(= épreuve)* a horse show ◆ **promotion par (voie de) ~** promotion by (competitive) examination ◆ **~ de beauté** beauty contest ◆ **~ d'entrée (à)** (competitive) entrance examination (for) ◆ **~ de recrutement** competitive entry examination ◆ **~ général** *competitive examination with prizes, open to secondary school children* ◆ **être présenté hors ~** to be shown outside the competition *(because of outstanding merit)* ◆ **être mis hors ~** to be declared ineligible to compete, to be disqualified ◆ **il est hors ~** *(fig)* he's in a class of his own
2 *(= participation)* aid, help ◆ **prêter son ~ à qch** to lend one's support to sth ◆ **avec le ~ de** *(participation)* with the participation of; *(aide)* with the support *ou* help *ou* assistance of ◆ **il a**

fallu le ~ des pompiers the firemen's help was needed

3 *(= rencontre)* ~ **de circonstances** combination of circumstances ◆ **un grand ~ de peuple** † a large concourse † *ou* throng of people

Concours

In France, the cultural significance of competitive examinations with a predetermined quota of successful candidates is considerable. Gruelling « classes préparatoires » after secondary school level are designed to prepare high-flying students for the « grandes écoles » entrance exams, and have tended to promote a competitive and elitist approach to learning in these schools. Other examples of the importance of **concours** are the competitive recruitment procedures for public sector teaching posts (« CAPES » and « agrégation »), civil service appointments in ministries, and even jobs in the Post Office.

concret, -ète /kɔ̃kʀɛ, ɛt/ ADJ *[situation, détail, objet]* concrete ◆ **esprit ~** practical mind ◆ **il en a tiré des avantages ~s** it gave him certain real *ou* positive advantages; → **musique** NM ◆ **le ~ et l'abstrait** the concrete and the abstract ◆ **ce que je veux, c'est du ~** I want something concrete

concrètement /kɔ̃kʀɛtmɑ̃/ ADV *(gén)* in concrete terms; *(= pratiquement)* in practical terms ◆ **je me représente très ~ la situation** I can visualize the situation very clearly ◆ **~, à quoi ça va servir ?** what practical use will it have?, in concrete terms, what use will it be?

concrétion /kɔ̃kʀesjɔ̃/ NF *(Géol, Méd)* concretion

concrétisation /kɔ̃kʀetizasjɔ̃/ NF *[de promesse]* realization

concrétiser /kɔ̃kʀetize/ ▸ conjug 1 ◂ VT to give concrete expression to VI *(Sport = marquer)* to score ◆ **~ avec qn*** *(= sortir avec qn)* to go out with sb VPR **se concrétiser** *[espoir, projet]* to materialize ◆ **ses promesses/menaces ne se sont pas concrétisées** his promises/threats didn't come to anything *ou* didn't materialize ◆ **le projet commence à se ~** the project is beginning to take shape

concubin, e /kɔ̃kybɛ̃, in/ NM,F 1 *(Jur)* cohabitant, cohabitee, common-law husband *(ou* wife) 2 († *ou hum)* lover NF **concubine** *(Hist)* concubine

concubinage /kɔ̃kybinaʒ/ NM cohabitation ◆ **ils vivent en ~** they're living together *ou* as husband and wife ◆ **~ notoire** *(Jur)* common-law marriage

concupiscence /kɔ̃kypisɑ̃s/ NF concupiscence

concupiscent, e /kɔ̃kypisɑ̃, ɑ̃t/ ADJ concupiscent

concurremment /kɔ̃kyʀamɑ̃/ ADV 1 *(= conjointement)* conjointly ◆ **il agit ~ avec le président** he acts conjointly with *ou* in conjunction with the president 2 *(= en même temps)* concurrently

concurrence /kɔ̃kyʀɑ̃s/ NF 1 *(gén)* competition ◆ **prix défiant toute ~** absolutely unbeatable price, rock-bottom price ◆ **~ déloyale** unfair trading *ou* competition ◆ **faire ~ à qn** to be in competition with sb ◆ **être en ~ avec qn** to be in competition with sb, to compete with sb 2 *(= limite)* **(jusqu')à ~ de ...** up to ...

concurrencer /kɔ̃kyʀɑ̃se/ ▸ conjug 3 ◂ VT to compete with ◆ **il nous concurrence dangereusement** he is a serious threat *ou* challenge to us ◆ **leurs produits risquent de ~ les nôtres** their products could well pose a serious threat *ou* challenge to ours

concurrent, e /kɔ̃kyʀɑ̃, ɑ̃t/ ADJ 1 *(= rival)* rival, competing 2 († *= concourant) [forces, actions]* concurrent, cooperative NM,F *(Comm, Sport)* competitor; *(Scol) [de concours]* candidate

concurrentiel, -elle /kɔ̃kyʀɑ̃sjɛl/ ADJ *[secteur, produit, prix]* competitive

concussion /kɔ̃kysjɔ̃/ NF misappropriation of public funds

concussionnaire /kɔ̃kysjɔnɛʀ/ ADJ embezzling *(épith)* NMF embezzler of public funds

condamnable /kɔ̃dɑnabl/ ADJ *[action, opinion]* reprehensible, blameworthy ◆ **il n'est pas ~ d'avoir pensé à ses intérêts** he cannot be blamed for having thought of his own interests

condamnation /kɔ̃dɑnasjɔ̃/ NF 1 *(Jur) [de coupable] (= action)* sentencing *(à* to; *pour* for); *(= peine)* sentence ◆ **il a 3 ~s à son actif** he already has 3 convictions ◆ **~ à mort** death sentence, sentence of death ◆ **~ à une amende** imposition of a fine ◆ **~ à 5 ans de prison** 5-year (prison) sentence ◆ **~ (aux travaux forcés) à perpétuité** life sentence (of hard labour) ◆ **~ aux dépens** order to pay costs ◆ **~ pour meurtre** sentence for murder 2 *[de livre, délit, conduite, idée]* condemnation 3 *(= faillite) [d'espoir, théorie, projet]* end ◆ **c'est la ~ du petit commerce** it means the end of *ou* it spells the end for the small trader 4 *(dans voiture) (= action)* locking; *(= système)* locking device ◆ **~ centralisée des portes** central-locking device

condamné, e /kɔ̃dɑne/ (ptp de **condamner**) NM,F sentenced person, convict; *(à mort)* condemned person ◆ **un ~ à mort s'est échappé** a man under sentence of death *ou* a condemned man has escaped ◆ **les malades ~s** the terminally ill; → **cigarette**

condamner /kɔ̃dɑne/ GRAMMAIRE ACTIVE 41 ▸ conjug 1 ◂ VT 1 *[+ coupable]* to sentence *(à* to; *pour* for); ◆ **~ à mort** to sentence to death ◆ **~ qn à une amende** to fine sb, to impose a fine on sb ◆ **~ qn à 5 ans de prison** to sentence sb to 5 years' imprisonment, to pass a 5-year (prison) sentence on sb ◆ **être condamné aux dépens** to be ordered to pay costs ◆ **~ qn par défaut/par contumace** to sentence sb by default/in his absence *ou* in absentia ◆ **~ pour meurtre** to sentence for murder ◆ **Serge Despins, plusieurs fois condamné pour vol ...** Serge Despins, several times convicted of theft ...

2 *(= interdire) [+ délit, livre]* to condemn ◆ **la loi condamne l'usage de stupéfiants** the law condemns the use of drugs ◆ **ces délits sont sévèrement condamnés** these offences carry heavy sentences *ou* penalties

3 *(= blâmer) [+ action, idées, impropriété]* to condemn ◆ **il ne faut pas le ~ d'avoir fait cela** you mustn't condemn *ou* blame him for doing that

4 *(= accuser)* to condemn ◆ **sa rougeur le condamne** the fact that he's blushing points to his guilt

5 *[+ malade]* to give up hope for; *[+ théorie, espoir]* to put an end to ◆ **ce projet est maintenant condamné** this project is now doomed ◆ **il était condamné depuis longtemps** there had been no hope for him *ou* he had been doomed for a long time ◆ **il est condamné par les médecins** the doctors have given up hope (for him)

6 *(= obliger, vouer)* **~ à** *[+ silence]* to condemn to ◆ **je suis condamné** *ou* **ça me condamne à me lever tôt** I'm obliged to get up early ◆ **condamné à sombrer dans l'oubli** doomed to sink into oblivion

7 *[+ porte, fenêtre] (gén)* to fill in, to block up; *(avec briques)* to brick up; *(avec planches)* to board up; *[+ pièce]* to lock up; *[+ portière de voiture]* to lock ◆ **~ sa porte à qn** *(fig)* to bar one's door to sb

condé /kɔ̃de/ NM *(arg Police = policier)* cop*; *(= accord)* deal *(which allows one to pursue illegal activities in exchange for information)*

condensable /kɔ̃dɑ̃sabl/ ADJ condensable

condensateur /kɔ̃dɑ̃satœʀ/ NM *(Élec)* capacitor, condenser; *(Opt)* condenser

condensation /kɔ̃dɑ̃sasjɔ̃/ NF condensation

condensé, e /kɔ̃dɑ̃se/ (ptp de **condenser**) ADJ *[gaz, vapeur, lait]* condensed; *[exposé, pensée]* condensed, compressed NM *(gén)* summary; *(Presse)* digest

condenser /kɔ̃dɑ̃se/ ▸ conjug 1 ◂ VT *[+ gaz, vapeur]* to condense; *[+ exposé, pensée]* to condense, to compress VPR **se condenser** *[vapeur]* to condense

condenseur /kɔ̃dɑ̃sœʀ/ NM *(Opt, Phys)* condenser

condescendance /kɔ̃desɑ̃dɑ̃s/ NF condescension ◆ **avec ~** condescendingly

condescendant, e /kɔ̃desɑ̃dɑ̃, ɑ̃t/ ADJ condescending

condescendre /kɔ̃desɑ̃dʀ/ ▸ conjug 41 ◂ **condescendre à** VT INDIR to condescend to ◆ **~ à faire qch** to condescend *ou* deign to do sth

condiment /kɔ̃dimɑ̃/ NM condiment *(including pickles, spices, and any other seasoning)*

condisciple /kɔ̃disipl/ NMF *(Scol)* schoolmate; *(Univ)* fellow student

condition /kɔ̃disjɔ̃/ NF 1 *(= circonstances)* **~s** conditions ◆ **~s atmosphériques/sociologiques** atmospheric/sociological conditions ◆ **~s de travail/vie** working/living conditions ◆ **dans ces ~s, je refuse** under these conditions, I refuse ◆ **dans les ~s actuelles** in *ou* under (the) present conditions ◆ **améliorer la ~ des travailleurs émigrés** to improve the lot of foreign workers

2 *(= stipulation) [de traité]* condition; *(= exigence) [d'acceptation]* condition, requirement ◆ **~ préalable** prerequisite ◆ **la ~ nécessaire et suffisante pour que ...** the necessary and sufficient condition for ... ◆ **~ sine qua non** sine qua non, necessary condition ◆ **l'honnêteté est la ~ du succès** honesty is the (prime) requirement for *ou* condition of success ◆ **dicter/poser ses ~s** to state/lay down one's conditions ◆ **il ne remplit pas les ~s requises (pour le poste)** he doesn't fulfil the requirements (for the job) ◆ **~s d'admission** terms *ou* conditions of admission *ou* entry *(dans* to); ◆ **sans ~(s)** *[capitulation]* unconditional; *[capituler]* unconditionally

3 *(Comm)* term ◆ **~s de vente/d'achat** terms of sale/of purchase ◆ **~s de paiement** terms (of payment) ◆ **obtenir des ~s intéressantes** to get favourable terms ◆ **faire ses ~s** to make *ou* name one's (own) terms ◆ **acheter/envoyer à** *ou* **sous ~** to buy/send on approval ◆ **dans les ~s normales du commerce** in the ordinary course of business

4 *(= état)* condition

◆ **en + condition** ◆ **en bonne ~** *[aliments, envoi]* in good condition ◆ **en bonne** *ou* **grande ~ (physique)** in good condition, fit ◆ **en mauvaise ~ (physique)** out of condition, unfit ◆ **mettre en ~** *[+ sportif]* to make *ou* get fit; *[+ candidat]* to prepare (mentally); *[+ spectateurs]* to condition ◆ **la mise en ~ des téléspectateurs** the conditioning of television viewers ◆ **se mettre en ~** *(avant un examen)* to prepare o.s. mentally ◆ **entrer/être en ~ chez qn** †† to enter sb's service/be in service with sb

5 *(= rang social)* station, condition ◆ **vivre selon sa ~** to live according to one's station ◆ **étudiant de ~ modeste** student from a modest home *ou* background ◆ **personne de ~** †† person of quality ◆ **la ~ féminine** women's position in society ◆ **la ~ ouvrière** the conditions of working-class life ◆ **la ~ de prê-**

tre the priesthood ◆ **la ~ d'artisan/d'intellectuel** the situation of the craftsman/intellectual

6 *(locutions)* **à une ~** on one condition ◆ **je le ferai, à la seule ~ que toi aussi tu fasses un effort** I'll do it but only on one condition - you have to make an effort as well ◆ **tu peux rester, à ~ d'être sage** *ou* **à ~ que tu sois sage** you can stay provided (that) *ou* so long as you're good ◆ **sous ~** conditionally

conditionné, e /kɔ̃disjɔne/ (ptp de **conditionner**) ADJ 1 *(= emballé)* packaged; *(= sous vide)* vacuum-packed 2 *(= influencé)* conditioned ◆ **réflexe ~** conditioned response *ou* reflex 3 *(= climatisé)* → **air**[1]

conditionnel, -elle /kɔ̃disjɔnɛl/ ADJ, NM *(gén)* conditional ◆ **réflexe ~** conditioned response *ou* reflex ◆ **au ~** *(Ling)* in the conditional ◆ **cette information est à mettre au ~** this information has still to be confirmed; → **liberté**

conditionnellement /kɔ̃disjɔnɛlmɑ̃/ ADV conditionally

conditionnement /kɔ̃disjɔnmɑ̃/ NM *(= emballage)* packaging; *[d'air, personne, textile, blé]* conditioning

conditionner /kɔ̃disjɔne/ ▸ conjug 1 ◂ VT *(= emballer)* to package; *(= influencer)* to condition; *[+ textiles, blé]* to condition ◆ **ceci conditionne notre départ** our departure is dependent on *ou* is conditioned by this

conditionneur, -euse /kɔ̃disjɔnœʀ, øz/ NM,F *(= emballeur)* packer NM *[de denrées]* packaging machine; *[d'air]* air conditioner; *(pour cheveux)* conditioner

condoléances /kɔ̃dɔleɑ̃s/ GRAMMAIRE ACTIVE 51.4 NFPL condolences ◆ **offrir** *ou* **faire ses ~ à qn** to offer sb one's sympathy *ou* condolences ◆ **toutes mes ~** (please accept) all my condolences *ou* my deepest sympathy ◆ **lettre de ~** letter of condolence

condom /kɔ̃dɔm/ NM condom

condominium /kɔ̃dɔminjɔm/ NM *(= souveraineté, logement)* condominium

condor /kɔ̃dɔʀ/ NM condor

conductance /kɔ̃dyktɑ̃s/ NF conductance

conducteur, -trice /kɔ̃dyktœʀ, tʀis/ ADJ *(Élec)* conductive, conducting; → **fil** NM,F *[de voiture, train]* driver; *[de machine]* operator ◆ **~ d'engins** heavy plant driver ◆ **~ d'hommes** leader ◆ **~ de travaux** clerk of works NM *(Élec)* conductor; (TV) continuity

> ⚠ Quand il désigne une personne, le mot **conducteur** ne se traduit pas par l'anglais **conductor**, qui a le sens de 'chef d'orchestre' ou 'contrôleur'.

conductibilité /kɔ̃dyktibilite/ NF conductivity

conductible /kɔ̃dyktibl/ ADJ conductive

conduction /kɔ̃dyksjɔ̃/ NF conduction

conductivité /kɔ̃dyktivite/ NF conductivity

conduire /kɔ̃dɥiʀ/ ▸ conjug 38 ◂ VT 1 *(= emmener)* **~ qn quelque part** to take sb somewhere; *(en voiture)* to take *ou* drive sb somewhere ◆ **~ un enfant à l'école/chez le médecin** to take a child to school/to the doctor ◆ **~ la voiture au garage** to take the car to the garage ◆ **~ les bêtes aux champs** to take *ou* drive the animals to the fields ◆ **~ qn à la gare** *(en voiture)* to take *ou* drive sb to the station; *(à pied)* to walk *ou* see sb to the station ◆ **il me conduisit à ma chambre** he showed me *ou* took me to my room

2 *(= guider)* to lead ◆ **il conduisit les hommes à l'assaut** he led the men into the attack ◆ **le guide nous conduisait** the guide was leading us ◆ **il nous a conduits à travers Paris** he guided us through Paris

3 *(= piloter) [+ véhicule]* to drive; *[+ embarcation]* to steer; *[+ avion]* to pilot; *[+ cheval] [cavalier]* to ride; *[cocher]* to drive ◆ **~ un cheval par la bride** to lead a horse by the bridle

4 *(en voiture : emploi absolu)* to drive ◆ **il conduit bien/mal** he is a good/bad driver, he drives well/badly; → **permis**

5 *(= mener)* **~ qn quelque part** *[véhicule]* to take sb somewhere; *[route, traces]* to lead *ou* take sb somewhere; *[études, événement]* to lead sb somewhere ◆ **où cela va-t-il nous ~ ?** where will all this lead us? ◆ **cela nous conduit à penser que ...** this leads us to believe that ... ◆ **cet escalier conduit à la cave** this staircase leads (down) to the cellar ◆ **où ce chemin conduit-il ?** where does this road lead *ou* go? ◆ **~ ses pas vers** *(littér)* to bend one's steps towards ◆ **cet article l'a conduit en prison** the article landed him in prison

6 *(= diriger) [+ affaires]* to run, to manage; *[+ travaux]* to supervise; *[+ pays]* to run, to lead; *[+ négociations, enquête]* to lead, to conduct; *[+ orchestre] [chef d'orchestre]* to conduct; *[premier violon]* to lead ◆ **les fouilles sont conduites par P. Brunel** the excavation is being led *ou* directed by P. Brunel

7 *(= transmettre) [+ chaleur, électricité]* to conduct; *(= transporter)* to carry ◆ **un aqueduc conduit l'eau à la ville** an aqueduct carries water to the town

VPR **se conduire** to behave ◆ **il sait se ~ (en société)** he knows how to behave (in polite company) ◆ **ce ne sont pas des façons de se ~** that's no way to behave ◆ **conduisez-vous comme il faut !** behave properly! ◆ **il s'est mal conduit** he behaved badly

conduit /kɔ̃dɥi/ NM 1 *(= tuyau)* conduit, pipe ◆ **~ de fumée** flue ◆ **~ d'air** *ou* **de ventilation** ventilation shaft ◆ **~ d'alimentation** supply pipe ◆ **~ d'aération** air duct 2 *(Anat)* duct, canal, meatus *(SPÉC)*

COMP **conduit auditif** auditory canal
conduit lacrymal tear duct
conduit urinaire ureter, urinary canal

conduite /kɔ̃dɥit/ NF 1 *(= pilotage) [de véhicule]* driving; *[d'embarcation]* steering; *[d'avion]* piloting ◆ **la ~ d'un gros camion demande de l'habileté** driving a big truck takes a lot of skill ◆ **~ accompagnée** *driving as a learner accompanied by an experienced driver* ◆ **~ en état d'ivresse** drunk driving, driving while under the influence (of alcohol) ◆ **en Angleterre la ~ est à gauche** in England you drive on the left ◆ **voiture avec ~ à gauche/à droite** left-hand-drive/right-hand-drive car ◆ **faire un brin de ~ à qn** * to go *ou* walk part of the way with sb, to walk along with sb for a bit *

2 *(= direction) [d'affaires]* running, management; *[de travaux]* supervision; *[de pays]* running, leading; *[de négociations, enquête]* leading, conducting; *(Littérat) [d'intrigue]* conducting ◆ **sous la ~ de** *[+ homme politique, capitaine]* under the leadership of; *[+ guide]* accompanied by; *[+ instituteur]* under the supervision of; *[+ chef d'orchestre]* under the baton *ou* leadership of

3 *(= comportement)* behaviour *(Brit)*, behavior *(US)*; *(Scol)* conduct ◆ **avoir une ~ bizarre** to behave strangely ◆ **quelle ~ adopter ?** what course of action shall we take? ◆ **zéro de ~** zero *ou* no marks *(Brit)* for conduct ◆ **relâché** *ou* **libéré pour bonne ~** *(Prison)* released for good behaviour; → **acheter, écart, ligne**[1]

4 *(= tuyau)* pipe ◆ **~ d'eau/de gaz** water/gas main

COMP **conduite d'échec** defeatist behaviour
conduite forcée *(Hydro-Élec)* pressure pipeline
conduite intérieure *(= voiture)* saloon (car) *(Brit)*, sedan *(US)*
conduite montante rising main

condyle /kɔ̃dil/ NM *(Anat)* condyle

condylome /kɔ̃dilom/ NM condyloma, genital wart

cône /kon/ NM *(gén, Sci)* cone ◆ **en forme de ~** cone-shaped ◆ **~ de déjection** alluvial cone ◆ **~ d'ombre/de lumière** cone of shadow/light

conf * /kɔ̃f/ NF abrév de **conférence**

confection /kɔ̃fɛksjɔ̃/ NF 1 *(= exécution) [d'appareil, vêtement]* making; *[de repas]* making, preparation, preparing ◆ **un plat de ma ~** a dish that I made *ou* prepared myself 2 *(Habillement)* **la ~** the clothing industry ◆ **être dans la ~** to be in the clothing business ◆ **vêtement de ~** ready-made garment ◆ **il achète tout en ~** he buys everything ready-to-wear *ou* off-the-peg *(Brit)* *ou* off-the-rack *(US)*; → **magasin**

confectionner /kɔ̃fɛksjɔne/ ▸ conjug 1 ◂ VT *[+ mets]* to prepare, to make; *[+ appareil, vêtement]* to make

confectionneur, -euse /kɔ̃fɛksjɔnœʀ, øz/ NM,F clothes manufacturer

confédéral, e (mpl **-aux**) /kɔ̃fedeʀal, o/ ADJ confederal

confédération /kɔ̃fedeʀasjɔ̃/ NF *(Pol)* confederation, confederacy; *(= syndicats)* confederation ◆ **la Confédération helvétique** the Swiss Confederation

confédéré, e /kɔ̃fedeʀe/ (ptp de **confédérer**) ADJ *[nations]* confederate NMPL *(Hist US)* ◆ **les Confédérés** the Confederates

confédérer /kɔ̃fedeʀe/ ▸ conjug 6 ◂ VT to confederate

conférence /kɔ̃feʀɑ̃s/ NF 1 *(= discours, exposé) (gén)* lecture, talk; *(Univ)* lecture ◆ **faire une ~ sur qch** to lecture on sth, to give a lecture on sth; → **salle, maître** 2 *(= colloque)* conference, meeting ◆ **être en ~** to be in conference *ou* in a *ou* at a meeting ◆ **~ au sommet** summit (meeting *ou* conference) ◆ **~ de presse** press conference 3 *(= poire)* conference pear

> ⚠ Au sens de 'discours', **conférence** ne se traduit par **conference**.

conférencier, -ière /kɔ̃feʀɑ̃sje, jɛʀ/ NM,F speaker, lecturer

conférer /kɔ̃feʀe/ ▸ conjug 6 ◂ VT *(= décerner) [+ dignité]* to confer (à on); *[+ baptême, ordres sacrés]* to give; *(frm = donner) [+ prestige, autorité]* to impart; *[+ droit]* to give (à to); ◆ **~ un certain sens/aspect à qch** to endow sth with a certain meaning/look, to give sth a certain meaning/look ◆ **ce titre lui confère un grand prestige** the title confers great prestige on him VI *(= s'entretenir)* to confer (sur on, about)

confesse /kɔ̃fɛs/ NF ◆ **être/aller à ~** to be at/go to confession

confesser /kɔ̃fese/ ▸ conjug 1 ◂ VT 1 *(= avouer) [+ péchés, erreur]* to confess ◆ **~ que ...** to confess that ... ◆ **~ sa foi** to confess one's faith 2 ◆ **~ qn** *(Rel)* to hear sb's confession, to confess sb; *(* = faire parler qn)* to draw the truth out of sb, to make sb talk ◆ **l'abbé X confesse de 4 à 6** Father X hears confession from 4 to 6 VPR **se confesser** *(Rel)* to go to confession ◆ **se ~ à** *[+ prêtre]* to confess to, to make confession to; *[+ ami]* to confess to ◆ **se ~ de** *[+ péchés, méfait]* to confess

confesseur /kɔ̃fesœʀ/ NM confessor

confession /kɔ̃fesjɔ̃/ NF *(= aveu)* confession; *(= acte du prêtre)* hearing of confession; *(= religion)* denomination; → **dieu**

confessionnal (pl **-aux**) /kɔ̃fesjɔnal, o/ NM confessional

confessionnel, -elle /kɔ̃fesjɔnɛl/ ADJ denominational ◆ **école ~le** denominational *ou* sectarian school ◆ **non ~** non denominational, nonsectarian

confetti /kɔ̃feti/ **NM** piece of confetti ◆ **des ~s** confetti *(NonC)* ◆ **tu peux en faire des ~s !*** *[+ contrat, chèque]* it's not worth the paper it's written on!

confiance /kɔ̃fjɑ̃s/ **NF** *(en l'honnêteté de qn)* confidence, trust; *(en la valeur de qn, le succès de qch, la solidité d'un appareil)* confidence, faith *(en* in); ◆ **avoir ~ en** *ou* **dans, faire ~ à** to have confidence *ou* faith in, to trust ◆ **quelqu'un en qui on peut avoir ~** someone you can rely on *ou* trust ◆ **je l'aurai, tu peux me faire ~ !** I'll get it – believe me! ◆ **voter la ~ (au gouvernement)** to pass a vote of confidence (in the government) ◆ **restaurer** *ou* **rétablir la ~** to restore peoples' *ou* public confidence ◆ **il faut avoir ~** one must have confidence ◆ **je n'ai pas ~ dans leur matériel** I have nc faith *ou* confidence in their equipment ◆ **il a toute ma ~** he has my complete trust *ou* confidence ◆ **mettre qn en ~** to win sb's trust ◆ **placer** *ou* **mettre sa ~ dans** to place *ou* put one's trust in ◆ **avec ~** *[se confier]* trustingly; *[espérer]* confidently ◆ **en (toute) ~, de ~** *[acheter]* with confidence ◆ **de ~** *[personne, maison]* trustworthy, reliable ◆ **c'est l'homme de ~ du ministre** he's the minister's right-hand man ◆ **poste de ~** position of trust ◆ **~ en soi** self-confidence ◆ **la ~ règne !** *(iro)* I can see you really trust me!; → **abus, inspirer, question**

confiant, e /kɔ̃fjɑ̃, jɑ̃t/ **ADJ** 1 *(= assuré, plein d'espoir)* confident; *(en soi-même)* (self-) confident 2 *(= sans défiance) [caractère, regard]* confiding

confidence /kɔ̃fidɑ̃s/ **NF** *(= secret)* confidence, little (personal) secret ◆ **je vais vous faire une ~** let me tell you a secret ◆ **faire des ~s à qn** to confide in sb ◆ **~ pour ~, je ne l'aime pas non plus** since we're speaking frankly, I don't like him either ◆ **en ~** in confidence ◆ **mettre qn dans la ~** to let sb into the secret ◆ **sur le ton de la ~** in a confidential tone (of voice) ◆ **~s sur l'oreiller** pillow talk

confident /kɔ̃fidɑ̃/ **NM** *(= personne)* confidant; *(= siège)* tête-à-tête, confidante

confidente /kɔ̃fidɑ̃t/ **NF** confidante

confidentialité /kɔ̃fidɑ̃sjalite/ **NF** confidentiality

confidentiel, -ielle /kɔ̃fidɑ̃sjɛl/ **ADJ** *(= secret)* confidential; *(sur une enveloppe)* private (and confidential); *(pour public limité) [roman]* for a narrow readership; *[film]* for a limited audience

confidentiellement /kɔ̃fidɑ̃sjɛlmɑ̃/ **ADV** confidentially

confier /kɔ̃fje/ ▸ conjug 7 ◂ **VT** 1 *(= dire en secret)* to confide *(à* to); ◆ **il me confie ses projets** he confides his plans to me, he tells me about his plans ◆ **il me confie tous ses secrets** he shares all his secrets with me, he tells me all his secrets ◆ **dans ce livre il confie ses joies et ses peines** in this book he tells of *ou* reveals his sorrows and his joys

2 *(= laisser aux soins de qn)* to entrust, to confide *(à* to); ◆ **~ qn/qch aux soins de qn** to leave sb/sth in sb's care, to entrust sb/sth to sb's care ◆ **~ qn/qch à la garde de qn** to leave sb to look after sb/sth, to entrust sb/sth to sb's safekeeping ◆ **je vous confie le soin de le faire** I'll leave you to do it, I entrust you with the task of doing it

VPR se confier 1 *(= dire un secret)* **se ~ à qn** to confide in sb ◆ **ils se confièrent l'un à l'autre leur chagrin** they confided their grief to each other

2 *(frm = se fier à)* **se ~ à** *ou* **en qn** to place o.s. in sb's hands

configuration /kɔ̃figyʀasjɔ̃/ **NF** 1 *(= aspect général)* (general) shape, configuration ◆ **la ~ des lieux** the layout of the premises ◆ **suivant la ~ du terrain** following the lie of the land 2 *(Ordin)* configuration ◆ **~ multipostes** multi-user system

configurer /kɔ̃figyʀe/ ▸ conjug 1 ◂ **VT** *(Ordin)* to configure

confiné, e /kɔ̃fine/ (ptp de **confiner**) **ADJ** 1 *(= enfermé)* **vivre ~ chez soi** to live shut away in one's own home 2 *(= renfermé) [atmosphère]* enclosed; *[air]* stale

confinement /kɔ̃finmɑ̃/ **NM** *[de malade]* confining; *[de déchets, site]* containment; *(Phys)* containment, confinement

confiner /kɔ̃fine/ ▸ conjug 1 ◂ **VT** *(= enfermer)* ◆ **~ qn à** *ou* **dans** to confine sb to *ou* in **VT INDIR confiner à** *(= toucher à) (lit)* to border on, tc adjoin; *(fig)* to border *ou* verge on **VPR se confiner** to confine o.s. *(à* to); ◆ **se ~ chez soi** tc confine o.s. to the house, to shut o.s. up at home

confins /kɔ̃fɛ̃/ **NMPL** *(= frontières)* borders; *(= partie extrême)* fringes ◆ **aux ~ de la Bretagne et de la Normandie/du rêve et de la réalité** on the borders of Brittany and Normandy/dream and reality ◆ **aux ~ de la Bretagne/la science** at the outermost *ou* furthermost bounds of Brittany/science ◆ **aux ~ de l'univers** in the far reaches of the universe

confire /kɔ̃fiʀ/ ▸ conjug 37 ◂ **VT** *(au sucre)* to preserve, to candy; *(au vinaigre)* to pickle; *(dans de la graisse)* to preserve; → **confit**

confirmand, e /kɔ̃fiʀmɑ̃, ɑ̃d/ **NM,F** confirmand *(SPÉC)*, confirmation candidate

confirmation /kɔ̃fiʀmasjɔ̃/ GRAMMAIRE ACTIVE 47.3 **NF** *(gén, Rel)* confirmation ◆ **en ~ de** confirming, in confirmation of ◆ **apporter ~ de** to confirm, to provide confirmation of ◆ **c'est la ~ de** it provides *ou* is confirmation of ◆ **j'en attends ~** I'm waiting for confirmation

confirmer /kɔ̃fiʀme/ GRAMMAIRE ACTIVE 46.5, 47.3, 48.3 ▸ conjug 1 ◂ **VT** *(gén, Rel)* to confirm ◆ **il m'a confirmé que ...** he confirmed that ... ◆ **je souhaite ~ ma réservation du ...** *(dans une lettre)* I wish to confirm my reservation of ... ◆ **cela l'a confirmé dans ses idées** it confirmed *ou* strengthened him in his ideas ◆ **~ qn dans ses fonctions** to confirm sb's appointment ◆ **la nouvelle se confirme** the news has been confirmed, there is some confirmation of the news; → **exception**

confiscable /kɔ̃fiskabl/ **ADJ** liable to confiscation *ou* seizure

confiscation /kɔ̃fiskasjɔ̃/ **NF** confiscation, seizure

confiserie /kɔ̃fizʀi/ **NF** *(= magasin)* confectioner's (shop), sweetshop *(Brit)*, candy store *(US)*; *(= métier)* confectionery; *(= bonbons)* confectionery *(NonC)*, sweets *(Brit)*, candy *(NonC) (US)* ◆ **une ~** a sweet *(Brit)*, a candy *(US)*

confiseur, -euse /kɔ̃fizœʀ, øz/ **NM,F** confectioner

confisquer /kɔ̃fiske/ ▸ conjug 1 ◂ **VT** *(gén, Jur)* to confiscate, to seize

confit, e /kɔ̃fi, it/ (ptp de **confire**) **ADJ** *[fruit]* crystallized, candied; *[cornichon]* pickled ◆ **gésiers ~s** gizzards preserved in fat ◆ **la salade est ~e** the salad has gone soggy ◆ **~ de** *ou* **en dévotion** steeped in piety **NM** ◆ **~ d'oie/de canard** goose/duck confit

confiture /kɔ̃fityʀ/ **NF** jam ◆ **~ de prunes/d'abricots** plum/apricot jam ◆ **~ d'oranges** (orange) marmalade ◆ **~ de citrons** lemon marmalade ◆ **~ de lait** *confectionery made of milk and sugar reduced to a thick cream* ◆ **faire des ~s** to make jam ◆ **donner de la ~ aux cochons** to throw pearls before swine

confiturerie /kɔ̃fityʀʀi/ **NF** jam factory

confiturier, -ière /kɔ̃fityʀje, jɛʀ/ **NM,F** jam *ou* preserves *(Brit)* maker **NM** *(= pot)* jam jar

conflagration /kɔ̃flagʀasjɔ̃/ **NF** *(frm = conflit)* cataclysm

conflictualité /kɔ̃fliktyalite/ **NF** conflict, conflictual situations

conflictuel, -elle /kɔ̃fliktyɛl/ **ADJ** *[pulsions, intérêts]* conflicting ◆ **situation ~le** situation of conflict ◆ **avoir des rapports ~s avec qn** to have a conflictual relationship with sb

conflit /kɔ̃fli/ **NM** conflict; *(= grève)* dispute ◆ **pour éviter le ~** to avoid (a) conflict *ou* a clash ◆ **entrer en ~ avec qn** to come into conflict with sb, to clash with sb ◆ **être en ~ avec qn** to be in conflict with sb, to clash with sb ◆ **~ d'intérêts** conflict *ou* clash of interests ◆ **le ~ des générations** the generation gap ◆ **~ armé** armed conflict ◆ **~ social, ~ du travail** industrial dispute ◆ **~s internes** infighting ◆ **~ de juridiction** *(Jur)* jurisdictional dispute

confluence /kɔ̃flyɑ̃s/ **NF** *[de cours d'eau]* confluence, flowing together; *(fig)* mingling, merging

confluent /kɔ̃flyɑ̃/ **NM** *(Géog)* confluence ◆ **au ~ de deux cultures** at the bridge of two cultures, where two cultures meet ◆ **au ~ du rêve et de la réalité** where dream meets reality

confluer /kɔ̃flye/ ▸ conjug 1 ◂ **VI** *[cours d'eau]* to join, to flow together; *(littér) [foule, troupes]* to converge *(vers* on); ◆ **~ avec** to flow into, to join

confondant, e /kɔ̃fɔ̃dɑ̃, ɑ̃t/ **ADJ** astounding

confondre /kɔ̃fɔ̃dʀ/ ▸ conjug 41 ◂ **VT** 1 *(= mêler) [+ choses, dates]* to mix up, to confuse ◆ **on confond toujours ces deux frères** people always mix up *ou* confuse the two brothers *ou* get the two brothers mixed up ◆ **les deux sœurs se ressemblent au point qu'on les confond** the two sisters are so alike that you take *ou* mistake one for the other ◆ **~ qch/qn avec qch/qn d'autre** to mistake sth/sb for sth/sb else ◆ **elle a confondu sa valise avec la mienne** she mistook my suitcase for hers ◆ **j'ai dû ~** I must have made a mistake, I must have been mistaken ◆ **mes réserves ne sont pas de la lâcheté, il ne faudrait pas ~** my reservations aren't cowardice, let there be no mistake about that *ou* you shouldn't confuse the two

2 *(= déconcerter)* to astound ◆ **il me confondit par l'étendue de ses connaissances** he astounded me with the extent of his knowledge ◆ **son insolence a de quoi vous ~** his insolence is astounding *ou* is enough to leave you speechless ◆ **je suis confondu devant** *ou* **de tant d'amabilité** I'm overcome *ou* overwhelmed by such kindness ◆ **être confondu de reconnaissance** to be overcome with gratitude

3 *(= démasquer) [+ ennemi, menteur]* to confound

4 *(= réunir, fusionner)* to join, to meet ◆ **deux rivières qui confondent leurs eaux** two rivers which flow together *ou* join ◆ **toutes classes d'âge/dépenses confondues** all age groups/expenses taken into account ◆ **les députés, toutes appartenances confondues** the deputies, irrespective of which party they belong to

VPR se confondre 1 *(= ne faire plus qu'un)* to merge; *(= se rejoindre)* to meet; *(= s'embrouiller)* to become confused ◆ **les silhouettes se confondaient dans la brume** the silhouettes merged (together) in the mist ◆ **les couleurs se confondent de loin** the colours merge in the distance ◆ **tout se confondait dans sa mémoire** everything became confused in his memory ◆ **nos intérêts se confondent** our interests are one and the same ◆ **les deux fleuves se confondent à cet endroit** the two rivers flow together *ou* join here

2 ◆ **se ~ en excuses** to apologize profusely ◆ **il se confondit en remerciements** he thanked me *(ou* them *etc)* profusely *ou* effusively

conformation /kɔ̃fɔʀmasjɔ̃/ **NF** conformation; → **vice**

conforme /kɔ̃fɔʀm/ **ADJ** 1 (= *semblable*) true (*à* to); ◆ ~ **à l'original/au modèle** true to the original/pattern ◆ **c'est ~ à l'échantillon** it matches the sample ◆ **c'est peu ~ à ce que j'ai dit** it bears little resemblance to what I said ◆ **ce n'est pas ~ à l'original** it does not match the original; → **copie**

2 (= *fidèle*) **être ~ à** [+ *norme, règle, commande*] to be in accordance with, to comply with; [+ *loi*] to be in accordance *ou* conformity with ◆ **l'exécution des travaux est ~ au plan prévu** the work is being carried out in accordance with the agreed plan ◆ **être ~ aux normes de sécurité** to conform to *ou* meet safety standards

3 (= *en harmonie avec*) ~ **à** [+ *promesse*] in keeping with, consonant with (*frm*) ◆ **un niveau de vie ~ à nos moyens** a standard of living in keeping *ou* consonant with (*frm*) our means ◆ **il a des vues ~s aux miennes** his views are in keeping with my own ◆ **ces mesures sont ~s à notre politique** these measures are in line with our policy ◆ **c'est ~ à ce que j'espérais** it is as I hoped

conformé, e /kɔ̃fɔʀme/ (ptp de **conformer**) **ADJ** [*corps, enfant*] ◆ **bien/mal** ~ well-/ill-formed ◆ **bizarrement** ~ strangely shaped *ou* formed

conformément /kɔ̃fɔʀmemɑ̃/ **conformément à LOC ADV** 1 (= *en respectant*) [+ *loi*] in accordance *ou* conformity with; [+ *plan*] in accordance with, according to ◆ **ce travail a été exécuté ~ au modèle/à l'original** this piece of work was done to conform to the pattern/original *ou* to match the pattern/original exactly 2 (= *suivant*) in accordance with ◆ ~ **à ce que j'avais promis/prédit** in accordance with what I had promised/predicted

conformer /kɔ̃fɔʀme/ ▸ conjug 1 ◂ **VT** (= *calquer*) ◆ ~ **qch à** to model sth on ◆ ~ **sa conduite à celle d'une autre personne** to model one's (own) conduct on somebody else's ◆ ~ **sa conduite à ses principes** to match one's conduct to one's principles **VPR** **se conformer** ◆ **se ~ à** to conform to

conformisme /kɔ̃fɔʀmism/ **NM** (*gén, Rel*) conformism

conformiste /kɔ̃fɔʀmist/ **ADJ, NMF** (*gén, Rel*) conformist

conformité /kɔ̃fɔʀmite/ **NF** 1 (= *identité*) similarity, correspondence (*à* to); ◆ **la ~ de deux choses** the similarity of *ou* between two things, the close correspondence of *ou* between two things

2 (= *fidélité*) faithfulness (*à* to); ◆ ~ **à la règle/aux ordres reçus** compliance with the rules/orders received ◆ **en ~ avec le plan prévu/avec les ordres reçus** in accordance *ou* conformity with the proposed plan/orders received ◆ **en ~ avec le modèle** in accordance with the pattern ◆ **certificat de ~** certificate of compliance

3 (= *harmonie*) conformity, agreement (*avec* with); ◆ **la ~ de nos vues sur la question, notre ~ de vues sur la question** the convergence of our views on the question ◆ **sa conduite est en ~ avec ses idées** his conduct is in keeping *ou* in conformity with his ideas

confort /kɔ̃fɔʀ/ **NM** comfort ◆ **villa tout ~** *ou* **avec (tout) le ~ moderne** villa with all modern conveniences *ou* mod cons (*Brit*) ◆ **il aime le** *ou* **son ~** he likes his creature comforts *ou* his comfort ◆ **dès que ça dérange son ~ personnel il refuse de nous aider** as soon as it inconveniences him *ou* puts him out he refuses to help us ◆ **pour notre ~ intellectuel** for our peace of mind ◆ ~ **psychologique** psychological well-being ◆ **améliorer le ~ d'écoute** to improve the sound quality ◆ **cette présentation apporte un grand ~ de lecture** this presentation makes for easy reading

confortable /kɔ̃fɔʀtabl/ **ADJ** 1 (= *douillet*) [*appartement*] comfortable, cosy; [*vêtement, vie*] comfortable, comfy* ◆ **peu ~** [*fauteuil*] rather uncomfortable; [*situation*] rather uncomfortable, awkward 2 (= *opulent*) [*fortune, retraite, situation, vie*] comfortable 3 (= *important*) [*majorité, marge*] comfortable ◆ **il dispose d'une avance ~ sur ses rivaux** he has a comfortable lead over his rivals

confortablement /kɔ̃fɔʀtabləmɑ̃/ **ADV** comfortably ◆ **vivre ~** (*dans le confort*) to live in comfort; (*dans la richesse*) to live very comfortably, to lead a comfortable existence

conforter /kɔ̃fɔʀte/ ▸ conjug 1 ◂ **VT** [+ *thèse*] to reinforce, to back up; [+ *détermination*] to reinforce ◆ **ceci me conforte dans mon analyse** this backs up *ou* reinforces my analysis

confraternel, -elle /kɔ̃fʀatɛʀnɛl/ **ADJ** [*relations, amitié*] between colleagues

confrère /kɔ̃fʀɛʀ/ **NM** [*de profession*] colleague; [*d'association*] fellow member ◆ **selon notre ~ Le Monde** (= *journal*) according to Le Monde

confrérie /kɔ̃fʀeʀi/ **NF** brotherhood

confrontation /kɔ̃fʀɔ̃tasjɔ̃/ **NF** 1 [*d'opinions, personnes*] confrontation; [*de textes*] comparison, collation ◆ **au cours de la ~ des témoins** when the witnesses were brought face to face 2 (= *conflit*) clash, confrontation

confronter /kɔ̃fʀɔ̃te/ ▸ conjug 1 ◂ **VT** (= *opposer*) [+ *opinions, personnes*] to confront; (= *comparer*) [+ *textes*] to compare, to collate ◆ **être confronté à** to be confronted with

confucianisme /kɔ̃fysjanism/ **NM** Confucianism

confucianiste /kɔ̃fysjanist/ **ADJ** Confucian **NMF** Confucian, Confucianist

Confucius /kɔ̃fysjys/ **NM** Confucius

confus, e /kɔ̃fy, yz/ **ADJ** 1 (= *peu clair*) [*bruit, texte, souvenir, mélange*] confused; [*esprit, personne, affaire*] confused, muddled 2 (= *honteux*) [*personne*] ashamed, embarrassed ◆ **il était ~ d'avoir fait cela/de son erreur** he was embarrassed at having done that/about his mistake ◆ **vous avez fait des folies, nous sommes ~ !** you've been far too kind, we're quite overwhelmed!

> ⚠ Au sens de 'honteux', **confus** ne se traduit pas par **confused**.

confusément /kɔ̃fyzemɑ̃/ **ADV** [*distinguer*] vaguely; [*comprendre, ressentir*] vaguely, in a confused way; [*parler*] unintelligibly, confusedly

confusion /kɔ̃fyzjɔ̃/ **NF** 1 (= *honte*) embarrassment, confusion ◆ **à ma grande ~** to my great embarrassment ◆ **rouge de ~** red *ou* blushing with embarrassment

2 (= *erreur*) [*de noms, personnes, dates*] mix-up, confusion (*de* in); ◆ **vous avez fait une ~** (*sur la personne*) you've made a mistake; (*sur des choses*) you've got things confused *ou* mixed up ◆ **cela peut prêter à ~** this could be confusing ◆ **pour éviter la ~ des genres entre économique et politique** to avoid bundling economics and politics together ◆ **ce genre d'émission entretient la ~ des genres entre divertissement et information** this kind of programme blurs the distinction between entertainment and news

3 (= *désordre*) [*d'esprits, idées*] confusion; [*d'assemblée, pièce, papiers*] confusion, disorder (*de* in); ◆ **ses idées sont dans la plus grande ~** his ideas are extremely confused ◆ **c'était dans une telle ~** it was in such confusion *ou* disorder ◆ **mettre** *ou* **jeter la ~ dans les esprits/l'assemblée** to throw people/the audience into confusion *ou* disarray ◆ ~ **mentale** mental confusion

4 (*Jur*) ~ **des dettes** confusion ◆ ~ **de part** *ou* **de paternité** doubt over paternity ◆ ~ **des peines** concurrency of sentences ◆ ~ **des pouvoirs** *non-separation of legislative, executive and judicial powers*

confusionnel, -elle /kɔ̃fyzjɔnɛl/ **ADJ** (*Psych*) [*délire, état*] confusional

confusionnisme /kɔ̃fyzjɔnism/ **NM** (*Psych*) *confused thinking of a child*; (*Pol*) *policy of spreading confusion in people's minds*

congé /kɔ̃ʒe/ **NM** 1 (= *vacances*) holiday (*Brit*), vacation (*US*); (= *arrêt momentané de travail*) leave (*NonC*); (*Mil* = *permission*) leave (*NonC*) ◆ **c'est son jour de ~** it's his day off ◆ **avoir ~ le mercredi** to have Wednesdays off, to be off on Wednesdays ◆ **quel jour avez-vous ~ ?** which day do you have off?, which day are you off? ◆ **j'ai pris deux semaines de ~ pour** *ou* **à Noël** I took two weeks off *ou* two weeks' leave at Christmas, I took two weeks' holiday (*Brit*) *ou* vacation (*US*) at Christmas ◆ **il me reste trois jours de ~ à prendre** I've got three days' holiday (*Brit*) *ou* vacation (*US*) still to come ◆ ~ **sans solde** unpaid leave

2 ◆ **en ~** [*écolier*] on holiday (*Brit*) *ou* vacation (*US*); [*salarié*] on holiday (*Brit*) *ou* vacation (*US*), on leave; [*soldat*] on leave ◆ **se mettre en ~ de son parti** (*fig*) to leave the party temporarily

3 (= *avis de départ*) notice; (= *renvoi*) notice (to quit *ou* leave) ◆ **mon locataire m'a donné son ~** my tenant gave me notice that he was leaving ◆ **donner (son) ~ à un locataire/employé** to give a tenant/an employee (his) notice ◆ **donner ~ huit jours à l'avance** to give a week's notice ◆ **il a demandé son ~** he has asked to leave

4 (= *adieu*) **prendre ~** to take one's leave (*de qn* of sb); ◆ **donner ~ à qn** (*en fin d'un entretien*) to dismiss sb

5 (*Admin* = *autorisation*) clearance certificate; [*de transports d'alcool*] release (*of alcohol from bond*) ◆ ~ **(de navigation)** clearance

COMP **congé annuel** annual holiday (*Brit*) *ou* vacation (*US*) *ou* leave

congé pour convenance personnelle ≃ compassionate leave

congé de conversion retraining period

congé (individuel) de formation (personal) training leave

congé de longue durée extended *ou* prolonged leave of absence

congé (de) maladie sick leave ◆ ~ **de longue maladie** prolonged *ou* extended sick leave

congé (de) maternité maternity leave

congé parental (d'éducation) (unpaid) extended maternity (*ou* paternity) leave

les congés payés (= *vacances*) (annual) paid holidays (*Brit*) *ou* vacation (*US*) *ou* leave; (*péj* = *vacanciers*) riff-raff (*péj*) on holiday (*Brit*) *ou* on vacation (*US*)

congés scolaires school holidays (*Brit*) *ou* vacation (*US*); → **sabbatique**

congédier /kɔ̃ʒedje/ ▸ conjug 7 ◂ **VT** to dismiss

congel * /kɔ̃ʒɛl/ **NM** abrév de **congélateur**

congelable /kɔ̃ʒlabl/ **ADJ** suitable for freezing

congélateur /kɔ̃ʒelatœʀ/ **NM** (= *meuble*) freezer, deep-freeze; (= *compartiment*) freezer compartment ◆ ~ **armoire** upright freezer ◆ ~ **bahut** chest freezer

congélation /kɔ̃ʒelasjɔ̃/ **NF** [*d'eau, aliment, embryon*] freezing; [*d'huile*] congealing ◆ **sac de ~** freezer bag; → **point¹**

congeler /kɔ̃ʒ(ə)le/ ▸ conjug 5 ◂ **VT** [+ *eau*] to freeze; [+ *aliments*] to (deep-)freeze; [+ *huile*] to congeal ◆ **produits congelés** frozen foods **VPR** **se congeler** to freeze

congélo * /kɔ̃ʒelo/ **NM** abrév de **congélateur**

congénère /kɔ̃ʒenɛʀ/ ADJ congeneric NMF (= *semblable*) fellow, fellow creature ◆ **toi et tes ~s** you and your like *ou* kind

congénital, e (mpl **-aux**) /kɔ̃ʒenital, o/ ADJ congenital ◆ **elle est optimiste, c'est ~** *(hum)* she's a born optimist

congère /kɔ̃ʒɛʀ/ NF snowdrift

congestif, -ive /kɔ̃ʒɛstif, iv/ ADJ congestive

congestion /kɔ̃ʒɛstjɔ̃/ NF congestion ◆ **~ (cérébrale)** stroke ◆ **~ (pulmonaire)** congestion of the lungs

congestionner /kɔ̃ʒɛstjɔne/ ▸ conjug 1 ◂ VT *[+ rue]* to congest; *[+ personne, visage]* to make flushed ◆ **être congestionné** *[personne, visage]* to be flushed; *[rue]* to be congested

conglomérat /kɔ̃glɔmeʀa/ NM *(Écon, Géol)* conglomerate; *(fig = amalgame)* conglomeration

conglomération /kɔ̃glɔmeʀasjɔ̃/ NF conglomeration

conglomérer /kɔ̃glɔmeʀe/ ▸ conjug 6 ◂ VT to conglomerate

Congo /kɔ̃go/ NM ◆ **le ~** (= *fleuve*) the Congo ◆ **au ~** in the Congo ◆ **la République démocratique du ~** the Democratic Republic of (the) Congo

congolais, e /kɔ̃gɔlɛ, ɛz/ ADJ Congolese NM,F **Congolais(e)** Congolese NM (= *gâteau*) coconut cake

congratulations /kɔ̃gʀatylasjɔ̃/ NFPL († *ou hum*) congratulations

congratuler /kɔ̃gʀatyle/ ▸ conjug 1 ◂ VT († *ou hum*) to congratulate

congre /kɔ̃gʀ/ NM conger (eel)

congrégation /kɔ̃gʀegasjɔ̃/ NF *(Rel)* congregation; *(fig)* assembly

congrès /kɔ̃gʀɛ/ NM *(gén)* congress; *(Pol = conférence)* conference ◆ **le Congrès** *(Pol US)* Congress ◆ **membre du Congrès** *(gén)* member of Congress; *(homme)* congressman; *(femme)* congresswoman

congressiste /kɔ̃gʀesist/ NMF *(gén)* participant at a congress; *(Pol)* participant at a conference

congru, e /kɔ̃gʀy/ ADJ 1 → **portion** 2 ⇒ **congruent**

congruence /kɔ̃gʀyɑ̃s/ NF *(Math)* congruence

congruent, e /kɔ̃gʀyɑ̃, ɑ̃t/ ADJ *(Math)* congruent

conifère /kɔnifɛʀ/ NM conifer

conique /kɔnik/ ADJ conical ◆ **de forme ~** cone-shaped, conical NF conic (section)

conjectural, e (mpl **-aux**) /kɔ̃ʒɛktyʀal, o/ ADJ conjectural

conjecture /kɔ̃ʒɛktyʀ/ NF conjecture ◆ **se perdre en ~s quant à qch** to lose o.s. in conjectures about sth ◆ **nous en sommes réduits aux ~s** we can only conjecture *ou* guess (about this)

conjecturer /kɔ̃ʒɛktyʀe/ ▸ conjug 1 ◂ VT *(frm)* *[+ causes, résultat]* to conjecture, to speculate about ◆ **~ que ...** to conjecture *ou* surmise that ...

conjoint, e /kɔ̃ʒwɛ̃, wɛ̃t/ ADJ *[démarche, action, débiteurs, legs]* joint *(épith)*; *[problèmes]* linked, related ◆ **financement ~** joint financing ◆ **degrés ~s** *(Mus)* conjunct degrees NM,F *(Admin = époux)* spouse ◆ **lui et sa ~e** he and his spouse ◆ **le maire a félicité les ~s** the mayor congratulated the couple ◆ **les (deux) ~s** the husband and wife ◆ **les futurs ~s** the bride and groom to be

conjointement /kɔ̃ʒwɛ̃tmɑ̃/ ADV jointly ◆ **~ avec** together with ◆ **la notice explicative vous sera expédiée ~ (avec l'appareil)** the explanatory leaflet will be enclosed (with the machine) ◆ **~ et solidairement** *(Jur)* jointly and severally

conjonctif, -ive /kɔ̃ʒɔ̃ktif, iv/ ADJ *(Gram)* conjunctive; *(Anat)* *[tissu]* connective NF **conjonctive** *(Anat)* conjunctiva

conjonction /kɔ̃ʒɔ̃ksjɔ̃/ NF 1 *(Astron, Gram)* conjunction ◆ **~ de coordination/de subordination** coordinating/subordinating conjunction 2 *(frm = union)* union, conjunction

conjonctivite /kɔ̃ʒɔ̃ktivit/ NF conjunctivitis

conjoncture /kɔ̃ʒɔ̃ktyʀ/ NF (= *circonstances*) situation, circumstances ◆ **dans la ~ (économique) actuelle** in the present (economic) situation *ou* circumstances ◆ **crise de ~** economic crisis ◆ **enquête de ~** study of the overall economic climate *ou* of the present state of the economy ◆ **institut de ~** economic(s) research institute

conjoncturel, -elle /kɔ̃ʒɔ̃ktyʀɛl/ ADJ *[phénomène, reprise]* linked to the present economic climate; *[situation, tendance, prévisions]* economic ◆ **chômage ~** cyclical unemployment ◆ **fluctuations ~les** current economic fluctuations

conjoncturiste /kɔ̃ʒɔ̃ktyʀist/ NMF economic analyst

conjugable /kɔ̃ʒygabl/ ADJ which can be conjugated

conjugaison /kɔ̃ʒygɛzɔ̃/ NF *(Bio, Gram)* conjugation; *(frm = union)* union, uniting ◆ **grâce à la ~ de nos efforts** thanks to our joint efforts

conjugal, e (mpl **-aux**) /kɔ̃ʒygal, o/ ADJ *[amour, union]* conjugal ◆ **devoir ~** conjugal duty ◆ **vie ~e** married *ou* conjugal life; → **domicile**

conjugalement /kɔ̃ʒygalmɑ̃/ ADV ◆ **vivre ~** to live (together) as a (lawfully) married couple

conjugalité /kɔ̃ʒygalite/ NF conjugality

conjugué, e /kɔ̃ʒyge/ (ptp de **conjuguer**) ADJ *(Bot, Math)* conjugate; *[efforts, actions]* joint, combined

conjuguer /kɔ̃ʒyge/ ▸ conjug 1 ◂ VT 1 *(Gram)* to conjugate 2 (= *combiner*) to combine ◆ **cette réforme, conjuguée avec une baisse des prix, devrait relancer l'économie** this reform, combined with a drop in prices, should kick-start the economy VPR **se conjuguer** 1 *[efforts, qualités]* to combine 2 *(Gram)* **ce verbe se conjugue avec 'avoir'** this verb is conjugated with 'avoir'

conjuration /kɔ̃ʒyʀasjɔ̃/ NF (= *complot*) conspiracy; (= *rite*) conjuration ◆ **c'est une véritable ~ !*** it's a conspiracy!, it's all a big plot!

conjuré, e /kɔ̃ʒyʀe/ (ptp de **conjurer**) NM,F conspirator

conjurer /kɔ̃ʒyʀe/ ▸ conjug 1 ◂ VT 1 (= *éviter*) *[+ danger, échec]* to avert 2 *(littér = exorciser)* *[+ démons]* to ward off, to cast out ◆ **essayer de ~ le sort** to try to ward off ill fortune 3 (= *implorer*) **~ qn de faire qch** to beseech *ou* entreat *ou* beg sb to do sth ◆ **je vous en conjure** I beseech *ou* entreat *ou* beg you 4 (†† = *conspirer*) *[+ mort, perte de qn]* to plot ◆ **~ contre qn** to plot *ou* conspire against sb VPR **se conjurer** (= *s'unir*) *[circonstances]* to conspire; *[conspirateurs]* to plot, to conspire *(contre* against); ◆ **vous vous êtes tous conjurés contre moi !** *(frm ou hum)* you're all conspiring against me!, you're all in league against me!

connaissable /kɔnɛsabl/ ADJ knowable

connaissance /kɔnɛsɑ̃s/ GRAMMAIRE ACTIVE 46.2 NF 1 (= *savoir*) **la ~** knowledge ◆ **la ~ intuitive/expérimentale** intuitive/experimental knowledge ◆ **sa ~ de l'anglais** his knowledge of English ◆ **il a une bonne ~ des affaires** he has a good *ou* sound knowledge of business matters ◆ **une profonde ~ du cœur humain** a deep understanding of *ou* insight into the human heart ◆ **la ~ de soi** self-knowledge

2 (= *choses connues, science*) **~s** knowledge ◆ **faire étalage de ses ~s** to display one's knowledge *ou* learning ◆ **approfondir/enrichir ses ~s** to deepen *ou* broaden/enhance one's knowledge ◆ **avoir** *ou* **posséder des ~s en** to have some knowledge of ◆ **c'est un garçon qui a des ~s** he's a knowledgeable fellow ◆ **il a de bonnes/vagues ~s en anglais** he has a good command of/a smattering of English ◆ **il a de vagues ~s en physique** he has a vague knowledge of *ou* a nodding acquaintance with physics

3 (= *personne*) acquaintance ◆ **c'est une vieille/simple ~** he is an old/a mere acquaintance ◆ **faire de nouvelles ~s** to make new acquaintances, to meet new people

4 (= *conscience, lucidité*) consciousness ◆ **être sans ~** to be unconscious ◆ **perdre ~** to lose consciousness ◆ **reprendre ~** to regain consciousness, to come to, to come round *(Brit)*

5 *(locutions)* **à ma/sa/leur ~** to (the best of) my/his/their knowledge, as far as I know/he knows/they know ◆ **pas à ma ~** not to my knowledge, not as far as I know ◆ **venir à la ~ de qn** to come to sb's knowledge ◆ **donner ~ de qch à qn** to inform *ou* notify sb of sth ◆ **porter qch à la ~ de qn** to notify sb of sth, to bring sth to sb's attention ◆ **avoir ~ d'un fait** to be aware of a fact ◆ **en (toute) ~ de cause** with full knowledge of the facts ◆ **nous sommes parmi gens de ~** we are among familiar faces ◆ **un visage de ~** a familiar face ◆ **en pays de ~** *(personnes)* among familiar faces; *(sujet)* on familiar ground *ou* territory ◆ **il avait amené quelqu'un de sa ~** he had brought along an acquaintance of his *ou* someone he knew ◆ **faire ~ avec qn, faire la ~ de qn** *(rencontrer)* to meet sb, to make sb's acquaintance; *(apprendre à connaître)* to get to know sb ◆ **(je suis) heureux de faire votre ~** (I am) pleased to meet you ◆ **prendre ~ de** *[+ lettre]* to read; *[+ faits]* to become acquainted with, to be informed of ◆ **nous avons fait ~ à Paris** we met in Paris ◆ **je leur ai fait faire ~** I introduced them (to each other)

connaissement /kɔnɛsmɑ̃/ NM bill of lading ◆ **~ sans réserves** clean bill of lading

connaisseur, -euse /kɔnɛsœʀ, øz/ ADJ *[coup d'œil, air]* expert NM,F connoisseur ◆ **être ~ en vins** to be a connoisseur of wines ◆ **il juge en ~** his opinion is that of a connoisseur

connaître /kɔnɛtʀ/ ▸ conjug 57 ◂ VT 1 *[+ date, nom, adresse]* to know; *[+ fait]* to know, to be acquainted with; *[+ personne]* *(gén)* to know, to be acquainted with; (= *rencontrer*) to meet ◆ **connaît-il la nouvelle ?** has he heard *ou* does he know the news? ◆ **vous connaissez la dernière (nouvelle) ?** have you heard the latest (news)? ◆ **connais-tu un bon restaurant ?** do you know of a good restaurant? ◆ **~ qn de vue/nom/réputation** to know sb by sight/by name/by reputation ◆ **chercher à ~ qn** to try to get to know sb ◆ **apprendre à ~ qn** to get to know sb ◆ **il l'a connu à l'université** he met *ou* knew him at university ◆ **je l'ai connu enfant** *ou* **tout petit** I knew him when he was a child; (= *je le vois encore*) I have known him since he was a child ◆ **si tu te conduis comme ça je ne te connais plus !** *(hum)* if you behave like that (I'll pretend) I'm not with you ◆ **je ne lui connaissais pas ce chapeau/ces talents** I didn't know he had that hat/these talents ◆ **je ne lui connais pas de défauts/d'ennemis** I'm not aware of his having any faults/enemies ◆ **tu le connais mal, c'est mal le ~** you're underestimating *ou* misjudging him

2 *[+ langue, science]* to know; *[+ méthode, auteur, texte]* to know, to be acquainted with ◆ **~ les oiseaux/les plantes** to know about birds/plants ◆ **tu connais la mécanique/la musi-**

que ? do you know anything *ou* much about engineering/music? ◆ ~ **un texte** to know a text, to be familiar with a text ◆ **il connaît son affaire** he knows what he's talking about ◆ **elle connaît son métier** she (really) knows her job ◆ **il en connaît un bout** * *ou* **un rayon** * he knows a thing or two about it * ◆ **un poète qui connaît la vie/l'amour** a poet who knows what life/love is *ou* knows (about) life/love ◆ **tu connais ce village ? – si je connais ! j'y suis né !** * do you know this village? – do I know it! I was born here! ◆ **il ne connaît pas grand-chose à cette machine** he doesn't know (very) much about this machine ◆ **il n'y connaît rien** he doesn't know anything *ou* a thing about it, he doesn't have a clue about it * ◆ **je ne connais pas bien les coutumes du pays** I'm not really familiar with *ou* I'm not (very) well acquainted with *ou* I'm not very well up on * the customs of the country ◆ **je connais la chanson** *ou* **la musique** * I've heard it all before ◆ **il ne connaît pas sa force** he doesn't know *ou* realize his own strength ◆ **il ne connaît pas son bonheur** *ou* **sa chance** he doesn't know how lucky he is ◆ **il ne connaît que son devoir** duty first is his motto

3 *(= éprouver)* *[+ faim, privations]* to know, to experience; *[+ crise, événement]* to experience; *[+ humiliations]* to experience, to suffer, to go through ◆ **il ne connaît pas la pitié** he knows no pity ◆ **ils ont connu des temps meilleurs** they have known *ou* seen better days ◆ **nous connaissons de tristes heures** we are going through sad times ◆ **le pays connaît une crise économique grave** the country is going through *ou* experiencing a serious economic crisis

4 *(= avoir)* *[+ succès]* to enjoy, to have; *[+ sort]* to experience ◆ ~ **un échec** to fail ◆ **sa patience ne connaît pas de bornes** his patience knows no bounds ◆ **cette règle ne connaît qu'une exception** there is only one exception to this rule ◆ **l'histoire de ce pays ne connaît qu'une tentative de coup d'État** in the history of this country there has only been one attempted coup

5 ◆ **faire** ~ *[+ idée, sentiment]* to make known; *[+ décision]* to announce, to make public ◆ **faire** ~ **qn à qn** to introduce sb to sb ◆ **cette pièce/ce traducteur l'a fait** ~ **en Angleterre** this play/translator brought him to the attention of the English public ◆ **il m'a fait** ~ **les joies de la pêche** he introduced me to *ou* initiated me in(to) the joys of fishing ◆ **se faire** ~ *(par le succès)* to make a name for o.s., to make one's name; *(aller voir qn)* to introduce o.s., to make o.s. known

6 *(locutions)* **ça le/me connaît !** * he knows/I know all about it! ◆ **je ne connais que lui/que ça !** do I know him/it! *, don't I know him/it! * ◆ **une bonne tasse de café après le repas, je ne connais que ça** there's nothing like a good cup of coffee after a meal ◆ **je ne le connais ni d'Ève ni d'Adam** I don't know him from Adam ◆ **je te connais comme si je t'avais fait** I know you inside out

VPR **se connaître** 1 ◆ **se** ~ **(soi-même)** to know o.s. ◆ **connais-toi toi-même** know thyself ◆ **il ne se connaît plus** *(fig)* he's beside himself *(with joy or rage etc)*

2 *(= se rencontrer)* to meet ◆ **ils se sont connus en Grèce** they met *ou* became acquainted in Greece

3 ◆ **s'y** ~ **en qch** to know (a lot) about sth, to be well up on * *ou* well versed in sth ◆ **il s'y connaît en voitures** he knows (all) about cars, he's an expert on cars ◆ **c'est de l'or ou je ne m'y connais pas** * unless I'm very much mistaken, this is gold ◆ **quand il s'agit d'embêter les autres, il s'y connaît !** * when it comes to annoying people he's an expert! *

VT INDIR **connaître de** *(Jur)* to take cognizance of

connard ‡ /kɔnaʀ/ NM bloody *(Brit)* idiot ‡, schmuck ‡ *(US)*

connarde ‡ /kɔnaʀd/, **connasse** ‡ /kɔnas/ NF (silly) bitch *‡ *ou* cow ‡ *(Brit)*

conne² ‡ /kɔn/ NF (silly) bitch *‡ *ou* cow ‡ *(Brit)* ◆ **quelle** ~ **je fais !** shit, what an idiot I am! ‡ ◆ **et comme une** ~, **j'ai accepté !** and like a bloody idiot *(Brit)* *ou* like a dumb bitch *(US)* I said yes! ‡

connecter /kɔnɛkte/ ▸ conjug 1 ◂ VT *(Élec, Ordin)* to connect *(à* to; *avec* with) VPR **se connecter** *(Ordin)* *(à la prise)* to get connected, to connect *(à* to); *(à un serveur)* to log on ◆ **se** ~ **sur Internet** to log onto *ou* into the Internet

connecteur /kɔnɛktœʀ/ NM *(Logique, Ling)* connective; *(Élec)* connector

Connecticut /kɔnɛktikət/ NM Connecticut

connectique /kɔnɛktik/ NF *(= industrie)* connector industry; *(= connexions)* connections, wiring

connectivité /kɔnɛktivite/ NF *(Ordin)* connectivity

connement ‡ /kɔnmɑ̃/ ADV stupidly ◆ **j'ai dit ça un peu** ~ it was a bit stupid of me to say that

connerie ‡ /kɔnʀi/ NF 1 *(NonC)* damned *ou* bloody *(Brit)* stupidity ‡ 2 *(= remarque, acte)* damned *ou* bloody *(Brit)* stupid thing to say *ou* do ‡; *(= livre, film)* bullshit *‡ *(NonC)*, bloody rubbish ‡ *(Brit)* *(NonC)* ◆ **arrête de dire des** ~**s** stop talking bullshit *‡ *ou* such bloody rubbish ‡ *(Brit)* ◆ **il a encore fait une** ~ he's gone and done another damned stupid thing ‡ ◆ **c'est de la** ~ **!** that's (a load of) bullshit! *‡ *ou* cobblers! ‡ *(Brit)*

connétable /kɔnetabl/ NM *(Hist)* constable

connexe /kɔnɛks/ ADJ (closely) related

connexion /kɔnɛksjɔ̃/ NF *(gén)* link, connection; *(Élec)* connection *(entre* between; *avec* with) ◆ ~ **Internet** Internet connection ◆ **le nombre d'heures de** ~ **sur le réseau** the number of hours people spend on the network ◆ **temps de** ~ connection time

connivence /kɔnivɑ̃s/ NF connivance ◆ **être/agir de** ~ **avec qn** to be/act in connivance with sb ◆ **un sourire de** ~ a smile of complicity ◆ **ils sont de** ~ they're in league with each other

connotatif, -ive /kɔ(n)nɔtatif, iv/ ADJ *(Ling)* *[sens]* connotative

connotation /kɔ(n)nɔtasjɔ̃/ NF connotation

connoter /kɔ(n)nɔte/ ▸ conjug 1 ◂ VT to connote, to imply; *(Ling)* to connote

connu, e /kɔny/ (ptp de **connaître**) ADJ *(= non ignoré)* *[terre, animal]* known; *(= célèbre)* *[idée, méthode, auteur, livre]* well-known *(épith)* ◆ **(bien)** ~ well-known *(épith)* ◆ **très** ~ very well known, famous ◆ **ces faits sont mal** ~**s** these facts are not well *ou* widely known ◆ **il est** ~ **comme le loup blanc** everybody knows him ◆ **chiffres non encore** ~**s** *(Stat)* figures not yet available; → **ni**

conque /kɔ̃k/ NF *(= coquille)* conch; *(Anat)* concha

conquérant, e /kɔ̃keʀɑ̃, ɑ̃t/ ADJ *[pays, peuple]* conquering; *[ardeur]* masterful; *[air, regard]* swaggering NM,F conqueror

conquérir /kɔ̃keʀiʀ/ ▸ conjug 21 ◂ VT *[+ pays, place forte, montagne]* to conquer; *[+ part de marché]* to capture; *(littér)* *[+ femme, cœur]* to conquer *(littér)*, to win; *(littér)* *[+ estime, respect]* to win, to gain; *[+ supérieur, personnage influent, public]* to win over ◆ **conquis à une doctrine** won over *ou* converted to a doctrine; → **pays¹**

conquête /kɔ̃kɛt/ NF conquest ◆ **faire la** ~ **de** *[+ pays, montagne]* to conquer; *[+ femme]* to conquer *(littér)*, to win; *[+ supérieur, personnage influent, électeurs]* to win over ◆ **s'élancer** *ou* **partir à la** ~ **de** *(gén)* to set out to conquer; *[+ record]* to set out to break ◆ **faire des** ~**s** *(hum)* to break a few hearts, to make a few conquests

conquis, e /kɔ̃ki, iz/ ptp de **conquérir**

conquistador /kɔ̃kistadɔʀ/ NM conquistador

consacré, e /kɔ̃sakʀe/ (ptp de **consacrer**) ADJ 1 *(= béni)* *[hostie, église]* consecrated; *[lieu]* consecrated, hallowed 2 *(= habituel, accepté)* *[coutume]* established, accepted; *[itinéraire, visite]* traditional; *[écrivain]* established, recognized ◆ **c'est l'expression** ~**e** it's the accepted way of saying it ◆ **selon la formule** ~**e** as the expression goes 3 *(= destiné à)* ~ **à** given over to ◆ **talents** ~**s à faire le bien** talents given over to *ou* dedicated to doing good

consacrer /kɔ̃sakʀe/ ▸ conjug 1 ◂ VT 1 ◆ ~ **à** *(= destiner, dédier à)* to devote to, to dedicate to; *(= affecter à, utiliser pour)* to devote to, to give (over) to ◆ ~ **son temps à faire qch** to devote one's time to doing sth ◆ ~ **sa vie à Dieu** to devote *ou* dedicate one's life to God ◆ **il consacre toutes ses forces/tout son temps à son travail** he devotes all his energies/time to his work, he gives all his energies/time (over) to his work ◆ **pouvez-vous me** ~ **un instant ?** can you spare me a moment? ◆ **se** ~ **à une profession/à Dieu** to dedicate *ou* devote o.s. to a profession/God, to give o.s. to a profession/God ◆ **il a consacré plusieurs articles à ce sujet** he devoted several articles to this subject

2 *(Rel)* *[+ reliques, lieu]* to consecrate, to hallow *(littér)*; *[+ église, évêque, hostie]* to consecrate ◆ **temple consacré à Apollon** temple dedicated to Apollo ◆ **leur mort a consacré cette terre** *(littér)* their death has made this hallowed ground

3 *(= entériner)* *[+ coutume, droit]* to establish; *[+ abus]* to sanction ◆ **expression consacrée par l'usage** expression sanctioned by use *ou* which has become accepted through use ◆ **consacré par le temps** time-honoured *(épith)* ◆ **la fuite de l'ennemi consacre notre victoire** the enemy's flight makes our victory complete

consanguin, e /kɔ̃sɑ̃gɛ̃, in/ ADJ ◆ **frère** ~ half-brother *(on the father's side)* ◆ **mariage** ~ intermarriage, marriage between blood relations ◆ **les mariages** ~**s sont à déconseiller** marriages between blood relations *ou* intermarrying should be discouraged NM,F ◆ **les** ~**s** blood relations

consanguinité /kɔ̃sɑ̃g(ɥ)inite/ NF *(du même père, d'ancêtre commun)* consanguinity; *(= union consanguine)* intermarrying

consciemment /kɔ̃sjamɑ̃/ ADV consciously, knowingly

conscience /kɔ̃sjɑ̃s/ NF 1 *(= faculté psychologique)* *(gén)* awareness, consciousness *(de* of); *(Philos, Psych)* consciousness ◆ ~ **de soi** self-awareness ◆ ~ **individuelle/collective/nationale/de classe** individual/collective/national/class consciousness ◆ ~ **politique/écologique** ecological/political awareness ◆ **avoir** ~ **que ...** to be aware *ou* conscious that ... ◆ **avoir** ~ **de sa faiblesse/de l'importance de qch** to be aware *ou* conscious of one's own weakness/of the importance of sth ◆ **avoir une** ~ **claire/aiguë de ses responsabilités** to be fully/keenly aware of one's responsibilities ◆ **prendre** ~ **de qch** to become aware of sth, to realize sth ◆ **il prit soudain** ~ **d'avoir dit ce qu'il ne fallait pas** he was suddenly aware that *ou* he suddenly realized that he had said something he shouldn't have ◆ **cela lui a donné** *ou* **fait prendre** ~ **de son importance** it made him aware of his importance, it made him realize how important he was ◆ **prise de** ~ awareness, realization ◆ **il faut qu'il y ait**

une prise de ~ du problème people must be made aware of the problem

2 (= *éveil*) consciousness ◆ **perdre/reprendre ~** to lose/regain consciousness

3 (= *faculté morale*) conscience ◆ **avoir la ~ tranquille/chargée, avoir bonne/mauvaise ~** to have a clear/guilty conscience ◆ **il n'a pas la ~ tranquille** he has a guilty *ou* an uneasy conscience, his conscience is troubling him ◆ **j'ai ma ~ pour moi** I have a clear conscience ◆ **avoir qch sur la ~** to have sth on one's conscience ◆ **donner bonne ~ à qn** to ease sb's conscience ◆ **donner mauvaise ~ à qn** to give sb a guilty *ou* bad conscience ◆ **se donner bonne ~** to salve *ou* ease one's conscience ◆ **agir selon sa ~** to act according to one's conscience *ou* as one's conscience dictates ◆ **étouffer les ~s** to stifle consciences *ou* people's conscience ◆ **en (toute) ~** in all conscience *ou* honesty ◆ **sans ~** without conscience ◆ **il a plusieurs morts/un mensonge sur la ~** he has several deaths/a lie on his conscience ◆ **son déjeuner lui est resté sur la ~*** his lunch is lying heavy on his stomach; → **acquit, objecteur**

4 ◆ **~ (professionnelle)** conscientiousness ◆ **faire un travail avec beaucoup de ~** to do a piece of work very conscientiously

consciencieusement /kɔ̃sjɑ̃sjøzmɑ̃/ **ADV** conscientiously

consciencieux, -ieuse /kɔ̃sjɑ̃sjø, jøz/ **ADJ** conscientious

conscient, e /kɔ̃sjɑ̃, jɑ̃t/ **ADJ** (= *non évanoui*) conscious; (= *lucide*) [*personne*] lucid; [*mouvement, décision*] conscious ◆ **~ de/que** conscious *ou* aware of/that **NM** (*Psych*) ◆ **le ~** the conscious

conscription /kɔ̃skʀipsjɔ̃/ **NF** conscription, draft (*US*)

conscrit /kɔ̃skʀi/ **NM** conscript, draftee (*US*)

consécration /kɔ̃sekʀasjɔ̃/ **NF** 1 (*Rel*) [*de personne*] consecration; [*de temple*] consecration, dedication (*à* to) 2 [*de coutume, droit, artiste*] establishment; [*d'abus*] sanctioning ◆ **la ~ du temps** time's sanction ◆ **cette exposition fut la ~ de son œuvre** this exhibition established his reputation as an artist ◆ **ce traité fut la ~ de sa politique** this treaty was the apotheosis of his policy ◆ **la ~ ultime** the ultimate accolade

consécutif, -ive /kɔ̃sekytif, iv/ **ADJ** (= *successif*) consecutive; (= *résultant*) consequential ◆ **pendant trois jours ~s** for three days running, for three consecutive days ◆ **elle a eu trois succès ~s** she had three hits in a row ◆ **sa blessure est consécutive à un accident** his injury is the result of an accident; → **proposition**

consécution /kɔ̃sekysjɔ̃/ **NF** consecution

consécutivement /kɔ̃sekytivmɑ̃/ **ADV** consecutively ◆ **elle eut ~ deux accidents** she had two consecutive accidents, she had two accidents in a row *ou* one after the other ◆ **~ à** following

conseil /kɔ̃sɛj/ **GRAMMAIRE ACTIVE 23.1, 29.2, 29.3, 38.3**

NM 1 (= *recommandation*) piece of advice, advice (*NonC*), counsel (*frm*); (= *simple suggestion*) hint ◆ **donner des ~s à qn** to give sb some advice ◆ **écouter/suivre le ~ *ou* les ~s de qn** to listen to/follow sb's advice ◆ **demander ~ à qn** to ask *ou* seek sb's advice, to ask sb for advice ◆ **prendre ~ de qn** to take advice from sb ◆ **je lui ai donné le ~ d'attendre** I advised him to wait ◆ **un petit ~** a word *ou* a few words *ou* a bit of advice ◆ **ne pars pas, c'est un ~ d'ami** don't go – that's (just) a friendly piece of advice ◆ **écoutez mon ~** take my advice, listen to my advice ◆ **un bon ~** a good *ou* sound piece of advice ◆ **un bon ~ : reposez-vous** a bit of advice: get some rest ◆ **ne suivez pas les ~s de la colère** don't let yourself be guided by anger ◆ **il est de bon ~** he gives good *ou* sound advice ◆ **un homme de bon ~** (*frm*) a man of sound advice ◆ **~s à ...** (*Admin, Comm*) advice to ... ◆ **~s à la ménagère/au débutant** hints *ou* tips for the housewife/the beginner; → **nuit**

2 (= *activité professionnelle*) consultancy ◆ **cabinet *ou* société de ~** consultancy *ou* consulting firm, firm of consultants ◆ **activité de ~** consultancy

3 (= *personne*) consultant, adviser (*en* in); ◆ **~ en brevets d'invention** patent engineer ◆ **~ fiscal** tax consultant ◆ **~ juridique** legal consultant *ou* adviser ◆ **~ en communication** communications *ou* media consultant ◆ **~ en propriété industrielle** patent lawyer *ou* attorney (*US*) ◆ **ingénieur(-)~** consulting engineer, engineering consultant ◆ **avocat-/esthéticienne-~** legal/beauty consultant

4 (= *assemblée*) [*d'entreprise*] board; [*d'organisme politique ou professionnel*] council, committee; (= *séance*) meeting ◆ **tenir ~** (= *se réunir*) to hold a meeting; (= *délibérer*) to deliberate

COMP **conseil d'administration** [*de société anonyme*] board of directors; [*d'hôpital, école*] board of governors

conseil de classe (*Scol*) staff meeting (*to discuss the progress of individual members of a class*)

conseil communal (*Belg*) ≃ local council

Conseil constitutionnel Constitutional Council

conseil départemental council of a (*ou* the) département

conseil de discipline (*Scol, Univ*) disciplinary committee

Conseil économique et social Economic and Social Council

conseil d'établissement (*Scol*) ≃ governing board (*Brit*), board of education (*US*)

Conseil d'État Council of State; (*Helv*) cantonal government

Conseil des États (*Helv*) *one of the two chambers of the Swiss federal government*

Conseil de l'Europe Council of Europe

Conseil européen European Council

conseil exécutif executive council

conseil de famille board of guardians

Conseil fédéral (*Helv*) *the executive of the Swiss federal government*

conseil général (French) departmental council, ≃ county council (*Brit*), county commission (*US*)

conseil de guerre (= *réunion*) war council; (= *tribunal*) court-martial ◆ **passer en ~ de guerre** to be court-martialled ◆ **faire passer qn en ~ de guerre** to court-martial sb

conseil législatif legislative council

Conseil des ministres (= *personnes*) (*en Grande-Bretagne*) Cabinet; (*en France*) (French) Cabinet, council of ministers; (= *réunion*) Cabinet meeting

conseil municipal town council

Conseil national (*Helv*) *one of the two chambers of the Swiss federal government*

Conseil national du patronat français *French national employers' federation*, ≃ Confederation of British Industry (*Brit*)

Conseil œcuménique des Églises World Council of Churches

le conseil de l'Ordre [*d'avocats*] *lawyers' governing body*, ≃ the Bar Council (*Brit*), the Bar (*US*); [*de médecins*] *doctors' governing body*, ≃ British Medical Association (*Brit*)

conseil des prud'hommes industrial arbitration court ≃ industrial tribunal

conseil régional regional council

conseil de révision (*Mil*) recruiting board, draft board (*US*)

Conseil de sécurité Security Council

Conseil supérieur de l'audiovisuel *French broadcasting regulatory body*, ≃ Independent Broadcasting Authority (*Brit*), Federal Communications Commission (*US*)

Conseil supérieur de la magistrature *French magistrates' council (which also hears appeals)*

conseil de surveillance supervisory board

conseil d'UFR (*Univ*) departmental (management) committee

conseil d'université university management committee, ≃ governing body (*Brit*), Board of Trustees *ou* Regents (*US*)

CONSEIL

The **Conseil constitutionnel** is made up of nine appointed members and the surviving former presidents of France. It ensures that the constitution is respected in matters of legislation and during elections.

The **Conseil d'État** examines bills before they are submitted to the **Conseil des ministres**. It is also the highest administrative court in the land, dealing with legal irregularities within public bodies and at government level.

The **Conseil régional**, **Conseil général**, **Conseil municipal** and **Conseil d'arrondissement** are elected local councils, respectively at the level of the « région », the « département », the « commune » and (in Paris, Lyons and Marseilles) the « arrondissement ». → **ARRONDISSEMENT, COMMUNE, DÉPARTEMENT, MAIRE, RÉGION**

conseiller[1] /kɔ̃seje/ **GRAMMAIRE ACTIVE 29**

▸ conjug 1 ◂ **VT** 1 (= *recommander*) [+ *méthode, bonne adresse*] to recommend (*à qn* to sb); ◆ **prix conseillé** recommended price ◆ **il conseille la prudence/le silence** he recommends *ou* counsels caution/silence ◆ **il m'a conseillé ce médecin** he advised me to go to this doctor, he recommended this doctor to me ◆ **~ à qn de faire qch** to advise sb to do sth ◆ **je vous conseille vivement de ...** I strongly advise you to ... ◆ **la peur/prudence lui conseilla de ...** fear/prudence prompted him to ... ◆ **il est conseillé de s'inscrire à l'avance** it is advisable to enrol in advance ◆ **il est conseillé aux parents de ...** parents are advised to ...

2 (= *guider*) to advise, to give advice to ◆ **~ un étudiant dans ses lectures** to advise a student in his reading ◆ **il a été bien/mal conseillé** he has been given good/bad advice, he has been well/badly advised

conseiller[2], **-ère** /kɔ̃seje, ɛʀ/ **NM,F** 1 (= *expert*) consultant, adviser (*en* in); (= *personne d'expérience*) counsellor, adviser ◆ **~ diplomatique/économique/technique** diplomatic/economic/technical adviser ◆ **~ financier** financial consultant *ou* adviser ◆ **il est ~ auprès du président** he is an adviser to the president ◆ **que ta conscience soit ta conseillère** may your conscience be your guide; → **colère**

2 (*Admin, Pol* = *fonctionnaire*) council member, councillor

COMP **conseiller conjugal** marriage counsellor

conseiller d'État senior member of the Council of State

conseiller général (French) departmental councillor

conseiller en image image consultant

conseiller matrimonial marriage guidance counsellor

conseiller municipal town councillor (*Brit*), city council man (*US*)

conseiller d'orientation (*Scol*) careers adviser (*Brit*), (school) counselor (*US*), guidance counselor (*US*)

conseiller pédagogique educational adviser

conseiller (principal) d'éducation year head (*Brit*), dean (*US*)

conseiller régional regional councillor

conseiller spécial special adviser

conseilleur, -euse /kɔ̃sɛjœʀ, øz/ NM,F *(péj)* dispenser of advice ◆ **les ~s ne sont pas les payeurs** *(Prov)* givers of advice don't pay the price

consensuel, -elle /kɔ̃sɑ̃sɥɛl/ ADJ *[programme, gouvernement, solution]* consensus *(épith)*; *[volonté, point de vue, société]* consensual; *[patron]* who seeks consensus; *[accord]* consensual ◆ **dans un esprit ~** in a spirit of consensus

consensus /kɔ̃sɛ̃sys/ NM consensus (of opinion) ◆ **~ politique/social/national** political/social/national consensus ◆ **cette évolution fait l'objet d'un très large ~** there is a broad consensus on this development ◆ **~ mou** *(hum, péj)* loose consensus

consentant, e /kɔ̃sɑ̃tɑ̃, ɑ̃t/ ADJ *[partenaire sexuel, otage, victime]* willing; *(Jur) [personnes, parties]* in agreement, agreeable ◆ **(entre) adultes ~s** (between) consenting adults ◆ **ce mariage ne peut avoir lieu que si les parents sont ~s** this marriage can only take place with the parents' consent *ou* if the parents consent to it

consentement /kɔ̃sɑ̃tmɑ̃/ NM consent ◆ **divorce par ~ mutuel** divorce by mutual consent ◆ **donner son ~ à qch** to consent to sth, to give one's consent to sth ◆ **le ~ universel** *(littér)* universal *ou* common assent

consentir /kɔ̃sɑ̃tiʀ/ GRAMMAIRE ACTIVE 36.2
▸ conjug 16 ◂ VI *(= accepter)* to agree, to consent (*à* to); ◆ **~ à faire qch** to agree to do(ing) sth ◆ **je consens à ce qu'il vienne** I consent *ou* agree to his coming ◆ **espérons qu'il va (y) ~** let's hope he'll agree *ou* consent to it; → **mot** VT *(= accorder) [+ permission, délai, prêt]* to grant (*à* to)

conséquemment /kɔ̃sekamɑ̃/ ADV *(littér = donc)* consequently; *(† ou littér = avec cohérence)* consequentially ◆ **~ à** as a result of

conséquence /kɔ̃sekɑ̃s/ NF 1 *(= effet, résultat)* consequence, outcome ◆ **cela pourrait avoir** *ou* **entraîner des ~s graves pour ...** this could have serious consequences for ... ◆ **cela a eu pour ~ de l'obliger à réfléchir** the result *ou* consequence of this was that he was forced to think again, he was forced to think again as a result ◆ **accepter/subir les ~s de ses actions** *ou* **de ses actes** to accept/suffer the consequences of one's actions ◆ **c'est une erreur grosse** *ou* **lourde de ~s** this mistake will have serious consequences *ou* repercussions ◆ **avoir d'heureuses ~s** to have a happy outcome

2 *(Philos = suite logique)* consequence; → **proposition, voie**

3 *(= conclusion, déduction)* inference, conclusion (*de* to be drawn from); ◆ **tirer les ~s** to draw conclusions *ou* inferences (*de* from)

4 *(locutions)* **cela ne tire** *ou* **ne porte** *ou* **ne prête pas à ~** *(= sans importance)* it's of no consequence; *(= sans suites fâcheuses)* it's unlikely there will be any repercussions

◆ **de conséquence** *[affaire, personne]* of (some) consequence *ou* importance

◆ **en conséquence** *(= donc)* consequently; *(= comme il convient)* accordingly

◆ **en conséquence de** *(= par suite de)* in consequence of, as a result of; *(= selon)* according to ◆ **en ~ de quoi, ...** as a result of which, ...

◆ **sans conséquence** *(= sans suite fâcheuse)* without repercussions; *(= sans importance)* of no consequence *ou* importance

conséquent, e /kɔ̃sekɑ̃, ɑ̃t/ GRAMMAIRE ACTIVE 44.1 ADJ 1 *(= logique)* logical, rational; *(= doué d'esprit de suite)* consistent ◆ **~ à** *(littér)* consistent with, in keeping *ou* conformity with ◆ **être ~ avec soi-même** to be consistent ◆ **~ dans ses actions** consistent in one's actions 2 *(* = important)* sizeable 3 *(Géol) [rivière, percée]* consequent 4 *(Mus)* **partie ~e** answer NM *(Ling, Logique, Math)* consequent

◆ **par conséquent** consequently, therefore NF **conséquente** *(Mus)* answer

conservateur, -trice /kɔ̃sɛʀvatœʀ, tʀis/ ADJ *(gén)* conservative; *(Pol Brit)* Conservative, Tory ◆ **le parti ~** *(Can)* the Progressive-Conservative Party *(Can)* NM,F 1 *(= gardien) [de musée]* curator; *[de bibliothèque]* librarian ◆ **~ des eaux et forêts** ≈ forestry commissioner ◆ **~ des hypothèques** ≈ land registrar 2 *(Pol)* conservative; *(Pol Brit)* Conservative, Tory; *(Can)* Conservative *(Can)* NM *(= produit chimique)* preservative; *(= réfrigérateur)* freezer compartment

conservation /kɔ̃sɛʀvasjɔ̃/ NF 1 *(= action) [d'aliments]* preserving; *[de monuments]* preserving, preservation; *[d'archives, accent, souplesse]* keeping; *[d'habitudes]* keeping up ◆ **date limite de ~** *(gén)* use-by date; *[d'aliments]* best-before date; → **instinct, long** 2 *(= état) [d'aliments, monuments]* preservation ◆ **en bon état de ~** *[fruits]* well-preserved; *[monument]* well-preserved, in a good state of preservation 3 *(Admin = charge)* ◆ **~ des eaux et forêts** ≈ Forestry Commission ◆ **~ des hypothèques** ≈ Land Registry

conservatisme /kɔ̃sɛʀvatism/ NM conservatism

conservatoire /kɔ̃sɛʀvatwaʀ/ ADJ *(Jur)* protective; → **saisie** NM school, academy *(of music, drama etc)* ◆ **le Conservatoire (de musique et de déclamation)** the (Paris) Conservatoire ◆ **le Conservatoire national des arts et métiers** *national school of engineering and technology*

conserve /kɔ̃sɛʀv/ NF 1 ◆ **les ~s** *(en boîtes)* canned *ou* tinned *(Brit)* food(s); *(en bocaux)* preserves ◆ **~s de viande/poisson** canned *ou* tinned *(Brit)* meat/fish ◆ **l'industrie de la ~** the canning industry ◆ **se nourrir de ~s** to live out of cans *ou* tins *(Brit)* ◆ **faire des ~s de haricots** to bottle beans ◆ **tu ne vas pas en faire des ~s !** * *(fig)* you're not going to hoard it away for ever!

◆ **en conserve** ◆ **légumes en ~** tinned *(Brit) ou* canned vegetables ◆ **mettre en ~** to can; → **boîte**

2 *(locution)*

◆ **de conserve** *(= ensemble) [naviguer]* in convoy; *[agir]* in concert

conserver /kɔ̃sɛʀve/ ▸ conjug 1 ◂ VT 1 *(= garder dans un endroit) [+ objets, papiers]* to keep ◆ **"conserver à l'abri de la lumière"** "keep *ou* store away from light" ◆ **"à conserver au froid"** "keep refrigerated"

2 *(= ne pas perdre) (gén)* to keep, to retain; *[+ usage, habitude]* to keep up; *[+ espoir]* to retain; *[+ qualité, droits]* to conserve, to retain; *(Sport) [+ titre]* to retain, to hold on to ◆ **~ son calme** to keep *ou* remain calm, to keep cool ◆ **ça conserve tout son sens** it retains its full meaning ◆ **~ la vie** to conserve life ◆ **il a conservé toute sa tête** he still has his wits about him, he's still all there* ◆ **~ l'allure** *(Naut)* to maintain speed ◆ **~ sa position** *(Naut)* to hold one's position ◆ **~ ses positions** *(Mil)* to hold its (*ou* their) positions

3 *(= maintenir en bon état) [+ aliments, santé, monument]* to preserve ◆ **la vie au grand air, ça conserve !** * the open-air life keeps you young ◆ **bien conservé pour son âge** well-preserved for one's age

4 *(Culin)* to preserve, to can; *(dans du vinaigre)* to pickle; *(en bocal)* to bottle

VPR **se conserver** *[aliments]* to keep

conserverie /kɔ̃sɛʀvəʀi/ NF *(= usine)* canning factory; *(= industrie)* canning industry

considérable /kɔ̃sideʀabl/ ADJ *(gén)* considerable; *[somme]* considerable, sizeable; *[foule]* sizeable; *[succès, changement, risque, dégâts, progrès]* considerable, significant; *[rôle]* major, significant; *[personnage]* eminent, important

considérablement /kɔ̃sideʀabləmɑ̃/ ADV considerably ◆ **ceci nous a ~ retardés** this delayed us considerably ◆ **ceci a ~ modifié la situation** this has changed things considerably

considérant /kɔ̃sideʀɑ̃/ NM *[de loi, jugement]* preamble

considération /kɔ̃sideʀasjɔ̃/ NF 1 *(= examen) [d'argument, problème]* consideration ◆ **ceci mérite ~** this is worth considering *ou* consideration *ou* looking into

◆ **en considération** ◆ **prendre qch en ~** to take sth into consideration *ou* account ◆ **la prise en ~ de qch** taking sth into consideration *ou* account ◆ **il faut prendre les enfants en ~** we must consider the children

◆ **en considération de** ◆ **en ~ de son âge** *(= en raison de)* because of *ou* given his age ◆ **en ~ de ce qui aurait pu se passer** *(= par rapport à)* considering what could have happened ◆ **en ~ des services rendus** for services rendered

2 *(= motif, aspect)* consideration, issue ◆ **n'entrons pas dans ces ~s** let's not go into these considerations ◆ **c'est une ~ dont nous n'avons pas à nous préoccuper** it's a question *ou* an issue we don't need to bother ourselves with ◆ **~s d'ordre personnel** personal considerations

3 *(= remarques, observations)* **~s** reflections ◆ **il se lança dans des ~s interminables sur la crise** he launched into lengthy reflections on the crisis

4 *(= respect)* esteem, respect ◆ **jouir de la ~ de tous** to enjoy everyone's esteem *ou* respect ◆ **par ~ pour** out of respect *ou* regard for; → **agréer**

◆ **sans considération** ◆ **sans ~ des conséquences** heedless *ou* regardless of the consequences ◆ **sans ~ d'âge ni de sexe** regardless of age or sex ◆ **ils agissent sans ~ pour l'opinion publique** they act with no thought for public opinion ◆ **des plans d'urbanisme sans ~ pour l'environnement** town planning that takes no account of the environment

considérer /kɔ̃sideʀe/ GRAMMAIRE ACTIVE 53.1
▸ conjug 6 ◂ VT 1 *(= envisager) [+ problème, situation]* to consider, to think about ◆ **il faut ~ (les) avantages et (les) inconvénients** one must consider *ou* take into account the advantages and disadvantages ◆ **considère bien ceci** think about this carefully ◆ **il ne considère que son intérêt** he only thinks about *ou* considers his own interests ◆ **tout bien considéré** all things considered, taking everything into consideration *ou* account ◆ **c'est à ~** *(pour en tenir compte)* this has to be considered *ou* borne in mind *ou* taken into account; *(à étudier)* this has to be gone into *ou* examined

2 ◆ **~ comme** *(= juger)* to consider (to be); *(= assimiler à)* to look upon as, to regard as, to consider (to be) ◆ **je le considère comme mon fils** I look upon him as *ou* regard him as my son, I consider him (to be) my son ◆ **je le considère comme intelligent** I consider him intelligent, I deem him to be intelligent *(frm)* ◆ **il se considère comme un personnage important** he sees himself as an important person, he considers himself (to be) an important person

3 *(= juger)* to consider, to deem *(frm)* ◆ **je le considère intelligent** I consider him intelligent, I deem him to be intelligent *(frm)* ◆ **je considère qu'il a raison** I consider that he is right ◆ **c'est très mal considéré (d'agir ainsi)** that's not an acceptable way to act, it's very bad form (to act like that) *(Brit)* ◆ **considérant que ...** *(gén)* considering that ...; *(Jur)* whereas ...

4 *(frm = regarder)* to consider, to study

5 *(= respecter : gén ptp)* to respect, to have a high regard for ◆ **il est très considéré** he is highly regarded *ou* respected, he is held in high regard *ou* high esteem ◆ **métier peu considéré** profession held in low esteem *ou* regard ◆ **le**

besoin d'être considéré the need to have people's respect *ou* esteem

consignataire /kɔ̃siɲatɛʀ/ **NM** *[de biens, marchandises]* consignee; *[de navire]* consignee, forwarding agent; *[de somme]* depositary

consignation /kɔ̃siɲasjɔ̃/ **NF** *(= dépôt d'argent)* deposit; *(= dépôt de marchandise)* consignment ◆ **la ~ d'un emballage** charging a deposit on a container ◆ **marchandises en ~** goods on consignment ◆ **~ à bord** *[de clandestins]* detention on board; → **caisse**

consigne /kɔ̃siɲ/ **NF** 1 *(= instructions)* instructions ◆ **c'est la ~** those are our instructions ◆ **la ~ c'est la ~** * orders are orders ◆ **donner/observer la ~** to give/follow instructions ◆ **j'ai reçu (la) ~ de ne laisser entrer personne** I've been given instructions not to let anyone in ◆ **ils n'ont pas donné de ~ de vote** they didn't give their supporters guidance on how to vote in the second round

2 *(pour les bagages)* left-luggage (office) *(Brit)*, checkroom *(US)* ◆ **~ automatique** (left-luggage) lockers

3 *(= somme remboursable)* deposit ◆ **il y a 50 cents de consigne ou une consigne de 50 cents sur la bouteille** there's a 50-cent deposit *ou* a deposit of 50 cents on the bottle, you get 50 cents back on the bottle

4 *(= punition) (Mil)* confinement to barracks; († : *Scol)* detention

consigné, e /kɔ̃siɲe/ (ptp de **consigner**) **ADJ** *[bouteille, emballage]* returnable ◆ **non ~** non-returnable

consigner /kɔ̃siɲe/ ▸ conjug 1 ◂ **VT** 1 *[+ fait, pensée, incident]* to record ◆ **~ qch par écrit** to put sth down in writing *ou* on paper

2 *(= interdire de sortir à) [+ troupe]* to confine to barracks; *[+ élève]* to give detention to, to keep in (after school); *[+ enfant]* to ground *; *(= interdire l'accès de) [+ salle, établissement]* to bar entrance to ◆ **consigné à la caserne** confined to barracks ◆ **établissement consigné aux militaires** establishment out of bounds to troops

3 *(= mettre en dépôt) [+ somme, marchandise]* to deposit; *[+ navire]* to consign; *[+ bagages]* to deposit *ou* put in the left-luggage (office) *(Brit) ou* checkroom *(US)*

4 *(= facturer provisoirement) [+ emballage, bouteille]* to put a deposit on ◆ **les bouteilles sont consignées 50 cents** there is a deposit of 50 cents on the bottles ◆ **je vous le consigne** I'm giving it to you on a deposit

consistance /kɔ̃sistɑ̃s/ **NF** *[de sauce, neige, terre]* consistency; *[de caractère]* strength ◆ **~ sirupeuse/élastique** syrupy/elastic consistency ◆ **manquer de ~** *[sauce]* to lack consistency; *[idée, personnage, texte, film]* to lack substance; *[rumeur]* to be unsupported by evidence ◆ **donner de la ~ à** *[+ pâte]* to give body to; *[+ rumeur]* to give strength to; *[+ idée, théorie]* to give substance to ◆ **prendre ~** *[liquide]* to thicken; *[idée, projet, texte, personnage]* to take shape ◆ **sans ~** *[caractère]* spineless, colourless; *[rumeur]* ill-founded, groundless; *[substance]* lacking in consistency *(attrib)* ◆ **cette rumeur prend de la ~** this rumour is gaining ground

consistant, e /kɔ̃sistɑ̃, ɑ̃t/ **ADJ** *[repas]* solid *(épith)*, substantial; *[nourriture]* solid *(épith)*; *[mélange, peinture, sirop]* thick; *[argument]* solid, sound ◆ **système ~** *(Logique)* consistent system

> ⚠ **consistant** se traduit rarement par le mot anglais **consistent**, qui a le sens de 'cohérent'.

consister /kɔ̃siste/ ▸ conjug 1 ◂ **VI** 1 *(= se composer de)* **~ en** to consist of, to be made up of ◆ **le village consiste en 30 maisons et une église** the village consists of *ou* is made up of 30 houses and a church ◆ **en quoi consiste votre travail ?** what does your work consist of? 2 *(= résider dans)* **~ dans** to consist in ◆ **leur salut consistait dans l'arrivée immédiate de renforts** their salvation lay in the immediate arrival of reinforcements ◆ **~ à faire** to consist in doing

consistoire /kɔ̃sistwaʀ/ **NM** consistory

consistorial, e (mpl **-iaux**) /kɔ̃sistɔʀjal, jo/ **ADJ** consistorial, consistorian **NM** consistorian

conso * /kɔ̃so/ **NF** (abrév de **consommation**) *(= boisson)* drink

consœur /kɔ̃sœʀ/ **NF** *(hum)* (female) colleague

consolable /kɔ̃sɔlabl/ **ADJ** consolable

consolant, e /kɔ̃sɔlɑ̃, ɑ̃t/ **ADJ** consoling, comforting

consolateur, -trice /kɔ̃sɔlatœʀ, tʀis/ **ADJ** consolatory **NM,F** *(littér)* comforter

consolation /kɔ̃sɔlasjɔ̃/ **NF** *(= action)* consoling, consolation; *(= réconfort)* consolation *(NonC)*, comfort *(NonC)*, solace *(NonC) (littér)* ◆ **nous prodiguant ses ~s** offering us comfort ◆ **paroles de ~** words of consolation *ou* comfort ◆ **elle est sa ~** she is his consolation *ou* comfort *ou* solace *(littér)* ◆ **il n'y a pas de dégâts, c'est une ~** there's no damage, that's one consolation ◆ **lot** *ou* **prix de ~** consolation prize

console /kɔ̃sɔl/ **NF** 1 *(= table)* console (table); *(Archit)* console 2 *[de harpe]* neck; *[d'orgue]* console; *(d'enregistrement)* console ◆ **~ de jeu** games console ◆ **~ de jeu vidéo** video game console ◆ **~ de mixage** mixing desk

consoler /kɔ̃sɔle/ ▸ conjug 1 ◂ **VT** *[+ personne]* to console; *[+ chagrin]* to soothe ◆ **ça me consolera de mes pertes** that will console me for my losses ◆ **je ne peux pas le ~ de sa peine** I cannot console *ou* comfort him in his grief ◆ **si ça peut te ~ ...** if it is of any consolation *ou* comfort to you ... ◆ **le temps console** time heals **VPR** **se consoler** to console o.s., to find consolation ◆ **se ~ d'une perte/de son échec** to be consoled for *ou* to get over a loss/one's failure ◆ **il s'est vite consolé avec une autre** *(hum)* he soon consoled himself with another woman ◆ **il ne s'en consolera jamais** he'll never get over it

consolidation /kɔ̃sɔlidasjɔ̃/ **NF** 1 *(gén) [de maison, table, mur]* strengthening, reinforcement; *(Méd) [de fracture]* setting 2 *[d'accord, acquis, amitié, parti, fortune]* consolidation; *[de monnaie]* strengthening ◆ **~ de l'unité européenne** strengthening of European unity 3 *(Fin)* funding ◆ **~ de la dette** debt funding *ou* consolidation

consolidé, e /kɔ̃sɔlide/ (ptp de **consolider**) **ADJ** 1 *(Fin) [bénéfice, bilan, chiffre d'affaires]* consolidated ◆ **dette ~e** *(gén)* consolidated debt; *(comptabilité publique)* funded debt ◆ **rente ~e** consolidated government stock, consols 2 *(Méd)* **la fracture est ~e** the fracture has healed, the bone has set ◆ **l'état du patient est ~** the patient's condition has stabilized *ou* is stable **NMPL** **consolidés** *(Fin)* consols

consolider /kɔ̃sɔlide/ ▸ conjug 1 ◂ **VT** 1 *[+ maison, table]* to strengthen, to reinforce; *[+ mur]* to reinforce; *(Méd) [+ fracture]* to set 2 *[+ accord, amitié, parti, fortune]* to consolidate; *(Écon) [+ monnaie]* to strengthen ◆ **~ sa position** to consolidate one's position ◆ **~ son avance** to extend one's lead 3 *(Fin) [+ rente, emprunt]* to guarantee; *[+ dette]* to fund **VPR** **se consolider** *[régime, parti]* to strengthen *ou* consolidate its position; *[fracture]* to set, to knit ◆ **la position de la gauche/droite s'est encore consolidée** the position of the left/right has been further consolidated *ou* strengthened

consommable /kɔ̃sɔmabl/ **ADJ** *[solide]* edible; *[liquide]* drinkable ◆ **cette viande n'est ~ que bouillie** this meat can only be eaten boiled **NM** *(gén, Ordin)* consumable

consommateur, -trice /kɔ̃sɔmatœʀ, tʀis/ **NM,F** *(= acheteur)* consumer; *(= client d'un café)* customer ◆ **les plus grands** *ou* **gros ~s de thé** the biggest *ou* largest consumers of tea ◆ **ce sont de gros ~s d'énergie/de médicaments** they consume a lot of energy/medicines ◆ **c'est un grand ~ de romans** he reads a lot of novels ◆ **défense/information des ~s** consumer protection/information **ADJ** ◆ **industrie consommatrice d'énergie/de pétrole** energy-consuming/oil-consuming industry ◆ **le premier pays ~ d'eau** the country with the highest water consumption

consommation /kɔ̃sɔmasjɔ̃/ **NF** 1 *[de nourriture, gaz, matière première, essence]* consumption ◆ **faire une grande ~ de** to get through *ou* use a lot of ◆ **~ aux 100 km** (fuel) consumption per 100 km, ≈ miles per gallon, gas mileage *(US)* ◆ **ampoule basse ~** low-energy light bulb

2 *(Écon)* **la ~** consumption ◆ **la ~ des ménages** household *ou* private consumption ◆ **la ~ intérieure** domestic consumption ◆ **~ ostentatoire** conspicuous consumption ◆ **de ~** *[biens, société]* consumer *(épith)* ◆ **produits de ~** consumables, consumer goods ◆ **article** *ou* **produit de ~ courante** *ou* **de grande ~** staple

3 *(dans un café) (= boisson)* drink; *(= commande)* order

4 *(frm) [de mariage]* consummation; *[de ruine]* confirmation; *[de crime]* perpetration ◆ **jusqu'à la ~ des siècles** *(littér)* until the end of time

consommé, e /kɔ̃sɔme/ (ptp de **consommer**) **ADJ** *[habileté]* consummate *(épith)*; *[écrivain, artiste]* accomplished ◆ **tableau qui témoigne d'un art ~** picture revealing consummate artistry **NM** *(Culin)* consommé ◆ **~ de poulet** chicken consommé, consommé of chicken

consommer /kɔ̃sɔme/ ▸ conjug 1 ◂ **VT** 1 *[+ nourriture]* to eat, to consume *(frm)*; *[+ boissons]* to drink, to consume *(frm)* ◆ **on consomme beaucoup de fruits chez nous** we eat a lot of fruit in our family ◆ **la France est le pays où l'on consomme** *ou* **où il se consomme le plus de vin** France is the country with the greatest wine consumption *ou* where the most wine is consumed *ou* drunk ◆ **il est interdit de ~ de l'alcool dans les bureaux** alcohol is not allowed *ou* may not be consumed in the office ◆ **"à consommer de préférence avant le"** "best before" ◆ **"à consommer avec modération"** "to be drunk in moderation"

2 *[+ combustible, matière première]* to use, to consume ◆ **cette machine consomme beaucoup d'eau** this machine uses (up) a lot of water ◆ **combien consommez-vous aux 100 km ?** how much do you use per 100 km?, what's your petrol *(Brit) ou* gas *(US)* consumption?, ≈ how many miles per gallon do you get? *(Brit)*, what's your gas mileage? *(US)* ◆ **elle consomme beaucoup d'huile** *[voiture]* it's heavy on oil, it uses a lot of oil

3 *(frm = accomplir) [+ acte sexuel]* to consummate; *[+ crime]* to perpetrate, to commit ◆ **le mariage n'a pas été consommé** the marriage has not been consummated ◆ **cela a consommé sa ruine** this finally confirmed his downfall ◆ **ce qui a consommé la rupture ...** what put the seal on the break-up ... ◆ **la rupture est consommée** the break-up is complete

consomption /kɔ̃sɔ̃psjɔ̃/ **NF** († *ou littér = dépérissement)* wasting; († *= tuberculose)* consumption †

consonance /kɔ̃sɔnɑ̃s/ **NF** consonance *(NonC)* ◆ **nom aux ~s étrangères/douces** foreign-sounding/sweet-sounding name

consonant, e /kɔ̃sɔnɑ̃, ɑ̃t/ **ADJ** consonant

consonantique /kɔ̃sɔnɑ̃tik/ **ADJ** consonantal, consonant *(épith)* ◆ **groupe ~** consonant cluster

consonantisme /kɔ̃sɔnɑtism/ NM consonant system

consonne /kɔ̃sɔn/ NF consonant ◆ ~ **d'appui** intrusive consonant ◆ ~ **de liaison** linking consonant

consort /kɔ̃sɔʀ/ ADJ → **prince** NMPL *(péj)* ◆ **Pierre Renaud et ~s** *(= acolytes)* Pierre Renaud and company, Pierre Renaud and his bunch* *(péj)*; *(= pareils)* Pierre Renaud and his like *(péj)*

consortial, e (mpl **-iaux**) /kɔ̃sɔʀsjal, jo/ ADJ *[prêt]* syndicated

consortium /kɔ̃sɔʀsjɔm/ NM consortium ◆ **former un ~ (de prêt)** to syndicate a loan, to form a loan consortium

conspirateur, -trice /kɔ̃spiʀatœʀ, tʀis/ ADJ conspiratorial NM,F conspirator, plotter

conspiration /kɔ̃spiʀasjɔ̃/ NF conspiracy, plot ◆ **c'est une véritable ~ !** it's a plot! ◆ **la Conspiration des poudres** *(Hist)* the Gunpowder Plot

conspirer /kɔ̃spiʀe/ ▸ conjug 1 ◂ VI *(= comploter)* to conspire, to plot *(contre* against*)* VT INDIR **conspirer à** *(= concourir à)* ~ **à faire qch** to conspire to do sth ◆ **tout semblait ~ à notre succès** everything seemed to be conspiring to bring about our success VT † *[+ mort, ruine de qn]* to conspire †, to plot

conspuer /kɔ̃spɥe/ ▸ conjug 1 ◂ VT to boo, to shout down

constamment /kɔ̃stamɑ̃/ ADV *(= sans trêve)* constantly, continuously; *(= très souvent)* constantly, continually

Constance /kɔ̃stɑ̃s/ N *(Géog)* Constance ◆ **le lac de ~** Lake Constance

constance /kɔ̃stɑ̃s/ NF **1** *(= permanence)* consistency, constancy **2** *(littér = persévérance, fidélité)* constancy, steadfastness ◆ **travailler avec ~** to work steadfastly ◆ **vous avez de la ~ !** *(iro)* you don't give up easily! **3** *(† = courage)* fortitude, steadfastness

constant, e /kɔ̃stɑ̃, ɑ̃t/ ADJ **1** *(= invariable)* constant; *(= continu)* constant, continuous; *(= très fréquent)* constant, continual ◆ **francs ~s** inflation-adjusted francs, constant francs **2** *(littér = persévérant) [effort]* steadfast; *[travail]* constant ◆ **être ~ dans ses efforts** to be steadfast *ou* constant in one's efforts NF **constante** **1** *(Math, Phys)* constant **2** *(= caractéristique)* permanent feature ◆ **une ~e de son caractère/sa politique** an abiding feature of his character/policies

Constantin /kɔ̃stɑ̃tɛ̃/ NM Constantine

Constantinople /kɔ̃stɑ̃tinɔpl/ N Constantinople

constat /kɔ̃sta/ NM **1** *(= procès-verbal)* ~ **(d'huissier)** affidavit drawn up by a bailiff ◆ ~ **(d'accident)** (accident) report ◆ ~ **(à l')amiable** *jointly-agreed statement for insurance purposes* ◆ ~ **d'adultère** recording of adultery ◆ ~ **de décès** death certificate **2** *(= constatation)* ~ **d'échec/d'impuissance** acknowledgement of failure/impotence ◆ **ce n'est pas une supposition, c'est un ~** it's not a supposition, it's a statement of fact ◆ **je suis forcé de faire le triste ~ que ...** I regret to have to say that ...

constatation /kɔ̃statasjɔ̃/ GRAMMAIRE ACTIVE 53.2 NF **1** *(NonC) [de fait]* noting, noticing; *[d'erreur]* seeing, noticing; *(frm) [d'effraction, état de fait, authenticité]* recording; *[de décès]* certifying **2** *(= observation)* observation ◆ **~s** *[d'enquête]* findings ◆ **c'est une simple ~ et non un reproche** it's just a statement of fact *ou* an observation, not a criticism ◆ **faire une ~** to make an observation ◆ **procéder aux ~s d'usage** *(Police)* to make a routine report

constater /kɔ̃state/ ▸ conjug 1 ◂ VT **1** *(= remarquer) [+ fait]* to note, to notice; *[+ erreur]* to see ◆ **il constata la disparition de son carnet** he noticed *ou* saw that his notebook had disappeared ◆ **je ne critique pas, je fais que ~** I'm not criticizing, I'm merely stating a fact ◆ **je constate que vous n'êtes pas pressé de tenir vos promesses** I see *ou* notice that you aren't in a hurry to keep your promises ◆ **vous pouvez ~ par vous-même les erreurs** you can see the mistakes for yourself **2** *(frm = consigner) [+ effraction, état de fait, authenticité, dégâts]* to record; *[+ décès]* to certify ◆ **le médecin a constaté le décès** the doctor certified that death had taken place *ou* occurred

constellation /kɔ̃stelasjɔ̃/ NF *(Astron)* constellation ◆ ~ **de** *(littér) [+ lumières, poètes]* constellation *ou* galaxy of ◆ **~s de satellites** satellite constellations

constellé, e /kɔ̃stele/ (ptp de **consteller**) ADJ ◆ ~ **(d'étoiles)** star-studded, star-spangled ◆ ~ **de** *[+ astres, joyaux, lumières]* spangled *ou* studded with; *[+ taches]* spotted *ou* dotted with

consteller /kɔ̃stele/ ▸ conjug 1 ◂ VT ◆ **des lumières constellaient le ciel** the sky was studded with lights ◆ **des taches constellaient le tapis** the carpet was spotted *ou* dotted with marks

consternant, e /kɔ̃stɛʀnɑ̃, ɑ̃t/ ADJ distressing ◆ **d'une bêtise ~e** incredibly stupid

consternation /kɔ̃stɛʀnasjɔ̃/ NF consternation, dismay

consterner /kɔ̃stɛʀne/ ▸ conjug 1 ◂ VT to dismay, to fill with dismay ◆ **avoir l'air consterné** to look dismayed ◆ **je suis absolument consterné par son attitude** his attitude fills me with dismay

constipation /kɔ̃stipasjɔ̃/ NF constipation

constipé, e /kɔ̃stipe/ (ptp de **constiper**) ADJ *(Méd)* constipated ◆ **avoir l'air** *ou* **être ~** *(péj = guindé)* to look stiff *ou* ill-at-ease

constiper /kɔ̃stipe/ ▸ conjug 1 ◂ VT to constipate

constituant, e /kɔ̃stitɥɑ̃, ɑ̃t/ ADJ **1** *[élément]* constituent **2** *(Pol)* **assemblée ~e** constituent assembly ◆ **l'Assemblée ~e** *(Hist)* the Constituent Assembly NM **1** *(Jur, Fin)* settlor; *(Gram)* constituent ◆ ~ **immédiat** immediate constituent ◆ **analyse en ~s immédiats** constituent analysis ◆ ~ **ultime** ultimate constituent **2** *(Hist)* **les ~s** the members of the Constituent Assembly NF **constituante** **1** *(au Québec) [d'université]* branch **2** *(Hist)* **la Constituante** the Constituent Assembly

constitué, e /kɔ̃stitɥe/ (ptp de **constituer**) ADJ **1** *(Méd)* **bien/mal ~** of sound/unsound constitution **2** *(Pol)* → **corps**

constituer /kɔ̃stitɥe/ ▸ conjug 1 ◂ VT **1** *(= fonder) [+ comité, ministère, gouvernement, société anonyme]* to set up, to form; *[+ bibliothèque]* to build up; *[+ collection]* to build up, to put together; *[+ dossier]* to make up, to put together

2 *(= composer)* to make up, to constitute, to compose ◆ **les pièces qui constituent cette collection** the pieces that (go to) make up *ou* that constitute this collection ◆ **sa collection est surtout constituée de porcelaines** his collection is made up *ou* is composed *ou* consists mainly of pieces of porcelain

3 *(= être, représenter)* to constitute ◆ **ceci constitue un délit/ne constitue pas un motif** that constitutes an offence/does not constitute a motive ◆ **ceci constitue toute ma fortune** this constitutes *ou* represents my entire fortune ◆ **ils constituent un groupe homogène** they make *ou* form a well-knit group

4 *(Jur = établir) [+ rente, pension, dot]* to settle *(à* on*)*; ◆ ~ **qn son héritier** to appoint sb one's heir

VPR **se constituer** ◆ **se ~ prisonnier** to give o.s. up ◆ **se ~ en société** to form o.s. into a company ◆ **se ~ un capital** to build (up) capital

constitutif, -ive /kɔ̃stitytif, iv/ ADJ constituent, component

constitution /kɔ̃stitysjɔ̃/ NF **1** *(NonC = création) [de comité, ministère, gouvernement, société anonyme]* setting-up, forming; *[de bibliothèque]* building-up; *[de collection]* building-up, putting together; *[de dossier]* making-up, putting together; *(Jur) [de rente, pension, dot]* settlement, settling; *[d'avocat]* retaining ◆ ~ **de stocks** stockpiling **2** *(= éléments) [de substance, ensemble, organisation]* make-up, composition; *[d'équipe, comité]* composition **3** *(= santé)* constitution ◆ **être de ~ délicate** to have a delicate constitution ◆ **il a une robuste ~** he has a sturdy constitution **4** *(Pol)* constitution ◆ **la Constitution française** the French constitution ◆ **c'est contraire à la ~** it's unconstitutional, it's against the constitution

constitutionnaliser /kɔ̃stitysjɔnalize/ ▸ conjug 1 ◂ VT to constitutionalize

constitutionnalité /kɔ̃stitysjɔnalite/ NF constitutionality

constitutionnel, -elle /kɔ̃stitysjɔnɛl/ ADJ constitutional; → **droit³**

constitutionnellement /kɔ̃stitysjɔnɛlmɑ̃/ ADV constitutionally

constricteur /kɔ̃stʀiktœʀ/ ADJ M, NM *(Anat)* ◆ **(muscle) ~** constrictor (muscle) ◆ **boa ~** boa constrictor

constrictif, -ive /kɔ̃stʀiktif, iv/ ADJ *(Phon)* constricted

constriction /kɔ̃stʀiksjɔ̃/ NF constriction

constrictor /kɔ̃stʀiktɔʀ/ ADJ M, NM ◆ **(boa) ~** (boa) constrictor

constructeur /kɔ̃stʀyktœʀ/ NM **1** *(= fabricant)* manufacturer ◆ ~ **automobile** *ou* **d'automobiles** car manufacturer *ou* maker ◆ ~ **de téléphones portables** mobile phone manufacturer ◆ ~ **de navires** shipbuilder **2** *(= bâtisseur)* builder

constructible /kɔ̃stʀyktibl/ ADJ ◆ **terrain ~** building land ◆ **zone/terrain non ~** *area/land where no building is permitted*

constructif, -ive /kɔ̃stʀyktif, iv/ ADJ constructive

construction /kɔ̃stʀyksjɔ̃/ NF **1** *(= action) [de machine, bâtiment, route, navire, chemin de fer]* building, construction; *[de théorie, phrase, intrigue]* construction ◆ **la ~ européenne** European construction ◆ **la ~ de l'immeuble/du navire a pris deux ans** building the flats/ship *ou* the construction of the flats/ship took two years, it took two years to build the flats/ship ◆ **la ~ automobile/navale/aéronautique est menacée** the car/shipbuilding/aircraft industry is under threat ◆ **ça va bien dans la ~** things are going well in the building trade *(Brit) ou* construction business ◆ **entreprise de ~** construction company ◆ **matériaux de ~** building materials ◆ **maison de ~ récente** newly *ou* recently built house ◆ **voiture de ~ française** French-built car ◆ **en (cours de) ~** under construction; → **jeu**

2 *(= structure) [de roman, thèse]* construction; *[de phrase]* structure ◆ **c'est une simple ~ de l'esprit** it's pure hypothesis

3 *(= édifice, bâtiment)* building, construction

4 *(Ling = expression, tournure)* construction, structure

5 *(Géom = figure)* figure, construction

constructivisme /kɔ̃stʀyktivism/ NM constructivism

constructiviste /kɔ̃stʀyktivist/ ADJ, NMF constructivist

construire /kɔ̃stʀɥiʀ/ ► conjug 38 ◄ VT 1 *[+ machine, bâtiment, route, navire, chemin de fer]* to build, to construct ◆ **ils font ~ à la campagne** they're having a house built in the countryside
2 *[+ théorie, phrase, intrigue]* to construct, to put together; *[+ équipe]* to put together, to make up; *[+ famille]* to start ◆ **~ un couple** to build a relationship ◆ **~ l'Europe** to build Europe ◆ **devoir bien construit** well-constructed essay
3 *[+ figure géométrique]* to construct
VPR **se construire** 1 *(= être bâti)* ◆ **ça s'est beaucoup construit ici depuis la guerre** there's been a lot of building here since the war ◆ **le quartier s'est construit en quelques mois** the district was built in a few months ◆ **l'Europe se construit peu à peu** Europe is gradually taking shape ◆ **le film se construit autour de deux personnages** the film is built around two characters
2 *[personnalité]* **un parent doit aider son enfant à se ~** parents should help children develop their personality
3 *(= créer)* **l'oiseau s'est construit un nid** the bird built itself a nest ◆ **il s'est construit un personnage** he created a personality for himself ◆ **ils se construisent une vie virtuelle** they are creating a virtual life for themselves
4 *(Gram)* **ça se construit avec le subjonctif** it takes the subjunctive, it takes a subjunctive construction

consubstantialité /kɔ̃sypstɑ̃sjalite/ NF consubstantiality

consubstantiation /kɔ̃sypstɑ̃sjasjɔ̃/ NF consubstantiation

consubstantiel, -elle /kɔ̃sypstɑ̃sjɛl/ ADJ consubstantial *(à, avec* with)

consul /kɔ̃syl/ NM consul ◆ **~ général** consul general ◆ **~ de France** French Consul

consulaire /kɔ̃sylɛʀ/ ADJ consular

consulat /kɔ̃syla/ NM 1 *(= bureaux)* consulate; *(= charge)* consulate, consulship 2 *(Hist)* **le Consulat** the Consulate

consultable /kɔ̃syltabl/ ADJ *(= disponible) [ouvrage, livre]* available for consultation, which may be consulted ◆ **cette carte est trop grande pour être aisément ~** *(= utilisable)* this map is too big to be used easily

consultant, e /kɔ̃syltɑ̃, ɑ̃t/ ADJ *[avocat]* consultant *(épith)* ◆ **médecin ~** consulting physician NM,F 1 *(= conseiller)* consultant ◆ **~ en relations publiques** public relations consultant 2 *(= patient)* patient

consultatif, -ive /kɔ̃syltatif, iv/ ADJ consultative, advisory ◆ **à titre ~** in an advisory capacity

consultation /kɔ̃syltasjɔ̃/ NF 1 *(= action)* consulting, consultation ◆ **pour faciliter la ~ du dictionnaire/de l'horaire** to make the dictionary/timetable easier to consult ◆ **après ~ de son agenda** having consulted his diary ◆ **d'une ~ difficile** *[livre]* difficult to use *ou* consult ◆ **~ électorale** *(= élection)* election; *(= référendum)* referendum ◆ **faire une ~ électorale** to ask the electorate's opinion, to go to the country *(Brit)*
2 *(= séance : chez le médecin, un expert)* consultation ◆ **aller à la ~** *(Méd)* to go to the surgery *(Brit) ou* doctor's office *(US)* ◆ **donner une ~** to give a consultation ◆ **les heures de ~** *(Méd)* consulting *ou* surgery *(Brit)* hours ◆ **service (hospitalier) de ~ externe** outpatients' department
3 *(= échange de vues)* consultation ◆ **être en ~ avec des spécialistes** to be in consultation with specialists
4 *(frm = avis donné)* professional advice *(NonC)*

consulter /kɔ̃sylte/ ► conjug 1 ◄ VT *[+ médecin, astrologue, base de données]* to consult; *[+ expert, avocat, ami, parents]* to consult, to seek advice from; *[+ dictionnaire, documents]* to consult, to refer to; *[+ courrier électronique, répondeur]* to check; *[+ boussole, baromètre, horaire]* to look at, to check ◆ **la population a été consultée par référendum** the people's opinion was canvassed in a referendum ◆ **ne ~ que sa raison/son intérêt** *(littér)* to be guided only by one's reason/self-interest, to look only to one's reason/self-interest VI *[médecin] (= recevoir)* to hold surgery *(Brit)*, to be in (the office) *(US)*; *(= conférer)* to hold a consultation VPR **se consulter** *(= s'entretenir)* to confer, to consult each other ◆ **ils se consultèrent du regard** they looked questioningly at each other

consumer /kɔ̃syme/ ► conjug 1 ◄ VT 1 *(= brûler)* to consume, to burn ◆ **l'incendie a tout consumé** the fire consumed *ou* wiped out everything ◆ **des débris à demi consumés** charred debris 2 *(= dévorer) [fièvre, mal]* to consume, to devour ◆ **consumé par l'ambition** consumed with *ou* devoured by ambition 3 *(littér = dépenser) [+ forces]* to expend; *[+ fortune]* to squander ◆ **il consume sa vie en plaisirs frivoles** he fritters away his life in idle pleasures VPR **se consumer** 1 *(= brûler)* **une bûche se consumait dans l'âtre** a log was burning away in the hearth 2 *(littér = dépérir)* to waste away ◆ **se ~ de chagrin/de désespoir** to waste away with sorrow/despair ◆ **il se consume à petit feu** he is slowly wasting away

consumérisme /kɔ̃symeʀism/ NM consumerism

consumériste /kɔ̃symeʀist/ ADJ, NMF consumerist

contact /kɔ̃takt/ NM 1 *(= toucher)* contact ◆ **le ~ de deux surfaces** contact between two surfaces ◆ **ça s'attrape par (le) ~** it can be caught through physical contact ◆ **le ~ de la soie est doux** silk is soft to the touch ◆ **au point de ~ des deux lignes** at the point of contact *ou* the meeting point of the two lines; → **lentille, verre**
2 *(électrique)* contact ◆ **mettre/couper le ~** *(en voiture)* to switch on/switch off the ignition ◆ **~ électrique** electrical contact ◆ **appuyer sur le ~** to press the contact button *ou* lever ◆ **~ !** *(avion)* contact!; *(auto-école)* switch on the ignition!; *(machine)* switch on! ◆ **il y a un faux ~** there's a bad connection, there's a wire loose; → **clé**
3 *(= rapport)* contact ◆ **il a beaucoup de ~s (avec l'étranger)** he has got a lot of contacts *ou* connections (abroad) ◆ **notre ~ à Moscou** our contact in Moscow ◆ **dès le premier ~, ils ...** from their first meeting, they ... ◆ **garder le ~ avec qn** to keep in touch *ou* contact with sb ◆ **elle a besoin de ~ humain** she needs human contact ◆ **j'ai un bon/mauvais ~ avec eux** my relations with them are good/bad, I have a good/bad relationship with them ◆ **"bon contact"** *(dans une offre d'emploi)* "ability to get on well with people" ◆ **être de ~ facile/difficile** to be easy/not very easy to talk to ◆ **établir/rompre le ~** *(Mil)* to make/break off contact *(avec* with); ◆ **faire des ~s** to network
4 *(locutions)*
♦ **au contact de** ◆ **au ~ de sa main** at the touch of his hand ◆ **métal qui s'oxyde au ~ de l'air/de l'eau** metal that oxidizes on contact with air/water ◆ **il est sans cesse au ~ des malades** he is in constant contact with patients ◆ **au ~ de ces jeunes gens il a acquis de l'assurance** through his contact *ou* association with these young people he has gained self-assurance ◆ **j'ai beaucoup appris au ~ de ces gens** I've learned a lot from being with those people
♦ **en contact** ◆ **entrer/être en ~** *[objets]* to come into/be in contact; *[fils électriques]* to make/be making contact ◆ **mettre en ~** *[+ objets]* to bring into contact ◆ **en ~ étroit avec** in close touch *ou* contact with ◆ **rester/être en ~** *(Radio)* to remain in/be in contact *(avec* with); *[client, ami]* to keep in/be in touch *(avec* with) to remain in/be in contact *(avec* with); ◆ **être en ~ radio avec qn** to be in radio contact with sb ◆ **mettre en ~** *[+ relations d'affaires]* to put in touch; *(Radio)* to put in contact ◆ **se mettre en ~ avec** to make contact with, to contact
♦ **prendre contact, entrer en contact** *(Radio)* to make contact *(avec* with); *[+ ami, clients]* to get in touch *ou* contact *(avec* with)
♦ **prise de contact** *(= première entrevue)* first meeting; *(Mil)* first contact
♦ **perdre (le) contact** *(Radio)* to lose contact *(avec* with); *[+ client, ami]* to lose touch *ou* contact *(avec* with); ◆ **il a perdu le ~ avec la réalité** he's lost touch with reality

contacter /kɔ̃takte/ GRAMMAIRE ACTIVE 48.2 ► conjug 1 ◄ VT to contact, to get in touch with

contagieux, -ieuse /kɔ̃taʒjø, jøz/ ADJ 1 *[maladie] (gén)* infectious, catching *(attrib)*; *[personne]* infectious 2 *[enthousiasme, peur, rire]* infectious, contagious; *[bonne humeur, optimisme]* infectious

> ⚠ Attention à ne pas traduire automatiquement **contagieux** par **contagious**, qui a le sens de 'communiqué par contact direct'.

contagion /kɔ̃taʒjɔ̃/ NF *(Méd)* contagion, contagiousness; *(fig)* infectiousness ◆ **pour éviter tout risque de ~** to avoid any risk of contagion ◆ **ils n'ont pas pu résister à la ~ de la crise financière** they couldn't escape the effects of the financial crisis ◆ **pour éviter la ~ de la violence dans les grandes villes** to prevent violence spreading further in the big cities

contagiosité /kɔ̃taʒjozite/ NF contagiousness

container /kɔ̃tɛnɛʀ/ NM ⇒ **conteneur**

contaminant, e /kɔ̃taminɑ̃, ɑ̃t/ ADJ infectious *(pour* to)

contaminateur, -trice /kɔ̃taminatœʀ, tʀis/ ADJ *[agent]* infectious; *[aiguille]* causing infection NM,F *(Méd)* contaminator

contamination /kɔ̃taminasjɔ̃/ NF 1 *(= contagion) [de personne]* infection, contamination; *(= pollution) [de cours d'eau, zone]* contamination ◆ **~ radioactive** radioactive contamination 2 *(littér : morale)* pollution 3 *(Ling)* contamination

contaminer /kɔ̃tamine/ ► conjug 1 ◄ VT 1 *(= infecter) [+ personne, animal]* to infect, to contaminate; *[+ aliment, linge]* to contaminate; *(= polluer) [+ cours d'eau, zone]* to contaminate 2 *(= influencer)* to corrupt ◆ **il s'est laissé ~ par le pessimisme ambiant** he gave in to the prevailing mood of pessimism

conte /kɔ̃t/ NM *(= récit)* tale, story; *(† ou littér = histoire mensongère)* (tall) story ◆ **les ~s pour enfants** children's stories ◆ **les ~s d'Andersen/de Grimm** Andersen's/Grimm's fairy tales
COMP **conte de fée** *(lit, fig)* fairy tale *ou* story
conte de Noël Christmas tale

contemplateur, -trice /kɔ̃tɑ̃platœʀ, tʀis/ NM,F contemplator

contemplatif, -ive /kɔ̃tɑ̃platif, iv/ ADJ *[air, esprit]* contemplative, meditative; *(Rel) [ordre]* contemplative NM *(Rel)* contemplative

contemplation /kɔ̃tɑ̃plasjɔ̃/ NF *(= action)* contemplation ◆ **la ~** *(Philos)* contemplation, meditation; *(Rel)* contemplation ◆ **rester en ~ devant qch** to stand gazing at sth

contempler /kɔ̃tɑ̃ple/ ► conjug 1 ◄ VT *(= regarder)* to contemplate, to gaze at VPR **se**

contempler ◆ **se ~ dans un miroir** to gaze at o.s. in a mirror

contemporain, e /kɔ̃tɑ̃pɔʀɛ̃, ɛn/ ADJ [1] *(= de la même époque) [personne]* contemporary; *[événement]* contemporaneous, contemporary *(de* with) [2] *(= actuel) [problème]* contemporary, present-day *(épith)*; *[art, mobilier, histoire]* contemporary NM,F contemporary *(de* of)

contemporanéité /kɔ̃tɑ̃pɔʀaneite/ NF contemporaneousness

contempteur, -trice /kɔ̃tɑ̃ptœʀ, tʀis/ NM,F *(littér)* denigrator

contenance /kɔ̃t(ə)nɑ̃s/ NF [1] *(= capacité) [de bouteille, réservoir]* capacity; *[de navire]* (carrying) capacity ◆ **avoir une ~ de 45 litres** to have a capacity of 45 litres, to hold 45 litres [2] *(= attitude)* bearing, attitude ◆ **~ humble/fière** humble/proud bearing ◆ **~ gênée** embarrassed attitude ◆ **il fumait pour se donner une ~** he was smoking to give an impression of composure *ou* to disguise his lack of composure ◆ **faire bonne ~ (devant)** to put on a bold front (in the face of) ◆ **perdre ~** to lose one's composure

contenant /kɔ̃t(ə)nɑ̃/ NM ◆ **le ~ (et le contenu)** the container (and the contents)

conteneur /kɔ̃t(ə)nœʀ/ NM container

contenir /kɔ̃t(ə)niʀ/ ▸ conjug 22 ◂ VT [1] *(= avoir une capacité de) [récipient]* to hold, to take; *[cinéma, avion, autocar]* to seat, to hold [2] *(= renfermer) [récipient, livre, minerai]* to contain ◆ **ce minerai contient beaucoup de fer** this ore contains a lot of iron *ou* has a lot of iron in it [3] *(= maîtriser) [+ surprise]* to contain; *[+ colère]* to contain, to suppress; *[+ sanglots, larmes]* to contain, to hold back; *[+ foule]* to contain, to restrain; *[+ inflation]* to control, to curb ◆ **~ l'ennemi** *(Mil)* to contain the enemy, to hold the enemy in check VPR **se contenir** to contain o.s., to control one's emotions

content, e /kɔ̃tɑ̃, ɑ̃t/ ADJ [1] *(= heureux)* pleased, glad, happy ◆ **avoir l'air ~** to look happy *ou* pleased ◆ **je serais ~ que vous veniez** I'd be pleased *ou* glad *ou* happy if you came ◆ **je suis ~ d'apprendre cela** I'm pleased to hear that ◆ **il était très ~ de ce changement** he was very pleased *ou* glad about the change ◆ **je suis très ~ ici** I'm very happy *ou* contented here ◆ **voilà, c'est cassé, tu es ~ ?** there, it's broken, are you happy *ou* satisfied now?

[2] ◆ **~ de** *(= satisfait de) [+ élève, voiture, situation]* pleased *ou* happy with ◆ **être ~ de peu** to be content with little, to be easily satisfied ◆ **être ~ de soi** to be pleased with o.s.

[3] ◆ **non ~ d'être/d'avoir fait ...** not content with being/with having done ...

NM ◆ **avoir (tout) son ~ de qch** to have had one's fill of sth

contentement /kɔ̃tɑ̃tmɑ̃/ NM [1] *(= état)* contentment, satisfaction ◆ **éprouver un profond ~ à la vue de ...** to feel great contentment *ou* deep satisfaction at the sight of ... ◆ **~ de soi** self-satisfaction ◆ **il a eu un sourire de ~** he smiled contentedly to himself [2] *(= action de contenter)* satisfaction, satisfying

contenter /kɔ̃tɑ̃te/ GRAMMAIRE ACTIVE 53.2 ▸ conjug 1 ◂

VT *[+ personne, besoin, envie, curiosité]* to satisfy ◆ **facile à ~** easy to please, easily pleased *ou* satisfied ◆ **cette explication l'a contenté** he was satisfied *ou* happy with this explanation, this explanation satisfied him ◆ **il est difficile de ~ tout le monde** it's difficult to please everyone

VPR **se contenter** ◆ **se ~ de qch/de faire qch** to content o.s. with sth/with doing sth ◆ **se ~ de peu/de ce qu'on a** to make do *ou* be content with very little/with what one has ◆ **il a dû se ~ d'un repas par jour/de manger les restes** he had to content himself *ou* make do with one meal a day/with eating the left-overs ◆ **contentez-vous d'écouter/de regarder** just listen/watch ◆ **il se contenta d'un sourire/de sourire** he merely gave a smile/smiled

contentieux, -ieuse /kɔ̃tɑ̃sjø, jøz/ ADJ *(Jur)* contentious NM *(= litige)* dispute, disagreement; *(Comm)* litigation; *(= service)* legal department ◆ **~ administratif/commercial** administrative/commercial actions *ou* litigation

contention /kɔ̃tɑ̃sjɔ̃/ NF *(Méd) (= procédé) [de membre, dents]* support; *(= appareil)* brace ◆ **de ~** *[collants, chaussettes]* support *(épith)*

contenu, e /kɔ̃t(ə)ny/ (ptp de **contenir**) ADJ *[colère, sentiments]* restrained, suppressed NM *[de récipient, dossier]* contents; *[de loi, texte]* content; *(Ling)* content ◆ **la table des matières indique le ~ du livre** the contents page shows what's in the book ◆ **le ~ subversif de ce livre** the subversive content of this book

conter /kɔ̃te/ ▸ conjug 1 ◂ VT *(frm) [+ histoire]* to recount, to relate ◆ **contez-nous vos malheurs** *(hum)* let's hear your problems, tell us all about your problems ◆ **que me contez-vous là ?** what are you trying to tell me? ◆ **il lui en a conté de belles !** he really spun him some yarns! * *ou* told him some incredible stories! ◆ **elle ne s'en laisse pas ~** she's not easily taken in, she doesn't let herself be taken in (easily) ◆ **il ne faut pas lui en ~** don't bother trying those stories on him, it's no use trying it on with him * *(Brit)* ◆ **~ fleurette à qn** († , *ou hum)* to whisper sweet nothings in sb's ear

contestable /kɔ̃tɛstabl/ ADJ *[théorie, idée]* questionable, disputable; *[raisonnement]* questionable, doubtful; *[attitude]* questionable

contestataire /kɔ̃tɛstatɛʀ/ ADJ *[journal, étudiants, tendances]* anti-establishment NMF ◆ **c'est un ~** he's anti-establishment *ou* anti-authority ◆ **les ~s ont été expulsés** the protesters were made to leave

contestateur, -trice /kɔ̃tɛstatœʀ, tʀis/ ADJ contentious

contestation /kɔ̃tɛstasjɔ̃/ NF [1] *(NonC = dénégation) [de succession, droit, compétence, résultats]* contesting; *[légitimité, bien-fondé]* questioning, challenging; *[de fait]* questioning, disputing, contesting; *[de décision]* challenging, disputing, contesting ◆ **il a été condamné pour ~ de crimes contre l'humanité** *(Jur)* he was sentenced for denying the existence of crimes against humanity [2] *(= objection)* dispute ◆ **il y a matière à ~** there are grounds for contention *ou* dispute ◆ **c'est sans ~ possible, il n'y a aucune ~ possible** it's beyond dispute [3] **la ~** *(gén, Pol) (= opposition)* protest ◆ **mouvement de ~** protest movement

conteste /kɔ̃tɛst/ **sans conteste** LOC ADV unquestionably, indisputably

contester /kɔ̃tɛste/ ▸ conjug 1 ◂ VT *(Jur) [+ succession, droit, compétence]* to contest; *[+ légitimité, bien-fondé]* to question, to challenge; *[+ fait]* to question, to dispute, to contest; *[+ décision]* to challenge, to dispute, to contest ◆ **~ les résultats électoraux** to contest *ou* challenge the election results ◆ **je ne conteste pas que vous ayez raison** I don't dispute that you're right ◆ **je ne lui conteste pas ce droit** I don't question *ou* dispute *ou* contest his right ◆ **ce roman/cet écrivain est très contesté** this novel/writer is very controversial

VI *(gén)* to take issue *(sur* over); *(Pol)* to protest ◆ **il ne conteste jamais** he never takes issue over anything ◆ **il conteste toujours sur des points de détail** he's always taking issue over points of detail ◆ **les jeunes ne pensent qu'à ~** all young people think about is protesting

conteur, -euse /kɔ̃tœʀ, øz/ NM,F *(= écrivain)* storywriter; *(= narrateur)* storyteller

contexte /kɔ̃tɛkst/ NM context ◆ **pris hors ~** taken out of context

contextuel, -elle /kɔ̃tɛkstɥɛl/ ADJ *(Ling)* contextual; *(Ordin) [aide en ligne]* context-sensitive

contexture /kɔ̃tɛkstyʀ/ NF *[d'organisme]* texture; *[d'œuvre]* structure

contigu, -uë /kɔ̃tigy/ ADJ *[maison, pièce, jardin]* adjoining, adjacent, contiguous *(frm)*; *[domaines, sujets]* (closely) related ◆ **être ~ à qch** to be adjacent *ou* next to sth

contiguïté /kɔ̃tigɥite/ NF *[de choses]* proximity, contiguity *(frm)*; *(fig) [de sujets]* relatedness ◆ **la ~ de ces deux sujets** the fact that the two subjects are (closely) related

continence /kɔ̃tinɑ̃s/ NF continence, continency

continent[1], e /kɔ̃tinɑ̃, ɑ̃t/ ADJ continent

continent[2] /kɔ̃tinɑ̃/ NM *(gén, Géog)* continent; *(par rapport à une île)* mainland ◆ **le ~ noir** the dark continent

continental, e (mpl **-aux**) /kɔ̃tinɑ̃tal, o/ ADJ *[région, climat]* continental; *(opposé à côtier, insulaire)* mainland *(épith)* ◆ **petit déjeuner ~** continental breakfast NM,F *(gén)* mainlander; *(= Européen)* Continental

continentalité /kɔ̃tinɑ̃talite/ NF continental character

contingence /kɔ̃tɛ̃ʒɑ̃s/ NF [1] *(Philos)* contingency [2] ◆ **les ~s** contingencies ◆ **il ne se soucie pas des ~s matérielles** he doesn't bother with the routine *ou* the chores of everyday life ◆ **les ~s de la vie** the (little) chance happenings of life ◆ **tenir compte des ~s** to take account of all contingencies *ou* eventualities

contingent, e /kɔ̃tɛ̃ʒɑ̃, ɑ̃t/ ADJ contingent NM [1] *(Mil = groupe)* contingent ◆ **le ~** *(en France) the conscripts called up for national service, the draft (US)* [2] *(Comm, Jur = quota)* quota [3] *(= part, contribution)* share

contingentement /kɔ̃tɛ̃ʒɑ̃tmɑ̃/ NM ◆ **le ~ des exportations/importations** the fixing *ou* establishing of export/import quotas, the placing of quotas on exports/imports

contingenter /kɔ̃tɛ̃ʒɑ̃te/ ▸ conjug 1 ◂ VT *[+ importations, exportations]* to place *ou* fix a quota on; *[+ produits, matière première]* to distribute by a system of quotas

continu, e /kɔ̃tiny/ ADJ *[mouvement, série, bruit]* continuous; *[ligne, silence]* unbroken, continuous; *[effort]* continuous, unremitting; *[souffrance]* endless; *(Math)* continuous ◆ **papier ~** *(Ordin)* continuous stationery; → **jet[1]**, **journée** NM *(Math, Philos, Phys)* continuum; *(Élec)* direct current

◆ **en continu** ◆ **utilisation en ~** continuous use ◆ **faire qch en ~ pendant cinq heures** to do sth continuously *ou* non-stop for five hours, to do sth for five hours non-stop ◆ **papier en ~** *(Ordin)* continuous stationery NF **continue** *(Phon)* continuant

continuateur, -trice /kɔ̃tinɥatœʀ, tʀis/ NM,F *(= successeur)* successor; *[d'œuvre littéraire]* continuator ◆ **les ~s de cette réforme** those who carried on *(ou* carry on *etc)* the reform

continuation /kɔ̃tinɥasjɔ̃/ NF continuation ◆ **nous comptons sur la ~ de cette entente** we count on the continuation of this agreement; → **bon[1]**

continuel, -elle /kɔ̃tinɥɛl/ ADJ *(= continu)* continuous; *(= très fréquent)* continual, constant ◆ **il lui fait des reproches ~s** he's always *ou* forever criticizing her

continuellement /kɔ̃tinɥɛlmɑ̃/ ADV *(= sans interruption)* continuously; *(= très fréquemment)* continually, constantly ◆ **elle se plaint ~** she's always *ou* she never stops complaining

continuer /kɔ̃tinɥe/ ▸ conjug 1 ◂ VT ① (= *poursuivre*) *[+ démarches, politique]* to continue (with), to carry on with; *[+ tradition]* to continue, to carry on; *[+ travaux, études]* to continue (with), to carry on with, to go on with ◆ ~ **son chemin** to continue on *ou* along one's way, to go on one's way ◆ ~ **l'œuvre de son maître** to carry on *ou* continue the work of one's master ◆ **Pompidou continua de Gaulle** Pompidou carried on *ou* continued where de Gaulle left off
② (= *prolonger*) *[+ droite, route]* to continue
VI ① *[bruit, spectacle, guerre]* to continue, to go on; *[voyageur]* to go on, to continue on one's way ◆ **je continuerai par le saumon** I'll have the salmon to follow ◆ **"mais" continua-t-il** "but", he went on *ou* continued ◆ **dis-le, continue !** go on, say it! ◆ **s'il continue, je vais …** * if he goes on *ou* keeps on *ou* continues, I'm going to … ◆ **si ça continue, je vais …** if this keeps up *ou* continues, I'm going to … ◆ **la route (se) continue jusqu'à la gare** the road goes (on) *ou* continues as far as the station ◆ **le chemin (se) continue par un sentier** the road turns into a path
② ◆ ~ **de** *ou* **à marcher/lire** to go on *ou* keep on *ou* continue walking/reading, to continue to walk/read, to walk/read on

continuité /kɔ̃tinɥite/ NF *[de politique, tradition]* continuation; *[d'action]* continuity ◆ **la ~ de l'État** the continuity of the state ◆ **assurer la ~ d'une politique** to ensure continuity in applying a policy, to ensure the continuation of a policy; → **solution**

continûment /kɔ̃tinymɑ̃/ ADV continuously

continuum /kɔ̃tinɥɔm/ NM continuum ◆ **le ~ espace-temps** the space-time continuum

contondant, e /kɔ̃tɔ̃dɑ̃, ɑt/ ADJ *[instrument]* blunt ◆ **arme ~e** blunt instrument

contorsion /kɔ̃tɔʀsjɔ̃/ NF contortion

contorsionner (se) /kɔ̃tɔʀsjɔne/ ▸ conjug 1 ◂ VPR *[acrobate]* to contort o.s.; *(péj)* to contort o.s. ◆ **il se contorsionnait pour essayer de se détacher** he was writhing about *ou* contorting himself in an attempt to get free

contorsionniste /kɔ̃tɔʀsjɔnist/ NMF contortionist

contour /kɔ̃tuʀ/ NM ① *[d'objet]* outline; *[de montagne, visage, corps]* outline, contour ◆ **crayon ~ des yeux** eyeliner ② ◆ **~s** *[de route, rivière]* windings

contourné, e /kɔ̃tuʀne/ (ptp de **contourner**) ADJ *(péj)* *[raisonnement, style]* tortuous; *(péj)* *[colonne, pied de table]* (over)elaborate

contournement /kɔ̃tuʀnəmɑ̃/ NM *[d'obstacle]* bypassing; *[de règle, difficulté]* circumventing, bypassing ◆ **le ~ de la ville** driving round *ou* skirting (round) *ou* bypassing the town ◆ **autoroute de ~** bypass

contourner /kɔ̃tuʀne/ ▸ conjug 1 ◂ VT ① *[+ ville]* to skirt (round), to bypass; *[+ montagne]* to skirt (round), to walk (*ou* drive *etc*) round; *[+ mur, véhicule]* to walk (*ou* drive *etc*) round; *[+ règle]* to circumvent; *[+ difficulté]* to get round ② (= *façonner*) *[+ arabesques]* to trace (out); *[+ vase]* to fashion ③ (= *déformer*) to twist, to contort

contraceptif, -ive /kɔ̃tʀasɛptif, iv/ ADJ, NM contraceptive

contraception /kɔ̃tʀasɛpsjɔ̃/ NF contraception ◆ **moyens de ~** methods of contraception, contraceptive methods ◆ **être sous ~ orale** to use oral contraception

contractant, e /kɔ̃tʀaktɑ̃, ɑt/ ADJ *(Jur)* contracting NM,F contracting party

contracté, e /kɔ̃tʀakte/ (ptp de **contracter**) ADJ ① *(Ling)* contracted ② *[personne, muscle]* tense

contracter¹ /kɔ̃tʀakte/ ▸ conjug 1 ◂ VT ① (= *raidir*) *[+ muscle]* to tense, to contract; *(fig)* *[+ personne]* to make tense ◆ **la peur lui contracta la gorge** fear gripped his throat ◆ **l'émotion lui contracta la gorge** his throat tightened with emotion ◆ **les traits contractés par la souffrance** his features contorted with pain ◆ **un sourire forcé contracta son visage** his face stiffened into a forced smile ② *(Phys)* ~ **un corps/fluide** (= *réduire*) to make a body/fluid contract VPR **se contracter** ① *[muscle]* to tense (up), to contract; *[gorge]* to tighten; *[traits, visage]* to tense (up); *[cœur]* to contract; *(Phys)* *[corps]* to contract ② *[personne]* to become tense ◆ **ne te contracte pas, sinon ça va te faire mal** don't tense up or it'll hurt ③ *[mot, syllabe]* to be (able to be) contracted

contracter² /kɔ̃tʀakte/ ▸ conjug 1 ◂ VT ① *[+ dette, obligation]* to contract, to incur; *[+ alliance]* to contract, to enter into ◆ ~ **une assurance** to take out an insurance policy ◆ ~ **un emprunt** to take out a loan ◆ ~ **mariage avec** *(Admin)* to contract (a) marriage with ② *[+ maladie]* to contract; *[+ manie]* to acquire, to contract

contractile /kɔ̃tʀaktil/ ADJ contractile

contractilité /kɔ̃tʀaktilite/ NF contractility

contraction /kɔ̃tʀaksjɔ̃/ NF ① (= *action*) *[de corps, liquide]* contraction; *[de muscle]* tensing, contraction ② (= *état*) *[de muscles, traits, visage]* tenseness ③ (= *spasme*) contraction ◆ **elle a des ~s** *[de femme enceinte]* she's having contractions ④ (= *résumé*) ~ **de texte** summary

contractualisation /kɔ̃tʀaktɥalizasjɔ̃/ NF *[d'accord, rapports]* formalization by contract ◆ **une politique de ~ des universités** a policy of setting up contract-based links between universities and the state

contractualiser /kɔ̃tʀaktɥalize/ ▸ conjug 1 ◂ VT ① *[+ personne]* to put on contract *(in a department of the public services)* ② *[+ accord, rapports]* to formalize by contract; *[+ université]* to set up contract-based links with

contractuel, -elle /kɔ̃tʀaktɥɛl/ ADJ *[obligation]* contractual; *[emploi]* under contract *(attrib)*; *[clause]* contract *(épith)*, in the contract *(attrib)* NM ◆ **(agent) ~** *(gén)* contract worker *(in the public sector)*; *(stationnement)* ≃ traffic warden *(Brit)*, traffic policeman *(US)*; *(sortie d'école)* ≃ lollipop man * *(Brit)*, crossing guard *(US)* NF **contractuelle** *(gén)* contract worker *(working for local authority)*; *(stationnement)* ≃ traffic warden *(Brit)*, meter maid * *(US)*; *(sortie d'école)* ≃ lollipop lady * *(Brit)*, crossing guard *(US)*

contractuellement /kɔ̃tʀaktɥɛlmɑ̃/ ADV by contract, contractually

contracture /kɔ̃tʀaktyʀ/ NF *(Archit)* contracture; *(Physiol)* spasm, (prolonged) contraction ◆ ~ **musculaire** cramp

contradicteur /kɔ̃tʀadiktœʀ/ NM opponent, contradictor

contradiction /kɔ̃tʀadiksjɔ̃/ NF ① *(NonC = contestation)* **porter la ~ dans un débat** to introduce counter-arguments in a debate, to add a dissenting voice to a debate ◆ **je ne supporte pas la ~** I can't bear to be contradicted; → **esprit**
② (= *discordance*) contradiction, inconsistency ◆ **texte plein de ~s** text full of contradictions *ou* inconsistencies ◆ **le monde est plein de ~s** the world is full of contradictions ◆ ~ **dans les termes** contradiction in terms ◆ **il y a ~ entre …** there is a contradiction between … ◆ **être en ~ avec soi-même** to contradict o.s. ◆ **il est en ~ avec ce qu'il a dit précédemment** he's contradicting what he said before ◆ **leurs témoignages sont en ~** their testimonies contradict each other

contradictoire /kɔ̃tʀadiktwaʀ/ ADJ *[idées, théories, récits, sentiments]* contradictory, conflicting ◆ **débat ~** debate ◆ **réunion politique ~** political meeting with an open debate ◆ ~ **à** in contradiction to, in conflict with ◆ **arrêt/jugement ~** *(Jur)* order/judgement given after due hearing of the parties

contradictoirement /kɔ̃tʀadiktwaʀmɑ̃/ ADV *(Jur)* after due hearing of the parties

contraignant, e /kɔ̃tʀɛɲɑ̃, ɑt/ ADJ *[mesures, législation, normes, règlement, système]* restrictive ◆ **des horaires de travail très ~s** very inconvenient working hours ◆ **mon travail est très ~** my work doesn't allow me much freedom ◆ **tu n'es pas ~ toi au moins !** you're very easy-going!

contraindre /kɔ̃tʀɛ̃dʀ/ ▸ conjug 52 ◂ VT ◆ ~ **qn à faire qch** to force *ou* compel sb to do sth ◆ **contraint à** *ou* **de démissionner** forced *ou* compelled to resign ◆ **il/cela m'a contraint au silence/au repos** he/this forced *ou* compelled me to be silent/to rest ◆ **par voie de justice** to constrain by law *(to pay debt)* VPR **se contraindre** to restrain o.s. ◆ **se ~ à être aimable** to force o.s. to be polite, to make o.s. be polite

contraint, e¹ /kɔ̃tʀɛ̃, ɛ̃t/ GRAMMAIRE ACTIVE 37.1, 48.3 (ptp de **contraindre**) ADJ ① (= *gêné*) constrained, forced ◆ **d'un air ~** with an air of constraint, constrainedly ② ◆ **~ et forcé** under duress *ou* compulsion

contrainte² /kɔ̃tʀɛ̃t/ NF ① (= *pression*) **elle ne m'a imposé aucune ~** she didn't put any pressure on me ◆ **pour moi ce n'est pas une ~, mais une volonté** it's not something I have to do, it's something I want to do ◆ **mon nouveau travail est bien payé, mais il y a beaucoup plus de ~s** my new job is well paid, but I have a lot less freedom ◆ **l'entreprise est soumise à une ~ de rentabilité par ses actionnaires** the company is under obligation to make a profit for its shareholders ◆ **par ~** *ou* **sous la ~** under duress ◆ **agir sous la ~** to act under duress
② (= *règle obligatoire*) constraint ◆ **~ administrative/budgétaire/juridique** administrative/budgetary/legal constraint ◆ **double ~** double bind ◆ **la seule ~ est qu'il faut payer d'avance** the only stipulation is that you have to pay in advance
③ (= *gêne*) constraint; *(Ling)* constraint ◆ **sans ~** unrestrainedly, without restraint *ou* constraint
④ *(Jur)* ~ **par corps** civil imprisonment
⑤ *(Phys)* stress

⚠ Au sens de 'pression', **contrainte** ne se traduit pas par **constraint**.

contraire /kɔ̃tʀɛʀ/ GRAMMAIRE ACTIVE 53.3
ADJ ① (= *inverse*) *[sens, effet, mouvement]* opposite; *(Naut)* *[vent]* contrary, adverse ◆ **dans le cas ~** otherwise; → **avis**
◆ **contraire à** *[+ loi]* against ◆ **c'est ~ à mes principes/intérêts** it is *ou* goes against my principles/interests ◆ ~ **à la santé** bad for the health ◆ **l'alcool m'est ~** alcohol doesn't agree with me ◆ **le sort lui fut ~** fate was against him
② (= *contradictoire*) *[opinions, propositions, intérêts]* conflicting
③ (= *nuisible*) *[forces, action]* contrary; *[destin]* adverse
NM *[de mot, concept]* opposite ◆ **c'est le ~ de son frère** he's the opposite of his brother ◆ **et pourtant c'est tout le ~** and yet it's just the reverse *ou* opposite ◆ **il fait toujours le ~ de ce qu'on lui dit** he always does the opposite of what he's told ◆ **je ne vous dis pas le ~** I'm not saying anything to the contrary, I'm not disputing *ou* denying it ◆ **il dit/promet tout et son ~** he says/promises anything and everything
◆ **au contraire** on the contrary ◆ **je ne te reproche rien, (bien** *ou* **tout) au ~** I'm not

criticising you at all, quite the reverse *ou* the opposite

♦ **au contraire de** unlike ♦ **au ~ des autres** unlike the others

contrairement /kɔ̃tʀɛʀmɑ̃/ **contrairement à** LOC ADV [*+ idées, apparences*] contrary to ♦ **~ à qn** unlike sb ♦ **~ aux autres** unlike the others

contralto /kɔ̃tʀalto/ NM contralto

contrapuntique /kɔ̃tʀapɔ̃tik/ ADJ (*Mus*) contrapuntal

contrariant, e /kɔ̃tʀaʀjɑ̃, jɑ̃t/ ADJ [*personne*] perverse, contrary; [*incident*] tiresome, annoying ♦ **tu n'es pas ~ !** you're very easy-going!

contrarier /kɔ̃tʀaʀje/ GRAMMAIRE ACTIVE 45.3 ▸ conjug 7 ◂ VT 1 (= *irriter*) to annoy; (= *ennuyer*) to bother ♦ **il cherche à vous ~** he's trying to annoy you 2 (= *gêner*) [*+ projets*] to frustrate, to thwart; [*+ amour*] to thwart ♦ **~ la marche d'un bateau** to impede a ship's progress ♦ **~ les mouvements de l'ennemi** to impede the enemy's movements ♦ **forces qui se contrarient** forces which act against each other ♦ **pour lui, la cuisine a été un don contrarié** his gift for cooking was never given a chance to develop 3 (= *contraster*) to alternate (for contrast) 4 [*+ gaucher*] to force to write with his (*ou* her) right hand

contrariété /kɔ̃tʀaʀjete/ NF (= *irritation*) annoyance, vexation ♦ **éprouver une ~** to feel annoyed *ou* vexed ♦ **un geste de ~** a gesture of annoyance ♦ **toutes ces ~s l'ont rendu furieux** all these annoyances *ou* vexations made him furious

contrastant, e /kɔ̃tʀastɑ̃, ɑt/ ADJ [*couleurs, figures, effets*] contrasting (*épith*)

contraste /kɔ̃tʀast/ GRAMMAIRE ACTIVE 32.1 NM (*gén, TV*) contrast ♦ **par ~** by contrast ♦ **faire ~ avec** to contrast with ♦ **en ~ avec** in contrast to ♦ **mettre en ~** to contrast

contrasté, e /kɔ̃tʀaste/ (ptp de **contraster**) ADJ [*composition, image, style*] full of contrasts; [*bilan, résultats*] uneven, mixed ♦ **une photographie trop/pas assez ~e** a photograph with too much/not enough contrast ♦ **couleurs très ~es** strongly contrasting colours ♦ **les marchés ont connu des évolutions très ~es** the markets have developed in very different ways

contraster /kɔ̃tʀaste/ ▸ conjug 1 ◂ VT [*+ photographie*] to give contrast to, to put contrast into ♦ **ce peintre contraste à peine son sujet** this painter hardly brings out his subject (at all) *ou* hardly makes his subject stand out ♦ **éléments contrastés** contrasting elements VI to contrast (*avec* with)

contrastif, -ive /kɔ̃tʀastif, iv/ ADJ (*Ling*) contrastive

contrat /kɔ̃tʀa/ NM 1 (= *convention, document*) contract, agreement ♦ **passer un ~ (avec qn)** to sign a contract (with sb) ♦ **~ de confiance** contract of trust

♦ **sous contrat** ♦ **être sous ~** [*employé*] to be under contract (*avec* to); ♦ **être employé sous ~** to be employed on contract ♦ **établissement privé (placé) sous ~ (d'association)** ≈ grant-aided school

2 (= *accord, pacte*) agreement ♦ **nous allons passer un ~ ensemble : si tu as ton examen, je te laisse partir en Afrique** let's make a deal: if you pass your exam, I'll let you go to Africa ♦ **réaliser** *ou* **remplir son ~** (*Bridge*) to make one's contract; (*fig*) to fulfil one's pledges ♦ **notre équipe a rempli son ~, elle a remporté tous ses matches** our team made good its promise and won all its matches

3 (*arg Crime*) contract ♦ **lancer un ~ contre qn** to take a contract out on sb; → **bridge**[1]

COMP **contrat d'achat** purchase contract
contrat administratif public service contract
contrat d'apprentissage apprenticeship contract
contrat d'assurance insurance contract
contrat collectif collective agreement
contrat conclu dans les conditions normales du commerce arm's length agreement
contrat à durée déterminée fixed-term contract
contrat à durée indéterminée permanent *ou* open-ended contract
contrat emploi-solidarité *government-sponsored work contract for the unemployed which includes professional training*
contrat de garantie guarantee, warranty
contrat initiative-emploi *incentive scheme to encourage employers to hire the long-term unemployed*
contrat de location (*pour locaux*) tenancy agreement (*Brit*), rental agreement (*US*); (*pour voiture*) rental agreement
contrat de louage de services contract for services
contrat de mariage marriage contract
contrat de qualification *short-term employment contract for 16-26 year olds with on-the-job training*
contrat de retour à l'emploi *former incentive scheme to encourage employers to hire the long-term unemployed*
contrat social (*Hist, Pol*) social contract *ou* compact
contrat de travail work contract
contrat de vente sales contract
contrat verbal verbal agreement
contrat de ville urban development programme

contravention /kɔ̃tʀavɑ̃sjɔ̃/ NF 1 (*Aut*) (*pour infraction au code*) fine; (*pour stationnement interdit*) (= *amende*) (parking) fine; (= *procès-verbal*) parking ticket ♦ **dresser ~ (à qn)** (*stationnement interdit*) to issue a parking ticket (to sb); (*autres infractions*) to fine sb, to book sb* (*Brit*) ♦ **prendre une ~*** to get a fine 2 (*Jur* = *infraction*) **~ à** contravention *ou* infraction of ♦ **être en (état de) ~** to be contravening the law ♦ **être en ~ à** to be in contravention of

contre /kɔ̃tʀ/ GRAMMAIRE ACTIVE 39.2, 53.4

PRÉP

> Pour des expressions comme **être furieux contre qn, joue contre joue** etc, cherchez aussi sous l'autre mot.

1 (*contact, juxtaposition*) against ♦ **se mettre ~ le mur** to stand against the wall ♦ **s'appuyer ~ un arbre** to lean against a tree ♦ **(la) face ~ terre** face downwards ♦ **pousse la table ~ la fenêtre** push the table (up) against the window ♦ **son garage est juste ~ notre maison** his garage is built onto our house ♦ **elle s'assit (tout) ~ lui** she sat down (right) next to *ou* beside him ♦ **il s'est cogné la tête ~ le mur** he banged his head against *ou* on the wall ♦ **les voitures étaient pare-chocs ~ pare-chocs** the cars were bumper to bumper

2 (*opposition, hostilité*) against ♦ **se battre/voter ~ qn** to fight/vote against sb ♦ **Poitiers ~ Lyon** (*Sport*) Poitiers versus Lyon ♦ **jeter une pierre ~ la fenêtre** to throw a stone at the window ♦ **agir ~ l'avis/les ordres de qn** to act against *ou* contrary to *ou* counter to sb's advice/orders ♦ **aller/nager ~ le courant** to go/swim against the current ♦ **acte ~ nature** unnatural act, act contrary to *ou* against nature ♦ **je n'ai rien ~ (cela)** *ou* **là ~** (*frm*) I have nothing against it ♦ **il a les ouvriers ~ lui** he's got the workers against him; → **envers**[1], **gré**, **vent**

3 (*défense, protection*) **s'abriter ~ le vent/la pluie** to take shelter from the wind/rain ♦ **des comprimés ~ la grippe** flu tablets, tablets for flu ♦ **s'assurer ~ les accidents/l'incendie** to insure (o.s.) against accidents/fire

4 (*échange*) (in exchange) for ♦ **échanger** *ou* **troquer qch ~** to exchange *ou* swap* sth for ♦ **donner qch ~** to give sth (in exchange) for ♦ **il a cédé ~ la promesse/l'assurance que ...** he agreed in return for the promise/assurance that ...

5 (*proportion, rapport*) **il y a un étudiant qui s'intéresse ~ neuf qui bâillent** for every one interested student there are nine who are bored ♦ **9 voix ~ 4** 9 votes to 4 ♦ **à 100 ~ 1** at 100 to 1

6 (*locution*)

♦ **par contre** on the other hand ♦ **il est beau, mais qu'est-ce qu'il est bête par ~ !** he's handsome, but he's so stupid!

ADV 1 (= *opposé à*) **je suis (tout à fait) ~ !** I'm (completely) against it!

2 (= *sur*) **appuyez-vous ~** lean against *ou* on it

NM 1 → **pour**

2 (= *riposte*) counter, retort; (*Billard*) rebound; (*Sport*) (= *contre-attaque*) counterattack; (= *blocage*) block; (*Cartes*) double ♦ **faire un ~** (*Rugby*) to charge down a kick ♦ **l'art du ~** the art of repartee

PRÉF ♦ **contre-** counter-, anti-

contre-accusation /kɔ̃tʀakyzasjɔ̃/ NF countercharge, counter-accusation

contre-alizé /kɔ̃tʀalize/ NM anti-trade (wind)

contre-allée /kɔ̃tʀale/ NF (*en ville*) service road (*Brit*), frontage road (*US*); (*dans un parc*) side path (*running parallel to the main drive*)

contre-amiral (pl **contre-amiraux**) /kɔ̃tʀamiʀal, o/ NM rear admiral

contre-analyse /kɔ̃tʀanaliz/ NF second analysis, counter-analysis

contre-attaque /kɔ̃tʀatak/ NF counter-attack

contre-attaquer /kɔ̃tʀatake/ ▸ conjug 1 ◂ VI to counter-attack

contrebalancer /kɔ̃tʀəbalɑ̃se/ ▸ conjug 3 ◂ VT 1 [*poids*] to counterbalance 2 (= *égaler, compenser*) to offset VPR **se contrebalancer** ♦ **je m'en contrebalance*** I don't give a damn‡

contrebande /kɔ̃tʀəbɑ̃d/ NF (= *activité*) smuggling; (= *marchandises*) contraband, smuggled goods ♦ **faire de la ~** to be involved in smuggling ♦ **faire la ~ du tabac** to smuggle tobacco ♦ **produits de ~** contraband (goods), smuggled goods

contrebandier, -ière /kɔ̃tʀəbɑ̃dje, jɛʀ/ NM,F smuggler ♦ **navire ~** smugglers' ship

contrebas /kɔ̃tʀəbɑ/ **en contrebas** LOC ADV (down) below ♦ **en ~ de** below

contrebasse /kɔ̃tʀəbɑs/ NF (= *instrument*) (double) bass; (= *musicien*) (double) bass player

contrebassiste /kɔ̃tʀəbɑsist/ NMF (double) bass player

contrebasson /kɔ̃tʀəbɑsɔ̃/ NM contrabassoon, double bassoon

contre-boutant /kɔ̃tʀəbutɑ̃/ NM (*en bois*) shore; (*en pierre*) buttress

contrebraquage /kɔ̃tʀəbʀakaʒ/ NM (*en dérapage*) steering into the skid (*NonC*) ♦ **grâce à ce ~ instantané** because he immediately steered into the skid

contrebraquer /kɔ̃tʀəbʀake/ ▸ conjug 1 ◂ VI (*en dérapant*) to steer into the skid; (*pour se garer*) to steer in the opposite direction

contrebutement /kɔ̃tʀəbytmɑ̃/ NM ⇒ **contre-boutant**

contrecarrer /kɔ̃tʀəkaʀe/ ▸ conjug 1 ◂ VT [*+ projets*] to thwart, to foil; † [*+ personne*] to thwart

contrechamp /kɔ̃tʀəʃɑ̃/ NM (*Ciné*) reverse angle (shot)

contrechant, contre-chant /kɔ̃tʀəʃɑ̃/ **NM** *(Mus)* descant, discant

contrechâssis /kɔ̃tʀəʃɑsi/ **NM** double (window) frame

contrechoc /kɔ̃tʀəʃɔk/ **NM** repercussions, after-effects ♦ **~ pétrolier** impact of the oil slump

contreclef /kɔ̃tʀəkle/ **NF** stone adjoining the keystone

contrecœur[1] /kɔ̃tʀəkœʀ/ **à contrecœur LOC ADV** reluctantly

contrecœur[2] /kɔ̃tʀəkœʀ/ **NM** 1 *(= fond de cheminée)* fire-back 2 *(Rail)* guardrail

contrecollé, e /kɔ̃tʀəkɔle/ **ADJ** *[cuir, laine]* foam-backed ♦ **bois ~** plywood

contrecoup /kɔ̃tʀəku/ **NM** 1 *(= ricochet) [de balle]* ricochet 2 *(= répercussion)* repercussions ♦ **ce pays subit le ~ de la crise** this country is suffering from the (after-) effects of the crisis ♦ **par ~** as an indirect consequence

contre-courant /kɔ̃tʀəkuʀɑ̃/ **NM** *[de cours d'eau]* counter-current

♦ **à contre-courant** *(lit)* upstream, against the current; *(fig)* against the current *ou* tide ♦ **aller à ~ de la tendance générale** to go against the (general) trend ♦ **ramer à ~** *(fig)* to swim against the tide

contre-culture /kɔ̃tʀəkyltyʀ/ **NF** counter-culture

contredanse /kɔ̃tʀədɑ̃s/ **NF** 1 * *(gén)* fine; *(pour stationnement interdit)* (parking) ticket 2 († † *= danse)* quadrille

contredire /kɔ̃tʀədiʀ/ ► **conjug 37** ◄ **VT** *[personne]* to contradict; *[faits]* to be at variance with, to refute **VPR se contredire** *[personne]* to contradict o.s.; *[témoins, témoignages]* to contradict each other

contredit /kɔ̃tʀədi/ **NM** *(frm)* ♦ **sans ~** unquestionably, without question

contrée /kɔ̃tʀe/ **NF** *(littér) (= pays)* land; *(= région)* region

contre-écrou (pl **contre-écrous**) /kɔ̃tʀekʀu/ **NM** lock nut

contre-électromotrice /kɔ̃tʀelɛktʀɔmɔtʀis/ **ADJ F** → **force**

contre-emploi /kɔ̃tʀɑ̃plwa/ **NM** ♦ **il joue** *ou* **est utilisé à ~** *[acteur]* he's cast against type

contre-enquête /kɔ̃tʀɑ̃kɛt/ **NF** counter-inquiry

contre-épreuve /kɔ̃tʀepʀœv/ **NF** *(Typo)* counter-proof; *(= vérification)* countercheck

contre-espionnage /kɔ̃tʀɛspjɔnaʒ/ **NM** counter-espionage

contre-essai /kɔ̃tʀesɛ/ **NM** control test, counter test

contre-étude /kɔ̃tʀetyd/ **NF** control study

contre-exemple /kɔ̃tʀegzɑ̃pl/ **NM** counter-example

contre-expert /kɔ̃tʀɛkspɛʀ/ **NM** *[de dommages]* second assessor; *[d'antiquité, bijou]* second valuer

contre-expertise /kɔ̃tʀɛkspɛʀtiz/ **NF** *[de dommages]* second assessment; *[d'antiquité, bijou]* second valuation

contrefaçon /kɔ̃tʀəfasɔ̃/ **NF** 1 *(NonC = falsification) [d'argent, signature]* counterfeiting, forgery, forging; *[de produits, édition]* counterfeiting; *[de disques compacts]* pirating ♦ **~ involontaire d'un brevet** innocent infringement of a patent ♦ **poursuivre qn en ~** to take legal action against sb for counterfeiting *ou* forgery 2 *(= faux) [d'édition]* unauthorized *ou* pirated edition; *[de produit]* imitation; *[de disque compact]* pirate copy; *[de billets, signature]* forgery, counterfeit ♦ **méfiez-vous des ~s** beware of imitations

contrefacteur /kɔ̃tʀəfaktœʀ/ **NM** forger, counterfeiter

contrefaire /kɔ̃tʀəfɛʀ/ ► **conjug 60** ◄ **VT** 1 *(littér = imiter)* to imitate; († *= parodier)* to mimic, to imitate 2 *(= déguiser) [+ voix, écriture]* to disguise 3 *(= falsifier) [+ argent, signature]* to counterfeit, to forge; *[+ produits, édition]* to counterfeit; *[+ brevet]* to infringe 4 († *= feindre) [+ douleur, folie]* to feign 5 *(= déformer)* to distort

contrefait, e /kɔ̃tʀəfɛ, ɛt/ (ptp de **contrefaire**) **ADJ** *(= difforme)* misshapen, deformed

contre-fenêtre /kɔ̃tʀəfənɛtʀ/ **NF** inner window *(of a double window)*

contre-fer /kɔ̃tʀəfɛʀ/ **NM** iron cap

contre-feu (pl **contre-feux**) /kɔ̃tʀəfø/ **NM** *(= plaque)* fire-back; *(= feu)* backfire

contreficher (se) * /kɔ̃tʀəfiʃe/ ► **conjug 1** ◄ **VPR** ♦ **je m'en contrefiche** I don't give a damn *

contrefil, contre-fil /kɔ̃tʀəfil/ **NM** *(Menuiserie)* ♦ **à ~** against the grain

contre-filet /kɔ̃tʀəfilɛ/ **NM** *(= morceau)* sirloin; *(= tranche)* sirloin steak

contrefort /kɔ̃tʀəfɔʀ/ **NM** 1 *(Archit) [de voûte, terrasse]* buttress 2 *[de chaussure]* stiffener 3 *(Géog) [d'arête]* spur ♦ **~s** *[de chaîne]* foothills

contrefoutre (se) * /kɔ̃tʀəfutʀ/ **VPR** ♦ **je m'en contrefous** I don't give a damn *

contre-fugue /kɔ̃tʀəfyg/ **NF** counterfugue

contre-gouvernement /kɔ̃tʀəguvɛʀnəmɑ̃/ **NM** shadow government, shadow cabinet *(surtout Brit)*

contre-haut /kɔ̃tʀəo/ **en contre-haut LOC ADV** above

contre-indication /kɔ̃tʀɛ̃dikasjɔ̃/ **NF** *(Méd, Pharm)* contraindication

contre-indiquer /kɔ̃tʀɛ̃dike/ ► **conjug 1** ◄ **VT** *(Méd)* to contraindicate ♦ **c'est contre-indiqué** *(gén)* it is not recommended

contre-insurrection /kɔ̃tʀɛ̃syʀɛksjɔ̃/ **NF** counterinsurgency

contre-interrogatoire /kɔ̃tʀɛteʀɔgatwaʀ/ **NM** cross-examination ♦ **faire subir un ~ à qn** to cross-examine sb

contre-jour /kɔ̃tʀəʒuʀ/ **NM** *(= éclairage)* backlighting *(NonC)*, contre-jour *(NonC)*; *(= photographie)* backlit *ou* contre-jour shot

♦ **à contre-jour** *[se profiler, se détacher]* against the sunlight; *[photographier]* into the light; *[travailler, coudre]* with one's back to the light

contremaître /kɔ̃tʀəmɛtʀ/ **NM** foreman

contremaîtresse /kɔ̃tʀəmɛtʀɛs/ **NF** forewoman

contre-manifestant, e /kɔ̃tʀəmanifɛstɑ̃, ɑ̃t/ **NM,F** counter demonstrator

contre-manifestation /kɔ̃tʀəmanifɛstasjɔ̃/ **NF** counter demonstration

contre-manifester /kɔ̃tʀəmanifɛste/ ► **conjug 1** ◄ **VI** to hold a counter demonstration

contremarche /kɔ̃tʀəmaʀʃ/ **NF** 1 *(Mil)* countermarch 2 *[de marche d'escalier]* riser

contremarque /kɔ̃tʀəmaʀk/ **NF** 1 *(Comm = marque)* countermark 2 *(Ciné, Théât = ticket)* ≈ voucher

contre-mesure /kɔ̃tʀəm(ə)zyʀ/ **NF** 1 *(= action)* countermeasure 2 *(Mus)* **à ~** against the beat, offbeat

contre-offensive /kɔ̃tʀɔfɑ̃siv/ **NF** counter-offensive

contre-offre /kɔ̃tʀɔfʀ/ **NF** counterbid, counter offer

contre-OPA /kɔ̃tʀɔpea/ **NF INV** counterbid, counter offer *(in a takeover battle)*

contre-ordre, contrordre /kɔ̃tʀɔʀdʀ/ **NM** counter order, countermand ♦ **ordres et ~s** orders and counter orders ♦ **il y a ~** there has been a change of orders ♦ **sauf ~** unless otherwise directed

contrepartie /kɔ̃tʀəpaʀti/ **NF** 1 *(gén = compensation)* compensation ♦ **moyennant ~ valable** *(Jur, Fin)* ≈ for a good and valuable consideration ♦ **obtenir de l'argent en ~** to get money in compensation ♦ **prendre qch sans ~** to take sth without offering compensation

♦ **en contrepartie** *(= en échange, en retour)* in return; *(= en revanche)* in compensation, to make up for it 2 *(littér = contre-pied)* opposing view 3 *(Comm) (= registre)* duplicate register; *(= écritures)* counterpart entries

contrepente, contre-pente /kɔ̃tʀəpɑ̃t/ **NF** opposite slope

contre-performance /kɔ̃tʀəpɛʀfɔʀmɑ̃s/ **NF** poor performance ♦ **sa ~ aux élections** his poor performance *ou* showing in the elections

contrepet /kɔ̃tʀəpɛ/ **NM, contrepèterie** /kɔ̃tʀəpetʀi/ **NF** spoonerism

contre-pied /kɔ̃tʀəpje/ **NM** 1 *[d'opinion, attitude]* (exact) opposite ♦ **prendre le ~** *(d'une opinion)* to take the opposing *ou* opposite view; *(d'une action)* to take the opposite course ♦ **il a pris le ~ de ce qu'on lui demandait** he did the exact opposite of what he was asked 2 *(Chasse)* **prendre le ~** to (run) heel 3 *(locution)*

♦ **à contre-pied** *(Sport)* on the wrong foot ♦ **prendre qn à ~** *(lit)* to wrong-foot sb; *(fig)* to wrong-foot sb, to catch sb off-guard ♦ **les électeurs ont pris à ~ les instituts de sondage** the voters foiled the predictions of the pollsters

contreplaqué /kɔ̃tʀəplake/ **NM** plywood

contre-plongée /kɔ̃tʀəplɔ̃ʒe/ **NF** low-angle shot ♦ **filmer en ~** to film from below

contrepoids /kɔ̃tʀəpwɑ/ **NM** *(lit)* counterweight, counterbalance; *[d'acrobate]* balancing-pole ♦ **faire ~** *(lit, fig)* to act as a counterbalance ♦ **porter un panier à chaque main pour faire ~** to carry a basket in each hand to balance oneself ♦ **servir de ~ à, apporter un ~ à** to counterbalance

contre-poil /kɔ̃tʀəpwal/ **à contre-poil LOC ADV** *(lit, fig)* the wrong way

contrepoint /kɔ̃tʀəpwɛ̃/ **NM** *(Mus)* counterpoint ♦ **en ~** *(lit, fig)* in counterpoint ♦ **thème joué en ~** theme played in counterpoint, contrapuntal theme ♦ **en ~ de** as a counterpoint to

contrepoison /kɔ̃tʀəpwazɔ̃/ **NM** antidote, counterpoison

contre-porte /kɔ̃tʀəpɔʀt/ **NF** *[de voiture]* inner door ♦ **dans la ~ du réfrigérateur** in the inside of the fridge door

contre-pouvoir /kɔ̃tʀəpuvwaʀ/ **NM** opposition force ♦ **les syndicats doivent jouer leur rôle de ~** the unions should fulfil their role in challenging established authority

contre-productif, -ive /kɔ̃tʀəpʀɔdyktif, iv/ **ADJ** counter-productive

contre-projet /kɔ̃tʀəpʀɔʒɛ/ **NM** counterplan

contre-propagande /kɔ̃tʀəpʀɔpagɑ̃d/ **NF** counter-propaganda

contre-proposition /kɔ̃tʀəpʀɔpozisjɔ̃/ **NF** counterproposal

contre-publicité /kɔ̃tʀəpyblisite/ **NF** adverse publicity ♦ **ça leur fait de la ~** it's bad *ou* adverse publicity for them

contrer /kɔ̃tʀe/ ► **conjug 1** ◄ **VT** 1 *[+ personne, menées]* to counter ♦ **se faire ~** to be countered *(par* by) 2 *(Cartes)* to double ♦ **~ un coup**

de pied *(Rugby)* to charge down a kick VI *(Cartes)* to double

contre-rail (pl **contre-rails**) /kɔ̃tʀəʀaj/ NM checkrail *(Brit)*, guard-rail

Contre-Réforme /kɔ̃tʀəʀefɔʀm/ NF *(Hist)* ◆ **la** ~ the Counter-Reformation

contre-révolution /kɔ̃tʀəʀevɔlysjɔ̃/ NF counter-revolution

contre-révolutionnaire /kɔ̃tʀəʀevɔlysjɔnɛʀ/ ADJ, NMF counter-revolutionary

contrescarpe /kɔ̃tʀɛskaʀp/ NF counterscarp

contreseing /kɔ̃tʀəsɛ̃/ NM countersignature

contresens /kɔ̃tʀəsɑ̃s/ NM *(= erreur)* misinterpretation; *(de traduction)* mistranslation; *(= absurdité)* nonsense *(NonC)*, piece of nonsense ◆ **faire un** ~ *(en traduction)* to mistranslate a word *(ou* a phrase); *(sur les intentions de qn)* to misinterpret sb totally

◆ **à contresens** *(sur la route)* the wrong way; *(Couture)* against the grain ◆ **à** ~ **de** against ◆ **il a pris mes paroles à** ~ he misinterpreted what I said

contresigner /kɔ̃tʀəsiɲe/ ▸ conjug 1 ◂ VT to countersign

contretemps /kɔ̃tʀətɑ̃/ NM 1 *(= complication, retard)* hitch, contretemps *(fml)* *(aussi hum)* 2 *(Mus)* off-beat rhythm

◆ **à contretemps** *(Mus)* off the beat; *(fig)* at an inopportune moment

contre-ténor /kɔ̃tʀətenɔʀ/ NM countertenor

contre-terrorisme /kɔ̃tʀəteʀɔʀism/ NM counterterrorism

contre-terroriste /kɔ̃tʀəteʀɔʀist/ ADJ, NMF counterterrorist

contre-torpilleur /kɔ̃tʀətɔʀpijœʀ/ NM destroyer

contre-ut /kɔ̃tʀyt/ NM INV top *ou* high C

contre-valeur /kɔ̃tʀəvalœʀ/ NF *(Fin, Écon)* exchange value

contrevenant, e /kɔ̃tʀəv(ə)nɑ̃, ɑt/ *(Jur)* ADJ offending NM,F offender

contrevenir /kɔ̃tʀəv(ə)niʀ/ ▸ conjug 22 ◂ **contrevenir à** VT INDIR *(Jur, littér)* *[+ loi, règlement]* to contravene

contrevent /kɔ̃tʀəvɑ̃/ NM 1 *(= volet)* shutter 2 *[de charpente]* brace, strut

contrevérité /kɔ̃tʀəveʀite/ NF untruth, falsehood

contrevirage /kɔ̃tʀəviʀaʒ/ NM *(Ski)* counter-turn

contre-visite /kɔ̃tʀəvizit/ NF *(gén)* follow-up inspection; *(Méd)* second examination

contre-voie /kɔ̃tʀəvwa/ NF opposite track *(of a railway line)* ◆ **à** ~ *(= en sens inverse)* on the wrong track; *(= du mauvais côté)* on the wrong side (of the train)

contribuable /kɔ̃tʀibɥabl/ NMF taxpayer ◆ **aux frais du** ~ at the taxpayer's expense

contribuer /kɔ̃tʀibɥe/ ▸ conjug 1 ◂ **contribuer à** VT INDIR *[+ résultat, effet]* to contribute to(wards); *[+ effort, dépense]* to contribute towards ◆ **de nombreux facteurs ont contribué au déclin de .../à réduire le ...** numerous factors contributed to(wards) the decline in .../to(wards) the reduction in the ... *ou* to reducing the ...

contributeur, -trice /kɔ̃tʀibytœʀ, tʀis/ ADJ contributing ◆ **les pays ~s de** *ou* **en troupes** the countries contributing troops NM,F contributor ◆ **~s de** *ou* **en troupes/de fonds** contributors of troops/funds ◆ **~s de l'ONU** UN contributors

contributif, -ive /kɔ̃tʀibytif, iv/ ADJ *(Jur)* *[part]* contributory ◆ **logiciel** ~ shareware

contribution /kɔ̃tʀibysjɔ̃/ NF 1 *(= participation)* contribution ◆ **apporter sa** ~ **à qch** to make one's contribution to sth ◆ **mettre qn à** ~ to call upon sb's services, to make use of sb ◆ **mettre qch à** ~ to make use of sth ◆ **tous les employés ont été mis à** ~ **pour terminer le projet** the entire staff were called on so the project would be finished on time

2 *(= impôts)* **~s** *(à la commune)* local taxes; *(à l'État)* taxes ◆ **~s directes/indirectes** direct/indirect taxation ◆ ~ **sociale généralisée** *supplementary social security contribution in aid of the underprivileged*

3 *(= administration)* **~s** tax office, ≃ Inland Revenue *(Brit)*, Internal Revenue Service *(US)* ◆ **travailler aux ~s** to work in the tax office, to work for *ou* in the Inland Revenue *(Brit)* *ou* Internal Revenue *(US)*

contrister /kɔ̃tʀiste/ ▸ conjug 1 ◂ VT *(littér)* to grieve, to sadden

contrit, e /kɔ̃tʀi, it/ ADJ contrite

contrition /kɔ̃tʀisjɔ̃/ NF contrition; → **acte**

contrôlable /kɔ̃tʀolabl/ ADJ *[opération]* that can be checked; *[affirmation]* that can be checked *ou* verified, verifiable; *[sentiment, inflation]* controllable ◆ **un billet** ~ **à l'arrivée** a ticket that is inspected *ou* checked on arrival ◆ **le débat était difficilement** ~ it was difficult to control the discussion

contrôle /kɔ̃tʀol/ NM 1 *(= vérification)* checking *(NonC)*, check ◆ ~ **antidopage** dope test ◆ ~ **des comptes** audit ◆ ~ **d'identité** identity check ◆ ~ **de police** police check ◆ ~ **de vitesse** speed check ◆ ~ **fiscal** tax inspection ◆ **le** ~ **des passeports** passport control ◆ ~ **des passeports !** passports please! ◆ **le** ~ **des billets s'effectue à bord** tickets are checked *ou* inspected on board ◆ ~ **de qualité** quality control ◆ ~ **sanitaire** health check ◆ ~ **automatique de gain** *(Élec)* automatic gain control ◆ **opérer** *ou* **faire des ~s** to do *ou* run checks *(ou* tests); → **visite**

2 *(= surveillance)* *[d'opérations, agissements, gestion]* controlling, supervising, supervision; *[de prix, loyers]* monitoring, controlling ◆ **exercer un** ~ **sévère sur les agissements de qn** to maintain strict control over sb's actions ◆ **sous** ~ **judiciaire** ≃ on probation ◆ **sous** ~ **médical** under medical supervision ◆ ~ **des changes/des prix** exchange/price control ◆ ~ **des naissances** birth control ◆ ~ **radar** *(sur route)* radar speed trap ◆ ~ **technique** *[de voiture]* MOT (test) *(Brit)*, inspection *(US)*

3 *(= maîtrise)* control ◆ ~ **de soi** self-control ◆ **garder/perdre le** ~ **de son véhicule** to remain in/lose control of one's vehicle ◆ **prendre le** ~ **d'une entreprise** to take control of *ou* take over a firm ◆ **prise de** ~ *[d'entreprise]* takeover ◆ **sous** ~ **étranger** *[firme]* foreign-owned; *[territoire]* under foreign control ◆ **sous** ~ **militaire** under military control ◆ **avoir une région sous son** ~ to be in control of a region, to have a region under one's control ◆ **ne t'inquiète pas, tout est sous** ~ don't worry, everything's under control

4 *(Scol = épreuve)* (written) test ◆ **le** ~ **continu** continuous assessment ◆ **le** ~ **des connaissances** pupil *ou* student assessment ◆ **avoir un** ~ **de chimie** to have a chemistry test

5 *(= bureau)* *(gén)* office; *(Théât)* booking office *(surtout Brit)*, reservation office *(US)*

6 *(Mil = registres)* **~s** rolls, lists ◆ **rayé des ~s de l'armée** removed from the army lists

7 *(= poinçon)* hallmark

> ⚠ Attention à ne pas traduire automatiquement **contrôle** par le mot anglais **control**, qui a le sens de 'surveillance'.

contrôler /kɔ̃tʀole/ ▸ conjug 1 ◂ VT 1 *(= vérifier)* *[+ billets, passeports]* to inspect, to check; *[+ comptes]* to check, to inspect; *[+ texte, traduction]* to check *(sur* against); *[+ régularité de qch]* to check; *[+ qualité]* to control, to check; *[+ affirmations, alibi]* to check, to verify; *[+ connaissances]* to test ◆ ~ **le bon fonctionnement d'un appareil** to check that a machine is working properly ◆ **il a été contrôlé positif** *(contrôle antidopage)* he failed a dope test, he returned a positive dope test

2 *(= surveiller)* *[+ opérations, agissements, gestion]* to control, to supervise; *[+ employés, travail]* to supervise; *[+ prix, loyers]* to monitor, to control

3 *(= maîtriser)* *[+ colère, réactions, nerfs, respiration]* to control; *[+ véhicule]* to control, to be in control of; *[+ situation]* to be in control of; *[+ zone, pays]* to be in control of; *[+ secteur, firme]* to control; *[+ ballon, skis, jeu]* to control ◆ **les rebelles contrôlent l'aéroport** the rebels have taken control of the airport ◆ **nous contrôlons cette société à 80%** we have an 80% (controlling) stake in this company

4 *(Orfèvrerie)* to hallmark

VPR **se contrôler** to control o.s. ◆ **il ne se contrôlait plus** he was no longer in control of himself

> ⚠ Attention à ne pas traduire automatiquement **contrôler** par **to control**, notamment au sens de 'vérifier'.

contrôleur, -euse /kɔ̃tʀolœʀ, øz/ NM,F 1 *(dans le train, le métro, le bus)* (ticket) inspector; *(sur le quai)* ticket collector ◆ ~ **aérien,** ~ **de la navigation aérienne** air-traffic controller 2 *[de comptabilité]* auditor; *[de contributions]* inspector ◆ ~ **de gestion** financial controller, management *ou* cost accountant 3 *[de mécanisme]* regulator; *[d'ordinateur]* controller ◆ ~ **de ronde** time-clock

contrordre /kɔ̃tʀɔʀdʀ/ NM ⇒ **contre-ordre**

controuvé, e /kɔ̃tʀuve/ ADJ *(littér)* *[fait, nouvelle]* fabricated; *[histoire, anecdote]* fabricated, concocted

controverse /kɔ̃tʀɔvɛʀs/ NF controversy ◆ **prêter à** ~ to be debatable

controversé, e /kɔ̃tʀɔvɛʀse/ ADJ ◆ **(très)** ~ *[théorie, question]* much debated; *[personne, article, film]* controversial

contumace /kɔ̃tymas/ ADJ absconding NF *(Jur)* contumacy, failure to appear in court ◆ **par** ~ in absentia, in his *(ou her etc)* absence ◆ **il a été condamné à mort par** ~ he was sentenced to death in absentia NMF absconder

contumax /kɔ̃tymaks/ NMF *person who fails to appear in court*

contus, e /kɔ̃ty, yz/ ADJ *(Méd)* *[membre]* bruised, contused

contusion /kɔ̃tyzjɔ̃/ NF bruise, contusion *(SPÉC)*

contusionner /kɔ̃tyzjɔne/ ▸ conjug 1 ◂ VT to bruise, to contuse *(SPÉC)* ◆ **son corps était tout contusionné** his body was covered in bruises

conurbation /kɔnyʀbasjɔ̃/ NF conurbation

convaincant, e /kɔ̃vɛ̃kɑ̃, ɑt/ GRAMMAIRE ACTIVE 53.4 ADJ convincing

convaincre /kɔ̃vɛ̃kʀ/ ▸ conjug 42 ◂ VT 1 *[+ personne sceptique]* to convince *(de qch* of sth); *[+ personne hésitante]* to persuade *(de faire qch* to do sth); ◆ **je ne suis pas convaincu par son explication** I'm not convinced by his explanation ◆ **il m'a convaincu de renoncer à cette idée** he persuaded *ou* convinced me to give up the idea, he talked me into giving up the idea ◆ **se laisser** ~ to let o.s. be persuaded ◆ **je ne demande qu'à me laisser** ~ I'm open to persuasion 2 *(= déclarer coupable)* ~ **qn de meurtre/trahison** to prove sb guilty of *ou* convict sb of murder/treason

convaincu, e /kɔ̃vɛ̃ky/ GRAMMAIRE ACTIVE 33.2, 43.1, 53.6 (ptp de **convaincre**) ADJ convinced

◆ **d'un ton** ~ with conviction ◆ **c'est un européen** ~ he's strongly pro-European

convalescence /kɔ̃valesɑ̃s/ NF convalescence ◆ **période de** ~ (period of) convalescence ◆ **maison de** ~ convalescent home

◆ **en convalescence** ◆ **être en** ~ to be convalescing ◆ **entrer en** ~ to start one's convalescence ◆ **une économie en** ~ a recovering economy ◆ **le pays est en** ~ the country is still recovering *ou* getting back on its feet

convalescent, e /kɔ̃valesɑ̃, ɑ̃t/ ADJ, NM,F convalescent

convecteur /kɔ̃vɛktœʀ/ NM convector (heater)

convection /kɔ̃vɛksjɔ̃/ NF convection

convenable /kɔ̃vnabl/ ADJ 1 (= *approprié*) *[parti]* fitting, suitable; *[moment, endroit]* fitting, suitable, appropriate 2 (= *décent*) *[manières]* acceptable, correct; *[vêtements]* decent, respectable; *[personne, famille]* respectable ◆ **peu** ~ *[manières]* improper, unseemly; *[vêtements]* unsuitable ◆ **ne montre pas du doigt, ce n'est pas** ~ don't point – it's not polite, it's bad manners to point 3 (= *acceptable*) *[devoir]* adequate, passable; *[salaire, logement]* decent, acceptable, adequate ◆ **des conditions de vie à peine** ~**s** barely adequate living conditions

convenablement /kɔ̃vnabləmɑ̃/ ADV *[placé, choisi]* suitably, appropriately; *[s'exprimer]* properly; *[payé, logé]* decently ◆ **je vous demande de travailler** ~ I'm asking you to do your work properly ◆ **s'habiller** ~ *(décemment)* to dress respectably *ou* properly; *(en fonction du temps)* to dress appropriately

convenance /kɔ̃vnɑ̃s/ NF 1 *(frm = ce qui convient)* **trouver qch à sa** ~ to find sth to one's liking, to find sth suitable ◆ **la chambre est-elle à votre** ~ **?** is the room to your liking? ◆ **le service est-il à votre** ~ **?** is the service to your satisfaction? ◆ **choisissez un jour à votre** ~ choose a day to suit you *ou* to suit your convenience ◆ **pour des raisons de** ~**(s) personnelle(s), pour** ~**s personnelles** for personal reasons; → **mariage** 2 (= *étiquette*) **les** ~**s** propriety, the proprieties ◆ **contraire aux** ~**s** contrary to the proprieties 3 *(littér = harmonie) [de goûts, caractères]* affinity; († = *caractère adéquat) [de terme, équipement]* appropriateness, suitability

convenir /kɔ̃vniʀ/ GRAMMAIRE ACTIVE 36.1 ▸ conjug 22 ◂

VT INDIR **convenir à** (= *être approprié à*) to suit, to be suitable for; (= *être utile à*) to suit, to be convenient for; (= *être agréable à*) to be agreeable to, to suit ◆ **ce chapeau ne convient pas à la circonstance** this hat is not suitable for the occasion *ou* does not suit the occasion ◆ **le climat ne lui convient pas** the climate doesn't suit him *ou* doesn't agree with him ◆ **oui, cette chambre me convient très bien** yes, this room suits me very well ◆ **cette maison convient à une personne seule** this house is suitable for a person living on their own ◆ **j'irai si cela me convient** I'll go if it is convenient (for me); *(ton péremptoire)* I'll go if it suits me ◆ **si l'heure/la date vous convient** if the time/date is convenient for you *ou* suits you ◆ **c'est tout à fait ce qui me convient** this is exactly what I need *ou* want ◆ **j'espère que cela vous conviendra** I hope you will find this acceptable, I hope this will be acceptable to you

VT INDIR **convenir de** 1 (= *avouer*) to admit (to), to acknowledge ◆ **tu as eu tort, conviens-en** you were wrong, admit it

2 (= *s'accorder sur*) to agree on ◆ ~ **d'une date/d'un lieu** to agree on a date/place ◆ **une date a été convenue** a date has been agreed ◆ **nous en avons convenu ensemble** we agreed on it together

VT **convenir que** (= *avouer*) to admit that, to acknowledge the fact that; (= *s'accorder sur*) to agree that ◆ **il est convenu que nous nous réunissons demain** it is agreed that we should meet tomorrow

VB IMPERS ◆ **il convient de faire** (= *il vaut mieux*) it is advisable to do; (= *il est bienséant de*) it would be proper to do ◆ **il convient d'être prudent** caution is advised, it is advisable to be cautious ◆ **il convient qu'elle remercie ses hôtes de leur hospitalité** it is proper *ou* right for her to thank her host and hostess for their hospitality ◆ **il convient de faire remarquer ...** *(frm)* we should point out ...

VPR **se convenir** *[personnes]* to be well-suited (to each other)

convent /kɔ̃vɑ̃/ NM *general assembly of Freemasons*

convention /kɔ̃vɑ̃sjɔ̃/ NF 1 (= *pacte*) *(gén)* agreement, covenant *(frm)*; *(Pol)* convention ◆ ~ **collective** collective agreement ◆ **cela n'entre pas dans nos** ~**s** that doesn't enter into our agreement 2 (= *accord tacite*) *(gén)* understanding; *(Art, Littérat)* convention ◆ **les** ~**s (sociales)** convention, social conventions ◆ **décor/personnage/langage de** ~ *(Littérat, Théât)* conventional set/character/language ◆ **mots/amabilité de** ~ conventional words/kindness 3 (= *assemblée*) *(Pol US)* convention ◆ **la Convention** *(Hist)* the Convention

conventionné, e /kɔ̃vɑ̃sjɔne/ ADJ *[établissement, médecin] linked to the state health scheme,* ≃ National Health *(Brit) (épith)*; *[prix]* government-regulated; *[prêt]* subsidized, low-interest *(épith)*

conventionnel, -elle /kɔ̃vɑ̃sjɔnɛl/ ADJ *(gén)* conventional; *(Jur) [acte, clause]* contractual NM *(Hist)* ◆ **les** ~**s** the members of the Convention

conventionnellement /kɔ̃vɑ̃sjɔnɛlmɑ̃/ ADV conventionally

conventionnement /kɔ̃vɑ̃sjɔnmɑ̃/ NM *state health service contract,* ≃ National Health *(Brit)* contract

conventionner (se) /kɔ̃vɑ̃sjɔne/ ▸ conjug 1 ◂ VPR *[médecin] to register as a practitioner within the state health scheme*

conventuel, -elle /kɔ̃vɑ̃tɥɛl/ ADJ *[vie, règle, monde, bâtiment] [de moines]* monastic; *[de nonnes]* convent *(épith)*, conventual; *[simplicité, paix]* monastic

convenu, e /kɔ̃vny/ (ptp de **convenir**) ADJ 1 (= *décidé*) *[heure, prix, mot]* agreed ◆ **comme** ~ as agreed ◆ **il a été** ~ **de se réunir toutes les semaines** it was agreed that we should meet every week ◆ **ce qu'il est** ~ **d'appeler la politesse** what people call politeness 2 *(péj = conventionnel)* conventional

convergence /kɔ̃vɛʀʒɑ̃s/ NF convergence ◆ **point de** ~ *(Sci, Math)* point of convergence; *(Pol)* point of agreement ◆ **nous avons des points de** ~ there are points on which we agree ◆ **le point de** ~ **entre les deux théories** the meeting point between the two theories ◆ **objectif/programme de** ~ convergence target/programme; → **critère**

convergent, e /kɔ̃vɛʀʒɑ̃, ɑ̃t/ ADJ convergent

converger /kɔ̃vɛʀʒe/ ▸ conjug 3 ◂ VI *[lignes, rayons, routes]* to converge ◆ ~ **sur** *[regards]* to focus on ◆ **nos pensées convergent sur le sujet** we think along the same lines on the subject

convers, e /kɔ̃vɛʀ, ɛʀs/ ADJ *(Rel)* lay *(épith)*

conversation /kɔ̃vɛʀsasjɔ̃/ NF 1 (= *entretien*) *(gén)* conversation; *(politique, diplomatique)* talk ◆ **la** ~ conversation ◆ ~ **téléphonique** (tele)phone conversation ◆ **en (grande)** ~ **avec** (deep) in conversation with ◆ **faire la** ~ **à** to make conversation with; → **frais²** 2 (= *art de parler*) conversation ◆ **avoir de la** ~ to be a good conversationalist ◆ **il n'a pas de** ~ he's got no conversation ◆ **elle a de la** ~ † she's well-stacked*, she has big breasts 3 (= *langage familier*) **dans la** ~ **courante** in informal *ou* conversational *ou* everyday speech ◆ **employer le style de la** ~ to use a conversational style

conversationnel, -elle /kɔ̃vɛʀsasjɔnɛl/ ADJ *(Ordin)* conversational

converser /kɔ̃vɛʀse/ ▸ conjug 1 ◂ VI to converse *(avec* with)

conversion /kɔ̃vɛʀsjɔ̃/ NF 1 *(à une religion)* conversion *(à* to; *en* into); *(à une théorie)* winning over *(à* to) conversion *(à* to) 2 *(Écon = reconversion) (professionnelle)* retraining; *(industrielle)* conversion ◆ **convention de** ~ retraining scheme 3 *[de chiffres, mesures, devises]* conversion ◆ **taux de** ~ conversion rate ◆ ~ **de dollars en euros** conversion of dollars into euros ◆ **faire une** ~ **de fractions en ...** to convert fractions into ... 4 (= *demi-tour*) *(Mil)* wheel; *(Ski)* kick turn 5 *(Ordin)* conversion 6 *(Psych)* conversion

converti, e /kɔ̃vɛʀti/ (ptp de **convertir**) ADJ converted NM,F convert; → **prêcher**

convertibilité /kɔ̃vɛʀtibilite/ NF convertibility

convertible /kɔ̃vɛʀtibl/ ADJ convertible *(en* into) NM (= *avion*) convertiplane; (= *canapé*) sofa bed, bed-settee *(Brit)*

convertir /kɔ̃vɛʀtiʀ/ ▸ conjug 2 ◂ VT 1 (= *rallier*) *(à une religion)* to convert *(à* to); *(à une théorie)* to win over, to convert *(à* to) 2 (= *transformer*) to convert *(en* into); ◆ ~ **une terre en blés** to turn a field over to wheat VPR **se convertir** (= *devenir croyant, changer de religion*) to convert; *(à une théorie)* to be converted *(à* to); ◆ **il s'est converti à l'islam** he converted to Islam

convertissage /kɔ̃vɛʀtisaʒ/ NM *(Métal)* conversion

convertissement /kɔ̃vɛʀtismɑ̃/ NM *(Fin)* conversion

convertisseur /kɔ̃vɛʀtisœʀ/ NM converter ◆ ~ **Bessemer** Bessemer converter ◆ ~ **d'images** image converter ◆ ~ **de couple** torque converter ◆ ~ **numérique** *(Ordin)* digitizer ◆ ~ **numérique analogique** digital-analogue converter ◆ ~ **francs-euros** franc-euro currency converter

convexe /kɔ̃vɛks/ ADJ convex

convexion /kɔ̃vɛksjɔ̃/ NF ⇒ **convection**

convexité /kɔ̃vɛksite/ NF convexity

conviction /kɔ̃viksjɔ̃/ NF 1 (= *certitude*) conviction, (firm) belief ◆ **j'en ai la** ~ I'm convinced of it ◆ **parler avec** ~ to speak with conviction 2 (= *sérieux, enthousiasme*) conviction ◆ **faire qch avec/sans** ~ to do sth with/without conviction ◆ **manquer de** ~ to lack conviction 3 (= *opinions*) ~**s** beliefs, convictions 4 → **pièce**

convier /kɔ̃vje/ GRAMMAIRE ACTIVE 52.1 ▸ conjug 7 ◂ VT *(frm)* ◆ ~ **à** *[+ soirée, concert]* to invite to ◆ ~ **qn à faire qch** *(pousser)* to urge sb to do sth; *(inviter)* to invite sb to do sth ◆ **la chaleur conviait à la baignade** the hot weather made it very tempting to swim

convive /kɔ̃viv/ NMF guest *(at a meal)*

convivial, e (mpl **-iaux**) /kɔ̃vivjal, jo/ ADJ *(gén) [ambiance, lieu]* friendly, convivial; *(Ordin)* user-friendly

convivialité /kɔ̃vivjalite/ NF (= *rapports*) social interaction; (= *jovialité*) friendliness, conviviality; *(Ordin)* user-friendliness

convoc * /kɔ̃vɔk/ NF abrév de **convocation**

convocation /kɔ̃vɔkasjɔ̃/ NF 1 (NonC) *[d'assemblée]* convening, convoking; *[de membre de club]* inviting; *[de témoin, prévenu, subordonné]* summoning ◆ **la** ~ **des membres doit se faire longtemps à l'avance** members must be invited a long time in advance ◆ **cette** ~ **chez le**

directeur l'intriguait he was intrigued to know why the chairman had asked to see him ◆ **la ~ des membres/candidats doit se faire par écrit** members/candidates must be given written notification to attend [2] *(= lettre, carte)* (written) notification to attend; *(Jur)* summons ◆ **je n'ai pas encore reçu ma ~** I haven't had notification yet

convoi /kɔ̃vwa/ **NM** [1] *(= cortège funèbre)* funeral procession [2] *(= train)* train ◆ **~ de marchandises** goods train [3] *[de véhicules, navires, prisonniers]* convoy [4] **~ exceptionnel** ≈ wide *(ou* long *ou* dangerous) load

convoiement /kɔ̃vwamɑ̃/ **NM** *(= escorte)* escorting; *(Mil, Naut)* escorting, convoying; *(= transport)* conveying

convoiter /kɔ̃vwate/ ▸ conjug 1 ◂ **VT** *[+ héritage, objet, poste]* to covet; *[+ personne]* to lust after ◆ **poste très convoité** highly-coveted job

convoitise /kɔ̃vwatiz/ **NF** *(= désir) (gén)* covetousness; *(pour une personne)* lust, desire ◆ **la ~ des richesses** the lust for wealth ◆ **la ~ de la chair** the lusts of the flesh ◆ **l'objet de sa ~** the object of his desire ◆ **regarder avec ~** *[+ objet]* to cast covetous looks at; *[+ personne]* to look *ou* gaze lustfully at ◆ **regard brillant de ~** covetous (*ou* lustful) look ◆ **l'objet des ~s de tous** the object of everyone's desire

convoler /kɔ̃vɔle/ ▸ conjug 1 ◂ **VI** († *ou hum*) ◆ **~ (en justes noces)** to be wed † *(aussi hum)*

convoquer /kɔ̃vɔke/ ▸ conjug 1 ◂ **VT** *[+ assemblée]* to convene, to convoke; *(= convier)* to invite (*à* to); *[+ témoin, prévenu, subordonné]* to summon ◆ **~ qn (pour une entrevue)** to call *ou* invite sb for an interview ◆ **~ un candidat (à un examen)** to send a candidate written notification (of an exam) ◆ **il va falloir ~ les membres** we're going to have to call a meeting of the members *ou* call the members together ◆ **as-tu été convoqué à la réunion ?** have you been invited to (attend) the meeting? ◆ **le président a convoqué la presse pour annoncer ...** the president called a press conference to announce ... ◆ **j'ai été convoqué à dix heures (pour mon oral)** I've been asked to attend at ten o'clock (for my oral) ◆ **le chef m'a convoqué** the boss sent for me *ou* asked to see me ◆ **le chef m'a convoqué dans son bureau** the boss called *ou* summoned me to his office ◆ **le juge m'a convoqué** I was summoned to appear before the judge, I was called before the judge

convoyage /kɔ̃vwajaʒ/ **NM** ⇒ **convoiement**

convoyer /kɔ̃vwaje/ ▸ conjug 8 ◂ **VT** *(= escorter)* to escort; *(Mil, Naut)* to escort, to convoy; *(= transporter)* to convey

convoyeur /kɔ̃vwajœʀ/ **NM** *(= navire)* convoy, escort ship; *(= personne)* escort; *(= tapis roulant)* conveyor ◆ **~ de fonds** security guard, Securicor ® guard *(Brit)*

convulser /kɔ̃vylse/ ▸ conjug 1 ◂ **VT** *[+ visage]* to convulse, to distort; *[+ corps]* to convulse ◆ **la douleur lui convulsa le visage** his face was distorted *ou* convulsed with pain ◆ **son visage se convulsait** his face was distorted

convulsif, -ive /kɔ̃vylsif, iv/ **ADJ** convulsive

convulsion /kɔ̃vylsjɔ̃/ **NF** *(gén, Méd, fig)* convulsion ◆ **le pays est en proie à des ~s politiques** the country is in political turmoil

convulsionnaire /kɔ̃vylsjɔnɛʀ/ **NMF** convulsionary

convulsionner /kɔ̃vylsjɔne/ ▸ conjug 1 ◂ **VT** to convulse ◆ **visage convulsionné** distorted *ou* convulsed face

convulsivement /kɔ̃vylsivmɑ̃/ **ADV** convulsively

coobligé, e /kɔɔbliʒe/ **NM,F** *(Jur)* joint obligor

cooccurrence /kɔɔkyʀɑ̃s/ **NF** *(Ling)* co-occurrence

cookie /kuki/ **NM** *(Internet, Culin)* cookie

cool* /kul/ **ADJ** *(f inv)* cool*

coolie /kuli/ **NM** coolie

coopé /kɔpe/ **NF** [1] abrév de **coopération** [2] (abrév de **coopérative**) co-op

coopérant, e /kɔɔpeʀɑ̃, ɑ̃t/ **ADJ** cooperative **NM** ≈ VSO volunteer, Peace Corps volunteer *(US)*

coopérateur, -trice /k(ɔ)ɔpeʀatœʀ, tʀis/ **ADJ** cooperative **NM,F** [1] *(= associé)* collaborator, cooperator [2] *(= membre d'une coopérative)* member of a cooperative, cooperator

coopératif, -ive /k(ɔ)ɔpeʀatif, iv/ **ADJ** cooperative **NF** **coopérative** *(= organisme)* cooperative; *(= magasin)* co-op ◆ **coopérative scolaire** school fund

coopération /kɔɔpeʀasjɔ̃/ **NF** [1] *(gén = collaboration)* cooperation ◆ **apporter sa ~ à une entreprise** to cooperate *ou* collaborate in an undertaking [2] *(Pol)* ≈ Voluntary Service Overseas *(Brit)*, VSO *(Brit)*, Peace Corps *(US) (usually as form of military service)* ◆ **il a été envoyé en Afrique comme professeur au titre de la ~** ≈ he was sent to Africa as a VSO teacher *(Brit)*, he was sent to Africa by the Peace Corps to be a teacher *(US)*

> **COOPÉRATION**
>
> The French government, through the ministère de la **Coopération**, provides aid to developing countries by setting up and supporting educational and training schemes abroad. → **SERVICE MILITAIRE**

coopératisme /k(ɔ)ɔpeʀatism/ **NM** *(Écon)* cooperation

coopérer /kɔɔpeʀe/ ▸ conjug 6 ◂ **VI** to cooperate **VT INDIR** **coopérer à** to cooperate in

cooptation /kɔɔptasjɔ̃/ **NF** coopting, cooptation

coopter /kɔɔpte/ ▸ conjug 1 ◂ **VT** to coopt

coordinateur, -trice /kɔɔʀdinatœʀ, tʀis/ **NM, F** ⇒ **coordonnateur**

coordination /kɔɔʀdinasjɔ̃/ **NF** *(gén, Ling)* coordination ◆ **~ ouvrière/étudiante** workers'/students' committee; → **conjonction**

coordonnant /kɔɔʀdɔnɑ̃/ **NM** *(Ling)* coordinating conjunction

coordonnateur, -trice /kɔɔʀdɔnatœʀ, tʀis/ **ADJ** coordinating **NM,F** coordinator

coordonné, e /kɔɔʀdɔne/ (ptp de **coordonner**) **ADJ** coordinated ◆ **(proposition) ~e** *(Ling)* coordinate clause ◆ **papiers peints ~s** matching wallpapers ◆ **vêtements ~s** coordinating separates **NMPL** **coordonnés** *(Habillement)* coordinates **NFPL** **coordonnées** *(Math)* coordinates ◆ **donnez-moi vos ~es** can I have your name and address *ou* your contact details please?

coordonner /kɔɔʀdɔne/ ▸ conjug 1 ◂ **VT** to coordinate

copain* /kɔpɛ̃/ **NM** *(= ami)* friend, mate* *(surtout Brit)*, buddy* *(surtout US)* ◆ **son ~** *(= amoureux)* her boyfriend ◆ **de bons ~s** good friends, great pals* ◆ **~ de régiment** army pal* *ou* buddy* ◆ **il est très ~ avec le patron** he's really in with the boss*, he's very pally* *(Brit)* with the boss ◆ **avec eux, c'est *ou* on est ~ ~** we're very chummy* *ou* dead pally‡ *(Brit)* with them ◆ **ils ont fait ~-copine** they really hit it off* ◆ **ils sont ~s comme cochons** they are great buddies*, they're as thick as thieves ◆ **les meilleurs postes sont toujours pour les petits ~s** *(péj)* they always give the best jobs to their cronies*, it's always jobs for the boys*

coparent /kopaʀɑ̃/ **NM** co-parent

coparentalité /kopaʀɑ̃talite/ **NF** co-parenting

coparticipant, e /kopaʀtisipɑ̃, ɑ̃t/ *(Jur)* **ADJ** in copartnership *ou* joint account **NM,F** copartner

coparticipation /kopaʀtisipasjɔ̃/ **NF** *(Jur)* copartnership ◆ **~ aux bénéfices** profit-sharing

copeau (pl **copeaux**) /kɔpo/ **NM** *[de bois]* shaving; *[de métal]* turning ◆ **brûler des ~x** to burn wood shavings ◆ **~x de chocolat/de parmesan** shaved chocolate/parmesan

Copenhague /kɔpənag/ **N** Copenhagen

Copernic /kɔpɛʀnik/ **NM** Copernicus

copernicien, -ienne /kɔpɛʀnisjɛ̃, jɛn/ **ADJ, NM,F** Copernican ◆ **révolution ~ne** Copernican revolution

copiage /kɔpjaʒ/ **NM** *(gén)* copying; *(Scol)* copying, cribbing

copie /kɔpi/ **NF** [1] *(= reproduction, exemplaire) [de diplôme, film]* copy; *[de tableau]* copy, reproduction; *[de sculpture, bijou]* copy, reproduction, replica ◆ **~ certifiée conforme** *(Admin)* certified copy ◆ **pour ~ conforme** *(Admin)* certified accurate ◆ **~ d'écran** *(Ordin)* screenshot ◆ **~ étalon** *(Ciné, TV)* master print ◆ **~ d'exploitation** *(Ciné)* release print ◆ **~ neuve** *(Ciné)* new copy ◆ **~ papier** *(Ordin)* hard copy ◆ **~ de sauvegarde** *(Ordin)* backup copy ◆ **prendre ~ de qch** to make a copy of sth ◆ **je vous ai mis en ~** I've copied it to you

[2] *(= action de copier)* copying

[3] *(= reproduction frauduleuse)* copy, imitation ◆ **pâle ~** pale imitation

[4] *(Scol) (= feuille de papier)* sheet (of paper), paper; *(= devoir)* exercise; *(= composition, examen)* paper, script ◆ **~ simple/double** single/double sheet (of paper) ◆ **~ d'examen** examination script ◆ **rendre *ou* remettre ~ blanche** to hand in a blank sheet of paper ◆ **rendre *ou* remettre sa ~** *(lit)* to hand in one's paper; *(fig)* to turn in one's report ◆ **revoir sa ~** *(fig)* to go back to the drawing board; → **mal²**

[5] *(Typo)* copy

[6] *(Presse)* copy; → **pisseur**

copier /kɔpje/ ▸ conjug 7 ◂ **VT** [1] *(= reproduire également) [+ écrit, texte, acte]* to copy, to make a copy of; *(Ordin)* to copy; *[+ tableau, sculpture]* to copy, to reproduce ◆ **~ qch au propre** to make a fair copy of sth, to copy sth out neatly ◆ **~ une leçon trois fois** to copy out a lesson three times ◆ **vous me la copierez !*** I won't forget that in a hurry!* ◆ **~ coller** *(Ordin)* to copy and paste [2] *(= reproduire frauduleusement) [+ tableau, sculpture, bijou, logiciel]* to copy, to make a copy of; *(Scol = tricher)* to copy, to crib ◆ **~ le voisin** to copy *ou* crib from one's neighbour [3] *(= imiter) [+ style, démarche, auteur]* to copy **VI** *(Scol = tricher)* to copy, to crib *(sur* from)

copieur, -ieuse /kɔpjœʀ, jøz/ **NM,F** *(Scol)* copier, cribber **NM** *(= machine)* copier

copieusement /kɔpjøzmɑ̃/ **ADV** *[manger, boire]* copiously, heartily; *[illustré, annoté]* copiously ◆ **repas ~ arrosé** meal generously washed down with wine ◆ **on s'est fait ~ arroser/engueuler‡** we got well and truly soaked/told off* ◆ **il s'est fait ~ siffler après son discours** the crowd booed and whistled loudly when he finished his speech

copieux, -ieuse /kɔpjø, jøz/ **ADJ** *[repas]* copious, hearty; *[portion]* generous; *[notes, exemples]* copious

copilote /kopilɔt/ **NMF** *[d'avion]* co-pilot; *[de voiture]* navigator

copin* /kɔpɛ̃/ **NM** ⇒ **copain**

copinage* /kɔpinaʒ/ **NM** *(péj)* pally* *(Brit) ou* buddy-buddy* *(surtout US)* relationship ◆ **obtenir qch par ~** to get sth through friendly contacts

copine* /kɔpin/ **NF** *(= amie)* friend; *(= amoureuse)* girlfriend ◆ **une ~ de ma mère** one of my mother's friends *ou* girlfriends ◆ **~ de classe**

school friend *ou* mate ◆ **elles sont très ~s** they're great friends ◆ **elle est très ~ avec le voisin** she's very friendly *ou* pally* *(Brit)* with the next-door neighbour

copiner* /kɔpine/ ▸ conjug 1 ◂ VI to be pally* *(Brit) ou* great buddies* *(surtout US) (avec* with)

copiste /kɔpist/ NMF *(Hist, Littérat)* copyist, transcriber

copossséder /kopɔsede/ ▸ conjug 6 ◂ VT to own jointly

copossession /kopɔsɛsjɔ̃/ NF co-ownership, joint ownership

copra(h) /kɔpʀa/ NM copra

coprésidence /kopʀezidɑ̃s/ NF co-presidency, co-chairmanship

coprésident /kopʀezidɑ̃/ NM co-president, co-chairman

coprésidente /kopʀezidɑ̃t/ NF co-president, co-chairwoman

coprin /kɔpʀɛ̃/ NM ink cap, coprinus *(SPÉC)*

coproducteur, -trice /kopʀɔdyktœʀ, tʀis/ NM,F co-producer

coproduction /kopʀɔdyksjɔ̃/ NF *(Ciné, TV)* coproduction, joint production ◆ **une ~ franco-italienne** a French-Italian co-production, a joint French-Italian production

coproduire /kopʀɔdɥiʀ/ ▸ conjug 38 ◂ VT to coproduce

coprophage /kɔpʀɔfaʒ/ ADJ coprophagous

copropriétaire /kopʀɔpʀijetɛʀ/ NMF co-owner, joint owner

copropriété /kopʀɔpʀijete/ NF (= *statut*) co-ownership, joint ownership; (= *propriétaires*) co-owners ◆ **immeuble en ~** block of flats *(Brit) ou* apartment building *(US)* in co-ownership, condominium *(US)*

copte /kɔpt/ ADJ Coptic NM (= *langue*) Coptic NMF **Copte** Copt

copulation /kɔpylasjɔ̃/ NF copulation

copule /kɔpyl/ NF *(Ling)* copulative verb, copula

copuler /kɔpyle/ ▸ conjug 1 ◂ VI to copulate

copyright /kɔpiʀajt/ NM copyright

coq[1] /kɔk/ NM *[de basse-cour]* cock, rooster; (= *girouette*) weather cock *ou* vane ◆ **~ faisan/de perdrix** (= *oiseau mâle*) cock pheasant/partridge ◆ **jeune ~** cockerel ◆ **~, poids ~** *(Boxe)* bantam-weight ◆ **être comme un ~ en pâte** to be in clover, to live the life of Riley ◆ **jambes** *ou* **mollets de ~** wiry legs ◆ **sauter** *ou* **passer du ~ à l'âne** to jump from one subject to another; → **chant**[1], **rouge**

COMP **coq de bruyère** *(grand)* capercaillie; *(petit)* black grouse

coq de combat fighting cock

le coq gaulois the French cockerel *(emblem of the French fighting spirit)*

coq nain bantam cock

coq de roche cock-of-the-rock

coq au vin coq au vin

coq[2] /kɔk/ NM *(Naut)* (ship's) cook

coq-à-l'âne /kɔkalɑn/ NM INV abrupt change of subject ◆ **faire un ~** to jump from one subject to another

coquard*, **coquart*** /kɔkaʀ/ NM black eye, shiner*

coque /kɔk/ NF 1 *[de bateau]* hull; *[d'avion]* fuselage; *[d'auto]* shell, body 2 *[de noix, amande]* shell; † *[d'œuf]* shell ◆ **œuf (à la) ~** *(Culin)* (soft-)boiled egg ◆ **~ de noix** *(Naut)* cockleshell 3 (= *mollusque*) cockle

coquelet /kɔklɛ/ NM *(Culin)* cockerel

coquelicot /kɔkliko/ NM poppy; → **rouge**

coqueluche /kɔklyʃ/ NF 1 *(Méd)* whooping cough 2 *(fig)* **être la ~ de** to be the idol *ou* darling of

coquemar /kɔkmaʀ/ NM cauldron, big kettle

coqueret /kɔkʀɛ/ NM Chinese lantern, winter *ou* ground cherry

coquerico /kɔk(ə)ʀiko/ NM, EXCL ⇒ **cocorico**

coquerie /kɔkʀi/ NF *(Naut)* (*à bord*) (ship's) galley, caboose *(Brit)*; (*à terre*) cookhouse

coquet, -ette /kɔkɛ, ɛt/ ADJ 1 (= *bien habillé*) smart, well turned-out; (= *soucieux de son apparence*) appearance-conscious, clothes-conscious ◆ **il est trop ~** he takes too much interest in his appearance, he is too clothes-conscious ◆ **il n'est pas ~** he doesn't take much interest in his appearance 2 († = *flirteur*) flirtatious 3 *[ville]* pretty, charming; *[logement]* charming; *[robe]* smart, stylish 4 (* : *intensif*) *[somme d'argent, revenu]* tidy* *(épith)* NF **coquette** ◆ **c'est une coquette** she's a coquette *ou* a flirt, she's very coquettish *ou* flirtatious ◆ **faire sa coquette** to play hard to get* ◆ **jouer les grandes coquettes** *(fig)* to flirt a lot, to be very coquettish

coquetier /kɔk(ə)tje/ NM egg cup ◆ **gagner** *ou* **décrocher le ~** †* to hit the jackpot*

coquettement /kɔkɛtmɑ̃/ ADV *[s'habiller]* smartly, stylishly; *[sourire]* coquettishly ◆ **un appartement ~ meublé** an elegantly furnished apartment

coquetterie /kɔkɛtʀi/ NF 1 (= *élégance*) *[de personne]* interest in one's appearance, consciousness of one's appearance; *[de toilette, coiffure]* smartness, stylishness 2 (= *galanterie*) coquetry, flirtatiousness *(NonC)* ◆ **il mettait sa ~ à marcher sans canne/parler sans notes** *(littér = amour propre)* he prided himself on *ou* made a point of walking without a stick/talking without notes 3 *(hum)* **avoir une ~ dans l'œil*** to have a cast in one's eye

coquillage /kɔkijaʒ/ NM (= *mollusque*) shellfish *(NonC)*; (= *coquille*) shell

coquillard* /kɔkijaʀ/ NM → **tamponner**

coquille /kɔkij/ NF 1 *[de mollusque, œuf, noix]* shell ◆ **rentrer dans/sortir de sa ~** *(fig)* to go *ou* withdraw into/come out of one's shell 2 (= *récipient*) (shell-shaped) dish, scallop ◆ **~ de poisson/crabe** (= *mets*) scallop of fish/crab, fish/crab served in scallop shells 3 (= *décoration*) scallop; *[d'épée]* coquille, shell 4 *(Typo)* misprint 5 *(Sport* = *protection)* box 6 *(Méd* = *plâtre)* spinal bed

COMP **coquille de beurre** shell of butter

coquille de noix* *(Naut)* cockleshell

coquille d'œuf (= *couleur*) eggshell *(épith)*

coquille Saint-Jacques (= *animal*) scallop; (= *carapace*) scallop shell

coquillettes /kɔkijɛt/ NFPL pasta shells

coquillier, -ière /kɔkije, jɛʀ/ ADJ conchiferous *(SPÉC)* NM † shell collection

coquin, e /kɔkɛ̃, in/ ADJ 1 (= *malicieux*) *[enfant, air]* mischievous ◆ **~ de sort !*** the devil!*, the deuce! †* 2 (= *polisson*) *[histoire, regard]* naughty, suggestive NM,F (= *enfant*) rascal, mischief ◆ **tu es un petit ~ !** you little monkey! *ou* rascal! NM († † = *gredin*) rascal, rogue NF **coquine** †† (= *débauchée*) loose woman, strumpet †

coquinerie /kɔkinʀi/ NF 1 (= *caractère*) *[d'enfant]* mischievousness; *[de gredin]* roguery 2 (= *action*) *[d'enfant]* mischievous trick; *[de personne peu honnête]* low-down trick

cor[1] /kɔʀ/ NM *(Mus)* horn ◆ **premier ~** principal horn

◆ **à cor et à cri** ◆ **réclamer** *ou* **demander qch/qn à ~ et à cri** to clamour for sth/sb ◆ **chasser à ~ et à cri** to hunt with the hounds

COMP **cor anglais** cor anglais *(Brit)*, English horn *(US)*

cor de basset basset horn

cor de chasse hunting horn

cor d'harmonie French horn

cor à pistons valve horn

cor[2] /kɔʀ/ NM *(Méd)* ◆ **~ (au pied)** corn

cor[3] /kɔʀ/ NM *[de cerf]* tine ◆ **un (cerf) 10 ~s** a 10-point stag, a 10-pointer

corail (pl **-aux**) /kɔʀaj, o/ NM coral ◆ **la mer de Corail** the Coral Sea ADJ INV 1 (= *couleur*) coral (pink) 2 ◆ **(train) Corail** ® ≈ express (train), inter-city train *(Brit)* 3 **serpent ~** coral snake

corallien, -ienne /kɔʀaljɛ̃, jɛn/ ADJ coralline *(littér)*, coral *(épith)*

corallin, e /kɔʀalɛ̃, in/ ADJ *(littér) [lèvre, coquille]* coralline *(littér)*, coral (red)

Coran /kɔʀɑ̃/ NM ◆ **le ~** the Koran

coranique /kɔʀanik/ ADJ Koranic

corbeau (pl **corbeaux**) /kɔʀbo/ NM 1 (= *oiseau*) *(terme générique)* crow ◆ **(grand) ~** raven ◆ **~ freux** rook 2 († *péj* = *prêtre*) black-coat † *(péj)*, priest 3 *(Archit)* corbel 4 (* = *diffamateur*) writer of poison-pen letters

corbeille /kɔʀbɛj/ NF 1 (= *panier*) basket; *(pour courrier)* tray; *(Ordin)* trash ◆ **vider la ~** to empty the trash ◆ **~ de fleurs/de fruits** basket of flowers/fruit ◆ **~ arrivée/départ** in/out tray ◆ **soutien-gorge ~** push-up bra

2 *(Théât)* (dress) circle

3 *(Archit) [de chapiteau]* bell, basket

4 ◆ **la ~** † *(Bourse)* the trading floor *ou* pit *(in Paris Stock Exchange)*

5 (= *parterre*) (round *ou* oval) flowerbed

COMP **corbeille d'argent** (= *plante*) sweet alyssum

corbeille à courrier mail tray

corbeille de mariage wedding presents ◆ **sa femme a apporté une fortune dans la ~ de mariage** his wife brought him a fortune when she married him ◆ **dans cette fusion, leur société apporte 10 millions d'euros dans la ~ de mariage** their company brings (a dowry of) 10 million euros to this merger

corbeille d'or (= *plante*) golden alyssum

corbeille à ouvrage workbasket

corbeille à pain breadbasket

corbeille à papier(s) wastepaper basket *ou* bin

corbillard /kɔʀbijaʀ/ NM hearse

cordage /kɔʀdaʒ/ NM 1 (= *corde, lien*) rope ◆ **~s** *(gén)* ropes, rigging; *(Naut : de voilure)* rigging 2 *[de raquette de tennis]* stringing

corde /kɔʀd/ NF 1 *(gén* = *câble, cordage)* rope ◆ **attacher qn avec une ~** *ou* **de la ~** to tie sb up with a (piece of) rope ◆ **attacher** *ou* **lier qn à un arbre avec une ~** to rope sb to a tree, to tie sb to a tree with a (piece of) rope ◆ **en ~, de ~** *[tapis]* whipcord *(épith)* ◆ **à semelle de ~** rope-soled ◆ **grimper** *ou* **monter à la ~** to climb a rope, to pull o.s. up a rope; → **danseur, sauter**

2 *(Mus)* string ◆ **instruments à ~s** stringed instruments ◆ **les ~s** the strings ◆ **orchestre/quatuor à ~s** string orchestra/quartet ◆ **~ à vide** open string ◆ **instrument à ~s pincées/frottées** plucked/bowed instrument ◆ **à ~s croisées** *[piano]* overstrung

3 *(Sport) [de raquette, arc]* string ◆ **être envoyé dans les ~s** *(Boxe)* to be thrown against the ropes

4 *[de funambule]* tightrope, high wire

5 *(Courses)* rails ◆ **à la ~** *(gén : sur piste)* on the inside; *(Courses)* on the rails *ou* the inside ◆ **prendre un virage à la ~** to hug a bend, to take a bend on the inside ◆ **prendre/tenir la ~** *(gén : sur piste)* to get on/be on the inside; *(Courses)* to get close to/be on the rails, to get on/be on the inside ◆ **c'est lui qui tient la ~** *(fig)* he's in with the best chance (of winning)

6 (= *trame d'un tissu*) thread; → **user**

7 *(Math)* chord

[8] († = *mesure)* cord
[9] *(locutions)* **mériter la ~** † to deserve to hang *ou* be hanged ◆ **il s'est mis la ~ au cou** *(= il s'est marié)* he's tied the knot, he's got hitched * ◆ **il a dû y aller la ~ au cou** *(humble, soumis)* he had to go cap in hand ◆ **être** *ou* **marcher** *ou* **danser sur la ~ raide** to walk a tightrope ◆ **politique de la ~ raide** brinkmanship ◆ **parler de (la) ~ dans la maison du pendu** to bring up a sore point, to make a tactless remark ◆ **avoir plus d'une ~** *ou* **plusieurs ~s à son arc** to have more than one string to one's bow ◆ **c'est dans ses ~s** it's right up his street *(Brit) ou* alley *(US)* ◆ **est-ce que c'est dans ses ~s ?** is he up to it? ◆ **ce n'est pas dans mes ~s** it's not my line (of country) ◆ **tirer sur la ~** to push one's luck a bit *, to go too far ◆ **toucher** *ou* **faire vibrer la ~ sensible** to touch the right chord ◆ **il pleut** *ou* **il tombe des ~s** * it's raining cats and dogs * *ou* bucketing (down) * *(Brit)*; → **sac¹**

COMP **corde cervicale** cervical nerve
corde dorsale spinal cord
corde à linge clothes line, washing line
corde lisse (climbing) rope
corde à nœuds knotted climbing rope
corde à *ou* **de piano** piano wire
corde de rappel abseiling rope
corde à sauter skipping rope, jump rope *(US)*
corde du tympan chorda tympani
cordes vocales vocal cords

cordeau (pl **cordeaux**) /kɔʀdo/ NM [1] *(= corde)* string, line ◆ **~ de jardinier** gardener's line ◆ **fait** *ou* **tiré au ~** *(fig)* as straight as a die [2] *(= mèche)* fuse ◆ **~ Bickford** Bickford fuse, safety fuse ◆ **~ détonant** detonator fuse [3] *(Pêche)* ledger line

cordée /kɔʀde/ NF [1] *[d'alpinistes]* climbers roped together ◆ **premier de ~** leader [2] *[de bois]* cord

cordelette /kɔʀdəlɛt/ NF cord

Cordelier /kɔʀdəlje/ NM *(= religieux)* Cordelier

cordelière /kɔʀdəljɛʀ/ NF [1] *(= corde)* cord [2] *(Archit)* cable moulding *(Brit) ou* molding *(US)* [3] *(= religieuse)* **Cordelière** Franciscan nun

corder /kɔʀde/ ► conjug 1 ◄ VT [1] *[+ chanvre, tabac]* to twist [2] *(= lier) [+ malle]* to tie up (with rope), to rope up [3] *(= mesurer) [+ bois]* to cord [4] *[+ raquette]* to string

corderie /kɔʀd(ə)ʀi/ NF *(= industrie)* ropemaking industry; *(= atelier)* rope factory

cordial, e (mpl **-iaux**) /kɔʀdjal, jo/ ADJ *[accueil]* hearty, warm, cordial; *[sentiment, personne]* warm; *[manières]* cordial; *[antipathie, haine]* cordial, hearty; → **entente** NM heart tonic, cordial

cordialement /kɔʀdjalmɑ̃/ ADV [1] *(gén)* ◆ **se serrer la main ~** to shake hands warmly ◆ **ils nous ont reçus très ~** they gave us a hearty *ou* very warm welcome ◆ **vous êtes tous ~ invités** you are all cordially invited ◆ **il la déteste ~** he cordially *ou* heartily detests her [2] *(en fin de lettre)* **~ (vôtre)** kind regards ◆ **bien ~** kindest regards

cordialité /kɔʀdjalite/ NF *[d'accueil]* warmth, cordiality; *[de sentiment, personne]* warmth; *[de manières]* cordiality ◆ **tout s'est passé dans la plus parfaite ~** it all went off in the most cordial fashion

cordier /kɔʀdje/ NM [1] *(= fabricant)* ropemaker [2] *(Mus)* tailpiece

cordillère /kɔʀdijɛʀ/ NF mountain range, cordillera ◆ **la ~ des Andes** the Andes cordillera ◆ **la ~ australienne** the Great Dividing Range

cordite /kɔʀdit/ NF cordite

cordon /kɔʀdɔ̃/ NM [1] *[de sonnette, rideau]* cord; *[de tablier]* tie; *[de sac, bourse]* string; *[de chaussures]* lace ◆ **~ de sonnette** bell-pull ◆ **tenir/délier/resserrer les ~s de la bourse** *(fig)* to hold/loosen/tighten the purse strings [2] *[de soldats]* cordon [3] *(Archit)* string-course, cordon [4] *(= décoration)* sash ◆ **~ du Saint-Esprit** ribbon of the order of the Holy Ghost ◆ **~ de la Légion d'honneur** sash *ou* cordon of the Légion d'Honneur

COMP **cordon Bickford** Bickford fuse, safety fuse
cordon bleu *(= cuisinier)* cordon-bleu cook; *(= décoration)* cordon bleu
cordon littoral offshore bar
cordon médullaire spinal cord
cordon ombilical *(lit, fig)* umbilical cord ◆ **couper** *ou* **rompre le ~ (ombilical)** *(fig)* to cut *ou* sever the umbilical cord
cordon sanitaire *(Méd, Pol)* quarantine line, cordon sanitaire

cordon-bleu (pl **cordons-bleus**) /kɔʀdɔ̃blø/ NM → **cordon**

cordonner /kɔʀdɔne/ ► conjug 1 ◄ VT *[+ soie, cheveux]* to twist

cordonnerie /kɔʀdɔnʀi/ NF *(= boutique)* shoe-repair shop, cobbler's †; *(= métier)* shoe-repairing

cordonnet /kɔʀdɔnɛ/ NM *(= petit cordon)* braid *(NonC)*, cord *(NonC)*; *(pour boutonnière)* buttonhole twist *(NonC)*

cordonnier, -ière /kɔʀdɔnje, jɛʀ/ NM,F *(= réparateur)* shoe-repairer, cobbler †; († = *fabricant)* shoemaker ◆ **les ~s sont toujours les plus mal chaussés** *(Prov)* the shoemaker's children always go barefoot *(Prov)*

Cordoue /kɔʀdu/ N Cordoba

coréalisateur, -trice /koʀealizatœʀ, tʀis/ NM,F *(Ciné, TV)* codirector

Corée /koʀe/ NF Korea ◆ **~ du Sud/du Nord** South/North Korea

coréen, -enne /koʀeɛ̃, ɛn/ ADJ Korean NM *(= langue)* Korean NM,F **Coréen(ne)** Korean

coreligionnaire /koʀ(ə)liʒjɔnɛʀ/ NMF co-religionist

coresponsabilité /koʀɛspɔ̃sabilite/ NF joint responsibility

coresponsable /koʀɛspɔ̃sabl/ ADJ *[personne]* co-responsible, jointly responsible *(de* for) NMF person sharing responsibility *(de* for)

Corfou /kɔʀfu/ N Corfu

coriace /kɔʀjas/ ADJ *(lit, fig)* tough ◆ **il est ~ en affaires** he's a hard-headed *ou* tough businessman

coriandre /kɔʀjɑ̃dʀ/ NF coriander

coricide /kɔʀisid/ NM corn remover

corindon /kɔʀɛ̃dɔ̃/ NM corundum

Corinthe /kɔʀɛ̃t/ N Corinth; → **raisin**

corinthien, -ienne /kɔʀɛ̃tjɛ̃, jɛn/ ADJ Corinthian

Coriolan /kɔʀjɔlɑ̃/ NM Coriolanus

cormier /kɔʀmje/ NM *(= arbre)* service tree; *(= bois)* service wood

cormoran /kɔʀmɔʀɑ̃/ NM cormorant ◆ **~ huppé** shag

cornac /kɔʀnak/ NM *[d'éléphant]* mahout, elephant driver

cornaline /kɔʀnalin/ NF carnelian

cornaquer * /kɔʀnake/ ► conjug 1 ◄ VT to show around ◆ **il m'a cornaqué à travers la ville** he showed me round the town

cornard ⁂ /kɔʀnaʀ/ NM cuckold †

corne /kɔʀn/ NF [1] *[d'escargot, vache]* horn; *[de cerf]* antler; *[de narval]* tusk ◆ **à ~s** horned ◆ **donner un coup de ~ à qn** to butt sb ◆ **blesser qn d'un coup de ~** to gore sb ◆ **avoir** *ou* **porter des ~s** * *(fig)* to be a cuckold † ◆ **sa femme lui fait porter des ~s** * his wife is unfaithful to him ◆ **faire les ~s à qn** to make a face at sb, to make a jeering gesture at sb; → **bête, taureau**
[2] *(= substance)* horn
[3] *(= instrument)* horn; *(Chasse)* hunting horn; († = *avertisseur)* hooter, horn
[4] *(= coin) [de page]* dog-ear ◆ **faire une ~ à la page d'un livre** to turn down the corner of the page in a book
[5] (* = *peau dure)* **avoir de la ~** to have patches of hard skin, to have calluses

COMP **corne d'abondance** horn of plenty, cornucopia
la corne de l'Afrique the Horn of Africa
corne de brume foghorn
corne à chaussures shoehorn
cornes de gazelle *(Culin) sugar-covered shortbread crescents*

cornée /kɔʀne/ NF cornea

cornéen, -enne /kɔʀneɛ̃, ɛn/ ADJ corneal; → **lentille**

corneille /kɔʀnɛj/ NF crow ◆ **~ mantelée** hooded crow ◆ **~ noire** carrion crow; → **bayer**

cornélien, -ienne /kɔʀneljɛ̃, jɛn/ ADJ *(Littérat)* Cornelian; *(fig) [situation] where love and duty conflict; [héros] who puts duty before everything*

cornemuse /kɔʀnəmyz/ NF bagpipes ◆ **joueur de ~** piper, bagpiper

corner¹ /kɔʀne/ ► conjug 1 ◄ VT [1] *[+ livre, carte]* to make *ou* get dog-eared; *[+ page]* to turn down the corner of [2] (†† = *claironner) [+ nouvelle]* to blare out ◆ **arrête de nous ~ (ça) aux oreilles !** * stop shouting about it! VI *[chasseur]* to sound a horn; † *[automobiliste]* to hoot *(Brit) ou* sound one's horn; *[sirène]* to sound

corner² /kɔʀnɛʀ/ NM *(Ftbl)* corner (kick) ◆ **tirer un ~** to take a corner (kick) ◆ **sortir en ~** to go out of play for a corner (kick)

cornet /kɔʀnɛ/ NM [1] *(= récipient)* **~ (de papier)** paper cone ◆ **~ de dragées/de frites** cornet *ou* paper cone of sweets/chips, ≈ bag of sweets/chips ◆ **~ de glace** ice-cream cone *ou* cornet *(Brit)* ◆ **mettre sa main en ~** to cup one's hand to one's ear [2] *(Belg = combiné téléphonique)* handset, receiver [3] *(Helv = sachet)* (paper *ou* plastic) bag [4] *(Mus) [d'orgue]* cornet stop

COMP **cornet acoustique** ear trumpet
cornet à dés dice cup
cornets du nez turbinate bones
cornet (à pistons) cornet
cornet de poste *ou* **de postillon** posthorn

cornette /kɔʀnɛt/ NF *[de religieuse]* cornet; *(Naut = pavillon)* burgee

cornettiste /kɔʀnetist/ NMF cornet player

corniaud /kɔʀnjo/ NM *(= chien)* mongrel; (⁂ = *imbécile)* nitwit *, twit * *(Brit)*

corniche /kɔʀniʃ/ NF [1] *(Archit = moulure)* cornice; *[de piédestal]* entablement [2] *(Alpinisme)* ledge ◆ **(route en) ~** coast road, cliff road [3] *[de neige]* cornice

cornichon /kɔʀniʃɔ̃/ NM [1] *(= concombre)* gherkin; *(en condiment)* gherkin *(Brit)*, pickle *(US)* [2] (* = *personne)* nitwit *, nincompoop * [3] *(arg Scol) pupil in the class preparing for Saint-Cyr*

cornière /kɔʀnjɛʀ/ NF *(= pièce métallique)* corner iron; *(= pièce d'écoulement)* valley

cornique /kɔʀnik/ ADJ Cornish NM *(= langue)* Cornish

corniste /kɔʀnist/ NMF horn player

Cornouaille /kɔʀnwaj/ NF ◆ **la ~** Cornouaille *(area of Brittany)*

Cornouailles /kɔʀnwaj/ NF ◆ **les ~** Cornwall

cornouiller /kɔʀnuje/ NM dogwood

cornu, e /kɔʀny/ ADJ *[animal, démon]* horned NF **cornue** *(= récipient)* retort; *(Tech = four)* retort

corollaire /kɔʀɔlɛʀ/ NM *(Logique, Math)* corollary; *(gén = conséquence)* consequence, corollary ◆ **et ceci a pour ~ ...** and this has as a consequence ..., and the corollary of this is ...

corolle /kɔʀɔl/ NF corolla

coron /kɔʀɔ̃/ NM *(= maison)* mining cottage; *(= quartier)* mining village

coronaire /kɔʀɔnɛʀ/ ADJ *(Anat)* coronary

coronarien, -ienne /kɔʀɔnaʀjɛ̃, jɛn/ ADJ *(Méd)* coronary

coronavirus /kɔʀɔnaviʀys/ NM coronavirus

corossol /kɔʀɔsɔl/ NM soursop

corporatif, -ive /kɔʀpɔʀatif, iv/ ADJ *[mouvement, système]* corporative; *[esprit]* corporate

corporation /kɔʀpɔʀasjɔ̃/ NF *[de notaires, médecins]* corporate body; *(Hist)* guild ◆ **dans notre ~** in our profession

corporatisme /kɔʀpɔʀatism/ NM corporatism

corporatiste /kɔʀpɔʀatist/ ADJ corporatist

corporel, -elle /kɔʀpɔʀɛl/ ADJ *[châtiment]* corporal; *[sévices]* physical; *[intégrité]* physical, bodily; *[accident]* involving physical injury; *[besoin]* bodily ◆ **lait ~** body lotion *ou* milk ◆ **bien ~** *(Jur)* corporeal property

corps /kɔʀ/ NM 1 *(Anat)* body; *(= cadavre)* corpse, (dead) body ◆ **le ~ humain** the human body ◆ **frissonner** *ou* **trembler de tout son ~** to tremble all over ◆ **jusqu'au milieu du ~** up to the waist ◆ **je n'ai rien dans le ~** I've had nothing to eat ◆ **robe près du ~** close-fitting dress; → **contrainte², diable**

2 *(Astron, Chim, Phys = objet, substance)* body ◆ **~ simples/composés** simple/compound bodies; → **chute**

3 *(= partie essentielle) [de bâtiment, lettre, article, ouvrage]* (main) body; *[de meuble]* main part, body; *[de pompe]* barrel; *(Typo)* body

4 *[de vêtement]* bodice; *[d'armure]* cors(e)let

5 *(= consistance) [d'étoffe, papier, vin]* body ◆ **ce vin a du ~** this wine is full-bodied *ou* has (got) body

6 *(= groupe)* body, corps; *(Mil)* corps ◆ **~ de sapeurs-pompiers** fire brigade ◆ **les grands ~ de l'État** the senior branches of the civil service; → **esprit**

7 *(= recueil de textes)* corpus, body ◆ **~ de doctrines** body of doctrines

8 *(locutions)* **se donner ~ et âme à qch** to give o.s. body and soul to sth ◆ **sombrer ~ et biens** *[bateau]* to go down with all hands; *[entreprise]* to sink without trace ◆ **perdu ~ et biens** lost with all hands ◆ **s'élancer** *ou* **se jeter à ~ perdu dans une entreprise/la mêlée** to throw o.s. wholeheartedly *ou* headlong into a venture/into the fray ◆ **donner ~ à qch** to give substance to sth ◆ **faire ~** *[idées]* to form one body *(avec* with); *[choses concrètes]* to be joined *(avec* to); ◆ **prendre ~** to take shape ◆ **s'ils veulent faire cela, il faudra qu'ils me passent sur le ~** if they want to do that, it'll be over my dead body ◆ **pour avoir ce qu'il veut, il vous passerait sur le ~** he'd trample you underfoot to get his own way ◆ **faire qch à son ~ défendant** to do sth against one's will *ou* unwillingly ◆ **mais qu'est-ce qu'il a dans le ~ ?** whatever's got into him? ◆ **j'aimerais bien savoir ce qu'il a dans le ~** I'd like to know what makes him tick ◆ **tenir au ~** *[aliment]* to be filling

COMP **corps d'armée** army corps

corps de ballet corps de ballet

corps de bâtiment main body (of a building)

corps caverneux erectile tissue (of the penis)

corps céleste celestial *ou* heavenly body

corps constitués constitutional bodies (of the state)

corps consulaire consular corps

corps à corps clinch ◆ **se battre (au) ~ à ~** to fight hand-to-hand

corps du délit *(Jur)* corpus delicti

le Corps diplomatique the Diplomatic Corps, the Foreign Service *(US)*

corps électoral electorate

le corps enseignant *(gén)* the teaching profession, teachers; *[de lycée, collège]* the teaching staff

corps étranger *(Méd)* foreign body

le Corps européen the Eurocorps

corps expéditionnaire task force

corps franc irregular force

corps de garde *(local)* guardroom; *(= troupe)* guard ◆ **plaisanteries de ~ de garde** *(péj)* barrack-room *ou* guardroom jokes

corps gras greasy substance, glyceride *(SPÉC)*

corps jaune *(Physiol)* yellow body, corpus luteum *(SPÉC)*

corps législatif legislative body

corps de logis main building, central building

le corps médical the medical profession

corps de métier trade association, guild

corps noir *(Phys)* black body

corps politique body politic

corps préfectoral prefects

corps social *(= société, acteurs sociaux)* society

corps strié *(Anat)* striate body

corps de troupe unit (of troops)

corps vitré *(Anat)* vitreous body

corps-mort (pl **corps-morts**) /kɔʀmɔʀ/ NM *(Naut)* mooring

corpulence /kɔʀpylɑ̃s/ NF stoutness, corpulence ◆ **(être) de forte/moyenne ~** (to be) of stout/medium build

corpulent, e /kɔʀpylɑ̃, ɑ̃t/ ADJ stout, corpulent

corpus /kɔʀpys/ NM *(gén, Jur, Ling)* corpus

corpusculaire /kɔʀpyskylɛʀ/ ADJ *(Anat, Phys)* corpuscular

corpuscule /kɔʀpyskyl/ NM *(Anat, Phys)* corpuscle

correct, e /kɔʀɛkt/ ADJ 1 *(= exact) [plan, copie]* accurate; *[phrase]* correct, right; *[emploi, fonctionnement]* proper, correct ◆ **~ !** *(en réponse)* correct!, right! 2 *(= convenable) [tenue]* proper, correct 3 *(= courtois) [conduite]* correct; *[personne]* polite ◆ **ce n'est pas très ~ de sa part** that's a bit rude of him 4 *(= honnête)* correct ◆ **il est ~ en affaires** he's very correct in business matters 5 *(= acceptable) [repas, hôtel, salaire]* reasonable, decent; → **politiquement**

correctement /kɔʀɛktəmɑ̃/ ADV *[fonctionner, se nourrir, s'habiller]* properly; *[parler, écrire]* properly, correctly; *[évaluer]* accurately; *[rémunérer]* decently, reasonably well ◆ **vivre ~** to live reasonably well

correcteur, -trice /kɔʀɛktœʀ, tʀis/ ADJ *[dispositif]* corrective; → **verre** NM,F *[d'examen]* examiner, marker *(Brit)*, grader *(US)*; *(Typo)* proofreader NM 1 *(Tech = dispositif)* corrector ◆ **~ de tonalité** tone control ◆ **~ d'orthographe** *ou* **orthographique** *(Ordin)* spellchecker ◆ **~ liquide** correcting fluid 2 *(= substance)* ◆ **~ d'acidité** acidity regulator

correctif, -ive /kɔʀɛktif, iv/ ADJ *[gymnastique, substance]* corrective NM 1 *(lit, fig = médicament)* corrective *(à* to) 2 *(= mise au point)* qualifying statement ◆ **apporter un ~ à qch** *(= corriger)* to rectify *ou* correct an error in sth; *(= ajouter une précision à)* to qualify sth 3 *(Ordin)* patch

correction /kɔʀɛksjɔ̃/ NF 1 *(NonC = action) [d'erreur, abus]* correction, putting right; *[de manuscrit]* correction, emendation; *[de mauvaise habitude]* correction; *(Naut) [de compas]* correction; *[de trajectoire]* correction; *[d'examen] (gén)* correcting; *(en notant)* marking *(Brit)*, grading *(US)*; *(Ordin) [de programme]* patching; *[de mise au point]* debugging ◆ **~ d'épreuves** *(Édition)* proofreading ◆ **apporter une ~ aux propos de qn** to amend what sb has said ◆ **la ~ des copies lui a pris toute la soirée** it took him all evening to correct *ou* mark the homework ◆ **j'ai fait la ~ du devoir avec les élèves** I went through the pupils' essays with them ◆ **après ~ des variations saisonnières** after seasonal adjustments; → **maison**

2 *(= surcharge, rature)* correction ◆ **~s d'auteur** *(Typo)* author's corrections *ou* emendations

3 *(= châtiment)* (corporal) punishment, thrashing ◆ **recevoir une bonne ~** to get a good hiding *ou* thrashing

4 *(NonC = exactitude) [de plan, copie]* accuracy; *[de phrase]* correctness; *[d'emploi, fonctionnement]* propriety, correctness

5 *(= bienséance) [de tenue]* propriety, correctness; *(= honnêteté) [de conduite, personne]* correctness; *(= courtoisie)* good manners ◆ **il a fait preuve d'une parfaite ~** he behaved impeccably ◆ **je l'ai fait par ~** it was the polite thing to do, it was only good manners

correctionnel, -elle /kɔʀɛksjɔnɛl/ ADJ ◆ **peine ~le** penalty *(imposed by courts)* ◆ **tribunal (de police) ~** ≈ magistrate's court *(dealing with criminal matters)* NF **correctionnelle** ≈ magistrate's court ◆ **passer en ~le** to go before the magistrate ◆ **il a frisé la ~le*** he almost ended up in court

Corrège /kɔʀɛʒ/ N ◆ **le ~** Correggio

corrélat /kɔʀela/ NM correlate

corrélatif, -ive /kɔʀelatif, iv/ ADJ, NM correlative

corrélation /kɔʀelasjɔ̃/ NF correlation ◆ **être en ~ étroite avec** to be closely related to *ou* connected with, to be in close correlation with ◆ **mettre en ~** to correlate

corréler /kɔʀele/ ▸ conjug 6 ◂ VT to correlate

correspondance /kɔʀɛspɔ̃dɑ̃s/ NF 1 *(= conformité)* correspondence, conformity; *(Archit = symétrie)* balance ◆ **~ de goûts/d'idées entre deux personnes** conformity of two people's tastes/ideas ◆ **être en parfaite ~ d'idées avec qn** to have ideas that correspond perfectly to sb's *ou* that are perfectly in tune with sb's

2 *(Math)* relation ◆ **~ biunivoque** one-to-one mapping, bijection

3 *(= échange de lettres)* correspondence ◆ **avoir** *ou* **entretenir une longue ~ avec qn** to engage in *ou* keep up a lengthy correspondence with sb ◆ **être en ~ commerciale avec qn** to have a business correspondence with sb ◆ **nous avons été en ~** we have corresponded, we have been in correspondence ◆ **être en ~ téléphonique avec qn** to be in touch by telephone with sb ◆ **cours par ~** correspondence course ◆ **il a appris le latin par ~** he learned Latin through a *ou* by correspondence course

4 *(= ensemble de lettres)* mail, post *(surtout Brit)*, correspondence; *(Littérat) [d'auteur]* correspondence; *(Presse)* letters to the Editor ◆ **il reçoit une volumineuse ~** he receives large quantities of mail ◆ **dépouiller/lire sa ~** to go through/read one's mail *ou* one's correspondence

5 *(= transports)* connection ◆ **~ ferroviaire/ d'autobus** rail/bus connection ◆ **attendre la ~** to wait for the connection ◆ **l'autobus n'assure pas la ~ avec le train** the bus does not connect with the train ◆ **"correspondance pour Paris, voie 3"** "connecting service to Paris, platform 3"

correspondancier, -ière /kɔʀɛspɔ̃dɑ̃sje, jɛʀ/ NM,F correspondence clerk

correspondant, e /kɔʀɛspɔ̃dɑ̃, ɑ̃t/ ADJ *(gén : qui va avec, par paires)* corresponding; *(Géom) [angles]* corresponding ◆ **ci-joint un chèque ~ à la facture** enclosed a cheque in the amount of *ou* in respect of *(Brit)* the invoice

NM,F 1 (gén, Presse) correspondent; (épistolaire) penfriend; (Banque) correspondent bank ◆ ~ **de guerre/à l'étranger** war/foreign correspondent ◆ **de notre ~ permanent à Londres** from our correspondent in London ◆ **(membre) ~** [de société savante] corresponding member
2 (Téléc) **mon ~** (= appelé) the person I was calling; (= appelant) the caller ◆ **le numéro de votre ~ a changé** the number you dialled has been changed ◆ **nous recherchons votre ~** we are trying to connect you ou to put you through
3 (Scol = responsable d'un interne) guardian (for child at boarding school)

correspondre /kɔʀɛspɔ̃dʀ/ GRAMMAIRE ACTIVE 32.4 ► conjug 41 ◄ VT INDIR **correspondre à** 1 (= s'accorder avec) [+ goûts] to suit; [+ capacités] to fit; [+ description] to correspond to, to fit ◆ **sa version des faits ne correspond pas à la réalité** his version of the facts doesn't square ou tally with what happened in reality 2 (= être l'équivalent de) [+ système, institutions, élément symétrique] to correspond to ◆ **le yard correspond au mètre** the yard corresponds to the metre VI 1 (= écrire) to correspond (avec with) 2 (= communiquer) [mers] to be linked; [chambres] to communicate (avec with) 3 (Transport) **~ avec** to connect with VPR **se correspondre** [chambres] to communicate (with one another); [éléments d'une symétrie] to correspond

corrida /kɔʀida/ NF bullfight ◆ **ça va être la ~ !*** all hell will break loose !*

corridor /kɔʀidɔʀ/ NM corridor, passage ◆ **~ humanitaire** humanitarian corridor ◆ **~ ferroviaire** rail corridor ◆ **~ de fluctuation** [de monnaie] fluctuation margin

corrigé /kɔʀiʒe/ NM (Scol) [d'exercice] correct version; [de traduction] fair copy ◆ **~s** (en fin de manuel) key to exercises; (livre du professeur) answer book; [d'examens] past papers

corriger /kɔʀiʒe/ ► conjug 3 ◄ VT 1 (= repérer les erreurs de) [+ manuscrit] to correct, to emend; (Typo) [+ épreuves] to correct, to (proof)read; (Scol) [+ examen, dictée] to correct; (en notant) to mark (Brit), to grade (US)
2 (= rectifier) [+ erreur, défaut] to correct, to put right; [+ théorie] to put right; [+ abus] to remedy, to put right; [+ manières] to improve; (Naut) [+ compas] to correct, to adjust; [+ trajectoire, vue, vision] to correct ◆ **~ ses actions** to mend one's ways ◆ **j'ai corrigé mon jugement sur lui** I've changed my opinion of him ◆ **~ l'injustice du sort** (frm) to mitigate the injustice of fate, to soften the blows of unjust Fate (littér) ◆ **corrigé des variations saisonnières** seasonally adjusted; → **tir**
3 (= guérir) **~ qn de** [+ défaut] to cure ou rid sb of ◆ **tu ne le corrigeras pas à son âge** it's too late to make him change his ways now
4 (= punir) to thrash
VPR **se corriger** (= devenir raisonnable) to mend one's ways ◆ **se ~ de** [+ défaut] to cure ou rid o.s. of

corrigible /kɔʀiʒibl/ ADJ rectifiable, which can be put right

corroboration /kɔʀbɔʀasjɔ̃/ NF corroboration

corroborer /kɔʀbɔʀe/ GRAMMAIRE ACTIVE 38.1 ► conjug 1 ◄ VT to corroborate

corrodant, e /kɔʀɔdɑ̃, ɑt/ ADJ, NM corrosive

corroder /kɔʀɔde/ ► conjug 1 ◄ VT [+ métal] to corrode, to eat into; (littér) [+ sentiments] to erode VPR **se corroder** [métal] to corrode

corrompre /kɔʀɔ̃pʀ/ ► conjug 41 ◄ VT 1 (= soudoyer) [+ témoin, fonctionnaire] to bribe, to corrupt 2 (frm = pervertir) [+ mœurs, esprit, jeunesse] to corrupt; [+ langage] to debase ◆ **mots corrompus par l'usage** words corrupted ou debased by usage 3 [+ air, eau, aliments] to taint; (Méd) [+ sang] to contaminate VPR **se corrompre** [mœurs, jeunesse] to become corrupt; [goût] to become debased; [aliments] to go off (Brit), to go bad

corrompu, e /kɔʀɔ̃py/ (ptp de **corrompre**) ADJ corrupt

corrosif, -ive /kɔʀozif, iv/ ADJ [acide, substance] corrosive; [ironie, œuvre, écrivain] caustic, scathing NM corrosive

corrosion /kɔʀozjɔ̃/ NF [de métaux] corrosion; [de rochers] erosion; [de volonté, bon sens] erosion

corroyage /kɔʀwajaʒ/ NM [de cuir] currying; [de métal] welding

corroyer /kɔʀwaje/ ► conjug 8 ◄ VT [+ cuir] to curry; [+ métal] to weld; [+ bois] to trim

corroyeur /kɔʀwajœʀ/ NM currier

corrupteur, -trice /kɔʀyptœʀ, tʀis/ ADJ (littér) [spectacle, journal] corrupting NM,F (= qui soudoie) briber; (littér = qui déprave) corrupter

corruptible /kɔʀyptibl/ ADJ (littér) [personne] corruptible; † [matière] perishable

corruption /kɔʀypsjɔ̃/ NF 1 (gén) corruption; (en soudoyant) bribery, corruption ◆ **~ active** bribery ◆ **~ passive** accepting bribes ◆ **~ de fonctionnaire** bribery of a public official 2 (= dépravation) [de mœurs, esprit, jeunesse, texte] corruption; [de langage] debasement 3 (= décomposition) [d'aliments] decomposition; [de sang] contamination

corsage /kɔʀsaʒ/ NM (= chemisier) blouse; [de robe] bodice

corsaire /kɔʀsɛʀ/ NM 1 (Hist = marin, navire) privateer 2 (= pirate) pirate, corsair 3 ◆ **(pantalon) ~** breeches

corse /kɔʀs/ ADJ Corsican NM (= langue) Corsican NMF **Corse** Corsican NF **Corse** Corsica

corsé, e /kɔʀse/ (ptp de **corser**) ADJ 1 [vin] full-bodied; [café] (= parfumé) full-flavoured (Brit) ou -flavored (US); (= fort) strong; [mets, sauce] spicy 2 (= scabreux) [histoire] spicy 3 (* intensif) [addition] high, steep* (attrib); [exercice, problème] tough

corselet /kɔʀsəlɛ/ NM (= cuirasse) cors(e)let; (= vêtement) corselet

corser /kɔʀse/ ► conjug 1 ◄ VT 1 [+ repas] to make spicier, to pep up*; [+ vin] to strengthen; [+ boisson] to spike; [+ assaisonnement] to pep up* 2 [+ difficulté] to intensify, to aggravate; [+ histoire, intrigue] to liven up VPR **se corser** ◆ **l'histoire** ou **l'affaire se corse !** the plot thickens! (hum) ◆ **le premier exercice est facile mais après ça se corse** the first exercise is easy but then it gets much tougher ◆ **les choses ont commencé à se ~ quand il a voulu discuter le prix** things started to get heated when he tried to haggle ◆ **ça se corse entre lui et sa femme** things are getting really tense between him and his wife

corset /kɔʀsɛ/ NM (= sous-vêtement) corset; (= pièce de costume) bodice ◆ **~ orthopédique** ou **médical** surgical corset

corseter /kɔʀsəte/ ► conjug 5 ◄ VT (lit) to corset; (fig = enserrer) to constrain, to constrict

corsetier, -ière /kɔʀsətje, jɛʀ/ NM,F corset-maker

corso /kɔʀso/ NM ◆ **~ (fleuri)** procession of floral floats

cortège /kɔʀtɛʒ/ NM [de fête] procession; [de président] cortège, retinue ◆ **~ nuptial** bridal procession ◆ **~ funèbre** funeral procession ou cortège ◆ **~ de** [+ manifestants, grévistes] procession of; (littér) [+ malheurs, faillites] trail of; [+ visions, souvenirs] succession of ◆ **la faillite et son ~ de licenciements** bankruptcy and the accompanying lay-offs

cortex /kɔʀtɛks/ NM cortex

cortical, e (mpl **-aux**) /kɔʀtikal, o/ ADJ (Anat, Bot) cortical

corticoïde /kɔʀtikɔid/ NM corticoid

corticostéroïde /kɔʀtikosteʀɔid/ NM corticosteroid

corticosurrénale /kɔʀtikosyʀenal/ ADJ F adrenocortical NF adrenal cortex

corticothérapie /kɔʀtikoteʀapi/ NF corticosteroid ou corticoid therapy

cortisone /kɔʀtizɔn/ NF cortisone

corvéable /kɔʀveabl/ ADJ (Hist) liable to the corvée, required to do unpaid labour ◆ **ils sont ~s à merci** they can be exploited at will; → **taillable**

corvée /kɔʀve/ NF 1 (Mil) (= travail) fatigue (duty); (= soldats) fatigue party ◆ **être de ~** to be on fatigue (duty) ◆ **~ de chiottes**‡ latrine duty ◆ **~ de vaisselle** (Mil) cookhouse fatigue; (hum) dishwashing duty ◆ **~ de ravitaillement** supply duty ◆ **~ de pommes de terre** ou **de patates*** spud-bashing (arg Mil) (NonC) ◆ **être de ~ de pommes de terre** ou **de patates*** to be on spud duty* 2 (= tâche pénible) chore, drudgery (NonC) ◆ **quelle ~ !** what drudgery!, what a chore! ◆ **quelle ~ ce type !*** that guy's such a pain!* 3 (Hist) corvée (statute labour) 4 (Can) voluntary work, bee* (US, Can)

corvette /kɔʀvɛt/ NF corvette; → **capitaine**

coryphée /kɔʀife/ NM (Théât) coryphaeus

coryza /kɔʀiza/ NM (Méd) coryza (SPÉC), head cold

COS /kɔs/ NM (abrév de **coefficient d'occupation des sols**) → **coefficient**

cosaque /kɔzak/ NM cossack

cosécante /kosekɑ̃t/ NF cosecant

cosignataire /kosiɲatɛʀ/ ADJ, NMF cosignatory

cosigner /kosiɲe/ ► conjug 1 ◄ VT [+ document] [une personne] to be a joint signatory to (frm); [deux personnes] to be joint signatories to (frm), to sign jointly ◆ **un document cosigné par X et Y** a document signed jointly by X and Y

cosinus /kosinys/ NM cosine

cosmétique /kɔsmetik/ ADJ, NM cosmetic NF ◆ **la ~** the cosmetics industry

cosmétologie /kɔsmetɔlɔʒi/ NF beauty care

cosmétologue /kɔsmetɔlɔg/ NMF cosmetics expert

cosmique /kɔsmik/ ADJ cosmic; → **rayon**

cosmogonie /kɔsmɔgɔni/ NF cosmogony

cosmogonique /kɔsmɔgɔnik/ ADJ cosmogonic(al), cosmogonal

cosmographie /kɔsmɔgʀafi/ NF cosmography

cosmographique /kɔsmɔgʀafik/ ADJ cosmographic

cosmologie /kɔsmɔlɔʒi/ NF cosmology

cosmologique /kɔsmɔlɔʒik/ ADJ cosmological

cosmologiste /kɔsmɔlɔʒist/ NMF cosmologist

cosmonaute /kɔsmɔnot/ NMF cosmonaut

cosmopolite /kɔsmɔpɔlit/ ADJ cosmopolitan

cosmopolitisme /kɔsmɔpɔlitism/ NM cosmopolitanism

cosmos /kɔsmos/ NM (= univers) cosmos; (= espace) (outer) space

cossard, e* /kɔsaʀ, aʀd/ ADJ lazy NM,F lazybones

cosse /kɔs/ NF 1 [de pois, haricots] pod, hull 2 (Élec) terminal spade tag ◆ **~ de batterie** [de voiture] battery lead connection 3 (* = flemme) lazy mood ◆ **avoir la ~** to feel as lazy as anything, to be in a lazy mood

cossu, e /kɔsy/ ADJ [personne] well-off, well-to-do; [maison] rich-looking, opulent(-looking)

costal, e (mpl **-aux**) /kɔstal, o/ ADJ (Anat) costal

costar(d) * /kɔstaʀ/ NM suit; → **tailler**

Costa Rica /kɔstaʀika/ NM Costa Rica

costaricain, e /kɔstaʀikɛ̃, ɛn/, **costaricien, -ienne** /kɔstaʀisjɛ̃, jɛn/ ADJ Costarican NM,F **Costaricain(e), Costaricien(ne)** Costarican

costaud, e * /kɔsto, od/ ADJ *[personne]* strong, sturdy; *[vin, tissu]* strong ◆ **une voiture ~** *ou* **~e** a sturdy car NM 1 *(= homme)* strong *ou* sturdy *ou* strapping man 2 ◆ **c'est du ~** *[alcool, tissu]* it's strong stuff; *[maison]* it's strongly built NF **costaude** strong *ou* sturdy *ou* strapping woman

costume /kɔstym/ NM 1 *(régional, traditionnel)* costume, dress ◆ **~ national** national costume *ou* dress ◆ **en ~ d'Adam/d'Ève** *(hum)* in his/her birthday suit *(hum)* 2 *(Ciné, Théât)* costume 3 *(= complet)* suit ◆ **~ deux/trois pièces** two-/three-piece suit ◆ **en ~-cravate** in a suit and tie COMP **costume de bain** bathing suit *ou* costume *(Brit)*
costume de cérémonie ceremonial dress *(NonC)*
costume de chasse hunting gear *(NonC)*
costume civil ordinary clothes
costume marin sailor suit

⚠ Au sens de 'complet', **costume** ne se traduit pas par le mot anglais **costume**.

costumé, e /kɔstyme/ (ptp de **costumer**) ADJ *[personne] (dans un bal)* in costume, in fancy dress *(Brit)*; *(au théâtre)* in costume; → **bal**

costumer /kɔstyme/ ► conjug 1 ◄ VT ◆ **~ qn en monstre/en Zorro** to dress sb up as a monster/as Zorro VPR **se costumer** *(= porter un déguisement)* to put on a costume *ou* fancy dress *(Brit)*; *[acteur]* to get into costume ◆ **se ~ en fée** to dress up as a fairy

costumier /kɔstymje/ NM *(= fabricant, loueur)* costumier, costumer; *(Théât = employé)* wardrobe master

costumière /kɔstymjɛʀ/ NF *(Théât)* wardrobe mistress

cosy /kozi/ ADJ *[atmosphère, confort, appartement]* cosy, snug

cosy(-corner) (pl **cosys** *ou* **cosy-corners**) /kozi(kɔʀnœʀ)/ NM corner divan *(with shelves attached)*

cotangente /kɔtɑ̃ʒɑ̃t/ NF cotangent

cotation /kɔtasjɔ̃/ NF *[de valeur boursière]* listing, quotation; *[de timbre, voiture]* valuation; *[de devoir scolaire]* marking *(Brit)*, grading *(US)* ◆ **~ en Bourse/au second marché/à New York** listing *ou* quotation on the stock exchange/on the second market/in New York ◆ **~ électronique** e-listing

cote /kɔt/ NF 1 *(= fixation du prix) [de valeur boursière]* quotation; *[de timbre, voiture d'occasion]* quoted value ◆ **~ officielle** *(Bourse = liste)* official list ◆ **consulter la ~** to look at the share prices ◆ **inscrit à la ~** quoted *(Brit)* *ou* listed *(US)* on the stock exchange list
2 *(= évaluation) [de devoir scolaire]* mark *(Brit)*, grade *(US)*; *(Courses) [de cheval]* odds *(de on)*; ◆ **la ~ de Banjo est de 3 contre 1** the odds on Banjo are 3 to 1
3 *(= popularité)* rating, standing ◆ **avoir une bonne** *ou* **grosse ~** to be (very) highly thought of, to be highly rated *(auprès de* by); ◆ **avoir la ~** * to be very popular *(auprès de* with) to be very well thought of *ou* highly rated *(auprès de* by); ◆ **elle a/n'a pas la ~** * **auprès du patron** she is/isn't in the boss's good books ◆ **~ de popularité** *ou* **de confiance** popularity *ou* approval rating ◆ **la ~ du président** the president's popularity rating
4 *(sur une carte = altitude)* spot height; *(sur un croquis = dimension)* dimension ◆ **il y a une ~ qui est effacée** one of the dimensions has been rubbed out ◆ **l'ennemi a atteint la ~ 215** the enemy reached hill 215 ◆ **les explorateurs ont atteint la ~ 4.550/-190** the explorers reached the 4,550-metre mark above sea level/190-metre mark below ground
5 *(= marque de classement) (gén)* classification mark, serial number *ou* mark; *[de livre de bibliothèque]* class(ification) mark *(Brit)*, call number *(US)*
6 *(= part)* ◆ **~ mobilière/foncière** *(Fin)* property/land assessment
COMP **cote d'alerte** *[de rivière]* danger mark *ou* level, flood level ◆ **atteindre la ~ d'alerte** *[de chômage, épidémie]* to reach *ou* hit crisis point
cote d'amour ◆ **sa ~ d'amour remonte/baisse** his popularity rating is rising/falling
cote mal taillée rough-and-ready solution

coté, e /kɔte/ (ptp de **coter**) ADJ ◆ **être très ~** to be highly thought of *ou* rated ◆ **il est mal ~** he's not very highly thought of ◆ **vin (très) ~** highly-rated wine

côte /kot/ NF 1 *(Anat)* rib ◆ **~s flottantes** floating ribs ◆ **vraie/fausse ~** true/false rib ◆ **on peut lui compter les ~s, on lui voit les ~s** he's all skin and bone ◆ **avoir les ~s en long** *(fig)* to feel stiff ◆ **se tenir les ~s (de rire)** *(fig)* to split one's sides (with laughter) ◆ **~ à ~** side by side; → **caresser**
2 *(Boucherie) [de bœuf]* rib; *[de veau, agneau, mouton, porc]* chop ◆ **~ première** loin chop; → **faux²**
3 *(= nervure) [de chou, coupole]* rib; *[de tissu]* rib, wale *(US)* ◆ **veste à ~s** ribbed jacket ◆ **velours à larges ~s** wide rib *ou* wide wale *(US)* corduroy, elephant cord ◆ **faire les poignets en ~s** *(Tricot)* to do the cuffs in rib(bing)
4 *(= pente) [de colline]* slope, hillside; *[de route]* hill ◆ **il a dû s'arrêter dans la ~** he had to stop on the hill ◆ **ne pas dépasser au sommet d'une ~** do not overtake when approaching the top of a hill *ou* on the brow of a hill *(Brit)* ◆ **en ~** *[démarrer]* on a hill; → **course, démarrage**
5 *(= littoral)* coast; *(= ligne du littoral)* coastline ◆ **les ~s de France** the French coast(s) *ou* coastline ◆ **la Côte (d'Azur)** the (French) Riviera ◆ **la ~ d'Émeraude** the northern coast of Brittany ◆ **la Côte-d'Ivoire** the Ivory Coast ◆ **~ rocheuse/découpée/basse** rocky/indented/low coastline ◆ **sur la ~** *ou* **les ~s, il fait plus frais** it is cooler along *ou* on *ou* at the coast ◆ **la route qui longe la ~** the coast road ◆ **aller à la ~** *(Naut)* to run ashore

côté /kote/ GRAMMAIRE ACTIVE 32.2, 53.3, 53.5 NM 1 *(= partie du corps)* side ◆ **être blessé au ~** to be wounded in the side ◆ **l'épée au ~** with his sword by his side ◆ **être couché sur le ~** to be lying on one's side ◆ **à son ~** at his side, beside him ◆ **aux ~s de** by the side of; → **point¹**
2 *(= face, partie latérale) [d'objet, route, feuille]* side ◆ **le ~ fermé, le petit ~** *(Sport)* the inside ◆ **le ~ ouvert, le grand ~** *(Sport)* the outside ◆ **changer de ~** *(Tennis)* to change ends ◆ **un navire sur le ~** *(Naut)* a ship on her beam-ends
3 *(= aspect)* side, point ◆ **le ~ pratique/théorique** the practical/theoretical side ◆ **les bons et les mauvais ~s** *(de qn)* the good and bad sides *ou* points; *(de qch)* the pros and cons ◆ **il a un ~ sympathique** there's a likeable side to him ◆ **son attitude/ce film a un ~ pervers** there's something perverse about his attitude/this film ◆ **prendre qch du bon/mauvais ~** to take sth well/badly ◆ **par certains ~s** in some respects *ou* ways ◆ **d'un ~ ... d'un autre ~ ...** *(alternative)* on (the) one hand ... on the other hand ...; *(hésitation)* in one respect *ou* way ... in another respect *ou* way ... ◆ **d'un ~ comme de l'autre** on both sides ◆ **(du) ~ santé tout va bien** * healthwise * *ou* as far as health is concerned everything is fine ◆ **~ argent, tout va bien** * all's well on the money side, moneywise * everything is fine
4 *(= parti, branche familiale)* side ◆ **de mon ~** on my side (of the family) ◆ **du ~ paternel** on his father's side
5 ◆ **~ du vent** windward side ◆ **~ sous le vent** leeward side ◆ **ils ne sont pas partis du bon ~** they didn't go the right way *ou* in the right direction
6 *(Théât)* ◆ **~ cour** stage left, prompt side *(Brit)* ◆ **~ jardin** stage right, opposite prompt side *(Brit)* ◆ **une chambre ~ rue** a bedroom overlooking the street
7 *(locutions)*
♦ **à côté** *(proximité)* near; *(= pièce ou maison adjacente)* next door; *(= en comparaison)* in comparison ◆ **la maison/les gens (d')à ~** the house/the people next door ◆ **nos voisins d'à ~** our next-door neighbours ◆ **l'hôtel est (tout) à ~** the hotel is near *ou* close by ◆ **elle a été très malade, ton rhume n'est rien à ~** she's been very ill, your cold is nothing in comparison ◆ **ils ont mal visé, les bombes sont tombées à ~** their aim was bad and the bombs went astray *ou* fell wide ◆ **je suis tombé à ~** *(= me suis trompé)* I got it all wrong
♦ **à côté de** *(= à proximité de)* next to, beside; *(= en comparaison de)* compared to, by comparison with, beside ◆ **on passe à ~ de beaucoup de choses en ne voyageant pas** you miss a lot by not travelling ◆ **il est à ~ de la plaque** * he hasn't got a clue * ◆ **à ~ de la cible** off target, wide of the target ◆ **il a répondu à ~ de la question** *(sans le faire exprès)* his answer was off the point; *(intentionnellement)* he avoided the question ◆ **leur maison est grande à ~ de la nôtre** their house is big compared to ours ◆ **il est paresseux, à ~ de ça il aime son travail** * he's lazy, but on the other hand he does like his work
♦ **de côté** *(= de biais) [marcher, regarder, se tourner]* sideways; *(= en réserve) [mettre, garder]* aside ◆ **regard de ~** sidelong look ◆ **porter son chapeau de ~** to wear one's hat (tilted) to *ou* on one side ◆ **mettre de l'argent de ~** to put money by *ou* aside ◆ **se jeter de ~** to leap aside *ou* to the *ou* to one side ◆ **laisser qn/qch de ~** to leave sb/sth to one side *ou* out ◆ **de ~ et d'autre** here and there
♦ **de + côté** ◆ **de ce ~-ci/-là** this/that way ◆ **de ce ~(-là)** *(fig)* in that respect ◆ **de l'autre ~** the other way, in the other direction ◆ **voir de quel ~ vient le vent** *(fig)* to see which way the wind is blowing ◆ **je l'ai entendu dire de divers ~s** I've heard it from several quarters *ou* sources ◆ **de chaque ~** *ou* **des deux ~s de la cheminée** on each side *ou* on both sides of the fireplace ◆ **il a sauté de l'autre ~ du mur/du ruisseau** he jumped over the wall/across the stream ◆ **le bruit vient de l'autre ~ de la rivière/de la pièce** the sound is coming from across *ou* from over the river *ou* from the other side of the river/from the other side of the room ◆ **de l'autre ~ de la forêt il y a des prés** on the other side of the forest *ou* beyond the forest there are meadows ◆ **de l'autre ~ de la barricade** *ou* **de la barrière** on the other side of the fence
♦ **de mon/ton/son** *etc* **côté** ◆ **de mon ~, je ferai tout pour l'aider** for my part, I'll do everything I can to help him ◆ **renseigne-toi de ton ~, je me renseignerai du mien** you find out what you can and I'll do the same
♦ **de tous côtés** ◆ **venir de tous ~s** to come from all directions ◆ **assiégé de tous ~s** besieged on *ou* from all sides ◆ **chercher qn de tous ~s** to look for sb everywhere *ou* all over the place, to search high and low for sb
♦ **du côté de** ◆ **nous habitons du ~ de la poste** we live over by the post office ◆ **le vent vient du ~ de la mer/du ~ opposé** the wind is blowing from the sea/from the opposite direction ◆ **ils se dirigeaient du ~ des prés/du ~ opposé** they were heading towards the meadows/in the opposite direction ◆ **se ranger** *ou*

se mettre du ~ du plus fort to side with the strongest ◆ **nous pourrions regarder du ~ de la littérature médiévale** we could take a look at medieval literature

coteau (pl **coteaux**) /kɔto/ NM (= *colline*) hill; (= *versant*) slope, hillside; → **flanc**

côtelé, e /kot(ə)le/ ADJ ribbed; → **velours**

côtelette /kotlɛt/ NF (*Culin*) cutlet ◆ **~s découvertes** middle neck chops ◆ **~s*** (= *côtes, flanc*) ribs, side

coter /kɔte/ ▸ conjug 1 ◂ VT 1 [+ *valeur boursière*] to quote, to list; [+ *timbre-poste, voiture d'occasion*] to quote the market price of; [+ *cheval*] to put odds on; (*Scol*) [+ *devoir*] to mark (*Brit*), to grade (*US*); [+ *film, roman*] to rate ◆ **coté en Bourse/au comptant** quoted *ou* listed on the stock exchange/on the spot market ◆ **être coté à l'Argus** to be listed (*in the secondhand car book*) 2 [+ *carte*] to put spot heights on; [+ *croquis*] to mark in the dimensions on 3 [+ *pièce de dossier*] to put a classification mark *ou* serial number *ou* serial mark on; [+ *livre de bibliothèque*] to put a class(ification) mark (*Brit*) *ou* call number (*US*) *ou* shelf-mark *ou* pressmark (*Brit*) on VI (*Bourse*) ◆ **valeur qui cote 50 €** share quoted *ou* listed at €50

coterie /kɔtʀi/ NF (*gén péj*) set ◆ **~ littéraire** literary coterie *ou* clique *ou* set

cothurne /kɔtyʀn/ NM buskin

côtier, -ière /kotje, jɛʀ/ ADJ [*pêche*] inshore; [*navigation, région, fleuve, ville*] coastal (*épith*) ◆ **(bateau) ~** coaster

cotillon /kɔtijɔ̃/ NM 1 (*serpentins etc*) **~s** party novelties (*confetti, streamers, paper hats etc*) 2 (†† = *jupon*) petticoat; → **courir** 3 (= *danse*) cotillion, cotillon

cotisant, e /kɔtizɑ̃, ɑ̃t/ NM,F [*de club, syndicat*] subscriber, contributor (*à* to); [*de Sécurité sociale, pension*] contributor (*à* to); ◆ **seuls les ~s y ont droit** only those who pay their subscriptions (*ou* dues *ou* contributions) qualify

cotisation /kɔtizasjɔ̃/ NF (= *quote-part*) [*de club*] subscription; [*de syndicat*] subscription, dues; [*de Sécurité sociale, pension, mutuelle*] contributions ◆ **la ~ est obligatoire** there is a mandatory subscription charge

cotiser /kɔtize/ ▸ conjug 1 ◂ VI (*dans un club*) to subscribe, to pay one's subscription; (*à la Sécurité sociale*) to pay one's contributions (*à* to); ◆ **tu as cotisé pour le cadeau ?** did you chip in* for the present? VPR **se cotiser** to club together ◆ **ils se sont cotisés pour lui faire un cadeau** they clubbed together to get him a present

côtoiement /kotwamɑ̃/ NM (= *contact*) [*de danger, artistes*] contact (*de* with)

coton /kɔtɔ̃/ NM 1 (= *plante, fil*) cotton ◆ **~ à broder** embroidery thread ◆ **~ à repriser** darning thread *ou* cotton ◆ **~ hydrophile** cotton wool (*Brit*), absorbent cotton (*US*) ◆ **robe de *ou* en ~** cotton dress 2 (= *tampon*) (cotton-wool (*Brit*) *ou* cotton (*US*)) swab ◆ **mets un ~ dans ton nez** put some *ou* a bit of cotton wool (*Brit*) *ou* cotton (*US*) in your nose 3 (*locutions*) **avoir du ~ dans les oreilles*** to be deaf, to have cloth ears* (*Brit*) ◆ **j'ai les bras/jambes en ~** my arms/legs feel like jelly *ou* cotton wool (*Brit*) ◆ **c'est ~*** it's tricky*; → **élever, filer**

cotonnade /kɔtɔnad/ NF cotton (fabric)

cotonneux, -euse /kɔtɔnø, øz/ ADJ 1 [*fruit, feuille*] downy 2 [*brouillard*] wispy; [*nuage*] fluffy, fleecy, cotton-wool (*Brit*) (*épith*); [*bruit*] muffled

cotonnier, -ière /kɔtɔnje, jɛʀ/ ADJ cotton (*épith*) NM (= *plante*) cotton plant

Coton-tige ® (pl **Cotons-tiges**) /kɔtɔ̃tiʒ/ NM cotton bud (*Brit*), Q-tip ®

côtoyer /kotwaje/ ▸ conjug 8 ◂ VT 1 (= *être à côté de*) to be next to; (= *fréquenter*) to mix with, to rub shoulders with ◆ **~ le danger** to flirt with danger 2 (= *longer*) (*en voiture, à pied etc*) to drive (*ou* walk *etc*) along *ou* alongside; [*rivière*] to run *ou* flow alongside; [*route*] to skirt, to run along *ou* alongside 3 (= *frôler*) [*procédé, situation*] to be bordering *ou* verging on ◆ **cela côtoie la malhonnêteté** that is bordering *ou* verging on dishonesty ◆ **il aime à ~ l'illégalité** he likes to do things that verge on illegality *ou* that come close to being illegal VPR **se côtoyer** [*individus*] to mix, to rub shoulders; [*genres, extrêmes*] to meet, to come close

cotre /kɔtʀ/ NM (*Naut*) cutter

cottage /kɔtedʒ/ NM cottage

cotte /kɔt/ NF 1 (*Hist*) **~ de mailles** coat of mail ◆ **~ d'armes** (= *tunique*) coat of arms (*surcoat*) 2 (= *salopette*) overalls, (pair of) dungarees (*Brit*); (†† = *jupe*) petticoat

cotutelle /kotytɛl/ NF joint guardianship

cotuteur, -trice /kotytœʀ, tʀis/ NM,F joint guardian

cotylédon /kɔtiledɔ̃/ NM (*Anat, Bot*) cotyledon

cou /ku/ NM (*Anat, Couture*) [*de bouteille*] neck ◆ **porter qch au ~ *ou* autour du ~** to wear sth round one's neck ◆ **elle a un vrai ~ de girafe** she's got a neck like a giraffe ◆ **avoir mal au ~** (*Helv : à la gorge*) to have a sore throat ◆ **jusqu'au ~** (*lit*) up to one's neck ◆ **endetté jusqu'au ~** up to one's eyes in debt ◆ **être impliqué jusqu'au ~ dans un scandale** to be heavily implicated in a scandal ◆ **il est impliqué jusqu'au ~** he's in it up to his neck* ◆ **sauter *ou* se jeter au ~ de qn** to throw one's arms around sb's neck, to fall on sb's neck; → **bride, casser, taureau** *etc*

couac /kwak/ NM (*Mus*) [*d'instrument*] false note, goose note (*Brit*); [*de voix*] false note ◆ **il y a eu des ~s pendant les discussions avec les syndicats** (*fig*) there were moments of friction during the talks with the unions

couard, couarde /kwaʀ, kwaʀd/ (*frm*) ADJ cowardly ◆ **il est trop ~ pour cela** he's too cowardly *ou* too much of a coward for that NM,F coward

couardise /kwaʀdiz/ NF (*frm*) cowardice

couchage /kuʃaʒ/ NM (= *matelas, draps*) bedding (*NonC*) ◆ **il faudra organiser le ~ en route** (= *installation*) we'll have to organize our sleeping arrangements on the way ◆ **matériel de ~** sleeping equipment, bedding ◆ **pour ~ 90/135** (= *matelas*) for mattress size 90/135 cm; → **sac¹**

couchant /kuʃɑ̃/ ADJ ◆ **soleil ~** setting sun ◆ **au soleil ~** at sunset *ou* sundown (*US*); → **chien** NM (= *ouest*) west; (= *aspect du ciel, à l'ouest*) sunset, sundown (*US*)

couche /kuʃ/ NF 1 (*gén*) layer; [*de peinture*] coat ◆ **ils avaient une ~ épaisse de crasse** they were covered in *ou* coated with dirt, they were covered in a thick layer of dirt ◆ **en tenir *ou* avoir une ~*** to be really thick* *ou* dumb* ◆ **la ~ d'ozone** the ozone layer ◆ **~s de l'atmosphère** layers *ou* strata of the atmosphere ◆ **~s ligneuses** (*Bot*) woody *ou* ligneous layers

2 (= *catégorie sociale*) level ◆ **dans toutes les ~s de la société** at all levels of society

3 (*pour cultures*) hotbed; → **champignon**

4 [*de bébé*] nappy (*Brit*), diaper (*US*) ◆ **~-culotte** disposable nappy (*Brit*) *ou* diaper (*US*)

5 (*littér* = *lit*) bed ◆ **une ~ de feuillage** a bed of leaves

NFPL **couches** (*Méd* = *accouchement*) confinement † ◆ **mourir en ~s** to die in childbirth ◆ **femme en ~s** woman in labour ◆ **elle a eu des ~s pénibles** she had a difficult confinement † *ou* labour; → **faux², relever, retour**

couché, e /kuʃe/ (ptp de **coucher**) ADJ 1 (= *étendu*) lying (down); (*au lit*) in bed ◆ **Rex, ~ !** lie down, Rex! ◆ **~ sur son guidon** bent over his handlebars 2 (= *penché*) [*écriture*] sloping, slanting 3 → **papier**

couche-dehors* /kuʃdəɔʀ/ NM INV down-and-out, homeless person

coucher /kuʃe/ ▸ conjug 1 ◂ VT 1 (= *mettre au lit*) to put to bed; (= *donner un lit à*) to put up ◆ **on peut vous ~** we can put you up, we can offer you a bed ◆ **nous pouvons ~ 4 personnes** we can put up *ou* sleep 4 people; → **nom**

2 (= *étendre*) [+ *blessé*] to lay out; [+ *échelle*] to lay down; [+ *bouteille*] to lay on its side ◆ **il y a un arbre couché en travers de la route** there's a tree lying across the road ◆ **la rafale a couché le bateau** the gust of wind made the boat keel over *ou* keeled the boat over ◆ **le vent a couché les blés** the wind has flattened the corn; → **joue**

3 (*frm* = *inscrire*) to inscribe ◆ **~ qn dans un testament** to name sb in a will ◆ **~ qn sur une liste** to inscribe *ou* include sb's name on a list ◆ **~ un article dans un contrat** to insert a clause into a contract

4 [+ *branches pour clôtures*] to layer

VI 1 (= *passer la nuit, séjourner*) to sleep ◆ **nous avons couché à l'hôtel/chez des amis** we spent the night at a hotel/with friends ◆ **nous couchions à l'hôtel/chez des amis** we were staying in a hotel/with friends ◆ **~ sous la tente** to sleep under canvas ◆ **il faudra qu'il couche par terre** he'll have to sleep on the floor ◆ **on peut ~ à 5 dans le bateau** the boat sleeps 5 ◆ **ma voiture couche dehors*** my car stays outside at night; → **étoile**

2 (* = *se coucher*) to go to bed ◆ **cela nous a fait ~ très tard** that kept us up very late

3 (* = *avoir des rapports sexuels*) **~ avec qn** to sleep *ou* go to bed with sb ◆ **ils couchent ensemble** they're sleeping together ◆ **avant le mariage, je ne couche pas** I don't believe in (having) sex before marriage

VPR **se coucher** 1 (= *aller au lit*) to go to bed ◆ **se ~ comme les poules** to go to bed early *ou* when the sun goes down ◆ **va te ~ !*** (*fig*) clear off!*; → **comme**

2 (= *s'étendre*) to lie down ◆ **il s'est couché sur l'enfant pour le protéger** he lay on top of the child to protect him ◆ **le gardien s'est couché sur le ballon** the goalkeeper smothered the ball ◆ **se ~ sur les avirons/le guidon** (*Sport*) to bend over the oars/the handlebars ◆ **un poteau s'est couché au travers de la route** there's a telegraph pole lying across the road ◆ **se ~ devant qn*** (*péj*) to crawl to sb, to grovel before sb

3 [*soleil, lune*] to set, to go down

4 (*Naut*) [*bateau*] to keel over

5 (*Cartes* = *s'incliner*) (*gén*) to throw in one's hand; (*Poker*) to fold

NM 1 (= *moment*) **surveiller le ~ des enfants** to see the children into bed ◆ **le ~ était toujours à 9 heures** bedtime was always at 9 o'clock ◆ **le ~ du roi** (*Hist*) the king's going-to-bed ceremony

2 († = *logement*) accommodation ◆ **le ~ et la nourriture** board and lodging

3 (= *tombée de la nuit*) **(au) ~ du soleil** (at) sunset *ou* sundown (*US*) ◆ **le soleil à son ~** the setting sun

coucherie /kuʃʀi/ NF (*gén pl : péj*) sleeping around (*NonC*)

couche-tard* /kuʃtaʀ/ NMF INV night owl*

couche-tôt* /kuʃto/ NMF INV ◆ **c'est un ~** he always goes to bed early

couchette /kuʃɛt/ NF (*Rail*) couchette, berth; (*Naut*) [*de voyageur*] couchette, berth; [*de marin*] bunk

coucheur /kuʃœʀ/ NM → **mauvais**

couci-couça* /kusikusa/ ADV so-so*

coucou /kuku/ NM ① (= oiseau) cuckoo; (= pendule) cuckoo clock ◆ **maigre comme un ~*** as thin as a rake ② (péj = avion) (old) crate* ③ (= fleur) cowslip ④ (* = bonjour) **faire un petit ~** to say hello (à to); ◆ **elle a fait un ~ à la caméra** she waved to the camera EXCL (à cache-cache) peek-a-boo!; (= bonjour) cooey!, hello! ◆ **~, c'est moi !** hi! ou hello!, it's me!

coude /kud/ NM ① (Anat = partie de la manche) elbow ◆ **~s au corps** (lit) (with one's) elbows in; [courir] at the double ◆ **se tenir** ou **serrer les ~s** to stick together ◆ **coup de ~** nudge ◆ **prendre un coup de ~ dans la figure** to get an elbow in the face ◆ **écarter qn d'un coup de ~** to elbow sb out of the way ◆ **d'un coup de ~ il attira son attention** he nudged him to attract his attention ◆ **donner un coup de ~ à qn** (légèrement) to give sb a nudge, to nudge sb; (plus brutalement) to elbow sb ◆ **~ à ~** [travailler] shoulder to shoulder, side by side ◆ **être au ~ à ~** [coureurs, candidats] to be neck and neck (avec with); ◆ **j'ai** ou **je garde votre dossier sous le ~** I am holding on to your file ◆ **j'ai toujours ce dictionnaire sous le ~** I always keep this dictionary handy; → **doigt, huile** etc
② [de rivière] bend, elbow; [de route, tuyau, barre] bend

coudé, e /kude/ (ptp de **couder**) ADJ [tuyau, barre] angled, bent at an angle, with a bend in it

coudée /kude/ NF († † = mesure) cubit † ◆ **avoir ses** ou **les ~s franches** (lit) to have elbow room; (fig) to have complete freedom of action ◆ **laisser les ~s franches à qn** to give sb complete freedom of action

cou-de-pied (pl **cous-de-pied**) /kud(ə)pje/ NM instep

couder /kude/ ▸ conjug 1 ◂ VT [+ tuyau, barre de fer] to put a bend in, to bend (at an angle)

coudoyer /kudwaje/ ▸ conjug 8 ◂ VT [+ gens] to rub shoulders with, to mix with, to come into contact with ◆ **dans cet article, la stupidité coudoie la mesquinerie** in this article, stupidity stands side by side with pettiness

coudre /kudʀ/ ▸ conjug 48 ◂ VT [+ pièces de tissu] to sew (together); [+ pièce, bouton] to sew on; [+ vêtement] to sew up, to stitch up; (Reliure) [+ cahiers] to stitch; (Méd) [+ plaie] to sew up, to stitch (up) ◆ **~ un bouton/une pièce à une veste** to sew a button/patch on a jacket ◆ **~ une semelle (à l'empeigne)** to stitch a sole (to the upper) ◆ **~ à la main/à la machine** to sew by hand/by machine; → **dé, machine**

coudrier /kudʀije/ NM hazel tree

Coué /kwe/ N ◆ **méthode ~** autosuggestion, Couéism (SPÉC) ◆ **il faut pratiquer** ou **utiliser la méthode ~** you need to try self-persuasion

couenne /kwan/ NF ① [de lard] rind; (Helv) [de fromage] rind ② (‡ = peau) hide* ③ (Méd) [de peau] membrane

couenneux, -euse /kwanø, øz/ ADJ → **angine**

couette /kwɛt/ NF ① (= couverture) continental quilt, duvet, comforter (US) ◆ **se mettre sous la ~** to go to bed, to turn in* ② [de cheveux] **~s** bunches

couffin /kufɛ̃/ NM [de bébé] Moses basket; († = cabas) (straw) basket

coug(o)uar /kugwaʀ/ NM cougar

couic /kwik/ EXCL erk!, squeak! ◆ **je n'y comprends que ~*** † * I don't understand a blooming* (Brit) ou darn* (US) thing ◆ **faire ~*** (= mourir) to croak‡, to snuff it*

couille‡‡ /kuj/ NF ① (= testicule) ball‡‡ ◆ **~s** balls‡‡, bollocks‡‡ (Brit) ◆ **avoir des ~s** (courage) to have balls‡‡ ◆ **c'est une ~ molle** he has no balls‡‡ ◆ **se faire des ~s en or** to get filthy rich‡ ◆ **tenir qn par les ~s** to have sb by the balls‡‡ ② (= erreur, problème) balls-up‡‡ (Brit), cock-up‡ (Brit), ball-up‡‡ (US) ◆ **faire une ~** to screw up‡, to fuck up‡‡ ◆ **je n'ai eu que des ~s cette semaine** it's been one cock-up‡‡ (Brit) ou balls-up‡‡ (Brit) ou ball-up‡‡ (US) after another this week ◆ **partir en ~** to go down the drain*

couillon‡ /kujɔ̃/ ADJ M damn‡ ou bloody (Brit)‡ stupid NM damn‡ ou bloody‡ (Brit) idiot ou cretin‡

couillonnade‡ /kujɔnad/ NF bullshit‡‡ (NonC) ◆ **c'est de la ~** it's a load of bullshit‡‡

couillonner‡ /kujɔne/ ▸ conjug 1 ◂ VT to con* ◆ **on t'a couillonné, tu t'es fait ~** you've been had* ou conned*

couinement /kwinmɑ̃/ NM [de porc, freins] squealing (NonC), squeal; [de souris etc] squeaking (NonC), squeak; [de porte, ressort] creaking (NonC); (péj) [de personne] whining (NonC), whine ◆ **pousser un ~** [porc] to squeal; [souris etc] to squeak

couiner* /kwine/ ▸ conjug 1 ◂ VI [porc, freins] to squeal; [souris etc] to squeak; [porte, ressort] to creak; (péj) [personne] to whine

coulage /kulaʒ/ NM ① [de cire, ciment] pouring; [de statue, cloche] casting ② (Écon) (= gaspillage) waste; (= vol) pilferage

coulant, e /kulɑ̃, ɑt/ ADJ ① [pâte] runny; [vin] smooth; [style] (free-)flowing, smooth; → **nœud** ② (* = indulgent) [personne] easy-going NM ① [de ceinture] sliding loop ② (Bot) runner

coule /kul/ NF (= capuchon) cowl ◆ **être à la ~** †* to know the ropes, to know the tricks of the trade

coulé, e /kule/ (ptp de **couler**) ADJ (jeu de bataille navale) ◆ **(touché) ~ !** she's gone under!; → **brasse** NM (Mus) slur; (Danse) glide; (Billard) follow NF **coulée** [de métal] casting ◆ **~e de lave** lava flow ◆ **~e de boue** mudslide ◆ **~e de neige** snowslide ◆ **il y a une ~e** [de peinture] the paint has run ◆ **il y a des/trois ~es** the paint has run (in several places)/in three places ◆ **~e verte** pedestrian zone (bordered with trees and grass)

coulemelle /kulmɛl/ NF parasol mushroom

couler /kule/ ▸ conjug 1 ◂ VI ① [liquide] to run, to flow; [sang, larmes] to flow; [fromage, bougie] to run; [rivière] to flow ◆ **la sueur coulait sur son visage** he had sweat running down his face; (plus fort) he had sweat pouring down his face ◆ **ton rimmel a coulé** your mascara has run ◆ **~ à flots** [vin, champagne] to be flowing freely ◆ **le sang a coulé** (fig) blood has been shed
② ◆ **faire ~** [+ eau] to run ◆ **faire ~ un bain** to run a bath, to run water for a bath ◆ **faire ~ le sang** (fig) to cause bloodshed ◆ **ça a fait ~ beaucoup d'encre** (fig) it has caused a lot of ink to flow ◆ **ça fera ~ de la salive** that'll set (the) tongues wagging
③ [robinet] to run; (= fuir) to leak; [récipient, stylo] to leak ◆ **ne laissez pas ~ les robinets** don't leave the taps (Brit) ou faucets (US) running ou on ◆ **il a le nez qui coule** his nose is running, he has a runny nose
④ [paroles] to flow; [roman, style] to flow (along) ◆ **~ de source** (= être clair) to be obvious; (= s'enchaîner) to follow naturally
⑤ [vie, temps] to slip by, to slip past
⑥ [bateau, personne] to sink; [entreprise] to go under, to fold ◆ **~ à pic** to sink straight to the bottom
VT ① [+ cire, ciment] to pour; [+ métal, statue, cloche] to cast ◆ **~ une bielle** (en voiture) to run a big end
② (= passer) **~ une existence paisible/des jours heureux** to enjoy a peaceful existence/happy days
③ [+ bateau] to sink, to send to the bottom; (= discréditer) [+ personne] to discredit; (* = faire échouer) [+ candidat] to bring down; [+ entreprise, firme] to wreck, to ruin ◆ **c'est son accent/l'épreuve de latin qui l'a coulé*** it was his accent/the Latin test that brought him down
④ (= glisser) [+ regard, sourire] to steal; [+ pièce de monnaie] to slip
⑤ (= filtrer) [+ liquide] to pour
VPR **se couler** ① (= se glisser) **se ~ dans/à travers** to slip into/through ◆ **se ~ dans un moule** [personne] to conform to a norm
② ◆ **se la ~ douce*** (= avoir la belle vie) to have it easy*, to have an easy time (of it)*; (= paresser) to take it easy

couleur /kulœʀ/ NF ① (= coloris) colour (Brit), color (US); (= nuance) shade, tint, hue (littér) ◆ **~s fondamentales/complémentaires** primary/complementary colours ◆ **une robe de ~ bleue** a blue dress ◆ **de ~ claire/sombre** light-/dark-coloured ◆ **une belle ~ rouge** a beautiful shade of red, a beautiful red colour ◆ **aux ~s délicates** delicately coloured, with delicate colours ◆ **film/cartes en ~s** colour film/postcards ◆ **vêtements noirs ou de ~** dark or colourful clothes ◆ **la ~, les ~s** (= linge de couleur) coloureds ◆ **je n'aime pas les ~s de la chambre** I don't like the colour scheme ou the colours in the bedroom ◆ **les feuilles prenaient une ~ dorée** the leaves were turning golden-brown ou taking on a golden-brown colour ◆ **se faire faire sa** ou **une ~** to have one's hair coloured; → **goût**
② (= peinture) paint ◆ **~s à l'eau** watercolours ◆ **~s à l'huile** oil colours, oil paint ◆ **boîte de ~s** paintbox, box of paints; → **crayon, marchand**
③ (= carnation) **~s** colour (Brit), color (US) ◆ **avoir des ~s** to have a good colour ◆ **perdre ses/(re)prendre des ~s** to lose/get back one's colour ◆ **tu as pris des ~s** (bronzage) you've caught the sun; → **changer, haut**
④ (= vigueur) colour (Brit), color (US) ◆ **ce récit a de la ~** this tale is very vivid ou colourful ◆ **sans ~** colourless
⑤ (= caractère) colour (Brit), color (US), flavour (Brit), flavor (US) ◆ **le poème prend soudain une ~ tragique** the poem suddenly takes on a tragic colour ou note
⑥ (Pol = étiquette) colour (Brit), color (US) ◆ **~ politique** political persuasion
⑦ (Cartes) suit; → **annoncer**
⑧ (Sport) **~s** [de club, écurie] colours (Brit), colors (US) ◆ **les ~s** (drapeau) the colours (Brit) ou colors (US)
⑨ ◆ **~ locale** local colour ◆ **ces costumes font très ~ locale** these costumes give plenty of local colour
⑩ (locutions) **homme/femme de ~** coloured man/woman ◆ **sous ~ de qch** under the guise of sth ◆ **sous ~ de faire** while pretending to do ◆ **montrer/présenter qch sous de fausses ~s** to show/present sth in a false light ◆ **décrire** ou **peindre qch sous les plus sombres/vives ~s** to paint the darkest/rosiest picture of sth, to paint sth in the darkest/rosiest colours ◆ **l'avenir se présente sous les plus sombres ~s** the future looks very dark ou looks very gloomy ◆ **elle n'a jamais vu la ~ de son argent*** she's never seen the colour of his money* ◆ **il m'a promis un cadeau mais je n'en ai jamais vu la ~*** he promised me a present but I've yet to see it; → **voir**
ADJ INV ◆ **yeux ~ d'azur** sky-blue eyes ◆ **tissu ~ cyclamen/mousse** cyclamen-coloured/moss-green material ◆ **~ chair** flesh-coloured, flesh (épith) ◆ **~ paille** straw-coloured

couleuvre /kulœvʀ/ NF ◆ **~ (à collier)** grass snake ◆ **~ lisse** smooth snake ◆ **~ vipérine** viperine snake; → **avaler**

couleuvrine /kulœvʀin/ NF (Hist) culverin

coulis /kuli/ ADJ M → **vent** NM ① (Culin) coulis ◆ **~ de framboise/de cassis/de tomates** raspberry/blackcurrant/tomato coulis ◆ **~ d'écre-**

visses crayfish bisque 2 *(Tech) (= mortier)* grout; *(= métal)* molten metal *(filler)*

coulissant, e /kulisɑ̃, ɑ̃t/ ADJ *[porte, panneau]* sliding *(épith)* ◆ **ceinture ~e** drawstring belt

coulisse /kulis/ NF 1 *(Théât : gén pl)* wings ◆ **en ~, dans les ~s** *(Théât)* in the wings; *(fig)* behind the scenes ◆ **les ~s de la politique** what goes on behind the political scenes ◆ **rester dans la ~** to work behind the scenes 2 *[de porte, tiroir]* runner; *[de rideau]* top hem; *[de robe]* casing; *(= panneau mobile)* sliding door; *(Tech = glissière)* slide ◆ **porte à ~** sliding door ◆ **regard en ~** sidelong glance *ou* look; → **pied, trombone** 3 († : *Bourse)* unofficial Stock Market

coulisseau (pl **coulisseaux**) /kuliso/ NM *[de tiroir]* runner; *(Tech)* slide

coulisser /kulise/ ▸ conjug 1 ◂ VT *[+ tiroir, porte]* to provide with runners; *[+ rideau]* to hem (the top of) ◆ **jupe coulissée** skirt with a drawstring waist VI *[porte, rideau, tiroir]* to slide, to run

coulissier † /kulisje/ NM unofficial broker

couloir /kulwaʀ/ NM *[de bâtiment]* corridor, passage; *[de wagon]* corridor; *[d'avion, train]* aisle; *[d'appareil de projection]* channel, track; *(Athlétisme, Natation)* lane; *(Tennis)* tramlines *(Brit)*, alley *(surtout US)*; *(Géog)* gully, couloir *(SPÉC)*; *(Ski)* corridor; *(pour bus, taxi)* lane ◆ **~ aérien** air (traffic) lane ◆ **~ humanitaire** safe *ou* humanitarian corridor ◆ **~ de navigation** shipping lane ◆ **~ d'avalanches** *(Géog)* avalanche corridor ◆ **le ~ rhodanien** *(Géog)* the Rhône corridor ◆ **bruits de ~(s)** *(Pol etc)* rumours ◆ **intrigues de ~(s)** *(Pol etc)* backstage manoeuvring

coulommiers /kulɔmje/ NM Coulommiers cheese *(soft cheese)*

coulpe /kulp/ NF *(littér ou hum)* ◆ **battre sa ~** to beat one's breast

coulure /kulyʀ/ NF 1 *[de vigne]* failure to set fruit 2 *(= trace) [de métal]* runoff ◆ **il y a des ~s** *[de peinture]* the paint has run (in several places)

coup /ku/

Lorsque **coup** est suivi d'un complément de nom désignant une partie du corps ou un instrument (**coup de main/pied/balai/marteau/téléphone, coup d'œil** etc), cherchez à ce nom.

NOM MASCULIN

1 [= heurt, choc] knock, blow; *(affectif)* blow, shock; *(marquant l'agression)* blow ◆ **il a pris un ~ sur la tête** *(= il s'est cogné)* he knocked *ou* hit *ou* banged his head, he was hit on the head; *(= on l'a frappé)* he was hit on the head, he got a blow on the head ◆ **la voiture a reçu un ~** the car has had a knock *(Brit)* *ou* bump ◆ **donner des ~s dans la porte** to bang *ou* hammer at the door ◆ **donner un ~ sec pour dégager qch** to give sth a sharp knock to release it ◆ **ça a porté un ~ sévère à leur moral** it dealt a severe blow to their morale ◆ **en prendre un (bon *ou* sacré *ou* sérieux) ~*** *[carrosserie]* to have a (nasty) bash* *(Brit)* *ou* bang; *[personne, confiance, moral]* to take a (nasty) blow *ou* a (real) knock ◆ **ça lui a fait *ou* fichu un ~*** it's given him a (bit of a) shock, it was a bit of a blow (for him) ◆ **~ dur** hard blow ◆ **il m'a donné un ~** he hit me ◆ **en venir aux ~s** to come to blows ◆ **les ~s tombaient dru *ou* pleuvaient** the blows rained down ◆ **~s et blessures** *(Jur)* assault and battery, aggravated assault; → **accuser, marquer**

2 [Sport = geste] *(Cricket, Golf, Tennis)* stroke; *(Boxe)* blow, punch; *(Tir)* shot; *(Échecs)* move; *(aux dés)* throw ◆ **il a fait 421 en deux ~s** he got 421 in two throws ◆ **~ droit** *(Tennis)* drive ◆ **~ droit croisé** *(Tennis)* cross-court drive ◆ **renvoyer la balle en ~ droit** to do a forehand drive ◆ **~ bas** *(Boxe)* blow *ou* punch below the belt; *(fig)* blow below the belt ◆ **c'était un ~ bas** that was below the belt ◆ **~ franc** *(Ftbl, Rugby)* free kick; *(Basket)* free-throw shot ◆ **tous les ~s sont permis** no holds barred ◆ **un ~ pour rien** *(lit)* a go for nothing, a free go ◆ **c'était un ~ pour rien** *(fig)* it was all for nothing; → **discuter, marquer**

3 [= habileté] **avoir le ~** to have the knack ◆ **attraper *ou* prendre le ~** to get the knack; → **main**

4 [effort] **en mettre un ~*** to pull out all the stops* ◆ **il en met un sacré ~*** he's really going at it

5 [= décharge, détonation] *[d'arme à feu]* shot ◆ **à six ~s** six-shot *(épith)* ◆ **il jouait avec le fusil quand le ~ est parti** he was playing with the rifle when it went off ◆ **faire ~ double** *(Chasse)* to do a right and left; *(fig)* to kill two birds with one stone; → **feu¹, grâce, tirer**

6 [= bruit de choc] knock; *(sec)* rap ◆ **il y eut un ~ à la porte** there was a knock at the door ◆ **sonner 3 ~s** to ring 3 times ◆ **les douze ~s de midi** the twelve strokes of noon ◆ **sur le ~ de minuit** at *ou* on the stroke of midnight ◆ **sur le ~ des 10-11 heures** around 10 or 11; → **frapper**

7 [= événement fortuit] **~ du sort *ou* du destin** blow dealt by fate ◆ **~ de chance *ou* de veine*, ~ de pot* *ou* de bol*** stroke *ou* piece of luck ◆ **~ de malchance** rotten luck; → **sale**

8 [* = action concertée, hasardeuse] *[de cambrioleurs]* job* ◆ **~ médiatique** media stunt ◆ **il est sur un ~** he's up to something ◆ **elle voulait cette maison, mais ils étaient plusieurs sur le ~** she wanted that house but there were several people after it ◆ **c'est un ~ à faire *ou* tenter** it's worth (having) a go* *ou* a bash* *(Brit)* ◆ **réussir un beau ~** to pull it off ◆ **il a manqué *ou* raté son ~** he blew it*, he didn't pull it off* ◆ **c'est un ~ à se tuer !*/à se faire virer !*** you could get yourself killed doing that!/fired for doing that! ◆ **c'est encore un ~ de 100 €*** that'll be another €100 to fork out*; → **cent¹, quatre**

♦ **dans le coup** ◆ **être dans le ~** *(impliqué)* to be in on it*; *(au courant)* to know all about it; *(expert)* to know what's what; *(à la page)* to be with it* ◆ **une grand-mère dans le ~** a with-it* *ou* hip* grandmother ◆ **mettre qn dans le ~** to get sb involved, to bring sb in ◆ **pendant le match, il n'était pas dans le ~** he wasn't really with it* during the match

♦ **valoir le coup** ◆ **ça vaut le ~** it's worth it ◆ **c'est un film qui vaut le ~** the film is worth seeing ◆ **cela valait le ~ d'essayer** it was worth trying *ou* a try ◆ **ça ne vaut pas le ~ de partir pour 2 jours** it's not worth going just for 2 days ◆ **elle vaut vraiment le ~ qu'on la forme*** it's really worth our while to train her

9 [= action contre qn] trick ◆ **~ monté** setup ◆ **c'est bien un ~ à lui** that's just like him *ou* typical of him ◆ **tu ne vas pas nous faire le ~ d'être malade** you're not going to go and be ill on us* ◆ **il nous fait le ~ chaque fois** he always does that ◆ **un ~ en vache*** a dirty trick* ◆ **faire un ~ en vache à qn*** to do the dirty on sb*, to pull a dirty trick on sb* ◆ **un ~ en traître** a stab in the back; → **mauvais, panne¹, sale**

10 [* = fois] time ◆ **à chaque ~, à tous (les) ~s, à tout ~** every time ◆ **à tous les ~s on gagne !** every one a winner! ◆ **du même ~** at the same time ◆ **pleurer/rire un bon ~** to have a good cry/laugh

♦ **au coup par coup** *[agir]* on an ad hoc basis; *[embaucher, acheter]* as and when the need arises ◆ **nous réglerons ce problème au ~ par ~** we'll deal with this problem as we go along

♦ **coup sur coup** in quick succession ◆ **deux victoires ~ sur ~, c'est bon pour l'équipe !** two wins one after the other *ou* two successive wins, that's good for the team!

♦ **d'un seul coup** ◆ **d'un seul ~, les lumières s'éteignirent** all at once *ou* all of a sudden the lights went out ◆ **il a sauté 4 marches d'un seul ~** he leaped *ou* took 4 steps in one go *ou* at a time

♦ **du premier coup, au premier coup** straight away, right away ◆ **il a eu son permis de conduire du premier ~** he got his driving licence first time round *ou* first go*

11 [* = quantité bue] **boire un ~** to have a drink *ou* something to drink ◆ **aller boire un ~** *(gén)* to go and have something to drink; *(au café)* to go for a drink ◆ **je te paie un ~ (à boire)** I'll buy you a drink ◆ **vous boirez bien un ~ de rouge avec nous ?** come and have a glass of red wine with us ◆ **il a bu un ~ de trop, il a un ~ dans le nez*** he's had one too many*, he's had one over the eight*

12 [** = partenaire sexuel] **être un bon ~** to be a good screw** *ou* fuck**

13 [locutions]

♦ **à coup(s) de** *(= au moyen de)* ◆ **la société boucle son budget à ~s de subventions** the firm manages to balance its budget by using *ou* through subsidies ◆ **réussir à ~ de publicité** to succeed through advertising

♦ **à coup sûr** *(= sûrement)* definitely

♦ **après coup** afterwards, after the event

♦ **du coup** as a result

♦ **pour le coup** ◆ **c'est pour le ~ qu'il se fâcherait** then he'd really get angry ◆ **là, pour le ~, il m'a étonné** he really surprised me there

♦ **sous le coup de** *(= sous l'effet de) [+ surprise, colère]* in the grip of ◆ **sous le ~ d'une forte émotion** in a highly emotional state, in the grip of a powerful emotion ◆ **être sous le ~ d'une condamnation** to have a current conviction ◆ **être sous le ~ d'une mesure d'expulsion** to be under an expulsion order ◆ **il est sous le ~ d'un mandat d'arrêt** there is a warrant out for his arrest ◆ **tomber sous le ~ de la loi** *[activité, acte]* to be a statutory offence

♦ **sur le coup** *(= instantanément)* outright ◆ **mourir sur le ~** *(assassinat)* to be killed outright; *(accident)* to die *ou* be killed instantly ◆ **sur le ~ je n'ai pas compris** at the time I didn't understand

♦ **tout à coup, tout d'un coup** all of a sudden, suddenly, all at once

---

coupable /kupabl/ ADJ 1 *(= fautif) [personne]* guilty *(de of)*; ◆ **il s'est rendu ~ de corruption** he was guilty of corruption; → **non, plaider** 2 *(= blâmable) [désirs, amour]* guilty *(épith)*; *[action, négligence]* culpable, reprehensible; *[faiblesse]* reprehensible NMF culprit, guilty party *(hum)* ◆ **le grand ~ c'est le jeu** the real culprit is gambling, gambling is chiefly to blame

coupage /kupaʒ/ NM *[de vin] (avec un autre vin)* blending *(NonC)*; *(avec de l'eau)* dilution *(NonC)*, diluting *(NonC)* ◆ **ce sont des ~s, ce sont des vins de ~** these are blended wines

coupant, e /kupɑ̃, ɑ̃t/ ADJ *[lame, brin d'herbe]* sharp(-edged); *[ton, réponse]* sharp

coupe¹ /kup/ NF 1 *(à dessert, à glace)* dish, bowl; *(= contenu)* dish(ful), bowl(ful); *(à boire)* goblet ◆ **une ~ de champagne** a glass of champagne ◆ **~ à fruits** *(= saladier)* fruit bowl; *(individuelle)* fruit dish, coupe ◆ **la ~ est pleine** *(fig)* I've had enough, that's the limit; → **boire, loin** 2 *(Sport = objet, épreuve)* cup ◆ **~ d'Europe/du monde** European/World cup ◆ **la ~ de France de football** the French football *(Brit)* *ou* soccer *(US)* cup ◆ **la Coupe des Coupes** the Cupwinners' Cup

coupe[2] /kup/ NF 1 *(Couture)* (= *action*) cutting(-out); (= *pièce de tissu*) length; (= *façon d'être coupé*) cut ◆ **robe de belle ~/de ~ sobre** beautifully/simply cut dress ◆ **~ nette** *ou* **franche** clean cut
2 *(Sylviculture)* (= *action*) cutting (down); (= *étendue de forêt*) felling area; (= *surface, tranche*) section
3 *[d'herbe]* cutting; *[de gâteau]* cutting up, slicing; *[de rôti]* carving, cutting up ◆ **fromage/beurre vendu à la ~** cheese/butter sold loose
4 *[de cheveux]* cutting ◆ **~ (de cheveux)** (hair) cut ◆ **~ au rasoir** razor-cut ◆ **faites-moi une ~ toute simple** just do something simple
5 *(pour examen au microscope)* section ◆ **~ histologique** histological section
6 (= *dessin, plan*) section ◆ **le navire vu en ~** a (cross) section of the ship ◆ **~ transversale** cross *ou* transversal section ◆ **~ longitudinale** longitudinal section
7 *(Littérat) [de vers]* break, caesura
8 *(Cartes)* cut, cutting *(NonC)* ◆ **jouer sous la ~ de qn** to lead (after sb has cut)
9 (= *réduction*) cut ◆ **faire des ~s dans qch** to make cuts in sth
10 *(locutions)* **être sous la ~ de qn** *[personne]* (= *être dominé*) to be under sb's thumb; *(hiérarchiquement)* to be under sb; *[entreprise, organisation]* to be under sb's control ◆ **tomber sous la ~ de qn** to fall prey to sb, to fall into sb's clutches
COMP **coupe claire** clear-cutting, clear-felling ◆ **faire des ~s claires dans qch** *(fig)* to make drastic cuts in sth
coupe d'ensemencement thinning (out) *(to allow space for sowing new trees)*
coupe réglée periodic felling ◆ **mettre en ~ réglée** *(fig)* to bleed systematically
coupe sombre (slight) thinning (out) ◆ **faire des ~s sombres dans** to make drastic cuts in ◆ **~s sombres dans le personnel** severe staff reductions *ou* cutbacks

coupé, e[1] /kupe/ (ptp de **couper**) ADJ 1 *[vêtement]* **bien/mal ~** well/badly cut 2 *[communications, routes]* cut off *(attrib)* 3 *[vin]* blended 4 (= *castré*) neutered NM (= *voiture, pas de danse*) coupé

coupe-chou(x)* (pl **coupe-choux**) /kupʃu/ NM (= *épée*) short sword; (= *rasoir*) open razor

coupe-cigare (pl **coupe-cigares**) /kupsigaʀ/ NM cigar cutter

coupe-circuit (pl **coupe-circuits**) /kupsiʀkɥi/ NM cutout, circuit breaker

coupe-coupe /kupkup/ NM INV machete

coupée[2] /kupe/ NF *(Naut)* gangway *(opening, with ladder)*; → **échelle**

coupe-faim (pl **coupe-faim(s)**) /kupfɛ̃/ NM appetite suppressant ◆ **le tabac a un effet ~** smoking takes away your appetite

coupe-feu (pl **coupe-feu(x)**) /kupfø/ NM (= *espace*) firebreak; (= *chose*) fireguard ◆ **porte ~** fire door

coupe-file (pl **coupe-files**) /kupfil/ NM (= *carte de priorité*) pass

coupe-frites /kupfʀit/ NM INV chip-cutter *ou* -slicer *(Brit)*, French-fry-cutter *ou* -slicer *(US)*

coupe-gorge (pl **coupe-gorge(s)**) /kupgɔʀʒ/ NM (= *quartier*) dangerous *ou* no-go area; (= *rue*) dangerous back-alley ◆ **ce café/cette banlieue est un vrai ~ !** you take your life in your hands when you go into that café/area!

coupe-jarret (pl **coupe-jarrets**) /kupʒaʀɛ/ NM († *ou hum*) cutthroat

coupe-légume(s) (pl **coupe-légumes**) /kuplegym/ NM vegetable-cutter

coupelle /kupɛl/ NF 1 (= *petite coupe*) (small) dish 2 *(Chim)* cupel

coupe-œufs /kupø/ NM INV egg-slicer

coupe-ongle(s) (pl **coupe-ongles**) /kupɔ̃gl/ NM (= *pince*) nail clippers; (= *ciseaux*) nail scissors

coupe-papier /kuppapje/ NM INV paper knife

couper /kupe/ GRAMMAIRE ACTIVE 54.7 ► conjug 1 ◄
VT 1 (= *sectionner*) to cut; *[+ bois]* to chop; *[+ arbre]* to cut down, to fell; (= *séparer*) to cut off; (= *découper*) *[+ rôti]* to carve, to cut up; (= *partager*) *[+ gâteau]* to cut, to slice; (= *entailler*) to slit; *(fig) [vent]* to sting ◆ **~ qch en (petits) morceaux** to cut sth up, to cut sth into (little) pieces ◆ **~ qch en tranches** to slice sth, to cut sth into slices ◆ **~ qch en deux** *(lit)* to cut sth in two *ou* in half ◆ **le parti/l'électorat est coupé en deux** the party is/the voters are split down the middle ◆ **le pays sera coupé en deux** *(Météo)* the country will be split in two ◆ **~ coller** *(Ordin)* to cut and paste ◆ **~ la gorge à qn** to slit *ou* cut sb's throat ◆ **~ la tête** *ou* **le cou à qn** to cut *ou* chop sb's head off ◆ **~ (les pages d')un livre** to slit open *ou* cut the pages of a book ◆ **livre non coupé** book with uncut pages ◆ **coupez-lui une tranche de pain** cut him a slice of bread ◆ **se faire ~ les cheveux** to get *ou* have one's hair cut, to have a haircut; → **six, tête, vif**
2 *(Couture) [+ vêtement]* to cut out; *[+ étoffe]* to cut
3 (= *retrancher*) *[+ passages inutiles]* to cut (out), to take out, to delete; (= *raccourcir*) *[+ émission]* to cut (down)
4 (= *arrêter*) *[+ eau, gaz, courant]* to cut off; *(au compteur)* to turn off; *[+ communications, route, pont]* to cut off; *[+ relations diplomatiques]* to cut off, to break off; *(Téléc)* to cut off; *[+ crédits]* to cut off; *(Ciné) [+ prise de vues]* to cut ◆ **coupez !** *(Ciné)* cut! ◆ **~ le contact** *ou* **l'allumage** *(en voiture)* to switch off the ignition ◆ **~ l'appétit à qn** *(un peu)* to take the edge off sb's appetite; *(complètement)* to spoil sb's appetite, to take away sb's appetite ◆ **~ la faim à qn** to take the edge off sb's hunger ◆ **~ la fièvre à qn** to bring down sb's fever ◆ **~ les ponts avec qn** *(fig)* to break off communications with sb ◆ **~ la retraite à qn** to cut *ou* block off sb's line of retreat ◆ **~ la route à qn** to cut sb off, to cut in front of sb ◆ **~ la route d'un véhicule** to cut a vehicle off ◆ **la route était coupée net par le bombardement** the road was completely cut off by the bombing ◆ **~ le vent** to cut out the wind ◆ **~ les vivres à qn** to cut off sb's means of subsistence
5 (= *interrompre*) **~ qn** to interrupt sb ◆ **~ la parole à qn** *[personne]* to cut sb short; *[émotion]* to leave *ou* render sb speechless ◆ **~ le sifflet*** *ou* **la chique*** **à qn** to shut sb up*, to take the wind out of sb's sails ◆ **ça te la coupe !*** that's shut you up!*
6 (= *rompre la continuité de*) *[+ voyage]* to break; *[+ journée]* to break up ◆ **nous nous arrêterons à Caen pour ~ le voyage** we'll stop at Caen to break the journey, we'll break the journey at Caen
7 (= *isoler*) **~ qn de qch** to cut sb off from sth
8 (= *traverser*) *[ligne]* to intersect, to cut; *[route]* to cut across, to cross ◆ **le chemin de fer coupe la route en 2 endroits** the railway cuts across *ou* crosses the road at 2 points
9 *(Cartes) [+ jeu]* to cut; (= *prendre avec l'atout*) to trump
10 *(Sport) [+ balle]* to slice, to undercut
11 (= *mélanger*) *[+ lait, vin]* *(à table)* to dilute, to add water to; *[+ vin]* *(à la production)* to blend ◆ **vin coupé d'eau** wine diluted with water
12 (= *castrer*) to neuter
13 *(locutions)* **~ les bras** *ou* **bras et jambes à qn** *[travail]* to wear sb out; *[nouvelle]* to knock sb for six* *(Brit)* *ou* for a loop* *(US)* ◆ **j'en ai les jambes coupées** I'm stunned ◆ **coupons la poire en deux** let's meet halfway ◆ **~ les cheveux en quatre** to split hairs, to quibble ◆ **~ la respiration à qn** *(lit)* to wind sb; *(fig)* to take sb's breath away; → **couteau, effet, herbe, souffle** *etc*
VT INDIR **couper à** (= *échapper à*) *[+ corvée]* to get out of ◆ **tu n'y couperas pas d'une amende** you won't get away without paying a fine, you won't get out of paying a fine ◆ **tu n'y couperas pas** you won't get out of it; → **court**[1]
VI 1 (= *être tranchant*) *[couteau, verre]* to cut; *[vent]* to be biting ◆ **ce couteau coupe bien** this knife cuts well *ou* has a good cutting edge
2 (= *prendre un raccourci*) **~ à travers champs** to cut across country *ou* the fields ◆ **~ au plus court** to go the quickest way ◆ **~ par un sentier/la forêt** to cut along a path/through the forest
3 *(Cartes)* (= *diviser le jeu*) to cut; (= *jouer atout*) to trump ◆ **~ à trèfle/à carreau** *etc* to trump with a club/diamond *etc*
VPR **se couper** 1 (= *s'entailler la peau*) to cut o.s.
2 (= *retrancher une partie de son corps*) **se ~ les cheveux/les ongles** to cut one's hair/nails
3 (= *être usé*) *[tissu]* to come apart; *[cuir]* to crack
4 (= *perdre contact*) ◆ **se ~ de** *[+ amis, famille, pays]* to cut o.s. off from, to cut all ties with
5 (= *se trahir*) to give o.s. away

couper-coller /kupekɔle/ NM *(Ordin)* ◆ **faire un ~** to cut and paste

couperet /kupʀɛ/ NM *[de boucher]* chopper, cleaver; *[de guillotine]* blade, knife ◆ **la décision est tombée comme un ~** the decision came as a bombshell *ou* was a bolt from the blue ◆ **date ~** cut-off date ◆ **match ~** decider, deciding match

couperose /kupʀoz/ NF blotches *(on the face)*, rosacea *(SPÉC)*

couperosé, e /kupʀoze/ ADJ blotchy, affected by rosacea *(SPÉC)*

coupeur, -euse /kupœʀ, øz/ NM,F *(Couture)* cutter ◆ **~ de tête** headhunter ◆ **~ de cheveux en quatre** hairsplitter, quibbler

coupe-vent (pl **coupe-vent(s)**) /kupvɑ̃/ NM (= *haie*) windbreak; (= *vêtement*) windcheater *(Brit)*, windbreaker *(US)*

couplage /kuplaʒ/ NM coupling

couple /kupl/ NM 1 (= *époux, amoureux, danseurs*) couple; (= *patineurs, animaux*) pair ◆ **le ~ Martin** the Martins ◆ **ils ont des problèmes de ~, leur ~ a des problèmes** they have problems with their relationship ◆ **l'épreuve en** *ou* **par ~s** *(Patinage)* the pairs (event) 2 *(Phys)* couple ◆ **~ moteur** torque ◆ **~ de torsion** torque 3 *[de navire]* (square) frame; *[d'avion]* frame ◆ **s'amarrer à ~** to moor alongside another boat; → **nage, nager** NF *ou* NM † ◆ **un** *ou* **une ~ de** (= *deux*) a couple of NF *(Chasse)* couple

couplé /kuple/ NM ◆ **(pari) ~** first and second place double *(on two horses in the same race)*

coupler /kuple/ ► conjug 1 ◄ VT 1 (= *combiner*) to combine *(à* with); ◆ **la baisse des prix, couplée à l'augmentation de la puissance des ordinateurs** falling prices combined with increased computer power 2 *[+ chiens de chasse]* to couple (together), to leash together 3 *[+ machines]* to couple together *ou* up; *[+ ordinateurs]* to interface *(avec* with); ◆ **télémètre couplé** *(Photo)* coupled rangefinder ◆ **bielles couplées** *(Rail)* coupling rods

couplet /kuplɛ/ NM (= *strophe*) verse; *(péj)* tirade ◆ **~s satiriques** (= *chanson*) satirical song ◆ **y aller de son ~ sur qch** to give a little speech about sth

coupleur /kuplœʀ/ NM *(Élec)* coupler ◆ **~ acoustique** *(Ordin)* acoustic coupler

coupole /kupɔl/ NF 1 *(Archit)* dome ◆ **petite ~** cupola, small dome ◆ **être reçu sous la Coupole** to become *ou* be made a member of the Académie française; → ACADÉMIE 2 *(Mil) [de char d'assaut]* revolving gun turret

coupon /kupɔ̃/ NM 1 (= *reste de tissu*) remnant; (= *rouleau*) roll 2 (*Fin*) ~ **(de dividende)** coupon ◆ **avec ~ attaché/détaché** cum-/ex-dividend ◆ **~ de rente** income coupon ◆ **~ zéro** zero coupon 3 (= *billet, ticket*) coupon ◆ **~ de théâtre** theatre ticket ◆ **~ hebdomadaire/mensuel** (*Transport*) ≃ weekly/monthly season ticket 4 (*Comm*) coupon, voucher ◆ **~ de réduction** coupon, cash premium voucher

coupon-réponse (pl **coupons-réponse**) /kupɔ̃repɔ̃s/ NM reply coupon

coupure /kupyʀ/ NF 1 (= *blessure, brèche*) cut 2 ◆ **~ (de presse** *ou* **de journal)** (newspaper) cutting, (newspaper) clipping 3 (= *suppression : dans un film, livre*) cut 4 (= *billet de banque*) note, bill (*US*) ◆ **petites/grosses ~s** small/big notes, notes of small/large denomination 5 (= *interruption*) ~ **(de courant)** power cut ◆ **il y aura des ~s ce soir** (*électricité*) there'll be power cuts tonight; (*gaz, eau*) the gas (*ou* water) will be cut off tonight 6 (= *arrêt, pause*) break ◆ **la ~ estivale** the summer break ◆ **~ publicitaire** commercial break 7 (= *division*) divide (*entre* between); ◆ **la ~ droite-gauche** (*Pol*) the left-right divide

cour /kuʀ/ NF 1 [*de bâtiment*] yard, courtyard ◆ **être sur (la) ~** to look onto the (back)yard ◆ **la ~ de la caserne** the barracks square ◆ **~ de cloître** cloister garth ◆ **~ d'école** schoolyard, playground ◆ **~ de ferme** farmyard ◆ **la ~ de la gare** the station forecourt ◆ **~ d'honneur** main courtyard ◆ **~ d'immeuble** courtyard of a block of flats (*Brit*) *ou* an apartment building (*US*) ◆ **~ intérieure** inner courtyard ◆ **~ de récréation** playground ◆ **la ~ des grands** (*lit*) the older children's playground ◆ **jouer dans la ~ des grands** (*fig*) to play with the big boys* *ou* in the major league (*US*); → **côté**

2 (*Jur*) court ◆ **Messieurs, la Cour !** ≃ all rise!, be upstanding in court! (*Brit*) ◆ **la Cour suprême** the Supreme Court; → **haut**

3 [*de roi*] court; [*de personnage puissant, célèbre*] following ◆ **vivre à la ~** to live at court ◆ **faire sa ~ à** [+ *roi*] to pay court to; [+ *supérieur, femme*] to pay one's respects to ◆ **être bien/mal en ~** to be in/out of favour (*auprès de qn* with sb); ◆ **homme/habit de ~** court gentleman/clothes ◆ **gens de ~** courtiers, people at court ◆ **c'est la ~ du roi Pétaud** it's absolute bedlam*

4 [*de femme*] (= *soupirants*) following; (= *essai de conquête*) wooing (*NonC*), courting (*NonC*) ◆ **faire la ~ à une femme** to woo *ou* court a woman ◆ **faire un brin de ~ à une femme*** to flirt a little with a woman

COMP **cour d'appel** ≃ Court of Appeal, appellate court (*US*)
cour d'assises ≃ Crown Court (*Brit*), Court of Assizes
cour de cassation Court of Cassation; (*final*) Court of Appeal
cour des comptes revenue court, ≃ Government Accounting Office (*US*)
cour de discipline budgétaire Budgetary and Financial Disciplinary Court
Cour européenne des droits de l'homme European Court of Human Rights
Cour européenne de justice European Court of Justice
Cour internationale de justice International Court of Justice
cour de justice court of justice
cour martiale court martial ◆ **passer en ~ martiale** to be court-martialled
la Cour des Miracles (*Hist*) *area of Paris famed for its disreputable population* ◆ **chez eux c'est une vraie ~ des miracles** (*fig*) their place is always full of shady characters ◆ **ce quartier est une vraie ~ des miracles** this is a very unsavoury area
Cour pénale internationale International Criminal Court
Cour de sûreté de l'État state security court

courage /kuʀaʒ/ NM 1 (= *bravoure*) courage, bravery, guts* ◆ **avoir du ~** to be brave *ou* courageous, to have guts* ◆ **~ physique/moral** physical/moral courage ◆ **se battre avec ~** to fight courageously *ou* with courage *ou* bravely ◆ **s'il y va, il a du ~ !** if he goes, it means he has guts!* ◆ **je n'ai pas eu le ~ de lui refuser** I didn't have the heart to refuse

2 (= *ardeur*) will, spirit ◆ **entreprendre une tâche/un travail avec ~** to undertake a task/job with a will ◆ **je voudrais finir ce travail, mais je ne m'en sens pas** *ou* **je n'en ai pas le ~** I'd like to get this work finished, but I don't feel up to it ◆ **je n'ai pas beaucoup de ~ ce soir** I don't feel up to much this evening ◆ **il se lève tous les jours à 5 heures ? – quel ~ !/il a du ~ !** he gets up at 5am every day? – what willpower!/he must have a lot of willpower! ◆ **un petit verre pour vous donner du ~*** just a little drink to buck you up*

3 (*locutions*) **~ ! nous y sommes presque !** cheer up! *ou* take heart! we're almost there! ◆ **avoir le ~ de ses opinions** to have the courage of one's convictions ◆ **prendre son ~ à deux mains** to take one's courage in both hands ◆ **perdre ~** to lose heart, to become discouraged ◆ **reprendre ~** to take fresh heart

courageusement /kuʀaʒøzmɑ̃/ ADV bravely, courageously ◆ **entreprendre ~ une tâche** to tackle a task with a will

courageux, -euse /kuʀaʒø, øz/ ADJ brave, courageous ◆ **il n'est pas très ~ pour l'étude** he's lazy when it comes to studying, he hasn't got much will for studying ◆ **je ne suis pas très ~ aujourd'hui** I don't feel up to very much today

couramment /kuʀamɑ̃/ ADV 1 (= *aisément*) fluently ◆ **parler le français ~** to speak French fluently *ou* fluent French 2 (= *souvent*) commonly ◆ **ce mot s'emploie ~** this word is in current *ou* common usage ◆ **ça se dit ~** it's a common *ou* an everyday expression ◆ **cela arrive ~** it's a common occurrence ◆ **cela se fait ~** it's quite a common thing to do, it's quite common practice

courant, e /kuʀɑ̃, ɑ̃t/ ADJ 1 (= *normal, habituel*) [*dépenses*] everyday, standard, ordinary; [*modèle, taille, marque*] standard ◆ **l'usage ~** everyday *ou* ordinary *ou* standard usage ◆ **en utilisant les procédés ~s on gagne du temps** it saves time to use the normal *ou* ordinary *ou* standard procedures ◆ **il nous suffit pour le travail ~** it's OK for routine work; → **vie**

2 (= *fréquent*) common ◆ **c'est un procédé ~** it's quite common practice *ou* quite a common procedure, it's quite commonplace ◆ **ce genre d'incident est très ~ ici** this kind of incident is very common here, this kind of thing is a common occurrence here

3 (= *en cours, actuel*) [*année, semaine*] current, present; (*Écon*) [*euros, prix*] current ◆ **votre lettre du 5 ~** (*Comm*) your letter of the 5th inst. *ou* instant *ou* of the 5th of this month; → **expédier, monnaie**

4 (= *qui court*) → **chien, compte, eau**

NM 1 [*de cours d'eau, mer, atmosphère*] current ◆ **~ (atmosphérique)** airstream, current ◆ **~ d'air** draught (*Brit*), draft (*US*) ◆ **plein de ~s d'air** very draughty ◆ **~ d'air froid/chaud** (*Météo*) cold/warm airstream ◆ **c'est un vrai ~ d'air** (*fig*) one minute he's there, the next he's gone ◆ **il y a trop de ~** the current's too strong ◆ **suivre le ~** (*lit*) to go with the current; (*fig*) to go with the stream, to follow the crowd ◆ **remonter le ~** (*lit*) to go against the current; (*fig*) to get back on one's feet

2 (= *déplacement*) [*de population, échanges commerciaux*] movement ◆ **~s de population** movements *ou* shifts of (the) population

3 (= *mouvement*) (*gén*) movement; [*d'opinion, pensée*] trend, current ◆ **les ~s de l'opinion** the trends of public opinion ◆ **un ~ de scepticisme/de sympathie** a wave of scepticism/sympathy ◆ **le ~ romantique/surréaliste** the romantic/surrealist movement

4 (*Élec*) current, power ◆ **~ continu/alternatif** direct/alternating current ◆ **couper le ~** to cut off the power ◆ **rétablir le ~** to put the power back on ◆ **on s'est rencontré un soir et le ~ est tout de suite passé** we met one evening and hit it off straight away* ◆ **le ~ ne passe pas entre nous** we don't get on ◆ **entre ce chanteur et le public le ~ passe très bien** this singer really gets through to his audience *ou* has a really good rapport with his audience; → **coupure, prise**[2]

5 (= *cours*) **dans le ~ de la semaine/du mois** in the course of the week/month ◆ **je dois le voir dans le ~ de la semaine** I'm to see him some time during the week ◆ **dans le ~ de la conversation** in the course of the conversation ◆ **le projet doit être fini ~ mai** the project is due to finish some time in May

6 (*locutions*)

◆ **au courant** ◆ **être au ~** (= *savoir la nouvelle*) to know (about it); (= *bien connaître la question*) to be well-informed ◆ **tu m'as l'air très** *ou* **bien au ~ de ce qu'il fait !** you seem to know a lot about *ou* to be very well-informed about what he's doing! ◆ **être au ~ de** [+ *accident, projet*] to know about; [+ *théories nouvelles*] to be well up on*, to be up to date on ◆ **mettre qn au ~ de** [+ *faits, affaire*] to tell sb about, to put sb in the picture about*, to fill sb in on*; [+ *méthodes nouvelles*] to bring sb up to date on ◆ **il s'est vite mis au ~ dans son nouvel emploi** he soon got the hang of things* in his new job ◆ **tenir qn au ~ de** [+ *faits, affaire*] to keep sb informed of *ou* posted about*; [+ *méthodes*] to keep sb up to date on ◆ **si jamais ça recommence, tenez-moi au ~** if it happens again let me know ◆ **s'abonner à une revue scientifique pour se tenir au ~** to subscribe to a science magazine to keep o.s. up to date

NF **courante** 1 (✻ = *diarrhée*) **la ~e** the runs✻

2 (*Mus* = *danse, air*) courante, courant

courbatu, e /kuʀbaty/ ADJ stiff, aching all over

courbature /kuʀbatyʀ/ NF ache ◆ **ce match de tennis m'a donné des ~s** I'm stiff *ou* aching all over after that game of tennis ◆ **plein de ~s** stiff *ou* aching all over

courbaturé, e /kuʀbatyʀe/ ADJ stiff, aching all over

courbe /kuʀb/ NF bend ◆ **le fleuve fait une ~ ici** the river curves here ◆ **~ de niveau** contour line ◆ **~ de température** temperature curve ◆ **une femme aux ~s très généreuses** a woman with generous curves ADJ curved

courber /kuʀbe/ ▸ conjug 1 ◂ VT 1 (= *plier*) [+ *branche, tige*] to bend ◆ **branches courbées sous le poids de la neige** branches bowed down with *ou* bent under the weight of the snow ◆ **l'âge l'avait courbé** he was bowed *ou* bent with age 2 (= *pencher*) **~ la tête** to bow *ou* bend one's head ◆ **courbant le front sur son livre** his head bent over a book ◆ **~ la tête** *ou* **le front** *ou* **le dos** (*fig*) to submit (*devant* to) → **échine** VI to bend ◆ **~ sous le poids** to bend under the weight VPR **se courber** 1 [*arbre, branche, poutre*] to bend, to curve 2 [*personne*] (*pour entrer, passer*) to bend (down), to stoop; (*signe d'humiliation*) to bow down; (*signe de déférence*) to bow (down) ◆ **il se courba pour le saluer** he greeted him with a bow ◆ **se ~ en deux** to bend (o.s.) double 3 (*littér* = *se soumettre*) to bow down (*devant* before)

courbette /kuʀbɛt/ **NF** 1 (= salut) low bow ◆ **faire des ~s à** ou **devant qn** (fig) to kowtow to sb, to bow and scrape to sb 2 [de cheval] curvet

courbure /kuʀbyʀ/ **NF** [de ligne, surface] curvature ◆ **~ rentrante/sortante/en S** inward/outward/S curve ◆ **~ du nez/des reins** curve of the nose/the back

courette /kuʀɛt/ **NF** (small) courtyard

coureur, -euse /kuʀœʀ, øz/ **NM,F** (= athlète) runner; (= cycliste) cyclist, competitor; (= pilote de course) driver, competitor ◆ **~ de fond/de demi-fond** long-distance/middle-distance runner ◆ **~ de 110 mètres haies** 110 metres hurdler

NM 1 **(oiseaux)** **~s** running birds

2 (péj = amateur de) **c'est un ~ de cafés/de bals** he hangs round (Brit) ou around cafés/dances ◆ **~ (de filles** ou **femmes** ou **jupons)** womanizer, skirt-chaser ◆ **il est assez ~** he's a bit of a womanizer ou a skirt-chaser ou a wolf*

NF **coureuse** (péj = débauchée) manhunter ◆ **elle est un peu coureuse** she's always chasing after men, she's a bit of a manhunter

COMP **coureur automobile** racing(-car) driver

coureur de ou **des bois** (Hist Can) trapper, coureur de bois (US, Can)

coureur cycliste racing cyclist

coureur de dot (péj) fortune-hunter

coureur motocycliste motorcycle ou motorbike racer

courge /kuʀʒ/ **NF** (= plante, fruit) gourd, squash (US, Can); (Culin) marrow (Brit), squash (US, Can); (*: péj) idiot, berk* (Brit)

courgette /kuʀʒɛt/ **NF** courgette (Brit), zucchini (US)

courir /kuʀiʀ/ ► conjug 11 ◄ **VI** 1 (gén, Athlétisme) to run; (courses automobiles, cyclisme) to race; (Courses) to run, to race ◆ **entrer/sortir en courant** to run in/out ◆ **se mettre à ~** to break into a run, to start to run, to start running ◆ **~ sur Ferrari** to race with Ferrari ◆ **il courait à toutes jambes** ou **à perdre haleine** he ran as fast as his legs could carry him ◆ **~ comme un dératé*** ou **ventre à terre** to run flat out ◆ **elle court comme un lapin** ou **lièvre** she runs ou can run like a hare ou the wind ◆ **le voleur court encore** ou **toujours** the thief is still at large ◆ **faire ~ un cheval** to race ou run a horse ◆ **il ne fait plus ~** he doesn't race ou run horses any more ◆ **un cheval trop vieux pour ~** a horse too old to race ou to be raced

2 (= se précipiter) to rush ◆ **~ chez le docteur/chercher le docteur** to rush ou run to the doctor's/for the doctor ◆ **je cours l'appeler** I'll go ou run and call him straight away (Brit) ou right away ◆ **ce spectacle fait ~ tout Paris** all Paris is rushing to see the show ◆ **faire qch en courant** to do sth in a rush ou hurry ◆ **elle m'a fait ~** she had me running all over the place ◆ **elle est toujours en train de ~** she's always rushing about ◆ **un petit mot en courant** just a (quick) note ou a few hurried lines ◆ **~ partout pour trouver qch** to hunt everywhere for sth ◆ **tu peux toujours ~ !*** you can (go) whistle for it!* ◆ **pour enlever les taches, tu peux toujours ~*** if you think you can get rid of those stains you've got another think coming*

3 (avec à, après, sur) **~ à l'échec/à une déception** to be heading ou headed for failure/a disappointment ◆ **~ à sa perte** ou **ruine** to be on the road to ruin ◆ **~ à la catastrophe** to be rushing headlong into disaster ◆ **~ après qch** to chase after sth ◆ **~ après un ballon** to run after a ball ◆ **l'autobus démarra et il courut après** the bus started and he ran after it ◆ **gardez cet argent pour l'instant, il ne court pas après** keep this money for now as he's not in any hurry ou rush for it ou he's not desperate for it ◆ **les épinards, je ne cours pas après*** I'm not that keen on spinach ◆ **~ après qn** (lit, fig) to run after sb ◆ **~ après les femmes** to be a womanizer ◆ **~ sur ses 60/70 ans** to be approaching ou pushing* ou getting on for 60/70 ◆ **~ sur le système** ou **le haricot à qn*** to get on sb's nerves* ou wick* (Brit)

4 [nuages] to speed, to race, to scud (littér); [ombres, reflets] to speed, to race; [eau] to rush; [chemin] to run ◆ **un frisson lui courut par tout le corps** a shiver went ou ran through his body ◆ **sa plume courait sur le papier** his pen was racing across the paper ◆ **laisser ~ ses doigts sur un clavier** to tinkle away at a piano

5 (= se répandre) **faire ~ une nouvelle** to spread a piece of news ◆ **le bruit court que ...** rumour has it that ..., there is a rumour that ..., the rumour is that ... ◆ **le bruit a récemment couru que ...** there has been a rumour going around that ... ◆ **il court sur leur compte de curieuses histoires** there are some strange stories going around about them

6 (= se passer) **l'année/le mois qui court** the current ou present year/month ◆ **laisser ~*** to let things alone ◆ **laisse ~ !*** forget it!*, drop it!*

7 (Naut) to sail

8 (Fin) [intérêt] to accrue; [bail] to run

VT 1 (Sport) [+ épreuve] to compete in ◆ **~ un 100 mètres** to run (in) ou compete in a 100 metres race ◆ **~ le Grand Prix** to race in the Grand Prix

2 (Chasse) **~ le cerf/le sanglier** to hunt stag/boar, to go staghunting/boarhunting; → **lièvre**

3 (= rechercher) [+ honneurs] to seek avidly ◆ **~ de grands dangers** (= s'exposer à) to be in great danger ◆ **~ les aventures** ou **l'aventure** to seek adventure ◆ **~ un (gros) risque** to run a (high ou serious) risk ◆ **~ sa chance** to try one's luck ◆ **il court le risque d'être accusé** he runs the risk of being accused ◆ **c'est un risque à ~** it's a risk we'll have to take ou run

4 (= parcourir) [+ mers, monde] to roam, to rove; [+ campagne, bois] to roam ou rove (through); (= faire le tour de) [+ magasins, bureaux] to go round ◆ **j'ai couru les agences toute la matinée** I've been going round the agencies all morning ◆ **~ les rues** (lit) to wander ou roam the streets; (fig) to be run-of-the-mill, to be nothing out of the ordinary ◆ **le vrai courage ne court pas les rues** real courage is hard to find ◆ **des gens comme lui, ça ne court pas les rues*** there aren't many like him

5 (= fréquenter) **~ les théâtres/les bals** to do the rounds of (all) the theatres/dances ◆ **~ les filles** to chase the girls ◆ **~ la gueuse** † to go wenching † ◆ **~ le guilledou** † ou **la prétentaine** † ou **le cotillon** to go gallivanting †, to go wenching †

6 (* = ennuyer) **~ qn** to bug sb*, to get up sb's nose* (Brit) ou on sb's wick* (Brit)

courlis /kuʀli/ **NM** curlew

couronne /kuʀɔn/ **NF** 1 [de fleurs] wreath, circlet ◆ **~ funéraire** ou **mortuaire** (funeral) wreath ◆ **~ de fleurs d'oranger** orange-blossom headdress, circlet of orange-blossom ◆ **~ de lauriers** laurel wreath, crown of laurels ◆ **~ d'épines** crown of thorns ◆ **en ~** in a ring; → **fleur** 2 (= diadème) [de roi, pape] crown; [de noble] coronet 3 (= autorité royale) **la ~** the Crown ◆ **la ~ d'Angleterre/de France** the crown of England/of France, the English/French crown ◆ **aspirer/prétendre à la ~** to aspire to/lay claim to the throne ou the crown ◆ **de la ~** [joyaux, colonie] crown (épith) 4 (= objet circulaire) crown; (= pain) ring-shaped loaf; [de dent] crown; (Archit, Astron) corona ◆ **~ dentée** [de moteur de voiture] crown wheel ◆ **la grande/petite ~** the outer/inner suburbs (of Paris) 5 (= monnaie) crown

couronnement /kuʀɔnmɑ̃/ **NM** 1 [de roi, empereur] coronation, crowning 2 [d'édifice, colonne] top, crown; [de mur] coping; [de toit] ridge 3 [de carrière, œuvre, recherche] crowning achievement

couronner /kuʀɔne/ ► conjug 1 ◄ **VT** 1 [+ souverain] to crown ◆ **on le couronna roi** he was crowned king, they crowned him king; → **tête**

2 [+ ouvrage, auteur] to award a prize to; (Hist) [+ lauréat, vainqueur] to crown with a laurel wreath

3 (littér = orner, ceindre) to crown; [diadème] [+ front] to encircle ◆ **couronné de fleurs** wreathed ou encircled with flowers ◆ **remparts qui couronnent la colline** ramparts which crown the hill ◆ **pic couronné de neige** snow-capped peak, peak crowned with snow

4 (= parachever) to crown ◆ **cela couronne son œuvre/sa carrière** that is the crowning achievement of his work/his career ◆ **et pour ~ le tout** (iro) and to crown it all ◆ **ses efforts ont été couronnés de succès** his efforts were successful ou crowned with success

5 [+ dent] to crown

VPR **se couronner** ◆ **se ~ (le genou)** [cheval] to graze its knee; [personne] to graze one's knee

courre /kuʀ/ **VT** → **chasse¹**

courriel /kuʀjɛl/ **NM** (Can) e-mail ◆ **envoyer qch par ~** to e-mail sth

courrier /kuʀje/ **NM** 1 (= lettres reçues) mail, post (Brit), letters; (= lettres à écrire) letters ◆ **le ~ de 11 heures** the 11 o'clock post (Brit) ou mail ◆ **avoir** ou **recevoir un ~ de ministre** to be inundated with mail ou letters, to have a huge postbag* (Brit) ◆ **"courrier arrivée/départ"** (sur bac) "in/out" ◆ **~ électronique** (Ordin) e-mail, electronic mail ◆ **envoyer qch par ~ électronique** to e-mail sth, to send sth by e-mail; → **retour**

2 † (= avion, bateau) mail; (Mil = estafette) courier; (de diligence) post ◆ **l'arrivée du ~ de Bogota** the arrival of the Bogota mail; → **long-courrier**

3 (Presse) (= rubrique) column; (= nom de journal) ≈ Mail ◆ **~ du cœur** problem page, agony column (Brit) ◆ **~ des lecteurs** letters to the Editor ◆ **~ littéraire** literary column ◆ **~ économique** financial page

> ⚠ **courrier** se traduit par **courier** uniquement au sens de 'estafette'.

courriériste /kuʀjeʀist/ **NMF** columnist

courroie /kuʀwa/ **NF** (= attache) strap; (dans mécanisme) belt ◆ **~ de transmission** driving belt ◆ **je ne suis qu'une simple ~ de transmission** I'm just a cog in the machine ou in the wheel ◆ **~ de ventilateur** fan belt

courroucé, e /kuʀuse/ (ptp de **courroucer**) **ADJ** (littér) wrathful, incensed

courroucer /kuʀuse/ ► conjug 3 ◄ (littér) **VT** to anger, to incense **VPR** **se courroucer** to become incensed

courroux /kuʀu/ **NM** (littér) ire (littér), wrath

cours /kuʀ/ **NM** 1 (= déroulement, Astron) course; [d'événements] course, run; [de saisons] course, progression; [de guerre, maladie] progress, course; [de pensées, idées] course ◆ **donner (libre) ~ à** [+ imagination] to give free rein to; [+ douleur] to give way to; [+ joie, sentiment] to give vent to, to give free expression to ◆ **il donna libre ~ à ses larmes** he let his tears flow freely; → **suivre**

2 [de rivière] (= cheminement) course; (= écoulement) flow ◆ **avoir un ~ rapide/régulier** to be fast-/smooth-flowing ◆ **sur une partie de son ~** on ou along part of its course ◆ **descendre le ~ de la Seine** to go down the Seine ◆ **~ d'eau** (gén) watercourse; (= ruisseau) stream; (= rivière) river

[3] *[de valeurs, matières premières]* price; *[de devises]* rate ◆ **avoir** ~ *[monnaie]* to be legal tender; *(fig)* to be current, to be in current use ◆ **avoir** ~ **légal** to be legal tender ◆ **ne plus avoir** ~ *[monnaie]* to be no longer legal tender, to be out of circulation; *[expression]* to be obsolete, to be no longer in use *ou* no longer current ◆ **ces plaisanteries n'ont plus** ~ **ici** jokes like that are no longer appreciated here ◆ ~ **d'ouverture** *(Bourse)* opening price ◆ ~ **de clôture, dernier** ~ closing price, latest quotations ◆ ~ **des devises** *ou* **du change** foreign exchange rate ◆ **au** ~ **(du jour)** at the price of the day ◆ **au** ~ **du marché** at (the) market price ◆ **le** ~ **des voitures d'occasion** the (selling) price of secondhand cars

[4] *(= leçon)* class; *(Univ = conférence)* lecture; *(= série de leçons)* course; *(= manuel)* coursebook, textbook ◆ ~ **de solfège/de danse** musical theory/dancing lesson ◆ ~ **de chimie** *(= leçon)* chemistry class *ou* lesson; *(= conférence)* chemistry lecture; *(= enseignement)* chemistry course; *(= manuel)* chemistry coursebook *ou* textbook ◆ ~ **de droit** *(= notes)* law (course) notes ◆ ~ **de répétition** *(Helv Mil)* two or three weeks of national service done each year ◆ **faire** *ou* **donner un** ~ **sur** to give a class *(ou* lecture *ou* course) on ◆ **il donne des** ~ **en fac*** he lectures at (the) university ◆ **qui vous fait** ~ **en anglais ?** who takes you for English?, who have you got for English? ◆ **je ne ferai pas** ~ **demain** I won't be teaching tomorrow ◆ **j'ai (un)** ~ **d'histoire à quatorze heures** I've got a history class at two o'clock ◆ ~ **accéléré** *(Univ)* crash course *(de* in); ◆ ~ **du soir** *(pl)* evening classes ◆ ~ **par correspondance** correspondence course ◆ ~ **de vacances** summer school, holiday course *(Brit)* ◆ ~ **intensif** intensive course *(de, en* in); ◆ **donner/prendre des** ~ **particuliers** to give/have private lessons *ou* tuition *(Brit)* ◆ ~ **particuliers de piano** private piano lessons

[5] *(Scol = établissement)* school ◆ ~ **privé** private school ◆ ~ **de jeunes filles** girls' school *ou* college ◆ ~ **de danse** dancing school

[6] *(Scol = enseignement primaire)* class ◆ ~ **préparatoire/élémentaire/moyen** *first/second or third/fourth or fifth year in primary school* ◆ ~ **complémentaire** *(Hist) final year in elementary school*

[7] *(= avenue)* walk

[8] *(locutions)*

◆ **au cours de** in the course of, during

◆ **en cours** *[année]* current *(épith)*; *[affaires]* in hand, in progress; *[essais]* in progress, under way

◆ **en cours de** in the process of ◆ **c'est en** ~ **de réparation/réfection** it's (in the process of) being repaired/rebuilt ◆ **le projet est en** ~ **d'étude** the project is under consideration ◆ **en** ~ **de route** *(lit, fig)* on the way ◆ **brevet en** ~ **d'agrément** *(Jur)* patent pending

course /kuʀs/ NF [1] *(= action de courir)* running ◆ **prendre sa** ~ *(littér)* to start running ◆ **le cheval, atteint d'une balle en pleine** ~ the horse, hit by a bullet in mid gallop ◆ **il le rattrapa à la** ~ he ran after him and caught up with him ◆ **quelle** ~ **pour attraper le bus !** I had to run like mad* to catch the bus! ◆ **la** ~ **folle de la voiture s'est terminée dans le ravin** the car careered out of control and ended up in the ravine ◆ **c'est la** ~* it's a race against the clock ◆ **depuis que le bébé est né, c'est la** ~* we've been run off our feet ever since the baby was born; → **pas[1]**

[2] *(= discipline)* racing ◆ **la** ~ **(à pied)** running ◆ **faire de la** ~ **pour s'entraîner** to go running to get fit ◆ **tu fais de la** ~ **?** do you race? ◆ **la** ~ **de fond/demi-fond** long-distance/middle-distance running ◆ **la** ~ **sur piste/route** track/road racing ◆ **faire la** ~ **avec qn** to race with sb ◆ **allez, on fait la** ~ **!** let's have a race!, I'll race you!; → **champ[1], écurie**

[3] *(= compétition)* race ◆ ~ **de fond/sur piste** long-distance/track race ◆ ~ **autour du monde (à la voile)** round-the-world (yacht) race ◆ **les** ~**s** *[de chevaux]* horse racing ◆ **aller aux** ~**s** to go to the races ◆ **parier aux** ~**s** to bet on the races ◆ **les** ~**s de lévriers** greyhound racing ◆ **être/ne plus être dans la** ~ *[candidat]* to be in the running/out of the running ◆ **il n'est plus dans la** ~* *(dépassé)* he's out of touch ◆ **pour rester dans la** ~**, les entreprises françaises doivent faire de gros efforts** French companies will have to make a big effort if they want to remain competitive

◆ **hors course** *[pilote, voiture]* out of the race; *[candidat]* out of the running ◆ **il a été mis hors** ~ *(Sport)* he was disqualified; *[candidat]* he was put out of the running; → **solitaire**

[4] *(pour l'obtention de qch)* race ◆ **la** ~ **aux armements** the arms race ◆ **la** ~ **à la présidence/à l'Élysée/au pouvoir** the race for the presidency/the Élysée/power ◆ **la** ~ **à la productivité** the drive to be ultraproductive ◆ **la** ~ **au diplôme** the rush to obtain as many diplomas as possible

[5] *(= voyage) (en autocar)* trip, journey *(Brit)*; *(en taxi)* ride ◆ **payer (le prix de) la** ~ to pay the fare ◆ **il n'a fait que 3** ~**s hier** *[taxi]* he only picked up *ou* had 3 fares yesterday

[6] *[de projectile]* flight; *[de navire]* rapid course; *[de nuages, ombres]* racing, swift passage; *[de temps]* swift passage, swift passing *(NonC)*; *[d'étoiles]* path

[7] *(= excursion) (à pied)* hike; *(= ascension)* climb

[8] *(= commission)* errand ◆ ~**s** *(dans un magasin)* shopping *(NonC)* ◆ **faire une** ~ to (go and) get something from the shop(s) *(Brit) ou* store(s) *(US)* ◆ **faire les** ~**s** to do the shopping ◆ **il est sorti faire des** ~**s** he has gone out to do *ou* get some shopping ◆ **j'ai quelques** ~**s à faire** I've got some shopping to do ◆ **les** ~**s sont sur la table** the shopping is on the table ◆ ~**s à domicile** home shopping

[9] *(Tech) [de pièce mobile]* movement; *[de piston]* stroke

◆ **à bout de course** *(Tech)* at full stroke

◆ **à** *ou* **en bout de course** *[institution, industrie, machine]* on its last legs*; *[personne]* on one's last legs*

◆ **en bout de course** *(= finalement)* at the end of the day, ultimately ◆ **nous n'intervenons qu'en bout de** ~ we only intervene in the final stage of the process; → **fin[2]**

[10] *[de corsaire]* privateering ◆ **faire la** ~ to privateer, to go privateering

COMP **course attelée** harness race
course automobile motor race
course de chevaux horse-race
course de côte *(dans course automobile)* hill climb
course d'école *(Helv)* school trip
course par étapes stage race
course de haies hurdling ◆ **faire de la** ~ **de haies** to hurdle
course hippique ⇒ **course de chevaux**
course d'obstacles *(Sport)* obstacle race; *(Hippisme)* steeplechase; *(fig)* obstacle course *ou* race
course d'orientation orienteering race
course de relais relay race
course en sac sack race
course de taureaux bullfight
course au trésor treasure hunt
course de trot trotting race
course au trot attelé harness race
course de vitesse sprint; → **montre[1]**

course-poursuite (pl **courses-poursuites**) /kuʀspuʀsɥit/ NF *(Cyclisme)* pursuit; *(après un voleur)* chase

courser* /kuʀse/ ► conjug 1 ◄ VT to chase *ou* hare* after

coursier[1] /kuʀsje/ NM *(littér = cheval)* charger *(littér)*, steed *(littér)*

coursier[2], -ière /kuʀsje, jɛʀ/ NM,F *(gén)* messenger, courier; *(à moto)* dispatch rider ◆ **on vous l'enverra par** ~ we'll send it to you by courier, we'll courier it over to you

coursive /kuʀsiv/ NF *(Naut)* gangway *(connecting cabins)*

court[1], e /kuʀ, kuʀt/ ADJ [1] *(gén)* short; *[introduction, séjour]* short, brief ◆ **de** ~**e durée** *[enthousiasme, ardeur]* short-lived ◆ **il connaît un chemin plus** ~ he knows a quicker *ou* shorter way ◆ **la journée m'a paru** ~**e** the day seemed to go very quickly *ou* to fly by ◆ **avoir l'haleine** *ou* **la respiration** ~**e** *ou* **le souffle** ~ to be out of *ou* short of breath; → **idée, manche[1], mémoire[1]**

[2] *(= insuffisant) [avance, majorité]* narrow, small ◆ **il lui a donné 10 jours, c'est** ~ he's given him 10 days, which is (a bit) on the short side *ou* which isn't very long ◆ **10 € pour le faire, c'est** ~* €10 for doing that – that's not very much *ou* that's a bit stingy* ◆ **20 minutes, c'est bien** ~ 20 minutes is a bit tight

[3] *(loc)* **tirer à la** ~**e paille** to draw lots *ou* straws *(US)* ◆ **à sa** ~**e honte** to his humiliation ◆ **d'une** ~**e tête** by a short head ◆ **prendre au plus** ~ to go the shortest way ◆ **aller au plus** ~ *(fig)* to cut corners

ADV [1] **elle s'habille très** ~ she wears very short skirts *(ou* dresses) ◆ **les cheveux coupés** ~ with short hair

[2] *(locutions)* **s'arrêter** ~ to stop short ◆ **couper** ~ **à** *[+ débat, rumeur, critiques]* to put a stop to ◆ **il faut faire** ~* *(= être concis)* you *(ou* we) need to be brief; *(= être rapide)* you'd *(ou* we'd) better make it quick* ◆ **prendre qn de** ~ to catch sb unawares *ou* on the hop* *(Brit)* ◆ **rester** *ou* **demeurer** ~ to be at a loss ◆ **tourner** ~ *[projet, débat]* to come to a sudden end; → **pendre**

◆ **à court de** short of ◆ **être à** ~ **d'argent/d'arguments** to be short of money/arguments ◆ **être à** ~ **d'idées** to be short of ideas

◆ **tout court** ◆ **appelez-moi Bob tout** ~ just call me Bob ◆ **ils veulent l'indépendance tout** ~ they want independence, nothing more and nothing less ◆ **il n'est pas un peu hypocrite, il est hypocrite tout** ~ he's not just a bit of a hypocrite - he's a hypocrite full stop *(Brit) ou* he's a hypocrite, period *(US)*

court[2] /kuʀ/ NM *(Sport)* (tennis) court ◆ ~ **central** centre court

courtage /kuʀtaʒ/ NM *(= métier)* brokerage; *(= commission)* commission ◆ **vendre par** ~ to sell through a broker; *[+ livres]* to sell door to door ◆ **maison** *ou* **société de** ~ brokerage company; → **vente**

courtaud, e /kuʀto, od/ ADJ [1] *[personne]* dumpy, squat [2] ◆ **(chien/cheval)** ~ docked and crop-eared dog/horse

court-bouillon (pl **courts-bouillons**) /kuʀbujɔ̃/ NM *(Culin)* court-bouillon ◆ **faire cuire qch au** ~ to cook sth in a court-bouillon

court-circuit (pl **courts-circuits**) /kuʀsiʀkɥi/ NM *(Élec)* short(-circuit)

court-circuitage* (pl **court-circuitages**) /kuʀsiʀkɥitaʒ/ NM *[de personne, service]* bypassing

court-circuiter /kuʀsiʀkɥite/ ► conjug 1 ◄ VT *(Élec)* to short(-circuit); *[+ personne]* to bypass, to go over the head of; *[+ service]* to bypass

courtepointe /kuʀtəpwɛ̃t/ NF counterpane

courtier, -ière /kuʀtje, jɛʀ/ NM,F broker ◆ ~ **d'assurances** *ou* **en assurances** insurance broker ◆ ~ **en vins** wine broker ◆ ~ **maritime** ship broker

courtilière /kuʀtiljɛʀ/ NF mole cricket

courtine /kuʀtin/ NF curtain

courtisan /kuʀtizɑ̃/ NM *(Hist)* courtier; *(fig)* sycophant ◆ **des manières de** ~ sycophantic ways

courtisane /kuʀtizan/ NF (*Hist, littér*) courtesan

courtiser /kuʀtize/ ▸ conjug 1 ◂ VT († *ou littér*) [*+ femme*] to woo, to court, to pay court to; (*= flatter*) to pay court to, to fawn on (*péj*)

court-jus* (pl **courts-jus**) /kuʀʒy/ NM short(-circuit)

court-métrage (pl **courts-métrages**) /kuʀmetʀaʒ/ NM → **métrage**

courtois, e /kuʀtwa, waz/ ADJ courteous; (*Littérat*) courtly

courtoisement /kuʀtwazmɑ̃/ ADV courteously

courtoisie /kuʀtwazi/ NF courtesy, courteousness ◆ **~ internationale** (*Jur*) comity of nations

court-vêtu, e (mpl **court-vêtus**) /kuʀvety/ ADJ wearing a short skirt *ou* dress

couru, e /kuʀy/ (ptp de **courir**) ADJ 1 [*restaurant, spectacle*] popular ◆ **ce festival est moins ~ que l'autre** this festival is less popular *ou* draws less of a crowd than the other one 2 ◆ **c'est ~ (d'avance)*** it's a foregone conclusion, it's a sure thing*, it's a (dead) cert* (*Brit*)

couscous /kuskus/ NM (*= plat*) couscous

couscoussier /kuskusje/ NM couscous-maker

cousette † /kuzɛt/ NF (*= ouvrière*) dressmaker's apprentice; (*= nécessaire*) sewing kit

cousin[1], e /kuzɛ̃, in/ NM,F cousin ◆ **~ germain** first cousin ◆ **~s issus de germains** second cousins ◆ **~s au 3e/4e degré** 3rd/4th cousins ◆ **ils sont un peu ~s** they are related (in some way) *ou* are distant relations; → **mode[1], petit, roi**

cousin[2] /kuzɛ̃/ NM (*= insecte*) cranefly, daddy longlegs (*Brit*)

cousinage † /kuzinaʒ/ NM (*entre germains*) cousinhood, cousinship; (*= vague parenté*) relationship

cousiner † /kuzine/ ▸ conjug 1 ◂ VI to be on familiar terms (*avec* with)

coussin /kusɛ̃/ NM [*de siège*] cushion; (*Tech*) [*de collier de cheval*] padding; (*Belg, Helv = oreiller*) pillow ◆ **~ d'air** air cushion

coussinet /kusinɛ/ NM 1 [*de siège, genoux*] (small) cushion; [*d'animal*] pad 2 (*Tech*) bearing ◆ **~ de tête de bielle** [*d'arbre de transmission*] big end bearing; [*de rail*] chair 3 (*Archit*) (volute) cushion

cousu, e /kuzy/ (ptp de **coudre**) ADJ sewn, stitched ◆ **être (tout) ~ d'or** (*fig*) to be extremely wealthy ◆ **c'est ~ de fil blanc** (*fig*) it's a blatant lie ◆ **~ main** (*lit*) handsewn, handstitched ◆ **c'est du ~ main*** (*fig*) it's top quality stuff ◆ **~ machine** machine-sewn; → **bouche, motus**

coût /ku/ NM (*lit, fig*) cost ◆ **le ~ de la vie** the cost of living ◆ **~ d'acquisition** original cost ◆ **~s de base** baseline costs ◆ **~ du crédit** credit charges ◆ **~ de distribution** distribution cost ◆ **~ d'investissement** capital cost ◆ **~ de production** production cost ◆ **~ salarial** wage(s) bill ◆ **~ d'utilisation** cost-in-use → **indice**

coûtant /kutɑ̃/ ADJ M ◆ **prix ~** cost price ◆ **vendre à prix ~** to sell at cost (price)

couteau (pl **couteaux**) /kuto/ NM 1 (*pour couper*) knife; [*de balance*] knife edge; (*= coquillage*) razor-shell (*Brit*), razor clam (*US*) ◆ **~ à beurre/dessert/fromage** butter/dessert/cheese knife ◆ **~ à pamplemousse/poisson/huîtres** grapefruit/fish/oyster knife ◆ **des frites (coupées) au ~** hand-cut chips ◆ **tartare (coupé) au ~** hand-chopped steak tartare; → **lame**

2 (*locutions*) **vous me mettez le ~ sous** *ou* **sur la gorge** you're holding a gun to my head ◆ **être à ~(x) tiré(s)** to be at daggers drawn (*avec* with); ◆ **remuer** *ou* **retourner le ~ dans la plaie** to twist the knife in the wound, to rub it in* ◆ **second ~** (*fig*) minor figure ◆ **ce ne sont que des seconds ~x** they're only the small fry

COMP **couteau de boucher** butcher's knife
couteau de chasse hunting knife
couteau de cuisine kitchen knife
couteau à découper carving knife
couteau à désosser boning knife
couteau électrique electric carving knife
couteau à éplucher, couteau à légumes (potato) peeler
couteau à pain breadknife
couteau à palette *ou* **de peintre** (*Art*) palette knife
couteau suisse Swiss army knife
couteau de table table knife; → **cran**

couteau-scie (pl **couteaux-scies**) /kutosi/ NM serrated knife

coutelas /kutlɑ/ NM (*= couteau*) large (kitchen) knife; (*= épée*) cutlass

coutelier, -ière /kutəlje, jɛʀ/ NM,F (*= fabricant, marchand*) cutler

coutellerie /kutɛlʀi/ NF (*= industrie*) cutlery industry; (*= atelier*) cutlery works; (*= magasin*) cutlery shop, cutler's (shop); (*= produits*) cutlery

coûter /kute/ ▸ conjug 1 ◂ VTI 1 (*financièrement*) to cost ◆ **combien ça coûte ?** how much is it?, how much does it cost? ◆ **ça coûte cher ?** is it expensive?, does it cost a lot? ◆ **ça m'a coûté 25 €** it cost me €25 ◆ **les vacances, ça coûte !*** holidays (*Brit*) *ou* vacations (*US*) are expensive *ou* cost a lot! ◆ **ça coûte une fortune** *ou* **les yeux de la tête*** it costs a fortune *ou* the earth* ◆ **ça coûte bonbon*** *ou* **la peau des fesses*** it costs an arm and a leg* ◆ **ça va lui ~ cher** (*lit*) it'll cost him a lot; [*erreur, impertinence*] he'll pay for that, it will cost him dear(ly) ◆ **ça coûtera ce que ça coûtera*** never mind the expense *ou* cost, hang the expense*

2 (*= être pénible*) ◆ **cette démarche me coûte** this is a painful step for me (to take) ◆ **il m'en coûte de refuser** it pains *ou* grieves me to have to refuse; → **premier**

3 (*= causer, valoir*) ◆ **ça m'a coûté bien des mois de travail** it cost me many months' work ◆ **ça lui a coûté la tête/la vie** it cost him his head/life ◆ **ça ne coûte rien d'essayer** it costs nothing to try ◆ **je sais ce qu'il en coûte** I know what it costs ◆ **tu pourrais le faire, pour ce que ça te coûte !** you could easily do it – it wouldn't make any difference to you *ou* it wouldn't put you to any trouble

◆ **coûte que coûte** at all costs, no matter what ◆ **il faut y arriver coûte que coûte** we must get there at all costs *ou* by hook or by crook

coûteux, -euse /kutø, øz/ ADJ [*objet, erreur*] costly, expensive; [*expérience*] painful ◆ **procédé ~ en temps/énergie** process costly in time/energy

coutil /kuti/ NM [*de vêtements*] drill, twill; [*de matelas*] ticking

coutre /kutʀ/ NM coulter (*Brit*), colter (*US*)

coutume /kutym/ NF 1 (*= usage : gén, Jur*) custom; (*Jur = recueil*) customary 2 (*= habitude*) **avoir ~ de** to be in the habit of ◆ **plus/moins que de ~** more/less than usual ◆ **comme de ~** as usual ◆ **selon sa ~** as is his custom *ou* wont; → **fois**

coutumier, -ière /kutymje, jɛʀ/ ADJ (*gén*) customary, usual; [*loi*] customary ◆ **droit ~** (*= concept*) customary law; (*= lois*) common law ◆ **il est ~ du fait** (*gén péj*) that is what he usually does, that's his usual trick* NM (*Jur*) customary

couture /kutyʀ/ NF 1 (*= action, ouvrage*) sewing; (*= profession*) dressmaking ◆ **faire de la ~** to sew ◆ **veste/robe (haute) ~** designer jacket/dress; → **haut, maison, point[2]** 2 (*= suite de points*) seam ◆ **sans ~(s)** seamless ◆ **faire une ~ à grands points** to tack *ou* baste a seam ◆ **~ apparente** *ou* **sellier** topstitching, overstitching ◆ **~ anglaise/plate** *ou* **rabattue** French/flat seam ◆ **regarder qch/qn sous toutes les ~s** to examine sth/sb from every angle; → **battre** 3 (*= cicatrice*) scar 4 (*= suture*) stitches

couturé, e /kutyʀe/ ADJ [*visage*] scarred

couturier /kutyʀje/ NM 1 (*= personne*) couturier, fashion designer ◆ **grand ~** top designer 2 (*Anat*) **(muscle) ~** sartorial muscle, sartorius

couturière /kutyʀjɛʀ/ NF 1 (*= personne*) dressmaker; (*en atelier*) dressmaker, seamstress † 2 (*Théât*) *rehearsal preceding the full dress rehearsal, when alterations are made to the costumes*

couvain /kuvɛ̃/ NM (*= œufs*) brood; (*= rayon*) brood cells

couvaison /kuvɛzɔ̃/ NF (*= période*) incubation; (*= action*) brooding, sitting

couvée /kuve/ NF [*de poussins*] brood, clutch; [*d'œufs*] clutch; [*d'enfants*] brood; → **naître**

couvent /kuvɑ̃/ NM 1 [*de sœurs*] convent; [*de moines*] monastery ◆ **entrer au ~** to enter a convent 2 (*= internat*) convent (school)

couventine /kuvɑ̃tin/ NF (*= religieuse*) conventual; (*= jeune fille élevée au couvent*) convent schoolgirl

couver /kuve/ ▸ conjug 1 ◂ VT 1 [*+ œufs*] [*poule*] to sit on; [*appareil*] to hatch ◆ **la poule était en train de ~** the hen was sitting on its eggs *ou* was brooding 2 [*+ enfant*] to be overcareful with, to cocoon; [*+ maladie*] to be getting, to be coming down with; [*+ vengeance*] to brew, to plot; [*+ révolte*] to plot ◆ **enfant couvé par sa mère** child cosseted by his mother, child brought up by an overcautious *ou* overprotective mother ◆ **~ qn/qch des yeux** *ou* **du regard** (*tendresse*) to gaze lovingly *ou* devotedly at sb/sth; (*convoitise*) to look covetously *ou* longingly at sb/sth VI [*feu, incendie*] to smoulder; [*haine, passion*] to smoulder, to simmer; [*émeute*] to be brewing; [*complot*] to be hatching ◆ **~ sous la cendre** (*lit*) to smoulder under the embers; [*passion*] to smoulder, to simmer; [*émeute*] to be brewing

couvercle /kuvɛʀkl/ NM [*de casserole, boîte, bocal*] lid; [*d'aérosol*] cap, top; (*qui se visse*) (screw-)cap, (screw-)top; (*Tech*) [*de piston*] cover

couvert, e[1] /kuvɛʀ, ɛʀt/ (ptp de **couvrir**) ADJ 1 (*= habillé*) covered (up) ◆ **il est trop ~ pour la saison** he's dressed too warmly for the time of year ◆ **il est resté ~ dans l'église** he kept his hat on inside the church

2 ◆ **~ de** [*+ boutons, taches*] covered in *ou* with ◆ **pics ~s de neige** snow-covered *ou* snow-clad (*littér*) peaks ◆ **~ de chaume** [*toit, maison*] thatched ◆ **le rosier est ~ de fleurs** the rosebush is a mass of *ou* is covered in flowers

3 (*= voilé*) [*ciel*] overcast ◆ **par temps ~** when the sky is overcast; → **mot**

4 [*rue, cour*] covered; [*piscine, court de tennis*] indoor (*épith*), indoors (*attrib*); → **marché**

5 (*= protégé par un supérieur, une assurance*) covered

6 [*syllabe*] closed

NM 1 (*= couteau, fourchette, cuillère, verre, assiette*) place setting ◆ **une ménagère de 12 ~s** a canteen of 12 place settings ◆ **~s** (*= couteaux, fourchettes, cuillères*) cutlery (*Brit*), flatware (*US*), silverware (*US*) ◆ **j'ai sorti les ~s en argent** I've brought out the silver *ou* the silver cutlery (*Brit*) ◆ **des ~s en plastique** plastic knives and forks

2 (*à table*) **mettre le ~** to lay *ou* set the table ◆ **mettre 4 ~s** to lay *ou* set 4 places, to lay *ou* set the table for 4 ◆ **table de 4 ~s** table laid *ou* set for 4 ◆ **mets un ~ de plus** lay *ou* set another place ◆ **il a toujours son ~ mis chez nous**

there's always a place for him at our table ◆ **remettre le ~** * *(fig)* to do it again; *(sexuellement)* to be at it again * ◆ **le vivre** *ou* **gîte et le ~** board *(Brit)* *ou* food *(US)* and lodging, room *ou* bed *(Brit)* and board

3 *(au restaurant = prix)* cover charge

4 *(= abri)* **sous le ~ d'un chêne** *(littér)* under the shelter of an oak tree ◆ **à ~ de la pluie** sheltered from the rain ◆ **être à ~** *(Mil)* to be under cover ◆ **se mettre à ~** *(Mil)* to get under *ou* take cover; *(fig)* to cover *ou* safeguard o.s.

5 *(= prétexte)* ◆ **sous (le) ~ de** under cover of ◆ **ils l'ont fait sous le ~ de leurs supérieurs** they did it by hiding behind the authority of their superiors ◆ **sous (le) ~ de la plaisanterie** under the guise of a joke ◆ **il a parlé sous le ~ de l'anonymat** he spoke anonymously ◆ **Monsieur le Ministre sous ~ de Monsieur le Recteur** the Minister through the person of the Director of Education ◆ **sous ~ de lutter contre la corruption, ils éliminent les ennemis du parti** under the pretext of fighting corruption, they are getting rid of the enemies of the party

couverte[2] /kuvɛʀt/ **NF** *(= émail)* glaze

couverture /kuvɛʀtyʀ/ **NF** 1 *(= literie)* blanket ◆ **~ de laine/chauffante** wool *ou* woollen/electric blanket ◆ **~ de voyage** travelling rug ◆ **tirer la ~ à soi** *(fig)* *(= s'attribuer tout le succès)* to take (all) the credit; *(= monopoliser la parole)* to hog the stage

2 *(= toiture)* roofing ◆ **~ de chaume** thatch, thatched roof ◆ **~ en tuiles** tiles, tiled roof

3 *[de cahier, livre]* cover; *(= jaquette)* dust cover ◆ **en ~** on the cover ◆ **première/quatrième de ~** (outside) front/back cover

4 *(Mil)* cover; *(= prétexte)* cover ◆ **troupes de ~** covering troops ◆ **~ aérienne** aerial cover

5 *(Fin)* cover, margin ◆ **~ sociale** social security cover *ou* coverage ◆ **~ médicale** medical *ou* health cover(age) ◆ **~ des risques** risk insurance coverage

6 *(Journalisme)* coverage ◆ **assurer la ~ d'un événement** to provide coverage of an event ◆ **~ médiatique** media coverage

7 *(Police)* **servir de ~ à qn** to cover sb

couveuse /kuvøz/ **NF** 1 *(= poule)* broody hen ◆ **~ (artificielle)** incubator 2 *[de bébé]* incubator ◆ **être en ~** to be in an incubator

couvrant, e /kuvʀɑ̃, ɑ̃t/ **ADJ** *[peinture, fond de teint]* that covers well **NF couvrante** * blanket, cover

couvre-chef (pl **couvre-chefs**) /kuvʀəʃɛf/ **NM** *(hum)* hat, headgear *(NonC)* *(hum)*

couvre-feu (pl **couvre-feux**) /kuvʀəfø/ **NM** curfew

couvre-lit (pl **couvre-lits**) /kuvʀəli/ **NM** bedspread, coverlet

couvre-livre (pl **couvre-livres**) /kuvʀəlivʀ/ **NM** book cover *ou* jacket

couvre-pied(s) (pl **couvre-pieds**) /kuvʀəpje/ **NM** quilt

couvre-plat (pl **couvre-plats**) /kuvʀəpla/ **NM** dish cover

couvre-théière (pl **couvre-théières**) /kuvʀətejɛʀ/ **NM** tea cosy

couvreur /kuvʀœʀ/ **NM** roofer

couvrir /kuvʀiʀ/ ▸ conjug 18 ◂ **VT** 1 *(gén)* *[+ livre, sol, chargement]* to cover *(de, avec* with); *[+ récipient]* to cover *(de, avec* with) to put the lid on; *(Jeux)* *[+ carte]* to cover ◆ **~ un toit d'ardoises/de chaume/de tuiles** to slate/thatch/tile a roof ◆ **des tableaux couvraient tout un mur** one whole wall was covered in pictures ◆ **~ le feu** to bank up the fire

2 *(= habiller)* to cover ◆ **couvre bien les enfants** wrap *ou* cover the children up well ◆ **un châle lui couvrait les épaules** she had a shawl around her shoulders

3 *(fig)* **~ qch/qn de** to cover sth/sb with *ou* in ◆ **couvert de bleus** bruised all over, covered in *ou* with bruises ◆ **~ qn de cadeaux** to shower sb with gifts, to shower gifts (up)on sb ◆ **~ qn de caresses/baisers** to cover *ou* shower sb with caresses/kisses ◆ **~ qn d'injures/d'éloges** to shower sb with insults/praise, to heap insults/praise on sb ◆ **cette aventure l'a couvert de ridicule** this affair has covered him with ridicule; → **boue**

4 *(= masquer)* *[+ son, voix]* to drown (out); *[+ énigme]* to conceal ◆ **le bruit de la rue couvrait la voix du conférencier** the noise from the street drowned (out) the lecturer's voice ◆ **~ son jeu** *(lit, fig)* to hold *ou* keep one's cards close to one's chest

5 *(= protéger)* to cover ◆ **~ qn de son corps** to cover *ou* shield sb with one's body ◆ **~ sa retraite** *(Mil)* to cover one's retreat ◆ **~ qn** *(fig)* to cover up for *ou* shield sb ◆ **couvre-moi !** *(lors d'une fusillade)* cover me! ◆ **~ une erreur** to cover up a mistake

6 *[+ frais, dépenses]* to cover; *[assurance]* to cover ◆ **pourriez-vous nous ~ de la somme de 100 € ?** *(Admin)* would you remit to us the sum of €100 ? ◆ **~ l'enchère de qn** to make a higher bid than sb

7 *(= parcourir)* *[+ kilomètres, distance]* to cover

8 *[+ animal femelle]* to cover

9 *(Journalisme)* *[+ événement]* to cover

VPR se couvrir 1 *(locution)*

◆ **se couvrir de** ◆ **se ~ de fleurs/feuilles** to come into bloom/leaf ◆ **les prés se couvrent de fleurs** the meadows are becoming a mass of flowers ◆ **se ~ de taches** to get covered with splashes ◆ **se ~ de boutons** to become covered in *ou* with spots ◆ **se ~ de gloire** to cover o.s. with glory ◆ **se ~ de honte/ridicule** to bring shame/ridicule upon o.s., to cover o.s. with shame/ridicule

2 *(= s'habiller)* to cover up, to wrap up; *(= mettre son chapeau)* to put on one's hat ◆ **il fait froid, couvrez-vous bien** it's cold so wrap *ou* cover (yourself) up well

3 *[ciel]* to become overcast, to cloud over ◆ **le temps se couvre** it's clouding over, the sky is *ou* it's becoming (very) overcast

4 *(Boxe, Escrime)* to cover o.s. ◆ **pour se ~** *(fig)* to cover *ou* shield himself

covalence /kovalɑ̃s/ **NF** *(Chim)* covalency, covalence *(US)* ◆ **liaison de ~** covalent bond

covalent, e /kovalɑ̃, ɑ̃t/ **ADJ** *(Chim)* covalent

cover-girl (pl **cover-girls**) /kɔvœʀgœʀl/ **NF** cover girl

covoiturage /kovwatyʀaʒ/ **NM** car sharing

cow-boy (pl **cow-boys**) /kobɔj/ **NM** cowboy ◆ **jouer aux ~s et aux Indiens** to play (at) cowboys and Indians

coxalgie /kɔksalʒi/ **NF** coxalgia

coyote /kɔjɔt/ **NM** *(= animal)* coyote

CP /sepe/ **NM** (abrév de **cours préparatoire**) → **cours**

CPAM /sepeaɛm/ **NF** (abrév de **caisse primaire d'assurance maladie**) → **caisse**

CQFD /sekyɛfde/ (abrév de **ce qu'il fallait démontrer**) QED

crabe /kʀɑb/ **NM** 1 *(= crustacé)* crab ◆ **marcher en ~** to walk crabwise *ou* crabways; → **panier** 2 *(= véhicule)* caterpillar-tracked vehicle

crac /kʀak/ **EXCL** *[de bois, glace]* crack; *[d'étoffe]* rip

crachat /kʀaʃa/ **NM** 1 *(gén)* spit *(NonC)*, spittle *(NonC)* ◆ **il a reçu un ~ dans la figure** someone spat in his face 2 († * = *plaque, insigne)* decoration

craché, e * /kʀaʃe/ (ptp de **cracher**) **ADJ** ◆ **c'est son père tout ~** he's the spitting image of his father ◆ **c'est lui tout ~** that's just like him, that's him all over *

crachement /kʀaʃmɑ̃/ **NM** 1 *(= expectoration)* spitting *(NonC)* ◆ **~ de sang** spitting of blood ◆ **~s de sang** spasms of spitting blood *ou* of blood-spitting 2 *(= projection)* *[de flammes, vapeur]* burst; *[d'étincelles]* shower 3 *(= bruit)* *[de radio, mitrailleuses]* crackling *(NonC)*, crackle

cracher /kʀaʃe/ ▸ conjug 1 ◂ **VI** 1 *(avec la bouche)* to spit ◆ **rincez-vous la bouche et crachez** rinse your mouth and spit it out ◆ **~ sur qn** *(lit)* to spit at sb; *(fig)* to spit on sb ◆ **il ne crache pas sur le caviar** * he doesn't turn his nose up at caviar ◆ **il ne faut pas ~ sur cette offre** * this offer is not to be sneezed at ◆ **il ne faut pas ~ dans la soupe** * don't bite the hand that feeds you ◆ **c'est comme si je crachais en l'air** * I might as well be whistling in the wind ◆ **~ au bassinet** * to cough up *

2 *[stylo, plume]* to splutter, to splotch; *[micro]* to crackle

VT 1 *[personne]* *[+ sang]* to spit; *[+ bouchée]* to spit out; *[+ injures]* to spit (out); ⁑ *[+ argent]* to cough up *, to stump up * *(Brit)* ◆ **~ ses poumons** ⁑ to cough up one's lungs ⁑; → **venin**

2 *[canon]* *[+ flammes]* to spit (out); *[+ projectiles]* to spit out; *[cheminée, volcan, dragon]* to belch (out) ◆ **le moteur crachait des étincelles** the engine was sending out showers of sparks ◆ **le tuyau crachait une eau brunâtre** the pipe was spitting out dirty brown water

cracheur, -euse /kʀaʃœʀ, øz/ **NM,F** ◆ **~ de feu** *ou* **de flammes** fire-eater

crachin /kʀaʃɛ̃/ **NM** drizzle

crachiner /kʀaʃine/ ▸ conjug 1 ◂ **VB IMPERS** to drizzle

crachoir /kʀaʃwaʀ/ **NM** spittoon, cuspidor *(US)* ◆ **tenir le ~** * to hold the floor ◆ **j'ai tenu le ~ à ma vieille tante tout l'après-midi** I had to sit and listen to my old aunt spouting all afternoon *

crachotement /kʀaʃɔtmɑ̃/ **NM** *[de haut-parleur, téléphone, radio]* crackling *(NonC)*, crackle; *[de robinet]* spluttering *(NonC)*

crachoter /kʀaʃɔte/ ▸ conjug 1 ◂ **VI** *[haut-parleur, téléphone, radio]* to crackle; *[robinet]* to splutter

crachouiller /kʀaʃuje/ ▸ conjug 1 ◂ **VI** *[personne]* to splutter

crack[1] /kʀak/ **NM** 1 *(= poulain)* crack *ou* star horse 2 *(* = as)* ace ◆ **un ~ en informatique** an ace *ou* a wizard * at computing ◆ **c'est un ~ au saut en longueur** he's a first-class long jumper

crack[2] /kʀak/ **NM** *(Drogue)* crack (cocaine)

cracking /kʀakiŋ/ **NM** *(Chim)* cracking

Cracovie /kʀakɔvi/ **N** Cracow

cracra ⁑ /kʀakʀa/ **ADJ INV**, **crade** ⁑ /kʀad/, **cradingue** ⁑ /kʀadɛ̃g/, **crado** ⁑ /kʀado/, **cradoque** ⁑ /kʀadɔk/ **ADJ** *[personne, vêtement]* dirty, scuzzy ⁑; *[endroit, meuble]* dirty, grotty * *(Brit)*; *[blague, remarque]* dirty

craie /kʀɛ/ **NF** *(= substance, bâtonnet)* chalk ◆ **~ de tailleur** tailor's chalk, French chalk ◆ **écrire qch à la ~ sur un mur** to chalk sth up on a wall

craignos ⁑ /kʀɛɲos/ **ADJ INV** *[personne, quartier]* shady *, dodgy * *(Brit)* ◆ **il est vraiment ~ ce type** he's a really freaky guy *

craindre /kʀɛ̃dʀ/ ▸ conjug 52 ◂ **VT** 1 *(= avoir peur)* *[personne]* to fear, to be afraid *ou* scared of ◆ **je ne crains pas la mort/la douleur** I'm not afraid of dying/pain ◆ **ne craignez rien** don't be afraid *ou* frightened ◆ **oui, je le crains !** yes, I'm afraid so! ◆ **je crains le pire** I fear the worst ◆ **il voulait se faire ~** he wanted to be feared

◆ **craindre de faire qch** to be afraid of doing sth ◆ **il craint de se faire mal** he's afraid of hurting himself ◆ **je ne crains pas de dire** que … I am not afraid of saying that … ◆ **je crains d'avoir bientôt à partir** I'm afraid *ou* I fear I may have to leave soon ◆ **craignant de manquer le train** afraid of missing *ou* afraid (that) he might miss the train

♦ **craindre que** to be afraid that, to fear that ◆ **je crains qu'il (n')attrape froid** I'm afraid (that) he might catch cold ◆ **ne craignez-vous pas qu'il arrive ?** aren't you afraid he'll come? *ou* he might come? ◆ **je crains qu'il (ne) se soit perdu** I'm afraid that he might *ou* may have got lost ◆ **il est à ~ que …** it is to be feared that … ◆ **je crains que vous ne vous trompiez** I fear you are mistaken

♦ **craindre pour** *[+ vie, réputation, personne]* to fear for ◆ **je crains pour mon emploi** I'm afraid I might lose my job

② *(= ne pas supporter)* ~ **le froid** to be easily damaged by (the) cold ◆ **"craint l'humidité/la chaleur"** "keep *ou* store in a dry place/cool place", "do not expose to a damp atmosphere/to heat" ◆ **vêtement qui ne craint rien** hard-wearing *ou* sturdy garment ◆ **c'est un vieux tapis, ça ne craint rien** don't worry, it's an old carpet ◆ **ces animaux craignent la chaleur** these animals can't stand the heat

VI ‡ ◆ **il craint, ce type** that guy's really creepy* ◆ **ça craint dans ce quartier** *(louche)* this is a really shady* *ou* dodgy *(Brit)** area; *(dangereux)* this is a really dangerous area ◆ **ça craint, leur émission** that programme's the pits‡ ◆ **s'il est élu, ça craint pour la démocratie** if he gets elected, it'll be a bad day for democracy

crainte /kʀɛ̃t/ GRAMMAIRE ACTIVE 44.1 NF ① *(= peur)* fear ◆ **la ~ de la maladie** *ou* **d'être malade l'arrête** fear of illness *ou* of being ill stops him ◆ **soyez sans ~, n'ayez ~** have no fear, never fear ◆ **j'ai des ~s à son sujet** I'm worried about him ◆ **sans ~** *[personne]* fearless; *[affronter, parler]* without fear, fearlessly ◆ **avec ~** fearfully ◆ **la ~ qu'on ne les entende** the fear that they might be overheard ◆ **la ~ est le commencement de la sagesse** *(Prov)* only the fool knows no fear

② *(locutions)* **dans la ~ de, par ~ de** for fear of ◆ **de ~ d'une erreur** for fear of (there being) a mistake, lest there be a mistake *(frm)* ◆ **(par) ~ d'être suivi, il courut** he ran for fear of being followed *ou* fearing that he might be followed ◆ **de ~ que …** for fear that …, fearing that … ◆ **de ~ qu'on ne le suive, il courut** he ran for fear of being followed *ou* fearing that he might be followed

craintif, -ive /kʀɛ̃tif, iv/ ADJ timid

craintivement /kʀɛ̃tivmɑ̃/ ADV timidly

cramé, e‡ /kʀame/ ADJ ① *(= brûlé)* burnt, burned *(US)* ② *(= saoul)* pissed‡; *(= drogué)* stoned‡ NM ◆ **ça sent le ~** *(lit)* I (can) smell burning; *(fig)* there's trouble brewing ◆ **ça a un goût de ~** it tastes burnt ◆ **ne mange pas le ~** don't eat the burnt bit(s)

cramer‡ /kʀame/ ▸ conjug 1 ◂ VI *[maison]* to burn down, to go up in flames; *[mobilier]* to go up in flames *ou* smoke; *[tissu, papier]* to burn ◆ **ça crame !** *(= il fait chaud)* it's roasting!* VT *(gén)* to burn; *[+ maison]* to burn down

cramoisi, e /kʀamwazi/ ADJ crimson

crampe /kʀɑ̃p/ NF cramp ◆ **avoir une ~ au mollet** to have cramp *(Brit)* *ou* a cramp *(US)* in one's calf ◆ **~ d'estomac** stomach cramp ◆ **la ~ de l'écrivain** *(hum)* writer's cramp *(hum)*

crampon /kʀɑ̃pɔ̃/ NM ① *(= outil)* cramp (iron), clamp ② *[de chaussures de rugby]* stud; *[de chaussures de course]* spike; *[de fer à cheval]* calk ◆ **~ (à glace)** *[d'alpiniste]* crampon ③ *(Bot)* tendril ④ *(* = personne)* leech ◆ **elle est ~** she clings like a leech, you can't shake her off

cramponnage /kʀɑ̃pɔnaʒ/ NM *(Alpinisme)* crampon technique, cramponning

cramponner /kʀɑ̃pɔne/ ▸ conjug 1 ◂ VT ① *(= fixer)* to cramp (together), to clamp (together) ② *(* fig)* to cling to VPR **se cramponner** *(pour ne pas tomber)* to hold on, to hang on; *(dans son travail)* to stick at it* ◆ **elle se cramponne** *(= ne vous lâche pas)* she clings like a leech, you can't shake her off; *(= ne veut pas mourir)* she's hanging on (to life) ◆ **se ~ à** *[+ branche, volant, bras]* to cling (on) to, to clutch, to hold on to; *[+ personne] (lit)* to cling (on) to; *(fig) [+ vie, espoir, personne]* to cling to

cran /kʀɑ̃/ NM ① *(pour accrocher, retenir) [de pièce dentée, crémaillère]* notch; *[d'arme à feu]* catch; *[de ceinture, courroie]* hole ◆ **hausser un rayon de plusieurs ~s** to raise a shelf a few notches *ou* holes ◆ **~ de sécurité** *ou* **de sûreté** safety catch ◆ **(couteau à) ~ d'arrêt** flick-knife

② *(Couture, Typo : servant de repère)* nick ◆ **~ de mire** bead

③ *[de cheveux]* wave ◆ **le coiffeur lui avait fait un ~** *ou* **des ~s** the hairdresser had put her hair in waves

④ *(* = courage)* guts* ◆ **elle a un drôle de ~*** she's got a lot of guts* *ou* bottle‡ *(Brit)* ◆ **il faut un sacré ~ pour oser dire ça** it takes a lot of guts* to say something like that

⑤ *(locutions)* **monter/descendre d'un ~** *(dans la hiérarchie)* to move up/come down a rung *ou* peg ◆ **elle est monté/descendu d'un ~ dans mon estime** she's gone up/down a notch *ou* peg in my estimation ◆ **être à ~** to be very edgy ◆ **ne le mets pas à ~** don't make him mad*

crâne[1] /kʀɑn/ NM *(Anat)* skull, cranium *(SPÉC)*; *(fig)* head ◆ **avoir mal au ~*** to have a splitting headache ◆ **avoir le ~ dur*** *(fig)* to be thick(skulled)* ◆ **il n'a rien dans le ~** he's really thick* ◆ **~ d'œuf*** *(= chauve)* bald man, baldy*; *(= intellectuel)* egghead; → **bourrage, bourrer, fracture**

crâne[2] † /kʀɑn/ ADJ gallant

crânement † /kʀɑnmɑ̃/ ADV gallantly

crâner* /kʀɑne/ ▸ conjug 1 ◂ VI to swank*, to show off*, to put on the dog* *(US)* ◆ **ce n'est pas la peine de ~** it's nothing to swank* *ou* show off* about

crânerie † /kʀɑnʀi/ NF gallantry

crâneur, -euse* /kʀɑnœʀ, øz/ NM,F swank*, show-off* ◆ **faire le** *ou* **son ~** to swank* *ou* show off* ◆ **elle est un peu crâneuse** she's a bit of a show-off*

crânien, -ienne /kʀɑnjɛ̃, jɛn/ ADJ cranial; → **boîte**

craniologie /kʀanjɔlɔʒi/ NF craniology

cranter /kʀɑ̃te/ ▸ conjug 1 ◂ VT *[+ pignon, roue]* to put notches in ◆ **~ ses cheveux** to put one's hair in waves ◆ **tige crantée** notched stem

crapahuter /kʀapayte/ ▸ conjug 1 ◂ VI ① *(arg Mil)* to yomp ◆ **on a crapahuté dans la montagne toute la journée** we trekked in the mountains all day ② * *(= faire l'amour)* to bonk‡

crapaud /kʀapo/ NM ① *(= animal)* toad ◆ **quel ~ ce type !** *(= très laid)* he's as ugly as sin!; → **bave, fauteuil, laid, piano**[1] ② * *(= gamin)* brat* ③ *[de diamant]* flaw

crapaud-buffle (pl **crapauds-buffles**) /kʀapobyfl/ NM buffalo frog

crapaudine /kʀapodin/ NF *[de tuyau]* grating; *[de gond]* gudgeon; *(= pierre)* toadstone

crapoter* /kʀapɔte/ ▸ conjug 1 ◂ VI *[fumeur]* ◆ **il crapote** he doesn't inhale

crapoteux, -euse* /kʀapɔtø, øz/ ADJ *[lieu]* murky, gloomy; *[personne]* grimy-looking

crapouillot /kʀapujo/ NM *(Hist Mil)* trench mortar

crapule /kʀapyl/ NF *(= escroc)* crook; *(†† = racaille)* riffraff, scum* ◆ **petite ~ !** *(à un enfant = coquin)* you little rascal!

crapulerie /kʀapylʀi/ NF ① *(= caractère)* villainy ② *(= acte)* villainy

crapuleux, -euse /kʀapylø, øz/ ADJ *[action]* villainous; *[vie]* dissolute; → **crime**

> ⚠ **crapuleux** ne se traduit pas par **crapulous**, qui a le sens de 'ivre'.

craquage /kʀakaʒ/ NM *(Chim)* cracking

craquant, e* /kʀakɑ̃, ɑ̃t/ ADJ *[biscuit]* crunchy; *(* = séduisant) [objet, personne]* gorgeous, lovely

craque‡ † /kʀak/ NF whopper‡, whopping lie* ◆ **tu m'as raconté des ~s** you've been trying to put one over on me

craquelé, e /kʀakle/ (ptp de **craqueler**) ADJ *[terre, chemin]* covered with cracks; *[glace, peinture, cuir]* cracked; *[objet en faïence]* crackled ◆ **des chaussures toutes ~es** cracked leather shoes

craqueler /kʀakle/ ▸ conjug 4 ◂ VT *[+ vernis, faïence, terre] [usure, âge]* to crack; *[artisan]* to crackle VPR **se craqueler** *[vernis, faïence, terre]* to crack

craquelure /kʀaklyʀ/ NF *(accidentelle)* crack ◆ **~s** *(volontaires) [de porcelaine, verre]* crackle (NonC); *[de tableau]* craquelure (NonC) *(SPÉC)* ◆ **couvert de ~s** covered in cracks

craquement /kʀakmɑ̃/ NM *(= bruit) [d'arbre, branche qui se rompt]* crack, snap; *[de plancher, boiserie]* creak; *[de feuilles sèches, neige]* crackle, crunch; *[de chaussures]* squeak ◆ **le ~ continuel des arbres/de la banquise** the constant creak of the trees/icefield

craquer /kʀake/ ▸ conjug 1 ◂ VI ① *(= produire un bruit) [parquet]* to creak, to squeak; *[feuilles mortes, disque]* to crackle; *[neige]* to crunch; *[chaussures]* to squeak; *[biscuit]* to crunch ◆ **faire ~ ses doigts** to crack one's fingers ◆ **faire ~ une allumette** to strike a match

② *(= céder) [bas]* to rip, to go* *(Brit)*; *[bois, couche de glace]* to crack; *[branche]* to crack, to snap ◆ **veste qui craque aux coutures** jacket which is coming apart at the seams; → **plein**

③ *(= s'écrouler) [entreprise, gouvernement]* to be falling apart (at the seams), to be on the verge of collapse; *[athlète]* to collapse; *[accusé, malade]* to break down, to collapse ◆ **ils ont craqué en deuxième mi-temps** they gave way in the second half ◆ **je craque*** *(= je n'en peux plus)* I've had enough; *(= je deviens fou)* I'm cracking up*; → **nerf**

④ *(* = être séduit)* **j'ai craqué** I couldn't resist it ◆ **j'ai craqué pour** *ou* **sur lui dès notre première rencontre** I fell for him the first time we met ◆ **il est à ~ !** he's irresistible!

VT ① *[+ pantalon]* to rip, to split ◆ **~ un bas*** to rip *ou* tear a stocking

② *[+ allumette]* to strike

③ *[+ produit pétrolier]* to crack

④ *[+ ordinateur]* to crack

crash* /kʀaʃ/ NM crash

crasher (se)* /kʀaʃe/ ▸ conjug 1 ◂ VPR *[voiture, train]* to crash; *[chauffeur, motard]* to have a crash; *[avion] (= s'écraser)* to crash; *(= atterrir)* to crash-land ◆ **il s'est crashé contre un arbre** he crashed into *ou* hit a tree ◆ **se ~ en moto/voiture** to crash one's motorbike/car

crassane /kʀasan/ NF ⇒ **passe-crassane**

crasse /kʀas/ NF ① *(= saleté)* grime, filth ② *(* = sale tour)* dirty trick* ◆ **faire une ~ à qn** to play a dirty trick on sb*, to do the dirty on sb* ③ *(Tech) (= scorie)* dross, scum, slag; *(= résidus)* scale ADJ *[ignorance, bêtise]* crass; *[paresse]* unashamed ◆ **être d'une ignorance ~** to be abysmally ignorant *ou* pig ignorant‡

crasseux, -euse /kʀasø, øz/ ADJ grimy, filthy

crassier /kʀasje/ NM slag heap

cratère /kʀatɛʀ/ NM crater

cravache /kʀavaʃ/ NF (riding) crop, quirt *(US)* ◆ **mener qn à la ~** to drive sb ruthlessly

cravacher /kʀavaʃe/ ► conjug 1 ◄ VT *[+ cheval]* to use the crop on, to whip, to quirt *(US)*; *[+ personne]* to strike with a riding crop; *(= rouer de coups)* to horsewhip VI *(* = foncer)* to belt along*; *(pour finir un travail)* to work like mad*, to pull out all the stops*

cravate /kʀavat/ NF 1 *[de chemise]* tie ◆ **~ de chanvre** *(hum)* hangman's rope ◆ **~ de commandeur de la Légion d'honneur** ribbon of commander of the Legion of Honour; → **épingle, jeter** 2 *(Lutte)* headlock; *(Rugby)* clothesline tackle 3 *(Naut)* sling

cravater /kʀavate/ ► conjug 1 ◄ VT 1 *(lit) [+ personne]* to put a tie on ◆ **cravaté de neuf** wearing a new tie ◆ **se ~** to put one's *ou* a tie on 2 *(= prendre au collet) (gén)* to grab round the neck; *(Lutte)* to put in a headlock; *(Rugby)* to do a high tackle on ◆ **se faire ~ par un journaliste** to be collared* *ou* buttonholed* by a journalist

crawl /kʀol/ NM *(= nage)* crawl ◆ **nager le ~** to do *ou* swim the crawl

crawler /kʀole/ ► conjug 1 ◄ VI to do *ou* swim the crawl ◆ **dos crawlé** backstroke

crayeux, -euse /kʀɛjø, øz/ ADJ *[terrain, substance]* chalky; *[teint]* chalk-white

crayon /kʀɛjɔ̃/ NM 1 *(pour écrire)* pencil ◆ **écrire au ~** to write with a pencil ◆ **écrivez cela au ~** write that in pencil ◆ **notes au ~** pencilled notes ◆ **avoir le ~ facile** to be good at drawing ◆ **coup de ~** pencil stroke ◆ **avoir un bon coup de ~** to be good at sketching

2 *(= bâtonnet)* pencil

3 *(Art) (= matière)* crayon; *(= dessin)* crayon (drawing) ◆ **colorier qch au ~** to crayon sth

COMP **crayon contour des lèvres** ⇒ **crayon à lèvres**
crayon contour des yeux ⇒ **crayon pour les yeux**
crayon de couleur crayon
crayon feutre felt-tip pen
crayon gomme pencil with rubber *(Brit) ou* eraser *(US)*
crayon gras soft lead pencil
crayon hémostatique styptic pencil
crayon khôl eyeliner (pencil)
crayon à lèvres lip pencil
crayon lithographique litho pen
crayon au nitrate d'argent silver-nitrate pencil, caustic pencil
crayon noir *ou* **à papier** lead pencil
crayon optique light pen
crayon à sourcils eyebrow pencil
crayon pour les yeux eyeliner (pencil)

crayonnage /kʀɛjɔnaʒ/ NM *(= gribouillage)* scribble, doodle; *(= dessin)* (pencil) drawing, sketch

crayonner /kʀɛjɔne/ ► conjug 1 ◄ VT 1 *[+ notes]* to scribble, to jot down (in pencil); *[+ dessin]* to sketch 2 *(péj = gribouiller) [+ traits]* to scribble; *[+ dessins]* to doodle

CRDP /seɛʀdepe/ NM (abrév de **Centre régional de documentation pédagogique**) → **centre**

CRDS /seɛʀdeɛs/ NF (abrév de **contribution au remboursement de la dette sociale**) → **remboursement**

créance /kʀeɑ̃s/ NF 1 *(Fin, Jur)* (financial) claim, debt *(seen from the creditor's point of view)*; *(= titre)* letter of credit ◆ **~ hypothécaire** mortgage loan *(seen from the creditor's point of view)* ◆ **~s** *(Fin)* accounts receivable ◆ **~ irrécouvrable** bad debt; → **lettre** 2 *(† ou littér = crédit, foi)* credence *(frm)* ◆ **donner ~ à qch** *(= rendre croyable)* to lend credibility to sth; *(= ajouter foi à)* to give credence to sth *(frm)*

créancier, -ière /kʀeɑ̃sje, jɛʀ/ NM,F creditor ◆ **~-gagiste** lienor ◆ **~ privilégié** preferential creditor

créateur, -trice /kʀeatœʀ, tʀis/ NM,F 1 *(gén, Rel)* creator ◆ **les ~s d'entreprise** people who set up companies ◆ **le Créateur** the Creator 2 *(= artiste)* designer ◆ **~ (de mode)** fashion designer ◆ **les grands ~s de meubles** the great furniture designers ◆ **~ publicitaire** commercial artist ADJ 1 *(= créatif)* creative 2 *(= générateur)* ◆ **un secteur ~ d'emplois** a sector which generates employment ◆ **cette solution sera créatrice d'emplois** this will help create *ou* generate new jobs

> ⚠ Au sens de 'artiste', **créateur** ne se traduit pas par **creator**.

créatif, -ive /kʀeatif, iv/ ADJ creative NM,F *(Publicité)* designer ◆ **c'est une créative** *(créativité)* she's very creative

créatine /kʀeatin/ NF creatine, creatin

créatinine /kʀeatinin/ NF creatinine

création /kʀeasjɔ̃/ NF 1 *(= invention, conception) [de style, produit]* creation; *(= chose créée)* creation ◆ **ses ~s les plus originales** his most original creations 2 *(= production, fondation) [d'empire, association]* creation, founding; *[de firme]* creation, setting up ◆ **la ~ d'emplois** job creation ◆ **il y a eu 200 ~s d'emplois/de postes** 200 jobs/posts were created ◆ **je travaille dans cette entreprise depuis sa ~** I've worked in this company since it was first set up ◆ **il y a eu plusieurs ~s d'entreprises** several new companies have been created ◆ **la Création** *(Rel)* (the) Creation ◆ **depuis la ~ du monde** since the world began 3 *(Théât) [de pièce]* first production ◆ **depuis la ~ du spectacle** since the show first opened 4 *(Phys)* **théorie de la ~ continue** steady-state theory

créationnisme /kʀeasjɔnism/ NM creationism

créationniste /kʀeasjɔnist/ ADJ creationistic NMF creationist

créativité /kʀeativite/ NF creativeness, creativity; *(Ling)* creativity

créature /kʀeatyʀ/ NF *(gén, péj)* creature

crécelle /kʀesɛl/ NF rattle; → **voix**

crécerelle /kʀes(ə)ʀɛl/ NF kestrel

crèche /kʀɛʃ/ NF 1 *(Rel : de Noël)* nativity scene, crib *(Brit)*, crèche *(US)* ◆ **~ vivante** living nativity (scene) 2 *(= établissement)* crèche, day nursery, day-care centre *(Brit) ou* center *(US)*, child care center *(US)* ◆ **~ familiale** *crèche in the home of a registered child minder* ◆ **~ parentale** *crèche run by parents* ◆ **mettre son bébé à la ~** to put one's baby in a crèche

crécher‡ /kʀeʃe/ ► conjug 6 ◄ VI to hang out* ◆ **je ne sais pas où ~ cette nuit** I don't know where I'm going to crash‡ *ou* kip down‡ *(Brit)* tonight ◆ **je crèche à Paris** *(= j'y habite)* I live in Paris

crédence /kʀedɑ̃s/ NF 1 *(= desserte)* credence 2 *(Rel)* credence table, credenza

crédibiliser /kʀedibilize/ ► conjug 1 ◄ VT *[+ histoire]* to back up, to give credibility to; *[+ candidature, situation financière]* to support ◆ **ceci crédibilise la gauche** this gives credibility to the Left

crédibilité /kʀedibilite/ NF credibility

crédible /kʀedibl/ GRAMMAIRE ACTIVE 53.6 ADJ credible ◆ **peu ~** *[discours, témoin]* unconvincing ◆ **il n'est plus très ~** he's lost his credibility

crédirentier, -ière /kʀediʀɑ̃tje, jɛʀ/ NM,F *recipient of an annuity*

crédit /kʀedi/ NM 1 *(= paiement différé)* credit ◆ **12 mois de ~** 12 months' credit ◆ **faire ~ à qn** to give sb credit ◆ **faites-moi ~, je vous paierai la semaine prochaine** let me have (it on) credit – I'll pay you next week ◆ **"la maison ne fait pas (de) crédit"** "we are unable to give credit to our customers", "no credit is given here" ◆ **"possibilités de crédit"** "credit (terms) available"

◆ **à crédit** ◆ **acheter/vendre qch à ~** to buy/sell sth on credit ◆ **ces gens qui achètent tout à ~** these people who buy everything on credit *ou* on time *(US)*; → **carte**

2 *(= prêt)* loan, credit ◆ **établissement de ~** credit institution ◆ **l'ouverture d'un ~** the granting of credit ◆ **~ à taux préférentiel** preferential credit ◆ **~ à taux fixe/révisable** fixed rate/adjustable rate loan ◆ **accorder/obtenir un ~** to grant/obtain credit ◆ **prendre un ~ sur dix ans** to take out a ten-year loan; → **lettre**

3 *(dans une raison sociale)* bank

4 *(= excédent d'un compte)* credit ◆ **porter une somme au ~ de qn** to credit sb *ou* sb's account with a sum, to credit a sum to sb *ou* sb's account

5 *(Pol : gén pl = fonds)* **~s** funds ◆ **~s publics** public funds ◆ **~s budgétaires** budget allocation ◆ **~s extraordinaires** extraordinary funds ◆ **débloquer un ~ de 35 millions de francs** to release 35 million francs of funding ◆ **les ~s alloués à la défense** the funds allocated to defence, defence funding

6 *(Can Univ = unité de valeur)* credit

7 *(= confiance)* credit; *(= réputation)* reputation ◆ **firme/client qui a du ~** creditworthy firm/client ◆ **jouir d'un très grand ~** to enjoy an excellent reputation ◆ **cette théorie connaît un grand ~** this theory is very widely accepted *(auprès de* by); ◆ **ça donne du ~ à ce qu'il affirme** that lends credibility to what he says ◆ **faire ~ à l'avenir** to put one's trust in the future, to have faith in the future ◆ **bonne action à mettre** *ou* **porter au ~ de qn** good deed which is to sb's credit *ou* which counts in sb's favour ◆ **perdre tout ~ auprès de qn** to lose all credit with sb, to lose sb's confidence ◆ **trouver ~ auprès de qn** *[racontars]* to find credence with sb *(frm)*; *[personne]* to win sb's confidence ◆ **il a utilisé son ~ auprès de lui pour ...** he used his influence with him to ...

COMP **crédit acheteur** buyer credit
crédit d'appoint standby credit
crédit bancaire bank credit
crédit en blanc loan without security
crédit à la consommation consumer credit
crédit documentaire documentary (letter of) credit
crédits d'enseignement *(Admin Scol)* government grant (to each school)
crédit à l'exportation export credit
crédit fournisseur supplier credit
crédit gratuit (interest-)free credit
crédit hypothécaire mortgage
crédit immobilier ≃ mortgage
crédit d'impôt tax credit
crédit municipal state-owned pawnshop *ou* pawnbroker's

crédit-bail (pl **crédits-bails**) /kʀedibaj/ NM *(= système)* leasing; *(= contrat)* lease, leasing agreement *ou* arrangement ◆ **acquérir qch en ~** to buy sth under a leasing agreement *ou* arrangement

créditer /kʀedite/ ► conjug 1 ◄ VT 1 *(Fin)* **~ qn/un compte de** *[+ somme]* to credit sb/an account with 2 *(Pol)* **il est crédité de 43% des voix** *ou* **des suffrages** he is expected to win 43% of the vote 3 *(= complimenter)* **~ qn de qch** to give sb credit for sth

créditeur, -trice /kʀeditœʀ, tʀis/ ADJ *[banque, pays]* creditor *(épith)* ◆ **compte/solde ~** credit account/balance ◆ **leur compte est de nouveau ~** their account is in credit *ou* in the black* again NM,F customer in credit

crédit-relais (pl **crédits-relais**) /kʀediʀ(ə)lɛ/ NM bridging loan

credo /kʀedo/ NM [1] *(Rel)* **le Credo** the (Apostle's) Creed [2] *(= principes)* credo, creed

crédule /kʀedyl/ ADJ credulous, gullible

crédulité /kʀedylite/ NF credulity, gullibility

créer /kʀee/ ▸ conjug 1 ◂ VT [1] *(= inventer, concevoir)* *[+ vêtement, bijou]* to create, to design; *[+ style, produit]* to create; *[+ mot]* to coin, to invent ◆ **il a créé cette histoire de toutes pièces** he made up the story from beginning to end ◆ **la joie de ~** the joy of making things *ou* creating something [2] *(= produire, fonder)* *[+ empire, association]* to create, to found; *[+ entreprise]* to create, to set up, to form; *[+ emplois]* to create ◆ **~ des ennuis/difficultés à qn** to create problems/difficulties for sb, to cause sb problems/difficulties ◆ **~ la surprise** to cause a surprise; → **événement, fonction, précédent** *etc* [3] *(Théât)* *[+ rôle]* to create; *[+ pièce]* to produce (for the first time) VPR **se créer** ◆ **se ~ une clientèle** to build up a clientele ◆ **se ~ des problèmes** to create *ou* make problems for o.s.

crémaillère /kʀemajɛʀ/ NF [1] *(= fête)* housewarming party; → **pendre** [2] *[de cheminée]* trammel [3] *(= mécanisme)* rack ◆ **chemin de fer à ~** rack railway, cog railway ◆ **engrenage/direction à ~** rack-and-pinion gear/steering

crémant /kʀemɑ̃/ ADJ M, NM cremant *(sparkling wine)*

crémation /kʀemasjɔ̃/ NF cremation

crématoire /kʀematwaʀ/ ADJ crematory; → **four** NM crematorium, crematory *(furnace)*

crématorium /kʀematɔʀjɔm/ NM crematorium

crème /kʀɛm/ NF [1] *(Culin)* *(= produit laitier)* cream; *(= peau sur le lait)* skin; *(= entremets)* cream dessert ◆ **~ d'asperges/de champignons/tomates** *(potage)* cream of asparagus/of mushroom/of tomato (soup) ◆ **~ de cassis** *(= liqueur)* crème de cassis ◆ **~ de marron** sweetened chestnut purée ◆ **fraises à la ~** strawberries and cream ◆ **gâteau à la ~** cream cake; → **chou¹, fromage** *etc*

[2] *(= produit pour la toilette, le nettoyage)* cream ◆ **~ de beauté** beauty cream ◆ **~ pour le visage/de jour/de nuit** face/day/night cream ◆ **~ pour les chaussures** shoe polish *ou* cream *(Brit)*

[3] *(= les meilleurs)* **la ~** the cream of the crop, the crème de la crème ◆ **c'est la ~ des pères** he's the best of (all) fathers ◆ **ses amis ce n'est pas la ~** his friends aren't exactly the cream of society *ou* the crème de la crème ◆ **ce garçon est vraiment une ~** he's such a sweetie*

ADJ INV cream(-coloured *(Brit)* *ou* -colored *(US)*)

NM *(= café au lait)* coffee with milk *ou* cream, white coffee *(Brit)* ◆ **un grand/petit ~** a large/small cup of white coffee

COMP **crème aigre** sour cream

crème anglaise *thin custard made with eggs*

crème antirides anti-wrinkle cream

crème au beurre butter cream

crème brûlée crème brûlée

crème (au) caramel crème caramel, caramel cream *ou* custard

crème démaquillante cleansing cream, make-up removing cream

crème épaisse ≈ double cream *(Brit)*, heavy cream *(US)*

crème fleurette ≈ single cream *(Brit)*, light cream *(US)*

crème fond de teint fluid foundation *ou* makeup

crème fouettée (sweetened) whipped cream

crème fraîche crème fraîche ◆ **~ fraîche épaisse** ≈ double cream *(Brit)*, heavy cream *(US)*

crème glacée ice cream

crème grasse dry-skin cream

crème de gruyère ≈ cheese spread

crème hydratante moisturizing cream, moisturizer

crème pâtissière confectioner's custard

crème à raser shaving cream

crème renversée cream mould *(Brit)*, cup custard *(US)*

crémerie /kʀɛmʀi/ NF *(= magasin)* dairy (shop) ◆ **changeons de ~*** let's push off* somewhere else, let's take our custom *(Brit)* *ou* business *(US)* elsewhere *(hum)*

crémeux, -euse /kʀemø, øz/ ADJ creamy

crémier, -ière /kʀemje, jɛʀ/ NM,F *person working in a dairy*

crémone /kʀemɔn/ NF window catch

créneau (pl **créneaux**) /kʀeno/ NM [1] *[de rempart]* crenel, crenelle; *(Mil)* *[de tranchée]* slit ◆ **les ~x** *(= forme)* the crenelations; *(= chemin de ronde)* the battlements ◆ **monter au ~ pour défendre sa politique** *(fig)* to leap to the defence of one's policies [2] *(pour se garer)* **faire un ~** to reverse into a parking space *(between two cars)* *(Brit)*, to parallel park *(US)* ◆ **j'ai raté mon ~** I've parked badly [3] *[de marché]* gap, niche; *[d'emploi du temps]* gap ◆ **~ (horaire)** *(TV)* (time) slot ◆ **~ publicitaire** advertising slot ◆ **il y a un ~ pour les voitures économiques** there is a niche *ou* a ready market for fuel-efficient cars ◆ **~ de lancement** *[de fusée]* (launch) window ◆ **trouver un bon ~** to find a good source of income ◆ **le karaoké constitue un ~ porteur pour les bars** karaoke is a good money-maker for bars

crénelage /kʀen(ə)laʒ/ NM *(Tech)* milling; *(Ordin)* aliasing

crénelé, e /kʀen(ə)le/ (ptp de **créneler**) ADJ *[mur, arête]* crenellated; *[feuille, bordure]* scalloped, crenate *(Bot)*

créneler /kʀen(ə)le/ ▸ conjug 4 ◂ VT [1] *[+ muraille]* to crenellate, to crenel; *[+ tranchée]* to make a slit in [2] *[+ roue]* to notch; *[+ pièce de monnaie]* to mill

crénom /kʀenɔ̃/ EXCL ◆ **~ de nom!** † confound it!, dash it all! *(surtout Brit)*

créole /kʀeɔl/ ADJ creole; → **riz** NM *(Ling)* Creole NMF Creole NF *(= boucle d'oreille)* large hoop earring

créolité /kʀeɔlite/ NF Creole identity

Créon /kʀeɔ̃/ NM Creon

créosote /kʀeɔzɔt/ NF creosote

crêpage /kʀɛpaʒ/ NM [1] *[de cheveux]* backcombing [2] ◆ **~ de chignon** * dust-up*, free-for-all, set-to* *(Brit)* [3] *[de tissu]* crimping

crêpe¹ /kʀɛp/ NF *(Culin)* pancake *(Brit)*, crêpe ◆ **faire sauter une ~** to toss a pancake ◆ **~ Suzette** crêpe suzette; → **dentelle, pâte, retourner**

crêpe² /kʀɛp/ NM [1] *(= tissu)* crepe, crêpe, crape ◆ **~ de Chine** crepe de Chine ◆ **~ georgette** georgette (crepe) ◆ **~ de soie** silk crepe [2] *(noir : de deuil)* black mourning crepe ◆ **voile de ~** mourning veil ◆ **porter un ~** *(au bras)* to wear a black armband; *(autour du chapeau)* to wear a black hatband; *(aux cheveux, au revers)* to wear a black ribbon [3] *(= matière)* **semelles (de) ~** crepe soles

crêper /kʀepe/ ▸ conjug 1 ◂ VT [1] *[+ cheveux]* to backcomb [2] *[+ tissu]* to crimp VPR **se crêper** ◆ **se ~ les cheveux** to backcomb one's hair ◆ **se ~ le chignon** * to tear each other's hair out, to have a dust-up* *ou* a set-to* *(Brit)*

crêperie /kʀɛpʀi/ NF crêperie, pancake house *ou* restaurant *(Brit)*

crépi, e /kʀepi/ (ptp de **crépir**) ADJ, NM roughcast

crêpier, -ière /kʀepje, jɛʀ/ NM,F *(= personne)* pancake *(Brit)* *ou* crêpe seller NF **crêpière** *(= plaque)* pancake *(Brit)* *ou* crêpe griddle; *(= poêle)* shallow frying pan *(for making pancakes)*

crépine /kʀepin/ NF [1] *[de tuyau]* strainer; *[de passementerie]* fringe [2] *(= membrane)* caul

crépinette /kʀepinɛt/ NF flat sausage *(in caul)*

crépir /kʀepiʀ/ ▸ conjug 2 ◂ VT to roughcast

crépissage /kʀepisaʒ/ NM roughcasting

crépitation /kʀepitasjɔ̃/ NF *[de feu, électricité]* crackling ◆ **~ osseuse** *(Méd)* crepitus ◆ **~ pulmonaire** crepitations

crépitement /kʀepitmɑ̃/ NM *[de feu, électricité]* crackling *(NonC)*; *[de chandelle, friture]* sputtering *(NonC)*, spluttering *(NonC)*; *[de pluie]* pattering *(NonC)*; *[de mitrailleuse]* rattle *(NonC)*; *[de grésil]* rattle *(NonC)*, patter *(NonC)* ◆ **sous le ~ des flashs** with flashguns going off all around

crépiter /kʀepite/ ▸ conjug 1 ◂ VI *[feu, électricité]* to crackle; *[chandelle, friture]* to sputter, to splutter; *[pluie]* to patter; *[flashs]* to go off; *[mitrailleuse]* to rattle out; *[grésil]* to rattle, to patter ◆ **les applaudissements crépitèrent** there was a ripple of applause

crépon /kʀepɔ̃/ NM ≈ seersucker; → **papier**

crépu, e /kʀepy/ ADJ *[cheveux]* frizzy ◆ **elle est toute ~e** her hair's all frizzy

crépusculaire /kʀepyskylɛʀ/ ADJ *(littér, Zool)* crepuscular ◆ **lumière ~** twilight glow

crépuscule /kʀepyskyl/ NM *(lit)* twilight, dusk; *(fig)* twilight ◆ **au ~** at twilight ◆ **au ~ de sa vie** in his twilight years

crescendo /kʀeʃɛndo/ ADV [1] *(Mus)* crescendo [2] ◆ **aller ~** *[vacarme, acclamations]* to rise in a crescendo, to grow louder and louder, to crescendo; *[colère, émotion]* to grow *ou* become ever greater NM *(Mus)* crescendo ◆ **le ~ de sa colère/de son émotion** the rising tide of his anger/emotion

cresson /kʀesɔ̃/ NM ◆ **~ (de fontaine)** watercress ◆ **~ des prés** cardamine, lady's-smock

cressonnette /kʀesɔnɛt/ NF cardamine, lady's-smock

cressonnière /kʀesɔnjɛʀ/ NF watercress bed

Crésus /kʀezys/ NM Croesus ◆ **je ne suis pas ~ !** I'm not made of money!; → **riche**

crésyl, Crésyl ® /kʀezil/ NM *type of disinfectant containing cresol*

crétacé, e /kʀetase/ ADJ Cretaceous NM ◆ **le ~** the Cretaceous period

crête /kʀɛt/ NF [1] *[de coq]* comb; *[d'oiseau]* crest; *[de batracien]* horn ◆ **~ de coq** cockscomb [2] *[de mur]* top; *[de toit]* ridge; *[de montagne]* ridge, crest; *[de vague]* crest; *[de graphique]* peak ◆ **la ~ du tibia** the edge *ou* crest *(SPÉC)* of the tibia, the shin ◆ **(ligne de) ~** *(Géog)* watershed

Crète /kʀɛt/ NF Crete

crétin, e /kʀetɛ̃, in/ ADJ *(péj)* cretinous*, idiotic, moronic* NM,F *(péj)* moron*, cretin*

crétinerie* /kʀetinʀi/ NF [1] *(= caractère)* idiocy, stupidity [2] *(= acte, parole)* idiotic *ou* stupid thing to do *ou* say

crétiniser /kʀetinize/ ▸ conjug 1 ◂ VT to turn into a moron* *ou* half-wit

crétinisme /kʀetinism/ NM *(Méd)* cretinism; *(péj)* idiocy, stupidity

crétois, e /kʀetwa, waz/ ADJ Cretan ◆ **régime ~** Cretan diet NM *(= langue)* Cretan NM,F **Crétois(e)** Cretan

cretonne /kʀətɔn/ NF cretonne

creusage /kʀøzaʒ/, **creusement** /kʀøzmɑ̃/ NM *[de fondations]* digging; *[de canal]* digging, cutting

creuser /kʀøze/ ▸ conjug 1 ◂ VT [1] *(= évider)* *[+ bois, falaise]* to hollow (out); *[+ sol, roc]* to make *ou* dig a hole in, to dig out; *(au marteau-*

piqueur) to drill a hole in ◆ ~ **la neige de ses mains** to dig out the snow with one's hands

2 *[+ puits]* to sink, to bore; *[+ fondations, mine]* to dig; *[+ canal]* to dig, to cut; *[+ tranchée, fosse]* to dig (out); *[+ sillon]* to plough *(Brit)*, to plow *(US)*; *[+ trou] (gén)* to dig, to make; *(au marteau-piqueur)* to drill ◆ ~ **un tunnel sous une montagne** to bore *ou* drive a tunnel under a mountain ◆ ~ **un terrier** to burrow, to make a burrow ◆ **la taupe creuse des galeries** moles make *ou* dig tunnels in the soil ◆ ~ **sa propre tombe** to dig one's own grave ◆ **ça a creusé un abîme** *ou* **un fossé entre eux** that has created *ou* thrown a great gulf between them

3 *(= approfondir) [+ problème, sujet]* to go into (deeply *ou* thoroughly), to look into (closely) ◆ **c'est une idée à** ~ it's something to be gone into (more deeply *ou* thoroughly), it's an idea worth pursuing ◆ **si on creuse un peu** *(fig)* if you scratch the surface

4 *(fig)* **la fatigue lui creusait les joues** he was so tired his face was gaunt ◆ **visage creusé de rides** face furrowed with wrinkles ◆ ~ **les reins** to draw o.s. up, to throw out one's chest ◆ **la promenade, ça creuse (l'estomac)** * walking gives you a real appetite ◆ ~ **l'écart** *(lit, fig)* to establish a convincing lead *(par rapport à* over)

VI *[personne]* to dig; *[lapin]* to burrow ◆ **il a fallu** ~ **beaucoup** *ou* **profond** we had to dig deep *(dans* into)

VPR se creuser 1 *[joues, visage]* to become gaunt *ou* hollow ◆ **la mer se creuse** there's a swell coming on ◆ **l'écart se creuse entre eux** *(lit, fig)* the gap between them is widening

2 * **se** ~ **(la cervelle** *ou* **la tête)** *[personne]* to rack *ou* cudgel one's brains ◆ **il ne s'est pas beaucoup creusé !** he didn't exactly put himself out *ou* overexert himself! ◆ **ils ne se sont pas beaucoup creusés pour trouver un cadeau** they didn't look very hard to find a present

creuset
/kʀøzɛ/ **NM** 1 *(= récipient)* crucible; *[de haut fourneau]* heart, crucible ◆ ~ **de verrerie** glassmaker's crucible 2 *(= lieu de brassage)* melting pot; *(littér = épreuve)* crucible, trial

Creutzfeldt-Jakob
/kʀɔjtsfɛldʒakɔb/ **N** ◆ **maladie de** ~ Creutzfeldt-Jakob disease, CJD

creux, creuse
/kʀø, kʀøz/ **ADJ** 1 *[arbre, dent]* hollow; *[toux, voix]* hollow, deep; *[son]* hollow; *[estomac]* empty ◆ **j'ai la tête** *ou* **la cervelle creuse** my mind's a blank; → **nez, sonner, ventre**

2 *(= concave) [surface]* concave, hollow; *[yeux]* deep-set, sunken; *[joue]* gaunt, hollow; *[visage]* gaunt ◆ **aux yeux** ~ hollow-eyed; → **assiette, chemin**

3 *(= vide de sens) [paroles]* empty, hollow; *[idées]* barren, futile; *[raisonnement]* weak, flimsy

4 *(= sans activité)* **les jours** ~ slack days ◆ **les heures creuses** *(gén)* slack periods; *(métro, électricité, téléphone)* off-peak periods ◆ **période creuse** *(gén)* slack period; *(Tourisme)* low season; → **classe**

NM 1 *(= cavité) [d'arbre]* hollow, hole; *[de rocher, dent]* cavity, hole ◆ **avoir un** ~ **(dans l'estomac)** * to feel *ou* be hungry *ou* peckish * *(Brit)*

2 *(= dépression)* hollow ◆ **être plein de** ~ **et de bosses** to be full of bumps and holes *ou* hollows ◆ **le** ~ **de la main** the hollow of one's hand ◆ **ça tient dans le** ~ **de la main** it's small enough to hold in your hand ◆ **des écureuils qui mangent dans le** ~ **de la main** squirrels which eat out of your hand ◆ **le** ~ **de l'aisselle** the armpit ◆ **le** ~ **de l'estomac** the pit of the stomach ◆ **le** ~ **de l'épaule** the hollow of one's shoulder ◆ **au** ~ **des reins** in the small of one's back; → **gravure**

3 *(= activité réduite)* slack period

4 *(Naut) [de voile]* belly; *[de vague]* trough ◆ **il y avait des** ~ **de 10 mètres** there were 10-metre-high waves, the waves were 10 metres high ◆ **être au** *ou* **dans le** ~ **de la vague** *(fig) [marché]* to have hit rock bottom; *[économie]* to be in the doldrums, to be at its lowest ebb; *[entreprise]* to be in the doldrums ◆ **il est au** *ou* **dans le** ~ **de la vague** his fortunes are at their lowest ebb

5 *(Art)* **graver en** ~ to do intaglio engraving

crevaison
/kʀəvɛzɔ̃/ **NF** *(en voiture)* puncture *(Brit)*, flat

crevant, e
* /kʀəvɑ̃, ɑ̃t/ **ADJ** *(= fatigant)* gruelling, killing * *(Brit)*; († *= amusant)* priceless *

crevasse
/kʀəvas/ **NF** *[de mur, rocher]* crack, fissure, crevice; *[de sol]* crack, fissure; *[de glacier]* crevasse; *[de peau]* crack ◆ **avoir des** ~**s aux mains** to have chapped hands

crevassé, e
/kʀəvase/ (ptp de **crevasser**) **ADJ** *[sol]* fissured; *[mains, peau]* chapped ◆ **glacier très** ~ glacier with a lot of crevasses

crevasser
/kʀəvase/ ▸ **conjug 1** ◂ **VT** *[+ sol]* to cause cracks *ou* fissures in, to crack; *[+ mains]* to chap **VPR se crevasser** *[sol]* to crack, to become cracked; *[mains]* to chap, to become *ou* get chapped

crevé, e
/kʀəve/ (ptp de **crever**) **ADJ** 1 *[pneu]* burst, punctured ◆ **j'ai un pneu (de)** ~ I've got a puncture *(Brit)*, I've got a flat tyre *(Brit) ou* tire *(US)*, I've got a flat * 2 ‡ *(= mort)* dead; *(= fatigué)* dead beat *, bushed *, exhausted, knackered ‡ *(Brit)* **NM** *(Couture)* slash ◆ **des manches à** ~**s** slashed sleeves

crève
‡ /kʀɛv/ **NF** (bad) cold ◆ **j'ai la** ~ I've got a bad cold ◆ **elle a attrapé** *ou* **chopé * la** ~ she's caught a bad cold

crève-cœur
(pl **crève-cœurs**) /kʀɛvkœʀ/ **NM** heartbreak

crève-la-faim
* /kʀɛvlafɛ̃/ **NMF INV** *(péj) (= miséreux)* miserable wretch; *(= clochard)* down-and-out

crever
/kʀəve/ ▸ **conjug 5** ◂ **VT** 1 *(= percer) [+ pneu]* to burst, to puncture; *[+ ballon]* to burst ◆ ~ **les yeux à qn** *(intentionnellement)* to gouge (out) *ou* put out sb's eyes; *(accidentellement)* to blind sb (in both eyes) ◆ **ça crève les yeux** it's as plain as the nose on your face ◆ **ça te crève les yeux !** it's staring you in the face! ◆ **le prix a crevé le plafond** the price has gone through the roof ◆ ~ **le cœur à qn** to break sb's heart ◆ **cet acteur crève l'écran** this actor has a tremendous screen presence

2 *(* = exténuer)* ~ **qn** *[personne]* to wear sb out, to work sb to death *; *[tâche, marche]* to wear sb out, to kill sb * ◆ ~ **un cheval** to ride *ou* work a horse into the ground *ou* to death

3 ‡ ~ **la faim** *ou* **la dalle** to be starving * *ou* famished * ◆ **on la crève ici !** they starve us here!

4 *(‡ = tuer)* to kill

VI 1 *(= s'ouvrir) [fruit, sac, abcès]* to burst ◆ **les nuages crevèrent** the clouds burst, the heavens opened ◆ **faire** ~ **du riz** *(Culin)* to boil rice until the grains burst *ou* split

2 *(péj = être plein de)* ~ **de** *[+ orgueil]* to be bursting *ou* puffed up with; *[+ jalousie]* to be full of, to be bursting with; *[+ dépit]* to be full of ◆ ~ **d'envie de faire qch** to be dying to do sth *; → **rire**

3 *(= mourir) [animal, plante]* to die (off); ‡ *[personne]* to die, to kick the bucket ‡, to snuff it ‡ *(Brit)* ◆ **un chien crevé** a dead dog ◆ ~ **de faim/froid** ‡ to starve/freeze to death ◆ **on crève de froid ici** * *(fig)* it's freezing (cold) in here ◆ **on crève de chaud ici** * it's boiling in here * ◆ **je crève de faim** * I'm starving * *ou* famished * *ou* ravenous ◆ **je crève de soif** * I'm dying of thirst *, I'm parched * ◆ ~ **d'ennui** * to be bored to tears *ou* death *, to be bored out of one's mind * ◆ **tu veux nous faire** ~ **!** * do you want to kill us or what! ◆ **faire** ~ **qn de soif** to make sb die of thirst ◆ **tu peux toujours** ~ **!** * get stuffed! ‡ ◆ **qu'ils crèvent !** * they can go and get stuffed! ‡

4 *[pneu, automobiliste]* to have a flat tyre *(Brit) ou* tire *(US)*, to have a puncture *(Brit)* ◆ **faire 10 000 km sans** ~ to drive 10,000 km without getting a flat * *ou* a puncture *(Brit)*

VPR se crever *(‡ = se fatiguer)* to kill o.s. * *(à faire* doing); ◆ **se** ~ **(au travail)** * *(gén)* to work o.s. to death; *[ménagère]* to work one's fingers to the bone * ◆ **se** ~ **le cul** *‡ to slog one's guts out ‡ *(à faire* doing); ◆ **je ne vais pas me** ~ **le cul à transporter toutes ces briques !** *‡ I'm not going to bust a gut ‡ *ou* to kill myself * carrying all those bricks around!

crevette
/kʀəvɛt/ **NF** ◆ ~ **(rose)** prawn ◆ ~ **grise** shrimp; → **filet**

crevettier
/kʀəvetje/ **NM** *(= filet)* shrimp net; *(= bateau)* shrimp boat

cri
/kʀi/ **NM** 1 *(= éclat de voix) [de personne]* cry, shout; *(très fort)* scream; *(ton aigu)* shriek, screech; *(= pleurs)* cry, scream; *(de douleur, de peur)* scream, cry, yell ◆ **le** ~ **du nouveau-né** the cry of the newborn baby ◆ **pousser des** ~**s de joie/triomphe** to cry out in joy/triumph ◆ ~ **de surprise** cry *ou* exclamation of surprise ◆ ~ **aigu** *ou* **perçant** piercing cry *ou* scream, shrill cry; *[d'animal]* squeal ◆ ~ **sourd** *ou* **étouffé** muffled cry *ou* shout ◆ **pousser un** ~ **de colère** to shout angrily ◆ **pousser un** ~ **de rage** to cry out in rage, to give a cry of rage ◆ **jeter** *ou* **pousser des** ~**s** to shout (out), to cry out ◆ **elle jeta un** ~ **de douleur** she cried out in pain, she gave a cry of pain ◆ **pousser des** ~**s d'orfraie** to scream, to shriek; → **étouffer**

2 *(= exclamation)* cry, shout ◆ ~ **d'alarme/d'approbation** cry *ou* shout of alarm/approval ◆ **le** ~ **des marchands ambulants** the hawkers' cries ◆ **marchant au** ~ **de "liberté"** marching to shouts *ou* cries of "freedom" ◆ **le** ~ **des opprimés** *(fig)* the cries of the oppressed ◆ **une tentative de suicide est souvent un** ~ **(de détresse)** *(fig)* a suicide attempt is often a cry for help ◆ **ce poème est un véritable** ~ **d'amour** this poem is a cry of love ◆ **le** ~ **de la conscience** *(fig)* the voice of conscience; → **haut**

3 *(terme générique)* noise; *[d'oiseau]* call; *[de canard]* quack; *[de cochon]* squeal ◆ **le** ~ **d'un animal** *(terme générique)* the noise an animal makes

4 *(littér = crissement)* squeal, screech

5 *(locutions)* **c'est le dernier** ~ it's the (very) latest thing ◆ **un ordinateur dernier** ~ a state-of-the-art computer ◆ **à grands** ~**s** vociferously

COMP cri du cœur heartfelt cry, cry from the heart, cri de cœur

cri de guerre *(lit)* war cry; *(fig)* slogan, war cry

cri primal primal scream

criaillement
/kʀijɑjmɑ̃/ **NM** 1 *(gén pl) [d'oie]* squawking *(NonC)*; *[de paon]* squawking *(NonC)*, screeching *(NonC)*; *[de bébé]* bawling *(NonC)*, squalling *(NonC)* 2 ⇒ **criailleries**

criailler
/kʀijɑje/ ▸ **conjug 1** ◂ **VI** 1 *[oie]* to squawk; *[paon]* to squawk, to screech; *[bébé]* to bawl, to squall 2 *(= rouspéter)* to grouse *, to grumble ◆ ~ **après qn** *(= houspiller)* to nag (at) sb

criailleries
/kʀijɑjʀi/ **NFPL** *(= rouspétance)* grousing * *(NonC)*, grumbling *(NonC)*; *(= houspillage)* nagging *(NonC)*

criailleur, -euse
/kʀijɑjœʀ, øz/ **ADJ** grouchy * **NM,F** *(= rouspéteur)* grouch *, grouser *

criant, e
/kʀijɑ̃, ɑ̃t/ **ADJ** *[erreur]* glaring *(épith)*; *[injustice]* rank *(épith)*, blatant, glaring *(épith)*; *[preuve]* striking *(épith)*, glaring *(épith)*; *[contraste, vérité]* striking *(épith)* ◆ **portrait** ~ **de vérité** amazingly true-to-life portrait

criard, e /kʀijaʀ, aʀd/ ADJ *(péj)* *[enfant]* yelling, squalling; *[oiseau]* squawking; *[son, voix]* piercing; *[couleurs, vêtement]* loud, garish

criblage /kʀiblaʒ/ NM *(= tamisage)* *[de graines]* sifting; *[de sable]* riddling, sifting; *[de minerai]* screening, jigging; *(= calibrage)* *[de fruits]* grading; *[de charbon]* riddling, screening

crible /kʀibl/ NM *(à main)* riddle; *(industriel)* screen, jig, jigger • **~ mécanique** screening machine

• **passer au crible** *(lit)* to riddle, to put through a riddle; *[+ idée, proposition]* to examine closely; *[+ déclaration, texte]* to go through with a fine-tooth comb; *[+ établissement]* to do a thorough investigation into

criblé, e /kʀible/ (ptp de **cribler**) **criblé de** LOC ADJ *[+ balles, flèches, trous]* riddled with; *[+ taches]* covered in • **visage ~ de boutons** face covered in spots *ou* pimples, spotty face • **~ de dettes** crippled with debts, up to one's eyes in debt

cribler /kʀible/ ► conjug 1 ◄ VT 1 *(= tamiser)* *[+ graines]* to sift; *[+ sable]* to riddle, to sift; *(= trier)* *[+ minerai]* to screen, to jig; *(= calibrer)* *[+ charbon]* to riddle, to screen; *[+ fruits]* to grade 2 *(= percer)* **~ qch/qn de balles/flèches** to riddle sth/sb with bullets/arrows • **~ qn de questions** *(= accabler)* to bombard sb with questions • **~ qn d'injures** to heap insults on sb

cribleur, -euse /kʀiblœʀ, øz/ NM,F *(= ouvrier)* *[de graines]* sifter; *[de fruits]* grader; *[de sable]* riddler, sifter; *[de charbon]* riddler, screener; *[de minerai]* screener, jigger NF **cribleuse** *(= machine)* sifter, sifting machine

cric /kʀik/ NM • **~ (d'automobile)** (car) jack • **soulever qch au ~** to jack sth up • **~ hydraulique** hydraulic jack • **~ à vis** screw jack

cric-crac /kʀikkʀak/ EXCL, NM *(gén)* creak; *(= bruit de clé)* click

cricket /kʀikɛt/ NM *(Sport)* cricket

cricoïde /kʀikɔid/ ADJ *(Anat)* cricoid NM • **le ~** the cricoid cartilage

cricri NM, **cri-cri** NM INV /kʀikʀi/ *(= cri du grillon)* chirping; *(* = grillon)* cricket

criée /kʀije/ NF 1 • **(vente à la) ~** (sale by) auction • **vendre des poissons à la ~** to auction fish, to sell fish by auction 2 *(= salle)* auction room, salesroom

crier /kʀije/ ► conjug 7 ◄ VI 1 *[personne]* to shout; *(très fort)* to scream; *(ton aigu)* to shriek, to screech; *(= vagir)* to cry, to scream; *(de douleur, peur)* to scream, to cry out, to yell (out) • **~ de douleur** to scream *ou* yell out in pain • **"oh non !" cria-t-il** "oh no!", he cried • **~ à tue-tête** *ou* **comme un sourd** *ou* **comme un putois** to shout one's head off • **tes parents vont ~** your parents are going to make a fuss • **tu ne peux pas parler sans ~ ?** do you have to shout?, can't you talk without shouting?

2 *[oiseau]* to call; *[canard]* to quack; *[cochon]* to squeal; *[dindon]* to gobble; *[hibou, singe]* to call, to screech, to hoot; *[mouette]* to cry; *[oie]* to honk; *[perroquet]* to squawk; *[souris]* to squeak

3 *(= grincer)* *[porte, plancher, roue]* to creak, to squeak; *[frein]* to squeal, to screech; *[chaussure, étoffe]* to squeak; *(fig)* *[couleur]* to scream, to shriek • **faire ~ la craie sur le tableau** to make the chalk squeak on the blackboard

4 *(avec prép)* **~ contre** *ou* **après* qn** to nag (at) *ou* scold sb, to go on at sb* • **~ contre qch** to shout about sth • **elle passe son temps à lui ~ après*** *ou* **dessus*** she's forever going on at him*, she's always shouting at him • **~ à la trahison/au scandale** to call it treason/a scandal, to start bandying words like treason/scandal about • **~ au miracle** to hail it as a miracle, to call it a miracle • **~ à l'assassin** *ou* **au meurtre** to shout "murder" • **~ au loup/au voleur** to cry wolf/thief • **quand il a demandé une augmentation de 50% son patron a crié au fou** when he asked for a 50% rise his boss called him a madman *ou* said he was crazy

VT 1 *[+ ordre, injures]* to shout (out), to yell (out); *(= proclamer)* *[+ mépris, indignation]* to proclaim; *[+ innocence]* to protest • **~ qch sur (tous) les toits** to shout *ou* proclaim sth from the rooftops *ou* housetops • **elle cria qu'elle en avait assez** she shouted that she had had enough; *(plus fort)* she screamed (out) that she had had enough • **~ à qn de se taire** *ou* **qu'il se taise** to shout at sb to be quiet

2 *(pour vendre)* **au coin de la rue, un gamin criait les éditions spéciales** at the street corner a kid was shouting out *ou* calling out the special editions

3 *(pour avertir, implorer)* **sans ~ gare** without a warning • **~ grâce** *(lit)* to beg for mercy; *(fig)* to beg for mercy *ou* a respite • **quand j'ai parlé de me lancer seul dans l'entreprise, ils ont crié casse-cou** when I spoke of going it alone, they said I was crazy; → **victoire**

⚠ Attention à ne pas traduire automatiquement **crier** par **to cry**.

crieur, -euse /kʀijœʀ, øz/ NM,F • **~ de journaux** newspaper seller • **~ public** *(Hist)* town crier

crime /kʀim/ NM 1 *(= meurtre)* murder • **il s'agit bien d'un ~** it's definitely (a case of) murder • **retourner sur les lieux du ~** to go back to the scene of the crime • **la victime/l'arme du ~** the murder victim/weapon • **~ de sang** murder • **~ crapuleux** foul crime • **~ passionnel** crime of passion, crime passionnel • **~ sexuel** sex murder *ou* crime • **le ~ parfait** the perfect crime • **cherchez à qui profite le ~** find someone with a motive

2 *(Jur = délit grave)* crime, offence, ≈ felony *(US)* • **~s et délits** crimes • **~ contre la sûreté de l'État** crime against state security • **~ de lèse-majesté** crime of lèse-majesté • **~ contre les mœurs** sexual offence, offence against public decency • **~ contre la paix** crime against peace • **~ contre un particulier** crime against a private individual • **~ contre nature** unnatural act, crime against nature • **~s de guerre** war crimes • **~ contre l'humanité** crime against humanity • **le ~ ne paie pas** *(Prov)* crime doesn't pay *(Prov)* → **syndicat**

3 *(sens affaibli)* crime • **c'est un ~ de faire** it's criminal *ou* a crime to do • **il est parti avant l'heure ? ce n'est pas un ~ !** he left early? well, that's hardly a crime!

4 *(† ou littér = péché, faute)* sin, crime

Crimée /kʀime/ NF • **la ~** the Crimea, the Crimean peninsula • **la guerre de ~** the Crimean War

criminalisation /kʀiminalizasjɔ̃/ NF criminalization

criminaliser /kʀiminalize/ ► conjug 1 ◄ VT *(Jur)* to criminalize

criminaliste /kʀiminalist/ NMF criminal lawyer

criminalité /kʀiminalite/ NF *(= actes criminels)* criminality, crime • **la ~ juvénile** juvenile criminality • **la grande/petite ~** serious/petty crime • **la ~ organisée** organized crime • **la ~ d'entreprise** corporate crime

criminel, -elle /kʀiminɛl/ ADJ *(gén, Jur)* *[acte, personne, procès]* criminal • **ce serait ~ de laisser ces fruits se perdre** *(sens affaibli)* it would be criminal *ou* a crime to let this fruit go to waste; → **incendie** NM,F *(= meurtrier)* murderer *(ou* murderess); *(Jur = auteur d'un délit grave)* criminal • **~ de guerre** war criminal • **voilà le ~** *(hum = coupable)* there's the culprit *ou* the guilty party NM *(juridiction)* • **avocat au ~** criminal lawyer • **poursuivre qn au ~** to take criminal proceedings against sb, to prosecute sb in a criminal court NF **criminelle** • **la ~le** *(= police)* the crime *ou* murder squad

criminellement /kʀiminɛlmɑ̃/ ADV *[agir]* criminally • **poursuivre qn ~** to take criminal proceedings against sb, to prosecute sb in a criminal court

criminogène /kʀiminɔʒɛn/ ADJ *[facteur]* encouraging criminality *ou* crime

criminologie /kʀiminɔlɔʒi/ NF criminology

criminologiste /kʀiminɔlɔʒist/, **criminologue** /kʀiminɔlɔg/ NMF criminologist

crin /kʀɛ̃/ NM 1 *(= poil)* *[de cheval]* hair (NonC); *[de matelas, balai]* horse hair • **~ végétal** vegetable (horse)hair; → **gant** 2 • **à tous ~s, à tout ~** *[conservateur, républicain]* diehard, dyed-in-the-wool • **révolutionnaire à tout ~** out-and-out revolutionary

crincrin* /kʀɛ̃kʀɛ̃/ NM *(péj)* *(= violon)* squeaky fiddle; *(= son)* squeaking, scraping

crinière /kʀinjɛʀ/ NF 1 *[d'animal]* mane 2 * *[de personne]* mane of hair, flowing mane • **elle avait une ~ rousse** she had a mane of red hair 3 *[de casque]* plume

crinoline /kʀinɔlin/ NF crinoline petticoat • **robe à ~** crinoline (dress)

crique /kʀik/ NF creek, inlet

criquet /kʀikɛ/ NM *(= insecte)* locust

crise /kʀiz/ NF 1 *(= bouleversement, Pol, Écon)* crisis • **en période de ~** in times of crisis *ou* of trouble • **pays/économie en (état de) ~** country/economy in (a state of) crisis • **la ~ de l'immobilier** the property market crisis • **~ financière/politique** financial/political crisis

2 *(Méd)* *[de rhumatisme, goutte]* attack; *[d'épilepsie, apoplexie]* fit • **~ de toux** fit *ou* bout of coughing • **cette affection survient par ~s** this illness manifests itself in recurrent bouts

3 *(= accès)* outburst, fit; *(= lubie)* fit • **~ de colère/rage/jalousie** fit of anger/rage/jealousy • **~ de rire** laughing fit • **être pris d'une ~ de rire** to be in fits (of laughter) • **la ~ (de rire) !*** what a scream!* • **j'ai été pris d'une ~ de rangement** I got a sudden urge to tidy the place up • **travailler par ~s** to work in fits and starts • **je vais au cinéma/je lis par ~s** I go through phases when I go to the cinema/I read a lot

4 *(* = colère)* rage, tantrum • **piquer** *ou* **faire une** *ou* **sa ~** to throw a tantrum *ou* a fit*, to fly off the handle

5 *(= pénurie)* shortage • **~ de main-d'œuvre** shortage of manpower

COMP **crise d'appendicite** attack of appendicitis
crise d'asthme asthma attack, attack of asthma
crise cardiaque heart attack
crise de confiance crisis of confidence, breakdown in trust
crise de conscience crisis of conscience
crise économique economic crisis, slump
crise d'épilepsie epileptic fit
crise de foie bilious attack, bad attack of indigestion
crise d'identité identity crisis
crise de larmes crying fit
crise du logement housing shortage
crise ministérielle cabinet crisis
crise morale moral crisis
crise de nerfs *(Méd)* fit of hysterics; *(caprice)* tantrum • **il nous a fait une ~ de nerfs parce qu'il ne voulait pas manger sa soupe** he threw a tantrum because he didn't want to eat his soup
crise du pétrole oil crisis
crise du pouvoir leadership crisis
crise de la quarantaine midlife crisis
crise religieuse crisis of belief

crispant, e /kʀispɑ̃, ɑ̃t/ ADJ *(= énervant)* irritating, aggravating*, annoying ◆ **ce qu'il est ~ !*** he really gets on my nerves!*, he's a real pain in the neck!*

crispation /kʀispasjɔ̃/ NF [1] *(= contraction) [de traits, visage]* tensing; *[de muscles]* contraction; *[de cuir]* shrivelling-up [2] *(= spasme)* twitch ◆ **des ~s nerveuses** nervous twitches *ou* twitching ◆ **une ~ douloureuse de la main** a painful twitching of the hand ◆ **donner des ~s à qn** *(fig)* to get on sb's nerves* [3] *(= nervosité)* state of tension ◆ **il y a certaines ~s au sein de l'équipe** there is some tension in the team ◆ **c'est un signe de ~ nationaliste** it shows that there is a resurgence in nationalism

crispé, e /kʀispe/ (ptp de **crisper**) ADJ *[sourire]* nervous, tense; *[personne]* tense, on edge *(attrib)*; *[style]* tense, awkward

crisper /kʀispe/ ▸ conjug 1 ◂ VT [1] *(= contracter) [+ muscles, membres]* to tense, to flex; *[+ poings]* to clench ◆ **la douleur crispait les visages** their faces were contorted with grief ◆ **les mains crispées sur le volant** clutching the wheel [2] *(= plisser) [+ cuir]* to shrivel (up) ◆ **le froid crispe la peau** the cold makes one's skin feel taut *ou* tight [3] *(* = agacer)* **~ qn** to get on sb's nerves* VPR **se crisper** *[visage]* to tense; *[sourire]* to become strained *ou* tense; *[poings]* to clench; *[personne]* to get edgy* *ou* tense ◆ **ses mains se crispèrent sur le manche de la pioche** his hands tightened on the pickaxe, he clutched the pickaxe

crispin /kʀispɛ̃/ NM ◆ **gants à ~** gauntlets

criss /kʀis/ NM kris, creese

crissement /kʀismɑ̃/ NM *[de neige, gravier]* crunch(ing) *(NonC)*; *[de pneus, freins]* screech(ing) *(NonC)*, squeal(ing) *(NonC)*; *[de soie, taffetas]* rustling *(NonC)*, rustle *(NonC)*; *[de cuir]* squeaking *(NonC)*; *[de plume]* scratching *(NonC)* ◆ **s'arrêter dans un ~ de pneus** to screech to a halt ◆ **le ~ de la craie sur le tableau** the squeaking of chalk on the blackboard

crisser /kʀise/ ▸ conjug 1 ◂ VI *[neige, gravier]* to crunch; *[pneus, freins]* to screech, to squeal; *[soie, taffetas]* to rustle; *[cuir]* to squeak; *[plume]* to scratch; *[craie]* to squeak

cristal (pl **-aux**) /kʀistal, o/ NM [1] *(Chim, Min)* crystal ◆ **~ (de roche)** rock crystal *(NonC)*, quartz *(NonC)* ◆ **~ (de plomb)** (lead) crystal ◆ **~ de Baccarat** Baccarat crystal ◆ **cristaux de givre** *(sur arbre)* ice crystals; *(sur vitre)* ice patterns ◆ **cristaux liquides** liquid crystals ◆ **écran à cristaux liquides** liquid crystal screen ◆ **de** *ou* **en ~** crystal *(épith)* ◆ **le ~ de sa voix, sa voix de ~** *(littér)* his crystal-clear voice ◆ **~ de Bohême** Bohemian crystal ◆ **~ d'Islande** Iceland spar; → **boule** [2] *(= objet)* crystal(ware) *(NonC)*, piece of crystal(ware) *ou* fine glassware ◆ **les cristaux du lustre** the crystal droplets of the chandelier [3] *(pour le nettoyage)* **cristaux (de soude)** washing soda

cristallerie /kʀistalʀi/ NF *(= fabrication)* crystal (glass-)making; *(= fabrique)* (crystal) glassworks; *(= objets)* crystal(ware), fine glassware

cristallier /kʀistalje/ NM *(Hist)* *(= chercheur)* crystal seeker; *(= ouvrier)* crystal engraver

cristallin, e /kʀistalɛ̃, in/ ADJ *(Min)* crystalline; *[son, voix]* crystal-clear; *[eau]* crystal(-clear), crystalline NM *(Anat)* crystalline lens

cristallisation /kʀistalizasjɔ̃/ NF *(lit, fig)* crystallization ◆ **pour éviter la ~ du débat autour de ce sujet** to stop the debate focusing on this issue

cristallisé, e /kʀistalize/ (ptp de **cristalliser**) ADJ *[minerai, sucre]* crystallized

cristalliser /kʀistalize/ ▸ conjug 1 ◂ VTI *(lit, fig)* to crystallize ◆ **cette réorganisation a cristallisé le mécontentement du personnel** this reorganisation has crystallized staff discontent VPR **se cristalliser** ◆ **le débat s'est cristallisé autour de la question de la sécurité** the debate focused on the issue of security

cristallisoir /kʀistalizwaʀ/ NM crystallizing dish

cristallographie /kʀistalɔgʀafi/ NF crystallography

cristallomancie /kʀistalomɑ̃si/ NF crystal-gazing, crystallomancy

criste-marine (pl **cristes-marines**) /kʀist(ə)maʀin/ NF (rock) samphire

critère /kʀitɛʀ/ NM [1] *(= référence)* criterion ◆ **son seul ~ est l'avis du parti** his only criterion is the opinion of the party ◆ **le style n'est pas le seul ~ pour juger de la valeur d'un roman** style is not the only yardstick *ou* criterion by which one can judge the value of a novel ◆ **~s de sélection** selection criteria

[2] *(= stipulation)* requirement ◆ **il n'y a pas de ~ d'âge** there are no special requirements as far as age is concerned ◆ **~s de qualité** quality requirements ◆ **~s de convergence** *(Europe)* convergence criteria ◆ **~s d'attribution d'un prêt** loan requirements ◆ **quels sont vos ~s de choix ?** what do you base your choices on?

[3] *(= preuve)* criterion ◆ **ce n'est pas un ~ suffisant pour prouver l'authenticité du document** this is not a good enough criterion on which to prove the document's authenticity ◆ **la richesse n'est pas un ~ de succès** wealth is not a criterion *ou* an indication of success

critérium /kʀiteʀjɔm/ NM [1] *(Cyclisme)* rally; *(Natation)* gala [2] † ⇒ **critère**

criticisme /kʀitisism/ NM *(Philos)* critical approach

critiquable /kʀitikabl/ ADJ *[attitude]* reprehensible; *[politique]* open to criticism *(attrib)* ◆ **les aspects les plus ~s de la procédure** the aspects of the procedure which are most open to criticism

critique[1] /kʀitik/ ADJ *(= alarmant) [situation, période]* critical; *(= décisif) [phase, situation, période]* crucial, critical; *(Sci) [vitesse, masse, point]* critical ◆ **dans les circonstances ~s, il perd la tête** in critical situations *ou* in emergencies *ou* in a crisis he loses his head; → **âge**

critique[2] /kʀitik/ ADJ [1] *(= qui analyse) [jugement, notes, édition]* critical; → **apparat, esprit** [2] *(= sévère)* critical, censorious *(frm)* ◆ **d'un œil ~** with a critical eye ◆ **il s'est montré très ~ (au sujet de ...)** he was very critical (of ...)

NF [1] *(= blâme)* criticism ◆ **il ne supporte pas la ~** *ou* **les ~s** he can't tolerate criticism ◆ **malgré les nombreuses ~s** despite the many criticisms ◆ **faire une ~ à (l'endroit de) qch/qn** to criticize sth/sb ◆ **une ~ que je lui ferais est qu'il ...** one criticism I would make of him is that he ... ◆ **la ~ est aisée** it's easy to criticize

[2] *(= analyse) [de texte, œuvre]* appreciation, critique; *[de livre, spectacle]* review ◆ **la ~** *(= art de juger)* criticism ◆ **la ~ littéraire/musicale** literary/music criticism ◆ **faire la ~ de** *[+ livre, film]* to review, to do a write-up on; *[+ poème]* to write an appreciation *ou* a critique of

[3] *(= personnes)* **la ~** the critics ◆ **la ~ a bien accueilli sa pièce** his play was well received by the critics

NMF *(= commentateur)* critic ◆ **~ d'art/de cinéma** art/cinema *ou* film critic ◆ **~ littéraire** literary critic

critiquer /kʀitike/ ▸ conjug 1 ◂ VT [1] *(= blâmer)* to criticize ◆ **il critique tout/tout le monde** he finds fault with *ou* criticizes everything/everybody [2] *(= juger) [+ livre, œuvre]* to assess, to make an appraisal of; *(= examiner)* to examine (critically)

croassement /kʀɔasmɑ̃/ NM caw, cawing *(NonC)*

croasser /kʀɔase/ ▸ conjug 1 ◂ VI to caw

croate /kʀɔat/ ADJ Croatian NM *(= langue)* Croat, Croatian NMF **Croate** Croat, Croatian

Croatie /kʀɔasi/ NF Croatia

croato-musulman, e /kʀɔatomyzylmɑ̃, an/ ADJ Muslim-Croat *(épith)*

crobard* /kʀɔbaʀ/ NM sketch

croc /kʀo/ NM [1] *(= dent)* fang ◆ **montrer les ~s** *[animal]* to bare its teeth, to show its teeth *ou* fangs; * *[personne]* to show one's teeth ◆ **avoir les ~s*** to be starving*, to be famished* [2] *(= objet)* hook ◆ **~ de boucherie/de marinier** meat/boat hook ◆ **~ à fumier** muck rake

croc-en-jambe (pl **crocs-en-jambe**) /kʀɔkɑ̃ʒɑ̃b/ NM ◆ **faire un ~ à qn** *(lit)* to trip sb (up); *(fig)* to trip sb up, to pull a fast one on sb* ◆ **un ~ me fit perdre l'équilibre** I was tripped up and lost my balance

croche /kʀɔʃ/ NF *(Mus)* quaver *(Brit)*, eighth (note) *(US)* ◆ **double ~** semiquaver *(Brit)*, sixteenth (note) *(US)* ◆ **triple/quadruple ~** demisemiquaver/hemidemisemiquaver *(Brit)*, thirty-second/sixty-fourth note *(US)*

croche-patte* (pl **croche-pattes**) /kʀɔʃpat/ NM ⇒ **croc-en-jambe**

croche-pied (pl **croche-pieds**) /kʀɔʃpje/ NM ⇒ **croc-en-jambe**

crochet /kʀɔʃɛ/ NM [1] *(= fer recourbé) (gén)* hook; *[de chiffonnier]* spiked stick; *[de patte de pantalon]* fastener, clip, fastening; *[de cambrioleur, serrurier]* picklock ◆ **~ d'attelage** *(Rail)* coupling ◆ **~ de boucherie** *ou* **de boucher** meat hook ◆ **~ à boutons** *ou* **bottines** buttonhook ◆ **vivre aux ~s de qn*** to live off sb, to sponge off* sb

[2] *(= aiguille)* crochet hook; *(= technique)* crochet ◆ **couverture au ~** crocheted blanket ◆ **faire du ~** to crochet ◆ **faire qch au ~** to crochet sth

[3] *(Boxe)* **~ du gauche/du droit** left/right hook

[4] *(= détour) [de véhicule]* sudden swerve; *[de route]* sudden turn; *[de voyage]* detour ◆ **il a fait un ~ pour éviter l'obstacle** he swerved to avoid the obstacle ◆ **faire un ~ par une ville** to make a detour through a town

[5] *(Typo)* **~s** square brackets ◆ **entre ~s** in square brackets

[6] *[de serpent]* fang

[7] *(Archit)* crocket

[8] † **~ radiophonique** *(Radio)* talent show

crochetage /kʀɔʃtaʒ/ NM *[de serrure]* picking

crocheter /kʀɔʃte/ ▸ conjug 5 ◂ VT [1] *[+ serrure]* to pick; *[+ porte]* to pick the lock on [2] *(= faire tomber)* to trip (up) [3] *(Tricot)* to crochet

crocheteur /kʀɔʃtœʀ/ NM *(= voleur)* picklock

crochu, e /kʀɔʃy/ ADJ *[nez]* hooked; *[mains, doigts]* claw-like ◆ **au nez ~** hook-nosed; → **atome**

croco* /kʀɔko/ NM (abrév de **crocodile**) crocodile skin ◆ **en ~** crocodile *(épith)*

crocodile /kʀɔkɔdil/ NM *(= animal, peau)* crocodile; *(Rail)* contact ramp ◆ **sac en ~** crocodile(-skin) handbag; → **larme**

crocus /kʀɔkys/ NM crocus

croire /kʀwaʀ/

▸ conjug 44 ◂

GRAMMAIRE ACTIVE 33.2, 53.5

1 VERBE TRANSITIF	4 VT INDIRECT
2 VERBE INTRANSITIF	5 VERBE PRONOMINAL
3 VT INDIRECT	

1 – VERBE TRANSITIF

= tenir pour vrai ou sincère *[+ personne, fait, histoire]* to believe ◆ **auriez-vous cru cela de lui ?**

would you have believed that of him? ◆ **le croira qui voudra, mais ...** believe it or not (but) ... ◆ **je veux bien le ~** I can quite *ou* well believe it ◆ **je n'en crois rien** I don't believe a word of it ◆ **croyez moi** believe me ; ◆ **non, mais qu'est-ce que vous croyez ?*** what do you imagine? ◆ **je ne suis pas celle que vous croyez !** I'm not that sort of person! → **fer, parole**

◆ **je te** *ou* **vous crois!** * you bet! *

◆ **croire** + *infinitif ou* **que** (= *penser estimer*) to believe, to think; (= *déduire*) to believe, to assume, to think ◆ **nous croyons qu'il a dit la vérité** we believe *ou* think that he told the truth ◆ **je n'arrive pas à ~ qu'il a réussi** I (just) can't believe he has succeeded ◆ **elle croyait avoir perdu son sac** she thought she had lost her bag ◆ **il a bien cru manquer son train** he really thought he would miss his train ◆ **il n'y avait pas de lumière, j'ai cru qu'ils étaient couchés** there was no light on so I thought *ou* assumed they had gone to bed ◆ **il a cru bien faire** he meant well, he thought he was doing the right thing *ou* acting for the best ◆ **je crois que oui** I think so ◆ **je crois que non** I don't think so, I think not ◆ **il n'est pas là ? – je crois que si** isn't he in? – (yes) I think he is ◆ **on ne croyait pas qu'il viendrait** we didn't think he'd come ◆ **elle ne croit pas/elle ne peut pas ~ qu'il mente** she doesn't think/ can't believe he is lying ◆ ; → **dire, rêver**

◆ **à croire que** ◆ **(c'est) à ~ qu'il est amoureux** you'd *ou* anyone would think he was in love ◆ **il est à ~ que ...** *(frm)* it is to be supposed *ou* presumed that ...

◆ **il faut croire que ...** * it would seem *ou* appear that ... ◆ **j'entends rien, faut ~ * que je deviens sourde** I can't hear a thing, I must be going deaf

◆ **faut pas ~ !** * make no mistake (about it)!

◆ **croire** + *adjectif, adverbe ou pronom* (= *juger, estimer*) to think, to believe, to consider; (= *supposer*) to think, to believe ◆ **croyez-vous cette réunion nécessaire ?** do you think *ou* believe this meeting is necessary?, do you consider this meeting (to be) necessary? ◆ **il n'a pas cru utile** *ou* **nécessaire de me prévenir** he didn't think it necessary to warn me ◆ **on a cru préférable de refuser** we thought it preferable for us to refuse, we thought that it would be better for us to refuse ◆ **on l'a cru mort** he was believed *ou* presumed (to be) dead ◆ **on les croyait en France** they were believed *ou* thought to be in France ◆ **je la croyais ailleurs/ avec vous** I thought she was somewhere else/ with you ◆ **où vous croyez-vous ?** where do you think you are? ◆ **tu ne peux pas ~** *ou* **vous ne sauriez ~** *(frm)* **combien il nous manque** you cannot (begin to) imagine how much we miss him

◆ **on croirait, on aurait cru** ◆ **on croirait une hirondelle** it looks like a swallow ◆ **on aurait cru (voir) un fantôme** he looked like a ghost ◆ **on croirait (entendre) une clarinette** it sounds like *ou* it could be a clarinet (playing) ◆ **on croirait entendre son père** it could (almost) be his father talking, you'd think it was his father talking ◆ **on croirait qu'elle ne comprend pas** she doesn't seem to understand, you might almost think she didn't understand

◆ **en croire qn** *ou* **qch** (= *s'en rapporter à*) ◆ **à l'en ~** to listen to *ou* hear him, if you (were to) go by what he says ◆ **s'il faut en ~ les journaux** if we (are to) go by what the papers say, if we are to believe the papers, if the papers are anything to go by ◆ **croyez-m'en** believe me ◆ **vous pouvez m'en ~, croyez-en mon expérience** (you can) take it from me, take it from one who knows ◆ **si vous m'en croyez** if you want my opinion ◆ **il n'en croyait pas ses oreilles/ses yeux** he couldn't believe his ears/ his eyes

2 - VERBE INTRANSITIF

Rel = avoir la foi to believe, to be a believer

3 - VT INDIRECT

croire à [+ *innocence de qn, vie éternelle, Père Noël*] to believe in; [+ *justice, médecine*] to have faith *ou* confidence in, to believe in; [+ *promesses*] to believe (in), to have faith in ◆ **il ne croit plus à rien** he no longer believes in anything ◆ **ses histoires, je n'y crois plus** I don't believe his stories any more ◆ **on a cru d'abord à un accident** at first they believed *ou* thought it was accident, at first they took it for an accident ◆ **pour faire ~ à un suicide** to make people think it was suicide, to give the impression *ou* appearance of (a) suicide ◆ **il ne croit pas à la guerre** (= *il pense qu'elle n'aura pas lieu*) he doesn't think *ou* believe there will be a war; (= *il pense qu'elle ne sert à rien*) he doesn't believe in war ◆ **non, mais tu crois au Père Noël !** you really do live in cloud-cuckoo land! *(Brit)*, you must believe in Santa Claus too! ◆ **c'est à n'y pas ~ !** it's beyond belief!, it's unbelievable!, it's hardly credible! ◆ **veuillez ~ à mes sentiments dévoués** *(frm : formule épistolaire)* yours sincerely

4 - VT INDIRECT

croire en to believe in ◆ **~ en Dieu** to believe in God ◆ **~ en qn** to believe in sb, to have faith *ou* confidence in sb

5 - VERBE PRONOMINAL

se croire

1 = penser être tel ou dans telle situation **se ~ fort/malin** to think one is strong/clever ◆ **il se croit un génie** he thinks he's a genius ◆ **elle se croit tout permis** she thinks she can do whatever she likes *ou* she can get away with anything ◆ **on se croirait en vacances** I feel as if I'm on holiday ◆ **on se croirait en Bretagne/été** it could almost be Brittany/summer ◆ **le patron lui a dit qu'elle avait un espoir de promotion et elle s'y croit déjà** * the boss told her she had a chance of promotion and she acts as if she'd already got it

2 = être prétentieux **qu'est-ce qu'il se croit, celui-là ?** who does he think he is?* ◆ **il s'y croit** * *(péj)* he thinks he's really something *

---

croisade /kʀwazad/ **NF** *(Hist, fig)* crusade ◆ **les Croisades** the (Holy) Crusades ◆ **la ~ des Albigeois** the Albigensian Crusade ◆ **partir en ~** *(lit)* to go on a crusade; *(fig)* to launch *ou* mount a crusade (*contre* against); ◆ **se lancer dans une ~ contre le chômage** to go on a crusade for job creation

croisé[1], e[1] /kʀwaze/ (ptp de **croiser**) **ADJ** [*veste*] double-breasted; [*rimes, vers*] alternate ◆ **race ~e** crossbreed ◆ **tissu ~** twill; → **bras, feu[1], mot** **NM** (= *étoffe*) twill

croisé[2] /kʀwaze/ **NM** *(Hist)* crusader

croisée[2] /kʀwaze/ **NF** 1 (= *jonction*) **~ de chemins** crossroads, crossing ◆ **à la ~ des chemins** *(fig)* at a crossroads ◆ **~ d'ogives** ribbed vault ◆ **~ du transept** transept crossing ◆ **leur musique est à la ~ de plusieurs cultures** their music is a blend of several cultural influences 2 *(littér = fenêtre)* window, casement *(littér)*

croisement /kʀwazmɑ̃/ **NM** 1 [*de fils, brins*] crossing ◆ **l'étroitesse de la route rendait impossible le ~ des véhicules** the narrowness of the road made it impossible for vehicles to pass (one another); → **feu[1]** 2 [*de races, espèces*] crossing *(NonC)*, crossbreeding *(NonC)*, interbreeding *(NonC)* (*avec* with); ◆ **faire des ~s de race** to rear *ou* produce crossbreeds, to cross(breed) ◆ **est-ce un ~ ?** *ou* **le produit d'un ~ ?** is it a cross(breed)? 3 (= *carrefour*) crossroads, junction ◆ **au ~ de la route et de la voie ferrée** where the road crosses the railway

croiser /kʀwaze/ ▸ conjug 1 ◂ **VT** 1 [+ *bras*] to fold, to cross; [+ *jambes*] to cross; [+ *fils, lignes*] to cross ◆ **elle croisa son châle sur sa poitrine** she folded her shawl across *ou* over her chest ◆ **les jambes croisées** cross-legged ◆ **~ les doigts** *(lit)* to cross one's fingers; *(fig)* to keep one's fingers crossed, to cross one's fingers ◆ **croisons les doigts !** *(fig)* fingers crossed! ◆ **je croise les doigts pour qu'il fasse beau** I'm keeping my fingers crossed that the weather will be good ◆ **~ le fer** *(lit, fig)* to cross swords (*avec* with); ◆ **se ~ les bras** *(fig)* to lounge around, to sit around idly

2 (= *couper*) [+ *route*] to cross, to cut across; [+ *ligne*] to cross, to cut across, to intersect

3 (= *passer à côté de*) [+ *véhicule, passant*] to pass ◆ **notre train a croisé le rapide** our train passed the express going in the other direction ◆ **son regard croisa le mien** his eyes met mine ◆ **je l'ai croisé plusieurs fois dans des réunions** I've seen him several times at meetings ◆ **j'ai croisé Jean dans la rue** I bumped into Jean in the street

4 (= *accoupler*) [+ *espèces, races*] to cross(breed), to interbreed (*avec* with); ◆ **l'âne peut se ~ avec le cheval** an ass can crossbred with a horse

5 *(Sport)* [+ *tir, coup droit*] to angle ◆ **passe croisée** diagonal pass

VI 1 *(Habillement)* **cette veste croise bien** that jacket has got a nice *ou* good overlap ◆ **cette saison les couturiers font ~ les vestes** this season fashion designers are making jackets double-breasted ◆ **il avait tellement grossi qu'il ne pouvait plus (faire) ~ sa veste** he'd got so fat that he couldn't get his jacket to fasten

2 *(Naut)* to cruise

VPR **se croiser** 1 [*chemins, lignes*] to cross, to cut (across) each other, to intersect ◆ **se ~ à angle droit** to cross at right angles ◆ **nos regards** *ou* **nos yeux se croisèrent** our eyes met ◆ **il a les yeux qui se croisent** * he's cross-eyed

2 [*personnes, véhicules*] to pass each other ◆ **ma lettre s'est croisée avec la tienne, nos lettres se sont croisées** my letter crossed yours (in the post), our letters crossed (in the post) ◆ **nous nous sommes croisés hier** we bumped *ou* ran into each other yesterday ◆ **nous nous sommes croisés plusieurs fois dans des réunions** we've seen each other several times at meetings

3 *(Hist)* to take the cross, to go on a crusade

croiseur /kʀwazœʀ/ **NM** (= *bateau*) cruiser

croisière /kʀwazjɛʀ/ **NF** cruise ◆ **partir en ~, faire une ~** to go on a cruise ◆ **être en ~** to be on a cruise ◆ **ce voilier est idéal pour la ~** this boat is ideal for cruising ◆ **allure** *ou* **régime** *ou* **rythme** *ou* **vitesse de ~** cruising speed

croisiériste /kʀwazjeʀist/ **NMF** (= *passager*) cruise passenger; (= *voyagiste*) cruise company

croisillon /kʀwazijɔ̃/ **NM** [*de croix, charpente*] crosspiece, crossbar; [*d'église*] transept ◆ **~s** [*de fenêtre*] lattice work; [*de tarte*] lattice; → **fenêtre**

croissance /kʀwasɑ̃s/ **NF** [*d'enfant, ville, industrie*] growth, development; [*de plante*] growth ◆ **~ économique** economic growth *ou* development ◆ **~ interne/externe** [*d'entreprise*] internal/external growth ◆ **~ molle** *(Écon)* soft growth ◆ **~ négative** *(Écon)* negative growth ◆ **~ zéro** zero (economic) growth ◆ **arrêté dans sa ~** stunted ◆ **maladie de ~** growth disease ◆ **entreprise en pleine ~** expanding company

croissant[1] /kʀwasɑ̃/ **NM** 1 (= *forme*) crescent ◆ **~ de lune** crescent of the moon ◆ **en ~** crescent-shaped 2 *(Culin)* croissant

croissant², e /kʀwasɑ̃, ɑ̃t/ ADJ *[nombre, tension]* growing, increasing, rising; *[chaleur]* rising; *[froid]* increasing; *(Math) [fonction]* increasing ◆ **aller ~** *[peur, enthousiasme]* to grow, to increase; *[bruit]* to grow *ou* get louder ◆ **le rythme ~ des accidents** the increasing number of accidents, the rising accident rate

croissanterie /kʀwasɑ̃tʀi/ NF croissant shop

Croissant-Rouge /kʀwasɑ̃ʀuʒ/ NM ◆ **le ~** the Red Crescent

croître /kʀwatʀ/ ▸ conjug 55 ◂ VI 1 *[enfant, plante]* to grow; *[ville]* to grow, to increase in size ◆ **~ en beauté/sagesse** to grow in beauty/wisdom ◆ **~ dans l'estime de qn** to rise *ou* grow in sb's esteem

2 *[ambition, bruit, quantité]* to grow, to increase ◆ **les jours croissent** the days are getting longer *ou* are lengthening ◆ **~ en nombre/volume** to increase in number/size *ou* volume ◆ **l'inquiétude sur son état de santé ne cessait de ~** there was increasing concern over the state of his health ◆ **son enthousiasme ne cessa de ~** he grew more and more enthusiastic ◆ **la chaleur ne faisait que ~** the heat got more and more intense, the temperature kept on rising

3 *[rivière]* to swell, to rise; *[lune]* to wax; *[vent]* to rise

4 *(locutions)* **croissez et multipliez !** *(Bible)* go forth and multiply! ◆ **ça ne fait que ~ et embellir !** *(iro)* (things are getting) better and better! *(iro)*

croix /kʀwa/ NF 1 *(gén)* cross ◆ **~ ansée** ansate cross ◆ **~ celtique/grecque/latine** Celtic/Greek/Latin cross ◆ **~ de Malte/de Saint-André** Maltese/St Andrew's cross ◆ **~ ancrée/fleuretée** cross moline/fleury *ou* flory ◆ **~ fleuronnée** *ou* **tréflée** cross tréflée ◆ **~ de Jérusalem** cross of Jerusalem ◆ **~ potencée** potent cross ◆ **en ~** crosswise, in the form of a cross ◆ **mettre des bâtons en ~** to lay sticks crosswise ◆ **être disposé en ~** to form a cross *ou* be arranged crosswise ◆ **chemins qui se coupent en ~** paths which cross at right angles (to one another) ◆ **mettre en ~, mettre à mort sur la ~** to crucify ◆ **mise en ~** crucifixion ◆ **mettre les bras en ~** to stretch one's arms out sideways ◆ **pour le faire sortir, c'est la ~ et la bannière*** it's the devil's own job *ou* a devil of a job to get him to go out* ◆ **~ de bois ~ de fer (, si je mens je vais en enfer)** cross my heart (and hope to die); → **chemin, signe**

2 *(= décoration)* cross; *(Scol = récompense)* prize, medal

3 *(= marque)* cross ◆ **faire** *ou* **mettre une ~ devant un nom** to put a cross in front of *ou* by a name ◆ **(appeler) les noms marqués d'une ~** (to call out) the names with a cross against *(Brit)* *ou* by *(US)* them ◆ **ta prime, tu peux faire une ~ dessus*** you might just as well forget all about your bonus *ou* write your bonus off* ◆ **si tu lui prêtes ton livre, tu peux faire une ~ dessus !*** if you lend him your book, you can say goodbye to it!* *ou* you can kiss it goodbye!* ◆ **il faut faire une ~ à la cheminée** *ou* **sur le calendrier** *(iro)* it's a red-letter day

4 *(= souffrance, épreuve)* cross, burden ◆ **chacun a** *ou* **porte sa ~** we all have our cross to bear

COMP **croix de fer** *(Gym)* crucifix
croix gammée swastika
Croix de guerre *(Mil)* Military Cross
croix de Lorraine cross of Lorraine
Croix-du-Sud Southern Cross

Croix-Rouge /kʀwaʀuʒ/ NF ◆ **la ~** the Red Cross

cromlech /kʀɔmlɛk/ NM cromlech

cromorne /kʀɔmɔʀn/ NF krumhorn

croquant¹ † /kʀɔkɑ̃/ NM *(péj)* yokel, (country) bumpkin

croquant², e /kʀɔkɑ̃, ɑ̃t/ ADJ crisp, crunchy NM *[de volaille]* gristle ◆ **le ~ de l'oreille** the cartilage in the ear

croque* /kʀɔk/ NM abrév de **croque-monsieur**

croque au sel /kʀɔkosɛl/ **à la croque au sel** LOC ADV with salt (and nothing else)

croque-madame /kʀɔkmadam/ NM INV *toasted ham and cheese sandwich with a fried egg on top*

croquembouche /kʀɔkɑ̃buʃ/ NM *pyramid of cream-filled choux pastry balls*

croque-mitaine (pl **croque-mitaines**) /kʀɔkmitɛn/ NM bog(e)y man, ogre ◆ **ce maître est un vrai ~** this schoolmaster is a real ogre

croque-monsieur /kʀɔkməsjø/ NM INV *toasted ham and cheese sandwich*

croque-mort* (pl **croque-morts**) /kʀɔkmɔʀ/ NM undertaker's *ou* mortician's *(US)* assistant ◆ **avoir un air de ~** to have a funereal look *ou* a face like an undertaker

croquenot* /kʀɔkno/ NM *(= chaussure)* clodhopper*

croquer /kʀɔke/ ▸ conjug 1 ◂ VT 1 *(= manger) [+ biscuits, noisettes, bonbons]* to crunch; *[+ fruit]* to bite into ◆ **Adam croqua la pomme** Adam took a bite out of the apple ◆ **à laisser fondre dans la bouche sans ~** to be sucked slowly and not chewed *ou* crunched ◆ **je ne peux pas ~ avec mon dentier** I can't bite properly with my dentures ◆ **~ la vie à pleines dents** to make the most of life; → **chocolat**

2 *(* = dépenser)* to squander ◆ **~ de l'argent** to squander money, to go through money like water* ◆ **~ un héritage** to squander *ou* blow* an inheritance

3 *(= dessiner)* to sketch ◆ **être (joli) à ~** to be as pretty as a picture, to look good enough to eat ◆ **tu es à ~ avec ce chapeau** you look good enough to eat in that hat

4 *(= camper) [+ personnage]* to sketch, to outline, to give a thumbnail sketch of

5 *(arg Crime)* **il en croque** *[indicateur]* he's a (copper's) nark*; *[policier]* he gets paid off*

VI 1 *[fruit]* to be crunchy; *[salade]* to be crisp ◆ **le sucre croque sous la dent** sugar is crunchy

2 *(= mordre)* to bite ◆ **~ dans une pomme** to bite into an apple

croquet /kʀɔkɛ/ NM *(Sport)* croquet

croquette /kʀɔkɛt/ NF *(Culin)* croquette ◆ **~s de chocolat** chocolate croquettes ◆ **~s pour chiens/chats** dry dogfood/catfood

croqueuse /kʀɔkøz/ NF ◆ **~ de diamants** gold digger, fortune-hunter

croquignolet, -ette* /kʀɔkiɲɔlɛ, ɛt/ ADJ *(= mignon)* sweet, cute*, dinky* ◆ **ça promet d'être ~** *(iro)* that sounds like great fun *(iro)*

croquis /kʀɔki/ NM *(= dessin)* (rough) sketch; *(= description)* sketch ◆ **faire un ~ de qch** to sketch sth, to make a (rough) sketch of sth ◆ **faire un rapide ~ de la situation** to give a rapid outline *ou* thumbnail sketch of the situation ◆ **~ d'audience** court-room sketches

crosne /kʀon/ NM Chinese artichoke

cross(-country) /kʀɔs(kuntʀi)/ NM *(= course) (à pied)* cross-country race *ou* run; *(Équitation)* cross-country race; *(= sport) (à pied)* cross-country racing *ou* running; *(Équitation)* cross-country racing ◆ **faire du ~(-country)** *(à pied)* to do cross-country running

crosse /kʀɔs/ NF 1 *(= poignée) [de fusil]* butt; *[de revolver]* grip ◆ **frapper qn à coups de ~** to hit sb with the butt of one's rifle ◆ **mettre** *ou* **lever la ~ en l'air** *(= se rendre)* to show the white flag, to lay down one's arms; *(= se mutiner)* to mutiny, to refuse to fight 2 *(= bâton) (Rel)* crook, crosier, crozier ◆ **~ de golf** *(Sport)* golf club ◆ **~ de hockey** hockey stick 3 *(= partie recourbée) [de violon]* head, scroll ◆ **~ de piston** cross-head ◆ **~ de l'aorte** arch of the aorta, aortic arch ◆ **~ de fougère** crosier *(of fern)* 4 ⁑ **chercher des ~s à qn** to pick a quarrel with sb ◆ **s'il me cherche des ~s** if he's looking for a chance to make trouble *ou* to pick a quarrel with me 5 *(Culin)* **~ de bœuf** knuckle of beef

crotale /kʀɔtal/ NM rattlesnake, rattler* *(US)*

crotchon /kʀɔtʃɔ̃/ NM *(Helv = entame)* crust

crotte /kʀɔt/ NF 1 *(= excrément) [de brebis, lapin, souris]* dropping ◆ **~ de nez*** bog(e)y⁑ *(Brit)*, booger⁑ *(US)* ◆ **son chien a déposé une ~ sur le palier** his dog has messed *ou* done its business on the landing ◆ **c'est plein de ~(s) de chien** it's covered in dog mess ◆ **c'est de la ~*** it's a load of (old) rubbish* ◆ **c'est pas de la ~*** it's not cheap rubbish ◆ **il ne se prend pas pour une ~*** he thinks he's God's gift to mankind *ou* the bee's knees* *(Brit)* ◆ **ma (petite) ~*** *(terme d'affection)* my little sausage* 2 *(= bonbon)* **~ de chocolat** chocolate 3 († = *boue)* mud EXCL * oh heck!*, blast (it)!* *(Brit)* ◆ **je te dis ~ !*** get lost!*

crotté, e /kʀɔte/ (ptp de **crotter**) ADJ *[chaussure, vêtement]* muddy, caked with *ou* covered in mud ◆ **il était tout ~** he was all covered in mud *ou* all muddy

crotter /kʀɔte/ ▸ conjug 1 ◂ VT to muddy VI *[chien]* to do its business, to mess

crottin /kʀɔtɛ̃/ NM 1 *[de cheval, âne]* droppings, dung *(NonC)*, manure *(NonC)* 2 *(= fromage) small, round goat's milk cheese*

crouillat ⁑*/kʀuja/, **crouille** ⁑*/kʀuj/ NM *(injurieux)* North African

croulant, e /kʀulɑ̃, ɑ̃t/ ADJ *[mur]* crumbling, tumbledown *(épith)*; *[maison]* ramshackle, tumbledown *(épith)*, crumbling; *[autorité, empire]* crumbling, tottering NM ◆ **vieux ~** ⁑ old fogey⁑, crumbly *(Brit)**

crouler /kʀule/ ▸ conjug 1 ◂ VI 1 *(= s'écrouler) [maison, mur]* to collapse, to fall down; *[masse de neige]* to collapse; *[terre]* to give (way); *[empire]* to collapse ◆ **le tremblement de terre a fait ~ les maisons** the earthquake has brought the houses down ◆ **nous avons réparé les murs qui croulaient** we've repaired the walls that were crumbling ◆ **la terre croulait sous ses pas** the ground gave (way) beneath *ou* under his feet ◆ **~ sous le poids de qch** *(fig)* to collapse under the weight of sth ◆ **la table croulait sous les livres** the table collapsed under the weight of the books

2 *(= être submergé)* **ils croulent sous les dettes** they are crippled by debts ◆ **il croule sous l'argent** he's rolling in money* ◆ **les employés croulent sous le travail** the employees are snowed under with work ◆ **nous croulons sous les demandes de réservation** we're snowed under with bookings ◆ **la salle croulait sous les applaudissements** the auditorium resounded with applause

croup /kʀup/ NM *(Méd)* croup ◆ **faux ~** spasmodic croup

croupe /kʀup/ NF 1 *[de cheval]* croup, crupper, rump, hindquarters ◆ **monter en ~** to ride pillion ◆ **il monta en ~ et ils partirent** he got on behind and off they went ◆ **il avait son ami en ~** he had his friend behind him (on the pillion) 2 * *[de personne]* rump* 3 *[de colline]* hilltop

croupetons /kʀuptɔ̃/ ADV ◆ **se tenir** *ou* **être à ~** to be crouching, to be squatting, to be down on one's haunches ◆ **se mettre à ~** to crouch *ou* squat down, to go down on one's haunches

croupi, e /kʀupi/ (ptp de **croupir**) ADJ *[eau]* stagnant

croupier, -ière¹ /kʀupje, jɛʀ/ NM,F croupier

croupière² /kʀupjɛʀ/ NF *(= harnais)* crupper ◆ **tailler des ~s à qn** † to put a spoke in sb's wheel

croupion /kʀupjɔ̃/ **NM** *[d'oiseau]* rump; *(Culin)* parson's nose, pope's nose *(US)*; (* *hum) [de personne]* rear (end)*, backside* ◆ **parlement/parti ~** *(péj)* rump parliament/party

croupir /kʀupiʀ/ ▸ conjug 2 ◂ **VI** *[eau]* to stagnate ◆ **feuilles qui croupissent dans la mare** leaves rotting in the pond ◆ ~ **dans son ignorance/dans le vice** to wallow *ou* remain sunk in one's own ignorance/in vice ◆ **je n'ai pas envie de ~ dans ce bled*** I don't want to stay and rot in this dump* ◆ ~ **en prison** to rot in prison

croupissant, e /kʀupisɑ̃, ɑ̃t/ **ADJ** *[eau]* stagnant ◆ **une vie ~e** a dreary existence

CROUS /kʀus/ **NM** (abrév de **centre régional des œuvres universitaires et scolaires**) → **centre**

croustade /kʀustad/ **NF** croustade

croustillant, e /kʀustijɑ̃, ɑ̃t/ **ADJ** 1 *[pain, pâte]* crusty; *[croissant, galette, chips]* crisp, crunchy 2 *(= grivois)* spicy

croustiller /kʀustije/ ▸ conjug 1 ◂ **VI** *[pain, pâte]* to be crusty; *[croissant, galette, chips]* to be crisp *ou* crunchy

croûte /kʀut/ **NF** 1 *[de pain, pâte]* crust; *[de fromage]* rind; *[de vol-au-vent]* case

◆ **en croûte** ◆ **jambon en ~** ham en croute ◆ **morue en ~ de pommes de terre** cod baked in a potato crust; → **pâté**

2 (* *= nourriture)* food, grub* ◆ **à la ~ !*** *(= venez manger)* come and get it!*, grub's up!* *(Brit)*, grub's on!* *(US)*; *(= allons manger)* let's go and eat!*; → **casser, gagner**

3 *(= couche)* layer; *(sur plaie)* scab; *(sur pot de peinture)* skin ◆ **couvert d'une ~ de glace** crusted with ice, covered with a crust *ou* a layer of ice ◆ **recouvert d'une ~ de boue** caked with mud ◆ ~ **calcaire** *ou* **de tartre** layer of scale *ou* fur ◆ **gratter des ~s de cire sur une table** to scrape candlewax off a table

4 *(= apparence)* ~ **de culture** veneer of culture ◆ ~ **de bêtise** (thick) layer of stupidity

5 ◆ ~ **(de cuir)** undressed leather *ou* hide ◆ **sac en ~** hide bag

6 *(péj = tableau)* lousy painting

7 *(péj = personne)* old fossil*

COMP **croûte aux champignons** mushrooms on toast

croûte au fromage cheese on toast, toasted cheese, ≃ Welsh rarebit *ou* rabbit

croûte de pain crust of bread ◆ **~s de pain** *(péj)* old crusts; *(quignons)* hunks *ou* chunks of bread

la croûte terrestre *(Géol)* the earth's crust

croûté, e /kʀute/ **ADJ** *(Ski)* ◆ **neige ~e** crusted snow

croûter* /kʀute/ ▸ conjug 1 ◂ **VI** to eat

croûteux, -euse /kʀutø, øz/ **ADJ** scabby, covered with scabs

croûton /kʀutɔ̃/ **NM** 1 *(= bout du pain)* crust; *(Culin)* crouton 2 *(péj)* **(vieux) ~** *(= personne)* fuddy-duddy*, old fossil*

croyable /kʀwajabl/ **ADJ** ◆ **ce n'est pas ~!** it's unbelievable!, it's incredible! ◆ **c'est à peine ~** it's hard to believe

croyance /kʀwajɑ̃s/ **NF** 1 *(= foi)* ~ **à** *ou* **en** belief in, faith in 2 *(= religion, opinion)* belief ◆ **~s religieuses** religious beliefs ◆ **la ~ populaire** folk *ou* conventional wisdom

croyant, e /kʀwajɑ̃, ɑ̃t/ **ADJ** ◆ **être ~** to be a believer ◆ **ne pas être ~** to be a non-believer **NM,F** believer ◆ **les ~s** people who believe in God

CRS /seɛʀɛs/ (abrév de **Compagnie républicaine de sécurité**) **NM** *member of the state security police* ≃ member of the riot police ◆ **les ~** ≃ the riot police **NF** *company of the state security police* ≃ riot police

cru[1], **e**[1] /kʀy/ **ADJ** 1 *(= non cuit) [aliments]* raw, uncooked ◆ **je ne vais pas te manger tout ~** I won't eat you ◆ **je l'aurais avalée** *ou* **mangée toute ~e*** *(= j'étais furieux)* I could have strangled *ou* murdered her*; *(= elle était belle à croquer)* she looked good enough to eat*; → **lait**

2 *(= non apprêté) [soie]* raw; *[chanvre, toile]* raw, untreated; *[métal]* crude, raw ◆ **cuir ~** untreated *ou* raw leather, rawhide

3 *[lumière, couleur]* harsh

4 *(= franc, réaliste) [mot]* forthright, blunt; *[description]* raw, blunt; *[réponse]* straight, blunt, forthright ◆ **je vous le dis tout ~** I'll tell you straight out*, I'll give it to you straight*

5 *(= choquant) [histoire, chanson, langage]* crude, coarse ◆ **parler ~** to speak coarsely *ou* crudely

6 *(Helv = humide et froid)* **il fait ~** it's cold and damp

7 *(locutions)* ◆ **à ~ construire à ~** to build without foundations ◆ **monter à ~** *(Équitation)* to ride bareback

cru[2] /kʀy/ **NM** 1 *(= vignoble)* vineyard ◆ **un vin d'un bon ~** a good vintage 2 *(= vin)* wine ◆ **un grand ~** a great wine; → **bouilleur** 3 *(locutions)* **du ~** local ◆ **les gens du ~** the locals ◆ **de son (propre) ~** of his own invention *ou* devising

cruauté /kʀyote/ **NF** 1 *[de personne, destin]* cruelty *(envers* to); *[de bête sauvage]* ferocity 2 *(= action)* (act of) cruelty, cruel act

cruche /kʀyʃ/ **NF** 1 *(= récipient)* jug *(Brit)*, pitcher *(US)*; *(= contenu)* jug(ful) *(Brit)*, pitcher(ful) *(US)* ◆ **tant va la ~ à l'eau qu'à la fin elle se casse** *(Prov)* if you keep playing with fire you must expect to get burnt 2 (* *= imbécile)* ass*, twit* *(Brit)* ◆ **ce qu'il est ~ !** he's such a ninny!*

cruchon /kʀyʃɔ̃/ **NM** *(= récipient)* small jug *(Brit) ou* pitcher *(US)*; *(= contenu)* small jug(ful) *(Brit) ou* pitcher(ful) *(US)*

crucial, e (mpl **-iaux**) /kʀysjal, jo/ **ADJ** crucial

crucifère /kʀysifɛʀ/ **ADJ** cruciferous

crucifiement /kʀysifimɑ̃/ **NM** crucifixion ◆ **le ~ de la chair** *(fig)* the crucifying of the flesh

crucifier /kʀysifje/ ▸ conjug 7 ◂ **VT** *(lit, fig)* to crucify

crucifix /kʀysifi/ **NM** crucifix

crucifixion /kʀysifiksjɔ̃/ **NF** crucifixion

cruciforme /kʀysifɔʀm/ **ADJ** cruciform ◆ **tournevis ~** Phillips screwdriver ® ◆ **vis ~** Phillips screw ®

cruciverbiste /kʀysivɛʀbist/ **NMF** *(= joueur)* crossword enthusiast; *(= inventeur)* crossword compiler

crudité /kʀydite/ **NF** 1 *[de langage]* crudeness, coarseness; *[de description]* bluntness; *[de lumière, couleur]* harshness, garishness 2 *(= propos)* **~s** coarse remarks, coarseness *(NonC)* ◆ **dire des ~s** to make coarse remarks 3 *(Culin)* **~s** raw vegetables ◆ **salade de ~s** ≃ mixed salad, crudités

crue[2] /kʀy/ **NF** *(= montée des eaux)* rise in the water level; *(= inondation)* flood ◆ **en ~** in spate ◆ **les ~s du Nil** the Nile floods ◆ **la fonte des neiges provoque des ~s subites** the spring thaw produces a sudden rise in river levels

cruel, -elle /kʀyɛl/ **ADJ** 1 *(= méchant) [personne, acte, paroles]* cruel; *[animal]* ferocious 2 *(= douloureux) [perte]* cruel; *[destin, sort, épreuve]* cruel, harsh; *[remords, froid, nécessité]* cruel, bitter; *[manque]* desperate, severe

cruellement /kʀyɛlmɑ̃/ **ADV** 1 *(= méchamment)* cruelly ◆ **traiter qn ~** to be cruel to sb, to treat sb cruelly 2 *(= douloureusement) [décevoir]* bitterly; *[souffrir]* terribly ◆ **manquer ~ de qch** to be desperately short of sth ◆ **l'argent fait ~ défaut** the lack of money is sorely felt ◆ ~ **éprouvé par ce deuil** sorely *ou* grievously distressed by this bereavement

crûment /kʀymɑ̃/ **ADV** *[dire, parler] (= nettement)* bluntly, forthrightly; *(= grossièrement)* crudely, coarsely ◆ **éclairer ~** to cast a harsh *ou* garish light over

crustacé /kʀystase/ **NM** shellfish *(pl inv) (crabs, lobsters and shrimps)*, crustacean *(SPÉC)* ◆ **~s** *(Culin)* seafood, shellfish

cryobiologie /kʀijɔbjɔlɔʒi/ **NF** cryobiology

cryochirurgie /kʀijɔʃiʀyʀʒi/ **NF** cryosurgery

cryoconservation /kʀijokɔ̃sɛʀvasjɔ̃/ **NF** cryogenic preservation

cryogénie /kʀijɔʒeni/ **NF** cryogenics *(sg)*

cryogénique /kʀijɔʒenik/ **ADJ** cryogenic ◆ **moteur ~** cryogenic (first-stage) engine ◆ **fusée à propulsion ~** cryogenicallypowered rocket

cryologie /kʀijɔlɔʒi/ **NF** cryogenics *(sg)*

cryptage /kʀiptaʒ/ **NM** *[de message, émission, données]* encryption

crypte /kʀipt/ **NF** *(Archit, Anat)* crypt

crypter /kʀipte/ ▸ conjug 1 ◂ **VT** *[+ message, émission, données]* to encrypt ◆ **chaîne/émission cryptée** encrypted channel/programme ◆ **données cryptées** encrypted *ou* scrambled data

cryptique /kʀiptik/ **ADJ** 1 *(= secret)* cryptic 2 *(Anat)* cryptal

cryptocommuniste † /kʀiptokɔmynist/ **NMF** crypto-communist

cryptogame /kʀiptɔgam/ **ADJ** cryptogamic **NM** *ou* **NF** cryptogam

cryptogramme /kʀiptɔgʀam/ **NM** cryptogram

cryptographie /kʀiptɔgʀafi/ **NF** cryptography, cryptology

cryptographique /kʀiptɔgʀafik/ **ADJ** cryptographic

crypton /kʀiptɔ̃/ **NM** ⇒ **krypton**

CSA /seɛsa/ **NM** (abrév de **Conseil supérieur de l'audiovisuel**) → **conseil**

CSCE /seɛssea/ **NF** (abrév de **Conférence sur la Sécurité et la Coopération en Europe**) CSCE

CSG /seɛsʒe/ **NF** (abrév de **contribution sociale généralisée**) → **contribution**

CSM /seɛsɛm/ **NM** (abrév de **Conseil supérieur de la magistrature**) → **conseil**

CSP /seɛspe/ **NF** (abrév de **catégorie socioprofessionnelle**) socio-professional category, SPC

Cuba /kyba/ **N** Cuba ◆ **à ~** in Cuba

cubage /kybaʒ/ **NM** 1 *(= action)* cubage 2 *(= volume)* cubage, cubature, cubic content ◆ ~ **d'air** air space

cubain, e /kybɛ̃, ɛn/ **ADJ** Cuban **NM,F** **Cubain(e)** Cuban

cube /kyb/ **NM** *(gén, Géom, Math)* cube; *[de jeu]* building block, (wooden) brick ◆ **le ~ de 2 est 8** *(Math)* 2 cubed is 8, the cube of 2 is 8 ◆ **élever au ~** to cube ◆ **gros ~*** *(= moto)* big bike* **ADJ** ◆ **centimètre/mètre ~** cubic centimetre/metre; → **cylindrée**

cuber /kybe/ ▸ conjug 1 ◂ **VT** *[+ nombre]* to cube; *[+ volume, solide]* to cube, to measure the volume of; *[+ espace]* to measure the cubic capacity of **VI** *[récipient]* ◆ ~ **20 litres** to have a cubic capacity of 20 litres ◆ **avec l'inflation leurs dépenses vont ~** * *(fig)* with inflation their expenses are going to mount up

cubique /kybik/ **ADJ** cubic; → **racine** **NF** *(Math = courbe)* cubic

cubisme /kybism/ **NM** Cubism

cubiste /kybist/ **ADJ, NMF** Cubist

cubitainer ® /kybitɛnɛʀ/ **NM** square plastic container *(for holding liquids)*

cubital, e (mpl **-aux**) /kybital, o/ ADJ ulnar

cubitus /kybitys/ NM ulna

cucu(l) * /kyky/ ADJ ◆ ~**(l) (la praline)** *[personne]* silly; *[film, livre]* corny*

cucurbitacée /kykyʀbitase/ NF cucurbitaceous plant, cucurbit ◆ **les ~s** the Cucurbitaceae *(SPÉC)*

cueillette /kœjɛt/ NF 1 *[de fleurs, fraises, mûres]* picking, gathering; *[de pommes, poires etc]* picking; *(Ethnologie)* gathering ◆ **la ~ du houblon/des pommes** hop-/apple-picking ◆ **ils vivent de la ~ et de la chasse** they are hunter-gatherers 2 *(= récolte)* harvest, crop ◆ **elle me montra sa ~** she showed me what she'd picked ◆ **quelle ~ !** what a harvest! *ou* crop! 3 *(Can) [de données]* collection

cueilleur, -euse /kœjœʀ, øz/ NM,F *[de fruits]* gatherer

cueillir /kœjiʀ/ ▸ conjug 12 ◂ VT 1 *[+ fleurs, fraises, mûres]* to pick; *(en quantité)* to gather; *[+ pommes, poires]* to pick ◆ ~ **les lauriers de la victoire** to win *ou* bring home the laurels (of victory) 2 *(= attraper) [+ ballon]* to catch; *[+ baiser]* to snatch, to steal ◆ **il est venu nous ~ à la gare*** he came to collect *ou* get us *ou* pick us up at the station ◆ **il m'a cueilli à froid** *(= pris au dépourvu)* he caught me off guard *ou* on the hop* *(Brit)* 3 *(* = arrêter)* to nab*, to catch ◆ **le voleur s'est fait ~ par la police*** the thief was *ou* got nabbed by the police*

cuesta /kwɛsta/ NF cuesta

cui-cui /kɥikɥi/ EXCL, NM tweet-tweet ◆ **faire ~** to go tweet-tweet

cuiller, cuillère /kɥijɛʀ/ NF 1 *(= ustensile)* spoon; *(= contenu)* spoonful ◆ **petite ~** *(à thé, à dessert)* teaspoon ◆ **faire manger qn à la ~** to spoonfeed sb ◆ **manger son dessert à la** *ou* **avec une ~** to use a spoon to eat one's dessert ◆ **service à la ~** *(Tennis)* underarm serve ◆ **servir à la ~** to serve underarm; → **dos, ramasser**

2 *(* = main)* **serrer la ~ à qn** to shake sb's paw*

3 *(Pêche)* spoon, spoonbait ◆ ~ **tournante** spinner ◆ **pêche à la ~** spoonbait fishing, fishing with a spoon(bait)

4 *(Tech) [de grenade]* (safety) catch

COMP **cuiller de bois** *(gén, Rugby)* wooden spoon ◆ **dans ce domaine, la France remporte la ~ de bois** France is the least successful in this field
cuiller à café coffee spoon, ≃ teaspoon ◆ **prenez une ~ à café de sirop** take a teaspoonful of cough mixture
cuiller à dessert dessertspoon
cuiller à moka (small) coffee spoon
cuiller à moutarde mustard spoon
cuiller à pot ladle ◆ **en deux** *ou* **trois coups de ~ à pot*** in two shakes of a lamb's tail*, in a flash, in no time (at all)
cuiller à soupe *(= ustensile)* soup spoon; *(pour mesurer)* tablespoon
cuiller de verrier (glassblower's) ladle

cuillerée /kɥijʀe/ NF spoonful ◆ ~ **à soupe** ≃ tablespoonful ◆ ~ **à café** ≃ teaspoonful

cuir /kɥiʀ/ NM 1 *(= peau apprêtée)* leather; *(= industrie, artisanat)* leathercraft, leatherwork; *(* = blouson)* leather jacket ◆ **ceinture/semelles de ~** leather belt/soles ◆ **objets** *ou* **articles en ~** leather articles *ou* goods ◆ **le style ~** the leather look; → **relier, tanner**

2 *(sur l'animal vivant, ou avant tannage)* hide; * *[de personne]* hide* ◆ **avoir le ~ dur** *(= être résistant)* to be as tough *ou* as hard as nails; *(= être insensible à la critique)* to be thick-skinned

3 *(* = faute de liaison)* incorrect liaison *(due to an intrusive z- or t-sound)*

4 *(arg Ftbl)* ball

COMP **cuir bouilli** cuir-bouilli
cuir brut rawhide
cuir chevelu *(Anat)* scalp
cuir de crocodile crocodile skin
cuir en croûte undressed leather
cuir à rasoir (barber's *ou* razor) strop
cuir suédé suede
cuir de vache cowhide
cuir de veau calfskin
cuir verni patent leather
cuir vert ⇒ **cuir brut**

cuirasse /kɥiʀas/ NF *(Hist) [de chevalier]* breastplate; *(Naut)* armour(-plate *ou* -plating) *(Brit)*, armor(-plate *ou* -plating) *(US)*; *[d'animal]* cuirass; *(fig)* armour *(Brit)*, armor *(US)*; → **défaut**

cuirassé, e /kɥiʀase/ (ptp de **cuirasser**) ADJ *[soldat]* breastplated; *[navire]* armour-plated *(Brit)*, armor-plated *(US)*, armoured *(Brit)*, armored *(US)* ◆ **être ~ contre qch** *(fig)* to be hardened against sth, to be proof against sth NM battleship

cuirasser /kɥiʀase/ ▸ conjug 1 ◂ VT *[+ chevalier]* to put a breastplate on; *[+ navire]* to armour-plate *(Brit)*, to armor-plate *(US)*; *(fig = endurcir)* to harden *(contre* against) VPR **se cuirasser** *(= s'endurcir)* to harden o.s. *(contre* against); ◆ **se ~ contre la douleur/l'émotion** to harden o.s. against suffering/emotion

cuirassier /kɥiʀasje/ NM *(Hist)* cuirassier; *(Mil = soldat)* (armoured *(Brit) ou* armored *(US)*) cavalryman ◆ **le 3e ~** *(= régiment)* the 3rd (armoured) cavalry

cuire /kɥiʀ/ ▸ conjug 38 ◂ VT 1 ◆ **(faire) ~** *[+ plat, dîner]* to cook ◆ ~ **à feu doux** *ou* **doucement** to cook gently *ou* slowly ◆ ~ **à petit feu** to simmer ◆ **laisser** *ou* **faire ~ à feu doux** *ou* **à petit feu pendant 20 minutes** (allow to) simmer *ou* cook gently for 20 minutes ◆ ~ **à la broche** to cook *ou* roast on the spit, to spit-roast ◆ ~ **au four** *[+ pain, gâteau, pommes]* to bake; *[+ viande]* to roast; *[+ pommes de terre]* to roast, to bake ◆ ~ **qch à la vapeur/au gril/à la poêle/à l'eau/à la casserole** to steam/grill/fry/boil/stew sth ◆ ~ **au beurre/à l'huile** to cook in butter/in oil ◆ **faites-le ~ dans son jus** cook *ou* stew it in its own juice ◆ **faire bien/peu ~ qch** to cook sth thoroughly *ou* well/slightly *ou* lightly ◆ **faire trop ~ qch** to overcook sth ◆ **ne pas faire assez ~ qch** to undercook sth ◆ **il l'a fait ~ à point** he cooked it to a turn; → **carotte, cuit, dur, œuf**

◆ **à cuire** *[chocolat]* cooking *(épith)*; *[prunes, poires]* stewing *(épith)* ◆ **pommes à ~** cooking apples

2 ◆ **four qui cuit mal la viande** oven which cooks *ou* does meat badly *ou* unevenly

3 *[+ briques, porcelaine]* to fire

VI 1 *[aliment]* to cook ◆ ~ **à gros bouillon(s)** to boil hard *ou* fast ◆ **le dîner cuit à feu doux** *ou* **à petit feu** the dinner is cooking gently *ou* is simmering *ou* is on low ◆ ~ **dans son jus** to cook in its own juice, to stew

2 *[personne]* ~ **au soleil** to roast in the sun ◆ ~ **dans son jus*** *(= avoir très chaud)* to be boiling* *ou* roasting*; *(= se morfondre)* to stew in one's own juice ◆ **on cuit ici !*** it's boiling (hot)* *ou* roasting* *ou* sweltering in here!

3 *(= brûler)* **les mains/yeux me cuisaient** my hands/eyes were smarting *ou* stinging ◆ **mon dos me cuit** my back is burning

4 *(frm)* **il lui en a cuit** he suffered for it, he had good reason to regret it ◆ **il vous en cuira** you'll rue the day *(frm)*

cuisant, e /kɥizɑ̃, ɑt/ ADJ 1 *[douleur]* smarting, sharp; *[blessure]* burning, stinging; *[froid]* bitter, biting 2 *[remarque]* caustic, stinging; *[échec, regret, défaite, souvenir]* bitter

cuisine /kɥizin/ NF 1 *(= pièce)* kitchen; *(= mobilier)* kitchen furniture *(NonC)*; *(Naut)* galley ◆ **les ~s** the kitchens ◆ **la mère est à la caisse et le fils en ~** *(dans un restaurant)* the mother works at the till and the son in the kitchen ◆ **studio avec coin-~** studio flat with kitchen area *ou* kitchenette ◆ **table/couteau de ~** kitchen table/knife; → **batterie, intégré, latin, livre^1^**

2 *(= art culinaire)* cookery, cooking; *(= préparation)* cooking; *(= nourriture apprêtée)* cooking, food ◆ ~ **allégée** *ou* **légère** *ou* **minceur** low-fat *ou* low-calorie foods ◆ **la ~ chinoise/italienne** Chinese/Italian food ◆ **faire la ~ au beurre/à l'huile** to cook with butter/oil ◆ **je ne supporte pas la ~ au beurre/à l'huile** I can't stand things cooked in butter/oil ◆ **apprendre la ~** to learn (how) to cook, to learn cookery *ou* cooking ◆ **la ~ prend du temps** cooking takes time ◆ **une ~ épicée** hot *ou* spicy dishes *ou* food ◆ **une ~ soignée** carefully prepared dishes *ou* food ◆ **la bonne ~** good cooking *ou* food ◆ **il est en train de faire la ~** he's busy cooking *ou* making the meal ◆ **chez eux, c'est le mari qui fait la ~** the husband does the cooking *ou* the husband is the cook in their house ◆ **savoir faire la ~, faire de la bonne ~** to be a good cook, to be good at cooking; → **nouveau**

3 *(= personnel) [de maison privée]* kitchen staff; *[de cantine]* kitchen *ou* catering staff

4 *(fig péj)* ~ **électorale** electoral schemings *ou* jiggery-pokery* *(Brit)* ◆ **je n'aime pas beaucoup sa petite ~** I'm not very fond of his underhand tricks *ou* his little fiddles *(Brit)* ◆ **faire sa petite ~** to do one's own thing

COMP **cuisine américaine** open-plan kitchen
cuisine bourgeoise (good) plain cooking *ou* fare
cuisine de cantine canteen food
la cuisine française French cooking *ou* cuisine
cuisine de restaurant restaurant meals *ou* food
cuisine roulante *(Mil)* field kitchen

cuisiner /kɥizine/ ▸ conjug 1 ◂ VT 1 *[+ plat]* to cook 2 *(= interroger)* * *[+ personne]* to grill*, to give the third degree to* ◆ **il m'a cuisiné pour savoir avec qui elle était partie** he gave me the third degree trying to find out who she had left with VI to cook ◆ **il cuisine bien** he's a good cook ◆ **ne la dérange pas quand elle cuisine** don't bother her when she's cooking

cuisinette /kɥizinɛt/ NF kitchenette

cuisinier, -ière /kɥizinje, jɛʀ/ NM,F *(= personne)* cook NF **cuisinière** *(à gaz, électrique)* stove, cooker *(Brit)*; *(à bois)* (kitchen) range, wood-burning stove ◆ **cuisinière à gaz** gas stove *ou* cooker *(Brit)* ◆ **cuisinière à charbon** solid-fuel stove; *(vieux modèle)* kitchen range *(Brit)*, stove *(US)*

cuissage /kɥisaʒ/ NM → **droit^3^**

cuissard /kɥisaʀ/ NM *[d'armure]* cuisse; *[de cycliste]* (cycling) shorts

cuissardes /kɥisaʀd/ NFPL *[de pêcheur]* waders; *[de femme]* thigh boots

cuisse /kɥis/ NF *(Anat)* thigh ◆ ~ **de mouton** *(Culin)* leg of mutton *ou* lamb ◆ ~ **de poulet** chicken leg ◆ ~**s de grenouilles** frogs' legs ◆ **il se croit sorti de la ~ de Jupiter*** he thinks he's God's gift to mankind ◆ **elle a la ~ légère*** she is generous with her favours *(euph)*

cuisseau (pl **cuisseaux**) /kɥiso/ NM haunch (of veal)

cuisse-madame (pl **cuisses-madame**) /kɥismadam/ NF *(= poire)* cuisse madame pear

cuissettes /kɥisɛt/ NFPL *(Helv = shorts)* shorts

cuisson /kɥisɔ̃/ NF 1 *[d'aliments]* cooking; *[de pain, gâteau]* baking; *[de gigot]* roasting ◆ **ceci demande une longue ~** this needs to be cooked *(ou* baked) for a long time ◆ **temps de ~** cooking time ◆ ~ **à la vapeur/au four** steam/oven cooking ◆ **la pâte gonfle à la ~** the dough rises as it bakes *ou* is baked ◆ **quelle ~ ?** *(au restaurant)* how would you like it cooked? 2 *[de* *briques, céramique]* firing [3] *(= sensation de brûlure)* stinging *ou* smarting sensation

cuissot /kɥiso/ NM haunch (of venison *ou* wild boar)

cuistance‡ /kɥistɑ̃s/ NF *(= préparation)* cooking, preparing the grub‡; *(= nourriture)* grub‡, nosh‡ *(Brit)*

cuistot * /kɥisto/ NM cook

cuistre † /kɥistʀ/ NM prig, priggish pedant

cuistrerie † /kɥistʀəʀi/ NF priggish pedantry

cuit, e[1] /kɥi, kɥit/ (ptp de **cuire**) ADJ [1] *[aliment, plat]* cooked; *[viande]* done *(attrib)*; *[pomme]* baked ◆ **bien** ~ well done ◆ **je voudrais une baguette bien ~e** I'd like a nice crisp baguette ◆ **trop** ~ overdone ◆ **pas assez** ~ underdone ◆ ~ **à point** *(= peu saignant)* medium-cooked; *(parfaitement)* done to a turn [2] *(* = perdu)* **il est** ~ *(= il va se faire prendre)* he's done for*, his goose is cooked*; *(= il va perdre)* it's all up *(Brit) ou* over for him, he's had it* ◆ **c'est ~ (pour ce soir)** we've had it (for tonight)* [3] *(* = ivre)* plastered‡, sloshed‡ [4] *(locutions)* **c'est du tout** ~* it's *ou* it'll be a cinch* *ou* a walkover* ◆ **il attend toujours que ça lui arrive** *ou* **tombe tout ~ (dans le bec)*** he expects everything to be handed to him on a plate

cuite[2] /kɥit/ NF [1] ‡ **prendre une** ~ to get plastered‡ *ou* sloshed‡ ◆ **il a pris une sacrée** ~ he got really plastered‡ *ou* roaring drunk* [2] *(Tech = cuisson)* firing

cuiter (se)‡ /kɥite/ ▸ conjug 1 ◂ VPR to get plastered‡ *ou* sloshed‡

cuit-vapeur /kɥivapœʀ/ NM INV steamer

cuivre /kɥivʀ/ NM [1] ◆ ~ **(rouge)** copper ◆ ~ **jaune** brass ◆ ~ **blanc** white copper ◆ **objets** *ou* **articles en** ~ copperware ◆ **casseroles à fond (de)** ~ copper-bottomed pans; → **gravure** [2] *(Art)* copperplate [3] *(= ustensiles)* ~**s** *(de cuivre)* copper; *(de cuivre et laiton)* brasses ◆ **faire (briller) les ~s** to do the brass *ou* the brasses [4] *(Mus)* brass instrument ◆ **les ~s** the brass (section) ◆ **orchestre de ~s** brass band

cuivré, e /kɥivʀe/ (ptp de **cuivrer**) ADJ *[reflets]* coppery; *[peau, teint]* bronzed; *[voix]* resonant, sonorous ◆ **cheveux aux reflets ~s** hair with copper glints *ou* lights in it

cuivrer /kɥivʀe/ ▸ conjug 1 ◂ VT *(Tech)* to copper(plate), to cover with copper; *[+ peau, teint]* to bronze

cuivreux, -euse /kɥivʀø, øz/ ADJ *(Chim)* cuprous ◆ **oxyde** ~ cuprous oxide, cuprite

cul /ky/ NM [1] *(** = fesses)* backside*, bum* *(Brit)*, arse** *(Brit)*, ass** *(US)* ◆ ~ **nu** bare-bottomed ◆ **il est tombé le ~ dans l'eau** he fell arse first in the water** *(Brit)*, he fell on his ass in the water** *(US)* ◆ **un coup de pied au** ~ a kick *ou* boot up the arse** *(Brit)*, a kick in the ass** *(US)* ◆ **gros** ~* *(camion)* heavy truck *ou* lorry *(Brit)*, rig; *(tabac)* ≃ shag; → **faux**[1], **feu**[1], **trou** *etc*

[2] *(Hist, Habillement)* **(faux)** ~ bustle

[3] *[de bouteille]* bottom ◆ **pousser une voiture au** ~* to give a car a shove

[4] *(**= amour physique)* **le** ~ sex ◆ **film de** ~ porn movie*, skinflick‡ ◆ **revue** *ou* **magazine de** ~ porn mag*; *(montrant des femmes)* girlie mag* ◆ **une histoire de** ~ *(= plaisanterie)* a dirty joke ◆ **il nous a raconté ses histoires de** ~ he told us all about his sexual exploits

[5] *(locutions)* **on l'a dans le** ~** that's really screwed us (up)** ◆ **je suis sur le** ~‡ *(= surpris)* I'm speechless, I'm gobsmacked‡ *(Brit)*; *(= fatigué)* I'm dead-beat* *ou* knackered‡ *(Brit)* ◆ **en tomber** *ou* **rester sur le** ~* to be taken aback, to be gobsmacked‡ *(Brit)* ◆ **montrer son** ~** to moon* ◆ **être comme** ~ **et chemise*** to be as thick as thieves *(avec* with); ◆ **tu peux te le mettre** *ou* **foutre au** ~ **!**** go fuck yourself!** ◆ **mon** ~ **!**** my arse!** *(Brit)*, my ass!** *(US)* ◆ **avoir le** ~ **bordé de nouilles****, **avoir du** ~** to be a lucky *ou* jammy *(Brit)* bastard‡ ◆ **parle à mon ~, ma tête est malade**** you don't give a fuck** about what I'm saying, do you? ◆ **il a fait** ~ **sec** he downed it *ou* his drink in one ◆ **allez, ~ sec !** come on, down in one! ◆ **tout était ~ par-dessus tête** everything was in a mess ◆ **renverser ~ par-dessus tête** to turn head over heels

ADJ *(‡ = stupide)* silly ◆ **qu'il est ~, ce type !** that guy's a real twerp‡ *ou* wally‡ *(Brit)*!

culasse /kylas/ NF [1] *[de moteur]* cylinder head; → **joint**[1] [2] *[de canon, fusil]* breech ◆ ~ **(mobile)** breechblock; → **bloc**

cul-bénit * (pl **culs-bénits**) /kybeni/ NM *(péj)* religious nut*

cul-blanc (pl **culs-blancs**) /kyblɑ̃/ NM wheatear

culbute /kylbyt/ NF [1] *(= cabriole)* somersault; *(= chute)* tumble, fall ◆ **faire une** ~ *(cabriole)* to (turn a) somersault; *(chute)* to (take a) tumble, to fall (head over heels) [2] *(* fig = faillite)* *[de ministère]* collapse, fall; *[de banque]* collapse ◆ **faire la** ~ *(= être ruiné)* *[banque]* to collapse; *[entreprise]* to go bust*; *[spéculateur]* to take a tumble, to come a cropper* *(Brit)*; *(= doubler ses gains)* to double one's money

culbuter /kylbyte/ ▸ conjug 1 ◂ VI *[personne]* to (take a) tumble, to fall (head over heels); *[chose]* to topple (over), to fall (over); *[voiture]* to somersault, to turn a somersault, to overturn ◆ **il a culbuté dans l'étang** he tumbled *ou* fell into the pond VT *[+ chaise]* to upset, to knock over; *[+ personne]* to knock over; *[+ ennemi]* to overwhelm; *[+ ministère]* to bring down, to topple; ‡ *[+ femme]* to lay‡, to screw**

culbuteur /kylbytœʀ/ NM [1] *[de moteur]* rocker arm [2] *[de benne]* tipper [3] *(= jouet)* tumbler

culbuto /kylbyto/ NM wobbly toy, Weeble ®

cul(-)de(-)basse-fosse (pl **culs-de-basse-fosse**) /kyd(ə)bɑsfos/ NM dungeon

cul-de-four (pl **culs-de-four**) /kyd(ə)fuʀ/ NM *(Archit)* cul-de-four

cul-de-jatte (pl **culs-de-jatte**) /kyd(ə)ʒat/ NM legless cripple

cul-de-lampe (pl **culs-de-lampe**) /kyd(ə)lɑ̃p/ NM *(Archit)* cul-de-lampe; *(Typo)* tailpiece

cul-de-poule /kyd(ə)pul/ **en cul-de-poule** LOC ADJ ◆ **avoir la bouche en** ~ to purse one's lips

cul-de-sac (pl **culs-de-sac**) /kyd(ə)sak/ NM *(= rue)* cul-de-sac, dead end; *(fig)* blind alley

culer /kyle/ ▸ conjug 1 ◂ VI *(Naut)* *[bateau]* to go astern; *[vent]* to veer astern ◆ **brasser à** ~ to brace aback

culinaire /kylinɛʀ/ ADJ culinary ◆ **l'art** ~ cookery

culminant, e /kylminɑ̃, ɑ̃t/ ADJ → **point**[1]

culminer /kylmine/ ▸ conjug 1 ◂ VI [1] *[sommet, massif]* to tower *(au-dessus de* above); ◆ ~ **à** to reach its highest point at ◆ **le Mont-Blanc culmine à 4 807 mètres** Mont Blanc reaches 4,807 metres at its highest point [2] *[colère, manifestation]* to come to a head; *[salaire, bénéfice, récession]* to peak, to reach a peak *(à* at); ◆ **la crise culmina avec l'abdication du roi** the crisis culminated in the king's abdication [3] *(Astron)* to reach its highest point

culot /kylo/ NM [1] *(* = effronterie)* nerve*, cheek* *(Brit)* ◆ **il a du** ~ he's got a nerve* *ou* cheek* *(Brit)* ◆ **tu ne manques pas de** ~ **!** you've got a nerve!* *ou* a cheek!* *(Brit)* ◆ **il y est allé au** ~ he bluffed his way through it [2] *[d'ampoule]* cap; *[de cartouche]* cap, base; *[de bougie]* body; *[d'obus, bombe]* base [3] *(= dépôt)* *[de pipe]* dottle; *[de creuset]* residue ◆ ~ **volcanique** *(Géog)* volcanic cone

culottage /kylɔtaʒ/ NM *[de pipe]* seasoning

culotte /kylɔt/ NF [1] *(= slip)* *[de femme]* pants *(Brit)*, knickers *(Brit)*, panties *(US)*; *[d'homme]* underpants ◆ **petite** ~ *[de femme]* panties ◆ **trois ~s** three pairs of underpants

[2] *(= pantalon)* trousers, pants *(US)*; *(Hist)* breeches; *(= short)* shorts

[3] *(Boucherie)* rump

[4] *(locutions)* **baisser (sa)** ~ *(lit)* to pull *ou* take one's knickers *(Brit) ou* panties *(US)* down; *(‡ fig)* to back down ◆ **c'est elle qui porte la** ~ she wears the trousers *ou* pants *(US)* ◆ **prendre une** ~* *(au jeu)* to lose one's shirt, to lose heavily ◆ **faire dans sa** ~ *(uriner)* to wet oneself *ou* one's pants; *(déféquer)* to dirty one's pants ◆ **trembler** *ou* **faire dans sa** ~‡, **mouiller sa** ~‡ *(fig)* to wet oneself‡, to pee one's pants‡ ◆ **il n'a rien dans la** ~ *(impuissant)* he can't get it up‡; *(lâche)* he has no balls** *ou* no guts‡

COMP **culotte de bain** † (swimming *ou* bathing) trunks
culotte(s) bouffante(s) jodhpurs
culotte(s) de cheval *(lit)* riding breeches ◆ **avoir une ~ de cheval** *(fig)* to have jodhpur thighs *ou* saddlebags
culotte(s) courte(s) short trousers *ou* pants *(US)* ◆ **j'étais encore en ~(s) courte(s)** I was still in short trousers *ou* short pants *(US)*
culotte de golf plus fours, knickerbockers
culotte(s) longue(s) long trousers *ou* pants *(US)*
culotte de peau *(péj Mil)* **une (vieille) ~ de peau** a colonel Blimp

culotté, e /kylɔte/ (ptp de **culotter**) ADJ [1] *(* = effronté)* cheeky* *(Brit)*, sassy* *(US)* [2] *[pipe]* seasoned; *[cuir]* mellowed

culotter /kylɔte/ ▸ conjug 1 ◂ VT [1] *[+ pipe, théière]* to season [2] *[+ enfant]* to put trousers on VPR **se culotter** [1] *[pipe]* to season [2] *[enfant]* to put one's trousers on

culottier, -ière † /kylɔtje, jɛʀ/ NM,F trouser maker, breeches maker †

culpabilisant, e /kylpabilizɑ̃, ɑ̃t/ ADJ *[discours, idée]* that induces feelings of guilt ◆ **c'est un peu ~ de laisser les enfants seuls** you feel a bit guilty about leaving the children on their own

culpabilisation /kylpabilizasjɔ̃/ NF *(= action)* making guilty; *(= état)* guilt

culpabiliser /kylpabilize/ ▸ conjug 1 ◂ VT ◆ ~ **qn** to make sb feel guilty VI **se culpabiliser** VPR to feel guilty, to blame o.s.

culpabilité /kylpabilite/ NF *(gén)* guilt; *(Jur)* guilt, culpability; → **sentiment**

cul-rouge (pl **culs-rouges**) /kyʀuʒ/ NM great spotted woodpecker

culte /kylt/ NM [1] *(= vénération)* worship ◆ **le ~ de Dieu** the worship of God ◆ **le ~ du feu/du soleil** fire-/sun-worship ◆ **avoir le ~ de** *[+ justice, tradition]* to make a cult *ou* religion of; *[+ argent]* to worship ◆ **avoir un ~ pour qn** to (hero-)worship sb ◆ **vouer** *ou* **rendre un ~ à qn/la mémoire de qn** to worship sb/sb's memory ◆ ~ **de la personnalité** personality cult ◆ **son ~ du secret** his cult of secrecy [2] *(= pratiques)* form of worship; *(= religion)* religion ◆ **le ~ catholique** the Catholic form of worship ◆ **les objets du** ~ liturgical objects ◆ **lieu de** ~ place of worship; → **denier, liberté, ministre** [3] *(= office protestant)* (church) service ◆ **assister au** ~ to attend a (church) service ADJ *[film, livre]* cult *(épith)* ◆ **c'est un groupe** ~ they're a cult band

cul-terreux * (pl **culs-terreux**) /kyteʀø/ NM *(péj)* yokel, country bumpkin, hick* *(US)*

cultivable /kyltivabl/ ADJ *[terre]* suitable for cultivation, cultivable

cultivar /kyltivaʀ/ NM cultivar

cultivateur, -trice /kyltivatœʀ, tʀis/ ADJ *[peuple]* agricultural, farming *(épith)* NM,F farmer NM *(= machine)* cultivator

cultivé, e /kyltive/ (ptp de **cultiver**) ADJ *(= instruit)* cultured, cultivated

cultiver /kyltive/ ▸ conjug 1 ◂ VT 1 *[+ champ]* to cultivate ◆ ~ **la terre** to cultivate the soil, to farm the land ◆ **terrains cultivés** cultivated land, land under cultivation 2 *[+ céréales, légumes, vigne]* to grow, to cultivate; *[+ moules, huîtres]* to breed, to farm 3 *(= exercer) [+ goût, don, image]* to cultivate ◆ ~ **son esprit** to improve *ou* cultivate one's mind 4 *(= pratiquer) [+ art, sciences, genre]* to cultivate ◆ ~ **l'esprit de famille** to have a strong sense of family ◆ **il cultive la grossièreté/le paradoxe** he goes out of his way to be rude/to do the unexpected 5 *(= fréquenter) [+ personne, amitié]* to cultivate ◆ **c'est une relation à** ~ it's a connection which should be cultivated VPR **se cultiver** to improve *ou* cultivate one's mind

cultuel, -elle /kyltɥɛl/ ADJ ◆ **édifices ~s** places of worship ◆ **association ~le** religious organization

culture /kyltyʀ/ NF 1 ◆ **la** ~ *(= connaissances)* culture ◆ **homme de** ~ man of culture, cultured man ◆ **il manque de** ~ he's not very cultured ◆ **la** ~ **occidentale** western culture ◆ ~ **scientifique** scientific knowledge *ou* education ◆ ~ **générale** general knowledge ◆ ~ **classique** classical culture *ou* education ◆ ~ **de masse** mass culture ◆ ~ **d'entreprise** corporate culture, house style

2 *[de champ]* cultivation; *[de légumes]* growing, cultivating, cultivation; *[de moules, huîtres]* breeding, farming ◆ **méthodes de** ~ farming methods, methods of cultivation ◆ ~ **mécanique** mechanized farming ◆ ~ **intensive/extensive** intensive/extensive farming ◆ **pays de moyenne/grande** ~ country with a medium-scale/large-scale farming industry ◆ ~ **maraîchère** market gardening ◆ ~ **fruitière** fruit farming ◆ **mettre en** ~ *[+ terre]* to bring under cultivation ◆ **j'ai deux cents hectares en** ~ I have two hundred hectares of farmland *ou* of land under cultivation

3 *(= espèce cultivée)* crop ◆ ~ **de rapport,** ~ **commerciale** cash crop ◆ ~ **vivrière** food crop

4 *(Bio)* culture ◆ ~ **microbienne/de tissus** microbe/tissue culture ◆ **mettre des tissus en** ~ to put tissue in a culture medium; → **bouillon**

NFPL **cultures** *(= terres cultivées)* land under cultivation, arable land

COMP **culture physique** physical culture *ou* training, PT ◆ **faire de la** ~ **physique** to do physical training

culturel, -elle /kyltyʀɛl/ ADJ cultural

culturellement /kyltyʀɛlmɑ̃/ ADV culturally

culturisme /kyltyʀism/ NM body-building

culturiste /kyltyʀist/ NMF body-builder

cumin /kymɛ̃/ NM *(= faux anis)* cumin; *(= carvi)* caraway; *(= graines)* cumin; *(de carvi)* caraway seeds

cumul /kymyl/ NM 1 *[de fonctions]* plurality; *[de salaires]* concurrent drawing ◆ **pour limiter le ~ des mandats** in order to limit the number of mandates that may be held at the same time *ou* concurrently 2 *(Jur) [de droits]* accumulation ◆ **avec ~ de peines** sentences to run consecutively ◆ ~ **d'infractions** combination of offences

cumulable /kymylabl/ ADJ *[fonctions]* which may be held concurrently *ou* simultaneously; *[traitements]* which may be drawn concurrently *ou* simultaneously ◆ **les réductions sur ces articles ne sont pas ~s** not more than one discount can be applied to each item

cumulard, e /kymylaʀ, aʀd/ NM,F *(péj) person drawing several salaries at the same time*

cumulatif, -ive /kymylatif, iv/ ADJ cumulative

cumulativement /kymylativmɑ̃/ ADV *[exercer des fonctions]* simultaneously, concurrently; *[purger des peines]* consecutively

cumuler /kymyle/ ▸ conjug 1 ◂ VT 1 *[+ fonctions]* to hold concurrently *ou* simultaneously; *[+ salaires]* to draw concurrently *ou* simultaneously ◆ ~ **deux traitements** to draw two separate salaries ◆ ~ **les fonctions de directeur et de comptable** to act simultaneously as manager and accountant, to hold concurrently the positions of manager and accountant ◆ ~ **plusieurs handicaps** to suffer from several handicaps 2 *(Jur) [+ droits]* to accumulate ◆ **calcul des intérêts cumulés** calculation of the interests accrued VPR **se cumuler** *[effets, handicaps, facteurs]* to accumulate ◆ **cette augmentation se cumulera avec celle de la TVA** this rise will come along on top of the increase in VAT

cumulonimbus /kymylonɛ̃bys/ NM cumulonimbus

cumulus /kymylys/ NM 1 *(= nuage)* cumulus ◆ ~ **de beau temps/d'orage** *(pl)* fine-weather/storm clouds 2 *(= chauffe-eau) (electric)* water heater

cunéiforme /kyneifɔʀm/ ADJ 1 *[écriture, caractère]* wedge-shaped, cuneiform *(SPÉC)* 2 *(Anat)* **les (os) ~s** the cuneiform bones *(of the tarsus)*

cunnilingus /kynilɛ̃gys/ NM cunnilingus

cupide /kypid/ ADJ *[air]* greedy; *[personne]* grasping, greedy, moneygrubbing

cupidement /kypidmɑ̃/ ADV greedily

cupidité /kypidite/ NF greed, greediness, cupidity *(littér)*

Cupidon /kypidɔ̃/ NM Cupid

cuprifère /kypʀifɛʀ/ ADJ copper-bearing, cupriferous *(SPÉC)*

cupule /kypyl/ NF *(Bot)* cupule; *[de gland]* (acorn) cup

curabilité /kyʀabilite/ NF curability

curable /kyʀabl/ ADJ curable

curaçao /kyʀaso/ NM curaçao

curage /kyʀaʒ/ NM *[de fossé, égout]* clearing- *ou* cleaning-out; *[de puits]* cleaning-out

curaillon* /kyʀajɔ̃/ NM *(péj)* priest

curare /kyʀaʀ/ NM curare

curatelle /kyʀatɛl/ NF *(Jur) [de mineur, aliéné]* guardianship; *[de succession]* trusteeship

curateur, -trice /kyʀatœʀ, tʀis/ NM,F *(Jur) [de mineur, aliéné]* guardian; *[de succession]* trustee

curatif, -ive /kyʀatif, iv/ ADJ curative

curcuma /kyʀkyma/ NM turmeric

cure[1] /kyʀ/ NF 1 *(= traitement)* course of treatment ◆ ~ **(thermale)** ≃ course of treatment *ou* a cure at a spa ◆ **faire une ~ (thermale) à Vichy, être en ~ à Vichy** to take the waters at Vichy ◆ **suivre une ~ d'amaigrissement** to go on a slimming course *(Brit)*, to have reducing treatment *(US)* ◆ **faire une ~ de sommeil** to have sleep therapy ◆ ~ **de thalassothérapie** course of thalassotherapy ◆ **la ~ (psychanalytique)** the talking cure; → **désintoxication**

2 *(= consommation) [d'aliments]* diet ◆ **j'ai fait une ~ de lecture/théâtre** I've done nothing but read/but go to the theatre ◆ **faire une ~ de fruits** to eat a lot of fruit, to go on a fruit diet

3 *(littér, hum)* **n'avoir ~ de qch** to care little about sth, to pay no attention to sth ◆ **il n'en a** ~ he's not worried about that, he pays no attention to that ◆ **je n'ai ~ de ces formalités** I've no time for these formalities, I can't be doing with these formalities

cure[2] /kyʀ/ NF *(Rel) (= fonction)* cure; *(= paroisse)* cure, ≃ living *(Brit)*; *(= maison)* presbytery, ≃ vicarage

curé /kyʀe/ NM parish priest ◆ ~ **de campagne** country priest ◆ **se faire** ~* to go in for the priesthood ◆ **les ~s** *(péj)* clerics, priests ◆ **élevé chez les ~s** brought up by priests *ou* clerics; → **bouffer², Monsieur**

cure-dent (pl **cure-dents**) /kyʀdɑ̃/ NM toothpick

curée /kyʀe/ NF 1 *(Chasse)* quarry ◆ **donner la ~ aux chiens** to give the quarry to the hounds 2 *(fig = ruée)* scramble (for the spoils) ◆ **se ruer** *ou* **aller à la** ~ to scramble for the spoils ◆ **les journalistes ont donné le signal de la** ~ *(attaque violente)* the press had everybody baying for his *(ou their etc)* blood

cure-ongle (pl **cure-ongles**) /kyʀɔ̃gl/ NM nailcleaner

cure-oreille (pl **cure-oreilles**) /kyʀɔʀɛj/ NM *(= coton-tige)* cotton bud *(Brit)*, Q-tip ® *(US)*

cure-pipe (pl **cure-pipes**) /kyʀpip/ NM pipe cleaner

curer /kyʀe/ ▸ conjug 1 ◂ VT 1 *[+ fossé, égout]* to clear *ou* clean out; *[+ puits]* to clean out; *[+ pipe]* to clean out, to scrape out 2 ◆ **se ~ les dents/le nez** to pick one's teeth/nose ◆ **se ~ les ongles/oreilles** to clean one's nails/ears

curetage /kyʀtaʒ/ NM curetting, curettage

cureter /kyʀte/ ▸ conjug 4 ◂ VT to curette

cureton* /kyʀtɔ̃/ NM *(péj)* priestling

curette /kyʀɛt/ NF *(Tech)* scraper; *(Méd)* curette

curie[1] /kyʀi/ NF *(Hist romaine)* curia; *(Rel)* Curia

curie[2] /kyʀi/ NM *(Phys)* curie

curieusement /kyʀjøzmɑ̃/ ADV *(= avec curiosité)* curiously; *(= étrangement)* strangely, curiously, oddly ◆ ~**, ils n'ont pas protesté** strangely *ou* oddly enough, they didn't protest

curieux, -ieuse /kyʀjø, jøz/ ADJ 1 *(= intéressé)* interested, curious ◆ **esprit** ~ inquiring mind ◆ ~ **de tout** curious about everything ◆ ~ **de mathématiques** interested in *ou* keen on *(Brit)* mathematics ◆ ~ **d'apprendre** interested in learning, keen to learn *(Brit)* ◆ **je serais ~ de voir/savoir** I'd be interested *ou* curious to see/know

2 *(= indiscret)* curious, inquisitive, nos(e)y* ◆ **jeter un regard ~ sur qch** to glance inquisitively *ou* curiously at sth

3 *(= bizarre)* strange, curious, odd ◆ **ce qui est ~, c'est que ...** the odd *ou* strange *ou* curious thing is that ...; → **bête, chose**

NM *(= étrangeté)* ◆ **le ~/le plus ~ de la chose** the funny *ou* strange thing/the funniest *ou* strangest thing about it

NM,F 1 *(= indiscret)* inquisitive person, nos(e)y parker*, busybody* ◆ **petite curieuse !** little nos(e)y parker!*, nos(e)y little thing!*

2 *(gén mpl = badaud)* (inquisitive) onlooker, bystander ◆ **éloigner les** ~ to move the bystanders along ◆ **venir en** ~ to come just for a look *ou* to have a look

curiosité /kyʀjozite/ NF 1 *(= intérêt)* curiosity ◆ **cette ~ de tout** this curiosity about everything ◆ **ayant eu la ~ d'essayer** having been curious enough to try ◆ **il n'a pas eu la ~ de vérifier** he didn't even bother to check

2 *(= indiscrétion)* curiosity, inquisitiveness, nosiness* ◆ ~ **malsaine** unhealthy curiosity ◆ **par (pure)** ~ out of (sheer) curiosity ◆ **avec** ~ curiously ◆ **la ~ est un vilain défaut** *(Prov)* curiosity killed the cat *(Prov)*

3 *(= site, monument)* curious *ou* unusual sight *ou* feature; *(= bibelot)* curio ◆ **les ~s de la ville** the (interesting *ou* unusual) sights of the town ◆ **magasin de ~s** curio *ou* curiosity shop ◆ **ce timbre est une ~ pour les amateurs** this stamp has curiosity value for collectors

4 (= *caractéristique*) oddity ◆ **c'est une des ~s de son esprit** it's one of the quirks *ou* oddities of his mind

curiste /kyʀist/ NMF person taking the waters (*at a spa*)

curium /kyʀjɔm/ NM curium

curling /kœʀliŋ/ NM curling

curriculum (vitæ) /kyʀikylɔm(vite)/ NM INV curriculum vitae, résumé (US)

curry /kyʀi/ NM curry ◆ **poulet au ~, ~ de poulet** curried chicken, chicken curry

curseur /kyʀsœʀ/ NM [*de règle*] slide, cursor; [*de fermeture éclair*] slider; [*d'ordinateur*] cursor

cursif, -ive /kyʀsif, iv/ ADJ 1 (= *lié*) [*écriture, lettre*] cursive ◆ **écrire en cursive** to write in cursive script 2 (= *rapide*) [*lecture, style*] cursory

cursus /kyʀsys/ NM (*Univ*) ≈ degree course; [*de carrière*] career path

curule /kyʀyl/ ADJ ◆ **chaise** ~ curule chair

curviligne /kyʀviliɲ/ ADJ curvilinear

customiser /kœstɔmize/ ► conjug 1 ◄ VT [+ *produit*] to customize

cutané, e /kytane/ ADJ skin (*épith*), cutaneous (*SPÉC*) ◆ **affection ~e** skin trouble

cuti* /kyti/ NF (abrév de **cuti-réaction**) → **virer**

cuticule /kytikyl/ NF [*d'animal, plante, peau*] cuticle

cuti-réaction /kytiʀeaksjɔ̃/ NF skin test ◆ **faire une** ~ to take a skin test

cutter /kœtœʀ/ NM (*petit*) craft knife; (*gros*) Stanley knife ®

cuvage /kyvaʒ/ NM, **cuvaison** /kyvezɔ̃/ NF [*de raisins*] fermentation (*in a vat*)

cuve /kyv/ NF [*de fermentation, teinture*] vat; [*de brasserie*] mash tun; [*de mazout*] tank; [*d'eau*] cistern, tank; [*de blanchissage*] laundry vat ◆ ~ **de développement** (*Photo*) developing tank

cuvée /kyve/ NF (= *contenu*) vatful; (= *cru, année*) vintage; [*d'étudiants, films*] crop ◆ **la ~ 1937** the 1937 vintage ◆ **une excellente** ~ (= *examen*) an excellent crop of graduates; → **tête**

cuver /kyve/ ► conjug 1 ◄ VT ◆ ~ **(son vin)** * to sleep it off * ◆ ~ **sa colère** to sleep (*ou* work *ou* walk) off one's anger VI [*vin, raisins*] to ferment

cuvette /kyvɛt/ NF 1 (= *récipient*) basin, bowl; (*pour la toilette*) washbowl; (*Photo*) dish ◆ ~ **de plastique** plastic bowl 2 [*de lavabo*] washbasin, basin; [*d'évier*] basin; [*de W.-C.*] pan 3 (*Géog*) basin 4 [*de baromètre*] cistern, cup 5 [*de montre*] cap

CV /seve/ GRAMMAIRE ACTIVE 46.2 NM 1 (abrév de **curriculum vitæ**) CV 2 (abrév de **cheval-vapeur**) hp

cyanose /sjanoz/ NF cyanosis

cyanosé, e /sjanoze/ ADJ cyanotic (*SPÉC*) ◆ **avoir le visage** ~ to be blue in the face

cyanure /sjanyʀ/ NM cyanid(e)

cyber(-) /sibɛʀ/ PRÉF e-, cyber(-) ◆ ~**boutique** cyberstore ◆ ~**casino** cybercasino, e-casino ◆ ~**consommateur** e-customer, cybercustomer

cybercafé, cyber-café (pl **cyber-cafés**) /sibɛʀkafe/ NM cybercafé

cybercitoyen, -enne /sibɛʀsitwajɛ̃, ɛn/ NM,F netizen

cybercrime /sibɛʀkʀim/ NM cybercrime

cybercriminalité /sibɛʀkʀiminalite/ NF cybercrime

cyberculture /sibɛʀkyltyʀ/ NF cyberculture

cyberespace /sibɛʀɛspas/ NM cyberspace

cybermonde /sibɛʀmɔ̃d/ NM cyberspace

cybernaute /sibɛʀnot/ NMF cybersurfer, cybernaut

cybernéticien, -ienne /sibɛʀnetisjɛ̃, jɛn/ NM,F cyberneticist

cybernétique /sibɛʀnetik/ NF cybernetics (*sg*)

cyberpunk* /sibɛʀpœk/ ADJ, NMF, NM cyberpunk

cyberspace /sibɛʀspas/ NM cyberspace

cybersquatter, cybersquatteur /sibɛʀskwatœʀ/ NM cybersquatter

cybersquatting /sibɛʀskwatiŋ/ NM cybersquatting

cyclable /siklabl/ ADJ ◆ **piste** ~ (*à la campagne*) cycle track *ou* path (*Brit*); (*en ville*) cycle lane

cyclamen /siklamɛn/ NM cyclamen

cycle[1] /sikl/ NM 1 (*Astron, Bio, Élec*) cycle ◆ ~ **du carbone/de l'azote** carbon/nitrogen cycle ◆ ~ **menstruel** *ou* **ovarien** menstrual *ou* ovarian cycle ◆ **le ~ infernal de la violence** the vicious circle of violence

2 (*Écon*) cycle ◆ ~ **de vie d'un produit** product life cycle

3 (*Littérat*) cycle ◆ **le ~ arthurien** the Arthurian cycle ◆ ~ **de chansons** song cycle

4 (*Scol*) ~ **(d'études)** academic cycle ◆ ~ **élémentaire** ≈ first five years of primary school (*Brit*), grades one through five (*US*) ◆ ~ **d'orientation** ≈ middle school (*transition classes*) ◆ ~ **long** *studies leading to the baccalauréat* ◆ ~ **court** *studies leading to vocational training instead of the baccalauréat* ◆ **premier/deuxième** ~ middle/upper school

5 (*Univ*) ~ **court** two-year vocational course (*taken after the baccalauréat*) ◆ ~ **long** higher education course ◆ **premier** ~ ≈ first and second year ◆ **deuxième** *ou* **second** ~ ≈ Final Honours ◆ **troisième** ~ ≈ postgraduate studies ◆ **diplôme de troisième** ~ ≈ postgraduate degree, PhD ◆ **étudiant de troisième** ~ ≈ postgraduate *ou* PhD student

6 (= *cours*) course ◆ ~ **de conférences** course of lectures ◆ ~ **de formation** training course

CYCLE

In France, primary and secondary education is split into four broad age-group divisions known as **cycles** (similar to « key stages » in Britain). « Le cycle élémentaire » corresponds to primary school, « le cycle d'observation » covers the first two years of « collège » (referred to as « sixième » and « cinquième »), and « le premier cycle » the final two years of « collège » (« quatrième » and « troisième »). « Le second cycle » corresponds to the three years spent at the « lycée » (referred to as « seconde », « première » and « terminale »).

Higher education in France has three **cycles**: « premier cycle » (up to « DEUG » level), « deuxième cycle » (up to « licence and maîtrise »), and « troisième cycle » (« doctorat », « DEA » and « DESS »). → COLLÈGE, LYCÉE

cycle[2] /sikl/ NM (= *bicyclette*) cycle ◆ **magasin de ~s** cycle shop ◆ **marchand de ~s** bicycle seller ◆ **tarif : ~s 10 €, automobiles 25 €** charge: cycles and motorcycles €10, cars €25

cyclique /siklik/ ADJ cyclic(al)

cyclisme /siklism/ NM cycling

cycliste /siklist/ ADJ ◆ **course/champion** ~ cycle race/champion ◆ **coureur** ~ racing cyclist NMF cyclist NM (= *short*) cycling shorts

cyclocross, cyclo-cross /siklokʀɔs/ NM INV (= *sport*) cyclo-cross; (= *épreuve*) cyclo-cross race

cycloïdal, e (mpl **-aux**) /siklɔidal, o/ ADJ cycloid(al)

cycloïde /siklɔid/ NF cycloid

cyclomoteur /siklomɔtœʀ/ NM moped, motorized bike *ou* bicycle

cyclomotoriste /siklomɔtɔʀist/ NMF moped rider

cyclonal, e (mpl **-aux**) /siklɔnal, o/ ADJ cyclonic

cyclone /siklon/ NM (= *typhon*) cyclone; (= *basse pression*) zone of low pressure; (= *vent violent*) hurricane; (*fig*) whirlwind ◆ **entrer comme un** ~ to sweep *ou* come in like a whirlwind; → **œil**

cyclonique /siklonik/ ADJ ⇒ **cyclonal**

cyclope /siklɔp/ NM 1 (*Myth*) **Cyclope** Cyclops 2 (= *crustacé*) cyclops

cyclopéen, -enne /siklɔpeɛ̃, ɛn/ ADJ (*Myth*) Cyclopean

cyclopousse /siklopus/ NM INV (bicycle-powered) rickshaw

cyclosporine /siklospɔʀin/ NF ⇒ **ciclosporine**

cyclothymie /siklotimi/ NF manic-depression, cyclothymia (*SPÉC*)

cyclothymique /siklotimik/ ADJ, NMF manic-depressive, cyclo-thymic (*SPÉC*)

cyclotourisme /siklotuʀism/ NM bicycle touring ◆ **faire du** ~ (*vacances*) to go on a cycling holiday

cyclotron /siklɔtʀɔ̃/ NM cyclotron

cygne /siɲ/ NM swan ◆ **jeune** ~ cygnet ◆ ~ **mâle** male swan, cob; → **chant[1]**

cylindre /silɛ̃dʀ/ NM 1 (*Géom*) cylinder ◆ ~ **droit/oblique** right (circular)/oblique (circular) cylinder ◆ ~ **de révolution** cylindrical solid of revolution 2 (= *rouleau*) roller; [*de rouleau-compresseur*] wheel, roller ◆ ~ **d'impression** printing cylinder; → **bureau, presse** 3 [*de moteur*] cylinder ◆ **moteur à 4 ~s en ligne** straight-4 engine ◆ **moteur à 6 ~s en V** V6 engine ◆ **moteur à 2 ~s opposés** flat-2 engine ◆ **une 6 ~s** a 6-cylinder (car)

cylindrée /silɛ̃dʀe/ NF capacity ◆ **une ~ de 1 600 cm³** a capacity of 1,600 ccs ◆ **une (voiture de) grosse/petite** ~ a big-/small-engined car ◆ **grosse** ~ (*arg Sport*) (= *personne*) top athlete; (= *équipe*) big-league team

cylindrer /silɛ̃dʀe/ ► conjug 1 ◄ VT (= *rouler*) [+ *métal*] to roll; [+ *papier*] to roll (up); (= *aplatir*) [+ *linge*] to press; [+ *route*] to roll

cylindrique /silɛ̃dʀik/ ADJ cylindrical

cymbale /sɛ̃bal/ NF cymbal

cymbalier /sɛ̃balje/ NM, **cymbaliste** /sɛ̃balist/ NMF cymbalist, cymbale(e)r

cymbalum /sɛ̃balɔm/ NM dulcimer, cymbalo

cynégétique /sineʒetik/ ADJ cynegetic NF cynegetics (*sg*)

cynique /sinik/ ADJ cynical; (*Philos*) Cynic NM cynic; (*Philos*) Cynic

cyniquement /sinikmɑ̃/ ADV cynically

cynisme /sinism/ NM cynicism; (*Philos*) Cynicism ◆ **il est d'un ~ !** he's so cynical!

cynocéphale /sinosefal/ NM dog-faced baboon, cynocephalus (*SPÉC*)

cynodrome /sinodʀom/ NM greyhound track

cynor(r)hodon /sinɔʀɔdɔ̃/ NM rosehip

cyprès /sipʀɛ/ NM cypress

cypriote /sipʀijɔt/ ADJ, NMF ⇒ **chypriote**

cyrillique /siʀilik/ ADJ Cyrillic

cystite /sistit/ NF cystitis (*NonC*)

Cythère /sitɛʀ/ NF Cythera

cytise /sitiz/ NM laburnum

cytogénéticien, -ienne /sitoʒenetisjɛ̃, jɛn/ NM,F cytogenetics specialist

cytogénétique /sitoʒenetik/ NF cytogenetics (*sg*)

cytologie /sitɔlɔʒi/ NF cytology

cytologique /sitɔlɔʒik/ ADJ cytological

cytomégalovirus /sitomegaloviʀys/ NM cytomegalovirus, CMV

cytoplasme /sitɔplasm/ NM cytoplasm

czar /tsaʀ/ NM ⇒ **tsar**

czarewitch /tsaʀevitʃ/ NM ⇒ **tsarévitch**

czariste /tsaʀist/ ADJ ⇒ **tsariste**

Dd

D, d /de/ NM (= *lettre*) D, d; → **système**

d' /d/ → **de[1], de[2]**

da /da/ INTERJ → **oui**

DAB /dab/ NM (abrév de **distributeur automatique de billets**) ATM

dab †⁑ /dab/ NM (= *père*) old man *, father

d'abord /dabɔʀ/ LOC ADV → **abord**

Dacca /daka/ N Dacca

d'accord /dakɔʀ/ LOC ADV, LOC ADJ → **accord**

Dacron ® /dakʀɔ̃/ NM Terylene ® *(Brit)*, Dacron ® *(US)*

dactyle /daktil/ NM [1] *(Poésie)* dactyl [2] (= *plante*) cocksfoot

dactylique /daktilik/ ADJ dactylic

dactylo /daktilo/ NF abrév de **dactylographe, dactylographie**

dactylographe † /daktilɔgʀaf/ NF typist

dactylographie /daktilɔgʀafi/ NF typing, typewriting ◆ **elle apprend la** ~ she's learning to type

dactylographier /daktilɔgʀafje/ ► conjug 7 ◄ VT to type (out)

dactylographique /daktilɔgʀafik/ ADJ typing *(épith)*

dactyloscopie /daktilɔskɔpi/ NF fingerprinting

dada[1] /dada/ NM [1] *(langage enfantin = cheval)* horsey *(langage enfantin)*, gee-gee *(Brit) (langage enfantin)* ◆ **viens faire à** ~ come and ride the horsey *ou* the gee-gee ◆ **jeu de ~s** ≃ ludo *(Brit)*, Parcheesi *(US)* [2] (= *marotte*) hobby-horse *(fig)* ◆ **enfourcher son** ~ to get on one's hobbyhorse, to launch o.s. on one's pet subject

dada[2] /dada/ ADJ *(Art, Littérat)* Dada, dada

dadais /dadɛ/ NM *(péj)* ◆ **un grand** ~ a great awkward lump of a man ◆ **espèce de grand ~ !** you great lump!

dadaïsme /dadaism/ NM Dadaism, Dada

dadaïste /dadaist/ ADJ Dadaist NMF Dadaist

DAF /daf/ NM (abrév de **directeur administratif et financier**) → **directeur**

dague /dag/ NF [1] (= *arme*) dagger [2] *[de cerf]* spike

daguerréotype /dageʀeɔtip/ NM daguerreotype

daguet /dagɛ/ NM young stag, brocket

dahlia /dalja/ NM dahlia

dahoméen, -enne /daɔmeɛ̃, ɛn/ ADJ Dahomean NM,F **Dahoméen(ne)** Dahomean

Dahomey /daɔme/ NM Dahomey

dahu /day/ NM *imaginary animal which gullible people are lured into chasing*

daigner /deɲe/ ► conjug 1 ◄ VT to deign, to condescend ◆ **il n'a même pas daigné nous regarder** he didn't even deign to look at us ◆ **daignez nous excuser** *(frm)* be so good as to excuse us

daim /dɛ̃/ NM [1] (= *animal*) *(gén)* (fallow) deer; *(mâle)* buck [2] (= *peau*) buckskin, doeskin; (= *cuir suédé*) suede ◆ **chaussures en** ~ suede shoes

daine /dɛn/ NF (fallow) doe

dais /dɛ/ NM canopy

Dakar /dakaʀ/ N Dakar

dakin, Dakin /dakɛ̃/ NM ◆ **solution** *ou* **eau de Dakin** Dakin's solution

Dakota /dakɔta/ NM Dakota ◆ ~ **du Nord/du Sud** North/South Dakota

dalaï-lama (pl **dalaï-lamas**) /dalailama/ NM Dalai Lama

Dalila /dalila/ NF Delilah

dallage /dalaʒ/ NM *(NonC = action)* paving, flagging; (= *surface, revêtement*) paving, pavement

dalle /dal/ NF [1] (= *pavement*) *[de trottoir]* paving stone, flag(stone); *(Constr)* slab ◆ ~ **flottante/de béton** floating/concrete slab ◆ **la** ~ **de couverture du parking** the concrete slab roof of the car park ◆ ~ **funéraire** tombstone ◆ ~ **de moquette** carpet tile ◆ **couler une** ~ to lay *ou* pour a concrete floor [2] *[de paroi de rocher]* slab [3] (* = *gosier*) **avoir la** ~ **en pente** to be a bit of a boozer⁑ ◆ **avoir** *ou* **crever la** ~ (= *avoir faim*) to be starving * *ou* famished *; → **rincer** [4]

◆ **que dalle**⁑ nothing at all, damn all⁑ *(Brit)* ◆ **j'y pige** *ou* **entrave que** ~ I don't get it *, I don't understand a bloody⁑ *(Brit)* thing ◆ **je n'y vois que** ~ I can't see a damn⁑ *ou* bloody⁑ *(Brit)* thing

daller /dale/ ► conjug 1 ◄ VT to pave, to lay paving stones *ou* flagstones on ◆ **cour dallée de marbre** courtyard paved with marble, marble courtyard

dalleur /dalœʀ/ NM flag layer, paviour

dalmate /dalmat/ ADJ Dalmatian NM (= *langue*) Dalmatian NMF **Dalmate** Dalmatian

Dalmatie /dalmasi/ NF Dalmatia

dalmatien, -ienne /dalmasjɛ̃, jɛn/ NM,F (= *chien*) dalmatian

daltonien, -ienne /daltɔnjɛ̃, jɛn/ ADJ colour-blind *(Brit)*, color-blind *(US)* NM,F colour-blind *(Brit) ou* color-blind *(US)* person

daltonisme /daltɔnism/ NM colour blindness *(Brit)*, color-blindness *(US)*, daltonism *(SPÉC)*

dam /dɑ̃, dam/ NM ◆ **au (grand)** ~ **de qn** to sb's great displeasure

Damas /damas/ N Damascus; → **chemin**

damas /dama(s)/ NM (= *tissu*) damask; (= *acier*) Damascus steel, damask; (= *prune*) damson

damasquinage /damaskinaʒ/ NM damascening

damasquiner /damaskine/ ► conjug 1 ◄ VT to damascene

damassé, e /damase/ ADJ, NM damask

dame /dam/ NF [1] (= *femme*) lady; (* = *épouse*) wife ◆ **il y a une** ~ **qui vous attend** there is a lady waiting for you ◆ **votre** ~ **m'a dit que** * … your wife told me that … ◆ **alors ma petite ~ !** * now then, dear! ◆ **vous savez, ma bonne ~ !** * you know, my dear! ◆ **la** ~ **Dubois** *(Jur)* Mrs Dubois ◆ **coiffeur pour ~s** ladies' hairdresser ◆ **de** ~ *[sac, manteau]* lady's ◆ **la Dame de fer** the Iron Lady ◆ **une vieille** ~ **indigne** *(hum)* an eccentric old lady ◆ **la finale ~s** *(Sport)* the women's final; → **vertu**

[2] *(de haute naissance)* lady ◆ **une grande** ~ (= *noble*) a highborn *ou* great lady; (= *artiste*) a great lady (*de* of); ◆ **la grande** ~ **du roman policier** the grande dame *ou* the doyenne of crime fiction ◆ **jouer les grandes ~s** to play the fine lady ◆ **les belles ~s des quartiers chic** the fashionable *ou* fine ladies from the posh districts ◆ **la première** ~ **de France** France's first lady ◆ **la** ~ **de ses pensées** *(hum)* his lady-love *(hum)* ◆ **la Vieille Dame du Quai Conti** the French Academy

[3] *(Cartes, Échecs)* queen; *(Dames)* crown; *(Jacquet)* piece, man ◆ **le jeu de ~s**, **les ~s** draughts *(sg) (Brit)*, checkers *(sg) (US)* ◆ **jouer aux ~s** to play draughts *(Brit) ou* checkers *(US)* ◆ **aller à** ~ *(Dames)* to make a crown; *(Échecs)* to make a queen ◆ **la** ~ **de pique** the queen of spades

[4] *(Tech = hie)* beetle, rammer; *(Naut)* rowlock

EXCL ◆ ~ **oui/non !** † why yes/no!, indeed yes/no!

COMP **dame blanche** (= *chouette*) barn owl
dame catéchiste catechism mistress, ≃ Sunday school teacher
dame de charité benefactress
dame de compagnie (lady's) companion
Dame Fortune Lady Luck
dame d'honneur lady-in-waiting
Dame Nature Mother Nature
dame patronnesse († *ou péj*) Lady Bountiful
dame pipi * lady toilet attendant

dame-jeanne (pl **dames-jeannes**) /damʒɑn/ NF demijohn

damer /dame/ ▸ conjug 1 ◂ VT 1 *[+ terre, neige, piste de ski]* to pack (down) 2 *[+ pion] (Dames)* to crown; *(Échecs)* to queen ◆ ~ **le pion à qn** *(fig)* to get the better of sb, to checkmate sb

dameuse /damøz/ NF *(Ski)* snow-grooming machine

damier /damje/ NM *(Dames)* draughtboard *(Brit)*, checkerboard *(US)*; *(= dessin)* check (pattern) ◆ **en damier, à damiers** *[motif]* chequered *(Brit)*, checkered *(US)* ◆ **tissu/foulard à ~s** checked *ou* check fabric/scarf ◆ **ville/rues en ~** town/streets in a grid pattern ◆ **les champs formaient un ~** the fields were laid out like a draughtboard *(Brit) ou* a checkerboard *(US)*

damnable /dɑnabl/ ADJ *(Rel)* damnable; *[passion, idée]* despicable, abominable

damnation /dɑnasjɔ̃/ NF damnation ◆ ~ **!** † damnation!, tarnation! † *(US)*; → **enfer**

damné, e /dɑne/ (ptp de **damner**) ADJ (*, *avant le nom = maudit)* cursed*, confounded* †; → **âme** NM,F damned person ◆ **les ~s** the damned; → **souffrir**

damner /dɑne/ ▸ conjug 1 ◂ VT to damn ◆ **faire ~ qn*** to drive sb mad* ◆ **c'est bon à faire ~ un saint*** *(hum)* it's so good it's wicked* ◆ **elle est belle à faire ~ un saint*** *(hum)* she's so lovely she would tempt a saint (in heaven)* VPR **se damner** to damn o.s. ◆ **être prêt à se ~ pour qn** to be prepared to do absolutely anything for sb ◆ **se ~ pour qch** to sell one's soul for sth ◆ **à se ~*** *(= merveilleux)* fabulous*

Damoclès /damɔklɛs/ NM Damocles; → **épée**

damoiseau (pl **damoiseaux**) /damwazo/ NM *(Hist)* page, squire; *(†, hum)* young beau †

damoiselle /damwazɛl/ NF *(Hist)* damsel †

dan /dan/ NM *(Arts martiaux)* dan ◆ **il est deuxième ~** he's a second dan

danaïde /danaid/ NF *(= papillon)* monarch butterfly

Danaïdes /danaid/ NFPL → **tonneau**

dancing /dɑ̃siŋ/ NM dance hall

> ⚠ **dancing** ne se traduit pas par le mot anglais **dancing**, qui désigne une action et non un lieu.

dandinement /dɑ̃dinmɑ̃/ NM *[de canard, personne]* waddle

dandiner (se) /dɑ̃dine/ ▸ conjug 1 ◂ VPR *[canard, personne]* to waddle ◆ **avancer** *ou* **marcher en se dandinant** to waddle along

dandy /dɑ̃di/ NM dandy

dandysme /dɑ̃dism/ NM dandyism

Danemark /danmaʀk/ NM Denmark

danger /dɑ̃ʒe/ NM danger ◆ **un grave ~ nous menace** we are in serious *ou* grave danger ◆ **courir un ~** to run a risk ◆ **en cas de ~** in case of emergency ◆ **il est hors de ~** he is out of danger, he is safe ◆ **ça ne présente aucun ~, c'est sans ~** it doesn't present any danger *(pour* to) it's quite safe *(pour* for); ◆ **il y aurait (du) ~ à faire cela** it would be dangerous to do that ◆ **cet automobiliste est un ~ public** that driver is a public menace ◆ **les ~s de la route** road hazards ◆ **attention ~ !** look out! ◆ **"danger de mort"** "danger of death" ◆ **(il n'y a) pas de ~ !*** no fear!* ◆ **pas de ~ qu'il vienne !*** there's no danger that he'll come

◆ **en danger** ◆ **être en ~** to be in danger ◆ **ses jours sont en ~** his life is in danger ◆ **mettre en ~** *[+ personne]* to put in danger; *[+ vie, espèce]* to endanger; *[+ chances, réputation, carrière]* to jeopardize ◆ **adolescents en ~ moral** teenagers in danger of being corrupted *ou* led astray ◆ **en ~ de** in danger of ◆ **il est en ~ de mort** he is in danger *ou* peril of his life ◆ **ce pays est en grand ~ de perdre son indépendance** this country is in grave danger of losing its independence

◆ **sans danger** *[opération, expérience]* safe; *[utiliser, agir]* safely

dangereusement /dɑ̃ʒʀøzmɑ̃/ ADV dangerously

dangereux, -euse /dɑ̃ʒʀø, øz/ ADJ *[route, ennemi, doctrine, animal]* dangerous *(pour* to); *[entreprise]* dangerous, hazardous, risky ◆ **~ à manipuler** dangerous to handle ◆ **zone dangereuse** danger zone ◆ **il joue un jeu ~** he's playing a dangerous game ◆ **"abus dangereux"** "to be taken in moderation"

dangerosité /dɑ̃ʒʀozite/ NF dangerousness

danois, e /danwa, waz/ ADJ Danish NM 1 *(= langue)* Danish 2 *(= chien)* **(grand) ~** Great Dane NM,F **Danois(e)** Dane

dans /dɑ̃/

PRÉPOSITION

1 [sans changement de lieu] in; *(= à l'intérieur de)* in, inside ◆ **il habite ~ Londres même/l'Est/le Jura** he lives in London itself/the East/the Jura ◆ **le ministère est ~ la rue de Grenelle** the ministry is in the rue de Grenelle ◆ **courir ~ l'herbe/les champs** to run around in *ou* run through the grass/fields ◆ **il a plu ~ toute la France** there has been rain throughout France ◆ **elle erra ~ la ville/les rues/la campagne** she wandered through *ou* round *ou* about the town/the streets/the countryside ◆ **ne marche pas ~ l'eau** don't walk in *ou* through the water ◆ **vous êtes ~ la bonne direction** you are going the right way *ou* in the right direction ◆ **ils ont voyagé ~ le même train/avion** they travelled on the same train/plane ◆ **cherche** *ou* **regarde ~ la boîte** look inside *ou* in the box ◆ **~ le fond/le bas/le haut de l'armoire** at *ou* in the back/the bottom/the top of the wardrobe ◆ **il reconnut le voleur ~ la foule/l'assistance** he recognized the thief in *ou* among the crowd/among the spectators ◆ **qu'est-ce qui a bien pu se passer ~ sa tête ?** what can he have been thinking of? ◆ **il avait ~ l'esprit** *ou* **l'idée que ...** he had a feeling that ... ◆ **elle avait ~ l'idée** *ou* **la tête de ...** she had a mind to ... ◆ **il y a de la tristesse ~ son regard/sourire** there's a certain sadness in his eyes/smile; → **fouiller, recevoir, tomber**[1] *etc*

2 [changement de lieu] into, to ◆ **s'enfoncer/pénétrer ~ la forêt** to plunge deep into/go into *ou* enter the forest ◆ **ils sont partis ~ la montagne** they have gone off into the mountains ◆ **mettre qch ~ un tiroir** to put sth in *ou* into a drawer ◆ **verser du vin ~ un verre** to pour wine into a glass ◆ **jeter l'eau sale ~ l'évier** to pour the dirty water down the sink

3 [= dans des limites de] within ◆ **~ le périmètre/un rayon très restreint** within the perimeter/a very restricted radius ◆ **ce n'est pas ~ ses projets** he's not planning to do *ou* on doing that

4 [indiquant l'action de prélever] out of, from ◆ **prendre qch ~ un tiroir** to take sth out of *ou* from a drawer ◆ **boire du café ~ une tasse/un verre** to drink coffee out of *ou* from a cup/glass ◆ **la chèvre lui mangeait ~ la main** the goat was eating out of his hand ◆ **le chien a mangé ~ mon assiette** the dog ate off my plate ◆ **bifteck ~ le filet** fillet steak ◆ **il l'a appris/copié ~ un livre** he learnt/copied it from *ou* out of a book

5 [= pendant] in ◆ **~ ma jeunesse/mon jeune temps** in my youth/my younger days ◆ **~ les siècles passés** in previous centuries ◆ **~ les mois à venir** in the months to come ◆ **~ le cours** *ou* **le courant de l'année** in the course of the year ◆ **il est ~ sa 6e année** he's in his 6th year; → **temps**[1], **vie**

6 [période ou délai dans l'avenir] in; *(= dans des limites de)* within, inside, in (the course of) ◆ **il part ~ deux jours/une semaine** he leaves in two days *ou* two days' time/a week *ou* a week's time ◆ **~ combien de temps serez-vous prêt ?** how long will it be before you are ready? ◆ **il sera là ~ une minute** *ou* **un instant** he'll be here in a minute ◆ **cela pourrait se faire ~ le mois/la semaine** it could be done within the month/week *ou* inside a month/week ◆ **il mourut ~ l'heure qui suivit** he died within the hour ◆ **je l'attends ~ la matinée/la nuit** I'm expecting him some time this morning/some time tonight, I'm expecting him some time in the course of the morning/night

7 [état, condition, manière] in ◆ **être ~ les affaires/l'industrie/le textile** to be in business/industry/textiles ◆ **vivre ~ la misère/la peur** to live in poverty/fear ◆ **vivre ~ l'oisiveté** to live a life of idleness ◆ **~ le brouillard/l'obscurité** in fog/darkness, in the fog/the dark ◆ **il n'est pas ~ le complot/le secret** he's not in on* the plot/the secret ◆ **je l'aime beaucoup ~ cette robe/ce rôle** I really like her in that dress/that part ◆ **et ~ tout cela, qu'est-ce que vous devenez ?** and with all this going on, how are things with you? ◆ **il est difficile de travailler ~ ce bruit/ces conditions** it's difficult to work with this noise/in these conditions ◆ **le camion passa ~ un bruit de ferraille** the truck rattled past ◆ **elles sortirent ~ un frou-frou de soie** they left in a rustle of silk ◆ **faire les choses ~ les règles** to work within the rules

8 [situation, cause] in, with ◆ **~ son effroi, elle poussa un cri** she cried out in fright ◆ **~ sa hâte il oublia son chapeau** in his haste he forgot his hat ◆ **~ ces conditions** *ou* **ce cas-là, je refuse** in that case *ou* if that's the way it is* I refuse ◆ **elle partit tôt, ~ l'espoir de trouver une place** she left early in the hope of getting *ou* hoping to get a seat ◆ **il l'a fait ~ ce but** he did it with this aim in view

9 [destination] **mettre son espoir ~ qn/qch** to pin one's hopes on sb/sth ◆ **avoir confiance ~ l'honnêteté de qn/le dollar** to have confidence in sb's honesty/the dollar

10 [locutions]

◆ **dans les** *(= environ) (prix)* (round) about, (something) in the region of; *(temps, grandeur)* (round) about, something like, some ◆ **cela vaut/coûte ~ les 10 €** it's worth/it costs in the region of €10 *ou* (round) about €10 ◆ **il faut compter ~ les 3 ou 4 mois** we'll have to allow something like 3 or 4 months *ou* some 3 or 4 months ◆ **il vous faut ~ les 3 mètres de tissu** you'll need something like 3 metres of fabric *ou* about *ou* some 3 metres of fabric ◆ **cette pièce fait ~ les 8 m²** this room is about *ou* some 8 m² ◆ **il a ~ les 30 ans** he's about 30, he's 30 or so

dansant, e /dɑ̃sɑ̃, ɑ̃t/ ADJ *[mouvement, lueur]* dancing; *[musique]* lively ◆ **thé ~** tea dance ◆ **soirée ~e** dance

danse /dɑ̃s/ NF 1 *(= valse, tango etc)* dance ◆ **la ~** *(= art)* dance; *(= action)* dancing ◆ **la ~ folklorique** folk *ou* country dancing ◆ **~ classique** ballet ◆ **~ contemporaine** contemporary dance ◆ **~ de salon** ballroom dance ◆ **la ~ du ventre** belly dancing ◆ **faire la ~ du ventre** to belly-dance, to do a belly dance ◆ **~ de guerre** war dance ◆ **~ macabre** danse macabre, dance of death ◆ **ouvrir la ~** to open the dancing ◆ **avoir la ~ de Saint-Guy** *(Méd)* to have St Vitus's dance; *(fig)* to have the fidgets ◆ **de ~** *[professeur, leçon]* dancing; *[musique]* dance ◆ **entrer dans la ~** *(lit)* to join in the dance *ou* dancing ◆ **s'il entre dans la ~ ...** *(fig)* if he decides to get involved *ou* to join in ...; → **mener, piste**

2 (* = volée) belting*, (good) hiding ◆ **filer** *ou* **flanquer une ~ à qn** to belt sb*, to give sb a (good) hiding

danser /dɑ̃se/ ▸ conjug 1 ◂ VI (*gén*) to dance; [*ombre, flamme*] to flicker, to dance; [*flotteur, bateau*] to bob (up and down), to dance ◆ **elle danse bien** she's a good dancer ◆ **faire ~ qn** to (have a) dance with sb ◆ **après dîner il nous a fait** ~ after dinner he got us dancing ◆ **voulez-vous ~ (avec moi) ?, vous dansez ?** shall we dance?, would you like to dance? ◆ **~ de joie** to dance for joy ◆ **à l'époque, on dansait devant le buffet** * (*fig*) those were lean times ◆ **les lignes dansaient devant mes yeux** the lines were dancing before my eyes ◆ **personne ne savait sur quel pied** ~ nobody knew what to do VT to dance ◆ **~ le tango** to dance the tango ◆ **~ un rock** to jive ◆ **elle danse "le Lac des cygnes"** she's dancing "Swan Lake"

danseur, -euse /dɑ̃sœʀ, øz/ NM,F (*gén*) dancer; (= *partenaire*) partner ◆ **~ classique** *ou* **de ballet** ballet dancer ◆ **~ étoile** (*Opéra*) principal dancer ◆ **danseuse étoile** prima ballerina ◆ **~ de corde** tightrope walker ◆ **~ de claquettes** tap dancer ◆ **~ mondain** *professional ballroom dancing host* NF **danseuse** ◆ **danseuse de cabaret** cabaret dancer ◆ **pédaler en danseuse** to pedal standing up ◆ **entretenir une danseuse** (*maîtresse*) to keep a mistress ◆ **l'État ne peut pas se permettre d'entretenir des danseuses** the state cannot afford to support unprofitable ventures ◆ **les voiliers de course, c'est sa danseuse** he spends all his money on racing yachts

dantesque /dɑ̃tɛsk/ ADJ Dantesque, Dantean

Danube /danyb/ NM Danube

DAO /deao/ NM (abrév de **dessin assisté par ordinateur**) CAD

daphnie /dafni/ NF daphnia

dard /daʀ/ NM [*d'animal*] sting; († , *Mil*) javelin, spear

Dardanelles /daʀdanɛl/ NFPL ◆ **les ~** the Dardanelles

darder /daʀde/ ▸ conjug 1 ◂ VT 1 (= *lancer*) [+ *flèche*] to shoot ◆ **le soleil dardait ses rayons sur la maison** the sun was beating down on the house ◆ **il darda un regard haineux sur son rival** he shot a look full of hate at his rival 2 (= *dresser*) [+ *piquants, épines*] to point ◆ **le clocher dardait sa flèche vers le ciel** the church spire thrust upwards into the sky

dare-dare * /daʀdaʀ/ LOC ADV double-quick * ◆ **accourir ~** to come running up double-quick * *ou* at the double

darne /daʀn/ NF [*de poisson*] steak

dartre /daʀtʀ/ NF dry patch, scurf (*NonC*)

darwinien, -ienne /daʀwinjɛ̃, jɛn/ ADJ Darwinian

darwinisme /daʀwinism/ NM Darwinism

darwiniste /daʀwinist/ ADJ, NMF Darwinist

DAT /deate/ NM (abrév de **Digital Audio Tape**) DAT

datable /databl/ ADJ dat(e)able ◆ **manuscrit facilement ~** manuscript which can easily be dated

DATAR /dataʀ/ NF (abrév de **Délégation à l'aménagement du territoire et à l'action régionale**) → **délégation**

datation /datasjɔ̃/ NF [*de contrat, manuscrit*] dating ◆ **~ au carbone 14** carbon dating

datcha /datʃa/ NF dacha

date /dat/ NF date ◆ **~ de naissance/mariage/paiement** date of birth/marriage/payment ◆ **~ d'exigibilité** due *ou* maturity date ◆ **~ de péremption/clôture** expiry/closing date ◆ **~ butoir** *ou* **limite** deadline ◆ **~ limite de consommation/de vente** use-by/sell-by date ◆ **~ limite de fraîcheur** *ou* **de conservation** best-before date ◆ **~ de valeur** [*de chèque*] processing date ◆ **pourriez-vous faire ce virement avec ~ de valeur le 15 juin ?** could you process this payment on 15 June? ◆ **la ~ à laquelle je vous ai vu** the day I saw you ◆ **j'ai pris ~ avec lui pour le 18 mai** I have set *ou* fixed a date with him for 18 May ◆ **cet événement fait ~ dans l'histoire** this event stands out in *ou* marks a milestone in history ◆ **sans ~** undated

◆ **à + date** ◆ **note ce rendez-vous à la ~ du 12 mai** note down this appointment for 12 May ◆ **à quelle ~ cela s'est-il produit ?** on what date did that occur? ◆ **à cette ~ il ne le savait pas encore** at that time he did not yet know about it ◆ **à cette ~-là il était déjà mort** by that time *ou* by then he was already dead ◆ **le comité se réunit à ~ fixe** the committee meets on a fixed *ou* set date

◆ **en date** ◆ **lettre en ~ du 23 mai** letter dated 23 May ◆ **le premier en ~** the first *ou* earliest ◆ **le dernier en ~** the latest *ou* most recent

◆ **de longue** *ou* **vieille date** [*amitié*] long-standing; [*ami*] long-standing, long-time ◆ **je le connais de longue ~** I've known him for a (very) long time ◆ **nous sommes des amis de longue ~** we go back a long way

◆ **de fraîche date** [*ami*] recent ◆ **arrivé de fraîche ~ à Paris** newly arrived in Paris

dater /date/ ▸ conjug 1 ◂ VT [+ *lettre, événement*] to date ◆ **lettre datée du 6/de Paris** letter dated the 6th/from Paris ◆ **non daté** undated VI 1 ◆ **~ de** (= *remonter à*) to date back to, to date from ◆ **ça ne date pas d'hier** *ou* **d'aujourd'hui** [*maladie*] it has been going a long time; [*amitié, situation*] it goes back a long way; [*objet*] it's far from new ◆ **à ~ de demain** as from tomorrow, from tomorrow onwards ◆ **de quand date votre dernière rencontre ?** when did you last meet? 2 (= *être important*) **cet événement a daté dans sa vie** this event marked a milestone in his life 3 (= *être démodé*) to be dated ◆ **ça commence à ~** it's beginning to date ◆ **le film est un peu daté** the film is a little dated

dateur /datœʀ/ NM [*de montre*] date indicator ◆ **(timbre** *ou* **tampon) ~** date stamp

datif, -ive /datif, iv/ ADJ, NM dative ◆ **au ~** in the dative

dation /dasjɔ̃/ NF (*Jur*) payment in kind; [*d'œuvres d'art*] donation

datte /dat/ NF date

dattier /datje/ NM date palm

datura /datyʀa/ NM datura

daube /dob/ NF 1 (= *viande*) stew, casserole ◆ **faire une ~** *ou* **de la viande en ~** to make a stew *ou* casserole ◆ **bœuf en ~** casserole of beef, beef stew 2 (* = *nullité*) **c'est de la ~** it's crap*

dauber /dobe/ ▸ conjug 1 ◂ VI 1 (*littér*) **~ sur qn/qch** to jeer (at) sb/sth ◆ **il serait facile de ~ sur nos erreurs** it would be easy to sneer *ou* scoff at our mistakes 2 (* = *puer*) **ça daube ici !** it stinks in here!

dauphin /dofɛ̃/ NM 1 (= *animal*) dolphin 2 (*Hist*) **le Dauphin** the Dauphin 3 (= *successeur*) heir apparent

Dauphine /dofin/ NF Dauphine, Dauphiness

dauphinois, e /dofinwa, waz/ ADJ of *ou* from the Dauphiné; → **gratin** NM,F **Dauphinois(e)** inhabitant *ou* native of the Dauphiné

daurade /dɔʀad/ NF gilthead bream, sea bream ◆ **~ rose** red sea bream ◆ **~ royale** gilthead bream

davantage /davɑ̃taʒ/ ADV 1 (= *plus*) [*gagner, acheter*] more; (*négatif*) any more; (*interrogatif*) (any) more ◆ **en voulez-vous ~ ?** would you like more? ◆ **bien/encore/même ~** much/still/even more ◆ **je n'en sais pas ~** I don't know anything more about it ◆ **il s'approcha ~** he drew closer *ou* nearer

◆ **davantage de** (some) more; (*négatif*) any more ◆ **vouloir ~ de pain/temps** to want (some) more bread/time ◆ **veux-tu ~ de viande ?** do you want (any *ou* some) more meat? ◆ **il n'en a pas voulu ~** he didn't want any more (of it)

◆ **davantage que** (= *plus*) more than; (= *plus longtemps*) longer than ◆ **tu te crois malin mais il l'est ~ (que toi)** you think you're sharp but he is more so than you *ou* but he is sharper (than you)

2 (= *plus longtemps*) longer; (*négatif, interrogatif*) any longer ◆ **sans s'attarder/rester ~** without lingering/staying any longer

3 (= *de plus en plus*) more and more ◆ **les prix augmentent chaque jour ~** prices go up more and more every day

David /david/ NM David

davier /davje/ NM (= *forceps*) forceps; (*Menuiserie*) cramp

db (abrév de **décibel**) dB, db

DCA /desea/ NF (abrév de **défense contre avions**) anti-aircraft defence

DDASS /das/ NF (abrév de **Direction départementale de l'action sanitaire et sociale**) local department of social services ◆ **un enfant de la ~** (*orphelin*) a state orphan; (*retiré de la garde de ses parents*) a child who has been taken into care (*Brit*), a child in court custody (*US*)

DDT /dedete/ NM (abrév de **dichloro-diphényl-trichloréthane**) DDT

de[1] /də/

Devant une voyelle ou un **h** muet = **d'**; contraction **de + le = du**; **de + les = des**.

Lorsque **de** fait partie d'une locution du type **décider de faire, content de qch, c'est l'occasion de, se nourrir de, s'aider de, de plus en plus** etc, reportez-vous à l'autre mot.

PRÉPOSITION

1 déplacement, provenance from ◆ **être/provenir/s'échapper ~** to be/come/escape from ◆ **sauter du toit** to jump off *ou* from the roof ◆ **~ sa fenêtre elle voit la mer** she can see the sea from her window ◆ **il arrive du Japon** he has just arrived from Japan ◆ **il y a une lettre ~ Paul** there's a letter from Paul ◆ **nous recevons des amis du Canada** we have friends from Canada staying (with us) ◆ **ce sont des gens ~ la campagne/la ville** they are people from the country/town ◆ **on apprend de Londres que ...** we hear *ou* it is announced from London that ... ◆ **des pommes ~ notre jardin** apples from our garden ◆ **le train/l'avion ~ Londres** the train/plane from London, the London train/plane ◆ **je l'ai vu en sortant ~ la maison** I saw him as I was coming out of the house

2 localisation in ◆ **les magasins ~ Londres/Paris** the shops in London/Paris, the London/Paris shops ◆ **les gens ~ ma rue** the people in my street ◆ **les voisins du 2e (étage)** the neighbours on the 2nd floor

3 destination for, to ◆ **le train/l'avion ~ Bruxelles** the Brussels train/plane, the train/plane for *ou* to Brussels ◆ **la route ~ Tours** the Tours road, the road for Tours

4 appartenance

Lorsque **de** sert à exprimer l'appartenance, il peut se traduire par **of** ; on préférera toutefois souvent le génitif lorsque le possesseur est une personne ou un pays, plus rarement une chose.

◆ **la maison ~ David/~ notre ami** David's/our friend's house ◆ **le mari ~ la reine d'Angle-**

terre the Queen of England's husband ◆ **la patte du chien** the dog's paw ◆ **le roi ~ France** the King of France ◆ **l'attitude du Canada** Canada's attitude, the attitude of Canada ◆ **un ami ~ mon père** a friend of my father's ◆ **c'est le médecin ~ mes cousins** he's my cousins' doctor ◆ **un ami ~ la famille** a friend of the family, a family friend ◆ **un programmeur d'IBM** *ou* **~ chez IBM** a programmer with IBM ◆ **ses collègues ~** *ou* **du bureau** his colleagues at work

Après un pluriel régulier ou un pluriel irrégulier se terminant par un **s**, l'apostrophe s'utilise toujours seule ; après un pluriel irrégulier ne se terminant pas par un **s, 's** est obligatoire.

◆ **la maison ~ nos amis** our friends' house ◆ **la loge des actrices** the actresses' dressing-room ◆ **les amis ~ nos enfants** our children's friends

Après un nom commun se terminant par **ss, 's** est obligatoire.

◆ **la loge ~ l'actrice** the actress's dressing-room

Après un nom propre se terminant par **s** ou **ss**, l'apostrophe peut être utilisée seule dans un registre plus soutenu.

◆ **la vie ~ Jésus** Jesus's life, Jesus' life ◆ **la maison ~ Wells/Burgess** Wells's/Burgess's house, Wells'/Burgess' house

Dans le cas où le possesseur est un inanimé, l'anglais juxtapose parfois les noms.

◆ **le pied ~ la table** the leg of the table, the table leg ◆ **le bouton ~ la porte** the door knob

5 caractérisation

Lorsque **de** est utilisé pour la caractérisation, il peut être traduit par **of**, mais l'anglais utilise souvent des tournures adjectivales.

(caractérisation par le contenu) ◆ **une bouteille ~ vin/lait** a bottle of wine/milk ◆ **une tasse ~ thé** a cup of tea ◆ **une pincée/cuillerée ~ sel** a pinch/spoonful of salt ◆ **une poignée ~ gens** a handful of people ◆ **une collection ~ timbres** a stamp collection ◆ **une boîte ~ bonbons** a box of sweets
(caractérisation par la matière) ◆ **vase ~ cristal** crystal vase ◆ **robe ~ soie** silk dress
(caractérisation par la qualité) ◆ **un homme ~ goût/d'une grande bonté** a man of taste/great kindness ◆ **quelque chose ~ beau/cher** something lovely/expensive ◆ **rien ~ neuf/d'intéressant** nothing new/interesting *ou* of interest
(caractérisation par la fonction) ◆ **il est professeur d'anglais** he's an English teacher *ou* a teacher of English
(caractérisation par le temps) ◆ **les romanciers du 20ᵉ siècle** 20th-century novelists, novelists of the 20th century ◆ **les journaux d'hier/du dimanche** yesterday's/the Sunday papers

◆ **de** + *participe passé* ◆ **il y a deux verres ~ cassés** there are two broken glasses *ou* glasses broken ◆ **il y a cinq enfants ~ disparus** five children are missing

6 valeur intensive **et elle ~ se moquer ~ nos efforts !** and she made fun of our efforts! ◆ **et lui d'ajouter : "jamais !"** "never!" he added

La valeur intensive de **de + article ou démonstratif** est souvent rendue par un adjectif ou un adverbe en anglais.

◆ **il est d'une bêtise !** he's so stupid!, he's incredibly stupid! ◆ **il a un ~ ces appétits !** he's got an incredible appetite ◆ **j'ai ~ ces douleurs !** I've got this terrible pain ◆ **elle a ~ ces initiatives !** some of the things she gets up to! ◆ **tu as ~ ces idées !** you have the strangest ideas sometimes!

7

Lorsque **de** introduit un nom en apposition, il est rarement traduit.

◆ **le jour ~ Noël** Christmas Day ◆ **le prénom ~ Paul est très courant** the name Paul is very common ◆ **le mot ~ "liberté"** the word "freedom" ◆ **cette saleté ~ temps nous gâche nos vacances** this rotten weather is spoiling our holiday ◆ **ton idiot ~ fils** that stupid son of yours ◆ **la ville ~ Paris** the city of Paris ◆ **le mois ~ juin** (the month of) June

8 suivi d'un nombre **~ six qu'ils étaient (au départ), ils ne sont plus que deux** of the original six there are only two left

Lorsque **de** est suivi d'une mesure, d'un poids, d'un âge, d'une durée, d'un montant etc, il est souvent rendu en anglais par une simple apposition.

◆ **un rôti ~ 2 kg** a 2-kilo joint ◆ **une table ~ 2 mètres ~ large** a table 2 metres wide *ou* in width ◆ **un enfant ~ 5 ans** a 5-year-old (child) ◆ **un bébé ~ 6 mois** a 6-month(-old) baby, a baby of 6 months ◆ **une attente ~ 2 heures** a 2-hour wait ◆ **un voyage ~ trois jours** a three-day journey ◆ **une promenade ~ 3 km/3 heures** a 3-km/3-hour walk ◆ **une pièce ~ 6 m²** a room 6 metres square ◆ **une plage ~ plusieurs kilomètres** a beach several kilometres long ◆ **un bébé ~ quelques mois** a baby just a few months old ◆ **il y aura une attente ~ quelques heures** there will be a few hours' wait, you will have to wait a few hours MAIS **un chèque ~ 20 €** a cheque for €20 ◆ **elle est plus grande que lui ~ 5 cm** she is 5 cm taller than he is, she is taller than him by 5 cm

9 agent animé by ◆ **un film ~ Fellini** a Fellini film, a film by Fellini ◆ **un concerto ~ Brahms** a concerto by Brahms, a Brahms concerto ◆ **le message a été compris ~ tous** the message was understood by everybody ◆ **c'est ~ qui ?** who is it by? ◆ **le poème n'est pas ~ moi** I didn't write the poem ◆ **c'est bien ~ lui ~ sortir sans manteau** it's just like him *ou* it's typical of him to go out without a coat

10 agent inanimé

Lorsque **de** introduit un agent inanimé, la traduction dépend étroitement du verbe ; reportez-vous à celui-ci.

◆ **couvert ~ boue/d'un drap** covered in mud/with a sheet ◆ **rempli ~ fumée** filled with smoke

11 = avec, manière, cause

Lorsque **de** signifie **avec, au moyen de, à l'aide de**, ou exprime la manière ou la cause, la traduction dépend étroitement du contexte ; reportez-vous au verbe ou au nom.

◆ **il l'attrapa ~ la main gauche** he caught it with his left hand ◆ **~ rien/d'un bout ~ bois, il peut faire des merveilles** he can make wonderful things out of nothing/a bit of wood ◆ **il les encourageait ~ la voix** he cheered them on ◆ **marcher d'un pas lent/d'un bon pas** to walk slowly/briskly ◆ **parler d'une voix émue/ferme** to speak emotionally/firmly *ou* in an emotional/a firm voice ◆ **regarder qn d'un air tendre** to look at sb tenderly, to give sb a tender look ◆ **rougir ~ dépit/~ honte** to blush with vexation/with *ou* for shame ◆ **~ colère, il la gifla** he slapped her in anger ◆ **être fatigué du voyage/~ répéter** to be tired from the journey/of repeating ◆ **elle rit ~ le voir si maladroit** she laughed to see him *ou* on seeing him so clumsy ◆ **contrarié ~ ce qu'il se montre si peu coopératif** annoyed at his being so uncooperative

12 = par, chaque **il gagne 15 € ~ l'heure** he earns €15 an hour *ou* per hour ◆ **ça coûte 8 € du mètre** it costs €8 a metre

13 = durant **~ jour/nuit** by day/night, during the day/the night ◆ **3 heures du matin/~ l'après-midi** 3 (o'clock) in the morning/afternoon, 3 am/pm

Notez l'emploi de **all** dans les phrases suivantes.

◆ **il n'a rien fait ~ la semaine/l'année** he hasn't done a thing all week/year ◆ **~ (toute) ma vie je n'ai entendu pareilles sottises** I've never heard such nonsense in all my life ◆ **je ne l'avais pas vu ~ la semaine/~ la soirée** I hadn't seen him all week/all evening

14 valeur emphatique **t'en as une, ~ moto ?*** have you got a motorbike? ◆ **moi j'en ai vu deux, ~ lions !*** I saw two lions, I did! ◆ **c'en est un, d'imbécile*** he's a real idiot

◆ **de ... à** from ... to
(dans l'espace) ◆ **~ chez moi à la gare, il y a 5 km** it's 5 km from my house to the station
(dans le temps) ◆ **je serai là ~ 6 à 8** I'll be there from 6 to 8 ◆ **du 2 au 7 mai** *(écrit)* from 2 to 7 May; *(parlé)* from the 2nd to the 7th of May ◆ **le magasin est ouvert du mardi au samedi** the shop is open from Tuesday to Saturday ◆ **d'une minute/d'un jour à l'autre** *(= très rapidement)* from one minute/day to the next; *(= incessamment, n'importe quand)* any minute/day now
(avec un âge, une durée, une estimation) ◆ **les enfants ~ 9 à 12 ans** children from 9 to 12, children between (the ages of) 9 and 12 ◆ **ça peut coûter ~ 20 à 30 €** it can cost from €20 to €30 *ou* between €20 and €30
(pour exprimer l'exhaustivité) ◆ **ils ont tout pris, des petites cuillères à l'armoire** they took everything, from the teaspoons to the wardrobe; → **ici, là**

◆ **de ... en** from ... to
(dans l'espace) ◆ **il va ~ village en village/~ porte en porte** he goes from village to village/from door to door
(dans le temps) ◆ **~ mois en mois/jour en jour** from month to month/day to day ◆ **le nombre diminue d'année en année** the number is decreasing year on year *ou* every year ◆ **~ minute en minute, l'espoir s'amenuisait** hope faded as the minutes went by
(dans une succession, une évolution) ◆ **il va d'échec en échec** he goes from one failure to the next ◆ **nous allions ~ surprise en surprise** we had one surprise after another

de² /də/

Devant une voyelle ou un **h** muet = **d'**
contraction **de** + **le** = **du**; **de** + **les** = **des**.

1 ARTICLE PARTITIF 2 ARTICLE INDÉFINI PL

1 - ARTICLE PARTITIF

1 dans une affirmation

de se traduit généralement par **some**, mais celui-ci peut être omis.

◆ **au déjeuner, nous avons eu du poulet** we had (some) chicken for lunch ◆ **j'ai du travail à faire** I've got (some) work to do ◆ **il but ~ l'eau au robinet** he drank some water from the tap ◆ **j'ai acheté des pommes/~ la viande** I bought some apples/some meat ◆ **j'ai acheté des fruits, des légumes et du vin** I bought (some) fruit, (some) vegetables and (some) wine ◆ **j'ai acheté ~ la laine** I bought some wool ◆ **il a joué du Chopin/des valses ~ Chopin** he played (some) Chopin/some Chopin waltzes ◆ **cela demande du courage/~ la patience** it takes (some) courage/patience ◆ **c'est du chantage/vol !** that's blackmail/robbery!

de ne se traduit pas lorsque l'on ne veut pas ou ne peut pas préciser la quantité.

◆ **boire du vin/~ la bière/~ l'eau** to drink wine/beer/water ◆ **ils vendent des pommes/~ la viande** they sell apples/meat ◆ **on peut acheter ~ la laine chez Dupont** you can buy wool at Dupont's ◆ **il mange des biscuits toute la journée** he eats biscuits all day ◆ **les ânes mangent du foin** donkeys eat hay MAIS **il y avait ~ l'agressivité dans ses paroles** there was something aggressive about what he said

Dans certaines expressions, **de** se traduit par l'article **a, an**.

◆ **faire du bruit** to make a noise ◆ **avoir ~ l'humour** to have a sense of humour

2 dans une interrogation, une hypothèse

de se traduit généralement par **any** ; **some** est utilisé si l'on s'attend à une réponse positive.

◆ **avez-vous du pain/des œufs à me passer ?** do you have any bread/eggs you could let me have?, I wonder if you could let me have some bread/eggs? ◆ **voulez-vous du pain/des œufs ?** would you like some bread/eggs? ◆ **vous ne voulez vraiment pas ~ vin ?** are you sure you don't want some *ou* any wine? ◆ **si on prenait ~ la bière/du vin ?** what about some beer/wine? ◆ **s'il y avait du pain, j'en mangerais** if there was some *ou* any bread, I'd eat it

Lorsqu'il s'agit d'une alternative, **de** ne se traduit généralement pas.

◆ **voulez-vous du thé ou du café ?** would you like tea or coffee?

3 dans une négation

de se traduit généralement par **any** ou **no**.

◆ **je n'ai pas acheté ~ pommes/~ laine** I didn't buy (any) apples/wool ◆ **il n'y a pas ~ pain** there's no bread, there isn't any bread

4 dans une comparaison **il y a du poète chez cet homme** he has something of the poet about him ◆ **il y a du puritain chez lui** he has something of the puritan about him, there's something puritanical about him ◆ **il y a du Fellini chez lui** his work is somewhat reminiscent of Fellini

2 – ARTICLE INDÉFINI PLURIEL

1 dans une affirmation

des, de peuvent se traduire par **some** mais ce dernier est souvent omis.

◆ **des enfants ont cassé les carreaux** some children have broken the window panes ◆ **il y a des vers dans le fromage** there are (some) maggots in the cheese ◆ **j'ai des voisins charmants** *ou* **~ charmants voisins** I've got (some) lovely neighbours ◆ **il y a des gens qui attendent** there are (some) people waiting ◆ **il y a des gens qui disent que ...** some people say that ... ◆ **elle a des taches ~ rousseur** she's got freckles ◆ **elle a ~ petites taches ~ rousseur sur les joues** she's got (some) little freckles on her cheeks

Lorsque le nom suivant **de** appartient à un ensemble d'éléments fixes, **some** ne peut être employé.

◆ **elle a ~ jolies mains/~ jolis doigts** she's got lovely hands/lovely fingers ◆ **il a ~ beaux enfants** he's got beautiful kids ◆ **il portait des lunettes** he was wearing glasses

Dans les oppositions, **de** ne se traduit pas.

◆ **elle élève des chats mais pas ~ chiens** she breeds cats but not dogs

2 dans une interrogation

des, de se traduisent par **any** ; **some** est utilisé lorsque l'on s'attend à une réponse positive.

◆ **as-tu rencontré des randonneurs ?** did you meet any hikers? ◆ **tu veux vraiment des livres pour ton anniversaire ?** do you really want (some) books for your birthday?

3 dans une négation

de se traduit par **any** ou **no**.

◆ **je n'ai pas ~ voisins** I haven't got any neighbours, I have no neighbours ◆ **il n'a pas eu ~ client ce matin** he hasn't had any customers this morning ◆ **je n'ai jamais vu ~ loups ici** I have never seen (any) wolves here MAIS **je n'ai jamais vu ~ loups** I've never seen a wolf

4 valeur intensive **elle est restée des mois et des mois sans nouvelles** she was without news for months and months, she went for months and months without news ◆ **j'ai attendu des heures** I waited (for) hours ◆ **nous n'avons pas fait des kilomètres** we didn't exactly walk miles ◆ **ils en ont cueilli des kilos (et des kilos)** they picked kilos (and kilos) ◆ **il y en a des qui exagèrent*** some people do exaggerate

dé /de/ NM 1 ◆ ~ **(à coudre)** thimble; *(= petit verre)* tiny glass ◆ **ça tient dans un ~ à coudre** *(fig)* it will fit into a thimble 2 *(Jeux)* dice ◆ **~s (à jouer)** dice ◆ **jouer aux ~s** to play dice ◆ **les ~s sont jetés** the die is cast ◆ **couper des carottes en ~s** to dice carrots ◆ **sur un coup de ~s** *(lit, fig)* on a throw of the dice ◆ **jouer son avenir sur un coup de ~s** to risk one's future on a throw of the dice, to (take a) gamble with one's future

DEA /deəa/ NM (abrév de **diplôme d'études approfondies**) → **diplôme**

deal /dil/ NM 1 *(Drogue)* drug dealing 2 *(* = transaction)* deal ◆ **passer un ~** to do *ou* strike a deal *(avec* with)

dealer[1] /dile/ ▸ conjug 1 ◂ VI *(Drogue)* to push drugs*

dealer[2] /dilœʀ/ NM *(Drogue)* (drug) dealer*

déambulateur /deɑ̃bylatœʀ/ NM walking frame, walker, zimmer (aid) ®

déambulatoire /deɑ̃bylatwaʀ/ NM ambulatory

déambuler /deɑ̃byle/ ▸ conjug 1 ◂ VI *(gén)* to wander; *[promeneur]* to stroll ◆ **j'aime ~ dans les rues de Paris** I like to stroll through the streets of Paris

déb* /dɛb/ NF (abrév de **débutante**) deb*

débâcle /debɑkl/ NF *[d'armée]* debacle, rout; *[de régime]* collapse; *[de glaces]* breaking up, debacle (SPÉC) ◆ **c'est une vraie ~ !** it's a complete disaster! ◆ **la ~ de la livre (face au dollar)** the collapse of the pound (against the dollar)

déballage /debalaʒ/ NM 1 *(= action) [d'objets]* unpacking 2 *[de marchandises]* display *(of loose goods)* 3 *(* = paroles, confession)* revelations ◆ **ce grand ~** all these revelations, this spate of revelations ◆ **ce ~ de linge sale** this public washing of dirty linen ◆ **ce ~ médiatique** these revelations in the media

déballer /debale/ ▸ conjug 1 ◂ VT *[+ objets]* to unpack; *[+ marchandises]* to display, to lay out; * *[+ histoires, souvenirs]* to let out; * *[+ sentiments]* to pour out, to give vent to; *(* péj) [+ connaissances]* to air *(péj)* ◆ **elle lui a tout déballé*** she poured out her heart to him

déballonner (se)‡ /debalɔne/ ▸ conjug 1 ◂ VPR to chicken out*

débandade /debɑ̃dad/ NF *(= déroute)* frantic retreat; *(= fin)* collapse; *(= confusion)* chaos ◆ **c'était la ~** it was total chaos ◆ **la ~ allemande devant les Russes** the frantic retreat of the Germans ahead of the Russians ◆ **la ~ de Manchester à Rotterdam** *(Sport)* Manchester's disastrous defeat at Rotterdam ◆ **c'est la ~ dans le camp des réformateurs** the reformist camp is in disarray

◆ **en débandade** ◆ **les soldats en ~** the fleeing soldiers ◆ **une foule en ~ (dans les rues)** a crowd fleeing in terror (through the streets) ◆ **les places boursières sont en ~** stock markets are in chaos

débander /debɑ̃de/ ▸ conjug 1 ◂ VT 1 *(Méd)* to unbandage, to take the bandages off ◆ **~ les yeux de qn** to remove a blindfold from sb's eyes 2 *[+ arc, ressort]* to relax, to slacken (off) VI *(‡ : sexuellement)* to lose one's hard-on*‡ ◆ **travailler 10 heures sans ~** *(fig)* to work 10 hours without letting up* VPR **se débander** *[armée, manifestants]* to scatter, to break up; *[arc, ressort]* to relax, to slacken

débaptiser /debatize/ ▸ conjug 1 ◂ VT to change the name of, to rename

débarbouillage /debaʀbujaʒ/ NM *[de visage]* quick wash, cat-lick* *(Brit)*

débarbouiller /debaʀbuje/ ▸ conjug 1 ◂ VT *[+ visage]* to give a quick wash *ou* cat-lick* *(Brit)* to VPR **se débarbouiller** to give one's face a quick wash *ou* a cat-lick* *(Brit)*

débarbouillette /debaʀbujɛt/ NF *(Can)* face cloth, flannel *(Brit)*, wash cloth *(US)*

débarcadère /debaʀkadɛʀ/ NM landing stage

débardage /debaʀdaʒ/ NM *(Naut)* unloading, unlading; *(Sylviculture)* skidding

débarder /debaʀde/ ▸ conjug 1 ◂ VT *(Naut)* to unload, to unlade; *(Sylviculture)* to skid

débardeur /debaʀdœʀ/ NM 1 *(Naut)* docker, stevedore; *(Sylviculture)* skidder 2 *(= vêtement, T-shirt)* singlet, sleeveless T-shirt; *(par-dessus une chemise)* tank top, slipover *(Brit)*

débarqué, e /debaʀke/ (ptp de **débarquer**) NM,F *(lit)* disembarked passenger ◆ **un nouveau ~ dans le service*** *(fig)* a new arrival in the department ADJ ◆ **un jeune auteur fraîchement ~ de sa province** a young writer just up *ou* newly arrived from the provinces

débarquement /debaʀkəmɑ̃/ NM *[de marchandises]* unloading, landing; *[de passagers]* disembarkation, landing; *[de troupes]* landing ◆ **navire** *ou* **péniche de ~** landing craft *(inv)* ◆ **le ~** *(Hist : en Normandie)* the Normandy landings

débarquer /debaʀke/ ▸ conjug 1 ◂ VT 1 *[+ marchandises]* to unload, to land; *[+ passagers]* to disembark, to land; *[+ troupes]* to land 2 *(* = congédier)* to fire, to sack* *(Brit)*, to kick out* ◆ **se faire ~** to get the push* *ou* sack* *(Brit)*, to get kicked out* VI 1 *(Aviat, Naut) [passagers]* to disembark *(de* from); *[troupes]* to land 2 *(* = arriver subitement)* to turn up ◆ **il a débarqué chez moi hier soir** he turned up at my place last night ◆ **j'ai débarqué à Paris quand j'avais 20 ans** I arrived in Paris when I was 20 3 *(* = ne pas être au courant)* **tu débarques !** where have you been?* ◆ **je n'en sais rien, je débarque** I don't know, that's the first I've heard of it

débarras /debaʀa/ NM 1 *(= pièce)* junk room, boxroom *(Brit)*; *(= placard, soupente)* junk cupboard, junk closet *(US)* 2 * **bon ~ !** good riddance! ◆ **il est parti, quel ~ !** thank goodness he's gone!

débarrasser /debaʀase/ ▸ conjug 1 ◂ VT 1 *[+ local]* to clear *(de* of); ◆ **~ (la table)** to clear the table ◆ **débarrasse le plancher !*** beat it!*, hop it!* *(Brit)* 2 ◆ **~ qn de** *[+ fardeau, manteau, chapeau]* to relieve sb of; *[+ habitude]* to break *ou* rid sb of; *[+ ennemi, mal]* to rid sb of; *[+ liens]* to release sb from ◆ **écris ces lettres tout de suite, tu en seras débarrassé** write those letters now to get them out of the way ◆ **je**

peux vous ~ ? can I take your coat (*ou* jacket *etc*)? VPR **se débarrasser** ◆ **se ~ de** *[+ objet, personne]* to get rid of, to rid o.s. of; *[+ mauvaise habitude]* to rid o.s. of; *(= ôter) [+ vêtement]* to take off, to remove ◆ **débarrassez-vous !** *[+ objets]* put your things down; *[+ manteau]* take your coat off

débat /deba/ NM *(= polémique)* debate; *(= discussion)* discussion, debate ◆ **~ intérieur** inner struggle ◆ **dîner-~** dinner debate ◆ **émission-~** *(TV)* televised *ou* television debate ◆ **~ de clôture** *(Parl)* ≃ adjournment debate ◆ **~ d'idées** ideological debate ◆ **ouvrir le ~** to open the debate ◆ **un grand ~ de société sur l'éthique médicale** a major public debate *ou* controversy about medical ethics ◆ **avec lui, il n'y a pas de ~ d'idées possible** with him there is no possibility of a discussion about ideas NMPL **débats** *(Jur, Pol = séance)* proceedings, debates ◆ **~s à huis clos** *(Jur)* hearing in camera

débâter /debɑte/ ▸ conjug 1 ◂ VT *[+ bête de somme]* to unsaddle

débâtir /debɑtiʀ/ ▸ conjug 2 ◂ VT *(Couture)* to take out *ou* remove the tacking *ou* basting

débatteur /debatœʀ/ NM debater

débattre /debatʀ/ ▸ conjug 41 ◂ VT *[+ problème, question]* to discuss, to debate; *[+ prix, clauses d'un traité]* to discuss ◆ **le prix reste à ~** the price has still to be discussed ◆ **à vendre 200 € à ~** *(petite annonce)* for sale: €200 or nearest offer VT INDIR **débattre de** *ou* **sur** *[+ question]* to discuss, to debate ◆ **les participants au sommet débattront du processus de paix** the participants at the summit will discuss the peace process VPR **se débattre** *(contre un adversaire)* to struggle *(contre* with); *(contre le courant)* to struggle *(contre* against); *(contre les difficultés)* to struggle *(contre* against; *avec* with) to wrestle *(contre* with); ◆ **se ~ comme un beau diable** *ou* **comme un forcené** to struggle like the very devil *ou* like one possessed

débauchage /deboʃaʒ/ NM *(= licenciement)* laying off, dismissal; *[de salarié d'une autre entreprise]* hiring away, poaching ◆ **il y a eu plusieurs ~s** *(licenciements)* there were several layoffs, several people were laid off; *(d'autres entreprises)* several people were hired away *ou* poached

débauche /deboʃ/ NF 1 *(= vice)* debauchery ◆ **mener une vie de ~, vivre dans la ~** to lead a debauched life *ou* a life of debauchery ◆ **scène de ~** scene of debauchery ◆ **incitation de mineurs à la ~** *(Jur)* corruption of minors; → **lieu¹** 2 *(= abondance)* **~ de** profusion *ou* abundance *ou* wealth of ◆ **~ de couleurs** riot of colour

débauché, e † /deboʃe/ (ptp de **débaucher**) ADJ *[personne, vie]* debauched NM,F debauched individual ◆ **c'est un ~** he leads a debauched life *ou* a life of debauchery

débaucher /deboʃe/ ▸ conjug 1 ◂ VT 1 *(= embaucher un salarié d'une autre entreprise)* to hire away, to poach *(de* from); *[chasseur de tête]* to headhunt ◆ **il s'est fait ~ par un chasseur de tête** he was head-hunted 2 *(= licencier)* to lay off, to make redundant *(Brit)* ◆ **on débauche dans ce secteur** a lot of people are being laid off *ou* made redundant in this sector ◆ **les usines qui débauchent** factories that are laying off workers 3 († *= détourner) (du droit chemin)* to debauch, to corrupt; *(* : d'une occupation)* to entice away, to tempt away; *(= inciter à la grève)* to incite to strike VI *(= sortir du travail)* to stop work for the day, to knock off*

débecter ‡ /debɛkte/ ▸ conjug 1 ◂ VT *(= dégoûter)* to disgust ◆ **ça me débecte** it makes me sick, it makes me want to throw up* *ou* to puke‡

débile /debil/ ADJ 1 *(= stupide *) [personne]* moronic*; *[film, discours, raisonnement]* pathetic*, stupid 2 *(= faible) [enfant]* sickly, weak; *[corps, membre]* weak, feeble; *[esprit]* feeble; *[santé]* frail, poor NMF *(Méd)* ◆ **~ mental** (mentally) retarded person ◆ **~ léger/moyen/profond** mildly/moderately/severely (mentally) retarded *ou* handicapped person ◆ **quel ~, celui-là !** *(péj)* what a moron!*

débilitant, e /debilitɑ̃, ɑ̃t/ ADJ *(= anémiant) [climat, régime]* debilitating, enervating; *(= déprimant) [atmosphère]* demoralizing; *(* = abêtissant) [travail]* mind-numbing; *[musique, spectacle]* mindless

débilité /debilite/ NF († *= faiblesse)* debility; *(péj) [de propos, attitude]* stupidity ◆ **~ mentale** mental retardation *ou* deficiency ◆ **enfant atteint d'une ~ légère** mildly (mentally) retarded *ou* handicapped child

débiliter /debilite/ ▸ conjug 1 ◂ VT *(= affaiblir) [climat, régime]* to debilitate, to enervate; *(= déprimer) [endroit, propos]* to demoralize

débinage * /debinaʒ/ NM knocking*, running down

débine †* /debin/ NF ◆ **être dans la ~** to be hard up, to be on one's uppers* *(Brit)* ◆ **tomber dans la ~** to fall on hard times

débiner * /debine/ ▸ conjug 1 ◂ VT *(= dénigrer) [+ personne]* to knock*, to run down VPR **se débiner** *(= se sauver)* to clear off*

débineur, -euse * /debinœʀ, øz/ NM,F backbiter*

débirentier, -ière /debiʀɑ̃tje, jɛʀ/ NM,F *(Jur)* payer of an annuity

débit /debi/ NM 1 *(Fin)* debit; *[de relevé de compte]* debit side ◆ **mettre** *ou* **porter 25 € au ~ de qn** to debit sb *ou* sb's account with €25, to charge €25 to sb's account ◆ **pouvez-vous me faire le** *ou* **mon ~ ?** can I pay for it please?

2 *(= rythme de vente)* turnover (of goods), sales ◆ **cet article a un bon/faible ~** this item sells well/poorly ◆ **n'achète pas ton fromage dans cette boutique, il n'y a pas assez de ~** don't buy your cheese in this shop, there isn't a quick enough turnover

3 *[de fleuve]* (rate of) flow; *[de gaz, électricité]* output; *[de pompe]* flow, outflow; *[de tuyau]* discharge; *[de machine]* output; *[de moyen de transport]* passenger flow; *(Ordin) [de données]* output ◆ **il n'y a pas assez de ~ au robinet** there is not enough pressure in the tap ◆ **~ cardiaque** *(Méd)* cardiac output ◆ **~ sanguin** blood flow (from the heart) ◆ **le haut ~** high-speed Internet access ◆ **connexion haut ~** high-speed connection

4 *(= élocution)* delivery ◆ **~ rapide/monotone** rapid/monotonous delivery ◆ **elle a un sacré ~** * she's a real chatterbox, she's a great talker*

5 *(Menuiserie)* cutting up, sawing up

COMP **débit de boissons** *(= petit bar ou café)* bar; *(Admin, terme générique)* drinking establishment

débit de tabac tobacconist's (shop) *(Brit)*, tobacco *ou* smoke shop *(US)*

débitable /debitabl/ ADJ *[bois]* which can be sawn *ou* cut up

débitant, e /debitɑ̃, ɑ̃t/ NM,F ◆ **~ (de boissons)** ≃ off-licence manager *(Brit)*, liquor store manager *(US)* ◆ **~ (de tabac)** tobacconist *(Brit)*, tobacco dealer *(US)*

débiter /debite/ ▸ conjug 1 ◂ VT 1 *[+ personne, compte]* to debit ◆ **j'ai été débité de 300 euros** 300 euros has been debited from my account 2 *(Comm) [+ marchandises]* to retail, to sell 3 *[usine, machine]* to produce; *(Ordin)* to output ◆ **ce fleuve/tuyau débite 3 m³/s** the flow of this river/through this pipe is 3 cu m per second 4 *(péj = dire) [+ sottises, banalités]* to utter, to mouth; *[+ insultes]* to pour forth; *[+ sermon]* to spout, to spiel off* *(US)*; *[+ rôle]* to churn out ◆ **il me débita tout cela sans s'arrêter** he poured all that out to me without stopping 5 *(= découper) [+ bois]* to cut up, to saw up *(en* into); *[+ viande]* to cut up

débiteur, -trice /debitœʀ, tʀis/ ADJ *(Fin) [compte, solde]* debit *(épith)* ◆ **mon compte est ~ (de 100 €)** my account has a debit balance (of €100) *ou* is (€100) in the red* ◆ **l'organisme ~** the organisation that owes the money ◆ **toute personne débitrice paiera des agios** account holders with a debit balance must pay charges NM,F *(Fin, fig)* debtor ◆ **~-gagiste** *(Jur)* lienee ◆ **être le ~ de qn** *(lit, fig)* to be indebted to sb, to be in sb's debt

déblai /deblɛ/ NM *(= nettoyage)* clearing; *(Tech = terrassement)* earth-moving, excavation NMPL **déblais** *(= gravats)* rubble, debris *(sg)*; *(= terre)* (excavated) earth

déblaiement /deblɛmɑ̃/ NM *[de chemin, espace]* clearing

déblatérer * /deblateʀe/ ▸ conjug 6 ◂ VI to rant and rave *(contre* about); ◆ **~ contre** *ou* **sur** *(= médire)* to go *ou* rant on about*

déblayage /deblɛjaʒ/ NM 1 ⇒ **déblaiement** 2 *(fig)* **le ~ d'une question** (doing) the spadework on a question

déblayer /debleje/ ▸ conjug 8 ◂ VT 1 *(= retirer) [+ décombres]* to clear away, to remove; *[+ neige]* to clear away; *(= dégager) [+ route, porte, espace]* to clear; *[+ pièce]* to clear up, to tidy up; *(= aplanir) [+ terrain]* to level off 2 *[+ travail]* to prepare, to do the spadework on ◆ **~ le terrain** *(avant des négociations, une réflexion)* to clear the ground *ou* the way ◆ **déblaye (le terrain) !** * *(= déguerpir)* get lost!*, shove off!*, push off!* *(Brit)*

déblocage /deblɔkaʒ/ NM 1 *[de crédits, fonds, aide, marchandises]* releasing; *[de prix, salaires, loyers]* unfreezing; *[de compte]* freeing 2 *[de machine]* unjamming; *[d'écrou, frein]* releasing; *[de route]* unblocking ◆ **ceci a permis le ~ de la situation/des négociations** this has broken the deadlock in the situation/the negotiations

débloquer /deblɔke/ ▸ conjug 1 ◂ VT 1 *[+ crédits, fonds, aide, marchandises]* to release; *[+ prix, salaires, loyers]* to unfreeze; *[+ compte]* to free 2 *[+ machine]* to unjam; *[+ écrou, freins]* to release; *[+ route]* to unblock; *[+ négociations, situation]* to break the deadlock in 3 ◆ **~ qn** *(= le rendre moins timide)* to bring sb out of their shell; *(* = désinhiber)* to rid sb of their complexes *ou* inhibitions VI ‡ *(= dire des bêtises)* to talk nonsense *ou* rot* *(Brit)*; *(= être fou)* to be off one's rocker* VPR **se débloquer** *[personne]* to loosen up ◆ **la situation commence à se ~** things are starting to get moving again

débobiner /debɔbine/ ▸ conjug 1 ◂ VT *(Couture)* to unwind, to wind off; *(Élec)* to unwind, to uncoil

déboguer /debɔge/ ▸ conjug 1 ◂ VT to debug

débogueur /debɔgœʀ/ NM debugger

déboires /debwaʀ/ NMPL *(= déceptions)* disappointments; *(= échecs)* setbacks; *(= ennuis)* trials, difficulties

déboisage /debwazaʒ/, **déboisement** /debwazmɑ̃/ NM *[de montagne, région]* deforestation; *[de forêt]* clearing

déboiser /debwaze/ ▸ conjug 1 ◂ VT *[+ montagne, région]* to deforest; *[+ forêt]* to clear of trees

déboîtement /debwatmɑ̃/ NM 1 *(Méd)* dislocation 2 *(en voiture) (du trottoir)* pulling out; *(d'une file)* changing lanes, pulling out

déboîter /debwate/ ▸ conjug 1 ◂ VT *[+ épaule, cheville, mâchoire]* to dislocate; *[+ porte]* to take off its hinges; *[+ tuyaux]* to disconnect; *[+ objet]* to dislodge, to knock out of place ◆ **se ~ l'épaule** to dislocate one's shoulder VI *(Aut) (du trottoir)* to pull out; *(d'une file)* to change lanes, to pull out; *(Mil)* to break rank

débonder /debɔ̃de/ ▸ conjug 1 ◂ VT *[+ tonneau]* to remove the bung *ou* stopper from; *[+ baignoire]* to pull the plug out of VPR **se débonder** *[personne]* to open one's heart, to pour out one's feelings

débonnaire /debɔnɛʀ/ ADJ *(= bon enfant)* easy-going, good-natured; *(† = trop bon, faible)* soft, weak ◆ **air** ~ kindly appearance

débordant, e /debɔʀdɑ̃, ɑ̃t/ ADJ 1 *[activité]* exuberant; *[enthousiasme, joie]* overflowing, unbounded; *[imagination]* overactive ◆ **elle était ~e de vie** she was bursting with vitality 2 *(Mil)* **mouvement** ~ outflanking manoeuvre

débordé, e /debɔʀde/ (ptp de **déborder**) ADJ ◆ ~ **(de travail)** snowed under with work, up to one's eyes in work ◆ **les hôpitaux sont ~s** the hospitals are unable to cope

débordement /debɔʀdəmɑ̃/ NM 1 *[de rivière, liquide]* overflowing *(NonC)*; *[de liquide en ébullition]* boiling over *(NonC)*; *(Ordin)* memory overflow; *(Mil, Sport)* outflanking *(NonC)* ◆ **le ~ du parti par la base** the outflanking of the party by the rank and file 2 *[de joie, violence]* outburst; *[d'énergie]* burst; *[de paroles, injures]* torrent, rush; *[d'activité]* explosion ◆ ~ **de vie** bubbling vitality NMPL **débordements** *(= excès)* excesses ◆ **afin d'éviter les ~s** *(dans une manifestation)* to prevent things from getting out of hand

déborder /debɔʀde/ ▸ conjug 1 ◂ VI 1 *[récipient, liquide]* to overflow; *[fleuve, rivière]* to burst its banks, to overflow; *[liquide bouillant]* to boil over ◆ **les pluies ont fait ~ le réservoir** the rains caused the reservoir to overflow ◆ **faire ~ le lait** to let the milk boil over ◆ **tasse/boîte pleine à ~** cup/box full to the brim *ou* to overflowing *(de* with); ◆ **l'eau a débordé du vase/de la casserole** the water has overflowed out of the vase/has boiled over ◆ **les vêtements débordaient de la valise** the clothes were spilling out of the suitcase ◆ **la foule débordait sur la chaussée** the crowd was overflowing onto the roadway ◆ **cela a fait ~ le vase, c'est la goutte qui a fait ~ le vase** *(fig)* that was the last straw, that was the straw that broke the camel's back ◆ **son cœur débordait, il fallait qu'il parle** his heart was (full to) overflowing and he just had to speak

2 *(en coloriant, en mettant du rouge à lèvres)* to go over the edge

3 *(fig)* ~ **de santé** to be bursting with health ◆ ~ **de joie** to be brimming over *ou* bubbling *ou* bursting with joy ◆ ~ **d'activité** *[lieu]* to be bustling *ou* buzzing with activity; *[personne]* to be bursting with vitality ◆ ~ **de vie** to be bursting with vitality ◆ ~ **d'imagination** to be full of imagination ◆ **son cœur débordait de reconnaissance** his heart was overflowing *ou* bursting with gratitude ◆ **il débordait de tendresse pour elle** his heart was overflowing with tenderness for her

VT 1 *(= dépasser) [+ enceinte, limites]* to extend beyond; *(Mil, Pol, Sport) [+ ennemi]* to outflank ◆ **leur maison déborde les autres** their house juts out from the others ◆ **la nappe doit ~ la table** the tablecloth should hang over the edge of the table ◆ **le conférencier/cette remarque déborde le cadre du sujet** the lecturer/that remark goes beyond the bounds of the subject ◆ **il a débordé (le temps imparti)** he has run over (the allotted time) ◆ **se laisser ~ sur la droite** *(Mil, Pol, Sport)* to allow o.s. to be outflanked on the right ◆ **le service d'ordre s'est laissé ~** the stewards were unable to cope

2 *[+ couvertures]* to untuck ◆ ~ **qn** to untuck sb *ou* sb's bed

3 *(Couture) [+ vêtement]* to remove the border from

VPR **se déborder** ◆ **il s'est débordé en dormant** he *ou* his bed came untucked in his sleep

débosseler /debɔs(ə)le/ ▸ conjug 4 ◂ VT *[+ carrosserie]* to beat *ou* hammer (back) into shape; *[+ chapeau] (à coups de poing)* to beat back into shape

débotté /debɔte/ **au débotté** LOC ADV *(littér)* ◆ **je ne peux pas répondre au ~** I can't answer off the cuff ◆ **prendre qn au ~** to catch sb unawares, to take sb by surprise ◆ **il m'a reçu au ~** he received me straight away

débotter /debɔte/ ▸ conjug 1 ◂ VT ◆ ~ **qn** to take off sb's boots VPR **se débotter** to take one's boots off

débouchage /debuʃaʒ/ NM *[de bouteille]* uncorking, opening; *[de tuyau]* unblocking

débouché /debuʃe/ NM 1 *(gén pl) (= marché, créneau)* outlet; *(= carrière)* opening, prospect ◆ **le câble offre de formidables ~s pour le journalisme d'investigation** cable TV offers great prospects for investigative journalism 2 *(= sortie, ouverture)* opening ◆ **au ~ de la vallée (dans la plaine)** where the valley opens out (into the plain) ◆ **au ~ de la rue** at the end of the street ◆ **la Suisse n'a aucun ~ sur la mer** Switzerland is landlocked

déboucher /debuʃe/ ▸ conjug 1 ◂ VT 1 *[+ lavabo, tuyau]* to unblock

2 *[+ bouteille de vin]* to uncork, to open; *[+ carafe, flacon]* to unstopper, to take the stopper out of; *[+ tube]* to uncap, to take the cap *ou* top off

VI to emerge, to come out ◆ ~ **de** *[personne, voiture]* to emerge from, to come out of ◆ ~ **sur** *ou* **dans** *[rue]* to run into, to open onto *ou* into; *[personne, voiture]* to come out onto *ou* into, to emerge onto *ou* into ◆ **sur quoi ces études débouchent-elles ?** what does this course lead on to? ◆ **les négociations ont débouché sur une impasse** the talks have reached an impasse *ou* a dead end ◆ ~ **sur des mesures concrètes** to result in *ou* lead to concrete measures ◆ **ne ~ sur rien** to lead nowhere ◆ **les discussions n'ont pas débouché** the discussions led nowhere

VPR **se déboucher** *[bouteille]* to come uncorked; *[tuyau]* to unblock, to come unblocked

déboucheur /debuʃœʀ/ NM caustic cleaner, Liquid Plumber ® *(US)*

débouchoir /debuʃwaʀ/ NM *[de lavabo]* plunger, plumber's helper *(US)*

déboucler /debukle/ ▸ conjug 1 ◂ VT *[+ ceinture]* to unbuckle, to undo ◆ **je suis toute débouclée** my hair has all gone straight, the curl has come out of my hair

déboulé /debule/ NM *(Danse)* déboulé; *(Courses)* charge ◆ **tirer un lapin au ~** *(Chasse)* to shoot a rabbit as it breaks cover

débouler /debule/ ▸ conjug 1 ◂ VI 1 *[lapin]* to bolt 2 *(* = surgir)* **attention, les voitures déboulent à toute vitesse ici** watch out, the cars come out of nowhere around here ◆ **le vélo déboula d'une rue adjacente** the bike shot out of a side street ◆ ~ **chez qn** to turn up at sb's home 3 *(= dégringoler)* to tumble down VT *(* = dévaler)* to charge down ◆ ~ **l'escalier** to come charging down the stairs *

déboulonnage /debulɔnaʒ/, **déboulonnement** /debulɔnmɑ̃/ NM 1 *(= dévissage)* removal of bolts *(de* from); *[de statue]* dismantling, taking down 2 * *[de personne] (= action de discréditer)* discrediting, debunking; *(= renvoi)* ousting

déboulonner /debulɔne/ ▸ conjug 1 ◂ VT 1 *(= dévisser)* to remove the bolts from, to take the bolts out of ◆ ~ **la statue de qn** *(lit)* to dismantle *ou* take down sb's statue; *(fig)* to knock sb off their pedestal 2 * *[+ personne] (= discréditer)* to discredit, to debunk; *(= renvoyer)* to oust

débourber /debuʀbe/ ▸ conjug 1 ◂ VT *[+ fossé]* to clear of mud, to clean out; *[+ canal]* to dredge; *[+ véhicule]* to pull out of the mud ◆ ~ **du vin** to decant wine

débourrage /debuʀaʒ/ NM *[de cheval]* breaking in

débourrer /debuʀe/ ▸ conjug 1 ◂ VT 1 *[+ cheval]* to break in 2 *[+ cuir]* to deburr 3 *[+ pipe]* to empty VI *[bourgeon]* to open out

débours /debuʀ/ NM *(= dépense)* outlay ◆ **pour rentrer dans ses ~** to recover one's outlay ◆ **sans ~ d'argent** without any financial outlay

déboursement /debuʀsəmɑ̃/ NM payment, disbursement *(frm)*

débourser /debuʀse/ ▸ conjug 1 ◂ VT to pay out ◆ **sans ~ un sou** without paying out a penny

déboussoler* /debusɔle/ ▸ conjug 1 ◂ VT to disorientate ◆ **il est complètement déboussolé** he is completely lost *ou* disorientated

debout /d(ə)bu/ ADV, ADJ INV 1 *[personne] (= en position verticale)* standing (up); *(= levé)* up ◆ **être** *ou* **se tenir ~** to stand ◆ **être ~** *(= levé)* to be up; *(= guéri)* to be up (and about) ◆ **se mettre ~** to stand up, to get up ◆ **il préfère être** *ou* **rester ~** he prefers to stand *ou* remain standing ◆ **hier, nous sommes restés ~ jusqu'à minuit** yesterday we stayed up till midnight ◆ **il l'aida à se (re)mettre ~** he helped him (back) up, he helped him (back) to his feet ◆ **leur fils se tient ~ maintenant** their son can stand (up) now ◆ **le plafond est si bas qu'on ne peut pas se tenir ~** the ceiling is so low that it's impossible to stand upright ◆ **il est très fatigué, il tient à peine ~** he's so tired he can hardly stand ◆ **je ne tiens plus ~** I'm fit *ou* ready to drop * ◆ **elle est ~ toute la journée** she's on her feet all day ◆ **ces gens ~ nous empêchent de voir** we can't see because of the people standing in front of us ◆ ~ **!** get up!, on your feet! ◆ ~ **là-dedans !** * get up, you guys *ou* you lot! * *(Brit)* ◆ **il veut mourir ~** *(fig)* he wants to die on his feet *ou* with his boots on; → **dormir, magistrature, place**

2 *[bouteille, meuble] (position habituelle)* standing up(right); *(position inhabituelle)* standing (up) on end ◆ **mettre qch ~** to stand sth up(right), to stand sth (up) on end ◆ **les tables, ~ le long du mur** the tables, standing (up) on end along the wall ◆ **mets les bouteilles ~** stand the bottles up(right) ◆ **tenir ~** *[objet]* to stay upright ◆ **je n'arrive pas à faire tenir le livre ~** I can't keep the book upright, I can't make the book stand *ou* stay up

3 *[édifice, mur]* standing *(attrib)* ◆ **ces institutions sont** *ou* **tiennent encore ~** *(fig)* these institutions are still going ◆ **cette théorie tient ~** this theory holds up *ou* holds water ◆ **ça ne tient pas ~** ce que tu dis what you say doesn't stand up ◆ **son histoire ne tient pas ~** his story doesn't make sense *ou* doesn't hold together

débouté /debute/ NM *(Jur)* ≈ nonsuit

déboutement /debutmɑ̃/ NM *(Jur)* ≈ nonsuiting

débouter /debute/ ▸ conjug 1 ◂ VT *(Jur)* ≈ to nonsuit ◆ ~ **qn de sa plainte** ≈ to nonsuit a plaintiff ◆ **être débouté de sa demande** to be ruled out of court, to see one's case dismissed by the court, ≈ to be nonsuited

déboutonner /debutɔne/ ▸ conjug 1 ◂ VT to unbutton, to undo VPR **se déboutonner** 1 *[personne]* to unbutton *ou* undo one's jacket *(ou* coat *etc)*; *[vêtement]* to come unbuttoned *ou* undone 2 *(* = se confier)* to open up *

débraillé, e /debʀaje/ (ptp de **débrailler**) ADJ *[tenue, personne]* untidy, slovenly-looking; *[manières]* slovenly; *[style]* sloppy, slipshod NM *[de tenue, manières]* slovenliness; *[de style]* sloppiness ◆ **être en ~** to be slovenly dressed

débrailler (se)* /debʀɑje/ ► conjug 1 ◄ VPR *[personne]* to loosen one's clothing

débranchement /debʀɑ̃ʃmɑ̃/ NM *(gén)* disconnecting; *[d'appareil électrique]* unplugging, disconnecting; *(Rail) [de wagons]* splitting up

débrancher /debʀɑ̃ʃe/ ► conjug 1 ◄ VT *[+ appareil électrique]* to unplug, to disconnect; *[+ prise]* to disconnect, to pull out; *[+ téléphone, perfusion]* to disconnect; *(Rail) [+ wagons]* to split up ◆ **ils l'ont débranché*** *[+ malade]* they switched him off* ◆ **quand il commence à en parler, on a du mal à le ~** * once he get's going on that subject there's no stopping him VI * *(= ne plus prêter attention)* to switch off* ◆ **débranche un peu, tu veux ?** *(= arrête de parler, de t'agiter)* why don't you give it a break?*

débrayage /debʀɛjaʒ/ NM 1 *(= objet) [de voiture]* clutch; *[d'appareil-photo]* release button 2 *(= action) [de moteur]* disengagement of the clutch, declutching *(Brit)*; *[d'appareil-photo]* releasing ◆ **faire un double ~** to double-declutch 3 *(= grève)* stoppage

débrayer /debʀeje/ ► conjug 8 ◄ VI 1 *(en voiture)* to disengage the clutch, to declutch *(Brit)*; *(sur une machine)* to operate the release mechanism 2 *(= faire grève)* to stop work, to come out on strike ◆ **le personnel a débrayé à 4 heures** the staff stopped work at 4 o'clock VT *[+ mécanisme]* to release

débridé, e /debʀide/ (ptp de **débrider**) ADJ unbridled, unrestrained

débridement /debʀidmɑ̃/ NM *[d'instincts]* unbridling, unleashing; *[de plaie]* lancing, incising

débrider /debʀide/ ► conjug 1 ◄ VT *[+ cheval]* to unbridle; *[+ volaille]* to untruss; *[+ plaie]* to lance, to incise ◆ **travailler sans ~** to work non-stop

débriefer /debʀife/ ► conjug 1 ◄ VT to debrief

débriefing /debʀifiŋ/ NM debriefing ◆ **faire un ~** to debrief

débris /debʀi/ NM 1 *(pl = morceaux)* fragments, pieces; *(= décombres)* debris *(sg)*; *(= détritus)* rubbish *(NonC)* ◆ **des ~ de métal** scraps of metal 2 *(pl : littér = restes) [de mort]* remains; *[de plat, repas]* left-overs, scraps; *[d'armée, fortune]* remains, remnants; *[d'État]* ruins; *[d'édifice]* ruins, remains 3 *(= éclat, fragment)* fragment 4 *(péj = personne)* **(vieux) ~** old wreck, old dodderer

débronzer /debʀɔ̃ze/ ► conjug 1 ◄ VI to lose one's tan

débrouillage /debʀujaʒ/ NM *[de fils]* disentangling, untangling; *[d'énigme]* unravelling

débrouillard, e /debʀujaʀ, aʀd/ ADJ *(= ingénieux)* resourceful; *(= malin)* smart NM,F ◆ **c'est un ~** he's resourceful *ou* smart

débrouillardise /debʀujaʀdiz/, **débrouille*** /debʀuj/ NF *(= ingéniosité)* resourcefulness; *(= astuce)* smartness

débrouillement /debʀujmɑ̃/ NM ⇒ **débrouillage**

débrouiller /debʀuje/ ► conjug 1 ◄ VT 1 *[+ fils]* to disentangle, to untangle; *[+ affaire]* to sort out; *[+ problème]* to sort out, to untangle; *[+ énigme]* to unravel

2 (* = *éduquer*) **~ qn** *(gén)* to teach sb how to look after himself *(ou* herself*)*; *(à l'école)* to teach sb the basics ◆ **~ qn en anglais/en informatique** to teach sb the basics *ou* give sb a grounding in English/computing

VPR **se débrouiller** to manage ◆ **débrouillez-vous** you'll have to manage on your own *ou* sort things out yourself ◆ **il m'a laissé me ~ tout seul** he left me to cope alone *ou* on my own ◆ **il a fallu qu'il se débrouille tout seul dans la vie** he had to cope on his own, he had to fend for himself ◆ **il s'est débrouillé pour obtenir la permission d'y aller** he somehow managed to get permission to go, he wangled* permission to go ◆ **c'est toi qui as fait l'erreur, maintenant débrouille-toi pour la réparer** you made the mistake so now you can sort it out yourself ◆ **il faudra bien nous en ~** we'll have to sort it out ◆ **pour les boissons, je me débrouillerai avec mon frère*** I'll look after *ou* I'll organize the drinks with my brother ◆ **elle se débrouille en allemand*** she can get by in German ◆ **il se débrouille bien en anglais*** he gets by fairly well in English ◆ **elle se débrouille bien*** *(= elle gagne bien sa vie)* she does well for herself

débroussaillage /debʀusɑjaʒ/, **débroussaillement** /debʀusɑjmɑ̃/ NM *[de terrain]* clearing *(de* of*)*; *[de problème]* spadework *(de* on*)*

débroussailler /debʀusɑje/ ► conjug 1 ◄ VT *[+ terrain]* to clear (of brushwood); *[+ problème]* to do the spadework on

débroussailleuse /debʀusɑjøz/ NF edge trimmer, Strimmer ® *(Brit)*, weedeater ® *(US)*

débucher /debyʃe/ ► conjug 1 ◄ VI *[animal]* to break cover VT to force to break cover

débudgétisation /debydʒetizasjɔ̃/ NF debudgeting

débudgétiser /debydʒetize/ ► conjug 1 ◄ VT to debudget

débusquer /debyske/ ► conjug 1 ◄ VT *[+ lièvre, cerf]* to drive out (from cover); *[+ oiseau]* to flush out, to drive out (from cover); *[+ personne]* to flush out

début /deby/ NM beginning, start; *[de discours]* beginning, opening ◆ **le chômage augmente, et ce n'est qu'un ~** unemployment is getting worse, and it's only the beginning ◆ **ce n'est pas mal pour un ~** it's not bad for a first attempt ◆ **j'ai un ~ de grippe** I've got the beginnings *ou* first signs of the flu ◆ **l'incident a déclenché un ~ de panique** the incident caused some initial panic ◆ **trouver un ~ de solution** to find the beginnings of a solution ◆ **il y a** *ou* **il faut un ~ à tout** there's a first time for everything ◆ **~ mai** at the beginning of May, in early May ◆ **dès le ~** from the outset *ou* the start *ou* the (very) beginning ◆ **du ~ à la fin** from beginning to end, from start to finish ◆ **en ~ de soirée** early on in the evening ◆ **salaire de ~** starting salary ◆ **les scènes du ~ sont très belles** the opening scenes are very beautiful

◆ **au + début** ◆ **au début** at first, in *ou* at the beginning ◆ **au ~ du mois prochain** early next month, at the beginning of next month ◆ **au tout ~ du siècle** right at the beginning of the century, at the very beginning of the century

NMPL **débuts** ◆ **ses ~s furent médiocres** he made an indifferent start ◆ **à mes ~s (dans ce métier)** when I started (in this job) ◆ **ce projet n'en est qu'à ses ~s** the project is still in its early stages ◆ **faire ses ~s dans le monde** to make one's début in society ◆ **faire ses ~s sur la scène** to make one's début *ou* one's first appearance on the stage

débutant, e /debytɑ̃, ɑt/ ADJ novice *(épith)* NM,F *(gén)* beginner, novice; *(Théât)* debutant actor ◆ **cours pour ~s** beginners' course ◆ **grand/faux ~ en anglais** absolute/false beginner in English NF **débutante** *(Théât)* debutant actress; *(dans la haute société)* debutante

débuter /debyte/ ► conjug 1 ◄ VI 1 *[personne]* to start (out) ◆ **~ bien/mal** to make a good/bad start, to start well/badly ◆ **il a débuté (dans la vie) comme livreur** he started (life) as a delivery boy ◆ **elle a débuté dans mon film** she made her début *ou* her first appearance in my film ◆ **il débute (dans le métier), soyez indulgent** he is just starting (in the business) so don't be too hard on him ◆ **l'orateur a débuté par des excuses** the speaker started (off) *ou* began *ou* opened by apologizing ◆ **~ dans le monde** to make one's début in society ◆ **pour ~** to start (off) with 2 *[livre, concert, manifestation]* to start, to begin, to open *(par, sur* with*)* VT *[+ semaine, réunion, discours]* to start, to begin, to open *(par, sur* with*)*; ◆ **il a bien débuté l'année** he has begun *ou* started the year well

deçà /dəsa/ ADV ◆ **en ~ de** *(= de ce côté-ci de)* (on) this side of; *(= en dessous de) [+ limite, prévisions]* below ◆ **en ~ du fleuve/de la montagne** this side of the river/of the mountain ◆ **tu vois la rivière, sa maison se trouve en ~** you see the river – his house is this side of it ◆ **en ~ d'une certaine intensité, on ne peut plus rien entendre** below a certain intensity, one can no longer hear anything ◆ **ce qu'il dit est très** *ou* **bien en ~ de la vérité** what he says is well short of the truth ◆ **en ~ de ses moyens** within his means ◆ **~, delà** †† here and there

déca* /deka/ NM (abrév de **décaféiné**) decaf*

déca- /deka/ PRÉF deca-

décabosser /dekabɔse/ ► conjug 1 ◄ VT *[+ chapeau] (à coups de poing)* to beat back into shape; *[+ carrosserie]* to beat *ou* hammer (back) into shape

décachetage /dekaʃtaʒ/ NM unsealing, opening

décacheter /dekaʃ(ə)te/ ► conjug 4 ◄ VT *[+ lettre]* to unseal, to open

décade /dekad/ NF *(= dix jours)* period of ten days; *(= décennie)* decade

décadenasser /dekadnase/ ► conjug 1 ◄ VT *[+ porte]* to unpadlock, to remove the padlock from

décadence /dekadɑ̃s/ NF *(= processus)* decline, decadence; *(= état)* decadence ◆ **la ~ de l'empire romain** the decline of the Roman empire ◆ **tomber en ~** to fall into decline; → **grandeur**

décadent, e /dekadɑ̃, ɑt/ ADJ decadent NM,F decadent

décaèdre /dekaɛdʀ/ ADJ decahedral NM decahedron

décaféiné, e /dekafeine/ (ptp de **décaféiner**) ADJ decaffeinated, caffeine-free NM decaffeinated coffee

décaféiner /dekafeine/ ► conjug 1 ◄ VT to decaffeinate

décagonal, e (mpl **-aux**) /dekagɔnal, o/ ADJ decagonal

décagone /dekagon/ NM decagon

décagramme /dekagʀam/ NM decagram(me)

décaissement /dekɛsmɑ̃/ NM payment, disbursement

décaisser /dekese/ ► conjug 1 ◄ VT *[+ argent]* to pay out; *[+ objet]* to uncrate, to unpack

décalage /dekalaʒ/ NM 1 *(= écart)* gap, interval; *(entre deux concepts)* gap, discrepancy; *(entre deux actions successives)* interval, time-lag *(entre* between*)*; ◆ **le ~ entre le rêve et la réalité** the gap between dream and reality ◆ **il y a un ~ entre le coup de feu et le bruit de la détonation** there is an interval *ou* a time-lag between firing and the sound of the shot ◆ **ses créations sont en ~ avec son époque/par rapport aux tendances actuelles** *(fig)* his designs are out of step with the times/with contemporary trends

2 *(= déplacement)* move forward *ou* back ◆ **il y a eu un ~ d'horaire/de date pour cette réunion** *(avance)* the time/date of this meeting has been brought forward; *(retard)* the time/date of this meeting has been put back

3 *(dans l'espace) (= avancée)* jutting out; *(= retrait)* standing back; *(= déplacement) [de meuble, objet]* shifting forward *ou* back

COMP **décalage horaire** time difference ◆ **le ~ horaire entre l'est et l'ouest des USA** the time difference between the east and west of the USA ◆ **(fatigue due au) ~ horaire** *(en avion)* jet lag ◆ **mal supporter le ~ horaire** to suffer from jet lag

décalaminage /dekalaminaʒ/ NM decarbonization, decoking *(Brit)*

décalaminer /dekalamine/ ▸ conjug 1 ◂ VT to decarbonize, to decoke *(Brit)*

décalcification /dekalsifikasjɔ̃/ NF decalcification

décalcifier VT, **se décalcifier** VPR /dekalsifje/ ▸ conjug 7 ◂ to decalcify

décalcomanie /dekalkɔmani/ NF transfer, decal ◆ **faire des ~s** to do transfers

décalé, e /dekale/ (ptp de **décaler**) ADJ [1] *(= non conventionnel) [humour]* quirky, off-beat; *[image]* unconventional, off-beat; *[personne] (marginal)* unconventional; *(en retard sur son temps)* out of touch ◆ **il est complètement ~ par rapport à la réalité** he's completely out of touch with reality [2] *(= irrégulier) [horaire]* irregular

décaler /dekale/ ▸ conjug 1 ◂ VT [1] *[+ horaire, départ, repas] (= avancer)* to bring *ou* move forward; *(= retarder)* to put back ◆ **décalé d'une heure** *(= avancé)* brought *ou* moved forward an hour; *(= retardé)* put back an hour [2] *[+ pupitre, meuble] (= avancer)* to move *ou* shift forward; *(= reculer)* to move *ou* shift back ◆ **décale le tableau (de 20 cm) vers la droite** move the picture (20 cm) to the right ◆ **une série d'immeubles décalés par rapport aux autres** a row of buildings out of line with *ou* jutting out from the others [3] *(= déséquilibrer)* **le buffet est décalé** the sideboard isn't straight VPR **se décaler** *[rythme]* to go out of sync* ◆ **décalez-vous d'un rang** move forward *(ou* back) a row ◆ **décalez-vous d'une place** move up a seat

décalitre /dekalitʀ/ NM decalitre *(Brit)*, decaliter *(US)*

décalogue /dekalɔg/ NM Decalogue

décalotter /dekalɔte/ ▸ conjug 1 ◂ VT *(gén)* to take the top off ◆ **~ le pénis** to pull back the foreskin

décalquer /dekalke/ ▸ conjug 1 ◂ VT *(= reproduire) (avec papier transparent)* to trace; *(par pression, à chaud)* to transfer; *(fig = imiter)* to copy

décamètre /dekamɛtʀ/ NM decametre *(Brit)*, decameter *(US)*

décamper * /dekɑ̃pe/ ▸ conjug 1 ◂ VI *(= déguerpir)* to clear out* *ou* off* ◆ **décampez d'ici !** clear off!*, scram!* ◆ **faire ~ qn** to chase sb out *(de* from)

décan /dekɑ̃/ NM *(Astrol)* decan

décanal, e (mpl **-aux**) /dekanal, o/ ADJ decanal

décanat /dekana/ NM *(= dignité, durée)* deanship

décaniller * /dekanije/ ▸ conjug 1 ◂ VI *(= partir)* to clear out* *ou* off* ◆ **il nous a fait ~** he sent us packing* *(de* from)

décantation /dekɑ̃tasjɔ̃/ NF *[de liquide, vin]* settling (and decanting) ◆ **bassin de ~** settling *ou* sedimentation tank

décanter /dekɑ̃te/ ▸ conjug 1 ◂ VT *[+ liquide, vin]* to settle, to allow to settle (and decant) ◆ **il faut laisser ~ ce liquide pendant une nuit** this liquid must be allowed to settle overnight ◆ **~ ses idées** to allow the dust to settle around one's ideas VPR **se décanter** *[liquide, vin]* to settle; *[idées]* to become clear ◆ **il faut laisser les choses se ~, après on verra** we'll have to let things clarify themselves *ou* we'll have to allow the dust to settle and then we'll see ◆ **attendre que la situation se décante** to wait until the situation becomes clearer

décanteur /dekɑ̃tœʀ/ NM *[de station d'épuration]* settling *ou* sedimentation tank

décapage /dekapaʒ/ NM *(gén)* cleaning, cleansing; *(à l'abrasif)* scouring; *(à l'acide)* pickling; *(à la brosse)* scrubbing; *(au papier de verre)* sanding; *(à la sableuse)* sandblasting; *(au chalumeau)* burning off; *[de peinture]* stripping

décapant /dekapɑ̃/ ADJ *[produit]* abrasive, caustic; *[humour, critique]* scathing, caustic NM *(= abrasif)* scouring agent, abrasive; *(pour peinture, vernis)* paint stripper; *(= acide)* pickle, acid solution

décaper /dekape/ ▸ conjug 1 ◂ VT *(gén)* to clean, to cleanse; *(à l'abrasif)* to scour; *(à l'acide)* to pickle; *(à la brosse)* to scrub; *(au papier de verre)* to sand; *(à la sableuse)* to sandblast; *(au chalumeau)* to burn off; *(= enlever la peinture)* to strip ◆ **décapez d'abord la surface pour enlever la rouille** first scrub the surface to remove the rust ◆ **un savon qui décape la peau** an abrasive soap ◆ **un humour qui décape** * scathing *ou* caustic humour ◆ **ça décape !** * it's strong stuff!

décapitation /dekapitasjɔ̃/ NF *[de personne]* beheading

décapiter /dekapite/ ▸ conjug 1 ◂ VT *[+ personne]* to behead; *(accidentellement)* to decapitate; *[+ arbre]* to top, to cut the top off ◆ **la police a décapité un réseau terroriste** the police have arrested the ringleaders of a terrorist network ◆ **à la suite de l'attentat le parti s'est trouvé décapité** the party was left leaderless *ou* without a leader as a result of the attack

décapode /dekapɔd/ NM decapod ◆ **les ~s** the Decapoda

décapotable /dekapɔtabl/ ADJ, NF ◆ **(voiture) ~** convertible

décapoter /dekapɔte/ ▸ conjug 1 ◂ VT ◆ **~ une voiture** to put down the top *ou* roof *(Brit)* of a car

décapsuler /dekapsyle/ ▸ conjug 1 ◂ VT [1] *[+ bouteille]* to take the cap *ou* top off [2] *(Méd) [+ rein]* to decapsulate

décapsuleur /dekapsylœʀ/ NM bottle-opener

décarcasser (se) * /dekaʀkase/ ▸ conjug 1 ◂ VPR to go to a lot of trouble *(pour faire* to do); ◆ **si tu veux des tickets, il faut que tu te décarcasses** if you want to get tickets, you'd better get a move on*

décarreler /dekaʀle/ ▸ conjug 4 ◂ VT to remove the tiles from

décarrer * /dekaʀe/ ▸ conjug 1 ◂ VI to split*, to make tracks*, to hit the road*

décasyllabe /dekasi(l)lab/ ADJ decasyllabic NM decasyllable

décasyllabique /dekasi(l)labik/ ADJ decasyllabic

décathlon /dekatlɔ̃/ NM decathlon

décathlonien /dekatlɔnjɛ̃/ NM decathlete

décati, e /dekati/ ADJ *(péj) [vieillard]* decrepit; *[visage]* aged; *[beauté]* faded; *[immeuble, façade]* shabby-looking

décatir /dekatiʀ/ ▸ conjug 2 ◂ VT *[+ étoffe]* to remove the gloss from VPR **se décatir** *[personne]* to become decrepit

décavé, e /dekave/ ADJ [1] *(= ruiné) [joueur]* ruined, cleaned out* *(attrib)*; * *[banquier]* ruined [2] *(* = hâve) [visage]* haggard, drawn

décéder /desede/ GRAMMAIRE ACTIVE 51.4 ▸ conjug 6 ◂ VI *(frm)* to die ◆ **M. Leblanc, décédé le 14 mai** Mr Leblanc, who died on 14 May ◆ **il est décédé depuis 20 ans** he died 20 years ago, he's been dead 20 years ◆ **les biens des personnes décédées** the property of deceased persons *ou* of those who have died

décelable /des(ə)labl/ ADJ detectable

déceler /des(ə)le/ ▸ conjug 5 ◂ VT [1] *(= repérer)* to detect ◆ **on a décelé des traces de poison** traces of poison have been detected ◆ **on peut ~ dans ce poème l'influence germanique** the Germanic influence can be discerned *ou* detected in this poem [2] *(= indiquer)* to indicate, to reveal

décélération /deseleʀasjɔ̃/ NF *[de véhicule]* deceleration ◆ **la ~ de la croissance économique** the slowdown in *ou* deceleration of economic growth

décélérer /deseleʀe/ ▸ conjug 1 ◂ VI *[véhicule]* to decelerate; *[investissements, rythme]* to slow down

décembre /desɑ̃bʀ/ NM December; *pour loc voir* **septembre**

décemment /desamɑ̃/ ADV *[vivre, se nourrir]* decently, properly; *[se conduire]* decently ◆ **je ne peux ~ pas accepter** it wouldn't be right for me *ou* proper of me to accept

décence /desɑ̃s/ NF *(= bienséance)* decency, propriety; *(= réserve)* (sense of) decency ◆ **il aurait pu avoir la ~ de ...** he could *ou* might have had the decency to ...

décennal, e (mpl **-aux**) /desenal, o/ ADJ decennial ◆ **garantie ~e** ten-year guarantee

décennie /deseni/ NF decade

décent, e /desɑ̃, ɑ̃t/ ADJ *(= bienséant)* decent, proper; *(= discret, digne)* proper; *(= acceptable) [logement, salaire]* decent; *[prix]* reasonable, fair ◆ **je vais mettre une robe pour être un peu plus ~e** I'm going to put on a dress to look a bit more decent ◆ **il eût été plus ~ de refuser** it would have been more proper to refuse

décentrage /desɑ̃tʀaʒ/ NM *(gén)* decentring *(Brit)*, decentering *(US)*; *(Opt)* decentration

décentralisateur, -trice /desɑ̃tʀalizatœʀ, tʀis/ ADJ decentralizing *(épith)*, decentralization *(épith)* NM,F advocate of decentralization

décentralisation /desɑ̃tʀalizasjɔ̃/ NF *(gén Pol)* decentralization

décentraliser /desɑ̃tʀalize/ ▸ conjug 1 ◂ VT *[+ administration, décisions]* to decentralize VPR **se décentraliser** *[d'usine]* to be decentralized

décentration /desɑ̃tʀasjɔ̃/ NF, **décentrement** /desɑ̃tʀəmɑ̃/ NM *(Opt)* decentration; *(= action)* decentring *(Brit)*, decentering *(US)*, throwing off centre

décentrer /desɑ̃tʀe/ ▸ conjug 1 ◂ VT to decentre *(Brit)*, to decenter *(US)*, to throw off centre VPR **se décentrer** to move off centre

déception /desɛpsjɔ̃/ NF disappointment ◆ **c'est la plus grande ~ de ma carrière** it's the worst disappointment of my whole career ◆ **~ sentimentale** unhappy love affair ◆ **j'ai eu la ~ de voir que ...** I was disappointed to see that ...

> ⚠ **déception** ne se traduit pas par le mot anglais **deception**, qui a le sens de 'duperie'.

décérébration /deseʀebʀasjɔ̃/ NF *(Physiol)* decerebration

décérébrer /deseʀebʀe/ ▸ conjug 6 ◂ VT *(lit)* to decerebrate; *(fig)* to make moronic

décernement /desɛʀnəmɑ̃/ NM awarding

décerner /desɛʀne/ ▸ conjug 1 ◂ VT [1] *[+ prix, récompense]* to give, to award; *[+ titre]* to award [2] *(Jur) [+ mandat d'arrêt, de dépôt]* to issue

décervelage /desɛʀvəlaʒ/ NM *(= abrutissement)* making moronic; *(= lavage de cerveau)* brainwashing ◆ **l'entreprise de ~ menée par la télévision** the way television turns people into morons

décerveler /desɛʀvəle/ ▸ conjug 4 ◂ VT *(= abrutir)* to make moronic; *(= laver le cerveau de)* to brainwash ◆ **machine à ~** *(allusion littéraire)* debraining machine; *(péj)* propaganda machine

décès /desɛ/ GRAMMAIRE ACTIVE 51.4 NM death ◆ **"fermé pour cause de décès"** "closed owing to bereavement"; → **acte**

décevant, e /des(ə)vɑ̃, ɑ̃t/ ADJ disappointing

décevoir /des(ə)vwaʀ/ ► conjug 28 ◄ VT *[+ personne]* to disappoint ◆ **êtes-vous déçu par le nouveau président ?** are you disappointed in the new president? ◆ **nous avons été très déçus de notre score face à la Nouvelle-Zélande** we were very disappointed by our score against New Zealand ◆ **ils ont été déçus de voir que la France refusait de les accueillir** they were disappointed to find that France would not receive them ◆ **le nouveau gouvernement n'a pas déçu** the new government has not been disappointing ◆ **je ne veux pas ~ vos espoirs** I don't want to dash your hopes ◆ **le gouvernement a déçu l'attente de l'opinion publique** the government failed to meet the public's expectations ◆ **~ en bien** *(Helv)* to turn out better than expected; → **déçu**

⚠ **décevoir** ne se traduit pas par **to deceive**, qui a le sens de 'tromper'.

déchaîné, e /deʃene/ (ptp de **déchaîner**) ADJ *[flots, éléments]* raging; *[passion]* unbridled, raging; *[personne]* wild; *[foule]* raging, wild; *[opinion publique]* furious ◆ **il est ~ contre moi** he is furious with me

déchaînement /deʃɛnmɑ̃/ NM [1] *[de fureur, passions, haine]* outburst, explosion ◆ **l'événement a provoqué un ~ de violence** the incident triggered an outburst of violence [2] *(= colère, violence)* (raging) fury ◆ **un tel ~ contre son fils** such an outburst of fury at his son ◆ **les ~s des médias/du public contre la réforme** angry outbursts from the media/the public against the reform

déchaîner /deʃene/ ► conjug 1 ◄ VT [1] *[+ tempête, violence, passions, colère]* to unleash; *[+ enthousiasme]* to arouse; *[+ opinion publique]* to rouse ◆ **~ l'hilarité générale** to cause great *ou* much hilarity ◆ **~ les huées/les cris/les rires** to raise a storm of booing/shouting/laughter ◆ **~ les critiques** to unleash a barrage of criticism [2] *[+ chien]* to unchain, to let loose VPR **se déchaîner** *[fureur, passions]* to explode; *[personne]* to fly into a rage; *[foule]* to go wild ◆ **il s'est déchaîné contre elle** he blew up at her *ou* let fly at her ◆ **la presse se déchaîna contre lui/cette décision** the press railed against him/the decision ◆ **la tempête se déchaînait** the storm was raging furiously

déchant /deʃɑ̃/ NM *(Mus)* descant

déchanter /deʃɑ̃te/ ► conjug 1 ◄ VI to become disillusioned *ou* disenchanted ◆ **il commence à ~** he is becoming (somewhat) disillusioned *ou* disenchanted

décharge /deʃaʀʒ/ NF [1] **~ (électrique)** electrical discharge ◆ **il a pris une ~ (électrique) dans les doigts** he got an electric shock in his fingers ◆ **~ d'adrénaline** *(Physiol)* rush of adrenalin ◆ **~ émotionnelle** *(Psych)* emotional release

[2] *(= salve)* volley of shots, salvo ◆ **on entendit le bruit de plusieurs ~s** a volley of shots was heard ◆ **il a reçu une ~ de chevrotines dans le dos** he was hit in the back by a volley of buckshot

[3] *(= libération) (Jur)* discharge; *(Hôpital) (= action)* discharge; *(= document)* discharge form ◆ **~ (de service)** *(Scol)* reduction in teaching load ◆ **il faut dire à sa ~ que ...** *(fig)* it must be said in his defence that ...; → **témoin**

[4] *(= reçu)* receipt ◆ **je vais signer la ~ pour ce colis** I'll sign the receipt for this parcel

[5] *(= dépôt)* **~ (publique** *ou* **municipale)** rubbish tip *ou* dump *(Brit)*, garbage dump *(US)* ◆ **la mise en ~ des déchets toxiques** the dumping of toxic waste; → **sauvage**

[6] *(Typo)* offset sheet

[7] *(Archit)* **voûte/arc de ~** relieving *ou* discharging vault/arch

déchargement /deʃaʀʒəmɑ̃/ NM *[de cargaison, véhicule, arme]* unloading ◆ **commencer le ~ d'un véhicule** to start unloading a vehicle

décharger /deʃaʀʒe/ ► conjug 3 ◄ VT [1] *[+ véhicule, animal]* to unload; *[+ bagages, marchandises]* to unload *(de* from); ◆ **je vais vous ~ : donnez-moi vos sacs/votre manteau** let me take your bags/your coat off you

[2] *(= soulager) [+ conscience, cœur]* to unburden, to disburden *(auprès de* to); ◆ **~ sa colère** *ou* **bile** *(littér)* to vent one's anger *ou* spleen *(sur qn* (up)on sb)

[3] *(Jur)* **~ un accusé** to discharge an accused person

[4] ◆ **~ qn de** *[+ dette]* to release sb from; *[+ impôt]* to exempt sb from; *[+ responsabilité, fonction, tâche]* to relieve sb of *ou* from ◆ **le juge a demandé à être déchargé du dossier** the judge asked to be taken off the case

[5] *[+ arme] (= enlever le chargeur)* to unload; *(= tirer)* to discharge, to fire ◆ **il déchargea son revolver sur la foule** he emptied his revolver into the crowd

[6] *(Élec)* to discharge

[7] *(Tech) [+ bassin]* to drain off the excess from; *[+ support, étai]* to take the load *ou* weight off

VI [1] *[tissu]* to lose its colour

[2] *(* = éjaculer)* to come*, to shoot one's load*

VPR **se décharger** [1] *(Élec) [pile, batterie]* to run down, to go flat

[2] ◆ **se ~ de** *[+ responsabilité, problème]* to offload, to pass off *(sur qn* onto sb); ◆ **il s'est déchargé sur moi du soin de prévenir sa mère** he offloaded the job of telling his mother onto me

[3] *(= être expulsé)* **l'excès de vapeur d'eau se décharge dans l'atmosphère** excess steam is released into the atmosphere

décharné, e /deʃaʀne/ (ptp de **décharner**) ADJ *[corps, membre]* all skin and bone *(attrib)*, emaciated; *[doigts]* bony, fleshless; *[visage]* fleshless, emaciated; *[squelette]* fleshless; *(fig) [paysage]* bare; *[style]* bald

décharner /deʃaʀne/ ► conjug 1 ◄ VT *(= amaigrir)* to emaciate ◆ **cette maladie l'a complètement décharné** this illness has left him completely emaciated

déchaussé, e /deʃose/ (ptp de **déchausser**) ADJ *[personne]* barefoot(ed); *[pied]* bare; *[carmélite]* discalced *(frm)*; *[dent, pavé]* loose; *[mur]* exposed

déchaussement /deʃosmɑ̃/ NM *[de dent]* loosening

déchausser /deʃose/ ► conjug 1 ◄ VT *[+ arbre]* to expose the roots of; *[+ mur]* to lay bare the foundations of ◆ **~ un enfant** to take a child's shoes off ◆ **~ ses skis** to take one's skis off VI *(Ski)* to lose one's skis VPR **se déchausser** *[personne]* to take one's shoes off; *[skieur]* to take one's skis off; *[dents]* to come *ou* work loose

dèche* /dɛʃ/ NF ◆ **on est dans la ~, c'est la ~** we're flat broke*

déchéance /deʃeɑ̃s/ NF [1] *(morale)* decay, decline; *(intellectuelle)* intellectual decline *ou* degeneration; *(physique)* degeneration; *(Rel)* fall; *[de civilisation]* decline, decay [2] *(Pol) [de souverain]* deposition, dethronement ◆ **~ de l'autorité parentale** *(Jur)* loss of parental rights [3] *(Fin)* **remboursement par ~ du terme** repayment by acceleration

déchet /deʃɛ/ NM [1] *(= reste) [de viande, tissu, métal]* scrap [2] *(gén, Comm = perte)* waste, loss ◆ **il y a du ~** *(dans une marchandise)* there is some waste *ou* wastage; *(dans un examen)* there are (some) failures, there is (some) wastage (of students) *(Brit)*; *(viande)* there's a lot of waste ◆ **~ de route** loss in transit [3] *(péj) (= raté)* failure, wash-out*, dead loss*; *(= épave)* wreck, dead-beat* ◆ **les ~s de l'humanité** the dregs *ou* scum of the earth NMPL **déchets** *(= restes, résidus) [de viande, métal, tissu]* scraps; *(= épluchures)* peelings; *(= ordures)* waste *(NonC)*, refuse *(NonC)*, rubbish *(NonC) (Brit)*; *(Physiol)* waste *(NonC)* ◆ **~s domestiques/industriels** household/industrial waste *ou* wastes *(US)* ◆ **~s nucléaires/radioactifs/toxiques** nuclear/radioactive/toxic waste

déchetterie /deʃɛtʀi/ NF waste collection centre *ou* site

déchiffonner /deʃifɔne/ ► conjug 1 ◄ VT to smooth out, to uncrease ◆ **sa robe s'est déchiffonnée toute seule** the creases have come out of her dress (on their own)

déchiffrable /deʃifʀabl/ ADJ *[message, écriture]* decipherable; *[code]* decodable, decipherable

déchiffrage /deʃifʀaʒ/, **déchiffrement** /deʃifʀəmɑ̃/ NM *[de message, hiéroglyphe]* deciphering; *[de code]* decoding; *[de code-barres]* scanning; *[d'écriture]* deciphering; *(Mus)* sight-reading

déchiffrer /deʃifʀe/ ► conjug 1 ◄ VT *[+ message, hiéroglyphe]* to decipher; *[+ code]* to decode; *[+ code-barres]* to scan; *[+ écriture]* to make out, to decipher; *(Mus)* to sight-read; *[+ énigme]* to unravel, to fathom; *[+ avenir]* to read; *[+ sentiment]* to read, to make out

déchiffreur, -euse /deʃifʀœʀ, øz/ NM,F *[de code]* decoder; *[d'inscriptions, message]* decipherer

déchiqueté, e /deʃikte/ (ptp de **déchiqueter**) ADJ *[montagne, relief, côte]* jagged, ragged; *[feuille]* jagged(-edged); *[corps]* mutilated

déchiqueter /deʃikte/ ► conjug 4 ◄ VT *[+ papier, tissu]* to tear to pieces *ou* shreds; *[+ viande, victime]* to pull *ou* tear to pieces ◆ **elle a été déchiquetée par le train/l'explosion** she was mangled by the train/blown to pieces by the explosion ◆ **déchiqueté par un lion** mauled *ou* savaged by a lion

déchiqueteur /deʃiktœʀ/ NM, **déchiqueteuse** /deʃik(ə)tøz/ NF *(= machine)* shredder

déchiqueture /deʃik(ə)tyʀ/ NF *[de tissu]* slash; *[de feuille]* notch ◆ **~s** *[de côte, montagne]* jagged *ou* ragged outline

déchirant, e /deʃiʀɑ̃, ɑ̃t/ ADJ *[cri, spectacle]* heartrending, harrowing; *[adieux]* heartbreaking

déchiré, e* /deʃiʀe/ (ptp de **déchirer**) ADJ ◆ **il était complètement ~** *(= ivre, drogué)* he was completely ripped*

déchirement /deʃiʀmɑ̃/ NM [1] *[de tissu]* tearing, ripping; *[de muscle, tendon]* tearing [2] *(= peine)* wrench, heartbreak ◆ **pour lui, l'exil fut un véritable ~** exile was a heartrending experience for him [3] ◆ **~s** *(= divisions)* rifts, splits

déchirer /deʃiʀe/ ► conjug 1 ◄ VT [1] *(= mettre en morceaux) [+ papier, lettre]* to tear up, to tear to pieces; *(= faire un accroc à) [+ vêtement]* to tear, to rip; *(= arracher) [+ page]* to tear out *(de* from); *(= ouvrir) [+ sac, enveloppe]* to tear open; *[+ bande de protection]* to tear off; *(= mutiler) [+ corps]* to tear to pieces ◆ **~ un papier/tissu en deux** to tear a piece of paper/cloth in two *ou* in half

[2] *(fig)* **leurs cris déchirèrent le silence** their cries rent pierced the silence ◆ **ce bruit me déchire les oreilles** that noise is ear-splitting ◆ **la toux lui déchirait la poitrine** his chest was racked by a terrible cough ◆ **un spectacle qui déchire (le cœur)** a heartrending *ou* harrowing sight ◆ **elle est déchirée par le remords/la douleur** she is torn by remorse/racked by pain ◆ **les dissensions continuent à ~ le pays** the country continues to be torn (apart) by dissension, dissension is still tearing the country apart ◆ **~ qn à belles dents** to

tear *ou* pull sb to pieces ◆ **ça déchire!*** *(= c'est génial)* it's great

VPR **se déchirer** 1 *[vêtement]* to tear, to rip; *[sac]* to burst ◆ **attention, tu vas te ~*** be careful, you'll tear your clothes ◆ **se ~ un muscle** to tear a muscle ◆ **se ~ les mains** to graze *ou* skin one's hands ◆ **son cœur se déchira** his heart broke ◆ **le pays se déchira en deux camps** the country was split into two camps

2 *(mutuellement)* to tear one another apart ◆ **ils ne cessent de se ~** they are constantly tearing each other apart

déchirure /deʃiʀyʀ/ NF *[de tissu]* tear, rip, rent; *[de ciel]* break *ou* gap in the clouds ◆ **~ musculaire** torn muscle ◆ **se faire une ~ musculaire** to tear a muscle ◆ **le chômage fait planer la menace d'une ~ sociale** unemployment threatens to rip society *ou* the social fabric apart ◆ **ce fut une ~ quand mon fils est parti** it was a real wrench when my son left

déchoir /deʃwaʀ/ ▸ conjug 25 ◂ *(frm)* VI 1 *[personne]* to lower o.s., to demean o.s. ◆ **ce serait ~ que d'accepter** you would be lowering *ou* demeaning yourself if you accepted ◆ **~ de son rang** to fall from rank 2 *[réputation, influence]* to decline, to wane VT ◆ **~ qn de sa nationalité/son titre** to strip *ou* deprive sb of their nationality/title ◆ **être déchu de ses droits** to be deprived of one's rights

déchristianisation /dekʀistjanizasjɔ̃/ NF dechristianization

déchristianiser /dekʀistjanize/ ▸ conjug 1 ◂ VT to dechristianize VPR **se déchristianiser** to become dechristianized

déchu, e /deʃy/ (ptp de **déchoir**) ADJ *[roi]* deposed, dethroned; *[président, champion]* deposed; *(Rel) [ange, humanité]* fallen

déci /desi/ NM *(Helv)* decilitre (of wine) ◆ **2 ~s de blanc** two decilitres of white wine

décibel /desibɛl/ NM decibel

décidé, e /deside/ (ptp de **décider**) ADJ 1 *(= résolu, volontaire)* determined; *[personne]* determined; *(= net, marqué)* ◆ **maintenant je suis ~** now I have made up my mind ◆ **il est bien ~ à agir** he is determined to act ◆ **il est ~ à tout** he is prepared to do anything ◆ **il était ~ à ce que ça change** he was determined that this should change ◆ **j'y suis tout à fait ~** I am quite determined (to do it) ◆ **avoir l'air ~** to look determined ◆ **les mesures sont ~es en comité** the measures are decided in committee 2 *(= fixé) [question]* settled, decided ◆ **bon, c'est ~** right, that's settled *ou* decided (then) ◆ **c'est une chose ~e** the matter is settled

décidément /desidemɑ̃/ ADV *(= manifestement)* obviously ◆ **oui, c'est ~ une question de chance** yes, obviously it's a matter of luck ◆ **~, il est fou** it's obvious he's mad ◆ **~, je perds toujours mes affaires !** oh, I'm always losing my things! ◆ **~, tu m'ennuies aujourd'hui** oh, you're really annoying me today

> ⚠ **décidément** ne se traduit pas par **decidedly**, qui a le sens de 'nettement', 'tout à fait'.

décider /deside/ GRAMMAIRE ACTIVE 35.2 ▸ conjug 1 ◂

VT 1 *[personne] (= déterminer, établir)* **~ qch** to decide on sth ◆ **~ que** to decide that ◆ **~ de faire qch** to decide to do sth ◆ **comment ~ qui a raison ?** how is one to decide who is right? ◆ **elle décida qu'elle devait démissionner** she decided *ou* came to the decision that she must resign ◆ **ils ont décidé la grève/de faire grève/de ne pas faire grève** they decided on a strike/to go on strike/against a strike *ou* not to go on strike ◆ **c'est à lui de ~** it's up to him to decide ◆ **c'est souvent lui qui décide pour les autres** he often decides for the others

2 *(= persuader) [personne]* to persuade; *[conseil, événement]* to decide, to convince ◆ **~ qn à faire qch** to persuade *ou* induce sb to do sth ◆ **c'est moi qui l'ai décidé à ce voyage** I'm the one who persuaded *ou* induced him to go on this trip ◆ **la bonne publicité décide les clients éventuels** good advertising wins over potential customers

3 *[chose] (= provoquer)* to cause, to bring about ◆ **ces scandales ont finalement décidé son renvoi** these scandals finally brought about *ou* caused his dismissal

VT INDIR **décider de** *(= être l'arbitre de)* to decide; *(= déterminer)* to decide, to determine ◆ **~ de l'importance/de l'urgence de qch** to decide on the *ou* as to the importance/urgency of sth, to decide how important/urgent sth is ◆ **les résultats de son examen décideront de sa carrière** the results of his exam will decide *ou* determine his career ◆ **le sort en a décidé autrement** fate has decided *ou* ordained *ou* decreed otherwise ◆ **ainsi en a décidé le gouvernement** this was the decision the government reached

VPR **se décider** 1 *[personne]* to come to *ou* make a decision, to make up one's mind ◆ **se ~ à qch** to decide on sth ◆ **se ~ à faire qch** to make up one's mind to do sth, to make the decision to do sth ◆ **je ne peux pas me ~ à lui mentir** I cannot bring myself to lie to him ◆ **se ~ pour qch** to decide on sth *ou* in favour of sth ◆ **allez, décide-toi !** come on, make up your mind!

2 *[problème, affaire]* to be decided *ou* settled *ou* resolved ◆ **la question se décide aujourd'hui** the question is being decided *ou* settled *ou* resolved today ◆ **leur départ s'est décidé très vite** they very quickly decided to leave

3 *(locutions)* * **est-ce qu'il va se ~ à faire beau ?** do you think it'll turn out fine after all? ◆ **ça ne veut pas se ~** it won't make up its mind* ◆ **la voiture ne se décide pas à partir** the car just won't start

décideur, -euse /desidœʀ, øz/ NM,F decision-maker ◆ **avoir un rôle de ~** to have a decision-making role

décidu, e /desidy/ ADJ *[forêt]* deciduous

décigramme /desigʀam/ NM decigram(me)

décilitre /desilitʀ/ NM decilitre *(Brit)*, deciliter *(US)*

décimal, e (mpl **-aux**) /desimal, o/ ADJ decimal NF **décimale** decimal place ◆ **nombre à quatre ~es** number given to four decimal places ◆ **jusqu'à la deuxième/troisième ~e** to two/three decimal places

décimalisation /desimalizasjɔ̃/ NF decimalization

décimation /desimasjɔ̃/ NF decimation

décimer /desime/ ▸ conjug 1 ◂ VT to decimate

décimètre /desimɛtʀ/ NM decimetre *(Brit)*, decimeter *(US)*

décisif, -ive /desizif, iv/ ADJ *[argument, combat]* decisive, conclusive; *[intervention, influence]* decisive; *[preuve]* conclusive; *[moment, rôle]* decisive, critical; *[ton]* decisive, authoritative ◆ **tournant ~** watershed ◆ **le facteur ~** the deciding factor ◆ **porter un coup ~ au terrorisme** to deal terrorism a decisive blow; → **jeu**

décision /desizjɔ̃/ NF 1 *(= choix)* decision ◆ **prendre une ~** to take *ou* make a decision ◆ **prendre la ~ de faire qch** to take *ou* make the decision to do sth ◆ **il n'a pas encore pris sa ~** he hasn't yet made his decision ◆ **le processus de prise de ~ dans l'entreprise** the decision-making process in the company ◆ **parvenir à une ~** to come to *ou* reach a decision ◆ **la ~ t'appartient** it's your decision, it's for you to decide ◆ **soumettre qch à la ~ de qn** to ask sb to make a decision about sth; → **pouvoir²**

2 *(= verdict)* decision ◆ **~ administrative/gouvernementale** administrative/government decision ◆ **par ~ judiciaire *ou* de justice** by court order ◆ **nommé à un poste de ~** appointed to a decision-making job ◆ **organe de ~** decision-making body ◆ **faire la ~** *(Sport)* to win the match ◆ **leurs trois voix ont fait la ~** their three votes swung the result

3 *(= qualité)* decision, decisiveness ◆ **montrer de la ~** to be decisive ◆ **avoir l'esprit de ~** to be decisive

décisionnaire /desizjɔnɛʀ/ ADJ *[organisme, pouvoir]* decision-making *(épith)* ◆ **il n'est pas ~** he's not the one who makes the decision NMF decision-maker

décisionnel, -elle /desizjɔnɛl/ ADJ *[rôle, responsabilité]* decision-making *(épith)*

déclamateur, -trice /deklamatœʀ, tʀis/ *(péj)* ADJ ranting, declamatory NM,F ranter, declaimer

déclamation /deklamasjɔ̃/ NF *(= art)* declamation (NonC); *(péj)* ranting (NonC), spouting (NonC) ◆ **toutes leurs belles ~s** all their ranting

déclamatoire /deklamatwaʀ/ ADJ 1 *(péj) [ton]* ranting, bombastic, declamatory; *[style]* bombastic, turgid 2 *[rythme]* declamatory

déclamer /deklame/ ▸ conjug 1 ◂ VT to declaim; *(péj)* to spout VI *(péj)* to rant ◆ **~ contre** *(littér)* to inveigh *ou* rail against

déclarable /deklaʀabl/ ADJ *[marchandise]* declarable, dutiable; *[revenus]* declarable

déclarant, e /deklaʀɑ̃, ɑ̃t/ NM,F *(Jur)* informant

déclaratif, -ive /deklaʀatif, iv/ ADJ *(Jur)* declaratory; *(Ling, Ordin)* declarative

déclaration /deklaʀasjɔ̃/ NF 1 *(= discours, commentaire)* statement; *(= aveu)* admission; *(= révélation)* revelation ◆ **dans une ~ télévisée** in a televised statement ◆ **le ministre n'a fait aucune ~** the minister did not make a statement ◆ **je n'ai aucune ~ à faire** I have no comment to make ◆ **selon sa propre ~, il était ivre** by his own admission he was drunk

2 *(= manifeste, proclamation, Ordin)* declaration ◆ **Déclaration (universelle) des droits de l'homme** (Universal) Declaration of Human Rights ◆ **Déclaration d'indépendance** *(Hist US)* Declaration of Independence ◆ **~ d'intention** declaration of intent ◆ **~ de principe** statement *ou* declaration of principle

3 *(= document) [de naissance, décès]* certificate; *[de vol, perte, changement de domicile]* notification ◆ **envoyer une ~ de changement de domicile** to send notification of change of address ◆ **faire une ~ d'accident** *(à l'assurance)* to file an accident claim; *(à la police)* to report an accident ◆ **~ en douane** customs declaration ◆ **~ de faillite** declaration of bankruptcy ◆ **~ de guerre** declaration of war ◆ **~ d'impôts *ou* de revenus** tax declaration; *(formulaire)* tax return (form) ◆ **faire sa ~ d'impôts** to fill in one's tax return (form) ◆ **~ d'utilité publique** public notice; → **IMPÔTS**

4 *(amoureuse)* **~ (d'amour)** declaration of love ◆ **faire une *ou* sa ~ à qn** to make a declaration of love to sb, to declare one's love to sb

> ⚠ Au sens de 'discours', **déclaration** ne se traduit pas par le mot anglais **declaration**.

LA DÉCLARATION DES DROITS DE L'HOMME ET DU CITOYEN

Written in 1789, this document is of great cultural and historical significance in France, reflecting as it does the Republican ideals upon which modern France is founded. Drawing on philosophical ideas that developed during the Enlightenment, it declares the natural and inalienable right of all people to freedom, ownership of property and equality before the law, as well as the universal right of all nations to sovereignty and the separation of powers. It has always been used as a basis for the French Constitution.

déclaratoire /deklaʀatwaʀ/ ADJ *(Jur)* declaratory

déclaré, e /deklaʀe/ (ptp de **déclarer**) ADJ *[opinion]* professed; *[athée, révolutionnaire]* declared, self-confessed; *[ennemi]* sworn, avowed; *[intention]* avowed, declared; *[travailleur]* registered, declared ◆ **revenus non ~s** undeclared income

déclarer /deklaʀe/ ▸ conjug 1 ◂ VT 1 *(= annoncer)* to announce, to state, to declare; *(= proclamer)* to declare; *(= avouer)* to admit, to confess to; *(= dire)* to say ◆ **"c'est un moment historique" déclara le ministre** "it's an historic moment", the minister declared ◆ **~ son amour (à qn)** to declare one's love (to sb), to make a declaration of love (to sb) ◆ **~ la guerre à une nation/à la pollution** to declare war on a nation/on pollution ◆ **le président déclara la séance levée** the chairman declared the meeting closed ◆ **~ qn coupable/innocent** to find sb guilty/innocent

◆ **déclarer que ...** to declare *ou* say that ... ◆ **je vous déclare que je n'y crois pas** I tell you I don't believe it ◆ **ils ont déclaré que nous avions menti** they claimed that we had lied

2 *(Admin) [+ marchandises, revenus, employés]* to declare; *[+ naissance, décès]* to register, to notify ◆ **le père doit aller ~ l'enfant à la mairie** the father has to go and register the child at the town hall ◆ **~ qn en faillite** to declare sb bankrupt ◆ **avez-vous quelque chose à ~ ?** *(Douane)* do you have anything to declare? ◆ **~ qch au-dessus/au-dessous de sa valeur** to overvalue/undervalue sth ◆ **rien à ~** nothing to declare

VPR **se déclarer** 1 *(= se prononcer)* to declare *ou* state one's opinion ◆ **se ~ en faveur de qch** to declare o.s. *ou* profess o.s. in favour of sth ◆ **se ~ pour/contre qch** to come out in favour of/against sth ◆ **il s'est déclaré l'auteur de ces poèmes/crimes** he stated that he had written the poems/committed the crimes ◆ **se ~ satisfait** to declare o.s. satisfied ◆ **il s'est déclaré prêt à signer ce document** he said he was ready *ou* declared himself ready to sign the document ◆ **se ~ incompétent** *(Jur)* to decline a jurisdiction

2 *(= apparaître) [incendie, épidémie]* to break out

3 *[amoureux]* to make a declaration of one's love, to declare *ou* avow *(littér)* one's love

déclassé, e /deklɑse/ (ptp de **déclasser**) ADJ 1 *[coureur]* relegated *(in the placing)*; *[hôtel, restaurant, vin]* downgraded ◆ **valeurs ~es** *(Bourse)* displaced stocks *ou* securities 2 *[fiche, livre]* out of order *(attrib)*

déclassement /deklɑsmɑ̃/ NM 1 *(social, dans une hiérarchie)* fall *ou* drop in status 2 *(Sport) [de coureur]* relegation *(in the placing)*; *(Rail) [de voyageur]* change of class; *(Admin) [d'hôtel]* downgrading; *[de monument]* delisting; *(Bourse) [de valeur]* displacement 3 *[de fiches, livres]* **pour éviter le ~** to stop things getting out of order

déclasser /deklɑse/ ▸ conjug 1 ◂ VT 1 *(socialement, dans une hiérarchie)* to lower in status ◆ **il estimait qu'on l'avait déclassé en le mettant dans l'équipe B** he felt that he had suffered a drop in status *ou* that he had been downgraded by being put in the B team ◆ **il se déclassait par de telles fréquentations** he was lowering himself socially *ou* demeaning himself by keeping such company 2 *(= rétrograder) (Sport) [+ coureur]* to relegate *(in the placing)*; *(Rail) [+ voyageur]* to put in second class; *(Admin) [+ hôtel]* to downgrade; *[+ monument]* to delist; *(Bourse) [+ valeur]* to displace 3 *(= déranger) [+ fiches, livres]* to get out of order, to put back in the wrong order

déclenchement /deklɑ̃ʃmɑ̃/ NM 1 *(= actionnement) [de ressort, mécanisme]* release; *[de sonnerie, alarme]* setting off, activating 2 *(= provocation) [d'insurrection]* launching, starting; *[de catastrophe, guerre, crise, grève, processus, polémique]* triggering *ou* sparking off; *[d'accouchement]* inducement ◆ **le rôle du psychisme dans le ~ de certaines maladies** the role of psychological factors in triggering certain illnesses 3 *(Mil) [de tir]* opening; *[d'attaque]* launching

déclencher /deklɑ̃ʃe/ ▸ conjug 1 ◂ VT 1 *(= actionner) [+ ressort, mécanisme]* to release; *[+ sonnerie, alarme]* to set off, to activate ◆ **ce bouton déclenche l'ouverture/la fermeture de la porte** this button opens/closes the door ◆ **faire la mise au point avant de ~** *(Photo)* to focus before releasing the shutter

2 *(= provoquer) [+ insurrection]* to launch, to start; *[+ catastrophe, guerre, crise, processus, polémique]* to trigger *ou* spark off; *[+ accouchement]* to induce ◆ **c'est ce mot qui a tout déclenché** this is the word which triggered everything off ◆ **~ une grève** *[meneur]* to launch *ou* start a strike; *[incident]* to trigger *ou* spark off a strike ◆ **ça m'a déclenché une sciatique** it gave me sciatica ◆ **quand je me penche ça me déclenche une douleur dans le dos** when I bend down my back hurts *ou* I get backache ◆ **ça a déclenché un fou rire général** it caused great hilarity

3 *(Mil) [+ tir]* to open; *[+ attaque]* to launch ◆ **~ l'offensive** to launch the offensive

VPR **se déclencher** *[ressort, mécanisme]* to release itself; *[sonnerie, alarme]* to go off; *[attaque, grève]* to start, to begin; *[catastrophe, crise, réaction nerveuse]* to be triggered off

déclencheur /deklɑ̃ʃœʀ/ NM *(= dispositif)* release mechanism; *[d'appareil photo]* shutter release ◆ **~ souple** cable release ◆ **~ automatique** *ou* **à retardement** self-timer ◆ **cet incident a servi de ~ à la crise** this incident sparked off *ou* triggered (off) the crisis

déclic /deklik/ NM *(= bruit)* click; *(= mécanisme)* trigger mechanism ◆ **ça a été le ~** *(mentalement)* it triggered something off in my *(ou his etc)* mind

déclin /deklɛ̃/ NM 1 *(gén)* decline; *[de malade, santé, vue]* deterioration; *[de talent, forces, beauté, sentiment]* waning, fading ◆ **~ de la production/de l'activité économique** decline in production/in economic activity ◆ **le ~ du parti** the party's decline, the decline of the party ◆ **le ~ du jour** the close of day ◆ **au ~ de la vie** *(littér)* in the twilight years ◆ **~ démographique** population decline

2 *(locutions)* **être à son ~** *[soleil]* to be setting; *[lune]* to be on the wane, to be waning ◆ **être sur le** *ou* **son ~** *[malade]* to be going downhill; *[acteur, homme politique]* to be on the decline *ou* on the wane ◆ **être en ~** *[talent, prestige]* to be on the decline *ou* on the wane; *[forces, intelligence, civilisation, art]* to be in decline *ou* on the wane; *[marché, secteur]* to be in decline ◆ **marché/industrie en ~** declining market/industry

déclinable /deklinabl/ ADJ 1 *(= adaptable)* **un espace architectural ~ à l'infini** an infinitely adaptable architectural space ◆ **une coupe de cheveux ~ en trois longueurs** a style that can be adapted to three different lengths of hair ◆ **ce produit est facilement ~** a whole range can easily be developed from this product 2 *(Gram)* declinable

déclinaison /deklinɛzɔ̃/ NF *(Ling)* declension; *(Astron, Phys)* declination

déclinant, e /deklinɑ̃, ɑ̃t/ ADJ *[pouvoir]* declining; *[santé]* declining, deteriorating; *[vue]* failing; *[prestige, popularité, forces]* waning, declining; *[beauté, sentiment]* fading

déclinatoire /deklinatwaʀ/ NM 1 *(= boussole)* surveyor's compass 2 *(Jur)* **~ (de compétence)** *(gén)* challenge to jurisdiction; *(fait par le tribunal)* declining *ou* denial of jurisdiction

décliner /dekline/ ▸ conjug 1 ◂ VT 1 *(frm = refuser) [+ offre, invitation, honneur]* to decline, to turn down, to refuse ◆ **la direction décline toute responsabilité en cas de perte ou de vol** the management accepts no responsibility *ou* refuses to accept responsibility for loss or theft of articles ◆ **~ la compétence de qn/la compétence d'une juridiction** *(Jur)* to refuse to recognize sb's competence/the competence of a court

2 *(Ling)* to decline ◆ **ce mot ne se décline pas** this word does not decline

3 *(frm = réciter)* **~ son identité** to give one's personal particulars ◆ **déclinez vos nom, prénoms, titres et qualités** state your name, forenames, qualifications and status

4 *(Comm) [+ produit]* to offer in a variety of forms ◆ **un rouge à lèvres décliné en cinq nuances** a lipstick available in *ou* that comes in five shades

VI 1 *(= s'affaiblir)* to decline; *[malade, santé, vue]* to deteriorate, to go downhill; *[talent, forces, beauté, sentiment]* to wane, to fade; *[prestige, popularité]* to wane, to fall off; *[production, ventes]* to fall, to be on the decline; *[marché, secteur]* to be on the decline ◆ **le revenu par habitant décline** per capita income is falling

2 *[jour]* to draw to a close; *[soleil]* to be setting, to go down; *[lune]* to wane, to be on the wane; *(Tech) [aiguille aimantée]* to deviate

VPR **se décliner** *[produit]* to come in a variety of forms ◆ **ce yaourt se décline en trois saveurs** this yoghurt is available in *ou* comes in three flavours

déclive /dekliv/ ADJ *[terrain]* inclined

déclivité /deklivite/ NF slope, incline, declivity *(frm)*

décloisonnement /deklwazɔnmɑ̃/ NM decompartmentalization

décloisonner /deklwazɔne/ ▸ conjug 1 ◂ VT to decompartmentalize

déclouer /deklue/ ▸ conjug 1 ◂ VT *[+ caisse]* to open; *[+ planche]* to remove

déco /deko/ ADJ INV (abrév de **décoratif**) → **art** NF (* abrév de **décoration**) ◆ **j'ai refait la ~ de ma chambre** I've redecorated my bedroom

décocher /dekɔʃe/ ▸ conjug 1 ◂ VT 1 *[+ flèche]* to shoot, to fire; *[+ coup de pied]* to give, to deliver; *[+ coup de poing]* to throw; *[+ ruade]* to let fly 2 *[+ œillade, regard]* to shoot, to flash, to dart; *[+ sourire]* to flash; *[+ remarque]* to fire, to let fly

décoction /dekɔksjɔ̃/ NF decoction, brew

décodage /dekɔdaʒ/ NM *[de code]* decoding, cracking; *(TV, Ordin, Ling)* decoding; *[de message]* deciphering ◆ **système de ~ numérique** digital decoding system

décoder /dekɔde/ ▸ conjug 1 ◂ VT *[+ code]* to decode, to break; *(TV, Ordin, Ling)* to decode; *[+ message]* to decipher; *(= comprendre) [+ poème, comportement]* to understand

décodeur /dekɔdœʀ/ NM *[de code]* (TV, Ordin, Ling) decoder; *[de message]* decipherer

décoffrage /dekɔfʀaʒ/ NM *(Constr)* removal of the formwork; → **brut**

décoffrer /dekɔfʀe/ ► conjug 1 ◄ VT (*Constr*) to remove the formwork from

décoiffer /dekwafe/ ► conjug 1 ◄ VT 1 (= *ébouriffer*) ~ **qn** to mess up sb's hair ◆ **il s'est/le vent l'a décoiffé** he/the wind has disarranged *ou* messed up his hair ◆ **je suis toute décoiffée** my hair is in a mess *ou* is (all) messed up ◆ **ça décoiffe !*** (*fig*) it really takes your breath away! 2 (= *ôter le chapeau*) ~ **qn** to take sb's hat off ◆ **il se décoiffa** he took his hat off 3 (*Tech*) [+ *obus*] to uncap

décoincement /dekwɛ̃smɑ̃/ NM (*gén*) unjamming, loosening (*de* of); (*Tech*) removal of the wedge (*de* from)

décoincer /dekwɛ̃se/ ► conjug 3 ◄ VT (*gén*) to unjam, to loosen ◆ ~ **qch** (*Tech*) to remove the wedge from sth ◆ ~ **qn*** to get sb to loosen up* VPR **se décoincer** [*objet*] to come loose; * [*personne*] to loosen up*

décolérer /dekɔleʀe/ ► conjug 6 ◄ VI ◆ **ne jamais** ~ to be always in a temper ◆ **il ne décolère pas depuis hier** he hasn't calmed down since yesterday, he's still angry from yesterday

décollage /dekɔlaʒ/ NM 1 [*d'avion*] takeoff; [*de fusée*] lift-off ◆ **au** ~ [*d'avion*] at take off; [*de fusée*] at lift-off 2 (*fig*) **depuis le** ~ **économique de la région** since the region's economy took off ◆ **le** ~ **de l'informatique n'a pas été facile** information technology had difficulty getting off the ground 3 [*de timbre*] unsticking; [*de papier peint*] stripping, peeling off

décollation /dekɔlasjɔ̃/ NF decapitation, beheading

décollectivisation /dekɔlɛktivizasjɔ̃/ NF [*d'agriculture, économie*] decollectivization

décollement /dekɔlmɑ̃/ NM [*de timbre*] unsticking; [*de rétine*] detachment ◆ **se faire faire un** ~ **de racines** (*Coiffure*) to have one's hair volumized

décoller /dekɔle/ ► conjug 1 ◄ VT 1 (*gén*) to unstick; (*en trempant*) [+ *timbre, étiquette*] to soak off; (*à la vapeur*) [+ *timbre, papier peint*] to steam off; [+ *lettre*] to steam open ◆ ~ **qn de*** [+ *livre, télévision*] to drag sb away from

2 (* = *se débarrasser de*) [+ *créanciers, poursuivants*] to shake off, to get rid of ◆ **je ne suis pas arrivé à m'en** ~ *ou* **le** ~ ! I couldn't manage to shake him off *ou* get rid of him!

VI 1 [*avion, pays*] to take off; [*fusée*] to lift off (*de* from); [*industrie*] to take off, to get off the ground

2 (* = *maigrir*) to lose weight

3 (* = *partir*) [*gêneur*] to budge, to shift; [*drogué*] to get off* ◆ **il n'a pas décollé (d'ici) pendant deux heures** he sat *ou* stayed here for two solid hours without budging* ◆ ~ **du peloton** (*Sport*) (*en avant*) to pull away from *ou* ahead of the pack; (*en arrière*) to fall *ou* drop behind the pack ◆ ~ **du réel** to escape from reality

VPR **se décoller** [*timbre*] to come unstuck; [*papier peint*] to peel; (*Méd*) [*rétine*] to become detached

décolletage /dekɔltaʒ/ NM 1 (= *forme*) (low-cut) neckline, décolletage; [*de robe*] (= *action*) cutting out of the neck 2 (*Agr*) [*de racines*] topping 3 (*Tech*) [*de pièces métalliques*] cutting (from the bar)

décolleté, e /dekɔlte/ (ptp de **décolleter**) ADJ [*robe*] low-necked, low-cut; [*femme*] wearing a low-cut dress; [*chaussure*] low-cut ◆ **robe ~e dans le dos** dress cut low at the back NM [*de robe*] low neck(line); [*de femme*] (bare) neck and shoulders; (*plongeant*) cleavage

COMP **décolleté bateau** bateau *ou* boat neck
décolleté en pointe V-neck
décolleté rond round-neck

décolleter /dekɔlte/ ► conjug 4 ◄ VT 1 [+ *robe*] to cut out the neck of 2 (*Agr*) [+ *racines*] to top 3 (*Tech*) [+ *pièces métalliques*] to cut (from the bar)

décolleuse /dekɔløz/ NF [*de papier peint*] steam stripper

décolonisateur, -trice /dekɔlɔnizatœʀ, tʀis/ ADJ decolonization (*épith*), decolonizing (*épith*) NM,F decolonizer

décolonisation /dekɔlɔnizasjɔ̃/ NF decolonization

décoloniser /dekɔlɔnize/ ► conjug 1 ◄ VT to decolonize

décolorant, e /dekɔlɔʀɑ̃, ɑ̃t/ ADJ decolorizing (*épith*), bleaching (*épith*) NM bleaching agent

décoloration /dekɔlɔʀasjɔ̃/ NF (*gén*) discolouration (*Brit*), discoloration (*US*); [*de tissu*] fading; [*de cheveux*] bleaching, lightening ◆ **se faire faire une** ~ (*gén*) to have one's hair lightened; (*en blond*) to have one's hair bleached

décoloré, e /dekɔlɔʀe/ (ptp de **décolorer**) ADJ [*vêtement*] faded; [*cheveux*] bleached, lightened; [*teint, lèvres*] pale, colourless (*Brit*), colorless (*US*) ◆ **une blonde ~e** a peroxide *ou* bleached *ou* bottle* blonde

décolorer /dekɔlɔʀe/ ► conjug 1 ◄ VT (*gén*) to discolour (*Brit*), to discolor (*US*); [+ *tissu*] [*soleil*] to fade; [*lavage*] to take the colour (*Brit*) *ou* color (*US*) out of, to fade; [+ *cheveux*] (*gén*) to lighten; (*en blond*) to bleach VPR **se décolorer** [*liquide*] to lose its colour (*Brit*) *ou* color (*US*); [*tissu*] to fade, to lose its colour (*Brit*) *ou* color (*US*) ◆ **elle s'est décolorée, elle s'est décoloré les cheveux** (*gén*) she has lightened her hair; (*en blond*) she has bleached her hair

décombres /dekɔ̃bʀ/ NMPL rubble, debris (*sg*); (*fig*) ruins ◆ **les ~ de l'empire/de l'économie soviétique** the ruins of the empire/the Soviet economy

décommander /dekɔmɑ̃de/ ► conjug 1 ◄ VT [+ *marchandise*] to cancel (an order for); [+ *invités*] to put off; [+ *invitation*] to cancel VPR **se décommander** to cancel one's appointment

décompactage /dekɔ̃paktaʒ/ NM (*Ordin*) decompressing

décompacter /dekɔ̃pakte/ ► conjug 1 ◄ VT (*Ordin*) to decompress

décompensation /dekɔ̃pɑ̃sasjɔ̃/ NF (*Méd*) (*physique*) decompensation; (*nerveuse*) (emotional) collapse

décompenser /dekɔ̃pɑ̃se/ ► conjug 1 ◄ VI (*Méd*) (*physiquement*) to decompensate; (*nerveusement*) to collapse (emotionally)

décomplexer /dekɔ̃plɛkse/ ► conjug 1 ◄ VT ◆ ~ **qn** to rid sb of their complexes *ou* hang-ups

décomposable /dekɔ̃pozabl(ə)/ ADJ (*Math*) [*nombre*] that can be factorized; (*Chim*) decomposable; (*Phys*) [*lumière*] that can be broken up, that can be split up; (*Tech*) [*forces*] resoluble

décomposer /dekɔ̃poze/ ► conjug 1 ◄ VT 1 (= *diviser*) (*gén*) to split up *ou* break up into its component parts; (*Ling*) [+ *phrase*] to break down, to split up; [+ *problème, idée*] to dissect, to break down ◆ **la prof de danse décomposa le mouvement devant nous** the dance teacher broke the movement up for us *ou* went through the movement slowly for us

2 (= *altérer*) [+ *visage*] to contort, to distort ◆ **la douleur décomposait ses traits** his face was contorted with pain ◆ **il était décomposé** he looked distraught

3 (= *putréfier*) [+ *viande*] to cause to decompose *ou* rot ◆ **la chaleur décomposait les cadavres** the heat was causing the corpses to decompose *ou* to decay

4 (*Tech*) [+ *forces*] to resolve; (*Math*) [+ *nombre*] to factorize, to express as a product of prime factors; (*Chim*) to decompose; (*Phys*) [+ *lumière*] to break up, to split up

VPR **se décomposer** 1 (= *pourrir*) [*viande*] to decompose, to rot; [*cadavre*] to decompose, to decay

2 (= *s'altérer*) [*visage*] to become distorted ◆ **à cette nouvelle son visage se décomposa** when he heard this news his face fell

3 (= *se diviser*) to be divided ◆ **se ~ en trois parties** to be divided *ou* broken up into three parts ◆ **cela se décompose de la façon suivante ...** it breaks down *ou* is divided up in the following way ... ◆ **la phrase se décompose en trois propositions** the sentence can be broken down *ou* split up into three clauses

4 (= *se déstructurer*) [*société*] to break down; [*fédération*] to break up

> ⚠ Attention à ne pas traduire automatiquement **décomposer** par **to decompose**, qui a le sens de 'pourrir'.

décomposeur /dekɔ̃pozœʀ/ NM (*Bio*) decomposer

décomposition /dekɔ̃pozisjɔ̃/ NF 1 (= *division*) (*gén*) splitting up, breaking up; (*Math*) [*de nombre*] factorization; (*Chim*) decomposition; (*Phys*) [*de lumière*] breaking up, splitting up; (*Tech*) [*de forces*] resolution; (*Ling*) [*de phrase*] breaking down, splitting up; [*de problème, idée*] dissection, breaking down ◆ **le calcul de l'impôt nécessite la ~ du revenu en tranches** income needs to be divided up into bands for tax calculation purposes 2 (= *pourriture*) decomposition, decay ◆ **cadavre en** ~ corpse in a state of decomposition *ou* decay 3 (= *déstructuration*) [*de société*] breakdown; [*de fédération*] breakup ◆ **société/système en complète** ~ society/system in decay

décompresser /dekɔ̃pʀese/ ► conjug 1 ◄ VT (*Tech, Ordin*) to decompress VI (* = *se détendre*) to unwind, to relax

décompresseur /dekɔ̃pʀesœʀ/ NM decompression tap; [*de voiture*] decompressor

décompression /dekɔ̃pʀesjɔ̃/ NF 1 (*Tech, Méd, Ordin*) decompression ◆ **soupape/chambre de** ~ decompression valve/chamber ◆ ~ **cardiaque** cardiac decompression 2 (* = *détente*) relaxation

décomprimer /dekɔ̃pʀime/ ► conjug 1 ◄ VT to decompress

décompte /dekɔ̃t/ NM 1 (= *calcul*) detailed account, breakdown 2 (= *déduction*) deduction ◆ **faire le ~ des points** to count up the points ◆ **faire le ~ des voix** to count the votes ◆ **vous voulez faire mon ~ ?** will you make out my bill (*Brit*) *ou* check? (*US*)

décompter /dekɔ̃te/ ► conjug 1 ◄ VT (= *défalquer*) to deduct (*de* from) VI [*horloge*] to strike *ou* chime at the wrong time

déconcentration /dekɔ̃sɑ̃tʀasjɔ̃/ NF 1 [*de personne*] loss of concentration 2 (*Admin, chim*) deconcentration

déconcentré, e /dekɔ̃sɑ̃tʀe/ (ptp de **déconcentrer**) ADJ 1 (*Admin, chim*) deconcentrated; [*crédits*] regional ◆ **des services ~s** deconcentrated services 2 [*personne*] **être** ~ to have lost (one's) concentration ◆ **j'étais un peu/très** ~ I wasn't really concentrating/wasn't concentrating at all

déconcentrer /dekɔ̃sɑ̃tʀe/ ► conjug 1 ◄ VT 1 [+ *institutions*] to deconcentrate ◆ **le ministre s'est engagé à ~ 200 emplois** the minister is committed to dispersing 200 jobs ◆ **les difficultés surgissent quand il s'agit de ~ les personnels** the difficulties arise when it comes to moving staff 2 (= *distraire*) **ça m'a déconcentré** it made me lose (my) concentration ◆ **tu me déconcentres !** you're putting me off! VPR **se déconcentrer** 1 [*personne*] to lose (one's) concentration [2] *[institution]* to deconcentrate

déconcertant, e /dekɔ̃sɛʀtɑ̃, ɑ̃t/ ADJ disconcerting

déconcerter /dekɔ̃sɛʀte/ ► conjug 1 ◄ VT (= *décontenancer*) to disconcert; (†† = *déjouer*) to thwart, to frustrate

déconditionner /dekɔ̃disjɔne/ ► conjug 1 ◄ VT to decondition

déconfit, e /dekɔ̃fi, it/ ADJ [1] (= *dépité*) *[personne, air, mine]* crestfallen, downcast ◆ **avoir la mine ~e** to look downcast *ou* crestfallen [2] (†† = *battu*) defeated, discomfited †

déconfiture * /dekɔ̃fityʀ/ NF (= *déroute*) *(gén)* failure, collapse; *[de parti, armée]* defeat; *(financière)* (financial) collapse, ruin ◆ **cette entreprise est en ~** the company is in a state of collapse

décongélation /dekɔ̃ʒelasjɔ̃/ NF defrosting, unfreezing

décongeler /dekɔ̃ʒ(ə)le/ ► conjug 5 ◄ VI *[aliment]* to defrost, to thaw VT *[+ aliment]* to defrost, to leave to thaw; *[+ sperme]* to thaw

décongestionnant, e /dekɔ̃ʒɛstjɔnɑ̃, ɑ̃t/ ADJ *[gel, crème]* decongestant; *(pour les jambes)* soothing cream

décongestionner /dekɔ̃ʒɛstjɔne/ ► conjug 1 ◄ VT *(Méd)* *[+ poumons, fosses nasales]* to decongest, to relieve congestion in; *[+ malade]* to relieve congestion in; *[+ rue, centre-ville]* to relieve congestion in; *[+ service, aéroport, université, administration]* to relieve the pressure on

déconnade ‡ /dekɔnad/ NF ◆ **il aime la franche ~** he likes to mess around * *ou* to fool around * ◆ **il se moquait d'elle pour la ~** he was teasing her for a laugh * *ou* just for the hell of it *

déconnecter /dekɔnɛkte/ ► conjug 1 ◄ VT [1] *(Élec)* to disconnect [2] *[+ problème]* to dissociate *(de* from); ◆ **il est complètement déconnecté de la réalité/de son pays d'origine** he's completely out of touch with reality/with his native country VI * *[personne]* to switch off * VPR **se déconnecter** *(Ordin)* to log off

déconner ‡ /dekɔne/ ► conjug 1 ◄ VI *[personne]* (= *faire des bêtises*) to mess around *, to fool around *; (= *dire des bêtises*) to talk nonsense; (= *plaisanter*) to joke, to kid *; *[machine]* to act up * ◆ **arrête de ~ !** stop messing around!, quit fooling! ◆ **sans ~, c'était super !** no joke *, it was great! ◆ **faut pas ~ !** come off it! *

déconneur ‡ /dekɔnœʀ/ NM ◆ **c'est un sacré ~** he'll do the craziest things for a laugh

déconneuse ‡ /dekɔnøz/ NF ◆ **c'est une sacrée ~** she'll do the craziest things for a laugh

déconnexion /dekɔnɛksjɔ̃/ NF disconnection; *(Ordin)* logging off

déconseiller /dekɔ̃seje/ GRAMMAIRE ACTIVE 29.2 ► conjug 1 ◄ VT to advise against ◆ **~ qch à qn/à qn de faire qch** to advise sb against sth/sb against doing sth ◆ **c'est déconseillé** it's not advisable, it's inadvisable ◆ **dans ce régime, le beurre est déconseillé** butter is not recommended in this diet

déconsidération /dekɔ̃sideʀasjɔ̃/ NF discredit, disrepute

déconsidérer /dekɔ̃sideʀe/ ► conjug 6 ◄ VT to discredit VPR **se déconsidérer** to discredit o.s. ◆ **il s'est déconsidéré en agissant ainsi** he has discredited himself *ou* brought discredit upon himself by behaving in this way

déconsigner /dekɔ̃siɲe/ ► conjug 1 ◄ VT [1] *[+ valise]* to collect from the left luggage office *(Brit)* *ou* the baggage checkroom *(US)*; *[+ bouteille]* to return the deposit on [2] *[+ troupes]* to release from confinement to barracks

déconsommation /dekɔ̃sɔmasjɔ̃/ NF *(Écon)* drop in consumption (of consumer goods) ◆ **on observe une tendance à la ~ des ménages** there is a growing tendency for households to buy less consumer goods

déconstruction /dekɔ̃stʀyksjɔ̃/ NF *[de concept, système]* deconstruction; *[de bâtiment]* dismantling

déconstruire /dekɔ̃stʀɥiʀ/ ► conjug 38 ◄ VT *[+ concept, système]* to deconstruct; *[+ bâtiment]* to dismantle

décontamination /dekɔ̃taminasjɔ̃/ NF decontamination

décontaminer /dekɔ̃tamine/ ► conjug 1 ◄ VT to decontaminate

décontenancer /dekɔ̃t(ə)nɑ̃se/ ► conjug 3 ◄ VT to disconcert VPR **se décontenancer** to lose one's composure

décontract * /dekɔ̃tʀakt/ ADJ INV laid-back *, cool *

décontractant, e /dekɔ̃tʀaktɑ̃, ɑ̃t/ ADJ *[ambiance, massage, médicament]* relaxing NM relaxant

décontracté, e /dekɔ̃tʀakte/ (ptp de **décontracter**) ADJ [1] *[muscles, corps]* relaxed [2] *[personne]* relaxed, laid-back *; (= *sans-gêne*) casual, offhand; *[atmosphère, attitude]* relaxed, laid-back *; *[vêtements, style]* casual

décontracter VT, **se décontracter** VPR /dekɔ̃tʀakte/ ► conjug 1 ◄ to relax

décontraction /dekɔ̃tʀaksjɔ̃/ NF [1] *[de muscle, corps]* relaxation [2] (= *désinvolture*) relaxed *ou* laid-back * attitude ◆ **sa ~ m'a étonné** I was amazed that he was so relaxed *ou* laid-back *

déconventionner /dekɔ̃vɑ̃sjɔne/ ► conjug 1 ◄ VT *[+ établissement, médecin]* to strike off the register *(for financial misconduct)*

déconvenue /dekɔ̃v(ə)ny/ NF (= *déception*) disappointment

décor /dekɔʀ/ NM [1] *(Théât)* **le ~, les ~s** the scenery *(NonC)*, the décor *(NonC)* ◆ **~ de cinéma** film set ◆ **on dirait un ~** *ou* **des ~s de théâtre** it looks like a stage setting *ou* a theatre set, it looks like scenery for a play ◆ **tourner en ~s naturels** to shoot on location ◆ **planter le ~** to set the scene ◆ **faire partie du ~** *(lit, fig)* to be part of the furniture ◆ **aller** *ou* **partir dans le ~** * *ou* **les ~s** * *[véhicule, conducteur]* to go off the road ◆ **envoyer qn dans le ~** * *ou* **les ~s** * to force sb off the road; → **changement, envers²**

[2] (= *paysage*) scenery; (= *arrière-plan*) setting; (= *intérieur de maison*) décor *(NonC)*, decoration ◆ **~ de montagnes** mountain scenery ◆ **dans un ~ de verdure** in a green setting ◆ **photographié dans son ~ habituel** photographed in his usual surroundings

décorateur, -trice /dekɔʀatœʀ, tʀis/ NM,F [1] *(d'intérieurs)* (interior) decorator; → **peintre** [2] *(Théât = architecte)* stage *ou* set designer; *(TV, Ciné)* set designer

décoratif, -ive /dekɔʀatif, iv/ ADJ *[ornement]* decorative, ornamental; *[arts, effet]* decorative ◆ **elle a un rôle purement ~** *(péj)* she has a purely decorative role

décoration /dekɔʀasjɔ̃/ NF [1] (= *action*) decoration [2] *(gén pl = ornement)* decorations; (= *ensemble des ornements*) decoration ◆ **~s de Noël** Christmas decorations [3] (= *médaille*) decoration

décorder (se) /dekɔʀde/ ► conjug 1 ◄ VPR *(Alpinisme)* to unrope

décoré, e /dekɔʀe/ (ptp de **décorer**) ADJ [1] (= *orné*) decorated ◆ **joliment ~** prettily decorated ◆ **richement ~** ornate, richly decorated ◆ **mur ~ de fresques** wall decorated with frescoes ◆ **un vase très ~** an ornate vase [2] (= *récompensé*) wearing a (military) decoration (*ou* decorations), decorated ◆ **un vieux monsieur très ~** an old man bedecked with medals and ribbons ◆ **les ~s de la Première Guerre mondiale** soldiers awarded (military) decorations *ou* decorated during the First World War

décorer /dekɔʀe/ ► conjug 1 ◄ VT [1] (= *embellir*) *(gén)* to decorate; *[+ robe]* to trim ◆ **~ une maison pour Noël** to decorate a house for Christmas ◆ **l'ensemblier qui a décoré leur maison** the interior decorator who did their house [2] (= *médailler*) to decorate *(de* with); ◆ **on va le ~** *(gén)* he is to be decorated; *(Légion d'honneur)* he is to be made a member of the Legion of Honour

décorner /dekɔʀne/ ► conjug 1 ◄ VT *[+ page]* to smooth out; *[+ animal]* to dehorn; → **vent**

décorticage /dekɔʀtikaʒ/ NM *[de crevettes, amandes]* shelling; *[de riz]* hulling, husking; *[de texte]* dissection

décortication /dekɔʀtikasjɔ̃/ NF *(Méd, Sylviculture)* decortication

décortiquer /dekɔʀtike/ ► conjug 1 ◄ VT [1] *[+ crevettes, amandes]* to shell; *[+ riz]* to hull, to husk; *[+ texte]* to dissect [2] *(Méd)* to decorticate [3] *(Sylviculture)* to remove the bark from

décorum /dekɔʀɔm/ NM ◆ **le ~** (= *convenances*) decorum; (= *étiquette*) etiquette

décote /dekɔt/ NF *(Fin)* *[de devises, valeur]* below par rating; *[d'impôts]* tax relief

découcher /dekuʃe/ ► conjug 1 ◄ VI to spend the night away from home

découdre /dekudʀ/ ► conjug 48 ◄ VT [1] *[+ vêtement]* to take the stitches out of, to unpick *(Brit)*; *[+ bouton]* to take off; *[+ couture]* to take out, to unpick *(Brit)* [2] ◆ **en ~** *(littér, hum = se battre)* to fight, to do battle *(avec* with) [3] *(Chasse)* to gore, to rip open VPR **se découdre** *[robe]* to come unstitched; *[bouton]* to come off; *[couture]* to come apart

découenné, e /dekwane/ ADJ ◆ **jambon ~** rindless bacon

découler /dekule/ GRAMMAIRE ACTIVE 53.4 ► conjug 1 ◄ VI (= *dériver*) to ensue, to follow *(de* from); ◆ **il découle de cela que ...** it ensues *ou* follows that ... ◆ **les changements qui en découleront seront considérables** the changes which will follow on from this will be considerable ◆ **la partition de l'Empire et les terribles massacres qui en ont découlé** the partition of the Empire and the terrible massacres which followed ◆ **des réductions de dépenses découleront de l'accord** the agreement will lead to a reduction in spending

découpage /dekupaʒ/ NM [1] *[de papier, gâteau]* cutting up; *[de viande]* carving; *[d'image, métal]* cutting out [2] (= *image*) cut-out ◆ **un cahier de ~s** a cut-out book ◆ **faire des ~s** to make cut-out figures [3] *(Ciné)* cutting [4] *(Pol)* **~ électoral** division into constituencies, distribution of constituencies *(Brit)*, ≃ apportionment *(US)*

découpe /dekup/ NF [1] *(Couture)* (= *coupe*) cut; (= *coupure*) cut-out [2] *[de bois, verre, carrelage]* cutting to shape ◆ **verre/bois à la ~** glass/wood cut to order

découpé, e /dekupe/ (ptp de **découper**) ADJ *[relief, sommets, côte]* jagged, indented; *[feuille]* jagged, serrated

découper /dekupe/ ► conjug 1 ◄ VT [1] *(Culin)* *[+ viande, volaille]* to carve, to cut; *[+ gâteau]* to cut ◆ **couteau/fourchette à ~** carving knife/fork [2] *[+ papier, tissu]* to cut up; *[+ bois, verre]* to cut to shape; *[+ images, métal]* to cut out ◆ **~ un article dans un magazine** to cut an article out of a magazine ◆ **"découpez suivant le pointillé"** "cut along the dotted line" ◆ **les indentations qui découpent la côte** the indentations which cut into the coastline; → **scie** VPR **se découper** [1] (= *se couper*) to be cut out ◆ **les**

biscuits se découpent avec des emporte-pièce you cut out the biscuits *(Brit) ou* cookies *(US)* with a cutter ◆ **l'identité ne se découpe pas en tranches** one's identity cannot be cut into neat pieces 2 *(= se détacher)* **sa silhouette se découpait dans la lumière** his figure stood out *ou* was outlined against the light

découpeur, -euse / dekupœʀ, øz / NM,F *(= personne) [de viande]* carver; *[de métal]* cutter; *[de bois]* jigsaw operator NF **découpeuse** *(= machine) (gén)* cutting machine; *[de bois]* fretsaw, jigsaw

découplage / dekuplaʒ / NM 1 *(Élec)* decoupling 2 *(= dissociation)* delinking, decoupling ◆ **le ~ croissance-emploi** the fact that there is no longer any connection between industrial growth and employment

découplé, e / dekuple / ADJ ◆ **bien ~** well-built

découpler / dekuple / ▸ conjug 1 ◂ VT *(Élec)* to decouple; *(Chasse)* to uncouple; *(= dissocier)* to delink, to decouple *(de* from); ◆ **le pays n'a pas voulu ~ son économie de celles de ses partenaires** the country did not want to delink its economy from that of its partners

découpure / dekupyʀ / NF 1 *(= forme, contour)* jagged *ou* indented outline 2 ◆ **~s** *(= échancrures) [de côte]* indentations; *[d'arête]* jagged *ou* indented edge *ou* outline; *[de dentelle, guirlande]* scalloped edge 3 *(= morceau)* bit *ou* piece *(that has been cut out)* ◆ **~s de papier** cut-out bits of paper

décourageant, e / dekuʀaʒɑ̃, ɑ̃t / ADJ *[nouvelle, situation]* discouraging; *[élève, travail]* unrewarding

découragement / dekuʀaʒmɑ̃ / NM despondency ◆ **un ~ profond** a feeling of deep despondency ◆ **le ~ gagne** there is a growing feeling of despondency ◆ **le ~ des enseignants** the demoralization felt by teachers

décourager / dekuʀaʒe / ▸ conjug 3 ◂ VT 1 *(= démoraliser)* to discourage, to dishearten ◆ **il ne faut pas se laisser ~ par un échec** one must not be discouraged *ou* disheartened by failure 2 *(= dissuader) [+ personne]* to discourage, to put off; *[+ chose]* to discourage ◆ **le gouvernement a tout fait pour ~ la spéculation** the government has done everything in its power to discourage speculation ◆ **pour ~ les malfaiteurs** to deter criminals ◆ **~ qn de qch/de faire qch** to discourage sb from sth/from doing sth, to put sb off sth/doing sth ◆ **~ qn d'une entreprise** to discourage *ou* deter sb from an undertaking, to put sb off an undertaking VPR **se décourager** to lose heart, to become disheartened *ou* discouraged ◆ **ne nous décourageons pas** let's not lose heart

découronner / dekuʀɔne / ▸ conjug 1 ◂ VT *[+ roi]* to dethrone, to depose ◆ **arbre découronné par la tempête** tree that has had its topmost branches blown off by the storm

décours / dekuʀ / NM 1 *(Astron)* wane ◆ **au ~ de la lune** when the moon is *(ou* was) waning 2 *(Méd)* regression ◆ **au ~ de la maladie** during the regression phase of the illness ◆ **au ~ de la fièvre** when the fever is *(ou* was) abating

décousu, e / dekuzy / (ptp de **découdre**) ADJ 1 *(Couture)* unstitched ◆ **couture ~e** seam that has come unstitched *ou* unsewn ◆ **ourlet ~** hem that has come down ◆ **ta robe est ~e à la manche** your dress is coming apart at the sleeve 2 *[style]* disjointed, desultory; *[idées]* disconnected, unconnected; *[dissertation, travail]* scrappy, disjointed; *[paroles, conversation]* disjointed, desultory NM *[de style]* disjointedness, desultoriness; *[d'idées, raisonnement]* disconnectedness

découvert, e[1] / dekuvɛʀ, ɛʀt / (ptp de **découvrir**) ADJ 1 *(= mis à nu) [épaules, corps, tête]* bare, uncovered *(attrib)*; → **visage**

2 *(= sans protection) [lieu]* open, exposed; *[piscine]* open-air *(épith)*, outdoor *(épith)* ◆ **en terrain ~** in open country *ou* terrain ◆ **allée ~e** open avenue

NM *(Fin) [de firme, compte]* overdraft; *[de caisse]* deficit; *[d'objet assuré]* uncovered amount *ou* sum ◆ **~ du Trésor** Treasury deficit ◆ **~ bancaire** bank overdraft ◆ **~ budgétaire/de trésorerie** budget/cash deficit ◆ **tirer de l'argent à ~** to overdraw one's account ◆ **mon compte est/je suis à ~** my account is/I am overdrawn ◆ **crédit à ~** unsecured credit ◆ **vendre à ~** to sell short ◆ **vente à ~** short sale

◆ **à découvert** ◆ **être à ~ dans un champ** to be exposed *ou* without cover in a field ◆ **la plage laissée à ~ par la marée** the beach left exposed by the tide ◆ **mettre qch à ~** to expose sth, to bring sth into the open ◆ **parler à ~** to speak frankly *ou* openly ◆ **agir à ~** to act openly

découverte[2] / dekuvɛʀt / NF 1 *(= action)* discovery; *(= objet)* find, discovery ◆ **aller *ou* partir à la ~ de** to go off to explore ◆ **jeune homme, il part à la ~ de l'Amérique** as a young man, he sets off to explore America ◆ **faire une ~** to make a discovery ◆ **faire la ~ de** to discover ◆ **montre-moi ta ~** show me what you've found ◆ **ce n'est pas une ~ !*** that's hardly news!, so what's new?* 2 *(Art, Photo)* background

découvreur, -euse / dekuvʀœʀ, øz / NM,F discoverer ◆ **~ de talents** talent scout

découvrir / dekuvʀiʀ / ▸ conjug 18 ◂ VT 1 *(= trouver) [+ trésor, loi scientifique, terre inconnue]* to discover; *[+ indices, complot]* to discover, to unearth; *[+ cause, vérité]* to discover, to find out, to unearth; *[+ personne cachée]* to discover, to find ◆ **~ que ...** to discover *ou* find out that ... ◆ **il veut ~ comment/pourquoi c'est arrivé** he wants to find out how/why it happened ◆ **je lui ai découvert des qualités insoupçonnées** I have discovered some unsuspected qualities in him ◆ **il a découvert l'amour à 50 ans** he found love at the age of 50 ◆ **il craint d'être découvert** *(percé à jour)* he is afraid of being found out, *(trouvé)* he is afraid of being found ◆ **quand ils découvriront le pot aux roses*** when they find out what's been going on

◆ **faire découvrir** ◆ **faire ~ la musique/la peinture à qn** to introduce sb to music/painting ◆ **ce livre vous fera ~ un Paris insolite** this book will show you Paris as few people see it ◆ **il m'a fait ~ un monde que je ne soupçonnais pas** he showed me a world I never knew existed

2 *(= enlever ce qui couvre, protège) [+ plat, casserole]* to take the lid *ou* cover off; *[+ voiture]* to open the roof of; *[+ statue]* to unveil; *(Échecs) [+ roi]* to uncover; *(Mil) [+ frontière]* to expose, to uncover; *[+ corps]* to uncover; *[+ membres, poitrine, épaules, tête]* to bare, to uncover; *(= mettre à jour) [+ ruines]* to uncover ◆ **elle enleva les housses et découvrit les meubles** she removed the dust sheets and uncovered the furniture ◆ **il découvrit son torse/avant-bras** he bared *ou* uncovered his torso/forearm ◆ **il resta découvert devant elle** he kept his hat off in her presence ◆ **ils découvrirent leur aile gauche** *(Mil)* they exposed their left wing, they left their left wing open to attack

3 *(= laisser voir)* to reveal ◆ **une robe qui découvre le dos** a dress cut low at the back ◆ **son sourire découvre des dents superbes** when he smiles he shows his beautiful teeth

4 *(= voir)* to see, to have a view of; *(Naut) [+ terre]* to sight ◆ **du haut de la falaise on découvre toute la baie** from the top of the cliff you have a view of the whole bay

5 *(= révéler, dévoiler) [+ projets, intentions, motifs]* to reveal, to disclose *(à qn* to sb); ◆ **~ son cœur** to lay bare *ou* open one's heart ◆ **~ son jeu** to show one's hand

VI *[mer]* to recede

VPR **se découvrir** 1 *(= ôter son chapeau)* to take off one's hat; *(= ôter ses habits)* to undress, to take off one's clothes; *(= perdre ses couvertures)* to throw off the bedclothes, to uncover o.s. ◆ **en altitude on doit se ~ le moins possible** at high altitudes you must keep covered up as much as possible; → **avril**

2 *(Boxe, Escrime)* to leave o.s. open; *(Mil, fig)* to expose o.s., to leave o.s. open to attack

3 *[ciel, temps]* to clear ◆ **ça va se ~** it will soon clear

4 *(= trouver)* **elle s'est découvert un cousin en Amérique/un talent pour la peinture** she found out *ou* discovered she had a cousin in America/a gift for painting ◆ **c'est dans les épreuves qu'on se découvre** one finds *ou* discovers one's true self in testing situations

décrassage / dekʀasaʒ /, **décrassement** / dekʀasmɑ̃ / NM *[d'objet boueux, graisseux]* cleaning; *[de chaudière]* cleaning, cleaning-out; *[de bougie de moteur]* cleaning-up ◆ **un bon ~*** *(= toilette)* a good scrubbing-down *ou* clean-up

décrasser / dekʀase / ▸ conjug 1 ◂ VT 1 *[+ enfant]* to scrub clean; *[+ objet boueux, graisseux]* to clean, to get the mud *(ou* grease *etc)* off; *(en frottant)* to scrub; *(en trempant)* to soak the dirt out of; *[+ chaudière]* to clean out, to clean; *[+ bougie de moteur]* to clean (up) ◆ **se ~** *[personne]* to give o.s. a good scrub, to clean o.s. up ◆ **se ~ le visage/les mains** to give one's face/hands a good clean ◆ **le bon air, ça décrasse les poumons** fresh air cleans out the lungs ◆ **rouler à cette vitesse, ça décrasse le moteur** driving at that speed gives the engine a good decoking *(Brit) ou* cleans the engine out well 2 *(fig = dégrossir)* to take the rough edges off

décrédibilisation / dekʀedibilizasjɔ̃ / NF loss of credibility

décrédibiliser / dekʀedibilize / ▸ conjug 1 ◂ VT *[+ personne, organisation]* to undermine the credibility of

décrêper / dekʀepe / ▸ conjug 1 ◂ VT *[+ cheveux]* to straighten

décrépir / dekʀepiʀ / ▸ conjug 2 ◂ VT *[+ mur]* to remove the roughcast from ◆ **façade décrépie** peeling façade VPR **se décrépir** *[mur]* to peel

décrépit, e / dekʀepi, it / ADJ *[personne]* decrepit; *[maison, mur]* dilapidated, decrepit

décrépitude / dekʀepityd / NF *[de personne]* decrepitude; *[de nation, institution, civilisation]* decay ◆ **tomber en ~** *[personne]* to become decrepit; *[nation]* to decay

decrescendo / dekʀeʃendo / ADV *(Mus)* decrescendo ◆ **sa réputation va ~** his reputation is declining *ou* waning NM *(Mus)* decrescendo

décret / dekʀɛ / NM *(Pol, Rel)* decree ◆ **~ d'application** *decree specifying how a law should be enforced* ◆ **gouverner par ~** to rule by decree ◆ **~-loi** government decree ◆ **les ~s de la Providence** *(littér)* the decrees of Providence

décréter / dekʀete / ▸ conjug 6 ◂ VT *[+ mobilisation]* to order; *[+ état d'urgence]* to declare; *[+ mesure]* to decree ◆ **le président a décrété la nomination d'un nouveau ministre** the president ordered the appointment of a new minister ◆ **~ que** *[gouvernement, patron]* to decree *ou* order that; *(Rel)* to ordain *ou* decree that ◆ **il a décrété qu'il ne mangerait plus de betteraves** he swore that he wouldn't eat beetroot any more ◆ **j'ai décrété que je n'irai pas** I have decided that I won't go

décrier / dekʀije / ▸ conjug 7 ◂ VT *[+ œuvre, mesure, principe, auteur]* to decry *(littér)*, to disparage, to downcry *(US)* ◆ **la chasteté, une vertu si décriée de nos jours** chastity, a much disparaged virtue nowadays ◆ **ces auteurs maintenant si décriés par la critique** these authors now so disparaged by the critics ◆ **il décria**

fort ma conduite he (strongly) censured my behaviour

décriminalisation /dekʀiminalizasjɔ̃/ NF decriminalization

décriminaliser /dekʀiminalize/ ► conjug 1 ◄ VT to decriminalize

décrire /dekʀiʀ/ ► conjug 39 ◄ VT 1 *(= dépeindre)* to describe 2 *[+ trajectoire]* to follow; *[+ cercle, ellipse]* to describe ◆ **l'oiseau/l'avion décrivait des cercles au-dessus de nos têtes** the bird/plane flew in circles overhead ◆ **la route décrit une courbe** the road makes *ou* follows a curve ◆ **le satellite décrit une ellipse** the satellite follows *ou* makes *ou* describes an elliptical orbit

décrispation /dekʀispasjɔ̃/ NF *(Pol)* easing of tension *(entre* between); ◆ **il y a des signes de ~ politique** there are signs that the political tension is easing

décrisper /dekʀispe/ ► conjug 1 ◄ VT *[+ situation]* to defuse; *[+ personne]* to relax ◆ **pour ~ les relations** to make relations less strained, to ease relations

décrochage /dekʀɔʃaʒ/ NM 1 *[de rideaux]* taking down, unhooking; *[de wagon]* uncoupling 2 *(Mil)* **opérer un ~** to disengage, to break off the action 3 *(Radio, TV)* switchover 4 *(Fin)* **le ~ du franc par rapport au mark** the decoupling *ou* unpegging of the franc from the mark 5 *(en avion)* stalling ◆ **faire un ~** to stall 6 *(Scol)* ◆ **être en situation de ~ scolaire** to be doing badly at school

décrochement /dekʀɔʃmɑ̃/ NM 1 *[de wagon]* uncoupling 2 *(Géol)* thrust fault, slide 3 *(Constr) (en retrait)* recess; *(en saillie)* projection ◆ **le mur présente un ~** *(en retrait)* the wall is recessed; *(en saillie)* the wall juts out 4 *(Fin)* ⇒ **décrochage d**

décrocher /dekʀɔʃe/ ► conjug 1 ◄ VT 1 *(= détacher) [+ tableau]* to take down; *[+ rideau]* to take down, to unhook; *[+ vêtement]* to take down, to take off the hook *ou* peg; *[+ fermoir]* to undo, to unclasp; *[+ poisson]* to unhook; *[+ wagon]* to uncouple ◆ **il n'a pas pu ~ son cerf-volant qui s'était pris dans l'arbre** he couldn't free *ou* unhook his kite which had got caught in the tree ◆ **~ le reste du peloton** *(Sport)* to leave the pack behind ◆ **~ le franc du mark** *(Fin)* to decouple *ou* unpeg the franc from the mark

2 *[+ téléphone] (pour répondre)* to pick up, to lift; *(pour l'empêcher de sonner)* to take off the hook ◆ **ne décroche pas !** don't answer it! ◆ **le téléphone est décroché** the telephone is off the hook

3 *(* = obtenir) [+ prix, contrat, poste, récompense]* to get, to land* ◆ **il a décroché une belle situation** he's landed a plum job* ◆ **~ le gros lot** *ou* **la timbale** *(lit, fig)* to hit the jackpot; → **lune, pompon**

VI 1 *(Mil)* to pull back, to break off the action; *[coureur]* to fall behind

2 * *(= abandonner, ne pas suivre)* to fall by the wayside, to fail to keep up; *(= se désintéresser)* to drop out, to opt out; *(= cesser d'écouter)* to switch off*

3 *(arg Drogue)* to come off

4 *(Fin)* **le franc a décroché du mark** *(= a perdu du terrain)* the franc lost ground against the mark

5 *(Radio, TV)* to go off the air

6 *(Aviat)* to stall

VPR **se décrocher** *[tableau, vêtement]* to fall down *ou* off; *[rideau]* to fall down, to come unhooked; *[fermoir]* to come undone; *[poisson]* to get unhooked; *[wagon]* to come uncoupled ◆ **le cerf-volant pris dans l'arbre s'est finalement décroché** the kite which had been caught in the tree finally came free; → **bâiller**

décroiser /dekʀwaze/ ► conjug 1 ◄ VT *[+ jambes]* to uncross; *[+ bras]* to unfold; *[+ fils]* to untwine, to untwist

décroissance /dekʀwasɑ̃s/ NF *(= diminution)* decline, decrease *(de* in)

décroissant, e /dekʀwasɑ̃, ɑ̃t/ ADJ *(gén)* decreasing, diminishing, declining; *[bruit]* fading; *[vitesse]* decreasing, falling ◆ **par ordre ~** in decreasing *ou* descending order

décroissement /dekʀwasmɑ̃/ NM *[de jours]* shortening; *[de lune]* waning

décroît /dekʀwa/ NM *[de lune]* ◆ **dans** *ou* **sur son ~** in its last quarter

décroître /dekʀwatʀ/ ► conjug 55 ◄ VI *[nombre, population, intensité, pouvoir]* to decrease, to diminish, to decline; *[eaux, fièvre]* to subside, to go down; *[popularité]* to decline, to drop; *[vitesse]* to drop; *[force]* to decline, to diminish, to fail; *[revenus]* to get less, to diminish; *[lune]* to wane; *[jours]* to get shorter; *[silhouette]* to get smaller and smaller; *[bruit]* to die away, to fade; *[lumière]* to fade, to grow fainter *ou* dimmer ◆ **ses forces vont (en) décroissant** his strength is failing *ou* gradually diminishing *ou* declining ◆ **cette ville a beaucoup décru en importance** this town has greatly declined in importance

décrotter /dekʀɔte/ ► conjug 1 ◄ VT *[+ chaussures]* to scrape the mud off; *(fig) [+ rustre]* to take the rough edges off

décrottoir /dekʀɔtwaʀ/ NM *(= lame)* mudscraper, shoescraper; *(= paillasson)* wire (door) mat

décrue /dekʀy/ NF *[d'eaux, rivière]* fall *ou* drop in level *(de* of); *[de taux d'intérêt]* drop *(de* in); *[de popularité]* decline, drop *(de* in); ◆ **la ~ des eaux atteint deux mètres** the water level *ou* flood-level has fallen *ou* dropped by two metres ◆ **au moment de la ~** when the water level drops

décryptage /dekʀiptaʒ/, **décryptement** /dekʀiptəmɑ̃/ NM deciphering; *(Ordin, TV)* decryption , unscrambling

décrypter /dekʀipte/ ► conjug 1 ◄ VT *(= décoder) [+ message, code, génome]* to decipher; *(Ordin, TV)* to decrypt ◆ **~ l'attitude de qn** *(= élucider)* to work sb out, to understand sb's attitude

déçu, e /desy/ (ptp de **décevoir**) ADJ disappointed ◆ **j'ai été très ~ d'apprendre que ...** I was very disappointed to find out that ... ◆ **elle ne va pas être ~e du voyage !*** *(iro)* she's going to be over the moon! * *(iro)*

de cujus /dekyʒys, dekujus/ NM INV *(Jur)* ◆ **le ~** the deceased

déculottée‡ /dekylɔte/ NF *(= défaite)* clobbering*, hammering* ◆ **prendre** *ou* **recevoir une ~** to get a hammering* *ou* clobbering*

déculotter /dekylɔte/ ► conjug 1 ◄ VT ◆ **~ qn** to take down sb's trousers VPR **se déculotter** *(lit)* to take down one's trousers; *(‡ = s'humilier)* to lie down and take it*

déculpabilisation /dekylpabilizasjɔ̃/ NF *[de personne]* removal of guilt feelings ◆ **la ~ du divorce** taking away the guilt associated with divorce

déculpabiliser /dekylpabilize/ ► conjug 1 ◄ VT ◆ **~ qn** to remove sb's guilt feelings ◆ **~ le divorce** to take away the guilt associated with divorce

déculturation /dekyltyʀasjɔ̃/ NF loss of cultural identity

décuple /dekypl/ ADJ tenfold ◆ **un revenu ~ du mien** an income ten times as large as mine NM ◆ **20 est le ~ de 2** 20 is ten times 2 ◆ **il gagne le ~ de ce que je gagne** he earns ten times what I earn ◆ **il me l'a rendu au ~** he paid me back tenfold

décuplement /dekypləmɑ̃/ NM *(lit)* tenfold increase ◆ **grâce au ~ de nos forces** thanks to our greatly increased strength

décupler /dekyple/ ► conjug 1 ◄ VTI to increase tenfold ◆ **la colère décuplait ses forces** anger gave him the strength of ten

dédaignable /dedeɲabl/ ADJ ◆ **ce n'est pas ~** it's not to be sniffed at

dédaigner /dedeɲe/ ► conjug 1 ◄ VT 1 *(= mépriser) [+ personne]* to despise, to look down on, to scorn; *[+ honneurs, richesse]* to scorn, to despise ◆ **il ne dédaigne pas de rire avec ses subordonnés** he doesn't consider it beneath him to joke with his subordinates ◆ **il ne dédaigne pas un verre de vin de temps à autre** he's not averse to the occasional glass of wine 2 *(= négliger) [+ offre, adversaire]* to spurn; *[+ menaces, insultes]* to disregard, to discount ◆ **ce n'est pas à ~** *(honneur, offre)* it's not to be sniffed at; *(danger, adversaire)* it can't just be shrugged off ◆ **il dédaigna de répondre/d'y aller** he did not deign to reply/go

dédaigneusement /dedeɲøzmɑ̃/ ADV disdainfully, scornfully, contemptuously

dédaigneux, -euse /dedeɲø, øz/ ADJ *[personne, air]* scornful, disdainful, contemptuous ◆ **~ de** contemptuous *ou* scornful *ou* disdainful of ◆ **il est ~ de plaire** *(littér)* he scorns to please

dédain /dedɛ̃/ NM contempt, scorn, disdain *(de* for); ◆ **sourire de ~** disdainful *ou* scornful smile

dédale /dedal/ NM 1 *[de rues, idées, lois]* maze 2 *(Myth)* **Dédale** Daedalus

dedans /dədɑ̃/ ADV 1 *(= à l'intérieur)* inside; *(= pas à l'air libre)* indoors, inside ◆ **voulez-vous dîner dehors ou ~ ?** do you want to have dinner outside or inside? *ou* outdoors or indoors? ◆ **au-~** inside ◆ **la maison est laide, mais** *ou* **au-~ c'est très joli** it's an ugly-looking house but it's lovely inside ◆ **nous sommes restés ~ toute la journée** we stayed in *ou* inside *ou* indoors all day ◆ **elle cherche son sac, tout son argent est ~** she is looking for her bag, it's got all her money in it ◆ **prenez ce fauteuil, on est bien ~** have this chair, you'll be comfortable in it *ou* you'll find it comfortable ◆ **de** *ou* **du ~ on n'entend rien** you can't hear a sound from inside ◆ **passez par ~ pour aller au jardin** go through the house to get to the garden ◆ **la crise ? on est en plein ~ !** the crisis? we're right in the middle of it!

2 *(locutions)* **être ~** *(Cartes)* to lose *(de* by); ◆ **mettre*** *ou* **ficher*** *ou* **foutre**‡ **qn ~** to get sb confused, to make sb get it wrong ◆ **il s'est fait mettre ~**‡ he got himself put away‡ *ou* put inside‡ ◆ **il s'est fichu*** *ou* **foutu**‡ **~** he got it all wrong* ◆ **un bus lui est rentré ~*** a bus hit him *ou* ran into him ◆ **il a dérapé, il y avait un arbre, il est rentré** *ou* **entré ~*** he skidded. there was a tree and he ran *ou* went *ou* crashed straight into it

◆ **en dedans** ◆ **fleur blanche en dehors et jaune en ~** *(= à l'intérieur)* a flower that's white (on the) outside and yellow (on the) inside ◆ **ces volets s'ouvrent en ~** *(= vers l'intérieur)* these shutters open inwards ◆ **avoir** *ou* **marcher les pieds en ~** to be pigeon-toed ◆ **ne marche pas les pieds en ~** don't walk with your feet turned in

NM *[d'objet, bâtiment]* inside ◆ **le coup a été préparé du ~** it's an inside job

dédicace /dedikas/ NF 1 *(imprimée)* dedication; *(manuscrite) [de livre, photo]* dedication, inscription *(à* to) 2 *[d'église]* consecration, dedication

dédicacer /dedikase/ ► conjug 3 ◄ VT *[+ livre, photo] (= signer)* to sign, to autograph *(à qn* for sb); *(= dédier)* to dedicate *(à* to)

> ⚠ Au sens de 'signer', **dédicacer** ne se traduit pas par **to dedicate**.

dédicataire /dedikatɛʀ/ NMF dedicatee

dédicatoire /dedikatwaʀ/ ADJ dedicatory, dedicative

dédié, e /dedje/ (ptp de **dédier**) ADJ *[équipement, ligne, ordinateur]* dedicated

dédier /dedje/ ► conjug 7 ◄ **dédier à** VT *(Rel)* to consecrate to, to dedicate to ◆ **~ ses efforts à** to devote ou dedicate one's efforts to ◆ **~ un livre à** to dedicate a book to

dédire (se) /dediʀ/ ► conjug 37 ◄ VPR [1] *(= manquer à ses engagements)* to go back on one's word ◆ **se ~ d'une promesse** to go back on a promise [2] *(= se rétracter)* to retract, to recant ◆ **se ~ d'une affirmation** to withdraw a statement, to retract (a statement); → **cochon**

dédit /dedi/ NM [1] *(= somme)* forfeit, penalty ◆ **un ~ de 5 000 €** a 5,000 euro penalty [2] *(= rétractation)* retraction; *(= manquement aux engagements)* failure to keep one's word; *(= non-paiement)* default ◆ **en cas de ~ il faut payer un supplément** in case of default a supplement must be paid

dédommagement /dedɔmaʒmɑ̃/ NM compensation ◆ **en ~, je lui ai donné une bouteille de vin** in compensation ou to make up for it, I gave him a bottle of wine ◆ **en ~ des dégâts** ou **à titre de ~ pour les dégâts, on va me donner 100 €** they will give me €100 in compensation for the damage ◆ **en ~ du mal que je vous donne** to make up for the trouble I'm causing you

dédommager /dedɔmaʒe/ ► conjug 3 ◄ VT *(= indemniser)* ◆ **~ qn** to compensate sb *(de* for) to give sb compensation *(de* for); ◆ **je l'ai dédommagé en lui donnant une bouteille de vin** I gave him a bottle of wine in compensation ou to make up for it ◆ **~ qn d'une perte** to compensate sb for a loss, to make good sb's loss ◆ **comment vous ~ du dérangement que je vous cause ?** how can I ever make up for the trouble I'm causing? ◆ **le succès le dédommage de toutes ses peines** his success is compensation ou compensates for all his troubles

dédoré, e /dedɔʀe/ (ptp de **dédorer**) ADJ *[bijou, tableau]* which has lost its gilt, tarnished; *(fig) [noblesse]* faded

dédorer /dedɔʀe/ ► conjug 1 ◄ VT to remove the gilt from

dédouanage /dedwanaʒ/, **dédouanement** /dedwanmɑ̃/ NM *(Comm)* clearing ou clearance through customs, customs clearance; * *[de personne]* clearing (the name of), putting in the clear*

dédouaner /dedwane/ ► conjug 1 ◄ VT *(Comm)* to clear through customs; *(* = réhabiliter) [+ personne]* to clear (the name of), to put in the clear* ◆ **marchandises dédouanées** duty-paid goods ◆ **se ~** to clear one's name

dédoublement /dedubləmɑ̃/ NM *[de classe]* dividing ou splitting in two; *[d'ongles]* splitting ◆ **le ~ d'un train** the running of a relief train ◆ **le ~ de la personnalité est un trouble grave** *(Psych)* having a split ou dual personality is a serious illness ◆ **souffrir d'un ~ de la personnalité** to suffer from a split ou dual personality

dédoubler /deduble/ ► conjug 1 ◄ VT [1] *[+ manteau]* to remove the lining of [2] *[+ classe]* to split ou divide in two; *[+ ficelle]* to separate the strands of ◆ **~ un train** to run ou put on a relief train ◆ **pour Noël on a dû ~ tous les trains** at Christmas they had to run additional trains on all services [3] *[+ couverture]* to unfold, to open out VPR **se dédoubler** *(= se déplier)* to unfold, to open out; *[ongles]* to split ◆ **dans les cas où la personnalité se dédouble** in cases of split ou dual personality ◆ **je ne peux pas me ~** * I can't be in two places at once ◆ **l'image se dédoublait dans l'eau** there was a double outline reflected in the water

dédramatisation /dedʀamatizasjɔ̃/ NF *(= minimisation) [événement, situation]* playing down the importance of ◆ **au gouvernement, le ton est à la ~** the government is trying to play things down ◆ **le patient fait un travail de ~ de sa maladie** the patient tries to come to terms with his illness

dédramatiser /dedʀamatize/ ► conjug 1 ◄ VT *[+ examen, opération]* to make less alarming ou awesome; *[+ problème]* to play down the importance of; *[+ débat]* to take the heat out of ◆ **il faut ~ la situation** we mustn't overdramatize the situation

déductible /dedyktibl/ ADJ *(Fin) [frais, somme]* deductible *(de* from); ◆ **~ du revenu imposable** tax-deductible ◆ **dépenses non ~s** non-deductible expenses

déductif, -ive /dedyktif, iv/ ADJ deductive

déduction /dedyksjɔ̃/ NF [1] *(= abattement)* deduction ◆ **~ fiscale** tax deduction ◆ **~ forfaitaire** standard deduction ◆ **~ faite de** after deducting, after deduction of ◆ **ça entre en ~ de ce que vous nous devez** that's deductible from what you owe us, that'll be taken off what you owe us [2] *(= forme de raisonnement)* deduction, inference; *(= conclusion)* conclusion, inference

déduire /dedɥiʀ/ ► conjug 38 ◄ VT [1] *(= soustraire)* to deduct *(de* from); ◆ **tous frais déduits** after deduction of expenses [2] *(= conclure)* to deduce, to infer *(de* from)

déesse /dees/ NF goddess ◆ **elle a un corps/port de ~** she's got the body/bearing of a goddess

de facto /defakto/ LOC ADV de facto ◆ **reconnaître qch ~** to give de facto recognition to sth ◆ **~, il devient président** he becomes de facto president

défaillance /defajɑ̃s/ NF [1] *(= évanouissement)* blackout; *(= faiblesse physique)* feeling of weakness ou faintness; *(= faiblesse morale)* weakness, failing ◆ **avoir une ~** *(évanouissement)* to faint, to have a blackout; *(faiblesse)* to feel faint ou weak ◆ **l'athlète a eu une ~ au troisième kilomètre** the athlete seemed to be in difficulty ou to be weakening at the third kilometre ◆ **il a eu plusieurs ~s ces derniers jours** he has had several weak spells these last few days ◆ **faire son devoir sans ~** to do one's duty without flinching

[2] *(= mauvais fonctionnement)* (mechanical) fault, failure, breakdown *(de* in); ◆ **l'accident était dû à une ~ de la machine** the accident was caused by a fault in the machine

[3] *(= insuffisance)* weakness ◆ **élève qui a des ~s (en histoire)** pupil who has certain shortcomings ou weak points (in history) ◆ **devant la ~ du gouvernement** faced with the weakness of the government ou the government's failure to act ◆ **mémoire sans ~** faultless memory

[4] *(Jur)* default ◆ **~ d'entreprise** bankruptcy

COMP **défaillance cardiaque** heart failure
défaillance mécanique mechanical fault
défaillance de mémoire lapse of memory

défaillant, e /defajɑ̃, ɑ̃t/ ADJ [1] *(= affaibli) [forces]* failing, declining; *[santé, mémoire, raison]* failing; *[courage, volonté]* faltering, weakening; *[cœur]* weak [2] *(= tremblant) [voix, pas]* unsteady, faltering; *[main]* unsteady [3] *(= près de s'évanouir) [personne]* weak, faint *(de* with) [4] *[matériel, installation]* faulty; *[pouvoir, gouvernement]* shaky [5] *(Jur) [partie, témoin]* defaulting ◆ **client ~** client who defaults ou has defaulted ◆ **candidat ~** candidate who fails (ou who has failed) to appear

défaillir /defajiʀ/ ► conjug 13 ◄ VI [1] *(= s'évanouir)* to faint ◆ **elle défaillait de bonheur/de faim** she felt faint with happiness/hunger [2] *(= faiblir) [forces]* to weaken, to fail; *[courage, volonté]* to falter, to weaken; *[mémoire]* to fail ◆ **faire son devoir sans ~** to do one's duty without flinching

défaire /defɛʀ/ ► conjug 60 ◄ VT [1] *(= démonter) [+ échafaudage]* to take down, to dismantle; *[+ installation électrique]* to dismantle; *[+ sapin de Noël]* to take down

[2] *(= découdre, dénouer) [+ couture, tricot]* to undo, to unpick *(Brit)*; *[+ écheveau]* to undo, to unravel, to unwind; *[+ corde, nœud, ruban]* to undo, to untie; *[+ cheveux, nattes]* to undo

[3] *(= ouvrir) [+ courroie, fermeture, robe]* to undo, to unfasten; *[+ valise]* to unpack ◆ **~ ses bagages** to unpack (one's luggage) ◆ **~ le lit** *(pour changer les draps)* to strip the bed; *(pour se coucher)* to pull back the sheets; *(mettre en désordre)* to unmake ou rumple the bed

[4] *(= détruire) [+ mariage]* to break up; *[+ contrat, traité]* to break ◆ **cela défit tous nos plans** it ruined all our plans ◆ **il (faisait et) défaisait les rois** he (made and) unmade kings ◆ **elle se plaît à ~ tout ce que j'essaie de faire pour elle** she takes pleasure in undoing everything I try to do for her ◆ **la maladie l'avait défait** his illness had left him shattered ◆ **la douleur défaisait ses traits** his face was contorted with pain

[5] *(= battre) (littér) [+ ennemi, armée]* to defeat

[6] *(= débarrasser) (littér)* **~ qn de** *[+ liens, gêneur]* to rid sb of, to relieve sb of, to deliver sb from *(littér)*; *[+ habitude]* to break sb of, to cure sb of, to rid sb of; *[+ défaut]* to cure sb of, to rid sb of

VPR **se défaire** [1] *[nœud, ficelle, coiffure]* to come undone; *[couture]* to come undone ou apart; *[légumes, viande] (à la cuisson)* to fall to pieces, to disintegrate; *[mariage, amitié]* to break up

[2] *(= se déformer)* **ses traits se défirent, son visage se défit** his face crumpled, his face twisted with grief *(ou pain etc)*

[3] *(locution)*

◆ **se défaire de** *(= se débarrasser de) [+ gêneur, vieillerie, odeur]* to get rid of; *[+ image, idée]* to put ou get out of one's mind; *[+ habitude]* to break ou cure o.s. of, to get rid of; *[+ défaut]* to cure o.s. of; *[+ souvenir]* to part with

défait, e[1] /defɛ, ɛt/ (ptp de **défaire**) ADJ [1] *[visage]* ravaged, haggard; *[cheveux]* tousled, dishevelled ◆ **il était complètement ~** he looked terribly haggard [2] *[lit]* unmade, rumpled [3] *[armée]* defeated

défaite[2] /defɛt/ NF *(Mil)* defeat; *(= échec)* defeat, failure ◆ **la ~ de notre équipe** our team's defeat ◆ **~ électorale** electoral defeat

défaitisme /defetism/ NM defeatism

défaitiste /defetist/ ADJ, NMF defeatist

défalcation /defalkasjɔ̃/ NF deduction ◆ **~ faite des frais** after deduction of expenses

défalquer /defalke/ ► conjug 1 ◄ VT to deduct

défatigant, e /defatigɑ̃, ɑ̃t/ ADJ *[lait, lotion]* soothing

défausse /defos/ NF *(Cartes)* discarding; *(fig)* prevarication ◆ **il excelle dans l'art de la ~** he excels the art of prevarication ◆ **pas question d'une ~ de l'État** there is no way the State can prevaricate

défausser (se) /defose/ ► conjug 1 ◄ VPR *(Cartes)* to discard, to throw out ou away ◆ **se ~ (d'une carte)** to discard ◆ **il s'est défaussé à trèfle** he discarded a club

défaut /defo/ NM [1] *[de pierre précieuse, métal]* flaw; *[d'étoffe, verre]* flaw, fault; *[de machine]* defect, fault; *[de bois]* blemish; *[de roman, tableau, système]* flaw, defect ◆ **sans ~** flawless, faultless

2 *[de personne]* fault, failing; *[de caractère]* defect, fault ◆ **chacun a ses petits ~s** we've all got our little faults *ou* our failings ◆ **il n'a aucun ~** he's perfect ◆ **la gourmandise n'est pas un gros ~** greediness isn't such a bad fault; → **curiosité**

3 *(= désavantage)* drawback ◆ **ce plan/cette voiture a ses ~s** this plan/car has its drawbacks ◆ **le ~ de** *ou* **avec* cette voiture, c'est que ...** the trouble *ou* snag* *ou* drawback with this car is that ...

4 *(= manque)* **~ de** *[+ raisonnement]* lack of; *[+ main-d'œuvre]* shortage of

5 *(locutions)*

◆ **faire défaut** *[temps, argent, talent]* to be lacking; *(Jur) [prévenu, témoin]* to default ◆ **la patience/le temps lui fait ~** he lacks patience/time ◆ **le courage lui a finalement fait ~** his courage failed him in the end ◆ **ses amis lui ont finalement fait ~** his friends let him down in the end ◆ **si ma mémoire ne me fait pas ~** if my memory serves me right

◆ **à défaut** ◆ **à ~ de** for lack *ou* want of ◆ **à ~ de vin, il boira du cidre** if there's no wine, he'll drink cider ◆ **elle cherche une table ovale, ou, à ~, ronde** she is looking for an oval table, or, failing that, a round one (will do)

◆ **en défaut** ◆ **être en ~** to be at fault *ou* in the wrong ◆ **c'est votre mémoire qui est en ~** it's your memory that's at fault ◆ **se mettre en ~** to put o.s. in the wrong ◆ **prendre qn en ~** to catch sb out ◆ **mettre les chiens en ~** *(Chasse)* to put the dogs off the scent

◆ **par défaut** by default ◆ **condamner/juger qn par ~** *(Jur)* to sentence/judge sb in absentia ◆ **calculer qch par ~** *(Math)* to calculate sth to the nearest decimal point ◆ **il pèche par ~** he doesn't try hard enough ◆ **le lecteur par ~** *(Ordin)* the default drive

COMP **défaut de comparution** *(Jur)* default, non-appearance, failure to appear
le défaut de la cuirasse *(lit, fig)* the chink in the armour
défaut d'élocution ⇒ **défaut de prononciation**
le défaut de l'épaule the hollow beneath the shoulder
défaut de fabrication manufacturing defect
défaut de masse *(Phys)* mass defect
défaut de paiement *(Jur)* default in payment, non-payment
défaut de prononciation speech impediment *ou* defect

défaut-congé (pl **défauts-congés**) /defokɔ̃ʒe/ NM *(Jur) dismissal of case through non-appearance of plaintiff*

défaveur /defavœʀ/ NF disfavour *(Brit)*, disfavor *(US) (auprès de* with); ◆ **être en ~** to be out of favour *(Brit) ou* favor *(US)*, to be in disfavour ◆ **s'attirer la ~ de** to incur the disfavour of

défavorable /defavɔʀabl/ ADJ unfavourable *(Brit)*, unfavorable *(US) (à* to); ◆ **voir qch d'un œil ~** to view sth with disfavour *(Brit) ou* disfavor *(US)*

défavorablement /defavɔʀabləmɑ̃/ ADV unfavourably

défavoriser /defavɔʀize/ ▸ conjug 1 ◂ VT *(= désavantager) [décision, loi]* to penalize; *[défaut, timidité]* to put at a disadvantage; *[examinateur, patron]* to put at an unfair disadvantage ◆ **il a défavorisé l'aîné** he treated the eldest less fairly (than the others) ◆ **j'ai été défavorisé par rapport aux autres candidats** I was put at an unfair disadvantage with respect to the other candidates ◆ **aider les couches les plus défavorisées de la population** to help the most underprivileged *ou* disadvantaged sections of the population

défécation /defekasjɔ̃/ NF *(Physiol)* defecation; *(Chim)* defecation, purification

défectif, -ive /defɛktif, iv/ ADJ *[verbe]* defective

défection /defɛksjɔ̃/ NF *[d'amis, alliés politiques]* desertion, defection; *[de troupes]* failure to give *ou* lend assistance; *[de candidats]* failure to attend *ou* appear; *[d'invités]* failure to appear ◆ **faire ~** *[partisans]* to fail to lend support; *[invités]* to fail to appear *ou* turn up ◆ **il y a eu plusieurs ~s** *(membres d'un parti)* a number of people have withdrawn their support; *(invités, candidats)* several people failed to appear

défectueux, -euse /defɛktɥø, øz/ ADJ *[matériel]* faulty, defective; *[raisonnement]* faulty

défectuosité /defɛktɥozite/ NF *(= état)* defectiveness, faultiness; *(= défaut)* imperfection, (slight) defect *ou* fault *(de* in)

défendable /defɑ̃dabl/ ADJ *(Mil) [ville]* defensible; *(= soutenable) [conduite]* defensible, justifiable; *[position]* tenable, defensible ◆ **il n'est pas ~** *(gén)* he has no excuse; *(Jur)* he cannot be defended

défendant /defɑ̃dɑ̃/ (prp de **défendre**) → **corps**

défendeur, -deresse /defɑ̃dœʀ, dʀɛs/ NM,F *(Jur)* defendant ◆ **~ en appel** respondent

défendre /defɑ̃dʀ/ ▸ conjug 41 ◂ VT 1 *(= protéger) (gén, Jur, Mil)* to defend; *(= soutenir) [+ personne, opinion]* to stand up for, to defend *(contre* against); *[+ cause]* to champion, to defend *(contre* against); ◆ **ville défendue par deux forts** town defended *ou* protected by two forts ◆ **~ son bifteck*** *(fig)* to stand up for one's rights, to defend one's livelihood

2 *(= interdire)* **~ qch à qn** to forbid sb sth ◆ **~ à qn de faire qch** *ou* **qu'il fasse qch** to forbid sb to do sth ◆ **le médecin lui défend le tabac/la mer** the doctor has forbidden him *ou* won't allow him to smoke/to go to the seaside ◆ **il m'en a défendu l'accès** he forbade me access to it ◆ **~ sa porte à qn** to bar one's door to sb, to refuse to allow sb in ◆ **ne fais pas ça, c'est défendu** don't do that, it's not allowed *ou* it's forbidden ◆ **il est défendu de fumer** smoking is prohibited *ou* not allowed ◆ **il est défendu de parler** talking is not allowed; → **fruit¹**

VPR **se défendre** 1 *(= se protéger) (gén, Jur, Mil)* to defend o.s. *(contre* against); *(contre brimades, critiques)* to stand up for o.s., to defend o.s. *(contre* against); ◆ **se ~ du froid/de la pluie** to protect o.s. from the cold/rain

2 *(* = se débrouiller)* to manage, to get along *ou* by ◆ **elle se défend au tennis/au piano** she's not bad at tennis/on the piano ◆ **il se défend bien/mal en affaires** he gets on *ou* does quite well/he doesn't do very well in business ◆ **il se défend** he gets along *ou* by, he can hold his own (quite well)

3 *(= se justifier)* **se ~ d'avoir fait qch** to deny doing *ou* having done sth ◆ **il se défendit d'être vexé/jaloux** he denied being *ou* that he was annoyed/jealous ◆ **sa position/son point de vue se défend** his position/point of view is quite defensible ◆ **ça se défend !** *(raisonnement)* it holds *ou* hangs together ◆ **il dit que ce serait trop cher, ça se défend** he says it would be too expensive and he has a point *ou* it's a fair point

4 ◆ **se ~ de** *(= s'empêcher de)* to refrain from ◆ **il ne pouvait se ~ d'un sentiment de pitié/gêne** he couldn't help feeling pity/embarrassment ◆ **elle ne put se ~ de sourire** she could not refrain from smiling, she couldn't suppress a smile

⚠ Au sens de 'interdire', **défendre** ne se traduit pas par **to defend**.

défenestration /defənɛstʀasjɔ̃/ NF defenestration

défenestrer /defənɛstʀe/ ▸ conjug 1 ◂ VT to throw out of the *(ou* a) window, to defenestrate *(frm)* VPR **se défenestrer** to throw o.s. out of a window

défense¹ /defɑ̃s/ NF 1 *(contre agression)* defence *(Brit)*, defense *(US)* ◆ **~s** *(= fortifications)* defences ◆ **~ nationale/antiaérienne** *ou* **contre avions/passive** national/anti-aircraft/civil defence ◆ **le budget de la ~ (nationale)** the (national) defence budget ◆ **les ~s d'une frontière** border defences ◆ **la ~ du pays** the country's defence *ou* protection ◆ **ligne de ~** line of defence ◆ **ouvrage de ~** fortification ◆ **prendre la ~ de qn** to stand up for sb, to defend sb

2 *(= protection) [de droits, environnement]* protection ◆ **la ~ des opprimés** the defence *ou* protection of the oppressed ◆ **la ~ de l'emploi** job protection

3 *(= résistance)* defence *(Brit)*, defense *(US)* ◆ **opposer une ~ courageuse** to put up a brave defence ◆ **mécanisme/instinct de ~** defence mechanism/instinct ◆ **moyens de ~** means of defence ◆ **~s immunitaires** immune defence system ◆ **sans ~** *(= trop faible)* defenceless; *(= non protégé)* unprotected ◆ **sans ~ contre les tentations** helpless *ou* defenceless against temptation; → **légitime**

4 *(Sport)* defence *(Brit)*, defense *(US)* ◆ **jouer en ~** to play in defence

5 *(Jur)* defence *(Brit)*, defense *(US)*; *(= avocat)* counsel for the defence *(Brit)*, defense attorney *(US)* ◆ **assurer la ~ d'un accusé** to conduct the case for the defence ◆ **la parole est à la ~** (the counsel for) the defence may now speak ◆ **qu'avez-vous à dire pour votre ~ ?** what have you to say in your defence?

6 *(= interdiction)* **"défense d'entrer"** "no entrance", "no entry", "no admittance" ◆ **"propriété privée, défense d'entrer"** "private property, no admittance *ou* keep out" ◆ **"danger : défense d'entrer"** "danger – keep out" ◆ **"défense de fumer/stationner"** "no smoking/parking", "smoking/parking prohibited" ◆ **"défense d'afficher"** "(stick *ou* post) no bills" ◆ **~ d'en parler à quiconque** it is forbidden to speak of it to anyone ◆ **il est sorti malgré ma ~** he went out in spite of the fact that I'd told him not to *ou* in spite of my having forbidden him to do so

défense² /defɑ̃s/ NF *[d'éléphant, morse, sanglier]* tusk

défenseur /defɑ̃sœʀ/ NM *(gén, Mil, Sport)* defender; *[de cause]* champion, defender; *[de doctrine]* advocate; *(Jur)* counsel for the defence *(Brit)*, defense attorney *(US)* ◆ **l'accusé et son ~** the accused and his counsel ◆ **~ de l'environnement** conservationist, preservationist; → **veuf**

défensif, -ive /defɑ̃sif, iv/ ADJ *(Mil, fig)* defensive NF **défensive** ◆ **la défensive** the defensive ◆ **être** *ou* **se tenir sur la défensive** to be on the defensive

déféquer /defeke/ ▸ conjug 6 ◂ VI *(Physiol)* to defecate VT *(Chim)* to defecate, to purify

déférence /defeʀɑ̃s/ NF deference ◆ **par ~ pour** in deference to

déférent, e /defeʀɑ̃, ɑ̃t/ ADJ deferential, deferent; → **canal**

déférer /defeʀe/ ▸ conjug 6 ◂ VT 1 *(Jur)* **~ une affaire** to refer a case to the court ◆ **~ un coupable à la justice** to hand a guilty person over to the law 2 *(= céder)* to defer *(à* to) 3 († *= conférer)* to confer *(à* on, upon)

déferlante /defɛʀlɑ̃t/ ADJ F, NF ◆ **(vague) ~** breaker ◆ **la ~ de films américains/de produits nouveaux** the flood of American films/of new products

déferlement /defɛʀləmɑ̃/ NM *[de vagues]* breaking; *[de violence]* surge, spread; *[de véhicules, touristes]* flood ◆ **ils étaient impuissants devant le ~ des troupes** they were powerless before the advancing tide of troops ◆ **ce ~ d'enthousiasme le surprit** this sudden wave of enthusiasm surprised him ◆ **le ~ de haine/des sentiments anti-catholiques dans tout le pays** the hatred/anti-Catholic feeling which has engulfed the country *ou* swept through the country

déferler /defɛʀle/ ▸ conjug 1 ◂ VI *[vagues]* to break ◆ **la violence/haine déferla sur le pays** violence/hatred swept through the country ◆ **les touristes déferlaient sur les plages** tourists were streaming onto the beaches ◆ **la foule déferla dans la rue/sur la place** the crowd flooded into the street/over the square VT *[+ voile, pavillon]* to unfurl

déferrer /defeʀe/ ▸ conjug 1 ◂ VT *[+ cheval]* to unshoe; *[+ porte]* to remove the iron plates from

défi /defi/ NM *(gén)* challenge; *(= bravade)* defiance ◆ **lancer un ~ à qn** to challenge sb ◆ **relever un ~** to take up *ou* accept a challenge ◆ **mettre qn au ~** to challenge *ou* defy sb *(de faire* to do); ◆ **c'est un ~ au bon sens** it defies common sense, it goes against common sense ◆ **d'un air** *ou* **d'un ton de ~** defiantly

défiance /defjɑ̃s/ NF mistrust, distrust ◆ **avec ~** with mistrust *ou* distrust, mistrustingly, distrustingly ◆ **sans ~** *[personne]* unsuspecting; *[agir, s'abandonner]* unsuspectingly ◆ **mettre qn en ~** to arouse sb's mistrust *ou* suspicions, to make sb suspicious

défiant, e /defjɑ̃, jɑ̃t/ ADJ mistrustful, distrustful

défibrillateur /defibʀijatœʀ/ NM defibrillator

défibrillation /defibʀijasjɔ̃/ NF defibrillation

déficeler /defis(ə)le/ ▸ conjug 4 ◂ VT to untie VPR **se déficeler** *[paquet]* to come untied *ou* undone

déficience /defisjɑ̃s/ NF *(Méd, fig)* deficiency ◆ **~ musculaire** muscular insufficiency ◆ **~ immunitaire** immunodeficiency ◆ **~ de mémoire** lapse of memory ◆ **~ mentale** *ou* **intellectuelle** mental deficiency ◆ **les ~s du système de production** the deficiencies in *ou* shortcomings of the production system

déficient, e /defisjɑ̃, jɑ̃t/ ADJ *[force, intelligence]* deficient; *[raisonnement]* weak; *[matériel]* faulty, defective ◆ **enfant ~** *(intellectuellement)* mentally deficient child; *(physiquement)* child with a physical disability, physically disabled *ou* handicapped child NM,F ◆ **~ mental/visuel** mentally/visually handicapped person ◆ **~ moteur** person with motor deficiencies

déficit /defisit/ NM 1 *(Fin)* deficit ◆ **être en ~** to be in deficit ◆ **le ~ budgétaire** the budget deficit ◆ **le ~ de notre commerce extérieur** the deficit in our foreign trade ◆ **~ de la balance des paiements** balance of payments deficit ◆ **~ commercial/d'exploitation** trade/operating deficit ◆ **~ de trésorerie** cash deficit ◆ **les ~s sociaux** the social security budget deficit 2 *[manque]* **~ de ressources** resource(s) gap ◆ **~ en main d'œuvre** labour *(Brit) ou* labor *(US)* shortage ◆ **~ en magnésium** *(Méd)* magnesium deficiency ◆ **~ psychologique/intellectuel** psychological/mental defect ◆ **~ immunitaire** immunodeficiency

déficitaire /defisitɛʀ/ ADJ *(Fin)* in deficit *(attrib)*; *[récolte]* poor; *[année]* poor *(en* in) bad *(en* for); ◆ **~ en** *[main-d'œuvre]* short of, deficient in ◆ **année ~ en blé** year showing a wheat shortage

défier /defje/ ▸ conjug 7 ◂ VT 1 *(= déclarer trop lâche)* to challenge *(à* to); ◆ **~ qn en combat singulier** to challenge sb to single combat ◆ **~ qn du regard** to give sb a challenging look ◆ **je te défie de sauter du grand plongeoir** I challenge *ou* dare you to jump off the top board ◆ **je t'en défie !** I dare you (to)!

2 *(= braver) [+ mort, adversité]* to defy, to brave; *[+ opinion publique]* to fly in the face of, to defy; *[+ autorité]* to defy, to challenge ◆ **je vous défie de faire la différence entre les deux produits** I defy you tell the difference between these two products ◆ **ça défie l'imagination !** it defies the imagination! * ◆ **à des prix qui défient toute concurrence** at absolutely unbeatable prices

VPR **se défier** *(littér)* **se ~ de** to distrust, to mistrust ◆ **je me défie de moi-même** I don't trust myself ◆ **défie-toi de ton caractère impulsif** beware of your impulsiveness ◆ **défie-toi de lui !** beware of him!, be on your guard against him!

> ⚠ **défier** se traduit par **to defy** uniquement au sens de 'braver'.

défigurement /defigyʀmɑ̃/ NM *[de vérité]* distortion; *[de texte, tableau]* mutilation; *[de visage]* disfigurement

défigurer /defigyʀe/ ▸ conjug 1 ◂ VT 1 *[blessure, maladie]* to disfigure; *[bouton, larmes] [+ visage]* to spoil ◆ **l'acné qui la défigurait** the acne that spoiled her looks 2 *(= altérer) [+ pensée, réalité, vérité]* to distort; *[+ texte, tableau]* to mutilate, to deface; *[+ monument]* to deface; *[+ paysage]* to disfigure, to mar, to spoil

défilé /defile/ NM 1 *(= cortège)* procession; *(= manifestation)* march; *(Mil)* march-past, parade ◆ **~ de mode** *ou* **de mannequins** fashion show ◆ **~ aérien** *(Mil)* flypast *(Brit)*, flyover *(US)* 2 *(= succession) [de visiteurs]* procession, stream; *[de voitures]* stream; *[d'impressions, pensées]* stream, succession 3 *(Géog)* (narrow) gorge, defile

défilement /defilmɑ̃/ NM *[de film]* projection; *[de bande magnétique]* unreeling, unwinding; *(Ordin)* scrolling ◆ **vitesse de ~** *(Ciné)* projection speed ◆ **~ horizontal/vertical** *(Ordin)* horizontal/vertical scrolling

défiler /defile/ ▸ conjug 1 ◂ VT 1 *[+ aiguille, perles]* to unthread; *[+ chiffons]* to shred

2 *(Mil) [+ troupes]* to put under cover *(from the enemy's fire)*

VI 1 *(Mil)* to march past, to parade; *[manifestants]* to march *(devant* past)

2 *[bande magnétique]* to unreel, to unwind; *[texte de téléprompteur]* to scroll ◆ **faire ~ un document** *(Ordin)* to scroll a document ◆ **faire ~ une bande magnétique** *(vers l'avant)* to forward a tape; *(vers l'arrière)* to rewind a tape ◆ **les souvenirs défilaient dans sa tête** a stream of memories passed through his mind ◆ **les visiteurs défilaient devant le mausolée** the visitors filed past the mausoleum ◆ **la semaine suivante tous les voisins défilèrent chez nous** the following week we were visited by all the neighbours one after the other ◆ **nous regardions le paysage qui défilait devant nos yeux** we watched the scenery pass by *ou (plus vite)* flash by

VPR **se défiler** 1 *[aiguille]* to come unthreaded; *[perles]* to come unstrung *ou* unthreaded

2 *(Mil)* to take cover *(from the enemy's fire)*

3 *(= s'éclipser)* to slip away *ou* off ◆ **il s'est défilé** *(= s'est dérobé)* he wriggled *ou* ducked out of it

défini, e /defini/ (ptp de **définir**) ADJ 1 *(= déterminé) [but]* definite, precise ◆ **terme bien ~** well-defined term 2 *(Gram) [article]* definite ◆ **passé ~** preterite

définir /definiʀ/ ▸ conjug 2 ◂ VT *[+ idée, sentiment, position]* to define; *(Géom, Gram)* to define; *[+ personne]* to define, to characterize; *[+ conditions]* to specify, to define ◆ **il se définit comme un humaniste** he defines himself as a humanist ◆ **notre politique se définit comme étant avant tout pragmatique** our policies can be defined as being essentially pragmatic

définissable /definisabl(ə)/ ADJ definable

définitif, -ive /definitif, iv/ GRAMMAIRE ACTIVE 53.4 ADJ 1 *(= final) [résultat, destination, résolution]* final; *[mesure, installation, victoire, fermeture]* permanent, definitive; *[solution]* definitive, final; *[étude, édition]* definitive; *[prix]* set, fixed ◆ **son départ était ~** he was leaving for good, his departure was final ◆ **les bâtiments provisoires sont vite devenus ~s** the temporary buildings quickly became permanent 2 *(= sans appel) [décision]* final; *[refus]* definite, decisive; *[argument]* conclusive ◆ **un jugement ~** a final judgment ◆ **et c'est ~ !** and that's that *ou* that's final! LOC ADV **en définitive** *(= à la fin)* eventually; *(= somme toute)* in fact, when all is said and done

définition /definisjɔ̃/ NF 1 *[de concept, mot]* definition; *[de mots croisés]* clue ◆ **par ~** by definition ◆ **~ de poste** job description 2 (TV) definition ◆ **la haute ~** high definition ◆ **(de) haute ~** high-definition *(épith)*

définitivement /definitivmɑ̃/ ADV *[partir, perdre, abandonner]* for good; *[résoudre, décider]* once and for all; *[adopter]* permanently; *[exclure, s'installer]* for good, permanently; *[nommer]* on a permanent basis, permanently

> ⚠ **définitivement** se traduit rarement par **definitively**, qui a le sens de 'avec certitude'.

définitoire /definitwaʀ/ ADJ *(Ling) [vocabulaire]* defining *(épith)*

défiscalisation /defiskalizasjɔ̃/ NF tax exemption

défiscaliser /defiskalize/ ▸ conjug 1 ◂ VT to exempt from tax(ation)

déflagration /deflagʀasjɔ̃/ NF *(gén)* explosion; *(Chim)* deflagration

déflagrer /deflagʀe/ ▸ conjug 1 ◂ VI to deflagrate

déflateur /deflatœʀ/ NM *(Fin)* deflator

déflation /deflasjɔ̃/ NF *(Écon, Fin)* deflation; *[d'effectifs]* reduction, cut *(de* in); ◆ **~ salariale** declining wage trend

déflationniste /deflasjɔnist/ ADJ *[politique, effets]* deflationary; *[économiste]* deflationist NMF deflationist

déflecteur /deflɛktœʀ/ NM *[de voiture]* quarter-light *(Brit)*, vent *(US)*; *(Tech) [de courant gazeux]* jet deflector; *[de compas]* deflector

défleurir /deflœʀiʀ/ ▸ conjug 2 ◂ *(littér)* VT *[+ buisson]* to remove the blossom from VI *[buisson]* to shed its flowers *ou* its blossom

déflexion /deflɛksjɔ̃/ NF deflection

déflocage /deflɔkaʒ/ NM *(Tech)* removal of asbestos ◆ **le ~ de l'immeuble a duré 6 mois** it took six months to remove the asbestos from the building

défloquer /deflɔke/ ▸ conjug 1 ◂ VT *[+ pièce, bâtiment]* to remove asbestos from

défloraison /deflɔʀɛzɔ̃/ NF *(Bot, littér)* falling of blossoms

défloration /deflɔʀasjɔ̃/ NF *[de jeune fille]* defloration

déflorer /deflɔʀe/ ▸ conjug 1 ◂ VT *[+ jeune fille]* to deflower; *(littér) [+ sujet, moments]* to spoil the charm of, to deflower *(littér)*

défoliant /defɔljɑ̃/ NM defoliant

défoliation /defɔljasjɔ̃/ NF defoliation

défolier /defɔlje/ ▸ conjug 7 ◂ VT to defoliate

défonçage /defɔ̃saʒ/, **défoncement** /defɔ̃smɑ̃/ NM *[de caisse, barque]* staving in; *[de porte, clôture]* smashing in *ou* down, staving in; *[de sommier, fauteuil]* breaking; *[de route, terrain] (par bulldozers, camions)* ripping *ou* ploughing *ou* breaking up; *(Agr)* deep-ploughing

défonce /defɔ̃s/ NF *(arg Drogue)* getting high* ◆ ~ **à la colle/aux solvants** getting high on glue/solvents ◆ **il était en pleine** ~ he was completely out of it*

défoncé, e /defɔ̃se/ (ptp de **défoncer**) ADJ 1 *[canapé, fauteuil]* sagging; *[chemin, route]* full of potholes *(attrib)* ◆ **un vieux fauteuil tout** ~ an old sunken armchair ◆ **sur des routes ~es** on roads full of potholes 2 *(arg Drogue)* high* ◆ **il était complètement** ~ he was completely out of it*, he was as high as a kite* NM,F *(= drogué)* junkie*, drug addict ◆ **un ~ au crack** a crack addict

défoncer /defɔ̃se/ ▸ conjug 3 ◂ VT *[+ caisse, barque]* to stave in, to knock *ou* smash the bottom out of; *[+ porte, clôture]* to smash in *ou* down, to stave in; *[+ sommier, fauteuil]* to break *ou* burst the springs of; *[+ route, terrain] [bulldozers, camions]* to rip *ou* plough *ou* break up; *(Agr)* to plough deeply, to deep-plough ◆ **il a eu le crâne défoncé** his skull was smashed in VPR **se défoncer** 1 *(* = travailler dur)* to work like a dog*, to work flat out* ◆ **se ~ pour qn/pour faire qch** to work like a dog* for sb/to do sth 2 *(arg Drogue)* to get high* *(à on)*

déforcer /defɔʀse/ ▸ conjug 3 ◂ VT *(Belg)* to dishearten

déforestation /defɔʀɛstasjɔ̃/ NF deforestation

déformant, e /defɔʀmɑ̃, ɑ̃t/ ADJ *[miroir, prisme]* distorting; *[rhumatisme]* crippling ◆ **le prisme ~ de ...** *(fig)* the distorting prism of ...

déformation /defɔʀmasjɔ̃/ NF 1 *[d'objet, métal]* bending (out of shape), distortion; *[de bois]* warping; *[de visage, image, vision]* distortion; *[de vérité, pensée]* distortion, misrepresentation; *[d'esprit]* warping ◆ **par une curieuse ~ d'esprit, il ...** by a strange twist in his character, he ... ◆ **désolé, c'est de la ~ professionnelle** sorry, I can't help it, it's my job ◆ **par ~ professionnelle** as a result of being so conditioned by one's job 2 *(Méd)* deformation ◆ **souffrir d'une ~ de la hanche** to have a hip deformity

déformer /defɔʀme/ ▸ conjug 1 ◂ VT *[+ objet, métal]* to bend (out of shape), to distort; *[+ bois]* to warp; *[+ chaussures, vêtements]* to stretch out of shape; *[+ corps]* to deform; *[+ visage, image, vision]* to distort; *[+ vérité, pensée]* to distort, to misrepresent; *[+ esprit]* to warp ◆ **vieillard au corps déformé** old man with a deformed *ou* misshapen body ◆ **veste déformée** jacket which has lost its shape *ou* has gone out of shape ◆ **pantalon (tout) déformé** trousers that have gone all baggy ◆ **traits déformés par la douleur** features contorted *ou* distorted by pain ◆ **mes propos ont été déformés** *(involontairement)* I've been misquoted; *(volontairement)* my words have been twisted ◆ **il est déformé par son métier** he has been conditioned by his job; → **chaussée**

VPR **se déformer** *[objet]* to be bent (out of shape), to lose its shape; *[métal]* to be bent (out of shape), to be distorted; *[bois]* to warp; *[vêtement]* to lose its shape

défoulement /defulmɑ̃/ NM *[d'instincts, sentiments]* (psychological) release ◆ **moyen de** ~ (psychological) outlet *ou* means of release ◆ **après les examens on a besoin de** ~ after the exams you need some kind of (psychological) release *ou* you need to let off steam*

défouler /defule/ ▸ conjug 1 ◂ VT ◆ **j'ai crié des injures, ça m'a défoulé** I shouted some abuse, it helped relieve my feelings *ou* helped me to get it out of my system* ◆ **ça (vous) défoule de courir** running helps you unwind *ou* relax VPR **se défouler** *(= se libérer de tensions)* to let off steam*; *(= se relaxer)* to relax, to unwind ◆ **se ~ sur qn/qch** to take it out on sb/sth

défourailler * /defuʀaje/ ▸ conjug 1 ◂ VI to draw (one's gun)

défourner /defuʀne/ ▸ conjug 1 ◂ VT *[+ pain]* to take out of the oven; *[+ poteries]* to take out of the kiln

défragmentation /defʀagmɑ̃tasjɔ̃/ NF *(Ordin) [de disque dur]* defragmentation

défragmenter /defʀagmɑ̃te/ ▸ conjug 1 ◂ VT *(Ordin) [+ disque dur]* to defragment

défraîchi, e /defʀeʃi/ (ptp de **défraîchir**) ADJ *[article]* shopsoiled; *[fleur, couleur]* faded; *[tissu] (= passé)* faded; *(= usé)* worn; *[humour, idée]* dated, stale *(péj)*

défraîchir /defʀeʃiʀ/ ▸ conjug 2 ◂ VT to take the freshness from VPR **se défraîchir** *[fleur, couleur]* to fade; *[tissu] (= passer)* to fade; *(= s'user)* to become worn

défraiement /defʀɛmɑ̃/ NM expenses ◆ **vous avez droit à un ~** you can claim expenses ◆ **les comédiens ne touchent qu'un ~** the actors only get their expenses

défrayer /defʀeje/ ▸ conjug 8 ◂ VT 1 *(= payer)* ~ **qn** to pay *ou* settle sb's expenses 2 *(= être en vedette)* ~ **la conversation** to be the main topic of conversation ◆ ~ **la chronique** to be widely talked about, to be in the news

défrichage /defʀiʃaʒ/, **défrichement** /defʀiʃmɑ̃/ NM *[de forêt, terrain]* clearing *(for cultivation)* ◆ **le ~ d'un sujet** the spadework (done) on a subject

défricher /defʀiʃe/ ▸ conjug 1 ◂ VT *[+ forêt, terrain]* to clear *(for cultivation)*; *[+ sujet, question]* to open up, to do the spadework on ◆ ~ **le terrain** *(fig)* to prepare the ground *ou* way, to clear the way

défricheur /defʀiʃœʀ/ NM *(lit)* land-clearer; *(fig)* pioneer

défriper /defʀipe/ ▸ conjug 1 ◂ VT to smooth out

défriser /defʀize/ ▸ conjug 1 ◂ VT 1 *[+ cheveux]* to straighten 2 *(* = contrarier) [+ personne]* to bug* ◆ **ce qui me défrise*** what bugs* *ou* gets* me ◆ **et alors ! ça te défrise ?*** so (what)?*, what's it to you?*

défroisser /defʀwase/ ▸ conjug 1 ◂ VT to smooth out

défroque /defʀɔk/ NF *(= frusques)* old cast-offs; *(= accoutrement)* getup*; *[de moine]* effects *(left by a dead monk)*

défroqué, e /defʀɔke/ (ptp de **défroquer**) ADJ defrocked, unfrocked NM defrocked *ou* unfrocked priest *(ou* monk)

défroquer /defʀɔke/ ▸ conjug 1 ◂ VT to defrock, to unfrock VI **se défroquer** VPR to give up the cloth, to renounce one's vows

défunt, e /defœ̃, œt/ ADJ *(frm) [personne]* late *(épith)*; *(littér) [espoir, année]* which is dead and gone; *(littér) [assemblée, projet]* defunct ◆ **son ~ père** his late father NM,F deceased

dégagé, e /degaʒe/ (ptp de **dégager**) ADJ 1 *[route]* clear; *[ciel]* clear, cloudless; *[espace, site]* open, clear; *[vue]* wide, open; *[front, nuque]* bare ◆ **c'est un peu trop ~ autour des oreilles** it's a bit short around the ears 2 *[air, allure, manières]* casual, jaunty; *[ton]* airy, casual NM *(Danse)* dégagé

dégagement /degaʒmɑ̃/ NM 1 *(= action de libérer) [de personne]* freeing, extricating; *[d'objet, main]* freeing; *(Mil) [de troupe, ville]* relief; *(Fin) [de crédits, titres]* release *(for a specific purpose)*; *[d'objet en gage]* redemption ◆ **ils ont procédé au ~ des blessés enfouis sous les décombres** they began to free the injured from the rubble ◆ **le ~ d'une promesse** going back on a promise

2 *(à l'accouchement)* expulsion, delivery ◆ ~ **de la tête** crowning

3 *(= production) [de fumée, gaz, chaleur]* emission, emanation; *[d'énergie]* release ◆ **un ~ de vapeurs toxiques** a discharge *ou* an emission of toxic fumes

4 *(Escrime)* disengagement; *(Ftbl, Rugby)* clearance ◆ **faire un ~ au pied/au poing** to kick/knock a ball clear ◆ **coup de pied de ~** kick downfield; *(en touche)* kick to touch

5 *(= espace libre) [de forêt]* clearing; *[d'appartement] (gén)* open space; *(= couloir)* passage; *(Tech) [de camion]* clearance, headroom

dégager /degaʒe/ ▸ conjug 3 ◂ VT 1 *(= libérer) [+ personne]* to free, to extricate; *[+ objet, main]* to free; *(Mil) [+ troupe, ville]* to relieve, to bring relief to; *(Fin) [+ crédits, titres]* to release *(for a specific purpose)*; *[+ objet en gage]* to redeem, to take out of pawn ◆ **on a dû ~ les blessés au chalumeau** the injured had to be cut loose *ou* free (from the wreckage) ◆ ~ **qn de sa promesse/d'une obligation** to release *ou* free sb from his promise/an obligation ◆ ~ **qn d'une dette** to cancel sb's debt ◆ ~ **sa responsabilité d'une affaire** to disclaim *ou* deny (all) responsibility in a matter ◆ **col/robe qui dégage le cou/les épaules** collar/dress which leaves the neck/shoulders bare

2 *[+ place, passage, table]* to clear *(de* of); *(Méd) [+ gorge, nez, poitrine]* to clear ◆ **je voudrais que ce soit bien dégagé derrière les oreilles** *(chez le coiffeur)* cut it nice and short around the ears ◆ **dégagez s'il vous plaît !** move away please! ◆ **dégage !*** clear off!*, buzz off!* ◆ **toutes ces vieilleries, à ~ !*** all these old things can go *ou* can be chucked out*

3 *(= exhaler) [+ odeur, fumée, gaz, chaleur]* to give off, to emit; *[+ enthousiasme]* to radiate ◆ **la maison dégageait une impression de tristesse** there was an aura of gloom about the house, the house had a gloomy feel about it

4 *(= extraire) [+ conclusion]* to draw; *[+ idée, sens]* to bring out; *[+ bénéfice, marge]* to show ◆ **l'entreprise a dégagé de gros profits cette année** the company showed a high profit this year ◆ **l'idée principale qu'on peut ~ de ce rapport** the main idea that can be drawn *ou* derived from this report ◆ **je vous laisse ~ la morale de cette histoire** I'll let you guess what the moral of the story is

5 *(Escrime) [+ épées]* to disengage; *(Ftbl, Rugby) [+ ballon]* to clear ◆ ~ **(le ballon) en touche** to clear the ball into touch, to kick (the ball) into touch

6 *(Danse)* to do a dégagé

VPR **se dégager** 1 *[personne]* to free *ou* extricate o.s., to get free; *(Mil) [troupe]* to extricate itself *(de* from); ◆ **se ~ de** *[+ dette]* to free o.s. of; *[+ obligation]* to free *ou* release o.s. from; *[+ affaire]* to get *ou* back out of; *[+ promesse]* to go back on ◆ **il s'est dégagé d'une situation très délicate** he extricated himself from a very tricky situation ◆ **j'ai une réunion mais je vais essayer de me ~** I have a meeting but I'll try to get out of it

2 *[ciel, rue, nez]* to clear; *[objet]* to appear ◆ **le sommet/la silhouette se dégagea du brouillard** the summit/the outline appeared out of the fog

3 *[odeur, fumée, gaz, chaleur]* to emanate, to be given off; *[enthousiasme]* to emanate, to radiate; *[impression]* to emanate *(de* from); ◆ **il se dégage d'elle une telle vitalité** she exudes such vitality

4 *[conclusion]* to be drawn; *[impression, idée, sens]* to emerge; *[morale]* to be drawn, to emerge *(de* from); ◆ **il se dégage de tout cela que ...** from all this it emerges that ...

dégaine * /degɛn/ NF ◆ **il a une drôle de ~** he's got an odd look about him ◆ **je n'aime pas leur ~** I don't like the look of them

dégainer /degene/ ▸ conjug 1 ◂ VT *[+ épée]* to unsheathe, to draw; *[+ pistolet]* to draw VI to draw one's sword *(ou* gun)

déganter (se) /degɑ̃te/ ▸ conjug 1 ◂ VPR to take off one's gloves ◆ **main dégantée** ungloved hand

dégarni, e /degaʀni/ (ptp de **dégarnir**) ADJ *[front, arbre, salle, rayon]* bare; *[compte en banque]* low; *[portefeuille]* empty; *[magasin]* low in stock; *[tête, personne]* balding ◆ **il est un peu ~ sur le dessus** he's a bit thin on top

dégarnir /degaʀniʀ/ ▸ conjug 2 ◂ VT *[+ maison, salle, vitrine]* to empty, to clear; *[+ compte en banque]* to drain, to draw heavily on; *(Mil)* *[+ ville, place]* to withdraw troops from ◆ **il faut ~ un peu le sapin de Noël** we should take some of the decorations off the Christmas tree VPR **se dégarnir** *[salle]* to empty; *[personne]* to go bald; *[arbre]* to lose its leaves; *[bois]* to become sparse; *[rayons d'un magasin]* to be cleaned out *ou* cleared; *[stock]* to run out, to be cleaned out ◆ **il se dégarnit sur le dessus/au niveau des tempes** he's getting a bit thin on top/he has a receding hairline

dégât /degɑ/ NM damage (NonC) ◆ **causer** *ou* **faire beaucoup de ~s** *[grêle, inondation, personne etc]* to cause *ou* do a lot of damage; *[alcool]* to do a lot of *ou* great harm ◆ **~ des eaux** *(Assurances)* water damage; → **limiter**

dégauchir /degoʃiʀ/ ▸ conjug 2 ◂ VT *[+ bois]* to surface; *[+ pierre]* to dress

dégauchissage /degoʃisaʒ/, **dégauchissement** /degoʃismɑ̃/ NM *[de bois]* surfacing; *[de pierre]* dressing

dégauchisseuse /degoʃisøz/ NF surface-planing machine

dégazage /degɑzaʒ/ NM *[de pétrolier]* emptying of fuel tanks ◆ **les pétroliers qui pratiquent le ~** oil tankers which empty their tanks

dégazer /degɑze/ ▸ conjug 1 ◂ VT to degas VI *[navire]* to empty its tanks

dégel /deʒɛl/ NM *(lit, fig)* thaw ◆ **tu attends le ~ ou quoi ?** * what on earth are you waiting for?, are you waiting for Christmas or what?; → **barrière**

dégelée * /deʒ(ə)le/ NF *(= coups)* thrashing, hiding, beating; *(= défaite)* thrashing * ◆ **recevoir une ~** *(coups)* to get a hiding; *(défaite)* to be thrashed *

dégeler /deʒ(ə)le/ ▸ conjug 5 ◂ VT 1 *[+ lac, terre]* to thaw (out); *[+ glace]* to thaw, to melt; * *[+ pieds, mains]* to thaw 2 * *[+ invité, réunion]* to thaw (out) ◆ **pour ~ l'atmosphère** to break the ice 3 *(Fin)* to unfreeze VI 1 *[neige, lac]* to thaw (out) 2 *[aliment]* **faire ~** to thaw, to leave to thaw VB IMPERS ◆ **ça dégèle** it's thawing VPR **se dégeler** *[personne] (lit)* to warm up, to get o.s. warmed up; *(fig)* to thaw (out); *[public]* to warm up

dégénératif, -ive /deʒeneʀatif, iv/ ADJ *[affection, maladie]* degenerative, wasting

dégénéré, e /deʒeneʀe/ (ptp de **dégénérer**) ADJ *(= abâtardi)* degenerate; († : *Psych)* defective ◆ **t'es complètement ~ !** * you're such a moron! * NM,F degenerate; († : *Psych)* defective; (*, *péj)* moron *

dégénérer /deʒeneʀe/ ▸ conjug 6 ◂ VI 1 *(= s'abâtardir)* *[race]* to degenerate; *[qualité]* to deteriorate 2 *(= mal tourner)* to degenerate *(en* into); ◆ **leur dispute a dégénéré en rixe** their quarrel degenerated into a brawl ◆ **un coup de froid qui dégénère en grippe** a chill which develops into flu ◆ **ça a rapidement dégénéré** *[débat, manifestation]* it soon got out of hand

dégénérescence /deʒeneʀesɑ̃s/ NF 1 *(physique, mentale)* degeneration; *(morale)* degeneracy 2 *(Méd, Bio, Phys)* degeneration

dégénérescent, e /deʒeneʀesɑ̃, ɑ̃t/ ADJ *(Méd)* degenerating, deteriorating

dégermer /deʒɛʀme/ ▸ conjug 1 ◂ VT to degerm, to remove the germ from

dégingandé, e * /deʒɛ̃gɑ̃de/ ADJ gangling, lanky

dégivrage /deʒivʀaʒ/ NM *[de réfrigérateur]* defrosting; *[d'avion, pare-brise]* de-icing ◆ **~ automatique** auto-defrost

dégivrer /deʒivʀe/ ▸ conjug 1 ◂ VT *[+ réfrigérateur]* to defrost; *[+ avion, pare-brise]* to de-ice ◆ **rétroviseur dégivrant** heated *ou* de-icer rearview mirror

dégivreur /deʒivʀœʀ/ NM *[de réfrigérateur]* defroster; *[d'avion, pare-brise]* de-icer

déglaçage /deglasaʒ/, **déglacement** /deglasmɑ̃/ NM 1 *(Culin)* deglazing ◆ **~ à la crème** deglazing with cream 2 *(Tech)* *[de papier]* removal of the glaze *(de* from) 3 *[de route]* removal of the ice *(de* from)

déglacer /deglase/ ▸ conjug 3 ◂ VT 1 *(Culin)* to deglaze ◆ **déglacez au vinaigre** deglaze with vinegar 2 *(Tech)* *[+ papier]* to remove the glaze from 3 *[+ route]* to remove the ice from

déglingue ⁑ /deglɛ̃g/ NF dilapidation, decay ◆ **il est au bord de la ~** he's on his last legs *

déglingué, e * /deglɛ̃ge/ (ptp de **déglinguer**) ADJ *[mécanisme]* kaput *; *[valise]* battered, broken; *[banlieue, ville]* dilapidated, run-down ◆ **la chaise était toute ~e** the chair was falling apart ◆ **une voiture toute ~e** a ramshackle car ◆ **nous vivons dans une société ~e** we live in a society that is coming apart at the seams *ou* that is falling apart

déglinguer * /deglɛ̃ge/ ▸ conjug 1 ◂ VT *[+ objet, appareil]* to bust * VPR **se déglinguer** *[appareil]* to be on the blink *; *[chaise]* to fall to pieces, to fall *ou* come apart; *[serrure, robinet]* to go bust * ◆ **se ~ l'estomac/la santé** to ruin one's stomach/one's health

déglutir /deglytiʀ/ ▸ conjug 2 ◂ VTI *(Méd)* to swallow

déglutition /deglytisjɔ̃/ NF *(Méd)* swallowing, deglutition *(SPÉC)*

dégobiller ⁑ /degɔbije/ ▸ conjug 1 ◂ VTI *(= vomir)* to puke ⁑

dégoiser * /degwaze/ ▸ conjug 1 ◂ VT *[+ boniments, discours]* to spout * ◆ **qu'est-ce qu'il dégoise ?** what is he rattling on about? * VI *(= parler)* to rattle on *, to go on (and on) * ◆ **~ sur le compte de qn** *(= médire)* to gossip about sb

dégommer ⁑ /degɔme/ ▸ conjug 1 ◂ VT 1 *(= dégrader)* to demote; *(= détrôner)* to unseat; *(= renvoyer)* to give the push to *, to fire, to sack * *(Brit)* ◆ **se faire ~** to get the push *, to be fired * *ou* sacked * *(Brit)* 2 *[+ avion]* to down *; *[+ quille]* to knock flying *; *[+ bille]* to knock out of the way; *[+ cible sur écran]* to zap *; *[+ cible sur stand de tir]* to hit

dégonflage /degɔ̃flaʒ/ NM 1 *[de pneu]* deflating 2 (⁑ = *lâcheté*) chickening out * ◆ **j'appelle ça du ~ !** that's what I call being chicken! *, that's what I call chickening out! *

dégonflard, e ⁑ /degɔ̃flaʀ, aʀd/ NM,F *(= lâche)* chicken *, yellow-belly *

dégonflé, e /degɔ̃fle/ (ptp de **dégonfler**) ADJ 1 *[+ pneu]* flat 2 (⁑ = *lâche*) chicken * *(attrib)*, yellow(-bellied) * NM,F yellow-belly *, chicken *

dégonflement /degɔ̃fləmɑ̃/ NM *[de ballon, pneu]* deflation; *[d'enflure]* reduction

dégonfler /degɔ̃fle/ ▸ conjug 1 ◂ VT *[+ pneu]* to let down, to let the air out of, to deflate; *[+ ballon]* to deflate, to let the air out of; *[+ enflure]* to reduce, to bring down; *[+ chiffres, statistiques]* to reduce, to bring down; *[+ effectif]* to reduce; *[+ mythe]* to debunk VI *[chiffre, effectifs]* to go down, to fall ◆ **ses yeux/jambes ont dégonflé** the swelling in his eyes/legs has gone down VPR **se dégonfler** 1 *[ballon, pneu]* to deflate, to go down; *[enflure]* to go down ◆ **se ~ comme une baudruche** *[espoir, illusion, promesse]* to fade (away); *[mouvement politique, parti]* to fizzle out 2 (⁑ = *avoir peur*) to chicken out *

dégorgement /degɔʀʒəmɑ̃/ NM 1 *(= débouchage)* *[d'évier, égout]* clearing out 2 *(= évacuation)* *[d'eau, bile]* discharge 3 *(= écoulement)* *[d'égout, rivière]* discharge; *[de gouttière]* discharge, overflow 4 *(Tech = lavage)* *[de cuir]* cleaning, cleansing; *[de laine]* scouring

dégorgeoir /degɔʀʒwaʀ/ NM *(= conduit d'évacuation)* overflow duct *ou* pipe; *(Pêche)* disgorger

dégorger /degɔʀʒe/ ▸ conjug 3 ◂ VT 1 *(= déboucher)* *[+ évier, égout]* to clear out 2 *(= déverser)* *[tuyau]* *[+ eau]* to discharge, to pour out; *[rue, train]* *[+ personnes]* to disgorge, to pour forth *ou* out *(dans* into) 3 *(Tech = laver)* *[+ cuir, étoffe]* to clean; *[+ laine]* to scour VI 1 *[étoffe]* to soak *(to release impurities)*; *(Culin)* *[viande]* to soak ◆ **faire ~** *[+ étoffe, viande]* to soak; *[+ escargots] to clean by soaking in salted water* ◆ **faites ~ le concombre** sprinkle the cucumber with salt and leave to drain 2 ◆ **~ dans** *[égout, gouttière]* to discharge into; *[rivière]* to discharge itself into VPR **se dégorger** *[eau]* to be discharged, to pour out *(dans* into); *[foule]* to pour forth *ou* out *(dans* into)

dégot(t)er * /degɔte/ ▸ conjug 1 ◂ VT *(= trouver)* to dig up *, to unearth, to find

dégoulinade /degulinad/ NF trickle

dégoulinement /degulinmɑ̃/ NM *(en filet)* trickling; *(goutte à goutte)* dripping

dégouliner /deguline/ ▸ conjug 1 ◂ VI *(en filet)* to trickle; *(goutte à goutte)* to drip ◆ **ça me dégouline dans le cou** it's dripping *ou* trickling down my neck ◆ **je dégoulinais (de sueur)** * I was dripping with sweat ◆ **gâteau dégoulinant de crème** cake oozing with cream ◆ **mélodrame dégoulinant de sentimentalité** melodrama full of treacly sentiment, cloyingly sentimental melodrama

dégoulinure /degulinyʀ/ NF ⇒ **dégoulinade**

dégoupiller /degupije/ ▸ conjug 1 ◂ VT *[+ grenade]* to pull the pin out of ◆ **grenade dégoupillée** unpinned grenade, grenade with the pin pulled out

dégourdi, e * /deguʀdi/ (ptp de **dégourdir**) ADJ *(= malin)* smart, resourceful, bright ◆ **il n'est pas très ~** he's pretty clueless * NM,F ◆ **c'est un ~** he knows what's what *, he's on the ball * ◆ **quel ~ tu fais !** *(iro)* you're a smart one! *ou* a bright one! *ou* a bright spark! * *(Brit)*

dégourdir /deguʀdiʀ/ ▸ conjug 2 ◂ VT *[+ membres] (ankylosés)* to bring the circulation back to; *(gelés)* to warm up; *(= donner plus d'aisance à)* *[+ personne]* to knock the rough edges off, to teach a thing or two to *; *(= réchauffer)* *[+ eau]* to warm (up) ◆ **le service militaire/habiter à Paris le dégourdira** military service/living in Paris will knock him into shape *ou* teach him a thing or two * ◆ **~ qn en anglais/en physique** to teach sb the basics of English/physics VPR **se dégourdir** ◆ **il est sorti pour se ~ un peu (les jambes)** he went out to stretch his legs a bit ◆ **elle s'est un peu dégourdie depuis l'an dernier** she seems to have learnt a thing or two * since last year

dégoût /degu/ NM 1 *(NonC = répugnance)* disgust (NonC) *(pour, de* for); ◆ **j'y repensais sans cesse avec ~** I kept thinking back to it with disgust ◆ **par ~** out of feelings of revulsion ◆ **cette attitude m'inspire un profond ~** I am absolutely disgusted by this attitude ◆ **mon ~ pour ce type de nourriture** the revulsion I feel for this sort of food ◆ **je peux manger des cerises jusqu'au ~** I can eat cherries till they come out of my ears ◆ **ce ~ de la vie m'étonnait** such world-weariness surprised me 2 *(= aversion)* dislike ◆ **ses ~s** the things he dislikes

dégoûtant, e /degutɑ̃, ɑt/ ADJ 1 *(= sale)* disgusting; *(= répugnant) [manie, image]* revolting 2 *(= ignoble, odieux)* disgusting ◆ **il a été ~ avec elle** the way he treated her was disgusting 3 *(= obscène, vicieux)* disgusting ◆ **il est vraiment ~ ce type !** he's so disgusting! NM,F (dirty) pig* ◆ **espèce de vieux ~ !*** *(vicieux)* you dirty old man!*

dégoûtation* /degutasjɔ̃/ NF *(= dégoût)* disgust ◆ **quelle ~ !** *(= saleté)* what a disgusting *ou* filthy mess!

dégoûté, e /degute/ (ptp de **dégoûter**) ADJ ◆ **je suis ~!** *(scandalisé)* I'm disgusted!; *(lassé)* I'm sick and tired of it! ◆ **~ de la vie** weary *ou* sick of life ◆ **il leur jeta un regard ~** he looked at them in disgust ◆ **il n'est pas ~ !** *(hum)* he's not (too) fussy! *ou* choosy! * NM,F ◆ **il a fait le ~** *(devant un mets, une offre)* he turned his nose up at it ◆ **ne fais pas le ~ !** don't be so fussy!

dégoûter /degute/ ► conjug 1 ◄ VT 1 *(= écœurer)* to disgust ◆ **cet homme me dégoûte** that man disgusts me *ou* fills me with disgust, I find that man disgusting *ou* revolting ◆ **ce plat me dégoûte** I find this food disgusting *ou* revolting ◆ **la vie me dégoûte** I'm weary *ou* sick of life

2 ◆ **~ qn de qch** *(= ôter l'envie de)* to put sb (right) off sth; *(= remplir de dégoût pour)* to make sb feel disgusted with sth ◆ **c'est à vous ~ d'être honnête** it's enough to put you (right) off being honest ◆ **si tu n'aimes pas ça, n'en dégoûte pas les autres** if you don't like it, don't put the others off ◆ **je suis dégoûté par ces procédés** I think this is a disgusting way to act ◆ **ça m'a dégoûté de fumer** it put me (right) off smoking

VPR **se dégoûter** ◆ **se ~ de qn/qch** to get sick of sb/sth ◆ **elle s'est dégoûtée du tabac** she's gone right off smoking ◆ **je me dégoûte d'avoir dit ça !** I'm disgusted with myself for having said that!

dégoutter /degute/ ► conjug 1 ◄ VI to drip ◆ **dégouttant de sueur** dripping with sweat ◆ **l'eau qui dégoutte du toit** the water dripping down from *ou* off the roof ◆ **dégouttant de pluie** dripping wet

dégradant, e /degʀadɑ̃, ɑt/ ADJ degrading

dégradation /degʀadasjɔ̃/ NF 1 *(= détérioration) [de mur, bâtiment] (par le vandalisme)* damage; *[de monument, façade]* defacement; *(par la pluie)* erosion; *[de roches]* erosion; *[de relations, situation, qualité, santé]* deterioration; *[de valeurs morales, forces]* decline; *[de personne] (= affaiblissement physique)* weakening; *[de temps]* worsening; *[de marché]* decline; *[de monnaie, pouvoir d'achat]* weakening, erosion ◆ **~s** *(= dégâts)* damage *(NonC)* ◆ **les ~s causées au bâtiment** the damage caused to the building ◆ **la ~ des données** the corruption of the data 2 *(= avilissement)* degradation, debasement; *[de qualité]* debasement; *[de beauté]* defiling, debasement 3 *(Mil)* demotion ◆ **~ civique** *(Jur)* loss of civil rights 4 *(Art) [de couleurs]* shading-off, gradation; *[de lumière]* gradation 5 *(Phys)* **la ~ de l'énergie** the degradation of energy

dégradé /degʀade/ NM 1 *(= nuance)* ◆ **~ de lumière** *(dans un tableau, une photo)* shading ◆ **un ~ de couleurs** shaded colours ◆ **un ~ de rouges** blended shades of red 2 *(Ciné)* grading 3 *(Coiffure)* layers, layered cut ◆ **couper en ~** to layer

dégrader /degʀade/ ► conjug 1 ◄ VT 1 *(Mil = destituer) [+ officier]* to demote

2 *(= avilir) [+ personne]* to degrade, to debase; *[+ qualité]* to debase; *[+ beauté]* to defile, to debase

3 *(= détériorer) [+ mur, bâtiment] [vandales]* to damage, to cause damage to; *[pluie]* to erode, to cause to deteriorate; *[+ monument, façade]* to deface, to damage; *(Géol) [+ roches]* to erode, to wear away; *[+ relations]* to damage ◆ **ils ont dégradé le matériel** they damaged the equipment ◆ **les quartiers dégradés** the rundown areas

4 *(Art) [+ couleurs]* to shade off; *[+ lumière]* to subdue ◆ **tons dégradés** shaded tones

5 *[+ cheveux]* to layer, to cut in layers

VPR **se dégrader** 1 *[personne] (= s'avilir moralement)* to degrade o.s., to debase o.s.; *(= s'affaiblir physiquement)* to lose one's physical powers

2 *(= empirer) [relations, situation, qualité, santé, bâtiment]* to deteriorate; *[valeurs morales, forces]* to decline; *[mémoire]* to fail; *[marché]* to weaken; *[monnaie]* to grow weaker; *[pouvoir d'achat]* to shrink ◆ **le temps se dégrade** the weather is deteriorating, there's a change for the worse in the weather

3 *(Art) [couleurs]* to shade off; *[lumière]* to become subdued

4 *(Sci) [énergie]* to become dissipated *ou* degraded

dégrafer /degʀafe/ ► conjug 1 ◄ VT *[+ vêtement]* to unfasten, to unhook, to undo; *[+ bracelet, ceinture, collier]* to unfasten, to undo; *[+ papiers]* to unstaple ◆ **tu peux me ~ ?** can you undo me? VPR **se dégrafer** *(accidentellement) [vêtement, collier]* to come undone; *[papiers]* to come apart; *(volontairement) [personne]* to unfasten *ou* unhook *ou* undo one's dress *etc*

dégrafeur /degʀafœʀ/ NM staple remover

dégraissage /degʀɛsaʒ/ NM 1 ◆ **le ~ d'un vêtement** dry-cleaning a garment ◆ **le ~ du bouillon** skimming (the fat off) the broth ◆ **"dégraissage et nettoyage à sec"** "dry cleaning" 2 *(Écon) [d'effectifs]* cutback, rundown *(de* in); ◆ **opérer un ~** *ou* **des ~s** to slim down *ou* cut back the workforce

dégraissant /degʀɛsɑ̃/ NM *(= produit)* spot remover

dégraisser /degʀese/ ► conjug 1 ◄ VT 1 *[+ vêtement]* to dry-clean 2 *(Culin) [+ bouillon]* to skim (the fat off); *[+ viande]* to remove the fat from, to cut the fat off ◆ **jambon dégraissé** extra-lean ham 3 *(Menuiserie) [+ bois]* to trim the edges of 4 *(Écon) [+ personnel, effectifs]* to cut back, to slim down

degré /dəgʀe/ NM 1 *(= niveau)* degree; *(= stade de développement)* stage; *(Admin = échelon)* grade ◆ **c'est le ~ zéro de la civilisation/politique** it's civilisation/politics in its most basic form ◆ **haut ~ de civilisation** high degree *ou* level of civilization ◆ **à un ~ avancé de** at an advanced stage of ◆ **mur de 6e ~** *(Alpinisme)* grade 6 wall ◆ **au plus haut ~** to the highest degree ◆ **avare au plus haut ~** miserly in the extreme ◆ **jusqu'à un certain ~** to some *ou* a certain extent *ou* degree, to a degree ◆ **à un ~ moindre, à un moindre ~** to a lesser degree *ou* extent ◆ **par ~(s)** by degrees ◆ **c'est le dernier ~ de la perfection/passion** it's the height of perfection/passion ◆ **il s'est montré grossier au dernier ~** he was extremely rude

2 *(Gram, Mus, Sci)* degree ◆ **équation du 1er/2e ~** equation of the 1st/2nd degree ◆ **il fait 20 ~s dans la chambre** it's 20 degrees (centigrade) in the room ◆ **la température a baissé/est montée de 2 ~s** the temperature has dropped/risen 2 degrees ◆ **~ centigrade/Fahrenheit/Celsius** degree centigrade/Fahrenheit/Celsius

3 *(= proportion)* ◆ **~ d'alcool d'une boisson** proof of an alcoholic drink ◆ **~ en alcool d'un liquide** percentage of alcohol in a liquid ◆ **alcool à 90 ~s** 90% proof alcohol, surgical spirit *(Brit)* ◆ **du cognac à 40 ~s** 70° proof cognac ◆ **ce vin fait (du) 11 ~s** this wine is 11° *(on Gay-Lussac scale)* ◆ **~ Baumé** degree Baumé

4 *(dans un classement)* degree ◆ **brûlure du premier/deuxième ~** *(Méd)* first/second degree burn ◆ **~ de parenté** *(Sociol)* degree of (family) relationship *ou* of kinship *(frm)* ◆ **cousins au premier ~** first cousins ◆ **parents au premier/deuxième ~** relatives of the first/second degree ◆ **prendre qch au premier ~** to take sth literally ◆ **prendre qch au deuxième** *ou* **second ~** to look below the surface of sth ◆ **c'est de l'humour au second ~** it's tongue-in-cheek (humour) ◆ **c'est à prendre au second ~** it's not to be taken literally

5 *(Scol)* **enseignement du premier/second ~** primary/secondary education ◆ **enseignant du premier/second ~** primary/secondary schoolteacher

6 *(littér = marche)* step ◆ **les ~s de l'échelle sociale** the rungs of the social ladder

dégressif, -ive /degʀesif, iv/ ADJ *[impôt]* degressive ◆ **appliquer un tarif ~** to use a sliding scale of charges

dégressivité /degʀesivite/ NF *[d'impôt]* degression

dégrèvement /degʀɛvmɑ̃/ NM 1 *(Fin)* **~ fiscal, ~s fiscaux** tax exemption *ou* relief ◆ **le ~ d'un produit** reduction of tax(es) on a product ◆ **le ~ d'une industrie** reduction of the tax burden on an industry ◆ **le ~ d'un contribuable** granting tax relief to a taxpayer 2 *(Jur) [d'hypothèque]* disencumbrance

dégrever /degʀəve/ ► conjug 5 ◄ VT *[+ produit]* to reduce the tax(es) on; *[+ industrie]* to reduce the tax burden on; *[+ contribuable]* to grant tax relief to; *[+ immeuble]* to disencumber

dégriffé, e /degʀife/ ADJ ◆ **robe ~e** unlabelled designer dress NM ◆ **magasin de ~s** designer seconds store ◆ **ils vendent du ~** they sell designer seconds

dégringolade /degʀɛ̃gɔlad/ NF *[de personne, objet]* fall; *[de prix, firme]* tumble; *(Bourse) [de cours, monnaie]* collapse ◆ **pour stopper la ~ des prix** to stop prices (from) collapsing ◆ **après son divorce, ça a été la ~** after his divorce he went downhill

dégringoler /degʀɛ̃gɔle/ ► conjug 1 ◄ VI 1 *[personne, objet]* to tumble (down), to fall ◆ **il a dégringolé jusqu'en bas** he tumbled all the way down, he came *ou* went tumbling down ◆ **elle a dégringolé du toit** she tumbled *ou* fell off the roof ◆ **elle a fait ~ toute la pile de livres** she toppled the whole pile of books over *ou* brought the whole pile of books (crashing) down ◆ **ça dégringole !*** *[pluie]* it's pouring (down) *ou* tipping down* *(Brit)* 2 *[monnaie, prix]* to collapse, to take a tumble; *[firme, réputation]* to tumble, to take a tumble ◆ **il a dégringolé (jusqu')à la 15e place/dans les sondages** he tumbled to 15th place/in the polls VT *[+ escalier, pente] (en courant)* to rush *ou* tear down; *(en tombant)* to tumble down

dégrippant /degʀipɑ̃/ NM penetrating oil

dégripper /degʀipe/ ► conjug 1 ◄ VT to unblock, to unchoke

dégrisement /degʀizmɑ̃/ NM *(lit, fig)* sobering up

dégriser /degʀize/ ► conjug 1 ◄ VT *(lit)* to sober up; *(fig)* to sober up, to bring back down to earth VPR **se dégriser** *(lit)* to sober up; *(fig)* to sober up, to come back down to earth

dégrossir /degʀosiʀ/ ► conjug 2 ◄ VT 1 *[+ bois]* to trim, to cut down to size; *[+ marbre]* to rough-hew 2 *[+ projet, travail]* to rough out, to work out roughly, to do the spadework on 3 *[+ personne]* to knock the rough edges off, to polish up ◆ **individu mal dégrossi** coarse *ou* unpolished *ou* unrefined individual ◆ **il s'est un peu dégrossi** he has lost some of his rough edges

dégrossissage /degʀosisaʒ/ NM *[de bois]* trimming; *[de marbre]* rough-hewing

dégrouiller (se)* /degʀuje/ ► conjug 1 ◄ VPR *(= se dépêcher)* to hurry up, to get a move on* ◆ **allez, dégrouille(-toi) !** come on, hurry up!

ou get a move on! * ◆ **se ~ de** *ou* **pour faire qch** to hurry to do sth

dégroupement /degʀupmɑ̃/ **NM** putting *ou* dividing into groups

dégrouper /degʀupe/ ► conjug 1 ◄ **VT** to put *ou* divide into groups

déguenillé, e /deg(ə)nije/ **[ADJ]** ragged, tattered **[NM,F]** ragamuffin

déguerpir * /degɛʀpiʀ/ ► conjug 2 ◄ **VI** *(= s'enfuir)* to clear off *, to scarper⁑ *(Brit)* ◆ **faire ~** *[+ ennemi]* to scatter; *[+ voleur]* to chase *ou* drive off

dégueu⁑ /degø/ **ADJ** abrév de **dégueulasse**

dégueulasse⁑ /degœlas/ **[ADJ]** [1] *(= crasseux, sale)* disgusting, filthy [2] *(= mauvais, injuste)* lousy *, rotten * ◆ **il a fait un temps ~** the weather was lousy * ◆ **c'est ~ de faire ça** that's a lousy * *ou* rotten * thing to do ◆ **il a vraiment été ~ avec elle** he was really rotten * to her ◆ **c'est pas ~** it's not bad at all [3] *(= vicieux)* disgusting ◆ **il est vraiment ~, ce type** he's a filthy swine⁑ **[NMF]** *[personne]* *(sale)* dirty pig⁑; *(mauvais, vicieux, homme)* swine⁑; *(femme)* bitch, cow⁑ *(Brit)* ◆ **c'est un gros ~** he's a lousy *ou* rotten swine⁑ ◆ **c'est un vieux ~** he's a dirty old man⁑

dégueulasser⁑ /degœlase/ ► conjug 1 ◄ **VT** *(= salir)* to mess up *

dégueuler⁑ /degœle/ ► conjug 1 ◄ **VTI** *(= vomir)* to throw up⁑, to puke⁑ ◆ **c'est à ~** it's enough to make you throw up⁑ *ou* puke⁑

dégueulis⁑ /degœli/ **NM** puke⁑

déguisé, e /degize/ (ptp de **déguiser**) **ADJ** [1] *(pour tromper)* in disguise *(attrib)*, disguised *(en* as); *(pour s'amuser)* in fancy dress *(Brit)*, in costume *(US)* ◆ **~ en Zorro** dressed up as Zorro [2] *[voix, écriture, subvention, chômage]* disguised; *[ambition, sentiment]* disguised, masked, veiled; *[prêt, accord]* backdoor *(épith)* ◆ **non ~** unconcealed, undisguised ◆ **à peine ~** thinly disguised ◆ **il parlait avec une hostilité à peine ~e** he spoke with thinly disguised hostility ◆ **les taxes ont augmenté sous une forme ~e** there have been hidden tax increases ◆ **impôt ~** hidden tax

déguisement /degizmɑ̃/ **NM** *(pour tromper)* disguise; *(pour s'amuser)* disguise, fancy dress *(Brit)*, costume *(US)* ◆ **sans ~** *(littér)* without disguise, openly

déguiser /degize/ ► conjug 1 ◄ **[VT]** *(gén)* *[+ voix, écriture, visage]* to disguise; *[+ pensée, ambition, vérité]* to disguise, to mask; *[+ poupée, enfant]* to dress up *(en* as); ◆ **je ne puis vous ~ ma surprise** I cannot conceal my surprise from you **[VPR]** **se déguiser** *(pour tromper)* to disguise o.s.; *(pour s'amuser)* to dress up, to put on fancy dress *(Brit)* ◆ **se ~ en Zorro** to dress up as a Zorro ◆ **se ~ en courant d'air** * to make o.s. scarce *

> ⚠ Au sens de 'costumer', **déguiser** ne se traduit pas par **to disguise**.

dégurgiter /degyʀʒite/ ► conjug 1 ◄ **VT** *[+ nourriture]* to vomit *ou* bring back (up); *[+ leçon]* to parrot, to regurgitate

dégustateur, -trice /degystatœʀ, tʀis/ **NM,F** *[de vin]* wine taster

dégustation /degystasjɔ̃/ **NF** *[de coquillages, fromages]* sampling; *[de vin]* tasting ◆ **"ici, dégustation d'huîtres à toute heure"** "oysters available at all times"; → **menu**[1]

déguster /degyste/ ► conjug 1 ◄ **[VT]** *[+ vins]* to taste; *[+ coquillages, fromages]* to sample; *[+ repas, café, spectacle]* to enjoy, to savour ◆ **as-tu fini ton café ? – non, je le déguste** have you finished your coffee? – no, I'm enjoying it *ou* savouring it **[VI]** *(* = souffrir)* ◆ **il a dégusté !** he didn't half have a rough time! * ◆ **j'ai une rage de dents, je déguste !** I've got toothache and I'm in agony * *ou* and it's killing me! *

déhanché, e /deɑ̃ʃe/ (ptp de **se déhancher**) **ADJ** *[démarche]* swaying; *[d'infirme]* lop-sided ◆ **il se tenait légèrement ~** he was standing with his weight on one leg

déhanchement /deɑ̃ʃmɑ̃/ **NM** *(= démarche)* swaying walk; *[d'infirme]* lop-sided walk; *(= posture)* standing with one's weight on one hip

déhancher (se) /deɑ̃ʃe/ ► conjug 1 ◄ **VPR** [1] *(en marchant)* to sway one's hips [2] *(immobile)* to stand with one's weight on one hip

dehors /dəɔʀ/ **[ADV]** *(= à l'extérieur)* outside; *(= à l'air libre)* outside, outdoors, out of doors; *(= pas chez soi)* out ◆ **attendez-le ~** wait for him outside ◆ **je serai ~ toute la journée** I'll be out all day ◆ **par beau temps, les enfants passent la journée ~** when it's fine, the children spend the day outdoors *ou* out of doors *ou* outside ◆ **il fait plus frais dedans que ~** it is cooler inside than out(side) *ou* indoors than out(doors) ◆ **cela ne se voit pas de ~** it can't be seen from (the) outside ◆ **passez par ~ pour aller au jardin** go round the outside (of the house) to get to the garden ◆ **dîner ~** *(dans le jardin)* to eat out of doors *ou* outside; *(au restaurant)* to eat *ou* dine out ◆ **jeter** *ou* **mettre** *ou* **ficher** * *ou* **foutre**⁑ **qn ~** *(gén)* to throw *ou* kick⁑ *ou* chuck⁑ sb out; *[patron]* to sack * *ou* fire * sb ◆ **mettre le nez** *ou* **le pied ~** to set foot outside ◆ **il fait un temps à ne pas mettre le nez ~** it's weather for staying indoors

◆ **au dehors** *ou* **au-dehors** *(= à l'extérieur)* outside ◆ **au ~, elle paraît calme, mais c'est une nerveuse** outwardly she looks relaxed, but actually she's quite highly strung ◆ **au ~, la situation est tendue** *(= à l'étranger)* outside the country, the situation is tense

◆ **en dehors** ◆ **avoir les pieds en ~** to have turned-out feet, to be splay-footed ◆ **marcher les pieds en ~** to walk with one's feet *ou* toes turned out, to walk splay-footed

◆ **en dehors de** *(lit)* outside; *(= sans rapport avec)*, irrelevant to; *(= excepté)* apart from ◆ **ce passage est en ~ du sujet** this passage is irrelevant (to the subject) ◆ **en ~ de cela, il n'y a rien de neuf** apart from that *ou* beyond that *ou* otherwise there's nothing new ◆ **cette tâche est en ~ de ses possibilités** this task is beyond his capabilities ◆ **il a voulu rester en ~ de cette affaire** he didn't want to get involved ◆ **en ~ de tout contrôle** *[fabriquer, exporter]* without any form of control

[NM] *(= extérieur)* outside ◆ **on n'entend pas les bruits du ~** you can't hear the noise from outside ◆ **l'air du ~** the fresh air ◆ **les détenus n'avaient aucune communication avec le ~** the prisoners had no contact with the outside world ◆ **ce sont certainement des gens du ~ qui ont commis ce vol** it must be outsiders *ou* people from outside who are responsible for the theft

[NMPL] **dehors** *(= apparences)* **les ~ sont trompeurs** appearances are deceptive ◆ **sous des ~ aimables, il est dur** under his friendly exterior, he's a hard man

déhoussable /deusabl/ **ADJ** with loose covers *(attrib)*

déicide /deisid/ **[ADJ]** deicidal **[NMF]** deicide **[NM]** *(= crime)* deicide

déictique /deiktik/ **NM** *(Ling)* deictic

déification /deifikasjɔ̃/ **NF** deification

déifier /deifje/ ► conjug 7 ◄ **VT** to deify

déisme /deism/ **NM** deism

déiste /deist/ **[ADJ]** deistic, deist **[NMF]** deist

déité /deite/ **NF** *(littér)* deity

déjà /deʒa/ **ADV** [1] *(= dès maintenant, dès ce moment)* already ◆ **il a ~ fini** he has finished already, he has already finished ◆ **est-il ~ parti ?** has he left already? ◆ **à trois heures il avait ~ écrit trois lettres** he'd already written three letters by three o'clock ◆ **~ à cette époque** even then ◆ **j'aurais ~ fini si tu ne me dérangeais pas tout le temps** I would have finished by now *ou* already if you didn't keep bothering me all the time ◆ **je l'aurais ~ dit si je n'avais pas craint de le vexer** I would have said it before now *ou* by now *ou* already if I hadn't been afraid of offending him

[2] *(= auparavant)* before, already ◆ **je suis sûr de l'avoir ~ rencontré** I'm sure I've met him before, I'm sure I've already met him ◆ **j'ai ~ fait ce genre de travail** I've done that sort of work before, I've already done that sort of work

◆ **déjà-vu** ◆ **c'est du ~-vu** we've seen it all before, it's old hat * ◆ **impression de ~-vu** sense *ou* feeling of déjà vu

[3] *(intensif)* **200 €, c'est ~ pas mal** * €200, that's not bad at all ◆ **30 tonnes, c'est ~ un gros camion** 30 tons, that's quite a big truck *ou* that's a fair-sized truck ◆ **il est ~ assez paresseux** he's lazy enough as it is ◆ **enfin, c'est ~ quelque chose !** anyway, it's better than nothing *ou* it's a start! ◆ **c'est ~ ça** that's something ◆ **~ que** * **je ne suis pas riche, s'il faut encore payer une amende ...** I'm not rich as it is but if I have to pay a fine as well ...

[4] *(* : interrogatif)* **qu'est-ce qu'il a dit, ~ ?** what was it he said again?, what did he say again? ◆ **c'est combien, ~ ?** how much is it again?, how much did you say it was again?; → **ores**

déjanté, e⁑ /deʒɑ̃te/ (ptp de **déjanter**) **ADJ** ◆ **tu es complètement ~!** you're off your rocker⁑ *ou* trolley⁑ *(Brit)*!

déjanter /deʒɑ̃te/ ► conjug 1 ◄ **[VT]** *[pneu]* to remove from its rim **[VI]** *(⁑ = devenir fou)* to go crazy * ◆ **non mais tu déjantes !** you must be off your rocker!⁑ *ou* trolley!⁑ *(Brit)* **[VPR]** **se déjanter** *[pneu]* to come off its rim

déjection /deʒɛksjɔ̃/ **NF** [1] *(Méd)* evacuation ◆ **~s** faeces, excrement ◆ **~s canines** dog mess [2] *(Géol)* **~s** ejecta *(SPÉC)*, ejectamenta *(SPÉC)*; → **cône**

déjeté, e /deʒ(ə)te/ **ADJ** *[position, mur, arbre, infirme]* lop-sided, crooked; *[colonne vertébrale]* twisted ◆ **il est tout ~** he's all lop-sided *ou* misshapen

déjeuner /deʒœne/ ► conjug 1 ◄ **[VI]** [1] *(gén : à midi)* to have lunch ◆ **nous avons déjeuné de fromage et de pain** we had bread and cheese for lunch ◆ **inviter qn à ~** to invite sb to lunch ◆ **rester à ~ chez qn** to stay and have lunch with sb, to stay for *ou* to lunch at sb's ◆ **viens ~ avec nous demain** come and have lunch with us tomorrow, come to lunch with us tomorrow ◆ **nous avons déjeuné sur l'herbe** we had a picnic lunch ◆ **ne pars pas sans ~** don't go before you've had your lunch

[2] *(le matin)* to have breakfast; → **pouce**

[NM] [1] *(= repas de midi)* *(gén)* lunch ◆ **~ d'affaires** business lunch ◆ **~ de travail** working lunch ◆ **~ sur l'herbe** picnic lunch ◆ **prendre son ~** to have lunch ◆ **j'ai eu du poulet à ~** I had chicken for lunch ◆ **j'ai ma mère à ~** I've got my mother coming for lunch

[2] *(Belg, Helv : du matin)* breakfast

[3] *(= tasse et soucoupe)* breakfast cup and saucer

[4] *(locution)* **ça a été un vrai ~ de soleil** *(vêtement, tissu)* it didn't take long to fade; *(objet)* it soon gave up the ghost *, it didn't last long; *(résolution)* it was a flash in the pan, it didn't last long

déjouer /deʒwe/ ► conjug 1 ◄ **VT** *[+ complot]* to foil, to thwart; *[+ plan]* to thwart, to frustrate; *[+ ruse]* to outsmart; *[+ surveillance]* to elude ◆ **~ les plans de l'ennemi** to frustrate the enemy in his plans, to confound the enemy's plans ◆ **j'ai déjoué ses plans** I thwarted his plans, I outwitted him

déjuger (se) /deʒyʒe/ ► conjug 3 ◄ VPR to go back on *ou* reverse one's decision

de jure /deʒyʀe/ LOC ADJ, LOC ADV de jure

delà /dəla/ ADV

♦ **au-delà** beyond ♦ **au-~ il y a l'Italie** beyond that is Italy ♦ **il a eu ce qu'il voulait et bien au-~** he had all he wanted and more (besides) ♦ **vous avez droit à dix bouteilles et pas au-~/mais au-~ vous payez une taxe** you're entitled to ten bottles and no more/but above that you pay duty ♦ **n'allez pas au-~** *(somme, prix)* don't go beyond *ou* over that figure (*ou* sum *etc*), don't exceed that figure (*ou* sum *etc*) ♦ **mes connaissances ne vont pas au-~** that's as far as my knowledge goes, that's the extent of my knowledge

♦ **par(-)delà** beyond ♦ **devant eux il y a le pont et par(-)~ l'ennemi** in front of them is the bridge and beyond that the enemy *ou* and on the other *ou* far side of it, the enemy

♦ **en delà** beyond, outside ♦ **la clôture était à 20 mètres et il se tenait un peu en ~** the fence was 20 metres away and he was standing just beyond it *ou* outside it → **deçà**

PRÉP

♦ **au delà de** *[+ lieu, frontière]* beyond, on the other side of; *[+ somme, limite]* over, above ♦ **au ~ des mers** *(littér)* overseas, beyond *ou* over the seas ♦ **ceci va au ~ de tout ce que nous espérions** this goes (far) beyond anything we hoped for ♦ **au ~ de la conscience/douleur** beyond consciousness/pain ♦ **aller au ~ de ses forces/moyens** to go beyond *ou* exceed one's strength/means

♦ **par delà** beyond ♦ **par ~ les mers** overseas, beyond *ou* over the seas ♦ **par ~ les apparences** beneath the surface ♦ **par ~ les siècles** across the centuries; → **par-delà**

délabré, e /delabʀe/ (ptp de **délabrer**) ADJ *[maison]* dilapidated, ramshackle *(épith)*, tumble-down *(épith)*; *[mobilier, matériel]* broken-down; *[santé]* ruined; *[mur]* crumbling, in ruins *(attrib)*; *[affaires]* in a poor *ou* sorry state *(attrib)*; *[fortune]* depleted

délabrement /delabʀəmɑ̃/ NM *[de maison]* dilapidation, decay, ruin; *[de santé, affaires]* poor *ou* sorry state; *[de vêtements]* raggedness; *[de mobilier, matériel, mur]* decay, ruin; *[de fortune]* depletion ♦ **état de ~** dilapidated state, state of decay *ou* ruin

délabrer /delabʀe/ ► conjug 1 ◄ VT *[+ maison]* to ruin; *[+ mobilier, matériel]* to spoil, to ruin; *[+ santé]* to ruin, to impair VPR **se délabrer** *[maison, mur, matériel]* to fall into decay; *[santé]* to break down; *[affaires]* to go to rack and ruin

délacer /delase/ ► conjug 3 ◄ VT *[+ chaussures]* to undo (the laces of); *[+ corset]* to unlace VPR **se délacer** *[chaussures]* to come undone

délai /delɛ/ GRAMMAIRE ACTIVE 47.2, 47.3

NM 1 (= *temps accordé*) time limit ♦ **c'est un ~ trop court pour ...** it's too short a time for ... ♦ **je vous donne trois mois, c'est un ~ impératif** I'll give you three months and that's the absolute limit ♦ **avant l'expiration du ~** before the deadline ♦ **dans le ~ imparti** *ou* **prescrit** within the allotted *ou* prescribed time, within the time laid down *ou* allotted ♦ **dans un ~ de six jours** within (a period of) six days ♦ **livrable dans un ~ de quinze jours** *(sur facture)* allow two weeks for delivery ♦ **vous êtes dans les ~s** you're within the time limit ♦ **ce sera fait dans les ~s** it'll be done within the time limit *ou* allotted time ♦ **observer** *ou* **respecter** *ou* **tenir les ~s** *[de travail]* to keep *ou* meet the deadline; *[de livraison]* to keep *ou* meet delivery dates ♦ **prolonger un ~** to extend a time limit *ou* a deadline

2 (= *période d'attente*) waiting period ♦ **il faut compter un ~ de huit jours** you'll have to allow a week

3 (= *sursis*) extension ♦ **un dernier ~ de dix jours** a final extension of ten days ♦ **accorder des ~s successifs** to allow further extensions ♦ **il va demander un ~ pour achever le travail** he's going to ask for more time to finish the job

4 *(locutions)* **à bref ~** *[prévenir]* at short notice; (= *très bientôt*) shortly, very soon ♦ **dans le(s) plus bref(s) ~(s), dans les meilleurs ~s** as soon *ou* as quickly as possible ♦ **il faut payer avant le 15, dernier ~** it must be paid by the 15th at the latest, the 15th is the deadline for payment ♦ **15 octobre, dernier ~ pour les inscriptions** 15 October is the closing *ou* final date for registration, registration must be completed by 15 October at the latest ♦ **sans ~** without delay, immediately

COMP **délai de carence** *(Fin, Jur)* waiting period *(before receiving social security payments)*
délai d'exécution *(pour un travail)* turnaround time
délai de fabrication production time
délai de grâce *(Fin, Jur)* grace period ♦ **un ~ de grâce de cinq jours** five days' grace
délai de livraison delivery time *ou* period
délai de paiement term of payment, time for payment
délai de préavis term *ou* period of notice
délai de prescription *(Jur)* limitation period
délai de réflexion *(avant réponse)* time to think; *(avant date limite de paiement)* cooling-off period
délai de rétractation cooling-off period
délai de rigueur final deadline ♦ **à remettre avant le 15 mai, ~ de rigueur** to be handed in before the final deadline of 15 May

⚠ **délai** se traduit rarement par **delay**, qui a le sens de 'retard'.

délai-congé (pl **délais-congés**) /delɛkɔ̃ʒe/ NM term *ou* period of notice

délaissement /delɛsmɑ̃/ NM (= *action*) abandonment, desertion; (= *état*) neglect, state of neglect *ou* abandonment; *(Jur)* relinquishment *ou* renunciation *(of a right)*

délaisser /delese/ ► conjug 1 ◄ VT 1 (= *abandonner*) *[+ famille, ami]* to abandon, to give up; *[+ travail]* to give up, to quit ♦ **épouse délaissée** deserted wife 2 (= *négliger*) *[+ famille, ami, travail]* to neglect ♦ **c'est un métier délaissé par les jeunes** young people don't go in for this kind of work ♦ **épouse/fillette délaissée** neglected wife/little girl 3 *(Jur)* *[+ droit]* to relinquish

délassant, e /delasɑ̃, ɑt/ ADJ *[massage, bain]* relaxing

délassement /delasmɑ̃/ NM (= *état*) relaxation, rest; (= *distraction*) relaxation

délasser /delase/ ► conjug 1 ◄ VT (= *reposer*) *[+ membres]* to refresh; (= *divertir*) *[+ personne, esprit]* to entertain ♦ **un bon bain, ça délasse** a good bath is very relaxing ♦ **c'est un livre qui délasse** it's an entertaining sort of book VPR **se délasser** (= *se détendre*) to relax *(en faisant qch* by doing sth)

délateur, -trice /delatœʀ, tʀis/ NM,F *(frm)* informer

délation /delasjɔ̃/ NF *(frm)* denouncement, informing ♦ **lettre de ~** denunciatory letter

délavage /delavaʒ/ NM 1 *[d'aquarelle]* watering down; *[de tissu, inscription]* fading 2 *[de terre]* waterlogging

délavé, e /delave/ (ptp de **délaver**) ADJ 1 *[tissu]* faded; *[inscription]* washed-out ♦ **jeans ~s** prewashed jeans ♦ **un ciel ~ après la pluie** a watery *ou* washed-out (blue) sky after rain 2 *[terre]* waterlogged

délaver /delave/ ► conjug 1 ◄ VT 1 *[+ aquarelle]* to water down; *[+ tissu, inscription]* to (cause to) fade *(by the action of water)* 2 *[+ terre]* to waterlog

Delaware /dəlawɛʀ/ NM Delaware

délayage /delɛjaʒ/ NM 1 *[de couleur]* thinning down; *[de farine, poudre]* mixing *(to a certain consistency)* *(dans* with) 2 *(fig péj)* *[d'idée]* dragging out, spinning out; *[de texte, exposé]* padding out ♦ **faire du ~** *(péj)* *[personne, écrivain]* to waffle* ♦ **son commentaire est un pur ~** his commentary is pure waffle*

délayer /deleje/ ► conjug 8 ◄ VT 1 *[+ couleur]* to thin down; *[+ farine, poudre]* to mix *(to a certain consistency)* *(dans* with); ♦ **~ 100 g de farine dans un litre d'eau** mix 100 g of flour with a litre of water 2 *(péj)* *[+ idée]* to drag out, to spin out; *[+ exposé]* to pad out ♦ **quelques idées habilement délayées** a few ideas cleverly spun out

Delco ® /dɛlko/ NM distributor; → **tête**

deleatur /deleatyʀ/ NM INV delete mark *ou* sign, deleatur *(SPÉC)*

délectable /delɛktabl/ ADJ delectable

délectation /delɛktasjɔ̃/ NF delight, delectation *(littér)*; *(Rel)* delight ♦ **avec ~** *[écouter]* with delight; *[boire]* with relish ♦ **~ morose** delectatio morosa

délecter /delɛkte/ ► conjug 1 ◄ VT *(littér)* to delight VPR **se délecter** ♦ **se ~ de qch/à faire** to delight *ou* revel *ou* take delight in sth/in doing ♦ **il se délectait** he was thoroughly enjoying it

délégataire /delegatɛʀ/ NMF proxy

délégation /delegasjɔ̃/ NF 1 (= *groupe*) delegation; (= *commission*) commission ♦ **ils sont allés en ~ voir le patron** they went as a delegation to see the boss

2 (= *mandat*) delegation ♦ **quand il est absent, sa secrétaire signe le courrier par ~** when he is away his secretary signs his letters on his authority ♦ **il agit par ~** *ou* **en vertu d'une ~** he is acting on somebody's authority ♦ **~ de créance** *(Jur)* assignment *ou* delegation of debt ♦ **~ de pouvoirs** delegation of powers ♦ **~ de solde** *(Mil)* assignment of pay *(to relatives)*

3 *(Admin* = *succursale)* branch, office(s) ♦ **Délégation générale pour l'armement** *state organization responsible for armament programmes* ♦ **Délégation à l'aménagement du territoire et à l'action régionale** *state organization for regional development*

délégué, e /delege/ (ptp de **déléguer**) NM,F (= *représentant*) *(gén)* representative; *(à une réunion, une conférence)* delegate ♦ **~ rectoral** *(Scol)* ≃ temporary teacher ♦ **~ de classe/de parents d'élèves** class/parents' representative ♦ **~ du personnel** staff representative ♦ **~ général** *[de parti politique]* deputy leader; *[d'association, organisme]* chief representative ♦ **~ syndical** union representative, shop steward *(Brit)*

ADJ delegated *(à* to); ♦ **membre ~** delegate ♦ **producteur ~** *(Ciné)* associate producer ♦ **~ à qch** *[adjoint, directeur]* responsible for sth; → **administrateur, juge, ministre**

> **DÉLÉGUÉS**
>
> At the start of the new school year in state « collèges » and « lycées », pupils elect two class representatives known as « délégués de classe », as well as two deputies. The role of the **délégués** is to represent the interest of the class as a whole by liaising with teachers and the school administration. At the end-of-term « conseils de classe », for example, the **délégués** are consulted during discussions on whether borderline pupils should move up to the next year, leave school or repeat the year. The **délégués** of the whole school elect two « délégués d'établissement » who attend the « conseil d'établissement », where they participate in discussions on the general running of the school and vote on decisions to be made.

déléguer /delege/ ▸ conjug 6 ◂ VT 1 *(= transmettre) [+ compétence, pouvoirs, responsabilité]* to delegate *(à* to); *(Jur) [+ créance]* to assign, to delegate ◆ **il faut savoir** ~ it's important to be able to delegate 2 *(= mandater) [+ personne]* to (appoint as a) delegate *(à* to)

délestage /delɛstaʒ/ NM *(= coupure de courant)* power cut; *(sur une route)* diversion; *[de ballon, navire]* removal of ballast *(de* from); ◆ **établir un itinéraire de** ~ to signpost an alternative route

délester /delɛste/ ▸ conjug 1 ◂ VT *[+ navire, ballon]* to remove ballast from, to unballast; *(Élec)* to cut off power from ◆ **on a délesté la N4** a diversion has been signposted on the N4 to relieve congestion ◆ ~ **qn d'un fardeau** to relieve sb of a burden ◆ ~ **qn de qch** * *(= voler qn)* to relieve sb of sth VPR **se délester** *[bateau, ballon]* to jettison ballast ◆ **se** ~ **de ses bombes** *[avion] (en cas de panne)* to jettison its bombs; *(sur l'objectif)* to release its bombs ◆ **elle se délesta de ses colis** she put down *ou* dropped her parcels ◆ **se** ~ **de ses responsabilités sur qn** to offload one's responsibilities on sb

délétère /deletɛʀ/ ADJ *[émanations, gaz]* noxious; *[influence, pouvoir]* pernicious, deleterious; *[effet]* deleterious; *[climat, ambiance]* poisonous

délétion /delesjɔ̃/ NF *(Bio)* deletion

Delhi /dɛli/ N Delhi

déliassage /deljasaʒ/ NM *(Ordin)* decollation

déliasser /deljase/ ▸ conjug 1 ◂ VT *(Ordin)* to decollate

délibérant, e /delibeʀɑ̃, ɑ̃t/ ADJ deliberative

délibératif, -ive /delibeʀatif, iv/ ADJ *[assemblée, conseil]* deliberative ◆ **avoir voix délibérative** to have voting rights

délibération /delibeʀasjɔ̃/ NF 1 *(= débat)* deliberation, debate ◆ ~**s** proceedings, deliberations ◆ **mettre une question en** ~ to debate *ou* deliberate (over *ou* upon) an issue ◆ **après** ~ **du jury** after the jury's due deliberation 2 *(= réflexion)* deliberation, consideration 3 *(= décision)* decision, resolution ◆ ~**s** resolutions ◆ **par** ~ **du jury** on the jury's recommendation

délibéré, e /delibeʀe/ (ptp de **délibérer**) ADJ *(= intentionnel)* deliberate; *(= assuré)* resolute, determined; → **propos** NM *(Jur)* deliberation *(of court at end of trial)* ◆ **mettre en** ~ *[+ jugement, affaire, décision, arrêté]* to adjourn for further consultation ◆ **mise en** ~ deliberation

délibérément /delibeʀemɑ̃/ ADV *(= volontairement)* deliberately, intentionally; *(= après avoir réfléchi)* with due consideration; *(= résolument)* resolutely

délibérer /delibeʀe/ ▸ conjug 6 ◂ VI *(= débattre) (gén)* to deliberate; *[jury]* to confer, to deliberate; *(= réfléchir)* to deliberate, to consider ◆ **après avoir mûrement délibéré** after having pondered the matter, after duly considering the matter ◆ ~ **sur une question** to deliberate (over *ou* upon) an issue VT INDIR **délibérer de** *(= décider)* ~ **de qch** to deliberate sth ◆ ~ **de faire qch** to decide *ou* resolve to do sth (after deliberation)

délicat, e /delika, at/ ADJ 1 *(= fin) [dentelle, parfum, forme, couleur]* delicate; *[fil, voile, facture, travail]* fine; *[mets]* subtle ◆ **un objet gravé de facture** ~**e** an intricately engraved object 2 *(= fragile) [tissu, fleur, enfant, santé]* delicate ◆ **il a la peau très** ~**e** he has very delicate *ou* sensitive skin ◆ **lotion pour peaux** ~**es** lotion for sensitive skins 3 *(= difficile) [situation, question, opération]* delicate, tricky; *[sujet]* delicate, sensitive ◆ **c'est** ~ **!** it's rather delicate! *ou* tricky! ◆ **c'est** ~ **de lui dire ça** it's a bit awkward to tell him that 4 *(= scrupuleux)* scrupulous ◆ **des procédés peu** ~**s** unscrupulous *ou* dishonest methods ◆ **il ne s'est pas montré très** ~ **envers vous** he hasn't behaved very fairly *ou* decently towards you 5 *(= raffiné) [sentiment, goût, esprit, style]* refined, delicate; *[attention]* thoughtful; *[geste]* delicate, thoughtful ◆ **ces propos conviennent peu à des oreilles** ~**es** this conversation isn't suitable for delicate *ou* sensitive ears ◆ **avoir le palais** ~ to have a discerning palate 6 *(= précis) [nuance]* subtle, fine, delicate; *[oreille]* sensitive, fine; *[travail]* fine, delicate 7 *(= léger) [toucher, touche]* gentle, delicate ◆ **prendre qch d'un geste** ~ to take sth gently *ou* delicately 8 *(= plein de tact)* tactful *(envers* to, towards) 9 *(= exigeant)* fussy, particular ◆ **il est** ~ **pour manger** he's fussy *ou* particular about his food ◆ **faire le** ~ *(nourriture)* to be particular *ou* fussy; *(spectacle)* to be squeamish; *(propos)* to act shocked

délicatement /delikatmɑ̃/ ADV 1 *[parfumé, coloré, ouvragé, préparé, exprimé]* delicately 2 *[poser, saisir]* gently; *[prélever]* carefully ◆ **incorporer** ~ **la crème fouettée** gently fold in the whipped cream

délicatesse /delikatɛs/ NF 1 *(= finesse) [de dentelle, parfum, couleur, forme]* delicacy; *[de mets]* subtlety; *[de fil, voile, facture, travail]* fineness 2 *(= fragilité) [de peau]* sensitiveness; *[de tissu]* delicacy 3 *(= scrupules) [de personne, procédés]* scrupulousness ◆ **sa manière d'agir manque de** ~ his behaviour is somewhat unscrupulous 4 *(= raffinement) [de sentiment, goût, esprit, style, geste]* refinement 5 *(= tact)* tact; *(= attentions)* thoughtfulness ◆ **par** ~ **il se retira** he withdrew tactfully 6 *(= précision) [de nuance]* subtlety; *[d'oreille]* sensitivity; *[de travail]* fineness 7 *(= légèreté)* gentleness ◆ **il prit le vase avec** ~ he picked up the vase gently *ou* delicately 8 *(= caractère complexe) [de situation, question]* awkwardness ◆ **être en** ~ **avec qn/la justice** *(frm)* to be at odds with sb/the law 9 *(gén pl = prévenances)* consideration (NonC), (kind) attentions ◆ **avoir des** ~**s pour qn** to show consideration for sb

délice /delis/ NM *(= plaisir)* delight ◆ **quel** ~ **de s'allonger au soleil !** what a delight to lie in the sun! ◆ **se plonger dans l'eau avec** ~ to jump into the water with sheer delight ◆ **ce dessert est un vrai** ~ this dessert is quite delightful *ou* delicious

délices /delis/ NFPL *(littér = plaisirs)* delights ◆ **les** ~ **de l'étude** the delights of study ◆ **toutes les** ~ **de la terre se trouvaient réunies là** every earthly delight was to be found there ◆ **faire ses** ~ **de qch** to take delight in sth ◆ **cette vie rustique ferait les** ~ **de mon père** this country life would delight my father

délicieusement /delisjøzmɑ̃/ ADV *(= d'une manière délicieuse)* exquisitely; *(= d'une manière charmante)* delightfully, exquisitely ◆ **s'enfoncer** ~ **dans les couvertures** to snuggle down under the covers with delight

délicieux, -ieuse /delisjø, jøz/ ADJ *[fruit]* delicious; *[goût]* delicious, delightful; *[lieu, personne, sensation, anecdote]* charming, delightful

délictuel, -elle /deliktɥɛl/ ADJ *[action]* criminal

délictueux, -euse /deliktɥø, øz/ ADJ *(Jur)* criminal ◆ **fait** ~ criminal act

délié, e /delje/ (ptp de **délier**) ADJ 1 *(= agile) [doigts]* nimble, agile; *[esprit]* astute, penetrating ◆ **avoir la langue** ~**e** to be very talkative 2 *(= fin) [taille]* slender; *[fil, écriture]* fine NM *[de lettre]* (thin) upstroke ◆ **les pleins et les** ~**s** the downstrokes and the upstrokes *(in handwriting)* ◆ **avoir un bon** ~ *(Mus)* to have a flowing *ou* an even touch

délier /delje/ ▸ conjug 7 ◂ VT 1 *[+ corde, paquet, prisonnier]* to untie; *[+ gerbe]* to unbind ◆ **déliez-lui les mains** untie his hands ◆ ~ **la langue de qn** to loosen sb's tongue; → **bourse** 2 *(= libérer)* ◆ ~ **qn de** *[+ obligation, serment]* to free *ou* release sb from; *(Rel) [+ péché]* to absolve sb from VPR **se délier** *[lien]* to come untied; *[prisonnier]* to untie o.s., to get (o.s.) free; *[langue]* to loosen ◆ **sous l'effet de l'alcool les langues se délient** alcohol loosens people's tongues ◆ **se** ~ **d'un serment** to free *ou* release o.s. from an oath

délimitation /delimitasjɔ̃/ NF *[de terrain, frontière]* delimitation; *[de sujet, rôle]* definition, delimitation; *[de responsabilités, attributions]* determination

délimiter /delimite/ ▸ conjug 1 ◂ VT *[+ terrain, frontière]* to delimit; *[+ sujet, rôle]* to define (the scope of), to delimit; *[+ responsabilités, attributions]* to determine

délinquance /delɛ̃kɑ̃s/ NF criminality ◆ ~ **juvénile** juvenile delinquency ◆ ~ **financière** financial crime ◆ ~ **routière** reckless driving ◆ **la petite/la grande** ~ petty/serious crime ◆ **acte de** ~ crime ◆ **il a sombré dans la** ~ he slid into crime

délinquant, e /delɛ̃kɑ̃, ɑ̃t/ ADJ delinquent ◆ **la jeunesse** ~**e** juvenile delinquents *ou* offenders NM,F delinquent, offender ◆ ~ **primaire** first offender ◆ ~ **en col blanc** white-collar criminal

déliquescence /delikesɑ̃s/ NF 1 *(Chim = action)* deliquescence 2 *(= décadence)* decay ◆ **en** ~ *[régime, structure]* in decline ◆ **société en complète** ~ society in a state of total decay ◆ **tomber en** ~ to fall into decay *ou* decline

déliquescent, e /delikesɑ̃, ɑ̃t/ ADJ 1 *(Chim)* deliquescent 2 *(= décadent) [régime, mœurs, société]* decaying; *[atmosphère]* devitalizing; *[esprit]* enfeebled; *[personne]* decrepit

délirant, e /deliʀɑ̃, ɑ̃t/ ADJ 1 *(= enthousiaste) [foule]* delirious; *[accueil]* rapturous ◆ **un public** ~ a frenzied audience ◆ **tu n'es pas d'un optimisme** ~ **!** you're not exactly overflowing with optimism! 2 *(= extravagant) [idée, architecture]* extraordinary, wild; *[prix, propos]* outrageous; *[comédie, film]* whacky * ◆ **ce projet est complètement** ~ **!** * this project is completely off the wall! * 3 *(Méd) [malade]* delirious ◆ **crise** ~**e** delirious episode

délire /deliʀ/ NM 1 *(Méd)* delirium ◆ **dans un accès de** ~ in a fit of delirium ◆ **être en plein** ~ to be totally delirious 2 *(= frénésie)* frenzy ◆ **sa passion allait jusqu'au** ~ his passion was almost frenzied ◆ **dans le** ~ **de son imagination** in his wild *ou* frenzied imagination ◆ **une foule en** ~ a frenzied crowd ◆ **quand l'acteur parut, ce fut le** *ou* **du** ~ * when the actor appeared the crowd went crazy

3 **c'est du ~ !** (= *chose extravagante*) it's crazy! ◆ **aux heures de pointe, c'est du ~ dans cette ville** it's absolute chaos *ou* sheer madness in the city at rush hour ◆ **c'est le ~ !*** (= *c'est super*) it's great!*

COMP **délire alcoolique** alcoholic mania
délire de grandeur delusions of grandeur
délire hallucinatoire hallucinatory delirium
délire de persécution persecution mania
délire poétique (*Littérat*) poetic frenzy

délirer /deliʀe/ ▸ conjug 1 ◂ VI [*malade*] to be delirious ◆ **~ de joie** to be delirious with joy ◆ **il délire !*** he's raving!*, he's out of his mind!* ◆ **~ sur qch** (= *en parler*) to jabber on* about sth ◆ **il délire complètement sur le rap** he's crazy* about rap music

delirium tremens /deliʀjɔmtʀemɛs/ NM delirium tremens

délit /deli/ NM (*gén*) crime, offence; (*Jur*) (criminal) offence, misdemeanor (*US*) ◆ **commettre un ~** to commit an offence ◆ **~ de fuite** failure to report an accident, hit-and-run offence ◆ **il a été arrêté pour ~ de faciès/de sale gueule** they arrested him because of the colour of his skin/because they didn't like the look of him ◆ **~ financier** financial crime ◆ **~ d'ingérence** abuse of office ◆ **~ d'initié** insider dealing *ou* trading ◆ **~ de presse** violation of the press laws ◆ **~ sexuel** sexual offence *ou* crime ◆ **être poursuivi pour ~ d'opinion** to be prosecuted for one's beliefs *ou* convictions; → **corps, flagrant**

déliter /delite/ ▸ conjug 1 ◂ VT [+ *pierre*] to cleave VPR **se déliter** (*lit*) to disintegrate (*because of exposure to moisture*); [*certitudes, valeurs*] to crumble; [*État, structure*] to fall apart

délivrance /delivʀɑ̃s/ NF 1 [*de prisonniers*] release; [*de pays*] deliverance, liberation 2 (= *soulagement*) relief ◆ **il est parti, quelle ~ !** he's gone - what a relief! 3 [*de passeport, reçu*] issue, delivery; [*d'ordonnance*] issue; [*de lettre, marchandise*] delivery ◆ **~ d'un brevet** issue of a patent 4 (*littér* = *accouchement*) delivery

délivrer /delivʀe/ ▸ conjug 1 ◂ VT 1 (= *libérer*) [+ *prisonnier, esclave*] to set free ◆ **~ qn de** [+ *rival*] to relieve *ou* rid sb of; [+ *liens, obligation*] to free sb from, to relieve sb of; [+ *crainte*] to relieve sb of ◆ **être délivré d'un grand poids** to be relieved of a great weight 2 (= *remettre*) [+ *passeport, reçu*] to issue; [+ *lettre, marchandise*] to deliver; [+ *brevet*] to grant; [+ *ordonnance*] to give, to issue; [+ *médicament*] [*pharmacien*] to dispense; (*Admin*) to sell; → **ordonnance** VPR **se délivrer** [*personne*] to free o.s. (*de* from)

délocalisable /delɔkalizabl/ ADJ [*emploi, entreprise*] that can be relocated

délocalisation /delɔkalizasjɔ̃/ NF relocation

délocaliser /delɔkalize/ ▸ conjug 1 ◂ VT [+ *activités, entreprise, emplois*] to relocate VPR **se délocaliser** ◆ **l'entreprise va se ~ à l'étranger** the company is going to relocate abroad

déloger /delɔʒe/ ▸ conjug 3 ◂ VT [+ *locataire*] to turn *ou* throw out; [+ *fugitif*] to flush out; [+ *lièvre*] to start; [+ *objet, ennemi*] to dislodge (*de* from) VI 1 (= *déguerpir*) to clear out ◆ **délogez de là !** clear out of there!* 2 (*Belg* = *découcher*) to spend the night away from home

déloguer (se) /delɔge/ VPR (*Ordin* = *se déconnecter*) to log off

déloquer (se) * /delɔke/ ▸ conjug 1 ◂ VPR (= *se déshabiller*) to strip off

déloyal, e (mpl **-aux**) /delwajal, o/ ADJ [*ami*] unfaithful, disloyal (*envers* towards); [*adversaire*] underhand; [*conduite*] disloyal, underhand; [*procédé*] unfair ◆ **concurrence ~e** unfair competition ◆ **un coup ~** (*Sport*) a foul

déloyalement /delwajalmɑ̃/ ADV disloyally

déloyauté /delwajote/ NF [*d'ami, conduite*] disloyalty (*envers* towards); [*d'adversaire*] underhandedness, unfairness; [*de procédé*] unfairness ◆ **actes de ~** disloyal acts

Delphes /dɛlf/ N Delphi

delphinarium /dɛlfinaʀjɔm/ NM dolphinarium

delphinium /dɛlfinjɔm/ NM delphinium

delta /dɛlta/ NM (*Géog, Ling*) delta ◆ **le ~ du Mékong** the Mekong delta ◆ **rayon ~** (*Phys*) delta ray ◆ **avion à ailes (en) ~** delta-winged aicraft; → **aile**

deltaïque /dɛltaik/ ADJ deltaic, delta (*épith*)

deltaplane ® /dɛltaplan/ NM (= *appareil*) hang-glider; (= *sport*) hang-gliding ◆ **faire du ~** to hang-glide, to go hang-gliding

deltoïde /dɛltɔid/ ADJ, NM deltoid

déluge /delyʒ/ NM (= *pluie*) downpour, deluge; [*de larmes, paroles, injures*] flood; [*de compliments, coups*] shower ◆ **le ~** (*Bible*) the Flood, the Deluge ◆ **ça date du ~, ça remonte au ~** it's ancient history ◆ **après moi le ~ !** I don't care what happens after I'm gone!, après moi le déluge!

déluré, e /delyʀe/ ADJ 1 (= *débrouillard*) smart, resourceful 2 (= *impertinent*) (*gén*) forward; [*fille*] saucy, sassy* (*US*) ◆ **sa sœur est un peu ~e** his sister is a bit wild

délurer /delyʀe/ ▸ conjug 1 ◂ VT (= *dégourdir*) to make smart *ou* resourceful, to teach a thing or two to*; (*péj*) to make forward *ou* pert VPR **se délurer** (= *se dégourdir*) to become smart *ou* resourceful; (*péj*) to become forward ◆ **il s'est déluré au régiment** he learnt a thing or two* in the army

démagnétisation /demaɲetizasjɔ̃/ NF demagnetization

démagnétiser /demaɲetize/ ▸ conjug 1 ◂ VT, **se démagnétiser** VPR to demagnetize

démago * /demago/ ADJ abrév de **démagogique** NMF abrév de **démagogue**

démagogie /demagɔʒi/ NF ◆ **il se garde de toute ~** he makes no attempt to court popularity ◆ **absoudre par ~ des actes de violence** to excuse acts of violence out of a desire to win popularity ◆ **le magazine s'adresse à un large public sans pour autant tomber dans la ~** the magazine addresses a wide readership without dumbing down

> ⚠ Attention à ne pas traduire automatiquement **démagogie** par **demagogy**, qui a des emplois spécifiques.

démagogique /demagɔʒik/ ADJ ◆ **ce n'est pas réaliste, c'est ~** it's not realistic, it's just designed to appeal to the public ◆ **son discours est rassurant, paternaliste, ~** what he says is soothing, paternalistic and calculated to appeal to public opinion ◆ **aucun parti n'a intérêt à faire de surenchère ~ à propos de l'immigration** it's not in the interest of any party to get involved in a demagogic slanging match about immigration

> ⚠ Attention à ne pas traduire automatiquement **démagogique** par **demagogic**, qui a des emplois spécifiques.

démagogue /demagɔg/ NMF demagogue ADJ ◆ **être ~** to be a demagogue

démaillage /demɑjaʒ/ NM [*de bas*] laddering (*Brit*), running (*US*); [*de tricot*] undoing, unravelling

démailler /demɑje/ ▸ conjug 1 ◂ VT [+ *bas*] to ladder (*Brit*), to run (*US*); [+ *filet*] to undo (the mesh of); [+ *tricot*] to undo, to unravel; [+ *chaîne*] to unlink, to separate the links of ◆ **ses bas sont démaillés** her stockings are laddered (*Brit*) *ou* have got ladders (*Brit*) *ou* have runs (*US*) in them VPR **se démailler** [*bas*] to ladder (*Brit*), to run (*US*); [*tricot, filet*] to unravel, to come unravelled ◆ **la chaîne s'est démaillée** the links of the chain have come apart

démailloter /demajɔte/ ▸ conjug 1 ◂ VT [+ *enfant*] to take the swaddling clothes off

demain /d(ə)mɛ̃/ ADV 1 (= *dans un jour*) tomorrow ◆ **~ matin** tomorrow morning ◆ **~ soir** tomorrow evening *ou* night ◆ **~ en huit/en quinze** a week/two weeks tomorrow ◆ **à dater *ou* à partir de ~** (as) from tomorrow, from tomorrow on ◆ **~ il fera jour** tomorrow is another day ◆ **ce n'est pas ~ la veille*, ce n'est pas pour ~*** that won't happen in a hurry ◆ **~ on rase gratis !*** it's jam tomorrow! ◆ **à ~** (*gén*) see you tomorrow; (= *je téléphonerai*) I'll talk to you tomorrow ◆ **d'ici (à) ~ tout peut changer** everything might be different by tomorrow; → **remettre** 2 (= *l'avenir*) **le monde de ~** the world of tomorrow, tomorrow's world ◆ **de quoi ~ sera-t-il fait ?** what will tomorrow's world hold for us?

démanché, e /demɑ̃ʃe/ (ptp de **démancher**) ADJ [*bras*] out of joint (*attrib*), dislocated; * [*objet*] loose; [*meuble*] rickety ◆ **le marteau est ~** the hammer has no handle *ou* has lost its handle NM (*Mus*) shift

démancher /demɑ̃ʃe/ ▸ conjug 1 ◂ VT [+ *outil*] to take the handle off; (* = *disloquer*) [+ *meuble*] to knock a leg off; [+ *bras*] to put out of joint, to dislocate VI (*Mus*) to shift VPR **se démancher** [*outil*] to lose its handle; [*bras*] to be put out of joint, to be dislocated; * [*meuble, objet*] to fall to bits *ou* pieces ◆ **se ~ le bras** to dislocate one's shoulder ◆ **se ~ le cou pour voir qch*** to crane one's neck to see sth

demande /d(ə)mɑ̃d/ NF 1 (= *requête*) request (*de qch* for sth); (= *revendication*) claim, demand (*de* for); (*Admin*) [*d'autorisation, naturalisation*] application (*de* for); [*de remboursement, dédommagement*] claim (*de* for); [*de renseignement*] enquiry; (*Cartes*) bid ◆ **faire une ~** (*gén*) to make a request ◆ **faire une ~ de remboursement** to make a claim, to claim ◆ **adressez votre ~ au ministère** apply to the ministry ◆ **remplir une ~** (*formulaire*) to fill in a claim form (*de* for); ◆ **~ d'adhésion** application for membership ◆ **~ d'asile** request *ou* application for asylum ◆ **~ de rançon** ransom demand ◆ **~ d'emploi** job application ◆ **"demandes d'emploi"** (*rubrique de journal*) "situations wanted" ◆ **~ (en mariage)** proposal (of marriage) ◆ **faire sa ~ (en mariage)** to propose ◆ **à *ou* sur la ~ de qn** at sb's request ◆ **à la ~, sur ~** (*gén*) on request; (*Admin*) on application ◆ **et maintenant, à la ~ générale ...** and now, by popular request ...
2 (*Écon*) **la ~** demand ◆ **pour répondre à la ~ (de pétrole/de fruits)** to meet the demand (for oil/fruit) ◆ **il y a une forte ~ de produits importés** imported goods are in great demand, there is a great *ou* high demand for imported goods
3 (*Jur*) **~ en divorce** divorce petition ◆ **~ en renvoi** request for remittal ◆ **~ principale/accessoire/subsidiaire** chief/secondary/contingency petition
4 (= *besoins*) [*de malade, enfant*] needs ◆ **~ d'affection** need for affection

> ⚠ Attention à ne pas traduire automatiquement **demande** par **demand**.

demandé, e /d(ə)mɑ̃de/ (ptp de **demander**) ADJ (*Comm*) in demand ◆ **cet article est très ~** this item is very much in demand, there is a great demand for this item ◆ **il est très ~** [*médecin, chanteur*] he is very much in demand ◆ **c'est une destination très ~e** it's a very popular destination

demander /d(ə)mɑ̃de/ GRAMMAIRE ACTIVE 28.2, 43.1, 53.6 ▸ conjug 1 ◂

VT [1] *(= solliciter) [+ chose, conseil, réponse, entrevue, volontaire]* to ask for; *(Admin, Jur) [+ délai, emploi, divorce]* to apply for; *[+ indemnité, remboursement]* to claim; *[+ réunion, enquête]* to call for, to ask for ♦ **~ qch à qn** to ask sb for sth ♦ **~ un service** *ou* **une faveur à qn** to ask sb a favour ♦ **~ la paix** to sue for peace ♦ **~ une permission** *(Mil)* to ask for *ou* request *(frm)* leave ♦ **~ la permission de faire qch** to ask *ou* request *(frm)* permission to do sth ♦ **~ aide et assistance** to request aid *(à* from*)*; ♦ **~ à voir qn/à parler à qn** to ask to see sb/to speak to sb ♦ **il a demandé à partir plus tôt** he has asked to leave earlier ♦ **~ à qn de faire** *ou* **qu'il fasse qch** to ask *ou* request *(frm)* sb to do sth ♦ **puis-je vous ~ (de me passer) du pain ?** would you mind passing me some bread? ♦ **vous n'avez qu'à ~, il n'y a qu'à ~** you only have to ask ♦ **que demande le peuple ?** *(hum)* what more could you ask for?; → **aumône, charité, pardon**

[2] *(= appeler) [+ médecin, prêtre, plombier]* to send for ♦ **le blessé demande un prêtre** the injured man is asking *ou* calling for a priest

[3] *(au téléphone, au bureau etc) [+ personne, numéro]* to ask for ♦ **demandez-moi M. Leblanc** *(au téléphone)* get me Mr Leblanc ♦ **qui demandez-vous ?** who do you wish to speak to? ♦ **on le demande au bureau/au téléphone** he is wanted at the office/on the phone, someone is asking for him at the office/on the phone ♦ **le patron vous demande** *ou* **demande après* vous** the boss wants to see you *ou* speak to you, the boss is asking to see you

[4] *(= désirer)* to be asking for, to want ♦ **ils demandent 10 € de l'heure et une semaine de congé** they are asking (for) €10 an hour and a week's holiday ♦ **le chat miaule, il demande son lait** the cat's mewing – he's asking for his milk ♦ **je demande à voir !*** I'll believe it when I see it! ♦ **il ne demande qu'à apprendre/à se laisser convaincre** all he wants is to learn/to be convinced, he's more than willing to learn/be convinced ♦ **il demande qu'on le laisse partir** he wants us to *ou* is asking us to let him go ♦ **tout ce que je demande, c'est qu'il vienne** all (that) I ask is that he should come ♦ **je ne demande pas mieux !** *ou* **que ça !** I'll be *ou* I'm only too pleased! ♦ **il ne demandera pas mieux que de vous aider** he'll be only too pleased to help you

[5] *(= s'enquérir de) [+ heure, nom, chemin]* to ask ♦ **~ l'heure à qn** to ask sb the time ♦ **je lui ai demandé son nom** I asked him his name ♦ **~ un renseignement à qn** to ask sb for some information ♦ **~ quand/comment/pourquoi c'est arrivé** to ask when/how/why it happened ♦ **~ des nouvelles de qn, ~ après qn*** to enquire *ou* ask after sb ♦ **"où est-il ?" demanda-t-elle** "where is he?", she asked ♦ **va ~ !** go and ask! ♦ **je ne t'ai rien demandé** I didn't ask you ♦ **je ne te demande rien** I'm not asking you ♦ **on ne t'a pas demandé l'heure (qu'il est)*** *ou* **ton avis*** who asked you?, who rattled your cage?** ♦ **je vous le demande !, je vous demande un peu !*** *(excl)* honestly!*

[6] *(= nécessiter) [travail, décision]* to require, to need ♦ **ça demande un effort** it requires an effort ♦ **ces plantes demandent beaucoup d'eau/à être arrosées** these plants need *ou* require a lot of water/watering ♦ **ce travail va (lui) ~ six heures** the job will take (him) 6 hours *ou* will require 6 hours, he'll need 6 hours to do the job ♦ **cette proposition demande réflexion** this proposal needs thinking over ♦ **cette proposition demande toute votre attention** this proposal calls for *ou* requires your full attention

[7] *(= exiger)* **~ qch à** *ou* **de qn** to ask sth of sb ♦ **~ beaucoup à** *ou* **de la vie/ses élèves** to ask a lot of life/of one's pupils ♦ **il ne faut pas trop lui en ~ !** you mustn't ask too much of him!

[8] *(Comm)* **ils (en) demandent 100 €** they are asking *ou* want €100 (for it) ♦ **ils m'en ont demandé 100 €** they asked (me) for €100 for it ♦ **ils demandent une vendeuse** *(= ils en cherchent une)* they're looking for a shop assistant ♦ **ils demandent 3 vendeuses** *(par annonce)* they are advertising for *ou* they want 3 shop assistants ♦ **on demande beaucoup de vendeuses en ce moment** shop assistants are very much in demand *ou* are in great demand just now ♦ **"on demande : électricien"** "electrician wanted *ou* required" ♦ **comme vous l'avez demandé dans votre lettre du 25 janvier** as requested in your letter of 25 January

VPR **se demander** [1] *(= hésiter, douter)* to wonder ♦ **on peut vraiment se ~** *ou* **c'est à se ~ s'il a perdu la tête** it makes you wonder if he isn't out of his mind ♦ **il se demande où aller/ce qu'il doit faire** he is wondering where to go/what to do ♦ **il se demanda : suis-je vraiment aussi bête ?** he asked himself *ou* wondered: am I really so stupid? ♦ **ils se demandent bien pourquoi il a démissionné** they can't think why he resigned, they really wonder why he resigned

[2] *(sens passif)* **ça ne se demande pas !** that's a stupid question!

> ⚠ Attention à ne pas traduire automatiquement **demander** par **to demand**, qui a le sens de 'exiger'.

demandeur[1], -deresse /d(ə)mɑ̃dœʀ, dʀɛs/ NM,F *(Jur)* plaintiff, complainant; *(en divorce)* petitioner ♦ **~ en appel** appellant ♦ **la partie demanderesse** the moving party

demandeur[2], -euse /d(ə)mɑ̃dœʀ, øz/ NM,F ♦ **~ d'emploi** person looking for work, job seeker ♦ **le nombre des ~s d'emploi a baissé** the number of job seekers has fallen ♦ **~ d'asile** asylum seeker ♦ **~ de visa** visa applicant ♦ **ils sont très ~s de nos produits** our goods are very popular with them ♦ **s'il existe un bon dictionnaire, je suis ~** if there's a good dictionary I'm interested

démangeaison /demɑ̃ʒɛzɔ̃/ NF itching *(NonC)*, itching sensation ♦ **avoir des ~s** to be itching ♦ **j'ai des ~s dans le dos** my back is itching ♦ **j'ai une ~** I've got an itch

démanger /demɑ̃ʒe/ ► conjug 3 ◄ VT [1] *(= gratter)* **son dos/son coup de soleil le** *ou* **lui démange** his back/sunburn itches *ou* is itching ♦ **où est-ce que ça (vous) démange ?** where does it itch? ♦ **ça (me) démange** it itches, it's making me itch [2] *(fig)* **ses poings le démangent** he's itching* for a fight ♦ **la main me démange** I'm itching* *ou* dying to hit him *(ou her etc)* ♦ **la langue me démange** I'm itching* *ou* dying to say something ♦ **ça me démange de faire ..., l'envie me démange de faire ...** I'm dying to do ... ♦ **ça me démangeait de lui dire** I was itching* to tell him

démantèlement /demɑ̃tɛlmɑ̃/ NM *(Mil) [de forteresse]* demolition, demolishing; *[d'armes, missiles, centrale nucléaire, entreprise, service]* dismantling; *[de gang, réseau d'espionnage, de trafiquants]* breaking up; *[d'empire]* dismantling, break-up

démanteler /demɑ̃t(ə)le/ ► conjug 5 ◄ VT *(Mil) [+ forteresse]* to demolish; *[+ armes, missiles, centrale nucléaire, entreprise, service]* to dismantle; *[+ gang, réseau d'espionnage, de trafiquants]* to break up; *[+ empire]* to dismantle, to break up

démantibuler* /demɑ̃tibyle/ ► conjug 1 ◄ VT *[+ objet]* to demolish, to break up VPR **se démantibuler** to fall apart ♦ **se ~ le bras** to dislocate one's shoulder

démaquillage /demakijaʒ/ NM ♦ **elle commença son ~** she started to take off *ou* remove her make-up ♦ **produit de ~** make-up remover ♦ **pour le ~ des yeux, ne jamais frotter** when removing eye make-up, don't rub your eyes

démaquillant, e /demakijɑ̃, ɑ̃t/ ADJ ♦ **lait** *(ou* **gel)** ~ make-up remover NM make-up remover ♦ **~ pour les yeux** eye make-up remover

démaquiller /demakije/ ► conjug 1 ◄ VT *[+ yeux, visage]* to remove the make-up from, to take the make-up off ♦ **~ qn** to take off *ou* remove sb's make-up VPR **se démaquiller** to take one's make-up off, to remove one's make-up ♦ **se ~ les yeux** to remove one's eye make-up

démarcage /demaʀkaʒ/ NM ⇒ **démarquage**

démarcatif, -ive /demaʀkatif, iv/ ADJ demarcating

démarcation /demaʀkasjɔ̃/ NF demarcation *(de, entre* between*)* → **ligne[1]**

démarchage /demaʀʃaʒ/ NM *(= vente de porte à porte)* door-to-door *ou* doorstep selling ♦ **~ téléphonique** cold calling ♦ **~ électoral** canvassing ♦ **faire du ~** *(de porte à porte)* to do door-to-door selling; *(par téléphone)* to work in telesales; *(Pol)* to canvass

démarche /demaʀʃ/ NF [1] *(= façon de marcher)* walk, gait ♦ **avoir une ~ pesante/gauche** to have a heavy/an awkward gait *ou* walk, to walk heavily/awkwardly

[2] *(= intervention)* step ♦ **faire une ~ auprès de qn (pour obtenir qch)** to approach sb (to obtain sth) ♦ **entreprendre des ~s auprès d'un service** to apply to a department ♦ **toutes nos ~s ont échoué** everything we tried failed ♦ **les ~s nécessaires pour obtenir un passeport** what you have to do to get a passport ♦ **l'idée de (faire) cette ~ m'effrayait** I was frightened at the idea of doing this ♦ **sa ~ m'a surpris** I was surprised by what he did ♦ **faire le test est une ~ volontaire qui ne peut être imposée à quelqu'un** having the test is voluntary and cannot be forced on anyone ♦ **par une ~ volontaire** voluntarily ♦ **la bonne ~ (consiste à faire qch)** the right approach (is to do sth)

[3] *(= attitude)* approach ♦ **sa ~ politique** his political approach

[4] *(= raisonnement)* reasoning ♦ **expliquez-moi votre ~** explain your reasoning to me ♦ **~ intellectuelle** reasoning

démarcher /demaʀʃe/ ► conjug 1 ◄ VT *[+ clients]* to canvass; *[+ produit]* to sell door-to-door

démarcheur, -euse /demaʀʃœʀ, øz/ NM,F *(= vendeur)* door-to-door salesman *(ou* saleswoman); *(Pol)* (door-to-door) canvasser

démarier /demaʀje/ ► conjug 7 ◄ VT *(Agr)* to thin out

démarquage /demaʀkaʒ/ NM *[de linge, argenterie]* removal of the identifying mark(s) *(de* on*)*; *[d'auteur, œuvre]* copying *(de* from*)*; ♦ **le ~ d'un joueur** *(Sport)* the drawing away of a player's marker ♦ **cet ouvrage est un ~ grossier** this work is a crude plagiarism *ou* copy

démarque /demaʀk/ NF *[d'article]* markdown, marking-down ♦ **~ inconnue** shortfall *(in stock)* ♦ **"deuxième démarque"** "further reductions"

démarqué, e /demaʀke/ (ptp de **démarquer**) ADJ *(Sport) [joueur]* unmarked ♦ **robe ~e** unlabelled designer dress

démarquer /demaʀke/ ► conjug 1 ◄ VT [1] *(= ôter une marque) [+ linge, argenterie]* to remove the (identifying) mark(s) from; *(Comm) (= solder)* to mark down; *(= retirer l'étiquette de)* to remove the (designer) label from [2] *(= copier) [+ œuvre, auteur]* to plagiarize, to copy [3] *(Sport) [+ joueur]* to draw a marker away from VPR **se démarquer** [1] *(Sport)* to lose *ou* shake off one's marker [2] ♦ **se ~ de** *(= marquer sa différence avec)* to distinguish *ou* differentiate o.s. from

démarrage /demaʀaʒ/ NM [1] *(= départ) [de véhicule]* moving off *(NonC)* ♦ **~ en trombe** shooting off *(NonC)* ♦ **il a calé au ~** he stalled as he moved off ♦ **secoués à chaque ~ du bus** shaken about every time the bus moved off

2 (= début) start ◆ **l'excellent/le difficile ~ de la campagne électorale** the excellent/difficult start to the electoral campaign
3 (Sport = accélération) [de coureur] pulling away (NonC) ◆ **il a placé un ~ à 100 m de l'arrivée** he put on a burst of speed ou he pulled away 100 metres from the finishing line ◆ **être lent au ~** * to be slow to get going
4 (= largage des amarres) casting off, unmooring
5 (= mise en marche) [de véhicule] starting ◆ **le ~ d'une affaire/campagne** getting a deal/a campaign off the ground
COMP **démarrage en côte** hill start
démarrage à la manivelle crank-starting

démarrer /demaʀe/ ► conjug 1 ◄ VI 1 [moteur, conducteur] to start (up); [véhicule] to move off; [affaire, campagne] to get under way, to get off the ground; [économie] to take off; [élève, débutant] to start off ◆ **l'affaire a bien démarré** the deal got off to a good start ou started off well ◆ **~ en trombe** to shoot off ◆ **faire ~** [+ véhicule] to start, to get started; [+ affaire, campagne] to get under way, to get off the ground ◆ **il a bien démarré en latin** he got off to a good start in Latin, he started off well in Latin; → **froid**
2 (= accélérer) [coureur] to pull away
3 (= larguer les amarres) to cast off, to unmoor
VT INDIR **démarrer de** (= démordre de) [+ idée, projet] to let go of ◆ **il ne veut pas ~ de son idée** he just won't let go of his idea
VT [+ véhicule] to start, to get started; (Naut) [+ embarcation] to cast off, to unmoor; * [+ travail] to get going on* ◆ **~ une affaire/une campagne** to get a deal/a campaign started ◆ **~ qn en anglais** to get sb started in English

démarreur /demaʀœʀ/ NM (Aut) starter

démasquer /demaske/ ► conjug 1 ◄ VT 1 (= dévoiler) [+ imposteur, espion, hypocrisie] to unmask; [+ plan] to unveil, to uncover 2 (= enlever le masque de) to unmask VPR **se démasquer** [imposteur] to drop one's mask; [personne déguisée] to take off one's mask

démâtage /demɑtaʒ/ NM dismasting

démâter /demɑte/ ► conjug 1 ◄ VT (involontairement) to dismast; (volontairement) to unstep the mast(s) of VI [bateau] to lose its mast(s), to be dismasted ◆ **j'ai démâté** my boat lost its mast(s)

dématérialisation /dematerjalizasjɔ̃/ NF dematerialization

dématérialiser (se) /dematerjalize/ ► conjug 1 ◄ VPR [transaction] to dematerialize ◆ **les frontières de l'Europe se dématérialisent** Europe's borders are becoming less and less visible

démazouter /demazute/ ► conjug 1 ◄ VT [+ plage] to remove the oil from

d'emblée /dɑ̃ble/ LOC ADV → **emblée**

démêlage /demelaʒ/ NM (lit, fig) disentangling, untangling

démêlant, e /demelɑ̃, ɑt/ ADJ (hair) conditioning NM (hair) conditioner

démêlé /demele/ NM (= dispute) dispute, quarrel ◆ **~s** (= ennuis) problems ◆ **il a eu des ~s avec la justice** he has fallen foul of the law ou has had some problems ou trouble with the law ◆ **il risque d'avoir des ~s avec l'administration** he's likely to have some trouble with the authorities

démêlement /demɛlmɑ̃/ NM ⇒ **démêlage**

démêler /demele/ ► conjug 1 ◄ VT 1 [+ ficelle, écheveau] to disentangle, to untangle; [+ cheveux] to untangle; (avec un peigne) to comb out 2 [+ problème, situation] to untangle, to sort out; [+ intentions, machinations] to unravel, to get to the bottom of ◆ **~ qch d'avec ou de** to distinguish ou tell sth from ◆ **~ le vrai du faux** to sort the truth out from the lies 3 (littér = débattre) **~ qch avec qn** to dispute sth with sb ◆ **je ne veux rien avoir à ~ avec lui** I do not wish to have to contend with him VPR **se démêler de** (= se tirer de) (littér) [+ embarras, difficultés] to disentangle o.s. from, to extricate o.s. from

démêloir /demɛlwaʀ/ NM (large-toothed) comb

démêlures /demelyʀ/ NFPL combings

démembrement /demɑ̃bʀəmɑ̃/ NM 1 [d'animal] dismemberment 2 [de pays, empire] dismemberment, break-up; [d'entreprise] asset-stripping

démembrer /demɑ̃bʀe/ ► conjug 1 ◄ VT 1 [+ animal] to dismember 2 [+ pays, empire] to dismember, to break up; [+ entreprise] to asset-strip

déménagement /demenaʒmɑ̃/ NM 1 [de meubles] moving, removal (Brit); [de pièce] emptying (of furniture) (NonC) ◆ **camion de ~** removal (Brit) ou moving (US) van ◆ **le ~ du mobilier s'est bien passé** moving the furniture ou the removal of the furniture went well ◆ **le ~ du laboratoire a posé des problèmes** moving the furniture out of the laboratory ou emptying the laboratory of (its) furniture proved to be no easy matter ◆ **ils ont fait quatre ~s en trois jours** they did four moves ou removals (Brit) in three days
2 (= changement de domicile) move, moving (house) (NonC); (= changement de bureau) move, moving (offices) (NonC) ◆ **faire un ~** to move (house) ◆ **on a dû perdre ça pendant le ~** we must have lost it during the move ◆ **trois ~s en une année, c'est trop** three moves in one year is too much, moving (house) three times in one year is too much

déménager /demenaʒe/ ► conjug 3 ◄ VT [+ meubles, affaires] to move; [+ maison, pièce] to move the furniture out of, to empty (of furniture) VI 1 (= changer de maison) to move (house); (= changer d'appartement) to move (into a new flat); (= changer de locaux) to move (offices) ◆ **~ à la cloche de bois** to sneak off in the middle of the night, to do a moonlight flit* (Brit) 2 (* = partir) to clear off* ◆ **allez, déménage !** buzz ou clear off!* ◆ **il nous a fait ~** he sent us packing* ◆ **avec elle, les dossiers ça déménage*** she gets through files like nobody's business* 3 (* = être fou) to be off one's rocker* 4 (* = être excellent) **il/ça déménage !** he's/it's brill!* (Brit) ou awesome!* (US)

déménageur /demenaʒœʀ/ NM (= entrepreneur) furniture remover (Brit), moving company (US); (= ouvrier) removal man (Brit), (furniture) mover (US) ◆ **il a une carrure de ~** he's built like a tank

démence /demɑ̃s/ NF (Méd) dementia; (Jur) mental disorder; (gén) madness, insanity ◆ **c'est de la ~** (fig) it's (sheer) madness ou lunacy, it's insane ◆ **~ précoce** (Méd) dementia praecox ◆ **~ sénile** (Méd) senile dementia

démener (se) /dem(ə)ne/ ► conjug 5 ◄ VPR (= se débattre) to thrash about, to struggle (violently); (= se dépenser) to exert o.s. ◆ **se ~ comme un beau diable** (pour se sauver) to thrash about ou struggle violently; (pour obtenir qch) to make a tremendous effort, to go to great lengths ◆ **si on se démène un peu on aura fini avant la nuit** if we put our backs into it a bit* we'll finish before nightfall ◆ **ils se démenèrent tant et si bien que …** they exerted themselves to such an extent that …, they made such a great effort that … ◆ **il faut que tu te démènes si tu veux des billets** you'll have to get a move on* if you want tickets

dément, e /demɑ̃, ɑt/ ADJ (= fou) mad, insane, crazy; (= incroyable) incredible, unbelievable; (* = extravagant) [type, musique] way-out*, weird*; [prix, projet] mad, crazy NM,F (= personne) lunatic, demented person

démenti /demɑ̃ti/ NM (= déclaration) denial, refutation; (apporté par les faits, les circonstances) refutation ◆ **opposer un ~ à** [+ nouvelle, allégations, rumeurs] to deny formally ◆ **publier un ~** to publish a denial ◆ **sa version des faits reste sans ~** his version of the facts remains uncontradicted ou unchallenged ◆ **son expression opposait un ~ à ses paroles** his expression belied his words

démentiel, -ielle /demɑ̃sjɛl/ ADJ 1 (Méd) dementia (épith) 2 [projet, prix] mad, crazy

démentir /demɑ̃tiʀ/ ► conjug 16 ◄ VT 1 [personne] [+ nouvelle, rumeur] to deny, to refute; [+ personne] to contradict ◆ **il dément ses principes par son attitude** his attitude contradicts his principles
2 [+ faits, témoignage] to refute; [+ apparences] to belie; [+ espoirs] to disappoint ◆ **la douceur de son sourire est démentie par la dureté de son regard** the hardness in her eyes belies the sweetness of her smile ◆ **les résultats ont démenti les pronostics** the results have contradicted the predictions
VPR **se démentir** (nég = cesser) **son amitié/sa fidélité ne s'est jamais démentie** his friendship/loyalty has never failed ◆ **c'est un roman dont le succès ne s'est jamais démenti** the novel has always maintained its popularity ◆ **leur intérêt pour ces mystères, qui ne s'est jamais démenti** their unfailing ou never-failing interest in these mysteries

démerdard, e* /demɛʀdaʀ, aʀd/ NM,F ◆ **c'est un ~** he knows how to look after himself ADJ ◆ **il est ~** he's a smart customer*, there are no flies on him (Brit) ◆ **il n'est pas ~ pour deux sous** he's really clueless*, he hasn't (got) a clue* ◆ **dans la vie il faut être ~** you have to learn to look out for yourself in life

démerde* /demɛʀd/ ADJ ⇒ **démerdard** NF ◆ **la ~** (= ingéniosité) resourcefulness; (= astuce) smartness ◆ **c'est le roi de la ~** he always knows how to wangle* things

démerder (se)* /demɛʀde/ ► conjug 1 ◄ VPR 1 (= se débrouiller) to manage ◆ **il sait se ~ dans la vie** he knows how to look after himself all right* ◆ **elle se démerde (pas mal) au ski/en peinture** she's pretty good at skiing/painting ◆ **si je m'étais mieux démerdé, j'aurais gagné** if I'd known how to handle things better, I'd have won ◆ **il s'est démerdé pour avoir une permission** he wangled himself some leave*, he wangled it so that he got some leave* 2 (= se tirer d'affaire) to get out of a mess ◆ **il a voulu y aller, maintenant qu'il se démerde tout seul** he wanted to go so now he can get out of his own bloody* (Brit) ou damn* mess

démérite /demeʀit/ NM (littér) demerit (littér), fault ◆ **où est son ~, dans ce cas ?** where is he at fault in this matter?, wherein lies his fault in this matter? (littér)

démériter /demeʀite/ ► conjug 1 ◄ VT INDIR **démériter de** [+ patrie, institution] to show o.s. unworthy of VI (Rel) to deserve to fall from grace ◆ **en quoi a-t-il démérité ?** how was he to blame? ◆ **il n'a pas démérité** he hasn't done anything blameworthy ◆ **l'équipe perdante n'a cependant pas démérité** the losing team nevertheless put up a creditable performance

démesure /dem(ə)zyʀ/ NF [de personnage] excessiveness, immoderation; [de propos, exigences, style] outrageousness ◆ **je hais la ~** I hate excess

démesuré, e /dem(ə)zyʀe/ ADJ [orgueil] overweening, excessive; [ambition, prétentions] overweening; [taille] disproportionate; [territoire, distances] vast, enormous; [membres] enormous

démesurément /dem(ə)zyʀemɑ̃/ ADV immoderately, inordinately; *[augmenter]* disproportionately ◆ ~ **long** disproportionately long

démettre /demɛtʀ/ ▸ conjug 56 ◂ VT 1 *(= disloquer) [+ articulation]* to dislocate 2 *(= révoquer)* ~ **qn de ses fonctions/son poste** to dismiss sb from his duties/post 3 *(Jur)* ~ **qn de son appel** to dismiss sb's appeal VPR **se démettre** 1 *(frm = démissionner)* to resign, to hand in one's resignation ◆ **se** ~ **de ses fonctions/son poste** to resign (from) one's duties/post 2 *(= se disloquer)* **se** ~ **le poignet/la cheville** to dislocate one's wrist/ankle, to put one's wrist/ankle out of joint

demeurant /d(ə)mœʀɑ̃/ **au demeurant** LOC ADV incidentally, by the way

demeure /d(ə)mœʀ/ NF *(= maison)* residence; *(littér = domicile)* residence, dwelling place *(littér)*

◆ **à demeure** *[installations]* permanent; *[domestique]* live-in, resident ◆ **s'installer à** ~ **dans une ville** to make one's permanent home *ou* settle permanently in a town ◆ **il ne faudrait pas qu'ils y restent à** ~ they mustn't stay there permanently

◆ **en demeure** ◆ **mettre qn en** ~ **de faire qch** to instruct *ou* order sb to do sth ◆ **mettre qn en** ~ **de payer/de partir** *(Jur)* to give sb notice to pay/to quit *ou* leave ◆ **mise en** ~ formal demand, notice

demeuré, e /d(ə)mœʀe/ (ptp de **demeurer**) ADJ half-witted ◆ **il est complètement** ~ he's an absolute half-wit NM,F half-wit

demeurer /d(ə)mœʀe/ ▸ conjug 1 ◂ VI 1 *(avec aux avoir)* ~ **quelque part** *(= habiter)* to live somewhere; *(= séjourner)* to stay somewhere ◆ **il demeure au 24 rue d'Ulm** he lives at number 24 (in the) rue d'Ulm 2 *(frm : avec aux être, avec attrib ou adv de lieu) (= rester, = subsister)* to remain ◆ ~ **fidèle/quelque part** to remain faithful/somewhere ◆ **il lui faut** ~ **couché** he must remain in bed ◆ **l'odeur demeurait dans la pièce** the smell lingered in the room ◆ **la conversation en est demeurée là** the conversation was taken no further *ou* was left at that 3 *(† = être transmis)* ~ **à qn** to be left to sb ◆ **la maison leur est demeurée de leur mère** the house was left to them by their mother, they inherited the house from their mother

demi[1] /d(ə)mi/ ADV half ◆ ~ **plein/nu** half-full/-naked

◆ **à demi** ◆ **il n'était qu'à** ~ **rassuré** he was only half reassured ◆ **il ne te croit qu'à** ~ he only half believes you ◆ **il a fait le travail à** ~ he has (only) done half the work, he has (only) half done the work ◆ **je ne fais pas les choses à** ~ I don't do things by halves ◆ **ouvrir une porte à** ~ to half open a door, to open a door halfway

demi[2], **e** /d(ə)mi/ ADJ *(après n : avec et, nominal)* ◆ **une livre/heure et** ~**e** one and a half pounds/hours, a pound/an hour and a half ◆ **un centimètre/kilo et** ~ one and a half centimetres/kilos, one centimetre/kilo and a half ◆ **à six heures et** ~**e** at half past six ◆ **deux fois et** ~**e plus grand/autant** two and a half times greater/as much; → **malin**

ADV, PRÉF 1 *(avant n = moitié)* **une** ~**-livre/-douzaine/-journée** half a pound/dozen/day, a half-pound/half-dozen/half-day ◆ **un** ~**-tour de clé** half a turn of the key, a half turn of the key ◆ **un** ~**-paquet** half a packet

2 *(avant n = incomplet)* **c'est un** ~**-succès** it's a partial success ◆ **une** ~**-vérité** a half-truth ◆ ~**-cécité** partial blindness ◆ ~**-pouvoir** partial power ◆ ~**-circulaire** *[canal]* semicircular

NM,F *(fonction pronominale)* ◆ **un** ~ (a) half ◆ **une bouteille ?** – **non, une** ~**e** one bottle? – no, (a) half *ou* no, half a bottle *ou* no, a half-bottle ◆ **deux** ~**s font un entier** two halves make a whole

NM 1 *(= bière)* glass of beer, ≃ half-pint, half* *(Brit)*; *(Helv = vin)* half a litre

2 *(Sport)* half-back ◆ ~ **gauche/droit** left/right half ◆ ~ **de mêlée** *(Rugby)* scrum half ◆ ~ **d'ouverture** *(Rugby)* stand-off half

NF **demie** *(à l'horloge)* **la** ~**e** the half-hour ◆ **la** ~**e a sonné** the half-hour has struck ◆ **c'est déjà la** ~**e** it's already half past ◆ **on part à la** ~**e** we're leaving at half past ◆ **le bus passe à la** ~**e** the bus comes by at half past (the hour), the bus comes by on the half-hour ◆ **la pendule sonne les heures et les** ~**es** the clock strikes the hours and the halves *ou* the half-hours

demiard /dəmjaʀ/ NM *(Can)* half-pint, 0.284 litre

demi-botte /d(ə)mibɔt/ NF calf-length boot

demi-bouteille /d(ə)mibutɛj/ NF half-bottle

demi-canton (pl **demi-cantons**) /d(ə)mikɑ̃tɔ̃/ NM *(en Suisse)* demicanton *(Swiss territorial subdivision)*

demi-cercle /d(ə)misɛʀkl/ NM *(= figure)* semicircle; *(= instrument)* protractor ◆ **en** ~ semicircular ◆ **se mettre en** ~ to make a semicircle, to stand *(ou* sit) in a semicircle

demi-colonne /d(ə)mikɔlɔn/ NF semi-column, demi-column, half-column

demi-deuil /d(ə)midœj/ NM half-mourning ◆ **poularde** ~ *(Culin) chicken served in a white sauce with black truffles*

demi-dieu (pl **demi-dieux**) /d(ə)midjø/ NM demigod

demi-douzaine /d(ə)miduzɛn/ NF ◆ **une** ~ half-a-dozen, a half-dozen ◆ **une** ~ **d'œufs** half-a-dozen eggs, a half-dozen eggs ◆ **une bonne** ~ **de voitures** a good half-a-dozen cars ◆ **cette** ~ **de joueurs** these half-a-dozen players

demi-droite /d(ə)midʀwat/ NF half-line, half-ray

demi-écrémé /dəmiekʀeme/ ADJ M, NM ◆ **(lait)** ~ semi-skimmed milk

demi-fin, e /d(ə)mifɛ̃, fin/ ADJ *[petit pois]* small; *[aiguille]* medium; *[or]* 12-carat

demi-finale /d(ə)mifinal/ NF semifinal ◆ **arriver en** ~ to reach the semifinals ◆ **éliminé en** ~ eliminated in the semifinal

demi-finaliste /d(ə)mifinalist/ NMF semifinalist

demi-fond /d(ə)mifɔ̃/ NM *(= discipline)* ◆ **le** ~ medium-distance *ou* middle-distance running; *(= épreuve)* medium-distance *ou* middle-distance race ◆ **coureur de** ~ medium-distance *ou* middle-distance runner

demi-frère /d(ə)mifʀɛʀ/ NM half-brother

demi-gros /d(ə)migʀo/ NM INV *(Comm)* retail-wholesale

demi-heure /d(ə)mijœʀ, dəmjœʀ/ NF ◆ **une** ~ half an hour, a half-hour ◆ **la première** ~ **a passé très lentement** the first half-hour went very slowly

demi-jour (pl **demi-jour(s)**) /d(ə)miʒuʀ/ NM *(gén)* half-light; *(= le soir)* twilight

demi-journée /d(ə)miʒuʀne/ NF ◆ **une** ~ half a day, a half-day ◆ **faire des** ~**s de ménage/couture** to work half-days cleaning/sewing ◆ **il travaille deux** ~**s par semaine** he works two half-days a week

démilitarisation /demilitaʀizasjɔ̃/ NF demilitarization

démilitariser /demilitaʀize/ ▸ conjug 1 ◂ VT to demilitarize

demi-litre /d(ə)militʀ/ NM ◆ **un** ~ **(de)** half a litre (of), a half-litre (of) ◆ **versez ce** ~ **de lait sur ...** pour this half-litre of milk over ...

demi-longueur /d(ə)milɔ̃gœʀ/ NF *(Sport)* ◆ **une** ~ half a length, a half-length ◆ **la** ~ **d'avance qui lui a valu le prix** the half-length lead that won him the prize

demi-lune /d(ə)milyn/ NF *(Mil)* demilune; *(Rail)* relief line ◆ **en** ~ semicircular, half-moon *(épith)* ADJ *[table, console]* semicircular ◆ **lunettes** ~**s** half-moon glasses

demi-mal (pl **demi-maux**) /d(ə)mimal, d(ə)mimo/ NM ◆ **il n'y a que** *ou* **ce n'est que** ~ it could have been worse, there's no great harm done

demi-mesure /d(ə)mim(ə)zyʀ/ NF 1 *(= compromis)* half-measure ◆ **ils ne se contenteront pas de** ~**s** they won't be satisfied with half-measures ◆ **elle n'aime pas les** ~**s** she doesn't do things by halves 2 *(Habillement)* **la** ~ semi-finished clothing ◆ **s'habiller en** ~ to buy semifinished clothing

demi-mondaine † /dəmimɔ̃dɛn/ NF demi-mondaine

demi-monde † /d(ə)mimɔ̃d/ NM demi-monde

demi-mot /d(ə)mimo/ **à demi-mot** LOC ADV without having to spell things out ◆ **se faire comprendre à** ~ to make o.s. understood without having to spell it out ◆ **ils se comprenaient à** ~ they didn't have to spell things out to each other

déminage /deminaʒ/ NM *[de terrain]* mine clearance; *[d'eaux]* minesweeping ◆ **équipe de** ~ *(pour mines)* mine-clearing team; *(pour bombes)* bomb disposal unit ◆ **opérations de** ~ mine-clearing operations

déminer /demine/ ▸ conjug 1 ◂ VT to clear of mines *(ou* bombs)

déminéralisation /demineʀalizasjɔ̃/ NF *(Tech)* demineralization

déminéraliser /demineʀalize/ ▸ conjug 1 ◂ VT *(Tech)* to demineralize; *(Méd)* to make deficient in essential minerals ◆ **eau déminéralisée** distilled *ou* demineralized water VPR **se déminéraliser** *(Méd)* to become deficient in essential minerals

démineur /deminœʀ/ NM *[de mines]* mine-clearing expert; *[de bombes]* bomb disposal expert

demi-pause /d(ə)mipoz/ NF *(Mus)* minim *(Brit) ou* half-note *(US)* rest

demi-pension /d(ə)mipɑ̃sjɔ̃/ NF *(à l'hôtel)* half-board *(Brit)*, bed and breakfast with an evening meal *(Brit)*, modified American plan *(US)*; *(Scol)* half-board ◆ **être en** ~ to take school lunches

demi-pensionnaire /d(ə)mipɑ̃sjɔnɛʀ/ NMF day pupil ◆ **être** ~ to take school lunches

demi-place /d(ə)miplas/ NF *(Transport)* half-fare; *(Ciné, Théât etc)* half-price ticket *ou* seat

demi-point (pl **demi-points**) /d(ə)mipwɛ̃/ NM *(Écon)* half point ◆ **abaisser un taux d'un** ~ to lower a rate by a half point *ou* by half a point

demi-pointe (pl **demi-pointes**) /d(ə)mipwɛ̃t/ NF *(Danse) (= position)* demi-pointe ◆ **(chausson de)** ~ ballet shoe ◆ **faire des** ~**s** to dance on points

demi-portion* /d(ə)mipɔʀsjɔ̃/ NF *(péj)* weed*, weedy person*

demi-queue /d(ə)mikø/ ADJ, NM ◆ **(piano)** ~ baby grand (piano)

demi-reliure /d(ə)miʀəljyʀ/ NF half-binding

démis, e /demi, iz/ (ptp de **démettre**) ADJ *[membre]* dislocated

demi-saison /d(ə)misɛzɔ̃/ NF spring *(ou* autumn), cool season ◆ **un manteau de** ~ a spring *(ou* an autumn) coat

demi-sang (pl **demi-sang(s)**) /d(ə)misɑ̃/ NM *(= cheval)* half-breed (horse)

demi-sel /d(ə)misɛl/ ADJ INV slightly salted ♦ **(fromage)** ~ slightly salted cream cheese NM († : *arg Crime*) small-time crook*

demi-siècle (pl **demi-siècles**) /d(ə)misjɛkl/ NM half-century ♦ **l'organisation fête son ~ d'existence** the organization is celebrating its fiftieth anniversary ♦ **les grands enjeux médicaux de ce dernier** ~ the big medical issues of the last fifty years *ou* half-century

demi-sœur /d(ə)misœʀ/ NF half-sister

demi-solde /d(ə)misɔld/ NF (*Mil*) half-pay

demi-sommeil /d(ə)misɔmɛj/ NM half-sleep ♦ **dans un ~ il entendit des rires** in his half-sleep, he heard laughter ♦ **le marché est en ~** the market is rather sluggish

demi-soupir /d(ə)misupiʀ/ NM (*Mus*) quaver (*Brit*) *ou* eighth note (*US*) rest

démission /demisjɔ̃/ NF (*d'un poste*) resignation; (*de ses responsabilités*) abdication ♦ **donner sa ~** to hand in *ou* tender (*frm*) one's resignation ♦ **la ~ des politiques/de la police** the politicians'/the police's failure to take responsibility ♦ **la ~ des parents** the abdication of parental responsibility

démissionnaire /demisjɔnɛʀ/ ADJ (= *en train de démissionner*) resigning; (= *qui a démissionné*) who has resigned NMF person resigning

démissionner /demisjɔne/ ▸ conjug 1 ◂ VI 1 [*employé*] to resign, to hand in one's notice ♦ **il a démissionné de ses fonctions de président** he resigned from his post as president 2 (= *abandonner*) [*parents, enseignants*] to give up VT ♦ ~ **qn*** to give sb his cards* (*Brit*) *ou* his pink slip* (*US*) ♦ **on l'a démissionné** they persuaded him to resign

demi-tarif /d(ə)mitaʀif/ NM half-price; (*Transport*) half-fare ♦ **billet d'avion (à)** ~ half-price *ou* half-fare plane ticket ♦ **voyager à ~** to travel (at) half-fare

demi-teinte /d(ə)mitɛ̃t/ NF (*Art*) halftone ♦ **en ~** (= *nuancé, discret*) [*film, déclaration, humour*] low-key ♦ **notre équipe a eu une saison en ~** (= *mitigé*) our team had a season with mixed results

demi-ton /d(ə)mitɔ̃/ NM (*Mus*) semitone, half step (*US*), half-tone (*US*)

demi-tonneau (pl **demi-tonneaux**) /d(ə)mitɔno/ NM (*en avion*) half flick roll (*Brit*), snap roll (*US*)

demi-tour /d(ə)mituʀ/ NM 1 (*lit, fig*) about-turn, U-turn; (*en voiture*) U-turn ♦ **faire un ~** to make an about-turn *ou* a U-turn ♦ **faire ~** (*fig*) to do a U-turn, to make an about-turn 2 (= *moitié d'un tour*) **le coureur a fini dernier, à un ~ de ses concurrents** the athlete finished last, half a lap behind the other competitors ♦ **il avait déjà bouclé un ~ du monde** he had already travelled halfway round the world

démiurge /demjyʀʒ/ NM demiurge

demi-vie /d(ə)mivi/ NF [*de radiation*] half-life

demi-vierge † /d(ə)mivjɛʀʒ/ NF virgin in name only

demi-volée /d(ə)mivɔle/ NF half-volley

demi-volte (pl **demi-voltes**) /d(ə)mivɔlt/ NF (*Équitation*) demivolt(e)

démo* /demo/ NF abrév de **démonstration**

démobilisateur, -trice /demɔbilizatœʀ, tʀis/ ADJ [*discours, mesure*] demobilizing, disarming

démobilisation /demɔbilizasjɔ̃/ NF (*Mil*) demobilization, demob* (*Brit*); (= *apathie*) apathy

démobiliser /demɔbilize/ ▸ conjug 1 ◂ VT (*Mil*) to demobilize, to demob* (*Brit*); (= *démotiver*) to demobilize ♦ **se ~** to become apathetic

démocrate /demɔkʀat/ ADJ democratic NMF democrat

démocrate-chrétien, -ienne (mpl **démocrates-chrétiens**) /demɔkʀatkʀetjɛ̃, jɛn/ ADJ, NM,F Christian Democrat

démocratie /demɔkʀasi/ NF democracy ♦ ~ **directe/représentative** direct/representative democracy ♦ ~ **libérale/sociale** liberal/social democracy ♦ ~ **populaire** people's democracy ♦ ~ **parlementaire/présidentielle** parliamentary/presidential democracy ♦ ~ **participative** participative democracy

démocratique /demɔkʀatik/ ADJ democratic ♦ **le Nouveau Parti Démocratique** (*Can*) the New Democratic Party

démocratiquement /demɔkʀatikmɑ̃/ ADV democratically

démocratisation /demɔkʀatizasjɔ̃/ NF democratization

démocratiser /demɔkʀatize/ ▸ conjug 1 ◂ VT to democratize VPR **se démocratiser** to become (more) democratic

démodé, e /demɔde/ (ptp de **se démoder**) ADJ [*vêtement, style*] old-fashioned; [*procédé, théorie*] outmoded, old-fashioned

démoder /demɔde/ ▸ conjug 1 ◂ VT [+ *principe*] to make obsolete; [+ *vêtement*] to make old-fashioned VPR **se démoder** [*vêtement, style*] to go out of fashion, to become old-fashioned; [*procédé, théorie*] to become outmoded *ou* old-fashioned

démodulateur /demɔdylatœʀ/ NM demodulator

démographe /demɔgʀaf/ NMF demographer

démographie /demɔgʀafi/ NF 1 (= *science*) demography 2 (= *chiffres de population*) population size ♦ ~ **galopante** massive population growth

démographique /demɔgʀafik/ ADJ demographic ♦ **poussée** ~ increase in population, population increase

demoiselle /d(ə)mwazɛl/ NF 1 (*frm, hum*) (*jeune*) young lady; (*d'un certain âge*) single lady, maiden lady ♦ **votre ~*** (*dial* : = *fille*) your daughter 2 (*Hist* = *noble*) young noblewoman 3 (= *insecte*) dragonfly 4 (= *outil*) rammer

COMP **demoiselle de compagnie** (lady's) companion

demoiselle d'honneur (*à un mariage*) bridesmaid; (*d'une reine*) maid of honour

démolir /demɔliʀ/ ▸ conjug 2 ◂ VT 1 [+ *maison, quartier*] to demolish, to pull down ♦ **on démolit beaucoup dans le quartier** they are pulling down *ou* demolishing a lot of houses *ou* they are doing a lot of demolition in the area 2 [+ *jouet, radio, voiture*] to wreck, to demolish, to smash up* ♦ **cet enfant démolit tout !** that child wrecks *ou* demolishes everything! ♦ **ces boissons vous démolissent l'estomac/la santé*** these drinks play havoc with *ou* ruin your stomach/health

3 [+ *autorité, influence*] to destroy; [+ *doctrine*] to demolish, to crush; [+ *espoir*] to crush, to shatter; [+ *foi*] to shatter, to destroy

4 * [+ *personne*] (= *épuiser*) to do for*, to do in*; (= *frapper*) to bash up*, to duff up* (*Brit*); (= *critiquer*) to tear to pieces, to slam*, to slate* (*Brit*) ♦ **ce travail/cette maladie l'avait démoli** this work/this illness had just about done for him* ♦ **je vais lui ~ le portrait** I'm going to smash his face in* ♦ **cette marche m'a complètement démoli** I'm whacked* *ou* shattered* (*Brit*) after that walk, that walk has done for me* *ou* shattered me* (*Brit*)

démolissage* /demɔlisaʒ/ NM (= *critique*) panning*, slating* (*Brit*)

démolisseur, -euse /demɔlisœʀ, øz/ NM,F (= *ouvrier*) demolition worker; (= *entrepreneur*) demolition contractor; [*de doctrine*] demolisher

démolition /demɔlisjɔ̃/ NF [*d'immeuble, quartier*] demolition, pulling down; [*de doctrine, idéal*] demolition, crushing ♦ **entreprise de ~** (*lit*) demolition company; [*de droits, institution*] demolition job (*de* on); ♦ **l'immeuble est en ~** the building is (in the course of) being demolished; → **chantier** NFPL **démolitions** (= *décombres*) debris (*sg*), ruins

démon /demɔ̃/ NM 1 (*Rel*) demon, fiend; (= *enfant*) devil, demon ♦ **sa femme est un vrai ~** his wife is a real harpy ♦ **le ~** the Devil ♦ **le ~ de midi** middle-aged lust ♦ **le ~ du jeu** gambling fever ♦ **le ~ de l'alcool** the demon drink ♦ **le ~ de la luxure/de la curiosité** the demon of lechery/curiosity ♦ **réveiller les vieux ~s du racisme** to reawaken the old demons of racism; → **possédé** 2 (*Myth*) genius, daemon ♦ **écoutant son ~ familier/son mauvais ~** listening to his familiar/evil spirit

démonétisation /demɔnetizasjɔ̃/ NF (*Fin*) demonetization, demonetarization

démonétiser /demɔnetize/ ▸ conjug 1 ◂ VT 1 (*Fin*) to demonetize, to demonetarize 2 (*fig*) [+ *théorie*] to devalue, to discredit; [+ *personne*] to discredit

démoniaque /demɔnjak/ ADJ diabolical, fiendish NMF person possessed by the devil *ou* by an evil spirit

démonisation /demɔnizasjɔ̃/ NF demonization

démoniser /demɔnize/ ▸ conjug 1 ◂ VT [+ *personne, pays, parti*] to demonize

démonisme /demɔnism/ NM demonism

démonologie /demɔnɔlɔʒi/ NF demonology

démonstrateur, -trice /demɔ̃stʀatœʀ, tʀis/ NM,F demonstrator (*of commercial products*)

démonstratif, -ive /demɔ̃stʀatif, iv/ ADJ 1 [*personne, caractère*] demonstrative ♦ **peu ~** undemonstrative 2 [*argument, preuve*] demonstrative, illustrative 3 (*Gram*) demonstrative NM (*Gram*) demonstrative

démonstration /demɔ̃stʀasjɔ̃/ NF 1 (*gén, Math*) [*de vérité, loi*] demonstration; [*de théorème*] proof ♦ **cette ~ est convaincante** this demonstration is convincing 2 [*de fonctionnement, appareil*] demonstration ♦ **faire une ~** to give a demonstration ♦ **faire la ~ d'un appareil** to demonstrate an appliance ♦ **appareil de ~** demonstration model ♦ **disquette de ~** (*Ordin*) demo disk 3 (= *manifestation*) [*de joie, tendresse*] demonstration, show, display ♦ **accueillir qn avec des ~s d'amitié** to welcome sb with a great show of friendship ♦ ~ **de force** (*Mil*) show of force ♦ ~ **aérienne/navale** (*Mil*) display of air/naval strength

démontable /demɔ̃tabl/ ADJ that can be dismantled ♦ **armoire ~** wardrobe that can be dismantled *ou* taken to pieces, knock-down wardrobe (*US*)

démontage /demɔ̃taʒ/ NM 1 [*d'installation, échafaudage, étagères*] taking down, dismantling; [*de tente*] taking down; [*de moteur, arme*] stripping; [*d'armoire, appareil, horloge*] dismantling, taking to pieces, taking apart ♦ **pièces perdues lors de ~s successifs** parts lost during successive dismantling operations ♦ **le ~ de la tente se fait en 5 minutes** it takes 5 minutes to take the tent down 2 [*de pneu, porte*] taking off 3 [*de raisonnement*] dissection, taking apart; (*pour contrecarrer*) demolishing

démonté, e /demɔ̃te/ (ptp de **démonter**) ADJ [*mer*] raging, wild; [*personne*] (= *déconcerté*) disconcerted

démonte-pneu (pl **démonte-pneus**) /demɔ̃t(ə)pnø/ NM tyre lever (*Brit*), tire iron (*US*)

démonter /demɔ̃te/ ▸ conjug 1 ◂ VT 1 [+ *installation, échafaudage, étagères*] to take down, to dismantle; [+ *tente*] to take down; [+ *moteur, arme*] to strip down; [+ *armoire, appareil, horloge*] to dis-

mantle, to take to pieces, to take apart; *[+ circuit électrique]* to dismantle
[2] *[+ pneu, porte]* to take off
[3] *(= déconcerter)* to disconcert ◆ **ça m'a complètement démonté** I was completely taken aback by that, that really disconcerted me ◆ **il ne se laisse jamais** ~ he never gets flustered, he always remains unruffled
[4] *[+ argumentation, raisonnement]* to dissect, to take apart; *(pour contrecarrer)* to demolish
[5] *(= désarçonner) [+ cavalier]* to throw, to unseat
VPR **se démonter** [1] *[assemblage, pièce] (accidentellement)* to come apart *ou* to pieces ◆ **est-ce que ça se démonte ?** can it be dismantled *ou* taken apart?
[2] *(= perdre son calme : gén nég)* to get flustered ◆ **répondre sans se** ~ to reply without getting flustered *ou* without losing one's cool ◆ **il ne se démonte pas pour si peu** he's not that easily flustered, it takes more than that to ruffle him

démontrable /demɔ̃tʀabl/ ADJ demonstrable

démontrer /demɔ̃tʀe/ GRAMMAIRE ACTIVE 53.4 ▸ conjug 1 ◂ VT *(= prouver) [+ loi, vérité]* to demonstrate; *[+ théorème]* to prove; *(= expliquer) [+ fonctionnement]* to demonstrate; *(= faire ressortir) [+ urgence, nécessité]* to show, to demonstrate ◆ ~ **l'égalité de deux triangles** to demonstrate *ou* prove *ou* show that two triangles are equal ◆ **sa hâte démontrait son inquiétude** his haste clearly indicated his anxiety ◆ **tout cela démontre l'urgence de ces réformes** all this shows *ou* demonstrates the urgency of these reforms

démoralisant, e /demɔʀalizɑ̃, ɑ̃t/ ADJ demoralizing

démoralisateur, -trice /demɔʀalizatœʀ, tʀis/ ADJ demoralizing

démoralisation /demɔʀalizasjɔ̃/ NF demoralization

démoraliser /demɔʀalize/ ▸ conjug 1 ◂ VT to demoralize VPR **se démoraliser** to lose heart, to become demoralized

démordre /demɔʀdʀ/ ▸ conjug 41 ◂ VI ◆ **il ne démord pas de son avis/sa décision** he is sticking to *ou* standing by his opinion/decision ◆ **il ne veut pas en** ~ he won't budge an inch, he's sticking to his guns

Démosthène /demɔstɛn/ NM Demosthenes

démotivant, e /demɔtivɑ̃, ɑ̃t/ ADJ demotivating

démotivation /demɔtivasjɔ̃/ NF loss of motivation, demotivation

démotiver /demɔtive/ ▸ conjug 1 ◂ VT ◆ ~ **qn** to demotivate sb, to take sb's motivation away ◆ **je suis totalement démotivé** I've lost all my motivation, I am *ou* I feel completely demotivated

démoucheté, e /demuʃte/ ADJ *[fleuret]* unbuttoned

démoulage /demulaʒ/ NM *[de statue]* removal from the mould; *[de flan, gâteau]* turning out ◆ **procédez au** ~ **du gâteau** turn out the cake

démouler /demule/ ▸ conjug 1 ◂ VT *[+ statue]* to remove from the mould; *[+ flan, gâteau]* to turn out

démoustiquer /demustike/ ▸ conjug 1 ◂ VT to clear *ou* rid of mosquitoes

démultiplicateur, -trice /demyltiplikatœʀ, tʀis/ ADJ reduction *(épith)*, reducing *(épith)* NM reduction system

démultiplication /demyltiplikasjɔ̃/ NF *(= procédé)* reduction; *(= rapport)* reduction ratio

démultiplier /demyltiplije/ ▸ conjug 7 ◂ VT *[+ force]* to reduce, to gear down; *[+ moyens]* to increase

démuni, e /demyni/ (ptp de **démunir**) ADJ [1] *(= sans ressources)* destitute ◆ **nous sommes ~s** *(sans argent)* we are destitute; *(sans défense)* we are powerless *(devant* in the face of) [2] *(= privé de)* ~ **de** without, lacking in ◆ ~ **d'ornements** unornamented, unadorned ◆ ~ **de protection** unprotected ◆ ~ **de talents/d'attraits** without talent/attraction, devoid of talent/charm ◆ ~ **d'intérêt** devoid of *ou* without interest, uninteresting ◆ ~ **de tout** destitute ◆ ~ **d'argent** penniless, without money ◆ ~ **de papiers d'identité** without identity papers NMPL **les démunis** the destitute ◆ **un centre d'hébergement pour les ~s** a hostel for the destitute

démunir /demyniʀ/ ▸ conjug 2 ◂ VT ◆ ~ **qn de** *[+ vivres]* to deprive sb of; *[+ ressources, argent]* to divest *ou* deprive sb of ◆ ~ **qch de** to divest sth of VPR **se démunir** *(financièrement)* to part with one's money ◆ **se** ~ **de** *(= se défaire de)* to part with, to give up

démystification /demistifikasjɔ̃/ NF *[de personne]* enlightenment; *(= banalisation)* demystification

démystifier /demistifje/ ▸ conjug 7 ◂ VT *(= détromper)* to enlighten, to disabuse; *(= banaliser)* to demystify, to take the mystery out of

démythification /demitifikasjɔ̃/ NF demythologization, demystification

démythifier /demitifje/ ▸ conjug 7 ◂ VT to demythologize, to demystify

dénasalisation /denazalizasjɔ̃/ NF denasalization

dénasaliser /denazalize/ ▸ conjug 1 ◂ VT to denasalize

dénatalité /denatalite/ NF fall *ou* decrease in the birth rate

dénationalisation /denasjɔnalizasjɔ̃/ NF denationalization

dénationaliser /denasjɔnalize/ ▸ conjug 1 ◂ VT to denationalize

dénatter /denate/ ▸ conjug 1 ◂ VT *[+ cheveux]* to unplait

dénaturation /denatyʀasjɔ̃/ NF *(Tech)* denaturation

dénaturé, e /denatyʀe/ (ptp de **dénaturer**) ADJ [1] *(Tech) [alcool, sel]* denatured [2] *[goût, mœurs, parents]* unnatural

dénaturer /denatyʀe/ ▸ conjug 1 ◂ VT [1] *[+ vérité, faits]* to distort, to misrepresent; *[+ propos]* to distort, to twist; *[+ intentions]* to misrepresent [2] *(Tech) [+ alcool, substance alimentaire]* to denature; *(= altérer) [+ goût, aliment]* to alter completely, to change the nature of

dénazification /denazifikasjɔ̃/ NF denazification

dendrite /dɑ̃dʀit, dɛ̃dʀit/ NF *(Géol, Anat)* dendrite

dénébuliser /denebylize/, **dénébuler** /denebyle/ ▸ conjug 1 ◂ VT to dispel the fog from

dénégation /denegasjɔ̃/ NF *(gén, Jur)* denial

déneigement /denɛʒmɑ̃/ NM snow-clearing (operation), snow removal

déneiger /deneʒe/ ▸ conjug 3 ◂ VT *[+ objet]* to clear of snow, to clear the snow from

déni /deni/ NM denial ◆ ~ **de justice** *(Jur)* denial of justice ◆ ~ **(de la réalité)** *(Psych)* denial ◆ **être dans le** ~ to be in denial

déniaiser /denjeze/ ▸ conjug 1 ◂ VT ◆ ~ **qn** *(= dégourdir qn)* to teach sb a thing or two; *(= dépuceler qn)* to take away sb's innocence VPR **se déniaiser** to learn about life, to lose one's innocence

dénicher /deniʃe/ ▸ conjug 1 ◂ VT [1] *(* = trouver) [+ objet]* to unearth; *[+ magasin, restaurant]* to discover; *[+ personne]* to track *ou* hunt down [2] *(= débusquer) [+ fugitif, animal]* to drive out (of hiding), to flush out [3] *(= enlever du nid) [+ œufs, oisillons]* to take out of the nest VI *[oiseau]* to leave the nest

dénicheur, -euse /deniʃœʀ, øz/ NM,F [1] **c'est un vrai ~ d'objets rares** he's really good at finding rare objects ◆ ~ **de talents** talent scout [2] *(d'oiseaux)* bird's-nester

denier /dənje/ NM [1] *(= monnaie) (Hist romaine)* denarius; *(Hist française)* denier ◆ **ça ne leur a pas coûté un** ~ † it didn't cost them a farthing *(Brit) ou* a cent *(US)* ◆ **l'ayant payé de ses propres ~s** having paid for it out of his own pocket ◆ **les trente ~s de Judas** Judas's thirty pieces of silver [2] *(= unité de poids d'un tissu)* denier ◆ **bas de 30 ~s** 30-denier stockings
COMP **le denier du culte** the contribution to parish costs *(paid yearly)*
les deniers publics *ou* **de l'État** public moneys *ou* monies

dénier /denje/ ▸ conjug 7 ◂ VT [1] *[+ responsabilité]* to deny, to disclaim; *[+ faute]* to deny [2] *(= refuser)* ~ **qch à qn** to deny *ou* refuse sb sth

dénigrement /denigʀəmɑ̃/ NM denigration, defamation ◆ **ce mot s'emploie par** ~ this word is used disparagingly ◆ **campagne de** ~ smear campaign

dénigrer /denigʀe/ ▸ conjug 1 ◂ VT to denigrate, to run down

denim /dənim/ NM denim

dénivelé NM, **dénivelée** NF /deniv(ə)le/ difference in height *(entre* between)

déniveler /deniv(ə)le/ ▸ conjug 4 ◂ VT *(= rendre inégal)* to make uneven; *(= abaisser)* to lower, to put on a lower level

dénivellation /denivelasjɔ̃/ NF, **dénivellement** /denivɛlmɑ̃/ NM [1] *(= pente)* slope; *(= cassis, creux)* unevenness *(NonC)*, dip [2] *(= différence de niveau)* difference in level *ou* altitude [3] *(NonC) (= fait de rendre inégal)* making uneven; *(= abaissement)* lowering, putting on a lower level

dénombrable /denɔ̃bʀabl/ ADJ countable ◆ **nom** ~ *(Ling)* countable *ou* count noun ◆ **non** ~ uncountable

dénombrement /denɔ̃bʀəmɑ̃/ NM counting ◆ ~ **de la population** population census *ou* count

dénombrer /denɔ̃bʀe/ ▸ conjug 1 ◂ VT *(= compter)* to count; *(= énumérer)* to enumerate, to list ◆ **on dénombre trois morts et cinq blessés** there are three dead and five wounded

dénominateur /denɔminatœʀ/ NM *(Math)* denominator ◆ **(plus petit)** ~ **commun** *(fig, Math)* (lowest) common denominator

dénominatif, -ive /denɔminatif, iv/ ADJ, NM denominative

dénomination /denɔminasjɔ̃/ NF *(= nom)* designation, appellation *(frm)*, denomination *(frm)*; *(= action)* denomination *(frm)*, naming

dénommé, e /denɔme/ (ptp de **dénommer**) ADJ *(parfois péj)* ◆ **le** ~ **X** a certain X, the man called X ◆ **on m'a présenté un** ~ **Dupont** I was introduced to a certain Mr Dupont, I was introduced to someone by the name of Dupont

dénommer /denɔme/ ▸ conjug 1 ◂ VT *(frm = donner un nom à)* to denominate *(frm)*, to name; *(= désigner)* to designate, to denote; *(Jur)* to name

dénoncer /denɔ̃se/ ▸ conjug 3 ◂ VT [1] *(= révéler) [+ coupable]* to denounce; *[+ forfait, abus]* to expose ◆ **sa hâte l'a dénoncé** his haste gave him away *ou* betrayed him ◆ ~ **qn à la police** to inform against sb, to give sb away to the police [2] *(= signaler publiquement) [+ danger, injustice]* to denounce [3] *(= annuler) [+ contrat, traité]* to denounce [4] *(littér = dénoter)* to announce, to indicate VPR **se dénoncer** *[criminel]* to give o.s.

up, to come forward ◆ **se ~ à la police** to give o.s. up to the police

dénonciateur, -trice /denɔ̃sjatœʀ, tʀis/ ADJ denunciatory, accusatory NM,F *[de criminel]* denouncer, informer; *[de forfait]* exposer ◆ **les ~s d'injustices/de malhonnêtetés** those who denounce injustices/dishonesty

dénonciation /denɔ̃sjasjɔ̃/ NF *[de criminel]* denunciation; *[de forfait, abus]* exposure *(NonC)*; *[de traité]* denunciation, denouncement; *[de contrat]* termination ◆ **emprisonné sur la ~ de qn** imprisoned on the strength of a denunciation by sb

dénotatif, -ive /denɔtatif, iv/ ADJ denotative

dénotation /denɔtasjɔ̃/ NF denotation

dénoter /denɔte/ ▸ conjug 1 ◂ VT to denote

dénouement /denumɑ̃/ NM *(Théât)* dénouement; *[d'affaire, aventure, intrigue]* outcome, conclusion ◆ **~ heureux** *[de film]* happy ending

dénouer /denwe/ ▸ conjug 1 ◂ VT 1 *[+ nœud, lien]* to untie, to undo; *[+ cravate]* to undo; *[+ cheveux]* to let down, to undo ◆ **les cheveux dénoués** with her hair (falling) loose 2 *[+ situation]* to untangle, to resolve; *[+ difficultés, intrigue]* to untangle, to unravel VPR **se dénouer** 1 *[lien, nœud]* to come untied, to come undone; *[cheveux]* to come undone, to come down; → **langue** 2 *[intrigue, situation]* to be resolved

dénoûment /denumɑ̃/ NM ⇒ **dénouement**

dénoyautage /denwajotaʒ/ NM *[de fruit]* stoning *(Brit)*, pitting *(US)*

dénoyauter /denwajote/ ▸ conjug 1 ◂ VT *[+ fruit]* to stone *(Brit)*, to pit *(US)*

dénoyauteur /denwajotœʀ/ NM stoner *(Brit)*, pitter *(US)*

denrée /dɑ̃ʀe/ NF commodity, foodstuff ◆ **~s alimentaires** foodstuffs ◆ **~s de base** basic foods ◆ **~s de consommation courante** basic consumer goods ◆ **~s périssables** perishable foods *ou* foodstuffs ◆ **l'honnêteté devient une ~ rare** honesty is in short supply these days

dense /dɑ̃s/ ADJ 1 *(gén, phys)* dense 2 *[circulation]* heavy 3 *(= complexe) [texte, livre]* complex; *[style]* compact, condensed

densifier /dɑ̃sifje/ ▸ conjug 7 ◂ VT to make denser VPR **se densifier** to get denser

densimètre /dɑ̃simɛtʀ/ NM densimeter

densité /dɑ̃site/ NF *(Démographie, Phys)* density; *[de brouillard]* denseness, thickness; *[de circulation]* heaviness; *[de foule]* denseness ◆ **région à forte/faible ~ de population** densely/sparsely populated area, area with a high/low population density ◆ **~ d'implantation** *(Ordin)* packing density

dent /dɑ̃/ NF 1 *[d'homme, animal]* tooth ◆ **~s du haut/du bas/de devant/du fond** upper/lower/front/back teeth ◆ **~ de lait/de sagesse** milk *ou* baby/wisdom tooth ◆ **~ définitive** *ou* **de remplacement** permanent *ou* second tooth ◆ **donner un coup de ~ à** to bite into, to take a bite at; → **arracher, brosse, faux²**

2 *[de herse, fourche, fourchette]* prong; *[de râteau]* tooth, prong; *[de scie, peigne]* tooth; *[de roue, engrenage]* tooth, cog; *[de feuille]* serration; *[d'arête rocheuse]* jag; *[de timbre]* perforation

◆ **en dents de scie** *[couteau]* serrated; *[montagne]* jagged *[graphique, carrière, évolution]* uneven; ◆ **évoluer en ~s de scie** to make uneven progress

3 *(locutions)* **avoir la ~** * to be hungry ◆ **avoir la ~ dure** to be scathing (in one's comments) *(envers* about); ◆ **avoir/garder une ~ contre qn** to have/hold a grudge against sb ◆ **avoir les ~s longues** *(= être ambitieux)* to be very ambitious, to have one's sights fixed high ◆ **avoir les ~s qui rayent le parquet** *(hum)* to have one's sights fixed high, to want it all * ◆ **montrer les ~s** *(lit, fig)* to bare one's teeth ◆ **être sur les ~s** *(fébrile)* to be keyed up; *(très occupé)* to be under great pressure ◆ **faire** *ou* **percer ses ~s** to teethe, to cut (one's) teeth ◆ **il vient de percer une ~** he has just cut a tooth ◆ **se faire les ~s** *[animal]* to cut its teeth; *(fig = s'exercer)* to cut one's teeth *(sur* on); ◆ **croquer/manger qch à belles ~s** to bite into sth/eat sth with gusto ◆ **manger du bout des ~s** to eat half-heartedly, to pick at one's food ◆ **parler/marmotter entre ses ~s** to talk/mumble between one's teeth ◆ **ils n'ont rien à se mettre sous la ~** they have nothing to eat ◆ **on voudrait bien quelque chose à se mettre sous la ~** we wouldn't say no to a bite to eat *ou* something to eat ◆ **il mange tout ce qui lui tombe sous la ~** he eats everything he can lay his hands on; → **armé, casser**

dentaire /dɑ̃tɛʀ/ ADJ dental ◆ **faire l'école ~** * to study dentistry; → **fil, formule, prothèse** NF ◆ **faire ~** * to study dentistry

dental, e (mpl **-aux**) /dɑ̃tal, o/ *(Ling)* ADJ dental NF **dentale** dental

dent-de-lion (pl **dents-de-lion**) /dɑ̃dəljɔ̃/ NF dandelion

denté, e /dɑ̃te/ ADJ *[roue]* toothed; *[feuille]* dentate; → **roue**

dentelé, e /dɑ̃t(ə)le/ (ptp de **denteler**) ADJ *[arête]* jagged; *[timbre]* perforated; *[contour, côte]* indented, jagged; *[feuille]* dentate; *[muscle]* serrate

denteler /dɑ̃t(ə)le/ ▸ conjug 4 ◂ VT *(Tech) [+ timbre-poste]* to perforate ◆ **l'érosion avait dentelé la côte** *(fig = découper)* erosion had indented the coastline *ou* had given the coast a jagged outline ◆ **les pics qui dentelaient l'horizon** the peaks that stood in a jagged line along the horizon

dentelle /dɑ̃tɛl/ NF lace *(NonC)* ◆ **de** *ou* **en ~** lace *(épith)* ◆ **~ à l'aiguille** *ou* **au point** needle-point lace ◆ **~ au(x) fuseau(x)** bobbin lace ◆ **~ de papier** lacy paper ◆ **~ de pierre** (stone) filigree ◆ **crêpe ~** thin pancake ◆ **il ne fait pas dans la ~** * he's not particular about details

dentellerie /dɑ̃tɛlʀi/ NF *(= fabrication)* lacemaking; *(Comm)* lace manufacture

dentellier, -ière /dɑ̃təlje, jɛʀ/ ADJ *[industrie]* lace *(épith)* NM,F lacemaker NF **dentellière** *(= machine)* lacemaking machine

dentelure /dɑ̃t(ə)lyʀ/ NF *[de timbre-poste]* perforations; *[de feuille]* serration; *[d'arête]* jagged outline ◆ **les ~s d'une côte** the indentations *ou* jagged outline of a coastline

dentier /dɑ̃tje/ NM dentures ◆ **porter un ~** to wear dentures

dentifrice /dɑ̃tifʀis/ NM toothpaste ADJ ◆ **eau ~** mouthwash ◆ **poudre ~** tooth powder ◆ **pâte ~** toothpaste

dentine /dɑ̃tin/ NF dentine

dentiste /dɑ̃tist/ NMF dentist; → **chirurgien**

dentisterie /dɑ̃tistəʀi/ NF dentistry

dentition /dɑ̃tisjɔ̃/ NF *(= dents)* teeth *(pl)*; *(= croissance)* dentition ◆ **~ de lait** milk *ou* baby teeth, deciduous dentition *(SPÉC)* ◆ **~ définitive** permanent teeth *ou* dentition *(SPÉC)*

denture /dɑ̃tyʀ/ NF *(humaine, animale)* 1 teeth *(pl)*, set of teeth, dentition *(SPÉC)* 2 *(Tech) [de roue]* teeth *(pl)*, cogs

dénucléarisation /denyklearizasjɔ̃/ NF denuclearization

dénucléariser /denykleaʀize/ ▸ conjug 1 ◂ VT to denuclearize ◆ **zone dénucléarisée** nuclear-free zone

dénudé, e /denyde/ (ptp de **dénuder**) ADJ *(gén)* bare; *[crâne]* bald; *[colline]* bare, bald

dénuder /denyde/ ▸ conjug 1 ◂ VT 1 *[+ fil]* to bare, to strip; *[+ os]* to strip 2 *[+ arbre, sol, colline]* to bare, to strip 3 *[+ bras, dos] [robe]* to leave bare; *[mouvement]* to bare VPR **se dénuder** 1 *[personne]* to strip (off) 2 *[colline, arbre]* to become bare, to be bared; *[crâne]* to be balding, to be going bald

dénudeur /denydœʀ/ NM ◆ **~ de fil** wire stripper

dénué, e /denɥe/ (ptp de **dénuer**) **dénué de** ADJ devoid of ◆ **~ de sens** unreasonable ◆ **~ d'intérêt** devoid of interest, uninteresting ◆ **~ de talent/d'imagination** lacking in *ou* without talent/imagination, untalented/unimaginative ◆ **il n'est pas ~ d'humour** he is not without a sense of humour ◆ **~ de tout** destitute ◆ **~ de tout fondement** completely unfounded *ou* groundless, entirely without foundation

dénuement /denymɑ̃/ NM *[de personne]* destitution ◆ **le ~ de la recherche/du système de soins** the impoverished state of research/of the care system ◆ **dans le ~ le plus total** in utter destitution

dénuer (se) /denɥe/ ▸ conjug 1 ◂ VPR *(littér)* to deprive o.s. *(de* of)

dénûment /denymɑ̃/ NM ⇒ **dénuement**

dénutri, e /denytʀi/ ADJ *[enfant]* malnourished ◆ **bébé gravement ~** severely malnourished baby

dénutrition /denytʀisjɔ̃/ NF undernutrition, undernourishment

déo * /deo/ NM abrév de **déodorant**

déodorant /deɔdɔʀɑ̃/ NM deodorant ADJ *[spray, stick]* deodorant

déontologie /deɔ̃tɔlɔʒi/ NF professional code of ethics, deontology *(SPÉC)*

déontologique /deɔ̃tɔlɔʒik/ ADJ ethical, deontological *(SPÉC)*

déontologue /deɔ̃tɔlɔg/ NMF deontologist

dép. (abrév de **département**) 1 *[d'organisme, entreprise]* dept 2 *(= division du territoire)* → **département**

dépailler /depɑje/ ▸ conjug 1 ◂ VT *[+ chaise]* to remove the straw seating from

dépannage /depanaʒ/ NM *[de véhicule, appareil]* fixing, repairing ◆ **ils ont fait trois ~s aujourd'hui** *(de véhicules)* they've dealt with three breakdowns today; *(d'appareils)* they've done three repair jobs today ◆ **camion de ~** breakdown lorry *(Brit)*, tow truck *(US)* ◆ **service de ~** *(pour véhicules)* breakdown service; *(pour appareils)* repair service ◆ **c'est une lampe/une bouilloire de ~** * it's a spare lamp/kettle ◆ **solution de ~** stopgap solution, temporary fix

dépanner /depane/ ▸ conjug 1 ◂ VT 1 *(= réparer) [+ véhicule, appareil]* to fix, to repair; *[+ automobiliste]* to fix the car of ◆ **j'ai dû me faire ~ sur l'autoroute** I had to call the breakdown service on the motorway 2 *(* = tirer d'embarras) [+ personne]* to help out ◆ **~ qn d'un ticket restaurant** to help sb out with a luncheon voucher ◆ **il m'avait donné 20 € pour me ~** he gave me €20 to tide me over *ou* to help me out ◆ **tu peux me ~ d'une cigarette ?** can you spare me a cigarette?

dépanneur /depanœʀ/ NM *(gén)* repairman; *(pour voitures)* breakdown mechanic; *(TV)* television engineer *ou* repairman; *(Can = épicerie)* convenience store

dépanneuse /depanøz/ NF breakdown lorry *(Brit)*, tow truck *(US)*, wrecker *(US)*

dépaqueter /depak(ə)te/ ▸ conjug 4 ◂ VT to unpack

déparasiter /depaʀazite/ ▸ conjug 1 ◂ VT *[+ poste de radio]* to fit a suppressor to; *[+ animal, local]* to rid of parasites

dépareillé, e /depaʀeje/ (ptp de **dépareiller**) ADJ *[collection]* incomplete; *[objet]* odd *(épith)* ◆ **articles ~s** oddments ◆ **couverts ~s** odd cutlery

dépareiller /depaʀeje/ ▸ conjug 1 ◂ VT *[+ collection, service de table]* to make incomplete, to spoil ◆ **en cassant cette assiette tu as dépareillé le service** you've spoilt the set now that you've broken that plate

déparer /depaʀe/ ▸ conjug 1 ◂ VT *[+ paysage]* to spoil, to disfigure, to mar; *[+ visage]* to disfigure; *[+ beauté, qualité]* to detract from, to mar ◆ **cette pièce ne déparerait pas ma collection** this piece would go well in my collection ◆ **cette lampe ne déparerait pas dans la chambre** this lamp wouldn't look bad in the bedroom

déparié, e /depaʀje/ (ptp de **déparier**) ADJ *[chaussures, gants]* odd *(épith)*

déparier /depaʀje/ ▸ conjug 7 ◂ VT *[+ chaussures, gants]* to split up

départ[1] /depaʀ/ NM 1 *[de voyageur, véhicule, excursion]* departure; *[de fusée]* launch; *(= endroit)* point of departure ◆ **observer le ~ du train** to watch the train leave ◆ **le ~ est à huit heures** the train *(ou* coach *etc)* leaves at eight o'clock ◆ **fixer l'heure/le jour de son ~** to set a time/day for one's departure ◆ **être sur le ~** to be about to leave *ou* go ◆ **excursions au ~ de Chamonix** excursions (departing) from Chamonix, (day) trips from Chamonix ◆ **"départ des grandes lignes"** *(Rail)* "main-line departures" ◆ **dès son ~ j'ai ...** as soon as he had left I ... ◆ **peu après mon ~ de l'hôtel** soon after I had left the hotel, soon after my departure from the hotel ◆ **c'est bientôt le ~ en vacances** we'll soon be off on holiday *(Brit) ou* vacation *(US)* ◆ **alors, c'est pour bientôt le grand ~ ?** when's the big trip then? ◆ **le ~ du train/bateau est imminent** the train/boat will be leaving any time now *ou* is about to depart ◆ **son ~ précipité** his hasty departure ◆ **il a essayé de reculer son ~ pour Glasgow** he tried to put off his trip to Glasgow, he tried to postpone his departure for Glasgow ◆ **la levée du matin est à sept heures et le ~ du courrier se fait à neuf heures** the morning collection is at seven and the mail leaves town at nine o'clock; → **tableau**

2 *(Sport)* start ◆ **un faux ~** *(lit, fig)* a false start ◆ **~ lancé/arrêté** flying/standing start ◆ **~ décalé** staggered start ◆ **donner le ~ aux coureurs** to give the runners the starting signal, to start the race ◆ **les coureurs se rassemblent au ~** the runners are assembling at the start ◆ **être au ~ d'une course, prendre le ~ d'une course** to take part in a race ◆ **47 concurrents ont pris le ~** 47 competitors took part in the race ◆ **prendre un bon/mauvais ~** *(lit, fig)* to get off to a good/bad start

3 *[de salarié, ministre]* leaving *(NonC)*, departure ◆ **le ministre annonça son ~** the minister announced that he was going to quit *ou* that he was leaving ◆ **demander le ~ d'un fonctionnaire** to demand the resignation of a civil servant ◆ **réduire le personnel par ~s naturels** to reduce the staff gradually by natural wastage ◆ **indemnité de ~** severance pay ◆ **~ anticipé** *ou* **en préretraite** early retirement ◆ **~ à la retraite** retirement ◆ **~ volontaire** *ou* **négocié** voluntary redundancy

4 *(= origine) [de processus, transformation]* start ◆ **au ~** at the start *ou* outset ◆ **de ~** *[hypothèse]* initial ◆ **salaire de ~** starting salary ◆ **de la langue de ~ à la langue d'arrivée** from the source language to the target language ◆ **il y a eu plusieurs ~s de feu** fire broke out in several places; → **point[1]**

départ[2] /depaʀ/ NM *(littér)* distinction *(entre* between); ◆ **faire le ~ entre le vrai et le faux** to draw *ou* make a distinction between truth and falsehood

départager /depaʀtaʒe/ ▸ conjug 3 ◂ VT *[+ concurrents]* to decide between; *[+ votes]* to settle, to decide; *(littér) [+ opinions]* to decide between; *(littér) [+ camps opposés]* to separate ◆ **~ l'assemblée** to settle the voting in the assembly

département /depaʀtəmɑ̃/ NM *[d'organisme, université, entreprise]* department; *(= division du territoire)* département *(administrative division)* ◆ **~ (ministériel)** ministry, department ◆ **le ~ d'État** *(aux USA)* the State Department ◆ **~ d'outre-mer** French overseas département

> **DÉPARTEMENT**
>
> Since 1790, France has been divided into 95 metropolitan **départements** and four overseas **départements**. Each is run by its own local council, the « conseil général », which has its headquarters in the principal town (« le chef-lieu du département »). Every **département** has a code number which appears as the first two figures of postcodes and the last two figures on vehicle registration plates. → **ARRONDISSEMENT, CANTON, COMMUNE, RÉGION, DOM-TOM**

départemental, e (mpl **-aux**) /depaʀtəmɑ̃tal, o/ ADJ *(gén)* departmental; *(Admin) of a département; (= ministériel)* ministerial ◆ **route ~e** secondary road NF **départementale** secondary road

départementalisation /depaʀtəmɑ̃talizasjɔ̃/ NF *(Admin) [de territoire]* giving the status of département to; *[de compétence]* devolution to the départements ◆ **la ~ des services judiciaires** basing legal services in the départements

départir /depaʀtiʀ/ ▸ conjug 16 ◂ VT *(†, littér = attribuer) [+ tâche]* to assign; *[+ faveur]* to accord *(frm)* VPR **se départir** ◆ **se ~ de** *(gén nég = abandonner) [+ ton, attitude]* to abandon, to depart from; *[+ sourire]* to drop ◆ **sans se ~ de sa prudence/sa bonne humeur** without abandoning his caution/his good humour ◆ **il a répondu sans se ~ de son calme** he answered without losing his composure

départiteur /depaʀtitœʀ/ NM ◆ **(juge) ~** arbitrator

dépassé, e /depɑse/ ADJ *(= périmé)* outmoded, old-fashioned, out of date; *(* = désorienté)* out of one's depth *(attrib)*

dépassement /depɑsmɑ̃/ NM 1 *(en voiture)* passing *(NonC)*, overtaking *(Brit) (NonC)* ◆ **tout ~ est dangereux** overtaking is always dangerous, it is always dangerous to overtake ◆ **"dépassement interdit"** "no overtaking" ◆ **après plusieurs ~s dangereux ...** after perilously overtaking several vehicles ...

2 *[de limite, prix] (= action)* exceeding; *(= excès)* excess ◆ **~ d'honoraires** charge exceeding the statutory fee ◆ **faire des ~s d'honoraires** to charge more than the statutory fee ◆ **il a eu une amende pour ~ de vitesse ou de la vitesse autorisée** he was fined for speeding *ou* for exceeding the speed limit

3 *(Fin)* **~ (de crédit)** overspending *(NonC)* ◆ **un ~ de crédit de 5 millions** overspending by 5 million francs ◆ **~ budgétaire** overspend on budget, overspending

4 **~ (de soi)** setting new targets (for oneself) ◆ **la notion de ~ de soi** the idea of setting new targets for oneself *ou* of seeking new challenges

dépasser /depɑse/ ▸ conjug 1 ◂ VT 1 *(= aller plus loin que) [+ endroit]* to pass, to go past; *[+ piste d'atterrissage]* to overshoot; *(= distancer) [+ véhicule, personne]* to pass, to overtake *(Brit)* ◆ **dépassez les feux et prenez la première rue à gauche** take the first on the left after the lights

2 *(= déborder de) [+ alignement] (horizontalement)* to jut out over, to overhang; *(verticalement)* to jut out above, to stand higher than ◆ **son succès a dépassé les frontières** his success has reached beyond *ou* transcended national boundaries

3 *(= excéder) [+ limite, quantité mesurable]* to exceed ◆ **~ qch en hauteur/largeur** to be higher *ou* taller/wider than sth, to exceed sth in height/width ◆ **il a dépassé son père (de 10 cm) maintenant** he's (10 cm) taller than his father now ◆ **cette plante a dépassé l'autre** this plant has outgrown the other one *ou* is now taller than the other one ◆ **~ en nombre** to outnumber ◆ **tout colis qui dépasse 20 kg/la limite (de poids)** all parcels in excess of *ou* exceeding *ou* over 20 kg/the (weight) limit ◆ **~ le nombre prévu** to be more than expected ◆ **la réunion ne devrait pas ~ trois heures** the meeting shouldn't go on longer than *ou* last longer than three hours, the meeting shouldn't exceed three hours (in length) ◆ **il ne veut pas ~ 75 €** he won't go above *ou* over €75 ◆ **ça va ~ 20 €** it'll be more than *ou* over €20 ◆ **elle a dépassé la quarantaine** she is over forty, she has turned forty ◆ **"ne pas dépasser la dose prescrite"** "do not exceed the prescribed dose" ◆ **le prix de cette maison dépasse nos moyens** this house is beyond our means *ou* is more than we can afford

4 *(= surpasser) [+ valeur, prévisions]* to exceed; *[+ réputation]* to outshine; *[+ rival]* to outmatch, to outstrip ◆ **~ qn en violence/intelligence** to be more violent/intelligent than sb, to surpass sb in violence/intelligence ◆ **pour la paresse/l'appétit il dépasse tout le monde** he beats everybody for laziness/appetite ◆ **il dépasse tous ses camarades** he is ahead of *ou* he surpasses all his friends ◆ **sa bêtise dépasse tout ce qu'on peut imaginer** his stupidity beggars belief, he's more stupid than you could possibly imagine ◆ **les résultats ont dépassé notre attente** the results exceeded *ou* surpassed our expectations ◆ **cela dépasse toutes mes espérances** it is beyond my wildest dreams, it is better than anything I had ever hoped for

5 *(= outrepasser) [+ moyens, instructions]* to go beyond; *[+ attributions]* to go beyond, to overstep; *[+ crédits]* to exceed ◆ **cela dépasse les bornes ou les limites ou la mesure** that's the absolute limit, that's going too far ◆ **il a dépassé les bornes ou la mesure** he has really gone too far *ou* overstepped the mark *ou* passed over the bounds *(US)* ◆ **cela a dépassé le stade de la plaisanterie** it has gone beyond a joke ◆ **les mots ont dû ~ sa pensée** he must have got carried away ◆ **cela dépasse mes forces/ma compétence** it's beyond my strength/capabilities ◆ **cela me dépasse** it's beyond me ◆ **il a dépassé ses forces** he has overtaxed himself *ou* overdone it

6 *(= dérouter)* **cela/cet argument me dépasse !** it/this argument is beyond me! ◆ **être dépassé (par les événements)** to be overtaken by events

VI 1 *(en voiture)* to overtake *(Brit)*, to pass *(US)* ◆ **"défense de dépasser"** "no overtaking" *(Brit)*, "no passing" *(US)*

2 *(= faire saillie) [bâtiment, tour]* to stick out; *[planche, balcon, rocher]* to stick out, to jut out, to protrude; *[clou]* to stick out; *[jupon]* to show *(de, sous* below); *[chemise]* to be hanging out *(de* of) to be untucked ◆ **il y a quelque chose qui dépasse du tiroir** something's sticking out *ou* hanging out of the drawer ◆ **leur chien a toujours un bout de langue qui dépasse** their dog always has the end of his tongue hanging out

VPR **se dépasser** to surpass o.s., to excel o.s.

dépassionner /depasjɔne/ ▸ conjug 1 ◂ VT *[+ débat]* to take the heat out of

dépatouiller (se) * /depatuje/ ▸ conjug 1 ◂ VPR ◆ **se ~ de** *[+ situation difficile]* to get out of ◆ **laisse-le se ~ !** leave him to *ou* let him get out of it on his own! ◆ **savoir se ~** to (manage to) get by

dépavage /depavaʒ/ NM removal of the cobbles *ou* cobblestones (*de* from)

dépaver /depave/ ▸ conjug 1 ◂ VT to dig up the cobbles *ou* cobblestones from

dépaysant, e /depeizɑ̃, ɑ̃t/ ADJ exotic ◆ **un restaurant au décor ~** a restaurant with an exotic décor ◆ **l'Inde est un pays ~** India is so different ◆ **j'ai passé un séjour très ~ en Inde** my stay in India provided me with a complete change of scene

dépaysé, e /depeize/ (ptp de **dépayser**) ADJ *(gén)* disoriented ◆ **je me sens très ~ ici** I feel very much like a fish out of water here, I feel very disoriented here, I don't feel at home at all here ◆ **il ne sera pas ~ dans notre service** he'll feel quite at home *ou* he won't feel at all out of place in our department

dépaysement /depeizmɑ̃/ NM *(= changement salutaire)* change of scene *ou* scenery; *(= désorientation)* disorientation, feeling of strangeness ◆ **partez en Inde, c'est le ~ assuré !** go to India, you're guaranteed exotic new surroundings!

dépayser /depeize/ ▸ conjug 1 ◂ VT *(= désorienter)* to disorientate, to disorient; *(= changer agréablement)* to give a change of scenery to, to give a welcome change of surroundings to ◆ **ce séjour m'a dépaysé** this stay has given me a change of scenery *ou* a welcome change of surroundings

dépeçage /depəsaʒ/, **dépècement** /depɛsmɑ̃/ NM *[d'animal] (par un boucher)* cutting up; *(par un fauve)* dismembering; *[de territoire, état]* carving up, dismembering; *[de groupe, entreprise]* carving up

dépecer /depəse/ ▸ conjug 5 ◂ VT *[− animal] [boucher]* to cut up; *[fauve]* to dismember, to tear limb from limb; *[+ territoire, état]* to carve up, to dismember; *[+ groupe, entreprise]* to carve up

dépêche /depɛʃ/ NF 1 *(Journalisme)* **~ (d'agence)** dispatch, agency *ou* wire *(US)* story ◆ **je reçois à l'instant une ~ de notre correspondant** I've just received a dispatch *ou* story from our correspondent 2 *(Admin)* dispatch ◆ **~ diplomatique** diplomatic dispatch 3 *(Téléc)* **~ (télégraphique)** telegram, wire *(US)* ◆ **envoyer une ~ à qn** to send sb a telegram *ou* wire *(US)*, to telegraph sb, to wire sb *(US)*

dépêcher /depeʃe/ ▸ conjug 1 ◂ VT to dispatch, to send *(auprès de* to) VPR **se dépêcher** to hurry ◆ **il se dépêchait** *(en marchant, courant)* he was hurrying (along); *(en travaillant)* he was hurrying ◆ **dépêche-toi !** hurry (up)!, (be) quick! ◆ **se ~ de faire qch** to hurry to do sth ◆ **dépêche-toi de les commander, il n'y en aura bientôt plus** hurry up and order them or there soon won't be any left

dépeigner /depeɲe/ ▸ conjug 1 ◂ VT ◆ **~ qn** to make sb's hair untidy, to ruffle sb's hair ◆ **dépeigné par le vent** with windswept hair ◆ **elle entra toute dépeignée** she came in with tousled *ou* dishevelled hair

dépeindre /depɛ̃dʀ/ ▸ conjug 52 ◂ VT to depict

dépenaillé, e /dep(ə)naje/ ADJ *[personne, vêtements] (= débraillé)* messy; *(= en haillons)* tattered, ragged; *[drapeau, livre]* tattered

dépénalisation /depenalizasjɔ̃/ NF *[de délit, drogue]* decriminalization

dépénaliser /depenalize/ ▸ conjug 1 ◂ VT to decriminalize

dépendance /depɑ̃dɑ̃s/ NF 1 *(= interdépendance)* dependence *(NonC)*, dependency ◆ **la ~ de qch vis-à-vis de qch d'autre** the dependence of sth (up)on sth else ◆ **un réseau subtil de ~s** a subtle network of dependencies *ou* interdependencies 2 *(= asservissement, subordination)* subordination *(à l'égard de* to); ◆ **la ~ de qn vis-à-vis de qn d'autre** the subordination of sb to sb else ◆ **être sous** *ou* **dans la ~ de qn** to be subordinate to sb 3 *(= bâtiment) [d'hôtel, château, ferme]* outbuilding, outhouse 4 *(Hist, Pol = territoire)* dependency 5 *(à une drogue, à l'alcool)* dependence, dependency *(à* on) addiction *(à* to) 6 *(Ling)* dependency

dépendant, e /depɑ̃dɑ̃, ɑ̃t/ ADJ 1 *(= non autonome)* dependent *(de* (up)on); ◆ **personnes âgées ~es** elderly dependants 2 *[drogué]* dependent *(à* on) addicted *(à* to)

dépendre /depɑ̃dʀ/ GRAMMAIRE ACTIVE 52.6
▸ conjug 41 ◂ VT INDIR **dépendre de** 1 *[décision, résultat, phénomène]* to depend (up)on, to be dependent (up)on

◆ **ça dépend** it all depends

◆ **ça dépend de** it depends on ◆ **ça dépend du temps** it depends on the weather ◆ **ça va ~ du temps** it'll depend on the weather

◆ **il dépend de qn de** *ou* **que** ◆ **il dépend de vous/de ceci que ...** it depends (up)on you/this whether ... ◆ **il ne dépend que de vous que ...** it depends entirely (up)on you whether ..., it's entirely up to you whether ... ◆ **il dépend de toi de réussir** it depends on you *ou* it's up to you whether you succeed (or not)

2 *(= être sous l'autorité de) [employé]* to be answerable to, to be responsible to; *[organisation]* to be dependent (up)on; *[territoire]* to be dependent (up)on, to be a dependency of ◆ **~ (financièrement) de ses parents** to be financially dependent (up)on one's parents ◆ **ce pays dépend économiquement de la France** this country is economically dependent (up)on France ◆ **je ne veux ~ de personne** I don't wish to be dependent (up)on anyone *ou* to have to depend (up)on anyone ◆ **ce terrain dépend de leur domaine** this piece of land is part of *ou* belongs to their property ◆ **ne ~ que de soi-même** to be answerable only to oneself

VT *[+ lustre, guirlandes, pendu]* to take down

> ⚠ Au sens de 'être sous l'autorité de', **dépendre de** ne se traduit pas par **to depend on**.

dépens /depɑ̃/ NMPL 1 *(Jur)* costs ◆ **être condamné aux ~** to be ordered to pay costs, to have costs awarded against one 2 ◆ **aux ~ de** at the expense of ◆ **rire aux ~ de qn** to (have a) laugh at sb's expense ◆ **vivre aux ~ de qn** to live off sb ◆ **je l'ai appris à mes ~** I learnt this to my cost *ou* at my expense ◆ **notre équipe s'est qualifiée aux ~ de Toulon** our team qualified after *ou* by beating Toulon

dépense /depɑ̃s/ NF 1 *(= argent dépensé, frais)* spending *(NonC)*, expense, expenditure *(NonC)*; *(= sortie)* outlay, expenditure *(NonC)* ◆ **une ~ de 300 €** an outlay *ou* expenditure of €300 ◆ **les ~s du ménage** household expenses ◆ **contrôler les ~s de qn** to control sb's expenditure *ou* spending ◆ **je n'aurais pas dû faire cette ~** I shouldn't have spent that money ◆ **j'hésite, c'est une grosse ~** I can't decide, it's a large outlay *ou* it's a lot to lay out ◆ **calculer ~s et recettes** to calculate expenditure and receipts ◆ **~s diverses** sundries ◆ **~s publiques** public *ou* government expenditure *ou* spending ◆ **les ~s de santé/militaires** health/military expenditure *ou* spending ◆ **~ d'investissement** *ou* **d'équipement** capital expenditure *(NonC)* ◆ **pousser qn à la ~** to make sb spend some money ◆ **faire la ~ d'une voiture** to lay out money *ou* spend money on a car ◆ **ne pas regarder à la ~** to spare no expense

2 *[d'électricité, essence]* consumption ◆ **~ physique** (physical) exercise

dépenser /depɑ̃se/ ▸ conjug 1 ◂ VT 1 *[+ argent]* to spend; *[+ électricité, essence]* to use ◆ **~ sans compter** to spend without counting the cost, to spend lavishly ◆ **elle dépense peu pour la nourriture** she doesn't spend much on food, she spends little on food

2 *[+ forces, énergie]* to expend, to use up; *[+ temps, jeunesse]* to spend, to use up ◆ **~ son trop-plein d'énergie** to use up one's surplus energy ◆ **vous dépensez inutilement votre salive** you're wasting your breath

VPR **se dépenser** *(= faire des efforts)* to exert o.s.; *(= se défouler)* to let off steam * ◆ **se ~ en démarches inutiles** to waste one's energies in useless procedures ◆ **pour ce projet il s'est dépensé sans compter** he has put all his energy *ou* energies into this project ◆ **les enfants ont besoin de se ~ physiquement** children need to expend their energy

dépensier, -ière /depɑ̃sje, jɛʀ/ ADJ, NM,F extravagant ◆ **c'est une dépensière, elle est dépensière** she's a spendthrift

déperdition /depɛʀdisjɔ̃/ NF *(Sci, gén)* loss

dépérir /depeʀiʀ/ ▸ conjug 2 ◂ VI *[personne]* to fade away, to waste away; *[santé, forces]* to fail, to decline; *[plante]* to wither; *[commerce]* to (be on the) decline, to fall off; *[affaire, région, économie]* to be in decline, to go downhill

dépérissement /depeʀismɑ̃/ NM *[de personne]* fading away, wasting away; *[de santé, forces]* failing, decline; *[de plante]* withering; *[de commerce]* decline, falling off; *[d'affaire, région, économie]* decline

déperlant, e /depɛʀlɑ̃, ɑ̃t/ ADJ *[tissu]* waterproof

dépersonnalisation /depɛʀsɔnalizasjɔ̃/ NF depersonalization

dépersonnaliser /depɛʀsɔnalize/ ▸ conjug 1 ◂ VT to depersonalize VPR **se dépersonnaliser** *[relations, débat]* to become impersonal *ou* depersonalized; *(Psych)* to become depersonalized

dépêtrer /depetʀe/ ▸ conjug 1 ◂ VT ◆ **~ qn de** *[+ bourbier, ronces, harnachement]* to extricate sb from, to free sb from; *[+ situation]* to extricate sb from, to get sb out of VPR **se dépêtrer** *(lit, fig)* to extricate o.s., to free o.s. ◆ **se ~ de** *[+ ronces, situation]* to extricate *ou* free o.s. from, to get out of; *[+ liens]* to free o.s. from; *[+ gêneur]* to get rid of

dépeuplement /depœpləmɑ̃/ NM *[de région, ville]* depopulation ◆ **le ~ de la rivière** the depletion of fish stocks in the river ◆ **le ~ des forêts** the disappearance of wildlife from forests

dépeupler /depœple/ ▸ conjug 1 ◂ VT 1 *[+ région, ville]* to depopulate ◆ **zones rurales dépeuplées** depopulated rural areas 2 *[+ rivière]* to deplete the fish stocks in; *[+ forêt]* to kill off the wildlife in VPR **se dépeupler** 1 *[région, ville]* to be depopulated ◆ **les campagnes se dépeuplent** the countryside is becoming depopulated 2 *[rivière]* to be depleted of fish; *[région, forêt]* to be emptied of wildlife

déphasage /defazaʒ/ NM *(Phys)* phase difference; *(* = perte de contact)* being out of touch ◆ **il y a ~ entre les syndicats et leurs dirigeants** the unions and their leaders are out of phase *ou* step

déphasé, e /defaze/ (ptp de **déphaser**) ADJ 1 *(Phys)* out of phase 2 *(* = désorienté)* **il était ~** he was out of step

déphaser /defaze/ ▸ conjug 1 ◂ VT 1 *(Phys)* to cause a phase difference in 2 *(* = désorienter)* to confuse, to disorientate

déphosphatation /defɔsfatasjɔ̃/ NF removal of phosphates (*de* from)

déphosphater /defɔsfate/ ▸ conjug 1 ◂ VT [+ eau] to remove phosphates from

dépiauter* /depjote/ ▸ conjug 1 ◂ VT [+ animal] to skin; [+ paquet] to undo; [+ texte] to pull to pieces

dépigmentation /depigmɑ̃tasjɔ̃/ NF depigmentation

dépilation /depilasjɔ̃/ NF (Méd) hair loss

dépilatoire /depilatwaʀ/ ADJ depilatory, hair-removing (épith) NM depilatory ou hair-removing cream

dépiler /depile/ ▸ conjug 1 ◂ VT (Méd) to cause hair loss to; (Tech) [+ peaux] to grain

dépiquer /depike/ ▸ conjug 1 ◂ VT (Couture) to unstitch, to unpick (Brit); (Agr) [+ laitue] to transplant; [+ blé] to thresh; [+ riz] to hull

dépistage /depistaʒ/ NM [de maladie, virus, dopage] screening (de for); ◆ **centre de ~ du sida** HIV testing centre ◆ **examen** ou **test de ~** screening test ◆ **test de ~ du sida** AIDS test

dépister /depiste/ ▸ conjug 1 ◂ VT 1 (Méd) [+ maladie, virus, dopage] to detect; (= faire passer un test à) to screen 2 (= détecter) [+ gibier, criminel] to track down; [+ influence, cause] to unearth, to detect

dépit /depi/ NM (= amertume) pique, (great) vexation ◆ **causer du ~ à qn** to vex sb greatly ◆ **il en a conçu du ~** he was very piqued at it ◆ **il l'a fait par ~** he did it out of pique ou in a fit of pique ◆ **par ~ amoureux elle a épousé le premier venu** she married the first man she met on the rebound*

◆ **en dépit de** in spite of, despite ◆ **faire qch en ~ du bon sens** to do sth any old how

dépité, e /depite/ (ptp de **dépiter**) ADJ (greatly) vexed, piqued

dépiter /depite/ ▸ conjug 1 ◂ VT to vex

dépitonner /depitɔne/ ▸ conjug 1 ◂ VTI (Alpinisme) to depeg

déplacé, e /deplase/ (ptp de **déplacer**) ADJ [présence] uncalled-for; [intervention, scrupule] misplaced, out of place (attrib); [remarque, propos] uncalled-for, out of place (attrib); → **personne**

déplacement /deplasmɑ̃/ NM 1 [d'objet, meuble] moving, shifting

2 (Méd) [d'articulation, os] displacement ◆ **~ de vertèbre** slipped disc ◆ **~ d'organe** organ displacement

3 [d'usine, fonctionnaire] transfer; [de collectivité] moving ◆ **le ~ forcé des populations** the forced movement ou transfer of people ◆ **j'ai demandé le ~ du rendez-vous** I asked for the appointment to be changed

4 [de pièce mobile] movement; [de substance] movement, displacement ◆ **~ d'air** displacement of air ◆ **~ de troupes** movement of troops

5 (= voyage) trip ◆ **les ~s coûtent cher** travelling ou travel is expensive ◆ **être en ~ (pour affaires)** to be away on business ◆ **ça vaut le ~*** it's worth the trip; → **frais²**

6 (Naut) displacement ◆ **~ de 10 000 tonnes** 10,000-ton displacement

7 (Psych) displacement

déplacer /deplase/ ▸ conjug 3 ◂ VT 1 (= bouger) [+ objet, meuble] to move, to shift ◆ **il déplace beaucoup d'air** (hum) he's all talk (and no action) ◆ **~ des montagnes** to move mountains

2 (Méd) [+ articulation, os] to displace

3 [+ usine, fonctionnaire] to transfer, to move; [+ collectivité] to move; [+ rendez-vous] to change ◆ **personnes déplacées** (Pol, Mil) displaced persons

4 (= attirer) **le spectacle a déplacé plus de 60 000 personnes** the show brought in ou drew more than 60,000 people

5 [+ problème, question] to shift the emphasis of

6 (Naut) to displace ◆ **navire qui déplace 10 000 tonnes** ship with a 10,000-ton displacement

VPR **se déplacer** 1 [pièce mobile] to move; [air, substance] to move, to be displaced

2 [personne] to move; (= circuler) to move (around); [animal] to move (along) ◆ **il ne se déplace qu'avec peine** he has difficulty getting about ◆ **il est interdit de se ~ pendant la classe** no moving around during class ◆ **pouvez-vous vous ~ sur la droite ?** can you move (over) to the right?

3 (= se déranger) [médecin] to come out ◆ **avec le téléachat on peut faire ses courses sans se ~** teleshopping means you can do your shopping in the comfort of your own home ◆ **il ne s'est même pas déplacé pour le mariage de sa sœur** he didn't even bother to go to his sister's wedding

4 (= voyager) to travel ◆ **il ne se déplace qu'en avion** he only travels by air ◆ **il se déplace fréquemment** he travels a lot, he's a frequent traveller

5 (Méd) [os] to be displaced ◆ **se ~ une articulation** to put a joint out, to displace a joint ◆ **se ~ une vertèbre** to slip a disc

déplafonnement /deplafɔnmɑ̃/ NM [de crédit] derestriction ◆ **ils réclament le ~ des cotisations** they are asking for the ceiling on contributions to be lifted

déplafonner /deplafɔne/ ▸ conjug 1 ◂ VT [+ crédit] to derestrict; [+ cotisations] to lift the ceiling on

déplaire /deplɛʀ/ GRAMMAIRE ACTIVE 34.3 ▸ conjug 54 ◂

VT INDIR 1 (= n'être pas aimé de) **il déplaît à tout le monde** he is disliked by everyone ◆ **cette mode/ville/femme me déplaît** I dislike ou I don't like ou I don't care for this fashion/town/woman ◆ **au bout d'un moment, cela risque de ~** after a while it can become disagreeable ou unpleasant ◆ **ça ne me déplairait pas de le faire** I wouldn't mind doing it ◆ **il me déplaît de faire ...** (frm) I dislike doing ... ◆ **il me déplairait d'avoir à vous renvoyer** (frm) I would be sorry to have to dismiss you

2 (= irriter) **~ à qn** to displease sb ◆ **il fait tout pour nous ~** he does all he can to displease us ◆ **ceci a profondément déplu** this gave profound ou great displeasure ◆ **il cherche à ~** he is trying to be disagreeable ou unpleasant

3 († ou hum) **c'est, ne t'en déplaise, beaucoup plus pratique** whether you like it or not, it's more practical ◆ **j'irai la voir, n'en déplaise à votre père** whatever your father's views on the matter, I shall go and see her

VPR **se déplaire** 1 (= être malheureux) ◆ **elle se déplaît ici/à la campagne** she dislikes it ou doesn't like it here/in the country ◆ **se ~ dans son nouvel emploi** to be unhappy in one's new job, to dislike one's new job

2 (mutuellement) **ils se sont déplu dès leur première rencontre** they disliked each other right from the start

déplaisant, e /deplɛzɑ̃, ɑ̃t/ ADJ disagreeable, unpleasant

déplaisir /deplezir/ NM (= contrariété) displeasure, annoyance ◆ **je le ferai sans ~** I'm quite willing ou happy to do it, I don't mind doing it ◆ **faire qch avec (le plus grand) ~** to do sth with (the greatest) displeasure

déplantage /deplɑ̃taʒ/ NM, **déplantation** /deplɑ̃tasjɔ̃/ NF [de plante] transplanting; [de plate-bande] digging up; [de piquet] pulling out

déplanter /deplɑ̃te/ ▸ conjug 1 ◂ VT 1 [+ plante] to transplant; [+ plate-bande] to dig up; [+ piquet] to pull out 2 [+ ordinateur] to get going again

déplâtrage /deplɑtʀaʒ/ NM ◆ **le ~ d'un mur** (Constr) stripping the plaster off a wall ◆ **le ~ d'un membre** (Méd) taking a limb out of plaster ou out of its (plaster) cast, taking a (plaster) cast off a limb

déplâtrer /deplɑtʀe/ ▸ conjug 1 ◂ VT (Constr) to strip the plaster off; (Méd) to take out of plaster, to take the (plaster) cast off ◆ **je me fais ~ lundi** I'm going to have my cast taken off on Monday

déplétion /deplesjɔ̃/ NF depletion

dépliage /deplijaʒ/ NM [de serviette, vêtement] unfolding; [de carte, journal, canapé-lit] opening out, unfolding

dépliant, e /deplijɑ̃, ijɑ̃t/ ADJ extendible NM (= prospectus) leaflet; (= grande page) fold-out page ◆ **~ touristique** travel brochure

déplier /deplije/ ▸ conjug 7 ◂ VT 1 [+ serviette, vêtement] to unfold; [+ carte routière, journal, canapé-lit] to open out, to unfold ◆ **~ les jambes** to stretch one's legs out 2 († = déballer) [+ paquet] to open out, to open up ◆ **~ sa marchandise** to spread (out) one's wares VPR **se déplier** [carte routière] to open out; [feuille d'arbre] to open out, to unfold ◆ **ça peut se ~, ça se déplie** it unfolds ou opens out, it can be unfolded ◆ **le canapé se déplie pour faire lit** the sofa opens out ou unfolds into a bed

déplissage /deplisaʒ/ NM [d'étoffe plissée] taking the pleats out of; (= défroissage) flattening (out), smoothing (out)

déplisser /deplise/ ▸ conjug 1 ◂ VT (= défaire les plis de) to take the pleats out of; (= défroisser) to flatten (out), to smooth (out); (littér) [+ front] to smooth VPR **se déplisser** [jupe] to come unpleated, to lose its pleats

déploiement /deplwamɑ̃/ NM [de voile, drapeau] unfurling; [d'ailes] spreading; [de troupes] deployment; [de richesses, forces, amabilité, talents] display ◆ **le ~ d'une force internationale** the deployment of an international force

déplomber /deplɔ̃be/ ▸ conjug 1 ◂ VT [+ colis, compteur] to unseal; [+ dent] to remove the filling from, to take the filling out of; (Ordin) to hack into, to gain unauthorized access to

déplorable /deplɔʀabl/ ADJ 1 (= regrettable) [incident, situation] deplorable 2 (= très mauvais) [conduite, gestion, notes] appalling, deplorable ◆ **sa chambre est dans un état ~** his room is in an appalling ou a terrible state

déplorablement /deplɔʀabləmɑ̃/ ADV deplorably

déploration /deplɔʀasjɔ̃/ NF (Art) ◆ **~ du Christ** lamentation

déplorer /deplɔʀe/ ▸ conjug 1 ◂ VT to lament ◆ **on déplore 5 morts** (unfortunately,) 5 people have died ◆ **on ne déplore aucune victime** there have been no deaths ou victims ◆ **ils déploraient que la presse ne les ait pas soutenus** they lamented the fact that the press had not lent them any support ◆ **nous déplorons le manque d'informations sur les arrestations** we are deeply concerned about the lack of information on the arrests

déployer /deplwaje/ ▸ conjug 8 ◂ VT 1 (= ouvrir) [+ carte, tissu] to open out, to spread out; [+ voile, drapeau] to unfurl; [+ ailes] to spread; [+ assortiment, échantillons] to spread out, to lay out 2 (Mil) [+ troupes, forces de police] to deploy ◆ **il a déployé ses troupes en éventail** he made his troops fan out 3 (= montrer, manifester) [+ richesses, fastes] to make a display of, to display; [+ talents, ressources, forces] to display, to exhibit ◆ **~ beaucoup d'activité** to be very active ◆ **~ beaucoup d'efforts/d'énergie** to expend a lot of effort/energy; → **rire** VPR **se déployer** [voile, drapeau] to unfurl; [ailes] to spread; [troupes] to deploy; [cortège] to spread out

déplumé, e /deplyme/ (ptp de **déplumer**) ADJ 1 [oiseau] featherless, that has lost its feathers 2 (* = chauve) bald ◆ **il est un peu ~ sur**

le dessus he's a bit thin on top ♦ **son crâne** ~ his bald *ou* hairless head 3 (* = *démuni*) broke*, skint* *(Brit)* ♦ **il s'est retrouvé complètement** ~ he ended up completely skint* *(Brit) ou* with no money at all

déplumer /deplyme/ ▸ conjug 1 ◂ **VT** † to pluck **VPR se déplumer** *[oiseau]* to moult, to lose its feathers; (* = *perdre ses cheveux)* to go bald, to lose one's hair

dépoétiser /depɔetize/ ▸ conjug 1 ◂ **VT** to take the romance out of, to make prosaic

dépoitraillé, e /depwatʀɑje/ **ADJ** *(péj)* ♦ **il était tout** ~ his shirt was open, revealing his chest

dépolarisant, e /depɔlaʀizɑ̃, ɑt/ **ADJ** depolarizing **NM** depolarizer

dépolarisation /depɔlaʀizasjɔ̃/ **NF** depolarization

dépolariser /depɔlaʀize/ ▸ conjug 1 ◂ **VT** to depolarize

dépoli, e /depɔli/ (ptp de **dépolir**) **ADJ** → **verre**

dépolir /depɔliʀ/ ▸ conjug 2 ◂ **VT** *[+ argent, étain]* to tarnish; *[+ verre]* to frost **VPR se dépolir** to tarnish

dépolissage /depɔlisaʒ/ **NM** *[d'argent, étain]* tarnishing; *[de verre]* frosting

dépolitisation /depɔlitizasjɔ̃/ **NF** depoliticization

dépolitiser /depɔlitize/ ▸ conjug 1 ◂ **VT** to depoliticize **VPR se dépolitiser** to become depoliticized

dépolluant, e /depɔlyɑ̃, ɑt/ **ADJ** *[produit]* depolluting, anti-pollutant **NM** depollutant, antipollutant

dépolluer /depɔlɥe/ ▸ conjug 1 ◂ **VT** to clean up, to rid *ou* clear of pollution

dépollution /depɔlysjɔ̃/ **NF** getting rid of pollution *(de* from); ♦ **la ~ des plages souillées par le mazout** the cleaning (up) of oil-polluted beaches

déponent, e /depɔnɑ̃, ɑt/ **ADJ** *(Ling)* deponent **NM** deponent (verb)

dépopulation /depɔpylasjɔ̃/ **NF** depopulation

déportation /depɔʀtasjɔ̃/ **NF** (= *exil)* deportation, transportation; (= *internement)* imprisonment (in a concentration camp) ♦ **ils sont morts en** ~ they died in the (Nazi concentration) camps

déporté, e /depɔʀte/ (ptp de **déporter**) **NM,F** (= *exilé)* deportee; (= *interné)* prisoner (in a concentration camp)

déportement /depɔʀtəmɑ̃/ **NM** 1 (= *embardée)* ~ **vers la gauche** swerve to the left 2 († = *écarts de conduite)* ~**s** misbehaviour *(Brit)*, misbehavior *(US)*

déporter /depɔʀte/ ▸ conjug 1 ◂ **VT** 1 *[+ personne]* (= *exiler)* to deport, to transport; (= *interner)* to send to a concentration camp 2 (= *faire dévier)* to carry off course ♦ **le vent l'a déporté** the wind carried *ou* blew him off course **VPR se déporter** *(en voiture)* to swerve ♦ **se ~ sur la gauche** to swerve to the left

déposant, e /depozɑ̃, ɑt/ **NM,F** 1 (= *épargnant)* depositor 2 *(Jur)* bailor; (= *témoin)* deponent

dépose /depoz/ **NF** *[de moquette]* lifting, taking up; *[de serrure, moteur]* taking out, removal; *[de rideau]* taking down ♦ **"dépose des passagers"** "setting down only"

déposer /depoze/ ▸ conjug 1 ◂ **VT** 1 (= *poser)* to put down, to set down; *[+ ordures]* to dump ♦ **"défense de déposer des ordures"** "no dumping", "no tipping" *(Brit)* ♦ ~ **les armes** to lay down (one's) arms ♦ ~ **un baiser sur le front de qn** *(littér)* to plant a kiss on sb's forehead

2 (= *laisser)* *[+ chose]* to leave; (= *conduire)* *[+ personne]* to drop ♦ ~ **sa carte** to leave one's card ♦ **on a déposé une lettre/un paquet pour vous** somebody left a letter/a parcel for you, somebody dropped a letter/a parcel in for you ♦ ~ **une valise à la consigne** to deposit *ou* leave a suitcase at the left-luggage office *(Brit) ou* baggage check *(US)* ♦ **je te dépose à la gare** I'll drop you (off) at the station ♦ **l'autobus le déposa à la gare** the bus dropped him *ou* set him down at the station ♦ **est-ce que je peux vous ~ quelque part ?** can I give you a lift *(Brit) ou* ride *(US)* anywhere?, can I drop you anywhere?

3 *(Fin)* *[+ argent, valeur]* to deposit ♦ ~ **de l'argent sur un compte** to put money into an account, to deposit money in an account

4 *(Admin, Jur)* *[+ plainte]* to lodge; *[+ réclamation]* to file; *[+ conclusions]* to present; *[+ brevet, marque de fabrique]* to register; *[+ projet de loi]* to bring in, to table *(Brit)*; *[+ rapport]* to send in, to file ♦ ~ **son bilan** to go into (voluntary) liquidation ♦ ~ **un préavis de grève** to give notice of strike action; → **marque**

5 (= *destituer)* *[+ souverain]* to depose

6 *[eau, vin]* *[+ sable, lie]* to deposit

7 (= *démonter)* *[+ tenture]* to take down; *[+ tapis]* to take up, to lift; *[+ serrure, moteur]* to take out, to remove

VI 1 *[liquide]* to form a sediment *ou* a deposit ♦ **laisser** ~ to leave to settle

2 *(Jur)* to give evidence, to testify

VPR se déposer *[poussière, lie]* to settle

dépositaire /depozitɛʀ/ **NMF** 1 *[d'objet confié]* depository; *[de secret, vérité]* possessor, guardian; *(Jur)* bailee ♦ ~ **public** *(Jur)* ≈ authorized depository ♦ ~ **légal** *(Fin)* escrow agent 2 *(Comm = agent)* agent *(de* for); ♦ ~ **exclusif** sole agent *(de* for); ♦ **nous ne sommes pas ~s** we are not agents for them, it's not a line we carry

déposition /depozisjɔ̃/ **NF** 1 *(Jur)* *(à un procès)* evidence *(NonC)*; *(écrite)* (sworn) statement, deposition ♦ **faire une** ~ *(à un procès)* to give evidence; *(écrite)* to write a statement ♦ **signer sa** ~ to sign one's statement *ou* deposition 2 *[de souverain]* deposition, deposing 3 *(Art)* ~ **de croix** Deposition

déposséder /depɔsede/ ▸ conjug 6 ◂ **VT** ♦ ~ **qn de** *[+ terres]* to dispossess sb of; *[+ place, biens]* to deprive sb of; *[+ charge]* to divest *ou* deprive sb of ♦ **ils se sentaient dépossédés** they felt dispossessed

dépossession /depɔsesjɔ̃/ **NF** *(de terres)* dispossession; *(d'une place, de biens)* deprivation; *(d'une charge)* divesting ♦ **leur sentiment de** ~ their feeling of being dispossessed ♦ ~ **de soi** *(littér)* loss of a sense of self

dépôt /depo/ **NM** 1 (= *action de déposer)* *[d'argent, valeurs]* deposit(ing) ♦ **le ~ des manteaux au vestiaire est obligatoire** coats must be left *ou* deposited in the cloakroom ♦ **le ~ d'une marque de fabrique** the registration of a trademark ♦ ~ **de bilan** (voluntary) liquidation ♦ ~ **légal** *(Jur)* registration of copyright ♦ **en ~ fiduciaire** *(Fin)* in escrow; → **mandat**

2 (= *garde)* **avoir qch en** ~ to hold sth in trust ♦ **confier qch en ~ à qn** to entrust sth to sb

3 (= *chose confiée)* **restituer un** ~ to return what has been entrusted to one ♦ ~ **sacré** sacred trust ♦ ~ **(bancaire)** *(Fin)* (bank) deposit ♦ ~ **à vue** *(Fin)* deposit on current account *(Brit)*, checking deposit *(US)* ♦ ~ **à terme** fixed term deposit; → **banque, compte**

4 (= *garantie)* deposit ♦ ~ **préalable** advance deposit ♦ **verser un** ~ to put down *ou* pay a deposit

5 (= *sédiment)* *[de liquide, lie]* sediment, deposit ♦ ~ **de sable** silt *(NonC)* ♦ ~ **de tartre** layer of sediment, fur *(Brit)* *(NonC)* ♦ **l'eau a formé un ~ calcaire dans la bouilloire** the water has formed a layer of sediment on the kettle *ou* has furred up the kettle *(Brit)*

6 (= *entrepôt)* warehouse, store; *[d'autobus]* depot, garage; *[de trains]* depot, shed; *(Mil)* depot

7 *(Comm)* **il y a un ~ de pain/de lait à l'épicerie** (= *point de vente)* bread/milk can be bought at the grocer's

8 (= *prison)* jail, prison ♦ **il a passé la nuit au** ~ he spent the night in the cells *ou* in jail

COMP dépôt d'essence petrol *(Brit) ou* gasoline *(US)* depot
dépôt de marchandises goods *(Brit) ou* freight *(US)* depot *ou* station
dépôt de munitions ammunition *ou* munitions dump
dépôt d'ordures (rubbish) dump *ou* tip *(Brit)*, garbage dump *(US)*

dépotage /depɔtaʒ/, **dépotement** /depɔtmɑ̃/ **NM** *[de plante]* transplanting; *[de liquide]* decanting

dépoter /depɔte/ ▸ conjug 1 ◂ **VT** *[+ plante]* to take out of the pot; *[+ liquide]* to decant

dépotoir /depɔtwaʀ/ **NM** 1 *(lit, fig = décharge)* dumping ground, (rubbish) dump *ou* tip *(Brit)*, garbage dump *(US)* ♦ **classe** ~ class of rejects ♦ **c'est devenu une banlieue** ~ it's become a suburban dumping ground 2 (= *usine)* sewage works

dépôt-vente (pl **dépôts-ventes**) /depovɑ̃t/ **NM** second-hand shop *(Brit) ou* store *(US)* *(where items are sold on commission)*

dépouille /depuj/ **NF** 1 (= *peau)* skin, hide; *[de mue d'insecte]* cast; *[de serpent]* slough 2 *(littér = cadavre)* ~ **(mortelle)** (mortal) remains 3 *(littér = butin)* ~**s** plunder, spoils 4 *(Pol US)* **système des ~s** spoils system

dépouillé, e /depuje/ (ptp de **dépouiller**) **ADJ** *[décor]* bare, austere; *[style]* plain ♦ ~ **de** *[poésie]* lacking in; *[ornements]* shorn *ou* stripped of ♦ **des vêtements au style simple, pur et** ~ clothes that are simple, classic and uncluttered ♦ **une maison élégante, au style** ~ an elegant, uncluttered house ♦ **les journaux télévisés sont revenus à un style ~ et prudent** the style of television news has reverted to being plain and careful

dépouillement /depujmɑ̃/ **NM** 1 (= *examen)* *[de comptes, journal, documents, courrier]* going through, perusal *(frm)*; *[d'auteur]* going through, studying ♦ **le ~ du courrier a pris trois heures** it took three hours to go through the mail ♦ **le ~ du scrutin** counting the votes ♦ **lors du** ~ when the votes are *(ou* were) being counted, during the count ♦ **pendant le ~ des données** while sifting through the data 2 (= *ascèse, pauvreté)* asceticism; (= *sobriété)* spareness, sobriety ♦ **vivre dans le** ~ to lead an ascetic life 3 (= *spoliation)* stripping

dépouiller /depuje/ ▸ conjug 1 ◂ **VT** 1 (= *examiner en détail)* *[+ comptes, documents, courrier]* to go through, to peruse; *[+ auteur]* to go through, to study (in detail) ♦ ~ **un scrutin** to count the votes

2 (= *écorcher)* to skin; (= *écorcer)* to bark, to strip the bark from

3 (= *priver)* ♦ ~ **qn de** *[+ vêtements]* to strip sb of; *[+ économies, honneurs]* to strip *ou* divest sb of; *[+ droits]* to strip *ou* deprive sb of ♦ ~ **qch de** *[+ ornements]* to strip *ou* divest *ou* denude sth of; *[+ feuilles, fleurs]* to strip *ou* denude sth of ♦ **un livre qui dépouille l'amour de son mystère** a book that strips *ou* divests love of its mystery

4 *(littér = dénuder)* to strip, to denude ♦ **le vent dépouille les arbres** the wind strips *ou* denudes the trees (of their leaves) ♦ **l'hiver dépouille les champs** winter lays the fields bare ♦ ~ **un autel** to remove the ornaments from an altar, to strip an altar (of its ornaments) ♦ ~ **son style** to strip one's style of all ornament

5 *(littér = spolier)* ~ **un voyageur** to despoil *(littér) ou* strip a traveller of his possessions ♦ ~ **un héritier** to deprive *ou* divest an heir of his

inheritance ◆ **il a dépouillé ses enfants** he's deprived *ou* stripped his children of everything ◆ **ils ont dépouillé le pays** they have plundered the country *ou* laid the country bare **VPR se dépouiller** 1 *(littér)* **se ~ de** *[+ vêtements]* to shed, to divest o.s. of; *[+ possessions]* to divest *ou* deprive o.s. of; *[+ arrogance]* to cast off *ou* aside, to divest o.s. of; *[arbre] [+ feuilles, fleurs]* to shed; *[pré] [+ verdure, fleurs]* to become stripped *ou* denuded of ◆ **les arbres se dépouillent (de leurs feuilles)** the trees are shedding their leaves ◆ **la campagne se dépouille (de son feuillage** *ou* **de sa verdure)** the countryside is losing *ou* shedding its greenery ◆ **son style s'était dépouillé de toute redondance** his style had been stripped *ou* shorn of all unnecessary repetition
2 *[animal qui mue]* to shed its skin

dépourvu, e /depuʀvy/ **ADJ** ◆ **~ de** without ◆ **être ~ de qch** to lack sth ◆ **~ de moyens** *ou* **de ressources** without means *ou* resources ◆ **les organisations humanitaires sont ~es de moyens** the humanitarian organizations lack money ◆ **une présence militaire ~e de moyens de dissuasion** a military presence which has no means of deterrence ◆ **cet article est totalement ~ d'intérêt** this article is not of the slightest interest ◆ **une réponse ~e d'ambiguïté** an unambiguous reply ◆ **~ de tout diplôme, il accomplit une carrière brillante** although he had no qualifications he had a very successful career ◆ **ce n'est pas une question totalement ~e de sens** this question is not entirely unreasonable ◆ **des gens ~s (de tout)** destitute people
NM ◆ **prendre qn au ~** to catch sb off their guard ◆ **il a été pris au ~ par cette question inattendue** he was caught off his guard by this unexpected question

dépoussiérage /depusjeʀaʒ/ **NM** *(lit)* dusting *(de of)*; *(fig) [d'administration, parti]* revamping *(de of)*

dépoussiérant /depusjeʀɑ̃/ **NM** anti-static furniture polish

dépoussiérer /depusjeʀe/ ▸ conjug 6 ◂ **VT** *(lit)* to dust; *(fig) [+ texte, institution]* to blow *ou* brush away the cobwebs from ◆ **~ l'image d'un parti** to revamp a party's image, to get rid of a party's old-fashioned image

dépravation /depʀavasjɔ̃/ **NF** (= *état*) depravity

dépravé, e /depʀave/ (ptp de **dépraver**) **ADJ** depraved **NM,F** depraved person

dépraver /depʀave/ ▸ conjug 1 ◂ **VT** to deprave ◆ **les mœurs se dépravent** morals are becoming depraved

dépréciateur, -trice /depʀesjatœʀ, tʀis/ **NM,F** disparager

dépréciatif, -ive /depʀesjatif, iv/ **ADJ** *[propos, jugement]* depreciatory, disparaging; *[mot, sens]* derogatory, disparaging

dépréciation /depʀesjasjɔ̃/ **NF** depreciation

déprécier /depʀesje/ ▸ conjug 7 ◂ **VT** (= *faire perdre de la valeur à*) to depreciate; (= *dénigrer*) to belittle, to disparage, to depreciate **VPR se déprécier** *[monnaie, objet]* to depreciate; *[personne]* to belittle o.s., to put o.s. down

déprédateur, -trice /depʀedatœʀ, tʀis/ **ADJ** (= *voleur*) plundering *(épith)*; (= *destructeur*) *[personne]* destructive ◆ **insectes ~s** insect pests **NM,F** (= *pilleur*) plunderer; (= *escroc*) embezzler; (= *vandale*) vandal

déprédation /depʀedasjɔ̃/ **NF** 1 *(gén pl)* (= *pillage*) plundering *(NonC)*, depredation *(frm)*; (= *dégâts*) damage *(NonC)*, depredation *(frm)* ◆ **commettre des ~s** to cause damage 2 *(Jur = détournement)* misappropriation, embezzlement

déprendre (se) /depʀɑ̃dʀ/ ▸ conjug 58 ◂ **VPR** *(littér)* ◆ **se ~ de** *[+ personne, chose]* to lose one's fondness for; *[+ habitude]* to lose

dépressif, -ive /depʀesif, iv/ **ADJ, NM,F** depressive

dépression /depʀesjɔ̃/ **NF** 1 ◆ **~ (de terrain)** depression; *(petite)* dip 2 *(Météo)* **~ (atmosphérique)** (atmospheric) depression, low ◆ **une ~ centrée sur le nord** an area of low pressure in the north 3 *(Psych = état)* depression ◆ **~ (nerveuse)** (nervous) breakdown ◆ **il a fait une ~** he had a (nervous) breakdown ◆ **elle fait de la ~** she suffers from depression 4 *(Écon)* **~ (économique)** (economic) depression *ou* slump

dépressionnaire /depʀesjɔnɛʀ/ **ADJ** *(Météo)* ◆ **zone ~** area of low pressure

dépressurisation /depʀesyʀizasjɔ̃/ **NF** depressurization ◆ **en cas de ~ de la cabine** should the pressure drop in the cabin

dépressuriser /depʀesyʀize/ ▸ conjug 1 ◂ **VT** to depressurize

déprimant, e /depʀimɑ̃, ɑ̃t/ **ADJ** *(moralement)* depressing; *(physiquement)* debilitating

déprime* /depʀim/ **NF** depression ◆ **faire de la ~** to be depressed ◆ **c'est la ~ dans les milieux financiers** financial circles are depressed ◆ **période de ~** low period

déprimé, e /depʀime/ (ptp de **déprimer**) **ADJ** 1 *[personne]* *(moralement)* depressed, low *(attrib)* 2 *[terrain]* low-lying

déprimer /depʀime/ ▸ conjug 1 ◂ **VT** 1 *(moralement)* to depress; *(physiquement)* to debilitate, to enervate 2 (= *enfoncer*) to depress **VI** * to be depressed, to feel down *

déprise /depʀiz/ **NF** ◆ **~ (agricole)** abandonment of farmland

De profundis /depʀɔfɔ̃dis/ **NM** de profundis

déprogrammation /depʀɔgʀamasjɔ̃/ **NF** cancellation

déprogrammer /depʀɔgʀame/ ▸ conjug 1 ◂ **VT** *(TV)* *(définitivement)* to take off the air; *(temporairement)* to cancel; *[+ magnétoscope]* to cancel the programming on; *[+ rendez-vous, visite]* to cancel

déprotéger /depʀɔteʒe/ ▸ conjug 6 et 3 ◂ **VT** *(Ordin)* to unprotect

dépucelage* /depys(ə)laʒ/ **NM** ◆ **~ d'une fille/ d'un garçon** taking of a girl's/boy's virginity

dépuceler* /depys(ə)le/ ▸ conjug 4 ◂ **VT** to take the virginity of ◆ **se faire ~** to lose one's virginity *ou* one's cherry ✻ ◆ **c'est lui qui l'a dépucelée** she lost it to him ✻

depuis /dəpɥi/

1 PRÉPOSITION 2 ADVERBE

1 - PRÉPOSITION

Notez l'emploi de **for** lorsque l'on parle d'une durée, et de **since** lorsque l'on parle d'un point de départ dans le temps.

Pour exprimer une durée, le présent français devient un parfait en anglais, et l'imparfait un pluperfect.

1 durée for ◆ **il est malade ~ une semaine** he has been ill for a week ◆ **il était malade ~ une semaine** he had been ill for a week ◆ **elle cherche du travail ~ plus d'un mois** she's been looking for a job for over *ou* more than a month ◆ **il est mort ~ deux ans** he has been dead (for) two years ◆ **il dormait ~ une heure quand le réveil a sonné** he had been sleeping *ou* asleep for an hour when the alarm went off ◆ **mort ~ longtemps** long since dead ◆ **nous n'avons pas été au théâtre ~ des siècles** we haven't been to the theatre for *ou* in ages

Dans les questions, **for** est généralement omis.

◆ **~ combien de temps travaillez-vous ici ? – ~ cinq ans** how long have you been working here? – five years ◆ **tu le connais ~ longtemps ? – ~ toujours** have you known him long? – I've known him all my life

2 point de départ dans le temps since ◆ **~ le 3 octobre** since 3 October ◆ **il attend ~ hier/ce matin** he has been waiting since yesterday/this morning ◆ **il attendait ~ lundi** he had been waiting since Monday ◆ **~ leur dispute ils ne se parlent/parlaient plus** they haven't/hadn't spoken to each other since their quarrel *ou* since they quarrelled ◆ **je ne l'ai pas vue ~ qu'elle/~ le jour où elle s'est cassé la jambe** I haven't seen her since she/since the day she broke her leg ◆ **elle joue du violon ~ son plus jeune âge** she has played the violin since early childhood ◆ **~ quand le connaissez-vous ?** how long have you known him? ◆ **~ quelle date êtes-vous ici ?** when did you arrive here? ◆ **~ cela** since then *ou* that time ◆ **~ lors** *(littér)* from that time forward *(littér)* ◆ **~ quand es-tu (devenu) expert sur la question ?** since when have you been an expert on the matter? ◆ **~ le matin jusqu'au soir** from morning till night

◆ **depuis peu** ◆ **~ peu elle a recommencé à sortir** lately *ou* recently she has started going out again ◆ **je la connaissais ~ peu quand elle est partie** I hadn't known her long *ou* I had known her (for) only a short time when she left

◆ **depuis que** since ◆ **~ qu'il habite ici, il n'a cessé de se plaindre** he hasn't stopped complaining since he moved here ◆ **~ qu'il est ministre il ne nous parle plus** now that he is *ou* since he became a minister he doesn't speak to us any more ◆ **~ qu'il avait appris son succès il désirait la féliciter** he'd been wanting to congratulate her ever since he heard of her success ◆ **~ que le monde est monde** since the beginning of time, from time immemorial

◆ **depuis le temps que** ◆ **~ le temps qu'il apprend le français, il devrait pouvoir le parler** considering how long he's been learning French, he ought to be able to speak it ◆ **~ le temps qu'il est ici, il ne nous a jamais dit un mot** in all the time he has been here he has never said a word to us ◆ **~ le temps qu'on ne s'était pas vus !** it's ages since we (last) saw each other!, long time no see! * ◆ **~ le temps que je voulais voir ce film !** I had been wanting to see that film for ages! *ou* for such a long time! ◆ **~ le temps que je dis que je vais lui écrire !** I've been saying I'll write to him for ages! ◆ **~ le temps qu'il essaie !** he has been trying long enough! ◆ **~ le temps que je te le dis !** I've told you often enough!

3 lieu (= *à partir de*) from ◆ **le concert est retransmis ~ Paris/nos studios** the concert is broadcast from Paris/our studios ◆ **nous roulons/roulions sous la pluie ~ Londres** it's been raining/it rained all the way from London ◆ **~ Nice il a fait le plein trois fois** he's filled up three times since Nice

4 rang, ordre from ◆ **~ le simple soldat jusqu'au général** from private (right up) to general ◆ **~ le premier jusqu'au dernier** from the first to the last ◆ **robes ~ 50 € jusqu'à ...** dresses from €50 to ..., dresses starting at €50 (and) going up to ... ◆ **~ 5 grammes jusqu'à ...** from 5 grammes (up) to ... ◆ **ils ont toutes les tailles ~ le 36** they have all sizes from 36 upwards

2 - ADVERBE

since then ◆ **~, nous sommes sans nouvelles** we've had no news since then ◆ **nous étions**

en vacances ensemble, je ne l'ai pas revu ~ we went on holiday together, but I haven't seen him since then

dépuratif, -ive /depyʀatif, iv/ **ADJ, NM** depurative

députation /depytasjɔ̃/ **NF** *(= envoi, groupe)* deputation, delegation; *(= mandat de député)* post of deputy • **candidat à la** ~ parliamentary candidate • **se présenter à la** ~ to stand *(Brit)* ou run *(US)* for parliament

député, e /depyte/ **NM,F** ① *(au parlement)* deputy; *(en Grande-Bretagne)* Member of Parliament, MP; *(aux États-Unis)* congressman, congresswoman • **elle a été élue** ~ **de Metz** she has been elected (as) deputy ou member for Metz • ~ **au Parlement européen,** ~ **européen** Member of the European Parliament, MEP • **le** ~**-maire de Rouen** the deputy and mayor of Rouen • ~ **en exercice** present incumbent, sitting member *(Brit)*

NM *(= envoyé d'un prince)* envoy; *(= envoyé d'une assemblée)* delegate

⚠ La traduction de **député** varie en fonction du système politique.

DÉPUTÉ

577 **députés**, elected in the « élections législatives » held every five years, make up the lower house of the French parliament (the « Assemblée nationale »). Each **député** represents a constituency (« circonscription »). Their role is comparable to that of Members of Parliament in Britain and Congressmen and women in the United States. → **ASSEMBLÉE NATIONALE, ÉLECTIONS, MAIRE**

députer /depyte/ ▸ conjug 1 ◂ **VT** • ~ **qn pour faire/aller** to delegate sb to do/go • ~ **qn à** ou **auprès d'une assemblée/auprès de qn** to send sb (as representative) to an assembly/to sb

déqualification /dekalifikasjɔ̃/ **NF** deskilling • **la** ~ **est de plus en plus courante** more and more people are being given jobs for which they are overqualified ou which don't match their qualifications

déqualifié, e /dekalifje/ (ptp de **déqualifier**) **ADJ** *[personnel, emploi]* deskilled

déqualifier /dekalifje/ ▸ conjug 7 ◂ **VT** *[+ personnel, emploi]* to deskill

der* /dɛʀ/ **NF** (abrév de **dernière**) • **dix de** ~ *(Cartes) ten points awarded for the last trick taken in belote* • **la** ~ **des** ~**s** *(gén)* the very last one; *(= guerre de 1914-1918)* the war to end all wars

déraciné, e /deʀasine/ (ptp de **déraciner**) **ADJ** *[personne]* rootless **NM,F** rootless person • **toute ma vie, je serai un** ~ I'll always feel rootless

déracinement /deʀasinmɑ̃/ **NM** *[d'arbre, personne]* uprooting; *[d'erreur, préjugé]* eradication • **il a souffert de ce** ~ he suffered as a result of being uprooted like this

déraciner /deʀasine/ ▸ conjug 1 ◂ **VT** *[+ arbre, personne]* to uproot; *[+ erreur]* to eradicate; *[+ préjugé]* to root out, to eradicate

déraillement /deʀɑjmɑ̃/ **NM** derailment

dérailler /deʀɑje/ ▸ conjug 1 ◂ **VI** ① *[train]* to be derailed, to go off ou leave the rails • **faire** ~ **un train** to derail a train • **faire** ~ **le processus de paix/les négociations** to derail the peace process/the negotiations ② * *(= divaguer)* to talk nonsense ou twaddle* *(Brit)*; *(= mal fonctionner)* to be on the blink*, to be up the spout* *(Brit)* • **tu dérailles !** *(= tu es fou)* you're nuts!*, you're off your rocker!*; *(= tu te trompes)* you're talking nonsense! • **son père déraille complètement** *(= être gâteux)* his father is completely gaga* ou has lost his marbles*

dérailleur /deʀɑjœʀ/ **NM** *[de bicyclette]* derailleur; *(Rail)* derailer, derailing stop

déraison /deʀɛzɔ̃/ **NF** *(littér)* insanity

déraisonnable /deʀɛzɔnabl/ **ADJ** unreasonable

déraisonnablement /deʀɛzɔnabləmɑ̃/ **ADV** unreasonably

déraisonner /deʀɛzɔne/ ▸ conjug 1 ◂ **VI** *(littér)* *(= dire des bêtises)* to talk nonsense; *(= être fou)* to rave

dérangé, e /deʀɑ̃ʒe/ (ptp de **déranger**) **ADJ** ① *(* = fou)* crazy • **il est complètement** ~ ! he's a real head case!*, he's nuts!* • **il a le cerveau** ou **l'esprit** ~ he's deranged ou unhinged ② *(= malade)* **il a l'estomac** ~ he has an upset stomach ou a stomach upset • **il est (un peu)** ~ *(= malade)* he has (a bit of) diarrhoea, his bowels are (a bit) loose ③ *[coiffure]* dishevelled, untidy • **mes papiers étaient tout** ~**s** my papers were all in a mess **NM,F** * nutcase*

dérangeant, e /deʀɑ̃ʒɑ̃, ɑt/ **ADJ** disturbing

dérangement /deʀɑ̃ʒmɑ̃/ GRAMMAIRE ACTIVE 54.7 **NM** ① *(= gêne)* trouble • **(toutes) mes excuses pour le** ~ my apologies for the trouble I'm causing ou for the inconvenience ② *(= déplacement)* **pour vous éviter un autre** ~ to save you another trip • **voilà 10 € pour votre** ~ here's €10 for coming ou for taking the trouble to come ③ *(= bouleversement)* *[d'affaires, papiers]* disorder (de in); • **en** ~ *[machine, téléphone]* out of order

déranger /deʀɑ̃ʒe/ GRAMMAIRE ACTIVE 36.1 ▸ conjug 3 ◂

VT ① *(= gêner, importuner)* to trouble, to bother; *(= surprendre)* *[+ animal, cambrioleur]* to disturb • **je ne vous dérange pas ?** am I disturbing you?, I hope I'm not disturbing you? • **les cambrioleurs ont été dérangés** the burglars were disturbed • **elle viendra vous voir demain, si cela ne vous dérange pas** she'll come and see you tomorrow, if that's all right by you* ou if that's no trouble to you • **elle ne veut pas** ~ **le médecin inutilement** she doesn't want to bother the doctor unnecessarily • **ne me dérangez pas toutes les cinq minutes** don't come bothering me every five minutes • ~ **qn dans son sommeil** to disturb sb's sleep • **on le dérange toutes les nuits en ce moment** he is disturbed every night at the moment • **ça vous dérange si je fume ?** do you mind ou will it bother you if I smoke? • **cela vous dérangerait-il de venir ?** would you mind coming? • **alors, ça te dérange ?*** what does it matter to you?, what's it to you?* • **"ne pas déranger"** "do not disturb" • **ses films dérangent** his films are disturbing

② *(= déplacer)* *[+ papiers]* to disturb, to mix ou muddle up; *[+ coiffure]* to ruffle, to mess up; *[+ vêtements]* to rumple, to disarrange

③ *(= dérégler)* *[+ projets, routine]* to disrupt, to upset; *[+ machine]* to put out of order • **les essais atomiques ont dérangé le temps** the nuclear tests have unsettled ou upset the weather • **ça lui a dérangé l'esprit** this has unsettled his mind

VPR se déranger ① *[médecin, réparateur]* to come out

② *(pour une démarche, une visite)* to go along, to come along • **sans vous** ~, **sur simple appel téléphonique, nous vous renseignons** without leaving your home, you can obtain information simply by telephoning us • **je me suis dérangé pour rien, c'était fermé** it was a waste of time going ou it was a wasted trip ou journey *(Brit)* – it was closed

③ *(= changer de place)* to move • **il s'est dérangé pour me laisser passer** he moved ou stepped aside to let me pass

④ *(= se gêner)* **surtout, ne vous dérangez pas pour moi** please don't put yourself out ou go to any inconvenience on my account

dérapage /deʀapaʒ/ **NM** ① *[de véhicule]* skid; *[de skis]* sideslipping; *[d'avion]* sideslip • **faire un** ~ to skid • **faire un** ~ **contrôlé** to do a controlled skid • **descendre une piste en** ~ *(Ski)* to sideslip down a slope ② *(fig)* *[de prix]* unexpected increase; *(= maladresse)* blunder, faux pas • ~**s budgétaires** overspending • **le** ~ **des dépenses publiques** government overspending • ~ **verbal** slip, verbal faux pas • **pour éviter tout** ~ **inflationniste** to prevent inflation from getting out of control

déraper /deʀape/ ▸ conjug 1 ◂ **VI** ① *[véhicule]* to skid; *[piéton, semelles, échelle]* to slip; *(Ski)* to sideslip • **ça dérape** *[chaussée]* it's slippery ② *[ancre]* to drag; *[bateau]* to trip her anchor ③ *(fig)* *[prix, salaires]* to get out of hand, to soar; *[conversation]* to veer onto slippery ground; *[personne]* to make a faux pas

dératé, e /deʀate/ **NM,F** → **courir**

dératisation /deʀatizasjɔ̃/ **NF** rat extermination

dératiser /deʀatize/ ▸ conjug 1 ◂ **VT** • ~ **un lieu** to exterminate the rats in a place, to rid a place of rats

derby /dɛʀbi/ **NM** *(Ftbl, Rugby)* derby; *(Équitation)* Derby; *(= chaussure) kind of lace-up shoe,* blucher *(US)*

derche** /dɛʀʃ/ **NM** arse** *(Brit)*, ass** *(US)* • **c'est un faux** ~ he's a two-faced bastard**

déréalisation /deʀealizasjɔ̃/ **NF** *(Psych)* derealization

déréaliser /deʀealize/ ▸ conjug 1 ◂ **VT** to derealize

derechef /dəʀəʃɛf/ **ADV** *(†† ou littér)* once more, once again

déréférencement /deʀefeʀɑ̃smɑ̃/ **NM** *[de produit]* withdrawal from sale

déréférencer /deʀefeʀɑ̃se/ ▸ conjug 3 ◂ **VT** *[+ produit]* to withdraw from sale

déréglé, e /deʀegle/ (ptp de **dérégler**) **ADJ** ① *(= détraqué)* *[mécanisme]* out of order *(attrib)*; *[esprit]* unsettled; *[habitudes, temps]* upset, unsettled; *[estomac, appétit, pouls]* upset • **les élucubrations de son imagination** ~**e** the ravings of his wild ou disordered imagination ② *(= corrompu)* *[vie, mœurs]* dissolute

dérèglement /deʀɛgləmɑ̃/ **NM** *[de machine, mécanisme]* disturbance; *[de pouls, estomac, temps]* upset; *[d'esprit]* unsettling *(NonC)*; *[de mœurs]* dissoluteness *(NonC)* • ~**s** *(littér)* *(= dépravations)* dissoluteness • ~ **hormonal** hormone imbalance

déréglementation /deʀɛgləmɑ̃tasjɔ̃/ **NF** deregulation

déréglementer /deʀɛgləmɑ̃te/ ▸ conjug 1 ◂ **VT** to deregulate

dérégler /deʀegle/ ▸ conjug 6 ◂ **VT** ① *(= détraquer)* *[+ mécanisme, machine]* to affect the workings of; *[+ esprit]* to unsettle; *[+ habitudes, temps]* to upset, to unsettle; *[+ estomac, appétit, pouls]* to upset; *[+ métabolisme]* to disrupt, to upset ② *(= corrompre)* *[+ vie, mœurs]* to make dissolute

VPR se dérégler ① *[mécanisme, machine, appareil]* to go wrong; *[pouls, estomac, temps]* to be upset; *[esprit]* to become unsettled • **cette montre se dérègle tout le temps** this watch keeps going wrong ② *(= se corrompre)* *[mœurs]* to become dissolute

dérégulation /deʀegylasjɔ̃/ **NF** *[de marché, secteur]* deregulation • ~ **économique/sociale** economic/social deregulation

déréguler /deʀegyle/ ▸ conjug 1 ◂ **VT** *[+ marché, secteur]* to deregulate

déréliction /deʀeliksjɔ̃/ NF *(Rel, littér)* dereliction

déremboursement /deʀɑ̃buʀs(ə)mɑ̃/ NM *(Admin)* ◆ **le ~ des médicaments** *cutting back on the reimbursement of medicines by the French Social Security system* ◆ **le gouvernement a annoncé des mesures de ~** the government have announced measures to cut back on the reimbursement of medicines

dérembourser /deʀɑ̃buʀse/ ► conjug 1 ◄ VT *[+ médicament]* to no longer reimburse the cost of

déresponsabiliser /deʀɛspɔ̃sabilize/ ► conjug 1 ◄ VT ◆ **~ qn** to take away sb's sense of responsibility ◆ **il est essentiel de ne pas les ~** it's essential not to take away their sense of responsibility ◆ **l'interventionnisme systématique et déresponsabilisant des pouvoirs publics** the authorities' constant interference, which destroys a sense of individual responsibility ◆ **les employés déresponsabilisés deviennent moins productifs** employees become less productive when they have less of a feeling of responsibility

dérider /deʀide/ ► conjug 1 ◄ VT *[+ personne]* to brighten up; *[+ front]* to uncrease VPR **se dérider** *[personne]* to cheer up; *[front]* to uncrease

dérision /deʀizjɔ̃/ NF derision, mockery ◆ **par ~** derisively, mockingly ◆ **de ~** *[parole, sourire]* of derision, derisive ◆ **esprit de ~** sense of mockery *ou* ridicule ◆ **tourner en ~** *(= ridiculiser)* to ridicule; *(= minimiser)* to make a mockery of

dérisoire /deʀizwaʀ/ ADJ *(gén)* derisory, pathetic, laughable ◆ **pour une somme ~** for a derisory sum

dérisoirement /deʀizwaʀmɑ̃/ ADV pathetically

dérivant /deʀivɑ̃/ ADJ M ◆ **filet ~** drift net

dérivatif, -ive /deʀivatif, iv/ ADJ derivative NM distraction ◆ **dans son travail il cherche un ~ à sa douleur** he throws himself into his work to try and take his mind off his grief

dérivation /deʀivasjɔ̃/ NF 1 *[de rivière]* diversion; *[de circulation routière]* diversion (Brit), detour (US); → **canal** 2 *(Ling, Math)* derivation ◆ **~ régressive** back formation 3 *(Élec)* shunt 4 *[d'avion, bateau]* drift, deviation

dérive /deʀiv/ NF 1 *(= déviation)* drift, leeway; *(= errance)* drift ◆ **~ sur bâbord** drift to port ◆ **navire en ~** ship adrift ◆ **~ des continents** continental drift ◆ **~ nord-atlantique** North Atlantic Drift

♦ **à la dérive** adrift ◆ **être à la ~** *[personne]* to be adrift, to be drifting ◆ **être à la ~** *[personne]* to be adrift, to be drifting ◆ **tout va à la ~** everything is going to the dogs *ou* is going downhill ◆ **partir à la ~** to go drifting off 2 *(= dispositif)* *[d'avion]* fin, vertical stabilizer (US); *[de bateau]* centre-board (Brit), center-board (US) 3 *(= abus)* excess, abuse; *(= évolution)* drift ◆ **~ droitière/totalitaire** drift towards the right/towards totalitarianism

dérivé, e /deʀive/ (ptp de **dériver**) ADJ *(gén, Chim, Math)* derived NM *(Chim, Ling, Math)* derivative; *(= produit)* by-product NF **dérivée** *(Math)* derivative

dériver /deʀive/ ► conjug 1 ◄ VT 1 *[+ rivière, circulation]* to divert 2 *(Chim, Ling, Math)* to derive 3 *(Élec)* to shunt 4 *(Tech = dériveter)* to unrivet VT INDIR **dériver de** to derive *ou* stem from; *(Ling)* to derive from, to be derived from, to be a derivative of VI *[avion, bateau]* to drift; *[orateur]* to wander *ou* drift (away) from the subject; *[marginal]* to be adrift, to be drifting ◆ **la conversation a dérivé sur ...** the conversation drifted onto ...

dériveur /deʀivœʀ/ NM *(= voile)* storm sail; *(= bateau)* sailing dinghy *(with centre-board)*

dermabrasion /dɛʀmabʀazjɔ̃/ NF dermabrasion

dermatite /dɛʀmatit/ NF dermatitis

dermato * /dɛʀmato/ NF abrév de **dermatologie** NMF abrév de **dermatologiste** *ou* **dermatologue**

dermatologie /dɛʀmatɔlɔʒi/ NF dermatology

dermatologique /dɛʀmatɔlɔʒik/ ADJ dermatological

dermatologue /dɛʀmatɔlɔg/, **dermatologiste** /dɛʀmatɔlɔʒist/ NMF dermatologist, skin specialist

dermatose /dɛʀmatoz/ NF dermatosis

derme /dɛʀm/ NM dermis

dermique /dɛʀmik/ ADJ dermic, dermal

dermite /dɛʀmit/ NF dermatitis

dernier, -ière /dɛʀnje, jɛʀ/ ADJ 1 *(dans le temps)* last ◆ **arriver ~** to come in last ◆ **arriver bon ~** to come in a long way behind the others ◆ **durant les ~s jours du mois** in the last few days of the month ◆ **l'artiste, dans ses dernières œuvres ...** the artist, in his final *ou* last works ... ◆ **les dernières années de sa vie** the last few years of his life ◆ **après un ~ regard/effort** after one last *ou* final look/effort ◆ **on prend un ~ verre ?** one last drink?, one for the road?

2 *(dans l'espace)* *[étage]* top *(épith)*; *[rang]* back *(épith)*; *[branche]* upper *(épith)*, highest ◆ **la dernière marche de l'escalier** *(en bas)* the bottom step; *(en haut)* the top step ◆ **le ~ mouchoir de la pile** *(dessus)* the top handkerchief in the pile; *(dessous)* the bottom handkerchief in the pile ◆ **en dernière page** *(Presse)* on the back page ◆ **les 100 dernières pages** the last 100 pages; → **jugement, premier**

3 *(dans une hiérarchie, un ordre)* *[élève]* bottom, last ◆ **être reçu ~** to come last *ou* bottom *(à* in); ◆ **il est toujours ~ (en classe)** he's always bottom (of the class), he's always last (in the class) ◆ **c'est bien la dernière personne à qui je demanderais !** he's the last person I'd ask!

4 *(= le plus récent)* *(gén avant n)* last, latest ◆ **son ~ roman** his latest *ou* last novel ◆ **ces ~s mois/jours** (during) the last *ou* past couple of *ou* few months/days ◆ **ces ~s incidents/événements** these latest *ou* most recent incidents/events; → **temps¹**

5 *(= précédent)* last, previous ◆ **les ~s propriétaires sont partis à l'étranger** the last *ou* previous owners went abroad ◆ **le ~ détenteur du record était américain** the last *ou* previous record holder was American ◆ **l'an/le mois ~** last year/month ◆ **samedi ~** last Saturday

6 *(= extrême)* **il a protesté avec la dernière énergie** he protested most vigorously *ou* with the utmost vigour ◆ **examiner qch dans les ~s détails** to study sth in the most minute *ou* in the minutest detail ◆ **c'est du ~ ridicule** it's utterly ridiculous, it's ridiculous in the extreme ◆ **c'est du ~ chic** it's the last word in elegance ◆ **c'est de la dernière importance** it is of the utmost importance ◆ **il est du ~ bien avec le patron** he's on the best of terms with his boss

7 *(= pire)* *[qualité]* lowest, poorest ◆ **c'était la dernière chose à faire !** that was the last thing to do!

8 *(= meilleur)* *[échelon, grade]* top, highest

9 *(évoquant la mort)* last ◆ **ses ~s moments** *ou* **instants** his last *ou* dying moments ◆ **jusqu'à mon ~ jour** until the day I die, until my dying day ◆ **je croyais que ma dernière heure était venue** I thought my last *ou* final hour had come ◆ **à sa dernière heure** on his deathbed ◆ **dans les ~s temps il ne s'alimentait plus** towards the end he stopped eating ◆ **rendre les ~s devoirs** *(littér, frm)* to pay one's last respects *(à* to); ◆ **accompagner qn à sa dernière demeure** to accompany sb to his final resting place ◆ **les dernières dispositions du défunt** the deceased's last will and testament; → **soupir**

NM,F 1 *(dans le temps)* last (one) ◆ **parler/sortir le ~** to speak/leave last ◆ **les ~s arrivés n'auront rien** the last ones to arrive *ou* the last arrivals will get nothing ◆ **~ entré, premier sorti** last in, first out ◆ **tu seras servi le ~** you'll be served last, you'll be the last to get served ◆ **elle a tendance à gâter son (petit) ~** she's inclined to spoil her youngest (child)

2 *(dans une hiérarchie, un ordre)* **il est le ~ de sa classe/de la liste** he's (at the) bottom of the class/list ◆ **il a été reçu dans les ~s** he was nearly bottom among those who passed the exam ◆ **ils ont été tués jusqu'au ~** they were all killed (right down) to the last man, every single one of them was killed ◆ **c'est la dernière à qui vous puissiez demander un service** she's the last person you can ask a favour of ◆ **il est le ~ à pouvoir** *ou* **qui puisse faire cela** he's the last person to be able to do that

♦ **ce dernier, cette dernière** the latter ◆ **enseignants et chercheurs étaient présents ; ces ~s ...** there were teachers and researchers there; the latter ... ◆ **Luc, Marc et Jean étaient là et ce ~ a dit que ...** Luc, Marc and Jean were there, and Jean said that ... ◆ **Paul, Pierre et Maud sont venus ; cette dernière ...** Paul, Pierre and Maud came; she ...; → **souci²**

3 *(péj : intensif)* **le ~ des imbéciles** an absolute imbecile, a complete and utter fool ◆ **le ~ des filous** an out-and-out scoundrel ◆ **c'est le ~ des ~s !** he's the lowest of the low!

NM *(= étage)* top floor *ou* storey (Brit) *ou* story (US)

♦ **en dernier** last ◆ **j'ai été servi en ~** I was served last, I was the last to be served

NF **dernière** 1 *(Théât)* last performance

2 *(* = nouvelle)* **vous connaissez la dernière ?** have you heard the latest?

dernièrement /dɛʀnjɛʀmɑ̃/ ADV *(= il y a peu de temps)* recently; *(= ces derniers temps)* lately, recently, of late

dernier-né, dernière-née (mpl **derniers-nés**) /dɛʀnjene, dɛʀnjɛʀne/ NM,F *(= enfant)* last-born, youngest child; *(= œuvre)* latest *ou* most recent creation ◆ **le ~ de leurs logiciels** the latest in their line of software

dérobade /deʀɔbad/ NF evasion; *(Équitation)* refusal ◆ **~ fiscale** tax evasion

dérobé, e /deʀɔbe/ (ptp de **dérober**) ADJ *[escalier, porte]* secret, hidden LOC ADV **à la dérobée** secretly, surreptitiously ◆ **regarder qn à la ~e** to give sb a surreptitious *ou* stealthy glance

dérober /deʀɔbe/ ► conjug 1 ◄ VT 1 *(= voler)* to steal ◆ **~ qch à qn** to steal sth from sb ◆ **~ un baiser (à qn)** to steal a kiss (from sb)

2 *(= cacher)* **~ qch à qn** to hide *ou* conceal sth from sb ◆ **une haie dérobait la palissade aux regards** a hedge hid *ou* screened the fence from sight, a hedge concealed the fence ◆ **~ qn à la justice/au danger/à la mort** to shield sb from justice/danger/death

3 *(littér = détourner)* *[+ regard, front]* to turn away

VPR **se dérober** 1 *(= refuser d'assumer)* to shy away ◆ **se ~ à son devoir/à ses obligations** to shy away from *ou* shirk one's duty/obligations ◆ **se ~ à une discussion** to shy away from a discussion ◆ **je lui ai posé la question mais il s'est dérobé** I put the question to him but he evaded *ou* side-stepped it

2 *(= se cacher de)* to hide, to conceal o.s. ◆ **se ~ aux regards** to hide from view ◆ **se ~ à la justice** to hide from justice ◆ **pour se ~ à la curiosité dont il était l'objet** in order to escape the curiosity surrounding him

[3] *(= se libérer)* to slip away ◆ **se ~ à l'étreinte de qn** to slip out of sb's arms ◆ **il voulut la prendre dans ses bras mais elle se déroba** he tried to take her in his arms but she shrank *ou* slipped away

[4] *(= s'effondrer) [sol]* to give way ◆ **ses genoux se dérobèrent (sous lui)** his knees gave way (beneath him)

[5] *(Équitation)* to refuse

dérocher /deʀɔʃe/ ▸ conjug 1 ◂ **VI se dérocher** **VPR** *[alpiniste]* to fall off (a rock face) **VT** *[+ métal]* to pickle; *[+ terrain]* to clear of rocks

dérogation /deʀɔgasjɔ̃/ **NF** (special) dispensation ◆ **ceci constitue une ~ par rapport à la loi** this constitutes a departure from the law ◆ **aucune ~ ne sera permise** no exemption will be granted, no special dispensation will be allowed ◆ **il a obtenu ceci par ~** he obtained this by special dispensation

dérogatoire /deʀɔgatwaʀ/ **ADJ** dispensatory, exceptional ◆ **appliquer un régime ~ à** to apply exceptional arrangements to *ou* in respect of ◆ **à titre ~** by special dispensation

déroger /deʀɔʒe/ ▸ conjug 3 ◂ **VI** [1] ~ **à qch** *(= enfreindre)* to go against sth, to depart from sth ◆ **~ aux règles** to depart from the rules ◆ **ce serait ~ à la règle établie** that would go against the established order *ou* procedure [2] *(= déchoir) (gén)* to lower o.s., to demean o.s.; *(Hist)* to lose rank and title

dérouillée⁑ /deʀuje/ **NF** thrashing, belting* ◆ **recevoir une ~** *(coups)* to get a thrashing *ou* belting*; *(défaite)* to get a thrashing* *ou* hammering*

dérouiller /deʀuje/ ▸ conjug 1 ◂ **VT** [1] *[+ métal]* to remove the rust from; *[+ mémoire]* to refresh ◆ **je vais me ~ les jambes** I'm going to stretch my legs [2] (⁑ *= battre)* to give a thrashing *ou* belting* to, to thrash **VI** (⁑ *= souffrir)* to have a hard time of it, to go through it* *(surtout Brit)*; *(= se faire battre)* to catch it*, to cop it⁑ *(Brit)* ◆ **j'ai une rage de dents, qu'est-ce que je dérouille !** I've got toothache, it's agony! * *ou* it's driving me mad! *ou* it's killing me! *

déroulant /deʀulɑ̃/ **ADJ M** ◆ **menu ~** pull-down menu

déroulement /deʀulmɑ̃/ **NM** [1] *(= fait de se passer)* ◆ **de carrière** career development ◆ **rappelez-moi le ~ des événements** go over the sequence of events for me again ◆ **pendant le ~ des opérations** during the course of (the) operations, while the operations were in progress ◆ **pendant le ~ du film** while the film was on, during the film ◆ **rien n'est venu troubler le ~ de la manifestation** the demonstration went off *ou* passed off without incident, nothing happened to disturb the course of the demonstration ◆ **veiller au bon ~ des élections** to make sure the elections go smoothly [2] *[de fil, bobine, film, bande magnétique]* unwinding; *[de cordage]* uncoiling; *[de carte]* unrolling

dérouler /deʀule/ ▸ conjug 1 ◂ **VT** [1] *[+ fil, bobine, pellicule, ruban]* to unwind; *[+ cordage]* to uncoil; *[+ carte, parchemin]* to unroll; *[+ tapis]* to roll out; *[+ store]* to roll down ◆ **~ le tapis rouge à qn** to roll out the red carpet for sb ◆ **la rivière déroule ses méandres** the river snakes *ou* winds along its tortuous course

[2] *(Tech) [+ tronc d'arbre]* to peel a veneer from

[3] *(= passer en revue)* **il déroula dans son esprit les événements de la veille** in his mind he went over *ou* through the events of the previous day

VPR se dérouler [1] *(= avoir lieu) (comme prévu)* to take place; *(accidentellement)* to happen, to occur ◆ **la ville où la cérémonie s'est déroulée** the town where the ceremony took place

[2] *(= progresser) [histoire]* to unfold, to develop ◆ **à mesure que l'histoire se déroulait** as the story unfolded *ou* developed

[3] *(= se passer)* to go (off) ◆ **la manifestation s'est déroulée dans le calme** the demonstration went off peacefully ◆ **comment s'est déroulé le match ?** how did the match go? ◆ **ça s'est bien déroulé** it went well ◆ **son existence se déroulait, calme et morne** his life went on *ou* pursued its course, dreary and uneventful ◆ **c'est là que toute ma vie s'est déroulée** that was where I spent my whole life

[4] *[fil, bobine, pellicule, ruban]* to unwind, to come unwound; *[bande magnétique]* to unwind; *[cordage]* to unreel, to uncoil; *[carte, drapeau, parchemin]* to unroll, to come unrolled; *[tapis]* to unroll; *[store]* to roll down ◆ **le paysage se déroulait devant nos yeux** the landscape unfolded before our eyes

dérouleur /deʀulœʀ/ **NM** *[de papier]* holder *[de papier absorbant]* dispenser

dérouleuse /deʀuløz/ **NF** *[pour bois]* unwinding machine; *(pour câbles)* cable drum

déroutant, e /deʀutɑ̃, ɑt/ **ADJ** disconcerting

déroute /deʀut/ **NF** *[d'armée, équipe]* rout; *[de régime, entreprise]* collapse ◆ **armée en ~** routed army ◆ **mettre en ~** *[+ armée]* to rout, to put to rout *ou* flight; *[+ adversaire]* to rout

déroutement /deʀutmɑ̃/ **NM** *[d'avion, bateau]* rerouting, diversion

dérouter /deʀute/ ▸ conjug 1 ◂ **VT** *[+ avion, navire]* to reroute, to divert; *[+ candidat, orateur]* to disconcert, to throw*; *[+ poursuivants, police]* to throw *ou* put off the scent

derrick /deʀik/ **NM** derrick

derrière /dɛʀjɛʀ/ **PRÉP** [1] *(= à l'arrière de, à la suite de)* behind ◆ **il se cache ~ le fauteuil** he's hiding behind the armchair ◆ **il avait les mains ~ le dos** he had his hands behind his back ◆ **sors de ~ le lit** come out from behind the bed ◆ **passe (par) ~ la maison** go round the back of *ou* round behind the house ◆ **marcher l'un ~ l'autre** to walk one behind the other ◆ **il a laissé les autres loin ~ lui** *(lit, fig)* he left the others far *ou* a long way behind (him) ◆ **disparaître ~ une colline** to disappear behind a hill

[2] *(fig)* behind ◆ **il faut chercher ~ les apparences** you must look beneath (outward) appearances ◆ **~ sa générosité se cache l'intérêt le plus sordide** behind his generosity lurks *ou* his generosity hides the most sordid self-interest ◆ **faire qch ~ (le dos de) qn** to do sth behind sb's back ◆ **dire du mal ~ (le dos de) qn** to say (unkind) things behind sb's back ◆ **il a laissé trois enfants ~ lui** he left three children ◆ **le président avait tout le pays ~ lui** the president had the whole country behind him *ou* had the backing of the whole country ◆ **ayez confiance, je suis ~ vous** take heart, I'll support you *ou* back you up *ou* I'm on your side ◆ **il laisse tout le monde ~ (lui) pour le talent/le courage** his talent/courage puts everyone else in the shade ◆ **il laisse tout le monde ~ en chimie** he's head and shoulders above *ou* miles ahead of the others in chemistry ◆ **il faut toujours être ~ lui** *ou* **son dos** you've always got to keep an eye on him ◆ **un vin de ~ les fagots*** an extra-special (little) wine ◆ **une bouteille de ~ les fagots*** a bottle of the best; → **idée**

[3] *(Naut) (dans le bateau)* aft, abaft; *(sur la mer)* astern of

ADV [1] *(= en arrière)* behind ◆ **vous êtes juste ~** you're just *ou* right behind (it *ou* us *etc*) ◆ **on l'a laissé (loin) ~** we (have) left him (far *ou* a long way) behind ◆ **il est assis trois rangs ~** he's sitting three rows back *ou* three rows behind (us *ou* them *etc*) ◆ **il a pris des places ~** he has got seats at the back ◆ **il a préféré monter ~** *(en voiture)* he preferred to sit in the back ◆ **chemisier qui se boutonne ~** blouse which buttons up *ou* does up at the back ◆ **passe le plateau ~** pass the tray back ◆ **regarde ~, on nous suit** look behind (you) *ou* look back - we're being followed ◆ **il est ~** he's behind (us *ou* them *etc*) ◆ **regarde ~** *(au fond de la voiture)* look in the back; *(derrière un objet)* look behind (it) ◆ **arrêtez de pousser, ~ !** stop pushing back there! ◆ **tu peux être sûr qu'il y a quelqu'un ~** *(fig)* you can be sure that there's somebody behind it (all)

[2] *(Naut) (dans le bateau)* aft, abaft; *(sur la mer)* astern

LOC ADV par-derrière ◆ **c'est fermé, entre** *ou* **passe par-~** it's locked, go in by the back *ou* go in the back way ◆ **attaquer par-~** *[+ ennemi]* to attack from behind *ou* from the rear; *[+ adversaire]* to attack from behind ◆ **dire du mal de qn par-~** to say (unkind) things behind sb's back ◆ **il fait tout par-~** he does everything behind people's backs *ou* in an underhand way

NM [1] *[de personne]* bottom, behind*; *[d'animal]* hindquarters, rump ◆ **donner un coup de pied au ~** *ou* **dans le ~ de qn** to give sb a kick in the behind* *ou* up the backside* *ou* in the pants* ◆ **quand j'ai eu 20 ans mon père m'a chassé à coups de pied dans le ~** when I was 20 my father sent me packing *ou* kicked me out*; → **botter**

[2] *[d'objet]* back; *[de maison]* back, rear ◆ **le ~ de la tête** the back of the head ◆ **habiter sur le ~** to live at the back (of the house) ◆ **roue de ~** back *ou* rear wheel ◆ **porte de ~** *[de maison]* back door; *[de véhicule]* back *ou* rear door; → **patte¹**

NMPL derrières † *[d'édifice]* back, rear; *[d'armée]* rear

derviche /dɛʀviʃ/ **NM** dervish ◆ **~ tourneur** whirling dervish

des /de/ → **de¹, de²**

dès /dɛ/ **PRÉP** [1] *(dans le temps)* from ◆ **dimanche il a commencé à pleuvoir ~ le matin** on Sunday it rained from the morning onwards *ou* it started raining in the morning ◆ **~ le 15 août nous ne travaillerons plus qu'à mi-temps** (as) from 15 August we will only be working part-time ◆ **~ le début** from the (very) start *ou* beginning, right from the start *ou* beginning ◆ **~ son retour il fera le nécessaire** as soon as he's back *ou* immediately upon his return he'll do what's necessary ◆ **~ son retour il commença à se plaindre** as soon as he was back *ou* from the moment he was back he started complaining ◆ **il se précipita vers la sortie ~ la fin du spectacle** as soon as *ou* immediately the performance was over he rushed towards the exit ◆ **~ l'époque romaine on connaissait le chauffage central** as early as *ou* as far back as Roman times people used central heating ◆ **~ son enfance il a collectionné les papillons** he has collected butterflies from (his) childhood *ou* ever since he was a child ◆ **on peut dire ~ maintenant** *ou* **à présent** it can be said here and now ◆ **~ l'abord/ce moment** from the very beginning *ou* the outset/that moment

[2] *(dans l'espace)* **~ Lyon il se mit à pleuvoir** we ran into rain *ou* it started to rain as *ou* when we got to Lyons ◆ **~ Lyon il a plu sans arrêt** it never stopped raining from Lyons onwards *ou* after Lyons ◆ **~ l'entrée vous êtes accueillis par des slogans publicitaires** advertising slogans hit you as soon as *ou* immediately you walk in the door ◆ **~ le seuil je sentis qu'il se passait quelque chose** as I walked in at the door I sensed that something was going on

[3] *(dans une gradation)* **~ sa première année il brilla en anglais** he was good at English right from the first year ◆ **~ le premier verre il roula sous la table** after the (very) first glass he collapsed under the table ◆ **~ la troisième**

chanson elle se mit à pleurer at the third song she started to cry

♦ **dès que** as soon as, immediately ◆ **~ qu'il aura fini il viendra** as soon as *ou* immediately he's finished he'll come

♦ **dès lors** *(= depuis lors)* from that moment *ou* time on, from then on; *(= conséquemment)* that being the case, consequently ◆ **~ lors il ne fuma plus** from that time on he never smoked again ◆ **~ lors il décida de ne plus fumer** at that moment he decided he wouldn't smoke any more ◆ **vous ne pouvez rien prouver contre lui, ~ lors vous devez le relâcher** you can prove nothing against him and that being the case *ou* and so you'll have to release him

♦ **dès lors que** *(temporel)* as soon as; *(= si)* if; *(= puisque)* since, as ◆ **~ lors que vous décidez de partir, nous ne pouvons plus rien pour vous** if you choose to go, we can do nothing more for you ◆ **~ lors qu'il a choisi de démissionner, il n'a plus droit à rien** since *ou* as he has decided to hand in his notice he is no longer entitled to anything ◆ **peu m'importe, ~ lors qu'ils sont heureux** I don't mind so long as they are happy

désabonnement /dezabɔnmɑ̃/ NM non-renewal *ou* cancellation of one's subscription

désabonner /dezabɔne/ ▸ conjug 1 ◂ VT ◆ **~ qn d'un journal** to cancel sb's subscription to a newspaper VPR **se désabonner** to cancel one's subscription, not to renew one's subscription

désabusé, e /dezabyze/ (ptp de **désabuser**) ADJ *[personne, air]* disenchanted, disillusioned; *(† = détrompé)* disabused, undeceived *(frm)* ◆ **geste ~** gesture of disillusion ◆ **"non" dit-il d'un ton ~** "no" he said in a disillusioned voice

désabusement /dezabyzmɑ̃/ NM disillusionment

désabuser /dezabyze/ ▸ conjug 1 ◂ VT to disabuse *(de* of) to undeceive *(frm) (de* of)

désacclimater /dezaklimate/ ▸ conjug 1 ◂ VT to disacclimatize

désaccord /dezakɔʀ/ NM 1 *(= mésentente)* discord ◆ **être en ~ avec sa famille/son temps** to be at odds *ou* at variance with one's family/time

2 *(= divergence) (entre personnes, points de vue)* disagreement; *(entre idées, intérêts)* conflict, clash ◆ **le ~ qui subsiste entre leurs intérêts** their unresolved conflict *ou* clash of interests ◆ **leurs intérêts sont en ~ avec les nôtres** their interests conflict *ou* clash with ours

3 *(= contradiction)* discrepancy ◆ **~ entre la théorie et la réalité** discrepancy between theory and reality ◆ **les deux versions de l'accident sont en ~ sur bien des points** the two versions of the accident conflict *ou* diverge on many points ◆ **ce qu'il dit est en ~ avec ce qu'il fait** he says one thing and does another, there is a discrepancy between what he says and what he does

désaccordé, e /dezakɔʀde/ (ptp de **désaccorder**) ADJ *[piano]* out of tune

désaccorder /dezakɔʀde/ ▸ conjug 1 ◂ VT *[+ piano]* to put out of tune VPR **se désaccorder** to go out of tune

désaccoupler /dezakuple/ ▸ conjug 1 ◂ VT *[+ wagons, chiens]* to uncouple; *(Élec)* to disconnect

désaccoutumance /dezakutymɑ̃s/ NF ◆ **~ de qch** losing the habit of (doing) sth ◆ **méthode utilisée dans les cures de ~ du tabac** method used in breaking nicotine dependency *ou* to wean smokers off nicotine

désaccoutumer /dezakutyme/ ▸ conjug 1 ◂ VT ◆ **~ qn de qch/de faire** to get sb out of the habit of sth/of doing VPR **se désaccoutumer** ◆ **se ~ de qch/de faire** to lose the habit of sth/of doing

désacralisation /desakʀalizasjɔ̃/ NF ◆ **la ~ de la fonction présidentielle** the removal of the mystique surrounding the presidency

désacraliser /desakʀalize/ ▸ conjug 1 ◂ VT *[+ institution, profession]* to take away the sacred aura of ◆ **la médecine se trouve désacralisée** medicine has lost its mystique ◆ **il désacralise tout** he debunks everything, nothing escapes his cynicism

désactiver /dezaktive/ ▸ conjug 1 ◂ VT *(= neutraliser) [+ engin explosif]* to deactivate; *[+ réseau d'espionnage]* to break up; *(Chim)* to deactivate; *(Phys Nucl)* to decontaminate; *(Ordin)* to disable

désadapté, e /dezadapte/ ▸ conjug 1 ◂ ADJ ◆ **personne ~e** misfit ◆ **le système judiciaire est ~ par rapport à son époque** the legal system has not moved with the times

désaffectation /dezafɛktasjɔ̃/ NF *[de lieu]* closing down; *[de somme d'argent]* withdrawal

désaffecté, e /dezafɛkte/ (ptp de **désaffecter**) ADJ *[usine, gare]* disused; *[église]* deconsecrated

désaffecter /dezafɛkte/ ▸ conjug 1 ◂ VT *[+ lieu]* to close down; *[+ somme d'argent]* to withdraw ◆ **l'école a été désaffectée pour en faire une prison** the school was closed down and converted into a prison

désaffection /dezafɛksjɔ̃/ NF *(gén)* loss of interest *(pour* in); *(Pol)* disaffection *(pour* with)

désaffectionner (se) † /dezafɛksjɔne/ ▸ conjug 1 ◂ VPR ◆ **se ~ de** to lose one's affection *ou* fondness for

désagréable /dezagʀeabl/ ADJ unpleasant ◆ **ce n'est pas ~** it's quite pleasant, it's not unpleasant

désagréablement /dezagʀeabləmɑ̃/ ADV unpleasantly

désagrégation /dezagʀegasjɔ̃/ NF *[de roche]* crumbling; *[d'État]* breakup; *(Psych)* disintegration (of the personality)

désagréger /dezagʀeʒe/ ▸ conjug 3 et 6 ◂ VT *[+ roches]* to crumble ◆ **pour ~ la cellulite** to break down cellulite ◆ **ça a désagrégé leur couple** it was the end of *ou* it broke up their relationship VPR **se désagréger** 1 *[cachet, sucre]* to break up, to disintegrate; *[roche]* to crumble 2 *[amitié, État]* to break up; *[couple]* to break *ou* split up

désagrément /dezagʀemɑ̃/ NM 1 *(gén pl = inconvénient, déboire)* annoyance, inconvenience, trouble *(NonC)* ◆ **malgré tous les ~s que cela entraîne** despite all the annoyances *ou* trouble it involves ◆ **c'est un des ~s de ce genre de métier** it's one of the inconveniences of *ou* it's part of the trouble with this kind of job ◆ **cette voiture m'a valu bien des ~s** this car has given me a great deal of trouble ◆ **"la direction vous prie d'excuser les désagréments causés par les travaux"** "the management apologizes for any inconvenience caused to customers during renovations" 2 *(frm = déplaisir)* displeasure ◆ **causer du ~ à qn** to cause sb displeasure

désaimantation /dezemɑ̃tasjɔ̃/ NF demagnetization

désaimanter /dezemɑ̃te/ ▸ conjug 1 ◂ VT to demagnetize

désaisonnaliser /desɛzɔnalize/ ▸ conjug 1 ◂ VT to make seasonal adjustments to ◆ **le chiffre du chômage, en données désaisonnalisées** the seasonally adjusted unemployment figure

désalpe /dezalp/ NF *(Helv) process of bringing cattle down from the high alps for winter*

désalper /dezalpe/ ▸ conjug 1 ◂ VI *(Helv) to bring cattle down from the high mountain pastures*

désaltérant, e /dezalteʀɑ̃, ɑ̃t/ ADJ thirst-quenching

désaltérer /dezalteʀe/ ▸ conjug 6 ◂ VT to quench the thirst of ◆ **le vin ne désaltère pas** wine does not quench your thirst *ou* stop you feeling thirsty VPR **se désaltérer** to quench one's thirst

désambiguïsation /dezɑ̃biguizasjɔ̃/ NF disambiguation

désambiguïser /dezɑ̃biguize/ ▸ conjug 1 ◂ VT to disambiguate

désamiantage /dezamjɑ̃taʒ/ NM removal of asbestos ◆ **le ~ du bâtiment a pris 3 mois** it took 3 months to remove the asbestos from the building

désamianter /dezamjɑ̃te/ ▸ conjug 1 ◂ VT *[+ bâtiment]* to remove asbestos from

désamorçage /dezamɔʀsaʒ/ NM 1 *[de fusée, pistolet]* removal of the primer (*de* from); *[de bombe, situation, conflit]* defusing 2 *[de dynamo]* failure

désamorcer /dezamɔʀse/ ▸ conjug 3 ◂ VT 1 *[+ fusée, pistolet]* to remove the primer from; *[+ bombe]* to defuse 2 *[+ pompe]* to drain 3 *[+ situation explosive, crise]* to defuse; *[+ mouvement de revendication]* to forestall

désamour /dezamuʀ/ NM *(gén)* disenchantment; *(entre deux amoureux)* falling out of love ◆ **le ~ des citoyens vis-à-vis de la politique** people's disillusionment *ou* disenchantment with politics ◆ **il a quitté son amie par ~** he left his girlfriend because he no longer loved her *ou* because he had fallen out of love with her

désaper* /desape/ ▸ conjug 1 ◂ VT to undress VPR **se désaper** to get undressed

désapparié, e /dezapaʀje/ (ptp de **désapparier**) ADJ ⇒ **déparié**

désapparier /dezapaʀje/ ▸ conjug 7 ◂ VT ⇒ **déparier**

désappointé, e /dezapwɛ̃te/ (ptp de **désappointer**) ADJ disappointed

désappointement /dezapwɛ̃tmɑ̃/ NM disappointment

désappointer /dezapwɛ̃te/ ▸ conjug 1 ◂ VT to disappoint

désapprendre /dezapʀɑ̃dʀ/ ▸ conjug 58 ◂ VT *(littér)* to forget; *(volontairement)* to unlearn ◆ **~ à faire qch** to forget how to do sth ◆ **ils ont dû ~ à être exigeants** they had to learn not to be so demanding

désapprobateur, -trice /dezapʀɔbatœʀ, tʀis/ ADJ disapproving

désapprobation /dezapʀɔbasjɔ̃/ NF disapproval, disapprobation *(frm)*

désapprouver /dezapʀuve/ GRAMMAIRE ACTIVE 41 ▸ conjug 1 ◂ VT *[+ acte, conduite]* to disapprove of ◆ **je le désapprouve de les inviter** I disagree with his inviting them, I disapprove of his inviting them ◆ **elle désapprouve qu'il vienne** she disapproves of his coming ◆ **le public désapprouva** the audience showed its disapproval

désarçonner /dezaʀsɔne/ ▸ conjug 1 ◂ VT *(= faire tomber) [cheval]* to throw, to unseat; *[adversaire]* to unseat, to unhorse; *(= déconcerter) [argument]* to throw*, to baffle ◆ **son calme/sa réponse me désarçonna** I was completely thrown* *ou* nonplussed by his calmness/reply

désargenté, e /dezaʀʒɑ̃te/ (ptp de **désargenter**) ADJ 1 *(= terni)* **couverts ~s** cutlery with the silver worn off 2 *(* = sans un sou)* broke* *(attrib)*, penniless ◆ **je suis ~ en ce moment** I'm a bit short of cash *ou* a bit strapped for cash* at the moment

désargenter /dezaʀʒɑ̃te/ ▸ conjug 1 ◂ VT 1 *[+ métal]* to rub *ou* wear the silver off 2 ◆ **~ qn**

* to leave sb broke* ou penniless VPR **se désargenter** ◆ **cette fourchette se désargente** the silver is wearing off this fork

désarmant, e /dezaʀmɑ̃, ɑ̃t/ ADJ disarming

désarmé, e /dezaʀme/ (ptp de **désarmer**) ADJ 1 *[pays, personne]* unarmed 2 *(fig = démuni)* helpless *(devant* before)

désarmement /dezaʀməmɑ̃/ NM 1 *[de personne, forteresse]* disarming; *[de pays]* disarmament 2 *[de navire]* laying up

désarmer /dezaʀme/ ▸ conjug 1 ◂ VT 1 *[+ adversaire, pays]* to disarm 2 *[+ mine]* to disarm, to defuse; *[+ fusil]* to unload; *(= mettre le cran de sûreté)* to put the safety catch on 3 *(Naut)* to lay up 4 *(= émouvoir) [sourire, réponse]* to disarm VI *[pays]* to disarm; *[haine]* to yield, to abate ◆ **il ne désarme pas contre son fils** he is unrelenting in his attitude towards his son ◆ **il ne désarme pas et veut intenter un nouveau procès** he won't give in and wants a new trial

désarrimage /dezaʀimaʒ/ NM shifting (of the cargo)

désarrimer /dezaʀime/ ▸ conjug 1 ◂ VT to shift, to cause to shift

désarroi /dezaʀwa/ NM *[de personne]* (feeling of) helplessness; *[d'armée, équipe]* confusion ◆ **ceci l'avait plongé dans le ~ le plus profond** this had left him feeling totally helpless and confused ◆ **être en plein ~** *[personne] (= être troublé)* to be utterly distraught; *(= se sentir impuissant)* to feel quite helpless; *[marché, pays]* to be in total disarray ◆ **sa mort laisse le pays en plein ~** his death has left the nation numb with grief, the entire nation is deeply distressed by his death

désarticulation /dezaʀtikylasjɔ̃/ NF *[de membre]* dislocation; *(en chirurgie)* disarticulation

désarticuler /dezaʀtikyle/ ▸ conjug 1 ◂ VT *[+ membre] (= déboîter)* to dislocate; *(= amputer)* to disarticulate; *[+ mécanisme]* to upset ◆ **il s'est désarticulé l'épaule** he dislocated his shoulder VPR **se désarticuler** *[acrobate]* to contort o.s.

désassemblage /dezasɑ̃blaʒ/ NM dismantling

désassembler /dezasɑ̃ble/ ▸ conjug 1 ◂ VT to dismantle, to take apart

désassorti, e /dezasɔʀti/ (ptp de **désassortir**) ADJ *[service de table]* unmatching, unmatched; *[+ assiettes etc]* odd *(épith)*; *[magasin, marchand]* poorly stocked

désassortir /dezasɔʀtiʀ/ ▸ conjug 2 ◂ VT *[+ service de table]* to break up, to spoil

désastre /dezastʀ/ NM *(lit, fig)* disaster ◆ **courir au ~** to be heading (straight) for disaster ◆ **les ~s causés par la tempête** the damage caused by the storm

désastreusement /dezastʀøzmɑ̃/ ADV disastrously

désastreux, -euse /dezastʀø, øz/ ADJ disastrous; *[état]* appalling

désavantage /dezavɑ̃taʒ/ NM *(= inconvénient)* disadvantage, drawback; *(= handicap)* disadvantage, handicap ◆ **avoir un ~ sur qn** to be at a disadvantage compared to sb ◆ **cela présente bien des ~s** it has many disadvantages *ou* drawbacks ◆ **être/tourner au ~ de qn** to be/turn to sb's disadvantage ◆ **malgré le ~ du terrain, ils ont gagné** they won even though the ground put them at a disadvantage

désavantager /dezavɑ̃taʒe/ ▸ conjug 3 ◂ VT to disadvantage, to put at a disadvantage ◆ **cette mesure nous désavantage par rapport aux autres** this measure puts us at a disadvantage compared to the others ◆ **cela désavantage les plus pauvres** this penalizes the very poor ◆ **nous sommes désavantagés par rapport à eux dans le domaine économique** in the economic field we are handicapped *ou* at a disadvantage compared to them ◆ **se sentir désavantagé par rapport à son frère** to feel unfavourably treated by comparison with one's brother, to feel one is treated less fairly than one's brother ◆ **les couches sociales les plus désavantagées** the most under-privileged *ou* disadvantaged sectors of society

désavantageusement /dezavɑ̃taʒøzmɑ̃/ ADV unfavourably, disadvantageously

désavantageux, -euse /dezavɑ̃taʒø, øz/ ADJ unfavourable, disadvantageous

désaveu /dezavø/ NM *(= rétractation)* retraction; *(= reniement) [d'opinion, propos]* disowning, disavowal *(frm)*; *(= blâme)* repudiation, disowning; *[de signature]* disclaiming, repudiation ◆ **encourir le ~ de qn** to be disowned by sb ◆ **~ de paternité** *(Jur)* repudiation *ou* denial of paternity

désavouer /dezavwe/ ▸ conjug 1 ◂ VT 1 *(= renier) [+ livre, opinion, propos]* to disown, to disavow *(frm)*; *[+ signature]* to disclaim; *[+ paternité]* to disclaim, to deny 2 *(= blâmer) [+ personne, action]* to disown

désaxé, e /dezakse/ (ptp de **désaxer**) ADJ *[personne]* unhinged NM,F lunatic ◆ **ce crime est l'œuvre d'un ~** this crime is the work of a lunatic *ou* a psychotic

désaxer /dezakse/ ▸ conjug 1 ◂ VT *[+ roue]* to put out of true; *[+ personne, esprit]* to unbalance, to unhinge

descellement /deselmɑ̃/ NM *[de pierre]* freeing; *[de grille]* pulling up; *[d'acte]* unsealing, breaking the seal on *ou* of

desceller /desele/ ▸ conjug 1 ◂ VT *(= arracher) [+ pierre]* to (pull) free; *[+ grille]* to pull up; *(= ouvrir) [+ acte]* to unseal, to break the seal on *ou* of VPR **se desceller** *[objet]* to come loose

descendance /desɑ̃dɑ̃s/ NF *(= enfants)* descendants; *(= origine)* descent, lineage *(frm)* ◆ **mourir sans ~** to die without issue

descendant, e /desɑ̃dɑ̃, ɑ̃t/ ADJ *[direction, chemin]* downward, descending; *(Mus) [gamme]* falling, descending; *(Mil) [garde]* coming off duty *(attrib)*; *(Rail) [voie, train]* down *(épith)*; *[bateau]* sailing downstream ◆ **marée ~e** ebb tide ◆ **à marée ~e** when the tide is going out *ou* on the ebb NM,F descendant *(de* of)

descendeur, -euse /desɑ̃dœʀ, øz/ NM,F *(Ski, Cyclisme)* downhill specialist *ou* racer, downhiller NM *(Alpinisme)* descender, abseil device

descendre /desɑ̃dʀ/ ▸ conjug 41 ◂ VI *(avec aux être)* 1 *(= aller vers le bas) [personne] (vu d'en haut)* to go down; *(vu d'en bas)* to come down *(à, vers* to; *dans* into); *[fleuve]* to flow down; *[oiseau]* to fly down; *[avion]* to come down, to descend ◆ **descends me voir** come down and see me ◆ **descends le prévenir** go down and warn him ◆ **~ à pied/à bicyclette/en voiture/en parachute** to walk/cycle/drive/parachute down ◆ **on descend par un sentier étroit** the way down is by a narrow path ◆ **~ en courant/en titubant** to run/stagger down ◆ **~ en train/par l'ascenseur** to go down by train/in the lift *(Brit) ou* elevator *(US)* ◆ **~ par la fenêtre** to get down through the window ◆ **nous sommes descendus en 10 minutes** we got down in 10 minutes ◆ **~ à Marseille** to go down to Marseilles ◆ **~ en ville** to go into town; → **arène, rappel, rue**[1]

2 *(d'un lieu élevé)* **~ de** *[+ toit, rocher, arbre]* to climb *ou* come down from; *[+ balançoire, manège]* to get off ◆ **il descendait de l'échelle** he was climbing *ou* coming down the ladder ◆ **il est descendu de sa chambre** he came down from his room ◆ **~ de la colline** to come *ou* climb *ou* walk down the hill ◆ **fais ~ le chien du fauteuil** get the dog (down) off the armchair ◆ **descends de ton nuage !*** come back (down) to earth!

3 *(d'un moyen de transport)* **~ de voiture/du train** to get out of the car/off *ou* out of the train, to alight from the car/train *(frm)* ◆ **"tout le monde descend !"** "all change!" ◆ **vous descendez (à la prochaine) ?** *(dans le métro, le bus)* are you getting off (at the next stop)? ◆ **beaucoup de passagers sont descendus à Lyon** a lot of people got off at Lyons ◆ **ça descend pas mal à Châtelet** a lot of people get off at Châtelet ◆ **~ à terre** to go ashore ◆ **~ de cheval** to dismount ◆ **~ de bicyclette** to get off one's bicycle

4 *(= atteindre)* **~ à** *ou* **jusqu'à** *[habits, cheveux]* to come down to ◆ **son manteau lui descendait jusqu'aux chevilles** his coat came down to his ankles

5 *(= loger)* **~ dans un hôtel** *ou* **à l'hôtel** to stay at *ou* put up at a hotel ◆ **~ chez des amis** to stay with friends

6 *(= s'étendre de haut en bas)* **~ en pente douce** *[colline, route]* to slope gently down ◆ **~ en pente raide** to drop *ou* fall away sharply ◆ **la route descend en tournant** *ou* **en lacets** the road winds downwards

7 *(= s'enfoncer)* **le puits descend à 60 mètres** the well goes down 60 metres

8 *(= tomber) [obscurité, neige]* to fall; *[soleil]* to go down, to sink ◆ **le brouillard descend sur la vallée** the fog is coming down over the valley ◆ **le soleil descend sur l'horizon** the sun is going down on the horizon ◆ **le soir descendait** night was falling ◆ **les impuretés descendent au fond** the impurities fall *ou* drop to the bottom ◆ **la neige descend en voltigeant** the snow is fluttering down ◆ **qu'est-ce que ça descend !, qu'est-ce qu'il descend !*** *[pluie]* it's pouring, it's tipping it down! * *(Brit)*; *[neige]* it's snowing really hard

9 *(= baisser) [baromètre, température]* to fall, to drop; *[mer, marée]* to go out, to ebb; *[prix]* to come down, to fall, to drop; *[valeurs boursières, cote de popularité]* to fall ◆ **il est descendu à la dixième place** he's fallen back into tenth position ◆ **l'équipe est descendue en seconde division** the team moved down into the second division ◆ **~ dans l'échelle sociale** to move down the social scale ◆ **faire ~ le taux d'inflation/le nombre des chômeurs** to bring down the inflation rate/the number of unemployed ◆ **dans le 200 m, il est descendu en dessous de** *ou* **sous les 21 secondes** in the 200 metres he brought his time down to less than 21 seconds ◆ **ma voix ne descend pas plus bas** my voice doesn't *ou* won't go any lower

10 *(= s'abaisser)* **~ dans l'estime de qn** to go down in sb's estimation ◆ **il est descendu bien bas/jusqu'à mendier** he has stooped very low/to begging

11 *(= faire irruption)* **la police est descendue dans cette boîte de nuit** the police raided the night club, there was a police raid on the night club

12 *(* = être avalé ou digéré)* **ça descend bien** *[vin, repas]* that goes down well, that goes down a treat * *(Brit)* ◆ **se promener pour faire ~ son déjeuner** to take a walk in order to help digest one's lunch ◆ **il a bu une bière pour faire ~ son sandwich** he washed his sandwich down with a beer

VT INDIR **descendre de** *(= avoir pour ancêtre)* to be descended from ◆ **l'homme descend du singe** man is descended from the apes

VT *(avec aux avoir)* 1 *(= parcourir vers le bas) [+ escalier, colline, pente]* to go down, to descend *(frm)* ◆ **~ l'escalier/les marches précipitamment** to dash downstairs/down the steps ◆ **la péniche descend le fleuve** the barge goes down the river ◆ **~ une rivière en canoë** to go down a river in a canoe, to canoe down a river ◆ **~ la rue en courant** to run down the street ◆ **~ une piste en slalom** to slalom down a slope ◆ **~ la gamme** *(Mus)* to go down the scale

2 (= porter, apporter en bas) [+ valise] to get down, to take down, to bring down; [+ meuble] to take down, to bring down ◆ **faire ~ ses bagages** to have one's luggage brought *ou* taken down ◆ **tu peux me ~ mes lunettes ?** can you bring my glasses down for me? ◆ **il faut ~ la poubelle tous les soirs** the rubbish *(Brit) ou* garbage *(US)* has to be taken down every night ◆ **~ des livres d'un rayon** to reach *ou* take books down from a shelf ◆ **je te descends en ville** I'll take *ou* drive you into town, I'll give you a lift into town ◆ **le bus me descend à ma porte** the bus drops me right outside my front door

3 *(= baisser)* [+ étagère, rayon] to lower ◆ **descends les stores** pull the blinds down, lower the blinds ◆ **~ une étagère d'un cran** to lower a shelf (by) a notch, to take a shelf down a notch

4 * *(= abattre)* [+ avion] to bring down, to shoot down; *(= tuer)* [+ personne] to do in*, to bump off* ◆ **le patron du bar s'est fait ~** the bar owner got himself done in* *ou* bumped off* ◆ **l'auteur s'est fait ~ en beauté (par la critique)** *(fig)* the author was shot down in flames (by the critics); → **flamme**

5 *(* = boire)* [+ bouteille] to down* ◆ **qu'est-ce qu'il descend !** he drinks like a fish! *

⚠ **descendre** se traduit rarement par **to descend** ; l'anglais préfère employer un verbe à particule.

descente /desɑ̃t/ NF 1 *(= action)* going down *(NonC)*, descent; *(en avion, d'une montagne)* descent ◆ **le téléphérique est tombé en panne dans la ~** the cable-car broke down on the *ou* its way down ◆ **en montagne, la ~ est plus fatigante que la montée** in mountaineering, coming down *ou* the descent is more tiring than going up *ou* the climb ◆ **la ~ dans le puits est dangereuse** it's dangerous to go down the well ◆ **accueillir qn à la ~ du train/bateau** to meet sb off the train/boat ◆ **à ma ~ de voiture** as I got out of the car ◆ **~ en feuille morte** *(en avion)* falling leaf ◆ **~ en tire-bouchon** *(en avion)* spiral dive ◆ **~ en parachute** parachute drop ◆ **l'épreuve de ~** *(Ski)* the downhill (race) ◆ **~ en slalom** slalom descent ◆ **~ en rappel** *(Alpinisme)* abseiling, roping down; → **tuyau**

2 *(= raid, incursion)* raid ◆ **~ de police** police raid ◆ **faire une ~ sur** *ou* **dans** to raid, to make a raid on ◆ **les enfants ont fait une ~ dans le frigidaire** * the children have raided the fridge

3 *(en portant)* **la ~ des bagages prend du temps** it takes time to bring down the luggage ◆ **pendant la ~ du tonneau à la cave** while taking the barrel down to the cellar

4 *(= partie descendante)* (downward) slope, incline ◆ **s'engager dans la ~** to go off on the downward slope ◆ **la ~ est rapide** it's a steep (downward) slope ◆ **freiner dans les ~s** to brake going downhill *ou* on the downhill ◆ **les freins ont lâché au milieu de la ~** the brakes went halfway down (the slope) ◆ **la ~ de la cave** the stairs *ou* steps down to the cellar ◆ **la ~ du garage** the slope down to the garage ◆ **il a une bonne ~** * he can really knock it back * *ou* put it away *

COMP **descente de croix** *(Art, Rel)* Deposition
descente aux enfers *(Rel, fig)* descent into hell
descente de lit bedside rug
descente d'organe *(Méd)* prolapse of an organ

⚠ Attention à ne pas traduire automatiquement **descente** par le mot anglais **descent**, qui a des emplois spécifiques et est d'un registre plus soutenu.

déscolarisation /deskɔlarizasjɔ̃/ NF ◆ **les enfants en voie de ~** children who are dropping out of the school system

déscolarisé, e /deskɔlarize/ ADJ ◆ **un enfant ~** a child who has dropped out of the school system

déscotcher * /deskɔtʃe/ ▸ conjug 1 ◂ VT ◆ **je n'ai pas réussi à le ~ de la télévision** I couldn't drag him away from the television

descriptible /dɛskriptibl/ ADJ ◆ **ce n'est pas ~** it's indescribable

descriptif, -ive /dɛskriptif, iv/ ADJ descriptive NM *(= brochure)* explanatory leaflet; *[de travaux]* specifications, specification sheet; *[de projet]* outline

description /dɛskripsjɔ̃/ NF description ◆ **faire la ~ de** to describe

descriptivisme /dɛskriptivism/ NM descriptivism

descriptiviste /dɛskriptivist/ NMF descriptivist

désectorisation /desɛktɔrizasjɔ̃/ NF *(Scol)* removal of catchment area *(Brit) ou* school district *(US)* boundaries

désectoriser /desɛktɔrize/ ▸ conjug 1 ◂ VT *(Scol)* ◆ **~ une région** to remove a region's catchment area *(Brit) ou* school district *(US)* boundaries

déségrégation /desegregasjɔ̃/ NF desegregation

désélectionner /deselɛksjɔne/ ▸ conjug 1 ◂ VT to deselect

désembourber /dezɑ̃burbe/ ▸ conjug 1 ◂ VT to get out of the mud

désembourgeoiser /dezɑ̃burʒwaze/ ▸ conjug 1 ◂ VT to make less bourgeois VPR **se désembourgeoiser** to become less bourgeois, to lose some of one's bourgeois habits *ou* attitudes

désembouteiller /dezɑ̃buteje/ ▸ conjug 1 ◂ VT [+ route] to unblock; [+ lignes téléphoniques] to unjam

désembuage /dezɑ̃bɥaʒ/ NM demisting

désembuer /dezɑ̃bɥe/ ▸ conjug 1 ◂ VT [+ vitre] to demist

désemparé, e /dezɑ̃pare/ (ptp de **désemparer**) ADJ 1 [personne, air] helpless, distraught 2 [navire] crippled

désemparer /dezɑ̃pare/ ▸ conjug 1 ◂ VI ◆ **sans ~** without stopping VT *(Naut)* to cripple

désemplir /dezɑ̃plir/ ▸ conjug 2 ◂ VT to empty VI ◆ **le magasin ne désemplit jamais** the shop is never empty *ou* is always full VPR **se désemplir** to empty *(de* of)

désencadrer /dezɑ̃kadre/ ▸ conjug 1 ◂ VT 1 [+ tableau] to take out of its frame 2 *(Écon)* **~ le crédit** to ease credit controls

désenchaîner /dezɑ̃ʃene/ ▸ conjug 1 ◂ VT to unchain, to unfetter *(frm)*

désenchantement /dezɑ̃ʃɑ̃tmɑ̃/ NM *(= désillusion)* disillusionment, disenchantment

désenchanter /dezɑ̃ʃɑ̃te/ ▸ conjug 1 ◂ VT 1 [+ personne] to disillusion, to disenchant 2 *(littér)* [+ activité] to dispel the charm of; *(†† = désensorceler)* to free from a *ou* the spell, to disenchant

désenclavement /dezɑ̃klavmɑ̃/ NM *[de région, quartier, ville]* opening up ◆ **cela a permis le ~ de la région** this has opened up the region

désenclaver /dezɑ̃klave/ ▸ conjug 1 ◂ VT [+ région, quartier] to open up

désencombrement /dezɑ̃kɔ̃brəmɑ̃/ NM reduction of congestion

désencombrer /dezɑ̃kɔ̃bre/ ▸ conjug 1 ◂ VT [+ passage] to clear

désencrasser /dezɑ̃krase/ ▸ conjug 1 ◂ VT to clean out

désencroûter * /dezɑ̃krute/ ▸ conjug 1 ◂ VT ◆ **~ qn** to get sb out of the *ou* a rut, to shake sb up * VPR **se désencroûter** to get (o.s.) out of the *ou* a rut, to shake o.s. up *

désendettement /dezɑ̃dɛtmɑ̃/ NM *[d'entreprise, pays]* reduction in debt ◆ **l'entreprise poursuit son ~** the company is progressively clearing its debts ◆ **une politique de ~ de l'État** a policy of reducing the national debt

désendetter /dezɑ̃dete/ ▸ conjug 1 ◂ VT *(= annuler la dette de)* to get out of debt; *(= réduire la dette)* to reduce the debt of VPR **se désendetter** to get (o.s.) out of debt

désenfiler /dezɑ̃file/ ▸ conjug 1 ◂ VT [+ aiguille] to unthread; [+ perles] to unstring ◆ **mon aiguille s'est désenfilée** my needle has come unthreaded

désenfler /dezɑ̃fle/ ▸ conjug 1 ◂ VI to go down, to become less swollen

désengagement /dezɑ̃gaʒmɑ̃/ NM *(gén, Mil)* withdrawal, disengagement; *(Fin)* disinvestment ◆ **le ~ progressif des forces militaires** the gradual withdrawal of military forces ◆ **le ~ de l'État** the withdrawal of state funding

désengager /dezɑ̃gaʒe/ ▸ conjug 3 ◂ VT [+ troupes] to disengage, to withdraw ◆ **~ qn d'une obligation** to free sb from an obligation VPR **se désengager** [troupes] to disengage, to withdraw; [entreprise, État] to withdraw, to pull out *(de* from)

désengorger /dezɑ̃gɔrʒe/ ▸ conjug 3 ◂ VT [+ tuyau] to unblock; [+ route] to relieve the traffic congestion on; [+ service] to relieve

désenivrer /dezɑ̃nivre/ ▸ conjug 1 ◂ VTI to sober up

désennuyer /dezɑ̃nɥije/ ▸ conjug 8 ◂ VT ◆ **~ qn** to relieve sb's boredom ◆ **la lecture désennuie** reading relieves (one's) boredom VPR **se désennuyer** to relieve the *ou* one's boredom

désensabler /dezɑ̃sable/ ▸ conjug 1 ◂ VT [+ voiture] to dig out of the sand; [+ chenal] to dredge

désensibilisant, e /desɑ̃sibilizɑ̃, ɑ̃t/ ADJ [produit] desensitizing

désensibilisation /desɑ̃sibilizasjɔ̃/ NF *(Méd, Photo, fig)* desensitization

désensibiliser /desɑ̃sibilize/ ▸ conjug 1 ◂ VT *(Méd, Photo, fig)* to desensitize ◆ **se faire ~ au pollen** *(Méd)* to be desensitized to pollen ◆ **des enfants totalement désensibilisés à la violence** children totally inured to violence

désensorceler /dezɑ̃sɔrsəle/ ▸ conjug 4 ◂ VT to free *ou* release from a *ou* the spell

désentortiller /dezɑ̃tɔrtije/ ▸ conjug 1 ◂ VT to disentangle, to unravel

désentraver /dezɑ̃trave/ ▸ conjug 1 ◂ VT to unshackle

désenvaser /dezɑ̃vaze/ ▸ conjug 1 ◂ VT *(= sortir)* to get out of the mud; *(= nettoyer)* to clean the mud off; [+ port, chenal] to dredge

désenvenimer /dezɑ̃vnime/ ▸ conjug 1 ◂ VT [+ plaie] to take the poison out of; [+ relations] to take the bitterness out of ◆ **pour ~ la situation** to defuse *ou* take the heat out of the situation

désenvoûtement /dezɑ̃vutmɑ̃/ NM release from a *ou* the spell

désenvoûter /dezɑ̃vute/ ▸ conjug 1 ◂ VT to free *ou* release from a *ou* the spell

désépaissir /dezepesir/ ▸ conjug 2 ◂ VT [+ cheveux] to thin (out); [+ sauce] to thin (down), to make thinner

désépargne /dezeparɲ/ NF ◆ **on enregistre une tendance à la ~** there is a tendency for people to save less

désépargner /dezeparɲe/ ▸ conjug 1 ◂ VI to save less

déséquilibrant, e /dezekilibʀɑ̃, ɑ̃t/ ADJ destabilizing

déséquilibre /dezekilibʀ/ NM (= *manque d'assise*) unsteadiness; (*dans un rapport de forces, de quantités*) imbalance (*entre* between); (*mental, nerveux*) unbalance, disequilibrium (*frm*) ◆ **l'armoire est en ~** the cupboard is unsteady ◆ **le budget est en ~** the budget is not balanced ◆ **~ commercial** trade gap *ou* imbalance

déséquilibré, e /dezekilibʀe/ (ptp de **déséquilibrer**) ADJ [*budget*] unbalanced; [*esprit*] disordered, unhinged NM,F unbalanced *ou* mentally disturbed person

déséquilibrer /dezekilibʀe/ ▸ conjug 1 ◂ VT (*lit*) to throw off balance; [+ *esprit, personne*] to unbalance; [+ *budget*] to create an imbalance in

désert, e /dezɛʀ, ɛʀt/ ADJ deserted; → **île** NM (*Géog*) desert; (*fig*) desert, wilderness ◆ **~ de Gobi/du Kalahari/d'Arabie** Gobi/Kalahari/Arabian Desert ◆ **~ culturel** cultural desert; → **prêcher, traversée**

déserter /dezɛʀte/ ▸ conjug 1 ◂ VT [+ *lieu*] to desert, to abandon ◆ **village déserté par ses habitants** village deserted *ou* abandoned by its inhabitants VI (*Mil, fig*) to desert

déserteur /dezɛʀtœʀ/ NM deserter ADJ M deserting

désertification /dezɛʀtifikasjɔ̃/ NF 1 (*Écol, Géog*) desertification 2 (*fig*) [*de campagnes, région*] depopulation ◆ **la ~ rurale** *ou* **des campagnes** rural depopulation

désertifier (se) /dezɛʀtifje/ ▸ conjug 7 ◂ VPR 1 (*Écol, Géog*) to turn into a desert ◆ **zone désertifiée** desertified area 2 [*campagnes, région*] to become depopulated ◆ **région désertifiée** depopulated area

désertion /dezɛʀsjɔ̃/ NF (*Mil, fig*) desertion

désertique /dezɛʀtik/ ADJ [*lieu*] (= *de sable*) desert (*épith*); (= *aride*) barren; [*climat, plante*] desert (*épith*)

désescalade /dezɛskalad/ NF 1 (*Mil*) de-escalation 2 (*Écon*) [*de taux*] de-escalation

désespérance /dezɛspeʀɑ̃s/ NF (*littér*) desperation, desperateness

désespérant, e /dezɛspeʀɑ̃, ɑ̃t/ ADJ [*lenteur, nouvelle, bêtise*] appalling; [*enfant*] hopeless; [*temps*] depressing ◆ **d'une naïveté ~e** hopelessly naïve

désespéré, e /dezɛspeʀe/ (ptp de **désespérer**) ADJ [*personne*] in despair (*attrib*), desperate; [*situation*] desperate, hopeless; [*cas*] hopeless; [*tentative*] desperate ◆ **appel/regard ~** cry/look of despair, desperate cry/look ◆ **je suis ~ d'avoir à le faire** (*sens affaibli*) I'm desperately sorry to have to do it NM,F desperate person, person in despair ◆ **la ~e s'est jetée dans la Seine** the woman committed suicide by jumping into the Seine

désespérément /dezɛspeʀemɑ̃/ ADV (= *avec acharnement*) desperately; (= *sans espoir de changement*) hopelessly ◆ **la salle restait ~ vide** the room remained hopelessly empty

désespérer /dezɛspeʀe/ ▸ conjug 6 ◂ VT (= *décourager*) to drive to despair ◆ **il désespère ses parents** he drives his parents to despair, he is the despair of his parents

VI (= *se décourager*) to despair, to lose hope, to give up hope ◆ **c'est à ~** it's enough to drive you to despair, it's hopeless

VT INDIR **désespérer de** to despair of ◆ **je désespère de toi/de la situation** I despair of you/of the situation ◆ **je désespère de son succès** I despair of his (ever) being successful ◆ **~ de faire qch** to have lost (all) hope *ou* have given up (all) hope of doing sth, to despair of doing sth ◆ **il désespère de leur faire entendre raison** he has lost all hope of making them see reason, he despairs of (ever) making them see reason ◆ **je ne désespère pas de les amener à signer** I haven't lost hope *ou* given up hope of getting them to sign

VPR **se désespérer** to despair ◆ **elle passe ses nuits à se ~** her nights are given over to despair

désespoir /dezɛspwaʀ/ NM (= *perte de l'espoir*) despair; (= *chagrin*) despair ◆ **il fait le ~ de ses parents** he is the despair of his parents ◆ **sa paresse fait mon ~** his laziness drives me to despair *ou* to desperation ◆ **sa supériorité fait le ~ des autres athlètes** his superiority makes other athletes despair ◆ **être au ~** to be in despair ◆ **je suis au ~ de ne pouvoir venir** (*sens affaibli*) I'm desperately sorry that I can't come ◆ **en ~ de cause, on fit appel au médecin** in desperation, we called in the doctor COMP **désespoir des peintres** (= *plante*) London pride, saxifrage

désétatisation /dezetatizasjɔ̃/ NF denationalization

désétatiser /dezetatize/ ▸ conjug 1 ◂ VT to denationalize

désexualiser /desɛksɥalize/ ▸ conjug 1 ◂ VT to desexualize

déshabillage /dezabijaʒ/ NM undressing

déshabillé /dezabije/ NM négligé

déshabiller /dezabije/ ▸ conjug 1 ◂ VT to undress ◆ **~ Pierre pour habiller Paul** (*fig*) to rob Peter to pay Paul VPR **se déshabiller** to undress, to take off one's clothes; (* = *ôter son manteau, sa veste*) to take off one's coat ◆ **déshabillez-vous dans l'entrée** leave your coat *ou* things in the hall

déshabituer /dezabitɥe/ ▸ conjug 1 ◂ VT ◆ **~ qn de (faire) qch** to get sb out of the habit of (doing) sth, to break sb of the habit of (doing) sth VPR **se déshabituer** ◆ **se ~ de qch/de faire qch** (*volontairement*) to get (o.s.) out of the habit *ou* break o.s. of the habit of sth/of doing sth; (*par inaction, inertie*) to get out of *ou* lose the habit of sth/of doing sth

désherbage /dezɛʀbaʒ/ NM weeding

désherbant /dezɛʀbɑ̃/ NM weed-killer

désherber /dezɛʀbe/ ▸ conjug 1 ◂ VT to weed

déshérence /dezeʀɑ̃s/ NF escheat ◆ **tomber en ~** to escheat

déshérité, e /dezeʀite/ (ptp de **déshériter**) ADJ (= *désavantagé*) [*quartier, région*] deprived; [*famille, population*] destitute, deprived, underprivileged ◆ **l'enfance ~e** deprived children NM,F ◆ **les ~s** the underprivileged

déshériter /dezeʀite/ ▸ conjug 1 ◂ VT [+ *héritier*] to disinherit

déshonnête /dezɔnɛt/ ADJ (*littér* = *impudique*) unseemly, immodest

déshonnêteté /dezɔnɛtte/ NF (*littér* = *impudeur*) unseemliness, immodesty

déshonneur /dezɔnœʀ/ NM disgrace, dishonour (*Brit*), dishonor (*US*) ◆ **il n'y a pas de ~ à avouer son échec** there's no disgrace in admitting one's failure

déshonorant, e /dezɔnɔʀɑ̃, ɑ̃t/ ADJ dishonourable (*Brit*), dishonorable (*US*), degrading

déshonorer /dezɔnɔʀe/ ▸ conjug 1 ◂ VT 1 (= *discréditer*) [+ *profession*] to disgrace, to dishonour (*Brit*), to dishonor (*US*); [+ *personne, famille*] to dishonour (*Brit*), to dishonor (*US*), to be a disgrace to, to bring disgrace on ◆ **il se croirait déshonoré de travailler** he would think it beneath him to work 2 † [+ *femme*] to dishonour (*Brit*), to dishonor (*US*) VPR **se déshonorer** to disgrace o.s.

déshumaniser /dezymanize/ ▸ conjug 1 ◂ VT to dehumanize

déshumidificateur /dezymidifikatœʀ/ NM dehumidifier

déshydratation /dezidʀatasjɔ̃/ NF dehydration

déshydraté, e /dezidʀate/ (ptp de **déshydrater**) ADJ [*peau, aliment*] dehydrated

déshydrater VT, **se déshydrater** VPR /dezidʀate/ ▸ conjug 1 ◂ to dehydrate

déshydrogénation /dezidʀɔʒenasjɔ̃/ NF dehydrogenation, dehydrogenization

déshydrogéner /dezidʀɔʒene/ ▸ conjug 6 ◂ VT to dehydrogenate, to dehydrogenize

déshypothéquer /dezipɔteke/ ▸ conjug 6 ◂ VT to free from mortgage

desiderata /dezideʀata/ NMPL (= *souhaits*) wishes, desiderata (*frm*)

design /dizajn/ NM ◆ **le ~** (= *activité*) design; (= *style*) the designer look; (= *mobilier*) designer furniture ◆ **le ~ industriel** industrial design ADJ INV designer ◆ **un modèle/briquet très ~** a designer model/lighter ◆ **un intérieur très ~** an interior full of designer furniture

désignation /deziɲasjɔ̃/ NF (= *appellation*) name, designation (*frm*); (= *élection*) naming, appointment, designation

designer /dizajnœʀ/ NM (= *décorateur*) designer

désigner /deziɲe/ ▸ conjug 1 ◂ VT 1 (= *montrer*) to point out, to indicate ◆ **~ qn du doigt** to point sb out ◆ **ces indices le désignent clairement comme coupable** these signs point clearly to his guilt ◆ **~ qch à l'attention de qn** to draw *ou* call sth to sb's attention ◆ **~ qch à l'admiration de qn** to point sth out for sb's admiration

2 (= *nommer*) to name, to appoint, to designate ◆ **le gouvernement a désigné un nouveau ministre** the government has named *ou* appointed a new minister ◆ **~ qn pour remplir une mission** to designate sb to undertake a mission ◆ **~ qn à un poste** to appoint sb to a post ◆ **que des volontaires se désignent !** volunteers step forward!, could we have some volunteers! ◆ **membre/successeur désigné** member/successor elect *ou* designate

3 (= *qualifier*) to mark out ◆ **sa hardiesse le désigne pour (faire) cette tentative** his boldness marks him out for this attempt ◆ **c'était le coupable désigné/la victime désignée** he was the classic culprit/victim ◆ **être tout désigné pour faire qch** [*personne*] to be cut out to do sth, to be altogether suited to doing sth ◆ **l'endroit est tout désigné pour ce genre de festival** the place is perfect for this kind of festival

4 (= *dénommer*) to designate, to refer to ◆ **~ qn par son nom** to refer to sb by (their) name ◆ **on désigne sous ce nom toutes les substances toxiques** this name designates all toxic substances ◆ **ces métaphores désignent toutes le héros** these metaphors all refer to the hero ◆ **les mots qui désignent des objets concrets** the words which denote *ou* designate concrete objects

désillusion /dezi(l)lyzjɔ̃/ NF disillusion

désillusionnement /dezi(l)lyzjɔnmɑ̃/ NM disillusionment

désillusionner /dezi(l)lyzjɔne/ ▸ conjug 1 ◂ VT to disillusion

désincarcération /dezɛ̃kaʀseʀasjɔ̃/ NF ◆ **la ~ des victimes a pris deux heures** it took two hours to cut the victims (free) from the wreckage

désincarcérer /dezɛ̃kaʀseʀe/ ▸ conjug 6 ◂ VT [+ *accidenté*] to free (*from a wrecked vehicle*)

désincarné, e /dezɛ̃kaʀne/ ADJ (*Rel*) [*âme*] disembodied ◆ **on dirait qu'il est ~** you'd think he wasn't flesh and blood

désincrustant, e /dezɛ̃kʀystɑ̃, ɑ̃t/ ADJ 1 (*Tech*) (de)scaling 2 [*crème, masque*] (deep) cleansing (*épith*) NM (*Tech*) (de)scaling agent

désincruster /dezɛ̃kʀyste/ ▸ conjug 1 ◂ VT [*+ chaudière*] to descale, to remove the fur (*Brit*) *ou* sediment (*US*) from; [*+ peau*] to cleanse

désindexation /dezɛ̃dɛksasjɔ̃/ NF de-indexation

désindexer /dezɛ̃dɛkse/ ▸ conjug 1 ◂ VT to de-index

désindustrialisation /dezɛ̃dystʀijalizasjɔ̃/ NF de-industrialization

désindustrialiser /dezɛ̃dystʀijalize/ ▸ conjug 1 ◂ VT to de-industrialize

désinence /dezinɑ̃s/ NF (*Ling*) ending, inflexion

désinentiel, -ielle /dezinɑ̃sjɛl/ ADJ inflexional

désinfectant, e /dezɛ̃fɛktɑ̃, ɑ̃t/ ADJ, NM disinfectant

désinfecter /dezɛ̃fɛkte/ ▸ conjug 1 ◂ VT to disinfect

désinfection /dezɛ̃fɛksjɔ̃/ NF disinfection

désinflation /dezɛ̃flasjɔ̃/ NF ⇒ **déflation**

désinformation /dezɛ̃fɔʀmasjɔ̃/ NF disinformation

désinformer /dezɛ̃fɔʀme/ ▸ conjug 1 ◂ VT to give false information to

désinhiber /dezinibe/ ▸ conjug 1 ◂ VT ◆ ~ **qn** to rid sb of his (*ou* her) inhibitions

désinhibition /dezinibisjɔ̃/ NF loss of inhibitions

désinsectisation /dezɛ̃sɛktizasjɔ̃/ NF spraying *ou* treatment with insecticide, ≈ pest control

désinsectiser /dezɛ̃sɛktize/ ▸ conjug 1 ◂ VT to spray *ou* treat with insecticide

désinsertion /dezɛ̃sɛʀsjɔ̃/ NF ◆ **la ~ sociale provoquée par le chômage** the social exclusion caused by unemployment

désinstallation /dezɛ̃stalasjɔ̃/ NF [*de logiciel*] deinstalling

désinstaller /dezɛ̃stale/ ▸ conjug 1 ◂ VT [*+ logiciel*] to deinstall

désintégration /dezɛ̃tegʀasjɔ̃/ NF [*de groupe*] splitting-up, breaking-up; [*d'État*] disintegration, breakup; [*de roche*] disintegration, breaking-up; [*de fusée*] self-destructing; (*Phys Nucl*) [*d'atome*] splitting ◆ **la ~ de la matière** the disintegration of matter

désintégrer /dezɛ̃tegʀe/ ▸ conjug 6 ◂ VT [*+ groupe*] to split up, to break up; [*+ État, roche*] to break up, to disintegrate; (*Phys Nucl*) [*+ atome, matière*] to disintegrate VPR **se désintégrer** [*groupe*] to split up, to break up; [*État*] to break up, to disintegrate; [*roche*] to disintegrate, to crumble, to break up; [*fusée*] to self-destruct; (*Phys Nucl*) to disintegrate

désintéressé, e /dezɛ̃teʀese/ (ptp de **désintéresser**) ADJ (= *généreux*) disinterested, unselfish; (= *impartial*) disinterested ◆ **elle n'était pas complètement ~e en l'invitant** she had an ulterior motive in inviting him

désintéressement /dezɛ̃teʀɛsmɑ̃/ NM 1 (= *générosité*) unselfishness, selflessness; (= *impartialité*) disinterestedness ◆ **avec ~** unselfishly 2 (*Fin*) [*de créancier*] paying off; [*d'associé*] buying out

désintéresser /dezɛ̃teʀese/ ▸ conjug 1 ◂ VT [*+ créancier*] to pay off; [*+ associé*] to buy out VPR **se désintéresser** ◆ **se ~ de** to lose interest in

désintérêt /dezɛ̃teʀɛ/ NM disinterest, lack of interest (*pour* in)

désintoxication /dezɛ̃tɔksikasjɔ̃/ NF (*Méd*) [*d'alcoolique*] detoxification, treatment for alcoholism; [*de drogué*] detoxification, treatment for drug addiction ◆ **il fait une** *ou* **est en cure de ~** [*alcoolique*] he's undergoing treatment for alcoholism, he's in detox*; [*drogué*] he's undergoing treatment for drug addiction, he's in detox* ◆ **centre de ~** detoxification centre (*Brit*) *ou* center (*US*)

désintoxiqué, e /dezɛ̃tɔksike/ (ptp de **désintoxiquer**) ADJ [*ancien alcoolique*] dried out, detoxed*; [*ancien drogué*] clean, detoxed*

désintoxiquer /dezɛ̃tɔksike/ ▸ conjug 1 ◂ VT 1 (*Méd*) [*+ alcoolique*] to treat for alcoholism, to detoxify, to dry out*; [*+ drogué*] to treat for drug addiction, to detoxify ◆ **il s'est fait ~** [*alcoolique*] he was treated for alcoholism; [*drogué*] he was treated for drug addiction 2 [*+ citadin, gros mangeur*] to cleanse the system of 3 (= *désaccoutumer*) **tu veux un café ? – non, j'essaie de me ~** do you want a coffee? – no, I'm trying to give it up ◆ **pour ~ les enfants de la télévision** to wean children off *ou* from the television ◆ **il faut ~ l'opinion publique** (= *déconditionner*) the record has to be set straight with the public

désinvestir /dezɛ̃vɛstiʀ/ ▸ conjug 2 ◂ VI 1 (*Écon*) to disinvest (*dans* in); ◆ **la société a désinvesti dans le secteur immobilier** the company has disinvested in *ou* withdrawn its investments from the real estate market 2 (*Psych*) to cease to invest o.s. VT (*Mil*) to lift the siege of VPR **se désinvestir** to lose interest (*de* in); ◆ **elle s'est complètement désinvestie de sa relation amoureuse/de son travail** she has completely lost interest in her relationship/her work, she no longer puts anything into her relationship/her work

désinvestissement /dezɛ̃vɛstismɑ̃/ NM 1 (*Écon*) disinvestment, withdrawal of investments ◆ **la société a procédé à des ~s dans ces secteurs** the company began to disinvest in *ou* to withdraw its investments from these areas 2 (*Psych*) loss of interest ◆ **on note chez certains cadres un grand ~** some managers are putting less and less of themselves into their jobs *ou* are less and less committed to their jobs

désinvolte /dezɛ̃vɔlt/ ADJ (= *sans gêne*) casual, offhand, airy; (= *à l'aise*) casual, relaxed

désinvolture /dezɛ̃vɔltyʀ/ NF casualness ◆ **avec ~** casually, in an offhand way

désir /deziʀ/ NM 1 (= *souhait*) wish, desire (*de qch* for sth); ◆ **le ~ de faire qch** the desire to do sth ◆ **vos ~s sont des ordres** your wish is my command ◆ **selon le ~ de qn** in accordance with sb's wishes ◆ **prendre ses ~s pour des réalités** to indulge in wishful thinking, to delude o.s. 2 (= *convoitise, sensualité*) desire (*de qch* for sth); ◆ **yeux brillants de ~** eyes burning with desire ◆ **éprouver du ~ pour qn** to feel desire for sb

désirabilité /deziʀabilite/ NF desirability

désirable /deziʀabl/ ADJ desirable ◆ **peu ~** undesirable

désirer /deziʀe/ GRAMMAIRE ACTIVE 48.1 ▸ conjug 1 ◂ VT 1 (= *vouloir*) to want ◆ **~ faire qch** to want *ou* wish to do sth ◆ **que désirez-vous ?** (*dans un magasin*) what would you like?, what can I do for you? ◆ **désirez-vous prendre du café ?** would you care for *ou* would you like some coffee? ◆ **Madame désire ?** (*dans une boutique*) can I help you, madam?; (*domestique*) yes, madam? ◆ **il désire que tu viennes tout de suite** he wants you to come at once ◆ **désirez-vous qu'on vous l'envoie ?** would you like it sent to you?

◇ **laisser à désirer** ◆ **la cuisine/son travail laisse à ~** the food/his work leaves something to be desired *ou* is not (quite) up to the mark* (*Brit*) ◆ **ça laisse beaucoup à ~** it leaves much *ou* a lot to be desired ◆ **la décoration ne laisse rien à ~** the decor is all that one could wish for *ou* leaves nothing to be desired

2 (*sexuellement*) to desire ◆ **se faire ~*** to play hard-to-get*

désireux, -euse /deziʀø, øz/ ADJ ◆ **~ de faire** anxious to do, desirous of doing (*frm*) ◆ **il est très ~ de faire votre connaissance** he is most anxious to make your acquaintance ◆ **ils sont peu ~ d'entamer les négociations** they aren't very eager to *ou* they are reluctant to start negotiations ◆ **~ de qch** avid for sth, desirous of sth (*frm*)

désistement /dezistəmɑ̃/ NM (*Jur, Pol*) withdrawal

désister (se) /deziste/ ▸ conjug 1 ◂ VPR 1 (*Pol*) to withdraw, to stand down (*Brit*) (*en faveur de qn* in sb's favour) 2 (*Jur*) **se ~ de** [*+ action, appel*] to withdraw

désobéir /dezɔbeiʀ/ ▸ conjug 2 ◂ VI to disobey ◆ **~ à qn/à un ordre** to disobey sb/an order ◆ **il désobéit tout le temps** he never does what he's told

désobéissance /dezɔbeisɑ̃s/ NF disobedience (*NonC*) (*à* to); ◆ **~ civile** civil disobedience

désobéissant, e /dezɔbeisɑ̃, ɑ̃t/ ADJ disobedient

désobligeamment /dezɔbliʒamɑ̃/ ADV (*frm*) [*répondre, se conduire*] disagreeably

désobligeance /dezɔbliʒɑ̃s/ NF (*frm*) disagreeableness

désobligeant, e /dezɔbliʒɑ̃, ɑ̃t/ ADJ rude ◆ **~ à l'égard de** *ou* **pour qn/qch** offensive to sb/sth

désobliger /dezɔbliʒe/ ▸ conjug 3 ◂ VT (*frm*) to offend

désocialisation /desɔsjalizasjɔ̃/ NF ◆ **la ~ des chômeurs de longue durée** the social exclusion of the long-term unemployed

désocialiser /desɔsjalize/ ▸ conjug 1 ◂ VT [*+ personne*] to turn into a social misfit *ou* outcast

désodé, e /desɔde/ ADJ [*régime*] sodium-free

désodorisant, e /dezɔdɔʀizɑ̃, ɑ̃t/ ADJ [*savon*] deodorizing (*épith*), deodorant (*épith*); [*filtre*] deodorizing (*épith*) ◆ **bombe ~e** air freshener NM (*pour le corps*) deodorant; (*pour l'air*) air freshener

désodoriser /dezɔdɔʀize/ ▸ conjug 1 ◂ VT to deodorize

désœuvré, e /dezœvʀe/ ADJ idle ◆ **il restait ~ pendant des heures** he did nothing *ou* he sat idle for hours on end ◆ **le voyant ~, elle lui a demandé de l'aider** seeing that he was at a loose end, she asked him to help her NM,F ◆ **pour occuper les ~s** to occupy people with nothing to do

désœuvrement /dezœvʀəmɑ̃/ NM idleness ◆ **lire par ~** to read for something to do *ou* for want of anything better to do

désolant, e /dezɔlɑ̃, ɑ̃t/ ADJ [*nouvelle, situation, spectacle*] distressing ◆ **cet enfant est vraiment ~** this child is absolutely hopeless ◆ **ce serait ~ qu'elle ne puisse pas venir** it would be a terrible shame *ou* such a pity if she couldn't come ◆ **il est ~ de bêtise/paresse** he's hopelessly *ou* desperately stupid/lazy

désolation /dezɔlasjɔ̃/ NF 1 (= *consternation*) distress, grief ◆ **être plongé dans la ~** to be plunged in grief ◆ **il fait la ~ de sa mère** he causes his mother great distress, he breaks his mother's heart 2 (= *dévastation*) desolation, devastation

désolé, e /dezɔle/ GRAMMAIRE ACTIVE 39.2, 45.1, 45.3, 48.1, 52.5 (ptp de **désoler**) ADJ 1 [*personne, air*] (= *contrit*) sorry ◆ **(je suis) ~ de vous avoir dérangé** (I'm) sorry to have disturbed you ◆ **~, je dois partir** sorry, I have to go ◆ **je suis ~ d'avoir appris que vous avez perdu votre mari** I am sorry to hear that you have lost your husband 2 [*endroit*] desolate

désoler /dezɔle/ ▸ conjug 1 ◂ VT [1] (*= affliger*) to distress, to grieve, to sadden; (*= contrarier*) to upset ◆ **cet enfant me désole !** I despair of that child! [2] (*littér = dévaster*) to desolate, to devastate VPR **se désoler** to be upset ◆ **inutile de vous ~** it's no use upsetting yourself

désolidariser /desɔlidaʀize/ ▸ conjug 1 ◂ VT (*gén*) to divide; [*+ parties d'un mécanisme*] to separate VPR **se désolidariser** [*syndicats*] to go in different directions ◆ **se ~ de** to dissociate o.s. from

désopilant, e /dezɔpilɑ̃, ɑ̃t/ ADJ hilarious

désordonné, e /dezɔʀdɔne/ ADJ [1] [*pièce, personne*] untidy; [*mouvements*] uncoordinated; [*combat, fuite*] disorderly; [*esprit*] muddled, disorganized ◆ **être ~ dans son travail** to be disorganized in one's work [2] (*littér*) [*vie*] disorderly; [*dépenses, imagination*] reckless, wild

désordre /dezɔʀdʀ/ NM [1] (*= état*) [*de pièce, vêtements, cheveux*] untidiness; [*d'affaires publiques, service*] disorderliness, disorder ◆ **il ne supporte pas le ~** he can't bear disorder *ou* untidiness ◆ **quel ~ !** what a mess! ◆ **il régnait dans la pièce un ~ indescriptible** the room was in a terrible mess ◆ **les mauvaises herbes sur la terrasse, ça fait ~*** the weeds on the terrace are rather unsightly, the terrace looks messy with weeds growing all over it ◆ **un service sans chef, ça fait ~*** it doesn't look good, having a department without a manager ◆ **dans le ~** in no particular order ◆ **mettre du ~ dans une pièce** to mess up a room

◆ **en désordre** ◆ **être en ~** [*pièce, affaires*] to be untidy *ou* in disorder *ou* in a mess; [*cheveux, vêtements*] to be untidy *ou* in a mess ◆ **mettre une pièce en ~** to mess up a room, to make a room untidy ◆ **jeter quelques idées en ~ sur le papier** to jot down a few random ideas; → **tiercé**

[2] (*= agitation*) disorder ◆ **des agitateurs ont semé le ~ dans l'armée** agitators spread unrest in the army ◆ **faire du ~ (dans la classe/dans un lieu public)** to cause a commotion *ou* a disturbance (in class/in a public place) ◆ **arrêté pour ~ sur la voie publique** arrested for disorderly conduct ◆ **jeter le ~ dans les esprits** to throw people's minds into confusion ◆ **c'est un facteur de ~** it's a disruptive influence

[3] (*littér = débauche*) dissoluteness, licentiousness ◆ **mener une vie de ~** to lead a dissolute *ou* licentious life ◆ **regretter les ~s de sa jeunesse** to regret the dissolute *ou* licentious ways of one's youth

[4] (*Méd*) **~ fonctionnel/hépatique** functional/liver disorder

NMPL **désordres** (*= émeutes*) disturbances, disorder (*NonC*) ◆ **de graves ~s ont éclaté** serious disturbances have broken out, there have been serious outbreaks of violence ◆ **~s monétaires/politiques** (*= perturbations*) monetary/political chaos

désorganisation /dezɔʀganizasjɔ̃/ NF disorganization

désorganiser /dezɔʀganize/ ▸ conjug 1 ◂ VT (*gén*) to disorganize; [*+ projet, service*] to disrupt, to disorganize ◆ **à cause de la grève, nos services sont désorganisés** our services have been disrupted by the strike

désorientation /dezɔʀjɑ̃tasjɔ̃/ NF disorientation

désorienté, e /dezɔʀjɑ̃te/ (ptp de **désorienter**) ADJ (*= égaré*) disorientated; (*= déconcerté*) bewildered, confused (*par* by)

désorienter /dezɔʀjɑ̃te/ ▸ conjug 1 ◂ VT (*= égarer*) to disorientate; (*= déconcerter*) to bewilder, to confuse

désormais /dezɔʀmɛ/ ADV (*au présent*) from now on, henceforth (*frm*); (*au passé*) from then on, henceforth (*frm*)

désossé, e /dezɔse/ (ptp de **désosser**) ADJ [*viande*] boned; (*fig*) [*personne*] supple

désossement /dezɔsmɑ̃/ NM [*de viande*] boning

désosser /dezɔse/ ▸ conjug 1 ◂ VT [*+ viande*] to bone; [*+ objet, texte*] to take to pieces; [*+ voiture*] to strip (down) VPR **se désosser** ◆ **acrobate qui se désosse** acrobat who can twist himself in every direction

désoxydant, e /dezɔksidɑ̃, ɑ̃t/ ADJ deoxidizing NM deoxidizer

désoxyder /dezɔkside/ ▸ conjug 1 ◂ VT to deoxidize

désoxyribonucléique /dezɔksiʀibɔnykleik/ ADJ desoxyribonucleic

desperado /despeʀado/ NM desperado

despote /dɛspɔt/ ADJ despotic NM (*lit, fig*) despot, tyrant

despotique /dɛspɔtik/ ADJ despotic

despotiquement /dɛspɔtikmɑ̃/ ADV despotically

despotisme /dɛspɔtism/ NM (*lit, fig*) despotism, tyranny

desquamation /dɛskwamasjɔ̃/ NF desquamation

desquamer /dɛskwame/ ▸ conjug 1 ◂ VT to remove (*in scales*) VI **se desquamer** VPR to flake off, to desquamate (*SPÉC*)

desquels, desquelles /dekɛl/ → **lequel**

DESS /deəɛsɛs/ NM (abrév de **diplôme d'études supérieures spécialisées**) → **diplôme**

dessaisir /desezir/ ▸ conjug 2 ◂ VT (*Jur*) ◆ **~ un tribunal d'une affaire** to remove a case from a court ◆ **être dessaisi du dossier** to be taken off the case VPR **se dessaisir** ◆ **se ~ de** to give up, to part with, to relinquish

dessaisissement /desezismɑ̃/ NM ◆ **~ d'un tribunal/juge (d'une affaire)** removal of a case from a court/judge

dessalage /desalaʒ/ NM [1] (*= chavirement*) capsizing, turning turtle* [2] ⇒ **dessalement**

dessalé, e* /desale/ (ptp de **dessaler**) ADJ (*= déluré*) ◆ **il est drôlement ~ depuis qu'il a fait son service militaire** he has really learnt a thing or two* since he did his military service

dessalement /desalmɑ̃/ NM [*d'eau de mer*] desalination; [*de poisson*] soaking

dessaler /desale/ ▸ conjug 1 ◂ VT [1] [*+ eau de mer*] to desalinate; [*+ poisson*] to soak (*to remove the salt*) ◆ **faire ~** *ou* **mettre à ~ de la viande** to put meat to soak [2] (** = délurer*) **~ qn** to teach sb a thing or two*, to teach sb about life VI (*Naut*) to capsize, to turn turtle* VPR **se dessaler** ◆ **il s'était dessalé au contact de ses camarades** he had learnt a thing or two* *ou* learnt about life through contact with his friends

dessangler /desɑ̃gle/ ▸ conjug 1 ◂ VT [*+ cheval*] to ungirth; [*+ paquetage*] to unstrap

dessaouler* /desule/ ▸ conjug 1 ◂ VTI ⇒ **dessoûler**

desséchant, e /deseʃɑ̃, ɑ̃t/ ADJ [*vent*] parching, drying; [*travail*] soul-destroying

dessèchement /desɛʃmɑ̃/ NM (*= action*) drying (out *ou* up), parching; (*= état*) dryness; (*= amaigrissement*) emaciation

dessécher /deseʃe/ ▸ conjug 6 ◂ VT [1] [*+ terre, végétation*] to dry out, to parch; [*+ plante, feuille*] to wither, to dry out ◆ **le vent dessèche la peau** the wind dries (out) the skin ◆ **la soif me dessèche la bouche** my mouth is dry *ou* parched ◆ **lèvres desséchées** parched lips ◆ **cheveux desséchés** dry and damaged hair [2] (*volontairement*) [*+ aliments*] to dry, to dehydrate, to desiccate [3] (*= racornir*) [*+ cœur*] to harden ◆ **l'amertume/la vie lui avait desséché le cœur** bitterness/life had hardened his heart *ou* left him stony-hearted ◆ **desséché par l'étude** fossilized by years of study VPR **se dessécher** [*terre*] to dry out, to become parched; [*plante, feuille*] to wither, to dry out; [*aliments*] to dry out, to go dry; [*bouche, lèvres*] to go dry, to become parched; [*peau*] to dry out

dessein /desɛ̃/ NM (*littér*) (*= intention*) intention, design; (*= projet*) plan ◆ **son ~ est** *ou* **il a le ~ de faire** he intends *ou* means to do ◆ **former le ~ de faire qch** to make up one's mind to do sth, to form a plan to do sth ◆ **avoir des ~s sur qn** to have designs on sb ◆ **c'est dans ce ~ que** it is with this in mind *ou* with this intention that ◆ **il est parti dans le ~ de** *ou* **à ~ de faire fortune** he went off meaning *ou* intending to make his fortune *ou* with the intention of making his fortune ◆ **faire qch à ~** to do sth intentionally *ou* deliberately *ou* on purpose

desseller /desele/ ▸ conjug 1 ◂ VT to unsaddle

desserrage /deseʀaʒ/ NM [*de vis, écrou*] unscrewing, undoing, loosening; [*de câble*] loosening, slackening; [*de frein*] releasing; [*de crédit*] relaxation

desserré, e /deseʀe/ (ptp de **desserrer**) ADJ [*vis, écrou*] loose, undone (*attrib*); [*ficelle*] loose, slack; [*cravate, ceinture, nœud*] loose; [*frein*] off (*attrib*), released (*attrib*)

desserrement /desɛʀmɑ̃/ NM [*de ficelle, câble*] loosening, slackening; [*de nœud, écrou, étau*] loosening; [*de frein*] releasing; [*d'étreinte, contrainte*] relaxation ◆ **~ de la politique monétaire** relaxation of *ou* in monetary policy

desserrer /deseʀe/ ▸ conjug 1 ◂ VT [1] [*+ nœud, ceinture, ficelle, écrou*] to loosen; [*+ poing, dents*] to unclench; [*+ frein*] to release, to take off; [*+ étreinte*] to relax, to loosen; [*+ objets alignés, mots, lignes*] to space out ◆ **~ sa ceinture de 2 crans** to let one's belt out 2 notches ◆ **~ les cordons de la bourse** (*fig*) to loosen the purse strings ◆ **il n'a pas desserré les dents de toute la soirée** he didn't say a word *ou* open his mouth all evening ◆ **~ l'étau** (*lit*) to loosen the vice; (*fig*) to loosen one's grip (*autour de* on) [2] (*Écon*) [*+ contrainte, politique monétaire*] to relax, to ease VPR **se desserrer** [*ficelle, câble*] to come loose, to slacken; [*nœud*] to come loose; [*écrou*] to work *ou* come loose; [*frein*] to release itself; [*étreinte*] to relax

dessert /desɛʀ/ NM dessert, pudding (*Brit*), sweet (*Brit*) ◆ **ils en sont au ~** they're on to the dessert

desserte /desɛʀt/ NF [1] (*= meuble*) sideboard [2] (*Transport*) **la ~ d'une localité par bateau** the servicing of an area by water transport ◆ **la ~ de la ville est assurée par un car** there is a bus service to the town ◆ **cette compagnie aérienne assure une ~ quotidienne entre ces deux villes** the airline operates a daily scheduled flight between these two cities [3] [*de prêtre*] cure

dessertir /desɛʀtiʀ/ ▸ conjug 2 ◂ VT to unset, to remove from its setting

desservant /desɛʀvɑ̃/ NM priest in charge

desservir[1] /desɛʀviʀ/ ▸ conjug 14 ◂ VT [1] [*+ repas, plat*] to clear away ◆ **vous pouvez ~ (la table)** you can clear away, you can clear the table [2] (*= nuire à*) [*+ personne, cause*] to do a disservice to; [*+ intérêts*] to harm ◆ **son mauvais caractère le dessert** his bad temper goes against him *ou* doesn't do him any favours ◆ **il m'a desservi auprès de mes amis** he turned my friends against me

desservir[2] /desɛʀviʀ/ ▸ conjug 14 ◂ VT [1] (*Transport*) to serve ◆ **le village est desservi par 3 autobus chaque jour** there is a bus service from the village *ou* a bus runs from the village 3 times daily ◆ **le village est desservi par 3 lignes d'autobus** the village is served by *ou* has 3 bus services ◆ **ville bien desservie** town well served by public transport [2] *[porte, couloir]* to lead to [3] *[prêtre]* to serve ◆ ~ **une paroisse** to minister to a parish

dessiccatif, -ive /desikatif, iv/ **ADJ** desiccative **NM** desiccant

dessiccation /desikasjɔ̃/ **NF** *(Chim)* desiccation; *[d'aliments]* drying, desiccation

dessiller /desije/ ▸ conjug 1 ◂ **VT** *(fig)* ◆ ~ **les yeux de** *ou* **à qn** to open sb's eyes ◆ **mes yeux se dessillèrent** my eyes were opened, the scales fell from my eyes *(Brit)*

dessin /desɛ̃/ **NM** [1] *(= image)* drawing ◆ **il a fait un (joli)** ~ he drew a (nice) picture, he did a (nice) drawing ◆ **il passe son temps à faire des ~s** he spends his time drawing ◆ **il fait toujours des petits ~s sur son cahier** he's always doodling on his exercise book ◆ ~ **à la plume/au fusain/au trait** pen-and-ink/charcoal/line drawing ◆ ~ **animé** cartoon (film) ◆ ~ **humoristique** cartoon *(in a newspaper or magazine)* ◆ ~ **publicitaire/de mode** advertisement/fashion drawing ◆ **il n'a rien compris, fais lui donc un ~ !*** *(hum)* he hasn't understood a word – explain it in words of one syllable *ou* you'll have to spell it out for him; → **carton**

[2] *(= art)* **le** ~ drawing ◆ **il est doué pour le** ~ he has a gift for drawing ◆ **école de** ~ *(Art)* art school; *(technique)* technical college (for draughtsmen) ◆ **professeur de** ~ art teacher ◆ ~ **technique** technical drawing ◆ ~ **de mode** fashion design ◆ ~ **industriel** draughtsmanship *(Brit)*, draftsmanship *(US)* ◆ **table/planche à** ~ drawing table/board ◆ ~ **assisté par ordinateur** computer-aided design

[3] *(= motif)* pattern, design ◆ **tissu avec des ~s jaunes** material with a yellow pattern on it ◆ **le ~ des veines sur la peau** the pattern of the veins on the skin

[4] *(= contour)* outline, line ◆ **la bouche a un joli** ~ the mouth has a good line *ou* is finely delineated

dessinateur, -trice /desinatœʀ, tʀis/ **NM,F** *(= artiste)* artist *(who draws)*; *(= technicien)* draughtsman *(Brit)*, draftsman *(US)*; *(= technicienne)* draughtswoman *(Brit)*, draftswoman *(US)* ◆ **son talent de** ~ his skill at drawing; *(professionnel)* his skill as a draughtsman ◆ ~ **humoristique** cartoonist ◆ ~ **de mode** fashion designer ◆ ~ **industriel** draughtsman *(Brit)*, draftsman *(US)* ◆ ~ **de publicité** commercial artist ◆ **~-cartographe** cartographic designer, cartographer ◆ ~ **concepteur** designer

dessiner /desine/ ▸ conjug 1 ◂ **VT** [1] *(Art)* to draw ◆ **il dessine bien** he's good at drawing, he draws well ◆ ~ **qch à grands traits** to draw a broad outline of sth ◆ ~ **au pochoir** to stencil ◆ ~ **au crayon/à l'encre** to draw in pencil/ink

[2] *(= faire le plan, la maquette de) [+ véhicule, meuble]* to design; *[+ plan d'une maison]* to draw; *[+ jardin]* to lay out, to landscape ◆ **une bouche/oreille bien dessinée** *(fig)* a finely delineated mouth/ear

[3] *[chose]* to make, to form ◆ **les champs dessinent un damier** the fields form *ou* are laid out like a checkerboard *ou* (a) patchwork ◆ **un vêtement qui dessine bien la taille** a garment that shows off the waist well

VPR **se dessiner** [1] *[contour, forme]* to stand out, to be outlined ◆ **des collines se dessinaient à l'horizon** hills stood out on the horizon

[2] *[tendance]* to become apparent; *[projet]* to take shape ◆ **on voit se ~ une tendance à l'autoritarisme** a tendency towards authoritarianism is becoming apparent *ou* is emerging ◆ **un sourire se dessina sur ses lèvres** a smile played *ou* formed on his lips

dessouder /desude/ ▸ conjug 1 ◂ **VT** [1] *[+ pièces métalliques]* to unsolder [2] *(✻ = tuer)* to bump off✻, to do in✻ **VPR** **se dessouder** *[pièces métalliques]* to come unsoldered ◆ **leur couple s'est dessoudé** they broke up

dessoûler* /desule/ ▸ conjug 1 ◂ **VTI** to sober up ◆ **il n'a pas dessoûlé depuis 2 jours** he's been drunk for the past 2 days, he's been on a bender✻ for the past 2 days

dessous /d(ə)su/ **ADV** *(= sous) [placer, passer, suspendre]* underneath; *(= plus bas)* below ◆ **mettez votre valise** ~ put your suitcase underneath (it) *ou* under it ◆ **soulevez ces dossiers, la liste est** ~ lift up those files – the list is underneath (them) *ou* under them *ou* beneath them ◆ **passez (par)** ~ go underneath (it) *ou* under it ◆ **tu as mal lu, il y a une note** ~ you misread it – there's a note underneath ◆ **retirer qch de ~ le lit/la table** to get sth from under(neath) *ou* beneath the bed/table ◆ **ils ont pris le buffet par (en)** ~ they took hold of the sideboard from underneath

◆ **au-dessous** below ◆ **ils habitent au-~** they live downstairs ◆ **des articles à 15 € et au-~** items at 15 euros and less *ou* below

◆ **au-dessous de** *(lit)* below, underneath; *[+ possibilités, limite]* below; *(= indigne de)* beneath ◆ **sa jupe lui descend au-~ du genou** her skirt comes down to below her knees *ou* reaches below her knees ◆ **les enfants au-~ de 7 ans ne paient pas** children under 7 don't pay, the under-sevens don't pay ◆ **20° au-~ de zéro** 20° below (zero) ◆ **il considère que c'est au-~ de lui de faire la vaisselle** he considers it beneath him to do the dishes ◆ **il est au-~ de sa tâche** *(incapable)* he's not up to the job ◆ **il est au-~ de tout !** he's the absolute limit!, he's the end! ◆ **le service est au-~ de tout** the service is hopeless *ou* a disgrace

◆ **en dessous** *(= sous)* underneath; *(= plus bas)* below; *(= hypocritement)* in an underhand *ou* underhanded *(US)* manner ◆ **en ~ de** below ◆ **il s'est glissé en** ~ he slid underneath ◆ **les locataires d'en** ~ the people who rent the flat below *ou* downstairs ◆ **jeter un coup d'œil en ~ à qn, regarder qn en** ~ to give sb a shifty look ◆ **faire qch en** ~ to do sth in an underhand *ou* underhanded *(US)* manner ◆ **il est très en ~ de la moyenne** he's well below (the) average

NM [1] *[d'objet]* bottom, underside; *[de pied]* sole; *[d'avion, voiture, animal]* underside; *[de tissu]* wrong side; *[de tapis]* back ◆ **le ~ de la table est poussiéreux** the table is dusty underneath ◆ **avoir le** ~ to get the worst of it, to come off worst

◆ **du dessous** *[feuille, drap]* bottom ◆ **les voisins du** ~ the downstairs neighbours, the people below (us *ou* them *etc*), the people downstairs (from us *ou* them *etc*) ◆ **à l'étage du** ~ on the floor below ◆ **les fruits du ~ sont moisis** the fruit at the bottom *ou* the fruit underneath is mouldy

[2] *(= côté secret)* **le ~ de l'affaire** *ou* **l'histoire** the hidden side of the affair ◆ **les ~ de la politique** the unseen *ou* hidden side of politics ◆ **connaître le ~ des cartes** to have inside information

[3] *(Habillement)* undergarment ◆ **les** ~ underwear, undies*

COMP **dessous de caisse** *[de voiture]* underbody

dessous de robe slip, petticoat

dessous de verre coaster

dessous-de-bouteille /d(ə)sud(ə)butɛj/ **NM INV** bottle mat

dessous-de-bras /d(ə)sud(ə)bʀɑ/ **NM INV** dress shield

dessous-de-plat /d(ə)sud(ə)pla/ **NM INV** table mat *(for hot serving dishes)*, hot pad *(US)*

dessous-de-table /d(ə)sud(ə)tabl/ **NM INV** bribe, under-the-counter payment, backhander*

dessus /d(ə)sy/ GRAMMAIRE ACTIVE 43.4

ADV *(= sur) [placer, poser, monter]* on top (of it); *[coller, écrire, fixer]* on it; *[passer, lancer]* over it; *(= plus haut)* above ◆ **mettez votre valise** ~ put your suitcase on top (of it) ◆ **regardez ces dossiers, la liste doit être** ~ have a look at those files - the list must be on top (of them) ◆ **il n'y a pas de timbre** ~ there's no stamp on it ◆ **c'est écrit** ~ it's written on it ◆ **montez** ~ *[+ tabouret, échelle]* get up on it ◆ **passez (par)** ~ go over it ◆ **il a sauté par** ~ he jumped over it ◆ **ôter qch de ~ la table** to take sth (from) off the table ◆ **il n'a même pas levé la tête de ~ son livre** he didn't even look up from his book, he didn't even take his eyes off his book ◆ **il lui a tapé/tiré** ~ he hit him/shot at him ◆ **il nous sont arrivés** *ou* **tombés** ~ **à l'improviste** they dropped in on us unexpectedly

◆ **au-dessus** above; *(= à l'étage supérieur)* upstairs; *(= posé sur)* on top; *(= plus cher)* over, above ◆ **pour le confort, il n'y a rien au-~** there's nothing to beat it for comfort

◆ **au-dessus de** *(= plus haut que)* above; *(= sur)* on top of; *[+ prix, limite]* over, above; *[+ possibilités]* beyond ◆ **la valise est au-~ de l'armoire** the suitcase is on top of the wardrobe ◆ **les enfants au-~ de 7 ans paient** children over 7 pay, the over-sevens pay ◆ **20° au-~ de zéro** 20° above zero ◆ **il n'y a pas d'articles au-~ de 25 €** there are no items over €25 ◆ **c'est au-~ de ce que je peux mettre** *(prix)* it's beyond my means, it's more than I can afford ◆ **cette tâche est au-~ de ses capacités** this task is beyond his capabilities ◆ **c'est au-~ de mes forces** it's too much for me ◆ **il ne voit rien au-~ de son fils** he thinks no one can hold a candle to his son ◆ **il est au-~ de ces petites mesquineries** he's above this kind of pettiness ◆ **être au-~ de tout soupçon/reproche** to be above suspicion/beyond reproach

◆ **en dessus** above ◆ **leur plumage est fauve en ~, blanc en dessous** their feathers are reddish brown above and white below ◆ **en ~ de** above ◆ **la France se situe un peu en ~ de la moyenne européenne** France is slightly above the European average

NM [1] *[d'objet, pied, tête]* top; *[de tissu]* right side ◆ **le ~ de la table est en marbre** the table-top *ou* the top of the table is marble ◆ **le ~ du panier** *(= les meilleurs)* the pick of the bunch; *(= l'élite sociale)* the upper crust

◆ **du dessus** *[feuille, drap]* top ◆ **les voisins du** ~ the upstairs neighbours, the people above (us *ou* them *etc*) *ou* upstairs (from us *ou* them *etc*) ◆ **à l'étage du** ~ on the floor above ◆ **les fraises du ~ sont plus belles** the strawberries on top are nicer ◆ **elle portait deux pulls, celui du ~ était bleu** she was wearing two jumpers and the top one was blue

[2] *(locutions)* **avoir/prendre le** ~ to have/get the upper hand ◆ **reprendre le** ~ to get over it ◆ **il a été très malade/déprimé mais il a repris le ~ rapidement** he was very ill/depressed but he soon got over it

COMP **dessus de cheminée** *(= tablette)* mantelpiece; *(= bibelots)* mantelpiece ornaments

dessus de table table runner

dessus-de-lit /d(ə)syd(ə)li/ **NM INV** bedspread

dessus-de-porte /d(ə)syd(ə)pɔʀt/ **NM INV** overdoor

DEST /deəɛste/ **NM** (abrév de **diplôme d'études supérieures techniques**) → **diplôme**

déstabilisant, e /destabilizɑ̃, ɑ̃t/, **déstabilisateur, -trice** /destabilizatœʀ, tʀis/ **ADJ** *[influence, événement]* destabilizing

déstabilisation /destabilizasjɔ̃/ **NF** destabilization

déstabiliser /destabilize/ ▸ conjug 1 ◂ **VT** to destabilize

déstalinisation /destalinizasjɔ̃/ **NF** destalinization

déstaliniser /destalinize/ ► conjug 1 ◄ VT to destalinize

destin /dɛstɛ̃/ NM (= *fatalité, sort*) fate; (= *existence, vocation*) destiny; (= *avenir*) future ♦ **le ~ de l'Europe** the future of Europe ♦ **le ~ contraire** ill-fortune ♦ **elle connut un ~ tragique** she met with a tragic end ♦ **c'est le ~ !** it was meant to be!

destinataire /dɛstinatɛʀ/ NMF [*de lettre*] addressee; [*de marchandise*] consignee; [*de mandat*] payee; (*Ling*) person addressed ♦ **remettre une lettre à son ~** to hand a letter to the person it is addressed to

destinateur /dɛstinatœʀ/ NM (*Ling*) speaker

destination /dɛstinasjɔ̃/ NF 1 (= *direction*) destination ♦ **à ~ de** [*avion, train, bateau*] to, bound for; [*voyageur*] travelling to; [*lettre*] sent to ♦ **arriver à ~** to reach one's *ou* its destination, to arrive (at one's *ou* its destination) ♦ **train/vol 702 à ~ de Paris** train number 702/flight (number) 702 to *ou* for Paris ♦ **partir pour une ~ inconnue/lointaine** to leave for an unknown/a faraway destination 2 (= *usage*) [*d'appareil, édifice, somme d'argent*] purpose ♦ **quelle ~ comptez-vous donner à cette somme/pièce ?** to what purpose do you intend to put this money/room?, what do you intend to use this money/room for? ♦ **on a rendu à ce local sa ~ première** these premises have been restored to their original purpose

destiné, e[1] /dɛstine/ (ptp de **destiner**) ADJ 1 (= *prévu pour*) ~ **à faire qch** intended *ou* meant to do sth ♦ **ces mesures sont ~es à freiner l'inflation** these measures are intended *ou* meant to curb inflation ♦ **cette pommade est ~e à guérir les brûlures** this ointment is intended for healing burns ♦ **livre ~ aux enfants** book (intended *ou* meant) for children ♦ **édifice ~ au culte** building intended for worship 2 (= *voué à*) ~ **à qch** destined for sth ♦ **~ à faire** destined to do ♦ **il était ~ à une brillante carrière** he was destined for a brilliant career ♦ **elle était ~e à mourir jeune** she was destined *ou* fated *ou* doomed to die young

destinée[2] /dɛstine/ NF (= *fatalité, sort*) fate; (= *existence, avenir, vocation*) destiny ♦ **unir sa ~ à celle de qn** to unite one's destiny with sb's ♦ **promis à de hautes ~s** destined for great things

destiner /dɛstine/ ► conjug 1 ◄ VT 1 (= *attribuer*) ~ **sa fortune à qn** to intend *ou* mean sb to have one's fortune, to intend that sb should have one's fortune ♦ **il vous destine ce poste** he intends *ou* means you to have this post ♦ **~ une allusion à qn** to intend an allusion for sb ♦ **~ un coup à qn** to aim a blow at sb ♦ **nous destinons ce livre à tous ceux qui souffrent** this book is intended *ou* meant for all who are suffering, we have written this book with all those who are suffering in mind ♦ **il ne put attraper le ballon qui lui était destiné** he couldn't catch the ball thrown to him ♦ **sans deviner le sort qui lui était destiné** not knowing what fate had in store for him ♦ **cette lettre t'était/ne t'était pas destinée** this letter was/was not (meant *ou* intended) for you

2 (= *affecter*) ~ **une somme à l'achat de qch** to intend to use a sum to buy sth, to earmark a sum for sth ♦ **~ un local à un usage précis** to intend a place to be used for a specific purpose, to have a specific use in mind for a place ♦ **les fonds seront destinés à la recherche** the money will be devoted to *ou* used for research

3 (= *vouer*) to destine ♦ **~ qn à une fonction** to destine sb for a post ♦ **sa famille la destinait à être médecin/à un vicomte** her family wanted her to be a doctor/wanted to marry her off to a viscount ♦ **sa bravoure le destinait à mourir de mort violente** his boldness marked him out *ou* destined him to die a violent death ♦ **il se destine à l'enseignement/à être ingénieur** he intends to go into teaching/to be an engineer, he has set his sights on teaching/being an engineer

destituer /dɛstitɥe/ ► conjug 1 ◄ VT [+ *ministre*] to dismiss; [+ *roi*] to depose; [+ *officier*] to discharge ♦ **~ un officier de son commandement** to relieve an officer of his command ♦ **~ qn de ses fonctions** to relieve sb of his duties

destitution /dɛstitysjɔ̃/ NF [*de ministre, fonctionnaire*] dismissal; [*d'officier*] discharge; [*de roi*] deposition

déstockage /destɔkaʒ/ NM destocking ♦ **« déstockage massif »** (*dans une vitrine*) "massive clearance sale"

déstocker /destɔke/ ► conjug 1 ◄ VT [+ *produit, or*] to sell off ♦ **vêtements déstockés** end-of-line garments VI to reduce stocks, to destock

déstresser /destʀese/ ► conjug 1 ◄ VTI **se déstresser** VPR to relax

destrier /dɛstʀije/ NM (*Hist*) charger

destroy* /dɛstʀɔj/ ADJ INV [*musique*] wild ♦ **il avait une allure complètement ~** he looked wild and wasted ♦ **l'égérie la plus ~ du rock américain** the grunge-queen of American rock

destroyer /dɛstʀwaje/ NM (*Naut*) destroyer

destructeur, -trice /dɛstʀyktœʀ, tʀis/ ADJ destructive ♦ **produits ~s d'ozone** products that deplete *ou* destroy the ozone layer, ozone-depleting *ou* -destroying products NM,F destroyer

destructible /dɛstʀyktibl/ ADJ destructible

destructif, -ive /dɛstʀyktif, iv/ ADJ destructive

destruction /dɛstʀyksjɔ̃/ NF (*gén*) destruction (*NonC*); [*de rats, insectes*] extermination (*NonC*) ♦ **les ~s causées par la guerre** the destruction caused by the war

déstructuration /destʀyktyʀasjɔ̃/ NF [*de texte*] taking apart, deconstruction ♦ **pour empêcher la ~ de l'esprit** (*Psych*) to prevent the mind from becoming destructured ♦ **la ~ de la société** the breakdown of social structures

déstructurer /destʀyktyʀe/ ► conjug 1 ◄ VT [+ *société, organisation*] to dismantle the structure of; [+ *texte*] to take apart, to deconstruct ♦ **veste déstructurée** unstructured jacket ♦ **~ l'emploi** to dismantle traditional job structures ♦ **des gens déstructurés par le chômage** people who have been devastated by unemployment VPR **se déstructurer** [*société*] to disintegrate, to come apart at the seams; [*esprit, personnalité*] to become destructured

désuet, -ète /dezɥɛ, ɛt/ ADJ (*gén*) outdated, antiquated, outmoded; [*charme*] old-fashioned, quaint; [*vêtement*] old-fashioned; [*mode*] outdated

désuétude /desɥetyd/ NF disuse, obsolescence, desuetude (*littér*) ♦ **tomber en ~** [*loi*] to fall into abeyance; [*expression, coutume*] to become obsolete, to fall into disuse

désuni, e /dezyni/ (ptp de **désunir**) ADJ [*couple, famille*] divided, disunited; [*mouvements*] uncoordinated; [*coureur, cheval*] off his stride (*attrib*) ♦ **l'équipe était un peu ~e** the team wasn't really working together

désunion /dezynjɔ̃/ NF [*de couple, parti*] disunity, dissension (*de* in)

désunir /dezyniʀ/ ► conjug 2 ◄ VT [+ *famille, couple*] to divide, to disunite, to break up; [+ *pierres, planches*] to separate VPR **se désunir** [*athlète*] to lose one's stride; [*cheval*] to lose its stride; [*équipe*] to lose its coordination

désynchronisation /desɛ̃kʀɔnizasjɔ̃/ NF desynchronization

désynchroniser /desɛ̃kʀɔnize/ ► conjug 1 ◄ VT to desynchronize

désyndicalisation /desɛ̃dikalizasjɔ̃/ NF decrease in union membership

détachable /detaʃabl/ ADJ detachable

détachage /detaʃaʒ/ NM (= *nettoyage*) stain removal

détachant /detaʃɑ̃/ ADJ stain-removing (*épith*) NM stain remover

détaché, e /detaʃe/ (ptp de **détacher**) ADJ 1 (= *indifférent*) detached ♦ **"peut-être", dit-il d'un ton ~** "maybe", he said with detachment ♦ **elle prit un air ~** she assumed an indifferent air 2 [*fonctionnaire*] on temporary assignment (*auprès de* to) on secondment (*Brit*) (*auprès de* to) 3 (*Mus*) detached; → **pièce**

détachement /detaʃmɑ̃/ NM 1 (= *indifférence*) detachment (*envers, à l'égard de* from); ♦ **regarder/dire qch avec ~** to look at/say sth with (an air of) detachment ♦ **le ~ qu'il montrait pour les biens matériels** the disregard he showed for material goods 2 (*Mil*) detachment 3 [*de fonctionnaire*] temporary assignment, secondment (*Brit*)

♦ **en détachement** ♦ **être en ~** to be on a temporary assignment *ou* on secondment (*Brit*) ♦ **en ~ à l'ambassade de France** on a temporary assignment at *ou* on secondment (*Brit*) to the French embassy

détacher[1] /detaʃe/ ► conjug 1 ◄ VT 1 (= *délier*) [+ *chien, cheval*] to untie, to let loose; [+ *prisonnier*] to untie, to unbind; [+ *paquet, objet*] to undo, to untie; [+ *wagon, remorque*] to take off, to detach ♦ **~ un wagon d'un convoi** to detach a carriage (*Brit*) *ou* car (*US*) from a train ♦ **il détacha la barque/le prisonnier de l'arbre** he untied the boat/the prisoner from the tree

2 (= *dénouer*) [+ *vêtement, ceinture*] to undo, to unfasten; [+ *lacet, nœud*] to undo, to untie; [+ *chaussure, chaîne*] to unfasten, to undo ♦ **il détacha la corde du poteau** he untied *ou* removed the rope from the post

3 (= *ôter*) [+ *peau, écorce*] to remove (*de* from) to take off; [+ *papier collé*] to remove, to unstick (*de* from); [+ *rideau, tableau*] to take down (*de* from); [+ *épingle*] to take out (*de* of) to remove; [+ *reçu, bon*] to tear out (*de* of) to detach (*de* from); ♦ **l'humidité avait détaché le papier** the paper had come unstuck because of the damp ♦ **~ des feuilles d'un bloc** to tear *ou* take some sheets out of a pad, to detach some sheets from a pad ♦ **~ un morceau de plâtre du mur** to remove a piece of plaster from the wall, to take a piece of plaster from *ou* off the wall ♦ **il détacha une pomme de l'arbre** he took an apple from the tree, he picked an apple off the tree ♦ **détachez bien les bras du corps** keep your arms well away from your body ♦ **il ne pouvait ~ son regard du spectacle** he could not take his eyes off the sight ♦ **"partie à détacher"** (*sur un coupon*) "tear off (this section)" ♦ **"détacher suivant le pointillé"** "tear off along the dotted line"

4 (= *envoyer*) [+ *personne*] to send, to dispatch; (= *affecter : à un ministère, une organisation*) to assign temporarily, to second (*Brit*) (*à* to); ♦ **il a été détaché auprès du Premier ministre** he was temporarily assigned *ou* he was seconded (*Brit*) to work with the Prime Minister

5 (= *mettre en relief*) [+ *lettres*] to separate; [+ *syllabes, mots*] to articulate, to separate; (*Peinture*) [+ *silhouette, contour*] to bring out, to make stand out; (*Mus*) [+ *notes*] to detach

6 (= *éloigner*) ~ **qn de qch/qn** to turn sb away from sth/sb ♦ **son cynisme a détaché de lui tous ses amis** his cynicism has turned his friends away from him

VPR **se détacher** 1 (= *se délier*) [*chien*] to free itself, to get loose (*de* from); [*prisonnier*] to free o.s., to get loose (*de* from); [*paquet*] to come undone *ou* untied; [*barque*] to come untied, to loose itself (*de* from); *[wagon]* to come off, to detach itself (*de* from); ◆ **la boule s'était détachée de l'arbre de Noël** the bobble had fallen off the Christmas tree

[2] (= *se dénouer*) *[ceinture, chaussure]* to come undone *ou* unfastened; *[lacet, ficelle]* to come undone *ou* untied

[3] (= *se séparer*) *[fruit, ficelle]* to come off; *[page]* to come loose, to come out; *[peau, écorce]* to come off; *[papier collé]* to come unstuck, to come off; *[épingle]* to come out, to fall out; *[rideau]* to come down ◆ **le papier s'était détaché à cause de l'humidité** the paper had come unstuck because of the damp ◆ **un bloc de pierre se détacha du rocher** a block of stone broke away from *ou* detached itself from the rock ◆ **l'écorce se détachait de l'arbre** the bark was coming off the tree *ou* was coming away from the tree ◆ **la capsule spatiale s'est détachée de la fusée** the space capsule has separated from *ou* come away from the rocket

[4] (*Sport*) *[coureur]* to pull *ou* break away (*de* from); ◆ **un petit groupe se détacha du reste des manifestants** a small group broke away from *ou* detached itself from the rest of the demonstrators

[5] (= *ressortir*) to stand out ◆ **la forêt se détache sur le ciel clair** the forest stands out against the clear sky

[6] (*fig*) ◆ **se ~ de** (= *renoncer à*) to turn one's back on, to renounce; (= *se désintéresser de*) to grow away from ◆ **se ~ des plaisirs de la vie** to turn one's back on *ou* renounce the pleasures of life ◆ **ils se sont détachés l'un de l'autre** they have grown apart

détacher² /detaʃe/ ► conjug 1 ◄ VT to remove the stains from, to clean ◆ **donner une robe à ~** to take a dress to be cleaned *ou* to the cleaner's ◆ **~ au savon/à la benzine** to clean with soap/benzine

détail /detaj/ NM [1] (= *particularité*) detail ◆ **dans les (moindres) ~s** in (minute) detail ◆ **se perdre dans les ~s** to lose o.s. in details ◆ **entrer dans les ~s** to go into detail(s) *ou* particulars ◆ **je n'ai pas remarqué ce ~** I didn't notice that detail *ou* point ◆ **c'est un ~ !** that's just a minor detail!; → **revue**

[2] (= *description précise*) *[de facture, compte]* breakdown ◆ **examiner le ~ d'un compte** to examine a breakdown of *ou* the particulars of an account ◆ **pourriez-vous nous faire le ~ de la facture/de ce que l'on vous doit ?** could you give us a breakdown of the invoice/of what we owe you? ◆ **il nous a fait le ~ de ses aventures** he gave us a detailed account *ou* a rundown* of his adventures ◆ **en ~, dans le ~** in detail ◆ **il ne fait pas de** *ou* **le ~ !*** he doesn't make any exceptions!, he doesn't discriminate!

[3] (*Comm*) retail ◆ **commerce/magasin/prix de ~** retail business/shop *ou* store/price ◆ **vendre au ~** *[+ marchandise, vin]* to (sell) retail; *[+ articles, couverts]* to sell separately ◆ **il fait le gros et le ~** he deals in wholesale and retail

> ⚠ **détail** se traduit par **detail** uniquement au sens de 'particularité'.

détaillant, e /detajɑ̃, ɑ̃t/ NM,F retailer, retail dealer

détaillé, e /detaje/ (ptp de **détailler**) ADJ *[récit, plan, explications]* detailed; *[facture]* itemized

détailler /detaje/ ► conjug 1 ◄ VT [1] (*Comm*) *[+ articles]* to sell separately; *[+ marchandise]* to (sell) retail ◆ **nous détaillons les services de table** we sell dinner services in separate pieces ◆ **est-ce que vous détaillez cette pièce de tissu ?** do you sell lengths of this piece of material? [2] (= *passer en revue*) *[+ plan]* to detail, to explain in detail; *[+ facture]* to itemize; *[+ récit]* to tell in detail; *[+ incidents, raisons]* to detail, to give details of ◆ **il m'a détaillé (de la tête aux pieds)** he examined me *ou* looked me over (from head to foot)

détaler /detale/ ► conjug 1 ◄ VI *[lapin]* to bolt; * *[personne]* to take off*, to clear off* ◆ **il a détalé comme un lapin** he bolted*, he skedaddled*

détartrage /detaʀtʀaʒ/ NM *[de dents]* scaling; *[de chaudière]* descaling; *[de lave-vaisselle, WC]* removal of limescale from ◆ **se faire faire un ~** to have one's teeth scaled (and polished)

détartrant /detaʀtʀɑ̃/ ADJ descaling NM descaling agent

détartrer /detaʀtʀe/ ► conjug 1 ◄ VT *[+ dents]* to scale (and polish); *[+ chaudière]* to descale; *[+ lave-vaisselle, WC]* to remove limescale from

détaxation /detaksasjɔ̃/ NF (= *réduction*) reduction in tax; (= *suppression*) removal of tax (*de* from)

détaxe /detaks/ NF (= *réduction*) reduction in tax; (= *suppression*) removal of tax (*de* from); (= *remboursement*) tax refund ◆ **~ à l'exportation** duty-free for export ◆ **marchandises en ~** duty-free *ou* tax-free goods

détaxer /detakse/ ► conjug 1 ◄ VT (= *réduire*) to reduce the tax on; (= *supprimer*) to remove the tax on, to take the tax off ◆ **produits détaxés** duty-free *ou* tax-free goods

détectable /detɛktabl/ ADJ detectable, detectible

détecter /detɛkte/ ► conjug 1 ◄ VT to detect

détecteur, -trice /detɛktœʀ, tʀis/ ADJ *[dispositif]* detecting (*épith*), detector (*épith*); *[lampe, organe]* detector (*épith*) NM detector ◆ **~ d'approche** intrusion-detection device ◆ **~ de faux billets** forged banknote detector ◆ **~ de fumée/de métaux** metal/smoke detector ◆ **~ de mensonges** polygraph, lie detector ◆ **~ de mines/particules** mine/particle detector

détection /detɛksjɔ̃/ NF detection ◆ **~ sous-marine/électromagnétique** underwater/electromagnetic detection

détective /detɛktiv/ NM ◆ **~ (privé)** private detective *ou* investigator, private eye*

déteindre /detɛ̃dʀ/ ► conjug 52 ◄ VI (*au lavage*) *[étoffe]* to run, to lose its colour; *[couleur]* to run, to come out; (*par l'humidité*) *[couleur]* to come off; (*au soleil*) *[étoffe]* to fade, to lose its colour; *[couleur]* to fade

◆ **déteindre sur** *[couleur]* to run into; (= *influencer*) *[trait de caractère]* to rub off on ◆ **le pantalon a déteint sur la chemise** some of the colour has come out of the trousers onto the shirt ◆ **elle a déteint sur sa fille** something of her character rubbed off on her daughter VT *[personne, produit]* to take the colour out of; *[soleil]* to fade, to take the colour out of

dételer /det(ə)le/ ► conjug 4 ◄ VT *[+ bœufs]* to unyoke; *[+ chevaux]* to unharness; *[+ voiture]* to unhitch; *[+ wagon]* to uncouple, to unhitch VI (* = *arrêter de travailler*) to knock off* ◆ **sans ~** *[travailler, faire qch]* without a break, non-stop

détendeur /detɑ̃dœʀ/ NM *[de bouteille de gaz, installation frigorifique]* regulator

détendre /detɑ̃dʀ/ ► conjug 41 ◄ VT [1] (= *relâcher*) *[+ ressort]* to release; *[+ corde]* to slacken, to loosen; (*Phys*) *[+ gaz]* to release the pressure of; *[+ corps, esprit]* to relax ◆ **~ ses jambes** to unbend one's legs ◆ **je vais me ~ les jambes** I'm going to stretch my legs

[2] (= *décontracter*) **ces vacances m'ont détendu** this holiday has relaxed me ◆ **pour ~ un peu ses nerfs** to calm *ou* soothe his nerves a little ◆ **pour ~ la situation/les relations** to relieve *ou* ease the situation/the tension in relations ◆ **il n'arrivait pas à ~ l'atmosphère** he couldn't ease the strained *ou* tense atmosphere ◆ **~ le climat social** to reduce social tensions

VPR **se détendre** [1] *[ressort]* to lose its tension; *[corde]* to become slack, to slacken; (*Phys*) *[gaz]* to be reduced in pressure

[2] *[visage, esprit, corps]* to relax; *[nerfs]* to calm down; *[atmosphère]* to become less tense ◆ **aller à la campagne pour se ~** to go to the country to relax *ou* to unwind ◆ **détendez-vous !** relax! ◆ **la situation internationale s'est détendue** the international situation has grown less tense *ou* has relaxed ◆ **pour que leurs rapports se détendent** to make their relations less strained

détendu, e /detɑ̃dy/ (ptp de **détendre**) ADJ *[personne, visage, atmosphère]* relaxed; *[câble]* slack; *[ressort]* unextended

détenir /det(ə)niʀ/ ► conjug 22 ◄ VT [1] *[+ record, grade, titres]* to hold; *[+ secret, objets volés]* to hold, to be in possession of, to have in one's possession; *[+ moyen]* to have (in one's possession) ◆ **~ le pouvoir** to be in power, to have *ou* hold the power ◆ **il détient la clé de l'énigme** he holds the key to the enigma ◆ **il détient 25% du capital de l'entreprise** he holds 25% of the company's capital [2] *[+ prisonnier]* to detain; *[+ otage]* to hold ◆ **il a été détenu dans un camp** he was held prisoner in a camp

détente /detɑ̃t/ NF [1] (= *délassement*) relaxation ◆ **avoir besoin de ~** to need to relax *ou* unwind ◆ **ce voyage a été une (bonne) ~** this trip has been (very) relaxing [2] (= *décrispation*) *[de relations]* easing (*dans* of); ◆ **la ~** (*Pol*) détente [3] (= *élan*) *[de sauteur]* spring; *[de lanceur]* thrust ◆ **ce sauteur a de la ~** *ou* **une bonne ~** this jumper has plenty of spring *ou* a powerful spring ◆ **d'une ~ rapide, il bondit sur sa victime** with a swift bound he leaped upon his victim [4] (= *relâchement*) *[de ressort, arc]* release; *[de corde]* slackening, loosening [5] (*lit, fig* = *gâchette*) trigger; → **dur** [6] (= *dispositif*) *[de pendule]* catch; *[de gaz]* reduction in pressure; *[de moteur à explosion]* expansion

détenteur, -trice /detɑ̃tœʀ, tʀis/ NM,F *[de secret]* keeper; *[de record, objet volé]* holder ◆ **le ~ du titre** the title-holder ◆ **les ~s de titres** the shareholders ◆ **un homme puissant, ~ de bien des secrets d'État** a powerful man, keeper of many state secrets

détention /detɑ̃sjɔ̃/ NF [1] (= *possession*) *[d'armes, drogue, faux passeport]* possession; *[de titres]* holding; (*Jur*) *[de bien]* holding [2] (= *captivité*) detention ◆ **en ~ provisoire** *ou* † **préventive** remanded in custody, on remand ◆ **mettre** *ou* **placer qn en ~ provisoire** to remand in custody, to put on remand ◆ **~ abusive** false imprisonment

détenu, e /det(ə)ny/ (ptp de **détenir**) NM,F prisoner ◆ **~ politique/de droit commun** political/ordinary prisoner ◆ **jeune ~** young offender (*in prison*)

détergent, e /detɛʀʒɑ̃, ɑ̃t/ ADJ, NM detergent

détérioration /deteʀjɔʀasjɔ̃/ NF *[d'objet]* damaging (*de* of) damage (*de* to); *[de matériel, bâtiment, santé, temps]* deterioration (*de* in); *[de relations, situation]* deterioration (*de* in) worsening (*de* in); ◆ **la ~ irréversible des muscles** the progressive wasting of the muscles ◆ **la ~ du niveau de vie** the deterioration *ou* decline in living standards ◆ **la ~ du climat économique** the deterioration in the economic climate

détériorer /deteʀjɔʀe/ ► conjug 1 ◄ VT *[+ objet]* to damage, to spoil; *[+ santé, bâtiment, relations]* to damage VPR **se détériorer** to deteriorate; *[relations, situation, climat économique]* to deteriorate, to worsen

déterminable /detɛʀminabl/ ADJ determinable

déterminant, e /detɛʀminɑ̃, ɑ̃t/ ADJ (= *décisif*) determining (*épith*); (= *prépondérant*) decisive ◆ **la taille est-elle un facteur ~ dans votre secteur ?** is size a determining factor in your line of business? ◆ **la qualité de la direction est l'élément ~ du succès d'une entreprise** the quality of the management is the decisive factor in a company's success ◆ **l'influence ~e d'une enfance perturbée** the decisive influence of a troubled childhood ◆ **ça a été ~** that was the decisive factor **NM** *(Ling)* determiner; *(Math, Bio)* determinant

déterminatif, -ive /detɛʀminatif, iv/ **ADJ** determinative; *[proposition]* defining *(épith)* **NM** determiner, determinative

détermination /detɛʀminasjɔ̃/ **NF** 1 *[de cause, sens]* determining, establishing; *[de date, quantité]* determining, fixing 2 *(= résolution)* decision, resolution 3 *(= fermeté)* determination ◆ **il le regarda avec ~** he looked at him determinedly *ou* with (an air of) determination 4 *(Philos)* determination

déterminé, e /detɛʀmine/ GRAMMAIRE ACTIVE 35.2 (ptp de **déterminer**) **ADJ** 1 *[personne, air]* determined, resolute 2 *(= précis) [but, intentions]* specific, definite; *(= spécifique) [quantité, distance, date]* determined, given *(épith)* 3 *(Philos) [phénomènes]* predetermined **NM** *(Gram)* determinatum

déterminer /detɛʀmine/ ▸ conjug 1 ◂ **VT** 1 *(= préciser) [+ cause, distance, sens d'un mot]* to determine, to establish; *[+ date, lieu, quantité]* to determine, to fix ◆ **~ par des calculs où une météorite va tomber** to calculate *ou* work out where a meteorite will fall 2 *(= décider)* to decide, to determine ◆ **~ qn à faire qch** to decide *ou* determine sb to do sth ◆ **ils se sont déterminés à agir** they have made up their minds *ou* resolved to act 3 *(= motiver) [+ chose]* to determine ◆ **c'est ce qui a déterminé mon choix** that's what decided me ◆ **ceci a déterminé d'importants retards** this brought about *ou* caused long delays 4 *(Gram)* to determine

déterminisme /detɛʀminism/ **NM** determinism

déterministe /detɛʀminist/ **ADJ** determinist(ic) **NMF** determinist

déterré, e /detɛʀe/ (ptp de **déterrer**) **NM,F** *(péj)* ◆ **avoir une tête** *ou* **une mine de ~** to look deathly pale *ou* like death warmed up* *(Brit) ou* warmed over* *(US)*

déterrer /detɛʀe/ ▸ conjug 1 ◂ **VT** *[+ objet enfoui]* to dig up, to unearth; *[+ arbre]* to uproot, to dig up; *[+ mort]* to dig up, to disinter; * *[+ vieil objet, bouquin]* to dig out*, to unearth

détersif, -ive /detɛʀsif, iv/ **ADJ, NM** detergent, detersive

détersion /detɛʀsjɔ̃/ **NF** cleaning

détestable /detɛstabl/ **ADJ** *[personne]* detestable; *[attitude]* appalling, dreadful; *[habitude, caractère]* foul ◆ **leur image de marque est ~** their public image is appalling ◆ **cela a fait une impression ~** it made a dreadful impression

détestablement /detɛstabləmɑ̃/ **ADV** *[jouer, chanter]* appallingly *ou* dreadfully badly

détestation /detɛstasjɔ̃/ **NF** *(littér)* *(= haine)* abhorrence ◆ **avoir de la ~ pour qn/qch** to abhor sb/sth

détester /detɛste/ GRAMMAIRE ACTIVE 34.3 ▸ conjug 1 ◂ **VT** to hate ◆ **il déteste la peinture/le fromage** he hates painting/cheese ◆ **elle déteste attendre/les enfants** she hates *ou* can't stand waiting/children ◆ **il déteste qu'on range son bureau/qu'on l'appelle Michou** he hates *ou* can't stand people tidying his desk/being called Michou ◆ **il ne déteste pas le chocolat** he's partial to chocolate ◆ **il ne déteste pas (de) faire parler de lui** he's not averse to having people talk about him

⚠ Attention à ne pas traduire automatiquement **détester** par **to detest**, qui est d'un registre plus soutenu.

déthéiné, e /deteine/ **ADJ** decaffeinated

détonant, e /detɔnɑ̃, ɑ̃t/ **ADJ** ◆ **cocktail** *ou* **mélange ~** *(lit, fig)* explosive mixture

détonateur /detɔnatœʀ/ **NM** detonator ◆ **être le ~ de** *(fig)* to trigger off

détonation /detɔnasjɔ̃/ **NF** *[de bombe, obus]* detonation, explosion; *[de fusil]* report, bang

détoner /detɔne/ ▸ conjug 1 ◂ **VI** to detonate, to explode

détonner /detɔne/ ▸ conjug 1 ◂ **VI** 1 *[couleurs]* to clash (with each other); *[meuble, bâtiment, personne]* to be out of place ◆ **ses manières vulgaires détonnent dans ce milieu raffiné** his vulgar manners are out of place in this refined milieu 2 *(Mus)* *(= sortir du ton)* to go out of tune; *(= chanter faux)* to sing out of tune

détordre /detɔʀdʀ/ ▸ conjug 41 ◂ **VT** to untwist ◆ **le câble s'est détordu** the cable came untwisted

détortiller /detɔʀtije/ ▸ conjug 1 ◂ **VT** to untwist

détour /detuʀ/ **NM** 1 *(= sinuosité)* bend, curve ◆ **la rivière fait des ~s** the river meanders ◆ **ce sentier est plein de ~s** this path is full of twists and turns, it's a very winding path

◆ **au détour de** ◆ **au ~ du chemin** at the bend in the path ◆ **on devine au ~ d'une phrase …** you begin to guess as you are reading … ◆ **au ~ de la conversation** in the course of the conversation ◆ **des personnes rencontrées au ~ de son enquête** people he met during the course of his investigation

2 *(= déviation)* detour ◆ **faire un ~** to make a detour *(par* via*)*; ◆ **le musée valait le ~** the museum was worth the detour *ou* was worth seeing; → **tour²**

3 *(= moyen indirect)* roundabout means; *(= circonlocution)* circumlocution ◆ **explique-toi sans ~(s)** just say straight out what you mean ◆ **user de longs ~s** *ou* **prendre beaucoup de ~s pour demander qch** to ask for sth in a very roundabout way ◆ **il ne s'embarrasse pas de ~s pour arriver à ses fins** he doesn't shilly-shally when it comes to getting what he wants

détourné, e /detuʀne/ (ptp de **détourner**) **ADJ** *[chemin]* roundabout *(épith)*; *[moyen]* roundabout *(épith)*, indirect; *[reproche]* indirect, oblique ◆ **je l'ai appris de façon ~e** I heard it in a roundabout way *ou* indirectly

détournement /detuʀnəmɑ̃/ **NM** *[de rivière]* diversion, rerouting ◆ **~ d'avion** hijacking, skyjacking* ◆ **~ de fonds** embezzlement, misappropriation of funds ◆ **~ de mineur** corruption of a minor ◆ **~ de pouvoir** abuse of power

détourner /detuʀne/ ▸ conjug 1 ◂ **VT** 1 *(= dévier) [+ route, ruisseau, circulation, convoi]* to divert, to reroute; *[+ bus] [pirate]* to hijack; *[+ avion] [pirate de l'air]* to hijack, to skyjack*; *[+ soupçon]* to divert *(sur* on to*)*; *[+ coup]* to parry, to ward off; *(Sport) [+ ballon, tir au but]* to deflect ◆ **~ l'attention de qn** to divert *ou* distract sb's attention ◆ **~ la conversation** to change the subject ◆ **pour ~ leur colère** to ward off *ou* avert their anger

2 *(= tourner d'un autre côté)* to turn away ◆ **~ les yeux** *ou* **le regard** to look away, to avert one's gaze ◆ **~ la tête** to turn one's head away

3 *(= écarter)* to divert ◆ **~ qn de sa route** *ou* **de son chemin** to divert sb, to take sb out of his way ◆ **si ça ne te détourne pas (de ton chemin) …** *(à un conducteur)* if it's not out of your way … ◆ **~ qn d'un projet/de faire qch** to dissuade sb from a plan/from doing sth, to put sb off a plan/off doing sth ◆ **~ qn de qn** to put sb off sb, to turn sb away from sb ◆ **~ qn du droit chemin** to lead sb astray, to lead sb off the straight and narrow ◆ **~ qn de son devoir** to lead sb away *ou* divert sb from his duty ◆ **pour le ~ de ses soucis** to divert him from his worries, to take his mind off his worries

4 *(= modifier l'objectif de) [+ loi, réglementation]* to twist ◆ **elle a détourné le sens de mes paroles** she twisted my words ◆ **il a su ~ le système à son profit** he managed to work the system to his advantage ◆ **~ un médicament de son usage normal** to use a drug for something it wasn't meant for

5 *(= voler) [+ fonds]* to embezzle, to misappropriate; *[+ marchandises]* to misappropriate

VPR se détourner to turn away *(de* from*)*; ◆ **se ~ de sa route** *(pour aller ailleurs)* to make a detour *ou* diversion; *(par erreur)* to go off the right road ◆ **il s'est détourné de tous ses amis** he has turned away *ou* aside from all his friends ◆ **le public s'est détourné de ce produit** the public have turned their backs on *ou* spurned this product

détracteur, -trice /detʀaktœʀ, tʀis/ **NM,F** critic, detractor *(frm)* **ADJ** disparaging

détraqué, e /detʀake/ (ptp de **détraquer**) **ADJ** *[machine]* broken down; * *[personne]* unhinged, cracked*; *[temps]* unsettled; *[nerfs, santé]* shaky; *[imagination]* unbalanced ◆ **cette horloge est ~e** this clock is on the blink* *ou* is bust* ◆ **il a l'estomac ~** he's got an upset stomach ◆ **avoir le cerveau ~*** to be unhinged *ou* cracked*, to have a screw loose* ◆ **c'est un ~*** he's a headcase*, he's off his head* ◆ **c'est un ~ sexuel** he's a pervert

détraquement /detʀakmɑ̃/ **NM** *[de machine]* breakdown; *[de santé, nerfs]* shakiness; *[d'économie]* shakiness, instability

détraquer /detʀake/ ▸ conjug 1 ◂ **VT** *[+ machine]* to put out of order; *[+ personne] (physiquement)* to put out of sorts; *[+ estomac]* * to upset; *[+ nerfs]* * to shake up, to upset ◆ **ces orages ont détraqué le temps** these storms have unsettled the weather ◆ **ce drame lui a détraqué le cerveau*** *ou* **l'a détraqué*** this tragedy unhinged him *ou* sent him out of his mind* **VPR se détraquer** *[machine]* to go wrong, to break down; *[estomac]* to be upset; *[économie]* to become unstable ◆ **le temps se détraque*** the weather is becoming unsettled ◆ **tout, dans sa vie, s'est soudain détraqué** suddenly everything started going wrong for him

détrempe¹ /detʀɑ̃p/ **NF** *(Peinture)* *(= substance) (gén)* distemper; *(à base d'œuf)* tempera; *(= tableau)* distemper *ou* tempera painting ◆ **peindre en** *ou* **à la ~** to paint in tempera *ou* distemper

détrempe² /detʀɑ̃p/ **NF** *[d'acier]* softening

détremper¹ /detʀɑ̃pe/ ▸ conjug 1 ◂ **VT** *(= délayer) [+ terre, pain]* to soak; *[+ couleurs]* to dilute, to water down; *[+ chaux]* to mix with water, to slake; *[+ mortier]* to mix with water, to temper ◆ **chemins détrempés** sodden *ou* waterlogged paths ◆ **ma chemise est détrempée** my shirt is soaking (wet) *ou* soaked

détremper² /detʀɑ̃pe/ ▸ conjug 1 ◂ **VT** *[+ acier]* to soften

détresse /detʀɛs/ **NF** 1 *(= sentiment)* distress ◆ **son cœur en ~** his anguished heart 2 *(= situation)* distress ◆ **être dans la ~** to be in distress ◆ **bateau/avion en ~** boat/plane in distress ◆ **entreprise en ~** business in dire straits ◆ **envoyer un appel/un signal de ~** to send out a distress call/signal; → **feu¹**

détricotage /detʀikɔtaʒ/ **NM** *(= démantèlement)* dismantling

détricoter /detʀikɔte/ ▸ conjug 1 ◂ **VT** *[+ pull, manche]* to unpick

détriment /detʀimɑ̃/ **au détriment de LOC PRÉP** to the detriment of

détritique /detʀitik/ ADJ *[roche]* detrital

détritivore /detʀitivɔʀ/ ADJ *[bactérie, insecte]* detritivorous

détritus /detʀity(s)/ NMPL litter *(NonC)*, rubbish *(NonC) (Brit)*; *(Méd)* detritus *(NonC)*

détroit /detʀwa/ NM *(Géog)* strait ◆ **le ~ de Gibraltar/du Bosphore** the Strait of Gibraltar/of the Bosphorus ◆ **le ~ de Magellan** the Magellan Strait

détromper /detʀɔ̃pe/ ▸ conjug 1 ◂ VT *[+ personne]* to disabuse *(de* of); ◆ **je croyais à cette histoire mais son frère m'a détrompé** I believed that story but his brother put me right VPR **se détromper** ◆ **détrompez-vous, il n'est pas venu** you're quite mistaken, he didn't come ◆ **si tu crois que je vais accepter, détrompe-toi !** if you think I'm going to accept you'll have to think again!

détrôner /detʀone/ ▸ conjug 1 ◂ VT *[+ souverain]* to dethrone, to depose; *(= supplanter) [+ champion]* to oust, to dethrone; *[+ mode, produit]* to supplant

détrousser /detʀuse/ ▸ conjug 1 ◂ VT *(† ou hum)* ◆ **~ qn** to rob sb

détrousseur /detʀusœʀ/ NM *(† ou hum)* robber

détruire /detʀɥiʀ/ ▸ conjug 38 ◂ VT 1 *(= ravager)* to destroy ◆ **un incendie a détruit l'hôtel** the hotel was destroyed by fire ◆ **la ville a été complètement détruite** the town was wiped out *ou* razed to the ground *ou* completely destroyed ◆ **cet enfant détruit tout** this child wrecks *ou* ruins everything *ou* smashes everything up ◆ **la tempête a détruit les récoltes** the storm has ruined the crops

2 *(= tuer) [+ animaux, insectes]* to destroy, to exterminate; *[+ armée]* to wipe out

3 *(= ruiner) [+ empire]* to destroy; *[+ santé, réputation]* to ruin, to wreck; *[+ sentiment]* to destroy, to kill; *[+ espoir, théorie, projet]* to ruin, to wreck, to put paid to *(Brit)* ◆ **cela détruit tous ses beaux arguments** that destroys *ou* puts paid to *(Brit)* all his fine arguments

VPR **se détruire** 1 *(soi-même)* **il a essayé de se ~** he tried to do away with himself

2 *(mutuellement) [personnes]* to destroy one another ◆ **les effets se détruisent** the effects cancel each other out

dette /dɛt/ NF 1 *(Fin)* debt ◆ **avoir des ~s** to be in debt, to have debts ◆ **faire des ~s** to get into debt, to run up debts ◆ **avoir 2 000 € de ~s** to be €2,000 in debt, to be in debt to the tune of €2,000 ◆ **~ de jeu, ~ d'honneur** a gambling *ou* gaming debt is a debt of honour ◆ **la ~ publique** *ou* **de l'État/extérieure** the national/foreign debt; → **reconnaissance** 2 *(morale)* debt ◆ **~ d'amitié/de reconnaissance** debt of friendship/gratitude ◆ **je suis en ~ envers vous** I am indebted to you ◆ **il a payé sa ~ envers la société** he has paid his debt to society ◆ **j'ai une ~ de reconnaissance envers vous** I am eternally grateful to you

DEUG /døg/ NM (abrév de **diplôme d'études universitaires générales**) → **diplôme**

DEUG, DEUST

French students sit their **DEUG** or their **DEUST** after two years of university study. Students can leave university after the **DEUG** or **DEUST**, which may be awarded with distinction, or proceed to the « licence ». The certificate obtained specifies the principal subject area studied. → DIPLÔMES

deuil /dœj/ NM 1 *(= perte)* bereavement ◆ **il a eu un ~ récemment** he was recently bereaved, he recently suffered a bereavement *(frm)*, there has recently been a death in his family

2 *(= affliction)* mourning *(NonC)*, grief ◆ **cela nous a plongés dans le ~** it has plunged us into mourning *ou* grief ◆ **si nous pouvons vous réconforter dans votre ~** if we can comfort you in your grief *ou* sorrow ◆ **décréter un ~ national de trois jours** to declare three days of national mourning

3 *(= vêtements)* mourning (clothes) ◆ **quitter le ~** to come out of mourning ◆ **prendre/porter le ~ d'un ami** to go into/be in mourning for a friend ◆ **porter le ~ de ses espoirs/illusions** to grieve for one's lost hopes/illusions

4 *(= durée)* mourning ◆ **le ~ du président dura un mois** the mourning for the president lasted a month

5 *(= cortège)* funeral procession ◆ **conduire** *ou* **mener le ~** to head the funeral procession, to be (the) chief mourner

◆ **en + deuil** ◆ **être/se mettre en ~** to be in/go into mourning ◆ **en grand ~** in deep mourning

◆ **faire son deuil de qch** to kiss sth goodbye*, to say goodbye to sth* ◆ **il n'arrive pas à faire le ~ de cette relation** he hasn't come to terms with the fact that they have split up ◆ **les vacances sont annulées, j'en ai fait mon ~** the holidays have been cancelled but I'm resigned to it *ou* it's no use crying about it

deus ex machina /deusɛksmakina/ NM deus ex machina

deusio * /døzjo/ ADV secondly

DEUST /døst/ NM (abrév de **diplôme d'études universitaires scientifiques et techniques**) → **diplôme**

deutérium /døteʀjɔm/ NM deuterium

Deutéronome /døteʀɔnɔm/ NM Deuteronomy

deux /dø/ ADJ INV 1 *(= nombre)* two ◆ **les ~ yeux/mains** *etc* both eyes/hands *etc* ◆ **ses ~ jambes** both his legs, his two legs ◆ **montrez-moi les ~** show me both (of them) *ou* the two of them ◆ **~ fois** twice, two times *(US)* ◆ **il ne peut être en ~ endroits/aux ~ endroits à la fois** he can't be in two places/in both places at once ◆ **je les ai vus tous (les) ~** I saw them both, I saw both of them, I saw the two of them ◆ **inflation à ~ chiffres** double-figure *ou* two-figure inflation ◆ **des ~ côtés de la rue** on both sides *ou* on either side of the street ◆ **tous les ~ jours/mois** every other *ou* every second day/month, every two days/months ◆ **habiter** *ou* **vivre à ~** to live together *ou* as a couple ◆ **~ t/l** *(gén)* two t's/l's; *(en épelant)* double t/l

2 *(= quelques)* a couple, a few ◆ **c'est à ~ pas/à ~ minutes d'ici** it's only a short distance/just a few minutes from here, it's only a stone's throw/only a couple of minutes from here ◆ **pouvez-vous attendre ~ (ou trois) minutes ?** could you wait two (or three) minutes? *ou* a couple of minutes? ◆ **vous y serez en ~ secondes** you'll be there in no time (at all) ◆ **j'ai ~ mots à vous dire** I want to have a word with you

3 *(= deuxième)* second ◆ **volume/acte ~** volume/act two ◆ **le ~ janvier** the second of January ◆ **Jacques II** James the Second; *pour autres loc voir* **six**

4 *(Mus)* **mesure à ~-~/à ~-quatre/à ~-huit** two-two/two-four/two-eight time

5 *(locutions)* **un homme entre ~ âges** a middle-aged man ◆ **pris entre ~ feux** caught in the crossfire ◆ **faire** *ou* **avoir ~ poids ~ mesures** to have double standards *ou* two sets of rules ◆ **être assis** *ou* **avoir le cul*** **entre ~ chaises** to be caught between two stools ◆ **~ précautions valent mieux qu'une** *(Prov)* better safe than sorry *(Prov)* ◆ **~ avis valent mieux qu'un** two heads are better than one *(Prov)* ◆ **en ~ temps, trois mouvements il l'a réparé*** he repaired it in no time *ou* before you could say Jack Robinson* *(hum)* ◆ **il ne reste pas les ~ pieds dans le même sabot** he doesn't just sit back and wait for things to happen

◆ **ça fait deux** ◆ **lui et les maths, ça fait ~ !*** he hasn't got a clue about maths ◆ **lui et la tendresse, ça fait ~ !*** he doesn't know the meaning of tenderness ◆ **essayer et réussir, ça fait ~** to try is one thing but to succeed is another thing altogether, to try and to succeed are two (entirely) different things

NM INV *(= chiffre)* two ◆ **le ~** *(Cartes, Dés)* the two, the deuce ◆ **couper en ~** to cut in two *ou* in half ◆ **marcher ~ par ~** *ou* **à ~** to walk two by two *ou* in pairs *ou* two abreast ◆ **à nous ~** *(= parlons sérieusement)* let's talk; *(= je m'occupe de vous)* I'm all yours; *(à un ennemi)* now let's fight it out!; *(à un appareil à réparer)* now let's see what we can do with you, now let's get you fixed ◆ **quand il y en a pour ~, il y en a pour trois** there's always enough to go around ◆ **il cuisine comme pas ~*** he's a hell of a cook* ◆ **elle est rapide comme pas ~*** she's damn quick* ◆ **quel bricoleur/gardien de but de mes ~ !**** what a crap** *ou* lousy* handyman/goalie!; *pour autres loc voir* **six** *et* **moins, pas**[1]

deuxième /døzjɛm/ ADJ, NMF second; *pour loc voir* **sixième** COMP **le Deuxième Bureau** *(Admin)* the intelligence branch *ou* service

deuxièmement /døzjɛmmɑ̃/ GRAMMAIRE ACTIVE 53.5 ADV second(ly)

deux-mâts /døma/ NM INV *(Naut)* two-master

deux-pièces /døpjɛs/ NM INV 1 *(= ensemble)* two-piece suit; *(= maillot)* two-piece (swimsuit) 2 *(= appartement)* two-room flat *(Brit) ou* apartment *(US)* ◆ **"à louer : deux-pièces cuisine"** "for rent: two-room flat with separate kitchen"

deux-points /døpwɛ̃/ NM INV colon

deux-ponts /døpɔ̃/ ADJ, NM INV *(= bateau)* two-decker; *(= avion)* double-decker

deux-roues /døʀu/ NM INV two-wheeled vehicle ◆ **~ motorisé** motorcycle

deux-temps /døtɑ̃/ ADJ INV *[moteur]* two-stroke NM INV *(= moteur)* two-stroke (engine); *(Mus)* half-common time

deuzio * /døzjo/ ADV secondly

dévaler /devale/ ▸ conjug 1 ◂ VT *(en courant)* to tear down, to hurtle down; *(en tombant)* to tumble down ◆ **il dévala les escaliers quatre à quatre** he tore *ou* hurtled down the stairs four at a time, he came tearing *ou* hurtling down the stairs four at a time VI *[rochers]* to hurtle down; *[lave]* to rush down, to gush down; *[terrain]* to fall away sharply ◆ **il a dévalé dans les escaliers et s'est cassé le bras** he tumbled down the stairs and broke his arm

dévaliser /devalize/ ▸ conjug 1 ◂ VT *[+ maison]* to burgle, to burglarize *(US)*; *[+ banque]* to rob ◆ **~ qn** to strip sb of what he has on him ◆ **~ un magasin** *[voleurs]* to burgle *ou* burglarize *(US)* a shop; *[clients]* to buy up a shop ◆ **~ le réfrigérateur** to raid the fridge

dévalorisant, e /devalɔʀizɑ̃, ɑ̃t/ ADJ *[emploi, tâche]* demeaning ◆ **cette expérience a été très ~e pour lui** this experience was very damaging to his sense of self-worth

dévalorisation /devalɔʀizasjɔ̃/ NF depreciation

dévaloriser /devalɔʀize/ ▸ conjug 1 ◂ VT *[+ marchandises, collection]* to reduce the value of; *[+ monnaie, diplôme]* to undermine the value of ◆ **son patron le dévalorise sans cesse** his boss is forever running *ou* putting him down ◆ **ce type de publicité dévalorise les femmes** this type of advertising degrades women ◆ **cette situation le dévalorise aux yeux de sa famille** this situation undermines his standing *ou* status in the eyes of his family VPR **se dévaloriser** *[monnaie, marchandise]* to fall in value, to depreciate; *[personne]* to run o.s. down ◆ **ce métier s'est dévalorisé** this profession has lost its prestige

dévaluation / devalɥasjɔ̃ / **NF** devaluation

dévaluer / devalɥe / ▸ conjug 1 ◂ **VT** *[+ monnaie, métier, diplôme]* to devalue, to devaluate *(US)*; *[+ rôle, statut]* to undermine **VPR** **se dévaluer** *[monnaie]* to devalue, to be devalued, to fall in value

devancement / d(ə)vɑ̃smɑ̃ / **NM** ◆ ~ **d'une échéance** payment in advance *ou* before time ◆ ~ **d'appel** *(Mil)* enlistment before call-up

devancer / d(ə)vɑ̃se / ▸ conjug 3 ◂ **VT** [1] *(= distancer) [+ coureur]* to get ahead of, to get in front of; *[+ concurrent, rival]* to get ahead of, to forestall ◆ **il m'a devancé de 3 minutes/de 3 points** he beat me by 3 minutes/3 points, he was 3 minutes/3 points ahead of me [2] *(= précéder)* to arrive before, to arrive ahead of ◆ **il m'a devancé au carrefour** he got to the crossroads before me ◆ ~ **son siècle** to be ahead of *ou* in advance of one's time [3] *(= aller au-devant de) [+ question, objection, désir]* to anticipate ◆ **j'allais le faire mais il m'a devancé** I was going to do it but he did it first *ou* got there first [4] *(= faire qch en avance)* ~ **l'appel** *(Mil)* to enlist before call-up ◆ ~ **la date d'un paiement** to make a payment before it is due

devancier, -ière / d(ə)vɑ̃sje, jɛʀ / **NM,F** predecessor

devant / d(ə)vɑ̃ / **PRÉP** [1] *(position = en face de)* in front of, before *(littér)*; *(mouvement = le long de)* past ◆ **ma voiture est ~ la porte** my car is (just) outside *ou* at the door ◆ ~ **nous se dressait un vieux chêne** before us *ou* in front of us stood an old oak tree ◆ **le bateau est ancré ~ le port** the boat is anchored outside the port ◆ **il est passé ~ moi sans me voir** he walked past me *ou* he passed me *ou* he went right by me without seeing me ◆ **elle était assise ~ la fenêtre** she was sitting at *ou* by the window ◆ **il est passé** *ou* **a filé ~ nous comme une flèche** he shot past us (like an arrow), he flashed past us ◆ **va-t-en de ~ la vitrine** move away from (in front of) the window ◆ **va-t-en de ~ la lumière** get out of the *ou* my light

[2] *(= en avant de) (proximité)* in front of; *(distance)* ahead of ◆ **il marchait ~ moi** he was walking in front of *ou* ahead of me ◆ **il est loin ~ nous** he is a long way ahead of us ◆ **regarde ~ toi** look in front of you *ou* straight ahead (of you) ◆ **il est ~ moi en classe** *(banc)* he sits in front of me at school; *(résultats)* he is ahead of me at *ou* in school ◆ **fuir ~ qn** to flee before *ou* from sb ◆ **(droit) ~ nous se dressait la muraille** the wall rose up (straight) in front of *ou* ahead of us ◆ **allez droit ~ vous, vous trouverez le village** go straight on *ou* ahead and you'll come to the village ◆ **aller droit ~ soi (sans s'occuper des autres)** *(fig)* to go straight on (regardless of others) ◆ **passe ~ moi si tu es pressé** you go first *ou* in front of me if you're in a hurry ◆ **elle est passée ~ moi chez le boucher** she pushed (in) in front of me at the butcher's ◆ **avoir du temps/de l'argent ~ soi** to have time/money to spare ◆ **il avait du temps ~ lui** he had time to spare, he had time on his hands ◆ **il a toute la vie ~ lui** he has his whole life ahead of him

[3] *(= en présence de)* before, in front of ◆ **s'incliner ~ qn** to bow before sb ◆ **comparaître ~ ses juges** to appear before one's judges ◆ **ne dis pas cela ~ les enfants/tout le monde** don't say that in front of the children/everyone ◆ **cela s'est passé juste ~ nous** *ou* **nos yeux** it happened before *ou* in front of our very eyes ◆ **imperturbable ~ le malheur d'autrui** unmoved by *ou* in the face of other people's misfortune ◆ **reculer ~ ses responsabilités** to shrink from one's responsibilities ◆ **par-~ notaire/Maître Durand** *(Jur)* in the presence of a notary/Maître Durand

[4] *(= face à)* faced with, in the face of; *(= étant donné)* in view of, considering ◆ ~ **la gravité de la situation** in view of *ou* considering the gravity of the situation ◆ **rester ferme ~ le danger** to stand fast in the face of danger ◆ **il ne sut quelle attitude prendre ~ ces faits** he did not know what line to adopt when faced *ou* confronted with these facts ◆ **tous égaux ~ la loi** everyone (is) equal in the eyes of the law

ADV [1] *(position)* in front ◆ **vous êtes juste ~** you're right in front of it ◆ **vous êtes passé ~** you came past *ou* by it ◆ **je suis garé juste ~** I'm parked just out at the front *ou* just outside ◆ **en passant ~, regarde si la boutique est ouverte** see if the shop is open as you go past ◆ **corsage qui se boutonne (par-)~** blouse which buttons up *ou* does up at the front ◆ **tu as mis ton pull ~ derrière** you've put your sweater on back-to-front *(Brit) ou* backwards *(US)* ◆ **entre par-~, la grille du jardin est fermé** go in the front, the garden gate is locked

[2] *(= en avant)* ahead, in front ◆ **il est parti ~** he went on ahead *ou* in advance ◆ **il est loin ~** he's a long way ahead ◆ **attention, obstacle (droit) ~ !** *(Naut)* stand by, hazard ahead! ◆ **il est assis 3 rangs ~** he's sitting 3 rows in front (of us) ◆ **fais passer le plateau ~** pass the tray forward ◆ **il a pris des places ~** he has got front seats *ou* seats at the front *ou* up front* ◆ **il a préféré monter ~** *(en voiture)* he preferred to sit in (the) front ◆ **marchez ~, les enfants** walk in front, children ◆ **passe ~, je te rejoindrai** go on ahead and I'll catch up with you ◆ **passe ~, il roule trop lentement** go past him *ou* overtake him *(Brit)*, he's going too slowly ◆ **passez ~, je ne suis pas pressé** after you *ou* you go first *ou* you go in front of me, I'm in no hurry

NM *[de maison, voiture, objet]* front; *[de bateau]* fore, bow(s) ◆ **habiter sur le ~** to live at the front (of the house *etc*) ◆ **de ~** *[roue, porte]* front

◆ **au-devant** ◆ **je l'ai vu de loin et je suis allé au-~ de lui** I saw him in the distance and went (out) to meet him ◆ **aller au-~ des désirs de qn** to anticipate sb's wishes ◆ **courir au-~ du danger** to court danger ◆ **aller au-~ des ennuis** *ou* **difficultés** to be asking for trouble ◆ **nous avons bien assez de problèmes sans aller au-~** we've got enough problems as it is without asking for more

◆ **prendre les devants** ◆ **voyant qu'il hésitait, j'ai pris les ~s pour lui parler** as he was hesitating I made the first move *ou* took the initiative and spoke to him ◆ **nous étions plusieurs sur cette affaire, j'ai dû prendre les ~s en offrant un contrat plus intéressant** there were several of us after the job so I had to pre-empt *ou* forestall the others and offer a more competitive contract ◆ **prendre les ~s en attaquant** *(Mil)* to launch a pre-emptive strike *ou* attack

devanture / d(ə)vɑ̃tyʀ / **NF** [1] *(= étalage)* display; *(= vitrine)* shop *ou* store *(US)* window ◆ **à la** *ou* **en ~** on display; *(dans la vitrine)* in the window [2] *(= façade)* (shop *ou* store) front

dévastateur, -trice / devastatœʀ, tʀis / **ADJ** *[torrent, orage]* devastating; *[passion]* destructive

dévastation / devastasjɔ̃ / **NF** devastation ◆ **les ~s de la guerre/de la tempête** the ravages of war/the storm, the devastation *ou* havoc wreaked by war/the storm

dévasté, e / devaste / (ptp de **dévaster**) **ADJ** *[pays, ville, cultures]* devastated; *[maison]* ruined; *[visage]* ravaged

dévaster / devaste / ▸ conjug 1 ◂ **VT** *[+ pays, ville, cultures]* to devastate, to lay waste; *[+ esprit, cœur]* to devastate, to ravage

déveine* / devɛn / **NF** rotten luck* ◆ **être dans la ~** to be down on one's luck *ou* out of luck ◆ **avoir la ~ de** to have the rotten luck to* ◆ **quelle ~ !** what rotten luck!*

développable / dev(ə)lɔpabl / **ADJ** *(gén, Géom)* developable

développé, e / dev(ə)lɔpe / (ptp de **développer**) **ADJ** *[pays]* developed; *[sens, intuition, musculature]* well-developed ◆ **bien/peu ~** well-developed/underdeveloped ◆ **sens olfactif très ~** highly developed sense of smell **NM** *(Haltérophilie)* press; *(Danse)* développé

développement / dev(ə)lɔpmɑ̃ / **NM** [1] *(= croissance) [d'intelligence, corps, science, maladie]* development; *[d'économie, affaire, commerce, région]* development, expansion, growth; *[de chômage]* growth ◆ **une affaire en plein ~** a fast-expanding *ou* fast-developing business ◆ **l'entreprise a connu un ~ important** the firm has expanded *ou* developed greatly *ou* has undergone a sizeable expansion ◆ **la crise a connu un ~ inattendu** the crisis has taken an unexpected turn, there has been an unexpected development in the crisis ◆ **principe du ~ durable** *(Écol)* principle of sustainable development; → **pays¹**

[2] *(= prolongement)* ◆ **~s** *[d'affaire, enquête]* developments ◆ **cette affaire pourrait connaître de nouveaux ~s** there could be some new developments in this affair

[3] *[de sujet]* exposition; *(Mus) [de thème]* development ◆ **entrer dans des ~s inutiles** to go into unnecessary details, to develop the subject unnecessarily

[4] *(= mise au point)* development ◆ **on évalue le ~ de ce missile à 1 milliard d'euros** it is estimated that it will cost 1 billion euros to develop this missile

[5] *(Photo)* developing, development, processing ◆ **appareil/photo à ~ instantané** instant camera/photograph

[6] *(Cyclisme)* **choisir un grand/petit ~** to choose a high/low gear

[7] *(Géom) [de solide]* development; *(Algèbre) [de fonction]* development; *[d'expression algébrique]* simplification

développer / dev(ə)lɔpe / GRAMMAIRE ACTIVE 53.2 ▸ conjug 1 ◂

VT [1] *[+ corps, muscle, intelligence, stratégie]* to develop; *[+ commerce, industrie]* to develop, to expand ◆ ~ **le goût de l'aventure chez les enfants** to bring out *ou* develop adventurousness in children ◆ **il faut ~ les échanges entre les pays** exchanges between countries must be developed

[2] *[+ récit, argument, projet]* to develop, to enlarge (up)on, to elaborate upon ◆ **il faut ~ ce paragraphe** this paragraph needs developing *ou* expanding

[3] *(Photo) [+ film]* to develop ◆ **envoyer une pellicule à ~** to send a film to be developed *ou* processed

[4] *(Méd) [+ maladie]* to develop

[5] *(= déballer) [+ paquet]* to unwrap

[6] *(= déployer) [+ parchemin]* to unroll; *[+ coupon]* to unfold; *[+ armée, troupes]* to deploy

[7] *(Math) [+ solide, fonction, série]* to develop; *[+ expression algébrique]* to simplify

[8] ◆ **vélo qui développe 6 mètres** bicycle which moves forward 6 metres for every complete revolution of the pedal

VPR **se développer** [1] *[personne, intelligence, plante]* to develop, to grow; *[entreprise]* to expand, to develop, to grow; *[pays, région]* to develop [2] *[armée]* to spread out [3] *[habitude]* to spread [4] *[maladie, symptôme]* to develop

développeur / dev(ə)lɔpœʀ / **NM** *(Photo, Ordin)* developer

devenir / dəv(ə)niʀ / ▸ conjug 22 ◂ **VI** [1] *(= passer d'un état à un autre)* to become ◆ ~ **capitaine/médecin** to become a captain/a doctor ◆ **cet enfant maladif est devenu un homme solide**

that sickly child has turned out *ou* turned into *ou* has become a strong man ◆ **il est devenu tout rouge** he turned *ou* went quite red ◆ **il devient de plus en plus agressif** he's becoming *ou* growing *ou* getting more and more aggressive ◆ ~ **vieux/grand** to grow *ou* get old/tall ◆ **arrête, tu deviens grossier** stop it, you're starting to be rude ◆ **c'est à ~ fou !** it's enough to drive you mad!

2 *(pour demander des nouvelles)* ◆ **bonjour, que devenez-vous?** * hullo, how are you doing * *ou* getting on? *(Brit)* ◆ **et Chantal, qu'est-ce qu'elle devient ?** how's Chantal these days? ◆ **qu'étais-tu devenu ? nous te cherchions partout** where were you ? we were looking for you everywhere ◆ **que sont devenues mes lunettes ?** where have my glasses gone *ou* got to? *(Brit)* ◆ **que sont devenus tes grands projets ?** what has become of your great plans? ◆ **que deviendrais-je sans toi ?** what(ever) would I do *ou* what(ever) would become of me without you? ◆ **qu'allons-nous ~ ?** what is going to happen to us?, what will become of us?

NM *(= progression)* evolution; *(= futur)* future ◆ **quel est le ~ de l'homme ?** what is man's destiny? ◆ **en ~** constantly evolving

déverbal (pl **-aux**) /devɛʀbal, o/ NM deverbal *(noun formed from verb)*

dévergondage /devɛʀgɔ̃daʒ/ NM licentious *ou* loose living

dévergondé, e /devɛʀgɔ̃de/ (ptp de **se dévergonder**) ADJ *[femme]* shameless, loose; *[homme]* wild; *[conversation]* licentious, bawdy ◆ **vie ~e** licentious *ou* loose living NM,F ◆ **c'est une ~e** she's a shameless hussy ◆ **c'est un ~** he leads a wild life

dévergonder /devɛʀgɔ̃de/ ▸ conjug 1 ◂ VT *[+ personne]* to debauch VPR **se dévergonder** to run wild, to get into bad ways

déverrouillage /deveʀujaʒ/ NM 1 *[de porte]* unbolting 2 *[de mécanisme, arme à feu]* unlocking

déverrouiller /deveʀuje/ ▸ conjug 1 ◂ VT 1 *[+ porte] (avec un verrou)* to unbolt; *(avec une serrure)* to unlock 2 *[+ mécanisme]* to unlock, to release; *[+ arme à feu]* to release the bolt of; *[+ train d'atterrissage]* to release ◆ **ils déverrouillent la grille des salaires** they are introducing greater flexibility into the salary structure ◆ **pour tenter de ~ le débat** to try and break the deadlock in the debate

devers /dəvɛʀ/ → **par-devers**

dévers /devɛʀ/ NM *[de route]* banking; *[de mur]* slant

déversement /devɛʀsəmɑ̃/ NM *[de liquide]* pouring (out); *[de sable, ordures]* tipping (out); *[de bombes]* unloading ◆ ~ **accidentel de pétrole** oil spill ◆ **le ~ en mer de déchets toxiques** the dumping of toxic waste at sea ◆ **le ~ de produits sur le marché européen** the dumping of goods onto the European market

déverser /devɛʀse/ ▸ conjug 1 ◂ VT 1 *[+ liquide]* to pour (out) ◆ **la rivière déverse ses eaux dans le lac** the river flows into the lake ◆ **une fenêtre ouverte déversait des flots de musique** strains of music wafted from an open window

2 *[+ sable, ordures]* to tip (out); *[+ bombes]* to unload ◆ ~ **des produits sur un marché** to dump *ou* unload products onto a market ◆ **le train déversa des milliers de banlieusards** the train disgorged *ou* discharged thousands of commuters ◆ **des tonnes de pommes de terre ont été déversées sur la route** tons of potatoes were dumped on the road

3 *(= épancher)* **il déversa toute sa colère sur moi** he poured out *ou* vented his anger on me ◆ ~ **des injures sur qn** to shower abuse on sb ◆ ~ **sa bile sur qn** to vent one's spleen on sb

VPR **se déverser** to pour (out) ◆ **la rivière se déverse dans le lac** the river flows into the lake ◆ **du trou se déversaient des torrents d'eaux boueuses** torrents of muddy water poured out of the hole ◆ **les produits qui se déversent sur le marché européen** the products being dumped *ou* unloaded onto the European market

déversoir /devɛʀswaʀ/ NM *[de canal]* overflow; *[de réservoir]* spillway, overflow; *(fig)* outlet

dévêtir /devetiʀ/ ▸ conjug 20 ◂ VT *[+ personne, poupée]* to undress ◆ ~ **un enfant** to undress a child, to take a child's clothes off VPR **se dévêtir** to undress, to get undressed, to take one's clothes off

déviance /devjɑ̃s/ NF *(Psych)* deviancy, deviance

déviant, e /devjɑ̃, jɑ̃t/ ADJ *[comportement]* deviant; *[discours, opinion]* dissenting NM,F deviant ◆ ~ **sexuel** sexual deviant

déviation /devjasjɔ̃/ NF 1 *[de circulation]* diversion *(Brit)*, detour *(US)* 2 *(= écart)* deviation ◆ ~ **par rapport à la norme** deviation from the norm ◆ **le parti l'a accusé de ~** he was accused of deviating from the party line ◆ **il n'admettra aucune ~ par rapport à ses objectifs** he will not be deflected from his goals 3 *(Méd) [d'organe]* inversion; *[d'utérus]* displacement; *[de colonne vertébrale]* curvature

> ⚠ **déviation** se traduit par le mot anglais **deviation** uniquement au sens de 'écart'.

déviationnisme /devjasjɔnism/ NM deviationism ◆ **faire du ~ de droite** to veer to the right

déviationniste /devjasjɔnist/ ADJ, NMF deviationist

dévidage /devidaʒ/ NM *(= déroulement) [de pelote, bobine]* unwinding; *(= mise en pelote) [de fil]* reeling

dévider /devide/ ▸ conjug 1 ◂ VT 1 *(= dérouler) [+ pelote, bobine]* to unwind; *[+ cordage, câble]* to unreel ◆ ~ **son chapelet** *(lit)* to tell one's beads ◆ ~ **un chapelet de clichés** to reel off a string of clichés ◆ **elle m'a dévidé tout son chapelet** * she gave me a catalogue of her woes 2 *(= mettre en pelote) [+ fil]* to wind into a ball *ou* skein; *[+ écheveau]* to wind up

dévideur /devidœʀ/ NM, **dévideuse** /devidøz/ NF *[de ruban adhésif]* dispenser

dévidoir /devidwaʀ/ NM *[de fil, tuyau]* reel; *[de câbles]* drum, reel

dévier /devje/ ▸ conjug 7 ◂ VI 1 *[aiguille magnétique]* to deviate; *[ballon, bateau, projectile]* to veer (off course), to turn (off course) ◆ **le ballon a dévié vers la gauche** the ball veered to the left ◆ **le poteau a fait ~ le ballon** the post deflected the ball ◆ **le vent nous a fait ~ (de notre route)** the wind blew us off course *ou* made us veer off course ◆ **nous avons dévié par rapport à notre route** we've gone off course, we're off course

2 *(fig) [doctrine]* to alter; *[conversation]* to turn *(sur* (on)to); ◆ **voyant que la conversation déviait dangereusement** seeing that the conversation was taking a dangerous turn ◆ **il fit ~ la conversation vers des sujets plus neutres** he turned *ou* diverted the conversation onto more neutral subjects ◆ **nous avons dévié par rapport au projet initial** we have moved away *ou* departed from the original plan ◆ **on m'accuse de ~ de ma ligne politique** I'm accused of straying from my political principles ◆ **rien ne me fera ~ de mes principes** nothing will turn me away from my principles

VT *[+ route, circulation]* to divert *(Brit)*, to detour *(US)*; *[+ projectile, coup]* to deflect, to divert ◆ **avoir la colonne vertébrale déviée** to have curvature of the spine

devin, devineresse /dəvɛ̃, dəvin(ə)ʀɛs/ NM,F soothsayer, seer ◆ **je ne suis pas ~** * I don't have second sight, I can't see into the future

devinable /d(ə)vinabl/ ADJ *[résultat]* foreseeable; *[énigme]* solvable; *[secret, raison]* that can be guessed, guessable

deviner /d(ə)vine/ ▸ conjug 1 ◂ VT 1 *[+ secret, raison]* to guess; *[+ énigme]* to solve; *[+ avenir]* to foresee, to foretell ◆ **devine pourquoi/qui** guess why/who ◆ **vous ne devinez pas ?** can't you guess? ◆ **tu devines le reste** you can imagine the rest ◆ ~ **qn** to read sb's mind ◆ **je crois ~ où il veut en venir** I think I know *ou* I think I can guess what he's getting at ◆ **rien ne laissait ~ leur liaison** nothing hinted that they were having an affair

2 *(= apercevoir)* to make out ◆ **je devinais son sourire dans la pénombre** I could make out his smile in the darkness ◆ **sa robe laissait ~ son corps souple** you could make out the contours of her lithe body through her dress ◆ **une silhouette se devinait à la place du conducteur** you could just make out a figure in the driver's seat ◆ **ses véritables sentiments se devinaient derrière son apparente indifférence** his true feelings showed through his apparent indifference

devineresse /dəvin(ə)ʀɛs/ NF → **devin**

devinette /d(ə)vinɛt/ NF riddle, conundrum ◆ **poser une ~ à qn** to ask *ou* set sb a riddle ◆ **jouer aux ~s** *(lit)* to play at riddles ◆ **arrête de jouer aux ~s** * stop playing guessing games *ou* talking in riddles

déviriliser /deviʀilize/ ▸ conjug 1 ◂ VT ◆ ~ **qn** to emasculate sb

devis /d(ə)vi/ NM estimate, quotation, quote ◆ ~ **descriptif/estimatif** detailed/preliminary estimate ◆ **faire faire des réparations sur ~** to have repairs carried out on the basis of an estimate ◆ **il a établi un ~ de 3 000 €** he drew up *ou* made out an estimate for €3,000

dévisager /devizaʒe/ ▸ conjug 3 ◂ VT to stare at, to look hard at

devise /dəviz/ NF 1 *(= monnaie)* currency ◆ ~ **forte** hard *ou* strong currency ◆ ~ **faible** soft *ou* weak currency ◆ **~s étrangères** foreign currency ◆ ~ **convertible** convertible currency ◆ **payer en ~s** to pay in foreign currency; → **cours** 2 *[de maison de commerce]* slogan; *[de parti]* motto, slogan ◆ **simplicité est ma ~** simplicity is my motto 3 *(Héraldique) (= formule)* motto; *(= figure emblématique)* device

deviser /dəvize/ ▸ conjug 1 ◂ VI *(littér)* to converse *(de* about, on)

dévissage /devisaʒ/ NM 1 *[de bouchon, couvercle, boulon]* unscrewing, undoing; *[d'ampoule électrique]* unscrewing 2 *[d'alpiniste]* fall

dévisser /devise/ ▸ conjug 1 ◂ VT *[+ bouchon, couvercle, boulon]* to unscrew, to undo; *[+ ampoule électrique]* to unscrew ◆ **se ~ la tête** *ou* **le cou** to crane one's neck VI *[alpiniste]* to fall

de visu /devizy/ LOC ADV ◆ **constater qch ~** to see sth for oneself ◆ **vérifier qch ~** to check sth personally

dévitalisation /devitalizasjɔ̃/ NF ◆ ~ **d'une dent** removal of a nerve from a tooth, devitalization *(SPÉC)* of a tooth

dévitaliser /devitalize/ ▸ conjug 1 ◂ VT *[+ dent]* to remove the nerve from, to devitalize *(SPÉC)*

dévoiement /devwamɑ̃/ NM *(littér) [de personne]* leading astray; *[d'idéal, principe]* corruption ◆ **ils réprouvaient les ~s du régime établi** they condemned the corrupt behaviour of the regime in power ◆ **il voit dans cette expérience un ~ pervers de la science** he regards this experiment as a perverse misuse of science

dévoilement /devwalmɑ̃/ NM 1 *[de statue, plaque commémorative]* unveiling 2 *[d'intentions, secret, vérité, identité, date]* revelation, disclosure; *[de projet]* unveiling, revealing; *[de complot, scandale]* exposure

dévoiler /devwale/ ▸ conjug 1 ◂ VT 1 *[+ statue, plaque commémorative]* to unveil ◆ ~ **ses charmes** *(hum)* to reveal one's charms 2 *[+ intentions, secret, vérité, identité, date]* to reveal, to disclose; *[+ projet]* to unveil, to reveal; *[+ complot, scandale]* to expose, to uncover ◆ ~ **son vrai visage** to show one's true face VPR **se dévoiler** *[femme]* to take off one's veil ◆ **le mystère s'est dévoilé** the mystery has been revealed *ou* unfolded

devoir /d(ə)vwaʀ/
▸ conjug 28 ◂
GRAMMAIRE ACTIVE 28.1, 28.2, 29, 36.3, 37.1, 37.2, 37.4, 41, 42.2

1 VERBE TRANSITIF
2 VERBE AUXILIAIRE
3 VERBE PRONOMINAL
4 NOM MASCULIN
5 NOM MASCULIN PLURIEL

1 - VERBE TRANSITIF

1 [= avoir à payer] *[+ chose, somme d'argent]* to owe ◆ ~ **qch à qn** to owe sb sth ◆ **elle (lui) doit 50 €/2 jours de travail** she owes (him) €50/2 days' work ◆ **il réclame seulement ce qui lui est dû** he is asking only for what he's owed *ou* for what is owing to him

2 [= être redevable de] ~ **qch à qn** to owe sth to sb, to owe sb sth ◆ **c'est à son courage qu'elle doit la vie** she owes her life to his courage, it's thanks to his courage that she's alive ◆ **je dois à mes parents d'avoir réussi** I have my parents to thank for my success, I owe my success to my parents ◆ **c'est à lui que l'on doit cette découverte** we have him to thank for this discovery, it is to him that we owe this discovery [MAIS] **à qui doit-on ce délicieux gâteau?** who do we have to thank for this delicious cake? ◆ **à qui doit-on la découverte du radium?** who discovered radium? ◆ **il ne veut rien ~ à personne** he doesn't want to be indebted to anyone ◆ **sa réussite ne doit rien au hasard** his success has nothing to do with luck

3 [= être tenu à] ~ **(l')obéissance à qn** to owe sb obedience ◆ **les enfants doivent le respect à leurs parents** children ought to respect their parents ◆ **il lui doit bien cela !** it's the least he can do for him! ◆ **avec les honneurs dus à son rang** with honours befitting his rank

2 - VERBE AUXILIAIRE

1 [obligation]

Lorsque **devoir** exprime une obligation, il se traduit généralement par **have to** ou la forme plus familière **have got to** lorsqu'il s'agit de contraintes extérieures ; notez que **have got to** ne s'utilise qu'au présent. Le verbe **must** a généralement une valeur plus impérative ; **must** étant défectif, on utilise **have to** aux temps où il ne se conjugue pas.

◆ **elle doit (absolument) partir ce soir** she (really) has to *ou* she (really) must go tonight, she's (really) got to go tonight ◆ **il avait promis, il devait le faire** he'd promised, so he had to do it ◆ **dois-je lui écrire tout de suite ?** must I *ou* do I have to *ou* have I got to write to him immediately? ◆ **vous ne devez pas entrer sans frapper** you are not to *ou* must not come in without knocking [MAIS] **il a cru ~ accepter** he thought he should accept ◆ **dois-je comprendre par là que ...** am I to understand from this that ...

2 [conseil, suggestion]

Lorsque **devoir** est au conditionnel et qu'il a donc un sens proche du conseil, de la suggestion ou qu'il introduit ce qu'il est raisonnable de supposer, il se traduit par **should** ou **ought to.**

◆ **tu devrais t'habiller plus chaudement** you should *ou* ought to dress more warmly ◆ **il aurait dû la prévenir** he should have *ou* ought to have warned her ◆ **il devrait maintenant connaître le chemin** he ought to *ou* should know the way by now

3 [fatalité]

Lorsque **devoir** exprime une fatalité ou le caractère très vraisemblable d'un événement, il se traduit généralement par **have to ou be bound to.**

◆ **nos chemins devaient se croiser un jour ou l'autre** our paths were bound to *ou* had to cross some time ◆ **cela devait arriver !** it was bound to happen!, it (just) had to happen! ◆ **on doit tous mourir un jour** we all have to die some time [MAIS] **les choses semblent ~ s'arranger/empirer** things seem to be sorting themselves out/getting worse

Notez l'emploi de **be to** dans les exemples suivants.

◆ **elle ne devait pas les revoir vivants** she was never to see them alive again ◆ **il devait devenir premier ministre trois mois plus tard** he was to become prime minister three months later

4 [prévision]

Lorsque **devoir** exprime une prévision, il est souvent traduit par **be going to.**

◆ **elle doit vous téléphoner demain** she's going to ring you tomorrow ◆ **il devait acheter une moto mais c'était trop cher** he was going to buy a motorbike but it was too expensive

Notez l'emploi de **be due to** et **be supposed to** dans les contextes où la notion de temps est importante.

◆ **son train doit** *ou* **devrait arriver dans cinq minutes** his train is due to arrive in five minutes ◆ **il devait partir à 6 heures mais ...** he was supposed to be leaving at 6 but ... ◆ **elle doit nous rejoindre ce soir** she's supposed to be joining us this evening ◆ **nous ne devions pas arriver avant 8 heures** we weren't supposed to come before 8

5 [probabilité, hypothèse]

Lorsque **devoir** exprime une probabilité, une hypothèse, il se traduit généralement par **must** dans les phrases affirmatives.

◆ **il doit faire froid ici en hiver** it must be cold here in winter ◆ **vous devez vous tromper** you must be mistaken ◆ **il a dû se tromper** *ou* **il doit s'être trompé de chemin** he must have lost his way ◆ **il devait être 6 heures quand il est sorti** it must have been 6 when he went out

Au conditionnel, on utilise **should** ou **ought to.**

◆ **ça devrait pouvoir se faire** it should be *ou* ought to be feasible ◆ **ça devrait tenir dans le coffre** it should go *ou* ought to go in the boot

Dans les phrases négatives, on utilise généralement **can't.**

◆ **elle ne doit pas être bête, vous savez** she can't be stupid, you know ◆ **il ne devait pas être loin du sommet quand il a abandonné** he can't have been far from the top when he gave up

6 [supposition] **dussé-je** *(frm)* **perdre de l'argent, j'irai jusqu'au procès** I'll go to court even if it means losing money

Notez l'emploi possible de **be to.**

◆ **même s'il devait** *ou* **dût-il** *(littér)* **être condamné, il refuserait de parler** even if he were (to be) found guilty he would refuse to talk

3 - VERBE PRONOMINAL

se devoir

1 [réciproque] **les époux se doivent (mutuellement) fidélité** husband and wife have a duty to be faithful to one another ◆ **nous nous devons la vérité** we owe it to each other to tell the truth

2 [locutions]

◆ **se devoir à qn/qch** ◆ **il se doit à sa famille** he has a duty to his family ◆ **quand on gagne un salaire pareil, on se doit à son métier** when you earn that much, you've got to be committed to your job

◆ **se devoir de** + *infinitif (= être obligé de)* ◆ **nous nous devons de le lui dire** it is our duty *ou* we are duty bound to tell him ◆ **l'ONU se devait de réagir/prendre des sanctions** the UN was duty bound to react/to introduce sanctions ◆ **je me devais de la prévenir** I owed it to myself to warn her ◆ **je me devais d'essayer** I had to try for my own sake ◆ **nos deux pays se doivent de coopérer davantage** our two countries must cooperate more ◆ **nous nous devons de satisfaire nos clients** we must satisfy our customers ◆ **pour être acceptée, la nouvelle procédure se devait d'être simple** the new procedure had to be simple if it was going to be accepted

◆ **comme il se doit/se devait** ◆ **j'en ai informé mon chef, comme il se doit** I informed my boss, of course ◆ **il a convié le ministre, comme il se devait** he invited the minister to attend, as was right and proper ◆ **on a fêté l'événement, comme il se doit** and naturally *ou* of course, we celebrated the event ◆ **le premier tome est consacré, comme il se doit, au Moyen Âge** not surprisingly, the first volume is devoted to the Middle Ages ◆ **comme il se doit en pareil cas, on a procédé à un vote** as is usual in these cases, we put it to a vote ◆ **ils ont été punis comme il se doit** they were duly punished ◆ **et il est arrivé en retard, comme il se doit !** *(hum)* and naturally he arrived late!

4 - NOM MASCULIN

1 [= obligation] duty ◆ **agir par ~** to act from a sense of duty ◆ **un homme de ~** a man of conscience *ou* with a sense of duty ◆ **accomplir** *ou* **faire** *ou* **remplir son ~** to carry out *ou* do one's duty *(envers* towards); ◆ **les ~s du citoyen/d'une charge** the duties of a citizen/a post ◆ **se faire un ~ de faire qch** to make it one's duty to do sth ◆ **il est de mon/ton/son** *etc* **~ de ...** it is my/your/his *etc* duty to ... ◆ **croire de son ~ de faire qch** to think *ou* feel it one's duty to do sth ◆ **~s religieux** religious duties

◆ **se mettre en devoir de** + *infinitif (frm)* ◆ **il se mit en ~ de répondre à la lettre** he proceeded to reply to the letter ◆ **il se mit immédiatement en ~ de le faire** he set about doing it immediately

2 [Scol] *(= dissertation)* essay, paper; *(= exercice) (fait à la maison)* homework *(NonC)*; *(fait en classe)* exercise ◆ **faire ses ~s** to do one's homework ◆ **~s de vacances** holiday homework ◆ **~ (à la) maison** homework *(NonC)* ◆ **~ sur table** *ou* **surveillé** (written) test

5 - NOM MASCULIN PLURIEL

devoirs († *ou hum* = *hommages)* respects ◆ **présenter ses ~s à qn** to pay one's respects to sb

dévoisé, e /devwaze/ ADJ *(Ling)* *[consonne]* devoiced

dévoisement /devwazmɑ̃/ NM *(Ling)* devoicing

dévolter /devɔlte/ ▸ conjug 1 ◂ VT to reduce the voltage of

dévolu, e /devɔly/ ADJ ◆ **être ~ à qn** *[succession, droits]* to be devolved upon *ou* to sb; *[charge]* to be handed down *ou* passed on to sb ◆ **le budget qui a été ~ à la recherche** the funds that have been allotted *ou* granted to research ◆ **la part de gâteau qui m'avait été ~e** the piece of cake that had been allotted to me ◆ **c'est à moi qu'il a été ~ de commencer** it fell to me to start ◆ **le sort qui lui sera ~** the fate that is in store for him NM ◆ **jeter son ~ sur qn/qch** to set one's heart on sb/sth

dévolution /devɔlysjɔ̃/ NF devolution

dévonien, -ienne /devɔnjɛ̃, jɛn/ ADJ Devonian NM ◆ **le ~** the Devonian

dévorant, e /devɔʀɑ̃, ɑ̃t/ ADJ *[faim]* raging *(épith)*; *[curiosité, soif]* burning *(épith)*; *[passion]* devouring *(épith)*, consuming *(épith)*; *(littér)* *[flammes]* all-consuming

dévorer /devɔʀe/ ▸ conjug 1 ◂ VT 1 (= *manger) [fauve]* to devour; *[personne]* to devour, to wolf down* ◆ **des limaces ont dévoré mes laitues** my lettuces have been eaten by slugs ◆ **cet enfant dévore !** this child has a huge appetite! ◆ **on est dévoré par les moustiques !** we're being eaten alive by mosquitoes! ◆ ~ **un livre** to devour a book ◆ ~ **qch à belles dents** to wolf sth down* ◆ ~ **qn/qch du regard** *ou* **des yeux** to eye sb/sth greedily *ou* hungrily ◆ ~ **qn de baisers** to smother sb with kisses ◆ **la barbe qui lui dévorait les joues** the beard that covered his face; → **loup**

2 (= *consumer)* to consume ◆ **le feu dévore le bâtiment** the building is being consumed by fire ◆ **il a dévoré sa fortune** he has consumed his (whole) fortune ◆ **voiture qui dévore les kilomètres** *ou* **la route** car which eats up the miles ◆ **c'est une tâche qui dévore tous mes loisirs** it's a task which takes up *ou* swallows up all my free time

3 *(littér* = *tourmenter) [jalousie, remords, soucis]* to consume, to devour; *[maladie]* to consume ◆ **la soif le dévorait** he had a burning *ou* raging thirst ◆ **être dévoré de remords/jalousie** to be eaten up with *ou* consumed with *ou* devoured by remorse/jealousy ◆ **dévoré par l'ambition** consumed with ambition

4 *(frm* = *cacher)* ~ **ses larmes** to choke back *ou* gulp back one's tears

⚠ Attention à ne pas traduire automatiquement **dévorer** par **to devour**, qui est d'un registre plus soutenu.

dévoreur, -euse /devɔʀœʀ, øz/ NM,F devourer ◆ **un ~ de livres** an avid reader ◆ **ce projet est un gros ~ de crédits** this project eats up money *ou* is a great drain on funds

dévot, e /devo, ɔt/ ADJ *(gén)* devout, pious; *(péj* = *bigot)* sanctimonious, churchy* NM,F *(gén)* deeply religious person; *(péj)* sanctimonious person ◆ **une vieille ~e** *(péj)* a churchy* *ou* sanctimonious old woman; → **faux²**

dévotement /devɔtmɑ̃/ ADV devoutly, piously

dévotion /devosjɔ̃/ NF 1 (= *piété)* devoutness, religious devotion; → **faux²** 2 (= *culte)* devotion ◆ **avoir une ~ pour qn** to worship sb ◆ **être à la ~ de qn** to be totally devoted to sb ◆ **il avait à sa ~ plusieurs employés** he had several totally devoted employees NFPL **dévotions** devotions ◆ **faire ses ~s** to perform one's devotions

dévoué, e /devwe/ (ptp de **se dévouer**) ADJ *[employé]* devoted, dedicated; *[époux, ami]* devoted ◆ **être ~ à qn/qch** to be devoted to sb/sth ◆ **votre ~ serviteur** †† *(formule de lettre)* your devoted servant; → **croire**

dévouement /devumɑ̃/ NM *[de mère, ami, voisin]* devotion; *[d'infirmière, sauveteur, soldat]* devotion, dedication ◆ ~ **à un parti** devotion to a party ◆ **avec ~** devotedly ◆ **avoir un ~ aveugle pour qn** to be blindly devoted to sb ◆ **elle a fait preuve d'un grand ~ pour lui/à leur cause** she showed great devotion to him/to their cause

dévouer (se) /devwe/ ▸ conjug 1 ◂ VPR 1 (= *se sacrifier)* to sacrifice o.s. ◆ **il se dévoue pour les autres** he sacrifices himself for others ◆ **c'est toujours moi qui me dévoue !** it's always me who makes the sacrifices! ◆ **personne ne veut le manger ? bon, je me dévoue** *(hum)* so nobody wants to eat it? all right, I'll be a martyr *(hum)* 2 (= *se consacrer à)* **se ~ à qn/qch** to devote *ou* dedicate o.s. to sb/sth

dévoyé, e /devwaje/ (ptp de **dévoyer**) ADJ *[personne]* depraved ◆ **un nationalisme ~** warped nationalism NM,F corrupt individual ◆ **une bande de jeunes ~s** a gang of young delinquents

dévoyer /devwaje/ ▸ conjug 8 ◂ VT to lead astray VPR **se dévoyer** to go astray

dextérité /dɛksteʀite/ NF skill, dexterity ◆ **avec ~** skilfully, dextrously, with dexterity

dextre /dɛkstʀ/ ADJ *[coquille]* dextral NF (††, *hum)* right hand

dextrine /dɛkstʀin/ NF dextrin(e)

dey /dɛ/ NM dey

dézipper /dezipe/ VT *[+ fichier]* to unzip

dézonage /dezɔnaʒ/ NM *[de DVD]* dezoning

dézoner /dezɔne/ ▸ conjug 1 ◂ VT *[+ DVD]* to dezone

DG /deʒe/ NM (abrév de **directeur général**) CEO NF (abrév de **direction générale**) (= *siège social)* head office; *(de l'UE)* DG

dg (abrév de **décigramme**) dg

DGA /deʒea/ NM (abrév de **directeur général adjoint**) → **directeur** NF (abrév de **Délégation générale pour l'armement**) → **délégation**

DGE /deʒeə/ NF (abrév de **dotation globale d'équipement**) *state contribution to local government budget*

DGI /deʒei/ NF abrév de **Direction générale des impôts**

DGSE /deʒeɛsə/ NF (abrév de **Direction générale de la sécurité extérieure**) ≈ MI6 *(Brit)*, CIA *(US)*

Dhaka /daka/ N Dhaka

dia /dja/ EXCL → **hue**

diabète /djabɛt/ NM diabetes *(sg)* ◆ **avoir du ~** to have diabetes ◆ ~ **insipide/sucré** diabetes insipidus/mellitus ◆ ~ **gras** maturity-onset diabetes ◆ ~ **maigre** insulin-dependent *ou* juvenile-onset diabetes

diabétique /djabetik/ ADJ, NMF diabetic

diabétologie /djabetɔlɔʒi/ NF study of diabetes

diabétologue /djabetɔlɔg/ NMF diabetes specialist

diable /djabl/ NM 1 *(Myth, Rel)* devil ◆ **le ~** the Devil ◆ **s'agiter comme un beau ~** to thrash about like the (very) devil ◆ **j'ai protesté comme un beau ~** I protested for all I was worth *ou* as loudly as I could ◆ **il a le ~ au corps** he's the very devil ◆ **faire le ~ à quatre** † to create the devil* of a rumpus ◆ **que le ~ l'emporte !** the devil take him!* ◆ **le ~ m'emporte si j'y comprends quelque chose !** the devil take me † *ou* the deuce † if I understand any of it!, I'll be damned if I understand it!* ◆ **c'est bien le ~ si on ne trouve pas à les loger** it would be most surprising if we couldn't find anywhere for them to stay ◆ **ce n'est pas le ~** it's not that bad ◆ **(fait) à la ~** (done) any old how ◆ **tirer le ~ par la queue*** to live from hand to mouth, to be on one's uppers *(Brit)* ◆ **se démener comme un ~ dans un bénitier** to be like a cat on a hot tin roof *ou* on hot bricks *(Brit)* ◆ **envoyer qn à tous les ~s** † to tell sb to go to the devil*; → **avocat¹, île**

2 *(dans excl)* **Diable !** † **c'est difficile !** it's dashed *ou* deuced difficult! † ◆ ~ **oui/non !** good gracious yes/no! ◆ **du ~ si je le sais !** the devil take me † *ou* the deuce † if I know! ◆ **allons, du courage que ~ !** cheer up, dash it!* † ◆ **où/quand/qui/pourquoi ~ ... ?** where/when/who/why the blazes* *ou* the devil* ...?

3 *(locutions)*

◆ **au diable** ◆ **être situé/habiter au ~ (vauvert)** to be/live miles from anywhere *ou* at the back of beyond *(Brit)* ◆ **envoyer qn au ~** to tell sb to go to the devil* ◆ **il peut aller au ~ !, qu'il aille au ~ !** he can go to the devil!* ◆ **au ~ l'avarice !** hang the expense! ◆ **au ~ le percepteur !** the devil take the tax collector!*

4 (* = *enfant)* devil, rogue ◆ **pauvre ~*** (= *personne)* poor devil *ou* wretch ◆ **grand ~*** tall fellow ◆ **c'est un bon/ce n'est pas un mauvais ~*** he's a nice/he's not a bad sort* *ou* fellow

5 *(en intensif)* **il fait un froid du ~** *ou* **de tous les ~s** it's fearfully *ou* fiendishly cold ◆ **il faisait un vent du ~** *ou* **de tous les ~s** there was the *ou* a devil* of a wind ◆ **on a eu un mal du ~ à le faire avouer** we had the *ou* a devil* of a job making him own up ◆ **il est menteur en ~** he is a deuced † *ou* damned* liar ◆ **il est courageux/robuste en ~** he is devilishly brave/strong ◆ **ce ~ d'homme** that wretched fellow ◆ **cette ~ d'affaire** this wretched business ◆ **avec ce ~ de temps on ne peut pas sortir** we can't go out in this wretched weather

6 (= *chariot)* hand truck ◆ ~ **(à ressort)** (= *jouet)* jack-in-the-box

7 (= *casserole)* earthenware braising pot

8 *(Culin)* **à la ~** in a piquant sauce, à la diable

diablement* /djɑbləmɑ̃/ ADV (= *très)* darned* ◆ **il y a ~ longtemps que ...** it's a heck* of a long time since ... ◆ **il m'a ~ surpris** he gave me a heck* of a surprise

diablerie /djɑbləʀi/ NF 1 (= *espièglerie)* roguishness; (= *acte)* mischief *(NonC)* ◆ **leurs ~s me feront devenir folle** their mischief will drive me mad 2 (†† = *machination)* machination, evil intrigue 3 (†† = *sorcellerie)* devilry 4 *(Théât) mystery play featuring devils*

diablesse /djɑblɛs/ NF (= *diable femelle)* she-devil; († = *mégère)* shrew, vixen; (* = *bonne femme)* wretched woman ◆ **cette enfant est une vraie ~** that child is a little devil

diablotin /djɑblɔtɛ̃/ NM *(lit, fig)* imp; (= *pétard)* (Christmas) cracker *(Brit)*, favor *(US)*

diabolique /djabɔlik/ ADJ diabolic(al), devilish

diaboliquement /djabɔlikmɑ̃/ ADV diabolically

diabolisation /djabɔlizasjɔ̃/ NF *[d'adversaire, ennemi]* demonization ◆ **la ~ du cannabis** the way cannabis is portrayed as an evil *ou* dangerous drug

diaboliser /djabɔlize/ ▸ conjug 1 ◂ VT *[+ personne, État]* to demonize

diabolo /djabɔlo/ NM (= *jouet)* diabolo ◆ ~ **grenadine/menthe** (= *boisson)* grenadine/mint (cordial) and lemonade

diachronie /djakʀɔni/ NF diachrony

diachronique /djakʀɔnik/ ADJ diachronic

diaclase /djaklɑz/ NF *(Géol)* joint *(in rock)*

diaconal, e (mpl **-aux**) /djakɔnal, o/ ADJ diaconal

diaconat /djakɔna/ NM diaconate

diaconesse /djakɔnɛs/ NF deaconess

diacre /djakʀ/ NM deacon

diacritique /djakʀitik/ ADJ diacritic(al) ◆ **signe ~** diacritic, diacritical mark NM diacritic, diacritical mark

diadème /djadɛm/ NM (*lit, fig = couronne*) diadem; (*= bijou*) tiara

diagnostic /djagnɔstik/ NM [*de médecin, expert*] diagnosis ◆ **~ prénatal** prenatal *ou* antenatal diagnosis ◆ **faire** *ou* **établir** *ou* **poser un ~** to make a diagnosis ◆ **erreur de ~** error in diagnosis ◆ **il a un bon ~** he's a good diagnostician ◆ **le ~ des économistes est pessimiste** the economists' diagnosis *ou* prognosis is pessimistic

diagnostique /djagnɔstik/ ADJ diagnostic

diagnostiquer /djagnɔstike/ ► conjug 1 ◄ VT (*lit, fig*) to diagnose

diagonal, e (mpl **-aux**) /djagɔnal, o/ ADJ diagonal NF **diagonale** diagonal ◆ **couper un tissu dans la ~e** to cut a fabric on the bias *ou* on the cross (*Brit*)

◆ **en diagonale** diagonally, crosswise ◆ **tirer un trait en ~e** to draw a line across the page ◆ **lire** *ou* **parcourir en ~e** to skim through

diagonalement /djagɔnalmɑ̃/ ADV diagonally

diagramme /djagʀam/ NM (*= schéma*) diagram; (*= courbe, graphique*) chart, graph ◆ **~ à barres** *ou* **à bâtons** *ou* **en tuyaux d'orgue** bar chart *ou* graph ◆ **~ sagittal/en arbre** sagittal/tree diagram ◆ **~ en secteurs** pie chart

dialectal, e (mpl **-aux**) /djalɛktal, o/ ADJ dialectal

dialecte /djalɛkt/ NM dialect; (*Helv = suisse allemand*) Swiss German

dialecticien, -ienne /djalɛktisjɛ̃, jɛn/ NM,F dialectician

dialectique /djalɛktik/ ADJ dialectic(al) NF dialectics (*sg*)

dialectiquement /djalɛktikmɑ̃/ ADV dialectically

dialectologie /djalɛktɔlɔʒi/ NF dialectology

dialogue /djalɔg/ NM (*gén*) dialogue, dialog (*US*) ◆ **le ~ social** the dialogue between employers (*ou* government) and trade unions ◆ **c'est un ~ de sourds** it's a dialogue of the deaf ◆ **c'est un ~ de sourds entre le syndicat et la direction** the union and the management are not listening to each other ◆ **sa volonté de ~** his willingness to engage in dialogue ◆ **c'est un homme de ~** he is a man who is open to dialogue *ou* who is prepared to discuss matters ◆ **il faut établir un ~ entre parents et enfants** it's important to get parents and children to talk to each other *ou* to get a dialogue going between parents and children

dialoguer /djalɔge/ ► conjug 1 ◄ VI to have talks, to enter into dialogue (*Brit*) *ou* dialog (*US*) ◆ **~ avec un ordinateur** to interact with a computer ◆ **il veut faire ~ syndicats et patronat** he wants to get unions and employers to enter into dialogue VT [*+ roman*] to put into dialogue (form)

dialoguiste /djalɔgist/ NMF dialogue writer, screen writer

dialyse /djaliz/ NF dialysis ◆ **~ rénale** kidney dialysis ◆ **être en ~** to be on dialysis ◆ **subir une ~** to have dialysis ◆ **patient sous ~** dialysis patient

dialysé, e /djalize/ (ptp de **dialyser**) ADJ ◆ **patient ~** dialysis patient NM,F dialysis patient

dialyser /djalize/ ► conjug 1 ◄ VT to dialyse (*Brit*), to dialyze (*US*)

dialyseur /djalizœʀ/ NM dialyser (*Brit*), dialyzer (*US*)

diam* /djam/ NM (abrév de **diamant**), diamond

diamant /djamɑ̃/ NM (*gén*) diamond ◆ **le ~ noir** (*fig*) the truffle; → **croqueuse**

diamantaire /djamɑ̃tɛʀ/ NM (*= tailleur*) diamond-cutter; (*= vendeur*) diamond merchant

diamanté, e /djamɑ̃te/ ADJ [*outil*] diamond (*épith*); (*littér*) [*eau, lumière*] glittering

diamantifère /djamɑ̃tifɛʀ/ ADJ diamond-bearing, diamantiferous (*SPÉC*)

diamétral, e (mpl **-aux**) /djametʀal, o/ ADJ diametral, diametric(al)

diamétralement /djametʀalmɑ̃/ ADV (*Géom*) diametrally, diametrically ◆ **points de vue ~ opposés** diametrically opposite *ou* opposed views

diamètre /djametʀ/ NM diameter ◆ **10 m de ~** 10 m in diameter

Diane /djan/ NF Diane, Diana ◆ **~ chasseresse** Diana the Huntress

diane /djan/ NF († *Mil*) reveille ◆ **sonner/battre la ~** to sound/beat the reveille

diantre † /djɑ̃tʀ/ EXCL (*aussi hum*) by Jove *ou* gad! ◆ **qui/pourquoi/comment ~ ... ?** who/why/how the deuce *ou* the devil ...?

diantrement /djɑ̃tʀəmɑ̃/ ADV (†, *hum*) devilish †, deuced †

diapason /djapazɔ̃/ NM 1 (*Mus*) (*= registre*) compass, range, diapason; (*= instrument*) (*en métal*) tuning fork, diapason; (*à vent*) pitch pipe, diapason ◆ **~ de Scheibler** tonometer 2 (*fig*) **être au ~ d'une situation** to be in tune with a situation ◆ **se mettre au ~ de qn** to get in tune with sb, to get onto sb's wavelength ◆ **il s'est vite mis au ~** he soon fell *ou* got in step with the others

diaphane /djafan/ ADJ [*tissu, vêtement*] see-through; [*parchemin, porcelaine*] translucent; [*mains*] diaphanous

diaphragme /djafʀagm/ NM [*d'appareil photo*] diaphragm; aperture ◆ **ouvrir de deux ~s** to open two stops

diaphragmer /djafʀagme/ ► conjug 1 ◄ VI (*Photo*) to adjust the aperture

diaphyse /djafiz/ NF (*Anat*) shaft

diapo* /djapo/ NF abrév de **diapositive**

diaporama /djapɔʀama/ NM slide show

diapositive /djapozitiv/ NF slide, transparency (*Brit*) ◆ **passer** *ou* **projeter des ~s** to show slides *ou* transparencies (*Brit*)

diapré, e /djapʀe/ (ptp de **diaprer**) ADJ mottled, variegated

diaprer /djapʀe/ ► conjug 1 ◄ VT (*littér*) to mottle, to variegate

diaprure /djapʀyʀ/ NF (*NonC, littér*) variegation, mottled effect

diarrhée /djaʀe/ NF diarrhoea (*Brit*) (*NonC*), diarrhea (*US*) (*NonC*) ◆ **avoir la ~** *ou* **des ~s** to have diarrhoea (*Brit*) *ou* diarrhea (*US*) ◆ **~ verbale*** (*péj*) verbal diarrhoea*

diarrhéique /djaʀeik/ ADJ diarrh(o)eal, diarrh(o)eic

diarthrose /djaʀtʀoz/ NF (*Anat*) hinge joint ◆ **~ rotatoire** pivot joint

diaspora /djaspɔʀa/ NF (*gén*) diaspora ◆ **la Diaspora (juive)** the (Jewish) Diaspora

diastase /djastɑz/ NF diastase

diastasique /djastɑzik/ ADJ diastatic, diastasic

diastole /djastɔl/ NF diastole

diathermie /djatɛʀmi/ NF diathermy, diathermia

diatomique /diatɔmik/ ADJ diatomic

diatonique /djatɔnik/ ADJ diatonic

diatribe /djatʀib/ NF diatribe ◆ **se lancer dans une longue ~ contre qn** to launch into a long diatribe against sb

dichotomie /dikɔtɔmi/ NF (*Bot, fig*) dichotomy

dichotomique /dikɔtɔmik/ ADJ ◆ **cela perpétue une vision ~ du monde** this perpetuates the view that the world is a dichotomy

dichromatique /dikʀɔmatik/ ADJ dichromatic

dico* /diko/ NM abrév de **dictionnaire**

dicotylédone /dikɔtiledɔn/ ADJ dicotyledonous NF dicotyledon

Dictaphone ® /diktafɔn/ NM Dictaphone ®

dictateur /diktatœʀ/ NM dictator ◆ **ton/allure de ~** dictatorial tone/manner

dictatorial, e (mpl **-iaux**) /diktatɔʀjal, jo/ ADJ dictatorial

dictature /diktatyʀ/ NF dictatorship ◆ **la ~ du prolétariat** dictatorship of the proletariat ◆ **~ militaire** military dictatorship ◆ **sous la ~ de** under the dictatorship of ◆ **c'est de la ~ !** (*fig*) this is tyranny!

dictée /dikte/ NF (*= action*) dictating, dictation; (*= exercice*) dictation ◆ **écrire qch sous la ~** to take down a dictation of sth ◆ **écrire sous la ~ de qn** to take down sb's dictation *ou* what sb dictates ◆ **~ musicale** musical dictation ◆ **les ~s de son cœur** (*littér*) the dictates of his heart

dicter /dikte/ ► conjug 1 ◄ VT [*+ lettre, action*] to dictate ◆ **ils nous ont dicté leurs conditions** they laid down *ou* dictated their conditions to us ◆ **les mesures que nous dicte la situation** the steps that the situation imposes upon us ◆ **il m'a dicté sa volonté** he imposed his will upon me ◆ **sa réponse (lui) est dictée par sa femme/par la peur** his reply was dictated by his wife/by fear ◆ **je n'aime pas qu'on me dicte ce que je dois faire !** I won't be dictated to! ◆ **une paix dictée par l'ennemi** peace on the enemy's terms

diction /diksjɔ̃/ NF (*= débit*) diction; (*= art*) speech ◆ **professeur/leçons de ~** speech lesson/speech teacher

dictionnaire /diksjɔnɛʀ/ NM dictionary ◆ **~ analogique** thesaurus ◆ **~ de langue/de rimes** language/rhyme dictionary ◆ **~ de données** (*Ordin*) data directory *ou* dictionary ◆ **~ électronique** electronic dictionary ◆ **~ encyclopédique/étymologique** encyclopaedic/etymological dictionary ◆ **~ géographique** gazetteer ◆ **~ des synonymes** dictionary of synonyms ◆ **c'est un vrai ~** *ou* **un ~ vivant** he's a walking encyclopaedia

dicton /diktɔ̃/ NM saying, dictum ◆ **il y a un ~ qui dit ...** there's a saying that goes ...

didacticiel /didaktisjɛl/ NM educational software (*NonC*), piece of educational software ◆ **des ~s** educational software

didactique /didaktik/ ADJ 1 (*= destiné à instruire*) [*ouvrage*] educational; [*exposé, style*] didactic ◆ **matériel ~** teaching aids 2 (*= savant*) [*mot, terme*] technical 3 (*Psych*) **psychanalyse ~** training analysis NF didactics (*sg*)

didactiquement /didaktikmɑ̃/ ADV didactically

didactisme /didaktism/ NM didacticism

didascalie /didaskali/ NF (*Théât*) stage direction

Didon /didɔ̃/ NF Dido

dièdre /djɛdʀ/ ADJ [*angle*] dihedral NM dihedron, dihedral; (*Alpinisme*) dièdre, corner

diérèse /djeʀɛz/ NF (*Ling*) di(a)eresis

dièse /djɛz/ NM (*gén*) hash mark *ou* sign; (*Mus*) sharp ◆ **fa/sol ~** F/G sharp

diesel /djezɛl/ NM diesel; (*= moteur*) diesel engine; (*= camion*) diesel lorry (*Brit*) *ou* truck ADJ diesel

diéser /djeze/ ▸ conjug 6 ◂ VT (*Mus*) to sharpen, to make sharp

diète[1] /djɛt/ NF (*Méd*) (*= jeûne*) starvation diet; (*= régime*) diet ◆ **~ lactée/végétale** milk/vegetarian diet ◆ **mettre qn à la ~** to put sb on a starvation diet ◆ **il est à la ~** he has been put on a starvation diet

diète[2] /djɛt/ NF (*Hist*) diet

diététicien, -ienne /djetetisjɛ̃, jɛn/ NM,F dietician, dietitian

diététique /djetetik/ ADJ [*restaurant, magasin*] health-food (*épith*) NF dietetics (*sg*)

dieu (pl **dieux**) /djø/ NM 1 (*= divinité, idole*) god ◆ **les ~x de l'Antiquité** the gods of Antiquity ◆ **le ~ Chronos** the god Chronos

2 (*dans le monothéisme*) **Dieu** God ◆ **le Dieu des chrétiens/musulmans** the God of the Christians/Muslims ◆ **Dieu le père** God the Father ◆ **c'est Dieu le père dans l'entreprise** (*hum*) he's God *ou* he's the big white chief in the company ◆ **une société/génération sans Dieu** a godless society/generation ◆ **le bon Dieu** the good *ou* dear Lord ◆ **donner/recevoir le bon Dieu** to offer/receive the Lord (in Sacrament) ◆ **on lui donnerait le bon Dieu sans confession** he looks as if butter wouldn't melt in his mouth ◆ **faire de qn son ~** to idolize *ou* worship sb, to put sb on a pedestal ◆ **il n'a ni ~ ni maître** he has neither lord nor master; → **âme, homme**

3 (*locutions*) **mon Dieu !** my God!, my goodness! ◆ **(grand) Dieu !, grands Dieux !** good God!, good heavens! ◆ **Dieu qu'il est beau/bête !** he's so good-looking/stupid! ◆ **mon Dieu oui, on pourrait ...** well yes, we could ... ◆ **Dieu vous bénisse !** God bless you! ◆ **que Dieu vous assiste !** may God be with you! ◆ **à Dieu ne plaise !, Dieu m'en garde !** God forbid! ◆ **Dieu vous entende/aide !** may God hear your prayer/help you! ◆ **Dieu seul le sait** God only *ou* alone knows ◆ **Dieu sait s'il est généreux/si nous avons essayé !** God knows he's generous/we've tried! ◆ **Dieu sait pourquoi elle l'a épousé** heaven *ou* God (only) knows why she married him ◆ **Dieu merci, Dieu soit loué !** (*frm*) thank God!, praise the Lord! ◆ **Dieu merci, il n'a pas plu** it didn't rain, thank goodness *ou* thank God *ou* thank heaven(s) ◆ **c'est pas Dieu possible !*** that's just not possible ◆ **à-Dieu-vat !** † (*entreprise risquée*) it's in God's hands; (*départ*) Godspeed ◆ **Dieu m'est témoin que je n'ai jamais ...** as God is my witness I have never ... ◆ **tu vas te taire bon Dieu !**⁑ for Christ's sake⁑ *ou* sakes⁑ (*US*) will you be quiet!; → **amour, grâce, plaire**

diffamant, e /difamɑ̃, ɑ̃t/ ADJ [*propos*] slanderous, defamatory; [*écrits*] libellous, defamatory

diffamateur, -trice /difamatœʀ, tʀis/ ADJ [*propos*] slanderous, defamatory; [*écrit*] libellous, defamatory NM,F slanderer

diffamation /difamasjɔ̃/ NF 1 (*NonC, gén*) defamation (of character); (*en paroles*) slander; (*par écrit*) libel ◆ **campagne de ~** smear campaign ◆ **procès en ~** action for slander (*ou* libel) ◆ **engager des poursuites en ~ contre qn** to sue sb for slander (*ou* libel) ◆ **il a été condamné pour ~ envers X** he was found guilty of slander (*ou* libel) against X *ou* of slandering (*ou* libelling) X 2 (*= propos*) slander (*NonC*); (*= pamphlet*) libel (*NonC*) ◆ **les ~s des journaux** the libellous reports in the newspapers

diffamatoire /difamatwaʀ/ ADJ (*gén*) defamatory; [*propos*] slanderous; [*écrit*] libellous ◆ **avoir un caractère ~** to be slanderous (*ou* libellous)

diffamer /difame/ ▸ conjug 1 ◂ VT (*en paroles*) to slander, to defame; (*par écrit*) to libel, to defame

différé, e /difeʀe/ (ptp de **différer**) ADJ (*TV*) (pre-)recorded NM ◆ **(émission en) ~** (pre-)recorded programme, recording ◆ **le match sera retransmis en ~** the match will be broadcast at a later time

différemment /difeʀamɑ̃/ ADV differently

différence /difeʀɑ̃s/ GRAMMAIRE ACTIVE 32.1, 32.4, 53.5 NF 1 (*gén*) difference ◆ **~ d'opinion** difference of opinion ◆ **~ d'âge/de prix** difference in age/price, age/price difference ◆ **ils ont neuf ans de ~** there are nine years between them ◆ **quelle ~ avec les autres !** what a difference from the others! ◆ **ne pas faire de ~** to make no distinction (*entre* between); ◆ **ils savent faire la ~ entre vérité et mensonge** they can tell the difference *ou* distinguish between truth and falsehood ◆ **c'est son service qui a fait la ~** (*Tennis*) it was his serve that made all the difference ◆ **il fait des ~s entre ses enfants** he doesn't treat all his children in the same way *ou* equally ◆ **tu auras à payer la ~** you will have to make up *ou* pay the difference ◆ **~ de buts** (*Ftbl*) goal difference

2 (*= identité*) **marquer sa ~** to assert one's (*ou* its) distinctive identity ◆ **il fait entendre sa ~ au sein du parti** he voices his dissent in the party

3 (*locutions*) **à la ~ de** unlike ◆ **à la ~** *ou* **à cette ~ que** except (for the fact) that

différenciateur, -trice /difeʀɑ̃sjatœʀ, tʀis/ ADJ differentiating, differential

différenciation /difeʀɑ̃sjasjɔ̃/ NF differentiation

différencié, e /difeʀɑ̃sje/ (ptp de **différencier**) ADJ (*Bio*) [*cellule, tissu*] differentiated; (*Sociol*) [*groupe ethnique*] diverse; (*Scol*) [*enseignement, filières*] specialized

différencier /difeʀɑ̃sje/ GRAMMAIRE ACTIVE 32.1 ▸ conjug 7 ◂ VT to differentiate VPR **se différencier** (*= être différent de*) to differ (*de* from); (*= devenir différent*) to become differentiated (*de* from); (*= se rendre différent*) to differentiate o.s. (*de* from)

différend /difeʀɑ̃/ NM difference of opinion, disagreement; (*Jur, Fin*) controversy ◆ **avoir un ~ avec qn** to have a difference of opinion with sb

différent, e /difeʀɑ̃, ɑ̃t/ GRAMMAIRE ACTIVE 53.3 ADJ 1 (*= dissemblable*) different (*de* from); ◆ **dans des circonstances ~es, je vous aurais aidé** if things had been different *ou* in other *ou* different circumstances, I would have helped you ◆ **chercher des solutions ~es** to try to find alternative *ou* other solutions 2 (*pl, gén avant n*) (*= divers*) different, various ◆ **à ~es reprises** on several different *ou* on various occasions ◆ **à ~es heures de la journée** at different times of the day ◆ **pour ~es raisons** for various *ou* diverse (*frm*) reasons

différentialisme /difeʀɑ̃sjalism/ NM differentialism

différentiation /difeʀɑ̃sjasjɔ̃/ NF (*Math*) differentiation

différentiel, -ielle /difeʀɑ̃sjɛl/ ADJ, NM (*gén*) differential ◆ **~ d'inflation** inflation differential NF **différentielle** differential

différentier /difeʀɑ̃sje/ ▸ conjug 7 ◂ VT (*Math*) to differentiate

différer /difeʀe/ ▸ conjug 6 ◂ VI 1 (*= être dissemblable*) to differ, to be different (*de* from; *en, par* in); ◆ **leur politique ne diffère en rien de celle de leurs prédécesseurs** their policy is no different *ou* is in no way different from their predecessors 2 (*= diverger*) to differ ◆ **elle et moi différons sur** *ou* **en tout** she and I differ about everything 3 (*= varier*) to differ, to vary ◆ **la mode diffère de pays à pays** fashions differ *ou* vary from one country to the next VT [*+ travail*] to postpone, to put off; [*+ jugement, paiement, départ*] to defer, to postpone ◆ **~ une décision** to defer *ou* postpone making *ou* put off making a decision ◆ **à quoi bon ~ plus longtemps ?** why delay any longer? ◆ **~ de** *ou* **à faire qch** (*frm*) to delay *ou* defer *ou* postpone doing sth; → **crédit**

difficile /difisil/ GRAMMAIRE ACTIVE 33.3, 43.4 ADJ 1 (*= ardu*) [*travail, problème*] difficult ◆ **il nous est ~ de prendre une décision tout de suite** it is difficult *ou* hard for us *ou* we find it difficult *ou* hard to make a decision straight away ◆ **il a eu un moment ~ lorsque sa femme est morte** he went through a difficult *ou* hard time when his wife died ◆ **il a trouvé l'expédition ~** he found the expedition hard going *ou* heavy going ◆ **~ à faire** difficult *ou* hard to do ◆ **morceau ~ (à jouer)** *ou* **d'exécution ~** difficult *ou* hard piece to play

2 (*= délicat*) [*position, situation*] difficult, awkward ◆ **ils ont des fins de mois ~s** they have a hard time making ends meet

3 [*personne*] (*= contrariant*) difficult, trying; (*= exigeant*) hard *ou* difficult to please (*attrib*), fussy ◆ **un enfant ~** a difficult *ou* a problem child ◆ **elle a un caractère ~** she's difficult *ou* awkward ◆ **elle est ~ pour ce qui est de** *ou* **en ce qui concerne la propreté** she's a stickler for cleanliness, she's very fussy *ou* particular about cleanliness ◆ **être** *ou* **se montrer ~ sur la nourriture** to be difficult *ou* fussy *ou* finicky about one's food ◆ **il ne faut pas être trop ~** *ou* **(trop) faire le ~** it's no good being too fussy *ou* over-fussy ◆ **cette chambre ne vous plaît pas ? vous êtes vraiment ~ !** don't you like this room? you really are hard *ou* difficult to please! ◆ **elle est ~ dans le choix de ses amis** she's very selective *ou* choosy* about her friends; → **vivre**[1]

4 [*banlieue, quartier*] tough

difficilement /difisilmɑ̃/ ADV [*marcher, s'exprimer*] with difficulty ◆ **c'est ~ visible/croyable** it's difficult *ou* hard to see/believe ◆ **il gagne ~ sa vie** he finds it difficult *ou* hard to earn a living ◆ **je vois ~ comment tu vas y arriver** I find it difficult to see how you're going to manage it

difficulté /difikylte/ NF 1 (*NonC*) difficulty ◆ **selon la ~ du travail** depending on how difficult the work is, according to the difficulty of the work ◆ **faire qch avec ~** to do sth with difficulty ◆ **avoir** *ou* **éprouver de la ~ à faire qch** to have difficulty (in) doing sth, to find it difficult *ou* hard to do sth ◆ **j'ai eu beaucoup de ~ à trouver des arguments** I had great difficulty finding *ou* I was hard put to find any arguments

◆ **en difficulté** ◆ **être** *ou* **se trouver en ~** [*personne*] to find o.s. in difficulty, to be in difficulties *ou* in trouble; [*entreprise*] to be having difficulties ◆ **avion/navire en ~** aircraft/ship in distress ◆ **couple en ~** couple with problems ◆ **enfant en ~** (*Scol*) child with learning difficulties; (*Psych*) child with emotional difficulties ◆ **mettre qn en ~** to put sb in a difficult position ◆ **notre gardien de but a été plusieurs fois en ~** our goalkeeper ran into trouble several times

2 (*= embarras, obstacle*) difficulty, problem; [*de texte, morceau de musique*] difficult passage, difficulty ◆ **il s'est heurté à de grosses ~s** he has come up against grave difficulties ◆ **cela ne fait** *ou* **ne présente aucune ~** that presents *ou* poses no problem ◆ **il y a une ~** there's a problem *ou* hitch* *ou* snag* ◆ **c'est là la ~** that's where the trouble lies, that's the difficulty ◆ **il a fait des ~s pour accepter nos conditions** he made *ou* raised difficulties about accepting our conditions ◆ **il n'a pas fait de ~s pour nous suivre** he followed us

without protest *ou* fuss ◆ **sans ~** easily, without any difficulty ◆ **en cas de ~** in case of difficulty

♦ **avoir des difficultés** ◆ **avoir des ~s pour faire qch** to have some difficulty (in) doing sth ◆ **enfant qui a des ~s (à l'école/en orthographe)** child who has difficulty *ou* difficulties (at school/with spelling) ◆ **avoir des ~s financières** to be in financial difficulties *ou* straits ◆ **ils ont des ~s avec leurs enfants** they have problems *ou* trouble with their children

difficultueux, -euse † /difikyltɥø, øz/ **ADJ** difficult, awkward

difforme /difɔʀm/ **ADJ** *[corps, membre, visage]* deformed, misshapen; *[arbre]* twisted

difformité /difɔʀmite/ **NF** deformity ◆ **présenter des ~s** to have deformities, to be deformed

diffracter /difʀakte/ ▸ conjug 1 ◂ **VT** to diffract

diffraction /difʀaksjɔ̃/ **NF** diffraction; → **réseau**

diffus, e /dify, yz/ **ADJ** *(gén)* diffuse; *[douleur]* diffuse, not localized

diffuser /difyze/ ▸ conjug 1 ◂ **VT** 1 *[+ lumière, chaleur]* to diffuse 2 *[+ rumeur, idée, nouvelle]* to spread; *[+ connaissances]* to disseminate, to spread ◆ **la police a diffusé le signalement du ravisseur** the police have issued a description of the kidnapper 3 *(Radio, TV) [+ émission]* to broadcast ◆ **le concert était diffusé en direct/en différé** the concert was broadcast live/was pre-recorded ◆ **des slogans diffusés par haut-parleur** slogans broadcast over a loudspeaker 4 *(= distribuer) [+ livres, revues]* to distribute; *[+ tracts]* to distribute, to circulate ◆ **hebdomadaire diffusé à 80 000 exemplaires** weekly magazine with a circulation of 80,000 **VI** *(Sci)* to diffuse **VPR se diffuser** *[chaleur, lumière]* to be diffused; *[rumeur, idée, nouvelle, phénomène]* to spread

diffuseur /difyzœʀ/ **NM** 1 *[de parfum]* diffuser *(for room fragrance)* ◆ **~ d'insecticide** electric mosquito killer 2 *(Presse = distributeur)* distributor 3 *(TV)* broadcaster 4 *(= personne qui propage un art, etc)* publicist 5 *[de moteur]* diffuser

diffusion /difyzjɔ̃/ **NF** 1 *[de lumière, chaleur]* diffusion 2 *[de rumeur, idée, nouvelle]* spreading; *[de connaissances]* dissemination, diffusion 3 *[d'émission]* broadcasting ◆ **des films en première ~** films being shown *ou* broadcast for the first time on television ◆ **~ numérique** digital broadcasting 4 *(= distribution) [de livres, revues]* distribution; *[de tracts]* distribution, circulation ◆ **journal de grande ~** large *ou* wide circulation paper ◆ **pour ~ restreinte** *[rapport] (gén)* restricted; *(secret d'État)* classified 5 *[de maladie, virus]* spread, spreading

digérer /diʒeʀe/ ▸ conjug 6 ◂ **VT** 1 *[+ aliment, connaissance]* to digest ◆ **je l'ai bien/mal digéré** I had no trouble/I had trouble digesting it ◆ **c'est du Marx mal digéré** it's ill-digested Marx 2 *(* = supporter) [+ insulte, attitude]* to stomach*, to put up with; *[+ échec, choc]* to accept, to come to terms with ◆ **je ne peux plus ~ son insolence** I won't put up with *ou* stand for his insolence any longer

digest /dajʒest, diʒɛst/ **NM** digest

digeste /diʒɛst/ **ADJ** *[aliment]* easily digested, easily digestible ◆ **c'est un livre peu ~*** this book's rather heavy going

digesteur /diʒɛstœʀ/ **NM** *(Chim)* digester

digestibilité /diʒɛstibilite/ **NF** digestibility

digestible /diʒɛstibl/ **ADJ** easily digested, easily digestible

digestif, -ive /diʒɛstif, iv/ **ADJ** digestive; → **tube** **NM** *(Méd)* digestive; *(= liqueur)* liqueur

digestion /diʒɛstjɔ̃/ **NF** digestion ◆ **j'ai une ~ difficile** I have trouble digesting, I have digestive problems

digicode ® /diʒikɔd/ **NM** (press-button) door-entry system ◆ **y a-t-il un ~ pour entrer chez toi ?** do you have a door code?

digit /diʒit/ **NM** *(Ordin) (= chiffre)* digit; *(= caractère)* character

digital, e[1] (mpl **-aux**) /diʒital, o/ **ADJ** *(gén)* digital; → **empreinte**[2]

digitale[2] /diʒital/ **NF** digitalis ◆ **~ pourprée** foxglove

digitaline /diʒitalin/ **NF** digitalin

digitalisation /diʒitalizasjɔ̃/ **NF** digitalisation

digitaliser /diʒitalize/ ▸ conjug 1 ◂ **VT** *[+ données, images]* to digitize ◆ **son digitalisé** digital sound

diglossie /diglɔsi/ **NF** diglossia

digne /diɲ/ **ADJ** 1 *(= auguste)* dignified ◆ **il avait un air très ~** he had a very dignified air (about him)

2 **~ de** *(= qui mérite) [+ admiration, intérêt]* worthy of, deserving (of) ◆ **~ de ce nom** worthy of the name ◆ **~ d'être remarqué** noteworthy ◆ **~ d'éloges** praiseworthy ◆ **~ de foi** trustworthy ◆ **~ de pitié** pitiable ◆ **~ d'envie** enviable ◆ **vous devez vous montrer ~s de représenter la France** you must show that you are fit *ou* worthy to represent France ◆ **livre à peine ~ d'être lu** book which is scarcely worth reading *ou* which scarcely deserves to be read ◆ **il n'est pas ~ de vivre** he's not fit to live ◆ **je ne suis pas ~ que vous m'offriez votre soutien** I am not worthy of your offering me your support *(littér)*

3 *(= à la hauteur)* worthy ◆ **son ~ fils/père/représentant** his worthy son/father/representative ◆ **tu es le ~ fils** *ou* **tu es ~ de ton père** *(lit, péj)* you're fit to be your father's son, you take after your father ◆ **avoir un adversaire ~ de soi** to have an opponent worthy of oneself ◆ **œuvre ~ de son auteur** work worthy of its author ◆ **avec une attitude peu ~ d'un juge** with an attitude little befitting a judge *ou* unworthy of a judge ◆ **un dessert ~ d'un si fin repas** a fitting dessert for such a fine meal

dignement /diɲ(ə)mɑ̃/ **ADV** 1 *(= noblement)* with dignity ◆ **garder ~ le silence** to maintain a dignified silence 2 *(= justement)* fittingly, justly ◆ **être ~ récompensé** to receive a fitting *ou* just reward, to be fittingly *ou* justly rewarded

dignitaire /diɲitɛʀ/ **NM** dignitary

dignité /diɲite/ **NF** 1 *(= noblesse)* dignity ◆ **la ~ du travail** the dignity of labour ◆ **la ~ de la personne humaine** human dignity ◆ **avoir de la ~** to be dignified, to have dignity ◆ **manquer de ~** to be lacking in dignity, to be undignified ◆ **c'est contraire à sa ~** *(hum)* it is beneath his dignity ◆ **elle entra, pleine de ~** she came in with great dignity 2 *(= fonction)* dignity ◆ **être élevé à la ~ de juge** to be promoted to the dignity *ou* rank of judge

digramme /digʀam/ **NM** digraph

digression /digʀesjɔ̃/ **NF** digression ◆ **faire une ~** to digress, to make a digression

digue /dig/ **NF** *(gén)* dyke, dike; *(pour protéger la côte)* sea wall; *(fig)* barrier ◆ **élever des ~s contre qch** to erect barriers against sth

diktat /diktat/ **NM** diktat

dilapidateur, -trice /dilapidatœʀ, tʀis/ **ADJ** wasteful **NM,F** spendthrift, squanderer ◆ **~ des fonds publics** embezzler of public funds

dilapidation /dilapidasjɔ̃/ **NF** *[d'héritage, fortune]* squandering; *[de fonds publics, biens]* embezzlement, misappropriation

dilapider /dilapide/ ▸ conjug 1 ◂ **VT** *[+ héritage, fortune]* to squander; *[+ énergie]* to waste; *[+ fonds publics, biens]* to embezzle, to misappropriate

dilatabilité /dilatabilite/ **NF** dilatability

dilatable /dilatabl/ **ADJ** *[corps]* dilatable

dilatant, e /dilatɑ̃, ɑ̃t/ **ADJ** dilative **NM** dilat(at)or

dilatateur, -trice /dilatatœʀ, tʀis/ **ADJ** dilative ◆ **muscle ~** dilator **NM** *(Méd)* dilator

dilatation /dilatasjɔ̃/ **NF** *[de pupille, narine, vaisseau, col de l'utérus]* dilation, dilatation; *[d'estomac]* distension; *[de métal, gaz, liquide]* expansion; *[de pneu]* swelling, distension ◆ **avoir une ~ d'estomac** to have a distended stomach

dilater /dilate/ ▸ conjug 1 ◂ **VT** *[+ pupille, narine, vaisseau, col de l'utérus, cœur]* to dilate; *[+ estomac]* to distend; *[+ métal, gaz, liquide]* to cause to expand; *[+ pneu]* to cause to swell **VPR se dilater** *[pupille, narine]* to dilate; *[estomac]* to distend; *[métal, gaz, liquide]* to expand; *[pneu]* to swell ◆ **se ~ les poumons** to open one's lungs ◆ **pupilles dilatées** dilated pupils ◆ **pores dilatés** enlarged pores ◆ **se ~ la rate** † to split one's sides (laughing)*

dilatoire /dilatwaʀ/ **ADJ** ◆ **manœuvres** *ou* **moyens ~s** delaying *ou* stalling tactics ◆ **donner une réponse ~** to play for time

dilemme /dilɛm/ **NM** dilemma ◆ **sortir du ~** to resolve the dilemma ◆ **enfermer qn dans un ~** to put sb in a dilemma

dilettante /diletɑ̃t/ **NMF** *(= amateur d'art)* dilettante; *(péj = amateur)* dilettante, dabbler ◆ **faire qch en ~** *(en amateur)* to dabble in sth; *(péj)* to do sth in an amateurish way

dilettantisme /diletɑ̃tism/ **NM** amateurishness ◆ **faire qch avec ~** to do sth in an amateurish way *ou* amateurishly

diligemment /diliʒamɑ̃/ **ADV** *(littér) (= avec soin)* diligently; *(= avec célérité)* promptly, speedily

diligence /diliʒɑ̃s/ **NF** 1 *(littér = soin)* diligence, conscientiousness ◆ **à la ~ du ministre** *(Jur)* at the minister's behest *(littér)* *ou* request 2 *(†, littér = empressement)* haste, dispatch ◆ **faire ~** to make haste, to hasten ◆ **en ~** posthaste †, speedily 3 *(Hist = voiture)* diligence, stagecoach

diligent, e /diliʒɑ̃, ɑ̃t/ **ADJ** *(littér)* 1 *(= actif) [serviteur]* prompt 2 *(= assidu) [employé, travail]* diligent, conscientious; *[soins, attention]* diligent, sedulous *(frm)*

diligenter /diliʒɑ̃te/ ▸ conjug 1 ◂ **VT** *(Admin)* ◆ **~ une enquête** to launch an immediate inquiry ◆ **~ une inspection** to carry out an (immediate) assessment

diluant /dilɥɑ̃/ **NM** thinner

diluer /dilɥe/ ▸ conjug 1 ◂ **VT** 1 *[+ liquide]* to dilute; *[+ peinture]* to thin (down); *(péj) [+ discours]* to pad out ◆ **alcool dilué** alcohol diluted with water ◆ **ce médicament se dilue dans l'eau** this medicine should be diluted with water 2 *[+ force, pouvoir]* to dilute, to weaken 3 *(Fin) [+ participation, capital, bénéfice]* to dilute ◆ **capital dilué** diluted capital

dilution /dilysjɔ̃/ **NF** 1 *[de liquide]* dilution; *[de peinture]* thinning (down); *(péj) [de discours]* padding out ◆ **à haute ~** highly diluted 2 *[de force, pouvoir]* dilution, weakening 3 *(Fin)* dilution

diluvien, -ienne /dilyvjɛ̃, jɛn/ **ADJ** *[pluie]* torrential; *(Bible) [époque]* diluvian

dimanche /dimɑ̃ʃ/ **NM** Sunday ◆ **le ~ des Rameaux/de Pâques** Palm/Easter Sunday ◆ **le ~ de Noël** the Sunday after Christmas ◆ **les ~s de l'Avent/de Carême** the Sundays in Advent/Lent ◆ **mettre son costume** *ou* **ses habits du ~** to put on one's Sunday clothes *ou* one's Sunday best ◆ **promenade/journal du ~** Sunday walk/(news)paper ◆ **peintre/sportif du ~** *(péj)* amateur *ou* spare-time painter/

sportsman ◆ **chauffeur du ~** Sunday driver ◆ **sauf ~ et jours fériés** Sundays and holidays excepted ◆ **ici, c'est pas tous les jours ~ !** life isn't always much fun here! ◆ **allez, encore un verre, c'est pas tous les jours ~ !** go on, have another, it's not every day we have an excuse for celebrating!; *pour autres loc voir* **samedi**

dîme /dim/ NF *(Hist)* tithe ◆ **lever une ~ sur qch** to tithe sth ◆ **payer la ~ du vin/des blés** to pay tithes *ou* the tithe on wine/corn ◆ **le grossiste/l'État prélève sa ~ (sur la marchandise)** *(fig)* the wholesaler takes his/the State takes its cut (on the goods)

dimension /dimɑ̃sjɔ̃/ NF 1 *(= taille)* *[de pièce, terrain]* size ◆ **avoir la même ~** to be the same size, to have the same dimensions ◆ **de grande/petite ~** large/small-sized, of large/small dimensions ◆ **faire une étagère à la ~ d'un recoin** to make a shelf to fit (into) an alcove
2 *(= mesure)* **~s** dimensions ◆ **quelles sont les ~s de la pièce ?** what are the dimensions *ou* measurements of the room?, what does the room measure? ◆ **ce placard est fait aux ~s du mur** the cupboard has been built to the dimensions of the wall *ou* built to fit the wall ◆ **mesurez-le dans la plus grande ~** measure it at the widest *ou* longest point ◆ **prendre la ~ de qn/d'un problème** to size sb/a problem up
3 *(= importance)* **une entreprise de ~ internationale** a company of international standing ◆ **une erreur de cette ~** a mistake of this magnitude ◆ **un repas à la ~ de son appétit** a meal commensurate with one's appetite ◆ **une tâche à la ~ de son talent** a task equal to *ou* commensurate with one's talent ◆ **il n'a pas la ~ d'un premier ministre** he hasn't got what it takes to be a prime minister
4 *(Philos, Phys)* dimension ◆ **la troisième/quatrième ~** the third/fourth dimension ◆ **à** *ou* **en 2/3 ~s** 2-/3-dimensional

dimensionner /dimɑ̃sjɔne/ ▸ conjug 1 ◂ VT to proportion ◆ **objet bien dimensionné** well-proportioned object

diminué, e /diminɥe/ (ptp de **diminuer**) ADJ 1 *(= affaibli)* **il est (très)** *ou* **c'est un homme (très) ~ depuis son accident** he's not (at all) the man he was since his accident ◆ **très ~ physiquement** in very poor health ◆ **très ~ mentalement** mentally much less alert 2 *(Mus)* diminished; *(Tricot)* *[vêtement]* fully-fashioned; *[rang de tricot]* decreased

diminuer /diminɥe/ ▸ conjug 1 ◂ VT 1 *(= réduire)* to reduce; *[+ durée, volume, nombre]* to reduce, to decrease; *[+ son]* to lower, to turn down; *[+ ardeur]* to dampen; *[+ chances de succès, intérêt]* to lessen, to reduce, to diminish ◆ **~ les effectifs** to cut staff ◆ **~ le plaisir de qn** to lessen sb's pleasure ◆ **~ les forces de qn** to diminish sb's strength
2 *(= affaiblir)* *[+ personne]* to weaken ◆ **ça l'a beaucoup diminué physiquement/moralement** it greatly weakened him physically/mentally
3 *(= rabaisser)* *[+ personne]* to belittle; *[+ mérite, talent]* to belittle, to depreciate
4 *(Tricot)* to decrease
VI 1 *[violence, intensité]* to diminish, to lessen; *[lumière]* to fade; *[bruit]* to die down; *[pluie]* to let up; *[orage]* to die down, to subside; *[intérêt, ardeur]* to decline, to decrease ◆ **le bruit diminue d'intensité** the noise is dying down ◆ **les combats diminuent d'intensité** the fighting is subsiding
2 *[effectifs, nombre, valeur, pression]* to decrease, to diminish, to fall; *[provisions]* to diminish, to run low; *[forces]* to decline, to diminish ◆ **~ de longueur/largeur** to grow shorter/narrower, to decrease in length/width ◆ **le (prix du) beurre a diminué** butter has gone *ou* come down *ou* dropped in price ◆ **ça a diminué de volume** it has got smaller ◆ **les jours diminuent** the days are growing shorter *ou* drawing in *(Brit)*
VPR **se diminuer** *(= se rabaisser)* ◆ **il cherche toujours à se ~** he's always putting himself down

> ⚠ Attention à ne pas traduire automatiquement **diminuer** par **to diminish** qui a des emplois spécifiques.

diminutif, -ive /diminytif, iv/ ADJ *[suffixe]* diminutive NM *(Ling)* diminutive; *(= petit nom)* pet name (*de* for) diminutive (*de* of)

diminution /diminysjɔ̃/ NF 1 *[de longueur, largeur, vitesse]* reduction, decreasing; *[de durée, volume, nombre, quantité]* reduction, decreasing; *[de prix, impôts, consommation, valeur]* reduction, bringing down, cutting back ◆ **il nous a consenti une petite ~** he gave us a small reduction ◆ **une ~ très nette du nombre des accidents** a marked decrease *ou* drop *ou* fall-off in the number of accidents ◆ **être en nette ~** to be falling rapidly
2 *[de chances de succès, plaisir, intérêt]* lessening, reduction; *[de violence, intensité]* diminishing, lessening
3 *[de lumière, bruit]* fading, diminishing; *[de circulation]* dying down; *[de pluie]* letting up, diminishing; *[d'orage]* dying down, dying away, subsiding; *[d'ardeur]* dying down, diminishing, decrease (*de* in)
4 *(Tricot)* decreasing ◆ **faire une ~** to decrease ◆ **commencer les ~s** to begin decreasing

dimorphe /dimɔʀf/ ADJ dimorphous, dimorphic

dimorphisme /dimɔʀfism/ NM dimorphism

DIN /din/ NM INV (abrév de **Deutsche Industrie Norm**) DIN ◆ **les ~ et les ASA** DIN and ASA standards

dinanderie /dinɑ̃dʀi/ NF *(= commerce)* copperware trade; *(= articles)* copperware

dinandier /dinɑ̃dje/ NM copperware manufacturer and retailer

dinar /dinaʀ/ NM dinar

dînatoire /dinatwaʀ/ ADJ *(frm)* ◆ **goûter ~** substantial afternoon meal, ≃ high tea *(Brit)* ◆ **buffet ~** ≃ buffet dinner

dinde /dɛ̃d/ NF 1 *(= oiseau)* turkey hen; *(Culin)* turkey ◆ **~ rôtie/de Noël** roast/Christmas turkey 2 *(péj = fille stupide)* silly little goose

dindon /dɛ̃dɔ̃/ NM 1 *(gén)* turkey; *(mâle)* turkey cock 2 *(* = homme sot)* **être le ~ (de la farce)** to be the fall guy*; → **pavaner**

dindonneau (pl **dindonneaux**) /dɛ̃dɔno/ NM *(= oiseau)* turkey poult; *(Culin)* turkey

dîner /dine/ ▸ conjug 1 ◂ VI 1 *(le soir)* to have dinner, to dine *(frm)* ◆ **~ aux chandelles** to have dinner *ou* to dine by candlelight ◆ **~ d'une tranche de pain** to have a slice of bread for dinner ◆ **avoir qn à ~** to have sb to dinner; → **dormir** 2 *(Can, Helv, Belg)* to have lunch NM 1 *(= repas du soir)* dinner ◆ **ils donnent un ~ demain** they are having a dinner party tomorrow ◆ **~ de famille/d'affaires** family/business dinner ◆ **~ en ville** (formal) dinner party ◆ **avant le ~** before dinner 2 *(Can, Helv, Belg)* lunch

dînette /dinɛt/ NF 1 *(= jeu d'enfants)* doll's tea party ◆ **jouer à la ~** to play at having a tea party ◆ **venez à la maison, on fera (la) ~*** come round and we'll have a bite to eat 2 *(= jouet)* **~ de poupée** doll's tea set, toy tea set

dîneur, -euse /dinœʀ, øz/ NM,F diner

ding /diŋ/ EXCL ding ◆ **~ dong !** ding dong!

dingo[1] /dɛ̃go/ NM *(= chien)* dingo

dingue* /dɛ̃g/, **dingo**[2] *† /dɛ̃go/ ADJ *[personne]* nuts*, crazy*, barmy* *(Brit)* ◆ **il y avait un bruit ~** it was incredibly noisy ◆ **tu verrais les prix, c'est ~ !** you should see the prices, they're crazy *ou* incredible! ◆ **un film ~** a really way-out* film ◆ **un vent ~** a hell of* a wind, an incredible wind ◆ **il est ~ de cette fille/de ce chanteur** he's crazy* *ou* mad* about that girl/singer NMF nutcase*, loony* ◆ **on devrait l'envoyer chez les ~s** he ought to be locked up *ou* to be sent to the loony bin* ◆ **c'est un ~ de la voiture/de la guitare** he's crazy* *ou* mad* about cars/guitar-playing

dinguer* /dɛ̃ge/ ▸ conjug 1 ◂ VI ◆ **aller ~** *[personne]* to fall flat on one's face, to go sprawling; *[chose]* to go crashing down, to go flying* ◆ **envoyer ~ qn** *(= faire tomber)* to send sb flying*; *(= chasser)* to tell sb to buzz off* *ou* push off* ◆ **envoyer ~ qch** to send sth flying*

dinguerie* /dɛ̃gʀi/ NF craziness, stupidity ◆ **toutes ces ~s** all these stupidities

dinosaure /dinozɔʀ/ NM *(lit, fig)* dinosaur

diocésain, e /djɔsezɛ̃, ɛn/ ADJ, NM,F diocesan

diocèse /djɔsɛz/ NM diocese

diode /djɔd/ NF diode

Diogène /djɔʒɛn/ NM Diogenes

dionysiaque /djɔnizjak/ ADJ Dionysian, Dionysiac ◆ **les ~s** the Dionysia

Dionysos /djɔnizɔs/ NM Dionysus, Dionysos

dioptrie /djɔptʀi/ NF dioptre

dioptrique /djɔptʀik/ ADJ dioptric(al) NF dioptrics *(sg)*

diorama /djɔʀama/ NM diorama

dioxine /diɔksin/ NF dioxin

dioxyde /diɔksid/ NM dioxide

diphasé, e /difaze/ ADJ diphase, diphasic, two-phase

diphtérie /difteʀi/ NF diphtheria

diphtérique /difteʀik/ ADJ diphther(it)ic, diphtherial

diphtongaison /diftɔ̃gɛzɔ̃/ NF diphthongization

diphtongue /diftɔ̃g/ NF diphthong

diphtonguer VT, **se diphtonguer** VPR /diftɔ̃ge/ ▸ conjug 1 ◂ to diphthongize

diplodocus /diplɔdɔkys/ NM diplodocus

diplômant, e /diplomɑ̃, ɑ̃t/ ADJ ◆ **formation ~e** *course leading to a qualification*, ≃ certificate course

diplomate /diplɔmat/ ADJ diplomatic NMF *(= ambassadeur, personne habile)* diplomat NM *(Culin)* ≃ trifle ◆ **~ au chocolat** ≃ chocolate charlotte russe

diplomatie /diplɔmasi/ NF *(lit, fig)* diplomacy ◆ **le personnel de la ~** the diplomatic staff ◆ **entrer dans la ~** to enter the diplomatic service ◆ **le chef de la ~ allemande** the head of the German diplomatic staff ◆ **faire preuve de ~ envers qn** to treat sb diplomatically, to be diplomatic towards sb ◆ **il a déployé des trésors de ~** he showed wonderful diplomatic skills

diplomatique /diplɔmatik/ ADJ diplomatic ◆ **c'est une maladie ~** it's a case of diplomatic toothache; → **valise**

diplomatiquement /diplɔmatikmɑ̃/ ADV *(Pol, fig)* diplomatically

diplôme /diplom/ NM *(= titre)* *(gén)* diploma, certificate; *(Univ)* ≃ degree ◆ **avoir des ~s** to have qualifications ◆ **~ d'études universitaires générales** *diploma taken after two years at university* ◆ **~ d'études approfondies** *post-graduate diploma taken before completing a PhD* ◆ **~ d'études supérieures spécialisées** *one-year post-graduate diploma in an applied subject* ◆ ~

d'études supérieures techniques *university post-graduate technical degree* ◆ ~ **d'études universitaires scientifiques et techniques** *qualification in science taken after two years at university* ◆ ~ **universitaire de technologie** *two-year qualification taken at a technical college after the baccalauréat*

DIPLÔMES

The initial university qualifications in France are the DEUG or DEUST (taken after two years, the latter in science and technology), and the « licence », taken after three years. The « maîtrise » follows the « licence », and is assessed mainly on the basis of a written dissertation known as a « mémoire ». Higher post-graduate study usually begins with a « DEA », a preparatory research qualification that precedes the « doctorat ».

diplômé, e /diplome/ (ptp de **diplômer**) ADJ qualified NM,F holder of a diploma ◆ **il est ~ d'Harvard** he has a Harvard degree, he has a degree from Harvard ◆ **jeune ~(e)** graduate

diplômer /diplome/ ▸ conjug 1 ◂ VT to award a diploma to

diplopie /diplɔpi/ NF double vision, diplopia (SPÉC)

dipôle /dipol/ NM (*Phys*) dipole; (*Élec*) dipole (aerial)

dipsomane /dipsɔman/ ADJ dipsomaniacal NMF dipsomaniac

dipsomanie /dipsɔmani/ NF dipsomania

diptère /diptɛʀ/ ADJ *[temple]* dipteral; *[insecte]* dipterous, dipteran NM (*= insecte*) dipteran ◆ **les ~s** dipterans, the Diptera (*SPÉC*)

diptyque /diptik/ NM (*Hist, Art = tablette*) diptych; (*= roman, film*) work in two parts

dir. abrév de **direction**

dircom * /diʀkɔm/ NMF abrév de **directeur, -trice de la communication**

dire /diʀ/

▸ conjug 37 ◂

GRAMMAIRE ACTIVE 28.1, 30, 53.1, 53.5

1 VERBE TRANSITIF
2 VERBE PRONOMINAL
3 NOM MASCULIN

1 - VERBE TRANSITIF

1 (gén = déclarer) to say ◆ **avez-vous quelque chose à ~ ?** have you got anything to say? ◆ **"j'ai froid", dit-il** "I'm cold", he said ◆ **on peut commencer ? – elle a dit oui** can we start? – she said yes *ou* she said we could ◆ **~ bonjour/quelques mots à qn** to say hello/a few words to sb ◆ **il m'a dit : "je comprends"** he said to me, "I understand" ◆ **que dites-vous ?, qu'est-ce que vous dites ?** (I beg your) pardon?, what did you say? ◆ **comment dit-on ça en anglais ?** what's the English for that?, how do you say that in English? ◆ **comme disent les spécialistes** as the experts say ◆ **~ ce que l'on pense** to speak one's mind, to say what one thinks ◆ **je ne fais que ~ tout haut ce que tout le monde pense tout bas** I'm only saying aloud what everyone else is thinking ◆ **je ne savais plus quoi ~** I was at a loss for words ◆ **il n'a pas dit un mot** he didn't say *ou* utter a (single) word ◆ **l'argent ne fait pas le bonheur, dit-on** money can't buy you happiness, as the saying goes *ou* as they say ◆ **qu'est-ce que les gens vont ~ ?, qu'en dira-t-on ?** whatever will people *ou* they say? ◆ **il sait ce qu'il dit** he knows what he's talking about ◆ **il ne sait pas ce qu'il dit** (*= il déraisonne*) he doesn't know what he's saying; (*= il ne sait pas de quoi il parle*) he doesn't know what he's talking about ◆ **à** *ou* **d'après ce qu'il dit** according to him, according to what he says ◆ **tu ne crois pas si bien ~ !** you don't know how right you are! ◆ **ce n'est pas une chose à ~** some things are better left unsaid ◆ **où va-t-il ? – il ne l'a pas dit** where's he going? – he didn't say ◆ **c'est à vous de ~** (*Cartes*) your call; → **bien, mal², parler**

◆ **dire que** to say that ◆ **~ à qn que ...** to tell sb that ..., to say to sb that ... ◆ **il dit qu'il nous a écrit** he says that he wrote to us ◆ **il a bien dit qu'il ne rentrerait pas** he did say that he would not be coming home ◆ **est-ce qu'il doit venir ? – elle dit que oui/que non** is he coming? – she says he is/he isn't *ou* she says so/not ◆ **la radio et les journaux avaient dit qu'il pleuvrait** the radio and the papers had said it would rain ◆ **vous nous dites dans votre lettre que ...** you tell us *ou* you say in your letter that ... ◆ **votre lettre/la loi dit clairement que ...** your letter/the law says clearly that *ou* clearly states that ... ◆ **qu'est-ce qui me dit que c'est vrai ?** how can I tell it's the truth?, how am I to know *ou* how do I know it's the truth?

◆ **on dit que ...** rumour has it that ..., they say that ...

◆ **que dis-je** ◆ **il a au moins 70 ans, que dis-je, plutôt 80** he must be at least 70 – what am I saying? – more like 80 ◆ **il est très économe, que dis-je, il est avare !** he's very thrifty, not to say mean!

◆ **ceci** *ou* **cela dit** (*avec restriction*) nevertheless, having said this; (*= à ces mots*) thereupon, having said this

◆ **cela va sans dire** it goes without saying

◆ **il va sans dire que ...** needless to say...

◆ **comme on dit, comme dit** *ou* **dirait l'autre** * as they say, so to speak

◆ **comme qui dirait** * as you might say ◆ **j'entends comme qui dirait des grognements** I can hear what sounds like groans ◆ **cette maison c'est comme qui dirait un énorme cube** the house looks a bit like a huge cube

◆ **comment dirais-je?** how shall I put it?

◆ **je ne te** *ou* **vous dis que ça!** * that's all I can say! ◆ **il nous a fait un dîner, je ne te dis que ça !** (*admiratif*) he made us one hell of a dinner! *

◆ **pour ne pas dire** ◆ **il est gros, pour ne pas ~ obèse** he's fat, not to say obese

◆ **soit dit en passant** by the way, let me say in passing, incidentally

2 (= communiquer) *[+ mensonges, nouvelle, adresse, nom]* to tell; *[+ sentiment]* to tell of, to express ◆ **~ qch à qn** to tell sb sth ◆ **il m'a dit quelque chose qui m'a fait rire** he told me something *ou* he said something to me that made me laugh ◆ **j'ai quelque chose à vous ~** there's something I want to tell you *ou* say to you ◆ **~ des bêtises** to talk nonsense ◆ **il nous a dit sa joie/son soulagement** he told us how happy/how relieved he was ◆ **je ne te le dirai pas deux fois** I won't tell you again ◆ **je suis sûr, je te dis !** * I'm certain, I tell you! ◆ **je vous l'avais bien dit !** I told you so!, didn't I tell you? ◆ **quelque chose me dit que ...** something tells me (that) ..., I've got the feeling (that) ... ◆ **rien ne dit que ...** there's nothing to say that ...; → **aventure**

◆ **entre nous soit dit, soit dit entre nous** (just) between the two of us, between you and me

◆ **pour mieux dire** ◆ **sa franchise, ou pour mieux ~ son manque de tact** his frankness, or rather his tactlessness

◆ **pour tout dire** actually, in fact ◆ **pour tout ~, ce film m'a paru sans intérêt** actually, I found the film totally uninteresting ◆ **il n'est pas bricoleur, pour tout ~ il a horreur des travaux manuels** he's not much of a handyman - in fact he hates manual work

3 (= ordonner, prévenir) to tell ◆ **dites-lui de partir/qu'il parte ce soir** tell him to go/that he must leave tonight ◆ **il a dit de venir tôt** he said we were to come *ou* he said to come* early, he told us to come early ◆ **fais ce qu'on te dit !** do as *ou* what you are told! ◆ **ça suffit, j'ai dit !** I said that's enough! ◆ **on nous a dit de l'attendre** we were told to wait for him; → **envoyer**

4 (= objecter) to say (*à, contre* against); ◆ **que veux-tu que je dise à** *ou* **contre ça ?** what can I say against that? ◆ **je n'ai rien à ~ sur son travail** I can't complain about his work ◆ **tu n'as rien à ~, tu aurais fait la même chose !** you can talk! you would have done exactly the same thing! ◆ **tais-toi, tu n'as rien à ~ !** be quiet, you're in no position to comment! ◆ **tu n'as rien à ~, tu es bien servi** you can't complain, you've done very well out of it

◆ **c'est pas pour dire** * ◆ **c'est pas pour ~, mais je l'ai bien réussi, ce gâteau !** I don't mean to boast, but I made a really good job of that cake! ◆ **c'est pas pour ~, mais il aurait pu m'inviter !** I don't mean to complain, but he could have invited me!

◆ **il n'y a pas à dire** *, **on ne peut pas dire** * there's no doubt about it, there's no getting away from it

5 (= réciter) *[+ poèmes]* to say, to recite; *[+ prière]* to say; *[+ rôle]* to speak ◆ **~ la messe** to say mass ◆ **l'acteur a très mal dit ce passage** the actor spoke the lines very badly; → **chapelet**

6 (= plaire) **ça vous dit de sortir ?** do you feel like going out?, do you fancy (*Brit*) going out? ◆ **ça ne me dit rien** I don't feel like it at all, it doesn't appeal to me at all, I don't fancy (*Brit*) it at all ◆ **il y a des fraises mais ça ne me dit pas** there are strawberries but I don't fancy them (*Brit*) *ou* I'm not in the mood for them ◆ **rien ne me dit en ce moment** I'm not in the mood for anything *ou* I don't feel like doing anything just now ◆ **si le cœur vous en dit** if you feel like it, if you feel so inclined

7 (= penser) to think ◆ **qu'est-ce que tu dis de ma robe ?** what do you think of *ou* how do you like my dress? ◆ **qu'est-ce que vous dites de ça ?** what do you think *ou* how do you feel about it?, what are your feelings on the subject? ◆ **qu'est-ce que vous diriez d'une promenade ?** what would you say to a walk?, how about a walk? ◆ **on dirait qu'il n'aime pas cette ville** he doesn't seem to like this town ◆ **on dirait qu'il le fait exprès !** you'd almost think he does it on purpose! ◆ **qui aurait dit qu'elle allait gagner ?** who would have thought (that) she would win? ◆ **on dirait qu'il va pleuvoir** it looks like rain ◆ **on dirait qu'il va pleurer** he looks as though he is going to cry ◆ **cette eau est noire, on dirait de l'encre** this water is black – it looks like ink ◆ **on dirait du poulet** it tastes like *ou* it's like chicken ◆ **on dirait du Brahms** it sounds like *ou* it's like Brahms ◆ **on dirait du parfum** it's like *ou* it smells like perfume ◆ **on dirait de la soie** it's like *ou* it feels like silk ◆ **qui l'eût dit !** who'd have thought it!

◆ **dire que ...!** (*dans une phrase exclamative*) ◆ **et ~ qu'il aurait pu se tuer !** to think he might have killed himself!

8 (= supposer, prétendre) **on le dit malade/à Londres** he's rumoured to be ill/in London ◆ **des gens dits cultivés** supposedly educated people

9 (= décider) **venez bientôt, disons demain** come soon, let's make it tomorrow *ou* (let's) say tomorrow ◆ **tout n'est pas dit** the last word has not been said, it isn't all over yet ◆ **il est dit ou il a été dit que je ne gagnerai jamais** I'm destined *ou* fated never to win ◆ **bon, c'est dit** *ou* **voilà qui est dit** right, that's settled *ou* it's all arranged ◆ **ce qui est**

dit est dit what's said is said ◆ **à l'heure dite** at the appointed time *ou* hour ◆ **au jour dit** on the appointed day; → **aussitôt, facile, tenir**

10 [= admettre] to say, to admit ◆ **il faut bien ~ que ...** I must say *ou* admit that ... ◆ **disons-le, il nous ennuie** let's be frank *ou* let's face it*, we find him boring

11 [= évoquer] **ce nom me dit quelque chose** this name rings a bell ◆ **ça ne me dit rien du tout** that doesn't mean a thing to me

12 [* = avoir tel aspect] **et tes plantations, qu'est-ce que ça dit ?** how are your plants doing? ◆ **pour l'instant, ça ne dit rien †, mais attendez que ce soit fini !** for the moment it doesn't look up to much*, but just wait until it's finished!

13 [= indiquer] to say, to show ◆ **ma montre dit 6 heures** my watch says 6 o'clock, it's 6 o'clock by my watch ◆ **son visage disait sa déception** his face gave away his disappointment, his disappointment was written all over his face; → **long**

14 [locutions] **tu me l'envoies, dis, cette lettre ?** you will send me that letter, won't you? ◆ **dis Papa, quand est-ce qu'on part ?** hey daddy, when are we going? ◆ **dis** *ou* **dites donc !** (*= à propos*) by the way; (*= holà*) hey!, say! (*US*) ◆ **c'est joli dis donc !** oh, isn't that pretty! ◆ **ça lui a rapporté 10 000 € – ben dis donc !*** that earned him €10,000 – goodness me *ou* well I never!* (*Brit*) ◆ **tu l'as dit (bouffi*) !** how right you are!, you said it! ◆ **quand je vous le disais !** I told you so!, what did I tell you! ◆ **c'est moi qui vous le dis** take my word for it ◆ **c'est vous qui le dites** that's what YOU say ◆ **c'est (vous) ~ s'il est content/s'il a eu peur** that just shows you how pleased he is/how frightened he was ◆ **c'est beaucoup/trop ~** that's saying a lot/too much ◆ **c'est peu ~** that's an understatement ◆ **et ce n'est pas peu ~ !, ce qui n'est pas peu ~ !** and that's really saying something! ◆ **c'est une superproduction hollywoodienne, c'est tout ~ !** it's a Hollywood spectacular, which says it all! ◆ **est-ce à ~ que ... ?** does that mean (that) ...? ◆ **qu'est-ce à ~ ?** (*frm*) what does that mean? ◆ **que tu dis (ou qu'il dit etc) !⁑** that's YOUR (*ou* HIS *etc*) story!, that's what YOU say (*ou* HE says *etc*)! ◆ **qui dit argent, dit problèmes** money means problems ◆ **à qui le dites-vous !** don't I know it!*, you're telling me!* ◆ **qui dit mieux ?** (*aux enchères*) any advance? ◆ **il a fait 50% de bénéfice, qui dit mieux ?** he made a 50% profit, you can't get much better than that, can you?

◆ **faire dire** ◆ **faire ~ qch à qn** to send word of sth to sb ◆ **faire ~ à qn de venir** to send for sb ◆ **faire ~ à qn qu'on a besoin de lui** to let sb know that he is needed ◆ **faire ~ à qn des choses (qu'il n'a pas dites)** to put words in sb's mouth ◆ **je ne vous le fais pas ~ !** you said it! ◆ **il ne se l'est pas fait ~ deux fois** he didn't need *ou* have to be told twice ◆ **elle partit sans se le faire ~ deux fois** she left without having to be told twice ◆ **sous la torture, on fait ~ aux gens ce qu'on veut** people can be made to say *ou* you can make people say anything under torture

◆ **laisser dire** to let people talk ◆ **laisse ~ !** let them talk!, never mind what they say! ◆ **je me suis laissé ~ que ...** I heard that ..., I was told that ...

◆ **vouloir dire** (*= signifier*) to mean ◆ **qu'est-ce que ça veut ~ ?** [*mot, texte*] what does that mean?; [*attitude de qn*] what does that imply? *ou* mean? ◆ **cette phrase ne veut rien ~** this sentence doesn't mean a thing ◆ **que veux-tu ~ par là ?** what do you mean? ◆ **ça ne veut pas ~ qu'il viendra** it doesn't mean (to say) that *ou* it doesn't follow that he'll come ◆ **ça veut tout ~ !** that says it all! ◆ **ça dit bien ce que ça veut ~** it means exactly *ou* just what it says ◆ **non mais, qu'est-ce que ça veut ~ de crier comme ça ?** what on earth is all this shouting about?

2 - VERBE PRONOMINAL

se dire

1 [= penser] to say to o.s ◆ **il se dit qu'il était inutile de rester** he said to himself that there was no point in staying ◆ **je me dis que j'aurais dû l'acheter** I feel now *ou* I'm thinking now that I should have bought it ◆ **il faut bien se ~ que ...** one has to realize *ou* accept that ...

2 [= se prétendre] to claim to be ◆ **il se dit malade** he claims to be ill *ou* that he is ill ◆ **elle se dit sa cousine** she claims to be his cousin, she says she is his cousin

3 [= se croire] **on se dirait en Grèce/au Moyen Âge** you'd think we were in Greece/back in the Middle Ages

4 [mutuellement] **elles se dirent au revoir** they said goodbye (to each other)

5 [= être dit] **ça ne se dit pas** (*inusité*) you don't say that; (*impoli*) it's not polite ◆ **cela ne se dit plus en français** the expression is no longer used *ou* in use in French ◆ **ça se dit de la même façon en anglais et en français** it's the same in English and in French ◆ **comment ça se dit en français ?** how do you say that in French? ◆ **se dit d'un objet/d'une personne** *etc* (*dans un dictionnaire*) of an object/a person *etc*

3 - NOM MASCULIN

[= déclaration] statement ◆ **d'après** *ou* **selon ses ~s** according to him *ou* to what he says ◆ **au ~ de, aux ~s de** according to ◆ **au ~ de** *ou* **selon le ~ de tous** by all accounts ◆ **leurs ~s ne concordent pas** (*Jur*) their statements do not agree

---

direct, e /diʀɛkt/ ADJ 1 (*= sans détour*) [*route, personne, reproche, regard*] direct; [*question*] direct, straight; [*allusion*] direct, pointed (*épith*) ◆ **c'est le chemin le plus ~** it's the most direct route ◆ **c'est ~ en bus** there's a bus that goes direct ◆ **il m'a parlé de manière très ~e, il a été très ~** he spoke to me in a very direct *ou* straightforward way, he didn't beat about the bush

2 (*= sans intermédiaire*) (*gén*) direct; [*cause, conséquence*] immediate, direct; (*Jur*) [*action*] direct ◆ **ses chefs ~s** his immediate superiors ◆ **vente ~e** direct selling ◆ **ligne téléphonique ~e** (*privée*) private *ou* direct line; (*automatique*) automatic dialling system ◆ **être en rapport** *ou* **en contact ~** *ou* **en relations ~es avec** to deal directly *ou* be in direct contact with ◆ **se mettre en rapport ~ avec qn** to contact sb *ou* make contact with sb directly ◆ **il n'y a pas de rapport** *ou* **lien ~ entre les deux faits** there is no direct connection *ou* link between the two facts ◆ **il a pris une part très ~e à cette affaire** he was directly involved in the deal

3 (*= absolu*) **en contradiction/opposition ~e avec** in direct contradiction/opposition to

4 (*Astron*) direct; (*Ling*) [*style, discours, objet*] direct; (*Logique*) [*proposition*] positive; → **complément**

5 (*Transport*) [*train*] through (*épith*), non-stop (*épith*); [*vol*] direct, non-stop (*épith*) ◆ **ce train est ~ jusqu'à Paris** this is a through *ou* non-stop train to Paris

NM 1 (*Rail*) express (train), fast *ou* non-stop train ◆ **le ~ Paris-Dijon** the Paris-Dijon express

2 (*Boxe*) jab ◆ **~ du gauche/du droit** straight left/right, left/right jab ◆ **il lui a envoyé un ~ dans l'estomac** he delivered a punch straight to his stomach

3 (*Radio, TV*) **c'est du ~** it's live ◆ **émission en ~** live broadcast ◆ **parler/faire un reportage en ~ de New York** to be speaking/reporting live from New York ◆ **ce sont les risques du ~** those are the risks of live broadcasting *ou* of broadcasting live

ADV * straight ◆ **tu fais la traduction ~ ?** do you translate straight off? ◆ **on l'a emmené ~ à l'hôpital** he was taken straight to hospital

directement /diʀɛktəmɑ̃/ ADV 1 (*= immédiatement*) straight, right away, straight away (*Brit*) ◆ **il est allé se coucher ~** he went straight *ou* directly to bed, he went to bed right *ou* straight (*Brit*) away ◆ **en rentrant il est allé ~ au réfrigérateur** when he came home he went straight to the fridge *ou* he made a beeline for the fridge

2 (*= sans détour*) straight, directly ◆ **cette rue mène ~ à la gare** this street leads straight to the station ◆ **cet escalier communique ~ avec la cave** this staircase leads straight *ou* directly to the cellar ◆ **il est entré ~ dans le vif du sujet** he came straight to the point

3 (*= personnellement*) directly ◆ **il m'a très ~ accusé de ce crime** he accused me of the crime straight out ◆ **sa bonne foi est ~ mise en cause** it's a direct challenge to his good faith ◆ **tout ceci ne me concerne pas ~ mais ...** none of this concerns me directly *ou* personally but ..., none of this is of any direct *ou* immediate concern to me but ... ◆ **les secteurs les plus ~ touchés par la crise** the sectors most directly *ou* immediately affected by the crisis

4 (*= sans intermédiaire*) direct, straight ◆ **adressez-vous ~ au patron** apply to the boss direct *ou* in person, go straight to the boss ◆ **j'ai été ~ le trouver pour le lui demander** I went straight to him to ask him about it ◆ **~ du producteur au consommateur** direct *ou* straight from the producer to the consumer ◆ **colis expédié ~ à l'acheteur** parcel sent direct to the buyer

5 (*= diamétralement*) (*lit*) directly; (*fig*) completely, utterly, directly ◆ **la maison ~ en face** the house directly *ou* straight opposite

directeur, -trice /diʀɛktœʀ, tʀis/ ADJ (*= dirigeant*) directing; (*= principal*) [*idée*] principal, main; [*principe*] guiding; [*force*] guiding, driving; (*Tech*) [*bielle*] driving; [*roue*] front ◆ **le taux ~ de la Banque de France** The Bank of France's key interest rate; → **comité, ligne¹, plan¹**

NM 1 (*= responsable, gérant*) [*de banque, usine*] manager; (*Admin*) head; (*Police*) ≃ chief constable (*Brit*), police chief (*US*); (*Ciné, TV*) director ◆ **~ général** [*d'entreprise*] general manager; (*au conseil d'administration*) managing director, chief executive officer; [*d'organisme international*] director general ◆ **~ général adjoint** assistant general manager ◆ **le ~ de l'UFR d'anglais** the head of the English department ◆ **~ des achats** *ou* **d'achat** chief buyer, purchasing manager

2 (*= administrateur, propriétaire*) director

3 ◆ **~ (d'école)** headmaster, principal (*US*)

NF **directrice** 1 [*d'entreprise*] manageress; (*= propriétaire*) director; (*Admin*) head

2 ◆ **directrice (d'école)** headmistress, principal (*US*)

3 (*Math*) directrix

COMP **directeur administratif et financier** financial and administrative director

directeur artistique artistic director

directeur de cabinet (*d'un ministre*) principal private secretary

directeur commercial commercial manager

directeur de la communication head of communications

directeur de conscience spiritual adviser

directeur financier financial director, chief financial officer

directeur gérant managing director

directeur de journal newspaper editor
directeur de la photographie director of photography
directeur de prison prison governor *(Brit)*, head warden *(US)*
directeur des programmes *(Radio, TV)* programme *(Brit) ou* program *(US)* director
directeur des ressources humaines human resources manager
directeur spirituel ⇒ **directeur de conscience**
directeur de théâtre theatre *(Brit) ou* theater *(US)* manager
directeur de thèse *(Univ)* supervisor *(Brit)*, (dissertation) director *(US)*
directeur des ventes sales manager

directif, -ive[1] /dirɛktif, iv/ **ADJ** directive ◆ **il est très ~** he's very directive, he's always telling people what to do ◆ **ne soyez pas trop ~** try not to exert too much control

direction /dirɛksjɔ̃/ **NF** 1 *(= sens)* direction; *(= route, chemin)* direction, way ◆ **vous n'êtes pas dans** *ou* **vous n'avez pas pris la bonne ~** you're not going the right way you're going in the wrong direction ◆ **dans quelle ~ est-il parti ?** which way did he go? ◆ **aller dans la ~ de** *ou* **en ~ de Paris, prendre la ~ de Paris** to go towards *ou* in the direction of Paris ◆ **prendre la ~ Châtelet** *(en métro)* take the line that goes to Châtelet ◆ **train/avion en ~ de ...** train/plane for *ou* going to ... ◆ **bateau en ~ de ...** ship bound *ou* heading for ... ◆ **nous devons chercher dans une autre ~** we must look in some other *ou* a different direction ◆ **l'enquête a pris une nouvelle ~** the inquiry has taken a new turn ◆ **dans toutes les ~s** in all directions ◆ **"autres directions"** *(panneau)* "all other routes" ◆ **"toutes directions"** "all routes"
2 *(= action de diriger) [d'entreprise, usine, théâtre]* management, running; *[de journal, pays, gouvernement, parti]* running; *[d'orchestre]* conducting; *(Ciné, Théât, TV) [d'acteurs]* directing; *[d'opération, manœuvre]* supervision ◆ **il a été chargé de** *ou* **on lui a confié la ~ de l'enquête/des travaux** he has been put in charge of the inquiry/the work ◆ **prendre la ~ de** *[+ service]* to become head of, to take over the running of; *[+ usine, entreprise]* to become manager of, to take over the running *ou* management of; *[+ équipe, travaux]* to take charge of, to take over the supervision of; *[+ mouvement, pays]* to become leader of, to take over the leadership of; *[+ débats]* to take control of; *[+ journal]* to take over the editorship of ◆ **~ par objectifs** management by objectives ◆ **prendre la ~ des opérations** to take charge *ou* control (of operations) ◆ **sous sa ~** under his leadership *(ou* management *etc)* ◆ **il a travaillé sous la ~ d'un spécialiste** he has worked under the supervision of an expert ◆ **il a fait ses études sous la ~ de M. Borel** he studied under M. Borel ◆ **orchestre (placé) sous la ~ de Luc Petit** orchestra conducted by Luc Petit
3 *(= fonction de responsable)* post of manager, managership; *(= fonction d'administrateur)* post of director, directorship; *[d'école]* headship, post of head *ou* principal *(US)*; *[de journal]* editorship, post of editor; *[de pays, gouvernement, parti]* leadership ◆ **on lui a offert la ~ de l'usine/d'une équipe de chercheurs** he was offered the post of factory manager/of head of a research team ◆ **on lui a donné la ~ générale** he was given the director-generalship
4 *(= personnel dirigeant) [d'usine, service, équipe]* management; *[de journal]* editorial board ◆ **la ~ générale/commerciale** the general/sales management ◆ **se plaindre à la ~** to make a complaint to the board *ou* the management ◆ **la ~ décline toute responsabilité** the management accepts no responsibility; → **changement**
5 *(= bureau) [d'usine]* manager's *(ou* director's) office; *[d'école]* headmaster's *(ou* headmistress's) office, principal's office *(US)*; *[de journal]* editor's office
6 *(= service)* department ◆ **la ~ des ressources humaines** the human resources department ◆ **adressez-vous à la ~ du personnel** apply to the personnel department ◆ **notre ~ générale est à Paris** our head office is in Paris ◆ **Direction générale** *(de l'UE)* Directorate General ◆ **la Direction de la surveillance du territoire** the counter-espionage services, ≃ MI5 *(Brit)*, the CIA *(US)* ◆ **Direction départementale de l'action sanitaire et sociale** ≃ social services ◆ **Direction générale des impôts** *government tax authority*
7 *(= mécanisme)* steering ◆ **~ assistée** power steering ◆ **il n'y a plus de ~** the steering has gone; → **rupture**

> ⚠ Dans le monde des affaires, **direction** ne se traduit pas par le mot anglais **direction**.

directionnel, -elle /dirɛksjɔnɛl/ **ADJ** directional

directive[2] /dirɛktiv/ **NF** *(gén pl)* directive, order, instruction ◆ **~ communautaire/européenne** Community/European directive

directoire /dirɛktwar/ **NM** 1 *[d'entreprise]* board of directors *ou* management ◆ **membre/président du ~** member/chairman of the board (of directors) 2 *(Hist)* **le Directoire** the (French) Directory, the Directoire ◆ **fauteuil/table ~** Directoire chair/table

directorat /dirɛktɔra/ **NM** *[d'administration]* directorship; *[d'entreprise]* managership; *[d'école]* headship, principalship *(US)*

directorial, e (mpl **-iaux**) /dirɛktɔrjal, jo/ **ADJ** *[fonction, responsabilité]* managerial; *(= du directoire)* of directors; *(Scol)* of headmaster *(ou* headmistress), of principal *(US)* ◆ **fauteuil/bureau ~** manager's *(ou* director's *ou* head's *ou* principal's *(US))* chair/office

directrice /dirɛktris/ **NF** → **directeur**

dirham /diram/ **NM** dirham

dirigeable /diriʒabl/ **ADJ, NM** ◆ **(ballon) ~** dirigible, airship

dirigeant, e /diriʒɑ̃, ɑ̃t/ **NM,F** *[de parti, syndicat, pays]* leader; *(= monarque, dictateur)* ruler ◆ **~ d'entreprise** company director; *(salarié)* company manager **ADJ** *[classe]* ruling

diriger /diriʒe/ ► conjug 3 ◄ **VT** 1 *[+ service]* to run, to be in charge of; *[+ entreprise, usine, théâtre]* to manage, to run; *[+ journal]* to run, to edit; *[+ pays] (gén)* to lead; *[dictateur, monarque]* to rule; *[+ mouvement, parti]* to lead; *[+ orchestre]* to conduct ◆ **mal ~ une entreprise** to mismanage a business, to run a business badly ◆ **savoir ~** to be a good manager *ou* leader ◆ **équipe bien/mal dirigée** team under good/poor leadership *ou* management, well-/badly-run team; → **économie**
2 *(= superviser) [+ opération, manœuvre]* to direct, to be in charge of; *[+ recherches, travaux]* to supervise, to oversee, to be in charge of
3 *(= mener) [+ enquête, procès]* to conduct; *[+ débat]* to conduct, to lead ◆ **a-t-il bien su ~ sa vie ?** did he manage to run his life properly? ◆ **cette idée dirige toute notre politique** this idea guides *ou* determines our whole policy ◆ **l'ambition dirige tous ses actes** he is entirely ruled by ambition
4 *(Mil)* **~ le tir** to direct the firing
5 *(= piloter) [+ voiture]* to steer; *[+ avion]* to pilot, to fly; *[+ bateau]* to steer, to navigate; *(= guider) [+ cheval] (de trait)* to steer; *(de selle)* to guide ◆ **bateau qui se dirige facilement** boat which is easy to steer
6 *(= acheminer) [+ marchandises, convoi]* to send *(vers, sur* to)
7 *(= orienter) [+ personnes]* to direct, to send *(sur, vers* to); ◆ **on m'a mal dirigé** I was misdirected *ou* sent the wrong way ◆ **~ ses pas vers un lieu** to make for *ou* make one's way to *ou* head for a place ◆ **la flèche est dirigée vers la gauche** the arrow is pointing left *ou* to(wards) the left ◆ **on devrait ~ ce garçon vers les sciences** we should advise this boy to specialize in science, we should guide this boy towards the sciences ◆ **cet élève a été mal dirigé** this pupil has been badly advised *ou* guided ◆ **nous dirigeons notre enquête/nos travaux dans une voie nouvelle** we are conducting *ou* directing our inquiry/carrying out *ou* directing our work along new lines ◆ **~ un article/une allusion contre qn/qch** to aim *ou* direct an article/an allusion at sb/sth ◆ **~ une critique contre qn/qch** to aim *ou* direct *ou* level a criticism at sb/sth ◆ **les poursuites dirigées contre lui** the proceedings brought against him
8 *(= braquer)* **~ une arme sur** to point *ou* level *ou* aim a weapon at ◆ **~ un canon/télescope sur** to train a gun/telescope on, to point a gun/telescope at ◆ **~ une lampe de poche/lumière sur** to shine a torch/light on ◆ **le pompier dirigea sa lance vers les flammes** the fireman aimed *ou* pointed his hose at *ou* trained his hose on the flames ◆ **~ son attention sur qn/qch** to turn one's attention to *ou* on sb/to sth ◆ **~ son regard** *ou* **ses yeux sur** *ou* **vers qch** to look towards *ou* in the direction of sth ◆ **son regard se dirigea vers elle** he turned his gaze towards *ou* on her
9 *(Ciné, Théât, TV) [+ acteurs]* to direct
VPR se diriger 1 ◆ **se ~ vers** *(= aller, avancer vers)* to make for, to head for, to make one's way towards ◆ **il se dirigea vers la sortie** he made his way towards *ou* made for the exit ◆ **le bateau/la voiture semblait se ~ vers le port** the boat/car seemed to be heading *ou* making for the harbour ◆ **l'avion se dirigea vers le nord** the plane flew *ou* headed northwards ◆ **se ~ droit sur qch/qn** to make a beeline *ou* make straight for sth/sb ◆ **nous nous dirigeons vers une solution/un match nul** we seem to be heading towards a solution/a draw ◆ **se ~ vers les sciences** *(Scol)* to specialize in science ◆ **se ~ vers une carrière juridique** to opt for *ou* be headed for a career in law
2 *(= se guider)* to find one's way ◆ **se ~ sur les étoiles/le soleil** to navigate by the stars/the sun ◆ **se ~ au radar** to navigate by radar ◆ **il n'est pas facile de se ~ dans le brouillard** it isn't easy to find one's way in the fog

dirigisme /diriʒism/ **NM** *(Écon)* interventionism, state intervention

dirigiste /diriʒist/ **ADJ, NMF** interventionist

dirlo /dirlo/ **NMF** (abrév de **directeur, -trice**) *(arg Scol)* head

disant /dizɑ̃/ → **soi-disant**

discal, e (mpl **-aux**) /diskal, o/ **ADJ** *(Méd)* of the intervertebral discs; → **hernie**

discernable /disɛrnabl/ **ADJ** discernible, detectable

discernement /disɛrnəmɑ̃/ **NM** 1 *(= sagesse)* judgment, discernment ◆ **manquer de ~** to be lacking in judgment *ou* discernment
◆ **sans discernement** *(= distinction)* without (making a) distinction ◆ **agir sans ~** *(à la légère)* to act without proper judgment 2 *(= action)* distinguishing, discriminating, distinction

discerner /disɛrne/ ► conjug 1 ◄ **VT** 1 *(= distinguer) [+ forme]* to discern, to make out, to perceive; *[+ bruit]* to detect, to hear, to make out; *[+ nuance]* to discern, to detect 2 *(= différencier)* to distinguish, to discriminate *(entre* between); ◆ **~ une couleur d'une** *ou* **d'avec une autre/le vrai du faux** to distinguish *ou* tell one colour from another/truth from falsehood

disciple /disipl/ NM (= *élève*) disciple; (= *adepte*) follower, disciple

disciplinable /disiplinabl/ ADJ disciplinable

disciplinaire /disiplinɛʀ/ ADJ disciplinary ◆ **au quartier** ~ in the punishment cells

disciplinairement /disiplinɛʀmɑ̃/ ADV ◆ **poursuivre qn** ~ to take disciplinary action against sb ◆ **le comportement** ~ **fautif d'un magistrat** behaviour by a magistrate that would lead to disciplinary action

discipline /disiplin/ NF 1 (= *règle*) discipline ◆ **une** ~ **de fer** an iron discipline ◆ ~ **de vote d'un parti** party discipline; *(Pol Brit)* party whip ◆ **elle n'a aucune** ~ she has no self-discipline ◆ **il s'entraîne tous les matins avec** ~ he makes himself train every morning ◆ **il fait régner la** ~ **dans sa classe** he imposes discipline on his class ◆ **s'imposer une** ~ **alimentaire** to be very strict *ou* careful about what one eats; → **compagnie, conseil** 2 (= *matière*) *(Scol, Univ)* subject, discipline; *(Sport)* sport ◆ ~ **olympique** Olympic sport ◆ **c'est le meilleur dans sa** ~ he's the best in his field

discipliné, e /disipline/ (ptp de **discipliner**) ADJ *[soldat]* well-disciplined; *[citoyen, peuple]* law-abiding; *[parti]* disciplined; *[enfant, élève]* well-behaved

discipliner /disipline/ ▸ conjug 1 ◂ VT *[+ soldats, élèves]* to discipline; *[+ impulsions]* to discipline, to control; *[+ cheveux]* to control, to keep tidy ◆ **cheveux difficiles à** ~ unruly *ou* unmanageable hair ◆ **il faut apprendre à se** ~ one must learn self-discipline *ou* to discipline oneself

disc-jockey (pl **disc-jockeys**) /disk(ə)ʒɔkɛ/ NM disc jockey, DJ

disco /disko/ ADJ *[musique]* disco NM ◆ **le** ~ disco music

discobole /diskɔbɔl/ NM discus thrower; *(Antiq)* discobolus

discographie /diskɔgʀafi/ NF discography ◆ **sa** ~ **est abondante** he's made a lot of records

discoïde /diskɔid/ ADJ discoid(al), disc- *ou* disk-shaped

discontinu, e /diskɔ̃tiny/ ADJ *(Ling, Math)* discontinuous; (= *intermittent*) *[trait]* broken; *[bruit, effort]* intermittent ◆ **bande** *ou* **ligne blanche** ~**e** *(sur route)* broken white line NM *(Philos)* discontinuity ◆ **en** ~ intermittently

discontinuer /diskɔ̃tinɥe/ ▸ conjug 1 ◂ VTI *(littér)* to discontinue, to cease, to stop ◆ **sans** ~ without stopping, without a break ◆ **pendant deux heures sans** ~ for two hours at a stretch *ou* without stopping *ou* without a break

discontinuité /diskɔ̃tinɥite/ NF discontinuity

disconvenir /diskɔ̃v(ə)niʀ/ ▸ conjug 22 ◂ VI *(littér = nier)* ◆ **je n'en disconviens pas** I don't deny it ◆ **il ne peut** ~ **que ce soit vrai** he cannot deny the truth of it *ou* that it's true

discophile /diskɔfil/ NMF record collector

discordance /diskɔʀdɑ̃s/ NF 1 *[de caractères]* conflict, clash; *[d'opinions]* difference, conflict; *[de sons]* discord *(NonC)*, discordance, dissonance; *[de couleurs]* clash(ing) *(NonC)* ◆ **leurs déclarations présentent des** ~**s graves** there were major discrepancies between their statements 2 *(Géol)* unconformability, discordance

discordant, e /diskɔʀdɑ̃, ɑ̃t/ ADJ 1 *[caractères, opinions, témoignages]* conflicting; *[sons, cris, bruits]* discordant, harsh; *[instruments]* out of tune; *[couleurs]* clashing, discordant ◆ **elle a une voix** ~**e** she has a harsh *ou* grating voice, her voice grates 2 *(Géol)* unconformable, discordant

discorde /diskɔʀd/ NF *(littér)* discord, dissension ◆ **mettre** *ou* **semer la** ~ to sow discord, to cause dissension *(chez, parmi* among) → **pomme**

discorder /diskɔʀde/ ▸ conjug 1 ◂ VI *[sons]* to be discordant; *[couleurs]* to clash; *[témoignages]* to conflict

discothécaire /diskɔtekɛʀ/ NMF record librarian

discothèque /diskɔtɛk/ NF 1 (= *club*) discotheque 2 (= *collection*) record collection 3 (= *bâtiment*) record library 4 (= *meuble*) record cabinet

discount /diskunt/ NM (= *rabais*) discount ◆ **billets/vols en** ~ discount tickets/flights ◆ **(magasin)** ~ discount store *ou* shop ◆ **à des prix** ~ at discount prices

discounter[1] /diskunte/ ▸ conjug 1 ◂ VT to discount, to sell at a discount ◆ **tout est discounté** everything is cut-price *ou* is at a discount price

discounter[2], **discounteur** /diskuntœʀ/ NM discount dealer

discoureur, -euse /diskuʀœʀ, øz/ NM,F *(péj)* speechifier, windbag *

discourir /diskuʀiʀ/ ▸ conjug 11 ◂ VI 1 (= *faire un discours*) to discourse *(frm)*, to expatiate *(frm)* *(sur, de* (up)on); *(péj)* to hold forth *(sur, de* on) to speechify 2 (= *bavarder*) to talk (away)

discours /diskuʀ/ NM 1 (= *allocution*) speech ◆ ~ **d'ouverture/de clôture** opening/closing speech *ou* address ◆ ~ **inaugural** inaugural address *ou* speech ◆ ~ **d'investiture** nomination speech ◆ ~**-programme** keynote speech ◆ ~ **du trône** Queen's (*ou* King's) speech, speech from the throne ◆ **sur l'état de l'Union** *(Pol US)* State of the Union Address ◆ **faire** *ou* **prononcer un** ~ to make *ou* deliver a speech ◆ **prononcer un** ~ **sur la tombe de qn** to deliver a funeral oration for sb

2 *(péj)* talking *(NonC)*, chatter *(NonC)* ◆ **tous ces beaux** ~ **n'y changeront rien** all these fine words *ou* all this fine talk won't make any difference ◆ **suis-moi sans faire de** ~ **!** follow me and don't argue! ◆ **que de** ~ **!** what a lot of fuss (about nothing)! ◆ **perdre son temps en** ~ to waste one's time talking ◆ **assez de** ~, **des faits !** that's enough talk, let's see some action! ◆ **elle me tenait des** ~ **sans fin sur la morale/la politique** she gave me endless lectures on morality/politics, she lectured me endlessly on morality/politics ◆ **il aime tenir de grands** ~ he likes to hold forth ◆ **elle m'a tenu des** ~ **à n'en plus finir** she went on and on as if she was never going to stop ◆ **un dessin vaut mieux qu'un long** ~ a picture is worth a thousand words

3 (= *idées exprimées*) views ◆ **le** ~ **des intellectuels/des extrémistes** the views expressed by intellectuals/extremists ◆ **le** ~ **dominant** the prevailing attitude *ou* view ◆ **c'est le** ~ **officiel** it's the official line ◆ **leur** ~ **rassurant/optimiste** their reassuring/optimistic words ◆ **changer de** ~ to change one's position ◆ **il tient rarement ce** ~ **en public** he seldom expresses these views in public ◆ **ce parti tient un** ~ **nouveau** the party is taking a new line ◆ **il m'a déjà tenu ce** ~ he's already told me that ◆ **ils tiennent tous le même** ~ they all say the same thing

4 ◆ **le** ~ (= *expression verbale*) speech; *(Ling, Rhétorique)* discourse; *(Philos = raisonnement)* discursive reasoning *ou* thinking ◆ **(au)** ~ **direct/indirect** *(Ling)* (in) direct/indirect *ou* reported speech ◆ **les parties du** ~ *(Ling)* the parts of speech; *(Rhétorique)* the parts of discourse

5 *(Philos = traité)* discourse, treatise

discourtois, e /diskuʀtwa, waz/ ADJ discourteous

discourtoisie /diskuʀtwazi/ NF *(littér)* discourtesy

discrédit /diskʀedi/ NM *[de personne]* discredit, disfavour; *[d'idée, théorie, œuvre]* discredit, disrepute ◆ **tomber dans le** ~ to fall into disrepute ◆ **être en** ~ to be discredited *ou* in disrepute ◆ **jeter le** ~ **sur qch/qn** to discredit sth/sb

discréditer /diskʀedite/ ▸ conjug 1 ◂ VT *[+ personne]* to discredit; *[+ théorie, œuvre]* to discredit, to bring into disrepute ◆ **c'est une opinion tout à fait discréditée de nos jours** it is an opinion which has gone right out of favour *ou* which is quite discredited nowadays VPR **se discréditer** *[idée, théorie]* to become discredited, to fall into disrepute; *[personne]* to bring discredit upon o.s., to discredit o.s. *(aux yeux de qn, auprès de qn* in sb's eyes)

discret, -ète /diskʀɛ, ɛt/ ADJ 1 (= *réservé, retenu*) discreet ◆ **soyez** ~, **ne lui parlez pas de sa défaite** mind what you say - don't mention his defeat to him 2 (= *qui n'attire pas l'attention*) *[personne, manière]* unobtrusive; *[parfum, maquillage]* discreet, light; *[vêtement]* plain, simple; *[endroit, couleur]* quiet; *[lumière]* subdued; *[parole, regard]* discreet ◆ **il lui remit un paquet sous emballage** ~ he handed her a parcel wrapped in plain paper ◆ **"envoi discret"** "sent under plain cover" ◆ **n'y a-t-il pas une façon plus discrète de m'avertir ?** couldn't you have told me in a more discreet way? 3 (= *qui garde les secrets*) discreet 4 *(Math) [quantité]* discrete; *(Phys) [fonction]* discontinuous; *(Ling) [unité]* discrete

discrètement /diskʀɛtmɑ̃/ ADV 1 (= *avec tact*) *[se tenir à l'écart, parler, reprocher]* discreetly, quietly ◆ **il a** ~ **fait allusion à ...** he gently hinted at ..., he made a discreet allusion to ... 2 (= *pour ne pas se faire remarquer*) discreetly; *[se maquiller]* lightly; *[s'habiller]* plainly, simply ◆ **il s'est éclipsé** ~ he made a discreet exit, he slipped away *ou* out quietly ◆ **parler** ~ **à l'oreille de qn** to have a quiet word in sb's ear, to have a discreet word with sb

discrétion /diskʀesjɔ̃/ NF 1 (= *fait de garder un secret*) discretion ◆ **"discrétion assurée"** "discretion assured" ◆ **j'aimerais que vous gardiez la plus grande** ~ **sur le sujet** I'd appreciate it if you could be as discreet as possible about this ◆ **ils se sont mariés dans la plus grande** ~ they had a very quiet wedding 2 (= *réserve*) *[de personne]* discretion, tact ◆ **sa** ~ **est exemplaire** he's a model of discretion *ou* tact 3 (= *modération*) *[de maquillage, parfum]* lightness; *[de vêtement]* plainness, simpleness ◆ **avec** ~ *[s'habiller]* soberly, plainly, simply; *[se conduire]* discreetly, unobtrusively; *[parler]* discreetly 4 *(littér = discernement)* discretion 5 *(locutions)* **vin/pain à** ~ unlimited wine/bread, as much wine/bread as you want ◆ **être à la** ~ **de qn** *(littér)* to be in sb's hands

discrétionnaire /diskʀesjɔnɛʀ/ ADJ discretionary

discriminant, e /diskʀiminɑ̃, ɑ̃t/ ADJ discriminating, distinguishing NM *(Math)* discriminant

discrimination /diskʀiminasjɔ̃/ NF discrimination *(contre, à l'égard de, envers* against); ◆ ~ **raciale/sexuelle** race *ou* racial/sex *ou* sexual discrimination ◆ **sans** ~ **d'âge ni de sexe** regardless of age or sex ◆ **ce métier est accessible à tous sans** ~ this profession is open to everyone without discrimination ◆ **tirer sans** ~ **(dans la foule)** to fire indiscriminately (into the crowd) ◆ ~ **positive** affirmative action

discriminatoire /diskʀiminatwaʀ/ ADJ *[mesures]* discriminatory, discriminating

discriminer /diskʀimine/ ▸ conjug 1 ◂ VT 1 *(littér = distinguer)* to distinguish ◆ **apprendre à** ~ **les méthodes** to learn how to discriminate *ou* distinguish between methods 2 *(surtout ptp)* *[+ personnes]* to discriminate against

disculpation /diskylpasjɔ̃/ NF exoneration, exculpation *(frm)*

disculper /diskylpe/ ▸ conjug 1 ◂ VT to exonerate, to exculpate *(frm) (de* from) VPR **se disculper** to exonerate o.s., to vindicate o.s., to exculpate o.s. *(frm) (auprès de qn* in sb's eyes)

discursif, -ive /diskyʀsif, iv/ ADJ discursive

discussion /diskysjɔ̃/ NF 1 *[de problème]* discussion *(de* of); *[de projet de loi]* debate *(de* on) discussion *(de* of); ◆ **mettre une question en ~** to bring a matter up for discussion ◆ **le projet de loi est en ~** the bill is being debated *ou* is under discussion 2 *(= débat)* discussion, debate; *(= pourparlers, échanges de vues)* discussion(s), talks; *(= conversation)* discussion, talk ◆ **les délégués sont en ~** the delegates are in conference ◆ **sans ~ possible** indisputably, undoubtedly ◆ **de la ~ jaillit la lumière** *(Prov)* truth is reached through discussion 3 *(= querelle)* argument, quarrel ◆ **avoir une violente ~ avec qn** to have a violent disagreement *ou* quarrel *ou* argument with sb ◆ **suis-moi et pas de ~s** follow me and don't argue *ou* no argument

discutable /diskytabl/ ADJ 1 *(= contestable)* debatable, questionable, arguable ◆ **il est compétent – c'est tout à fait ~** he's competent – that's debatable 2 *(= mauvais, douteux) [goût]* doubtful, questionable

discutailler* /diskytɑje/ ▸ conjug 1 ◂ VI *(péj) (= bavarder)* to chat (away), to natter (away)* *(Brit)*; *(= débattre sans fin)* to argue *(sur* over) to go on* *(sur* about); *(= ergoter)* to wrangle, to quibble *(sur* over); ◆ **~ dans le vide** to argue *ou* quibble over nothing

discute‡ /diskyt/ NF ◆ **taper la ~** to have a chin-wag*

discuté, e /diskyte/ (ptp de **discuter**) ADJ *(= contesté)* ◆ **ministre très ~** very controversial minister ◆ **question très ~e** vexed question, much debated *ou* disputed question ◆ **théorie très ~e** very *ou* highly controversial theory

discuter /diskyte/ ▸ conjug 1 ◂ VT 1 *(= débattre) [+ problème]* to discuss; *[+ projet de loi]* to debate, to discuss; *[+ prix]* to argue about, to haggle over ◆ **cette question se discute actuellement au Parlement** this issue is now being debated *ou* discussed in Parliament ◆ **~ le coup*** *ou* **le bout de gras*** *(= bavarder)* to have a chat *ou* natter* *(Brit)*; *(= parlementer)* to argue away

2 *(= contester) [+ ordre, droits de qn]* to question, to dispute ◆ **ça se discute, ça peut se ~** that's debatable ◆ **cela ne se discute pas** the question doesn't even arise

VI 1 *(= être en conférence)* to have a discussion, to confer *(avec* with); *(= parler)* to talk *(avec* with); *(= parlementer)* to argue *(avec* with); ◆ **~ de** *ou* **sur qch** to discuss sth ◆ **~ (de) politique/(d') affaires** to discuss *ou* talk politics/business ◆ **on ne peut pas ~ avec lui !** you just can't argue with him!, there's no arguing with him!

2 *(= protester)* to argue ◆ **suivez-moi sans ~** follow me and don't argue *ou* no argument ◆ **il a obéi sans ~** he obeyed without question ◆ **pour moi c'est décidé, il n'y a pas à ~** my mind's made up about it and that's that *ou* and that's final *ou* and there's nothing further to be said

3 *(= débattre)* **~ de** *ou* **sur** *[+ question, problème]* to discuss, to debate ◆ **ensuite, nous avons discuté du prix** then we discussed the price ◆ **~ sur le cas de qn** to discuss *ou* debate sb's case ◆ **j'en ai discuté avec lui et il est d'accord** I have discussed the matter *ou* talked the matter over with him and he agrees ◆ **vous discutez sur des points sans importance** you are arguing about *ou* niggling over trifles ◆ **~ du sexe des anges** *(hum)* to discuss futilities, to discuss how many angels can dance *ou* sit on the head of a pin *(hum)*

disert, e /dizɛʀ, ɛʀt/ ADJ *(frm, hum)* talkative ◆ **il s'est montré peu ~ sur ses intentions** he was less than *ou* not very forthcoming about his intentions

disette /dizɛt/ NF 1 *(= manque) [de vivres, idées]* scarcity, shortage, dearth 2 *(= famine)* food shortage, scarcity (of food)

diseur, -euse /dizœʀ, øz/ NM,F ◆ **diseuse de bonne aventure** fortune-teller ◆ **~ de bons mots** wit, wag

disgrâce /disgʀɑs/ NF 1 *(= défaveur, déchéance)* disgrace ◆ **encourir** *ou* **mériter la ~ de qn** to incur sb's disfavour *(Brit) ou* disfavor *(US) ou* displeasure ◆ **être en ~ auprès de** to be out of favour *(Brit) ou* favor *(US)* with ◆ **tomber en ~** to fall into disgrace 2 († *= malheur)* misfortune ◆ **pour comble de ~** most unfortunately of all

disgracié, e /disgʀasje/ (ptp de **disgracier**) ADJ *(= en disgrâce)* in disgrace, disgraced; *(frm = laid)* ill-favoured *(Brit) ou* -favored *(US)*, ugly

disgracier /disgʀasje/ ▸ conjug 7 ◂ VT to disgrace, to dismiss from favour *(Brit) ou* favor *(US)*

disgracieux, -ieuse /disgʀasjø, jøz/ ADJ *[geste]* inelegant, awkward; *[démarche]* inelegant, awkward, ungainly; *[visage]* ugly; *[forme, objet]* unsightly

disharmonie /dizaʀmɔni, disaʀmɔni/ NF disharmony

disjoindre /disʒwɛ̃dʀ(ə)/ ▸ conjug 49 ◂ VT *[+ planches, tôles, tuiles]* to take apart, to separate; *[+ tuyaux]* to disconnect, to take apart; *[+ pierres]* to break apart; *[+ problèmes]* to separate, to split; *(Jur) [+ causes]* to deal with *ou* hear separately VPR **se disjoindre** *[planches, tôles, tuiles]* to come apart *ou* loose, to separate; *[tuyaux, pierres]* to come apart

disjoint, e /disʒwɛ̃, wɛ̃t/ (ptp de **disjoindre**) ADJ ◆ **ces deux questions sont ~es** these two matters are not connected ◆ **planches/tuiles ~es** planks/tiles which are coming apart *ou* loose, loose planks/tiles ◆ **tuyaux ~s** pipes which have come apart *ou* undone

disjoncter /disʒɔ̃kte/ ▸ conjug 1 ◂ VT *[+ courant]* to cut off, to disconnect VI 1 *(Élec)* **ça a disjoncté** the trip-switch has gone 2 * *[personne]* to crack up*, to lose it* ◆ **cette musique la fait carrément ~** she really goes crazy* when she listens to that music

disjoncteur /disʒɔ̃ktœʀ/ NM *(Élec)* circuit-breaker, cutout

disjonctif, -ive /disʒɔ̃ktif, iv/ ADJ disjunctive NF **disjonctive** disjunctive

disjonction /disʒɔ̃ksjɔ̃/ NF *(gén, Logique)* disjunction; *(Jur)* separation

dislocation /dislɔkasjɔ̃/ NF 1 *(Méd) [d'articulation]* dislocation 2 *[de machine, meuble] (= démontage)* dismantling; *(= casse)* smashing, breaking up 3 *[de rassemblement, cortège]* dispersal, breaking up; *[de troupes]* dispersal, scattering 4 *[de pays, empire]* dismantling, breaking up ◆ **~ de la cellule familiale** breakdown of the family unit 5 *(Géol)* fault

disloquer /dislɔke/ ▸ conjug 1 ◂ VT 1 *(Méd) [+ articulation]* to dislocate, to put out of joint ◆ **avoir l'épaule disloquée** to have a dislocated shoulder

2 *(= démonter) [+ machine, meuble]* to dismantle, to take apart *ou* to pieces; *(= casser)* to smash, to break up ◆ **la chaise est toute disloquée** the chair's completely broken

3 *(= disperser) [+ rassemblement, cortège]* to disperse, to break up; *[+ troupes]* to disperse, to scatter

4 *(= démembrer) [+ pays, empire]* to dismantle, to break up ◆ **les familles disloquées par la guerre** families broken up *ou* torn apart by war

VPR **se disloquer** 1 ◆ **se ~ le bras** to dislocate one's arm, to put one's arm out of joint ◆ **son épaule s'est disloquée** he has dislocated his shoulder

2 *[meuble]* to come apart, to fall to pieces

3 *[troupes]* to disperse, to scatter; *[cortège]* to disperse, to break *ou* split up

4 *[empire]* to break up, to disintegrate

disparaître /dispaʀɛtʀ/ ▸ conjug 57 ◂ VI 1 *(= s'en aller, devenir invisible)* to disappear, to vanish ◆ **il disparut au coin de la rue/dans la foule** he disappeared *ou* vanished round the corner of the street/into the crowd ◆ **~ discrètement** to slip away quietly ◆ **~ furtivement** to sneak away *ou* out ◆ **je ne veux pas le voir, je disparais** I don't want to see him so I'll just slip away *ou* so I'll be off ◆ **le voilà, disparais !** there he is, make yourself scarce!* ◆ **~ aux regards** to vanish out of sight, to disappear from view ◆ **~ à l'horizon** *[soleil]* to disappear *ou* vanish *ou* sink below the horizon; *[bateau]* to vanish *ou* disappear over the horizon ◆ **l'arbre disparut dans le brouillard** the tree vanished *ou* was swallowed up in the fog ◆ **le bâtiment disparaît sous le lierre** the building is (half-) hidden under the ivy

◆ **faire disparaître** *[+ objet] (gén)* to remove, to hide away *ou* out of sight; *[prestidigitateur]* to make vanish *ou* disappear; *[+ document]* to dispose of, to get rid of; *[+ tache, trace, obstacle, difficulté]* to remove; *[+ personne]* to eliminate, to get rid of, to do away with*; *[+ crainte]* to dispel, to eliminate ◆ **cela a fait ~ la douleur/la rougeur** it made the pain/red mark go away, it got rid of the pain/all trace of the red mark ◆ **le voleur fit ~ le bijou dans sa poche** the thief concealed the jewel *ou* hid the jewel in his pocket ◆ **il prenait de gros morceaux de pain qu'il faisait ~ dans sa bouche** he was taking large hunks of bread and cramming them into his mouth ◆ **ils firent ~ toute trace de leur passage** they destroyed *ou* removed all trace of their visit ◆ **faire ~ une inscription** *[temps]* to erase *ou* efface *ou* wear away an inscription; *[personne]* to erase *ou* wipe out *ou* remove an inscription

2 *(= être porté manquant) [personne]* to disappear, to go missing *(Brit)*; *[objet]* to disappear ◆ **il a disparu de son domicile** he is missing *ou* has gone missing *(Brit) ou* has disappeared from home ◆ **trois voitures ont disparu (du garage)** three cars have disappeared *ou* are missing *ou* have gone (from the garage) ◆ **~ sans laisser de traces** to disappear *ou* vanish without trace ◆ **il a disparu de la circulation*** he dropped out of circulation

3 *(= passer, s'effacer) [joie, crainte, sourire]* to disappear, to vanish, to evaporate; *[rougeur, douleur, cicatrice]* to disappear, to vanish, to go away; *(graduellement)* to fade; *[jeunesse]* to vanish, to be lost; *[brouillard]* to lift

4 *(= mourir) [race, civilisation]* to die (out), to vanish; *[coutume]* to die out, to disappear; *[personne]* to die; *(= se perdre) [navire]* to sink, to be lost ◆ **si je venais à ~, tu n'aurais pas de soucis matériels** if I were to die, you wouldn't have any financial worries ◆ **tout le charme de la Belle Époque disparaît avec elle** all the charm of the Belle Époque dies *ou* vanishes with her ◆ **~ en mer** to be lost at sea ◆ **~ corps et biens** *(Naut)* to go down with all hands

disparate /dispaʀat/ ADJ *[éléments]* disparate; *[objets, mobilier]* disparate, ill-assorted; *[couple, couleurs]* ill-assorted, badly matched

disparité /dispaʀite/ NF *[d'éléments, salaires]* disparity *(de* in); *[d'objets, couleurs]* mismatch (NonC) *(de* of)

disparition /dispaʀisjɔ̃/ NF 1 *[de personne]* disappearance; *[de cicatrice, rougeur] (gén)* disappearance; *(graduelle)* fading; *[de brouillard]* lifting; *[de soleil]* sinking, setting; *[de tache, obstacle]* disappearance, removal ◆ **la ~ de la**

douleur sera immédiate the pain will be relieved *ou* will go away *ou* vanish immediately 2 *(= mort, perte)* *[de personne]* death; *[d'espèce]* extinction, disappearance; *[de coutume, langue]* disappearance, dying out; *[d'objet, bateau]* loss, disappearance ◆ **menacé** *ou* **en voie de** ~ *[espèce]* endangered; *[civilisation, langue, tradition]* dying, fast disappearing; *[emploi, métier]* dying ◆ **cette espèce est en voie de** ~ *(animaux)* this species is becoming extinct *ou* is dying out, this is an endangered species; *(fig)* they're a dying breed

disparu, e /dispaʀy/ (ptp de **disparaître**) ADJ 1 *(= révolu)* *[monde, époque]* bygone *(épith)*, vanished; *[bonheur, jeunesse]* lost

2 *(= effacé)* **une lueur menaçante, aussitôt ~e, brilla dans ses yeux** a dangerous gleam flickered and died in his eyes, his eyes glinted dangerously for a brief moment ◆ **un sentiment d'espoir, bientôt ~, l'anima un court instant** hope filled him for a brief moment only to fade again

3 *(= mort)* *[personne]* dead, deceased; *[espèce]* extinct; *[race, coutume, langue]* vanished, dead, extinct; *(= dont on est sans nouvelles)* *[victime]* missing ◆ **il a été porté** ~ *(Mil)* he has been reported missing; *(dans une catastrophe)* he is missing, believed dead ◆ **marin ~ en mer** sailor lost at sea

NM,F *(= mort)* dead person; *(= dont on a perdu la trace)* missing person ◆ **le cher** ~ the dear departed ◆ **l'incendie a fait cinq morts et trois ~s** the fire left five people dead and three unaccounted for *ou* missing

dispatcher[1] /dispatʃe/ ▸ conjug 1 ◂ VT to dispatch

dispatcher[2]**, dispatcheur** /dispatʃœʀ/ NM dispatcher

dispatching /dispatʃiŋ/ NM *(gén)* dispatching; *[de courrier]* routing, dispatching

dispendieusement /dispɑ̃djøzmɑ̃/ ADV *(frm)* *[vivre]* extravagantly, expensively

dispendieux, -ieuse /dispɑ̃djø, jøz/ ADJ 1 *(frm)* *[goûts, luxe]* extravagant, expensive 2 *(Can)* *(= cher)* expensive

dispensaire /dispɑ̃sɛʀ/ NM community *(Brit)* *ou* free *(US)* clinic, health centre *(Brit)* *ou* center *(US)*, people's dispensary

dispensateur, -trice /dispɑ̃satœʀ, tʀis/ *(littér)* ADJ dispensing NM,F dispenser

dispense /dispɑ̃s/ NF 1 *(= exemption, Rel)* exemption *(de* from) dispensation *(de* from) 2 *(= permission)* special permission ◆ ~ **d'âge pour passer un examen** permission to sit an exam under the statutory age limit ◆ ~ **de recherche d'emploi** *(pour un chômeur)* exemption from the actively seeking work rule ◆ ~ **du service militaire/d'un examen** exemption from military service/from an exam

dispenser /dispɑ̃se/ ▸ conjug 1 ◂ VT 1 *(= exempter)* to exempt, to excuse *(de faire* from doing; *de qch* from sth); ◆ ~ **qn d'un vœu** *(Rel)* to release sb from a vow ◆ **je vous dispense de vos réflexions** I can do without your comments, you can spare me your comments ◆ **dispensez-moi d'en dire plus** *(frm)* spare me the necessity of saying any more ◆ **se faire** ~ to get exempted ◆ **il est dispensé de gymnastique** he's excused from gym

2 *(littér = distribuer)* *[+ bienfaits]* to dispense; *[+ charme]* to radiate; *[+ lumière]* to dispense, to give out ◆ ~ **des soins à un malade** to give medical care to a patient

VPR **se dispenser** ◆ **se ~ de** *[+ corvée]* to avoid, to get out of; *[+ remarque]* to refrain from ◆ **se ~ de faire qch** to get out of doing sth, not to bother doing sth ◆ **il peut se ~ de travailler** he doesn't need to work, he has no need to work ◆ **je me dispenserais bien d'y aller** I'd gladly save myself the bother of going if I could ◆ **il s'est dispensé de s'excuser** *(iro)* he didn't see any necessity for excusing himself

dispersant, e /dispɛʀsɑ̃, ɑ̃t/ ADJ dispersive NM dispersant

dispersé, e /dispɛʀse/ (ptp de **disperser**) ADJ *[habitat, famille]* scattered ◆ **en ordre** ~ in a disorganised manner ◆ **leur actionnariat est très** ~ they have many small shareholders ◆ **nos efforts sont trop ~s** our efforts aren't focused enough ◆ **il est trop** ~ *[élève]* he tries to do too many things at once

disperser /dispɛʀse/ ▸ conjug 1 ◂ VT 1 *[+ papiers, feuilles]* to scatter; *[+ brouillard, pétrole]* to disperse, to break up; *[+ collection]* to break up ◆ ~ **les cendres de qn** to scatter sb's ashes 2 *[+ forces]* to dissipate; *[+ foule, ennemi]* to scatter, to disperse ◆ ~ **l'attention de qn** to distract sb ◆ **il ne faut pas ~ tes efforts** you shouldn't spread yourself too thin ◆ **tous nos amis sont maintenant dispersés** all our friends are now scattered VPR **se disperser** *[foule]* to scatter, to disperse, to break up; *[élève, artiste]* to overdiversify ◆ **ne vous dispersez pas trop !** don't spread yourself too thin!, don't attempt to do too many things at once!

dispersion /dispɛʀsjɔ̃/ NF 1 *(Chim, Phys, Stat)* dispersion; *[de papiers, feuilles]* scattering; *[de brouillard, pétrole]* dispersal, breaking up; *[de collection]* breaking up 2 *[de forces]* dissipation; *[de foule, ennemi]* scattering, dispersal ◆ **évitez la ~ dans votre travail** don't attempt to do too many things at once

disponibilité /disponibilite/ NF *[de choses]* availability ◆ ~ **des biens** *(Jur)* *(faculté du possesseur)* ability to transfer one's property; *(caractère des possessions)* transferability of property ◆ **en fonction des ~s** *ou* **de la ~ de chacun** depending on each person's availability ◆ **~s** *(Fin)* available funds, liquid assets

♦ **mettre en disponibilité** *[+ fonctionnaire]* to free from duty temporarily, to grant leave of absence to; *[+ officier]* to place on reserve

♦ **mise en disponibilité** *[de fonctionnaire]* leave of absence; *[d'officier]* transfer to reserve duty 4 *[d'élève, esprit, auditoire]* alertness, receptiveness ◆ ~ **d'esprit** alertness *ou* receptiveness of mind

disponible /disponibl/ GRAMMAIRE ACTIVE 46.3

ADJ 1 *[appartement, fonds, produit]* available ◆ **avez-vous des places ~s pour ce soir ?** are there any seats (available) for this evening? ◆ **il n'y a plus une seule place** ~ there's not a single seat left *ou* not one spare seat ◆ **je ne suis pas ~ ce soir** I'm not free tonight ◆ **elle est toujours ~ pour écouter ses amis** she's always ready to listen to her friends ◆ **biens ~s** *(Jur)* transferable property 2 *(Admin)* **fonctionnaire** ~ civil servant on leave of absence *ou* temporarily freed from duty ◆ **officier** ~ officer on reserve 3 *[élève, esprit, auditoire]* alert, receptive NM *(Fin)* available assets *ou* funds

dispos, e /dispo, oz/ ADJ *[personne]* refreshed, in good form *(attrib)*, full of energy *(attrib)* ◆ **avoir l'esprit** ~ to have a fresh mind; → **frais**[1]

disposé, e /dispoze/ (ptp de **disposer**) ADJ 1 *(= prêt)* **être ~ à faire qch** to be willing *ou* prepared to do sth ◆ **être peu ~ à faire** to be unwilling to do, not to be prepared to do 2 ◆ **bien/mal** ~ in a good/bad mood ◆ **bien/mal ~ à l'égard de** *ou* **pour** *ou* **envers qn** well-disposed/ill-disposed towards sb 3 *[terrain]* situated, sited ◆ **bâtiments ~s face à la mer** buildings facing the sea ◆ **pièces bien/mal ~es** well/badly laid-out rooms

disposer /dispoze/ ▸ conjug 1 ◂ VT 1 *(= arranger)* *[+ personnes, meubles, fleurs]* to arrange; *[+ couverts]* to set, to lay ◆ ~ **des troupes sur le terrain** to draw up *ou* range troops on the battlefield ◆ ~ **des objets en ligne/en cercle** to place *ou* lay *ou* arrange things in a row/in a circle ◆ **on avait disposé le buffet dans le jardin** they had laid out *ou* set out the buffet in the garden

2 *(= engager)* ◆ ~ **qn à faire/à qch** to incline *ou* dispose *(frm)* sb to do/towards sth; *(frm = préparer à)* to prepare sb to do/for sth ◆ **cela ne dispose pas à l'optimisme** it doesn't exactly make you feel optimistic

VI *(frm = partir)* to leave ◆ **vous pouvez** ~ you may leave *ou* go (now), that will be all

VT INDIR **disposer de** *(= avoir l'usage de)* to have at one's disposal; *(= avoir)* to have ◆ ~ **d'une voiture** to have a car (at one's disposal) ◆ ~ **d'une somme d'argent** to have a sum of money at one's disposal *ou* available ◆ **il disposait de quelques heures pour visiter Lille** he had a few hours to visit Lille ◆ **je ne dispose que de quelques minutes** I've only got a few minutes ◆ **il peut ~ de son temps** his time is his own, he can do what he likes with his time ◆ **avec les moyens dont il dispose** with the means at his disposal *ou* available to him ◆ **si vous voulez vous pouvez en** ~ if you wish you can use it ◆ ~ **d'un domaine (par testament)** *(Jur)* to dispose of an estate (in one's will) ◆ **il se croit autorisé à ~ de ses amis** he thinks his friends are just there to do his bidding ◆ **droit des peuples à ~ d'eux-mêmes** right of nations to self-determination ◆ **le droit de chacun à ~ de son corps** *(pendant sa vie)* the individual's right to own and control his own body; *(après sa mort)* the individual's right to determine what shall be done to his body

VPR **se disposer** ◆ **se ~ à faire** *(= se préparer à)* to prepare to do, to be about to do ◆ **il se disposait à quitter le bureau** he was about to *ou* was preparing to *ou* was getting ready to leave the office

> ⚠ **disposer de** se traduit rarement par **to dispose of**, qui veut dire 'se débarrasser de'.

dispositif /dispozitif/ NM 1 *(= mécanisme)* device, mechanism ◆ ~ **d'alarme** alarm *ou* warning device ◆ ~ **de contrôle** control mechanism ◆ ~ **de sécurité** safety device ◆ ~ **scénique** *(Opéra, Théât)* set ◆ ~ **intra-utérin** *(Méd)* intrauterine (contraceptive) device, IUD

2 *(= moyens prévus)* plan (of action) ◆ ~ **d'attaque** *(Mil)* plan of attack ◆ ~ **de combat** *(Mil)* fighting plan ◆ ~ **de contrôle** control system ◆ ~ **de défense** *(Mil)* defence *(Brit)* *ou* defense *(US)* system ◆ ~ **législatif** legislation, laws ◆ ~ **de lutte contre le chômage** measures to combat unemployment ◆ ~ **de lutte contre l'incendie** fire-fighting system *ou* arrangements ◆ **renforcer/alléger le ~ militaire** to increase/decrease the military presence ◆ **un important ~ de sécurité a été mis en place à la frontière** a major security operation has been mounted on the border ◆ ~ **de surveillance** surveillance *ou* monitoring system

3 *(Jur)* *[de jugement]* pronouncement; *[de loi]* purview

disposition /dispozisjɔ̃/ GRAMMAIRE ACTIVE 46.3

NF 1 *(= arrangement, action)* arrangement, arranging, placing; *(= résultat)* arrangement, layout ◆ **selon la ~ des pions/des joueurs** according to how the pawns/players are placed ◆ **ils ont changé la ~ des objets dans la vitrine** they have changed the arrangement *ou* layout of the things in the window ◆ **la ~ des lieux/pièces** the layout of the premises/rooms

2 *(= usage)* disposal ◆ **avoir la libre ~ de qch** *(Jur)* to have free disposal of sth, to be free to dispose of sth ◆ **mettre qch/être à la ~ de qn** to put sth/be at sb's disposal ◆ **la maison/la bibliothèque est à votre** ~ the house/library is at your disposal, you can have the run of the house/library ◆ **les moyens (mis) à notre** ~

sont insuffisants we have insufficient means at our disposal ◆ **je me mets** *ou* **tiens à votre entière ~ pour de plus amples renseignements** I am entirely at your disposal *ou* service should you require further information ◆ **il a été mis à la ~ de la justice** *(Jur)* he was handed over to the law

3 *(= mesure)* measure ◆ **~s** *(= préparatifs)* arrangements, preparations; *(= précautions)* measures, precautions, steps ◆ **prendre des** *ou* **ses ~s pour que qch soit fait** to make arrangements *ou* take steps to have sth done *ou* for sth to be done ◆ **prendre ses ~s pour partir** to make arrangements for *ou* prepare for one's departure ◆ **nous avons prévu des ~s spéciales** we have arranged for special steps *ou* measures *ou* precautions to be taken

4 *(= manière d'être)* mood, humour, frame of mind ◆ **être dans de bonnes/mauvaises ~s** to be in a good/bad mood, to be in (a) good/bad humour ◆ **être dans de bonnes ~s pour faire qch** to be in the right mood to do sth, to be in the right frame of mind for doing sth ◆ **être dans les meilleures ~s** to be in the best of moods ◆ **être dans de bonnes/de mauvaises/les meilleures ~s à l'égard de qn** to feel well-disposed/ill-disposed/very well-disposed towards sb ◆ **est-il toujours dans les mêmes ~s à l'égard de ce projet/candidat ?** does he still feel the same way about this plan/candidate? ◆ **~ d'esprit** mood, state *ou* frame of mind

5 *(= tendance)* *[de personne]* predisposition, tendency; *[d'objet]* tendency *(à* to); ◆ **avoir une ~ au rhumatisme** to have a tendency to rheumatism ◆ **ce bateau a une curieuse/fâcheuse ~ à ...** this boat has a strange/an annoying tendency to ...

6 *(Jur)* clause ◆ **~s testamentaires** provisions of a will, testamentary provisions; → **dernier**

NFPL **dispositions** *(= inclinations, aptitudes)* bent, aptitude, natural ability ◆ **avoir des ~s pour la musique/les langues/le tennis** to have a special aptitude for *ou* a gift for music/languages/tennis

disproportion /disprɔpɔrsjɔ̃/ **NF** disproportion *(entre* between; *de* in)

disproportionné, e /disprɔpɔrsjɔne/ **ADJ** disproportionate *(par rapport à, avec* to) out of (all) proportion *(par rapport à, avec* to, with); ◆ **il a une tête ~e** his head is out of proportion with his body

dispute /dispyt/ **NF** 1 *(= querelle)* argument, quarrel ◆ **~ d'amoureux** lovers' tiff *ou* quarrel ◆ **tu cherches la ~ !** you're looking for an argument! ◆ **c'est leur principal sujet de ~** it's a major bone of contention between them 2 *(†† = débat polémique)* debate, dispute

disputé, e /dispyte/ (ptp de **disputer**) **ADJ** ◆ **très ~** *[course, élection, siège]* hotly *ou* closely contested; *[match]* close, closely fought; *[marché]* competitive

disputer /dispyte/ ▸ **conjug 1** ◂ **VT** 1 *(= contester)* **~ qch/qn à qn** to fight with sb for *ou* over sth/sb ◆ **~ la victoire/la première place à son rival** to fight for victory/for first place with one's rival, to fight one's rival for victory/first place ◆ **elle essaya de lui ~ la gloire de son invention** she tried to rob him of the glory of his invention ◆ **le ~ en beauté/en grandeur à qn** *(littér)* to vie with *ou* rival sb in beauty/greatness ◆ **~ le terrain** *(Mil)* to fight for every inch of ground; *(fig)* to fight every inch of the way

2 *(= livrer)* *[+ combat]* to fight; *[+ match]* to play ◆ **le match a été disputé** *ou* **s'est disputé en Angleterre** the match was played *ou* took place in England

3 *(= gronder)* to tell off*, to tick off* *(Brit)* ◆ **se faire ~ par son père** to get a telling-off* *ou* ticking-off* *(Brit)* from one's father

VPR **se disputer** 1 *(= se quereller)* to quarrel, to argue, to have a quarrel *ou* an argument *(avec* with); ◆ **il s'est disputé avec son oncle** *(= s'est querellé avec lui)* he quarrelled *ou* had a quarrel *ou* an argument with his uncle; *(= s'est brouillé avec lui)* he fell out with his uncle

2 *(= se battre pour)* **se ~ qch** to fight over sth, to contest sth ◆ **deux chiens se disputent un os** two dogs are fighting over a bone ◆ **deux candidats se disputent un siège à l'Académie** there are two contenders for *ou* two candidates are contesting a seat at the Academy

disquaire /diskɛʀ/ **NMF** *(= commerçant)* record dealer

disqualification /diskalifikasjɔ̃/ **NF** *(Sport)* disqualification

disqualifier /diskalifje/ ▸ **conjug 7** ◂ **VT** 1 *(Sport = exclure)* to disqualify 2 *(= discréditer)* to dishonour *(Brit)*, to dishonor *(US)*, to bring discredit on ◆ **il s'est disqualifié aux yeux de l'opinion** he has destroyed people's trust in him *ou* people's good opinion of him

disque /disk/ **NM** 1 *(gén, Méd, Photo)* disc, disk *(surtout US)* ◆ **~ d'embrayage** clutch plate ◆ **~ de stationnement** parking disc ◆ **~ à démaquiller** make-up remover pad; → **frein** 2 *(Sport)* discus 3 *(Mus) (gén, en vinyle)* record ◆ **~ compact** compact disc, CD ◆ **~ (compact) audio/interactif/laser/vidéo** audio (compact)/interactive/laser/video disc ◆ **~ d'or/de platine** gold/platinum disc ◆ **mettre/passer un ~** *(compact)* to put on/play a CD; *(vinyle)* to put on/play a record ◆ **ça vient de sortir en ~ compact** it's just come out on compact disc *ou* CD; → **changer** 4 *(Ordin)* disk, disc ◆ **~ dur/souple/optique** hard/floppy/optical disk ◆ **~ optique compact** compact optical disk ◆ **~ optique numérique** digital optical disk

disquette /diskɛt/ **NF** *(Ordin)* floppy (disk *ou* disc), diskette

dissection /disɛksjɔ̃/ **NF** dissection ◆ **de ~** *[instrument, table]* dissecting, dissection

dissemblable /disɑ̃blabl/ **ADJ** dissimilar, different *(de* from, to)

dissemblance /disɑ̃blɑ̃s/ **NF** dissimilarity, difference *(de* in)

dissémination /diseminasjɔ̃/ **NF** 1 *(= action)* *[de graines]* scattering; *[de troupes, maisons, usines]* scattering, spreading; *[d'idées]* dissemination 2 *(= état)* *[de maisons, points de vente]* scattered layout *ou* distribution ◆ **à cause de la ~ de notre famille** because our family is scattered

disséminer /disemine/ ▸ **conjug 1** ◂ **VT** *[+ graines]* to scatter; *[+ troupes, maisons]* to scatter, to spread (out); *[+ idées]* to disseminate ◆ **les points de vente sont très disséminés** the (sales) outlets are widely scattered *ou* thinly distributed ◆ **des milliers de familles de réfugiés sont disséminées dans les villages** thousands of refugee families are dispersed among the villages **VPR se disséminer** *[graines]* to scatter; *[personnes]* to spread (out) ◆ **les pique-niqueurs se disséminèrent aux quatre coins de la forêt** the picnickers spread out *ou* scattered to the four corners of the forest

dissension /disɑ̃sjɔ̃/ **NF** dissension *(entre, au sein de* between, within)

dissentiment /disɑ̃timɑ̃/ **NM** disagreement, difference of opinion

disséquer /diseke/ ▸ **conjug 6** ◂ **VT** *[+ cadavre, plante]* to dissect; *[+ texte, problème]* to dissect, to analyze minutely

dissert* /disɛʀt/ **NF** (abrév de **dissertation**) essay

dissertation /disɛʀtasjɔ̃/ **NF** *(Scol, hum)* essay; *(péj : †† = traité)* dissertation

disserter /disɛʀte/ ▸ **conjug 1** ◂ **VI** 1 *(Scol)* **~ sur** *(= parler)* to speak on; *(= écrire)* to write an essay on 2 *(péj)* to hold forth *(de, sur* about, on)

dissidence /disidɑ̃s/ **NF** *(= sécession)* *(Pol)* dissidence, rebellion; *(Rel)* dissent; *(= dissidents)* dissidents, rebels; *(littér = divergence)* disagreement, dissidence ◆ **entrer en ~ contre** *[+ régime]* to rebel against; *[+ parti]* to break away from ◆ **rejoindre la ~** to join the dissidents *ou* the rebels

dissident, e /disidɑ̃, ɑ̃t/ **ADJ** *(Pol)* dissident; *(Rel)* dissenting ◆ **groupe ~** breakaway *ou* splinter group ◆ **une fraction ~e de cette organisation terroriste** a dissident minority in this terrorist organization ◆ **une voix ~e à l'intérieur du parti** a dissenting voice within the party ◆ **un candidat socialiste ~** a socialist candidate who has broken away from the party **NM,F** *(Pol)* dissident, rebel; *(Rel)* dissenter

dissimilitude /disimilityd/ **NF** dissimilarity

dissimulateur, -trice /disimylatœʀ, tʀis/ **ADJ** dissembling **NM,F** dissembler

dissimulation /disimylasjɔ̃/ **NF** *(NonC)* *(= duplicité)* dissimulation, dissembling; *(= cachotterie)* dissimulation *(NonC)*, dissembling *(NonC)*; *(= action de cacher)* concealment ◆ **agir avec ~** to act in an underhand way ◆ **~ d'actif** *(Jur)* (fraudulent) concealment of assets ◆ **~ de salariés** *(Jur)* non-declaration of workers ◆ **~ de preuve(s)** withholding of evidence

dissimulé, e /disimyle/ (ptp de **dissimuler**) **ADJ** ◆ **sentiments mal ~s** ill-concealed feelings ◆ **avec un plaisir non ~** with undisguised glee *ou* pleasure

dissimuler /disimyle/ ▸ **conjug 1** ◂ **VT** *(= cacher)* *[+ objet, personne, sentiment, difficulté]* to conceal, to hide *(à qn* from sb); *(Fin)* *[+ bénéfices]* to conceal ◆ **son visage dissimulé par un foulard** her face hidden by a scarf ◆ **ces arbustes dissimulent la cabane** the shrubs hide the shed from view ◆ **il sait bien ~** he's good at pretending *ou* dissembling *(frm)* ◆ **il parvenait mal à ~ son impatience/son envie de rire** he had great difficulty concealing *ou* hiding his annoyance/his urge to laugh ◆ **je ne vous dissimulerai pas qu'il y a de gros problèmes** I won't disguise *ou* conceal the fact that there are serious problems

VPR se dissimuler to conceal *ou* hide o.s. ◆ **il essaie de se ~ la vérité/qu'il a tort** he's trying to close his eyes to the truth/to the fact that he's wrong, he's trying to conceal the truth from himself/to conceal from himself the fact that he's wrong

dissipateur, -trice /disipatœʀ, tʀis/ **NM,F** *(littér)* spendthrift, squanderer *(Brit)*

dissipation /disipasjɔ̃/ **NF** 1 *(= indiscipline)* misbehaviour *(Brit)*, misbehavior *(US)*, unruliness; *(littér = débauche)* dissipation ◆ **une vie de ~** a dissipated life, a life of dissipation 2 *(= dilapidation)* *[de fortune]* squandering, dissipation; *(= folle dépense)* extravagance 3 *[de fumée, nuages]* dissipation, dispersal; *[de brouillard]* clearing, lifting; *[de craintes]* dispelling ◆ **après ~ des brouillards matinaux** after the early morning fog has lifted *ou* cleared

dissipé, e /disipe/ (ptp de **dissiper**) **ADJ** *[élève]* undisciplined, unruly; *[vie]* dissolute, dissipated

dissiper /disipe/ ▸ **conjug 1** ◂ **VT** 1 *(= chasser)* *[+ brouillard, fumée]* to dispel, to disperse, to clear away; *[+ nuages]* to break up, to disperse; *[+ soupçon, crainte]* to dissipate, to dispel; *[+ malentendu]* to clear up 2 *(= dilapider)* *[+ fortune]* to squander, to fritter away, to dissipate; *(littér)* *[+ jeunesse]* to waste, to dissipate, to idle away 3 ◆ **~ qn** to lead sb astray *ou* into bad ways ◆ **il dissipe ses camarades en classe** he is a distracting influence on *ou* he distracts his classmates 4 *(Sci)* to dissipate **VPR se dissiper**

① *(= disparaître) [fumée]* to drift away, to disperse; *[nuages]* to break (up), to disperse; *[brouillard]* to clear, to lift, to disperse; *[inquiétude]* to vanish, to melt away; *[malaise, fatigue]* to disappear, to go away, to wear off ② *[élève]* to become undisciplined *ou* unruly, to misbehave

dissociable /disɔsjabl/ ADJ *[molécules]* dissociable, separable; *[problèmes]* separable

dissociation /disɔsjasjɔ̃/ NF *[de molécules, problèmes]* dissociation, separation

dissocier /disɔsje/ ▸ conjug 7 ◂ VT *[+ molécules, problèmes]* to dissociate VPR **se dissocier** *[éléments, groupe, équipe]* to break up, to split up ◆ **nous tenons à nous ~ de ces groupes/vues** we are anxious to dissociate ourselves from these groups/views

dissolu, e /disɔly/ ADJ dissolute

dissolution /disɔlysjɔ̃/ NF ① *(Jur) [d'assemblée, gouvernement, mariage]* dissolution; *[d'association, groupe, parti]* dissolution, disbanding ◆ **prononcer la ~ de** *[+ mariage]* to dissolve; *[+ parti, groupement]* to disband ② *(= désagrégation) [de groupe, association]* breaking-up, splitting-up; *[d'empire]* crumbling, decay, dissolution ◆ **l'unité nationale est en pleine ~** national unity is crumbling *ou* disintegrating *ou* falling apart ③ *[de sucre]* dissolving ◆ **jusqu'à ~ complète du cachet** until the tablet has completely dissolved ④ *(= colle)* rubber solution ⑤ *(littér = débauche)* dissoluteness, dissipation

dissolvant, e /disɔlvɑ̃, ɑ̃t/ ADJ solvent NM *(= produit)* solvent ◆ **~ (gras)** *(pour les ongles)* nail polish *ou* varnish remover

dissonance /disɔnɑ̃s/ NF *(Mus = intervalle)* dissonance, discord; *[de couleurs, styles]* mismatch; *(fig)* clash; *(= manque d'harmonie)* discord, dissonance ◆ **des ~s de tons dans un tableau** clashes of colour in a painting

dissonant, e /disɔnɑ̃, ɑ̃t/ ADJ *[sons, accord]* dissonant, discordant; *[couleurs]* clashing *(épith)*

dissoudre /disudʀ/ ▸ conjug 51 ◂ VT ① *[+ sel]* to dissolve ◆ **(faire) ~ du sucre** to dissolve sugar ② *(Jur, Pol) [+ assemblée, gouvernement]* to dissolve; *[+ parti, groupement, association]* to disband; *[+ mariage]* to dissolve VPR **se dissoudre** ① *[sel, sucre]* to dissolve, to be dissolved ② *[association]* to disband

dissuader /disɥade/ ▸ conjug 1 ◂ VT ◆ **~ qn de faire qch** to persuade sb not to do sth; *[circonstances]* to deter sb from doing sth ◆ **il m'a dissuadé d'y aller** he talked me out of going, he persuaded me not to go ◆ **rien ne pouvait l'en ~** nothing could dissuade him

dissuasif, -ive /disɥazif, iv/ ADJ deterrent *(épith)* ◆ **avoir un effet ~ sur** to have a deterrent effect on ◆ **à un prix ~** at a prohibitive price

dissuasion /disɥazjɔ̃/ NF *(gén)* dissuasion; *(Mil)* deterrence ◆ **la ~ nucléaire** nuclear deterrence ◆ **de ~** *[mesures, force, stratégie]* deterrent

dissyllabe /disi(l)lab/ ADJ disyllabic NM disyllable

dissyllabique /disi(l)labik/ ADJ disyllabic

dissymétrie /disimetʀi/ NF dissymmetry

dissymétrique /disimetʀik/ ADJ dissymmetric(al)

distance /distɑ̃s/ NF ① *(= éloignement, intervalle, trajet)* distance ◆ **~ focale** *(Photo)* focal length ◆ **~ de freinage** braking distance ◆ **respectez les ~s (de freinage)** keep your distance ◆ **parcourir de grandes/petites ~s** to cover great/small distances ◆ **il est meilleur sur les grandes ~s** *(Sport)* he's better over long distances ◆ **quelle ~ parcourue depuis son dernier roman !** what a long way *ou* how far he has come since his last novel!

② *(= écart)* gap ◆ **la ~ qui sépare deux générations/points de vue** the gap between *ou* which separates two generations/points of view ◆ **la guerre a mis une grande ~ entre ces deux peuples** the war has left a great gulf between these two nations

③ *(locutions)* **garder ses ~s** to keep one's distance *(vis à vis de* from); ◆ **prendre ses ~s** *(Mil)* to form open order; *(Scol etc)* to space out; *(fig)* to stand aloof *(à l'égard de* from) to distance o.s. *(par rapport à* from); ◆ **les syndicats ont pris leurs ~s vis-à-vis du gouvernement** the unions have distanced themselves from the government ◆ **tenir la ~** *[coureur]* to go *ou* do *ou* cover the distance, to last *ou* stay the course; *[conférencier]* to stay *ou* last the course ◆ **à deux ou trois ans de ~ je m'en souviens encore** two or three years later I can still remember it ◆ **nés à quelques années de ~** born within a few years of one another, born a few years apart ◆ **de ~ en ~** at intervals, here and there ◆ **téléphone/communication/vol longue ~** long-distance (tele)phone/call/flight

♦ **à distance** *(dans l'espace)* at *ou* from a distance, from afar; *(dans le temps)* at *ou* from a distance ◆ **le prestidigitateur fait bouger des objets à ~** the conjurer moves objects from a distance ◆ **mettre en marche à ~** *[+ appareil]* to switch on by remote control ◆ **tenir qn à ~** to keep sb at a distance *ou* at arm's length ◆ **se tenir à ~** to keep one's distance, to stand aloof

♦ **à + distance** ◆ **à quelle ~ est la gare ?** how far (away) is the station?, what's the distance to the station? ◆ **se tenir à une respectueuse ~ de** to keep *ou* stay a respectful distance from ◆ **habiter à une grande ~/à quelques kilomètres de ~** to live a great distance away *ou* a long way away/a few kilometres away *(de* from); ◆ **à grande ~** *[détection]* long-range *(épith)*, at long range; *[apercevoir]* from a long way off *ou* away ◆ **entendre un bruit/distinguer qch à une ~ de 30 mètres** to hear a noise/make out sth from a distance of 30 metres *ou* from 30 metres away

distancer /distɑ̃se/ ▸ conjug 3 ◂ VT ① *[+ coureur]* to outrun, to outdistance, to leave behind; *[+ voiture]* to outdistance, to leave behind; *[+ concurrent, élève]* to outstrip, to outclass, to leave behind ◆ **se laisser** *ou* **se faire ~** to be left behind, to be outdistanced *(par* by); ◆ **ne nous laissons pas ~** let's not fall behind *ou* be left behind ② *(Sport = disqualifier)* to disqualify

distanciation /distɑ̃sjasjɔ̃/ NF distance ◆ **sa ~ par rapport aux événements** the way he has distanced himself from events

distancier (se) /distɑ̃sje/ ▸ conjug 7 ◂ VPR to distance o.s. *(de* from)

distant, e /distɑ̃, ɑ̃t/ ADJ ① *[lieu]* far-off, faraway, distant; *[événement]* distant, far-off ◆ **~ de la gare** far away from the station ◆ **une ville ~e de 10 km** a town 10 km away ◆ **deux villes ~es de 10 km (l'une de l'autre)** two towns 10 km apart *ou* 10 km away from one another ② *[attitude]* distant, aloof; *[voix]* distant ◆ **il s'est montré très ~** he was very stand-offish

distendre /distɑ̃dʀ/ ▸ conjug 41 ◂ VT *[+ peau]* to distend; *[+ corde, pull, col]* to stretch VPR **se distendre** *[lien]* to slacken, to become looser; *[ventre, peau]* to distend, to become distended *ou* bloated

distendu, e /distɑ̃dy/ (ptp de **distendre**) ADJ *[ventre]* distended, bloated; *[corde]* slack, loose; *[élastique, ressort]* slack

distension /distɑ̃sjɔ̃/ NF *[de peau, estomac]* distension; *[de corde]* slackening, loosening

distillat /distila/ NM *(Chim)* distillate

distillateur /distilatœʀ/ NM *(= personne)* distiller

distillation /distilasjɔ̃/ NF distillation, distilling

distiller /distile/ ▸ conjug 1 ◂ VT *[+ alcool]* to distil; *[+ suc]* to elaborate; *[+ ennui]* to exude ◆ **eau distillée** distilled water VI *(Sci)* to distil

distillerie /distilʀi/ NF *(= usine)* distillery; *(= industrie)* distilling

distinct, e /distɛ̃(kt), ɛ̃kt/ ADJ ① *(= indépendant)* distinct, separate *(de* from) ② *(= net)* distinct, clear

distinctement /distɛ̃ktəmɑ̃/ ADV distinctly, clearly

distinctif, -ive /distɛ̃ktif, iv/ ADJ distinctive

distinction /distɛ̃ksjɔ̃/ NF ① *(= différentiation)* distinction ◆ **faire la ~ entre** to make a distinction between ◆ **sans ~** without distinction ◆ **sans ~ de race/d'âge** irrespective of race/age, without distinction of race/age ② *(= décoration, honneur)* distinction ③ *(= raffinement)* distinction, refinement ◆ **il a de la ~** he is very distinguished *ou* refined, he has great distinction ④ *(= éminence)* distinction, eminence ◆ **un pianiste de la plus haute ~** *(frm)* a pianist of the highest distinction

distinguable /distɛ̃gabl/ ADJ distinguishable *(de* from)

distingué, e /distɛ̃ge/ (ptp de **distinguer**) ADJ ① *(= élégant, bien élevé) [personne]* distinguished; *[allure]* elegant, refined, distinguished ◆ **il a l'air très ~** he looks very distinguished, he has a very distinguished look about him ◆ **ça fait très ~** it's very distinguished; → **agréer** ② *(= illustre)* distinguished, eminent ◆ **notre ~ collègue, le professeur Campbell** our distinguished *ou* eminent colleague, Professor Campbell

distinguer /distɛ̃ge/ ▸ conjug 1 ◂ VT ① *(= percevoir) [+ objet, bruit]* to make out, to distinguish ◆ **~ qn dans la foule** to pick out *ou* spot sb in the crowd ◆ **on commença à ~ les collines à travers la brume** the hills began to be visible through the mist ◆ **il distingue mal sans lunettes** he can't see very well without his glasses

② *(= différencier)* to distinguish ◆ **~ une chose d'une autre** *ou* **d'avec une autre** to distinguish *ou* tell one thing from another ◆ **savoir ~ les oiseaux/plantes** to be able to distinguish different species of birds/plants ◆ **les deux sœurs sont difficiles à ~ (l'une de l'autre)** the two sisters are difficult to tell apart ◆ **~ le bien du mal/un Picasso d'un** *ou* **d'avec un Braque** to tell good from evil/a Picasso from a Braque, to distinguish between good and evil/between a Picasso and a Braque ◆ **tu la distingueras à sa veste rouge** you will recognize her *ou* pick her out by her red jacket ◆ **distinguons, il y a chanteur et chanteur** we must make a distinction, there are good singers and bad singers

③ *(= rendre différent)* to distinguish, to set apart *(de* from) to mark off ◆ **c'est son accent qui le distingue des autres** it is his accent which distinguishes him from *ou* makes him different from the others *ou* which sets him apart

④ *(frm) (= choisir)* to single out; *(= honorer)* to honour *(Brit)*, to honor *(US)* ◆ **on l'a distingué pour faire le discours d'adieu** he was singled out to make the farewell speech ◆ **l'Académie française a distingué X pour son œuvre poétique** the Académie Française has honoured X for his works of poetry

VPR **se distinguer** ① *(= différer)* to distinguish o.s., to be distinguished *(de* from); ◆ **ces objets se distinguent par** *ou* **grâce à leur couleur** these objects can be distinguished by their colour ◆ **les deux frères se distinguent (l'un de l'autre) par leur taille** you can tell the two brothers apart by their (different) height ◆ **il se distingue par son accent/sa démarche** his accent/his walk makes him stand out *ou* makes him seem quite different

2 *(= se signaler, réussir)* to distinguish o.s. ◆ **se ~ (pendant une guerre) par son courage** to distinguish o.s. (in a war) by one's courage ◆ **il s'est distingué par ses découvertes en physique** he has become famous for *ou* from his discoveries in physics, he's made a name for himself by his discoveries in physics ◆ **il se distingue par son absence** *(hum)* he is noticeable *ou* conspicuous by his absence ◆ **il s'est particulièrement distingué en latin** he has done particularly well *ou* he has particularly distinguished himself in Latin

distinguo /distɛ̃go/ **NM** *(= nuance)* distinction ◆ **faire le ~ entre l'homme et l'animal** to make a distinction between humans and animals

distique /distik/ **NM** distich

distordre **VT**, **se distordre** **VPR** /distɔʀdʀ/ ▸ conjug 41 ◂ to twist, to distort

distorsion /distɔʀsjɔ̃/ **NF** 1 *(gén, Anat, Téléc)* distortion ◆ **la ~ des faits/de la réalité** distortion of the facts/of reality ◆ **~ de concurrence** *(Écon)* distortion of competition ◆ **~ du temps** time warp 2 *(= déséquilibre : entre des chiffres, salaires, taux)* imbalance *(entre* between); ◆ **la ~ entre les textes et la réalité** *(= décalage)* the discrepancy between the texts and reality

distractif, -ive /distʀaktif, iv/ **ADJ** entertaining

distraction /distʀaksjɔ̃/ **NF** 1 *(= inattention)* absent-mindedness, lack of attention ◆ **j'ai eu une ~** my concentration lapsed, my attention wandered ◆ **cette ~ lui a coûté la vie** this one lapse in concentration cost him his life ◆ **les ~s proverbiales des savants** the proverbial absent-mindedness of scientists 2 *(= passe-temps)* leisure *ou* recreational activity, pastime ◆ **ça manque de ~** there's not much in the way of entertainment ◆ **c'est sa seule ~** it's his only form of entertainment 3 *(Jur = vol)* abstraction ◆ **~ de fonds** misappropriation of funds

distraire /distʀɛʀ/ ▸ conjug 50 ◂ **VT** 1 *(= divertir)* to entertain, to amuse 2 *(= déranger)* to distract, to divert *(de* from); ◆ **~ l'attention de qn** to distract sb's attention ◆ **il distrait ses camarades** he distracts his friends ◆ **se laisser facilement ~ de son travail** to be easily distracted from one's work ◆ **~ qn de ses soucis** to take sb's mind off his worries 3 *(frm = voler)* to abstract *(de* from); ◆ **~ des fonds** to misappropriate funds **VPR** **se distraire** to amuse o.s., to enjoy o.s. ◆ **je vais au cinéma, j'ai besoin de me ~** I'm going to the cinema, I need a break ◆ **je lis des romans pour me ~** I read novels for entertainment

distrait, e /distʀɛ, ɛt/ (ptp de **distraire**) **ADJ** *[personne, caractère]* absent-minded ◆ **d'un air ~** distractedly ◆ **il n'y a prêté qu'une attention ~e** he wasn't giving it his full attention ◆ **d'une oreille ~e** with only half an ear, abstractedly ◆ **je l'ai lu d'un œil ~** I glanced through it

distraitement /distʀɛtmɑ̃/ **ADV** absent-mindedly, distractedly

distrayant, e /distʀɛjɑ̃, ɑ̃t/ **ADJ** entertaining ◆ **les romans policiers sont d'une lecture ~e** detective stories are entertaining

distribuer /distʀibɥe/ ▸ conjug 1 ◂ **VT** 1 *(= donner)* *[+ objets]* to distribute, to give out, to hand out; *[+ vivres]* to distribute, to share out; *[+ courrier]* to deliver; *[+ récompense]* to present; *(Fin) [+ actions]* to allot; *[+ travail]* to distribute; *[+ argent, dividendes]* to distribute, to hand out; *[+ cartes]* to deal (out); *[+ ordres]* to hand out, to deal out; *[+ coups]* to deal, to deliver; *[+ saluts, sourires, enseignement]* to dispense *(à* to); ◆ **~ les rôles d'une pièce** to cast a play ◆ **~ des claques à qn** to slap sb

2 *(= répartir)* to distribute, to arrange; *(Typo) [+ caractères]* to distribute ◆ **on distribue ces plantes en quatre espèces** these plants are divided into four species ◆ **savoir ~ son temps** to know how to allocate *ou* divide (up) one's time ◆ **comment les pièces sont-elles distribuées ?** how are the rooms set out? *ou* laid out? ◆ **~ les masses dans un tableau** to arrange *ou* distribute the masses in a picture ◆ **mon emploi du temps est mal distribué** my schedule is badly arranged

3 *(= amener)* to distribute, to carry ◆ **~ l'eau dans les villages** to distribute *ou* carry *ou* supply water to villages ◆ **le sang est distribué dans tout le corps par le cœur** blood is pumped *ou* carried round the body by the heart ◆ **chaîne de télévision distribuée par câble** cable television channel

4 *[+ film, produit]* to distribute

distributeur, -trice /distʀibytœʀ, tʀis/ **ADJ** *[compagnie, entreprise]* distributing ◆ **société distributrice de films** film distribution company, film distributor **NM,F** *(= agent commercial)* distributor ◆ **~ d'essence** petrol company ◆ **~ de films** film distributor **NM** *(= appareil)* machine; *[de savon, papier absorbant]* dispenser; *(dans moteur)* distributor ◆ **~ (automatique)** vending machine ◆ **~ de boissons/préservatifs** drinks/condom(-vending) machine, drinks/condom dispenser ◆ **~ (automatique) de billets** *(Banque)* cash dispenser *ou* machine, automatic *ou* automated teller machine; *(Rail)* (automatic) ticket machine ◆ **~ d'engrais** *(Agr)* manure- *ou* muck-spreader

distributif, -ive /distʀibytif, iv/ **ADJ** distributive

distribution /distʀibysjɔ̃/ **NF** 1 *[d'objets]* distribution, giving out, handing out; *[de vivres]* distribution, sharing out; *[d'argent, dividendes]* distribution; *[de cartes]* deal; *[de courrier]* delivery; *(Fin) [d'actions]* allotment ◆ **la ~ du travail sera faite suivant l'âge** the work will be shared out *ou* allotted *ou* allocated according to age ◆ **~ gratuite** free gifts ◆ **(jour de la) ~ des prix** prize giving (day)

2 *(= répartition)* distribution, arrangement; *(Ling)* distribution ◆ **la ~ des mots dans une phrase** the distribution of words in a sentence ◆ **la ~ des meubles dans une pièce** the arrangement of the furniture in a room ◆ **cet appartement a une bonne/mauvaise ~ (des pièces)** the flat is well/badly laid out ◆ **ce résultat a conduit à une nouvelle ~ des cartes** this result has shifted *ou* altered the balance of power *ou* has put a new complexion on the situation

3 *(= acteurs)* cast ◆ **~ par ordre d'entrée en scène** cast *ou* characters in order of appearance ◆ **qui est responsable de la ~ de cette pièce ?** who's in charge of casting this play?

4 *[d'eau, électricité]* supply ◆ **~ par câble/par satellite** (TV) cable/satellite distribution

5 *[de livres, films]* distribution ◆ **réseau de ~** distribution network ◆ **la grande ~** mass marketing

6 *(dans moteur)* distribution

distributionnel, -elle /distʀibysjɔnɛl/ **ADJ** distributional

distributivement /distʀibytivmɑ̃/ **ADV** distributively

distributivité /distʀibytivite/ **NF** distributiveness

district /distʀikt/ **NM** district ◆ **~ urbain** urban district

dit, e /di, dit/ (ptp de **dire**) **ADJ** 1 *(= appelé)* **Louis XIV, ~ le Roi Soleil** Louis XIV, known as the Sun King ◆ **Jean Petit, ~ le Chacal** Jean Petit, also known as the Jackal *ou* aka *ou* alias the Jackal ◆ **une émission ~e culturelle** a so-called cultural programme 2 *(= fixé)* **à l'heure ~e** at the appointed time *ou* hour ◆ **le jour ~** on the appointed day **NM** *(Psych)* ◆ **le ~ et le non-~** what is said and what is left unsaid

dithyrambe /ditiʀɑ̃b/ **NM** 1 *(= poème)* dithyramb 2 *(= éloge)* panegyric, eulogy

dithyrambique /ditiʀɑ̃bik/ **ADJ** *[paroles]* laudatory, eulogistic; *[éloges]* extravagant; *(Littérat)* dithyrambic ◆ **une critique ~** a rave review

dito /dito/ **ADV** *(Comm)* ditto

DIU /deiy/ **NM** (abrév de **dispositif intra-utérin**) IUD

diurèse /djyʀɛz/ **NF** *(Physiol)* diuresis

diurétique /djyʀetik/ **ADJ, NM** diuretic

diurne /djyʀn/ **ADJ** diurnal

diva /diva/ **NF** (†, *aussi hum)* diva, prima donna ◆ **elle a des caprices de ~** she's a bit of a prima donna

divagation /divagasjɔ̃/ **NF** *(gén pl)* *(= délire)* wandering, rambling; *(= bêtises)* raving

divaguer /divage/ ▸ conjug 1 ◂ **VI** *(= délirer)* to ramble; *(= dire des bêtises)* to rave ◆ **il commence à ~** he's beginning to ramble ◆ **tu divagues !** you're off your head! *

divan /divɑ̃/ **NM** divan ◆ **le ~ du psychanalyste** the psychoanalyst's couch

dive /div/ **ADJ F** ◆ **la ~ bouteille** the bottle, drink ◆ **il aime la ~ bouteille** he likes his drink

divergence /divɛʀʒɑ̃s/ **NF** 1 *[d'opinions]* divergence, difference; *[de témoignages]* discrepancy 2 *(Opt, Phys Nucl)* divergence

divergent, e /divɛʀʒɑ̃, ɑ̃t/ **ADJ** 1 *[opinions]* divergent, differing; *[témoignages]* differing 2 *(Opt, Phys Nucl)* divergent; → **strabisme**

diverger /divɛʀʒe/ GRAMMAIRE ACTIVE 39.1 ▸ conjug 3 ◂ **VI** 1 *[opinions]* to diverge, to differ; *[témoignages]* to differ 2 *[chemins, rayons]* to diverge 3 *(Phys Nucl)* to go critical

divers, e /divɛʀ, ɛʀs/ **ADJ** 1 *(pl)* *(= varié)* *[couleurs, opinions]* various; *[coutumes]* diverse; *(= différent)* *[sens d'un mot, moments, occupations]* different, various ◆ **frais ~, dépenses ~es** sundries, miscellaneous expenses ◆ **ses dons/écrits ~ et variés** his many and various talents/writings ◆ **elle a suivi des traitements ~ et variés** *(hum)* she has undergone all manner of treatments; → **fait¹** 2 *(pl = plusieurs)* various, several ◆ **~es personnes m'en ont parlé** various *ou* several people have spoken to me about it 3 *(littér = changeant)* *[spectacle]* varied, changing *(épith)*

diversement /divɛʀsəmɑ̃/ **ADV** in various ways ◆ **son livre a été ~ accueilli** his book has had a mixed reception ◆ **son discours a été ~ apprécié** there were mixed reactions to his speech

diversification /divɛʀsifikasjɔ̃/ **NF** diversification ◆ **l'entreprise poursuit la ~ de ses activités** the company is continuing to diversify (its activities)

diversifier /divɛʀsifje/ ▸ conjug 7 ◂ **VT** *[+ méthodes, exercices]* to vary; *[+ activités, centres d'intérêt, production]* to diversify ◆ **une économie/une gamme de produits diversifiée** a varied *ou* diversified economy/range of products **VPR** **se diversifier** *[entreprise]* to diversify; *[activités]* to be diversified; *[clientèle, public]* to become more diverse ◆ **nous devons nous ~ davantage** we must diversify more

diversion /divɛʀsjɔ̃/ **NF** *(Mil, littér)* diversion ◆ **faire ~** to create a diversion

diversité /divɛʀsite/ **NF** *(= grand nombre)* range, variety; *(= variété)* variety, diversity

divertir /divɛʀtiʀ/ ▸ conjug 2 ◂ **VT** 1 *(= amuser)* to amuse, to entertain 2 *(Jur)* **~ des fonds/une succession** *(= détourner)* to misappropriate funds/an inheritance **VPR** **se divertir** *(= se distraire)* to amuse o.s.; *(= prendre du bon temps)* to enjoy o.s. ◆ **se ~ de qn** *(littér)* to make fun of sb, to laugh at sb

divertissant, e /divɛʀtisɑ̃, ɑ̃t/ ADJ *(= qui fait rire)* amusing; *(= qui occupe agréablement)* entertaining

divertissement /divɛʀtismɑ̃/ NM 1 *(NonC = action de distraire)* entertainment ◆ **la boxe est un ~ populaire** boxing is a popular form of entertainment ◆ **le spectacle est organisé pour le ~ des touristes** the show is put on to entertain the tourists ◆ **émission de ~** light-entertainment programme 2 *(= distraction, passe-temps)* entertainment ◆ **le jazz était considéré d'abord comme un ~** jazz was considered as being primarily entertainment ◆ **les ~s sont rares dans ce village** there isn't much to do in this village, there's not much by way of entertainment in this village 3 *(Mus)* divertimento, divertissement 4 *(††, Philos)* distraction

dividende /dividɑ̃d/ NM *(Fin, Math)* dividend ◆ **~ sous forme d'actions** share *ou* stock dividend ◆ **~ prioritaire** preferential *ou* preference dividend ◆ **avec ~** cum div(idend), dividend on *(US)* ◆ **sans ~** ex div(idend), dividend off *(US)*

divin, e /divɛ̃, in/ ADJ 1 *[caractère, justice, service]* divine ◆ **la loi ~e** divine law, the law of God ◆ **le ~ Achille** the divine Achilles ◆ **la ~e Providence** divine Providence ◆ **notre ~ Sauveur** our Divine Saviour ◆ **notre ~ Père** our heavenly Father ◆ **l'amour ~** divine *ou* heavenly love ◆ **le sens du ~** the sense of the divine; → **bonté, droit³** 2 *(= excellent) [poésie, beauté, mets, robe, temps]* divine, heavenly

divinateur, -trice /divinatœʀ, tʀis/ ADJ divining, foreseeing NM,F †† diviner, soothsayer

divination /divinasjɔ̃/ NF divination

divinatoire /divinatwaʀ/ ADJ *[science]* divinatory

divinement /divinmɑ̃/ ADV divinely

divinisation /divinizasjɔ̃/ NF deification

diviniser /divinize/ ► conjug 1 ◄ VT to deify

divinité /divinite/ NF *(= essence divine)* divinity; *(lit, fig = dieu)* deity, divinity

diviser /divize/ ► conjug 1 ◄ VT 1 *(= fractionner) (gén)* to divide; *[+ tâche, ressources]* to share out, to split up; *[+ gâteau]* to cut up, to divide up ◆ **~ une somme en trois/en trois parties** to divide *ou* split a sum of money in three/into three parts ◆ **~ une somme entre plusieurs personnes** to share (out) *ou* divide (out) a sum among several people ◆ **le pays est divisé en deux par des montagnes** the country is split *ou* divided in two by mountains ◆ **~ un groupe en plusieurs équipes** to split a group up into several teams

2 *(= désunir) [+ famille, adversaires]* to divide, to set at variance ◆ **"diviser pour (mieux) régner"** "divide and rule" ◆ **une famille divisée** a broken family ◆ **les historiens sont très divisés à ce sujet** historians are very divided on this subject ◆ **l'opinion est divisée en deux par cette affaire** opinion is split *ou* divided over this affair

3 *(† = séparer)* to divide, to separate ◆ **un rideau divise la chambre d'avec le salon** *ou* **du salon** a curtain separates the bedroom (off) from the drawing room

4 *(Math)* to divide ◆ **~ 4 par 2** to divide 4 by 2

VPR **se diviser** 1 *(= se scinder) [groupe, cellules]* to split up, to divide (*en* into)

2 *(= se ramifier) [route]* to fork, to divide; *[tronc d'arbre]* to fork ◆ **ce livre se divise en plusieurs chapitres** this book is divided into several chapters

diviseur /divizœʀ/ NM 1 *(Math)* divisor ◆ **nombre/fraction ~** divisor number/fraction ◆ **plus grand commun ~** highest common factor ◆ **~ de fréquence** *(Élec)* frequency divider 2 *(= personne)* divisive force *ou* influence

divisibilité /divizibilite/ NF divisibility

divisible /divizibl/ ADJ divisible ◆ **le nombre est ~ par 2** the number is divisible by *ou* can be divided by 2

division /divizjɔ̃/ NF 1 *(Math)* division ◆ **faire une ~** to do a division (sum) 2 *(= désaccord)* division ◆ **il y a une ~ au sein du parti** there's a split *ou* rift within the party ◆ **semer la ~** to sow discord (*entre* among) 3 *(Ftbl etc)* division ◆ **~ d'honneur** 4th division ◆ **club de première/deuxième ~** first/second division club ◆ **ils sont montés en première ~** they've gone up to *ou* have been promoted to the first division 4 *(Mil, Admin)* division ◆ **~ blindée/d'infanterie** armoured/infantry division; → **général²** 5 *(= fractionnement)* division; *(= partage)* sharing out, division (*en* into); ◆ **~ du travail** division of labour ◆ **~ cellulaire** cellular division 6 *(= graduation)* division 7 *(= partie, compartiment)* division; *(= branche) [de science]* division

divisionnaire /divizjɔnɛʀ/ ADJ divisional NM *(† Mil)* major-general ◆ **(commissaire) ~** *(Police)* ≃ chief superintendent *(Brit)*, police chief *(US)*

divorce /divɔʀs/ NM *(lit, fig)* divorce (*avec, d'avec* from; *entre* between); ◆ **demander le ~** *(gén)* to ask for a divorce; *(Jur)* to sue for (a) divorce ◆ **obtenir le ~** to obtain *ou* get a divorce ◆ **~ par consentement mutuel** divorce by consent *(Brit)*, no-fault divorce *(US)* ◆ **les enfants du ~** children of divorced parents *ou* of divorce

divorcé, e /divɔʀse/ (ptp de **divorcer**) ADJ *(lit, fig)* divorced (*de* from) NM,F divorcee

divorcer /divɔʀse/ ► conjug 3 ◄ VI 1 *[personne]* to get a divorce; *[couple]* to get divorced ◆ **~ d'avec sa femme/son mari** to divorce one's wife/one's husband 2 *(fig)* to break (*d'avec, de* with)

divulgateur, -trice /divylgatœʀ, tʀis/ NM,F divulger

divulgation /divylgasjɔ̃/ NF disclosure

divulguer /divylge/ ► conjug 1 ◄ VT to divulge, to disclose

dix /dis/ ADJ INV, NM INV ten ◆ **les ~ commandements** the Ten Commandments ◆ **elle a eu ~ sur ~** *(Scol)* she got ten out of ten, she got full marks *(Brit)* ◆ **avoir ~ dixièmes à chaque œil** to have twenty-twenty vision ◆ **répéter/recommencer ~ fois la même chose** to repeat/start the same thing over and over (again); *pour autres loc voir* **six**

dix-huit /dizɥit/ ADJ INV, NM INV eighteen ◆ **un (golf) ~ trous** an eighteen-hole golf course

dix-huitième /dizɥitjɛm/ ADJ, NMF eighteenth ◆ **un fauteuil fin ~** a late eighteenth-century armchair

dixième /dizjɛm/ ADJ, NMF tenth ◆ **je ne sais pas le ~ de ce qu'il sait** I don't know one tenth *ou* a tenth of the things he knows

dixièmement /dizjɛmmɑ̃/ ADV tenthly, in (the) tenth place

dixit /diksit/ LOC VERB dixit

dix-neuf /diznœf/ ADJ INV, NM INV nineteen

dix-neuvième /diznœvjɛm/ ADJ, NMF nineteenth ◆ **les romans du ~** nineteenth-century novels

dix-sept /di(s)sɛt/ ADJ INV, NM INV seventeen

dix-septième /di(s)sɛtjɛm/ ADJ, NMF seventeenth ◆ **les auteurs du ~** seventeenth-century writers

dizain /dizɛ̃/ NM ten-line poem

dizaine /dizɛn/ NF *(= dix)* ten; *(= quantité voisine de dix)* about ten, ten or so ◆ **des ~s de fois** dozens of times, over and over again ◆ **les ~s** *(= colonne)* the tens column

DJ /didʒi/ NM (abrév de **disque-jockey**) DJ

Djakarta /dʒakaʀta/ N Jakarta, Djakarta

djebel /dʒebɛl/ NM jebel

djellaba /dʒɛ(l)laba/ NF jellaba

Djibouti /dʒibuti/ NM Djibouti, Djibouti

djiboutien, -ienne /dʒibusjɛ̃, jɛn/ ADJ of *ou* from Djibouti NM,F **Djiboutien(ne)** inhabitant *ou* native of Djibouti

djihad /dʒi(j)ad/ NF jihad, jehad ◆ **le Djihad islamique** Islamic Jihad

djihadiste /dʒi(j)adist/ NMF jihadist

djinn /dʒin/ NM jinn, djinn

dl (abrév de **décilitre**) dl

DM (abrév de **Deutsche Mark**) DM

dm (abrév de **décimètre**) dm

do /do/ NM INV *(Mus) (= note)* C; *(en chantant la gamme)* doh ◆ **le ~ du milieu du piano** middle C

doberman /dɔbɛʀman/ NM Doberman pinscher

doc* /dɔk/ NF abrév de **documentation**

docile /dɔsil/ ADJ *[personne, caractère]* docile, obedient; *[animal]* docile; *[cheveux]* manageable

docilement /dɔsilmɑ̃/ ADV docilely, obediently

docilité /dɔsilite/ NF docility, obedience

docimologie /dɔsimɔlɔʒi/ NF (statistical) analysis of test *ou* exam results

dock /dɔk/ NM 1 *(= bassin)* dock; *(= cale de construction)* dockyard ◆ **~ de carénage/flottant** dry/floating dock 2 *(= hangar, bâtiment)* warehouse

docker /dɔkɛʀ/ NM docker, stevedore

docte /dɔkt/ ADJ *(littér, hum)* learned

doctement /dɔktəmɑ̃/ ADV *(littér, hum)* learnedly

docteur /dɔktœʀ/ NM 1 *(Méd)* doctor ◆ **~ en médecine** doctor of medicine ◆ **aller chez le ~** to go to the doctor's ◆ **le ~ Lebrun** Dr Lebrun 2 *(Univ)* doctor (*ès, en* of); ◆ **maintenant que tu es ~** *(Univ)* now you've got your doctorate *ou* PhD ◆ **Monsieur Leroux, ~ ès lettres** Dr Leroux, PhD ◆ **les ~s de l'Église** *(Rel)* the Doctors of the Church

doctoral, e (mpl **-aux**) /dɔktɔʀal, o/ ADJ 1 *(Univ)* doctoral ◆ **école ~e** graduate school *(US)* 2 *(péj = pédant) [ton, air]* pompous

doctorant, e /dɔktɔʀɑ̃, ɑ̃t/ NM,F PhD student *(Brit)*, doctoral student *(US)*

doctorat /dɔktɔʀa/ NM doctorate (*ès, en* in); ◆ **~ de 3ᵉ cycle, ~ d'État** doctorate, PhD; → **DIPLÔMES**

doctoresse /dɔktɔʀɛs/ NF woman *ou* lady doctor

doctrinaire /dɔktʀinɛʀ/ ADJ *(= dogmatique)* doctrinaire; *(= sentencieux)* pompous, sententious NMF doctrinarian

doctrinal, e (mpl **-aux**) /dɔktʀinal, o/ ADJ doctrinal

doctrine /dɔktʀin/ NF doctrine

docu* /dɔky/ NM (abrév de **documentaire**) documentary ◆ **~-soap** docu-soap

docudrame /dɔkydʀam/ NM docudrama

document /dɔkymɑ̃/ NM document ◆ **nous avons des ~s le prouvant** we have documentary evidence, we have documents to prove it ◆ **~s de travail** working documents ◆ **~ de référence** *ou* **d'information** background paper ◆ **~s d'expédition** dispatch documents ◆ **~s d'archives** archives; *(Ciné, TV)* archive footage *(NonC)* *ou* material *(NonC)* ◆ **~ administratif unique** Single Administrative Document

documentaire /dɔkymɑ̃tɛʀ/ ADJ *[intérêt]* documentary ◆ **à titre** ~ for your (*ou* his *etc*) information ◆ **logiciel** ~ documentation software (*NonC*) NM (= *film*) documentary (film)

documentaliste /dɔkymɑ̃talist/ NMF (*Presse, TV*) researcher; (*Scol*) librarian; (*dans une entreprise*) archivist

documentariste /dɔkymɑ̃taʀist/ NMF documentary maker

documentation /dɔkymɑ̃tasjɔ̃/ NF (= *brochures*) information, literature; (*Presse, TV* = *service*) research department

documenter /dɔkymɑ̃te/ ▸ conjug 1 ◂ VT *[+ situation, conditions, conflit]* to document ◆ **bien documenté** *[rapport, cas]* well-documented; *[article, livre]* well-researched; *[+ personne]* well-informed VPR **se documenter** to gather information *ou* material (*sur* on, about)

dodécaèdre /dɔdekaɛdʀ/ NM dodecahedron

dodécagonal, e (mpl **-aux**) /dɔdekagɔnal, o/ ADJ dodecagonal

dodécagone /dɔdekagɔn/ NM dodecagon

dodécaphonique /dɔdekafɔnik/ ADJ dodecaphonic

dodécaphonisme /dɔdekafɔnism/ NM dodecaphony

dodécaphoniste /dɔdekafɔnist/ ADJ *[compositeur, œuvre]* dodecaphonic NMF dodecaphonist

dodeliner /dɔd(ə)line/ ▸ conjug 1 ◂ VI ◆ **il dodelinait de la tête** his head was nodding gently ◆ **sa tête dodelinait par instants** his head would nod every now and again

dodo[1] /dodo/ NM (*langage enfantin*) (= *sommeil*) sleep, beddy-byes (*langage enfantin*) ◆ **faire** ~ to be asleep ◆ **il est temps d'aller au** ~ *ou* **d'aller faire** ~ it's time to go to beddy-byes (*langage enfantin*) ◆ **(fais)** ~ **!** come on, sleepy-time! ◆ **un bon gros/un petit** ~ a nice long/a short sleep

dodo[2] /dodo/ NM (= *oiseau*) dodo

Dodoma /dodoma/ N Dodoma

dodu, e /dɔdy/ ADJ *[personne, poule, bras]* plump; *[enfant, joue]* chubby

doge /dɔʒ/ NM doge

dogmatique /dɔgmatik/ ADJ dogmatic

dogmatiquement /dɔgmatikmɑ̃/ ADV dogmatically

dogmatiser /dɔgmatize/ ▸ conjug 1 ◂ VI to dogmatize

dogmatisme /dɔgmatism/ NM dogmatism

dogme /dɔgm/ NM (*lit, fig*) dogma ◆ **le** ~ (*Rel*) the dogma

dogon /dɔgɔ̃/ ADJ *[art, pays]* Dogon NMF **Dogon** Dogon ◆ **les Dogons** the Dogon people

dogue /dɔg/ NM (= *chien*) ◆ ~ **(anglais)** mastiff ◆ ~ **allemand** German mastiff

doigt /dwa/ NM 1 *[de main, gant]* finger; *[d'animal]* digit ◆ ~ **de pied** toe ◆ **le petit** ~ the little finger ◆ **se mettre** *ou* **se fourrer*** **les ~s dans le nez** to pick one's nose ◆ **le ~ de Dieu** the hand of God ◆ **montrer qn du** ~ (*lit*) to point sb out; (*fig*) to point the finger at sb ◆ **désigner qn d'un ~ accusateur** to point an accusing finger at sb; → **bague, bout, compter** *etc*

2 (= *mesure*) **raccourcir une jupe de 2/3 ~s** to shorten a skirt by 1 inch/2 inches ◆ **un ~ de vin** a drop of wine ◆ **un ~ de whisky/vodka** a finger of whisky/vodka

3 (*locutions*) **avoir des ~s de fée** *[couturière, tricoteuse]* to have nimble fingers; *[infirmière]* to have gentle hands ◆ **il ne fait rien de ses dix ~s** he's an idle *ou* a lazy good-for-nothing, he's bone idle (*Brit*) ◆ **il ne sait rien faire de ses dix ~s** he's useless ◆ **faire marcher** *ou* **mener qn au ~ et à l'œil** to keep a tight rein on sb ◆ **avec lui, ils obéissent au ~ et à l'œil** with him, they have to toe the line ◆ **le (petit) ~ sur la couture du pantalon** (*lit*) standing to attention ◆ **c'est devenu un employé modèle, le petit ~ sur la couture du pantalon** he's become a model employee, always ready to jump to attention ◆ **mon petit ~ me l'a dit** a little bird told me ◆ **se mettre** *ou* **se fourrer*** **le ~ dans l'œil (jusqu'au coude)** to be kidding o.s.* ◆ **là tu te mets** *ou* **te fourres*** **le ~ dans l'œil** you've got another think coming* ◆ **il n'a pas levé** *ou* **bougé** *ou* **remué le petit ~ pour nous aider** he didn't lift a finger to help us ◆ **mettre le ~ sur le problème** to put one's finger on the problem ◆ **mettre le ~ sur la plaie** (*fig*) to touch a raw nerve ◆ **toucher du ~** (*lit*) to touch sth (with one's finger); *[+ réalité, sentiment, difficulté]* to grasp fully ◆ **faire toucher du ~ qch (à qn)** (*fig*) to bring sth home (to sb) ◆ **mettre le ~ dans l'engrenage** to get involved ◆ **filer** *ou* **glisser entre les ~s de qn** to slip through sb's fingers ◆ **ils sont unis comme les (deux) ~s de la main** they're joined at the hip*, they're very close ◆ **je le ferais les ~s dans le nez*** I could do it standing on my head *ou* with my eyes closed ◆ **il a gagné les ~s dans le nez*** he won hands down* ◆ **avoir un morceau de musique dans les ~s** to know a piece of music like the back of one's hand ◆ **avoir les ~s de pied en éventail*** to have one's feet up ◆ **être à deux ~s** *ou* **un ~ de faire** to come very close to doing ◆ **il a été à deux ~s de la mort/de réussir** he was within an ace *ou* an inch of death/of succeeding ◆ **la balle est passée à un ~ de sa tête** the bullet passed within a hairbreadth *ou* an inch of his head ◆ **c'est la pratique du ~ mouillé** it's guess work

doigté /dwate/ NM 1 (*Mus*) (= *jeu des doigts*) fingering technique; (= *position des doigts*) fingering 2 *[de chirurgien, dactylo, pianiste]* touch; (= *tact*) diplomacy, tact ◆ **avoir du** ~ (*lit*) to be nimble-fingered; (*fig*) to be tactful ◆ **manquer de** ~ to be heavy-handed ◆ **il faudra du ~ pour mener à bien cette négociation** a certain amount of diplomacy will be needed to bring these negotiations to a successful conclusion

doigter /dwate/ ▸ conjug 1 ◂ VTI (*Mus*) to finger

doigtier /dwatje/ NM fingerstall

doit /dwa/ NM debit ◆ ~ **et avoir** debit and credit

dojo /dɔʒo/ NM dojo

dol /dɔl/ NM (*Jur*) fraud, wilful misrepresentation (*SPÉC*)

dolby ® /dɔlbi/ NM Dolby ®

dolce vita /dɔltʃevita/ NF dolce vita

doléances /dɔleɑ̃s/ NFPL (= *plaintes*) complaints; (= *réclamations*) grievances

dolent, e /dɔlɑ̃, ɑt/ ADJ (*littér*) doleful, mournful

doline /dɔlin/ NF doline

dollar /dɔlaʀ/ NM dollar ◆ ~ **australien/canadien** Australian/Canadian dollar ◆ ~ **titre** security dollar

dollarisation /dɔlaʀizasjɔ̃/ NF *[d'économie, échanges]* dollarization

dolman /dɔlmɑ̃/ NM (*Hist* = *veste*) dolman

dolmen /dɔlmɛn/ NM dolmen

dolomie /dɔlɔmi/, **dolomite** /dɔlɔmit/ NF dolomite ◆ **les Dolomites** the Dolomites

dolomitique /dɔlɔmitik/ ADJ dolomitic

DOM /dɔm/ NM (abrév de **département d'outre-mer**) → **département**

Dom /dɔ̃/ NM (= *titre*) Dom

domaine /dɔmɛn/ NM 1 (= *propriété*) estate, property ◆ **le ~ de la couronne** Crown lands *ou* property ◆ **le ~ (de l'État)** (*Jur*) (= *propriété*) state(-owned) property; (= *service*) the state property department ◆ **dans le ~ public/privé** in the public/private domain, in public/private ownership ◆ **ses œuvres sont maintenant tombées dans le ~ public** his works are now out of copyright ◆ **la salle de jeux est le ~ des enfants** the playroom belongs to the children; → **skiable** 2 (= *sphère*) field, domain, sphere ◆ **ce n'est pas (de) mon** ~ it's not my field *ou* sphere ◆ **dans tous les ~s** in every domain *ou* field ◆ ~ **d'activité stratégique** (*Gestion*) strategic business unit ◆ ~ **réservé** (*fig*) preserve 3 (*dans un dictionnaire*) field ◆ **indication de** ~ field label

domanial, e (mpl **-iaux**) /dɔmanjal, jo/ ADJ (= *d'un domaine privé*) belonging to a private estate; (= *d'un domaine public*) national (*épith*), state (*épith*)

dôme /dom/ NM (= *voûte*) dome; (= *cathédrale*) cathedral ◆ **le ~ du ciel** (*littér*) the vault of heaven ◆ **un ~ de verdure** a canopy of foliage *ou* greenery ◆ ~ **volcanique** volcanic dome

domestication /dɔmɛstikasjɔ̃/ NF (= *action*) domestication, domesticating; (= *résultat*) domestication

domesticité /dɔmɛstisite/ NF 1 (= *condition de domestique*) domestic service 2 (= *personnel*) (domestic) staff, household ◆ **une nombreuse** ~ a large staff of servants 3 *[d'animal]* domesticity

domestique /dɔmɛstik/ NMF servant ◆ **les ~s** the servants, the staff (of servants) ◆ **je ne suis pas ton ~ !** I'm not your servant! ADJ 1 (= *ménager*) *[travaux]* domestic, household (*épith*); *[soucis, querelle]* domestic, family (*épith*) ◆ **accidents ~s** accidents in the home ◆ **déchets ~s** kitchen waste *ou* wastes (*US*) ◆ **les dieux ~s** the household gods 2 *[marché, consommation]* domestic, home (*épith*) 3 *[animal]* domestic ◆ **les animaux ~s** (*gén*) domestic animals; (= *animaux de compagnie*) pets

domestiquer /dɔmɛstike/ ▸ conjug 1 ◂ VT *[+ animal]* to domesticate; *[+ énergie solaire, marée, vent]* to harness

domicile /dɔmisil/ NM place of residence, home; (*sur formulaire*) address; *[de société]* domicile ◆ ~ **légal** official domicile ◆ ~ **conjugal/parental** marital/parental home ◆ **dernier ~ connu** last known address ◆ **sans ~ fixe** of no fixed abode

◆ **à domicile** ◆ **je vous l'apporterai à** ~ I'll bring it to your home ◆ **le travail** *ou* **l'emploi à** ~ homeworking ◆ **il cherche du travail à** ~ he's looking for work at home ◆ **travailler à** ~ to work at *ou* from home ◆ **"réparations à domicile"** "home repairs carried out" ◆ **service de courses à** ~ home delivery service ◆ **la banque à** ~ home banking ◆ **le cinéma à** ~ home cinema ◆ **jouer à** ~ (*Sport*) to play at home

domiciliaire /dɔmisiljɛʀ/ ADJ domiciliary, house (*épith*)

domiciliataire /dɔmisiljatɛʀ/ NM paying agent

domiciliation /dɔmisiljasjɔ̃/ NF *[de personne, données]* address; *[de société]* registered address ◆ **leurs ~s bancaires** the address of their banks

domicilier /dɔmisilje/ ▸ conjug 7 ◂ VT *[+ facture]* to pay by banker's order ◆ **être domicilié** to be domiciled (*Admin*), to have one's home (*à* in); ◆ **je me suis fait ~ à Lyon** I gave Lyons as my official address *ou* place of residence ◆ **faire ~ ses factures** to have one's bills paid by banker's order

domien, -ienne /dɔmjɛ̃, jɛn/ ADJ from the French overseas departments NM, F **Domien(ne)** person from the French overseas departments

dominance /dɔminɑ̃s/ NF *[de gène]* dominance

dominant, e /dɔminɑ̃, ɑt/ ADJ *[pays, rôle]* dominant; *[idéologie, opinion, vent]* prevailing (*épith*); *[idée, trait]* dominant, main (*épith*); *[passion]* ruling *(épith)*; *[problème, préoccupation]* main *(épith)*, chief *(épith)*; *[position]* dominating *(épith)*, leading *(épith)*; *(Bio, Jur)* dominant NF **dominante** *(= caractéristique)* dominant characteristic; *(= couleur)* dominant *ou* predominant colour; *(Mus)* dominant ◆ **tableau à ~e rouge** painting with red as the dominant *ou* predominant colour ◆ **septième de ~e** *(Mus)* dominant seventh chord

dominateur, -trice /dɔminatœʀ, tʀis/ ADJ *[personne, caractère]* domineering, overbearing; *[voix, geste, regard]* imperious; *[pays]* dominating *(épith)*; *[passion]* ruling *(épith)* NM,F *(littér)* ruler

domination /dɔminasjɔ̃/ NF 1 *(Pol = autorité)* domination; *(fig = emprise)* domination, influence ◆ **la ~ de la Gaule (par Rome)** the domination of Gaul (by Rome) ◆ **la ~ de Rome (sur la Gaule)** Roman rule *ou* domination (over Gaul) ◆ **les pays sous (la) ~ britannique** countries under British rule *ou* domination *ou* dominion ◆ **tomber sous la ~ de** to fall *ou* come under the domination of ◆ **exercer sa ~ sur qn** to exert one's influence on sb, to hold sway over sb ◆ **exercer une ~ morale sur qn** to exert a moral influence on sb ◆ **un besoin insatiable de ~** an insatiable need to dominate ◆ **~ de soi-même** self-control, self-possession 2 *(Rel)* **~s** dominations

dominer /dɔmine/ ▸ conjug 1 ◂ VT 1 *(= être maître de)* *[+ personne, pays]* to dominate ◆ **il voulait ~ le monde** he wanted to rule the world ◆ **ces enfants sont dominés par leur père** these children are kept down *ou* dominated by their father ◆ **il se laisse ~ par sa femme** he's dominated by his wife, he's under his wife's sway ◆ **se laisser ~ par ses passions** to let o.s. be ruled by one's passions ◆ **elle ne sait pas ~ ses élèves** she can't keep her pupils in order *ou* under control, she can't keep control over her pupils

2 *(= surpasser)* *[+ adversaire, concurrent]* to outclass, to tower above ◆ **il domine de loin les autres étudiants** he is way ahead of the other students ◆ **écrivain qui domine son siècle** writer who dominates his century ◆ **se faire ~ par l'équipe adverse** to be dominated *ou* outclassed by the opposing team ◆ **parler fort pour ~ le bruit de la rue** to speak loudly to be heard above the noise from the street ◆ **chez lui cette passion domine toutes les autres** this is his overriding passion ◆ **le problème de la pollution domine tous les autres** the problem of pollution overshadows all others

3 *(= être le meilleur dans)* *[+ course, match, marché]* to dominate

4 *(= maîtriser)* *[+ sentiment]* to control, to master, to overcome; *[+ problème]* to overcome, to master; *[+ sujet]* to master; *[+ situation]* to dominate, to master ◆ **elle ne put ~ son trouble** she couldn't overcome her confusion

5 *(= diriger, gouverner)* to dominate, to govern ◆ **l'idée maîtresse/la préoccupation qui domine toute son œuvre** the key idea/the main concern which dominates his whole work

6 *(= surplomber)* to tower above, to dominate ◆ **rocher/terrasse qui domine la mer** rock/terrace which overlooks the sea ◆ **la tour domine la ville** the tower dominates the town ◆ **il dominait la foule de sa haute taille** he towered above the crowd with his great height ◆ **de là-haut on domine la vallée** from up there you look down over the whole valley

VI 1 *(= être le meilleur)* *[nation]* to hold sway; *[orateur, concurrent]* to be in the dominant position; *(Sport)* *[équipe]* to be in the dominant position, to be on top; *[coureur]* to be in a commanding position ◆ **l'Angleterre a dominé sur les mers pendant des siècles** England ruled the seas *ou* held dominion over the seas for centuries ◆ **dans les débats, il domine nettement** in debates, he clearly has the edge on everyone else *ou* he's definitely the strongest speaker ◆ **leur équipe a dominé pendant tout le match** their team was on top throughout the match ◆ **ce coureur a dominé pendant les premiers kilomètres** this runner was out in front for the first few kilometres ◆ **~ de la tête et des épaules** *(fig)* to be head and shoulders above the others

2 *(= prédominer)* *[caractère, défaut, qualité]* to predominate; *[idée, théorie]* to prevail; *[préoccupation, intérêt]* to be dominant, to predominate; *[parfum]* to predominate; *[couleur]* to stand out, to predominate ◆ **c'est l'ambition qui domine chez lui** ambition is his dominant characteristic ◆ **c'est le jaune qui domine** it is yellow which stands out *ou* which is the predominant colour

VPR **se dominer** to control o.s., to keep o.s. under control ◆ **il ne sait pas se ~** he has no self-control

dominicain, e /dɔminikɛ̃, ɛn/ ADJ *(Géog, Rel)* Dominican ◆ **République ~e** Dominican Republic NM,F **Dominicain(e)** 1 *(Rel)* Dominican 2 *(Géog)* Dominican

dominical, e (mpl **-aux**) /dɔminikal, o/ ADJ Sunday *(épith)*; → **repos**

dominion /dɔminjɔn/ NM *(Pol Brit)* dominion *(of the British Commonwealth)*

Dominique /dɔminik/ NF *(Géog)* ◆ **la ~** Dominica

domino /dɔmino/ NM 1 *(= jeu)* domino ◆ **les ~s** dominoes *(sg)* ◆ **un jeu de ~s** a domino set ◆ **la théorie des ~s** *(Pol)* the domino theory ◆ **l'effet ~** the domino effect 2 *(= costume)* domino 3 *(Élec)* connecting block

dommage /dɔmaʒ/ GRAMMAIRE ACTIVE 45.3

NM 1 *(= préjudice)* harm *(NonC)*, injury ◆ **causer un ~ à qn** to cause *ou* do sb harm ◆ **pour réparer le ~ que je vous ai causé** to repair the injury I've done you ◆ **s'en tirer sans ~(s)** to emerge *ou* escape unscathed ◆ **~ causé avec intention de nuire** *(Jur)* malicious damage

2 *(locutions)* **c'est ~ !, quel ~ !** what a pity! *ou* shame! ◆ **il est vraiment ~ que ...** it's such a pity *ou* it's a great pity that ... ◆ **(c'est *ou* quel) ~ que tu ne puisses pas venir** it's a *ou* what a pity *ou* shame (that) you can't come ◆ **le spectacle était formidable, ~ pour les absents !** the show was fantastic, too bad for those who missed it! ◆ **ça ne te plaît pas ? c'est bien ~ !** *(iro)* you don't like it? well, that really is a shame! *(iro)*

NMPL **dommages** *(= ravages)* damage *(NonC)* ◆ **causer des ~s aux récoltes** to damage *ou* cause damage to the crops ◆ **les ~s sont inestimables** there is incalculable damage

COMP **dommage(s) corporel(s)** physical injury

dommages de guerre war damages

dommages et intérêts damages ◆ **il réclame 1 000 € de ~s et intérêts** he is claiming €1,000 (in) damages

dommage(s) matériel(s) material damage

dommageable /dɔmaʒabl/ ADJ harmful *(à* to)

dommages-intérêts /dɔmaʒɛ̃teʀɛ/ NMPL *(Jur)* damages

domotique /dɔmɔtik/ NF home automation

domptable /dɔ̃(p)tabl/ ADJ tam(e)able

domptage /dɔ̃(p)taʒ/ NM taming

dompter /dɔ̃(p)te/ ▸ conjug 1 ◂ VT *[+ fauve]* to tame; *[+ cheval]* to break in; *[+ enfant insoumis]* to subdue; *[+ rebelles]* to put down, to subdue; *[+ sentiments, passions]* to master, to control, to overcome; *[+ nature, fleuve]* to tame

dompteur, -euse /dɔ̃(p)tœʀ, øz/ NM,F *(gén)* tamer, trainer ◆ **~ (de lions)** lion-tamer

DOM-TOM /dɔmtɔm/ NMPL (abrév de **départements et territoires d'outre-mer**) *French overseas departments and territories*

DOM-TOM, ROM AND COM

There are four « Départements d'outre-mer »: Guadeloupe, Martinique, La Réunion and French Guyana (« Guyane »). They are run in the same way as metropolitan « départements » and their inhabitants are French citizens. In administrative terms they are also "Régions", and in this regard are also referred to as ROM ("Régions d'outre-mer").

The term "Dom-Tom" is still commonly used but the term « Territoire d'outre-mer » has been superseded by that of "Collectivité d'outre-mer" (COM). The COM include French Polynesia, Wallis-and-Futuna, Saint-Pierre-et-Miquelon and Mayotte. They are independent, but each is supervised by a representative of the French government.

Don /dɔ̃/ NM 1 *(Géog)* Don 2 *(= titre)* Don

don /dɔ̃/ NM 1 *(= aptitude)* gift, talent ◆ **~s littéraires** literary gifts *ou* talents ◆ **avoir un ~ pour** to have a gift *ou* talent for ◆ **avoir le ~ des maths** to have a gift for maths ◆ **avoir des ~s** to be gifted *ou* talented ◆ **elle a le ~ de m'énerver** she has a knack *ou* a genius for getting on my nerves ◆ **cette proposition n'a pas eu le ~ de lui plaire** this proposal was not destined to *ou* didn't happen to please him

2 *(= cadeau)* gift; *(= offrande)* donation ◆ **~ en argent** cash donation ◆ **~ en nature** donation in kind ◆ **~ d'organes** donation of organs ◆ **les ~s de la terre** *(littér)* the gifts of the earth ◆ **faire ~ de** *[+ fortune, maison]* to donate ◆ **je lui ai fait ~ de ce livre** I made him a present *ou* gift of that book, I gave him that book as a gift ◆ **cette tâche exige le ~ de soi** this task demands real self-sacrifice ◆ **faire (le) ~ de sa vie pour sauver qn** to give one's life to save sb, to lay down one's life for sb ◆ **c'est un ~ du ciel** *(fig)* it's a godsend

Doña /dɔɲa/ NF Doña

donataire /dɔnatɛʀ/ NMF donee

donateur, -trice /dɔnatœʀ, tʀis/ NM,F donor

donation /dɔnasjɔ̃/ NF *(Jur)* ≃ settlement ◆ **faire une ~ à qn** to make a settlement on sb ◆ **~ entre vifs** donation inter vivos

donation-partage (pl **donations-partages**) /dɔnasjɔ̃partaʒ/ NF *(Jur)* inter vivos settlement, deed of gift

donc /dɔ̃k *en tête de proposition ou devant voyelle ; ailleurs*/ dɔ̃/ GRAMMAIRE ACTIVE 44.1 CONJ 1 *(= par conséquent)* therefore, so, thus; *(= après une digression)* so, then ◆ **il partit ~ avec ses amis et ...** so he left with his friends and ... ◆ **je n'étais pas d'accord, ~ j'ai refusé** I didn't agree (and) so I refused *ou* and I therefore refused ◆ **j'ai raté le train, ~ je n'ai pas pu venir** I missed the train and was thus not able to come *ou* and so I couldn't come ◆ **si ce n'est pas la variole c'est ~ la rougeole** if it's not smallpox then it's measles

2 *(intensif : marque la surprise)* then, so ◆ **c'était ~ un espion ?** he was a spy then?, so he was a spy? ◆ **voilà ~ ce dont il s'agissait** that's what it was (all) about then, so that's what it was (all) about

3 *(de renforcement)* **allons ~ !** come on!, come now! ◆ **écoute-moi ~** do listen to me ◆ **demande-lui ~** go on, ask him ◆ **tais-toi ~ !** do be quiet! ◆ **regardez ~ ça comme c'est joli** just look at that, isn't it pretty? ◆ **pensez ~ !** just imagine *ou* think! ◆ **comment ~ ?** how do you mean? ◆ **quoi ~ ?** what was that?, what did you say? ◆ **dis ~, dites ~** *(introduit une question)* tell me, I say; *(introduit un avertissement, une in-*

jonction) look (here) ...; *(ton indigné)* well really ... ◆ **non mais dis ~, ne te gêne pas !** well, don't mind me! ◆ **dites ~, où l'avez-vous mis ?** I say, where did you put it? ◆ **tiens ~ !** well, well!, I say! ◆ **et moi** ~ me too!

dondon* /dɔ̃dɔ̃/ **NF** big *ou* fat woman (*ou* girl) ◆ **une grosse** ~ a big lump* of a woman (*ou* girl)

donf /dɔ̃f/ **à donf LOC ADJ** * ◆ **rouler à** ~ to drive like crazy* ◆ **on s'est éclaté à** ~ we had a fantastic time* ◆ **elle est jolie ? – à ~ !** is she pretty? – fantastic! *

donjon /dɔ̃ʒɔ̃/ **NM** keep, donjon

don Juan /dɔ̃ʒɥɑ̃/ **NM** Don Juan

donjuanesque /dɔ̃ʒɥanɛsk/ **ADJ** of Don Juan, typical of Don Juan ◆ **un vieux marquis** ~ an elderly marquis and Don Juan

donjuanisme /dɔ̃ʒɥanism/ **NM** Don Juanism

donnant-donnant, donnant, donnant /dɔnɑ̃dɔnɑ̃/ **NM** quid pro quo ◆ **stratégie/principe du** ~ strategy/principle of quid pro quo ◆ **les belligérants ont insisté sur le** ~ the belligerents insisted on a quid pro quo arrangement **LOC ADV** ◆ **avec lui, c'est donnant, donnant** he always wants something in return ◆ **donnant, donnant : je te prête mon livre, tu me prêtes ton stylo** fair's fair - I lend you my book and you lend me your pen

donne /dɔn/ **NF** *(Cartes)* deal; *(fig)* (= *situation*) order ◆ **à vous la** ~ your deal ◆ **faire la** ~ to deal (out) the cards ◆ **il y a fausse** ~ it's a misdeal ◆ **la nouvelle ~ politique** the new political order ◆ **cela change complètement la** ~ it puts a new light on everything

donné, e /dɔne/ **GRAMMAIRE ACTIVE 44.1** (ptp de **donner**) **ADJ** 1 (= *déterminé*) *[lieu, date]* given, fixed; → **moment**

◆ **étant donné** ◆ **étant ~ la situation** in view of *ou* given *ou* considering the situation ◆ **étant ~ que tu es parti** seeing *ou* given that you left

2 (= *pas cher* *) (dirt) cheap*

NF donnée 1 *(Math, Sci) [de problème]* datum ◆ **~es** data ◆ **selon les ~es corrigées des variations saisonnières** *(Écon)* according to the seasonally adjusted figures ◆ **le taux de chômage en ~es corrigées des variations saisonnières** the seasonally adjusted unemployment rate 2 (= *chose connue*) piece of information ◆ **~es** facts, particulars ◆ **manquer de ~es** to be short of facts ◆ **modifier les ~es du problème** to redefine the problem **NM** ◆ **le ~, c'est ...** the facts of the situation are ...

donner /dɔne/

► conjug 1 ◄

1 VERBE TRANSITIF	4 VT INDIRECT
2 VERBE INTRANSITIF	5 VERBE PRONOMINAL
3 VT INDIRECT	

1 - VERBE TRANSITIF

1 = offrir **~ qch à qn** to give sth to sb, to give sb sth ◆ **je le lui ai donné** I gave it to him ◆ **~ son cœur/son amitié (à qn)** to give one's heart/one's friendship (to sb) ◆ **~ à manger/boire à qn** to give sb something to eat/drink ◆ **~ son corps à la science** to donate one's body to science ◆ **il a donné ses tableaux au Louvre** he donated his paintings to the Louvre ◆ **~ sa vie/son temps pour une cause** to give (up) one's life/one's time for a cause ◆ **~ qch pour** *ou* **contre qch d'autre** to give sth in exchange for sth else, to exchange sth for sth else ◆ **en ~ à qn pour son argent** to give sb their money's worth ◆ **on ne les vend pas, on les donne** we're not selling them, we're giving them away ◆ **j'ai déjà donné !** *(hum = on ne m'y reprendra plus !)* I've been there! ◆ **~ c'est ~ (, reprendre c'est voler)** *(Prov)* a gift is a gift ◆ **qui donne aux pauvres prête à Dieu** *(Prov)* charity will be rewarded in heaven; → **change, matière, sang**

2 = remettre, confier to give, to hand; *[+ copie d'examen]* to hand in, to give in ◆ **~ quelque chose à faire à qn** to give sb something to do ◆ **je donnerai la lettre au concierge** I shall give the letter to the caretaker ◆ **donnez-moi les outils** give me *ou* hand me *ou* pass me the tools ◆ **donnez-moi un kilo d'oranges** I'd like a kilo of oranges ◆ **~ ses chaussures à ressemeler/au cordonnier** to take one's shoes (in) to be resoled/to the shoe-repair shop

3 = accorder *[+ moyen, occasion]* to give; *[+ permission, interview]* to grant, to give; *[+ prix, décoration, subvention]* to award, to give ◆ **donnez-moi le temps d'y réfléchir** give me time to think about it ◆ **on lui a donné 24 heures pour quitter le pays** he was given 24 hours to leave the country ◆ **le médecin lui donne trois mois (à vivre)** the doctor has given him three months (to live) ◆ **~ sa fille en mariage à qn** to give one's daughter to sb in marriage ◆ **il m'a été donné d'assister à cet événement historique** I was privileged enough to be there when this historic event took place ◆ **il ou ça n'est pas donné à tout le monde de ...** not everyone is lucky *ou* fortunate enough to ... ◆ **l'intelligence n'est pas donnée à tout le monde** not everyone is gifted with intelligence ◆ **je vous le donne en cent** *ou* **en mille !*** you'll never guess (in a million years)!; → **dieu**

4 = administrer *[+ médicament, bain]* to give; *(Rel) [+ communion]* to give; *[+ sacrement]* to administer ◆ **~ une punition à qn** to punish sb ◆ **~ un baiser/un coup de pied à qn** to give sb a kiss/a kick ◆ **~ un coup de balai à la pièce** to give the room a quick sweep ◆ **~ un coup de chiffon à la pièce** to flick a duster over the room, to give the room a quick dust

5 = céder *[+ vieux vêtements]* to give away ◆ **~ sa place à une dame** to give up one's seat to a lady ◆ **je donnerais beaucoup pour savoir** I would give a lot to know; → **langue**

6 = distribuer to hand out, to give out; *[+ cartes]* to deal (out) ◆ **c'est à vous de ~** *(Cartes)* it's your deal

7 = communiquer, indiquer *[+ description, détails, idée, avis]* to give; *[+ sujet de devoir]* to set ◆ **il lui a donné l'ordre de partir** he has ordered him to go ◆ **pouvez-vous me ~ l'heure ?** can you tell me the time?; → **alarme, alerte**

8 = causer *[+ plaisir, courage]* to give (*à* to); *[+ peine, mal]* to cause, to give (*à* to); ◆ **ça donne chaud/froid/soif/faim** it makes you (feel) hot/cold/thirsty/hungry ◆ **~ le vertige/le mal de mer (à qn)** to make sb (feel) giddy/seasick ◆ **ça donne des maux de tête** it causes headaches *ou* gives you headaches ◆ **mangez ça, ça va vous ~ des forces** eat this, it'll give you some energy *ou* it'll make you feel stronger ◆ **rajoute des fines herbes, ça donnera du goût** add some herbs to give it some flavour; → **appétit**

9 = organiser *[+ réception, bal]* to give, to hold (*à* for); *[+ film]* to show; *[+ pièce]* to perform, to put on

10 = conférer *[+ poids, valeur]* to add, to give; *[+ importance]* to give ◆ **le brouillard donne un air triste à la ville** the fog makes the town look really dismal

11 = attribuer **quel âge lui donnez-vous ?** how old would you say he was? ◆ **je lui donne 50 ans** I'd say he was 50; → **raison, tort**

12 locutions

◆ **donner à** + *infinitif* (= *faire*) ◆ **cela m'a donné à penser que ...** it made me think that ... ◆ **tout donne à croire que ...** everything points to the fact that ... ◆ **ces événements nous ont donné (beaucoup) à réfléchir** these events have given us (much) food for thought *ou* have really set us thinking ◆ **c'est ce qu'on m'a donné à entendre** that's what I was given to understand *ou* led to believe ◆ **~ à rire** to be laughable

◆ **donner qch/qn pour** (= *présenter comme*) ◆ **~ un fait pour certain** to present a fact as a certainty ◆ **on le donne pour un homme habile** he is said *ou* made out to be a clever man ◆ **il se donne pour un tireur d'élite** he makes himself out *ou* claims to be a crack shot ◆ **on l'a donné pour mort** he was given up for dead ◆ **on m'a dit qu'il démissionnait, je te le donne pour ce que ça vaut*** for what it's worth, somebody told me he's resigning

13 Mus *[+ le la, la note, le ton]* to give

14 = produire *[+ fruits, récolte]* to yield; *[+ résultat]* to produce ◆ **cette vigne donne un très bon vin** this vine produces a very good wine ◆ **elle lui a donné un fils** she gave *ou* bore him a son ◆ **cet écrivain donne un livre tous les ans** this writer produces a book every year ◆ **cette méthode ne donne rien** this method is totally ineffective ◆ **j'ai essayé de le convaincre, mais ça n'a pas donné grand-chose** I tried to convince him, but without much success ◆ **qu'est-ce que ça donne ?*** (= *qu'en penses-tu*) how's that?, what do you think?; (= *comment ça se passe*) how's it going? ◆ **essaie la robe, pour que je voie ce que ça donne** try the dress on so I can see what it looks like

15 * = dénoncer *[+ complice]* to squeal *ou* grass on*, to shop* *(Brit)*

2 - VERBE INTRANSITIF

1 = frapper **le voilier est allé ~ sur les rochers** the boat ran onto *ou* struck the rocks ◆ **le soleil donne en plein sur la voiture** the sun is beating down on *ou* shining right onto the car ◆ **~ de la tête contre une porte** to knock *ou* bump one's head against a door ◆ **je ne sais plus où ~ de la tête** I don't know which way to turn

2 = attaquer to attack ◆ **l'artillerie va ~** the artillery is going to fire ◆ **faites ~ la garde !** send in the guards!

3 = produire to yield ◆ **les pommiers ont bien donné cette année** the apple trees have produced a good crop *ou* given a good yield this year ◆ **cet arbre ne donnera pas avant trois ans** this tree won't bear fruit for three years ◆ **les tomates donnent à plein** it is the height of the tomato season ◆ **la radio donne à plein** *(fig)* the radio is turned right up ◆ **ça donne !*** (= *l'ambiance est fantastique*) it's cool* *ou* magic* *ou* brill!*

3 - VT INDIRECT

donner dans ◆ **~ dans le piège de la propagande communiste** to fall for communist propaganda ◆ **elle a donné dans le roman à la fin de sa vie** she took to writing novels at the end of her life ◆ **si vous donnez dans le luxueux, optez pour ...** if luxury is what you're after, go for ... ◆ **~ dans le snobisme** to be rather snobbish, to have a tendency to be snobbish; → **panneau**

4 - VT INDIRECT

donner sur (= *s'ouvrir sur*) *[pièce, porte]* to give onto, to open onto; *[fenêtre]* to overlook, to open onto, to look onto ◆ **la maison donne sur la mer** the house faces *ou* looks onto the sea

5 - VERBE PRONOMINAL

se donner

1 = se consacrer **se ~ à** *[+ cause, parti, travail]* to devote o.s. to

2 = agir avec énergie **il s'est donné à fond** he gave his all ◆ **il se donne pour réussir dans la vie** he works hard to succeed in life

3 [sexuellement] **elle s'est donnée à lui** † she gave herself to him

4 [= donner à soi-même] **donne-toi un coup de peigne** give your hair a quick comb, run a comb through your hair ◆ **se ~ bien du mal** *ou* **de la peine** to go to a lot of trouble ◆ **il s'est donné la peine de me prévenir** he took the trouble to warn me ◆ **se ~ bonne conscience** to ease *ou* soothe one's conscience ◆ **elle se donne des airs de jeune fille naïve** she makes herself out to be an innocent young thing ◆ **se ~ un maire/un président** to choose a mayor/a president ◆ **il s'est donné 6 mois pour fonder son entreprise** he gave *ou* allowed himself 6 months to set up the company ◆ **s'en ~ (à cœur joie)** to have a whale of a time*, to have the time of one's life ◆ **se la ~** to show off; → **cœur**

5 [= échanger] **ils se donnaient des baisers** they were kissing each other ◆ **ils se sont donné des coups/des nouvelles** they exchanged blows/news; → **main, rendez-vous,** *etc*

6 [= être joué, montré] *[pièce]* to be on; *[film]* to be on, to be showing

donneur, -euse /dɔnœʀ, øz/ **NM,F** 1 *(gén)* giver ◆ **~ de leçons** *(péj)* sermonizer *(péj)* ◆ **~ de conseils** person who hands out advice ◆ **~ d'ordre** *(Comm)* principal ◆ **le tribunal a condamné l'un des ~s d'ordres de la purification ethnique** the court sentenced one of the people who gave the order for ethnic cleansing *ou* who ordered ethnic cleansing 2 *[d'organe]* donor ◆ **~ de sang/de sperme** blood/sperm donor ◆ **~ universel** universal donor 3 *(Cartes)* dealer 4 *(* = dénonciateur)* squealer*, grass*, informer

Don Quichotte /dɔ̃kiʃɔt/ **NM** Don Quixote

don-quichottisme /dɔ̃kiʃɔtism/ **NM** quixotism

dont /dɔ̃/ **PRON REL** 1 *(provenant d'un complément de nom : indique la possession, la qualité etc)* whose, of which; *(antécédent humain)* whose ◆ **la femme ~ vous apercevez le chapeau** the woman whose hat you can see ◆ **c'est un pays ~ j'aime le climat** it's a country whose climate I like *ou* which has a climate I like ◆ **un vagabond ~ les chaussures laissaient voir les doigts de pied** a tramp whose toes showed through his shoes ◆ **les enfants ~ la mère travaille sont plus indépendants** children whose mothers go out to work *ou* children with working mothers are more independent ◆ **l'histoire, ~ voici l'essentiel, est ...** the story, of which these are the main points, is ...

2 *(indiquant la partie d'un tout)* **il y a eu plusieurs blessés, ~ son frère** there were several casualties, among which *ou* among whom was his brother *ou* including his brother ◆ **des livres ~ j'ai lu une dizaine environ/~ une dizaine sont reliés** books of which I have read about ten/of which about ten are bound ◆ **ils ont trois filles ~ deux sont mariées** they have three daughters, two of whom are married *ou* of whom two are married, they have three daughters, two of them married ◆ **il a écrit deux romans ~ un est autobiographique** he has written two novels one of which is autobiographical

3 *(indique la manière, la provenance)* **la façon ~ elle marche/s'habille** the way (in which) she walks/dresses, her way of walking/dressing ◆ **la pièce ~ il sort** the room (which) he is coming out of *ou* out of which he is coming ◆ **mines ~ on extrait de l'or** mines from which gold is extracted, mines (that) gold is extracted from ◆ **la classe sociale ~ elle est issue** the social class (which) she came from; → aussi **de¹**

4 *(provenant d'un complément prépositionnel d'adjectif, de verbe : voir aussi les adjectifs et verbes en question)* **l'outil ~ il se sert** the tool (which) he is using ◆ **la maladie ~ elle souffre** the illness she suffers from *ou* from which she suffers ◆ **le vase ~ la maison m'a fait cadeau** the vase (which) the firm gave me, the vase with which the firm presented me ◆ **le film/l'acteur ~ elle parle tant** the film/actor she talks so much about *ou* about which/whom she talks so much ◆ **voilà ce ~ il faut vous assurer** that is what you must make sure of *ou* about ◆ **l'accident ~ il a été responsable** the accident he was responsible for *ou* for which he was responsible ◆ **le collier/l'enfant ~ elle est si fière** the necklace/child she is so proud of *ou* of which/whom she is so proud

donzelle /dɔ̃zɛl/ **NF** *(péj)* young madam *(péj)*

dopage /dɔpaʒ/ **NM** doping ◆ **l'athlète a été disqualifié pour ~** the athlete was disqualified for a doping offence *ou* for failing a dope test

dopamine /dɔpamin/ **NF** dopamine

dopant, e /dɔpɑ̃, ɑ̃t/ **ADJ** ◆ **produit ~** drug **NM** drug

dope /dɔp/ **NF** *(arg Drogue)* dope *(arg)*

doper /dɔpe/ ▸ **conjug 1** ◂ **VT** *[+ athlète, cheval]* to dope; *[+ économie, ventes]* to boost ◆ **semi-conducteur dopé** doped semiconductor **VPR** **se doper** to take drugs ◆ **il se dope aux amphétamines** he takes amphetamines

doping /dɔpiŋ/ **NM** ⇒ **dopage**

Doppler /dɔplɛʀ/ **NM** Doppler test ◆ **se faire faire un ~** to have a Doppler test ◆ **effet ~(-Fizeau)** Doppler effect

dorade /dɔʀad/ **NF** ⇒ **daurade**

Dordogne /dɔʀdɔɲ/ **NF** ◆ **la ~** the Dordogne

doré, e /dɔʀe/ (ptp de **dorer**) **ADJ** 1 *(= couvert d'une dorure)* gilt, gilded ◆ **~ sur tranche** gilt-edged, with gilded edges 2 *(= couleur d'or) [peau]* bronzed, tanned; *[blé, cheveux, lumière]* golden; *[gâteau, viande]* browned ◆ **des rêves ~s** *(fig)* golden dreams ◆ **~ comme les blés** golden-blond, flaxen; → **jeunesse** **NM** 1 *(= dorure)* gilt, gilding ◆ **le ~ du vase s'en va** the gilt *ou* gilding is coming off the vase 2 *(Can = poisson)* yellow pike, wall-eyed pike **NF** **dorée** John Dory, dory

dorénavant /dɔʀenavɑ̃/ **ADV** *(dans le futur)* from now on, henceforth *(frm)*; *(dans le passé)* from then on

dorer /dɔʀe/ ▸ **conjug 1** ◂ **VT** 1 *(= couvrir d'or) [+ objet]* to gild ◆ **faire ~ un cadre** to have a frame gilded ◆ **~ la pilule à qn*** *(fig)* to sugar *ou* sweeten the pill for sb 2 *(Culin) [+ gâteau]* to glaze *(with egg yolk)* ◆ **le four dore bien la viande** the oven browns the meat well 3 *[soleil] [+ peau]* to bronze, to tan ◆ **le soleil dore les blés** *(littér)* the sun turns the corn gold ◆ **le soleil dore les dunes** the sun tinges the dunes with gold **VI** *(Culin) [rôti]* to brown ◆ **faire ~ un poulet** to brown a chicken **VPR** **se dorer** *(= bronzer)* **se ~ au soleil, se ~ la pilule*** to lie (and get brown) in the sun, to sunbathe

d'ores et déjà /dɔʀzedeʒa/ **ADV** → **ores**

doreur, -euse /dɔʀœʀ, øz/ **NM,F** gilder

dorien, -ienne /dɔʀjɛ̃, jɛn/ **ADJ** *(Géog)* Dorian, Doric; *[dialecte]* Doric; *(Mus) [mode]* Dorian **NM** *(= dialecte)* Doric (dialect)

dorique /dɔʀik/ **ADJ, NM** Doric

dorlotement /dɔʀlɔtmɑ̃/ **NM** pampering, (molly)coddling, cosseting

dorloter /dɔʀlɔte/ ▸ **conjug 1** ◂ **VT** to pamper ◆ **il est trop dorloté** he's mollycoddled ◆ **se faire ~** to be pampered *ou* cosseted **VPR** **se dorloter** to pamper o.s.

dormance /dɔʀmɑ̃s/ **NF** *(Bot, Méd)* dormancy ◆ **la ~ cancéreuse** dormancy of cancer cells

dormant, e /dɔʀmɑ̃, ɑ̃t/ **ADJ** *[eau]* still; *(Tech) [châssis]* fixed ◆ **compte ~** *(Jur, Fin)* dormant account ◆ **agent ~** *(Espionnage)* sleeper **NM** *[de porte, châssis]* casing, frame; *[de bateau]* standing end

dormeur, -euse /dɔʀmœʀ, øz/ **NM,F** sleeper ◆ **c'est un gros** *ou* **grand ~** he likes his sleep, he's a real sleepyhead* **NM** *(= crabe)* (common *ou* edible) crab **NF** **dormeuse** († = *boucle d'oreille)* stud (earring) **ADJ** *[poupée]* with eyes that shut

dormir /dɔʀmiʀ/ ▸ **conjug 16** ◂ **VI** 1 *(gén)* to sleep; *(= être en train de dormir)* to be asleep, to be sleeping ◆ **~ d'un sommeil léger/lourd** to sleep lightly/heavily ◆ **parler en dormant** to talk in one's sleep ◆ **il dormait d'un sommeil agité** he was tossing and turning in his sleep ◆ **je n'ai pas dormi de la nuit/de trois jours** I haven't slept a wink (all night)/for three days ◆ **avoir envie de ~** to feel sleepy ◆ **essayez de ~ un peu** try to get some sleep ◆ **ça m'empêche de ~** *[café]* it keeps me awake; *[soucis]* I'm losing sleep over it ◆ **ce n'est pas ça qui va m'empêcher de ~** I'm not going to lose any sleep over that ◆ **il n'en dort pas** *ou* **plus** he's losing sleep over it, he can't sleep for thinking of it

2 *(= rester inactif) [eau]* to be still; *[argent, capital]* to lie idle; *[machines]* to be *ou* lie idle; *[nature, forêt]* to be still, to be asleep ◆ **tout dormait dans la maison/ville** everything was quiet *ou* still in the house/town ◆ **la brute qui dormait en lui** the beast within *ou* inside ◆ **investis ton capital plutôt que de le laisser ~** invest your capital rather than leave it idle ◆ **ce n'est pas le moment de ~ !** this is no time for slacking *ou* idling! ◆ **il dormait sur son travail** he wasn't concentrating on his work ◆ **voilà six ans que le projet dort dans un tiroir** the project has been lying dormant *ou* has been in mothballs* for six years; → **pire**

3 *(locutions)* **je dors debout** I'm asleep on my feet, I can't keep my eyes open ◆ **une histoire à ~ debout** a cock-and-bull story ◆ **~ (de) son dernier sommeil** *(frm)* to sleep one's last sleep ◆ **~ comme un bienheureux** to sleep like a baby ◆ **~ comme un loir** *ou* **une marmotte** *ou* **une souche** *ou* **un sonneur** to sleep like a log ◆ **ne ~ que d'un œil** to sleep with one eye open ◆ **il dort à poings fermés** he is sound *ou* fast asleep, he's dead to the world* ◆ **cette nuit je vais ~ à poings fermés** I'm going to sleep very soundly tonight ◆ **~ du sommeil du juste** to sleep the sleep of the just ◆ **~ tranquille** *ou* **sur ses deux oreilles** *(sans soucis)* to sleep soundly; *(sans danger)* to sleep safely (in one's bed) ◆ **qui dort dîne** *(Prov)* he who sleeps forgets his hunger

dormitif, -ive /dɔʀmitif, iv/ **ADJ** soporific

dorsal, e (mpl **-aux**) /dɔʀsal, o/ **ADJ** *(gén)* dorsal; *[douleur]* back *(épith)*; → **épine, parachute** **NF** **dorsale** 1 *(Ling)* dorsal consonant 2 *(Géog)* ridge ◆ **~e barométrique** *(Météo)* ridge of high pressure

dortoir /dɔʀtwaʀ/ **NM** dormitory ◆ **banlieue(-)~** dormitory *ou* bedroom (US) suburb

dorure /dɔʀyʀ/ **NF** 1 *(= couche d'or)* gilt, gilding ◆ **uniforme couvert de ~s** uniform covered in gold decorations 2 *(= action)* gilding

doryphore /dɔʀifɔʀ/ **NM** Colorado beetle

DOS, Dos ® /dɔs/ **NM** (abrév de **Disc Operating System**) DOS ®

dos /do/ **NM** 1 *[d'être animé, main, vêtement, siège, page]* back; *[de livre]* spine; *[de lame, couteau]* blunt edge ◆ **avoir le ~ rond** to be round-shouldered ◆ **couché sur le ~** lying on one's (*ou* its) back ◆ **écrire au ~ d'une lettre/enveloppe** to write on the back of a letter/an envelope ◆ **robe décolletée dans le ~** low-backed dress ◆ **"voir au dos"** "see over *ou* overleaf" ◆ **aller à ~ d'âne/de chameau** to ride on a donkey/a camel ◆ **les vivres sont portés à ~ de chameau/d'homme** the supplies are carried by camel/men ◆ **ils partirent, sac au** ~ they set off, (with) their rucksacks on their backs ◆ **avoir les cheveux dans le** ~ to wear one's hair loose ◆ **(vu) de** ~ **il a une allure jeune** (seen) from behind *ou* from the back he looks quite young ◆ **le chat fait le gros** ~ the cat is arching its back

2 *(= nage)* ~ **(crawlé)** backstroke

3 *(locutions)* **il s'est mis tout le monde à** ~ he has turned everybody against him ◆ **être** ~ **à** ~ to be back to back ◆ **renvoyer deux adversaires** ~ **à** ~ to send away *ou* dismiss two opponents without pronouncing in favour of either ◆ **le train/ta mère a bon** ~* *(fig)* (that's right) blame the train/your mother *(iro)* ◆ **il n'y va pas avec le** ~ **de la cuiller*** he certainly doesn't go in for half-measures*, there are no half-measures with him ◆ **faire qch dans** *ou* **derrière le** ~ **de qn** to do sth behind sb's back ◆ **nous avions la mer/l'ennemi dans le** ~ we had the sea/the enemy behind us *ou* at our back(s) ◆ **on l'a dans le** ~ **!*** we've had it!* ◆ **j'ai toujours mon patron sur le** ~ my boss is always breathing down my neck *ou* is always standing over me ◆ **mettre qch sur le** ~ **de qn** *[+ responsabilité]* to saddle sb with sth, to make sb shoulder the responsibility for sth; *[+ accusation]* to pin sth on sb ◆ **il s'est mis une sale affaire sur le** ~ he has got himself mixed up in a nasty bit of business ◆ **faire des affaires sur le** ~ **de qn** to do a bit of business at sb's expense ◆ **il a tout pris sur le** ~* he bore the brunt of the whole thing ◆ **je n'ai rien à me mettre sur le** ~ I haven't a thing to wear ◆ **tomber sur le** ~ **de qn** *(= arriver à l'improviste)* to drop in on sb, to pay sb an unexpected visit; *(= attaquer) (physiquement)* to fall on sb, to go for sb; *(en paroles)* to jump down sb's throat, to go for sb ◆ **tourner le** ~ **à** to turn one's back on ◆ **avoir le** ~ **tourné à la mer/à la porte** to have one's back to the sea/door ◆ **dès qu'il a le** ~ **tourné** as soon as his back is turned; → **froid, laine, plein**

COMP **dos brisé** *(Reliure)* hollow *ou* open *ou* loose back

dosage /dozaʒ/ NM 1 *[de mélange]* correct proportioning, mixture ◆ **se tromper dans le** ~ **d'un cocktail/d'une solution chimique** to mix a cocktail/a chemical solution in the wrong proportions 2 *(= équilibre)* **tout est question de** ~ it's all a matter of striking a balance *ou* the right balance ◆ **un savant** ~ **de prudence et d'audace** a judicious combination of caution and audacity 3 *(= action) [d'ingrédient, élément]* measuring out; *[de remède]* dosage

dos-d'âne /dodɑn/ NM INV hump ◆ **pont en** ~ humpback bridge

dose /doz/ NF 1 *(Pharm)* dose ◆ ~ **mortelle** lethal dose ◆ **absorber une** ~ **excessive de barbituriques** to take an overdose of barbiturates ◆ **s'en tenir à la** ~ **prescrite** to keep to the prescribed dose *ou* dosage

2 *(= proportion) [d'ingrédient, élément]* amount, quantity ◆ **il a eu sa** ~ **quotidienne** *(hum)* he has had his daily dose *ou* fix* *(hum)* ◆ **forcer la** ~ *(fig)* to overdo it, to overstep the mark ◆ **introduire une petite** ~ **d'ironie dans un récit** to introduce a touch of irony into a story ◆ **pour faire cela, il faut une** ~ **de courage peu commune** you need an extraordinary amount of courage to do that ◆ **affligé d'une forte** ~ **de stupidité** afflicted with more than one's fair share of stupidity ◆ **j'aime bien la poésie/ce chanteur mais seulement par petites** ~**s** *ou* **à petites** ~**s** I like poetry/that singer but only in small doses ◆ **le travail, c'est bien mais à** ~**s homéopathiques** *(hum)* work's fine but only in small doses

◆ **en avoir sa dose*** to have had more than one's share ◆ **les mecs, elle en a eu sa** ~* she's had enough of men ◆ **les ennuis, elle en aura sa** ~ **!** she'll have more than her share of trouble!

doser /doze/ ▸ conjug 1 ◂ VT 1 *(= mesurer) [+ ingrédient, élément]* to measure out; *[+ remède]* to measure out a dose of 2 *(= proportionner) [+ mélange]* to proportion correctly, to mix in the correct proportions ◆ **mal** ~ **un cocktail/une solution chimique** to mix a cocktail/a chemical solution in the wrong proportions ◆ **gélules dosées à 100 mg** 100 mg capsules ◆ **pilule faiblement dosée (en œstrogènes)** low-dose (oestrogen) pill 3 *(= équilibrer)* to strike a balance between; *[+ exercices, difficultés]* to grade ◆ **il faut savoir** ~ **compréhension et sévérité** you must strike a balance *ou* the right balance between understanding and severity ◆ ~ **ses efforts** to pace o.s. ◆ **cet auteur sait** ~ **l'ironie** this author has a gift for using irony in just the right amounts

dosette /dozɛt/ NF *[de moutarde, sauce]* sachet

doseur /dozœʀ/ NM measure ◆ **bouchon** ~ measuring cap ◆ **flacon** ~ pump dispenser

dosimètre /dozimɛtʀ/ NM dosimeter

dossard /dosaʀ/ NM *(Sport)* number *(worn by competitor)* ◆ **avec le** ~ **numéro 9** wearing number 9

dosseret /dosʀɛ/ NM headboard

dossier /dosje/ NM 1 *[de siège]* back

2 *(= documents)* file, dossier ◆ ~ **d'inscription** *(Scol, Univ)* registration forms ◆ ~ **médical** medical file *ou* records ◆ ~ **de presse** press kit ◆ ~ **scolaire** school record, student file *(US)* ◆ **constituer un** ~ **sur qn** to draw up a file on sb ◆ **connaître** *ou* **posséder ses** ~**s** to know what one is about, to know what's what ◆ **être sélectionné sur** ~ to be selected on the basis of one's application

3 *(Jur) (= affaire)* case; *(= papiers)* case file ◆ **il n'y a rien dans le** ~ the case has no substance ◆ **ils ont fermé le** ~ they closed the case ◆ **verser une pièce au** ~ to add a piece of evidence to the case file

4 *(= question à traiter)* issue, question; *(Scol, Univ = travail de recherche)* project ◆ **le** ~ **agricole** the agriculture issue ◆ **le** ~ **brûlant de l'immigration** the burning *ou* highly sensitive issue of immigration ◆ **ils ont un** ~ **à faire sur les ours** they've got to do a project on bears

5 *(Presse = article)* special report *(sur* on) survey *(sur* of); ◆ ~ **spécial sur la Mafia** *(TV)* special programme *(Brit) ou* program *(US)* on the Mafia

6 *(= classeur)* file, folder

dot /dɔt/ NF *[de mariage]* dowry ◆ **apporter qch en** ~ to bring a dowry of sth, to bring sth as one's dowry; → **coureur**

dotal, e (mpl **-aux**) /dɔtal, o/ ADJ dotal, dowry *(épith)*

dotation /dɔtasjɔ̃/ NF *(Jur) [d'institution]* endowment; *(Hist) [de fonctionnaire, dignitaire]* emolument; *(Admin = allocation)* grant ◆ **l'État a diminué les** ~**s en capital des entreprises publiques** the government has reduced subsidies to state-owned companies

doter /dɔte/ ▸ conjug 1 ◂ VT 1 *(= pourvoir)* ◆ ~ **qn/qch de** to equip sb/sth with ◆ **la nature l'avait doté d'un grand talent** nature had endowed him with great talent, nature had bestowed great talent upon him ◆ **doté de** *[équipement, matériel, dispositif]* equipped with; *[talent, courage, pouvoir]* endowed with 2 *(Jur) [+ fille à marier]* to provide with a dowry; *[+ institution]* to endow; *(Hist) [+ fonctionnaire, dignitaire]* to endow with an emolument; *(Admin) [+ université, organisme]* to grant money to, to give a grant to ◆ **richement dotée** *[fille]* with a handsome dowry; *[compétition]* with big prizemoney

douaire /dwɛʀ/ NM dower

douairière /dwɛʀjɛʀ/ NF dowager

douane /dwan/ NF 1 *(= service)* Customs ◆ **les** ~**s britanniques** British Customs ◆ **il est employé aux** ~**s** *ou* **à la** ~ he's employed in the Customs department ◆ **marchandises (entreposées) en** ~ bonded goods, goods in bond ◆ **zone/port sous** ~ zone/port under the authority of the Customs 2 *(= lieu)* customs ◆ **poste** *ou* **bureau de** ~ customs house ◆ **passer (à) la** ~ *(à l'aéroport etc)* to go through customs ◆ **la visite de la** ~ *(dans le train)* the customs check ◆ **il s'est fait contrôler à la** ~ he was stopped by customs (officers) *ou* at customs, he had his baggage checked *ou* examined by customs (officers) 3 *(= argent)* ◆ **(droits de)** ~ customs duty *ou* dues, duty ◆ **exempté de** ~ duty-free, non-dutiable

douanier, -ière /dwanje, jɛʀ/ NM,F customs officer ADJ customs *(épith)*; → **barrière, union**

doublage /dublaʒ/ NM 1 *[de film]* dubbing ◆ **le** ~ **d'un acteur** *(voix)* dubbing an actor; *(rôle)* using a double for an actor 2 *[de vêtement, paroi, boîte, tableau]* lining; *(Naut) [de coque]* sheathing 3 *[de somme, quantité, lettre]* doubling 4 *[de fil]* doubling; *[de revêtement]* doubling, laying double; *[de couverture]* doubling, folding (in half)

double /dubl/ ADJ 1 *(gén)* double; *[inconvénient, avantage]* double, twofold ◆ **feuille** ~ double sheet (of paper) ◆ ~ **whisky** double *ou* large whisky ◆ **le prix est** ~ **de ce qu'il était** the price is double *ou* twice what it was ◆ **vous avez fait une** ~ **erreur** you have made two mistakes ◆ **faire qch en** ~ **exemplaire** to make two copies of sth, to do sth in duplicate ◆ **à** ~ **action** *[rasoir]* dual-action; *[crème]* double-acting; *[shampooing]* two-in-one ◆ **ustensile à** ~ **usage** dual-purpose utensil ◆ **faire** ~ **emploi** to be redundant ◆ **cet appareil fait maintenant** ~ **emploi avec l'ancien** this appliance makes the old one redundant ◆ **"à vendre voiture, cause double emploi"** "for sale: car, surplus to requirements" ◆ **fermer une porte à** ~ **tour** to double-lock a door ◆ **enfermer qn à** ~ **tour** to put sb under lock and key ◆ **à** ~ **tranchant** *(lit, fig)* double-edged, two-edged ◆ **boîte/valise à** ~ **fond** box/case with a false bottom ◆ **foyer à** ~ **revenu** dual-income *ou* double-income household ◆ **mettre un fil (en)** ~ to use a double thread ◆ **mettre une couverture (en)** ~ to put a blanket on double ◆ **en** ~ **aveugle** double-blind *(épith)*; → **bouchée², coup**

2 *(= qui a des aspects opposés) [vie, aspect]* double ◆ **à** ~ **face** *[tissu]* reversible; *[adhésif]* double-sided ◆ **accusé de jouer un** ~ **jeu** accused of double-dealing *ou* of playing a double game *(Brit)* ◆ **phrase à** ~ **sens** *ou* **entente** sentence with a double meaning ◆ **mener une** ~ **vie** to lead a double life ◆ **personnage à personnalité** ~ person with a dual personality *ou* a Jekyll-and-Hyde personality; → **agent**

NM 1 *(= quantité)* **manger/gagner le** ~ **(de qn)** to eat/earn twice as much (as sb) *ou* double the amount (that sb does) ◆ **il pèse le** ~ **de vous** he's twice your weight, he weighs twice as much as you do ◆ **4 est le** ~ **de 2** 4 is two times *ou* twice 2 ◆ **c'est le** ~ **du prix normal** it is twice *ou* double the normal price ◆ **c'est le** ~ **de la distance Paris-Lyon** it's twice *ou* double the distance from Paris to Lyons ◆ **hier il a mis le** ~ **de temps à faire ce travail** yesterday he took twice as long *ou* double the time to do this job ◆ **nous attendons le** ~ **de gens** we expect twice as many people *ou* double the number of people ◆ **plier qch en** ~ to fold sth in half *ou* in two; → **quitte**

2 *(= copie, duplicata) [de facture, acte]* copy; *[de timbre]* duplicate, double; *[de personne]* double; *[d'objet d'art]* replica, exact copy ◆ **se faire faire un** ~ **de clé** to have a second key cut ◆ **avoir des timbres en** ~ to have duplicates *ou* doubles *ou*

two of a stamp ◆ **il a tous les documents/ toutes les photos en** ~ he has copies of all the documents/all the photos ◆ **on a tout en ~, pour plus de sûreté** we have two of everything to be on the safe side

3 *(Sport)* doubles ◆ **le ~ dames/messieurs/ mixte** the ladies'/men's/mixed doubles ◆ **faire un ~, jouer en** ~ to play a doubles match

4 *(Jeux) [de dés, dominos]* double ◆ **faire un** ~ to throw a double ◆ **~-six** double six ◆ **~-blanc** double blank

ADV *[payer, compter]* double

COMP **double allumage** *(Tech)* NM dual ignition
double barre *(Mus)* NF double bar
doubles cordes *(Mus)* NFPL double stopping
double dièse *(Mus)* NM double sharp
double fenêtre NF double window
double nœud NM double knot
double page NF double page (spread)
doubles rideaux NMPL double curtains *(Brit) ou* drapes *(US)*

doublé, e /duble/ (ptp de **doubler**) ADJ 1 *[vêtement]* lined *(de* with); ◆ ~ **de cuir/cuivre** *[boîte, paroi]* lined with leather/copper ◆ **non** ~ unlined ◆ ~ **de fourrure** fur-lined ◆ ~ **(de) coton/ nylon** cotton/nylon-lined, lined with cotton/ nylon 2 ~ **de** (= *qui est aussi)* as well as ◆ **c'est un savant** ~ **d'un pédagogue** he's a teacher as well as a scholar NM 1 *(Sport, fig = victoire, réussite)* double; *(Chasse = coup double)* right and left 2 *(Orfèvrerie)* rolled gold 3 *(Mus)* turn

double-cliquer /dubləklike/ ► conjug 1 ◄ VI to double-click *(sur* on)

double-crème (pl **doubles-crèmes**) /dubləkʀɛm/ NM cream cheese

double-croche (pl **doubles-croches**) /dubləkʀɔʃ/ NF semiquaver *(Brit)*, sixteenth note *(US)*

double-décimètre (pl **doubles-décimètres**) /dublədesimɛtʀ/ NM (20 cm) rule

doublement /dubləmɑ̃/ ADV (= *pour deux raisons)* for two reasons; (= *à un degré double)* doubly NM 1 *[de somme, quantité, lettre]* doubling 2 *[de feuille]* doubling, folding (in half); *[de fil]* doubling 3 *[de véhicule]* passing, overtaking *(Brit)*

double-mètre (pl **doubles-mètres**) /dubləmɛtʀ/ NM two-metre *(Brit) ou* -meter *(US)* rule

doubler /duble/ ► conjug 1 ◄ VT 1 (= *augmenter) [+ fortune, dose, longueur, salaire]* to double ◆ ~ **le pas** to quicken one's pace, to speed up ◆ **il a doublé son poids** he has doubled in weight

2 (= *mettre en double) [+ fil, ficelle]* to double; *[+ revêtement]* to double, to lay double; *[+ couverture]* to double, to fold (in half)

3 *(Scol) [+ classe, année]* to repeat

4 *[+ film, acteur]* to dub ◆ ~ **(la voix de) qn** to dub sb, to dub sb's voice

5 *(Théât, Ciné = remplacer)* to understudy, to act as an understudy for; *(dans une scène dangereuse)* to stand in for ◆ **il s'est fait** ~ **par un cascadeur** a stuntman stood in for him

6 (= *revêtir) [+ boîte, paroi, tableau, veste]* to line *(de* with); ◆ ~ **une veste de fourrure** to line a jacket with fur

7 (= *dépasser) [+ véhicule]* to pass, to overtake *(Brit)*; *(Naut) [+ cap]* to round ◆ **il a doublé ce cap important** *(fig)* he has got over this important hurdle *ou* turned this important corner ◆ ~ **le cap des 50 ans** to turn 50, to pass the 50 mark

8 (* = *tromper)* ~ **qn** to pull a fast one on sb*, to double-cross sb

VI 1 *[nombre, quantité, prix]* to double, to increase twofold ◆ ~ **de poids/valeur** to double in weight/value ◆ **le nombre des crimes a doublé** the number of crimes has doubled *ou* increased twofold

2 *[automobiliste]* to pass, to overtake *(Brit)*

VPR **se doubler** ◆ **se** ~ **de** to be coupled with ◆ **chez lui le sens de l'honneur se double de courage** with him a sense of honour is coupled with *ou* goes hand in hand with courage ◆ **ce dispositif se double d'un système d'alarme** this device works *ou* functions in conjunction with an alarm system

doublet /dublɛ/ NM *(Ling, Orfèvrerie)* doublet

doubleur, -euse /dublœʀ, øz/ NM,F *(Ciné)* dubber

doublon /dublɔ̃/ NM 1 (= *monnaie)* doubloon 2 (= *redondance)* duplication 3 *(Typo)* double

doublonner /dublɔne/ ► conjug 1 ◄ VI ◆ ~ **avec** to duplicate

doublure /dublyʀ/ NF 1 (= *étoffe)* lining 2 *(Théât)* understudy; *(Ciné)* stand-in; *(pour scènes dangereuses)* stuntman *(ou* stuntwoman)

douce /dus/ ADJ F, NF → **doux**

douceâtre /dusɑtʀ/ ADJ *[odeur]* sickly sweet

doucement /dusmɑ̃/ ADV 1 (= *légèrement) [toucher, prendre, soulever]* gently; *[frapper, parler]* gently, softly; *[éclairer]* softly ◆ **marcher** ~ to tread carefully *ou* softly ◆ **allez-y** ~ **!*** easy *ou* gently does it!*, go easy!*

2 (= *graduellement) [monter, progresser]* gently, gradually; (= *lentement) [rouler, avancer]* slowly; *[démarrer]* smoothly ◆ **la route monte/descend** ~ the road climbs/descends gradually *ou* goes gently up/down ◆ **la température monte/descend** ~ the temperature is slowly *ou* gradually rising/falling

3 (* = *plus ou moins bien)* so-so* ◆ **comment allez-vous ? – (tout)** ~ how are you? – so-so*

4 (* = *en cachette)* **s'amuser** ~ **de voir qn dans l'embarras** to have a quiet laugh* (to o.s.) at seeing sb in difficulties ◆ **ça me fait** ~ **rigoler !** it makes me want to laugh!

EXCL gently!, easy! ◆ ~ **avec le whisky !** go easy on the whisky!*, careful with the whisky! ◆ ~ **les basses !*** take it easy!*, go easy!*

doucereux, -euse /dus(ə)ʀø, øz/ ADJ *[goût, saveur]* sickly sweet; *(péj) [ton, paroles]* sugary, honeyed; *(péj) [personne, manières]* suave, smooth*

doucet, -ette /dusɛ, ɛt/ ADJ † meek, mild NF **doucette** (= *plante)* corn-salad, lamb's lettuce

doucettement* /dusɛtmɑ̃/ ADV *[commencer, avancer]* gently; *[vivre]* quietly

douceur /dusœʀ/ NF 1 *[de peau, tissu]* softness, smoothness; *[de matelas, brosse, suspension]* softness

2 *[de temps, climat, température, saison]* mildness; *[de brise]* gentleness

3 (= *goût sucré) [de fruit, liqueur, saveur]* sweetness; (= *goût faible) [de fromage, tabac, moutarde, piment]* mildness

4 *[de son, musique, voix]* sweetness, gentleness; *[de parfum]* sweetness; *[de lumière, couleur]* softness

5 (= *modération) [de pente]* gentleness

6 (= *affabilité, gentillesse) [de caractère, personne, sourire, geste]* gentleness ◆ **c'est un homme d'une grande** ~ he's a very gentle man ◆ **elle est d'une** ~ **angélique** she's as sweet as an angel ◆ **prendre qn par la** ~ to deal gently with sb; *(pour convaincre)* to use gentle persuasion on sb ◆ ~ **de vivre** gentle way of life

7 *(gén pl)* (= *sucrerie)* sweet; (= *flatterie)* sweet talk *(NonC)* ◆ **les ~s de l'amitié** the (sweet) pleasures of friendship

LOC ADJ **en douceur** LOC ADV *[démarrage]* smooth *[démarrer]* smoothly; *[commencer, manœuvrer]* gently ◆ **il faut y aller en** ~ we must go about it gently ◆ **ça s'est passé en** ~ it went off smoothly; → **atterrissage**

Douchanbe /duʃɑ̃be/ N Dushanbe

douche /duʃ/ NF 1 (= *jet, système)* shower ◆ **prendre une** ~ to have *ou* take a shower ◆ **passer à la** ~ to go for a shower ◆ **il est sous la** ~ he's in the *ou* having a shower 2 (= *salle)* **~s** shower room, showers 3 * (= *déception)* let-down*, bummer*; (= *réprimande)* (good) telling-off* *ou* ticking-off* *(Brit)*; (= *averse, arrosage)* soaking, drenching ◆ **on a pris une bonne** ~ we got drenched *ou* soaked ◆ **ça nous a fait l'effet d'une** ~ **(froide) quand nous l'avons appris** it was a real let-down* when we found out COMP **douche écossaise** *(lit)* alternately hot and cold shower ◆ **ça a été la** ~ **écossaise*** *(fig)* it came as a bit of a blow *ou* shock

doucher /duʃe/ ► conjug 1 ◄ VT 1 ◆ ~ **qn** to give sb a shower ◆ **se faire** ~ *(par l'averse)* to get a soaking, to get soaked *ou* drenched; († * = *se faire réprimander)* to get a (good) telling-off* *ou* ticking-off* *(Brit)* 2 *[+ espoirs, enthousiasme]* to dampen ◆ **ce qu'il m'a dit, ça m'a douché*** what he said really knocked me back* VPR **se doucher** to have *ou* take a shower

douchette /duʃɛt/ NF *[de douche]* shower rose; *(pour codes-barres)* bar-code reader *ou* scanner

doudou[1] * /dudu/ NF *(terme des Antilles)* (= *femme)* woman; (= *jeune fille)* girl

doudou[2] /dudu/ NM *(langage enfantin)* ≈ security blanket

doudoune /dudun/ NF 1 (= *anorak)* down jacket 2 (* = *sein)* boob*, breast

doué, e /dwe/ (ptp de **douer**) ADJ 1 (= *talentueux)* gifted, talented *(en* in); ◆ **être** ~ **pour** to have a gift for ◆ **il n'est pas** ~* *(iro)* he's not exactly bright *ou* clever ◆ ~ **sur le plan scolaire** academically able 2 (= *pourvu)* ~ **de** *[+ vie, raison]* endowed with; *[+ intelligence, talent, mémoire]* blessed with, endowed with

douer /dwe/ ► conjug 1 ◄ VT **douer qn de** *[+ vie, raison]* to endow sb with; *[+ intelligence, talent, mémoire]* to bless sb with, to endow sb with

douille /duj/ NF *[de cartouche]* (cartridge) case, cartridge; *[de fil électrique]* (electric light) socket; *[de manche]* socket; *(Culin)* piping socket ◆ ~ **à vis/à baïonnette** *(Élec)* screw/bayonet socket

douiller* /duje/ ► conjug 1 ◄ VI (= *payer cher)* to pay through the nose*, to fork out* a lot ◆ **ça douille** it's damn expensive *ou* pricey*

douillet, -ette /dujɛ, ɛt/ ADJ 1 (= *sensible à la douleur) [personne]* soft *(péj)* ◆ **je suis** ~ I can't stand pain ◆ **je ne suis pas** ~ I can take it 2 (= *confortable) [maison, atmosphère]* cosy, snug; *[nid, lit, vie]* soft, cosy NF **douillette** † *[d'ecclésiastique]* (clerical) overcoat; *[de bébé]* quilted coat

douillettement /dujɛtmɑ̃/ ADV cosily, snugly

douleur /dulœʀ/ GRAMMAIRE ACTIVE 51.4 NF 1 *(physique)* pain ◆ **~s rhumatismales** rheumatic pains ◆ **~s dorsales** backache *(NonC)*, back pains ◆ **les ~s (de l'accouchement)** labour *(Brit) ou* labor *(US)* pains ◆ **j'ai une** ~ **dans le bras** I have a sore arm, I have a pain in my arm, my arm hurts ◆ **mes vieilles ~s me font souffrir** my old aches and pains are bothering me; → **accouchement**

2 *(morale)* grief, distress ◆ **il a eu la** ~ **de perdre son frère** he had the distress of *ou* had to suffer the grief of losing his brother ◆ **"nous avons la douleur de vous faire part du décès de ..."** "it is our sad duty to tell you *ou* it is with great sorrow that we have to tell you of the death of ..." ◆ **"nous avons la douleur d'ap-**

prendre que ..." "it is with great sorrow that we've learned that ..." ◆ **j'ai compris ma ~** * *(fig)* I realized my mistake, I could have kicked myself * ◆ **les grandes ~s sont muettes** *(Prov)* great sorrow is often silent

douloureusement /duluʀøzmɑ̃/ ADV painfully ◆ **une perte de pouvoir d'achat ~ ressentie** the loss of purchasing power that makes itself painfully felt

douloureux, -euse /duluʀø, øz/ ADJ 1 *[sensation, maladie, opération, membre]* painful 2 *[perte]* grievous, distressing; *[décision, spectacle]* painful, distressing, harrowing; *[séparation, circonstances, moment]* painful, distressing; *[regard, expression]* sorrowful NF **douloureuse** (*, *hum*) *(= addition)* bill *(Brit)*, check *(US)*; *(= facture)* bill ◆ **apportez-nous la douloureuse** what's the damage? *, let's hear the worst *

douma /duma/ NF duma

doute /dut/ GRAMMAIRE ACTIVE 42.1, 43.1, 53.6 NM 1 *(= état d'incertitude)* doubt, uncertainty; *(Philos, Rel)* doubt ◆ **être dans le ~** to be doubtful *ou* uncertain ◆ **laisser qn dans le ~** to leave sb in a state of uncertainty ◆ **être dans le ~ au sujet de qch** to be in doubt *ou* doubtful *ou* uncertain about sth ◆ **le ~ l'envahit** he was overcome by doubt ◆ **le ~ n'est plus permis quant à...** there is no more room for doubt concerning... ◆ **un air de ~** a doubtful air

2 *(= soupçon, perplexité)* doubt ◆ **je n'ai pas le moindre ~ à ce sujet** I haven't the slightest doubt about it ◆ **avoir des** *ou* **ses ~s sur** *ou* **au sujet de qch/qn** to have misgivings *ou* (one's) doubts about sth/sb ◆ **malgré tout, j'ai des ~s** nevertheless, I have my doubts ◆ **il a émis des ~s à propos de ...** he expressed (his) doubts *ou* misgivings about ... ◆ **un ~ plane sur l'affaire** a certain amount of *ou* an element of doubt hangs over the matter

3 *(locutions)* **dans le ~, abstiens-toi** *(Prov)* when in doubt, don't! ◆ **il ne fait aucun ~ que ...** there is (absolutely) no doubt that ..., there is no question that ... ◆ **ceci ne fait aucun ~** there is no doubt *ou* question about it ◆ **il est hors de ~ qu'il a raison** he's undoubtedly right, it's beyond doubt that he's right ◆ **mettre hors de ~** *[+ authenticité]* to prove beyond doubt ◆ **nul ~ que ...** (there is) no doubt that ...

◆ **sans doute** *(= vraisemblablement)* doubtless, no doubt, probably ◆ **sans ~ s'est-il trompé** he's doubtless *ou* no doubt mistaken ◆ **tu viendras demain ? – sans ~** are you coming tomorrow – yes, probably *ou* most likely ◆ **sans (aucun** *ou* **nul) ~** *(= incontestablement)* without (a) doubt, undoubtedly

◆ **en doute** ◆ **mettre en ~** *[+ affirmation, honnêteté de qn]* to question, to challenge, to cast doubt on ◆ **mettre en ~ que ...** to question whether ...

douter /dute/ GRAMMAIRE ACTIVE 43.1 ▸ conjug 1 ◂ VT INDIR **douter de** 1 *(sentiment d'incertitude)* *[+ identité, authenticité, existence de qch]* to doubt, to question, to have doubts as to; *[+ réussite]* to be doubtful of ◆ **au début il le croyait, maintenant il doute** at first he believed it, but now he's not so sure ◆ **il le dit mais j'en doute** he says so but I have my doubts *ou* but I doubt it ◆ **il a dit la vérité, n'en doutez pas** he's telling the truth, you can be sure of that *ou* there's no doubt about that ◆ **je doute d'avoir jamais fait/dit cela** I doubt that I ever did/said that ◆ **je n'ai jamais douté du résultat** I never had any doubts about *ou* as to the result ◆ **je doute qu'il vienne** I doubt (if *ou* whether) he'll come ◆ **je ne doute pas qu'il le fera** *ou* **ne le fasse** I don't doubt *ou* I dare say that he'll do it ◆ **à n'en pas ~** *(= sans aucun doute)* without (a) doubt; *(= vraisemblablement)* doubtless, no doubt ◆ **~ si** *(littér)* to doubt whether

2 *(Philos, Rel : esprit de réfutation)* **~ de** *[+ dogme]* to have *ou* entertain *(frm)* doubts about, to doubt ◆ **mieux vaut ~ que tout accepter** it is better to doubt than to accept everything

3 *(sentiment de méfiance)* **~ de** *[+ allié, sincérité de qn]* to have (one's) doubts about, to doubt ◆ **je n'ai jamais douté de vous** I never doubted you, I never had any doubts about you ◆ **~ de la parole de qn** to doubt sb's word ◆ **il ne doute de rien !** * he's got some nerve! * ◆ **il doute de lui(-même)** he has feelings of self-doubt ◆ **je te dis que c'était lundi – ah, tu me fais ~ de moi, j'étais sûr que c'était mardi** I tell you it was Monday – oh, I was sure it was Tuesday, but now you're making me wonder

VPR **se douter** ◆ **se ~ de qch** to suspect sth ◆ **je me doute de son inquiétude quand il apprendra la nouvelle** I can (just) imagine his anxiety when he learns the news ◆ **je ne m'en suis jamais douté** I never guessed *ou* suspected it for a moment ◆ **ça, je m'en doutais depuis longtemps** I've thought so *ou* thought as much *ou* suspected as much for a long time ◆ **j'étais (bien) loin de me ~ que ...** little did I know that ... ◆ **se ~ que** to suspect that, to have an idea that ◆ **il ne se doutait pas qu'elle serait là** he had no idea *ou* hadn't suspected (that) she would be there ◆ **je me doute qu'il a dû accepter** I expect *ou* imagine that he must have accepted ◆ **qu'il soit fâché, je m'en doute** I can well imagine that he's angry ◆ **on s'en serait douté !** * surprise, surprise! *(iro)*

douteux, -euse /dutø, øz/ ADJ 1 *(= incertain)* *[fait]* doubtful, questionable, uncertain; *[résultat, issue]* doubtful, uncertain; *[sens, date, réponse]* doubtful ◆ **il est ~ que ...** it is doubtful *ou* questionable that *ou* whether ... ◆ **il n'est pas ~ que ...** there is no doubt that ... ◆ **d'origine douteuse** of uncertain *ou* doubtful origin 2 *(péj)* *(= médiocre)* *[raisonnement, propreté, qualité, mœurs]* doubtful, dubious, questionable; *(= peu solide ou peu propre)* *[vêtements, individu, aliment]* dubious-looking; *[amarrage, passerelle]* shaky, dubious-looking ◆ **d'un goût ~** *[décoration, cravate, plaisanterie]* in doubtful *ou* questionable *ou* dubious taste

douve /duv/ NF 1 *(Agr)* drainage ditch; *(Équitation)* water jump ◆ **~(s)** *[de château]* moat 2 *[de tonneau]* stave

3 *(= parasite)* fluke ◆ **~ du foie** liver fluke

Douvres /duvʀ/ N Dover

doux, douce /du, dus/ ADJ 1 *(= lisse, souple)* *[peau, tissu]* soft, smooth; *[matelas, suspension, brosse]* soft; → **fer, lime**

2 *[eau]* *(= non calcaire)* soft; *(= non salé)* fresh

3 *(= clément)* *[temps, climat, température]* mild; *[brise, chaleur]* gentle ◆ **il fait ~ aujourd'hui** it's mild today

4 *(au goût)* *(= sucré)* *[fruit, saveur, liqueur]* sweet; *(= pas fort)* *[moutarde, fromage, tabac, piment]* mild ◆ **~ comme le miel** as sweet as honey; → **orange, patate**

5 *(à l'ouïe, la vue)* *[son, musique, accents]* sweet, gentle; *[voix]* soft, gentle; *[lumière, couleur]* soft, mellow, subdued ◆ **un nom aux consonances douces** a mellifluous *ou* sweet-sounding name

6 *(= modéré)* *[pente, montée]* gentle, gradual ◆ **en pente douce** gently sloping ◆ **nous pratiquons des prix très ~** our prices are easy on the pocket; → **drogue, feu¹, médecine** *etc*

7 *(= non brutal, gentil)* *[caractère, manières, reproche]* mild, gentle; *[personne, sourire]* gentle; *[punition]* mild ◆ **il a l'air ~** he looks gentle ◆ **elle a eu une mort douce** she died peacefully ◆ **il est ~ comme un agneau** he's as gentle *ou* meek *(Brit)* as a lamb ◆ **d'un geste très ~** very gently; → **œil**

8 *(gén avant nom)* *(= agréable)* *[victoire, revanche, repos, tranquillité]* sweet; *[parfum, souvenirs, pensées]* sweet, agreeable, pleasant ◆ **cette pensée lui était douce** this thought gave him great pleasure ◆ **qu'il m'était ~ de repenser à ces moments** what pleasure it gave me *ou* how pleasant *ou* agreeable for me to think over those moments; → **billet, couler, folie**

LOC ADV **en douce** * on the quiet, on the q.t. *

LOC ADV **tout doux** ◆ **ça va tout ~** * things are going so-so * ◆ **tout ~ !** († *ou hum*) gently (now)!, careful (now)!; → **filer**

NM,F *(parfois péj)* *(= personne douce)* mild (-natured) person

NF **douce** (†, *aussi hum* = *amoureuse*) sweetheart †

doux-amer, douce-amère (mpl **doux-amers**, fpl **douces-amères**) /du(z)amɛʀ, dusamɛʀ/ ADJ *(lit, fig)* bittersweet NF **douce-amère** *(= plante)* woody nightshade, bittersweet

douzain /duzɛ̃/ NM *(Poésie)* twelve-line poem; *(Hist = monnaie)* douzain

douzaine /duzɛn/ NF *(= douze)* dozen ◆ **une ~** *(= environ douze)* about twelve, a dozen (or so) ◆ **une ~ d'huîtres/d'œufs** a dozen oysters/eggs ◆ **il y a une ~ d'années** about twelve years ago, twelve or so years ago ◆ **elle a une ~ d'années** she's about twelve ◆ **vendre qch à la ~** to sell sth by the dozen ◆ **il y en a à la ~** *(fig)* there are dozens of them; → **treize**

douze /duz/ ADJ INV twelve ◆ **~ douzaines** *(Comm)* a gross, twelve dozen; *pour autres loc voir* **six** NM INV twelve ◆ **les Douze** *(Hist)* the Twelve; *pour autres loc voir* **six**

douzième /duzjɛm/ ADJ, NMF twelfth; *pour loc voir* **sixième**

douzièmement /duzjɛmmɑ̃/ ADV in twelfth place, twelfthly

Dow Jones /dodʒɔns/ NM *(Bourse)* ◆ **le ~, l'indice ~** the Dow Jones (index)

doyen, -enne /dwajɛ̃, jɛn/ NM,F *(Rel, Univ)* ≈ dean; *[d'équipe, groupe]* most senior member ◆ **~ (d'âge)** *[d'assemblée, corps constitué]* most senior member, doyen ◆ **la doyenne des Français** France's oldest citizen

doyenné /dwajene/ NM *(Rel)* *(= circonscription)* deanery; *(= charge)* deanery, deanship NF *(= poire)* ◆ **~ (du comice)** comice (pear)

dpi /depei/ NMPL (abrév de **dots per inch**) dpi

DPLG /depeelʒe/ ADJ (abrév de **diplômé par le gouvernement**) ◆ **ingénieur ~** (state) certified engineer

Dr (abrév de **docteur**) Dr

drachme /dʀakm/ NF drachma

draconien, -ienne /dʀakɔnjɛ̃, jɛn/ ADJ *[loi]* draconian; *[mesure]* drastic, draconian; *[régime alimentaire]* strict

dragage /dʀagaʒ/ NM *(pour nettoyer)* dredging; *(pour trouver qch)* dragging ◆ **~ des mines** minesweeping

dragée /dʀaʒe/ NF 1 *(= friandise)* sugared almond; *(Méd)* sugar-coated pill 2 *(= plomb de chasse)* small shot; (* = *balle*) slug *, bullet 3 *(Agr)* dredge 4 *(locution)* **tenir la ~ haute à qn** to hold out on sb

dragéifier /dʀaʒeifje/ ▸ conjug 7 ◂ VT to sugar, to coat with sugar ◆ **comprimé dragéifié** sugared *ou* sugar-coated tablet

drageon /dʀaʒɔ̃/ NM *(Bot)* sucker

dragon /dʀagɔ̃/ NM 1 *(Myth, fig)* dragon ◆ **~ volant** flying lizard *ou* dragon ◆ **~ de Komodo** Komodo dragon ◆ **un ~ de vertu** a dragon of virtue 2 *(Hist Mil)* dragoon

dragonnade /dʀagɔnad/ NF *(Hist)* dragonnade

dragonne /dʀagɔn/ NF *[d'épée]* sword-knot; *[de parapluie]* loop *(for wrist)*; *[de bâton de ski]* wrist-strap; *(Alpinisme)* wrist loop

dragonnier /dʀagɔnje/ NM dragon tree

dragster /dʀagstɛʀ/ NM dragster

drague /dʀag/ NF [1] *(Pêche)* dragnet [2] *(Tech)* *(= machine)* dredge; *(= navire, ponton)* dredger [3] *(* : pour séduire)* **la ~** trying to pick people up*, chatting people up* *(Brit)*

draguer /dʀage/ ► conjug 1 ◄ VT [1] *(* : pour séduire)* **~ qn** to try and pick sb up*, to chat sb up* *(Brit)* ◆ **elle s'est fait ~ par un mec** some guy tried to pick her up* [2] *[+ rivière, port, canal]* *(pour nettoyer)* to dredge; *(pour trouver qch)* to drag; *[+ mines]* to sweep [3] *(Pêche)* to dredge for [4] **~ (le fond)** *[ancre]* to drag VI * to try and pick up* girls *(ou* guys), to chat up* *(Brit)* girls *(ou* guys), to be on the pull* *(Brit)* *ou* make* *(US)* ◆ **~ en voiture** to go cruising*, to go kerb-crawling ◆ **~ dans les boîtes** *(gén)* to go to night-clubs to try and pick somebody up; *[homosexuel]* to go cruising (in night-clubs)*

dragueur[1] /dʀagœʀ/ NM *(= pêcheur)* dragnet fisherman; *(= ouvrier)* dredger; *(= bateau)* dredger ◆ **~ de mines** minesweeper

dragueur[2], **-euse*** /dʀagœʀ, øz/ NM,F ◆ **c'est un sacré ~** he's a great one for trying to pick up* girls *ou* women ◆ **quelle dragueuse !** she's always trying to pick up guys

drain /dʀɛ̃/ NM *(Agr)* (underground) drain; *(Méd, Élec)* drain ◆ **poser un ~ à qn** to insert a drain in sb

drainage /dʀɛnaʒ/ NM [1] *[de marais, sol]* drainage [2] *(Méd)* drainage ◆ **~ lymphatique** lymphatic drainage [3] *[de main-d'œuvre, capitaux]* drain

draine /dʀɛn/ NF mistlethrush

drainer /dʀene/ ► conjug 1 ◄ VT [1] *[+ marais, sol]* to drain [2] *(Méd)* *[+ plaie, rein]* to drain [3] *(= attirer)* *[+ main-d'œuvre, capitaux]* to bring in; *[+ public, clientèle]* to attract ◆ **~ l'épargne vers l'immobilier** to encourage savers to invest in real estate

draisienne /dʀɛzjɛn/ NF *(Hist)* dandy horse

draisine /dʀɛzin/ NF *(Rail)* track motorcar *(Brit)*, gang car *(US)*, handcar *(US)*

drakkar /dʀakaʀ/ NM longship

Dralon® /dʀalɔ̃/ NM Dralon®

dramatique /dʀamatik/ ADJ [1] *(= grave)* tragic ◆ **ce n'est pas ~ !** it's not the end of the world! ◆ **la situation est ~** it's a terrible situation [2] *(Théât)* **artiste ~** stage actor *(ou* actress) ◆ **auteur ~** playwright, dramatist ◆ **centre ~** drama school ◆ **critique ~** drama critic; → **art, comédie** [3] *(= épique)* *[récit, puissance, intensité]* dramatic NF *(TV)* ◆ **~** (television) play *ou* drama

> ⚠ Au sens de 'grave', 'terrible', **dramatique** ne se traduit pas par **dramatic**.

dramatiquement /dʀamatikmɑ̃/ ADV [1] *(= beaucoup)* dramatically [2] *(= de façon épique)* dramatically; *(= tragiquement)* tragically

dramatisation /dʀamatizasjɔ̃/ NF dramatization

dramatiser /dʀamatize/ ► conjug 1 ◄ VT to dramatize ◆ **il ne faut pas ~ (la situation)** you shouldn't dramatize things

dramaturge /dʀamatyʀʒ/ NMF dramatist, playwright

dramaturgie /dʀamatyʀʒi/ NF *(= art)* dramatic art; *(= traité)* treatise on dramatic art

drame /dʀam/ NM [1] *(Théât)* *(= genre littéraire)* drama; *(= œuvre)* play, drama [2] *(= événement tragique)* tragedy ◆ **le ~ du tunnel du Mont-Blanc** the tragedy in the Mont-Blanc tunnel ◆ **~ de la jalousie** drama of jealousy, crime of passion ◆ **la farce tournait au ~** the joke was going tragically wrong ◆ **faire un ~ de qch** to make a drama out of sth ◆ **n'en faites pas un ~** don't make such a fuss *ou* to-do* about it ◆ **ce n'est pas un ~ !** it's not the end of the world!

> ⚠ Au sens de 'événement tragique', **drame** ne se traduit pas par l'anglais **drama**.

drap /dʀa/ NM [1] *(= pièce de tissu)* **~ (de lit)** sheet ◆ **~s de soie/nylon** silk/nylon sheets ◆ **~ de dessus/dessous** top/bottom sheet ◆ **~ de bain** bath sheet ◆ **~ de plage** beach towel ◆ **~ mortuaire** *ou* **funéraire** pall ◆ **être dans les ~s** to be between the sheets ◆ **être dans de beaux** *ou* **sales ~s** *(fig)* to be in a right fix* *ou* mess* ◆ **tu m'as mis dans de beaux ~s** you got me in a right fix*, you really landed me in it* [2] *(= tissu)* woollen cloth

drapé, e /dʀape/ (ptp de **draper**) ADJ draped ◆ **tambours ~s** muffled drums NM ◆ **le ~ d'un rideau** *etc* the hang *ou* drape of a curtain *etc*

drapeau (pl **drapeaux**) /dʀapo/ NM [1] *(gén)* flag ◆ **le ~ tricolore** the (French) tricolour ◆ **le ~ blanc/rouge** the white/red flag ◆ **hisser le ~ blanc** to wave the white flag ◆ **~ à damier** *(Courses)* chequered *(Brit)* *ou* checkered *(US)* flag ◆ **~ de trou** *(Golf)* pin ◆ **le respect du ~** respect for the flag ◆ **être sous les ~x** *(Mil)* to be doing one's military service ◆ **le ~ de la liberté** the flag of liberty ◆ **mettre son ~ dans sa poche** *(fig)* to keep one's views well hidden [2] *(Aviat, Naut)* **en ~** feathered ◆ **mettre une hélice en ~** to feather a propeller

draper /dʀape/ ► conjug 1 ◄ VT [1] *(= habiller)* to drape ◆ **un foulard de soie drapait ses épaules** a silk scarf was draped over her shoulders, her shoulders were draped in a silk scarf [2] *(Textiles)* *[+ étoffe de laine]* to process VPR **se draper** ◆ **se ~ dans** to drape o.s. in ◆ **se ~ dans sa dignité** to stand on one's dignity ◆ **se ~ dans sa vertu/son honnêteté** to cloak o.s. in one's virtue/one's honesty

draperie /dʀapʀi/ NF *(= tenture)* drapery, hanging; *(Comm)* drapery, cloth; *(Art)* drapery

drap-housse (pl **draps-housses**) /dʀaus/ NM fitted sheet

drapier, -ière /dʀapje, jɛʀ/ ADJ ◆ **industrie drapière** clothing industry ◆ **ouvrier ~** cloth-worker NM *(= fabricant)* (woollen) cloth manufacturer ◆ **(marchand) ~** clothier, draper *(Brit)*

drastique /dʀastik/ ADJ *(Méd, gén)* drastic

drave* /dʀav/ NF *(Can Hist)* *[de bois]* drive, rafting

draver* /dʀave/ ► conjug 1 ◄ VT *(Can Hist)* *[+ bois]* to drive, to raft

draveur* /dʀavœʀ/ NM *(Can Hist)* (log *ou* timber) driver, raftsman

dravidien, -ienne /dʀavidjɛ̃, jɛn/ ADJ, NM Dravidian

dreadlocks /dʀɛdlɔks/ NFPL dreadlocks

Dresde /dʀɛzd/ N Dresden

dressage /dʀesaʒ/ NM [1] *[d'animal sauvage]* taming; *[de jeune cheval]* breaking in; *(pour le cirque)* *[de chien, cheval]* training; * *[de recrue]* knocking *ou* licking into shape* ◆ **épreuve de ~** *(Équitation)* dressage event [2] *[de tente]* pitching; *[d'échafaudage]* erection, putting up [3] *[de pierre, planche, tôle]* dressing

dresser /dʀese/ ► conjug 1 ◄ VT [1] *(= établir)* *[+ inventaire, liste]* to draw up, to make out; *[+ plan, carte]* to draw up ◆ **~ un acte** *(Jur)* to draw up a deed ◆ **il a dressé un bilan encourageant de la situation** he gave an encouraging review of the situation *ou* an encouraging run-down* on the situation

[2] *(= ériger)* *[+ monument, statue, échafaudage]* to put up, to erect; *[+ barrière, échelle]* to put up, to set up; *[+ tente]* to pitch, to put up; *[+ mât]* to raise, to put up, to erect; *[+ lit]* to put up ◆ **nous avons dressé un buffet dans le jardin** we laid out a buffet in the garden ◆ **~ le couvert** *ou* **la table** to lay *ou* set the table ◆ **dressez les filets sur un plat** *(Culin)* arrange the fillets on a dish

[3] *(= lever)* *[+ tête]* to raise, to lift; *[+ menton]* to stick out ◆ **~ l'oreille** *(fig)* to prick up one's ears ◆ **~ l'oreille** *ou* **ses oreilles** *[chien]* to prick up *ou* cock (up) its ears ◆ **faire ~ les cheveux sur la tête à qn** to make sb's hair stand on end ◆ **une histoire à faire ~ les cheveux sur la tête** a spine-chilling *ou* spine-tingling tale, a tale to make your hair stand on end

[4] *(= braquer)* **~ qn contre** to set sb against

[5] *(= dompter)* *[+ animal sauvage]* to tame; *[+ jeune cheval]* to break (in); *(pour le cirque)* *[+ chien, cheval]* to train ◆ **~ un chien à rapporter** to train a dog to retrieve

[6] *(* = mater)* *[+ recrue]* to knock *ou* lick into shape* ◆ **ça le dressera !** that will knock *ou* lick him into shape* ◆ **~ un enfant** to teach a child his place ◆ **les enfants/les élèves, ça se dresse !** children/pupils should be taught their place! ◆ **enfant mal dressé** badly brought-up child

[7] *(Tech)* *[+ pierre, planche, tôle]* to dress

VPR **se dresser** [1] *[personne]* *(debout)* to stand up; *(assis)* to sit up (straight) ◆ **se ~ sur la pointe des pieds** to stand on tiptoe ◆ **se ~ de toute sa taille** to draw o.s. up to one's full height ◆ **se ~ sur ses pattes de derrière** *[cheval]* to rear (up); *[autre animal]* to stand up on its hind legs; → **ergot**

[2] *[cheveux]* to stand on end; *[oreille]* to prick up

[3] *[statue, bâtiment, obstacle]* to stand; *(de façon imposante, menaçante)* to tower (up) ◆ **un navire se dressa soudain dans le brouillard** a ship suddenly loomed (up) out of the fog

[4] *(= s'insurger)* to rise up *(contre, face à* against)

dresseur, -euse /dʀesœʀ, øz/ NM,F *(gén)* trainer; *[d'animaux sauvages]* tamer ◆ **~ de lions** lion tamer ◆ **~ de chevaux** *(débourrage)* horse-breaker; *(dans un cirque)* horse-trainer

dressing /dʀesiŋ/, **dressing-room** (pl **dressing-rooms** /dʀesiŋʀum/) NM dressing room

dressoir /dʀeswaʀ/ NM dresser

dreyfusard, e /dʀefyzaʀ, aʀd/ ADJ *(Hist)* supporting *ou* defending Dreyfus NM,F supporter *ou* defender of Dreyfus

DRH /deɛʀaʃ/ NF (abrév de **direction des ressources humaines**) → **direction** NMF (abrév de **directeur, -trice des ressources humaines**) → **directeur, -trice**

dribble /dʀibl/ NM *(Sport)* dribble

dribbler /dʀible/ ► conjug 1 ◄ *(Sport)* VI to dribble VT *[+ ballon]* to dribble; *[+ joueur]* to dribble past *ou* round

drill[1] /dʀil/ NM *(= singe)* drill

drill[2] /dʀil/ NM *(Scol etc = exercice)* drill

drille[1] /dʀij/ NM † ◆ **bon** *ou* **joyeux ~** jolly fellow, cheerful character

drille[2] /dʀij/ NF *(= outil)* hand-drill

dring /dʀiŋ/ EXCL, NM ding, ding-a-ling

drisse /dʀis/ NF *(Naut)* halyard

drive /dʀajv/ NM *(Golf, Ordin)* drive

driver[1] /dʀajve, dʀive/ ► conjug 1 ◄ VT *[jockey]* to drive VI *(Golf)* to drive

driver[2], **driveur** /dʀajvœʀ, dʀivœʀ/ NM *(Équitation, Golf, Ordin)* driver

drogue /dʀɔg/ NF [1] *(= stupéfiant)* drug ◆ **la ~** drugs ◆ **une ~ dure/douce** a hard/soft drug; → **trafic** [2] *(fig, o.f)* *(Pharm)* drug; *(péj)* patent medicine, quack remedy *(péj)* ◆ **le café est une ~** coffee is a drug

drogué, e /dʀɔge/ (ptp de **droguer**) NM,F drug addict

droguer /dʀɔge/ ► conjug 1 ◄ VT [1] *(péj)* *[+ malade]* to dose up *(péj)*; *(† Méd)* to give drugs to [2] *[+ victime]* to drug VPR **se droguer** [1] *(péj : de médicaments)* to dose o.s. (up) *(de* with) [2] *(de stupéfiants)* to take drugs ◆ **il se drogue** he's on drugs, he's taking drugs ◆ **se ~ à la cocaïne** to be on *ou* take cocaine

droguerie /dʀɔgʀi/ **NF** (*= magasin*) hardware shop; (*= commerce*) hardware trade

droguet /dʀɔgɛ/ **NM** (*= étoffe*) drugget

droguiste /dʀɔgist/ **NMF** owner *ou* keeper of a hardware shop

droit[1], e[1] /dʀwa, dʀwat/ **ADJ** (*après nom : opposé à gauche*) [*main, bras, jambe*] right; [*poche, chaussure*] right(-hand) ◆ **du côté ~** on the right-hand side; → **bras, centre, main**

NM (*Boxe = coup*) right ◆ **direct du ~** (*= poing*) straight right ◆ **crochet du ~** right hook

NF droite 1 (*opposé à la gauche*) **la ~e** the right (side), the right-hand side ◆ **à ~e** on the right; (*direction*) to the right ◆ **troisième rue à ~e** third street on the right ◆ **à ma/sa ~e** on my/his right (hand), on my/his right(-hand) side ◆ **le tiroir/chemin de ~e** the right-hand drawer/path ◆ **il ne connaît pas sa ~e de sa gauche** he can't tell (his) right from (his) left ◆ **à ~e de la fenêtre** to the right of the window ◆ **de ~e à gauche** from right to left ◆ **à ~e et à gauche, de ~e et de gauche** this way and that ◆ **il a couru à ~e et à gauche pour se renseigner** he tried everywhere *ou* all over the place to get some information ◆ **c'est ce qu'on entend dire de ~e et de gauche** that's what one hears from all sides *ou* quarters

2 (*sur une route*) **la ~e** the right ◆ **rouler à ~e** to drive on the right (-hand side of the road) ◆ **garder** *ou* **tenir sa ~e** to keep to the right; → **conduite**

3 (*Pol*) **la ~e** the right (wing) ◆ **candidat/idées de ~e** right-wing candidate/ideas ◆ **un homme de ~e** a man of the right ◆ **membre de la ~e** right-winger ◆ **elle est très à ~e** she's very right-wing ◆ **la ~e est divisée** the right wing is split; → **extrême**

4 (*Boxe = coup*) right

droit[2], e[2] /dʀwa, dʀwat/ **ADJ** 1 (*= sans déviation, non courbe*) [*barre, ligne, route, nez*] straight ◆ **ça fait 4 km en ligne ~e** it's 4 km as the crow flies ◆ **cela vient en ~e ligne de ...** (*fig*) that comes straight *ou* direct from ... ◆ **le ~ chemin** (*Rel*) the straight and narrow ◆ **~ fil** (*Couture*) straight grain ◆ **cette décision s'inscrit dans le ~ fil de leur politique** this decision is totally in keeping with *ou* in line with their policy; → **coup**

2 (*= vertical, non penché*) [*arbre, mur*] upright, straight; (*Géom*) [*prisme, cylindre, cône*] right; [*écriture*] upright ◆ **ce tableau n'est pas ~** this picture isn't (hanging) straight ◆ **est-ce que mon chapeau est ~ ?** is my hat (on) straight? ◆ **jupe ~e** straight skirt ◆ **veston ~** single-breasted jacket ◆ **tiens ta tasse ~e** hold your cup straight *ou* level ◆ **être ~ comme un pieu** *ou* **un piquet** (*péj, hum*) to be as stiff as a poker *ou* ramrod (*péj*) ◆ **être ~ comme un i** to have a very upright posture, to hold o.s. very erect ◆ **se tenir ~ comme un i** to stand bolt upright *ou* very erect ◆ **tiens-toi ~** (*debout*) stand up (straight); (*assis*) sit up (straight); → **angle**

3 (*= honnête, loyal*) [*personne*] upright, straight(-forward)

4 (*= sensé*) [*jugement*] sound, sane

NF droite (*Géom*) straight line

ADV [*viser, couper, marcher*] straight ◆ **aller/marcher ~ devant soi** to go/walk straight ahead ◆ **écrire ~** to have upright handwriting ◆ **c'est ~ devant vous** it's straight ahead of you *ou* right in front of you ◆ **aller ~ à la faillite** to be heading *ou* headed straight for bankruptcy ◆ **aller ~ au but** *ou* **au fait** (*fig*) to go straight to the point ◆ **cela lui est allé ~ au cœur** (*fig*) it went straight to his heart; → **marcher**

droit[3] /dʀwa/ **GRAMMAIRE ACTIVE 36, 37.4**

NM 1 (*= prérogative*) right ◆ **~ de pêche/chasse** fishing/hunting rights ◆ **~ du sang/du sol** *right to nationality based on parentage/on place of birth* ◆ **les ~s du sang** (*fig*) rights of kinship ◆ **le ~ des peuples à disposer d'eux-mêmes** the right of peoples to self-determination ◆ **le ~ à l'enfant** the right to have a child ◆ **le ~ du plus fort** the law of the jungle ◆ **avoir le ~ de faire** (*gén : simple permission, possibilité*) to be allowed to do; (*Admin, Jur : autorisation*) to have the right to do ◆ **avoir le ~ pour soi** to have right on one's side ◆ **avoir ~ à** [*+ allocation*] to be entitled to, to be eligible for; [*+ critique*] to come in for ◆ **il a eu ~ à une bonne raclée** */**réprimande** (*hum*) he got *ou* earned himself a good hiding/telling-off* ◆ **avoir (le) ~ de vie ou de mort sur** to have (the) power of life and death over ◆ **avoir ~ de regard sur** [*+ documents*] to have the right to examine *ou* to inspect; [*+ affaires, choix, décision*] to have a say in ◆ **avoir ~ de regard dans la comptabilité** (*Fin, Jur*) to be entitled to have access to the books and records ◆ **avoir des ~s sur** to have rights over ◆ **il n'a aucun ~ sur ce terrain** he has no right to this land ◆ **cette carte vous donne ~ à des places gratuites** this card entitles you to free seats ◆ **être en ~ de faire** to have a *ou* the right to do, to be entitled to do ◆ **on est en ~ de se demander pourquoi ...** (*fig*) one has every right *ou* one is entitled to wonder why ... ◆ **être dans son (bon) ~** to be (quite) within one's rights ◆ **faire ~ à** [*+ requête*] to grant, to accede to ◆ **l'humour ne perd jamais ses ~s** there is always a place for humour ◆ **c'est (bien) votre ~** you've every right to do so, you are perfectly entitled to do so, you're perfectly within your rights ◆ **à bon ~** with good reason, legitimately ◆ **membre de ~** ex officio member ◆ **monarque de ~ divin** monarch by divine right ◆ **cela lui revient de ~** it's his by right(s), it is rightfully his ◆ **de quel ~ est-il entré ?** what right did he have *ou* what gave him the right to come in? ◆ **de ~ comme de fait** both legitimately and effectively ◆ **être membre de plein ~** to be a fully-fledged member ◆ **réclamer qch de plein ~** to claim sth as one's right; → **force, qui**

2 **le ~** (*Jur*) law ◆ **faire son ~** (*Univ*) to study law ◆ **~ civil/pénal** civil/criminal law ◆ **~ constitutionnel/international** constitutional/international law ◆ **~ canon** canon law ◆ **~ romain** Roman law ◆ **~ privé/public** private/public law ◆ **~ coutumier** (*= concept*) customary law; (*= lois*) common law ◆ **~ écrit** statute law ◆ **~ administratif/commercial/fiscal/du travail** administrative/commercial/tax/employment law ◆ **~ des affaires** company *ou* corporate law ◆ **le ~ des gens** the law of nations ◆ **~ de la famille** family law ◆ **une société de ~ anglais** a firm that comes under English law

3 (*gén pl = taxe*) duty, tax; (*d'inscription etc*) fee(s) ◆ **~ d'entrée** entrance (fee) ◆ **~s d'inscription/d'enregistrement** enrolment/registration fee(s) ◆ **~s portuaires** *ou* **de port** harbour fees *ou* dues ◆ **exempt de ~s** duty-free ◆ **passible de ~s** liable to duty, dutiable

COMP droit d'aînesse birthright
droit d'asile right of asylum
droit d'auteur (*= propriété artistique, littéraire*) copyright ◆ **~s d'auteur** (*= rémunération*) royalties
droit de cité (*fig*) ◆ **avoir ~ de cité parmi/dans** to be established among/in
droits civils civil rights
droits civiques civic rights
droit commun ◆ **condamné/délit de ~ commun** common law criminal/crime
droits compensatoires (*Fin*) countervailing duties
droit de cuissage (*Hist*) droit du seigneur; (*hum*) *right to subject employees to sexual harassment*
droits de douane customs duties
les droits de la femme women's rights ◆ **les ~s de la femme mariée** the rights of married women *ou* a married woman
droit de gage (*Jur*) lien
droit de garde [*d'enfant*] custody
droit de grâce right of reprieve
le droit de grève the right to strike
les droits de l'homme human rights
droit d'initiative (*Pol*) *citizens' right to initiate legislation (in Switzerland etc)*
droit de mutation (*Fin*) transfer tax
les droits naturels natural rights
droit de passage right of way, easement (*US*)
droit de propriété right of property ◆ **nous avons un ~ de propriété sur notre corps** we should have jurisdiction over our own bodies
droit réel (*Jur*) title
droit de réponse right of reply
droits de reproduction reproduction rights ◆ **"tous droits (de reproduction) réservés"** "all rights reserved"
droit de souscription application right
droits de succession inheritance tax
droit de timbre stamp duty
droits de tirage spéciaux special drawing rights
droit d'usage (*Jur*) right of user
droit de visite (*Jur*) (right of) access
le droit de vote the right to vote, the vote, franchise

droitement /dʀwatmɑ̃/ **ADV** [*agir, parler*] uprightly, honestly; [*juger*] soundly

droitier, -ière /dʀwatje, jɛʀ/ **ADJ** (*= non gaucher*) right-handed; (*Pol*) right-wing **NM,F** right-handed person; (*Pol*) right-winger ◆ **c'est un ~** (*Tennis etc*) he's a right-handed player *ou* a right-hander

droiture /dʀwatyʀ/ **NF** [*de personne*] uprightness, honesty; [*de conscience*] honesty ◆ **~ de caractère** uprightness, rectitude (of character)

drolatique /dʀɔlatik/ **ADJ** (*littér*) comical, droll

drôle /dʀol/ **ADJ** 1 (*= amusant*) [*situation, accoutrement*] funny, comical, amusing; (*= spirituel*) [*personne*] funny, amusing ◆ **je ne trouve pas ça ~** I don't find that funny *ou* amusing ◆ **la vie n'est pas ~** life's no joke ◆ **tu es ~, je ne pouvais pourtant pas l'insulter !*** you must be joking *ou* kidding – I could hardly insult him!; → **histoire**

2 (*= bizarre*) funny, strange ◆ **c'est ~, j'aurais juré l'avoir rangé** that's funny *ou* strange, I could have sworn I had put it away ◆ **avoir un ~ d'air** to look funny *ou* peculiar *ou* strange ◆ **un ~ de type** a strange *ou* peculiar fellow, an oddbod* ◆ **c'est un ~ de numéro** he's a bit of a character ◆ **une ~ d'idée/d'odeur** a funny *ou* strange *ou* peculiar idea/smell ◆ **il a fait une ~ de tête !** he pulled a wry *ou* funny face! ◆ **la ~ de guerre** (*Hist*) the Phoney War ◆ **se sentir tout ~** to feel funny *ou* strange *ou* peculiar ◆ **ça me fait (tout) ~ (de le voir)*** it gives me a funny *ou* strange *ou* odd feeling (to see him)

3 (* *: intensif*) **un ~ d'orage** a fantastic* *ou* terrific* storm ◆ **de ~s de muscles/progrès** fantastic* *ou* terrific* muscles/progress ◆ **une ~ de correction** a hell of a punishment* ◆ **on en a vu de ~s pendant la guerre** we had a hard time (of it) during the war

NM (*dial = gamin*) child, kid*; († *: péj = coquin*) scamp, rascal

drôlement /dʀolmɑ̃/ **ADV** 1 (*= bizarrement*) strangely ◆ **il m'a regardé ~** he gave me a strange *ou* funny look 2 (** = extrêmement*) **~ bon/sage** awfully *ou* terribly good/well-behaved ◆ **il fait ~ froid** it's awfully *ou* terribly cold, it isn't half cold* ◆ **il est ~ musclé** he's really muscular, he's got a lot of muscle* ◆ **il est ~ culotté** he's got some cheek*, he hasn't half got a cheek* (*Brit*) ◆ **il a ~ changé** he really has changed, he's changed an awful lot* ◆ **ça lui a fait ~ plaisir** it pleased him no end* 3 (*= spirituellement*) funnily, comically, amusingly

drôlerie /dʀolʀi/ NF 1 (NonC) funniness, drollness ◆ **la ~ de la situation m'échappe** I don't see *ou* I fail to see what's so funny *ou* amusing ◆ **c'est d'une ~ !** it's so funny *ou* comical! 2 (*= propos, action*) funny *ou* amusing thing (to say *ou* do)

drôlesse † /dʀolɛs/ NF (*péj*) hussy † (*péj*)

dromadaire /dʀɔmadɛʀ/ NM dromedary

dronte /dʀɔ̃t/ NM dodo

drop /dʀɔp/, **drop-goal** (pl **drop-goals**) /dʀɔpgol/ NM (*= coup de pied*) drop kick; (*= but*) drop goal ◆ **passer un ~** to score a drop goal

drosophile /dʀozɔfil/ NF fruit fly, drosophila (SPÉC)

drosser /dʀɔse/ ▸ conjug 1 ◂ VT (*Naut*) [*vent, courant*] to drive (*contre* onto, against)

dru, e /dʀy/ ADJ [*herbe*] thick; [*barbe*] thick, bushy; [*haie*] thick, dense; [*pluie*] heavy ADV [*pousser*] thickly, densely; [*tomber*] [*pluie*] heavily, fast; [*coups*] thick and fast

drug(-)store (pl **drug(-)stores**) /dʀœgstɔʀ/ NM drugstore

druide /dʀɥid/ NM druid

druidesse /dʀɥidɛs/ NF druidess

druidique /dʀɥidik/ ADJ druidic

druidisme /dʀɥidism/ NM druidism

drupe /dʀyp/ NF drupe

druze /dʀyz/ ADJ Drusean, Drusian NMPL **Druzes** ◆ **les Druzes** the Druse *ou* Druze

dryade /dʀijad/ NF (*Myth*) dryad, wood-nymph; (*= plante*) dryas

DST /deɛste/ NF (abrév de **Direction de la surveillance du territoire**) ≈ MI5 (*Brit*), CIA (*US*)

DT /dete/ NM (abrév de **diphtérie, tétanos**) *vaccine against diphtheria and tetanus*

du /dy/ ART PARTITIF → **de²** PRÉP + ART DÉF → **de¹**

dû, due /dy/ GRAMMAIRE ACTIVE 47.5 (ptp de **devoir**) ADJ (*= à restituer*) owing, owed; (*= arrivé à échéance*) due ◆ **la somme due** the sum owing *ou* owed, the sum due ◆ **la somme qui lui est due** the sum owing *ou* owed *ou* due to him; → **chose, port²**

◆ **dû à** due to ◆ **ces troubles sont dus à ...** these troubles are due to ...

◆ **en (bonne et) due forme** in due form NM due; (*= somme d'argent*) dues

dual, e /dɥal/ ADJ [*économie, système*] dual ◆ **société ~e** two-tier society

dualisme /dɥalism/ NM dualism

dualiste /dɥalist/ ADJ dualistic NMF dualist

dualité /dɥalite/ NF duality

Dubaï, Dubay /dybaj/ N Dubai

dubitatif, -ive /dybitatif, iv/ ADJ doubtful ◆ **d'un air ~** doubtfully

dubitativement /dybitativmɑ̃/ ADV doubtfully

Dublin /dyblɛ̃/ N Dublin

dublinois, e /dyblinwa, waz/ ADJ of *ou* from Dublin NM,F **Dublinois(e)** Dubliner

duc /dyk/ NM duke

ducal, e (mpl **-aux**) /dykal, o/ ADJ ducal

ducasse /dykas/ NF (*Belg*) fair

ducat /dyka/ NM ducat

duché /dyʃe/ NM (*= fonction*) dukedom; (*= territoire*) dukedom, duchy

duchesse /dyʃɛs/ NF 1 (*= noble*) duchess ◆ **elle fait la** *ou* **sa ~** (*péj*) she's playing the grand lady *ou* putting on airs 2 ◆ **(poire) ~** Duchesse pear

ductile /dyktil/ ADJ ductile

ductilité /dyktilite/ NF ductility

dudit /dydi/, **de ladite** /dəladit/ (mpl **desdits** /dedi/) (fpl **desdites** /dedit/) ADJ (*Jur, hum*) of the aforementioned, of the said ◆ **le propriétaire ~ édifice/chien** the owner of the aforementioned *ou* said building/dog

duègne /dɥɛɲ/ NF duenna

duel¹ /dɥɛl/ NM duel ◆ **provoquer qn en ~** to challenge sb to a duel ◆ **se battre en ~** to fight a duel (*avec* with); ◆ **deux malheureux bouts de viande se battaient en ~ au fond du plat** (*péj*) there were just two measly bits of meat on the plate ◆ **~ oratoire** verbal duel *ou* battle ◆ **~ d'artillerie** artillery battle

duel² /dɥɛl/ NM (*Ling*) dual (number)

duelliste /dɥelist/ NM duellist

duettiste /dɥetist/ NMF duettist

duffle-coat (pl **duffle-coats**), **duffel-coat** (pl **duffel-coats**) /dœfœlkot/ NM duffel coat

dugong /dygɔ̃g/ NM dugong

dulcinée /dylsine/ NF (†, *aussi hum*) lady-love † (*aussi hum*)

dum-dum /dumdum/ NF INV ◆ **(balle) ~** dum-dum (bullet)

dûment /dymɑ̃/ ADV duly

dumping /dœmpiŋ/ NM (*Écon*) dumping ◆ **faire du ~** to dump goods ◆ **~ social** social dumping

dune /dyn/ NF dune ◆ **~ de sable** sand dune

dunette /dynɛt/ NF (*Naut*) poop deck

Dunkerque /dœ̃kɛʀk/ N Dunkirk

duo /dɥo/ NM (*Mus*) duet; (*Théât*) double act, duo; [*de plaisantins*] pair, duo; (*= dialogue*) exchange ◆ **chanter en ~** to sing a duet ◆ **~ de poissons sur lit de poireaux** (*sur menu*) two types of fish on a bed of leeks

> ⚠ Au sens musical, **duo** ne se traduit pas par le mot anglais **duo**.

duodécimal, e (mpl **-aux**) /dɥɔdesimal, o/ ADJ duodecimal

duodénal, e (mpl **-aux**) /dɥɔdenal, o/ ADJ duodenal

duodénum /dɥɔdenɔm/ NM duodenum

duopole /dɥɔpɔl/ NM duopoly

dupe /dyp/ NF dupe ◆ **prendre pour ~** to fool, to take in, to dupe ◆ **être la ~ de qn** to be taken in *ou* fooled by sb; → **jeu, marché** ADJ ◆ **être ~ (de)** to be taken in (by), to be fooled (by) ◆ **je ne** *ou* **n'en suis pas ~** I'm not taken in (by it), he (*ou* it *etc*) doesn't fool me

duper /dype/ ▸ conjug 1 ◂ VT to dupe, to deceive, to fool VPR **se duper** ◆ **se ~ (soi-même)** to deceive o.s.

duperie /dypʀi/ NF (*= tromperie*) dupery (*NonC*), deception

duplex /dyplɛks/ ADJ INV (*Téléc*) duplex, two-way NM (*= appartement*) split-level apartment, duplex (*US*); (*Can*) duplex (house), maisonette ◆ **(émission en) ~** (*Téléc*) link-up

duplicata /dyplikata/ NM INV (*Admin, Jur*) duplicate

duplicateur /dyplikatœʀ/ NM duplicator, duplicating machine

duplication /dyplikasjɔ̃/ NF (*Math*) duplication; (*Bio*) doubling; [*de ADN*] replication; [*d'enregistrement*] duplication

duplicité /dyplisite/ NF duplicity

dupliquer /dyplike/ ▸ conjug 1 ◂ VT to duplicate

duquel /dykɛl/ → **lequel**

dur, e /dyʀ/ ADJ 1 [*roche, métal, lit, crayon, sol*] hard; [*carton, col, brosse*] stiff; [*viande*] tough; [*porte, serrure, levier*] stiff ◆ **être ~ d'oreille, être ~ de la feuille *, avoir l'oreille ~e** † to be hard of hearing ◆ **~ comme le roc** as hard as (a) rock, rock-hard; → **blé, œuf, pain** *etc*

2 [*problème, travail, parcours*] hard, stiff, tough ◆ **~ à manier/digérer/croire** hard to handle/digest/believe ◆ **leur fils est un enfant très ~** their son is a very difficult child ◆ **être ~ à la détente *** (*= avare*) to be tight-fisted *; (*= difficile à persuader*) to be pigheaded; (*= obtus*) to be slow on the uptake *

3 [*climat, lumière, punition, combat*] harsh, hard; [*couleur, épreuve*] harsh; [*leçon*] hard; (*= âpre*) [*vin, cidre*] harsh; (*= calcaire*) [*eau*] hard ◆ **il lui est ~ d'avoir à partir** it's hard for him to have to leave ◆ **ce sont des vérités ~es à avaler** *ou* **digérer *** these are hard truths to take ◆ **la vie est ~e** it's a hard life, life's no bed of roses ◆ **~ ! *** *ou* **~, ~ ! *** not easy! ◆ **les temps sont ~s** (*souvent hum*) times are hard ◆ **il nous mène la vie ~e** he makes life difficult for us, he gives us a hard time ◆ **le plus ~ est passé** the worst is over; → **coup**

4 (*= sévère*) [*personne, voix, regard, traits, visage*] hard, harsh, severe; [*loi, critique*] harsh, severe ◆ **être ~ avec** *ou* **pour** *ou* **envers qn** to be harsh with sb, to be hard on sb; → **dent, école**

5 (*= insensible, cruel*) [*personne*] hard(-hearted) ◆ **il a le cœur ~** he's a hard-hearted man, he has a heart of stone

6 (*= endurant*) **être ~ au mal** *ou* **à la douleur** to be tough ◆ **être ~ à la peine** *ou* **à l'ouvrage** to be a tireless *ou* hard worker; → **peau**

7 (*= sans concession*) uncompromising ◆ **le gouvernement adopte une ligne ~e sur le commerce international** the government is taking a hard line on *ou* a hardline stance on international trade; → **pur**

ADV * [*travailler, frapper*] hard ◆ **le soleil tape ~** the sun is beating down ◆ **le vent souffle ~** the wind is blowing hard *ou* strongly ◆ **croire à qch ~ comme fer** to have a blind belief in sth

NM 1 (* *= résistant*) tough one; (*= meneur, casseur*) tough nut *, tough guy *; (*gén, Pol = intransigeant*) hard-liner ◆ **c'est un ~ au cœur tendre** his bark is worse than his bite ◆ **c'est un ~ à cuire** *ou* **un ~ de ~ *** he's a hard nut to crack * ◆ **jouer les ~s** to act the tough guy *, to act tough

2 (*locution*) **c'est du ~ *** it's solid *ou* tough stuff, it's sturdy

◆ **en dur** ◆ **construire en ~** to build a permanent structure ◆ **une construction en ~** a permanent structure ◆ **un court (de tennis) en ~** a hard court

3 [*de corde*] tension ◆ **~ !** (*Alpinisme*) pull tight!

NF **dure** 1 * **c'est une ~e** (*= résistante*) she's a tough one; (*= meneuse*) she's a hard one

2 (*loc*) **coucher sur la ~e** to sleep on the ground, to sleep rough (*surtout Brit*)

◆ **à la dure** ◆ **être élevé à la ~e** to be brought up the hard way ◆ **vivre à la ~e** to live rough

3 (* : *loc*) **en dire de ~es à qn** to give sb a good telling-off * ◆ **en entendre de ~es** (*= reproches*) to get a good telling-off * *ou* ticking-off * (*Brit*) ◆ **en voir de ~es** to have a hard time (of it) * ◆ **en faire voir de ~es à qn** to give sb a hard time (of it) *

durabilité /dyʀabilite/ NF (*gén*) durability; [*de produit*] life span

durable /dyʀabl/ ADJ [*croissance, développement, reprise*] lasting; [*solution, paix*] lasting, durable; [*bonheur, monument, souvenir, succès*] lasting, enduring; [*emploi*] long-term (*épith*); → **bien**

durablement /dyʀabləmɑ̃/ ADV [*s'installer*] on a long-term basis ◆ **bâtir ~** to build something to last ◆ **bâti ~** built to last

duraille* /dyʀaj/ ADJ [*problème*] tough, hard; [*matelas, viande*] hard

duralumin ® /dyʀalymɛ̃/ NM Duralumin ®

durant /dyʀɑ̃/ PRÉP 1 (*= pendant*) for ◆ **il peut rêvasser ~ des heures** *ou* **des heures ~** he can daydream for hours (on end) ◆ **deux heures ~** for (a full *ou* whole) two hours ◆ **des années ~**

for years (and years) ◆ **sa vie** ~ throughout his life, for as long as he lived (*ou* lives) 2 (*= au cours de*) during, in the course of ◆ ~ **le spectacle** during the show ◆ **il a plu** ~ **la nuit** it rained in (the course of) *ou* during the night

duratif, -ive /dyʀatif, iv/ **ADJ** durative

durcir /dyʀsiʀ/ ► conjug 2 ◄ **VT** *[+ attitude]* to harden; *[+ contrôle, embargo, sanctions]* to tighten ◆ ~ **ses positions** to take a tougher stand ◆ ~ **un mouvement de grève** to step up strike action ◆ **il a durci son discours** he has taken a tougher stand **VI** **se durcir** **VPR** *[sol, colle, visage, attitude, ton]* to harden; *[mouvement de grève]* to become more firmly entrenched; *[conflit]* to become more serious

durcissement /dyʀsismɑ̃/ **NM** *[d'attitude, positions]* hardening; *[de sanctions, embargo]* tightening ◆ ~ **des mouvements de grève** stepping up of strike action

durcisseur /dyʀsisœʀ/ **NM** hardener

durée /dyʀe/ **NF** 1 *[de spectacle, opération]* duration, length; *[de bail]* term; *[de prêt]* period; *[de matériau, pile, ampoule]* life; *(Mus) [de note]* value ◆ **la** ~ **d'une mode dépend de ...** how long a fashion lasts depends on ... ◆ **je m'étonne de la** ~ **de ce spectacle** I'm amazed at how long this show is ◆ **pour une** ~ **illimitée** for an unlimited length of time, for an unlimited period ◆ **pendant une** ~ **d'un mois** for (the period of) one month ◆ **pour la** ~ **des négociations** while negotiations continue, for the duration of the negotiations ◆ **pendant la** ~ **des réparations** for the duration of repairs, while repairs are being carried out ◆ **de courte** ~ *[séjour]* short; *[bonheur, répit]* short-lived ◆ **(de) longue** ~ *[effet]* long-lasting *(épith)*; *[contrat, chômage, visa]* long-term *(épith)*; *[pile]* long-life *(épith)*, long-lasting *(épith)* ◆ ~ **de vie utile** useful life

2 (*= permanence*) continuance ◆ **il n'osait croire à la** ~ **de cette prospérité** he didn't dare to believe that this prosperity would last *ou* to believe in the continuance of this prosperity

3 *(Philos)* duration

> ⚠ Attention à ne pas traduire automatiquement **durée** par **duration** ; l'anglais préfère des tournures verbales.

durement /dyʀmɑ̃/ **ADV** 1 (*= sévèrement*) harshly, severely; (*= brutalement*) harshly ◆ **élever qn** ~ to bring sb up the hard way ◆ **parler** ~ **à qn** to speak harshly *ou* severely to sb ◆ **la manifestation a été** ~ **réprimée** the demonstration was suppressed using force 2 (*= cruellement*) *[éprouvé, ressenti]* sorely ◆ **région** ~ **touchée par la crise** region hard hit by the recession

dure-mère (pl **dures-mères**) /dyʀmɛʀ/ **NF** *(Anat)* dura mater

durer /dyʀe/ ► conjug 1 ◄ **VI** 1 (*= avoir une durée de*) to last ◆ **combien de temps cela dure-t-il ?** how long does it last? ◆ **l'effet dure deux minutes/mois** the effect lasts (for) two minutes/months ◆ **le festival dure (pendant) deux semaines** the festival lasts (for) two weeks

2 (*= se prolonger*) *[mode, maladie, tempête]* to last ◆ **la fête a duré toute la nuit/jusqu'au matin** the party went on *ou* lasted all night/until morning ◆ **sa maladie dure depuis deux mois** he has been ill for two months (now), his illness has lasted for two months (now) ◆ **ça fait deux mois que ça dure** it has been going on *ou* it has lasted for two months (now) ◆ **ça n'a que trop duré !** it's gone on too long already! ◆ **ça va** ~ **longtemps, cette plaisanterie ?** how much longer is this joke going to go on? *ou* continue? ◆ **ça durera ce que ça durera** I don't know if it'll last, it might last and it might not ◆ **ça ne peut plus** ~ **!** this can't go on (any longer)! ◆ **elle dure, leur conversation !** they've been talking for ages! ◆ **faire** ~ **un travail** to prolong *ou* spin out* *(Brit)* a job ◆ **faire** ~ **le plaisir** *(iro)* to prolong the agony ◆ **le temps me dure** *(littér)* time hangs heavy on my hands ◆ **l'inaction me dure** *(littér)* I am growing impatient at this inactivity; → **pourvu**²

3 *(littér = subsister) [coutume]* to linger on; *(péj) [mourant]* to hang on *(péj)*, to linger on

4 (*= se conserver*) *[matériau, vêtement, outil]* to last ◆ **faire** ~ **des chaussures** to make shoes last ◆ **cette somme doit te** ~ **un mois** this money will have to last you a month

dureté /dyʀte/ **NF** 1 *[de roche, métal, lit, crayon]* hardness; *[de carton, col, brosse]* stiffness; *[de viande]* toughness 2 *[de problème, travail, parcours]* hardness, stiffness, toughness ◆ **la** ~ **des temps** the hard times we live in ◆ **la** ~ **de la vie quotidienne** the harshness of daily life 3 *[de climat, lumière, punition, combat]* harshness, hardness; *[de vin, cidre]* harshness 4 (*= sévérité*) *[de personne, voix, regard, traits, visage]* hardness, harshness, severity; *[de loi, critique]* harshness, severity ◆ **sa** ~ **de ton m'a surpris** his harsh tone surprised me 5 (*= insensibilité, cruauté*) ~ **(de cœur)** hard-heartedness ◆ **traiter qn avec** ~ to treat sb harshly 6 *[d'eau]* hardness ◆ **tester la** ~ **de l'eau** to test how hard the water is

durian /dyʀjɑ̃, dyʀjan/ **NM** (*= arbre*) durian; (*= fruit*) durian (fruit)

durillon /dyʀijɔ̃/ **NM** *(aux mains)* callus, hard skin *(NonC)*; *(aux pieds)* callus, corn

durit ®, durite /dyʀit/ **NF** (radiator) hose ◆ **il a pété une** ~ * *(fig)* he flipped his lid *

DUT /deyte/ **NM** (abrév de **diplôme universitaire de technologie**) → **diplôme**

duty-free /djutifʀi/ **ADJ** duty-free **NM** duty-free (shop) ◆ **en** ~ duty-free ◆ **j'ai acheté du parfum en** ~ I bought some duty-free perfume, I bought some perfume in the duty-free

duvet /dyvɛ/ **NM** 1 *[d'oiseau, fruit, joues]* down 2 (*= sac de couchage*) (down-filled) sleeping bag 3 (*Helv = couette*) duvet

duveté, e /dyv(ə)te/ **ADJ** *[pêche, joue]* downy ◆ **elle avait la lèvre** ~**e** she had a faint moustache

duveter (se) /dyv(ə)te/ ► conjug 5 ◄ **VPR** to become downy

duveteux, -euse /dyv(ə)tø, øz/ **ADJ** downy

DVD /devede/ **NM** (abrév de **digital versatile disc**) DVD ◆ ~**-A** DVD-A ◆ **lecteur** ~ DVD drive ◆ ~ **multiangle** multi-angle DVD ◆ ~ **musicale** music DVD ◆ ~**-RAM** DVD-RAM ◆ ~**-ROM** DVD-ROM ◆ ~**-RW** DVD-RW

dynamique /dinamik/ **ADJ** *(Phys, gén)* dynamic; → **cadre** **NF** 1 *(Phys, Mus)* dynamics *(sg)* ◆ **la** ~ **de groupe** *(Sociol)* group dynamics 2 (*= processus*) ◆ **nous sommes dans une** ~ **de croissance** we are in a growth phase ◆ **relancer la** ~ **de croissance** to get (the process of) growth going ◆ **créer une** ~ **de croissance** to create growth ◆ **accélérer la** ~ **de paix** to speed up the peace process ◆ **la** ~ **en cours** the current state of affairs

dynamiquement /dinamikmɑ̃/ **ADV** dynamically

dynamisant, e /dinamizɑ̃, ɑ̃t/ **ADJ** *[effet, changement]* stimulating

dynamisation /dinamizasjɔ̃/ **NF** *[de secteur, marché]* stimulation

dynamiser /dinamize/ ► conjug 1 ◄ **VT** *[+ économie, marché]* to stimulate, to give a boost to; *[+ personnel]* to energize; *[+ affiche, image de marque]* to make more dynamic; *(Méd) [+ médicament]* to potentiate *(SPÉC)*

dynamisme /dinamism/ **NM** *(Philos, gén)* dynamism

dynamitage /dinamitaʒ/ **NM** dynamiting

dynamite /dinamit/ **NF** dynamite ◆ **faire sauter qch à la** ~ to blow sth up with dynamite ◆ **c'est de la** ~ **!*** *(fig)* it's dynamite!

dynamiter /dinamite/ ► conjug 1 ◄ **VT** *(lit)* to dynamite, to blow up with dynamite; *[+ certitudes, mythe]* to explode

dynamiteur, -euse /dinamitœʀ, øz/ **NM,F** dynamiter

dynamo /dinamo/ **NF** dynamo

dynamoélectrique /dinamoelɛktʀik/ **ADJ** dynamoelectric

dynamogène /dinamɔʒɛn/, **dynamogénique** /dinamɔʒenik/ **ADJ** dynamogenic

dynamographe /dinamɔgʀaf/ **NM** dynamograph

dynamomètre /dinamɔmɛtʀ/ **NM** dynamometer

dynamométrique /dinamɔmetʀik/ **ADJ** dynamometric; → **clé**

dynastie /dinasti/ **NF** dynasty

dynastique /dinastik/ **ADJ** dynastic

dyne /din/ **NF** dyne

dysenterie /disɑ̃tʀi/ **NF** dysentery

dysentérique /disɑ̃teʀik/ **ADJ** dysenteric

dysfonction /disfɔ̃ksjɔ̃/ **NF** dysfunction ◆ **de très graves ~s sont apparues dans le département** serious failures have been apparent in the department

dysfonctionnel, -elle /disfɔ̃ksjɔnɛl/ **ADJ** dysfunctional

dysfonctionnement /disfɔ̃ksjɔnmɑ̃/ **NM** *(Méd)* dysfunction ◆ **il n'y a pas eu de** ~ **dans les procédures d'alerte** no failure was found in the warning systems, the warning systems were found to be functioning properly ◆ **il y a des ~s dans la gestion du service** there are problems in the management of the department ◆ **chaque fois qu'il y a un** ~**, on demande la démission d'un ministre** every time something goes wrong there are calls for a minister to resign

dysfonctionner /disfɔ̃ksjɔne/ ► conjug 1 ◄ **VI** to become dysfunctional

dysgraphie /disgʀafi/ **NF** dysgraphia

dysharmonie /disaʀmɔni/ **NF** ⇒ **disharmonie**

dyslexie /dislɛksi/ **NF** dyslexia

dyslexique /dislɛksik/ **ADJ, NMF** dyslexic

dysménorrhée /dismenɔʀe/ **NF** dysmenorrhoea, painful periods

dyspareunie /dispaʀøni/ **NF** dyspareunia

dyspepsie /dispɛpsi/ **NF** dyspepsia

dyspepsique /dispɛpsik/, **dyspeptique** /dispɛptik/ **ADJ, NMF** dyspeptic

dysphasie /disfazi/ **NF** dysphasia

dysplasie /displazi/ **NF** *(Méd)* dysplasia

dyspnée /dispne/ **NF** dyspnoea *(Brit)*, dyspnea *(US)*

dysprosium /dispʀozjɔm/ **NM** dysprosium

dystrophie /distʀofi/ **NF** ◆ ~ **musculaire progressive** muscular dystrophy

E e

E¹, e /ə/ **NM** (= *lettre*) E, e ◆ **e dans l'o** o and e joined together, o and e ligature

E² (abrév de **Est**) E

e- /i/ **PRÉF** (= *électronique*) e- ◆ **~entreprise** e-business

EAO /əao/ **NM** (abrév de **enseignement assisté par ordinateur**) CAI, CAL

EAU /əay/ **NMPL** (abrév de **Émirats arabes unis**) UAE

eau (pl **eaux**) /o/ **NF** 1 (*gén*) water; (= *pluie*) rain ◆ **sans ~** *[alcool]* neat, straight ◆ **cuire à l'~** to boil ◆ **se passer les mains à l'~** to rinse one's hands, to give one's hands a quick wash ◆ **passer qch sous l'~** to give sth a quick rinse ◆ **laver à grande ~** *[+ sol]* to wash *ou* sluice down; (*avec un tuyau*) to hose down; *[+ légumes]* to wash thoroughly ◆ **port en ~ profonde** deep-water port ◆ **que d'~, que d'~ !** (*hum*) it's coming down in buckets* *ou* in torrents!

2 (*Bijouterie*) water ◆ **diamant de la plus belle ~** diamond of the first water ◆ **un escroc de la plus belle ~** an out-and-out crook ◆ **de la même ~** (*fig*) of the same ilk

3 (*locutions*) **tout cela apporte de l'~ à son moulin** it's all grist to his mill ◆ **aller sur l'~** (*Naut*) (= *flotter*) to be buoyant; (= *naviguer*) to sail ◆ **aller à l'~** to go for a dip* ◆ **j'en avais l'~ à la bouche** my mouth was watering, it made my mouth water ◆ **être en ~** to be bathed in perspiration *ou* sweat ◆ **faire de l'~** (*Naut, Rail*) to take on (a supply of) water ◆ **faire ~ (de toutes parts)** to leak (like a sieve) ◆ **mettre à l'~** (*Naut*) to launch ◆ **mise à l'~** launch, launching ◆ **se mettre à l'~** (= *nager*) to get into the water; (= *être sobre*) to go on the wagon*, to keep off alcohol ◆ **mettre de l'~ dans son vin** (*lit*) to water down one's wine; (= *modérer ses prétentions*) to climb down; (= *faire des concessions*) to make concessions ◆ **prendre l'~** *[chaussures, objet]* to let in water; *[projet]* to founder ◆ **il passera** *ou* **coulera beaucoup d'~ sous les ponts avant que ...** it will be a long time before ... ◆ **porter de l'~ à la rivière** (*Prov*) to carry coals to Newcastle (*Prov*) ◆ **l'~ va à la rivière** (*Prov*) money makes money, to him that has shall more be given ◆ **s'en aller** *ou* **tourner en ~ de boudin*** to flop ◆ **notre projet est (tombé) à l'~** our project has fallen through ◆ **il y a de l'~ dans le gaz*** things aren't running too smoothly ◆ **ils sont comme l'~ et le feu** they're as different as night and day *ou* as chalk and cheese (*Brit*)

NFPL eaux 1 *[de fleuve]* **hautes ~x** high water ◆ **basses ~x** (*lit*) low water ◆ **pendant les basses ~x** when the waters are low, when the water level is low ◆ **en période de basses ~x** (*fig*) when the economy is at a low ebb, during a period of economic stagnation ◆ **être dans les ~x d'un navire** (*Naut*) to be in the wake of a ship ◆ **nager** *ou* **naviguer en ~x troubles** (*fig*) to move in shady circles ◆ **dans ces ~x-là*** or thereabouts ◆ **entre deux ~x** just below the surface ◆ **nager entre deux ~x** (*fig*) to keep a foot in both camps, to run with the hare and hunt with the hounds

2 (*Méd*) **elle a perdu les ~x** her waters have broken

3 (*station thermale*) **prendre les ~x** † to take the waters; → **ville**

4 (*Admin*) **la Compagnie des Eaux et de l'Ozone** the French water utility

COMP eau bénite holy water
eau blanche lead acetate, sugar of lead
eau de Cologne eau de Cologne, cologne
eau courante running water
eau de cuisson cooking water
eau douce fresh water
eau écarlate ® (liquid) stain remover
eau d'érable maple sap (*Can*)
eau de fleur d'oranger orange-flower water
les Eaux et Forêts ≃ the Forestry Commission (*Brit*), the Forest Service (*US*)
eau gazeuse sparkling (mineral) water
eaux grasses swill, slops
eaux internationales international waters
eau de Javel bleach
eau lourde heavy water
eau de mélisse melissa water
eaux ménagères (household) waste water
eau de mer sea water
eaux mères mother liquids
eau minérale mineral water
eau oxygénée hydrogen peroxide
eau de parfum eau de parfum
eau plate plain *ou* still water
eau de pluie rainwater
eau potable drinking water
eaux profondes deep waters
eau de refroidissement cooling water
eaux résiduaires waste water
eau du robinet tap water
eau de rose rose water ◆ **roman/histoire à l'~ de rose** sentimental *ou* schmaltzy* novel/story
eau rougie wine and water
eaux de ruissellement run-off water
eau salée salt water
eau savonneuse soapy water
eau de Seltz soda (water), seltzer water (*US*)
eau de source spring water
eaux superficielles, eaux de surface surface water(s)
eaux territoriales territorial waters ◆ **dans les ~x territoriales françaises** in French (territorial) waters
eaux thermales thermal springs *ou* waters
eau de toilette eau de toilette, toilet water
eaux usées waste water
eau de vaisselle dishwater, washing-up (*Brit*) water

eau-de-vie (pl **eaux-de-vie**) /od(ə)vi/ **NF** ≃ brandy ◆ **~ de prune/poire** plum/pear brandy ◆ **cerises à l'~** cherries in brandy

eau-forte (pl **eaux-fortes**) /ofɔʀt/ **NF** (*Art*) etching; (*Chim*) aqua fortis

ébahi, e /ebai/ (ptp de **ébahir**) **ADJ** astounded

ébahir /ebaiʀ/ ► conjug 2 ◄ **VT** to astound **VPR s'ébahir** to wonder (*de voir* at seeing)

ébahissement /ebaismɑ̃/ **NM** astonishment, amazement

ébarber /ebaʀbe/ ► conjug 1 ◄ **VT** *[+ papier, poisson]* to trim; *[+ métal]* to (de)burr, to trim; *[+ plante]* to clip, to trim

ébats /eba/ **NMPL** frolics ◆ **~ amoureux** *ou* **sexuels** lovemaking

ébattre (s') /ebatʀ/ ► conjug 41 ◄ **VPR** *[animaux]* to frolic, to frisk, to gambol (about); *[enfants]* to play *ou* romp about, to frolic

ébaubi, e /ebobi/ (ptp de **s'ébaubir**) **ADJ** (†, *hum*) bowled over, flabbergasted (*de* at); ◆ **être tout ~** to be agog (*devant* at)

ébaubir (s') /ebobiʀ/ ► conjug 2 ◄ **VPR** (†, *hum*) to wonder (*de voir* at seeing)

ébauche /eboʃ/ **NF** *[de livre]* skeleton, outline; *[de tableau, dessin]* draft, sketch; *[de statue]* rough shape; *[de projet, roman]* (rough) outline ◆ **une ~ de sourire** the ghost of a smile ◆ **l'~ d'un geste** a slight movement ◆ **ce n'est que la première ~** this is just a rough draft ◆ **c'est encore à l'état d'~** it's still in the early stages ◆ **l'~ d'une amitié** the beginnings of a friendship ◆ **il a proposé l'~ d'une solution** he offered the beginnings of a solution

ébaucher /eboʃe/ ► conjug 1 ◄ **VT** 1 (= *esquisser*) *[+ livre, plan, tableau]* to sketch out; *[+ statue]* to rough out; *[+ programme, solution]* to outline 2 (= *commencer*) *[+ amitié, conversation]* to start up; *[+ relations]* to open up ◆ **~ un sourire** to give a faint smile ◆ **~ un geste** to start to make a movement 3 (= *dégrossir*) *[+ poutre]* to rough-hew; *[+ pierre]* to rough-hew, to boast; *[+ diamant]* to begin to cut **VPR s'ébaucher** *[plan]* to form, to take shape *ou* form; *[livre]* to take shape *ou* form; *[amitié]* to form; *[conversation]* to start; *[relations]* to open up ◆ **une solution s'ébauche lentement** a solution is gradually taking shape ◆ **une idée à peine ébauchée** the bare bones *ou* the mere outline of an idea

ébaudir VT, **s'ébaudir** VPR /ebodiʀ/ ► conjug 2 ◄ (†, *hum*) to rejoice (*de, à* over, at)

ébène /ebɛn/ NF ebony ◆ **cheveux/table d'~** ebony hair/table; → **bois**

ébénier /ebenje/ NM ebony (tree); → **faux²**

ébéniste /ebenist/ NMF cabinetmaker

ébénisterie /ebenist(ə)ʀi/ NF (= *métier*) cabinet-making; (= *façon, meuble*) cabinetwork

éberlué, e /ebɛʀlɥe/ (ptp de **éberluer**) ADJ flabbergasted, dumbfounded ◆ **il avait un regard ~** he looked dazed

éberluer /ebɛʀlɥe/ ► conjug 1 ◄ VT to flabbergast, to dumbfound

éblouir /ebluiʀ/ ► conjug 2 ◄ VT (*lit, fig*) to dazzle

éblouissant, e /ebluisɑ̃, ɑ̃t/ ADJ (*lit, fig*) dazzling ◆ **~ de talent/de beauté** dazzlingly talented/beautiful

éblouissement /ebluismɑ̃/ NM [1] [*de lampe*] dazzle [2] (= *émerveillement*) bedazzlement; (= *spectacle*) dazzling sight [3] (*Méd*) **avoir un ~** to have a dizzy spell

ébonite /ebɔnit/ NF vulcanite, ebonite

éborgner /ebɔʀɲe/ ► conjug 1 ◄ VT ◆ **~ qn** to blind sb in one eye, to put *ou* poke sb's eye out ◆ **j'ai failli m'~ contre la cheminée** * I nearly put *ou* poked my eye out on the corner of the mantelpiece

éboueur /ebwœʀ/ NM dustman (*Brit*), refuse collector (*Brit Admin*), garbage man *ou* collector (*US*), sanitation man (*US Admin*)

ébouillanter /ebujɑ̃te/ ► conjug 1 ◄ VT (*gén*) to scald; [*+ légumes*] to scald, to blanch; [*+ théière*] to warm VPR **s'ébouillanter** to scald o.s.

éboulement /ebulmɑ̃/ NM [1] [*de falaise*] (*progressif*) crumbling; (*soudain*) collapsing; [*de mur, toit*] falling in, caving in ◆ **~ de rochers** rock fall ◆ **~ de terrain** landslide, landslip [2] (= *éboulis*) heap of rocks (*ou* earth)

ébouler /ebule/ ► conjug 1 ◄ VT to cause to collapse *ou* crumble, to bring down VI **s'ébouler** VPR [*pente, falaise*] (*progressivement*) to crumble; (*soudainement*) to collapse; [*mur, toit*] to fall in, to cave in; [*terre*] to slip, to slide

éboulis /ebuli/ NM mass of fallen rocks (*ou* earth) ◆ **pente couverte d'~** scree-covered slope

ébouriffant, e * /ebuʀifɑ̃, ɑ̃t/ ADJ [*vitesse, prix*] hair-raising

ébouriffé, e /ebuʀife/ (ptp de **ébouriffer**) ADJ [*cheveux*] tousled, dishevelled; [*plumes, poils*] ruffled; [*personne*] dishevelled ◆ **il était tout ~** his hair was all tousled *ou* dishevelled

ébouriffer /ebuʀife/ ► conjug 1 ◄ VT [1] [*+ cheveux*] to tousle, to ruffle; [*+ plumes, poil*] to ruffle [2] (* = *surprendre*) to amaze, to astound

ébrancher /ebʀɑ̃ʃe/ ► conjug 1 ◄ VT to prune, to lop (the branches off)

ébranchoir /ebʀɑ̃ʃwaʀ/ NM billhook

ébranlement /ebʀɑ̃lmɑ̃/ NM [1] (= *tremblement*) shaking [2] (= *affaiblissement*) [*de confiance, gouvernement*] weakening [3] (= *choc*) shock ◆ **l'~ provoqué par cette nouvelle** the shock caused by the news

ébranler /ebʀɑ̃le/ ► conjug 1 ◄ VT [1] (= *faire trembler*) [*+ vitres, mur, sol*] to shake [2] (= *troubler*) to shake ◆ **le monde entier a été ébranlé par cette nouvelle** the whole world was shaken by the news ◆ **la nouvelle a ébranlé les esprits** people were shaken by the news ◆ **ces paroles l'ont ébranlé** he was very shaken by what he heard ◆ **se laisser ~ par qch** to allow o.s. to be swayed by sth [3] (= *affaiblir*) [*+ résolution, confiance, gouvernement*] to shake; [*+ santé*] to affect; [*+ conviction, marché*] to undermine ◆ **ça a fortement ébranlé ses nerfs** it has shattered his nerves VPR **s'ébranler** [*train, véhicule, cortège*] to move off, to set off; [*cloche*] to start swinging

ébrécher /ebʀeʃe/ ► conjug 6 ◄ VT [*+ assiette*] to chip; [*+ lame*] to nick; [*+ fortune*] [*personne*] to break into; [*achat*] to make a hole *ou* a dent in

ébréchure /ebʀeʃyʀ/ NF [*d'assiette*] chip; [*de lame*] nick

ébriété /ebʀijete/ NF (*frm*) intoxication, inebriation ◆ **en état d'~** intoxicated, inebriated

ébrouement /ebʀumɑ̃/ NM [*de cheval*] snort

ébrouer (s') /ebʀue/ ► conjug 1 ◄ VPR [1] [*cheval*] to snort [2] [*personne, chien, oiseau*] to shake o.s.

ébruiter /ebʀɥite/ ► conjug 1 ◄ VT [*+ nouvelle, rumeur*] to spread; [*+ secret*] to divulge, to disclose VPR **s'ébruiter** ◆ **il ne faut pas que ça s'ébruite** people mustn't get to know about this ◆ **pour que rien ne s'ébruite** so that nothing leaks out ◆ **l'affaire s'est ébruitée** news of the affair got out

ébullition /ebylisjɔ̃/ NF [*d'eau*] boiling; (= *agitation*) turmoil ◆ **au moment de/avant l'~** as/before boiling point is reached, as/before it begins to boil ◆ **porter à ~** (*dans une recette*) bring to the boil ◆ **maintenir à ~ trois minutes** boil for three minutes

◆ **en ébullition** ◆ **être en ~** [*liquide*] to be boiling; [*ville, pays, maison*] to be in turmoil; [*personne*] (*par la surexcitation*) to be bubbling over with excitement; (*par la colère*) to be seething (with anger)

écaillage /ekajaʒ/ NM [1] [*de poisson*] scaling [2] [*d'huîtres*] opening [3] [*de peinture*] flaking, peeling

écaille /ekaj/ NF [*de poisson, reptile, bourgeon, pomme de pin*] scale; [*de tortue, huître*] shell; [*d'oignon*] layer, scale; [*de peinture sèche*] flake ◆ **lunettes (à monture) d'~** tortoise shell *ou* horn-rimmed glasses ◆ **en ~** tortoiseshell (*épith*) ◆ **les ~s lui sont tombées des yeux** (*frm*) the scales fell from his eyes ◆ **chat ~** tortoiseshell (cat)

écaillé, e /ekaje/ (ptp de **écailler¹**) ADJ [*peinture, surface*] chipped, flaking; [*façade*] peeling, flaking; [*baignoire*] chipped; [*poisson*] scaled

écailler¹ /ekaje/ ► conjug 1 ◄ VT [1] [*+ poisson*] to scale [2] [*+ huîtres*] to open [3] [*+ peinture*] to chip VPR **s'écailler** [*peinture*] to flake (off), to peel (off), to chip; [*vernis à ongles*] to chip

écailler², -ère /ekaje, jɛʀ/ NM,F (= *marchand*) oyster seller; (= *restaurateur*) owner of an oyster bar

écailleux, -euse /ekajø, øz/ ADJ [*poisson, peau*] scaly; [*peinture, ardoise*] flaky, flaking

écaillure /ekajyʀ/ NF [1] (= *morceau de peinture*) chip, flake; (= *surface écaillée*) chipped *ou* flaking patch [2] [*de poisson*] scales

écale /ekal/ NF [*de noix*] husk

écaler /ekale/ ► conjug 1 ◄ VT [*+ noix*] to husk; [*+ œuf dur*] to peel

écarlate /ekaʀlat/ ADJ scarlet ◆ **devenir ~** (*de honte*) to turn scarlet *ou* crimson (*de* with) → **eau** NF scarlet

écarquiller /ekaʀkije/ ► conjug 1 ◄ VT ◆ **~ les yeux** to stare wide-eyed (*devant* at)

écart /ekaʀ/ NM [1] [*d'objets*] distance, space, gap; [*de dates*] interval, gap; [*de chiffres, températures*] difference; [*d'opinions*] difference, divergence; [*d'explications*] discrepancy, disparity (*entre* between); ◆ **~ par rapport à la règle** deviation *ou* departure from the rule ◆ **il y a un ~ important de prix entre …** there's a big difference in price between … ◆ **il y a un gros ~ d'âge entre eux** there's a big age gap *ou* age difference between them ◆ **ils ont 11 ans d'~** there are 11 years between them ◆ **réduire l'~ entre** (*lit, fig*) to narrow *ou* close the gap between ◆ **réduire l'~ à la marque** (*Sport*) to narrow *ou* close the gap ◆ **faire un ~** [*cheval apeuré*] to shy; [*voiture*] to swerve; [*personne surprise*] to jump out of the way, to leap aside ◆ **faire un ~ de régime** to allow o.s. a break *ou* a lapse in one's diet ◆ **grand ~** (*Gym, Danse*) splits (*sg*); (*fig*) balancing act ◆ **faire le grand ~** (*lit*) to do the splits; (*fig*) to do a balancing act

[2] (*Cartes*) discard

[3] (*Admin* = *hameau*) hamlet

[4] (*locutions*)

◆ **à l'écart** ◆ **être à l'~** [*hameau*] to be out of the way *ou* isolated ◆ **tirer qn à l'~** to take sb aside *ou* to one side ◆ **mettre** *ou* **tenir qn à l'~** (= *empêcher de participer*) to keep sb in the background, to keep sb out of things; (= *empêcher d'approcher*) to keep *ou* hold sb back ◆ **se tenir** *ou* **rester à l'~** (= *s'isoler*) to stand *ou* remain aloof, to stand apart; (= *ne pas approcher*) to stay in the background, to keep out of the way; (= *ne pas participer*) to stay on the sidelines, to keep out of things

◆ **à l'écart de** ◆ **la maison est à l'~ de la route** the house is (well) off the road ◆ **ils habitent un peu à l'~ du village** they live just outside the village ◆ **tenir qn à l'~ d'un lieu** to keep sb (well) away from a place ◆ **tenir qn à l'~ d'une affaire** to keep sb out of a deal ◆ **se tenir** *ou* **rester à l'~ des autres** to keep out of the way of the others ◆ **se tenir** *ou* **rester à l'~ d'une affaire/de la politique** to steer clear of *ou* keep out of an affair/out of politics

COMP **écart de conduite** misdemeanour
écart d'inflation inflation differential
écart de jeunesse youthful misdemeanour
écart de langage strong *ou* bad language (*NonC*) ◆ **faire un ~ de langage** to use unacceptable language
écart type standard deviation

écarté, e /ekaʀte/ (ptp de **écarter**) ADJ [*lieu, hameau*] remote, isolated, out-of-the-way; [*yeux*] set far apart ◆ **avoir les dents ~es** to have gap(py) teeth, to have gaps between one's teeth ◆ **il se tenait debout, les jambes ~es/les bras ~s** he stood with his feet apart/with his arms outspread NM (*Cartes*) écarté

écartèlement /ekaʀtɛlmɑ̃/ NM (*Hist* = *supplice*) quartering; (= *tiraillement*) agonizing struggle

écarteler /ekaʀtəle/ ► conjug 5 ◄ VT (*Hist* = *supplicier*) to quarter; (= *tirailler*) to tear apart ◆ **écartelé entre ses obligations familiales et professionnelles** torn between family and professional obligations

écartement /ekaʀtəmɑ̃/ NM space, distance, gap (*de, entre* between); ◆ **~ (des rails)** [*de voie ferrée*] gauge ◆ **~ des essieux** [*de véhicule*] wheelbase

écarter /ekaʀte/ ► conjug 1 ◄ VT [1] (= *séparer*) [*+ objets*] to move apart, to move away from each other; [*+ bras, jambes*] to open, to spread; [*+ doigts*] to spread (open), to part; [*+ rideaux*] to draw (back) ◆ **il écarta la foule pour passer** he pushed his way through the crowd

[2] (= *exclure*) [*+ objection, solution*] to dismiss, to set *ou* brush aside; [*+ idée*] to dismiss, to rule out; [*+ candidature*] to dismiss, to turn down; [*+ personne*] (*d'une liste*) to remove, to strike off; (*d'une équipe*) to remove, to exclude (*de* from)

[3] (= *éloigner*) [*+ meuble*] to move away, to push away *ou* back; [*+ foule, personne*] to push back (*de* from) to push aside ◆ **elle essaie d'~ son mari de ses parents** (= *brouiller*) she's trying to cut her husband off from his parents ◆ **~ qn de la tentation** to keep sb (away) from temptation ◆ **tout danger est maintenant écarté** the danger's passed now ◆ **ce chemin nous écarte du village** this road takes *ou* leads us away from the village ◆ **ça nous écarte de notre propos** this is getting us off the subject ◆ **ça**

l'écarte de l'étude it distracts him from his studies

4 *(Cartes)* to discard

VPR **s'écarter** 1 *(= se séparer) [foule]* to draw aside, to part; *[nuages]* to part ◆ **la foule s'écarta pour le laisser passer** the crowd drew aside *ou* parted to let him through

2 *(= s'éloigner)* to withdraw, to move away, to step back *(de* from); ◆ **la foule s'écarta du lieu de l'accident** the crowd moved away from the scene of the accident ◆ **écartez-vous !** (move) out of the way! ◆ **s'~ de sa route** to stray *ou* wander from one's path ◆ **avec ce chemin nous nous écartons** this path is taking us out of our way ◆ **les deux routes s'écartent l'une de l'autre** the two roads diverge ◆ **s'~ du droit chemin** *(fig)* to wander from the straight and narrow ◆ **le mur s'écarte dangereusement de la verticale** the wall is dangerously out of plumb ◆ **s'~ de la norme** to deviate *ou* depart from the norm ◆ **s'~ d'un sujet** to stray *ou* wander from a subject ◆ **nous nous écartons !** we are getting away from the point!

écarteur /ekaʀtœʀ/ NM *(Méd)* retractor

ecchymose /ekimoz/ NF bruise, ecchymosis *(SPÉC)*

Ecclésiaste /eklezjast/ NM ◆ **(le livre de) l'~** (the Book of) Ecclesiastes

ecclésiastique /eklezjastik/ ADJ *[vie, charge]* ecclesiastical; *[revenus]* church *(épith)*; → **habit** NM ecclesiastic, clergyman

écervelé, e /esɛʀvəle/ ADJ *(= étourdi)* scatterbrained, birdbrained NM,F scatterbrain, birdbrain

échafaud /eʃafo/ NM 1 *(pour l'exécution)* scaffold ◆ **monter à l'~** to mount the scaffold ◆ **finir sur l'~** to die on the scaffold ◆ **tu finiras sur l'~** † you'll end up on the gallows ◆ **il risque l'~** he's risking his neck 2 *(†† = estrade)* platform, stand

échafaudage /eʃafodaʒ/ NM 1 *(Constr)* scaffolding *(NonC)* ◆ **ils ont mis un ~** they have put up scaffolding 2 *(= pile) [d'objets]* heap, pile 3 *(= élaboration) [de fortune]* building up, amassing; *[de théorie]* building up, construction ◆ **l'~ financier de cette affaire** the financial framework of the deal

échafauder /eʃafode/ ▸ conjug 1 ◂ VT 1 *[+ fortune]* to build (up), to amass; *[+ projet]* to construct, to build; *[+ théorie]* to construct, to build up ◆ **il a échafaudé toute une histoire pour ne pas venir** he made up *ou* fabricated a whole story so he wouldn't have to come 2 *(= empiler)* to pile up, to stack up VI *(= ériger des échafaudages)* to put up *ou* erect scaffolding

échalas /eʃala/ NM *(= perche)* stake, pole; *(* = personne)* beanpole*

échalier /eʃalje/ NM *(= échelle)* stile; *(= clôture)* gate

échalote /eʃalɔt/ NF shallot

échancré, e /eʃɑ̃kʀe/ (ptp de **échancrer**) ADJ *[côte]* indented, jagged; *[feuille]* serrated, jagged ◆ **robe ~e dans le dos** dress cut low in the back ◆ **robe très ~e sur le devant** dress with a plunging neckline

échancrer /eʃɑ̃kʀe/ ▸ conjug 1 ◂ VT *[+ robe]* *(devant)* to cut (out) a neckline in; *(dans le dos)* to cut (out) the back of; *[+ manche]* to widen the top of, to widen at the top

échancrure /eʃɑ̃kʀyʀ/ NF *[de robe]* neckline; *[de côte]* indentation; *[de feuille]* serration

échange /eʃɑ̃ʒ/ GRAMMAIRE ACTIVE 44.1

NM 1 *(gén, Échecs, Sci)* exchange *(avec* with); *(= troc)* swap, trade off *(entre* between); ◆ **~ de prisonniers** exchange of prisoners ◆ **programme d'~ de seringues** needle *ou* syringe exchange scheme ◆ **~ de vues** exchange of views ◆ **~s de coups avec la police** scuffles with the police ◆ **de vifs ~s entre des orateurs** heated exchanges between speakers ◆ **nous avons de bons ~s entre collègues** there's good communication between colleagues here ◆ **c'est un ~ de bons procédés** it's an exchange of favours, one good turn deserves another ◆ **~ standard** standard part replacement ◆ **faire l'~ standard d'un moteur** to replace an engine by a standard one

2 *(locutions)* ◆ **faire (l')~ de qch** to swap *ou* exchange sth ◆ **on a fait ~** we've done a swap *ou* an exchange ◆ **ils ont fait (l')~ de leurs maisons** they've swapped houses ◆ **faire ~** *(Échecs)* to exchange pieces

◆ **en échange** *(= par contre)* on the other hand; *(= en guise de troc)* in exchange; *(= pour compenser)* to make up for it

◆ **en échange de** in exchange for, in return for

3 *(= relations)* exchange ◆ **~ culturel** cultural exchange ◆ **~ scolaire/universitaire** school/university *ou* academic exchange

4 *(Tennis, Ping-Pong)* rally ◆ **faire des ~s** to have a knock-up, to knock up

NMPL *(Écon)* ◆ **~s (commerciaux)** trade, trading ◆ **le volume des ~s** the volume of trade ◆ **~s extérieurs/internationaux** foreign/international trade ◆ **dès les premiers ~s entre banques** as soon as trading between banks got under way

échangeabilité /eʃɑ̃ʒabilite/ NF exchangeability

échangeable /eʃɑ̃ʒabl/ ADJ exchangeable *(contre* for)

échanger /eʃɑ̃ʒe/ ▸ conjug 3 ◂ VT 1 *(= troquer)* to exchange, to swap *(contre* for; *avec* with); ◆ **"articles ni repris ni échangés"** "goods can neither be returned nor exchanged" ◆ **ce titre s'échange à 200 dollars** *(Bourse)* this security is traded at $200 2 *[+ idées, regards, lettres, coups]* to exchange; *[+ injures]* to trade, to exchange ◆ **ils ont échangé des remerciements** they thanked one another ◆ **~ des balles** *(Tennis, Ping-Pong)* to have a knock-up, to knock up

échangeur /eʃɑ̃ʒœʀ/ NM 1 *(= route)* interchange 2 *(Tech)* **~ (de chaleur** *ou* **thermique)** heat exchanger ◆ **~ d'ions** *(Chim)* ion exchanger

échangisme /eʃɑ̃ʒism/ NM *(gén)* partner-swapping; *(d'épouses)* wife-swapping

échangiste /eʃɑ̃ʒist/ ADJ *[club, soirée]* partner-swapping ◆ **couples ~s** couples who engage in partner-swapping, swingers* NMF partner-swapper, swinger*

échanson /eʃɑ̃sɔ̃/ NM *(Hist)* cupbearer; *(hum)* wine waiter

échantillon /eʃɑ̃tijɔ̃/ NM *(Stat, Ordin)* sample; *[de parfum, crème] (pour tester)* tester; *(en cadeau)* sample; *(fig)* example ◆ **~ de tissu** fabric sample, swatch (of material) ◆ **choisir un tissu sur ~** to choose a material from a sample *ou* swatch ◆ **catalogue** *ou* **livre d'~s** swatch book ◆ **~ de sang** *(Méd)* blood sample *ou* specimen ◆ **~ représentatif** *[de personnes sondées]* cross-section, representative sample ◆ **prendre** *ou* **prélever des ~s de** to take samples of, to sample

échantillonnage /eʃɑ̃tijɔnaʒ/ NM 1 *(= collection)* range *ou* selection of samples ◆ **~ d'outils** selection of tools ◆ **~ de tissus** swatch ◆ **le festival représente un ~ intéressant du jeune cinéma français** the festival brings together an interesting cross-section of young French film directors 2 *(Stat, Ordin, Mus)* sampling ◆ **~ par couches** *ou* **par strates** stratified sampling ◆ **~ au hasard** random sampling ◆ **l'~ de la population a été fait de manière rigoureuse** the population samples were very carefully selected

échantillonner /eʃɑ̃tijɔne/ ▸ conjug 1 ◂ VT *(Stat, Ordin, Mus)* to sample; *[+ population à sonder]* to take a sample of

échappatoire /eʃapatwaʀ/ NF *(= faux-fuyant)* way out ◆ **sa réponse n'était qu'une ~** his answer was just a way of evading the issue ◆ **il nous faut trouver une ~** we need to find a way out ◆ **il n'y a pas d'~ à la guerre** there's no way of avoiding war; → **clause**

échappé, e /eʃape/ (ptp de **échapper**) NM,F 1 *(Sport)* breakaway ◆ **les ~s** the breakaway group 2 *(†† ou hum)* **~ de l'asile** bedlamite † NF **échappée** 1 *(Sport)* breakaway ◆ **échappée solitaire** solo breakaway ◆ **il ne faisait pas partie de l'échappée** he wasn't in the breakaway group ◆ **faire une échappée de 100 km** to be ahead of the pack for 100 km 2 *(= vue)* vista; *(= rayon de soleil)* gleam 3 *[d'escalier]* headroom

échappement /eʃapmɑ̃/ NM 1 *[de véhicule]* exhaust (system) ◆ **rouler en ~ libre** to drive without a silencer *(Brit) ou* a muffler *(US)* ◆ **soupape d'~** exhaust valve; → **pot** 2 *[de mécanisme]* escapement 3 *(Ordin)* escape

échapper /eʃape/ ▸ conjug 1 ◂ VI

◆ **échapper à** ◆ **un cri de douleur lui échappa** he let out *ou* gave a cry of pain ◆ **un gros mot lui a échappé** he let slip *ou* let out a swearword ◆ **je ne voulais pas le dire mais ça m'a échappé** I didn't mean to say it but it just slipped out

◆ **échapper de** ◆ **~ des mains de qn** to slip out of *ou* slip from sb's hands ◆ **~ des lèvres de qn** *[cri, parole]* to burst from sb's lips

◆ **laisser échapper** *[+ gros mot]* to let out, to let slip; *[+ cri]* to let out, to give; *[+ objet]* to let slip, to drop; *[+ secret]* to let out; *[+ occasion]* to let slip, to let go; *[+ détail, faute]* to overlook ◆ **laisser ~ un prisonnier** to let a prisoner escape *ou* get away

◆ **faire échapper** ◆ **faire ~ un prisonnier** to help a prisoner (to) escape *ou* get out ◆ **il a fait ~ l'oiseau** he let the bird out

◆ **l'échapper belle** ◆ **il l'a échappé belle** he had a narrow escape, it was a close shave (for him)

VT INDIR **échapper à** 1 *[+ danger, destin, punition, mort]* to escape; *[+ poursuivants] (en fuyant)* to escape (from), to get away from; *(par ruse)* to evade, to elude; *[+ obligations, responsabilités]* to evade; *[+ corvée]* to get out of; *[+ ennuis]* to avoid ◆ **~ aux recherches** to escape detection ◆ **~ à l'impôt** *(Écon) (par privilège)* to be exempt from tax; *(illégalement)* to evade *ou* dodge* tax, to avoid paying tax ◆ **~ à la règle** to be an exception to the rule ◆ **cela échappe à toute tentative de définition** it defies definition ◆ **il échappe à tout contrôle** he is beyond (any) control ◆ **cela échappe à notre juridiction** *(Jur)* it is outside *ou* beyond our jurisdiction ◆ **tu ne m'échapperas pas !** *(lit)* you won't get away from me!; *(fig)* you won't get off as easily as that!, I'll get you yet! ◆ **son fils lui échappe** *(gén)* her son is slipping from her clutches; *(en grandissant)* her son is growing away from her ◆ **essaie d'~ pour quelques jours à ton travail** try and get away from work for a few days ◆ **~ à la vue** *ou* **aux regards de qn** to escape sb's notice ◆ **nous n'échapperons pas à une tasse de thé** *(hum)* we won't get away without having a cup of tea

2 *(= être oublié)* **~ à l'esprit de qn** to escape sb ◆ **son nom m'échappe** his name escapes me *ou* has slipped my mind ◆ **ce détail m'avait échappé** this detail had escaped my attention, I had overlooked this detail ◆ **ce détail ne lui a pas échappé** this detail was not lost on him ◆ **ce qu'il a dit m'a échappé** *(= je n'ai pas entendu)* I didn't catch what he said; *(= je n'ai pas compris)* I didn't understand what he said ◆ **ça a échappé à mon attention** it escaped my notice ◆ **l'opportunité d'une telle mesure m'échappe** I can't see *ou* I fail to see the point

of such a measure ◆ **l'intérêt de la chose m'échappe** I don't see the point ◆ **rien ne lui échappe** *(= il voit tout)* nothing escapes him, he doesn't miss a thing

VPR s'échapper ① *[prisonnier]* to escape *(de* from) to break out *(de* of); *[cheval]* to get out *(de* of); *[oiseau]* to fly away; *[cri]* to escape, to burst *(de* from); ◆ **l'oiseau s'est échappé de la cage** the bird got out of *ou* escaped from the cage ◆ **la voiture réussit à s'~ malgré la foule** the car got away in spite of the crowd ◆ **je m'échappe un instant pour préparer le dîner** I'll slip away for a moment *ou* I must leave you for a moment to get dinner ready ◆ **j'ai pu m'~ du bureau de bonne heure** I managed to get away *ou* slip out early from the office ◆ **le coureur s'est échappé dans la côte** *(Sport)* the runner drew ahead *ou* pulled away on the uphill stretch

② *[gaz]* to escape, to leak; *[odeur, lumière]* to come, to issue *(littér) (de* from); ◆ **de la fumée s'échappait de la cheminée** smoke was coming from *ou* out of the chimney ◆ **l'eau s'est échappée de la casserole** the water boiled over ◆ **des flammes s'échappaient du toit** flames were coming out of the roof

écharde /eʃaʀd/ NF splinter

écharpe /eʃaʀp/ NF *(= cache-nez)* scarf; *(= bandage)* sling; *[de maire]* sash ◆ **porter** *ou* **avoir le bras en** ~ to have one's arm in a sling ◆ **prendre une voiture en** ~ to hit a car broadside *ou* sideways on *(Brit)*

écharper /eʃaʀpe/ ▸ conjug 1 ◂ VT *(lit, fig)* to tear to pieces ◆ **se faire** ~ to be torn to pieces

échasse /eʃas/ NF *(= objet, oiseau)* stilt ◆ **marcher avec des ~s** to walk on stilts ◆ **être monté sur des ~s** *(hum)* to have long legs

échassier /eʃasje/ NM wading bird, wader *(Brit)*

échauder /eʃode/ ▸ conjug 1 ◂ VT ① *(= faire réfléchir)* ~ **qn** to teach sb a lesson ◆ **se faire** ~ to burn one's fingers, to get one's fingers burnt; → **chat** ② *(= laver à l'eau chaude)* ≈ wash in hot water; *(= ébouillanter)* to scald; *[+ théière]* to warm

échauffement /eʃofmɑ̃/ NM ① *(Sport)* warm-up ◆ **exercices/séance d'**~ warm-up exercises/session ② *[de terre]* heating; *[de moteur]* overheating ③ *(† = constipation)* constipation; *(= inflammation)* inflammation; *[de sang]* overheating

échauffer /eʃofe/ ▸ conjug 1 ◂ VT ① *[+ moteur, machine]* to overheat ◆ **il était échauffé par la course, la course l'avait échauffé** he was hot after the race ② *[+ imagination]* to fire, to excite ◆ **cette remarque a échauffé le débat** this remark made for a heated discussion ◆ **après une heure de discussion les esprits étaient très échauffés** after arguing for an hour people were getting very heated *ou* worked up* ◆ **tu commences à m'~ * (les oreilles** *ou* **la bile** †) you're getting on my nerves *ou* wick* *(Brit)* ③ *(† : Méd)* ~ **la peau** to inflame the skin ◆ **je suis un peu échauffé** I'm a bit constipated **VPR s'échauffer** ① *(Sport)* to warm up ② *(= s'animer) [personne]* to become heated, to get worked up*; *[conversation]* to become heated

échauffourée /eʃofuʀe/ NF *(avec la police)* brawl, clash; *(Mil)* skirmish

échauguette /eʃogɛt/ NF bartizan, watchtower

èche /ɛʃ/ NF *(Pêche)* bait

échéance /eʃeɑ̃s/ NF ① *(= date limite) [de délai]* expiration *ou* expiry *(Brit)* date; *[de bon, action]* maturity date; *[de traite, emprunt]* redemption date; *[de loyer]* date of payment; *[de facture, dette]* due date, settlement date *(Bourse)* settling day ◆ **~s politiques** elections ◆ **payable à l'**~ payable when due ◆ **venir à** ~ to fall due

② *(= règlements à effectuer)* **l'~ de fin de mois** the end-of-month payments ◆ **faire face à ses ~s** to meet one's financial obligations *ou* commitments ◆ **avoir de lourdes ~s** to be heavily committed, to have heavy financial commitments

③ *(= laps de temps)* term ◆ **à longue** ~ in the long run *ou* term ◆ **à courte** *ou* **brève** ~ before long ◆ **à plus ou moins brève** *ou* **longue** ~ sooner or later ◆ **à longue/courte** ~ *[traite]* long-/short-term *(épith)*; *[bon]* long-/short-dated

échéancier /eʃeɑ̃sje/ NM *[d'effets]* billbook; *[d'emprunt]* schedule of repayments; *[de travaux]* schedule

échéant /eʃeɑ̃, ɑ̃t/ ADJ M → **cas**

échec[1] /eʃɛk/ NM ① *(= insuccès)* failure; *(= défaite)* defeat; *(= revers)* setback ◆ **subir un** ~ *(gén)* to suffer a setback; *(Mil)* to suffer a defeat ◆ **son troisième ~ dans une élection** his third defeat in an election ◆ **l'~ des pourparlers** the breakdown in *ou* the failure of the talks ◆ **après l'~ des négociations** after negotiations broke down ◆ **sa tentative s'est soldée par un** ~ his attempt has failed *ou* has ended in failure ◆ **voué à l'**~ bound to fail, doomed to failure ◆ **avoir une conduite d'**~ *(Psych)* to be self-defeating ◆ **être/mettre qn en situation** *ou* **position d'**~ to be in/put sb in a hopeless *ou* no-win situation ◆ **l'~ scolaire** academic failure ◆ **des élèves en situation d'~ scolaire** children who perform poorly at school

② *(locutions)* **tenir qn en** ~ to hold sb in check ◆ **faire ~ à qn** to foil sb

échec[2] /eʃɛk/ NM *(Jeux)* ◆ **les ~s** chess ◆ **jeu d'~s** *(= échiquier)* chessboard; *(= pièces)* chessmen ◆ **jouer aux ~s** to play chess ◆ **mettre/être en** ~ to put/be in check ◆ **faire ~ au roi** to put the king in check ◆ ~ **au roi !** check! ◆ ~ **et mat** checkmate ◆ **faire ~ et mat** to checkmate

échelle /eʃɛl/ NF ① *(= objet)* ladder ◆ **courte** ~ *(= appui)* leg up, boost *(US)* ◆ **faire la courte ~ à qn** to give sb a leg up *ou* a boost *(US)* ◆ **la grande ~ (des pompiers)** the (firemen's) turntable ladder ◆ **faire grimper** *ou* **monter qn à l'**~ *(= le faire marcher)* to pull sb's leg*, to have sb on* *(Brit)* ◆ **il a grimpé à** *ou* **est monté à l'~** * he fell for it, he was taken in (by it) ◆ **il n'y a plus qu'à tirer l'**~ *(= renoncer)* we may as well give it up ◆ **après lui, il n'y a plus qu'à tirer l'**~ nobody can hold a candle to him, he's the best by a long shot

② *(= dimension)* scale ◆ **à l'~ (de) 1/100 000** on a scale of 1 to 100,000 ◆ **croquis à l'~** scale drawing ◆ **le dessin est/n'est pas à l'~** the drawing is/is not to scale ◆ **carte à grande/petite** ~ large-/small-scale map ◆ **sur une grande** ~ on a large scale ◆ **à l'~ nationale/mondiale** on a national/world(wide) scale ◆ **un monde à l'~ de l'homme** a world on a human scale ◆ **à l'~ de la firme** *(et non d'une seule usine)* at the level of the firm as a whole; *(en rapport avec son importance)* in proportion to the firm's size *(ou requirements etc)*

③ *[de bas, collant]* run, ladder *(Brit)*

④ *(dans les cheveux)* **faire des ~s à qn** to cut sb's hair all unevenly

⑤ *(= gradation, Mus)* scale; *(= hiérarchie)* ladder, scale ◆ **être au sommet de l'~** *[poste]* to be at the top of the ladder; *[salaire]* to be at the top of the scale

COMP **les échelles de Barbarie** the Ports of the Barbary Coast
échelle de Beaufort Beaufort scale
échelle chromatique chromatic scale
échelle de corde rope ladder
échelle coulissante extending *ou* extension ladder
échelle de coupée accommodation ladder
échelle double high stepladder
échelle de gravité *[d'accidents nucléaires]* international nuclear event scale
échelle d'incendie fire escape
l'échelle de Jacob *(Bible)* Jacob's ladder
les échelles du Levant the Ports of the Levant
échelle de meunier (wooden) step ladder
échelle mobile *[de pompiers]* extending ladder; *(Écon)* sliding scale
échelle de Richter Richter scale
échelle des salaires salary scale
échelle à saumons salmon ladder
échelle sociale social scale *ou* ladder
échelle des traitements ⇒ **échelle des salaires**
échelle des valeurs scale of values

échelon /eʃ(ə)lɔ̃/ NM ① *[d'échelle]* rung; *[de hiérarchie]* step, grade ◆ **fonctionnaire au 8e ~** official on grade 8 (of the salary scale) ◆ **être au dernier/premier** ~ *(Admin)* to be on the highest/lowest grade ◆ **monter d'un ~ dans la hiérarchie** to go up one step in the hierarchy ◆ **grimper rapidement les ~s** to climb the career ladder quickly ② *(= niveau)* level ◆ **à l'~ national** at the national level ◆ **à tous les ~s** at every level ③ *(Mil = troupe)* echelon

échelonnement /eʃ(ə)lɔnmɑ̃/ NM ① *[d'objets]* spacing out, spreading out ②, *[de paiements]* spreading *(sur* over); *[de congés, vacances]* staggering *(sur* over) ③ *[d'exercices] (dans la complexité)* grading; *(dans le temps)* gradual introduction

échelonner /eʃ(ə)lɔne/ ▸ conjug 1 ◂ VT ① *[+ objets]* to space out, to spread out, to place at intervals *(sur* over); ◆ **les bouées sont échelonnées à 50 mètres l'une de l'autre** the buoys are spaced *ou* placed 50 metres apart ◆ **les membres du service d'ordre sont échelonnés tout au long du parcours** the police are positioned *ou* stationed at intervals all along the route ◆ **les bâtiments s'échelonnent sur 3 km** the buildings are spaced out over 3 km ② *[+ paiements]* to spread (out) *(sur* over); *[+ congés, vacances]* to stagger *(sur* over) ③ *[+ exercices, difficultés] (dans la complexité)* to grade; *(dans le temps)* to introduce gradually ④ *(Mil)* to place in echelon, to echelon

échenilloir /eʃ(ə)nijwaʀ/ NM billhook, pruning hook

écheveau (pl **écheveaux**) /eʃ(ə)vo/ NM skein, hank; *(fig)* tangle, web

échevelé, e /eʃəv(ə)le/ (ptp de **écheveler**) ADJ *[course, danse, rythme]* wild, frenzied ◆ **il était tout** ~ his hair was all dishevelled

écheveler /eʃəv(ə)le/ ▸ conjug 4 ◂ VT *(littér) [+ personne]* to dishevel the hair of

échevin /eʃ(ə)vɛ̃/ NM *(Hist)* alderman, principal county magistrate; *(en Belgique)* deputy burgomaster; *(au Canada)* municipal councillor, alderman

échiffer* /eʃife/ ▸ conjug 1 ◂ VT *(Can)* to tease, to unravel

échine /eʃin/ NF ① *(Anat)* backbone, spine; *(Culin)* loin, chine ◆ **côte de porc dans l'~** pork loin chop ◆ **il a l'~ souple** *(fig)* he kowtows to his superiors, he's a bit of a doormat ◆ **plier** *ou* **courber l'~** to submit *(devant* to) ② *(Archit)* echinus

échiner (s') /eʃine/ ▸ conjug 1 ◂ VPR *(= travailler dur)* to work o.s. to death *ou* into the ground *(à faire qch* doing sth) ◆ **je m'échine à lui dire que c'est impossible** I've told him time and time again it can't be done

échiquier /eʃikje/ NM *(Échecs)* chessboard ◆ **l'~ politique/économique** the political/economic scene ◆ **notre place sur l'~ mondial** our place in the field *ou* on the scene of world affairs ◆ **en** ~ in a chequered pattern ◆ **l'Échiquier** *(Pol Brit)* the Exchequer

écho /eko/ NM ① *(= son)* echo ◆ **il y a de l'~** *(lit, fig)* there's an echo ◆ **"toujours", répondit-il en ~** "always", he echoed

2 *(= nouvelle, réponse)* **avez-vous eu des ~s de la réunion ?** did you get any inkling of what went on at the meeting?, did anything come back to you from the meeting? ◆ **se faire l'~ de** *[+ souhaits, opinions, inquiétudes]* to echo, to repeat; *[+ rumeurs]* to repeat, to spread ◆ **sa proposition est restée sans ~** his suggestion wasn't taken up, nothing further came of his suggestion ◆ **l'~ donné par les médias à cette nouvelle** the coverage *ou* publicity given to this news item by the media ◆ **cette nouvelle n'a eu aucun ~ dans la presse** this item got no coverage *ou* was not mentioned in the press ◆ **trouver un ~ (chez)** to find an echo (among)
3 *(Presse = nouvelle)* miscellaneous news item, item of gossip ◆ **(rubrique des) ~s** gossip column

échographie /ekɔgʀafi/ NF *(= technique)* ultrasound; *(= examen)* ultrasound (scan), sonogram *(US)* ◆ **passer une ~** to have an ultrasound (scan) *ou* a sonogram *(US)* ◆ **à l'~** on the ultrasound, on the sonogram *(US)*

> ⚠ Attention à ne pas traduire automatiquement **échographie** par le mot anglais **echography**, qui est d'un emploi peu courant.

échographier /ekɔgʀafje/ ► conjug 7 ◄ VT ◆ **~ qn** to give sb an ultrasound (scan)

échographique /ekɔgʀafik/ ADJ *[étude, compte rendu]* ultrasound *(épith)*, ultrasonographic ◆ **guidage ~** ultrasound guidance

échoir /eʃwaʀ/ VI 1 *(littér)* **~ (en partage) à qn** to fall to sb's share *ou* lot ◆ **il vous échoit de …** it falls to you to … 2 *[loyer, dettes]* to fall due; *[délai]* to expire

échoppe † /eʃɔp/ NF *(= boutique)* workshop; *(sur un marché)* stall, booth

échotier, -ière /ekɔtje, jɛʀ/ NM,F gossip columnist

échouage /eʃwaʒ/, **échouement** /eʃumɑ̃/ NM *(Naut) (= état)* state of being aground; *(= action)* grounding, running aground

échouer /eʃwe/ ► conjug 1 ◄ VI 1 *[personne]* to fail ◆ **~ à un examen/dans une tentative** to fail an exam/in an attempt
2 *[tentative]* to fail; *[plan]* to fail, to fall through
◆ **faire échouer** *[+ complot]* to foil; *[+ projet]* to wreck, to ruin ◆ **faire ~ les plans de l'ennemi** to foil the enemy's plans, to thwart the enemy in his plans ◆ **on a fait ~ leur tentative** they were foiled in their attempt
3 *(= aboutir)* to end up ◆ **nous avons échoué dans un petit hôtel** we ended up *ou* landed up in a small hotel
4 *[bateau]* to run aground; *[débris d'épave]* to be washed up; *[baleine]* to be beached ◆ **le bateau s'est échoué** *ou* **a échoué sur un écueil** the boat ran onto a reef ◆ **le bateau s'est échoué** *ou* **a échoué sur un banc de sable** the boat ran aground on *ou* ran onto a sandbank ◆ **bateau échoué** boat lying high and dry
VT *(Naut) (accidentellement)* to ground; *(volontairement)* to beach ◆ **il a échoué sa barque sur un écueil** he ran his boat onto a reef
VPR **s'échouer** → vi 4

échu, e /eʃy/ (ptp de **échoir**) ADJ *(Fin)* due, outstanding ◆ **intérêts ~s** outstanding interest ◆ **billets ~s** bills overdue ◆ **obligations ~es** matured bonds ◆ **effet non ~** unmatured bill ◆ **à terme ~** at the expiry date, when the fixed period has expired ◆ **les loyers sont versés à terme ~** rents are paid at the end of each rental period

écimer /esime/ ► conjug 1 ◄ VT *[+ arbre]* to pollard, to poll

éclaboussement /eklabusmɑ̃/ NM splash

éclabousser /eklabuse/ ► conjug 1 ◄ VT 1 *(= salir)* to splash, to spatter ◆ **~ de sang** to spatter with blood ◆ **~ qn de son luxe** *(éblouir)* to dazzle sb with a show of wealth; *(humilier)* to overwhelm sb with a show of wealth 2 *(moralement)* ◆ **~ qn** *[affaire, scandale]* to tarnish sb's reputation ◆ **ils ont été éclaboussés par le scandale** they have been tainted by the scandal, their reputations have been tarnished by the scandal

éclaboussure /eklabusyʀ/ NF *[de boue]* splash; *[de sang]* spatter; *(sur la réputation)* stain, smear, blot ◆ **il y a des ~s sur la glace** there are smears *ou* spots on the mirror

éclair /eklɛʀ/ NM 1 *(= foudre)* flash of lightning; *(Photo)* flash ◆ **il y a des ~s** there's lightning, there are flashes of lightning ◆ **~s de chaleur** summer lightning ◆ **~ de magnésium** magnesium flash
2 *[d'intelligence, génie]* flash, spark ◆ **~ de malice** mischievous glint ◆ **dans un ~ de lucidité** in a moment *ou* flash of lucidity ◆ **ses yeux lançaient des ~s (de colère)** her eyes blazed with anger
3 *(locutions)* **comme un ~** like a flash, like greased lightning* ◆ **passer comme un ~** *[coureur]* to flash past *ou* by; *[moment]* to fly by ◆ **en un ~** in a flash, in a split second; → **rapide**
4 *(= pâtisserie)* éclair
ADJ INV *[attaque, victoire]* lightning *(épith)*; *[visite]* lightning *(épith)*, flying *(épith)*; *(Échecs) [partie]* lightning *(épith)* ◆ **voyage ~** flying visit ◆ **raid ~** *(en avion)* blitz raid; *(par militaires)* hit-and-run raid ◆ **son passage ~ au pouvoir** his brief spell in power; → **fermeture, guerre**

éclairage /eklɛʀaʒ/ NM 1 *(artificiel)* lighting; *(= niveau de luminosité)* light (level) ◆ **sous cet ~** in this light ◆ **~ à l'électricité** electric lighting ◆ **~ au néon** neon lighting ◆ **~ direct/indirect/d'ambiance** direct/indirect *ou* concealed/subdued lighting ◆ **l'~ est insuffisant pour faire une bonne photo** there isn't enough light to take a good photograph ◆ **les ~s** *(Théât, Ciné) (= projecteurs)* the lights; *(= effets de lumière)* the lighting effects ◆ **l'~** *ou* **les ~s du Tintoret** *(Art)* Tintoretto's use of light
2 *(= action d'éclairer)* lighting ◆ **l'~ public** *ou* **des rues** street lighting
3 *(= point de vue)* light ◆ **sous cet ~** in this light ◆ **donner** *ou* **apporter un nouvel ~ à qch** to shed *ou* cast new light on sth ◆ **apporter un ~ intéressant/différent sur qch** to give an interesting/different perspective to sth ◆ **ces informations apportent un premier ~ sur ce qui s'est passé** this information provides us with a first indication of what happened

éclairagiste /eklɛʀaʒist/ NMF *(Théât)* electrician; *(Ciné)* lighting engineer

éclairant, e /eklɛʀɑ̃, ɑ̃t/ ADJ *(lit) [pouvoir, propriétés]* lighting *(épith)*; *(fig)* illuminating, enlightening; → **fusée**

éclaircie /eklɛʀsi/ NF 1 *(Météo)* bright interval, sunny spell 2 *(dans la vie)* bright spot; *(dans une situation)* upturn, upswing

éclaircir /eklɛʀsiʀ/ ► conjug 2 ◄ VT 1 *[+ teinte]* to lighten; *[+ pièce]* to brighten up, to make brighter ◆ **cela éclaircit le teint** it brightens the complexion 2 *(= désépaissir) [+ soupe]* to make thinner, to thin (down); *[+ plantes]* to thin (out); *[+ arbres, cheveux]* to thin 3 *[+ mystère]* to clear up, to solve; *[+ question, pensée, situation]* to clarify, to make clear; *[+ meurtre]* to solve ◆ **pouvez-vous nous ~ sur ce point ?** can you enlighten us on this point? VPR **s'éclaircir** 1 *[ciel]* to clear; *[temps]* to clear up ◆ **s'~ la voix** *ou* **la gorge** to clear one's throat 2 *[arbres, foule]* to thin out; *[cheveux]* to thin, to get thinner ◆ **les rangs de leurs alliés se sont éclaircis** their allies are getting thin on the ground 3 *[idées, situation]* to become clearer; *[mystère]* to be solved *ou* explained

éclaircissant, e /eklɛʀsisɑ̃, ɑ̃t/ ADJ ◆ **shampooing ~** shampoo for lightening the hair

éclaircissement /eklɛʀsismɑ̃/ NM 1 *[de mystère]* solving, clearing up; *[de texte obscur]* clarification; *(= explication)* explanation ◆ **j'exige des ~s sur votre attitude** I demand some explanation of your attitude ◆ **demande d'~** *(Jur)* request for clarification 2 *[de cheveux]* **se faire faire un ~** to have one's hair lightened

éclairé, e /eklɛʀe/ (ptp de **éclairer**) ADJ *[public, minorité, avis, despote]* enlightened; *[conseil]* knowledgeable ◆ **un amateur ~** an informed amateur ◆ **l'opération réclame le consentement ~ du patient** the operation requires the patient's informed consent

éclairement /eklɛʀmɑ̃/ NM *(Phys)* illumination

éclairer /eklɛʀe/ ► conjug 1 ◄ VT 1 *[lampe]* to light (up); *[soleil]* to shine (down) on ◆ **une seule fenêtre était éclairée** there was a light in only one window, only one window was lit up ◆ **café éclairé au néon** café with neon lights ◆ **une grande baie éclairait l'entrée** a large bay window brought light into the hall ◆ **ce papier peint éclaire le couloir** this wallpaper makes the passage look lighter *ou* brighter ◆ **deux grands yeux éclairaient son visage** *(littér)* her large eyes seemed to light up her face ◆ **un sourire éclaira son visage** a smile lit up his face ◆ **bien/mal éclairé** well-/badly-lit
2 *[+ problème, situation]* to throw *ou* shed light on, to clarify; *[+ auteur, texte]* to throw light on ◆ **~ qch d'un jour nouveau** to shed *ou* cast new light on sth
3 ◆ **~ qn** *(= montrer le chemin)* to light the way for sb; *(= renseigner)* to enlighten sb *(sur* about); ◆ **~ la lanterne de qn** to put sb in the picture*
4 *(Mil)* **~ le terrain** to reconnoitre *(Brit) ou* reconnoiter *(US)* the area, to scout the area ◆ **~ un régiment** to reconnoitre *(Brit) ou* reconnoiter *(US)* for a regiment ◆ **~ la route** to scout out the route
VI ◆ **~ bien/mal** to give a good/poor light
VPR **s'éclairer** 1 *[rue]* to be lit; *[visage]* to light up, to brighten (up)
2 *[situation]* to get clearer ◆ **tout s'éclaire !** it's all becoming clear!
3 ◆ **s'~ à l'électricité** to have electric light ◆ **s'~ à la bougie** to use candlelight ◆ **prends une lampe pour t'~** take a lamp to light the way

éclaireur /eklɛʀœʀ/ NM 1 *(Mil)* scout ◆ **avion ~** reconnaissance plane ◆ **partir en ~** *(lit)* to go and scout around; *(fig)* to go on ahead 2 *(Scoutisme)* (boy) scout

éclaireuse /eklɛʀøz/ NF (girl) guide *(Brit)*, girl scout *(US)*

éclat /ekla/ NM 1 *[d'os, verre]* splinter, fragment; *[de bois]* splinter, sliver; *[de grenade, pierre]* fragment ◆ **~ d'obus** piece of shrapnel ◆ **des ~s d'obus** shrapnel; → **voler**[1]
2 *[de lumière, métal, soleil]* brightness, brilliance; *(aveuglant)* glare; *[de diamant, pierreries]* flash, brilliance, sparkle; *[de couleur]* brightness, vividness; *[de braise]* glow; *[de vernis]* shine, gloss; *[de satin, bronze]* sheen; *[de perle]* lustre ◆ **l'~ des phares** *(Aut)* the glare of the headlights ◆ **l'~ (des lumières) de la rampe** *(Théât)* the blaze *ou* glare of the footlights
3 *[de yeux]* brightness, sparkle; *[de teint, beauté]* radiance ◆ **dans tout l'~ de sa jeunesse** in the full radiance *ou* bloom of her youth ◆ **perdre son ~** *[personne]* to lose one's sparkle ◆ **pour retrouver l'~ de votre sourire** to put the sparkle back into your smile

[4] *[de cérémonie]* glamour (Brit), glamor (US), splendour (Brit), splendor (US); *[de nom]* fame; *[de richesse, époque]* brilliance, glamour (Brit), glamor (US); *[de personnage]* glamour (Brit), glamor (US) ◆ **donner de l'~ à qch** to lend glamour to sth ◆ **réception donnée avec ~** sumptuous *ou* dazzling reception ◆ **ça s'est déroulé sans ~** it passed off quietly *ou* without fuss ◆ **sans ~** *[personnalité, interprétation]* lacklustre (Brit), lackluster (US) ◆ **coup** *ou* **action d'~** (= *exploit)* (glorious) feat

[5] (= *scandale)* fuss (NonC), commotion (NonC) ◆ **faire un ~** *ou* **un coup d'~** to make *ou* cause a fuss, to create a commotion

[6] (= *bruit)* **~s de voix** shouts ◆ **sans ~ de voix** without voices being raised ◆ **avec un soudain ~ de colère** in a sudden blaze of anger ◆ **~ de rire** roar *ou* burst of laughter ◆ **on l'accueillit avec des ~s de rire** his arrival was greeted with roars *ou* shouts of laughter ◆ **"oui", dit-il dans un ~ de rire** "yes", he said with a peal of laughter

éclatant, e /eklatɑ̃, ɑ̃t/ ADJ [1] *[lumière]* bright, brilliant; (= *aveuglant)* glaring; *[couleur]* bright, vivid; *[feu, soleil]* blazing; *[blancheur]* dazzling ◆ **des murs ~s de blancheur** dazzling white walls [2] *[teint]* radiant; *[beauté, sourire]* dazzling ◆ **~ de santé** radiant with health ◆ **la santé ~e de l'économie** the excellent state of health of the economy [3] *[succès]* dazzling, resounding; *[revanche]* shattering, devastating; *[victoire]* resounding; *[gloire]* shining; *[vérité]* manifest, self-evident; *[exemple]* striking, shining; *[mensonge]* blatant ◆ **cela démontre de façon ~e que ...** this provides striking proof that ... [4] *[rire, bruit]* loud; *[voix]* loud, ringing; *[musique]* blaring (péj), loud [5] ⁑ *[fête, musique]* super, fab* (Brit)

éclate⁑ /eklat/ NF ◆ **c'est l'~ totale** it's brilliant*

éclaté, e /eklate/ ADJ [1] *[initiatives, marché]* fragmented; *[paysage politique]* confused, fragmented ◆ **des enfants issus de familles ~es** children from broken homes [2] ◆ **j'étais ~ (de rire)*** I was splitting my sides (with laughter)* NM exploded view

éclatement /eklatmɑ̃/ NM *[de bombe, mine]* explosion; *[d'obus]* bursting, explosion; *[de pneu, ballon]* bursting; *[de veine]* rupture; *[de parti, fédération, coalition]* break-up, split (de in); *[de marché]* fragmentation ◆ **à cause de l'~ d'un pneu** as a result of a burst tyre ◆ **l'~ d'une bombe/d'un obus le couvrit de terre** an exploding bomb/shell covered him with earth ◆ **au moment de l'~ du conflit** when the conflict broke out ◆ **l'~ des familles favorise la délinquance** broken homes contribute to delinquency

éclater /eklate/ ► conjug 1 ◄ VI [1] *[mine, bombe]* to explode, to blow up; *[obus]* to burst, to explode; *[veine]* to rupture; *[bourgeon]* to burst open; *[pneu, chaudière]* to burst; *[verre]* to splinter, to shatter; *[parti, ville, services, structures familiales]* to break up ◆ **j'ai cru que ma tête allait ~** I thought my head was going to burst

[2] *[crise, dispute, incendie, épidémie, guerre, polémique]* to break out; *[orage, scandale, nouvelle]* to break ◆ **des troubles ont éclaté dans la capitale** unrest has broken out in the capital ◆ **la nouvelle a éclaté comme un coup de tonnerre** the news came as *ou* was a bolt from the blue, the news was a real bombshell

[3] (= *retentir)* **des cris ont éclaté** shouts were raised ◆ **une détonation éclata** there was an explosion ◆ **une fanfare éclata** there was a sudden flourish of trumpets ◆ **un coup de fusil a éclaté** there was the crack of a rifle ◆ **un coup de tonnerre éclata** there was a sudden peal of thunder ◆ **des rires/des applaudissements ont éclaté** there was a roar of laughter/a burst of applause, laughter/applause broke out

[4] (= *se manifester) [vérité, bonne foi]* to shine out, to shine forth (littér); *[mauvaise foi]* to be blatant ◆ **sa joie** *ou* **la joie éclate dans ses yeux/sur son visage** his eyes are/face is shining with joy

[5] ◆ **~ de rire** to burst out laughing ◆ **il éclata (de rage)** he exploded (with rage) ◆ **~ en menaces** *ou* **en reproches** to inveigh *(contre* against) to rail *(contre* at, against); ◆ **~ en sanglots** to burst into tears ◆ **nous avons éclaté en protestations devant sa décision** we protested angrily at his decision

[6] ◆ **faire ~** *[+ mine]* to detonate, to blow up; *[+ bombe, obus]* to explode; *[+ poudrière]* to blow up; *[+ pétard]* to let *ou* set off; *[+ ballon]* to burst; *[+ tuyau]* to burst, to crack; *[+ verre]* to shatter, to splinter ◆ **cette remarque l'a fait ~ (de colère)** he exploded at this remark ◆ **faire** *ou* **laisser ~ sa joie** to give free rein to one's joy ◆ **faire** *ou* **laisser ~ sa colère** to give vent to one's anger

VT ⁑ ◆ **je vais l'~, je vais lui ~ la tête** (= *frapper)* I'm going to smash his face in⁑

VPR **s'éclater** ⁑ (= *se défouler)* to have a ball* ◆ **s'~ à faire** *ou* **en faisant qch** to get one's kicks* doing sth

éclateur /eklatœʀ/ NM *(Élec)* spark gap

éclectique /eklɛktik/ ADJ eclectic

éclectisme /eklɛktism/ NM eclecticism

éclipse /eklips/ NF *(Astron, fig)* eclipse ◆ **~ partielle/totale (de soleil/lune)** partial/total eclipse (of the sun/moon) ◆ **~ annulaire** annular eclipse ◆ **carrière à ~s** career with ups and downs ◆ **personnalité à ~s** public figure who comes and goes, figure who is in and out of the public eye

éclipser /eklipse/ ► conjug 1 ◄ VT *(Astron)* to eclipse; *[événement, gloire]* to eclipse, to overshadow; *[personne]* to eclipse, to overshadow, to outshine VPR **s'éclipser** *[personne]* to slip away, to slip out

éclisse /eklis/ NF *(Méd)* splint; *(Rail)* fishplate; *[de violon]* rib; *(à fromage)* wicker tray

éclisser /eklise/ ► conjug 1 ◄ VT *(Méd)* to splint, to put in splints; *(Rail)* to join with fishplates

éclopé, e /eklɔpe/ ADJ *[personne]* limping, lame; *[cheval]* lame NM,F *(hum) (dans une bagarre)* (slightly) wounded person; *(dans un accident)* (slightly) injured person

éclore /eklɔʀ/ ► conjug 45 ◄ VI [1] *[œuf]* to hatch; *[poussin, larve]* to hatch (out) ◆ **faire ~** *[+ œuf]* to hatch [2] *[plan, idée]* to take form; *[association, secte]* to appear [3] *[fleur]* to open; *(littér) [amour, talent, jour]* to be born ◆ **fleur à peine éclose/fraîche éclose** budding/fresh-blown flower ◆ **faire ~** *[+ sentiment]* to kindle; *[+ qualités]* to draw forth

éclosion /eklozjɔ̃/ NF [1] *[d'œuf, poussin, larve]* hatching [2] *[d'idée]* forming; *[d'association, secte]* appearance [3] *[de fleur]* opening; *(littér) [d'amour, talent, jour]* birth, dawn

écluse /eklyz/ NF *(Naut)* lock ◆ **porte d'~** lock gate ◆ **lâcher** *ou* **ouvrir les ~s** * *(fig)* to turn on the waterworks*

éclusée /eklyze/ NF sluice *(amount of water contained in a lock)*

écluser /eklyze/ ► conjug 1 ◄ VT [1] (⁑ = *boire)* to down*, to knock back⁑ ◆ **qu'est-ce qu'il a éclusé !** he really knocked it back!⁑ [2] *[+ canal]* to lock, to sluice; *[+ bateau]* to lock

éclusier, -ière /eklyzje, jɛʀ/ NM,F lock keeper

écobilan /ekobilɑ̃/ NM life-cycle analysis

écodéveloppement /ekodevlɔpmɑ̃/ NM ecodevelopment

écoemballage /ekoɑ̃balaʒ/ NM eco-packaging

écœurant, e /ekœʀɑ̃, ɑ̃t/ ADJ [1] *[gâteau, boisson, goût, odeur]* sickly ◆ **les sauces à la crème, je trouve ça ~** I find cream sauces too rich [2] *[conduite]* disgusting, sickening; *[personne]* loathsome; *[richesse]* obscene; *[talent, succès]* sickening ◆ **elle a une chance ~e** she is so lucky it makes you sick *ou* it's sickening

écœurement /ekœʀmɑ̃/ NM (= *dégoût) (lit)* nausea; *(fig)* disgust; (= *lassitude)* disillusionment, discouragement ◆ **manger/boire jusqu'à ~** to eat/drink until one feels sick

écœurer /ekœʀe/ ► conjug 1 ◄ VT ◆ **~ qn** *[gâteau, boisson]* to make sb feel sick; *[conduite, personne]* to disgust sb, to nauseate sb, to make sb sick; *[avantage, chance]* to make sb sick, to sicken sb; *[échec, déception]* to discourage sb, to sicken sb ◆ **le foie gras m'écœure un peu** I find foie gras a bit too rich

éco-industrie (pl **éco-industries**) /ekoɛ̃dystʀi/ NF green-technology industry

écolabel /ekolabɛl/ NM eco-label

école /ekɔl/ NF [1] (= *établissement)* school ◆ **avion-/navire-~** training plane/ship ◆ **ferme-~** teaching farm ◆ **l'~ reprend dans une semaine** school starts again in a week's time ◆ **aller à l'~** *[élève]* to go to school; *[visiteur]* to go to the school ◆ **envoyer** *ou* **mettre un enfant à l'~** to send a child to school ◆ **grande ~** *(Univ) prestigious higher education institute with competitive entrance examination* ◆ **il va/est à la grande ~** * *(école primaire)* he goes to/is at primary school

[2] (= *enseignement)* schooling; (= *système scolaire)* school system ◆ **l'~ gratuite** free education ◆ **l'~ en France** the French school system ◆ **les partisans de l'~ laïque** the supporters of secular state education ◆ **elle fait l'~ depuis 15 ans** † she's been teaching for 15 years

[3] *(Art, Philos)* school ◆ **un tableau/peintre de l'~ florentine** a painting/painter of the Florentine School ◆ **querelle d'~s** petty quarrel between factions ◆ **son œuvre est une ~ de courage/de vertu** his work presents us with an inspiring model of courage/virtue ◆ **la lexicographie est une ~ de rigueur** you learn to be very rigorous when doing lexicography

[4] *(locutions)* **être à bonne ~** to be in good hands ◆ **il a été à dure** *ou* **rude ~** he learned about life the hard way ◆ **à l'~ de qn** under sb's guidance ◆ **apprendre la vie à l'~ de la pauvreté** to be schooled by poverty ◆ **faire l'~ buissonnière** to play truant (Brit) *ou* hooky (US) ◆ **faire ~** *[personne]* to acquire a following; *[théorie]* to gain widespread acceptance ◆ **il est de la vieille ~** he belongs to *ou* is one of the old school

COMP **école de l'air** flying school

école d'application *(Mil)* officers' training school

école des Beaux-Arts ≃ art college

École centrale (des arts et manufactures) *prestigious college of engineering*

école de commerce business school ◆ **elle a fait une ~ de commerce** she went to business school

école de conduite driving school

école de danse *(gén)* dancing school; *(classique)* ballet school

école de dessin art school

école élémentaire elementary school

école enfantine *(Helv)* nursery school

école hôtelière catering school, hotel management school

école libre sectarian *ou* denominational school

école militaire military academy

École nationale d'administration *prestigious college training senior civil servants*

École nationale supérieure de chimie *national college of chemical engineering*

École nationale supérieure d'ingénieurs *national college of engineering*

école de neige ski school

École normale ≃ teacher training college

École normale supérieure *grande école for training of teachers*
école de pensée school of thought
école de police police academy
école de recrues *(Helv Mil)* military service
école secondaire *(Helv)* secondary school
école de secrétariat secretarial college; → **haut**; → GRANDES ÉCOLES

ÉCOLE NATIONALE D'ADMINISTRATION

The « École nationale d'administration » or « ENA », in Strasbourg (formerly in Paris), is a competitive-entrance college training top civil servants such as diplomats, « préfets » and « inspecteurs des finances ». Because so many ministers and high-ranking decision-makers are « énarques » (ex-students of ENA), the school has often been criticized for exercising too much influence, and French political life is perceived by some as being monopolised by the so-called « énarchie ». → CONCOURS

écolier /ekɔlje/ NM schoolboy; (= *novice*) novice ◆ **papier (format)** ~ exercise (book) paper; → **chemin**

écolière /ekɔljɛʀ/ NF schoolgirl

écolo* /ekolo/ ADJ (abrév de **écologique, écologiste**) ◆ **il est très** ~ he's very ecology-minded, he's an eco-freak* NMF (abrév de **écologiste**) ecologist

écologie /ekɔlɔʒi/ NF ecology

écologique /ekɔlɔʒik/ ADJ 1 *[catastrophe]* ecological, environmental; *[équilibre]* ecological 2 *[produit]* eco-friendly, environmentally friendly 3 *(Pol) [association]* ecological, environmentalist; *[discours, politique]* on ecological issues; *[conscience, préoccupation]* ecological ◆ **mouvement** ~ ecological *ou* ecology *ou* green movement, ecomovement ◆ **la cause** ~ the green cause

écologisme /ekɔlɔʒism/ NM environmentalism

écologiste /ekɔlɔʒist/ ADJ *[candidat]* green *(épith)*, ecological *(épith)*, ecologist *(épith)*; *[vote]* green *(épith)*; *[action, idée]* green *(épith)*, ecologist *(épith)*, ecology *(épith)* ◆ **militant** ~ green *ou* ecology activist ◆ **mouvement** ~ ecological *ou* ecology *ou* green movement, ecomovement NMF (= *spécialiste d'écologie*) ecologist, environmentalist; *(Pol)* ecologist; (= *partisan*) environmentalist

écologue /ekɔlɔg/ NMF ecology expert, ecologist ◆ **ingénieur** ~ ecological engineer

écomusée /ekomyze/ NM eco-museum

éconduire /ekɔ̃dɥiʀ/ ► conjug 38 ◄ VT *[+ visiteur]* to dismiss; *[+ soupirant]* to reject; *[+ solliciteur]* to turn away

éconocroques‡ /ekɔnɔkʀɔk/ NFPL savings

économat /ekɔnɔma/ NM (= *fonction*) bursarship, stewardship; (= *bureau*) bursar's office, steward's office; (= *magasin*) staff cooperative *ou* store

économe /ekɔnɔm/ ADJ thrifty ◆ **elle est très** ~ she's very careful with money ◆ **être** ~ **de son temps/ses efforts** to be sparing of one's time/efforts ◆ **il n'est jamais** ~ **de conseils** he's always full of advice ◆ **une production de plus en plus** ~ **de main-d'œuvre** a system of production which requires less and less manpower ◆ **une gestion** ~ **des ressources énergétiques** careful management of energy resources NMF bursar, steward NM ◆ **(couteau)** ~ (vegetable) peeler, paring knife

économétrie /ekɔnɔmetʀi/ NF econometrics *(sg)*

économétrique /ekɔnɔmetʀik/ ADJ econometric

économie /ekɔnɔmi/ NF 1 (= *science*) economics *(sg)* ◆ **elle fait des études d'**~ she's studying economics ◆ **il est étudiant en** ~ he's an economics student ◆ ~ **domestique** *(Scol)* home economics

2 *(Pol = système)* economy ◆ ~ **politique/monétaire** political/cash economy ◆ ~ **de troc** barter economy ◆ ~ **dirigée** state-controlled *ou* centrally-planned economy ◆ ~ **de marché** free market *ou* free enterprise economy ◆ **nouvelle** ~ new economy ◆ ~ **souterraine** underground economy

3 *(NonC = épargne)* economy, thrift ◆ **par** ~ for the sake of economy ◆ **il a le sens de l'**~ he's careful with money, he's thrifty

4 (= *gain*) saving ◆ **faire une** ~ **de temps/d'argent** to save time/money ◆ **représenter une** ~ **de temps** to represent a saving in time ◆ **procédé permettant une** ~ **de temps/de main-d'œuvre** time-saving/labour-saving process ◆ **elle fait l'**~ **d'un repas par jour** she goes *ou* does without one meal a day ◆ **on aurait pu faire l'**~ **de ces négociations** we could have dispensed with the negotiations ◆ **j'ai fait l'**~ **d'une visite** I've saved myself a visit ◆ **avec une grande** ~ **de moyens** with very restricted *ou* limited means ◆ ~ **d'échelle** economy of scale

5 *[de livre]* arrangement; *[de projet]* organization

NFPL **économies** (= *gains*) savings ◆ **avoir des** ~**s** to have (some) savings, to have some money saved up ◆ **faire des** ~**s** to save up, to put money by ◆ **faire des** ~**s de chauffage** to economize on heating ◆ **les** ~**s d'énergie sont nécessaires** energy conservation is essential ◆ **réaliser d'importantes** ~**s d'énergie** to make significant energy savings ◆ ~**s budgétaires** budget savings ◆ **il n'y a pas de petites** ~**s** every little helps look after the pennies and the pounds will look after themselves *(Brit)* *(Prov)* ◆ **faire des** ~**s de bouts de chandelle** *(péj)* to make cheeseparing economies

> ⚠ Au sens de 'science économique', **économie** ne se traduit pas par le mot anglais **economy**.

économique /ekɔnɔmik/ ADJ 1 *(Écon)* economic 2 (= *bon marché*) economical; *[voiture]* fuel-efficient ◆ **cycle** ~ *[de machine à laver]* economy cycle ◆ **classe** ~ economy class

économiquement /ekɔnɔmikmɑ̃/ ADV economically ◆ **les** ~ **faibles** the lower-income groups

économiser /ekɔnɔmize/ ► conjug 1 ◄ VT *[+ électricité]* to economize on, to save on; *[+ énergie]* to conserve, to save; *[+ temps]* to save; *[+ argent]* to save up, to put aside ◆ ~ **ses forces** to save one's strength ◆ ~ **sur le chauffage** to economize on *ou* cut down on heating ◆ **économise ta salive** *ou* **tes paroles** don't waste your breath

économiseur /ekɔnɔmizœʀ/ NM ◆ ~ **(de carburant)** fuel-saving device ◆ ~ **d'écran** screen saver

économisme /ekɔnɔmism/ NM economism

économiste /ekɔnɔmist/ NMF economist

écope /ekɔp/ NF *(Naut)* bailer, baler, scoop

écoper /ekɔpe/ ► conjug 1 ◄ VTI 1 *(Naut)* to bail *ou* bale (out) 2 (* = *prendre*) ~ **(d')une punition** to catch it*, to get it*, to cop it‡ *(Brit)* ◆ ~ **de trois ans de prison*** to get a three-year sentence, to be sent down for three years* ◆ **c'est moi qui ai écopé** I was the one that took the rap* ◆ **il a écopé pour les autres** he took the rap for the others*

écoproduit /ekopʀɔdɥi/ NM environmentally-friendly *ou* eco-friendly product

écorce /ekɔʀs/ NF *[d'arbre]* bark; *[d'orange]* peel, skin ◆ **l'**~ **terrestre** *(Géol)* the earth's crust ◆ **canot d'**~ *(Can)* bark canoe

écorcer /ekɔʀse/ ► conjug 3 ◄ VT *[+ fruit]* to peel; *[+ arbre]* to bark, to strip the bark from

écorché /ekɔʀʃe/ NM *[de corps]* écorché; (= *dessin technique*) cut-away (diagram) ◆ **c'est un** ~ **vif** *(fig)* he's a tormented soul

écorchement /ekɔʀʃəmɑ̃/ NM *[d'animal]* skinning

écorcher /ekɔʀʃe/ ► conjug 1 ◄ VT 1 (= *dépecer*) *[+ animal]* to skin ◆ **écorché vif** flayed alive 2 (= *égratigner*) *[+ peau, visage]* to scratch, to graze; *[+ genoux]* to graze, to scrape ◆ **il s'est écorché les genoux** he grazed his knees 3 *(par frottement)* to chafe, to rub; *[+ cheval]* to gall 4 *[+ mot, nom]* to mispronounce ◆ **il écorche l'allemand** his German's terrible 5 († = *escroquer*) ~ **le client** to fleece* one's customers 6 ◆ ~ **les oreilles de qn** *[bruit]* to grate on sb's ears; *[personne]* to hurt sb's ears ◆ ~ **ça t'écorcherait la gueule**‡ **de dire merci ?** would it kill you to say thank you?

écorchure /ekɔʀʃyʀ/ NF *[de peau, visage]* scratch, graze; *[de genou]* graze

éco-recharge (pl **éco-recharges**) /ekoʀ(ə)ʃaʀʒ/ NF eco-refill

écorner /ekɔʀne/ ► conjug 1 ◄ VT *[+ meuble]* to chip the corner of; *[+ livre]* to turn down the corner of; *[+ économies, fortune]* to make a hole *ou* a dent in ◆ **livre tout écorné** dog-eared book

écornifler* † /ekɔʀnifle/ ► conjug 1 ◄ VT to cadge, to scrounge (*chez qn* from sb)

écornifleur, -euse* † /ekɔʀniflœʀ, øz/ NM,F cadger, scrounger

écossais, e /ekɔsɛ, ɛz/ ADJ *(gén)* Scottish, Scots *(épith)*; *[whisky]* Scotch; *[tissu]* tartan; → **douche** NM 1 ◆ **Écossais** Scot, Scotsman ◆ **les Écossais** the Scots 2 (= *dialecte anglais*) Scots; (= *dialecte gaélique*) Gaelic 3 (= *tissu*) tartan (cloth) NF **Écossaise** Scot, Scotswoman

Écosse /ekɔs/ NF Scotland

écosser /ekɔse/ ► conjug 1 ◄ VT to shell, to pod ◆ **petits pois à** ~ peas in the pod; → **haricot**

écosystème /ekosistɛm/ NM ecosystem

écot /eko/ NM (= *quote-part*) share (of a bill) ◆ **chacun de nous a payé son** ~ we all paid our share

écotaxe /ekotaks/ NF eco(-)tax

écotoxicologie /ekotɔksikɔlɔʒi/ NF ecotoxicology

écoulement /ekulmɑ̃/ NM 1 *[d'eau]* flow ◆ **tuyau/fossé d'**~ drainage pipe/ditch ◆ ~ **d'air** air flow 2 *[d'humeur, pus]* discharge ◆ ~ **de sang** flow of blood, bleeding 3 *[de foule]* dispersal; *[de temps]* passage, passing ◆ **l'**~ **des voitures** the flow of traffic 4 (= *vente*) selling ◆ **articles d'**~ **facile** quick-selling *ou* fast-moving articles

écouler /ekule/ ► conjug 1 ◄ VT (= *vendre*) to sell ◆ ~ **des faux billets** to dispose of counterfeit money ◆ **on n'arrive pas à** ~ **ce stock** this stock isn't moving *ou* selling, we can't shift this stock ◆ **nous avons écoulé tout notre stock** we've cleared all our stock

VPR **s'écouler** 1 *[liquide]* (= *suinter*) to seep *ou* ooze (out); (= *fuir*) to leak (out); (= *couler*) to flow (out); *[pus]* to ooze out ◆ **s'**~ **à grands flots** to pour out

2 *[temps]* to pass (by), to go by; *[argent]* to disappear, to melt away; *[foule]* to disperse, to drift away ◆ **en réfléchissant sur sa vie écoulée** thinking over his past life ◆ **10 ans s'étaient écoulés** 10 years had passed *ou* had elapsed *ou* had gone by ◆ **les fonds s'écoulent vite** funds are rapidly disappearing

3 (= *se vendre*) to sell ◆ **marchandise qui s'écoule bien** quick-selling *ou* fast-moving

item ◆ **nos produits se sont bien écoulés** our products have sold well

écourter /ekuʀte/ ▸ conjug 1 ◂ VT [+ *bâton*] to shorten; [+ *visite, attente, supplice, adieux*] to cut short, to shorten; [+ *texte, discours*] to shorten, to cut down; [+ *queue*] to dock

écoutant, e /ekutɑ̃, ɑt/ NM,F telephone counsellor

écoute /ekut/ NF 1 (= *attention*) **ces personnes recherchent un réconfort, une ~** what these people are looking for is some consolation and a sympathetic ear ◆ **une ~ attentive du patient peut ...** listening attentively to what the patient has to say can ...

2 **être aux ~s** † to be listening (*de* to); (= *épier*) to listen in, to eavesdrop (*de* on); (= *être aux aguets*) to be on the look-out (*de* for) to keep one's ears open (*de* for)

3 (*Radio*) listening (*de* to); ◆ **se mettre à** *ou* **prendre l'~** to tune in ◆ **nous restons à l'~** we are staying tuned ◆ **reprendre l'~** to retune ◆ **heures de grande ~** (*Radio*) peak listening hours; (*TV*) prime time, peak viewing hours ◆ **avoir une grande ~** (*Radio, TV*) to have a large audience ◆ **avoir une grande ~ féminine** to have a large female audience *ou* a large number of women listeners *ou* viewers ◆ **indice d'~** audience ratings

4 (*Mil, Police*) **~s téléphoniques** phone-tapping ◆ **ils sont sur ~(s)** their phone is being tapped ◆ **mettre qn sur ~(s)** to tap sb's phone ◆ **la mise sur ~(s) du ministre** tapping the minister's phone; → **table**

5 (*Mus*) **pour une meilleure ~** for better sound quality; → **confort**

6 (*Naut*) sheet

7 [*de sanglier*] **~s** ears

8 (*locution*)

◆ **être à l'écoute de** [+ *radio*] to be tuned in to, to be listening to; [+ *opinion publique, pays*] to be in touch with, to listen to; [+ *enfant, revendications*] to listen to; [+ *marché*] to have one's finger on the pulse of ◆ **il faut être à l'~ de son corps** you should listen to what your body is telling you ◆ **soyez à l'~ de votre partenaire** be in touch with your partner's needs

écouter /ekute/ ▸ conjug 1 ◂ VT 1 [+ *discours, chanteur, radio, disque*] to listen to ◆ **écoute !** listen! ◆ **(allô, oui) j'écoute** hello! ◆ **j'ai été ~ sa conférence** I went to hear his lecture ◆ **écoutons ce qu'il dit** let's listen to *ou* hear what he has to say ◆ **~ qn jusqu'au bout** to hear sb out ◆ **~ qch/qn secrètement** to eavesdrop on sth/sb ◆ **~ qn parler** to hear sb speak ◆ **savoir ~** to be a good listener ◆ **~ aux portes** to eavesdrop ◆ **~ de toutes ses oreilles** to be all ears, to listen with both ears ◆ **n'~ que d'une oreille** to listen with only half an ear ◆ **faire ~ un disque/une chanson à qn** to play sb a record/a song

2 [+ *justification, confidence*] to listen to; (*Jur, Rel*) to hear ◆ **écoute-moi au moins !** at least listen to *ou* hear what I have to say!

3 [+ *conseil*] to listen to, to take notice of ◆ **écoute-moi** listen to me ◆ **refuser d'~ un conseil** to turn a deaf ear to advice, to disregard a piece of advice ◆ **bon, écoute !** look!, listen! ◆ **aide-moi, écoute !** come on – help me! ◆ **écoute, c'est bien simple** look *ou* listen – it's quite simple ◆ **il se fait ~ du ministre** he has the ear of the minister ◆ **c'est quelqu'un de très écouté** his opinion is highly valued ◆ **ses conseils sont très écoutés** his advice is greatly valued *ou* greatly sought after

4 (= *obéir à*) to listen to ◆ **~ ses parents** to listen to *ou* obey one's parents ◆ **vas-tu (m')~ !** will you listen to me! ◆ **faire ~ qn** to get sb to listen ◆ **son père saura le faire ~** his father will get him to do as he's told ◆ **il sait se faire ~** he's good at getting people to do what he says ◆ **~ ses envies/son cœur** to be guided by one's desires/one's heart ◆ **il faut apprendre à ~ son corps** you must listen to what your body is telling you ◆ **n'écoutant que son courage** letting (his) courage be his only guide

VPR **s'écouter** [*malade*] **elle s'écoute trop** she coddles herself ◆ **si je m'écoutais je n'irais pas** if I were to take my own advice I wouldn't go ◆ **s'~ parler** to savour one's words ◆ **il aime s'~ parler** he loves the sound of his own voice

écouteur, -euse /ekutœʀ, øz/ NM,F (*littér* = *personne*) (*attentif*) listener; (*indiscret*) eavesdropper NM [*de téléphone*] earpiece ◆ **~s** (*Radio*) earphones, headphones

écoutille /ekutij/ NF (*Naut*) hatch(way)

écouvillon /ekuvijɔ̃/ NM [*de fusil*] swab; [*de bouteille*] (bottle-)brush; [*de boulanger*] scuffle

écouvillonner /ekuvijɔne/ ▸ conjug 1 ◂ VT [+ *fusil*] to swab; [+ *bouteille, four*] to clean

écovillage /ekovilaʒ/ NM eco-village

écrabouiller * /ekʀabuje/ ▸ conjug 1 ◂ VT to squash, to crush ◆ **se faire ~ par une voiture** to get flattened *ou* crushed by a car

écran /ekʀɑ̃/ NM 1 (*gén*) screen ◆ **ce mur fait ~ et nous isole du froid/du bruit** this wall screens *ou* shields us from the cold/noise, this wall acts as a screen *ou* shield against the cold/noise ◆ **faire ~ à qn** (= *abriter*) to screen *ou* shelter sb; (= *gêner*) to get in sb's way; (= *éclipser*) to stand in sb's way ◆ **son renom me fait ~** he puts me in the shade because he's so famous ◆ **~ de fumée/de protection** smoke/protective screen ◆ **~ de verdure** screen of foliage ◆ **~ publicitaire** advertising slot ◆ **~ solaire** (= *crème*) sun screen ◆ **~ total** total sunblock

2 (*Ordin, TV*) screen ◆ **télévision grand ~** large-screen television ◆ **~ cathodique** cathode-ray screen ◆ **~ de contrôle** monitor (screen) ◆ **~ plasma** plasma screen ◆ **~ plat** flat screen ◆ **~ pleine page** (*Ordin*) full page display ◆ **~ réflectif** reflective screen ◆ **~ vidéo** video screen ◆ **~ de visualisation** (visual) display screen ◆ **~ tactile** touch-sensitive screen ◆ **~ 16/9e** wide screen ◆ **le petit ~** (= *télévision*) the small screen, television ◆ **une vedette du petit ~** a television *ou* TV star ◆ **travailler sur ~** (*Ordin*) to work on screen

3 (*Ciné*) **~ (de cinéma)** (= *toile*) screen ◆ **~ de projection** projector screen ◆ **sur ~ géant** on a giant screen ◆ **porter un roman à l'~** to adapt a novel for the screen ◆ **prochainement sur vos ~s** coming soon to a cinema near you ◆ **ce film sera la semaine prochaine sur les ~s londoniens** this film will open *ou* be showing next week in London ◆ **le grand ~** (= *le cinéma*) the big *ou* silver screen ◆ **sur grand ~** on the big screen ◆ **une vedette de l'~** *ou* **du grand ~** a star of the silver screen, a film *ou* movie (*US*) star

écrasant, e /ekʀazɑ̃, ɑt/ ADJ [*impôts, mépris, poids*] crushing; [*preuve, responsabilité, nombre*] overwhelming; [*travail*] gruelling, back-breaking; [*défaite, supériorité*] crushing, overwhelming; [*chaleur*] overpowering, overwhelming ◆ **majorité/victoire ~e** (*Pol*) landslide *ou* crushing majority/victory

écrasé, e /ekʀaze/ (ptp de **écraser**) ADJ [*nez*] flat, squashed; [*perspective, relief*] dwarfed

écrasement /ekʀazmɑ̃/ NM 1 [*d'objet, révolte, ennemi*] crushing 2 (*Ordin*) [*de données, fichier*] overwriting

écraser /ekʀaze/ ▸ conjug 1 ◂ VT 1 (*gén*) to crush; [+ *mouche*] to squash; [+ *mégot*] to stub out; (*en purée*) to mash; (*en poudre*) to grind (*en* to); (*au pilon*) to pound; (*pour le jus*) to squeeze; (*en aplatissant*) to flatten (out); (*en piétinant*) to trample down; (*Tennis*) [+ *balle*] to flatten, to kill ◆ **~ sous la dent** [+ *biscuit*] to crunch; [+ *noix*] to crush between one's teeth ◆ **écrasé par la foule** squashed *ou* crushed in the crowd ◆ **aïe, vous m'écrasez les pieds !** ouch, you're standing *ou* treading on my feet! ◆ **~ la pédale d'accélérateur** * to step on it *

2 (= *tuer*) [*voiture, train*] to run over; [*avalanche*] to crush ◆ **il s'est fait ~ par une voiture** he was run over by a car

3 (= *accabler*) to crush ◆ **nous sommes écrasés d'impôts** we are overburdened *ou* crushed by taxation ◆ **il nous écrase de son mépris** he crushes us with his scornful attitude ◆ **écrasé de chaleur** overcome by the heat ◆ **écrasé de sommeil/de douleur** overcome by sleep/with grief ◆ **écrasé de travail** snowed under with * *ou* overloaded with work

4 (= *vaincre*) [+ *ennemi*] to crush; [+ *rébellion*] to crush, to suppress, to put down ◆ **notre équipe a été écrasée** *ou* **s'est fait ~** we were hammered * *ou* we were beaten hollow (*Brit*)

5 (*Ordin*) [+ *données, fichiers*] to overwrite

VI 1 (* = *ne pas insister*) to drop the subject ◆ **oh écrase !** oh shut up! * *ou* belt up! ‡ (*Brit*)

2 (= *dormir*) ◆ **en ~** ‡ to sleep like a log *

VPR **s'écraser** 1 [*avion, voiture*] to crash (*contre* into, against; *sur* on); [*objet, corps*] to be crushed (*contre* on, against)

2 [*foule*] to be *ou* get crushed (*dans* in); ◆ **on s'écrase pour en acheter** they're falling over each other *ou* they're rushing to buy them ◆ **on s'écrase devant les cinémas** there's a great crush to get into the cinemas

3 (‡ = *ne pas protester*) to pipe down * ◆ **il s'écrase toujours devant son chef** he never says a word when the boss is around ◆ **il a intérêt à s'~ !** he'd better keep quiet!

écraseur, -euse * /ekʀazœʀ, øz/ NM,F (= *chauffard*) roadhog *

écrémage /ekʀemaʒ/ NM 1 [*de lait*] skimming 2 (*fig*) creaming off

écrémer /ekʀeme/ ▸ conjug 6 ◂ VT 1 [+ *lait*] to skim ◆ **lait écrémé** skimmed milk 2 [+ *candidats*] to cream off the best from

écrémeuse /ekʀemøz/ NF creamer, (cream) separator

écrêter /ekʀete/ ▸ conjug 1 ◂ VT (= *niveler*) to lop

écrevisse /ekʀəvis/ NF (freshwater) crayfish (*Brit*), crawfish (*US*); → **rouge**

écrier (s') /ekʀije/ ▸ conjug 7 ◂ VPR to exclaim, to cry out

écrin /ekʀɛ̃/ NM (= *coffret*) case, box ◆ **niché dans un ~ de verdure** (*littér*) nestling in a green setting ◆ **le musée est un merveilleux ~ pour ces œuvres** the museum is a wonderful showcase for these works

écrire /ekʀiʀ/ GRAMMAIRE ACTIVE 48.1, 48.2 ▸ conjug 39 ◂

VT 1 (*gén*) [+ *mots, livres*] to write; (= *orthographier*) to spell; (= *inscrire, marquer*) to write down ◆ **je lui ai écrit que je viendrais** I wrote and told him I would be coming ◆ **~ des commentaires au crayon** to pencil in comments, to make notes *ou* comments in pencil

2 (*locutions*) **c'était écrit** it was bound to happen, it was inevitable ◆ **il est écrit que je ne pourrai jamais y arriver !** I'm fated *ou* doomed never to succeed! ◆ **c'est écrit sur sa figure** it's written all over his face ◆ **c'est écrit noir sur blanc** *ou* **en toutes lettres** it's written in black and white

VI (*gén*) to write; (= *être écrivain*) to be a writer, to write ◆ **vous écrivez très mal** your writing is really bad ◆ **~ gros/fin** [*personne*] to have large/small (hand)writing; [*stylo*] to have a thick/fine nib ◆ **~ au crayon/à l'encre** to write in pencil/in ink

VPR **s'écrire** [*personnes*] to write to each other ◆ **comment ça s'écrit ?** how do you spell it? ◆ **ça s'écrit comme ça se prononce** it's spelt how it sounds, you write it the same way as you pronounce it

écrit, e /ekʀi, it/ (ptp de **écrire**) ADJ ◆ **épreuve ~e** *(Scol)* written exam *ou* paper ◆ **le texte/scénario est très ~** it's a very carefully written *ou* crafted text/script NM *(= ouvrage)* piece of writing, written work; *(= examen)* written exam *ou* paper; *(Jur)* document ◆ **par ~** in writing ◆ **être bon à l'~** *(Scol)* to do well in the written papers

écriteau (pl **écriteaux**) /ekʀito/ NM notice, sign

écritoire /ekʀitwaʀ/ NF writing case

écriture /ekʀityʀ/ NF 1 *(à la main)* (hand)writing *(NonC)* ◆ **il a une belle ~** he has beautiful (hand)writing ◆ **~ de chat** spidery (hand) writing 2 *(= alphabet)* writing *(NonC)*, script ◆ **~ hiéroglyphique** hieroglyphic writing ◆ **~ phonétique** phonetic script 3 *(fig = composition)* composition ◆ **~ chorégraphique** choreographic composition ◆ **~ scénique** stage composition 4 *(littér = style)* writing *(NonC)* 5 *(= rédaction)* writing ◆ **se consacrer à l'~ (de romans)** to devote one's time to writing (novels) ◆ **~ automatique** *(Littérat)* automatic writing 6 *(Fin)* entry ◆ **passer une ~** to make an entry 7 *(Rel)* **les (Saintes) Écritures, l'Écriture (sainte)** Scripture, the Scriptures, (the) Holy Writ NFPL **écritures** *(= comptes)* accounts, books ◆ **employé aux ~s** ledger clerk ◆ **tenir les ~s** to keep the books

écrivailler /ekʀivaje/ ▸ conjug 1 ◂ VI *(péj)* to scribble

écrivailleur, -euse /ekʀivajœʀ, øz/ NM,F, **écrivaillon** /ekʀivajɔ̃/ NM *(péj)* scribbler

écrivain /ekʀivɛ̃/ NM writer ◆ **femme-~** woman writer ◆ **~ public** (public) letter-writer

écrivassier, -ière /ekʀivasje, jɛʀ/ NM,F ⇒ **écrivailleur, -euse**

écrou /ekʀu/ NM 1 *(à visser)* nut ◆ **~ à ailettes** wing nut 2 *(Jur)* commitment, committal, mittimus *(SPÉC)* ◆ **mettre qn sous ~** to enter sb on the prison register ◆ **mise sous ~** entering on the prison register ◆ **sous les ~s** in prison; → **levée²**

écrouelles †† /ekʀuɛl/ NFPL scrofula

écrouer /ekʀue/ ▸ conjug 1 ◂ VT *(= incarcérer)* to imprison, to lock away (in prison) ◆ **il a été écroué sous le numéro 3489** he was entered on the prison register under the number 3489

écroulé, e /ekʀule/ (ptp de **s'écrouler**) ADJ 1 *[maison, mur]* ruined ◆ **à moitié ~** half-ruined, tumbledown *(épith)*, dilapidated 2 ◆ **être ~* (de rire)** to be doubled up with laughter

écroulement /ekʀulmɑ̃/ NM collapse ◆ **l'explosion a provoqué l'~ du toit** the explosion caused the roof to collapse *ou* cave in

écrouler (s') /ekʀule/ ▸ conjug 1 ◂ VPR 1 *[mur]* to fall (down), to collapse; *[rocher]* to fall; *[toit]* to collapse, to cave in, to fall in; *(Rugby) [mêlée]* to collapse 2 *[empire]* to collapse, to crumble; *[entreprise]* to collapse, to crash; *[prix, cours]* to collapse, to plummet; *[espoir, théorie]* to collapse ◆ **tous nos projets se sont écroulés** all our plans have fallen through 3 *[personne] (= tomber)* to collapse; *(* = s'endormir)* to fall fast asleep; *[coureur, candidat]* to collapse ◆ **s'~ de sommeil/de fatigue** to be overcome with *ou* collapse with sleepiness/weariness ◆ **il s'écroula dans un fauteuil*** he flopped down *ou* collapsed into an armchair ◆ **être près de s'~** to be on the verge of collapse

écru, e /ekʀy/ ADJ *[tissu]* raw, in its natural state; *[vêtement]* ecru ◆ **couleur ~e** ecru ◆ **toile ~e** unbleached linen ◆ **soie ~e** raw silk *(before dyeing)*

ecstasy /ɛkstazi/ NF ecstasy

ectoplasme /ɛktoplasm/ NM ectoplasm

écu /eky/ NM *(= monnaie ancienne, papier)* crown; *(= monnaie européenne)* ecu; *(Hist = bouclier)* shield

écubier /ekybje/ NM hawse-hole

écueil /ekœj/ NM *(lit)* reef, shelf; *(= pierre d'achoppement)* stumbling block; *(= piège, danger)* pitfall

écuelle /ekɥɛl/ NF *(= assiette creuse) (pour chien)* bowl; *(= contenu)* bowlful; *(Hist)* platter

éculé, e /ekyle/ (ptp de **éculer**) ADJ *[chaussure]* down-at-heel; *[plaisanterie]* hackneyed, worn; *[mot]* overused

éculer /ekyle/ ▸ conjug 1 ◂ VT *[+ chaussure]* to wear down at the heel VPR **s'éculer** *[plaisanterie]* to wear thin; *[mot]* to be overused

écumage /ekymaʒ/ NM skimming

écumant, e /ekymɑ̃, ɑ̃t/ ADJ *[mer, torrent, vague]* foamy; *[lait]* frothy; *[bouche]* foaming

écume /ekym/ NF *[de mer]* foam; *[de bouche, bière]* foam, froth; *[de métal]* dross; *[de confiture, bouillon]* scum; *[de savon, cheval]* lather ◆ **pipe en ~ de mer** meerschaum pipe ◆ **l'~ de la société** *(péj)* the scum *ou* dregs of society

écumer /ekyme/ ▸ conjug 1 ◂ VT 1 *[+ bouillon]* to skim; *[+ confiture]* to take the scum off, to skim; *[+ métal]* to scum 2 *(= piller)* to clean out, to plunder ◆ **~ les mers** to scour the seas ◆ **~ la ville à la recherche de** to scour the town in search of VI *[mer, confiture]* to foam; *[métal]* to scum; *[bouche, liquide]* to froth, to foam; *[cheval]* to lather ◆ **~ (de rage)** to foam *ou* froth at the mouth *(fig)*, to foam with rage

écumeur /ekymœʀ/ NM *(Hist)* ◆ **~ des mers** *(hum)* pirate, buccaneer

écumeux, -euse /ekymø, øz/ ADJ foamy, frothy

écumoire /ekymwaʀ/ NF skimmer ◆ **troué comme une ~** riddled with holes

écureuil /ekyʀœj/ NM squirrel ◆ **~ roux/gris** red/grey squirrel ◆ **~ de Corée** chipmunk ◆ **~ volant** flying squirrel

écurie /ekyʀi/ NF *[de chevaux, cyclistes etc]* stable; *(péj = endroit sale)* pigsty ◆ **mettre un cheval à l'~** to stable a horse ◆ **~ de course** racing stable ◆ **nettoyer les ~s d'Augias** to clean the Augean stables; → **sentir**

écusson /ekysɔ̃/ NM *(= insigne)* badge; *(Mil)* tab; *(Héraldique)* escutcheon; *[de serrure]* escutcheon; *[d'insecte]* scutellum ◆ **(greffe en) ~** *(Agr)* shield-graft

écuyer /ekɥije/ NM 1 *(= cavalier)* rider, horseman; *(= professeur d'équitation)* riding master ◆ **~ de cirque** circus rider 2 *(Hist) (d'un chevalier)* squire; *(à la cour)* equerry

écuyère /ekɥijɛʀ/ NF rider, horsewoman ◆ **~ de cirque** circus rider ◆ **bottes à l'~** riding boots

eczéma /ɛgzema/ NM eczema ◆ **avoir** *ou* **faire de l'~** to have eczema

eczémateux, -euse /ɛgzematø, øz/ ADJ eczematous, eczema *(épith)*

édam /edam/ NM *(= fromage)* Edam

edelweiss /edɛlvɛs, edɛlvajs/ NM edelweiss

Éden /edɛn/ NM ◆ **l'~ , le jardin d'~** (the garden of) Eden

édenté, e /edɑ̃te/ (ptp de **édenter**) ADJ *(totalement)* toothless; *(partiellement)* gap-toothed NM edentate mammal ◆ **les ~s** edentate mammals, the Edentata *(SPÉC)*

édenter /edɑ̃te/ ▸ conjug 1 ◂ VT to break the teeth of

EDF /ədeɛf/ NF (abrév de **Électricité de France**) ◆ **l'~** the French Electricity Board ◆ **l'~-GDF** the French Electricity and Gas Board

édicter /edikte/ ▸ conjug 1 ◂ VT *[+ loi]* to enact, to decree; *[+ peine]* to decree

édicule /edikyl/ NM *(hum = cabinets)* public lavatory *ou* convenience *(Brit)*, (public) rest room *(US)*; *(= kiosque)* kiosk

édifiant, e /edifjɑ̃, jɑ̃t/ ADJ *[livre, conduite, histoire]* edifying; *[exemple]* salutary

édification /edifikasjɔ̃/ NF *[de bâtiment]* erection, construction; *[de personne]* edification *(frm)*, enlightenment

édifice /edifis/ NM building, edifice *(frm)* ◆ **~ public** public building ◆ **l'~ social** the social structure *ou* fabric

édifier /edifje/ ▸ conjug 7 ◂ VT 1 *[+ maison]* to build, to construct, to erect; *[+ fortune, empire]* to build (up); *[+ système]* to build, to develop 2 *(moralement)* to edify *(frm)*, to enlighten

édile /edil/ NM *(frm, hum)* (town) councillor

Édimbourg /edɛ̃buʀ/ N Edinburgh

édit /edi/ NM *(Hist)* edict ◆ **l'Édit de Nantes** the Edict of Nantes

éditer /edite/ ▸ conjug 1 ◂ VT *(= publier)* to publish; *[+ disques]* to produce; *(= annoter, présenter)* to edit

éditeur, -trice /editœʀ, tʀis/ NM,F *(= annotateur)* editor NM 1 *(= personne ou entreprise qui publie)* publisher ◆ **~ de disques** record producer 2 *(Ordin)* **~ de textes** text editor

> ⚠ Au sens de 'personne ou entreprise qui publie', **éditeur** ne se traduit pas par le mot anglais **editor**.

édition /edisjɔ̃/ NF 1 *(= action de publier)* publishing; *[de disques]* production ◆ **travailler dans l'~** to be in publishing *ou* in the publishing business ◆ **l'~ électronique** electronic publishing

2 *(= livre, journal)* edition ◆ **~ spéciale** *(= journal)* special edition; *(= magazine)* special issue ◆ **"édition spéciale !"** *(cri du vendeur)* "extra! extra!" ◆ **~ de 5 heures** *(= journal)* five o'clock edition ◆ **notre ~ de 13 heures** *(Radio, TV = informations)* our 1 o'clock news bulletin ◆ **dernière ~** *(Presse)* late edition; *(TV)* late news bulletin ◆ **deuxième/troisième ~ !*** *(hum)* for the second/third time!

3 *(= annotation)* editing; *(= texte)* edition ◆ **établir l'~ critique d'un texte** to produce a critical edition of a text ◆ **~ revue et corrigée/revue et augmentée** revised/revised and enlarged edition

4 *(Ordin)* editing

> ⚠ Au sens de 'action de publier', **édition** ne se traduit pas par le mot anglais **edition**.

édito* /edito/ NM abrév de **éditorial**

éditorial, e (mpl **-iaux**) /editɔʀjal, jo/ ADJ *[comité, politique, projet]* editorial ◆ **il y a un superbe travail ~** it's beautifully edited NM leading article, leader, editorial

éditorialiste /editɔʀjalist/ NMF leader *ou* editorial writer

Édouard /edwaʀ/ NM Edward ◆ **~ le Confesseur** Edward the Confessor

édredon /edʀədɔ̃/ NM eiderdown

éducable /edykabl/ ADJ educable, teachable

éducateur, -trice /edykatœʀ, tʀis/ ADJ educational NM,F *(gén)* teacher; *(en prison)* tutor, instructor; *(= théoricien)* educationalist ◆ **~ spécialisé** *(gén)* teacher of children with special needs; *[de maison de jeunes]* youth worker ◆ **~ sportif** sports teacher

éducatif, -ive /edykatif, iv/ ADJ *[rôle, valeur, processus]* educational, educative; *[chaîne, programme, jeu]* educational ◆ **système ~** education system ◆ **équipe éducative** *(Scol)* teaching staff; *[de services sociaux]* (social services) support team

éducation /edykasjɔ̃/ NF 1 *(= enseignement)* education ◆ **les problèmes de l'~** educational problems ◆ **j'ai fait mon ~ à Paris** I was educated *ou* I went to school in Paris ◆ **j'ai fait**

mon ~ musicale à Paris I studied music in Paris ◆ **il a reçu une bonne** ~ he had a good education ◆ **il a reçu une ~ religieuse** he had a religious upbringing ◆ **toute une ~ à refaire !** *(hum)* you've got a few things to learn! ◆ **~ manuelle et technique** technical education *(Brit)*, industrial arts *(US)* ◆ **l'Éducation nationale** *(= système)* state education; *(= ministère)* the Ministry *(Brit)* *ou* Department *(US)* of Education ◆ **~ religieuse** religious education ◆ **~ civique** civic education, civics *(sg)* ◆ **~ permanente** continuing education ◆ **~ physique et sportive** physical training *ou* education, PE ◆ **~ sexuelle** sex education ◆ **le roman raconte l'~ sentimentale d'un jeune homme** the novel recounts a young man's first experience of love; → **maison, ministère** *etc*

[2] *(= discipline familiale)* upbringing

[3] *(= bonnes manières)* **avoir de l'~** to be well brought up ◆ **manquer d'~** to be badly brought up, to be ill-mannered ◆ **sans ~** ill-mannered

[4] *[de goût, volonté]* training

ÉDUCATION NATIONALE

The French state education system is the responsibility of the « Ministre de l'Éducation nationale ». Schools administration at local level is the responsibility of the « recteur d'académie ».

State education in France is divided into four levels: « maternelle » (for children 2-6 years old), « primaire » (including « école élémentaire » and « école primaire », for 7 to 11-year-olds), « secondaire » (including collège and « lycée », for 12 to 18-year-olds) and « supérieur » (universities and other higher education establishments).

State education as a whole is designed to follow key republican principles, the concept of « laïcité » (secular education) being of particular significance. Private education (mainly in Catholic schools) is structured in a similar way to the state system.

→ **ACADÉMIE, COLLÈGE, CONCOURS, DIPLÔMES, LYCÉE**

édulcorant, e /edylkɔʀɑ̃, ɑ̃t/ ADJ sweetening NM sweetener ◆ **sans ~** unsweetened

édulcorer /edylkɔʀe/ ▸ conjug 1 ◂ VT [1] *(= expurger)* *[+ doctrine, propos]* to water down; *[+ texte osé]* to tone down ◆ **ils ont adopté une version édulcorée des thèses de l'extrême droite** they have adopted a toned-down version of the ideas of the far right ◆ **il a beaucoup édulcoré les passages violents du livre** he has really toned down the violent parts of the book [2] *(Pharm)* to sweeten

éduquer /edyke/ ▸ conjug 1 ◂ VT *[+ enfant]* *(à l'école)* to educate; *(à la maison)* to bring up, to raise; *[+ peuple]* to educate; *[+ goût, volonté, œil, oreille]* to train ◆ **bien éduqué** well-mannered, well-bred, well brought up ◆ **mal éduqué** ill-mannered, ill-bred, badly brought up

EEE /əəə/ NM (abrév de **espace économique européen**) EEA

effaçable /efasabl/ ADJ *[inscription]* erasable

effacé, e /efase/ (ptp de **effacer**) ADJ [1] *[couleur]* *(= qui a passé)* faded; *(= sans éclat)* subdued [2] *[personne, manières]* unassuming, self-effacing; *[vie]* retiring; *[rôle]* unobtrusive [3] *[menton]* receding; *[poitrine]* flat ◆ **en position ~e** *(Escrime)* sideways (on)

effacement /efasmɑ̃/ NM [1] *[d'inscription, faute, souvenir]* obliteration, effacing; *[de bande magnétique]* erasing; *[de craintes]* dispelling; *(Ling)* deletion ◆ **~ du corps/des épaules** *(Escrime)* drawing o.s./one's shoulders in ◆ **l'~ progressif des frontières** the gradual elimination of borders [2] *[de personne]* *(par modestie)* unassuming *ou* self-effacing manner ◆ **son ~ progressif au profit du jeune sous-directeur** the way in which he was gradually being eclipsed by the young deputy director

effacer /efase/ ▸ conjug 3 ◂ VT [1] *(= enlever)* *[+ inscription, traces]* to erase, to obliterate, to efface; *[+ bande magnétique, fichier]* to erase; *[+ tableau noir]* to clean, to wipe; *(à la gomme)* to erase, to rub out *(Brit)*; *(à l'éponge)* to wipe off, to sponge off; *(en lavant)* to wash off *ou* out; *(au chiffon)* to wipe off, to rub out; *(Ling)* to delete ◆ **cette gomme efface bien** this is a good rubber *(Brit)* *ou* eraser *(US)*, this rubber *(Brit)* *ou* eraser *(US)* works well ◆ **prends un chiffon pour** ~ use a cloth to rub it out *ou* wipe it off ◆ **un chemin à demi effacé** a barely distinguishable track

[2] *[+ mauvaise impression, souvenir]* to erase, to efface; *[+ faute]* to erase, to obliterate; *[+ craintes]* to dispel ◆ **pour ~ vos rides** to smooth out your wrinkles ◆ **on efface tout et on recommence** *(on oublie le passé)* we'll let bygones be bygones, we'll wipe the slate clean; *(on reprend à zéro)* let's go back to square one, let's make a fresh start ◆ **tenter d'~ son passé** to try to blot out one's past ◆ **le temps efface tout** everything fades in *ou* with time ◆ **ce moyen de communication efface les frontières** this means of communication cuts across borders

[3] *(= éclipser)* to outshine, to eclipse

[4] *(Sport)* *[+ adversaire]* to smash

[5] **~ le corps** *(Escrime)* to stand sideways on; *(gén)* to draw o.s. in ◆ **effacez les épaules !** shoulders back! ◆ **effacez le ventre !** stomach in!

VPR **s'effacer** [1] *[inscription]* to wear away; *[couleurs]* to fade; *[sourire]* to fade, to die ◆ **le crayon s'efface mieux que l'encre** it is easier to erase *ou* rub out *(Brit)* pencil than ink, pencil erases *ou* rubs out *(Brit)* more easily than ink ◆ **les frontières s'effacent** borders are coming down *ou* disappearing

[2] *[crainte, impression, souvenir]* to fade, to diminish ◆ **tout s'efface avec le temps** everything fades in *ou* with time ◆ **un mauvais souvenir qui s'efface difficilement** an unpleasant memory that is hard to forget *ou* that is slow to fade

[3] *(= s'écarter)* to move aside, to step back *ou* aside; *(= se faire discret)* to keep in the background; *(= se retirer)* to withdraw ◆ **l'auteur s'efface derrière ses personnages** the author hides behind his characters ◆ **elle s'efface le plus possible** she keeps (herself) in the background as much as possible ◆ **s'~ devant** *ou* **au profit de qn** to step aside in favour of sb ◆ **le romantisme s'efface devant** *ou* **derrière le réalisme** romanticism is giving way to realism

effaceur /efasœʀ/ NM ◆ **~ d'encre** (ink) eraser pen

effarant, e /efaʀɑ̃, ɑ̃t/ ADJ *[prix]* outrageous; *[vitesse]* alarming, breathtaking; *[bêtise]* astounding, incredible

effaré, e /efaʀe/ (ptp de **effarer**) ADJ alarmed *(attrib)* *(de* by, at) aghast *(attrib)* *(de* at); ◆ **son regard ~** his wild eyes, his look of alarm

effarement /efaʀmɑ̃/ NM alarm, trepidation

effarer /efaʀe/ ▸ conjug 1 ◂ VT *(= alarmer)* to alarm ◆ **cette bêtise/hausse des prix m'effare** *(= stupéfier)* I find such stupidity/this rise in prices most alarming

effaroucher /efaʀuʃe/ ▸ conjug 1 ◂ VT *(= alarmer)* *[+ animal]* to frighten away *ou* off, to scare away *ou* off; *[+ personne timide]* to frighten, to scare; *(= choquer)* to shock, to upset VPR **s'effaroucher** *(par timidité)* *[animal, personne]* to shy *(de* at) to take fright *(de* at); *(par pudeur)* to be shocked *ou* upset *(de* by)

effectif, -ive /efɛktif, iv/ ADJ *[aide]* real *(épith)*, positive *(épith)*; *[travail]* actual *(épith)*, real *(épith)*; *(Fin)* *[capital]* real *(épith)* ◆ **le couvre-feu sera ~ à partir de 22 heures** the curfew will take effect *ou* become effective as from 10pm

NM *[d'armée]* strength *(NonC)*; *[de classe]* size, (total) number of pupils; *[de parti]* size; *[d'entreprise]* staff, workforce ◆ **~s** *(Mil)* numbers, strength ◆ **l'école n'a jamais atteint son ~ ou l'~ prévu** the school has never reached its full complement ◆ **l'~ de la classe a triplé en deux ans** the (total) number of pupils in the class has *ou* the (size of the) class has trebled in two years ◆ **l'~ est au complet** *(Mil)* we are at full strength *ou* up to strength ◆ **augmenter ses ~s** *[parti, lycée]* to increase its numbers; *[entreprise]* to increase its workforce ◆ **l'usine a un ~ de 70 personnes** the factory has 70 people on the payroll *ou* has a workforce of 70 ◆ **maintenir le niveau des ~s** to keep up manning levels

effectivement /efɛktivmɑ̃/ ADV [1] *(= réellement)* actually, really ◆ **cet incident s'est ~ produit** the incident really did happen *ou* actually happened ◆ **heures ~ travaillées** hours actually worked [2] *(= en effet)* actually, in fact; *(dans une réponse = oui)* quite, indeed ◆ **c'est ~ plus rapide** it's true that it's faster ◆ **n'y a-t-il pas risque de conflit ? – ~ !** isn't there a risk of conflict? – there is indeed! ◆ **~, quand ce phénomène se produit ...** indeed *ou* in fact, when this phenomenon occurs ...

⚠ **effectivement** ne se traduit pas par **effectively**, qui veut dire 'efficacement'.

effectivité /efɛktivite/ NF *(frm)* *[d'action, démarche, aide, travail]* effectiveness, efficacy

effectuer /efɛktɥe/ ▸ conjug 1 ◂ VT *[+ manœuvre, opération, mission, réparation]* to carry out; *[+ expérience]* to carry out, to perform; *[+ mouvement, geste]* to make; *[+ paiement]* to make, to effect; *[+ trajet]* to make, to complete; *[+ reprise économique]* to undergo, to stage ◆ **le franc/le coureur a effectué une remontée spectaculaire** the franc/the runner made *ou* staged a spectacular recovery VPR **s'effectuer** ◆ **le trajet s'effectue en 2 heures** the journey takes 2 hours (to complete) ◆ **le paiement peut s'~ de deux façons** payment may be made in two ways ◆ **le rapatriement des prisonniers s'est effectué sans incident** the repatriation of the prisoners went off without a hitch ◆ **la rentrée scolaire s'est effectuée dans de bonnes conditions** the new school year got off to a good start

efféminé, e /efemine/ ADJ effeminate

efféminer /efemine/ ▸ conjug 1 ◂ VT *[+ personne]* to make effeminate; *[+ peuple, pensée]* to emasculate ◆ **s'~** to become effeminate

effervescence /efɛʀvesɑ̃s/ NF *(lit)* effervescence; *(fig)* agitation ◆ **mettre la ville en ~** to plunge the town into a turmoil ◆ **être en ~** to be bubbling with excitement ◆ **l'~ révolutionnaire** the stirrings of revolution

effervescent, e /efɛʀvesɑ̃, ɑ̃t/ ADJ *(lit)* effervescent; *(fig)* agitated, in turmoil *(attrib)*

effet /efɛ/

1 NOM MASCULIN	3 LOCUTION ADVERBIALE
2 NOM MASCULIN PLURIEL	4 COMPOSÉS

1 - NOM MASCULIN

[1] [= résultat] *[d'action, médicament]* effect ◆ **~ pervers** pernicious effect ◆ **c'est un ~ de son inexpérience** it is because of *ou* a result of his inexperience ◆ **c'est l'~ du hasard** it's pure chance, it is the result of chance ◆ **avoir** *ou* **produire beaucoup d'~/l'~ voulu** to have *ou* produce a considerable effect/the desired ef-

fect ◆ **ces livres ont un ~ nocif sur la jeunesse** these books have a harmful effect on young people ◆ **créer un ~ de surprise** to create a surprise ◆ **il espérait créer un ~ de surprise** he was hoping to surprise them (*ou* us *etc*) ◆ **avoir pour ~ de faire qch** to have the effect of doing sth ◆ **avoir pour ~ une augmentation/diminution de** to result in an increase/a decrease in ◆ **faire** ~ *[médicament]* to take effect ◆ **le médicament (me) fait de l'~/a fait son ~** the medicine works (on me)/has worked ◆ **la bière me fait beaucoup d'~** beer goes straight to my head ◆ **la bière ne me fait aucun ~** beer has no effect on me ◆ **être** *ou* **rester sans ~** to be ineffective, to have no effect ◆ **ces mesures sont demeurées sans ~** these measures had no effect *ou* were ineffective; → **relation**

2 = impression impression ◆ **faire** *ou* **produire un ~ considérable/déplorable (sur qn)** to make a great/dreadful impression (on sb) ◆ **il a fait** *ou* **produit son petit ~** he managed to cause a bit of a stir *ou* a minor sensation ◆ **il aime faire de l'~** he likes to create a stir ◆ **c'est tout l'~ que ça te fait ?** is that all it means to you?, is that all you feel about it? ◆ **quel ~ ça te fait d'être revenu ?** what does it feel like *ou* how does it feel to be back? ◆ **ça m'a fait un drôle d'~ de le revoir après si longtemps** I found it strange seeing him again after so long ◆ **cela m'a fait de l'~ de le voir dans cet état** it really affected me *ou* it gave me quite a turn to see him in that state ◆ **faire bon/mauvais ~ sur qn** to make a good/bad impression on sb ◆ **il m'a fait bon ~** he made a good impression on me, I was favourably impressed by him ◆ **ce tableau fait bon ~/beaucoup d'~ ici** this picture is quite/very effective here ◆ **il me fait l'~ d'(être) une belle crapule** he strikes me as being a real crook, he seems like a real crook to me; → **bœuf**

3 = artifice, procédé effect ◆ **~ de contraste/de style/comique** contrasting/stylistic/comic effect ◆ **~ d'optique** visual effect ◆ **~s de lumière** *(au théâtre)* lighting effects; *(naturels, sur l'eau)* play of light *(NonC)* ◆ **~s spéciaux** *(Ciné)* special effects ◆ **rechercher les ~s** *ou* **l'~** to strive for effect ◆ **soigner ses ~s** to take great trouble over one's effects ◆ **elle lui a coupé ses ~s** she stole his thunder ◆ **manquer** *ou* **rater son ~** *[personne]* to spoil one's effect; *[plaisanterie]* to fall flat, to misfire ◆ **faire des ~s de voix** to use one's voice to dramatic effect, to make dramatic use of one's voice ◆ **il fait des ~s de manches** *[avocat]* he waves his arms about in a most dramatic fashion

4 Phys, Tech effect ◆ **machine à simple/double ~** single-/double-effect machine; → **boomerang, larsen, placebo, secondaire**

5 Sport spin ◆ **donner de l'~ à une balle** to put spin on a ball ◆ **tu as mis trop d'~** you've put too much spin on the ball

6 Admin, Jur **augmentation de salaire avec ~ rétroactif au 1er janvier** payrise backdated to 1 January, retrospective payrise from 1 January ◆ **prendre ~ à la date de** to take effect from, to be operative from ◆ **à l'~ de** in order to

7 Comm = valeur **~ bancaire, ~ de commerce** bill of exchange ◆ **~ à vue** sight bill, demand note ◆ **~ au porteur** bill payable to bearer ◆ **~s à payer** notes payable ◆ **~s à recevoir** bills receivable ◆ **~s publics** government securities

8 locution **mettre à ~** to put into operation *ou* effect

◆ **à cet effet** ◆ **utilisez la boîte prévue à cet ~** use the box provided ◆ **un bâtiment construit à cet ~** a building designed for that purpose

◆ **sous l'effet de** *[+ alcool]* under the effect(s) *ou* influence of; *[+ drogue]* under the effect(s) of ◆ **sous l'~ de la colère il me frappa** in his anger he hit me

2 - NOM MASCULIN PLURIEL

effets (= *affaires, vêtements*) things, clothes ◆ **~s personnels** personal effects

3 - LOCUTION ADVERBIALE

en effet

1 introduit une explication because ◆ **cette voiture me plaît beaucoup, en ~, elle est rapide et confortable** I like this car very much because it's fast and comfortable

2 = effectivement **cela me plaît beaucoup, en ~** yes (indeed), I like it very much ◆ **c'est en ~ plus rapide** it's true that it's faster

3 dans une réponse **étiez-vous absent mardi dernier ? – en ~, j'avais la grippe** were you absent last Tuesday? – yes (I was) *ou* that's right, I had flu ◆ **tu ne travaillais pas ? – en ~** you weren't working? – no, I wasn't as it happens

4 - COMPOSÉS

effet d'annonce ◆ **c'est un ~ d'annonce** it's hype ◆ **créer un ~ d'annonce** to create hype
effet papillon butterfly effect
effet retard *[de médicament]* delayed action
effet de serre greenhouse effect
effet de souffle blast ◆ **bombe à ~ de souffle** blast bomb
effet tunnel tunnel effect; → **domino, gaz, levier**

effeuillage /efœjaʒ/ NM *(Agr)* thinning-out of leaves; *(hum)* striptease

effeuiller /efœje/ ▸ conjug 1 ◂ VT *[+ arbre, branche] [arboriculteur]* to thin out the leaves of; *[vent]* to blow the leaves off ◆ **~ une branche/une fleur** *(par jeu)* to pull *ou* pick the leaves off a branch/the petals off a flower ◆ **~ la marguerite** to play "she-loves-me, she-loves-me-not" VPR **s'effeuiller** *[arbre]* to shed *ou* lose its leaves

effeuilleuse /efœjøz/ NF *(hum = strip-teaseuse)* stripper

efficace /efikas/ ADJ *[remède, mesure]* effective; *[personne, machine]* efficient; → **grâce**

efficacement /efikasmɑ̃/ ADV efficiently, effectively

efficacité /efikasite/ NF *[de remède, mesure]* effectiveness; *[de personne, machine]* efficiency

efficience /efisjɑ̃s/ NF efficiency

efficient, e /efisjɑ̃, jɑt/ ADJ efficient

effigie /efiʒi/ NF effigy ◆ **à l'~ de** depicting ◆ **des autocollants à l'~ de Céline Dion** Céline Dion stickers ◆ **à l'~ du logo de l'entreprise** bearing the company logo ◆ **en ~** in effigy

effilé, e /efile/ ADJ *[doigt, silhouette]* slender; *[pointe, outil]* highly-sharpened; *[carrosserie]* streamlined; *[tissu]* frayed ◆ **amandes ~es** flaked almonds ◆ **poulet ~** oven-ready chicken NM *[de jupe, serviette]* fringe

effiler /efile/ ▸ conjug 1 ◂ VT 1 *[+ objet]* to taper; *[+ lignes, forme]* to streamline 2 *[+ étoffe]* to fray; *[+ cheveux]* to thin (out) VPR **s'effiler** *[objet]* to taper; *[étoffe]* to fray

effilochage /efilɔʃaʒ/ NM fraying

effilocher /efilɔʃe/ ▸ conjug 1 ◂ VT *[+ tissu]* to fray VPR **s'effilocher** to fray ◆ **veste effilochée** frayed jacket

efflanqué, e /eflɑ̃ke/ ADJ raw-boned ◆ **c'était un cheval ~** the horse was just skin and bones

effleurement /eflœʀmɑ̃/ NM (= *frôlement*) light touch; *(Ordin)* touch ◆ **elle sentit sur son bras l'~ d'une main** she felt the light touch of a hand on her arm, she felt a hand brush against her arm ◆ **massage par ~** effleurage ◆ **écran/touche à ~** touch-sensitive screen/key

effleurer /eflœʀe/ ▸ conjug 1 ◂ VT 1 (= *frôler*) to touch lightly, to brush (against); (= *érafler*) to graze; *[+ sujet]* to touch (lightly) on *ou* upon, to skim over; *(Ordin)* to touch ◆ **les oiseaux effleuraient l'eau** the birds skimmed (across) the water ◆ **une idée lui effleura l'esprit** an idea crossed his mind ◆ **ça ne m'a pas effleuré** it didn't cross my mind, it didn't occur to me ◆ **ayant oublié le désir qui l'avait effleuré** having forgotten his fleeting desire 2 *[+ cuir]* to buff

efflorescence /eflɔʀesɑ̃s/ NF *(Bot, Chim)* efflorescence

effluent, e /eflyɑ̃, ɑt/ ADJ effluent NM *(Géog)* effluent ◆ **~ urbain** urban effluent ◆ **~s radioactifs** radioactive effluent *(NonC)* *ou* discharges

effluves /eflyv/ NMPL *(littér)* *(agréables)* fragrance; *(désagréables)* smell, effluvia *(frm)*

effondré, e /efɔ̃dʀe/ (ptp de **s'effondrer**) ADJ *(gén = abattu)* shattered, crushed *(de* by); ◆ **~ de douleur** prostrate with grief ◆ **les parents ~s** the grief-stricken parents

effondrement /efɔ̃dʀəmɑ̃/ NM 1 *[de mur, édifice]* collapse ◆ **ça a provoqué l'~ du plancher** it caused the floor to cave in *ou* collapse 2 *[d'empire, entreprise]* collapse, fall; *[de prix, marché]* collapse 3 (= *abattement*) utter dejection

effondrer /efɔ̃dʀe/ ▸ conjug 1 ◂ VT *(Rugby)* *[+ mêlée]* to collapse VPR **s'effondrer** 1 *[toit, plancher]* to collapse, to cave in, to fall in; *[mur]* to collapse, to fall down; *[terre]* to fall away, to collapse; *[pont]* to collapse; *(Rugby)* *[mêlée]* to collapse 2 *[empire, projet]* to collapse; *[prix, marché]* to collapse, to plummet; *[argument]* to collapse, to fall to pieces; *[espoirs]* to be dashed; *[rêves]* to come to nothing 3 *[personne]* to collapse; *(fig)* *[accusé]* to break down ◆ **elle s'est effondrée en larmes** she dissolved *ou* collapsed into tears, she broke down and wept ◆ **effondré sur sa chaise** slumped on his chair

efforcer (s') /efɔʀse/ ▸ conjug 3 ◂ VPR ◆ **s'~ de faire qch** to try hard *ou* endeavour to do sth, to do one's best to do sth ◆ **il s'efforçait à une politesse dont personne n'était dupe** *(littér)* he was striving to remain polite but he convinced nobody ◆ **ils s'efforçaient en vain** *(littér)* they were striving in vain

effort /efɔʀ/ NM 1 *(physique, intellectuel)* effort ◆ **après bien des ~s** after much exertion *ou* effort ◆ **la récompense de nos ~s** the reward for our efforts ◆ **nécessiter un (gros) ~ financier** to require a (large) financial outlay ◆ **l'~ financier de la France dans le domaine de l'énergie** France's investment in the field of energy ◆ **~ de guerre** war effort ◆ **~ de volonté** effort of will ◆ **cela demande un ~ de réflexion** that requires careful thought ◆ **cela demande un ~ d'attention** you have to make an effort to concentrate ◆ **faire un ~** to make an effort ◆ **faire un ~ de mémoire** to make an effort *ou* try hard to remember ◆ **tu dois faire un ~ d'imagination** you should try to use your imagination ◆ **faire de gros ~s pour réussir** to make a great effort *ou* great efforts to succeed, to try very hard to succeed ◆ **faire un ~ sur soi-même pour rester calme** to make an effort *ou* force o.s. to stay calm ◆ **faire un ~ financier en faveur des petites entreprises** to give financial help to small businesses ◆ **tu dois faire un peu plus d'~s** you must try a bit harder ◆ **faire l'~ de** to make the effort to ◆ **faire porter son** *ou* **l'~ sur** to concentrate one's efforts on ◆ **plier sous l'~** to bend with the effort ◆ **il est resté en deçà de son ~** *(Sport)* he didn't go all out, he didn't stretch himself to his limit ◆ **encore un ~** just a little more effort ◆ **sans ~** effortlessly, easily ◆ **avec ~** with some effort; → **moindre**

[2] *(Tech)* stress, strain ◆ ~ **de torsion** torsional stress ◆ ~ **de traction** traction, pull ◆ **l'~ que subissent les fondations** the strain on the foundations

effraction /efʀaksjɔ̃/ NF *(Jur)* breaking and entering ◆ **entrer par** ~ to break in ◆ **ils sont entrés par ~ dans la maison** they broke into the house ◆ ~ **informatique** (computer) hacking; → **vol²**

effraie /efʀɛ/ NF ◆ **(chouette)** ~ barn-owl

effrangé, e /efʀɑ̃ʒe/ (ptp de **effranger**) ADJ fringed; (= *effiloché*) frayed

effranger /efʀɑ̃ʒe/ ► conjug 3 ◄ VT to fringe *(by fraying)* VPR **s'effranger** to fray ◆ **ces manches s'effrangent** these sleeves are fraying (at the edges)

effrayant, e /efʀɛjɑ̃, ɑ̃t/ ADJ (= *qui fait peur*) frightening; (= *alarmant*) alarming

effrayé, e /efʀeje/ (ptp de **effrayer**) ADJ frightened, scared ◆ **il me regarda d'un air** ~ he looked at me in alarm

effrayer /efʀeje/ ► conjug 8 ◄ VT (= *faire peur à*) to frighten, to scare VPR **s'effrayer** to be frightened *ou* scared *ou* afraid (**de** of)

effréné, e /efʀene/ ADJ *[spéculation]* rampant ◆ **la consommation ~e** rampant consumerism ◆ **ils se sont engagés dans une course ~e à la productivité** they went all out to increase productivity ◆ **la recherche ~e du profit** the reckless pursuit of profit ◆ **se livrer à une concurrence ~e** to compete savagely ◆ **à un rythme** ~ at a furious pace ◆ **les fusions se sont succédé à un rythme** ~ it was just one merger after another

effritement /efʀitmɑ̃/ NM *[de roche]* crumbling; *[de valeurs morales, majorité]* crumbling; *[de monnaie]* erosion; *[de fortune, valeurs boursières]* dwindling; *[de relation]* disintegration

effriter /efʀite/ ► conjug 1 ◄ VT *[+ biscuit, sucre]* to crumble; *[+ roche, falaise]* to cause to crumble VPR **s'effriter** *[roche]* to crumble; *[valeurs, marché]* to decline; *[majorité électorale]* to crumble; *[fortune]* to dwindle; *[consensus]* to crack; *[relation]* to disintegrate, to fall apart ◆ **son avance s'effrite** *(Sport)* he's losing his lead ◆ **la livre s'effrite face au dollar** *(Bourse)* sterling is falling against the dollar ◆ **Radio Soleil voit son audience s'~** Radio Soleil is losing listeners

effroi /efʀwa/ NM *(littér)* terror, dread ◆ **saisi d'~** terror-stricken

effronté, e /efʀɔ̃te/ ADJ *[personne, air, réponse]* insolent, impudent, cheeky *(Brit)*, sassy *(US)*; *[mensonge, menteur]* barefaced *(épith)*, shameless NM,F insolent *ou* impudent person ◆ **petit ~ !** you cheeky *(Brit)* *ou* sassy *(US)* little thing!

effrontément /efʀɔ̃temɑ̃/ ADV *[mentir]* brazenly; *[sourire]* impudently, cheekily *(Brit)*

effronterie /efʀɔ̃tʀi/ NF *[de réponse, personne]* insolence, impudence, cheek *(Brit)*; *[de mensonge]* shamelessness, effrontery

effroyable /efʀwajabl/ ADJ appalling, horrifying

effroyablement /efʀwajabləmɑ̃/ ADV appallingly, horrifyingly

effusion /efyzjɔ̃/ NF *[de tendresse]* outpouring ◆ **après ces ~s** after all this effusiveness ◆ **remercier qn avec** ~ to thank sb effusively ◆ ~ **de sang** bloodshed

égailler (s') /egaje/ ► conjug 1 ◄ VPR to scatter, to disperse

égal, e (mpl **-aux**) /egal, o/ GRAMMAIRE ACTIVE 34.5

ADJ [1] (= *de même valeur*) equal (**à** to); ◆ **de poids** ~ of equal weight ◆ **à poids** ~ weight for weight ◆ **à nombre/prix** ~ for the same number/price ◆ **égaux en nombre** equal in numbers ◆ **à ~e distance de deux points** equidistant *ou* exactly halfway between two points ◆ **Orléans est à ~e distance de Tours et de Paris** Orléans is equidistant from Tours and Paris *ou* is the same distance from Tours as from Paris ◆ **Tours et Paris sont à ~e distance d'Orléans** Tours and Paris are the same distance from *ou* are equidistant from Orléans ◆ **d'adresse/d'audace ~e** of equal skill/boldness, equally skilful/bold ◆ **toutes choses ~es par ailleurs** all *ou* other things being equal; → **signe**

[2] (= *sans variation*) *[justice]* even, unvarying; *[climat]* equable, unchanging; *[terrain]* even, level; *[bruit, rumeur, vent]* steady ◆ **de caractère** ~ even-tempered ◆ **marcher d'un pas** ~ to walk with a regular *ou* an even step

[3] *(locutions)* **ça m'est** ~ (= *je n'y attache pas d'importance*) I don't mind, it's all one *ou* the same to me; (= *je m'en fiche*) I don't care ◆ **pense ce que tu veux, ça m'est bien** ~ you can think what you like, I really don't care ◆ **tout lui est** ~ he doesn't feel strongly about anything ◆ **c'est ~, il aurait pu m'écrire** all the same *ou* be that as it may, he might have written ◆ **sa probité n'a d'~e que sa générosité** his integrity is matched *ou* equalled only by his generosity ◆ **rester ~ à soi-même** to remain true to form; → **arme, jeu**

NM,F [1] (= *personne*) equal ◆ **il ne fréquente que ses égaux** he only associates with his equals

[2] *(locutions)* **il a traité d'~ à ~ avec moi** he treated me as his *ou* an equal ◆ **nous parlions d'~ à ~** we talked to each other as equals ◆ **sa probité est à l'~ de sa générosité** his generosity is equalled *ou* matched by his integrity ◆ **c'est une vraie mégère à l'~ de sa mère** she's a real shrew just like her mother ◆ **sans** ~ *[beauté, courage]* matchless, unequalled, peerless

égalable /egalabl/ ADJ ◆ **difficilement** ~ difficult to equal *ou* match

également /egalmɑ̃/ ADV [1] (= *aussi*) also, too, as well ◆ **elle lui a ~ parlé** *(elle aussi)* she also *ou* too spoke to him; *(à lui aussi)* she spoke to him as well *ou* too [2] (= *sans aspérités*) evenly; (= *sans préférence*) equally

égaler /egale/ ► conjug 1 ◄ VT [1] *[+ personne, record]* to equal (**en** in); ◆ **2 plus 2 égalent 4** *(Math)* 2 plus 2 equals 4 ◆ **personne ne l'a encore égalé en adresse** so far there has been no one to equal *ou* match his skill, so far no one has matched him for skill ◆ **son intégrité égale sa générosité** his generosity is matched *ou* equalled by his integrity, his integrity matches *ou* equals his generosity [2] (= *comparer*) ~ **qn à** to rank sb with ◆ **c'est un bon compositeur mais je ne l'égalerais pas à Ravel** he's a good composer but I wouldn't rank him with *ou* put him beside Ravel [3] († = *rendre égal*) **la mort égale tous les êtres** death is the great leveller VPR **s'égaler** ◆ **s'~ à** (= *se montrer l'égal de*) to equal, to be equal to; (= *se comparer à*) to liken o.s. to, to compare o.s. to

égalisateur, -trice /egalizatœʀ, tʀis/ ADJ equalizing *(Brit)*, tying *(US)* ◆ **le but** ~ *(Sport)* the equalizer *(Brit)*, the tying goal *(US)* ◆ **le jeu** ~ *(Tennis)* the game which evened (up) the score

égalisation /egalizasjɔ̃/ NF *(Sport)* equalization *(Brit)*, tying *(US)*; *[de sol, revenus]* levelling ◆ **c'est l'~** *(Sport)* they've scored the equalizer *(Brit)* *ou* the tying goal *(US)*, they've equalized *(Brit)* *ou* tied *(US)*

égaliser /egalize/ ► conjug 1 ◄ VT *[+ chances]* to equalize, to make equal; *[+ cheveux]* to straighten up; *[+ sol, revenus]* to level (out) VI *(Sport)* to equalize *(Brit)*, to tie *(US)* VPR **s'égaliser** *[chances]* to become (more) equal; *[sol]* to level (out), to become (more) level

égaliseur /egalizœʀ/ NM ◆ ~ **graphique** graphic equalizer

égalitaire /egalitɛʀ/ ADJ egalitarian

égalitarisme /egalitaʀism/ NM egalitarianism

égalitariste /egalitaʀist/ ADJ, NMF egalitarian

égalité /egalite/ GRAMMAIRE ACTIVE 32.4 NF [1] *[d'hommes]* equality; *(Math)* identity ◆ **comparatif d'~** *(Gram)* comparative of similar degree ◆ ~ **des chances** equal opportunities, equality of opportunity [2] *[de climat]* equableness, equability; *[de pouls]* regularity; *[de surface]* evenness, levelness ◆ ~ **d'humeur** evenness of temper, equableness ◆ ~ **d'âme** equanimity [3] *(Tennis)* **"égalité !"** "deuce!"

◆ **à égalité** ◆ **être à** ~ *(après un but)* to be equal; *(fin du match)* to draw *(Brit)*, to tie *(US)*; *(Tennis : à 40/40)* to be at deuce ◆ **ils sont à** ~ *(Sport)* the score is *ou* the scores are even ◆ **à ~ de qualification on prend le plus âgé** in the case of equal qualifications we take the oldest

égard /egaʀ/ NM [1] (= *respect*) **~s** consideration ◆ **il la reçut avec de grands ~s** he welcomed her with every *ou* great consideration ◆ **être plein d'~s pour qn, avoir beaucoup d'~s pour qn** to be very considerate towards sb, to show great consideration for sb ◆ **manquer d'~s envers qn** to be inconsiderate to(wards) sb, to show a lack of consideration for sb ◆ **vous n'avez aucun ~ pour votre matériel** you have no respect for your equipment

[2] *(locutions)* **avoir ~ à qch** to take sth into account *ou* consideration ◆ **par ~ pour** out of consideration for ◆ **sans ~ pour** without regard for, without consideration for ◆ **à bien des ~s, à maints ~s** in many respects ◆ **à tous (les) ~s** in all respects

◆ **eu égard à** in view of, considering

◆ **à l'égard de** ◆ **aimable à l'~ des enfants** *(envers)* friendly towards children ◆ **des mesures ont été prises à son** ~ *(contre)* measures have been taken against him ◆ **à l'~ de ce que vous me dites ...** *(en ce qui concerne)* concerning *ou* regarding *ou* with regard to what you're saying ...

égaré, e /egaʀe/ (ptp de **égarer**) ADJ [1] *[voyageur]* lost; *[animal]* stray *(épith)*, lost; → **brebis** [2] *[air, regard]* distraught, wild

égarement /egaʀmɑ̃/ NM *(littér = trouble affectif)* distraction ◆ **dans un moment d'~** in a moment of distraction NMPL **égarements** *(littér = dérèglements)* aberrations ◆ **elle est revenue de ses ~s** she's seen the error of her ways

égarer /egaʀe/ ► conjug 1 ◄ VT [1] *[+ voyageur]* to lead out of his way; *[+ enquêteurs]* to mislead; *(moralement)* *[+ jeunes, esprits]* to lead astray ◆ **la douleur vous égare** *(frm)* you are distraught *ou* distracted with grief

[2] *[+ objet]* to mislay

VPR **s'égarer** [1] *[voyageur]* to lose one's way, to get lost; *[animal]* *(gén)* to get lost; *(du troupeau)* to stray; *[colis, lettre]* to get lost, to go astray; *[discussion, auteur]* to wander from the point ◆ **ne nous égarons pas !** let's stick to the point!, let's not wander from the point! ◆ **il s'égare dans des détails** he loses himself *ou* he gets lost in details ◆ **une espèce d'original égaré dans notre siècle** an eccentric individual who seems out of place in the age we live in ◆ **s'~ du droit chemin** *(fig, Rel)* to wander *ou* stray from the straight and narrow ◆ **quelques votes d'extrême droite se sont égarés sur ce candidat socialiste** a few votes from the far right have been lost to the socialist candidate

[2] (= *perdre la raison*) to lose one's reason ◆ **mon esprit s'égare à cette pensée** the thought of it makes me feel quite distraught

égayer /egeje/ ► conjug 8 ◄ VT *[+ personne]* to cheer up; *[+ pièce]* to brighten up; *[+ conversation]* to enliven VPR **s'égayer** to have fun ◆ **s'~ aux dépens de qn** to amuse o.s. at sb's expense ◆ **s'~ à voir ...** to be highly amused *ou* entertained at seeing ...

Égée /eʒe/ ADJ ◆ **la mer** ~ the Aegean Sea ◆ **les îles de la mer** ~ the Aegean Islands

égérie /eʒeʀi/ **NF** 1 *[de poète]* muse ◆ **c'est la nouvelle ~ de Chanel** *(= mannequin)* she's Chanel's new icon ◆ **une ~ du cinéma américain** an American movie queen ◆ **elle est l'~ du président** the president looks to her for inspiration ◆ **la police a arrêté l'~ de la bande** the police have arrested the woman who was the brains behind the gang 2 ◆ **Égérie** *(Hist)* Egeria

égide /eʒid/ **sous l'égide de LOC PRÉP** under the aegis of

églantier /eglɑ̃tje/ **NM** wild *ou* dog rose *(plant)*

églantine /eglɑ̃tin/ **NF** wild *ou* dog rose *(flower)*, eglantine

églefin /egləfɛ̃/ **NM** haddock

église /egliz/ **NF** 1 *(= bâtiment)* church ◆ **aller à l'~** to go to church ◆ **il est à l'~** *(pour l'office)* he's at *ou* in church; *(en curieux)* he's in the church ◆ **se marier à l'~** to get married in church, to have a church wedding ◆ **à l'~ Ste Marie** at St Mary's (church) 2 ◆ **l'Église** *(= secte, clergé)* the Church ◆ **l'Église anglicane** the Church of England, the Anglican Church ◆ **l'Église catholique** the Church of Rome, the Roman Catholic Church ◆ **l'Église réformée** the Reformed Church ◆ **l'Église orthodoxe** the Orthodox Church ◆ **l'Église de France/Rome** The Church of France/Rome ◆ **l'Église militante/triomphante** the Church militant/triumphant; → **gens¹, homme**

églogue /eglɔg/ **NF** eclogue

ego /ego/ **NM** *(Philos, Psych)* ego ◆ **il a un ~ démesuré** he has an inflated ego

égocentrique /egosɑ̃tʀik/ **ADJ** egocentric, self-centred **NMF** egocentric *ou* self-centred person

égocentrisme /egosɑ̃tʀism/ **NM** *(gén)* egocentricity, self-centredness; *(Psych)* egocentricity

égocentriste /egosɑ̃tʀist/ **ADJ, NMF** ⇒ **égocentrique**

égoïne /egɔin/ **NF** ◆ **(scie) ~** handsaw

égoïsme /egɔism/ **NM** selfishness, egoism

égoïste /egɔist/ **ADJ** selfish, egoistic **NMF** selfish person, egoist

égoïstement /egɔistəmɑ̃/ **ADV** selfishly, egoistically

égorgement /egɔʀʒəmɑ̃/ **NM** ◆ **l'~ d'un mouton** slitting *ou* cutting a sheep's throat

égorger /egɔʀʒe/ ► conjug 3 ◄ **VT** *(lit)* to slit *ou* cut the throat of; * *[+ débiteur, client]* to bleed white

égorgeur, -euse /egɔʀʒœʀ, øz/ **NM,F** cut-throat

égosiller (s') /egozije/ ► conjug 1 ◄ **VPR** *(= crier)* to shout o.s. hoarse; *(= chanter fort)* to sing at the top of one's voice *ou* lungs (US)

égotisme /egɔtism/ **NM** egotism

égotiste /egɔtist/ *(littér)* **ADJ** egotistic(al) **NMF** egotist

égout /egu/ **NM** sewer ◆ **réseau** *ou* **système d'~s** sewerage system ◆ **eaux d'~** sewage ◆ **aller à l'~** *[d'eaux usées]* to go down the drain ◆ **~ pluvial** storm drain *ou* sewer

égoutier /egutje/ **NM** sewer worker

égoutter /egute/ ► conjug 1 ◄ **VT** *[+ légumes] (avec une passoire)* to strain; *[+ linge] (en le tordant)* to wring out; *[+ fromage]* to drain **VI** *[vaisselle]* to drain; *[linge, eau]* to drip ◆ **faire ~ l'eau** to drain off the water ◆ **mettre le linge à ~** to hang up the washing to drip ◆ **ne l'essore pas, laisse-le ~** don't wring it out, leave it to drip dry **VPR s'égoutter** *[arbre, linge, eau]* to drip; *[vaisselle]* to drain

égouttoir /egutwaʀ/ **NM** *[de vaisselle] (intégré dans l'évier)* draining *(Brit) ou* drain *(US)* board; *(mobile)* draining rack *(Brit)*, drainer *(US)*, dish rack *(US)*; *[de légumes]* strainer, colander

égratigner /egʀatiɲe/ ► conjug 1 ◄ **VT** *[+ peau]* to scratch, to graze; *[+ genou]* to graze, to scrape; *(fig) [+ adversaire]* to have a dig at ◆ **il s'est égratigné le genou** he grazed his knee ◆ **le film/l'auteur s'est fait ~ par la critique** the film/the author was given a bit of a rough ride by the critics

égratignure /egʀatiɲyʀ/ **NF** *[de peau]* scratch, graze; *[de genou]* graze, scrape ◆ **il s'en est sorti sans une ~** he came out of it without a scratch ◆ **ce n'était qu'une ~ faite à son amour-propre** it just dented his self-esteem

égrènement /egʀɛnmɑ̃/ **NM** ◆ **l'~ des heures/minutes** marking out the hours/minutes ◆ **l'~ des hameaux le long de la vallée** *(littér)* the hamlets dotted along the valley

égrener /egʀəne/ ► conjug 5 ◄ **VT** 1 *[+ pois]* to shell, to pod; *[+ blé, maïs, épi]* to shell; *[+ coton]* to gin; *[+ grappe]* to pick grapes off ◆ **~ des raisins** to pick grapes off the bunch 2 *(fig)* ◆ **~ son chapelet** to tell one's beads † *(aussi littér)*, to say the rosary ◆ **la pendule égrène les heures** the clock marks out the hours ◆ **~ la liste de ses succès** to go through a list of one's successes **VPR s'égrener** *[raisins]* to drop off the bunch; *[blé]* to drop off the stalk; *[rire]* to break out ◆ **les maisons s'égrenaient le long de la route** the houses were dotted along the road ◆ **les notes du piano s'égrenaient dans le silence** the notes of the piano fell one by one in the silence

égreneuse /egʀənøz/ **NF** *[de céréales]* cornsheller; *[de coton]* gin

égrillard, e /egʀijaʀ, aʀd/ **ADJ** *[ton, regard]* ribald; *[plaisanterie, rire, propos]* ribald, bawdy

Égypte /eʒipt/ **NF** Egypt ◆ **la basse/haute ~** Lower/Upper Egypt ◆ **la République arabe d'~** the Arab Republic of Egypt

égyptien, -ienne /eʒipsjɛ̃, jɛn/ **ADJ** Egyptian **NM,F Égyptien(ne)** Egyptian

égyptologie /eʒiptɔlɔʒi/ **NF** Egyptology

égyptologue /eʒiptɔlɔg/ **NMF** Egyptologist

eh /e/ **EXCL** hey! ◆ **~ oui !/non !** I'm afraid so!/not! ◆ **~ bien** well

éhonté, e /eɔ̃te/ **ADJ** *[action]* shameless, brazen; *[menteur, mensonge]* shameless, barefaced, brazen

eider /ɛdɛʀ/ **NM** eider

Eiffel /efɛl/ **N** ◆ **la tour ~** the Eiffel Tower

einsteinien, -ienne /ɛnstajnjɛ̃, jɛn/ **ADJ** Einsteinian

einsteinium /ɛnstenjɔm/ **NM** einsteinium

Eire /ɛʀ/ **NF** Eire

éjaculateur /eʒakylatœʀ/ **NM** ◆ **être un ~ précoce** to suffer from premature ejaculation, to be a premature ejaculator

éjaculation /eʒakylasjɔ̃/ **NF** ejaculation ◆ **~ précoce** premature ejaculation

éjaculer /eʒakyle/ ► conjug 1 ◄ **VI** to ejaculate

éjectable /eʒɛktabl/ **ADJ** → **siège¹**

éjecter /eʒɛkte/ ► conjug 1 ◄ **VT** 1 to eject ◆ **le choc l'a éjecté de la voiture** he was thrown out of the car 2 * *(= congédier)* to sack *; *(= expulser)* to kick out * ◆ **se faire ~** *(de son travail)* to get the sack *; *(d'une boîte de nuit)* to get kicked out * **VPR s'éjecter** *[pilote]* to eject

éjection /eʒɛksjɔ̃/ **NF** ejection *(*= licenciement)* sacking *

élaboration /elabɔʀasjɔ̃/ **NF** *[de plan, système]* working-out, elaboration; *[de bile, sève, aliments]* elaboration

élaboré, e /elabɔʀe/ (ptp de **élaborer**) **ADJ** *(= sophistiqué) [théorie, savoir]* elaborate; *[cuisine, coiffure, système]* elaborate, sophisticated

élaborer /elabɔʀe/ ► conjug 1 ◄ **VT** *[+ plan, système, solution]* to work out, to elaborate; *[+ document]* to draw up; *[+ bile, sève, aliments]* to elaborate

élagage /elagaʒ/ **NM** *(lit, fig)* pruning

élaguer /elage/ ► conjug 1 ◄ **VT** *(lit, fig)* to prune

élagueur, -euse /elagœʀ, øz/ **NM,F** pruner

élan¹ /elɑ̃/ **NM** *(= animal)* elk, moose

élan² /elɑ̃/ **NM** 1 *(= vitesse acquise)* momentum; *[de sauteur, joueur]* run up ◆ **prendre son ~** to take a run up ◆ **prendre de l'~** *[sauteur, joueur]* to take a run up; *[coureur]* to gather speed; *[mouvement, campagne]* to gather momentum ◆ **perdre son ~** to lose one's *(ou* its) momentum ◆ **saut avec/sans ~** running/standing jump ◆ **il a continué dans** *ou* **sur son ~** he continued to run at the same pace *ou* speed ◆ **emporté par son ~, il n'a pas pu s'arrêter à temps** he was going so fast he couldn't stop ◆ **emportée par son ~, elle a eu des paroles malheureuses** she got carried away and said some unfortunate things ◆ **rien ne peut l'arrêter dans son ~** *(= dans sa carrière, son projet)* nothing can stop him now ◆ **je vais te donner de l'~ !*** you're going to get a slap!

2 *(= accès)* **dans un ~ d'enthousiasme/de générosité/de colère** in a fit of enthusiasm/of generosity/of anger ◆ **il eut un ~ de tendresse pour elle** he felt a surge of affection for her ◆ **les ~s lyriques de l'orateur** the lyrical outbursts of the speaker ◆ **maîtriser les ~s de son cœur** to control the impulses of one's heart ◆ **'bien sûr !' dit-il avec ~** 'of course!', he exclaimed

3 *(= ardeur)* fervour *(Brit)*, fervor *(US)* ◆ **~ patriotique/révolutionnaire** patriotic/revolutionary fervour

4 *(= dynamisme)* boost ◆ **redonner de l'~** *ou* **donner un nouvel ~ à une politique/une institution/l'économie** to give new impetus to a policy/an institution/the economy ◆ **l'~ vital** the life force

élancé, e /elɑ̃se/ (ptp de **élancer**) **ADJ** *[clocher, colonne, taille, personne]* slender

élancement /elɑ̃smɑ̃/ **NM** *(Méd)* shooting *ou* sharp pain

élancer /elɑ̃se/ ► conjug 3 ◄ **VT** *(littér)* ◆ **le clocher élance sa flèche vers le ciel** the church steeple soars up *ou* thrusts upwards into the sky

VI *[blessure]* to give shooting *ou* sharp pains ◆ **mon doigt m'élance** I get shooting *ou* sharp pains in my finger

VPR s'élancer 1 *(= se précipiter)* to rush forward; *(= prendre son élan)* to take a run up ◆ **s'~ au-dehors** to rush *ou* dash outside ◆ **s'~ comme une flèche vers** to dart towards ◆ **s'~ d'un bond sur** to leap onto ◆ **s'~ au secours de qn** to rush *ou* dash to help sb ◆ **s'~ à la poursuite de qn** to rush off in pursuit of sb, to dash after sb ◆ **s'~ vers qn** to leap *ou* dash towards sb ◆ **s'~ sur qn** to hurl *ou* throw o.s. at sb, to rush at sb ◆ **s'~ à l'assaut d'une montagne/forteresse** to launch an attack on a mountain/fortress

2 *(littér = se dresser)* to soar *ou* thrust (upwards) ◆ **la tour s'élance vers le ciel** the tower soars *ou* thrusts up into the sky

élargir /elaʀʒiʀ/ ► conjug 2 ◄ **VT** 1 *(pour agrandir) [+ rue]* to widen; *[+ robe]* to let out; *[+ chaussures]* to stretch, to widen; *(= déformer) [+ vêtement, chaussures]* to stretch ◆ **ça lui élargit la taille** it makes her look bigger round the waist ◆ **une veste qui élargit les épaules** a jacket that makes the shoulders look broader *ou* wider 2 *[+ débat, connaissances]* to broaden, to widen ◆ **majorité élargie** *(Pol)* increased majority ◆ ~ **son horizon** to enlarge *ou* widen one's horizons ◆ ~ **son champ d'action** to extend one's field of operations 3 *(Jur = libérer)* to release, to free **VPR s'élargir** *[vêtement]* to stretch; *[route]* to widen, to get wider; *[esprit, débat]* to broaden; *[idées]* to broaden, to widen

élargissement /elaʀʒismɑ̃/ **NM** 1 *(= agrandissement) [de rue]* widening; *[de robe]* letting out; *[de chaussures]* stretching, widening 2 *[de débat, connaissances]* broadening, widening ◆ **elle réclame un ~ de ses pouvoirs** she wants her powers to be extended 3 *(Jur = libération)* release, freeing

élasthanne /elastan/ **NM** spandex ®, elastane ® *(Brit)*

élasticité /elastisite/ **NF** 1 *[d'objet]* elasticity; *[de démarche]* springiness; *(Écon) [d'offre, demande]* elasticity 2 *[de sens, esprit, principes]* flexibility; *(péj) [de conscience]* accommodating nature; *[de règlement]* elasticity, flexibility

élastine /elastin/ **NF** elastin

élastique /elastik/ **ADJ** 1 *[objet]* elastic; *[démarche]* springy; *(Écon) [offre, demande]* elastic ◆ **taille ~** *(Couture)* elasticated *(Brit) ou* elasticized *(US)* waist 2 *[sens, esprit, principes]* flexible; *(péj) [conscience]* accommodating; *[règlement]* elastic, flexible **NM** 1 *(de bureau)* elastic *ou* rubber band; → **lâcher** 2 *(pour couture, jeu etc)* elastic *(NonC)*; *(Sport)* bungee cord ◆ **en ~** elasticated, elastic; → **saut**

élastiqué, e /elastike/ **ADJ** *[encolure, ceinture, manche, taille]* elasticated *(Brit)*, elasticized *(US)*; *[pantalon]* with an elasticated *(Brit) ou* elasticized *(US)* waist

élastomère /elastɔmɛʀ/ **NM** elastomer ◆ **en ~** *[chaussures]* man-made

Elbe /ɛlb/ **N** ◆ **l'île d'~** (the island of) Elba ◆ **l'~** *(= fleuve)* the Elbe

Eldorado /ɛldoʀado/ **NM** El Dorado

électeur, -trice /elɛktœʀ, tʀis/ **NM,F** 1 *(Pol, gén)* voter, elector; *(dans une circonscription)* constituent ◆ **le député et ses ~s** ≈ the member of parliament and his constituents ◆ **les ~s** *(corps électoral)* the electorate, the voters ◆ **grand ~** *(en France) elector who votes in the elections for the French Senate; (aux USA)* presidential elector 2 *(Hist)* **Électeur** Elector ◆ **Électrice** Electress; → **SÉNAT**

électif, -ive /elɛktif, iv/ **ADJ** *(Pol)* elective

élection /elɛksjɔ̃/ **NF** 1 *(Pol, gén)* election ◆ **jour des ~s** polling *ou* election day ◆ **se présenter aux ~s** to stand *(Brit) ou* run *(US)* as a candidate (in the election) ◆ ~ **présidentielle** presidential election ◆ ~ **partielle** ≈ by(e)-election ◆ **~s législatives** legislative elections, ≈ general election ◆ **~s municipales/cantonales** municipal/cantonal elections ◆ **~s régionales** regional elections

2 *(littér = choix)* choice ◆ **lieu/patrie d'~** place/country of one's (own) choosing *ou* choice ◆ **la France est une patrie** *ou* **terre d'~ pour les poètes** France is a country much favoured by poets ◆ ~ **de domicile** *(Jur)* choice of residence

> **ÉLECTIONS**
>
> Presidential elections and legislative elections (for the « députés » who make up the « Assemblée nationale ») take place every five years in France. Elections for one third of the « Sénat » are held every three years, but these are collegiate and only « grands électeurs » (high-ranking officials and party representatives) vote in them.
>
> There are two kinds of local election in France, and both are held every six years. They are the « élections cantonales » in which people vote for the « Conseil régional » and « Conseil général », and the « élections municipales » for the « Conseil municipal » (or the « Conseil d'arrondissement » in Paris, Marseille and Lyon).
>
> All public elections take place on a Sunday in France, usually in school halls and « mairies ». → **CANTON, COMMUNE, DÉPARTEMENT** *etc*

électoral, e (mpl **-aux**) /elɛktɔʀal, o/ **ADJ** *[affiche, réunion]* election *(épith)* ◆ **campagne ~e** election *ou* electoral campaign ◆ **pendant la période ~e** during election time, during the run-up to the election ◆ **il m'a promis son soutien ~** he promised me his backing in the election; → **agent, circonscription, corps**

électoralisme /elɛktɔʀalism/ **NM** electioneering

électoraliste /elɛktɔʀalist/ **ADJ** electioneering

électorat /elɛktɔʀa/ **NM** 1 *(= électeurs)* electorate; *(dans une circonscription)* constituency; *(= droit de vote)* franchise ◆ **l'~ socialiste** the voters for the socialist party, the socialist vote 2 *(Hist = principauté)* electorate

Électre /elɛktʀ/ **NF** Electra

électricien, -ienne /elɛktʀisjɛ̃, jɛn/ **NM,F** electrician

électricité /elɛktʀisite/ **NF** electricity ◆ **allumer l'~** to turn the light on ◆ **ça marche à l'~** it runs on electricity, it's electrically operated ◆ **refaire l'~** to rewire the house (*ou* shop *etc*) ◆ **être sans ~** *(gén)* to have no electricity; *(suite à une panne, à une grève)* to be without power ◆ ~ **statique** static electricity ◆ **l'~ d'origine nucléaire** nuclear(-generated) electricity ◆ ~ **atmosphérique** atmospherics ◆ **il y a de l'~ dans l'air** * the atmosphere is electric; → **panne**[1]

électrification /elɛktʀifikasjɔ̃/ **NF** electrification

électrifier /elɛktʀifje/ ► conjug 7 ◄ **VT** to electrify ◆ ~ **un village** to bring electricity *ou* electric power to a village

électrique /elɛktʀik/ **ADJ** *(lit)* electric(al); *(fig)* electric ◆ **atmosphère ~** highly-charged atmosphere ◆ **bleu ~** electric blue ◆ **j'ai les cheveux ~s** * I've got static (electricity) in my hair

électriquement /elɛktʀikmɑ̃/ **ADV** electrically

électrisable /elɛktʀizabl/ **ADJ** *[foule]* easily roused; *[substance]* chargeable, electrifiable

électrisant, e /elɛktʀizɑ̃, ɑ̃t/ **ADJ** *[discours, contact]* electrifying

électrisation /elɛktʀizasjɔ̃/ **NF** *[de substance]* charging, electrifying

électriser /elɛktʀize/ ► conjug 1 ◄ **VT** *[+ substance]* to charge, to electrify; *[+ public]* to electrify

électroacoustique, électro-acoustique (pl **électro-acoustiques**) /elɛktʀoakustik/ **ADJ** electroacoustic **NF** acoustoelectronics *(sg)*, electroacoustics *(sg)*

électro-aimant (pl **électro-aimants**) /elɛktʀoɛmɑ̃/ **NM** electromagnet

électrocardiogramme /elɛktʀokaʀdjɔgʀam/ **NM** electrocardiogram ◆ **faire un ~ à qn** to give sb an electrocardiogram *ou* an ECG

électrocardiographe /elɛktʀokaʀdjɔgʀaf/ **NM** electrocardiograph

électrocardiographie /elɛktʀokaʀdjɔgʀafi/ **NF** electrocardiography

électrochimie /elɛktʀoʃimi/ **NF** electrochemistry

électrochimique /elɛktʀoʃimik/ **ADJ** electrochemical

électrochoc /elɛktʀoʃɔk/ **NM** *(= procédé)* electric shock treatment, electroconvulsive therapy *(SPÉC)* ◆ **on lui a fait des ~s** he was given electric shock treatment *ou* ECT ◆ **sa proposition a provoqué un ~** his proposal sent shock waves through the country

électrocuter /elɛktʀokyte/ ► conjug 1 ◄ **VT** to electrocute **VPR s'électrocuter** to electrocute o.s.

électrocution /elɛktʀokysjɔ̃/ **NF** electrocution

électrode /elɛktʀɔd/ **NF** electrode

électrodynamique /elɛktʀodinamik/ **ADJ** electrodynamic **NF** electrodynamics *(sg)*

électro-encéphalogramme (pl **électro-encéphalogrammes**) /elɛktʀoɑ̃sefalɔgʀam/ **NM** electroencephalogram

électro-encéphalographie (pl **électro-encéphalographies**) /elɛktʀoɑ̃sefalɔgʀafi/ **NF** electroencephalography

électrogène /elɛktʀoʒɛn/ **ADJ** *[animal, organe]* electrogenic; → **groupe**

électrolyse /elɛktʀoliz/ **NF** electrolysis

électrolyser /elɛktʀolize/ ► conjug 1 ◄ **VT** to electrolyse

électrolyseur /elɛktʀolizœʀ/ **NM** electrolyser

électrolyte /elɛktʀolit/ **NM** electrolyte

électrolytique /elɛktʀolitik/ **ADJ** electrolytic(al)

électromagnétique /elɛktʀomaɲetik/ **ADJ** electromagnetic

électromagnétisme /elɛktʀomaɲetism/ **NM** electromagnetism

électromécanicien, -ienne /elɛktʀomekanisjɛ̃, jɛn/ **NM,F** electromechanical engineer

électromécanique /elɛktʀomekanik/ **ADJ** electromechanical **NF** electromechanical engineering

électroménager /elɛktʀomenaʒe/ **ADJ** ◆ **appareil ~** (household *ou* domestic) electrical appliance **NM** ◆ **l'~** *(= appareils)* (household *ou* domestic) electrical appliances; *(= industrie)* the electrical goods industry ◆ **le petit/gros ~** small/large electrical appliances ◆ **magasin d'~** electrical goods shop *(Brit) ou* store *(US)*

électrométallurgie /elɛktʀometalyʀʒi/ **NF** electrometallurgy

électrométallurgique /elɛktʀometalyʀʒik/ **ADJ** electrometallurgical

électromètre /elɛktʀomɛtʀ/ **NM** electrometer

électromoteur, -trice /elɛktʀomotœʀ, tʀis/ **ADJ** electromotive **NM** electric motor, electromotor

électron /elɛktʀɔ̃/ **NM** electron

électronégatif, -ive /elɛktʀonegatif, iv/ **ADJ** electronegative

électronicien, -ienne /elɛktʀonisjɛ̃, jɛn/ **NM,F** electronics engineer

électronique /elɛktʀɔnik/ **ADJ** *(gén)* electronic; *[microscope]* electron *(épith)* ◆ **groupe/industrie ~** electronics group/industry; → **adresse**[1], **autoroute, courrier, dictionnaire** **NF** electronics *(sg)*

électronucléaire /elɛktʀɔnykleɛʀ/ ADJ nuclear power (*épith*) NM ◆ **l'~** nuclear power

électrophone /elɛktʀɔfɔn/ NM record player

électropositif, -ive /elɛktʀopozitif, iv/ ADJ electropositive

électrostatique /elɛktʀostatik/ ADJ electrostatic NF electrostatics (*sg*)

électrotechnicien, -ienne /elɛktʀotɛknisjɛ̃, jɛn/ NM,F electrotechnician

électrotechnique /elɛktʀotɛknik/ ADJ electrotechnical ◆ **institut ~** institute of electrical engineering *ou* of electrotechnology NF (*= science*) electrical engineering, electrotechnology, electrotechnics (*sg*); (*= secteur*) electrical engineering

électrothérapie /elɛktʀoteʀapi/ NF electrotherapy

élégamment /elegamɑ̃/ ADV elegantly

élégance /elegɑ̃s/ NF 1 [*de personne, toilette*] elegance, stylishness ◆ **l'~ féminine** feminine elegance 2 [*de conduite*] generosity; [*de solution*] elegance, neatness ◆ **~s (de style)** ornaments (of style) ◆ **perdre avec ~** to be a good loser ◆ **concours d'~** *parade of elegant women in beautiful cars* ◆ **il aurait pu avoir l'~ de s'excuser** he might have had the good grace to apologize

élégant, e /elegɑ̃, ɑ̃t/ ADJ 1 [*personne, toilette*] elegant, stylish ◆ **tu es très ~ habillé comme ça** you're looking very elegant 2 [*conduite*] generous; [*solution*] elegant, neat ◆ **user de procédés peu ~s** to use crude methods ◆ **c'était une façon ~e de le remettre à sa place** it was a neat way of putting him in his place NM († *= dandy*) elegant *ou* stylish man, man of fashion NF **élégante** † elegant *ou* stylish woman, woman of fashion

élégiaque /eleʒjak/ ADJ elegiac

élégie /eleʒi/ NF elegy

élément /elemɑ̃/ NM 1 [*de structure, ensemble*] element, component; [*de problème*] element; [*de mélange*] ingredient, element; [*de réussite*] factor, element; [*d'appareil*] part, component ◆ **~ comique (d'un roman)** comic element (of a novel)

2 (*= meuble*) unit ◆ **~s de rangement** storage units ◆ **~s de cuisine/de bibliothèque** kitchen/bookshelf units

3 (*Mil*) **~s blindés/aéroportés** armoured/airborne units

4 (*Chim*) element ◆ **l'~ hydrogène** the element hydrogen

5 [*de pile, batterie*] cell

6 (*= fait*) fact ◆ **nous manquons d'~s** we lack information *ou* facts ◆ **aucun ~ nouveau n'est survenu** there have been no new developments, no new facts have come to light ◆ **~s de tir** (*Mil*) range data

7 (*Comptabilité, Fin*) item ◆ **après/hors ~s exceptionnels** after/before extraordinary items

8 (*= individu*) **c'est le meilleur ~ de ma classe** he's the best pupil in my class ◆ **bons et mauvais ~s** good and bad elements ◆ **~s subversifs/ennemis** subversive/hostile elements

9 (*= milieu*) element ◆ **les quatre ~s** the four elements ◆ **les ~s (naturels)** the elements ◆ **l'~ liquide** the liquid element ◆ **quand on parle d'électronique il est dans son ~** * when you talk about electronics he's in his element ◆ **parmi ces artistes il ne se sentait pas dans son ~** he didn't feel at home *ou* he felt like a fish out of water among those artists

NMPL **éléments** (*= rudiments*) basic principles, rudiments, elements ◆ **il a quelques ~s de chimie** he has some elementary knowledge of chemistry ◆ **"Éléments de Mécanique"** (*titre d'ouvrage*) "Elementary Mechanics"

élémentaire /elemɑ̃tɛʀ/ ADJ 1 (*= facile*) [*problème*] elementary; (*= de base*) [*notion*] elementary, basic; [*forme*] rudimentary, basic; (*Scol*) [*cours, niveau*] elementary; (*= évident*) [*précaution*] elementary, basic ◆ **c'est ~ !** it's elementary! ◆ **~, mon cher Watson !** elementary, my dear Watson! ◆ **cela relève de la plus ~ courtoisie** it's only good manners 2 (*Chim*) elemental ◆ **particules ~s** elementary *ou* fundamental particles

Éléonore /eleɔnɔʀ/ NF Eleanor

éléphant /elefɑ̃/ NM elephant ◆ **~ femelle** cow elephant ◆ **~ d'Asie/d'Afrique** Indian/African elephant ◆ **~ de mer** sea elephant, elephant seal ◆ **comme un ~ dans un magasin de porcelaine** like a bull in a china shop ◆ **les ~s du parti** (*fig*) the party old guard

éléphanteau (pl **éléphanteaux**) /elefɑ̃to/ NM elephant calf, baby elephant

éléphantesque /elefɑ̃tɛsk/ ADJ (*= énorme*) elephantine, gigantic

éléphantiasis /elefɑ̃tjazis/ NM elephantiasis

élevage /el(ə)vaʒ/ NM 1 [*de bétail*] rearing, breeding; [*de chiens, porcs, chevaux, vers à soie*] breeding; [*de volailles*] farming ◆ **l'~ (du bétail)** cattle breeding *ou* rearing ◆ **l'~ des abeilles** beekeeping ◆ **~ intensif de porcs/poulets** intensive farming of pigs/chickens ◆ **faire de l'~** to breed *ou* rear cattle ◆ **faire l'~ de** [*+ bétail*] to rear, to breed; [*+ chiens, porcs, chevaux, vers à soie*] to breed; [*+ abeilles*] to keep ◆ **région ou pays d'~** cattle-rearing *ou* -breeding area ◆ **truite/saumon d'~** farmed trout/salmon 2 (*= ferme*) [*de bétail*] cattle farm ◆ **~ de poulets/de truites** poultry/trout farm ◆ **~ de chiens** breeding kennels

élévateur, -trice /elevatœʀ, tʀis/ ADJ, NM,F ◆ **(muscle) ~** elevator ◆ **(appareil) ~** elevator ◆ **(appareil *ou* transformateur) ~ de tension** (*Élec*) step-up transformer; → **chariot**

élévation /elevasjɔ̃/ NF 1 (*= action d'élever*) [*de rempart, statue*] putting up, erection; [*d'objet, niveau*] raising; [*de pensée, âme*] elevation ◆ **~ d'un nombre au carré** (*Math*) squaring of a number ◆ **~ d'un nombre à une puissance** (*Math*) raising of a number to a power ◆ **son ~ au rang de capitaine** his being raised *ou* elevated to the rank of captain, his elevation to the rank of captain 2 (*= action de s'élever*) [*de température, niveau*] rise (*de* in) 3 (*Rel*) **l'~** the Elevation 4 (*= tertre*) elevation, mound ◆ **~ de terrain** rise 5 (*Archit, Géom = coupe, plan*) elevation 6 (*= noblesse*) [*de pensée, style*] elevation, loftiness

élevé, e /el(ə)ve/ (ptp de **élever**) ADJ 1 [*prix, niveau, température*] high; [*pertes*] heavy ◆ **peu ~** [*prix, niveau*] low; [*pertes*] slight ◆ **dommages-intérêts ~s** (*Jur*) substantial damages 2 [*cime, arbre*] tall; [*colline*] high 3 [*rang, grade*] high, elevated ◆ **être de condition ~e** (*frm*) to be of high birth ◆ **occuper une position ~e** to hold a high position, to be high-ranking 4 (*= noble*) [*pensée, style*] elevated, lofty; [*principes*] high ◆ **avoir une conception ~e de qch** to have a lofty view of sth 5 (*= éduqué*) **bien ~** well-mannered ◆ **mal ~** (*= rustre*) bad-mannered, ill-mannered; (*= impoli*) rude, impolite ◆ **espèce de mal ~ !** you rude thing! ◆ **c'est mal ~ de parler en mangeant** it's bad manners *ou* it's rude to talk with your mouth full

élève /elɛv/ NMF (*gén*) pupil, student; (*Grande École*) student; (*Mil*) cadet ◆ **~ professeur** student teacher, trainee teacher ◆ **~ infirmière** student nurse ◆ **~ officier** officer cadet ◆ **~-officier de réserve** officer cadet

élever /el(ə)ve/ ▸ conjug 5 ◂ VT 1 (*= éduquer*) [*+ enfant*] to bring up, to raise ◆ **il a été élevé dans du coton** he had a sheltered upbringing, he was wrapped (up) in cotton wool as a child (*Brit*) ◆ **elle a été élevée selon des principes stricts** she had a strict upbringing ◆ **son fils est élevé maintenant** his son is grown-up now

2 (*= faire l'élevage de*) [*+ bétail*] to rear, to breed; [*+ chiens, porcs, chevaux, vers à soie*] to breed; [*+ abeilles*] to keep; [*+ volailles*] to farm; [*+ vin*] to produce ◆ **vin élevé dans nos chais** wine matured in our cellars

3 (*= dresser*) [*+ rempart, mur, statue*] to put up, to erect, to raise ◆ **la maison élevait sa masse sombre** (*littér*) the dark mass of the house rose up *ou* reared up (*littér*) ◆ **~ des objections/des protestations** to raise objections/a protest ◆ **~ des critiques** to make criticisms

4 (*= hausser*) [*+ édifice*] to raise, to make higher ◆ **~ une maison d'un étage** to raise a house by one storey, to make a house one storey higher

5 (*= lever, mettre plus haut*) [*+ poids, objet*] to lift (up), to raise; [*+ niveau, taux, prix*] to raise; [*+ voix*] to raise; (*littér*) [*+ yeux, bras*] to raise, to lift (up) ◆ **pompe qui élève l'eau** pump which raises water

6 [*+ débat*] to raise the tone of ◆ **musique qui élève l'âme** elevating *ou* uplifting music ◆ **élevons nos cœurs vers le Seigneur** (*Rel*) let us lift up our hearts unto the Lord

7 (*= promouvoir*) to raise, to elevate ◆ **il a été élevé au grade de capitaine** he was raised *ou* elevated to the rank of captain ◆ **chez eux l'abstinence est élevée à la hauteur d'une institution** they've given abstinence the status of an institution, they have made abstinence a way of life

8 (*Math*) **~ une perpendiculaire** to raise a perpendicular ◆ **~ un nombre à la puissance 5** to raise a number to the power of 5 ◆ **~ un nombre au carré** to square a number

VPR **s'élever** 1 (*= augmenter*) [*température, niveau, prix*] to rise, to go up ◆ **le niveau des élèves/de vie s'est élevé** the standard of the pupils/of living has risen *ou* improved

2 (*= se dresser*) [*montagne, tour*] to rise ◆ **la tour s'élève à 50 mètres au-dessus du sol** the tower is 50 metres tall ◆ **un mur s'élevait entre ces deux jardins** a wall stood between the two gardens ◆ **la cime s'élève majestueusement au-dessus des forêts** the peak rises (up) *ou* towers majestically above the forests

3 (*= monter*) [*avion*] to go up, to ascend; [*oiseau*] to fly up, to ascend ◆ **l'avion s'élevait régulièrement** the plane was climbing *ou* ascending steadily ◆ **la pensée s'élève vers l'absolu** thought soars *ou* ascends towards the absolute ◆ **l'âme s'élève vers Dieu** the soul ascends to(wards) God ◆ **le ton s'élève, les voix s'élèvent** voices are beginning to rise ◆ **s'~ au-dessus des querelles** to rise above petty quarrels

4 [*objections, doutes*] to be raised, to arise ◆ **sa voix s'éleva dans le silence** his voice broke the silence ◆ **aucune voix ne s'éleva en sa faveur** not a (single) voice was raised in his favour

5 (*dans la société*) to rise ◆ **s'~ jusqu'au sommet de l'échelle** to climb to the top of the ladder ◆ **s'~ à la force du poignet/par son seul travail** to work one's way up unaided/by the sweat of one's brow

6 (*= protester*) **s'~ contre** to rise up against

7 (*= se bâtir*) to go up, to be put up *ou* erected ◆ **la maison s'élève peu à peu** the house is going up bit by bit *ou* is gradually going up

8 (*= se monter*) **s'~ à** [*prix, pertes*] to total, to add up to, to amount to

éleveur, -euse /el(ə)vœʀ, øz/ NM,F (*Agr*) stockbreeder; [*de vin*] producer ◆ **~ (de bétail)** cattle breeder *ou* rearer ◆ **~ de chiens/chevaux/porcs** dog/horse/pig breeder ◆ **~ de volailles** poultry farmer ◆ **~ de vers à soie** silkworm breeder, sericulturist (*SPÉC*) ◆ **~ d'abeilles** beekeeper; → **propriétaire** NF **éleveuse** (*pour poussins*) brooder

elfe /ɛlf/ NM elf

élider VT, **s'élider** VPR /elide/ ► conjug 1 ◄ to elide ◆ **article élidé** elided article

Élie /eli/ NM Elijah

éligibilité /eliʒibilite/ NF eligibility (*à* for)

éligible /eliʒibl/ ADJ eligible (*à* for)

élimé, e /elime/ (ptp de **élimer**) ADJ *[vêtement, tissu]* threadbare, worn ◆ **manteau un peu ~** rather worn overcoat ◆ **chemise ~e au col/aux poignets** shirt with a frayed collar/with frayed cuffs

élimer /elime/ ► conjug 1 ◄ VT *[+ vêtement, tissu]* to wear thin VPR **s'élimer** *[vêtement, tissu]* to wear thin, to become threadbare

élimination /eliminasjɔ̃/ NF *(gén)* elimination ◆ **procéder par ~** to work by a process of elimination

éliminatoire /eliminatwaʀ/ ADJ *[match, épreuve]* qualifying *(épith)*; *[note, temps]* disqualifying *(épith)* ◆ **les phases ~s de la Coupe du monde** the qualifying stages of the World Cup NFPL **éliminatoires** *(Sport)* qualifying heats

éliminer /elimine/ ► conjug 1 ◄ VT *(gén, Math, Méd)* to eliminate; *[+ possibilité]* to rule out, to eliminate; *[+ données secondaires]* to discard, to eliminate ◆ **éliminé au second tour** *(Pol)* eliminated in the second ballot ◆ **être éliminé à l'oral** to be eliminated in *ou* to fail (in) the oral ◆ **éliminé !** *(Jeux)* you're out! ◆ **éliminé en quart de finale** knocked out *ou* eliminated in the quarter finals ◆ **les petits exploitants seront éliminés du marché** small farmers will be forced out of the market ◆ **boire de l'eau minérale fait ~** drinking mineral water cleans out the system

élire /eliʀ/ ► conjug 43 ◄ VT to elect ◆ **il a été élu président** he was elected president, he was voted in as president ◆ **~ domicile** to take up residence (*à, dans* in)

Élisabeth /elizabɛt/ NF Elizabeth

élisabéthain, e /elizabetɛ̃, ɛn/ ADJ Elizabethan NM,F **Élisabéthain(e)** Elizabethan

Élisée /elize/ NM Elisha

élision /elizjɔ̃/ NF elision

élitaire /elitɛʀ/ ADJ *[club, festival]* exclusive

élite /elit/ NF [1] (= *groupe*) elite, élite ◆ **l'~ de** the cream *ou* elite of ◆ **les ~s (de la nation)** the elite (of the nation) ◆ **être** *ou* **personnalité d'~** exceptional person ◆ **corps/cavalerie d'~** *(Mil)* crack corps/cavalry ◆ **soldat d'~** elite soldier ◆ **joueur/pilote d'~** ace player/pilot ◆ **tireur d'~** crack shot ◆ **troupes d'~** elite *ou* crack troops ◆ **école d'~** elite school [2] *(Imprim)* **caractères ~** elite (type)

élitisme /elitism/ NM elitism ◆ **faire de l'~** to be elitist

élitiste /elitist/ ADJ, NMF elitist

élixir /eliksiʀ/ NM elixir ◆ **~ de longue vie** elixir of life ◆ **~ d'amour** love potion, elixir of love

elle /ɛl/ PRON PERS F [1] *(fonction sujet, personne)* she; *(chose)* it; *(nation)* it, she; *(animal, bébé)* she, it ◆ **~s** they ◆ **~ est couturière** she is a dressmaker ◆ **prends cette chaise, ~ est plus confortable** have this chair - it's more comfortable ◆ **je me méfie de sa chienne, ~ mord** I don't trust his dog - she *ou* it bites ◆ **~, furieuse, a refusé** furious, she refused ◆ **la Suisse a décidé qu'~ resterait neutre** Switzerland decided that it *ou* she would remain neutral ◆ **qu'est-ce qu'ils ont dit ? – ~, rien** what did they say? – she said nothing ◆ **il est venu mais pas ~/~s** he came but she/they didn't, he came but not her/them ◆ **~ partie, j'ai pu travailler** with her gone *ou* after she had gone I was able to work ◆ **~, n'aurait jamais fait ça** she would never have done that ◆ **~, renoncer ? ce n'est pas son genre** her give up? it wouldn't be like her; → aussi **même**

[2] *(fonction objet, souvent emphatique, personne)* her; *(chose)* it; *(nation)* it, her; *(animal)* her, it ◆ **~s** them ◆ **il n'admire qu'~** he only admires her, she's the only one he admires ◆ **je les ai bien vus, ~ et lui** I definitely saw both *ou* the two of them ◆ **la revoir ~ ? jamais !** see her again? never!

[3] *(emphatique avec qui, que)* **c'est ~ qui me l'a dit** she was the one who *ou* that told me ◆ **ce fut ~ qui lança le mouvement** she was the one *ou* it was her that launched the movement ◆ **voilà la pluie, et ~ qui est sortie sans manteau !** here comes the rain and to think she has gone out without a coat! *ou* and there she is out without a coat! ◆ **chasse cette chienne, c'est ~ qui m'a mordu** chase that dog away, it's the one that bit me ◆ **c'est ~ que j'avais invitée** it was her I had invited ◆ **c'est à ~ que je veux parler** it's her I want to speak to, I want to speak to her ◆ **il y a une chouette dans le bois, c'est ~ que j'ai entendue cette nuit** there's an owl in the wood - that's what I heard last night

[4] *(avec prép, personne)* her; *(animal)* her, it; *(chose)* it ◆ **ce livre est à ~** this book belongs to her *ou* is hers ◆ **ces livres sont à ~s** these books belong to them *ou* are theirs ◆ **c'est à ~ de décider** it's up to her to decide, it's her decision ◆ **c'est gentil à ~ d'avoir écrit** it was kind of her to write ◆ **un ami à ~** a friend of hers, one of her friends ◆ **~ ne pense qu'à ~** she only thinks of herself ◆ **~ a une maison à ~** she has a house of her own ◆ **ses enfants à ~** her children ◆ **qu'est-ce qu'il ferait sans ~ ?** what would he do without her? ◆ **ce poème n'est pas d'~** this poem is not by her ◆ **il veut une photo d'~** he wants a photo of her

[5] *(dans comparaisons, sujet)* she; *(objet)* her ◆ **il est plus grand qu'~/~s** he is taller than she is/they are *ou* than her/them ◆ **je le connais aussi bien qu'~** *(aussi bien que je la connais)* I know him as well as (I know) her; *(aussi bien qu'elle le connaît)* I know him as well as she does ◆ **ne faites pas comme ~** don't do as *ou* what she does, don't do like her *

[6] *(interrog, emphatique : gén non traduit)* **Alice est-~ rentrée ?** is Alice back? ◆ **sa lettre est-~ arrivée ?** has his letter come? ◆ **les infirmières sont-~s bien payées ?** are nurses well paid? ◆ **tu sais, ta tante, ~ n'est pas très aimable !** you know, your aunt isn't very nice!

ellébore /elebɔʀ/ NM hellebore

elle-même (pl **elles-mêmes**) /ɛlmɛm/ PRON → **même**

ellipse /elips/ NF *(Géom)* ellipse; *(Ling)* ellipsis

ellipsoïde /elipsɔid/ NM ellipsoid ADJ *(Géom)* elliptical

elliptique /eliptik/ ADJ *(Géom)* elliptic(al); *(Ling)* elliptical ◆ **il a fait une réponse assez ~** he gave a somewhat succinct reply ◆ **il a été très ~ à ce propos** he was tight-lipped about the matter

elliptiquement /eliptikmɑ̃/ ADV *(Ling)* elliptically

élocution /elɔkysjɔ̃/ NF (= *débit*) delivery; (= *clarté*) diction ◆ **défaut d'~** speech impediment *ou* defect ◆ **professeur d'~** elocution teacher

éloge /elɔʒ/ NM [1] (= *louange*) praise ◆ **couvert d'~s** showered with praise ◆ **digne d'~** praiseworthy, commendable ◆ **faire des ~s à qn** to praise sb; → **tarir** [2] (= *apologie*) praise ◆ **faire l'~ de** to praise, to speak (very) highly of ◆ **son ~ n'est plus à faire** I do not need to add to the praise he has already received ◆ **c'est le plus bel ~ à lui faire** it's the highest praise one can give him ◆ **faire son propre ~** to sing one's own praises, to blow one's own trumpet * *(Brit) ou* horn * *(US)* ◆ **l'~ que vous avez fait de cette œuvre** your praise *ou* commendation of this work [3] *(littér = panégyrique)* eulogy ◆ **prononcer l'~ funèbre de qn** to deliver a funeral oration for sb

élogieusement /elɔʒjøzmɑ̃/ ADV ◆ **parler ~ de qn** to speak very highly *ou* most favourably of

élogieux, -ieuse /elɔʒjø, jøz/ ADJ laudatory, eulogistic(al) ◆ **parler de qn/qch en termes ~** to speak very highly of sb/sth, to speak of sb/sth in the most laudatory terms

éloigné, e /elwaɲe/ (ptp de **éloigner**) ADJ [1] *(dans l'espace)* distant, remote ◆ **les deux écoles ne sont pas très ~es (l'une de l'autre)** the two schools are not very far away from each other *ou* not very far apart ◆ **est-ce très ~ de la gare ? – oui, c'est très ~** is it a long way from the station? – yes, it's a long way ◆ **~ de 3 km** 3 km away ◆ **le village est trop ~ pour qu'on puisse y aller à pied** the village is too far away to walk *ou* isn't within walking distance

[2] *(dans le temps)* *[époque, événement, échéance]* distant (*de* from) remote (*de* from); ◆ **dans un avenir peu ~** in the not-too-distant future, in the near future

[3] *[parent]* distant; *[ancêtre]* remote ◆ **la famille ~e** distant relatives

[4] *(locutions)*

◆ **être éloigné de** (= *être sans rapport avec*) to be far from, to be a long way from ◆ **sa version est très ~e de la vérité** his version is very far from the truth ◆ **les prévisions étaient très ~s de la réalité** the forecasts were a long way off the mark ◆ **ces statistiques sont très ~es de la réalité** these statistics bear no relation to reality *ou* do not reflect reality ◆ **un sentiment pas très ~ de la haine** a feeling not far removed from hatred ◆ **rien n'est plus ~ de mes pensées** nothing is *ou* could be further from my thoughts ◆ **je suis fort ~ de ses positions** my point of view is very far removed from his ◆ **certains hommes politiques sont très ~s des préoccupations des gens** some politicians have little idea of people's real concerns

◆ **tenir éloigné de** to keep away from ◆ **cette conférence m'a tenu ~ de chez moi** the conference kept me away from home ◆ **se tenir ~ du feu** to keep away from *ou* clear of the fire ◆ **se tenir ~ du danger/des querelles** to steer *ou* keep clear of danger/of quarrels

éloignement /elwaɲmɑ̃/ NM [1] (= *action d'éloigner*) *[de personne indésirable]* taking away, removal; *[de soupçons]* removal, averting; *[d'échéance]* putting off, postponement ◆ **leur ~ de la cour, ordonné par le roi** their having been ordered away *ou* their banishment from the court by the king ◆ **~ du territoire** expulsion ◆ **il prône l'~ des délinquants** he advocates the forcible removal of young offenders

[2] (= *action de s'éloigner*) *[d'être aimé]* estrangement ◆ **son ~ des affaires** his progressive disinvolvement with business

[3] (= *état spatial, temporel*) distance ◆ **l'~ rapetisse les objets** distance makes objects (look) smaller ◆ **notre ~ de Paris complique le travail** our being so far from Paris makes the work more complicated ◆ **la région souffre de cet ~ géographique** the region suffers from being so remote ◆ **en amour, l'~ rapproche** absence makes the heart grow fonder *(Prov)* ◆ **avec l'~, on juge mieux les événements** it is easier to judge events from a distance

éloigner /elwaɲe/ ► conjug 1 ◄ VT [1] *[+ objet]* to move away, to take away (*de* from); ◆ **éloigne ce coussin du radiateur** move *ou* take that cushion away from the radiator ◆ **la lentille éloigne les objets** the lens makes objects look further away than they really are

[2] *[+ personne]* **~ qn de** *[+ endroit, activité, tentations]* to take sb away from, to remove sb from;

[+ être aimé, compagnons] to estrange sb from; *(= exiler, écarter)* to send sb away from ◆ ~ **les curieux du lieu d'un accident** to move onlookers *ou* bystanders away from the scene of an accident ◆ **ce chemin nous éloigne du village** this path takes *ou* leads us away from the village ◆ **il veut ~ les jeunes délinquants de leurs cités** he wants to forcibly remove young offenders from the areas where they live ◆ **allumer du feu pour ~ les bêtes sauvages** to light a fire to keep off the wild animals ◆ **son penchant pour la boisson a éloigné ses amis** his drinking lost him his friends *ou* made his friends drift away from him

3 *[+ souvenir, idée]* to banish, to dismiss; *[+ crainte]* to remove, to dismiss; *[+ danger]* to ward off, to remove; *[+ soupçons]* to remove, to avert (*de* from); ◆ **ces résultats ont éloigné la perspective d'une baisse des taux d'intérêt** these figures have made the prospect of a cut in interest rates less likely

4 *(= espacer) [+ visites]* to make less frequent, to space out

VPR **s'éloigner** 1 *[objet, véhicule en mouvement]* to move away; *[cycliste]* to ride away; *[orage]* to go away, to pass; *[bruit]* to go away, to grow fainter ◆ **le village s'éloignait et finit par disparaître dans la brume** the village got further (and further) away *ou* grew more and more distant and finally disappeared in the mist

2 *[personne] (par prudence)* to go away (*de* from); *(par pudeur, discrétion)* to go away, to withdraw (*de* from); ◆ **s'~ de** *[+ être aimé, compagnons]* to become estranged from, to grow away from; *[+ sujet traité]* to wander from; *[+ position, objectif]* to move away from; *[+ devoir]* to swerve *ou* deviate from ◆ **éloigne-toi du feu** come away from the fire ◆ **s'~ en courant/en hâte** to run/hurry away *ou* off ◆ **éloignez-vous, ça risque d'éclater !** move away *ou* stand back, it might explode! ◆ **ne t'éloigne pas trop** don't go (too) far (away) ◆ **il suffit de s'~ de quelques kilomètres pour se retrouver à la campagne** the countryside is just a few kilometres away, you only have to go a few kilometres to get to the countryside ◆ **là vous vous éloignez du sujet** you're wandering from *ou* getting off the point *ou* subject ◆ **je la sentais s'~ de moi** I felt her growing away from me ◆ **le gouvernement s'éloigne des objectifs qu'il s'était fixés** the government is retreating from the targets it set itself ◆ **s'~ du droit chemin** to stray *ou* wander from the straight and narrow ◆ **s'~ de la vérité** to wander from the truth

3 *[souvenir, échéance]* to grow more (and more) distant *ou* remote; *[danger]* to pass, to go away; *[craintes]* to go away

élongation /elɔ̃gasjɔ̃/ NF 1 *(Méd)* strained *ou* pulled muscle ◆ **les ~s font très mal** straining *ou* pulling a muscle is very painful, a pulled muscle is very painful ◆ **se faire une ~** to strain *ou* pull a muscle ◆ **je me suis fait une ~ à la jambe** I've strained *ou* pulled a muscle in my leg 2 *(Astron)* elongation; *(Phys)* displacement

éloquemment /elɔkamɑ̃/ ADV eloquently

éloquence /elɔkɑ̃s/ NF eloquence ◆ **avec ~** eloquently ◆ **il m'a fallu toute mon ~ pour la convaincre** I needed all the eloquence I could muster to convince her ◆ **l'~ de ces chiffres rend tout commentaire superflu** these figures speak for themselves *ou* need no comment

éloquent, e /elɔkɑ̃, ɑ̃t/ ADJ *[orateur, discours, geste]* eloquent; *[exemple]* clear ◆ **ces chiffres sont ~s** these figures speak for themselves ◆ **une étreinte plus ~e que toute parole** an embrace that spoke louder than any words, an embrace more eloquent *ou* meaningful than any words ◆ **un silence ~** a silence that speaks volumes, a meaningful *ou* an eloquent silence

élu, e /ely/ (ptp de **élire**) ADJ *(Rel)* chosen; *(Pol)* elected NM,F 1 *(Pol) (= député)* elected member, ≃ member of parliament, M.P. *(Brit)*; *(= conseiller)* elected representative, councillor ◆ **les nouveaux ~s** the newly elected members, the newly elected councillors ◆ **les ~s locaux** the local *ou* town councillors ◆ **les citoyens et leurs ~s** the citizens and their elected representatives 2 *(hum = fiancé)* **l'~ de son cœur** her beloved ◆ **quelle est l'heureuse ~e ?** who's the lucky girl? 3 *(Rel)* **les Élus** the Chosen ones, the Elect ◆ **être l'~ de Dieu** to be chosen by God

élucidation /elysidasjɔ̃/ NF elucidation

élucider /elyside/ ► conjug 1 ◄ VT to clear up, to elucidate

élucubrations /elykybʀasjɔ̃/ NFPL *(péj)* wild imaginings

élucubrer /elykybʀe/ ► conjug 1 ◄ VT *(péj)* to dream up

éluder /elyde/ ► conjug 1 ◄ VT *[+ difficulté]* to evade, to elude; *[+ loi, problème]* to evade, to dodge

élusif, -ive /elyzif, iv/ ADJ *(frm)* elusive

Élysée /elize/ NM *(Myth)* ◆ **l'~** the Elysium ◆ **(le palais de) l'~** the Élysée palace *(official residence of the French President)*; → **champ**[1]

élyséen, -enne /elizeɛ̃, ɛn/ ADJ *(Myth)* Elysian; *(Pol française)* of the Élysée palace

élytre /elitʀ/ NM wing case, elytron *(SPÉC)*

émaciation /emasjasjɔ̃/ NF emaciation

émacié, e /emasje/ (ptp de **émacier**) ADJ *[corps, visage]* emaciated, wasted; *[personne]* emaciated

émacier /emasje/ ► conjug 7 ◄ VT to emaciate VPR **s'émacier** to become emaciated *ou* wasted

émail (pl **-aux**) /emaj, o/ NM *(= substance)* enamel; *(= objet)* piece of enamel, enamel; *(Hér)* colour ◆ **en** *ou* **d'~** enamel(led) ◆ **cendrier en émaux** enamelled ashtray ◆ **peinture sur ~** enamel painting ◆ **faire des émaux** to do enamel work

e-mail /imɛl/ NM e-mail ◆ **envoyer qch par ~** to e-mail sth

émaillage /emajaʒ/ NM enamelling

émaillé, e /emaje/ (ptp de **émailler**) ADJ 1 *(lit)* enamelled 2 ◆ **~ de** *(= parsemé de) [+ étoiles]* spangled *ou* studded with; *[+ fautes, citations]* peppered *ou* dotted with ◆ **voyage ~ d'incidents** journey punctuated by unforeseen incidents

émailler /emaje/ ► conjug 1 ◄ VT 1 *(lit)* to enamel 2 *(= parsemer) [étoiles]* to stud, to spangle ◆ **~ un texte de citations/d'erreurs** to pepper a text with quotations/errors

émailleur, -euse /emajœʀ, øz/ NM,F enameller, enamellist

émanation /emanasjɔ̃/ NF 1 ◆ **~s** *(= odeurs)* smells, emanations ◆ **~s fétides** fetid emanations ◆ **~s volcaniques** volatiles ◆ **~s toxiques** toxic fumes 2 *(= produit)* product ◆ **le pouvoir est l'~ du peuple** power issues from the people, power is a product of the will of the people 3 *(Phys)* emanation; *(Rel)* procession

émancipateur, -trice /emɑ̃sipatœʀ, tʀis/ ADJ liberating, emancipatory NM,F liberator, emancipator

émancipation /emɑ̃sipasjɔ̃/ NF *(Jur)* emancipation; *[de colonie, femme]* liberation, emancipation

émancipé, e /emɑ̃sipe/ (ptp de **émanciper**) ADJ emancipated, liberated

émanciper /emɑ̃sipe/ ► conjug 1 ◄ VT *(Jur)* to emancipate; *[+ femme]* to emancipate, to liberate; *[+ esprit]* to liberate, to (set) free VPR **s'émanciper** *[femme]* to become emancipated *ou* liberated, to liberate o.s.; *[esprit, art]* to become liberated, to liberate *ou* free itself

émaner /emane/ ► conjug 1 ◄ **émaner de** VT INDIR *(Pol, Rel) [pouvoir]* to issue from; *[ordres, note]* to come from, to be issued by; *[chaleur, lumière, odeur]* to emanate *ou* issue *ou* come from; *[charme]* to emanate from

émargement /emaʀʒəmɑ̃/ NM 1 *(NonC)* signing; *(= annotation)* annotating ◆ **feuille d'~** *(= feuille de paye)* paysheet; *(= feuille de présence)* attendance sheet 2 *(= signature)* signature; *(= annotation)* annotation

émarger /emaʀʒe/ ► conjug 3 ◄ VT 1 *(frm) (= signer)* to sign; *(= mettre ses initiales)* to initial 2 *(= annoter)* to annotate 3 *(Typo)* to trim VI 1 *(† = toucher son salaire)* to draw one's salary ◆ **à combien émarge-t-il par mois ?** what is his monthly salary? 2 *(= recevoir)* **~ d'une certaine somme à un budget** to receive a certain sum out of a budget

émasculation /emaskylasjɔ̃/ NF *(lit, fig)* emasculation

émasculer /emaskyle/ ► conjug 1 ◄ VT *(lit, fig)* to emasculate

emballage /ɑ̃balaʒ/ NM 1 *(= action d'emballer) (dans un carton)* packing(-up), packaging; *(dans du papier)* wrapping(-up) 2 *(Comm) (= boîte, carton)* package, packaging *(NonC)*; *(= papier)* wrapping *(NonC)* ◆ **carton d'~, ~ carton** cardboard packaging ◆ **~ perdu** throwaway packaging ◆ **produit sous ~ (plastique)** plastic-wrapped product

emballant, e* /ɑ̃balɑ̃, ɑ̃t/ ADJ *(gén au nég)* thrilling ◆ **ce n'est pas un film/un projet très ~** it's not a very inspiring film/project

emballement /ɑ̃balmɑ̃/ NM 1 * *(= enthousiasme)* flight of enthusiasm; *(= colère)* flash of anger ◆ **méfiez-vous de ses ~s** *(= passade)* beware of his (sudden) crazes* 2 *[de moteur]* racing; *[de cheval]* bolting 3 *(Écon)* **cela a provoqué l'~ du dollar/de l'économie** it caused the dollar/the economy to race out of control

emballer /ɑ̃bale/ ► conjug 1 ◄ VT 1 *(= empaqueter) (dans un carton, de la toile)* to pack (up); *(dans du papier)* to wrap (up) ◆ **emballé sous vide** vacuum-packed ◆ **emballez, c'est pesé !** * *(fig)* it's a deal!* 2 *(‡ = arrêter)* to run in*, to nick‡ *(Brit)* 3 *[+ moteur]* to race 4 *(* = enthousiasmer)* ◆ **ça m'a emballé** I loved it ◆ **l'idée n'avait pas l'air de l'~** he didn't seem too keen on the idea ◆ **je n'ai pas été très emballé par ce film** the film didn't do much for me* 5 *(‡ = séduire) [+ personne]* to pick up*, to get off with* VPR **s'emballer** 1 * *[personne] (enthousiasme)* to get *ou* be carried away*; *(colère)* to fly off the handle* 2 *[moteur]* to race; *[cheval]* to bolt ◆ **cheval emballé** runaway *ou* bolting horse 3 *[économie, monnaie]* to race out of control

emballeur, -euse /ɑ̃balœʀ, øz/ NM,F packer

embarcadère /ɑ̃baʀkadɛʀ/ NM landing stage, pier

embarcation /ɑ̃baʀkasjɔ̃/ NF (small) boat, (small) craft *(pl inv)*

embardée /ɑ̃baʀde/ NF *(en voiture)* swerve; *(dans un bateau)* yaw ◆ **faire une ~** *(en voiture)* to swerve; *(dans un bateau)* to yaw

embargo /ɑ̃baʀgo/ NM embargo *(à l'encontre de, contre* against); ◆ **~ économique/commercial/total** economic/trade/total embargo ◆ **pétrolier/militaire** oil/military embargo ◆ **imposer un ~ sur qch, mettre l'~ sur qch** to impose *ou* put an embargo on sth, to embargo sth ◆ **lever l'~ (mis sur qch/un pays)** to lift *ou* raise the embargo (on sb/a country) ◆ **pays/marchandises sous ~** country/goods (placed) under embargo

embarqué, e /ɑ̃baʀke/ ADJ *[équipement automobile]* in-car; ◆ **multimédia** ~ in car multimedia

embarquement /ɑ̃baʀkəmɑ̃/ NM *[de marchandises]* loading; *[de passagers] (en bateau)* embarkation, boarding; *(en avion, en train)* boarding ◆ **vol 134, ~ porte 9** flight 134 now boarding at gate 9 ◆ **carte d'~** boarding pass *ou* card

embarquer /ɑ̃baʀke/ ► conjug 1 ◄ VT 1 *[+ passagers]* to embark, to take on board ◆ **je l'ai embarqué dans le train*** I saw him onto the train, I put him on the train
2 *[+ cargaison] (en train, gén)* to load; *(en bateau)* to load, to ship ◆ **le navire embarque des paquets d'eau** the boat is taking in *ou* shipping water
3 *‡ (= emporter)* to cart off*, to lug off*; *(= voler)* to pinch*, to nick‡ *(Brit)*; *(pour emprisonner)* to cart off* *ou* away* ◆ **se faire ~ par la police** to get picked up by the police*
4 *(* = entraîner)* ~ **qn dans** to get sb mixed up in *ou* involved in, to involve sb in ◆ **il s'est laissé ~ dans une sale histoire** he has got (himself) mixed up in *ou* involved in a nasty bit of business ◆ **une affaire bien/mal embarquée** an affair that has got off to a good/bad start
VI 1 *(= partir en voyage)* to embark ◆ **il a embarqué** *ou* **il s'est embarqué hier pour le Maroc** he sailed for Morocco yesterday
2 *(= monter à bord)* to board, to go aboard *ou* on board
3 *(Naut)* **le navire embarque, la mer embarque** we are *ou* the boat is shipping water
VPR **s'embarquer** 1 → vi 1
2 ◆ **s'~ dans*** *[+ aventure, affaire]* to embark (up)on, to launch into; *[+ affaire louche]* to get mixed up in *ou* involved in

embarras /ɑ̃baʀa/ NM 1 *(= ennui)* trouble ◆ **cela constitue un ~ supplémentaire** that's yet another problem ◆ **je ne veux pas être un ~ pour vous** I don't want to be a nuisance to you, I don't want to bother you ◆ **causer** *ou* **faire toutes sortes d'~ à qn** to give *ou* cause sb no end* of trouble *ou* bother ◆ **ne vous mettez pas dans l'~ pour moi** don't put yourself out *ou* go to any trouble for me
2 *(= gêne)* confusion, embarrassment ◆ **dit-il avec ~** he said in some confusion *ou* with (some) embarrassment ◆ **il remarqua mon ~ pour répondre** he noticed that I was at a loss for a reply *ou* that I was stuck* for a reply
3 *(= situation délicate)* **mettre** *ou* **plonger qn dans l'~** to put sb in an awkward position *ou* on the spot* ◆ **tirer qn d'~** to get *ou* help sb out of an awkward position *ou* out of a predicament ◆ **être dans l'~** *(en mauvaise position)* to be in a predicament *ou* an awkward position; *(dans un dilemme)* to be in a quandary *ou* in a dilemma
4 *(= gêne financière)* ~ **(d'argent** *ou* **financiers)** financial difficulties, money worries ◆ **être dans l'~** to be in financial straits *ou* difficulties, to be short of money
5 *(Méd)* ~ **gastrique** upset stomach, stomach upset
6 *(† = encombrement)* ~ **de circulation** *ou* **de voitures** (road) congestion *(NonC)*, traffic holdup ◆ **les ~ de Paris** the congestion in the streets of Paris
7 *(= chichis, façons)* **faire des ~** to make a fuss ◆ **c'est un faiseur d'~** he's a fusspot*, he's always making a fuss
8 *(locution)* **avoir l'~ du choix, n'avoir que l'~ du choix** to be spoilt for choice

embarrassant, e /ɑ̃baʀasɑ̃, ɑ̃t/ ADJ 1 *[situation]* embarrassing, uncomfortable; *[problème]* awkward, thorny ◆ **c'est ~ de devoir lui dire** it's embarrassing to have to tell him 2 *[paquets]* cumbersome, awkward ◆ **ce que cet enfant peut être ~ !** that child is always in the way!

embarrassé, e /ɑ̃baʀase/ (ptp de **embarrasser**) ADJ 1 *(= gêné) [personne]* embarrassed, ill-at-ease *(attrib)*; *[sourire]* embarrassed, uneasy ◆ **être ~ de sa personne** to feel self-conscious ◆ **je serais bien ~ de choisir entre les deux** I'd really be at a loss *ou* I'd be hard put to choose between the two 2 *(= peu clair) [explication, phrase]* muddled, confused 3 *(Méd)* **avoir l'estomac ~** to have an upset stomach ◆ **j'ai la langue ~e** my tongue is coated 4 *(= encombré) [table, corridor]* cluttered (up) ◆ **j'ai les mains ~es** my hands are full

embarrasser /ɑ̃baʀase/ ► conjug 1 ◄ VT 1 *(= encombrer) [paquets]* to clutter (up); *[vêtements]* to hinder, to hamper ◆ **enlève ce manteau qui t'embarrasse** take that coat off – you'll be more comfortable without it ◆ **je ne t'embarrasse pas au moins ?** are you sure I'm not bothering you? *ou* I'm not in your way?
2 *(= désorienter)* ~ **qn par des questions indiscrètes** to embarrass sb with indiscreet questions ◆ **sa demande m'embarrasse** his request puts me in a predicament *ou* an awkward position *ou* on the spot* ◆ **ça m'embarrasse de te le dire mais ...** I don't like to tell you this but ... ◆ **il y a quelque chose qui m'embarrasse là-dedans** there's something about it that bothers *ou* worries me
3 *(Méd)* ~ **l'estomac** to lie heavy on the stomach
VPR **s'embarrasser** 1 *(= s'encombrer)* **s'~ de** *[+ paquets, compagnon]* to burden o.s. with ◆ **il s'embarrasse dans ses explications** *(fig)* he gets in a muddle with his explanations, he ties himself in knots* trying to explain things
2 *(= se soucier)* to trouble o.s. *(de* about) to be troubled *(de* by); ◆ **sans s'~ des détails** without troubling *ou* worrying about the details ◆ **il ne s'embarrasse pas de scrupules** he doesn't let scruples get in his way

embastillement /ɑ̃bastijmɑ̃/ NM *(††, hum)* imprisonment

embastiller /ɑ̃bastije/ ► conjug 1 ◄ VT *(††, hum)* to imprison

embauche /ɑ̃boʃ/ NF *(= action d'embaucher)* taking on, hiring; *(= travail disponible)* vacancy ◆ **ils devront recourir à l'~ cet été** they will have to start taking people on *ou* hiring new staff this summer ◆ **la surqualification peut être un obstacle à l'~** being overqualified can be an obstacle to finding employment ◆ **est-ce qu'il y a de l'~ ?** are there any vacancies?, are you taking anyone on? *ou* hiring anyone? ◆ **il n'y a pas d'~ (chez eux)** they're not hiring, they're not taking anybody on ◆ **bureau d'~** employment office ◆ **salaire d'~** starting salary ◆ **quelles sont les conditions d'~ ?** what kind of package are you *(ou* are they) offering? ◆ **aide(s)** *ou* **prime(s) à l'~** employment incentive(s) ◆ **le questionnaire leur est remis à l'~** they are given the questionnaire when they start work *ou* on their first day at work

embaucher /ɑ̃boʃe/ ► conjug 1 ◄ VT to take on, to hire ◆ **il s'est fait ~ par l'entreprise** he was taken on *ou* hired by the company ◆ **je t'embauche pour écosser les petits pois** I'll put you to work shelling the peas, you've got yourself a job shelling the peas ◆ **s'~ comme peintre** to get o.s. taken on *ou* hired as a painter ◆ **on embauche** *[entreprise]* we are recruiting new staff, we have vacancies (for new staff) ◆ **le nouvel embauché** the new recruit *ou* employee VI *(= commencer le travail)* to start work

embaucheur, -euse /ɑ̃boʃœʀ, øz/ NM,F employment *ou* labour *(Brit)* contractor

embauchoir /ɑ̃boʃwaʀ/ NM shoetree

embaumé, e /ɑ̃bome/ (ptp de **embaumer**) ADJ *[air]* fragrant, balmy *(littér)*

embaumement /ɑ̃bommɑ̃/ NM embalming

embaumer /ɑ̃bome/ ► conjug 1 ◄ VT 1 *[+ cadavre]* to embalm 2 *(= parfumer)* **le lilas embaumait l'air** the scent of lilac hung heavy in the air 3 *(= avoir l'odeur de)* to smell of ◆ **l'air embaumait le lilas** the air was fragrant *ou* balmy *(littér)* with the scent of lilac VI *[fleur]* to give out a fragrance, to be fragrant; *[jardin]* to be fragrant; *[mets]* to fill the air with a nice smell; *[fromage]* to smell strong ◆ **ça n'embaume pas !*** it doesn't smell too sweet!

embaumeur, -euse /ɑ̃bomœʀ, øz/ NM,F embalmer

embellie /ɑ̃beli/ NF *[de temps]* slight improvement *(de* in); *[d'économie]* slight improvement *ou* upturn *(de* in)

embellir /ɑ̃beliʀ/ ► conjug 2 ◄ VT *[+ personne, jardin]* to beautify, to make more attractive; *[+ ville]* to smarten up *(Brit)*, to give a face-lift to*; *[+ vérité, récit]* to embellish VI *[personne]* to grow lovelier *ou* more attractive, to grow in beauty *(littér)*

embellissement /ɑ̃belismɑ̃/ NM *[de récit, vérité]* embellishment ◆ **les récents ~s de la ville** the recent improvements to the town, the recent face-lift the town has been given*

embellisseur /ɑ̃belisœʀ/ ADJ M ◆ **shampooing ~** beauty shampoo

emberlificoter* /ɑ̃bɛʀlifikɔte/ ► conjug 1 ◄ VT *(= enjôler)* to get round*; *(= embrouiller)* to mix up*, to muddle (up); *(= duper)* to hoodwink*, to bamboozle* VPR **s'emberlificoter** *(dans un vêtement)* to get tangled *ou* caught up *(dans* in); ◆ **il s'emberlificote dans ses explications** he gets in a terrible muddle *ou* he gets himself tied up in knots with his explanations*

embêtant, e /ɑ̃bɛtɑ̃, ɑ̃t/ ADJ *(gén)* annoying; *[situation, problème]* awkward, tricky ◆ **c'est ~ !** *(ennuyeux)* what a nuisance!, how annoying!; *(alarmant)* it's worrying! ◆ **j'ai oublié de lui dire – !** I forgot to tell him – oh dear!

embêté, e /ɑ̃bete/ (ptp de **embêter**) ADJ ◆ **je suis très ~** *(= je ne sais pas quoi faire)* I'm in a real state, I just don't know what to do ◆ **elle a eu l'air ~ quand je lui ai demandé ça** she looked embarrassed when I asked her that ◆ **je suis très ~, je ne pourrai vous donner la réponse que dans trois jours** I'm really sorry, I can't give you an answer for another three days

embêtement /ɑ̃bɛtmɑ̃/ NM problem, trouble ◆ **causer des ~s à qn** to make trouble for sb ◆ **ce chien/four ne m'a causé que des ~s** this dog/oven has brought me nothing but trouble

embêter /ɑ̃bete/ ► conjug 1 ◄ VT *(= gêner, préoccuper)* to bother, to worry; *(= importuner)* to pester, to bother; *(= irriter)* to annoy; *(= lasser)* to bore
VPR **s'embêter** 1 *(= se morfondre)* to be bored, to be fed up* ◆ **qu'est-ce qu'on s'embête ici !** it's so boring *ou* such a drag* here! 2 *(= s'embarrasser)* to bother o.s. *(à faire* doing); ◆ **ne t'embête pas avec ça** don't bother *ou* worry about that ◆ **pourquoi s'~ à le réparer ?** why go to all the trouble *ou* bother of repairing it?, why bother yourself repairing it? ◆ **il ne s'embête pas !** *(= il a de la chance)* he does all right for himself!*; *(= il ne se gêne pas)* he's got a nerve!*

embeurrée /ɑ̃bøʀe/ NF ◆ ~ **de choux** cabbage cooked in butter

emblaver /ɑ̃blave/ ► conjug 1 ◄ VT to sow *(with a cereal crop)*

emblavure /ɑ̃blavyʀ/ NF field *(sown with a cereal crop)*

emblée /ɑ̃ble/ **d'emblée** LOC ADV straightaway, right away, at once ◆ **détester qn d'~** to detest sb on sight, to take an instant dislike to sb

emblématique /ɑ̃blematik/ ADJ *(lit)* emblematic; *(fig)* symbolic ◆ **c'est la figure ~ de l'opposition** he's the figurehead of the opposition

◆ **un personnage ~ du football français** a French football icon

emblème /ɑ̃blɛm/ **NM** *(lit)* emblem; *(fig)* symbol, emblem

embobiner* /ɑ̃bɔbine/ ▸ conjug 1 ◂ **VT** *(= enjôler)* to get round*; *(= embrouiller)* to mix up*, to muddle (up); *(= duper)* to hoodwink*, to bamboozle* ◆ **elle sait ~ son père** she can twist her father round her little finger, she knows how to get round her father

emboîtement /ɑ̃bwatmɑ̃/ **NM** fitting, interlocking

emboîter /ɑ̃bwate/ ▸ conjug 1 ◂ **VT** 1 *[+ pièces, parties]* to fit together, to fit into each other; *[+ livre]* to case ◆ **~ qch dans** to fit sth into 2 ◆ **~ le pas à qn** *(lit)* to follow close behind sb *ou* close on sb's heels; *(= imiter)* to follow suit **VPR** **s'emboîter** *[pièces]* to fit together, to fit into each other ◆ **ces deux pièces s'emboîtent exactement** these two parts fit together exactly ◆ **des chaises qui peuvent s'~ pour le rangement** chairs that can be stacked (together) when not in use

embolie /ɑ̃bɔli/ **NF** embolism ◆ **~ gazeuse/pulmonaire** air/pulmonary embolism ◆ **faire une ~** to have an embolism

embonpoint /ɑ̃bɔ̃pwɛ̃/ **NM** stoutness, portliness ◆ **avoir/prendre de l'~** to be/become rather stout

embossage /ɑ̃bɔsaʒ/ **NM** fore and aft mooring

embosser /ɑ̃bɔse/ ▸ conjug 1 ◂ **VT** 1 *[+ navire]* to moor fore and aft 2 *[+ carte]* to emboss

embouché, e /ɑ̃buʃe/ (ptp de **emboucher**) **ADJ** ◆ **mal ~** *(= grossier)* foul-mouthed; *(= de mauvaise humeur)* in a foul mood

emboucher /ɑ̃buʃe/ ▸ conjug 1 ◂ **VT** *[+ instrument]* to raise to one's lips ◆ **~ un cheval** to put the bit in a horse's mouth ◆ **~ les trompettes de la victoire/du nationalisme** *(fig)* to launch into triumphalist/nationalist rhetoric

embouchure /ɑ̃buʃyʀ/ **NF** *[de fleuve]* mouth; *[de mors]* mouthpiece; *(Mus)* mouthpiece, embouchure

embourber /ɑ̃buʀbe/ ▸ conjug 1 ◂ **VT** ◆ **~ une voiture** to get a car stuck in the mud **VPR** **s'embourber** *[voiture]* to get stuck in the mud, to get bogged down (in the mud) ◆ **notre voiture s'est embourbée dans le marais** our car got stuck in *ou* got bogged down in the marsh ◆ **s'~ dans** *[+ détails]* to get bogged down in; *[+ monotonie]* to sink into

embourgeoisement /ɑ̃buʀʒwazmɑ̃/ **NM** *[de personne, parti]* adoption of middle-class attitudes

embourgeoiser /ɑ̃buʀʒwaze/ ▸ conjug 1 ◂ **VPR** **s'embourgeoiser** *[parti, personne]* to become middle-class, to adopt a middle-class outlook; *[quartier]* to become middle-class **VT** *[+ personne]* to make middle-class (in outlook)

embout /ɑ̃bu/ **NM** *[de canne]* tip, ferrule; *[de tuyau]* nozzle

embouteillage /ɑ̃butɛjaʒ/ **NM** 1 *(sur route)* traffic jam, (traffic) holdup 2 († *= mise en bouteilles)* bottling

embouteiller /ɑ̃buteje/ ▸ conjug 1 ◂ **VT** *(Aut)* to jam, to block; *[+ lignes téléphoniques]* to block; † *[+ vin, lait]* to bottle ◆ **les routes sont très embouteillées** the roads are very congested

emboutir /ɑ̃butiʀ/ ▸ conjug 2 ◂ **VT** *[+ métal]* to stamp; *[+ véhicule]* to crash *ou* run into ◆ **avoir une aile emboutie** to have a dented *ou* damaged wing ◆ **il s'est fait ~ par une voiture** he was hit by another car

emboutisseur, -euse /ɑ̃butisœʀ, øz/ **NM,F** *(= personne)* stamper **NF** **emboutisseuse** *(= machine)* stamping press *ou* machine

embranchement /ɑ̃bʀɑ̃ʃmɑ̃/ **NM** 1 *[de voies, routes, tuyaux]* junction ◆ **à l'~ des deux routes** where the road forks 2 *(= route)* side road, branch road; *(Rail = voie)* branch line; *(= tuyau)* branch pipe; *(= rivière)* embranchment 3 *(= catégorie d'animaux ou de plantes)* branch

embrancher /ɑ̃bʀɑ̃ʃe/ ▸ conjug 1 ◂ **VT** *[+ tuyaux, voies]* to join (up) ◆ **~ qch sur** to join sth (up) to **VPR** **s'embrancher** *[tuyaux, voies]* to join (up) ◆ **s'~ sur** to join (up) to

embrasement /ɑ̃bʀazmɑ̃/ **NM** 1 *(littér = incendie)* fire, conflagration *(frm)* ◆ **ce qui a provoqué l'~ de la maison** what set the house on fire ◆ **l'~ du ciel au couchant** the blazing *ou* fiery sky at sunset ◆ **des ~s soudains** *(lueurs)* sudden blazes of light 2 *[de pays]* unrest ◆ **l'~ des esprits** the stirring *ou* rousing of people's passions

embraser /ɑ̃bʀaze/ ▸ conjug 1 ◂ **VT** 1 *(littér)* *[+ maison, forêt]* to set ablaze, to set fire to; *[+ ciel]* to set aglow *ou* ablaze 2 *[+ pays]* to cause unrest in **VPR** **s'embraser** 1 *(littér)* *[maison]* to blaze up, to flare up; *[ciel]* to flare up, to be set ablaze *(de* with); *[cœur]* to become inflamed, to be fired *(de* with) 2 *[pays]* to be thrown into a state of unrest

embrassade /ɑ̃bʀasad/ **NF** *(gén pl)* hugging and kissing *(NonC)*

embrasse /ɑ̃bʀas/ **NF** tieback ◆ **rideaux à ~s** curtains with tiebacks

embrassement /ɑ̃bʀasmɑ̃/ **NM** *(littér)* ⇒ **embrassade**

embrasser /ɑ̃bʀase/ GRAMMAIRE ACTIVE 48.2 ▸ conjug 1 ◂ **VT** 1 *(= donner un baiser à)* to kiss ◆ **~ qn à pleine bouche** to kiss sb (full) on the lips ◆ **je t'embrasse** *(en fin de lettre)* with love; *(au téléphone)* big kiss 2 († *ou frm = étreindre)* to embrace ◆ **qui trop embrasse mal étreint** *(Prov)* you shouldn't bite off more than you can chew; → **rime** 3 *(frm = choisir)* *[+ doctrine, cause]* to embrace, to espouse *(frm)*; *[+ carrière]* to take up, to enter upon 4 *(= couvrir)* *[+ problèmes, sujets]* to encompass, to embrace ◆ **il embrassa la plaine du regard** *(littér)* he surveyed the plain **VPR** **s'embrasser** to kiss (each other)

> ⚠ Au sens de 'donner un baiser à', **embrasser** ne se traduit pas par **to embrace**.

embrasure /ɑ̃bʀazyʀ/ **NF** *(Constr = créneau)* embrasure ◆ **il se tenait dans l'~ de la porte/la fenêtre** he stood in the doorway/the window

embrayage /ɑ̃bʀɛjaʒ/ **NM** 1 *(= mécanisme)* clutch 2 *(= action)* engaging *ou* letting out *(Brit)* the clutch, clutching *(US)*

embrayer /ɑ̃bʀeje/ ▸ conjug 8 ◂ **VT** *[+ véhicule, mécanisme]* to put into gear **VI** *[automobiliste]* to engage *ou* let out *(Brit)* the clutch, to clutch *(US)* ◆ **~ sur** *[+ sujet]* to switch to

embrigadement /ɑ̃bʀigadmɑ̃/ **NM** *(= endoctrinement)* indoctrination; *(= recrutement)* recruitment *(dans* into)

embrigader /ɑ̃bʀigade/ ▸ conjug 1 ◂ **VT** *(péj)* *(= endoctriner)* to indoctrinate; *(= recruter)* to recruit *(dans* into)

embringuer* /ɑ̃bʀɛ̃ge/ ▸ conjug 1 ◂ **VT** to mix up, to involve ◆ **il s'est laissé ~ dans une sale histoire** he got (himself) mixed up *ou* involved in some nasty business

embrocation /ɑ̃bʀɔkasjɔ̃/ **NF** embrocation

embrocher /ɑ̃bʀɔʃe/ ▸ conjug 1 ◂ **VT** *(Culin)* *(sur broche)* to spit, to put on a spit; *(sur brochette)* to skewer ◆ **~ qn** *(fig : avec une épée)* to run sb through ◆ **il m'a embroché avec son parapluie** he ran into me with his umbrella

embrouillage /ɑ̃bʀujaʒ/ **NM** ⇒ **embrouillement**

embrouillamini* /ɑ̃bʀujamini/ **NM** muddle, jumble

embrouille* /ɑ̃bʀuj/ **NF** ◆ **il y a de l'~ là-dessous** there's something funny at the bottom of this ◆ **toutes ces ~s** all this carry-on* ◆ **il y a eu une ~ administrative** there was an administrative mix-up*

embrouillé, e /ɑ̃bʀuje/ (ptp de **embrouiller**) **ADJ** *[style, problème, idées]* muddled, confused; *[papiers]* muddled, mixed-up

embrouillement /ɑ̃bʀujmɑ̃/ **NM** muddle ◆ **l'~ de ses explications** his muddled explanations

embrouiller /ɑ̃bʀuje/ ▸ conjug 1 ◂ **VT** 1 *[+ fils]* to tangle (up), to snarl up; *[+ affaire, problème]* to muddle (up), to confuse 2 *[+ personne]* to muddle, to confuse, to mix up **VPR** **s'embrouiller** 1 *[idées, style, situation]* to become muddled *ou* confused 2 *[personne]* to get in a muddle, to become confused *ou* muddled ◆ **s'~ dans un discours/ses explications** to get in a muddle with a speech/with one's explanations

embroussaillé, e /ɑ̃bʀusaje/ **ADJ** *[chemin]* overgrown; *[barbe, sourcils, cheveux]* bushy, shaggy

embrumer /ɑ̃bʀyme/ ▸ conjug 1 ◂ **VT** *(littér)* to mist over, to cloud over *(de* with); *(fig)* to cloud *(de* with); ◆ **à l'horizon embrumé** on the misty *ou* hazy horizon ◆ **l'esprit embrumé par l'alcool** his mind fuddled *ou* clouded with drink

embruns /ɑ̃bʀœ̃/ **NMPL** sea spray *(NonC)*, spindrift *(NonC)*

embryogenèse /ɑ̃bʀijoʒənɛz/ **NF** embryogeny, embryogenesis

embryologie /ɑ̃bʀijɔlɔʒi/ **NF** embryology

embryologique /ɑ̃bʀijɔlɔʒik/ **ADJ** embryologic(al)

embryologiste /ɑ̃bʀijɔlɔʒist/ **NMF** embryologist

embryon /ɑ̃bʀijɔ̃/ **NM** *(lit, fig)* embryo ◆ **à l'état d'~** *(fig)* in embryo, in an embryonic state ◆ **un ~ de réseau/gouvernement** an embryonic network/government

embryonnaire /ɑ̃bʀijɔnɛʀ/ **ADJ** *(Méd, fig)* embryonic ◆ **à l'état ~** *(fig)* in embryo, in an embryonic state

embûche /ɑ̃byʃ/ **NF** pitfall, trap ◆ **semé d'~s** treacherous, full of pitfalls *ou* traps

embuer /ɑ̃bɥe/ ▸ conjug 1 ◂ **VT** to mist (up), to mist over ◆ **vitre embuée** misted(-up) window pane ◆ **yeux embués de larmes** eyes misted (over) *ou* clouded with tears

embuscade /ɑ̃byskad/ **NF** ambush ◆ **être *ou* se tenir en ~** to lie in ambush ◆ **tendre une ~ à qn** to set (up) *ou* lay an ambush for sb ◆ **tomber dans une ~** *(Mil)* to fall into an ambush; *(tendue par des brigands)* to fall into an ambush, to be waylaid

embusqué, e /ɑ̃byske/ (ptp de **embusquer**) **ADJ** ◆ **être ~** *[soldats]* to lie *ou* wait in ambush; → **tireur** **NM** *(arg Mil)* shirker

embusquer (s') /ɑ̃byske/ ▸ conjug 1 ◂ **VPR** to lie *ou* wait in ambush

éméché, e* /emeʃe/ **ADJ** tipsy*, merry*

émeraude /em(ə)ʀod/ **NF, ADJ INV** emerald

émergence /emɛʀʒɑ̃s/ **NF** *(gén)* emergence ◆ **(point d')~ d'une source** source of a spring

émergent, e /emɛʀʒɑ̃, ɑ̃t/ **ADJ** 1 *(= en développement)* *[marché, économie, démocratie, besoins]* emerging ◆ **pays ~s** emerging countries 2 *(Géol, Opt, Phys)* emergent

émerger /emɛʀʒe/ ▸ conjug 3 ◂ **VI** 1 *(= apparaître)* to emerge ◆ **il émergea de sa chambre** he emerged from his room ◆ **le sommet émergea du brouillard** the summit rose out of *ou* emerged from the fog 2 *(* = se réveiller)* to surface [3] *(= faire saillie) [rocher, fait, artiste]* to stand out [4] *(d'une situation difficile)* to begin to see light at the end of the tunnel

émeri /em(ə)ʀi/ NM emery ♦ **toile** *ou* **papier** ~ emery paper; → **bouché**

émerillon /em(ə)ʀijɔ̃/ NM [1] *(= oiseau)* merlin [2] *(= dispositif)* swivel

émérite /emeʀit/ ADJ *(= chevronné)* highly skilled, outstanding ♦ **professeur** ~ professor emeritus, emeritus professor

émersion /emɛʀsjɔ̃/ NF emersion

émerveillement /emɛʀvɛjmɑ̃/ NM *(= sentiment)* wonder; *(= vision, sons)* wonderful thing, marvel

émerveiller /emɛʀveje/ ▸ conjug 1 ◂ VT to fill with wonder VPR **s'émerveiller** to be filled with wonder ♦ **s'~ de** to marvel at, to be filled with wonder at

émétique /emetik/ ADJ, NM emetic

émetteur, -trice /emetœʀ, tʀis/ ADJ [1] *(Radio)* transmitting; → **poste²**, **station** [2] *(Fin)* issuing *(épith)* ♦ **banque émettrice** issuing bank NM *(Radio)* transmitter ♦ **~-récepteur** transmitter-receiver, transceiver NM,F *(Fin)* issuer

émettre /emɛtʀ/ ▸ conjug 56 ◂ VT [1] *[+ lumière] [lampe]* to give (out), to send out; *(Phys)* to emit; *[+ son, radiation, liquide]* to give out, to send out, to emit; *[+ odeur]* to give off [2] *(Radio, TV)* to transmit; *[+ avion, bateau]* to send out ♦ **son bateau n'émet plus** he's no longer sending out signals ♦ ~ **sur ondes courtes** to broadcast *ou* transmit on shortwave [3] *(Fin) [+ monnaie, actions]* to issue; *[+ emprunt]* to issue, to float; *[+ chèque]* to draw [4] *[+ idée, hypothèse, doute]* to voice, to put forward

émeu /emø/ NM emu

émeute /emøt/ NF riot ♦ **~s** riots, rioting

émeutier, -ière /emøtje, jɛʀ/ NM,F rioter

émiettement /emjɛtmɑ̃/ NM *[de pain, terre]* crumbling; *[de territoire]* breaking up, splitting up; *[de pouvoir, responsabilités]* dispersion; *[d'énergie, effort, temps]* dissipation; *[de fortune]* frittering away

émietter /emjete/ ▸ conjug 1 ◂ VT *[+ pain, terre]* to crumble; *[+ territoire]* to break up, to split up; *[+ pouvoir, responsabilités]* to disperse; *[+ énergie, effort, temps]* to dissipate VPR **s'émietter** *[pain, terre]* to crumble; *[pouvoir]* to disperse; *[énergie, existence]* to dissipate; *[fortune]* to be frittered *ou* whittled away

émigrant, e /emigʀɑ̃, ɑ̃t/ NM,F emigrant

émigration /emigʀasjɔ̃/ NF emigration

émigré, e /emigʀe/ (ptp de **émigrer**) NM,F *(Hist)* émigré; *(Pol)* expatriate, émigré ♦ **(travailleur)** ~ migrant worker

émigrer /emigʀe/ ▸ conjug 1 ◂ VI *[personnes]* to emigrate; *[animaux]* to migrate

émincé /emɛ̃se/ NM *(= plat)* émincé; *(= tranche)* sliver, thin slice ♦ ~ **de veau/de foie de veau** émincé of veal/calves' liver

émincer /emɛ̃se/ ▸ conjug 3 ◂ VT to slice thinly, to cut into slivers *ou* thin slices

éminemment /eminamɑ̃/ ADV eminently

éminence /eminɑ̃s/ NF [1] *[de terrain]* knoll, hill; *(Méd)* protuberance [2] *[de qualité, rang]* distinction, eminence [3] *(= cardinal)* Eminence ♦ **Son/Votre Éminence** his/your Eminence ♦ **l'~ grise** *(fig)* the power behind the throne, the éminence grise

éminent, e /eminɑ̃, ɑ̃t/ ADJ distinguished, eminent ♦ **mon ~ collègue** *(frm)* my learned *ou* distinguished colleague

émir /emiʀ/ NM emir

émirat /emiʀa/ NM emirate ♦ **les Émirats arabes unis** the United Arab Emirates

émissaire /emisɛʀ/ NM *(= personne)* emissary; → **bouc**

émission /emisjɔ̃/ NF [1] *(Phys) [de son, lumière, signaux]* emission ♦ **source d'~ (de lumière/chaleur)** (emitting) source (of light/heat) [2] *(Radio, TV) (= transmission de sons, d'images)* broadcasting; *(= programme)* broadcast, programme *(Brit)*, program *(US)* ♦ ~ **télévisée/radiophonique** television/radio programme *ou* broadcast ♦ ~ **(de télévision) par câble** cablecast ♦ **les ~s de la semaine** this week's programmes ♦ **"nos émissions sont terminées"** "that's the end of today's broadcasts *ou* programmes *ou* broadcasting" [3] *[de monnaie, actions, emprunt]* issue, flotation; *[de chèque]* drawing ♦ **monopole d'~** monopoly of issue ♦ **cours d'~** issue par ♦ **prix d'~** offering price; → **banque** [4] *[d'idée, hypothèse]* voicing, putting forward [5] *(Physiol)* ~ **d'urine/de sperme** emission of urine/semen [6] *(Phon)* ~ **de voix** utterance

emmagasiner /ɑ̃magazine/ ▸ conjug 1 ◂ VT *(gén = amasser)* to store up, to accumulate; *[+ chaleur]* to store; *[+ souvenirs, connaissances]* to amass, to accumulate; *(= stocker)* to store, to put into store, to warehouse

emmailloter /ɑ̃majɔte/ ▸ conjug 1 ◂ VT *[+ doigt, pied]* to bind (up), to bandage; *[+ enfant]* to wrap up

emmanché, e †* /ɑ̃mɑ̃ʃe/ (ptp de **emmancher**) NM,F *(= crétin)* twit*, jerk*, berk* *(Brit)*

emmanchement /ɑ̃mɑ̃ʃmɑ̃/ NM *[d'outil]* fitting of a handle *(de* to, on, onto)

emmancher /ɑ̃mɑ̃ʃe/ ▸ conjug 1 ◂ VT *[+ pelle]* to fix *ou* put a handle on ♦ ~ **une affaire*** to get a deal going, to set up a deal ♦ **l'affaire s'emmanche mal*** things are getting off to a bad start ♦ **l'affaire est bien/mal emmanchée*** the deal has got off to a good/bad start

emmanchure /ɑ̃mɑ̃ʃyʀ/ NF armhole

Emmaüs /emays/ N Emmaus

EMMAÜS

This is the name of a well-known charity founded in 1949 by l'abbé Pierre that provides help for homeless people. It is partly financed by the proceeds of jumble sales organized by a community of volunteers known as « les chiffonniers d'Emmaüs ».

emmêlement /ɑ̃mɛlmɑ̃/ NM *(= action)* tangling; *(= état)* tangle, muddle

emmêler /ɑ̃mele/ ▸ conjug 1 ◂ VT *[+ cheveux]* to tangle (up), to knot; *[+ fil]* to tangle (up), to entangle, to muddle up; *[+ affaire]* to confuse, to muddle ♦ **tes cheveux sont tout emmêlés** your hair is all tangled ♦ **tu emmêles tout** you're getting everything mixed up *ou* muddled (up) *ou* confused VPR **s'emmêler** *[corde, cheveux]* to tangle, to get in a tangle ♦ **s'~ les pieds dans le tapis** to get one's feet caught in the carpet ♦ **s'~ dans ses explications** to get in a muddle with one's explanations ♦ **s'~ les pieds*** *ou* **crayons*** *ou* **pinceaux*** *ou* **pédales*** to get all confused, to get in a right muddle* *(Brit)* ♦ **tout s'emmêle dans ma tête** everything's muddled up *ou* confused in my head

emménagement /ɑ̃menaʒmɑ̃/ NM moving in *(NonC)* ♦ **au moment de leur ~ dans la nouvelle maison** when they moved into the new house

emménager /ɑ̃menaʒe/ ▸ conjug 3 ◂ VI to move in ♦ ~ **dans** to move into

emmener /ɑ̃m(ə)ne/ ▸ conjug 5 ◂ VT [1] *[+ personne] (comme otage)* to take away; *(comme invité, compagnon)* to take (along) ♦ ~ **qn au cinéma** to take sb to the cinema ♦ ~ **qn en prison** to take sb (away *ou* off) to prison ♦ ~ **qn en promenade** *ou* **faire une promenade** to take sb (off) for a walk ♦ ~ **déjeuner qn** to take sb out to *ou* for lunch ♦ **voulez-vous que je vous emmène (en voiture) ?** shall I give you *ou* would you like a lift *(Brit)* *ou* ride *(US)*? [2] *(* = emporter) [+ chose]* to take ♦ **tu vas ~ cette grosse valise ?** are you going to take that huge suitcase (with you)? [3] *(Mil, Sport = guider) [+ équipe, troupe]* to lead

emment(h)al /emɛtal/ NM Emmenthal (cheese)

emmerdant, e* /ɑ̃mɛʀdɑ̃, ɑ̃t/ ADJ [1] *(= irritant, gênant)* damned *ou* bloody *(Brit)* annoying* ♦ **elle n'est pas trop ~e** she isn't too much of a pain* [2] *(= ennuyeux)* damned *ou* bloody *(Brit)* boring* ♦ **qu'est-ce qu'il est ~ avec ses histoires** what a damned *ou* bloody *(Brit)* bore *ou* pain (in the neck) he is with his stories*

emmerde* /ɑ̃mɛʀd/ NF ⇒ **emmerdement**

emmerdement* /ɑ̃mɛʀdəmɑ̃/ NM hassle* ♦ **quel ~ !** what a damned *ou* bloody *(Brit)* nuisance!* ♦ **j'ai eu tellement d'~s avec cette voiture** that car has given me so much damned *ou* bloody *(Brit)* trouble* ♦ **je n'ai que des ~s en ce moment** it's just one damned *ou* bloody *(Brit)* hassle after the other at the moment* ♦ **ça risque de m'attirer des ~s** it's likely to get me into hot water* *ou* to land me in the shit**

emmerder* /ɑ̃mɛʀde/ ▸ conjug 1 ◂ VT ♦ ~ **qn** *(= irriter)* to bug sb*, to get on sb's nerves; *(= préoccuper, contrarier)* to bug sb*, to bother sb; *(= lasser)* to bore the pants off sb*, to bore sb stiff* *ou* to death*; *(= mettre dans l'embarras)* to get sb into trouble, to land sb in it* ♦ **on n'a pas fini d'être emmerdé avec ça** we haven't heard the last of it ♦ **je suis drôlement emmerdé** I'm in deep trouble*, I'm really in the shit** ♦ **il m'emmerde à la fin, avec ses questions** he really bugs me* *ou* gets up my nose* *(Brit)* with his questions ♦ **ça m'emmerde qu'il ne puisse pas venir** it's a damned nuisance* *ou* a hell of a nuisance* that he can't come ♦ **je les emmerde !** to hell with them!*, bugger them!** *(Brit)*

VPR **s'emmerder** *(= s'ennuyer)* to be bored stiff* *ou* to death*; *(= s'embarrasser)* to put o.s. out ♦ **ne t'emmerde pas avec ça** don't bother *ou* worry about that ♦ **je me suis drôlement emmerdé à réparer ce poste !** I really put myself out repairing that damned* radio! ♦ **on ne s'emmerde pas avec eux !** there's never a dull moment with them! ♦ **tu ne t'emmerdes pas !** you've got a damn* nerve *ou* cheek! ♦ **elle a trois voitures – dis donc, elle ne s'emmerde pas !** she has three cars – (it's) all right for some!*

emmerdeur, -euse* /ɑ̃mɛʀdœʀ, øz/ NM,F damned nuisance*, pain in the neck*

emmieller /ɑ̃mjele/ ▸ conjug 1 ◂ VT [1] *[+ tisane]* to sweeten with honey [2] *(* = ennuyer)* ~ **qn** to bug sb* ♦ **je suis drôlement emmiellé** I'm in a bit of a fix*, I've run into a spot of bother* *(Brit)* [3] *(= enjôler) [+ personne]* to soft-soap*, to cajole

emmitoufler /ɑ̃mitufle/ ▸ conjug 1 ◂ VT to wrap up (warmly), to muffle up ♦ **s'~ (dans un manteau)** to wrap o.s. up (in a coat)

emmouscailler* † /ɑ̃muskaje/ ▸ conjug 1 ◂ VT ♦ ~ **qn** *(= irriter)* to bug sb*; *(= préoccuper)* to bother sb; *(= mettre dans l'embarras)* to land sb in the soup* ♦ **être bien emmouscaillé** to be in deep trouble* *ou* in a real mess ♦ **s'~ à faire qch** to go to the bother of doing sth

emmurer /ɑ̃myʀe/ ▸ conjug 1 ◂ VT *(lit)* to wall up, to immure *(frm)* ♦ **emmuré vivant** walled up alive ♦ **s'~ dans** *[+ silence, sentiment]* to retreat into ♦ **emmuré dans ses convictions** entrenched in his convictions

émoi /emwa/ NM (littér) (= trouble) agitation, emotion; (de joie) excitement; (= tumulte) commotion ◆ **doux ~** pleasant agitation ◆ **l'affaire a suscité un grand ~ dans le pays** the affair plunged the country into turmoil ◆ **dit-elle non sans ~** she said with some confusion ◆ **en ~** [cœur] in a flutter (attrib); [sens] agitated, excited ◆ **la rue était en ~** the street was in turmoil

émollient, e /emɔljɑ̃, jɑ̃t/ ADJ, NM emollient

émoluments /emɔlymɑ̃/ NMPL (Admin) [d'officier ministériel] fees, emoluments (frm); [d'employé] remuneration, emoluments (frm)

émondage /emɔ̃daʒ/ NM [d'arbre] pruning, trimming

émonder /emɔ̃de/ ▸ conjug 1 ◂ VT [+ arbre] to prune, to trim; [+ amandes] to blanch

émondeur, -euse /emɔ̃dœʀ, øz/ NM,F (= personne) pruner

émondoir /emɔ̃dwaʀ/ NM pruning hook

émoticône /emɔtikon/ NM emoticon

émotif, -ive /emɔtif, iv/ ADJ 1 [personne, choc, réaction] emotional ◆ **charge émotive** emotional charge 2 (Ling) emotive NM,F emotional person ◆ **c'est un ~** he's very emotional

émotion /emosjɔ̃/ NF 1 (= sentiment) emotion; (= peur) fright ◆ **ils ont évité l'accident mais l'~ a été grande** they avoided an accident but it gave them a bad fright ◆ **ce scandale a suscité une vive ~ dans le pays** this scandal has caused a real stir in the country ◆ **pour nous remettre de nos ~s ...** to get over all the excitement ou commotion ... ◆ **pour les amateurs d'~s fortes** for those who are looking for thrills, for thrill-seekers ◆ **grand moment d'~** very ou highly emotional moment ◆ **c'est avec une grande ~ que nous recevons ...** it is with great pleasure that we welcome ... 2 (= sensibilité) emotion, feeling ◆ **parler avec ~** to speak with emotion ou feeling, to speak feelingly (de about); ◆ **se laisser gagner par l'~** to get emotional

émotionnel, -elle /emosjɔnɛl/ ADJ emotional

émotionner* /emosjɔne/ ▸ conjug 1 ◂ VT to upset ◆ **j'en suis encore tout émotionné** it gave me quite a turn*, I'm still upset about it VPR **s'émotionner** to get worked up*, to get upset (de about)

émotivité /emɔtivite/ NF emotionalism

émoulu, e /emuly/ ADJ → **frais¹**

émoussé, e /emuse/ (ptp de **émousser**) ADJ [couteau] blunt; [goût, sensibilité] blunted, dulled

émousser /emuse/ ▸ conjug 1 ◂ VT [+ couteau] to blunt; [+ appétit] to take the edge off; [+ souvenir, désir] to dull VPR **s'émousser** [intérêt, enthousiasme] to wane; [talent] to lose its fine edge

émoustillant, e* /emustijɑ̃, ɑ̃t/ ADJ [présence] tantalizing, titillating; [propos] titillating

émoustiller* /emustije/ ▸ conjug 1 ◂ VT to titillate, to tantalize

émouvant, e /emuvɑ̃, ɑ̃t/ ADJ (nuance de compassion) moving, touching; (nuance d'admiration) stirring

émouvoir /emuvwaʀ/ ▸ conjug 27 ◂ VT 1 [+ personne] (gén) to move, to stir; (= perturber) to disturb; (= indigner) to rouse (the indignation of); (= effrayer) to disturb, to worry, to upset ◆ **leur attitude ne l'émut/leurs menaces ne l'émurent pas le moins du monde** their attitude/threats didn't disturb ou worry ou upset him in the slightest ◆ **plus ému qu'il ne voulait l'admettre par ce baiser** more aroused than he wished to admit by this kiss ◆ **leur misère l'émouvait profondément** their wretchedness moved him deeply ou upset him greatly ◆ **~ qn jusqu'aux larmes** to move sb to tears ◆ **se laisser ~ par des prières** to be moved by entreaties, to let o.s. be swayed by entreaties ◆ **encore tout ému d'avoir frôlé l'accident/de cette rencontre** still very shaken ou greatly upset at having been so close to an accident/over that encounter

2 (littér) [+ colère] to arouse ◆ **~ la pitié de qn** to move sb to pity, to arouse sb's pity

VPR **s'émouvoir** (gén) to be moved, to be stirred; (= être perturbé) to be disturbed; (= s'inquiéter) to be ou get worried, to be ou get upset ◆ **il ne s'émeut de rien** nothing upsets him ◆ **dit-il sans s'~** he said calmly ou impassively ◆ **s'~ à la vue de qch** to be moved at the sight of sth ◆ **le pays entier s'est ému de l'affaire** the affair aroused the indignation of the whole country ◆ **le gouvernement s'en est ému** the government was roused to action

empailler /ɑ̃paje/ ▸ conjug 1 ◂ VT [+ animal] to stuff; [+ chaise] to bottom (with straw)

empailleur, -euse /ɑ̃pajœʀ, øz/ NM,F [de chaise] chair-bottomer; [d'animal] taxidermist

empalement /ɑ̃palmɑ̃/ NM impalement

empaler /ɑ̃pale/ ▸ conjug 1 ◂ VT (= supplicier) to impale; (= embrocher) to put on a spit VPR **s'empaler** to impale o.s. (sur on)

empan /ɑ̃pɑ̃/ NM (Hist = mesure) span

empanaché, e /ɑ̃panaʃe/ ADJ plumed

empanner /ɑ̃pane/ ▸ conjug 1 ◂ VI (Naut) to gibe (Brit), to jibe (US)

empaquetage /ɑ̃paktaʒ/ NM (gén) wrapping (up); (Comm = conditionnement) packing, packaging

empaqueter /ɑ̃pakte/ ▸ conjug 4 ◂ VT (gén) to wrap (up); (Comm = conditionner) to pack, to package

emparer (s') /ɑ̃paʀe/ ▸ conjug 1 ◂ VPR 1 ◆ **s'~ de** [+ objet] to seize ou grab (hold of); [+ butin] to seize, to grab; [+ otage] to seize; [+ conversation, sujet] to take over; [+ prétexte] to seize (up)on; (Mil) [+ ville, territoire, ennemi, pouvoir] to seize ◆ **s'~ des moyens de production/d'information** to take over ou seize the means of production/the information networks ◆ **ils se sont emparés du caissier** they grabbed (hold of) the cashier ◆ **s'~ du ballon** (Rugby) to get possession (of the ball) ◆ **les journaux se sont emparés de l'affaire** the papers picked up the story 2 ◆ **s'~ de** [jalousie, colère, remords] to take possession of, to take ou lay hold of ◆ **cette obsession s'empara de son esprit** his mind was taken over by this obsession ◆ **une grande peur s'empara d'elle** she suddenly became very afraid

empâté, e /ɑ̃pate/ (ptp de **empâter**) ADJ [visage] fleshy, bloated; [personne, silhouette] heavy; [langue] coated; [voix] slurred

empâtement /ɑ̃patmɑ̃/ NM 1 [de personne, silhouette, visage] thickening-out, fattening-out; [de traits] thickening 2 (Peinture) impasto

empâter /ɑ̃pate/ ▸ conjug 1 ◂ VT [+ langue, bouche] to coat, to fur (up) (Brit); [+ traits] to thicken, to coarsen ◆ **la maladie l'a empâté** his illness has made him put on weight VPR **s'empâter** [personne, silhouette, visage] to thicken out, to fatten out; [traits] to thicken, to grow fleshy; [voix] to become thick

empathie /ɑ̃pati/ NF empathy

empathique /ɑ̃patik/ ADJ empath(et)ic

empattement /ɑ̃patmɑ̃/ NM (Constr) footing; [de voiture] wheelbase; (Typo) serif

empêché, e /ɑ̃peʃe/ (ptp de **empêcher**) ADJ 1 (= retenu) detained, held up ◆ **~ par ses obligations, il n'a pas pu venir** because of his commitments he was prevented from coming 2 (= embarrassé) **avoir l'air ~** to look ou seem embarrassed ou ill-at-ease 3 † **tu es bien ~ de me le dire** you seem at a (complete) loss to know what to tell me ◆ **je serais bien ~ de vous le dire** I'd be hard put (to it) to tell you, I'd be at a loss to know what to tell you

empêchement /ɑ̃pɛʃmɑ̃/ NM (= obstacle) (unexpected) obstacle ou difficulty, hitch; (Jur) impediment ◆ **il n'est pas venu, il a eu un ~** he couldn't come – something cropped up ◆ **en cas d'~** if there's a hitch, if something crops up

empêcher /ɑ̃peʃe/ ▸ conjug 1 ◂ VT 1 [+ chose, action] to prevent, to stop ◆ **~ que qch (ne) se produise, ~ qch de se produire** to prevent sth from happening, to stop sth happening ◆ **~ que qn (ne) fasse qch** to prevent sb from doing sth, to stop sb (from) doing sth

2 ◆ **~ qn de faire qch** to prevent sb from doing sth, to stop sb (from) doing sth ◆ **rien ne nous empêche de partir** there's nothing stopping us (from) going ou preventing us from going ◆ **~ qn de sortir/d'entrer** to prevent sb from ou stop sb going out/coming in, to keep sb in/out ◆ **s'il veut le faire, on ne peut pas l'en ~ ou l'~** if he wants to do it, we can't prevent him (from doing it) ou stop him (doing it) ◆ **ça ne m'empêche pas de dormir** (lit) it doesn't prevent me from sleeping ou stop me sleeping ou keep me awake; (fig) I don't lose any sleep over it

3 (locutions) **qu'est-ce qui empêche (qu'on le fasse) ?** what's there to stop us (doing it)? ou to prevent us (from doing it)?, what's stopping us (doing it)? * ◆ **qu'est-ce que ça empêche ?*** what odds* ou difference does that make? ◆ **ça n'empêche rien*** it makes no odds* ou no difference ◆ **(il) n'empêche qu'il a tort** all the same ou be that as it may, he's wrong ◆ **j'ai peut-être tort, n'empêche, il a un certain culot !*** maybe I'm wrong, but all the same ou even so he's got a nerve!*

VPR **s'empêcher** 1 (littér) **s'~ de faire qch** to stop o.s. (from) doing sth, to refrain from doing sth ◆ **par politesse, il s'empêcha de bâiller** out of politeness he stifled a yawn ou he stopped himself yawning

2 ◆ **il n'a pas pu s'~ de rire** he couldn't help laughing, he couldn't stop himself (from) laughing ◆ **je ne peux m'~ de penser que ...** I cannot help thinking that ... ◆ **je n'ai pu m'en ~** I couldn't help it, I couldn't stop myself

empêcheur, -euse /ɑ̃pɛʃœʀ, øz/ NM,F ◆ **~ de danser ou de tourner en rond** (= trouble-fête) spoilsport; (= gêneur) troublemaker

empeigne /ɑ̃pɛɲ/ NF [de chaussure] upper ◆ **quelle gueule ou face d'~ !**‡ (péj) what a jerk‡ ou a prat‡ (Brit)!

empennage /ɑ̃penaʒ/ NM [d'avion] stabilizer, tailplane (Brit); [de flèche] (= action) feathering; (= plumes) feathers, fletchings

empenner /ɑ̃pene/ ▸ conjug 1 ◂ VT [+ flèche] to feather, to fledge

empereur /ɑ̃pʀœʀ/ NM emperor ◆ **l'~ à la barbe fleurie** Charlemagne

empesé, e /ɑ̃pəze/ (ptp de **empeser**) ADJ [col] starched; (péj) [personne, air] stiff, starchy

empeser /ɑ̃pəze/ ▸ conjug 5 ◂ VT to starch

empester /ɑ̃pɛste/ ▸ conjug 1 ◂ VT (= sentir) [+ odeur, fumée] to stink of, to reek of; (= empuantir) [+ pièce] to stink out (de with) to make stink (de of); (littér = empoisonner) to poison, to taint (de with); ◆ **ça empeste ici** it stinks in here, there's a foul smell in here

empêtrer (s') /ɑ̃petʀe/ ▸ conjug 1 ◂ VPR ◆ **s'~ dans** (lit) to get tangled up in, to get entangled in, to get caught up in; [+ mensonges] to get o.s. tangled up in; [+ affaire] to get (o.s.) involved in, to get (o.s.) mixed up in ◆ **s'~ dans des explications** to tie o.s. up in knots trying to explain*, to get tangled up in one's explanations

emphase /ɑ̃fɑz/ NF 1 (= *pompe*) bombast, pomposity ◆ **avec ~** bombastically, pompously ◆ **sans ~** in a straightforward manner, simply 2 († = *force d'expression*) vigour

emphatique /ɑ̃fatik/ ADJ 1 (= *grandiloquent*) bombastic, pompous 2 (*Ling*) emphatic

emphysémateux, -euse /ɑ̃fizematø, øz/ ADJ emphysematous NM,F emphysema sufferer

emphysème /ɑ̃fizɛm/ NM emphysema

empiècement /ɑ̃pjɛsmɑ̃/ NM [*de corsage*] yoke

empierrement /ɑ̃pjɛʀmɑ̃/ NM 1 (= *action*) [*de route*] metalling (*Brit*), gravelling (*US*); [*de voie de chemin de fer*] ballasting; [*de bassin, cour, fossé*] lining with stones 2 (= *pierres*) [*de route*] roadbed, road metal (*Brit*); [*de chemin de fer*] ballast

empierrer /ɑ̃pjeʀe/ ▸ conjug 1 ◂ VT [*+ route*] to metal (*Brit*), to gravel (*US*); [*+ voie de chemin de fer*] to ballast; [*+ bassin, cour, fossé*] to line with stones

empiètement /ɑ̃pjɛtmɑ̃/ NM (*sur territoire, mer, route*) encroachment (*sur* on); (*sur droits, libertés*) infringement (*sur* of) encroachment (*sur* on); (*sur des attributions*) trespassing (*sur* on)

empiéter /ɑ̃pjete/ ▸ conjug 6 ◂ **empiéter sur** VT INDIR [*+ territoire, mer, route*] to encroach (up)on; [*+ droit, liberté*] to infringe, to encroach (up)on; [*+ domaine, attributions*] to encroach (up)on, to trespass on ◆ **~ sur un couloir** (*Athlétisme*) to run into a lane

empiffrer (s')* /ɑ̃pifʀe/ ▸ conjug 1 ◂ VPR to stuff one's face*, to stuff o.s.* (*de* with)

empilable /ɑ̃pilabl/ ADJ [*siège*] stackable

empilage /ɑ̃pilaʒ/, **empilement** /ɑ̃pilmɑ̃/ NM (= *action*) piling up, stacking up; (= *pile*) pile, stack

empiler /ɑ̃pile/ ▸ conjug 1 ◂ VT 1 (= *mettre en pile*) to pile (up), to stack (up) 2 (* = *voler*) to rook*, to do* (*Brit*) (*de* out of) ◆ **se faire ~** to be had* *ou* done* (*Brit*) VPR **s'empiler** 1 (= *s'amonceler*) to be piled up (*sur* on) 2 (= *s'entasser*) **s'~ dans** [*+ local, véhicule*] to squeeze *ou* pile into

empire /ɑ̃piʀ/ NM 1 (*Pol, fig*) empire ◆ **~ colonial/industriel/financier** colonial/industrial/financial empire ◆ **pas pour un ~ !** not for all the tea in China!, not for all the world! ◆ **premier/second Empire** First/Second Empire ◆ **pendule Empire** Empire clock
2 (= *autorité, emprise*) influence, authority ◆ **avoir de l'~ sur** to have influence *ou* a hold on *ou* over, to hold sway over ◆ **prendre de l'~ sur** to gain influence *ou* a hold over ◆ **exercer son ~ sur** to exert one's authority over, to use one's influence on *ou* over ◆ **~ sur soi-même** self-control
◆ **sous l'empire de** [*+ peur, colère*] in the grip of; [*+ jalousie*] possessed by ◆ **sous l'~ de la boisson** under the influence of alcohol
COMP **l'Empire byzantin** the Byzantine Empire
l'Empire du Milieu the Middle Kingdom
l'Empire romain d'Occident/d'Orient the Western/Eastern Roman Empire
l'Empire du Soleil-Levant the Land of the Rising Sun

empirer /ɑ̃piʀe/ ▸ conjug 1 ◂ VI to get worse, to deteriorate VT to make worse, to worsen

empirique /ɑ̃piʀik/ ADJ (*Philos, Phys*) empirical; († † *Méd*) empiric NM († † *Méd*) empiric

empiriquement /ɑ̃piʀikmɑ̃/ ADV empirically

empirisme /ɑ̃piʀism/ NM empiricism

empiriste /ɑ̃piʀist/ ADJ, NMF (*Philos, Phys*) empiricist; († † *Méd*) empiric

emplacement /ɑ̃plasmɑ̃/ NM (= *endroit*) place; (= *site*) site; (*pour construire*) site, location; [*de parking*] parking space ◆ **à** *ou* **sur l'~ d'une ancienne cité romaine** on the site of an ancient Roman city ◆ **pour indiquer l'~ du chemin** to show the location of the path ◆ **~ publicitaire** (*sur un mur*) advertising site *ou* space (*NonC*); (*dans un journal*) advertising space (*NonC*)

emplafonner* /ɑ̃plafɔne/ ▸ conjug 1 ◂ VT to slam* *ou* smash* into ◆ **il s'est fait ~ par un camion** a lorry slammed* *ou* smashed* into his car *ou* him

emplâtre /ɑ̃plɑtʀ/ NM (*Méd*) plaster; (* = *personne*) (great) lump*, clot* ◆ **ce plat vous fait un ~ sur l'estomac*** this kind of food lies heavy on your stomach; → **jambe**

emplette † /ɑ̃plɛt/ NF purchase ◆ **faire l'~ de qch** to purchase sth ◆ **faire des** *ou* **quelques ~s** to do some shopping, to make some purchases

emplir /ɑ̃pliʀ/ ▸ conjug 2 ◂ VT († , *littér*) 1 [*+ verre, récipient*] to fill (up) (*de* with) 2 [*foule, meubles*] to fill VPR **s'emplir** ◆ **s'~ de** to fill with ◆ **la pièce s'emplissait de lumière/de gens** the room was filling with light/people

emploi /ɑ̃plwa/ NM 1 (= *poste, travail*) job ◆ **l'~** (*Écon*) employment ◆ **créer de nouveaux ~s** to create new jobs ◆ **la situation de l'~** the employment situation ◆ **plein(-)~** full employment ◆ **~s de service** service jobs; → **demande, offre, proximité**
2 (= *mode d'utilisation*) [*d'appareil, produit*] use; [*de mot, expression*] use, usage ◆ **un ~ nouveau de cet appareil** a new use for this piece of equipment ◆ **divers ~s d'un mot** different uses of a word ◆ **c'est un ~ très rare de cette expression** it's a very rare use *ou* usage of this expression; → **mode²**
3 (= *usage*) use ◆ **je n'en ai pas l'~** I have no use for it ◆ **l'~ qu'il fait de son argent/temps** how he uses his money/time, the use he makes of his money/time; → **double**
4 (*Théât* = *rôle*) role, part ◆ **avoir le physique** *ou* **la tête de l'~*** to look the part
5 (*locutions*)
◆ **sans emploi** (= *sans travail*) unemployed; (= *inutilisé*) unused
COMP **emploi-jeune** ◆ **la création de 3 500 ~s-jeunes** the creation of 3,500 jobs for young people
emploi du temps time-table, schedule; (*Scol*) timetable ◆ **~ du temps chargé** heavy *ou* busy timetable, busy schedule

employabilité /ɑ̃plwajabilite/ NF [*de personne*] employability

employable /ɑ̃plwajabl/ ADJ [*appareil, produit*] usable, employable; [*personne*] employable

employé, e /ɑ̃plwaje/ (ptp de **employer**) NM,F employee ◆ **~ de banque** bank employee *ou* clerk ◆ **~ de commerce** business employee ◆ **~ de bureau** office worker *ou* clerk ◆ **~ municipal** council worker *ou* employee ◆ **~ des postes/des chemins de fer/du gaz** postal/railway (*Brit*) *ou* railroad (*US*)/gas worker ◆ **on a sonné, c'est l'~ du gaz** there's someone at the door – it's the gasman* ◆ **~ de maison** domestic employee ◆ **les ~s de cette firme** the staff *ou* employees of this firm

employer /ɑ̃plwaje/ ▸ conjug 8 ◂ VT 1 (= *utiliser*) to use, to employ ◆ **~ toute son énergie à faire qch** to apply *ou* devote all one's energies to doing sth ◆ **~ son temps à faire qch/à qch** to spend one's time doing sth/on sth ◆ **~ son argent à faire qch/à qch** to spend *ou* use one's money doing sth/on sth ◆ **bien ~** [*+ temps, argent*] to put to good use, to make good use of; [*+ mot, expression*] to use properly *ou* correctly ◆ **mal ~** [*+ temps, argent*] to misuse; [*+ mot, expression*] to misuse, to use wrongly *ou* incorrectly ◆ **ce procédé emploie énormément de matières premières** this process uses (up) huge amounts of raw materials
2 (= *faire travailler*) [*+ main-d'œuvre*] to employ ◆ **ils l'emploient comme vendeur/à trier le courrier** they employ him as a salesman/to sort the mail ◆ **il est mal employé à ce poste** he has been given the wrong sort of job *ou* is not suited to the post ◆ **il est employé par cette société** he is employed by that firm, he is on the staff of that firm
VPR **s'employer** ◆ **s'~ à faire qch/à qch** to apply *ou* devote o.s. to doing sth/to sth

employeur, -euse /ɑ̃plwajœʀ, øz/ GRAMMAIRE ACTIVE 46.3 NM,F employer

emplumé, e /ɑ̃plyme/ ADJ feathered, plumed

empocher* /ɑ̃pɔʃe/ ▸ conjug 1 ◂ VT (= *mettre en poche*) to pocket; (= *obtenir*) [*+ argent*] to pocket; [*+ prix*] to carry off; [*+ médaille*] to win

empoignade /ɑ̃pwaɲad/ NF (= *bagarre*) fight; (= *altercation*) argument, row (*Brit*)

empoigne /ɑ̃pwaɲ/ NF → **foire**

empoigner /ɑ̃pwaɲe/ ▸ conjug 1 ◂ VT 1 (= *saisir*) to grasp, to grab (hold of) 2 (= *émouvoir*) to grip VPR **s'empoigner** * (= *se battre*) to fight, to have a go at one another*

empois /ɑ̃pwa/ NM starch (*for linen etc*)

empoisonnant, e* /ɑ̃pwazɔnɑ̃, ɑt/ ADJ (= *irritant*) irritating; (= *contrariant*) annoying, aggravating* ◆ **il est ~ avec ses questions** he's so irritating *ou* he's such a nuisance *ou* such a pain* with his questions

empoisonnement /ɑ̃pwazɔnmɑ̃/ NM (*Méd*) poisoning

empoisonner /ɑ̃pwazɔne/ ▸ conjug 1 ◂ VT 1 (= *intoxiquer, tuer*) **~ qn** [*assassin*] to poison sb; [*aliments avariés*] to give sb food poisoning ◆ **empoisonné à la strychnine** poisoned with strychnine ◆ **flèches empoisonnées** poisoned arrows ◆ **propos empoisonnés** poisonous words; → **cadeau**
2 (= *altérer*) [*+ relations, vie politique*] to poison; [*+ air*] to stink out ◆ **elle empoisonne la vie de ses proches** she's making her family's life a misery
3 (* = *ennuyer*) **~ qn** [*gêneur*] to get on sb's nerves; [*contretemps*] to annoy sb, to bug sb* ◆ **il m'empoisonne avec ses jérémiades** his constant complaints really get on my nerves ◆ **il est bien empoisonné maintenant** he's in a real mess now*
VPR **s'empoisonner** 1 (*lit*) to poison o.s.; (*par intoxication alimentaire*) to get food poisoning
2 (* = *s'ennuyer*) to be bored stiff* *ou* to death* ◆ **qu'est-ce qu'on s'empoisonne** this is such a drag* ◆ **s'~ (l'existence) à faire qch** (= *s'embarrasser*) to go to the trouble *ou* bother of doing sth

empoisonneur, -euse /ɑ̃pwazɔnœʀ, øz/ NM,F 1 (*lit*) poisoner 2 (* = *gêneur*) pain in the neck*

empoissonner /ɑ̃pwasɔne/ ▸ conjug 1 ◂ VT to stock with fish

emporté, e /ɑ̃pɔʀte/ (ptp de **emporter**) ADJ [*caractère, personne*] quick-tempered, hot-tempered; [*ton, air*] angry

emportement /ɑ̃pɔʀtəmɑ̃/ NM fit of anger, rage, anger (*NonC*) ◆ **avec ~** angrily ◆ **aimer qn avec ~** (*littér*) to love sb passionately, to be madly in love with sb

emporte-pièce /ɑ̃pɔʀt(ə)pjɛs/ NM INV (= *outil*) punch; (*Culin*) pastry cutter
◆ **à l'emporte-pièce** [*déclaration, jugement*] cut-and-dried

emporter /ɑ̃pɔʀte/ ▸ conjug 1 ◂ VT 1 (= *prendre comme bagage*) [*+ vivres, vêtements*] to take ◆ **emportez des vêtements chauds** take warm clothes (with you) ◆ **j'emporte de quoi écrire** I'm taking something to write with ◆ **si vous gagnez, vous pouvez l'~ (avec vous)** if you win, you can take it away (with you) ◆ **plats chauds/boissons à ~** *ou (Helv)* **à l'~** take-away *(Brit) ou* take-out *(US)* hot meals/drinks, hot meals/drinks to go *(US)* ◆ **~ un secret dans la tombe** to take *ou* carry a secret to the grave ◆ **il ne l'emportera pas en** *ou* **au paradis !** he'll soon be smiling on the other side of his face!

2 *(= enlever) [+ objet inutile]* to take away, to remove; *[+ prisonniers]* to take away; *[+ blessés]* to carry *ou* take away; *(* = dérober)* to take ◆ **emportez ces papiers/vêtements, nous n'en avons plus besoin** take those papers/clothes away, we don't need them any more ◆ **ils ont emporté l'argenterie !** they've made off with * *ou* taken the silver!; → **diable**

3 *(= entraîner) [courant, vent]* to sweep along, to carry along; *[navire, train]* to carry along; *[imagination, colère]* to carry away; *[enthousiasme]* to carry away *ou* along, to sweep along ◆ **le courant emportait leur embarcation** the current swept *ou* carried their boat along ◆ **emporté par son élan** carried *ou* borne along by his own momentum ◆ **emporté par son imagination/enthousiasme** carried away by his imagination/enthusiasm ◆ **se laisser ~ par la colère** to lose one's temper ◆ **le train qui m'emportait vers de nouveaux horizons** the train which carried *ou* bore me away towards new horizons

4 *(= arracher) [+ jambe, bras]* to take off; *[+ cheminée, toit]* to blow away *ou* off; *[+ pont, berge]* to wash away, to carry away; *(euph = tuer) [maladie]* to carry off ◆ **l'obus lui a emporté le bras gauche** the shell blew off *ou* took off his left arm ◆ **pont emporté par le torrent** bridge swept *ou* carried away by the flood ◆ **la vague a emporté trois passagers** the wave washed *ou* swept three passengers overboard ◆ **ça emporte la bouche** *ou* **la gueule** ‡ it takes the roof of your mouth off *

5 *(= gagner) [+ prix]* to carry off; *(Mil) [+ position]* to take, to win ◆ **~ la décision** to carry *ou* win the day ◆ **~ l'adhésion de qn** to win sb over

6 *(locutions)* ◆ **l'~ (sur)** *[personne]* to gain *ou* get the upper hand (over); *[solution, méthode]* to prevail (over) ◆ **il a fini par l'~** he finally gained *ou* got the upper hand, he finally came out on top ◆ **il l'a emporté (sur Sampras) 6-4/7-5/6-2** *(Tennis)* he won (against Sampras) 6-4/7-5/6-2 ◆ **il va l'~ sur son adversaire** he's going to get the better of his opponent ◆ **la modération/cette solution finit par l'~** moderation/this solution prevailed in the end *ou* finally won the day ◆ **cette méthode l'emporte sur l'autre** this method has the edge on the other one *ou* is more satisfactory than the other one ◆ **cette voiture l'emporte sur ses concurrents sur tous les plans** this car outperforms its competitors on every score ◆ **il l'emporte sur ses concurrents en adresse** he outmatches his opponents in skill, his opponents can't match *ou* rival him for skill

VPR **s'emporter** 1 *(= s'irriter)* to lose one's temper *(contre* with) to blow up * *(contre* at)

2 *(= s'emballer) [cheval]* to bolt ◆ **faire (s')~ son cheval** to make one's horse bolt

empoté, e * /ɑ̃pɔte/ **ADJ** awkward, clumsy **NM,F** *(péj)* awkward lump *

empourprer /ɑ̃puʀpʀe/ ▸ conjug 1 ◂ **VT** *[+ visage, ciel]* to turn crimson **VPR** **s'empourprer** *[visage]* to flush, to turn crimson; *[ciel]* to turn crimson

empoussiérer /ɑ̃pusjeʀe/ ▸ conjug 6 ◂ **VT** to cover with dust, to make dusty

empreindre /ɑ̃pʀɛ̃dʀ/ ▸ conjug 52 ◂ *(littér)* **VT** *(= imprimer)* to imprint; *(fig) (= marquer)* to stamp; *(= nuancer)* to tinge *(de* with) **VPR** **s'empreindre** ◆ **s'~ de** *[+ mélancolie]* to be tinged with

empreint, e[1] /ɑ̃pʀɛ̃, ɛ̃t/ (ptp de **empreindre**) **ADJ** **empreint de** *[nostalgie, tristesse, regret, jalousie]* tinged with; *[autorité]* marked *ou* stamped with; *[menaces]* fraught *ou* heavy with ◆ **~ de mystère/poésie** with a certain mysterious/poetic quality ◆ **d'un ton ~ de gravité** in a somewhat solemn voice ◆ **dire qch d'un ton ~ de respect** to say sth respectfully

empreinte[2] /ɑ̃pʀɛ̃t/ **NF** 1 *(lit, gén)* imprint, impression; *[d'animal]* track ◆ **~ (de pas)** footprint ◆ **~s (digitales)** (finger)prints ◆ **~ génétique** genetic fingerprint ◆ **~ vocale** voiceprint ◆ **prendre l'~ d'une dent** to take an impression of a tooth ◆ **relever** *ou* **prendre des ~s digitales** to take fingerprints 2 *(= influence)* stamp, mark ◆ **laisser une ~ indélébile sur qn** to make a lasting impression on sb ◆ **son œuvre laissera son ~ dans ce siècle** his work will leave its mark on this century

empressé, e /ɑ̃pʀese/ (ptp de **s'empresser**) **ADJ** 1 *(= prévenant) [infirmière, serveur]* attentive; *[aide]* willing; *(gén péj) [admirateur, prétendant]* assiduous, overattentive; *[subordonné]* overanxious to please *(attrib)*, overzealous ◆ **faire l'~ (auprès d'une femme)** to be overattentive (towards a woman) 2 *(littér = marquant de la hâte)* eager ◆ **~ à faire qch** eager *ou* anxious to do sth

empressement /ɑ̃pʀesmɑ̃/ **NM** 1 *(= prévenance) [d'infirmière, serveur]* attentiveness; *[d'aide]* willingness; *(gén péj) [d'admirateur, prétendant]* overzealousness, overattentiveness; *[de subordonné]* overzealousness ◆ **son ~ auprès des femmes** the way he fusses around women, his overattentiveness towards women ◆ **il me servait avec ~** he waited upon me attentively 2 *(= hâte)* eagerness, anxiousness ◆ **son ~ à partir me paraît suspect** his eagerness *ou* anxiousness to leave seems suspicious to me ◆ **il montrait peu d'~ à ...** he seemed in no hurry to ..., he was obviously not anxious to ... ◆ **il s'exécuta avec ~** he complied eagerly

empresser (s') /ɑ̃pʀese/ ▸ conjug 1 ◂ **VPR** 1 *(= s'affairer)* to bustle about; *(péj)* to fuss about *ou* around, to bustle about *ou* around ◆ **s'~ auprès** *ou* **autour de** *[+ blessé, invité]* to surround with attentions; *[+ femme courtisée]* to dance attendance upon, to fuss around ◆ **ils s'empressèrent autour de la victime** they rushed to help *ou* assist the victim ◆ **ils s'empressaient auprès de l'actrice** they surrounded the actress with attentions 2 *(= se hâter)* **s'~ de faire qch** to hasten to do sth

emprise /ɑ̃pʀiz/ **NF** 1 *(= influence)* hold, ascendancy *(sur* over); ◆ **avoir beaucoup d'~ sur qn** to hold sway over sb

◆ **sous l'emprise de** ◆ **sous l'~ de la colère** in the grip of anger, gripped by anger ◆ **sous l'~ de l'alcool/de la drogue** under the influence of alcohol/of drugs 2 *(Jur = mainmise)* expropriation

emprisonnement /ɑ̃pʀizɔnmɑ̃/ **NM** imprisonment ◆ **condamné à 10 ans d'~** sentenced to 10 years in prison, given a 10-year prison sentence

emprisonner /ɑ̃pʀizɔne/ ▸ conjug 1 ◂ **VT** 1 *(en prison)* to imprison, to put in prison *ou* jail, to jail; *(dans une chambre, un couvent)* to shut up, to imprison 2 *[vêtement]* to confine; *[doctrine, milieu]* to trap ◆ **ce corset lui emprisonne la taille** this corset grips her too tightly around the waist ◆ **~ qn dans un système/un raisonnement** to trap sb within a system/by a piece of reasoning ◆ **emprisonné dans ses habitudes/la routine** imprisoned within *ou* a prisoner of his habits/routine

emprunt /ɑ̃pʀœ̃/ **NM** 1 *(= action d'emprunter) [d'argent, objet]* borrowing ◆ **ce n'était pas un vol, mais seulement un ~** it wasn't really stealing, only borrowing ◆ **recourir à l'~** *(Fin)* to resort to borrowing *ou* to a loan

2 *(= demande, somme)* loan ◆ **ses ~s successifs l'ont mis en difficulté** successive borrowing has *ou* his successive loans have put him in difficulty ◆ **~ d'État/public** government/public loan ◆ **~ du Trésor (américain)** (American *ou* US) Treasury bond ◆ **~ à 5%** loan at 5% (interest) ◆ **~s russes** Soviet loans ◆ **faire un ~ d'un million à une banque** to take out a loan of one million from a bank, to borrow a million from a bank ◆ **faire un ~ pour payer sa voiture** to borrow money *ou* take out a loan to pay for one's car

3 *(Littérat, Ling)* borrowing; *(= terme)* loan word, borrowed word, borrowing ◆ **c'est un ~ à l'anglais** it's a loan word *ou* borrowing from English

4 ◆ **d'~** *[nom, autorité]* assumed; *[matériel]* borrowed

emprunté, e /ɑ̃pʀœ̃te/ (ptp de **emprunter**) **ADJ** 1 *(= gauche) [air, personne]* ill-at-ease *(attrib)*, self-conscious, awkward 2 *(= artificiel) [gloire, éclat]* sham, feigned

emprunter /ɑ̃pʀœ̃te/ ▸ conjug 1 ◂ **VT** 1 *[+ argent, objet]* to borrow *(à* from) 2 *[+ mot, expression] (directement)* to borrow, to take *(à* from); *(par dérivation)* to derive, to take *(à* from); *[+ nom, autorité]* to assume, to take on; *[+ idée]* to borrow, to take *(à* from); ◆ **cette pièce emprunte son sujet à l'actualité** this play is based on a topical subject ◆ **métaphores empruntées à la musique** metaphors derived from music ◆ **mot emprunté à l'anglais** loan word from English 3 *[+ escalier, route]* to take; *[+ itinéraire]* to follow ◆ **"empruntez le passage souterrain"** "use the underpass" ◆ **les trains n'empruntent plus cette ligne** trains don't run on this line any more

emprunteur, -euse /ɑ̃pʀœ̃tœʀ, øz/ **NM,F** borrower

empuantir /ɑ̃pɥɑ̃tiʀ/ ▸ conjug 2 ◂ **VT** to stink out *(de* with)

empyrée /ɑ̃piʀe/ **NM** empyrean

EMT † /əɛmte/ **NF** (abrév de **éducation manuelle et technique**) → **éducation**

ému, e /emy/ (ptp de **émouvoir**) **ADJ** *[personne] (compassion)* moved; *(gratitude)* touched; *(joie)* excited; *(timidité, peur)* nervous, agitated; *[air]* filled with emotion; *[voix]* emotional, trembling with emotion; *[souvenirs]* tender, touching ◆ **~ jusqu'aux larmes** moved to tears *(devant* by); ◆ **très ~ lors de la remise des prix** very excited *ou* agitated at the prize giving ◆ **encore tout ~, il la remercia** still quite overcome *ou* still (feeling) very touched, he thanked her ◆ **dit-il d'une voix ~e** he said with emotion ◆ **trop ~ pour les remercier/leur annoncer la nouvelle** too overcome to thank them/announce the news to them

émulateur /emylatœʀ/ **NM** *(Ordin)* emulator

émulation /emylasjɔ̃/ **NF** *(gén, Ordin)* emulation ◆ **esprit d'~** spirit of competition, competitive spirit

émule /emyl/ **NMF** *(littér) (= imitateur)* emulator; *(= égal)* equal ◆ **ce fripon et ses ~s** *(péj)* this scoundrel and his like ◆ **être l'~ de qn** to emulate sb ◆ **il fait des ~s** people emulate him

émuler /emyle/ ▸ conjug 1 ◂ **VT** *(Ordin)* to emulate

émulsif, -ive /emylsif, iv/ **ADJ** *(Pharm)* emulsive; *(Chim)* emulsifying **NM** emulsifier

émulsifiant, e /emylsifjɑ̃, jɑ̃t/ **ADJ** emulsifying **NM** emulsifier

émulsion /emylsjɔ̃/ **NF** emulsion

émulsionner /emylsjɔne/ ▸ conjug 1 ◂ **VT** to emulsify

EN (abrév de **Éducation nationale**) → **éducation**

en[1] /ɑ̃/

> Lorsque **en** se trouve dans des expressions figées telles que **avoir confiance en qn, se mettre en tête de, couper qch en dés** etc, reportez-vous à l'autre mot.

PRÉPOSITION

1 [dans l'espace, lieu où l'on est] in; *(lieu où l'on va)* to ♦ **vivre ~ France/Normandie** to live in France/Normandy ♦ **aller** *ou* **partir ~ Angleterre/Normandie** to go to England/Normandy ♦ **il habite ~ banlieue/ville** he lives in the suburbs/the town ♦ **être ~ ville** to be in town ♦ **aller ~ ville** to go (in)to town ♦ **les objets ~ vitrine** the items in the window ♦ **il voyage ~ Grèce/Corse** he's travelling around Greece/Corsica

♦ **en** *+ pronom personnel* ♦ **~ lui-même, il n'y croit pas** deep down *ou* in his heart of hearts he doesn't believe it ♦ **je me disais ~ moi-même que ...** I was thinking to myself that ... ♦ **ce que j'aime ~ lui, c'est son courage** what I like about him is his courage ♦ **on voit ~ lui un futur champion du monde** they see him as a future world champion

2 [dans le temps] in ♦ **~ semaine** in *ou* during the week ♦ **~ soirée** in the evening ♦ **~ automne/été/mars/1999** in autumn/summer/March/1999 ♦ **il peut le faire ~ 3 jours** he can do it in 3 days ♦ **~ 6 ans je lui ai parlé deux fois** in (all of) 6 years I've spoken to him twice; → **de**[1]

3 [avec moyen de transport] **~ taxi/train/avion** by taxi/train *ou* rail/air ♦ **faire une promenade ~ bateau/voiture** to go for a trip in a boat/car, to go for a boat-/car-trip ♦ **ils y sont allés ~ voiture** they went by car ♦ **ils y sont allés ~ Rolls-Royce** they went in a Rolls-Royce ♦ **ils sont arrivés ~ voiture** they arrived in a car ♦ **je suis malade ~ bateau/~ voiture** I get seasick/carsick ♦ **il y est allé ~ pousse-pousse** he went there in a *ou* by rickshaw

> Notez que l'anglais emploie souvent un verbe spécifique.

♦ **aller à Londres ~ avion** to fly to London ♦ **ils ont remonté le fleuve ~ pirogue** they canoed up the river, they rowed up the river in a canoe

4 [= habillé de] in ♦ **être ~ noir/blanc** to be (dressed) in black/white, to be wearing black/white ♦ **elle est arrivée ~ manteau de fourrure** she arrived wearing *ou* in a fur coat ♦ **la femme ~ manteau de fourrure** the woman in the fur coat *ou* with a fur coat on ♦ **il était ~ chemise/pyjama** he was wearing a shirt/wearing pyjamas ♦ **être ~ chaussettes** to be in one's stockinged feet ♦ **elle était ~ bergère** she was disguised *ou* dressed as a shepherdess

5 [description, présentation] in ♦ **~ cercle/rang** in a circle/row ♦ **enregistré ~ stéréo** recorded in stereo ♦ **ils y vont ~ groupe** they are going in a group ♦ **l'œuvre de Proust ~ six volumes** Proust's works in six volumes ♦ **une pièce ~ trois actes** a three-act play, a play in three acts ♦ **ça se vend ~ boîtes de douze** they are sold in boxes of twelve ♦ **c'est écrit ~ anglais/vers/prose/lettres d'or** it's written in English/verse/prose/gold letters ♦ **image ~ trois dimensions** 3-D image, image in 3-D

♦ **en** *+ adjectif* ♦ **nous avons le même article ~ vert** we have the same item in green

♦ **en** *+ comparatif* ♦ **c'est son frère ~ mieux** he's like his brother, only better ♦ **c'est son père ~ plus jeune/petit** he's just like his father only younger/smaller, he's a younger/smaller version of his father ♦ **je veux la même valise ~ plus grand** I want the same suitcase only bigger *ou* only in a bigger size

6 [= composé de, fait de] **le plat est ~ or/argent** the dish is made of gold/silver ♦ **l'escalier sera ~ marbre** the staircase will be (in *ou* made of) marble ♦ **~ quoi est-ce** *ou* **c'est fait ?, c'est ~ quoi ?*** what's it made of?

> Notez qu'en anglais le substantif est souvent utilisé en apposition comme adjectif.

♦ **une bague ~ or/argent** a gold/silver ring ♦ **une table ~ acajou** a mahogany table ♦ **une jupe ~ soie imprimée** a printed silk skirt, a skirt made (out) of printed silk

7 [transformation] into ♦ **se changer ~** to change into ♦ **convertir/transformer qch ~** to convert/transform sth into ♦ **traduire ~ italien** to translate into Italian ♦ **casser qch ~ morceaux** to break sth in(to) pieces

8 [= comme] **agir ~ tyran/lâche** to act like a tyrant/coward ♦ **c'est ~ expert qu'il ~ a parlé** he spoke as an expert ♦ **~ bon politicien (qu'il est), il ...** good politician that he is, he ..., being the skilled politician he is, he ... ♦ **je le lui ai donné ~ cadeau/souvenir** I gave it to him as a present/souvenir

9 [= concernant] **~ politique/art/musique** in politics/art/music ♦ **~ affaires, il faut de l'audace** you have to take risks in business ♦ **je n'y connais rien ~ informatique** I don't know anything about computers ♦ **ce que je préfère ~ musique, c'est ...** what I like best in the way of music is ... ♦ **être bon** *ou* **fort ~ géographie** to be good at geography ♦ **diplôme ~ droit/histoire** law/history degree

10 [mesure] in ♦ **mesurer ~ mètres** to measure in metres ♦ **compter ~ euros** to count in euros ♦ **ce tissu se fait ~ 140 (cm)** this material comes in 140 cm width ♦ **nous avons ce manteau ~ trois tailles** we have this coat in three sizes

11 [locutions]

♦ **en** *+ participe présent*

(manière) ♦ **il me regarda ~ fronçant les sourcils** he looked at me with a frown ♦ **"je ne sais pas", dit-il ~ haussant les épaules** "I don't know" he said with a shrug ♦ **endormir un enfant ~ le berçant/chantant** to rock/sing a child to sleep

> Avec un verbe de mouvement ou d'énonciation, l'anglais préfèrera souvent un verbe suivi éventuellement d'une préposition.

♦ **monter/entrer ~ courant** to run up/in ♦ **sortir ~ rampant/boitant** to crawl/limp out ♦ **dire qch ~ murmurant/criant** to murmur/shout sth

> Là où le français emploie **en** suivi d'un verbe au participe présent pour exprimer la simultanéité, l'anglais utilise une proposition temporelle ou une forme en **ing**.

♦ **fermez la porte ~ sortant** shut the door as *ou* when you go out ♦ **elle est arrivée ~ chantant** she was singing when she arrived ♦ **j'ai écrit une lettre (tout) ~ vous attendant** I wrote a letter while I was waiting for you ♦ **il s'est endormi ~ lisant le journal** he fell asleep (while) reading the newspaper, he fell asleep over the newspaper ♦ **il s'est coupé ~ essayant d'ouvrir une boîte** he cut himself trying to open a tin ♦ **~ apprenant la nouvelle, elle s'est évanouie** she fainted when she heard the news ♦ **il a buté ~ montant dans l'autobus** he tripped as he got onto *ou* getting onto the bus [MAIS] **il a fait une folie ~ achetant cette bague** it was very extravagant of him to buy this ring

(nuance causale) by ♦ **~ disant cela, il s'est fait des ennemis** he made enemies by saying that ♦ **~ refusant de coopérer, vous risquez de tout perdre** by refusing to cooperate, you risk losing everything

♦ **en être à**

(= avoir atteint) ♦ **~ être à la page 9** to be at page 9, to have reached page 9 ♦ **où ~ est-il de** *ou* **dans ses études ?** how far has he got with his studies?, what point has he reached in his studies? ♦ **il ~ est à sa troisième année de médecine** he has reached his third year in medicine ♦ **l'affaire ~ est là** that's how the matter stands, that's as far as it's got ♦ **je ne sais plus où j'~ suis** I feel totally lost

(= se voir réduit à) ♦ **j'~ suis à me demander si** I'm beginning to wonder if, I've come to wonder if, I've got to wondering if* ♦ **il ~ est à mendier** he has come down to *ou* stooped to begging, he has been reduced to begging

en[2] /ɑ̃/

1 *(lieu)* **quand va-t-il à Nice ? – il ~ revient** when is he off to Nice? – he's just (come) back ♦ **elle était tombée dans une crevasse, on a eu du mal à l'~ sortir** she had fallen into a crevasse and they had difficulty *ou* trouble (in) getting her out (of it) ♦ **le bénéfice qu'il ~ a tiré** the profit he got out of it *ou* from it ♦ **il faut ~ tirer une conclusion** we must draw a conclusion (from it) ♦ **où ~ sommes-nous ?** *(livre, leçon)* where have we got (up) to?, where are we?; *(situation)* where do we stand?

2 *(cause, agent, instrument)* **je suis si inquiet que je n'~ dors pas** I can't sleep for worrying, I am so worried that I can't sleep ♦ **il saisit sa canne et l'~ frappa** he seized his stick and struck her with it ♦ **ce n'est pas moi qui ~ perdrai le sommeil** I won't lose any sleep over it ♦ **quelle histoire ! nous ~ avons beaucoup ri** what a business! we had a good laugh over *ou* about it ♦ **~ mourir** *(maladie)* to die of it; *(blessure)* to die because of it *ou* as a result of it ♦ **elle ~ est aimée** she is loved by him

3 *(complément de vb, d'adj, de n)* **rendez-moi mon stylo, j'~ ai besoin** give me back my pen – I need it ♦ **qu'est-ce que tu ~ feras ?** what will you do with it (*ou* them)? ♦ **c'est une bonne classe, les professeurs ~ sont contents** they are a good class and the teachers are pleased with them ♦ **elle, mentir ? elle ~ est incapable** she couldn't lie if she tried ♦ **elle a réussi et elle n'~ est pas peu fière** she has been successful and she is more than a little proud of herself *ou* of it ♦ **il ne fume plus, il ~ a perdu l'habitude** he doesn't smoke any more – he has got out of *ou* has lost the habit ♦ **sa décision m'inquiète car j'~ connais tous les dangers** her decision worries me because I am aware of all the dangers *ou* of all its possible dangers ♦ **je t'~ donne/offre 5 €** I'll give/offer you €5 for it

4 *(quantitatif, indéf)* of it, of them *(souvent omis)* ♦ **si vous aimez les pommes, prenez-~ plusieurs** if you like apples, take several ♦ **il avait bien des lettres à écrire mais il n'~ a pas écrit la moitié/beaucoup** he had a lot of letters to write but he hasn't written half of them/many (of them) ♦ **le vin est bon mais il n'y ~ a pas beaucoup** the wine is good but there isn't much (of it) ♦ **si j'~ avais** if I had any ♦ **voulez-vous du pain/des pommes ? il y ~ a encore** would you like some bread/some apples? we have still got some (left) ♦ **il n'y ~ a plus** *(pain)* there isn't any left, there's none left; *(pommes)* there aren't any left, there are none left ♦ **si vous cherchez un crayon, vous ~ trouverez des douzaines/un dans le tiroir** if you are looking for a pencil you will find dozens (of them)/one in the drawer ♦ **élevé dans le village, j'~ connaissais tous les habitants** having been brought up in the village I knew all its inhabitants ♦ **a-t-elle des poupées ? – oui, elle ~ a deux/trop/de belles** has she any dolls? – yes, she has two/too many/some lovely ones ♦ **nous avons du vin, j'~ ai acheté une bouteille hier** we have some wine, I bought a bottle yesterday ♦ **des souris ici ? nous n'~ avons jamais vu** mice here? we've never seen any ♦ **il ~ aime une autre** he loves another *(littér)*, he loves somebody else

5 *(renforcement : non traduit)* **il s'~ souviendra de cette réception** he'll certainly remember

that party • **je n'~ vois pas, moi, de places libres** well (I must say), I don't see any empty seats • **tu ~ as eu de beaux jouets à Noël !** well you did get some lovely toys *ou* what lovely toys you got for Christmas!; → **accroire, aussi, entendre, venir** *etc*

ENA /ena/ NF (abrév de **École nationale d'administration**) → **école**

enamouré, e /enamuʀe/ (ptp de **s'enamourer**) ADJ *[regard]* adoring

enamourer (s') †† /enamuʀe, ɑ̃namuʀe/ ► conjug 1 ◄ VPR • **s'~ de** to become enamoured of

énarchie /enaʀʃi/ NF *power of the énarques*

énarque /enaʀk/ NMF énarque *(student or former student of the École nationale d'administration)*

énarthrose /enaʀtʀoz/ NF socket joint

en-avant /ɑ̃navɑ̃/ NM INV *(Rugby)* forward pass, knock on

en-but /ɑ̃by(t)/ NM INV *(Rugby)* in-goal area

encablure /ɑ̃kablyʀ/ NF cable's length • **à 3 ~s de ...** 3 cables' length away from ...

encadré /ɑ̃kadʀe/ (ptp de **encadrer**) NM box

encadrement /ɑ̃kadʀəmɑ̃/ NM 1 *(NonC) [de tableau]* framing • **"tous travaux d'encadrement"** "all framing (work) undertaken" 2 *(NonC) [d'étudiants, débutants, recrues]* training, supervision 3 *(= embrasure) [de porte, fenêtre]* frame • **il se tenait dans l'~ de la porte** he stood in the doorway 4 *(= cadre)* frame • **cet ~ conviendrait mieux au sujet** this frame would be more appropriate to the subject 5 *(Admin) (= instructeurs)* training personnel; *(= cadres)* managerial staff 6 *(Écon)* ~ **du crédit** credit restriction

encadrer /ɑ̃kadʀe/ ► conjug 1 ◄ VT 1 *[+ tableau]* to frame • **c'est à ~ !** *(iro)* that's priceless!, that's one to remember!

2 *(= instruire) [+ étudiants, débutants, recrues]* to train (and supervise); *(= contrôler) [+ enfant]* to take in hand; *[+ équipe sportive, employés]* to manage; *(Écon) [+ crédit]* to restrict; *[+ prix, loyers]* to control

3 *(= entourer) [+ cour, plaine, visage]* to frame, to surround; *[+ prisonnier]* to surround; *(par deux personnes)* to flank • **les collines qui encadrent la plaine** the hills surrounding the plain • **encadré de ses gardes du corps** surrounded by his bodyguards • **l'accusé, encadré de deux gendarmes** the accused, flanked by two policemen

4 (*, *gén nég = supporter*) **je ne peux pas l'~** I can't stick* *ou* stand* him

5 *(Mil) [+ objectif]* to straddle

6 (* *= heurter) [+ véhicule, maison]* to smash into • **il s'est fait ~*** someone smashed into his car

VPR **s'encadrer** 1 *(= apparaître) [visage, silhouette]* to appear

2 * *(en voiture)* to crash one's car *(dans* into)

encadreur, -euse /ɑ̃kadʀœʀ, øz/ NM,F (picture) framer

encager /ɑ̃kaʒe/ ► conjug 3 ◄ VT *[+ animal, oiseau]* to cage (up)

encagoulé, e /ɑ̃kagule/ ADJ *[moine]* cowled; *[pénitent]* hooded, cowled; *[bandit, visage]* hooded, masked

encaissable /ɑ̃kɛsabl/ ADJ cashable, encashable *(Brit)*

encaisse /ɑ̃kɛs/ NF cash in hand, cash balance • ~ **métallique** gold and silver reserves • ~ **or** gold reserves

encaissé, e /ɑ̃kese/ (ptp de **encaisser**) ADJ *[vallée]* deep, steep-sided; *[rivière]* hemmed in by steep banks *ou* hills; *[route]* hemmed in by steep hills

encaissement /ɑ̃kɛsmɑ̃/ NM 1 *[d'argent, loyer]* collection, receipt; *[de facture]* receipt of payment *(de* for); *[de chèque]* cashing; *[d'effet de commerce]* collection 2 *[de vallée]* depth, steepsidedness • **l'~ de la route/rivière faisait que le pont ne voyait jamais le soleil** the steep hills hemming in the road/river stopped the sun from ever reaching the bridge

encaisser /ɑ̃kese/ ► conjug 1 ◄ VT 1 *[+ argent, loyer]* to collect, to receive; *[+ facture]* to receive payment for; *[+ chèque]* to cash; *[+ effet de commerce]* to collect

2 * *[+ coups, affront, défaite]* to take • **savoir ~** *[boxeur]* to be able to take a lot of beating *ou* punishment; *(dans la vie)* to know how to roll with the punches • **qu'est-ce qu'il a encaissé !** *(coups)* what a hammering he got!*, what a beating he took!; *(injures, réprimande)* what a hammering he got!*, he certainly got what for!*

3 (*, *gén nég = supporter*) **je ne peux pas ~ ce type** I can't stand* that guy • **il n'a pas encaissé cette décision** he couldn't stomach* the decision • **il n'a pas encaissé cette remarque** he didn't appreciate that remark one little bit*

4 *(Tech) [+ route, fleuve, voie ferrée]* to embank • **les montagnes qui encaissent la vallée** the mountains on either side of the valley • **la route s'encaisse entre les collines** the road is hemmed in by the hills

5 *[+ objets]* to pack in(to) boxes; *[+ plantes]* to plant in boxes *ou* tubs

encaisseur /ɑ̃kɛsœʀ/ NM collector *(of debts etc)*

encalminé, e /ɑ̃kalmine/ ADJ *[navire]* becalmed

encan /ɑ̃kɑ̃/ NM • **mettre** *ou* **vendre à l'~** to sell off by auction

encanaillement /ɑ̃kanajmɑ̃/ NM mixing with the riffraff

encanailler (s') /ɑ̃kanaje/ ► conjug 1 ◄ VPR *(hum)* to mix with the riffraff, to slum it* • **son style/langage s'encanaille** his style/language is becoming vulgar

encapuchonner /ɑ̃kapyʃɔne/ ► conjug 1 ◄ VT • ~ **un enfant** to put a child's hood up • **la tête encapuchonnée** hooded • **un groupe de bambins encapuchonnés** a group of toddlers snug in their hoods

encart /ɑ̃kaʀ/ NM *(Typo)* insert, inset • ~ **publicitaire** publicity *ou* advertising insert

encarté, e /ɑ̃kaʀte/ ADJ *(Pol) [militant]* card-carrying *(épith)* • **être ~ à un parti** to be a card-carrying member of a party

encarter /ɑ̃kaʀte/ ► conjug 1 ◄ VT *(Typo)* to insert, to inset • **le supplément télé est encarté dans le magazine** the TV listings are enclosed as an insert in the magazine

en-cas /ɑ̃ka/ NM INV *(= nourriture)* snack

encaserner /ɑ̃kazɛʀne/ ► conjug 1 ◄ VT to quarter *ou* lodge in barracks

encastrable /ɑ̃kastʀabl/ ADJ *[four, lave-vaisselle]* slot-in *(Brit) (épith)*, ready to be installed *(US) (attrib)*

encastré, e /ɑ̃kastʀe/ (ptp de **encastrer**) ADJ *[four, placard]* built-in • **spot ~ dans le plafond** recessed spotlight • **baignoire ~e (dans le sol)** sunken bath • **une église ~e entre deux gratte-ciel** a church hemmed *ou* boxed in between two skyscrapers • **de gros blocs ~s dans la neige/le sol** great blocks sunk in *ou* embedded in the snow/ground

encastrement /ɑ̃kastʀəmɑ̃/ NM *[d'interrupteur]* flush fitting; *[d'armoire, rayonnage]* recessed fitting

encastrer /ɑ̃kastʀe/ ► conjug 1 ◄ VT *(dans un mur)* to embed *(dans* in(to)) to sink *(dans* into); *[+ interrupteur]* to fit flush *(dans* with); *[+ rayonnages, armoire]* to recess *(dans* into) to fit *(dans* into); *(dans un boîtier) [+ pièce]* to fit *(dans* into); • **tous les boutons sont encastrés dans le mur** all the switches are flush with the wall • **l'aquarium est encastré dans le mur** the aquarium is built into the wall • **la voiture s'est encastrée sous le train** the car jammed itself underneath the train • **ces pièces s'encastrent l'une dans l'autre/dans le boîtier** these parts fit exactly into each other/into the case

encaustique /ɑ̃kostik/ NF wax polish

encaustiquer /ɑ̃kostike/ ► conjug 1 ◄ VT to polish, to wax

enceindre /ɑ̃sɛ̃dʀ/ ► conjug 52 ◄ VT *(gén ptp)* to encircle, to surround *(de* with); • **enceint de** encircled *ou* surrounded by

enceinte[1] /ɑ̃sɛ̃t/ ADJ F pregnant, expecting* *(attrib)* • **tomber/se retrouver ~** to get *ou* become/find o.s. pregnant • **femme ~** pregnant woman, expectant mother • **~ de cinq mois** five months pregnant • **j'étais ~ de Paul** *(= Paul était le bébé)* I was pregnant with *ou* was expecting Paul; *(= Paul était le père)* I was pregnant by Paul • **il l'a mise ~** he got *ou* made her pregnant • **~ jusqu'aux yeux*** very pregnant*

enceinte[2] /ɑ̃sɛ̃t/ NF 1 *(= mur)* wall; *(= palissade)* enclosure, fence • **une ~ de fossés défendait la place** the position was surrounded by defensive ditches *ou* was defended by surrounding ditches • **mur d'~** outer walls 2 *(= espace clos)* enclosure; *[de couvent]* precinct • **dans l'~ de la ville** within *ou* inside the town • **dans l'~ du tribunal** in(side) the court room • **dans l'~ de cet établissement** within *ou* in(side) this establishment • **~ militaire** military area *ou* zone • **~ de confinement** *(Phys)* protective shield 3 • **~ (acoustique)** speaker

encens /ɑ̃sɑ̃/ NM incense • **l'or, l'~ et la myrrhe** *(Bible)* gold, frankincense and myrrh • **l'~ des louanges/de leur flatterie** the heady wine of praise/of their flattery

encensement /ɑ̃sɑ̃smɑ̃/ NM 1 *(Rel)* incensing 2 *(= louanges)* praising *(NonC)* to the skies

encenser /ɑ̃sɑ̃se/ ► conjug 1 ◄ VT 1 *(= louanger)* to heap *ou* shower praise (up)on, to praise to the skies 2 *(Rel)* to incense

encenseur, -euse /ɑ̃sɑ̃sœʀ, øz/ NM,F *(Rel)* thurifer, censer-bearer; *(fig, †)* flatterer

encensoir /ɑ̃sɑ̃swaʀ/ NM censer, thurible • **manier l'~** *(péj)* to pour out flattery, to heap on the praise • **coups d'~** *(fig)* excessive flattery

encéphale /ɑ̃sefal/ NM encephalon

encéphalique /ɑ̃sefalik/ ADJ encephalic

encéphalite /ɑ̃sefalit/ NF encephalitis

encéphalogramme /ɑ̃sefalɔgʀam/ NM encephalogram

encéphalopathie /ɑ̃sefalɔpati/ NF encephalopathy • **~ bovine spongiforme** BSE, bovine spongiform encephalopathy *(SPÉC)*

encerclement /ɑ̃sɛʀkləmɑ̃/ NM *(par des murs)* surrounding, encircling; *(par l'armée, la police)* surrounding

encercler /ɑ̃sɛʀkle/ ► conjug 1 ◄ VT *[murs]* to surround, to encircle; *[armée, police]* to surround

enchaîné /ɑ̃ʃene/ NM *(Ciné)* change; → **fondu**

enchaînement /ɑ̃ʃɛnmɑ̃/ NM 1 *(= suite logique) [d'épisodes, preuves]* linking • **l'~ de la violence** the spiral of violence 2 *[de scènes, séquences] (= action)* linking; *(= résultat)* link 3 *(= série) [de circonstances]* sequence, series, string • **~ d'événements** chain *ou* series *ou* string *ou* sequence of events 4 *(Danse)* enchaînement • **faire un ~** *(Gym)* to do a sequence of movements • **un bel ~** a fluid sequence of movements • **~ des accords** *(Mus)* chord progression

enchaîner /ɑ̃ʃene/ ► conjug 1 ◄ VT 1 (= lier) [+ animal] to chain up; [+ prisonnier] to put in chains, to chain up ◆ ~ **qn à un arbre** to chain sb to a tree ◆ **enchaînés l'un à l'autre** chained together
2 (littér) [secret, souvenir, sentiment] to bind ◆ **l'amour enchaîne les cœurs** love binds hearts (together) ◆ **ses souvenirs l'enchaînaient à ce lieu** his memories tied ou bound ou chained him to this place
3 (= asservir) [+ peuple] to enslave; [+ presse] to muzzle, to gag ◆ ~ **la liberté** to put freedom in chains
4 (= assembler) [+ faits, épisodes, séquences] to connect, to link (together ou up); [+ paragraphes, pensées, mots] to link (together ou up), to string together ◆ **incapable d'~ deux pensées** incapable of stringing two thoughts together ◆ **elle enchaînait réunion sur réunion** she had meeting after meeting ou one meeting after another ◆ ~ **(la scène suivante)** (Ciné) to change to ou move on to the next scene ◆ **on va ~ les dernières scènes** (Ciné) we'll carry on with the last scenes, we'll go on to the last scenes
VI (Ciné, Théât) to move on ou carry on (Brit) (to the next scene) ◆ **sans laisser à Anne le temps de répondre, Paul enchaîna : "d'abord ..."** without giving Anne the time to reply, Paul went on ou continued: "first ..." ◆ **on enchaîne, enchaînons** (Théât) let's keep going ou carry on; (Ciné) let's keep rolling; (* : dans un débat) let's go on ou carry on, let's continue
VPR **s'enchaîner** [épisodes, séquences] to follow on from each other, to be linked (together); [preuves, faits] to be linked (together) ◆ **tout s'enchaîne** it's all linked ou connected, it all ties up ◆ **paragraphes/raisonnements qui s'enchaînent bien** welllinked paragraphs/pieces of reasoning

enchanté, e /ɑ̃ʃɑ̃te/ GRAMMAIRE ACTIVE 38.3 (ptp de **enchanter**) ADJ 1 (= ravi) enchanted (de by) delighted (de with); ◆ ~ **(de vous connaître)** how do you do?, (I'm) very pleased to meet you 2 (= magique) [forêt, demeure] enchanted

enchantement /ɑ̃ʃɑ̃tmɑ̃/ NM 1 (= action) enchantment; (= effet) (magic) spell, enchantment ◆ **comme par** ~ as if by magic 2 (= ravissement) delight, enchantment ◆ **ce spectacle fut un** ~ it was an enchanting ou a delightful sight ◆ **être dans l'~** to be enchanted ou delighted

enchanter /ɑ̃ʃɑ̃te/ ► conjug 1 ◄ VT 1 (= ensorceler) to enchant, to bewitch 2 (= ravir) to enchant, to delight ◆ **ça ne m'enchante pas beaucoup** I'm not exactly taken with it, it doesn't exactly thrill me VPR **s'enchanter** (littér) to rejoice (de at)

enchanteur, -teresse /ɑ̃ʃɑ̃tœʀ, tʀɛs/ ADJ enchanting, bewitching NM (= sorcier) enchanter; (fig) charmer NF **enchanteresse** enchantress

enchâssement /ɑ̃ʃɑsmɑ̃/ NM 1 [de pierre] setting (dans in) 2 (Ling) embedding

enchâsser /ɑ̃ʃɑse/ ► conjug 1 ◄ VT (gén) to set (dans in); (Ling) to embed ◆ ~ **une citation dans un texte** (littér) to insert a quotation into a text VPR **s'enchâsser** (l'un dans l'autre) to fit exactly together ◆ **s'~ dans** to fit exactly into

enchère /ɑ̃ʃɛʀ/ NF bid ◆ **faire une** ~ to bid, to make a bid ◆ **faire monter les ~s** (lit) to raise ou push up the bidding; (fig) to raise ou up the stakes ou the ante ◆ **les deux entreprises le veulent mais il laisse monter les ~s** the two companies want him but he's waiting for the highest possible bid ◆ **le système des ~s** (Cartes) the bidding system NFPL **enchères** ◆ **mettre qch aux ~s (publiques)** to put sth up for auction ◆ **le tableau a été mis aux ~s** the picture was put up for auction ou went under the hammer ◆ **vendre aux ~s** to sell by auction ◆ **acheté aux ~s** bought at an auction (sale); → **vente**

enchérir /ɑ̃ʃeʀiʀ/ ► conjug 2 ◄ VI 1 (lit) ~ **sur une offre** to make a higher bid ◆ ~ **sur qn** to bid higher than sb, to make a higher bid than sb ◆ ~ **sur (l'offre d') une somme** to go higher than ou go above ou go over an amount 2 (fig) ~ **sur** to go further than, to go beyond, to go one better than

enchérissement † /ɑ̃ʃeʀismɑ̃/ NM ⇒ **renchérissement**

enchérisseur, -euse /ɑ̃ʃeʀisœʀ, øz/ NM,F bidder

enchevêtrement /ɑ̃ʃ(ə)vɛtʀəmɑ̃/ NM [de ficelles, branches] entanglement; [de situation] confusion ◆ **l'~ de ses idées** the confusion ou muddle his ideas were in ◆ **un ~ de branches barrait la route** a tangle of branches blocked the way

enchevêtrer /ɑ̃ʃ(ə)vetʀe/ ► conjug 1 ◄ VT [+ ficelle] to tangle (up), to entangle, to muddle up; [+ idées, intrigue] to confuse, to muddle VPR **s'enchevêtrer** 1 [ficelles] to get in a tangle, to become entangled, to tangle; [branches] to become entangled ◆ **s'~ dans des cordes** to get caught up ou tangled up in ropes 2 [situations, paroles] to become confused ou muddled ◆ **mots qui s'enchevêtrent les uns dans les autres** words that run into each other ◆ **s'~ dans ses explications** to tie o.s. up in knots* explaining (something), to get tangled up in one's explanations

enchifrené, e † /ɑ̃ʃifʀəne/ ADJ [nez] blocked up

enclave /ɑ̃klav/ NF (lit, fig) enclave

enclavement /ɑ̃klavmɑ̃/ NM (= action) enclosing, hemming in ◆ **l'~ de la région par les montagnes** (= état) the way the region is enclosed by ou hemmed-in by mountains ◆ **cette province souffre de son ~** this province suffers from its isolation ou from its hemmed-in position

enclaver /ɑ̃klave/ ► conjug 1 ◄ VT 1 (= entourer) to enclose, to hem in ◆ **terrain complètement enclavé dans un grand domaine** piece of land completely enclosed within ou hemmed in by a large property ◆ **pays enclavé** landlocked country 2 (= encastrer) ~ **l'un dans l'autre** to fit together, to interlock ◆ ~ **dans** to fit into 3 (= insérer) ~ **entre** to insert between

enclenchement /ɑ̃klɑ̃ʃmɑ̃/ NM 1 (Tech) (= action) engaging; (= état) engagement; (= dispositif) interlock 2 (= début) start ◆ **l'~ du processus de paix** the start of the peace process ◆ **cela a provoqué l'~ d'une spirale déflationniste** this has set off a deflationary spiral

enclencher /ɑ̃klɑ̃ʃe/ ► conjug 1 ◄ VT [+ mécanisme] to engage; [+ affaire, processus] to get under way, to set in motion ◆ **j'ai laissé une vitesse enclenchée** I left the car in gear ◆ **l'affaire est enclenchée** things are under way VPR **s'enclencher** [mécanisme] to engage; [processus] to get under way

enclin, e /ɑ̃klɛ̃, in/ ADJ ◆ ~ **à qch/à faire qch** inclined ou prone to sth/to do sth

enclore /ɑ̃klɔʀ/ ► conjug 45 ◄ VT to enclose, to shut in ◆ ~ **qch d'une haie/d'une palissade/d'un mur** to hedge/fence/wall sth in

enclos /ɑ̃klo/ NM (= terrain, clôture) enclosure; [de chevaux] paddock; [de moutons] pen, fold

enclume /ɑ̃klym/ NF anvil; [de voiture] engine block; (Anat) anvil (bone), incus (SPÉC)

encoche /ɑ̃kɔʃ/ NF (gén) notch; [de flèche] nock ◆ **faire une ~ à** ou **sur qch** to notch sth, to make a notch in sth

encocher /ɑ̃kɔʃe/ ► conjug 1 ◄ VT (gén) to notch; [+ flèche] to nock

encodage /ɑ̃kɔdaʒ/ NM encoding

encoder /ɑ̃kɔde/ ► conjug 1 ◄ VT to encode

encodeur /ɑ̃kɔdœʀ/ NM encoder

encoignure /ɑ̃kɔɲyʀ/ NF 1 (= coin) corner 2 (= meuble) corner cupboard

encoller /ɑ̃kɔle/ ► conjug 1 ◄ VT to paste

encolure /ɑ̃kɔlyʀ/ NF [de cheval, personne, robe] neck; (= tour de cou) collar size ◆ **battre d'une ~** (Équitation) to beat by a neck

encombrant, e /ɑ̃kɔ̃bʀɑ̃, ɑt/ ADJ [paquet] cumbersome, unwieldy, bulky; [présence] burdensome, inhibiting ◆ **cet enfant est très ~** this child is a real nuisance ◆ **c'est devenu un collaborateur ~** he's become a bit of a liability

encombre /ɑ̃kɔ̃bʀ/ **sans encombre** LOC ADV without mishap ou incident

encombré, e /ɑ̃kɔ̃bʀe/ (ptp de **encombrer**) ADJ 1 [pièce] cluttered (up); [passage] obstructed; [lignes téléphoniques] jammed, overloaded; [profession] overcrowded; [marché] glutted ◆ **table ~e de papiers** table cluttered ou littered with papers ◆ **les bras ~s de paquets** his arms laden with parcels ◆ **j'ai les bronches ~es** my chest is congested ◆ **le parking est très ~** the car park is very full 2 (= embouteillé) [espace aérien, route] congested

encombrement /ɑ̃kɔ̃bʀəmɑ̃/ GRAMMAIRE ACTIVE 27.5 NM 1 (= obstruction) [de bronches] congestion ◆ **à cause de l'~ des lignes téléphoniques** because the telephone lines are jammed ou overloaded ◆ **l'~ du couloir rendait le passage malaisé** all the clutter in the corridor made it difficult to get through ◆ **un ~ de vieux meubles** a clutter ou jumble of old furniture 2 (= embouteillage) traffic jam, congestion (NonC) ◆ **être pris dans un ~** to be stuck in a traffic jam 3 (= volume) bulk; (= taille) size; [d'ordinateur] footprint ◆ **objet de faible ~** compact ou small objet ◆ **l'~ au sol de la tente est de 10 m²** the surface area of this tent is 10m² ◆ **l'~ sur le disque/de la mémoire** (Ordin) the amount of space used on the disk/in the memory

encombrer /ɑ̃kɔ̃bʀe/ ► conjug 1 ◄ VT 1 [+ pièce] to clutter (up) (de with); [+ couloir] to obstruct (de with); [+ rue] to congest; [+ lignes téléphoniques] to jam; [+ marché] to glut (de with); ◆ **ces fichiers encombrent le disque** (Ordin) these files are using up too much space on the disk ◆ ~ **le passage** to block the way, to be in the way ◆ **toutes ces informations inutiles encombrent ma mémoire** my mind is cluttered (up) with all this useless information
2 [personne] **il m'encombre plus qu'il ne m'aide** he's more of a hindrance than a help (to me) ◆ **je ne veux pas vous ~** (être à votre charge) I don't want to be a burden to you; (empiéter sur votre espace) I don't want to get in your way ◆ **ces boîtes m'encombrent** (je les porte) I'm loaded down with these boxes; (elles gênent le passage) these boxes are in my way
VPR **s'encombrer** ◆ **s'~ de** [+ paquets] to load o.s. down with; [+ enfants] to burden ou saddle* o.s. with ◆ **il ne s'encombre pas de scrupules** he's not overburdened with scruples, he's not unscrupulous

encontre /ɑ̃kɔ̃tʀ/ LOC PRÉP **à l'encontre de** (= contre) against, counter to; (= au contraire de) contrary to ◆ **aller à l'~ de** [+ décision, faits] to go against, to run counter to ◆ **je n'irai pas à l'~ de ce qu'il veut/fait** I won't go against his wishes/what he does ◆ **cela va à l'~ du but recherché** it's counterproductive, it defeats the purpose ◆ **action qui va à l'~ du but recherché** self-defeating ou counterproductive action ◆ **à l'~ de ce qu'il dit, mon opinion est que ...** contrary to what he says, my opinion is that ... LOC ADV **à l'encontre** in opposition, against it ◆ **je n'irai pas à l'~** I won't go against it

encor /ɑ̃kɔʀ/ ADV (††, Poésie) ⇒ **encore**

encorbellement /ɑ̃kɔʀbɛlmɑ̃/ NM *(Archit)* corbelled construction ◆ **fenêtre en ~** oriel window ◆ **balcon en ~** corbelled balcony

encorder /ɑ̃kɔʀde/ ► conjug 1 ◄ VT to rope up VPR **s'encorder** to rope up ◆ **les alpinistes s'encordent** the climbers are roping themselves together *ou* are roping up

encore /ɑ̃kɔʀ/ ADV 1 *(= toujours)* still ◆ **il restait ~ quelques personnes** there were still a few people left ◆ **il en était ~ au brouillon** he was still working on the draft ◆ **tu en es ~ là !** *(péj)* haven't you got beyond *ou* past that yet! ◆ **il n'est ~ qu'en première année/que caporal** he's still only in the first year/a corporal ◆ **il n'est ~ que 8 heures** it's (still) only 8 o'clock ◆ **le malfaiteur court ~** the criminal is still at large ◆ **ça ne s'était ~ jamais vu** it had never happened before ◆ **il reste une question non ~ résolue** one thing remains to be settled

♦ **pas encore** not yet ◆ **il n'est pas ~ prêt** he's not ready yet, he's not yet ready ◆ **ça ne s'était pas ~ vu** it had never happened before

2 *(= pas plus tard que)* only ◆ **~ ce matin** *ou* **ce matin ~, il semblait bien portant** only this morning he seemed quite well ◆ **il me le disait ~ hier** *ou* **hier ~** he was saying that to me only yesterday

3 *(= de nouveau)* again ◆ **~ une fois** (once) again, once more, one more time ◆ **~ une fois, je n'affirme rien** but there again, I'm not absolutely positive about it ◆ **~ une fois non !** how many times do I have to tell you - no! ◆ **ça s'est ~ défait** it has come undone (yet) again ◆ **il a ~ laissé la porte ouverte** he has left the door open (yet) again ◆ **elle a ~ acheté un nouveau chapeau** she has bought yet another new hat ◆ **~ vous !** (not) you again! ◆ **c'était Léo au téléphone – ~ !** it was Léo on the phone – again! ◆ **quoi ~ ?, qu'y a-t-il ~ ?** what's the matter with you this time?, what is it this time *ou* now?

♦ **encore et encore** again and again

4 *(= de plus, en plus)* more ◆ **~ un !** yet another!, one more! ◆ **~ un rhume** (yet) another cold ◆ **~ une tasse ?** another cup? ◆ **vous prendrez bien ~ quelque chose ?** *ou* **quelque chose ~ ?** surely you'll have something more? *ou* something else? ◆ **~ un peu de thé ?** a little more tea?, (any) more tea? ◆ **~ quelques gâteaux ?** (some *ou* any) more cakes? ◆ **j'en veux ~** I want some more ◆ **~ un mot, avant de terminer** (just) one more word before I finish ◆ **que te faut-il ~ ?** what else *ou* more do you want? ◆ **qu'est-ce que j'oublie ~ ?** what else have I forgotten? ◆ **qui y avait-il ~ ?** who else was there? ◆ **pendant ~ deux jours** for another two days, for two more days ◆ **il y a ~ quelques jours avant de partir** there are a few (more) days to go before we leave ◆ **~ un fou du volant !** (yet) another roadhog! ◆ **en voilà ~ deux** here are two more *ou* another two ◆ **mais ~ ?** is that all?, what else?

5 *(avec compar)* even ◆ **il fait ~ plus froid qu'hier** it's even *ou* still colder than yesterday ◆ **il fait ~ moins chaud qu'hier** it's even cooler than it was yesterday ◆ **il est ~ plus grand que moi** he is even taller than I am ◆ **ils veulent l'agrandir ~ (plus)** they want to make it even *ou* still larger, they want to enlarge it even further ◆ **~ pire, pire ~** even *ou* still worse, worse and worse ◆ **~ autant** as much again *(que* as)

6 *(= aussi)* too, also, as well ◆ **ce n'est pas seulement triste, mais ~ ridicule** it's not just sad, it's also ridiculous

7 *(valeur restrictive)* even then, even at that ◆ **~ ne sait-il pas tout** even then he doesn't know everything, and he doesn't even know everything (at that) ◆ **il en est sûrement capable, ~ faut-il le faire** he's obviously capable, but whether he does it or not is another matter ◆ **~ une chance** *ou* **~ heureux qu'il ne se soit pas plaint au patron** (still) at least he didn't complain to the boss, let's think ourselves lucky that he didn't complain to the boss

♦ **et encore** ◆ **on t'en donnera peut-être 10 €, et ~** they might give you €10 for it, if that ◆ **c'est passable, et ~ !** it's passable but only just! ◆ **et ~, ça n'a pas été sans mal** and even that wasn't easy

♦ **si encore** if only ◆ **si ~ je savais où ça se trouve, j'irais bien** if only I knew where it was, I would willingly go

♦ **encore que** *(littér = quoique)* even though ◆ **~ que je n'en sache rien** though I don't really know ◆ **ça devrait être faisable, ~ que ...** * it should be feasible, though come to think of it ...

encorner /ɑ̃kɔʀne/ ► conjug 1 ◄ VT to gore

encornet /ɑ̃kɔʀnɛ/ NM squid

encoubler (s') /ɑ̃kuble/ VPR *(Helv = trébucher)* to trip

encourageant, e /ɑ̃kuʀaʒɑ̃, ɑ̃t/ ADJ encouraging

encouragement /ɑ̃kuʀaʒmɑ̃/ NM 1 *(= soutien)* encouragement ◆ **message/mot d'~** message/word of encouragement ◆ **il est arrivé sur scène sous les ~s du public** he came on stage to shouts of encouragement from *ou* to the cheers of the audience 2 *(Pol, Écon = avantage financier)* encouragement, incentive ◆ **mesures d'~** incentive measures ◆ **multiplier les ~s à l'épargne** to offer more incentives for people to save

encourager /ɑ̃kuʀaʒe/ ► conjug 3 ◄ VT 1 *(gén)* to encourage *(à faire* to do); *[+ équipe]* to cheer ◆ **~ qn au meurtre** to encourage sb to commit murder, to incite sb to murder ◆ **~ qn du geste et de la voix** to cheer sb on ◆ **encouragé par ses camarades, il a joué un vilain tour au professeur** egged on *ou* encouraged by his classmates, he played a nasty trick on the teacher 2 *(Pol, Écon) [+ emploi, investissement, production]* to encourage

encourir /ɑ̃kuʀiʀ/ ► conjug 11 ◄ VT *[+ amende, frais]* to incur; *[+ mépris, reproche, punition]* to bring upon o.s., to incur

encours, en-cours /ɑ̃kuʀ/ NM INV *(= effets)* outstanding discounted bills; *(= dettes)* outstanding debt

encrage /ɑ̃kʀaʒ/ NM inking

encrassement /ɑ̃kʀasmɑ̃/ NM *[d'arme]* fouling (up); *[de cheminée, bougie de moteur]* sooting up; *[de piston, poêle, tuyau, machine]* clogging (up), fouling up

encrasser /ɑ̃kʀase/ ► conjug 1 ◄ VT 1 *[+ arme]* to foul (up); *[+ cheminée, bougie de moteur]* to soot up; *[+ piston, poêle, tuyau, machine]* to clog (up), to foul up 2 *(= salir)* to make filthy, to (make) dirty ◆ **ongles encrassés de cambouis** nails encrusted *ou* filthy with engine grease VPR **s'encrasser** *(gén)* to get dirty; *[arme]* to foul (up); *[cheminée, bougie de moteur]* to soot up; *[piston, poêle, tuyau, machine]* to clog (up), to foul up; *[filtre]* to clog up

encre /ɑ̃kʀ/ NF 1 *(pour écrire)* ink; *(en poudre, pour imprimante)* toner ◆ **écrire à l'~** to write in ink ◆ **d'un noir d'~** as black as ink, ink(y) black ◆ **de sa plus belle ~** *(littér)* in his best style; → **bouteille, couler, sang** 2 *[de calamar, pieuvre]* ink ◆ **calmars à l'~** *(Culin)* squid cooked in ink

COMP **encre blanche** white ink
encre de Chine Indian ink *(Brit)*, India ink *(US)*
encre d'imprimerie printing ink
encre sympathique invisible ink

encrer /ɑ̃kʀe/ ► conjug 1 ◄ VT to ink

encreur /ɑ̃kʀœʀ/ ADJ M *[rouleau, tampon]* inking NM inker

encrier /ɑ̃kʀije/ NM *(= bouteille)* inkpot *(Brit)*, ink bottle *(US)*; *(décoratif)* inkstand; *(encastré)* inkwell

encroûté, e * /ɑ̃kʀute/ (ptp de **encroûter**) ADJ ◆ **être ~** to stagnate, to be in a rut ◆ **quel ~ tu fais !** you're really stagnating!, you're really in a rut!

encroûtement /ɑ̃kʀutmɑ̃/ NM 1 *[de personne]* getting into a rut ◆ **essayons de le tirer de son ~** let's try and get him out of his rut 2 *[d'objet]* encrusting, crusting over

encroûter /ɑ̃kʀute/ ► conjug 1 ◄ VT *(= entartrer)* to encrust, to crust over VPR **s'encroûter** 1 * *[personne]* to stagnate, to get into a rut ◆ **s'~ dans** *[+ habitudes, préjugés]* to become entrenched in ◆ **s'~ dans la vie de province** to get into the rut of provincial life 2 *[objet]* to crust over, to form a crust

encryptage /ɑ̃kʀiptaʒ/ NM *[de données]* encrypting

encrypter /ɑ̃kʀipte/ ► conjug 1 ◄ VT *[+ données]* to encrypt

enculé **/ɑ̃kyle/ NM dickhead **

enculer ** /ɑ̃kyle/ ► conjug 1 ◄ VT to fuck ** *(implying anal sex)* ◆ **va te faire ~ !** fuck off! ** ◆ **ils enculent les mouches** they're nit-picking *

encyclique /ɑ̃siklik/ ADJ, NF ◆ **(lettre) ~** encyclical

encyclopédie /ɑ̃siklɔpedi/ NF encyclopedia, encyclopaedia *(Brit)*

encyclopédique /ɑ̃siklɔpedik/ ADJ encyclopedic, encyclopaedic *(Brit)*

encyclopédiste /ɑ̃siklɔpedist/ NMF *(Hist)* encyclopedist, encyclopaedist *(Brit)*

endémie /ɑ̃demi/ NF endemic disease

endémique /ɑ̃demik/ ADJ *(Méd, fig)* endemic

endetté, e /ɑ̃dete/ (ptp de **endetter**) ADJ in debt *(attrib)* ◆ **l'entreprise est ~e à hauteur de 3 millions d'euros** the company has a debt amounting to 3 million euros ◆ **très ~** heavily *ou* deep in debt ◆ **l'un des pays les plus ~s** one of the biggest *ou* largest debtor countries ◆ **(très) ~ envers qn** *(frm)* (greatly) indebted to sb

endettement /ɑ̃dɛtmɑ̃/ NM *(= dette)* debt ◆ **notre ~ extérieur** our foreign debt ◆ **causer l'~ d'une l'entreprise** to put a company in debt ◆ **le fort ~ des ménages** the high level of household debt ◆ **notre ~ envers la banque** our indebtedness to the bank

endetter /ɑ̃dete/ ► conjug 1 ◄ VT to put into debt VPR **s'endetter** *[particulier, entreprise]* to get into debt ◆ **s'~ sur dix ans** to take out a loan over ten years *ou* a ten-year loan

endeuiller /ɑ̃dœje/ ► conjug 1 ◄ VT *[+ personne, pays] (= toucher par une mort)* to plunge into mourning; *(= attrister)* to plunge into grief; *[+ épreuve sportive, manifestation]* to cast a pall over; *(littér) [+ paysage]* to make (look) dismal, to give a dismal aspect to

endiablé, e /ɑ̃djable/ ADJ *[danse, rythme]* boisterous, furious; *[course]* furious, wild; *[personne]* boisterous

endiguer /ɑ̃dige/ ► conjug 1 ◄ VT 1 *[+ fleuve]* to dyke (up) 2 *[+ foule, invasion]* to hold back, to contain; *[+ révolte]* to check, to contain; *[+ sentiments, progrès]* to check, to hold back; *[+ inflation, chômage]* to curb

endimanché, e /ɑ̃dimɑ̃ʃe/ (ptp de **s'endimancher**) ADJ *[personne]* (all done up) in one's Sunday best; *[style]* fancy, florid ◆ **il a l'air ~** *(péj)* he's terribly overdressed

endimancher (s') /ɑ̃dimɑ̃ʃe/ ► conjug 1 ◄ VPR to put on one's Sunday best

endive /ɑ̃div/ NF chicory *(Brit) (NonC)*, endive *(US)* ◆ **cinq ~s** five pieces *ou* heads of chicory *(Brit)*, five endives *(US)*

endocarde /ɑ̃dɔkaʀd/ NM endocardium

endocardite /ɑ̃dɔkaʀdit/ NF endocarditis

endocarpe /ɑ̃dɔkaʀp/ NM endocarp

endocrine /ɑ̃dɔkʀin/ ADJ ♦ **glande ~** endocrine (gland)

endocrinien, -ienne /ɑ̃dɔkʀinjɛ̃, jɛn/ ADJ endocrinal, endocrinous

endocrinologie /ɑ̃dɔkʀinɔlɔʒi/ NF endocrinology

endocrinologue /ɑ̃dɔkʀinɔlɔg/, **endocrinologiste** /ɑ̃dɔkʀinɔlɔʒist/ NMF endocrinologist

endoctrinement /ɑ̃dɔktʀinmɑ̃/ NM indoctrination

endoctriner /ɑ̃dɔktʀine/ ▸ conjug 1 ◂ VT to indoctrinate

endoderme /ɑ̃dɔdɛʀm/ NM endoderm

endogamie /ɑ̃dɔgami/ NF endogamy

endogène /ɑ̃dɔʒɛn/ ADJ endogenous

endolori, e /ɑ̃dɔlɔʀi/ ADJ painful, aching, sore

endomètre /ɑ̃dɔmɛtʀ/ NM endometrium

endométriose /ɑ̃dɔmetʀijoz/ NF endometriosis

endommagement /ɑ̃dɔmaʒmɑ̃/ NM damaging

endommager /ɑ̃dɔmaʒe/ ▸ conjug 3 ◂ VT to damage

endomorphine /ɑ̃dɔmɔʀfin/ NF ⇒ **endorphine**

endormeur, -euse /ɑ̃dɔʀmœʀ, øz/ NM,F *(péj = trompeur)* beguiler

endormi, e /ɑ̃dɔʀmi/ (ptp de **endormir**) ADJ 1 *(lit) [personne]* sleeping, asleep *(attrib)* 2 *(= apathique)* sluggish; *(= engourdi)* numb; *(= assoupi) [passion]* dormant; *[facultés]* dulled; *[ville, rue]* sleepy, drowsy ♦ **j'ai la main tout ~e** my hand has gone to sleep *ou* is completely numb ♦ **à moitié ~** half asleep ♦ **quel ~ !** what a sleepyhead!

endormir /ɑ̃dɔʀmiʀ/ ▸ conjug 16 ◂ VT 1 *[somnifère, discours]* to put *ou* send to sleep; *(en berçant)* to send *ou* lull to sleep ♦ **elle chantait pour l'~** she used to sing him to sleep

2 *(* = ennuyer)* to send to sleep*, to bore stiff*

3 *(= anesthésier)* to put to sleep, to put under*, to anaesthetize; *(= hypnotiser)* to hypnotise, to put under*

4 *(= dissiper) [+ douleur]* to deaden; *[+ soupçons]* to allay, to lull

5 *(= tromper)* to take in ♦ **se laisser ~ par des promesses** to let o.s. be taken in by promises ♦ **n'essaie pas de m'~!** don't try to pull the wool over my eyes!

VPR **s'endormir** 1 *[personne]* to go to sleep, to fall asleep, to drop off to sleep

2 *(= se relâcher)* to let up, to slacken off ♦ **ce n'est pas le moment de nous ~** now is not the time to slow up *ou* slacken off ♦ **allons, ne vous endormez pas !** come on, don't go to sleep on the job!*; → **laurier**

3 *[rue, ville]* to fall asleep; *[passion, douleur]* to subside, to die down; *[facultés]* to go to sleep*

4 *(euph = mourir)* to go to sleep, to pass away

endormissement /ɑ̃dɔʀmismɑ̃/ NM ♦ **médicament qui facilite l'~** medicine which helps one to sleep, sleep-inducing medicine ♦ **au moment de l'~** as one falls asleep

endorphine /ɑ̃dɔʀfin/ NF endorphin

endos /ɑ̃do/ NM endorsement

endoscope /ɑ̃dɔskɔp/ NM endoscope

endoscopie /ɑ̃dɔskɔpi/ NF endoscopy

endoscopique /ɑ̃dɔskɔpik/ ADJ endoscopic

endosmose /ɑ̃dɔsmoz/ NF endosmosis

endossable /ɑ̃dosabl/ ADJ *(Fin)* endorsable

endossataire /ɑ̃dosatɛʀ/ NMF endorsee

endossement /ɑ̃dosmɑ̃/ NM endorsement

endosser /ɑ̃dose/ ▸ conjug 1 ◂ VT 1 *(= revêtir) [+ vêtement]* to put on ♦ **~ l'uniforme/la soutane** *(= devenir soldat/prêtre)* to enter the army/the Church 2 *(= assumer) [+ responsabilité]* to take, to shoulder *(de* for); ♦ **il a voulu me faire ~ son erreur** he wanted me to take *ou* shoulder the responsibility for his mistake 3 *(Fin)* to endorse

endosseur /ɑ̃dosœʀ/ NM endorser

endothermique /ɑ̃dotɛʀmik/ ADJ endothermic

endroit /ɑ̃dʀwa/ NM 1 *(= localité, partie du corps)* place, spot; *(= lieu de rangement, partie d'objet)* place ♦ **un ~ idéal pour le pique-nique/une usine** an ideal spot *ou* place for a picnic/a factory ♦ **je l'ai mis au même ~** I put it in the same place ♦ **manteau usé à plusieurs ~s** coat worn in several places, coat with several worn patches ♦ **à** *ou* **en quel ~ ?** where(abouts)?, where exactly? ♦ **les gens de l'~** the local people, the locals*; → **petit**

2 *[de livre, récit]* passage, part ♦ **à quel ~ du récit t'es-tu arrêté ?** what part of the story did you stop at? ♦ **il arrêta sa lecture à cet ~** he stopped reading at that point

3 *(locutions)* **à l'~ où** *(lieu)* (at the place) where; *(dans un livre, un film)* at the part *ou* bit where ♦ **de/vers l'~ où** from/to (the place) where ♦ **en quelque ~ que ce soit** wherever it may be ♦ **en plusieurs ~s** in several places ♦ **par ~s** in places ♦ **au bon ~** in *ou* at the right place; *(littér)*

♦ **à l'endroit de** *(= à l'égard de)* towards ♦ **ses sentiments à mon ~** his feelings about me

4 *(= bon côté)* right side ♦ **faites les diminutions sur l'~** *(Tricot)* decrease on the knit row

♦ **à l'endroit** *[vêtement]* the right way round; *[objet posé]* the right way round; *(verticalement)* the right way up ♦ **remets tes chaussettes à l'~** put your socks on the right way out ♦ **une maille à l'~, une maille à l'envers** *(Tricot)* knit one – purl one, one plain – one purl ♦ **tout à l'~** *(Tricot)* knit every row

enduire /ɑ̃dɥiʀ/ ▸ conjug 38 ◂ VT 1 *[personne, appareil]* **~ une surface de** *[+ peinture, vernis, colle]* to coat a surface with; *[+ huile, boue]* to coat *ou* smear a surface with ♦ **~ ses cheveux de brillantine** to grease one's hair with brilliantine, to plaster brilliantine on one's hair ♦ **surface enduite d'une substance visqueuse** surface coated *ou* smeared with a sticky substance ♦ **s'~ de crème** to cover o.s. with cream 2 *[substance]* to coat ♦ **la colle qui enduit le papier** the glue coating the paper

enduit /ɑ̃dɥi/ NM *(pour recouvrir, lisser)* coating; *(pour boucher)* filler

endurable /ɑ̃dyʀabl/ ADJ endurable, bearable

endurance /ɑ̃dyʀɑ̃s/ NF *(moral)* endurance; *(physique)* stamina, endurance ♦ **coureur qui a de l'~** runner with stamina *ou* staying power

endurant, e /ɑ̃dyʀɑ̃, ɑ̃t/ ADJ tough, hardy ♦ **peu** *ou* **pas très ~** † *(= patient)* not very patient *(avec* with)

endurci, e /ɑ̃dyʀsi/ (ptp de **endurcir**) ADJ *[cœur]* hardened; *[personne]* hardened, hard-hearted ♦ **criminel ~** hardened criminal ♦ **célibataire ~** confirmed bachelor

endurcir /ɑ̃dyʀsiʀ/ ▸ conjug 2 ◂ VT *(physiquement)* to toughen; *(psychologiquement)* to harden VPR **s'endurcir** *(physiquement)* to become tough; *(moralement)* to harden, to become hardened ♦ **s'~ à la douleur** to become hardened *ou* inured to pain

endurcissement /ɑ̃dyʀsismɑ̃/ NM 1 *(= action) [de corps]* toughening; *[d'âme]* hardening 2 *(= état) [de corps]* toughness; *[d'âme]* hardness ♦ **~ à la douleur** resistance to pain

endurer /ɑ̃dyʀe/ ▸ conjug 1 ◂ VT to endure, to bear ♦ **~ de faire qch** to bear to do sth ♦ **il fait froid, on endure un pull** it's cold, you need a pullover

enduro /ɑ̃dyʀo/ NM enduro, trial

Énée /ene/ NM Aeneas

Énéide /eneid/ NF ♦ **l'~** the Aeneid

énergéticien, -ienne /enɛʀʒetisjɛ̃, jɛn/ NM,F energetics specialist

énergétique /enɛʀʒetik/ ADJ 1 *(Écon, Phys) [besoins, politique, ressources]* energy *(épith)* ♦ **nos dépenses ~s** our fuel *ou* energy bill 2 *(Physiol) [aliment]* energy-giving, energizing; *[valeur]* energy *(épith)* ♦ **aliment très ~** high-energy food ♦ **dépense ~** energy expenditure NF energetics *(sg)*

énergie /enɛʀʒi/ NF 1 *(= force physique)* energy ♦ **dépenser beaucoup d'~ à faire qch** to expend *ou* use up a great deal of energy doing sth ♦ **j'ai besoin de toute mon ~** I need all my energy ♦ **nettoyer/frotter avec ~** to clean/rub energetically ♦ **être** *ou* **se sentir sans ~** to be *ou* feel lacking in energy, to be *ou* feel unenergetic ♦ **avec l'~ du désespoir** with the strength born of despair

2 *(= fermeté, ressort moral)* spirit, vigour *(Brit)*, vigor *(US)* ♦ **protester/refuser avec ~** to protest/refuse energetically *ou* vigorously *ou* forcefully ♦ **mobiliser toutes les ~s d'un pays** to mobilize all a country's resources ♦ **l'~ de son style/d'un terme** *(littér)* the vigour *ou* energy of his style/of a term

3 *(Écon, Phys)* energy; *(Tech)* power, energy ♦ **réaction qui libère de l'~** reaction that releases energy ♦ **l'~ fournie par le moteur** the power supplied by the motor ♦ **consommation d'~** *[de moteur, véhicule]* power consumption; *[d'industrie, pays]* energy consumption ♦ **source d'~** source of energy

COMP **énergie atomique** atomic energy
énergie cinétique kinetic energy
les énergies douces alternative energy
énergie électrique electrical power *ou* energy
énergie éolienne wind power *ou* energy
les énergies fossiles fossil fuels
énergie mécanique mechanical power *ou* energy
énergies nouvelles new energy sources
énergie nucléaire nuclear power *ou* energy
énergie potentielle potential energy
énergie psychique psychic energy
énergies renouvelables renewable energy sources
énergie solaire solar energy *ou* power
les énergies de substitution substitute fuels
énergie thermique thermal energy
énergie vitale vital energy *ou* force

énergique /enɛʀʒik/ ADJ 1 *(physiquement) [personne]* energetic; *[mouvement, geste, effort]* vigorous, energetic 2 *(moralement) [personne, style]* vigorous, energetic; *[intervention]* forceful, vigorous; *[protestation]* vigorous, fierce; *[mesures]* drastic, stringent; *[punition]* severe, harsh; *[médicament]* powerful, strong

énergiquement /enɛʀʒikmɑ̃/ ADV *[agir, parler]* energetically; *[refuser]* emphatically; *[condamner]* vigorously

énergisant, e /enɛʀʒizɑ̃, ɑ̃t/ ADJ energizing ♦ **boisson ~e** energy drink NM energizer, tonic

énergivore /enɛʀʒivɔʀ/ ADJ *[secteur, activité, produit]* energy-guzzling

énergumène /enɛʀgymɛn/ NMF *(gén)* bizarre individual; *(= fou)* maniac ♦ **qu'est-ce que c'est que cet ~ ?** who's that nutcase?*

énervant, e /enɛʀvɑ̃, ɑ̃t/ ADJ (= *agaçant*) irritating, annoying

énervé, e /enɛʀve/ (ptp de **énerver**) ADJ (= *agacé*) irritated, annoyed; (= *agité*) nervous, edgy* (*Brit*)

énervement /enɛʀvəmɑ̃/ NM (= *agacement*) irritation, annoyance; (= *agitation*) nervousness, edginess* (*Brit*) ◆ **après les ~s du départ** after the upsets of the departure

énerver /enɛʀve/ ▸ conjug 1 ◂ VT ◆ **~ qn** (= *agiter*) to overexcite sb; (= *agacer*) to irritate sb, to annoy sb, to get on sb's nerves* ◆ **ça m'énerve** it really gets on my nerves* ◆ **le vin blanc énerve** white wine is bad for your nerves VPR **s'énerver** to get excited*, to get worked up* ◆ **ne t'énerve pas !*** don't get all worked up!*, take it easy! ◆ **ne t'énerve pas pour cela** don't let it get to you*

enfance /ɑ̃fɑ̃s/ NF 1 (= *jeunesse*) childhood; [*de garçon*] boyhood; [*de fille*] girlhood; (= *début*) infancy ◆ **petite ~** infancy ◆ **science encore dans son ~** science still in its infancy ◆ **c'est l'~ de l'art** it's child's play *ou* kid's stuff*; → **retomber** 2 (= *enfants*) children (*pl*) ◆ **la naïveté de l'~** the naivety of children *ou* of childhood ◆ **l'~ déshéritée** deprived children

enfant /ɑ̃fɑ̃/ NMF 1 (*gén*) child; (= *garçon*) (little) boy; (= *fille*) (little) girl ◆ **quand il était ~** when he was a child, as a child ◆ **il se souvenait que, tout ~, il avait une fois ...** he remembered that, while still *ou* only a child, he had once ... ◆ **c'est un grand ~** (*fig*) he's such a child, he's a big kid* ◆ **il est resté très ~** he has remained very childlike ◆ **faire l'~** to behave childishly, to behave like a child ◆ **ne faites pas l'~** don't be (so) childish, stop behaving like a child; → **bon[1], bonne[2], jardin**

2 (= *descendant*) child ◆ **sans ~** childless ◆ **M. Leblanc, décédé sans ~** Mr Leblanc who died childless *ou* without issue (*frm*) ◆ **faire un ~ à une femme*** to get a woman pregnant ◆ **elle a fait un ~ dans le dos à son mari*** she got pregnant without telling her husband; (= *lui a fait un mauvais coup*) she did the dirty on her husband * ◆ **ce livre est son ~** this book is his baby; → **attendre**

3 (= *originaire*) **c'est un ~ du pays/de la ville** he's a native of these parts/of the town ◆ **~ de l'Auvergne/de Paris** child of the Auvergne/of Paris ◆ **un ~ du peuple** a (true) child of the people

4 (* = *adulte*) **les ~s !** folks*, guys* ◆ **bonne nouvelle, les ~s !** good news, folks! * *ou* guys! *

COMP **enfant de l'amour** love child
enfant de la balle child of the theatre (*ou* circus *etc*)
enfant bleu (*Méd*) blue baby
enfant de chœur (*Rel*) altar boy ◆ **il me prend pour un ~ de chœur !*** (*ingénu*) he thinks I'm still wet behind the ears!* ◆ **ce n'est pas un ~ de chœur !*** he's no angel!*
enfant gâté spoilt child ◆ **c'était l'~ gâté du service** he was the blue-eyed boy of the department
l'Enfant Jésus (*Rel*) the baby Jesus
enfants de Marie (*Rel*) children of Mary ◆ **c'est une ~ de Marie** (*lit*) she's in the children of Mary; (* : *ingénue*) she's a real innocent ◆ **ce n'est pas une ~ de Marie !** she's no cherub!*, she's no innocent!
enfant naturel natural child
enfant prodige child prodigy
enfant prodigue (*Bible, fig*) prodigal son
enfant terrible (*lit*) unruly child; (*fig*) enfant terrible
enfant de troupe child reared by the army
enfant trouvé foundling
enfant unique only child ◆ **famille à ~ unique** one-child family, family with one child

enfantement /ɑ̃fɑ̃tmɑ̃/ NM († , *Bible* = *accouchement*) childbirth; (*littér*) [*d'œuvre*] giving birth (*de* to)

enfanter /ɑ̃fɑ̃te/ ▸ conjug 1 ◂ VT († , *Bible* = *mettre au monde*) to give birth to, to bring forth (*littér, Bible*); (*littér*) (= *élaborer*) to give birth to (*littér*) VI to give birth, to be delivered (*littér, Bible*)

enfantillage /ɑ̃fɑ̃tijaʒ/ NM childishness (*NonC*) ◆ **se livrer à des ~s** to do childish things, to behave childishly ◆ **c'est de l'~** you're just being childish ◆ **arrête ces ~s !** don't be so childish!

enfantin, e /ɑ̃fɑ̃tɛ̃, in/ ADJ (= *typique de l'enfance*) [*joie, naïveté, confiance*] childlike, childish; (= *puéril*) [*attitude, réaction*] childish, infantile ◆ **c'est ~** (*facile*) it's simple, it's child's play*, it's dead easy* (*Brit*) ◆ **rire/jeu ~** (*propre à l'enfant*) child's laugh/game ◆ **ses amours ~es** his childhood loves; → **classe, langage**

enfariné, e /ɑ̃faʀine/ ADJ (*lit*) dredged with flour ◆ **arriver la gueule ~e*** *ou* **le bec ~*** to breeze in*

enfer /ɑ̃fɛʀ/ NM 1 (*Rel*) **l'~** hell, Hell ◆ **les Enfers** (*Myth*) Hell, the Underworld ◆ **l'~ est pavé de bonnes intentions** (*Prov*) the road to hell is paved with good intentions (*Prov*)
◆ **d'enfer** [*bruit, vision*] hellish, infernal; [*vie, rythme*] hellish ◆ **feu d'~** raging fire ◆ **jouer un jeu d'~** to play for very high stakes ◆ **chevaucher à un train d'~** to ride hell (*Brit*) *ou* hellbent (*US*) for leather* ◆ **rouler à un train d'~** to tear along at breakneck speed ◆ **la pièce est menée à un rythme d'~** the play goes along at a furious pace ◆ **c'est d'~ !** it's magic!* ◆ **sa copine est d'~*** his girlfriend is a real stunner*

2 (*fig*) hell ◆ **cette usine est un ~** this factory is (absolute) hell ◆ **cette vie est un ~** it's a hellish life ◆ **l'~ de l'alcoolisme** the hellish world of alcoholism ◆ **vivre un véritable ~** to go through a living hell

3 [*de bibliothèque*] forbidden books department

EXCL ◆ **~ et damnation!*** hell and damnation!*

enfermement /ɑ̃fɛʀməmɑ̃/ NM (*lit*) confinement ◆ **son ~ dans le silence** (*volontaire*) his retreat into silence; (*involontaire*) his silent isolation

enfermer /ɑ̃fɛʀme/ ▸ conjug 1 ◂ VT 1 (= *mettre sous clé*) [*+ enfant puni, témoin gênant*] to shut up, to lock up; (*par erreur*) to lock in; [*+ prisonnier*] to shut up *ou* away, to lock up; * [*+ aliéné*] to lock up*; [*+ objet précieux*] to lock away *ou* up; [*+ animaux*] to shut up (*dans* in); ◆ **~ qch dans** [*+ coffre*] to lock sth away *ou* up in; [*+ boîte, sac*] to shut sth up *ou* away in ◆ **il est bon à ~*** he ought to be locked up* *ou* certified*, he's certifiable* ◆ **ils ont dû l'~ à clé** they had to lock him in ◆ **ne reste pas enfermé par ce beau temps** don't stay indoors *ou* inside in this lovely weather

2 (= *emprisonner*) to imprison; (*dans un dilemme*) to trap ◆ **l'école enferme la créativité dans un carcan de conventions** school traps *ou* imprisons *ou* confines creativity in a straitjacket of convention ◆ **~ le savoir dans des livres inaccessibles** to shut *ou* lock knowledge away in inaccessible books

3 (*littér* = *contenir, entourer*) to enclose, to shut in ◆ **les collines qui enfermaient le vallon** the hills that shut in *ou* enclosed the valley

4 (*Sport*) [*+ concurrent*] to hem *ou* box in

VPR **s'enfermer** 1 (*lit*) to shut o.s. up *ou* in ◆ **il s'est enfermé dans sa chambre** he shut himself away *ou* up in his room ◆ **zut, je me suis enfermé !** (*à l'intérieur*) damn, I've locked myself in!; (*à l'extérieur*) damn, I've locked myself out! ◆ **il s'est enfermé à clé dans son bureau** he has locked himself (away) in his office ◆ **ils se sont enfermés dans le bureau pour discuter** they have closeted themselves in the office *ou* shut themselves away in the office to have a discussion ◆ **elle s'enferme toute la journée** she stays shut up indoors all day long

2 ◆ **s'~ dans** [*+ mutisme*] to retreat into; [*+ rôle, attitude*] to stick to ◆ **s'~ dans sa décision** to keep *ou* stick stubbornly *ou* rigidly to one's decision ◆ **s'~ dans un système** to lock o.s. into a rigid pattern of behaviour

enferrer (s') /ɑ̃feʀe/ ▸ conjug 1 ◂ VPR 1 (= *s'embrouiller*) to tie o.s. up in knots* ◆ **s'~ dans ses contradictions/ses mensonges** to tie *ou* tangle o.s. up in one's own contradictions/one's lies, to ensnare o.s. in the mesh of one's own contradictions/lies ◆ **s'~ dans une analyse/une explication** to tie o.s. up in knots* trying to make an analysis/trying to explain ◆ **il s'enferre de plus en plus** he's getting himself in more and more of a mess *ou* into deeper and deeper water 2 (= *s'empaler*) to spike o.s. (*sur* on)

enfeu /ɑ̃fø/ NM funereal recess

enfiévré, e /ɑ̃fjevʀe/ (ptp de **enfiévrer**) ADJ [*atmosphère*] feverish; [*paroles*] impassioned

enfiévrer /ɑ̃fjevʀe/ ▸ conjug 6 ◂ VT 1 [*+ imagination*] to fire, to stir up; [*+ esprits*] to rouse; [*+ assistance*] to inflame, to rouse 2 [*+ malade*] to make feverish; [*+ visage, joues*] to inflame

enfilade /ɑ̃filad/ NF (= *série*) ◆ **une ~ de** [*maisons*] a row *ou* string of; [*colonnes, couloirs*] a row *ou* series of ◆ **pièces/couloirs en ~** series of linked rooms/corridors ◆ **maisons en ~** houses in a row ◆ **prendre en ~** (*Mil*) to rake, to enfilade (*SPÉC*) ◆ **prendre les rues en ~** [*conducteur*] to go from one street to the next ◆ **tir d'~** (*Mil*) raking, enfilading (*SPÉC*)

enfiler /ɑ̃file/ ▸ conjug 1 ◂ VT 1 [*+ aiguille*] to thread; [*+ perles*] to string, to thread ◆ **on n'est pas là pour ~ des perles*** let's get on with it*, let's get down to it* *ou* to business ◆ **~ des anneaux sur une tringle** to slip rings onto a rod

2 (* = *passer*) [*+ vêtement*] to slip on, to put on

3 (* = *fourrer*) **~ qch dans qch** to stick* *ou* shove* sth into sth

4 (= *s'engager dans*) [*+ ruelle, chemin*] to take; [*+ corridor*] to enter, to take ◆ **il tourna à gauche et enfila la rue de la Gare** he turned left into Rue de la Gare, he turned left and took the Rue de la Gare

5 (**: *sexuellement*) to screw**, to shag** (*Brit*)

VPR **s'enfiler** 1 (= *s'engager dans*) **s'~ dans** [*+ escalier, couloir, ruelle*] to disappear into

2 (* = *consommer*) [*+ verre de vin*] to knock back*, to down*; [*+ nourriture*] to wolf down*; [*+ corvée*] to land o.s. with*, to get lumbered with* *ou* landed with*

enfin /ɑ̃fɛ̃/ GRAMMAIRE ACTIVE 53.2, 53.5 ADV 1 (= *à la fin, finalement*) at last, finally ◆ **il y est ~ arrivé** he has finally succeeded, he has succeeded at last ◆ **quand va-t-il ~ y arriver ?** when on earth is he going to manage it? ◆ **~, après bien des efforts, ils y arrivèrent** eventually, after much effort, they managed it, after much effort they finally *ou* eventually managed it ◆ **~ seuls !** alone at last! ◆ **~, ils se sont décidés !** they've made up their minds at last! ◆ **~ ça va commencer !** at long last it's going to begin!

2 (= *en dernier lieu*) lastly, finally ◆ **on y trouvait des noisetiers, des framboisiers, ~ des champignons de toutes sortes** there were hazel trees, raspberry bushes and all kinds of mushrooms as well ◆ **~, je voudrais te remercier pour ...** finally, I'd like to thank you for ... ◆ **... ensuite des manuels et des ouvrages de référence, ~ et surtout, des dictionnaires** ... and next manuals and reference works, and last but not least *ou* and last but by no means least, dictionaries

3 (= *en conclusion*) in short, in a word ◆ **rien n'était prêt, ~ (bref), la vraie pagaille !** no-

thing was ready – in actual fact, it was absolute chaos! *ou* it was absolute chaos, in fact!

4 *(restrictif = disons, ou plutôt)* well ◆ **elle était assez grosse, ~, potelée** she was rather fat, well, chubby ◆ **pas exactement, ~, dans un sens, oui** not exactly, well – in a way, yes

5 *(= somme toute)* after all ◆ **c'est un élève qui, ~, n'est pas bête** he's not a stupid pupil after all ◆ **c'est une méthode qui, ~, a fait ses preuves** it's a well-tried method after all

◆ **car enfin** because (after all) ◆ **on va lui donner l'argent, car ~ il l'a bien mérité** we're going to give him the money because he deserves it

6 *(= toutefois)* still ◆ **~, si ça vous plaît/si vous le voulez, prenez-le** still, if you like it/if you want it, take it ◆ **moi je veux bien, ~ ...!** I don't mind, but ...!

◆ **mais enfin** but ◆ **j'irai, mais ~ ce ne sera pas de gaieté de cœur** I'll go, but not willingly

7 *(valeur exclamative)* **~ ! que veux-tu y faire !** anyway *ou* still, what can you do! ◆ **~, tu aurais pu le faire !** all the same *ou* even so, you could have done it! ◆ **(mais) ~ ! je viens de te le dire !** but I've just told you!, (but) for goodness sake*, I've just told you! ◆ **~ ! un grand garçon comme toi !** oh, come on, a big boy like you! ◆ **c'est son père, ~ !** he is his father, after all! ◆ **~ quoi ! ce n'est pas si difficile !** oh come on, it's not that difficult!

enflammé, e /ɑ̃flame/ (ptp de **enflammer**) ADJ 1 *[allumette, torche]* burning, blazing, ablaze *(attrib)*; *[ciel]* ablaze *(attrib)*, blazing, flaming 2 *[visage, yeux]* blazing, ablaze *(attrib)*; *[caractère]* fiery, ardent, passionate; *[esprit]* afire *(attrib)*, burning, on fire *(attrib)*; *[paroles]* inflamed, fiery, ardent; *[déclaration]* impassioned, passionate, ardent 3 *[plaie]* inflamed

enflammer /ɑ̃flame/ ▸ conjug 1 ◂ VT 1 *(= mettre le feu à) [+ bois]* to set on fire, to set fire to; *[+ allumette]* to strike; *(littér) [+ ciel]* to set ablaze 2 *(= exciter) [+ visage, regard]* to set ablaze; *[+ colère, désir, foule]* to inflame; *[+ imagination]* to fire, to kindle; *[+ esprit]* to set on fire 3 *[+ plaie]* to inflame VPR **s'enflammer** 1 *(= prendre feu)* to catch fire, to ignite ◆ **le bois sec s'enflamme bien** dry wood catches fire *ou* ignites *ou* kindles easily 2 *[visage, regard]* to blaze; *[sentiment, désir]* to flare up; *[imagination]* to be fired; *[orateur]* to become inflamed *ou* impassioned ◆ **s'~ (de colère)** to flare up (in anger)

enflé, e /ɑ̃fle/ (ptp de **enfler**) ADJ *[membre]* swollen; *[style]* bombastic, turgid NM,F *(* = imbécile)* jerk*, twit* *(Brit)*, clot* *(Brit)*

enfler /ɑ̃fle/ ▸ conjug 1 ◂ VT 1 *[+ membre]* to cause to swell (up), to make swell (up); *(littér) [+ voiles]* to fill, to swell; *(littér) [+ fleuve]* to (cause to) swell; *[+ voix]* to raise; *[+ addition, facture]* to inflate ◆ **~ son style** to adopt a bombastic *ou* turgid style 2 *(* = voler)* **~ qn** to diddle* *ou* do* sb *(de* out of*)* ◆ **se faire ~ de 10 €*** to be done out of 10 euros* VI *(lit) [membre]* to become swollen, to swell (up); *(* = prendre du poids)* to fill out VPR **s'enfler** 1 *[voix]* to rise; *[style]* to become bombastic *ou* turgid; *[son]* to swell 2 *(littér) [fleuve]* to swell, to become swollen; *[vagues]* to surge, to swell; *[voiles]* to fill (out), to swell (out)

enflure /ɑ̃flyʀ/ NF 1 *(Méd)* swelling 2 *[de style]* turgidity 3 *(* = imbécile)* jerk*, twit*, clot* *(Brit)*

enfoiré, e * /ɑ̃fwaʀe/ NM,F *(= homme)* bastard**; *(= femme)* bitch**

enfoncé, e /ɑ̃fɔ̃se/ (ptp de **enfoncer**) ADJ *[yeux]* deep-set; *[recoin]* deep ◆ **il avait la tête ~e dans les épaules** his head was sunk between his shoulders

enfoncement /ɑ̃fɔ̃smɑ̃/ NM 1 *(= action d'enfoncer) [de pieu]* driving in; *[de porte]* breaking down *ou* open; *[de lignes ennemies]* breaking through ◆ **il souffre d'un ~ de la cage thoracique/de la boîte crânienne** *(Méd)* he has crushed ribs/a fractured skull 2 *(= action de s'enfoncer) [de sol]* giving way; *[de fondations]* sinking ◆ **cet ~ progressif dans le vice/la misère** this gradual slide into vice/poverty 3 *(= recoin) [de mur]* recess, nook ◆ **dissimulé dans un ~ de la muraille** hidden in a recess *ou* nook in the wall ◆ **chalet enfoui dans un ~ du vallon** chalet tucked away in a corner of the valley

enfoncer /ɑ̃fɔ̃se/ ▸ conjug 3 ◂ VT 1 *(= faire pénétrer) [+ pieu, clou]* to drive (well) in; *[+ épingle, punaise]* to stick (well) in, to push (well) in ◆ **~ un pieu dans** to drive a stake in(to) ◆ **~ une épingle dans** to stick *ou* push a pin in(to) ◆ **~ un couteau dans** to thrust *ou* plunge a knife into ◆ **~ qch à coups de marteau** to hammer sth in, to knock sth in with a hammer ◆ **~ le clou** *(fig)* to hammer it in, to drive the point home

2 *(= mettre)* **~ les mains dans ses poches** to thrust *ou* dig one's hands (deep) into one's pockets ◆ **~ son chapeau jusqu'aux yeux** to ram *ou* pull one's hat (right) down over one's eyes ◆ **il lui enfonça sa canne dans les côtes** he prodded *ou* poked *ou* stuck him in the ribs with his walking stick ◆ **qui a bien pu lui ~ ça dans le crâne ?** *ou* **la tête ?** who on earth put that idea into his head? ◆ **ça les a enfoncés davantage dans les frais** it involved them in even greater expense

3 *(= défoncer) [+ porte]* to break open *ou* down; *[+ véhicule]* to smash in; *[+ lignes ennemies]* to break through ◆ **~ le plancher** to make the floor give way *ou* cave in, to cause the floor to give way *ou* cave in ◆ **le choc lui a enfoncé les côtes** the blow smashed his rib cage *ou* his ribs ◆ **il a eu les côtes enfoncées** he had his ribs broken, his ribs were broken *ou* smashed ◆ **le devant de sa voiture a été enfoncé** the front of his car has been smashed *ou* bashed* in ◆ **~ une porte ouverte** *ou* **des portes ouvertes** *(fig)* to state the obvious ◆ **c'est ~ une porte ouverte que d'affirmer ...** it's stating the obvious to say ...

4 * *(= battre)* to beat hollow*, to hammer*; *(= surpasser)* to lick* ◆ **ils se sont fait ~ !** they got beaten hollow!*, they got hammered!* ◆ **il les enfonce tous** he's got them all licked* ◆ **~ son complice** *(causer la perte de)* to put all the blame on one's accomplice ◆ **~ un candidat** to destroy a candidate

VI 1 *(= pénétrer)* to sink in ◆ **attention, on enfonce ici** careful, you'll sink in here ◆ **on enfonçait dans la neige jusqu'aux cuisses** we sank up to our thighs in the snow

2 *(= céder) [sol]* to yield, to give way ◆ **ça enfonce sous le poids du corps** it yields beneath the weight of the body

VPR **s'enfoncer** 1 *[lame, projectile]* **s'~ dans** to plunge *ou* sink into ◆ **l'éclat d'obus s'est enfoncé dans le mur** the shell fragment embedded itself in the wall ◆ **j'ai une épine enfoncée sous l'ongle** I've got a thorn stuck under my nail

2 *(= disparaître) (dans l'eau, la vase etc)* to sink *(dans* into, in*)*; ◆ **s'~ dans** *[+ forêt, rue, brume]* to disappear into; *[+ fauteuil, coussins]* to sink deep into, to sink back in(to); *[+ misère]* to sink into, to be plunged into; *[+ vice, rêverie]* to plunge into, to sink into ◆ **chemin qui s'enfonce dans les bois** path which disappears into the woods ◆ **je le regardais s'~, impuissant à le secourir** I watched him sinking (in), powerless to help him ◆ **s'~ sous les couvertures** to bury o.s. under *ou* snuggle down under the covers ◆ **il s'est enfoncé jusqu'au cou dans une sale histoire** he's up to his neck in a nasty bit of business ◆ **à mentir, tu ne fais que t'~ davantage** by lying, you're just getting yourself into deeper and deeper water *ou* into more and more of a mess

3 *(= céder)* to give way ◆ **le sol s'enfonce sous nos pas** the ground is giving way *ou* caving in beneath us ◆ **les coussins s'enfoncèrent sous son poids** the cushions sank under his weight

4 *(= faire pénétrer)* **s'~ une arête dans la gorge** to get a bone stuck in one's throat ◆ **s'~ une aiguille dans la main** to stick *ou* run a needle into one's hand ◆ **enfoncez-vous bien ça dans le crâne*** now get this firmly into your head

enfonceur, -euse /ɑ̃fɔ̃sœʀ, øz/ NM,F *(hum)* ◆ **c'est un ~ de porte(s) ouverte(s)** he's always stating the obvious

enfouir /ɑ̃fwiʀ/ ▸ conjug 2 ◂ VT *(gén)* to bury *(dans* in*)*; ◆ **il l'a enfoui dans sa poche** he tucked it (away) in his pocket ◆ **chalet enfoui dans la neige** chalet buried beneath the snow ◆ **la photo était enfouie sous des livres** the photo was buried under *ou* beneath a pile of books VPR **s'enfouir** ◆ **s'~ dans/sous** to bury o.s. *(ou* itself*)* in/under ◆ **s'~ sous les draps** to bury o.s. *ou* burrow beneath the covers

enfouissement /ɑ̃fwismɑ̃/ NM burying ◆ **site d'~ de déchets industriels** landfill site for industrial waste

enfourcher /ɑ̃fuʀʃe/ ▸ conjug 1 ◂ VT *[+ cheval, bicyclette]* to mount, to get on ◆ **~ son dada** to get on one's hobby-horse

enfourner /ɑ̃fuʀne/ ▸ conjug 1 ◂ VT 1 *[+ plat]* to put in the oven; *[+ poterie]* to put in the kiln 2 *(* = avaler)* to guzzle down, to gulp down, to wolf down 3 *(* = enfoncer)* **~ qch dans qch** to shove* *ou* stuff* sth into sth VPR **s'enfourner** ◆ **s'~ dans** *[personne]* to dive into; *[foule]* to rush into

enfreindre /ɑ̃fʀɛ̃dʀ/ ▸ conjug 52 ◂ VT *(frm)* to infringe, to break

enfuir (s') /ɑ̃fɥiʀ/ ▸ conjug 17 ◂ VPR *(= se sauver)* to run away, to run off, to flee *(chez, dans* to*)*; *(= s'échapper)* to run away, to escape *(de* from*)*; *(littér) [temps, souffrance]* to fly away *(littér)*, to flee *(littér)*

enfumer /ɑ̃fyme/ ▸ conjug 1 ◂ VT *[+ pièce]* to fill with smoke; *[+ personne, renard, ruche]* to smoke out ◆ **atmosphère/pièce enfumée** smoky atmosphere/room ◆ **tu nous enfumes avec ta cigarette** you're smoking us out

enfutailler /ɑ̃fytaje/, **enfûter** /ɑ̃fyte/ ▸ conjug 1 ◂ VT to cask

engagé, e /ɑ̃gaʒe/ (ptp de **engager**) ADJ 1 *[écrivain, littérature]* (politically) committed ◆ **non ~** *(Pol)* uncommitted 2 *(Archit) [colonne]* engaged 3 *[match]* hard-fought NM 1 *(= soldat)* enlisted man ◆ **~ volontaire** volunteer 2 *(Sport) (= coureur)* entrant, competitor; *(= cheval)* runner

engageant, e /ɑ̃gaʒɑ̃, ɑ̃t/ ADJ *[air, sourire]* engaging, winning, appealing; *[proposition]* attractive, appealing, tempting; *[repas, gâteau]* tempting, inviting ◆ **elle a eu des paroles ~es** what she said sounded most appealing

engagement /ɑ̃gaʒmɑ̃/ NM 1 *(= promesse)* commitment, promise; *(= accord)* agreement, undertaking ◆ **sans ~ de votre part** without obligation *ou* commitment on your part ◆ **signer un ~** to sign an undertaking *ou* agreement ◆ **prendre l'~ de** to make a commitment to, to undertake to ◆ **manquer à ses ~s** to fail to honour one's commitments, to fail to keep one's promises ◆ **faire face à/tenir** *ou* **honorer ses ~s** to fulfil/honour one's commitments *ou* promises

2 *(= embauche) [d'ouvrier]* taking on, engaging; *(= recrutement) [de soldats]* enlistment ◆ **lettre d'~** letter of appointment

3 *(Théât = contrat)* engagement; *(Sport = inscription pour un match, un combat)* entry ◆ **artiste sans ~** out-of-work actor

4 *(Fin) [de capitaux]* investing; *[de dépenses]* incurring ◆ **~s financiers** financial commit-

ments *ou* liabilities ◆ **cela a nécessité l'~ de nouveaux frais** this incurred further expenses ◆ **faire face à ses ~s (financiers)** to meet one's (financial) commitments

5 (= *amorce*) [*de débat, négociations*] opening, start

6 (*Sport*) (= *coup d'envoi*) kick-off; (*Boxe*) attack; (*Escrime*) engagement; (*Ping-Pong*) service

7 (*Mil*) [*de combat*] engaging; [*de troupes fraîches*] throwing in, engaging ◆ **tué dans un ~** killed in an engagement

8 (= *prise de position*) commitment (*dans* to); ◆ **~ personnel/politique/militaire** personal/political/military commitment ◆ **politique de non-~** policy of non-commitment

9 (= *mise en gage*) [*de montre*] pawning

10 (= *encouragement*) encouragement ◆ **c'est un ~ à persévérer** it encourages one to persevere

11 (= *introduction*) [*de clé*] introduction, insertion (*dans* in, into); [*de voiture*] entry (*dans* into)

12 (*Méd*) [*de fœtus*] engagement

engager /ɑ̃gaʒe/ GRAMMAIRE ACTIVE 33.3, 52.6 ▸ conjug 3 ◂

VT 1 (= *lier*) to bind, to commit ◆ **nos promesses nous engagent** we are bound to honour our promises, we are bound by our promises ◆ **ça l'engagerait trop** that would commit him too far ◆ **ça n'engage à rien** it doesn't commit you to anything ◆ **~ sa parole** *ou* **son honneur** to give *ou* pledge one's word (of honour)

2 (= *embaucher*) [+ *ouvrier*] to take on, to hire; [+ *artiste*] to engage ◆ **je vous engage (à mon service)** you've got the job, you're hired

3 (= *entraîner*) to involve ◆ **ça l'a engagé dans de gros frais/dans une affaire louche** it involved him in great expense/in a shady deal ◆ **le pays est engagé dans une politique d'inflation** the country is pursuing an inflationary policy

4 (= *encourager*) **~ qn à faire qch** to urge *ou* encourage sb to do sth ◆ **je vous engage à la circonspection** I advise you to be very cautious

5 (= *introduire*) to insert (*dans* in, into); (*Naut*) [+ *ancre*] to foul ◆ **il engagea sa clé dans la serrure** he fitted *ou* inserted his key into the lock ◆ **~ sa voiture dans une ruelle** to enter a lane, to drive into a lane ◆ **c'était à lui de passer puisqu'il était engagé** [*automobiliste*] it was up to him to go since he had already pulled out ◆ **~ le fer** (*Escrime*) to engage, to cross blades

6 (= *amorcer*) [+ *discussion*] to open, to start (up); [+ *négociations*] to enter into; [+ *procédure*] to instigate (*contre* against); ◆ **~ la conversation** to engage in conversation, to start up a conversation (*avec* with); ◆ **l'affaire semble bien/mal engagée** things seem to have got off to a good/bad start ◆ **~ le combat contre l'ennemi** to engage the enemy, to join battle with the enemy †

7 (= *mettre en gage*) to pawn, to put in pawn; (= *investir*) to invest, to lay out ◆ **les frais engagés** the expenses incurred

8 (*Sport*) [+ *concurrents*] to enter ◆ **15 chevaux sont engagés dans cette course** 15 horses are running in this race ◆ **~ la partie** to begin the match ◆ **la partie est bien engagée** the match is well under way

9 (*Mil*) [+ *recrues*] to enlist; [+ *troupes fraîches*] to throw in, to bring in, to engage ◆ **~ toutes ses forces dans la bataille** to throw all one's troops into the battle

VPR **s'engager** 1 (= *promettre*) to commit o.s. ◆ **s'~ à faire qch** to commit o.s. to doing sth, to undertake *ou* promise to do sth ◆ **il n'a pas voulu s'~ trop** he didn't want to commit himself (too far) *ou* to stick his neck out too far *

◆ **sais-tu à quoi tu t'engages ?** do you know what you're letting yourself in for? *ou* what you're committing yourself to?

2 (= *s'embaucher*) to take a job (*chez* with); ◆ **il s'est engagé comme garçon de courses** he took a job as an errand boy, he got himself taken on as an errand boy

3 (= *se lancer*) **s'~ dans** [+ *frais*] to incur; [+ *discussion, pourparlers*] to enter into; [+ *affaire, entreprise*] to become involved in ◆ **le pays s'engage dans une politique dangereuse** the country is embarking on a dangerous policy *ou* is steering a dangerous course ◆ **le pays s'est engagé dans la voie des réformes/du capitalisme** the country is on the road to reform/to capitalism ◆ **ne nous engageons pas dans cette voie-là** let's not go down that particular road

4 (= *s'emboîter*) **s'~ dans** to engage into, to fit into ◆ **s'~ dans** (= *pénétrer*) [*véhicule*] to enter, to turn into; [*piéton*] to take, to turn into ◆ **s'~ sur la chaussée** to step (out) onto the road ◆ **la voiture s'engagea sous le pont** the car drove under the bridge ◆ **j'avais la priorité puisque je m'étais engagé (dans la rue)** I had (the) right of way since I had already pulled out (into the street)

5 (= *s'amorcer*) [*pourparlers*] to begin, to start (up), to get under way ◆ **une conversation s'engagea entre eux** they struck up a conversation

6 (*Sport*) to enter (one's name) (*dans* for)

7 (*Mil*) [*recrues*] to enlist ◆ **s'~ dans l'armée de l'air** to join the air force ◆ **le combat s'engagea avec vigueur** the fight began briskly ◆ **s'~ dans la bataille** to join in the fighting

8 (*Littérat, Pol* = *prendre position*) to commit o.s.

engazonner /ɑ̃gazɔne/ ▸ conjug 1 ◂ VT (= *recouvrir*) to turf; (= *ensemencer*) to plant with grass

engeance † /ɑ̃ʒɑ̃s/ NF (*péj*) mob, crew ◆ **quelle ~ !** they're such a pain! *

engelure /ɑ̃ʒ(ə)lyʀ/ NF chilblain

engendrement /ɑ̃ʒɑ̃dʀəmɑ̃/ NM [*d'enfant*] begetting, fathering

engendrer /ɑ̃ʒɑ̃dʀe/ ▸ conjug 1 ◂ VT 1 [+ *colère, problèmes, tensions, violence*] to cause ◆ **ils n'engendrent pas la mélancolie** they're (always) a good laugh * 2 (*frm*) [+ *enfant*] to beget, to father 3 (*Ling, Math, Phys*) to generate

engin /ɑ̃ʒɛ̃/ NM (= *machine*) machine; (= *outil*) instrument, tool; (= *véhicule*) heavy vehicle; (= *avion*) aircraft; (* = *objet*) contraption *, gadget; (= *bombe*) bomb, device ◆ **"attention : sortie d'engins"** "heavy plant crossing", "beware – lorries turning" (*Brit*)

COMP **engin balistique** ballistic missile
engin blindé armoured vehicle
engin explosif explosive device
engins de guerre † engines of war † (*aussi littér*)
engin spatial space vehicle
engins (spéciaux) missiles
engin de terrassement earth-mover

englober /ɑ̃glɔbe/ ▸ conjug 1 ◂ VT (= *inclure*) to include, to encompass (*dans* in); (= *annexer*) to take in, to incorporate

engloutir /ɑ̃glutiʀ/ ▸ conjug 2 ◂ VT [+ *nourriture*] to gobble up, to gulp *ou* wolf down; [+ *navire*] to engulf, to swallow up; [+ *fortune*] [*personne*] to squander; [*dépenses*] to eat *ou* swallow up ◆ **qu'est-ce qu'il peut ~ !** * it's amazing what he puts away! * ◆ **la ville a été engloutie par un tremblement de terre** the town was swallowed up *ou* engulfed by an earthquake VPR **s'engloutir** [*navire*] to be engulfed

engloutissement /ɑ̃glutismɑ̃/ NM [*de nourriture*] gobbling up; [*de navire*] engulfing; [*de fortune*] squandering

engluer /ɑ̃glye/ ▸ conjug 1 ◂ VT [+ *arbre, oiseau*] to lime VPR **s'engluer** [*oiseau*] to get caught *ou* stuck in (bird) lime ◆ **s'~ les doigts** to get one's fingers sticky ◆ **s'~ dans ses problèmes/une situation** to get bogged down in one's problems/a situation

engoncer /ɑ̃gɔ̃se/ ▸ conjug 3 ◂ VT to restrict, to cramp ◆ **ce manteau l'engonce** he looks cramped in that coat, that coat restricts his movements ◆ **engoncé dans ses vêtements** (looking) cramped in his clothes ◆ **le cou engoncé dans un gros col** his neck (stiffly) encased in a big collar ◆ **engoncé dans cette petite vie bourgeoise** cooped up in this petty middle-class life

engorgement /ɑ̃gɔʀʒəmɑ̃/ NM [*de tuyau*] obstruction, clogging, blocking (*de* of); (*Méd*) engorgement; [*de marché*] glut (*de* in)

engorger /ɑ̃gɔʀʒe/ ▸ conjug 3 ◂ VT [+ *tuyau*] to obstruct, to clog, to block; (*Méd*) to engorge; [+ *marché*] to glut, to saturate VPR **s'engorger** [*tuyau*] to become blocked; [*route*] to get congested; [*marché*] to become glutted *ou* saturated

engouement /ɑ̃gumɑ̃/ NM (*pour qn*) infatuation, fancy (*pour* for); (*pour qch*) fad, craze (*pour* for); ◆ **~ passager** passing fancy, brief craze

engouer (s') /ɑ̃gwe/ ▸ conjug 1 ◂ VPR ◆ **s'~ de** *ou* **pour qch** to develop a passion for sth ◆ **s'~ de qn** to become infatuated with sb

engouffrer /ɑ̃gufʀe/ ▸ conjug 1 ◂ VT [+ *charbon*] to shovel (*dans* into); * [+ *fortune*] to swallow up, to devour; * [+ *nourriture*] to gobble up, to gulp down, to wolf down ◆ **qu'est-ce qu'il peut ~ !** * it's amazing what he puts away! * VPR **s'engouffrer** [*vent*] to rush, to sweep; [*flot, foule*] to surge, to rush; [*personne*] to rush, to dive; [*navire*] to sink (*dans* into) ◆ **s'~ dans la brèche** to step into the breach

engoulevent /ɑ̃gul(ə)vɑ̃/ NM ◆ **~ (d'Europe)** nightjar, goatsucker (*US*) ◆ **~ (d'Amérique)** nighthawk

engourdi, e /ɑ̃guʀdi/ (ptp de **engourdir**) ADJ [*membre*] numb; [*esprit*] dull, dulled ◆ **j'ai la main ~e** my hand is numb *ou* has gone to sleep *ou* gone dead

engourdir /ɑ̃guʀdiʀ/ ▸ conjug 2 ◂ VT 1 [+ *membres*] to numb, to make numb ◆ **être engourdi par le froid** [+ *membre*] to be numb with cold; [+ *animal*] to be sluggish with the cold 2 [+ *esprit*] to dull, to blunt; [+ *douleur*] to deaden, to dull ◆ **la chaleur et le vin l'engourdissaient** the heat and the wine were making him sleepy *ou* drowsy VPR **s'engourdir** [*corps*] to become *ou* go numb; [*bras, jambe*] to become *ou* go numb, to go to sleep, to go dead; [*esprit*] to grow dull *ou* sluggish

engourdissement /ɑ̃guʀdismɑ̃/ NM 1 (= *état*) [*de membre, corps*] numbness; [*d'esprit*] (= *torpeur*) sleepiness, drowsiness; (= *affaiblissement*) dullness 2 (= *action*) [*de membre*] numbing; [*d'esprit*] dulling

engrais /ɑ̃gʀɛ/ NM 1 (*chimique*) fertilizer; (*animal*) manure ◆ **~ vert** green manure ◆ **~ azoté** nitrogen fertilizer 2 (= *engraissement*) **mettre un animal à l'~** to fatten up an animal

engraissement /ɑ̃gʀɛsmɑ̃/, **engraissage** /ɑ̃gʀɛsaʒ/ NM [*de bœufs*] fattening (up); [*de volailles*] cramming

engraisser /ɑ̃gʀese/ ▸ conjug 1 ◂ VT [+ *animal*] to fatten (up); [+ *terre*] to manure, to fertilize; * [+ *personne*] to fatten up ◆ **quel pique-assiette, c'est nous qui devons l'~** * we seem to be expected to feed this scrounger * *ou* provide for this scrounger * ◆ **~ l'État** * to enrich the state VI * [*personne*] to get fat(ter), to put on weight VPR **s'engraisser** ◆ **l'État s'engraisse sur le dos du contribuable** the state grows fat at the taxpayer's expense

engrangement /ɑ̃gʀɑ̃ʒmɑ̃/ NM [*de foin*] gathering in, garnering (*littér*)

engranger /ɑ̃gʀɑ̃ʒe/ ▸ conjug 3 ◂ VT [+ *foin, moisson*] to gather *ou* get in, to garner (*littér*);

[+ bénéfices] to reap, to rake in*; *[+ connaissances]* to amass, to store (up)

engrenage /ɑ̃gʀənaʒ/ **NM** gears, gearing; *[d'événements]* chain ◆ **~ à chevrons** double helical gearing ◆ **quand on est pris dans l'~** *(fig)* when one is caught up in the system ◆ **l'~ de la violence** the spiral of violence; → **doigt**

engrosser‡ /ɑ̃gʀose/ ▸ conjug 1 ◂ **VT** ◆ **~ qn** to knock sb up*‡, to get sb pregnant ◆ **se faire ~** to get (o.s.) knocked up*‡, to get (o.s.) pregnant *(par* by)

engueulade‡ /ɑ̃gœlad/ **NF** *(= dispute)* row, slanging match* *(Brit)*; *(= réprimande)* bawling out‡, rocket‡ *(Brit)* ◆ **passer une ~ à qn** to bawl sb out‡, to give sb a rocket‡ *(Brit)* ◆ **avoir une ~ avec qn** to have a screaming match *ou* a row *ou* slanging match* *(Brit)* with sb ◆ **lettre d'~** stinking letter‡

engueuler‡ /ɑ̃gœle/ ▸ conjug 1 ◂ **VT** ◆ **~ qn** to bawl sb out‡, to give sb a rocket‡ *(Brit)* ◆ **se faire ~** to get bawled out‡, to get a rocket‡ *(Brit)*; → **poisson** **VPR** **s'engueuler** to have a row *ou* slanging match* *(Brit)* *(avec* with)

enguirlander /ɑ̃giʀlɑ̃de/ ▸ conjug 1 ◂ **VT** [1] (* *= disputer*) **~ qn** to give sb a telling-off* *ou* ticking-off* *(Brit)*, to tear sb off a strip‡ *(Brit)* ◆ **se faire ~** to get a telling-off* *ou* ticking-off* *(Brit)*, to get torn off a strip‡ *(Brit)* [2] *(= orner)* to garland

enhardir /ɑ̃aʀdiʀ/ ▸ conjug 2 ◂ **VT** to make bolder ◆ **enhardi par** emboldened by **VPR** **s'enhardir** to become *ou* get bolder ◆ **s'~ (jusqu')à dire** to make so bold as to say, to be bold enough to say

enharmonique /ɑ̃naʀmɔnik/ **ADJ** enharmonic

énième /enjɛm/ **ADJ** ⇒ **n-ième**

énigmatique /enigmatik/ **ADJ** enigmatic

énigmatiquement /enigmatikmɑ̃/ **ADV** enigmatically

énigme /enigm/ **NF** *(= mystère)* enigma, riddle; *(= jeu)* riddle, puzzle ◆ **tu es une ~ pour moi** you are an enigma to *ou* for me ◆ **trouver la clé** *ou* **le mot de l'~** to find the key *ou* clue to the puzzle *ou* riddle ◆ **parler par ~s** to speak in riddles

enivrant, e /ɑ̃nivʀɑ̃, ɑ̃t/ **ADJ** *[parfum, vin, succès]* heady, intoxicating; *[beauté]* intoxicating; *[vitesse]* intoxicating, dizzying

enivrement /ɑ̃nivʀəmɑ̃/ **NM** († *= ivresse*) intoxication; *(fig = exaltation)* exhilaration ◆ **l'~ du succès** the intoxication of success

enivrer /ɑ̃nivʀe/ ▸ conjug 1 ◂ **VT** *(lit)* to intoxicate, to make drunk; *(fig)* to intoxicate ◆ **le parfum m'enivrait** I was intoxicated by the perfume **VPR** **s'enivrer** *(lit)* to get drunk *(de* on) to become intoxicated *(de* with); *(fig)* to become intoxicated *(de* with); ◆ **il passe son temps à s'~** he spends all his time getting drunk ◆ **s'~ de mots** to get drunk on words ◆ **enivré de succès** intoxicated with *ou* by success

enjambée /ɑ̃ʒɑ̃be/ **NF** stride ◆ **d'une ~** in a stride ◆ **faire de grandes ~s** to stride out, to take big *ou* long strides ◆ **il allait à grandes ~s vers …** he was striding (along) towards …

enjambement /ɑ̃ʒɑ̃bmɑ̃/ **NM** *(Littérat)* enjambement; *(Bio)* crossing-over

enjamber /ɑ̃ʒɑ̃be/ ▸ conjug 1 ◂ **VT** *[+ obstacle]* to stride *ou* step over; *[+ fossé]* to step *ou* stride across; *[pont]* to span, to straddle, to stretch across ◆ **il enjamba la rampe et s'assit dessus** he sat down astride the banister

enjeu (pl **enjeux**) /ɑ̃ʒø/ **NM** *[de pari]* stake, stakes *(de* in); *(fig)* issue ◆ **quel est le véritable ~ de ces élections ?** what is the real issue in these elections? ◆ **c'est un match sans ~** nothing is at stake in this match ◆ **les OGM constituent des ~x économiques considérables** the economic stakes involved in GMOs are huge ◆ **la sécurité est devenue un ~ politique de taille** security has become an important political issue

enjoindre /ɑ̃ʒwɛ̃dʀ/ ▸ conjug 49 ◂ **VT** *(frm)* ◆ **~ à qn de faire** to enjoin *ou* charge sb to do *(frm)*

enjôlement /ɑ̃ʒolmɑ̃/ **NM** bewitching

enjôler /ɑ̃ʒole/ ▸ conjug 1 ◂ **VT** *(= ensorceler)* to bewitch; *(= amadouer)* to get round ◆ **elle a si bien su l'~ qu'il a accepté** she coaxed *ou* wheedled *ou* cajoled him into accepting it

enjôleur, -euse /ɑ̃ʒolœʀ, øz/ **ADJ** *[sourire, paroles]* coaxing, wheedling, winning **NM,F** *(= charmeur)* coaxer, wheedler; *(= escroc)* twister **NF** **enjôleuse** *(= séductrice)* wily woman

enjolivement /ɑ̃ʒɔlivmɑ̃/ **NM** [1] *(= action) [d'objet]* embellishment; *[de réalité, récit]* embroidering, embellishment [2] *(= ornement)* embellishment, adornment ◆ **les ~s apportés aux faits par le narrateur** the narrator's embellishment of the facts

enjoliver /ɑ̃ʒɔlive/ ▸ conjug 1 ◂ **VT** *[+ objet]* to embellish; *[+ réalité, récit]* to embroider, to embellish

enjoliveur /ɑ̃ʒɔlivœʀ/ **NM** *[de roue]* hub cap, wheel trim

enjolivure /ɑ̃ʒɔlivyʀ/ **NF** ⇒ **enjolivement**

enjoué, e /ɑ̃ʒwe/ **ADJ** cheerful ◆ **d'un ton ~** cheerfully, in a cheerful way

enjouement /ɑ̃ʒumɑ̃/ **NM** cheerfulness

enkystement /ɑ̃kistəmɑ̃/ **NM** encystment

enkyster (s') /ɑ̃kiste/ ▸ conjug 1 ◂ **VPR** to encyst ◆ **ça s'est enkysté** it's turned into a cyst

enlacement /ɑ̃lasmɑ̃/ **NM** *(= étreinte)* embrace; *(= enchevêtrement)* intertwining, interlacing

enlacer /ɑ̃lase/ ▸ conjug 3 ◂ **VT** [1] *(= étreindre)* to embrace, to clasp, to hug ◆ **le danseur enlaça sa cavalière** the dancer put his arm round his partner's waist [2] *(= enchevêtrer) [+ fils]* to intertwine, to interlace [3] *(= entourer) [lianes]* to wind round, to enlace, to entwine **VPR** **s'enlacer** [1] *[amants]* to embrace, to hug each other; *[lutteurs]* to take hold of each other, to clasp each other ◆ **amoureux enlacés** lovers clasped in each other's arms *ou* clasped in a fond embrace [2] *(= s'entrecroiser)* to intertwine, to interlace ◆ **fils inextricablement enlacés** hopelessly tangled threads [3] *[lianes]* **s'~ autour de** to twine round, to wind round

enlaidir /ɑ̃lediʀ/ ▸ conjug 2 ◂ **VT** *[+ personne]* to make look ugly; *[+ paysage]* to deface, to ruin ◆ **cette coiffure l'enlaidit** that hair style makes her look very plain *ou* rather ugly **VI** *[personne]* to become ugly **VPR** **s'enlaidir** to make o.s. look ugly

enlaidissement /ɑ̃ledismɑ̃/ **NM** ◆ **l'~ du paysage** the way the countryside is being defaced *ou* ruined

enlevé, e /ɑ̃l(ə)ve/ (ptp de **enlever**) **ADJ** *[récit]* spirited; *[scène, morceau de musique]* played with spirit *ou* brio; → **trot**

enlèvement /ɑ̃lɛvmɑ̃/ **NM** [1] *[de personne]* kidnapping, abduction ◆ **~ de bébé** baby snatching ◆ **"l'Enlèvement des Sabines"** *(Art)* "the Rape of the Sabine Women" [2] *[de meuble, objet]* removal, taking *ou* carrying away; *[de tache]* removal; *[d'organe]* removal; *[d'ordures]* collection, clearing (away); *[de bagages, marchandises]* collection; *[de voiture en infraction]* towing away [3] *(Mil) [de position]* capture, taking

enlever /ɑ̃l(ə)ve/ ▸ conjug 5 ◂ **VT** [1] *(gén)* to remove; *[+ couvercle]* to remove, to lift (off); *[+ meuble]* to remove, to take away; *[+ étiquette, housse]* to remove, to take off; *[+ tache]* to remove; *(en frottant ou lavant etc)* to brush *ou* wash *etc* out *ou* off; *[+ tapis]* to take up, to remove; *[+ lustre, tableau]* to take down; *[+ peau de fruit]* to take off, to peel off, to remove; *[+ mauvaises herbes]* to clear, to remove; *[+ organe]* to remove, to take out ◆ **se faire ~ une dent** to have a tooth out *ou* pulled *(US)* ◆ **enlève tes mains de tes poches/de là** take your hands out of your pockets/off there, remove your hands from your pockets/from there ◆ **~ le couvert** to clear the table ◆ **enlève tes coudes de la table** take your elbows off the table

[2] *[+ vêtements]* to take off, to remove ◆ **il enleva son chapeau pour dire bonjour** he raised his hat in greeting ◆ **j'enlève ma robe pour mettre quelque chose de plus confortable** I'll just slip out of this dress into something more comfortable, I'll just take off this dress and put on something more comfortable

[3] ◆ **~ à qn** *[+ objet, argent]* to take (away) from sb ◆ **on lui a enlevé son commandement** he was relieved of his command ◆ **on lui a enlevé la garde de l'enfant** the child was taken *ou* removed from his care ◆ **ça lui enlèvera peut-être le goût de recommencer** perhaps that'll cure him of trying that again, perhaps that'll make him think twice before he does it again ◆ **ça n'enlève rien à son mérite** that doesn't in any way detract from his worth ◆ **pour vous ~ tout scrupule** in order to dispel your misgivings ◆ **enlève-toi cette idée de la tête** get that idea out of your head ◆ **cela lui a enlevé son dernier espoir** it took away his last hope

[4] *(= emporter) [+ objet, meuble]* to take away, to carry away, to remove; *[+ ordures]* to collect, to clear (away); *[+ voiture en infraction]* to tow away ◆ **il a fait ~ ses vieux meubles** he had his old furniture taken away ◆ **il fut enlevé dans les airs** he was borne (up) *ou* lifted (up) into the air ◆ **il a été enlevé par un mal foudroyant** *(frm)* he was borne off by a sudden illness ◆ **la mort nous l'a enlevé** *(littér)* death has snatched *ou* taken him from us

[5] *(= kidnapper)* to kidnap, to abduct ◆ **se faire ~ par son amant** to elope with one's lover, to be carried off by one's lover ◆ **je vous enlève votre femme pour quelques instants** *(hum)* I'll just steal *ou* borrow your wife for a moment (if I may) *(hum)*

[6] *(= remporter) [+ siège d'élu, victoire]* to win; *[+ titre de champion]* to win, to take; *(Mil) [+ position]* to capture, to take ◆ **il a facilement enlevé la course** he won the race easily ◆ **elle enlève tous les suffrages** she wins everyone's sympathies, she wins everyone over ◆ **~ la décision** to carry the day ◆ **~ une affaire** *(tractation)* to pull off a deal; *(commande)* to get *ou* secure an order; *(marchandise)* to carry off *ou* get away with a bargain ◆ **ça a été vite enlevé** *(marchandise)* it sold *ou* went quickly, it was snapped up; (* *: travail)* it was done in no time *ou* in a jiffy*

[7] *(Mus) [+ morceau, mouvement]* to play with spirit *ou* brio

[8] *(Sport) [+ cheval]* to urge on

[9] *(= enthousiasmer) [+ public]* to fill with enthusiasm

VPR **s'enlever** [1] *[tache]* to come out, to come off; *(en brossant ou lavant etc)* to brush *ou* wash *etc* out *ou* off; *[peinture, peau, écorce]* to peel off, to come off ◆ **enlève-toi de là*** get out of the way*, mind out of the way! * *(Brit)* ◆ **comment est-ce que ça s'enlève ?** *[étiquette, housse]* how do you remove it *ou* take it off?; *[vêtement]* how do you get out of it *ou* take it off?

[2] *(Sport)* **le cheval s'enlève sur l'obstacle** *(= sauter)* the horse takes off to clear the obstacle

[3] († *= se vendre*) to sell

enlisement /ɑ̃lizmɑ̃/ **NM** ◆ **causer l'~ d'un bateau** to cause a ship to get stuck in the mud (*ou* sand *etc*)

enliser /ɑ̃lize/ ▸ conjug 1 ◂ **VT** ◆ **~ sa voiture** to get one's car stuck in the mud (*ou* sand *etc*) **VPR** **s'enliser** [1] *(dans le sable)* to sink *(dans* into) to get stuck (*dans* in) [2] (*dans les détails*) to get bogged down (*dans* in); ◆ **s'~ (dans la monotonie)** to sink into *ou* get bogged down in a monotonous routine ◆ **en mentant, tu t'enlises davantage** you're getting in deeper and deeper (water) with your lies

enluminer /ɑ̃lymine/ ▸ conjug 1 ◂ VT [*+ manuscrit*] to illuminate

enlumineur, -euse /ɑ̃lyminœʀ, øz/ NM,F illuminator

enluminure /ɑ̃lyminyʀ/ NF illumination

enneigé, e /ɑ̃neʒe/ ADJ [*pente, montagne*] snowy, snow-covered; [*sommet*] snow-capped; [*maison*] snowbound, snowed up (*attrib*); [*col, route*] blocked by snow, snowed up (*attrib*), snowbound

enneigement /ɑ̃nɛʒmɑ̃/ NM snow coverage ◆ **à cause du faible ~** because of the poor snow coverage ◆ **bulletin d'~** snow report ◆ **conditions d'~** snow conditions

ennemi, e /ɛn(ə)mi/ ADJ (*Mil*) enemy (*épith*); (= *hostile*) hostile ◆ **en pays ~** in enemy territory NM,F [1] (= *adversaire*) enemy, foe † (*aussi littér*) ◆ **se faire des ~s** to make enemies (for o.s.) ◆ **se faire un ~ de qn** to make an enemy of sb ◆ **passer à l'~** to go over to the enemy ◆ **~ public numéro un** public enemy number one [2] ◆ **être ~ de qch** to be opposed to sth, to be against sth ◆ **être ~ de la poésie/de la musique** to be strongly averse to poetry/music ◆ **la hâte est l'ennemie de la précision** speed and accuracy don't mix *ou* don't go together more haste less speed (*Prov*) → **mieux**

ennoblir /ɑ̃nɔbliʀ/ ▸ conjug 2 ◂ VT (*moralement*) to ennoble

ennoblissement /ɑ̃nɔblismɑ̃/ NM (*moral*) ennoblement

ennuager (s') /ɑ̃nɥaʒe/ ▸ conjug 3 ◂ VPR (*littér*) [*ciel*] to cloud over ◆ **ennuagé** cloudy, clouded

ennui /ɑ̃nɥi/ NM [1] (= *désœuvrement*) boredom; (*littér* = *spleen*) ennui (*littér*), world-weariness; (= *monotonie*) tedium, tediousness ◆ **écouter avec ~** to listen wearily ◆ **c'est à mourir d'~** it's enough to bore you to tears *ou* death * *ou* to bore you stiff *

[2] (= *tracas*) trouble, worry, problem ◆ **avoir des ~s** to have problems, to be in difficulty ◆ **il a eu des ~s avec la police** he's been in trouble with the police ◆ **avoir des ~s de santé** to be troubled with bad health, to have problems with one's health ◆ **~s d'argent** money worries ◆ **elle a des tas d'~s** she has a great many worries, she has more than her share of troubles ◆ **faire** *ou* **créer** *ou* **causer des ~s à qn** to make trouble for sb ◆ **ça peut lui attirer des ~s** that could get him into trouble *ou* hot water * ◆ **j'ai eu un ~ avec mon vélo** I had some trouble *ou* bother with my bike, something went wrong with my bike ◆ **si ça vous cause le moindre ~** if it is in any way inconvenient to you ◆ **l'~, c'est que ...** the trouble *ou* the hitch is that ...

[3] (*littér*, †† = *peine*) grief

ennuyant, e /ɑ̃nɥijɑ̃, ɑ̃t/ ADJ († , *Can*) ⇒ **ennuyeux**

ennuyé, e /ɑ̃nɥije/ (ptp de **ennuyer**) ADJ (= *préoccupé*) worried, bothered (*de* about); (= *contrarié*) annoyed, put out (*de* at, about)

ennuyer /ɑ̃nɥije/ GRAMMAIRE ACTIVE 36.1 ▸ conjug 8 ◂

VT [1] (= *lasser*) to bore, to weary ◆ **ce spectacle m'a profondément ennuyé** I was thoroughly bored by the show ◆ **cela (vous) ennuie à force** it palls (on you) *ou* it gets boring in the long run

[2] (= *préoccuper*) to worry; (= *importuner*) to bother, to put out ◆ **il y a quelque chose qui m'ennuie là-dedans** there's something that worries *ou* bothers me about it ◆ **ça m'ennuierait beaucoup de te voir fâché** I should be really upset to see you cross ◆ **ça m'ennuie de te le dire, mais ...** I'm sorry to have to tell you but ..., I hate to say it but ... ◆ **ça m'ennuierait beaucoup d'y aller** it would really put me out to go ◆ **si cela ne vous ennuie pas trop** if it wouldn't put you to any trouble *ou* inconvenience, if you wouldn't mind ◆ **je ne voudrais pas vous ~** I don't want to put you to any trouble *ou* inconvenience, I don't want to bother you *ou* put you out ◆ **ça m'ennuie, ce que tu me demandes de faire** what you're asking me to do is rather awkward *ou* a nuisance

[3] (= *irriter*) **~ qn** to annoy sb, to get on sb's nerves ◆ **tu m'ennuies avec tes jérémiades** I'm tired of your constant complaints, you're getting on my nerves with your constant complaints

VPR **s'ennuyer** [1] (= *se morfondre*) to be bored (*de, à* with); ◆ **il s'ennuie à faire un travail monotone** he's getting bored doing a humdrum job ◆ **s'~ à mourir** to be bored to tears *ou* to death *, to be bored stiff * ◆ **on ne s'ennuie jamais avec lui** there's never a dull moment when he's around

[2] ◆ **s'~ de qn** to miss sb

ennuyeux, -euse /ɑ̃nɥijø, øz/ ADJ [1] (= *lassant*) [*personne, spectacle, livre*] boring, tedious; [*travail*] boring, tedious, wearisome ◆ **~ comme la pluie** deadly dull, dull as ditchwater (*Brit*) [2] (= *qui importune*) annoying, tiresome; (= *préoccupant*) worrying ◆ **ce qui t'arrive est bien ~** this is a very annoying *ou* tiresome thing to happen to you

énoncé /enɔ̃se/ NM [1] (= *termes*) [*de sujet scolaire*] wording; [*de problème*] terms; [*de loi*] terms, wording ◆ **pendant l'~ du sujet** while the subject is being read out [2] (*Ling*) utterance

énoncer /enɔ̃se/ ▸ conjug 3 ◂ VT [*+ idée*] to express; [*+ faits, conditions*] to state, to set out, to set forth ◆ **pour m'~ plus clairement** († , *littér*) to express myself more clearly, to put it more clearly; → **concevoir**

énonciatif, -ive /enɔ̃sjatif, iv/ ADJ (*Ling*) [*phrase*] enunciative

énonciation /enɔ̃sjasjɔ̃/ NF [*de faits*] statement; (*Ling*) enunciation

enorgueillir /ɑ̃nɔʀgœjiʀ/ ▸ conjug 2 ◂ VT to make proud VPR **s'enorgueillir** ◆ **s'~ de** (= *être fier de*) to pride o.s. on, to boast about; (= *avoir*) to boast ◆ **la ville s'enorgueillit de deux opéras** the town boasts two opera houses

énorme /enɔʀm/ ADJ [1] (= *très grand*) enormous, huge; (*Météo*) [*mer*] phenomenal ◆ **mensonge ~** enormous *ou* whopping * lie, whopper * ◆ **ça lui a fait un bien ~** it's done him a great deal *ou* a world *ou* a power * (*Brit*) of good [2] (= *exceptionnel*) amazing ◆ **c'est un type ~ !*** he's an amazing guy! ◆ **c'est ~ ce qu'ils ont fait !** what they've done is absolutely amazing! ◆ **il a accepté, c'est déjà ~** he has accepted and that's quite something

énormément /enɔʀmemɑ̃/ ADV (= *beaucoup*) enormously, tremendously, hugely ◆ **ça m'a ~ amusé** I was greatly *ou* hugely amused by it ◆ **ça m'a ~ déçu** it greatly disappointed me, I was tremendously *ou* greatly disappointed by it ◆ **il boit ~** he drinks an enormous *ou* a huge amount

◆ **énormément de** [*d'argent, eau, bruit*] an enormous *ou* a huge amount of, a great deal of ◆ **~ de gens** a great many people

énormité /enɔʀmite/ NF [1] [*de poids, somme*] hugeness; [*de demande, injustice*] enormity [2] (= *propos inconvenant*) outrageous remark; (= *erreur*) big blunder, howler *

enquérir (s') /ɑ̃keʀiʀ/ ▸ conjug 21 ◂ VPR to inquire, to enquire, to ask (*de* about); ◆ **s'~ (de la santé) de qn** to ask *ou* inquire after sb *ou* after sb's health ◆ **je m'en suis enquis à la mairie** I inquired at the town hall about it ◆ **je m'en suis enquis auprès de lui** I asked him about it

enquête /ɑ̃kɛt/ NF (*gén, Jur*) inquiry, enquiry; (*après un décès*) inquest; (*Police*) investigation; (*Comm, Sociol* = *sondage*) survey, (opinion) poll ◆ **ouvrir une ~** (*Jur*) to set up *ou* open an inquiry ◆ **faire une ~** (*Police*) to make an investigation, to make investigations, to investigate; (*Comm, Sociol*) to do *ou* conduct a survey (*sur* on); ◆ **mener** *ou* **conduire une ~** (*Police*) to be in charge of *ou* lead an investigation ◆ **j'ai fait** *ou* **mené ma petite ~** I've done a little investigating (myself), I've done a little private investigation ◆ **~ administrative** public inquiry (*into planning proposals etc*) ◆ **~ parlementaire** parliamentary inquiry (*by parliamentary committee*) ◆ **~ statistique** statistical survey ◆ **~ préliminaire** preliminary inquiry ◆ **commission d'~** commission of inquiry ◆ **"notre grande enquête"** (*Presse*) "our big investigation *ou* survey *ou* inquiry"

enquêter /ɑ̃kete/ ▸ conjug 1 ◂ VI (*Jur*) to hold an inquiry (*sur* on); (*Police*) to investigate; (*Comm, Sociol*) to conduct a survey (*sur* on); ◆ **ils vont ~ sur l'origine de ces fonds** they'll investigate the origin of these funds *ou* carry out an investigation into the origin of these funds

enquêteur /ɑ̃kɛtœʀ/ NM [1] (*Police*) officer in charge of *ou* leading the investigation ◆ **les ~s poursuivent leurs recherches** the police are continuing their investigations ◆ **les ~s sont aidés par la population du village** the police are being helped in their inquiries *ou* investigations by the villagers ◆ **un des ~s a été abattu** one of the officers involved in the investigation was shot dead [2] (*Comm, Sociol*) investigator; (*pour sondages*) pollster, interviewer ◆ **des ~s sont venus dans le village** some people doing *ou* conducting a survey came to the village

enquêteuse /ɑ̃kɛtøz/ NF (*Police*) officer in charge of *ou* leading an investigation; (*Sociol*) ⇒ **enquêtrice**

enquêtrice /ɑ̃kɛtʀis/ NF (*Comm, Sociol*) investigator; (*pour sondages*) pollster, interviewer; → aussi **enquêteur**

enquiquinant, e * /ɑ̃kikinɑ̃, ɑ̃t/ ADJ (= *qui importune*) annoying, irritating; (= *préoccupant*) worrying; (= *lassant*) boring

enquiquinement * /ɑ̃kikinmɑ̃/ NM ◆ **quel ~!** what a darned *ou* flipping (*Brit*) nuisance! * ◆ **j'ai eu tellement d'~s avec cette voiture** I had so many darned *ou* flipping (*Brit*) problems with that car *

enquiquiner * /ɑ̃kikine/ ▸ conjug 1 ◂ VT (= *importuner*) to annoy, to bother; (= *préoccuper*) to worry; (= *lasser*) to bore VPR **s'enquiquiner** (= *se morfondre*) to be fed up *, to be bored ◆ **s'~ à faire** (= *se donner du mal*) to go to a heck of a lot of trouble to do *, to put o.s. out to do ◆ **ne t'enquiquine pas avec ça** don't bother (yourself) with that

enquiquineur, -euse * /ɑ̃kikinœʀ, øz/ NM,F pest *, pain in the neck *

enracinement /ɑ̃ʀasinmɑ̃/ NM [1] [*d'idée, arbre*] taking root [2] [*d'immigrant*] settling

enraciner /ɑ̃ʀasine/ ▸ conjug 1 ◂ VT [*+ arbre*] to root; [*+ idée*] to fix, to cause to take root ◆ **solidement enraciné** [*+ préjugé*] deep-rooted, firmly *ou* deeply entrenched; [*+ famille*] firmly rooted *ou* fixed; [*+ arbre*] well-rooted VPR **s'enraciner** [*arbre, préjugé*] to take root; [*importun*] to settle o.s. down; [*immigrant*] to put down roots, to settle

enragé, e /ɑ̃ʀaʒe/ (ptp de **enrager**) ADJ [1] (* = *passionné*) [*chasseur, joueur*] keen ◆ **être ~ de** to be mad * *ou* crazy about *, to be mad keen on * (*Brit*) ◆ **un ~ de la voiture** a car fanatic [2] (= *en* *colère)* furious ◆ **les ~s de Mai 68** the rebels of May '68 ③ *[animal])* rabid; → **vache**

enrageant, e /ɑ̃ʀaʒɑ̃, ɑ̃t/ ADJ annoying, infuriating ◆ **c'est vraiment ~ de devoir partir si tôt** it's a real pain* *ou* it's really annoying having to leave so early

enrager /ɑ̃ʀaʒe/ ► conjug 3 ◄ VI ① ◆ **faire ~ qn*** *(= taquiner)* to tease sb; *(= importuner)* to pester sb ② *(frm)* to be furious, to be in a rage ◆ **j'enrage d'avoir fait cette erreur** I'm furious at having made this mistake ◆ **il enrageait dans son coin** he was fretting and fuming

enraiement /ɑ̃ʀɛmɑ̃/ NM ⇒ **enrayement**

enrayage /ɑ̃ʀejaʒ/ NM *[de machine, arme]* jamming

enrayement /ɑ̃ʀejmɑ̃/ NM *[de maladie, évolution]* checking; *[de chômage, inflation]* checking, curbing

enrayer /ɑ̃ʀeje/ ► conjug 8 ◄ VT ① *[+ maladie, évolution]* to check; *[+ chômage, inflation]* to check, to curb; *[+ machine, arme]* to jam ② *[+ roue]* to spoke VPR **s'enrayer** *[machine, arme]* to jam

enrégimenter /ɑ̃ʀeʒimɑ̃te/ ► conjug 1 ◄ VT ① *(péj : dans un parti)* to enlist, to enrol ◆ **se laisser ~ dans** *[+ parti]* to let o.s. be dragooned into ② († *Mil)* to enlist

enregistrable /ɑ̃ʀ(ə)ʒistʀabl/ ADJ *[CD, disquette]* recordable; *[CD-Rom]* writeable

enregistrement /ɑ̃ʀ(ə)ʒistʀəmɑ̃/ NM ① *[de fait, son, souvenir]* recording ② *(= disque, bande)* recording ◆ **~ vidéo/magnétique** video/tape recording ③ *(Jur) [d'acte]* registration ◆ **l'Enregistrement** the Registration Department *(for legal transactions)* ◆ **droits** *ou* **frais d'~** registration fees ④ *(Transport)* **~ des bagages** *(à l'aéroport)* check-in; *(à la gare)* registration of luggage ◆ **se présenter à l'~** to go to the check-in desk ◆ **comptoir d'~** check-in desk

enregistrer /ɑ̃ʀ(ə)ʒistʀe/ ► conjug 1 ◄ VT ① *(sur bande)* to record, to tape; *(sur CD, en studio)* to record; *(sur magnétoscope)* to record, to video(-tape) ◆ **vous écoutez un message enregistré** *(Téléc)* this is a recorded message

② *(Jur) [+ acte, demande]* to register; *(Comm) [+ commande]* to enter, to book

③ *[+ profit, perte]* to show ◆ **nous avons enregistré de bonnes ventes** we've had good sales ◆ **ils ont enregistré un bénéfice de 5 millions** they showed a profit of 5 million ◆ **le PIB a enregistré une hausse de 12%** the GDP has shown *ou* recorded an increase of 12%

④ *(= constater)* **on enregistre une progression de l'épidémie** the epidemic is spreading ◆ **on enregistre une amélioration de la situation** we have seen *ou* there has been an improvement in the situation ◆ **la plus forte hausse enregistrée** the biggest rise recorded *ou* on record

⑤ *(= mémoriser) [+ information]* to take in ◆ **d'accord, j'enregistre*** *ou* **c'est enregistré*** all right, I'll make *ou* I've made a mental note of it *ou* I'll bear it in mind

⑥ *(Transport)* **(faire) ~ ses bagages** *(à l'aéroport)* to check in (one's luggage); *(à la gare)* to register one's luggage

enregistreur, -euse /ɑ̃ʀ(ə)ʒistʀœʀ, øz/ ADJ *[appareil]* recording; → **caisse** NM *(= instrument)* recorder, recording device ◆ **~ de vol** flight recorder ◆ **~ de temps** time recorder

enrhumé, e /ɑ̃ʀyme/ (ptp de **enrhumer**) ADJ ◆ **être ~** to have a cold ◆ **je suis un peu/très ~** I have a bit of a cold/a terrible *ou* bad cold

enrhumer /ɑ̃ʀyme/ ► conjug 1 ◄ VT to give a cold to VPR **s'enrhumer** to catch a cold

enrichi, e /ɑ̃ʀiʃi/ (ptp de **enrichir**) ADJ ① *(péj)* nouveau riche ② *[pain]* enriched; *[lessive]* improved *(de* with); ◆ **shampooing formule ~e** enriched formula shampoo; → **uranium**

enrichir /ɑ̃ʀiʃiʀ/ ► conjug 2 ◄ VT *[+ œuvre, esprit, langue, collection]* to enrich; *[+ catalogue]* to expand; *(financièrement)* to make rich VPR **s'enrichir** *(financièrement)* to get *ou* grow rich; *[esprit]* to grow richer *(de* in); *[collection]* to be enriched *(de* with); ◆ **leur collection s'enrichit d'année en année** their collection is becoming richer from year to year ◆ **notre catalogue s'est enrichi de cent nouveaux titres** a hundred new titles have been added to our catalogue

enrichissant, e /ɑ̃ʀiʃisɑ̃, ɑ̃t/ ADJ *[expérience]* rewarding ◆ **ce stage a été très ~ pour moi** I got a lot out of the course ◆ **j'ai trouvé ça très ~** it was very rewarding

enrichissement /ɑ̃ʀiʃismɑ̃/ NM enrichment *(NonC)*

enrobage /ɑ̃ʀɔbaʒ/, **enrobement** /ɑ̃ʀɔbmɑ̃/ NM coating

enrobé, e /ɑ̃ʀɔbe/ (ptp de **enrober**) ADJ *(= empâté) [personne]* plump

enrober /ɑ̃ʀɔbe/ ► conjug 1 ◄ VT *[+ bonbon, comprimé]* to coat *(de* with); *[+ paroles]* to wrap up *(de* in)

enrochement /ɑ̃ʀɔʃmɑ̃/ NM rip-rap

enrôlé /ɑ̃ʀole/ NM recruit

enrôlement /ɑ̃ʀolmɑ̃/ NM *(Mil)* enlistment; *(dans un parti)* enrolment, signing up

enrôler VT, **s'enrôler** VPR /ɑ̃ʀole/ ► conjug 1 ◄ *(Mil)* to enlist; *(dans un parti)* to enrol, to sign up

enroué, e /ɑ̃ʀwe/ (ptp de **enrouer**) ADJ ◆ **être ~** to be hoarse, to have a hoarse *ou* husky voice ◆ **j'ai la voix ~e** my voice is hoarse *ou* husky

enrouement /ɑ̃ʀumɑ̃/ NM hoarseness, huskiness

enrouer /ɑ̃ʀwe/ ► conjug 1 ◄ VT *[froid, cris]* to make hoarse VPR **s'enrouer** *(par le froid)* to go hoarse *ou* husky; *(en criant)* to make o.s. hoarse ◆ **s'~ à force de chanter** to sing o.s. hoarse

enroulement /ɑ̃ʀulmɑ̃/ NM ① *(NonC) [de tapis]* rolling up; *[de cheveux]* coiling; *[de corde, ruban, fil]* winding *(sur, autour de* round); *[de bobine]* winding ② *(Archit, Art)* volute, scroll, whorl ③ *(Élec)* coil

enrouler /ɑ̃ʀule/ ► conjug 1 ◄ VT *[+ tapis]* to roll up; *[+ cheveux]* to coil; *[+ corde, ruban, fil]* to wind *(sur, autour de* round); *[+ bobine]* to wind ◆ **~ une feuille autour de/dans** to roll a sheet of paper round/up in VPR **s'enrouler** *[serpent]* to coil up; *[film, fil]* to wind ◆ **s'~ dans une couverture** to wrap *ou* roll o.s. up in a blanket

enrouleur, -euse /ɑ̃ʀulœʀ, øz/ ADJ *[mécanisme, cylindre]* winding NM *[de tuyau d'arrosage]* drum ◆ **(galet) ~** idle pulley, idler ◆ **~ (automatique) de cordon** automatic cord winder ◆ **laisse à ~** retractable lead; → **ceinture**

enrubanner /ɑ̃ʀybane/ ► conjug 1 ◄ VT to decorate *ou* trim with ribbon(s); *(en attachant)* to tie up *ou* do up with (a) ribbon

ENS /eɛnɛs/ NF (abrév de **École normale supérieure**) → **école**

ensablement /ɑ̃sabləmɑ̃/ NM ① *[de port]* silting-up; *[de tuyau]* choking *ou* blocking (with sand); *[de bateau]* stranding; *[de voiture]* getting stuck (in the sand) ② *(= tas de sable) (formé par le vent)* (sand) dune; *(formé par l'eau)* sandbank

ensabler /ɑ̃sable/ ► conjug 1 ◄ VT *[+ port]* to silt up, to sand up; *[+ tuyau]* to choke *ou* block with sand; *[+ bateau]* to strand (on a sandbank); *[+ voiture]* to get stuck (in the sand) VPR **s'ensabler** *[port]* to silt up; *[bateau, voiture]* to get stuck in the sand ◆ **je m'étais ensablé jusqu'aux essieux** my car had sunk into the sand up to the axles

ensacher /ɑ̃saʃe/ ► conjug 1 ◄ VT to bag, to pack (into bags)

ensanglanter /ɑ̃sɑ̃glɑ̃te/ ► conjug 1 ◄ VT *[+ visage]* to cover with blood; *[+ vêtement]* to soak with blood ◆ **manche ensanglantée** blood-soaked sleeve ◆ **~ un pays** to bathe a country in blood ◆ **l'accident qui a ensanglanté la course** the accident which cast a tragic shadow over the race ◆ **l'attentat qui a ensanglanté la visite du président** the terrorist attack which brought an element of bloodshed to the president's visit

enseignant, e /ɑ̃sɛɲɑ̃, ɑ̃t/ ADJ teaching; → **corps** NM,F teacher ◆ **~-chercheur** teacher and researcher ◆ **poste d'~** teaching position *ou* post *ou* job ◆ **les ~s de l'école** the teaching staff *ou* the teachers at the school

enseigne /ɑ̃sɛɲ/ NF ① *(Comm)* (shop) sign ◆ **~ lumineuse** neon sign ◆ **"à l'enseigne du Lion Noir"** *(restaurant)* "the Black Lion" ◆ **loger à l'~ du Lion Noir** †† to put up at (the sign of) the Black Lion † ② *(Mil, Naut)* ensign ◆ **(défiler) ~s déployées** (to march) with colours flying ③ *(littér)* **à telle(s) ~(s) que ...** so much so that ... NM ① *(Hist)* ensign ② ◆ **~ de vaisseau** *(de 1re classe)* lieutenant; *(de 2e classe)* sub-lieutenant *(Brit)*, ensign *(US)*

enseignement /ɑ̃sɛɲ(ə)mɑ̃/ NM ① *(= cours, leçons)* education, instruction ◆ **recevoir un ~ dans une discipline** to receive instruction in a subject ◆ **~ assisté par ordinateur** computer-aided instruction ◆ **~ général** general education ◆ **~ obligatoire** compulsory education ◆ **~ musical** musical education ◆ **~ agricole** agricultural training ◆ **~ des langues** language teaching ◆ **~ ménager** home economics *(sg)* ◆ **~ mixte** coeducation ◆ **~ par correspondance** correspondence courses ◆ **~ à distance** distance learning ◆ **~ professionnel** professional *ou* vocational training ◆ **~ programmé** programmed learning ◆ **~ spécialisé** special education *ou* schooling ◆ **~ technique** technical education, industrial arts *(US)*

② *(= système scolaire)* education ◆ **l'~ en France** (the system of) education in France ◆ **~ primaire** *ou* **du premier degré/secondaire** *ou* **du second degré** primary/secondary education ◆ **~ supérieur/universitaire** higher/university education ◆ **~ libre/privé/ public** denominational/private/state education ◆ **l'~ public et gratuit** free public education; → **ÉDUCATION NATIONALE**

③ *(= art d'enseigner)* teaching ◆ **~ moderne** modern (methods of) teaching

④ *(= carrière)* **l'~** the teaching profession, teaching ◆ **entrer dans l'~** to enter the teaching profession, to go into teaching ◆ **être dans l'~** to be a teacher, to be a member of the teaching profession

⑤ *(= leçon donnée par l'expérience)* teaching, lesson ◆ **on peut en tirer plusieurs ~s** it has taught us several things, we can draw several lessons from it ◆ **les ~s du Christ** the teachings of Christ

enseigner /ɑ̃seɲe/ ► conjug 1 ◄ VT to teach ◆ **~ qch à qn** to teach sb sth ◆ **~ à qn à faire qch** to teach sb (how) to do sth

ensemble¹ /ɑ̃sɑ̃bl/ ADV ① *(= l'un avec l'autre)* together ◆ **ils sont partis ~** they left together ◆ **tous ~** all together

② *(= simultanément) (deux personnes)* together, both at once; *(plusieurs)* together, at the same time ◆ **ils ont répondu ~** *(deux)* they both answered together *ou* at once; *(plusieurs)* they all answered together *ou* at the same time, they answered all together

③ *(littér = à la fois)* **tout ~** *(deux)* both, at once; *(plus de deux)* at (one and) the same time ◆ **il était tout ~ triste et joyeux** he was both *ou* at once sad and happy

④ ◆ **aller ~** *[objets]* to go together; *[idées]* to go together *ou* hand in hand ◆ **aller bien ~** *[couple]* to be well-matched; *[escrocs]* to make a pretty *ou* a fine pair; *(plus de deux)* to make a fine bunch ◆ **l'armoire et la table ne vont pas**

(bien) ~ *ou* **vont mal** ~ the wardrobe and the table don't go (very well) together
[5] *[personnes]* **être bien** ~ to get along *ou* on *(Brit)* well (together) ◆ **ils sont mal** ~ they don't get along *ou* on *(Brit)* (well) (together)

ensemble² /ɑ̃sɑ̃bl/ **NM** [1] *(= totalité)* whole ◆ **former un ~ harmonieux** to form a harmonious whole ◆ **l'~ du personnel** the entire *ou* whole staff ◆ **on reconnaît cette substance à l'~ de ses propriétés** you can identify this substance from all its various properties
[2] *(= groupement) [de personnes]* set, group, body; *[d'objets, poèmes]* set, collection; *[de faits]* set, series; *[de meubles]* suite; *[de lois]* body, corpus ◆ **tout un ~ de choses** a whole combination of things ◆ **bel ~ architectural** fine architectural grouping ◆ **~ immobilier de 500 logements** residential complex with 500 housing units ◆ **grand ~** high-rise estate
[3] *(Mus)* ensemble ◆ **~ instrumental/vocal** instrumental/vocal ensemble
[4] *(Math)* set ◆ **~ vide** empty set ◆ **théorie des ~s** set theory
[5] *(Couture)* outfit, suit, ensemble ◆ **~ de ville** town suit ◆ **~ de voyage** travelling outfit ◆ **~ de plage** beach ensemble *ou* outfit ◆ **~ pantalon** trouser suit, pantsuit
[6] *(locutions)* **d'~** *[vue, étude]* overall, comprehensive, general; *[impression]* overall, general ◆ **mouvement d'~** ensemble movement
◆ **dans + ensemble** ◆ **les spectateurs dans leur ~** the audience as a whole ◆ **examiner la question dans son ~** to examine the question in its entirety *ou* as a whole
◆ **dans l'ensemble** on the whole, in the main, by and large ◆ **dans l'~ nous sommes d'accord** basically we agree
◆ **avec ensemble** *[répondre]* as one, with one accord

ensemblier /ɑ̃sɑ̃blije/ **NM** *(= décorateur)* interior designer; *(Ciné)* assistant (set) designer; *(= entreprise)* factory design consultancy

ensemencement /ɑ̃s(ə)mɑ̃smɑ̃/ **NM** sowing

ensemencer /ɑ̃s(ə)mɑ̃se/ ► conjug 3 ◄ **VT** *(Agr)* to sow *(de, en* with*)*; *(Bio)* to culture

enserrer /ɑ̃seʀe/ ► conjug 1 ◄ **VT** *[vêtement]* to hug tightly; *(dans ses bras)* to hold, to clasp ◆ **vallée enserrée par des montagnes** valley shut in *ou* hemmed in by mountains

ensevelir /ɑ̃səv(ə)liʀ/ ► conjug 2 ◄ **VT** *(frm = enterrer)* to bury; *(d'un linceul)* to shroud *(de* in*)*; *[+ peine, honte]* to hide, to bury; *[avalanche, décombres]* to bury ◆ **enseveli sous la neige/la lave** buried beneath the snow/lava

ensevelissement /ɑ̃səv(ə)lismɑ̃/ **NM** *(gén)* burying; *(dans un linceul)* shrouding

ENSI /ɛnsi/ **NF** (abrév de **École nationale supérieure d'ingénieurs**) → **école**

ensilage /ɑ̃silaʒ/ **NM** *(= aliment)* silage; *(= processus)* silage-making

ensiler /ɑ̃sile/ ► conjug 1 ◄ **VT** to ensilage, to ensile

en-soi /ɑ̃swa/ **NM** *(Philos)* en-soi

ensoleillé, e /ɑ̃sɔleje/ (ptp de **ensoleiller**) **ADJ** sunny

ensoleillement /ɑ̃sɔlɛjmɑ̃/ **NM** *(= durée)* period *ou* hours of sunshine ◆ **ce versant jouit d'un ~ exceptionnel** this side of the mountain gets a lot of sunshine ◆ **'~ moyen'** *(sur étiquette de plantes)* 'moderate sunlight'

ensoleiller /ɑ̃sɔleje/ ► conjug 1 ◄ **VT** *(lit)* to fill with *ou* bathe in sunshine *ou* sunlight; *(fig)* to brighten, to light up

ensommeillé, e /ɑ̃sɔmeje/ **ADJ** sleepy, drowsy

ensorcelant, e /ɑ̃sɔʀsəlɑ̃, ɑ̃t/ **ADJ** *[regard, sourire]* bewitching; *[personne]* bewitching, captivating; *[paroles, roman, œuvre, rythme, musique]* spellbinding

ensorceler /ɑ̃sɔʀsəle/ ► conjug 4 ◄ **VT** *(lit, fig)* to bewitch, to put *ou* cast a spell on *ou* over

ensorceleur, -euse /ɑ̃sɔʀsəlœʀ, øz/ **ADJ** bewitching, spellbinding **NM** *(lit)* sorcerer, enchanter; *(fig)* charmer **NF** **ensorceleuse** *(lit)* witch, enchantress, sorceress; *(fig = femme)* enchantress; *(hum = enfant)* charmer

ensorcellement /ɑ̃sɔʀsɛlmɑ̃/ **NM** *(= action)* bewitching, bewitchment; *(= charme)* charm, enchantment

ensuite /ɑ̃sɥit/ GRAMMAIRE ACTIVE 53.2 **ADV** *(= puis)* then, next; *(= par la suite)* afterwards, later ◆ **il nous dit ~ que ...** then *ou* next he said that ... ◆ **d'accord mais ~ ?** all right but what now? *ou* what next? *ou* then what? ◆ **il se mit à crier, ~ de quoi il claqua la porte** he started shouting, after which *ou* and after that he slammed the door ◆ **je le reçois d'abord et je vous verrai ~** I'll meet him first and I'll see you after *ou* afterwards

ensuivre (s') /ɑ̃sɥivʀ/ ► conjug 40 ◄ **VPR** to follow, to ensue ◆ **il s'ensuit que** it follows that ◆ **et tout ce qui s'ensuit** and all that goes with it ◆ **torturé jusqu'à ce que mort s'ensuive** tortured to death

ensuqué, e* /ɑ̃syke/ **ADJ** droopy

entablement /ɑ̃tabləmɑ̃/ **NM** entablature

entacher /ɑ̃taʃe/ ► conjug 1 ◄ **VT** *[+ honneur]* to soil, to sully, to taint; *[+ joie]* to taint, to blemish ◆ **entaché de nullité** *(Jur)* null and void ◆ **entaché d'erreurs** spoilt *ou* marred by mistakes

entaille /ɑ̃taj/ **NF** [1] *(sur le corps, gén)* cut; *(profonde)* gash; *(petite)* nick ◆ **se faire une ~** to cut o.s. [2] *(sur un objet)* notch; *(allongée)* groove; *(dans une falaise)* gash

entailler /ɑ̃taje/ ► conjug 1 ◄ **VT** *[+ corps] (gén)* to cut; *(profondément)* to gash; *(légèrement)* to nick; *[+ objet]* to notch ◆ **carrière qui entaille la colline** quarry which cuts a gash in the hill ◆ **s'~ la main** to cut *ou* gash one's hand

entame /ɑ̃tam/ **NF** *(= tranche)* first slice; *(Cartes)* first card

entamer /ɑ̃tame/ ► conjug 1 ◄ **VT** [1] *[+ pain, jambon]* to start (on); *[+ tonneau]* to broach, to tap; *[+ bouteille, boîte, sac]* to start, to open; *[+ tissu]* to cut into; *[+ patrimoine]* to make a hole in, to dip into ◆ **mes économies sont bien entamées** it has made a big dent *ou* hole in my savings ◆ **la boîte est à peine entamée** the box has hardly been touched
[2] *(= inciser) [+ chair, tissu]* to cut (into); *[+ métal]* to cut *ou* bite into
[3] *(= amorcer) [+ journée, livre]* to start; *[+ travail]* to start on; *[+ négociations, discussion]* to start, to open; *[+ poursuites]* to institute, to initiate ◆ **la journée est déjà bien entamée** we are already well into the day, the day is already quite far advanced
[4] *(= ébranler) [+ résistance]* to wear down, to break down; *[+ conviction]* to shake, to weaken; *[+ optimisme, moral]* to wear down
[5] *(= salir) [+ réputation]* to damage, to harm, to cast a slur on
[6] *(Cartes = commencer)* ~ **la partie** to open the game ◆ **c'est à toi d'~** it's you to lead ◆ **~ d'un pique** *(enchères)* to open (with) one spade; *(partie)* to lead a spade

entartage /ɑ̃taʀtaʒ/ **NM** custard pie attack

entarter /ɑ̃taʀte/ ► conjug 1 ◄ **VT** *[+ personne]* to throw a custard pie at

entarteur /ɑ̃taʀtœʀ/ **NM** *prankster who throws custard pies at celebrities*

entartrage /ɑ̃taʀtʀaʒ/ **NM** *[de chaudière, tuyau, bouilloire]* scaling, furring-up *(Brit)*; *[de dents]* scaling

entartrer /ɑ̃taʀtʀe/ ► conjug 1 ◄ **VT** *[+ chaudière, tuyau, bouilloire]* to scale, to fur up *(Brit)*; *[+ dents]* to scale **VPR** **s'entartrer** *[chaudière, tuyau, bouilloire]* to scale, to fur up *(Brit)*; *[dents]* to get covered in tartar

entassement /ɑ̃tasmɑ̃/ **NM** [1] *(= action) [d'objets]* piling up, heaping up; *[de personnes]* cramming in, packing together [2] *(= tas)* pile, heap

entasser /ɑ̃tase/ ► conjug 1 ◄ **VT** [1] *(= amonceler) [+ objets, arguments]* to pile up, to heap up *(sur* onto*)* [2] *(= tasser) [+ personnes, objets]* to cram, to pack *(dans* into*)* **VPR** **s'entasser** *(= s'amonceler) [déchets, erreurs]* to pile up; *[personnes]* to cram, to pack *(dans* into*)*; ◆ **ils s'entassent à 10 dans cette pièce** there are 10 of them crammed *ou* packed into that room ◆ **s'~ sur la plage** to pack onto the beach

ente /ɑ̃t/ **NF** *(Agr)* graft

entendement /ɑ̃tɑ̃dmɑ̃/ **NM** *(Philos)* understanding ◆ **cela dépasse l'~** that's beyond all understanding *ou* comprehension ◆ **perdre l'~** *(frm)* to lose one's reason

entendeur /ɑ̃tɑ̃dœʀ/ **NM** ◆ **à bon ~, salut** a word to the wise is enough

entendre /ɑ̃tɑ̃dʀ/ ► conjug 41 ◄ **VT** [1] *(= percevoir) [+ voix, bruit]* to hear ◆ **il entendit du bruit** he heard a noise ◆ **il entend mal de l'oreille droite** he can't hear very well with his right ear ◆ **il ne l'entend pas de cette oreille** *(fig)* he's not prepared to accept that ◆ **il entendit parler quelqu'un** he heard somebody speak ◆ **j'entendais quelqu'un parler** *ou* **parler quelqu'un** I heard *ou* could hear somebody talking ◆ **faire ~ un son** to make a sound ◆ **elle fit ~ sa voix mélodieuse, sa voix mélodieuse se fit ~** her sweet voice was heard ◆ **faire ~ sa voix** *ou* **se faire ~ dans un débat** to make oneself heard in a debate ◆ **qu'est-ce que j'entends ?** what did you say?, am I hearing right? ◆ **tu vas être sage, tu entends !** *(menace)* you're to be good, do you hear (me)! ◆ **ce qu'il faut ~ tout de même !*** really – the things you hear! *ou* the things people say! ◆ **il vaut mieux ~ ça que d'être sourd !*** really, the things you hear! *; → **voler¹**
[2] *(par ouï-dire)* ~ **parler de qn/qch** to hear of *ou* about sb/sth ◆ **j'en ai vaguement entendu parler** I did vaguely hear something about *ou* of it ◆ **on n'entend plus parler de lui** you don't hear anything of him these days, you never hear of him any more ◆ **il ne veut pas en ~ parler** *(fig)* he won't hear of it ◆ **~ dire que ...** to hear it said that ... ◆ **d'après ce que j'ai entendu dire** from what I have heard, by all accounts ◆ **on entend dire que ...** it is said *ou* rumoured that ..., rumour has it that ... ◆ **on entend dire des choses étranges** there are strange rumours going about ◆ **je l'ai entendu dire que ...** I heard him say that ...
[3] *(= écouter)* to hear, to listen to ◆ **le patron a entendu les syndicats pendant une heure** the boss listened to *ou* heard the unions for an hour ◆ **j'ai entendu son discours jusqu'au bout** I listened right to the end of his speech ◆ **~ les témoins** *(Jur)* to hear the witnesses ◆ **à l'~, c'est lui qui a tout fait** to hear him talk *ou* to listen to him you'd think he had done everything ◆ **il ne veut rien ~** he doesn't want to hear *ou* know about it, he just won't listen ◆ **il raconte à qui veut l'~ que c'est lui qui l'a quittée** he tells anyone who'll listen that he's the one who left her ◆ **si ça continue, il va m'~ !** *(menace)* if he doesn't stop I'll give him a piece of my mind!; → **messe, raison**
[4] *(frm = comprendre)* to understand ◆ **oui, j'entends bien, mais ...** yes, I fully *ou* quite understand but ... ◆ **je vous entends** I see what you mean, now I understand (you) ◆ **il n'entend rien à la musique** he doesn't know the first thing *ou* he doesn't have the first idea about music ◆ **il n'entend pas la plaisanterie** † he can't take a joke, he doesn't know how to take a joke ◆ **laisser ~ à qn que ..., donner à ~ à qn que ...** *(= faire comprendre)* to give sb to under-

stand that ...; *(= donner l'impression que ...)* to let it be understood that ..., to give sb the impression that ...; → **malice, pire**

5 *(frm avec infin = vouloir)* to intend, to mean ◆ **j'entends bien y aller** I certainly intend *ou* mean to go ◆ **faites comme vous l'entendez** do as you see fit *ou* think best ◆ **j'entends être obéi** *ou* **qu'on m'obéisse** I intend *ou* mean to be obeyed, I will be obeyed ◆ **j'entends ne pas céder, je n'entends pas céder** I have no intention of giving in

6 *(= vouloir dire)* to mean ◆ **qu'entendez-vous par là ?** what do you mean by that? ◆ **entendez-vous par là que ... ?** are you trying to say that ...?, do you mean that ...?

VPR **s'entendre** 1 *(soi-même)* **je me suis entendu à la radio** I heard myself on the radio ◆ **tu ne t'entends pas !** you don't know what you're saying!

2 *(= être d'accord, s'accorder)* to agree ◆ **ils se sont entendus sur plusieurs points** they have agreed on several points ◆ **hier tu m'as dit le contraire, il faudrait s'~ !** yesterday you told me exactly the opposite, make up your mind!

3 *(= sympathiser)* to get on ◆ **ils ne s'entendent pas** they don't get along ou on *(Brit)* (together *ou* with each other) ◆ **ils s'entendent à merveille** they get along *ou* on *(Brit)* extremely well (together *ou* with each other), they get on like a house on fire *(Brit)*; → **larron**

4 *(= s'y connaître)* **s'y ~ pour** *ou* **s'~ à** *(frm)* **faire qch** to be very good at doing sth ◆ **il s'y entend !** he knows what he's doing!, he knows his onions! * *(Brit) ou* stuff! *

5 *(= se comprendre)* **quand je dis magnifique, je m'entends, disons que c'est très joli** when I say it's magnificent, what I really mean is that it's very attractive ◆ **il le fera, moyennant finances, (cela) s'entend** he will do it – for a fee, of course *ou* naturally ◆ **entendons-nous bien !** let's be quite clear about *ou* on this, let's make quite sure we understand one another ◆ **ça peut s'~ différemment suivant les contextes** that can be taken to mean different things depending on the context

6 *(= être entendu)* **le bruit s'entendait depuis la route** the noise could be heard *ou* was audible from the road ◆ **cette expression ne s'entend plus guère** *(fig)* that phrase is hardly ever used *ou* heard nowadays, you hardly ever hear that phrase nowadays ◆ **on ne s'entend plus ici** you can't hear yourself think in here

entendu, e /ɑ̃tɑ̃dy/ (ptp de **entendre**) ADJ 1 *(= convenu)* agreed ◆ **étant ~ que** it being understood *ou* agreed that, since ◆ **il est bien ~ que vous n'en dites rien** of course it's understood *ou* it must be understood that you make no mention of it ◆ **c'est (bien) ~, n'est-ce pas ?** that's (all) agreed, isn't it? ◆ **(c'est) ~ !** right!, agreed!, right-oh! * *(Brit)*

◆ **bien entendu** *(= évidemment)* of course ◆ **(comme de) bien ~, tu dormais !** as I might have known *ou* expected (you to be), you were asleep! 2 *(concessif)* all right, granted, so we all agree ◆ **c'est ~** *ou* **c'est une affaire ~e, il t'a poussé** all right, so he pushed you 3 *(= complice) [sourire, air]* knowing ◆ **d'un air ~** with a knowing look, knowingly 4 *(†† = habile)* competent

enténébrer /ɑ̃tenebʀe/ ► conjug 6 ◄ VT *(littér) [+ salle]* to make dark *ou* gloomy; *[+ vie, voyage]* to cast a shadow over

entente /ɑ̃tɑ̃t/ NF 1 *(= amitié)* harmony, understanding; *(= alliance)* understanding ◆ **politique d'~ avec un pays** policy of friendship with a country ◆ **l'Entente cordiale** the Entente Cordiale ◆ **la Triple Entente** the Triple Alliance ◆ **vivre en bonne ~** to live in harmony *ou* harmoniously ◆ **vivre en bonne ~ avec les voisins** to be on good terms with the neighbours 2 *(= accord)* agreement, understanding; *(Écon = cartel)* combine ◆ **~s illicites** illegal agreements *ou* arrangements ◆ **faire une demande d'~ préalable** *to request the Social Security to agree to help with costs before one is treated* 3 *(= connaissance)* grasp, understanding; *(= habileté)* skill; → **double**

enter /ɑ̃te/ ► conjug 1 ◄ VT *(Agr)* to graft

entérinement /ɑ̃teʀinmɑ̃/ NM ratification, confirmation

entériner /ɑ̃teʀine/ ► conjug 1 ◄ VT to ratify, to confirm

entérite /ɑ̃teʀit/ NF enteritis

enterrement /ɑ̃tɛʀmɑ̃/ NM 1 *(= action) [de mort]* burial; *[d'espoir]* end, death 2 *(= cérémonie)* funeral, burial (service); *(= convoi)* funeral procession ◆ **~ civil/religieux** non-religious/religious burial (service) *ou* funeral ◆ **faire** *ou* **avoir une tête** *ou* **mine d'~** * to look down in the mouth *, to look gloomy *ou* glum ◆ **il a eu un ~ de première classe** *(hum) [politicien, cadre]* he was shunted off into the wings

enterrer /ɑ̃teʀe/ ► conjug 1 ◄ VT 1 *(= inhumer)* to bury, to inter *(frm)* ◆ **hier il a enterré sa mère** yesterday he attended his mother's burial *ou* funeral ◆ **on l'enterre ce matin** he is being buried this morning ◆ **tu nous enterreras tous !** you'll outlive us all! ◆ **s'~ dans un trou perdu** to bury o.s. in the sticks *ou* in the back of beyond *(Brit)* 2 *(= enfouir) [+ os, trésor]* to bury 3 *(= oublier) [+ projet]* to lay aside, to forget about; *[+ scandale]* to hush up; *[+ espoir]* to forget about ◆ **enterrons cette querelle** (let's) let bygones be bygones ◆ **c'est une querelle enterrée depuis longtemps** that quarrel has long since been (dead and) buried ◆ **~ son passé** to put one's past behind one ◆ **~ sa vie de garçon** to have *ou* throw a stag party (before one's wedding)

entêtant, e /ɑ̃tɛtɑ̃, ɑ̃t/ ADJ *[vin, parfum]* heady *(épith)*, which goes to the head

en-tête (pl **en-têtes**) /ɑ̃tɛt/ NM heading; *(Ordin)* header ◆ **papier à lettres à ~** headed notepaper

entêté, e /ɑ̃tete/ (ptp de **entêter**) ADJ stubborn, pigheaded * NM,F mule, stubborn individual ◆ **quel ~ tu fais !** you're so stubborn!

entêtement /ɑ̃tɛtmɑ̃/ NM *(= obstination)* stubbornness, pigheadedness *; *(= persévérance)* doggedness

entêter /ɑ̃tete/ ► conjug 1 ◄ VT *[vin, parfum]* to go to the head of ◆ **ce parfum entête** this perfume goes to your head VPR **s'entêter** to persist *(dans qch* in sth; *à faire qch* in doing sth)

enthousiasmant, e /ɑ̃tuzjasmɑ̃, ɑ̃t/ ADJ *[spectacle, livre, idée]* exciting, exhilarating

enthousiasme /ɑ̃tuzjasm/ GRAMMAIRE ACTIVE 40.2 NM enthusiasm ◆ **avec ~** enthusiastically, with enthusiasm ◆ **avoir des ~s soudains** to have sudden fits of enthusiasm *ou* sudden crazes

enthousiasmer /ɑ̃tuzjasme/ GRAMMAIRE ACTIVE 34.3 ► conjug 1 ◄ VT to fill with enthusiasm VPR **s'enthousiasmer** to be *ou* get enthusiastic *(pour* about, over); ◆ **il s'enthousiasma tout de suite pour ...** he was immediately enthusiastic about *ou* over ..., he was immediately filled with enthusiasm for ... ◆ **c'est quelqu'un qui s'enthousiasme facilement** he's easily carried away *(pour* by)

enthousiaste /ɑ̃tuzjast/ ADJ enthusiastic *(de* about, over) NMF enthusiast

entichement /ɑ̃tiʃmɑ̃/ NM *(pour une personne)* infatuation *(pour, de* for, with); *(pour une chose)* passion, craze *(de, pour* for)

enticher (s') /ɑ̃tiʃe/ ► conjug 1 ◄ VPR *(frm, péj)* ◆ **s'~ de** *[+ personne]* to become infatuated *ou* besotted *(Brit)* with; *[+ activité, théorie]* to get completely hooked * on

entier, -ière /ɑ̃tje, jɛʀ/ ADJ 1 *(= total) [quantité, prix]* whole, full; *[surface, endroit, année]* whole, entire ◆ **boire une bouteille entière** to drink a whole *ou* full *ou* an entire bottle ◆ **payer place entière** *(Théât)* to pay the full price; *(Rail)* to pay the full fare *ou* price ◆ **une heure entière** a whole hour ◆ **des heures entières** for hours (on end *ou* together) ◆ **dans le monde ~** in the whole *ou* entire world, throughout the world ◆ **dans la France entière** throughout France, in the whole of France; → **nombre**

◆ **tout entier** *(= complètement)* entirely, completely ◆ **je m'y suis consacré tout ~** I devoted all my energies to it ◆ **le pays tout ~** the whole country

2 *(= intact) [objet, vertu]* intact; *(Vét = non châtré)* entire ◆ **aucune assiette n'était entière** there wasn't one unbroken plate ◆ **la question reste entière** the question still remains unresolved ◆ **c'est un miracle qu'il en soit sorti ~** it's a miracle he escaped unscathed *ou* in one piece

3 *(= absolu) [liberté, confiance]* absolute, complete ◆ **mon accord plein et ~** my full *ou* entire (and) wholehearted agreement ◆ **donner entière satisfaction** to give complete satisfaction

4 *(= sans demi-mesure) [personne, caractère]* uncompromising; *[opinion]* strong

5 *[lait]* whole, full cream

NM *(Math)* whole, integer; *(Ordin)* integer ◆ **deux demis font un ~** two halves make a whole ◆ **la nation dans son ~** the nation as a whole, the entire nation

◆ **en entier** totally, in its entirety ◆ **occupé en ~ par des bureaux** totally occupied by offices, occupied in its entirety by offices ◆ **boire une bouteille en ~** to drink a whole *ou* a full *ou* an entire bottle ◆ **lire/voir qch en ~** to read/see the whole of sth, to read/watch sth right through

entièrement /ɑ̃tjɛʀmɑ̃/ ADV completely ◆ **je suis ~ d'accord avec vous** I fully *ou* entirely agree with you ◆ **la ville a été ~ détruite** the town was wholly *ou* entirely destroyed ◆ **c'est ~ fait main** it's completely hand-made ◆ **ce site Internet est ~ consacré au bricolage** this website is devoted exclusively to home improvements ◆ **je m'y suis ~ consacré** I devoted all my energies to it

entièreté /ɑ̃tjɛʀte/ NF entirety

entité /ɑ̃tite/ NF entity

entoiler /ɑ̃twale/ ► conjug 1 ◄ VT *[+ estampe]* to mount on canvas; *[+ vêtement]* to stiffen (with canvas)

entôler * /ɑ̃tole/ ► conjug 1 ◄ VT to con *, to fleece * *(de* of) to do * *(Brit) (de* out of)

entomologie /ɑ̃tɔmɔlɔʒi/ NF entomology

entomologique /ɑ̃tɔmɔlɔʒik/ ADJ entomological

entomologiste /ɑ̃tɔmɔlɔʒist/ NMF entomologist

entonner /ɑ̃tɔne/ ► conjug 1 ◄ VT ◆ **~ une chanson** to break into song, to strike up a song, to start singing ◆ **~ des louanges au sujet de qn** to start singing sb's praises ◆ **~ un psaume** to strike up a psalm, to start singing a psalm

entonnoir /ɑ̃tɔnwaʀ/ NM *(Culin)* funnel; *(Géog)* swallow hole, doline; *(= trou) [d'obus]* shell-hole; *[de bombe]* crater ◆ **en ~** *[forme, conduit]* funnel-shaped

entorse /ɑ̃tɔʀs/ NF 1 *(Méd)* sprain ◆ **se faire une ~ au poignet** to sprain one's wrist 2 *[de loi]* infringement *(à* of); ◆ **faire une ~ à** *[+ vérité]* to twist; *[+ habitudes, régime]* to break

◆ **faire une ~ au règlement** to bend *ou* stretch the rules

entortillement /ɑ̃tɔʀtijmɑ̃/ **NM** (= *action*) twisting, winding, twining; (= *état*) entwinement

entortiller /ɑ̃tɔʀtije/ ▸ conjug 1 ◂ **VT** 1 [*+ ruban*] to twist, to twine, to wind; [*+ bonbons*] to wrap (up) 2 * (= *enjôler*) to get round, to wheedle, to cajole; (= *embrouiller*) to mix up, to muddle (up); (= *duper*) to hoodwink* **VPR** **s'entortiller** [*liane*] to twist, to wind, to twine ◆ **s'~ dans ses réponses** to tie o.s. in knots* with one's answers ◆ **s'~ dans les couvertures** (*volontairement*) to wrap *ou* roll o.s. up in the blankets; (*involontairement*) to get caught up *ou* tangled up *ou* entangled in the blankets

entour /ɑ̃tuʀ/ **NM** (*littér*) ◆ **les ~s de qch** the surroundings of sth ◆ **à l'~ de qch** around sth

entourage /ɑ̃tuʀaʒ/ **NM** 1 (= *famille*) family circle; (= *compagnie*) (*gén*) set, circle; [*de roi, président*] entourage ◆ **les gens de son ~/dans l'~ du président** people around him/around the president 2 (= *bordure*) [*de fenêtre*] frame, surround (*Brit*); [*de massif floral*] border, surround (*Brit*)

entouré, e /ɑ̃tuʀe/ (ptp de **entourer**) **ADJ** 1 (= *admiré*) popular ◆ **cette jeune femme est très ~e** this young woman is the centre of attraction ◆ **pendant cette épreuve il était très ~** during this difficult time many people rallied around (him) ◆ **c'est un titre très ~** (*Bourse*) everyone's rallying around that stock 2 (= *encerclé*) ~ **de** surrounded with *ou* by

entourer /ɑ̃tuʀe/ ▸ conjug 1 ◂ **VT** 1 (= *mettre autour*) ~ **de** to surround with ◆ **~ un champ d'une clôture** to put a fence round a field, to surround a field with a fence ◆ **il entoura ses épaules d'un châle** he put *ou* wrapped a shawl (a)round her shoulders ◆ **~ qn de ses bras** to put one's arms (a)round sb

2 (= *être autour*) (*gén*) to surround; [*cadre*] to frame, to surround; [*couverture, écharpe*] to be round; [*soldats*] to surround, to encircle ◆ **le monde qui nous entoure** the world around *ou* about us, the world that surrounds us

3 (= *soutenir*) [*+ personne souffrante*] to rally round ◆ **~ qn de son affection** to surround sb with love

VPR **s'entourer** ◆ **s'~ de** [*+ amis, gardes du corps, luxe*] to surround o.s. with ◆ **s'~ de mystère** to surround o.s. with *ou* shroud o.s. in mystery ◆ **s'~ de précautions** to take elaborate precautions ◆ **nous voulons nous ~ de toutes les garanties** we wish to have *ou* avail ourselves of all possible guarantees

entourloupe * /ɑ̃tuʀlup/, **entourloupette** * /ɑ̃tuʀlupɛt/ **NF** mean *ou* rotten* trick ◆ **faire une ~ à qn** to play a (rotten* *ou* mean) trick on sb

entournure /ɑ̃tuʀnyʀ/ **NF** armhole; → **gêné**

entracte /ɑ̃tʀakt/ **NM** 1 (= *pause*) (*Théât*) interval, interlude, intermission (*US*); (*Ciné*) interval, intermission; (*fig* = *interruption*) interlude, break 2 (*Théât* = *divertissement*) entr'acte, interlude

entraide /ɑ̃tʀɛd/ **NF** mutual aid ◆ **~ judiciaire internationale** international judicial cooperation ◆ **service d'~** (*Admin*) support service

entraider (s') /ɑ̃tʀede/ ▸ conjug 1 ◂ **VPR** to help one another *ou* each other

entrailles /ɑ̃tʀɑj/ **NFPL** 1 [*d'animaux*] entrails, guts 2 (*littér*) [*de personne*] entrails; (= *ventre maternel*) womb ◆ **sans ~** (*fig*) heartless, unfeeling ◆ **la faim le mordait aux ~** hunger gnawed at him *ou* at his guts ◆ **spectacle qui vous prend aux ~** *ou* **qui vous remue les ~** sight that shakes your very soul *ou* shakes you to the core 3 (*littér*) [*d'édifice, terre*] bowels, depths

entrain /ɑ̃tʀɛ̃/ **NM** [*de personne*] spirit, drive; [*de réunion*] spirit, liveliness, go ◆ **avec ~** [*répondre, travailler*] enthusiastically; [*manger*] with gusto, heartily ◆ **sans ~** [*travailler*] half-heartedly, unenthusiastically ◆ **être plein d'~, avoir de l'~** to have plenty of *ou* be full of drive *ou* go* ◆ **ça manque d'~** (*soirée*) it's not exactly lively, it's a bit dead*

entraînant, e /ɑ̃tʀɛnɑ̃, ɑ̃t/ **ADJ** [*paroles, musique*] stirring, rousing; [*rythme*] brisk, lively

entraînement /ɑ̃tʀɛnmɑ̃/ **NM** 1 (= *action*) [*de roue, bielle*] driving; [*d'athlète*] training, coaching; [*de cheval*] training ◆ **~ à chaîne** chain drive 2 (= *impulsion, force*) [*de passions*] (driving) force, impetus; [*d'habitude*] force ◆ **des ~s dangereux** dangerous impulses 3 (*Sport* = *préparation, exercice*) training (*NonC*) ◆ **deux heures d'~ chaque matin** two hours of training every morning ◆ **course/terrain d'~** training race/ground ◆ **manquer d'~** to be out of training ◆ **il a de l'~** he's highly trained ◆ **il est à l'~** he's in a training session, he's training ◆ **il est à l'~ de rugby** he's at rugby practice ◆ **il s'est blessé à l'~** he hurt himself at *ou* while training *ou* during a training session ◆ **j'ai de l'~ !** (*hum*) I've had lots of practice!

entraîner /ɑ̃tʀene/ ▸ conjug 1 ◂ **VT** 1 (*lit*) (= *charrier*) [*+ épave, objets arrachés*] to carry *ou* drag along; (*Tech* = *mouvoir*) [*+ machine*] to drive; (= *tirer*) [*+ wagons*] to pull ◆ **le courant les entraîna vers les rapides** the current carried *ou* dragged *ou* swept them along towards the rapids ◆ **le poids de ses habits l'entraîna vers le fond** the weight of his clothes dragged him (down) towards the bottom ◆ **il entraîna son camarade dans sa chute** he pulled *ou* dragged his friend down in his fall

2 (= *emmener*) [*+ personne*] to take (off) (*vers* towards); ◆ **il m'entraîna vers la sortie/dans un coin** he dragged *ou* took me (off) towards the exit/into a corner ◆ **il les entraîna à sa suite vers ...** he took them (along *ou* off) with him towards ...

3 (= *influencer*) to lead ◆ **~ qn à voler qch** to get sb to steal sth ◆ **~ ses camarades à boire/dans la débauche** to lead one's friends into drinking/bad ways ◆ **se laisser ~ par ses camarades** to let o.s. be led by one's friends ◆ **cela l'a entraîné à de grosses dépenses** that meant great expense for him, that led him into great expense

4 (= *causer*) to bring about, to lead to; (= *impliquer*) to entail, to mean ◆ **ceci a entraîné des compressions budgétaires** this has brought about *ou* led to budgetary restraints ◆ **si je vous comprends bien, ceci entraîne la perte de nos avantages** if I understand you, this will mean *ou* will entail the loss of our advantages

5 (= *emporter*) [*rythme*] to carry along; [*passion, enthousiasme*] to carry away ◆ **son enthousiasme l'a entraîné trop loin** his enthusiasm carried him too far ◆ **se laisser ~ (par ses passions)** to (let o.s.) get *ou* be carried away (by one's passions)

6 (= *préparer*) [*+ athlète*] to train, to coach; [*+ cheval*] to train (*à* for)

VPR **s'entraîner** to practise; (*Sport*) to train ◆ **où est-il ? – il s'entraîne au stade** where is he? – he's (doing some) training at the stadium ◆ **s'~ à la course/pour le championnat** to get in training *ou* to train for running/for the championship ◆ **s'~ à faire qch** to practise doing sth ◆ **s'~ à faire un certain mouvement** to practise a certain movement, to work on a certain movement ◆ **entraînez-vous à respirer lentement** practise breathing slowly

entraîneur /ɑ̃tʀɛnœʀ/ **NM** [*de cheval*] trainer; [*d'équipe, coureur, boxeur*] coach, trainer ◆ **un ~ d'hommes** (*littér*) a leader of men

entraîneuse /ɑ̃tʀɛnøz/ **NF** [*de bar*] hostess; (*Sport*) coach, trainer

entrant, e /ɑ̃tʀɑ̃, ɑ̃t/ **NM,F** (*gén pl*) ◆ **les ~s** the people coming (*ou* going) in

entrapercevoir /ɑ̃tʀapɛʀsəvwaʀ/ ▸ conjug 28 ◂ **VT** to catch a (brief) glimpse of

entrave /ɑ̃tʀav/ **NF** 1 (= *obstacle*) hindrance (*à* to); ◆ **~ à la circulation** hindrance to traffic ◆ **~ à la liberté d'expression** constraint upon *ou* obstacle to freedom of expression ◆ **sans ~** [*liberté, bonheur*] total ◆ **vivre sans ~s** to lead an unfettered existence 2 [*d'animal*] hobble, fetter, shackle ◆ **~s** [*de prisonnier*] chains, fetters (*littér*) ◆ **se débarrasser des ~s de la rime** (*littér*) to free o.s. from the shackles *ou* fetters of rhyme (*littér*)

entravé, e /ɑ̃tʀave/ (ptp de **entraver**) **ADJ** [*voyelle*] checked ◆ **jupe ~e** pencil skirt

entraver /ɑ̃tʀave/ ▸ conjug 1 ◂ **VT** 1 (= *gêner*) [*+ circulation*] to hold up; [*+ mouvements*] to hamper, to hinder; [*+ action, plans, processus*] to hinder, to hamper, to impede ◆ **~ la carrière de qn** to hinder sb in his career 2 [*+ animal*] to hobble, to shackle, to fetter; [*+ prisonnier*] to chain (up), to fetter (*littér*) 3 (*‡* = *comprendre*) to get‡ ◆ **je n'y entrave que couic** *ou* **que dalle** I just don't get it‡, I don't twig (it) at all‡ (*Brit*)

entre /ɑ̃tʀ/ **PRÉP** 1 (= *à mi-chemin de, dans l'intervalle de*) [*+ objets, dates, opinions*] between ◆ **~ le vert et le jaune** between green and yellow ◆ **~ la vie et la mort** between life and death ◆ **~ ciel et terre** between heaven and earth ◆ **vous l'aimez saignant, à point ou ~ les deux ?** do you like it rare, medium or between the two? *ou* or in-between? ◆ **la vérité est ~ les deux** the truth is somewhere between the two *ou* somewhere in between; → **lire**[1]

2 (= *entouré par*) [*+ murs*] within, between; [*+ montagnes*] among, between ◆ **enfermé ~ quatre murs** (*fig*) shut in ◆ **encaissé ~ les hautes parois** enclosed between the high walls

3 (= *au milieu de, parmi*) [*+ objets épars, personnes*] among, amongst ◆ **il aperçut un objet brillant ~ les pierres** he saw an object shining among(st) the stones ◆ **choisir ~ plusieurs choses** to choose from among *ou* between several things ◆ **il hésita ~ plusieurs routes** he hesitated between several roads ◆ **je le compte ~ mes amis** (*frm*) I number him among my friends ◆ **l'un d'~ eux** one of them ◆ **plusieurs d'~ nous** several of us, several of our number (*frm*) ◆ **intelligent ~ tous** supremely intelligent ◆ **problème difficile ~ tous** inordinately *ou* particularly difficult problem ◆ **cette heure ~ toutes** this (hour) of all hours ◆ **je le reconnaîtrais ~ tous** I would know *ou* recognize him anywhere ◆ **c'est le meilleur ~ tous mes amis** he's the best friend I have ◆ **il l'a partagé ~ tous ses amis** he shared it out among all his friends

◆ **entre autres** ◆ **lui, ~ autres, n'est pas d'accord** he, for one *ou* among others, doesn't agree ◆ **~ autres (choses)** among other things ◆ **~ autres (personnes)** among others ◆ **il est, ~ autres, musicien et poète** he is, among other things, a musician and a poet ◆ **il m'a dit ~ autres que le projet avait été abandonné** one of the things he told me was that the project had been abandoned

4 (= *dans*) in, into ◆ **j'ai eu ce livre ~ les mains** I had that book in my (very) hands ◆ **prendre ~ ses bras** to take in one's arms ◆ **ma vie est ~ vos mains** my life is *ou* lies in your hands ◆ **tomber ~ les mains de l'ennemi/d'escrocs** to fall into the hands of the enemy/of crooks

5 (= *à travers*) through, between ◆ **je l'ai aperçu ~ les branches** I saw it through *ou* between the branches

6 (*indiquant une relation, deux choses*) between; (*plus de deux*) among ◆ **rapports ~ deux personnes/choses** relationship between two people/things ◆ **nous sommes ~ nous** *ou* **~ amis**

we're all friends here, we're among friends ◆ ~ **nous** between you and me, between ourselves ◆ ~ **nous c'est à la vie, à la mort** we are *ou* shall be friends for life ◆ ~ **eux 4** among the 4 of them ◆ **qu'y a-t-il exactement ~ eux ?** what exactly is there between them? ◆ **il n'y a rien de commun ~ eux** they have nothing in common *ou* no common ground ◆ **ils se marient ~ eux** they intermarry ◆ **ils préfèrent rester ~ eux** they prefer to keep (themselves) to themselves *ou* to be on their own ◆ **ils se sont entendus ~ eux** they reached a mutual agreement ◆ **entendez-vous ~ vous** sort it out among yourselves ◆ **ils se sont disputés ~ eux** they have quarrelled (with each other *ou* with one another) ◆ **laissons-les se battre ~ eux** let's leave them to fight it out (between *ou* among themselves) ◆ **on ne va pas se battre ~ nous** we're not going to fight (among ourselves)

entrebâillement /ɑ̃tʀəbɑjmɑ̃/ **NM** ◆ **dans/par l'~ de la porte** in/through the half-open door

entrebâiller /ɑ̃tʀəbɑje/ ▸ conjug 1 ◂ **VT** to half-open ◆ **la porte est entrebâillée** the door is ajar *ou* half-open

entrebâilleur /ɑ̃tʀəbɑjœʀ/ **NM** door chain

entrechat /ɑ̃tʀəʃa/ **NM** *(Danse)* entrechat; *(hum = saut)* leap, spring ◆ **faire des ~s** *(Danse)* to do entrechats; *(hum)* to leap about

entrechoquement /ɑ̃tʀəʃɔkmɑ̃/ **NM** *(gén)* knocking, banging; *[de verres]* clinking; *[de dents]* chattering; *[d'épées]* clashing

entrechoquer /ɑ̃tʀəʃɔke/ ▸ conjug 1 ◂ **VT** *(gén)* to knock *ou* bang together; *[+ verres]* to clink *ou* chink (together) **VPR** **s'entrechoquer** *(gén)* to knock *ou* bang together; *[verres]* to clink *ou* chink (together); *[dents]* to chatter; *[épées]* to clash *ou* clang together; *[idées, mots]* to jostle together

entrecôte /ɑ̃tʀəkot/ **NF** entrecôte steak, rib steak

entrecouper /ɑ̃tʀəkupe/ ▸ conjug 1 ◂ **VT** ◆ ~ **de** *[+ citations]* to intersperse *ou* pepper with; *[+ rires, sarcasmes]* to interrupt with; *[+ haltes]* to interrupt with, to break with ◆ **voix entrecoupée de sanglots** voice broken with sobs ◆ **parler d'une voix entrecoupée** to speak in a broken voice, to have a catch in one's voice as one speaks **VPR** **s'entrecouper** *[lignes]* to intersect, to cut across each other

entrecroisement /ɑ̃tʀəkʀwazmɑ̃/ **NM** *[de fils, branches]* intertwining; *[de lignes, routes]* intersecting

entrecroiser **VT**, **s'entrecroiser** **VPR** /ɑ̃tʀəkʀwaze/ ▸ conjug 1 ◂ *[fils, branches]* to intertwine; *[lignes, routes]* to intersect

entre-déchirer (s') /ɑ̃tʀədeʃiʀe/ ▸ conjug 1 ◂ **VPR** *(littér)* to tear one another *ou* each other to pieces

entre-deux /ɑ̃tʀədø/ **NM INV** 1 *(= intervalle)* intervening period, period in between 2 *(Sport)* jump ball 3 *(Couture)* ~ **de dentelle** lace insert

entre-deux-guerres /ɑ̃tʀədøgɛʀ/ **NM INV** ◆ **l'~** the interwar years *ou* period ◆ **pendant l'~** between the wars, in *ou* during the interwar years *ou* period

entre-dévorer (s') /ɑ̃tʀədevɔʀe/ ▸ conjug 1 ◂ **VPR** *(littér)* to tear one another *ou* each other to pieces

entrée /ɑ̃tʀe/ **NF** 1 *(= arrivée) [de personne] (gén)* entry, entrance; *(dans pays, ville)* entry; *[de véhicule, bateau, armée occupante]* entry ◆ **à son ~, tous se sont tus** as he came *ou* walked in *ou* entered, everybody fell silent ◆ **à son ~ dans le salon** as he came *ou* walked into *ou* entered the lounge ◆ **elle a fait une ~ remarquée** she made quite an entrance, she made a dramatic entrance ◆ **faire son ~ dans le salon** to enter the lounge ◆ **l'~ en gare du train** the train's entry into the station ◆ **l'~ au port du navire** the ship's entry into the port ◆ **~ illégale dans un pays** illegal entry into a country

2 *(Théât)* **faire son ~** to make one's entry *ou* entrance ◆ **rater son ~** *(sur scène)* to miss one's entrance; *(première réplique)* to miss one's cue

3 *(= accès)* entry, admission *(de, dans* to); ◆ **"entrée"** *(sur pancarte)* "way in" ◆ **"entrée libre"** *(dans boutique)* "come in and look round"; *(dans musée)* "admission free" ◆ **"entrée interdite"** "no admittance", "no entry" ◆ **"entrée interdite à tout véhicule"** "vehicles prohibited" ◆ **l'~ est gratuite/payante** there is no admission charge/there is an admission charge ◆ **on lui a refusé l'~ de l'amphithéâtre** he was refused admission *ou* entrance *ou* entry to the lecture hall

4 *[de marchandises]* entry; *[de capital]* inflow ◆ **droits d'~** import duties

5 *(dans un domaine, un milieu)* entry; *(dans un club)* entry, admission ◆ **l'~ de la Finlande dans l'Union européenne** Finland's entry into *ou* admission to the European Union ◆ **se voir refuser son ~ dans un club/une école** to be refused admission *ou* entry to a club/school, to be rejected by a club/school ◆ **l'~ des jeunes dans la vie active est souvent difficile** young people often find it difficult to enter the job market ◆ **ce parti a fait une ~ fracassante sur la scène politique** this party burst onto the political scene ◆ **ce produit/l'entreprise a fait une ~ discrète sur le marché** the product/company has crept onto the market ◆ **il a fait une ~ discrète au gouvernement** he entered the government unobtrusively ◆ **faire son ~ dans le monde** † *[débutante]* to come out †, to make one's début in society; → **concours, examen**

6 *(= billet)* ticket ◆ **j'ai pris 2 ~s** I got 2 tickets ◆ **billet d'~** entrance ticket ◆ **les ~s couvriront tous les frais** the receipts *ou* takings will cover all expenses ◆ **ils ont fait 10 000 ~s** they sold 10,000 tickets ◆ **le film a fait 200 000 ~s** 200,000 people went to see the film

7 *(= porte, portail)* entry, entrance; *[de tunnel, port, grotte]* entry, entrance, mouth ◆ **~ principale** main entrance

8 *(= vestibule)* entrance (hall)

9 *(Tech) [de fluide, air]* entry

10 *(= début)* outset; *(Mus = motif)* entry ◆ **à l'~ de l'hiver/de la belle saison** as winter/the warm weather set (*ou* sets *etc*) in, at the onset *ou* beginning of winter/the warm weather ◆ **produit d'~ de gamme** entry-level product

◆ **d'entrée de jeu** from the outset

11 *(Culin) (= mets)* first course, starter *(Brit)*; *(sur menu)* starter *(Brit)*, entrée *(Brit)*, appetizer *(US)*

12 *(Comm, Stat)* entry; *(Lexicographie = mot)* headword *(Brit)*, entry word *(US)* ◆ **tableau à double ~** double-entry table

13 *(Ordin)* input ◆ **~-sortie** input-output

NFPL **entrées** ◆ **avoir ses ~s auprès de qn** to have free *ou* easy access to sb ◆ **il a ses ~s au gouvernement** he has privileged access to government ministers

COMP **entrée d'air** *(Tech)* air inlet

entrée des artistes stage door

entrée de service *[d'hôtel]* service *ou* tradesmen's entrance; *[de villa]* tradesmen's entrance

entre-égorger (s') /ɑ̃tʀegɔʀʒe/ ▸ conjug 3 ◂ **VPR** to cut each other's *ou* one another's throats

entrefaites /ɑ̃tʀəfɛt/ **sur ces entrefaites** **LOC ADV** *(= à ce moment-là)* at that moment, at this juncture

entrefer /ɑ̃tʀəfɛʀ/ **NM** air-gap

entrefilet /ɑ̃tʀəfilɛ/ **NM** *(= petit article)* paragraph

entregent /ɑ̃tʀəʒɑ̃/ **NM** savoir-faire ◆ **avoir de l'~** to have a good manner with people

entrejambe /ɑ̃tʀəʒɑ̃b/ **NM** *(Couture, euph)* crotch

entrelacement /ɑ̃tʀəlasmɑ̃/ **NM** *(= action, état)* intertwining, interlacing ◆ **un ~ de branches** a network *ou* crisscross of branches

entrelacer **VT**, **s'entrelacer** **VPR** /ɑ̃tʀəlase/ ▸ conjug 3 ◂ to intertwine, to interlace ◆ **lettres entrelacées** intertwined *ou* interlaced letters ◆ **intrigues entrelacées** intertwined *ou* interwoven plots ◆ **voluptueusement entrelacés** locked in a sensual embrace ◆ **écran à balayage entrelacé/non entrelacé** *(Ordin)* screen with interleaved *ou* interlaced scanning/non-interleaved *ou* non-interlaced scanning

entrelacs /ɑ̃tʀəla/ **NM** *(Archit)* interlacing *(NonC)*; *(Peinture)* interlace *(NonC)*

entrelardé, e /ɑ̃tʀəlaʀde/ (ptp de **entrelarder**) **ADJ** *(= gras) [viande]* streaked with fat

entrelarder /ɑ̃tʀəlaʀde/ ▸ conjug 1 ◂ **VT** *(Culin)* to lard ◆ ~ **de citations** to (inter)lard *ou* intersperse with quotations

entremêler /ɑ̃tʀəmele/ ▸ conjug 1 ◂ **VT** 1 *[+ choses]* to (inter)mingle, to intermix ◆ ~ **des scènes tragiques et des scènes comiques** to (inter)mingle *ou* intermix tragic and comic scenes 2 *(= truffer de)* ~ **un récit de** to intersperse *ou* pepper a tale with **VPR** **s'entremêler** *[branches, cheveux]* to become entangled *(à* with); *[idées]* to become intermingled

entremets /ɑ̃tʀəmɛ/ **NM** dessert *(made with cream)*

entremetteur /ɑ̃tʀəmɛtœʀ/ **NM** 1 *(péj) (gén)* go-between; *(= proxénète)* procurer, go-between 2 *(= intermédiaire)* mediator, go-between

entremetteuse /ɑ̃tʀəmɛtøz/ **NF** *(péj) (gén)* go-between; *(= proxénète)* procuress, go-between

entremettre (s') /ɑ̃tʀəmɛtʀ/ ▸ conjug 56 ◂ **VPR** 1 *(dans une querelle)* to act as mediator, to mediate, to intervene *(dans* in); *(péj)* to interfere *(dans* in) 2 *(= intercéder)* to intercede *(auprès de* with)

entremise /ɑ̃tʀəmiz/ **NF** intervention ◆ **offrir son ~** to offer to act as mediator *ou* to mediate ◆ **grâce à son ~** thanks to his intervention ◆ **apprendre qch par l'~ de qn** to hear about sth through sb

entrepont /ɑ̃tʀəpɔ̃/ **NM** *(Naut)* steerage ◆ **dans l'~** in steerage

entreposage /ɑ̃tʀəpozaʒ/ **NM** storing, storage

entreposer /ɑ̃tʀəpoze/ ▸ conjug 1 ◂ **VT** *(gén)* to store, to put into storage; *(en douane)* to put in a bonded warehouse

entrepôt /ɑ̃tʀəpo/ **NM** *(gén)* warehouse; *(Douane)* bonded warehouse; *(= ville, port)* entrepôt

entreprenant, e /ɑ̃tʀəpʀənɑ̃, ɑt/ **ADJ** *(gén)* enterprising; *(sexuellement)* forward

entreprendre /ɑ̃tʀəpʀɑ̃dʀ/ ▸ conjug 58 ◂ **VT** 1 *(= commencer)* to begin *ou* start (upon); *[+ travail, démarche]* to set about; *[+ voyage]* to set out (up)on; *[+ procès]* to start up 2 *(= se lancer dans) [+ voyage, travail, recherches]* to undertake, to embark upon, to launch upon ◆ ~ **de faire qch** to undertake to do sth ◆ **la peur d'~** the fear of undertaking things 3 *[+ personne]* († *= courtiser)* to woo †, to court †; *(pour raconter une histoire)* to buttonhole, to collar*; *(pour poser des questions)* to tackle ◆ **il m'entreprit sur le sujet de …** he tackled me on the question of …

entrepreneur, -euse /ɑ̃tʀəpʀənœʀ, øz/ **NM,F** 1 *(= patron)* businessman; *(en menuiserie etc)* contractor ◆ ~ **(en *ou* de bâtiment)** building contractor ◆ ~ **de travaux publics** civil engineering contractor ◆ ~ **de transports** haulage contractor *(Brit)*, trucking firm *(US)* ◆ **~ de pompes funèbres** undertaker, funeral director *(Brit)*, mortician *(US)* 2 *(= brasseur d'affaires)* entrepreneur

entrepreneurial, e (mpl -iaux) /ɑ̃tʀəpʀənøʀjal, jo/ **ADJ** entrepreneurial

entreprise /ɑ̃tʀəpʀiz/ **GRAMMAIRE ACTIVE 46.1** **NF**

1 *(= firme)* firm, company ◆ **la grande ~ se porte mieux en France** big companies *ou* firms are doing better in France ◆ **~ agricole/familiale** farming/family business ◆ **~ de construction** building firm ◆ **~ de camionnage** *ou* **de transport** haulage firm *(Brit)*, trucker *(US)* ◆ **~ de déménagement** removal *(Brit)* *ou* moving *(US)* firm ◆ **~ de pompes funèbres** undertaker's *(Brit)*, funeral director's *(Brit)*, funeral parlor *(US)* ◆ **~ publique** state-owned company ◆ **~ de service public** public utility ◆ **~ de travaux publics** civil engineering firm ◆ **dirigeant d'~** company director ◆ **accords d'~** company agreements ◆ **financement des ~s** corporate financing; → **chef[1], culture**

2 *(= secteur d'activité)* **l'~** business ◆ **le monde de l'~** the business world

3 *(= dessein)* undertaking, venture, enterprise ◆ **se livrer à une ~ de démoralisation** to set out to demoralize sb; → **esprit, libre**

4 *(hum : envers une femme)* **~s** advances

entrer /ɑ̃tʀe/

▸ conjug 1 ◂

1 VERBE INTRANSITIF 2 VERBE TRANSITIF

1 - VERBE INTRANSITIF

avec auxilaire être

1 gén *(vu du dehors)* to go in, to enter; *(vu du dedans)* to come in, to enter; *(à pied)* to walk in; *(en voiture)* to drive in; *[véhicule]* to drive in, to go *ou* come in, to enter ◆ **~ dans** *[+ pièce, jardin]* to go *ou* come into, to enter; *[+ voiture]* to get in(to); *[+ région, pays] [voyageurs]* to go *ou* come into, to enter; *[armée]* to enter ◆ **entrez !** come in! ◆ **entre donc !** come on in! ◆ **qu'il entre !** tell him to come in, show him in ◆ **entrons voir** let's go in and see ◆ **je ne fais qu'~ et sortir** I can't stop ◆ **les gens entraient et sortaient** people were going *ou* coming in and out ◆ **c'est à gauche en entrant** it's on the left as you go in ◆ **il entra discrètement** he came in *ou* entered discreetly, he slipped in ◆ **~ chez qn** to come *(ou* go) into sb's house ◆ **je suis entré chez eux en passant** I called in *ou* dropped in at their house ◆ **je suis entré chez le fleuriste** I went to *ou* I called in at the florist's ◆ **~ en courant** to run in, to come running in ◆ **~ en boitant** to limp in, to come limping in, to come in limping ◆ **ils sont entrés par la porte de la cave/par la fenêtre** they got in *ou* entered by the cellar door/the window ◆ **~ sans payer** to get in without paying ◆ **entrez sans frapper** come *ou* go *ou* walk straight in (without knocking); → **gare[1], scène,** *etc*

◆ **laisser entrer** *[+ visiteur, intrus]* to let in; *[+ lumière, air]* to let in, to allow in; *(involontairement) [+ eau, air, poussière]* to let in ◆ **ne laisse ~ personne** don't let anybody in ◆ **laisser ~ qn dans** *[+ pièce]* to let sb into; *[+ pays]* to let sb into *ou* enter, to allow sb into *ou* to enter ◆ **on l'a laissé ~ au parti/club/dans l'armée** they've let him into *ou* let him join the party/club/army

◆ **faire entrer** *(= introduire) [+ invité, visiteur, client]* to show in; *[+ pièce, tenon, objet à emballer]* to fit in; *(en fraude) [+ marchandises, immigrants]* to smuggle in, to take *ou* bring in; *[+ accusé, témoin]* to bring in, to call ◆ **faire ~ la voiture dans le garage** to get the car into the garage ◆ **il me fit ~ dans la cellule** he showed me into the cell ◆ **faire ~ une clé dans la serrure** to insert *ou* fit a key in the lock ◆ **il m'a fait ~ dans leur club/au jury** *(m'a persuadé)* he had me join *ou* got me to join their club/the panel; *(a fait jouer son influence)* he got me into their club/onto the panel, he helped me join their club/the panel; *(m'a contraint)* he made me join their club/the panel ◆ **on l'a fait ~ comme serveur/livreur** they got him taken on as a waiter/delivery boy ◆ **faire ~ qch de force dans un emballage** to force *ou* stuff sth into a package ◆ **son roman nous fait ~ dans un univers fantastique** his novel takes us into a fantasy world

2 Comm *[marchandises, devises]* to enter ◆ **tout ce qui entre (dans le pays) est soumis à une taxe** everything entering (the country) is subject to duty ◆ **~ sur un marché** *[entreprise]* to enter a market ◆ **~ dans un fichier** *(Ordin)* *(légalement)* to enter a file, to get into a file; *(illégalement)* to hack into a file ◆ **appuyez sur (la touche) "entrer"** *(sur ordinateur)* press "enter" *ou* "return"

3 = s'enfoncer **la boule est entrée dans le trou** the ball went into the hole ◆ **le tenon entre dans la mortaise** the tenon fits into the mortice ◆ **la balle est entrée dans le poumon gauche/le montant de la porte** the bullet went into *ou* lodged itself in the left lung/the doorframe ◆ **son coude m'entrait dans les côtes** his elbow was digging into my ribs ◆ **l'eau entre (à l'intérieur) par le toit** the water gets *ou* comes in through the roof ◆ **l'air/la lumière entre dans la pièce** air/light comes into *ou* enters the room ◆ **pour que l'air/la lumière puisse ~** to allow air/light to enter *ou* get in ◆ **le vent entre de partout** the wind blows in everywhere ◆ **~ dans l'eau** *[baigneur]* to get into the water; *(en marchant)* to wade into the water; *[embarcation]* to enter the water ◆ **~ dans le bain** to get into the bath ◆ **~ dans le brouillard** *[randonneurs, avion]* to enter *ou* hit* fog ◆ **la rage/jalousie est entrée dans son cœur** his heart filled with rage/jealousy ◆ **l'argent entre dans les caisses** money is coming in ◆ **à force d'explications ça finira par ~*** explain it for long enough and it'll sink in ◆ **alors ces maths, ça entre ?*** are you getting the hang of maths then?*; → **beurre**

4 = tenir **ça n'entre pas dans la boîte** it won't go *ou* fit into the box ◆ **ça n'entre pas** it won't go *ou* fit in ◆ **nous n'entrerons jamais tous dans ta voiture** we're never all get *ou* fit into your car ◆ **il faut que je perde 3 kg pour ~ dans cette robe** I'll have to lose 3 kilos if I want to get *ou* fit into this dress

5 = devenir membre de **~ dans** *[+ club, parti, entreprise]* to join; *[+ groupe]* to go *ou* come into; *[+ métier]* to go into ◆ **~ dans l'Union européenne** to join the European Union ◆ **~ dans la magistrature** to become a magistrate, to enter the magistracy ◆ **~ dans l'armée** to join the army ◆ **~ dans les affaires** to go into business ◆ **~ à l'hôpital/en maison de retraite** to go into hospital/a retirement home ◆ **~ en religion** to become a monk *(ou* a nun) ◆ **elle entre en dernière année** *(Scol)* she's just going into her final year ◆ **~ à l'université/au lycée** to go to university *ou* college/secondary school ◆ **~ au service de qn** to enter sb's service ◆ **~ dans l'histoire** to go down in history ◆ **il veut ~ dans le livre Guinness des records** he wants to get into the Guinness Book of Records; → **jeu, légende, scène, usage**

6 = heurter **~ dans** *[+ arbre, poteau]* to go *ou* crash into

7 = être une composante de **~ dans** *[+ catégorie]* to fall into, to come into; *[+ mélange]* to go into ◆ **les substances qui entrent dans ce mélange** the substances which go into *ou* make up this mixture ◆ **tous ces frais entrent dans le prix de revient** all these costs (go to) make up the cost price ◆ **ces chiffres n'entrent pas dans nos statistiques** these figures are not included in our statistics ◆ **il y entre un peu de jalousie** a bit of jealousy comes into it ◆ **ça n'entre pas du tout dans son mode de réflexion** that's not something he thinks about ◆ **ça n'entre pas dans mes intentions** I don't have any intention of doing so; → **ligne[1]**

8 = commencer **~ dans** *[+ phase, période]* to enter (into) ◆ **~ dans une profonde rêverie/une colère noire** to go (off) into a deep daydream/a towering rage ◆ **~ dans la vie active, ~ dans le monde du travail** to begin one's working life ◆ **~ dans la cinquantaine** to turn fifty; → **danse, contact, fonction, guerre, relation, vigueur**

9 = aborder **~ dans** *[+ sujet, discussion]* to enter into ◆ **sans ~ dans les détails/ces considérations** without going into details/these considerations ◆ **il est entré dans des considérations futiles** he raised some trivial points ◆ **je n'arrive pas à ~ dans ce roman** I can't get into this novel ◆ **en quelques phrases, on entre dans la psychologie du héros** in just a few sentences you get right into the main character's mind; → **vif**

2 - VERBE TRANSITIF

avec auxiliaire avoir

1 Ordin *[+ données]* to key in ◆ **entrez votre code secret** key in *ou* enter your PIN (number)

2 + marchandises *(par la douane)* to take *ou* bring in, to import; *(en contrebande)* to take *ou* bring in, to smuggle in

3 = faire pénétrer **les bras dans les manches** to put one's arms into the sleeves

4 = faire s'ajuster *[+ pièce]* to make fit *(dans qch* in sth); ◆ **comment allez-vous ~ cette armoire dans la chambre ?** how are you going to get that wardrobe into the bedroom?

entresol /ɑ̃tʀəsɔl/ **NM** entresol, mezzanine *(between ground floor and first floor)*

entre-temps /ɑ̃tʀətɑ̃/ **ADV** meanwhile, (in the) meantime **NM** ◆ **dans l'~** meanwhile, (in the) meantime

entretenir /ɑ̃tʀət(ə)niʀ/ ▸ conjug 22 ◂ **VT** 1 *(= conserver en bon état) [+ propriété, bâtiment]* to maintain, to see to the upkeep of, to look after; *[+ vêtement]* to look after; *[+ route, machine]* to maintain ◆ **~ un jardin** to look after a garden ◆ **maison difficile à ~** house which is difficult to clean

2 *(= faire vivre) [+ famille]* to support, to keep, to maintain; *[+ maîtresse]* to keep, to support; *[+ armée]* to keep, to maintain; *[+ troupe de théâtre]* to support ◆ **se faire ~ par qn** to be kept *ou* supported by sb

3 *(= faire durer) [+ souvenir]* to keep alive; *[+ amitié]* to keep alive, to keep going; *[+ haine]* to fuel ◆ **j'entretiens de grands espoirs** I have high hopes ◆ **~ l'inquiétude de qn** to keep sb feeling uneasy, to keep sb in a state of anxiety ◆ **~ des rapports suivis avec qn** to be in constant contact with sb ◆ **~ une correspondance suivie avec qn** to keep up a regular correspondence with sb, to correspond regularly with sb ◆ **~ l'illusion que ...** to maintain the illusion that ... ◆ **l'air marin entretient une perpétuelle humidité** the sea air maintains a constant level of humidity ◆ **~ le feu** to keep the fire going *ou* burning ◆ **il m'a entretenu dans l'erreur** he didn't disabuse me (of it) ◆ **j'entretiens des craintes à son sujet** I am somewhat anxious about him ◆ **~ sa forme** to keep o.s. in (good) shape, to keep (o.s.) fit

4 *(frm = converser)* **~ qn** to converse with *ou* speak to sb ◆ **il m'a entretenu pendant une heure** we conversed for an hour, he conversed with me for an hour ◆ **il a entretenu l'auditoire de ses voyages** he addressed the audience *ou* spoke to the audience about his travels

VPR **s'entretenir** 1 *(= converser)* **s'~ avec qn** to converse with *ou* speak to sb *(de* about); ◆ **ils s'entretenaient à voix basse** they were conversing in hushed tones

2 *(= pourvoir à ses besoins)* to support o.s., to be self-supporting ◆ **il s'entretient tout seul maintenant** he is completely self-supporting now, he supports himself entirely on his own now

3 *(= prendre soin de soi)* **s'~ (en bonne forme)** to keep o.s. in (good) shape, to keep (o.s.) fit

> ⚠ **entretenir** se traduit rarement par **to entertain**, qui a le sens de 'amuser' ou 'recevoir'.

entretenu, e /ɑ̃tʀət(ə)ny/ (ptp de **entretenir**) ADJ *[personne]* kept *(épith)* ◆ **jardin bien/mal ~** well-/badly-kept garden, well-/badly-tended garden ◆ **maison bien ~e** *(propre et rangée)* well-kept house; *(en bon état)* house in a good state of repair, well-maintained house ◆ **maison mal ~e** *(sale et mal rangée)* badly-kept house; *(en mauvais état)* house in a bad state of repair, badly-maintained house

entretien /ɑ̃tʀətjɛ̃/ GRAMMAIRE ACTIVE 46.3, 46.5 NM

1 *(= conservation) [de jardin, maison]* upkeep; *[de route]* maintenance, upkeep; *[de machine]* maintenance ◆ **cher à l'~** expensive to maintain ◆ **d'un ~ facile** *[vêtement]* easy to look after; *[surface]* easy to clean; *[voiture, appareil]* easy to maintain ◆ **visite d'~** service ◆ **agent d'~** cleaning operative ◆ **l'~, le service d'~** *(maintenance)* the maintenance services; *(nettoiement)* the cleaning service; → **produit**

2 *(= aide à la subsistance) [de famille, étudiant]* keep, support; *[d'armée, corps de ballet]* maintenance, keep ◆ **pourvoir à l'~ de** *[+ famille]* to keep, to support, to maintain; *[+ armée]* to keep, to maintain

3 *(= conversation)* conversation; *(= entrevue)* interview; *(= discussion)* discussion ◆ **~(s)** *(Pol)* talks, discussions ◆ **~ télévisé** televised interview ◆ **~ téléphonique** telephone conversation ◆ **~ d'embauche** job interview ◆ **passer un ~** to have an interview ◆ **nous aurons un ~ à Francfort avec nos collègues** we shall be having discussions in Frankfurt with our colleagues ◆ **il est en ~** *(gén)* he's seeing someone, he's with someone; *(avec un candidat)* he's interviewing ◆ **~ de sortie** exit interview

entretoise /ɑ̃tʀətwaz/ NF *[de charpente]* diagonal *ou* angle brace, cross strut *ou* tie; *[de machine]* cross arm

entre(-)tuer (s') /ɑ̃tʀətɥe/ ► conjug 1 ◄ VPR to kill one another *ou* each other

entrevoir /ɑ̃tʀəvwaʀ/ ► conjug 30 ◄ VT 1 *(= voir indistinctement)* to make out; *(= pressentir) [+ objections, solutions, complications]* to foresee, to anticipate; *[+ amélioration]* to glimpse ◆ **je commence à ~ la vérité** I'm beginning to see the truth, I'm beginning to have an inkling of the truth ◆ **~ la lumière au bout du tunnel** *(lit, fig)* to see (the) light at the end of the tunnel 2 *(= apercevoir brièvement) (gén)* to catch a glimpse of, to catch sight of; *[+ visiteur]* to see briefly ◆ **vous n'avez fait qu'~ les difficultés** you have only half seen the difficulties

entrevue /ɑ̃tʀəvy/ NF *(= discussion)* meeting; *(= audience)* interview; *(Pol)* talks, discussions, meeting ◆ **se présenter à** *ou* **pour une ~** to come for *ou* to an interview

entrisme /ɑ̃tʀism/ NM entryism

entriste /ɑ̃tʀist/ ADJ, NMF entryist

entropie /ɑ̃tʀɔpi/ NF entropy

entrouvert, e /ɑ̃tʀuvɛʀ, ɛʀt/ (ptp de **entrouvrir**) ADJ *(gén)* half-open; *[fenêtre, porte]* ajar *(attrib)*, half-open ◆ **ses lèvres ~es** her parted lips

entrouvrir /ɑ̃tʀuvʀiʀ/ ► conjug 18 ◄ VT to half-open VPR **s'entrouvrir** *(gén)* to half-open; *[lèvres]* to part

entuber‡ /ɑ̃tybe/ ► conjug 1 ◄ VT *(= duper)* to con‡, to do* *(Brit)* ◆ **se faire ~** to be conned‡ *ou* be done* *(Brit)* ◆ **il m'a entubé de 10 €** he did *ou* diddled* me out of €10

enturbanné, e /ɑ̃tyʀbane/ ADJ turbaned

énucléation /enykleasjɔ̃/ NF *(Méd)* enucleation; *[de fruit]* pitting, stoning *(Brit)*

énucléer /enyklee/ ► conjug 1 ◄ VT *(Méd)* to enucleate; *[+ fruit]* to pit, to stone

énumératif, -ive /enymeʀatif, iv/ ADJ enumerative

énumération /enymeʀasjɔ̃/ NF enumeration, listing

énumérer /enymeʀe/ ► conjug 6 ◄ VT to enumerate, to list

énurésie /enyʀezi/ NF enuresis

énurétique /enyʀetik/ ADJ enuretic NMF enuretic person

env. (abrév de **environ**) approx.

envahir /ɑ̃vaiʀ/ ► conjug 2 ◄ VT 1 *(Mil, gén)* to invade, to overrun; *[douleur, sentiment]* to overcome, to sweep through ◆ **le sommeil l'envahissait** he was overcome by sleep, sleep was creeping *ou* stealing over him ◆ **le jardin est envahi par les orties** the garden is overrun *ou* overgrown with nettles ◆ **la foule envahit la place** the crowd swarmed *ou* swept into the square ◆ **cette mode a déjà envahi le pays** this fashion has already swept across the country *ou* taken the country by storm ◆ **leurs produits envahissent notre marché** our market is becoming flooded *ou* overrun with their products 2 *(gén hum)* **~ qn** *(= déranger)* to invade sb's privacy, to intrude on sb's privacy

envahissant, e /ɑ̃vaisɑ̃, ɑ̃t/ ADJ *[personne, présence]* intrusive; *[enfant]* demanding; *[passion]* all-consuming; *[odeur, goût]* strong, pervasive

envahissement /ɑ̃vaismɑ̃/ NM invasion

envahisseur /ɑ̃vaisœʀ/ ADJ M invading NM invader

envasement /ɑ̃vazmɑ̃/ NM *[de port]* silting up

envaser /ɑ̃vaze/ ► conjug 1 ◄ VT *[+ port]* to silt up VPR **s'envaser** *[port]* to silt up; *[bateau]* to stick in the mud; *[épave]* to sink in(to) the mud

enveloppant, e /ɑ̃v(ə)lɔpɑ̃, ɑ̃t/ ADJ enveloping *(épith)*; *(Mil)* surrounding *(épith)*, encircling *(épith)* ◆ **mouvement ~** encircling movement

enveloppe /ɑ̃v(ə)lɔp/ NF 1 *(= pli postal)* envelope ◆ **~ gommée/autocollante** *ou* **auto-adhésive** stick-down/self-seal envelope ◆ **~ rembourrée** *ou* **matelassée** padded bag ◆ **~ à fenêtre** window envelope ◆ **sous ~** *[envoyer]* under cover ◆ **mettre une lettre sous ~** to put a letter in an envelope

2 *(= emballage) (gén)* covering; *(en papier, toile)* wrapping; *(= gaine) [de graine]* husk; *[d'organe]* covering membrane; *[de pneu]* cover, casing; *[de dirigeable]* envelope; *[de chaudière]* lagging, jacket ◆ **dans une ~ de métal** in a metal casing

3 *(= apparence)* outward appearance, exterior ◆ **un cœur d'or sous une rude ~** a heart of gold beneath a rough exterior

4 *(littér = corps)* **il a quitté son ~ mortelle** he has shuffled off *ou* shed his mortal coil *(littér)*

5 *(Math)* envelope

6 *(= somme d'argent)* sum of money; *(= crédits)* budget ◆ **toucher une ~** *(pot-de-vin)* to get a bribe; *(gratification)* to get a bonus; *(départ en retraite)* to get a golden handshake ◆ **~ de départ** gratuity ◆ **~ budgétaire** budget ◆ **l'~ de la recherche** the research budget ◆ **le projet a reçu une ~ de 10 millions** the project was budgeted at 10 million

enveloppement /ɑ̃v(ə)lɔpmɑ̃/ NM 1 *(Méd)* *(= action)* packing; *(= emplâtre)* pack ◆ **~ d'algues** seaweed wrap 2 *(Mil) [d'ennemi]* surrounding, encirclement ◆ **manœuvre d'~** pincer *ou* encircling movement

envelopper /ɑ̃v(ə)lɔpe/ ► conjug 1 ◄ VT 1 *[+ objet, enfant]* to wrap (up) ◆ **voulez-vous que je vous l'enveloppe ?** shall I wrap it up for you? ◆ **elle est assez enveloppée** *(hum)* she's well-padded* ◆ **c'était très bien enveloppé** * *(propos)* it was phrased nicely

2 *(= voiler) [+ pensée, parole]* to veil

3 *(gén littér = entourer) [brume]* to envelop, to shroud ◆ **le silence enveloppe la ville** the town is wrapped *ou* shrouded in silence ◆ **la lumière enveloppe la campagne** the countryside is bathed in light ◆ **événement enveloppé de mystère** event shrouded *ou* veiled in mystery ◆ **~ qn du regard** to gaze at sb ◆ **il l'enveloppa d'un regard tendre** he gave her a long loving look ◆ **il enveloppa la plaine du regard** he took in the plain with his gaze, his eyes swept the plain ◆ **~ qn de son affection** to envelop sb in one's affection, to surround sb with one's affection ◆ **~ dans sa réprobation** † to include in one's disapproval

4 *(Mil) [+ ennemi]* to surround, to encircle

VPR **s'envelopper** *(dans une couverture, un châle)* to wrap o.s. *(dans* in); ◆ **il s'enveloppa dans une cape** he wrapped *ou* swathed himself in a cape ◆ **il s'enveloppa dans sa dignité** *(hum)* he assumed an air of dignity

envenimement /ɑ̃v(ə)nimmɑ̃/ NM *[de plaie]* poisoning; *[de querelle]* embittering; *[de situation]* worsening

envenimer /ɑ̃v(ə)nime/ ► conjug 1 ◄ VT *[+ plaie]* to make septic, to poison; *[+ querelle]* to inflame, to fan the flames of; *[+ situation]* to inflame, to aggravate VPR **s'envenimer** *[plaie]* to go septic, to fester; *[querelle, situation]* to grow more bitter *ou* acrimonious

envergure /ɑ̃vɛʀgyʀ/ NF 1 *[d'oiseau, avion]* wingspan; *[de voile]* breadth 2 *[de personne]* calibre; *[d'entreprise]* scale, scope; *[d'intelligence]* scope, range ◆ **prendre de l'~** *[entreprise, projet]* to expand ◆ **ce projet manque d'~** this project is not far-reaching enough ◆ **personnage sans ~** insignificant figure ◆ **il a l'~ d'un chef d'État** he has the calibre *ou* stature of a head of state ◆ **d'~, de grande ~** *[entreprise]* large-scale *(épith)*; *[auteur, politicien]* of great stature; *[projet, réforme]* far-reaching; *[opération]* large-scale *(épith)*, ambitious ◆ **projet d'~ européenne** project of European dimensions

envers[1] /ɑ̃vɛʀ/ PRÉP towards, to ◆ **cruel/traître ~ qn** cruel/a traitor to sb ◆ **~ et contre tous** *ou* **tout** in the face of *ou* despite all opposition ◆ **son attitude ~ moi** his attitude towards *ou* to me ◆ **son dédain ~ les biens matériels** his disdain for *ou* of material possessions ◆ **sa patience ~ elle** his patience with her

envers[2] /ɑ̃vɛʀ/ NM *[d'étoffe]* wrong side; *[de vêtement]* wrong side, inside; *[de papier]* back; *[de médaille]* reverse (side); *[de feuille d'arbre]* underside; *[de peau d'animal]* inside ◆ **sur l'~** *(Tricot)* on the wrong side ◆ **l'~ et l'endroit** the wrong (side) and the right side ◆ **quand on connaît l'~ du décor** *ou* **du tableau** *(fig)* when you know what is going on underneath it all, when you know the other side of the picture

◆ **à l'envers** *(verticalement)* upside down, wrong side up; *(dans l'ordre inverse)* backwards ◆ **mettre sa chemise à l'~** *(devant derrière)* to put one's shirt on back to front; *(dedans dehors)* to put one's shirt on inside out ◆ **il a mis la maison à l'~** * he turned the house upside down *ou* inside out ◆ **tout marche** *ou* **va à l'~** everything is haywire *ou* is upside down *ou* is going wrong ◆ **faire qch à l'~** *(fig) (à rebours)* to do sth the wrong way round; *(mal)* to do sth all wrong ◆ **elle avait la tête à l'~** *(fig)* her mind was in a whirl; → **maille, monde**

envi /ɑ̃vi/ **à l'envi** LOC ADV *(littér)* *[répéter]* over and over again ◆ **ils dénoncent ces abus à l'~** they ceaselessly condemn these abuses ◆ **je pourrais multiplier les exemples à l'~** I could reel off a whole string of examples

enviable /ɑ̃vjabl/ ADJ enviable ◆ **peu ~** unenviable

envie /ɑ̃vi/ GRAMMAIRE ACTIVE 35.4 NF 1 *(= désir)* desire *(de qch* for sth); *(plus fort)* craving, longing *(de qch* for sth); ◆ **cette ~ de changement lui passa vite** he soon lost this desire *ou* longing for change ◆ **avoir ~ de qch/qn** to want sth/sb ◆ **j'ai ~ de ce livre** I want *ou* would like that book ◆ **je n'ai pas ~ de lui** I don't want him ◆ **avoir une ~ de chocolat** to have a craving *ou* longing for chocolate ◆ **avoir des ~s de vacances** to feel like a holiday ◆ **j'ai des ~s de meurtre** I could kill somebody, I feel like killing somebody ◆ **des ~s de femme enceinte** pregnant woman's cravings ◆ **elle a des ~s de femme enceinte** *(fig)* she has sudden cravings ◆ **ce gâteau me fait ~** I like the look of that cake, I fancy *(Brit)* that cake ◆ **si ça te fait ~** if you like, if you feel like it ◆ **je vais lui faire passer l'~ de recommencer** * I'll make sure he won't feel like doing that again in a hurry ◆ **l'~ l'a pris de** *ou* **il lui a pris l'~ d'y aller** he suddenly felt like *ou* fancied *(Brit)* going there, he suddenly felt the urge to go there

2 ◆ **avoir ~ de faire qch** to want to do sth, to feel like doing sth ◆ **j'ai ~ d'y aller** I feel like going, I would like to go ◆ **je n'ai aucune ~ de le revoir** I have absolutely no desire to see him again ◆ **avoir bien/presque ~ de faire qch** to have a good *ou* great mind/half a mind to do sth ◆ **avoir ~ de rire** to feel like laughing ◆ **avoir ~ de vomir** to feel sick, to feel like vomiting ◆ **cela lui a donné (l')~ de rire** it made him want to laugh ◆ **j'ai ~ qu'il s'en aille** I would like him to go away, I wish he would go away; → **mourir**

3 *(euph)* **avoir ~** * to need the toilet *ou* the loo * *(Brit)* ◆ **être pris d'une ~ pressante** to have a sudden urge to go to the toilet, to be taken short * *(Brit)*; → **pisser**

4 *(= convoitise)* envy ◆ **mon bonheur lui fait ~** he envies my happiness, my happiness makes him envious (of me) ◆ **ça fait ~** it makes you envious ◆ **regarder qch avec (un œil d')~, jeter des regards d'~ sur qch** to look enviously at sth, to cast envious eyes *ou* glances at sth ◆ **digne d'~** enviable ◆ **il vaut mieux faire ~ que pitié** *(Prov)* *(gén)* it's better to be envied than pitied; *(pour personne grosse)* it's better to be a bit on the plump side than too thin

5 *(Anat)* *(sur la peau)* birthmark; *(autour des ongles)* hangnail

envier /ɑ̃vje/ ▸ conjug 7 ◂ VT *[+ personne, bonheur]* to envy, to be envious of ◆ **je vous envie votre maison** I envy you your house, I wish I had a house like yours ◆ **je vous envie (de pouvoir le faire)** I envy you *ou* I'm envious of you (being able to do it) ◆ **ce pays n'a rien à ~ au nôtre** *(il est mieux)* that country has no cause to be jealous of us; *(il est aussi mauvais)* that country is just as badly off as we are, there's nothing to choose between that country and ours

envieusement /ɑ̃vjøzmɑ̃/ ADV enviously

envieux, -ieuse /ɑ̃vjø, jøz/ ADJ envious ◆ **être ~ de** to be envious of, to envy NM,F envious person ◆ **faire des ~** to excite *ou* arouse envy

environ /ɑ̃viʀɔ̃/ ADV about, or thereabouts, or so ◆ **c'est à 100 km ~ d'ici** it's about 100 km from here, it's 100 km or so from here ◆ **il était ~ 3 heures** it was about 3 o'clock, it was 3 o'clock or thereabouts NMPL **les environs** *[de ville]* surroundings; *(= la banlieue)* outskirts ◆ **les ~s sont superbes** the surrounding area is gorgeous

◆ **dans les environs, aux environs** in the vicinity *ou* neighbourhood ◆ **qu'y a-t-il à voir dans les ~s ?** what is there to see around here?

◆ **aux environs de** ◆ **il habite aux ~s de Lille** he lives in the Lille area ◆ **aux ~s de 3 heures** 3 o'clock or thereabouts, some time around 3 o'clock, (round) about *(Brit)* 3 o'clock ◆ **aux ~s de 1 000 €** in the region of €1,000

environnant, e /ɑ̃viʀɔnɑ̃, ɑ̃t/ ADJ surrounding

environnement /ɑ̃viʀɔnmɑ̃/ NM *(gén, Écol, Ordin)* environment ◆ **~ économique/international/fiscal** economic/international/tax environment ◆ **~ familial** family background

environnemental, e (pl **-aux**) /ɑ̃viʀɔnmɑ̃tal, o/ ADJ environmental

environnementaliste /ɑ̃viʀɔnmɑ̃talist(ə)/ NMF environmentalist

environner /ɑ̃viʀɔne/ ▸ conjug 1 ◂ VT to surround, to encircle ◆ **s'~ d'experts** to surround o.s. with experts

envisageable /ɑ̃vizaʒabl/ ADJ conceivable

envisager /ɑ̃vizaʒe/ GRAMMAIRE ACTIVE 35.3, 53.3 ▸ conjug 3 ◂ VT 1 *(= considérer)* to view, to envisage, to contemplate ◆ **il envisage l'avenir de manière pessimiste** he views *ou* contemplates the future with pessimism, he has a pessimistic view of the future 2 *(= prévoir)* to envisage, to consider ◆ **~ de faire** to be thinking of doing, to consider *ou* contemplate doing ◆ **nous envisageons des transformations** we are thinking of *ou* envisaging changes ◆ **nous n'avions pas envisagé cela** we hadn't envisaged that ◆ **on ne peut raisonnablement ~ qu'il accepte** he cannot reasonably be expected to accept

envoi /ɑ̃vwa/ NM 1 *(NonC)* *[de colis, lettre]* sending (off); *[de vœux, amitiés, message radio]* sending; *[de marchandises]* dispatching, sending off; *(par bateau)* shipment; *[d'argent]* sending, remittance ◆ **faire un ~ de vivres** to send (a consignment of) supplies ◆ **faire un ~ de fonds** to remit cash ◆ **~ contre remboursement** cash on delivery ◆ **l'~ des couleurs** the hoisting of the colours ◆ **coup d'~** *(Sport)* kickoff; *[de festival]* start, opening; *[de série d'événements]* start, beginning ◆ **le spectacle qui donnera le coup d'~ du festival** the show which will kick off * *ou* open the festival 2 *(= colis)* parcel ◆ **~ de bouteilles** consignment of bottles ◆ **"envoi en nombre"** "mass mailing" 3 *(Littérat)* envoi

envol /ɑ̃vɔl/ NM *[d'oiseau]* taking flight *ou* wing; *[d'avion]* takeoff; *[d'âme, pensée]* flight ◆ **prendre son ~** *[d'oiseau]* to take flight *ou* wing; *[d'avion]* to take off; *[de pensée]* to soar, to take off

envolée /ɑ̃vɔle/ NF 1 *(dans un discours, un texte)* flight ◆ **~ oratoire/poétique** flight of oratory/poetry ◆ **dans une belle ~ lyrique, il a décrit les vertus du système** he waxed lyrical about the virtues of the system 2 *(= augmentation)* *[de chômage, prix, monnaie]* surge *(de* in); ◆ **l'~ de leur parti dans les sondages** their party's dramatic *ou* meteoric rise in the polls 3 *[d'oiseaux]* flight

envoler (s') /ɑ̃vɔle/ ▸ conjug 1 ◂ VPR 1 *[oiseau]* to fly away; *[avion]* to take off ◆ **je m'envole pour Tokyo dans deux heures** my flight leaves *ou* I take off for Tokyo in two hours 2 *(= être emporté)* *[chapeau]* to blow off, to be blown off; *[fumée, feuille, papiers]* to blow away 3 *(= passer)* *[temps]* to fly (past *ou* by); *[espoirs]* to vanish (into thin air); *(* = disparaître)* *[portefeuille, personne]* to disappear *ou* vanish (into thin air) 4 *(= augmenter)* *[prix, cours, chômage]* to soar ◆ **il s'est envolé dans les sondages** his popularity rating has soared in the opinion polls

envoûtant, e /ɑ̃vutɑ̃, ɑ̃t/ ADJ entrancing, bewitching, spellbinding

envoûtement /ɑ̃vutmɑ̃/ NM bewitchment

envoûter /ɑ̃vute/ ▸ conjug 1 ◂ VT to bewitch, to cast a spell on ◆ **être envoûté par qn** to be under sb's spell

envoûteur /ɑ̃vutœʀ/ NM sorcerer

envoûteuse /ɑ̃vutøz/ NF witch, sorceress

envoyé, e /ɑ̃vwaje/ (ptp de **envoyer**) ADJ *[remarque, réponse]* ◆ **(bien) ~** well-aimed, sharp ◆ **ça, c'est ~ !** well said!, well done! NM,F *(gén)* messenger; *(Pol)* envoy; *(Presse)* correspondent ◆ **notre ~ spécial** *(Presse)* our special correspondent ◆ **un ~ du ministère** a government official ◆ **vous êtes l'~ du ciel !** you're heaven-sent!

envoyer /ɑ̃vwaje/ GRAMMAIRE ACTIVE 47.1, 48.1 ▸ conjug 8 ◂

VT 1 *[+ colis, lettre]* to send (off); *[+ vœux, amitiés, message radio]* to send; *[+ marchandises]* to dispatch, to send off; *(par bateau)* to ship; *[+ argent]* to send, to remit *(Admin)* ◆ **~ sa démission** to send in one's resignation ◆ **~ sa candidature** to send in one's *ou* an application ◆ **n'envoyez pas d'argent par la poste** do not send money by post ◆ **envoie-moi un mot** drop me a line *

2 *[+ personne]* *(gén)* to send; *(en vacances, en courses)* to send (off) *(chez, auprès de* to); *(en mission)* *[+ émissaire, troupes]* to dispatch, to send out; *(de médecin à médecin)* to refer ◆ **envoie David à l'épicerie/aux nouvelles** send David to the grocer's/to see if there's any news ◆ **ils l'avaient envoyé chez sa grand-mère pour les vacances** they had sent him (off) to his grandmother's for the holidays ◆ **~ qn à la mort** to send sb to their death; → **monde**

3 *(= lancer)* *[+ objet]* to throw, to fling; *(avec force)* to hurl; *[+ obus]* to fire; *[+ signaux]* to send (out); *(Sport)* *[+ ballon]* to send ◆ **~ des baisers à qn** to blow sb kisses ◆ **~ des sourires à qn** to smile at sb ◆ **~ des coups de pied/poing à qn** to kick/punch sb ◆ **ne m'envoie pas ta fumée dans les yeux** don't blow (your) smoke in(to) my eyes ◆ **il le lui a envoyé dans les dents** ‡ *ou* **les gencives** ‡ he really let him have it! * ◆ **~ le ballon au fond des filets** *(Ftbl)* to put *ou* send the ball into the back of the net ◆ **~ qn à terre** *ou* **au tapis** to knock sb down, to knock sb to the ground, to floor sb ◆ **~ un homme sur la Lune** to send a man to the moon ◆ **~ par le fond** *(Naut)* to send down *ou* to the bottom

4 *(Mil)* **~ les couleurs** to run up *ou* hoist the colours

5 *(locutions)* **~ chercher qn/qch** to send for sb/sth ◆ **~ promener qn** * *ou* **balader qn** *, **~ qn coucher** *, **~ qn sur les roses** * to send sb packing *, to send sb about their business ◆ **~ valser** *ou* **dinguer qch** * to send sth flying * ◆ **il a tout envoyé promener** * he chucked the whole thing in ◆ **il ne le lui a pas envoyé dire** * he gave it to him straight *, he told him straight to his face

VPR **s'envoyer** ‡ *(= subir, prendre)* *[+ corvée]* to get stuck * *ou* landed * with; *[+ bouteille]* to knock back *; *[+ nourriture]* to scoff * ◆ **je m'enverrais des gifles** * I could kick myself * ◆ **s'~ une fille/un mec** to have it off *(Brit)* *ou* get off *(US)* with a girl/a guy ‡, to make it with a girl/a guy ‡ ◆ **s'~ en l'air** to have it off ‡ *(Brit)*, to get some ‡ *(US)*

envoyeur, -euse /ɑ̃vwajœʀ, øz/ NM,F sender; → **retour**

enzymatique /ɑ̃zimatik/ ADJ enzymatic, enzymic

enzyme /ɑ̃zim/ NM *ou* NF enzyme ◆ **~ de restriction** restriction enzyme

éocène /eɔsɛn/ ADJ Eocene NM ◆ **l'~** the Eocene

Éole /eɔl/ NM Aeolus

éolien, -ienne /eɔljɛ̃, jɛn/ ADJ wind *(épith)*, aeolian *(littér)*; → **énergie, harpe** NF **éolienne** windmill, windpump

EOR /eoœʀ/ NM (abrév de **élève officier de réserve**) → **élève**

éosine /eozin/ NF eosin

épagneul, e /epaɲœl/ NM,F spaniel ♦ ~ **breton** Brittany spaniel

épais, -aisse /epɛ, ɛs/ ADJ 1 *(gén) [chevelure, peinture]* thick; *[neige]* thick, deep; *[barbe]* bushy, thick; *[silence]* deep; *[personne, corps]* thickset; *[nuit]* pitch-black ♦ **cloison épaisse de 5 cm** partition 5 cm thick ♦ **j'ai la langue épaisse** my tongue is coated *ou* furred up *(Brit)* ♦ **au plus ~ de la forêt** in the depths of the forest ♦ **tu n'es pas bien ~** you're not exactly fat 2 *(péj = inhabile) [esprit]* dull; *[personne]* dense, thick(headed); *[mensonge, plaisanterie]* clumsy ADV ♦ **semer ~** to sow thick *ou* thickly ♦ **il n'y en a pas ~ !*** there's not much of it!

épaisseur /epɛsœʀ/ NF 1 *(gén)* thickness; *[de neige, silence]* depth ♦ **la neige a un mètre d'~** there is a metre of snow, the snow is a metre deep ♦ **creuser une niche dans l'~ d'un mur** to hollow out a niche in a wall 2 *(= couche)* layer, thickness ♦ **prenez deux ~s de tissu** take two thicknesses *ou* a double thickness of material ♦ **plier une couverture en double ~** to fold a blanket double 3 *(= richesse) [d'œuvre]* substance, depth; *[de personne]* depth ♦ **ce personnage manque d'~** this character lacks depth *ou* is rather flat

épaissir /epesiʀ/ ▸ conjug 2 ◂ VT *[+ substance]* to thicken; *[+ mystère]* to deepen ♦ **l'air était épaissi par les fumées** the air was thick with smoke ♦ **l'âge lui épaissit les traits** his features are becoming coarse with age ♦ **ce manteau m'épaissit beaucoup** this coat makes me look much broader *ou* fatter VI to get thicker, to thicken ♦ **il a beaucoup épaissi** he has filled out a lot VPR **s'épaissir** *[substance, brouillard]* to thicken, to get thicker; *[chevelure, feuillage]* to get thicker; *[ténèbres]* to deepen ♦ **sa taille s'épaissit** his waist is getting thicker, he's getting stouter around the waist ♦ **le mystère s'épaissit** the mystery deepens, the plot thickens

épaississant, e /epesisɑ̃, ɑ̃t/ ADJ thickening NM thickener

épaississement /epesismɑ̃/ NM thickening

épanchement /epɑ̃ʃmɑ̃/ NM *[de sang]* effusion; *[de sentiments]* outpouring ♦ **avoir un ~ de synovie** *(Méd)* to have water on the knee

épancher /epɑ̃ʃe/ ▸ conjug 1 ◂ VT *[+ sentiments] (irrités)* to give vent to, to vent; *(tendres)* to pour forth VPR **s'épancher** *[personne]* to open one's heart, to pour out one's feelings *(auprès de* to); *[sang]* to pour out

épandage /epɑ̃daʒ/ NM *(Agr)* manure spreading, manuring

épandre /epɑ̃dʀ/ ▸ conjug 41 ◂ VT († , *littér*) *[+ liquide, tendresse]* to pour forth *(littér)*; *(Agr) [+ fumier]* to spread VPR **s'épandre** *(littér)* to spread

épanoui, e /epanwi/ (ptp de **épanouir**) ADJ *[fleur]* in full bloom *(attrib)*; *[visage, sourire]* radiant, beaming *(épith)*; *[personne]* totally fulfilled *(attrib)* ♦ **c'est quelqu'un de très ~** he's very much at one with himself *ou* with the world

épanouir /epanwiʀ/ ▸ conjug 2 ◂ VT *(littér) [+ fleur]* to open out; *[+ branches, pétales]* to open *ou* spread out; *[+ visage]* to light up ♦ **la maternité l'a épanouie** she really blossomed when she became a mother VPR **s'épanouir** *[fleur]* to bloom, to come out, to open up *ou* out; *[visage]* to light up; *[personne]* to blossom, to bloom; *[vase]* to open out, to curve outwards ♦ **à cette nouvelle il s'épanouit** his face lit up at the news ♦ **s'~ dans sa profession** to find one's profession very fulfilling

épanouissant, e /epanwisɑ̃, ɑ̃t/ ADJ totally fulfilling

épanouissement /epanwismɑ̃/ NM *[de fleur]* blooming, coming out, opening up *ou* out; *[de visage]* lighting up; *[de personne]* blossoming, blooming ♦ **c'est une industrie en plein ~** it's a booming industry

épargnant, e /epaʀɲɑ̃, ɑ̃t/ NM,F saver, investor ♦ **petits ~s** small savers *ou* investors

épargne /epaʀɲ/ NF *(= somme)* savings ♦ **l'~** *(= action d'épargner)* saving ♦ **~ de temps/d'argent** saving of time/money ♦ **~ forcée/longue/liquide** forced/long-term/liquid savings ♦ **~-logement** home-buyers' savings scheme ♦ **~-retraite** retirement savings scheme ♦ **~ salariale** employee savings plan; → **caisse, compte, plan¹**

épargner /epaʀɲe/ ▸ conjug 1 ◂ VT 1 *(= économiser) [+ argent, nourriture, temps, forces]* to save ♦ **~ 10 € sur une somme** to save €10 out of a sum ♦ **~ sur la nourriture** to save *ou* make a saving on food ♦ **ils n'ont pas épargné le poivre !*** they haven't stinted *ou* skimped on the pepper! ♦ **~ pour ses vieux jours** to save (up) for one's old age, to put something aside for one's old age ♦ **je n'épargnerai rien pour le faire** I'll spare nothing to get it done ♦ **il n'a pas épargné sa peine** he spared no effort *(pour* to) 2 *(= éviter)* ~ **qch à qn** to spare sb sth ♦ **je vous épargne les détails** I'll spare you the details ♦ **pour t'~ des explications inutiles** to spare you useless explanations ♦ **pour m'~ la peine de venir** to save *ou* spare myself the bother of coming 3 *(= ménager) [+ ennemi]* to spare ♦ **l'épidémie a épargné cette région** that region was spared the epidemic

éparpillement /epaʀpijmɑ̃/ NM *(= action) [d'objets]* scattering; *[de troupes]* dispersal; *[de points de vente]* distribution, scattering; *[d'efforts, talent]* dissipation; *(= état) [de troupes, succursales]* dispersal ♦ **l'~ des maisons rendait les communications très difficiles** the fact that the houses were so scattered made communications difficult

éparpiller /epaʀpije/ ▸ conjug 1 ◂ VT *[+ objets, cendres]* to scatter; *[+ troupes]* to disperse; *[+ points de vente]* to distribute, to scatter; *[+ efforts, talent]* to dissipate VPR **s'éparpiller** 1 *[feuilles, foule]* to scatter ♦ **maisons qui s'éparpillent dans la campagne** houses dotted about the countryside 2 *[personne]* **il s'éparpille beaucoup trop** he spreads himself too thin ♦ **tu t'es trop éparpillé dans tes lectures/recherches** you've spread yourself too thin in your reading/research

épars, e /epaʀ, aʀs/ ADJ *(littér)* scattered

épatant, e* /epatɑ̃, ɑ̃t/ ADJ great*

épate* /epat/ NF *(péj)* ♦ **l'~** showing off* ♦ **faire de l'~** to show off*

épaté, e /epate/ (ptp de **épater**) ADJ *[vase]* flat-bottomed; *[nez]* flat

épatement /epatmɑ̃/ NM 1 *[de nez]* flatness 2 (* *= surprise*) amazement

épater /epate/ ▸ conjug 1 ◂ VT * *(= étonner)* to amaze, to stagger*; *(= impressionner)* to impress ♦ **pour ~ le bourgeois** to shake *ou* shock middle-class attitudes ♦ **ça t'épate, hein !** how about that!*, what do you think of that!; → **galerie** VPR **s'épater** *[objet, colonne]* to spread out

épaulard /epolaʀ/ NM killer whale

épaule /epol/ NF shoulder ♦ **large d'~s** broad-shouldered ♦ **~ d'agneau** shoulder of lamb ♦ **donner un coup d'~ à qn** to knock *ou* bump sb with one's shoulder ♦ **tout repose sur vos ~s** everything rests on your shoulders ♦ **il n'ont pas les ~s assez larges** *ou* **solides** *(financièrement)* they are not in a strong enough financial position; → **hausser, tête**

épaulé-jeté (pl **épaulés-jetés**) /epoleʒ(ə)te/ NM clean-and-jerk ♦ **il soulève 150 kg à l'~** he can do a clean-and-jerk using 150 kg

épaulement /epolmɑ̃/ NM *(= mur)* retaining wall; *(= rempart)* breastwork, epaulement; *(Géol)* escarpment

épauler /epole/ ▸ conjug 1 ◂ VT 1 *[+ personne]* to back up, to support ♦ **il faut s'~ dans la vie** people must help *ou* support each other in life ♦ **il a été bien épaulé par son frère** his brother gave him a lot of help *ou* support 2 *[+ fusil]* to raise (to the shoulder) ♦ **il épaula puis tira** he took aim *ou* he raised his rifle and fired 3 *[+ mur]* to support, to retain 4 *[+ vêtement]* to add shoulder pads to

épaulette /epolɛt/ NF *(Mil)* epaulette; *(= bretelle)* shoulder strap; *(= rembourrage d'un vêtement)* shoulder pad

épave /epav/ NF 1 *(= navire, voiture)* wreck; *(= débris)* piece of wreckage, wreckage *(NonC)*; *(= déchets)* flotsam (and jetsam) *(NonC)* 2 *(Jur = objet perdu)* derelict 3 *(= restes)* ruins; *(= loque humaine)* human wreck

épée /epe/ NF 1 *(= arme)* sword; *(Escrime)* épée ♦ **~ de Damoclès** Sword of Damocles ♦ **l'~ nue** *ou* **à la main** with drawn sword ♦ **c'est un coup d'~ dans l'eau** it's a complete waste of time; → **cape, noblesse, rein** 2 *(= escrimeur)* swordsman; *(= escrimeuse)* swordswoman

épeiche /epɛʃ/ NF great spotted woodpecker

épeichette /epɛʃɛt/ NF lesser-spotted woodpecker

épeire /epɛʀ/ NF garden spider

épéiste /epeist/ NMF épéeist

épeler /ep(ə)le/ ▸ conjug 4 ◂ VT *[+ mot]* to spell; *[+ texte]* to spell out

épépiner /epepine/ ▸ conjug 1 ◂ VT to deseed, to seed ♦ **raisins épépinés** seedless grapes

éperdu, e /epɛʀdy/ ADJ 1 *[personne]* distraught, overcome ♦ **~ de douleur/de terreur** distraught *ou* frantic *ou* out of one's mind with grief/terror ♦ **~ de joie** overcome *ou* beside o.s. with joy 2 *[gratitude]* boundless; *[regard]* wild, distraught; *[amour]* passionate; *[fuite]* headlong, frantic ♦ **désir/besoin ~ de bonheur** frantic desire for/need of happiness

éperdument /epɛʀdymɑ̃/ ADV *[crier, travailler]* frantically, desperately; *[aimer]* passionately, madly ♦ **je m'en moque ~** I couldn't care less

éperlan /epɛʀlɑ̃/ NM smelt ♦ **friture d'~s** fried whitebait

éperon /ep(ə)ʀɔ̃/ NM *[de cavalier, coq, montagne]* spur; *(Naut) [de galère]* ram; *[de pont]* cutwater ♦ **~ rocheux** rocky outcrop *ou* spur

éperonner /ep(ə)ʀɔne/ ▸ conjug 1 ◂ VT *[+ cheval]* to spur (on); *[+ navire]* to ram; *[+ personne]* to spur on

épervier /epɛʀvje/ NM 1 *(Orn)* sparrowhawk 2 *(= filet)* cast(ing) net

éphèbe /efɛb/ NM *(Hist)* ephebe; *(iro, péj)* beautiful young man

éphémère /efemɛʀ/ ADJ *[bonheur, succès]* fleeting, short-lived, ephemeral *(frm)*; *[moment]* fleeting; *[mouvement, règne, publication]* short-lived ♦ **le caractère ~ de la gloire** the transient nature of fame ♦ **~ ministre, il ...** having made a brief appearance as a minister, he ... NM mayfly, ephemera *(SPÉC)*

éphéméride /efemeʀid/ NF 1 *(= calendrier)* block calendar, tear-off calendar 2 *(Astron)* **~s** *(= tables)* ephemeris *(sg)*

Éphèse /efɛz/ N Ephesus

épi /epi/ NM 1 *[de blé, maïs]* ear; *[de fleur]* spike; *[de cheveux]* tuft ◆ **les blés sont en ~s** the corn is in the ear 2 *(= jetée)* breakwater, groyne, groin 3 *(Aut)* **être garé en ~** to be parked at an angle to the kerb 4 ◆ **~ de faîtage** finial

épice /epis/ NF spice ◆ **quatre ~s** allspice; → **pain**

épicé, e /epise/ (ptp de **épicer**) ADJ *[viande, plat]* highly spiced, spicy; *[goût]* spicy; *[histoire]* spicy, juicy*

épicéa /episea/ NM spruce

épicentre /episɑ̃tʀ/ NM epicentre

épicer /epise/ ▸ conjug 3 ◂ VT *[+ mets]* to spice; *[+ histoire]* to add spice to

épicerie /episʀi/ NF *(= magasin)* grocery, grocer's (shop *(Brit)* ou store *(US)*); *(= nourriture)* groceries; *(= métier)* grocery trade ◆ **rayon ~** grocery stand ou counter ◆ **aller à l'~** to go to the grocer's ou grocery ◆ **~ fine** ≈ delicatessen

épicier, -ière /episje, jɛʀ/ NM,F *(gén)* grocer; *(en fruits et légumes)* greengrocer *(Brit)*, grocer *(US)*; *(péj)* ◆ **d'~** *[idées, mentalité]* small-town *(épith)*, parochial

Épicure /epikyʀ/ NM Epicurus

épicurien, -ienne /epikyʀjɛ̃, jɛn/ ADJ, NM,F *(= gourmet)* epicurean; *(Philos)* Epicurean

épicurisme /epikyʀism/ NM epicureanism

épidémie /epidemi/ NF epidemic ◆ **~ de grippe** flu epidemic

épidémiologie /epidemjɔlɔʒi/ NF epidemiology

épidémiologique /epidemjɔlɔʒik/ ADJ epidemiological

épidémique /epidemik/ ADJ *(lit)* epidemic; *(fig)* contagious, catching *(attrib)*

épiderme /epidɛʀm/ NM epidermis *(SPÉC)*, skin ◆ **elle a l'~ délicat** she has delicate skin

épidermique /epidɛʀmik/ ADJ 1 *(Anat)* skin *(épith)*, epidermal *(SPÉC)*, epidermic *(SPÉC)* ◆ **blessure ~** (surface) scratch, skin wound 2 *(fig) [réaction]* instinctive, visceral ◆ **je le déteste, c'est ~** I hate him, I just can't help it

épididyme /epididim/ NM epididymis

épier /epje/ ▸ conjug 7 ◂ VT *[+ personne]* to spy on; *[+ geste]* to watch closely; *[+ bruit]* to listen out for; *[+ occasion]* to be on the look-out for, to look (out) for, to watch for

épieu /epjø/ NM spear

épigastre /epigastʀ/ NM epigastrium

épiglotte /epiglɔt/ NF epiglottis

épigone /epigɔn/ NM *(Littérat)* epigone

épigramme /epigʀam/ NF epigram

épigraphe /epigʀaf/ NF epigraph ◆ **mettre un vers en ~** to use a line as an epigraph

épigraphique /epigʀafik/ ADJ epigraphic

épilateur /epilatœʀ/ NM hair remover

épilation /epilasjɔ̃/ NF removal of (unwanted) hair; *[de sourcils]* plucking ◆ **~ à la cire** waxing ◆ **~ électrique** hair removal by electrolysis

épilatoire /epilatwaʀ/ ADJ depilatory, hair-removing *(épith)*

épilepsie /epilɛpsi/ NF epilepsy

épileptique /epilɛptik/ ADJ, NMF epileptic

épiler /epile/ ▸ conjug 1 ◂ VT *[+ jambes]* to remove the hair from; *[+ sourcils]* to pluck ◆ **se faire ~ les aisselles** to have one's underarm hair removed VPR **s'épiler** ◆ **elle s'épilait les jambes** she was removing the hair(s) from her legs ◆ **s'~ les jambes à la cire** to wax one's legs ◆ **s'~ les sourcils** to pluck one's eyebrows

épilogue /epilɔg/ NM *(Littérat)* epilogue; *(fig)* conclusion, dénouement

épiloguer /epilɔge/ ▸ conjug 1 ◂ VI *(parfois péj)* to hold forth *(sur* on) to go on* *(sur* about) to expatiate *(frm) (sur* upon)

épinard /epinaʀ/ NM *(Bot)* spinach ◆ **~s** *(Culin)* spinach *(NonC)*; → **beurre**

épine /epin/ NF 1 *[de buisson, rose]* thorn; *[de hérisson, oursin]* spine, prickle; *[de porc-épic]* quill ◆ **~ dorsale** backbone ◆ **vous m'enlevez une belle ~ du pied** you have got me out of a spot* 2 *(= arbre)* thorn bush ◆ **~ blanche** hawthorn ◆ **~ noire** blackthorn

épinette /epinɛt/ NF 1 *(Mus)* spinet 2 *(Can)* spruce ◆ **~ blanche/noire** white/black spruce ◆ **~ rouge** tamarack, hackmatack 3 *(Agr)* coop

épineux, -euse /epinø, øz/ ADJ *[plante]* thorny, prickly; *[problème]* thorny, tricky, ticklish; *[situation]* tricky, ticklish, sensitive; *[caractère]* prickly, touchy NM prickly shrub ou bush

épinglage /epɛ̃glaʒ/ NM pinning

épingle /epɛ̃gl/ NF pin ◆ **~ à chapeau** hatpin ◆ **~ à cheveux** hairpin ◆ **virage en ~ à cheveux** hairpin bend *(Brit)* ou curve *(US)* ◆ **~ de cravate** tie clip, tiepin ◆ **~ à linge** clothes peg *(Brit)* ou pin *(US)* ◆ **~ de nourrice ou de sûreté** safety pin; *(grand modèle)* nappy *(Brit)* ou diaper *(US)* pin ◆ **tirer son ~ du jeu** *(= bien manœuvrer)* to play one's game well; *(= s'en sortir à temps)* to extricate o.s.; → **monter², quatre**

épingler /epɛ̃gle/ ▸ conjug 1 ◂ VT 1 *(= attacher)* to pin (on) *(à, sur* to); ◆ **~ ses cheveux** to pin up one's hair ◆ **~ une robe** *(Couture)* to pin up a dress 2 *(* = arrêter)* to nab*, to nick* *(Brit)* ◆ **se faire ~** to get nabbed* ou nicked* *(Brit)* 3 *(= dénoncer)* to slam*, to criticize (severely) ◆ **il a épinglé le gouvernement** he laid into* ou slammed* the government, he took a swipe at the government

épinglette /epɛ̃glɛt/ NF lapel badge

épinière /epinjɛʀ/ ADJ F → **moelle**

épinoche /epinɔʃ/ NF stickleback

Épiphanie /epifani/ NF ◆ **l'~** Epiphany, Twelfth Night ◆ **à l'~** at Epiphany, on ou at Twelfth Night

épiphénomène /epifenɔmɛn/ NM epiphenomenon ◆ **c'est un ~** *(= non essentiel)* it's purely incidental

épiphyse /epifiz/ NF epiphysis

épiphyte /epifit/ ADJ epiphytic(al), epiphytal NM epiphyte

épique /epik/ ADJ *(lit, fig)* epic; *(hum)* epic, dramatic

épiscopal, e (mpl **-aux**) /episkɔpal, o/ ADJ episcopal ◆ **palais ~** Bishop's ou episcopal palace

épiscopalien, -ienne /episkɔpaljɛ̃, jɛn/ ADJ episcopalian ◆ **l'Église épiscopalienne** the Episcopal Church

épiscopat /episkɔpa/ NM episcopate, episcopacy

épiscope /episkɔp/ NM episcope *(Brit)*, opaque projector *(US)*

épisiotomie /epizjɔtɔmi/ NF episiotomy

épisode /epizɔd/ NM 1 *(gén)* episode ◆ **roman/film à ~s** serial ◆ **ce nouvel ~ de l'affaire Paloma** the latest development in the Paloma case ◆ **j'ai dû rater un ~** * I must have missed something 2 *(Méd)* **~ dépressif/infectieux** depressive/infectious phase

épisodique /epizɔdik/ ADJ 1 *(= occasionnel) [événement]* occasional; *[rôle]* fleeting, transitory ◆ **de façon ~** occasionally ◆ **nous avons eu une relation ~ pendant deux ans** we had an on-off relationship for two years ◆ **faire des apparitions ~s** to show up from time to time ou once in a while ◆ **sa présence ~ au sein de la commission** his occasional presence on the committee 2 *(= secondaire) [événement]* minor, of secondary importance; *[personnage]* minor, secondary

épisodiquement /epizɔdikmɑ̃/ ADV occasionally

épisser /epise/ ▸ conjug 1 ◂ VT to splice

épissoir /episwaʀ/ NM marlin(e) spike, splicing fid

épissure /episyʀ/ NF splice ◆ **on a dû faire une ~** we had to splice the two bits together

épistémologie /epistemɔlɔʒi/ NF *(Philos)* epistemology; *(Sci)* epistemics *(sg)*

épistémologique /epistemɔlɔʒik/ ADJ epistemological

épistolaire /epistɔlɛʀ/ ADJ *[style]* epistolary ◆ **être en relations ~s avec qn** to correspond with sb, to be in correspondence with sb

épistolier, -ière /epistɔlje, jɛʀ/ NM,F *(littér)* letter writer

épitaphe /epitaf/ NF epitaph

épithélial, e (mpl **-iaux**) /epiteljal, jo/ ADJ epithelial

épithélium /epiteljɔm/ NM épithelium

épithète /epitɛt/ NF 1 *(Gram)* attribute ◆ **adjectif ~** attributive adjective 2 *(= qualificatif)* epithet

épître /epitʀ/ NF epistle

épizootie /epizɔɔti, epizooti/ NF epizootic (disease)

éploré, e /eplɔʀe/ ADJ *(littér) [visage]* bathed in tears; *[personne]* tearful, weeping, in tears *(attrib)*; *[voix]* tearful

épluchage /eplyʃaʒ/ NM 1 *[de fruits, légumes, crevettes]* peeling; *[de salade, radis]* cleaning 2 *[de journaux, comptes]* dissection

épluche-légumes /eplyʃlegym/ NM INV (potato) peeler

éplucher /eplyʃe/ ▸ conjug 1 ◂ VT 1 *[+ fruits, légumes, crevettes]* to peel; *[+ salade, radis]* to clean 2 *[+ journaux, comptes]* to go over with a fine-tooth comb, to dissect

épluchette /eplyʃɛt/ NF *(Can)* corn-husking bee ou party

éplucheur, -euse /eplyʃœʀ, øz/ ADJ, NM ◆ **(couteau) ~** (potato) peeler NM,F *(= personne)* peeler; *(péj)* faultfinder NF **éplucheuse** *(= machine)* potato-peeler

épluchure /eplyʃyʀ/ NF ◆ **~ de pomme de terre** *etc* piece of potato *etc* peeling ◆ **~s** peelings

EPO /əpeo/ NM (abrév de **érythropoïétine**) EPO

épointer /epwɛ̃te/ ▸ conjug 1 ◂ VT *[+ aiguille]* to blunt ◆ **crayon épointé** blunt pencil

éponge /epɔ̃ʒ/ NF 1 *(gén)* sponge ◆ **passer un coup d'~ sur qch** to give sth a (quick) sponge, to wipe sth with a sponge ◆ **passons l'~ !** *(fig)* let's let bygones be bygones!, let's forget all about it! ◆ **passons l'~ sur cette vieille querelle !** let's forget all about that old quarrel!, let's put that old quarrel behind us! ◆ **jeter l'~** *(Boxe, fig)* to throw in the sponge ou towel ◆ **~ métallique** scouring pad, scourer ◆ **~ végétale** loofah *(Brit)*, luffa *(US)*; → **boire** 2 **(tissu) ~** (terry) towelling 3 *(* = ivrogne)* drunk*, drunkard

éponger /epɔ̃ʒe/ ▸ conjug 3 ◂ VT *[+ liquide]* to mop ou sponge up; *[+ plancher, visage]* to mop; *[+ dette]* to soak up, to absorb ◆ **s'~ le front** to mop one's brow

éponyme /epɔnim/ ADJ *(frm)* eponymous *(frm)* ◆ **le héros ~ de la pièce** the play's eponymous hero ◆ **la chanson ~ de l'album** the title track of the album NM eponym

épopée /epɔpe/ NF *(lit, fig)* epic

époque /epɔk/ NF 1 *(gén)* time ◆ **les chansons de l'~** the songs of the time ou day ◆ **j'étais jeune à l'~** I was young at the time ◆ **à cette**

~(-là) at that time ◆ **à l'~ où nous sommes** in this day and age ◆ **être de son ~** to be in tune with one's time ◆ **quelle ~ !** what times these are! ◆ **nous vivons une drôle d'~** these are strange times we're living in ◆ **l'accordéon, les bals populaires, toute une ~ !** accordions, open-air dances - a bygone era!

2 *(Hist)* age, era, epoch ◆ **chaque ~ a ses problèmes** every era has its problems ◆ **l'~ révolutionnaire** the revolutionary era *ou* age *ou* epoch ◆ **à l'~ des Grecs** at the time of *ou* in the age of the Greeks ◆ **la Belle Époque** the Belle Époque, ≈ the Edwardian era ◆ **cette invention a fait ~** it was an epoch-making invention ◆ **il s'est trompé d'~** he was born in the wrong century ◆ **à toutes les ~s** in every era ◆ **documents d'~** contemporary (historical) documents ◆ **sur instruments d'~** *(Mus)* on period *ou* authentic instruments

3 *(Géol)* period ◆ **à l'~ glaciaire** in the ice age

4 *(Art = style)* period ◆ **tableaux de la même ~** pictures of *ou* from the same period ◆ **meubles d'~** antique *ou* period furniture ◆ **ce vase n'est pas d'~** this vase isn't a genuine antique

épouiller /epuje/ ▸ conjug 1 ◂ **VT** to delouse

époumoner (s') /epumɔne/ ▸ conjug 1 ◂ **VPR** to shout o.s. hoarse ◆ **il s'époumonait à chanter** he was singing himself hoarse

épousailles /epuzɑj/ **NFPL** († *ou hum*) nuptials † *(aussi hum)*

épouse /epuz/ **NF** wife, spouse *(frm ou hum)* ◆ **voulez-vous prendre pour ~ Jeanne Dumont ?** do you take Jeanne Dumont to be your lawful wedded wife?

épousée /epuze/ **NF** († *ou dial*) bride

épouser /epuze/ ▸ conjug 1 ◂ **VT** 1 *[+ personne]* to marry, to wed †; *[+ idée]* to embrace, to espouse *(frm)*; *[+ cause]* to espouse *(frm)*, to take up ◆ **une grosse fortune** to marry into money 2 *[vêtement]* to mould, to hug; *[route, tracé]* to follow; *(étroitement)* to hug ◆ **cette robe épouse parfaitement les formes du corps** this dress moulds the curves of the body perfectly **VPR s'épouser** *(littér) [personnes]* to marry, to wed *(littér)*

épousseter /epuste/ ▸ conjug 4 ◂ **VT** *(= nettoyer)* to dust; *(= enlever)* to dust *ou* flick off

époustouflant, e* /epustuflɑ̃, ɑt/ **ADJ** staggering, amazing

époustoufler* /epustufle/ ▸ conjug 1 ◂ **VT** to stagger, to flabbergast

épouvantable /epuvɑ̃tabl/ **ADJ** *(gén)* terrible, dreadful; *(= très choquant)* appalling ◆ **il a un caractère ~** he has a foul temper

épouvantablement /epuvɑ̃tabləmɑ̃/ **ADV** terribly, dreadfully

épouvantail /epuvɑ̃taj/ **NM** 1 *(à oiseaux)* scarecrow 2 *(= spectre)* spectre ◆ **l'~ de la guerre/du chômage** the spectre of war/unemployment ◆ **ils se servaient du communisme comme d'un ~** they were raising the bogeyman of communism 3 *(péj = personne)* scruff* ◆ **j'ai l'air d'un ~ dans cette robe** I look a fright *(Brit) ou* like a scarecrow in this dress

épouvante /epuvɑ̃t/ **NF** terror, (great) fear ◆ **saisi d'~** terror-stricken ◆ **il voyait arriver ce moment avec ~** he saw with dread the moment approaching ◆ **roman/film d'~** horror story/film

épouvanter /epuvɑ̃te/ ▸ conjug 1 ◂ **VT** to terrify, to appal, to frighten ◆ **s'~ de qch** to be appalled *ou* horrified by sth

époux /epu/ **NM** husband, spouse *(frm ou hum)* ◆ **les ~** the (married) couple, the husband and wife ◆ **les ~ Durand** the Durands, Mr and Mrs Durand ◆ **voulez-vous prendre pour ~ Jean Legrand ?** do you take Jean Legrand to be your lawful wedded husband?

époxy /epɔksi/ **ADJ INV** epoxy ◆ **résine ~** epoxy resin

époxyde /epɔksid/ **NM** epoxide

éprendre (s') /epʀɑ̃dʀ/ ▸ conjug 58 ◂ **VPR** *(littér)* ◆ **s'~ de** to fall in love with, to become enamoured of *(littér)*

épreuve /epʀœv/ **NF** 1 *(= essai)* test ◆ **~ de résistance** strength test ◆ **~ de résistance au choc/à la chaleur** impact/heat test ◆ **~ de force** trial of strength, confrontation ◆ **~ de vérité** litmus *ou* acid test *(fig)* ◆ **faire l'~ d'un métal** to test a metal; → **rude**

2 *(= malheur)* ordeal, trial, hardship ◆ **subir de rudes ~s** to suffer great hardships, to undergo great trials *ou* ordeals ◆ **savoir réagir dans l'~** to cope well in the face of adversity

3 *(Scol)* test ◆ **corriger les ~s d'un examen** to mark the examination papers ◆ **~ orale** oral test ◆ **~ écrite** written test *ou* paper

4 *(Sport)* event ◆ **~ de sélection** heat ◆ **~ contre la montre** time trial ◆ **~s sur piste** track events ◆ **~ d'endurance** *[de personne]* test of endurance, endurance test; *(en voiture)* endurance test

5 *(Typo)* proof ◆ **premières/secondes ~s** first/second proofs ◆ **corriger les ~s d'un livre** to proofread a book, to correct the proofs of a book

6 *(Photo)* print; *(= gravure)* proof ◆ **~ (par) contact** contact print ◆ **~s (de tournage)** *(Ciné)* rushes

7 *(Hist : initiatique)* ordeal ◆ **~ du feu** ordeal by fire

8 *(locutions)*

◆ **à l'épreuve** ◆ **mettre à l'~** to put to the test ◆ **mise à l'~** *(Jur)* ≈ probation

◆ **à l'épreuve de** ◆ **gilet à l'~ des balles** bulletproof vest ◆ **à l'~ du feu** fireproof ◆ **résister à l'~ du temps** to stand the test of time

◆ **à toute épreuve** *[amitié, foi]* staunch; *[mur]* solid as a rock ◆ **il a un courage à toute ~** he has unfailing courage, his courage is equal to anything

épris, e /epʀi, iz/ (ptp de **s'éprendre**) **ADJ** *(frm)* *(d'une personne)* smitten (*de* with) enamoured *(littér)* (*de* of) in love (*de* with); ◆ **être ~ de justice/liberté** to have a great love of justice/liberty ◆ **~ d'histoire** enamoured of history

éprouvant, e /epʀuvɑ̃, ɑt/ **ADJ** *[travail, climat]* trying, testing ◆ **~ pour les nerfs** nerve-racking

éprouvé, e /epʀuve/ (ptp de **éprouver**) **ADJ** *(= sûr) [moyen, remède]* well-tried, proven; *[spécialiste, qualités]* (well-)proven; *[ami]* staunch, true, steadfast

éprouver /epʀuve/ ▸ conjug 1 ◂ **VT** 1 *(= ressentir) [+ sensation, sentiment]* to feel, to experience 2 *(= subir) [+ perte]* to suffer, to sustain; *[+ difficultés]* to meet with, to experience 3 *(= tester) [+ métal]* to test; *[+ personne]* to put to the test, to test 4 *(frm = affliger)* to afflict, to distress ◆ **très éprouvé par la maladie** sorely afflicted by illness *(frm)* ◆ **la ville a été durement éprouvée pendant la guerre** the city suffered greatly during the war

éprouvette /epʀuvɛt/ **NF** test tube; → **bébé**

EPS /əpeɛs/ **NF** (abrév de **éducation physique et sportive**) PE, PT

epsilon /ɛpsilɔn/ **NM** epsilon

épuisant, e /epɥizɑ̃, ɑt/ **ADJ** exhausting

épuisé, e /epɥize/ (ptp de **épuiser**) **ADJ** *[personne, cheval, corps]* exhausted, worn-out; *[article vendu]* sold out *(attrib)*; *[stocks]* exhausted *(attrib)*; *[livre]* out of print ◆ **~ de fatigue** exhausted, tired out, worn-out

épuisement /epɥizmɑ̃/ **NM** exhaustion ◆ **devant l'~ de ses finances** seeing that his money had run out ◆ **jusqu'à ~ des stocks** while stocks last ◆ **jusqu'à l'~ du filon** until the seam is (*ou* was) worked out ◆ **faire marcher qn jusqu'à (l')~** to make sb walk till he drops (with exhaustion) ◆ **dans un grand état d'~** in a completely *ou* an utterly exhausted state, in a state of complete *ou* utter exhaustion

épuiser /epɥize/ ▸ conjug 1 ◂ **VT** *[+ personne]* to exhaust, to tire out, to wear out; *[+ terre, sujet]* to exhaust; *[+ réserves, munitions]* to use up, to exhaust; *[+ filon]* to exhaust, to work out; *[+ patience]* to wear out, to exhaust **VPR s'épuiser** *[réserves]* to run out; *[source]* to dry up; *[personne]* to exhaust o.s., to wear o.s. out, to tire o.s. out *(à faire qch* doing sth); ◆ **les stocks s'étaient épuisés** the stocks had run out ◆ **ses forces s'épuisent peu à peu** his strength is gradually failing ◆ **je m'épuise à vous le répéter** I'm sick and tired of telling you

épuisette /epɥizɛt/ **NF** *(Pêche)* landing net; *(à crevettes)* shrimping net

épurateur /epyʀatœʀ/ **NM** purifier

épuration /epyʀasjɔ̃/ **NF** *[d'eau, huile]* purification; *[de langue, goût, style]* refinement, refining; *(Pol)* purge ◆ **station d'~ des eaux** water purification plant

épure /epyʀ/ **NF** working drawing

épuré, e /epyʀe/ **ADJ** *[style, décor]* uncluttered; *[lignes]* clean ◆ **la forme ~e de la sculpture** the sculpture's clean lines

épurer /epyʀe/ ▸ conjug 1 ◂ **VT** *[+ eau, huile]* to purify; *[+ langue, goût, style]* to refine; *(Pol)* to purge

équanimité /ekwanimite/ **NF** *(frm)* equanimity

équarrir /ekaʀiʀ/ ▸ conjug 2 ◂ **VT** 1 *[+ pierre, tronc]* to square (off) ◆ **poutre mal équarrie** rough-hewn beam 2 *[+ animal]* to cut up

équarrissage /ekaʀisaʒ/ **NM** 1 *[de pierre, tronc]* squaring (off) 2 *[d'animal]* quartering, cutting up ◆ **envoyer un animal à l'~** to send an animal to the abattoir

équarrisseur /ekaʀisœʀ/ **NM** *(gén)* renderer; *[de chevaux]* knacker *(Brit)*

Équateur /ekwatœʀ/ **NM** *(= pays)* ◆ **(la république de l')~** (the Republic of) Ecuador

équateur /ekwatœʀ/ **NM** equator ◆ **sous l'~** at *ou* on the equator

équation /ekwasjɔ̃/ **NF** 1 *(Math)* equation ◆ **~ du premier/second degré** simple/quadratic equation ◆ **mettre en ~** to put in an equation 2 *(fig)* equation ◆ **l'~ politique** the political equation ◆ **~ personnelle** *(Psych)* personal equation

équatorial, e (mpl **-iaux**) /ekwatɔʀjal, jo/ **ADJ** equatorial **NM** *(Astron)* equatorial (telescope)

équatorien, -ienne /ekwatɔʀjɛ̃, jɛn/ **ADJ** Ecuadorian, Ecuadoran **NM,F Équatorien(ne)** Ecuadorian, Ecuadoran

équerre /ekɛʀ/ **NF** *(pour tracer)* (set) square; *(de soutien)* brace ◆ **double ~** T-square ◆ **en ~** at right angles ◆ **ce tableau n'est pas d'~** this picture isn't straight *ou* level

équestre /ekɛstʀ/ **ADJ** *[statue, activités]* equestrian ◆ **centre ~** riding school ◆ **le sport ~** equestrian sport, horse-riding

équeuter /ekøte/ ▸ conjug 1 ◂ **VT** *[+ cerises]* to remove the stalk from, to pull the stalk off; *[+ fraises]* to hull

équi(-) /ekɥi/ **PRÉF** equi(-) ◆ **~ possible** equally possible

équidé /ekide/ **NM** member of the horse family ◆ **les ~s** the Equidae *(SPÉC)*

équidistance /ekɥidistɑ̃s/ **NF** equidistance ◆ **à ~ de Paris et de Dijon** half-way between Paris and Dijon

équidistant, e /ekɥidistɑ̃, ɑt/ **ADJ** equidistant (*de* between)

équilatéral, e (mpl **-aux**) /ekɥilateʀal, o/ **ADJ** *(lit)* equilateral ◆ **ça m'est complètement ~** †‡ I don't give a damn‡

équilibrage /ekilibʀaʒ/ **NM** *[de roues]* balancing

équilibrant, e /ekilibʀɑ̃, ɑ̃t/ **ADJ** stabilizing *(épith)* ◆ **shampooing ~** shampoo which restores the hair's natural balance

équilibre /ekilibʀ/ **NM** 1 *(gén) [de corps, objet]* balance, equilibrium ◆ **perdre/garder l'~** to lose/keep one's balance ◆ **avoir le sens de l'~** to have a (good) sense of balance ◆ **~ stable/instable** stable/unstable equilibrium ◆ **exercice/tour d'~** balancing exercise/act
◆ **en équilibre** ◆ **se tenir** *ou* **être en ~ (sur)** *[personne]* to balance (on); *[objet]* to be balanced (on) ◆ **mettre qch en ~** to balance sth *(sur* on); ◆ **en ~ instable sur le bord du verre** precariously balanced on the edge of the glass
2 *(Psych)* **~ (mental)** (mental) equilibrium, (mental) stability ◆ **il manque d'~** he's rather unstable
3 *(= harmonie) [de couple]* harmony; *[d'activités]* balance, equilibrium ◆ **préserver les grands ~s économiques** to keep the economy on a sound footing
4 *(Écon, Pol)* balance; *[de course aux armements]* parity ◆ **~ budgétaire/économique** balance in the budget/economy ◆ **budget en ~** balanced budget ◆ **atteindre l'~ financier** to break even (financially) ◆ **~ des pouvoirs** balance of power ◆ **~ politique** political balance ◆ **l'~ du monde** the world balance of power ◆ **~ de la terreur** balance of terror
5 *(Sci)* equilibrium ◆ **solution en ~** *(Chim)* balanced solution
6 *(Archit, Mus, Peinture)* balance

équilibré, e /ekilibʀe/ (ptp de **équilibrer**) **ADJ** *[personne]* stable, well-balanced, level-headed; *[régime alimentaire]* (well-)balanced; *[esprit]* well-balanced; *[vie]* well-regulated, regular ◆ **mal ~** unstable, unbalanced

équilibrer /ekilibʀe/ ► conjug 1 ◄ **VT** 1 *(= contrebalancer) [+ forces, poids, poussée]* to counterbalance ◆ **les avantages et les inconvénients s'équilibrent** the advantages and the disadvantages counterbalance each other *ou* cancel each other out 2 *(= mettre en équilibre) [+ balance]* to equilibrate, to balance; *[+ charge, embarcation, avion, roues]* to balance; *(Archit, Art)* to balance 3 *(= harmoniser) [+ emploi du temps, budget, pouvoirs]* to balance ◆ **~ qn** *(fig)* to restore sb's mental equilibrium

équilibriste /ekilibʀist/ **NMF** *(= funambule)* tightrope walker

équille /ekij/ **NF** sand eel

équin, e /ekɛ̃, in/ **ADJ** *(gén)* equine ◆ **pied bot ~** *(Méd)* talipes equinus

équinoxe /ekinɔks/ **NM** equinox ◆ **marée d'~** equinoctial tide ◆ **~ de printemps/d'automne** spring/autumn equinox

équinoxial, e (mpl **-iaux**) /ekinɔksjal, jo/ **ADJ** equinoctial

équipage /ekipaʒ/ **NM** 1 *[d'avion]* (air)crew; *[de bateau]* crew; → **homme, rôle** 2 *(* = attirail)* gear* *(NonC)* 3 † *[de seigneur, chevaux]* equipage † ◆ **~ à deux/à quatre chevaux** carriage and pair/and four ◆ **en grand ~** in state, in grand *ou* great style 4 *(Tech)* equipment *(NonC)*, gear *(NonC)*

équipe /ekip/ **NF** 1 *(Sport)* team; *[de rameurs]* crew ◆ **jeu** *ou* **sport d'~** team game ◆ **jouer en** *ou* **par ~s** to play in teams ◆ **il joue en ~ de France** he plays for the French team; → **esprit** 2 *(= groupe)* team ◆ **~ de chercheurs** research team, team of researchers ◆ **~ de secours** *ou* **de sauveteurs** *ou* **de sauvetage** rescue party *ou* squad *ou* team ◆ **~ pédagogique** teaching staff ◆ **l'~ de jour/de 8 heures** *(dans usine)* the day/8 o'clock shift ◆ **travailler en** *ou* **par ~s** to work in teams; *(sur un chantier)* to work in gangs; *(dans usine)* to work in shifts ◆ **on travaille en ~** we work as a team ◆ **faire ~ avec** to team up with; → **chef**¹ 3 *(* = bande)* team; *(péj)* bunch*, crew* ◆ **c'est la fine ~** they're a right bunch*

équipée /ekipe/ **NF** *[de prisonnier]* escape, flight; *[d'aventurier]* undertaking, venture; *[de promeneur, écolier]* jaunt ◆ **aller là-bas, c'est tout une ~** it's quite a palaver getting there ◆ **la folle ~ des terroristes** the mad dash of the terrorists

équipement /ekipmɑ̃/ **NM** 1 *(= matériel)* equipment ◆ **l'~ complet du skieur** a complete set of skiing equipment 2 *(= aménagement)* **~ électrique** electrical fittings ◆ **~ hôtelier** hotel facilities *ou* amenities ◆ **~ industriel** industrial plant ◆ **~s collectifs** *(Admin)* community facilities *ou* amenities ◆ **prime** *ou* **subvention d'~** equipment grant 3 *(= action)* equipping ◆ **assurer l'~ de qch** to equip sth

équipementier /ekipmɑ̃tje/ **NM** components manufacturer ◆ **~ automobile** car *ou* auto *(US)* parts manufacturer

équiper /ekipe/ ► conjug 1 ◄ **VT** *[+ troupe]* to equip *(de* with); *[+ local]* to equip, to fit out *(de* with); *[+ usine]* to tool up; *[+ ville, pays]* to equip, to provide *(de* with); *[+ sportif]* to equip, to fit out, to kit out *(Brit) (de* with); ◆ **cuisine tout équipée** fully equipped kitchen ◆ **~ une machine d'un dispositif de sécurité** to fit a machine with a safety device **VPR** **s'équiper** *[usine]* to tool up; *[personne]* to equip o.s. *(de, en* with); *[sportif]* to equip o.s., to kit o.s. out *(Brit)*, to get o.s. kitted out *(Brit)* ◆ **l'école s'équipe en micro-ordinateurs** the school is acquiring some computers

équipier, -ière /ekipje, jɛʀ/ **NM,F** *(Sport)* team member; *(= rameur)* crew member; *(dans la restauration rapide)* fast food worker

équiprobable /ekɥipʀɔbabl/ **ADJ** equiprobable

équitable /ekitabl/ **ADJ** *[partage, jugement]* equitable, fair; *[personne]* impartial, fair(-minded)

équitablement /ekitabləmɑ̃/ **ADV** equitably, fairly

équitation /ekitasjɔ̃/ **NF** (horse-)riding, equitation *(frm)* ◆ **faire de l'~** to go horse-riding ◆ **école d'~** riding school

équité /ekite/ **NF** equity ◆ **avec ~** equitably, fairly

équivalence /ekivalɑ̃s/ **NF** *(gén)* equivalence ◆ **diplômes étrangers admis en ~** *(Univ)* recognized foreign diplomas ◆ **demande d'~** *request for an equivalent rating of one's degree* ◆ **j'ai eu ma licence par ~** I obtained my degree by being granted an equivalent rating of my qualifications *ou* by transfer of credits

équivalent, e /ekivalɑ̃, ɑ̃t/ **GRAMMAIRE ACTIVE 32.4** **ADJ** equivalent *(à* to); ◆ **ces solutions sont ~es** these solutions are equivalent ◆ **à prix ~, ce produit est meilleur** for the same *ou* equivalent price this is the better product **NM** *(= chose semblable, mot)* equivalent *(de* of); ◆ **vous ne trouverez l'~ nulle part** you won't find the *ou* its like *ou* equivalent anywhere ◆ **~ pétrole** fuel oil equivalent ◆ **~ clavier** *(Ordin)* keyboard equivalent

équivaloir /ekivalwaʀ/ ► conjug 29 ◄ **VI** *(lit) [quantité]* to be equivalent *(à* to); *[effet]* to be equivalent *(à* to) to amount *(à* to); ◆ **ça équivaut à dire que ...** it amounts to *ou* is equivalent *ou* tantamount to saying that ... **VPR** **s'équivaloir** to be the same ◆ **ça s'équivaut** it amounts to the same thing

équivoque /ekivɔk/ **ADJ** *(= ambigu)* equivocal, ambiguous; *(= louche)* dubious, questionable **NF** *(= ambiguïté)* equivocation, ambiguity; *(= incertitude)* doubt; *(= malentendu)* misunderstanding ◆ **conduite sans ~** unequivocal *ou* unambiguous behaviour ◆ **pour lever l'~** to remove any doubt (on the matter)

érable /eʀabl/ **NM** maple (tree) ◆ **~ du Canada** *ou* **à sucre** silver maple

érablière /eʀablijɛʀ/ **NF** maple grove

éradication /eʀadikasjɔ̃/ **NF** eradication

éradiquer /eʀadike/ ► conjug 1 ◄ **VT** to eradicate

éraflement /eʀɑfləmɑ̃/ **NM** scratching

érafler /eʀɑfle/ ► conjug 1 ◄ **VT** *[+ peau, genou]* to scratch, to graze; *[+ surface]* to scratch, to scrape

éraflure /eʀɑflyʀ/ **NF** *(sur peau)* scratch, graze; *(sur objet)* scratch, scrape (mark)

éraillé, e /eʀɑje/ (ptp de **érailler**) **ADJ** *[voix]* rasping, hoarse, croaking *(épith)*

éraillement /eʀɑjmɑ̃/ **NM** *[de voix]* hoarseness

érailler /eʀɑje/ ► conjug 1 ◄ **VT** *[+ voix]* to make hoarse; *(= rayer) [+ surface]* to scratch ◆ **s'~ la voix** to ruin one's voice

Érasme /eʀasm/ **NM** ◆ **~ (de Rotterdam)** Erasmus

erbium /ɛʀbjɔm/ **NM** erbium

ère /ɛʀ/ **NF** era ◆ **400 avant notre ~** 400 BC ◆ **en l'an 1600 de notre ~** in the year of our Lord 1600, in the year 1600 AD ◆ **l'~ chrétienne** the Christian era ◆ **~ secondaire/tertiaire** secondary/tertiary era ◆ **les ~s géologiques** the geological eras ◆ **une ~ nouvelle commence** it's the beginning *ou* dawn of a new era ◆ **l'~ Mitterrand/Thatcher** the Mitterrand/Thatcher era ◆ **l'~ atomique/glaciaire/spatiale** the atomic/ice/space age

érectile /eʀɛktil/ **ADJ** erectile

érection /eʀɛksjɔ̃/ **NF** 1 *[de monument]* erection, raising; *(fig)* establishment, setting-up 2 *(Physiol)* erection ◆ **avoir une ~** to have an erection

éreintant, e /eʀɛ̃tɑ̃, ɑ̃t/ **ADJ** *[travail]* exhausting, backbreaking

éreintement /eʀɛ̃tmɑ̃/ **NM** *(= épuisement)* exhaustion; *(= critique)* savage attack *(de* on) panning*, slating* *(Brit)*

éreinter /eʀɛ̃te/ ► conjug 1 ◄ **VT** 1 *(= épuiser) [+ animal]* to exhaust; * *[+ personne]* to shatter*, to wear out ◆ **être éreinté** to be shattered* *ou* all in* *ou* worn out ◆ **s'~ à faire qch** to wear o.s. out doing sth 2 *(= critiquer) [+ auteur, œuvre]* to pull to pieces, to pan*, to slate* *(Brit)*

érémiste /'eʀemist/ **NMF** *person receiving welfare payment*, ≃ person on income support *(Brit)*, person on welfare *(US)*

Erevan /əʀəvɑ̃/ **N** Yerevan

erg /ɛʀg/ **NM** *(Géog, Phys)* erg

ergatif, -ive /ɛʀgatif, iv/ **ADJ, NM** *(Gram)* ergative

ergol /ɛʀgɔl/ **NM** propellant

ergonome /ɛʀgɔnɔm/ **NMF** ergonomist

ergonomie /ɛʀgɔnɔmi/ **NF** ergonomics *(sg)*

ergonomique /ɛʀgɔnɔmik/ **ADJ** ergonomic(al)

ergonomiste /ɛʀgɔnɔmist/ **NMF** ergonomist

ergot /ɛʀgo/ **NM** 1 *[de coq]* spur; *[de chien]* dewclaw ◆ **monter** *ou* **se dresser sur ses ~s** *(fig)* to get one's hackles up 2 *[de blé]* ergot 3 *(Tech)* lug

ergotage /ɛʀgɔtaʒ/ **NM** quibbling *(NonC)*, cavilling *(NonC)*, petty argument

ergoter /ɛʀgɔte/ ► conjug 1 ◄ **VI** to quibble *(sur* about) to cavil *(sur* at)

ergoteur, -euse /ɛʀgɔtœʀ, øz/ **NM,F** quibbler, hairsplitter

ergothérapeute /ɛʀgoteʀapøt/ **NMF** occupational therapist

ergothérapie /ɛʀgoteʀapi/ **NF** occupational therapy

Érié /eʀje/ **N** ◆ **le lac ~** Lake Erie

ériger /eʀiʒe/ ► conjug 3 ◄ VT (*frm*) [*+ monument, bâtiment*] to erect; [*+ société*] to set up, to establish ◆ ~ **le dogmatisme en vertu** to make a virtue of dogmatism ◆ ~ **un criminel en héros** to set a criminal up as a hero ◆ **il s'érige en maître/juge** he sets himself up as a master/ judge

ermitage /ɛʀmitaʒ/ NM (*d'ermite*) hermitage; (*fig*) retreat

ermite /ɛʀmit/ NM hermit

éroder /eʀɔde/ ► conjug 1 ◄ VT to erode

érogène /eʀɔʒɛn/ ADJ erogenous

Éros /eʀos/ NM (*Myth*) Eros ◆ **l'éros** (*Psych*) Eros

érosif, -ive /eʀozif, iv/ ADJ erosive

érosion /eʀozjɔ̃/ NF (*lit, fig*) erosion ◆ ~ **monétaire** (monetary) depreciation

érotique /eʀɔtik/ ADJ erotic

érotiquement /eʀɔtikmɑ̃/ ADV erotically

érotisation /eʀɔtizasjɔ̃/ NF eroticization

érotiser /eʀɔtize/ ► conjug 1 ◄ VT to eroticize

érotisme /eʀɔtism/ NM eroticism

érotomane /eʀɔtɔman/ NMF erotomaniac

errance /eʀɑ̃s/ NF (*littér*) wandering, roaming

errant, e /eʀɑ̃, ɑ̃t/ ADJ (*gén*) wandering ◆ **chien** ~ stray dog; → **chevalier, juif**

errata /eʀata/ NM PL errata

erratique /eʀatik/ ADJ (*Géol, Méd*) erratic

erratum /eʀatɔm/ (pl **errata**) /eʀata/ NM erratum

erre /ɛʀ/ NF [1] (*Naut*) headway (*made after the engines have stopped*) ◆ **se laisser glisser sur son** ~, **courir sur son** ~ (*fig*) to drift along [2] (*Vénerie*) ~**s** tracks

errements /ɛʀmɑ̃/ NMPL (*littér*) erring ways, bad habits

errer /eʀe/ ► conjug 1 ◄ VI (*littér*) [1] [*voyageur*] to wander, to roam; [*regard*] to rove, to roam, to wander (*sur* over); [*pensée*] to wander, to stray ◆ **un sourire errait sur ses lèvres** a smile played on his lips [2] (*= se tromper*) to err

erreur /eʀœʀ/ GRAMMAIRE ACTIVE 45.2, 45.4 NF [1] (*gén*) mistake, error; (*Stat*) error ◆ ~ **matérielle** technical error ◆ ~ **d'écriture** clerical error ◆ ~ **de calcul** mistake in calculation, miscalculation ◆ **faire une** ~ **de date** to make a mistake in *ou* be mistaken about the date ◆ ~ **d'impression**, ~ **typographique** misprint, typographical error ◆ ~ **de sens** wrong meaning ◆ ~ **de traduction** mistranslation ◆ ~ **(de) tactique** tactical error ◆ ~ **de jugement** error of judgment ◆ ~ **système** (*Ordin*) system error [2] (*locutions*) **par suite d'une** ~ due to an error *ou* a mistake ◆ **sauf** ~ unless I'm (very much) mistaken ◆ **sauf** ~ **ou omission** errors and omissions excepted ◆ **par** ~ by mistake ◆ **cherchez l'~ !** (*hum*) spot the deliberate mistake! ◆ ~ **profonde !, grave** ~ **!** not at all!, absolutely not! ◆ **commettre** *ou* **faire une** ~, **tomber dans l'~** to make a mistake *ou* an error (*sur* about); ◆ **faire** ~, **être dans l'~** to be wrong *ou* mistaken ◆ **vous faites** ~ (*Téléc*) you've got the wrong number ◆ **il y a** ~ there's been a mistake *ou* there's some mistake ◆ **il n'y a pas d'~ (possible)** there's no mistake! ◆ **ce serait une** ~ **de croire que ...** it would be a mistake *ou* be wrong to think that ..., you would be mistaken in thinking that ... ◆ **il n'a pas droit à l'~** he's got to get it right ◆ **l'~ est humaine** to err is human ◆ **il y a** ~ **sur la personne** you've *etc* got the wrong person ◆ **cherchez l'~ !** (*hum*) spot the deliberate mistake! [3] (*= dérèglements*) ~**s** errors, lapses ◆ ~**s de jeunesse** youthful indiscretions ◆ **retomber dans les** ~**s du passé** to lapse (back) into bad habits [4] (*Jur*) ~ **judiciaire** miscarriage of justice

erroné, e /eʀɔne/ ADJ erroneous

ersatz /ɛʀzats/ NM (*lit, fig*) ersatz, substitute ◆ ~ **de café** ersatz coffee

erse[1] /ɛʀs/ NM, ADJ (*= langue*) Erse

erse[2] /ɛʀs/ NF (*= anneau*) grommet

éructation /eʀyktasjɔ̃/ NF (*frm*) eructation (*frm*)

éructer /eʀykte/ ► conjug 1 ◄ VI (*frm*) to eructate (*frm*)

érudit, e /eʀydi, it/ ADJ erudite, learned, scholarly NM,F erudite *ou* learned person, scholar

érudition /eʀydisjɔ̃/ NF erudition, scholarship

éruptif, -ive /eʀyptif, iv/ ADJ eruptive

éruption /eʀypsjɔ̃/ NF [1] (*Géol*) eruption ◆ ~ **(solaire)** solar flare ◆ **volcan en** ~ erupting volcano ◆ **entrer en** ~ to erupt [2] (*Méd*) ~ **de boutons** outbreak of spots ◆ ~ **cutanée** (skin) rash [3] (*= manifestation*) ~ **de violence** outbreak *ou* outburst of violence

érysipèle /eʀizipɛl/ NM erysipelas

érythème /eʀitɛm/ NM rash ◆ ~ **fessier** nappy (*Brit*) *ou* diaper (*US*) rash ◆ ~ **solaire** sunburn

Érythrée /eʀitʀe/ NF Eritrea

érythrocyte /eʀitʀɔsit/ NM erythrocyte

érythromycine /eʀitʀɔmisin/ NF erythromycin

ès /ɛs/ PRÉP ◆ **licencié** ~ **lettres/sciences** ≈ Bachelor of Arts/Science ◆ **docteur** ~ **lettres** ≈ PhD ◆ ~ **qualités** [*agir, être invité*] in one's official capacity ◆ **membre** ~ **qualités** ex officio member

Ésaü /ezay/ NM Esau

esbigner (s')‡ † /ɛsbiɲe/ ► conjug 1 ◄ VPR to skedaddle*, to clear off*

esbroufe* /ɛsbʀuf/ NF ◆ **faire de l'~** to show off ◆ **il essaie de nous la faire à l'~** he's shooting us a line‡, he's bluffing

esbroufeur, -euse* /ɛsbʀufœʀ, øz/ NM,F big talker*

escabeau (pl **escabeaux**) /ɛskabo/ NM (*= tabouret*) (wooden) stool; (*= échelle*) stepladder, pair of steps (*Brit*) ◆ **tu me prêtes ton** ~ **?** can I borrow your stepladder? *ou* your steps (*Brit*)?

escadre /ɛskadʀ/ NF (*Naut*) squadron ◆ ~ **(aérienne)** wing

escadrille /ɛskadʀij/ NF flight, ≈ squadron ◆ ~ **de chasse** fighter squadron

escadron /ɛskadʀɔ̃/ NM (*Mil*) squadron; (*= bande*) bunch*, crowd ◆ ~ **de gendarmerie** platoon of gendarmes ◆ ~ **de la mort** death squad

escagasser* /ɛskagase/ ► conjug 1 ◄ VT (*terme du Midi*) (*= assommer*) to knock senseless, to stun; (*= ennuyer, agacer*) to bore to death* ◆ **ils l'ont escagassé d'un grand coup sur la tête** they landed him a blow to the head that knocked him senseless ◆ **tu m'escagasses avec tes questions** you're being a real pain* with your questions

escalade /ɛskalad/ NF [1] (*= action*) [*de montagne, rocher*] climbing; [*de mur*] climbing, scaling; (*Hist*) [*de forteresse*] scaling ◆ **partir faire l'~ d'une montagne** to set off to climb a mountain [2] (*Sport*) **l'~** (rock) climbing ◆ ~ **libre** free climbing ◆ ~ **artificielle** aid *ou* peg *ou* artificial climbing ◆ **une belle** ~ a beautiful climb ◆ **faire de l'~** to go (rock) climbing [3] (*= aggravation*) escalation ◆ **on craint une** ~ **de la violence en France** an escalation of violence is feared in France ◆ **pour éviter l'~** to stop things getting out of control

escalader /ɛskalade/ ► conjug 1 ◄ VT [*+ montagne, rocher*] to climb; [*+ mur*] to climb, to scale; (*Hist*) [*+ forteresse*] to scale

escalator /ɛskalatɔʀ/ NM escalator

escale /ɛskal/ NF [1] (*= endroit*) (*en bateau*) port of call; (*en avion*) stop ◆ **faire** ~ **à** (*en bateau*) to call at, to put in at; (*en avion*) to stop over at [2] (*= temps d'arrêt*) (*en bateau*) call; (*en avion*) stop(over); (*brève*) touchdown ◆ **vol sans** ~ nonstop flight ◆ **faire une** ~ **à Marseille** (*en bateau*) to put in at Marseilles; (*en avion*) to stop (over) at Marseilles ◆ ~ **technique** (*en avion*) refuelling stop

escalier /ɛskalje/ NM (*= marches*) stairs; (*à l'extérieur*) stairs, steps; (*= cage*) staircase, stairway ◆ **assis dans l'~** sitting on the stairs ◆ **grand** ~ main staircase ◆ ~ **en colimaçon** spiral staircase ◆ **montée en** ~ (*Ski*) side-stepping (*NonC*) ◆ **il m'a fait des** ~**s dans les cheveux*** he's cut my hair all unevenly; → **esprit**

COMP **escalier d'honneur** grand staircase

escalier mécanique *ou* **roulant** escalator

escalier de secours fire escape

escalier de service [*de maison*] backstairs, servants' stairs; [*d'hôtel*] service stairs

escalope /ɛskalɔp/ NF escalope ◆ ~ **cordon-bleu** *breaded veal escalope or turkey breast stuffed with ham and cheese*

escaloper /ɛskalɔpe/ ► conjug 1 ◄ VT [*+ volaille, poisson*] to cut into escalopes

escamotable /ɛskamɔtabl/ ADJ [*train d'atterrissage, antenne*] retractable; [*lit, siège*] collapsible, foldaway (*épith*); [*escalier*] foldaway (*épith*)

escamotage /ɛskamɔtaʒ/ NM [1] [*de cartes*] conjuring away [2] [*de difficulté*] evading, getting *ou* skirting round; [*de question*] dodging, evading; [*de mot*] skipping [3] * [*de portefeuille*] filching*, pinching* [4] [*de train d'atterrissage*] retraction

escamoter /ɛskamɔte/ ► conjug 1 ◄ VT [1] (*= faire disparaître*) [*+ cartes etc*] to conjure away [2] [*+ difficulté*] to evade, to get round, to skirt round; [*+ question*] to dodge, to evade; [*+ mot, repas*] to skip [3] (* *= voler*) [*+ portefeuille*] to filch*, to pinch* [4] [*+ train d'atterrissage*] to retract

escamoteur, -euse † /ɛskamɔtœʀ, øz/ NM,F (*= prestidigitateur*) conjurer

escampette* /ɛskɑ̃pɛt/ NF → **poudre**

escapade /ɛskapad/ NF ◆ **faire une** ~ [*d'écolier*] to run away *ou* off, to do a bunk‡ (*Brit*) ◆ **on a fait une petite** ~ **ce week-end** we went for a little trip this weekend ◆ ~ **de trois jours** (*Tourisme*) three-day break

escarbille /ɛskaʀbij/ NF bit of grit

escarboucle /ɛskaʀbukl/ NF (*= pierre*) carbuncle

escarcelle /ɛskaʀsɛl/ NF (†† *= portefeuille*) moneybag ◆ **tomber dans l'~ de qn** (*hum*) [*argent, prime*] to wind up in sb's pocket; [*entreprise*] to get caught in sb's net

escargot /ɛskaʀgo/ NM (*Zool*) snail; (* *= lambin*) slowcoach* (*Brit*), slowpoke* (*US*) ◆ **avancer comme un** ~ *ou* **à une allure d'~** to go at a snail's pace ◆ ~ **de mer** whelk ◆ **opération** ~ (*= manifestation*) go-slow (*Brit*), slow-down (*US*)

escargotière /ɛskaʀgɔtjɛʀ/ NF (*= parc*) snail farm; (*= plat*) snail-dish

escarmouche /ɛskaʀmuʃ/ NF (*lit, fig*) skirmish

escarpé, e /ɛskaʀpe/ ADJ steep

escarpement /ɛskaʀpəmɑ̃/ NM (*= côte*) steep slope, escarpment (SPÉC); (*= raideur*) steepness ◆ ~ **de faille** (*Géol*) fault scarp

escarpin /ɛskaʀpɛ̃/ NM low-fronted shoe, court shoe (*Brit*), pump (*US*)

escarpolette † /ɛskaʀpɔlɛt/ NF (= *balançoire*) swing; (*Alpinisme*) etrier (*Brit*), stirrup (*US*)

escarre /ɛskaʀ/ NF bedsore, decubitus ulcer (*SPÉC*)

Escaut /ɛsko/ NM ◆ **l'~** the Scheldt

eschatologie /ɛskatɔlɔʒi/ NF eschatology

Eschyle /eʃil/ NM Aeschylus

escient /ɛsjɑ̃/ NM ◆ **à bon ~** advisedly ◆ **à mauvais ~** ill-advisedly ◆ **utiliser qch à bon ~** to use sth wisely ◆ **les statistiques peuvent être utilisées à mauvais ~** statistics can be misused

esclaffer (s') /ɛsklafe/ ▸ conjug 1 ◂ VPR to burst out laughing, to guffaw

esclandre /ɛsklɑ̃dʀ/ NM (= *scandale*) scene; (*public*) scandal ◆ **faire** *ou* **causer un ~** (*scandale*) to make a scene; (*public*) to cause *ou* create a scandal

esclavage /ɛsklavaʒ/ NM slavery, bondage (*littér*) ◆ **réduire en ~** to enslave ◆ **tomber en ~** to become enslaved ◆ **c'est de l'~ !** (*fig*) it's sheer slavery!

esclavagisme /ɛsklavaʒism/ NM proslavery

esclavagiste /ɛsklavaʒist/ ADJ proslavery (*épith*) ◆ **États ~s** slave states NMF person in favour of slavery; (*fig*) slave driver

esclave /ɛsklav/ NMF slave (*de qn/qch* to sb/sth); ◆ **vie d'~** slave's life, life of slavery ◆ **être ~ de la mode/d'une habitude** to be a slave of fashion/to habit ◆ **devenir l'~ de qn** to become enslaved to sb ◆ **se rendre ~ de qch** to become a slave to sth

escogriffe /ɛskɔgʀif/ NM ◆ **(grand) ~** (great) beanpole*, string bean* (*US*)

escomptable /ɛskɔ̃tabl/ ADJ (*Banque*) discountable

escompte /ɛskɔ̃t/ NM (*Banque*) discount ◆ **présenter à l'~** to tender *ou* remit for discount

escompter /ɛskɔ̃te/ ▸ conjug 1 ◂ VT (*Banque*) to discount; (*fig*) to expect ◆ **~ faire qch** to expect to do sth, to reckon *ou* count on doing sth

escompteur /ɛskɔ̃tœʀ/ NM discounter

escopette † /ɛskɔpɛt/ NF blunderbuss

escorte /ɛskɔʀt/ NF (*gén, Mil, Naut*) escort; (= *suite*) escort, retinue ◆ **(toute) une ~ de** (*fig*) a whole train *ou* suite of ◆ **sous bonne ~** under escort ◆ **faire ~ à** to escort

escorter /ɛskɔʀte/ ▸ conjug 1 ◂ VT to escort ◆ **il est toujours escorté de jolies femmes** he's always surrounded by pretty women

escorteur /ɛskɔʀtœʀ/ NM ◆ **(navire) ~** escort (ship)

escouade /ɛskwad/ NF (*Mil*) squad; [*d'ouvriers*] gang, squad; (= *groupe de gens*) group, squad

escrime /ɛskʀim/ NF fencing ◆ **faire de l'~** to fence

escrimer (s') * /ɛskʀime/ ▸ conjug 1 ◂ VPR ◆ **s'~ à faire qch** to wear *ou* knock* o.s. out doing sth ◆ **s'~ sur qch** to struggle away at sth

escrimeur, -euse /ɛskʀimœʀ, øz/ NM,F (*Sport*) fencer

escroc /ɛskʀo/ NM crook, swindler, con man*

escroquer /ɛskʀɔke/ ▸ conjug 1 ◂ VT to swindle, to con* ◆ **~ qn de qch** to swindle sb out of sth, to swindle *ou* con* sth out of sb ◆ **se faire ~ par qn** to be swindled *ou* conned* by sb

escroquerie /ɛskʀɔkʀi/ NF (*gén*) swindle, swindling (*NonC*); (*Jur*) fraud ◆ **être victime d'une ~** (*gén*) to be swindled; (*Jur*) to be a victim of fraud ◆ **8 € pour un café, c'est de l'~** €8 for a coffee, that's a rip-off* *ou* that's daylight (*Brit*) *ou* highway (*US*) robbery ◆ **~ intellectuelle** intellectual fraud

escudo /ɛskydo/ NM escudo

Esculape /ɛskylap/ NM Aesculapius

esgourde †* /ɛsguʀd/ NF ear, lug* (*Brit*) ◆ **ouvre bien tes ~s** pin back your lugholes* (*Brit*), listen up

Ésope /ezɔp/ NM Aesop

ésotérique /ezɔteʀik/ ADJ esoteric

ésotérisme /ezɔteʀism/ NM esotericism

espace[1] /ɛspas/ NM 1 (*gén*) space ◆ **~-temps** space-time ◆ **~ disque** (*Ordin*) disk space ◆ **c'est un bel ~** (*musée, salle*) it's a beautiful space ◆ **l'~ public/urbain** public/urban space ◆ **l'~ publicitaire** advertising space ◆ **la musique est pour moi un ~ de liberté** music is an area in which I can express myself freely

2 (= *zone géographique*) area ◆ **l'~ monétaire européen** the European monetary area, Euroland ◆ **l'~ francophone** French-speaking countries

3 (= *place*) space, room ◆ **avoir assez d'~ pour bouger/vivre** to have enough room to move/live ◆ **manquer d'~** to lack space, to be short of space *ou* room

4 (= *intervalle*) space ◆ **~ de temps** space of time ◆ **~ parcouru** distance covered, interval (of time) ◆ **laisser de l'~** to leave some space ◆ **laisser un ~** to leave a space *ou* gap (*entre* between)

◆ **en l'espace de** ◆ **en l'~ de trois minutes** within (the space of) three minutes ◆ **en l'~ d'un instant** in no time at all

COMP **l'espace aérien** air space

l'Espace économique européen the European Economic Area

l'espace Schengen the Schengen area

espaces verts parks

espace vital (*Hist*) lebensraum; (*fig*) personal space

espace[2] /ɛspas/ NF (*Typo*) (= *tige*) quad; (= *blanc*) space

espacé, e /ɛspase/ (ptp de **espacer**) ADJ [*arbres, objets*] spaced (out) ◆ **elle a mis des bibelots sur l'étagère, bien ~s** she placed ornaments on the shelves, setting them neatly apart ◆ **des crises assez régulièrement ~es** attacks occurring at fairly regular intervals ◆ **ses visites sont très ~es ces temps-ci** his visits are few and far between these days ◆ **réunions ~es de huit à dix jours** meetings taking place every eight to ten days

espacement /ɛspasmɑ̃/ NM (= *action*) spacing out; (= *résultat*) spacing ◆ **devant l'~ de ses visites** in view of the growing infrequency of his visits

espacer /ɛspase/ ▸ conjug 3 ◂ VT [+ *objets*] to space out; [+ *visites*] to space out, to make less frequent VPR **s'espacer** [*visites, symptômes*] to become less frequent

espadon /ɛspadɔ̃/ NM swordfish

espadrille /ɛspadʀij/ NF espadrille

Espagne /ɛspaɲ/ NF Spain; → **château, grand**

espagnol, e /ɛspaɲɔl/ ADJ Spanish NM 1 (= *langue*) Spanish 2 ◆ **Espagnol** Spanish man, Spaniard ◆ **les Espagnols** the Spanish, the Spaniards NF **Espagnole** Spanish woman, Spaniard

espagnolette /ɛspaɲɔlɛt/ NF (window) catch ◆ **fenêtre fermée à l'~** window resting on the catch

espalier /ɛspalje/ NM (*Agr*) espalier; (*Sport*) wall bars ◆ **arbre en ~** espaliered tree

espar /ɛspaʀ/ NM (*Naut*) spar

espèce /ɛspɛs/ NF 1 (*Bio*) species ◆ **~s** species ◆ **~ humaine** human race ◆ **~ animale/végétale** animal/plant species; → **propagation**

2 (= *sorte*) sort, kind, type ◆ **de toute ~** of all kinds *ou* sorts *ou* types ◆ **ça n'a aucune ~ d'importance** that is of absolutely no importance *ou* not of the slightest importance ◆ **c'est une ~ de boîte** it's a kind *ou* sort of box ◆ **un voyou de la pire ~** a hoodlum of the worst kind *ou* sort; → **cas**

3 (*, *péj*) **une** *ou* **un ~ d'excentrique est venu** some eccentric turned up ◆ **qu'est-ce que c'est que cette** *ou* **cet ~ de crétin ?** who's this stupid twit?* *ou* idiot? ◆ **~ de maladroit !** you clumsy oaf!* *ou* clot!* (*Brit*)

4 (*Fin*) **~s** cash ◆ **versement en ~s** payment in cash *ou* in specie (*SPÉC*) ◆ **en ~s sonnantes et trébuchantes** († , *hum*) in coin of the realm (*hum*)

5 (*Philos, Rel*) species ◆ **les Saintes Espèces** the Eucharistic *ou* sacred species; → **communier**

6 (*locutions*)

◆ **en l'espèce** in the case in point

◆ **sous les espèces de** in the form of

espérance /ɛspeʀɑ̃s/ NF 1 (= *espoir*) hope (*de* for) expectation(s) ◆ **l'~** (*Rel, gén*) hope ◆ **au delà de toute ~** beyond all expectations ◆ **ça a dépassé toutes nos ~s** it was far more than we'd hoped for ◆ **contre toute ~** against all expectations *ou* hope, contrary to expectation(s) ◆ **avoir** *ou* **nourrir de grandes ~s** to have *ou* cherish great hopes ◆ **bâtir** *ou* **fonder des ~s sur** to build *ou* base one's hopes on ◆ **mettre son ~** *ou* **ses ~s en** *ou* **dans** to pin one's hopes on 2 (= *sujet d'espoir*) hope ◆ **c'est là toute mon ~** that is my greatest hope, it's what I hope for most 3 (*Sociol*) **~ de vie** life expectancy

espérantiste /ɛspeʀɑ̃tist/ ADJ, NMF Esperantist

espéranto /ɛspeʀɑ̃to/ NM Esperanto

espérer /ɛspeʀe/ GRAMMAIRE ACTIVE 31, 35.2 ▸ conjug 6 ◂

VT (= *souhaiter*) [+ *succès, récompense, aide*] to hope for ◆ **~ réussir** to hope to succeed ◆ **~ que** to hope that ◆ **nous ne vous espérions plus** we'd given up (all) hope of seeing you, we'd given up on you ◆ **je n'en espérais pas tant** I wasn't hoping *ou* I hadn't dared to hope for as much ◆ **viendra-t-il ? – je l'espère (bien)** *ou* **j'espère (bien)** will he come? – I (certainly) hope so ◆ **ceci (nous) laisse** *ou* **fait ~ un succès rapide** this gives us hope *ou* makes us hopeful of quick success ◆ **n'espérez pas qu'il change d'avis** there is no point in hoping he'll change his mind ◆ **j'espère bien n'avoir rien oublié** I hope I haven't forgotten anything

VI (= *avoir confiance*) to have faith ◆ **il faut ~** you must have faith ◆ **~ en** [+ *Dieu, honnêteté de qn, bienfaiteur*] to have faith in, to trust in

esperluette /ɛspɛʀlɥɛt/ NF ampersand

espiègle /ɛspjɛgl/ ADJ [*enfant*] mischievous, impish; [*air*] roguish, mischievous NMF imp, monkey*

espièglerie /ɛspjɛgləʀi/ NF 1 (= *caractère*) [*d'enfant*] mischievousness, impishness; [*d'air*] roguishness, mischievousness 2 (= *tour*) piece of mischief, prank

espion, -ionne /ɛspjɔ̃, jɔn/ NM,F spy

espionite /ɛspjɔnit/ NF spy mania

espionnage /ɛspjɔnaʒ/ NM espionage, spying ◆ **film/roman d'~** spy film/novel *ou* thriller ◆ **~ industriel** industrial espionage

espionner /ɛspjɔne/ ▸ conjug 1 ◂ VT [+ *personne, actions*] to spy ◆ **~ pour le compte de qn** to spy for sb

espionnite /ɛspjɔnit/ NF ⇒ **espionite**

esplanade /ɛsplanad/ NF esplanade

espoir /ɛspwaʀ/ NM 1 (= *espérance*) hope ◆ **~s chimériques** wild hopes ◆ **dans l'~ de vous voir bientôt** hoping to see you soon, in the hope of seeing you soon ◆ **avoir l'~/le ferme ~ que** to be hopeful/very hopeful that ◆ **il n'y a plus d'~** all hope is lost *ou* there's no longer any hope ◆ **avoir bon ~ de faire/que** to have great hopes of doing/that, to be confident of doing/that ◆ **reprendre** ~ to (begin to) feel hopeful again, to take heart once more ◆ **sans** ~ *[amour, situation]* hopeless ◆ **aimer sans** ~ to love without hope ◆ **l'~ fait vivre** *(gén)* hope keeps us going; *(hum)* there's always hope ◆ **tous les ~s sont permis** there's no limit to what we can hope for; → **lueur, rayon**

2 *(= personne)* hope ◆ **vous êtes mon dernier** ~ you are my last hope ◆ **les jeunes ~s du ski/de la chanson** the young hopefuls of the skiing/singing world ◆ **un des grands ~s de la boxe française** one of the great hopes in French boxing, one of France's great boxing hopes

esprit /ɛspʀi/ NM 1 *(gén, = pensée)* mind ◆ **l'~ humain** the mind of man, the human mind *ou* intellect ◆ **se reporter en** ~ *ou* **par l'~ à** to cast one's mind back to ◆ **avoir l'~ large/étroit** to be broad-/narrow-minded ◆ **avoir l'~ vif/lent** to be quick-/slow-witted ◆ **vivacité/lenteur d'~** quickness/slowness of wit *ou* mind ◆ **avoir l'~ clair** to have a clear head *ou* mind ◆ **avoir l'~ mal tourné** to have a dirty mind, to have that sort of mind *(Brit)* ◆ **il a l'~ ailleurs** his mind is elsewhere *ou* on other things ◆ **où ai-je l'~ ?** what am I thinking of? ◆ **j'ai l'~ plus libre maintenant** my mind is freer now ◆ **il n'a pas l'~ à ce qu'il fait** his mind is not on what he's doing ◆ **je n'ai pas l'~ à rire** I'm not in the mood for laughing ◆ **dans mon ~ ça voulait dire ...** to my mind it meant ... ◆ **l'~ est fort** *ou* **prompt, mais la chair est faible** *(hum)* the spirit is willing but the flesh is weak ◆ **il m'est venu à l'~ que ...** it crossed my mind that ..., it occurred to me that ... ◆ **un ~ sain dans un corps sain** *(Prov)* a healthy *ou* sound mind in a healthy body; → **aventure, disposition, état, faible**

2 *(= humour)* wit ◆ **avoir de l'~** to be witty ◆ **faire de l'~** to try to be witty *ou* funny ◆ **manquer d'~** to lack sparkle *ou* wit; → **femme, mot, trait**

3 *(= être humain)* **son pouvoir sur les ~s/jeunes ~s** his power over people's minds/young minds ◆ **il joue les ~s forts** he claims to be a rational man ◆ **c'est un ~ subtil** he is a shrewd man, he has a shrewd mind ◆ **un des plus grands ~s du siècle** one of the greatest minds of the century ◆ **bel ~** wit ◆ **faire le bel ~** to show off one's wit ◆ **les grands** *ou* **beaux ~s se rencontrent** great minds think alike

4 *(Rel, Spiritisme)* spirit ◆ **~, es-tu là ?** is (there) anybody there? ◆ **je ne suis pas un pur ~** I'm flesh and blood (and I have to eat)

5 *[de loi, époque, texte]* spirit

6 *(= aptitude)* **avoir l'~ mathématique/d'analyse/d'entreprise** to have a mathematical/an analytical/an enterprising mind ◆ **avoir l'~ critique** to be critical, to have a critical mind ◆ **avoir l'~ de critique** to like criticizing for its own sake ◆ **avoir l'~ de synthèse** to have a global approach ◆ **avoir le bon ~ de** to have enough sense to, to have the (good) sense to

7 *(= attitude)* spirit ◆ **l'~ de cette classe** *ou* **qui règne dans cette classe** the (general) attitude of this class ◆ **~ de révolte/sacrifice** spirit of rebellion/sacrifice ◆ **dans un ~ de conciliation** in a spirit of conciliation ◆ **comprenez l'~ dans lequel je le dis** you must understand the spirit in which I say it ◆ **avoir mauvais ~** to be negative about things ◆ **faire du mauvais ~** to make snide remarks

8 *(Ling)* ~ **doux/rude** smooth/rough breathing

COMP **esprit de caste** class consciousness
esprits chagrins *(péj)* fault-finders ◆ **il y aura toujours des ~s chagrins pour critiquer** there'll always be miserable people who'll find fault
esprit de chapelle cliquishness
esprit de clan clannishness
esprit de clocher parochialism ◆ **avoir l'~ de clocher** to have a small-town mentality
esprit de compétition competitive spirit
esprit de contradiction argumentativeness ◆ **il a l'~ de contradiction** he likes to contradict people just for the sake of it
esprit de corps esprit de corps
esprit d'équipe team spirit
esprit d'escalier ◆ **tu as l'~ d'escalier** you never think of an answer until it's too late
esprit de famille family feeling; *(péj)* clannishness
esprit frappeur poltergeist
esprit malin *ou* **du mal** evil spirit
l'Esprit saint *(Rel)* the Holy Spirit *ou* Ghost
esprit de suite consistency *(of thought)*
esprit de système methodical *ou* systematic mind; → **conquête, initiative, ouverture**

esprit-de-bois /ɛspʀidbwa/ NM wood alcohol

esprit-de-sel /ɛspʀidsɛl/ NM spirits of salt

esprit-de-vin /ɛspʀidvɛ̃/ NM spirits of wine

esquif /ɛskif/ NM *(littér)* boat ◆ **frêle** ~ frail barque *(littér)*

esquille /ɛskij/ NF splinter (of bone)

esquimau, -aude (mpl **esquimaux**) /ɛskimo, od/ ADJ Eskimo ◆ **chien** ~ husky NM 1 *(= langue)* Eskimo 2 *(® = glace)* choc-ice *(Brit)*, ice-cream bar *(US)* NM,F **Esquimau(de)** Eskimo

esquintant, e* /ɛskɛ̃tɑ̃, ɑ̃t/ ADJ exhausting

esquinter* /ɛskɛ̃te/ ▸ conjug 1 ◂ VT 1 *(= abîmer) [+ objet]* to mess up*; *[+ yeux]* to do in*, to ruin; *[+ santé]* to ruin; *[+ adversaire]* to beat up, to bash up*; *[+ voiture]* to smash up ◆ **se faire ~ par une voiture** *[automobiliste]* to have *ou* get one's car bashed* *ou* smashed into by another; *[cycliste, piéton]* to get badly bashed up* by a car ◆ **aile esquintée** *[de voiture]* damaged *ou* dented wing ◆ **vieux râteau tout esquinté** battered old rake

2 *(= critiquer) [+ film, livre]* to pull to pieces, to pan*, to slate* *(Brit)*

VPR **s'esquinter** *(= se fatiguer)* to tire *ou* knock* o.s. out; *(= se blesser)* to hurt o.s. ◆ **s'~ le bras** to hurt one's arm ◆ **s'~ à travailler** to work o.s. to death, to work o.s. into the ground ◆ **s'~ à étudier** to wear o.s. out studying, to work o.s. into the ground studying ◆ **s'~ les yeux (à lire)** to strain one's eyes (reading)

esquisse /ɛskis/ NF *(Peinture)* sketch; *[de projet]* outline, sketch; *[de geste, sourire]* beginnings, suggestion

esquisser /ɛskise/ ▸ conjug 1 ◂ VT *(Peinture)* to sketch (out); *[+ projet]* to outline, to sketch ◆ ~ **un geste** to make a slight *ou* vague gesture, to half-make a gesture ◆ ~ **un pas de danse** to have a quick dance ◆ **un sourire à peine esquissé** the ghost of a smile, the faintest of smiles ◆ **un certain progrès commence à s'~** one can begin to detect some progress

esquive /ɛskiv/ NF *(Boxe)* dodge; *(en politique)* evasion, sidestepping *(NonC)* ◆ **il est passé maître dans l'art de l'~** he's a past master in the art of sidestepping *ou* dodging his opponents *(ou* the issue)

esquiver /ɛskive/ ▸ conjug 1 ◂ VT *[+ difficulté, piège, danger, responsabilité]* to evade; *[+ coup, question]* to dodge, to evade; *[+ personne]* to elude, to evade; *[+ obligation]* to shirk, to dodge
VPR **s'esquiver** to slip *ou* sneak away

essai /esɛ/ NM 1 *(= mise à l'épreuve) [de produit]* testing; *[de voiture]* trying out, testing ◆ **faire l'~ de** *[+ produit]* to try out; *[+ nouvelle voiture]* to test drive, to try (out) ◆ **nous avons procédé par ~s et erreurs** we did it by trial and error; → **banc, bout**

2 *(= test)* test ◆ **~s nucléaires** nuclear tests ◆ **~s** *(= tests techniques de voiture ou d'avion)* trials ◆ **~s de résistance** resistance tests

3 *(= tentative)* attempt, try; *(Sport)* attempt ◆ **faire plusieurs ~s** to have several tries, to make *ou* have several attempts ◆ **faire des ~s infructueux** to make fruitless attempts ◆ **où en sont tes ~s de plantations ?** how are your efforts at growing things *ou* your attempts at gardening progressing? ◆ **ce n'est pas mal pour un premier ~** that's not bad for a first try *ou* attempt *ou* go ◆ **se livrer à des forages d'~** *[compagnie pétrolière]* to test drill

◆ **coup d'essai** first attempt ◆ **huit ans après ce coup d'~, il écrit un second roman** eight years after this first attempt, he wrote a second novel ◆ **il n'en est pas à son coup d'~** it's not a novice

◆ **à l'essai** ◆ **être à l'~** *[personne]* to be on trial ◆ **c'est à l'~** *[procédé]* it's being tried out *ou* tested ◆ **prendre qn à l'~** to take sb on for a trial period *ou* on a trial basis ◆ **mettre à l'~** to test (out), to put to the test ◆ **mise à l'~** *[de procédé]* test; → **ballon¹, bout, période**

4 *(Rugby)* try ◆ **marquer un ~** to score a try

5 *(Littérat)* essay

6 *(Tech) [d'or, argent]* assay

essaim /esɛ̃/ NM *(lit, fig)* swarm ◆ ~ **de jeunes filles** bevy *ou* gaggle of girls

essaimage /esemaʒ/ NM *[d'abeilles]* swarming; *[de famille]* scattering; *[de firme] (= développement)* spreading, expansion; *(= séparation)* hiving off

essaimer /eseme/ ▸ conjug 1 ◂ VI *[abeilles]* to swarm; *[famille]* to scatter; *[firme] (= se développer)* to spread, to expand; *(= se séparer)* to hive off

essayage /esejaʒ/ NM *(Couture)* fitting, trying on; → **cabine, salon**

essayer /eseje/ ▸ conjug 8 ◂ VT 1 *(= mettre à l'épreuve) [+ produit]* to test (out), to try (out); *[+ médicament, vaccin]* to try out; *[+ voiture]* to test ◆ **venez ~ notre nouveau modèle** come and test drive *ou* try (out) our new model ◆ **~ sa force/son talent** to try *ou* test one's strength/skill

2 *(= utiliser pour la première fois) [+ voiture, produit]* to try (out) ◆ **avez-vous essayé le nouveau boucher ?*** have you tried the new butcher('s)?; → **adopter**

3 *[+ vêtement]* to try on ◆ **il faut que je vous l'essaie** I must try it on you

4 *(= tenter) [+ méthode]* to try ◆ **~ de faire** to try *ou* attempt to do ◆ **as-tu essayé les petites annonces ?** have you tried the classified ads? ◆ **essaie de le faire** try to do it, try and do it ◆ **il a essayé de s'échapper** he attempted *ou* tried to run away ◆ **je vais ~** I'll try, I'll have a go *ou* a try *ou* a shot (at it) ◆ **essaie un coup*** have a crack at it*, have a bash (at it)* ◆ **essaie un peu pour voir** *(si tu y arrives)* have a try *ou* a go and see; *(* si tu l'oses)* just you try!*, just let me see you try it! ◆ **n'essaie pas de ruser avec moi** don't try being clever with me, don't try it on with me* *(Brit)*

5 *(Tech) [+ or, argent]* to assay

VPR **s'essayer** ◆ **s'~ à qch/à faire** to try one's hand at sth/at doing, to have a go at sth/at doing

essayeur, -euse /esejœʀ, øz/ NM,F *(Couture)* fitter; *(Tech)* assayer

essayiste /esejist/ NMF essayist

esse /ɛs/ NF *(= crochet)* hook; *(= goupille)* linchpin; *[de violon]* sound-hole

ESSEC /esɛk/ NF (abrév de **École supérieure des sciences économiques et commerciales**) *grande école for management and business students*

essence /esɑ̃s/ NF 1 *(= carburant)* petrol *(Brit)*, gas(oline) *(US)*; *(= solvant)* spirit ◆ **~ minérale** mineral oil ◆ **~ ordinaire** two-star petrol *(Brit)*, regular gas *(US)* ◆ **~ sans plomb** unleaded petrol *(Brit)*, unleaded gas *(US)* ◆ **~ de térében-**

thine turpentine ◆ **à** ~ petrol-driven (*Brit*), gasoline-powered (*US*) ◆ **prendre** *ou* **faire*** **de l'**~ to get petrol (*Brit*) *ou* gas (*US*), to fill up with petrol (*Brit*) *ou* gas (*US*); → **distributeur, panne**[1]

2 (*= extrait*) [*de plantes*] essential oil, essence; [*d'aliments*] essence ◆ ~ **de vanille/de violette/de café** vanilla/violet/coffee essence ◆ ~ **de citron/de rose** lemon/rose oil ◆ ~ **de lavande** lavender essence *ou* oil

3 (*= fondement*) [*de conversation, question, doctrine*] gist, essence; [*de livre*] gist; (*Philos*) essence; (*littér*) ◆ **par** ~ in essence, essentially

4 (*= espèce*) [*d'arbres*] species ◆ ~ **à feuilles persistantes** evergreen species ◆ **se croire d'une** ~ **supérieure** (*littér*) to think of o.s. as a superior being *ou* as of a superior species

essentiel, -elle /esɑ̃sjɛl/ GRAMMAIRE ACTIVE 37.1, 53.2

ADJ 1 (*= indispensable*) essential ◆ **ces formalités sont essentielles** these formalities are essential (*à* to; *pour* for)

2 (*= de base*) essential, basic, main (*épith*) ◆ ~ **à** essential to; → **huile**

NM 1 ◆ **l'**~ (*= objets nécessaires*) the basic essentials; (*= points principaux*) the essentials, the essential *ou* basic points ◆ **c'est l'**~ that's the main thing ◆ **l'**~ **est de ...** the main *ou* important thing is to ... ◆ **vous avez oublié l'**~ **: le coût** you've forgotten the most important thing: the cost ◆ **je suis passé à côté de l'**~ (*dans ma vie, ma carrière*) I've missed out on the most important things

2 ◆ **l'**~ **de** [*+ conversation*] the main part of; [*+ fortune*] the best *ou* main part of, the bulk of ◆ **l'**~ **de ce qu'il dit** most of what he says ◆ **l'**~ **de leur temps** the best part of their time

essentiellement /esɑ̃sjɛlmɑ̃/ ADV (*gén*) basically, essentially, mainly; (*= en majorité*) essentially, mainly; (*Philos*) essentially ◆ **c'est** ~ **grâce à .../dû à ...** it is basically *ou* essentially thanks to .../due to ...

esseulé, e /esœle/ ADJ (*littér*) forsaken (*littér*), forlorn (*littér*)

essieu (pl **essieux**) /esjø/ NM axle(-tree)

essor /esɔʀ/ NM (*frm = envol*) [*d'oiseau, imagination*] flight; (*= croissance*) [*d'entreprise, pays*] rapid development *ou* expansion; [*d'art, civilisation*] blossoming ◆ **entreprise en plein** ~ firm in full expansion ◆ **prendre son** ~ [*d'oiseau*] to soar up into the sky; [*de société*] to develop *ou* expand rapidly ◆ **le cinéma connaît un nouvel** ~ the cinema is enjoying a new boom

essorage /esɔʀaʒ/ NM (*avec essoreuse à rouleaux*) wringing; (*à la main*) wringing out; (*par la force centrifuge*) spin-drying ◆ **mettre sur la position "essorage"** to put on "spin" ◆ ~ **court/doux** *ou* **léger** short/gentle spin

essorer /esɔʀe/ ▸ conjug 1 ◂ VT (*avec essoreuse à rouleaux*) to wring; (*à la main*) to wring out; (*par la force centrifuge*) to spin-dry

essoreuse /esɔʀøz/ NF (*à rouleaux*) wringer, mangle; (*à tambour*) spin-dryer ◆ ~ **à salade** salad spinner

essoufflement /esufləmɑ̃/ NM breathlessness (*NonC*), shortness of breath (*NonC*); [*de mouvement*] running out of steam

essouffler /esufle/ ▸ conjug 1 ◂ VT to make breathless, to wind ◆ **il était essoufflé** he was out of breath *ou* winded *ou* puffed* (*Brit*) VPR **s'essouffler** [*coureur*] to get out of breath, to get puffed* (*Brit*); [*roman, travail*] to tail off, to fall off; [*romancier*] to exhaust o.s. *ou* one's talent, to dry up*; [*reprise économique, mouvement de grève*] to run out of steam

essuie /esɥi/ NM (*Belg*) (*pour les mains*) hand towel; (*= serviette de bain*) bath towel; (*= torchon*) cloth

essuie-glace (pl **essuie-glaces**) /esɥiglas/ NM windscreen (*Brit*) *ou* windshield (*US*) wiper ◆ ~ **arrière** rear windscreen wiper ◆ ~ **à balayage intermittent** intermittent wiper

essuie-mains /esɥimɛ̃/ NM INV hand towel

essuie-meuble(s) (pl **essuie-meubles**) /esyimœbl/ NM duster

essuie-tout /esɥitu/ NM INV kitchen paper (*Brit*), paper towels (*US*), Scott towels ® (*US*)

essuie-verre(s) (pl **essuie-verres**) /esɥivɛʀ/ NM glass cloth

essuyage /esɥijaʒ/ NM [*d'objet mouillé, assiettes*] wiping, drying; [*de sol, surface mouillée*] wiping, mopping; [*de tableau noir*] cleaning, wiping; [*de surface poussiéreuse*] dusting; [*de liquide*] wiping up, mopping up

essuyer /esɥije/ ▸ conjug 8 ◂ VT 1 (*= nettoyer*) [*+ objet mouillé, assiettes*] to wipe, to dry; [*+ sol, surface mouillée*] to wipe, to mop; [*+ tableau noir*] to clean, to wipe; [*+ surface poussiéreuse*] to dust; [*+ liquide*] to wipe up, to mop up ◆ **essuie-toi les pieds** *ou* **essuie tes pieds avant d'entrer** wipe your feet before you come in ◆ ~ **la vaisselle** to dry the dishes, to do the drying-up (*Brit*) ◆ **le tableau est mal essuyé** the blackboard hasn't been cleaned *ou* wiped properly ◆ **nous avons essuyé les plâtres*** we had all the initial problems to put up with

2 (*= subir*) [*+ pertes, reproches, échec, insultes*] to endure; [*+ refus*] to meet with; [*+ tempête*] to weather, to ride out ◆ ~ **le feu de l'ennemi** to come under enemy fire ◆ ~ **un coup de feu** to be shot at

VPR **s'essuyer** [*personne*] to dry o.s. ◆ **s'**~ **les mains** to dry one's hands ◆ **s'**~ **la bouche** to wipe one's mouth ◆ **s'**~ **les pieds** (*= sécher*) to dry one's feet; (*= nettoyer*) to wipe one's feet

est /ɛst/ NM INV 1 (*= point cardinal*) east ◆ **le vent d'**~ the east wind ◆ **un vent d'**~ an east (erly) wind, an easterly (*Naut*) ◆ **le vent tourne/est à l'**~ the wind is veering east (wards) *ou* towards the east/is blowing from the east ◆ **regarder vers l'**~ to look east(wards) *ou* towards the east ◆ **le soleil se lève à l'**~ the sun rises in the east ◆ **à l'**~ **de** east of, to the east of ◆ **la maison est exposée plein** ~ the house faces *ou* looks due east ◆ **d'**~ **en ouest** from east to west

2 (*= régions orientales*) east ◆ **l'Est** (*Pol*) the East ◆ **la France de l'Est, l'**~ **(de la France)** the East (of France) ◆ **les pays/le bloc de l'Est** the Eastern countries/bloc ◆ **l'Europe de l'Est** Eastern Europe

ADJ INV [*région, partie*] eastern; [*entrée, paroi*] east; [*versant, côte*] east(ern); [*côté*] east (ward); [*direction*] eastward, easterly; → **longitude**

estacade /ɛstakad/ NF landing stage

estafette /ɛstafɛt/ NF (*Mil*) courier; (*= camionnette*) van

estafilade /ɛstafilad/ NF gash, slash

est-allemand, e (mpl **est-allemands**) /ɛstalmɑ̃, ɑ̃d/ (*Hist*) ADJ East German NM,F **Est-Allemand(e)** East German

estaminet † /ɛstaminɛ/ NM tavern; (*péj*) pothouse † (*péj*), (low) dive (*péj*)

estampage /ɛstɑ̃paʒ/ NM 1 († * = *escroquerie*) fleecing, swindling ◆ **c'est de l'**~ it's a plain swindle 2 (*Tech*) stamping

estampe /ɛstɑ̃p/ NF (*= image*) engraving, print; (*= outil*) stamp ◆ ~ **japonaise** Japanese print ◆ **venez voir mes** ~**s japonaises** (*euph, hum*) you must let me show you my etchings (*hum*)

estamper /ɛstɑ̃pe/ ▸ conjug 1 ◂ VT 1 († * = *voler*) to fleece, to swindle ◆ **se faire** ~ to be fleeced *ou* swindled 2 (*Tech*) to stamp

estampeur, -euse /ɛstɑ̃pœʀ, øz/ NM,F 1 * swindler, shark* 2 (*Tech*) stamper

estampillage /ɛstɑ̃pijaʒ/ NM stamping, marking

estampille /ɛstɑ̃pij/ NF stamp

estampiller /ɛstɑ̃pije/ ▸ conjug 1 ◂ VT to stamp

estarie /ɛstaʀi/ NF (*Naut*) lay-days

ester[1] /ɛste/ VI (*s'emploie uniquement à l'infinitif*) ◆ ~ **en justice** [*plaignant*] to go to court; [*accusé*] to appear

ester[2] /ɛstɛʀ/ NM (*Chim*) ester ◆ ~ **de colza** rape methyl ester

esthète /ɛstɛt/ NMF aesthete (*Brit*), esthete (*US*)

esthéticien, -ienne /ɛstetisjɛ̃, jɛn/ NM,F (*de salon de beauté*) beautician; (*Art*) aesthetician (*Brit*), esthetician (*US*)

esthétique /ɛstetik/ ADJ 1 (*= beau*) attractive ◆ **ce bâtiment n'a rien d'**~ there is nothing attractive about this building; → **chirurgie, soin** 2 [*jugement, sentiment*] aesthetic (*Brit*), esthetic (*US*) ◆ **sens** ~ aesthetic sense NF [*de visage, pose*] aesthetic (*Brit*) *ou* esthetic (*US*) quality, attractiveness ◆ **l'**~ (*= discipline*) aesthetics (*sg*), esthetics (*US*) (*sg*) ◆ **l'**~ **industrielle** industrial design ◆ **juste pour l'**~ just for overall effect

esthétiquement /ɛstetikmɑ̃/ ADV aesthetically (*Brit*), esthetically (*US*)

esthétisant, e /ɛstetizɑ̃, ɑ̃t/ ADJ (*péj*) [*caractère, film*] mannered

esthétisme /ɛstetism/ NM 1 (*= doctrine, discours*) aestheticism (*Brit*), estheticism (*US*) 2 (*= qualités esthétiques*) aesthetic (*Brit*) *ou* esthetic (*US*) qualities ◆ **l'**~ **du film** the film's aesthetic qualities ◆ **l'**~ **japonais** the Japanese aesthetic 3 (*= formalisme*) formalism ◆ **d'un** ~ **excessif** too formalistic

estimable /ɛstimabl/ ADJ 1 (*frm = digne d'estime*) respectable, estimable (*frm*), worthy (*frm*) 2 (*= déterminable*) assessable, calculable ◆ **ces dégâts sont difficilement** ~**s** it is difficult to assess the extent of this damage

estimatif, -ive /ɛstimatif, iv/ ADJ [*coût, valeur*] estimated, appraised ◆ **état** ~ estimated statement

estimation /ɛstimasjɔ̃/ NF 1 (*= évaluation*) [*d'objet*] appraisal, valuation; [*de dégâts, prix*] assessment, estimation; [*de distance, quantité*] estimation, reckoning; [*de propriété*] valuation, assessment 2 (*= chiffre donné*) estimate, estimation ◆ **d'après mes** ~**s** according to my estimations *ou* reckonings ◆ ~ **des coûts** cost estimate 3 (*= sondage d'opinion, prévision*) ~**s** projections

estime /ɛstim/ GRAMMAIRE ACTIVE 40.4 NF (*= considération*) esteem, respect, regard ◆ **jouir d'une grande** ~ to be highly respected *ou* regarded, to be held in high esteem *ou* regard ◆ **il a baissé dans mon** ~ he has gone down in my estimation *ou* in my esteem ◆ **ce succès mérite l'**~ **de tous** this success deserves the respect of everyone ◆ **avoir de l'**~ **pour** to have (a) great esteem *ou* respect *ou* great regard for ◆ **tenir en piètre** ~ to have little regard *ou* respect for

◆ **à l'estime** ◆ **naviguer à l'**~ (*Naut*) to sail by dead reckoning; (*fig*) to sail in the dark ◆ **calculer à l'**~ to make a rough estimate; → **succès**

estimer /ɛstime/ ▸ conjug 1 ◂ VT 1 (*= expertiser*) [*+ objet, propriété*] to appraise, to value, to assess; [*+ dégâts*] to assess, to estimate, to evaluate (*à* at); ◆ **faire** ~ **un bijou** to have a piece of jewellery valued *ou* appraised ◆ **cette bague est estimée à 3 000** € this ring is valued at €3,000

2 (*= calculer approximativement*) [*+ prix*] to assess, to estimate, to evaluate (*à* at); [*+ distance, quantité*] to estimate, to reckon ◆ **les pertes sont estimées à 2 000 morts** 2,000 people are estimated to have died, an estimated 2,000 people have died, the number of those dead is estimated at *ou* put at 2,000 ◆ **j'estime sa**

vitesse à 80 km/h I reckon his speed to be 80 km/h, I would put his speed at 80 km/h

3 *(= respecter) [+ personne]* to esteem, to hold in esteem *ou* high esteem *ou* regard, to respect ◆ **estimé de tous** respected *ou* esteemed *ou* highly regarded by everyone ◆ **notre estimé collègue** our esteemed colleague ◆ **savoir se faire ~** to know how to win people's respect *ou* regard *ou* esteem

4 *(= faire cas de) [+ qualité]* to appreciate ◆ **j'estime beaucoup sa loyauté** I greatly value his loyalty ◆ **c'est un plat très estimé** this dish is considered a great delicacy

5 *(= considérer)* **~ que ...** to consider *ou* judge *ou* reckon that ... ◆ **j'estime qu'il est de mon devoir de ...** I consider it *ou* judge it *ou* deem it † (to be) my duty to ... ◆ **il estime que vous avez tort de faire cela** he considers it wrong for you to do that ◆ **il estime avoir raison** he considers he is right *ou* in the right ◆ **nous estimons nécessaire de dire/que** we consider it *ou* judge it *ou* deem it † necessary to say/that ◆ **~ inutile de faire** to see no point in doing, to consider it pointless to do ◆ **s'~ heureux d'avoir/que** to consider o.s. fortunate to have/that

estivage /ɛstivaʒ/ **NM** *summering of cattle on mountain pastures*

estival, e (mpl **-aux**) /ɛstival, o/ **ADJ** *(lit)* summer *(épith)*; *(= agréable) [temps, température]* summery ◆ **station ~e** summer resort ◆ **la période ~e** the summer season *ou* months

estivant, e /ɛstivɑ̃, ɑ̃t/ **NM,F** holiday-maker *(Brit)*, vacationer *(US)*, summer visitor

est-nord-est /ɛstnɔʀɛst/ **ADJ INV, NM INV** east-north-east

estoc /ɛstɔk/ **NM** → **frapper**

estocade /ɛstɔkad/ **NF** *(Tauromachie)* death-blow, final thrust ◆ **donner l'~ à un taureau** to deal a bull the death-blow ◆ **donner l'~ à une personne/un projet** to give *ou* deal the finishing blow to a person/a plan

estomac /ɛstɔma/ **NM** 1 *(= organe)* stomach ◆ **avoir mal à l'~** to have (a) stomach ache *ou* tummy ache* ◆ **partir l'~ creux** *ou* **vide** to set off on an empty stomach ◆ **avoir l'~ plein** *ou* **bien rempli** to be full (up), to have eaten one's fill ◆ **j'ai l'~ dans les talons** I'm starving *ou* famished ◆ **avoir un ~ d'autruche** to have a cast-iron stomach ◆ **prendre de l'~*** to develop a paunch; → **aigreur, creux, rester** 2

⁑ **avoir de l'~** *(= avoir du culot)* to have a nerve; *(= avoir du courage)* to have guts* ◆ **il la lui a fait à l'~** he bluffed him

estomaquer* /ɛstɔmake/ ► conjug 1 ◄ **VT** to flabbergast, to stagger

estompe /ɛstɔ̃p/ **NF** *(Art)* stump

estompé, e /ɛstɔ̃pe/ (ptp de **estomper**) **ADJ** *(= voilé) [couleurs, image]* blurred, soft

estomper /ɛstɔ̃pe/ ► conjug 1 ◄ **VT** *(Art) [+ dessin]* to stump *(SPÉC)*, to shade off *(with a stump)*; *(= voiler) [+ contours, souvenir]* to blur, to dim, to soften **VPR s'estomper** *[contours, souvenir]* to fade; *[différences]* to become less marked ◆ **la côte s'estompait dans la brume** the coastline faded into the mist

Estonie /ɛstɔni/ **NF** Estonia

estonien, -ienne /ɛstɔnjɛ̃, jɛn/ **ADJ** Estonian **NM** *(= langue)* Estonian **NM,F Estonien(ne)** Estonian

estouffade /ɛstufad/ **NF** *(Culin)* ◆ **~ de bœuf** ≈ beef stew ◆ **c'est de l'~** *(fig)* it's very stodgy

estourbir* /ɛstuʀbiʀ/ ► conjug 2 ◄ **VT** *(= assommer)* to stun; *(= tuer)* to do in⁑, to bump off⁑

estrade /ɛstʀad/ **NF** platform

estradiol /ɛstʀadjɔl/ **NM** ⇒ **œstradiol**

estragon /ɛstʀagɔ̃/ **NM** tarragon

estran /ɛstʀɑ̃/ **NM** foreshore

estrapade /ɛstʀapad/ **NF** strappado

estrogène /ɛstʀɔʒɛn/ **NM** → **œstrogène**

estropié, e /ɛstʀɔpje/ (ptp de **estropier**) **NM,F** cripple, maimed person

estropier /ɛstʀɔpje/ ► conjug 7 ◄ **VT** 1 *[+ personne]* to cripple, to disable, to maim 2 *[+ texte, citation]* to twist, to distort, to mangle; *[+ nom]* to mutilate, to mangle; *[+ langue étrangère, morceau de musique]* to mangle, to murder

est-sud-est /ɛstsydɛst/ **ADJ INV, NM INV** east-south-east

estuaire /ɛstɥɛʀ/ **NM** estuary; *(en Écosse)* firth ◆ **l'~ de la Seine** the Seine estuary

estudiantin, e /ɛstydjɑ̃tɛ̃, in/ **ADJ** student *(épith)*

esturgeon /ɛstyʀʒɔ̃/ **NM** sturgeon

et /e/ **CONJ** 1 *(lie des termes)* and ◆ **c'est vert ~ rouge** it's green and red ◆ **pour piano ~ orchestre** for piano and orchestra ◆ **je n'ai rien vu, ~ toi ?** I didn't see anything, did you? *ou* what about you? ◆ **j'aime beaucoup ça, ~ vous ?** I'm very fond of that, aren't you? *ou* what about you?, I like that very much – do you? ◆ **je n'aime pas ça ~ lui non plus** I don't like that and nor does he *ou* and he doesn't either ◆ **Chantal y alla, ~ Madeleine** *(littér)* Chantal went, as did Madeleine ◆ **une belle ~ grande maison** a beautiful, big house ◆ **il y a mensonge ~ mensonge** *(littér)* there are lies and lies, there's lying and lying ◆ **je suis né à Genève ~ mes parents aussi** I was born in Geneva and so were my parents, I was born in Geneva, as were my parents

2 *(lie des propositions)* and ◆ **j'ai payé ~ je suis parti** I paid and left ◆ **il est travailleur ~ ne boit pas** he works hard and (he) doesn't drink ◆ **lui ~ moi nous nous entendons bien** he and I get along well ◆ **~ lui ~ vous l'avez dit** he and you have both said so, both he and you have said so ◆ **2 ~ 2 font 4** 2 and 2 make 4 ◆ **il ne peut ~ ne doit pas y aller** he cannot and must not go ◆ **il a ri ~ ri/pleuré ~ pleuré** *(répétition)* he laughed and laughed/cried and cried ◆ **je ne l'approuve pas ~ ne l'approuverai jamais** I don't approve of it and (I) never shall *ou* will ◆ **plus j'en mange ~ plus j'en ai envie** the more of it I eat the more I want

3 *(valeur emphatique)* **~ alors/ensuite/après ?** and so/then/afterwards? ◆ **~ alors ?** *(= peu importe)* so (what)?* ◆ **~ moi alors ?** (and) what about me then? ◆ **~ puis** and then ◆ **~ puis (après) ?*** so (what)?* ◆ **~ moi, je peux venir ?** can I come too? ◆ **~ vous osez revenir ?** *(indignation)* and you dare (to) come back? ◆ **~ lui alors qu'est-ce qu'il va dire ?** what's he going to say? ◆ **~ ces livres que tu devais me prêter ?** what about these books (then) *ou* and what's happened to these books that you were supposed to lend me? ◆ **~ vous, vous y allez ?** and what about you, are you going? ◆ **~ si nous y allions aussi ?** what about (us) going as well?, why don't we go too? ◆ **~ voilà !** and there you are! ◆ **~ voilà que le voisin revient ...** and then the next-door neighbour comes back ... ◆ **~ voici qu'arrive notre ami** (and) along comes our friend ◆ **~ alors eux, voyant cela, ils sont partis** (and) so, seeing that, they left ◆ **~ lui de sourire/se fâcher** *(littér)* whereupon he smiled/grew angry ◆ **~ d'un il est paresseux, ~ de deux il est menteur** for one thing he's lazy, and for another thing he's a liar

4 ◆ **vingt/trente ~ un** twenty-/thirty-one ◆ **à midi/deux heures ~ quart** at (a) quarter past twelve/two ◆ **le vingt ~ unième** the twenty-first; → **mille¹**

ETA /ətea/ **NF** (abrév de **Euzkadi Ta Azkatasunra**) ETA

êta /ɛta/ **NM** eta

étable /etabl/ **NF** cowshed

établi /etabli/ **NM** (work) bench

établir /etabliʀ/ ► conjug 2 ◄ **VT** 1 *(= installer dans un lieu) [+ immeuble]* to put up, to erect; *[+ usine]* to set up; *[+ liaisons, communications]* to establish, to set up; *[+ empire]* to build, to found ◆ **~ son domicile** *ou* **sa demeure à** to set up house in, to make one's home in ◆ **l'ennemi a établi son camp/son quartier général dans le village** the enemy has pitched camp/has set up its headquarters in the village

2 *(= instaurer) [+ usage]* to establish, to institute; *[+ gouvernement]* to form, to set up; *[+ impôt]* to introduce, to bring in; *[+ règlement]* to lay down, to establish; *[+ normes]* to establish

3 *(= asseoir) [+ démonstration]* to base *(sur on)*; *[+ réputation]* to found, to base *(sur on)*; *[+ droits]* to establish; *[+ fortune]* to found *(sur on)*; ◆ **~ son pouvoir sur la force** to found *ou* base one's power on force

4 *(= faire régner) [+ autorité, paix]* to establish *(sur over)*; ◆ **~ son pouvoir sur un pays** to get control of a country, to establish control over a country

5 *(= dresser) [+ liste, devis]* to draw up, to make out; *[+ programme]* to arrange; *[+ facture, chèque]* to make out; *[+ plans]* to draw up, to draft; *[+ prix]* to fix, to work out

6 *(= montrer) [+ fait, comparaison]* to establish ◆ **~ l'innocence de qn** to establish sb's innocence ◆ **il est établi que ...** it's an established fact that ...

7 *(= nouer) [+ relations]* to establish ◆ **ils ont établi une amitié solide** they have established a firm friendship

8 *(Sport)* **~ un record** to set (up) *ou* establish a record

9 † *[+ personne]* **il a cinq enfants à ~** he has five children to set up in life ◆ **il a établi son fils médecin** he has set his son up *ou* established his son in medical practice

VPR s'établir 1 *(= s'installer dans un lieu) [jeune couple]* to settle ◆ **une usine s'est établie dans le village** a factory has been set up *ou* they've set up a factory in the village ◆ **l'ennemi s'est établi sur la colline** the enemy has taken up position on the hill

2 *(= s'instaurer)* **l'usage s'est établi de ...** it has become customary to ...

3 *(= prendre un emploi)* **s'~ boulanger** to set o.s. up as a baker ◆ **il s'est établi médecin** he has established himself *ou* set himself up in medical practice ◆ **s'~ à son compte** to set up one's own business

4 *(= régner) [pouvoir, régime]* to become established ◆ **son pouvoir s'est établi sur le pays** his rule has become (firmly) established throughout the country ◆ **un grand silence s'établit, il s'établit un grand silence** there was a great silence, a great silence fell ◆ **un consensus a fini par s'~** a consensus was eventually reached

5 *(= se nouer) [amitié, contacts]* to develop, to be established ◆ **une amitié solide s'est établie entre eux** a firm friendship has developed *ou* has been established between them

établissement /etablismɑ̃/ **NM** 1 *(= bâtiment)* establishment; *(= société)* establishment, firm, company; *(= institution)* institution; *(= hôtel)* hotel ◆ **~ (scolaire)** school ◆ **~ hospitalier** hospital ◆ **~ pénitentiaire** prison ◆ **~ religieux** religious institution ◆ **~ bancaire** bank ◆ **avec les compliments des ~s Minot** with the compliments of Minot and Co.

2 *(= mise en place) [d'immeuble]* putting up, erecting; *[d'empire]* building, founding; *[de programme]* arranging; *[de relations, autorité]* establishing *(sur over)*; *[de fortune]* founding *(sur on)*; *[d'usine, liaisons, communications]* setting up, establishing, institution; *[de gouvernement]* setting up, forming; *[de règlement]* laying down, establishing, institution; *[de droits]* establish-

ing; *[de liste]* drawing up, making out; *[de facture, chèque]* making out; *[de plans]* drawing up, drafting; *[de prix]* fixing, working out; *[de fait, comparaison]* establishing; *[personne] (dans un emploi)* setting up, establishing; *(dans un lieu)* settling; *[de pouvoir, régime]* establishment; *[d'amitié, contacts]* development, establishment ◆ **ils préconisent l'~ de relations diplomatiques** they call for the establishment of diplomatic relations, they wish to establish diplomatic relations ◆ **l'~ d'une paix durable dans la région** the establishment of a lasting peace in the area
3 *(= colonie)* settlement

étage /etaʒ/ NM 1 *[de bâtiment]* floor, storey *(Brit)*, story *(US)* ◆ **au premier** ~ *(en France)* on the first floor *(Brit)*, on the second floor *(US)*; *(au Canada)* on the ground floor *(Brit)*, on the first floor *(US)* ◆ **maison à** *ou* **de deux ~s** three-storeyed *(Brit) ou* -storied *(US)* house, house with three floors ◆ **monter à l'~** to go upstairs ◆ **monter à l'~ supérieur** to go to the next floor up ◆ **il grimpa trois ~s** he went up *ou* walked up three floors *ou* flights ◆ **les trois ~s de la tour Eiffel** the three levels of the Eiffel Tower
2 *[de fusée]* stage; *[de mine]* level; *[de jardin]* terrace, level; *[de gâteau]* tier ◆ **~s de végétation** *(Géog)* levels of vegetation ◆ **~ de pression** *(Tech)* pressure stage
3 ◆ **de bas** ~ († *= humble)* lowborn; *(péj = médiocre)* poor, second-rate ◆ **ce sont des trafiquants de bas** ~ they are low-level *ou* common dealers

étagement /etaʒmɑ̃/ NM *[de vignobles]* terracing

étager /etaʒe/ ▸ conjug 3 ◂ VT *[+ objets]* to set out in tiered rows, to lay out in tiers VPR **s'étager** *[jardins, maisons]* to rise in tiers *ou* terraces ◆ **la foule s'étage sur les gradins** the crowd is gathered on the terraces *ou* the steps ◆ **vignobles étagés sur la colline** vines in terraced rows on the hillside

étagère /etaʒɛʀ/ NF *(= tablette, rayon)* shelf ◆ **~s** *(= meuble)* shelves

étai /etɛ/ NM *(= support)* stay, prop, strut; *(Naut = cordage)* stay

étaiement /etɛmɑ̃/ NM ⇒ **étayage**

étain /etɛ̃/ NM *(Min)* tin; *(Orfèvrerie) (= matière)* pewter; *(= objet)* piece of pewterware, pewterware *(NonC)* ◆ **pot en** *ou* **d'~** pewter pot; → **papier**

étal (pl **étals**) /etal/ NM *[de boucherie, marché]* stall

étalage /etalaʒ/ NM 1 *(Comm) (= action)* display, displaying; *(= devanture)* shop window, show window, display window; *(= tréteaux)* stall, stand; *(= articles exposés)* display ◆ **présentation de l'~** window dressing ◆ **disposer l'~** to dress the window, to do the window display ◆ **chemise qui a fait l'~** shop-soiled shirt ◆ **droit d'~** stallage; → **vol²** 2 *(= déploiement) [de luxe, connaissances]* display, show ◆ **faire ~ de** *[+ luxe, savoir]* to flaunt, to show off, to parade; *[+ malheurs]* to make a show of 3 *(Métal)* **~s** bosh 4 *[de fibres textiles]* roving

étalagiste /etalaʒist/ NMF *(= décorateur)* window dresser; († *= marchand)* stallkeeper

étale /etal/ ADJ *[mer]* slack; *[vent, situation]* steady ◆ **navire** ~ becalmed ship NF *[de mer]* slack (water)

étalement /etalmɑ̃/ NM 1 *[de papiers, objets]* spreading *(sur* over); *[de journal, tissu]* spreading out *(sur* on); *(Comm) [de marchandise]* displaying, laying out, spreading out *(sur* on) 2 *[de beurre]* spreading *(sur* on); *[de peinture, crème solaire]* application 3 *[de paiements]* spreading, staggering *(sur* over); *[de vacances]* staggering *(sur* over); *[de travaux, opération]* spreading *(sur* over)

étaler /etale/ ▸ conjug 1 ◂ VT 1 *(= déployer) [+ papiers, objets]* to spread *(sur* over); *[+ journal, tissu]* to spread out *(sur* on); *[+ marchandise]* to display, to lay out, to spread out *(sur* on); ◆ **~ son jeu** *ou* **ses cartes** *(Cartes)* to display *ou* lay down one's hand *ou* one's cards
2 *(= étendre) [+ beurre, colle]* to spread *(sur* on); *[+ peinture]* to apply, to put on; *[+ crème solaire]* to apply, to smooth on; *(Culin) [+ pâte]* to roll out ◆ **une peinture qui s'étale bien** paint that is easy to apply
3 *(= répartir) [+ paiements]* to spread, to stagger *(sur* over); *[+ vacances]* to stagger *(sur* over); *[+ travaux, opération]* to spread *(sur* over); ◆ **étalez vos envois** *(Poste)* space out your consignments ◆ **les vacances/paiements s'étalent sur quatre mois** holidays/payments are staggered *ou* spread over a period of four months
4 *[+ luxe, savoir, richesse]* to parade, to flaunt, to show off; *[+ malheurs]* to make a show of; *[+ secrets]* to give away, to disclose ◆ **il faut toujours qu'il étale sa science** he doesn't miss an opportunity to display his knowledge ◆ **il aime à en** ~ * he likes to cause a stir
5 *(* = frapper)* to floor, to lay out ◆ **se faire ~ à un examen** to flunk * an exam ◆ **on s'est fait ~** *(Sport)* we got a real hammering *
VPR **s'étaler** 1 *[plaine, cultures]* to stretch out, to spread out ◆ **le titre s'étale sur trois colonnes** the headline is spread *ou* splashed across three columns
2 *[richesse, vanité]* to be flaunted; *[vaniteux]* to flaunt o.s. ◆ **son ignominie s'étale au grand jour** his ignominy is plain for all to see
3 *(= se vautrer)* **s'~ sur un divan** to sprawl *ou* lounge on a divan ◆ **étalé sur le tapis** sprawling on *ou* stretched out on the carpet ◆ **tu t'étales ! je n'ai plus de place sur la table !** stop spreading yourself, you're not leaving me any room
4 *(* = tomber)* **s'~ (par terre)** to fall flat on the ground, to come a cropper * *(Brit)* ◆ **attention, tu vas t'~ !** look out, you're going to fall flat on your face! *
5 *(* = échouer)* **s'~ à un examen/en chimie** to flunk * an exam/one's chemistry exam

étalon¹ /etalɔ̃/ NM *(= cheval)* stallion

étalon² /etalɔ̃/ NM *(= mesure)* standard; *(fig)* yardstick ◆ **kilogramme/balance** ~ standard kilogram/scales ◆ **~-or** *(Écon)* gold standard ◆ **c'est devenu l'~ de la beauté** it has become the yardstick by which we measure beauty ◆ **copie** ~ *(Ciné)* master print; → **mètre**

étalonnage /etalɔnaʒ/, **étalonnement** /etalɔnmɑ̃/ NM 1 *(= graduation)* calibration 2 *(= vérification)* standardization

étalonner /etalɔne/ ▸ conjug 1 ◂ VT 1 *(= graduer)* to calibrate 2 *(= vérifier)* to standardize 3 *[+ test]* to set the standards for

étambot /etɑ̃bo/ NM stern-post

étamer /etame/ ▸ conjug 1 ◂ VT *(gén)* to tin, to tinplate; *[+ glace]* to silver ◆ **cuivre étamé** tinned copper

étameur /etamœʀ/ NM tinsmith

étamine /etamin/ NF *(Bot)* stamen; *(= tissu)* muslin; *(pour laitage)* cheesecloth, butter muslin *(Brit)*

étanche /etɑ̃ʃ/ ADJ *[vêtements, chaussures, montre]* waterproof; *[bateau, compartiment]* watertight; *[cuve]* leakproof; *[toit, mur]* impervious, impermeable; *(fig)* watertight ◆ **~ à l'air** airtight ◆ **enduit** ~ sealant ◆ **la montre est ~ à 30 mètres** the watch is waterproof to a depth of 30 metres, the watch is water-resistant to 30 metres; → **cloison**

étanchéité /etɑ̃ʃeite/ NF *(à l'eau) [de bateau, compartiment]* watertightness ◆ **pour assurer son ~** *[de vêtement, montre]* to make sure it is waterproof ◆ **tester l'~ d'une montre** to test how waterproof *ou* water-resistant a watch is ◆ **~ (à l'air)** airtightness

étancher /etɑ̃ʃe/ ▸ conjug 1 ◂ VT 1 *[+ sang]* to staunch, to stem; *(littér) [+ larmes]* to dry, to stem; *(littér) [+ soif]* to quench, to slake; *(Naut) [+ voie d'eau]* to stop (up) 2 *(= rendre étanche)* to make watertight; *[+ écoulement, source]* to dam up, to stem

étançon /etɑ̃sɔ̃/ NM stanchion, shore, prop

étançonner /etɑ̃sɔne/ ▸ conjug 1 ◂ VT to shore up, to prop up

étang /etɑ̃/ NM pond; *(grand)* lake

étape /etap/ NF 1 *(= trajet) (gén, Sport)* stage, leg; *(= lieu d'arrêt) (gén)* stop, stopping place; *(Sport)* stopover point, staging point ◆ **faire ~ à** to stop off at, to break the journey at *(Brit)* ◆ **par petites ~s** in easy stages ◆ **~ de ravitaillement** staging post ◆ **ville-~** *(Cyclisme)* stopover town ◆ **Valence est une ville-~ entre Lyon et Nice** Valence is a stopping-off point *ou* place between Lyons and Nice 2 *(= phase)* stage; *(= palier)* stage, step ◆ **les ~s de sa vie** the various stages of his life; → **brûler**

état /eta/ NM 1 *(= condition physique)* state, condition ◆ **dans un tel ~ d'épuisement** in such a state of exhaustion ◆ **bon ~ général** good general state of health ◆ **~ (de santé)** health ◆ **en ~ d'ivresse** *ou* **d'ébriété** under the influence (of alcohol) ◆ **il n'est pas en ~ de le faire** he's in no condition *ou* (fit) state to do it ◆ **dans quel ~ es-tu ! tu saignes !** what a state you're in! you're bleeding! ◆ **être dans un triste ~** to be in a sad *ou* sorry state
2 *(= condition psychique)* state ◆ **être dans un grand ~ de nervosité** to be in a state of extreme nervousness, to be extremely nervous ◆ **il ne faut pas te mettre dans un ~ pareil** *ou* **des ~s pareils** you mustn't get yourself into such a state ◆ **être dans tous ses ~s** to be beside o.s. (with anger *ou* anxiety *etc*), to be all worked up *, to be in a terrible state ◆ **ça l'a mis dans tous ses ~s** that got him all worked up * *ou* into a terrible state ◆ **il n'était pas dans son ~ normal** he wasn't his usual *ou* normal self ◆ **être dans un ~ second** to be in a trance, to be spaced out * ◆ **je ne suis pas en ~ de le recevoir** I'm in no fit state to receive him
3 *[de chose abstraite]* state; *(Chim) [de corps]* state ◆ **~ liquide/solide/gazeux** liquid/solid/gaseous state ◆ **dans l'~ actuel de nos connaissances** in the present state of our knowledge, as our knowledge stands at (the) present ◆ **dans l'~ actuel des choses** as things stand at present ◆ **réduit à l'~ de cendres** reduced to cinders ◆ **quel est l'~ de la question ?** how do things stand?
4 *[d'objet, article d'occasion]* condition, state ◆ **en bon/mauvais ~** in good/poor *ou* bad condition ◆ **en ~** in (working) order ◆ **en ~ de naviguer** sea-worthy ◆ **en (parfait) ~ de marche** in (perfect) working order ◆ **remettre en ~** *[+ voiture]* to repair, to do up *; *[+ maison]* to renovate, to do up * ◆ **tenir en ~** *[+ voiture]* to maintain in good order, to keep in good repair; *[+ maison]* to keep in good repair, to look after ◆ **sucre/pétrole à l'~ brut** sugar/oil in its raw *ou* unrefined *ou* crude state ◆ **à l'~ (de) neuf** as good as new ◆ **remettre qch en l'~** to put sth back *ou* leave sth as it was
5 *(= nation)* **État** state ◆ **un État de droit** a constitutional state ◆ **être un État dans l'État** to be a law unto itself ◆ **les États pontificaux** *ou* **de l'Église** the Papal States ◆ **coup d'État** coup (d'État) ◆ **l'État-patron** the state as an employer ◆ **l'État-providence** the welfare state; → **affaire, chef¹**
6 † *(= métier)* profession, trade; *(= statut social)* station ◆ **l'~ militaire** the military profession ◆ **boucher/tailleur de son ~** a butcher/tailor by trade ◆ **donner un ~ à qn** to set sb up in a

trade ♦ **honteux de son ~** ashamed of his station in life †

7 *(= registre, comptes)* statement, account; *(= inventaire)* inventory ♦ **faire un ~ des recettes** to draw up a statement *ou* an account of the takings ♦ **~ appréciatif** evaluation, estimation ♦ **~ vérifié des comptes** audited statement of accounts

8 *(locutions)* **faire ~ de** *[+ ses services]* to instance; *[+ craintes, intentions]* to state; *[+ conversation, rumeur]* to report ♦ **en tout ~ de cause** anyway, in any case ♦ **c'est un ~ de fait** it is an established *ou* irrefutable fact ♦ **dans un ~ intéressant** *(hum)* in an interesting condition, in the family way* ♦ **à l'~ latent** in a latent state ♦ **en ~ de péché (mortel)** *(Rel)* in a state of (mortal) sin

COMP **état d'alerte** *(Mil)* state of alert
état d'âme mood, frame of mind ♦ **avoir des ~s d'âme** *(scrupules)* to have scruples *ou* qualms; *(hésitation)* to have doubts
état d'apesanteur weightlessness ♦ **être en ~ d'apesanteur** to be weightless ♦ **expérience en ~ d'apesanteur** experiment carried out under conditions of weightlessness
état de choc ♦ **être en ~ de choc** to be in (a state of) shock
état de choses state of affairs, situation
état civil civil status ♦ **(le bureau de) l'~ civil** the registry office *(Brit)*, the Public Records Office *(US)*
état de conscience *(Psych)* state of consciousness
état de crise state of crisis
état d'esprit frame *ou* state of mind
les états *ou* **États généraux** *(Hist)* the States General ♦ **réunir les États généraux de l'université/de la santé** to organize a convention on university/health issues
état de grâce *(Rel)* state of grace ♦ **en ~ de grâce** *(fig)* inspired
état de guerre state of war
état des lieux inventory of fixtures
l'état de nature the natural state
états de service service record
état de siège state of siege
état d'urgence state of emergency ♦ **décréter l'~ d'urgence** to declare a state of emergency
état de veille waking state

étatique /etatik/ **ADJ** state *(épith)* ♦ **système ~** system of state control ♦ **l'appareil ~** the state apparatus

étatisation /etatizasjɔ̃/ **NF** *(= doctrine)* state control ♦ **~ d'une entreprise** placing of a concern under direct state control, takeover of a concern by the state

étatiser /etatize/ ▸ **conjug 1** ◂ **VT** to establish state control over, to put *ou* bring under state control ♦ **économie/entreprise étatisée** state-controlled economy/firm

étatisme /etatism/ **NM** state socialism, state *ou* government control

étatiste /etatist/ **ADJ** *[système, doctrine]* of state control **NMF** partisan of state control, state socialist

état-major (pl **états-majors**) /etamaʒɔʀ/ **NM** 1 *(Mil)* *(= officiers)* staff; *(= bureaux)* staff headquarters ♦ **officier d'~** staff officer; → **chef¹** 2 *[de parti politique]* administrative staff; *[d'entreprise]* top *ou* senior management

état-nation (pl **états-nations**) /etanasjɔ̃/ **NM** nation-state

États-Unis /etazyni/ **NMPL** ♦ **les ~ (d'Amérique)** the United States (of America) ♦ **les ~ d'Europe** the United States of Europe

étau (pl **étaux**) /eto/ **NM** *(= outil)* vice ♦ **~ limeur** shaper ♦ **l'~ se resserre (autour des coupables)** the noose is tightening (around the guilty men) ♦ **se trouver pris (comme) dans un ~** to find o.s. caught in a stranglehold ♦ **j'ai la tête comme dans un ~** I feel like my head's in a vice

étayage /etɛjaʒ/, **étayement** /etɛjmɑ̃/ **NM** 1 *[de mur]* propping up, shoring up 2 *[de théorie]* support(ing), backing up 3 *[de régime, société]* support(ing), propping up

étayer /eteje/ ▸ **conjug 8** ◂ **VT** 1 *[+ mur]* to prop up, to shore up 2 *[+ argumentation, hypothèse, théorie]* to support, to back up; *[+ accusations]* to substantiate, to back up; *[+ soupçons]* to confirm ♦ **pour ~ ses dires, il a pris plusieurs exemples** he used several examples to back up what he said ♦ **les preuves nécessaires pour ~ le dossier de l'accusation** the evidence required to back up *ou* support the prosecution's case

etc /ɛtseteʀa/ **LOC** (abrév de **et cætera**) etc

et cætera, et cetera /ɛtseteʀa/ **LOC** etcetera, and so on (and so forth)

été /ete/ **NM** summer(time) ♦ **~ de la Saint-Martin, ~ indien, ~ des Indiens** *(Can)* Indian summer ♦ **~ comme hiver** summer and winter alike ♦ **en ~** in (the) summer(time) ♦ **jour d'~** summer's day ♦ **mois d'~** summer month ♦ **résidence d'~** summer residence

éteignoir /etɛɲwaʀ/ **NM** 1 *[de bougie]* extinguisher 2 († = *rabat-joie*) wet blanket, killjoy

éteindre /etɛ̃dʀ/ GRAMMAIRE ACTIVE 51.4 ▸ **conjug 52** ◂

VT 1 *[+ incendie, poêle]* to put out, to extinguish; *[+ bougie]* to blow out; *(avec éteignoir)* to snuff out; *[+ cigarette]* to put out, to extinguish *(frm)*; *(en l'écrasant)* to stub out

2 *[+ gaz, lampe]* to switch off, to put out, to turn off; *[+ électricité, chauffage, radio]* to turn off, to switch off ♦ **éteins dans la cuisine** switch off the light(s) in the kitchen

3 *[+ pièce, endroit]* to put out *ou* turn off the lights in ♦ **sa fenêtre était éteinte** his window was dark, there was no light at *ou* in his window

4 *[+ colère]* to subdue, to quell; *[+ amour, envie]* to kill; *[+ soif]* to quench, to slake

5 *[+ dette]* to extinguish

VPR s'éteindre 1 *[cigarette, feu, gaz]* to go out ♦ **la fenêtre s'est éteinte** the light at the window went out, the window went dark

2 *[agonisant]* to pass away, to die ♦ **famille qui s'est éteinte** family which has died out

3 *[colère]* to abate, to evaporate; *[amour, envie]* to die, to fade

éteint, e /etɛ̃, ɛ̃t/ (ptp de **éteindre**) **ADJ** *[couleur]* faded; *[race, volcan]* extinct; *[regard]* dull, lacklustre; *[voix]* feeble, faint, dying; *(* = *épuisé)* exhausted, tired out ♦ **chaux ~e** slaked lime ♦ **c'est un homme ~ maintenant** his spirit is broken now, he's a broken man now

étendard /etɑ̃daʀ/ **NM** 1 *(= drapeau, fig)* standard ♦ **brandir** *ou* **lever l'~ de la révolte** to raise the standard of revolt 2 *(Bot)* standard, vexillum *(SPÉC)*

étendoir /etɑ̃dwaʀ/ **NM** *(= corde)* clothes *ou* washing line; *(sur pied)* clotheshorse

étendre /etɑ̃dʀ/ ▸ **conjug 41** ◂ **VT** 1 *(= étaler)* *[+ journal, tissu]* to spread out, to open out; *[+ tapis]* to roll out; *[+ beurre]* to spread; *[+ pâte]* to roll out; *[+ bras, jambes, blessé]* to stretch out; *[+ ailes]* to spread; *(Ling) [+ sens]* to stretch, to extend ♦ **~ le linge** *(sur un fil)* to hang out the washing ♦ **veux-tu ~ le bras pour me passer ...** would you mind reaching out and passing me ...

2 * *[+ adversaire]* *(= frapper)* to floor, to lay out; *(= vaincre)* to thrash*, to knock out; *[+ candidat]* *(Scol)* to fail, to clobber*; *(Pol)* to hammer* ♦ **se faire ~** *[adversaire]* to be laid out cold, to be flattened*; *[candidat]* *(Scol)* to flunk it*; *(Pol)* to be hammered* ♦ **il s'est fait ~ en anglais** he flunked* his English exam

3 *(= agrandir)* *[+ pouvoirs]* to extend *(sur* over); *[+ fortune]* to increase; *[+ connaissances, cercle d'amis, recherches]* to broaden ♦ **~ ses activités** *[firme]* to expand ♦ **~ son action à d'autres domaines** to extend *ou* widen one's action to other fields ♦ **~ une idée à une autre** to extend one idea to (cover) another, to apply one idea to another

4 *(= diluer)* *[+ vin]* to dilute; *[+ sauce]* to thin *(de* with); ♦ **étendu d'eau** watered down

VPR s'étendre 1 *(= s'allonger)* to stretch out *(sur* on); *(= se reposer)* to lie down, to have a lie down *(Brit)*; *(en expliquant)* to elaborate ♦ **s'~ sur son lit** to stretch out *ou* lie down on one's bed

2 *(= insister)* **s'~ sur un sujet** to elaborate on *ou* enlarge on a subject ♦ **ne nous étendons pas là-dessus** let's not dwell on that ♦ **si je m'étends un peu là-dessus, c'est que c'est important** if I'm going on about it a bit, it's because it's important

3 *(= occuper un espace, une période)* *[côte, forêt]* to stretch (out), to extend; *[cortège]* to stretch (out) *(jusqu'à* as far as, to); *[vacances, travaux]* to stretch, to extend *(sur* over); ♦ **la plaine s'étendait à perte de vue** the plain stretched (away) as far as the eye could see

4 *(= augmenter)* *[brouillard, épidémie]* to spread; *[parti politique]* to expand; *[ville]* to spread, to expand; *[pouvoirs, domaine, fortune]* to increase, to expand; *[cercle d'amis]* to expand, to widen; *[recherches]* to broaden in scope; *[connaissances, vocabulaire]* to increase, to widen

5 *(= s'appliquer)* *[loi, avis]* to apply *(à* to); ♦ **sa bonté s'étend à tous** his kindness extends to everyone ♦ **cette mesure s'étend à tous les citoyens** this measure applies *ou* is applicable to *ou* covers all citizens ♦ **la domination romaine s'est étendue sur tout le monde méditerranéen** Roman rule spread *ou* expanded throughout the Mediterranean world

6 *(= s'étaler)* *[substance]* to spread ♦ **cette peinture s'étend facilement** this paint goes on *ou* spreads easily

étendu, e¹ /etɑ̃dy/ (ptp de **étendre**) **ADJ** 1 *(= vaste)* *[ville]* sprawling *(épith)*, spread out *(attrib)*; *[domaine]* extensive, large; *[connaissances, pouvoirs]* extensive, wide, wide-ranging; *[vue]* wide, extensive; *[vocabulaire]* wide, large, extensive; *[sens d'un mot]* broad *(épith)*, wide; *[dégâts]* extensive, widespread; *[famille]* extended 2 *(= allongé)* *[personne, jambes]* stretched out ♦ **~ sur l'herbe** lying *ou* stretched out on the grass ♦ **~ les bras en croix** spreadeagled ♦ **le cadavre, ~ sur le sol** the corpse, stretched (out) on the ground

étendue² /etɑ̃dy/ **NF** 1 *(= surface)* area, expanse ♦ **pays d'une grande ~** country with a large surface area *ou* which covers a large area ♦ **sur une ~ de 16 km** over an expanse *ou* area of 16 km ♦ **sur toute l'~ de la province** throughout the whole province, throughout the length and breadth of the province ♦ **grande ~ de sable** large stretch *ou* expanse of sand ♦ **surpris par l'~ de ce territoire** amazed at the sheer size *ou* extent of the territory

2 *(= durée)* *[de vie]* duration, length ♦ **sur une ~ de trois ans** over a period of three years

3 *(= importance)* *[de pouvoir, dégâts]* extent; *[de connaissances, recherches]* range, scope, extent ♦ **pouvoir/culture d'une grande ~** wide *ou* wide-ranging *ou* extensive power/culture ♦ **devant l'~ du désastre** faced with the scale of the disaster

4 *(Mus)* *[de voix]* compass, range; *[d'instrument]* range

5 *(Philos)* *[de matière]* extension, extent

éternel, -elle /etɛʀnɛl/ **ADJ** 1 *(Philos, Rel)* eternal ♦ **je ne suis pas ~ !** I won't live forever! ♦ **la vie éternelle** eternal *ou* everlasting life 2 *(= sans fin)* eternal, everlasting, endless ♦ **ma reconnaissance sera éternelle** I'll be eternally grateful to you; → **neige** 3 *(= perpétuel)* perpetual, eternal ◆ **c'est un ~ insatisfait** he's never happy with anything, he's perpetually *ou* eternally dissatisfied ◆ **c'est l'~ problème de ...** it's the eternal problem of ... 4 *(* = inamovible : avant n)* inevitable ◆ **il était là, son ~ chapeau sur la tête** there he was, wearing the same old hat NM 1 *(Rel)* **l'Éternel** the Eternal, the Everlasting; *(Bible)* the Lord ◆ **grand joueur devant l'Éternel** *(hum)* inveterate gambler 2 ◆ **l'~ féminin** the eternal feminine *ou* woman

éternellement /etɛʀnɛlmɑ̃/ ADV eternally; *[attendre, durer, rester]* forever ◆ **~ jeune** forever young

éterniser /etɛʀnize/ ▸ conjug 1 ◂ VT 1 *[+ débats, supplice, situation]* to drag out, to draw out 2 *(littér) [+ nom, mémoire]* to immortalize, to perpetuate VPR **s'éterniser** *[situation, débat, attente]* to drag on, to go on and on; *[visiteur]* to stay *ou* linger too long, to linger on ◆ **le jury s'éternise** the jury is taking ages ◆ **on ne peut pas s'~ ici** we can't stay here for ever ◆ **ne nous éternisons pas sur ce sujet** let's not dwell forever on that subject

éternité /etɛʀnite/ NF eternity ◆ **cela fait une ~ *ou* des ~s que je ne l'avais rencontré** it's ages *ou* donkey's years* *(Brit)* since I'd met him, I hadn't met him in ages ◆ **il y a des ~s que tu m'as promis cela** you promised me that ages ago, it's ages since you promised me that ◆ **ça a duré une ~** it lasted for ages ◆ **ça va durer une ~** it'll take forever ◆ **de toute ~** from the beginning of time, from time immemorial ◆ **pour l'~** for all eternity, eternally

éternuement /etɛʀnymɑ̃/ NM sneeze

éternuer /etɛʀnɥe/ ▸ conjug 1 ◂ VI to sneeze

étêter /etete/ ▸ conjug 1 ◂ VT *[+ arbre]* to pollard, to poll; *[+ clou, poisson]* to cut the head off

éthane /etan/ NM ethane

éthanol /etanɔl/ NM ethanol

éther /etɛʀ/ NM *(Chim)* ether

éthéré, e /eteʀe/ ADJ *(Chim, littér)* ethereal

Ethernet /etɛʀnɛt/ NM Ethernet

éthéromane /eteʀɔman/ NMF ether addict

éthéromanie /eteʀɔmani/ NF addiction to ether

Éthiopie /etjɔpi/ NF Ethiopia

éthiopien, -ienne /etjɔpjɛ̃, jɛn/ ADJ Ethiopian NM,F **Éthiopien(ne)** Ethiopian

éthique /etik/ ADJ ethical NF *(Philos)* ethics *(sg)*; *(= code moral)* moral code, code of ethics

ethmoïde /ɛtmɔid/ NM ethmoid

ethnicité /ɛtnisite/ NF ethnicity

ethnie /ɛtni/ NF ethnic group

ethnique /ɛtnik/ ADJ ethnic ◆ **minorité ~** ethnic minority ◆ **nettoyage *ou* purification ~** ethnic cleansing

ethnocentrisme /ɛtnosɑ̃tʀism/ NM ethnocentrism

ethnographe /ɛtnɔgʀaf/ NMF ethnographer

ethnographie /ɛtnɔgʀafi/ NF ethnography

ethnographique /ɛtnɔgʀafik/ ADJ ethnographic(al)

ethnolinguistique /ɛtnolɛ̃gɥistik/ NF ethnolinguistics *(sg)*

ethnologie /ɛtnɔlɔʒi/ NF ethnology

ethnologique /ɛtnɔlɔʒik/ ADJ ethnologic(al)

ethnologue /ɛtnɔlɔg/ NMF ethnologist

ethnomusicologie /ɛtnɔmyzikɔlɔʒi/ NF ethnomusicology

ethnomusicologue /ɛtnɔmyzikɔlɔg/ NMF ethnomusicologist

éthologie /etɔlɔʒi/ NF ethology

éthologique /etɔlɔʒik/ ADJ ethological

éthologiste /etɔlɔʒist/ NMF ethologist

éthologue /etɔlɔg/ NMF ethologist

éthyle /etil/ NM ethyl

éthylène /etilɛn/ NM ethylene

éthylique /etilik/ ADJ *[coma]* alcoholic; *[délire]* alcohol-induced ◆ **alcool ~** ethyl alcohol ◆ **gastrite ~** alcoholic gastritis NMF alcoholic

éthylisme /etilism/ NM alcoholism ◆ **crise d'~** alcoholic fit

éthylomètre /etilɔmɛtʀ/ NM ⇒ **éthylotest**

éthylotest /etilɔtɛst/ NM Breathalyser ® *(Brit)*, Breathalyzer ® *(US)*

étiage /etjaʒ/ NM *(= baisse)* low water *(NonC) (of a river)*; *(= niveau)* low-water level; *(= marque)* low-water mark

étincelant, e /etɛ̃s(ə)lɑ̃, ɑ̃t/ ADJ 1 *[lame, métal]* gleaming; *[étoile]* glittering, twinkling; *[diamant]* sparkling, glittering ◆ **~ de propreté** sparkling clean 2 *[yeux] (de colère)* flashing; *(de joie)* shining 3 *[conversation]* scintillating, brilliant; *[beauté]* dazzling ◆ **il a été ~** he was brilliant

étinceler /etɛ̃s(ə)le/ ▸ conjug 4 ◂ VI 1 *[lame, métal]* to gleam; *[étoile]* to glitter, to twinkle; *[diamant]* to sparkle, to glitter ◆ **la mer étincelle au soleil** the sea is sparkling *ou* glittering in the sun ◆ **~ de mille feux** *(littér) [soleil, nuit, bague]* to glitter with a myriad lights *(littér)* 2 *[yeux]* **~ de colère** to glitter *ou* flash with anger ◆ **~ de joie** to sparkle *ou* shine with joy 3 *[conversation, esprit, intelligence]* to sparkle; *[beauté]* to sparkle, to shine

étincelle /etɛ̃sɛl/ NF 1 *(= parcelle incandescente)* spark ◆ **~ électrique** electric spark ◆ **jeter des ~s** to throw out sparks ◆ **c'est l'~ qui a mis le feu aux poudres** *(fig)* it was this which sparked off *ou* touched off the incident ◆ **faire des ~s*** *(= se distinguer)* to scintillate, to shine ◆ **ça va faire des ~s*** *(= exploser)* sparks will fly 2 *[de lame, regard]* flash, glitter ◆ **jeter *ou* lancer des ~s** *[diamant, regard]* to flash 3 *[de raison, intelligence]* gleam, flicker, glimmer ◆ **~ de génie** spark *ou* flash of genius

étincellement /etɛ̃sɛlmɑ̃/ NM 1 *[de lame]* gleam *(NonC)*; *[d'étoile]* glitter *(NonC)*, twinkling *(NonC)*; *[de diamant]* sparkle *(NonC)*, glitter *(NonC)* 2 *[de yeux] (de colère)* flashing *(NonC)*; *(de joie)* sparkle *(NonC)*, shining *(NonC)*

étiolement /etjɔlmɑ̃/ NM 1 *[de plante]* blanching, etiolation *(SPÉC)* 2 *[de personne, intelligence]* decline

étioler /etjɔle/ ▸ conjug 1 ◂ VT 1 *[+ plante]* to blanch, to etiolate *(SPÉC)* 2 *[+ personne]* to weaken, to make sickly VPR **s'étioler** 1 *[plante]* to wilt 2 *[personne]* to languish, to decline; *[intelligence]* to decline

étiologie /etjɔlɔʒi/ NF etiology

étiologique /etjɔlɔʒik/ ADJ etiological

étique /etik/ ADJ skinny, bony

étiquetage /etik(ə)taʒ/ NM *[de paquet]* labelling; *[de prix]* marking, labelling

étiqueter /etik(ə)te/ ▸ conjug 4 ◂ VT *[+ paquet]* to label; *[+ prix]* to mark, to label; *[+ personne]* to label, to classify *(comme* as); ◆ **il étiquette toujours les gens** he's always putting people in little boxes, he's always pigeonholing people *(Brit)*

étiqueteur /etik(ə)tœʀ/ NM *(Ordin)* tagger

étiquette /etikɛt/ NF 1 *(sur paquet, Ordin)* label; *(de prix)* price tag ◆ **~ autocollante** self-stick *ou* self-adhesive *ou* stick-on label ◆ **~ politique** political label ◆ **les sans ~** *(Pol)* the independents ◆ **mettre une ~ à qn** *(fig)* to label sb, to stick a label on sb, to pigeonhole sb *(Brit)* 2 *(= protocole)* **l'~** etiquette

étirable /etiʀabl/ ADJ → **film**

étirement /etiʀmɑ̃/ NM stretching ◆ **exercice d'~** stretching exercise ◆ **faire des ~s** to do stretching exercises *ou* stretches

étirer /etiʀe/ ▸ conjug 1 ◂ VT *[+ peaux]* to stretch; *[+ métal, verre]* to draw (out) ◆ **~ ses membres** to stretch one's limbs VPR **s'étirer** *[personne]* to stretch; *[vêtement]* to stretch; *[convoi]* to stretch out; *[route]* to stretch out *ou* away

Etna /ɛtna/ NM ◆ **l'~** Etna, Mount Etna

étoffe /etɔf/ NF 1 *(= tissu)* material, fabric; *[de livre]* material, stuff 2 *(fig)* **avoir l'~ de** to have the makings of, to be cut out to be ◆ **avoir l'~ d'un héros** to be of the stuff heroes are made of, to have the makings of a hero ◆ **il a de l'~** *[personne]* he has a strong personality; *[roman]* it's really meaty ◆ **manquer d'~** *[personne]* to lack personality; *[roman]* to lack substance

étoffé, e /etɔfe/ (ptp de **étoffer**) ADJ *[personne]* fleshy; *[discours]* meaty; *[catalogue, bibliothèque, palmarès]* substantial; *[équipe]* beefed up*, strengthened ◆ **carnet de commandes bien ~** full order book ◆ **volumes (de transactions) ~s** *(Bourse)* heavy trading ◆ **dans un marché ~ de 404 600 titres** in a market buoyed up *ou* bolstered by 404,600 bonds

étoffer /etɔfe/ ▸ conjug 1 ◂ VT *[+ style]* to enrich; *[+ discours, personnage]* to fill out, to flesh out; *[+ répertoire]* to extend; *[+ équipe]* to beef up*, to strengthen *(de* with); *[+ carnet de commandes]* to fill out ◆ **~ ses sourcils au crayon** to fill out one's eyebrows with eyebrow pencil VPR **s'étoffer** *[personne]* to fill out, to thicken, to get thicker; *[carnet de commandes]* to fill up

étoile /etwal/ NF 1 *(Astron)* star ◆ **~ filante** shooting star ◆ **~ polaire** pole star, north star ◆ **~ du berger *ou* du soir** evening star ◆ **~ du matin** morning star, daystar ◆ **~ de David** star of David ◆ **~ jaune** *(Hist)* yellow star ◆ **semé d'~s** starry, star-studded ◆ **sans ~** starless ◆ **à la clarté des ~s** by starlight ◆ **dormir *ou* coucher à la belle ~** to sleep out in the open, to sleep under the stars

2 *(= dessin, objet)* star; *(= fêlure)* crack ◆ **général à deux ~s** two-star general ◆ **trois ~s** *[cognac, restaurant]* three-star *(épith)* ◆ **un trois ~s** *(= restaurant)* a three-star restaurant; *(= hôtel)* a three-star hotel ◆ **moteur en ~** radial engine

3 *(Ciné, Danse)* star ◆ **~ du cinéma** film star, movie star *(US)* ◆ **~ de la danse** dancing star ◆ **~ montante** rising *ou* up-and-coming star

4 *(= destinée)* **avoir foi en son ~** to trust one's lucky star, to trust to one's luck ◆ **être né sous une bonne/mauvaise ~** to be born under a lucky/an unlucky star ◆ **son ~ a pâli** his star has faded

COMP **étoile d'argent** *(= plante)* edelweiss

étoile de mer starfish

étoiler /etwale/ ▸ conjug 1 ◂ VT 1 *(= parsemer)* to stud *(de* with); ◆ **nuit étoilée** starry *ou* starlit night ◆ **ciel étoilé** starry *ou* star-studded sky 2 *(= fêler) (gén)* to crack; *[+ pare-brise]* to craze

étole /etɔl/ NF *(Rel, gén)* stole

étonnamment /etɔnamɑ̃/ ADV surprisingly; *(plus fort)* amazingly, astonishingly

étonnant, e /etɔnɑ̃, ɑ̃t/ ADJ 1 *(= surprenant)* surprising; *(plus fort)* amazing, astonishing ◆ **rien d'~ à cela, cela n'a rien d'~** no wonder, there's nothing (so) surprising about that 2 *(= remarquable) [personne]* amazing, incredible ◆ **vous êtes ~ !** you're incredible *ou* amazing! NM ◆ **l'~ est que** the astonishing *ou* amazing thing *ou* fact is that, what's astonishing *ou* amazing is that

étonné, e /etɔne/ (ptp de **étonner**) ADJ surprised; *(plus fort)* amazed, astonished ◆ **il a pris un air ~ *ou* a fait l'~ quand je lui ai dit** he acted surprised when I told him ◆ **je ne serais**

pas autrement ~ I wouldn't be that surprised ◆ **j'ai été très ~ de l'apprendre** I was really surprised *ou* I was amazed to hear that ◆ **sous les yeux ~s du public** before the astonished gaze of the audience ◆ **il a été le premier ~ de sa réussite/de réussir** nobody was more surprised than he was at his success/to have succeeded

étonnement /etɔnmɑ̃/ NM surprise; *(plus fort)* amazement, astonishment (*devant* at); ◆ **à mon grand ~** to my amazement *ou* astonishment ◆ **quel ne fut pas mon ~ quand je le vis !** imagine my surprise when I saw him!

étonner /etɔne/ ▸ conjug 1 ◂ VT to surprise; *(plus fort)* to amaze, to astonish ◆ **ça m'étonne que ...** I am surprised that ..., it surprises me that ... ◆ **ça ne m'étonne pas** I'm not surprised, it doesn't surprise me (*que* that) ◆ **vous serez étonnés du résultat** you'll be surprised by *ou* at the result ◆ **ça m'étonnerait** I should be very surprised ◆ **tu m'étonnes !*** *(iro)* you don't say!* *(iro)* VPR **s'étonner** to be surprised; *(plus fort)* to be amazed (*de qch* at sth; *de voir qch* at seeing sth); ◆ **je m'étonne que ...** I am surprised that ..., it surprises me that ... ◆ **il ne faut pas s'~ si ...** it's hardly surprising that ...

étouffant, e /etufɑ̃, ɑ̃t/ ADJ stifling

étouffe-chrétien* /etufkʀetjɛ̃/ NM INV ◆ **c'est de l'~** *ou* **un ~** it's stodgy

étouffée /etufe/ **à l'étouffée** LOC ADV ◆ **cuire à l'~** *[poisson, légumes, viande]* to steam LOC ADJ *[poisson, légumes, viande]* steamed

étouffement /etufmɑ̃/ NM [1] *(= mort)* suffocation ◆ **tuer qn par ~** to kill sb by suffocating *ou* smothering him ◆ **mourir d'~** to die of suffocation [2] *(Méd)* **sensation d'~** feeling of suffocation *ou* breathlessness ◆ **avoir des ~s** to have fits of breathlessness [3] *(= action) [de scandale]* hushing-up; *[de rumeurs]* suppression, stifling; *[de révolte]* quelling, suppression; *[de scrupules]* stifling, overcoming [4] *[de pas]* muffling

étouffer /etufe/ ▸ conjug 1 ◂ VT [1] *[assassin]* to suffocate, to smother; *[chaleur, atmosphère]* to suffocate, to stifle; *[sanglots, colère, aliment]* to choke; *(fig)* to stifle, to suffocate ◆ **mourir étouffé** to die of suffocation, to suffocate to death ◆ **~ qn de baisers** to smother sb with kisses ◆ **les scrupules ne l'étouffent pas** he isn't hampered *ou* overburdened by scruples, he doesn't let scruples cramp his style ◆ **ce n'est pas la politesse qui l'étouffe !*** politeness is not his forte! *ou* his strong suit! ◆ **ça l'étoufferait de dire merci** it would kill him to say thank you ◆ **plantes qui étouffent les autres** plants which choke *ou* smother others

[2] *[+ bruit]* to muffle, to deaden; *[+ bâillement]* to stifle, to smother, to suppress; *[+ sanglots, cris]* to smother, to choke back, to stifle ◆ **~ un juron** to stop o.s. swearing ◆ **rires étouffés** suppressed *ou* smothered laughter ◆ **dit-il d'une voix étouffée** he said in a low *ou* hushed tone ◆ **voix étouffées** *(discrètes)* subdued voices; *(confuses)* muffled voices

[3] *[+ scandale, affaire]* to hush up, to keep quiet; *[+ rumeurs, scrupules, sentiments]* to smother, to suppress, to stifle; *[+ révolte]* to put down, to quell, to suppress

[4] *[+ flammes]* to smother, to extinguish, to quench *(littér)* ◆ **~ un feu** to put out *ou* smother a fire

VI *(= mourir étouffé)* to die of suffocation, to suffocate to death; *(= être mal à l'aise)* to feel stifled, to suffocate ◆ **~ de colère/de rire** to choke with anger/with laughter ◆ **~ de chaleur** to be stifled, to be overcome with the heat ◆ **on étouffe dans cette pièce** it's stifling in here, the heat is suffocating *ou* overpowering in here

VPR **s'étouffer** *(gén)* to suffocate ◆ **s'~ en mangeant** to choke on something

étouffoir /etufwaʀ/ NM *(Mus)* damper ◆ **quel ~ ici !*** it's very stuffy in here!

étoupe /etup/ NF *(de lin, chanvre)* tow; *(de cordages)* oakum

étourderie /etuʀdəʀi/ NF *(= caractère)* absentmindedness ◆ **(faute d')~** *(= bévue)* careless mistake *ou* blunder ◆ **agir par ~** to act without thinking *ou* carelessly

étourdi, e /etuʀdi/ (ptp de **étourdir**) ADJ *[personne, action]* scatterbrained, absent-minded NM,F scatterbrain ◆ **agir en ~** to act without thinking *ou* carelessly

étourdiment /etuʀdimɑ̃/ ADV carelessly, rashly

étourdir /etuʀdiʀ/ ▸ conjug 2 ◂ VT [1] *(= assommer)* to stun, to daze [2] ◆ **~ qn** *[bruit]* to deafen sb; *[succès, parfum, vin]* to go to sb's head ◆ **l'altitude m'étourdit** heights make me dizzy *ou* giddy, I've no head for heights *(Brit)* ◆ **ce vacarme m'étourdit** this row is deafening ◆ **ce mouvement m'étourdit** this movement makes my head spin *ou* makes me feel quite dizzy VPR **s'étourdir** ◆ **il s'étourdit par la boisson** he drowns his sorrows in drink ◆ **il s'étourdit par les plaisirs** he tries to forget *ou* to deaden his sorrows by living a life of pleasure ◆ **il s'étourdit pour oublier** he keeps up a whirl of activity to forget ◆ **s'~ de paroles** to get drunk on words, to be carried away by the sound of one's own voice

étourdissant, e /etuʀdisɑ̃, ɑ̃t/ ADJ *[bruit]* deafening, earsplitting; *[succès]* staggering, stunning; *[beauté]* stunning ◆ **à un rythme ~** at a tremendous *ou* breakneck pace ◆ **~ de beauté** stunningly beautiful

étourdissement /etuʀdismɑ̃/ NM [1] *(= syncope)* blackout; *(= vertige)* dizzy spell, fit of giddiness ◆ **ça me donne des ~s** it makes me feel dizzy, it makes my head swim* *ou* spin [2] *(littér = surprise)* surprise [3] *(littér = griserie)* exhilaration, intoxication

étourneau (pl **étourneaux**) /etuʀno/ NM [1] *(= oiseau)* starling [2] *(* = distrait)* scatterbrain, featherbrain *(Brit)*, birdbrain *(US)*

étrange /etʀɑ̃ʒ/ ADJ strange, odd, peculiar ◆ **et chose ~** strangely *ou* funnily enough, the odd thing is ◆ **aussi ~ que cela puisse paraître** strange as it may seem ◆ **cela n'a rien d'~** there is nothing strange about *ou* in that NM ◆ **l'~** the bizarre ◆ **l'~ dans tout cela, c'est que ...** the odd *ou* strange *ou* funny thing is that ...

étrangement /etʀɑ̃ʒmɑ̃/ ADV *(= bizarrement)* strangely, oddly; *(= étonnamment)* surprisingly, amazingly ◆ **ressembler ~ à** to be surprisingly *ou* amazingly *ou* suspiciously like

étranger, -ère /etʀɑ̃ʒe, ɛʀ/ ADJ [1] *(= d'un autre pays)* foreign; *(Pol) [politique, affaires]* foreign ◆ **être ~ au pays** to be a foreigner ◆ **visiteurs ~s** foreign visitors, visitors from abroad

[2] *(= d'un autre groupe)* strange, unknown (*à* to); ◆ **être ~ à un groupe** not to belong to a group, be an outsider ◆ **il est ~ à notre famille** he is not a relative of ours, he is not a member of our family ◆ **"entrée interdite à toute personne étrangère à l'établissement** *ou* **au service"** "no entry for unauthorized persons", "no unauthorized entry"

[3] *(= inconnu) [nom, usage, milieu]* strange, unfamiliar (*à* to); *[idée]* strange, odd ◆ **son nom/son visage ne m'est pas ~** his name/face is not unknown *ou* not unfamiliar to me ◆ **cette personne/technique lui est étrangère** this person/technique is unfamiliar *ou* unknown to him, he is unfamiliar *ou* unacquainted with this person/technique ◆ **ce sentiment ne lui est pas ~** this feeling is not unknown to him; → **corps**

[4] *(= extérieur) [donnée, fait]* extraneous (*à* to); ◆ **~ au sujet** irrelevant (to the subject), beside the point ◆ **il est ~ au complot** he is not involved *ou* mixed up in the plot, he has nothing to do with the plot

NM,F [1] *(d'un autre pays)* foreigner; *(péj, Admin)* alien ◆ **une étrangère** a foreign woman ◆ **c'est une étrangère** she's a foreigner

[2] *(= inconnu)* stranger; *(à un groupe)* outsider, stranger

NM *(= pays)* ◆ **l'~** foreign countries, foreign parts ◆ **vivre/voyager à l'~** to live/travel abroad ◆ **rédacteur pour l'~** foreign editor ◆ **nouvelles de l'~** *(Journalisme)* news from abroad

étrangeté /etʀɑ̃ʒte/ NF *(= caractère) [de conduite]* strangeness, oddness; *(= fait ou événement bizarre)* odd *ou* strange fact *(ou event etc)*

étranglé, e /etʀɑ̃gle/ (ptp de **étrangler**) ADJ [1] *[voix]* tight, strangled ◆ **elle a poussé un petit cri ~** she let out a strangled little cry [2] *(= resserré)* **taille ~e** tightly constricted waist

étranglement /etʀɑ̃gləmɑ̃/ NM [1] *[de victime]* strangulation; *(Hist = supplice)* garotting; *[de presse, libertés]* stifling [2] *[de vallée]* neck; *[de rue]* bottleneck, narrowing; *[de taille, tuyau]* constriction [3] *[de voix]* strain, tightness [4] *(Méd)* strangulation [5] *(Sport)* stranglehold ◆ **faire un ~ à qn** to get sb in a stranglehold

étrangler /etʀɑ̃gle/ ▸ conjug 1 ◂ VT [1] *(= tuer) [+ personne]* to strangle, to choke, to throttle; *[+ poulet]* to wring the neck of; *(Hist = supplicier)* to garotte ◆ **mourir étranglé (par son écharpe)** to be strangled (by one's scarf) ◆ **cette cravate m'étrangle** this tie is choking *ou* throttling me; → **hernie**

[2] *[rage]* to choke ◆ **la fureur l'étranglait** he was choking with rage ◆ **voix étranglée par l'émotion** voice choked with emotion

[3] *[+ presse, libertés]* to stifle ◆ **taxes qui étranglent les commerçants** taxes which cripple shopkeepers

[4] *(= resserrer)* to squeeze (tightly)

VPR **s'étrangler** [1] *[personne]* to strangle o.s. ◆ **elle s'est étranglée accidentellement** she was strangled accidentally, she accidentally strangled herself ◆ **s'~ de rire/colère** to choke with laughter/anger ◆ **s'~ en mangeant** to choke on something

[2] *[voix, sanglots]* to catch in one's throat ◆ **un cri s'étrangla dans sa gorge** a cry caught *ou* died in his throat

[3] *[rue, couloir]* to narrow (down), to make a bottleneck

étrangleur, -euse /etʀɑ̃glœʀ, øz/ ADJ M ◆ **collier ~** choke chain NM,F strangler

étrave /etʀav/ NF *(Naut)* stem

être /ɛtʀ/
▸ conjug 61 ◂

1 VERBE COPULE	4 VERBE IMPERSONNEL
2 VERBE AUXILIAIRE	5 NOM MASCULIN
3 VERBE INTRANSITIF	

Pour les expressions figées telles que **être sur le point de, être en colère, étant donné que, il est de règle de** etc, reportez-vous au nom ou au verbe ; pour les expressions telles que **c'est à relire, être en robe, en être à, être pour faire qch** etc, reportez-vous à la préposition.

1 - VERBE COPULE

[1] pour qualifier to be ◆ **le ciel est bleu** the sky is blue ◆ **elle veut ~ médecin** she wants to be a doctor ◆ **soyez sages !** be good! ◆ **tu n'es qu'un enfant** you are only a child ◆ **si j'étais vous, je lui parlerais** if I were you I'd speak to her ◆ **il est tout pour elle** he's everything to her, he means the world to her ◆ **il n'est plus rien pour moi** he doesn't mean anything to me

any more ◆ **nous sommes dix à vouloir partir** ten of us want to go

2 pour indiquer la date **nous sommes** *ou* **on est le 12 janvier** it's the 12 January ◆ **on était en juillet** it was (in) July ◆ **quel jour sommes-nous ?** *(date)* what's the date today?, what's today's date?; *(jour)* what day is it (today)?

3 appartenance, participation à une activité

◆ **être de** ◆ **nous sommes de la même religion** we are of the same faith ◆ ~ **de la fête/de l'expédition** to take part in the celebration/in the expedition ◆ ~ **de noce/de baptême** to be at a wedding/christening ◆ **je ne serai pas du voyage** I won't be going ◆ **elle est des nôtres** *(= elle vient avec nous)* she's coming with us; *(= elle appartient à notre groupe, à la même communauté d'esprit)* she's one of us ◆ **je ne pourrai pas ~ des vôtres jeudi** I won't be able to come on Thursday ◆ **serez-vous des nôtres demain ?** will you be coming tomorrow?

◆ **en être** ◆ **vous en êtes ?** are you taking part? ◆ **il y avait une conférence, et bien sûr elle en était** there was a conference, and of course she was there ◆ **il en est*, c'en est une*** *(péj = homosexuel)* he's one of them* *(péj)*

2 - VERBE AUXILIAIRE

être se traduit par **have** pour former les temps composés de verbes intransitifs ou pronominaux ; ne pas oublier toutefois qu'un passé composé peut être rendu par un prétérit en anglais.

◆ **est-il déjà passé ?** has he been already? ◆ **nous étions montés** we had gone upstairs ◆ **il est passé hier** he came yesterday ◆ **elle serait tombée** she would *ou* might have fallen ◆ **il s'est assis** he sat down ◆ **ils s'étaient écrit** they had written to each other

être se traduit par **be** pour former le passif ; notez l'emploi du present perfect pour rendre certains présents français.

◆ ~ **donné/fabriqué par ...** to be given/made by ... ◆ **il est soutenu par son patron** he is backed up by his boss ◆ **l'eau est changée tous les jours** the water is changed every day ◆ **il a été blessé dans un accident** he was injured in an accident ◆ **elle n'a pas été invitée** she hasn't been invited ◆ **le contrat est signé** the contract has been signed ◆ **la maison est vendue** the house has been sold

3 - VERBE INTRANSITIF

1 = exister to be ◆ **je pense, donc je suis** I think, therefore I am ◆ **elle n'est plus** she is no more ◆ **le temps n'est plus où ...** the time is past when ... ◆ **que la lumière soit** let there be light ◆ **un menteur s'il en est** a liar if ever there was one ◆ **le meilleur homme qui soit** the kindest man imaginable

2 = se trouver to be ◆ **il est maintenant à Lille/au Japon** he is now in Lille/in Japan ◆ **le village est à 10 km d'ici** the village is 10 km from here ◆ **les verres étaient dans le placard** the glasses were in the cupboard ◆ **où étais-tu ?** where were you? ◆ **je suis à la page 25** I've got to *ou* reached page 25, I'm up to page 25

3

La tournure familière **avoir été** signifiant **être allé** est rendue par **be** sauf lorsque l'on a un prétérit en anglais ; dans ce cas, on utilise **go**.

◆ **il n'avait jamais été à Londres** he'd never been to London ◆ **as-tu déjà été à l'étranger ? – oui j'ai été en Italie l'an dernier** have you ever been abroad? – yes I went to Italy last year ◆ **elle a été lui téléphoner** *(elle est partie)* she's gone to phone him; *(elle est revenue)* she's been to phone him ◆ **elle a été lui téléphoner à 3 heures** she went to phone him at 3 o'clock ◆ **il a été dire que c'était de ma faute** he went and said that it was my fault

4 littér **il s'en fut la voir** he went to see her ◆ **elle s'en fut, furieuse** she left in a terrible rage

4 - VERBE IMPERSONNEL

1 gén **to be**

◆ **il est** + *adjectif* ◆ **il est étrange que ...** it's odd that ... ◆ **il fut facile de le convaincre** it was easy to convince him ◆ **il serait très agréable de voyager** it would be very nice to travel

2 pour dire l'heure **quelle heure est-il ?** what time is it? ◆ **il est 10 heures** it's 10 o'clock ◆ **il n'était pas encore 8 heures quand il est arrivé** it wasn't (even) 8 o'clock when he arrived ◆ **il n'était pas encore 10 heures que la place était pleine de monde** it wasn't (even) 10 o'clock and the square was already full of people

3 littér = il y a

◆ **il est** + *nom singulier* there is

◆ **il est** + *nom pluriel* there are ◆ **il est un pays où ...** there is a country where ... ◆ **il est des gens qui ...** there are people who ... ◆ **il n'est pas un jour sans que ...** not a single day passes without ... ◆ **il était une fois ...** once upon a time there was ...

4 autres locutions

◆ **c'est, ce sont** + *nom ou pronom* ◆ **c'est le médecin** *(en désignant)* he's *ou* that's the doctor; *(au téléphone, à la porte)* it's the doctor ◆ **c'est la plus intelligente de la classe** she's the most intelligent girl in the class ◆ **c'est la camionnette du boucher** it's *ou* that's the butcher's van ◆ **c'est une voiture rapide** it's a fast car ◆ **ce sont des mannequins/de bons souvenirs** they are models/happy memories

Notez l'emploi possible d'un auxiliaire en anglais pour traduire les propositions tronquées. Pour la forme **qui est-ce qui**, reportez-vous à **qui**.

◆ **qui a crié ? – c'est lui** who shouted? – he did *ou* it was him ◆ **qui le fera ? – c'est moi** who'll do it? – I will

◆ **c'est** + *adjectif* it is ◆ **c'est impossible** it's impossible ◆ **c'était bruyant/formidable** it was noisy/wonderful ◆ **c'est vrai** it's *ou* that's true ◆ **ça c'est vrai !** that's true ◆ **c'est vrai que ...** it's true that ...

Pour traduire des tournures emphatiques mettant en relief un sujet ou un complément, on peut employer soit un pronom suivi d'une relative, soit l'accent tonique.

◆ **c'est ... qui** ◆ **c'est le vent qui a emporté la toiture** it was the wind that blew the roof off ◆ **c'est eux*** *ou* **ce sont eux** *ou* **c'étaient eux qui mentaient** they are the ones who *ou* it's they who were lying ◆ **c'est toi qui le dis !** that's what YOU say! ◆ **c'est lui qui me l'a dit** he's the one who told me, he told me ◆ **c'est elle qui a voulu** SHE wanted it

◆ **c'est ... que** ◆ **c'est une bonne voiture que vous avez là** that's a good car you've got there ◆ **c'est ici que je l'ai trouvé** this is where I found it ◆ **c'était elle que je voulais rencontrer** she was the one I wanted to meet ◆ **ne partez pas, c'est à vous que je veux parler** don't go, it's you I want to talk to ◆ **c'est moi qu'on attendait** I was the one they were waiting for, it was me they were waiting for

Notez que l'anglais n'emploie pas de tournure avec le sujet réel antéposé.

◆ **voler, c'est quelque chose que je ne ferai jamais** stealing is something I'll never do

◆ **c'est que** *(pour expliquer)* ◆ **quand il écrit, c'est qu'il a besoin d'argent** when he writes, it's because he needs money ◆ **c'est qu'elle n'entend rien, la pauvre !** but the poor woman can't hear a thing!, but she can't hear, poor woman! ◆ **c'est que je le connais bien !** I know him so well! ◆ **c'est qu'elle n'a pas d'argent** it's because *ou* just that she has no money; *(exclamatif)* but she has no money!

◆ **ce n'est pas que** ◆ **ce n'est pas qu'il soit beau !** it's not that he's good-looking! ◆ **ce n'est pas qu'elle soit bête, mais elle est paresseuse** it's not that she's stupid, she's just lazy

◆ **est-ce que**

La forme interrogative **est-ce que** est rendue en anglais par l'auxiliaire suivi du pronom.

◆ **est-ce que tu m'entends ?** can you hear me? ◆ **est-ce que c'est/c'était vrai ?** is/was it true? ◆ **est-ce que vous saviez ?** did you know? ◆ **est-ce que c'est toi qui l'as battu ?** was it you who beat him? ◆ **quand est-ce que ce sera réparé ?** when will it be fixed? ◆ **où est-ce que tu l'as mis ?** where have you put it?

◆ **n'est-ce pas**

La forme interrogative **n'est-ce pas**, qui demande une confirmation, est rendue en anglais par l'auxiliaire suivi du pronom ; cette tournure est négative si la proposition est affirmative et inversement.

◆ **vous viendrez, n'est-ce pas ?** you will come, won't you?, you are coming, aren't you? ◆ **n'est-ce pas qu'il a promis ?** he did promise, didn't he? ◆ **il fait beau, n'est-ce pas ?** it's a lovely day, isn't it? ◆ **elle n'est pas partie, n'est-ce pas ?** she hasn't left, has she?

Notez les traductions possibles de la valeur intensive de **n'est-ce pas**.

◆ **le problème, n'est-ce pas, reste entier** you see the problem still hasn't been solved ◆ **ce n'est pas moi, n'est-ce pas, qui vais lui dire** I'm certainly not going to tell him ◆ **mais moi, n'est-ce pas, je ne suis qu'un raté** but I'm just a failure, aren't I?

5 pour exprimer la supposition **si ce n'était** were it not for, if it were not for, but for ◆ **n'était son orgueil** *(littér)* were it not for *ou* but for his pride, if it were not for his pride ◆ **ne serait-ce que pour quelques jours** if (it were) only for a few days ◆ **ne serait-ce que pour nous ennuyer** if only to annoy us

5 - NOM MASCULIN

1 gén *(Sci)* being ◆ ~ **humain/animé/vivant** human/animate/living being

2 = individu person ◆ **les ~s qui nous sont chers** our loved ones, those who are dear to us ◆ **un ~ cher** a loved one ◆ **c'était un ~ merveilleux** he was a wonderful person

3 = âme **il l'aimait de tout son ~** he loved her with all his heart ◆ **au plus profond de notre ~** deep down in our hearts ◆ **tout son ~ se révoltait** his whole being rebelled

4 Philos **l'~** being ◆ **l'Être suprême** the Supreme Being

étreindre /etʀɛ̃dʀ/ ► conjug 52 ◄ **VT** 1 *(frm) (dans ses bras) [+ ami]* to embrace, to hug, to clasp in one's arms; *[+ ennemi]* to seize, to grasp; *(avec les mains)* to clutch, to grip, to grasp ◆ **les deux amis s'étreignirent** the two friends embraced each other; → **embrasser** 2 *[douleur]* to grip

étreinte /etʀɛ̃t/ **NF** *(frm) [d'ami]* embrace, hug; *[d'ennemi]* stranglehold, grip; *[de main, douleur]* clutch, grip, grasp ◆ **l'armée resserre son ~ autour de ...** the army is tightening its grip round ...

étrenner /etʀene/ ▸ conjug 1 ◂ VT to use (*ou* wear *etc*) for the first time VI († * = *écoper*) to catch it*, to cop it* (*Brit*), to get it*

étrennes /etʀɛn/ NFPL (*à un enfant*) New Year's gift, Christmas present; (*au facteur etc*) ≈ Christmas box ◆ **que veux-tu pour tes ~ ?** what would you like for Christmas? *ou* as a Christmas present? ◆ **donner ses ~ à la femme de ménage** to give a Christmas box to the cleaning lady

étrier /etʀije/ NM (*Équitation, Constr, Méd*) stirrup; (*Anat*) stirrup bone, stapes (*SPÉC*); (*Alpinisme*) étrier (*Brit*), stirrup (*US*) ◆ **boire le coup de l'~** * (*gén*) to have one for the road*; [*cavalier*] to have a stirrup cup; → **pied, vider**

étrille /etʀij/ NF (= *brosse*) currycomb; (= *crabe*) velvet swimming crab

étriller /etʀije/ ▸ conjug 1 ◂ VT 1 [*+ cheval*] to curry(-comb) 2 (†, *hum* = *rosser*) to trounce †

étripage /etʀipaʒ/ NM gutting

étriper /etʀipe/ ▸ conjug 1 ◂ VT [*+ lapin*] to disembowel, to gut; [*+ volaille*] to draw; [*+ poisson*] to gut; * [*+ adversaire*] to cut open, to hack about (*Brit*) VPR **s'étriper** * to make mincemeat of each other*, to tear each other's guts out*

étriqué, e /etʀike/ (ptp de **étriquer**) ADJ [*vêtement, budget*] tight; [*esprit, conception, victoire, vision, vie*] narrow; [*marché*] tiny ◆ **il fait tout ~ dans son manteau** his coat looks far too small for him ◆ **le cadre ~ de ce domaine d'études** the narrow confines of this field (of study)

étriquer /etʀike/ ▸ conjug 1 ◂ VT ◆ **ce vêtement l'étrique** this garment is too tight-fitting for him

étrivière /etʀivjɛʀ/ NF stirrup leather

étroit, e /etʀwa, wat/ ADJ 1 [*rue, fenêtre, ruban*] narrow; [*espace*] narrow, cramped, confined; [*vêtement, chaussure*] tight ◆ **nous avons une marge de manœuvre très ~e** we have very little room for manoeuvre ◆ **être ~ des hanches** *ou* **du bassin** to have narrow hips
2 (= *borné*) [*vues*] narrow, limited ◆ **être ~ d'esprit** to be narrow-minded
3 (= *intime*) [*amitié*] close (*épith*); [*liens*] close (*épith*), intimate (*épith*) ◆ **en collaboration ~e avec ...** in close collaboration with ...
4 (= *strict*) [*surveillance*] close (*épith*), strict (*épith*); [*coordination, subordination*] strict (*épith*)
5 (*Ling*) [*acception*] narrow (*épith*), strict (*épith*), restricted ◆ **au sens ~ du terme** in the narrow *ou* strict sense of the term
6 (= *serré*) [*nœud, étreinte*] tight
LOC ADV **à l'étroit** cramped ◆ **vivre** *ou* **être logé à l'~** to live in cramped *ou* confined conditions ◆ **être à l'~ dans ses vêtements** to be wearing clothes that are too small, to be bursting out of one's clothes ◆ **il se sent un peu à l'~** (*dans un département, un parti*) he feels a bit cramped

étroitement /etʀwatmɑ̃/ ADV [*lier, unir*] closely; [*obéir*] strictly; [*surveiller*] closely, strictly; [*tenir*] tightly ◆ **être ~ logé** to live in cramped *ou* confined conditions

étroitesse /etʀwatɛs/ NF 1 [*de rue, fenêtre, espace, hanches*] narrowness ◆ **à cause de l'~ de ce logement** because of the cramped accommodation here 2 [*de vues*] narrowness ◆ **~ (d'esprit)** narrow-mindedness

étron /etʀɔ̃/ NM (*hum*) (piece of) excrement, turd**

Étrurie /etʀyʀi/ NF Etruria

étrusque /etʀysk/ ADJ Etruscan NM (= *langue*) Etruscan NMF **Étrusque** Etruscan

étude /etyd/ NF 1 (= *action*) (*gén*) study ◆ **l'~ d'un instrument** (*Mus*) the study of an instrument, learning to play an instrument ◆ **ce projet est à l'~** this project is under consideration *ou* is being studied ◆ **mettre un projet à l'~, procéder à l'~ d'un projet** to investigate *ou* go into *ou* study a project ◆ **avoir le goût de l'~** to like study *ou* studying ◆ **une ~ gratuite de vos besoins** a free assessment of your needs ◆ **voyage/frais d'~** study trip/costs ◆ **~ de marché** (*Écon*) market research (*NonC*) ◆ **~ de cas** case study ◆ **~ complémentaire** (*Fin*) follow-up study; → **bureau**
2 (*Scol, Univ*) **~s** studies ◆ **~s secondaires/supérieures** secondary/higher education ◆ **faire ses ~s à Paris** to study in Paris, to be educated in Paris ◆ **travailler pour payer ses ~s** to work to pay for one's education ◆ **faire des ~s de droit** to study law ◆ **quand je faisais mes ~s** when I was studying
3 (= *ouvrage*) study; (*Écon, Sci*) paper, study; (*Littérat*) study, essay ◆ **~s de fleurs** (*Art*) studies of flowers ◆ **~s pour piano** (*Mus*) studies *ou* études for (the) piano
4 (*Scol*) **(salle d')~** study *ou* prep room, private study room (*Brit*), study hall (*US*) ◆ **l'~ (du soir)** preparation, prep* (*Brit*) ◆ **~ surveillée** (supervised) study period (*Brit*), study hall (*US*) ◆ **être en ~** to have a study period ◆ **mettre des élèves en ~** to leave pupils to study on their own
5 (*Jur*) (= *bureau*) office; (= *charge, clientèle*) practice

étudiant, e /etydjɑ̃, jɑ̃t/ ADJ [*vie, problèmes, allures*] student (*épith*) NM,F student ◆ **~ en médecine/en lettres** medical/arts student ◆ **~ de première année** first-year student *ou* undergraduate, fresher (*Brit*), freshman (*US*) ◆ **~ de troisième cycle** post-graduate (student)

étudié, e /etydje/ (ptp de **étudier**) ADJ 1 (= *calculé*) [*jeu de scène*] studied; [*coupe, conception*] carefully designed; [*prix*] competitive, keen (*épith*) (*Brit*) ◆ **à des prix très ~s** at the lowest possible *ou* the keenest (*Brit*) prices ◆ **maison d'une conception très ~e** very carefully *ou* thoughtfully designed house 2 (= *affecté*) [*allure*] studied; [*sentiments*] affected, assumed

étudier /etydje/ GRAMMAIRE ACTIVE 53.2 ▸ conjug 7 ◂
VT 1 (= *apprendre*) [*+ matière*] (*gén*) to study; (*Univ*) to study, to read (*Brit*); [*+ instrument*] to study, to learn to play; (*Scol*) [*+ leçon*] to learn; [*+ texte, auteur*] to study ◆ **s'amuser au lieu d'~** to have a good time instead of studying
2 (= *examiner*) [*+ projet, possibilités*] to study, to examine, to go into; [*+ dossier, cas*] to study, to examine ◆ **~ une proposition sous tous ses aspects** to study a proposal from every angle ◆ **~ qch de près** to study sth closely, to make a close study of sth, to take a close look at sth
3 (= *observer*) [*+ terrain, adversaire*] to study, to observe closely; [*+ visage*] to study, to examine ◆ **je sentais qu'il m'étudiait constamment** I sensed that he was observing me all the time
4 (= *concevoir*) [*+ procédé, dispositif*] to devise; [*+ machine, coupe*] to design ◆ **c'est étudié pour*** that's what it's for
5 (= *calculer*) [*+ gestes, ton, effets*] to study, to calculate
VPR **s'étudier** (= *s'analyser*) to analyse o.s., to be introspective; (= *se regarder*) to study o.s. *ou* one's appearance ◆ **les deux adversaires s'étudiaient** the two opponents studied *ou* observed each other closely

étui /etɥi/ NM [*de violon, cigares*] case; [*de parapluie*] cover; [*de revolver*] holster ◆ **~ à lunettes** spectacle *ou* glasses case

étuve /etyv/ NF (= *bains*) steamroom; (*de désinfection*) sterilizer; (= *incubateur*) incubator ◆ **quelle ~ !** (*fig*) it's like a sauna in here!

étuvée /etyve/ **à l'étuvée** LOC ADV ◆ **cuire à l'~** [*+ poisson, légumes, viande*] to braise LOC ADJ [*poisson, légumes, viande*] braised

étuver /etyve/ ▸ conjug 1 ◂ VT 1 [*+ poisson, légumes*] to steam; [*+ viande*] to braise 2 (= *stériliser*) to sterilize

étymologie /etimɔlɔʒi/ NF etymology

étymologique /etimɔlɔʒik/ ADJ etymological

étymologiquement /etimɔlɔʒikmɑ̃/ ADV etymologically

étymologiste /etimɔlɔʒist/ NMF etymologist

étymon /etimɔ̃/ NM etymon

eu, e /y/ ptp de **avoir**

E.-U.(A.) NMPL (abrév de **États-Unis (d'Amérique)**) US(A)

eucalyptus /økaliptys/ NM eucalyptus

eucharistie /økaʀisti/ NF ◆ **l'Eucharistie, l'~** the Eucharist

eucharistique /økaʀistik/ ADJ eucharistic

Euclide /øklid/ NM Euclid

euclidien, -ienne /øklidjɛ̃, jɛn/ ADJ Euclidean

eudiomètre /ødjɔmɛtʀ/ NM eudiometer

eugénique /øʒenik/ NF eugenics (*sg*) ADJ eugenic

eugénisme /øʒenism/ NM eugenics (*sg*)

euh /ø/ EXCL er

eunuque /ønyk/ NM eunuch

euphémique /øfemik/ ADJ euphemistic(al)

euphémiquement /øfemikmɑ̃/ ADV euphemistically

euphémisme /øfemism/ NM euphemism

euphonie /øfɔni/ NF euphony

euphonique /øfɔnik/ ADJ euphonious, euphonic

euphoniquement /øfɔnikmɑ̃/ ADV euphoniously, euphonically

euphonium /øfɔnjɔm/ NM euphonium

euphorbe /øfɔʀb/ NF euphorbia, spurge

euphorie /øfɔʀi/ NF euphoria

euphorique /øfɔʀik/ ADJ euphoric

euphorisant, e /øfɔʀizɑ̃, ɑ̃t/ ADJ [*effet, nouvelle*] exhilarating NM ◆ **(médicament) ~** anti-depressant, pep pill*

euphoriser /øfɔʀize/ ▸ conjug 1 ◂ VT to make exhilarated

Euphrate /øfʀat/ NM ◆ **l'~** the Euphrates

eurafricain, e /øʀafʀikɛ̃, ɛn/ ADJ Eurafrican NM,F **Eurafricain(e)** Eurafrican

eurasiatique /øʀazjatik/ ADJ Eurasian NMF **Eurasiatique** Eurasian

Eurasie /øʀazi/ NF Eurasia

eurasien, -ienne /øʀazjɛ̃, jɛn/ ADJ Eurasian NM,F **Eurasien(ne)** Eurasian

EURATOM /øʀatɔm/ NF (abrév de **European Atomic Energy Commission**) EURATOM

eurêka /øʀeka/ EXCL eureka!

Euripide /øʀipid/ NM Euripides

euristique /øʀistik/ ADJ, NF ⇒ **heuristique**

euro /øʀo/ NM (= *monnaie*) euro

euro-américain, e (pl **euro-américains**) /øʀoameʀikɛ̃, ɛn/ ADJ Euro-American ◆ **alliance de défense ~e** Euro-American defence alliance

eurocentrisme /øʀosɑ̃tʀism/ NM (*péj*) Eurocentrism ◆ **nous sommes accusés d'~** we are accused of being Eurocentric *ou* of Eurocentrism

eurochèque /øʀɔʃɛk/ NM Eurocheque

eurocommunisme /øʀɔkɔmynism/ NM Eurocommunism

Eurocorps /øʀɔkɔʀ/ NM ◆ **l'~** the Eurocorps

eurocrate /øʀɔkʀat/ NMF Eurocrat

eurocratie /øʀɔkʀasi/ NF Eurocracy

eurodéputé /øʀodepyte/ NM Euro-MP

eurodevise /øʀɔdəviz/ NF Eurocurrency

eurodollar /øʀodɔlaʀ/ NM Eurodollar

eurofranc /øʀofʀɑ̃/ NM *(Fin)* eurofranc

Euroland /øʀolɑ̃d/ NM Euroland

euromissile /øʀomisil/ NM European missile

euro-obligations /øʀoɔbligasjɔ̃/ NF Eurobond

Europe /øʀɔp/ NF Europe ◆ **l'~ centrale/occidentale** central/Western Europe ◆ **l'~ de l'est** Eastern Europe ◆ **l'~ des quinze** the fifteen countries of the European Union ◆ **l'~ politique** political union in Europe ◆ **l'~ verte** European agriculture ◆ **il faut construire l'~ sociale** we must strive to build a Europe with a common social policy

européanisation /øʀɔpeanizasjɔ̃/ NF Europeanization

européaniser /øʀɔpeanize/ ▸ conjug 1 ◂ VT to Europeanize VPR **s'européaniser** to become Europeanized

européen, -enne /øʀɔpeɛ̃, ɛn/ ADJ European ◆ **les (élections) européennes** the European elections NM,F **Européen(ne)** *(Géog)* European; *(= partisan de l'Union européenne)* European, pro-European

europessimisme /øʀopesimism/ NM Europessimism

europhile /øʀofil/ ADJ, NMF Europhile

Europol /øʀɔpɔl/ N Europol

euroscepticisme /øʀosɛptisism/ NM Euroscepticism

eurosceptique /øʀosɛptik/ ADJ Eurosceptic(al) NMF Eurosceptic

Eurostar ® /øʀɔstaʀ/ NM Eurostar ® ◆ **voyager en ~** to travel by Eurostar

Eurovision /øʀɔvizjɔ̃/ NF Eurovision

Eurydice /øʀidis/ NF Eurydice

eurythmie /øʀitmi/ NF *(Mus)* eurhythmy; *(Méd)* eurhythmia

Eustache /østaʃ/ NM Eustace; → **trompe**

euthanasie /øtanazi/ NF euthanasia

eutrophisation /øtʀɔfizasjɔ̃/ NF eutrophication

eux /ø/ PRON PERS [1] *(sujet)* they ◆ **si j'étais ~** if I were *ou* was them, if I were they *(frm)* ◆ **nous y allons, ~ non** *ou* **pas ~** we are going but they aren't *ou* they're not *ou* not them ◆ **~ mentir ? ce n'est pas possible** them tell a lie? I can't believe it ◆ **ce sont ~ qui répondront** they are the ones who will reply, they'll reply ◆ **~ ils n'ont rien à dire** they've got nothing to say ◆ **ils l'ont bien fait, ~** they did it all right ◆ **~, pauvres innocents, ne l'ont jamais su** they, poor fools, never knew; → **même**
[2] *(objet)* them ◆ **il n'obéit qu'à ~** they are the only ones he obeys, he'll only obey them ◆ **les aider, ~ ? jamais !** help them? never!
[3] *(avec prép)* **à ~ tout seuls, ils ont tout acheté** they bought everything all on their own ◆ **cette maison est-elle à ~ ?** does this house belong to them?, is this house theirs? ◆ **ils ont cette grande maison pour ~ seuls** they have this big house all to themselves ◆ **ils ne pensent qu'à ~, ces égoïstes** these selfish people only think of themselves

eux-mêmes /ømɛm/ PRON → **même**

E.V. † /əve/ (abrév de **en ville**) by hand

évacuateur, -trice /evakɥatœʀ, tʀis/ ADJ evacuation *(épith)* NM sluice

évacuation /evakɥasjɔ̃/ NF *[de pays, personnes]* evacuation; *[de liquide]* draining; *(Méd)* evacuation ◆ **procéder à l'~ de** to evacuate

évacué, e /evakɥe/ (ptp de **évacuer**) NM,F evacuee

évacuer /evakɥe/ ▸ conjug 1 ◂ VT *[+ pays, ville, population]* to evacuate; *[+ salle, maison]* to evacuate, to clear; *(Méd)* to evacuate, to discharge; *[+ liquide]* to drain (off); * *[+ problème]* to dispose of ◆ **faire ~** *[+ salle, bâtiment]* to clear

évadé, e /evade/ (ptp de **s'évader**) NM,F escapee, escaped prisoner

évader (s') /evade/ ▸ conjug 1 ◂ VPR [1] *[prisonnier]* to escape *(de* from); ◆ **faire ~ qn** to help sb (to) escape [2] *(pour se distraire)* **s'~ de la réalité** to escape from reality ◆ **la musique me permet de m'~** music is an escape for me ◆ **j'ai besoin de m'~** *(= partir)* I need to get away from it all

évaluable /evalɥabl/ ADJ assessable ◆ **difficilement ~** difficult to assess *ou* evaluate

évaluation /evalɥasjɔ̃/ NF [1] *(= expertise) [de maison, bijou]* appraisal, evaluation, assessment, valuation; *[de dégâts, prix]* assessment, evaluation ◆ **~ des risques** risk assessment [2] *(approximative) [de fortune, nombre, distance]* estimation, assessment [3] *(= appréciation) [de besoins, risques, conséquences]* assessment [4] *[d'élève]* assessment ◆ **entretien d'~** *(en entreprise) [d'employé]* appraisal

évaluer /evalɥe/ ▸ conjug 1 ◂ VT [1] *(= expertiser) [+ maison, bijou]* to value (*à* at); *[+ dégâts, prix]* to assess, to evaluate (*à* at); ◆ **faire ~ qch par un expert** *[+ bijou, voiture]* to have sth valued by an expert ◆ **ils ont fait ~ les dégâts par un professionnel** they had an expert assess the damage [2] *(= juger approximativement) [+ fortune, nombre, distance]* to estimate, to assess (*à* at); ◆ **on évalue à 60 000 le nombre des réfugiés** there are an estimated 60,000 refugees, the number of refugees is estimated at *ou* put at 60,000 [3] *(= apprécier) [+ risques, besoins, conséquences]* to assess ◆ **bien/mal ~ qch** to be correct/mistaken in one's assessment of sth ◆ **j'ai mal évalué la distance** I misjudged the distance [4] *[+ élève, employé]* to assess

évanescence /evanesɑ̃s/ NF evanescence

évanescent, e /evanesɑ̃, ɑ̃t/ ADJ *(littér)* evanescent

évangélique /evɑ̃ʒelik/ ADJ evangelic(al)

évangélisateur, -trice /evɑ̃ʒelizatœʀ, tʀis/ ADJ evangelistic NM,F evangelist

évangélisation /evɑ̃ʒelizasjɔ̃/ NF evangelization

évangéliser /evɑ̃ʒelize/ ▸ conjug 1 ◂ VT to evangelize

évangélisme /evɑ̃ʒelism/ NM evangelism

évangéliste /evɑ̃ʒelist/ NM evangelist; *(Bible)* Evangelist

évangile /evɑ̃ʒil/ NM [1] *(Rel)* **l'Évangile** the Gospel ◆ **l'Évangile selon saint Jean** the Gospel according to St John ◆ **l'~ du jour** the gospel for the day, the day's reading from the gospel ◆ **les Évangiles synoptiques** the synoptic Gospels [2] *(fig)* gospel ◆ **c'est parole d'~** it's (the) gospel truth, it's gospel

évanoui, e /evanwi/ (ptp de **s'évanouir**) ADJ *[blessé]* unconscious ◆ **tomber ~** to faint, to pass out

évanouir (s') /evanwiʀ/ ▸ conjug 2 ◂ VPR *[personne]* to faint *(de* from) to pass out *(de* with) to black out *; *[rêves, apparition, craintes]* to vanish, to disappear

évanouissement /evanwismɑ̃/ NM [1] *(= syncope)* fainting fit, blackout [2] *[de rêves, apparition, craintes]* disappearance, fading

évaporation /evapɔʀasjɔ̃/ NF evaporation

évaporé, e /evapɔʀe/ (ptp de **évaporer**) ADJ *(péj) [personne]* giddy, scatterbrained, featherbrained *(Brit)* NM,F scatterbrain, featherbrain *(Brit)*, birdbrain

évaporer /evapɔʀe/ ▸ conjug 1 ◂ VTI ◆ **(faire) ~** to evaporate VPR **s'évaporer** *(lit)* to evaporate; *(* = disparaître)* to vanish *ou* disappear (into thin air)

évasé, e /evɑze/ (ptp de **évaser**) ADJ *[vallée, conduit]* which widens *ou* opens out; *[manches, jupe, pantalon]* flared ◆ **verre à bords ~s** glass with a curving *ou* bell-shaped rim

évasement /evɑzmɑ̃/ NM *[de passage, tuyau]* opening out; *[de manche, jupe]* flare ◆ **à cause de l'~ de la vallée** because of the way the valley opens out

évaser /evɑze/ ▸ conjug 1 ◂ VT *[+ tuyau, ouverture]* to widen, to open out; *[+ manche, jupe]* to flare VPR **s'évaser** *[passage, tuyau]* to open out; *[manche, jupe]* to flare

évasif, -ive /evazif, iv/ ADJ evasive

évasion /evazjɔ̃/ NF [1] *[de prisonnier]* escape *(de* from) [2] *(= divertissement)* **l'~** escape; *(= tendance)* escapism ◆ **littérature d'~** escapist literature ◆ **besoin d'~** need to escape ◆ **rechercher l'~ dans la drogue** to seek escape in drugs
COMP **évasion des capitaux** flight of capital
évasion fiscale tax evasion

> ⚠ **évasion** se traduit par **evasion** uniquement au sens fiscal.

évasivement /evazivmɑ̃/ ADV evasively

Ève /ɛv/ NF Eve; *(hum)* ◆ **en tenue d'~** in the altogether *, in one's birthday suit; → **connaître**

évêché /eveʃe/ NM *(= région)* bishopric; *(= palais)* bishop's palace; *(= ville)* cathedral town

éveil /evɛj/ NM *(littér) [de dormeur, intelligence]* awakening; *[d'amour]* awakening, dawning; *[de soupçons, jalousie]* arousing ◆ **être en ~** *[personne]* to be on the alert *ou* on the qui vive; *[sens]* to be alert *ou* wide awake, to be aroused ◆ **donner l'~** to raise the alarm *ou* alert ◆ **mettre qn en ~, donner l'~ à qn** to alert *ou* arouse sb's suspicions, to put sb on his guard ◆ **activités d'~** *(Scol)* early-learning activities

éveillé, e /eveje/ (ptp de **éveiller**) ADJ *(= alerte) [enfant, esprit, air]* alert, sharp, bright; *(= à l'état de veille)* (wide-)awake ◆ **tenir qn ~** to keep sb awake ◆ **rêve** *ou* **songe ~** daydream

éveiller /eveje/ ▸ conjug 1 ◂ VT [1] *(littér) (= réveiller)* to awaken, to waken [2] *(= faire naître) [+ curiosité, sentiment, souvenirs]* to arouse, to awaken; *[+ passion]* to kindle, to arouse ◆ **pour ne pas ~ l'attention** so as not to attract attention ◆ **sans ~ les soupçons** without arousing suspicion [3] *(= développer) [+ esprit]* to stimulate ◆ **~ l'intelligence de l'enfant** to awaken the child's intelligence VPR **s'éveiller** [1] *(= se réveiller) (lit)* to wake up, to awaken, to waken; *[ville, nature]* to come to life, to wake (up) [2] *(= naître) [sentiment, curiosité, soupçons]* to be aroused; *[amour]* to dawn, to be aroused *ou* born [3] *(= se développer) [intelligence, esprit]* to develop [4] *(littér = ressentir)* **s'~ à** *[+ amour]* to awaken to

événement, évènement /evɛnmɑ̃/ NM [1] *(gén)* event ◆ **semaine chargée en ~s** eventful week, action-packed week ◆ **l'~ de la semaine** the main story *ou* news of the week ◆ **faire** *ou* **créer l'~** *[personne, film]* to make a splash, to be big news ◆ **c'est un véritable ~ quand il dit merci** *(hum)* it's quite an event *ou* occasion when he says thank you ◆ **les ~s de mai 68** the events of May 1968 ◆ **les ~s d'Algérie** *the Algerian war of independence* ◆ **livre(-)/film(-)~** blockbuster; → **dépasser, heureux, tournure** [2] *(Ordin)* event

événementiel, -ielle /evɛnmɑ̃sjɛl/ ADJ factual ◆ **histoire événementielle** history of events ◆ **ils sont spécialisés dans la communication**

~le they specialize in organizing publicity events

évent /evɑ̃/ **NM** *[de baleine]* blowhole, spout (hole), spiracle *(SPÉC)*

éventail /evɑ̃taj/ **NM** 1 *(= instrument)* fan ◆ **en ~** *[objet]* fan-shaped; *[plusieurs objets]* fanned out ◆ **se déployer en ~** *(Mil)* to fan out; → **doigt, voûte** 2 *(= gamme) [de produits, prix, mesures]* range ◆ **~ des salaires** salary range, wage range *ou* spread *(US)* ◆ **l'~ politique** the political spectrum ◆ **il y a tout un ~/un large ~ de possibilités** there is a whole range/a wide range of possibilities

éventaire /evɑ̃tɛʀ/ **NM** *(= corbeille)* tray, basket; *(= étalage)* stall, stand

éventé, e /evɑ̃te/ (ptp de **éventer**) **ADJ** 1 *(= exposé au vent)* windy ◆ **rue très ~e** very windy *ou* exposed street 2 *[parfum, vin]* stale, musty; *[bière]* stale, flat 3 *(= connu)* well-known ◆ **c'est un truc*** **~** it's a well-known *ou* a rather obvious trick ◆ **le secret est ~** the secret is out

éventer /evɑ̃te/ ▸ conjug 1 ◂ **VT** 1 *(= rafraîchir)* to air; *(avec un éventail)* to fan 2 *[+ secret]* to let out; *[+ complot]* to discover **VPR s'éventer** 1 *[bière]* to go flat; *[vin, parfum]* to go stale *ou* musty 2 *(avec éventail)* to fan o.s. ◆ **s'~ avec un journal** to fan o.s. with a newspaper

éventration /evɑ̃tʀasjɔ̃/ **NF** *(Méd)* rupture

éventrer /evɑ̃tʀe/ ▸ conjug 1 ◂ **VT** 1 *(avec un couteau)* to disembowel; *(d'un coup de corne)* to gore 2 *[+ boîte, sac]* to tear open; *[+ muraille, coffre]* to smash open; *[+ matelas]* to rip open **VPR s'éventrer** *[boîte, sac]* to burst open; *[personne]* to rip one's stomach open ◆ **le bateau s'est éventré sur les rochers** the ship's hull was ripped open on the rocks

éventreur /evɑ̃tʀœʀ/ **NM** ripper ◆ **Jack l'Éventreur** Jack the Ripper

éventualité /evɑ̃tɥalite/ **NF** 1 *(= hypothèse)* possibility ◆ **dans cette ~** if this happens, should that arise ◆ **dans l'~ d'un refus de sa part** should he refuse, in the event of his refusal 2 *(= circonstance)* eventuality, contingency, possibility ◆ **pour parer à toute ~** to guard against all eventualities

éventuel, -elle /evɑ̃tɥɛl/ **ADJ** *(= possible)* possible; *[client, revenu]* potential ◆ **l'achat ~ d'un ordinateur** the possibility of buying a computer ◆ **ils ont évoqué l'~le reprise des pourparlers** they have mentioned the possible resumption of talks

> ⚠ **éventuel** ne se traduit pas par le mot anglais **eventual**, qui a le sens de 'final'.

éventuellement /evɑ̃tɥɛlmɑ̃/ **ADV** possibly ◆ **~, nous pourrions ...** we could possibly *ou* perhaps ... ◆ **~ je prendrai ma voiture** I may take my car ◆ **tu vas l'inviter ? – ~** are you going to invite him? – maybe

> ⚠ **éventuellement** ne se traduit pas par **eventually**, qui a le sens de 'finalement'.

évêque /evɛk/ **NM** bishop ◆ **~ suffragant** suffragan (bishop)

Everest /ev(ə)ʀɛst/ **NM** ◆ **le mont ~, l'~** Mount Everest

évertuer (s') /evɛʀtɥe/ ▸ conjug 1 ◂ **VPR** *(= s'efforcer de)* ◆ **s'~ à faire** to strive to do, to do one's utmost to do ◆ **j'ai eu beau m'~ à lui expliquer ...** no matter how hard I tried to explain to him ...

éviction /eviksjɔ̃/ **NF** *(Jur)* eviction; *[de rival]* ousting, supplanting ◆ **procéder à l'~ de** *[+ locataires]* to evict ◆ **~ scolaire** *temporary suspension from school of a child with an infectious illness*

évidage /evidaʒ/, **évidement** /evidmɑ̃/ **NM** hollowing-out, scooping-out

évidemment /evidamɑ̃/ **ADV** 1 *(= bien sûr)* of course, obviously ◆ **(bien) ~ !** of course! ◆ **~ que j'irai !** of course I'll go! 2 *(frm = d'une manière certaine)* obviously ◆ **il l'aura ~ prévenue** obviously he will have told her

> ⚠ **évidemment** ne se traduit pas par **evidently**, qui a le sens de 'apparemment'.

évidence /evidɑ̃s/ GRAMMAIRE ACTIVE 53.1, 53.6 **NF** 1 *(= caractère flagrant)* **c'est l'~ même !** it's quite *ou* perfectly obvious! ◆ **se rendre à l'~** to face the facts ◆ **nier l'~** to deny the obvious *ou* the facts ◆ **son incompétence est d'une telle ~ que ...** his incompetence is so obvious that ...
2 *(= fait)* obvious fact ◆ **trois ~s se dégagent de ce discours** this speech brings three obvious facts to light ◆ **pour moi c'est une ~** to me it's obvious ◆ **c'est une ~ que de le dire** it's stating the obvious
3 *(locutions)*
◆ **en évidence** ◆ **laissez les clés bien en ~ sur la table** put the keys where they can be seen on the table ◆ **la lettre était bien en ~ sur le bureau** the letter was in full view on the desk ◆ **essayez de ne pas laisser en ~ vos objets de valeur** try not to leave your valuables lying around ◆ **c'était un personnage très en ~ dans les années 20** he was very much in the public eye in the 20s ◆ **mettre en ~** *[+ fait] (= montrer)* to show; *(= souligner)* to emphasize; *(= révéler)* to reveal; *[+ personne]* to bring to the fore ◆ **se mettre en ~** to make one's presence felt ◆ **ce test met en ~ la présence d'anticorps** the test reveals the presence of antibodies ◆ **depuis la mise en ~ du rôle de la pollution dans l'effet de serre** since the role of pollution in the greenhouse effect has been demonstrated
◆ **de toute évidence** quite obviously *ou* evidently
◆ **contre toute évidence** against all the evidence

> ⚠ Attention à ne pas traduire automatiquement **évidence** par le mot anglais **evidence**, qui a le sens de 'preuve'.

évident, e /evidɑ̃, ɑ̃t/ **ADJ** 1 *(= flagrant, manifeste)* obvious, evident ◆ **il est ~ que** it is obvious *ou* evident that ◆ **il est ~ qu'ils s'aiment** it's obvious that they're in love, they're obviously in love
2 *(= certain)* **elle va démissionner, c'est ~** it's obvious she's going to resign ◆ **ils vont perdre – rien de plus ~ !** they're going to lose – that's quite obvious!; *(au négatif)* ◆ **c'est lui qui va gagner – ce n'est pas si ~** he's going to win – that's not certain ◆ **il n'est pas du tout ~ qu'elle vienne** it's not at all certain that she'll come ◆ **rien de moins ~ !** nothing could be less certain!
3 *(= simple) (au négatif)* **ce n'est pas ~ !*** *(= ce n'est pas si simple)* it's not that easy *ou* simple! ◆ **c'est pas ~ à traduire** it's not easy to translate

> ⚠ Au sens de 'certain' ou 'simple', **évident** ne se traduit pas par le mot anglais **evident**.

évider /evide/ ▸ conjug 1 ◂ **VT** to hollow out, to scoop out; *[+ pomme]* to core

évier /evje/ **NM** sink ◆ **~ (à) un bac/deux bacs** single/double sink

évincement /evɛ̃smɑ̃/ **NM** *[de rival]* ousting, supplanting

évincer /evɛ̃se/ ▸ conjug 3 ◂ **VT** *[+ concurrent]* to oust, to supplant; *(Jur) [+ locataire]* to evict

éviscérer /eviseʀe/ ▸ conjug 6 ◂ **VT** to eviscerate

évitable /evitabl/ **ADJ** avoidable ◆ **difficilement ~** hard to avoid

évitage /evitaʒ/ **NM** *(Naut) (= mouvement)* swinging; *(= espace)* swinging room

évitement /evitmɑ̃/ **NM** *[de risque, véhicule]* avoidance ◆ **voie d'~** *(Transport)* loop line ◆ **gare d'~** station with a loop line ◆ **manœuvre d'~** *(en voiture, en avion)* evasive action ◆ **réaction** *ou* **comportement d'~** *(Bio, Psych)* avoidance behaviour

éviter /evite/ GRAMMAIRE ACTIVE 29.2, 29.3 ▸ conjug 1 ◂
VT 1 *[+ coup, projectile]* to avoid, to dodge; *[+ obstacle, danger, maladie, situation]* to avoid, to steer clear of; *[+ gêneur, créancier]* to avoid, to keep clear of, to evade; *[+ regard]* to avoid, to evade ◆ **~ qu'une situation n'empire** to prevent a situation from getting worse, to avoid a deterioration in a situation ◆ **~ d'être repéré** to escape detection, to avoid being detected
2 *[+ erreur, méthode]* to avoid ◆ **~ de faire qch** to avoid doing sth ◆ **~ le sel** to avoid *ou* keep off salt ◆ **on lui a conseillé d'~ la marche** he has been advised to avoid walking *ou* advised against walking ◆ **évite de m'interrompre/de dire des bêtises** try not to interrupt me/say anything stupid
3 ◆ **~ qch à qn** to spare *ou* save sb sth ◆ **ça lui a évité d'avoir à se déplacer** that spared *ou* saved him the bother *ou* trouble of going
VI *(Naut)* to swing
VPR s'éviter 1 *(= se fuir)* to avoid each other *ou* one another ◆ **ils s'évitaient depuis quelque temps** they had been avoiding each other *ou* keeping clear of each other for some time
2 ◆ **s'~ qch** to avoid sth ◆ **je voudrais m'~ le trajet** I'd rather not have to make the trip, I'd like to save myself the trip ◆ **s'~ toute fatigue** to spare o.s. any fatigue, to save o.s. from getting at all tired

évocateur, -trice /evɔkatœʀ, tʀis/ **ADJ** evocative, suggestive *(de* of*)*

évocation /evɔkasjɔ̃/ **NF** 1 *[de souvenirs, faits]* evocation, recalling; *[de scène, idée]* conjuring-up, evocation ◆ **ces ~s la faisaient s'attendrir** she became more tender as she recalled these memories ◆ **la simple ~ de cette question** the mere mention of this issue ◆ **pouvoir** *ou* **puissance d'~ d'un mot** evocative *ou* suggestive power of a word 2 *(littér) [de démons]* evocation, calling-up, conjuring-up

évolué, e /evɔlɥe/ (ptp de **évoluer**) **ADJ** *[peuple, civilisation]* (highly) developed, advanced; *[personne]* broad-minded, enlightened; *[espèce animale]* evolved; *[procédé, industrie, technologie]* advanced; *(Ordin) [langage]* high-level ◆ **jeune fille ~e** *(hum)* liberated young woman

évoluer /evɔlɥe/ ▸ conjug 1 ◂ **VI** 1 *(= changer) [civilisation, idées, marché, situation, technique]* to evolve, to develop; *[personne, goûts]* to change; *[maladie, tumeur]* to develop; *[espèce]* to evolve ◆ **la situation évolue/n'évolue pas dans le bon sens** the situation is/isn't moving in the right direction ◆ **voyons comment les choses vont ~** let's wait and see how things develop ◆ **faire ~** *[+ situation, société]* to bring about some change in; *[+ réglementation]* to make changes to; *(Ordin) [+ matériel]* to upgrade 2 *(professionnellement) [personne]* to advance 3 *(= se mouvoir) [danseur]* to move about; *[avion]* to fly around, to wheel about; *[bateau à voile]* to sail around; *[troupes]* to manoeuvre *(Brit)*, to maneuvre *(US)* ◆ **le monde dans lequel il évolue** the world in which he moves

évolutif, -ive /evɔlytif, iv/ **ADJ** *(gén, Bio)* evolutionary, evolutional; *[maladie, processus]* progressive; *[poste]* with potential (for advancement *ou* promotion); *[ordinateur]* upgradeable ◆ **l'histoire évolutive de cette espèce** the evolutionary history of this species ◆ **compte tenu de la situation très évolutive** given the fact that the situation is changing all the time

◆ **on élargira l'Europe de manière évolutive** Europe will be enlarged step by step *ou* gradually; → **ski**

évolution /evɔlysjɔ̃/ **NF** [1] *(= changement) [de civilisation, idées, situation, technique]* evolution, development; *[de goûts]* change; *[de maladie, tumeur]* development; *[d'espèce]* evolution ◆ **il faut tenir compte de l'~ du marché/des prix** market/price trends have to be taken into account ◆ **~ positive** *(gén)* positive development; *(économique)* improvement ◆ **théorie de l'~** *(Bio)* theory of evolution [2] *(professionnelle)* **~ de carrière** career advancement **NFPL évolutions** *(= mouvements)* movements ◆ **il regardait les ~s du danseur/de l'avion** he watched the dancer as he moved about gracefully/the plane as it wheeled *ou* circled overhead ◆ **les ~s des troupes** troop manoeuvres *(Brit) ou* maneuvers *(US)*

évolutionnisme /evɔlysjɔnism/ **NM** evolutionism

évolutionniste /evɔlysjɔnist/ **ADJ** evolutionary **NMF** evolutionist

évolutivité /evɔlytivite/ **NF** [1] *[de maladie]* progressive nature ◆ **pour évaluer l'~ du cancer** to assess to what extent the cancer is likely to progress *ou* develop [2] *[de matériel informatique]* upgradeability

évoquer /evɔke/ ▸ **conjug 1** ◂ **VT** [1] *(= remémorer) [+ souvenirs]* to recall, to call up, to evoke; *[+ fait, événement]* to evoke, to recall; *[+ mémoire d'un défunt]* to recall [2] *(= faire penser à) [+ scène, idée]* to call to mind, to evoke, to conjure up ◆ **ça évoque mon enfance** it reminds me of my childhood [3] *(= effleurer) [+ problème, sujet]* to touch on, to bring up [4] *(littér = invoquer) [+ démons]* to evoke, to call up, to conjure up [5] *(Jur)* to transfer to a higher court

evzone /ɛvzɔn, ɛvzon/ **NM** evzone

ex* /ɛks/ **NMF** ex*

ex. (abrév de **exemple**) ◆ **par ~** eg, e.g.

ex- /ɛks/ **PRÉF** ex- ◆ **l'~URSS** former soviet Union

exacerbation /ɛgzasɛʀbasjɔ̃/ **NF** *[de tensions]* exacerbation; *[de concurrence]* intensification ◆ **pour éviter l'~ nationaliste** to prevent the heightening *ou* exacerbation of nationalist tensions

exacerber /ɛgzasɛʀbe/ ▸ **conjug 1** ◂ **VT** *[+ douleur]* to aggravate, to exacerbate; *[+ émotion, passion]* to intensify, to heighten; *[+ problème, tensions]* to exacerbate; *[+ concurrence]* to intensify ◆ **sensibilité exacerbée** heightened sensibility **VPR s'exacerber** *[concurrence, passion]* to become more intense, to intensify; *[tensions]* to increase, to be heightened; *[polémique]* to become more intense

exact, e /ɛgza(kt), ɛgzakt(ə)/ **ADJ** [1] *(= fidèle) [reproduction, compte rendu]* exact, accurate ◆ **réplique ~e** exact *ou* faithful replica ◆ **c'est l'~e vérité** that's the absolute truth

[2] *(= correct) [définition, raisonnement]* correct, exact; *[réponse, calcul]* correct, right ◆ **ce n'est pas le terme ~** that's not the right word ◆ **est-il ~ que ... ?** is it right *ou* correct *ou* true that ...? ◆ **ce n'est pas tout à fait ~** that's not quite right *ou* accurate, that's not altogether correct ◆ **~ !** absolutely!, exactly!

[3] *(= précis) [dimension, nombre, valeur]* exact, precise; *[donnée]* accurate, precise, correct; *[pendule]* accurate, right ◆ **l'heure ~e** the right *ou* exact *ou* correct time ◆ **la nature ~e de son travail** the precise nature of his work; → **science**

[4] *(= ponctuel)* punctual, on time ◆ **c'est quelqu'un de très ~ d'habitude** he's usually on time *ou* very punctual ◆ **être ~ à un rendez-vous** to arrive at an appointment on time, to arrive punctually for an appointment

[5] *(littér) [discipline]* exact, rigorous, strict; *[obéissance]* rigorous, strict, scrupulous

exactement /ɛgzaktəmɑ̃/ GRAMMAIRE ACTIVE 40.1, 40.2 **ADV** [1] *(gén)* exactly ◆ **c'est à 57 km ~** it's exactly *ou* precisely 57 km away ◆ **au troisième top, il sera ~ huit heures** at the third stroke, it will be eight o'clock precisely ◆ **c'est ~ ce que je pensais** that's exactly *ou* just *ou* precisely what I was thinking ◆ **ce n'est pas ~ un expert** *(hum)* he's not exactly an expert [2] *(= tout à fait)* exactly ◆ **oui, ~ !** yes, exactly! *ou* precisely!

exaction /ɛgzaksjɔ̃/ **NF** *(littér = extorsion)* exaction **NFPL exactions** *(= abus de pouvoir)* abuses (of power); *(= violences)* acts of violence, violent acts

exactitude /ɛgzaktityd/ **NF** [1] *(= fidélité) [de reproduction, compte rendu]* exactness, exactitude *(frm)*, accuracy [2] *(= justesse) [de définition, raisonnement]* correctness, exactness; *[de réponse, calcul]* correctness ◆ **je ne mets pas en doute l'~ de vos informations** I'm not saying your information is wrong [3] *(= précision) [de dimension, nombre, valeur]* exactness, precision; *[de donnée]* accuracy, precision, correctness; *[de pendule]* accuracy [4] *(= ponctualité)* punctuality ◆ **l'~ est la politesse des rois** *(Prov)* punctuality is the essence of courtesy [5] *(littér = minutie)* exactitude

ex æquo /ɛgzeko/ **ADJ INV** *(Scol, Sport)* placed equal *(attrib)* ◆ **ils sont ~** they tied **NM INV** ◆ **les ~** those who are *(ou* were) placed equal ◆ **il y a deux ~ pour la deuxième place** there is a tie for second place **ADV** ◆ **être (classé) premier ~** to be placed first equal *ou* joint first, to tie for first place

exagération /ɛgzaʒeʀasjɔ̃/ **NF** *(gén)* exaggeration ◆ **on peut dire sans ~ que ...** one can say without any exaggeration *ou* without exaggerating that ... ◆ **il est sévère sans ~** he's severe without taking it to extremes ◆ **on lui a reproché des ~s dans sa biographie** he has been accused of exaggerating in his biography

exagéré, e /ɛgzaʒeʀe/ (ptp de **exagérer**) **ADJ** *(= excessif) [dépenses, optimisme]* excessive; *(= surfait, amplifié) [commentaires]* exaggerated ◆ **donner une importance ~e à** to exaggerate the importance of ◆ **je suis peut-être d'un optimisme ~** maybe I'm being overly optimistic ◆ **venir se plaindre après ça, c'est un peu ~** it was too much *ou* a bit much* *(Brit)* to come and complain after all that ◆ **il serait ~ de dire** it would be an exaggeration *ou* an overstatement to say, it would be going too far to say ◆ **la polémique a pris des proportions ~es** the controversy has been blown out of all proportion

exagérément /ɛgzaʒeʀemɑ̃/ **ADV** *[cher]* excessively; *[optimiste, méfiant, simpliste]* overly, excessively

exagérer /ɛgzaʒeʀe/ GRAMMAIRE ACTIVE 53.1, 53.6 ▸ **conjug 6** ◂ **VT** *(gén)* to exaggerate ◆ **on a beaucoup exagéré leur rôle** their role has been hugely exaggerated **VI** [1] *(en paroles)* to exaggerate ◆ **n'exagérons rien !** let's not exaggerate! ◆ **sans ~, ça a duré trois heures** without any exaggeration *ou* I'm not exaggerating, it lasted three hours [2] *(en action)* to go too far ◆ **quand même il exagère !** really he goes too far *ou* oversteps the mark! ◆ **500 € pour ça ? – ils exagèrent !** €500 for that? – they must be joking *ou* that's a bit steep! ◆ **joue le personnage plus passionné, mais sans ~** make the character more passionate but don't overdo it **VPR s'exagérer** *[+ difficultés]* to exaggerate; *[+ plaisirs, avantages]* to exaggerate, to overrate

exaltant, e /ɛgzaltɑ̃, ɑt/ **ADJ** *[vie, aventure]* exciting, thrilling

exaltation /ɛgzaltasjɔ̃/ **NF** [1] *(= surexcitation)* intense excitement; *(joyeuse)* elation; *(Psych)* overexcitement ◆ **~ mystique** exaltation [2] *(littér = glorification)* extolling, praising, exalting [3] *(Rel)* **~ de la Sainte Croix** Exaltation of the Cross

exalté, e /ɛgzalte/ (ptp de **exalter**) **ADJ** *[imagination]* wild, vivid; *[esprit]* excited **NM,F** *(= impétueux)* hothead; *(= fanatique)* fanatic

exalter /ɛgzalte/ ▸ **conjug 1** ◂ **VT** [1] *(= surexciter) [+ esprit, imagination]* to fire ◆ **exalté par cette nouvelle** *(très excité)* excited by *ou* keyed up with excitement over this piece of news; *(euphorique)* elated *ou* overjoyed by *ou* at this piece of news [2] *(= glorifier)* to extol, to praise, to exalt **VPR s'exalter** to get excited, to get carried away

exam* /ɛgzam/ **NM** (abrév de **examen**) exam

examen /ɛgzamɛ̃/ GRAMMAIRE ACTIVE 53.2

NM [1] *(= action d'étudier, d'analyser) (gén)* examination; *[de question, demande, cas, projet de loi]* examination, consideration; *[de possibilité]* examination, investigation ◆ **l'~ détaillé** *ou* **minutieux du rapport ...** detailed *ou* close examination of the report ... ◆ **la question est à l'~** the matter is under consideration ◆ **son argument ne résiste pas à l'~** his argument doesn't stand up to scrutiny ◆ **procéder à l'~ de** *[+ demande, question]* to consider, to look into; *[+ ordre du jour]* to go through ◆ **le livre vous sera envoyé en ~ gratuit** the book will be sent to you on approval

[2] *(Jur)* **mettre qn en ~** to indict sb *(pour* for); ◆ **mise en ~** indictment ◆ **il a demandé la mise en ~ de Luc Dufour** he asked that Luc Dufour be indicted

[3] *(Méd)* **~ (médical)** *[de patient]* (medical) examination; *(= analyse de sang etc)* (medical) test ◆ **l'~ clinique** clinical examination ◆ **se faire faire des ~s** to have some tests done ◆ **subir un ~ médical complet** to undergo *ou* have a complete *ou* thorough checkup, to have a thorough medical examination

[4] *(Scol)* exam, examination ◆ **~ écrit/oral** written/oral examination ◆ **passer un ~** to take *ou* sit *(Brit)* an exam; → **rattrapage**

COMP examen blanc *(Scol)* mock exam *(Brit)*, practice test *(US)*

examen de conscience self-examination; *(Rel)* examination of conscience ◆ **faire son ~ de conscience** to examine one's conscience, to take stock of o.s.

examen de passage *(Scol)* end-of-year exam *(Brit)*, final exam *(US)*; *(fig)* ultimate test ◆ **il a réussi son ~ de passage** he has proved himself, he has passed the ultimate test

examen prénuptial *(Méd)* pre-marital examination

examen de santé (medical) check-up

examen spécial d'entrée à l'université university entrance examination

examen spectroscopique *(Sci)* spectroscopic examination

examen de la vue *(Méd)* eye *ou* sight test ◆ **passer un ~ de la vue** to have one's eyes tested

examinateur, -trice /ɛgzaminatœʀ, tʀis/ **NM,F** examiner ◆ **~ extérieur/à l'oral** external/oral examiner

examiner /ɛgzamine/ GRAMMAIRE ACTIVE 53.1, 53.2 ▸ **conjug 1** ◂

VT [1] *(= analyser) [+ document, faits, situation]* to examine, to take a look at; *[+ possibilité]* to examine, to investigate; *[+ question, demande, cas]* to consider, to look into; *[+ comptes, dossier]* to examine, to go through; *[+ projet de loi]* to discuss ◆ **~ qch dans le** *ou* **en détail** to examine sth in detail ◆ **~ qch de près** to look closely at sth, to take a close look at sth ◆ **~ qch de plus près** to take a closer look at sth

[2] *(= regarder) [+ objet, personne, visage]* to examine; *[+ ciel, horizon]* to scan; *[+ appartement, pièce]* to look over, to have a (close) look round *(Brit)* ◆ **~ les lieux** to look over the place, to have a look round *(Brit)* ◆ **~ qn de la tête aux**

pieds to look sb up and down (contemptuously)

3 *(Méd)* *[+ malade]* to examine ◆ **se faire ~ par un spécialiste** to be examined by a specialist

VPR **s'examiner** *[personne]* to examine o.s. ◆ **s'~ devant la glace** to examine o.s. in the mirror ◆ **ils s'examinaient à la dérobée** they were looking at each other furtively

exanthème /ɛgzɑ̃tɛm/ NM exanthem

exarque /ɛgzaʀk/ NM exarch

exaspérant, e /ɛgzaspeʀɑ̃, ɑ̃t/ ADJ exasperating

exaspération /ɛgzaspeʀasjɔ̃/ NF exasperation

exaspérer /ɛgzaspeʀe/ ▸ conjug 6 ◂ VT 1 *(= irriter)* to exasperate 2 *(littér = aviver)* *[+ douleur]* to exacerbate, to aggravate; *[+ émotion, désir]* to exacerbate

exaucement /ɛgzosmɑ̃/ NM *[de vœu]* fulfilment, granting; *[de prière]* granting

exaucer /ɛgzose/ ▸ conjug 3 ◂ VT *[+ vœu]* to fulfil, to grant; *(Rel)* *[+ prière]* to grant, to answer ◆ **~ qn** to grant sb's wish, to answer sb's prayer

ex cathedra /ɛkskatedʀa/ ADV ex cathedra

excavateur /ɛkskavatœʀ/ NM *(= machine)* excavator, mechanical digger *(Brit)*, steam shovel *(US)*

excavation /ɛkskavasjɔ̃/ NF *(= trou)* excavation ◆ **~ naturelle** natural hollow *(ou cave etc)*; *(= creusement)* excavation

excavatrice /ɛkskavatʀis/ NF ⇒ **excavateur**

excaver /ɛkskave/ ▸ conjug 1 ◂ VT to excavate

excédant, e /ɛksedɑ̃, ɑ̃t/ ADJ *(= énervant)* exasperating, infuriating

excédent /ɛksedɑ̃/ NM surplus *(sur over)*; ◆ **~ de la balance des paiements** balance of payments surplus ◆ **~ budgétaire/commercial** budget/trade surplus ◆ **~ (du commerce) extérieur** foreign trade surplus, external surplus ◆ **~ de trésorerie** cash surplus ◆ **~ de poids/bagages** excess weight/luggage *ou* baggage ◆ **il y a 2 kg d'~** *ou* **en ~** it's 2 kg over (weight) ◆ **budget en ~** surplus budget ◆ **payer 30 € d'~** to pay €30 excess charge; → **recette**

excédentaire /ɛksedɑ̃tɛʀ/ ADJ *[graisse, réserves]* excess *(épith)*; *[production]* surplus *(épith)*, excess *(épith)*; *[balance commerciale]* positive ◆ **budget ~** surplus budget ◆ **la production est ~** production is over target ◆ **leur balance commerciale est fortement ~** they have a huge trade surplus ◆ **les régions ~s en céréales** regions with a grain surplus

excéder /ɛksede/ ▸ conjug 6 ◂ VT 1 *(= dépasser)* *[+ longueur, temps, prix]* to exceed, to be greater than ◆ **le prix excédait (de beaucoup) ses moyens** the price was (way *ou* far) beyond *ou* far exceeded his means ◆ **les avantages excèdent les inconvénients** the advantages outweigh the disadvantages ◆ **l'apprentissage n'excède pas trois ans** the apprenticeship doesn't last more than three years *ou* lasts no more than *ou* does not exceed three years

2 *(= outrepasser)* *[+ pouvoir, droits]* to overstep, to exceed, to go beyond; *[+ forces]* to overtax

3 *(gén pass = accabler)* to exhaust, to weigh down, to weary ◆ **excédé de fatigue** overcome by tiredness, exhausted, tired out ◆ **excédé de travail** overworked

4 *(gén pass = agacer)* to exasperate, to irritate, to infuriate ◆ **je suis excédé** I'm furious ◆ **tu m'excèdes avec tes jérémiades !** your whining irritates me!, you exasperate me with your moaning!

excellemment /ɛkselamɑ̃/ ADV *(littér)* excellently

excellence /ɛkselɑ̃s/ NF 1 *(littér)* excellence

◆ **par excellence** ◆ **il est le poète surréaliste par ~** he is the surrealist poet par excellence ◆ **il aime la musique par ~** he loves music above all else 2 ◆ **Son Excellence** His *(ou* Her) Excellency ◆ **merci (Votre) Excellence** thank you, Your Excellency

excellent, e /ɛkselɑ̃, ɑ̃t/ ADJ excellent

exceller /ɛksele/ ▸ conjug 1 ◂ VI to excel *(dans ou en qch* at *ou* in sth; *à faire* in doing)

excentré, e /ɛksɑ̃tʀe/ ADJ 1 *[quartier, région]* outlying *(épith)* ◆ **le magasin est trop ~ pour fidéliser une clientèle** the shop is (located) too far out (of town) to attract regular customers 2 *(Tech)* *[pièce]* off-centre *(Brit)*, off-center *(US)*

excentricité /ɛksɑ̃tʀisite/ NF *(gén, Math, Astron)* eccentricity; *[de quartier]* outlying location

excentrique /ɛksɑ̃tʀik/ ADJ *[personne]* *(Math)* *[cercle]* eccentric; *[quartier]* outlying *(épith)* NMF eccentric, crank *(péj)*

excepté, e /ɛksɛpte/ (ptp de **excepter**) ADJ ◆ **il n'a plus de famille sa mère ~e** he has no family left apart from *ou* aside from *(US)* *ou* except his mother, excluding his mother he has no family left PRÉP except, but for, apart from, aside from *(US)* ◆ **~ quand** except *ou* apart from when ◆ **~ que** except that ◆ **tous ~ sa mère** everyone but his mother, everyone except for *ou* aside from *(US)* his mother

excepter /ɛksɛpte/ ▸ conjug 1 ◂ VT to except *(de* from) to make an exception of ◆ **sans ~ personne** without excluding anyone, no one excepted

exception /ɛksɛpsjɔ̃/ NF 1 *(= dérogation)* exception ◆ **à quelques ~s près** with a few exceptions ◆ **c'est l'~ qui confirme la règle** it's the exception which proves the rule

◆ **d'exception** *[tribunal]* special; *[régime, mesure]* special, exceptional 2 *(Jur)* objection, plea ◆ **~ péremptoire** ≈ demurrer 3 *(locutions)* **faire une ~ à** *[+ règle]* to make an exception to ◆ **faire ~ (à la règle)** to be an exception (to the rule) ◆ **faire ~ de** to make an exception of

◆ **exception faite de, à l'exception de** except for, apart from, aside from *(US)*, with the exception of

◆ **sans exception** without exception

◆ **sauf exception** allowing for exceptions

exceptionnel, -elle /ɛksɛpsjɔnɛl/ ADJ *(= rare)* exceptional ◆ **offre exceptionnelle** *(sur produit)* special offer, special *(US)* ◆ **fait ~, il a accepté** he accepted for once ◆ **d'un talent ~** exceptionally talented; → **élément** NM ◆ **l'~** the exceptional

exceptionnellement /ɛksɛpsjɔnɛlmɑ̃/ ADV 1 *(= à titre d'exception)* **ils se sont réunis ~ un dimanche** contrary to their general practice *ou* in this particular instance they met on a Sunday ◆ **le magasin sera ~ ouvert dimanche** the store will open on Sunday just for this week *ou* for this week only ◆ **~, je vous recevrai lundi** just this once I will see you on Monday 2 *[difficile, élevé, fort]* exceptionally

excès /ɛksɛ/ NM 1 *[d'argent]* excess, surplus; *[de marchandises, produits]* glut, surplus ◆ **il y a un ~ d'acide** *(= il en reste)* there is some acid left over *ou* some excess acid; *(= il y en a trop)* there is too much acid ◆ **~ de cholestérol dans le sang** excess of cholesterol in the blood ◆ **~ de précautions** excessive care *ou* precautions ◆ **~ de zèle** overzealousness; → **pécher**

2 *(gén, Méd, Pol = abus)* excess ◆ **des ~ de langage** extreme *ou* immoderate language ◆ **tomber dans l'~** to go to extremes ◆ **tomber dans l'~ inverse** to go to the opposite extreme ◆ **~ de boisson** overindulgence in drink, intemperance ◆ **des ~ de table** overindulgence at (the) table, surfeit of (good) food ◆ **faire des ~ de table** to overindulge, to eat too much ◆ **se laisser aller à des ~** to go overboard* ◆ **je me suis trompé, par ~ de confiance en moi/d'optimisme** I made a mistake by being overconfident/over-optimistic

3 *(locutions)* **il est sévère, mais sans ~** he's strict, but not excessively so ◆ **l'~ en tout est un défaut** *(Prov)* everything in moderation

◆ **(jusqu')à l'excès** to excess, excessively, inordinately ◆ **généreux à l'~** inordinately generous, overgenerous, generous to a fault

◆ **avec excès** to excess, excessively ◆ **il fait tout avec ~** he does everything to excess, he is excessive in everything he does ◆ **boire avec ~** to drink to excess *ou* excessively ◆ **dépenser avec ~** to be excessive in one's spending

COMP **excès de pouvoir** *(Jur)* abuse of power, actions ultra vires *(SPÉC)*

excès de vitesse *(en conduisant)* breaking *ou* exceeding the speed limit, speeding ◆ **coupable de plusieurs ~ de vitesse** guilty of having broken *ou* of exceeding the speed limit on several occasions

excessif, -ive /ɛksesif, iv/ ADJ 1 *[+ colère, enthousiasme, prix]* excessive; *[+ fierté]* excessive, inordinate ◆ **des horaires de travail ~s** excessively long working hours ◆ **300 €, c'est ~ !** €300, that's far too much! ◆ **50 €, ce n'est vraiment pas ~ !** €50 isn't what you'd call expensive! 2 *[+ personne]* **elle est excessive (en tout)** she's a woman of extremes, she takes everything to extremes *ou* too far

excessivement /ɛksesivmɑ̃/ ADV *(gén)* excessively; *[cher, fier]* excessively, inordinately ◆ **~ difficile/grave** extremely difficult/serious

exciper /ɛksipe/ ▸ conjug 1 ◂ **exciper de** VT INDIR *(frm)* *[+ bonne foi, précédent]* to plead

excipient /ɛksipjɑ̃/ NM excipient

exciser /ɛksize/ ▸ conjug 1 ◂ VT to excise

excision /ɛksizjɔ̃/ NF excision

excitabilité /ɛksitabilite/ NF *(Bio)* excitability

excitable /ɛksitabl/ ADJ excitable, easily excited

excitant, e /ɛksitɑ̃, ɑ̃t/ ADJ 1 *(= enthousiasmant)* *[idée, livre, projet]* exciting ◆ **ce n'est pas très ~ !** it's not very exciting! 2 *(= stimulant)* *[effet, substance]* stimulating 3 *(sexuellement)* arousing, sexy NM stimulant

excitation /ɛksitasjɔ̃/ NF 1 *(= enthousiasme, nervosité)* excitement ◆ **dans un état de grande ~** in a state of great excitement 2 *(= désir)* **~ (sexuelle)** (sexual) excitement *ou* arousal 3 *(Méd)* *[de nerf, muscle]* excitation, stimulation; *(Élec)* *[d'électro-aimant]* excitation 4 *(Jur = incitation)* **~ à** incitement to ◆ **~ des mineurs à la débauche** incitement of minors to immoral behaviour

excité, e /ɛksite/ (ptp de **exciter**) ADJ 1 (* *= enthousiasmé)* excited ◆ **il ne semblait pas très ~ à l'idée de me revoir*** he didn't seem too thrilled at the idea of *ou* too wild* about seeing me again; → **puce** 2 *(= nerveux)* *[animal]* restless; *[enfant]* excitable ◆ **des soldats, très ~s, ont commencé à tirer** some of the soldiers were very jumpy* and started to shoot 3 (* *= irrité)* worked-up 4 *(sexuellement)* excited NM,F * *(= impétueux)* hothead; *(= fanatique)* fanatic ◆ **une poignée d'~s** a bunch of hotheads ◆ **ne fais pas attention, c'est un ~** don't take any notice, he gets carried away

exciter /ɛksite/ ▸ conjug 1 ◂ VT 1 *(= provoquer)* *[+ intérêt, désir]* to (a)rouse; *[+ curiosité]* to rouse, to excite; *[+ imagination]* to stimulate, to fire, to stir; *[+ appétit]* to whet, to stimulate ◆ **tous ses sens étaient excités** all his senses were aroused

2 *(= aviver)* *[+ colère, douleur, ardeur]* to intensify, to increase ◆ **cela ne fit qu'~ sa colère** that only increased *ou* intensified his anger, that only made him even more angry

3 *(= enthousiasmer)* *[+ personne]* to thrill ◆ **ça ne m'excite guère d'y aller** I'm not exactly thrilled at the thought of going
4 *(= rendre nerveux)* ~ **un animal/un enfant** to get an animal/a child excited ◆ **le vent les excite** the wind makes them restless ◆ **le café, ça m'excite trop** coffee makes me too nervous *ou* hyper *
5 *(sexuellement)* to arouse *ou* excite (sexually)
6 *(* = irriter)* *[situation, réunion]* to get worked-up ◆ **il commence à m'~** he's getting on my nerves
7 *(= encourager)* to urge on, to spur on ◆ **excitant ses chiens de la voix** urging on *ou* spurring on his dogs with shouts, shouting to urge on his dogs ◆ **~ qn contre qn** to set sb against sb
8 *(= inciter)* ~ **à** to exhort to, to incite to, to urge to ◆ **~ qn à faire qch** to push sb into doing sth, to provoke *ou* urge sb to do sth ◆ **~ des soldats au combat** to incite *ou* exhort soldiers to combat *ou* battle
9 *(Méd)* *[+ nerf, muscle]* to stimulate, to excite; *(Élec, Phys)* *[+ électro-aimant, noyau]* to excite
VPR **s'exciter** 1 * *(= s'enthousiasmer)* to get excited *(sur, à propos de* about, over) to get carried away; *(= devenir nerveux)* to get worked up *, to get in a flap *; *(= se fâcher)* to get annoyed ◆ **pas la peine de t'~ (bêtement) !** calm down!
2 *(sexuellement)* to become (sexually) excited, to be (sexually) aroused

exclamatif, -ive /ɛksklamatif, iv/ ADJ exclamatory

exclamation /ɛksklamasjɔ̃/ NF exclamation; → **point**[1]

exclamer (s') /ɛksklame/ ► conjug 1 ◄ VPR to exclaim ◆ **"dommage !" s'exclama-t-il** "what a pity!", he exclaimed ◆ **s'~ de colère/d'admiration** *(littér)* to exclaim *ou* cry out in anger/admiration ◆ **s'~ sur qch** *(littér = protester)* to shout *ou* make a fuss about sth

exclu, e /ɛkskly/ ADJ 1 *(= non accepté)* *[personne]* excluded ◆ **se sentir ~ de la société** to feel excluded from society 2 *(= excepté)* **tous les jours, mardi ~** every day, except Tuesday 3 *(= hors de question)* **c'est tout à fait ~** it's completely out of the question ◆ **aucune hypothèse n'est ~e** no possibility has been ruled out ◆ **il n'est pas ~ que ...** it is not impossible that ... ◆ **une défaite n'est pas ~e** defeat cannot be ruled out NM,F ◆ **les ~s (de la société)** victims of social exclusion ◆ **les ~s de la croissance économique** those left out of the economic boom

exclure /ɛksklyʀ/ ► conjug 35 ◄ VT 1 *(= chasser)* *(d'un parti, d'une équipe)* to expel; *(d'un club)* to expel, to ban; *(temporairement)* to suspend; *(d'une école)* to expel, to exclude; *(temporairement)* to suspend, to exclude; *(d'une université)* to expel, to send down *(Brit)* *(de* from) 2 *(= écarter)* *[+ solution]* to exclude, to rule out; *[+ hypothèse]* to dismiss, to rule out ◆ **~ qch de son régime** to cut sth out of one's diet 3 *(= être incompatible avec)* *[fait]* to preclude VPR **s'exclure** ◆ **s'~ mutuellement** *[idées]* to be mutually exclusive; *[actions, mesures]* to be (mutually) incompatible

exclusif, -ive[1] /ɛksklyzif, iv/ ADJ 1 *[privilège]* exclusive *(épith)* ◆ **à l'usage/au profit ~ de** for the sole use/benefit of ◆ **pour mon usage ~** for my use alone ◆ **dans le but ~ de faire ...** with the sole *ou* exclusive aim of doing ...
2 *[droits, distributeur]* sole *(épith)*, exclusive *(épith)*; *[représentant]* sole *(épith)*; *[photo, reportage, fabrication]* exclusive *(épith)*
3 *(Math, Logique)* exclusive ◆ **le ou ~** the exclusive or
4 *(dans ses sentiments)* **il lui porte un amour ~** he loves her to the exclusion of all others, he loves her alone ◆ **elle est exclusive en amour** she's a one-man woman ◆ **il a un caractère (trop) ~** he's (too) exclusive in his relationships ◆ **très ~ dans ses amitiés** very selective *ou* exclusive in his friendships ◆ **très ~ dans ses goûts** very selective in his tastes

exclusion /ɛksklyzjɔ̃/ NF 1 *(= expulsion)* *[de parti, équipe, club]* expulsion; *(temporaire)* suspension; *[d'école]* expulsion, exclusion; *(temporaire)* suspension, exclusion *(de* from) → **zone**
◆ **à l'exclusion de** *(= en écartant)* to the exclusion of; *(= sauf)* with the exclusion *ou* exception of ◆ **aimer les pommes à l'~ de tous les autres fruits** to love apples to the exclusion of all other fruit ◆ **il peut manger de tous les fruits à l'~ des pommes** he can eat any fruit excluding apples *ou* with the exclusion *ou* exception of apples 2 *(= marginalisation)* **l'~ (sociale)** social exclusion ◆ **personne en voie d'~** person who is in danger of becoming a social outcast

exclusive[2] /ɛksklyziv/ NF *(frm)* bar, debarment ◆ **tous sans ~** with none debarred ◆ **frapper qn d'~, prononcer l'~ contre qn** to debar sb

exclusivement /ɛksklyzivmɑ̃/ ADV 1 *(= seulement)* exclusively, solely ◆ **~ réservé au personnel** reserved for staff only 2 *(= non inclus)* **du 10 au 15 du mois ~** from the 10th to the 15th exclusive 3 *(littér = de manière entière ou absolue)* exclusively

exclusivité /ɛksklyzivite/ NF 1 *(= droits exclusifs)* exclusive rights ◆ **avoir l'~ de la couverture d'un événement** to have (the) exclusive coverage of an event ◆ **avoir l'~ de la distribution de qch** to have exclusive distribution rights to sth ◆ **il n'en a pas l'~** *(fig)* he's not the only one to have it, he hasn't (got) a monopoly on it *
◆ **contrat d'~** exclusive contract
◆ **en + exclusivité** ◆ **en ~ dans notre journal** exclusive to our paper ◆ **films en première ~** new releases ◆ **ce film passe en ~ à** this film is showing only *ou* exclusively at
2 *(= reportage)* *(gén)* exclusive; *(à sensation)* scoop ◆ **c'est une ~ de notre maison** it's made *(ou* sold) exclusively by our company, it's exclusive to our company
3 *[de sentiment]* **l'~ en amour est rare** it is rare for somebody to love one person alone

excommunication /ɛkskɔmynikasjɔ̃/ NF excommunication

excommunier /ɛkskɔmynje/ ► conjug 7 ◄ VT to excommunicate

excrément /ɛkskʀemɑ̃/ NM excrement *(NonC)* ◆ **~s** excrement, faeces

excrémenteux, -euse /ɛkskʀemɑ̃tø, øz/, **excrémentiel, -elle** /ɛkskʀemɑ̃sjɛl/ ADJ excremental, excrementitious

excréter /ɛkskʀete/ ► conjug 6 ◄ VT to excrete

excréteur, -trice /ɛkskʀetœʀ, tʀis/ ADJ excretory

excrétion /ɛkskʀesjɔ̃/ NF excretion ◆ **~s** excreta

excrétoire /ɛkskʀetwaʀ/ ADJ ⇒ **excréteur**

excroissance /ɛkskʀwasɑ̃s/ NF *(Méd)* excrescence, outgrowth; *(fig)* outgrowth, development

excursion /ɛkskyʀsjɔ̃/ NF *(en car)* excursion, (sightseeing) trip; *(en voiture)* drive; *(à vélo)* ride; *(à pied)* walk, hike ◆ **~ en mer** boat trip ◆ **~ de trois jours** three-day tour *ou* (sightseeing) trip ◆ **partir en ~** *ou* **faire une ~** *(en car)* to go on an excursion *ou* a trip; *(en voiture)* to go for a drive; *(à vélo)* to go for a ride; *(à pied)* to go on a walk *ou* hike, to go walking *ou* hiking

excursionner /ɛkskyʀsjɔne/ ► conjug 1 ◄ VI to go on an excursion *ou* trip

excursionniste /ɛkskyʀsjɔnist/ NMF *(en car)* (day) tripper *(Brit)*, traveler *(US)*; *(à pied)* hiker, walker

excusable /ɛkskyzabl/ ADJ *[acte]* excusable, forgivable ◆ **il n'est pas ~** what he did is unforgivable

excuse /ɛkskyz/ GRAMMAIRE ACTIVE 45.1, 45.2 NF 1 *(= prétexte)* excuse ◆ **bonne/mauvaise ~** good/poor *ou* lame excuse ◆ **sans ~** inexcusable ◆ **il a pris pour ~ qu'il avait à travailler** he made *ou* gave the excuse that he had work to do, he used his work as an excuse ◆ **~s légales** *(Jur)* lawful *ou* legal excuses ◆ **la belle ~ !** *(iro)* that's a fine excuse! *(iro)*; → **mot** 2 ◆ **~s** *(= regrets)* apology ◆ **faire des ~s, présenter ses ~s** to apologize, to offer one's apologies *(à* to); ◆ **je vous dois des ~s** I owe you an apology ◆ **exiger des ~s** to demand an apology ◆ **mille ~s** do forgive me, I'm so sorry ◆ **faites ~** *(* ou hum)* excuse me, 'scuse me * 3 *(Tarot)* excuse

excuser /ɛkskyze/ GRAMMAIRE ACTIVE 45.1 ► conjug 1 ◄
VT 1 *(= pardonner)* *[+ personne, faute]* to excuse, to forgive ◆ **veuillez ~ mon retard** please excuse my being late *ou* my lateness, I do apologize for being late ◆ **je vous prie de l'~** please excuse *ou* forgive him ◆ **veuillez m'~** *(frm)*, **je vous prie de m'~** I beg your pardon, please forgive me *(pour avoir fait* for having done); ◆ **excusez-moi** excuse me, I'm sorry ◆ **je m'excuse** * (I'm) sorry ◆ **excusez-moi de vous le dire mais ...** excuse *ou* forgive *ou* pardon my saying so but ... ◆ **excusez-moi de ne pas venir** excuse my not coming, I'm sorry I can't come ◆ **vous êtes tout excusé** please don't apologize, you are quite forgiven ◆ **excusez-moi, vous avez l'heure s'il vous plaît ?** excuse me, have you got the time please? ◆ **ils ont invité 500 personnes, excusez du peu !** * they invited 500 people if you please! * ◆ **vous invitez 500 personnes ? excusez du peu !** * you're inviting 500 people? is that all? *(iro)*
2 *(= justifier)* to excuse ◆ **cette explication n'excuse rien** this explanation is no excuse
3 *(= dispenser)* to excuse ◆ **il a demandé à être excusé pour la réunion de demain** he asked to be excused from tomorrow's meeting ◆ **se faire ~** to ask to be excused ◆ **"M. Dupont : (absent) excusé"** "Mr Dupont has sent an apology", "apologies for absence received from Mr Dupont"
VPR **s'excuser** to apologize *(de qch* for sth); ◆ **(aller) s'~ auprès de qn** to apologize to sb ◆ **qui s'excuse s'accuse** *(Prov)* apologizing is a way of admitting one's guilt

exécrable /ɛgzekʀabl/ ADJ atrocious, execrable

exécrablement /ɛgzekʀabləmɑ̃/ ADV atrociously, execrably

exécration /ɛgzekʀasjɔ̃/ NF *(littér = haine)* execration, loathing ◆ **avoir qch en ~** to hold sth in abhorrence

exécrer /ɛgzekʀe/ ► conjug 6 ◄ VT to loathe, to abhor, to execrate

exécutable /ɛgzekytabl/ ADJ *[tâche]* possible, manageable; *[projet]* workable, feasible; *(Ordin)* *[fichier]* executable

exécutant, e /ɛgzekytɑ̃, ɑt/ NM,F *(Mus)* performer, executant; *(péj = agent)* underling ◆ **il n'est qu'un ~** he just carries out orders, he's just an underling

exécuter /ɛgzekyte/ ► conjug 1 ◄ VT 1 *(= accomplir)* *[+ plan, ordre, mouvements]* to execute, to carry out; *[+ projet, mission]* to execute, to carry out, to accomplish; *[+ promesse]* to fulfil, to carry out; *[+ travail]* to do, to execute; *[+ tâche]* to execute, to discharge, to perform ◆ **travail exécuté à la hâte** work done in a hurry ◆ **il a fait ~ des travaux dans sa maison** he had some work done on his house
2 *(= réaliser)* *[+ objet]* to make; *[+ tableau]* to paint, to execute

3 *(= préparer) [+ ordonnance]* to make up; *[+ commande]* to fulfil, to carry out ◆ **faire ~ une ordonnance** to have a prescription made up

4 *(Mus) [+ morceau]* to perform, to play ◆ **brillamment exécuté** brilliantly executed *ou* played

5 *(= tuer)* to execute

6 *(= vaincre)* to trounce; *(= critiquer)* to demolish

7 *(Jur) [+ traité, loi, décret]* to enforce; *[+ contrat]* to perform; *[+ débiteur]* to distrain upon

8 *(Ordin) [+ programme]* to run; *[+ instruction]* to carry out

VPR **s'exécuter** *(en s'excusant)* to comply; *(en payant)* to pay up ◆ **je lui demandai de s'excuser et il finit par s'~** I asked him to apologize and finally he complied *ou* did ◆ **au moment de l'addition, il s'exécuta de mauvaise grâce** when the time came to settle the bill he paid up with bad grace

exécuteur, -trice /ɛgzekytœʀ, tʀis/ NM,F *[d'arrêt, décret]* enforcer NM *(Hist)* ◆ **~ (des hautes œuvres)** executioner ◆ **~ des basses œuvres** *(péj = homme de main)* henchman ◆ **~ (testamentaire)** *(Jur) (= homme)* executor; *(= femme)* executrix

exécutif, -ive /ɛgzekytif, iv/ ADJ ◆ **pouvoir ~** executive power NM ◆ **l'~** the executive

exécution /ɛgzekysjɔ̃/ NF 1 *(= accomplissement) [de plan, ordre, mouvement]* execution; *[de projet, mission]* execution, accomplishment; *[de promesse]* fulfilment; *[de travail, tâche]* execution ◆ **l'~ des travaux a été ralentie** the work has been slowed down *ou* delayed ◆ **~ !** get on with it!

◆ **mettre à exécution** *[+ projet, idées, menaces]* to carry out

◆ **mise à exécution** *[de loi]* enforcement ◆ **pour empêcher la mise à ~ de cette menace** to prevent the threat from being carried out; → **voie**

2 *(= réalisation) [d'objet]* production; *[de tableau]* execution

3 *(= préparation) [de commande]* fulfilment, carrying out; *[d'ordonnance]* making up

4 *(Mus) [de morceau]* performance ◆ **d'une ~ difficile** difficult to play

5 *(= mise à mort)* execution ◆ **~ capitale/sommaire** capital/summary execution

6 *(Jur) [de traité, loi, décret]* enforcement; *[de contrat]* performance ◆ **en ~ de la loi** in compliance *ou* accordance with the law

7 *(Ordin) [de programme]* running; *[d'instruction]* carrying out

exécutoire /ɛgzekytwaʀ/ ADJ *(Jur)* executory, enforceable ◆ **mesure ~ pour chaque partie contractante** measure binding on each contracting party

exégèse /ɛgzeʒɛz/ NF exegesis ◆ **faire l'~ d'un discours politique** to analyse a political speech

exégète /ɛgzeʒɛt/ NM exegete

exemplaire /ɛgzɑ̃plɛʀ/ ADJ *[mère]* model *(épith)*, exemplary; *[punition]* exemplary ◆ **infliger une punition ~ à qn** to make an example of sb (by punishing them) NM 1 *[de livre, formulaire]* copy ◆ **en deux ~s** in duplicate ◆ **en trois ~s** in triplicate ◆ **25 ~s de cet avion ont été vendus** 25 aeroplanes of this type have been sold; → **tirer** 2 *(= échantillon)* specimen, example

exemplairement /ɛgzɑ̃plɛʀmɑ̃/ ADV in an exemplary fashion

exemplarité /ɛgzɑ̃plaʀite/ NF exemplary nature

exemple /ɛgzɑ̃pl/ GRAMMAIRE ACTIVE 53.1, 53.5 NM 1 *(= modèle)* example ◆ **l'~ de leur faillite/de sa sœur lui sera bien utile** their failure/his sister will be a useful example for him ◆ **il est l'~ de la vertu/l'honnêteté** he sets an example of virtue/honesty, he is a model of virtue/honesty ◆ **citer qn/qch en ~** to quote sb/sth as an example ◆ **donner l'~ de l'honnêteté/de ce qu'il faut faire** to give *ou* set an example of honesty/of what to do ◆ **donner l'~** to set an example ◆ **suivre l'~ de qn** to follow sb's example ◆ **prendre ~ sur qn** to take sb as a model ◆ **servir d'~ à qn** to serve as an example to sb ◆ **faire un ~ de qn** *(punir)* to make an example of sb ◆ **il faut absolument faire un ~** we must make an example of somebody ◆ **il faut les punir pour l'~** they must be punished as an example *ou* as a deterrent to others; → **prêcher**

◆ **à l'exemple de** like ◆ **à l'~ de son père** just like his father

◆ **par exemple** *(explicatif)* for example *ou* instance ◆ **(ça) par ~ !** *(surprise)* well I never!, my word!; *(indignation)* honestly!, well really!

2 *(= cas, spécimen)* example ◆ **un bel ~ du gothique flamboyant** a fine example of flamboyant gothic ◆ **il en existe plusieurs : ~, le rat musqué** there are several, for example *ou* for instance the muskrat ◆ **être d'une bêtise/avarice sans ~** *(frm)* to be of unparalleled stupidity/meanness

exemplification /ɛgzɑ̃plifikasjɔ̃/ NF exemplification

exemplifier /ɛgzɑ̃plifje/ ► conjug 7 ◄ VT to exemplify

exempt, e /ɛgzɑ̃, ɑ̃(p)t/ ADJ 1 *(= dispensé de)* **~ de** *[+ service militaire, corvée, impôts]* exempt from ◆ **~ de taxes** tax-free, duty-free ◆ **~ de TVA** zero-rated for VAT 2 *(= dépourvu de)* **~ de** *[+ vent, dangers, arrogance, erreurs]* free from ◆ **entreprise ~e de dangers** danger-free undertaking, undertaking free from all danger ◆ **d'un ton qui n'était pas ~ d'humour** in a voice which was not without humour, with the faintest tinge of humour in his voice NM *(Hist : Mil, Police)* exempt

exempté, e /ɛgzɑ̃(p)te/ NM,F *(Mil)* *person who is exempt from military service*

exempter /ɛgzɑ̃(p)te/ ► conjug 1 ◄ VT 1 *(= dispenser)* to exempt (de from) 2 *(= préserver de)* **~ qn de** *[+ soucis]* to save sb from

exemption /ɛgzɑ̃psjɔ̃/ NF exemption

exerçant, e /ɛgzɛʀsɑ̃, ɑ̃t/ ADJ ◆ **médecin ~** practising doctor

exercé, e /ɛgzɛʀse/ (ptp de **exercer**) ADJ *[œil, oreille]* keen, trained; *[personne]* experienced

exercer /ɛgzɛʀse/ ► conjug 3 ◄ VT 1 *(= pratiquer) [+ métier]* to have; *[+ fonction]* to fulfil, to exercise; *[+ talents]* to exercise; *(littér) [+ charité, hospitalité]* to exercise, to practise ◆ **dans le métier que j'exerce** *[médecin, avocat]* in my profession *ou* job ◆ **il exerce encore** he's still practising *ou* in practice

2 *[+ droit, pouvoir]* to exercise *(sur* over); *[+ contrôle, influence]* to exert, to exercise *(sur* over); *[+ représailles]* to take *(sur* on); *[+ poussée, pression]* to exert *(sur* on) ◆ **~ des pressions sur qn** to bring pressure to bear on sb, to exert pressure on sb ◆ **~ ses sarcasmes contre qn** to use one's sarcasm on sb, to make sb the butt of one's sarcasm ◆ **~ des poursuites contre qn** to bring an action against sb

3 *(= aguerrir) [+ corps, esprit, mémoire, voix]* to train, to exercise *(à* to, for); ◆ **~ des élèves à lire** *ou* **à la lecture** to get pupils to practise their reading ◆ **~ un chien à rapporter le journal** to train a dog to bring back the newspaper

4 *(= éprouver) [+ sagacité, habileté]* to tax; *[+ patience]* to try, to tax

VPR **s'exercer** 1 *[pianiste, sportif]* to practise ◆ **s'~ à** *[+ technique, mouvement]* to practise ◆ **s'~ à la patience** to learn how to be patient ◆ **s'~ à faire qch** to practise doing sth

2 *(Phys)* **les forces qui s'exercent sur le levier** the force exerted on the lever

exercice /ɛgzɛʀsis/ NM 1 *(= pratique) [de métier]* practice; *[de droit]* exercising; *[de facultés]* exercise ◆ **l'~ du pouvoir** the exercise of power ◆ **après 40 ans d'~** after 40 years in practice ◆ **condamné pour ~ illégal de la médecine** sentenced for practising medicine illegally *ou* for the illegal practice of medicine ◆ **dans l'~ de ses fonctions** in the exercise *ou* execution *ou* discharge of his duties

◆ **en exercice** ◆ **être en ~** *[médecin]* to be in practice; *[juge, fonctionnaire]* to be in *ou* hold office ◆ **juge en ~** sitting judge ◆ **président en ~** serving chairman ◆ **entrer en ~** to take up *ou* assume one's duties

2 *(= activité physique)* **l'~ (physique)** (physical) exercise ◆ **prendre †** *ou* **faire de l'~** to take some exercise

3 *(Mil)* **l'~** exercises, drill ◆ **aller à l'~** to go on exercises ◆ **faire l'~** to drill, to be at drill

4 *(Mus, Scol, Sport = travail d'entraînement)* exercise ◆ **~ pour piano** piano exercise ◆ **~ de prononciation** pronunciation exercise *ou* drill ◆ **~ d'application** practise *ou* application exercise ◆ **~s au sol** *(Gym)* floor exercises ◆ **~ d'évacuation** fire drill ◆ **l'interview est un ~ difficile** interviewing is a difficult business; → **cahier**

5 *(Admin, Fin = période)* year ◆ **l'~ 1996** the 1996 fiscal *ou* tax year

COMP **exercices d'assouplissement** limbering up exercises, bending and stretching exercises

exercice budgétaire budgetary year

exercice comptable accounting year

exercice du culte religious worship

exercice fiscal fiscal *ou* tax year

exercice de style *(Littérat)* stylistic composition; *(fig)* exercise in style

exercices de tir *(Mil)* shooting drill *ou* practice

exerciseur /ɛgzɛʀsizœʀ/ NM *(gén)* exercise machine; *(pour poitrine)* chest expander

exergue /ɛgzɛʀg/ NM *[de texte]* ◆ **porter qch en ~** to bear sth as an epigraph ◆ **cette médaille porte en ~ l'inscription …** *(lit)* this medal is inscribed below … ◆ **mettre en ~** *(= mettre en évidence) [+ idée, phrase]* to bring out, to underline ◆ **mettre une citation en ~ à un chapitre** to head a chapter with a quotation, to put in a quotation as (an) epigraph to a chapter ◆ **mettre un proverbe en ~ à un tableau** to inscribe a painting with a proverb

exfoliant, e /ɛksfɔljɑ̃, jɑ̃t/ ADJ exfoliating *(épith)*

exfoliation /ɛksfɔljasjɔ̃/ NF exfoliation

exfolier /ɛksfɔlje/ ► conjug 7 ◄ VT *[+ peau]* to exfoliate VPR **s'exfolier** *[peau, os, roche, bois]* to exfoliate

exhalaison /ɛgzalɛzɔ̃/ NF *(littér) (désagréable)* exhalation; *(agréable)* fragrance, exhalation

exhalation /ɛgzalasjɔ̃/ NF *(Physiol)* exhalation

exhaler /ɛgzale/ ► conjug 1 ◄ VT *(littér)* 1 *[+ odeur, vapeur]* to exhale, to give off 2 *[+ soupir]* to breathe; *[+ plainte]* to utter, to give forth *(littér)*; *[+ joie, douleur]* to give vent *ou* expression to 3 *(Physiol = souffler)* to exhale VPR **s'exhaler** *[odeur]* to rise (up) *(de* from); ◆ **un soupir s'exhala de ses lèvres** a sigh rose from his lips

exhaussement /ɛgzosmɑ̃/ NM raising

exhausser /ɛgzose/ ► conjug 1 ◄ VT *[+ construction]* to raise (up) ◆ **~ une maison d'un étage** to add a floor to a house

exhausteur /ɛgzostœʀ/ NM ◆ **~ de goût** *ou* **de saveur** flavour enhancer

exhaustif, -ive /ɛgzostif, iv/ ADJ exhaustive ◆ **c'est une liste non exhaustive** it's not an exhaustive list ◆ **de manière exhaustive**

[analyser] exhaustively ◆ **décrire qch de manière exhaustive** to give a comprehensive description of sth

exhaustivement /ɛgzostivmɑ̃/ ADV exhaustively

exhaustivité /ɛgzostivite/ NF exhaustiveness ◆ **la liste ne prétend pas à l'~** the list doesn't claim to be exhaustive

exhiber /ɛgzibe/ ▸ conjug 1 ◂ VT 1 *(frm) (= produire) [+ document, passeport]* to present, to show, to produce 2 *(= montrer au public) [+ animal]* to show, to exhibit 3 *(péj) [+ partie du corps]* to show off, to display; *[+ savoir, richesse, diplômes]* to display, to show off, to flaunt VPR **s'exhiber** 1 *(péj) (= parader)* to show o.s. off (in public), to parade around 2 *[exhibitionniste]* to expose o.s.

exhibition /ɛgzibisjɔ̃/ NF 1 *(Sport)* **match (d')~** exhibition match 2 *[de partie du corps]* showing off 3 *[d'animal]* exhibiting, showing; *(= concours)* show 4 *(= comportement)* outrageous behaviour (NonC) 5 *(frm) [de document, passeport]* presentation, production

exhibitionnisme /ɛgzibisjɔnism/ NM exhibitionism

exhibitionniste /ɛgzibisjɔnist/ NMF exhibitionist ◆ **il est un peu ~** he's a bit of an exhibitionist

exhortation /ɛgzɔʀtasjɔ̃/ NF exhortation

exhorter /ɛgzɔʀte/ ▸ conjug 1 ◂ VT to exhort *(à faire* to do; *à qch* to sth) to urge *(à faire* to do)

exhumation /ɛgzymasjɔ̃/ NF *[de corps]* exhumation; *[de ruines, vestiges]* excavation; *[de faits, vieux livres]* unearthing, digging up *ou* out; *[de souvenirs]* recollection, recalling

exhumer /ɛgzyme/ ▸ conjug 1 ◂ VT *[+ corps]* to exhume; *[+ ruines, vestiges]* to excavate; *[+ faits, vieux livres]* to unearth, to dig up *ou* out; *[+ souvenirs]* to recall

exigeant, e /ɛgziʒɑ̃, ɑt/ ADJ *[client, public, enfant]* demanding, hard to please *(attrib)*; *[parents, patron, travail, amour]* demanding, exacting; *[œuvre]* demanding ◆ **je ne suis pas ~*, donnez-moi 10 €** I'm not asking for much - give me €10 ◆ **il est très ~ envers lui-même** he sets very high standards for himself ◆ **les consommateurs sont devenus plus ~s en matière de prix/sur la qualité** consumers are demanding better prices/quality

exigence /ɛgziʒɑ̃s/ NF 1 *(gén pl = revendication, condition)* demand, requirement ◆ **produit satisfaisant à toutes les ~s** product which meets all requirements ◆ **répondre aux ~s de qualité** to meet quality requirements ◆ **les ~s du marché** the demands of the market ◆ **~s (salariales)** salary expectations ◆ **~s démocratiques** demands for democracy 2 *(= caractère) [de client]* demanding nature; *[de maître]* strictness ◆ **il est d'une ~ insupportable** he's impossibly demanding ◆ **son ~ de rigueur** his requirement *ou* demand for accuracy ◆ **~ morale** high moral standards

exiger /ɛgziʒe/ GRAMMAIRE ACTIVE 35.4, 37.1, 37.3 ▸ conjug 3 ◂ VT 1 *(= réclamer)* to demand, to require *(qch de qn* sth of *ou* from sb) to insist on *(qch de qn* sth from sb); ◆ **j'exige de le faire** I insist on doing it ◆ **j'exige que vous le fassiez** I insist on your doing it, I demand *ou* insist that you do it ◆ **j'exige (de vous) des excuses** I demand an apology (from you), I insist on an apology (from you) ◆ **la loi l'exige** the law requires *ou* demands it ◆ **des titres universitaires sont exigés pour ce poste** university degrees are required *ou* needed *ou* are a requirement for this post ◆ **trop ~ de ses forces** to overtax one's strength 2 *(= nécessiter)* to require, to call for ◆ **cette plante exige beaucoup d'eau** this plant needs *ou* requires a lot of water

exigibilité /ɛgziʒibilite/ NF *[de dette]* payability ◆ **~s** current liabilities

exigible /ɛgziʒibl/ ADJ *[dette]* payable, due for payment ◆ **~ le 15 mai** payable *ou* due on 15 May

exigu, -uë /ɛgzigy/ ADJ *[lieu]* cramped, exiguous *(littér)*; *[ressources]* scanty, meagre, exiguous *(littér)*; *(Écon) [marché]* limited

exiguïté /ɛgzigɥite/ NF *[de lieu]* smallness; *[de ressources]* scantiness, meagreness, exiguity *(littér)*; *(Écon) [de marché]* limited size

exil /ɛgzil/ NM exile ◆ **~ volontaire** voluntary *ou* self-imposed exile ◆ **deux années d'~** two years in *ou* of exile ◆ **lieu d'~** place of exile ◆ **en ~** *[personne]* in exile *(attrib)*, exiled; *[vivre]* in exile ◆ **envoyer qn en ~** to send sb into exile, to exile sb

exilé, e /ɛgzile/ (ptp de **exiler**) NM,F exile *(de* from); ◆ **~ politique/volontaire** political/voluntary exile

exiler /ɛgzile/ ▸ conjug 1 ◂ VT 1 *(Pol)* to exile 2 *(littér)* to banish ◆ **se sentir exilé (loin de)** to feel like an outcast *ou* exile (far from) ◆ **une note exilée en bas de page** a note tucked away at the bottom of the page VPR **s'exiler** 1 *(Pol)* to go into exile 2 **s'~ à la campagne** to bury o.s. in the country ◆ **s'~ en Australie** to exile o.s. to Australia, to take o.s. off to Australia ◆ **s'~ loin du monde** to cut o.s. off from the world

existant, e /ɛgzistɑ̃, ɑt/ ADJ *[coutume, loi, prix]* existing NM ◆ **l'~** *(gén)* what already exists; *(= stock)* the existing stock; *(= circonstances)* the existing circumstances

existence /ɛgzistɑ̃s/ NF 1 *(Philos, Rel = présence)* existence 2 *(= vie quotidienne)* existence, life ◆ **dans l'~** in life ◆ **cette coutume a plusieurs siècles d'~** this custom has existed *ou* has been in existence for several centuries; → **moyen²**

existentialisme /ɛgzistɑ̃sjalism/ NM existentialism

existentialiste /ɛgzistɑ̃sjalist/ ADJ, NMF existentialist

existentiel, -ielle /ɛgzistɑ̃sjɛl/ ADJ existential ◆ **arrête de te poser des questions ~les !** stop worrying about the meaning of life!

exister /ɛgziste/ ▸ conjug 1 ◂ VI 1 *(= vivre)* to exist ◆ **il se contente d'~** *(péj)* he is content with just getting by *ou* just existing

2 *(= être réel)* to exist, to be ◆ **pour lui, la peur n'existe pas** there is no such thing as fear *ou* fear doesn't exist as far as he is concerned ◆ **quoi que vous pensiez, le bonheur ça existe** whatever you may say, there is such a thing as happiness

3 *(= se trouver)* to be, to be found ◆ **la vie existe-t-elle sur Mars ?** is there life on Mars? ◆ **produit qui existe en magasin** product (to be) found in shops ◆ **ce modèle existe-t-il en rose ?** is this model available in pink? ◆ **le costume régional n'existe plus guère** regional dress is scarcely ever (to be) found *ou* seen these days ◆ **les bateaux à aubes n'existent plus/existent encore** paddle steamers no longer/still exist ◆ **il existe encore une copie** there is still one copy extant *ou* in existence ◆ **pourquoi monter à pied ? les ascenseurs ça existe !** why walk up? there are lifts, you know! *ou* lifts have been invented! ◆ **si Hélène/la machine à café n'existait pas, il faudrait l'inventer !** *(hum)* if Hélène/the coffee machine didn't exist, we would have to invent her/it!

VB IMPERS *(= il y a)* ◆ **il existe** *(avec sg)* there is; *(avec pl)* there are ◆ **il n'existe pas de meilleur exemple** there is no better example ◆ **il existe des bégonias de plusieurs couleurs** begonias come *ou* are found in several colours

exit /ɛgzit/ VI, NM *(Théât)* exit ◆ **~ le directeur** *(hum)* out goes the manager, exit the manager ◆ **~ les pauses-café** *(hum)* no more coffee breaks, that's the end of the coffee breaks

ex-libris /ɛkslibʀis/ NM INV ex-libris

ex nihilo /ɛksniilo/ ADV ex nihilo

exo* /ɛgzo/ NM (abrév de **exercice**) exercise

exocet /ɛgzɔsɛ/ NM 1 *(= poisson)* flying fish 2 ® *(= missile)* exocet ®

exode /ɛgzɔd/ NM *(lit, fig)* exodus ◆ **l'~** *(Hist) the flight of civilians from the north of France during the German invasion in 1940* ◆ **l'Exode** *(Bible)* the Exodus ◆ **(le livre de) l'Exode** (the Book of) Exodus ◆ **~ rural** drift from the land, rural exodus ◆ **~ des cerveaux** brain drain ◆ **~ des capitaux** flight *ou* outflow of capital

exogame /ɛgzɔgam/ ADJ exogamous, exogamic

exogamie /ɛgzɔgami/ NF exogamy

exogène /ɛgzɔʒɛn/ ADJ exogenous

exonération /ɛgzɔneʀasjɔ̃/ NF exemption *(de* from); ◆ **~ fiscale** *ou* **d'impôt** tax exemption

exonérer /ɛgzɔneʀe/ ▸ conjug 6 ◂ VT to exempt *(de* from); ◆ **placement à 3,5% exonéré d'impôts** investment at 3.5% free of tax ◆ **les plus-values seront fiscalement exonérées** capital gains will be tax-exempt *ou* will be exempted from tax

exorbitant, e /ɛgzɔʀbitɑ̃, ɑt/ ADJ *[prix, demande, prétention]* exorbitant, outrageous; *[privilèges]* scandalous

exorbité, e /ɛgzɔʀbite/ ADJ *[yeux]* bulging *(de* with)

exorcisation /ɛgzɔʀsizasjɔ̃/ NF exorcizing

exorciser /ɛgzɔʀsize/ ▸ conjug 1 ◂ VT to exorcize

exorciseur /ɛgzɔʀsizœʀ/ NM exorcizer

exorcisme /ɛgzɔʀsism/ NM exorcism

exorciste /ɛgzɔʀsist/ NM exorcist

exorde /ɛgzɔʀd/ NM introduction, exordium *(SPÉC)*

exosmose /ɛgzɔsmoz/ NF exosmosis

exotique /ɛgzɔtik/ ADJ exotic

exotisme /ɛgzɔtism/ NM exoticism ◆ **aimer l'~** to love all that is exotic

expansé, e /ɛkspɑ̃se/ ADJ expanded

expansibilité /ɛkspɑ̃sibilite/ NF expansibility

expansible /ɛkspɑ̃sibl/ ADJ expansible

expansif, -ive /ɛkspɑ̃sif, iv/ ADJ 1 *(de caractère)* expansive, out-going ◆ **il s'est montré peu ~** he was not very forthcoming *ou* communicative 2 *(Phys)* expansionary

expansion /ɛkspɑ̃sjɔ̃/ NF 1 *(= extension)* expansion ◆ **l'~ d'une doctrine** the spreading of a doctrine ◆ **~ économique** economic expansion ◆ **~ démographique** population growth ◆ **en pleine ~** *[marché, économie, secteur]* booming, fast-expanding ◆ **univers en ~** expanding universe 2 *(= effusion)* expansiveness (NonC), effusiveness (NonC)

expansionnisme /ɛkspɑ̃sjɔnism/ NM expansionism

expansionniste /ɛkspɑ̃sjɔnist/ ADJ *(Écon, Math, Phys)* expansionary; *(Pol : péj)* expansionist NMF *(Pol)* expansionist

expansivité /ɛkspɑ̃sivite/ NF expansiveness

expatriation /ɛkspatʀijasjɔ̃/ NF expatriation

expatrié, e /ɛkspatʀije/ (ptp de **expatrier**) NM,F expatriate

expatrier /ɛkspatʀije/ ▸ conjug 7 ◂ VT to expatriate VPR **s'expatrier** to expatriate o.s., to leave one's country

expectative /ɛkspɛktativ/ NF *(= incertitude)* state of uncertainty; *(= attente prudente)* cautious approach ◆ **être** *ou* **rester dans l'~** *(incertitude)* to be still waiting *ou* hanging on (to hear *ou* see *etc*); *(attente prudente)* to hold back, to wait and see

expectorant, e /ɛkspɛktɔʀɑ̃, ɑ̃t/ ADJ, NM expectorant

expectoration /ɛkspɛktɔʀasjɔ̃/ NF expectoration

expectorer /ɛkspɛktɔʀe/ ► conjug 1 ◄ VTI to expectorate

expédient, e /ɛkspedjɑ̃, jɑ̃t/ ADJ *(frm)* expedient NM expedient ◆ **vivre d'~s** *[personne]* to live by one's wits

expédier /ɛkspedje/ GRAMMAIRE ACTIVE 47.3 ► conjug 7 ◄ VT 1 *[+ lettre, paquet]* to send, to dispatch ◆ **~ par la poste** to send through the post *ou* mail ◆ **~ par le train** to send by rail *ou* train ◆ **~ par bateau** *[+ lettres, colis]* to send surface mail; *[+ matières premières]* to ship, to send by sea ◆ **je l'ai expédié en vacances chez sa grand-mère*** I sent *ou* packed* him off to his grandmother's for the holidays; → **monde** 2 * *[+ client, visiteur]* to dismiss ◆ **~ une affaire** to dispose of *ou* dispatch a matter, to get a matter over with ◆ **~ son déjeuner en cinq minutes** to polish off* one's lunch in five minutes 3 *(Admin)* **~ les affaires courantes** to dispose of *ou* dispatch day-to-day matters

expéditeur, -trice /ɛkspeditœʀ, tʀis/ ADJ dispatching, forwarding NM,F *[de courrier]* sender, addresser, addressor; *[de marchandises]* consignor, shipper; → **retour**

expéditif, -ive /ɛkspeditif, iv/ ADJ *[personne]* quick, expeditious; *[méthode, solution]* expeditious; *[justice, licenciement, procès, procédure]* summary; *[victoire]* easy ◆ **il a des jugements un peu ~s** he tends to jump to conclusions

expédition /ɛkspedisjɔ̃/ NF 1 *(Mil) (= voyage, raid)* expedition ◆ **~ de police** police raid ◆ **partir en ~** to set off on an expedition ◆ **quelle ~ !** *(fig)* what an expedition!, what a palaver! 2 *(= action) [de lettre, vivres, renforts]* dispatch; *[de colis]* dispatch, shipping; *(par bateau)* shipping ◆ **notre service ~** our shipping department 3 *(= paquet)* consignment, shipment; *(par bateau)* shipment 4 *(Admin)* **l'~ des affaires courantes** the dispatching of day-to-day matters

expéditionnaire /ɛkspedisjɔnɛʀ/ ADJ *(Mil)* expeditionary NMF *(Comm)* forwarding agent; *(Admin)* copyist

expéditivement /ɛkspeditivmɑ̃/ ADV expeditiously

expérience /ɛkspeʀjɑ̃s/ GRAMMAIRE ACTIVE 46.2 NF 1 *(= pratique)* experience ◆ **avoir de l'~** to have experience, to be experienced (*en* in); ◆ **avoir l'~ du monde** *(frm)* to have experience of the world, to know the ways of the world ◆ **sans ~** inexperienced ◆ **il est sans ~ de la vie** he has no experience of life ◆ **savoir par ~** to know by *ou* from experience ◆ **il a une longue ~ de l'enseignement** he has a lot of teaching experience

2 *(= aventure humaine)* experience ◆ **~ amoureuse** *ou* **sexuelle** sexual experience ◆ **tente l'~, tu verras bien** try it and see ◆ **faire l'~ de qch** to experience sth ◆ **ils ont fait une ~ de vie communautaire** they experimented with communal living

3 *(= test scientifique)* experiment ◆ **vérité/fait d'~** experimental truth/fact ◆ **faire une ~ sur un cobaye** to do *ou* carry out an experiment on a guinea-pig

> ⚠ Au sens de 'test scientifique', **expérience** ne se traduit pas par le mot anglais **experience**.

expérimental, e (mpl **-aux**) /ɛkspeʀimɑ̃tal, o/ ADJ experimental ◆ **à titre ~** on a trial *ou* an experimental basis

expérimentalement /ɛkspeʀimɑ̃talmɑ̃/ ADV experimentally

expérimentateur, -trice /ɛkspeʀimɑ̃tatœʀ, tʀis/ NM,F *(gén)* experimenter; *(Sci)* bench scientist

expérimentation /ɛkspeʀimɑ̃tasjɔ̃/ NF experimentation ◆ **~ animale** *(= pratique)* animal experimentation; *(= expériences, tests)* animal experiments

expérimenté, e /ɛkspeʀimɑ̃te/ (ptp de **expérimenter**) ADJ experienced (*en, dans* in)

expérimenter /ɛkspeʀimɑ̃te/ ► conjug 1 ◄ VT *[+ appareil]* to test; *[+ remède]* to experiment with, to try out; *[+ méthode]* to test out, to try out ◆ **~ en laboratoire** to experiment *ou* do experiments in a laboratory

expert, e /ɛkspɛʀ, ɛʀt/ ADJ *[personne]* expert, skilled (*en* in; *à* at); *[mains, œil]* expert ◆ **être ~ en la matière** to be an expert on the subject; → **système** NM *(= connaisseur)* expert (*en* in, at) connoisseur (*en* in, of); *(= spécialiste)* expert; *(d'assurances après dégâts)* assessor; *(d'objet de valeur)* valuer, assessor; *(Naut)* surveyor ◆ **médecin(-)~** medical expert ◆ **géomètre(-)~** ≈ chartered surveyor

expert-comptable /ɛkspɛʀkɔ̃tabl/, **experte-comptable** /ɛkspɛʀtkɔ̃tabl/ (mpl **experts-comptables**) NM,F chartered accountant *(Brit)*, certified public accountant *(US)*

expertise /ɛkspɛʀtiz/ NF 1 *(= évaluation) [de bijou]* valuation; *[de dégâts]* assessment ◆ **~ d'avarie** damage survey ◆ **~ comptable** chartered accountancy *(Brit)* ◆ **~ psychiatrique** psychiatric examination ◆ **(rapport d')~** valuer's *ou* assessor's *ou* expert's report 2 *(= compétence)* expertise ◆ **notre ~ technique dans ce domaine** our technical expertise in this field

expertiser /ɛkspɛʀtize/ ► conjug 1 ◄ VT *[+ bijou]* to value, to evaluate; *[+ dégâts]* to assess, to evaluate ◆ **faire ~ un diamant** to have a diamond valued

expiable /ɛkspjabl/ ADJ expiable

expiation /ɛkspjasjɔ̃/ NF expiation (*de* of) atonement (*de* for); ◆ **en ~ de ses crimes** in expiation of *ou* atonement for his crimes

expiatoire /ɛkspjatwaʀ/ ADJ expiatory

expier /ɛkspje/ ► conjug 7 ◄ VT *[+ péchés, crime]* to expiate, to atone for ◆ **~ une imprudence** *(fig)* to pay for an imprudent act

expirant, e /ɛkspiʀɑ̃, ɑ̃t/ ADJ dying

expiration /ɛkspiʀasjɔ̃/ NF 1 *(= terme)* expiration, expiry *(Brit)* ◆ **venir à ~** to expire ◆ **à l'~ du délai** when the deadline expires 2 *(= respiration)* expiration, exhalation ◆ **une profonde ~** a complete exhalation

expirer /ɛkspiʀe/ ► conjug 1 ◄ VT *[+ air]* to breathe out, to exhale, to expire *(SPÉC)* VI 1 *[délai, passeport]* to expire ◆ **le contrat/la carte expire le 5 mai** the contract/the card expires on 5 May 2 *(frm = mourir)* to expire 3 *(= respirer)* to exhale, to breathe out ◆ **expirez lentement !** breathe out slowly!

explétif, -ive /ɛkspletif, iv/ ADJ expletive ◆ **le ne ~** "ne" used as an expletive NM expletive

explicable /ɛksplikabl/ ADJ explicable, explainable ◆ **difficilement ~** difficult to explain

explicatif, -ive /ɛksplikatif, iv/ ADJ explanatory ◆ **une notice explicative accompagne l'appareil** the machine comes with an explanatory leaflet ◆ **proposition relative explicative** *(Gram)* non-restrictive relative clause

explication /ɛksplikasjɔ̃/ GRAMMAIRE ACTIVE 53.4 NF 1 *[de méthode, phénomène]* explanation (*de* of); ◆ **~s** *(= marche à suivre)* instructions 2 *(= justification)* explanation (*de* for); ◆ **votre conduite demande des ~s** your conduct requires some explanation ◆ **j'exige des ~s** I demand an explanation 3 *(= discussion)* discussion; *(= dispute)* argument; *(= bagarre)* fight ◆ **j'ai eu une petite ~ avec lui** I had a bit of an argument with him 4 *(Scol) [d'auteur, passage]* commentary (*de* on) analysis (*de* of); ◆ **~ de texte** critical analysis *ou* appreciation of a text, textual analysis

explicitation /ɛksplisitasjɔ̃/ NF *[de symbole]* making explicit, explaining, clarifying ◆ **faire un effort d'~** to try to explain in more detail

explicite /ɛksplisit/ ADJ *[clause, terme]* explicit ◆ **il n'a pas été très ~ sur ce point** he wasn't very clear on that point

explicitement /ɛksplisitmɑ̃/ ADV explicitly

expliciter /ɛksplisite/ ► conjug 1 ◄ VT *[+ clause]* to make explicit; *[+ pensée]* to explain, to clarify

expliquer /ɛksplike/ ► conjug 1 ◄ VT 1 *(= faire comprendre)* to explain ◆ **il m'a expliqué comment faire** he told me *ou* explained to me how to do it ◆ **je lui ai expliqué qu'il avait tort** I pointed out to him *ou* explained to him that he was wrong ◆ **explique-moi comment/pourquoi** explain how/why, tell me how/why ◆ **il m'a expliqué le pourquoi du comment** he explained to me the how and the why of it

2 *(= rendre compte de)* to account for, to explain ◆ **cela explique qu'il ne soit pas venu** that explains why he didn't come, that accounts for his not coming

3 *(Scol) [+ texte]* to comment on, to criticize, to analyse ◆ **~ un passage de Flaubert** to give a critical analysis *ou* a critical appreciation *ou* a critical interpretation of a passage from Flaubert

VPR **s'expliquer** 1 *(= donner des précisions)* to explain o.s., to make o.s. clear ◆ **je m'explique** let me explain, let me make myself clear ◆ **le président s'explique** the president gives his reasons ◆ **s'~ sur ses projets** to talk about *ou* explain one's plans ◆ **s'~ devant qn** to justify o.s. to sb, to explain one's actions to sb

2 *(= comprendre)* to understand ◆ **je ne m'explique pas bien qu'il soit parti** I can't see *ou* understand *ou* it isn't at all clear to me why he should have left

3 *(= être compréhensible)* **son retard s'explique par le mauvais temps** his lateness is explained by the bad weather, the bad weather accounts for *ou* explains his lateness ◆ **leur attitude s'explique : ils n'ont pas reçu notre lettre** that explains their attitude: they didn't get our letter ◆ **tout s'explique !** it's all clear now!, I see it all now!

4 *(= parler clairement)* **s'~ bien/mal** to express o.s. well/badly ◆ **je me suis peut-être mal expliqué** perhaps I have expressed myself badly, perhaps I didn't make myself (quite) clear

5 ◆ **s'~ avec qn** *(= discuter)* to have a talk with sb; *(= se disputer, se battre)* to have it out with sb* ◆ **va t'~ avec lui** go and sort it out with him ◆ **après s'être longuement expliqués ils sont tombés d'accord** after having discussed the matter *ou* after having talked the matter over for a long time they finally reached an agreement ◆ **ils sont allés s'~ dehors*** they went to fight it out outside *ou* to finish it off outside ◆ **s'~ à coups de fusil** to shoot it out

exploit /ɛksplwa/ NM exploit, feat, achievement ◆ **quel ~ !** what a feat! *ou* an achievement! ◆ **~s amoureux** amorous exploits ◆ **~ sportif** sporting achievement *ou* feat ◆ **il a réussi l'~ d'arriver le premier** he came first, which was quite an achievement ◆ **~ d'huissier** writ

exploitable /ɛksplwatabl/ ADJ *(gén)* exploitable ◆ **des données immédiatement ~s** data that can be used immediately ◆ **ces craintes sont facilement ~s en période électorale** these fears can easily be exploited during an election period

exploitant, e /ɛksplwatɑ̃, ɑ̃t/ NM,F 1 *(= fermier)* ~ **(agricole)** farmer ◆ **petit** ~ **(agricole)** small farmer, smallholder *(Brit)* ◆ ~ **forestier** forestry developer 2 *(Ciné) (= propriétaire)* cinema owner; *(= gérant)* cinema manager

exploitation /ɛksplwatasjɔ̃/ NF 1 *(= action) [de mine, sol]* working, exploitation; *[d'entreprise]* running, operating ◆ **mettre en** ~ *[+ domaine, ressources]* to exploit, to develop ◆ **frais/méthodes d'**~ running *ou* operating costs/methods ◆ **satellite en** ~ working satellite ◆ **copie d'**~ *(Ciné)* release print; → **visa**

2 *(= entreprise)* ~ **familiale** family business ◆ ~ **(agricole)** farm ◆ **petite** ~ **(agricole)** small farm, smallholding *(Brit)* ◆ ~ **vinicole** vineyard ◆ ~ **commerciale/industrielle** business/industrial concern ◆ ~ **minière** mine ◆ ~ **forestière** commercial forest

3 *[d'idée, situation, renseignement]* exploiting, using ◆ **la libre** ~ **de l'information** the free use of information

4 *(= abus)* exploitation ◆ **l'**~ **de l'homme par l'homme** man's exploitation of man *ou* of his fellow man ◆ **l'**~ **sexuelle des enfants** sexual exploitation of children

exploité, e /ɛksplwate/ (ptp de **exploiter**) ADJ *[personne]* exploited ◆ **terres non ~es** unfarmed land ◆ **richesses non ~es** unexploited *ou* untapped riches ◆ **un créneau peu** ~ a niche in the market that has not been fully tapped *ou* exploited NM,F exploited person

exploiter /ɛksplwate/ ► conjug 1 ◄ VT 1 *[+ mine]* to work, to exploit; *[+ sol, terres]* to farm, to work; *[+ entreprise]* to run, to operate; *[+ ligne aérienne, réseau]* to operate; *[+ brevet]* to use; *[+ ressources]* to exploit 2 *[+ idée, situation]* to exploit, to make the most of; *[+ don]* to make use of; *[+ personne, bonté, crédulité]* to exploit; *[+ avantage]* to capitalize on, to exploit ◆ **ils exploitent la xénophobie à des fins politiques** they're capitalizing on *ou* exploiting xenophobia for political ends

exploiteur, -euse /ɛksplwatœʀ, øz/ NM,F exploiter

explorateur, -trice /ɛksplɔʀatœʀ, tʀis/ NM,F *(= personne)* explorer

exploration /ɛksplɔʀasjɔ̃/ NF *(gén)* exploration; *[de possibilité, problème]* investigation, examination, exploration; *(Méd)* exploration ◆ ~ **spatiale** space exploration

exploratoire /ɛksplɔʀatwaʀ/ ADJ exploratory

explorer /ɛksplɔʀe/ ► conjug 1 ◄ VT *(gén)* to explore; *[+ possibilité, problème]* to investigate, to examine, to explore; *(Méd)* to explore

exploser /ɛksploze/ ► conjug 1 ◄ VI 1 *[bombe, chaudière]* to explode, to blow up; *[gaz]* to explode ◆ **j'ai cru que ma tête allait** ~ I thought my head was going to explode *ou* burst ◆ **faire** ~ *[+ bombe]* to explode, to detonate; *[+ bâtiment]* to blow up; *[+ monopole, système, coalition]* to break up; *[+ contraintes]* to sweep away 2 *[de sentiments]* ~ **(de colère)** to blow up, to explode (with anger) ◆ **laisser** ~ **sa colère** to give vent to one's anger ◆ ~ **de joie** to go wild with joy 3 *(= augmenter) [chômage, demande, production, prix]* to soar, to rocket; *[marché]* to boom 4 *(* = abîmer) [+ objet]* to smash up ◆ **il s'est explosé le genou** he did his knee in* ◆ **je vais lui** ~ **la gueule**** I'm going to smash his face in**

explosible /ɛksplozibl/ ADJ *[mélange]* explosive

explosif, -ive /ɛksplozif, iv/ ADJ 1 *[engin, charge]* explosive; → **cocktail, mélange** 2 *[dossier, rapport, sujet]* highly sensitive; *[situation, climat]* explosive ◆ **une affaire politiquement explosive** a politically explosive issue 3 *[croissance]* explosive NM explosive ◆ **attentat à l'**~ bomb attack

explosion /ɛksplozjɔ̃/ NF 1 *[de bombe, gaz, chaudière]* explosion; → **moteur**[1] 2 *[de joie, violence]* outburst, explosion; *[de dépenses, nombre]* explosion, dramatic rise *(de* in); ◆ ~ **de colère** angry outburst, explosion of anger ◆ ~ **démographique** population explosion ◆ ~ **sociale** outburst *ou* explosion of social unrest

expo* /ɛkspo/ NF abrév de **exposition**

exponentiel, -ielle /ɛkspɔnɑ̃sjɛl/ ADJ exponential

export /ɛkspɔʀ/ NM (abrév de **exportation**) export ◆ **se lancer dans l'**~ to go into exports ◆ **les bénéfices réalisés à l'**~ profits earned on exports

exportable /ɛkspɔʀtabl/ ADJ exportable

exportateur, -trice /ɛkspɔʀtatœʀ, tʀis/ ADJ export *(épith)*, exporting ◆ **pays** ~ exporting country ◆ **être** ~ **de** to export, to be an exporter of NM,F exporter ◆ ~ **de pétrole** oil exporter

exportation /ɛkspɔʀtasjɔ̃/ NF *(= action)* export, exportation; *(= produit)* export ◆ **faire de l'**~ to be in the export business ◆ **produit d'**~ export product

exporter /ɛkspɔʀte/ ► conjug 1 ◄ VT *(Comm, Ordin)* to export ◆ **notre mode s'exporte bien/mal** our fashions are popular/not very popular abroad

exposant, e /ɛkspozɑ̃, ɑ̃t/ NM,F *[de foire, salon]* exhibitor NM *(Math)* exponent ◆ **chiffre en** ~ superscript number

exposé /ɛkspoze/ NM *(= action)* account, statement, exposition *(frm)*; *(= conférence)* talk; *(Scol) (oral)* presentation; *(écrit)* (written) paper ◆ **faire un** ~ **oral sur** to give a presentation on ◆ **faire un** ~ **de la situation** to give an account *ou* overview of the situation ◆ ~ **des motifs** *(Jur)* preamble *(in bill, stating grounds for its adoption)*

exposer /ɛkspoze/ ► conjug 1 ◄ VT 1 *(= exhiber) [+ marchandises]* to put on display, to display; *[+ tableaux]* to exhibit, to show ◆ **ce peintre expose dans leur galerie** that painter shows *ou* exhibits at their gallery ◆ **exposé en vitrine** on display ◆ **les œuvres exposées** the works on show ◆ **son corps est exposé dans l'église** *(frm)* he is lying in state in the church

2 *(= expliquer) [+ faits, raisons]* to set out, to state; *[+ griefs]* to air; *[+ idées, théories]* to expound, to set out; *[+ situation]* to explain

3 *(= soumettre)* ~ **qn à qch** to expose sb to sth ◆ **ils ont été exposés à des doses massives de radiations** they were exposed to massive doses of radiation

4 *(= mettre en danger) [+ vie, réputation]* to risk ◆ **c'est une personnalité très exposée** his position makes him an easy target for criticism ◆ **sa conduite l'expose à des reproches** his behaviour lays him open to censure

5 *(= orienter, présenter)* to expose; *(Photo)* to expose ◆ ~ **au soleil/aux regards** to expose to sunlight/to view ◆ **maison exposée au sud** house facing (due) south, house with a southern aspect ◆ **maison bien exposée** house with a good aspect ◆ **endroit très exposé** *(au vent, à l'ennemi)* very exposed place

6 *(Littérat) [+ action]* to set out; *(Mus) [+ thème]* to introduce

VPR **s'exposer** to expose o.s. ◆ **s'**~ **à** *[+ danger, reproches, poursuites]* to expose o.s. to, to lay o.s. open to ◆ **s'**~ **au soleil** to expose o.s. to the sun

exposition /ɛkspozisjɔ̃/ NF 1 *(= foire, salon)* exhibition, show ◆ **l'Exposition universelle** the World Fair ◆ **faire une** ~ *[visiteur]* to go to an exhibition; *[artiste]* to put on an exhibition 2 *(= orientation) [de maison]* aspect ◆ **nous avons une** ~ **plein sud** our house faces south *ou* has a southerly aspect *(frm)* 3 *(à des radiations, à la chaleur)* exposure *(à* to); ◆ **évitez les ~s prolongées au soleil** avoid prolonged exposure to the sun 4 *(Photo)* exposure 5 *[de marchandises]* display; *[de faits, raisons, situation, idées]* exposition; *[de condamné, enfant]* exposure ◆ **grande** ~ **de blanc** *(Comm)* special linen week *ou* event 6 *(Littérat, Mus)* exposition ◆ **scène d'**~ expository *ou* introductory scene

exposition-vente (pl **expositions-ventes**) /ɛkspozisjɔ̃vɑ̃t/ NF *[d'art]* art show *(with works on display for sale)*; *[d'artisanat]* craft fair

expo-vente* (pl **expos-ventes**) /ɛkspovɑ̃t/ NF abrév de **exposition-vente**

exprès[1] /ɛkspʀɛ/ GRAMMAIRE ACTIVE 45.4 ADV *(= spécialement)* specially; *(= intentionnellement)* on purpose, deliberately, intentionally ◆ **venir (tout)** ~ **pour** to come specially to ◆ **il l'a fait** ~ he did it on purpose *ou* deliberately *ou* intentionally ◆ **il ne l'a pas fait** ~ he didn't do it on purpose, he didn't mean to do it ◆ **c'est fait** ~ it's meant to be like that, it's deliberate ◆ **comme par un fait** ~ almost as if it was meant to happen

exprès[2], **-esse** /ɛkspʀɛs/ ADJ *[interdiction, ordre]* formal, express; *(Jur) [clause]* express NM, ADJ INV ◆ **(lettre/colis)** ~ express *(Brit) ou* special delivery *(US)* letter/parcel ◆ **(messager)** ~ † express messenger ◆ **envoyer qch en** ~ to send sth by express post *(Brit) ou* special delivery *(US)*, to send sth express *(Brit)*

express /ɛkspʀɛs/ ADJ, NM 1 ◆ **(train)** ~ fast train 2 *(= café)* espresso (coffee)

expressément /ɛkspʀesemɑ̃/ ADV *(= formellement) [dire, interdire]* expressly; *(= spécialement) [fait, conçu]* specially ◆ **il ne l'a pas dit** ~ he didn't say it in so many words

expressif, -ive /ɛkspʀesif, iv/ ADJ *[geste, regard]* expressive, meaningful; *[physionomie]* expressive; *[langage]* expressive, vivid; *[silence]* eloquent

expression /ɛkspʀesjɔ̃/ NF 1 *(gén)* expression ◆ **au-delà de toute** ~ beyond (all) expression, inexpressible ◆ **visage plein d'~/sans** ~ expressive/expressionless face ◆ **jouer avec beaucoup d'**~ to play with great feeling *ou* expression ◆ ~ **corporelle** music and movement ◆ **journal d'**~ **française/anglaise** French/English-language newspaper; → **agréer, liberté, moyen**[2]**, réduire** 2 *(Math = formule)* expression; *(Gram = locution)* phrase, expression ◆ ~ **figée** set *ou* fixed expression, set phrase ◆ ~ **toute faite** stock phrase ◆ ~ **nominale** nominal ◆ **réduit à sa plus simple** ~ reduced to its simplest terms *ou* expression

expressionnisme /ɛkspʀesjɔnism/ NM expressionism

expressionniste /ɛkspʀesjɔnist/ ADJ expressionist *(épith)*, expressionistic NMF expressionist

expressivement /ɛkspʀesivmɑ̃/ ADV expressively

expressivité /ɛkspʀesivite/ NF expressiveness

expresso /ɛkspʀeso/ NM *(= café)* espresso ◆ **machine/cafetière (à)** ~ espresso machine/coffee maker

exprimable /ɛkspʀimabl/ ADJ expressible ◆ **c'est difficilement** ~ it's hard to put it into words *ou* to express ◆ **cette opinion n'est pas** ~ **publiquement** this view cannot be expressed publicly

exprimer /ɛkspʀime/ ► conjug 1 ◄ VT 1 *(= signifier)* to express; *[+ pensée]* to express, to give expression *ou* utterance to *(frm)*; *[+ opinion]* to voice, to express ◆ **mots qui expriment un sens** words which express *ou* convey a meaning ◆ **regards qui expriment la colère** looks which express *ou* indicate anger ◆ **œuvre qui exprime parfaitement l'artiste** work which expresses the artist completely

2 *(Écon, Math)* to express ◆ **somme exprimée en euros** sum expressed in euros ◆ **le signe + exprime l'addition** the sign + indicates *ou* stands for addition

3 *(littér) [+ jus]* to press *ou* squeeze out

VPR **s'exprimer** to express o.s. ◆ **s'~ par gestes** to use gestures to express o.s. ◆ **je me suis peut-être mal exprimé** perhaps I have expressed myself badly, I may not have made myself clear ◆ **si je peux m'~ ainsi** if I may put it like that ◆ **il faut permettre au talent de s'~** talent must be allowed free expression *ou* to express itself ◆ **la joie s'exprima sur son visage** (his) joy showed in his expression, his face expressed his joy

expropriation /ɛkspʀɔpʀijasjɔ̃/ NF *(= action)* expropriation, compulsory purchase *(Brit)*; *(= arrêté)* expropriation order, compulsory purchase order *(Brit)*

exproprier /ɛkspʀɔpʀije/ ► conjug 7 ◄ VT *[+ propriété]* to expropriate, to place a compulsory purchase order on *(Brit)* ◆ **ils ont été expropriés** their property has been expropriated, they have had a compulsory purchase order made on their property

expulsable /ɛkspylsabl/ ADJ *[locataire]* liable to be evicted; *[immigré clandestin]* liable to be deported

expulser /ɛkspylse/ ► conjug 1 ◄ VT 1 *(gén)* *[+ élève]* to expel *(de* from); *[+ étranger]* to deport, to expel *(de* from); *[+ locataire]* to evict *(de* from) to throw out *(de* of); *(Sport)* *[+ joueur]* to send off; *[+ manifestant]* to eject *(de* from) to throw out, to turn out *(de* of) 2 *(Anat)* *[+ déchets]* to evacuate, to excrete; *[+ placenta]* to deliver

expulsion /ɛkspylsjɔ̃/ NF 1 *(gén)* *[d'élève]* expulsion *(de* from); *[d'étranger]* deportation, expulsion *(de* from); *[de locataire]* eviction *(de* from); *[de joueur]* sending off; *[de manifestant]* ejection *(de* from) 2 *(Anat)* *[de déchets]* evacuation, excretion; *[de placenta]* delivery

expurger /ɛkspyʀʒe/ ► conjug 3 ◄ VT to expurgate, to bowdlerize ◆ **version expurgée** sanitized *ou* expurgated *ou* bowdlerized version

exquis, -ise /ɛkski, iz/ ADJ *[plat, choix, politesse]* exquisite; *[personne, temps]* delightful; *(Méd)* *[douleur]* exquisite

exsangue /ɛksɑ̃g/ ADJ *[visage, lèvres]* bloodless; *[économie]* battered ◆ **le pays est ~** the country is on its knees ◆ **les guerres ont laissé le pays ~** wars have bled the country white

exsudation /ɛksydasjɔ̃/ NF *(frm)* exudation *(frm)*

exsuder /ɛksyde/ ► conjug 1 ◄ VTI *(frm, lit)* to exude ◆ **son visage exsude la joie** his face radiates joy

extase /ɛkstɑz/ NF *(Rel)* ecstasy; *(sexuelle)* climax; *(fig)* ecstasy, rapture ◆ **il est en ~ devant sa fille** he is rapturous about his daughter, he goes into raptures over his daughter ◆ **tomber/rester en ~ devant un tableau** to go into ecstasies at/stand in ecstasy before a painting

extasié, e /ɛkstɑzje/ (ptp de **s'extasier**) ADJ ecstatic, enraptured

extasier (s') /ɛkstɑzje/ ► conjug 7 ◄ VPR to go into ecstasies *ou* raptures *(devant, sur* over)

extatique /ɛkstatik/ ADJ ecstatic, enraptured

extenseur /ɛkstɑ̃sœʀ/ ADJ ◆ **(muscle) ~** extensor NM *(Sport)* chest expander

extensibilité /ɛkstɑ̃sibilite/ NF extensibility

extensible /ɛkstɑ̃sibl/ ADJ *[matière]* extensible; *[définition]* extendable ◆ **le budget de l'État n'est pas ~ à l'infini** the state budget is not inexhaustible

extensif, -ive /ɛkstɑ̃sif, iv/ ADJ 1 *(Agr)* *[culture, élevage]* extensive, non-intensive 2 *(fig)* *[conception, interprétation, sens]* broad; *[usage, lecture]* wide, extensive

extension /ɛkstɑ̃sjɔ̃/ NF 1 *(= étirement)* *[de ressort]* stretching; *[de membre]* *(gén)* stretching, extension; *(Méd)* traction ◆ **le ressort atteint son ~ maximum** the spring is fully stretched *ou* is stretched to its maximum ◆ **être en ~** *[personne]* to be stretching; *[bras]* to be stretched out *ou* extended ◆ **en ~ sur la pointe des pieds, levez les bras** stand on tiptoe and raise your arms 2 *(= augmentation)* *[d'épidémie, grève, incendie]* extension, spreading; *[de commerce, domaine]* expansion; *[de pouvoirs]* extension, expansion ◆ **prendre de l'~** *[épidémie]* to spread; *[entreprise]* to expand 3 *(= élargissement)* *[de loi, mesure, sens d'un mot]* extension *(à* to); *(Logique)* extension ◆ **par ~ (de sens)** by extension 4 *(Ordin)* extension; → **carte**

exténuant, e /ɛkstenɥɑ̃, ɑ̃t/ ADJ exhausting

exténuer /ɛkstenɥe/ ► conjug 1 ◄ VT to exhaust, to tire out VPR **s'exténuer** to exhaust o.s., to tire o.s. out *(à faire qch* doing sth)

> ⚠ **exténuer** ne se traduit pas par **to extenuate**, qui a le sens de 'atténuer'.

extérieur, e /ɛksteʀjœʀ/ ADJ 1 *(à un lieu)* *[paroi]* outer, outside, exterior; *[escalier, WC]* outside; *[quartier, cour, boulevard]* outer; *[bruit]* external, outside; *[décoration]* exterior, outside; *[collaborateur]* outside ◆ **apparence ~e** *[de personne]* outward appearance; *[de maison]* outside

2 *(à l'individu)* *[monde, influences]* external, outside; *[activité, intérêt]* outside; *[réalité]* external ◆ **manifestation ~e de colère** outward show *ou* display of anger

3 *(= étranger)* *[commerce, vente]* external, foreign; *[politique, nouvelles]* foreign

4 *(= superficiel)* *[amabilité]* surface *(épith)*, superficial ◆ **sa gaieté est toute ~e** his gaiety is all on the surface *ou* all an outward display

5 *(= sans relation avec)* **être ~ à une question** to be external to *ou* outside a question, to be beyond the scope of a question ◆ **c'est tout à fait ~ à moi** it has nothing to do with me, it doesn't concern me in the least ◆ **rester ~ à un conflit** to stay *ou* keep out of a conflict ◆ **"interdit à toute personne extérieure à l'usine/au chantier"** "factory employees/site workers only", "no entry for unauthorized personnel"

6 *(Géom)* *[angle]* exterior

NM 1 *[d'objet, maison]* outside, exterior; *[de piste, circuit]* outside ◆ **il l'a débordé par l'~** *[joueur]* he overtook him on the outside ◆ **juger qch de l'~** *(d'après son apparence)* to judge sth by appearances; *(en tant que profane)* to judge sth from the outside

◆ **à l'extérieur** *(= au dehors)* outside ◆ **travailler à l'~** *(hors de chez soi)* to work outside the home ◆ **il a été recruté à l'~** *(de l'entreprise)* he was recruited from outside ◆ **téléphoner à l'~** to make an outside *ou* external call ◆ **jouer à l'~** to play an away match, to play away ◆ **c'est à l'~ (de la ville)** it's outside (the town)

2 ◆ **l'~** *(gén)* the outside world; *(= pays étrangers)* foreign countries ◆ **vendre beaucoup à l'~** to sell a lot abroad *ou* to foreign countries ◆ **nouvelles de l'~** news from abroad

3 *(frm = apparence)* exterior, (outward) appearance

NMPL **extérieurs** *(Ciné)* location shots ◆ **tourner en ~s** to shoot on location

extérieurement /ɛksteʀjœʀmɑ̃/ ADV 1 *(= du dehors)* on the outside, externally 2 *(= en apparence)* on the surface, outwardly

extériorisation /ɛksteʀjɔʀizasjɔ̃/ NF *[de sentiment]* display, outward expression; *(Psych)* externalization, exteriorization

extérioriser /ɛksteʀjɔʀize/ ► conjug 1 ◄ VT *[+ sentiment]* to show, to express; *(Psych)* to exteriorize, to externalize VPR **s'extérioriser** *[personne]* to express o.s.; *[sentiment]* to be expressed

extériorité /ɛksteʀjɔʀite/ NF *(Philos)* exteriority

exterminateur, -trice /ɛkstɛʀminatœʀ, tʀis/ ADJ exterminating; → **ange** NM,F exterminator

extermination /ɛkstɛʀminasjɔ̃/ NF extermination; → **camp**

exterminer /ɛkstɛʀmine/ ► conjug 1 ◄ VT *(lit, fig)* to exterminate, to wipe out

externalisation /ɛkstɛʀnalizasjɔ̃/ NF *[d'activité, service]* outsourcing

externaliser /ɛkstɛʀnalize/ ► conjug 1 ◄ VT *[+ activité, service]* to outsource

externat /ɛkstɛʀna/ NM *(Scol)* day school ◆ **faire son ~ à** *(Méd)* to be a non-resident student *ou* an extern *(US)* at

externe /ɛkstɛʀn/ ADJ *[surface]* external, outer; *[angle]* exterior; *[candidature, recrutement, croissance]* external NMF *(= élève)* day pupil ◆ **~ (des hôpitaux)** non-resident student at a teaching hospital, extern *(US)*

exterritorialité /ɛksteʀitɔʀjalite/ NF exterritoriality

extincteur, -trice /ɛkstɛ̃ktœʀ, tʀis/ ADJ extinguishing NM (fire) extinguisher

extinction /ɛkstɛ̃ksjɔ̃/ NF *[d'incendie, lumières]* extinction, extinguishing, putting out; *[de peuple]* extinction, dying out; *[de dette, droit]* extinguishment ◆ **~ de voix** loss of voice, aphonia *(SPÉC)* ◆ **avoir une ~ de voix** to lose one's voice ◆ **avant l'~ des feux** *(Mil, fig)* before lights out ◆ **espèce en voie d'~** endangered species

extirpation /ɛkstiʀpasjɔ̃/ NF *(littér)* *[d'abus, vice]* eradication; *[de polype, tumeur]* extirpation; *[de plante]* uprooting, pulling up

extirper /ɛkstiʀpe/ ► conjug 1 ◄ VT *(littér)* *[+ abus, vice]* to eradicate, to root out; *[+ polype, tumeur]* to extirpate; *[+ herbes]* to uproot, to pull up ◆ **elle a extirpé un chéquier de son sac** * she rooted around in her handbag and pulled out a chequebook ◆ **impossible de lui ~ une parole !** * it's impossible to drag *ou* get a word out of him! ◆ **~ qn de son lit** * to drag *ou* haul sb out of bed VPR **s'extirper** ◆ **s'~ de son manteau** to extricate o.s. from one's coat ◆ **s'~ du lit** to drag o.s. out of bed

extorquer /ɛkstɔʀke/ ► conjug 1 ◄ VT *[+ argent]* to extort; *[+ aveu, promesse]* to extract, to extort *(à qn* from sb); ◆ **ils lui ont extorqué une signature** they forced a signature out of him

extorqueur, -euse /ɛkstɔʀkœʀ, øz/ NM,F extortioner

extorsion /ɛkstɔʀsjɔ̃/ NF extortion ◆ **~ de fonds** extortion of money

extra /ɛkstʀa/ NM *(= serveur)* catering assistant; *(= gâterie)* (special) treat ◆ **s'offrir un ~** to give o.s. a treat, to treat o.s. to something special ADJ INV *(Comm = supérieur)* *[fromage, vin]* first-rate, extra-special; *[tissu]* top-quality; *(* = excellent)* *[film, personne, week-end]* fantastic, terrific *, great * ◆ **de qualité ~** of the finest *ou* best quality

extraconjugal, e (mpl **-aux**) /ɛkstʀakɔ̃ʒygal, o/ ADJ extramarital

extracteur /ɛkstʀaktœʀ/ NM extractor

extractif, -ive /ɛkstʀaktif, iv/ ADJ *[industrie]* extractive, mining

extraction /ɛkstʀaksjɔ̃/ NF 1 *[de pétrole, données]* extraction; *[de charbon]* mining; *[de marbre]* quarrying 2 *(Math, Méd)* extraction 3 († *= origine)* extraction *(frm)* ◆ **de haute/basse ~** of high/low birth

extrader /ɛkstʀade/ ► conjug 1 ◄ VT to extradite

extradition /ɛkstʀadisjɔ̃/ NF extradition

extrafin, e, extra-fin, e /ɛkstʀafɛ̃, fin/ ADJ *[haricots, petits pois]* super-fine; *[aiguille]* extra fine

extrafort, extra-fort, e /ɛkstʀafɔʀ, fɔʀt/ ADJ *[carton, moutarde]* extra-strong NM *(Couture)* binding

extraire /ɛkstʀɛʀ/ ▸ conjug 50 ◂ VT 1 *[+ minerai, pétrole, données]* to extract; *[+ charbon]* to mine; *[+ marbre]* to quarry 2 *[+ gaz, jus]* to extract; *(en pressant)* to squeeze out; *(en tordant)* to wring out 3 *[+ dent]* to extract, to pull out; *[+ clou]* to pull out; *[+ racine carrée]* to extract; *[+ balle]* to extract, to remove (*de* from) 4 ◆ **~ de** *[+ placard, poche]* to take *ou* bring out of; *[+ avalanche, prison]* to rescue from, to get out of ◆ **passage extrait d'un livre** passage taken from a book VPR **s'extraire** ◆ **s'~ de son manteau** to extricate o.s. from one's coat ◆ **s'~ de sa voiture** to climb out of one's car

extrait /ɛkstʀɛ/ NM 1 *[de discours, journal]* extract; *[d'auteur, film, livre]* extract, excerpt; *[de chanson]* excerpt ◆ **~ de naissance/baptême** birth/baptismal certificate ◆ **~ de compte** abstract of accounts ◆ **un court ~ de l'émission** a clip from the programme 2 *[de plante]* essence ◆ **~ de viande** meat extract

extrajudiciaire /ɛkstʀaʒydisjɛʀ/ ADJ *(Jur) [exécution]* extrajudicial

extralégal, e (mpl **-aux**) /ɛkstʀalegal, o/ ADJ extra-legal

extralinguistique /ɛkstʀalɛ̃gɥistik/ ADJ extralinguistic

extra-lucide, extralucide /ɛkstʀalysid/ ADJ, NMF clairvoyant

extra-marital, e (mpl **-aux**) /ɛkstʀamaʀital, o/ ADJ extra-marital

extra-muros /ɛkstʀamyʀos/ ADJ INV extramural ◆ **un campus ~** a campus outside town ◆ **Paris ~** outer Paris ADV outside the town

extranet /ɛkstʀanɛt/ NM extranet

extraordinaire /ɛkstʀaɔʀdinɛʀ/ ADJ 1 *(= étrange) [costume, événement, opinions]* extraordinary ◆ **l'~, c'est que …** the extraordinary thing is that … 2 *(= exceptionnel) [beauté, force]* extraordinary, exceptional, outstanding; *[succès]* resounding ◆ **ce roman n'est pas ~** this isn't a particularly great novel 3 *(Pol) [assemblée, mesures, moyens]* extraordinary, special; → **ambassadeur** 4 ◆ **si par ~** if by some unlikely chance ◆ **quand par ~** on those rare occasions when

extraordinairement /ɛkstʀaɔʀdinɛʀmɑ̃/ ADV *(= exceptionnellement)* extraordinarily, exceptionally; *(= d'une manière étrange)* extraordinarily

extraparlementaire /ɛkstʀapaʀləmɑ̃tɛʀ/ ADJ extra-parliamentary

extraplat, e /ɛkstʀapla, at/ ADJ *[télévision, montre, calculatrice]* slimline ◆ **télévision à écran ~** flat screen television

extrapolation /ɛkstʀapɔlasjɔ̃/ NF extrapolation

extrapoler /ɛkstʀapɔle/ ▸ conjug 1 ◂ VTI to extrapolate (*à partir de* from)

extrascolaire /ɛkstʀaskɔlɛʀ/ ADJ *[activités]* extracurricular

extrasensible /ɛkstʀasɑ̃sibl/ ADJ extrasensible *(frm)*, that cannot be perceived by the senses

extrasensoriel, -ielle /ɛkstʀasɑ̃sɔʀjɛl/ ADJ *[perception]* extrasensory

extrasystole /ɛkstʀasistɔl/ NF extrasystole

extraterrestre /ɛkstʀateʀɛstʀ/ ADJ extraterrestrial NMF extra-terrestrial, alien

extraterritorialité /ɛkstʀateʀitɔʀjalite/ NF extraterritoriality

extra-utérin, e (mpl **extra-utérins**) /ɛkstʀayteʀɛ̃, in/ ADJ extrauterine ◆ **grossesse ~e** ectopic pregnancy

extravagance /ɛkstʀavagɑ̃s/ NF 1 *(= caractère) [de costume, conduite]* eccentricity, extravagance 2 *(= acte)* eccentric *ou* extravagant behaviour *(NonC)* ◆ **dire des ~s** to talk wildly *ou* extravagantly

extravagant, e /ɛkstʀavagɑ̃, ɑ̃t/ ADJ *[idée, théorie]* extravagant, wild, crazy; *[prix]* outrageous, excessive

extraversion /ɛkstʀavɛʀsjɔ̃/ NF extroversion

extraverti, e /ɛkstʀavɛʀti/ ADJ, NM,F extrovert

extrême /ɛkstʀɛm/ ADJ 1 *(le plus éloigné)* extreme, furthest ◆ **à l'~ bout de la table** at the far *ou* furthest end of the table, at the very end of the table ◆ **dans son ~ jeunesse** in his very young days, in his earliest youth ◆ **à l'~ opposé** at the opposite extreme ◆ **l'~ droite/gauche** *(Pol)* the far right/left

2 *(le plus intense)* extreme, utmost ◆ **dans la misère ~** in extreme *ou* the utmost poverty ◆ **c'est avec un plaisir ~ que** it is with the greatest *ou* the utmost pleasure that ◆ **il m'a reçu avec une ~ amabilité** he received me in the friendliest possible way *ou* with the utmost kindness ◆ **il fait une chaleur ~** it is extremely hot ◆ **d'une pâleur/difficulté ~** extremely pale/difficult; → **rigueur, urgence**

3 *(après n = excessif, radical) [théories, moyens]* extreme ◆ **ça l'a conduit à des mesures ~s** that drove him into taking drastic *ou* extreme steps ◆ **il a un caractère ~** he tends to go to extremes, he is an extremist by nature

NM extreme ◆ **les ~s se touchent** extremes meet ◆ **passer d'un ~ à l'autre** to go from one extreme to the other *ou* to another

◆ **(jusqu')à l'extrême** in the extreme, to an extreme degree ◆ **cela lui répugnait à l'~** he was extremely loath to do it ◆ **noircir une situation à l'~** to paint the blackest possible picture of a situation ◆ **scrupuleux à l'~** scrupulous to a fault

extrêmement /ɛkstʀɛmmɑ̃/ ADV extremely, exceedingly

extrême-onction (pl **extrêmes-onctions**) /ɛkstʀɛmɔ̃ksjɔ̃/ NF Extreme Unction

Extrême-Orient /ɛkstʀɛmɔʀjɑ̃/ NM INV Far East

extrême-oriental, e (mpl **extrême-orientaux**) /ɛkstʀɛmɔʀjɑ̃tal, o/ ADJ far eastern, oriental NM,F **Extrême-Oriental(e)** person from the Far East

extrémisme /ɛkstʀemism/ NM extremism

extrémiste /ɛkstʀemist/ ADJ, NMF extremist

extrémité /ɛkstʀemite/ NF 1 *(= bout) (gén)* end; *[d'aiguille]* point; *[d'objet mince]* tip; *[de village, île]* extremity, limit; *[de péninsule]* head 2 *(frm = situation critique)* plight, straits ◆ **être dans la pénible ~ de devoir** to be in the unfortunate necessity of having to ◆ **réduit à la dernière ~** in the most dire plight *ou* straits ◆ **être à toute ~, être à la dernière ~** to be on the point of death 3 *(frm = action excessive)* extremes, extreme lengths ◆ **se porter à une ~** *ou* **à des ~s** to go to extremes ◆ **pousser qn à une ~** *ou* **à des ~s** to push *ou* drive sb to extremes *ou* into taking extreme action ◆ **se livrer à des ~s (sur qn)** to assault sb ◆ **d'une ~ dans l'autre** from one extreme to another 4 *(= pieds et mains)* **~s** extremities

extrinsèque /ɛkstʀɛ̃sɛk/ ADJ extrinsic

extruder /ɛkstʀyde/ ▸ conjug 1 ◂ VT to extrude

extrusion /ɛkstʀyzjɔ̃/ NF extrusion

exubérance /ɛgzybeʀɑ̃s/ NF *(= caractère)* exuberance *(NonC)*; *(= action)* exuberant behaviour *(NonC)* *(ou* talk *(NonC)* etc) ◆ **parler avec ~** to speak exuberantly

exubérant, e /ɛgzybeʀɑ̃, ɑ̃t/ ADJ *(gén)* exuberant

exultation /ɛgzyltasjɔ̃/ NF exultation

exulter /ɛgzylte/ ▸ conjug 1 ◂ VI to exult

exutoire /ɛgzytwaʀ/ NM *(Tech)* outlet; *(= dérivatif)* outlet (*à* for)

ex-voto /ɛksvoto/ NM INV thanksgiving *ou* commemorative plaque

eye-liner (pl **eye-liners**) /ajlajnœʀ/ NM eyeliner

Ézéchiel /ezekjɛl/ NM Ezekiel ◆ **(le livre d') ~** (the Book of) Ezekiel

F¹, f /ɛf/ **NM** *(= lettre)* F, f ◆ **un F2** *(= appartement)* a 2-roomed flat *(Brit) ou* apartment *(surtout US)*

F² [1] (abrév de **franc**) F, fr [2] (abrév de **Fahrenheit**) F [3] abrév de **frère**

fa /fa/ **NM INV** *(Mus)* F; *(en chantant la gamme)* fa; → **clé**

FAB /ɛfabe/ (abrév de **franco à bord**) FOB

fable /fɑbl/ **NF** *(= genre)* fable; *(= légende)* fable, legend; *(= mensonge)* tale, story ◆ **quelle ~ va-t-il inventer ?** what yarn will he spin? ◆ **cette rumeur est une pure ~** this rumour is completely unfounded *ou* untrue ◆ **être la ~ de toute la ville** † to be the laughing stock of the whole town

fabliau (pl **fabliaux**) /fablijo/ **NM** fabliau

fablier /fablije/ **NM** book of fables

fabricant, e /fabʀikɑ̃, ɑ̃t/ **NM,F** manufacturer ◆ **un gros ~ d'ordinateurs** a big computer manufacturer ◆ **~ de pneus** tyre-maker *(Brit)*, tire-maker *(US)*

fabricateur, -trice /fabʀikatœʀ, tʀis/ **NM,F** *[de fausse monnaie, faux papiers]* counterfeiter, forger; *[de fausses nouvelles]* fabricator

fabrication /fabʀikasjɔ̃/ **NF** [1] *(industrielle)* manufacture, manufacturing; *(artisanale, personnelle)* making ◆ **la ~ industrielle/en série** factory *ou* industrial/mass production ◆ **~ par lots** batch production ◆ **de ~ française** made in France, French-made ◆ **de ~ étrangère** foreign-made ◆ **de ~ locale** made locally ◆ **c'est une ~ maison** * it's home-made ◆ **de bonne ~** well-made, of good *ou* high-quality workmanship ◆ **~ assistée par ordinateur** computer-aided manufacturing ◆ **une robe de sa ~** a dress of her own making, a dress she made herself; → **artisanal, défaut, procédé** *etc* [2] *[de faux]* forging; *[de fausses nouvelles]* fabricating, making up ◆ **~ de fausse monnaie** counterfeiting *ou* forging money

fabrique /fabʀik/ **NF** [1] *(= établissement)* factory ◆ **~ de gants** glove factory ◆ **~ de papier** paper mill; → **marque, prix** [2] *(littér = facture)* workmanship ◆ **de bonne ~** well-made, of good *ou* high-quality workmanship

fabriquer /fabʀike/ ► conjug 1 ◄ **VT** [1] *(industriellement)* to manufacture; *(de façon artisanale, chez soi)* to make; *[+ cellules, anticorps]* to make, to produce; *[+ faux document]* to forge; *[+ fausses nouvelles, fausses preuves]* to fabricate, to make up; *[+ incident, histoire]* to invent, to make up ◆ **~ de la fausse monnaie** to counterfeit *ou* forge money ◆ **~ en série** to mass-produce ◆ **~ industriellement** to manufacture, to produce industrially ◆ **~ de façon artisanale** to handcraft, to make *ou* produce on a small scale ◆ **c'est une histoire fabriquée de toutes pièces** this story is made up from start to finish *ou* is a complete fabrication ◆ **il s'est fabriqué un personnage de prophète** he created *ou* invented a prophet-like character for himself ◆ **il s'est fabriqué un poste de radio/une cabane** he built *ou* made himself a radio set/a shed

[2] *(* = faire)* to do ◆ **qu'est-ce qu'il fabrique ?** what (on earth) is he doing? *ou* is he up to?* ◆ **quelquefois, je me demande ce que je fabrique ici !** sometimes I wonder what on earth I'm doing here!

fabulateur, -trice /fabylatœʀ, tʀis/ **NM,F** storyteller

fabulation /fabylasjɔ̃/ **NF** *(= fait d'imaginer)* fantasizing; *(= fait de mentir)* storytelling; *(= fable)* tale, fable; *(= mensonge)* story, yarn, tale

fabuler /fabyle/ ► conjug 1 ◄ **VI** to make up *ou* invent stories ◆ **tu fabules!** * you're talking rubbish! *

fabuleusement /fabyløzmɑ̃/ **ADV** fabulously, fantastically

fabuleux, -euse /fabylø, øz/ **ADJ** [1] *(= prodigieux)* fabulous ◆ **il est d'une hypocrisie, c'est ~ !** it's amazing what a hypocrite he is! [2] *(= des temps anciens, de la mythologie)* mythical, legendary; *(= de la légende, du merveilleux)* fabulous

fabuliste /fabylist/ **NM** writer of fables *ou* tales

fac * /fak/ **NF** (abrév de **faculté**) → **faculté 1**

façade /fasad/ **NF** [1] *(= devant de maison) (gén)* façade, front, frontage; *(Archéol)* façade; *(= côté de maison)* side; *[de magasin]* front, frontage ◆ **~ latérale** side wall ◆ **~ ouest** west side *ou* wall ◆ **la ~ arrière de la maison** the back of the house ◆ **les ~s des magasins** the shop fronts ◆ **3 pièces en ~** 3 rooms at *ou* facing the front ◆ **sur la ~ atlantique** *(Météo)* along the Atlantic shoreline

[2] *(= apparence)* façade, appearance; *(= couverture)* cover ◆ **~ de respectabilité/de vertu** façade *ou* outward show *ou* appearance of respectability/virtue ◆ **ce n'est qu'une ~** it's just a front *ou* façade, it's a mere façade *ou* pretence ◆ **de ~** *[luxe]* apparent; *[optimisme]* fake ◆ **maintenir une unité de ~** to preserve an appearance *ou* outward show of unity ◆ **pour la ~** for the sake of appearances, for appearances' sake ◆ **ce restaurant est une ~ qui cache un tripot clandestin** this restaurant is a cover for an illegal dive *

[3] *(* = visage)* **se refaire la ~** *(= se maquiller)* to redo one's face*; *(= se faire faire un lifting)* to have a face-lift ◆ **il va te démolir la ~** he's going to smash your face in*

face /fas/ **NF** [1] *(frm, Méd = visage)* face ◆ **les blessés de la ~** people with facial injuries ◆ **tomber ~ contre terre** to fall flat on the ground *ou* flat on one's face ◆ **se prosterner ~ contre terre** to prostrate o.s. with one's face to the ground ◆ **~ de rat/de singe*** rat/monkey face* ◆ **sauver/perdre la ~** to save/lose face ◆ **opération destinée à sauver la ~** face-saving move; → **voiler¹**

[2] *(= côté) [d'objet, organe]* side; *[de médaille, pièce de monnaie]* front, obverse; *(Math) [de cube, figure]* side, face; *(Alpinisme)* face, wall ◆ **~ A/B** *[de disque]* A-/B-side ◆ **la ~ interne des cuisses** the inner thighs ◆ **la ~ cachée de la lune** the dark side of the moon ◆ **examiner un objet/une question sous** *ou* **sur toutes ses ~s** to examine an object/a problem from all sides ◆ **question à double ~** two-sided question ◆ **la pièce est tombée sur ~** *ou* **côté ~** the coin fell face up ◆ **~ ! ** *(jeu de pile ou face)* heads!; → **pile**

[3] *(= aspect)* face ◆ **la ~ changeante des choses** the changing face of things ◆ **changer la ~ du monde** to change the face of the world ◆ **le monde a changé de ~** (the face of) the world has changed

[4] *(littér = surface)* **la ~ de la terre** *ou* **du globe** the face of the earth ◆ **la ~ de l'océan** the surface of the ocean

[5] *(locutions)*

◆ **faire face** to face up to things ◆ **faire ~ à** *[+ lieu, objet, personne]* to face, to be opposite; *[+ épreuve, adversaire, obligation, concurrence]* to face; *[+ dette, engagement]* to honour *(Brit) ou* honor *(US)* ◆ **ils ne disposent pas de fonds suffisants pour faire ~ à la situation** they have insufficient funds to deal with the situation ◆ **il a dû faire ~ à des dépenses élevées** he has been faced with *ou* he has had to face considerable expense

◆ **se faire face** *[maisons]* to be facing *ou* opposite each other; *[adversaires]* to be face to face

◆ **face à** *(physiquement)* facing; *(moralement)* faced with; *(= contre)* against ◆ **il était ~ à moi** he was facing me ◆ **~ à ces problèmes, il se sentait impuissant** faced with *ou* in the face of such problems, he felt helpless ◆ **~ à cette situation, que peut la diplomatie ?** what can diplomacy do when faced with such a situation? ◆ **il a fait part de son inquiétude ~ à la baisse de l'euro** he spoke of his concern about the fall in the euro ◆ **l'euro reste ferme ~ au dollar** the euro remains stable against the dollar ◆ **la science est impuissante ~ à ce virus** science is powerless against this virus ◆ **leur victoire/défaite ~ à l'Islande** their victory over/defeat against Iceland

♦ **face à face** *[lieux, objets]* opposite *ou* facing each other; *[personnes, animaux]* face to face, facing each other ♦ **~ à ~ avec** *[+ lieu, objet]* opposite, facing; *[+ personne, animal]* face to face with ♦ **~ à ~ avec une difficulté** faced with *ou* up against a difficulty

♦ **à la face de** ♦ **il éclata de rire à la ~ de son professeur** he laughed in his teacher's face ♦ **proclamer qch à la ~ du monde** to proclaim sth to the whole world

♦ **en face** *(= de l'autre côté de la rue)* across the street, opposite, over the road ♦ **j'habite en ~** I live across the street *ou* over the road *ou* opposite ♦ **la maison d'en ~** the house across the street *ou* over the road *ou* opposite ♦ **le trottoir d'en ~** the opposite pavement ♦ **la dame d'en ~** the lady (from) across the street *ou* (from) over the road, the lady opposite ♦ **regarder qn (bien) en ~** to look sb (straight) in the face ♦ **je lui ai dit en ~ ce que je pensais d'elle** I told her to her face what I thought of her ♦ **regarder la mort en ~** to look death in the face ♦ **il faut voir les choses en ~** one must see things as they are, one must face facts ♦ **avoir le soleil en ~** to have the sun in one's eyes

♦ **en face de** *(= en vis-à-vis de)* opposite; *(= en présence de)* in front of ♦ **au banquet, on les a mis l'un en ~ de l'autre** *ou* **en ~ l'un de l'autre** they were placed opposite each other at the banquet ♦ **ils étaient l'un en ~ de l'autre** they were sitting (*ou* standing) opposite each other ♦ **il n'ose rien dire en ~ de son patron** he daren't say anything in front of his boss ♦ **ne te mets pas en ~ de moi/de ma lumière** don't stand in my way/in my light ♦ **se trouver en ~ d'un danger/problème** to be confronted *ou* faced with a danger/problem ♦ **mettre qn en ~ de ses responsabilités** to make sb face up to their responsibilities ♦ **en ~ de cela** *(= cependant)* on the other hand

♦ **de face** *[portrait]* full-face; *[nu, portrait en pied]* full-frontal; *[attaque]* (full-)frontal; *[place] (au théâtre)* in the centre *(Brit) ou* center *(US)* ♦ **un personnage/cheval de ~** the front view of a person/horse ♦ **avoir une vue de ~ sur qch** to have a front view of sth ♦ **voir qn de ~** to see sb face on ♦ **vu/filmé de ~** seen/filmed from the front ♦ **attaquer de ~** to make a frontal attack on, to attack from the front ♦ **un vent de ~** a facing wind ♦ **avoir le vent de ~** to have the wind in one's face

face-à-face /fasafas/ **NM INV** *(= rencontre)* (face-to-face) meeting *ou* encounter; *(= rivalité)* showdown; *(= conflit)* confrontation ♦ **~ télévisé** one-to-one *ou* face-to-face TV debate ♦ **le ~ Bordeaux-Nantes** *(Sport)* the encounter between Bordeaux and Nantes

face-à-main (pl **faces-à-main**) /fasamɛ̃/ **NM** lorgnette

facétie /fasesi/ **NF** *(= drôlerie)* joke; *(= farce)* prank, trick ♦ **faire des ~s** to play pranks *ou* tricks ♦ **dire des ~s** to crack jokes

facétieusement /fasesjøzmɑ̃/ **ADV** mischievously

facétieux, -ieuse /fasesjø, jøz/ **ADJ** *[personne, caractère]* mischievous

facette /fasɛt/ **NF** (lit, fig) facet ♦ **à ~s** *[pierre]* faceted; *[caractère, personnage]* multi-faceted, many-sided; *[histoire, réalité]* multifaceted ♦ **yeux à ~s** compound eyes ♦ **étudier un problème sous toutes ses ~s** to examine a problem from every angle

facetter /fasete/ ▸ **conjug 1** ◂ **VT** to facet

fâché, e /fɑʃe/ (ptp de **fâcher**) **ADJ** 1 *(= en colère)* angry, cross *(surtout Brit) (contre* with); ♦ **elle a l'air ~(e)** she looks angry *ou* cross *(surtout Brit)* ♦ **tu n'es pas ~, au moins ?** you're not angry *ou* cross *(surtout Brit)*, are you?

2 *(= brouillé)* **ils sont ~s** they have fallen out ♦ **elle est ~e avec moi** she has fallen out with me ♦ **nous sommes ~s à mort** we can't stand the sight of each other, we are mortal enemies ♦ **il est ~ avec les chiffres** *(hum)* he's hopeless with numbers ♦ **il est ~ avec l'orthographe** *(hum)* he can't spell to save his life ♦ **il est ~ avec son peigne** *(hum)* his hair has never seen a comb

3 *(= contrarié)* sorry *(de qch* about sth); ♦ **je suis ~ de ne pas pouvoir vous aider** *(frm)* I'm sorry that I can't help you ♦ **je ne suis pas ~ d'avoir fini ce travail** I'm not sorry to have finished this job ♦ **je ne serais pas ~ que vous me laissiez tranquille** *(hum)* I wouldn't mind being left alone *ou* in peace, I wouldn't object to a bit of peace and quiet

fâcher /fɑʃe/ ▸ **conjug 1** ◂ **VT** 1 *(= mettre en colère)* to anger, to make angry, to vex ♦ **tu ne réussiras qu'à le ~ davantage** you will only make him more angry *ou* angrier 2 *(frm = contrarier)* to grieve *(frm)*, to distress ♦ **cette triste nouvelle me fâche beaucoup** this sad news grieves me *(frm) ou* greatly distresses me **VPR se fâcher** 1 *(= se mettre en colère)* to get angry *ou* cross *(surtout Brit)*, to lose one's temper ♦ **se ~ contre qn/pour** *ou* **au sujet de qch** to get angry *ou* annoyed with sb/about *ou* over sth ♦ **va au lit ou je me fâche !** go to bed or I'll get angry! ♦ **si tu continues, je vais me ~ tout rouge*** *(hum)* if you go on like that, I'll get really angry *ou* cross *(surtout Brit)* 2 *(= se brouiller)* to quarrel, to fall out *(avec* with)

fâcherie /fɑʃʀi/ **NF** *(= brouille)* quarrel

fâcheusement /fɑʃøzmɑ̃/ **ADV** *[survenir]* (most) unfortunately *ou* awkwardly ♦ **~ surpris** (most) unpleasantly surprised

fâcheux, -euse /fɑʃø, øz/ **ADJ** unfortunate, regrettable ♦ **il est ~ qu'il ne soit pas venu** it's unfortunate *ou* a pity that he didn't come ♦ **le ~ dans tout ça c'est que ...** the unfortunate thing about it is that ... **NM,F** *(littér = importun)* bore

facho* /faʃo/ **ADJ, NMF** (abrév de **fasciste**) *(péj)* fascist ♦ **il est un peu ~** he's a bit of a fascist

facial, e (mpl **facials** *ou* **-iaux**) /fasjal, jo/ **ADJ** facial; → **angle**

faciès /fasjɛs/ **NM** 1 *(= visage)* features; *(Ethnol, Méd)* facies; → **délit** 2 *(Bot, Géog)* facies

facile /fasil/ **ADJ** 1 *(= aisé) [travail, problème, succès, proie]* easy ♦ **un livre ~ à lire** an easy book to read ♦ **c'est** *ou* **il est ~ de ...** it's easy to ... ♦ **~ d'emploi, ~ à utiliser** easy to use ♦ **~ d'accès, d'accès ~** easy to reach *ou* get to, of easy access ♦ **avoir la vie ~** to have an easy life ♦ **ils ne lui rendent pas la vie ~** they don't make life easy for him ♦ **c'est ~ à dire !** that's easy to say! ♦ **plus ~ à dire qu'à faire** easier said than done ♦ **c'est trop ~ de s'indigner** it's too easy to get indignant ♦ **ce n'est pas si ~** it's not as simple as that ♦ **~ comme tout*** *ou* **comme bonjour*** (as) easy as pie*, dead easy*

2 *(= spontané)* **avoir la parole ~** *(= parler aisément)* to be a fluent *ou* an articulate speaker; *(= parler volontiers)* to have a ready tongue *ou* the gift of the gab* ♦ **il a la plume ~** *(= écrire aisément)* he has an eloquent pen; *(= être toujours prêt à écrire)* he finds it easy to write, writing comes easily to him ♦ **avoir la larme ~** to be quick to cry, to be easily moved to tears ♦ **il a l'argent ~*** he's very casual about money, money just slips through his fingers ♦ **l'argent ~** easy money ♦ **avoir la gâchette ~** to be trigger-happy ♦ **il a le couteau ~** he's all too quick to use his knife, he's very ready with his knife

3 *(péj = superficiel)* **effet/ironie ~** facile effect/irony ♦ **littérature ~** cheap literature

4 *[caractère]* easy-going ♦ **il est d'humeur ~** he's easy-going ♦ **il est ~ à vivre/contenter** he's easy to get along with *ou* on with *(Brit)*/to please ♦ **il n'est pas ~ tous les jours** he's not always easy to get along with *ou* on with *(Brit)* ♦ **il n'est pas ~ en affaires** he's a tough businessman, he drives a hard bargain ♦ **ce n'est pas un adversaire ~** he's a formidable adversary ♦ **c'est un bébé très ~** he's a very easy baby

5 *(péj) [femme]* loose *(épith)* ♦ **une fille ~** a woman of easy virtue

ADV * *(= facilement)* easily; *(= au moins)* at least, easily ♦ **il y est arrivé ~** he managed it easily ♦ **il fait du 200 km/h ~** he's doing at least 200 km/h ♦ **elle a 50 ans ~** she's at least *ou* easily 50

facilement /fasilmɑ̃/ **ADV** easily ♦ **médicament ~ toléré par l'organisme** medicine easily *ou* readily tolerated by the body ♦ **il se fâche ~** he loses his temper easily, he's quick to lose his temper, he's quick-tempered ♦ **on met ~ 10 jours*** it takes 10 days easily *ou* at least 10 days

facilité /fasilite/ **NF** 1 *(= simplicité) [de devoir, problème, travail]* easiness ♦ **aimer la ~** to like things that are easy *ou* simple ♦ **tâche d'une grande ~** extremely easy *ou* straightforward task ♦ **d'une grande ~ d'emploi** *[outil]* very easy to use; *[logiciel]* very user-friendly

2 *(= aisance) [de succès, victoire]* ease; *[d'expression, style]* fluency, ease ♦ **il a choisi la ~ en ne venant pas** he took the easy way out by not coming ♦ **réussir qch avec ~** to manage sth with ease *ou* easily ♦ **la ~ avec laquelle il a appris le piano** the ease with which he learnt the piano ♦ **il travaille avec ~** he works with ease ♦ **il s'exprime avec ~** *ou* **avec une grande ~ de parole** he expresses himself with (great) fluency *ou* ease *ou* fluently; → **solution**

3 *(= aptitude)* ability, aptitude ♦ **cet élève a beaucoup de ~** this pupil has great ability *ou* aptitude ♦ **il a beaucoup de ~ pour les langues** he has a great aptitude *ou* facility for languages

4 *(gén pl = possibilité)* facility ♦ **avoir la ~/toutes (les) ~s de** *ou* **pour faire qch** to have the/every opportunity to do sth *ou* of doing sth ♦ **~s de transport** transport facilities ♦ **~s d'accès à un lieu/à des services** easy access *ou* ease of access to a place/services ♦ **~s de crédit** credit facilities *ou* terms ♦ **~s de paiement** easy terms ♦ **consentir des ~s de caisse** to grant an overdraft facility

5 *(= tendance)* tendency ♦ **il a une certaine ~ à se mettre en colère** he has a tendency to lose his temper

6 *(littér = complaisance)* readiness ♦ **il a une grande ~ à croire ce que l'on raconte/à se plier à une règle** he has a great tendency *ou* is very ready to believe what people tell him/to comply with the rules

faciliter /fasilite/ ▸ **conjug 1** ◂ **VT** *(gén)* to make easier, to facilitate ♦ **ça ne va pas ~ les choses** that's not going to make matters *ou* things (any) easier, that's not going to ease matters ♦ **pour lui ~ sa mission/la tâche** to make his mission/work easier, to make the mission/work easier for him

façon /fasɔ̃/ **NF** 1 *(= manière)* way, manner ♦ **voilà la ~ dont il procède** this is how *ou* the way he does it ♦ **il s'y prend de** *ou* **d'une ~ curieuse** he has a strange way of going about things ♦ **de quelle ~ est-ce arrivé ?** how did it happen? ♦ **il faut le faire de la ~ suivante** you must do it in the following way *ou* as follows ♦ **je le ferai à ma ~** I shall do it my own way ♦ **il raconte l'histoire à sa ~** he tells the story in his own way ♦ **à la ~ de** like ♦ **à la ~ d'un enfant** like a child, as a child would do ♦ **sa ~ d'agir/de répondre** the way he behaves/answers, his way of behaving/answering ♦ **c'est une ~ de parler** it's (just) a figure of speech ♦ **je vais lui dire ma ~ de penser** *(point de vue)* I'll tell him what I think about it *ou* how I feel about it; *(colère)* I'll give him a piece of my mind, I'll tell him what I think about it ♦ **c'est une ~ de voir (les choses)** it's one way of seeing things *ou* of looking at things ♦ **la ~ de**

donner vaut mieux que ce qu'on donne *(Prov)* it's the thought that counts

2 *(locutions)* **rosser qn de (la) belle ~** †† to give sb a sound thrashing ◆ **d'une certaine ~, c'est vrai** it is true in a way *ou* in some ways ◆ **de cette ~, tu n'auras rien à payer** that way, you won't have to pay anything ◆ **d'une ~ ou d'une autre** somehow or other, one way or another ◆ **en aucune ~** in no way ◆ **de quelque ~ qu'il s'y prenne** however *ou* no matter how he goes about it ◆ **et sans plus de ~s** and without further ado

◆ **de ma/sa** *etc* **façon** ◆ **je vais lui jouer un tour de ma ~** I'm going to play a trick of my own on him ◆ **un poème de ma ~** a poem written by me ◆ **un plat de ma ~** a dish of my own making *ou* made by me

◆ **d'une façon générale** generally speaking, as a general rule

◆ **de la même façon** in the same way ◆ **il a réagi de la même ~ que l'an dernier** he reacted (in the same way) as he did last year ◆ **il n'a pas réagi de la même ~ que son frère** he didn't react in the same way as his brother, his reaction was different from his brother's

◆ **de toute(s) façon(s)** in any case, at any rate, anyway

◆ **de façon à** ◆ **de ~ à ne pas le déranger** so as not to disturb him ◆ **de ~ à ce qu'il puisse regarder** so that he can see

◆ **de (telle) façon que ...** in such a way that ... ◆ **de (telle) ~ qu'il puisse regarder** so that he can see

◆ **sans façon** ◆ **accepter sans ~** to accept without fuss ◆ **il est sans ~** he's unaffected ◆ **merci, sans ~** no thanks, really *ou* honestly ◆ **repas sans ~** simple *ou* unpretentious meal

3 *(Couture)* *[de robe]* cut, making-up *(Brit)* ◆ **payer la ~** to pay for the tailoring *ou* making-up *(Brit)* ◆ **le travail à ~** tailoring, dressmaking ◆ **travailler à ~** to (hand) tailor *ou* make up *(Brit)* customers' own material ◆ **tailleur à ~** bespoke tailor *(Brit)*, custom tailor *(US)* ◆ **vêtements à ~** tailor-made garments, bespoke garments *(Brit)*

4 *(= imitation)* **veste ~ daim/cuir** jacket in imitation suede/leather ◆ **châle ~ cachemire** cashmere-style shawl ◆ **bijoux ~ antique** old-fashioned *ou* antique style jewellery ◆ **gigot ~ chevreuil** leg of lamb cooked like *ou* done like venison

5 *(Agr)* tillage ◆ **donner une ~ à la terre** to till the land

6 *(Artisanat)* *(= fabrication)* making, crafting; *(= facture)* workmanship, craftsmanship ◆ **payer la ~** to pay for the workmanship

7 *(† = genre)* **une ~ de maître d'hôtel** a head waiter of sorts ◆ **une ~ de roman** a novel of sorts

NFPL **façons** manners, behaviour *(Brit)*, behavior *(US)* ◆ **ses ~s me déplaisent profondément** I find his manners extremely unpleasant, I don't like his behaviour at all ◆ **en voilà des ~s !** what a way to behave!, that's no way to behave! ◆ **faire des ~s** *(minauderies)* to put on airs and graces; *(chichis)* to make a fuss

faconde /fakɔ̃d/ NF *(littér)* loquaciousness ◆ **avoir de la ~** to be very loquacious ◆ **quelle ~ !** what a talker!, he's *(ou* she's) got the gift of the gab! *

façonnage /fasɔnaʒ/ NM 1 *[d'argile, métal]* shaping, fashioning; *[de tronc d'arbre, bloc de pierre]* hewing, shaping 2 *[de pièce, clé]* *(industriel)* manufacturing; *(artisanal)* making, crafting; *[de chapeau, robe, statuette]* fashioning, making 3 *(Imprim)* forwarding

façonnement /fasɔnmɑ̃/ NM *[d'esprits, caractère]* moulding *(Brit)*, molding *(US)*, shaping, forming

façonner /fasɔne/ ► conjug 1 ◄ VT 1 *[+ argile, métal]* to shape, to fashion; *[+ tronc d'arbre, bloc de pierre]* to hew, to shape; *[+ terre]* to till 2 *[+ pièce, clé]* *(industriellement)* to manufacture; *(artisanalement)* to make, to craft; *[+ chapeau, robe, statuette]* to fashion, to make 3 *[+ caractère, personne]* to mould *(Brit)*, to mold *(US)*, to shape, to form ◆ **l'éducation puritaine qui a façonné son enfance** the puritanical upbringing that shaped his childhood

façonnier, -ière /fasɔnje, jɛʀ/ NM,F *(= fabricant)* manufacturer

fac-similé (pl **fac-similés**) /faksimile/ NM facsimile

factage /faktaʒ/ NM *(= transport)* cartage, forwarding ◆ **entreprise de ~** parcel delivery company, transport company ◆ **frais de ~** cartage, delivery charge, carriage

facteur /faktœʀ/ NM 1 *(Poste)* postman *(Brit)*, mailman *(US)*; → **factrice** 2 *(= élément, Math)* factor *(de, dans* in); ◆ **le ~ chance/prix/humain** the chance/price/human factor ◆ **~ de risque** risk factor ◆ **~ de croissance** *(Méd)* growth factor ◆ **le libre-échange a été un ~ de croissance** *(Écon)* free trade has been a factor in economic growth ◆ **~ commun** *(Math, gén)* common factor ◆ **mettre en ~s** to factorize ◆ **mise en ~s** factorization ◆ **~ Rhésus** Rhesus *ou* Rh factor 3 *(= fabricant)* **~ de pianos** piano maker ◆ **~ d'orgues** organ builder

factice /faktis/ ADJ *[marbre, beauté]* artificial; *[cuir, bijou]* imitation *(épith)*, artificial; *[barbe]* false; *[bouteilles, articles exposés]* dummy *(épith)*; *[enthousiasme, amabilité]* false, feigned ◆ **tout semblait ~, le marbre du sol et la civilité des employés** everything seemed phoney * *ou* artificial, from the marble floor to the politeness of the staff ◆ **ils vivent dans un monde ~** they live in an artificial world NM *(= objet)* dummy

factieux, -ieuse /faksjø, jøz/ ADJ factious, seditious NM,F seditionary

faction /faksjɔ̃/ NF 1 *(= groupe factieux)* faction 2 *(= garde)* *[de sentinelle]* sentry duty, guard duty; *[de soldat]* guard duty; *[de personne qui attend]* long watch ◆ **être de** *ou* **en ~** *[soldat]* to be on guard (duty), to stand guard; *[sentinelle]* to be on guard (duty) *ou* (sentry) duty, to stand guard; *[personne qui attend]* to keep *ou* stand watch ◆ **mettre qn de ~** to put sb on guard (duty) 3 *(= période de travail)* (eight hour) shift

factionnaire /faksjɔnɛʀ/ NM *(= sentinelle, garde)* sentry *ou* guard (on duty) NMF *(= ouvrier)* shift worker

factitif, -ive /faktitif, iv/ ADJ *(Ling)* factitive, causative

factoriel, -ielle /faktɔʀjɛl/ ADJ *(Math)* factorial ◆ **analyse factorielle** factor analysis NF **factorielle** *(Math)* factorial

factoring /faktɔʀiŋ/ NM factoring

factorisation /faktɔʀizasjɔ̃/ NF factorization

factoriser /faktɔʀize/ ► conjug 1 ◄ VT to factorize

factotum /faktɔtɔm/ NM *(= homme à tout faire)* odd-job man, general handyman, (general) factotum *(hum)*; *(péj = larbin)* gofer *, (general) dogsbody *(Brit)* *(péj)*

factrice /faktʀis/ NF *(Poste)* postwoman *(Brit)*, mailwoman *(US)*

factuel, -elle /faktɥɛl/ ADJ factual

factum /faktɔm/ NM *(littér)* lampoon

facturation /faktyʀasjɔ̃/ NF *(= opération)* invoicing, billing; *(= bureau)* invoice office ◆ **~ détaillée** itemized billing

facture /faktyʀ/ GRAMMAIRE ACTIVE 47.5 NF 1 *(= note)* *(gén)* bill; *(Comm)* invoice ◆ **~ d'électricité/de téléphone** electricity/(tele)phone bill ◆ **notre ~ pétrolière/énergétique** *(Écon)* the nation's oil/energy bill ◆ **fausse ~** false invoice ◆ **l'affaire des fausses ~s** *(Pol)* *scandal involving the use of false invoices to fund French political parties* ◆ **établir une ~** to make out a bill *ou* an invoice ◆ **qui va payer la ~ ?** *(fig)* who will foot the bill?; → **pro forma** 2 *(= manière, style)* *[d'objet]* workmanship, craftsmanship; *[de roman, symphonie]* construction; *[d'artiste]* technique ◆ **roman de ~ classique/originale** classic/original novel ◆ **meubles de bonne/belle ~** well-made/beautifully made furniture 3 *[d'instrument de musique]* making

facturer /faktyʀe/ ► conjug 1 ◄ VT *(= établir une facture pour)* to invoice; *(= compter)* to charge (for), to put on the bill, to include in the bill ◆ **~ qch 200 € (à qn)** to charge *ou* bill (sb) €200 for sth ◆ **~ l'emballage** to charge for the packing, to include the packing in the bill

facturette /faktyʀɛt/ NF credit card slip

facturier /faktyʀje/ NM *(= registre)* invoice register; *(= employé)* invoice clerk

facturière /faktyʀjɛʀ/ NF *(= employée)* invoice clerk; *(= machine)* invoicing machine, biller *(US)*

facultatif, -ive /fakyltatif, iv/ ADJ *[travail, cours]* optional; *[halte, arrêt]* request *(épith)* ◆ **option** *ou* **matière facultative** optional subject, elective (subject) *(US)* ◆ **épreuve facultative** *(d'un examen)* optional paper ◆ **la réponse à cette question est tout à fait facultative** there is no obligation to answer this question

facultativement /fakyltativmɑ̃/ ADV optionally

faculté /fakylte/ NF 1 *(Univ)* faculty ◆ **la ~ des Lettres/de Médecine** the Faculty of Arts/Medicine, the Arts/Medical Faculty *(Brit)*, the School *ou* College of Arts/Medicine *(US)* ◆ **Faculté des Arts/Sciences** *(Can)* Faculty of Arts/Science ◆ **Faculté des études supérieures** *(au Québec)* graduate and postgraduate studies ◆ **quand j'étais en ~** *ou* **à la ~** when I was at university *ou* college *ou* school *(US)* ◆ **professeur de ~** university professor ◆ **la Faculté me défend le tabac** *(hum)* I'm not allowed to smoke on doctor's orders

2 *(= don)* faculty; *(= pouvoir)* power; *(= propriété)* property ◆ **avoir une grande ~ de concentration** to have great powers of concentration *ou* a great faculty for concentration ◆ **avoir la ~ de marcher/de la préhension** to have the ability to walk/grasp, to have the power of walking/grasping ◆ **~s** *(= aptitudes intellectuelles)* faculties ◆ **ce problème dépasse mes ~s** this problem is beyond my powers ◆ **jouir de** *ou* **avoir toutes ses ~s** to be in full possession of one's faculties, to have all one's faculties

3 *(= droit)* right, option; *(= possibilité)* power, freedom, possibility ◆ **le propriétaire a la ~ de vendre son bien** the owner has the right to sell *ou* the option of selling his property ◆ **je te laisse la ~ de choisir** I'll give you the freedom to choose *ou* the possibility *ou* option of choosing ◆ **le Premier ministre a la ~ de révoquer certains fonctionnaires** *(frm)* the Prime Minister has the faculty *ou* power of dismissing certain civil servants ◆ **l'acheteur aura la ~ de décider** the buyer shall have the option to decide

fada * /fada/ ADJ *(= fou)* cracked *, crackers * *(attrib)*, barmy * *(Brit)* NM crackpot *

fadaise /fadɛz/ NF *(littér : gén pl)* *(= bagatelle)* trifle ◆ **dire des ~s** *(= platitude)* to mouth insipid *ou* empty phrases

fadasse /fadas/ ADJ *(péj)* *[plat, boisson]* tasteless, insipid; *[couleur, style, propos]* wishy-washy, insipid ◆ **des cheveux d'un blond ~** dull blond hair

fade /fad/ ADJ *[goût, odeur]* insipid, bland; *[soupe, cuisine]* tasteless, insipid; *[lumière, teinte]* dull;

[compliment, plaisanterie] tame, insipid; *[décor, visage, individu, conversation, style]* dull, insipid; *[politesses, amabilité]* insipid ◆ **l'odeur ~ du sang** the sickly smell of blood ◆ **des cheveux d'un blond ~** dull blond hair

fader (se)* /fade/ ▸ conjug 1 ◂ VPR *[+ corvée, personne]* to get landed with*, to get lumbered with* *(Brit)*

fadeur /fadœʀ/ NF 1 *[de soupe, cuisine]* tastelessness, insipidness; *[de goût]* insipidness, blandness; *[de lumière, teinte]* dullness; *[de compliment, plaisanterie, conversation, style]* dullness, insipidness; *[de politesses, amabilité]* insipidness; *[d'odeur]* sickliness 2 *(† = platitude)* **~s** sweet nothings, bland compliments ◆ **dire des ~s à une dame** to say sweet nothings to *ou* pay bland compliments to a lady

fading /fadiŋ/ NM *(Radio)* fading

faf * /faf/ ADJ, NMF (abrév de **fasciste**) *(péj)* fascist

fagot /fago/ NM bundle of sticks *ou* firewood; → **derrière, sentir**

fagoter /fagɔte/ ▸ conjug 1 ◂ VT *(péj = accoutrer)* *[+ enfant]* to dress up, to rig out* *(Brit)* ◆ **il est drôlement fagoté** *(déguisé)* he's wearing the strangest getup* *ou* rig-out* *(Brit)*; *(mal habillé)* he's really oddly dressed VPR **se fagoter** to dress o.s., to rig o.s. out* *(Brit)* *(en as a)*

Fahrenheit /faʀɛnajt/ ADJ, NM Fahrenheit ◆ **32 degrés ~** 32 degrees Fahrenheit

FAI /ɛfai/ NM (abrév de **fournisseur d'accès à internet**) ISP

faiblard, e* /fɛblaʀ, aʀd/ ADJ *(péj)* *(en classe)* weak, on the slow *ou* weak side *(attrib)*; *(physiquement)* (rather) feeble; *[argument, démonstration]* feeble, weak; *[lumière]* weak NM,F weakling

faible /fɛbl/ GRAMMAIRE ACTIVE 34.2

ADJ 1 *(physiquement)* weak; *[monnaie]* weak, soft ◆ **je me sens encore très ~ sur mes jambes** I still feel very shaky on my legs ◆ **avoir le cœur ~** to have a weak heart; → **économiquement, sexe**

2 *(moralement)* weak ◆ **il est ~ de caractère** he has a weak character ◆ **il est trop ~ avec elle/ses élèves** he's too soft with her/with his pupils

3 *(en importance)* *[rendement, revenu, demande]* low, poor; *[marge]* small; *[débit]* slow; *[quantité]* small, slight; *[écart, différence]* slight, small; *[espoir]* faint, slight, slender; *[avantage]* slight ◆ **il a de ~s chances de s'en tirer** *(optimiste)* he has a slight chance of pulling through; *(pessimiste)* his chances of pulling through are slight *ou* slim ◆ **à une vitesse plus ~** more slowly ◆ **à une ~ hauteur** low down, not very high up ◆ **à une ~ profondeur** not far below the surface ◆ **à une ~ majorité** *(Pol)* by a narrow *ou* slight majority ◆ **pays à ~ natalité** country with a low birth rate

4 *(en qualité)* *[élève]* weak; *[expression, devoir, style]* weak, poor; *[raisonnement, argument]* weak, poor, feeble ◆ **il est ~ en français** he's weak *ou* poor at *ou* in French ◆ **le côté ~ de ce raisonnement** the weak side of this argument; → **esprit, point**[1]**, temps**[1]

5 *(en intensité)* *[pouls, voix]* weak, faint, feeble; *[lumière]* dim, weak, faint; *[bruit, odeur]* faint, slight; *[résistance, protestation]* mild, weak; *[vent]* light, faint ◆ **vent ~ à modéré** wind light to moderate ◆ **~ en alcool** low in alcohol ◆ **à ~ teneur en sucre/cuivre** with a low sugar/copper content ◆ **c'est un escroc, et le terme est ~** he's a crook, and that's putting it mildly *ou* and that's an understatement ◆ **vous n'avez qu'une ~ idée de sa puissance** you have only a slight *ou* faint idea of his power

6 *(Ling)* *[conjugaison, verbe]* weak

NM 1 *(= personne)* weak person ◆ **les ~s et les opprimés** the weak *ou* feeble and the oppressed ◆ **un ~ d'esprit** a feeble-minded person ◆ **c'est un ~, elle en fait ce qu'elle veut** he's a weakling – she does what she wants with him

2 *(† = déficience)* weak point ◆ **le ~ de ce livre, ce sont les dialogues** the dialogues are the weak point in this book

3 *(= penchant)* weakness ◆ **il a un ~ pour le chocolat** he has a weakness for chocolate ◆ **il a un ~ pour sa fille** he has a soft spot for his daughter

faiblement /fɛbləmɑ̃/ ADV 1 *(= avec peine)* weakly ◆ **la demande reprend ~** demand is picking up slightly 2 *(= peu)* *[éclairer]* dimly; *[augmenter]* slightly ◆ **~ alcoolisé/gazéifié** slightly alcoholic/gaseous ◆ **~ éclairé** dimly *ou* poorly lit ◆ **zones ~ peuplées** sparsely populated areas

faiblesse /fɛblɛs/ NF 1 *(physique)* weakness ◆ **sa ~ de constitution** his weak *ou* frail constitution ◆ **il a une ~ dans le bras gauche** he has a weakness in his left arm

2 *(morale)* weakness ◆ **sa ~ de caractère** his weak character, his weakness of character ◆ **avoir la ~ d'accepter** to be weak enough to accept ◆ **sa ~ à l'égard de son frère** his softness *ou* weakness towards his brother ◆ **chacun a ses petites ~s** we all have our little foibles *ou* weaknesses *ou* failings

3 *(= niveau peu élevé)* **la ~ de la demande** the low level of demand ◆ **la ~ du revenu par habitant** the low per capita income

4 *(Bourse)* *[de monnaie, cours, marché]* weakness

5 *(= médiocrité)* *[d'argument, raisonnement]* feebleness, weakness; *[d'œuvre]* weakness ◆ **sa ~ en anglais est un vrai problème** the fact that he's so weak in English is a real problem

6 *(= défaut)* weak point, weakness ◆ **le film/l'intrigue présente quelques ~s** the film/the plot has several weak points *ou* weaknesses

faiblir /fɛbliʀ/ ▸ conjug 2 ◂ VI 1 *[malade, branche]* to get weaker, to weaken; *[cœur, vue, intelligence]* to fail; *[forces, courage]* to fail, to flag, to give out; *[influence]* to wane, to fall off; *[résolution, autorité]* to weaken ◆ **elle a faibli à la vue du sang/à sa vue** she felt weak *ou* faint when she saw the blood/when she saw him ◆ **il a faibli devant leurs prières** he weakened *ou* relented in the face of their pleas ◆ **pièce qui faiblit au 3e acte** play that falls off *ou* weakens in the 3rd act ◆ **la première ligne a faibli sous le choc** the front line weakened under the impact ◆ **ce n'est pas le moment de ~ !** don't give up now!

2 *[voix]* to weaken, to get weaker *ou* fainter; *[bruit, protestation]* to die down; *[lumière]* to dim, to get dimmer *ou* fainter; *[pouls]* to weaken, to get weaker; *[vent]* to drop, to abate; *[rendement]* to slacken (off); *[intensité, espoir]* to diminish, to decrease; *[résistance, demande]* to weaken, to slacken; *[chances]* to weaken, to run out ◆ **l'écart faiblit entre eux** the gap is closing *ou* narrowing between them

faïence /fajɑ̃s/ NF *(= substance)* (glazed) earthenware; *(= objets)* crockery *(NonC)*, earthenware *(NonC)*; *(= vase, objet)* piece of earthenware, earthenware *(NonC)* ◆ **assiette en/carreau de ~** earthenware plate/tile ◆ **~ fine** china ◆ **~ de Delft** delft, delftware; → **chien**

faïencerie /fajɑ̃sʀi/ NF earthenware factory

faïencier, -ière /fajɑ̃sje, jɛʀ/ ADJ earthenware *(épith)* NM,F *(= fabricant)* earthenware maker; *(= marchand)* earthenware seller

faignant, e /fɛɲɑ̃, ɑ̃t/ ADJ, NM,F ⇒ **fainéant, e**

faille[1] /faj/ NF *(Géol)* fault; *(fig = point faible)* flaw, weakness; *(= cassure)* rift ◆ **il y a une ~ dans votre raisonnement** there's a flaw in your argument ◆ **ce qui a causé une ~ dans leur amitié ...** what caused a rift in their friendship ... *ou* a rift between them ... ◆ **sans ~** *[fidélité, soutien]* unfailing, unwavering; *[organisation]* faultless, impeccable; *[volonté, détermination]* unfailing; → **ligne**[1]

faille[2] /faj/ → **falloir**

failli[1] /faji/ ptp de **faillir**

failli[2]**, e** /faji/ ADJ, NM,F *(Comm)* bankrupt

faillibilité /fajibilite/ NF fallibility

faillible /fajibl/ ADJ fallible

faillir /fajiʀ/ ▸ conjug 2 ◂ VI 1 *(= manquer)* **j'ai failli tomber/réussir** I almost *ou* very nearly fell/succeeded, I all but fell/succeeded ◆ **il a failli se faire écraser** he almost *ou* very nearly got run over, he narrowly missed getting run over ◆ **j'ai failli attendre** *(iro)* I hope you didn't rush on my account *(iro)*

2 *(frm)* ◆ **~ à** *(= manquer à)* *[+ engagement, mission]* to fail in; *[+ promesse, parole]* to fail to keep ◆ **il a failli/n'a pas failli à la tradition** he broke with/kept with *ou* to tradition ◆ **il n'a pas failli à sa parole** he was true to *ou* kept his word ◆ **le cœur lui faillit** † his heart missed a beat ◆ **le cœur** *ou* **le courage lui faillit** † his courage failed him ◆ **il résista jusqu'au bout sans ~** he resisted unfailingly *ou* unflinchingly to the end ◆ **ne pas ~ à sa réputation** to live up to one's reputation

3 *(†† ou hum = fauter)* to lapse

faillite /fajit/ NF 1 *[d'entreprise]* bankruptcy 2 *(= échec)* *[d'espoir, tentative, méthode]* collapse, failure ◆ **la ~ du gouvernement en matière économique** the government's failure on the economic front 3 *(locutions)* **en ~** *[entreprise]* bankrupt ◆ **être en ~** to be bankrupt ◆ **faire ~** *[entreprise]* to go bankrupt; *(fig)* to collapse ◆ **faire une ~ de 800 000 €** to go bankrupt with debts of €800,000 ◆ **déclarer/mettre qn en ~** to declare *ou* adjudge/make sb bankrupt ◆ **se déclarer en ~** to file (a petition) for bankruptcy

COMP **faillite frauduleuse** fraudulent bankruptcy

faillite personnelle personal bankruptcy

faillite simple bankruptcy

faim /fɛ̃/ NF 1 *(= envie de manger)* hunger ◆ **avoir (très** *ou* **grand †) ~** to be (very) hungry ◆ **j'ai une ~ de loup** *ou* **une de ces ~s*** I'm ravenous *ou* famished *ou* starving* ◆ **je n'ai plus ~** *(après un repas)* I'm (quite) full; *(plus envie de manger)* I'm not hungry any more ◆ **manger sans ~** *(sans besoin réel)* to eat for the sake of eating; *(sans appétit)* to pick at one's food, to toy with one's food ◆ **manger à sa ~** to eat one's fill ◆ **ça m'a donné ~** it made me hungry ◆ **il fait ~*** we're hungry ◆ **la ~ dans le monde** world hunger ◆ **la ~ fait sortir** *ou* **chasse le loup du bois** *(Prov)* hunger will drive him out; → **crever, mourir** *etc*

2 *(= besoin)* hunger ◆ **avoir ~ de** *[+ honneur, tendresse, justice]* to hunger for, to crave (for) ◆ **sa ~ de richesses** his hunger *ou* yearning for wealth ◆ **son discours a laissé les journalistes sur leur ~** his speech left the journalists hungry for more *ou* unsatisfied; → **rester**

faîne /fɛn/ NF beechnut ◆ **~s (tombées)** beechmast *(NonC)*

fainéant, e /fɛneɑ̃, ɑ̃t/ ADJ lazy, idle, bone idle*; → **roi** NM,F idler, loafer, lazybones*

fainéanter /fɛneɑ̃te/ ▸ conjug 1 ◂ VI to idle *ou* loaf about

fainéantise /fɛneɑ̃tiz/ NF laziness, idleness

faire /fɛʀ/

▸ conjug 60 ◂

1 VERBE TRANSITIF	4 VERBE SUBSTITUT
2 VERBE INTRANSITIF	5 VERBE AUXILIAIRE
3 VERBE IMPERSONNEL	6 VERBE PRONOMINAL

Lorsque **faire** est suivi d'un nom dans une expression figée telle que **faire une faute, faire une promesse, se faire des idées** etc, cherchez sous le nom.

1 - VERBE TRANSITIF

1

Lorsque **faire** est utilisé pour parler d'une activité non précisée, ou qu'il remplace un verbe plus spécifique, il se traduit par **do**.

◆ **que fais-tu ce soir ?** what are you doing tonight? ◆ **j'ai beaucoup/je n'ai rien à ~** I have a lot/nothing to do ◆ **ils sont en retard, qu'est-ce qu'ils peuvent bien ~ ?** they're late – what on earth are they doing? *ou* what are they up to?* ◆ **que voulez-vous qu'on y fasse ?** what do you expect us to do (about it)? ◆ **~ ses chaussures/l'argenterie/la chambre** to do one's shoes/the silver/the bedroom

2

Lorsque **faire** veut dire **créer, être l'auteur de**, il se traduit souvent par **make** ou par un verbe plus spécifique ; cherchez sous le nom.

◆ **~ un film** to make *ou* do a film ◆ **~ un tableau** to do a painting, to paint a picture ◆ **~ un plan** to make *ou* draw a map ◆ **fais-moi un joli chat** *(dessin)* do a nice cat for me; *(pâte à modeler)* make a nice cat for me

3 = fabriquer, produire *[+ meuble, voiture]* to make; *[+ mur, nid]* to make, to build; *[+ maison]* to build; *[+ blé, betteraves]* to grow ◆ **ils font du mouton*** they raise sheep ◆ **cette école fait de bons ingénieurs** the school turns out good engineers

4 Culin

Dans le sens de **préparer, confectionner, faire** peut se traduire par **do** de façon assez vague, mais **make** est beaucoup plus courant.

◆ **~ de la confiture/du vin/un cocktail** to make jam/wine/a cocktail ◆ **elle fait du lapin ce soir** she's doing rabbit tonight ◆ **je vais ~ quelques pommes de terre** I'll do a few potatoes

5 Sport *[+ football, tennis, rugby]* to play; *[+ sport de combat]* to do; → **natation, ski** *etc*

6 Scol *[+ matière, roman, auteur]* to do ◆ **~ l'école hôtelière** to go to a catering school

7 Mus *(= jouer)* to play; *(= s'entraîner)* to practise ◆ **~ du piano/du violon** to play the piano/the violin ◆ **va ~ ton piano*** go and practise your piano

8 Méd *[+ diabète, tension]* to have ◆ **il m'a encore fait une otite** he's gone and got another ear infection*

9 = parcourir, visiter to do ◆ **~ 10 km** to do *ou* cover 10 km ◆ **~ 100 km/h** to do 100 km/h ◆ **~ Rome/la Grèce en trois jours** to do Rome/Greece in three days ◆ **on a fait Lyon-Paris en cinq heures** we did Lyons to Paris in five hours

10 = chercher dans **j'ai fait tous les placards/toutes les pièces, je ne l'ai pas trouvé** I looked in all the cupboards/in every room but I didn't find it ◆ **il a fait toute la ville pour en trouver** he's been all over town looking for some ◆ **j'ai fait toutes les librairies mais sans succès** I went round all the bookshops but I didn't have any luck

11 = vendre **~ l'épicerie** to sell groceries ◆ **nous ne faisons pas les boutons/cette marque** we don't do *ou* stock *ou* carry *(US)* buttons/that make ◆ **je vous fais ce fauteuil (à) 90 €** I'll let you have this armchair for €90

12 = mesurer, peser, coûter **la cuisine fait 6 mètres de large** the kitchen is 6 metres wide ◆ **il fait 23 degrés** it is 23 degrees ◆ **ce rôti fait bien 3 kg** this joint weighs *ou* is a good 3 kg ◆ **ça fait encore loin jusqu'à Paris** it's still a long way to Paris ◆ **combien fait cette chaise ?** how much is this chair? ◆ **cette table fera un bon prix** this table will go for *ou* will fetch a high price ◆ **ça nous fera 1 000 €** *(dépense)* it will cost us €1,000; *(gain)* it will give *ou* bring us €1,000

13 dans un calcul to make ◆ **24 en tout, ce qui en fait 2 chacun** 24 altogether, which makes 2 each ◆ **deux et deux font quatre** two and two make four ◆ **cela fait combien en tout ?** how much does that make altogether?

14 Gram **"canal" fait "canaux" au pluriel** the plural of "canal" is "canaux" ◆ **qu'est-ce ça fait au subjonctif ?** what's the subjunctive?

15 = imiter **il a fait celui qui ne comprenait pas** he pretended not to understand ◆ **ne fais pas l'enfant/l'idiot** don't be so childish/so stupid ◆ **il fait bien le train** he does a really good imitation of a train

16 = faire fonction de, servir de *[personne]* to be; *(Théât)* to play; *[objet]* to be used as, to serve as ◆ **tu fais l'arbitre ?** will you be referee? ◆ **il fait le fantôme dans "Hamlet"** he plays the ghost in "Hamlet" ◆ **une vieille malle faisait table basse** an old trunk was being used as a coffee table ◆ **la cuisine fait salle à manger** the kitchen doubles as *ou* is used as *ou* serves as a dining room MAIS **cette branche fera une bonne canne** this branch will make a nice walking stick ◆ **cet hôtel fait aussi restaurant** the hotel has its own restaurant ◆ **cette montre fait aussi boussole** this watch doubles as a compass

17 = être, constituer **quel imbécile je fais !** what a fool I am! ◆ **ils font un beau couple** they make such a lovely couple ◆ **il veut ~ médecin** he wants to be a doctor ◆ **il fera un bon musicien** he'll make a good musician

18 = avoir la forme de, ressembler à to look like ◆ **ça fait comme une cloche** it looks a bit like a bell

19 = représenter to make out ◆ **on le fait plus riche qu'il n'est** he's made out *ou* people make him out to be richer than he is

20 = dire to say ◆ **"vraiment ?" fit-il** "really?", he said ◆ **il fit un "ah" de surprise** "ah", he said, surprised ◆ **le chat fait miaou** the cat goes *ou* says miaow

21 = agir sur **qu'est-ce qu'on lui fait à l'hôpital ?** what's he gone into hospital for? ◆ **qu'est-ce que tu as fait à ton frère ?** what have you been doing to your brother? ◆ **ils ne peuvent rien me ~** they can't do anything to me ◆ **on ne me la fait pas à moi !*** I wasn't born yesterday!

22 = constituer to make ◆ **cela fait la richesse du pays** that's what makes the country rich ◆ **c'est ce qui fait tout son charme** that's what makes him so charming

23 = importer **qu'est-ce que cela peut bien te ~ ?** what's it to you? ◆ **qu'est-ce que ça fait ?** so what?* ◆ **la mort de son père ne lui a rien fait** he was completely unaffected by his father's death ◆ **cela ne vous ferait rien de sortir ?** would you mind leaving the room?

◆ **faire + de** + *complément (= utiliser)* to do with ◆ **qu'as-tu fait de ta vie ?** what have you done with your life? ◆ **je ne sais pas quoi ~ de mon temps libre** I don't know what to do with my spare time ◆ **qu'avez-vous fait de votre sac/de vos enfants ?** what have you done with your bag/your children? ◆ **qu'ai-je bien pu ~ de mes lunettes ?** what on earth have I done with my glasses? ◆ **la vie a fait de lui un aigri** life has made him a bitter man ◆ **il a fait d'une grange une demeure agréable** he has turned *ou* made a barn into a comfortable home ◆ **il veut en ~ un avocat** he wants to make a lawyer of him

◆ **ne faire que** *(constamment)* ◆ **il ne fait que se plaindre** he's always *ou* forever complaining ◆ **il ne fait que bavarder** he won't stop chattering, he does nothing but chatter *(seulement)* ◆ **je ne fais que dire la vérité** I'm only telling the truth ◆ **je ne fais que passer** I'm just passing ◆ **je ne fais que d'arriver** *(récemment)* I've only just come

◆ **n'avoir que faire de** ◆ **je n'ai que ~ de vos conseils !** I don't need your advice! ◆ **je n'ai que ~ de gens comme lui !** I have no use for people like him!

2 - VERBE INTRANSITIF

1 = agir, procéder **~ vite** to act quickly ◆ **faites vite !** be quick (about it)! ◆ **faites comme chez vous** *(aussi hum)* make yourself at home

2 = durer **ce chapeau (me) fera encore un hiver** this hat will do *ou* last me another winter

3 = paraître to look ◆ **ce vase fait bien sur la table** the vase looks nice on the table ◆ **~ vieux/jeune** *[personne]* to look old/young (for one's age) ◆ **elle fait très femme** she looks very grown-up

4 * besoins naturels *[personne]* to go; *[animal]* to do its business ◆ **as-tu fait ce matin ?** have you been this morning?

3 - VERBE IMPERSONNEL

Lorsque **faire** est suivi d'une expression de temps et exprime une durée écoulée, on utilise généralement **since** ou **for** ; **for** se construit avec le present perfect ou le pluperfect.

◆ **cela fait deux ans/très longtemps que je ne l'ai pas vu** it's two years/a very long time since I last saw him, I haven't seen him for two years/for a very long time ◆ **ça fait trois ans qu'il est parti** it's three years since he left, he's been gone (for) three years

◆ **ce qui fait que ..., ça fait que ...** *(= ce qui implique que)* that means ... ◆ **ça fait que nous devons partir** that *ou* which means we have to go ◆ **et ça fait qu'il est arrivé en retard** and that meant he arrived late

4 - VERBE SUBSTITUT

to do ◆ **il travaille mieux que je ne fais** he works better than I do ◆ **as-tu payé la note ? – non, c'est lui qui l'a fait** did you pay the bill? – no, he did ◆ **puis-je téléphoner ? – faites, je vous en prie** could I use the phone? – (yes) please do *ou* (yes) by all means ◆ **n'en faites rien !** (please) don't! ◆ **je n'en ferai rien !** I'll do nothing of the sort!

5 - VERBE AUXILIAIRE

◆ **faire** + *infinitif*

1 = provoquer un acte, une situation to make ◆ **l'idée m'a fait sourire** the thought made me smile ◆ **ça m'a fait pleurer** it made me cry ◆ **ma mère me faisait manger des épinards quand j'étais petit** my mother made me eat spinach when I was little ◆ **il lui a fait boire du whisky** *(pour la remonter)* he got her to drink some whisky, he made her drink some whisky; *(pour qu'elle goûte)* he gave her some whisky to drink MAIS **ce genre de musique me fait dormir** that kind of music puts me to sleep ◆ **j'ai fait démarrer la voiture** I got the car going *ou* started

2 = aider to help ◆ **~ traverser la rue à un aveugle** to help a blind man across the road ◆ **je lui ai fait ~ ses devoirs** I helped him with his homework MAIS **~ manger un patient** to feed a patient

3 = laisser volontairement **~ entrer qn** *(qn que l'on attendait)* to let sb in; *(qn que l'on attendait pas)* to ask sb in ◆ **~ venir** *[+ employé]* to send for; *[+ médecin]* to call ◆ **~ entrer/sortir le chien** to let the dog in/out ◆ **faites entrer le patient** ask the patient to come in

4

Lorsque **faire** signifie **laisser involontairement**, sa traduction dépend étroitement du contexte ; reportez-vous au second verbe.

◆ **il a fait déborder le lait** he let the milk boil over ◆ **elle a fait s'échapper le chien** she let the dog out ◆ **il a fait glisser son frère** he (accidentally) made his brother slip over ◆ **elle a fait tomber une tasse** she dropped a cup

5 = donner une tâche à exécuter ~ ~ **qch par qn** to have sth done (*ou* made) by sb ◆ ~ ~ **qch à qn** (*gén*) to get sb to do (*ou* to make) sth, to have sb do (*ou* make) sth (*surtout US*); (*en le forçant*) to make sb do sth ◆ **(se)** ~ ~ **une robe** to have a dress made ◆ ~ **réparer une voiture/une montre** to have a car/a watch repaired ◆ ~ ~ **la vaisselle à qn** to get sb to do *ou* have sb do (*surtout US*) the dishes ◆ **elle a fait lire les enfants** she made the children read, she got the children to read ◆ **il m'a fait ouvrir le coffre-fort** he made me open the safe

6 - VERBE PRONOMINAL

se faire

1 pour soi **il se fait la cuisine** he cooks for himself ◆ **il s'est fait beaucoup d'amis/d'ennemis** he has made himself a great many friends/enemies ◆ **on s'est fait un restaurant/un film** * we went to a restaurant/the cinema

2 * = gagner to make ◆ **il se fait 7 000 € par mois** he makes €7,000 a month

3 = mûrir, évoluer [*fromage*] to ripen, to mature; [*vin*] to mature ◆ **il s'est fait tout seul** [*personne*] he's a self-made man

4 = être accompli **les choses finissent toujours par se** ~ things always get done in the end ◆ **rien ne se fera sans son aide** nothing will get done without his help ◆ **si ça doit se** ~**, ça se fera sans moi** if it's going to happen, it'll happen without me

5 = convenir **ça se fait d'offrir des fleurs à un homme ?** is it done *ou* OK to give flowers to a man? ◆ **cela ne se fait pas** it's not done ◆ **mais tu sais, ça se fait de vivre ensemble sans être marié !** people do live together without being married, you know!

6 = être courant, à la mode **les jupes longues se font beaucoup cette année** long skirts are in this year *ou* are being worn a lot this year ◆ **ça se fait encore ce style-là ?** are people still wearing that style? ◆ **ça se fait de plus en plus, ces chaussures** more and more people are wearing these shoes

7 sexuellement **se** ~ **qn**‡ to have sb‡

8 ‡ = agresser to get* ◆ **un jour, je me le ferai !** I'll get him one of these days*

9 * = cambrioler [*+ banque, bijouterie*] to do*

10 = se passer (*gén avec subjonctif*) **il peut/il pourrait se** ~ **qu'il pleuve** it may/it might (well) rain ◆ **comment se fait-il qu'il soit absent ?, comment ça se fait qu'il est absent ?*** how come he's not here?*

◆ **se faire** + *adjectif*
(= *devenir involontairement*) to get, to become ◆ **se** ~ **vieux** to be getting old ◆ **il se faisait tard** it was getting late ◆ **il se fit violent** he became violent
(= *devenir volontairement*) ◆ **se** ~ **beau** to make o.s. beautiful ◆ **il se fit menaçant** he became threatening ◆ **elle se fit implorante** she started pleading ◆ **sa voix se fit plus douce** his voice became softer
(= *faire semblant d'être*) to make o.s. out to be ◆ **il se fait plus bête qu'il n'est** he makes himself out to be more stupid than he really is

◆ **se faire** + *infinitif*

Lorsque cette tournure implique un ordre, elle se traduit généralement par **have + verbe** ; lorsqu'elle implique une demande polie, elle se traduit par **ask** ou **get + verbe**.

◆ **il se faisait apporter le journal tous les matins** he had the paper brought to him every morning ◆ **il s'est fait ouvrir par le voisin** he got his neighbour to let him in ◆ **elle s'est fait apporter un sandwich** she got somebody to bring her a sandwich ◆ **fais-toi expliquer le règlement** ask someone to explain the rules to you

Notez les différentes traductions possibles et en particulier l'emploi de la forme passive en anglais lorsque **se faire + infinitif** exprime une action subie par quelqu'un ; reportez-vous à l'autre verbe.

◆ **il s'est fait frapper par deux jeunes** he was hit by two youths, two youths hit him ◆ **elle s'est fait renvoyer** she was sacked ◆ **tu vas te** ~ **gronder** you'll get yourself into trouble, you'll get yourself told off*

◆ **se faire à** (= *s'habituer à*) to get *ou* become used to ◆ **il ne peut pas se** ~ **au climat** he can't get used to the climate

◆ **(il) faut se le/la/les faire !** ‡ ◆ **(il) faut se le** ~ **!** [*+ travail*] it's a hell of a chore!*, it's really heavy going!‡; [*+ personne*] he's a real pain in the neck!*

◆ **s'en faire** (= *s'angoisser*) to worry ◆ **il ne s'en fait pas** he doesn't worry; (= *a du culot*) he's got a nerve! ◆ **je viens de m'acheter un bateau – dis donc, tu t'en fais pas toi !** I've just bought a boat – you lucky devil!*

faire-part /fɛʀpaʀ/ **NM INV** announcement (of birth *ou* marriage *ou* death) ◆ ~ **de mariage** wedding announcement; (*avec carton d'invitation*) wedding invitation

faire-valoir /fɛʀvalwaʀ/ **NM INV** 1 (*Agr*) farming, working (of land) ◆ ~ **direct/indirect** farming by the owner/tenant 2 (= *personne*) foil; (*dans une comédie*) stooge ◆ **son mari lui sert de** ~ her husband serves as a foil to her

fair-play /fɛʀple/ **NM INV** fair play **ADJ INV** ◆ **être** ~ to play fair ◆ **c'est un joueur** ~ he plays fair

faisabilité /fəzabilite/ **NF** feasibility ◆ **étude de** ~ feasibility study

faisable /fəzabl/ GRAMMAIRE ACTIVE 39.2 **ADJ** feasible ◆ **est-ce** ~ **en deux jours ?** can it be done in two days? ◆ **est-ce** ~ **à pied ?** can it be done on foot?

faisan /fəzɑ̃/ **NM** 1 (= *oiseau*) (*gén*) pheasant; (*mâle*) cock pheasant ◆ ~ **doré** golden pheasant 2 († = *escroc*) shark

faisandé, e /fəzɑ̃de/ (ptp de **faisander**) **ADJ** 1 (*Culin*) [*gibier*] well hung; (*désagréablement*) high ◆ **je n'aime pas le** ~ I don't like high game ◆ **viande trop** ~**e** meat which has hung for too long 2 (*péj*, †) [*littérature, société*] corrupt, decadent; [*milieu*] crooked

faisandeau (pl **faisandeaux**) /fəzɑ̃do/ **NM** young pheasant

faisander /fəzɑ̃de/ ► conjug 1 ◄ **VT** (*Culin*) ◆ **(faire** *ou* **laisser)** ~ to hang **VPR se faisander** to become high

faisanderie /fəzɑ̃dʀi/ **NF** pheasantry

faisane /fəzan/ **NF, ADJ F** ◆ **(poule)** ~ hen pheasant

faisceau (pl **faisceaux**) /fɛso/ **NM** 1 (= *fagot*) bundle ◆ ~ **de preuves** (= *réseau*) body of evidence ◆ ~ **de faits/raisons** range of facts/reasons ◆ **nouer en** ~**x** to tie into bundles 2 (*Mil*) ~**x (d'armes)** stack (of arms) ◆ **mettre en** ~**x** [*fusils*] to stack ◆ **former/rompre les** ~**x** to stack/unstack arms 3 (*Phys*) beam 4 (*Antiq, Hist*) ~**x** (= *emblème*) fasces

COMP faisceau d'électrons *ou* **électronique** electron beam
faisceau hertzien electro-magnetic wave
faisceau laser laser beam
faisceau lumineux *ou* **de lumière** beam of light
faisceau musculaire fasciculus *ou* fascicule of muscle fibres
faisceau nerveux fasciculus *ou* fascicule of nerve fibres
faisceau de particules particle beam

faiseur, -euse /fəzœʀ, øz/ **NM,F** ◆ ~ **de** † [*+ monuments, meubles*] maker of; (*hum, péj*) [*+ romans, tableaux, opéras*] producer of **NM** († *péj*) (= *hâbleur*) show-off; (= *escroc*) shark ◆ **(bon)** ~ (*frm* = *tailleur*) good tailor

COMP faiseuse d'anges backstreet abortionist
faiseur de bons mots punster, wag
faiseur d'embarras fusspot (*Brit*), fussbudget (*US*)
faiseur d'intrigues (*péj*) schemer
faiseur de littérature (*péj*) scribbler
faiseur de marché (*Bourse*) market maker
faiseur de mariages matchmaker
faiseur de miracles miracle-worker
faiseur de phrases (*péj*) speechifier
faiseur de vers (*péj*) poetaster (*péj*), versifier

faisselle /fɛsɛl/ **NF** (= *passoire*) cheese strainer; (= *fromage*) fromage frais (*packed in its own strainer*)

fait[1] /fɛ/ GRAMMAIRE ACTIVE 44.1, 53.6

NM 1 (= *événement*) event, occurrence; (= *donnée*) fact; (= *phénomène*) phenomenon ◆ **il s'agit d'un** ~ **courant/rare** this is a common/rare occurrence *ou* event ◆ **aucun** ~ **nouveau n'est survenu** no new facts have come to light, there have been no new developments ◆ **il me faut des** ~**s concrets** I must have facts *ou* concrete evidence ◆ **reconnaissez-vous les** ~**s ?** (*Jur*) do you accept the facts? ◆ **les** ~**s qui lui sont reprochés** (*Jur*) the charges (brought) against him ◆ **ces** ~**s remontent à 3 ans** these events go back 3 years ◆ **il s'est produit un** ~ **curieux** a strange thing has happened ◆ **s'incliner devant les** ~**s** to bow to (the) facts ◆ **les** ~**s marquants de ces dix dernières années** the key events of the last ten years; → **erreur, état, gestion, incriminer**

2 (= *acte*) **le** ~ **de manger/bouger** the fact of eating/moving, eating/moving ◆ **être puni pour** ~ **d'insoumission** (*Jur, Mil*) to be punished for (an act of) insubordination; → **haut**

3 (*pour exprimer la cause*) **c'est le** ~ **du hasard** it's a matter of chance ◆ **c'est le** ~ **de son inexpérience** it's because of *ou* owing to his inexperience, it comes of his inexperience ◆ **par le** ~ in fact ◆ **par ce** ~ by this very fact ◆ **par le** ~ **même que/de** by the very fact that/of ◆ **par le (simple)** ~ **de** by the simple fact of ◆ **par le** ~ **même de son obstination** because of *ou* by his very obstinacy, by the very fact of his obstinacy

4 (*locutions*) **le** ~ **est que** the fact is that ◆ **le** ~ **que** the fact that ◆ **les** ~**s sont là** *ou* **sont têtus** there's no denying the facts, the facts speak for themselves ◆ **le** ~ **est là** that's the fact of the matter ◆ **être le** ~ **de** (= *être typique de*) to be typical *ou* characteristic of; (= *être le résultat de*) to be the result of ◆ **de son (propre)** ~ through *ou* by his (own) doing ◆ **c'est un** ~ that's a fact ◆ **c'est un** ~ **que** it's a fact that ◆ **dire son** ~ **à qn** to tell sb what's what, to talk straight to sb, to give sb a piece of one's mind ◆ **prendre** ~ **et cause pour qn** to fight for sb's cause ◆ **de ce** ~ therefore, for this reason ◆ **du** ~ **de sa démission, du** ~ **qu'il a démissionné** on account of *ou* as a result of his resignation

◆ **au fait** (= *à propos*) by the way ◆ **au** ~ **!** (= *à l'essentiel*) come to the point! ◆ **aller droit/en venir au** ~ to go straight/get to the point ◆ **au** ~ **de** (= *au courant*) conversant *ou* acquainted with, informed of ◆ **mettre qn au ~ (d'une affaire)** to acquaint *ou* familiarize sb with the facts (of a matter), to inform sb of the facts (of a matter)

◆ **de fait** *[gouvernement, dictature]* de facto; (= *en vérité*) in fact ◆ **il est de ~ que** it is a fact that

◆ **en fait** in (actual) fact, in point of fact, as a matter of fact

◆ **en fait de** (= *en guise de*) by way of; (= *en matière de*) as regards, in the way of ◆ **en ~ de repas on a eu droit à un sandwich** we were allowed a sandwich by way of a meal ◆ **en ~ de spécialiste, c'est plutôt un charlatan !** as for being an expert, charlatan more like! *

COMP fait accompli fait accompli ◆ **mettre qn devant le ~ accompli, pratiquer avec qn la politique du ~ accompli** to present sb with a fait accompli

fait d'armes feat of arms

fait divers (= *nouvelle*) (short) news item; (= *événement insignifiant*) trivial event ◆ **"faits divers"** (= *rubrique*) "(news) in brief"

faits et gestes actions, doings ◆ **épier les moindres ~s et gestes de qn** to watch sb's every move

faits de guerre acts of war

fait de langue fait de langue, language event

fait de parole fait de parole, speech event

le fait du prince the government fiat ◆ **c'est le ~ du prince** there's no going against authority

faits de résistance acts of resistance

fait², faite /fɛ, fɛt/ (ptp de **faire**) ADJ 1 ◆ **être ~ pour** to be made *ou* meant for ◆ **voitures ~es pour la course** cars (specially) made *ou* designed *ou* conceived for racing ◆ **ces chaussures ne sont pas ~es pour la marche** these are not proper walking shoes, these shoes are not suitable *ou* designed for walking in ◆ **c'est ~ pour** * that's what it's for ◆ **ce que tu lui as dit l'a énervé – c'était ~ pour** * what you said annoyed him – it was meant to ◆ **ceci n'est pas ~ pour lui plaire** this is not going to *ou* is not likely to please him ◆ **ce discours n'est pas ~ pour le rassurer** this is not the kind of speech to reassure him, this sort of speech isn't likely to reassure him ◆ **il est ~ pour être médecin** he's got the makings of a doctor ◆ **il n'est pas ~ pour être professeur** he's not cut out to be a teacher ◆ **ils sont ~s l'un pour l'autre** they are made for each other

2 (= *fini*) **c'en est ~ de notre vie calme** that's the end of our quiet life, it's goodbye to peace and quiet ◆ **c'en est ~ de moi** I'm done for*, I've had it* ◆ **c'est toujours ça de ~** that's one job done, that's one thing out of the way

3 (= *constitué*) **bien ~** *[femme]* shapely; *[homme]* well-built ◆ **avoir la jambe/main bien ~e** to have shapely *ou* nice legs/pretty *ou* nice hands ◆ **le monde est ainsi ~** that's the way of the world ◆ **les gens sont ainsi ~s que** people are such that ◆ **comment est-il ~ ?** what is he like?, what does he look like? ◆ **regarde comme tu es ~ !** * look at the state of you!*, what a sight you are!

4 (= *mûr*) *[personne]* mature; *[fromage]* ripe ◆ **fromage ~ à cœur** fully ripened cheese

5 (= *maquillé*) made-up ◆ **avoir les yeux ~s** to have one's eyes made up ◆ **avoir les ongles ~s** to have painted nails

6 ◆ **tout ~** *[objet, idée, solution]* ready-made ◆ **vêtements tout ~s** ready-made *ou* ready-to-wear clothes; → **expression, phrase**

7 (*locutions*) **il est ~ (comme un rat)** * he's in for it now*, he's cornered ◆ **c'est bien ~ pour toi !** it serves you right!, you asked for it!* ◆ **c'est bien ~ (pour eux) !** it serves them right! ◆ **ce n'est ni ~ ni à faire** it's a botched job*; → **vite**

faîtage /fɛtaʒ/ NM (= *poutre*) ridgepole; (= *couverture*) roofing; (*littér* = *toit*) roof

faîte /fɛt/ NM 1 (= *poutre*) ridgepole 2 (= *sommet*) *[de montagne]* summit; *[d'arbre]* top; *[de maison]* rooftop ◆ **~ du toit** rooftop; → **ligne¹** 3 (= *summum*) **~ de la gloire** pinnacle *ou* height of glory ◆ **parvenu au ~ des honneurs** having attained the highest honours

faîtière /fɛtjɛʀ/ ADJ F, NF ◆ **(tuile) ~** ridge tile ◆ **lucarne ~** skylight

faitout NM, **fait-tout** NM INV /fɛtu/ stewpot

faix /fɛ/ NM († *ou littér*) burden ◆ **sous le ~** under the weight *ou* burden (*de* of)

fakir /fakiʀ/ NM (*Rel*) fakir; (*Music-Hall*) wizard

falaise /falɛz/ NF cliff

falbalas /falbala/ NMPL frills and flounces, furbelows; (*péj*) frippery (*NonC*) (*péj*), furbelows (*péj*)

Falkland(s) /folklɑ̃d/ NPL ◆ **les (îles) ~(s)** the Falkland Islands, the Falklands ◆ **la guerre des ~(s)** the Falklands war

fallacieusement /fa(l)lasjøzmɑ̃/ ADV *[promettre]* deceptively

fallacieux, -ieuse /fa(l)lasjø, jøz/ ADJ *[apparence]* deceptive; *[arguments, raisonnement]* fallacious; *[accusation, promesse, appellation]* false; *[espoir]* illusory, delusive ◆ **il est entré sous un prétexte ~** he got in under false pretences ◆ **ils nous ont présenté l'image fallacieuse d'un pays paisible** they gave us a false image of the country as a peaceful place

falloir /falwaʀ/

► conjug 29 ◄

GRAMMAIRE ACTIVE 37.1, 37.2

1 VERBE IMPERSONNEL 2 VERBE PRONOMINAL

1 – VERBE IMPERSONNEL

1 besoin, nécessité

Lorsque **falloir** exprime un besoin ou une nécessité, il se traduit généralement par **need** ; il a alors pour sujet la personne, exprimée ou non en français, qui a besoin de quelque chose ; si l'on ne veut ou ne peut pas mentionner cette personne en anglais, **falloir** se traduit le plus souvent par **take**.

◆ **falloir** + *nom ou pronom* ◆ **il va ~ 10 000 €** we're going to need €10,000 ◆ **il faut du temps/de l'argent pour faire cela** it takes time/money to do that, you need time/money to do that ◆ **faut-il aussi de l'ail ?** do we need *ou* want garlic as well? ◆ **c'est juste ce qu'il faut** (*outil etc*) that's just what we need *ou* want; (*en quantité*) that's just the right amount ◆ **c'est plus qu'il n'en faut** that's more than we need ◆ **trois mètres de tissu ? – oui, il faudra au moins ça** three metres of material? – yes, we'll need *ou* want at least that much ◆ **trois heures ? – oh oui, il faut bien ça** three hours? – yes, it'll take at least that long ◆ **il n'en faut pas beaucoup pour qu'il se mette à pleurer** it doesn't take much to make him cry ◆ **il lui faut quelqu'un pour l'aider** he needs somebody to help him ◆ **une bonne fessée, voilà ce qu'il lui faut !** what he needs *ou* wants is a good hiding! ◆ **il ne me faut pas plus de dix minutes pour y aller** it won't take me more than ten minutes to get there ◆ **et avec ça, vous faut-il autre chose ?** (is there) anything else? ◆ **s'il le faut** if necessary, if need be ◆ **il vous le faut pour quand ?** when do you need it for? ◆ **il t'en faut combien ?** how many (*ou* much) do you need? ◆ **il a fait ce qu'il fallait pour la rendre heureuse/pour l'énerver** he did just the right thing to make her happy/to annoy her ◆ **il me faudrait trois steaks, s'il vous plaît** I'd like three steaks, please ◆ **il me le faut absolument** *ou* **à tout prix** I absolutely must have it, I've absolutely got to have it

◆ **falloir** + *infinitif* ◆ **faut-il réserver à l'avance ?** do you have to *ou* need to book in advance?, is it necessary to book in advance? ◆ **il vous faut tourner à gauche ici** you need *ou* want to turn left here ◆ **il faudrait avoir plus de temps** we need more time ◆ **il faut bien vivre/manger** you have to live/eat

2 obligation

Lorsque **falloir** exprime une obligation, il se traduit généralement par **have to** ou la forme plus familière **have got to** lorsqu'il s'agit de contraintes extérieures. Le verbe **must** a généralement une valeur plus impérative ; attention, **must** étant un verbe défectif, on utilise **have to** aux temps où il se ne conjugue pas.

◆ **tu pars déjà ? – il le faut** are you leaving already? – I have to *ou* I've got to ◆ **je le ferai s'il le faut** I'll do it if I have to *ou* if I must ◆ **il a bien fallu !** I (*ou* we *etc*) had to!

◆ **falloir** + *infinitif* ◆ **il va ~ le faire** we'll have to do it, it'll have to be done ◆ **il faut opérer** they're (*ou* we're *etc*) going to have to operate ◆ **il m'a fallu obéir** I had to do as I was told ◆ **que vous fallait-il faire ?** (*frm*) what did you have to do? ◆ **c'est dans le règlement, il faut le faire** those are the rules, you must do it ◆ **à l'époque, il fallait porter l'uniforme** in those days you had to wear a uniform ◆ **que faut-il leur dire ?** what should I (*ou* we *etc*) tell them?

◆ **falloir que** + *subjonctif* ◆ **il va ~ qu'il parte bientôt** he'll have to go soon ◆ **allez, il faut que je parte !** right, I must go! ◆ **il faut que tu y ailles, c'était ce qu'on avait prévu** you have to go *ou* you must go, that was the arrangement ◆ **il faudra bien que tu me le dises un jour** you'll have to tell me some time

3 suggestion, conseil, exhortation

Lorsque **falloir** est utilisé pour exprimer une suggestion, un conseil ou une exhortation au présent, il se traduit souvent par **must** ; au passé, au conditionnel ou dans une phrase négative, il se traduit généralement par **should** ou **ought to**.

◆ **il faut voir ce spectacle** you must see this show ◆ **il faut m'excuser, je ne savais pas** you must excuse me, I didn't know ◆ **il faut que vous veniez nous voir à Toulouse !** you must come and see us in Toulouse! ◆ **il faut vous dire que ...** I must *ou* I have to tell you that ... ◆ **il faut éviter de tirer des conclusions hâtives** it's important to *ou* we must avoid jumping to conclusions ◆ **dans pareil cas, il faut surtout rester calme** in cases like these, it's very important to stay calm *ou* you must above all stay calm ◆ **des fleurs ! il ne fallait pas !** flowers! you shouldn't have! ◆ **il fallait me le dire** you ought to *ou* should have told me ◆ **il ne fallait pas faire ça, c'est tout** you shouldn't have done it and that's all there is to it ◆ **il aurait fallu lui téléphoner** you (*ou* we *etc*) should have phoned him MAIS **il s'est mis en colère – il faut le comprendre** he got angry – that's understandable ◆ **il faudrait que tu viennes m'aider** I'm going to need your help ◆ **faudrait pas qu'il essaie** * he'd better not try *

4 probabilité, hypothèse

Lorsque **falloir** exprime une probabilité, une hypothèse, il se traduit généralement par **must** dans les phrases affirmatives ; **must** étant défectif, on utilise **have to** aux temps où il ne se conjugue pas.

◆ **falloir + être** ◆ **il faut être fou pour parler comme ça** you (*ou* he *etc*) must be mad to talk like that ◆ **il fallait être désespéré pour faire ça** they must have been desperate to do something like that MAIS **il ne faut pas être intel-**

ligent pour dire ça that's a pretty stupid thing to say ◆ faut-il donc être bête! some people are so *ou* really stupid! ◆ faut (pas) être gonflé! * it takes some nerve! *

◆ **falloir que** + *subjonctif* ◆ **il faut que tu te sois trompé** you must have made a mistake ◆ **faut-il qu'il soit bête !** he must be so *ou* really stupid!

5 dans des exclamatives, exprimant l'admiration ou l'agacement **il faut entendre ce qu'ils disent sur elle !** you should hear the sort of things they say about her! ◆ **il faut l'entendre chanter !** you should hear him sing! ◆ **faut dire qu'il est culotté** * you've got to *ou* you must admit he's got a nerve ◆ **(il) faut le faire !** *(admiratif)* that takes some doing!; (*, *péj)* that takes some beating! ◆ **ce qu'il faut entendre !** the things you hear! ◆ **quand faut y aller faut y aller !** * a man's gotta do what a man's gotta do! *

6 fatalité

◆ **falloir que** + *subjonctif* ◆ **il a fallu qu'elle l'apprenne** she WOULD have to hear about it ◆ **il a fallu qu'il arrive à ce moment-là** of course, he had to arrive just then ◆ **il fallait bien que ça arrive** it was bound to happen ◆ **il faut toujours qu'elle se trouve des excuses** she always has to find some excuse ◆ **faut-il toujours que tu te plaignes ?** do you always have to complain?

7 locutions ◆ **elle a ce qu'il faut** * *(hum)* she's got what it takes * ◆ **il faut ce qu'il faut** * you've got to do things properly ◆ **il faut de tout pour faire un monde** it takes all sorts to make a world

◆ **il faut/fallait/faudrait + voir** ◆ **il faut voir !** *(réserve)* we'll have to see! ◆ **elle danse superbement, il faut (la) voir !** you should see her dance, it's wonderful! ◆ **(il) faut le voir pour le croire** it has to be seen to be believed ◆ **faudrait voir à voir !** * come on! *, come off it! * ◆ **(il) faudrait voir à faire/ne pas faire ...** * you'd better make sure you do/don't do ... ◆ **son travail est fait faut voir (comme) !** * *ou* **(il) faut voir comment !** * you should see what a job he's made of it! ◆ **il faut voir comment tu t'y prends, aussi !** look at how you're going about it though! ◆ **il faut voir comment il s'habille !** you should see the way he dresses! ◆ **(il) faudrait voir à ne pas nous ennuyer !** * you'd better see you don't cause us any trouble! *

2 - VERBE PRONOMINAL

s'en falloir

◆ **s'en falloir de** ◆ **j'ai raté le train, il s'en est fallu de 5 minutes** I missed the train by 5 minutes ◆ **il ne s'en fallait que de 10 € pour qu'il ait la somme** he was only *ou* just €10 short of the full amount ◆ **il s'en est fallu de peu (pour) que ça (n')arrive** it came very close to happening, it very nearly happened ◆ **elle ne l'a pas injurié, mais il s'en est fallu de peu** she very nearly insulted him

◆ **loin s'en faut!, tant s'en faut!, il s'en faut (de beaucoup)!** far from it! ◆ **il s'en faut de beaucoup qu'il soit heureux** he is far from being happy, he is by no means happy

◆ **peu s'en faut** ◆ **il a fini, ou peu s'en faut** he has as good as finished, he has just about finished ◆ **ça m'a coûté 500 € ou peu s'en faut** it cost me the best part of €500, it cost me very nearly €500 ◆ **peu s'en est fallu (pour) qu'il pleure** he almost wept, he very nearly wept

---

falot[1] /falo/ NM 1 *(= lanterne)* lantern 2 *(arg Mil = tribunal militaire)* court martial

falot[2], **e** /falo, ɔt/ ADJ *[personne]* colourless *(Brit)*, colorless *(US)*; *[lumière]* wan, pale

falsifiable /falsifjabl/ ADJ *[document, papiers d'identité, signature]* forgeable; *[écriture]* that can be copied easily

falsificateur, -trice /falsifikatœʀ, tʀis/ NM,F *[de document, signature]* forger ◆ **les ~s de l'histoire** those who distort history, the distorters of history

falsification /falsifikasjɔ̃/ NF *[de comptes, faits, document]* falsification; *[de signature]* forgery, forging; *[d'aliment]* doctoring, adulteration

falsifier /falsifje/ ► conjug 7 ◄ VT *[+ comptes, faits, document]* to falsify; *[+ signature]* to forge; *[+ aliment]* to doctor, to adulterate

falzar * /falzaʀ/ NM (pair of) trousers, (pair of) pants *(US)*

famé, e /fame/ **mal famé** LOC ADJ disreputable

famélique /famelik/ ADJ scrawny, scraggy, rawboned

fameusement * /famøzmɑ̃/ ADV *(= très)* remarkably, really ◆ **c'est ~ bon** it's remarkably *ou* really good

fameux, -euse /famø, øz/ ADJ 1 (* : *après n = de qualité) [mets, vin]* first-rate, first-class

2 ◆ **pas ~** * *[mets, travail, temps]* not too good, not so great *; *[roman, auteur]* no great shakes *, not up to much * *(Brit)* ◆ **et le temps pour demain ? – pas ~** and tomorrow's weather? – not all that good *ou* not up to much * *(Brit)* ◆ **il n'est pas ~ en latin** he's not too good *ou* not all that good at Latin

3 *(avant n : intensif)* real ◆ **c'est un ~ trajet/problème/travail** it's quite a *ou* one hell of a * journey/problem/piece of work ◆ **c'est une fameuse erreur/raclée** it's quite a *ou* it's a real mistake/thrashing ◆ **un ~ salaud** * a downright *ou* an out-and-out *ou* a real bastard ** ◆ **une fameuse assiettée** a huge *ou* great plateful ◆ **c'est un ~ gaillard** *(bien bâti)* he's a strapping fellow; *(chaud lapin)* he's one for the ladies, he's a bit of a lad * *(Brit)*

4 *(avant n = bon) [idée, voiture]* first-rate, great *, fine ◆ **c'est une fameuse aubaine** it's a real *ou* great stroke of luck ◆ **il a fait un ~ travail** he's done a first-class *ou* first-rate *ou* fine job ◆ **elle était fameuse, ton idée !** what a bright *ou* great * idea you had!

5 (* : *avant n = fonction de référence)* famous ◆ **quel est le nom de cette fameuse rue ?** what's the name of that (famous) street? ◆ **ah, c'est ce ~ Paul dont tu m'as tant parlé** so this is the famous Paul you've told me so much about ◆ **c'est ça, sa fameuse honnêteté** so this is his much-vaunted honesty

6 *(après n = célèbre)* famous *(pour, par* for)

familial, e (mpl **-iaux**) /familjal, jo/ ADJ *[problème]* family *(épith)*, domestic *(épith)*; *[liens, vie, entreprise, ambiance]* family *(épith)*; *[boîte, paquet]* family-size(d); *[modèle de voiture]* family *(épith)*; → **aide**[2], **allocation** NF **familiale** (family) estate car *(Brit)*, station wagon *(US)*

familialiste /familjalist/ ADJ *[mouvement, modèle, groupe]* promoting family values

familiarisation /familjaʀizasjɔ̃/ NF familiarization

familiariser /familjaʀize/ ► conjug 1 ◄ VT ◆ **~ qn avec** to familiarize sb with, to get sb used to VPR **se familiariser** to familiarize o.s. ◆ **se ~ avec** *[+ lieu, personne, méthode, langue]* to familiarize o.s. with, to get to know, to become acquainted with; *[+ bruit, danger]* to get used *ou* accustomed to ◆ **ses pieds, peu familiarisés avec le sol rocailleux** his feet, unused *ou* unaccustomed to the stony ground

familiarité /familjaʀite/ NF 1 *(= bonhomie)* familiarity; *(= désinvolture)* offhandedness, (over)familiarity 2 *(= privautés)* **~s** familiarities ◆ **cessez ces ~s** stop these familiarities, stop taking liberties 3 *(= habitude)* **~ avec** *[+ langue, auteur, méthode]* familiarity with 4 *(= atmosphère amicale)* informality ◆ **dans la ~ de** *(littér)* on familiar terms with

familier, -ière /familje, jɛʀ/ ADJ 1 *(= bien connu) [problème, spectacle, objet]* familiar ◆ **sa voix/cette technique m'est familière** I'm familiar with his voice/this technique, his voice/this technique is familiar *ou* well-known to me ◆ **la langue anglaise lui est devenue familière** he has become (thoroughly) familiar with *ou* at home with the English language

2 *(= routinier) [tâche]* familiar ◆ **cette attitude lui est familière** this is a typical attitude of his ◆ **le mensonge lui était devenu ~** lying had become quite a habit of his *ou* had become almost second nature to him

3 *(= amical) [entretien, atmosphère]* informal, friendly, casual

4 *(= désinvolte) [personne]* (over)familiar; *[surnom]* familiar; *[ton, remarque]* (over)familiar, offhand; *[attitude, manières]* offhand ◆ **il devient vite ~** he soon gets too familiar ◆ **(trop) ~ avec ses supérieurs/ses clients/les femmes** overfamiliar with his superiors/his customers/women

5 *(= non recherché) [mot]* informal, colloquial; *[style, registre]* informal, conversational, colloquial ◆ **expression familière** colloquialism, colloquial phrase *ou* expression

6 *[divinités]* household *(épith)*; → **démon**

NM *[de club, théâtre]* regular visitor *(de* to); ◆ **le crime a été commis par un ~ (de la maison)** the crime was committed by a regular visitor to the house

familièrement /familjɛʀmɑ̃/ ADV *(= amicalement) [s'entretenir]* informally; *(= cavalièrement) [se conduire]* familiarly; *(= sans recherche) [s'exprimer]* informally, colloquially ◆ **comme on dit ~** as you say colloquially *ou* in conversation ◆ **le ficus elastica, ~ appelé caoutchouc** ficus elastica, commonly known as the rubber plant ◆ **il te parle un peu (trop) ~** he's being a bit too familiar with you

famille /famij/ NF 1 *(gén)* family ◆ **~ éloignée/proche** distant/close family *ou* relations *ou* relatives ◆ **avez-vous de la ~ à Londres ?** do you have any family *ou* relations *ou* relatives in London? ◆ **on a prévenu la ~** the relatives *ou* the next of kin *(Admin)* have been informed ◆ **~ d'accueil** host family ◆ **~ nombreuse** large family ◆ **la ~ étendue/nucléaire** the extended/nuclear family ◆ **elle promenait (toute) sa petite ~** * she was taking her (entire) brood * for a walk ◆ **comment va la petite ~ ?** how are the little ones? ◆ **entrer dans une ~** to become part of a family ◆ **leur mariage a consacré son entrée dans la ~** their marriage made him an official member of the family ◆ **elle fait partie de la ~, elle est de la ~** she is part *ou* one of the family ◆ **c'est une ~ de musiciens** they're a family of musicians; → **monoparental, recomposé**

2 *[de plantes, langues]* family ◆ **la ~ des cuivres** the brass family ◆ **~ de mots** word family ◆ **~ de produits** family of products, product family ◆ **ils sont de la même ~ politique** they're of the same political persuasion

3 *(locutions)* **de bonne ~** from a good family *ou* background ◆ **il est sans ~** he has no family ◆ **un (petit) bridge des ~s** * a quiet *ou* cosy little game of bridge ◆ **il est très ~** * he's very family-oriented, he's a real family man ◆ **de ~** *[possessions, réunion, dîner]* family *(épith)* ◆ **tableau de ~** *(= peinture)* family portrait; *(= spectacle)* family scene; *(légué par les ancêtres)* family heirloom ◆ **c'est de ~, ça tient de ~** it runs in the family

◆ **en famille** *(= avec la famille)* with the family; *(= comme une famille)* as a family ◆ **tout se passe en ~** it's all kept in the family ◆ **il vaut mieux régler ce problème en ~** it's best to sort this problem out within the family ◆ **passer ses vacances en ~** to spend one's holidays with the family

famine /famin/ **NF** (= *épidémie*) famine, starvation (*NonC*) ◆ **nous allons à la ~** we are heading for starvation, we are going to starve ◆ **crier ~** to complain that the wolf is at the door; → **salaire**

fan * /fan/ **NM,F** (= *admirateur*) fan

fana * /fana/ (abrév de **fanatique**) **ADJ** crazy * (*de* about) mad keen * (*Brit*) (*de* on) **NMF** fanatic ◆ **~ de ski/de varappe** skiing/rock-climbing fanatic ◆ **~ d'informatique/de cinéma** computer/cinema buff * ◆ **~ d'écologie** eco-freak *

fanage /fanaʒ/ **NM** tossing, turning, tedding

fanal (pl **-aux**) /fanal, o/ **NM** (= *feu*) [*de train*] headlight, headlamp; [*de mât*] lantern; (= *phare*) beacon, lantern; (= *lanterne à main*) lantern, lamp

fanatique /fanatik/ **ADJ** fanatical (*de* about) **NMF** (*gén, Sport*) fanatic; (*Pol, Rel*) fanatic, zealot ◆ **~ du ski/du football/des échecs** skiing/football/chess fanatic

fanatiquement /fanatikmɑ̃/ **ADV** fanatically

fanatisation /fanatizasjɔ̃/ **NF** rousing to fanaticism, fanaticization (*frm*)

fanatiser /fanatize/ ► conjug 1 ◄ **VT** to rouse to fanaticism, to fanaticize (*frm*)

fanatisme /fanatism/ **NM** fanaticism

fan-club (pl **fan-clubs**) /fanklœb/ **NM** [*de vedette*] fan club ◆ **il fait partie de mon ~** (*hum*) he's one of my fans

fane /fan/ **NF** (*surtout pl*) [*de légume*] top ◆ **~s de carottes/radis** carrot/radish tops ◆ **~s de haricots/pommes de terre** bean/potato haulms

fané, e /fane/ (ptp de **faner**) **ADJ** [*fleur, bouquet*] withered, wilted; [*couleur, teint, beauté, étoffe*] faded

faner /fane/ ► conjug 1 ◄ **VI** (*littér*) to make hay **VT** [1] [+ *herbe*] to toss, to turn, to ted ◆ **on fane (l'herbe) après la fauchaison** the tossing *ou* turning of the hay *ou* the tedding is done after the mowing [2] (*littér*) [+ *couleur, beauté*] to fade ◆ **femme que l'âge a fanée** woman whose looks have faded **VPR** **se faner** [*plante*] to fade, to wither, to wilt; [*peau*] to wither; [*teint, beauté, couleur*] to fade

faneur, -euse /fanœʀ, øz/ **NM,F** (= *ouvrier*) haymaker **NF** **faneuse** (= *machine*) tedder

fanfare /fɑ̃faʀ/ **NF** [1] (= *orchestre*) brass band ◆ **la ~ du régiment** the regimental band
[2] (= *musique*) fanfare ◆ **~ de clairons** fanfare of bugles ◆ **~ de trompettes** flourish *ou* fanfare of trumpets ◆ **des ~s éclatèrent** there was the sound of fanfares
◆ **en fanfare** [*réveil, départ*] clamorous, tumultuous; [*réveiller, partir*] noisily, with a great commotion ◆ **il est arrivé en ~** (*avec bruit*) he came in noisily *ou* with a great commotion; (*fièrement*) he came in triumphantly ◆ **l'entreprise a fait son entrée en ~ sur le marché** the company came onto the market with *ou* amid much fanfare ◆ **c'est le retour en ~ de la mode des années 60** sixties fashion is making a spectacular comeback *ou* is back with a vengeance ◆ **le plan a été annoncé en grande ~ en avril** the plan was announced with *ou* amid much fanfare in April

fanfaron, -onne /fɑ̃faʀɔ̃, ɔn/ **ADJ** [*personne, attitude*] boastful; [*air, propos*] bragging, boastful ◆ **il avait un petit air ~** he was quite full of himself, he looked very pleased with himself **NM,F** braggart ◆ **faire le ~** to brag, to boast

fanfaronnade /fɑ̃faʀɔnad/ **NF** bragging (*NonC*), boasting (*NonC*), boast ◆ **arrête tes ~s** stop boasting

fanfaronner /fɑ̃faʀɔne/ ► conjug 1 ◄ **VI** to brag, to boast

fanfreluche /fɑ̃fʀəlyʃ/ **NF** (*sur rideau, ameublement*) trimming ◆ **robe ornée de ~s** dress trimmed with frills and flounces

fange /fɑ̃ʒ/ **NF** (*littér*) mire (*littér*); → **traîner, vautrer (se)**

fanion /fanjɔ̃/ **NM** [*de vélo, club, bateau*] pennant; (*Rugby*) flag; (*Ski*) pennant ◆ **~ de commandement** (*Mil*) commanding officer's pennant

fanon /fanɔ̃/ **NM** [1] [*de baleine*] plate of whalebone *ou* baleen; (= *matière*) whalebone (*NonC*) [2] [*de cheval*] fetlock [3] [*de bœuf*] dewlap; [*de dindon*] wattle

fantaisie /fɑ̃tezi/ **NF** [1] (= *caprice*) whim ◆ **elle se plie à toutes ses ~s, elle lui passe toutes ses ~s** she gives in to his every whim ◆ **s'offrir une ~ en allant** *ou* **s'offrir la ~ d'aller au restaurant** to give o.s. a treat by having a meal out *ou* by eating out ◆ **je me suis payé une petite ~** (*bibelot, bijou, gadget*) I bought myself a little present
[2] (= *extravagance*) extravagance ◆ **ces ~s vestimentaires** such extravagance *ou* extravagances of dress ◆ **bijoux de ~** costume jewellery
[3] (*littér* = *bon plaisir*) **il agit selon** *ou* **il n'en fait qu'à sa ~** he does as the fancy takes him ◆ **il lui a pris la ~ de ...** he took it into his head to ... ◆ **à votre ~** as it may please you
[4] (= *imagination*) imagination ◆ **être plein de ~** to be full of imagination, to be imaginative ◆ **manquer de ~** [*vie*] to be monotonous *ou* uneventful; [*personne*] to be lacking in imagination *ou* be unimaginative
[5] (*en adj*) **boucles d'oreilles ~** (*originales*) fancy *ou* novelty earrings; (*imitation*) imitation gold (*ou* silver *etc*) earrings ◆ **bijoux ~** costume jewellery ◆ **rideaux ~** fancy curtains ◆ **boutons ~** fancy *ou* novelty buttons ◆ **kirsch ~** kirsch-flavoured brandy
[6] (= *œuvre*) (*Littérat*) fantasy; (*Mus*) fantasy, fantasia

fantaisiste /fɑ̃tezist/ **ADJ** [1] [*nouvelle, explication*] fanciful; [*horaires*] unpredictable ◆ **il a annoncé des chiffres de chômage tout à fait ~s** the unemployment figures he announced were pure fantasy [2] [*personne*] (= *farceur*) whimsical; (= *capricieux*) fanciful; (= *peu sérieux*) unreliable; (= *bizarre*) eccentric, unorthodox **NMF** [1] (*Théât*) variety artist *ou* entertainer [2] (= *original*) eccentric, oddball *

fantasmagorie /fɑ̃tasmagɔʀi/ **NF** phantasmagoria

fantasmagorique /fɑ̃tasmagɔʀik/ **ADJ** phantasmagorical

fantasmatique /fɑ̃tasmatik/ **ADJ** [*rêve, vision*] fantastical

fantasme /fɑ̃tasm/ **NM** fantasy ◆ **il vit dans ses ~s** he lives in a fantasy world

fantasmer /fɑ̃tasme/ ► conjug 1 ◄ **VI** to fantasize (*sur* about) **VT** to fantasize about

fantasque /fɑ̃task/ **ADJ** (*littér*) [*personne, humeur*] whimsical, capricious; [*chose*] weird, fantastic

fantassin /fɑ̃tasɛ̃/ **NM** foot soldier, infantryman ◆ **2 000 ~s** 2,000 foot *ou* infantry

fantastique /fɑ̃tastik/ **ADJ** [1] * (= *excellent*) fantastic *, terrific *, great *; (= *énorme, incroyable*) fantastic *, incredible ◆ **tu es vraiment ~ ! tu crois que c'est facile ?** you are incredible! do you think this is easy? [2] (= *étrange*) [*atmosphère*] weird, eerie; [*rêve*] weird, fantastic ◆ **conte ~** tale of fantasy *ou* of the supernatural ◆ **roman ~** (*gén*) fantasy; (= *romantique*) Gothic novel ◆ **film ~** fantasy film ◆ **le cinéma ~** science fiction, horror and fantasy films **NM** ◆ **le ~** the fantastic, the uncanny; (*Littérat*) (*gén*) fantasy, the fantastic; (*romantique*) Gothic literature; (*Ciné*) science fiction, horror and fantasy

fantastiquement /fɑ̃tastikmɑ̃/ **ADV** fantastically

fantoche /fɑ̃tɔʃ/ **NM, ADJ** puppet ◆ **gouvernement ~** puppet government

fantomatique /fɑ̃tɔmatik/ **ADJ** ghostly

fantôme /fɑ̃tom/ **NM** (= *spectre*) ghost, phantom ◆ **les ~s du passé** ghosts from the past ◆ **ce n'est plus qu'un ~** (= *personne amaigrie*) he's a shadow of his former self **ADJ** [*société*] dummy, bogus ◆ **salarié ~** ghost *ou* phantom employee ◆ **bateau ~** ghost *ou* phantom ship ◆ **train/ville ~** ghost train/town ◆ **étudiants ~s** *students who do not attend classes* ◆ **membre ~** (*Méd*) phantom limb ◆ **image ~** (*Phys*) ghost ◆ **cabinet/gouvernement ~** (*Pol*) shadow cabinet/government; → **vaisseau**

fanzine /fɑ̃zin/ **NM** fanzine

FAO /ɛfao/ **NF** [1] (abrév de **fabrication assistée par ordinateur**) CAM [2] (abrév de **Food and Agriculture Organization**) FAO

faon /fɑ̃/ **NM** fawn

faquin †† /fakɛ̃/ **NM** wretch, rascal

far /faʀ/ **NM** ◆ **~ (breton)** custard flan with prunes ◆ **~ aux poires** custard flan with pears

farad /faʀad/ **NM** farad

faraday /faʀadɛ/ **NM** faraday

faramineux, -euse * /faʀaminø, øz/ **ADJ** [*bêtise, inconscience*] staggering *, fantastic *, mind-boggling *; [*prix, somme, salaire, coût*] astronomical *; [*projet, vitesse*] fantastic * ◆ **toi et tes idées faramineuses !** you and your brilliant ideas!

farandole /faʀɑ̃dɔl/ **NF** (= *danse*) farandole ◆ **la ~ des desserts** a selection of desserts

faraud, e † /faʀo, od/ **ADJ** boastful ◆ **tu n'es plus si ~** you are no longer quite so boastful *ou* full of yourself *ou* pleased with yourself **NM,F** braggart ◆ **faire le ~** to brag, to boast

farce[1] /faʀs/ **NF** [1] (= *tour*) practical joke, prank, hoax ◆ **faire une ~ à qn** to play a practical joke *ou* a prank on sb ◆ **~s (et) attrapes** (= *objets*) (assorted) tricks ◆ **magasin de ~s-attrapes** joke (and novelty) shop [2] (*fig, Théât*) farce ◆ **grosse ~** slapstick comedy ◆ **ce procès est une ~** this trial is a farce; → **dindon**

farce[2] /faʀs/ **NF** (*Culin*) (*gén*) stuffing; (*à la viande*) forcemeat

farceur, -euse /faʀsœʀ, øz/ **NM,F** (= *facétieux*) (*en actes*) practical joker, prankster; (*en paroles*) joker, wag; (*péj* = *fumiste*) clown (*péj*) ◆ **sacré ~ !** you're (*ou* he's *etc*) a sly *ou* crafty one! **ADJ** (= *espiègle*) mischievous ◆ **il est très ~** he likes playing tricks *ou* practical jokes

farcir /faʀsiʀ/ ► conjug 2 ◄ **VT** [1] (*Culin*) to stuff ◆ **tomates farcies** stuffed tomatoes
[2] (*fig*) **farci de fautes** crammed *ou* littered with mistakes ◆ **j'en ai la tête farcie** I've had about as much as I can take
VPR **se farcir** [1] (*péj*) **se ~ la mémoire** *ou* **la tête de** to fill one's head with
[2] ‡ [+ *lessive, travail, personne*] to get stuck *ou* landed with *; [+ *bouteille*] to knock back *, to polish off *; [+ *gâteaux*] to gobble down *, to guzzle *, to scoff * (*Brit*) ◆ **se ~ une fille/un mec** ** to make it with ‡ a girl/a guy, to have it off with ‡ (*Brit*) a girl/a guy ◆ **il faudra se ~ ton cousin pendant 3 jours** we'll have to put up with your cousin for 3 days ◆ **il faut se le ~ !** [+ *importun*] he's a real pain (in the neck)! *; [+ *livre*] it's really heavy going! ◆ **je me suis farci le voyage à pied** I bloody well ‡ walked the whole way

fard /faʀ/ **NM** (= *maquillage*) make-up; († = *poudre*) rouge †, paint ◆ **~ (gras)** [*d'acteur*] greasepaint ◆ **~ à joues** blusher ◆ **~ à paupières** eye shadow ◆ **sans ~** [*parler*] openly; [*élégance*] unpretentious, simple; → **piquer**

fardé, e /faʀde/ (ptp de **farder**) **ADJ** [*personne*] wearing make-up ◆ **elle est trop ~e** she's wearing too much make-up ◆ **elle avait les**

paupières/joues ~es she was wearing eyeshadow/blusher ◆ **elle avait les lèvres ~es** she was wearing lipstick

fardeau (pl **fardeaux**) /faʀdo/ NM (*lit*) load, burden (*littér*); (*fig*) burden ◆ **sous le ~ de** under the weight *ou* burden of ◆ **il a traîné** *ou* **porté ce ~ toute sa vie** he carried *ou* bore this burden all his life

farder /faʀde/ ▸ conjug 1 ◂ VT 1 (*Théât*) [+ *acteur*] to make up; †† [+ *visage*] to rouge †, to paint 2 [+ *bilan, marchandise*] to dress up; (*littér*) [+ *vérité*] to disguise, to mask, to veil VPR **se farder** (= *se maquiller*) to make (o.s.) up; († = *se poudrer*) to paint one's face †; [*acteur*] to make up

farfadet /faʀfadɛ/ NM sprite, elf

farfelu, e* /faʀfəly/ ADJ [*idée, projet*] harebrained; [*personne, conduite*] eccentric, scatty* (*Brit*) NM,F eccentric

farfouiller* /faʀfuje/ ▸ conjug 1 ◂ VI to rummage about (*dans* in)

faribole /faʀibɔl/ NF (*littér*) (piece of) nonsense ◆ **conter des ~s** to talk nonsense *ou* twaddle (*Brit*) ◆ **~s (que tout cela) !** (stuff and) nonsense!, fiddlesticks! †*, poppycock! †*

farine /faʀin/ NF [*de blé*] flour ◆ **de (la) même ~** (*littér*) of the same ilk; → **fleur, rouler**

COMP **farines animales** bone meal
farine d'avoine oatmeal
farine de blé ⇒ **farine de froment**
farine complète wheatmeal *ou* whole wheat *ou* wholemeal (*Brit*) flour
farine de froment wheat flour
farine à gâteaux cake flour
farine de gruau fine wheat flour
farine lactée baby cereal
farine de lin linseed meal
farine de maïs cornflour (*Brit*), cornstarch (*US*)
farine de manioc cassava, manioc flour
farine de moutarde mustard powder
farine de poisson fish meal
farine de riz rice flour
farine de sarrasin buckwheat flour
farine de seigle rye flour
farine tamisée sifted flour

fariner /faʀine/ ▸ conjug 1 ◂ VT to flour ◆ **moule beurré et fariné** buttered and floured tin (*Brit*) *ou* pan (*US*)

farineux, -euse /faʀinø, øz/ ADJ [*consistance, aspect, goût*] floury, chalky; [*chocolat*] powdery, chalky; [*fromage*] chalky; [*pomme de terre*] floury; [*pomme*] dry, mushy NM starchy food, starch ◆ **les ~** starchy foods, starches

farniente /faʀnjɛnte/ NM idle life, idleness ◆ **faire du ~ sur la plage** to lounge *ou* laze on the beach

farouche /faʀuʃ/ ADJ 1 (= *timide*) [*personne, animal*] shy, timid; (= *peu sociable*) [*voisin*] unsociable ◆ **ces daims ne sont pas ~s** these deer are not a bit shy *ou* timid *ou* are quite tame ◆ **elle n'est pas ~** (*péj*) she's no shrinking violet 2 (= *acharné*) [*opposition, attachement, adversaire*] fierce; [*volonté*] unshakeable, inflexible; [*énergie*] irrepressible; [*partisan, défenseur*] staunch; [*haine, ennemi*] bitter; (= *hostile*) [*regard*] fierce, hostile 3 (= *indompté*) savage, wild

farouchement /faʀuʃmɑ̃/ ADV fiercely ◆ **nier ~ qch** to deny sth fiercely *ou* vehemently

farsi /faʀsi/ NM Farsi

fart /faʀt/ NM (ski) wax ◆ **~ de montée** climbing wax

fartage /faʀtaʒ/ NM [*de skis*] waxing

farter /faʀte/ ▸ conjug 1 ◂ VT [+ *skis*] to wax

Far-West, Far West /faʀwɛst/ NM INV ◆ **le ~** the Wild West

fascicule /fasikyl/ NM part, instalment, fascicule (*SPÉC*) ◆ **ce livre est vendu avec un ~ d'exercices** this book is sold with a manual of exercises ◆ **~ de mobilisation** (*Mil*) instructions for mobilization

fascinant, e /fasinɑ̃, ɑ̃t/ ADJ (*gén*) fascinating; [*beauté*] bewitching, fascinating

fascination /fasinasjɔ̃/ NF fascination ◆ **exercer une grande ~** to exert (a) great fascination (*sur* on, over) to have (a) great fascination (*sur* for)

fascine /fasin/ NF (= *fagot*) faggot (*of brushwood*); (*Constr*) fascine

fasciner[1] /fasine/ ▸ conjug 1 ◂ VT (*gén*) to fascinate; (= *soumettre à son charme*) to bewitch ◆ **il s'est laissé ~ par cette idéologie** he allowed himself to come under the spell of this ideology ◆ **être fasciné par le pouvoir** to be fascinated *ou* mesmerized by power

fasciner[2] /fasine/ ▸ conjug 1 ◂ VT (*Constr*) to line with fascines

fascisant, e /faʃizɑ̃, ɑ̃t/ ADJ fascistic

fascisation /faʃizasjɔ̃/ NF fascistization

fascisme /faʃism/ NM fascism

fasciste /faʃist/ ADJ, NMF fascist

faste[1] /fast/ NM splendour (*Brit*), splendor (*US*), pomp ◆ **sans ~** [*cérémonie*] simple, low-key; [*célébrer*] quietly, simply

faste[2] /fast/ ADJ (*littér*) [*année, période*] (= *de chance*) lucky; (= *prospère*) prosperous ◆ **jour ~** lucky day

fastes /fast/ NMPL (= *annales*) annals

fast-food (pl **fast-foods**) /fastfud/ NM (= *restaurant*) fast-food restaurant; (= *restauration*) fast food

fastidieusement /fastidjøzmɑ̃/ ADV tediously, tiresomely, boringly

> ⚠ **fastidieusement** ne se traduit pas par **fastidiously**, qui a le sens de 'méticuleusement'.

fastidieux, -ieuse /fastidjø, jøz/ ADJ tedious, boring; [*travail*] tedious ◆ **long et ~** long and boring ◆ **il serait ~ de les énumérer** it would be tedious to list them

> ⚠ **fastidieux** ne se traduit pas par **fastidious**, qui a le sens de 'méticuleux'.

fastoche* /fastɔʃ/ ADJ dead easy* ◆ **c'est vachement ~ !** it's dead easy* *ou* a cinch!*

fastueusement /fastɥøzmɑ̃/ ADV sumptuously, luxuriously ◆ **recevoir qn ~** (*pour dîner*) to entertain sb lavishly; (*à son arrivée*) to give sb a lavish reception

fastueux, -euse /fastɥø, øz/ ADJ sumptuous, luxurious ◆ **réception fastueuse** lavish reception ◆ **mener une vie fastueuse** to lead a sumptuous *ou* luxurious existence, to live a life of great luxury

fat † /fa(t)/ ADJ conceited, smug, complacent NM conceited *ou* smug *ou* complacent person

fatal, e (mpl **fatals**) /fatal/ ADJ 1 (= *funeste*) [*accident, issue*] fatal; [*coup*] fatal, deadly ◆ **erreur ~e !** fatal error *ou* mistake! ◆ **être ~ à qn** [*chute, accident*] to kill sb; [*erreur, bêtise*] to prove fatal *ou* disastrous for *ou* to sb 2 (= *inévitable*) inevitable ◆ **c'était ~** it was inevitable, it was bound to happen ◆ **il était ~ qu'elle le fasse** she was bound *ou* fated to do it, it was inevitable that she should do it 3 (= *marqué par le destin*) [*instant, heure*] fatal, fateful; → **femme**

fatalement /fatalmɑ̃/ ADV (= *inévitablement*) inevitably ◆ **~, il est tombé !** inevitably, he fell! ◆ **il y aura ~ des conséquences** inevitably, there will be consequences ◆ **ça devait ~ arriver** it was bound *ou* fated to happen

> ⚠ **fatalement** ne se traduit pas par **fatally**, qui a le sens de 'mortellement'.

fatalisme /fatalism/ NM fatalism

fataliste /fatalist/ ADJ fatalistic NMF fatalist

fatalité /fatalite/ NF 1 (= *destin*) fate, fatality (*littér*) ◆ **être poursuivi par la ~** to be pursued by fate ◆ **c'est la ~** it's fate 2 (= *nécessité*) **le chômage est-il une ~ ?** is unemployment inevitable? ◆ **par quelle ~ se sont-ils rencontrés ?** by what terrible *ou* unfortunate coincidence did they meet? 3 (= *caractère inévitable*) inevitability ◆ **la ~ de la mort/de cet événement** the inevitability of death/this event

fatidique /fatidik/ ADJ (= *lourd de conséquences*) [*décision, paroles*] fateful; (= *crucial*) [*moment*] fatal, fateful ◆ **la date ~** the fateful day ◆ **le chômage a passé la barre** *ou* **le seuil ~ des 10%** unemployment has passed the critical 10% threshold ◆ **enfin, le jour ~ est arrivé** at last the fateful day arrived ◆ **puis vint la question ~ : qui allait faire le travail ?** then came the big question *ou* the sixty-four thousand dollar question*: who was going to do the work?

fatigabilité /fatigabilite/ NF [*de personne*] fatigability

fatigant, e /fatigɑ̃, ɑ̃t/ ADJ (= *épuisant*) tiring; (= *agaçant*) [*personne*] annoying, tiresome, tedious; [*conversation*] tiresome, tedious ◆ **c'est ~ pour la vue** it's tiring *ou* a strain on the eyes ◆ **c'est ~ pour le cœur** it's a strain on the heart ◆ **tu es vraiment ~ avec tes questions** you really are annoying *ou* tiresome *ou* a nuisance with your questions ◆ **c'est ~ de devoir toujours tout répéter** it's annoying *ou* tiresome *ou* a nuisance to have to repeat everything all the time

fatigue /fatig/ NF 1 [*de personne*] (*gén*) tiredness; (*Méd*) fatigue ◆ **tomber** *ou* **être mort de ~** (*fig*) to be dead tired*, to be exhausted ◆ **il a voulu nous épargner cette ~** he wanted to save *ou* spare us the strain ◆ **dans un état d'extrême** *ou* **de grande ~** in a state of utter exhaustion ◆ **se remettre des ~s du voyage** to get over the strain *ou* the tiring effects of the journey ◆ **pour se reposer de la ~ du voyage** to rest after a tiring journey ◆ **cette ~ dans le bras gauche** this weakness in the left arm ◆ **~ oculaire** *ou* **visuelle** eyestrain; → **recru** 2 (*Tech*) fatigue ◆ **la ~ des métaux** metal fatigue

fatigué, e /fatige/ (ptp de **fatiguer**) ADJ 1 [*personne, voix*] tired; [*traits, membres*] tired; [*cœur*] strained, overworked; [*cerveau*] overtaxed, overworked; [*estomac, foie*] upset ◆ **il a les bras ~s** his arms are tired ◆ **j'ai les yeux ~s** my eyes are tired *ou* strained ◆ **~ par le voyage** tired after travelling ◆ **il est né ~** (*péj*) he's bone-lazy *ou* bone-idle (*Brit*) 2 ◆ **~ de** tired of ◆ **~ de la vie** tired of life *ou* living ◆ **je suis ~ de me répéter** I'm tired of repeating myself 3 [*poutre, joint, moteur, habits*] worn

fatiguer /fatige/ ▸ conjug 1 ◂ VT 1 [+ *personne*] [*effort, maladie, études*] to make tired, to tire; [*professeur, patron*] to overwork ◆ **ces efforts fatiguent, à la longue** all this effort tires *ou* wears you out in the end ◆ **ça fatigue les yeux/le cœur/l'organisme** it is *ou* puts a strain on the eyes/heart/whole body ◆ **se ~ les yeux/le cœur** to strain one's eyes/heart

2 [+ *animal, objet, cheval*] to tire, to put a strain on; [*cavalier*] to overwork; [+ *moteur*] to put (a) strain on, to strain; [+ *poutre, pièce*] to put (a) strain on; [+ *chaussures, vêtement*] to wear out; [+ *sol*] to exhaust, to impoverish

3 (= *agacer*) to annoy; (= *lasser*) to wear out ◆ **tu commences à me ~** you're beginning to annoy me ◆ **tu me fatigues avec tes questions !** you're getting on my nerves with all your questions! ◆ **il vous fatigue avec ses problèmes !** his problems are enough to tire anybody out!

4 [+ *salade*] to toss

VI *[moteur]* to labour *(Brit)*, to labor *(US)*, to strain; *[poutre, pièce, joint]* to become strained, to show (signs of) strain; *[personne]* to tire, to grow tired *ou* weary ◆ **je commence à ~** I'm starting to get tired

VPR **se fatiguer** 1 *(physiquement)* to get tired ◆ **se ~ à faire qch** to tire o.s. out doing sth ◆ **il ne s'est pas trop fatigué** *(iro)* he didn't overdo it, he didn't kill himself*

2 *(= se lasser de)* **se ~ de qch/de faire** to get tired *ou* weary of sth/of doing

3 *(= s'évertuer à)* **se ~ à répéter/expliquer** to wear o.s. out repeating /explaining ◆ **ne te fatigue pas** *ou* **pas la peine de te ~, il est borné*** he's just dim so don't waste your time *ou* your breath

fatras /fatʀa/ **NM** *[de choses]* jumble; *[d'idées]* jumble, hotchpotch *(Brit)*, hodgepodge *(US)*

fatuité /fatɥite/ **NF** self-complacency, selfconceit, smugness

fatwa /fatwa/ **NF** fatwa ◆ **prononcer une ~ contre qn** to declare *ou* issue a fatwa against sb

faubourg /fobuʀ/ **NM** (inner) suburb ◆ **avoir l'accent des ~s** to have a working-class Paris accent

faubourien, -ienne /fobuʀjɛ̃, jɛn/ **ADJ** *[accent, manières]* working-class Paris

fauchage /foʃaʒ/ **NM** *[de blé]* reaping; *[de champs, prés]* mowing; *[d'herbe] (avec une faux)* scything, mowing, cutting; *(mécanique)* mowing, cutting

fauchaison /foʃɛzɔ̃/ **NF** 1 *(= époque) [de pré]* mowing (time), reaping (time); *[de blés]* reaping (time) 2 *(= action)* ⇒ **fauchage**

fauche /foʃ/ **NF** 1 *(* = vol)* thieving ◆ **il y a beaucoup de ~** a lot of thieving goes on ◆ **lutter contre la ~ dans les supermarchés** to combat shoplifting *ou* thieving in supermarkets 2 †† ⇒ **fauchaison**

fauché, e* /foʃe/ (ptp de **faucher**) **ADJ** *(= sans argent)* (flat *ou* dead) broke* *(attrib)*, hard up*, stony-broke* *(Brit) (attrib)* ◆ **il est ~ comme les blés** he hasn't got a penny to his name, he hasn't got a bean* *(Brit) ou* a brass farthing *(Brit)* ◆ **c'est un éternel ~** he's permanently broke*, he never has a penny ◆ **avec toi, on n'est pas ~ !** *(iro)* you're a dead loss!*, you're a fat lot of good!* *(Brit)*

faucher /foʃe/ ▸ conjug 1 ◂ **VT** 1 *[+ blé]* to reap; *[+ champs, prés]* to mow, to reap; *[+ herbe] (avec une faux)* to scythe, to mow, to cut; *(mécanique-ment)* to mow, to cut 2 *(= abattre) [vent]* to flatten; *[véhicule]* to knock over *ou* down, to mow down; *[tir]* to mow down; *[explosion]* to flatten, to blow over; *(Ftbl)* to bring down ◆ **la mort l'a fauché en pleine jeunesse** he was cut down in his prime ◆ **ils ont été fauchés par un obus de mortier** they were blown up by a shell ◆ **avoir une jambe fauchée par un train** to have a leg cut off *ou* taken off by a train 3 *(* = voler)* to swipe*, to pinch* *(Brit)*, to nick* *(Brit)* ◆ **elle fauche dans les magasins** she pinches* things from shops **VI** *[cheval]* to dish

faucheur, -euse /foʃœʀ, øz/ **NM,F** *(= personne)* mower, reaper **NM** ⇒ **faucheux** **NF** **faucheuse** *(= machine)* reaper, mower ◆ **la Faucheuse** *(littér = mort)* the (Grim) Reaper

faucheux /foʃø/ **NM** harvestman *(Brit)*, harvest spider, daddy-longlegs *(US)*

faucille /fosij/ **NF** sickle ◆ **la ~ et le marteau** the hammer and sickle

faucon /fokɔ̃/ **NM** *(lit)* falcon, hawk; *(Pol)* hawk ◆ **~ crécerelle** kestrel ◆ **~ pèlerin** peregrine falcon ◆ **chasser au ~** to hawk ◆ **chasse au ~** hawking

fauconneau (pl **fauconneaux**) /fokɔno/ **NM** young falcon *ou* hawk

fauconnerie /fokɔnʀi/ **NF** *(= art)* falconry; *(= chasse)* hawking, falconry; *(= lieu)* hawk house

fauconnier /fokɔnje/ **NM** falconer, hawker

faufil /fofil/ **NM** tacking *ou* basting thread

faufilage /fofilaʒ/ **NM** tacking, basting

faufiler /fofile/ ▸ conjug 1 ◂ **VT** to tack, to baste **VPR** **se faufiler** ◆ **se ~ dans** to worm *ou* inch *ou* edge one's way into ◆ **se ~ entre** to dodge in and out of, to thread one's way through ◆ **se ~ parmi la foule** to worm *ou* inch *ou* thread one's way through the crowd, to slip through the crowd ◆ **se ~ entre les** *ou* **au milieu des voitures** to nip *ou* dodge in and out of the traffic, to thread one's way through the traffic ◆ **il se faufila à l'intérieur/au dehors** he wormed *ou* inched *ou* edged his way in/out

faune[1] /fon/ **NM** *(Myth)* faun

faune[2] /fon/ **NF** *(= animaux)* wildlife, fauna; *(péj = personnes)* bunch, crowd ◆ **la ~ et la flore** the flora and fauna ◆ **la ~ marine** marine fauna *ou* animal life ◆ **toute une ~** *(= animaux)* a wide variety of wildlife; ◆ **il y avait toute une ~ devant la gare** *(= gens bizarres)* there was a strange-looking crowd of people in front of the station

faunesque /fonɛsk/ **ADJ** faunlike

faussaire /fosɛʀ/ **NMF** forger

fausse /fos/ **ADJ F** → **faux**[2]

faussement /fosmɑ̃/ **ADV** *[accuser]* wrongly, wrongfully; *[croire]* wrongly, erroneously, falsely ◆ **~ modeste** falsely modest ◆ **~ intéressé** pretending to be interested ◆ **d'un ton ~ indifférent** in a tone of feigned indifference, in a deceptively detached tone of voice

fausser /fose/ ▸ conjug 1 ◂ **VT** 1 *[+ calcul, statistique, fait]* to distort, to alter; *[+ réalité, pensée]* to distort, to pervert; *[+ sens d'un mot]* to distort; *[+ esprit]* to unsettle, to disturb; *[+ jugement]* to distort

◆ **fausser compagnie à qn** to give sb the slip, to slip *ou* sneak away from sb ◆ **vous nous avez de nouveau faussé compagnie hier soir** you gave us the slip again last night, you sneaked *ou* slipped off again last night 2 *[+ clé]* to bend; *[+ serrure]* to break; *[+ poulie, manivelle, charnière]* to buckle, to bend; *[+ essieu, volant, hélice, lame]* to warp, to buckle, to bend ◆ **soudain il se troubla, sa voix se faussa** suddenly he became flustered and his voice became strained

fausset[1] /fosɛ/ **NM** falsetto (voice) ◆ **d'une voix de ~** in a falsetto voice

fausset[2] /fosɛ/ **NM** *[de tonneau]* spigot

fausseté /foste/ **NF** 1 *[d'idée, accusation, dogme]* falseness, falsity 2 *[de caractère, personne]* duplicity, deceitfulness 3 *(† = propos mensonger)* falsity †, falsehood

Faust /fost/ **NM** Faust

faustien, -ienne /fostjɛ̃, jɛn/ **ADJ** Faustian, of Faust

faut /fo/ → **falloir**

faute /fot/ GRAMMAIRE ACTIVE 44.1, 45.2

NF 1 *(= erreur)* mistake, error ◆ **faire** *ou* **commettre une ~** to make a mistake *ou* an error ◆ **~ de grammaire** grammatical mistake *ou* error ◆ **~ de ponctuation** mistake in punctuation, error of punctuation ◆ **~ de prononciation** mispronunciation ◆ **faire des ~s de prononciation** to mispronounce words ◆ **dictée sans ~** error-free dictation

2 *(= mauvaise action)* misdeed; *(Jur)* offence; *(† = péché de chair)* lapse (from virtue), sin (of the flesh) ◆ **commettre une ~** *(gén)* to do something wrong; *(† = péché de chair)* to sin ◆ **une ~ contre** *ou* **envers la religion** a sin *ou* transgression against religion

3 *(Sport)* foul; *(Tennis)* fault ◆ **le joueur a fait une ~** the player committed a foul ◆ **faire une ~ sur qn** to foul sb ◆ **faire une ~ de filet** *(Volley)* to make contact with the net ◆ **faire une ~ de main** to handle the ball ◆ **~ personnelle** *(Basket)* personal foul ◆ **~ de pied** *(Tennis)* foot fault ◆ **faire une ~ de pied** to foot-fault ◆ **faire une double ~ (de service)** *(Tennis)* to serve a double fault, to double-fault ◆ **~ !** *(pour un joueur)* foul!; *(pour la balle)* fault! ◆ **la balle est ~** *(Tennis)* the ball was out; → **parcours, sans-faute**

4 *(= responsabilité)* fault ◆ **par la ~ de Richard/sa ~** because of Richard/him ◆ **c'est (de) la ~ de** *ou* **à* Richard/(de) sa ~** it's Richard's fault/his fault ◆ **la ~ lui en revient** the fault lies with him ◆ **à qui la ~ ?** whose fault is it?, who is to blame? ◆ **c'est la ~ à pas de chance*** it's just bad *ou* hard luck

5 *(locutions)* **~ avouée est à demi** *ou* **à moitié pardonnée** *(Prov)* a sin confessed is a sin half pardoned ◆ **il ne se fait pas ~ de faire** *(littér)* he doesn't shy from *ou* at doing, he doesn't fail to do ◆ **il ne se fit pas ~ d'en parler** *(littér)* he didn't miss a chance to talk about it

◆ **en faute** ◆ **être/se sentir en ~** to be/feel at fault *ou* in the wrong ◆ **prendre qn en ~** to catch sb out

◆ **faute de** for *ou* through lack of ◆ **~ d'argent** for want of money ◆ **~ de temps** for *ou* through lack of time ◆ **~ de mieux** for lack of *ou* want of anything better ◆ **~ de quoi** failing which, otherwise ◆ **relâché ~ de preuves** released for *ou* through lack of evidence ◆ **~ de réponse sous huitaine** failing a reply within a week, if we receive no reply within a week ◆ **~ d'avis contraire** unless otherwise informed ◆ **~ d'y être allé, je ...** since I didn't go, I ... ◆ **je n'y suis pas arrivé, mais ce n'est pas ~ d'avoir essayé** I didn't manage to do it but it wasn't for want *ou* lack of trying ◆ **le combat cessa ~ de combattants** the battle died down, there being nobody left to carry on the fight ◆ **~ de grives, on mange des merles** *(Prov)* you have to cut your coat according to your cloth *(Prov)* beggars can't be choosers *(Prov)*

COMP **faute d'accord** *(Ling)* mistake in (the) agreement

faute de calcul miscalculation, error in calculation

faute de carres *(Ski)* edging mistake

faute civile *(Jur)* civil wrong

faute de conduite *(en voiture) (= erreur)* driving error; *(= infraction)* driving offence

faute d'étourderie ⇒ **faute d'inattention**

faute de français grammatical mistake *(in French)*

faute de frappe typing error

faute de goût error of taste

faute grave *(professionnelle)* gross misconduct *(NonC)*

faute d'impression misprint

faute d'inattention careless *ou* thoughtless mistake

faute d'orthographe spelling mistake

faute pénale *(Jur)* criminal offence

faute professionnelle professional misconduct *(NonC)*

faute de service *(Admin)* act of (administrative) negligence

fauter † /fote/ ▸ conjug 1 ◂ **VI** *[femme]* to sin

fauteuil /fotœj/ **NM** *(gén)* armchair; *(avec dos rembourré, moderne)* easy chair, armchair; *[de président]* chair; *[de théâtre, académicien]* seat ◆ **occuper le ~** *(= siéger comme président)* to be in the chair ◆ **il s'est installé dans le ~ de la présidence/du maire** he became chairman/mayor ◆ **il est arrivé dans un ~*** he romped home*, he walked it* *(Brit)*

COMP **fauteuil de balcon** *(Théât)* balcony seat, seat in the dress circle ◆ **~s de balcon** *(= région de la salle)* dress circle

fauteuil à bascule rocking chair

fauteuil club (big) leather armchair

fauteuil crapaud squat armchair
fauteuil de dentiste dentist's chair
fauteuil de jardin garden chair
fauteuil d'orchestre *(Théât)* seat in the front *ou* orchestra stalls *(Brit) ou* the orchestra *(US)* ◆ **~s d'orchestre** *(= région de la salle)* front *ou* orchestra stalls *(Brit)*, orchestra *(US)*
fauteuil à oreillettes winged chair
fauteuil pivotant swivel chair
fauteuil pliant folding chair
fauteuil roulant wheelchair
fauteuil tournant ⇒ **fauteuil pivotant**; → **voltaire**

fauteur /fotœʀ/ **NM** ◆ **~ de troubles** *ou* **de désordre** troublemaker, mischief-maker, rabble-rouser ◆ **~ de guerre** warmonger

fautif, -ive /fotif, iv/ **ADJ** 1 *[conducteur]* at fault *(attrib)*, in the wrong *(attrib)*; *[élève, enfant]* guilty ◆ **il se sentait ~** he felt he was at fault *ou* in the wrong, he felt guilty 2 *[texte, liste, calcul]* faulty, incorrect; *[citation]* incorrect, inaccurate; *(littér) [mémoire]* poor, faulty **NM,F** ◆ **c'est moi le ~** I'm the one to blame *ou* the guilty one *ou* the culprit

fautivement /fotivmɑ̃/ **ADV** by mistake, in error

fauve /fov/ **ADJ** 1 *[tissu, couleur]* tawny, fawn-coloured *(Brit) ou* -colored *(US)*); *(littér) [odeur]* musky; → **bête** 2 *(Art)* **période ~** Fauvist period **NM** 1 *(= animal)* wildcat ◆ **la chasse aux ~s** big-game hunting ◆ **les (grands) ~s** the big cats ◆ **ça sent le ~ ici** * there's a strong smell of BO in here*, it really stinks (of sweat) in here* 2 *(= couleur)* fawn 3 *(Art)* Fauvist, painter of the Fauvist school ◆ **les Fauves** the Fauvists *ou* Fauves

fauverie /fovʀi/ **NF** big-cat house

fauvette /fovɛt/ **NF** warbler ◆ **~ d'hiver** *ou* **des haies** hedge sparrow, dunnock ◆ **~ des marais** sedge warbler ◆ **~ des roseaux** reed warbler

fauvisme /fovism/ **NM** Fauvism

faux[1] /fo/ **NF** *(Agr)* scythe; *(Anat)* falx

faux[2], **fausse** /fo, fos/ **GRAMMAIRE ACTIVE 53.6**
ADJ 1 *(= imité) [argent, billet]* forged, fake; *[marbre, bijoux, meuble] (= en toc)* imitation *(épith)*; *(pour duper)* false, fake; *[documents, signature]* false, fake, forged; *[tableau]* fake ◆ **fausse pièce** forged *ou* fake coin, dud* ◆ **une fausse carte** a trick card ◆ **~ papiers** false papers, forged identity papers ◆ **fausse monnaie** forged currency ◆ **fausse perle** artificial *ou* imitation pearl ◆ **c'est du ~ Renaissance** it's mock-Renaissance ◆ **il peint des ~ Picasso** he does Picasso forgeries; → **facture**
2 *(= postiche) [dent, nez]* false
3 *(= simulé) [bonhomie, colère, désespoir, modestie]* feigned ◆ **un ~ air de prude** an air of false modesty ◆ **fausse dévotion** false piety
4 *(= mensonger) [déclaration, promesse, prétexte]* false, spurious *(frm)* ◆ **c'est ~** it's wrong *ou* untrue
5 *(= prétendu) [médecin, policier, étudiant]* bogus; *[écrivain]* sham *(épith)* ◆ **un ~ intellectuel/savant** a pseudo-intellectual/-scientist ◆ **~ chômeur** false claimant
6 *(= fourbe) [personne, attitude]* false, deceitful; *[regard]* deceitful
7 *(= inexact) [calcul, numéro, rue]* wrong; *[idée]* wrong, mistaken; *[affirmation, faits]* wrong, untrue; *[instrument de mesure]* inaccurate, faulty; *[instrument de musique, voix]* out of tune; *[raisonnement, vers]* faulty ◆ **c'est ~** *[résultat]* that's wrong; *[fait]* that's wrong *ou* untrue ◆ **il est ~ (de dire) qu'il y soit allé** it's wrong *ou* incorrect to say that he went, it's not true (to say) that he went ◆ **dire quelque chose de ~** to say something (that's) wrong *ou* untrue ◆ **faire fausse route** *(lit)* to go the wrong way, to take the wrong road; *(fig)* to be on the wrong track ◆ **faire un ~ pas** *(lit)* to trip (over), to stumble; *(fig)* to make a foolish mistake; *(par manque de tact)* to make a faux pas ◆ **avoir tout ~** * *(gén = avoir tort)* to get it all wrong; *(à un examen)* to get everything wrong
8 *(= non fondé) [espoir, rumeur, soupçons, principe]* false ◆ **avoir de fausses craintes** to have groundless *ou* ill-founded fears
9 *(= gênant, ambigu) [position, situation, atmosphère]* awkward, false
NM 1 *(= mensonge, Philos)* **le ~** falsehood ◆ **plaider** *ou* **prêcher le ~ pour savoir le vrai** to tell a lie (in order) to get at the truth
2 *(= contrefaçon)* forgery; *(= tableau, meuble, document)* fake, forgery ◆ **faire un ~** to do a forgery ◆ **pour ~ et usage de ~** for forgery and the use of forgeries ◆ **~ en écriture** false entry; → **inscrire**
ADV 1 *[chanter, jouer]* out of tune, off key; → **sonner**
2 *(locutions)* **tomber à ~** to come at the wrong moment ◆ **accuser qn à ~** to accuse sb unjustly *ou* wrongly; → **porter**
COMP faux acacia locust tree, false acacia
fausse alerte false alarm
faux ami *(= traître)* false friend; *(Ling)* false friend, faux ami, deceptive cognate
faux bond ◆ **faire ~ bond à qn** to let sb down, to leave sb in the lurch
faux bourdon *(= insecte)* drone
faux bruit false rumour
faux chignon hairpiece
faux col *[de chemise]* detachable collar; *[de bière]* head
fausses côtes false ribs
fausse couche miscarriage ◆ **faire une fausse couche** to have a miscarriage, to miscarry
faux cul ** *(= homme)* two-faced bastard**; *(= femme)* two-faced bitch**
faux départ *(lit, fig)* false start
faux derche ⇒ **faux cul**
faux dévot, fausse dévote NM,F pharisee
faux ébénier laburnum
fausse fenêtre blind window
fausse fourrure fake *ou* fun fur
faux frais PL extras, incidental expenses
faux frère false friend
faux jeton * two-faced person
fausse joie vain joy
faux jour ◆ **il y a un ~ jour** there's a reflection that makes it difficult to see properly ◆ **sous un ~ jour** in a false light
faux mouvement awkward movement ◆ **j'ai fait un ~ mouvement et maintenant j'ai un torticolis** I turned round too quickly and now I've got a crick in my neck
faux nom false *ou* assumed name
fausse note *(Mus)* wrong note; *(fig)* sour note ◆ **sans une fausse note** *(fig)* without a sour note, smoothly
fausse nouvelle false report
faux ongles false nails
faux ourlet false hem
fausse piste *(lit, fig)* wrong track
faux plafond false ceiling
faux plat *(= montée)* slight incline; *(= creux)* dip (in the road)
faux pli crease
fausse porte false door
faux problème non-problem, non-issue
fausse pudeur false modesty
faux seins falsies*
faux serment false oath
fausse sortie *(Théât)* sham exit ◆ **il a fait une fausse sortie** *(fig)* he made a pretence of leaving
faux témoignage *(= déposition mensongère)* false evidence *(NonC)*; *(= délit)* perjury
faux témoin lying witness

faux-bourdon (pl **faux-bourdons**) /foburdɔ̃/ **NM** *(Mus)* faux bourdon

faux-filet (pl **faux-filets**) /fofilɛ/ **NM** sirloin

faux-fuyant (pl **faux-fuyants**) /fofɥijɑ̃/ **NM** prevarication, evasion, equivocation ◆ **assez de ~s** stop dodging *ou* evading the issue, stop hedging *ou* prevaricating ◆ **user de ~s** to equivocate, to prevaricate, to evade the issue ◆ **dire qch sans ~s** to say sth without beating about the bush

faux-monnayeur (pl **faux-monnayeurs**) /fomɔnɛjœʀ/ **NM** forger, counterfeiter

faux(-)pont (pl **faux(-)ponts**) /fopɔ̃/ **NM** *(Naut)* orlop deck

faux-semblant (pl **faux-semblants**) /fosɑ̃blɑ̃/ **NM** sham, pretence ◆ **user de ~s** to put up a pretence

faux(-)sens /fosɑ̃s/ **NM INV** mistranslation

faux(-)titre (pl **faux(-)titres**) /fotitʀ/ **NM** half-title, bastard title

favela /favela/ **NF** favela

faveur[1] /favœʀ/ **GRAMMAIRE ACTIVE 53.2 NF** 1 *(frm = gentillesse)* favour *(Brit)*, favor *(US)* ◆ **faites-moi la ~ de ...** would you be so kind as to ... ◆ **fais-moi une ~** do me a favour ◆ **obtenir qch par ~** to get sth as a favour ◆ **par ~ spéciale (de la direction)** by special favour (of the management)
2 *(= considération)* favour *(Brit)*, favor *(US)* ◆ **avoir la ~ du ministre** *(littér, hum)* to be in favour with the minister ◆ **gagner/perdre la ~ du public** to win/lose public favour, to find favour/fall out of favour with the public ◆ **être en ~** *(littér)* to be in favour *(auprès de qn* with sb)
3 *(littér, hum)* **~s** favours *(Brit)*, favors *(US)* ◆ **elle lui a refusé ses ~s** she refused him her favours ◆ **elle lui a accordé ses dernières ~s** she bestowed her (ultimate) favours upon him *(littér) (aussi hum)*
4 *(locutions)* **de ~** *[prix, taux]* preferential, special ◆ **billet de ~** complimentary ticket ◆ **régime** *ou* **traitement de ~** preferential treatment
◆ **à la faveur de** thanks to, owing to ◆ **à la ~ de la nuit** under cover of darkness *ou* the night
◆ **en faveur de** *(= à cause de)* in consideration of, on account of; *(= au profit de)* in favour of, for; *(= dans un but charitable)* in aid of, on behalf of, for ◆ **en ma/sa ~** in my/his *(ou* her) favour

faveur[2] /favœʀ/ **NF** *(= ruban)* ribbon, favour *(Brit)*, favor *(US)*

favorable /favɔʀabl/ **GRAMMAIRE ACTIVE 40.2 ADJ**
1 *(= propice) [moment, occasion]* right, favourable *(Brit)*, favorable *(US)*; *[terrain, position, vent]* favourable *(Brit)*, favorable *(US)* ◆ **par temps ~** in favourable weather ◆ **se montrer sous un jour ~** to show o.s. in a favourable light ◆ **un projet ~ à l'emploi** a scheme designed to promote employment
2 *(exprimant l'accord)* **avoir un préjugé ~ envers** to be biased in favour of, to be favourably disposed towards ◆ **jouir d'un préjugé ~** to be favourably thought of ◆ **recevoir un accueil ~** to meet with a favourable reception ◆ **prêter une oreille ~ à** to lend a sympathetic *ou* kindly ear to ◆ **voir qch d'un œil ~** to view sth favourably *ou* with a favourable eye ◆ **le change nous est ~** the exchange rate is in our favour ◆ **je ne suis pas ~ à cette solution** I'm not in favour of that solution ◆ **ils ne sont pas ~s à sa candidature** they do not support his candidacy ◆ **ils ont donné un avis ~** they gave their approval ◆ **ils ont donné** *ou* **émis un avis ~ au projet** they came down *ou* decided in favour of the project

favorablement /favɔʀabləmɑ̃/ **ADV** favourably *(Brit)*, favorably *(US)*

favori, -ite /favɔʀi, it/ **GRAMMAIRE ACTIVE 34.3 ADJ** favourite *(Brit)*, favorite *(US)* **NM** 1 *(= préféré, gagnant probable)* favourite ◆ **le ~ des jeunes** the favourite with *ou* of young people ◆ **ils sont partis ~s** *(Sport)* they started off favourites ◆ **c'est le grand ~ de la course** he's the firm favourite for the race 2 *(Hist)* king's favourite *(Brit)* ou favorite *(US)* NMPL **favoris** side whiskers, sideburns, sideboards *(Brit)* NF **favorite** *(gén)* favourite *(Brit)*, favorite *(US)*; *(Hist)* king's favourite ou mistress

favorisant, e /favɔʀizɑ̃, ɑt/ ADJ *(Méd)* ◆ **facteurs ~s** predisposing factors

favoriser /favɔʀize/ ▸ conjug 1 ◂ VT 1 *(= avantager) [+ candidat, ambitions, commerce, parti]* to favour *(Brit)*, to favor *(US)* ◆ **les événements l'ont favorisé** events favoured him ou were to his advantage ◆ **la fortune le favorise** luck is on his side ◆ **les classes les plus favorisées** the most fortunate ou favoured classes 2 *(= faciliter) [+ dialogue, intégration]* to favour *(Brit)*, to favor *(US)*; *[+ développement]* to favour *(Brit)*, to favor *(US)*, to encourage ◆ **ceci a favorisé sa fuite** this helped him to escape ◆ **ces facteurs favorisent l'apparition du cancer** these factors contribute to the development of cancer ◆ **la hausse des salaires ne favorise pas l'emploi** raising salaries is not good for jobs

favorite /favɔʀit/ NF → **favori**

favoritisme /favɔʀitism/ NM favouritism *(Brit)*, favoritism *(US)* ◆ **faire du ~** to show favouritism

fax /faks/ NM *(= machine)* fax (machine); *(= document)* fax ◆ **envoyer par ~** to send by fax, to fax ◆ **~-modem** fax modem

faxer /fakse/ ▸ conjug 1 ◂ VT to fax

fayot /fajo/ NM 1 *(* Culin)* bean 2 *(* péj = lèche-bottes)* bootlicker, crawler*, brown-nose* *(US)*

fayo(t)tage* /fajɔtaʒ/ NM *(péj)* bootlicking, crawling*, brown-nosing* *(US)*

fayo(t)ter* /fajɔte/ ▸ conjug 1 ◂ VI *(péj = faire du zèle)* to crawl*, to suck up*, to brown-nose* *(US)*

FB (abrév de **franc belge**) → **franc²**

FBI /ɛfbiaj/ NM (abrév de **Federal Bureau of Investigation**) FBI

Fco abrév de **franco**

féal, e (mpl **-aux**) /feal, o/ ADJ †† loyal, trusty NM,F *(littér, hum)* loyal supporter

fébrifuge /febʀifyʒ/ ADJ, NM febrifuge, antipyretic

fébrile /febʀil/ ADJ *(lit, fig)* feverish, febrile *(frm)*

fébrilement /febʀilmɑ̃/ ADV *[s'activer, attendre]* feverishly

fébrilité /febʀilite/ NF feverishness

fécal, e (mpl **-aux**) /fekal, o/ ADJ faecal ◆ **matières ~es** faeces

fèces /fɛs/ NFPL faeces

fécond, e /fekɔ̃, ɔd/ ADJ 1 *(= non stérile) [femelle, fleur]* fertile 2 *(= prolifique) [auteur]* prolific 3 *(= fertile) [période]* productive; *[imagination]* fertile; *[dialogue, sujet, idée]* fruitful; *[esprit]* creative, fertile; *(littér) [terre]* fruitful, rich ◆ **une journée ~e en événements** an eventful day ◆ **ce fut une période ~e en innovations** it was a highly innovative period

fécondable /fekɔ̃dabl(ə)/ ADJ *[ovule]* capable of being fertilized; *[femme, femelle]* capable of becoming pregnant

fécondateur, -trice /fekɔ̃datœʀ, tʀis/ ADJ *(littér)* fertilizing

fécondation /fekɔ̃dasjɔ̃/ NF *[de femme]* impregnation; *[d'animal]* insemination, fertilization; *[de fleur]* pollination, fertilization ◆ **~ in vitro** in vitro fertilization ◆ **~ in vitro et transfert d'embryon** zygote intra-fallopian transfer

féconder /fekɔ̃de/ ▸ conjug 1 ◂ VT *[+ femme]* to make pregnant, to impregnate; *[+ animal]* to inseminate, to fertilize; *[+ fleur]* to pollinate, to fertilize; *(littér) [+ terre]* to make fruitful; *(littér) [+ esprit]* to enrich

fécondité /fekɔ̃dite/ NF *(lit)* fertility, fecundity *(littér)*; *[de terre, sujet, idée]* fruitfulness, richness, fecundity *(littér)* ◆ **les pays à forte/faible ~** countries with a high/low fertility rate

fécule /fekyl/ NF starch ◆ **~ (de pommes de terre)** potato flour

féculent, e /fekylɑ̃, ɑt/ ADJ starchy NM starchy food, starch

FED /ɛfəde/ NM (abrév de **Fonds européen de développement**) EDF

fedayin /fedajin/ NM *(surtout au pl)* fedayee

fédéral, e (mpl **-aux**) /fedeʀal, o/ ADJ federal ◆ **le français ~** *(Helv)* French showing the influence of German

fédéraliser /fedeʀalize/ ▸ conjug 1 ◂ VT to federalize

fédéralisme /fedeʀalism/ NM federalism

fédéraliste /fedeʀalist/ ADJ, NMF federalist

fédérateur, -trice /fedeʀatœʀ, tʀis/ ADJ federative NM,F unifier

fédératif, -ive /fedeʀatif, iv/ ADJ federative

fédération /fedeʀasjɔ̃/ NF federation ◆ **~ syndicale** trade union ◆ **Fédération syndicale mondiale** World Federation of Trade Unions ◆ **la Fédération de Russie** the Russian Federation

fédéré, e /fedeʀe/ (ptp de **fédérer**) ADJ federate

fédérer /fedeʀe/ ▸ conjug 6 ◂ VT to federate

fée /fe/ NF fairy ◆ **une vraie ~ du logis** *(hum)* a real homebody ◆ **la ~ Carabosse** the wicked fairy; → **conte, doigt**

feed-back /fidbak/ NM INV feedback

feeder /fidœʀ/ NM *(Tech)* feeder

feeling /filiŋ/ NM feeling ◆ **faire qch au ~** to do sth intuitively

féerie /fe(e)ʀi/ NF 1 *(Ciné, Théât)* extravaganza, spectacular *(incorporating features from pantomime)* 2 *(littér = vision enchanteresse)* **la ~ des soirées d'été/d'un ballet** the enchantment of summer evenings/of a ballet ◆ **la ~ à jamais perdue de l'enfance** the fairy-tale world of childhood which is gone forever

féerique /fe(e)ʀik/ ADJ magical

feignant, e /fɛɲɑ̃, ɑt/ ADJ, NM,F ⇒ **fainéant, e**

feindre /fɛ̃dʀ/ ▸ conjug 52 ◂ VT *(= simuler) [+ enthousiasme, ignorance, innocence]* to feign ◆ **~ la colère** to pretend to be angry, to feign anger ◆ **~ d'être/de faire** to pretend to be/do ◆ **il feint de ne pas comprendre** he pretends not to understand ◆ **~ de dormir** to feign sleep, to pretend to be asleep VI *(frm)* to dissemble, to dissimulate ◆ **inutile de ~ (avec moi)** no use pretending (with me)

feint, e¹ /fɛ̃, fɛ̃t/ (ptp de **feindre**) ADJ 1 *[émotion, maladie]* feigned, affected ◆ **non ~** *[plaisir, larmes]* genuine 2 *(Archit) [arcade, fenêtre, porte]* false

feinte² /fɛ̃t/ NF 1 *(= manœuvre) (gén)* dummy move; *(Ftbl, Rugby)* dummy *(Brit)*, fake *(US)*; *(Boxe, Escrime)* feint ◆ **faire une ~** *(Rugby)* to dummy *(Brit)*, to fake *(US)* ◆ **~ de passe** *(Rugby)* dummy *(Brit)* ou fake *(US)* pass ◆ **~ de corps** dodge 2 *(littér) (= ruse)* sham *(NonC)*, pretence ◆ **agir/parler sans ~** to act/speak without dissimulation

feinter /fɛ̃te/ ▸ conjug 1 ◂ VT 1 *(Ftbl, Rugby)* to dummy *(Brit)* ou fake *(US)* (one's way past); *(Boxe, Escrime)* to feint at 2 *(* = duper)* to trick, to fool, to take in ◆ **j'ai été feinté** I've been had* ou taken in VI *(Escrime)* to feint

feldspath /fɛldspat/ NM fel(d)spar

fêlé, e /fele/ (ptp de **fêler**) ADJ 1 *[assiette, voix]* cracked 2 *(* = fou)* **être ~** *[personne]* to have a screw loose* ◆ **elle est complètement ~e** she's completely nuts* ou cracked* ◆ **il a le cerveau ~** ou **la tête ~e** he's cracked* ou crackers* NM,F *(* = personne)* crackpot*, nutcase*

fêler /fele/ ▸ conjug 1 ◂ VT to crack VPR **se fêler** to crack ◆ **se ~ le bras** to crack a bone in one's arm

félicitations /felisitasjɔ̃/ GRAMMAIRE ACTIVE 50.6, 51 NFPL congratulations *(pour* on*)*; ◆ **~ !** congratulations! ◆ **faire ses ~ à qn pour** to congratulate sb on ◆ **avec les ~ du jury** *(Scol, Univ)* highly commended, summa cum laude

félicité /felisite/ NF *(littér, Rel)* bliss *(NonC)*

féliciter /felisite/ GRAMMAIRE ACTIVE 40.4, 50.6 ▸ conjug 1 ◂ VT to congratulate *(qn de ou sur qch* sb on sth*)*; ◆ **je vous félicite !** *(iro)* congratulations! *(iro)*, well done! *(iro)* ◆ **eh bien je ne vous félicite pas** you don't get any praise for that VPR **se féliciter** to congratulate o.s. *(de* on*)* to be very glad ou pleased *(de* about*)*; ◆ **je n'y suis pas allé et je m'en félicite** I didn't go and I'm glad ou very pleased I didn't ◆ **il se félicitait d'avoir refusé d'y aller** he was congratulating himself on having refused to go

félidé /felide/ NM feline, felid *(SPÉC)* ◆ **les ~s** the Felidae *(SPÉC)*

félin, e /felɛ̃, in/ ADJ *[allure, grâce]* feline, catlike ◆ **la race ~e** cats, the cat family NM feline ◆ **les ~s** cats, the cat family ◆ **les grands ~s** the big cats

fellah /fela/ NM fellah

fellation /felasjɔ̃/ NF fellatio(n) ◆ **faire une ~ à qn** to perform fellatio on sb

fellinien, -ienne /felinjɛ̃, jɛn/ ADJ *[fantaisie]* Felliniesque ◆ **des femmes à la silhouette fellinienne** full-bodied ou buxom women

félon, -onne /felɔ̃, ɔn/ *(frm)* ADJ perfidious *(frm)*, disloyal, treacherous NM *(aussi hum)* traitor NF **félonne** *(aussi hum)* traitress

félonie /felɔni/ NF *(frm) (= caractère)* perfidy *(frm)*, disloyalty; *(= acte)* act of treachery, perfidy

felouque /fəluk/ NF felucca

fêlure /felyʀ/ NF *(lit, fig)* crack; *(affective)* rift

femelle /fəmɛl/ ADJ female ◆ **panthère ~** female panther ◆ **merle ~** hen-blackbird, female blackbird ◆ **éléphant ~** cow elephant, female elephant ◆ **prise ~** female plug NF female

féminin, e /feminɛ̃, in/ ADJ 1 *[personne, traits]* feminine; *[hormone, corps, population, sexe, sport, tennis, tournoi]* female; *[silhouette]* womanly; *[mode, magazine, épreuve sportive, équipe]* women's ◆ **elle est peu ~e** she's not very feminine ◆ **elle est déjà très ~e** she's already quite a young woman ◆ **il a des traits assez ~s** he has rather feminine features ◆ **premier rôle ~** female lead ◆ **ses conquêtes ~es** his conquests ◆ **la condition ~e** the condition of women ◆ **le taux d'activité ~** the number of women in work; → **éternel, intuition, presse** 2 *(Ling)* feminine; → **rime** *etc*
NM *(Ling)* feminine ◆ **au ~** in the feminine ◆ **ce mot est du ~** this word is feminine

> ⚠ Attention à ne pas traduire automatiquement l'adjectif **féminin** par **feminine** ; la traduction varie en fonction du contexte.

féminisant, e /feminizɑ̃, ɑt/ ADJ feminizing

féminisation /feminizasjɔ̃/ NF feminization

féminiser /feminize/ ▸ conjug 1 ◂ VT *(Bio)* to feminize; *(Ling)* to make feminine, to put in the feminine; *(= rendre efféminé)* to make effeminate ◆ **~ une profession** to increase the number of women in a profession ◆ **profession féminisée** largely female profession ◆ **c'est un secteur féminisé à 80%** women make up 80% of the workforce in this sector

VPR **se féminiser** *(Bio)* to feminize; *(= devenir efféminé)* to become effeminate ◆ **la profession se féminise** an increasing number of women are entering the profession

féminisme /feminism/ NM feminism

féministe /feminist/ ADJ, NMF feminist

féminité /feminite/ NF femininity

femme /fam/ NF 1 *(= individu)* woman ◆ **la** ~ *(= espèce)* woman ◆ **une jeune** ~ a young woman ◆ **c'est la ~ de sa vie** she is his one true love *ou* the love of his life ◆ **elle n'est pas ~ à faire ceci** she's not the type (of woman) to do that ◆ **ce que ~ veut ...** what a woman wants ... ◆ **les ~s et les enfants d'abord !** women and children first! ◆ **une ~-enfant** a childlike woman ◆ **souvent ~ varie (bien fol est qui s'y fie)** *(Prov)* woman is fickle

2 *(= épouse)* wife ◆ **prendre qn pour** ~ † to take sb as one's wife † ◆ **chercher/prendre** ~ † to seek/take a wife †

3 *(profession)* ~ **médecin** woman *ou* lady doctor ◆ **professeur** ~ woman *ou* female teacher

4 *(Jur)* **la ~ Dupuis** Mrs Dupuis

ADJ INV ◆ **être/devenir** ~ *(nubile)* to have reached *ou* attained/reach *ou* attain womanhood; *(n'être plus vierge)* to be/become a woman ◆ **être très** ~ *(féminine)* to be very much a woman, to be very womanly

COMP **femme d'affaires** businesswoman
femme auteur authoress
femme battue battered woman
femme de chambre *(dans un hôtel)* chambermaid; *(de qn)* (lady's) maid
femme de charge † housekeeper
femme entretenue († *péj*) kept woman
femme d'esprit woman of wit and learning
femme fatale femme fatale
la femme au foyer the housewife, the woman (who stays) at home
femme galante † loose woman, courtesan
femme d'intérieur housewife ◆ **être ~ d'intérieur** to take pride in one's home, to be houseproud *(Brit)*
femme de lettres woman of letters
femme de mauvaise vie † loose woman
femme de ménage domestic help, cleaning lady
femme du monde society woman
femme de service *(nettoyage)* cleaner; *(cantine)* dinner lady
femme soldat woman soldier
femme de tête strong-minded intellectual woman; → **vertu**

femmelette /famlɛt/ NF *(péj) (= homme)* weakling; *(= femme)* frail female

femme-objet (pl **femmes-objets**) /famɔbʒɛ/ NF (woman as a) sex object ◆ **elle refuse d'être une** ~ she refuses to be treated as a sex object

fémoral, e (mpl **-aux**) /femɔʀal, o/ ADJ femoral

fémur /femyʀ/ NM thighbone, femur *(SPÉC)*; → **col**

FEN /fɛn/ NF (abrév de **Fédération de l'éducation nationale**) *confederation of teachers' unions*

fenaison /fənɛzɔ̃/ NF *(= époque)* haymaking time; *(= action)* haymaking

fendant /fɑ̃dɑ̃/ NM Swiss white wine *(from the Valais region)*

fendard[1] ⁑ /fɑ̃daʀ/ NM (pair of) trousers, (pair of) pants *(US)*

fendard[2], **e** ⁑ /fɑ̃daʀ, aʀd/ ADJ hilarious ◆ **ce film est vraiment** ~ that film's a real scream *

fendart ⁑ /fɑ̃daʀ/ NM ⇒ **fendard**[1]

fendillé, e /fɑ̃dije/ (ptp de **fendiller**) ADJ *[glace, plâtre, porcelaine, terre, vernis]* crazed; *[bois]* sprung; *[lèvres, peau]* chapped

fendillement /fɑ̃dijmɑ̃/ NM *[de glace, plâtre, porcelaine, terre, vernis]* crazing; *[de bois]* springing; *[de lèvres, peau]* chapping

fendiller /fɑ̃dije/ ▸ conjug 1 ◂ VT *[+ glace, plâtre, porcelaine, terre, vernis]* to craze; *[+ bois]* to spring; *[+ lèvres, peau]* to chap VPR **se fendiller** *[glace, plâtre, porcelaine, terre, vernis]* to craze (over); *[bois]* to spring; *[lèvres, peau]* to chap

fendoir /fɑ̃dwaʀ/ NM chopper, cleaver

fendre /fɑ̃dʀ/ ▸ conjug 41 ◂ VT 1 *[personne] (= couper en deux) [+ bûche, ardoise]* to split; *[+ tissu]* to slit, to slash ◆ ~ **du bois** to chop wood ◆ **il lui a fendu le crâne** he split his skull open

2 *[éléments, cataclysme, accident] [+ rochers]* to cleave; *[+ mur, plâtre, meuble]* to crack ◆ **cette chute lui a fendu le crâne** the fall cracked *ou* split his skull open; → **geler**

3 *(= pénétrer)* to cut *ou* slice through, to cleave through *(littér)* ◆ ~ **les flots/l'air** to cleave through *(littér)* the waves/air ◆ **le soc fend la terre** the ploughshare cuts through the earth ◆ ~ **la foule** to push *ou* cleave *(littér)* one's way through the crowd

4 *(Habillement) [+ jupe]* to put a slit in; *[+ veste]* to put a vent in; *[+ manche]* to put a slash in

5 *(locutions)* **ce récit me fend le cœur** *ou* **l'âme** this story breaks my heart *ou* makes my heart bleed ◆ **spectacle à vous ~ le cœur** heartrending *ou* heartbreaking sight ◆ **soupirs à ~ l'âme** heartrending *ou* heartbreaking sighs

VPR **se fendre** 1 *(= se fissurer)* to crack

2 *[+ partie du corps]* **il s'est fendu le crâne** he has cracked his skull open ◆ **se ~ la lèvre** to cut one's lip ◆ **se ~ la pipe**⁑ *ou* **la pêche**⁑ *ou* **la poire**⁑ *ou* **la gueule***⁑ *(= rire)* to laugh one's head off, to split one's sides *; *(= s'amuser)* to have a good laugh

3 *(Escrime)* to lunge

4 ⁑ **se ~ de** *[+ somme]* to shell out *; *[+ bouteille, cadeau]* to lash out on * ◆ **il ne s'est pas fendu !** he didn't exactly break himself! *

fendu, e /fɑ̃dy/ (ptp de **fendre**) ADJ 1 *[crâne]* cracked; *[lèvre]* cut; *[manche]* slashed; *[veste]* with a vent; *[jupe]* slit ◆ **la bouche ~e jusqu'aux oreilles** grinning from ear to ear 2 (* = *hilare*) **j'étais** ~ I fell about (laughing) *, I cracked up *

fenestrage /fənɛstʀaʒ/ NM ⇒ **fenêtrage**

fenestration /fənɛstʀasjɔ̃/ NF *(Archit, Méd)* fenestration

fenêtrage /fənɛtʀaʒ/ NM *(Archit)* windows, fenestration *(SPÉC)*

fenêtre /f(ə)nɛtʀ/ NF 1 *(gén)* window ◆ **regarder/sauter par la** ~ to look out of *ou* through/jump out of the window ◆ **se mettre à la** ~ *(se diriger vers)* to go to the window; *(s'asseoir)* to sit by the window ◆ **coin** ~ window seat, seat by the window ◆ ~ **à guillotine** sash window ◆ ~ **à battants/à meneaux** casement/mullioned window ◆ ~ **à croisillons** lattice window ◆ ~ **en saillie** bow window, bay window ◆ ~ **à tabatière** skylight ◆ ~ **d'observation** *(Ciné)* port, (projectionist's) window ◆ **c'est une ~ ouverte sur ...** *(fig)* it's a window on ...; → **faux**[2]

2 *[d'enveloppe]* window; *[de formulaire]* space

3 *(Ordin)* window ◆ ~ **de dialogue** dialogue box ◆ ~ **d'aide/d'édition** help/text-editing window ◆ ~ **active** active window

4 *(Anat : dans l'oreille)* fenestra

5 *(Espace)* ~ **de lancement** launch window ◆ ~ **météo** *(Naut)* weather window

fenêtrer /fənetʀe/ ▸ conjug 1 ◂ VT *(Archit)* to make windows in

fenil /fəni(l)/ NM hayloft

fennec /fenɛk/ NM fennec

fenouil /fənuj/ NM fennel

fente /fɑ̃t/ NF 1 *[de mur, terre, rocher]* crack, fissure, cleft; *[de bois]* crack, split 2 *[de volet, palissade]* slit; *[de boîte à lettres]* slot, opening; *[de tirelire]* slit, slot; *[de tête d'une vis]* groove, slot; *[de jupe]* slit; *[de veste]* vent; *[de pèlerine, cape]* slit, armhole; *(Anat)* fissure 3 *(Escrime)* lunge

fenugrec /fənygʀɛk/ NM fenugreek

féodal, e (mpl **-aux**) /feɔdal, o/ ADJ feudal NM feudal lord

féodaliser /feɔdalize/ ▸ conjug 1 ◂ VT to feudalize

féodalisme /feɔdalism/ NM feudalism

féodalité /feɔdalite/ NF *(Hist)* feudal system, feudalism

fer /fɛʀ/ NM 1 *(= métal)* iron ◆ **de** ~ *(lit, fig)* iron *(épith)* ◆ **volonté de** ~ will of iron, iron will ◆ **croire qch dur comme** ~ * to believe sth firmly, to be absolutely convinced of sth; → **âge, chemin, fil** *etc*

2 *(= barre, poutre)* iron girder ◆ ~ **en T/U** T/U girder

3 *(= embout) [de cheval]* shoe; *[de chaussure]* steel tip; *[de club de golf]* iron; *[de flèche, lance]* head, point; *[de rabot]* blade, iron ◆ **mettre un ~ à un cheval** to shoe a horse ◆ **avoir plusieurs ~s au feu** to have several irons in the fire; → **plaie, quatre**

4 *(= outil) (pour repasser)* iron; *[de relieur]* blocking stamp ◆ **donner un coup de ~ à qch** to run the iron over sth, to give sth an iron; *(plus soigneusement)* to press sth

5 *(= arme)* **engager/croiser le** ~ *(Escrime)* to engage/cross swords ◆ **par le ~ et par le feu** by fire and by sword

6 († † = *chaînes*) **~s** chains, fetters, irons ◆ **mettre un prisonnier aux ~s** to clap a prisoner in irons ◆ **être dans les ~s** *(littér)* to be in chains *ou* irons

7 ◆ **~s** †† *(Méd)* forceps

COMP **fer à béton** *(Constr)* steel reinforcement bar
fer à cheval *(lit, fig)* horseshoe ◆ **en ~ à cheval** *[table, bâtiment]* horseshoe-shaped, U-shaped ◆ **disposer qch en ~ à cheval** to arrange sth in a U-shape
fer doux soft iron
fer forgé wrought iron
fer à friser curling tongs
fer à gaufrer goffering iron
fer de lance *(fig)* spearhead
fer à repasser *(électrique)* (electric) iron; *(ancien modèle)* (flat) iron; *(* : pour cartes bancaires)* credit-card machine; → **nager**
fer rouge brand, branding iron ◆ **marquer au ~ rouge** to brand
fer à souder soldering iron
fer à vapeur steam iron

féra /feʀa/ NF *(= poisson)* féra, ferra *(species of fish from lake Geneva)*

fer-blanc (pl **fers-blancs**) /fɛʀblɑ̃/ NM tin(plate) ◆ **une boîte en** *ou* **de** ~ a (tin) can

ferblanterie /fɛʀblɑ̃tʀi/ NF *(= métier)* tinplate making; *(= produit)* tinware; *(= commerce)* tin trade; *(= boutique)* ironmonger's (shop) *(Brit)*, hardware store *(US)*

ferblantier /fɛʀblɑ̃tje/ NM *(= fabricant)* tinsmith; *(= vendeur)* ironmonger *(Brit)*, hardware dealer *(US)* ◆ **ouvrier** ~ tinplate worker

féria /feʀja/ NF feria *(Spanish and Southern French festival)*

férié, e /feʀje/ ADJ ◆ **jour** ~ public holiday, official holiday ◆ **le lundi suivant est** ~ the following Monday is a holiday

férir /feʀiʀ/ ◆ **sans coup férir** LOC ADV without meeting *ou* encountering any opposition

ferler /fɛʀle/ ▸ conjug 1 ◂ VT *(Naut)* to furl

fermage /fɛʀmaʒ/ NM *(= procédé)* tenant farming; *(= loyer)* (farm) rent

ferme[1] /fɛʀm/ ADJ 1 *[chair, fruit]* firm; *[sol]* firm, solid ♦ **cette viande est un peu ~** this meat is a bit tough ♦ **pour des cuisses plus ~s** to tone up the thigh muscles; → **terre**
2 *(= assuré) [main, écriture]* steady, firm; *[voix]* firm; *[style, exécution, trait]* confident, assured; *[marché, cours]* steady ♦ **être ~ sur ses jambes** to be steady on one's legs *ou* feet ♦ **marcher d'un pas ~** to walk with a firm stride *ou* step ♦ **rester ~ dans l'adversité** to remain steadfast in adversity
3 *(= déterminé) [personne, ton]* firm; *[décision, résolution, prise de position]* firm, definite ♦ **avec la ~ intention de faire qch** with the firm intention of doing sth
4 *(= irrévocable) [achat, vente]* firm; *[acheteur, vendeur]* firm, definite ♦ **prix ~s et définitifs** *(Bourse)* firm prices ♦ **ces prix sont ~s** these prices are binding ♦ **"prix : 200 000 € ferme"** "price: €200,000 (not negotiable)"
ADV 1 *(*: intensif) [travailler, cogner]* hard ♦ **boire ~** to drink hard, to be a hard drinker ♦ **discuter ~** to discuss vigorously ♦ **s'ennuyer ~** to be bored stiff*; → **tenir**
2 *[acheter, vendre]* definitely
3 *(Jur)* **condamné à sept ans (de prison) ~** sentenced to seven years imprisonment without remission

ferme[2] /fɛʀm/ NF 1 *(= domaine)* farm; *(= habitation)* farmhouse ♦ **~ collective** collective farm ♦ **~ d'élevage** cattle(-breeding) farm ♦ **~ marine** fish farm; → **cour, fille, valet** 2 *(Jur = contrat)* farm lease; *(Hist = perception)* farming *(of taxes)* ♦ **donner à ~** *[+ terres]* to let, to farm out ♦ **prendre à ~** *[+ terres]* to farm (on lease)

ferme[3] /fɛʀm/ NF *(Constr)* roof timbers, truss

ferme[4] /fɛʀm/ EXCL ♦ **la ~ !**‡ shut up!‡, shut your mouth!‡, pipe down!*; → aussi **fermer**

fermé, e /fɛʀme/ (ptp de **fermer**) ADJ 1 *[porte, magasin, valise]* shut, closed; *[col, route]* closed; *[espace]* closed-in; *[voiture]* locked; *[angle]* narrow; *[voyelle]* close(d), high; *[syllabe]* closed; *[série, ensemble]* closed; *[robinet]* off *(attrib)*; *[chemise]* fastened *(attrib)*, done up *(attrib)* ♦ **la porte est ~e à clé** the door is locked ♦ **la station est ~e au public** the station is closed to the public ♦ **pratiquer un jeu ~** *(Ftbl)* to play a tight game 2 *[milieu, club]* exclusive, select ♦ **cette carrière lui est ~e** this career is not open to him *ou* is closed to him ♦ **économie ~e** closed economy 3 *[visage, air]* inscrutable, impenetrable; *[caractère, personne]* uncommunicative 4 ♦ **être ~ à** *[+ sentiment, qualité]* to be impervious to *ou* untouched by *ou* closed to; *[+ science, art]* to have no interest in

fermement /fɛʀməmɑ̃/ ADV *(lit, fig)* firmly

ferment /fɛʀmɑ̃/ NM *(= micro-organisme)* ferment, fermenting agent, leaven *(NonC)*; *(fig)* ferment *(NonC)* ♦ **~ lactique** starter culture

fermentation /fɛʀmɑ̃tasjɔ̃/ NF fermentation ♦ **en ~** fermenting

fermenté, e /fɛʀmɑ̃te/ (ptp de **fermenter**) ADJ *[aliment, boisson]* fermented ♦ **bière non ~e** unfermented beer ♦ **cidre très peu ~** barely fermented cider

fermenter /fɛʀmɑ̃te/ ► conjug 1 ◄ VI to ferment ♦ **faire ~** to ferment

fermer /fɛʀme/ ► conjug 1 ◄ VT 1 *[+ porte, fenêtre, tiroir, paquet]* to close, to shut; *[+ fichier; boîte de dialogue]* to close ; *[+ rideaux]* to draw, to close; *[+ store]* to pull down, to close; *[+ magasin, café, musée] (le soir)* to shut, to close; *(pour cause de vacances)* to shut (up), to close ♦ **~ à clé** *[+ porte]* to lock; *[+ chambre]* to lock (up) ♦ **~ au verrou** to bolt ♦ **il ferma violemment la porte** he slammed the door (shut) ♦ **~ (la porte) à double tour** to double-lock the door ♦ **~ la porte au nez de qn** to shut *ou* slam the door in sb's face ♦ **~ sa porte** *ou* **sa maison à qn** *(fig)* to close one's door to sb ♦ **maintenant, toutes les portes lui sont fermées** all doors are closed to him now ♦ **~ la porte aux abus** to close the door to abuses ♦ **va ~** go and close *ou* shut the door ♦ **on ferme !** (it's) closing time!, we're closing! ♦ **on ferme en juillet** we close in July, we're closed *ou* shut in July ♦ **on ferme un jour par semaine** we close *ou* shut one day a week, we are closed one day a week; → **parenthèse**
2 *[+ yeux, bouche, paupières]* to close, to shut ♦ **la ferme**‡, **ferme-la**‡ shut *ou* belt up‡ ♦ **je n'ai pas fermé l'œil de la nuit** I didn't get a wink of sleep *ou* I didn't sleep a wink all night ♦ **~ les yeux** *(fig)* to turn a blind eye, to look the other way ♦ **~ les yeux sur** *[+ misère, scandale]* to close *ou* shut one's eyes to; *[+ abus, fraude, défaut]* to turn a blind eye to ♦ **~ son cœur à la pitié** to close one's heart to pity
3 *[+ canif, livre, éventail]* to close, to shut; *[+ lettre]* to close; *[+ parapluie]* to close, to shut; *[+ main, poing]* to close; *[+ manteau, gilet]* to do up, to fasten
4 *(= boucher) [+ chemin, passage]* to block, to bar; *[+ accès]* to shut off, to close off ♦ **des montagnes fermaient l'horizon** mountains blocked off the horizon ♦ **le champ était fermé par une haie** the field had a hedge round it ♦ **~ le jeu** *(Sport)* to tighten up play
5 *(= interdire l'accès de) [+ frontière, col, route]* to close; *[+ aéroport]* to close (down), to shut (down)
6 *(= cesser l'exploitation de) [+ magasin, restaurant, école]* to close (down), to shut (down) ♦ **~ boutique** to close down, to shut up shop ♦ **obliger qn à ~ (boutique)** to put sb out of business ♦ **ils ont dû ~ pour raisons financières** they had to close down *ou* cease trading because of financial difficulties
7 *(= arrêter) [+ liste, souscription, compte en banque, débat]* to close ♦ **~ la marche** to bring up the rear ♦ **~ le cortège** to bring up the rear of the procession
8 *[+ gaz, électricité, radio]* to turn off, to switch off; *[+ eau, robinet]* to turn off; *[+ lumière]* to turn off *ou* out, to switch off; *[+ vanne]* to close
VI 1 *[fenêtre, porte, boîte]* to close, to shut ♦ **cette porte/boîte ferme mal** this door/box doesn't close *ou* shut properly ♦ **ce robinet ferme mal** this tap doesn't turn off properly
2 *[magasin] (le soir)* to close, to shut; *(définitivement, pour les vacances)* to close down, to shut down ♦ **ça ferme à 7 heures** they close *ou* shut at 7 o'clock
VPR **se fermer** 1 *[porte, fenêtre, livre]* to close, to shut; *[fleur, coquillage]* to close (up); *[blessure]* to close (up); *[paupières, yeux]* to close, to shut ♦ **ça se ferme par devant** it does up *ou* fastens at the front ♦ **l'avenir se fermait devant lui** the future was closing before him ♦ **quand on essaie de lui expliquer ça, son esprit se ferme** when you try to explain it to him he closes his mind to it ♦ **son cœur se fermait à la vue de cette misère** he refused to be moved *ou* touched by the sight of this poverty ♦ **son visage se ferma** his face became expressionless ♦ **pays qui se ferme aux produits étrangers** country which closes its markets to foreign products
2 *[personne]* **se ~ à la pitié/l'amour** to close one's heart *ou* mind to pity/love ♦ **il se ferme tout de suite** he just clams up* *ou* closes up

fermeté /fɛʀməte/ NF 1 *[de chair, fruit, sol]* firmness 2 *(= assurance) [de main, écriture]* steadiness, firmness; *[de voix]* firmness; *[de style, exécution, trait]* confidence, assurance 3 *(= détermination)* firmness ♦ **avec ~** firmly, resolutely 4 *(= autorité)* firmness ♦ **il manque de ~ avec son fils** he's not firm enough with his son ♦ **elle lui a parlé avec beaucoup de ~** she spoke to him very firmly 5 *(Bourse)* firmness

fermette /fɛʀmɛt/ NF (small) farmhouse

fermeture /fɛʀmətyʀ/ NF 1 *[de porte]* **la ~ est automatique** the doors close automatically ♦ **"ne pas gêner la fermeture des portes"** "do not obstruct the doors (when closing)"
2 *[de magasin, musée, aéroport, route]* closing ♦ **les jours de ~ du magasin** the days when the shop is closed ♦ **~ annuelle** *(gén)* annual closure; *(sur la devanture)* closed for the holidays ♦ **à (l'heure de) la ~** at closing time ♦ **"fermeture pour (cause de) travaux"** "closed for repairs (*ou* redecoration *ou* refurbishment etc)" ♦ **faire la ~** *(Comm)* to close ♦ **on a fait la ~** *(clients d'un bar)* we stayed until closing time ♦ **la ~ de la chasse** the end of the hunting season
3 *(= cessation d'activité) [de magasin, restaurant, école]* closing down, closure ♦ **~ définitive** permanent closure
4 *(Comptabilité)* closing
5 *(= mécanisme) [de coffre-fort]* catch, latch; *[de vêtement]* fastener, fastening; *[de sac]* fastener, catch, clasp ♦ **~ à glissière**, **~ éclair** ® zip (fastener) *(Brit)*, zipper *(US)*

fermier, -ière /fɛʀmje, jɛʀ/ ADJ ♦ **poulet ~** ≈ free-range chicken, farm chicken ♦ **beurre ~** dairy butter ♦ **fromage ~** farmhouse cheese
NM 1 *(= cultivateur) (gén)* farmer; *(= locataire)* tenant farmer 2 *(Hist)* **~ général** farmer general
NF **fermière** farmer's wife; *(indépendante)* (woman) farmer

fermium /fɛʀmjɔm/ NM fermium

fermoir /fɛʀmwaʀ/ NM *[de livre, collier, sac]* clasp

féroce /feʀɔs/ ADJ 1 *[animal, regard, personne]* ferocious, fierce; → **bête** 2 *(fig) [répression, critique]* fierce, savage; *[envie]* savage, raging; *[appétit]* ferocious, ravenous; *[concurrence]* fierce, harsh, cut-throat ♦ **une satire ~ de la société** a ferocious social satire ♦ **avec une joie ~** with savage joy

férocement /feʀɔsmɑ̃/ ADV ferociously ♦ **un marché ~ compétitif** a ferociously competitive market

férocité /feʀɔsite/ NF *[d'animal, regard, personne]* ferocity, ferociousness, fierceness; *[de répression, critique]* fierceness, savagery; *[de satire, appétit]* ferociousness; *[de concurrence]* fierceness

Féroé /feʀɔe/ N ♦ **les îles ~** the Fa(e)roe Islands

ferrage /feʀaʒ/ NM *[de cheval]* shoeing

ferraillage /feʀɑjaʒ/ NM *(Constr)* (iron) framework

ferraille /feʀɑj/ NF 1 *(= déchets de fer)* scrap (iron), old iron ♦ **tas de ~** scrap heap ♦ **bruit de ~** clanking *ou* rattling noise ♦ **mettre une voiture à la ~** to scrap a car, to send a car for scrap ♦ **bon à mettre à la ~** ≈ good *ou* fit for the scrap heap ♦ **la voiture n'était plus qu'un amas de ~** the car was no more than a heap of twisted metal 2 *(* = monnaie)* small *ou* loose change

ferrailler /feʀɑje/ ► conjug 1 ◄ VI *(lit)* to clash swords ♦ **~ contre** *[+ injustice, préjugés]* to fight against ♦ **~ avec qn** *(= se disputer)* to cross swords with sb

ferrailleur /feʀɑjœʀ/ NM 1 *(= marchand de ferraille)* scrap (metal) merchant 2 *(†† péj)* swashbuckler

Ferrare /feʀaʀ/ NF Ferrara

ferrate /feʀat/ NM ferrate

ferré, e /feʀe/ (ptp de **ferrer**) ADJ 1 *[canne, bâton]* steel-tipped; *[chaussure]* hobnailed; *[lacet]* tagged; *[cheval]* shod; *[roue]* steel-rimmed ♦ **à bout ~** *[canne, bâton]* with a steel *ou* metal tip, steel-tipped; → **voie** 2 *(* = calé)* clued up* *(en, sur* about); ♦ **être ~ sur un sujet** to be well up* in a subject *ou* hot* at a subject, to know a subject inside out

ferrement /fɛʀmɑ̃/ NM 1 (= *garniture*) iron fitment 2 ⇒ **ferrage**

ferrer /feʀe/ ▸ conjug 1 ◂ VT 1 [+ *cheval*] to shoe; [+ *roue*] to rim with steel; [+ *chaussure*] to nail; [+ *lacet*] to tag; [+ *bâton*] to tip, to fit a metal tip to; [+ *porte*] to fit with iron corners 2 [+ *poisson*] to strike

ferret /feʀɛ/ NM 1 [*de lacet*] (metal) tag 2 (*Minér*) ~ **d'Espagne** red haematite

ferreux, -euse /feʀø, øz/ ADJ ferrous

ferrique /feʀik/ ADJ ferric

ferrite /feʀit/ NF ferrite

ferro- /feʀɔ/ PRÉF (*Chim, Phys*) ferro-

ferro-alliage (pl **ferro-alliages**) /feʀɔaljaʒ/ NM iron alloy

ferronnerie /feʀɔnʀi/ NF (= *atelier*) ironworks; (= *métier*) ironwork; (= *objets*) ironwork, ironware ◆ **faire de la ~ d'art** to be a craftsman in wrought iron ◆ **grille en ~** wrought-iron gate ◆ **c'est un beau travail de ~** that's a fine piece of wrought iron work

ferronnier /feʀɔnje/ NM (= *artisan*) craftsman in (wrought) iron; (= *commerçant*) ironware merchant ◆ **~ d'art** craftsman in wrought iron

ferroutage /feʀutaʒ/ NM (*Rail*) piggyback

ferrouter /feʀute/ ▸ conjug 1 ◂ VT (*Rail*) to piggyback

ferroviaire /feʀɔvjɛʀ/ ADJ [*réseau, trafic*] railway (*épith*) (*Brit*), railroad (*épith*) (*US*), rail (*épith*); [*transport*] rail (*épith*)

ferrugineux, -euse /feʀyʒinø, øz/ ADJ [*roche*] ferruginous, iron-bearing; [*eau, source*] chalybeate, iron-bearing

ferrure /feʀyʀ/ NF 1 (= *charnière*) (ornamental) hinge ◆ **~s** [*de porte*] (door) fittings 2 [*de cheval*] shoeing

ferry (pl **ferries**) /feʀi/ NM abrév de **ferry-boat**

ferry-boat (pl **ferry-boats**) /feʀibot/ NM [*de voitures*] (car) ferry; [*de trains*] (train) ferry

fertile /fɛʀtil/ ADJ fertile ◆ **l'affaire a été ~ en rebondissements** the affair triggered off a whole series of events ◆ **journée ~ en événements/en émotions** eventful/emotion-packed day

fertilisant, e /fɛʀtilizɑ̃, ɑ̃t/ ADJ fertilizing

fertilisation /fɛʀtilizasjɔ̃/ NF fertilization

fertiliser /fɛʀtilize/ ▸ conjug 1 ◂ VT to fertilize

fertilité /fɛʀtilite/ NF (*lit, fig*) fertility

féru, e /feʀy/ ADJ (*frm*) ◆ **être ~ de** to be very interested in *ou* keen on (*Brit*) ◆ **c'est un ~ d'informatique** he's a computer buff* ◆ **les ~s d'histoire** history buffs*

férule /feʀyl/ NF (*Hist Scol*) ferula (*wooden batten used formerly to punish schoolboys*) ◆ **être sous la ~ de qn** (*fig*) to be under sb's (firm *ou* iron) rule

fervent, e /fɛʀvɑ̃, ɑ̃t/ ADJ fervent, ardent ◆ **un catholique ~** a devout Catholic ◆ **son admiration ~e pour l'écrivain** his deep admiration for the writer NM,F devotee ◆ **~ de musique** music lover, devotee of music

ferveur /fɛʀvœʀ/ NF fervour (*Brit*), fervor (*US*), ardour (*Brit*), ardor (*US*) ◆ **avec ~** fervently, ardently

fesse /fɛs/ NF 1 (*Anat*) buttock ◆ **les ~s** the buttocks, the bottom, the backside* ◆ **coup de pied aux ~s*** kick up the backside* *ou* in the pants* ◆ **gare à tes ~s*** watch out or you'll get spanked ◆ **le bébé a les ~s rouges** the baby's got a bit of nappy (*Brit*) *ou* diaper (*US*) rash ◆ **on a les flics aux ~s*** the cops are on our tail* ◆ **où je pose mes ~s ?*** where can I park myself?*; → **pousser, serrer** 2 (‡ = *sexe*) **il y a de la ~ dans ce film** there's a lot of bare flesh *ou* there are a lot of tits and bums‡ in that film ◆ **magazine de ~s** girlie *ou* porn magazine* ◆ **histoire de ~s** dirty story

fessée /fese/ NF spanking, smack on the bottom ◆ **je vais te donner une ~** I'm going to smack your bottom

fesse-mathieu †† (pl **fesse-mathieux**) /fɛsmatjø/ NM skinflint

fesser /fese/ ▸ conjug 1 ◂ VT to give a spanking to, to spank

fessier, -ière /fesje, jɛʀ/ ADJ ◆ **les (muscles) ~s** the buttock muscles NM (*Anat*) gluteus (*SPÉC*)

festif, -ive /fɛstif, iv/ ADJ festive

festin /fɛstɛ̃/ NM feast ◆ **c'était un vrai ~** it was a real feast

festival (pl **festivals**) /fɛstival/ NM (*Mus, Théât*) festival ◆ **ce fut un vrai ~ (de talents) !** what a brilliant display (of talent) it was!

festivalier, -ière /fɛstivalje, jɛʀ/ NM,F festival-goer

festivités /fɛstivite/ NFPL (*gén*) festivities; (* = *repas joyeux*) festivities, merrymaking ◆ **les ~ du couronnement** the coronation festivities *ou* celebrations

festoiement /fɛstwamɑ̃/ NM feasting

feston /fɛstɔ̃/ NM (= *guirlande, Archit*) festoon; (*Couture*) scallop ◆ **à ~** scalloped; → **point²**

festonner /fɛstɔne/ ▸ conjug 1 ◂ VT [+ *façade*] to festoon; [+ *robe*] to scallop

festoyer /fɛstwaje/ ▸ conjug 8 ◂ VI to feast

feta /feta/ NF feta (cheese)

fêtard, e* /fɛtaʀ, aʀd/ NM,F (*péj*) reveller ◆ **réveillé par une bande de ~s** woken up by a band of merrymakers *ou* revellers

fête /fɛt/ GRAMMAIRE ACTIVE 50.2

NF 1 (= *réception*) party ◆ **donner une ~** to give *ou* throw a party ◆ **faire une ~ (pour son anniversaire** *etc*) to have a (birthday *etc*) party ◆ **les ~s en l'honneur d'un souverain étranger** the celebrations in honour of a foreign monarch ◆ **~s galantes** (*Art*) scenes of gallantry, fêtes galantes

2 (= *commémoration*) (*religieuse*) feast; (*civile*) holiday ◆ **la Toussaint est la ~ de tous les saints** All Saints' Day is the feast of all the saints ◆ **le 11 novembre est la ~ de la Victoire** 11 November is the day we celebrate the Victory (in the First World War) ◆ **Noël est la ~ des enfants** Christmas is for children

3 (= *jour du prénom*) name day, saint's day ◆ **la ~ de la Saint-Jean** Saint John's day ◆ **souhaiter sa** *ou* **bonne ~ à qn** to wish sb a happy name day

4 (= *congé*) holiday ◆ **les ~s (de fin d'année)** the (Christmas and New Year) celebrations *ou* holidays ◆ **demain c'est ~** tomorrow is a holiday

5 (= *foire*) fair; (= *kermesse*) fête, fair; (= *exposition, salon*) festival, show ◆ **~ paroissiale/communale** parish/local fête *ou* fair ◆ **~ de la bière/du jambon** beer/ham festival ◆ **~ de l'aviation** air show ◆ **~ de la moisson** harvest festival ◆ **~ de la vendange** festival of the grape harvest ◆ **c'est la ~ au village** the fair is on in the village ◆ **la ~ de la ville a lieu le premier dimanche de mai** the town festival takes place on the first Sunday in May; → **comité, jour** *etc*

6 (= *allégresse collective*) **la ~** celebration ◆ **c'est la ~ !** everyone's celebrating!, everyone's in a festive mood! ◆ **c'est la ~ chez nos voisins** our neighbours are celebrating ◆ **toute la ville était en ~** the whole town was celebrating ◆ **la foule en ~** the festive crowd ◆ **air/atmosphère de ~** festive air/atmosphere

7 (*locutions*) **hier il était à la ~** he had a field day yesterday, it was his day yesterday ◆ **je n'étais pas à la ~** it was no picnic (for me)*, I was feeling pretty uncomfortable ◆ **il n'avait jamais été à pareille ~** he was having the time of his life ◆ **être de la ~** to be one of the party ◆ **ça va être ta ~ ‡** you've got it coming to you*, you're going to get it in the neck‡ ◆ **faire sa ~ à qn‡** to bash sb up‡ ◆ **faire la ~*** to live it up*, to have a wild time ◆ **faire ~ à qn** to give sb a warm welcome *ou* reception ◆ **le chien fit ~ à son maître** the dog made a fuss of its master ◆ **elle se faisait une ~ d'y aller/de cette rencontre** she was really looking forward to going/to this meeting ◆ **ce n'est pas tous les jours ~** it's not everyday that we have an excuse to celebrate

COMP **fête carillonnée** great feast day
fête de charité charity bazaar *ou* fair
fête de famille family celebration
fête fixe fixed festival
fête foraine fun fair
la fête du Grand Pardon the Day of Atonement
fête légale public holiday
la fête des Mères Mother's Day, Mothering Sunday (*Brit*)
fête mobile movable feast
la fête des Morts All Souls' Day
fête nationale (*gén*) national holiday; (*en France*) Bastille Day; (*aux États-Unis*) Independence Day; (*au Canada*) Confederation Day; (*en Irlande*) St Patrick's Day
la fête des Pères Father's Day
la fête des Rois Twelfth Night
la fête du travail Labour Day
fête de village village fête

FÊTES LÉGALES

Holidays to which employees are entitled in addition to their paid leave in France are as follows:

Religious holidays: Christmas Day, New Year's Day, Easter Monday, Ascension Day, Pentecost, Assumption (15 August) and All Saints' Day (1 November).

Other holidays: 1 May (la fête du travail), 8 May (commemorating the end of the Second World War), 14 July (Bastille Day) and 11 November (Armistice Day).

When a holiday falls on a Tuesday or a Thursday, many people take an extra day off to fill in the gap before or after the weekend. Doing this is called « faire le pont ».

Fête-Dieu (pl **Fêtes-Dieu**) /fɛtdjø/ NF ◆ **la ~** Corpus Christi

fêter /fete/ GRAMMAIRE ACTIVE 52.2 ▸ conjug 1 ◂ VT [+ *anniversaire, victoire*] to celebrate; [+ *personne*] to fête ◆ **il faut ~ cela !** this calls for a celebration!

fétiche /fetiʃ/ NM (*lit*) fetish; (= *mascotte*) mascot ◆ **son acteur/son équipe ~** his favourite actor/team ◆ **film/roman ~** cult film/novel

fétichiser /fetiʃize/ ▸ conjug 1 ◂ VT to fetishize

fétichisme /fetiʃism/ NM fetishism

fétichiste /fetiʃist/ ADJ, NMF fetishist

fétide /fetid/ ADJ fetid

fétidité /fetidite/ NF fetidness

fétu /fety/ NM ◆ **~ (de paille)** wisp of straw ◆ **emporté comme un ~ (de paille)** [*avion, pont*] swept away as if it were weightless; [*personne*] swept along helplessly

fétuque /fetyk/ NF *ou* m fescue (grass)

feu¹ /fø/

GRAMMAIRE ACTIVE 36.1

1 NOM MASCULIN
2 ADJECTIF INVARIABLE
3 COMPOSÉS

1 - NOM MASCULIN

1 (= source de chaleur) fire ♦ ~ **de bois/tourbe** wood/peat fire ♦ **allumer/faire un** ~ to light/make a fire ♦ **faire du** ~ to have *ou* make a fire ♦ **jeter qch au** ~ to throw sth on the fire ♦ **un ~ d'enfer brûlait dans la cheminée** a fire blazed brightly *ou* a hot fire blazed in the fireplace ♦ **sur un ~ de braises** on glowing embers ♦ **avez-vous du ~ ?** *(pour un fumeur)* have you got a light? ♦ **donner du ~ à qn** to give sb a light ♦ **le ~ éternel** *(Rel)* eternal fire (and damnation) ♦ **l'épreuve du ~** *(Hist)* ordeal by fire ♦ **une soirée du ~ de Dieu*** a fantastic evening ♦ **avoir le ~ au derrière*** *ou* **aux fesses*** *ou* **au cul**** *(= être pressé)* to be in a hell of a hurry*; *(sexuellement)* to be really horny** ♦ **faire ~ des quatre fers** *(littér) [cheval]* to run like lightning, to make the sparks fly; *[personne]* to go all out, to pull out all the stops* ♦ **faire ~ de tout bois** to use all available means *ou* all the means at one's disposal ♦ **jeter** *ou* **lancer ~ et flammes** to breathe fire and fury, to be in a towering rage ♦ **pousser les ~x** *(Naut)* to stoke the boiler ♦ **il faut pousser les ~x pour réduire les inégalités sociales** we must speed up the process of reducing social inequalities; → **coin, long**

2 (= incendie) fire ♦ **mettre le ~ à qch** *(lit)* to set fire to sth, to set sth on fire ♦ **l'assassinat a mis le ~ au pays** the assassination has plunged the country into chaos *ou* turmoil ♦ **ça a mis le ~ aux poudres** it sparked things off ♦ **prendre ~** *[maison, forêt]* to catch fire ♦ **il prend ~ facilement dans la discussion** he's apt to get carried away in arguments ♦ **le ~ a pris dans la grange** fire has broken out in the barn ♦ **au ~ !** fire! ♦ **il y a le ~** there's a fire ♦ **il y a le ~ au grenier !** the attic's on fire! ♦ **il n'y a pas le ~ (au lac) !*** there's no panic!*

♦ **à feu et à sang** ♦ **mettre une ville à ~ et à sang** to put a town to fire and sword ♦ **la région est à ~ et à sang** the region is being torn apart *ou* laid waste by war

♦ **en feu** on fire *(attrib)* ♦ **devant la maison en ~** in front of the burning house ♦ **le piment m'a mis la bouche en ~** the chilli made my mouth burn ♦ **il avait les joues en ~** his cheeks were on fire

3 (Culin = brûleur) burner; *(= plaque électrique)* burner, ring *(Brit)* ♦ **cuisinière à trois ~x** stove with three burners *ou* rings *(Brit)* ♦ **faire cuire à ~ doux/vif** *(sur brûleur ou plaque)* to cook over *ou* on a low/high heat; *(au four)* to cook in a low/hot oven ♦ **plat qui va au ~** *ou* **sur le ~** fireproof dish ♦ **mettre qch/être sur le ~** to put sth/be on the stove ♦ **sur le ~** *(= en préparation)* in the pipeline

♦ **à petit feu** *[cuire]* gently; *[empoisonner]* slowly (but surely) ♦ **tuer** *ou* **faire mourir qn à petit ~** to kill sb by inches

4

♦ **mettre à feu** *[+ fusée]* to fire off; *[+ charge explosive, bombe]* to set off, to trigger; *[+ moteur]* to fire

♦ **mise à feu** *[de fusée, moteur]* firing; *[d'explosif, bombe]* setting off, triggering ♦ **au moment de la mise à ~ de la fusée** at blast-off

5 (= sensation de brûlure, de chaleur) **j'ai le ~ aux joues** my cheeks are burning ♦ **le ~ lui monta au visage** the blood rushed to his face ♦ **le ~ du rasoir** shaving rash, razor burn ♦ **le bébé a des ~x de dents** the baby's cutting a tooth *ou* teething

6 (= ardeur) fire ♦ **plein de ~** full of fire ♦ **parler avec ~** to speak passionately ♦ **un tempérament de ~** a fiery temperament ♦ **avoir du ~ dans les veines** to have fire in one's blood ♦ **avoir le ~ sacré** to burn with zeal ♦ **dans le ~ de l'action/de la discussion** in the heat of (the) action/the discussion

♦ **tout feu tout flamme** wildly enthusiastic, burning with enthusiasm

7 (Mil = tir) fire; *(= combat)* action ♦ **faire ~** to fire ♦ **~ ! fire!** ♦ **à volonté !** fire at will! ♦ **sous le ~ de l'ennemi** under enemy fire ♦ **~ nourri/rasant/roulant** sustained/grazing/running fire ♦ **un ~ roulant de questions** a barrage of questions ♦ **des ~x croisés** crossfire ♦ **être pris entre deux ~x** *(lit, fig)* to be caught in the crossfire ♦ **aller au ~** to go to the firing line ♦ **tué au ~** killed in action; → **arme, baptême**

8

♦ **coup de feu** *(d'une arme)* (gun)shot ♦ **il a reçu un coup de ~** he has been shot ♦ **faire le coup de ~ avec qn** to fight alongside sb ♦ **c'est le coup de ~** *(fig = précipitation, bousculade)* it's all go* ♦ **ma pizza a eu un coup de ~** my pizza's a bit burnt

9 (= revolver) *(arg Crime)* gun, shooter*, rod** *(US)*

10 (= signal lumineux) light ♦ **le ~ était (au) rouge** the lights were (on) red ♦ **s'arrêter aux ~x** to stop at the lights ♦ **naviguer/rouler tous ~x éteints** to sail/drive without lights ♦ **les ~x de la côte** the lights of the shore

11 (= éclairage) light ♦ **les ~x de la rampe** the footlights ♦ **pleins ~x sur ...** spotlight on ... ♦ **être sous le ~ des projecteurs** *(lit)* to be in the glare of the spotlights; *(fig)* to be in the limelight ♦ **les ~x de l'actualité sont braqués sur eux** they are under *ou* in the full glare of the media spotlight

12 (littér = éclat) **les ~x d'une pierre précieuse** the fire of a precious stone ♦ **les diamants jetaient mille ~x** the diamonds were sparkling ♦ **le ~ de son regard** his fiery gaze

13 (littér = lumière) **les ~x de la nuit** the lights in the night ♦ **les ~x du couchant** the fiery glow of sunset ♦ **les ~x de la ville** the lights of the town ♦ **les ~x de l'été** *(= chaleur)* the summer heat

14 (†† = maison) hearth †, homestead ♦ **un hameau de 15 ~x** a hamlet of 15 homesteads

♦ **sans feu ni lieu** *(littér)* with neither hearth nor home †

2 - ADJECTIF INVARIABLE

flame-coloured ♦ **rouge ~** flame red ♦ **chien noir et ~** black and tan dog

3 - COMPOSÉS

feu antibrouillard fog light *ou* lamp
feu arrière tail light, rear light *(Brit)*
feu d'artifice firework display, fireworks ♦ **un beau ~ d'artifice** beautiful fireworks ♦ **le texte est un ~ d'artifice d'images et de métaphores** the text is a virtuoso display of imagery and metaphor
feu de Bengale Bengal light
feu de brouillard ⇒ **feu antibrouillard**
feu de brousse bush fire
feu de camp campfire
feu de cheminée *(= flambée)* fire; *(= incendie)* chimney fire
feu clignotant flashing light
feux de croisement dipped headlights *(Brit)*, low beams *(US)*
feux de détresse hazard (warning) lights
feu follet *(lit, fig)* will-o'-the-wisp
feu de forêt forest fire
feu grégeois Greek fire
feu de joie bonfire
feu orange amber light *(Brit)*, yellow light *(US)*
feu de paille *(fig)* flash in the pan
feu de plancher* *(= pantalon)* high-riders*, clam-diggers*
feu de position sidelight
feux de recul reversing lights *(Brit)*, back-up lights *(US)*
feu rouge *(couleur)* red light; *(= objet)* traffic light ♦ **tournez au prochain ~ rouge** turn at the next set of traffic lights
feux de route headlamps *ou* headlights on full beam
feux de la Saint-Jean *bonfires lit to celebrate the summer solstice*
feux de signalisation traffic lights
feux de stationnement parking lights
feu de stop stop *ou* brake light
feux tricolores traffic lights
feu vert green light ♦ **donner le ~ vert à qn/qch** *(fig)* to give sb/sth the green light *ou* the go-ahead

feu², e /fø/ **ADJ** ♦ ~ **ma tante, ma ~e tante** *(frm)* my late aunt

feuillage /fœjaʒ/ **NM** *(sur l'arbre)* foliage *(NonC)*; *(coupé)* greenery *(NonC)* ♦ **les oiseaux gazouillaient dans le ~** *ou* **les ~s** the birds were twittering among the leaves *ou* the foliage

feuillaison /fœjɛzɔ̃/ **NF** leafing, foliation *(SPÉC)* ♦ **à l'époque de la ~** when the trees come into leaf

feuille /fœj/ **NF** 1 *[d'arbre, plante]* leaf; *(littér = pétale)* petal ♦ ~ **de laurier** bay leaf ♦ **à ~s caduques/persistantes** deciduous/evergreen; → **trèfle, trembler**

2 *[de papier, plastique, bois, ardoise, acier]* sheet ♦ **les ~s d'un cahier** the leaves of an exercise book ♦ **or en ~s** gold leaf ♦ **doré à la ~ d'or** gilded with gold leaf ♦ **bonnes ~s** *(Imprim)* advance sheets ♦ **alimentation ~ à ~** sheet feed ♦ **une ~ d'aluminium** *(Culin)* (a sheet of) aluminium foil

3 *(= bulletin)* slip; *(= formulaire)* form; *(= journal)* paper ♦ ~ **à scandales*** scandal sheet ♦ ~ **d'appel** *(Scol)* daily register (sheet) *(Brit)*, attendance sheet *(US)*

4 *(Ordin)* ~ **de programmation** work *ou* coding sheet ♦ ~ **de style** style sheet ♦ ~ **de calcul** spread sheet

5 *(* = oreille)* ear, lug* *(Brit)* ♦ **dur de la ~** hard of hearing

COMP **feuille de chêne** *(Bot)* oak-leaf; *(Mil)* general's insignia
feuille de chou *(péj = journal)* rag
feuille de garde endpaper
feuille d'impôt tax form *ou* slip
feuille d'impression folded sheet
feuille de maladie *form given by doctor to patient for forwarding to the Social Security*
feuille morte dead leaf ♦ **descendre en ~ morte** *(en avion)* to do the falling leaf
feuille de paye *ou* **paie** pay slip
feuille de présence attendance sheet
feuille de route *(Mil)* travel warrant
feuille de soins ⇒ **feuille de maladie**
feuille de température temperature chart
feuilles de thé tea leaves
feuille de vigne vine leaf; *(sur sculpture)* fig leaf
feuille volante loose sheet; → **oreille**

feuille-morte /fœjmɔʀt/ **ADJ INV** *(= couleur)* russet

feuillet /fœjɛ/ **NM** 1 *[de cahier, livre]* leaf, page; *[de bois]* layer ♦ **~s embryonnaires** *(Bio)* germ layers 2 *[de ruminants]* omasum, manyplies

feuilleté, e /fœjte/ (ptp de **feuilleter**) **ADJ** *[roche]* foliated; *[verre, pare-brise]* laminated **NM** *(= pâtisserie)* ≃ Danish pastry ♦ ~ **au jambon/aux amandes** ham/almond pastry

feuilleter /fœjte/ ▸ conjug 4 ◂ **VT** 1 *[+ pages, livre]* to leaf *ou* flick *ou* flip through; *(= lire rapidement)* to leaf *ou* skim *ou* glance through 2 *(Culin)* *[+ pâte]* to turn and roll

feuilleton /fœjtɔ̃/ **NM** *(Presse, Radio, TV)* serial ♦ ~ **télévisé** television serial; *(populaire et de longue durée)* soap (opera) ♦ **publié en ~** serialized ♦ **ses amours, c'est un véritable ~** his love life is like a soap opera ♦ ~ **judiciaire** *(fig)* judicial saga

feuilletoniste /fœjtɔnist/ **NMF** serial writer

feuillette /fœjɛt/ NF cask, barrel *(containing 114-140 litres)*

feuillu, e /fœjy/ ADJ leafy NM broad-leaved tree

feuillure /fœjyʀ/ NF rebate, rabbet

feulement /følmɑ̃/ NM growl

feuler /føle/ ► conjug 1 ◄ VI to growl

feutrage /føtʀaʒ/ NM felting

feutre /føtʀ/ NM *(= tissu)* felt; *(= chapeau)* felt hat, trilby *(Brit)*, fedora *(US)*; *(= stylo)* felt-tip (pen), felt pen

feutré, e /føtʀe/ (ptp de **feutrer**) ADJ 1 *[étoffe, surface]* felt-like, felt *(épith)*; *[lainage]* matted 2 *[atmosphère, bruit]* muffled ◆ **marcher à pas ~s** to walk with a muffled tread, to pad along *ou* about ◆ **elle descendit l'escalier à pas ~s** she crept down the stairs

feutrer /føtʀe/ ► conjug 1 ◄ VT 1 *(= garnir de feutre)* to line with felt; *(= mettre en feutre)* to mat 2 *(= amortir)* *[+ bruit]* to muffle VI to felt VPR **se feutrer** to felt, to mat ◆ **mon pull-over s'est feutré** my jumper has gone all matted *ou* has felted

feutrine /føtʀin/ NF (lightweight) felt

fève /fɛv/ NF 1 *(= plante, graine)* broad bean ◆ **~ de cacao** cocoa bean 2 *[de galette]* charm *(hidden in cake for Twelfth Night)*; → **LES ROIS** 3 *(*: Can)* bean ◆ **~s jaunes** wax beans ◆ **~s vertes** string *ou* French beans ◆ **~s au lard** pork and beans

février /fevʀije/ NM February; *pour loc voir* **septembre**

fez /fɛz/ NM fez

FF 1 (abrév de **franc français**) FF 2 (abrév de **frères**) bros

FFI /ɛfɛfi/ NFPL (abrév de **Forces françaises de l'intérieur**) → **force**

FFL /ɛfɛfɛl/ NFPL (abrév de **Forces françaises libres**) → **force**

Fg abrév de **faubourg**

fi /fi/ EXCL († †, *hum*) bah!, pooh! ◆ **faire ~ de** *[+ loi, conventions, conseils]* to flout; *[+ danger]* to snap one's fingers at

fiabiliser /fjabilize/ ► conjug 1 ◄ VT *[+ machine]* to make (more) reliable; *[+ méthode]* to make (more) accurate *ou* reliable

fiabilité /fjabilite/ NF *[de chiffres]* accuracy, reliability; *[de personnel]* reliability, dependability; *[de machine]* reliability

fiable /fjabl/ ADJ *[chiffres, données, méthode]* accurate, reliable; *[personne]* reliable, dependable; *[information, machine, produit]* reliable

fiacre /fjakʀ/ NM (hackney) cab *ou* carriage, hackney

fiançailles /fjɑ̃saj/ GRAMMAIRE ACTIVE 51.2 NFPL engagement, betrothal *(littér)* ◆ **ils m'ont invité à leurs ~** they invited me to their engagement party

fiancé, e /fjɑ̃se/ GRAMMAIRE ACTIVE 51.2 ADJ engaged NM *(= homme)* fiancé ◆ **les ~s** *(= couple)* the engaged couple NF **fiancée** fiancée

fiancer /fjɑ̃se/ ► conjug 3 ◄ VT to betroth *(littér)* *(avec, à* to) VPR **se fiancer** to become *ou* get engaged *ou* betrothed *(littér)* *(avec, à* to)

fiasco /fjasko/ NM fiasco ◆ **être un ~** to be a fiasco ◆ **faire (un) ~** *[personne]* to fail miserably; *[négociations, projet]* to end in a fiasco

fiasque /fjask/ NF wine flask

fibranne /fibʀan/ NF bonded fibre

fibre /fibʀ/ NF 1 *(lit : gén)* fibre *(Brit)*, fiber *(US)* ◆ **dans le sens des ~s** with the grain ◆ **~ de bois/carbone** wood/carbon fibre ◆ **~s musculaires** muscle fibres ◆ **~s nerveuses** nerve fibres ◆ **~ de verre** fibreglass *(Brit)*, fiberglass *(US)*, Fiberglas ® *(US)* ◆ **~ optique** *(= câble)* optical fibre; *(= procédé)* fibre optics ◆ **câble en ~s optiques** fibre-optic cable ◆ **riche en ~s (alimentaires)** high in (dietary) fibre 2 *(= âme)* **avoir la ~ maternelle/militaire** to be a born mother/soldier ◆ **faire vibrer la ~ patriotique** to play on *ou* stir patriotic feelings ◆ **sa ~ paternelle n'est pas très développée** he's lacking in paternal feelings

fibreux, -euse /fibʀø, øz/ ADJ *[texture]* fibrous; *[viande]* stringy

fibrillation /fibʀijasjɔ̃/ NF fibrillation

fibrille /fibʀij/ NF fibril, fibrilla

fibrine /fibʀin/ NF fibrin

fibrinogène /fibʀinɔʒɛn/ NM fibrinogen

fibroblaste /fibʀoblast/ NM fibroblast

fibrociment ® /fibʀosimɑ̃/ NM fibrocement

fibromateux, -euse /fibʀɔmatø, øz/ ADJ fibromatous

fibrome /fibʀom/ NM fibroid, fibroma

fibroscope /fibʀɔskɔp/ NM fibrescope *(Brit)*, fiberscope *(US)*

fibroscopie /fibʀɔskɔpi/ NF *endoscopy produced by fibroscope*

fibule /fibyl/ NF *(= broche)* fibula

ficaire /fikɛʀ/ NF lesser celandine

ficelage /fis(ə)laʒ/ NM *(= action)* tying (up); *(= liens)* string

ficeler /fis(ə)le/ ► conjug 4 ◄ VT 1 *[+ paquet, rôti, prisonnier]* to tie up ◆ **ficelé comme un saucisson** tied up in a bundle 2 *(* = habiller)* to get up*, to rig out* *(Brit)* ◆ **ta mère t'a drôlement ficelé !** that's some get-up* *ou* rig-out* *(Brit)* your mother has put you in! ◆ **c'est bien ficelé** *[scénario, film]* it's well put together

ficelle /fisɛl/ NF 1 *(= matière)* string; *(= morceau)* piece *ou* length of string; *(= pain)* stick (of French bread); *(arg Mil)* stripe *(of officer)* 2 *(locutions)* **tirer les ~s** to pull the strings ◆ **connaître les ~s du métier** to know the tricks of the trade, to know the ropes ◆ **la ~ est un peu grosse** you can see right through it

fichage /fiʃaʒ/ NM ◆ **le ~ de la population** filing *ou* recording information on the population

fiche¹ /fiʃ/ NF 1 *(= carte)* (index) card; *(= feuille)* sheet, slip; *(= formulaire)* form ◆ **~ client** customer card ◆ **~ d'état civil** *record of civil status,* ≃ birth and marriage certificate ◆ **~ d'inscription** enrolment form ◆ **~ perforée** perforated card ◆ **~ cartonnée** index card ◆ **~ de paye** *ou* **de paie** pay slip ◆ **~ de police** police record ◆ **~ technique** specification sheet ◆ **mettre en ~** to index ◆ **~-cuisine/-tricot** *[de magazine]* (pull-out) recipe/knitting pattern card; → **signalétique** 2 *(= cheville)* pin, peg; *(Élec)* *(= broche)* pin; *(= prise)* plug

fiche²* /fiʃ/ VB → **ficher²**

ficher¹ /fiʃe/ ► conjug 1 ◄ VT 1 *(= mettre en fiche)* *[+ renseignements]* to file; *[+ suspects]* to put on file ◆ **tous les meneurs sont fichés à la police** the police have files on all subversives 2 *(= enfoncer)* to stick in, to drive in ◆ **~ qch en terre** to drive sth into the ground ◆ **j'ai une arête fichée dans le gosier** I've got a fishbone stuck in my throat, a fishbone has got stuck in my throat

ficher²* /fiʃe/ ► conjug 1 ◄ (ptp courant **fichu**) VT 1 *(= faire)* to do ◆ **qu'est-ce qu'il fiche, il est déjà 8 heures** what on earth *ou* what the heck* is he doing *ou* is he up to* – it's already 8 o'clock ◆ **qu'est-ce que tu as fichu aujourd'hui ?** what have you been up to* *ou* what have you done today? ◆ **il n'a rien fichu de la journée** he hasn't done a thing *ou* a stroke *(Brit)* all day* ◆ **(pour) ce que j'en ai à fiche, de leurs histoires** I couldn't care less about what they're up to*

2 *(= donner)* to give ◆ **~ une trempe à qn** to give sb a slap in the face ◆ **ça me fiche la trouille** it gives me the jitters* *ou* the willies* ◆ **cette odeur/musique me fiche la migraine** that smell/music is giving me a damn⁑ *ou* blinking* *(Brit)* headache ◆ **fiche-moi la paix !** leave me alone! ◆ **eux, faire ça ? je t'en fiche !** you think they'd do that? not a hope!* *ou* you'll be lucky!* ◆ **ça va nous ~ la poisse** that'll bring us bad luck *ou* put a jinx* on us ◆ **je vous fiche mon billet que ...** I bet you anything (you like) *ou* my bottom dollar* that ... ◆ **qui est-ce qui m'a fichu un idiot pareil !** how stupid can you get!*, of all the blinking *(Brit)* idiots!*

3 *(= mettre)* to put ◆ **fiche-le dans le tiroir** stick* *ou* bung* *(Brit)* it in the drawer ◆ **~ qn à la porte** to chuck* *ou* kick* sb out ◆ **se faire ~ ou fiche à la porte** to get o.s. chucked* *ou* kicked* out, to get the push* *ou* the sack* ◆ **~ qch par la fenêtre/à la corbeille** to chuck* sth out of the window/in the wastebasket ◆ **ce médicament me fiche à plat** this medicine knocks me right out* *ou* knocks me for six* ◆ **il a fiché le vase par terre** *(qui était posé)* he knocked the vase off; *(qu'il avait dans les mains)* he dropped the vase ◆ **ça fiche tout par terre** *(fig)* that mucks* *ou* messes everything up ◆ **~ qn dedans** *(= emprisonner)* to put sb inside*; *(= faire se tromper)* to get sb all confused ◆ **ça m'a fichu en colère** that made me really *ou* hopping mad*; → **air²**

4 ◆ **~ le camp** to clear off*, to shove off⁑, to push off* ◆ **fiche-moi le camp !** clear off!*, push off!*

VPR **se ficher** 1 *(= se mettre)* **attention, tu vas te ~ ce truc dans l'œil** careful, you're going to stick that thing in your eye ◆ **se ~ qch dans le crâne** to get sth into one's head *ou* noddle* ◆ **je me suis fichu dedans** I (really) boobed⁑ ◆ **se ~ par terre** to go sprawling, to come a cropper* *(Brit)* ◆ **il s'est fichu en l'air avec sa voiture** he smashed himself up* in his car

2 ◆ **se ~ de qn** *(= rire de)* to make fun of sb; *(= raconter des histoires à)* to pull sb's leg ◆ **se ~ de qch** to make fun of sth ◆ **se ~ de qn/de qch/de faire qch** *(= être indifférent)* not to give a darn about sb/about sth/about doing sth*, not to care two hoots about sb/about sth/about doing sth* ◆ **laisse-le tomber, tu vois bien qu'il se fiche de toi** drop him – it's perfectly obvious that he's leading you on* *ou* he couldn't care less about you ◆ **ils se fichent de nous, 8 € pour une bière !** what (on earth) do they take us for *ou* they really must think we're idiots, €8 for a beer! ◆ **il se fiche de nous, c'est la troisième fois qu'il se décommande** he's giving us the runaround* *ou* really messing us about* *(Brit)* – that's the third time he has cancelled his appointment ◆ **il se fiche du monde !** he's the absolute limit!* ◆ **là, ils ne se sont vraiment pas fichus de nous** they really did us proud! ◆ **je m'en fiche pas mal !** I couldn't care less!, I don't give a damn!* ◆ **il s'en fiche comme de sa première chemise** *ou* **comme de l'an quarante** he couldn't care two hoots* (about it), what the heck does he care!*

3 ⁑ **va te faire fiche !** get lost!*, go to blazes!*, take a running jump!* ◆ **j'ai essayé, mais je t'en fiche** *ou* **va te faire fiche ! ça n'a pas marché** I did try but blow me* *(Brit)*, it didn't work, I did try but I'll be darned* *(US)* if it worked

fichier /fiʃje/ NM *(gén, Ordin)* file; *[de bibliothèque]* catalogue *(Brit)*, catalog *(US)* ◆ **~ d'adresses** mailing list ◆ **~ ASCII** ASCII file ◆ **~ (des) clients** customer file ◆ **~ (informatisé)** data file ◆ **~ de travail** *(Ordin)* scratch *ou* work file ◆ **~ système** system file ◆ **~ (de) texte** text file

fichiste † /fiʃist(ə)/ NMF filing clerk

fichtre* † /fiʃtʀ/ EXCL *(étonnement, admiration)* gosh!*, by Jove! †* ◆ **~ non !** gosh* *ou* goodness, no!

fichtrement * † /fiʃtʀəmɑ̃/ ADV darned*, dashed* *(Brit)* • **ça a coûté ~ cher** it was darned *ou* dashed *(Brit)* expensive*

fichu[1] /fiʃy/ NM (head)scarf; *(Hist : couvrant le corsage)* fichu

fichu[2], **e** * /fiʃy/ (ptp de **ficher**[2]) ADJ 1 *(avant n)* *(= sale) [métier, idée]* wretched*, lousy*; *(= mauvais)* rotten*, lousy*, foul*; *(= sacré)* one heck of a*, a heck of a* • **avec ce ~ temps on ne peut rien faire** with this lousy* *ou* wretched* weather we can't do a thing • **il fait un ~ temps** what rotten* *ou* lousy* *ou* foul* weather • **il a un ~ caractère** he's got a rotten* *ou* lousy* temper • **il y a une ~e différence** there's one heck of a *ou* a heck of a difference*

2 *(après n = perdu, détruit) [malade, vêtement]* done for*; *[appareil]* done for*, bust* • **il/ce veston est ~** he/this jacket has had it* *ou* is done for* • **avec ce temps, le pique-nique est ~** with weather like this, we've had it for the picnic*

3 *(= habillé)* got up*, rigged out* *(Brit)* • **regarde comme il est ~ !** look at the way he's got up! * *ou* rigged out! * *(Brit)* • **il est ~ comme l'as de pique** he looks like a scarecrow

4 *(= bâti, conçu)* **elle est bien ~e** she's well put together*, she's got a nice body • **cet appareil/ce livre est bien ~** this is a clever little gadget/book • **cet appareil/ce livre est mal ~** this gadget/book is hopeless *ou* useless • **il est tout mal ~** he's a fright • **comment c'est ~ ce truc ?** how does this thing work?

5 • **être mal ~** *ou* **pas bien ~** *[malade]* to feel rotten*, to be under the weather* *ou* out of sorts*; *(euph) [femme]* to have the curse*, to be on the rag‡ *(US)*

6 *(= capable)* **il est ~ d'y aller, tel que je le connais** knowing him he's quite capable of going • **il n'est (même) pas ~ de réparer ça** he can't even mend the darned thing*

fictif, -ive /fiktif, iv/ ADJ 1 *(= imaginaire)* fictitious, imaginary • **naturellement, tout ceci est ~** of course this is all fictitious *ou* imaginary 2 *(= faux) [nom, adresse, facture]* false • **des emplois ~s** bogus jobs • **il a reçu un salaire ~** he received a salary for a bogus job • **c'était des prestations fictives** the services were never actually provided 3 *(Fin) [prêt, actifs, contrat]* fictitious • **valeur fictive** *[monnaie]* face value

fiction /fiksjɔ̃/ NF 1 *(= imagination)* fiction, imagination • **cette perspective est encore du domaine de la ~** this prospect still belongs in the realms of fiction • **livre de ~** work of fiction 2 *(= fait imaginé)* invention; *(= situation imaginaire)* fiction; *(= roman)* (work of) fiction, fictional work; *(= film de télévision)* TV drama; *(= mythe)* illusion, myth • **heureusement, ce que je vous décris est une ~** fortunately all that I've been telling you is imaginary

fictivement /fiktivmɑ̃/ ADV *(= faussement)* • **il était ~ employé par la société** he had a bogus job with the company • **facturer ~ des prestations à une société** to present a company with false invoices for services

ficus /fikys/ NM ficus

fidéicommis /fideikɔmi/ NM *(= régime)* trust; *(= fonction)* trusteeship

fidéicommissaire /fideikɔmisɛʀ/ NM trustee

fidèle /fidɛl/ ADJ 1 *(= loyal) (gén)* faithful, loyal; *[époux]* faithful • **~ serviteur/épée** trusty *ou* loyal servant/sword • **demeurer ~ au poste** *(lit, fig)* to be loyal *ou* faithful to one's post • **rester ~ à** *[+ personne]* to remain faithful to; *[+ promesse]* to be *ou* remain faithful to, to keep; *[+ principe, idée]* to remain true *ou* faithful to, to stand by; *[+ habitude, mode]* to keep to; *[+ marque, produit]* to remain loyal to, to stay *ou* stick* with • **être ~ à une tradition** to remain faithful to *ou* to follow a tradition • **~ à la tradition, ...** in keeping with tradition, ... • **~ à ses convictions, il ...** true to his convictions, he ... • **être ~ à soi-même** to be true to o.s. • **~ à lui-même *ou* à son habitude, il est arrivé en retard** true to form *ou* true to character he arrived late

2 *(= habituel) [lecteur, client]* regular, faithful • **nous informons nos ~s clients que ...** we wish to inform our customers that ...

3 *(= exact) [historien, narrateur, son, reproduction]* faithful; *[souvenir, récit, portrait, traduction]* faithful, accurate; *[mémoire, appareil, montre]* accurate, reliable • **sa description est ~ à la réalité** his description is a true *ou* an accurate picture of the situation

NMF 1 *(Rel)* believer • **les ~s** *(= croyants)* the faithful; *(= assemblée)* the congregation

2 *(= client)* regular (customer); *(= lecteur)* regular (reader) • **je suis un ~ de votre émission depuis 10 ans** I have been a regular listener to *(ou* viewer of) your programme for 10 years

3 *(= adepte) [de doctrine, mode, écrivain]* follower, devotee

fidèlement /fidɛlmɑ̃/ ADV 1 *(= conformément à la réalité)* faithfully, accurately • **le combat est ~ décrit dans ce livre** the fight is accurately *ou* faithfully described in this book • **ces images reproduisent ~ ce qui se passe dans la réalité** these pictures are an accurate reflection of reality • **mes propos ont été ~ rapportés** what I said was accurately reported 2 *(= loyalement)* faithfully, loyally 3 *(= régulièrement)* faithfully, regularly • **j'écoute ~ vos émissions depuis 10 ans** I have been listening to your programmes regularly *ou* I have been a regular listener to your programmes for the past 10 years 4 *(= scrupuleusement)* faithfully

fidélisation /fidelizasjɔ̃/ NF • **~ de la clientèle** development of customer loyalty

fidéliser /fidelize/ ▸ conjug 1 ◂ VT • **~ sa clientèle/son personnel** to establish *ou* develop customer/staff loyalty • **~ un public** to build up a loyal audience

fidélité /fidelite/ NF 1 *(= loyauté) (gén)* faithfulness, loyalty; *[de conjoint, lecteur, client]* faithfulness; *(à un produit, un parti)* loyalty, fidelity • **la ~ (conjugale)** fidelity; → **carte, jurer** 2 *(= exactitude) [d'historien, narrateur, son, reproduction]* faithfulness; *[de souvenir, récit, portrait, traduction]* faithfulness, accuracy; *[de mémoire, appareil, montre]* accuracy, reliability

Fidji /fidʒi/ NFPL • **les (îles) ~** Fiji, the Fiji Islands

fidjien, -ienne /fidʒjɛ̃, jɛn/ ADJ Fiji, Fijian NM,F **Fidjien(ne)** Fiji, Fijian

fiduciaire /fidysjɛʀ/ ADJ fiduciary • **circulation ~** fiduciary circulation • **héritier ~** heir, trustee • **monnaie ~** fiat *ou* paper money • **société ~** trust company NM *(Jur)* trustee NF *(= société)* trust company

fiducie /fidysi/ NF trust • **société de ~** trust company

fief /fjɛf/ NM *(Hist)* fief; *(= zone d'influence) [de firme, organisation]* preserve; *[de parti, secte]* stronghold; *(hum = domaine)* private kingdom • **~ (électoral)** electoral stronghold • **ce bureau est son ~** *(hum)* this office is his kingdom

fieffé, e /fjefe/ ADJ • **un ~ menteur** a downright liar • **un ~ réactionnaire** a dyed-in-the-wool reactionary • **il m'a rendu un ~ service** he did me a huge favour

fiel /fjɛl/ NM *(lit)* gall • **propos pleins de ~** words filled with venom *ou* gall

fielleux, -euse /fjɛlø, øz/ ADJ venomous, spiteful

fiente /fjɑ̃t/ NF *[d'oiseau]* droppings

fienter /fjɑ̃te/ ▸ conjug 1 ◂ VI to leave droppings

fier, fière /fjɛʀ/ ADJ 1 *(= arrogant)* proud • **~ comme Artaban *ou* comme un coq *ou* comme un paon** (as) proud as a peacock • **trop ~ pour accepter** too proud to accept • **faire le ~** *(= être méprisant)* to be aloof, to give o.s. airs; *(= faire le brave)* to be full of o.s. • **c'est quelqu'un de pas ~** * he's not stuck-up* • **devant le danger, il n'était plus si ~** when he found himself faced with danger, he wasn't so full of himself any more; → **fier-à-bras**

2 *(littér = noble) [âme, démarche]* proud, noble • **avoir fière allure** to cut a fine figure, to cut a dash

3 • **~ de qch/de faire qch** proud of sth/to do sth • **elle est fière de sa beauté** she's proud of her beauty • **toute fière de sortir avec son papa** as proud as could be to be going out with her daddy • **il n'y a pas de quoi être ~** there's nothing to feel proud about *ou* to be proud of *ou* to boast about • **je n'étais pas ~ de moi** I didn't feel very proud of myself, I felt pretty small* • **elle est fière qu'il ait réussi** she's proud he has succeeded • **il n'était pas peu ~** he was really proud

4 *(intensif : avant n)* **~ imbécile** first-class *ou* prize* idiot • **fière canaille** out-and-out *ou* downright scoundrel • **il a un ~ toupet** he has the devil of a nerve* *ou* cheek* *(Brit)* • **je te dois une fière chandelle** I'm terribly indebted to you

5 *(littér = fougueux) [cheval]* mettlesome • **le ~ Aquilon** the harsh *ou* chill north wind

fier (se) /fje/ ▸ conjug 7 ◂ VPR 1 *(loyauté)* **se ~ à** *[+ allié, promesses, discrétion]* to trust • **on ne peut pas se ~ à lui** you can't trust him, he's not to be trusted, he can't be trusted • **ne vous fiez pas à ce qu'il dit** don't go by *ou* trust what he says • **il a l'air calme mais il ne faut pas s'y ~** he looks calm but that's nothing to go by 2 *(fiabilité)* **se ~ à** *[+ appareil, collaborateur, instinct, mémoire]* to trust, to rely on; *[+ destin, hasard]* to trust to • **ne te fie pas à ta mémoire, prends des notes** don't trust to memory, make notes

fier-à-bras (pl **fiers-à-bras**) /fjɛʀabʀɑ/ NM braggart

fièrement /fjɛʀmɑ̃/ ADV *(= dignement)* proudly

fiérot, e * /fjeʀo, ɔt/ ADJ cocky* • **faire le ~** to show off* • **tout ~ (d'avoir gagné/de son succès)** as pleased as Punch (about winning/about *ou* at his success)

fierté /fjɛʀte/ NF *(gén)* pride; *(péj = arrogance)* pride, haughtiness • **tirer ~ de** to get a sense of pride from • **sa ~ est d'avoir réussi tout seul** he takes pride in having succeeded all on his own • **son jardin est sa ~** his garden is his pride and joy • **je n'ai pas accepté son aide, j'ai ma ~ !** I didn't accept his help – I have my pride!

fiesta * /fjɛsta/ NF rave-up* • **faire la *ou* une ~** to have a rave-up*

fieu /fjø/ NM († *ou dial*) son, lad

fièvre /fjɛvʀ/ NF 1 *(= température)* fever, temperature • **accès de ~** bout of fever • **avoir (de) la ~/beaucoup de ~** to have *ou* run a temperature/a high temperature • **avoir 39 de ~** to have a temperature of 104(°F) *ou* 39(°C) • **une ~ de cheval*** a raging fever • **il a les yeux brillants de ~** his eyes are bright with fever; → **bouton**

2 *(= maladie)* fever • **~ jaune/typhoïde** yellow/typhoid fever • **~ hémorragique** haemorrhagic fever • **~ aphteuse** foot-and-mouth disease • **~ quarte** †† quartan fever *ou* ague • **avoir les ~s** † to have marsh fever • **~ acheteuse** *(hum)* compulsive shopping

3 *(= agitation)* fever, excitement • **parler avec ~** to speak excitedly • **dans la ~ du départ** in the heat of departure, in the excitement of going away • **la ~ de l'or/des élections** gold/election fever • **pays saisi par la ~ du nationa-**

lisme country caught in the grip of nationalist fervour

4 (= *envie*) fever ◆ **être pris d'une ~ d'écrire** to be seized with a frenzied *ou* feverish urge to write

fiévreusement /fjevʀøzmɑ̃/ ADV feverishly, excitedly

fiévreux, -euse /fjevʀø, øz/ ADJ (*Méd, fig*) feverish

FIFA /fifa/ NF (abrév de **Fédération internationale de football association**) FIFA

fifille * † /fifij/ NF (*terme affectueux*) ◆ **viens par ici,** ~ come here, my little girl *ou* sweetheart ◆ **~ à sa maman** (*péj*) mummy's (*Brit*) *ou* mommy's (*US*) little girl

fifre /fifʀ/ NM (= *instrument*) fife; (= *joueur*) fife player

fifrelin † /fifʀəlɛ̃/ NM ◆ **ça ne vaut pas un** ~ it's not worth a brass farthing (*Brit*) *ou* nickel (*US*)

fifty-fifty * /fiftififti/ LOC ADV ◆ **faire** ~ to go fifty-fifty*, to go Dutch* ◆ **on partage, ~ ?** shall we go fifty-fifty* *ou* Dutch*?

figé, e /fiʒe/ (ptp de **figer**) ADJ [*style*] stilted; [*manières*] stiff, constrained; [*société, mœurs*] rigid, ossified; [*attitude, sourire*] set, fixed; [*forme, expression*] set ◆ **une société ~e dans la tradition** a hidebound society ◆ **le village semble ~ dans le temps** the village seems to be stuck in a timewarp ◆ **être ~ dans des structures anciennes** to be set rigidly in outdated structures

figement /fiʒmɑ̃/ NM [*d'huile, sauce*] congealing; [*de sang*] clotting, coagulation, congealing

figer /fiʒe/ ▸ conjug 3 ◂ VT [+ *huile, sauce*] to congeal; [+ *sang*] to clot, to coagulate, to congeal ◆ **le cri le figea sur place** the scream froze *ou* rooted him to the spot ◆ **figé par la peur** terror-stricken ◆ **histoire à vous ~ le sang** bloodcurdling story, story to make one's blood run cold ◆ **des corps figés par la mort** rigid corpses VI [*sauce, huile*] to congeal; [*sang*] to clot, to coagulate, to congeal VPR **se figer** [*sauce, huile*] to congeal; [*sang*] to clot, to coagulate, to congeal; [*sourire, regard*] to freeze; [*visage*] to stiffen, to freeze ◆ **il se figea au garde-à-vous** he stood rigidly to attention ◆ **son sang se figea dans ses veines** his blood froze in his veins

fignolage * /fiɲɔlaʒ/ NM touching up, polishing ◆ **on a pratiquement terminé, le reste c'est du** ~ just a few more finishing touches and we'll be done

fignoler * /fiɲɔle/ ▸ conjug 1 ◂ VT (= *soigner*) to polish up, to put the finishing touches to ◆ **c'est du travail fignolé** that's a really neat job

fignoleur, -euse /fiɲɔlœʀ, øz/ NM,F meticulous worker, perfectionist

figue /fig/ NF fig ◆ **~ de Barbarie** prickly pear ◆ **~ de mer** (edible) sea squirt

figuier /figje/ NM fig tree ◆ **~ de Barbarie** prickly pear ◆ **~ banian** banyan tree

figurant, e /figyʀɑ̃, ɑ̃t/ NM,F (*Ciné*) extra; (*Théât*) walk-on, supernumerary; (*fig*) (= *pantin*) puppet, cipher; (= *complice*) stooge ◆ **avoir un rôle de** ~ (*dans un comité, une conférence*) to play a minor part, to be a mere onlooker; (*dans un crime*) to be a stooge; (*Ciné*) to be an extra; (*Théât*) to have a walk-on part

figuratif, -ive /figyʀatif, iv/ ADJ 1 (*Art*) representational, figurative 2 [*plan, écriture*] figurative NM,F representational *ou* figurative artist

figuration /figyʀasjɔ̃/ NF 1 (*Théât*) (= *métier*) playing walk-on parts; (= *rôle*) walk-on (part); (= *figurants*) walk-on actors; (*Ciné*) (= *métier*) working as an extra; (= *rôle*) extra part; (= *figurants*) extras ◆ **faire de la** ~ (*Théât*) to do walk-on parts; (*Ciné*) to work as an extra 2 (= *représentation*) representation

figure /figyʀ/ NF 1 (= *visage*) face; (= *mine*) face, countenance (*frm*) ◆ **sa ~ s'allongea** his face fell ◆ **elle lui a jeté** *ou* **lancé ses lettres à la ~** she threw his letters in his face ◆ **il lui a jeté** *ou* **lancé à la ~ qu'elle en était incapable** he told her to her face that she wasn't up to it; → **casser**

2 (= *personnage*) figure ◆ **~ équestre** equestrian figure ◆ **les grandes ~s de l'histoire** the great figures of history ◆ **les ~s** (*Cartes*) the court *ou* face cards

3 (= *image*) illustration, picture; (*Danse, Ling, Patinage*) figure; (*Math* = *tracé*) diagram, figure ◆ **~ géométrique** geometrical figure ◆ **faire une** ~ to draw a diagram

4 (*locutions*) **faire ~ de favori** to be generally thought of *ou* be looked on as the favourite ◆ **faire ~ d'idiot** to look a fool ◆ **faire ~ dans le monde** †† to cut a figure in society † ◆ **faire bonne** ~ to put up a good show ◆ **faire pâle ~** to pale into insignificance (*à côté de* beside, next to); ◆ **faire triste** *ou* **piètre** ~ to cut a sorry figure, to look a sorry sight ◆ **il n'a plus ~ humaine** he is disfigured beyond recognition ◆ **prendre** ~ [*construction, projet*] to take shape

COMP **figure de ballet** balletic figure
figure chorégraphique choreographic figure
figures imposées (*Patinage*) compulsory figures ◆ **ça fait partie des ~s imposées** (*fig*) it's part of the compulsory ritual
figures libres (*Patinage*) freestyle (skating)
figure mélodique figure
figure de proue (*Naut*) figurehead; (= *chef*) key figure, figurehead
figure de rhétorique rhetorical figure
figure de style stylistic device

figuré, e /figyʀe/ (ptp de **figurer**) ADJ [*langage, style, sens*] figurative; [*prononciation*] symbolized; [*plan, représentation*] diagrammatic; (*Archit*) figured ◆ **mot employé au** ~ word used figuratively *ou* in the figurative ◆ **au propre comme au** ~ both literally and figuratively, in the literal as well as the figurative sense

figurer /figyʀe/ ▸ conjug 1 ◂ VT to represent ◆ **le peintre l'avait figuré sous les traits de Zeus** the painter had shown *ou* represented him in the guise of Zeus ◆ **la scène figure un palais** the scene is a palace ◆ **la balance figure la justice** scales are the symbol of justice

VI 1 (= *être mentionné*) to appear ◆ **mon frère figure parmi les gagnants** my brother is listed among the winners *ou* is in the list of winners ◆ **son nom figure en bonne place/ne figure pas parmi les gagnants** his name is high up among/does not appear among the winners ◆ **~ sur une liste/dans l'annuaire** to appear on a list/in the directory ◆ **cet article ne figure plus sur votre catalogue** this item is no longer featured *ou* listed in your catalogue

2 (*Théât*) to have a walk-on part; (*Ciné*) to be an extra

VPR **se figurer** to imagine ◆ **figurez-vous une grande maison** picture *ou* imagine a big house ◆ **si tu te figures que tu vas gagner …** if you think *ou* imagine you're going to win … ◆ **figurez-vous que j'allais justement vous téléphoner** it so happens I was just about to phone you ◆ **je ne tiens pas à y aller, figure-toi !** believe it or not, I've no particular desire to go! ◆ **tu ne peux pas te ~ comme il est bête** you wouldn't believe *ou* you can't imagine how stupid he is

figurine /figyʀin/ NF figurine

fil /fil/ NM 1 (= *brin*) [*de coton, nylon*] thread; [*de laine*] yarn; [*de cuivre, acier*] wire; [*de haricot, marionnette*] string; [*d'araignée*] thread; [*d'appareil électrique*] cord ◆ **haricots pleins de ~s/sans ~s** stringy/stringless beans ◆ **~ de trame/de chaîne** weft/warp yarn ◆ **tu as tiré un ~ à ton manteau** you have pulled a thread in your coat ◆ **j'ai tiré un ~ à mon collant** I've laddered my tights (*Brit*), my hose have a run in them (*US*) ◆ **il suffit de tirer un ~ et on découvre l'ampleur du scandale** you only have to scratch the surface to see the true scale of the scandal ◆ **n'avoir plus un ~ de sec** to be soaked through ◆ **~ (à linge)** (washing *ou* clothes) line ◆ **~ (à pêche)** (fishing) line

2 (= *téléphone*) **j'ai ta mère au bout du** ~ I have your mother on the line *ou* phone

◆ **coup de fil** * (phone) call ◆ **donner** *ou* **passer un coup de ~ à qn** * to give sb a ring *ou* call *ou* buzz*, to call *ou* phone *ou* ring (*Brit*) sb (up) ◆ **il faut que je passe un coup de ~** * I've got to make a phone call

3 (= *lin*) linen ◆ **chemise de ~** linen shirt ◆ **chaussettes pur ~ (d'Écosse)** lisle socks

4 (= *sens*) [*de bois, viande*] grain ◆ **couper dans le sens du ~** to cut with the grain ◆ **dans le sens contraire du ~** against the grain; → **droit²**

5 (= *tranchant*) edge ◆ **donner du ~ à un rasoir** to sharpen a razor ◆ **être sur le ~ du rasoir** to be on the razor's edge *ou* on a razor-edge ◆ **passer un prisonnier au ~ de l'épée** to put a prisoner to the sword

6 (= *cours*) [*de discours, pensée*] thread ◆ **suivre/interrompre le ~ d'un discours/de ses pensées** to follow/interrupt the thread of a speech/of one's thoughts ◆ **tu m'as interrompu et j'ai perdu le ~** you've interrupted me and I've lost the thread ◆ **au ~ des jours/des ans** with the passing days/years, as the days/years go (*ou* went) by ◆ **raconter sa vie au ~ de ses souvenirs** to reminisce about one's life ◆ **suivre le ~ de l'eau** to follow the current ◆ **le bateau/papier s'en allait au ~ de l'eau** the boat/paper was drifting away with the stream *ou* current

7 (*locutions*) **mince comme un ~** (as) thin as a rake ◆ **donner du ~ à retordre à qn** to make life difficult for sb ◆ **avoir un ~ à la patte*** to be tied down ◆ **ne tenir qu'à un ~** to hang by a thread ◆ **de ~ en aiguille** one thing leading to another, gradually

COMP **fil d'Ariane** (*Myth*) Ariadne's thread; (*fig*) vital lead
fil conducteur [*d'enquête*] vital lead; [*de récit*] main theme *ou* thread
fil à coudre (sewing) thread
fil à couper le beurre cheesewire
fil dentaire dental floss
fil de discussion (*Internet*) discussion thread
fil électrique electric wire
fil de fer wire ◆ **avoir les jambes comme des ~s de fer** to have legs like matchsticks
fil de fer barbelé barbed wire
fil à plomb plumbline
fil rouge ◆ **le ~ rouge de ses émissions** the common theme linking his programmes
fil de soie dentaire ⇒ **fil dentaire**
fil à souder soldering wire
fil de terre earth wire (*Brit*), ground wire (*US*)
fils de la vierge gossamer (*NonC*), gossamer threads; → **inventer**

fil-à-fil /filafil/ NM INV (= *tissu*) pepper-and-salt (fabric)

filage /filaʒ/ NM [*de laine*] spinning; (*Ciné*) ghost image; (*Théât*) run-through

filament /filamɑ̃/ NM (*Bio, Élec*) filament; [*de glu, bave*] strand, thread

filamenteux, -euse /filamɑ̃tø, øz/ ADJ filamentous

filandière /filɑ̃djɛʀ/ NF (hand-)spinner

filandreux, -euse /filɑ̃dʀø, øz/ ADJ *[viande, légume]* stringy; *[scénario, récit]* incoherent

filant, e /filɑ, ɑt/ ADJ *[liquide]* free-flowing; *(Culin)* runny; *(Méd) [pouls]* very weak; → **étoile**

filao /filao/ NM casuarina, beefwood

filasse /filas/ NF tow ◆ **~ de chanvre/lin** hemp/flax tow ADJ INV ◆ **cheveux (blond) ~** tow-coloured hair ◆ **aux cheveux (blond) ~** tow-haired, tow-headed

filateur /filatœʀ/ NM mill owner

filature /filatyʀ/ NF 1 (= *action de filer la laine, etc*) spinning; (= *usine*) mill 2 (= *surveillance*) shadowing *(NonC)*, tailing* *(NonC)* ◆ **prendre qn en ~** to shadow *ou* tail* sb

fildeferiste, fil-de-fériste (pl **fil-de-féristes**) /fildəfeʀist/ NMF high-wire artist

file /fil/ NF *[de personnes, objets]* line ◆ **~ (d'attente)** queue *(Brit)*, line *(US)* ◆ **~ d'attente** *(d'impression)* print queue ◆ **~ de voitures** *(en stationnement)* line of cars; *(roulant)* line *ou* stream of cars ◆ **se mettre sur** *ou* **prendre la ~ de gauche** *(en voiture)* to move into the left-hand lane ◆ **se garer en double ~** to double-park ◆ **il est en double ~** he's double-parked ◆ **prendre la ~** to join the queue *(Brit) ou* the line *(US)*

◆ **à la file, en file** ◆ **se mettre à la ~** to join the queue *(Brit) ou* the line *(US)* ◆ **se mettre en ~** to line up ◆ **marcher à la ~** *ou* **en ~** to walk in line ◆ **entrer/sortir en ~** *ou* **à la ~** to file in/out ◆ **en ~ indienne** in single file ◆ **chanter plusieurs chansons à la ~** to sing several songs in a row *ou* in succession *ou* one after the other

filé /file/ (ptp de **filer**) NM (= *fil*) thread, yarn ◆ **~ d'or/d'argent** golden/silver thread

filer /file/ ► conjug 1 ◄ VT 1 *[+ laine, coton, acier, verre]* to spin; *[araignée, chenille]* to spin ◆ **~ un mauvais coton** *(au physique)* to be in a bad way; *(au moral)* to get into bad ways ◆ **verre/sucre filé** spun glass/sugar

2 (= *prolonger*) *[+ image, métaphore]* to spin out, to extend; *[+ son, note]* to draw out ◆ **~ le parfait amour** to spin out love's sweet dream ◆ **~ une pièce de théâtre** to run through a play

3 *(Police = suivre)* to shadow, to tail* ◆ **~ le train à qn*** to be hard *ou* close on sb's heels ◆ **j'ai quitté la salle et il m'a filé le train*** I left the room and he followed after me

4 *(Naut) [+ amarre]* to veer out ◆ **navire qui file 20 nœuds** ship doing 20 knots

5 (* = *donner*) **~ qch à qn** to give sth to sb, to give sb sth ◆ **il m'a filé son rhume** he's given me his cold ◆ **~ un coup de poing à qn** to punch sb, to give sb a punch ◆ **file-toi un coup de peigne** run a comb through your hair

6 (= *démailler*) *[+ bas, collant]* to get a run in, to ladder *(Brit)*

VI 1 *[liquide]* to run, to trickle; *[fromage fondu]* to go stringy; *[sirop]* to thread; *[lampe, flamme]* to smoke ◆ **il faisait ~ du sable entre ses doigts** he was running *ou* trickling sand through his fingers

2 (* = *courir, passer*) *[personne]* to fly, to dash; *[temps]* to fly (by) ◆ **~ bon train/comme le vent/à toute allure** to go at a fair speed/like the wind/at top speed ◆ **il fila comme une flèche devant nous** he darted *ou* zoomed* straight past us ◆ **~ à la poste/voir qn** to dash to the post office/to see sb

3 (* = *s'en aller*) to go off ◆ **le voleur avait déjà filé** the thief had already made off* ◆ **il faut que je file** I must dash *ou* fly* ◆ **file dans ta chambre** off to your room with you ◆ **allez, file, garnement !** clear off, you little pest!* ◆ **~ à l'anglaise** to run off *ou* away, to take French leave *(Brit)* ◆ **~ entre les doigts de qn** *[poisson]* to slip between sb's fingers; *[voleur, argent]* to slip through sb's fingers ◆ **les billets de 20 €, ça file vite** 20 euro notes disappear in no time ◆ **~ doux** to toe the line

4 (= *se démailler*) *[maille]* to run; *[bas, collant]* to run, to ladder *(Brit)* ◆ **mon collant a filé** I've got a run *ou* ladder in my tights *(Brit)*, my hose have a run in them *(US)*

5 *[monnaie]* to slide, to slip ◆ **laisser ~ le dollar** to let the dollar slide

filet /filɛ/ NM 1 (= *petite quantité*) *[d'eau, sang]* dribble, trickle; *[de fumée]* wisp; *[de lumière]* (thin) shaft; (= *trait*) thin line ◆ **il avait un ~ de voix** he had a reedy voice ◆ **mettez un ~ de vinaigre** add a drop *ou* a dash of vinegar ◆ **arrosez d'un ~ d'huile d'olive** drizzle with olive oil

2 *[de poisson]* fillet; *[de viande]* fillet *(Brit) ou* filet *(US)* steak ◆ **donnez-moi un rôti dans le ~** I'd like some fillet *(Brit) ou* filet *(US)* of beef ◆ **~ mignon** (pork) tenderloin ◆ **~ américain** *(Belg)* steak tartare

3 (= *nervure*) *[de langue]* frenum; *[de pas de vis]* thread; *(Typo)* rule; *(Archit)* fillet, list(el) ◆ **~s nerveux** nerve endings

4 *(Pêche, Sport)* net ◆ **~ (à provisions)** string bag ◆ **~ (à bagages)** (luggage) rack ◆ **~ à crevettes/à papillons/à cheveux** shrimping/butterfly/hair net ◆ **~ à poissons** *ou* **de pêche** fishing net, fishnet *(US)* ◆ **~ dérivant** drift net ◆ **envoyer la balle au fond des ~s** *(Ftbl)* to send the ball into the back of the net ◆ **~ !** *(Tennis)* let! ◆ **envoyer la balle dans le ~** *(Tennis)* to put the ball into the net, to net the ball ◆ **monter au ~** *(Tennis)* to go up to the net ◆ **il a dû monter au ~ pour défendre son projet** *(fig)* he had to stick his neck out to defend his proposal ◆ **travailler sans ~** *[acrobates]* to perform without a safety net; *(fig)* to be out on one's own ◆ **tendre un ~** *[chasseur]* to set a snare; *[police]* to set a trap ◆ **le ~ se resserre** the net is closing in *ou* tightening ◆ **coup de ~** *(fig)* haul ◆ **attirer qn dans ses ~s** *(fig)* to ensnare sb

filetage /filtaʒ/ NM (= *action*) thread cutting, threading; *[de pas de vis]* thread

fileter /filte/ ► conjug 5 ◄ VT 1 *[+ vis, tuyau]* to thread; (= *étirer*) *[+ métal]* to draw ◆ **tissu violet fileté d'or** purple cloth shot through with gold threads 2 *(Culin) [+ poisson]* to fillet

fileur, -euse /filœʀ, øz/ NM,F spinner

filial, e[1] (mpl **-iaux**) /filjal, jo/ ADJ filial

filiale[2] /filjal/ NF ◆ **(société) ~** subsidiary (company) ◆ **~ commune** joint venture ◆ **~ à 100%** wholly-owned subsidiary ◆ **~ de distribution/vente** distribution/sales subsidiary

filiation /filjasjɔ̃/ NF *[de personnes]* filiation; *[d'idées, mots]* relation ◆ **être issu de qn par ~ directe** to be a direct descendant of sb

filière /filjɛʀ/ NF 1 (= *succession d'étapes*) *[de carrière]* path; *[d'administration]* channels, procedures ◆ **la ~ administrative** the administrative procedures *ou* channels ◆ **passer par** *ou* **suivre la ~ pour devenir directeur** to work one's way up to become a director ◆ **il a suivi la ~ classique pour devenir professeur** he followed the classic route into teaching ◆ **de nouvelles ~s sont offertes aux jeunes ingénieurs** new paths are open to young engineers

2 *(Scol, Univ = domaine d'études spécifique)* course, subjects ◆ **~s technologiques/scientifiques/artistiques** technology/science/arts courses ◆ **nouvelles ~s** new subjects ◆ **suivre une ~ courte/longue** to do a short/long course

3 (= *réseau*) network ◆ **les policiers ont réussi à remonter toute la ~** the police have managed to trace the network right through to the man at the top ◆ **de nouvelles ~s pour le passage de la drogue** new channels for drug trafficking

4 *(Écon = secteur d'activité)* industry ◆ **~ bois/pêche/agroalimentaire** timber/fishing/food-processing industry ◆ **ce pays a choisi la ~ nucléaire** this country chose the nuclear(-power) option *ou* opted to use nuclear power

5 *(Phys Nucl)* **~ à eau légère/à eau pressurisée** light-water/pressurized water reactor technology

6 *(Tech) (pour étirer)* drawplate; *(pour fileter)* screwing die

7 *[d'araignée, chenille]* spinneret

filiforme /filifɔʀm/ ADJ *[antenne, patte]* thread-like, filiform *(SPÉC)*; *[jambes]* long and slender; *[corps]* lanky; *(Méd) [pouls]* thready

filigrane /filigʀan/ NM *[de papier, billet]* watermark; *[d'objet]* filigree

◆ **en filigrane** *(lit)* as a watermark ◆ **ce projet apparaît** *ou* **est inscrit en ~ dans le texte** this project is hinted at in the text ◆ **cette possibilité est inscrite en ~ dans la loi** this possibility is implicit in the law ◆ **sa haine apparaissait en ~ dans ses paroles** there was veiled hatred in his words ◆ **la frustration qui apparaît en ~ dans ses toiles** the sense of frustration that runs through his paintings

filigraner /filigʀane/ ► conjug 1 ◄ VT *[+ papier, billet]* to watermark; *[+ objet]* to filigree

filin /filɛ̃/ NM rope

fille /fij/ NF 1 *(dans une famille)* daughter ◆ **la ~ de la maison** the daughter of the house ◆ **la ~ Martin** *(souvent péj)* the Martin girl ◆ **la peur, ~ de la lâcheté** *(littér)* fear, the daughter of cowardice ◆ **oui, ma ~** *(Rel)* yes, my child ◆ **c'est bien la ~ de son père/de sa mère** she's very much her father's/her mother's daughter, she's just like her father/her mother; → **jouer**

2 (= *enfant*) girl; (= *femme*) woman; († = *vierge*) maid † ◆ **c'est une grande/petite ~** she's a big/little girl ◆ **elle est belle ~** she's a good-looking girl ◆ **c'est une bonne** *ou* **brave ~** she's a nice girl *ou* a good sort ◆ **elle n'est pas ~ à se laisser faire** she's not the type to let herself *ou* the type of girl who lets herself be messed about ◆ **être encore/rester ~** † to be still/stay unmarried ◆ **mourir ~** † to die an old maid; → **jeune, vieux**

3 († = *servante*) **~ de ferme** farm girl ◆ **~ d'auberge/de cuisine** serving/kitchen maid ◆ **ma ~** †† my girl

4 († *péj* = *prostituée*) whore ◆ **~ en carte** registered prostitute

COMP **fille d'Ève** daughter of Eve
fille d'honneur *(Hist)* maid of honour
fille de joie prostitute
fille publique streetwalker
fille des rues streetwalker
fille de salle *(restaurant)* waitress; *(hôpital)* ward orderly
fille à soldats *(péj †)* soldiers' whore
fille soumise † registered prostitute

fille-mère † (pl **filles-mères**) /fijmɛʀ/ NF *(péj)* unmarried mother

fillette /fijɛt/ NF 1 (= *petite fille*) (little) girl ◆ **rayon ~s** girls' department ◆ **elle chausse du 42 ~*** *(hum)* her feet are like boats* 2 (= *bouteille*) ≈ (half-)bottle

filleul /fijœl/ NM godson, godchild; (= *personne parrainée*) sponsoree ◆ **~ de guerre** adoptive son (in wartime)

filleule /fijœl/ NF goddaughter, godchild; (= *personne parrainée*) sponsoree

film /film/ NM 1 *(Ciné)* (= *pellicule*) film; (= *œuvre*) film, movie *(surtout US)* ◆ **le ~ fantastique/d'avant-garde** *(genre)* fantasy/avant-garde films ◆ **le grand ~** † the feature (film) ◆ **repasser le ~ des événements de la journée** *(fig)* to go over the sequence of the day's events ◆ **il n'a rien compris au ~*** *(fig)* he didn't get it at all; → **métrage**

2 (= *mince couche*) film ◆ **~ alimentaire** *ou* **étirable** *(transparent)* Clingfilm ® *(Brit)*, clingwrap *(Brit)*, Saran Wrap ® *(US)* ◆ **~ plastique de congélation** freezer film

COMP **film d'animation** animated film
film d'archives archive film
film documentaire documentary (film)
film d'épouvante ⇒ **film d'horreur**
film de guerre war film
film d'horreur horror film
film muet silent film
film noir film noir
film parlant talking film, talkie*
film policier detective film
film publicitaire (= *publicité*) advertising film; (= *film promotionnel*) promotional film
film à sketches film made up of sketches; → **action[1], aventure, espionnage**

filmage /filmaʒ/ NM *[de personne, paysage]* filming; *[de film, scène]* filming, shooting

filmer /filme/ ▸ conjug 1 ◂ VT *[+ personne, paysage]* to film; *[+ film, scène]* to film, to shoot ◆ **théâtre filmé** film drama

filmique /filmik/ ADJ film *(épith)*, cinematic ◆ **l'œuvre ~ de Renoir** Renoir's film work

filmographie /filmɔgʀafi/ NF filmography

filmologie /filmɔlɔʒi/ NF film studies

filoguidé, e /filogide/ ADJ wire-guided

filon /filɔ̃/ NM 1 *(Minér)* vein, seam ◆ **il exploite ce ~ depuis des années** he's worked that seam for years 2 *(= opportunité, secteur)* **trouver le ~** * to strike it lucky *ou* rich ◆ **ils ont flairé le (bon) ~** they're on to something good ◆ **on n'a pas fait de recherches sur ce sujet, c'est un ~ qu'il faudrait exploiter** no research has been done on that subject - it's a line worth developing ◆ **c'est un bon ~** * *[métier]* it's a cushy number*; *[secteur lucratif]* there's a lot of money to be made in it

filou /filu/ NM (= *escroc*) crook, swindler; (= *enfant espiègle*) rascal

filouter* /filute/ ▸ conjug 1 ◂ VT *[+ personne]* to cheat, to do* *(Brit)*, to diddle* *(Brit)*; *[+ argent, objets]* to snaffle*, to filch* ◆ **il m'a filouté (de) 5 €** he's cheated *ou* diddled *(Brit)* me out of 5 euros* VI (= *tricher*) to cheat ◆ **il est difficile de ~ avec le fisc** it's hard to cheat *ou* diddle *(Brit)* the taxman*

filouterie /filutʀi/ NF fraud *(NonC)*, swindling *(NonC)*

fils /fis/ NM son ◆ **le ~ de la maison** the son of the house ◆ **M. Martin ~** young Mr Martin ◆ **Martin ~** *(Comm)* Mr Martin junior ◆ **Martin et Fils** *(Comm)* Martin and Son (*ou* Sons) ◆ **le ~ Martin** the Martin boy ◆ **elle est venue avec ses deux ~** she came with her two sons *ou* boys ◆ **c'est bien le ~ de son père** he's very much his father's son, he's just like his father ◆ **les ~ de la France/de Charlemagne** *(frm)* the sons of France/of Charlemagne ◆ **être le ~ de ses œuvres** *(frm)* to be a self-made man ◆ **oui, mon ~** *(Rel)* yes, my son ◆ **le Fils de l'homme/de Dieu** *(Rel)* the Son of Man/of God
COMP **fils de famille** young man of means *ou* with money
fils de garce** †, **fils de pute**** son of a bitch**
fils spirituel spiritual son; → **papa**

filtrage /filtʀaʒ/ NM *[de liquide, données]* filtering; *(Élec)* filtration; *[de nouvelles, spectateurs]* screening

filtrant, e /filtʀɑ̃, ɑ̃t/ ADJ *[substance]* filtering *(épith)*; *[verre]* filter *(épith)* ◆ **barrage ~** *(sur route)* roadblock *(letting through a few vehicles)* ◆ **virus ~** filterable virus ◆ **le pouvoir ~ de ces lunettes de soleil** the way these sunglasses filter sunlight

filtrat /filtʀa/ NM filtrate

filtration /filtʀasjɔ̃/ NF *[de liquide]* filtering, filtration

filtre /filtʀ/ NM *(gén)* filter; *[de cigarette]* filter tip ◆ **~ à café** coffee filter ◆ **papier-~** filter paper ◆ **cigarette à bout ~** filter-tipped cigarette ◆ **"avec ou sans filtre ?"** "tipped or plain?" ◆ **~ à air/huile/essence** air/oil/fuel filter ◆ **~ anti-UV** UV filter ◆ **~ solaire** sunscreen

filtrer /filtʀe/ ▸ conjug 1 ◂ VT *[+ liquide, lumière, son, données]* to filter; *[+ nouvelles, spectateurs, appels téléphoniques]* to screen VI *[liquide]* to filter (through), to seep through; *[lumière, son]* to filter through; *[information]* to leak out, to filter through ◆ **rien n'a filtré de leur conversation** none of their conversation got out

fin[1], fine[1] /fɛ̃, fin/ ADJ 1 (= *mince*) *[tranche, couche, papier, tissu]* thin; *[cheveux, sable, poudre, papier de verre]* fine; *[pointe, pinceau]* fine; *[bec d'oiseau]* thin, pointed; *[lame]* sharp, keen; *[écriture]* small; *[taille, doigt, jambe]* slender, slim ◆ **plume ~e** fine-nibbed pen ◆ **petits pois ~s/très ~s** high-quality/top-quality garden peas ◆ **une petite pluie ~e** a fine drizzle; → **peigne, sel**
2 (= *raffiné, supérieur*) *[lingerie, porcelaine, travail]* fine, delicate; *[traits, visage, or, pierres]* fine; *[silhouette, membres]* neat, shapely; *[produits, aliments]* high-class, top-quality; *[mets]* choice, exquisite; *[chaussures]* fine-leather ◆ **faire un repas ~** to have a gourmet meal ◆ **vins ~s** fine wines ◆ **perles ~es** real pearls ◆ **~e fleur de froment** finest wheat flour ◆ **la ~e fleur de l'armée française** the pride *ou* flower of the French army ◆ **le ~ du ~** the last word *ou* the ultimate (*de* in) → **épicerie, partie[2]**
3 (= *très sensible*) *[vue, ouïe]* sharp, keen; *[goût, odorat]* fine, discriminating ◆ **avoir l'oreille** *ou* **l'ouïe ~e** to have a keen ear, to have keen hearing; → **nez**
4 (= *subtil*) *[personne]* astute; *[esprit, observation]* shrewd, sharp; *[allusion, nuance]* subtle; *[sourire]* wise, shrewd ◆ **faire des plaisanteries ~es sur qch** to joke wittily about sth ◆ **il n'est pas très ~** he's not very bright ◆ **ce n'est pas très ~ de sa part** that's not very clever of him ◆ **comme c'est ~ !** *(iro)* (that's) very clever! *(iro)* ◆ **c'est ~ ce que tu as fait !** *(iro)* that was clever of you! *(iro)* ◆ **il se croit plus ~ que les autres** he thinks he's smarter than everybody else ◆ **bien ~ qui pourrait le dire !** who knows! ◆ **tu as l'air ~ !** you look a right idiot!* ◆ **jouer au plus ~ avec qn** to try to outsmart sb
5 *(avant n = habile)* expert ◆ **~ connaisseur** connoisseur ◆ **~e cuisinière** skilled cook ◆ **~ gourmet, ~e bouche** *ou* **gueule*** gourmet ◆ **~e lame** expert swordsman ◆ **~ stratège** expert strategist ◆ **~ tireur** crack shot
6 *(avant n : intensif)* **au ~ fond de la campagne** right in the heart of the country, in the depths of the country ◆ **au ~ fond du tiroir** right at the back of the drawer ◆ **du ~ fond de ma mémoire** from the depths *ou* recesses of my memory ◆ **savoir le ~ mot de l'histoire** to know the real story
ADV *[moudre, tailler]* finely; *(Billard)* fine ◆ **écrire ~** to write small ◆ **~ prêt** quite *ou* all ready ◆ **~ soûl** dead *ou* blind drunk*
COMP **fines herbes** (sweet) herbs, fines herbes
fin limier (keen) sleuth
fine mouche, fin renard sharp customer; → aussi **adj 5**

fin[2] /fɛ̃/ GRAMMAIRE ACTIVE 53.4
NF 1 *(gén)* end; *[d'année, réunion]* end, close; *[de compétition]* end, finish, close ◆ **"Fin"** *[de film, roman]* "The End" ◆ **vers** *ou* **sur la ~** towards the end ◆ **le quatrième en partant de** *ou* **en commençant par la ~** the fourth from the end, the last but three *(Brit)* ◆ **~ juin, à la ~ (de) juin** at the end of June ◆ **~ courant** *(Comm)* at the end of the current month ◆ **jusqu'à la ~** to the very end ◆ **jusqu'à la ~ des temps** *ou* **des siècles** until the end of time ◆ **la ~ du monde** the end of the world ◆ **avoir des ~s de mois difficiles** to have difficulty making ends meet ◆ **en ~ de semaine** towards *ou* at the end of the week ◆ **on n'en verra jamais la ~** we'll never see the end of this ◆ **à la ~ il a réussi à se décider** he eventually managed *ou* in the end he managed to make up his mind ◆ **tu m'ennuies, à la ~ !*** you're beginning to get on my nerves! ◆ **en ~ d'après-midi** towards the end of the afternoon, in the late afternoon ◆ **en ~ de liste** at the end of the list ◆ **en ~ de compte** (= *tout bien considéré*) when all is said and done, in the end, at the end of the day; (= *en conclusion*) in the end, finally ◆ **sans ~** *[discussion, guerre, histoire]* endless, never-ending; *[errer, tourner]* endlessly ◆ **arriver en ~ de course** *[vis]* to screw home; *[piston]* to complete its stroke; *[batterie]* to wear out; * *[personne]* to be worn out, to come to the end of the road ◆ **en ~ de séance** *(Bourse)* at the close ◆ **un chômeur en ~ de droits, un ~ de droits*** *an unemployed person no longer entitled to benefit* ◆ **prendre ~** *[réunion]* to come to an end; *[contrat]* to terminate, to expire (*le* on); ◆ **être sur sa ~, toucher à** *ou* **tirer à sa ~** to be coming to an end, to be drawing to a close ◆ **on arrive à la ~ du spectacle** we're getting near the end of the show ◆ **mettre ~ à** to put an end to, to end ◆ **mettre ~ à ses jours** to put an end to one's life ◆ **mener qch à bonne ~** to bring sth to a successful conclusion, to carry sth off successfully ◆ **faire une ~** † (= *se marier*) to settle down; → **début, mot** *etc*
2 (= *ruine*) end ◆ **c'est la ~ de tous mes espoirs** that's the end of all my hopes ◆ **c'est la ~ de tout !*** *ou* **des haricots !*** that's the last straw!
3 (= *mort*) end, death ◆ **avoir une ~ tragique** to die a tragic death, to meet a tragic end ◆ **il a eu une belle ~** he had a fine end ◆ **la ~ approche** the end is near
4 (= *but*) end, aim, purpose; *(Philos)* end ◆ **~ en soi** end in itself ◆ **il est arrivé** *ou* **parvenu à ses ~s** he achieved his aim *ou* ends ◆ **à cette ~** to this end, with this end *ou* aim in view ◆ **à quelle ~ faites-vous cela ?** what is your purpose *ou* aim in doing that? ◆ **c'est à plusieurs ~s** it has a variety of uses ◆ **à seule ~ de faire** for the sole purpose of doing ◆ **à toutes ~s utiles** *(frm)* for your information ◆ **aux ~s de la présente loi** *(Jur)* for the purposes of this Act ◆ **la ~ justifie les moyens** *(Prov)* the end justifies the means
COMP **fin d'exercice** *(Comptabilité)* end of the financial year
fin de section *[d'autobus]* stage limit, fare stage
fin de semaine *(Can)* weekend
fin de série (= *produit*) end-of-line stock *(NonC)*
fin de siècle *(péj)* ADJ INV decadent, fin de siècle; → **non-recevoir**

final, e[1] (mpl **finals** *ou* **-aux**) /final, o/ ADJ 1 (= *terminal*) final ◆ **la scène ~e** the final *ou* last scene ◆ **quand le coup de sifflet ~ a retenti** when the final whistle went *ou* blew; → **point[1]** 2 (= *marquant la finalité : Ling, Philos*) final ◆ **proposition ~e** *(Ling)* purpose *ou* final clause ◆ **au** *ou* **en ~** in the end

finale[2] /final/ NF 1 *(Sport)* final ◆ **quart de ~** quarterfinal ◆ **demi-~** semifinal ◆ **huitième/seizième de ~** third/second round *(in a six-round tournament)* ◆ **elle a joué la ~** she played in the final ◆ **ils sont arrivés en ~** they're through to the final 2 (= *syllabe*) final *ou* last syllable; (= *voyelle*) final *ou* last vowel

finale[3] /final/ NM *(Mus)* finale

finalement /finalmɑ̃/ ADV *(gén)* 1 (= *à la fin*) in the end, finally ◆ **ils se sont ~ réconciliés** in the end they were reconciled ◆ **il a ~ décidé de s'abstenir** in the end he decided to abstain; *(après hésitation, réflexion)* he finally decided to abstain 2 (= *en fin de compte*) after all ◆ **ce n'est pas si mal ~** it's not so bad after all ◆ **~ je ne suis pas plus avancé** I've ended up no further forward

⚠ Au sens de 'en fin de compte', **finalement** ne se traduit pas par **finally**.

finalisation /finalizasjɔ̃/ NF *[d'accord, contrat]* finalization ◆ **un protocole en voie de ~** a protocol in the process of being finalized

finaliser /finalize/ ▸ conjug 1 ◂ VT [1] *(= achever)* to finalize [2] *(= orienter)* to target

finalisme /finalism/ NM finalism

finaliste /finalist/ ADJ *(Philos)* finalist NMF *(Philos, Sport)* finalist

finalité /finalite/ NF *(= but)* end, aim; *(= fonction)* purpose, function

finance /finɑ̃s/ NF [1] *(Pol = recettes et dépenses)* **~s** finances ◆ **les Finances** *(= administration)* the Ministry of Finance, ≃ the Treasury, the Exchequer *(Brit)*, the Treasury Department *(US)* ◆ **il est aux Finances** *(employé)* he works at the Ministry of Finance; *(ministre)* he is Minister of Finance ◆ **~s publiques** public funds ◆ **l'état de mes ~s*** the state of my finances, my financial state ◆ **les ou mes ~s sont à sec*** I'm right out of funds*; → **loi, ministre** [2] *(Fin)* finance ◆ **la (haute) ~** *(= activité)* (high) finance; *(= personnes)* (top) financiers ◆ **le monde de la ~** the financial world ◆ **il est dans la ~** he's in banking *ou* finance; → **moyennant**

financement /finɑ̃smɑ̃/ NM financing ◆ **plan de ~** financial plan ◆ **~ à court/long terme** short-/long-term financing ◆ **~-relais** bridge *ou* interim financing ◆ **~ à taux fixe** fixed-rate financing ◆ **~ par emprunt** debt financing

financer /finɑ̃se/ ▸ conjug 3 ◂ VT to finance VI * to fork out*

financier, -ière /finɑ̃sje, jɛʀ/ ADJ [1] *(Fin)* financial ◆ **soucis ~s** money *ou* financial worries; → **place** [2] *(Culin)* **(sauce) financière** sauce financière NM *(Fin)* financier; *(Culin)* almond sponge finger

financièrement /finɑ̃sjɛʀmɑ̃/ ADV financially

finasser* /finase/ ▸ conjug 1 ◂ VI to use trickery ◆ **inutile de ~ avec moi !** there's no point trying to use your tricks on me!

finasserie* /finasʀi/ NF trick, dodge*, ruse

finasseur, -euse /finasœʀ, øz/, **finassier, -ière** /finasje, jɛʀ/ NM,F trickster, dodger*

finaud, e /fino, od/ ADJ wily NM,F ◆ **c'est un petit ~** he's a crafty one*, there are no flies on him*, he's nobody's fool

finauderie /finodʀi/ NF *(= caractère)* wiliness, guile; *(= action)* wile, dodge* *(Brit)*

fine[2] /fin/ NF [1] *(= alcool)* liqueur brandy ◆ **~ Champagne** fine champagne cognac [2] *(= huître)* **~ de claire** green oyster

finement /finmɑ̃/ ADV *[ciselé, brodé]* finely, delicately; *[faire remarquer]* subtly; *[agir, manœuvrer]* cleverly, shrewdly

finesse /fines/ NF [1] *(= minceur) [de cheveux, poudre, pointe]* fineness; *[de lame]* keenness, sharpness; *[d'écriture]* smallness; *[de taille]* slenderness, slimness; *[de couche, papier]* thinness [2] *(= raffinement) [de broderie, porcelaine, travail, traits]* delicacy, fineness; *[d'aliments, mets]* refinement ◆ **son visage est d'une grande ~** he has very refined *ou* delicate features ◆ **un plat d'une grande ~** a very refined dish [3] *(= sensibilité) [de sens]* sharpness, sensitivity; *[de vue, odorat, goût, ouïe]* sharpness, keenness [4] *(= subtilité) [de personne]* sensitivity; *[d'esprit, observation, allusion]* subtlety NFPL **finesses** *[de langue, art]* niceties, finer points; *[d'affaire]* ins and outs ◆ **il connaît toutes les ~s** he knows all the ins and outs

finette /finɛt/ NF brushed cotton

fini, e /fini/ (ptp de **finir**) ADJ [1] *(= terminé)* finished, over ◆ **tout est ~ entre nous** it's all over between us, we're finished, we're through* ◆ **~e la rigolade !*** the party* *ou* the fun is over! ◆ **(c'est) ~ de rire maintenant** the fun *ou* joke is over now ◆ **ça n'est pas un peu ~ ce bruit* ?** will you stop that noise! [2] *(* = fichu) [acteur, homme politique, chose]* finished ◆ **il est ~** he's finished, he's a has-been* [3] *(= usiné, raffiné)* finished ◆ **costume bien/mal ~** well-/badly-finished suit [4] *(péj = complet) [menteur, escroc, salaud]* out-and-out, downright; *[ivrogne, bon à rien]* absolute, complete [5] *(Math, Philos, Ling)* finite ◆ **grammaire à états ~s** finite state grammar NM *[d'ouvrage]* finish ◆ **ça manque de ~** it needs a few finishing touches

finir /finiʀ/ ▸ conjug 2 ◂ VT [1] *(= achever) [+ travail, études, parcours]* to finish, to complete; *(= clôturer) [+ discours, affaire]* to finish, to end, to conclude ◆ **finis ton travail ou de travailler avant de partir** finish your work before you leave ◆ **il a fini ses jours à Paris** he ended his days in Paris ◆ **~ son verre** to finish one's glass, to drink up ◆ **finis ton pain !** finish your bread!, eat up your bread! ◆ **il finira (d'user) sa veste en jardinant** he can wear out his old jacket (doing the) gardening ◆ **il a fini son temps** *[soldat, prisonnier]* he has done *ou* served his time

[2] *(= arrêter)* to stop *(de faire* doing); ◆ **finissez donc !** do stop it! ◆ **finissez de vous plaindre !** stop complaining! ◆ **vous n'avez pas fini de vous chamailler ?** haven't you quite finished squabbling? ◆ **tu as fini de m'embêter ?** have you quite finished?

[3] *(= parachever) [+ œuvre d'art, meuble, mécanisme]* to put the finishing touches to

VI [1] *(= se terminer)* to finish, to end ◆ **le cours finit à deux heures** the class finishes *ou* ends at two ◆ **les vacances finissent demain** the holidays end *ou* are over tomorrow ◆ **la réunion/le jour finissait** the meeting/the day was drawing to a close ◆ **le sentier finit ici** the path ends *ou* comes to an end here ◆ **il est temps que cela finisse** it is time it (was) stopped ◆ **ce film finit bien** this film has a happy ending ◆ **tout cela va mal ~** it will all end in disaster ◆ **et pour ~** and finally

◆ **finir en qch** to end in sth ◆ **ça finit en pointe/en chemin de terre** it ends in a point/in a dirt track ◆ **mots finissant en -ble** words ending in *ou* with -ble

◆ **finir par** ◆ **~ par une dispute/un concert** to end in an argument/with a concert ◆ **ils vont ~ par avoir des ennuis** they'll end up getting into trouble ◆ **il a fini par se décider** he finally *ou* eventually made up his mind, he made up his mind in the end ◆ **tu finis par m'ennuyer** you're beginning to annoy me ◆ **ça finira bien par s'arranger** it'll work out all right in the end *ou* eventually

◆ **en finir** ◆ **en ~ avec qch/qn** to have *ou* be done with sth/sb ◆ **il faut en ~ avec cette situation** we'll have to put an end to this situation ◆ **nous en aurons bientôt fini** we'll soon be finished with it, we'll soon have it over and done with ◆ **quand en auras-tu fini avec tes jérémiades ?** when will you ever stop moaning? ◆ **je vais lui parler pour qu'on en finisse** I'll talk to him so that we can get the matter settled ◆ **qui n'en finit pas, à n'en plus ~** *[route, discours, discussion]* never-ending, endless ◆ **elle n'en finit pas de se préparer** she takes ages to get ready ◆ **on n'en aurait jamais fini de raconter ses bêtises** you could go on for ever talking about the stupid things he's done ◆ **il a des jambes qui n'en finissent pas** he's all legs*

[2] *[personne]* to finish up, to end up ◆ **il finira mal** he will come to a bad end ◆ **il a fini directeur/en prison** he ended up as (a) director/in prison ◆ **~ dans la misère** to end one's days in poverty, to end up in poverty ◆ **~ troisième/cinquième** *(Sport)* finish third/fifth

[3] *(= mourir)* to die ◆ **il a fini dans un accident de voiture** he died in a car accident

finish /finiʃ/ NM *(Sport)* finish ◆ **combat au ~** fight to the finish ◆ **il a du ~ ou un bon ~** he has good finish

finissage /finisaʒ/ NM *(Couture, Tech)* finishing

finissant, e /finisɑ̃, ɑ̃t/ ADJ *[règne, siècle, millénaire]* that is (*ou* was) drawing to an end; *[pouvoir, monarchie, république, régime]* declining ◆ **la lumière du jour ~** the dusky light ◆ **le soleil de l'été ~** the sun of late summer

finisseur, -euse /finisœʀ, øz/ NM,F [1] *(Couture, Tech)* finisher [2] *(Sport)* good *ou* strong finisher

finition /finisjɔ̃/ NF *(= action)* finishing; *(= résultat)* finish ◆ **la ~ est parfaite** the finish is perfect ◆ **faire les ~s** *(Couture)* to finish off; *(Tricot)* to sew up ◆ **travaux de ~** *(Constr)* finishing off

finitude /finityd/ NF finiteness

finlandais, e /fɛ̃lɑ̃dɛ, ɛz/ ADJ Finnish NM *(Ling)* Finnish NM,F **Finlandais(e)** Finn

Finlande /fɛ̃lɑ̃d/ NF Finland

finlandisation /fɛ̃lɑ̃dizasjɔ̃/ NF Finlandization

finnois, e /finwa, waz/ ADJ Finnish NM *(= langue)* Finnish NM,F **Finnois(e)** Finn

finno-ougrien, -ienne /finougʀijɛ̃, ijɛn/ ADJ, NM *(= langue)* Finno-Ugric, Finno-Ugrian

fiole /fjɔl/ NF *(= flacon)* phial, flask; *(* = tête)* face, mug*

fiord /fjɔʀ(d)/ NM ⇒ **fjord**

fioriture /fjɔʀityʀ/ NF *[de dessin]* flourish; *(Mus)* fioritura ◆ **~s de style** flourishes *ou* embellishments of style ◆ **sans ~s** plain, unadorned, unembellished; *[répondre]* in no uncertain terms

fioul /fjul/ NM ⇒ **fuel**

firmament /fiʀmamɑ̃/ NM *(littér)* firmament *(littér)* ◆ **au ~** in the firmament ◆ **elle a été propulsée au ~ des stars** she shot to stardom ◆ **leurs noms brillent au ~ de la couture** they are some of the top names in the fashion world

firme /fiʀm/ NF firm

FIS /fis/ NM (abrév de **Front islamique de** *ou* **du Salut**) FIS

fisc /fisk/ NM tax department, ≃ Inland Revenue *(Brit)*, Internal Revenue Service *(US)* ◆ **agent du ~** tax official ◆ **avoir des ennuis avec le ~** to have problems with the taxman*, to have tax problems

fiscal, e (mpl **-aux**) /fiskal, o/ ADJ *(gén)* fiscal; *[abattement, avantage]* tax *(épith)* ◆ **l'année ~e** the tax *ou* fiscal year ◆ **politique ~e** tax *ou* fiscal policy; → **abri, fraude, paradis**

fiscalement /fiskalmɑ̃/ ADV fiscally ◆ **c'est ~ avantageux** it's advantageous from a tax point of view ◆ **~ domicilié en France** resident in France for tax purposes

fiscalisation /fiskalizasjɔ̃/ NF *[de revenus]* making subject to tax; *[de prestation sociale]* funding by taxation

fiscaliser /fiskalize/ ▸ conjug 1 ◂ VT *[+ revenus]* to make subject to tax; *[+ prestation sociale]* to fund by taxation

fiscaliste /fiskalist/ NMF tax consultant *ou* adviser *ou* expert ◆ **avocat ~** tax lawyer

fiscalité /fiskalite/ NF *(= système)* tax system; *(= impôts)* taxation, taxes

fish-eye (pl **fish-eyes**) /fiʃaj, fiʃajz/ NM fish-eye lens

fissa* /fisa/ ADV ◆ **faire ~** to get a move on*

fissible /fisibl/ ADJ fissile, fissionable

fissile /fisil/ ADJ *(Géol)* tending to split; *(Phys)* fissile, fissionable

fission /fisjɔ̃/ NF fission ◆ **~ de l'atome** atomic fission, splitting of the atom

fissuration /fisyʀasjɔ̃/ NF *(NonC)* fissuring, cracking, splitting ◆ **des ~s ont été observées sur les tuyaux** cracks were seen in the pipes

fissure /fisyʀ/ NF *(lit)* crack, fissure; *(fig)* crack; *(Anat)* fissure ◆ **des ~s sont apparues dans la coalition** cracks have appeared in the coalition

fissurer /fisyʀe/ ▸ conjug 1 ◂ VT to crack, to fissure; *(fig)* to split VPR **se fissurer** to crack, to fissure; *(fig)* to crack

fiston * /fistɔ̃/ NM son ◆ **dis-moi,** ~ tell me, son *ou* sonny *

fistulaire /fistylɛʀ/ ADJ fistular

fistule /fistyl/ NF fistula

fistuleux, -euse /fistylø, øz/ ADJ fistulous

fitness /fitnɛs/ NM *(Sport)* fitness ◆ **centre de ~** fitness centre *ou* club ◆ **salle de ~** gym

FIV /ɛfive/ NF (abrév de **fécondation in vitro**) IVF

five o'clock † /fajvɔklɔk/ NM *(hum)* (afternoon) tea

FIVETE, Fivete /fivɛt/ NF (abrév de **fécondation in vitro et transfert d'embryon**) ZIFT

fixage /fiksaʒ/ NM *[de couleurs, prix]* fixing

fixateur /fiksatœʀ/ NM *(Art)* fixative; *(Coiffure)* (= *laque*) hair spray; (= *crème*) hair cream; *(avant la mise en plis)* setting lotion; *(Photo)* fixer

fixatif /fiksatif/ NM fixative; *(Can* = *laque)* hair spray

fixation /fiksasjɔ̃/ NF 1 *(Chim, Psych, Zool)* fixation; *(Photo)* fixing ◆ **faire une ~ sur qch** to have a fixation about sth 2 (= *attache*) fastening ◆ **~s (de sécurité)** *(Ski)* (safety) bindings ◆ **~s de randonnée** *(Ski)* touring bindings 3 *[de peuple]* settling 4 *[de salaires, date]* fixing 5 ◆ **gel coiffant à ~ forte/souple** firm hold/soft hold hair gel

fixe /fiks/ ADJ 1 (= *immobile*) *[point, panneau]* fixed; *[personnel]* permanent; *[emploi]* permanent, steady; *[regard]* vacant, fixed ◆ **regarder qn les yeux ~s** to gaze *ou* look fixedly *ou* intently at sb ◆ **~ !** *(commandement)* eyes front! ; → **barre, téléphone** 2 (= *prédéterminé*) *[revenu]* fixed; *[jour, date]* fixed, set ◆ **à heure ~** at set times; → **prix** 3 (= *inaltérable*) *[couleur]* fast, permanent ◆ **encre bleu ~** permanent blue ink; → **beau, idée** NM 1 (= *salaire*) basic *ou* fixed salary 2 *(arg Drogue)* fix ◆ **se faire un ~** to get a fix 3 * (= *téléphone fixe*) landline phone

fixe-chaussette (pl **fixe-chaussettes**) /fiksəʃosɛt/ NM garter, suspender *(Brit)*

fixement /fiksəmɑ̃/ ADV *[regarder]* fixedly

fixer /fikse/ ▸ conjug 1 ◂ VT 1 (= *attacher*) to fix, to fasten (*à, sur* to); ◆ **~ qch dans sa mémoire** to fix sth firmly in one's memory

2 (= *décider*) *[+ date]* to set, to arrange, to fix ◆ **~ la date/l'heure d'un rendez-vous** to set *ou* arrange *ou* fix the date/the time for a meeting ◆ **mon choix s'est fixé sur celui-ci** I settled *ou* decided on this one ◆ **je ne suis pas encore fixé sur ce que je ferai** I haven't made up my mind what to do yet, I haven't got any fixed plans in mind yet ◆ **avez-vous fixé le jour de votre départ ?** have you decided what day you are leaving (on)? ◆ **à l'heure fixée** at the agreed *ou* appointed time ◆ **au jour fixé** on the appointed day

3 *[+ regard, attention]* to fix ◆ **~ les yeux sur qn/qch, ~ qn/qch du regard** to stare at sb/sth ◆ **il la fixa longuement** he stared at her, he looked hard at her ◆ **mon regard se fixa sur lui** I fixed my gaze on him ◆ **tous les regards étaient fixés sur lui** all eyes were on him ◆ **~ son attention sur** to focus *ou* fix one's attention on

4 (= *déterminer*) *[+ prix, impôt, délai]* to set, to fix; *[+ règle, principe]* to lay down, to determine; *[+ idées]* to clarify, to sort out; *[+ conditions]* to lay down, to set ◆ **les droits et les devoirs fixés par la loi** the rights and responsibilities laid down *ou* determined by law ◆ **~ ses idées sur le papier** to set one's ideas down on paper ◆ **mot fixé par l'usage** word fixed by usage ◆ **l'orthographe s'est fixée** the spelling became fixed

5 (= *renseigner*) **~ qn sur qch** * to put sb in the picture about sth *, to enlighten sb as to sth ◆ **être fixé sur le compte de qn** to be wise to sb *, to have sb weighed up * *(Brit)* ◆ **alors, tu es fixé maintenant ?** * have you got the picture now? *

6 (= *stabiliser*) **~ qn** to make sb settle (down) ◆ **seul le mariage pourra le ~** marriage is the only thing that will make him settle down

7 *(Photo)* to fix

VPR **se fixer** 1 (= *s'installer*) to settle ◆ **il s'est fixé à Lyon** he settled in Lyon

2 (= *s'assigner*) **se ~ un objectif** to set o.s. a target ◆ **je me suis fixé fin mai pour terminer** I've decided the end of May is my deadline

fixing /fiksiŋ/ NM *(Fin)* fixing

fixité /fiksite/ NF *[d'opinions]* fixedness; *[de regard]* fixedness, steadiness

fjord /fjɔʀ(d)/ NM fiord, fjord

Fl (abrév de **florin**) fl

flac /flak/ EXCL splash! ◆ **faire (un) ~** to splash

flaccidité /flaksidite/ NF flabbiness, flaccidity

flacon /flakɔ̃/ NM (small) bottle; *(Chim)* flask ◆ **~ à parfum** perfume bottle

flafla * /flafla/ NM ◆ **faire des ~s** to show off ◆ **sans ~** without fuss (and bother)

flagada * /flagada/ ADJ INV ◆ **être ~** to be washed-out *

flagellateur, -trice /flaʒelatœʀ, tʀis/ NM,F flogger, flagellator

flagellation /flaʒelasjɔ̃/ NF *(gén)* flogging; *(Rel)* flagellation, scourging; (= *pratique sexuelle*) flagellation

flagelle /flaʒɛl/ NM flagellum

flagellé, e /flaʒele/ (ptp de **flageller**) ADJ, NM *[organisme]* flagellate

flageller /flaʒele/ ▸ conjug 1 ◂ VT *(gén)* to flog; *(Rel)* to flagellate, to scourge; *(fig)* to flay

flageolant, e /flaʒɔlɑ̃, ɑ̃t/ ADJ shaky, trembling

flageoler /flaʒɔle/ ▸ conjug 1 ◂ VI ◆ **il flageolait (sur ses jambes), ses jambes flageolaient** *(de faiblesse, de fatigue)* his legs were giving way, his legs were trembling *ou* shaking; *(de peur)* he was quaking at the knees, his legs were trembling *ou* shaking

flageolet /flaʒɔlɛ/ NM 1 *(Mus)* flageolet 2 (= *haricot*) flageolet, dwarf kidney bean

flagorner /flagɔʀne/ ▸ conjug 1 ◂ VT *(frm, hum)* to toady to, to fawn upon

flagornerie /flagɔʀnəʀi/ NF *(frm, hum)* toadying *(NonC)*, fawning *(NonC)*, sycophancy *(NonC)*

flagorneur, -euse /flagɔʀnœʀ, øz/ *(frm, hum)* ADJ toadying, fawning, sycophantic NM,F toady, sycophant

flagrance /flagʀɑ̃s/ NF *(Jur)* blatancy

flagrant, e /flagʀɑ̃, ɑ̃t/ ADJ *[violation, erreur, injustice, exemple]* flagrant, blatant; *[inégalités, manque]* glaring; *[preuve]* clear; *[mensonge]* blatant ◆ **prendre qn en ~ délit** to catch sb red-handed *ou* in the act *ou* in flagrante delicto *(SPÉC)* ◆ **pris en ~ délit de mensonge** caught lying ◆ **il ment, c'est ~ !** it's obvious he's lying! ◆ **les cas les plus ~s d'injustice** the most blatant cases of injustice

flair /flɛʀ/ NM *[de chien]* sense of smell, nose; *[de personne]* intuition, sixth sense ◆ **avoir du ~** *[chien]* to have a good nose; *[personne]* to have intuition *ou* a sixth sense ◆ **pour les investissements, il a du ~** he has a (good) nose for investments ◆ **son manque de ~ politique** his lack of political acumen

flairer /fleʀe/ ▸ conjug 1 ◂ VT 1 (= *humer*) to smell (at), to sniff (at); *(Chasse)* to scent 2 (= *deviner*) to sense ◆ **il a tout de suite flairé que quelque chose n'allait pas** he immediately sensed that something wasn't right ◆ **~ quelque chose de louche** to smell a rat ◆ **~ le danger** to sense *ou* scent danger ◆ **~ le vent** to see which way the wind is blowing, to read the wind

flamand, e /flamɑ̃, ɑ̃d/ ADJ Flemish NM 1 (= *langue*) Flemish 2 ◆ **Flamand** Fleming, Flemish man ◆ **les Flamands** the Flemish NF **Flamande** Fleming, Flemish woman

flamant /flamɑ̃/ NM flamingo ◆ **~ rose** (pink) flamingo

flambage /flɑ̃baʒ/ NM 1 *[de volaille]* singeing; *[d'instrument]* sterilizing *(in a flame)* 2 *(Tech)* (= *déformation*) buckling

flambant, e /flɑ̃bɑ̃, ɑ̃t/ ADJ (= *qui brûle*) burning; (* = *superbe*) great * ◆ **~ neuf** brand new

flambart * †, **flambard** * † /flɑ̃baʀ/ NM swankpot * ◆ **faire le** *ou* **son ~** to swank *

flambé, e[1] * /flɑ̃be/ (ptp de **flamber**) ADJ *[personne]* finished ◆ **il est ~ !** he's had it! * ◆ **l'affaire est ~e !** it's all over! *

flambeau (pl **flambeaux**) /flɑ̃bo/ NM 1 (= *torche*) (flaming) torch ◆ **aux ~x** *[dîner, défiler]* by torchlight ◆ **marche aux ~x** torchlight *ou* torchlit procession; → **retraite** 2 *(fig)* torch ◆ **passer le ~ à qn** to pass on *ou* hand on the torch to sb ◆ **reprendre le ~** to take up the torch 3 (= *chandelier*) candlestick

flambée[2] /flɑ̃be/ NF 1 (= *feu*) blazing fire ◆ **faire une ~ dans la cheminée** to make *ou* light a fire in the fireplace 2 *[de violence]* outburst; *[de cours, prix]* explosion ◆ **~ de colère** angry outburst, flare-up ◆ **la ~ de la Bourse** the sudden rise in the stock exchange

flambement /flɑ̃bmɑ̃/ NM *(Tech)* (= *déformation*) buckling

flamber /flɑ̃be/ ▸ conjug 1 ◂ VI 1 *[bois]* to burn; *[feu, incendie]* to blaze ◆ **la maison a flambé en quelques minutes** in a few minutes the house was burnt to the ground 2 * *[joueur]* to gamble huge sums, to play for high stakes 3 *[cours, prix, Bourse]* to shoot up, to rocket 4 (* = *crâner*) to show off VT 1 *(Culin)* to flambé ◆ **bananes flambées** bananas flambé 2 *[+ volaille, cheveux]* to singe; *[+ aiguille, instrument de chirurgie]* to sterilize *(in a flame)*

flambeur, -euse * /flɑ̃bœʀ, øz/ NM,F big-time gambler ◆ **quel ~ !** (= *frimeur*) he's really flash with his money! *

flamboiement /flɑ̃bwamɑ̃/ NM *[de flammes]* blaze, blazing; *[de lumière]* blaze; *[de yeux]* flash, gleam ◆ **dans un ~ de couleurs** in a blaze of colour

flamboyant, e /flɑ̃bwajɑ̃, ɑ̃t/ ADJ 1 *[feu, lumière, ciel, soleil]* blazing; *[yeux]* flashing, blazing; *[couleur]* flaming; *[regard]* fiery; *[épée, armure]* gleaming, flashing 2 *(Archit)* flamboyant NM 1 *(Archit)* flamboyant style 2 (= *arbre*) flamboyant, royal poinciana

flamboyer /flɑ̃bwaje/ ▸ conjug 8 ◂ VI *[flamme, soleil, ciel]* to blaze; *[yeux]* to flash, to blaze; *[couleur]* to flame; *[épée, armure]* to gleam, to flash

flamenco /flamɛnko/, **flamenca** /flamɛnka/ ADJ *[fête, chants]* flamenco ◆ **guitare flamenca** *ou* ~ flamenco guitar NM flamenco

flamiche /flamiʃ/ NF leek pie

flamingant, e /flamɛ̃gɑ̃, ɑ̃t/ ADJ Flemish-speaking NM,F **Flamingant(e)** Flemish speaker; (Pol) Flemish nationalist

flamme /flɑm/ NF 1 (*lit*) flame ◆ **être en ~s, être la proie des ~s** to be ablaze *ou* on fire *ou* in flames ◆ **dévoré par les ~s** consumed by fire *ou* the flames ◆ **la ~ olympique** the Olympic flame ◆ **les ~s de l'enfer** the flames *ou* fires of hell ◆ **descendre (qch/qn) en ~s*** to shoot (sth/sb) down in flames 2 (= *ardeur*) fire, fervour (*Brit*), fervor (*US*) ◆ **discours plein de ~** passionate *ou* fiery speech ◆ **jeune homme plein de ~** young man full of fire 3 (= *éclat*) fire, brilliance ◆ **la ~ de ses yeux** *ou* **de son regard** his flashing *ou* blazing eyes 4 (*littér ou hum* = *amour*) love, ardour (*Brit*), ardor (*US*) ◆ **il lui a déclaré sa ~** he declared his undying love to her 5 (= *drapeau*) pennant, pennon 6 (*Poste*) postal logo

flammé, e /flɑme/ ADJ [*céramique*] flambé

flammèche /flamɛʃ/ NF (flying) spark

flan /flɑ̃/ NM 1 (*Culin*) custard tart 2 (*Tech*) [*d'imprimeur*] flong; [*de monnaie*] blank, flan; [*de disque*] mould 3 * **c'est du ~ !** it's a load of hooey! *; → **rond**

flanc /flɑ̃/ NM 1 [*de personne*] side; [*d'animal*] side, flank ◆ **l'enfant qu'elle portait dans son ~** († , *littér*) the child she was carrying in her womb ◆ **être couché sur le ~** to be lying on one's side ◆ **tirer au ~*** to shirk, to skive* (*Brit*) ◆ **être sur le ~** (= *malade*) to be laid up; (= *fatigué*) to be all in* ◆ **cette grippe m'a mis sur le ~** this flu has really knocked me out*; → **battre** 2 [*de navire*] side; [*d'armée, bastion, écu*] flank; [*de montagne*] slope, side ◆ **à ~ de coteau** *ou* **de colline** on the hillside ◆ **prendre de ~** (*fig, Naut*) to catch broadside on; (*Mil*) to attack on the flank; → **prêter**

flancher* /flɑ̃ʃe/ ► conjug 1 ◄ VI [*cœur*] to give out, to pack up* (*Brit*); [*troupes*] to give way ◆ **sa mémoire a flanché** his memory failed him ◆ **c'est le moral qui a flanché** he lost his nerve ◆ **il a flanché en math** he fell down *ou* came down in maths ◆ **sans ~** without flinching ◆ **ce n'est pas le moment de ~** this is no time for weakness

flanchet /flɑ̃ʃɛ/ NM (*Boucherie*) flank

Flandre /flɑ̃dʀ/ NF ◆ **la ~, les ~s** Flanders

flanelle /flanɛl/ NF flannel ◆ **~ de coton** cotton flannel ◆ **pantalon de ~ grise** grey flannel trousers, grey flannels

flâner /flɑne/ ► conjug 1 ◄ VI to stroll; (*péj*) to hang about, to lounge about ◆ **va chercher du pain, et sans ~ !** go and get some bread, and don't hang about! *ou* and be quick about it!

flânerie /flɑnʀi/ NF stroll ◆ **perdre son temps en ~s** (*péj*) to waste one's time lounging about

flâneur, -euse /flɑnœʀ, øz/ ADJ idle NM,F stroller; (*péj*) idler, loafer

flanquer[1] /flɑ̃ke/ ► conjug 1 ◄ VT to flank ◆ **la boutique qui flanque la maison** the shop adjoining *ou* flanking the house ◆ **flanqué de ses gardes du corps** flanked by his bodyguards ◆ **il est toujours flanqué de sa mère** (*péj*) he always has his mother in tow*

flanquer[2]* /flɑ̃ke/ ► conjug 1 ◄ VT 1 (= *jeter*) **~ qch par terre** (*lit*) to fling sth to the ground; (*fig*) to knock sth on the head*, to put paid to sth (*Brit*) ◆ **~ qn par terre** to fling sb to the ground ◆ **~ qn à la porte** to chuck sb out*; (= *licencier*) to fire sb, to sack sb* (*Brit*), to give sb the sack* (*Brit*) ◆ **~ tout en l'air** to chuck* *ou* pack it all in* (*Brit*) 2 (= *donner*) **~ une gifle à qn** give sb a slap *ou* a clout* (*Brit*) ◆ **~ la trouille à qn** to give sb a scare, to put the wind up sb* (*Brit*) VPR **se flanquer** ◆ **se ~ par terre** to fall flat on one's face

flapi, e* /flapi/ ADJ washed-out*

flaque /flak/ NF ◆ **~ de sang/d'huile** pool of blood/oil ◆ **~ d'eau** (*petite*) puddle; (*grande*) pool of water

flash (pl **flashs** *ou* **flashes**) /flaʃ/ NM 1 (*Photo*) flash ◆ **au ~** using a flash, with a flash ◆ **~ anti-yeux rouges** flash with a red-eye reduction feature 2 (*Radio, TV*) **~ (d'informations)** newsflash ◆ **~ publicitaire** (*Radio*) commercial break 3 ◆ **avoir un ~** (*arg Drogue*) to be on a high*; (= *se souvenir*) to have a flashback

flash-back (pl **flash-back** *ou* **flashs-back** *ou* **flashes-back**) /flaʃbak/ NM flashback

flasher* /flaʃe/ ► conjug 1 ◄ VI ◆ **j'ai flashé pour** *ou* **sur cette robe** I fell in love with this dress ◆ **à chaque fois que je le vois, je flashe** *ou* **il me fait ~** every time I see him I go weak at the knees *ou* my heart skips a beat

flashmètre /flaʃmɛtʀ/ NM flash meter

flasque[1] /flask/ ADJ [*peau*] flaccid, flabby; [*ventre*] flabby

flasque[2] /flask/ NF (= *bouteille*) flask

flatté, e /flate/ (ptp de **flatter**) ADJ [*portrait*] flattering

flatter /flate/ ► conjug 1 ◄ VT 1 (= *flagorner*) to flatter ◆ **~ servilement** *ou* **bassement qn** to fawn on sb, to toady to sb ◆ **cette photo la flatte** this photo flatters her ◆ **sans vous ~** without meaning to flatter you

2 (= *faire plaisir*) [*compliment, décoration*] to flatter, to gratify ◆ **je suis très flatté de cet honneur** I am most flattered by this honour ◆ **cela le flatte dans son orgueil, cela flatte son orgueil** it flatters his pride

3 (*frm* = *favoriser*) [+ *manie, goûts*] to pander to; [+ *vice, passion*] to encourage

4 (*littér* = *tromper*) **~ qn d'un espoir** to hold out false hopes to sb

5 (*frm* = *charmer*) [+ *oreille, regard*] to delight, to be pleasing to; [+ *goût*] to flatter ◆ **~ le palais** to delight the taste buds

6 (*frm* = *caresser*) to stroke

VPR **se flatter** (*frm*) 1 (= *prétendre*) **se ~ de faire qch** to claim *ou* profess to be able to do sth ◆ **il se flatte de tout comprendre** he professes to understand everything ◆ **je me flatte d'avoir quelque influence sur lui** I like to think that I have some influence over him ◆ **je me flatte de m'y connaître un peu en informatique** I flatter myself that I know a little about computers

2 (= *s'enorgueillir*) **se ~ de qch** to pride o.s. on sth ◆ **elle se flatte de son succès** she prides herself on her success ◆ **et je m'en flatte !** and I'm proud of it!

3 (= *se leurrer*) to delude o.s. ◆ **se ~ d'un vain espoir** to cherish a forlorn hope ◆ **s'il croit réussir, il se flatte !** if he thinks he can succeed, he's deluding himself!

flatterie /flatʀi/ NF flattery (*NonC*) ◆ **vile ~** (*littér, hum*) base flattery

flatteur, -euse /flatœʀ, øz/ ADJ flattering ◆ **comparaison flatteuse** flattering comparison ◆ **faire un tableau ~ de la situation** to paint a rosy picture of the situation ◆ **ce n'est pas ~ !** that's not very flattering! NM,F flatterer ◆ **vil ~** (*littér, hum*) base flatterer

flatulence /flatylɑ̃s/ NF wind, flatulence

flatulent, e /flatylɑ̃, ɑ̃t/ ADJ flatulent

flatuosité /flatɥozite/ NF (*Méd*) flatus (*SPÉC*) ◆ **avoir des ~s** to have wind

fléau (pl **fléaux**) /fleo/ NM 1 (= *calamité*) scourge, curse ◆ **le chômage est un véritable ~ social** unemployment is the scourge of society ◆ **quel ~, ce type !*** that guy's such a pest!* 2 [*de balance*] beam; (*Agr*) flail

fléchage /fleʃaʒ/ NM signposting (*with arrows*)

flèche[1] /flɛʃ/ NF 1 (= *arme*) arrow; (*Ordin*) arrow ◆ **~ en caoutchouc** rubber-tipped dart ◆ **les ~s de l'Amour** *ou* **de Cupidon** Cupid's darts *ou* arrows ◆ **monter en ~** [*avion*] to soar; [*prix*] to soar, to rocket ◆ **il monte en ~** [*chanteur*] he's on the up and up, he's rocketing to fame ◆ **les prix sont montés en ~** prices have soared *ou* shot up *ou* rocketed ◆ **la montée en ~ des prix** the surge in prices ◆ **partir comme une ~** to set off like a shot ◆ **il est passé devant nous comme une ~** he shot past us ◆ **ce n'est pas une ~ !*** he's no Einstein!* ◆ **se trouver en ~** *ou* **prendre une position en ~ dans un débat** to take up an extreme position in a debate ◆ **leur équipe se trouve en ~ dans la recherche génétique** their team is at the cutting edge of genetic research

2 (= *critique*) **diriger ses ~s contre qn** to direct one's shafts against sb ◆ **la ~ du Parthe** (*Hist*) the Parthian shot ◆ **c'était la ~ du Parthe** (*fig*) it was his parting shot ◆ **faire ~ de tout bois** to use all available means

3 (= *direction*) (direction) arrow, pointer

4 [*d'église*] spire; [*de grue*] jib; [*de mât*] pole; [*d'affût, canon*] trail; [*de balance*] pointer, needle; [*de charrue*] beam; [*d'attelage*] pole ◆ **atteler en ~** to drive tandem ◆ **cheval de ~** lead horse

COMP **flèche lumineuse** (*sur l'écran*) arrow; (= *torche*) arrow pointer

flèche[2] /flɛʃ/ NF (*Culin*) flitch

fléché, e /fleʃe/ (ptp de **flécher**) ADJ ◆ **parcours ~** route marked *ou* signposted with arrows ◆ **croix ~e** crosslet; → **mot**

flécher /fleʃe/ ► conjug 1 ◄ VT to mark (with arrows) ◆ **ils ont fléché le parcours** they marked the route (out) with arrows, they put arrows along the route

fléchette /fleʃɛt/ NF dart ◆ **jouer aux ~s** to play darts

fléchi, e /fleʃi/ (ptp de **fléchir**) ADJ 1 (= *plié*) [*bras, jambe, genou*] bent, flexed; [*corps*] bent ◆ **avec les jambes légèrement ~es** with the legs slightly bent *ou* flexed 2 (*Ling*) inflected

fléchir /fleʃiʀ/ ► conjug 2 ◄ VT 1 (= *plier*) to bend; (*Méd*) [+ *articulation*] to flex ◆ **~ le genou devant qn** to go down on one knee in front of sb

2 (= *faire céder*) [+ *personne*] to sway; [+ *colère*] to soothe ◆ **il s'est laissé ~** he let himself be swayed

VI 1 (= *plier*) (*gén*) to bend; [*planches*] to sag, to bend; [*poutre, genoux*] to sag ◆ **ses jambes** *ou* **ses genoux fléchirent** his legs gave way

2 (= *faiblir*) [*armée*] to give ground, to yield; [*volonté*] to weaken ◆ **sans ~** with unflinching determination

3 (= *diminuer*) [*attention*] to flag; [*recettes, talent, nombre*] to fall off; [*cours de Bourse*] to ease, to drop; [*monnaie*] to weaken, to drop ◆ **la courbe de l'inflation fléchit** there is a downturn in inflation ◆ **les pétrolières ont fléchi en début de séance** (*Bourse*) oils were down *ou* dropped slightly in early trading

4 (= *céder*) to yield, to soften ◆ **il fléchit devant leurs prières** he yielded to their entreaties

5 (*Ling*) **forme fléchie** inflected form

fléchissement /fleʃismɑ̃/ NM 1 [*objet, membre*] bending; (*Méd*) [*d'articulation*] flexing 2 [*d'armée*] yielding; [*de volonté*] weakening 3 [*d'attention*] flagging; [*de recettes, talent, nombre*] falling off; [*de cours de Bourse*] easing off (*de* of) drop (*de* in); [*de monnaie*] weakening, dropping (*de* of); [*de natalité, exportations*] drop (*de* in)

fléchisseur /fleʃisœʀ/ ADJ M, NM (*Anat*) ◆ **(muscle) ~** flexor

flegmatique /flɛgmatik/ ADJ phlegmatic

flegme /flɛgm/ NM composure, phlegm ◆ **il perdit son ~** he lost his composure *ou* cool* ◆ **le ~ britannique** (*hum*) the British stiff upper lip

flémingite* /flemɛ̃ʒit/ NF *(hum)* bone idleness ◆ **il a une ~ aiguë** he's suffering from acute inertia *(hum)*

flemmard, e* /flemaʀ, aʀd/ ADJ workshy, bone-idle* *(Brit)* NM,F idler, lazybones

flemmarder* /flemaʀde/ ► conjug 1 ◄ VI to loaf about, to lounge about

flemmardise* /flemaʀdiz/ NF laziness, idleness

flemme* /flɛm/ NF laziness ◆ **j'ai la ~ de le faire** I can't be bothered ◆ **tirer sa ~** to idle around, to loaf about

fléole /fleɔl/ NF ◆ **~ des prés** timothy

flet /flɛ/ NM flounder

flétan /fletɑ̃/ NM halibut

flétri, e /fletʀi/ (ptp de **flétrir**[1]) ADJ *[feuille, fleur]* withered, wilted; *[peau, visage]* withered; *[beauté]* faded

flétrir[1] /fletʀiʀ/ ► conjug 2 ◄ VT (= *faner*) to wither, to fade ◆ **l'âge a flétri son visage** his face is wizened with age VPR **se flétrir** *[fleur]* to wither, to wilt; *[beauté]* to fade; *[peau, visage]* to become wizened; *[cœur]* to wither

flétrir[2] /fletʀiʀ/ ► conjug 2 ◄ VT 1 (= *stigmatiser*) *[+ personne, conduite]* to condemn; *[+ réputation]* to blacken 2 *(Hist)* to brand

flétrissement /fletʀismɑ̃/ NM *[de fleur]* withering, wilting; *[de peau]* withering; *[de beauté]* fading

flétrissure[1] /fletʀisyʀ/ NF *[de fleur, peau]* withering; *[de teint]* fading

flétrissure[2] /fletʀisyʀ/ NF 1 *[de réputation, honneur]* stain, blemish (*à* on) 2 *(Hist)* brand

fleur /flœʀ/ NF 1 *(Bot)* flower; *[d'arbre]* blossom ◆ **en ~(s)** *[plante]* in bloom, in flower; *[arbre]* in blossom, in flower ◆ **papier à ~s** flowered *ou* flower-patterned *ou* flowery paper ◆ **assiette à ~s** flower-patterned *ou* flowery plate ◆ **chapeau à ~s** flowery hat ◆ **"ni fleurs ni couronnes"** "no flowers by request"

2 *[de cuir]* grain side ◆ **cuir pleine ~** finest quality leather

3 (= *le meilleur*) **la ~ de** the flower of ◆ **à** *ou* **dans la ~ de l'âge** in the prime of life, in one's prime ◆ **perdre sa ~** († , *hum*) to lose one's honour † *(aussi hum)*; → **fin**[1]

4 *(locutions)* **comme une ~*** (= *sans effort*) without trying; (= *sans prévenir*) unexpectedly ◆ **il est arrivé le premier comme une ~** he romped home ◆ **à ~ de terre** just above the ground ◆ **un écueil à ~ d'eau** a reef just above the water *ou* which just breaks the surface of the water ◆ **j'ai les nerfs à ~ de peau** I'm all on edge, my nerves are all on edge ◆ **il a une sensibilité à ~ de peau** he's very touchy ◆ **avoir les yeux à ~ de tête** to have protruding eyes ◆ **faire une ~ à qn*** to do sb a favour *ou* a good turn ◆ **lancer des ~s à qn, couvrir qn de ~s** *(fig)* to shower praise on sb ◆ **s'envoyer des ~s** *(réfléchi)* to pat o.s. on the back*; *(réciproque)* to pat each other on the back* ◆ **~ bleue** *(hum)* naïvely sentimental ◆ **il est resté ~ bleue en vieillissant** even in his old age he is still a bit of a romantic ◆ **ils sont partis la ~ au fusil** they went to battle full of innocent enthusiasm

COMP **fleurs des champs** wild flowers
fleur de farine fine wheat flour
fleurs de givre frost patterns
fleur de lis (= *emblème*) fleur-de-lis
fleur(s) d'oranger orange blossom
fleur(s) de pommier apple blossom
fleurs de rhétorique flowers of rhetoric
fleur de sel *best quality unrefined salt*
fleur de soufre flowers of sulphur *(Brit) ou* sulfur *(US)*

fleuraison /flœʀɛzɔ̃/ NF ⇒ **floraison**

fleurdelisé, e /flœʀdəlize/ ADJ decorated with fleurs-de-lis ◆ **croix ~e** fleurettée *ou* fleurty cross NM *(Can)* ◆ **le ~** the Quebec flag

fleurer /flœʀe/ ► conjug 1 ◄ VT *(littér)* to have the scent of, to smell of ◆ **ça fleure bon le pain grillé** there's a lovely smell of toast ◆ **~ bon la lavande** to smell (sweetly) of lavender ◆ **sa musique fleure bon l'exotisme** his music has an exotic feel to it

fleuret /flœʀɛ/ NM (= *épée*) foil ◆ **propos à ~s mouchetés** discussion full of barbed remarks

fleurette † /flœʀɛt/ NF *(hum)* floweret; → **conter, crème**

fleuri, e /flœʀi/ (ptp de **fleurir**) ADJ 1 *[fleur]* in bloom; *[branche]* in blossom; *[jardin, pré]* in flower *ou* bloom; *[tissu, papier]* flowered, flowery; *[appartement, table]* decorated *ou* decked with flowers ◆ **à la boutonnière ~e** *(avec une fleur)* wearing *ou* sporting a flower in his buttonhole; *(avec une décoration)* wearing a decoration on his lapel ◆ **"Annecy, ville fleurie"** "Annecy, town in bloom" 2 *[teint]* florid; *[style]* flowery, florid ◆ **barbe ~e** *(hum)* flowing white beard 3 *[croûte de fromage]* mouldy

fleurir /flœʀiʀ/ ► conjug 2 ◄ VI 1 *[arbre]* to blossom, to (come into) flower; *[fleur]* to flower, to (come into) bloom; *(littér)* *[qualité, sentiment]* to blossom *(littér)* ◆ **un sourire fleurit sur ses lèvres** a smile appeared on his lips 2 (imparfait **florissait**) *[commerce, arts]* to flourish, to prosper, to thrive VT *[+ salon]* to decorate *ou* deck with flowers ◆ **~ une tombe/un mort** to put flowers on a grave/on sb's grave ◆ **~ sa boutonnière** to put a flower in one's buttonhole ◆ **un ruban fleurissait (à) sa boutonnière** he was wearing a decoration on his lapel ◆ **fleurissez-vous, mesdames, fleurissez-vous !** † treat yourselves to some flowers, ladies!, buy yourselves a buttonhole *(Brit) ou* boutonnière *(US)*, ladies!

fleuriste /flœʀist/ NMF (= *personne*) florist; (= *boutique*) florist's (shop), flower shop

fleuron /flœʀɔ̃/ NM *[de couronne]* floweret; *[de bâtiment]* finial; *(Bot)* floret; *[de collection]* jewel; *(Écon)* flagship ◆ **c'est le plus beau ~ de ma collection** it's the jewel of my collection ◆ **l'un des ~s de l'industrie française** a flagship French industry

fleuve /flœv/ NM *(lit)* river *(flowing into the sea)* ◆ **~ de boue/de lave** river of mud/of lava ◆ **le ~ Jaune** the Yellow River ◆ **~ de larmes** flood of tears ◆ **~ de sang** river of blood ◆ **sa vie n'a pas été un long ~ tranquille** *(hum)* his life hasn't been a bed of roses ADJ INV *[discours, film]* marathon *(épith)*

flexibilisation /flɛksibilizasjɔ̃/ NF *[de temps de travail, salaires, marché du travail]* increased flexibility ◆ **nous allons vers une plus grande ~ du temps de travail** working hours are becoming increasingly flexible

flexibiliser /flɛksibilize/ ► conjug 1 ◄ VT *[+ méthode, horaires]* to make more flexible

flexibilité /flɛksibilite/ NF flexibility ◆ **la ~ de l'emploi** flexibility in employment

flexible /flɛksibl/ ADJ *[métal]* flexible, pliable, pliant; *[branche, roseau]* pliable, pliant; *[caractère]* (= *accommodant*) flexible, adaptable; (= *malléable*) pliant, pliable ◆ **taux de change ~** floating exchange rate ◆ **atelier** *ou* **usine ~** flexible manufacturing system, FMS; → **horaire** NM (= *câble*) flexible coupling; (= *tuyau*) flexible tubing *ou* hose

flexion /flɛksjɔ̃/ NF 1 (= *courbure*) *[de ressort, lame d'acier]* flexion, bending; *[de poutre, pièce]* bending, sagging ◆ **résistance à la ~** bending strength 2 *[de membre, articulation]* flexing *(NonC)*, bending *(NonC)*; *(Ski)* knee-bend ◆ **faire plusieurs ~s du bras/du corps** to flex the arm/bend the body several times 3 *(Ling)* inflection, inflexion ◆ **langue à ~** inflecting *ou* inflected language

flexionnel, -elle /flɛksjɔnɛl/ ADJ *[désinence]* inflexional, inflectional, inflected ◆ **langue flexionnelle** inflecting *ou* inflected language

flexueux, -euse /flɛksɥø, øz/ ADJ flexuous, flexuose

flexuosité /flɛksɥozite/ NF flexuosity

flexure /flɛksyʀ/ NF flexure

flibuste /flibyst/ NF (= *piraterie*) freebooting, buccaneering; (= *pirates*) freebooters, buccaneers

flibustier /flibystje/ NM (= *pirate*) freebooter, buccaneer; († = *escroc*) swindler, crook

flic* /flik/ NM cop*, policeman ◆ **les ~s** the cops*, the police ◆ **une femme ~** a policewoman

flicage‡ /flikaʒ/ NM *[de quartier]* heavy policing ◆ **le ~ des ouvriers par la direction** the way the management keeps tabs on the workers

flicaille‡ /flikɑj/ NF ◆ **la ~** the fuzz‡, the pigs‡, the filth‡ *(Brit)*

flicard‡ /flikaʀ/ NM cop*

flic flac /flikflak/ NM, EXCL plop, splash ◆ **le ~ des vagues** the lapping of the waves ◆ **ses chaussures faisaient ~ dans la boue** his shoes went splash splash through the mud

flingue‡ /flɛ̃g/ NM gun, rifle

flinguer‡ /flɛ̃ge/ ► conjug 1 ◄ VT 1 (= *tuer*) *[+ personne]* to gun down, to put a bullet in, to shoot up* *(US)* ◆ **il y a de quoi se ~ !** it's enough to make you want to shoot yourself! 2 (= *détruire*) *[+ appareil]* to bust‡; *[+ voiture]* to smash (up)‡, to total* *(US)* 3 (= *critiquer*) to shoot down in flames* *(Brit)*, to shoot down* *(US)*

flingueur‡ /flɛ̃gœʀ/ NM (= *tueur à gages*) hitman*, contract killer ◆ **c'est un ~** (= *il a la gâchette facile*) he's trigger-happy*

flingueuse‡ /flɛ̃gøz/ NF contract killer

flint(-glass) /flint(glas)/ NM flint glass

flip[1]* /flip/ NM *(arg Drogue)* (fit of) depression ◆ **un jour de ~** a day on a downer*

flip[2] /flip/ NM ◆ **porto ~** egg flip *(with port)*

flippant, e‡ /flipɑ̃, ɑt/ ADJ *[situation, film]* grim*, depressing; *[personne]* depressing

flipper[1] /flipœʀ/ NM (= *billard électrique*) pinball machine ◆ **jouer au ~** to play pinball

flipper[2]* /flipe/ ► conjug 1 ◄ VI *(fig, Drogue)* to freak out*; (= *être déprimé*) to feel down* ◆ **son examen la fait ~** she's freaking out* at the thought of her exam

fliqué, e‡ /flike/ ADJ *[endroit]* full of *ou* crawling with cops* ◆ **le coin est très ~** the place is full of *ou* crawling with cops*

fliquer‡ /flike/ ► conjug 1 ◄ VT 1 *[police]* *[+ quartier]* to bring the cops* into 2 *[+ personne]* to keep under close surveillance ◆ **ma mère n'arrête pas de me ~** my mother watches my every move

flirt /flœʀt/ NM 1 (= *action*) flirting *(NonC)*; (= *amourette*) flirtation, brief romance; (= *rapprochement*) flirtation ◆ **avoir un ~ avec qn** to have a brief romance with sb 2 (= *amoureux*) boyfriend (*ou* girlfriend) ◆ **un de mes anciens ~s** an old flame of mine

> ⚠ **flirt** ne se traduit pas par le mot anglais **flirt**, qui désigne une personne.

flirter /flœʀte/ ► conjug 1 ◄ VI to flirt ◆ **~ avec qn** (= *fréquenter*) to go around with sb ◆ **~ avec** *[+ idée, parti]* to flirt with ◆ **le taux de chômage flirte avec la barre des 10%** unemployment is hovering around 10% ◆ **il a beaucoup flirté avec le cinéma avant de passer au théâtre** he did quite a bit of work in the cinema before becoming involved in theatre ◆ **des jeunes qui flirtent avec la mort** young people who court death

flirteur, -euse † /flœʀtœʀ, øz/ ADJ flirtatious NM,F flirt

FLN /ɛfɛlɛn/ NM (abrév de **Front de libération nationale**) FLN

FLNC /ɛfɛlɛnse/ NM (abrév de **Front de libération nationale de la Corse**) → **front**

floc /flɔk/ NM, EXCL plop, splash ◆ **faire ~** to splash, to (go) plop

flocage /flɔkaʒ/ NM flocking ~ **à l'amiante** asbestos flocking

flocon /flɔkɔ̃/ NM *[d'écume]* fleck; *[de laine]* flock ◆ **~ de neige** snowflake ◆ **~s d'avoine** oatflakes, rolled oats ◆ **~s de maïs** cornflakes ◆ **la neige tombe à gros ~s** the snow is falling in big flakes ◆ **purée en ~s** instant mashed potato

floconneux, -euse /flɔkɔnø, øz/ ADJ *[nuage, étoffe]* fluffy; *[écume, substance, liquide]* frothy

flonflons /flɔ̃flɔ̃/ NMPL *(gén)* oompah, oompahpah ◆ **les ~ de la musique foraine** the pom-pom of the fairground music

flop* /flɔp/ NM flop* ◆ **sa tournée a fait un ~** his tour was a real flop*

flopée* /flɔpe/ NF ◆ **une ~ de** loads of*, masses of ◆ **il y a une ~** *ou* **des ~s de touristes** there are loads* *ou* masses of tourists ◆ **elle a une ~ d'enfants** she's got loads* of children

floqué, e /flɔke/ ADJ *[moquette, papier, tissu]* flock *(épith)*, flocked ◆ **plafond ~ à l'amiante** ceiling insulated with asbestos flocking

floraison /flɔʀɛzɔ̃/ NF 1 *(lit)* *(= épanouissement)* flowering, blossoming; *(= époque)* flowering time ◆ **rosiers qui ont plusieurs ~s** rosebushes which have several flowerings *ou* which flower several times a year 2 *[de talents]* flowering, blossoming; *[d'affiches, articles]* rash, crop

floral, e (mpl **-aux**) /flɔʀal, o/ ADJ 1 *(gén)* flower *(épith)* ◆ **art ~** flower arranging ◆ **composition ~e** flower arrangement ◆ **exposition ~e** flower show ◆ **parc ~** flower garden 2 *(Bot)* *[enveloppe, organes]* floral

floralies /flɔʀali/ NFPL flower show

flore /flɔʀ/ NF *(= plantes)* flora; *(= livre)* plant guide ◆ **~ intestinale** intestinal flora

floréal /flɔʀeal/ NM Floreal *(eighth month in the French Republican calendar)*

Florence /flɔʀɑ̃s/ N *(= ville)* Florence

florentin, e /flɔʀɑ̃tɛ̃, in/ ADJ Florentine NM *(= dialecte)* Florentine dialect NM,F **Florentin(e)** Florentine

florès /flɔʀɛs/ NM *(littér, hum)* ◆ **faire ~** *[personne]* to shine, to enjoy great success; *[théorie]* to be in vogue

floriculture /flɔʀikyltyʀ/ NF flower-growing, floriculture *(SPÉC)*

Floride /flɔʀid/ NF Florida

florifère /flɔʀifɛʀ/ ADJ *(= qui a des fleurs)* flower-bearing ◆ **cette variété est très ~** this variety produces a lot of flowers *ou* flowers abundantly

florilège /flɔʀilɛʒ/ NM anthology

florin /flɔʀɛ̃/ NM florin

florissant, e /flɔʀisɑ̃, ɑ̃t/ ADJ *[pays, économie, théorie]* flourishing; *[santé, teint]* blooming

flot /flo/ NM 1 *(littér)* **~s** *[de lac, mer]* waves ◆ **les ~s** the waves ◆ **voguer sur les ~s bleus** to sail the ocean blue

2 *(= grande quantité)* *[de lumière, boue, sang, véhicules]* stream; *[de paroles, informations, images]* stream, flood; *[de souvenirs, larmes, lettres]* flood ◆ **un ~** *ou* **des ~s de rubans/dentelle** a cascade of ribbons/lace ◆ **les ~s de sa chevelure** her flowing locks *ou* mane *(littér)*

3 *(= marée)* **le ~** the floodtide, the incoming tide

4 *(locutions)*

◆ **à flot** ◆ **être à ~** *[bateau]* to be afloat; *[entreprise]* to be on an even keel; *[personne]* to have one's head above water ◆ **remettre à ~** *[+ bateau]* to refloat; *[+ entreprise]* to bring back onto an even keel ◆ **ces mesures devraient permettre la remise à ~ de l'économie** these measures should help get the economy back onto an even keel ◆ **classes de remise à ~** *(Scol)* remedial classes ◆ **mettre à ~** *(lit, fig)* to launch ◆ **la mise à ~ d'un bateau** the launching of a ship

◆ **à (grands) flots** in streams *ou* torrents ◆ **le vin coulait à ~s** the wine flowed like water ◆ **l'argent coule à ~s** there's plenty of money around ◆ **la lumière entre à ~s** light is streaming in *ou* flooding in *ou* pouring in

flottabilité /flɔtabilite/ NF buoyancy

flottable /flɔtabl/ ADJ *[bois, objet]* buoyant; *[rivière]* floatable

flottage /flɔtaʒ/ NM floating *(of logs down a river)*

flottaison /flɔtɛzɔ̃/ NF 1 *(Naut)* **(ligne de) ~** waterline ◆ **~ en charge** load line, Plimsoll line 2 *(Fin)* flotation, floatation

flottant, e /flɔtɑ̃, ɑ̃t/ ADJ 1 *[bois, glace, mine]* floating; *[brume]* drifting; *(Ordin)* *[virgule]* floating; → **île** 2 *[cheveux, cape]* flowing; *[vêtement]* loose 3 *[capitaux, taux de change, dette]* floating; *[effectifs]* fluctuating ◆ **électorat ~** floating voters 4 *[caractère, esprit]* irresolute, vacillating ◆ **rester ~** to be unable to make up one's mind (*devant* when faced with) 5 *[côte, rein]* floating NM 1 *(= short)* shorts ◆ **son ~ est usé** his shorts are worn out ◆ **deux ~s** two pairs of shorts 2 *(Fin)* float

flotte /flɔt/ NF 1 *[d'avions, bateaux]* fleet ◆ **~ aérienne** air fleet ◆ **~ de guerre** naval fleet ◆ **~ marchande** *ou* **de commerce** merchant fleet 2 * *(= pluie)* rain; *(= eau)* water ◆ **son café, c'est de la ~** *(péj)* his coffee's like dishwater 3 *(= flotteur)* float

flottement /flɔtmɑ̃/ NM 1 *(= hésitation)* wavering, hesitation ◆ **on observa un certain ~ dans la foule** the crowd seemed to hesitate ◆ **il y a eu un ~ électoral important** there was strong evidence *ou* a strong element of indecision among voters 2 *(Mil : dans les rangs)* swaying, sway 3 *(= relâchement)* *(dans une œuvre, copie)* vagueness, imprecision; *(dans le travail)* unevenness (*dans* in); ◆ **le ~ de son esprit/imagination** his wandering mind/roving imagination 4 *(= ondulation)* *[de fanion]* fluttering ◆ **le ~ du drapeau dans le vent** the fluttering *ou* flapping of the flag in the wind 5 *(Fin)* floating

flotter /flɔte/ ▸ conjug 1 ◂ VI 1 *(sur l'eau)* to float ◆ **faire ~ qch sur l'eau** to float sth on the water 2 *[brume]* to drift, to hang; *[parfum]* to hang; *[cheveux]* to stream (out); *[drapeau]* to fly; *[fanion]* to flutter ◆ **~ au vent** *[cape, écharpe]* to flap *ou* flutter in the wind ◆ **un drapeau flottait sur le bâtiment** a flag was flying over *ou* from the building 3 *(= être trop grand)* *[vêtement]* to hang loose ◆ **il flotte dans ses vêtements** his clothes are too big for him 4 *(littér = errer)* *[pensée, imagination]* to wander, to rove ◆ **un sourire flottait sur ses lèvres** a smile hovered on *ou* played about his lips 5 *(= hésiter)* to waver, to hesitate 6 *(Fin)* *[devise]* to float ◆ **faire ~** to float VB IMPERS (* = *pleuvoir*) to rain VT *[+ bois]* to float (down a waterway)

flotteur /flɔtœʀ/ NM *[de filet, hydravion, carburateur, trimaran]* float; *[de chasse d'eau]* ballcock *(Brit)*, floater *(US)*

flottille /flɔtij/ NF *[de bateaux]* flotilla; *[d'avions]* squadron

flou, e /flu/ ADJ 1 *[dessin, trait]* blurred; *[image, contour]* hazy, vague; *[photo]* blurred, fuzzy, out of focus; *[couleur]* soft 2 *[robe]* loose(-fitting); *[coiffure]* soft 3 *[idée, pensée, théorie]* woolly, vague; *(Ordin)* *[logique]* fuzzy NM *[de photo, tableau]* fuzziness; *[de couleur]* softness; *[de robe]* looseness; *[de contours]* haziness ◆ **le ~ de son esprit** the vagueness of his mind ◆ **le ~ artistique** *(lit)* soft focus ◆ **c'est le ~ artistique** *(fig)* it's all very vague ◆ **~ juridique** vagueness of the law ◆ **sur ses intentions, il est resté dans le ~** he remained vague about his intentions

flouer* /flue/ ▸ conjug 1 ◂ VT *(= duper)* to swindle, to diddle* *(Brit)* ◆ **se faire ~** to be had*

flouse‡ †, **flouze**‡ † /fluz/ NM *(= argent)* bread‡, dough‡, lolly‡

fluctuant, e /flyktɥɑ̃, ɑ̃t/ ADJ *[prix, monnaie]* fluctuating; *[humeur]* changing

fluctuation /flyktɥasjɔ̃/ NF *[de prix]* fluctuation; *[d'opinion publique]* swing, fluctuation (*de* in); ◆ **~s du marché** market fluctuations

fluctuer /flyktɥe/ ▸ conjug 1 ◂ VI to fluctuate

fluet, -ette /flyɛ, ɛt/ ADJ *[corps]* slight, slender; *[personne]* slightly built, slender; *[taille, membre, doigt]* slender, slim; *[voix]* thin, reedy, piping

fluide /flɥid/ ADJ *[liquide, substance]* fluid; *[style, mouvement]* fluid, flowing; *[ligne, silhouette, robe]* flowing; *(Écon)* *[main-d'œuvre]* flexible ◆ **la circulation est ~** the traffic is moving freely ◆ **la situation politique reste ~** the political situation remains fluid NM 1 *(= gaz, liquide)* fluid ◆ **~ de refroidissement** coolant 2 *(= pouvoir)* (mysterious) power ◆ **il a du ~, il a un ~ magnétique** he has mysterious powers

fluidification /flɥidifikasjɔ̃/ NF fluidification, fluxing

fluidifier /flɥidifje/ ▸ conjug 7 ◂ VT to fluidify, to flux

fluidité /flɥidite/ NF *[de liquide, style]* fluidity; *[de ligne, silhouette]* flow; *[de circulation]* free flow; *(Écon)* *[de main-d'œuvre]* flexibility

fluo* /flyo/ ADJ INV (abrév de **fluorescent**) fluorescent ◆ **vert/rose ~** fluorescent green/pink

fluor /flyɔʀ/ NM fluorine ◆ **dentifrice au ~** fluoride toothpaste

fluoré, e /flyɔʀe/ ADJ *[dentifrice]* fluoride *(épith)*; *[eau]* fluoridated

fluorescéine /flyɔʀesein/ NF fluorescein

fluorescence /flyɔʀesɑ̃s/ NF fluorescence

fluorescent, e /flyɔʀesɑ̃, ɑ̃t/ ADJ fluorescent ◆ **écran/tube ~** fluorescent screen/lamp

fluorine /flyɔʀin/ NF fluorspar, fluorite, calcium fluoride

fluorure /flyɔʀyʀ/ NM fluoride

flush /flœʃ/ NM *(Cartes)* flush

flûte /flyt/ NF 1 *(= instrument)* flute ◆ **petite ~** piccolo 2 *(= verre)* flute (glass) ◆ **une ~ de champagne** a flute of champagne 3 *(= pain)* baguette, French stick *(Brit)* 4 *(= jambes)* **~s*** legs, pins* *(Brit)*, gams* *(US)* ◆ **se tirer les ~s** †‡ to leg it*, to scarper*; → **jouer** EXCL * drat!*

COMP **flûte basse** bass flute
flûte à bec recorder
flûte à champagne champagne flute
flûte de Pan panpipes
flûte traversière flute

flûté, e /flyte/ ADJ *[voix]* fluty

flûteau (pl **flûteaux**) /flyto/, **flûtiau** (pl **flûtiaux**) /flytjo/ NM *(= flûte)* penny whistle, reed pipe; *(= mirliton)* kazoo

flûtiste /flytist/ NMF flautist, flutist *(US)*

fluvial, e (mpl **-iaux**) /flyvjal, jo/ ADJ *[eaux, pêche, navigation, trafic]* river *(épith)*; *[érosion]* fluvial *(épith)*

fluvioglaciaire /flyvjoglasjɛʀ/ ADJ fluvioglacial

flux /fly/ NM ① (= *grande quantité*) *[d'argent, paroles]* flood; *[de récriminations]* spate; *[de personnes]* influx ◆ ~ **de capitaux** *(Écon)* capital flow ◆ ~ **monétaire** flow of money ◆ ~ **de trésorerie** cash flow ◆ **travailler en ~ tendus** *(Comm)* to use just-in-time methods ② (= *marée*) **le ~** the floodtide, the incoming tide ◆ **le ~ et le reflux** the ebb and flow ③ *(Phys)* flux, flow ◆ ~ **électrique/magnétique/lumineux** electric/magnetic/luminous flux ④ *(Méd)* ~ **de sang** flow of blood ◆ ~ **menstruel** menstrual flow ⑤ *(Ordin)* ~ **de données** data flow

fluxion /flyksjɔ̃/ NF *(Méd)* swelling, inflammation; *(dentaire)* gumboil ◆ ~ **de poitrine** pneumonia

FM /ɛfɛm/ NM (abrév de **fusil-mitrailleur**) MG NF (abrév de **fréquence modulée**) FM

FMI /ɛfɛmi/ NM (abrév de **Fonds monétaire international**) IMF

FN /ɛfɛn/ NM (abrév de **Front national**) → **front**

FNE /ɛfɛnə/ NM (abrév de **Fonds national de l'emploi**) → **fonds**

FNSEA /ɛfɛnɛsəa/ NF (abrév de **Fédération nationale des syndicats d'exploitants agricoles**) *French farmers' union*

FO /ɛfo/ NF (abrév de **Force ouvrière**) *French trade union*

foc /fɔk/ NM jib ◆ **grand/petit ~** outer/inner jib ◆ ~ **d'artimon** mizzen-topmast staysail

focal, e (mpl **-aux**) /fɔkal, o/ ADJ focal ◆ **point ~** focal point NF **focale** *(Géom, Opt)* focal distance *ou* length

focalisation /fɔkalizasjɔ̃/ NF focus (*sur* on); ◆ **les raisons de la ~ de l'opinion publique sur le chômage** the reasons why public attention is focused on unemployment

focaliser /fɔkalize/ ▸ conjug 1 ◂ VT *(fig, Phys)* to focus (*sur* on) VPR **se focaliser** *[personne]* to focus; *[attention]* to be focused (*sur* on)

foehn /føn/ NM ① *(Météo)* foehn ② *(Helv)* hairdryer

foène, foëne /fwɛn/ NF pronged harpoon, fishgig

fœtal, e (mpl **-aux**) /fetal, o/ ADJ foetal, fetal

fœtus /fetys/ NM foetus, fetus

fofolle /fɔfɔl/ ADJ F → **foufou**

foi /fwa/ NF ① (= *croyance*) faith ◆ **avoir la ~** to have faith ◆ **perdre la ~** to lose one's faith ◆ **il faut avoir la ~ !** * you've got to be (really) dedicated! ◆ **il n'y a que la ~ qui sauve !** faith is a marvellous thing! ◆ **la ~ transporte** *ou* **fait bouger les montagnes** faith can move mountains ◆ **la ~ du charbonnier** blind faith ◆ **sans ~ ni loi** fearing neither God nor man; → **article, profession**

② (= *confiance*) faith, trust ◆ **avoir ~ en Dieu** to have faith *ou* trust in God ◆ **avoir ~ en qn/qch/l'avenir** to have faith in sb/sth/the future ◆ **digne de ~** *[témoin]* reliable, trustworthy; *[témoignage]* reliable; → **ajouter**

③ (= *assurance*) word ◆ **respecter la ~ jurée** to honour one's word ◆ ~ **d'honnête homme !** on my word as a gentleman!, on my word of honour! ◆ **cette lettre en fait ~** this letter proves it ◆ **les deux textes feront ~** *(Jur)* both texts shall be deemed authentic ◆ **sous la ~ du serment** under *ou* on oath ◆ **sur la ~ de vagues rumeurs** on the strength of vague rumours ◆ **sur la ~ des témoins** on the word *ou* testimony of witnesses ◆ **en ~ de quoi j'ai décidé …** *(gén)* on the strength of which I have decided …; *(Jur)* in witness whereof I have decided … ◆ **être de bonne ~** to be sincere *ou* honest ◆ **c'était de bonne ~** it was done *(ou* said *etc)* in good faith ◆ **faire qch en toute bonne ~** to do sth in all good faith ◆ **en toute bonne ~ je l'ignore** honestly I don't know ◆ **la mauvaise ~** *(gén)* dishonesty; *(Philos)* bad faith, mauvaise foi ◆ **tu es de mauvaise ~** you're being dishonest; → **cachet**

④ ◆ **ma ~ …** well … ◆ **ma ~, c'est comme ça, mon vieux** * well, that's how it is, old man ◆ **ça, ma ~, je n'en sais rien** well, I don't know anything about that ◆ **c'est ma ~ vrai que …** well it's certainly *ou* undeniably true that …

foie /fwa/ NM liver ◆ ~ **de veau/de volaille** calves'/chicken liver ◆ **avoir mal au ~** to have a stomach ache ◆ **avoir une crise de ~** to have a bad stomach upset ◆ **avoir les ~s** ‡ to be scared to death * COMP **foie gras** foie gras

foie-de-bœuf (pl **foies-de-bœuf**) /fwadbœf/ NM beefsteak fungus

foil /fɔjl/ NM *(Naut)* (hydro)foil

foin[1] /fwɛ̃/ NM hay ◆ **faire les ~s** to make hay ◆ **à l'époque des ~s** in the haymaking season ◆ ~ **d'artichaut** choke ◆ **faire du ~** * (= *faire un scandale*) to kick up a fuss; (= *faire du bruit*) to make a row *ou* racket; → **rhume**

foin[2] /fwɛ̃/ EXCL (††, *hum*) ◆ ~ **des soucis d'argent/des créanciers !** a plague on money worries/on creditors!, the devil take money worries/creditors!

foire /fwaʀ/ NF ① (= *marché*) fair; (= *exposition commerciale*) trade fair; (= *fête foraine*) (fun) fair ◆ ~ **agricole** agricultural show ◆ ~ **aux bestiaux** cattle fair *ou* market ◆ ~ **exposition** exposition, expo; → **larron** ② *(locutions)* **avoir la ~** †‡ to have the runs * *ou* trots * ◆ **faire la ~** * to whoop it up * ◆ **il aime faire la ~** he's a party animal *, he loves partying * ◆ **c'est la ~ ici !, c'est une vraie ~ !** * it's bedlam in here! * ◆ ~ **d'empoigne** free-for-all COMP **foire aux questions** *(Internet)* frequently asked questions

foirer /fwaʀe/ ▸ conjug 1 ◂ VI * *[vis]* to slip; *[obus]* to fail to go off; ‡ *[projet]* to fall through, to bomb * *(US)* ◆ **il a tout fait ~** he ballsed *(Brit) ou* balled *(US)* everything up ‡ VT (‡ = *rater*) to flunk * ◆ **j'ai foiré l'histoire** I flunked history *

foireux, -euse ‡ /fwaʀø, øz/ ADJ († = *peureux*) yellow(-bellied) *, chicken * *(attrib)*; (= *raté*) *[idée, projet]* useless ◆ **ce projet/film est ~** this project/film is a washout *

fois /fwa/ NF ① *(gén)* time ◆ **une ~** once ◆ **deux ~** twice ◆ **trois ~** three times ◆ **une ~, deux ~, trois ~, adjugé !** *(aux enchères)* going, going, gone! ◆ **pour la (toute) première ~** for the (very) first time ◆ **quand je l'ai vu pour la première/dernière ~** when I first/last saw him, the first/last time I saw him ◆ **cette ~-ci/-là** this/that time ◆ **c'est bon** *ou* **ça va pour cette ~** I'll let you off this time *ou* (just) this once ◆ **une seule ~** only once ◆ **elle ne s'est trompée qu'une seule ~** she only got it wrong once ◆ **cela a été payé en une seule ~** it was paid for in one go ◆ **c'est la seule ~ que …** it's the only time that … ◆ **plusieurs ~** several times, a number of times ◆ **peu de ~** on few occasions ◆ **bien des ~, maintes (et maintes) ~** many a time, many times ◆ **autant de ~ que** as often as, as many times as ◆ **y regarder à deux** *ou* **à plusieurs ~ avant d'acheter qch** to think twice *ou* very hard before buying sth ◆ **s'y prendre à** *ou* **en deux/plusieurs ~ pour faire qch** to take two/several attempts *ou* goes to do sth ◆ **payer en plusieurs ~** to pay in several instalments ◆ **frapper qn par deux/trois ~** to hit sb twice/three times ◆ **je suis trois ~ grand-père** I am a grandfather three times over ◆ **vous avez mille ~ raison** you're absolutely right; → **autre, cent**[1]**, encore** *etc*

② *(dans un calcul)* **une ~** once ◆ **deux ~** twice, two times ◆ **trois/quatre ~** three/four times ◆ **une ~ tous les deux jours** once every two days, every other *ou* second day ◆ **trois ~ par an, trois ~ l'an** † three times a year ◆ **neuf ~ sur dix** nine times out of ten ◆ **quatre ~ plus d'eau/de voitures** four times as much water/as many cars ◆ **quatre ~ moins d'eau** four times less water, a quarter as much water ◆ **quatre ~ moins de voitures** four times fewer cars, a quarter as many cars ◆ **3 ~ 5 (font 15)** *(Math)* 3 times 5 (is *ou* makes 15) ◆ **il avait trois ~ rien** *(argent)* he had hardly any money; *(blessure)* there was hardly a scratch on him ◆ **et encore merci ! – oh, c'est trois ~ rien !** and thanks again! – oh, please don't mention it!

③ *(locutions)*

◆ **une fois** once ◆ **il était une ~ …, il y avait une ~ …** once upon a time there was … ◆ **pour une ~ !** for once! ◆ **en une ~** at one go ◆ **une (bonne) ~ pour toutes** once and for all ◆ **il faudrait qu'il pleuve une bonne ~** what's needed is a good downpour ◆ **une ~ (qu'il sera) parti** once he has left ◆ **une ~ qu'il n'était pas là** once *ou* on one occasion when he wasn't there ◆ **viens ici une ~** *(Belg)* just come over here ◆ **une ~ n'est pas coutume** *(Prov)* just the once won't hurt

◆ **une nouvelle fois** once again ◆ **cela démontre une nouvelle ~ l'inefficacité du système** it shows once again how inefficient the system is

◆ **à la fois** ◆ **ne répondez pas tous à la ~** don't all answer at once ◆ **c'est à la ~ drôle et grave** it's both funny and serious ◆ **il est à la ~ metteur en scène et romancier** he's both a director and novelist ◆ **il était à la ~ grand, gros et fort** he was tall, fat and strong ◆ **faire deux choses à la ~** to do two things at once *ou* at the same time ◆ **l'appareil permet à la ~ de téléphoner et d'accéder à Internet** the device allows you to make phone calls and access the Internet at the same time

◆ **des fois** * (= *parfois*) sometimes ◆ **des ~, il est très méchant** he can be very nasty at times, sometimes he's pretty nasty ◆ **si des ~ vous le rencontrez** if you should happen *ou* chance to meet him ◆ **non mais, des ~ !** *(scandalisé)* do you mind!; *(en plaisantant)* you must be joking! ◆ **non mais des ~, pour qui te prends-tu ?** look here, who do you think you are! ◆ **des ~ que** (just) in case ◆ **attendons, des ~ qu'il viendrait** let's wait in case he comes ◆ **allons-y, des ~ qu'il resterait des places** let's go – there may be some seats left

foison /fwazɔ̃/ NF ◆ **une ~ de** any number of ◆ **il existe une ~ d'ouvrages sur le sujet** there are any number of books on the subject

◆ **à foison** ◆ **il y a du poisson/des légumes à ~** there is an abundance of fish/of vegetables, there is fish/there are vegetables in plenty ◆ **il y en avait à ~ au marché** there was plenty of it *(ou* there were plenty of them) at the market

foisonnant, e /fwazɔnɑ̃, ɑ̃t/ ADJ *[végétation]* luxuriant, lush; *[documentation]* abundant, lavish ◆ **une œuvre ~e** a rich and diverse oeuvre ◆ **un roman ~** a rich and lively novel

foisonnement /fwazɔnmɑ̃/ NM (= *abondance*) profusion, abundance ◆ **le ~ culturel des années 70** the cultural explosion that took place in the 70s ◆ **le ~ d'idées qu'on trouve dans ses romans** the wealth of ideas in his novels

foisonner /fwazɔne/ ▸ conjug 1 ◂ VI to abound ◆ **pays qui foisonne de** *ou* **en talents** country which has a profusion *ou* an abundance of talented people *ou* which is teeming with talented people ◆ **texte foisonnant d'idées/de fautes** text teeming with ideas/with mistakes

fol /fɔl/ ADJ M → **fou**

folâtre /fɔlɑtʀ/ ADJ *[enfant]* playful, frolicsome; *[jeux]* lively; *[caractère]* lively, sprightly ◆ **il n'est pas d'humeur ~** *(frm, hum)* he's not in a very playful mood

folâtrer /fɔlɑtʀe/ ▸ conjug 1 ◂ VI *[enfants]* to frolic, to romp; *[chiots, poulains]* to gambol, to frolic, to frisk ◆ **au lieu de ~ tu ferais mieux de travailler** you should do some work instead of fooling around

folâtrerie /fɔlɑtʀəʀi/ NF *(littér)* (NonC = caractère) playfulness; (= action) frolicking (NonC), romping (NonC), gambolling (NonC)

foldingue * /fɔldɛ̃g/ ADJ *[personne]* nuts*, crazy*; *[soirée, musique]* wild ◆ **tu es complètement ~ !** you're nuts!* *ou* crazy!* NMF nutcase* ◆ **les ~s de l'informatique** computer fanatics *ou* freaks*

foliacé, e /fɔljase/ ADJ foliated, foliaceous

foliation /fɔljasjɔ̃/ NF (= *développement*) foliation, leafing; (= *disposition*) leaf arrangement

folichon, -onne * /fɔliʃɔ̃, ɔn/ ADJ *(gén nég)* pleasant, interesting, exciting ◆ **aller à ce dîner, ça n'a rien de ~** going to this dinner won't be much fun *ou* won't be very exciting ◆ **la vie n'est pas toujours folichonne avec lui** life's not always fun with him

folie /fɔli/ NF 1 (= *maladie*) madness, insanity, lunacy ◆ **il a un petit grain de ~*** there's something eccentric about him ◆ **~ furieuse** *(Méd)* raving madness ◆ **c'est de la ~ douce** *ou* **pure** *ou* **furieuse** it's utter *ou* sheer madness *ou* lunacy ◆ **~ meurtrière** killing frenzy ◆ **c'était un coup de ~** it was a moment's madness ◆ **avoir la ~ des grandeurs** to have delusions of grandeur ◆ **il a la ~ des timbres-poste** he's mad* *ou* crazy* about stamps ◆ **aimer qn à la ~** to be madly in love with sb, to love sb to distraction ◆ **il a eu la ~ de refuser** he was mad enough *ou* crazy enough to refuse ◆ **c'est ~ d'y aller** it would be pure folly to go there ◆ **sortir en mer par un temps pareil, c'est de la ~ !** it's sheer madness going out to sea in weather like that!

◆ **en folie** *[public]* wild ◆ **les soldats en ~ ont tout saccagé** the soldiers went mad and ransacked the place ◆ **un monde en ~** a world gone mad

◆ **de folie** * *(fig = extraordinaire)* amazing, incredible

2 (= *bêtise, erreur, dépense*) extravagance ◆ **il a fait des ~s dans sa jeunesse** he had his fling *ou* a really wild time in his youth ◆ **des ~s de jeunesse** youthful indiscretions ◆ **ils ont fait une ~ en achetant cette voiture** they were mad *ou* crazy to buy that car ◆ **vous avez fait des ~s en achetant ce cadeau** you have been far too extravagant in buying this present ◆ **il ferait des ~s pour elle** he would do anything for her ◆ **il ferait des ~s pour la revoir** he'd give anything to see her again ◆ **je ferais des ~s pour un morceau de fromage** *(hum)* I'd give *ou* do anything for a piece of cheese ◆ **une nouvelle ~ de sa part** *(dépense)* another of his extravagances; *(projet)* another of his hare-brained schemes

3 *(Hist Archit)* folly

folié, e /fɔlje/ ADJ foliate

folingue * /fɔlɛ̃g/ ADJ nuts*, crazy*

folio /fɔljo/ NM folio

foliole /fɔljɔl/ NF *(Bot)* leaflet

folioter /fɔljɔte/ ▸ conjug 1 ◂ VT to folio

folique /fɔlik/ ADJ ◆ **acide ~** folic acid

folk /fɔlk/ NM folk music ADJ ◆ **chanteur/musique ~** folk singer/music COMP **folk song** folk music

folklo * /fɔlklo/ ADJ (abrév de **folklorique**) (= *excentrique*) weird, outlandish ◆ **c'est un peu ~ chez lui** his house is a bit weird ◆ **cette soirée, c'était ~** it was a really way-out* *ou* whacky* party

folklore /fɔlklɔʀ/ NM folklore ◆ **c'est du ~ !*** *(péj) (ridicule, dépassé)* it's all terribly quaint ◆ **le ~ habituel des visites princières** *(péj)* the usual razzmatazz of royal visits

folklorique /fɔlklɔʀik/ ADJ 1 *[chant, costume]* folk *(épith)* 2 (* = *excentrique*) *[personne, tenue, ambiance]* weird, outlandish ◆ **la réunion a été assez ~** the meeting was pretty bizarre

folle /fɔl/ ADJ F, NF → **fou**

follement /fɔlmɑ̃/ ADV 1 (= *très, énormément*) *[original, ambitieux, content, intéressant, drôle]* incredibly ◆ **on s'est ~ amusé** we had a fantastic time* ◆ **il désire ~ lui parler** he's dying* to speak to her, he desperately wants to speak to her 2 *[espérer]* desperately; *[dépenser]* madly ◆ **~ amoureux** madly in love, head over heels in love ◆ **il se lança ~ à leur poursuite** he dashed after them in mad pursuit ◆ **avant de te lancer ~ dans cette aventure** before rushing headlong into *ou* jumping feet first into this business

follet, -ette /fɔlɛ, ɛt/ ADJ (= *étourdi*) scatterbrained; → **feu¹, poil**

folliculaire /fɔlikylɛʀ/ ADJ follicular

follicule /fɔlikyl/ NM follicle

folliculine /fɔlikylin/ NF oestrone

fomentateur, -trice /fɔmɑ̃tatœʀ, tʀis/ NM,F troublemaker, agitator ◆ **les ~s des grèves** the people behind the strikes, the people who instigated the strikes

fomentation /fɔmɑ̃tasjɔ̃/ NF fomenting, fomentation

fomenter /fɔmɑ̃te/ ▸ conjug 1 ◂ VT *(lit, fig)* to foment, to stir up

foncé, e /fɔ̃se/ (ptp de **foncer²**) ADJ *[couleur] (gén)* dark; *(tons pastels)* deep ◆ **à la peau ~e** dark-skinned

foncer¹ /fɔ̃se/ ▸ conjug 3 ◂ VI 1 (* = *aller à vive allure*) *[conducteur, voiture]* to tear* *ou* belt* *(Brit)* along; *[coureur]* to charge* *ou* tear* along; *(dans un travail)* to get a move on* ◆ **maintenant, il faut que je fonce** I must dash *ou* fly* now ◆ **fonce le chercher** go and fetch him straight away *(Brit) ou* right away *(US)* ◆ **il a foncé chez le directeur** he rushed off to see the manager ◆ **allez, fonce !** come on, hurry up!

2 * (= *être dynamique*) to have drive; (= *aller de l'avant*) to go for it*

3 (= *se précipiter*) to charge (*vers* at; *dans* into); ◆ **~ sur** *ou* **vers l'ennemi/l'obstacle** to charge at *ou* make a rush at the enemy/the obstacle ◆ **le camion a foncé sur moi** the truck drove straight at me ◆ **~ sur un objet** *(lit, fig)* to make straight for *ou* make a beeline for an object ◆ **~ dans la foule** *[taureau, police]* to charge into the crowd; *[camion]* to plough into the crowd ◆ **~ (tête baissée) dans la porte/dans le piège** to walk straight into the door/straight *ou* headlong into the trap ◆ **~ dans le brouillard** *(fig)* to forge ahead regardless *ou* in the dark ◆ **la police a foncé dans le tas*** the police charged (into the crowd)

foncer² /fɔ̃se/ ▸ conjug 3 ◂ VT *[+ couleur]* to make darker VI *[liquide, couleur, cheveux]* to turn *ou* go darker

foncer³ /fɔ̃se/ ▸ conjug 3 ◂ VT *[+ tonneau]* to bottom; *[+ puits]* to sink, to bore; *(Culin) [+ moule]* to line

fonceur, -euse * /fɔ̃sœʀ, øz/ NM,F go-getter* ◆ **c'est un ~** he's a go-getter*, he's got tremendous drive

foncier, -ière /fɔ̃sje, jɛʀ/ ADJ 1 *[impôt]* property *(épith)*, land *(épith)*; *[noblesse, propriété]* landed *(épith)*; *[problème, politique]* (relating to) land ownership ◆ **propriétaire ~** property owner ◆ **revenus ~s** income from property 2 *[qualité, différence]* fundamental, basic ◆ **la malhonnêteté foncière de ces pratiques** the fundamental *ou* basic dishonesty of these practices ◆ **être d'une foncière malhonnêteté** to be fundamentally dishonest NM ◆ **le ~** real estate

foncièrement /fɔ̃sjɛʀmɑ̃/ ADV fundamentally

fonction /fɔ̃ksjɔ̃/ NF 1 (= *métier*) post, office ◆ **~s** (= *tâches*) office, duties ◆ **entrer en ~(s), prendre ses ~s** *[employé]* to take up one's post; *[maire, président]* to come into *ou* take office, to take up one's post ◆ **depuis son entrée en ~(s)** *ou* **sa prise de ~(s)** since he came into *ou* took office ◆ **ça n'entre pas dans mes ~s** it's not part of my duties ◆ **de par ses ~s** by virtue of his office ◆ **être en ~** to be in office ◆ **la ~ publique** the civil service ◆ **logement de ~** *(gén)* company accommodation; *[de concierge, fonctionnaire]* on-site accommodation *(with low or free rent)* ◆ **avoir une voiture de ~** *(gén)* to have a car that goes with one's job; *(firme privée)* to have a company car; → **démettre, exercice**

2 (= *rôle*) *(gén, Gram, Ordin)* function ◆ **~ biologique** biological function ◆ **remplir une ~** to fulfil a function ◆ **cet organe a pour ~ de ..., la ~ de cet organe est de ...** the function of this organ is to ... ◆ **avoir** *ou* **faire ~ de sujet** *(Gram)* to function *ou* act as a subject

3 *(Math)* **~ (algébrique)** (algebraic) function ◆ **~ acide** *(Chim)* acid(ic) function ◆ **être ~ de** *(Math)* to be a function of

4 *(locutions)* **faire ~ de directeur/d'ambassadeur** to act as manager/as ambassador ◆ **il n'y a pas de porte, ce rideau en fait ~** there is no door but this curtain serves the purpose ◆ **sa réussite est ~ de son travail** his success depends on how well he works

◆ **en fonction de** according to ◆ **salaire en ~ des diplômes** salary according to *ou* commensurate with qualifications

> ⚠ Quand il renvoie à un métier ou à une charge, **fonction** ne se traduit pas par le mot anglais **function**.

> **FONCTION PUBLIQUE**
>
> The term **la fonction publique** has great cultural significance in France, and covers a much broader range of activities than the English term 'civil service'. There are almost three million « fonctionnaires » (also known as « agents de l'État ») in France. They include teachers, social services staff, post office workers and employees of the French rail service.
>
> Recruitment for jobs in the **fonction publique** is by competitive examination, and successful candidates gain the official status of « titulaire ». Because this status theoretically guarantees total job security, « fonctionnaires » are sometimes stereotyped as being unfairly privileged compared to private sector employees. → **CONCOURS**

fonctionnaire /fɔ̃ksjɔnɛʀ/ NMF *(gén)* state employee; *(dans l'administration) [de ministère]* government official, civil servant; *[de municipalité]* local government officer *ou* official ◆ **haut ~** high-ranking *ou* top-ranking civil servant, senior official ◆ **petit ~** minor (public) official ◆ **les ~s de l'enseignement** state-employed teachers ◆ **~ de (la) police** police officer, officer of the law ◆ **il a une mentalité de ~** *(péj)* he has the mentality of a petty bureaucrat ◆ **c'est un vrai ~** he's a petty bureaucrat *ou* a real jobsworth* *(Brit)*

fonctionnalisme /fɔ̃ksjɔnalism/ NM functionalism

fonctionnaliste /fɔ̃ksjɔnalist/ ADJ, NMF functionalist

fonctionnalité /fɔ̃ksjɔnalite/ NF *(gén)* practicality; *(Ordin)* functionality

fonctionnariat /fɔ̃ksjɔnaʀja/ NM state employee status

fonctionnarisation /fɔ̃ksjɔnaʀizasjɔ̃/ NF ◆ **la ~ de la médecine** the state takeover of medicine ◆ **le gouvernement propose la ~ des médecins** the government proposes taking doctors into the public service *ou* making doctors employees of the state

fonctionnariser /fɔ̃ksjɔnaʀize/ ► conjug 1 ◄ VT ◆ **~ qn** to make sb an employee of the state; *(dans l'administration)* to take sb into the public service ◆ **~ un service** to take over a service (to be run by the state)

fonctionnarisme /fɔ̃ksjɔnaʀism/ NM *(péj)* officialdom ◆ **c'est le règne du ~** bureaucracy rules, officialdom has taken over

fonctionnel, -elle /fɔ̃ksjɔnɛl/ ADJ functional ◆ **mot ~** *(Ling)* function word NM staff manager ◆ **les ~s et les opérationnels** managers and operatives, staff and line

fonctionnellement /fɔ̃ksjɔnɛlmɑ̃/ ADV functionally

fonctionnement /fɔ̃ksjɔnmɑ̃/ NM *[d'appareil]* functioning; *[d'entreprise, institution]* operation, running; *(Méd) [d'organisme]* functioning ◆ **expliquer le ~ d'un moteur** to explain how a motor works ◆ **en parfait ~** in perfect working order ◆ **pour assurer le (bon) ~ de l'appareil** to keep the machine in (good) working order ◆ **pour assurer le (bon) ~ du service** to ensure the smooth running of the department ◆ **panne due au mauvais ~ du carburateur** breakdown due to a fault *ou* a malfunction in the carburettor ◆ **pendant le ~ de l'appareil** while the machine is in operation *ou* is running ◆ **budget de ~** operating budget ◆ **dépenses** *ou* **frais de ~** running costs ◆ **~ en réseau** *(Ordin)* networking

fonctionner /fɔ̃ksjɔne/ ► conjug 1 ◄ VI *[mécanisme, machine]* to work, to function; *[entreprise]* to function, to operate; * *[personne]* to function, to operate ◆ **faire ~** *[+ machine]* to operate ◆ **je n'ai jamais vraiment compris comment il fonctionne*** I've never really understood what makes him tick* ◆ **notre téléphone/télévision fonctionne mal** there's something wrong with our phone/television, our phone/television isn't working properly ◆ **le courrier fonctionne mal** the mail isn't reliable ◆ **ça ne fonctionne pas** it's out of order, it's not working ◆ **sais-tu faire ~ la machine à laver ?** do you know how to work the washing machine? ◆ **~ au gaz/à l'énergie solaire/sur piles** to be gas-powered/solar-powered/battery-operated, to run on gas/on solar power/on batteries ◆ **il a du mal à ~ au sein d'une équipe** he doesn't work well in a team

fond /fɔ̃/ NM 1 *[de récipient, vallée]* bottom; *[d'armoire]* back; *[de jardin]* bottom, far end; *[de pièce]* far end, back; *[d'utérus]* fundus ◆ **le ~** *(Min)* the (coal) face ◆ **travailler au ~** *(Min)* to work at *ou* on the (coal) face ◆ **être/tomber au ~ de l'eau** to be at/fall to the bottom of the water ◆ **le ~ de la gorge** the back of the throat ◆ **les mots lui sont restés au ~ de la gorge** the words stuck in his throat ◆ **envoyer un navire par le ~** to send a ship to the bottom ◆ **y a-t-il beaucoup de ~ ?** is it very deep? ◆ **l'épave repose par 10 mètres de ~** the wreck is lying 10 metres down ◆ **les grands ~s** the ocean depths ◆ **à ~ de cale** *(Naut)* (down) in the hold; (* = *vite*) at top speed ◆ **au ~ du couloir** at the far end of the corridor ◆ **au ~ de la boutique** at the back of the shop ◆ **ancré au ~ de la baie** anchored at the (far) end of the bay ◆ **village perdu au ~ de la province** village in the depths *ou* heart of the country ◆ **venir du ~ des âges** *[dynastie, réflexe, sagesse]* to be age-old ◆ **sans ~** *(lit, fig)* bottomless; → **double, fin**[1]

2 *(= tréfonds)* **le ~ de son cœur est pur** deep down his heart is pure ◆ **savoir lire au ~ des cœurs** to be able to see deep (down) into people's hearts ◆ **merci du ~ du cœur** I thank you from the bottom of my heart ◆ **il pensait au ~ de son cœur** *ou* **de lui(-même) que ...** deep down he thought that ..., in his heart of hearts he thought that ... ◆ **vous avez deviné/je vais vous dire le ~ de ma pensée** you have guessed/I shall tell you what I really think *ou* what my feelings really are ◆ **regarder qn au ~ des yeux** to look deep into sb's eyes ◆ **il a un bon ~, il n'a pas un mauvais ~** he's basically a good person, he's a good person at heart *ou* bottom ◆ **il y a chez lui un ~ d'honnêteté/de méchanceté** there's a streak of honesty/of maliciousness in him ◆ **il y a un ~ de vérité dans ce qu'il dit** there's an element of truth in what he says ◆ **toucher le ~** *(lit)* to touch the bottom; *(fig) [personne]* to hit rock bottom; *[récession, productivité]* to bottom out ◆ **j'ai touché le ~ du désespoir** I hit rock bottom

3 *(= essentiel) [d'affaire, question, débat]* heart ◆ **c'est là le ~ du problème** that's the heart *ou* root *ou* core of the problem ◆ **aller au ~ du problème** to get to the heart *ou* root of the problem ◆ **aller au ~ des choses** to do things thoroughly ◆ **il faut aller jusqu'au ~ de cette histoire** we must get to the root of this business ◆ **débat de ~** fundamental discussion ◆ **problème de ~** basic *ou* fundamental problem ◆ **ouvrage de ~** basic work ◆ **article de ~** *(Presse)* feature article

4 *(= contenu)* content ◆ **le ~ et la forme** content and form ◆ **le ~ de l'affaire** *(Jur)* the substance of the case

5 *(= arrière-plan) [de tableau, situation]* background ◆ **~ sonore** *ou* **musical** background music ◆ **blanc sur ~ noir** white on a black background ◆ **avec cette sombre perspective pour ~** with this gloomy prospect in the background; → **bruit, toile**

6 *(= petite quantité)* drop ◆ **versez-m'en juste un ~ (de verre)** pour me just a drop ◆ **ils ont vidé les ~s de bouteilles** they emptied what was left in the bottles *ou* the dregs from the bottles ◆ **il va falloir racler** *ou* **gratter** *ou* **faire les ~s de tiroirs** we'll have to scrape together what we can

7 *(= lie)* sediment, deposit

8 *(Sport)* **le ~** long-distance running ◆ **de ~** *[course, coureur]* long-distance *(épith)*; → **ski**

9 *[de chapeau]* crown; *[de pantalon]* seat ◆ **c'est là que j'ai usé mes ~s de culotte** that's where I spent my early school years

10 *(locutions)* **le ~ de l'air est frais** it's a bit chilly, there's a nip in the air

◆ **à fond** ◆ **étudier une question à ~** to study a question thoroughly *ou* in depth ◆ **il est soutenu à ~ par ses amis** his friends back him up all the way ◆ **il exploite à ~ la situation** he's exploiting the situation to the full ◆ **il joue à ~ de son charisme** he makes full use of his charisma ◆ **il se donne à ~ dans son travail** he really throws himself into his work ◆ **il connaît le sujet à ~** he knows the subject inside out ◆ **visser un boulon à ~** to screw a bolt (right) home ◆ **respirer à ~** to breathe deeply ◆ **à ~ de train, à ~ la caisse*, à ~ les manettes*** at top speed

◆ **au fond, dans le fond** *(= sous les apparences)* basically, at bottom; *(= en fait)* basically, really, in fact ◆ **il n'est pas méchant au ~** he's not a bad sort at heart ◆ **il fait semblant d'être désolé, mais dans le ~ il est bien content** he makes out he's upset but he's quite pleased really *ou* but deep down he's quite pleased ◆ **dans le ~** *ou* **au ~, ça ne change pas grand-chose** basically, it makes no great difference, it makes no great difference really ◆ **ce n'est pas si stupide, au ~** it's not such a bad idea after all

◆ **de fond en comble** *[fouiller]* from top to bottom; *[détruire]* completely, utterly ◆ **ce retard bouleverse mes plans de ~ en comble** this delay throws my plans right out, this delay completely overturns my plans

COMP **fond d'artichaut** artichoke heart
fond de court *(Tennis)* **jeu/joueur de ~ de court** baseline game/player
fond d'écran *(Ordin)* wallpaper
fond de magasin *(= invendus)* leftover stock
les fonds marins the sea bed
fond d'œil fundus ◆ **faire un ~ d'œil à qn** to look into the back of sb's eye, to perform a funduscopy on sb *(SPÉC)*
fond de portefeuille *(Bourse)* portfolio base
fond de robe slip
fond de tarte *(= pâte)* pastry base; *(= crème)* custard base
fond de teint foundation (cream)

fondamental, e (mpl **-aux**) /fɔ̃damɑ̃tal, o/ GRAMMAIRE ACTIVE 53.2 ADJ *(= essentiel) [question, recherche, changement]* fundamental, basic; *[vocabulaire]* basic; *[couleurs]* primary; *(= foncier) [égoïsme, incompréhension]* basic, inherent, fundamental ◆ **son ~, note ~e** fundamental (note) ◆ **matière ~e** *(Scol)* core subject *(Brit)* NF **fondamentale** *(Mus)* root, fundamental (note) NMPL **fondamentaux** *(= principes, bases)* fundamentals

fondamentalement /fɔ̃damɑ̃talmɑ̃/ ADV fundamentally

fondamentalisme /fɔ̃damɑ̃talism/ NM fundamentalism

fondamentaliste /fɔ̃damɑ̃talist/ ADJ, NMF fundamentalist

fondant, e /fɔ̃dɑ, ɑt/ ADJ *[neige]* thawing, melting; *[fruit]* luscious; *[viande]* tender, melt-in-the-mouth *(épith)* ◆ **température de la glace ~e** temperature of melting ice ◆ **bonbon ~** fondant ◆ **chocolat ~** high-quality plain chocolate NM *(Chim)* flux; *(= bonbon, Culin)* fondant ◆ **~ au chocolat** *(= gâteau)* chocolate fondant cake

fondateur, -trice /fɔ̃datœʀ, tʀis/ ADJ *[mythe, texte, idée]* founding; → **père** NM,F founder; *(Jur, Fin) [de société]* incorporator

fondation /fɔ̃dasjɔ̃/ NF *(= action, institut)* foundation ◆ **~s** *(Constr)* foundations

fondé, e /fɔ̃de/ (ptp de **fonder**) ADJ 1 *[crainte, réclamation]* well-founded, justified ◆ **bien ~** well-founded, fully justified ◆ **mal ~** ill-founded, groundless ◆ **ce qu'il dit n'est pas ~** there are no grounds *ou* there is no justification for what he says ◆ **~ sur des ouï-dire** based on hearsay 2 ◆ **être ~ à faire/croire/dire qch** to have good reason to do/believe/say sth, to have (good) grounds for doing/believing/saying sth NM ◆ **~ (de pouvoir)** *(Jur)* authorized representative; *(= cadre bancaire)* senior banking executive

fondement /fɔ̃dmɑ̃/ NM 1 *(= base)* foundation ◆ **~ d'une action en justice** cause of action ◆ **sans ~** without foundation, unfounded, groundless ◆ **jeter les ~s de qch** to lay the foundations of sth 2 *(hum = derrière)* posterior *(hum)*, backside; *(= fond de pantalon)* trouser seat

fonder /fɔ̃de/ ► conjug 1 ◄ VT 1 *(= créer) [+ ville, parti, prix littéraire]* to found; *[+ commerce]* to set up; *[+ famille]* to start ◆ **~ un foyer** to set up home and start a family ◆ **"maison fondée en 1850"** *(magasin)* "Established 1850" 2 *(= baser)* to base, to found *(sur on)*; ◆ **~ sa richesse sur qch** to build one's wealth on sth ◆ **~ une théorie sur qch** to base a theory on sth ◆ **~ tous ses espoirs sur qch/qn** to place *ou* pin all one's hopes on sth/sb 3 *(= justifier) [+ réclamation]* to justify VPR **se fonder** ◆ **se ~ sur** *[personne]* to go by, to go on, to base o.s. on; *[théorie, décision]* to be based on ◆ **sur quoi vous fondez-vous pour l'affirmer ?** what grounds do you have for saying this?

fonderie /fɔ̃dʀi/ NF 1 *(= usine d'extraction)* smelting works; *(= atelier de moulage)* foundry 2 *(= action)* founding, casting

fondeur, -euse /fɔ̃dœʀ, øz/ NM,F *(Ski)* cross-country skier NM *(Métal) (= industriel)* foundry owner; *(= ouvrier)* foundry worker

fondre /fɔ̃dʀ/ ▸ conjug 41 ◂ VT 1 *(= liquéfier) [+ substance]* to melt; *[+ argenterie, objet de bronze]* to melt down; *[+ minerai]* to smelt; *[+ neige]* to melt, to thaw
2 *(= diminuer, attendrir) [+ dureté, résolution]* to melt
3 *(= couler) [+ cloche, statue]* to cast, to found
4 *(= réunir)* to combine, to fuse together, to merge *(en* into*)*
5 *(Peinture) [+ couleur, ton]* to merge, to blend
VI 1 *(à la chaleur, gén)* to melt; *[neige]* to melt, to thaw; *(dans l'eau)* to dissolve ◆ **faire** ~ *[+ beurre]* to melt; *[+ graisse]* to render down; *[+ sel, sucre]* to dissolve; *[+ neige]* to melt, to thaw ◆ **ça fond dans la bouche** it melts in your mouth
2 *[colère, résolution]* to melt away; *[provisions, réserves]* to vanish ◆ ~ **comme neige au soleil** to melt away ◆ **l'argent fond entre ses mains** money runs through his fingers, he spends money like water ◆ **cela fit ~ sa colère** at that his anger melted away ◆ ~ **en larmes** to dissolve *ou* burst into tears
3 *(* = maigrir)* to slim down ◆ **j'ai fondu de 5 kg** I've lost 5 kg
4 *(* = s'attendrir)* to melt ◆ **j'ai fondu** my heart melted, I melted ◆ **son sourire me fait ~, je fonds devant son sourire** his smile makes me melt *ou* makes me go weak at the knees
5 *(= s'abattre)* ~ **sur qn** *[vautour, ennemi]* to swoop down on sb; *[malheurs]* to sweep down on sb
VPR **se fondre** 1 *(= se réunir) [cortèges, courants]* to merge *(en* into*)*
2 *(= disparaître)* **se ~ dans la nuit/brume** to fade (away) *ou* merge into the night/mist ◆ **se ~ dans la masse** *ou* **foule** *[personne]* to melt into the crowd ◆ **ce détail se fond dans la masse** this detail is lost among the rest ◆ **se ~ dans le décor** *[personne]* to melt into the background; *[appareil, objet]* to blend in with the decor

fondrière /fɔ̃dʀijɛʀ/ NF pothole

fonds /fɔ̃/ NM 1 *(Comm)* ~ **de commerce** *(lit)* business; *(fig = source de revenus)* moneymaker ◆ **il possède le ~ mais pas les murs** he owns the business but not the property ◆ **vendre son** ~ to sell up ◆ ~ **de terre** land *(NonC)*
2 *(= ressources) [de musée, bibliothèque]* collection ◆ **ce pays a un ~ folklorique très riche** this country has a rich folk heritage ◆ ~ **de secours/de solidarité/d'amortissement** relief/solidarity/sinking fund ◆ ~ **de garantie** guarantee fund ◆ **Fonds national de l'emploi** *French state fund to provide retraining and redundancy payments for the unemployed* ◆ **Fonds européen de coopération monétaire** European Monetary Cooperation Fund ◆ **Fonds européen de développement** European Development Fund ◆ **Fonds social européen** European Social Fund ◆ **le Fonds monétaire international** the International Monetary Fund
3 *(= organisme)* ~ **commun de placement** investment *ou* mutual fund ◆ ~ **de développement économique et social** fund for economic and social development ◆ ~ **de pension** pension fund ◆ ~ **de prévoyance** contingency fund *ou* reserve ◆ ~ **régulateur** buffer fund ◆ ~ **de retraite** pension fund ◆ ~ **de stabilisation des changes** (currency) stabilization fund, Foreign Exchange Equalization Account *(Brit)*
4 *(Fin : souvent pl) (= argent)* money; *(= capital)* funds, capital; *(pour une dépense précise)* funds ◆ **pour transporter les ~** to transport the money ◆ **investir des ~ importants dans qch** to invest large sums of money *ou* a large amount of capital in sth ◆ **réunir les ~ nécessaires à un achat** to raise the necessary funds for a purchase ◆ **mise de ~** capital outlay ◆ **faire une mise de ~** to lay out capital ◆ **mise de ~ initiale** initial (capital) outlay ◆ **ne pas être/être en ~** to be out of/be in funds ◆ **je lui ai prêté de l'argent, ça a été à ~ perdus** I lent him some money, but I never saw it again *ou* but I never got it back ◆ ~ **de caisse** cash in hand ◆ ~ **de roulement** *(gén)* working capital; *[de syndic]* contingency fund ◆ ~ **bloqués** frozen assets ◆ ~ **disponibles** liquid assets ◆ ~ **d'État** government securities ◆ ~ **propres** shareholders' equity, stockholders' equity *(US)*, equity capital ◆ ~ **publics** *(Bourse)* government stock *ou* securities; *(= recettes de l'État)* public funds *ou* money ◆ ~ **secrets** secret funds; → **appel, bailleur, détournement**

fondu, e /fɔ̃dy/ (ptp de **fondre**) ADJ 1 *(= liquide) [beurre]* melted; *[métal]* molten ◆ **neige ~e** slush; → **fromage**
2 *(Métal)* **statue de bronze ~** *(= moulé)* cast bronze statue
3 *(= flou, estompé) [contours]* blurred, hazy; *[couleurs]* blending
4 *(* = fou)* nuts *, loopy * ◆ **t'es complètement ~ !** you're nuts! *
NM,F * ◆ **c'est un ~ de jazz/télévision** *(= fanatique)* he's a jazz/television freak *
NM 1 *(Peinture) [de couleurs]* blend ◆ **le ~ de ce tableau me plaît** I like the way the colours blend in this picture
2 *(Ciné)* ~ **(enchaîné)** dissolve, fade in-fade out ◆ **fermeture en ~, ~ en fermeture** fade-out ◆ **ouverture en ~, ~ en ouverture** fade-in ◆ **faire un ~ au noir** to fade to black
NF **fondue** *(Culin)* **~e (savoyarde)** (cheese) fondue ◆ **~e bourguignonne** fondue bourguignonne, meat fondue ◆ **~e de poireaux/tomates** leek/tomato fondue

fongible /fɔ̃ʒibl/ ADJ fungible

fongicide /fɔ̃ʒisid/ ADJ fungicidal NM fungicide

fontaine /fɔ̃tɛn/ NF *(ornementale)* fountain; *(naturelle)* spring; *(murale)* fountain; *(= distributeur d'eau potable) (à jet d'eau)* drinking fountain; *(avec gobelets)* water dispenser ◆ **cette petite, c'est une vraie ~** * *(hum)* she's a real little crybaby ◆ **il ne faut pas dire ~ je ne boirai pas de ton eau** *(Prov)* never say never, you never know; → **jouvence**

fontainier /fɔ̃tenje/ NM hydraulic engineer

fontanelle /fɔ̃tanɛl/ NF fontanel(le)

fonte /fɔ̃t/ NF 1 *(= action) [de substance]* melting; *[d'argenterie, objet de bronze]* melting down; *[de minerai]* smelting; *[de neige]* melting, thawing; *[de cloche, statue]* casting, founding ◆ **à la ~ des neiges** when the thaw comes, when the snow melts *ou* thaws 2 *(= métal)* cast iron ◆ ~ **brute** pig-iron ◆ **en ~** *[tuyau, radiateur]* cast-iron *(épith)* 3 *(Typo)* font 4 *(Agr)* ~ **des semis** damping off

fontes /fɔ̃t/ NFPL holsters *(on saddle)*

fonts /fɔ̃/ NMPL ◆ ~ **baptismaux** (baptismal) font ◆ **tenir un enfant sur les ~ baptismaux** to be godfather *(ou* godmother) to a child

foot * /fut/ NM abrév de **football**

football /futbol/ NM football *(Brit)*, soccer ◆ ~ **américain** American football *(Brit)*, football *(US)* ◆ **jouer au ~** to play football; → **ballon¹**

footballeur, -euse /futbolœʀ, øz/ NM,F footballer *(Brit)*, football *(Brit) ou* soccer player

footballistique /futbolistik/ ADJ soccer *(épith)*, football *(épith) (Brit)*

footeux, -euse * /futø, øz/ NM,F *(= joueur)* football *ou* soccer player; *(= amateur)* football *ou* soccer enthusiast

footing /futiŋ/ NM jogging *(NonC)* ◆ **faire du ~** to go jogging ◆ **faire un (petit) ~** to go for a (little) jog

for /fɔʀ/ NM ◆ **dans** *ou* **en mon ~ intérieur** in my heart of hearts, deep down inside

forage /fɔʀaʒ/ NM *[de roche, paroi]* drilling, boring; *[de puits]* sinking, boring ◆ **effectuer plusieurs ~s** to drill several bare holes ◆ **se livrer à des ~s d'exploration** to test-drill ◆ **faire des ~s de prospection pétrolière** to prospect for oil, to wildcat *(US)*

forain, e /fɔʀɛ̃, ɛn/ ADJ fairground *(épith)*, carnival *(US) (épith)*; → **baraque, fête** NM *(= acteur)* (fairground) entertainer ◆ **(marchand) ~** *(= commerçant)* stallholder ◆ **les ~s** *(fête foraine)* fairground people, carnies * *(US)*

forban /fɔʀbɑ̃/ NM *(Hist = pirate)* pirate; *(= escroc)* shark, crook

forçage /fɔʀsaʒ/ NM *(Agr)* forcing

forçat /fɔʀsa/ NM *(= bagnard)* convict; *(= galérien, fig)* galley slave ◆ **travailler comme un ~** to work like a slave ◆ **c'est une vie de ~** it's sheer slavery

force /fɔʀs/ GRAMMAIRE ACTIVE 43.4
NF 1 *(= vigueur)* strength ◆ **avoir de la ~** to be strong ◆ **avoir de la ~ dans les bras** to have strong arms ◆ **je n'ai plus la ~ de parler** I have no strength left to talk ◆ **il ne connaît pas sa ~** he doesn't know his own strength ◆ **à la ~ du poignet** *[grimper]* using only one's arms; *[obtenir qch, réussir]* by the sweat of one's brow ◆ **cet effort l'avait laissé sans ~** the effort had left him completely drained ◆ **c'est une ~ de la nature** he's a real Goliath ◆ **dans la ~ de l'âge** in the prime of life ◆ ~ **morale/intellectuelle** moral/intellectual strength ◆ **c'est ce qui fait sa ~** that is where his great strength lies ◆ **bracelet** *ou* **poignet de ~** (leather) wristband; → **bout, union**
2 *(= violence)* force ◆ **recourir/céder à la ~** to resort to/give in to force ◆ **employer la ~ brutale** *ou* **brute** to use brute force ◆ **la ~ prime le droit** might is right
3 *(= ressources physiques)* **~s** strength ◆ **reprendre des ~s** to get one's strength back, to regain one's strength ◆ **ses ~s l'ont trahi** his strength failed *ou* deserted him ◆ **c'est au-dessus de mes ~s** it's too much for me, it's beyond me ◆ **frapper de toutes ses ~s** to hit as hard as one can *ou* with all one's might ◆ **désirer qch de toutes ses ~s** to want sth with all one's heart
4 *[de coup, vent]* force; *[d'argument]* strength, force; *[de sentiment, alcool, médicament]* strength ◆ **vent de ~ 4** force 4 wind ◆ **dans toute la ~ du terme** in the fullest *ou* strongest sense of the word ◆ **la ~ de l'évidence** the weight of evidence ◆ **la ~ de l'habitude** force of habit ◆ **par la ~ des choses** *(gén)* by force of circumstance; *(= nécessairement)* inevitably ◆ **les ~s naturelles** *ou* **de la nature** the forces of nature ◆ **les ~s aveugles du destin** the blind forces of fate ◆ **les ~s vives du pays** the lifeblood of the country ◆ **avoir ~ de loi** to have force of law; → **cas, idée-force, ligne¹**
5 *(Mil)* strength ◆ **~s** forces ◆ **notre ~ navale** our naval strength ◆ **les ~s de l'opposition** *(Pol)* the opposition forces ◆ **armée d'une ~ de 10 000 hommes** army with a strength of 10,000 men
6 *(= valeur)* **les deux joueurs sont de la même ~** the two players are evenly *ou* well matched ◆ **ces deux cartes sont de la même ~** these two cards have the same value ◆ **il est de première ~ au bridge** he's a first-class bridge player, he's first-rate at bridge ◆ **il est de ~ à le faire** he's equal to it, he's up to (doing) it * ◆ **tu n'es pas de ~ à lutter avec lui** you're no match for him ◆ **à ~s égales, à égalité de ~s** on equal terms
7 *(Phys)* force ◆ ~ **de gravité** force of gravity ◆ ~ **centripète/centrifuge** centripetal/centrifugal force
8 *(Typo) [de corps, caractère]* size

⑨ *(locutions)* ~ **nous est/lui est d'accepter** we have/he has no choice but to accept, we are/he is forced to accept ◆ ~ **m'est de reconnaître que ...** I am forced *ou* obliged to recognize that ... ◆ ~ **(nous) est de constater que ...** we have to admit that ... ◆ **affirmer avec** ~ to insist, to state firmly ◆ **insister avec** ~ **sur un point** to emphasize a point strongly ◆ **vouloir à toute** ~ to want absolutely *ou* at all costs ◆ **faire** ~ **de rames** *(Naut)* to ply the oars ◆ **faire** ~ **de voiles** *(Naut)* to cram on sail; → **tour²**

♦ **à force** ◆ **à** ~ **de chercher on va bien trouver** if we keep on looking we'll end up finding it ◆ **à** ~ **de gentillesse** by dint of kindness ◆ **à** ~**, tu vas le casser** you'll end up breaking it

♦ **de force, par force** ◆ **faire entrer qch de** ~ **dans qch** to cram *ou* force sth into sth ◆ **faire entrer qn de** ~ *ou* **par la** ~ **dans qch** to force sb into sth ◆ **obtenir qch par** ~ to get sth by *ou* through force ◆ **enlever qch de** ~ **à qn** to remove sth forcibly from sb, to take sth from sb by force ◆ **entrer de** ~ **chez qn** to force one's way into *ou* force an entry into sb's house ◆ **être en position de** ~ to be in a position of strength

♦ **en force** ◆ **attaquer/arriver** *ou* **venir en** ~ to attack/arrive in force ◆ **la montée en** ~ **du chômage** the dramatic rise in unemployment ◆ **passer un obstacle en** ~ *(Sport)* to get past an obstacle by sheer effort

♦ **coup de force** *(= coup d'état)* coup; *(= action militaire)* offensive action; *(pour racheter une entreprise)* hostile takeover ◆ **ils craignent un coup de** ~ **de l'aile droite de leur parti** they fear that the right wing will try to take over the party *ou* will make a play for power

ADV *(† hum)* many, a goodly number of *(hum)* ◆ **boire** ~ **bouteilles** to drink a goodly number of bottles ◆ **avec** ~ **remerciements** with profuse thanks

COMP **force d'âme** fortitude, moral strength
la force armée the army, the military
les forces armées the armed forces
force de caractère strength of character
force de dissuasion deterrent power
force d'extraction extraction force
les Forces françaises de l'intérieur *Resistance forces operating within France during World War II*
les Forces françaises libres the Free French (Forces *ou* Army)
force de frappe strike force
force d'inertie force of inertia
force d'interposition intervention force
forces d'intervention *(Mil, Police)* rapid deployment force
forces de maintien de la paix peace-keeping force(s)
force nucléaire stratégique strategic nuclear force
les forces de l'ordre, les forces de police the police ◆ **d'importantes ~s de police** large contingents *ou* numbers of police
la force publique, les forces de sécurité the police
force de vente sales force

forcé, e /fɔʀse/ (ptp de **forcer**) **ADJ** ① *(= imposé)* *[cours, mariage]* forced; *(= poussé)* *[comparaison]* forced ◆ **atterrissage** ~ forced *ou* emergency landing ◆ **prendre un bain** ~ to take an unintended dip ◆ **conséquence ~e** inevitable consequence; → **marche¹, travail¹** ② *(= feint)* *[rire, sourire]* forced; *[amabilité]* affected, put-on ③ *(= évident)* **c'est** ~ * there's no way round it, it's inevitable ◆ **je suis malade – c'est ~, tu as mangé trop de chocolat !** I'm ill – of course you are, you've eaten too much chocolate! ◆ **c'est** ~ **que tu sois en retard** it's obvious you're going to be late

forcement /fɔʀsəmɑ̃/ **NM** forcing

forcément /fɔʀsemɑ̃/ **ADV** inevitably ◆ **ça devait** ~ **arriver** it was bound to happen, it was inevitable ◆ **il le savait ~, puisqu'on le lui a dit** he obviously knew, because he'd been told ◆ **il est enrhumé – ~, il ne se couvre pas** he's got a cold – of course he has, he doesn't dress warmly enough ◆ **c'est voué à l'échec – pas** ~ it's bound to fail – not necessarily ◆ **c'est** ~ **vrai/plus simple** it has to be true/simpler ◆ **il a** ~ **raison** he must be right

forcené, e /fɔʀsəne/ **ADJ** *(= fou)* deranged, out of one's wits *(attrib) ou* mind *(attrib)*; *(= acharné)* *[ardeur, travail]* frenzied; *(= fanatique)* *[joueur, travailleur]* frenzied; *[partisan, critique]* fanatical **NM,F** maniac ◆ **travailler comme un** ~ to work like a maniac * ◆ ~ **du travail** *(hum)* workaholic * ◆ **les ~s du vélo/de la canne à pêche** *(hum)* cycling/angling fanatics

forceps /fɔʀsɛps/ **NM** pair of forceps, forceps *(pl)* ◆ **accouchement au** ~ forceps delivery

forcer /fɔʀse/ ► conjug 3 ◄ **VT** ① *(= contraindre)* to force, to compel ◆ ~ **qn à faire qch** to force sb to do sth, to make sb do sth ◆ **il est forcé de garder le lit** he is forced to stay in bed ◆ **il a essayé de me** ~ **la main** he tried to force my hand ◆ ~ **qn au silence/à des démarches/à la démission** to force sb to keep silent/to take action/to resign

② *(= faire céder)* *[+ coffre, serrure, barrage]* to force; *[+ porte, tiroir]* to force (open); *[+ blocus]* to run; *[+ ville]* to take by force ◆ ~ **le passage** to force one's way through ◆ ~ **la porte** to force one's way in ◆ ~ **la porte de qn** to force one's way into sb's home ◆ ~ **la consigne** to bypass orders ◆ **sa conduite force le respect/l'admiration** his behaviour commands respect/admiration ◆ **il a réussi à** ~ **la décision** he managed to settle *ou* decide the outcome

③ *(= traquer)* *[+ cerf, lièvre]* to run *ou* hunt down; *[+ ennemi]* to track down ◆ **la police a forcé les bandits dans leur repaire** the police tracked the gangsters down to their hideout

④ *(= pousser)* *[+ cheval]* to override; *[+ fruits, plantes]* to force; *[+ talent, voix]* to strain; *[+ allure]* to increase; *[+ destin]* to tempt, to brave ◆ **votre interprétation force le sens du texte** your interpretation stretches the meaning of the text ◆ ~ **sa nature** *(timidité)* to overcome one's shyness; *(volonté)* to force o.s. ◆ ~ **le pas** to quicken one's pace ◆ **il a forcé la dose** * *ou* **la note** * he overdid it ◆ ~ **le trait** *(= exagérer)* to exaggerate

VI to overdo it ◆ **j'ai voulu ~, et je me suis claqué un muscle** I overdid it and pulled a muscle ◆ **il a gagné sans** ~ * he had no trouble winning, he won easily ◆ **ne force pas, tu vas casser la corde** don't force it or you'll break the rope ◆ **arrête de tirer, tu vois bien que ça force** stop pulling, can't you see it's jammed? ◆ ~ **sur ses rames** to strain at the oars ◆ **il force un peu trop sur l'alcool** * once he starts drinking he doesn't know when to stop ◆ **il avait un peu trop forcé sur l'alcool** * he'd had a few too many *

VPR **se forcer** to force o.s., to make an effort *(pour faire* to do); ◆ **il se force à travailler** he forces himself to work, he makes himself work ◆ **elle se force pour manger** she forces herself to eat

forces /fɔʀs/ **NMPL** *(= ciseaux)* shears

forcing /fɔʀsiŋ/ **NM** *(gén, Boxe)* pressure *(auprès de* with); ◆ **faire le** ~ to pile on the pressure ◆ **on a dû faire le** ~ **pour avoir le contrat** we had to put on a lot of pressure *ou* we really had to push to get the contract ◆ **on a dû faire le** ~ **pour combler notre retard** we had to pull out all the stops to make up the time ◆ **négociations menées au** ~ negotiations conducted under pressure

> ⚠ **forcing** ne se traduit pas par le mot anglais **forcing**.

forcir /fɔʀsiʀ/ ► conjug 2 ◄ **VI** *[personne]* to broaden out; *[vent]* to strengthen

forclore /fɔʀklɔʀ/ ► conjug 45 ◄ **VT** *(Jur)* to debar ◆ **il s'est laissé** ~ he didn't make his claim within the prescribed time limit

forclusion /fɔʀklyzjɔ̃/ **NF** *(Jur)* debarment

forer /fɔʀe/ ► conjug 1 ◄ **VT** *[+ roche, paroi]* to drill, to bore; *[+ puits]* to drill, to sink, to bore

forestier, -ière /fɔʀɛstje, jɛʀ/ **ADJ** *[région, végétation, chemin]* forest *(épith)* ◆ **exploitation forestière** *(= activité)* forestry, lumbering; *(= lieu)* forestry site ◆ **perdreau (à la) forestière** *(Culin)* partridge (cooked) with mushrooms; → **garde²** **NM** forester

foret /fɔʀɛ/ **NM** *(= outil)* drill

forêt /fɔʀɛ/ **NF** *(lit, fig)* forest ◆ ~ **vierge** virgin forest ◆ ~ **pluviale** rain forest ◆ ~ **tropicale** tropical (rain) forest ◆ ~ **domaniale** national *ou* state-owned forest ◆ **~-galerie** gallery forest; → **arbre, eau**

forêt-noire (pl **forêts-noires**) /fɔʀɛnwaʀ/ **NF** ① *(Culin)* Black Forest gâteau ② ◆ **la Forêt-Noire** *(Géog)* the Black Forest

foreuse /fɔʀøz/ **NF** drill

forfaire /fɔʀfɛʀ/ ► conjug 60 ◄ **VI** *(frm)* ◆ ~ **à qch** to be false to sth, to betray sth ◆ ~ **à l'honneur** to forsake honour

forfait /fɔʀfɛ/ **NM** ① *(= prix fixe)* fixed *ou* set price; *(= prix tout compris)* all-inclusive price; *(= ensemble de prestations)* package ◆ **travailler au** *ou* **à** ~ to work for a flat rate *ou* a fixed sum ◆ **notre nouveau ~-vacances** our new package tour *ou* holiday *(Brit)* ◆ ~ **avion-hôtel** flight and hotel package ◆ ~ **hôtelier** hotel package ◆ **~-skieur(s)** ski-pass ◆ **être au (régime du)** ~ *(impôts)* to be taxed on estimated income ② *(Sport = abandon)* withdrawal ◆ **gagner par** ~ to win by default ◆ **déclarer** ~ *(Sport)* to withdraw; *(fig)* to give up ③ *(littér = crime)* crime

forfaitaire /fɔʀfɛtɛʀ/ **ADJ** *(= fixe)* fixed, set; *(= tout compris)* inclusive ◆ **montant** ~ lump *ou* fixed sum ◆ **indemnité** ~ inclusive payment, lump sum payment ◆ **prix** ~ fixed *ou* set price

forfaitairement /fɔʀfɛtɛʀmɑ̃/ **ADV** *[payer, évaluer]* on an inclusive basis, inclusively ◆ **une pension calculée** ~ an all-inclusive pension

forfaitiser /fɔʀfɛtize/ ► conjug 1 ◄ **VT** ◆ ~ **les coûts** to charge a flat rate ◆ **les communications locales sont forfaitisées** there is a flat-rate charge for local calls ◆ **la consommation d'eau est forfaitisée à 10 euros par mois** there is a standard charge of 10 euros a month for water

forfaiture /fɔʀfɛtyʀ/ **NF** *(Jur)* abuse of authority; *(Hist)* felony; *(littér = crime)* act of treachery

forfanterie /fɔʀfɑ̃tʀi/ **NF** *(= caractère)* boastfulness; *(= acte)* bragging *(NonC)*

forge /fɔʀʒ/ **NF** *(= atelier)* forge, smithy; *(= fourneau)* forge ◆ **~s** *(† = fonderie)* ironworks; → **maître**

forger /fɔʀʒe/ ► conjug 3 ◄ **VT** ① *[+ métal]* to forge; *(littér)* ◆ ~ **des liens** to forge links ◆ ~ **les fers** *ou* **les chaînes de qn** to enslave *ou* enchain sb ◆ **c'est en forgeant qu'on devient forgeron** *(Prov)* practice makes perfect *(Prov)* → **fer** ② *(= aguerrir)* *[+ caractère]* to form, to mould ③ *(= inventer)* *[+ mot]* to coin; *[+ exemple, prétexte]* to make up; *[+ histoire, mensonge, plan]* to concoct ◆ **cette histoire est forgée de toutes pièces** this story is a complete fabrication

VPR **se forger** ◆ **il s'est forgé une réputation d'homme sévère** he has won *ou* earned himself the reputation of being a stern man ◆ **se** ~ **un idéal** to create an ideal for o.s. ◆ **se** ~ **des illusions** to build up illusions

forgeron /fɔʀʒəʀɔ̃/ **NM** blacksmith, smith; → **forger**

formalisation /fɔʀmalizasjɔ̃/ **NF** formalization

formaliser /fɔʀmalize/ ▸ conjug 1 ◂ **VT** to formalize **VPR se formaliser** to take offence (*de* at)

formalisme /fɔʀmalism/ **NM** 1 (*péj*) formality ◆ **pas de ~ ici** we don't stand on ceremony here ◆ **s'encombrer de ~** to weigh o.s. down with formalities 2 (*Art, Philos, Math*) formalism

formaliste /fɔʀmalist/ **ADJ** 1 (*péj*) formalistic 2 (*Art, Philos*) formalist **NMF** formalist

formalité /fɔʀmalite/ **NF** (*Admin*) formality ◆ **les ~s à accomplir** *ou* **à remplir** the necessary procedures, the procedures involved ◆ **pas de ~s entre nous, appelle-moi Maud** no need to be formal, call me Maud ◆ **ce n'est qu'une ~** (*fig*) it's a mere formality ◆ **sans autre ~** (*fig*) without any more *ou* further ado

formant /fɔʀmɑ̃/ **NM** (*Ling, Phon*) formant

format /fɔʀma/ **NM** [*de livre*] format, size; [*de papier, objet*] size; (*Ordin*) format ◆ **papier ~ A4** A4 paper ◆ **~ portrait** *ou* **à la française** (*Ordin*) portrait ◆ **~ paysage** *ou* **à l'italienne** landscape ◆ **~ de données** (*Ordin*) data format ◆ **photo (en) petit ~** small format print ◆ **enveloppe grand ~** large envelope ◆ **les petits/grands ~s** (*livres*) small/large (format) books ◆ **il aime les blondes et préfère les petits ~s** (*fig, hum*) he likes blondes, preferably of the petite variety; → **poche²**

formatage /fɔʀmataʒ/ **NM** formatting

formater /fɔʀmate/ ▸ conjug 1 ◂ **VT** (*Ordin*) to format

formateur, -trice /fɔʀmatœʀ, tʀis/ **ADJ** [*élément, expérience*] formative; [*stage*] training **NM,F** trainer

formatif, -ive /fɔʀmatif, iv/ **ADJ** [*langue*] inflected; [*préfixe*] formative **NF formative** (*Ling*) formative

formation /fɔʀmasjɔ̃/ **NF** 1 (= *apprentissage*) training; (= *stage, cours*) training course ◆ **il a reçu une ~ littéraire** he received a literary education ◆ **~ des maîtres, ~ pédagogique** teacher training, teacher education (*US*) ◆ **sa ~ d'ingénieur** his training as an engineer ◆ **je suis juriste de ~** I trained as a lawyer ◆ **~ professionnelle** vocational training ◆ **~ permanente** continuing education ◆ **~ continue (au sein de l'entreprise)** (in-house) training ◆ **~ alternée** *ou* **en alternance** [*de salarié*] ≃ block-release training; [*d'élève en apprentissage*] *school course combined with work experience* ◆ **~ courte/longue** short/long training course ◆ **stage de ~ accélérée** intensive (training) course, crash course ◆ **centre de ~** training centre ◆ **suivre une ~ en informatique** to do a computer (training) course; → **tas**

2 (= *développement*) [*de gouvernement, croûte, fruits*] formation, forming ◆ **à (l'époque de) la ~** [*de fruit*] when forming; [*d'enfant*] at puberty ◆ **en voie** *ou* **en cours de ~** being formed, in the process of formation ◆ **la ~ des mots** word formation ◆ **la ~ du caractère** the forming *ou* moulding of character

3 (*gén, Mil* = *groupe*) formation ◆ **voler en ~** to fly in formation ◆ **~ serrée** close formation ◆ **~ musicale** music group ◆ **~ politique** political grouping *ou* formation

> ⚠ Au sens de 'apprentissage' ou 'stage', **formation** ne se traduit pas par le mot anglais **formation**.

forme /fɔʀm/ **NF** 1 (= *contour, apparence*) shape, form ◆ **cet objet est de ~ ronde/carrée** this object is round/square (in shape) ◆ **en ~ de poire/cloche** pear-/bell-shaped ◆ **elle a des ~s gracieuses** she has a graceful figure ◆ **elle prend des ~s** she's filling out ◆ **vêtement qui moule les ~s** clinging *ou* figure-hugging garment ◆ **une ~ apparut dans la nuit** a form *ou* figure *ou* shape appeared out of the darkness ◆ **n'avoir plus ~ humaine** to be unrecognizable ◆ **sans ~** [*chapeau*] shapeless; [*pensée*] formless ◆ **prendre la ~ d'un rectangle** to take the form *ou* shape of a rectangle ◆ **prendre la ~ d'un entretien** to take the form of an interview ◆ **prendre ~** [*statue, projet*] to take shape ◆ **sous ~ de comprimés** in tablet form ◆ **sous la ~ d'un vieillard** in the guise of *ou* as an old man ◆ **sous toutes ses ~s** in all its forms

2 (= *genre*) [*de civilisation, gouvernement*] form ◆ **~ d'énergie** form of energy ◆ **~ de vie** (= *présence effective*) form of life, life form; (= *coutumes*) way of life ◆ **une ~ de pensée différente de la nôtre** a way of thinking different from our own ◆ **les animaux ont-ils une ~ d'intelligence ?** do animals have a form of intelligence?

3 (*Art, Jur, Littérat, Philos*) form ◆ **soigner la ~** to be careful about form ◆ **mettre en ~** [+ *texte*] to finalize the presentation *ou* layout of; [+ *idées*] to formulate ◆ **poème à ~ fixe** fixed-form poem ◆ **poème en ~ d'acrostiche** poem forming an acrostic ◆ **de pure ~** [*aide, soutien*] token (*épith*), nominal ◆ **remarques de pure ~** purely formal remarks ◆ **pour la ~** as a matter of form, for form's sake ◆ **en bonne (et due) ~** in due form ◆ **faites une réclamation en ~** put in a formal request ◆ **sans autre ~ de procès** without further ado; → **fond, vice**

4 (*Ling*) form ◆ **mettre à la ~ passive** to put in the passive ◆ **~ contractée** contracted form ◆ **~ de base** base form

5 (= *moule*) mould; (*Typo*) forme (*Brit*), form (*US*); [*de cordonnier*] last; [*de couturier*] (dress) form; (= *partie de chapeau*) crown ◆ **mise en ~** (*Typo*) imposition; (*Ordin*) layout

6 (*gén, Sport*) **~ (physique)** form, fitness ◆ **être en (pleine** *ou* **grande) ~, tenir la ~** * (*gén*) to be in (great) form, to be in *ou* on top form; (*physiquement*) to be very fit ◆ **il n'est pas en ~, il n'a pas la ~** * (*gén*) he's not on form, he's off form; (*physiquement*) he's not very fit, he's unfit ◆ **baisse de ~** loss of form ◆ **retrouver la ~** to get back into shape, to get fit again ◆ **ce n'est pas la grande ~** * I'm (*ou* he's *etc*) not feeling too good * ◆ **centre de remise en ~** ≃ health spa; → **péter**

7 (*Mus*) **~ sonate** sonata form

8 (*Naut*) **~ de radoub** *ou* **sèche** dry *ou* graving dock

NFPL formes (= *convenances*) proprieties, conventions ◆ **respecter les ~s** to respect the proprieties *ou* conventions ◆ **refuser en y mettant des ~s** to decline as tactfully as possible ◆ **faire une demande dans les ~s** to make a request in the correct form

formé, e /fɔʀme/ (ptp de **former**) **ADJ** 1 [*jeune fille*] pubescent; [*fruit, épi*] formed ◆ **cette jeune fille est ~e maintenant** this girl is fully developed now 2 [*goût, jugement*] (well-) developed ◆ **son jugement n'est pas encore ~** his judgment is as yet unformed

formel, -elle /fɔʀmɛl/ **ADJ** 1 (= *catégorique*) definite, positive ◆ **dans l'intention formelle de refuser** with the definite intention of refusing ◆ **il a l'obligation formelle de le faire** he is obliged to do so ◆ **interdiction formelle d'en parler à quiconque** you mustn't talk about this to anyone ◆ **je suis ~ !** I'm absolutely sure! 2 (*Art, Philos*) formal 3 (= *extérieur*) [*politesse*] formal

> ⚠ Au sens de 'catégorique', **formel** ne se traduit pas par le mot anglais **formal**.

formellement /fɔʀmɛlmɑ̃/ **ADV** 1 (= *catégoriquement*) [*démentir, contester*] categorically; [*identifier*] positively; [*interdire*] strictly 2 (= *officiellement*) [*demander*] formally; [*condamner*] officially 3 (*Art, Philos*) formally

> ⚠ Au sens de 'catégoriquement', **formellement** ne se traduit pas par **formally**.

former /fɔʀme/ ▸ conjug 1 ◂ **VT** 1 (= *éduquer*) [+ *soldats, ingénieurs*] to train; [+ *intelligence, caractère, goût*] to form, to develop ◆ **les voyages forment la jeunesse** travel broadens the mind ◆ **le personnel est peu formé** the staff is relatively untrained

2 [+ *gouvernement*] to form; [+ *entreprise, équipe*] to set up; [+ *liens d'amitié*] to form, to create; [+ *croûte, dépôt*] to form ◆ **il s'est formé des liens entre nous** bonds have formed *ou* been created between us ◆ **le cône que forme la révolution d'un triangle** the cone formed by the revolution of a triangle

3 [+ *collection*] to form, to build up; [+ *convoi*] to form; [+ *forme verbale*] to form, to make up ◆ **~ correctement ses phrases** to form proper sentences ◆ **phrase bien formée** well-formed sentence ◆ **phrase mal formée** ill-formed sentence ◆ **le train n'est pas encore formé** they haven't made up the train yet

4 (= *être le composant de*) to make up, to form ◆ **article formé de trois paragraphes** article made up of *ou* consisting of three paragraphs ◆ **ceci forme un tout** this forms a whole ◆ **ils forment un beau couple** they make a nice couple

5 (= *dessiner*) to make, to form ◆ **ça forme un rond** it makes *ou* forms a circle ◆ **la route forme des lacets** the road winds ◆ **il forme bien/mal ses lettres** he forms his letters well/badly

6 ◆ **~ l'idée** *ou* **le projet de faire qch** to form *ou* have the idea of doing sth ◆ **nous formons des vœux pour votre réussite** we wish you every success

VPR se former 1 (= *se rassembler*) to form, to gather ◆ **des nuages se forment à l'horizon** clouds are forming *ou* gathering on the horizon ◆ **se ~ en cortège** to form a procession ◆ **il s'est formé un attroupement** a crowd gathered *ou* formed ◆ **l'armée se forma en carré** *ou* **forma le carré** the army took up a square formation

2 [*dépôt, croûte*] to form

3 (= *apprendre un métier*) to train o.s.; (= *éduquer son goût, son caractère*) to educate o.s.

4 (= *se développer*) [*goût, caractère, intelligence*] to form, to develop; [*fruit*] to form ◆ **les fruits commencent à se ~ sur l'arbre** the fruit is beginning to form on the tree

> ⚠ Quand il s'agit de la formation d'une personne, **former** ne se traduit pas par **to form**.

Formica ® /fɔʀmika/ **NM** Formica ® ◆ **table en ~** Formica table

formidable /fɔʀmidabl/ **ADJ** 1 (= *très important*) [*coup, obstacle, bruit*] tremendous 2 (* = *très bien*) fantastic *, great * 3 (* = *incroyable*) incredible ◆ **c'est tout de même ~ qu'on ne me dise jamais rien !** it's a bit much * that nobody ever tells me anything! ◆ **il est ~ : il convoque une réunion et il est en retard !** he's marvellous (*iro*) *ou* incredible - he calls a meeting and then he's late! 4 (*littér* = *effrayant*) fearsome

formidablement /fɔʀmidabləmɑ̃/ **ADV** (= *très bien*) fantastically * ◆ **on s'est ~ amusé** we had a fantastic time * ◆ **comment ça a marché ? – ~ !** how did it go? – great * *ou* fantastic! *

formique /fɔʀmik/ **ADJ** formic

formol /fɔʀmɔl/ **NM** formalin, formol

formosan, e /fɔʀmozɑ̃, an/ **ADJ** Formosan **NM,F Formosan(e)** Formosan

Formose /fɔʀmoz/ **NF** Formosa

formulable /fɔʀmylabl/ ADJ which can be formulated ◆ **difficilement ~** difficult to formulate

formulaire /fɔʀmylɛʀ/ NM 1 *(à remplir)* form ◆ **~ de demande** application form ◆ **~ E111** form E111 2 *[de pharmaciens, notaires]* formulary

formulation /fɔʀmylasjɔ̃/ NF *[de plainte, requête]* formulation, wording; *[de sentiment]* formulation, expression; *[d'ordonnance, acte notarié]* drawing up; *(Chim, Math)* formulation ◆ **changer la ~ d'une demande** to change the way an application is formulated, to change the wording of an application

formule /fɔʀmyl/ NF 1 *(Chim, Math)* formula ◆ **~ dentaire** dentition, dental formula

2 *(= expression)* phrase, expression; *(magique, prescrite par l'étiquette)* formula ◆ **~ heureuse** happy turn of phrase ◆ **~ de politesse** polite phrase; *(en fin de lettre)* letter ending ◆ **~ publicitaire** advertising slogan ◆ **~ toute faite** ready-made phrase ◆ **~ incantatoire** incantation; → **consacré**

3 *(= méthode)* system, way ◆ **~ de paiement** method of payment ◆ **~ de vacances** holiday programme *ou* schedule ◆ **trouver la bonne ~** to hit on *ou* find the right formula ◆ **c'est la ~ idéale pour des vacances avec de jeunes enfants** it's the ideal solution for going on holiday with young children ◆ **~ à 12 €** *(dans un restaurant)* 12 euro menu ◆ **ils proposent différentes ~s de location/de crédit** they offer several different rental/credit options

4 *(= formulaire)* form ◆ **~ de chèque** *cheque and stub*

5 *(Courses automobiles)* **la ~ 1/2/3** Formula One/Two/Three ◆ **une (voiture de) ~ 1** a Formula-One car

formuler /fɔʀmyle/ ► conjug 1 ◄ VT *[+ exigences, plainte, requête, demande, proposition, recommandation]* to make, to formulate *(frm)*; *[+ critiques, sentiment, souhaits]* to express; *[+ accusation]* to make; *[+ ordonnance, acte notarié]* to draw up ◆ **il a mal formulé sa question** he didn't word *ou* phrase his question very well

fornicateur, -trice /fɔʀnikatœʀ, tʀis/ NM,F *(littér, hum)* fornicator

fornication /fɔʀnikasjɔ̃/ NF *(littér, hum)* fornication

forniquer /fɔʀnike/ ► conjug 1 ◄ VI *(littér, hum)* to fornicate

FORPRONU, Forpronu /fɔʀpʀɔny/ NF (abrév de **Force de protection des Nations unies**) ◆ **la ~** Unprofor

fors †† /fɔʀ/ PRÉP save, except

forsythia /fɔʀsisja/ NM forsythia

fort¹, e¹ /fɔʀ, fɔʀt/

1 ADJECTIF 2 ADVERBE

1 - ADJECTIF

1 = puissant *[personne, État, lunettes, monnaie]* strong ◆ **il est ~ comme un bœuf** *ou* **un Turc** he's as strong as an ox *ou* a horse ◆ **il est de ~e constitution** he has a strong constitution ◆ **le dollar est une monnaie ~e** the dollar is a strong *ou* hard currency ◆ **la dame est plus ~e que le valet** *(Cartes)* the queen is higher than the jack ◆ **c'est plus ~ que moi** I can't help it ◆ **il est ~ en gueule** * he's loud-mouthed * *ou* a loudmouth *; → **partie²**

◆ **fort de** ◆ **une armée ~e de 20 000 hommes** an army 20,000 strong ◆ **une équipe ~e de 15 personnes** a team of 15 people ◆ **~ de leur soutien/de cette garantie** armed with their support/with this guarantee ◆ **~ de son expérience, il ...** wiser for this experience, he ... ◆ **être ~ de son bon droit** to be confident of one's rights

2 euph = gros *[personne]* stout, large; *[hanches]* broad, wide, large; *[poitrine]* large, ample; *[nez]* big ◆ **il s'habille au rayon (pour) hommes ~s** he gets his clothes from the outsize department ◆ **elle est un peu ~e des hanches** she has rather wide *ou* broad *ou* large hips, she's a bit broad in the beam *

3 = solide, résistant *[carton]* strong, stout; *[colle]* strong; → **château, place**

4 = intense *[lumière, rythme, battements]* strong; *[bruit, voix]* loud; *[sentiments]* strong, intense; *[dégoût, crainte]* great; *[impression]* great, strong; *[colère, douleur, chaleur]* great, intense; *[fièvre]* high ◆ **une ~e grippe** a bad bout of flu ◆ **une œuvre ~e** a powerful work ◆ **il y a quelques moments ~s dans son film** there are some powerful scenes in his film ◆ **au sens ~ du terme** in the strongest sense of the term ◆ **génie ? le terme est un peu ~ !** a genius? I wouldn't go so far as to say that!; → **envie, temps¹**

5 = marqué *[pente]* pronounced, steep; *[accent]* strong, marked, pronounced; *[goût, odeur, moutarde, café]* strong

6 = violent *[secousse, coup]* hard; *[houle, pluies]* heavy; *[vent]* strong, high ◆ **mer ~e/très ~e** *(Météo marine)* rough/very rough sea

7 = excessif **c'est trop ~ !** that's too much!, that's going too far! ◆ **c'est un peu ~ (de café)** * that's a bit much *, that's going a bit (too) far * ◆ **génie ! le mot est un peu ~** genius is a bit strong a word ◆ **elle est ~e celle-là !** *, **c'est plus ~ que de jouer au bouchon !** * that beats everything! *, that takes the biscuit! * *(Brit)* ◆ **et le plus ~** *ou* **et ce qu'il y a de plus ~, c'est que ...** and the best (part) of it is that ...

8 = important *[somme]* large, great; *[hausse, baisse, différence]* big, great; *[dose, augmentation]* large, big; *[consommation]* high ◆ **vin ~ en alcool** strong wine, wine with a high alcohol content; → **prix**

9 = courageux, obstiné *[personne]* strong ◆ **être ~ dans l'adversité** to be strong *ou* to stand firm in (the face of) adversity ◆ **âme ~e** steadfast soul ◆ **esprit ~** † freethinker ◆ **c'est une ~e tête** he (*ou* she) is a rebel

10 = doué good *(en, à* at) able ◆ **il est ~ en histoire/aux échecs** he's good at history/at chess ◆ **il est très ~ !** he's very good (at it)! ◆ **être ~ sur un sujet** to be well up on * *ou* good at a subject ◆ **il a trouvé plus ~ que lui** he has (more than) found *ou* met his match ◆ **quand il s'agit de critiquer, il est ~ !** he can criticize all right!, he's very good at criticizing! ◆ **ce n'est pas très ~ (de sa part)** * that's not very clever *ou* bright of him ◆ **c'est trop ~ pour moi** it's beyond me; → **point¹**

11 Ling **consonne ~e** hard consonant ◆ **forme ~e** strong form; → **verbe**

2 - ADVERBE

1 = intensément *[lancer, serrer, souffler]* hard ◆ **frapper ~** *(bruit)* to knock loudly; *(force)* to knock *ou* hit hard ◆ **sentir ~** to have a strong smell, to smell strong ◆ **respirez bien ~** breathe deeply, take a deep breath ◆ **son cœur battait très ~** his heart was pounding *ou* was beating hard ◆ **le feu marche trop ~** the fire is burning too fast ◆ **tu y vas un peu ~ tout de même** * even so, you're overdoing it a bit * *ou* going a bit far * ◆ **tu as fait ~ !** * that was a bit much! * ◆ **comment vont les affaires ? – ça ne va pas ~** * how is business? – it's not going too well

2 = bruyamment *[parler, crier]* loudly, loud ◆ **parlez plus ~** speak up *ou* louder ◆ **mets la radio moins/plus ~** turn the radio down/up

3 littér = beaucoup greatly ◆ **cela me déplaît ~** that displeases me greatly *ou* a great deal ◆ **j'en doute ~** I very much doubt it ◆ **il y tient ~** he sets great store by it ◆ **j'ai ~ à faire avec lui** I have a hard job with him, I've got my work cut out with him

4 frm = très *[simple, différent, rare, ancien]* extremely, very; *[aimable]* most; *[mécontent, intéressant]* most, highly ◆ **il est ~ apprécié de ses chefs** he is highly regarded by his bosses ◆ **il est ~ inquiet** he is very *ou* most anxious ◆ **c'est ~ bon** it is very *ou* exceedingly good, it is most excellent ◆ **il y avait ~ peu de monde** there were very few people; → **aise**

◆ **fort bien** *[dessiné, dit, conservé]* extremely well ◆ **tu sais ~ bien que ...** you know very well *ou* full well that ... ◆ **nous avons été ~ bien accueillis** we were made most welcome ◆ **je peux ~ bien le faire moi-même/m'en passer** I can quite easily do it myself/do without it ◆ **~ bien !** very good!, excellent! ◆ **tu refuses ? ~ bien, tu l'auras voulu** you refuse? very well, on your own head be it

5 locutions

◆ **se faire fort de** ◆ **nos champions se font ~ de gagner** our champions are confident they will win *ou* confident of winning ◆ **je me fais ~ de le réparer** I'm (quite) sure I can mend it, I can mend it, don't worry *ou* you'll see

fort² /fɔʀ/ NM 1 *(= forteresse)* fort 2 *(= personne)* **le ~ l'emporte toujours contre le faible** the strong will always win against the weak ◆ **un ~ en thème** *(péj Scol)* an egghead *, a swot * *(Brit)*; → **raison** 3 *(= spécialité)* strong point, forte ◆ **l'amabilité n'est pas son ~** kindness is not his strong point *ou* his forte LOC PRÉP **au fort de** *(littér)* *[+ été]* at the height of; *[+ hiver]* in the depths of ◆ **au plus ~ du combat** *(lieu)* in the thick of the battle; *(intensité)* when the battle was at its most intense, at the height of the battle COMP **fort des Halles** market porter

Fort-de-France /fɔʀdəfʀɑ̃s/ N Fort-de-France

forte² /fɔʀte/ ADV *(Mus)* forte

fortement /fɔʀtəmɑ̃/ ADV *[conseiller]* strongly; *[tenir]* fast, tight(ly); *[frapper]* hard; *[serrer]* hard, tight(ly) ◆ **il est ~ probable que ...** it is highly *ou* most probable that ... ◆ **~ marqué/attiré** strongly marked/attracted ◆ **il en est ~ question** it is being seriously considered ◆ **j'espère ~ que vous le pourrez** I very much hope that you will be able to ◆ **boiter ~** to have a pronounced limp, to limp badly ◆ **il est ~ intéressé par l'affaire** he is highly *ou* most interested in the matter

forteresse /fɔʀtəʀɛs/ NF *(lit)* fortress, stronghold; *(fig)* stronghold ◆ **la ~ Europe** Fortress Europe ◆ **ils voient leur pays comme une ~ assiégée** they regard their country as being under siege ◆ **une mentalité de ~ assiégée** a siege mentality

fortiche * /fɔʀtiʃ/ ADJ *[personne]* terrific *, great * *(en* at)

fortifiant, e /fɔʀtifjɑ̃, jɑ̃t/ ADJ *[médicament, boisson]* fortifying; *[air]* invigorating, bracing; *(littér)* *[exemple, lecture]* uplifting NM *(Pharm)* tonic

fortification /fɔʀtifikasjɔ̃/ NF fortification

fortifier /fɔʀtifje/ ► conjug 7 ◄ VT *[+ corps, âme]* to strengthen, to fortify; *[+ position, opinion, impression]* to strengthen; *[+ ville]* to fortify ◆ **l'air marin fortifie** (the) sea air is invigorating *ou* bracing ◆ **cela m'a fortifié dans mes résolutions** that strengthened my resolve VPR **se fortifier** *(Mil)* to fortify itself; *[opinion, amitié, position]* to grow stronger, to be strengthened; *[santé]* to grow more robust

fortin /fɔʀtɛ̃/ NM (small) fort

fortiori /fɔʀsjɔʀi/ → **a fortiori**

fortran /fɔʀtʀɑ̃/ NM Fortran, FORTRAN

fortuit, e /fɔʀtɥi, it/ ADJ *[événement, circonstance, remarque, rencontre, coïncidence]* chance *(épith)*, fortuitous *(frm)*; *[découverte]* accidental, fortuitous *(frm)*, chance *(épith)* ◆ **la simultanéité des deux faits n'est pas totalement ~e** the fact that the two things happened at the same time was not completely accidental *ou* was not entirely a coincidence *ou* was not entirely fortuitous ◆ **c'était tout à fait ~** it was quite accidental, it happened quite by chance; → **ressemblance**

fortuitement /fɔʀtɥitmɑ̃/ ADV by chance, fortuitously *(frm)*

fortune /fɔʀtyn/ NF 1 (= *richesse*) fortune ◆ **situation de ~** financial situation ◆ **ça vaut** *ou* **coûte une (petite) ~** it costs a fortune ◆ **cet homme est l'une des plus grosses ~s de la région** that man is one of the wealthiest in the area ◆ **avoir de la ~** to be independently wealthy ◆ **faire ~** to make one's fortune *(dans* in); ◆ **le mot a fait ~** the word has really caught on; → **impôt, revers**

2 (= *chance*) luck *(NonC)*, fortune *(NonC)*; (= *destinée*) fortune ◆ **chercher ~** to seek one's fortune ◆ **connaître des ~s diverses** *(sujet pluriel)* to enjoy varying fortunes; *(sujet singulier)* to have varying luck ◆ **il a eu la (bonne) ~ de le rencontrer** he was fortunate enough to meet him, he had the good fortune to meet him ◆ **ayant eu la mauvaise ~ de le rencontrer** having had the misfortune *ou* the ill-fortune to meet him ◆ **faire contre mauvaise ~ bon cœur** to make the best of it ◆ **venez dîner à la ~ du pot** come to dinner and take pot luck with us ◆ **~s de mer** *(Jur, Naut)* sea risks, perils of the sea ◆ **la ~ sourit aux audacieux** *(Prov)* fortune favours the brave ◆ **de ~** *[abri, embarcation, réparation, moyen]* makeshift; *[installation]* makeshift, rough-and-ready; *[compagnon]* chance *(épith)* ◆ **mât/gouvernail de ~** jury mast/rudder

3 *(Naut)* **~ (carrée)** crossjack

fortuné, e /fɔʀtyne/ ADJ (= *riche*) wealthy, well-off; *(littér = heureux)* fortunate

forum /fɔʀɔm/ NM (= *place, colloque*) forum ◆ **~ de discussion** *(Internet)* chat room ◆ **participer à un ~ de discussion** to chat

fosse /fos/ NF (= *trou*) pit; (= *tombe*) grave; *(Sport : pour le saut)* (sand)pit; *(Anat)* fossa

COMP **fosse d'aisances** cesspool
fosse commune common *ou* communal grave
fosse à fumier manure pit
fosse aux lions *(lit, fig)* lions' den
fosse marine ocean trench
fosses nasales nasal fossae
fosse d'orchestre orchestra pit
fosse aux ours bear pit
fosse à purin slurry pit
fosse septique septic tank

fossé /fose/ NM 1 *(dans le sol)* ditch ◆ **~ d'irrigation** irrigation channel *ou* ditch ◆ **~ antichar** anti-tank ditch 2 (= *écart*) gap ◆ **~ culturel** cultural gap ◆ **le ~ des** *ou* **entre les générations** the generation gap ◆ **le ~ entre riches et pauvres se creuse** the gap between rich and poor is widening ◆ **un ~ les sépare** a gulf lies between them

fossette /fosɛt/ NF dimple

fossile /fosil/ NM *(lit, fig)* fossil ADJ *[combustibles, énergie]* fossil *(épith)*; *[société]* fossilized; → **rayonnement**

fossilisation /fosilizasjɔ̃/ NF fossilization

fossiliser /fosilize/ ► conjug 1 ◄ VT *(lit, fig)* to fossilize ◆ **nous ne devons pas ~ notre langue** we mustn't let our language become fossilized VPR **se fossiliser** to fossilize, to become fossilized ◆ **des plantes fossilisées** fossilized plants

fossoyeur /foswajœʀ/ NM gravedigger ◆ **les ~s de notre société** those who precipitate the decline of society ◆ **ils considèrent que la monnaie unique sera le ~ de l'emploi** they think the single currency will be disastrous for employment

fou, folle /fu, fɔl/ (*m : devant voyelle ou h muet* fol) ADJ 1 *(Méd)* mad, insane; *(gén)* mad, crazy ◆ **~ à lier, ~ furieux** raving mad ◆ **il est devenu subitement ~** he suddenly went mad *ou* crazy ◆ **ça l'a rendu ~** *(lit, fig)* it drove him mad *ou* crazy ◆ **c'est à devenir ~** it's enough to drive you mad *ou* crazy ◆ **~ de colère/de désir/de chagrin** out of one's mind with anger/with desire/with grief ◆ **~ de joie** delirious *ou* out of one's mind with joy ◆ **~ d'amour (pour), amoureux ~ (de)** madly in love (with) ◆ **elle est folle de lui/de ce musicien** she's mad* *ou* crazy* about him/about that musician ◆ **tu es complètement ~ de refuser** you're completely mad *ou* absolutely crazy to refuse ◆ **y aller ? (je ne suis) pas si ~ !** go there?, I'm not that crazy! ◆ **pas folle, la guêpe*** he's *(ou* she's) no fool! ◆ **elle est folle de son corps*** *(hum)* she's sex-mad*

2 (= *insensé*) *[terreur, rage, course]* mad, wild; *[amour, joie, espoir]* mad, insane; *[idée, désir, tentative, dépense]* mad, insane, crazy; *[audace]* insane; *[imagination]* wild, insane; *[regard, gestes]* wild, crazed ◆ **avoir le ~ rire** to have the giggles ◆ **prix ~s sur les chemises** shirts at give-away prices ◆ **folle jeunesse** (†, *hum*) wild youth ◆ **folle enchère** irresponsible bid

3 (* = *énorme*) *[courage, énergie, succès]* fantastic*, terrific, tremendous; *[peur]* terrific, tremendous ◆ **j'ai une envie folle de chocolat/d'y aller** I'm dying for some chocolate/to go ◆ **j'ai eu un mal ~ pour venir** I had a terrific *ou* terrible job* getting here ◆ **tu as mis un temps ~** it took you ages* ◆ **gagner/dépenser un argent ~** to earn/spend loads of money* ◆ **payer un prix ~** to pay a ridiculous *ou* an astronomical price ◆ **rouler à une vitesse folle** to drive at a tremendous speed ◆ **il y a un monde ~** it's really crowded ◆ **c'est ~ ce qu'il y a comme monde** it's incredible how many people there are ◆ **c'est ~ ce qu'on s'amuse !** we're having such a great *ou* fantastic time!* ◆ **c'est ~ ce qu'il a changé** it's incredible *ou* unbelievable how much he has changed ◆ **c'est ~ ce que tu me racontes là !** I can't believe what you're telling me!

4 (= *déréglé*) *[boussole, aiguille]* erratic; *[camion, cheval]* runaway *(épith)*; *[mèche de cheveux]* stray, unruly ◆ **elle a les cheveux ~s** her hair's all over the place ◆ **folle avoine** wild oats; → **herbe, patte[1]**

NM 1 *(Méd, fig)* madman, lunatic ◆ **arrêtez de faire les ~s** stop messing *ou* fooling about* ◆ **ce jeune ~** this young lunatic ◆ **espèce de vieux ~** you silly old fool; → **histoire, maison, plus**

◆ **comme un fou** ◆ **courir comme un ~** to run like a madman *ou* lunatic ◆ **travailler comme un ~** to work like mad* *ou* crazy* ◆ **il faut se battre comme un ~ pour réussir dans cette profession** you have to fight like crazy* to succeed in this profession

2 (* = *fanatique*) fanatic ◆ **c'est un ~ de jazz/tennis** he's a jazz/tennis fanatic

3 *(Échecs)* bishop

4 *(Hist = bouffon)* jester, fool ◆ **le ~ du roi** the king's fool, the court jester

5 (= *oiseau*) **~ (de Bassan)** gannet

NF **folle** 1 *(Méd, fig)* madwoman, lunatic ◆ **cette vieille folle** that old madwoman, that mad old woman ◆ **la folle du logis** *(littér)* the imagination

2 (*, *péj = homosexuel*) **(grande) folle** queen*

foucade /fukad/ NF *(littér)* caprice, whim, passing fancy; (= *emportement*) outburst

foudre[1] /fudʀ/ NF *(Météo)* lightning; *(Myth)* thunderbolt ◆ **frappé par la ~** struck by lightning ◆ **la ~ est tombée sur la maison** the house was struck by lightning ◆ **comme la ~, avec la rapidité de la ~** like lightning, as quick as a flash ◆ **ce fut le coup de ~** it was love at first sight ◆ **j'ai eu le coup de ~ pour Julie** I fell head over heels in love with Julie ◆ **elle a eu le coup de ~ pour l'Écosse** she fell in love with Scotland NFPL (= *colère*) ◆ **~s** *(Rel)* anathema *(sg)* ◆ **il s'est attiré les ~s de l'opposition** he provoked an angry response from the opposition

foudre[2] /fudʀ/ NM (†, *hum*) ◆ **~ de guerre** outstanding *ou* great leader (in war) ◆ **ce n'est pas un ~ de guerre** he's no firebrand ◆ **~ d'éloquence** brilliant orator

foudre[3] /fudʀ/ NM (= *tonneau*) tun

foudroiement /fudʀwamɑ̃/ NM striking (by lightning)

foudroyant, e /fudʀwajɑ̃, ɑt/ ADJ *[progrès, vitesse, attaque]* lightning *(épith)*; *[poison, maladie]* violent *(épith)*; *[mort]* instant; *[succès]* stunning *(épith)* ◆ **une nouvelle ~e** a devastating piece of news ◆ **il lui lança un regard ~** he looked daggers at him

foudroyer /fudʀwaje/ ► conjug 8 ◄ VT *[foudre]* to strike; *[coup de feu, maladie, malheur]* to strike down ◆ **il a été foudroyé** he was struck by lightning ◆ **la décharge électrique la foudroya** the electric shock killed her ◆ **cette nouvelle le foudroya** he was thunderstruck by the news ◆ **~ qn du regard** to look daggers at sb, to glare at sb ◆ **dans le champ il y avait un arbre foudroyé** in the field was a tree that had been struck by lightning

fouet /fwɛ/ NM 1 (= *cravache*) whip; *(Culin = batteur)* whisk ◆ **donner le ~ à qn** to give sb a whipping *ou* flogging; → **plein**

◆ **coup de fouet** *(lit)* lash; *(fig)* boost ◆ **donner un coup de ~ à l'économie** to stimulate the economy, to give the economy a boost, to kick-start the economy ◆ **le café/la douche froide lui a donné un coup de ~** the coffee/the cold shower perked him up 2 *[d'aile, queue]* tip

fouettard /fwetaʀ/ ADJ → **père**

fouetté, e /fwete/ (ptp de **fouetter**) ADJ ◆ **crème ~e** whipped cream NM *(Danse)* fouetté

fouettement /fwɛtmɑ̃/ NM *[de pluie]* lashing

fouetter /fwete/ ► conjug 1 ◄ VT 1 *[+ personne]* to whip, to flog; *[+ cheval]* to whip; *(Culin) [+ crème]* to whip; *[+ blanc d'œuf]* to whisk ◆ **la pluie fouettait les vitres** the rain lashed against the window panes ◆ **le vent le fouettait au visage** the wind whipped his face ◆ **fouette cocher !** *(hum)* don't spare the horses! *(hum)*; → **chat** 2 (= *stimuler*) *[+ imagination]* to fire; *[+ désir]* to whip up ◆ **l'air frais fouette le sang** fresh air is a real tonic VI 1 ◆ **la pluie fouettait contre les vitres** the rain lashed against the window panes 2 (⁑ = *avoir peur*) to be scared stiff* *ou* to death* 3 (⁑ = *puer*) to reek, to stink ◆ **ça fouette ici !** there's one hell of a stench *ou* stink in here!⁑

foufou, fofolle* /fufu, fɔfɔl/ ADJ crazy, scatty* *(Brit)*

foufoune⁑ /fufun/, **foufounette⁑** /fufunɛt/ NF pussy*⁑, fanny*⁑ *(Brit)*

fougasse /fugas/ NF (= *galette*) focaccia; (= *pain brioché*) ≃ brioche

fougère /fuʒɛʀ/ NF fern ◆ **clairière envahie de ~s** clearing overgrown with bracken ◆ **~ arborescente** tree fern

fougue /fug/ NF *[de personne]* spirit; *[de discours, attaque]* fieriness ◆ **plein de ~** *[orateur, réponse]* fiery; *[cheval]* mettlesome, fiery ◆ **la ~ de la jeunesse** the hotheadedness of youth ◆ **avec ~** spiritedly

fougueusement /fugøzmɑ̃/ ADV spiritedly ◆ **se ruer ~ sur qn** to hurl o.s. impetuously at sb

fougueux, -euse /fugø, øz/ ADJ *[réponse, tempérament, orateur]* fiery; *[jeunesse]* hot-headed, fiery; *[cheval]* mettlesome, fiery; *[attaque]* spirited

fouille /fuj/ NF 1 *[de personne]* searching, frisking; *[de maison, bagages]* search, searching ◆ **~ corporelle** body search 2 *(Archéol)* **~s** excavation(s), dig* ◆ **faire des ~s** to carry out excavations 3 *(Constr) (= action)* excavation; *(= lieu)* excavation (site) 4 *(* = poche)* pocket ◆ **s'en mettre plein les ~s** *(= gagner de l'argent)* to make a packet*

fouillé, e /fuje/ (ptp de **fouiller**) ADJ *[analyse, étude]* detailed, in-depth *(épith)*, thorough ◆ **fronton très ~** finely detailed pediment

fouille-merde * /fujmɛʀd/ NMF INV muckraker, shit-stirrer*

fouiller /fuje/ ▸ conjug 1 ◂ VT *[+ pièce, mémoire]* to search; *[+ personne]* to search, to frisk; *[+ poches]* to search, to go ou rummage through; *[+ région, bois]* to search, to scour, to comb; *[+ question]* to go (deeply) into; *[+ sol]* to dig; *[+ terrain]* to excavate, to dig up; *[+ bas-relief]* to undercut ◆ **on a fouillé mes bagages à la frontières** my bags were searched at the border ◆ **il fouillait l'horizon avec ses jumelles** he scanned ou searched the horizon with his binoculars ◆ **il fouilla l'obscurité des yeux** he peered into the darkness ◆ **il le fouilla du regard** he gave him a searching look ◆ **étude/analyse très fouillée** very detailed study/analysis ◆ **rinceaux très fouillés** finely detailed mouldings
VI ◆ **~ dans** *[+ tiroir, armoire]* to rummage in, to dig about in; *[+ poches, bagages]* to go ou rummage through; *[+ mémoire]* to delve into, to search ◆ **qui a fouillé dans mes affaires ?** who's been rummaging about in my things? ◆ **~ dans les archives** to delve into the files ◆ **~ dans le passé de qn** to delve into sb's past
VPR **se fouiller** to go through one's pockets ◆ **tu peux toujours te ~ !** * no way!*, nothing doing!*

fouilleur, -euse /fujœʀ, øz/ NM,F 1 *(Archéol)* digger 2 *(Police)* searcher, frisker* NF **fouilleuse** *(= charrue)* subsoil plough *(Brit)* ou plow *(US)*

fouillis /fuji/ NM *[de papiers, objets]* jumble, muddle; *[de branchages]* tangle; *[d'idées]* jumble, hotchpotch *(Brit)*, hodgepodge *(US)* ◆ **faire du ~** *(dans une pièce) [personne]* to make a mess; *[objets]* to look a mess, to look messy ◆ **sa chambre est en ~** his room is a dreadful mess ◆ **il régnait un ~ indescriptible** everything was in an indescribable mess ◆ **il est très ~** * he's very untidy ◆ **un exposé ~** * a muddled account

fouinard, e * /fwinaʀ, aʀd/ ADJ, NM,F ⇒ **fouineur, -euse**

fouine /fwin/ NF *(= animal)* stone marten ◆ **c'est une vraie ~** *(fig)* he's a real snoop(er)* *(péj)* ◆ **visage ou tête de ~** weasel face

fouiner /fwine/ ▸ conjug 1 ◂ VI *(péj)* to nose around ou about ◆ **je n'aime pas qu'on fouine dans mes affaires** I don't like people nosing ou ferreting about in my things ◆ **il est toujours à ~ partout** he's always poking his nose into things

fouineur, -euse /fwinœʀ, øz/ *(péj)* ADJ prying, nosey* NM,F nosey parker*, snoop(er)*

fouir /fwiʀ/ ▸ conjug 2 ◂ VT to dig

fouisseur, -euse /fwisœʀ, øz/ ADJ burrowing, fossorial *(SPÉC)* NM burrower, fossorial animal *(SPÉC)*

foulage /fulaʒ/ NM *[de raisin]* pressing; *[de drap]* fulling; *[de cuir]* tanning

foulant, e * /fulɑ̃, ɑ̃t/ ADJ ◆ **ce n'est pas trop ~** it won't kill you *(ou him etc)* *; → **pompe¹**

foulard /fulaʀ/ NM 1 *(= écharpe) (carré)* (head-)scarf; *(long)* scarf ◆ **~ islamique** chador 2 *(= tissu)* foulard

foule /ful/ NF 1 *(gén)* crowd; *(péj = populace)* mob ◆ **la ~** *(= le peuple)* the masses ◆ **une ~ hurlante** a howling mob ◆ **la ~ et l'élite** the masses and the élite ◆ **la ~ des badauds** the crowd of onlookers; → **psychologie** 2 *(locutions)* **il y avait ~ à la réunion** there were lots of people at the meeting ◆ **il n'y avait pas ~ !** there was hardly anyone there! ◆ **une ~ de** *[+ livres, questions]* masses* ou loads* of ◆ **il y avait une ~ de gens** there was a crowd ou there were crowds of people ◆ **une ~ de gens pensent que c'est faux** lots ou masses* of people think it's wrong ◆ **j'ai une ~ de choses à te dire** I've got loads* ou masses* (of things) to tell you ◆ **ils vinrent en ~ à l'exposition** they flocked to the exhibition ◆ **les idées me venaient en ~** my head was teeming with ideas

foulée /fule/ NF *[de cheval, coureur]* stride; *[d'animal sauvage]* spoor ◆ **suivre qn dans la ~, être dans la ~ de qn** *(Sport)* to follow (close) on sb's heels ◆ **courir à petites ~s** *(Sport)* to jog ou trot along ◆ **dans la ~ je vais repeindre le couloir** I'll paint the corridor while I'm at it

fouler /fule/ ▸ conjug 1 ◂ VT *[+ raisins]* to press; *[+ drap]* to full; *[+ cuir]* to tan ◆ **~ le sol de sa patrie** *(littér)* to walk upon ou tread (upon) native soil ◆ **~ aux pieds quelque chose de sacré** to trample something sacred underfoot, to trample on something sacred VPR **se fouler** 1 ◆ **se ~ la cheville/le poignet** to sprain one's ankle/one's wrist 2 *(* = travailler dur)* **il ne se foule pas beaucoup, il ne se foule pas la rate** he doesn't exactly overtax himself ou strain himself ◆ **ils ne se sont pas foulés !** they didn't exactly go to a lot of trouble!

fouleur, -euse /fulœʀ, øz/ NM,F *[de drap]* fuller; *[de cuir]* tanner

fouloir /fulwaʀ/ NM *[de drap]* fulling mill; *[de cuir]* tanning drum

foulon /fulɔ̃/ NM → **terre**

foulque /fulk/ NF coot

foultitude * /fultityd/ NF ◆ **une ~ de** heaps of*, loads of*, masses of* ◆ **j'ai une ~ de choses à faire** I've got a thousand and one things ou heaps* ou masses* of things to do

foulure /fulyʀ/ NF sprain ◆ **se faire une ~ à la cheville/au poignet** to sprain one's ankle/one's wrist

four /fuʀ/ NM 1 *[de boulangerie, cuisinière]* oven; *[de potier]* kiln; *[d'usine]* furnace ◆ **~ à céramique/à émaux** pottery/enamelling kiln ◆ **cuire au ~** *[+ gâteau]* to bake; *[+ viande]* to roast ◆ **plat allant au ~** ovenproof ou fireproof dish ◆ **poisson cuit au ~** baked fish ◆ **il a ouvert la bouche comme un ~** * he opened his great cavern of a mouth ◆ **je ne peux pas être au ~ et au moulin** I can't be in two places at once; → **banal², noir**
2 *(Théât)* flop, fiasco ◆ **cette pièce est ou a fait un ~** the play is a complete flop
3 *(= gâteau)* **(petit) ~** small pastry, petit four ◆ **petits ~s frais** miniature pastries ◆ **petits ~s salés** savoury appetizers *(bite-size pizzas, quiches etc)*
COMP **four à air pulsé** fan(-assisted) oven
four à catalyse catalyc oven
four à chaux lime kiln
four crématoire *[de crématorium]* crematorium ou crematory (furnace) ◆ **les ~s crématoires** *(Hist)* the ovens *(in Nazi concentration camps)*
four électrique *(gén)* electric oven; *(industriel)* electric furnace
four à pain baker's oven
four à pyrolyse pyrolytic oven
four solaire solar furnace; → **micro-onde**

fourbe /fuʀb/ ADJ *[personne, caractère, air, regard]* deceitful, treacherous ◆ **c'est un ~** he's deceitful ou treacherous

fourberie /fuʀbəʀi/ NF *(littér) (= nature)* deceitfulness, treachery; *(= acte, geste)* deceit, treachery ◆ **à cause de ses ~s** because of his treachery ou deceit

fourbi * /fuʀbi/ NM *(= attirail)* gear* *(NonC)*, clobber* *(NonC) (Brit)*; *(= fouillis)* mess ◆ **canne à pêche, hameçons et tout le ~** fishing rod, hooks and all the rest of the gear ◆ **partir en vacances avec le bébé, ça va en faire du ou un ~** going on holiday with the baby will mean taking a whole heap of gear* with us

fourbir /fuʀbiʀ/ ▸ conjug 2 ◂ VT *[+ arme]* to polish, to furbish ◆ **~ ses armes** *(fig)* to prepare for battle, to get ready for the fray

fourbissage /fuʀbisaʒ/ NM polishing, furbishing

fourbu, e /fuʀby/ ADJ exhausted

fourche /fuʀʃ/ NF 1 *(pour le foin)* pitchfork; *(pour bêcher)* fork 2 *[d'arbre, chemin, bicyclette]* fork; *[de pantalon, jambes]* crotch; *[de cheveu]* split end ◆ **la route faisait une ~** the road forked 3 *(Hist)* **les Fourches Caudines** the Caudine Forks ◆ **passer sous les ~s Caudines** *(frm)* to be subjected to stringent checks 4 *(Belg = temps libre)* break

fourcher /fuʀʃe/ ▸ conjug 1 ◂ VI *[arbre, chemin]* † to fork ◆ **avoir les cheveux qui fourchent** to have split ends ◆ **ma langue a fourché** it was a slip of the tongue

fourchette /fuʀʃɛt/ NF 1 *(pour manger)* fork ◆ **~ à gâteaux/à huîtres** pastry/oyster fork ◆ **manger avec la ~ d'Adam** *(hum)* to eat with one's fingers ◆ **il a une bonne ~ ou un bon coup de ~** he has a hearty appetite, he's a good ou hearty eater 2 *[d'oiseau]* wishbone; *[de cheval]* frog; *(Aut)* selector fork; *(Tech)* fork ◆ **~ vulvaire** *(Anat)* fourchette ◆ **~ sternale** *(Anat)* suprasternal notch 3 *(Stat)* margin ◆ **la ~ se rétrécit** the margin is narrowing ◆ **~ d'âge** age bracket ◆ **~ d'imposition** tax bracket ou band ◆ **~ de prix** price range 4 *(Échecs)* fork ◆ **prendre la dame en ~** *(Cartes)* to finesse the queen

fourchu, e /fuʀʃy/ ADJ *[arbre, chemin]* forked; *[menton]* jutting *(épith)* ◆ **animal au pied ~** cloven-hoofed animal ◆ **elle a les cheveux ~s** she's got split ends; → **langue**

fourgon /fuʀgɔ̃/ NM *(= wagon)* wag(g)on; *(= camion)* (large) van, lorry *(Brit)*; *(= diligence)* coach, carriage; *(= tisonnier)* poker ◆ **~ à bagages** luggage van ◆ **~ à bestiaux** cattle truck ◆ **~ blindé** armoured van ◆ **~ cellulaire** prison ou police van *(Brit)*, patrol wagon *(US)* ◆ **~ de déménagement** removal *(Brit)* ou moving *(US)* van ◆ **~ funéraire ou mortuaire** hearse ◆ **~ de munitions** munitions wagon ◆ **~ postal** mail van ◆ **~ de queue** rear brake van ◆ **~ de vivres** *(Mil)* supply wagon

fourgonner /fuʀgɔne/ ▸ conjug 1 ◂ VT *[+ poêle, feu]* to poke, to rake VI *(* : parmi des objets)* to rummage about, to poke about ◆ **je l'entendais qui fourgonnait dans la cuisine/dans le placard** I heard him rummaging ou poking about in the kitchen/in the cupboard

fourgonnette /fuʀgɔnɛt/ NF (small) van, delivery van

fourgue /fuʀg/ *(arg Crime)* NM *(= personne)* fence* NF *(= trafic)* fencing*; *(= marchandise)* fenced goods*

fourguer * /fuʀge/ ▸ conjug 1 ◂ VT *(= vendre) [+ mauvaise marchandise]* to flog* *(à to)* to unload* *(à onto)*; *(= donner)* to unload *(à onto)*; ◆ **il**

m'a fourgué aux flics * (= *dénoncer*) he squealed on me to the cops *

fouriérisme /fuʀjeʀism/ NM Fourierism

fouriériste /fuʀjeʀist/ ADJ Fourieristic NMF Fourierist, Fourierite

fourme /fuʀm/ NF *type of French blue-veined cheese*

fourmi /fuʀmi/ NF 1 (= *insecte*) ant; (= *personne affairée*) beaver ◆ ~ **noire/rouge/volante** black/red/flying ant ◆ ~ **maçonne** builder *ou* worker ant ◆ **avoir des ~s dans les jambes** to have pins and needles in one's legs ◆ **vus de si haut les gens ont l'air de ~s** seen from so high up the people look like ants ◆ **elle s'affaire comme une ~** she bustles about as busy as a bee ◆ **tu es plutôt ~ ou plutôt cigale ?** do you put money aside or does it burn a hole in your pocket?; → **travail**[1] 2 (*arg Drogue*) small-time runner, mule (*arg*)

fourmilier /fuʀmilje/ NM anteater

fourmilière /fuʀmiljɛʀ/ NF (= *monticule*) ant-hill; (= *nid*) ants' nest; (*fig*) hive of activity ◆ **cette ville/ce bureau est une (vraie) ~** this town/this office is a hive of activity

fourmilion /fuʀmiljɔ̃/ NM antlion, doodlebug (*US*)

fourmillant, e /fuʀmijɑ̃, jɑ̃t/ ADJ [*foule*] milling, swarming; [*cité*] teeming

fourmillement /fuʀmijmɑ̃/ NM 1 [*d'insectes, personnes*] swarming ◆ **le ~ de la rue** the swarming *ou* milling crowds in the street ◆ **un ~ d'insectes** a mass of swarming insects ◆ **un ~ d'idées** a welter of ideas 2 (*gén pl*) **~s** (= *picotement*) pins and needles

fourmiller /fuʀmije/ ▸ conjug 1 ◂ VI [*insectes, personnes*] to swarm ◆ **dissertation où fourmillent les erreurs** essay riddled with mistakes ◆ ~ **de** [+ *insectes, personnes*] to be swarming *ou* crawling *ou* teeming with; [+ *idées, erreurs*] to be teeming with

fournaise /fuʀnɛz/ NF (= *feu*) blaze, blazing fire; (= *endroit surchauffé*) furnace, oven

fourneau (pl **fourneaux**) /fuʀno/ NM 1 († = *cuisinière, poêle*) stove ◆ **être aux ~x** to do the cooking 2 [*de forge, chaufferie*] furnace; [*de pipe*] bowl ◆ ~ **de mine** blast hole; → **haut**

fournée /fuʀne/ NF (*lit, fig*) batch

fourni, e /fuʀni/ (ptp de **fournir**) ADJ [*herbe*] luxuriant, lush; [*cheveux*] thick, abundant; [*barbe, sourcils*] bushy, thick ◆ **chevelure peu ~e** sparse *ou* thin head of hair ◆ **carte bien ~e** extensive menu ◆ **boutique bien ~e** well-stocked shop

fournil /fuʀni/ NM bakery, bakehouse

fourniment * /fuʀnimɑ̃/ NM gear * (*NonC*), clobber ⁑ (*NonC*) (*Brit*) ◆ **il va falloir emporter tout un ~** we'll have to take a whole heap of gear * *ou* stuff *

fournir /fuʀniʀ/ ▸ conjug 2 ◂ VT 1 (= *approvisionner*) [+ *client, restaurant*] to supply ◆ ~ **qn en viande/légumes** to supply sb with meat/vegetables

2 (= *procurer*) [+ *matériel, main-d'œuvre*] to supply, to provide; [+ *preuves, secours*] to supply, to furnish; [+ *renseignements*] to supply, to provide, to furnish; [+ *pièce d'identité*] to produce; [+ *prétexte, exemple*] to give, to supply ◆ ~ **qch à qn** to supply *ou* provide sb with sth ◆ ~ **à qn l'occasion/les moyens de faire qch** to provide sb with the opportunity of doing sth/the means to do sth ◆ ~ **du travail à qn** to provide sb with work ◆ ~ **le vivre et le couvert** to provide board and lodging

3 (= *produire*) [+ *effort*] to put in; [+ *prestation*] to give; [+ *récolte*] to supply ◆ ~ **un gros effort** to put in a lot of effort, to make a great deal of effort

4 (*Cartes*) ~ **(une carte)** to follow suit ◆ ~ **à cœur** to follow suit in hearts

VT INDIR **fournir à** † [+ *besoins*] to provide for; [+ *dépense, frais*] to defray ◆ **ses parents fournissent à son entretien** his parents give him his keep *ou* provide for his maintenance

VPR **se fournir** to provide o.s. (*de* with); ◆ **se ~ en** *ou* **de charbon** to get (in) supplies of coal ◆ **je me fournis toujours chez le même épicier** I always buy *ou* get my groceries from the same place, I always shop at the same grocer's

fournisseur /fuʀnisœʀ/ NM [*d'entreprise*] supplier; (= *détaillant*) retailer, stockist (*Brit*) ◆ ~ **exclusif** sole supplier ◆ ~ **de viande/papier** supplier *ou* purveyor (*frm*) of meat/paper, meat/paper supplier ◆ ~ **d'accès** (*Internet*) access *ou* service provider ◆ **les pays ~s de la France** countries that supply France (with goods *ou* imports) ◆ **les ~s de l'armée** army contractors ◆ **chez votre ~ habituel** at your local retailer('s) *ou* stockist('s) (*Brit*) ◆ **nos ~s manquent de matière première** our suppliers are out of raw materials

fourniture /fuʀnityʀ/ NF 1 (= *action*) [*de matériel, marchandises*] supply(ing), provision 2 (= *objet*) **~s (de bureau)** office supplies, stationery ◆ **~s scolaires** school stationery

fourrage /fuʀaʒ/ NM (*Agr*) fodder, forage ◆ ~ **vert** silage

fourrager[1] /fuʀaʒe/ ▸ conjug 3 ◂ **fourrager dans** VT INDIR [+ *papiers, tiroir*] to rummage through, to dig about in

fourrager[2], **-ère**[1] /fuʀaʒe, ɛʀ/ ADJ ◆ **plante/betterave/culture fourragère** fodder plant/beet/crop ◆ **céréales fourragères** feed grains

fourragère[2] /fuʀaʒɛʀ/ NF 1 (*Mil*) fourragère 2 (= *champ*) fodder *ou* forage field; (= *charrette*) haywagon

fourre /fuʀ/ NF (*Helv* = *taie*) pillowcase, pillowslip; [*d'édredon*] cover; (= *chemise cartonnée ou plastifiée*) folder; [*de livre*] (dust) jacket *ou* cover; [*de disque*] sleeve, jacket (*US*)

fourré[1] /fuʀe/ NM thicket ◆ **se cacher dans les ~s** to hide in the bushes

fourré[2], **e** /fuʀe/ (ptp de **fourrer**) ADJ [*bonbon, chocolat*] filled; [*manteau, gants*] fur-lined; (= *molletonné*) fleecy-lined ◆ ~ **d'hermine** ermine-lined ◆ **chocolats ~s** chocolate creams ◆ **gâteau ~ à la crème** cream(-filled) cake ◆ **tablette de chocolat ~ à la crème** bar of cream-filled chocolate ◆ **coup ~** underhand trick

fourreau (pl **fourreaux**) /fuʀo/ NM 1 [*d'épée*] sheath, scabbard; [*de parapluie*] cover ◆ **mettre au/tirer du ~ son épée** to sheathe/unsheathe one's sword 2 ◆ **(robe) ~** sheath dress

fourrer /fuʀe/ ▸ conjug 1 ◂ VT 1 * (= *enfoncer*) to stick *, to shove *, to stuff *; (= *mettre*) to stick * ◆ **où ai-je bien pu le ~ ?** where on earth *ou* the heck * did I put it? ◆ ~ **ses mains dans ses poches** to stuff * *ou* stick * *ou* shove * one's hands in one's pockets ◆ ~ **qch dans un sac** to stuff * *ou* shove * sth into a bag ◆ **qui t'a fourré ça dans le crâne ?** who put that (idea) into your head? ◆ ~ **son nez partout/dans les affaires des autres** to poke *ou* stick * one's nose into everything/into other people's business ◆ ~ **qn dans le pétrin** to land sb in the soup * *ou* in it * (*Brit*) ◆ ~ **qn en prison** to stick sb in prison *

2 [+ *gâteau*] to fill; [+ *manteau*] to line (with fur)

VPR **se fourrer** * 1 ◆ **se ~ une idée dans la tête** to get an idea into one's head ◆ **il s'est fourré dans la tête que ...** he has got it into his head that ...

2 ◆ **se ~ dans un coin** to go into a corner ◆ **se ~ sous la table** to get under the table ◆ **où a-t-il encore été se ~ ?** where has he got to now? ◆ **il ne savait plus où se ~** he didn't know where to put himself ◆ **tu es toujours fourré dans mes pattes !** you're always getting under my feet! ◆ **il est toujours fourré chez eux** he's always round at their place ◆ **son ballon est allé se ~ dans la niche du chien** his ball ended up in *ou* landed in the dog kennel; → **doigt, guêpier**

fourre-tout /fuʀtu/ NM INV (= *pièce*) junk room; (= *placard*) junk cupboard; (= *sac*) holdall ◆ **sa chambre est un vrai ~** his bedroom is an absolute dump * *ou* tip * (*Brit*) ◆ **sa dissertation/son livre est un vrai ~** (*péj*) his essay/his book is a real hotchpotch (*Brit*) *ou* hodgepodge (*US*) of ideas ◆ **un discours/une loi ~** a rag-bag of a speech/law

fourreur /fuʀœʀ/ NM furrier

fourrier /fuʀje/ NM (*littér* = *propagateur*) ◆ **ils accusent l'ancien roi d'avoir été le ~ du communisme dans ce pays** they accuse the former king of having paved the way for communism in the country; → **sergent**[1]

fourrière /fuʀjɛʀ/ NF pound; [*de chiens*] dog pound ◆ **emmener une voiture à la ~** to tow away a car, to impound a car

fourrure /fuʀyʀ/ NF (= *pelage*) coat; (= *matériau, manteau*) fur

fourvoiement /fuʀvwamɑ̃/ NM (*littér*) mistake

fourvoyer /fuʀvwaje/ ▸ conjug 8 ◂ VT ◆ ~ **qn** [*personne*] to get sb lost, to mislead sb; [*mauvais renseignement*] to mislead sb; [*mauvais exemple*] to lead sb astray VPR **se fourvoyer** (= *s'égarer*) to lose one's way; (= *se tromper*) to go astray ◆ **se ~ dans un quartier inconnu** to stray into an unknown district (by mistake) ◆ **dans quelle aventure s'est-il encore fourvoyé ?** what has he got involved in now? ◆ **il s'est complètement fourvoyé en faisant son problème** he has gone completely wrong *ou* completely off the track with his problem

foutaise ⁑ /futɛz/ NF ◆ **(des) ~s !, (c'est de la) ~ !** (that's) bullshit! *⁑, that's crap! *⁑ ◆ **dire des ~s** to talk bullshit *⁑ *ou* crap *⁑ ◆ **se disputer pour une ~** *ou* **des ~s** to quarrel over nothing

foutoir ⁑ /futwaʀ/ NM damned ⁑ *ou* bloody ⁑ (*Brit*) shambles (*sg*) ◆ **sa chambre est un vrai ~** his bedroom is a pigsty *ou* a dump * *ou* a bloody shambles ⁑ (*Brit*)

foutre ⁑ /futʀ/ VT 1 (= *faire*) to do ◆ **qu'est-ce qu'il fout, il est déjà 8 heures** what the hell ⁑ is he doing *ou* up to – it's already 8 o'clock ◆ **il n'a rien foutu de la journée** he hasn't done a damned ⁑ *ou* bloody ⁑ (*Brit*) thing all day, he's done damn all ⁑ *ou* bugger all *⁑ (*Brit*) today ◆ **j'en n'ai rien à ~ de leurs histoires** I don't give a damn ⁑ about what they're up to ◆ **qu'est-ce que ça peut me ~ ?, qu'est-ce que j'en ai à ~ ?** what the hell do I care? ⁑

2 (= *donner*) ~ **une raclée à qn** to beat the hell out of sb ⁑ ◆ ~ **une gifle à qn** to belt sb one * ◆ **ça me fout la trouille** it gives me the willies * *ou* creeps * ◆ **fous-moi la paix !** lay off! ⁑, bugger off! *⁑ (*Brit*) ◆ **je croyais qu'il avait compris mais je t'en fous !** I thought he'd understood but he damn well hadn't! ⁑ ◆ **qu'est-ce qui m'a foutu un idiot pareil !** of all the flaming idiots! * ◆ **je t'en foutrai des amis comme ça !** who the hell needs friends like that? ⁑ ◆ **je t'en foutrai, moi, du champagne !** I'll give you goddam ⁑ *ou* bloody ⁑ (*Brit*) champagne!

3 (= *mettre*) **fous-le là/dans ta poche** shove * it in here/in your pocket ◆ **c'est lui qui a foutu le feu** he was the one who set fire to the place ◆ ~ **qn à la porte** to give sb the boot *, to kick sb out * ◆ **il a foutu le vase par terre** (*qui était posé*) he knocked the vase off, he sent the vase flying * (*Brit*); (*qu'il avait dans les mains*) he dropped the vase ◆ **ça fout tout par terre** that screws *⁑ *ou* buggers *⁑ (*Brit*) everything up ◆ **ça l'a foutu en rogne** that made him as mad as

hell‡ ◆ **ça la fout mal** it looks pretty bad*; → **bordel, merde**

[4] ◆ **~ le camp** *[personne]* to split*, to bugger off*** *(Brit)*; *[bouton, rimmel, vis]* to come off ◆ **fous-moi le camp !** get lost!‡, bugger off!***(Brit)*, sod off!***(Brit)* ◆ **tout fout le camp** everything's falling apart *ou* going to hell‡

VPR se foutre [1] *(= se mettre)* **je me suis foutu dedans** I really screwed up***◆ **tu vas te ~ par terre** you're going to fall flat on your face ◆ **se ~ dans une sale affaire** to get mixed up in a messy business ◆ **ils se sont foutu sur la gueule** they beat (the) hell out of each other‡

[2] *(= se moquer)* **se ~ de qn/qch** to take the mickey* *ou* piss***(Brit)* out of sb/sth; *(= être indifférent)* not to give a damn about sb/sth‡ ◆ **se ~ de qn** *(= dépasser les bornes)* to mess* *ou* muck* *(Brit)* sb about ◆ **25 € pour ça, ils se foutent de nous** *ou* **du monde** €25 for that! – what the hell do they take us for!‡ ◆ **ça, je m'en fous pas mal** I couldn't give a damn‡ about that ◆ **je me fous qu'il parte ou qu'il reste** I couldn't give a damn‡ whether he goes or stays ◆ **tu te fous de ma gueule ?** *(= tu te moques de moi)* are you making fun of me?, are you taking the piss?***(Brit)*; *(= tu me fais marcher)* are you having *(Brit)* ou putting *(US)* me on?* ◆ **quelle belle bague ! il s'est pas foutu de toi !** what a beautiful ring! he really treats you right!* ◆ **du champagne et du caviar ! elle ne s'est pas foutue de nous !** champagne and caviar! she's really done us proud!

[3] *** **va te faire ~ !** fuck off!***, fuck you!***, bugger off!***(Brit)*, get stuffed!‡ *(Brit)* ◆ **je lui ai bien demandé, mais va te faire ~ : il n'a jamais voulu** I did ask him but no fucking***way would he do it

[4] ◆ **se ~ à faire qch** to start to do sth ◆ **il s'est foutu à chialer** he started to blubber*

foutre² †***/futʀ/ **EXCL, ADV** damnation!‡, bloody hell!‡ *(Brit)* ◆ **je n'en sais ~ rien !** I haven't got a fucking***clue!

foutrement‡ /futʀəmɑ̃/ **ADV** damn‡, bloody‡ *(Brit)* ◆ **il s'est ~ bien défendu** he stood up for himself damn well‡ *ou* bloody well‡ *(Brit)*

foutriquet †* /futʀikɛ/ **NM** *(péj)* nobody, little runt*

foutu, e‡ /futy/ (ptp de **foutre**) **ADJ** [1] *(avant n : intensif)* *[objet, appareil, personne]* damned‡, bloody‡ *(Brit)*; *(= mauvais)* *[temps, pays, travail]* damned awful‡, bloody awful *(Brit)*‡ ◆ **il a un ~ caractère** he's got one hell of a temper‡

[2] *(après n)* *[malade, vêtement]* done for* *(attrib)*; *[appareil]* bust*, buggered‡ *(Brit)* ◆ **il est ~** he's had it* ◆ **c'est ~ pour mon avancement** there *ou* bang* goes my promotion

[3] *(= habillé)* got up*, rigged out*

[4] *(= bâti, conçu)* **bien/mal ~** *[appareil, émission, documentaire]* well-/badly-made; *[manuel]* well-/badly-written ◆ **montre-moi comment c'est ~** show me what it looks like ◆ **elle est bien ~e** she's got a nice body

[5] *(= malade)* **être mal** *ou* **pas bien ~** to feel lousy*, to feel bloody‡ *(Brit)* awful

[6] *(= capable)* **il est ~ de le faire** he's quite likely *ou* liable to go and do it ◆ **il est même pas ~ de réparer ça** he can't even mend the damned thing‡

fox(-terrier) (pl **fox(-terriers)**) /fɔks(tɛʀje)/ **NM** fox terrier

fox(-trot) /fɔks(tʀɔt)/ **NM INV** foxtrot

fox-hound (pl **fox-hounds**) /fɔksaund/ **NM** fox-hound

foyer /fwaje/ **NM** [1] *(frm) (= maison)* home; *(= famille)* family ◆ **~ uni** close *ou* united family ◆ **les joies du ~** the joys of family life ◆ **revenir au ~** to come back home ◆ **un jeune ~** a young couple ◆ **~ fiscal** *household (as defined for tax purposes)*; → **femme, fonder, renvoyer**

[2] *[de locomotive, chaudière]* firebox; *(= âtre)* hearth, fireplace; *(= dalle)* hearth(stone)

[3] *(= résidence) [de vieillards, soldats]* home; *[de jeunes]* hostel; *[d'étudiants]* hostel, hall ◆ **~ éducatif** special (residential) school ◆ **~ socio-éducatif** community home ◆ **~ d'étudiants** students' hall (of residence) *ou* hostel

[4] *(= lieu de réunion) [de jeunes, retraités]* club; *(Théât)* foyer ◆ **~ des artistes** greenroom ◆ **~ des jeunes** youth club

[5] *(Math, Opt, Phys)* focus ◆ **à ~ variable** variable-focus *(épith)* ◆ **verres à double ~** bifocal lenses

[6] ◆ **~ de** *[+ incendie]* seat of, centre of; *[+ lumière, infection]* source of; *[+ agitation]* centre of ◆ **~ d'extrémistes** centre of extremist activities

FP (abrév de **franchise postale**) → **franchise**

FR3 † /ɛfɛʀtʀwa/ (abrév de **France Régions 3**) *former name of the third French television channel (now called France 3)*

frac /fʀak/ **NM** tails, tail coat ◆ **être en ~** to be in tails, to be wearing a tail coat

fracas /fʀaka/ **NM** *[d'objet qui tombe]* crash; *[de train, tonnerre, vagues]* roar; *[de bataille]* din ◆ **tomber avec ~** to fall with a crash, to come crashing down ◆ **la nouvelle a été annoncée à grand ~** the news was announced amid a blaze of publicity ◆ **démissionner avec ~** to resign dramatically ◆ **ils ont quitté la conférence avec ~** they stormed out of the conference; → **perte**

fracassant, e /fʀakasɑ̃, ɑt/ **ADJ** *[bruit]* thunderous, deafening; *[nouvelle]* shattering, staggering, sensational; *[déclaration]* sensational; *[succès]* resounding, thundering *(épith)*

fracasser /fʀakase/ ► conjug 1 ◄ **VT** *[+ objet, mâchoire, épaule]* to smash, to shatter; *[+ porte]* to smash (down), to shatter ◆ **il est fracassé‡** *(= saoul)* he's pissed‡; *(= drogué)* he's stoned‡ **VPR se fracasser** ◆ **se ~ contre** *ou* **sur qch** *[vagues]* to crash against sth; *[bateau, véhicule]* to be smashed (to pieces) against sth ◆ **la voiture est allée se ~ contre l'arbre** the car smashed *ou* crashed into the tree

fractal, e /fʀaktal/ **ADJ** fractal **NF fractale** fractal

fraction /fʀaksjɔ̃/ **NF** *(Math)* fraction; *[de groupe, somme, terrain]* part ◆ **en une ~ de seconde** in a fraction of a second, in a split second ◆ **par ~ de 3 jours/de 10 unités** for every 3-day period/10 units ◆ **une ~ importante du groupe** a large proportion of the group

fractionnaire /fʀaksjɔnɛʀ/ **ADJ** *[nombre]* fractional ◆ **livre ~** *(Comm)* day book

fractionné, e /fʀaksjɔne/ (ptp de **fractionner**) **ADJ** *(Chim) [distillation, cristallisation]* fractional; *[groupe de personnes]* fragmented ◆ **mon emploi du temps est trop ~** my timetable is too disjointed *ou* fragmented ◆ **paiement ~** payment in instalments *(Brit) ou* installments, installment payment *(US)*

fractionnel, -elle /fʀaksjɔnɛl/ **ADJ** *[attitude, menées]* divisive

fractionnement /fʀaksjɔnmɑ̃/ **NM** splitting up, division ◆ **~ d'actions** *(Bourse)* stock splitting

fractionner /fʀaksjɔne/ ► conjug 1 ◄ **VT** *[+ groupe, somme, travail]* to divide (up), to split up **VPR se fractionner** *[groupe]* to split up, to divide

fracture /fʀaktyʀ/ **NF** [1] *(Géol, Méd)* fracture ◆ **~ du crâne** fractured skull ◆ **~ ouverte** open fracture ◆ **~s multiples** multiple fractures [2] *(= écart)* split *(entre* between); ◆ **la ~ sociale** the gap between the haves and the have-nots ◆ **ceci ne réduira pas la ~ entre syndicats et patronat** this will not heal the rift *ou* split between unions and employers ◆ **cette question constitue la ligne de ~ entre la droite et la gauche** left and right are split over this issue

fracturer /fʀaktyʀe/ ► conjug 1 ◄ **VT** *(Géol, Méd)* to fracture; *[+ serrure]* to break (open); *[+ coffre-fort, porte]* to break open ◆ **il s'est fracturé la jambe** he's fractured his leg

fragile /fʀaʒil/ **ADJ** [1] *[corps, vase]* fragile; *[organe, peau, tissu]* delicate; *[cheveux]* brittle; *[surface, revêtement]* easily damaged ◆ **"attention fragile"** *(sur étiquette)* "fragile, handle with care" [2] *(fig) [économie, prospérité, santé, bonheur, paix]* fragile; *[preuve, argument]* flimsy; *[équilibre]* delicate ◆ **ne soyez pas trop brusque, elle est encore ~** don't be too rough with her - she's still rather fragile ◆ **avoir l'estomac ~, être ~ de l'estomac** to have a weak stomach ◆ **être de constitution ~** to have a weak constitution

fragilisation /fʀaʒilizasjɔ̃/ **NF** weakening ◆ **c'est un facteur de ~ de l'entreprise** this is a factor that might undermine *ou* weaken the company ◆ **cela entraîne la ~ des liens parents-enfants** this puts a great strain on the relationship between parents and children

fragiliser /fʀaʒilize/ ► conjug 1 ◄ **VT** *[+ position, secteur]* to weaken; *[+ personne]* to make vulnerable; *[+ régime politique]* to undermine, to weaken ◆ **des familles fragilisées par le chômage** families made vulnerable by unemployment ◆ **des maires fragilisés par les affaires** mayors whose position has been weakened by political scandals

fragilité /fʀaʒilite/ **NF** *[de corps, vase]* fragility; *[d'organe, peau]* delicacy; *[de cheveux]* brittleness; *[de santé]* fragility, frailty; *[de construction, économie, preuve, argument]* flimsiness, frailty; *[de bonheur, paix]* frailty, flimsiness, fragility; *[de gloire]* fragility; *[de pouvoir, prospérité]* fragility, flimsiness

fragment /fʀagmɑ̃/ **NM** [1] *[de vase, roche, papier]* fragment, bit, piece; *[d'os, vitre]* fragment, splinter, bit [2] *[de conversation]* bit, snatch; *[de chanson]* snatch; *[de lettre]* bit, part; *[de roman]* *(= bribe)* fragment; *(= extrait)* passage, extract

fragmentaire /fʀagmɑ̃tɛʀ/ **ADJ** *[connaissances]* sketchy, patchy; *[données]* fragmentary ◆ **nous avons une vue très ~ des choses** we have only a sketchy *ou* an incomplete picture of the situation

fragmentation /fʀagmɑ̃tasjɔ̃/ **NF** *[de matière]* breaking up, fragmentation; *[d'État, terrain]* fragmentation, splitting up, breaking up; *[d'étude, travail, livre, somme]* splitting up, division; *[de disque dur]* fragmentation → **bombe**

fragmenter /fʀagmɑ̃te/ ► conjug 1 ◄ **VT** *[+ matière]* to break up, to fragment; *[+ État, terrain]* to fragment, to split up, to break up; *[+ étude, travail, livre, somme]* to split up, to divide (up); *[+ disque dur]* to fragment ◆ **nous vivons dans une société fragmentée**; we live in a fragmented society ◆ **avoir une vision fragmentée du monde** to have a fragmented view of the world ◆ **ce travail est trop fragmenté** this work is too fragmented **VPR se fragmenter** *[roches]* to fragment, to break up

fragrance /fʀagʀɑ̃s/ **NF** *(littér)* fragrance

frai /fʀɛ/ **NM** *(= œufs)* spawn; *(= alevins)* fry; *(= époque)* spawning season; *(ponte)* spawning

fraîche /fʀɛʃ/ **ADJ, NF** → **frais¹**

fraîchement /fʀɛʃmɑ̃/ **ADV** [1] *(= récemment)* freshly, newly ◆ **~ arrivé** newly *ou* just arrived ◆ **fruit ~ cueilli** freshly picked fruit ◆ **amitié ~ nouée** newly-formed friendship [2] *(= froidement)* *[accueillir]* coolly ◆ **comment ça va ? – ~ !*** how are you? – a bit chilly!*

fraîcheur /fʀɛʃœʀ/ **NF** [1] *[de boisson]* coolness; *[de pièce]* *(agréable)* coolness; *(trop froid)* chilliness ◆ **la ~ du soir/de la nuit** the cool of the evening/of the night ◆ **chercher un peu de ~** to look for a cool spot *ou* place ◆ **ce déodorant procure une agréable sensation de ~** this deodorant leaves you feeling pleasantly cool ② *[d'accueil]* coolness, chilliness ③ *[d'âme]* purity; *[de sentiment, jeunesse, teint]* freshness; *[de couleurs]* freshness, crispness ④ *[d'aliment]* freshness ◆ **de première ~** very fresh

fraîchir /fʀeʃiʀ/ ▸ conjug 2 ◂ **VI** *[temps, température]* to get cooler; *[vent]* to freshen

frais¹, fraîche /fʀɛ, fʀɛʃ/ **ADJ** ① *(= légèrement froid) [eau, endroit]* cool; *[vent]* cool, fresh ◆ **vent ~** *(Météo marine)* strong breeze

② *(= sans cordialité) [accueil]* chilly, cool

③ *(= sain, éclatant) [couleur]* fresh, clear, crisp; *[joues, teint]* fresh; *[parfum]* fresh; *[haleine]* fresh, sweet; *[voix]* clear; *[joie, âme, histoire d'amour]* pure ◆ **ses vêtements ne sont plus très ~** his clothes don't look very fresh ◆ **un peu d'air ~** a breath of *ou* a little fresh air

④ *(= récent) [plaie]* fresh; *[traces, souvenir]* recent, fresh; *[peinture]* wet, fresh; *[nouvelles]* recent ◆ **l'encre est encore fraîche** the ink is still wet; → **date**

⑤ *(opposé à sec, en conserve) [poisson, légumes, lait, pâtes]* fresh; *[œuf]* fresh, new-laid; *[pain]* new, fresh; → **chair**

⑥ *(= jeune, reposé) [troupes]* fresh ◆ **~ et dispos** fresh (as a daisy) ◆ **~ comme un gardon** bright as a button ◆ **je ne suis pas très ~ ce matin** I'm feeling a bit seedy this morning ◆ **fraîche comme une rose** *ou* **la rosée** as fresh as a daisy ◆ **elle est encore très fraîche pour son âge** she's very young-looking for her age

⑦ **argent ~** *(disponible)* ready cash; *(à investir)* fresh money

⑧ *(* = en difficulté)* **eh bien, on est ~ !** *ou* **nous voilà ~ !** well, we're in a fine mess now! *

ADV ① ◆ **il fait ~** *(agréable)* it's cool; *(froid)* it's chilly ◆ **en été, il faut boire ~** in summer you need cool *ou* cold drinks ◆ **"servir frais"** "serve cold *ou* chilled"

② *(= récemment)* newly ◆ **herbe ~** *ou* **fraîche coupée** newly *ou* freshly cut grass ◆ **~ émoulu de l'université** fresh from *ou* newly graduated from university ◆ **~ débarqué de sa province** fresh *ou* newly up from the country ◆ **habillé/rasé de ~** freshly changed/shaven

NM ① *(= fraîcheur)* **prendre le ~** to take a breath of fresh air ◆ **mettre (qch) au ~** *(lit)* to put (sth) in a cool place ◆ **mettre qn au ~** * *(en prison)* to put sb in the cooler * ◆ **le linge sent le ~** the washing smells lovely and fresh

② *(Météo marine)* **joli** *ou* **bon ~** strong breeze ◆ **grand ~** near gale

③ **le ~** *(= produits frais)* fresh produce

NF fraîche ◆ **(sortir) à la fraîche** (to go out) in the cool of evening

frais² /fʀɛ/ **NMPL** ① *(gén = débours)* expenses, costs; *(facturés)* charges; *(Admin = droits)* charges, fee(s) ◆ **tous ~ compris** inclusive of all costs ◆ **voyage d'affaires tous ~ payés** business trip with all expenses paid ◆ **tous ~ payés** *(Comm)* after costs ◆ **faire de grands ~** to go to great expense ◆ **ça m'a fait beaucoup de ~** it cost me a great deal of money ◆ **avoir de gros ~** to have heavy outgoings; → **arrêter, faux²**

② *(locutions)* **se mettre en ~** *(lit)* to go to great expense ◆ **se mettre en ~ pour qn/pour recevoir qn** to put o.s. out for sb/to entertain sb ◆ **faire les ~ de la conversation** *(parler)* to keep the conversation going; *(en être le sujet)* to be the (main) topic of conversation ◆ **nous ne voulons pas faire les ~ de cette erreur** we do not want to have to pay for this mistake ◆ **rentrer dans** *ou* **faire ses ~** to recover one's expenses ◆ **j'ai essayé d'être aimable mais j'en ai été pour mes ~** I tried to be friendly but I might just as well have spared myself the trouble ◆ **aux ~ de la maison** at the firm's expense ◆ **à ses ~** at one's own expense ◆ **aux ~ de la princesse** * *(de l'État)* at the taxpayer's expense; *(de l'entreprise)* at the firm's expense; *(= gratuitement)* with all expenses paid ◆ **à grands ~** at great expense ◆ **il se l'est procuré à grands ~** he acquired it at great expense, he paid a great deal for it ◆ **il se l'est procuré à moindre(s) ~** it didn't cost him a lot, he paid very little for it ◆ **à peu de ~** cheaply ◆ **il s'en est tiré à peu de ~** he got off lightly

COMP frais d'agence agency fees
frais d'avocats solicitors' *ou* legal fees
frais bancaires banking charges
frais de démarrage start-up costs
frais de déplacement travelling expenses *ou* costs
frais divers miscellaneous expenses, sundries
frais d'encaissement collection charges
frais d'enregistrement registration fee(s)
frais d'entretien *[de jardin, maison]* (cost of) upkeep; *[de machine, équipement]* maintenance costs
frais d'envoi, frais d'expédition forwarding charges
frais d'exploitation running costs
frais financiers *(gén)* interest charges; *[de crédit]* loan charges
frais fixes fixed *ou* standing charges *ou* expenses *ou* costs
frais de fonctionnement running *ou* upkeep costs
frais de garde *[d'enfant]* childminding fees *ou* costs; *[de malade]* nursing fees; *(Fin)* management charges
frais généraux overheads *(Brit)*, overhead *(US)*
frais de gestion *(= charges)* running costs; *(= prix d'un service)* management fees; *(Fin)* management charges
frais d'hébergement accommodation costs *ou* expenses *ou* fees
frais d'hospitalisation hospital fees *ou* expenses
frais d'hôtel hotel expenses
frais d'inscription registration fees
frais de justice (legal) costs
frais de logement accommodation expenses *ou* costs
frais de main-d'œuvre labour costs
frais de manutention handling charges
frais médicaux medical costs *ou* expenses *ou* fees
frais de notaire legal fees
frais de personnel staff(ing) costs
frais de port et d'emballage postage and packing
frais de premier établissement start-up costs, organization expenses
frais professionnels business expenses
frais réels *(Impôts)* allowable expenses
frais de représentation entertainment expenses
frais de scolarité *(à l'école, au lycée)* school fees *(Brit)*, tuition (fees) *(US)*; *(pour un étudiant)* tuition (fees)
frais de timbre stamp charges
frais de transport transportation costs; → **étude, installation**

fraisage /fʀɛzaʒ/ **NM** *(pour agrandir)* reaming; *(pour mettre une vis)* countersinking; *(pour usiner)* milling

fraise /fʀɛz/ **NF** ① *(= fruit)* strawberry ◆ **~ des bois** wild strawberry; → **sucrer** ② *(Tech) (pour agrandir un trou)* reamer; *(pour trou de vis)* countersink (bit); *[de métallurgiste]* milling-cutter; *[de dentiste]* drill ③ *(Boucherie)* ◆ **~ de veau/de porc** calf's/pig's caul ④ *(Hist = col)* ruff, fraise; *[de dindon]* wattle ⑤ *(Méd)* strawberry mark ⑥ *(* = visage)* face; → **ramener** **ADJ INV** *[couleur]* strawberry pink

fraiser /fʀeze/ ▸ conjug 1 ◂ **VT** *(= agrandir)* to ream; *(pour mettre une vis)* to countersink; *(= usiner)* to mill ◆ **à tête fraisée** countersunk

fraiseur /fʀɛzœʀ/ **NM** milling-machine operator

fraiseuse /fʀɛzøz/ **NF** ① *(= machine)* milling machine ② *(= ouvrière)* (woman) milling-machine operator

fraisier /fʀezje/ **NM** ① *(= plante)* strawberry plant ② *(= gâteau)* strawberry gateau

fraisure /fʀezyʀ/ **NF** countersink, countersunk hole

framboise /fʀɑ̃bwaz/ **NF** *(= fruit)* raspberry; *(= liqueur)* raspberry liqueur

framboisier /fʀɑ̃bwazje/ **NM** ① *(= plante)* raspberry bush ◆ **~s** raspberry canes *ou* bushes ② *(= gâteau)* raspberry gateau

franc¹, franche /fʀɑ̃, fʀɑ̃ʃ/ **ADJ** ① *(= loyal) [personne, réponse]* frank, straightforward; *[entretien, entrevue]* frank, candid; *[rire]* hearty; *[gaieté]* open ◆ **pour être ~ avec vous** to be frank with you ◆ **~ comme l'or, ~ du collier** straight as a die; → **jouer**

② *(= net) [situation]* clear-cut; *[différence]* clear; *[cassure]* clean; *[hostilité, répugnance]* unconcealed; *[couleur]* clear, pure ◆ **accord ~ et massif** overwhelming *ou* unequivocal acceptance ◆ **5 jours ~s** *(Jur)* 5 clear days

③ *(péj = total) [imbécile]* utter, downright, absolute; *[canaille]* downright, out-and-out, absolute; *[ingratitude]* downright, sheer ◆ **c'est une franche comédie/grossièreté** it's downright *ou* utterly hilarious/rude, it's sheer comedy/rudeness

④ *(= libre) [zone, ville, port]* free ◆ **boutique franche** duty-free shop ◆ **~ de** *(Comm)* free of ◆ **(livré) ~ de port** *[marchandises]* carriage-paid; *[paquet]* post-free, postage paid ◆ **~ d'avaries communes/particulières** free of general/particular average; → **corps, coudée, coup**

⑤ *(Agr)* **(arbre) ~ (de pied)** cultivar ◆ **greffer sur ~** to graft onto a cultivar

ADV ◆ **à vous parler ~** to be frank with you ◆ **je vous le dis tout ~** I'm being frank *ou* candid with you

franc² /fʀɑ̃/ **NM** *(= monnaie)* franc ◆ **ancien/nouveau ~** old/new franc ◆ **~ lourd** revalued franc ◆ **~ constant** constant *ou* inflation-adjusted franc ◆ **~ courant** franc at the current rate ◆ **~ belge/français/suisse** Belgian/French/Swiss franc ◆ **~ CFA** CFA franc *(unit of currency used in certain African states)* ◆ **le ~ fort** the strong franc ◆ **demander/obtenir le ~ symbolique** to demand/obtain token damages ◆ **racheter une entreprise pour le** *ou* **un ~ symbolique** to buy up a company for a nominal *ou* token sum ◆ **trois ~s six sous** peanuts *, next to nothing

franc³, franque /fʀɑ̃, fʀɑ̃k/ **ADJ** Frankish **NM Franc** Frank **NF Franque** Frank

français, e /fʀɑ̃sɛ, ɛz/ **ADJ** French **ADV** ◆ **acheter ~** to buy French (products) ◆ **boire/rouler ~** to buy French wine/cars **NM** ① *(= langue)* French ◆ **tu ne comprends pas le ~ ?** * ≃ don't you understand (plain) English? ◆ **c'est une faute de ~** ≃ it's a grammatical mistake ② ◆ **Français** Frenchman ◆ **les Français** *(= gens)* the French, French people; *(= hommes)* Frenchmen ◆ **le Français moyen** the average Frenchman, the man in the street **NF française** ① ◆ **Française** Frenchwoman ② ◆ **à la ~e** *[démocratie, socialisme, capitalisme]* French-style, à la française; *[humour]* French; → **jardin**

franc-bord (pl **francs-bords**) /fʀɑ̃bɔʀ/ **NM** *(Naut)* freeboard

franc-comtois, e (mpl **francs-comtois**) /fʀɑ̃kɔ̃twa, az/ **ADJ** of *ou* from Franche-Comté

NM,F Franc-Comtois(e) inhabitant *ou* native of Franche-Comté

France /fʀɑ̃s/ **NF** France ◆ **histoire/équipe/ambassade de ~** French history/team/embassy ◆ **le roi de ~** the King of France ◆ **la ~ libre** *(Hist)* free France ◆ **la ~ d'en bas** ordinary French people ◆ **la ~ d'en haut** the privileged classes (in France) ◆ **~2/3** *(TV) state-owned channels on French television;* → **profond, vieux**

France Télévision

There are two state-owned television channels in France: France 2 and France 3, a regionally-based channel. Broadly speaking, France 2 is a general-interest and light entertainment channel, while France 3 offers more cultural and educational viewing and local news programmes.

Francfort /fʀɑ̃kfɔʀ/ **N** Frankfurt ◆ **~-sur-le-Main** Frankfurt am Main; → **saucisse**

franchement /fʀɑ̃ʃmɑ̃/ **ADV** 1 *(= honnêtement) [parler, répondre]* frankly; *[agir]* openly ◆ **pour vous parler ~** to be frank (with you) ◆ **avouez ~ que …** you've got to admit that … ◆ **~ ! j'en ai assez !** quite frankly, I've had enough! ◆ **il y a des gens, ~ !** really! *ou* honestly! some people! ◆ **~ non** frankly no

2 *(= sans hésiter) [entrer, frapper]* boldly ◆ **il entra ~** he strode in, he walked straight *ou* boldly in ◆ **appuyez-vous ~ sur moi** put all your weight on me, lean hard on me ◆ **allez-y ~** *(explication)* get straight to the point, say it straight out; *(manœuvre)* go right ahead

3 *(= sans ambiguïté)* clearly; *(= nettement)* definitely ◆ **je lui ai posé la question ~** I put the question to him straight ◆ **dis-moi ~ ce que tu veux** tell me straight out *ou* clearly what you want ◆ **c'est ~ rouge** it's clearly *ou* quite obviously red ◆ **c'est ~ au-dessous de la moyenne** it's well below average

4 *(intensif = tout à fait) [mauvais, laid]* utterly, downright, really; *[bon]* really; *[impossible]* downright, utterly; *[irréparable]* completely, absolutely ◆ **ça m'a ~ dégoûté** it really *ou* utterly disgusted me ◆ **ça s'est ~ mal passé** it went really badly ◆ **on s'est ~ bien amusé** we really *ou* thoroughly enjoyed ourselves ◆ **c'est ~ trop (cher)** it's far too expensive

franchir /fʀɑ̃ʃiʀ/ ▸ conjug 2 ◂ **VT** *[+ obstacle]* to clear, to get over; *[+ fossé]* to clear, to jump over; *[+ rue, rivière, ligne d'arrivée]* to cross; *[+ seuil]* to cross, to step across; *[+ porte]* to go through; *[+ distance]* to cover; *[+ mur du son]* to break (through); *[+ difficulté]* to get over, to surmount; *[+ borne, limite]* to overstep, to go beyond ◆ **~ les mers** *(littér)* to cross the sea ◆ **~ le Rubicon** to cross the Rubicon ◆ **il lui reste 10 mètres à ~** he still has 10 metres to go ◆ **~ le cap de la soixantaine** to turn sixty ◆ **le pays vient de ~ un cap important** the country has just passed an important milestone ◆ **ne pas réussir à ~ la barre de …** *[chiffres, vote]* to be *ou* fall short of … ◆ **sa renommée a franchi les frontières** his fame has spread far and wide ◆ **l'historien, franchissant quelques siècles …** the historian, passing over a few centuries …

franchisage /fʀɑ̃ʃizaʒ/ **NM** franchising

franchise /fʀɑ̃ʃiz/ **NF** 1 *(= sincérité) [de personne, réponse]* frankness, straightforwardness, candour *(Brit)*, candor *(US)* ◆ **en toute ~** quite frankly 2 *(= exemption) (gén)* exemption; *(Hist) [de ville]* franchise ◆ **~ fiscale** tax exemption ◆ **~ (douanière)** exemption from (customs) duties ◆ **colis en ~** duty-free parcel ◆ **importer qch en ~** to import sth duty-free ◆ **"franchise postale"** ≃ official paid ◆ **~ de bagages** baggage allowance 3 *(Assurances)* excess *(Brit)*, deductible *(US)* 4 *(Comm)* franchise ◆ **agent/magasin en ~** franchised dealer/shop *(Brit) ou* store *(US)*

> ⚠ Au sens de 'sincérité', **franchise** ne se traduit pas par le mot anglais **franchise**.

franchisé, e /fʀɑ̃ʃize/ **ADJ** ◆ **boutique ~e** franchised outlet **NM,F** franchisee

franchiser /fʀɑ̃ʃize/ ▸ conjug 1 ◂ **VT** to franchise

franchiseur /fʀɑ̃ʃizœʀ/ **NM** franchisor

franchissable /fʀɑ̃ʃisabl/ **ADJ** surmountable

franchissement /fʀɑ̃ʃismɑ̃/ **NM** *[d'obstacle]* clearing; *[de rivière, seuil]* crossing; *[de limite]* overstepping

franchouillard, e* /fʀɑ̃ʃujaʀ, aʀd/ *(péj)* **ADJ** typically French **NM** typically narrow-minded Frenchman **NF franchouillarde** typically narrow-minded French woman

francilien, -ienne /fʀɑ̃siljɛ̃, jɛn/ **ADJ** from *ou* of the Île-de-France **NM,F Francilien(ne)** inhabitant of the Île-de-France **NF Francilienne** ◆ **la Francilienne** *(= autoroute) motorway that encircles the Parisian region*

francique /fʀɑ̃sik/ **NM** Frankish

francisation /fʀɑ̃sizasjɔ̃/ **NF** *(Ling)* gallicizing, Frenchifying; *(Naut) [de navire]* registration as French

franciscain, e /fʀɑ̃siskɛ̃, ɛn/ **ADJ, NM,F** Franciscan

franciser /fʀɑ̃size/ ▸ conjug 1 ◂ **VT** *(Ling)* to gallicize, to Frenchify; *(Naut)* to register as French ◆ **il a francisé son nom** he made his name sound more French, he Frenchified his name

francisque /fʀɑ̃sisk/ **NF** francisc

francité /fʀɑ̃site/ **NF** Frenchness

francium /fʀɑ̃sjɔm/ **NM** francium

franc-jeu /fʀɑ̃ʒø/ **NM** *(Sport)* fair-play ◆ **jouer ~** *(fig)* to play fair

franc-maçon, -onne (mpl **francs-maçons**, fpl **franc-maçonnes**) /fʀɑ̃masɔ̃, ɔn/ **NM,F** freemason **ADJ** ◆ **loge ~ne** masonic lodge, freemasons' lodge ◆ **la solidarité ~ne** freemason solidarity

franc-maçonnerie (pl **franc-maçonneries**) /fʀɑ̃masɔnʀi/ **NF** freemasonry

franco /fʀɑ̃ko/ **ADV** ◆ **~ (de port)** *[marchandise]* carriage-paid; *[colis]* postage paid ◆ **~ de port et d'emballage** free of charge ◆ **~ à bord/sur wagon** free on board/on rail ◆ **~ (le) long du bord** free alongside ship ◆ **~ (le long du) quai** free alongside quay ◆ **y aller ~*** *(explication)* to go straight to the point, to come straight out with it*; *(coup, manœuvre)* to go right ahead

franco- /fʀɑ̃ko/ **PRÉF** Franco- ◆ **les relations ~britanniques** Franco-British relations ◆ **le sommet ~allemand** the Franco-German summit

franco-canadien, -ienne /fʀɑ̃kokanadjɛ̃, jɛn/ **ADJ, NM,F** French Canadian

franco-français, e /fʀɑ̃kofʀɑ̃sɛ, ɛz/ **ADJ** purely French; *(péj)* typically French

François /fʀɑ̃swa/ **NM** Francis ◆ **saint ~ d'Assise** Saint Francis of Assisi

francophile /fʀɑ̃kɔfil/ **ADJ, NMF** francophile

francophilie /fʀɑ̃kɔfili/ **NF** francophilia

francophobe /fʀɑ̃kɔfɔb/ **ADJ, NMF** francophobe

francophobie /fʀɑ̃kɔfɔbi/ **NF** francophobia

francophone /fʀɑ̃kɔfɔn/ **ADJ** French-speaking; *(Can)* primarily French-speaking **NMF** (native) French speaker; *(Can)* Francophone *(Can)*

francophonie /fʀɑ̃kɔfɔni/ **NF** French-speaking world

franco-québécois /fʀɑ̃kɔkebekwa/ **NM** Quebec French

franc-parler /fʀɑ̃paʀle/ **NM INV** outspokenness ◆ **avoir son ~** to speak one's mind, to be outspoken

franc-tireur (pl **francs-tireurs**) /fʀɑ̃tiʀœʀ/ **NM** 1 *(Mil) (= combattant)* irregular, franc tireur; *(= tireur isolé)* sniper 2 *(fig)* maverick ◆ **un ~ de la politique** a maverick politician ◆ **faire qch/agir en ~** to do sth/act independently *ou* off one's own bat *(Brit)*

frange /fʀɑ̃ʒ/ **NF** 1 *[de tissu]* fringe; *[de cheveux]* fringe *(Brit)*, bangs *(US)* ◆ **une ~ de lumière** a band of light ◆ **~s d'interférence** interference fringes ◆ **~s synoviales** synovial folds *ou* fringes 2 *(= limite) [de conscience, sommeil]* threshold 3 *(= minorité)* fringe (group) ◆ **toute une ~ de la population** a whole swathe *ou* chunk of the population

franger /fʀɑ̃ʒe/ ▸ conjug 3 ◂ **VT** *(gén ptp)* to fringe *(de* with)

frangin* /fʀɑ̃ʒɛ̃/ **NM** brother

frangine* /fʀɑ̃ʒin/ **NF** sister

frangipane /fʀɑ̃ʒipan/ **NF** *(Culin)* almond paste, frangipane ◆ **gâteau fourré à la ~** frangipane (pastry)

frangipanier /fʀɑ̃ʒipanje/ **NM** frangipani (tree)

franglais /fʀɑ̃glɛ/ **NM** Franglais

franque /fʀɑ̃k/ **ADJ, NF** → **franc³**

franquette* /fʀɑ̃kɛt/ **à la bonne franquette LOC ADV** *[inviter]* informally; *[recevoir]* without any fuss ◆ **venez déjeuner, ce sera à la bonne ~** come and have lunch with us – it'll be a simple meal *ou* it won't be anything special ◆ **on a dîné à la bonne ~** we had an informal *ou* a potluck *(US)* dinner

franquisme /fʀɑ̃kism/ **NM** Francoism

franquiste /fʀɑ̃kist/ **ADJ** pro-Franco **NMF** Franco supporter

fransquillon /fʀɑ̃skijɔ̃/ **NM** *(Belg péj)* French Belgian

frap(p)adingue‡ /fʀapadɛ̃g/ **ADJ** crazy* **NMF** nutcase*

frappant, e /fʀapɑ̃, ɑ̃t/ **ADJ** striking; → **argument**

frappe /fʀap/ **NF** 1 *[de monnaie, médaille] (= action)* striking; *(= empreinte)* stamp, impression 2 *[de dactylo, pianiste]* touch; *[de machine à écrire] (= souplesse)* touch; *(= impression)* typeface ◆ **la lettre est à la ~** the letter is being typed (out) ◆ **c'est la première ~** it's the top copy; → **faute, vitesse** 3 *(péj = voyou)* **petite ~** young hoodlum *ou* thug 4 *(Sport) [de boxeur]* punch; *[de footballeur]* kick; *[de joueur de tennis]* stroke ◆ **il a une bonne ~ de balle** *[footballeur]* he kicks the ball well, he has a good kick; *[joueur de tennis]* he strikes *ou* hits the ball well 5 *(Mil)* (military) strike ◆ **~ aérienne** airstrike ◆ **~ en second** second strike; → **chirurgical, force**

frappé, e /fʀape/ (ptp de **frapper**) **ADJ** 1 *(= saisi)* struck ◆ **~ de panique** panic-stricken ◆ **~ de stupeur** thunderstruck ◆ **j'ai été (très) ~ d'entendre/de voir que …** I was (quite) amazed to hear/to see that … 2 *[champagne, café]* iced ◆ **boire un vin bien ~** to drink a wine well chilled 3 *(* = fou)* touched* *(attrib)*, crazy* 4 *[velours]* embossed; → **coin**

frappement /fʀapmɑ̃/ **NM** striking

frapper /fʀape/ ▸ conjug 1 ◂ **VT** 1 *(= cogner) [+ personne, surface] (avec le poing, un projectile)* to hit, to strike; *(avec un couteau)* to stab, to strike; *[+ cordes, clavier]* to strike ◆ **~ qn à coups de poing/de pied** to punch/kick sb ◆ **~ le sol du pied** to stamp (one's foot) on the ground ◆ **~ d'estoc et de taille** *(Hist)* to cut and thrust ◆ **~ les trois coups** *(Théât)* to give *ou* sound the three knocks *(to announce the start of a performance)* ◆ **la pluie/la lumière frappait le mur** the rain lashed (against)/the light fell on the wall ◆ **~ un grand coup** *(fig)* to pull out all the stops ♦ **le gouvernement a décidé de ~ un grand coup contre la corruption** the government has decided to crack down on corruption ♦ **frappé à mort** fatally *ou* mortally wounded

2 *(= affecter) [maladie]* to strike (down); *[mesures, impôts, crise, récession, chômage]* to hit; *[embargo]* to strike ♦ **frappé par le malheur** stricken by misfortune ♦ **ce deuil le frappe cruellement** this bereavement is a cruel blow to him ♦ **il a été frappé de cécité à la suite d'un accident** he was blinded after an accident ♦ **les pays les plus frappés par la crise** the countries worst hit by the crisis ♦ **cet impôt frappe lourdement les petits commerçants** this tax is hitting small businesses hard ♦ **le pays a été frappé de sanctions économiques** the country was hit by economic sanctions ♦ **~ qn d'une amende/d'un impôt** to impose a fine/a tax on sb ♦ **contrat/jugement frappé de nullité** contract/judgment declared null and void ♦ **frappé par la loi de 1920** guilty of breaking the 1920 law; → **nullité**

3 *(= étonner, choquer) [coïncidence, détail]* to strike ♦ **j'ai été frappé par leur ressemblance** I was struck by how similar they looked ♦ **on est frappé par la qualité des images** the quality of the pictures is quite striking ♦ **son énergie a frappé tout le monde** everybody was struck by his energy ♦ **ce qui (me) frappe** what strikes me ♦ **ce qui a frappé mon regard/mon oreille** what caught my eye/reached my ears ♦ **rien ne vous a frappé quand vous êtes entré ?** didn't anything strike you as odd when you went in? ♦ **j'ai été frappé d'entendre cela** I was surprised to hear that ♦ **~ l'imagination** to catch *ou* fire the imagination

4 *[+ monnaie, médaille]* to strike

5 *(= glacer) [+ champagne, vin]* to put on ice, to chill; *[+ café]* to ice

VI to strike *(sur* on; *contre* against) ♦ **~ du poing sur la table** to bang one's fist on the table ♦ **~ sur la table avec une règle** to tap the table with a ruler; *(plus fort)* to bang on the table with a ruler ♦ **~ dans ses mains** to clap one's hands ♦ **~ du pied** to stamp (one's foot) ♦ **~ à la porte** *(lit, fig)* to knock on *ou* at the door ♦ **on a frappé** there was a knock at the door ♦ **frappez avant d'entrer** knock before you go in *ou* enter ♦ **~ à toutes les portes** to try every door ♦ **~ dur** *ou* **fort** *ou* **sec*** to hit hard ♦ **~ fort** *(pour impressionner)* to pull out all the stops; → **entrer**

VPR **se frapper** 1 ♦ **se ~ la poitrine** to beat one's breast ♦ **se ~ le front** to tap one's forehead

2 *(* = se tracasser)* to get (o.s.) worked up, to get (o.s.) into a state*

frappeur, -euse /fʀapœʀ, øz/ ADJ ♦ **esprit ~** poltergeist NM,F *[de monnaie]* striker

frasil /fʀazi(l)/ NM *(Can)* frazil *(Can)*

frasque /fʀask/ NF *(gén pl)* escapade ♦ **faire des ~s** to get up to mischief ♦ **~s de jeunesse** youthful indiscretions

fraternel, -elle /fʀatɛʀnɛl/ ADJ brotherly, fraternal ♦ **amour ~** brotherly love ♦ **liens ~s** brotherhood ♦ **tendre une main fraternelle à qn** *(fig)* to hold out the hand of friendship to sb

fraternellement /fʀatɛʀnɛlmɑ̃/ ADV in a brotherly way, fraternally

fraternisation /fʀatɛʀnizasjɔ̃/ NF fraternization, fraternizing ♦ **élan de ~** surge of brotherly feeling

fraterniser /fʀatɛʀnize/ ► conjug 1 ◄ VI *[pays, personnes]* to fraternize *(avec* with)

fraternité /fʀatɛʀnite/ NF 1 *(= amitié)* brotherhood *(NonC)*, fraternity *(NonC)* ♦ **~ d'esprit** kinship *ou* brotherhood of spirit; → **liberté** 2 *(Rel)* fraternity, brotherhood

fratricide /fʀatʀisid/ ADJ fratricidal NMF fratricide NM *(= crime)* fratricide

fratrie /fʀatʀi/ NF set of siblings, sibship *(SPÉC)* ♦ **il est le deuxième enfant d'une ~ de huit** he is the second child in a family of eight, he is the second of eight siblings

fraude /fʀod/ NF *(gén)* fraud *(NonC)*; *(à un examen)* cheating ♦ **en ~** *[fabriquer, vendre]* fraudulently; *[lire, fumer]* secretly ♦ **passer qch/faire passer qn en ~** to smuggle sth/sb in ♦ **~ électorale** electoral fraud, ballot rigging ♦ **~ fiscale** tax evasion

frauder /fʀode/ ► conjug 1 ◄ VT to defraud, to cheat ♦ **~ le fisc** to evade taxation VI *(gén, Scol)* to cheat ♦ **~ sur la quantité/qualité** to cheat over the quantity/quality ♦ **~ sur le poids** to cheat on the weight ♦ **il fraude souvent dans l'autobus** he often takes the bus without paying

fraudeur, -euse /fʀodœʀ, øz/ NM,F *(gén)* person guilty of fraud; *(à la douane)* smuggler; *(envers le fisc)* tax evader; *(dans le métro)* fare dodger ♦ **les ~s seront sanctionnés** *(Scol)* cheating *ou* candidates who cheat will be punished ♦ **il est ~** he has a tendency to cheat

frauduleusement /fʀodyløzmɑ̃/ ADV fraudulently

frauduleux, -euse /fʀodylø, øz/ ADJ *[pratiques, concurrence]* fraudulent ♦ **sans intention frauduleuse de ma part** with no fraudulent intention *ou* no intention of cheating on my part

frayer /fʀeje/ ► conjug 8 ◄ VT *[+ chemin]* to open up, to clear ♦ **~ le passage à qn** to clear the way for sb ♦ **~ la voie à** *(fig)* to pave the way for VPR **se frayer** ♦ **se ~ un passage (dans la foule)** to force *ou* elbow one's way through (the crowd) ♦ **se ~ un chemin dans la jungle** to cut a path through the jungle ♦ **se ~ un chemin vers les honneurs** to work one's way up to fame VI 1 *[poisson]* to spawn 2 ♦ **~ avec** *[+ personne]* to mix *ou* associate *ou* rub shoulders with; *[+ jeune fille]* to go out with

frayeur /fʀɛjœʀ/ NF fright ♦ **tu m'as fait une de ces ~s !** you gave me a dreadful fright! ♦ **cri de ~** (frightened) scream ♦ **se remettre de ses ~s** to recover from one's fright

fredaine /fʀədɛn/ NF mischief *(NonC)*, escapade, prank ♦ **faire des ~s** to be up to mischief

Frédéric /fʀedeʀik/ NM Frederick ♦ **~ le Grand** Frederick the Great

fredonnement /fʀədɔnmɑ̃/ NM humming

fredonner /fʀədɔne/ ► conjug 1 ◄ VT to hum ♦ **elle fredonnait dans la cuisine** she was humming (away) (to herself) in the kitchen

free-lance (pl **free-lances**) /fʀilɑ̃s/ ADJ INV freelance NMF freelance(r) ♦ **travailler en ~** to work freelance, to do freelance work

freesia /fʀezja/ NM freesia

Freetown /fʀitaun/ N Freetown

freezer /fʀizœʀ/ NM freezing *ou* ice-making compartment, freezer

frégate /fʀegat/ NF *(Hist, Mil, Naut)* frigate; *(Zool)* frigate bird; → **capitaine**

frein /fʀɛ̃/ NM 1 *(gén, fig)* brake ♦ **~ avant/arrière** front/rear brake ♦ **mets le ~** put the brake on ♦ **mettre un ~ à** *[+ inflation, colère, ambitions]* to put a brake on, to curb, to check ♦ **c'est un ~ à l'expansion** it acts as a brake on expansion ♦ **sans ~** *[imagination, curiosité]* unbridled, unchecked; → **bloquer, ronger**

♦ **coup de frein** *(lit)* brake; *(fig)* brake, curb ♦ **"coup de frein sur les salaires"** *(titre de presse)* "pay curb" ♦ **donner un coup de ~** to brake ♦ **donner un coup de ~ à** *[+ dépenses, inflation]* to put a brake on, to curb, to check; *[+ importations]* to stem

2 *(Anat)* fraenum *(Brit)*, frenum *(US)*

3 *[de cheval]* bit

COMP **frein aérodynamique**, **frein à air comprimé** air brake
frein à disques disc brake
frein à mâchoire ⇒ **frein à tambour**
frein à main handbrake
frein moteur engine braking ♦ **"utilisez votre frein moteur"** "engage low gear"
frein à pied footbrake
frein à tambour drum brake

freinage /fʀɛnaʒ/ NM *(= usage des freins)* braking; *[d'expansion, dépenses, inflation]* curbing ♦ **dispositif de ~** braking system ♦ **traces de ~** tyre marks *(caused by braking)* ♦ **un bon ~** good braking

freiner /fʀene/ ► conjug 1 ◄ VT *[+ véhicule]* to pull up, to slow down; *[+ progression, coureur]* to slow down, to hold up; *[+ progrès, évolution]* to put a brake on, to check; *[+ expansion, dépenses, inflation]* to put a brake on, to curb, to check; *[+ importations]* to stem; *[+ chômage]* to curb, to check; *[+ enthousiasme, joie]* to check, to put a damper on ♦ **il faut que je me freine** I have to cut down *(dans* on) VI *(dans un véhicule)* to brake; *(à ski, en patins)* to slow down ♦ **~ à bloc** *ou* **à mort*** to jam *ou* slam on the brakes ♦ **~ des quatre fers** *(lit, fig)* to jam *ou* slam on the brakes

frelaté, e /fʀəlate/ (ptp de **frelater**) ADJ 1 *[aliment, huile, vin, drogue]* adulterated 2 *(péj = malsain) [+ atmosphère]* false; *[mode de vie]* degenerate ♦ **un milieu ~** a dubious *ou* slightly corrupt milieu

frelater /fʀəlate/ ► conjug 1 ◄ VT *[+ vin, aliment]* to adulterate

frêle /fʀɛl/ ADJ *[tige, charpente]* flimsy, frail, fragile; *[personne, corps]* frail, fragile; *[voix]* thin, frail ♦ **de ~s espérances** *(littér)* frail *ou* flimsy hopes

frelon /fʀəlɔ̃/ NM hornet

freluquet /fʀəlykɛ/ NM *(péj)* whippersnapper

frémir /fʀemiʀ/ ► conjug 2 ◄ VI 1 *(de peur)* to quake, to tremble, to shudder; *(d'horreur)* to shudder, to shiver; *(de fièvre, froid)* to shiver; *(de colère)* to shake, to tremble, to quiver; *(d'impatience, de plaisir, d'espoir)* to quiver, to tremble *(de* with) ♦ **ça me fait ~** it makes me shudder ♦ **il frémit de tout son être** his whole being quivered *ou* trembled ♦ **histoire à vous faire ~** spine-chilling tale 2 *[lèvres, feuillage]* to tremble, to quiver; *[narine, aile, corde]* to quiver; *[eau chaude]* to simmer

frémissant, e /fʀemisɑ̃, ɑ̃t/ ADJ *(de peur)* quaking, trembling, shuddering; *(d'horreur)* shuddering, shivering; *(de fièvre, froid)* shivering; *(de colère)* shaking, trembling, quivering; *(d'impatience, de plaisir, d'espoir)* quivering, trembling ♦ **une voix ~e de colère** a voice shaking *ou* trembling *ou* quivering with anger ♦ **eau ~e** simmering water ♦ **sensibilité ~e** quivering sensitivity ♦ **naseaux ~s** quivering *ou* flaring nostrils

frémissement /fʀemismɑ̃/ NM 1 *[de corps]* trembling; *[de lèvres, narines]* quivering, trembling; *(de fièvre, de froid)* shivering; *(de peur, de colère, d'impatience, de plaisir, d'espoir)* trembling ♦ **un long ~ parcourut son corps** a shiver ran the length of his body ♦ **un ~ parcourut la salle** a quiver ran through the room 2 *[de feuillage]* trembling *(NonC)*, quivering *(NonC)*; *[d'aile, corde]* quivering *(NonC)*; *[d'eau chaude]* simmering *(NonC)* 3 *(= reprise)* **un ~ de l'économie** signs of economic recovery ♦ **des ~s dans l'opinion publique** signs of renewed public interest ♦ **il y a eu un ~ des valeurs françaises** French securities perked up a little

french cancan /fʀɛnʃkɑ̃kɑ̃/ NM (French) cancan

frêne /fʀɛn/ NM *(= arbre)* ash (tree); *(= bois)* ash

frénésie /fʀenezi/ NF frenzy ♦ **avec ~** *[travailler, applaudir]* frenetically, furiously

frénétique /fʀenetik/ ADJ *[applaudissements, rythme]* frenzied, frenetic; *[passion]* frenzied, wild; *[activité]* frantic

frénétiquement /fʀenetikmɑ̃/ ADV *[travailler, applaudir]* frenetically, furiously

Fréon ® /fʀeɔ̃/ NM Freon ®

fréquemment /fʀekamɑ̃/ ADV frequently, often

fréquence /fʀekɑ̃s/ NF 1 *(gén)* frequency ◆ **la ~ des accidents a diminué** accidents have become less frequent ◆ **~ cardiaque** *(Méd)* heart rate ◆ **~ d'achat** purchase rate 2 *(Phys, Élec)* frequency ◆ **haute/basse ~** high/low frequency ◆ **~ radio** radio frequency *ou* band ◆ **~ sonore** sound frequency ◆ **~ d'horloge** *(Ordin)* clock rate; → **modulation**

fréquent, e /fʀekɑ̃, ɑ̃t/ ADJ frequent ◆ **c'est le cas le plus ~** this is more often the case ◆ **il est ~ de voir ...** it is not uncommon to see ... ◆ **il est peu ~ qu'un président tienne ce discours** a president rarely makes such statements ◆ **ça arrive, mais ce n'est pas très ~** it does happen, but not very often

fréquentable /fʀekɑ̃tabl/ ADJ ◆ **sont-ils ~s ?** are they the sort of people one can associate with?

fréquentatif, -ive /fʀekɑ̃tatif, iv/ ADJ frequentative

fréquentation /fʀekɑ̃tasjɔ̃/ NF 1 *(= action)* **la ~ des églises/écoles** church/school attendance ◆ **la ~ des salles de cinéma augmente** the number of people going to the cinema is rising, more and more people are going to the cinema ◆ **la ~ de ces gens** associating *ou* frequent contact with these people ◆ **la ~ des auteurs classiques** acquaintance with classical authors 2 *(gén pl = relation)* company *(NonC)*, associate ◆ **~s douteuses** dubious company *ou* associates ◆ **il a de mauvaises ~s** he's mixing with the wrong kind *ou* sort of people, he's in with a bad crowd ◆ **ce n'est pas une ~ pour toi** you shouldn't go around with people like that

fréquenté, e /fʀekɑ̃te/ (ptp de **fréquenter**) ADJ *[lieu, établissement]* busy ◆ **très ~** very busy ◆ **c'est un établissement bien/mal ~** the right/wrong kind of people go there ◆ **l'endroit est moins ~ qu'avant** not as many people go there now

fréquenter /fʀekɑ̃te/ ▸ conjug 1 ◂ VT 1 *[+ lieu]* to go to, to frequent *(frm)* ◆ **je fréquente peu les musées** I don't go to museums very often ◆ **il fréquente plus les cafés que les cours** he's in cafés more often than at lectures 2 *[+ voisins]* to do things with; *(littér)* *[+ auteurs classiques]* to keep company with ◆ **~ la bonne société** to move in fashionable circles ◆ **il les fréquente peu** he doesn't see them very often ◆ **il fréquentait assidûment les milieux de l'art** he spent a lot of time with people from the art world 3 († = *courtiser*) to go around with VPR **se fréquenter** ◆ **nous nous fréquentons beaucoup** we see quite a lot of each other, we see each other quite often *ou* frequently ◆ **ces jeunes gens se fréquentent depuis un an** † those young people have been going around together for a year now

frère /fʀɛʀ/ NM 1 *(gén, fig)* brother ◆ **partager en ~s** to share like brothers ◆ **alors, vieux ~ !** * well, old pal! * *ou* mate! * *(Brit) ou* buddy! * *(US)* ◆ **j'ai trouvé le ~ de ce vase** * I found a vase to match this one ◆ **~s d'armes** brothers in arms ◆ **partis/peuples ~s** sister parties/countries ◆ **~s de sang** blood-brothers ◆ **ils sont devenus (des) ~s ennemis** they've become rivals ◆ **Dupont & Frères** *(entreprise)* Dupont & Bros; → **faux²**

2 *(Rel)* *(gén)* brother; *(= moine)* brother, friar ◆ **les hommes sont tous ~s** all men are brothers ◆ **mes (bien chers) ~s** *(Rel)* (dearly beloved) brethren ◆ **~ lai** lay brother ◆ **~ mendiant** mendicant friar ◆ **~ Antoine** Brother Antoine, Friar Antoine ◆ **les ~s maçons** *ou* **trois-points** * the Freemasons ◆ **on l'a mis en pension chez les ~s** he has been sent to a Catholic boarding school

frérot * /fʀeʀo/ NM kid brother *, little brother ◆ **salut ~ !** hello little brother!

fresque /fʀɛsk/ NF *(Art)* fresco; *(Littérat)* portrait; *(= description)* panorama ◆ **peindre à ~** to paint in fresco ◆ **ce film est une ~ historique** the film is a sweeping historical epic

fresquiste /fʀeskist/ NMF fresco painter

fret /fʀɛ(t)/ NM *(= prix)* *(par avion, bateau)* freight(age); *(par camion)* carriage; *(= cargaison)* *(par avion, bateau)* freight, cargo; *(par camion)* load ◆ **~ d'aller** outward freight ◆ **~ de retour** inward *ou* home *ou* return freight ◆ **~ aérien** air freight ◆ **prendre à ~** to charter

fréter /fʀete/ ▸ conjug 6 ◂ VT *(gén = prendre à fret)* to charter; *(Naut = donner à fret)* to freight

fréteur /fʀetœʀ/ NM *(Naut)* owner ◆ **~ et affréteur** owner and charterer

frétillant, e /fʀetijɑ̃, ɑ̃t/ ADJ *[poisson]* wriggling; *[personne]* lively ◆ **~ d'impatience** fidgeting *ou* quivering with impatience

frétillement /fʀetijmɑ̃/ NM *[de poisson]* wriggling *(NonC)* ◆ **~ d'impatience** quiver of impatience

frétiller /fʀetije/ ▸ conjug 1 ◂ VI *[poisson]* to wriggle; *[personne]* to wriggle, to fidget ◆ **le chien frétillait de la queue** the dog was wagging its tail ◆ **~ d'impatience** to fidget *ou* quiver with impatience ◆ **~ de joie** to be quivering *ou* quiver with joy ◆ **elle frétille de l'arrière-train** *(hum, péj)* she's wiggling her bottom *(hum)*

fretin /fʀətɛ̃/ NM *(= poissons)* fry; *(= personnes, choses négligeables)* small fry; → **menu²**

freudien, -ienne /fʀødjɛ̃, jɛn/ ADJ, NM,F Freudian

freudisme /fʀødism/ NM Freudianism

freux /fʀø/ NM rook

friabilité /fʀijabilite/ NF *[de roche, sol]* crumbly nature, flakiness, friability *(SPÉC)*

friable /fʀijabl/ ADJ *[roche, sol]* crumbly, flaky, friable *(SPÉC)*; *(Culin)* *[pâte]* crumbly

friand, e /fʀijɑ̃, ɑ̃d/ ADJ ◆ **~ de** *[+ lait, miel, bonbons]* partial to, fond of; *[+ compliments]* fond of NM *(= pâté)* (minced) meat pie ≃ sausage roll *(Brit)*; *(sucré)* small almond cake ◆ **~ au fromage** cheese puff

friandise /fʀijɑ̃diz/ NF titbit, delicacy, sweetmeat † ◆ **~s** *(= bonbons)* sweets *(Brit)*, candy *(NonC)* *(US)*

fric * /fʀik/ NM *(= argent)* money, cash * ◆ **il a du ~** he's loaded * ◆ **elle se fait beaucoup de ~** she makes a packet * ◆ **je n'ai plus de ~** *(temporairement)* I'm out of cash *; *(définitivement)* I'm broke *

fricandeau (pl **fricandeaux**) /fʀikɑ̃do/ NM fricandeau

fricassée /fʀikase/ NF fricassee ◆ **~ de poulet** chicken fricassee ◆ **faire cuire en ~** to fricassee

fricasser /fʀikase/ ▸ conjug 1 ◂ VT to fricassee

fricative /fʀikativ/ ADJ F, NF fricative

fric-frac † * (pl **fric-frac(s)**) /fʀikfʀak/ NM break-in

friche /fʀiʃ/ NF fallow land *(NonC)* ◆ **en ~** *(lit)* (lying) fallow ◆ **être en ~** *(Agr)* to lie fallow; *[talent, intelligence]* to go to waste; *[économie, pays]* to be neglected ◆ **laisser qch en ~** *(Agr)* to let sth lie fallow; *[talent, intelligence]* to let sth go to waste; *[économie, pays]* to neglect ◆ **le projet est resté en ~ pendant 5 ans** the project has been shelved *ou* has been on ice for 5 years ◆ **~ industrielle** industrial wasteland

frichti * /fʀiʃti/, **fricot** † * /fʀiko/ NM food, grub * *(NonC)* ◆ **préparer son ~** to do the cooking

fricoter * /fʀikɔte/ ▸ conjug 1 ◂ VT *(lit, fig)* to cook up * ◆ **qu'est-ce qu'il fricote ?** what's he cooking up? *, what's he up to? * VI *(= trafiquer)* to get involved in some shady business ◆ **~ avec qn** *(= s'associer)* to have dealings with sb; *(= avoir une liaison)* to sleep with sb

friction /fʀiksjɔ̃/ NF friction; *(= massage)* rub, rubdown; *(chez le coiffeur)* scalp massage ◆ **voiture à ~** *(Jeux)* friction car ◆ **point de ~** *(lit, fig)* point of friction ◆ **les taux d'intérêt, éternel point de ~ entre ces deux pays** interest rates, an eternal bone of contention between the two countries

frictionnel, -elle /fʀiksjɔnɛl/ ADJ frictional ◆ **chômage ~** frictional unemployment

frictionner /fʀiksjɔne/ ▸ conjug 1 ◂ VT to rub ◆ **se ~ après un bain** to rub o.s. down after a bath

frigidaire ® /fʀiʒidɛʀ/ NM refrigerator, fridge

frigide /fʀiʒid/ ADJ frigid

frigidité /fʀiʒidite/ NF frigidity

frigo * /fʀigo/ NM fridge, refrigerator

frigorifier /fʀigɔʀifje/ ▸ conjug 7 ◂ VT *(lit)* to refrigerate ◆ **être frigorifié** * *(= avoir froid)* to be frozen stiff

frigorifique /fʀigɔʀifik/ ADJ *[mélange]* refrigerating *(épith)*; *[camion, wagon]* refrigerator *(épith)*; → **armoire**

frigoriste /fʀigɔʀist/ NMF refrigeration engineer

frileusement /fʀiløzmɑ̃/ ADV ◆ **~ serrés l'un contre l'autre** huddled close together to keep warm *ou* against the cold ◆ **~ enfouis sous les couvertures** huddled under the blankets to keep warm

frileux, -euse /fʀilø, øz/ ADJ 1 *[personne]* sensitive to (the) cold; *[geste, posture]* shivery ◆ **il est très ~** he feels the cold easily, he is very sensitive to (the) cold ◆ **elle se couvrit de son châle d'un geste ~** with a shiver she pulled her shawl around her 2 *(= trop prudent)* *[boursier]* overcautious; *[marché]* nervous

frilosité /fʀilozite/ NF 1 *[de personne]* sensitivity to the cold 2 *[de boursier]* overcautiousness; *[de marché]* nervousness

frimaire /fʀimɛʀ/ NM Frimaire *(third month in the French Republican calendar)*

frimas /fʀima/ NMPL *(littér)* wintry weather

frime * /fʀim/ NF ◆ **c'est de la ~** it's all put on * ◆ **c'est pour la ~** it's all *ou* just for show ◆ **taper la ~** to show off

frimer * /fʀime/ ▸ conjug 1 ◂ VI to show off *

frimeur, -euse * /fʀimœʀ, øz/ NM,F show-off * ◆ **il est très ~** he's a real show-off *

frimousse /fʀimus/ NF 1 *(= visage)* (sweet) little face 2 *(= symbole)* emotion

fringale * /fʀɛ̃gal/ NF *(= faim)* raging hunger ◆ **une ~ de** *(= désir)* a craving for ◆ **j'ai la ~** I'm ravenous * *ou* famished * *ou* starving *

fringant, e /fʀɛ̃gɑ̃, ɑ̃t/ ADJ *[cheval]* frisky, high-spirited; *[personne, allure]* dashing

fringue * /fʀɛ̃g/ NF garment ◆ **je me suis acheté une ~** I bought myself something to wear ◆ **des ~s** clothes ◆ **elle a toujours de belles ~s** she always has such great clothes * *ou* such fantastic gear *

fringué, e * /fʀɛ̃ge/ (ptp de **(se) fringuer**) ADJ dressed, done up * ◆ **bien/mal ~** well-/badly-dressed ◆ **vise un peu comme elle est ~e !** look what she's got on!, look what she's done up in! *

fringuer* /fʀɛ̃ge/ ▸ conjug 1 ◂ VPR **se fringuer** (= s'habiller) to get dressed; (= s'habiller élégamment) to doll (o.s.) up*, to do o.s. up* ◆ **il ne sait pas se** ~ he's got no dress sense VT to dress

fripe* /fʀip/ NF ◆ **la** ~ (= commerce) the clothing trade, the rag trade* (Brit); (d'occasion) the secondhand clothes business NFPL **fripes** (= vêtements) clothes; (d'occasion) secondhand clothes

friper /fʀipe/ ▸ conjug 1 ◂ VT to crumple (up), to crush ◆ **ça se fripe facilement** it crumples ou crushes easily ◆ **des habits tout fripés** badly crumpled ou rumpled clothes ◆ **visage tout fripé** crumpled face

friperie /fʀipʀi/ NF (= boutique) secondhand clothes shop (Brit) ou store (US)

fripier, -ière /fʀipje, jɛʀ/ NM,F secondhand clothes dealer

fripon, -onne /fʀipɔ̃, ɔn/ ADJ [air, allure, yeux] mischievous, cheeky (Brit); [nez] saucy, pert NM,F († = gredin) knave †, rascally fellow †; (*: nuance affectueuse) rascal, rogue ◆ **petit** ~ **!** you little rascal!

friponnerie /fʀipɔnʀi/ NF (= acte) mischief (NonC), prank ◆ **les ~s de ce gamin** the mischief this little imp gets up to

fripouille /fʀipuj/ NF (péj) rogue, scoundrel ◆ **petite** ~ **!*** (nuance affectueuse) you little devil!*

fripouillerie /fʀipujʀi/ NF roguishness

friqué, e* /fʀike/ ADJ loaded*, filthy rich* ◆ **je ne suis pas très** ~ **en ce moment** I'm not exactly loaded* at the moment, I'm a bit hard-up* at the moment

frire /fʀiʀ/ VT (Culin) to fry; (en friteuse) to deep-fry; → **pâte, poêle¹** VI ◆ **(faire)** ~ to fry; (en friteuse) to deep-fry ◆ **on frit sur la plage*** it's baking (hot)* on the beach

frisbee ® /fʀizbi/ NM Frisbee ®

frise /fʀiz/ NF (Archit, Art) frieze; (Théât) border; → **cheval**

frisé, e /fʀize/ (ptp de **friser**) ADJ [cheveux] (very) curly; [personne, animal] curly-haired ◆ **il est tout** ~ he has very curly hair ◆ ~ **comme un mouton** curly-headed ou -haired, frizzy-haired; → **chou¹** NM (* injurieux = Allemand) Fritz* (injurieux), Jerry* (injurieux) NF **frisée** (= chicorée) curly endive

friser /fʀize/ ▸ conjug 1 ◂ VT 1 [+ cheveux] to curl; [+ moustache] to twirl ◆ ~ **qn** to curl sb's hair; → **fer** 2 (= frôler) [+ surface] to graze, to skim; [+ catastrophe, mort] to be within a hair's breadth of, to be within an ace of; [+ insolence, ridicule] to border on, to verge on ◆ ~ **la soixantaine** to be getting on for sixty, to be close to sixty VI [cheveux] to curl, to be curly; [personne] to have curly hair ◆ **faire** ~ **ses cheveux** to make one's hair go curly; (chez le coiffeur) to have one's hair curled VPR **se friser** to curl one's hair ◆ **se faire** ~ (par un coiffeur) to have one's hair curled

frisette /fʀizɛt/ NF 1 (= cheveux) little curl, little ringlet 2 (= lambris) panel ◆ ~ **de pin** pine panel

frison¹ /fʀizɔ̃/ NM 1 (= mèche) little curl ou ringlet (around face or neck) 2 (= copeaux) ~**s** wood shavings (used for packing)

frison², -onne /fʀizɔ̃, ɔn/ ADJ Frisian, Friesian NM (= langue) Frisian, Friesian NM,F **Frison(ne)** Frisian, Friesian NF **frisonne** ◆ **(vache) frisonne** Frisian, Friesian (cow)

frisottant, e /fʀizɔtɑ̃, ɑ̃t/ ADJ frizzy, tightly curled

frisotter /fʀizɔte/ ▸ conjug 1 ◂ VT to crimp, to frizz VI to frizz ◆ **ses cheveux frisottent quand il pleut** his hair goes all frizzy when it rains

frisottis /fʀizɔti/ NM little curl, little ringlet

frisquet, -ette* /fʀiskɛ, ɛt/ ADJ [vent] chilly ◆ **il fait** ~ it's chilly, there's a chill ou nip in the air

frisson /fʀisɔ̃/ NM [de froid, fièvre] shiver; [de répulsion, peur] shudder, shiver; [de volupté] thrill, shiver, quiver ◆ **elle fut prise** ou **saisie d'un** ~ a sudden shiver ran through her ◆ **la fièvre me donne des ~s** this fever is making me shiver ou is giving me the shivers* ◆ **ça me donne le** ~ it gives me the creeps* ou the shivers*, it makes me shudder ◆ **le** ~ **des herbes sous le vent** the quivering of the grass in the wind ◆ **ça a été le grand** ~ (hum) (gén) it was a real thrill*; (sexuel) the earth moved

frissonnement /fʀisɔnmɑ̃/ NM 1 (de peur) quaking, trembling, shuddering; (d'horreur) shuddering, shivering; (de fièvre, de froid) shivering; (de volupté, de désir) quivering, trembling ◆ **un long** ~ **parcourut son corps** a shiver ran the length of his body 2 [de feuillage] quivering, trembling, rustling; [de lac] rippling

frissonner /fʀisɔne/ ▸ conjug 1 ◂ VI 1 (de peur) to quake, to tremble, to shudder; (d'horreur) to shudder, to shiver; (de fièvre, froid) to shiver; (de volupté, désir) to quiver, to tremble (de with); ◆ **le vent le fit** ~ the wind made him shiver 2 [feuillage] to quiver, to tremble, to rustle; [lac] to ripple

frit, e¹ /fʀi, fʀit/ (ptp de **frire**) ADJ (Culin) fried ◆ **ils sont ~s*** (= fichu, perdu) they've had it*, their goose is cooked*, their number's up*

frite² /fʀit/ NF 1 (Culin : gén pl) **(pommes)** ~**s** French fries, chips (Brit), fries (surtout US) 2 (* = forme) **avoir la** ~ to be feeling great*, to be full of beans* (Brit) ◆ **en ce moment, elle n'a pas la** ~ she's a bit down* at the moment ◆ **ça va te donner la** ~ that'll perk you up ou put the wind back in your sails* 3 (* = tape) **faire une** ~ **à qn** to slap sb on the bottom

friter (se)* /fʀite/ ▸ conjug 1 ◂ VPR [personnes] (= se disputer) to have a row; (= se battre) to have a set-to* ou scrap* ◆ **il adore provoquer et se** ~ he loves provoking people and getting into scraps*

friterie /fʀitʀi/ NF (= boutique) ≈ chip shop (Brit), hamburger stand (US)

friteuse /fʀitøz/ NF deep fryer, chip pan (Brit) ◆ ~ **électrique** electric fryer

fritillaire /fʀitilɛʀ/ ADJ fritillary

fritons /fʀitɔ̃/ NMPL pork (ou goose) scratchings

friture /fʀityʀ/ NF 1 (Culin) (= méthode) frying; (= graisse) (deep) fat (for frying); (= poisson, mets) fried fish (NonC ou pl) ◆ **(petite)** ~ small fish ◆ ~ **de goujons** (dish of) fried gudgeon 2 * (Radio) crackle, crackling (NonC) ◆ **il y a de la** ~ **sur la ligne** (Téléc) there's interference on the line, the line is a bit crackly

fritz* /fʀits/ NM INV (injurieux = Allemand) Fritz* (injurieux), Jerry* (injurieux)

frivole /fʀivɔl/ ADJ [personne] frivolous; [occupation, argument] frivolous, trivial

frivolement /fʀivɔlmɑ̃/ ADV frivolously

frivolité /fʀivɔlite/ NF 1 [de personne] frivolity, frivolousness; [d'occupation, argument] frivolousness, triviality 2 ◆ ~**s** († = articles) fancy goods

froc /fʀɔk/ NM 1 (Rel) frock, habit ◆ **porter le** ~ to be a monk, to wear the habit of a monk ◆ **jeter le** ~ **aux orties** to leave the priesthood 2 (* = pantalon) (pair of) trousers, (pair of) pants (US) 3 (*: locutions) **faire dans son** ~ to be shitting** ou wetting* o.s. ◆ **baisser son** ~ to take it lying down* ◆ **ils baissent leur** ~ **devant le chef** they just lie down and take it from the boss*

froid, e /fʀwa, fʀwad/ ADJ [personne, repas, décor, couleur, moteur] cold; [manières, accueil] cold, chilly; [détermination, calcul] cold, cool ◆ **colère** ~**e** cold ou controlled anger ◆ **il fait assez** ~ it's rather cold ◆ **d'un ton** ~ coldly ◆ **ça me laisse** ~ it leaves me cold ◆ **garder la tête** ~**e** to keep cool, to keep a cool head ◆ ~ **comme le marbre** as cold as marble ◆ **à table ! ça va être** ~ come and get it! it's getting cold; → **battre, sueur** etc

NM 1 ◆ **le** ~ (gén) the cold; (= industrie) refrigeration ◆ **j'ai** ~ I'm cold ◆ **j'ai** ~ **aux pieds** my feet are cold ◆ **il fait** ~**/un** ~ **de canard*** ou **de loup*** it's cold/freezing cold ou perishing* ◆ **ça me donne** ~ it makes me (feel) cold ◆ **ça me fait** ~ **dans le dos** (lit) it gives me a cold back, it makes my back cold; (fig) it sends shivers down my spine ◆ **prendre** ou **attraper (un coup de)** ~ to catch cold ou a chill ◆ **vague** ou **coup de** ~ cold spell ◆ **les grands ~s** the cold of winter ◆ **n'avoir pas** ~ **aux yeux** [homme d'affaires, aventurier] to be venturesome ou adventurous; [enfant] to have plenty of pluck; → **craindre, jeter, mourir**

◆ **à froid** ◆ **laminer à** ~ to cold-roll ◆ **souder à** ~ to cold-weld ◆ **"laver à froid", "lavage à froid"** "wash in cold water" ◆ **démarrer à** ~ to start (from) cold ◆ **démarrage à** ~ cold start ou starting (US) ◆ **opérer à** ~ (Méd) to perform cold surgery; (fig) to let things cool down before acting ◆ **parler à** ~ **de qch** (fig) to speak coldly ou coolly of sth ◆ **prendre** ou **cueillir qn à** ~ * (fig) to catch sb unawares ou off guard

2 (= brouille) coolness (NonC) ◆ **malgré le** ~ **qu'il y avait entre eux** despite the coolness that existed between them ◆ **nous sommes en** ~ things are a bit strained between us

froidement /fʀwadmɑ̃/ ADV [accueillir, remercier] coldly, coolly; [calculer, réfléchir] coolly; [tuer] cold-bloodedly, in cold blood ◆ **il me reçut** ~ I got a cold ou chilly reception (from him), he greeted me coldly ◆ **meurtre accompli** ~ cold-blooded murder ◆ **comment vas-tu ? –** ~ **!** (hum) how are you? – cold!

froideur /fʀwadœʀ/ NF [de personne, sentiments] coldness; [de manières, accueil] coldness, chilliness ◆ **recevoir qn avec** ~ to give sb a cold ou chilly ou cool reception, to greet sb coldly ◆ **contempler qch avec** ~ to contemplate sth coldly ou coolly ◆ **la** ~ **de son cœur** (littér) her coldness of heart

froidure † /fʀwadyʀ/ NF cold

froissement /fʀwasmɑ̃/ NM 1 [de tissu] crumpling, creasing 2 (= bruit) rustle, rustling (NonC) ◆ **des ~s soyeux** the sound of rustling silk 3 (Méd) ~ **(d'un muscle)** (muscular) strain 4 (littér = vexation) ~ **(d'amour-propre)** blow to sb's pride

froisser /fʀwase/ ▸ conjug 1 ◂ VT 1 [+ tissu] to crumple, to crease; [+ habit] to crumple, to rumple, to crease; [+ papier] to screw up, to crumple; [+ herbe] to crush ◆ **il froissa la lettre et la jeta** he screwed up the letter and threw it away 2 [+ personne] to hurt, to offend ◆ **ça l'a froissé dans son orgueil** that wounded ou hurt his pride VPR **se froisser** [tissu] to crease, to crumple; [personne] to take offence, to take umbrage (de at); ◆ **se** ~ **un muscle** (Méd) to strain a muscle

frôlement /fʀolmɑ̃/ NM (= contact) light touch, light contact (NonC); (= bruit) rustle, rustling (NonC) ◆ **le** ~ **des corps dans l'obscurité** the light contact of bodies brushing against each other in the darkness

frôler /fʀole/ ▸ conjug 1 ◂ VT 1 (= toucher) to brush against; (= passer près de) to skim ◆ **le projectile le frôla** the projectile skimmed past him ◆ **l'automobiliste frôla le réverbère** the driver just missed the lamppost ◆ **le dollar a frôlé la barre des 1,5** € the dollar came very close to the 1.5 euro mark ◆ ~ **la mort/la catastrophe** to come within a hair's breadth ou an ace of death/a catastrophe ◆ ~ **la victoire** to come close to victory ◆ **le thermomètre a**

frôlé les 40 degrés temperatures were in the upper 30's 2 (= confiner à) to verge ou border on ◆ ça frôle l'indécence it verges on the indecent VPR se frôler [personnes] to brush against one another ◆ les deux voitures se sont frôlées the two cars just missed each other

fromage /fʀɔmaʒ/ NM cheese ◆ **biscuit/omelette/soufflé au ~** cheese biscuit/omelette/soufflé ◆ **nouilles au ~** pasta with cheese ◆ **il en a fait tout un ~*** he made a great song and dance ou a big fuss about it; → **cloche, plateau, poire**
COMP **fromage blanc** fromage blanc
fromage de chèvre goat's milk cheese
fromage à la crème cream cheese
fromage fermenté fermented cheese
fromage fondu cheese spread
fromage frais fromage frais
fromage gras full-fat cheese
fromage maigre low-fat cheese
fromage à pâte cuite cooked cheese
fromage à pâte dure hard cheese
fromage à pâte molle soft cheese
fromage à pâte persillée veined cheese
fromage râpé grated cheese
fromage à tartiner cheese spread
fromage de tête pork brawn, headcheese (US)

fromager, -ère /fʀɔmaʒe, ɛʀ/ ADJ [industrie, commerce, production] cheese (épith) ◆ **association fromagère** cheese producers' association NM 1 (= fabricant) cheese maker; (= marchand) cheese seller 2 (= arbre) kapok tree

fromagerie /fʀɔmaʒʀi/ NF cheese dairy

froment /fʀɔmɑ̃/ NM wheat

from(e)ton‡ /fʀɔmtɔ̃/ NM cheese

fronce /fʀɔ̃s/ NF gather ◆ **~s** gathers, gathering (NonC) ◆ **faire des ~s à une jupe** to gather a skirt ◆ **ça fait des ~s** it's all puckered

froncement /fʀɔ̃smɑ̃/ NM ◆ **~ de sourcils** frown

froncer /fʀɔ̃se/ ► conjug 3 ◄ VT (Couture) to gather ◆ **~ les sourcils** to frown, to knit one's brows

frondaison /fʀɔ̃dɛzɔ̃/ NF (= feuillage) foliage (NonC)

fronde[1] /fʀɔ̃d/ NF (= arme) sling; (= jouet) catapult (Brit), slingshot (US)

fronde[2] /fʀɔ̃d/ NF (= révolte) revolt ◆ **esprit/vent de ~** spirit/wind of revolt ou insurrection ◆ **la Fronde** (Hist) the Fronde

fronde[3] /fʀɔ̃d/ NF (Bot) frond

fronder /fʀɔ̃de/ ► conjug 1 ◄ VT (= railler) to lampoon, to satirize

frondeur, -euse /fʀɔ̃dœʀ, øz/ ADJ [tempérament] rebellious ◆ **les esprits ~s** rebellious spirits NM,F (Pol) rebel

front /fʀɔ̃/ NM 1 (Anat) forehead, brow; (littér) [de bâtiment] façade, front ◆ **il peut marcher le ~ haut** he can hold his head (up) high ◆ **la honte sur son ~** (littér) the shame on his brow (littér) ou face; → **courber, frapper**
2 (Météo, Mil, Pol) front ◆ **aller ou monter au ~** to go to the front, to go into action ◆ **tué au ~** killed in action ◆ **le ~ ennemi** the enemy front ◆ **le Front islamique de ou du Salut** the Islamic Salvation Front ◆ **le Front populaire** the Popular Front ◆ **le Front national** the National Front ◆ **le Front de libération nationale de la Corse** the Corsican liberation front ◆ **le ~ du refus** (fig) organized resistance
3 (Min) ~ **(de taille)** (gén) face; [de houillère] coalface
4 (locutions) **avoir le ~ de faire qch** (littér) to have the effrontery ou front to do sth
◆ **de front** ◆ **attaque de ~** frontal attack ◆ **choc de ~** head-on crash ◆ **attaquer qn de ~** (lit, fig) to attack sb head-on ◆ **se heurter de ~** (lit) to collide head-on; (fig) to clash head-on ◆ **marcher (à) trois de ~** to walk three abreast ◆ **mener plusieurs tâches de ~** to have several tasks in hand ou on the go (at one time) ◆ **aborder de ~ un problème** to tackle a problem head-on
◆ **faire front** ◆ **il va falloir faire ~** you'll (ou we'll etc) have to face up to it ou to things ◆ **faire ~ à l'ennemi/aux difficultés** to face up ou stand up to the enemy/difficulties ◆ **faire ~ commun contre qn/qch** to join forces against sb/sth, to take a united stand against sb/sth
COMP **front de mer** (sea) front

frontal, e (mpl **-aux**) /fʀɔ̃tal, o/ ADJ [collision, concurrence] head-on; [attaque] frontal, head-on; (Anat, Géom) frontal ◆ **lave-linge à chargement ~** front-loader, front-loading washing machine ◆ **choc ~** (lit) head-on crash ou collision; (fig) head-on clash NM ◆ **(os) ~** frontal (bone)

frontalier, -ière /fʀɔ̃talje, jɛʀ/ ADJ [ville, zone] border (épith), frontier (épith) ◆ **travailleurs ~s** people who cross the border every day to work NM,F inhabitant of the border ou frontier zone

frontière /fʀɔ̃tjɛʀ/ NF (Géog, Pol) border, frontier ◆ **à l'intérieur et au-delà de nos ~s** at home and abroad ◆ **~ naturelle/linguistique** natural/linguistic boundary ◆ **faire reculer les ~s du savoir/d'une science** to push back the frontiers ou boundaries of knowledge/of a science ◆ **à la ~ du rêve et de la réalité** on the dividing line between dream and reality; → **incident** ADJ INV ◆ **ville/zone ~** frontier ou border town/zone; → **garde**[1], **poste**[2]

frontispice /fʀɔ̃tispis/ NM frontispiece

frontiste /fʀɔ̃tist/ (Pol) ADJ (= du Front National) National Front NMF National Front supporter

fronton /fʀɔ̃tɔ̃/ NM (Archit) pediment; (à la pelote basque) (front) wall

frottement /fʀɔtmɑ̃/ NM (= action) rubbing; (= bruit) rubbing (NonC), rubbing noise, scraping (NonC), scraping noise; (Tech = friction) friction ◆ **il y a des ~s entre eux** (= désaccord) there's friction between them

frotter /fʀɔte/ ► conjug 1 ◄ VT 1 (gén) [+ peau, membre] to rub; [+ cheval] to rub down ◆ **frotte tes mains avec du savon** scrub your hands with soap ◆ **~ son doigt sur la table** to rub one's finger on the table ◆ **~ une allumette** to strike a match ◆ **pain frotté d'ail** bread rubbed with garlic
2 (pour nettoyer) [+ cuivres, meubles] to rub (up), to shine; [+ plancher, casserole, linge, pomme de terre] to scrub; [+ chaussures] (pour cirer) to rub (up), to shine; (pour enlever la terre) to scrape
3 († , hum) ◆ **les oreilles à qn** to box sb's ears ◆ **je vais te ~ l'échine** I'm going to beat you black and blue
VI to rub, to scrape ◆ **la porte frotte (contre le plancher)** the door is rubbing ou scraping (against the floor)
VPR **se frotter** 1 (= se laver) to rub o.s. ◆ **se ~ les mains** (lit, fig) to rub one's hands
2 ◆ **se ~ à** (= fréquenter) **se ~ à la bonne société** to rub shoulders with high society ◆ **se ~ à qn** (= attaquer) to cross swords with sb ◆ **il vaut mieux ne pas s'y ~** I wouldn't cross swords with him ◆ **qui s'y frotte s'y pique** (Prov) if you cross swords with him you do so at your peril

frottis /fʀɔti/ NM 1 (Méd) smear ◆ **se faire faire un ~ (cervico-)vaginal** to have a cervical ou Pap (US) smear 2 (Art) scumble

frottoir /fʀɔtwaʀ/ NM (à allumettes) friction strip; (pour le parquet) (long-handled) brush

froufrou /fʀufʀu/ NM 1 (= bruit) rustle, rustling (NonC), swish (NonC) ◆ **faire ~** to rustle, to swish 2 (= dentelles) **des ~s** frills

froufroutant, e /fʀufʀutɑ̃, ɑt/ ADJ rustling, swishing

froufroutement /fʀufʀutmɑ̃/ NM rustle, rustling (NonC), swish (NonC)

froufrouter /fʀufʀute/ ► conjug 1 ◄ VI to rustle, to swish

froussard, e* /fʀusaʀ, aʀd/ (péj) ADJ chicken* (attrib), yellow-bellied* (épith) NM,F chicken*, coward

frousse* /fʀus/ NF fright ◆ **avoir la ~** to be scared (to death) ou scared stiff* ◆ **quand il a sonné j'ai eu la ~** when he rang I really got a fright ou the wind up* (Brit) ◆ **ça lui a fichu la ~** that really gave him a fright ou put the wind up him* (Brit)

fructidor /fʀyktidɔʀ/ NM Fructidor (twelfth month in the French Republican calendar)

fructifère /fʀyktifɛʀ/ ADJ fruit-bearing, fructiferous

fructification /fʀyktifikasjɔ̃/ NF fructification

fructifier /fʀyktifje/ ► conjug 7 ◄ VI [arbre] to bear fruit; [terre] to be productive; [idée] to bear fruit; [investissement] to yield a profit ◆ **faire ~ son argent** to make one's money work for one

fructose /fʀyktoz/ NM fructose

fructueusement /fʀyktɥøzmɑ̃/ ADV fruitfully, profitably

fructueux, -euse /fʀyktɥø, øz/ ADJ [lectures, spéculation] fruitful, profitable; [collaboration, recherches] fruitful; [commerce] profitable

frugal, e (mpl **-aux**) /fʀygal, o/ ADJ frugal

frugalement /fʀygalmɑ̃/ ADV frugally

frugalité /fʀygalite/ NF frugality

fruit[1] /fʀɥi/ NM 1 (gén) fruit (NonC) ◆ **il y a des ~s/trois ~s dans la coupe** there is some fruit/there are three pieces of fruit in the bowl ◆ **passez-moi un ~** pass me some fruit ou a piece of fruit
2 (= espèce) fruit ◆ **l'orange et la banane sont des ~s** the orange and the banana are kinds of fruit ou are fruits; → **pâte, salade**
3 (littér = produit) fruit(s) ◆ **les ~s de la terre/de son travail** the fruits of the earth/of one's work ◆ **c'est le ~ de l'expérience/d'un gros travail** (= résultat) it is the fruit of experience/of much work ◆ **cet enfant est le ~ de leur union** this child is the fruit of their union (littér) ◆ **porter ses ~s** to bear fruit ◆ **avec ~** fruitfully, profitably, with profit ◆ **sans ~** fruitlessly, to no avail
COMP **fruits des bois** fruits of the forest
fruits confits candied ou glacé fruits
fruit défendu forbidden fruit
fruits déguisés prunes ou dates stuffed with marzipan
fruits de mer seafood(s)
fruit de la passion passion fruit
fruits rafraîchis fresh fruit salad
fruits rouges red berries
fruit sec (séché) dried fruit (NonC)

fruit[2] /fʀɥi/ NM [de mur] batter ◆ **donner du ~ à** to batter

fruité, e /fʀɥite/ ADJ fruity

fruiterie /fʀɥitʀi/ NF fruit (and vegetable) store, fruiterer's (shop) (Brit)

fruiticulteur, -trice /fʀɥitikyltœʀ, tʀis/ NM,F fruit farmer

fruitier, -ière /fʀɥitje, jɛʀ/ ADJ fruit (épith) NM,F (= marchand de fruits) fruit seller, fruiterer (Brit), greengrocer (Brit); (= fromager) cheese maker NF **fruitière** (= fromagerie) cheese dairy (in Savoy, Jura)

frusques /fʀysk/ NFPL (péj) (= vêtements) gear* (NonC), togs*, clobber‡ (NonC) (Brit); (= vieux vêtements) rags

fruste /fʀyst/ ADJ [art, style] crude, unpolished; [manières, personne] coarse

frustrant, e /fʀystʀɑ̃, ɑ̃t/ ADJ frustrating

frustration /fʀystʀasjɔ̃/ **NF** *(Psych)* frustration

frustré, e /fʀystʀe/ (ptp de **frustrer**) **ADJ, NM,F** *(gén, Psych)* frustrated ◆ **c'est un ~** he's frustrated

frustrer /fʀystʀe/ ▸ conjug 1 ◂ **VT** 1 *(= priver)* ~ **qn de** *[+ satisfaction]* to deprive sb of, to do sb out of*; *(Jur) [+ biens]* to defraud sb of ◆ ~ **qn dans ses espoirs/efforts** to thwart *ou* frustrate sb's hopes/efforts, to thwart sb in his hopes/efforts ◆ ~ **qn au profit d'un autre** *(Jur)* to defraud one party by favouring another 2 *(= décevoir) [+ attente, espoir]* to thwart, to frustrate 3 *(Psych)* to frustrate

FS (abrév de **franc suisse**) SF

FSE /efesə/ **NM** (abrév de **Fonds social européen**) ESF

fuchsia /fyʃja/ **ADJ INV, NM** fuchsia ◆ **(rose)** ~ fuchsia

fuchsine /fyksin/ **NF** fuchsin(e)

fucus /fykys/ **NM** wrack, fucus *(SPÉC)* ◆ ~ **vésiculeux** bladderwrack

fuel /fjul/ **NM** *(= carburant)* fuel oil ◆ ~ **domestique** domestic *ou* heating oil

fugace /fygas/ **ADJ** *[parfum, impression, lueur]* fleeting; *[beauté, fraîcheur]* fleeting, transient; *[bonheur]* transient

fugacité /fygasite/ **NF** *[de parfum, impression, lueur]* fleetingness; *[de beauté, fraîcheur]* fleetingness, transience

fugitif, -ive /fyʒitif, iv/ **ADJ** 1 *(= qui fuit) [esclave, prisonnier]* fugitive *(épith)*, runaway *(épith)* 2 *(= passager) [vision, impression, instant]* fleeting; *[beauté, bonheur]* fleeting, transient, short-lived **NM,F** fugitive

fugitivement /fyʒitivmɑ̃/ **ADV** *[entrevoir]* fleetingly

fugue /fyg/ **NF** 1 *(= fuite)* running away *(NonC)* ◆ **faire une** ~ to run away, to abscond *(Admin)* ◆ **il a fait plusieurs ~s** he ran away several times ◆ ~ **amoureuse** elopement 2 *(Mus)* fugue

fuguer* /fyge/ ▸ conjug 1 ◂ **VI** to run away *ou* off

fugueur, -euse /fygœʀ, øz/ **NM,F** absconder *(Admin)*, runaway ◆ **élève** ~ pupil who keeps running away

fuir /fɥiʀ/ ▸ conjug 17 ◂ **VT** 1 *(= éviter) [+ personne, danger]* to avoid, to shun; *[+ obligation, responsabilité]* to evade, to shirk ◆ ~ **qn/qch comme la peste** to avoid sb/sth like the plague ◆ **le sommeil/la tranquillité me fuit** sleep/quiet eludes me ◆ ~ **le monde** *(littér)* to flee society, to withdraw from the world ◆ **l'homme se fuit** *(littér)* man flees from his inner self

2 *(= s'enfuir de) [+ patrie, bourreaux]* to flee from, to run away from, to fly from *(littér)*

VI 1 *(= s'enfuir) [prisonnier]* to run away, to escape; *[troupes]* to take flight, to flee *(devant* from); *[femme] (avec un amant)* to run off; *(pour se marier)* to elope *(avec* with); ◆ **faire** ~ *(= mettre en fuite)* to put to flight; *(= chasser)* to chase off *ou* away ◆ **laid à faire** ~ repulsively ugly ◆ ~ **devant** *[+ danger, obligations]* to run away from ◆ **il a fui chez ses parents** he has fled to his parents

2 *(littér = passer rapidement) [esquif]* to speed along, to glide swiftly along; *[heures, saison]* to fly by, to slip by; *[horizon, paysage]* to recede ◆ **l'été a fui si rapidement** the summer flew by

3 *(= s'échapper) [gaz]* to leak, to escape; *[liquide]* to leak; *(= n'être pas étanche) [récipient, robinet]* to leak

fuite /fɥit/ **NF** 1 *[de fugitif]* flight, escape; *[de prisonnier]* escape; *[d'amants]* flight; *(pour se marier)* elopement ◆ **dans sa** ~ as he ran away ◆ **sa ~ devant toute responsabilité** his evasion of all responsibility ◆ **prendre la** ~ *[personne]* to run away, to take flight *(frm)*; *[conducteur, voiture]* to drive away ◆ **renversé par un automobiliste qui a pris la** ~ knocked down by a hit-and-run driver ◆ **chercher la ~ dans le sommeil/la drogue** to seek escape in sleep/in drugs; → **délit**

◆ **en fuite** *[malfaiteur]* on the run; *[véhicule]* runaway *(épith)* ◆ **les prisonniers sont en ~** the prisoners are on the run ◆ **l'évadé est toujours en ~** the escaped prisoner is still on the run ◆ **mettre qn en ~** to put sb to flight ◆ **capitaux en ~** flight capital

2 *(= perte de liquide)* leak, leakage ◆ ~ **de gaz/d'huile** gas/oil leak ◆ **avaries dues à des ~s** damage due to *ou* caused by leakage

3 *(= trou) [de récipient, tuyau]* leak

4 *(= indiscrétion)* leak ◆ **il y a eu des ~s à l'examen** some exam questions have been leaked

5 *(Art)* **point de ~** vanishing point

6 *(littér) (= passage) [de temps, heures, saisons]* (swift) passage *ou* passing

COMP **fuite en avant** blindly forging ahead ◆ **(pour stopper) cette ~ en avant dans la guerre/la violence** (to stop) this headlong rush into war/violence

fuite des capitaux capital flight, flight of capital

fuite des cerveaux brain drain

Fuji-Yama /fuʒijama/ **NM** Mount Fuji, Fujiyama, Fuji-san

fulgurance /fylgyʀɑ̃s/ **NF** *(frm) [de progrès, processus]* lightning *ou* dazzling speed; *[de plaisir, douleur]* searing intensity

fulgurant, e /fylgyʀɑ̃, ɑ̃t/ **ADJ** *[vitesse, progrès]* lightning *(épith)*, dazzling; *[succès, carrière]* dazzling; *[ascension]* meteoric; *[réplique]* lightning *(épith)*; *[regard]* blazing *(épith)*, flashing *(épith)* ◆ **une douleur ~e me traversa le corps** a searing pain flashed *ou* shot through my body ◆ **une clarté ~e illumina le ciel** a blinding flash lit up the sky

fulguration /fylgyʀasjɔ̃/ **NF** *(= éclair)* flash (of lightning); *(= thérapie)* fulguration ◆ **il revit son enfance dans une** ~ childhood memories flashed through his mind

fulgurer /fylgyʀe/ ▸ conjug 1 ◂ **VI** to flash

fuligineux, -euse /fyliʒinø, øz/ **ADJ** *(littér) [couleur, flamme]* sooty

fuligule /fyligyl/ **NM** ◆ ~ **(morillon)** tufted duck

full /ful/ **NM** *(Cartes)* full house ◆ ~ **aux as/rois** full house to aces/kings

fulmar /fylmaʀ/ **NM** fulmar

fulminant, e /fylminɑ̃, ɑ̃t/ **ADJ** 1 *[personne]* enraged, livid; *[lettre, réponse, regard]* angry and threatening ◆ ~ **de colère** enraged, livid (with anger) 2 *(= détonant) [mélange]* explosive ◆ **poudre ~e** fulminating powder ◆ **capsule ~e** percussion cap ◆ **sels ~s** explosive salts *(of fulminic acid)*

fulminate /fylminat/ **NM** fulminate

fulmination /fylminasjɔ̃/ **NF** 1 *(= malédictions)* ~**s** fulminations 2 *(Rel)* fulmination

fulminer /fylmine/ ▸ conjug 1 ◂ **VT** *[+ reproches, insultes]* to thunder forth; *(Rel)* to fulminate **VI** 1 *(= pester)* to thunder forth ◆ ~ **contre** to fulminate *ou* thunder forth against 2 *(Chim)* to fulminate, to detonate

fulminique /fylminik/ **ADJ** ◆ **acide** ~ fulminic acid

fumage /fymaʒ/ **NM** *(Culin) [de saucissons]* smoking, curing *(by smoking)*; *(Agr) [de terre]* manuring, dunging

fumant, e /fymɑ̃, ɑ̃t/ **ADJ** 1 *(= chaud) [cendres, cratère]* smoking; *[soupe, corps, naseaux]* steaming; *(Chim)* fuming ◆ **un coup** ~ *(fig)* a master stroke 2 *(* = en colère) [patron]* fuming* *(attrib)* ◆ ~ **de colère** fuming with anger*

fumasse* /fymas/ **ADJ** *(= en colère)* fuming* *(attrib)*

fumé, e[1] /fyme/ (ptp de **fumer**) **ADJ** *[jambon, saumon, verre]* smoked ◆ **verres ~s** *(lunettes)* tinted lenses ◆ **aimer le** ~ to like smoked food; → **lard**

fume-cigare (pl **fume-cigares**) /fymsigaʀ/ **NM** cigar holder

fume-cigarette (pl **fume-cigarettes**) /fymsigaʀet/ **NM** cigarette holder

fumée[2] /fyme/ **NF** 1 *[de combustion]* smoke ◆ ~ **de tabac/de cigarettes** tobacco/cigarette smoke ◆ **la ~ ne vous gêne pas ?** do you mind my smoking? ◆ **sans** ~ *[combustible]* smokeless; → **avaler, noir, rideau** 2 *(= vapeur) [de soupe, étang, corps, naseaux]* steam ◆ **les ~s de l'alcool** *ou* **de l'ivresse** the vapours of alcohol 3 *(locutions)* **partir** *ou* **s'en aller en** ~ to go up in smoke, to fizzle out ◆ **il n'y a pas de ~ sans feu** *(Prov)* there's no smoke without fire *(Prov)*

fumer /fyme/ ▸ conjug 1 ◂ **VI** 1 *[fumeur]* to smoke ◆ ~ **comme un sapeur** *ou* **un pompier** *ou* **une locomotive** to smoke like a chimney; → **défense**[1] 2 *[volcan, cheminée, cendres, lampe]* to smoke; *[soupe, étang, corps]* to steam; *[produit chimique]* to emit *ou* give off fumes, to fume 3 *(* = être en colère)* to be fuming* ◆ **il fumait de rage** he was fuming with rage* **VT** 1 *[+ tabac, hachisch]* to smoke ◆ ~ **la cigarette/le cigare/la pipe** to smoke cigarettes/cigars/a pipe ◆ **elle est allée en ~ une dehors*** she went outside to have a cigarette *ou* a smoke* ◆ **il fumait cigarette sur cigarette** he was chainsmoking 2 *(Culin) [+ aliments]* to smoke, to cure *(by smoking)* 3 *(Agr) [+ sol, terre]* to manure

fumerie /fymʀi/ **NF** ◆ ~ **(d'opium)** opium den

fumerolle /fymʀɔl/ **NF** *(gén pl) (= gaz)* smoke and gas *(emanating from a volcano)*; *(= fumée)* wisp of smoke

fumet /fyme/ **NM** *[de plat, viande]* aroma; *[de vin]* bouquet, aroma; *(Vénerie)* scent

fumeterre /fymtɛʀ/ **NF** fumitory

fumette* /fymɛt/ **NF** *(= drogue)* smoke* ◆ **la** ~ *(= action)* smoking*

fumeur, -euse /fymœʀ, øz/ **NM,F** smoker ◆ **(compartiment) ~s** *(Rail)* smoking compartment *(Brit) ou* car *(US)*, smoker ◆ ~ **d'opium/de pipe** opium/pipe smoker

fumeux, -euse /fymø, øz/ **ADJ** 1 *(= confus) [idées, explication]* hazy, woolly; *[esprit]* woolly; *[théoricien]* woolly-minded 2 *(avec de la fumée) [flamme, clarté]* smoky; *(avec de la vapeur) [horizon, plaine]* hazy, misty

fumier /fymje/ **NM** 1 *(= engrais)* dung, manure ◆ ~ **de cheval** horse-dung *ou* -manure ◆ **tas de** ~ dunghill, dung *ou* muck *ou* manure heap 2 *(** péj = salaud)* bastard**, shit**

fumigateur /fymigatœʀ/ **NM** *(Agr, Méd = appareil)* fumigator

fumigation /fymigasjɔ̃/ **NF** fumigation

fumigatoire /fymigatwaʀ/ **ADJ** fumigating, fumigatory

fumigène /fymiʒɛn/ **ADJ** *[engin, grenade]* smoke *(épith)* ◆ **(appareil)** ~ *(Agr)* smoke apparatus

fumiste /fymist/ **NM** *(= réparateur, installateur)* heating mechanic; *(= ramoneur)* chimney sweep **NMF** *(* péj = paresseux)* shirker, skiver* *(Brit)* **ADJ** *[attitude] (de paresseux)* shirking; *(de plaisantin)* phoney* ◆ **il est un peu (sur les bords)** he's a bit of a shirker *ou* skiver* *(Brit)*

fumisterie /fymistəʀi/ **NF** 1 *(péj)* **c'est une** *ou* **de la** ~ it's a fraud *ou* a con* 2 *(= établissement)* (heating mechanic's) workshop; *(= métier)* stove-building

fumoir /fymwaʀ/ NM (= *salon*) smoking room; (*pour fumer viandes, poissons*) smokehouse

fumure /fymyʀ/ NF manuring; (= *substance*) manure (NonC)

fun[1] * /fœn/ ADJ (= *amusant, excitant*) fun (*épith*) ◆ **c'est ~ !** it's fun! NM (= *amusement*) ◆ **le ~** fun ◆ **je suis mannequin, c'est le ~ !** I'm a model, it's great fun! ◆ **ils ont tout cassé, juste pour le ~** they smashed up everything, just for the fun *ou* hell‡ of it

fun[2] /fœn/ NM abrév de **funboard**

Funafuti /funafuti/ N Funafuti

funambule /fynɑ̃byl/ NMF tightrope walker, funambulist (*SPÉC*)

funboard /fœnbɔʀd/ NM (= *planche*) short windsurfing board *ou* sailboard; (= *sport*) windsurfing

funèbre /fynɛbʀ/ ADJ 1 (= *de l'enterrement*) [*service, marche, oraison*] funeral (*épith*); [*cérémonie, éloge, discours*] funeral (*épith*), funerary (*épith*) ◆ **air ~** dirge; → **entrepreneur, pompe**², **veillée** 2 (= *lugubre*) [*mélodie*] mournful, doleful; [*ton, silence, allure*] lugubrious, funereal; [*atmosphère, couleur, décor*] gloomy, dismal

funérailles /fyneʀɑj/ NFPL (*frm* = *enterrement*) funeral, obsequies (*littér*)

funéraire /fyneʀɛʀ/ ADJ [*dalle, monument, urne*] funeral (*épith*), funerary (*épith*) ◆ **pierre ~** gravestone ◆ **salon ~** (*Can*) funeral home, funeral parlour (*Brit*) *ou* parlor (*US*)

funérarium /fyneʀaʀjɔm/ NM funeral home, funeral parlour (*Brit*) *ou* parlor (*US*)

funeste /fynɛst/ ADJ 1 (= *désastreux*) [*erreur*] disastrous, grievous; [*conseil, décision*] disastrous, harmful; [*influence*] baleful, baneful, harmful; [*suite, conséquence*] dire, disastrous ◆ **le jour ~ où je l'ai rencontré** the fateful *ou* ill-fated day when I met him ◆ **politique ~ aux intérêts du pays** policy harmful to the country's interests 2 (= *de mort*) [*pressentiment, vision*] deathly (*épith*), of death 3 (*littér* = *mortel*) [*accident*] fatal; [*coup*] fatal, lethal, deadly, mortal

funiculaire /fynikylɛʀ/ NM funicular (railway)

funk /fœnk/ ADJ funk (*épith*), funky NM funk

funky /fœnki/ ADJ funky

fur /fyʀ/ NM

◆ **au fur et à mesure** [*classer, nettoyer*] as one goes along; [*dépenser*] as fast as one earns ◆ **il vaut mieux leur donner leur argent de poche au ~ et à mesure qu'en une fois** it's better to give them their pocket money as they need it rather than all in one go ◆ **le frigo se vidait au ~ et à mesure** the fridge was emptied as fast as it was stocked up ◆ **passe-moi les assiettes au ~ et à mesure** pass the plates to me as you go along

◆ **au fur et à mesure que** ◆ **donnez-les-nous au ~ et à mesure que vous les recevez** give them to us as (soon as) you receive them ◆ **nous dépensions tout notre argent au ~ et à mesure que nous le gagnions** we spent all our money as fast as we earned it

◆ **au fur et à mesure de** ◆ **au ~ et à mesure de leur progression** as they advanced, the further they advanced ◆ **prenez-en au ~ et à mesure de vos besoins** take some as and when you need them, help yourselves as you find you need them

furax‡ /fyʀaks/ ADJ INV (= *furieux*) livid* (*attrib*), hopping mad* (*attrib*) (*Brit*)

furet /fyʀɛ/ NM (= *animal*) ferret; (= *jeu*) pass-the-slipper

fureter /fyʀ(ə)te/ ▸ conjug 5 ◂ VI (= *regarder*) to nose *ou* ferret about; (= *fouiller*) to rummage (about)

fureteur, -euse /fyʀ(ə)tœʀ, øz/ ADJ [*regard, enfant*] prying, inquisitive NM,F snooper

fureur /fyʀœʀ/ NF 1 (= *colère*) fury; (= *accès de colère*) fit of rage ◆ **crise** *ou* **accès de ~** fit of rage, furious outburst ◆ **être pris de ~** to fly into a rage (*contre qn* at sb); ◆ **être/entrer en ~** to be/become infuriated *ou* enraged ◆ **être/entrer dans une ~ noire** to be in/go *ou* fly into a towering rage ◆ **mettre en ~** to infuriate, to enrage ◆ **se mettre dans des ~s folles** to have mad fits of rage, to fly into wild fits of anger

2 (= *violence*) [*de passion*] violence, fury; [*de combat, attaque*] fury, fierceness; [*de tempête, flots, vents*] fury

3 (= *passion*) **la ~ du jeu** a passion *ou* mania for gambling ◆ **il a la ~ de la vitesse/de lire** he has a mania for speed/reading ◆ **la ~ de vivre** the lust *ou* passion for life

4 (*littér* = *transe*) frenzy ◆ **~ prophétique** prophetic frenzy ◆ **~ poétique** poetic ecstasy *ou* frenzy

5 (*locutions*) **avec ~** (= *avec rage*) furiously; (= *à la folie*) wildly, madly, passionately ◆ **faire ~** to be all the rage

furibard, e * /fyʀibaʀ, aʀd/ ADJ livid* (*attrib*), hopping mad* (*attrib*) (*Brit*)

furibond, e /fyʀibɔ̃, ɔ̃d/ ADJ [*personne*] furious, livid* (*attrib*); [*colère*] wild, furious; [*ton, voix, yeux*] enraged, furious ◆ **il lui a lancé un regard ~** he glared at him

furie /fyʀi/ NF 1 (*péj* = *mégère*) shrew, termagant; (*Myth*) Fury 2 (= *violence*) [*d'attaque, combat*] fury, fierceness, furiousness; [*de tempête, flots*] fury; [*de passions*] violence, fury 3 (= *passion*) **la ~ du jeu** a passion *ou* mania for gambling 4 (= *colère*) fury 5 (*locutions*) **en ~** [*personne*] infuriated, enraged, in a rage (*attrib*); [*mer*] raging; [*tigre*] enraged ◆ **mettre qn en ~** to infuriate sb, to enrage sb

furieusement /fyʀjøzmɑ̃/ ADV (= *avec fureur*) [*attaquer*] furiously; [*répondre*] angrily; (*gén hum* = *extrêmement*) [*ressembler*] amazingly, tremendously ◆ **j'ai ~ envie d'une glace** I'm dying for* an ice cream

furieux, -ieuse /fyʀjø, jøz/ ADJ 1 (= *violent*) [*combat, résistance*] furious, fierce; [*tempête*] raging, furious, violent ◆ **avoir une furieuse envie de faire qch** to be dying to do sth*; → **folie, fou** 2 (= *en colère*) [*personne*] furious (*contre* with, at); [*ton, geste*] furious ◆ **taureau ~** raging bull ◆ **rendre qn ~** to infuriate *ou* enrage sb ◆ **le taureau, rendu ~ par la foule** the bull, driven wild by the crowd ◆ **elle est furieuse de n'avoir pas été invitée** she's furious that she wasn't invited *ou* at not having been invited ◆ **il est ~ que je lui aie menti** he is furious with *ou* at me for having lied to him 3 (*gén hum* = *fort*) [*envie, coup*] almighty* (*épith*), tremendous

furoncle /fyʀɔ̃kl/ NM boil, furuncle (*SPÉC*)

furonculose /fyʀɔ̃kyloz/ NF (recurrent) boils, furunculosis (*SPÉC*)

furtif, -ive /fyʀtif, iv/ ADJ [*coup d'œil, geste*] furtive, stealthy; [*joie*] secret; → **avion**

furtivement /fyʀtivmɑ̃/ ADV furtively, stealthily

fusain /fyzɛ̃/ NM 1 (= *crayon*) charcoal (crayon); (= *croquis*) charcoal (drawing) ◆ **tracé au ~** charcoal(-drawn), (drawn) in charcoal 2 (= *arbrisseau*) spindle-tree ◆

fusant, e /fyzɑ̃, ɑ̃t/ ADJ ◆ **obus ~** time shell ◆ **tir ~** air burst

fuseau (pl **fuseaux**) /fyzo/ NM 1 [*de fileuse*] spindle; [*de dentellière*] bobbin 2 ◆ **(pantalon) ~, ~x** stretch ski pants (*Brit*), stirrup pants (*US*) 3 (*Anat, Bio*) spindle 4 (*locutions*) **en (forme de) ~** [*colonne*] spindle-shaped; [*cuisses, jambes*] slender ◆ **arbuste taillé en ~** shrub shaped into a cone 5 ◆ **~ horaire** time zone ◆ **changer de ~ horaire** to cross time zones

fusée /fyze/ NF 1 (*spatiale*) (space) rocket; (*missile*) rocket, missile ◆ **~ air-air/sol-air** air-to-air/ground-to-air missile 2 [*de feu d'artifice*] rocket; [*d'obus, mine*] fuse ◆ **partir comme une ~** to set off like a rocket, to whizz off 3 [*d'essieu*] spindle; (*dans voiture*) stub axle; [*de montre*] fusee

COMP **fusée antichar** anti-tank rocket
fusée de détresse distress rocket
fusée éclairante flare
fusée à étages multi-stage rocket
fusée interplanétaire (interplanetary) space rocket
fusée de lancement launch vehicle

fusée-engin (pl **fusées-engins**) /fyzeɑ̃ʒɛ̃/ NF rocket shell

fusée-sonde (pl **fusées-sondes**) /fyzesɔ̃d/ NF rocket-powered space probe

fuselage /fyz(ə)laʒ/ NM [*d'avion*] fuselage

fuselé, e /fyz(ə)le/ ADJ [*colonne*] spindle-shaped; [*doigts*] tapering, slender; [*cuisses, jambes*] slender

fuser /fyze/ ▸ conjug 1 ◂ VI 1 [*cris, rires*] to burst forth; [*questions*] to come from all sides; [*liquide, vapeur*] to gush *ou* spurt out; [*étincelles*] to fly (out); [*lumière*] to stream out *ou* forth ◆ **les plaisanteries fusaient** the jokes came thick and fast ◆ **les insultes fusaient de toutes parts** insults were flying from all sides 2 (*Tech*) [*bougie*] to run; [*pile*] to sweat; [*poudre*] to burn out

fusible /fyzibl/ ADJ fusible NM 1 (= *fil*) fuse (wire); (= *fiche*) fuse ◆ **les ~s ont sauté** the fuses have blown 2 (= *personne*) fall guy ◆ **j'ai servi de ~** I was used as a fall guy

fusiforme /fyzifɔʀm/ ADJ spindle-shaped, fusiform (*SPÉC*)

fusil /fyzi/ NM 1 (= *arme*) (*de guerre, à canon rayé*) rifle, gun; (*de chasse, à canon lisse*) shotgun, gun ◆ **c'est un bon ~** (= *chasseur*) he's a good shot ◆ **un groupe de 30 ~s** († *Mil*) a group of 30 riflemen *ou* rifles ◆ **changer son ~ d'épaule** (*fig*) to have a change of heart ◆ **coup de ~** gun shot, rifle shot ◆ **c'est le coup de ~** (= *c'est cher*) the prices are extortionate

2 (= *allume-gaz*) gas lighter; (= *instrument à aiguiser*) steel

COMP **fusil à air comprimé** airgun
fusil d'assaut assault rifle
fusil automatique automatic rifle
fusil à canon rayé rifle, rifled gun
fusil à canon scié sawn-off (*Brit*) *ou* sawed-off (*US*) shotgun
fusil de chasse shotgun, hunting gun
fusil à deux coups double-barrelled *ou* twin-barrel rifle
fusil de guerre army rifle
fusil à harpon harpoon gun
fusil à lunette rifle with telescopic sight
fusil à pompe pump-action shotgun
fusil à répétition repeating rifle
fusil sous-marin (underwater) speargun

fusilier /fyzilje/ NM rifleman, fusilier; (*Hist*) fusilier ◆ **les ~s** (= *régiment*) the rifles; (*Hist*) the fusiliers ◆ **~ marin** marine

fusillade /fyzijad/ NF (= *bruit*) fusillade (*frm*), gunfire (*NonC*), shooting (*NonC*); (= *combat*) shoot-out, shooting battle; (= *exécution*) shooting

fusiller /fyzije/ ▸ conjug 1 ◂ VT 1 (= *exécuter*) to shoot ◆ **~ qn du regard** to look daggers at sb 2 (* = *casser*) to bust* 3 (* = *dépenser*) to blow‡

fusilleur /fyzijœʀ/ NM member of a firing squad

fusil-mitrailleur (pl **fusils-mitrailleurs**) /fyzimitʀajœʀ/ NM machine gun

fusion /fyzjɔ̃/ NF 1 [*de métal*] melting, fusion; [*de glace*] melting, thawing ◆ **en ~** [*métal*] molten ◆ **au moment de l'entrée en ~** when melting point is reached 2 (*Bio, Phys*) fusion ◆ **~ nucléaire/chromosomique** nuclear/

chromosome fusion 3 *[de cœurs, esprits, races]* fusion; *[de partis]* merging, combining; *[de systèmes, philosophies]* blending, merging, uniting 4 *[de sociétés]* merger, amalgamation; *[de fichiers]* merging ◆ ~ **absorption** takeover ◆ ~ **acquisition** acquisition and merger

fusionnel, -elle /fuzjɔnɛl/ ADJ *(Psych)* *[rapport]* intensely close; *[amour]* based on a very close bond ◆ **une relation trop fusionnelle avec la mère** a relationship with the mother that is too close *ou* too intense

fusionnement /fyzjɔnmɑ̃/ NM *(Comm)* merger, amalgamation; *(Pol)* merging, combining

fusionner /fyzjɔne/ ► conjug 1 ◄ VTI to merge; *[sociétés]* to merge, to amalgamate

fustanelle /fystanɛl/ NF fustanella

fustigation /fystigasjɔ̃/ NF 1 *(littér)* *[d'adversaire]* flaying; *[de pratiques, mœurs]* censuring, denouncing, denunciation 2 *(†† = flagellation)* birching, thrashing

fustiger /fystiʒe/ ► conjug 3 ◄ VT 1 *(littér)* *[+ adversaire]* to flay; *[+ pratiques, mœurs]* to censure, to denounce ◆ **ses sketches fustigent la société actuelle** his sketches are a scathing attack on modern society 2 *(†† = fouetter)* to birch, to thrash

fut* /fyt/ NM (abrév de **futal**) trousers *(Brit)*, pants *(US)*

fût /fy/ NM 1 *[d'arbre]* bole, trunk; *[de colonne]* shaft; *[de fusil]* stock 2 *(= tonneau)* barrel, cask

futaie /fytɛ/ NF *(= groupe d'arbres)* cluster of (tall) trees; *(= forêt)* forest *(of tall trees)*; *(Sylviculture)* plantation of trees *(for timber)* ◆ **haute** ~ mature (standing) timber ◆ **arbre de haute** ~ mature tree

futaille /fytɑj/ NF *(= barrique)* barrel, cask

futaine /fytɛn/ NF *(= tissu)* fustian

futal* (pl **futals**) /fytal/, **fute*** /fyt/ NM trousers *(Brit)*, pants *(US)*

futé, e /fyte/ ADJ wily, crafty, cunning, sly ◆ **c'est une petite ~e** she's a sly little minx ◆ **il n'est pas très** ~ he's not very bright

fute-fute* /fytfyt/ ADJ ◆ **il n'est pas (très)** ~ he's not very bright

futile /fytil/ ADJ *[prétexte, raison, question, préoccupation]* trifling, trivial; *[exercice]* futile; *[personne, esprit]* frivolous ◆ **l'univers ~ de la mode** the frivolous world of fashion

futilement /fytilmɑ̃/ ADV *(= frivolement)* frivolously

futilité /fytilite/ NF 1 *[d'entreprise, tentative]* futility, pointlessness; *[de raison, souci, occupation, propos]* triviality; *[de personne, esprit]* triviality, frivolousness 2 *(= propos, action)* **~s** trivialities ◆ **dire des ~s** to talk about trivia ◆ **ils ont passé leur journée à des ~s** they frittered the day away

futon /fytɔ̃/ NM futon

futsal /futsal/ NM *(= football en salle)* indoor football

futur, e /fytyʀ/ ADJ *(= prochain)* *[génération, désastres, besoins]* future *(épith)* ◆ **dans la vie ~e** *(Rel)* in the afterlife, in the hereafter ◆ ~ **mari** husband-to-be ◆ **les ~s époux** the bride-and-groom-to-be ◆ **tout pour la ~e maman** everything for the mother-to-be ◆ ~ **collègue/directeur** future colleague/director ◆ ~ **client** prospective customer ◆ ~ **président/champion** *(en herbe)* budding *ou* future president/champion NM 1 *(= avenir)* future 2 *(Ling)* **le ~ (simple)** the future (tense) ◆ **le ~ proche** the immediate future ◆ **le ~ antérieur** *ou* **du passé** the future perfect *ou* anterior 3 *(† = fiancé)* fiancé, husband-to-be, intended † NF **future** *(† = fiancée)* fiancée, wife-to-be, intended †

futurisme /fytyʀism/ NM futurism

futuriste /fytyʀist/ NMF futurist ADJ futuristic

futurologie /fytyʀɔlɔʒi/ NF futurology

futurologue /fytyʀɔlɔg/ NMF futurist, futurologist

fuyant, e /fɥijɑ̃, ɑt/ ADJ 1 *(= insaisissable)* *[regard, air]* evasive; *[personne, caractère]* elusive, evasive 2 *(= en retrait)* *[menton, front]* receding *(épith)* 3 *(littér = fugitif)* *[ombre, vision]* fleeting *(épith)* 4 *(Art)* *[vues, lignes]* receding *(épith)*, vanishing *(épith)*; *[perspective]* vanishing *(épith)*

fuyard, e /fɥijaʀ, aʀd/ NM,F runaway

Gg

G[1], g[1] /ʒe/ NM (= *lettre*) G, g ◆ **le G-8** the G8 nations, the Group of Eight ◆ **point G** (*Anat*) G spot

G[2] [1] (abrév de **Giga**) G [2] (= *constante de gravitation*) G [3] (*Anat*) ◆ **point G** G spot

g[2] [1] (abrév de **gramme**) g [2] (*Phys* = *accélération*) g

gabardine /gabaʀdin/ NF (= *tissu*) gabardine; (= *manteau*) gabardine (raincoat)

gabarit /gabaʀi/ NM [1] (= *dimension*) [*d'objet, véhicule*] size [2] * [*de personne*] (= *taille*) size, build; (= *valeur*) calibre (*Brit*), caliber (*US*) ◆ **ce n'est pas le petit ~ !** he's not exactly small! ◆ **du même ~** of the same build ◆ **il n'a pas le ~ d'un directeur commercial** he hasn't got what it takes *ou* he isn't of the right calibre to be a sales manager [3] (= *appareil de mesure*) gauge, gage (*US*); (= *maquette*) template ◆ **~ de chargement** (*Rail*) loading gauge

gabegie /gabʒi/ NF (*péj*) (= *gâchis*) waste (*due to bad management*); (= *désordre*) chaos ◆ **c'est une vraie ~ !** it's a real mess!, it's total chaos!

gabelle /gabɛl/ NF (*Hist* = *impôt*) salt tax, gabelle

gabelou /gablu/ NM (*Hist*) salt-tax collector; (*péj*) customs officer

gabier /gabje/ NM (*Naut*) topman

Gabon /gabɔ̃/ NM ◆ **le ~** (the) Gabon

gabonais, e /gabɔnɛ, ɛz/ ADJ Gabonese NM,F **Gabonais(e)** Gabonese

gâchage /gɑʃaʒ/ NM [1] [*de plâtre*] tempering; [*de mortier*] mixing [2] [*d'argent, talent, temps*] wasting

gâche /gɑʃ/ NF [1] [*de maçon*] (plasterer's) trowel [2] [*de serrure*] striking plate, strike (plate)

gâcher /gɑʃe/ ▸ conjug 1 ◂ VT [1] [*+ argent, temps*] to waste, to fritter away; [*+ nourriture, occasion, talent*] to waste; [*+ travail*] to botch ◆ **~ sa vie** to fritter away *ou* waste one's life ◆ **une vie gâchée** a wasted *ou* misspent life [2] [*+ plâtre*] to temper; [*+ mortier*] to mix [3] (= *gâter*) (*gén*) to spoil; [*+ jeunesse, séjour, chances*] to ruin ◆ **il nous a gâché le** *ou* **notre plaisir** he spoiled it for us ◆ **je ne veux pas lui ~ sa joie** I don't want to spoil his happiness ◆ **il gâche le métier** he spoils it for others (*by selling cheap or working for a low salary*)

gâchette /gɑʃɛt/ NF [*d'arme*] trigger; [*de serrure*] tumbler ◆ **appuyer** *ou* **presser sur la ~** to pull the trigger ◆ **il a la ~ facile** he's trigger-happy ◆ **une bonne ~** (= *tireur*) a good shot ◆ **la meilleure ~ de l'Ouest** the fastest gun in the West

gâchis /gɑʃi/ NM [1] (= *désordre*) mess ◆ **tu as fait un beau ~ !** you've made a real mess of it! [2] (= *gaspillage*) [*d'argent, nourriture, sentiments*] waste (*NonC*) ◆ **je ne supporte pas le ~** I hate waste *ou* wastefulness ◆ **quel ~ !** what a waste! [3] (= *mortier*) mortar

gadget /gadʒɛt/ NM (= *chose*) thingummy* (*Brit*), gizmo* (*US*); (= *jouet, ustensile*) gadget; (= *procédé, trouvaille*) gimmick ◆ **cette loi n'est qu'un ~** that law is just a token measure

gadgétiser /gadʒetize/ ▸ conjug 1 ◂ VT to equip with gadgets

gadin * /gadɛ̃/ NM ◆ **prendre** *ou* **ramasser un ~** to fall flat on one's face, to come a cropper* (*Brit*)

gadoue /gadu/ NF (= *boue*) mud, sludge; (= *neige*) slush; (= *engrais*) night soil

GAEC /gaɛk/ NM (abrév de **groupement agricole d'exploitation en commun**) → **groupement**

gaélique /gaelik/ ADJ Gaelic NM (= *langue*) Gaelic

gaffe /gaf/ NF [1] (= *bévue*) blunder, boob* (*Brit*) ◆ **faire une ~** (*action*) to make a blunder *ou* a boob* (*Brit*); (*parole*) to put one's foot in it*, to say the wrong thing, to drop a clanger* (*Brit*) [2] (= *perche*) (*Naut*) boat hook; (*Pêche*) gaff [3] (*locution*)

◆ **faire gaffe** * (= *être attentionné*) to pay attention (*à* to); ◆ **fais ~ !** watch out!, be careful! ◆ **fais ~ à toi** watch yourself

gaffer /gafe/ ▸ conjug 1 ◂ VI (*bévue*) to blunder, to boob* (*Brit*); (*paroles*) to put one's foot in it*, to drop a clanger* (*Brit*) ◆ **j'ai gaffé ?** have I put my foot in it?, did I say the wrong thing? VT [1] (*Naut*) to hook; (*Pêche*) to gaff [2] (†* = *regarder*) **gaffe un peu la fille !** get a load of her!* VPR **se gaffer** (*Helv* = *faire attention*) * to be careful ◆ **gaffe-toi !** watch out!

gaffeur, -euse /gafœʀ, øz/ NM,F blunderer ◆ **il est drôlement ~ !** he's always putting his foot in it!*

gag /gag/ NM (*gén, Ciné, Théât*) gag ◆ **ce n'est pas un ~** it's not a joke ◆ **le ~, c'est qu'il va falloir s'en servir** the funniest part of it is that we'll have to use it

gaga * /gaga/ ADJ [*vieillard*] gaga*, senile ◆ **sa fille le rend ~** he's putty in his daughter's hands, his daughter can wind him round her little finger ◆ **être ~ de qn** to be crazy* *ou* nuts* about sb

gage /gaʒ/ NM [1] (*à un créancier, arbitre*) security; (*à un prêteur*) pledge ◆ **mettre qch en ~ (chez le prêteur)** to pawn sth (at the pawnbroker's) ◆ **laisser qch en ~** to leave sth as (a) security; → **prêteur**

[2] (= *garantie*) guarantee ◆ **sa bonne forme physique est un ~ de succès** his fitness will guarantee him success *ou* assure him of success

[3] (= *témoignage*) proof (*NonC*), evidence (*NonC*) ◆ **donner des ~s de sa sincérité/de son talent** to give proof *ou* evidence of one's sincerity/one's talent ◆ **donner des ~s de (sa) bonne volonté** to make several gestures of goodwill ◆ **donner à qn un ~ d'amour/de fidélité** to give sb a token of one's love/of one's faithfulness ◆ **en ~ de notre amitié/de ma bonne foi** as a token *ou* in token of our friendship/of my good faith

[4] (*Jeux*) forfeit ◆ **avoir un ~** to have a forfeit

[5] († = *salaire*) **~s** wages ◆ **être aux ~s de qn** (*gén*) to be employed by sb; (*péj*) to be in the pay of sb; → **tueur**

gager /gaʒe/ ▸ conjug 3 ◂ VT [1] (*frm* = *parier*) **~ que** to wager that, to bet that ◆ **gageons que ..., je gage que ...** I bet (you) that ... [2] [*+ emprunt*] to guarantee

gageure /gaʒyʀ/ NF [1] (= *entreprise difficile*) **c'est une véritable ~ que de vouloir tenter seul cette ascension** it's attempting the impossible to try to do this climb alone ◆ **c'était une ~ de vouloir adapter ce roman à l'écran** adapting the book for the screen was a seemingly impossible challenge ◆ **cela relevait de la ~** it was a seemingly impossible task ◆ **il a réussi** *ou* **tenu la ~ de battre le tenant du titre** he achieved the tremendous feat of defeating the reigning champion [2] (†† = *pari*) wager

gagnable /gaɲabl/ ADJ winnable ◆ **les circonscriptions ~s par la gauche** the constituencies that the left could win

gagnant, e /gaɲɑ̃, ɑ̃t/ ADJ [*numéro, combinaison, équipe, point, ticket*] winning (*épith*) ◆ **on donne ce concurrent ~** this competitor is expected to win ◆ **il joue** *ou* **part ~ dans cette affaire** he's bound to win *ou* come out on top in this deal ◆ **tu es ~** you can't lose ◆ **la partie ~e** (*Jur*) the prevailing party ◆ **service ~** (*Tennis*) winning serve NM,F winner

gagne * /gaɲ/ NF (*Sport*) ◆ **la ~** the will *ou* drive to win ◆ **ce joueur est venu pour la ~** this player has come intent on winning

gagne-pain * /gaɲpɛ̃/ NM INV source of income ◆ **c'est son ~** it's his bread and butter*

gagne-petit /gaɲpəti/ NM INV (= *qui gagne peu*) low wage earner ◆ **c'est un ~** (*péj*) he's just out to make a quick buck

gagner /gaɲe/ ▸ conjug 1 ◂ VT 1 (= *acquérir par le travail*) to earn ◆ ~ **sa vie** to earn one's living (*en faisant* (by) doing); ◆ **elle gagne mal sa vie** she doesn't earn much ◆ **elle gagne bien sa vie** she earns a good living ◆ **elle gagne bien** * she earns good money * ◆ ~ **son pain** to earn one's daily bread ◆ ~ **de l'argent** (*par le travail*) to earn *ou* make money; (*dans une affaire*) to make money ◆ ~ **de quoi vivre** to earn a living ◆ ~ **gros** to make a lot of money ◆ **il ne gagne pas des mille et des cents** * he doesn't exactly earn a fortune ◆ ~ **sa croûte** * *ou* **son bifteck** * to earn one's crust *ou* one's bread and butter ◆ **il gagne bien sa croûte dans cet emploi** * he earns a good wage in that job ◆ **j'ai gagné ma journée** (*iro*) that really made my day (*iro*)

2 (= *mériter*) to earn ◆ **il a bien gagné ses vacances** he's really earned his holiday

3 (= *acquérir par le hasard*) [+ *prix, somme*] to win ◆ ~ **le gros lot** (*lit, fig*) to hit *ou* win the jackpot

4 (= *obtenir*) [+ *réputation*] to gain; [+ *parts de marché*] to win ◆ **avoir tout à** ~ **et rien à perdre** to have everything to gain and nothing to lose ◆ **vous n'y gagnerez rien** you'll gain nothing by it ◆ **vous n'y gagnerez rien de bon** you'll get nothing out of it ◆ **vous y gagnerez d'être tranquille** at least you'll get some peace and quiet that way ◆ **chercher à** ~ **du temps** (= *aller plus vite*) to try to save time; (= *temporiser*) to play for time, to try to gain time ◆ **cela fait** ~ **beaucoup de temps** it saves a lot *ou* a great deal of time, it's very time-saving ◆ ~ **de la place** to save space ◆ **c'est toujours ça de gagné !** that's always something! ◆ **c'est toujours 10 € de gagné** at least that's €10 saved *ou* that's saved us €10 ◆ **en jouant sur l'épaisseur, on peut** ~ **sur la quantité** by adjusting the thickness, we can gain in quantity ◆ **à sortir par ce temps, vous y gagnerez un bon rhume** you'll get nothing but a bad cold going out in this weather ◆ **je n'y ai gagné que des ennuis** I only made trouble for myself, I only succeeded in making things difficult for myself ◆ **s'il dit oui, c'est gagné** if he says yes, then everything will be all right

5 (= *augmenter de*) ~ **dix centimètres** [*plante, enfant*] to grow ten centimetres ◆ **l'indice CAC 40 gagne 4 points** the CAC 40 index is up 4 points ◆ **il gagne 3 points dans les sondages** he gains 3 points in the opinion polls

6 (= *être vainqueur de*) [+ *élection, bataille, procès, pari, course*] to win; (*arg Sport*) [+ *joueur*] to beat ◆ **le match/procès n'est pas gagné** the match/trial hasn't been won yet ◆ **ce n'est pas gagné d'avance** it's far from certain ◆ ~ **haut la main** to win hands down ◆ ~ **qn aux échecs** to beat sb at chess ◆ ~ **qn de vitesse** to catch up on sb

7 (= *se concilier*) [+ *gardiens, témoins*] to win over ◆ ~ **l'estime/le cœur de qn** to win sb's esteem *ou* regard/heart ◆ ~ **la confiance de qn** to win *ou* gain sb's confidence ◆ **savoir se** ~ **des amis/des partisans** to know how to win friends/supporters ◆ **se laisser** ~ **par les prières de qn** to be won over by sb's prayers ◆ ~ **qn à une cause** to win sb over to a cause ◆ ~ **qn à sa cause** to win sb over

8 (= *envahir*) to spread to ◆ **le sommeil les gagnait** sleep was creeping over them *ou* was gradually overcoming them ◆ **la gangrène gagne la jambe** the gangrene is spreading to his leg ◆ **le froid les gagnait** they were beginning to feel the cold ◆ **le feu gagna rapidement les rues voisines** the fire quickly spread to the neighbouring streets ◆ **l'eau/l'ennemi gagne du terrain** the water/the enemy is gaining ground ◆ **la grève gagne tous les secteurs** the strike is gaining ground in *ou* is spreading to all sectors

9 (= *atteindre*) [+ *lieu, frontière, refuge*] to reach ◆ ~ **le port** to reach port ◆ ~ **le large** (*Naut*) to get out into the open sea

VI 1 (= *être vainqueur*) to win ◆ ~ **aux courses** to win on the horses *ou* at the races ◆ **il a gagné aux courses hier** he won on the horses *ou* had a win at the races yesterday ◆ **il gagne sur tous les tableaux** he's winning all the way *ou* on all fronts ◆ **eh bien, tu as gagné !** (*iro*) well, you got what you asked for! * ◆ **à tous les coups on gagne !** (*à la foire*) every one a winner!; (*gén*) you can't lose!

2 (= *trouver un avantage*) **vous y gagnez** it's in your interest, it's to your advantage ◆ **vous gagnerez à ce que personne ne le sache** it'll be to your advantage *ou* it will be better for you if nobody knows about it ◆ **qu'est-ce que j'y gagne ?** what do I get out of it? *ou* gain from it?, what's in it for me? ◆ **vous gagneriez à partir en groupe** you'd be better off going in a group ◆ **tu aurais gagné à te taire !** you would have done better to keep quiet! ◆ **elle a gagné au change** she ended up better off

3 (= *s'améliorer*) ~ **en hauteur** to increase in height ◆ **son style gagne en force ce qu'il perd en élégance** his style gains in vigour what it loses in elegance ◆ **ce vin gagnera à vieillir** this wine will improve with age ◆ **il gagne à être connu** he improves on acquaintance ◆ **ce roman gagne à être relu** this novel gains by a second reading, this novel is better at a second reading

4 (= *s'étendre*) [*incendie, épidémie*] to spread, to gain ground ◆ **la mer gagne sur les falaises** the sea is encroaching *ou* advancing on the cliffs

gagneur, -euse /gaɲœʀ, øz/ NM,F (= *battant*) go-getter * ◆ **avoir un tempérament de** ~ to be a born winner NF **gagneuse** ** (= *prostituée*) whore **, hooker **

gai, e /ge/ ADJ 1 [*personne, vie*] cheerful, happy; [*voix, visage*] cheerful, happy, cheery; [*caractère, roman, conversation, musique*] cheerful ◆ **le** ~ **Paris** gay Paris ◆ **c'est un** ~ **luron** he's a cheery *ou* happy fellow ◆ ~ **comme un pinson** happy as a lark ◆ **tu n'as pas l'air (bien)** ~ you don't look too happy 2 (*euph* = *ivre*) merry, tipsy; → **vin** 3 [*robe*] bright; [*couleur, pièce*] bright, cheerful ◆ **on va peindre la chambre en jaune pour faire** ~ we're going to paint the bedroom yellow to brighten it up 4 (*iro* = *amusant*) **j'ai oublié mon parapluie, c'est** ~ **!** that's great *, I've forgotten my umbrella! (*iro*) ◆ **ça va être** ~, **un week-end avec lui !** the weekend's going to be great fun with him around! (*iro*) 5 (= *homosexuel*) gay NM (= *homosexuel*) gay

gaiement /gemɑ̃/ ADV 1 (= *joyeusement*) cheerfully, merrily 2 (= *avec entrain*) **allons-y** ~ **!** come on then, let's get on with it! ◆ **il va recommencer** ~ **à faire les mêmes bêtises** he'll blithely *ou* gaily start the same old tricks again

gaieté /gete/ NF [*de personne, caractère, roman, conversation*] cheerfulness, gaiety; [*de couleur*] brightness ◆ **plein de** ~ cheerful ◆ **perdre/retrouver sa** ~ to lose/recover one's good spirits ◆ **ses films sont rarement d'une** ~ **folle** his films are not exactly cheerful ◆ **ce n'est pas de** ~ **de cœur qu'il accepta** he wasn't exactly happy about accepting, it was with some reluctance that he accepted ◆ **voilà les** ~**s de la province** (*iro*) those are the joys *ou* delights of living in a provincial town (*iro*)

gaillard¹, e /gajaʀ, aʀd/ ADJ 1 (= *alerte*) [*personne*] strong; [*allure*] lively, springy, sprightly ◆ **vieillard encore** ~ sprightly *ou* spry old man 2 (= *grivois*) [*propos*] bawdy, ribald NM 1 (= *costaud*) **(robuste *ou* grand *ou* beau)** ~ strapping fellow *ou* lad 2 (* = *type*) fellow, guy *, chap * (*Brit*) ◆ **toi, mon** ~, **je t'ai à l'œil !** I've got my eye on you, chum! * *ou* mate! * (*Brit*) NF **gaillarde** (= *femme forte*) strapping wench * *ou* woman

gaillard² /gajaʀ/ NM (*Naut*) ◆ ~ **d'avant** forecastle (head), fo'c'sle ◆ ~ **d'arrière** quarter-deck

gaillardement /gajaʀdəmɑ̃/ ADV (= *avec bonne humeur*) cheerfully; (= *sans faiblir*) bravely, gallantly ◆ **ils attaquèrent la côte** ~ they set off energetically *ou* stoutly up the hill ◆ **il porte** ~ **sa soixantaine** he's a sprightly *ou* vigorous sixty-year-old

gaillardise /gajaʀdiz/ NF bawdy *ou* ribald remark

gaîment /gemɑ̃/ ADV ⇒ **gaiement**

gain /gɛ̃/ NM 1 (= *salaire*) (*gén*) earnings; [*d'ouvrier*] earnings, wages, wage ◆ **pour un** ~ **modeste** for a modest wage

2 (= *lucre*) **le** ~ gain; → **appât**

3 (= *bénéfice*) [*de société*] profit; (*au jeu*) winnings ◆ **faire un** ~ **de 2 milliards** to make a profit of 2 billion ◆ **se retirer sur son** ~ (*au jeu*) to pull out with one's winnings intact; (*spéculation*) to retire on one's profits *ou* with what one has made

4 (= *économie*) saving ◆ **le** ~ **d'argent/de place est énorme** it saves a considerable amount of money/space ◆ **ça permet un** ~ **de temps** it saves time ◆ **ce procédé permet un** ~ **de 50 minutes/d'électricité** this procedure saves 50 minutes/electricity

5 (= *avantage matériel*) gain ◆ ~ **de productivité** productivity gain ◆ ~ **de pouvoir d'achat** increase in purchasing power ◆ ~**s territoriaux** territorial gains

6 (= *obtention*) [*de match, bataille, procès*] winning; [*de fortune, voix d'électeurs*] gaining ◆ ~ **de poids** weight gain ◆ **ce** ~ **de trois sièges leur donne la majorité** winning *ou* gaining these three seats has given them a majority ◆ **l'action a terminé la séance sur un** ~ **de 2 points** the share was up (by) 2 points at close of trading

7 (*Élec*) gain, amplification ◆ **contrôle automatique de** ~ automatic gain control

8 (*locutions*) **avoir *ou* obtenir** ~ **de cause** (*Jur*) to win the case; (*fig*) to be proved right ◆ **on ne voulait pas me rembourser mais j'ai fini par avoir** ~ **de cause** they didn't want to reimburse me but in the end I won my claim ◆ **donner** ~ **de cause à qn** (*Jur*) to decide in sb's favour; (*fig*) to pronounce sb right

gainant, e /genɑ̃, ɑ̃t/ ADJ [*collant, culotte*] body-shaping

gaine /gɛn/ NF 1 (*Habillement*) girdle ◆ ~ **culotte** panty girdle 2 (= *fourreau*) (*Anat, Bot*) sheath; [*d'obus*] priming tube ◆ ~ **d'aération** *ou* **de ventilation** ventilation shaft 3 (= *piédestal*) plinth

gainer /gene/ ▸ conjug 1 ◂ VT (*gén*) to cover; [+ *fil électrique*] to sheathe; [+ *voile*] to put into a sailbag ◆ **jambes gainées de soie** legs sheathed in silk ◆ **objet gainé de cuir** leather-covered *ou* -cased object

gaîté /gete/ NF ⇒ **gaieté**

gala /gala/ NM official reception; (*pour collecter des fonds*) fund-raising reception ◆ ~ **de bienfaisance** charity gala ◆ **de** ~ [*soirée, représentation*] gala (*épith*) ◆ **tenue de** ~ full evening dress

Galaad /galaad/ NM Galahad

galactique /galaktik/ ADJ galactic

galactophore /galaktɔfɔʀ/ ADJ ◆ **canal/glande** ~ milk duct/gland

Galalithe ® /galalit/ N Galalith ®

galamment /galamɑ̃/ ADV courteously, gallantly ◆ **se conduire** ~ to behave courteously *ou* gallantly *ou* in a gentlemanly fashion

galandage /galɑ̃daʒ/ NM (brick) partition

galant, e /galɑ̃, ɑ̃t/ ADJ 1 (= *courtois*) gallant, courteous, gentlemanly ◆ **soyez** ~, **ouvrez-lui**

la porte be a gentleman and open the door for her ◆ **c'est un ~ homme** he is a gentleman ◆ **femme ~e** (†, *péj*) courtesan 2 *[ton, humeur, propos]* flirtatious, gallant; *[scène, tableau]* amorous, romantic; *[conte]* racy, spicy; *[poésie]* amorous, courtly ◆ **en ~e compagnie** *[homme]* with a lady friend; *[femme]* with a gentleman friend ◆ **rendez-vous ~** tryst **NM** (††, *hum = soupirant*) gallant (††), suitor (††), admirer † *(aussi hum)*

galanterie / galɑ̃tʀi / **NF** *(= courtoisie)* gallantry, chivalry; *(= propos)* gallant remark

galantine / galɑ̃tin / **NF** galantine

Galapagos / galapagɔs / **NFPL** ◆ **les (îles) ~** the Galapagos (Islands)

galapiat † / galapja / **NM** *(= polisson)* rapscallion †, scamp

Galatée / galate / **NF** Galatea

Galates / galat / **NMPL** *(Bible)* Galatians

galaxie / galaksi / **NF** *(Astron)* galaxy; *(= monde, domaine)* world, universe ◆ **la Galaxie** the Galaxy

galbe / galb / **NM** *[de meuble, visage, cuisse]* curve ◆ **cuisses d'un ~ parfait** shapely thighs

galbé, e / galbe / (ptp de **galber**) **ADJ** *[meuble]* with curved outlines; *[mollet]* rounded ◆ **bien ~** *[corps]* curvaceous, shapely; *[objet]* beautifully shaped

galber / galbe / ► conjug 1 ◄ **VT** to shape *(into curves)*, to curve

gale / gal / **NF** 1 *(Méd)* scabies, itch; *[de chien, chat]* mange; *[de mouton]* scab; *(Bot)* scab ◆ **tu peux boire dans mon verre, je n'ai pas la ~ !*** you can drink out of my glass, you won't catch anything! 2 *(= personne)* nasty character, nasty piece of work* ◆ **il est mauvais** *ou* **méchant comme la ~** he's a really nasty piece of work*

galée / gale / **NF** *(Typo)* galley

galéjade / galeʒad / **NF** tall story

galéjer / galeʒe / ► conjug 6 ◄ **VI** to spin a yarn ◆ **oh, tu galèjes !** that's a tall story!

galène / galɛn / **NF** galena, galenite

galère / galɛʀ / **NF** 1 *(Hist = bateau)* galley ◆ **~ réale** royal galley ◆ **envoyer/condamner qn aux ~s** to send/sentence sb to the galleys ◆ **qu'est-il allé faire dans cette ~ ?** why on earth did he have to get involved in that business? ◆ **dans quelle ~ me suis-je embarqué !** whatever have I let myself in for?; → **voguer** 2 (* *= ennui, problème*) **quelle ~ !, c'est (la) ~ !** what a drag * *ou* pain *! ◆ **rien n'allait dans ma vie, c'était (vraiment) la ~** nothing was going right for me, it was hell * *ou* it was the pits* ◆ **j'ai connu des années de ~** I went through some difficult years *ou* years of hardship ◆ **une journée/un voyage ~ *** a hellish * day/trip, a nightmare of a day/trip

galérer * / galeʀe / ► conjug 6 ◄ **VI** 1 *(= travailler dur)* to sweat blood *, to slog * *(Brit)* 2 *(= avoir des difficultés)* to have a lot of hassle *, to have a hard time of it * ◆ **il a galéré pendant des années avant d'être reconnu** he struggled for years before gaining recognition

galerie / galʀi / **NF** 1 *(= couloir) (gén)* gallery; *[de mine]* gallery, level; *[de fourmilière]* gallery; *[de taupinière]* tunnel 2 *(Art) (= magasin)* gallery; *(= salle de musée)* room, gallery; *(= collection)* collection 3 *(Théât = balcon)* circle ◆ **premières/deuxièmes ~s** dress/upper circle ◆ **les troisièmes ~s** the gallery, the gods * *(Brit)* 4 *(= public)* gallery, audience ◆ **il a dit cela pour la ~** he said that for appearances' sake ◆ **pour épater la ~** to show off * *ou* impress people; → **amuser** 5 *[de voiture]* roof rack; *(Archit = balustrade)* gallery

COMP **galerie d'art** art gallery

la galerie des Glaces *(Archit)* the Hall of Mirrors

galerie marchande shopping arcade, shopping mall *(US)*

galerie de peinture picture *ou* art gallery

galerie de portraits *(Littérat)* collection of pen portraits

galerie de tableaux ⇒ **galerie de peinture**

galérien / galeʀjɛ̃ / **NM** *(Hist)* galley slave; *(= SDF)* homeless person ◆ **travailler comme un ~** to work like a (galley) slave

galeriste / galʀist / **NMF** gallery owner

galet / galɛ / **NM** 1 *(= pierre)* pebble ◆ **~s** shingle, pebbles ◆ **plage de ~s** shingle beach 2 *(= roue)* wheel, roller

galetas / galta / **NM** *(= mansarde)* garret; *(= taudis)* hovel

galette / galɛt / **NF** 1 *(Culin) (= gâteau) round, flat biscuit; (Naut)* ship's biscuit ◆ **~ (de sarrasin)** *(= crêpe)* (buckwheat) pancake ◆ **~ de maïs** tortilla ◆ **~ de pommes de terre** potato pancake ◆ **~ des Rois** *cake eaten in France on Twelfth Night*; → **plat¹**; → LES ROIS 2 *(Ciné)* roll 3 (* *= argent*) dough*, bread*, lolly* *(Brit)* ◆ **il a de la ~** he's loaded*, he's rolling in money * 4 (* *= disque compact, CD-Rom*) disk

galeux, -euse / galø, øz / **ADJ** 1 *[personne]* affected with scabies, scabious *(SPÉC)*; *[chien]* mangy; *[mouton, plante, arbre]* scabby; *[plaie]* caused by scabies *ou* the itch; *[éruption]* scabious ◆ **il m'a traité comme un chien ~** he treated me like dirt *ou* as if I was the scum of the earth; → **brebis** 2 *(= sordide) [murs]* peeling, flaking; *[pièce, quartier]* squalid, dingy, seedy **NM,F** *(= personne méprisable)* scum ◆ **pour lui je suis un ~** as far as he's concerned I'm the lowest of the low *ou* the scum of the earth

galhauban / galobɑ̃ / **NM** backstay

Galice / galis / **NF** Galicia *(in Spain)*

Galien / galjɛ̃ / **NM** Galen

Galilée¹ / galile / **NM** Galileo

Galilée² / galile / **NF** Galilee ◆ **la mer de ~** the Sea of Galilee

galiléen¹, -enne¹ / galileɛ̃, ɛn / *(Géog)* **ADJ** Galilean **NM,F** **Galiléen(ne)** Galilean

galiléen², -enne² / galileɛ̃, ɛn / **ADJ** *(Phys, Astron)* Galilean ◆ **satellites ~s** Galilean satellites *ou* moons

galimatias / galimatja / **NM** *(= propos)* gibberish *(NonC)*, twaddle *(Brit) (NonC)*; *(= écrit)* tedious nonsense *(NonC)*, twaddle *(Brit) (NonC)*

galion / galjɔ̃ / **NM** galleon

galipette * / galipɛt / **NF** *(= cabriole)* somersault ◆ **~s** *(hum = ébats)* bedroom romps *(hum)* ◆ **faire des ~s** *(cabrioles)* to somersault, to do somersaults; *(hum : ébats)* to have a romp

galle / gal / **NF** gall ◆ **~ du chêne** oak apple; → **noix**

Galles / gal / **NFPL** → **pays¹, prince**

gallican, e / ga(l)likɑ̃, an / **ADJ, NM,F** Gallican

gallicanisme / ga(l)likanism / **NM** Gallicanism

gallicisme / ga(l)lisism / **NM** *(= idiotisme)* French idiom; *(dans une langue étrangère = calque)* gallicism

gallinacé / galinase / **NM** member of the chicken family, gallinaceous bird *(SPÉC)*; *(hum = poulet)* chicken

gallique / galik / **ADJ** gallic

gallium / galjɔm / **NM** gallium

gallois, e / galwa, waz / **ADJ** Welsh **NM** 1 *(= langue)* Welsh 2 ◆ **Gallois** Welshman ◆ **les Gallois** the Welsh **NF** **Galloise** Welshwoman

gallon / galɔ̃ / **NM** gallon ◆ **~ canadien** *ou* **impérial** *(Can)* Imperial gallon *(4.545 litres)* ◆ **~ américain** US gallon *(3.785 litres)*

gallo-romain, e (mpl **gallo-romains**) / ga(l)loʀɔmɛ̃, ɛn / **ADJ** Gallo-Roman **NM,F** **Gallo-Romain(e)** Gallo-Roman

galoche / galɔʃ / **NF** 1 *(= sabot)* clog; *(= chaussure) wooden-soled shoe*; → **menton** 2 *(Naut)* snatch block

galon / galɔ̃ / **NM** 1 *(Couture)* braid *(NonC)*, piece of braid; *(Mil)* stripe ◆ **il a gagné ses ~s d'homme d'État/de professeur en faisant ...** he earned *ou* won his stripes as a statesman/as a teacher doing ... ◆ **prendre du ~** to get promotion *(Brit)*, to get a promotion *(US)* 2 *(Can)* measuring tape, tape measure

galonné, e / galɔne / (ptp de **galonner**) **ADJ** *(Mil) [manche, uniforme]* with stripes on **NM** *(Mil)* ◆ **un ~ *** a brass hat *

galonner / galɔne / ► conjug 1 ◄ **VT** *[vêtement]* to trim with braid ◆ **robe galonnée d'or** dress trimmed with gold braid

galop / galo / **NM** 1 *(gén)* gallop ◆ **~ d'essai** *(lit)* trial gallop; *(fig)* trial run ◆ **j'ai fait un ~ de quelques minutes** I galloped for a few minutes ◆ **cheval au ~** galloping horse ◆ **prendre le ~, se mettre au ~** to break into a gallop ◆ **mettre son cheval au ~** to put one's horse into a gallop ◆ **partir au ~** *[cheval]* to set off at a gallop; *[personne]* to take off like a shot ◆ **nous avons dîné au ~** we bolted down our dinner ◆ **va chercher tes affaires au ~ !** go and get your things at *(Brit) ou* on *(US)* the double! *ou* and make it snappy! * ◆ **au petit ~** at a canter ◆ **au grand ~** at full gallop ◆ **au triple ~** *[partir, arriver]* at top speed ◆ **elle a rappliqué au triple ~ *** she came in like a shot * 2 *(= danse)* gallopade

galopade / galɔpad / **NF** *(Équitation)* hand gallop; *(= course précipitée)* stampede

galopant, e / galɔpɑ̃, ɑ̃t / **ADJ** *[inflation]* galloping, runaway; *[corruption, criminalité]* rampant ◆ **une croissance démographique ~e** soaring population growth

galoper / galɔpe / ► conjug 1 ◄ **VI** *[cheval]* to gallop; *[imagination]* to run wild, to run riot; *[enfant]* to run ◆ **~ ventre à terre** to gallop flat out *, to go at full gallop ◆ **les enfants galopent dans les couloirs** the children are charging *ou* haring * *(Brit)* along the corridors ◆ **j'ai galopé toute la journée !** * I've been rushing around *ou* haring * *(Brit)* around all day! ◆ **faire ~ qn** *(= presser qn)* to rush sb

galopin * / galɔpɛ̃ / **NM** *(= polisson)* urchin, ragamuffin ◆ **petit ~ !** you little rascal! *ou* ragamuffin!

galuchat / galyʃa / **NM** shagreen

galure * / galyʀ /, **galurin** * / galyʀɛ̃ / **NM** *(= chapeau)* hat, headgear * *(NonC)*

galvaniser / galvanize / ► conjug 1 ◄ **VT** *(Tech)* to galvanize; *(= stimuler) [+ troupes, équipe, foule]* to galvanize (into action) ◆ **pour ~ les énergies** to galvanize people into action

galvanomètre / galvanɔmɛtʀ / **NM** galvanometer

galvanoplastie / galvanoplasti / **NF** *(= reproduction)* electrotyping; *(= dépôt)* electroplating

galvaudé, e / galvode / (ptp de **galvauder**) **ADJ** *[expression]* trite, hackneyed; *[mot]* overused

galvauder / galvode / ► conjug 1 ◄ **VT** *[+ réputation, image]* to tarnish, to sully; *[+ nom]* to bring into disrepute; *[+ talent]* to waste; *[+ expression, mot]* to overuse **VPR** **se galvauder** *(= s'avilir)* to demean o.s., to lower o.s., to compromise o.s.; *[expression]* to become hackneyed; *[mot]* to become trivialized (through overuse)

gambade / gɑ̃bad / **NF** leap, caper ◆ **faire des ~s** *[personne, enfant]* to leap (about), to caper (about), to prance about; *[animal]* to gambol, to leap (about), to frisk about

gambader / gɑ̃bade / ► conjug 1 ◄ **VI** *[animal]* to gambol, to leap (about), to frisk about; *[personne, enfant]* to leap (about), to caper (about), to prance about; *[esprit]* to flit *ou* jump from one idea to another ◆ ~ **de joie** to jump for joy

gambas /gɑ̃bas/ NFPL Mediterranean prawns, gambas

gambe /gɑ̃b/ NF → **viole**

gamberge * /gɑ̃bɛʀʒ/ NF ◆ **la** ~ *(= réflexion)* hard thinking; *(= soucis)* brooding

gamberger * /gɑ̃bɛʀʒe/ ▸ conjug 3 ◂ VI *(= réfléchir)* to think hard; *(= se faire du souci)* to brood ◆ **ça gamberge là-dedans !** your brain is really working overtime! *

gambette /gɑ̃bɛt/ NF *(* = jambe)* leg ◆ **jouer des ~s** to run away, to take to one's heels NM *(= oiseau)* redshank

Gambie /gɑ̃bi/ NF ◆ **la** ~ *(= pays)* The Gambia; *(= fleuve)* the Gambia

gambien, -ienne /gɑ̃bjɛ̃, jɛn/ ADJ Gambian NM,F **Gambien(ne)** Gambian

gambit /gɑ̃bi/ NM *(Échecs)* gambit

gamelle /gamɛl/ NF *[de soldat]* mess tin *(Brit) ou* kit *(US)*; *[d'ouvrier, campeur]* billy-can, billy; *[de chien]* bowl; *(hum = assiette)* dish, plate ◆ **(se) ramasser** *ou* **(se) prendre une** ~ * to fall flat on one's face, to come a cropper * *(Brit)*

gamète /gamɛt/ NM gamete

gamin, e /gamɛ̃, in/ ADJ *(= puéril)* childish; *(= espiègle)* mischievous, playful NM,F *(* = enfant)* kid * ◆ **quand j'étais** ~ when I was a kid * ◆ ~ **des rues/de Paris** street/Paris urchin ◆ **quel** ~ **(tu fais) !** you're so childish!

gaminerie /gaminʀi/ NF *(= espièglerie)* playfulness *(NonC)*; *(= puérilité)* childishness *(NonC)*; *(= farce)* prank ◆ **faire des ~s** to play (mischievous) pranks, to be childish ◆ **arrête tes ~s** stop being so childish

gamma /ga(m)ma/ NM gamma; → **rayon**

gammaglobulines /ga(m)maglɔbylin/ NFPL gamma globulins

gamme /gam/ NF 1 *(= série)* range; *[d'émotions, sentiments]* range, variety ◆ **toute la** ~ the whole range ◆ **produit d'entrée/de milieu de** ~ entry-level/mid-range product ◆ **haut de** ~ *[produit, voiture, magazine, hôtel]* top-of-the-range; *[clientèle, tourisme]* upmarket ◆ **bas de** ~ *[produit, voiture, hôtel]* bottom-of-the-range; *[clientèle, tourisme]* downmarket ◆ **le très haut de** ~ **en chaînes hi-fi** the very top of the range in sound systems 2 *(Mus)* scale ◆ **faire des ~s** *[musicien]* to practise scales ◆ **il a fait ses ~s à la télévision** *(fig)* he cut his teeth in television

gammée /game/ ADJ F → **croix**

ganache /ganaʃ/ NF 1 *(* †)* **(vieille)** ~ *(= imbécile)* (old) fool, (old) duffer * 2 *[de cheval]* lower jaw 3 *(Culin)* ganache

Gand /gɑ̃/ N Ghent

gandin † /gɑ̃dɛ̃/ NM *(péj)* dandy

gang /gɑ̃g/ NM gang *(of crooks)*

Gange /gɑ̃ʒ/ NM ◆ **le** ~ the Ganges

ganglion /gɑ̃glijɔ̃/ NM ganglion ◆ ~ **lymphatique** lymph node ◆ **il a des ~s** he has swollen glands

gangrène /gɑ̃gʀɛn/ NF *(Méd)* gangrene; *(fig)* blight ◆ **avoir la** ~ to have gangrene ◆ **la** ~ **de la corruption** the cancer of corruption

gangrener /gɑ̃gʀəne/, **gangréner** /gɑ̃gʀene/ ▸ conjug 5 ◂ VT 1 *(Méd)* to gangrene 2 *(= corrompre)* to blight ◆ **société gangrenée** society in decay ◆ **la corruption gangrène tout le système** corruption is eating away at *ou* poisoning the entire system ◆ **la violence gangrène tous les rapports sociaux** violence poisons all social relationships VPR **se gangrener** to go gangrenous ◆ **blessure qui se gangrène** wound which is going gangrenous ◆ **membre gangrené** gangrenous limb

gangreneux, -euse /gɑ̃gʀənø, øz/, **gangréneux, -euse** /gɑ̃gʀenø, øz/ ADJ gangrenous

gangster /gɑ̃gstɛʀ/ NM *(= criminel)* gangster, mobster *(US)*; *(péj = escroc)* shark, swindler, crook

gangstérisme /gɑ̃gsteʀism/ NM gangsterism

gangue /gɑ̃g/ NF *[de minerai, pierre]* gangue; *(= carcan)* strait jacket ◆ ~ **de boue** coating *ou* layer of mud

ganja /gɑ̃dʒa/ NF ganja

ganse /gɑ̃s/ NF braid *(NonC)*

ganser /gɑ̃se/ ▸ conjug 1 ◂ VT to braid ◆ **veste gansée de noir** jacket with black braiding

gant /gɑ̃/ NM 1 *(gén)* glove ◆ **~s de caoutchouc** rubber gloves

2 *(locutions)* **remettre les ~s** * to take up boxing again ◆ **cette robe lui va comme un** ~ that dress fits her like a glove ◆ **ton idée/ce rôle lui va comme un** ~ your idea/this role suits him down to the ground ◆ **je ne vais pas prendre des ~s avec lui** I'm not going to pull my punches with him ◆ **tu ferais mieux de prendre des ~s avec lui** you'd better handle him with kid gloves ◆ **il va falloir prendre des ~s pour lui annoncer la nouvelle** we'll have to break the news to him gently ◆ **jeter/relever le** ~ *(lit, fig)* to throw down/take up the gauntlet; → **main, retourner**

COMP **gants de boxe** boxing gloves
gants de chirurgien surgical gloves
gant de crin massage glove
gant de cuisine oven glove
gant de données data glove
gant de jardinage gardening glove
gant de toilette ≃ facecloth *(Brit)*, (face) flannel *(Brit)*, wash cloth *(US)*

gantelet /gɑ̃t(ə)lɛ/ NM *(Mil, Sport)* gauntlet; *[d'artisan]* hand leather

ganter /gɑ̃te/ ▸ conjug 1 ◂ VT *[+ main, personne]* to fit with gloves, to put gloves on ◆ **ganté de cuir** wearing leather gloves ◆ **main gantée de cuir** leather-gloved hand VI ◆ ~ **du 7** to take (a) size 7 in gloves VPR **se ganter** to put on one's gloves

ganterie /gɑ̃tʀi/ NF *(= usine)* glove factory; *(= magasin)* glove shop; *(= commerce)* glove trade; *(= industrie)* glove-making industry

gantier, -ière /gɑ̃tje, jɛʀ/ NM,F glover

garage /gaʀaʒ/ NM garage ◆ **as-tu mis la voiture au** ~ **?** have you put the car in the garage? *ou* away?

COMP **garage d'autobus** bus depot *ou* garage
garage d'avions hangar
garage de *ou* **à bicyclettes** bicycle shed
garage de canots boathouse; → **voie**

garagiste /gaʀaʒist/ NMF *(= propriétaire)* garage owner; *(= mécanicien)* garage mechanic ◆ **le** ~ **m'a dit que ...** the man at the garage *ou* the mechanic told me that ... ◆ **emmener sa voiture chez le** ~ to take one's car to the garage

garance /gaʀɑ̃s/ NF *(= plante, teinture)* madder ADJ INV madder(-coloured)

garant, e /gaʀɑ̃, ɑ̃t/ NM,F *(gén)* *(= personne, état)* guarantor *(de* for); ◆ **servir de** ~ **à qn** *[personne]* to stand surety for sb, to act as guarantor for sb; *[honneur, parole]* to be sb's guarantee ◆ **être** *ou* **se porter** ~ **de qch** *(Jur)* to be answerable *ou* responsible for sth; *(gén)* *(= assurer)* to guarantee sth ◆ **la banque centrale sera la ~e de la stabilité de l'euro** the central bank will guarantee the stability of the euro

garanti, e[1] /gaʀɑ̃ti/ (ptp de **garantir**) ADJ guaranteed ◆ ~ **étanche/trois ans** guaranteed waterproof/for three years ◆ ~ **pièces et main-d'œuvre** guaranteed for parts and labour ◆ ~ **pure laine** warranted *ou* guaranteed pure wool ◆ **c'est** ~ **pour cinq ans** it carries a five-year guarantee, it is guaranteed for five years ◆ **il va refuser, c'est** ~ **(sur facture)** * he'll refuse – it's for sure *ou* it's a cert * *(Brit)*, you can bet your life he'll refuse * ◆ **c'est la migraine ~e** * you're bound to get *ou* it's a surefire way of getting * a headache

garantie[2] /gaʀɑ̃ti/ NF 1 *(Comm)* guarantee ◆ **sous** ~ under guarantee; → **bon², contrat**

2 *(= assurance)* guarantee, guaranty *(SPÉC)*; *(= gage)* security, surety; *(= protection)* safeguard ◆ **ils nous ont donné leur** ~ **que ...** they gave us their guarantee that ... ◆ **si on a la** ~ **qu'ils se conduiront bien** if we have a guarantee *ou* a firm undertaking *(Brit)* that they'll behave ◆ **servir de** ~ *[bijoux]* to act as a surety *ou* security *ou* guarantee; *[otages]* to be used as a security; *[honneur]* to be a guarantee ◆ **donner des ~s** to give guarantees ◆ **il faut prendre des ~s** we have to find sureties *ou* get guarantees ◆ **cette entreprise présente toutes les ~s de sérieux** there is every indication that the firm is reliable ◆ **c'est une** ~ **de succès** it's a guarantee of success ◆ **c'est une** ~ **contre le chômage/l'inflation** it's a safeguard against unemployment/inflation

3 *(= caution)* **donner sa** ~ **à** to guarantee, to stand security *ou* surety for, to be guarantor for

4 *[de police d'assurance]* cover *(NonC)*

5 *(locutions)* **je vous dis ça, mais c'est sans** ~ I can't vouch for what I'm telling you, I can't guarantee that what I'm telling you is right ◆ **j'essaierai de le faire pour jeudi mais sans** ~ I'll try and get it done for Thursday but I can't guarantee it *ou* I'm not making any promises ◆ **ils ont bien voulu essayer de le faire, sans** ~ **de succès** they were quite willing to try and do it, but they couldn't guarantee success

COMP **garantie constitutionnelle** constitutional guarantee
garantie de l'emploi job security
garantie d'exécution performance bond
garanties individuelles guarantees of individual liberties
garantie d'intérêt guaranteed interest
garantie de paiement guarantee of payment

garantir /gaʀɑ̃tiʀ/ GRAMMAIRE ACTIVE 42.1 ▸ conjug 2 ◂ VT 1 *(gén = assurer)* to guarantee; *[+ emprunt]* to guarantee, to secure ◆ ~ **que** to assure *ou* guarantee that ◆ **se** ~ **contre** *[+ vol, incendie, risque]* to insure *ou* cover o.s. against ◆ **je te garantis que ça ne se passera pas comme ça !** * I can assure you things won't turn out like that! ◆ **le poulet sera tendre, le boucher me l'a garanti** the chicken will be tender – the butcher assured me it would be ◆ **je te garantis le fait** I can vouch for the fact 2 *(= protéger)* ~ **qch de** to protect sth from ◆ **se** ~ **les yeux (du soleil)** to protect one's eyes (from the sun) ◆ **se** ~ **contre la pollution/dévaluation** to guard against pollution/currency devaluation

garce ‡ /gaʀs/ NF *(péj)* *(= méchante)* bitch *‡; *(= dévergondée)* slut ‡, tart ‡ *(Brit)* ◆ **qu'est-ce que tu es** ~ **!** you're such a bitch! *‡ ◆ ~ **de tondeuse !** damned ‡ *ou* bloody ‡ *(Brit)* mower!

garçon /gaʀsɔ̃/ NM 1 *(= enfant, fils)* boy ◆ **tu es un grand** ~ **maintenant** you're a big boy now ◆ **traiter qn comme un petit** ~ to treat sb like a child *ou* a little boy ◆ **à côté d'eux, on est des petits ~s** compared with them we're only beginners ◆ **cette fille est un** ~ **manqué** *ou* **un vrai** ~ this girl is a real tomboy

2 *(= jeune homme)* young man ◆ **il est beau** *ou* **joli** ~ he's good looking, he's a good-looking guy * *ou* young man ◆ **eh bien mon** ~ **...** *(hum)* well my boy ... ◆ **c'est un brave** ~ he's a good sort *ou* a nice fellow ◆ **ce** ~ **ira loin** that young man will go far; → **mauvais**

3 (= *commis*) (shop) assistant ◆ ~ **boulanger/boucher** baker's/butcher's assistant; (= *jeune homme*) baker's/butcher's boy ◆ ~ **coiffeur** hairdresser's assistant *ou* junior
4 (= *serveur*) waiter
5 († = *célibataire*) bachelor ◆ **être/rester** ~ to be/remain single *ou* a bachelor ◆ **vivre en** ~ to lead a bachelor's life; → **enterrer, vie, vieux**
COMP **garçon d'ascenseur** lift (*Brit*) *ou* elevator (*US*) attendant; (= *jeune homme*) lift (*Brit*) *ou* elevator (*US*) boy
garçon de bureau † office assistant
garçon de cabine cabin boy
garçon de café waiter
garçon de courses messenger; (= *jeune homme*) errand boy
garçon d'écurie stable boy *ou* lad (*Brit*)
garçon d'étage boots (*sg*) (*Brit*), bellhop (*US*)
garçon de ferme farm hand
garçon d'honneur best man
garçon de laboratoire laboratory assistant
garçon livreur delivery man; (= *jeune homme*) delivery boy
garçon de recettes bank messenger
garçon de salle waiter

garçonne /gaʀsɔn/ **à la garçonne** LOC ADJ, LOC ADV ◆ **coupe** *ou* **coiffure à la** ~ urchin cut ◆ **être coiffée à la** ~ to have an urchin cut

garçonnet /gaʀsɔnɛ/ NM small boy ◆ **taille** ~ boy's size ◆ **rayon** ~ boys' department

garçonnière /gaʀsɔnjɛʀ/ NF bachelor flat (*Brit*) *ou* apartment (*US*)

Garde /gaʀd/ N ◆ **le lac de** ~ Lake Garda

garde[1] /gaʀd/ NF 1 (= *surveillance*) **on lui avait confié la** ~ **des bagages/des prisonniers** he had been put in charge of the luggage/the prisoners, he had been given the job of looking after *ou* of guarding the luggage/the prisoners ◆ **il s'est chargé de la** ~ **des bagages/des prisonniers** he undertook to look after *ou* to guard *ou* to keep an eye on the luggage/the prisoners ◆ **la** ~ **des frontières est assurée par ...** the task *ou* job of guarding the frontiers is carried out by ... ◆ **confier qch/qn à la** ~ **de qn** to entrust sth/sb to sb's care, to leave sth/sb in sb's care ◆ **être sous la** ~ **de la police** to be under police guard ◆ **être/mettre qn sous bonne** ~ to be/put sb under guard
2 (*Jur : après divorce*) custody ◆ **elle a eu la** ~ **des enfants** she got *ou* was given (the) custody of the children ◆ ~ **alternée/conjointe** alternating/joint custody
3 (= *veille*) [*de soldat*] guard duty; [*d'infirmière*] ward duty; [*de médecin*] duty period ◆ **sa** ~ **a duré douze heures** (*soldat*) he was on guard duty for 12 hours; (*médecin, infirmier*) he was on duty for 12 hours ◆ **assurer 15 ~s par mois** [*médecin*] to be on call *ou* on duty 15 times a month ◆ **(être) de** ~ [*infirmière, sentinelle*] (to be) on duty; [*médecin, pharmacien*] (to be) on call *ou* on duty ◆ **pharmacie de** ~ duty chemist (*Brit*) *ou* pharmacist (*US*) ◆ **quel est le médecin de** ~ **?** who is the doctor on call?; → **chien, monter**[1], **poste**[2]
4 (= *conservation*) **être de bonne** ~ [*aliment, boisson*] to keep well ◆ **vin de** ~ wine for laying down, wine that will benefit from being kept
5 (= *groupe, escorte*) guard ◆ ~ **rapprochée** [*de président*] personal bodyguard ◆ ~ **descendante/montante** old/relief guard; → **corps, relever** *etc*
6 (= *infirmière*) nurse ◆ ~ **de jour/de nuit** day/night nurse
7 (*Boxe, Escrime*) guard ◆ **~s** (*Escrime*) positions ◆ **avoir/tenir la** ~ **haute** to have/keep one's guard up ◆ **fermer/ouvrir sa** ~ to close/open one's guard ◆ **baisser sa** ~ (*lit*) to lower one's guard; (*fig*) to drop one's guard
8 [*d'épée*] hilt, guard ◆ **jusqu'à la** ~ (*lit*) (up) to the hilt
9 (*Typo*) **(page de)** ~ flyleaf
10 [*de serrure*] **~s** wards
11 (= *espace*) ~ **au sol** [*de voiture*] ground clearance; [*d'avion*] vertical clearance ◆ ~ **au toit** headroom ◆ ~ **d'embrayage** clutch linkage *ou* pedal play ◆ **laisser une** ~ **suffisante à la pédale** to allow enough play on the pedal
12 (*Cartes*) **avoir la** ~ **à cœur** to have a stop (*Brit*) *ou* covering card (*US*) in hearts
13 (*locutions*) **être/se mettre/se tenir sur ses ~s** to be/put o.s./stay on one's guard ◆ **n'avoir** ~ **de faire** (*littér*) to take good care not to do, to make sure one doesn't do ◆ **faire bonne** ~ to keep a close watch
◆ **en + garde** ◆ **en** ~ **!** (*Escrime*) on guard! ◆ **se mettre en** ~ to take one's guard ◆ **mettre qn en** ~ to put sb on his guard, to warn sb (*contre* against); ◆ **mise en** ~ warning ◆ **prendre en** ~ [+ *enfant, animal*] to take into one's care, to look after ◆ **ils nous ont laissé leur enfant en** ~ they left their child in our care ◆ **Dieu vous ait en sa (sainte)** ~ (may) God be with you
◆ **prendre garde** ◆ **prendre** ~ **de** *ou* **à ne pas faire** to be careful *ou* take care not to do ◆ **prenez** ~ **de (ne pas) tomber** be careful *ou* take care you don't fall *ou* not to fall, mind you don't fall (*Brit*) ◆ **prends** ~ **!** (*exhortation*) watch out!; (*menace*) watch it! * ◆ **prends** ~ **à toi** watch yourself, take care ◆ **prends** ~ **aux voitures** be careful of *ou* watch out for *ou* mind the cars ◆ **sans prendre** ~ **au danger** without considering *ou* heeding the danger ◆ **sans y prendre** ~ without realizing it
COMP **garde d'enfants** (= *personne*) child minder (*Brit*), day-care worker (*US*); (= *activité*) child minding (*Brit*), day care (*US*)
garde d'honneur guard of honour
garde impériale Imperial Guard
garde judiciaire legal surveillance (*of impounded property*)
garde juridique legal liability
garde mobile anti-riot police
garde municipale *municipal guard*
garde pontificale Papal Guard
garde républicaine Republican Guard
garde à vue ≃ police custody ◆ **être mis** *ou* **placé en** ~ **à vue** ≃ to be kept in police custody, to be held for questioning

garde[2] /gaʀd/ NM 1 [*de locaux, prisonnier*] guard; [*de domaine, château*] warden (*Brit*), keeper (*US*); [*de jardin public*] keeper 2 (*Mil* = *soldat*) guardsman; (*Hist*) guard, guardsman; (= *sentinelle*) guard
COMP **garde champêtre** rural policeman
garde du corps bodyguard
garde forestier ≃ forest warden (*Brit*), (park) ranger (*US*), forester
garde impérial imperial guard *ou* guardsman
garde maritime coastguard
garde mobile member of the anti-riot police
garde municipal municipal guard *ou* guardsman
garde pontifical papal guard *ou* guardsman
garde républicain Republican guard *ou* guardsman, member of the Republican Guard
garde rouge Red Guard
Garde des Sceaux French Minister of Justice, ≃ Lord Chancellor (*Brit*), Attorney General (*US*); (*Hist*) ≃ Keeper of the Seals; → aussi **garder**

gardé, e /gaʀde/ (ptp de **garder**) ADJ ◆ **passage à niveau ~/non** ~ manned/unmanned level crossing ◆ **cabane ~e/non ~e** (*Alpinisme*) hut with/without resident warden; → **chasse**[1], **proportion**

garde-à-vous /gaʀdavu/ NM INV (*Mil*) (= *action*) standing to attention (*NonC*); (= *cri*) order to stand to attention ◆ ~ **fixe !** attention! ◆ **ils exécutèrent des** ~ **impeccables** they stood to attention faultlessly ◆ **rester/se mettre au** ~ (*Mil, fig*) to stand at/stand to attention

garde-barrière (pl **gardes-barrières**) /gaʀd(ə)baʀjɛʀ/ NMF level-crossing keeper

garde-boue /gaʀdəbu/ NM INV mudguard (*Brit*), fender (*US*)

garde-chasse (pl **gardes-chasse(s)**) /gaʀdəʃas/ NM gamekeeper

garde-chiourme (pl **gardes-chiourme**) /gaʀdəʃjuʀm/ NM (*Hist*) warder (*of galley slaves*); (*fig*) martinet

garde-corps /gaʀdəkɔʀ/ NM INV (*Naut*) lifeline, manrope; (= *rambarde*) (*en fer*) railing; (*en pierre*) parapet

garde-côte (pl **garde-côtes**) /gaʀdəkot/ NM (= *navire*) (*Mil*) coastguard ship; (= *vedette garde-pêche*) fisheries protection launch *ou* craft; (= *personne*) coastguard

garde-feu (pl **garde-feu(x)**) /gaʀdəfø/ NM fireguard

garde-fou (pl **garde-fous**) /gaʀdəfu/ NM (*en fer*) railing; (*en pierre*) parapet; (*fig*) safeguard (*contre, à* against); ◆ **servir de** ~ to act as a safeguard

garde-frein (pl **gardes-frein(s)**) /gaʀdəfʀɛ̃/ NM guard, brakeman

garde-frontière (pl **gardes-frontières**) /gaʀd(ə)fʀɔ̃tjɛʀ/ NMF border guard

garde-magasin (pl **gardes-magasins**) /gaʀd(ə)magazɛ̃/ NM (*Mil*) ≃ quartermaster; (= *magasinier*) warehouseman

garde-malade (pl **gardes-malades**) /gaʀd(ə)malad/ NMF home nurse

garde-manger /gaʀd(ə)mɑ̃ʒe/ NM INV (= *armoire*) meat safe (*Brit*), cooler (*US*); (= *pièce*) pantry, larder

garde-meuble (pl **garde-meubles**) /gaʀdəmœbl/ NM storehouse, furniture depository (*Brit*) ◆ **mettre une armoire au** ~ to put a wardrobe in storage *ou* in store (*Brit*)

gardénal ® /gaʀdenal/ NM phenobarbitone (*Brit*), phenobarbital (*US*), Luminal ®

gardénia /gaʀdenja/ NM gardenia

garde-pêche /gaʀdəpɛʃ/ NM (= *personne*) water bailiff (*Brit*), fish (and game) warden (*US*) NM INV (= *frégate*) fisheries protection vessel ◆ **vedette** ~ fisheries protection launch *ou* craft

garde-port (pl **gardes-ports**) /gaʀdəpɔʀ/ NM wharf master, harbour master

garder /gaʀde/ ► conjug 1 ◄ VT 1 (= *surveiller*) [+ *enfants, magasin*] to look after, to mind; [+ *bestiaux*] to look after, to guard; [+ *bagages*] to look after, to watch over; [+ *trésor, prisonnier*] to guard, to watch over; (= *défendre*) [+ *frontière, passage, porte*] to guard ◆ **le chien garde la maison** the dog guards the house ◆ ~ **des enfants** (*métier*) to be a child minder (*Brit*) *ou* day-care worker (*US*) ◆ **garde ma valise pendant que j'achète un livre** look after *ou* keep an eye on my suitcase while I buy a book ◆ **on n'a pas gardé les cochons ensemble !** * you've got a nerve(, we hardly know each other)! * ◆ **toutes les issues sont gardées** all the exits are guarded, a watch is being kept on all the exits ◆ **une statue gardait l'entrée** a statue stood at the entrance *ou* guarded the entrance
2 (= *ne pas quitter*) ~ **la chambre** to stay in *ou* keep to one's room ◆ ~ **le lit** to stay in bed ◆ **un rhume lui a fait** ~ **la chambre** he stayed in his room because of his cold, his cold kept him at home *ou* in his room
3 [+ *denrées, marchandises, papiers*] to keep ◆ **gardez la monnaie** keep the change ◆ **ces fleurs ne gardent pas leur parfum** these flowers lose their scent ◆ **il garde tout** he holds on to everything, he never throws anything out ◆ **il ne peut rien** ~ (*gén*) he can't keep anything; (= *il vomit*) he can't keep anything down

4 *(= conserver sur soi) [+ vêtement]* to keep on ◆ **gardez donc votre chapeau** do keep your hat on

5 *(= retenir) [+ personne, employé, client]* to keep; *[police]* to detain ◆ ~ **qn à vue** *(Jur)* ≈ to keep sb in custody ◆ ~ **qn à déjeuner** to have sb stay for lunch ◆ ~ **un élève en retenue** to keep a pupil in, to keep a pupil in detention ◆ **il m'a gardé une heure au téléphone** he kept me on the phone for an hour

6 *(= mettre de côté)* to keep, to put aside *ou* to one side; *(= réserver) [+ place] (pendant absence)* to keep (*à, pour* for); *(avant l'arrivée d'une personne)* to save, to keep (*à, pour* for); ◆ **je lui ai gardé une côtelette pour ce soir** I've kept *ou* saved a chop for him for tonight ◆ **j'ai gardé de la soupe pour demain** I've kept *ou* saved *ou* I've put aside some soup for tomorrow ◆ ~ **le meilleur pour la fin** to keep the best till the end ◆ ~ **une poire pour la soif** to keep *ou* save something for a rainy day; → **chien, dent**

7 *(= maintenir)* to keep ◆ ~ **les yeux baissés/la tête haute** to keep one's eyes down/one's head up ◆ ~ **un chien enfermé/en laisse** to keep a dog shut in/on a leash

8 *(= ne pas révéler)* to keep ◆ ~ **le secret** to keep the secret ◆ ~ **ses pensées pour soi** to keep one's thoughts to oneself ◆ **gardez cela pour vous** keep it to yourself, keep it under your hat* ◆ **gardez vos réflexions** *ou* **remarques pour vous** keep your comments to yourself

9 *(= conserver) [+ souplesse, élasticité, fraîcheur]* to keep, to retain; *[+ jeunesse, droits, facultés]* to retain; *[+ habitudes, apparences]* to keep up; *[+ emploi]* to keep ◆ **il a gardé toutes ses facultés** *ou* **toute sa tête** he still has all his faculties, he's still in full possession of his faculties ◆ ~ **le jeûne** to observe *ou* keep the fast ◆ ~ **son calme** to keep *ou* remain calm ◆ ~ **la tête froide** to keep a cool head, to keep one's head ◆ ~ **ses distances** to keep one's distance ◆ ~ **un bon souvenir de qch** to have happy memories of sth ◆ ~ **sa raison** to keep one's sanity ◆ ~ **le silence** to keep silent *ou* silence ◆ ~ **l'espoir** to keep hoping ◆ ~ **l'anonymat** to remain anonymous ◆ ~ **la ligne** to keep one's figure ◆ ~ **rancune à qn** to bear sb a grudge ◆ **j'ai eu du mal à** ~ **mon sérieux** I had a job keeping *ou* to keep a straight face ◆ ~ **les idées claires** to keep a clear head

10 *(= protéger)* ~ **qn de l'erreur/de ses amis** to save sb from error/from his friends ◆ **ça vous gardera du froid** it'll protect you from the cold ◆ **Dieu** *ou* **le Ciel vous garde** God be with you ◆ **la châsse qui garde ces reliques** the shrine which houses these relics

VPR **se garder** 1 *[denrées]* to keep ◆ **ça se garde bien** it keeps well

2 ◆ **se** ~ **de qch** *(= se défier de)* to beware of *ou* be wary of sth; *(= se protéger de)* to protect o.s. from sth, to guard against sth ◆ **gardez-vous de décisions trop promptes/de vos amis** beware *ou* be wary of hasty decisions/of your own friends ◆ **se** ~ **de faire qch** to be careful not to do sth ◆ **elle s'est bien gardée de le prévenir** she was very careful not to tell him, she carefully avoided telling him ◆ **vous allez lui parler ? – je m'en garderai bien !** are you going to speak to him? – that's one thing I won't do! *ou* that's the last thing I'd do!

garderie /gardəri/ NF ◆ ~ **(d'enfants)** *(jeunes enfants)* day nursery *(Brit)*, day-care center *(US)*; *(Scol)* ≈ after-school club *(Brit)*, after-school center *(US) (child-minding service operating outside school hours while parents are working)*

garde-robe (pl **garde-robes**) /gardərɔb/ NF *(= habits)* wardrobe ◆ **il faut que je renouvelle ma** ~ I need a whole new wardrobe

gardeur, -euse /gardœr, øz/ NM, F ◆ ~ **de troupeaux** herdsman ◆ ~ **de vaches** cowherd ◆ ~ **de chèvres** goatherd ◆ ~ **de cochons** swineherd

garde-voie (pl **gardes-voies**) /gardəvwa/ NM *(Rail)* line guard

gardian /gardjɑ̃/ NM herdsman *(in the Camargue)*

gardien, -ienne /gardjɛ̃, jɛn/ NM,F 1 *[de propriété, château]* warden *(Brit)*, keeper *(US)*; *[d'usine, locaux]* guard; *[d'hôtel]* attendant; *[de cimetière]* caretaker, keeper; *[de jardin public, zoo]* keeper; *[de réserve naturelle]* warden; *[de prisonnier]* guard; *[de bovins]* cowherd

2 *(= défenseur)* guardian, protector ◆ **la constitution, gardienne des libertés** the constitution, protector *ou* guardian of freedom ◆ **les ~s de la Constitution** the guardians of the Constitution; → **ange**

COMP **gardien(ne) (de but)** goalkeeper, goalie*

gardienne (d'enfants) child minder *(Brit)*, day-care worker *(US)*

gardien(-ne) (d'immeuble) caretaker *(of a block of flats) (Brit)*, (apartment house) manager *(US)*

gardien(ne) de musée museum attendant

gardien de nuit night watchman

gardien de la paix policeman, patrolman *(US)*

gardienne de la paix policewoman, patrolwoman *(US)*

gardien(ne) de phare lighthouse keeper

gardien (de prison) prison officer *(Brit) ou* guard *(US)*

gardienne (de prison) prison officer *ou* wardress *(Brit) ou* guard *(US)*

gardien du temple *(fig)* keeper of the flame

gardiennage /gardjenaʒ/ NM *[d'immeuble]* caretaking; *[de locaux]* guarding; *[de port]* security ◆ ~ **électronique** electronic surveillance ◆ **société de** ~ **et de surveillance** security company

gardon /gardɔ̃/ NM roach; → **frais**[1]

gare[1] /gar/ NF *(Rail)* station ◆ ~ **d'arrivée/de départ** station of arrival/of departure ◆ ~ **de marchandises/de voyageurs** goods *(Brit) ou* freight *(US)*/passenger station ◆ **le train entre/est en** ~ the train is coming in/is in ◆ **l'express de Dijon entre en** ~ **sur la voie 6** the express from Dijon is now approaching platform 6 ◆ **littérature/roman de** ~ *(péj)* pulp literature/novel; → **chef**[1]

COMP **gare fluviale** canal *ou* river basin

gare de fret cargo terminal

gare maritime harbour station

gare routière *[de camions]* haulage depot; *[d'autocars]* coach *(Brit) ou* bus *(US)* station

gare de triage marshalling yard

gare[2]* /gar/ EXCL *(= attention)* ◆ ~ **à toi !,** ~ **à tes fesses !**‡ (just) watch it!* ◆ ~ **à toi** *ou* **à tes fesses**‡ **si tu recommences !** you'll be in for it if you do that again!* ◆ ~ **au premier qui bouge !** whoever makes the first move will be in trouble!, the first one to move will be for it!* *(Brit)* ◆ **et fais ce que je dis, sinon** ~ **!** and do what I say, or else!* ◆ ~ **à ne pas recommencer !** just make sure you don't do it again! ◆ **la porte est basse,** ~ **à ta tête** it's a low door so (be) careful you don't bang your head *ou* mind *(Brit)* (you don't bang) your head ◆ ~ **aux conséquences/à ce type** beware of the consequences/of him; → **crier**

garenne /garɛn/ NF rabbit warren; → **lapin**

NM wild rabbit

garer /gare/ ► conjug 1 ◄ VT *[+ véhicule]* to park; *[+ train]* to put into a siding; *[+ embarcation]* to dock; *[+ récolte]* to (put into) store VPR **se garer**

1 *[automobiliste]* to park 2 *(= se ranger de côté) [véhicule, automobiliste]* to draw into the side, to pull over; *[piéton]* to move aside, to get out of the way 3 *(* = éviter)* **se** ~ **de qch/qn** to avoid sth/sb, to steer clear of sth/sb

Gargantua /gargɑ̃tɥa/ NM Gargantua ◆ **c'est un** ~ he has a gargantuan *ou* gigantic appetite

gargantuesque /gargɑ̃tɥɛsk/ ADJ *[appétit, repas]* gargantuan, gigantic

gargariser (se) /gargarize/ ► conjug 1 ◄ VPR to gargle ◆ **se** ~ **de** *(péj = se vanter de)* to crow over *ou* about ◆ **se** ~ **de grands mots** to revel in big words

gargarisme /gargarism/ NM gargle ◆ **se faire un** ~ to gargle

gargote /gargɔt/ NF *(péj)* cheap restaurant *ou* eating-house, greasy spoon*

gargotier, -ière /gargɔtje, jɛr/ NM,F *(= aubergiste)* owner of a greasy spoon*

gargouille /garguj/ NF *(Archit)* gargoyle; *(Constr)* waterspout

gargouillement /gargujmɑ̃/ NM ⇒ **gargouillis**

gargouiller /garguje/ ► conjug 1 ◄ VI *[eau]* to gurgle; *[intestin]* to rumble

gargouillis /garguji/ NM *(gén pl) [d'eau]* gurgling *(NonC)*; *[d'intestin]* rumbling *(NonC)* ◆ **faire des** ~ *[eau]* to gurgle; *[intestin]* to rumble

gargoulette /gargulɛt/ NF *(= vase)* earthenware water jug

garnement /garnəmɑ̃/ NM *(= gamin)* (young) imp; *(= adolescent)* tearaway *(Brit)*, hellion *(US)* ◆ **petit** ~ **!** you little rascal!

garni, e /garni/ (ptp de **garnir**) ADJ 1 *(= rempli)* **bien** ~ *[réfrigérateur, bibliothèque]* well-stocked; *[bourse]* well-lined; *[+ portefeuille]* well-filled, well-lined ◆ **il a encore une chevelure bien ~e** he has still got a good head of hair 2 *[plat, viande] (de légumes)* served with vegetables; *(de frites)* served with French fries *ou* chips *(Brit)* ◆ **cette entrecôte est bien ~e** there's a generous helping of French fries *ou* chips *(Brit)* with this steak; → **bouquet**[1], **choucroute** 3 († = *meublé) [chambre]* furnished NM † furnished accommodation *ou* rooms *(for renting)*

garnir /garnir/ ► conjug 2 ◄ VT 1 *(= protéger, équiper)* ~ **de** to fit out with ◆ ~ **une porte d'acier** to fit *ou* reinforce a door with steel plate ◆ ~ **une canne d'un embout** to put a tip on the end of a walking stick ◆ ~ **une muraille de canons** to range cannons along a wall ◆ ~ **une boîte de tissu** to line a box with material ◆ ~ **un mur de pointes** to arm a wall with spikes, to set spikes along a wall ◆ **mur garni de canons/pointes** wall bristling with cannons/spikes

2 *[chose] (= couvrir)* **l'acier qui garnit la porte** the steel plate covering the door ◆ **les canons qui garnissent la muraille** the cannons lining the wall *ou* ranged along the wall ◆ **des pointes garnissent le mur** there are spikes set in the wall ◆ **le cuir qui garnit la poignée** the leather covering the handle ◆ **coffret garni de velours** casket lined with velvet, velvet-lined casket

3 *(= approvisionner) [+ boîte, caisse]* to fill *(de* with); *[+ réfrigérateur]* to stock *(de* with); *[+ chaudière]* to stoke *(de* with); *[+ hameçon]* to bait *(de* with); ◆ **le cuisinier garnissait les plats de charcuterie** the cook was setting out *ou* putting cold meat on the plates ◆ ~ **de livres une bibliothèque** to stock *ou* fill (the shelves of) a library with books ◆ ~ **les remparts** *(Mil)* to garrison the ramparts

4 *(= remplir) [+ boîte]* to fill; *(= recouvrir) [+ surface, rayon]* to cover, to fill ◆ **une foule dense garnissait les trottoirs** a dense crowd covered *ou* packed the pavements ◆ **les chocolats qui garnissaient la boîte** the chocolates which filled the box ◆ **boîte garnie de chocolats** box full of chocolates ◆ **plats garnis de tranches de viande** plates filled with *ou* full of slices of meat

5 [+ siège] (= canner) to cane; (= rembourrer) to pad
6 (= enjoliver) [+ vêtement] to trim; [+ étagère] to decorate; [+ aliment] to garnish (de with); ◆ ~ **une jupe d'un volant** to trim a skirt with a frill ◆ ~ **une table de fleurs** to decorate a table with flowers ◆ **les bibelots qui garnissent la cheminée** the trinkets which decorate the mantelpiece ◆ **des plats joliment garnis de charcuterie** plates nicely laid out with cold meat ◆ **des côtelettes garnies de cresson** chops garnished with cress
VPR **se garnir** [salle, pièce] to fill up (de with); ◆ **la salle commençait à se** ~ the room was beginning to fill up

garnison /gaʀnizɔ̃/ NF (= troupes) garrison ◆ **(ville de)** ~ garrison town ◆ **vie de** ~ garrison life ◆ **être en** ~ **à, tenir** ~ **à** to be stationed *ou* garrisoned at

garniture /gaʀnityʀ/ NF 1 (= décoration) [de robe, chapeau] trimming (NonC); [de table] set of table linen; [de coffret] lining ◆ ~ **intérieure** [de voiture] upholstery, interior trim
2 (Culin) (= légumes) vegetables; (= sauce à vol-au-vent) filling ◆ **servi avec** ~ served with vegetables, vegetables included ◆ **pour la** ~**, vous avez des carottes ou des pois** you have a choice of carrots or peas as a vegetable
3 (Typo) furniture
4 (Tech = protection) [de chaudière] lagging (NonC); [de boîte] covering (NonC) ◆ **avec** ~ **de caoutchouc/cuir** with rubber/leather fittings *ou* fitments ◆ ~ **d'embrayage/de frein** clutch/brake lining ◆ **changer les** ~**s de freins** to reline the brakes, to change the brake linings
COMP **garniture de cheminée** mantelpiece ornaments
garniture de foyer (set of) fire irons
garniture de lit (set of) bed linen
garniture périodique sanitary towel (Brit) *ou* napkin (US)
garniture de toilette toilet set

Garonne /gaʀɔn/ NF ◆ **la** ~ the Garonne

garrigue /gaʀig/ NF garrigue, scrubland (*typical of the Mediterranean landscape*)

garrot /gaʀo/ NM [de cheval] withers; (Méd) tourniquet; (= supplice) garrotte ◆ **poser un** ~ to apply a tourniquet (à qn to sb)

garrotter /gaʀɔte/ ► conjug 1 ◄ VT (= attacher) to tie up; († = censurer) [+ presse] to gag

gars * /gɑ/ NM 1 (= enfant, fils) boy, lad (Brit) ◆ **les petits** ~ **du quartier** the local youths ◆ **dis-moi mon** ~ tell me son *ou* sonny * 2 (= type) guy *, bloke * (Brit) ◆ **un drôle de** ~ an odd guy *ou* customer * ◆ **allons-y, les** ~ **!** come on, guys * *ou* lads * (Brit)!

Gascogne /gaskɔɲ/ NF Gascony; → **golfe**

gascon, -onne /gaskɔ̃, ɔn/ ADJ Gascon NM (= dialecte) Gascon NM,F **Gascon(ne)** Gascon; → **promesse**

gasconnade /gaskɔnad/ NF (littér = vantardise) boasting (NonC), bragging (NonC)

gasoil, gas-oil /gazwal, gɑzɔjl/ NM diesel oil

gaspacho /gaspatʃo/ NM gazpacho

gaspillage /gaspijaʒ/ NM (= action) wasting; (= résultat) waste ◆ **quel** ~ **!** what a waste! ◆ **un immense** ~ **des ressources naturelles** an enormous waste of natural resources

gaspiller /gaspije/ ► conjug 1 ◄ VT [+ eau, nourriture, temps, ressources] to waste; [+ fortune, argent, dons, talent] to waste, to squander ◆ **il gaspille inutilement ses forces/son énergie** he's wasting his strength/energy ◆ **qu'est-ce que tu gaspilles !** you're so wasteful!

gaspilleur, -euse /gaspijœʀ, øz/ ADJ wasteful NM,F [d'eau, nourriture, temps, dons] waster; [de fortune] squanderer ◆ **quel** ~ he's so wasteful

gastéropode /gasteʀɔpɔd/ NM gastropod ◆ ~**s** Gastropoda (SPÉC)

gastralgie /gastʀalʒi/ NF stomach pains, gastralgia (SPÉC)

gastrine /gastʀin/ NF gastrin

gastrique /gastʀik/ ADJ gastric; → **embarras**

gastrite /gastʀit/ NF gastritis

gastro-duodénal, e (mpl **-aux**) /gastʀodɥɔdenal, o/ ADJ gastro-duodenal

gastroentérite /gastʀoɑ̃teʀit/ NF gastroenteritis (NonC)

gastroentérologie /gastʀoɑ̃teʀɔlɔʒi/ NF gastroenterology

gastroentérologue /gastʀoɑ̃teʀɔlɔg/ NMF gastroenterologist

gastro-intestinal, e (mpl **-aux**) /gastʀoɛ̃tɛstinal, o/ ADJ gastrointestinal

gastronome /gastʀɔnɔm/ NMF gourmet, gastronome

gastronomie /gastʀɔnɔmi/ NF gastronomy

gastronomique /gastʀɔnɔmik/ ADJ gastronomic; → **menu**[1]**, restaurant**

gastroplastie /gastʀoplasti/ NF gastroplasty, stomach stapling

gâté, e /gɑte/ (ptp de **gâter**) ADJ [enfant, fruit] spoilt ◆ **dent** ~**e** bad tooth ◆ **avoir les dents** ~**es** to have bad teeth

gâteau (pl **gâteaux**) /gɑto/ NM 1 (= pâtisserie) cake; (= génoise fourrée, forêt-noire) gateau; (Helv = tarte) tart ◆ ~ **d'anniversaire/aux amandes** birthday/almond cake ◆ ~**x (à) apéritif** (small) savoury biscuits, appetizers ◆ ~**x secs** biscuits (Brit), cookies (US) ◆ ~ **de semoule/ de riz** semolina/rice pudding; → **petit**
2 (** = butin, héritage) loot** ◆ **se partager le** ~ to share out the loot** ◆ **vouloir sa part du** ~ to want one's share of the loot** *ou* a fair share of the cake *ou* a piece of the pie * (US)
3 ◆ **c'est du** ~ * it's a piece of cake * *ou* a doddle * (Brit), it's a snap * (US) ◆ **pour lui, c'est du** ~ * it's a piece of cake for him *, that's pie * to him (US) ◆ **c'est pas du** ~ * it's no picnic *
4 (de plâtre) cake ◆ ~ **de miel** *ou* **de cire** honeycomb
ADJ INV (* = indulgent) soft ◆ **c'est un papa** ~ he's a real softie * of a dad

gâter /gɑte/ ► conjug 1 ◄ VT 1 (= abîmer) [+ paysage, visage, plaisir, goût] to ruin, to spoil; [+ esprit, jugement] to have a harmful effect on ◆ **la chaleur a gâté la viande** the heat has made the meat go bad *ou* go off (Brit) ◆ **tu vas te** ~ **les dents** you'll ruin your teeth ◆ **et, ce qui ne gâte rien, elle est jolie** and she's pretty to boot, and she's pretty, which is an added bonus *ou* is even better
2 (= choyer) [+ enfant] to spoil ◆ **nous avons été gâtés cette année, il a fait très beau** we've been really lucky *ou* we've been spoilt this year – the weather has been lovely ◆ **il pleut, on est gâté !** (iro) just our luck! – it's raining! ◆ **il n'est pas gâté par la nature** he hasn't been blessed by nature ◆ **la vie ne l'a pas gâté** life hasn't been very kind to him
VPR **se gâter** [viande] to go bad, to go off (Brit); [fruit] to go bad; [temps] to change (for the worse), to take a turn for the worse; [ambiance, relations] to take a turn for the worse ◆ **le temps va se** ~ the weather's going to change for the worse *ou* going to break ◆ **ça commence** *ou* **les choses commencent à se** ~ **(entre eux)** things are beginning to go wrong (between them) ◆ **mon père vient de rentrer, ça va se** ~ **!** my father has just come in and there's going to be trouble! *ou* things are going to turn nasty!

gâterie /gɑtʀi/ NF little treat ◆ **je me suis payé une petite** ~ (objet) I've treated myself to a little something, I've bought myself a little present; (sucrerie) I've bought myself a little treat

gâte-sauce (pl **gâte-sauces**) /gɑtsos/ NM (= apprenti) kitchen boy; (péj) bad cook

gâteux, -euse * /gɑtø, øz/ ADJ (= sénile) [vieillard] senile, gaga *, doddering ◆ **il l'aime tellement qu'il en est** ~ he's really quite besotted with her, he's dotty * (Brit) about her ◆ **son petit-fils l'a rendu** ~ he's gone soft * over his grandson NM ◆ **(vieux)** ~ (= sénile) dotard, doddering old man; (péj = radoteur, imbécile) silly old duffer * NF ◆ **(vieille) gâteuse** (= sénile) doddering old woman; (péj) silly old bag * *ou* woman

gâtifier * /gɑtifje/ ► conjug 7 ◄ VI to go soft in the head *

gâtisme /gɑtism/ NM [de vieillard] senility; [de personne stupide] idiocy, stupidity

GATT /gat/ NM (abrév de **General Agreement on Tariffs and Trade**) GATT

gatter * /gate/ ► conjug 1 ◄ VI (Helv Scol) to play truant

gauche[1] /goʃ/ ADJ (après nom) [bras, chaussure, côté, rive] left ◆ **du côté** ~ on the left(-hand) side ◆ **habiter au troisième** ~ to live on the third floor on the left; → **arme, lever**[1]**, main, marier**
NM (Boxe) (= coup) left ◆ **direct du** ~ (= poing) straight left ◆ **crochet du** ~ left hook
NF 1 (= côté) **la** ~ the left (side), the left-hand side ◆ **à** ~ on the left; (direction) to the left ◆ **à ma/sa** ~ on my/his left, on my/his left-hand side ◆ **le tiroir/chemin de** ~ the left-hand drawer/path ◆ **rouler à** ~ *ou* **sur la** ~ to drive on the left ◆ **de** ~ **à droite** from left to right ◆ **mettre de l'argent à** ~ †* to put money aside (on the quiet); *pour autres loc voir* **droit**[1]
2 (Pol) **la** ~ the left ◆ **la** ~ **caviar** champagne socialists ◆ **la** ~ **plurielle** *generic name for the French Left, which is made up of various different parties* ◆ **les** ~**s** the parties of the left ◆ **homme de** ~ man of the left, left-winger ◆ **candidat/idées de** ~ left-wing candidate/ideas ◆ **elle est très à** ~ she's very left-wing

gauche[2] /goʃ/ ADJ 1 (= maladroit) [personne, style, geste] awkward, clumsy; (= emprunté) [air, manière] awkward, gauche 2 (= tordu) [planche, règle] warped; (Math = courbe) [surface] skew

gauchement /goʃmɑ̃/ ADV clumsily, awkwardly

gaucher, -ère /goʃe, ɛʀ/ ADJ left-handed NM,F left-handed person; (Sport) left-hander ◆ ~ **contrarié** *left-handed person forced to use his right hand*

gaucherie /goʃʀi/ NF [d'allure] awkwardness (NonC); [d'action, expression] clumsiness (NonC); (= acte) awkward *ou* clumsy behaviour (NonC); (Méd) sinistral tendency ◆ **une** ~ **de style** a clumsy turn of phrase

gauchir /goʃiʀ/ ► conjug 2 ◄ VT 1 (Aviation, Menuiserie) to warp 2 [+ idée, fait] to distort, to misrepresent; [+ esprit] to warp 3 (Pol) ~ **sa position** to swing further to the left ◆ **elle a gauchi son discours** she's become more left-wing in what she says VI **se gauchir** VPR (= se déformer) to warp

gauchisant, e /goʃizɑ̃, ɑt/ ADJ [auteur] with left-wing *ou* leftist tendencies; [théorie] with a left-wing *ou* leftish bias

gauchisme /goʃism/ NM leftism

gauchissement /goʃismɑ̃/ NM 1 (Aviation, Menuiserie) warping 2 [d'idée, fait] distortion, misrepresentation; [d'esprit] warping

gauchiste /goʃist/ ADJ leftist (épith) NMF leftist

gaucho[1] * /goʃo/ (péj Pol) ADJ left-wing (épith) NMF lefty *, left-winger

gaucho[2] /go(t)ʃo/ NM (= gardien de troupeaux) gaucho

gaudriole * /godʀijɔl/ NF 1 (= *débauche*) **il aime la ~** he likes a bit of slap and tickle * 2 (= *propos*) dirty joke

gaufrage /gofʀaʒ/ NM *[de papier, cuir]* (*en relief*) embossing (*NonC*); (*en creux*) figuring (*NonC*); *[de tissu]* goffering (*NonC*)

gaufre /gofʀ/ NF (*Culin*) waffle; (*en cire*) honeycomb; → **moule**[1]

gaufrer /gofʀe/ ▸ conjug 1 ◂ VT *[+ papier, cuir]* (*en relief*) to emboss; (*en creux*) to figure; *[+ tissu]* to goffer ◆ **papier gaufré** embossed paper; → **fer**

gaufrerie /gofʀəʀi/ NF (*Can*) waffle shop

gaufrette /gofʀɛt/ NF wafer

gaufrier /gofʀije/ NM waffle iron

gaufrure /gofʀyʀ/ NF *[de papier, cuir]* (*en relief*) embossing (*NonC*), embossed design; (*en creux*) figuring (*NonC*); *[de papier]* goffering (*NonC*)

Gaule /gol/ NF Gaul

gaule /gol/ NF (= *perche*) (long) pole; (*Pêche*) fishing rod

gauler /gole/ ▸ conjug 1 ◂ VT *[+ arbre]* to beat (*using a long pole to bring down the fruit or nuts*); *[+ fruits, noix]* to bring down, to shake down (*with a pole*) ◆ **se faire ~** * to get caught; (*par la police*) to get nabbed * *ou* nicked * (*Brit*)

gaullien, -ienne /goljɛ̃, jɛn/ ADJ de Gaullian

gaullisme /golism/ NM Gaullism

gaulliste /golist/ ADJ, NMF Gaullist

gaulois, e /golwa, waz/ ADJ 1 (= *de Gaule*) Gallic; (*hum* = *français*) French 2 (= *grivois*) bawdy ◆ **esprit ~** (broad *ou* bawdy) Gallic humour NM (= *langue*) Gaulish NM,F **Gaulois(e)** Gaul; → **moustache** NF **Gauloise** ® (= *cigarette*) Gauloise

gauloisement /golwazmɑ̃/ ADV bawdily

gauloiserie /golwazʀi/ NF (= *propos*) broad *ou* bawdy story (*ou* joke); (= *caractère grivois*) bawdiness

gauss /gos/ NM (*Phys*) gauss

gausser (se) /gose/ ▸ conjug 1 ◂ VPR (*littér*) (= *se moquer*) to laugh (and make fun), to mock ◆ **vous vous gaussez !** you jest! ◆ **se ~ de** to deride, to make mock of (*littér*), to poke fun at

gavage /gavaʒ/ NM (*Agr*) force-feeding; (*Méd*) forced feeding, gavage

gave /gav/ NM mountain stream (*in the Pyrenees*)

gaver /gave/ ▸ conjug 1 ◂ VT *[+ animal]* to force-feed; *[+ personne]* to fill up (*de* with); ◆ **je suis gavé !** I'm full (up)!, I'm full to bursting! * ◆ **on les gave de connaissances inutiles** they cram their heads with useless knowledge ◆ **on nous gave de séries télévisées/de publicité** we're fed a non-stop diet of television serials/of advertisements ◆ **ça me gave** * it really hacks me off * VPR **se gaver** ◆ **se ~ de** *[+ nourriture]* to stuff o.s. with, to gorge o.s. on; *[+ romans]* to devour ◆ **il se gave de films** he's a real film buff * *ou* addict ◆ **si tu te gaves maintenant, tu ne pourras plus rien manger au moment du dîner** if you go stuffing yourself * *ou* filling yourself up now, you won't be able to eat anything at dinner time

gaveur, -euse /gavœʀ, øz/ NM,F (= *personne*) force-feeder NF **gaveuse** (= *machine*) automatic force-feeder

gavial /gavjal/ NM gavial, g(h)arial

gavotte /gavɔt/ NF gavotte

gavroche /gavʀɔʃ/ NM street urchin (*in Paris*)

gay * /gɛ/ ADJ, NM gay

gaz /gɑz/ NM INV 1 (*Chim*) gas; *[de boisson]* fizz ◆ **le ~ (domestique)** (domestic) gas (*NonC*) ◆ **les ~** (*Mil*) gas ◆ **l'employé du ~** the gasman ◆ **se chauffer au ~** to have gas(-fired) heating ◆ **s'éclairer au ~** to have *ou* use gas lighting ◆ **faire la cuisine au ~** to cook with gas ◆ **vous avez le ~ ?** do you have gas?, are you on gas? (*Brit*) ◆ **il s'est suicidé au ~** he gassed himself ◆ **suicide au ~** (suicide by) gassing ◆ **mettre les ~** * (*en voiture*) to put one's foot down * (*Brit*), to step on the gas * (*US*); (*en avion*) to throttle up ◆ **rouler (à) pleins ~** * to drive flat out * ◆ **remettre les ~** (*Aviat*) to pull *ou* nose up ◆ **on prend une bière mais vite fait sur le ~** * let's have a beer but a quick one * *ou* a quickie *; → **bec, chambre, eau**
2 (*euph* = *pet*) wind (*NonC*) ◆ **avoir des ~** to have wind

COMP **gaz d'admission** (*dans moteur*) air-fuel mixture
gaz asphyxiant poison gas
gaz en bouteille bottled gas
gaz carbonique carbon dioxide
gaz de combat poison gas (*for use in warfare*)
gaz d'échappement exhaust gas
gaz d'éclairage † ⇒ **gaz de ville**
gaz hilarant laughing gas
gaz des houillères firedamp (*NonC*)
gaz lacrymogène teargas
gaz des marais marsh gas
gaz moutarde (*Mil*) mustard gas
gaz naturel natural gas
gaz neurotoxique nerve gas
gaz parfait perfect *ou* ideal gas
gaz de pétrole liquéfié liquid petroleum gas
gaz poivre pepper gas
gaz propulseur propellant
gaz rare rare gas
gaz sulfureux sulphur dioxide
gaz de ville town gas

Gaza /gaza/ N ◆ **la bande** *ou* **le territoire de ~** the Gaza Strip

gazage /gɑzaʒ/ NM *[de tissus, personnes]* gassing

gaze /gɑz/ NF gauze ◆ **compresse de ~** gauze (compress) ◆ **robe de ~** gauze dress

gazé, e /gɑze/ (ptp de **gazer**) ADJ (*Mil*) gassed NM,F gas victim ◆ **les ~s de 14-18** the (poison) gas victims of the 1914-18 war

gazéification /gɑzeifikasjɔ̃/ NF (*Chim*) gasification; *[d'eau minérale]* aeration

gazéifier /gɑzeifje/ ▸ conjug 7 ◂ VT (*Chim*) to gasify; *[+ eau minérale]* to aerate ◆ **eau minérale gazéifiée** sparkling mineral water

gazelle /gazɛl/ NF gazelle ◆ **c'est une vraie ~ !** she's so graceful and lithe!; → **corne**

gazer /gɑze/ ▸ conjug 1 ◂ VI (* = *aller, marcher*) ◆ **ça gaze ?** (*affaires, santé*) how's things? *, how goes it? *; (*travail*) how goes it? *, how's it going? * ◆ **ça gaze avec ta belle-mère ?** how's it going with your mother-in-law?, are you getting on OK with your mother-in-law? * ◆ **ça a/ça n'a pas gazé ?** did it/didn't it go OK? * ◆ **ça ne gaze pas fort** (*santé*) I'm not feeling so *ou* too great *; (*affaires*) things aren't going too well ◆ **il y a quelque chose qui ne gaze pas** there's something slightly fishy about it, there's something wrong somewhere VT *[+ tissu, personne]* to gas

gazetier, -ière /gaz(ə)tje, jɛʀ/ NM,F († † *ou hum*) journalist

gazette /gazɛt/ NF († †, *hum, littér*) newspaper ◆ **c'est dans la ~ locale** (*hum*) it's in the local rag ◆ **c'est une vraie ~** he's a mine of information about the latest (local) gossip ◆ **faire la ~** to give a rundown * (*de* on)

gazeux, -euse /gɑzø, øz/ ADJ (*Chim*) gaseous ◆ **boisson gazeuse** fizzy drink (*Brit*), soda (*US*), pop (*US*); → **eau**

gazier, -ière /gɑzje, jɛʀ/ ADJ gas (*épith*) NM (= *employé*) gasman

gazinière /gɑzinjɛʀ/ NF gas cooker

gazoduc /gɑzodyk/ NM gas main, gas pipeline

gazogène /gɑzɔʒɛn/ NM gas generator

gazole /gazɔl/ NM diesel oil

gazoline /gazɔlin/ NF gasoline, gasolene

gazomètre /gɑzɔmɛtʀ/ NM gasholder, gasometer

gazon /gɑzɔ̃/ NM (= *pelouse*) lawn ◆ **le ~** (= *herbe*) turf (*NonC*), grass (*NonC*) ◆ **motte de ~** turf, sod ◆ **~ anglais** (*pelouse*) well-kept lawn

gazonné, e /gɑzɔne/ ADJ grassy

gazonner /gɑzɔne/ ▸ conjug 1 ◂ VT *[+ talus, terrain]* to plant with grass, to turf

gazouillement /gazujmɑ̃/ NM *[d'oiseau]* chirping (*NonC*); *[de ruisseau]* babbling (*NonC*); *[de bébé]* gurgling (*NonC*) ◆ **j'entendais le ~ des oiseaux/du bébé** I could hear the birds chirping/the baby gurgling ◆ **bercé par le ~ du ruisseau** lulled by the babbling brook

gazouiller /gazuje/ ▸ conjug 1 ◂ VI *[oiseau]* to chirp, to warble; *[ruisseau]* to babble; *[bébé]* to babble, to gurgle

gazouilleur, -euse /gazujœʀ, øz/ ADJ *[oiseau]* chirping, warbling; *[ruisseau]* babbling; *[bébé]* babbling, gurgling

gazouillis /gazuji/ NM *[d'oiseau]* chirping, warbling; *[de ruisseau]* babbling; *[de bébé]* babbling, gurgling

GB /ʒebe/ (abrév de **Grande-Bretagne**) GB

gdb * /ʒedebe/ NF (abrév de **gueule de bois**) ◆ **avoir la ~** to have a hangover

GDF /ʒedeɛf/ NM (abrév de **Gaz de France**) *French gas company*

geai /ʒɛ/ NM jay

géant, e /ʒeɑ̃, ɑt/ ADJ *[objet]* gigantic; *[animal, plante]* gigantic, giant (*épith*); *[paquet, carton]* giant-size (*épith*), giant (*épith*); *[étoile, écran]* giant (*épith*) ◆ **c'est ~ !** * it's great! * NM (= *homme, firme*) giant; (*Pol*) giant power ◆ **les ~s de la route** the great cycling champions; → **pas**[1] NF **géante** (= *femme*) giantess; (= *étoile*) giant star

géhenne /ʒeɛn/ NF (*Bible* = *enfer*) Gehenna

geignard, e * /ʒɛɲaʀ, aʀd/ ADJ *[personne]* moaning; *[voix]* whingeing, whining; *[musique]* whining NM,F moaner

geignement /ʒɛɲmɑ̃/ NM moaning (*NonC*)

geindre /ʒɛ̃dʀ/ ▸ conjug 52 ◂ VI 1 (= *gémir*) to groan, to moan (*de* with) 2 (* = *pleurnicher*) to moan ◆ **il geint tout le temps** he never stops moaning *ou* complaining 3 (*littér*) *[vent, instrument de musique]* to moan; *[parquet]* to creak ◆ **le vent faisait ~ les peupliers/le gréement** the poplars/the rigging groaned *ou* moaned in the wind

geisha /gɛʃa/ NF geisha (girl)

gel /ʒɛl/ NM 1 (= *temps*) frost ◆ **un jour de ~** one frosty day ◆ **plantes tuées par le ~** plants killed by (the) frost 2 (= *glace*) frost ◆ **"craint le gel"** "keep away from extreme cold" 3 *[de crédits, licenciements]* freeze ◆ **~ des terres** set-aside ◆ **protester contre le ~ des salaires** to protest against the wage freeze ◆ **ils réclament le ~ du programme nucléaire** they are calling for a freeze on the nuclear programme 4 (= *substance*) gel ◆ **~ (de) douche** shower gel ◆ **~ coiffant** *ou* **structurant** hair (styling) gel

gélatine /ʒelatin/ NF gelatine

gélatineux, -euse /ʒelatinø, øz/ ADJ jelly-like, gelatinous

gelé, e[1] /ʒ(ə)le/ (ptp de **geler**) ADJ 1 (= *qui a gelé*) *[eau, rivière]* frozen, iced-over; *[sol, tuyau]* frozen 2 (= *très froid*) ice-cold ◆ **j'ai les mains ~es** my hands are frozen *ou* freezing ◆ **je suis ~** I'm frozen (stiff) *ou* freezing 3 (= *endommagé, détruit*) *[plante]* damaged by frost; *[membre]* frostbitten ◆ **ils sont morts ~s** they froze to death, they died of exposure 4 *[crédits, prix,* *projet]* frozen; *[négociations]* suspended; *[terres agricoles]* set aside

gelée² /ʒ(ə)le/ NF 1 *(= gel)* frost ◆ ~ **blanche** white frost, hoarfrost 2 *(Culin) [de fruits, viande, volaille]* jelly ◆ **poulet/œuf en** ~ chicken/egg in aspic *ou* jelly ◆ ~ **de framboises** raspberry jelly *(Brit) ou* Jell-O ® *(US) ou* jello *(US)* ◆ ~ **royale** royal jelly

geler /ʒ(ə)le/ ▸ conjug 5 ◂ VT 1 *[+ eau, rivière]* to freeze (over); *[+ buée]* to turn to ice; *[+ sol, tuyau]* to freeze

2 *(= endommager)* **le froid a gelé les bourgeons** the buds were nipped *ou* damaged by frost ◆ **le froid lui a gelé les mains** he got frostbite in both hands

3 *[+ prix, crédits, salaires, projet]* to freeze; *[+ terres]* to set aside; *[+ négociations]* to suspend

4 *(= mettre mal à l'aise) [+ assistance]* to chill, to send a chill through

VPR **se geler** * *(= avoir froid)* to freeze ◆ **on gèle ici** we're *ou* it's freezing here ◆ **on se les gèle**‡ it's damned‡ *ou* bloody‡ *(Brit)* freezing, it's brass monkey weather‡ *(Brit)* ◆ **vous allez vous ~, à l'attendre** you'll get frozen stiff waiting for him

VI 1 *[eau, lac]* to freeze (over), to ice over; *[sol, linge, conduit]* to freeze; *[récoltes]* to be attacked *ou* blighted *ou* nipped by frost; *[doigt, membre]* to be freezing, to be frozen ◆ **les salades ont gelé sur pied** the lettuces have frozen on their stalks

2 *(= avoir froid)* to be frozen, to be freezing ◆ **on gèle ici** we're *ou* it's freezing here

3 *(dans un jeu)* **je chauffe ? – non, tu gèles** am I getting warmer? – no, you're freezing

VB IMPERS ◆ **il gèle** it's freezing ◆ **il a gelé dur** *ou* **à pierre fendre** *(littér)* it froze hard, there was a hard frost ◆ **il a gelé blanc** there was a white icy frost

gélifiant /ʒelifjɑ̃/ NM gelling agent

gélifier /ʒelifje/ ▸ conjug 7 ◂ VT ◆ ~ **qch** to make sth gel VPR **se gélifier** to gel

gélinotte /ʒelinɔt/ NF ◆ ~ **(des bois)** hazel grouse, hazel hen ◆ ~ **d'Écosse** red grouse ◆ ~ **blanche** willow grouse

gélose /ʒeloz/ NF agar-agar

gélule /ʒelyl/ NF *(Pharm)* capsule

gelure /ʒ(ə)lyʀ/ NF *(Méd)* frostbite *(NonC)*

Gémeaux /ʒemo/ NMPL *(Astron)* Gemini ◆ **il est (du signe des)** ~ he's (a) Gemini

gémellaire /ʒemelɛʀ/ ADJ twin *(épith)*

gémellité /ʒemelite, ʒemɛllite/ NF twinship ◆ **taux de** ~ incidence of twin births ◆ **les cas de vraie/fausse** ~ cases of identical twin/ non-identical twin births

gémination /ʒeminasjɔ̃/ NF gemination

géminé, e /ʒemine/ ADJ *(Ling) [consonne]* geminate; *(Archit)* twin *(épith)*, gemeled *(SPÉC)*; *(Bio)* geminate NF **géminée** *(Ling)* geminate

gémir /ʒemiʀ/ ▸ conjug 2 ◂ VI 1 *(= geindre)* to groan, to moan *(de* with); ◆ ~ **sur son sort** to bemoan one's fate ◆ ~ **sous l'oppression** *(littér)* to groan under oppression 2 *(= grincer) [ressort, gonds, plancher]* to creak; *[vent]* to moan ◆ **les gonds de la porte gémissaient horriblement** the door hinges made a terrible creaking noise 3 *[colombe]* to coo

gémissant, e /ʒemisɑ̃, ɑ̃t/ ADJ *[voix]* groaning, moaning; *[gonds, plancher]* creaking

gémissement /ʒemismɑ̃/ NM *[de voix]* groan, moan; *(prolongé)* groaning *(NonC)*, moaning *(NonC)*; *[de meuble]* creaking *(NonC)*; *[de vent]* moaning *(NonC)*; *[de colombe]* cooing

gemmage /ʒemaʒ/ NM tapping *(of pine trees)*

gemmail (pl **-aux**) /ʒemaj, o/ NM non-leaded stained glass

gemme /ʒɛm/ NF 1 *(Minér)* gem(stone); → **sel** 2 *(= résine de pin)* (pine) resin

gemmer /ʒeme/ ▸ conjug 1 ◂ VT to tap *(pine trees)*

gémonies /ʒemɔni/ NFPL *(littér)* ◆ **vouer** *ou* **traîner qn/qch aux** ~ to subject sb/sth to *ou* hold sb/sth up to public obloquy

gênant, e /ʒɛnɑ̃, ɑ̃t/ ADJ 1 *(= irritant)* **tu es/c'est vraiment** ~ you're/it's a real nuisance ◆ **ce n'est pas** ~ it's OK, it doesn't matter 2 *(= embarrassant) [question, détails, révélations, regard, présence]* embarrassing; *[situation, moment]* awkward, embarrassing; *[meuble, talons]* awkward ◆ **ce sont les symptômes les plus ~s** these are the most troublesome symptoms

gencive /ʒɑ̃siv/ NF *(Anat)* gum ◆ **il a pris un coup dans les ~s** * he got a sock on the jaw * *ou* a kick in the teeth * ◆ **prends ça dans les ~s !** * take that! ◆ **il faut voir ce qu'elle lui a envoyé dans les ~s !** * you should have heard the way she let fly at him! ◆ **je lui ai envoyé dans les ~s que ...** I told him to his face that ...

gendarme /ʒɑ̃daʀm/ NM 1 *(= policier)* policeman, police officer; *(en France)* gendarme; *(Hist, Mil)* horseman; *(= soldat)* soldier, man-at-arms ◆ **faire le** ~ to play the role of policeman ◆ **sa femme est un vrai** ~ *(hum)* his wife's a real battle-axe * ◆ **jouer aux ~s et aux voleurs** to play cops and robbers ◆ ~ **mobile** member of the anti-riot police ◆ **le ~ de la Bourse** the French stock exchange watchdog; → **chapeau, peur** 2 *(= punaise)* fire bug 3 *(Alpinisme)* gendarme *(SPÉC)*, pinnacle 4 († * *= hareng)* bloater *(Brit)*, salt herring *(US)* 5 ~ **couché** *(= ralentisseur)* speed bump, sleeping policeman *(Brit)*

gendarmer (se) /ʒɑ̃daʀme/ ▸ conjug 1 ◂ VPR ◆ **il faut se ~ pour qu'elle aille se coucher/pour la faire manger** you really have to take quite a strong line (with her) *ou* you really have to lay down the law to get her to go to bed/to get her to eat

gendarmerie /ʒɑ̃daʀməʀi/ NF *(= police)* police force, constabulary *(in countryside and small towns)*; *(en France)* Gendarmerie; *(= bureaux)* police station *(in countryside and small town)*; *(= caserne)* gendarmes' *ou* Gendarmerie barracks, police barracks; *(Hist, Mil = cavalerie)* heavy cavalry *ou* horse; *(= garde royale)* royal guard ◆ ~ **mobile** anti-riot police ◆ **la ~ nationale** the national Gendarmerie ◆ ~ **maritime** coastguard

gendre /ʒɑ̃dʀ/ NM son-in-law

gêne /ʒɛn/ NF 1 *(= malaise physique)* discomfort ◆ ~ **respiratoire** breathing *ou* respiratory problems ◆ **il ressentait une certaine ~ à respirer** he experienced some *ou* a certain difficulty in breathing

2 *(= désagrément, dérangement)* trouble, bother ◆ **je ne voudrais vous causer aucune** ~ I wouldn't like to put you to any trouble *ou* bother, I wouldn't want to be a nuisance; *(péj)* some people only think of their own comfort ◆ **"nous vous prions de bien vouloir excuser la gêne occasionnée durant les travaux"** "we apologize to customers for any inconvenience caused during the renovations" ◆ **où il y a de la ~, il n'y a pas de plaisir** *(Prov)* comfort comes first, there's no sense in being uncomfortable

3 *(= manque d'argent)* financial difficulties *ou* straits ◆ **vivre dans la ~/dans une grande ~** to be in financial difficulties *ou* straits/in great financial difficulties *ou* dire (financial) straits

4 *(= confusion, trouble)* embarrassment ◆ **un moment de ~** a moment of embarrassment ◆ **j'éprouve de la ~ devant lui** I feel embarrassed *ou* self-conscious in his presence ◆ **il éprouva de la ~ à lui avouer cela** he felt embarrassed admitting *ou* to admit that to her

gêné, e /ʒene/ (ptp de **gêner**) ADJ 1 *(= à court d'argent)* short (of money) *(attrib)* ◆ **être ~ aux entournures** * to be short of money *ou* hard up * 2 *(= embarrassé) [personne, sourire, air]* embarrassed, self-conscious; *[silence]* uncomfortable, embarrassed, awkward ◆ **j'étais ~ !** I was (so) embarrassed!, I felt (so) awkward! *ou* uncomfortable! ◆ **il n'est pas ~ !** he's got a nerve! * ◆ **ce sont les plus ~s qui s'en vont !** *(hum)* if you want to leave, no one's stopping you! 3 *(physiquement)* uncomfortable ◆ **êtes-vous ~ pour respirer ?** do you have trouble (in) breathing? ◆ **je suis ~e dans cette robe** I'm uncomfortable in this dress

gène /ʒɛn/ NM gene ◆ ~ **dominant/récessif** dominant/recessive gene

généalogie /ʒenealɔʒi/ NF *[de famille]* ancestry, genealogy; *[d'animaux]* pedigree; *(Bio) [d'espèces]* genealogy; *(= sujet d'études)* genealogy ◆ **faire** *ou* **dresser la ~ de qn** to trace sb's ancestry *ou* genealogy

généalogique /ʒenealɔʒik/ ADJ genealogical; → **arbre**

généalogiste /ʒenealɔʒist/ NMF genealogist

génépi /ʒenepi/ NM *(= plante)* wormwood, absinthe; *(= liqueur)* absinth(e)

gêner /ʒene/ ▸ conjug 1 ◂ VT 1 *(physiquement) [fumée, bruit]* to bother; *[vêtement étroit, obstacle]* to hamper ◆ **cela vous gêne-t-il si je fume ?** do you mind if I smoke?, does it bother you if I smoke? ◆ ~ **le passage** to be in the way ◆ **ça me gêne** *ou* **c'est gênant pour respirer/pour écrire** it hampers my breathing/hampers me when I write ◆ **le bruit me gêne pour travailler** noise bothers me *ou* disturbs me when I'm trying to work ◆ **son complet le gêne aux entournures** * his suit is uncomfortable *ou* constricting ◆ **ces papiers me gênent** these papers are in my way ◆ **ces travaux gênent la circulation** these roadworks are disrupting the (flow of) traffic

2 *(= déranger) [+ personne]* to bother, to put out; *[+ projet]* to hamper, to hinder ◆ **je crains de ~** I am afraid to bother people *ou* put people out, I'm afraid of being a nuisance ◆ **je ne voudrais pas (vous) ~** I don't want to bother you *ou* put you out *ou* be in the way ◆ **j'espère que ça ne vous gêne pas d'y aller** I hope it won't inconvenience you *ou* put you out to go ◆ **cela vous gênerait de ne pas fumer ?** would you mind not smoking? ◆ **ce qui me gêne (dans cette histoire), c'est que ...** what bothers me (in this business) is that ... ◆ **et alors, ça te gêne ?** * so what? *, what's it to you? *

3 *(financièrement)* to put in financial difficulties ◆ **ces dépenses vont les ~ considérablement** *ou* **vont les ~ aux entournures** * these expenses are really going to put them in financial difficulties *ou* make things tight for them *ou* make them hard up *

4 *(= mettre mal à l'aise)* to make feel ill-at-ease *ou* uncomfortable ◆ **ça me gêne de vous dire ça mais ...** I hate to tell you but ... ◆ **ça me gêne de me déshabiller chez le médecin** I find it embarrassing to get undressed at the doctor's ◆ **sa présence me gêne** I feel uncomfortable when he's around, his presence *ou* he makes me feel uncomfortable ◆ **son regard la gênait** his glance made her feel ill-at-ease *ou* uncomfortable ◆ **cela le gêne qu'on fasse tout le travail pour lui** it embarrasses him to have all the work done for him, he feels awkward about having all the work done for him

VPR **se gêner** 1 *(= se contraindre)* to put o.s. out ◆ **ne vous gênez pas pour moi** don't mind me, don't put yourself out for me ◆ **ne vous gênez pas !** *(iro)* do you mind! ◆ **il ne faut pas vous ~ avec moi** don't stand on ceremony with me ◆ **non mais ! je vais me ~ !** why shouldn't I! ◆ **il y en a qui ne se gênent pas !** some people just don't care! ◆ **il ne s'est pas gêné pour le lui dire** he told him straight out, he made no bones about telling him

2 *(dans un lieu)* **on se gêne à trois dans ce bureau** this office is too small for the three of us

général[1], **e** (mpl **-aux**) /ʒeneʀal, o/ ADJ 1 *(= d'ensemble) [vue]* general; *(= vague) [idée]* general ◆ **un tableau ~ de la situation** a general *ou* an overall picture of the situation ◆ **remarques d'ordre très ~** comments of a very general nature ◆ **se lancer dans des considérations ~es sur le temps** to venture some general remarks about the weather ◆ **d'une façon** *ou* **manière ~e** in general, generally; *(précédant une affirmation)* generally *ou* broadly speaking; → **règle**

2 *(= total, global) [assemblée, grève]* general ◆ **dans l'intérêt ~** *(= commun)* in the general *ou* common interest ◆ **cette opinion est devenue ~e** this is now a widely shared *ou* generally held opinion ◆ **devenir ~** *[crise, peur]* to become widespread ◆ **la mêlée devint ~e** the fight turned into a free-for-all ◆ **à l'indignation/la surprise ~e** to everyone's indignation/surprise ◆ **à la demande ~e** in response to popular demand; → **concours, état, médecine**

3 *(Admin = principal)* general *(épith)*; → **directeur, fermier, président, secrétaire**

NM *(Philos)* ◆ **le ~** the general ◆ **aller du ~ au particulier** to go from the general to the particular

LOC ADV **en général** *(= habituellement)* usually, generally, in general; *(= de façon générale)* generally, in general ◆ **je parle en ~** I'm speaking in general terms *ou* generally

NF **générale** 1 *(Théât)* **(répétition) ~e** dress rehearsal

2 *(Mil)* **battre** *ou* **sonner la ~e** to call to arms

général[2], **e** (mpl **-aux**) /ʒeneʀal, o/ NM *(Mil)* general ◆ **oui mon ~** yes sir *ou* general NF **générale** *(= épouse)* general's wife; → **Madame**

COMP **général d'armée** general; *(dans l'armée de l'air)* air chief marshal *(Brit)*, general *(US)*
général de brigade brigadier *(Brit)*, brigadier general *(US)*
général de brigade aérienne air commodore *(Brit)*, brigadier general *(US)*
général en chef general-in-chief, general-in-command
général de corps aérien air marshal *(Brit)*, lieutenant general *(US)*
général de corps d'armée lieutenant-general
général de division major general
général de division aérienne air vice marshal *(Brit)*, major general *(US)*

généralement /ʒeneʀalmɑ̃/ GRAMMAIRE ACTIVE 53.1 ADV generally ◆ **il est ~ chez lui après 8 heures** he's generally *ou* usually at home after 8 o'clock ◆ **coutume assez ~ répandue** fairly widespread custom ◆ **plus ~, ce genre de phénomène s'accompagne de ...** more generally *ou* commonly *ou* usually, this type of phenomenon is accompanied by ...

généralisable /ʒeneʀalizabl/ ADJ *[mesure, observation]* which can be applied generally ◆ **cela n'est pas ~ à l'ensemble du pays** this is not true of the whole country

généralisateur, -trice /ʒeneʀalizatœʀ, tʀis/ ADJ ◆ **il tient un discours ~** he makes a lot of generalizations ◆ **des commentaires ~s** generalizations ◆ **tendance généralisatrice** tendency to generalize *ou* towards generalization

généralisation /ʒeneʀalizasjɔ̃/ NF 1 *(= extension) [d'infection, corruption, pratique]* spread *(à to)*; ◆ **la ~ du cancer** the spread of the cancer ◆ **il y a un risque de ~ du conflit** there's a risk that the conflict will become widespread ◆ **il a refusé la ~ de cette mesure** he refused to allow the measure to be applied more widely ◆ **la ~ de l'usage des antibiotiques** the ever more widespread use of antibiotics 2 *(= énoncé)* generalization ◆ **~s hâtives/abusives** sweeping/excessive generalizations

généraliser /ʒeneʀalize/ ► conjug 1 ◄ VT 1 *(= étendre) [+ méthode]* to put *ou* bring into general *ou* widespread use ◆ **~ l'usage d'un produit** to bring a product into general use 2 *(= globaliser)* to generalize ◆ **il ne faut pas ~** we mustn't generalize VPR **se généraliser** *[infection]* to spread, to become generalized; *[corruption]* to become widespread; *[conflit]* to spread; *[procédé]* to become widespread, to come into general use ◆ **l'usage du produit s'est généralisé** the use of this product has become widespread, this product has come into general use ◆ **crise généralisée** general crisis ◆ **il a un cancer généralisé** the cancer has spread throughout his whole body ◆ **infection généralisée** systemic infection

généralissime /ʒeneʀalisim/ NM generalissimo

généraliste /ʒeneʀalist/ ADJ *[chaîne, radio, télévision, quotidien]* general-interest *(épith)*; *[formation]* general; *[ingénieur]* non-specialized ◆ **les banques ~s** the high-street banks ◆ **notre radio conservera sa vocation ~** our radio station will continue to cater for a general audience NM *(= non-spécialiste)* generalist ◆ **(médecin) ~** general *ou* family practitioner, GP *(Brit)*

généralité /ʒeneʀalite/ NF 1 *(= presque totalité)* majority ◆ **ce n'est pas une ~** that's not the case in general ◆ **dans la ~ des cas** in the majority of cases, in most cases 2 *(= caractère général) [d'affirmation]* general nature NFPL **généralités** *(= introduction)* general points; *(péj = banalités)* general remarks, generalities

générateur, -trice /ʒeneʀatœʀ, tʀis/ ADJ *[force]* generating; *[fonction]* generative, generating ◆ **secteur ~ d'emplois** job-generating sector ◆ **activité génératrice de profits** profit-making activity, activity that generates profit ◆ **un climat familial ~ d'angoisse** an unhappy family atmosphere NM *(= dispositif)* generator ◆ **~ nucléaire** nuclear generator ◆ **~ électrique/de particules/de programme** electric/particle/program generator ◆ **~ de vapeur** steam boiler NF **génératrice** 1 *(Élec)* generator 2 *(Math)* generating line, generatrix

génératif, -ive /ʒeneʀatif, iv/ ADJ *(Ling)* generative ◆ **grammaire générative** generative grammar

génération /ʒeneʀasjɔ̃/ NF generation ◆ **depuis des ~s** for generations ◆ **la ~ actuelle/montante** the present-day/rising generation ◆ **la jeune ~** the younger generation ◆ **~ spontanée** spontaneous generation ◆ **ordinateur/immigré de la deuxième/troisième ~** second-/third-generation computer/immigrant

générationnel, -elle /ʒeneʀasjɔnɛl/ ADJ 1 *(= des générations)* **le clivage ~** the generation gap 2 *(Marketing)* generational

générer /ʒeneʀe/ ► conjug 6 ◄ VT to generate

généreusement /ʒeneʀøzmɑ̃/ ADV generously ◆ **accueilli ~** warmly welcomed

généreux, -euse /ʒeneʀø, øz/ ADJ 1 *(= large) [personne, pourboire, part de nourriture]* generous ◆ **être ~ de son temps** to be generous with one's time ◆ **c'est très ~ de sa part** it's very generous of him ◆ **se montrer ~ envers qn** to be generous with sb ◆ **faire le ~** to act generous* 2 *(= noble, désintéressé) [personne, sentiment, idée]* noble 3 *(= riche) [sol]* productive, fertile 4 *[vin]* generous, full-bodied 5 *[poitrine]* ample ◆ **décolleté ~** plunging neckline ◆ **formes généreuses** generous curves

générique /ʒeneʀik/ ADJ 1 generic; *[produit]* unbranded, no-name *(épith)*; *[médicament]* generic ◆ **terme ~** generic term ◆ **adresse ~** *(Internet)* generic address ◆ **(nom de) domaine ~** *(Internet)* generic domain (name) 2 *(Ciné)* **chanson ~** theme song NM 1 *(= liste des participants) [de film, émission]* credits ◆ **être au ~** to feature *ou* be in the credits 2 *(= musique de film)* theme music 3 *(= médicament)* generic (drug)

générosité /ʒeneʀozite/ NF 1 *(= libéralité) [de pourboire, personne]* generosity ◆ **avec ~** generously 2 *(= noblesse) [d'acte, caractère]* generosity; *[d'âme, sentiment]* nobility; *[d'adversaire]* generosity, magnanimity ◆ **avoir la ~ de** to be generous enough to, to have the generosity to 3 *(= largesses)* **~s** kindnesses

Gênes /ʒɛn/ N Genoa

genèse /ʒənɛz/ NF *(= élaboration)* genesis *(frm)* ◆ **(le livre de) la Genèse** (the Book of) Genesis ◆ **ce texte éclaire la ~ de l'œuvre** this piece helps us to understand how the work came into being ◆ **la ~ du projet remonte à 1985** the project came into being in 1985

genet /ʒ(ə)nɛ/ NM *(= cheval)* jennet

genêt /ʒ(ə)nɛ/ NM *(= plante)* broom

généticien, -ienne /ʒenetisjɛ̃, jɛn/ NM,F geneticist

génétique /ʒenetik/ ADJ genetic ◆ **carte ~** genetic *ou* gene map ◆ **affection d'origine ~** genetically-transmitted disease; → **manipulation** NF genetics *(sg)* ◆ **~ des populations** population genetics

génétiquement /ʒenetikmɑ̃/ ADV genetically; → **organisme**

genette /ʒ(ə)nɛt/ NF genet(t)e

gêneur, -euse /ʒɛnœʀ, øz/ NM,F *(= importun)* intruder ◆ **supprimer un ~** *(= représentant un obstacle)* to do away with a person who is *ou* stands in one's way

Genève /ʒ(ə)nɛv/ N Geneva

genevois, e /ʒən(ə)vwa, waz/ ADJ Genevan NM,F **Genevois(e)** Genevan

genévrier /ʒənevʀije/ NM juniper

génial, e (mpl **-iaux**) /ʒenjal, jo/ ADJ 1 *(= inspiré) [écrivain]* of genius; *[plan, idée, invention]* inspired ◆ **plan d'une conception ~e** inspired idea, brilliantly thought out idea 2 *(* = formidable) [atmosphère, soirée]* fantastic*, great*; *[personne]* great*; *[plan]* brilliant*, great* ◆ **c'est ~ !** that's great!* *ou* fantastic!* ◆ **physiquement, il n'est pas ~ mais ...** he's not up to much physically but ... ◆ **ce n'est pas ~ !** *(idée)* that's not very clever!; *(film)* it's not brilliant!*

> ⚠ **génial** ne se traduit pas par le mot anglais **genial**, qui a le sens de 'cordial'.

génialement /ʒenjalmɑ̃/ ADV with genius, brilliantly

génie /ʒeni/ NM 1 *(= aptitude supérieure)* genius ◆ **avoir du ~** to have genius ◆ **éclair** *ou* **trait de ~** stroke of genius ◆ **de ~** *[découverte]* brilliant ◆ **homme de ~** man of genius ◆ **idée de ~** brainwave, brilliant idea

2 *(= personne)* genius ◆ **ce n'est pas un ~ !** he's no genius! ◆ **~ méconnu** unrecognized genius

3 *(= talent)* genius ◆ **avoir le ~ des affaires** to have a genius for business ◆ **avoir le ~ du mal** to have an evil bent ◆ **il a le ~ de** *ou* **pour dire ce qu'il ne faut pas** he has a genius for saying the wrong thing

4 *(= spécificité)* genius *(frm)* ◆ **le ~ de la langue française** the genius of the French language

5 *(= allégorie, être mythique)* spirit; *[de contes arabes]* genie ◆ **le ~ de la liberté** the spirit of liberty ◆ **le ~ de la lampe** the genie of the lamp ◆ **~ des airs/des eaux** spirit of the air/

waters ♦ **être le bon/mauvais ~ de qn** to be sb's good/evil genius
[6] *(Mil)* **le ~** ≈ the Engineers ♦ **soldat du ~** sapper, engineer ♦ **faire son service dans le ~** to do one's service in the Engineers
[7] *(= technique)* engineering ♦ **~ atomique/chimique/électronique** atomic/chemical/electronic engineering
COMP **génie civil** *(branche)* civil engineering; *(corps)* civil engineers
génie génétique genetic engineering
génie industriel industrial engineering
génie informatique computer engineering
génie logiciel software engineering
génie maritime *(branche)* marine engineering; *(corps)* marine engineers *(under state command)*
génie mécanique mechanical engineering
génie militaire *(branche)* military engineering; *(corps)* ≈ Engineers
génie rural agricultural engineering; → **ingénieur**

genièvre /ʒənjɛvʀ/ NM *(= boisson)* Dutch gin, Hollands (gin) *(Brit)*, genever *(Brit)*; *(= arbre)* juniper; *(= fruit)* juniper berry ♦ **baies de ~** juniper berries

génique /ʒenik/ ADJ gene *(épith)* ♦ **thérapie ~** gene therapy ♦ **traitement ~** genetic treatment

génisse /ʒenis/ NF heifer ♦ **foie de ~** cow's liver

génital, e (mpl **-aux**) /ʒenital, o/ ADJ genital ♦ **organes génitaux, parties ~es** genitals, genital organs, genitalia

géniteur, -trice /ʒenitœʀ, tʀis/ NM,F *(hum = parent)* parent NM *(= animal reproducteur)* sire

génitif /ʒenitif/ NM genitive (case) ♦ **au ~** in the genitive ♦ **~ absolu** genitive absolute

génito-urinaire (pl **génito-urinaires**) /ʒenitoyʀinɛʀ/ ADJ genito-urinary

génocidaire /ʒenɔsidɛʀ/ ADJ genocidal

génocide /ʒenɔsid/ NM genocide

génois, e /ʒenwa, waz/ ADJ Genoese NM,F **Génois(e)** Genoese NM *(Naut)* genoa (jib) NF **génoise** *(Culin)* sponge cake; *(Archit)* eaves consisting of decorative tiles

génome /ʒenom/ NM genom(e) ♦ **~ humain** human genome

génotype /ʒenotip/ NM genotype

genou (pl **genoux**) /ʒ(ə)nu/ NM [1] *(partie du corps, d'un vêtement)* knee ♦ **avoir les ~x cagneux** *ou* **rentrants** to be knock-kneed ♦ **mes ~x se dérobèrent sous moi** my legs gave way under me ♦ **des jeans troués aux ~x** jeans with holes at the knees, jeans that are out at the knees ♦ **dans la vase jusqu'aux ~x** up to one's knees *ou* knee-deep in mud
[2] *(= cuisses)* **~x** lap ♦ **avoir/prendre qn sur ses ~x** to have/take sb on one's knee *ou* lap ♦ **écrire sur ses ~x** to write on one's lap
[3] *(locutions)* **il me donna un coup de ~ dans le ventre** he kneed me in the stomach ♦ **il me donna un coup de ~ pour me réveiller** he nudged me with his knee to wake me up ♦ **faire du ~ à qn*** to play footsie with sb* ♦ **tomber aux ~x de qn** to fall at sb's feet, to go down on one's knees to sb ♦ **fléchir** *ou* **plier** *ou* **ployer le ~ devant qn** *(littér)* to bend the knee to sb ♦ **mettre (un) ~ à terre** to go down on one knee
♦ **à genoux** ♦ **il était à ~x** he was kneeling, he was on his knees ♦ **être à ~x devant qn** *(fig)* to idolize *ou* worship sb ♦ **se mettre à ~x** to kneel down, to go down on one's knees ♦ **se mettre à ~x devant qn** *(fig)* to go down on one's knees to sb ♦ **c'est à se mettre à ~x !*** it's out of this world!* ♦ **tomber/se jeter à ~x** to fall/throw o.s. to one's knees ♦ **demander qch à ~x** to ask for sth on bended knee, to go down on one's knees for sth ♦ **je te demande pardon à ~x** I beg you to forgive me
♦ **sur les genoux*** ♦ **être sur les ~x** *[personne]* to be ready to drop; *[pays]* to be on its knees* ♦ **ça m'a mis sur les ~x** it wore me out

genouillère /ʒ(ə)nujɛʀ/ NF *(Méd)* knee support; *(Sport)* kneepad, kneecap

genre /ʒɑ̃ʀ/ GRAMMAIRE ACTIVE 34.3 NM [1] *(= espèce)* kind, type, sort ♦ **~ de vie** lifestyle, way of life ♦ **elle n'est pas du ~ à se laisser faire** she's not the type *ou* kind *ou* sort to let people push her around ♦ **ce n'est pas son ~ de ne pas répondre** it's not like him not to answer ♦ **donner des augmentations, ce n'est pas leur ~** it's not their style to give pay rises ♦ **c'est bien son ~ !** that's just like him! ♦ **tu vois le ~ !** you know the type *ou* sort! ♦ **les rousses, ce n'est pas mon ~** redheads aren't my type ♦ **c'est le ~ grognon*** he's the grumpy sort* ♦ **un type (du) ~ homme d'affaires*** a businessman type ♦ **une maison ~ chalet*** a chalet-style house ♦ **il n'est pas mal dans son ~** he's quite attractive in his own way ♦ **ce qui se fait de mieux dans le ~** the best of its kind ♦ **réparations en tout ~** *ou* **en tous ~s** all kinds of repairs *ou* repair work undertaken ♦ **quelque chose de ce ~** *ou* **du même ~** something of the kind, that sort of thing ♦ **des remarques de ce ~** remarks *ou* comments like that *ou* of that nature ♦ **il a écrit un ~ de roman** he wrote a novel of sorts *ou* a sort of novel ♦ **plaisanterie d'un ~ douteux** doubtful joke ♦ **dans le ~ film d'action ce n'est pas mal** as action films go, it's not bad; → **unique**
[2] *(= allure)* appearance ♦ **avoir bon/mauvais ~** to look respectable/disreputable ♦ **je n'aime pas son ~** I don't like his style ♦ **il a un drôle de ~** he's a bit weird ♦ **avoir le ~ bohème/artiste** to be a Bohemian/an arty type ♦ **avoir un ~ prétentieux** to have a pretentious manner ♦ **faire du ~** to stand on ceremony ♦ **c'est un ~ qu'il se donne** it's (just) something *ou* an air he puts on ♦ **il aime se donner un ~** he likes to stand out *ou* to be a bit different ♦ **ce n'est pas le ~ de la maison*** that's just not the way we (*ou* they *etc*) do things
[3] *(Art, Littérat, Mus)* genre ♦ **tableau de ~** *(Peinture)* genre painting ♦ **œuvre dans le ~ ancien/italien** work in the old/Italian style *ou* genre ♦ **ses tableaux/romans sont d'un ~ un peu particulier** the style of his paintings/novels is slightly unusual
[4] *(Gram)* gender ♦ **s'accorder en ~** to agree in gender
[5] *(Philos, Sci)* genus ♦ **le ~ humain** mankind, the human race

gens[1] /ʒɑ̃/ NMPL [1] *(gén)* people ♦ **il faut savoir prendre les ~** you've got to know how to handle people ♦ **les ~ sont fous !** people are crazy (at times)! ♦ **les ~ de la ville** townspeople, townsfolk ♦ **les ~ du pays** *ou* **du coin*** the local people, the locals* ♦ **ce ne sont pas ~ à raconter des histoires** they're not the kind *ou* type *ou* sort of people to tell stories; → **droit[3], jeune, monde**
[2] *(locutions, avec accord féminin de l'adjectif antéposé)* **ce sont de petites ~** they are people of modest means ♦ **vieilles/braves ~** old/good people *ou* folk* ♦ **honnêtes ~** honest people ♦ **écoutez bonnes ~** *(hum)* harken, ye people *(hum)*
[3] *(†, hum = serviteurs)* servants ♦ **il appela ses ~** he called his servants
COMP **gens d'armes** *(Hist)* men-at-arms †
les gens d'Église the clergy
gens d'épée *(Hist)* soldiers *(of the aristocracy)*
gens de lettres men of letters
les gens de loi † the legal profession
gens de maison domestic servants
gens de mer sailors, seafarers
les gens de robe *(Hist)* the legal profession
gens de service ⇒ **gens de maison**
les gens du théâtre the acting profession, theatrical people
les gens du voyage *(= gitans)* travellers

gens[2] /ʒɛ̃s/ NF *(Antiq)* gens

gent /ʒɑ̃(t)/ NF *(†† ou hum)* race, tribe ♦ **la ~ canine** the canine race ♦ **la ~ féminine/masculine** the male/female sex

gentiane /ʒɑ̃sjan/ NF gentian

gentil, -ille /ʒɑ̃ti, ij/ GRAMMAIRE ACTIVE 49, 52.4
ADJ [1] *(= aimable)* kind, nice *(avec, pour* to); ♦ **il a toujours un mot ~ pour chacun** he always has a kind word for everyone *ou* to say to everyone ♦ **vous serez ~ de me le rendre** would you mind giving it back to me ♦ **c'est ~ à toi** *ou* **de ta part de ...** it's very kind *ou* nice *ou* good of you to ... ♦ **tu es ~ tout plein*** you're so sweet ♦ **tout ça, c'est bien ~ mais ...** that's (all) very nice *ou* well but ... ♦ **elle est bien gentille avec ses histoires mais ...** what she has to say is all very well *ou* nice but ... ♦ **sois ~, va me le chercher** be a dear and go and get it for me
[2] *(= sage)* good ♦ **il n'a pas été ~** he hasn't been a good boy ♦ **sois ~, je reviens bientôt** be good, I'll be back soon
[3] *(= plaisant) [visage, endroit]* nice, pleasant ♦ **une gentille petite robe/fille** a nice little dress/girl ♦ **c'est ~ comme tout chez vous** you've got a lovely little place ♦ **c'est ~ sans plus** it's OK but it's nothing special
[4] *(= rondelet) [somme]* tidy, fair
NM *(Hist, Rel)* gentile

> ⚠ **gentil** ne se traduit pas par **gentle**, qui a le sens de 'doux'.

gentilé /ʒɑ̃tile/ NM gentilic

gentilhomme /ʒɑ̃tijɔm/ (pl **gentilshommes** /ʒɑ̃tizɔm/) NM *(Hist, fig)* gentleman ♦ **~ campagnard** country squire

gentilhommière /ʒɑ̃tijɔmjɛʀ/ NF (small) country seat, (small) manor house

gentillesse /ʒɑ̃tijɛs/ NF [1] *(= amabilité)* kindness ♦ **être d'une grande ~** to be very kind *(avec qn* to sb); ♦ **me ferez-vous** *ou* **auriez-vous la ~ de faire ...** would you be so kind as to do *ou* kind enough to do ... [2] *(= faveur)* favour *(Brit)*, favor *(US)*, kindness ♦ **remercier qn de toutes ses ~s** to thank sb for all his kindness(es) ♦ **une ~ en vaut une autre** one good turn deserves another ♦ **il me disait des ~s** he said kind *ou* nice things to me

gentillet, -ette /ʒɑ̃tijɛ, ɛt/ ADJ ♦ **c'est ~** *(= mignon) [appartement]* it's a nice little place; *(péj = insignifiant) [film, roman]* it's nice enough (but it's nothing special)

gentiment /ʒɑ̃timɑ̃/ ADV *(= aimablement)* kindly; *(= gracieusement)* nicely; *(= doucement)* gently ♦ **ils jouaient ~** they were playing nicely *ou* like good children ♦ **on m'a ~ fait comprendre que ...** *(iro)* they made it quite clear to me that ...

gentleman /ʒɑ̃tləman/ (pl **gentlemen** /dʒɑ̃tləmɛn/) NM gentleman ♦ **~-farmer** gentleman-farmer

gentleman's agreement /dʒɛntləmansagʀimɛnt/, **gentlemen's agreement** /dʒɛntləmɛnsagʀimɛnt/ NM gentleman's *ou* gentlemen's agreement

génuflexion /ʒenyflɛksjɔ̃/ NF *(Rel)* genuflexion ♦ **faire une ~** to make a genuflexion, to genuflect

géo* /ʒeo/ NF abrév de **géographie**

géochimie /ʒeoʃimi/ NF geochemistry

géode /ʒeɔd/ NF [1] *(Minér)* geode [2] *(= bâtiment)* geodesic dome

géodésie /ʒeɔdezi/ NF geodesy

géodésique /ʒeɔdezik/ ADJ geodesic ◆ **point ~** triangulation point ◆ **ligne ~** geodesic line NF geodesic

géodynamique /ʒeodinamik/ ADJ geodynamic NF geodynamics *(sg)*

géographe /ʒeɔgʀaf/ NMF geographer

géographie /ʒeɔgʀafi/ NF geography ◆ **~ humaine/économique/physique** human/economic/physical geography

géographique /ʒeɔgʀafik/ ADJ geographic(al); → **dictionnaire**

géographiquement /ʒeɔgʀafikmɑ̃/ ADV geographically

geôle /ʒol/ NF *(littér)* jail, gaol *(Brit)*

geôlier, -ière /ʒolje, jɛʀ/ NM,F *(littér)* jailer, gaoler *(Brit)*

géologie /ʒeɔlɔʒi/ NF geology

géologique /ʒeɔlɔʒik/ ADJ geological

géologue /ʒeɔlɔg/ NMF geologist

géomagnétique /ʒeomaɲetik/ ADJ geomagnetic

géomagnétisme /ʒeomaɲetism/ NM geomagnetism

géomancie /ʒeɔmɑ̃si/ NF geomancy

géomancien, -ienne /ʒeɔmɑ̃sjɛ̃, jɛn/ NM,F geomancer

géomètre /ʒeɔmɛtʀ/ NM 1 *(= arpenteur)* surveyor 2 *(= phalène)* emerald, geometrid *(SPÉC)*

géométrie /ʒeɔmetʀi/ NF *(= science)* geometry; *(= livre)* geometry book ◆ **~ descriptive/plane/analytique** descriptive/plane/analytical geometry ◆ **~ dans l'espace** solid geometry
◆ **à géométrie variable** ◆ **aile à ~ variable** *(Aviat)* variable-geometry *ou* swing wing ◆ **l'Europe à ~ variable** variable-geometry Europe ◆ **c'est une justice à ~ variable** it's one rule for some and another for the rest

géométrique /ʒeɔmetʀik/ ADJ geometric(al); → **lieu¹, progression**

géométriquement /ʒeɔmetʀikmɑ̃/ ADV geometrically

géomorphologie /ʒeomɔʀfɔlɔʒi/ NF geomorphology

géophysicien, -ienne /ʒeofizisjɛ̃, jɛn/ NM,F geophysicist

géophysique /ʒeofizik/ ADJ geophysical NF geophysics *(sg)*

géopolitique /ʒeopɔlitik/ ADJ geopolitical NF geopolitics *(sg)*

Georgetown /ʒɔʀʒtaun/ N Georgetown

georgette /ʒɔʀʒɛt/ NF → **crêpe²**

Géorgie /ʒeɔʀʒi/ NF Georgia ◆ **~ du Sud** South Georgia

géorgien, -ienne /ʒeɔʀʒjɛ̃, jɛn/ ADJ Georgian NM *(= langue)* Georgian NM,F **Géorgien(ne)** Georgian

géorgique /ʒeɔʀʒik/ ADJ *(Hist Littérat)* georgic

géosciences /ʒeosjɑ̃s/ NFPL geosciences

géostationnaire /ʒeostasjɔnɛʀ/ ADJ geostationary

géostratégie /ʒeostʀateʒi/ NF geostrategy

géostratégique /ʒeostʀateʒik/ ADJ geostrategic

géosynclinal (pl **-aux**) /ʒeosɛ̃klinal, o/ NM geosyncline

géothermie /ʒeotɛʀmi/ NF geothermal science

géothermique /ʒeotɛʀmik/ ADJ geothermal

gérable /ʒeʀabl/ ADJ manageable ◆ **difficilement ~** hard to handle ◆ **le club sportif n'est plus ~** the sports club has become unmanageable ◆ **la situation n'est plus ~** the situation is out of control *ou* is out of hand

gérance /ʒeʀɑ̃s/ NF *[de commerce, immeuble]* management ◆ **il assure la ~ d'une usine** he manages a factory ◆ **au cours de sa ~** while he was manager ◆ **prendre un commerce en ~** to take over the management of a business ◆ **il a mis son commerce en ~** he has appointed a manager for his business ◆ **être en ~ libre** *[entreprise]* to be run by a manager ◆ **~ salariée** salaried management

géranium /ʒeʀanjɔm/ NM geranium ◆ **~-lierre** ivy(-leaved) geranium

gérant /ʒeʀɑ̃/ NM *[d'usine, café, magasin, banque]* manager; *[d'immeuble]* managing agent, factor *(Écos)*; *[de journal]* managing editor ◆ **~ de portefeuilles** portfolio manager

gérante /ʒeʀɑ̃t/ NF *[d'usine, café, magasin, banque]* manager; *[d'immeuble]* managing agent; *[de journal]* managing editor

gerbage /ʒɛʀbaʒ/ NM 1 *(Agr)* binding, sheaving 2 *[de marchandises]* stacking, piling ◆ **"gerbage interdit"** "do not stack"

gerbe /ʒɛʀb/ NF *[de blé]* sheaf; *[d'osier]* bundle; *[de fleurs]* spray; *[d'étincelles]* shower, burst; *[d'écume]* shower, flurry ◆ **déposer une ~ sur une tombe** to place a spray of flowers on a grave ◆ **~ d'eau** spray *ou* shower of water ◆ **~ de flammes** *ou* **de feu** jet *ou* burst of flame

gerber /ʒɛʀbe/ ▸ conjug 1 ◂ VT 1 *(Agr)* to bind into sheaves, to sheave 2 *[+ marchandises]* to stack, to pile VI *(*‡* = vomir)* to throw up‡, to puke (up)‡ ◆ **il me fait ~, ce mec** that guy makes me want to throw up‡ ◆ **c'était à ~** it was crap‡

gerbera /ʒɛʀbeʀa/ NM gerbera

gerbeur /ʒɛʀbœʀ/ NM stacking *ou* pallet truck

gerbille /ʒɛʀbij/ NF gerbil

gerboise /ʒɛʀbwaz/ NF jerboa

gercer /ʒɛʀse/ ▸ conjug 3 ◂ VT *[+ peau, lèvres]* to chap, to crack; *[+ sol]* to crack ◆ **avoir les lèvres toutes gercées** to have badly chapped lips ◆ **j'ai les mains gercées** my hands are all cracked VI **se gercer** VPR *[peau, lèvres]* to chap, to crack; *[sol]* to crack

gerçure /ʒɛʀsyʀ/ NF *(gén)* (small) crack ◆ **pour éviter les ~s** to avoid chapping

gérer /ʒeʀe/ ▸ conjug 6 ◂ VT *[+ entreprise, projet]* to manage, to run; *[+ pays]* to run; *[+ carrière, budget, temps, données, biens, fortune]* to manage ◆ **il gère bien ses affaires** he manages his affairs well ◆ **il a mal géré son affaire** he has mismanaged his business, he has managed his business badly ◆ **~ la crise** *(Pol)* to handle *ou* control the crisis

gerfaut /ʒɛʀfo/ NM gyrfalcon

gériatre /ʒeʀjatʀ/ NMF geriatrician

gériatrie /ʒeʀjatʀi/ NF geriatrics *(sg)*

gériatrique /ʒeʀjatʀik/ ADJ geriatric

germain, e /ʒɛʀmɛ̃, ɛn/ ADJ 1 → **cousin¹** 2 *(Hist)* German NM,F *(Hist)* ◆ **Germain(e)** German

Germanie /ʒɛʀmani/ NF *(Hist)* Germania

germanique /ʒɛʀmanik/ ADJ Germanic NM *(= langue)* Germanic NMF **Germanique** Germanic

germanisant, e /ʒɛʀmanizɑ̃, ɑ̃t/ NM,F ⇒ **germaniste**

germanisation /ʒɛʀmanizasjɔ̃/ NF germanization

germaniser /ʒɛʀmanize/ ▸ conjug 1 ◂ VT to germanize

germanisme /ʒɛʀmanism/ NM *(Ling)* germanism

germaniste /ʒɛʀmanist/ NMF German scholar, germanist

germanium /ʒɛʀmanjɔm/ NM germanium

germanophile /ʒɛʀmanɔfil/ ADJ, NMF germanophil(e)

germanophilie /ʒɛʀmanɔfili/ NF germanophilia

germanophobe /ʒɛʀmanɔfɔb/ ADJ germanophobic NMF germanophobe

germanophobie /ʒɛʀmanɔfɔbi/ NF germanophobia

germanophone /ʒɛʀmanɔfɔn/ ADJ *[personne]* German-speaking; *[littérature]* German-language *(épith)*, in German *(attrib)* NMF German speaker

germe /ʒɛʀm/ NM 1 *(Bio) [d'embryon, graine]* germ; *[d'œuf]* germinal disc; *[de pomme de terre]* eye ◆ **~s de blé** wheatgerm *(NonC)* ◆ **~s de soja** (soya) bean sprouts ◆ **~ dentaire** tooth bud; → **porteur** 2 *(= source) [de maladie, erreur, vie]* seed ◆ **~ d'une idée** germ of an idea ◆ **avoir ou contenir en ~** to contain in embryo, to contain the seeds of ◆ **l'idée était en ~ depuis longtemps** the idea had existed in embryo for a long time 3 *(Méd = microbe)* germ ◆ **~s pathogènes** pathogenic bacteria

germer /ʒɛʀme/ ▸ conjug 1 ◂ VI *[bulbe, graine]* to sprout, to germinate; *[idée]* to form, to germinate *(frm)* ◆ **pommes de terre germées** sprouting potatoes ◆ **l'idée a commencé à ~ dans ma tête** the idea began to form in my mind

germicide /ʒɛʀmisid/ ADJ germicidal NM germicide

germinal¹, e (mpl **-aux**) /ʒɛʀminal, o/ ADJ germinal

germinal² /ʒɛʀminal/ NM Germinal *(seventh month in the French Republican calendar)*

germinateur, -trice /ʒɛʀminatœʀ, tʀis/ ADJ germinative

germinatif, -ive /ʒɛʀminatif, iv/ ADJ germinal

germination /ʒɛʀminasjɔ̃/ NF *(Bot, fig)* germination ◆ **en ~** *[plante]* germinating

germoir /ʒɛʀmwaʀ/ NM *(pour graines)* seed tray; *[de brasserie]* maltings *(sg)*

gérondif /ʒeʀɔ̃dif/ NM *(latin, avec être)* gerundive; *(complément de nom)* gerund; *(français)* gerund

gérontocratie /ʒeʀɔ̃tɔkʀasi/ NF gerontocracy

gérontocratique /ʒeʀɔ̃tɔkʀatik/ ADJ gerontocratic

gérontologie /ʒeʀɔ̃tɔlɔʒi/ NF gerontology

gérontologique /ʒeʀɔ̃tɔlɔʒik/ ADJ gerontological

gérontologiste /ʒeʀɔ̃tɔlɔʒist/, **gérontologue** /ʒeʀɔ̃tɔlɔg/ NMF gerontologist

gérontophile /ʒeʀɔ̃tɔfil/ NMF gerontophile, gerontophiliac

gérontophilie /ʒeʀɔ̃tɔfili/ NF gerontophilia

gésier /ʒezje/ NM gizzard

gésine /ʒezin/ NF ◆ **être en ~** † *(= accoucher)* to be in labour *(Brit)* *ou* labor *(US)*

gésir /ʒeziʀ/ VI *[personne]* to be lying (down), to lie (down); *[arbres, objets]* to lie ◆ **il gisait sur le sol** he was lying *ou* lay on the ground ◆ **là gît le problème** therein lies the problem ◆ **c'est là que gît le lièvre** *(fig)* there's the rub

gestaltisme /gɛʃtaltism/ NM Gestalt (psychology)

gestation /ʒɛstasjɔ̃/ NF gestation ◆ **en ~** *(lit)* in gestation ◆ **être en ~** *[roman, projet]* to be in preparation, to be in the pipeline

geste¹ /ʒɛst/ NM 1 *(= mouvement)* gesture ◆ **~ d'approbation/d'effroi** gesture of approval/of terror ◆ **~ maladroit** *ou* **malheureux** clumsy gesture *ou* movement ◆ **pas un ~ ou je tire !** one move and I'll shoot! ◆ **il parlait en faisant de grands ~s** he waved his hands about as he spoke ◆ **il refusa d'un ~** he made a gesture of refusal, he gestured his refusal ◆ **il le fit entrer d'un ~** he motioned *ou* gestured *ou* waved to him to come in ◆ **il lui indiqua la porte d'un ~** with a gesture he showed him the door ◆ **faire un ~ de la main** to gesture with one's hand, to give a wave (of one's hand) ◆ **s'exprimer par ~s** to use one's hands to express o.s. ◆ **il ne fit pas un ~ pour l'aider** *(fig)* he didn't lift a finger *ou* make a move to help him ◆ **tu n'as qu'un ~ à faire pour qu'il revienne** *(fig)* just say the word *ou* you only have to say the word and he'll come back; → **fait¹, joindre**

2 *(= action)* gesture ◆ **quelle précision dans le ~ de l'horloger** what precision there is in every move of the watchmaker's hand ◆ **c'est un ~ très difficile** it's very difficult to do ◆ **c'est un ~ quotidien** it's something you do every day ◆ **trier les ordures, c'est un ~ simple** sorting rubbish is an easy thing to do ◆ **il maîtrise parfaitement tous les ~s techniques** he has great technical skill ◆ **le ~ du service** *(Tennis)* service (action) ◆ **des ~s de bonne volonté** goodwill gestures ◆ **~ de défi/de conciliation** gesture of defiance/of reconciliation ◆ **~ politique** political gesture ◆ **un ~ symbolique** a token gesture ◆ **beau ~** noble deed ◆ **un ~ désespéré** a desperate act ◆ **dans un ~ de désespoir** in sheer despair ◆ **comment expliquer ce ~ ?** how can we explain what he (*ou* she *etc*) did? ◆ **faire un ~ commercial** *(= faire une remise)* to offer a reduction ◆ **faire un (petit) ~** to make a (small) gesture

geste² /ʒɛst/ NF *(Littérat)* gest(e); → **chanson**

gesticulation /ʒɛstikylasjɔ̃/ NF gesticulation, gesticulating *(NonC)*

gesticuler /ʒɛstikyle/ ▸ conjug 1 ◂ VI to gesticulate

gestion /ʒɛstjɔ̃/ NF *[d'entreprise, projet]* management, running; *[de pays]* running; *[de biens, carrière, temps, déchets]* management ◆ **mauvaise ~** mismanagement, bad management ◆ **~ administrative** administration, administrative management ◆ **~ de portefeuilles** portfolio management ◆ **~ des stocks** stock *(Brit)* ou inventory *(US)* control ◆ **~ des ressources humaines** human resources management ◆ **~ de fichiers/mémoire/base de données** file/memory/database management ◆ **~ de la production assistée par ordinateur** computer-assisted production management ◆ **la ~ quotidienne de l'entreprise** the day-to-day running of the company ◆ **la ~ des affaires publiques** the conduct of public affairs ◆ **~ du temps** time management

gestionnaire /ʒɛstjɔnɛʀ/ ADJ administrative, management *(épith)* NMF administrator ◆ **~ de portefeuilles** portfolio manager NM *(Ordin)* manager ◆ **~ de base de données/de fichiers/de programmes** database/file/program manager ◆ **~ de mémoire/de réseau** memory/network manager ◆ **~ d'écran** screen monitor ◆ **~ d'impression** print monitor *ou* manager ◆ **~ de périphériques** device driver

gestuel, -elle /ʒɛstɥɛl/ ADJ gestural NF **gestuelle** body movements

Gethsemani /ʒetsəmani/ N Gethsemane

geyser /ʒɛzɛʀ/ NM geyser

Ghana /gana/ NM Ghana

ghanéen, -enne /ganeɛ̃, ɛn/ ADJ Ghanaian NM,F **Ghanéen(ne)** Ghanaian

ghetto /geto/ NM *(lit, fig)* ghetto ◆ **cité-~** inner-city ghetto ◆ **banlieue-~** run-down suburban area

ghilde /gild/ NF ⇒ **guilde**

GI /dʒiaj/ NM (abrév de **Government Issue**) *(= soldat américain)* GI

gibbeux, -euse /ʒibø, øz/ ADJ *(Astron, littér)* gibbous, gibbose

gibbon /ʒibɔ̃/ NM gibbon

gibbosité /ʒibozite/ NF *(Astron, Méd, littér)* hump, gibbosity *(SPÉC)*

gibecière /ʒib(ə)sjɛʀ/ NF *(gén)* (leather) shoulder bag; *[de chasseur]* gamebag; † *[d'écolier]* satchel

gibelin /ʒiblɛ̃/ NM *(Hist)* Ghibelline

gibelotte /ʒiblɔt/ NF *fricassee of game in wine*

giberne /ʒibɛʀn/ NF cartridge pouch

gibet /ʒibɛ/ NM gibbet, gallows ◆ **condamner qn au ~** *(Hist)* to condemn sb to death by hanging, to condemn sb to the gallows

gibier /ʒibje/ NM 1 *(Chasse)* game ◆ **gros/menu ~** big/small game ◆ **~ d'eau** waterfowl ◆ **~ à poil** game animals ◆ **~ à plume** game birds 2 *(= personne)* prey ◆ **les policiers attendaient leur ~** the policemen awaited their prey ◆ **~ de potence** gallows bird ◆ **le gros ~** big game

giboulée /ʒibule/ NF (sudden) shower, sudden downpour ◆ **~ de mars** ≈ April shower

giboyeux, -euse /ʒibwajø, øz/ ADJ *[pays, forêt]* abounding in game, well-stocked with game

Gibraltar /ʒibʀaltaʀ/ NM Gibraltar

gibus /ʒibys/ NM opera hat

GIC /ʒeise/ NM (abrév de **grand invalide civil**) ◆ **macaron ~** disabled sticker; → **invalide**

giclée /ʒikle/ NF spurt, squirt

gicler /ʒikle/ ▸ conjug 1 ◂ VI 1 *(= jaillir)* to spurt, to squirt ◆ **faire ~ de l'eau d'un robinet** to squirt water from a tap ◆ **le véhicule a fait ~ de l'eau à son passage** the vehicle sent up a spray of water as it went past 2 *(** = être expulsé) [+ personne]* to be given the bum's rush**, to get the boot**; *[+ objet]* to be tossed (out) *ou* chucked* (out)

gicleur /ʒiklœʀ/ NM *(Aut)* jet ◆ **~ de ralenti** idle, slow-running jet *(Brit)*

GIE /ʒeiə/ NM (abrév de **groupement d'intérêt économique**) → **groupement**

gifle /ʒifl/ NF *(lit)* slap (in the face), smack (on the face); *(fig)* slap in the face ◆ **donner** *ou* **filer*** *ou* **flanquer*** *ou* **allonger* une ~ à qn** to slap sb in the face, to give sb a slap in the face

gifler /ʒifle/ ▸ conjug 1 ◂ VT to slap (in the face) ◆ **~ qn** to slap *ou* smack sb's face, to slap sb in the face ◆ **visage giflé par la grêle** face lashed by (the) hail

GIG /ʒeiʒe/ NM (abrév de **grand invalide de guerre**) → **invalide**

giga... /ʒiga/ PRÉF giga... ◆ **gigahertz** gigahertz ◆ **gigaoctet** gigabyte ◆ **gigawatt** gigawatt

gigantesque /ʒigɑ̃tɛsk/ ADJ huge, gigantic

gigantisme /ʒigɑ̃tism/ NM *(Méd)* gigantism; *(= grandeur)* gigantic size *ou* proportions ◆ **ville/entreprise atteinte de ~** city/firm that suffers from overexpansion on a gigantic scale

GIGN /ʒeiʒeen/ NM (abrév de **Groupe d'intervention de la Gendarmerie nationale**) *special task force of the Gendarmerie,* ≈ SAS *(Brit)*, SWAT *(US)*

gigogne /ʒigɔɲ/ ADJ ◆ **c'est un dossier-~** the case is full of surprises; → **lit, poupée, table**

gigolette /ʒigɔlɛt/ NF *(Culin)* ◆ **~ de canard/de dinde** leg of duck/of turkey

gigolo* /ʒigɔlo/ NM gigolo

gigot /ʒigo/ NM ◆ **~ de mouton/d'agneau** leg of mutton/lamb ◆ **~ de chevreuil** haunch of venison ◆ **une tranche de ~** a slice off the leg of mutton *ou* lamb *etc*, a slice off the joint ◆ **elle a de bons ~s*** she has nice sturdy legs; → **manche¹**

gigoter* /ʒigɔte/ ▸ conjug 1 ◂ VI to wriggle (about)

gigoteuse /ʒigɔtøz/ NF sleeper, Babygro ® *(Brit)*

gigue /ʒig/ NF *(Mus)* gigue; *(= danse)* jig ◆ **~s*** *(= jambes)* legs ◆ **grande ~** *(péj = fille)* beanpole* *(Brit)*, string bean* *(US)* ◆ **~ de chevreuil** haunch of venison

gilde /gild/ NF ⇒ **guilde**

gilet /ʒilɛ/ NM *(de complet)* waistcoat *(Brit)*, vest *(US)*; *(= cardigan)* cardigan ◆ **~ (de corps** *ou* **de peau)** vest *(Brit)*, undershirt *(US)* ◆ **~ pare-balles** bulletproof jacket, flak jacket* ◆ **~ de sauvetage** *(gén)* life jacket; *(dans avion)* life vest; → **pleurer**

giletier, -ière /ʒil(ə)tje, jɛʀ/ NM,F waistcoat *(Brit)* *ou* vest *(US)* maker

gin /dʒin/ NM gin ◆ **~ tonic** gin and tonic

gingembre /ʒɛ̃ʒɑ̃bʀ/ NM ginger ◆ **racine de ~** root ginger *(NonC)*, ginger root *(NonC)*

gingival, e (mpl **-aux**) /ʒɛ̃ʒival, o/ ADJ gingival ◆ **pâte ~e** gum ointment

gingivite /ʒɛ̃ʒivit/ NF inflammation of the gums, gingivitis *(SPÉC)*

ginkgo /ʒiŋko/ NM ginkgo

gin-rami, gin-rummy /dʒinʀami/ NM gin rummy

ginseng /ʒinsɛŋ/ NM ginseng

girafe /ʒiʀaf/ NF *(= animal)* giraffe; *(péj = personne)* beanpole* *(Brit)*, string bean* *(US)*; *(Ciné)* boom; → **peigner**

girafeau /ʒiʀafo/, **girafon** /ʒiʀafɔ̃/ NM baby giraffe

girandole /ʒiʀɑ̃dɔl/ NF *(= chandelier)* candelabra, girandole; *(= feu d'artifice, guirlande lumineuse)* girandole

girasol /ʒiʀasɔl/ NM girasol

giration /ʒiʀasjɔ̃/ NF gyration

giratoire /ʒiʀatwaʀ/ ADJ gyrating, gyratory; → **sens**

girelle /ʒiʀɛl/ NF rainbow wrasse

girl /gœʀl/ NF chorus girl

girofle /ʒiʀɔfl/ NM clove; → **clou**

giroflée /ʒiʀɔfle/ NF wallflower, gillyflower; *(vivace)* stock ◆ **~ à cinq feuilles*** *(= gifle)* slap in the face

giroflier /ʒiʀɔflije/ NM clove tree

girolle /ʒiʀɔl/ NF chanterelle

giron /ʒiʀɔ̃/ NM *(= genoux)* lap; *(= sein)* bosom ◆ **après son retour dans le ~ familial** *(personne)* since his return to the fold ◆ **l'entreprise a quitté le ~ du groupe** the company is no longer part of the group ◆ **passer dans le ~ de l'État** *[entreprise]* to be nationalized ◆ **l'entreprise reste dans le ~ de l'État** the company continues to be state-run

Gironde /ʒiʀɔ̃d/ NF ◆ **la ~** the Gironde

gironde †* /ʒiʀɔ̃, ɔ̃d/ ADJ F buxom, well-padded*

girondin, e /ʒiʀɔ̃dɛ̃, in/ ADJ *(Géog)* from the Gironde; *(Hist)* Girondist NM,F *(Géog)* inhabitant *ou* native of the Gironde NM *(Hist)* Girondist

girouette /ʒiʀwɛt/ NF weather vane *ou* cock ◆ **c'est une vraie ~** *(fig)* he changes (his mind) with the weather, he changes his mind depending on which way the wind is blowing

gisait, gisaient /ʒizɛ/ → **gésir**

gisant, e /ʒizɑ̃, ɑ̃t/ ADJ lying NM *(Art)* recumbent statue *(on tomb)*

gisement /ʒizmɑ̃/ NM 1 *(Minér)* deposit ◆ **~ de pétrole** oilfield ◆ **~ houiller** coal seam ◆ **~ gazier** gas field 2 *[de clientèle]* pool ◆ **~ d'emplois** source of jobs *ou* employment ◆ **pour trouver des ~s de productivité/d'économies** to find opportunities for increasing productivity/cutting costs 3 *(Naut)* bearing

gisent /ʒiz/, **gît** /ʒi/ → **gésir**

gitan, e /ʒitɑ̃, an/ ADJ gipsy *(épith)* NM,F **Gitan(e)** gipsy **Gitane** ® NF (= *cigarette)* Gitane *(cigarette)*

gîte[1] /ʒit/ NM 1 (= *abri)* shelter; († = *maison)* home; *(Tourisme)* gîte, self-catering cottage *ou* flat ◆ **rentrer au** ~ to return home ◆ **ils lui donnent le** ~ **et le couvert** they give him room and board *ou* board and lodging *(Brit)* ◆ ~ **d'étape** *(pour randonneurs)* lodge ◆ ~ **rural** (country) gîte, self-catering cottage (in the country) 2 *(Chasse) [de lièvre]* form 3 *(Boucherie)* ~ **(à la noix)** topside *(Brit)*, bottom round *(US)* ◆ ~-~ shin *(Brit)*, shank *(US)* 4 *(Minér)* deposit

gîte[2] /ʒit/ NF *(Naut = emplacement d'épave)* bed *(of a sunken ship)* ◆ **donner de la** ~ to list, to heel

gîter /ʒite/ ▸ conjug 1 ◂ VI *(littér)* to lodge; *(Naut)* (= *pencher)* to list, to heel; (= *être échoué)* to be aground

givrage /ʒivʀaʒ/ NM *[d'avion]* icing

givrant, e /ʒivʀɑ̃, ɑ̃t/ ADJ → **brouillard**

givre /ʒivʀ/ NM 1 (= *gelée blanche)* (hoar) frost, rime *(SPÉC)*; → **fleur** 2 *(Chim)* crystallization

givré, e /ʒivʀe/ (ptp de **givrer**) ADJ 1 *[arbre]* covered in frost; *[fenêtre, hélice]* iced-up; *[verre]* frosted ◆ **orange** ~**e** orange sorbet served in the (orange) skin 2 * (= *ivre)* plastered‡; (= *fou)* cracked*, nuts*, bonkers‡ *(Brit)* ◆ **devenir complètement** ~ to go completely off one's head *ou* rocker‡

givrer VT, **se givrer** VPR /ʒivʀe/ ▸ conjug 1 ◂ *[pare-brise, aile d'avion]* to ice up

glabre /glabʀ/ ADJ (= *imberbe)* hairless; (= *rasé)* clean-shaven; *(Bot)* glabrous

glaçage /glasaʒ/ NM *[de viande, papier, étoffe]* glazing; *[de gâteau]* (au sucre) icing; *(au blanc d'œuf)* glazing

glaçant, e /glasɑ̃, ɑ̃t/ ADJ *[attitude, accueil, ton]* frosty, chilly; *[humour]* icy

glace[1] /glas/ NF 1 (= *eau congelée)* ice *(NonC)* ◆ ~ **pilée** crushed ice ◆ **sports de** ~ ice sports ◆ **briser** *ou* **rompre la** ~ *(lit, fig)* to break the ice; → **compartiment, hockey, saint** *etc* 2 ◆ **de** ~ (= *insensible, peu chaleureux) [accueil]* icy, frosty; *[expression, visage]* stony, frosty ◆ **rester de** ~ to remain unmoved 3 *(Culin)* (= *dessert)* ice cream; *(pour pâtisserie = glaçage)* royal icing, frosting *(US)* ◆ ~ **à l'eau** water ice *(Brit)*, sherbet *(US)* ◆ ~ **à la crème** dairy ice cream ◆ ~ **à la vanille/au café** vanilla/coffee ice cream ◆ ~ **(à l')italienne** soft ice cream; → **sucre** NFPL **glaces** *(Géog)* ice sheet(s), ice field(s) ◆ ~**s flottantes** drift ice, ice floe(s) ◆ **canal bloqué par les** ~**s** canal blocked with ice *ou* with ice floes ◆ **bateau pris dans les** ~**s** icebound ship

glace[2] /glas/ NF 1 (= *miroir)* mirror ◆ ~ **à main** hand mirror; → **armoire, tain** 2 (= *verre)* plate glass *(NonC)*; (= *plaque)* sheet of (plate) glass ◆ **la** ~ **d'une vitrine** the glass of a shop window 3 *[de véhicule]* (= *vitre)* window 4 *(Bijouterie)* white speckle

glacé, e /glase/ (ptp de **glacer**) ADJ *[neige, lac]* frozen; *[vent, eau, chambre]* icy, freezing; *[boisson]* icy, ice-cold; *[cuir, tissu]* glazed; *[fruit]* glacé; *[accueil, attitude, sourire]* frosty, chilly ◆ **je suis** ~ I'm frozen (stiff), I'm chilled to the bone ◆ **j'ai les mains** ~**es** my hands are frozen *ou* freezing ◆ **à servir** ~ to be served iced *ou* ice-cold ◆ **café/chocolat** ~ iced coffee/chocolate; → **crème, marron**[1]**, papier**

glacer /glase/ ▸ conjug 3 ◂ VT 1 *[+ liquide]* (= *geler)* to freeze; (= *rafraîchir)* to chill, to ice ◆ **mettre des boissons à** ~ to put some drinks to chill

2 *[+ personne, membres]* to make freezing, to freeze ◆ **ce vent glace les oreilles** your ears freeze with this wind ◆ **ce vent vous glace** it's a freezing *ou* perishing *(Brit)* (cold) wind, this wind chills you to the bone

3 ◆ ~ **qn** (= *intimider)* to turn sb cold, to chill sb; (= *paralyser)* to make sb's blood run cold ◆ **cela l'a glacé d'horreur** *ou* **d'épouvante** he was frozen with terror at this ◆ ~ **le sang de qn** to make sb's blood run cold, to chill sb's blood ◆ **cette réponse lui glaça le cœur** *(littér)* this reply turned his heart to ice ◆ **son attitude vous glace** he has a chilling way about him

4 *[+ viande, papier, étoffe]* to glaze; *[+ gâteau] (au sucre)* to ice; *(au blanc d'œuf)* to glaze

VPR **se glacer** *[eau]* to freeze ◆ **mon sang se glaça dans mes veines** my blood ran cold *ou* my blood froze in my veins ◆ **son sourire/son expression se glaça** his smile/expression froze

glaceuse /glasøz/ NF glazing machine

glaciaire /glasjɛʀ/ ADJ *[période, calotte]* ice *(épith)*; *[relief, régime, vallée, érosion]* glacial NM ◆ **le** ~ the glacial, the ice age

glaciairiste /glasjɛʀist/ NMF ice climber

glacial, e (mpl **glacials** *ou* **glaciaux**) /glasjal, jo/ ADJ 1 *[froid]* icy, freezing *(épith)*; *[nuit, pluie, vent]* icy, freezing (cold); → **océan** 2 *[accueil, silence, regard]* frosty, icy ◆ **c'est quelqu'un de** ~ he's a real cold fish, he's a real iceberg ◆ **"non", dit-elle d'un ton** ~ "no", she said frostily *ou* icily

glaciation /glasjasjɔ̃/ NF glaciation

glacier /glasje/ NM 1 *(Géog)* glacier 2 (= *fabricant)* ice-cream maker; (= *vendeur)* ice-cream man; → **pâtissier**

glacière /glasjɛʀ/ NF icebox, cool box ◆ **c'est une vraie** ~ **ici !** it's like a fridge *ou* an icebox in here!

glaciériste /glasjeʀist/ NMF ⇒ **glaciairiste**

glaciologie /glasjɔlɔʒi/ NF glaciology

glaciologue /glasjɔlɔg/ NMF glaciologist

glacis /glasi/ NM 1 *(Art)* glaze 2 *(Archit)* weathering; *(Géog, Mil)* glacis

glaçon /glasɔ̃/ NM *[de rivière]* block of ice; *[de toit]* icicle; *[de boisson]* ice cube; *(péj = personne)* cold fish ◆ **avec ou sans** ~ **?** *(boisson)* with or without ice? ◆ **mes pieds sont comme des** ~**s** my feet are like blocks of ice

gladiateur /gladjatœʀ/ NM gladiator

glagla * /glagla/ **à glagla** LOC EXCL it's freezing!

glaïeul /glajœl/ NM gladiola, gladiolus ◆ **des** ~**s** gladioli

glaire /glɛʀ/ NF *[d'œuf]* white; *(Méd)* phlegm ◆ ~ **cervicale** cervical mucus

glaireux, -euse /glɛʀø, øz/ ADJ slimy

glaise /glɛz/ NF clay; → **terre**

glaiseux, -euse /glɛzø, øz/ ADJ clayey

glaisière /glɛzjɛʀ/ NF clay pit

glaive /glɛv/ NM two-edged sword ◆ **le** ~ **de la justice** *(littér)* the sword of justice ◆ **le** ~ **et la balance** the sword and the scales

glamour /glamuʀ/ ADJ INV *[personne, tenue, photo]* glamorous; *[émission]* glitzy* NM ◆ **le** ~ glamour

glanage /glanaʒ/ NM gleaning

gland /glɑ̃/ NM *(Bot)* acorn; *(Anat)* glans; (= *ornement)* tassel ◆ **quel** ~ **!** (*‡ = *imbécile)* what a prick!*‡

glande /glɑ̃d/ NF gland ◆ **avoir des** ~**s** *(Méd)* to have swollen glands ◆ **avoir les** ~**s**‡ (= *être en colère)* to be really *ou* hopping *(Brit)* mad*; (= *être anxieux)* to be all wound-up*

glander‡ /glɑ̃de/ ▸ conjug 1 ◂ VI (= *traînailler)* to fart around*‡ *(Brit)*, to footle about* *(Brit)*, to screw around‡ *(US)*; (= *attendre)* to hang around*, to kick one's heels* *(Brit)* ◆ **j'en ai rien à** ~ I don't give *ou* care a damn‡ ◆ **qu'est-ce que tu glandes ?** what the hell are you doing?‡

glandeur, -euse‡ /glɑ̃dœʀ, øz/ NM,F layabout*, shirker ◆ **c'est un vrai** ~ he's a lazy bastard*‡ *ou* slob‡

glandouiller‡ /glɑ̃duje/ ▸ conjug 1 ◂ VI ⇒ **glander**

glandulaire /glɑ̃dylɛʀ/ ADJ glandular

glane /glan/ NF 1 (= *glanage)* gleaning 2 (= *chapelet)* ~ **d'oignons/d'ail** string of onions/of garlic

glaner /glane/ ▸ conjug 1 ◂ VT *(lit, fig)* to glean

glaneur, -euse /glanœʀ, øz/ NM,F gleaner

glapir /glapiʀ/ ▸ conjug 2 ◂ VI *[renard]* to bark; *[chien]* to yap, to yelp; *(péj) [personne]* to yelp, to squeal VT *[+ insultes]* to scream

glapissement /glapismɑ̃/ NM *[de renard]* barking; *[de chien]* yapping, yelping ◆ ~**s** *[personne en colère]* shouting

glas /glɑ/ NM knell *(NonC)*, toll *(NonC)* ◆ **on sonne le** ~ the bell is tolling, they are tolling the knell *ou* bell ◆ **sonner le** ~ **de** *(fig)* to toll *ou* sound the knell of

glasnost /glasnɔst/ NF *(Hist)* glasnost ◆ **le parti est en train de faire sa** ~ the party is pursuing a policy of glasnost *ou* openness

glaucome /glokom/ NM glaucoma

glauque /glok/ ADJ 1 (= *vert-bleu)* blue-green 2 (*, *péj = louche) [quartier, hôtel]* shabby; *[atmosphère]* murky; *[individu]* shifty, shady 3 (= *lugubre)* dreary

glaviot‡ /glavjo/ NM gob of spit‡

glavioter‡ /glavjɔte/ ▸ conjug 1 ◂ VI to spit, to gob‡ *(Brit)*

glèbe /glɛb/ NF *(Hist, littér)* glebe

glissade /glisad/ NF 1 ◆ **faire une** ~ *(par jeu)* to slide; (= *tomber)* to slip; (= *déraper)* to skid ◆ ~ **sur l'aile** *(en avion)* sideslip ◆ **il fit une** ~ **mortelle** he slipped and was fatally injured ◆ **faire des** ~**s sur la glace** to slide on the ice ◆ **la** ~ **du dollar** the slide of the dollar 2 *(Danse)* glissade

glissage /glisaʒ/ NM sledging *(of wood)*

glissant, e /glisɑ̃, ɑ̃t/ ADJ *[sol, savon, poisson]* slippery; *(Fin) [taux]* floating ◆ **sur un mois** ~ over a period of thirty days; → **terrain**

glisse /glis/ NF *(Ski)* glide ◆ **sports de** ~ *sports which involve sliding or gliding (eg skiing, surfing, skating)*

glissé, e /glise/ (ptp de **glisser**) ADJ, NM ◆ **(pas)** ~ glissé

glissement /glismɑ̃/ NM *[de porte, rideau, pièce]* sliding; *[de bateau]* gliding; *(Ski, Phon)* glide; *[de prix]* slide ◆ ~ **électoral (à gauche)** electoral swing *ou* move (to the left) ◆ ~ **de sens** shift in meaning ◆ ~ **de terrain** landslide, landslip ◆ **le récent** ~ **de la Bourse** the recent downturn in the stock exchange

glisser /glise/ ▸ conjug 1 ◂ VI 1 (= *avancer)* to slide along; *[voilier, nuages, patineurs]* to glide along; *[fer à repasser]* to slide along ◆ **le bateau glissait sur les eaux** the boat glided over the water ◆ **avec ce fart, on glisse bien** *(Ski)* you slide *ou* glide easily with this wax, this wax slides *ou* glides easily ◆ **il fit** ~ **le fauteuil sur le sol** he slid the armchair across the floor

2 (= *tomber)* to slide ◆ **ils glissèrent le long de la pente dans le ravin** they slid down the slope into the gully ◆ **il se laissa** ~ **le long du mur** he slid down the wall ◆ **une larme glissa le long de sa joue** a tear trickled *ou* slid down his cheek ◆ **d'un geste maladroit il fit** ~ **le paquet dans le ravin** with a clumsy movement he sent the parcel sliding down into the gully ◆ **il fit** ~ **l'argent dans sa poche** he slipped the money into his pocket

3 *(péj = dériver)* to slip ◆ **le pays glisse vers l'anarchie** the country is slipping *ou* sliding into anarchy ◆ **le pays glisse vers la droite** the country is moving *ou* swinging towards the right ◆ **il glisse dans la délinquance** he's slipping into crime

4 *(= déraper) [personne, objet]* to slip; *[véhicule, pneus]* to skid ◆ **il a glissé sur la glace et il est tombé** he slipped on the ice and fell ◆ **son pied a glissé** his foot slipped

5 *(= être glissant) [parquet]* to be slippery ◆ **attention, ça glisse** be careful, it's slippery (underfoot)

6 *(= coulisser) [tiroir, rideau]* to slide; *[curseur, anneau]* to slide (along) ◆ **ces tiroirs ne glissent pas bien** these drawers don't slide (in and out) easily

7 *(= s'échapper)* ~ **de la table/de la poêle** to slide off the table/out of the frying pan ◆ ~ **des mains** to slip out of one's hands ◆ **le voleur leur a glissé entre les mains** the thief slipped (right) through their fingers

8 *(= effleurer)* ~ **sur** *[+ sujet]* to skate over ◆ **ses doigts glissaient sur les touches** his fingers slipped over the keys ◆ **les reproches glissent sur lui (comme l'eau sur les plumes d'un canard)** criticism is like water off a duck's back to him ◆ **glissons !** let's not dwell on that! ◆ **la balle glissa sur le blindage** the bullet glanced off the armour plating ◆ **son regard glissa d'un objet à l'autre** he glanced from one object to another, his eyes slipped from one object to another ◆ **glissez, mortels, n'appuyez pas !** *(Prov)* enough said!

VT *(= introduire)* ◆ ~ **qch sous/dans qch** to slip *ou* slide sth under/into sth ◆ ~ **une lettre sous la porte** to slip *ou* slide a letter under the door ◆ **il me glissa un billet dans la main** he slipped a note into my hand ◆ ~ **un mot à l'oreille de qn** to whisper a word in sb's ear ◆ **il glisse toujours des proverbes dans sa conversation** he's always slipping proverbs into his conversation ◆ **il me glissa un regard en coulisse** he gave me a sidelong glance ◆ **il me glissa que ...** he whispered to me that ...

VPR **se glisser** 1 *[personne, animal]* **se ~ quelque part** to slip somewhere ◆ **le chien s'est glissé sous le lit/derrière l'armoire** the dog crept under the bed/behind the cupboard ◆ **se ~ dans les draps** to slip between the sheets ◆ **le voleur a réussi à se ~ dans la maison** the thief managed to sneak *ou* slip into the house ◆ **il a réussi à se ~ jusqu'au premier rang** he managed to edge *ou* worm his way to the front *ou* to slip through to the front

2 ◆ **se ~ dans** *[erreur, sentiment]* to creep into ◆ **l'inquiétude/le soupçon se glissa en lui/dans son cœur** anxiety/suspicion stole over him/into his heart ◆ **une erreur s'est glissée dans le texte** a mistake has slipped *ou* crept into the text

glissière /glisjɛʀ/ NF slide *ou* sliding channel; *[de siège d'auto]* runner ◆ **porte/panneau à ~** sliding door/panel ◆ ~ **de sécurité** *(sur une route)* crash barrier; → **fermeture**

glissoire /gliswaʀ/ NF *(= piste)* slide *(on ice or snow)*

global, e (mpl **-aux**) /glɔbal, o/ ADJ 1 *(= total) [montant, coût, budget]* total; *[accord, politique, stratégie]* comprehensive, general; *[baisse, offre, résultat, résumé, idée]* overall; *[perspective, vue, vision]* overall, comprehensive ◆ **c'est un prix ~** it's an all-inclusive price ◆ **offre ~e** *(Comm)* package ◆ **méthode ~e** word recognition method *(to teach reading)* 2 *(= mondial) [économie, marché]* global; → **village**

NM **au global** overall

> ⚠ **global** se traduit par le mot anglais **global** uniquement au sens de 'mondial'.

globalement /glɔbalmɑ̃/ ADV 1 *(= dans l'ensemble)* on the whole ◆ **je suis ~ satisfait de son travail** on the whole I find his work satisfactory ◆ ~ **nous sommes tous d'accord** on the whole we agree ◆ ~, **nos ventes ont diminué** our overall sales have fallen 2 *(= en bloc)* globally ◆ **traiter un problème ~** to take a holistic approach to a problem

globalisant, e /glɔbalizɑ̃, ɑ̃t/, **globalisateur, -trice** /glɔbalizatœʀ, tʀis/ ADJ *[analyse, approche, vision]* global ◆ **nous refusons tout discours ~ sur la toxicomanie** we will not accept sweeping generalizations about drug addiction

globalisation /glɔbalizasjɔ̃/ NF *(= mondialisation)* globalization

globaliser /glɔbalize/ ▸ conjug 1 ◂ VT 1 *(= mondialiser) [+ conflit, problème]* to globalize 2 *(= appréhender dans leur ensemble) [+ problèmes, raisons]* to consider from an overall *ou* a global perspective, to consider in their entirety VI *(= généraliser)* to generalize ◆ **les médias ont trop tendance à ~** the media tend to make sweeping generalizations VPR **se globaliser** *[économie, marché]* to become globalized *ou* global

globalité /glɔbalite/ NF global nature ◆ **regardons le problème dans sa ~** let us look at the problem from every angle

globe /glɔb/ NM 1 *(= sphère, monde)* globe ◆ ~ **oculaire** eyeball ◆ **le ~ terrestre** the globe, the earth ◆ **faire le tour du ~** to go around the world ◆ **le conflit pourrait s'étendre à tout le ~** the conflict could spread worldwide 2 *(pour recouvrir)* glass cover, globe ◆ **mettre qn/qch sous ~** *(fig)* to keep sb/sth in a glass case, to keep sb/sth in cotton wool *(Brit)*

globe-trotter (pl **globe-trotters**) /glɔbtʀɔtœʀ/ NM globe-trotter

globine /glɔbin/ NF globin

globulaire /glɔbylɛʀ/ ADJ *(= sphérique)* global; *(Physiol)* corpuscular; → **numération**

globule /glɔbyl/ NM *(gén, Chim)* globule; *(Physiol)* corpuscle ◆ **~s rouges/blancs** red/white corpuscles

globuleux, -euse /glɔbylø, øz/ ADJ *[forme]* globular; *[œil]* protruding

globuline /glɔbylin/ NF globulin

glockenspiel /glɔkœnʃpil/ NM glockenspiel

gloire /glwaʀ/ NF 1 *(= renommée)* glory, fame; *[de vedette]* stardom, fame ◆ ~ **littéraire** literary fame ◆ **être au sommet de la ~** to be at the height of one's fame ◆ **il s'est couvert de ~** he covered himself in glory ◆ **elle a eu son heure de ~** she has had her hour of glory ◆ **(faire qch) pour la ~** (to do sth) for the glory of it ◆ **faire la ~ de qn/qch** to make sb/sth famous ◆ **ce n'est pas la ~** * it's nothing to write home about *

2 *(= distinction)* **sa plus grande ~ a été de faire ...** his greatest distinction *ou* his greatest claim to fame was to do ... ◆ **s'attribuer toute la ~ de qch** to give o.s. all the credit for sth, to take all the glory for sth ◆ **se faire** *ou* **tirer ~ de qch** to revel *ou* glory in sth

3 *(littér, Rel = éclat)* glory ◆ **la ~ de Rome/de Dieu** the glory of Rome/of God ◆ **le trône/le séjour de ~** the throne/the Kingdom of Glory

4 *(= louange)* glory, praise ◆ ~ **à Dieu** glory to God, praise be to God ◆ ~ **à tous ceux qui ont donné leur vie** glory to all those who gave their lives ◆ **disons-le à sa ~** it must be said in praise of him ◆ **poème/chant à la ~ de qn/qch** poem/song in praise of sb/sth ◆ **célébrer** *ou* **chanter la ~ de qn/qch** to sing the praises of sb/sth; → **rendre**

5 *(personne = célébrité)* celebrity ◆ **toutes les ~s de la région étaient là** *(hum)* all the worthies *(hum) ou* notables of the region were there ◆ **cette pièce est la ~ du musée** this piece is the pride of the museum

6 *(Art = auréole)* glory ◆ **Christ en ~** Christ in majesty

gloria[1] /glɔʀja/ NM INV *(Rel)* Gloria

gloria[2] † /glɔʀja/ NM *(= boisson)* laced coffee, spiked coffee *(US)*

gloriette /glɔʀjɛt/ NF 1 *(= pavillon)* gazebo 2 *(= volière)* aviary

glorieusement /glɔʀjøzmɑ̃/ ADV gloriously

glorieux, -ieuse /glɔʀjø, jøz/ ADJ *[exploit, mort, personne, passé]* glorious; *[air, ton]* triumphant ◆ **tout ~ de sa richesse/de pouvoir dire ...** *(littér, péj)* glorying in *ou* priding himself on his wealth/on being able to say ... ◆ **tes résultats ne sont pas très ~** * your results aren't too great * ◆ **ce n'est pas très ~ !** it's nothing to be proud of! ◆ **les Trois Glorieuses** *(Hist)* Les Trois Glorieuses *(the three-day July revolution of 1830)* ◆ **les Trente Glorieuses** *(Hist) the thirty-year boom period after World War II*

glorification /glɔʀifikasjɔ̃/ NF glorification

glorifier /glɔʀifje/ ▸ conjug 7 ◂ VT to glorify, to extol ◆ ~ **Dieu** to glorify God VPR **se glorifier** ◆ **se ~ de** to glory in, to take great pride in

gloriole /glɔʀjɔl/ NF misplaced vanity, vainglory *(littér)* ◆ **faire qch par ~** to do sth out of (misplaced) vanity *ou* out of vainglory *(littér)*

glose /gloz/ NF *(= annotation, commentaire)* gloss

gloser /gloze/ ▸ conjug 1 ◂ VT to annotate, to gloss VI to ramble on *(sur about)*

glossaire /glɔsɛʀ/ NM glossary

glossématique /glɔsematik/ NF glossematics *(sg)*

glossine /glɔsin/ NF glossina

glossolalie /glɔsɔlali/ NF glossolalia

glottal, e (mpl **-aux**) /glɔtal, o/ ADJ glottal

glotte /glɔt/ NF glottis ◆ **coup de ~** glottal stop

glouglou /gluglu/ NM 1 *[d'eau]* gurgling, glug-glug ◆ **faire ~** to gurgle, to go glug-glug 2 *[de dindon]* gobbling, gobble-gobble ◆ **faire ~** to gobble, to go gobble-gobble

glouglouter /gluglute/ ▸ conjug 1 ◂ VI *[eau]* to gurgle; *[dindon]* to gobble

gloussement /glusmɑ̃/ NM *[de poule]* clucking; *(péj) [de personne]* chuckle ◆ **pousser des ~s de satisfaction** to chuckle with satisfaction

glousser /gluse/ ▸ conjug 1 ◂ VI *[poule]* to cluck; *(péj) [personne]* to chuckle

glouton, -onne /glutɔ̃, ɔn/ ADJ *[personne]* gluttonous, greedy; *[appétit]* voracious NM,F glutton NM *(= animal)* wolverine

gloutonnement /glutɔnmɑ̃/ ADV *[manger]* gluttonously, greedily; *[lire]* voraciously ◆ **avalant ~ son repas** wolfing (down) his meal, gulping his meal down

gloutonnerie /glutɔnʀi/ NF gluttony, greed

gloxinia /glɔksinja/ NM gloxinia

glu /gly/ NF *(pour prendre les oiseaux)* birdlime ◆ **prendre les oiseaux à la ~** to lime birds ◆ **on dirait de la ~, c'est comme de la ~** it's like glue ◆ **quelle ~, ce type !** * *(= personne)* the guy's such a leech! *

gluant, e /glyɑ̃, ɑ̃t/ ADJ *[substance]* sticky; *(= répugnant) [personne]* slimy

glucide /glysid/ NM carbohydrate

glucidique /glysidik/ ADJ carbohydrate *(épith)*

glucose /glykoz/ NM glucose

glucosé, e /glykoze/ ADJ *[eau, sérum]* containing glucose

glutamate /glytamat/ NM glutamate

gluten /glytɛn/ NM gluten

glutineux, -euse /glytinø, øz/ ADJ *[aliment]* glutinous

glycémie /glisemi/ NF glycaemia (Brit), glycemia (US)

glycérine /gliseʀin/ NF glycerin(e), glycerol (SPÉC)

glycériné, e /gliseʀine/ ADJ ◆ **joint** ~ glycerin(e)-coated joint ◆ **savon** ~ glycerin(e) soap

glycérique /gliseʀik/ ADJ ◆ **acide** ~ glyceric acid

glycérol /gliseʀɔl/ NM glycerin(e), glycerol (SPÉC)

glycérophtalique /gliseʀɔftalik/ ADJ [peinture] oil-based

glycine /glisin/ NF 1 (= plante) wisteria, wistaria 2 (= acide) glycine

glycocolle /glikokɔl/ NM glycine

glycogène /glikoʒɛn/ NM glycogen

glycol /glikɔl/ NM glycol

glyphe /glif/ NM glyph

GMT /ʒeɛmte/ (abrév de **Greenwich Mean Time**) GMT ◆ **à 15 heures** ~ at fifteen (hundred) hours GMT

gnangnan* /ɲɑ̃ɲɑ̃/ ADJ INV [film, roman] silly; [histoire d'amour] soppy* ◆ **qu'est-ce qu'il est ~ !** he's such a drip! * NMF drip*

gneiss /gnɛs/ NM gneiss

gniard* /ɲaʀ/ NM brat*

gniôle* /ɲol/ NF ⇒ **gnôle**

GNL /ʒeɛnɛl/ NM (abrév de **gaz naturel liquéfié**) LNG

gnocchi /ɲɔki/ NM gnocchi (NonC)

gnognote* /ɲɔɲɔt/ NF ◆ **c'est de la ~ !** it's rubbish! ◆ **c'est pas de la ~ !** that's really something!* ◆ **100 € ? c'est de la ~ pour lui** €100? that's nothing ou peanuts* to him

gnôle* /ɲol/ NF (= eau-de-vie) hooch* ◆ **un petit verre de** ~ a snifter*, a dram*

gnome /gnom/ NM gnome

gnomique /gnɔmik/ ADJ gnomic

gnon* /ɲɔ̃/ NM (= coup) blow, bash*; (= marque) dent, bump ◆ **prendre un** ~ [personne] to get bashed* ou walloped*; [voiture] to get bashed* ou dented

gnose /gnoz/ NF gnosis

gnosticisme /gnɔstisism/ NM gnosticism

gnostique /gnɔstik/ ADJ, NMF gnostic

gnou /gnu/ NM gnu, wildebeest

gnouf* /ɲuf/ NM (arg Crime) clink*, nick* (Brit) ◆ **au** ~ in the clink* ou nick* (Brit)

GO (abrév de **grandes ondes**) LW

Go (abrév de **gigaoctet**) Gb

go /go/ NM ◆ **(jeu de)** ~ go LOC ADV **tout de go** ◆ **dire qch tout de** ~ to say sth straight out ◆ **il est entré tout de** ~ he went straight in

goal /gol/ NM goalkeeper, goalie*

goal-average (pl **goal-averages**) /golaveʀaʒ/ NM (Sport) goal difference ◆ **ils l'emportent au** ~ they win on goal difference

gobelet /gɔblɛ/ NM [d'enfant, pique-nique] beaker; (en étain, verre, argent) tumbler; [de dés] cup ◆ ~ **en plastique/papier** plastic/paper cup

Gobelins /gɔb(ə)lɛ̃/ NMPL ◆ **la manufacture des** ~ the Gobelins tapestry workshop ◆ **tapisserie des** ~ Gobelin tapestry

gobe-mouche (pl **gobe-mouches**) /gɔbmuʃ/ NM 1 (= oiseau) flycatcher ◆ ~ **gris** spotted flycatcher 2 († = crédule) gullible person ◆ **c'est un** ~ he'd swallow anything

gober /gɔbe/ ▸ conjug 1 ◂ VT [+ huître, œuf] to swallow (whole); * [+ mensonge, histoire] to swallow hook, line and sinker ◆ **je ne peux pas le** ~* I can't stand him ◆ **ne reste pas là à ~ les mouches** don't just stand there gawping ◆ **il te ferait ~ n'importe quoi*** he'd have you believe anything

goberger (se)* /gɔbɛʀʒe/ ▸ conjug 3 ◂ VPR (= faire bonne chère) to indulge o.s.; (= prendre ses aises) to pamper o.s.

gobie /gɔbi/ NM goby

godailler /gɔdɑje/ ▸ conjug 1 ◂ VI ⇒ **goder**

godasse* /gɔdas/ NF shoe

godelureau † (pl **godelureaux**) /gɔd(ə)lyʀo/ NM (young) dandy; (péj) ladies' man

godemiché /gɔdmiʃe/ NM dildo

goder /gɔde/ ▸ conjug 1 ◂ VI [vêtement] to pucker, to be puckered; [papier peint] to have bubbles ou bulges in it ◆ **sa jupe godait de partout** her skirt was all puckered

godet /gɔdɛ/ NM 1 (gén = récipient) jar, pot; (à peinture) pot ◆ **viens boire un ~ avec nous*** come and have a drink ou a jar* (Brit) with us 2 (Couture) gore ◆ **jupe à ~s** gored skirt 3 (= auge) bucket

godiche* /gɔdiʃ/ ADJ lumpish, oafish ◆ **quelle ~, ce garçon !** what an awkward lump ou what a clumsy oaf that boy is!

godille /gɔdij/ NF 1 [de bateau] scull; (Ski) wedeln ◆ **descendre en** ~ to wedeln 2 (péj) **à la** ~* [système] crummy*, ropey* (Brit); [jambe, bras] bad, dicky* (Brit)

godiller /gɔdije/ ▸ conjug 1 ◂ VI (en bateau) to scull; (Ski) to wedeln, to use the wedeln technique

godillot* /gɔdijo/ NM (= chaussure) clodhopper*, clumpy shoe; († , péj : Pol) unquestioning ou ardent supporter

goéland /gɔelɑ̃/ NM seagull, gull ◆ ~ **cendré** common gull ◆ ~ **argenté** herring gull

goélette /gɔelɛt/ NF schooner

goémon /gɔemɔ̃/ NM wrack

goglu /gɔgly/ NM (Can) bobolink, ricebird

gogo[1]* /gogo/ NM (= personne crédule) sucker*, mug* ◆ **c'est bon pour les ~s** it's a con*, it's a mug's game* (Brit)

gogo[2]* /gogo/ **à gogo** LOC ADV (= en abondance) galore ◆ **on avait du vin à** ~ we had wine galore ◆ **des fraises, il y en a à** ~ there are plenty of ou loads of strawberries

gogol* /gogɔl/ NM idiot

goguenard, e /gɔg(ə)naʀ, aʀd/ ADJ mocking

goguenardise /gɔg(ə)naʀdiz/ NF mocking

goguenots* /gɔg(ə)no/, **gogues*** /gɔg/ NMPL (= toilettes) bog* (Brit), loo* (Brit), john* (US)

goguette* /gɔgɛt/ NF ◆ **des touristes en** ~ tourists out for a good time

goinfre* /gwɛ̃fʀ/ ADJ, NM ◆ **il est ~, c'est un** ~ he's a greedy pig* ou a greedy guts* (Brit) ◆ **arrête de manger comme un** ~ stop making a pig of yourself*

goinfrer (se) /gwɛ̃fʀe/ ▸ conjug 1 ◂ VPR (gén) to stuff o.s.*; (manger salement) to make a pig of o.s.* ◆ **se ~ de gâteaux** to pig* ou gorge o.s. on cakes

goinfrerie /gwɛ̃fʀəʀi/ NF piggery*, piggishness*

goitre /gwatʀ/ NM goitre

goitreux, -euse /gwatʀø, øz/ ADJ goitrous NM,F person suffering from goitre

golden /gɔldɛn/ NF INV Golden Delicious

golem /gɔlɛm/ NM golem

golf /gɔlf/ NM (= sport) golf; (= terrain) golf course ou links ◆ ~ **miniature** miniature golf ◆ **culottes** ou **pantalon de** ~ plus fours ◆ **jouer au** ou **faire du** ~ to play golf ◆ **faire un** ~ to play a round ou game of golf; → **joueur**

golfe /gɔlf/ NM gulf; (petit) bay ◆ **le ~ de Bengale/de Gascogne** the Bay of Bengal/of Biscay ◆ **le ~ du Lion/du Mexique** the Gulf of Lions/of Mexico ◆ **le ~ Persique** the Persian Gulf ◆ **les États du Golfe** the Gulf States; → **guerre**

golfeur, -euse /gɔlfœʀ, øz/ NM,F golfer

Golgotha /gɔlgɔta/ NM ◆ **le** ~ Golgotha

Goliath /gɔljat/ NM Goliath ◆ **c'était David contre** ~ it was David versus Goliath

gomina ® /gɔmina/ NF hair cream, Brylcreem ®

gominer (se) /gɔmine/ ▸ conjug 1 ◂ VPR to put hair cream on, to Brylcreem ® ◆ **cheveux gominés** slicked-back hair, hair slicked back with Brylcreem ®

gommage /gɔmaʒ/ NM 1 (= exfoliation) exfoliation ◆ **se faire un** ~ (visage) to use a facial scrub; (corps) to use a body scrub 2 [de mot, trait] rubbing-out, erasing; [de ride, souvenir, différence] erasing; [d'aspérités] smoothing out 3 (= encollage) gumming

gommant, e /gɔmɑ̃, ɑ̃t/ ADJ [crème] exfoliating ◆ **soin** ~ (gén) body scrub; (pour le visage) facial scrub

gomme /gɔm/ NF (= substance) gum; (Méd) gumma; (Bot) gummosis; (pour effacer) rubber (Brit), eraser (US) ◆ **mettre la** ~* [conducteur] to give it full throttle*, to step on the gas* (US); [ouvrier] to work flat out* ◆ **à la** ~* [outil, système, idée] pathetic*, crummy*; [renseignement] useless, hopeless; → **boule**

COMP **gomme adragante** tragacanth
gomme arabique gum arabic
gomme à encre ink rubber (Brit) ou eraser (US)
gomme laque lac
gomme à mâcher chewing gum

gomme-gutte (pl **gommes-guttes**) /gɔmgyt/ NF gamboge, cambogia

gommer /gɔme/ ▸ conjug 1 ◂ VT 1 [+ mot, trait] to rub out, to erase; [+ souvenir] to erase; [+ ride] to smooth away, to erase; [+ différence] to smooth ou iron out, to erase; [+ fatigue] to take away; [+ aspérités] to smooth out 2 (= encoller) to gum ◆ **gommé** [enveloppe, papier] gummed 3 [+ peau] to exfoliate

gomme-résine (pl **gommes-résines**) /gɔmʀezin/ NF gum resin

gommette /gɔmɛt/ NF coloured sticky label

gommeux, -euse /gɔmø, øz/ ADJ [arbre] gum-yielding (épith); [substance] sticky; [lésion] gummatous NM († * = jeune prétentieux) pretentious (young) dandy

gommier /gɔmje/ NM gum tree

Gomorrhe /gɔmɔʀ/ N Gomorrah; → **Sodome**

gonade /gɔnad/ NF gonad

gonadotrope /gɔnadɔtʀɔp/ ADJ gonadotropic

gonadotrophine /gɔnadotʀɔfin/, **gonadotropine** /gɔnadotʀɔpin/ NF gonadotropin

gond /gɔ̃/ NM hinge ◆ **sortir de ses ~s** [porte] to come off its hinges; [personne] to fly off the handle ◆ **jeter** ou **mettre qn hors de ses ~s** to make sb wild with rage

gondolage /gɔ̃dɔlaʒ/ NM ⇒ **gondolement**

gondole /gɔ̃dɔl/ NF (= bateau) gondola; [de supermarché] (supermarket) shelf, gondola ◆ **tête de** ~ end display

gondolement /gɔ̃dɔlmɑ̃/ NM [de papier] crinkling; [de planche] warping; [de tôle] buckling

gondoler /gɔ̃dɔle/ ▸ conjug 1 ◂ VI [papier] to crinkle, to go crinkly; [planche] to warp; [tôle] to buckle ◆ **du papier peint tout gondolé** wallpaper that is all crinkled ou crinkly ◆ **le disque**

est complètement gondolé the record is all *ou* completely warped VPR **se gondoler** 1 *[papier]* to crinkle; *[planche]* to warp; *[tôle]* to buckle 2 *(* = rire)* to split one's sides laughing*, to crease up*

gondolier, -ière /gɔ̃dɔlje, jɛʀ/ NM,F *(= batelier)* gondolier; *(dans un supermarché)* shelf stocker

gonfalon /gɔ̃falɔ̃/ NM gonfalon

gonfalonier /gɔ̃falɔnje/ NM gonfalonier

gonflable /gɔ̃flabl/ ADJ *[ballon, matelas, piscine]* inflatable ◆ **coussin** *ou* **sac** ~ *(dans voiture)* air bag; → **poupée**

gonflage /gɔ̃flaʒ/ NM inflating *(NonC)*, inflation *(NonC)* ◆ **vérifier le ~ des pneus** to check the air in the tyres *(Brit) ou* tires *(US)*

gonflant, e /gɔ̃flɑ̃, ɑt/ ADJ 1 *[coiffure]* bouffant 2 *(* = irritant)* damned* *ou* bloody* *(Brit)* irritating ◆ **il est ~ avec ses histoires** he's a real pain (in the neck)* the way he goes on NM ◆ **donner du ~ à ses cheveux** to give one's hair body

gonflé, e /gɔ̃fle/ (ptp de **gonfler**) ADJ 1 *[yeux, visage, pieds, chevilles]* puffy, swollen; *[ventre] (par la maladie)* distended, swollen; *(par un repas)* blown-out, bloated ◆ **il a les joues bien ~es** he has chubby *ou* plump cheeks ◆ **je me sens un peu ~** I feel a bit bloated 2 * **il est ~ !** *(= courageux)* he's got some nerve!*; *(= impertinent)* he's got a nerve!* *ou* a cheek!* *(Brit)* ◆ **être ~ à bloc** to be raring to go*

gonflement /gɔ̃fləmɑ̃/ NM *[de ballon, pneu]* inflation; *[de visage, ventre]* swelling; *[de prix, résultats]* inflation; *[d'effectifs] (= augmentation)* swelling; *(= exagération)* exaggeration ◆ **le ~ de son estomac m'inquiétait** his swollen stomach worried me ◆ **le ~ de la masse monétaire** the increase in the money supply ◆ **le ~ de la dette publique** the expansion of *ou* the increase in the public debt

gonfler /gɔ̃fle/ ► conjug 1 ◄ VT 1 *[+ pneu, ballon] (avec une pompe)* to pump up, to inflate; *(en soufflant)* to blow up, to inflate; *[+ aérostat]* to inflate; *[+ joues, narines]* to puff out; *[+ poumons]* to fill *(de* with); ◆ **les pluies ont gonflé la rivière** the rain has swollen the river *ou* caused the river to swell ◆ **le vent gonfle les voiles** the wind fills (out) *ou* swells the sails ◆ **un paquet gonflait sa poche** his pocket was bulging with a package ◆ **un soupir gonflait sa poitrine** he heaved a great sigh ◆ **éponge gonflée d'eau** sponge swollen with water ◆ **la bière me gonfle** *ou* **me fait ~ l'estomac** beer blows out my stomach, beer makes me feel bloated *ou* makes my stomach bloated ◆ **il avait les yeux gonflés par le manque de sommeil** his eyes were puffy *ou* swollen with lack of sleep

2 *(= dilater)* to swell ◆ **ses succès l'ont gonflé d'orgueil** his successes have made his head swell *ou* made him puffed up (with pride) ◆ **l'orgueil gonfle son cœur** his heart is swollen with pride ◆ **l'espoir/le chagrin lui gonflait le cœur** his heart was swelling *ou* bursting with hope/was heavy with sorrow ◆ **cœur gonflé de joie/d'indignation** heart bursting with joy/indignation ◆ **il nous les gonfle !*** he's a pain in the neck* *ou* butt!* *(surtout US)*

3 *(= grossir) [+ prix, résultat]* to inflate; *[+ effectif] (= augmenter)* to swell; *(= exagérer)* to exaggerate; *[+ moteur]* to soup up* ◆ **on a gonflé l'importance de l'incident** the incident has been blown up out of (all) proportion, they have exaggerated the importance of the incident ◆ **chiffres gonflés** inflated *ou* exaggerated figures

VI *(= enfler) [genou, cheville]* to swell (up); *[bois]* to swell; *(Culin) [pâte]* to rise ◆ **faire ~ le riz/les lentilles** to leave the rice/lentils to swell, to soak the rice/lentils ◆ **faire ~ ses cheveux** to give one's hair (some) body

VPR **se gonfler** 1 *[rivière]* to swell; *[poitrine]* to swell, to expand; *[voiles]* to swell, to fill (out)

2 ◆ **se ~ (d'orgueil)** to be puffed up (with pride), to be bloated with pride ◆ **son cœur se gonfle de tristesse/d'espoir** his heart is heavy (with sorrow)/is bursting with hope

gonflette * /gɔ̃flɛt/ NF *(péj)* body building (exercises) ◆ **faire de la ~** *(Sport)* to pump iron*; *(fig = exagérer)* to exaggerate, to lay it on thick*

gonfleur /gɔ̃flœʀ/ NM air pump

gong /gɔ̃(g)/ NM *(Mus)* gong; *(Boxe)* bell; → **sauver**

goniomètre /gɔnjɔmɛtʀ/ NM goniometer

goniométrie /gɔnjɔmetʀi/ NF goniometry

goniométrique /gɔnjɔmetʀik/ ADJ goniometric(al)

gonococcie /gɔnɔkɔksi/ NF gonorrhoea *(Brit)*, gonorrhea *(US)*

gonocoque /gɔnɔkɔk/ NM gonococcus

gonzesse* /gɔ̃zɛs/ NF *(péj)* bird* *(Brit)*, chick* *(US)* ◆ **c'est une vraie ~** *(péj : efféminé)* he's a real sissy*

gordien /gɔʀdjɛ̃/ ADJ M → **nœud**

gore /gɔʀ/ ADJ *[film, livre]* gory NM gore

goret /gɔʀɛ/ NM piglet ◆ **petit ~ !** *(à un enfant)* you dirty little pig!*, you mucky (little) pup!* *(Brit)*

Gore-Tex ® /gɔʀtɛks/ NM Gore-Tex ®

gorge /gɔʀʒ/ NF 1 *[de personne] (= cou, gosier)* throat; *(littér = seins)* breast, bosom *(littér)*; *[d'oiseau] (= poitrine)* breast; *(= gosier)* throat ◆ **rire à pleine ~** *ou* **à ~ déployée** to roar with laughter, to laugh heartily ◆ **chanter à pleine ~** *ou* **à ~ déployée** to sing at the top of one's voice; → **chat, couteau** *etc*

2 *(= vallée, défilé)* gorge ◆ **les ~s du Tarn** the gorges of the Tarn

3 *(= rainure) [de moulure, poulie]* groove; *[de serrure]* tumbler

4 *(locutions)* **prendre qn à la ~** *[créancier]* to put a gun to sb's head; *[agresseur]* to grab sb by the throat; *[fumée, odeur]* to catch *ou* get in sb's throat; *[peur]* to grip sb by the throat ◆ **tenir qn à la ~** *(lit)* to hold sb by the throat; *(= l'avoir à sa merci)* to have a stranglehold on sb, to have sb by the throat ◆ **l'os lui est resté dans la** *ou* **en travers de la ~** the bone (got) stuck in his throat ◆ **ça lui est resté dans la** *ou* **en travers de la ~** *(= il n'a pas aimé)* he found it hard to take *ou* swallow; *(= il n'a pas osé le dire)* it *ou* the words stuck in his throat ◆ **faire des ~s chaudes de qch** to laugh sth to scorn ◆ **je lui enfoncerai** *ou* **ferai rentrer ses mots dans la ~** I'll make him eat his words ◆ **faire rendre ~ à qn** to force sb to give back ill-gotten gains

gorge-de-pigeon /gɔʀʒ(ə)dəpiʒɔ̃/ ADJ INV dapple-grey

gorgée /gɔʀʒe/ NF mouthful ◆ **boire à petites ~s** to take little sips ◆ **boire à grandes ~s** to drink in gulps ◆ **boire son vin à grandes/petites ~s** to gulp down/sip one's wine ◆ **vider un verre d'une seule ~** to empty a glass in one gulp, down a glass in one*

gorger /gɔʀʒe/ ► conjug 3 ◄ VT *(gén)* to fill *(de* with); *[+ animal]* to force-feed ◆ **~ qn de pâtisseries** to fill sb up *ou* stuff* sb with cakes ◆ **terre/éponge gorgée d'eau** earth/sponge saturated with *ou* full of water ◆ **fruits gorgés de soleil** sun-kissed fruit VPR **se gorger** ◆ **se ~ de nourriture** to gorge o.s., to stuff o.s.* (with food) ◆ **se ~ de gâteaux** to gorge o.s. on *ou* with cakes ◆ **éponge qui se gorge d'eau** sponge which soaks up water

Gorgone /gɔʀgɔn/ NF *(Myth)* Gorgon ◆ **gorgone** *(= corail)* gorgonia

gorgonzola /gɔʀgɔ̃zɔla/ NM Gorgonzola

gorille /gɔʀij/ NM *(= animal)* gorilla; *(* = garde du corps)* bodyguard, heavy*

Gorki /gɔʀki/ NM Gorky

gosier /gozje/ NM *(Anat)* throat; *(* = gorge)* throat, gullet ◆ **crier à plein ~** to shout at the top of one's voice, to shout one's head off ◆ **chanter à plein ~** to sing at the top of one's voice ◆ **avoir le ~ sec*** to be parched* ◆ **ça m'est resté en travers du ~*** *(lit)* it (got) stuck in my throat; *(fig)* I found it hard to take; → **humecter**

gospel /gɔspɛl/ NM gospel (music)

gosse* /gɔs/ NMF kid* ◆ **sale ~** little brat* ◆ **elle est restée très ~** she's still a kid at heart* ◆ **~ des rues** street urchin ◆ **~ de riche(s)** *(péj)* (spoilt) rich kid *ou* brat* ◆ **il est beau ~*** he's a good-looker*

Goth /gɔt/ NMF Goth

gotha /gɔta/ NM *(= aristocratie)* high society ◆ **le ~ de la finance/de la publicité** the financial/advertising bigwigs*

gothique /gɔtik/ ADJ *[architecture, style]* Gothic ◆ **écriture ~** Gothic script NM ◆ **le ~** the Gothic ◆ **le ~ flamboyant/perpendiculaire** Flamboyant/Perpendicular Gothic

gotique /gɔtik/ NM *(= langue)* Gothic

gouache /gwaʃ/ NF *(= matière)* gouache, poster paint; *(= tableau)* gouache

gouaille /gwɑj/ NF cheeky *ou* cocky* humour

gouailleur, -euse /gwɑjœʀ, øz/ ADJ cheeky, cocky*

gouape* /gwap/ NF thug

gouda /guda/ NM Gouda

Goudjerate /gudʒeʀat/ NM ⇒ **Guj(a)rât**

goudron /gudʀɔ̃/ NM tar ◆ **~ de houille** coal tar ◆ **~ végétal** *ou* **de bois** wood tar ◆ **"goudrons : 15 mg"** *(sur un paquet de cigarettes)* ≈ 15 mg tar

goudronnage /gudʀɔnaʒ/ NM tarring

goudronner /gudʀɔne/ ► conjug 1 ◄ VT *[+ route, toile]* to tar

goudronneux, -euse /gudʀɔnø, øz/ ADJ tarry

gouffre /gufʀ/ NM *(Géog)* abyss, gulf, chasm ◆ **un ~ nous sépare** there's a gulf between us ◆ **le ~ de l'oubli** the depths of oblivion ◆ **c'est un ~ d'ignorance/de bêtise** he's abysmally ignorant/utterly stupid ◆ **c'est un ~ (financier)** it just swallows up money, it's a bottomless pit ◆ **nous sommes au bord du ~** we are on the brink of the abyss ◆ **entre la théorie et la pratique, il y a un ~** there's a huge gap between theory and practice

gouge /guʒ/ NF gouge

gougnafier* /guɲafje/ NM bungling idiot*

gouine* /gwin/ NF dyke*

goujat, e /guʒa, at/ ADJ boorish, churlish NM boor, churl

goujaterie /guʒatʀi/ NF boorishness

goujon /guʒɔ̃/ NM 1 *(= poisson)* gudgeon; 2 *(Tech = cheville)* pin

goulache, goulasch /gulaʃ/ NM *ou* NF goulash

goulafre* /gulafʀ/ ADJ, NMF *(Belg)* ◆ **il est ~, c'est un ~** he's a greedy pig*

goulag /gulag/ NM Gulag

goule /gul/ NF ghoul

goulée /gule/ NF *[de liquide]* gulp; *[de solide]* big mouthful ◆ **prendre une ~ d'air frais** *(gorgée)* to take in a lungful of fresh air; *(* : bol d'air)* to get some fresh air

goulet / gulɛ / NM *(Naut)* narrows, bottleneck *(at entrance of harbour)*; *(Géog)* gully ◆ **~ d'étranglement** bottleneck

gouleyant, e / gulɛjɑ̃, ɑ̃t / ADJ lively

goulot / gulo / NM *[de bouteille]* neck ◆ **boire au ~** to drink straight from the bottle ◆ **~ d'étranglement** bottleneck

goulotte / gulɔt / NF *(Archit)* channel; *(Tech)* chute, inclined channel

goulu, e / guly / ADJ *[personne]* greedy, gluttonous; *[regards]* greedy NM,F glutton

goulûment / gulymɑ̃ / ADV greedily, gluttonously

goumier / gumje / NM *(Hist) Moroccan soldier in the French army*

goupil †† / gupi(l) / NM fox

goupille / gupij / NF *(Tech)* pin

goupillé, e * / gupije / (ptp de **goupiller**) ADJ *(= arrangé)* ◆ **bien/mal ~** *[machine, plan, procédé]* well/badly thought out ◆ **comment est-ce ~, ce mécanisme ?** how does this thing work?

goupiller / gupije / ▸ conjug 1 ◂ VT 1 *(* = combiner)* to fix * ◆ **il a bien goupillé son affaire** he did alright for himself there * 2 *(= fixer avec une goupille)* to pin VPR **se goupiller** * *(= s'arranger)* **comment est-ce que ça se goupille pour demain ?** what's the plan for tomorrow? ◆ **ça s'est bien/mal goupillé, notre plan** our plan came off * (all right)/didn't come off * ◆ **tout ça a l'air de se ~ plutôt bien** it all seems to be going pretty well ◆ **ça se goupille plutôt mal, cette histoire de déménagement** this removal business is a bit of a shambles *

goupillon / gupijɔ̃ / NM *(Rel)* (holy water) sprinkler, aspergillum; *(à bouteille)* bottle brush; → **sabre**

gourance ‡ / guʀɑ̃s /, **gourante** ‡ / guʀɑ̃t / NF cock-up ‡, boob * *(Brit)* ◆ **faire une ~** to make a cock-up ‡ *ou* a boob * *(Brit)*, to goof up ‡ *(US)*

gourbi / guʀbi / NM *(arabe)* shack; *(* = taudis)* slum

gourd, e[1] / guʀ, guʀd / ADJ *(par le froid)* numb (with cold); *(= maladroit, mal à l'aise)* awkward

gourde[2] / guʀd / NF 1 *(= fruit)* gourd; *[d'eau, alcool]* flask 2 *(* = empoté)* dope *, clot * *(Brit)*, dumbbell * *(US)* ADJ *(* = bête)* dopey *, gormless * *(Brit)*; *(= maladroit)* clumsy

gourde[3] / guʀd / NF *(Fin)* gourde

gourdin / guʀdɛ̃ / NM club, bludgeon ◆ **assommer qn à coups de ~** to club *ou* bludgeon sb

gourer (se) ‡ / guʀe / ▸ conjug 1 ◂ VPR to boob * *(Brit)*, to goof up ‡ *(US)* ◆ **se ~ de jour** to get the day wrong ◆ **je me suis gouré de numéro de téléphone** I dialled the wrong number ◆ **on s'est gouré de rue** we went to the wrong street ◆ **je me suis gouré dans mes calculs** I made a cock-up in ‡ *ou* I goofed up ‡ *(US)* my calculations

gourgandine †† * / guʀgɑ̃din / NF hussy † *

gourmand, e / guʀmɑ̃, ɑ̃d / ADJ 1 *[personne]* fond of food ◆ **il est ~ comme un chat** he likes good food but he's fussy about what he eats ◆ **je suis très ~** I'm very fond of my food; *(pour les sucreries)* I've got a sweet tooth ◆ **être ~ de** *[+ sucreries]* to be fond of; *[+ nouveautés]* to be avid for ◆ **regarder qch d'un œil ~** to eye sth greedily

2 *(Culin)* ◆ **une cuisine ~e** gourmet food ◆ **menu ~** gourmet menu

3 *(= sensuel) [bouche]* voluptuous

4 *(= exigeant)* **cette voiture est (très) ~e (en carburant)** this car's a gas-guzzler, this car's heavy on petrol *(Brit) ou* gas *(US)* ◆ **c'est une activité (très) ~e en capitaux/en énergie** it's (very) capital/energy-intensive ◆ **des applications informatiques de plus en plus ~es en mémoire** computer applications requiring more and more power

5 *(Agr)* **branche ~e** sucker

NM,F gourmand *(frm)* ◆ **c'est une ~e** she's very fond of her food; *(pour les sucreries)* she's got a sweet tooth ◆ **tu n'es qu'un ~ !** *(enfant)* you greedy thing!

NM *(Agr)* sucker

gourmander / guʀmɑ̃de / ▸ conjug 1 ◂ VT *(littér)* to rebuke, to berate *(littér)*

gourmandise / guʀmɑ̃diz / NF *(gén)* fondness of food; *(péj)* greed, greediness; *(Rel = péché)* gluttony ◆ **elle regardait le gâteau avec ~** she eyed the cake greedily NFPL **gourmandises** delicacies, sweetmeats †

gourme / guʀm / NF († : *Méd)* impetigo; *(= maladie du cheval)* strangles *(sg)* ◆ **jeter sa ~** to sow one's wild oats

gourmé, e / guʀme / ADJ *(littér)* starchy, stiff

gourmet / guʀmɛ / NM gourmet, epicure; → **fin**[1]

gourmette / guʀmɛt / NF *[de cheval]* curb chain; *[de poignet]* chain bracelet

gourou / guʀu / NM guru

gousse / gus / NF *[de vanille, petits pois]* pod ◆ **~ d'ail** clove of garlic

gousset / gusɛ / NM *[de gilet, pantalon]* fob; *[de slip]* gusset; *(Tech = pièce d'assemblage)* gusset; → **montre**[1]

goût / gu / NM 1 *(= sens)* taste ◆ **amer au ~** bitter to the taste

2 *(= saveur)* taste ◆ **cela a un ~ de moisi** it tastes mouldy ◆ **ça a bon/mauvais ~** it tastes good/nasty, it has a nice/bad taste ◆ **la soupe a un ~** the soup tastes funny *ou* has a funny taste ◆ **plat sans ~** tasteless *ou* flavourless dish ◆ **ça a un ~ de fraise** it tastes of strawberries ◆ **yaourt ~ vanille** vanilla-flavoured yoghurt ◆ **donner du ~ à qch** *[épice, condiment]* to add (a bit of) flavour to sth ◆ **la vie n'a plus de ~ pour lui** he no longer has any taste for life, he has lost his taste for life ◆ **ses souvenirs ont un ~ amer** he has bitter memories ◆ **cette rétrospective a un ~ de nostalgie** this retrospective has a nostalgic feel *ou* flavour ◆ **ça a un ~ de revenez-y** * it makes you want seconds, it's very more-ish * *(Brit)*

3 *(= jugement)* taste ◆ **(bon) ~** (good) taste ◆ **avoir du/manquer de ~** to have/lack taste ◆ **avoir un ~ vulgaire** to have vulgar tastes ◆ **le ~ ne s'apprend pas** taste is something you're born with ◆ **faire qch sans/avec ~** to do something tastelessly/tastefully ◆ **elle s'habille avec beaucoup de ~** she has very good taste in clothes, she has very good dress sense ◆ **homme/femme de ~** man/woman of taste; → **faute**

4 *[vêtement, ameublement]* **de bon ~** tasteful, in good taste *(attrib)* ◆ **de mauvais ~** tasteless, in bad *ou* poor taste *(attrib)* ◆ **c'est une plaisanterie de mauvais ~** this joke is in bad taste ◆ **il serait de mauvais ~/d'un ~ douteux de faire** it would be in bad *ou* poor/doubtful taste to do ◆ **il serait de bon ~ d'y aller/qu'il se mette à travailler** *(hum)* it mightn't be a bad idea to go/if he started doing some work

5 *(= penchant)* taste, liking *(de, pour* for); ◆ **salez à votre ~** salt (according) to taste ◆ **il a peu de ~ pour ce genre de travail** this sort of work is not to his taste *ou* liking *ou* is not his cup of tea * ◆ **il n'a aucun ~ pour les sciences** science subjects don't appeal to him ◆ **il a le ~ de l'ordre** he likes order ◆ **il a le ~ du risque** he likes taking risks ◆ **faire qch par ~** to do sth from inclination *ou* because one has a taste for it ◆ **prendre ~ à qch** to get *ou* acquire a taste for sth, to get to like sth ◆ **elle a repris ~ à la vie/la danse** she has started to enjoy life/dancing again ◆ **il n'avait ~ à rien** he didn't feel like doing anything ◆ **à mon/son ~** for my/his liking *ou* taste(s) ◆ **ce n'est pas du ~ de chacun** it's not to everybody's taste ◆ **ses déclarations n'ont pas été du ~ de ses alliés politiques** what he said didn't go down well with his political allies, his political allies didn't like the sound of what he said ◆ **cela m'a mis en ~** that gave me a taste for it ◆ **est-ce à votre ~ ?** is it to your taste? ◆ **c'est tout à fait à mon ~** this is very much to my taste ◆ **il la trouve à son ~** she suits his taste ◆ **faire passer le ~ du pain à qn** * to wipe the smile off sb's face; *(= tuer)* to do sb in *, to bump sb off *; → **chacun**

6 *(= tendances)* **~s** tastes ◆ **avoir des ~s de luxe/modestes** to have expensive/simple tastes ◆ **des ~s et des couleurs (on ne discute pas)** *(Prov)* there's no accounting for taste(s) ◆ **tous les ~s sont dans la nature** *(Prov)* it takes all sorts to make a world

7 *(= style)* style ◆ **dans le ~ classique/de X** in the classical style/the style of X ◆ **ou quelque chose dans ce ~-là** * or something of that sort ◆ **au ~ du jour** in keeping with the style of the day *ou* with current tastes ◆ **il s'est mis au ~ du jour** he has brought himself into line with current tastes ◆ **chanson remise au ~ du jour** song brought up to date

goûter[1] / gute / ▸ conjug 1 ◂ VT 1 *[+ aliment]* to taste ◆ **goûte-le, pour voir si c'est assez salé** taste it and see if there's enough salt

2 *[+ repos, spectacle]* to enjoy, to savour *(Brit)*, to savor *(US)*

3 *(littér) [+ écrivain, œuvre, plaisanterie]* to appreciate ◆ **il ne goûte pas l'art abstrait** he doesn't appreciate abstract art, abstract art isn't to his taste

4 *(Belg) [aliment]* to taste of

VT INDIR **goûter à** *[+ aliment, plaisir]* to taste, to sample; *[+ indépendance, liberté]* to taste ◆ **il y a à peine goûté** he's hardly touched it ◆ **voulez-vous ~ à mon gâteau ?** would you like to try *ou* sample my cake? ◆ **goûtez-y** *[+ vin]* have a sip *ou* taste, taste it; *[+ plat]* have a taste, taste it

VT INDIR **goûter de** *(= faire l'expérience de)* to have a taste of, to taste ◆ **il a goûté de la vie militaire/de la prison** he has had a taste of army/prison life, he has tasted army/prison life

VI 1 *(= faire une collation)* to have tea *(Brit)*, to have an afterschool snack *(US)* ◆ **emporter à ~** to take an afterschool snack ◆ **inviter des enfants à ~** to ask children to tea *(Brit)*, to invite children for a snack *(US)*

2 *(Belg) [aliment]* to taste good

goûter[2] / gute / NM *[d'enfants]* (afterschool) snack; *[d'adultes]* afternoon tea ◆ **donner un ~ d'enfants** to give *ou* have a children's (tea) party *(Brit)*, to invite children for a snack *(US)* ◆ **l'heure du ~** (afternoon) snack time

goûteur, -euse / gutœʀ, øz / NM,F ◆ **~ d'eau/de vin** water/wine taster

goûteux, -euse / gutø, øz / ADJ *[vin, viande]* flavoursome *(Brit)*, flavorful *(US)*

goutte / gut / NF 1 *(lit, fig)* drop ◆ **~ de rosée** dewdrop ◆ **~ de sueur** bead of sweat ◆ **suer à grosses ~s** to be streaming with sweat ◆ **pleuvoir à grosses ~s** to rain heavily ◆ **il est tombé quelques ~s** there were a few spots *ou* drops of rain ◆ **du lait ? – une ~** milk? – just a drop ◆ **il n'y en a plus une ~** there's not a drop left ◆ **tomber ~ à ~** to drip

2 *(Pharm)* **~s** drops ◆ **~s pour les yeux/le nez** eye/nose drops

3 *(* = eau-de-vie)* brandy

4 *(††, hum)* **je n'y vois/entends ~** *(= rien)* I see/hear not a thing † *(aussi hum)*

5 *(Méd)* gout

6 *(loc)* **avoir la ~ au nez** to have a dripping *ou* runny nose ◆ **passer entre les ~s** *(de pluie)* to run between the drops; *(fig)* to come through without a scratch

COMP **goutte d'eau** drop of water; *(Bijouterie)* drop, droplet ◆ **c'est une ~ d'eau dans la mer** it's a drop in the ocean *(Brit) ou* in the bucket *(US)* ◆ **c'est la ~ (d'eau) qui fait déborder le vase** it's the last straw, it's the straw that breaks the camel's back; → **ressembler**

goutte-à-goutte /gutagut/ NM INV *(Méd)* drip *(Brit)*, IV *(US)* ◆ **alimenter qn au ~** to put sb on a drip *(Brit) ou* on an IV *(US)*, to drip-feed sb *(Brit)*

gouttelette /gut(ə)lɛt/ NF droplet

goutter /gute/ ▸ conjug 1 ◂ VI to drip *(de* from)

goutteux, -euse /gutø, øz/ ADJ *(Méd)* gouty

gouttière /gutjɛʀ/ NF *(horizontale)* gutter; *(verticale)* drainpipe; *[de voiture]* rain gutter; *(Méd)* (plaster) cast; *(Anat : sur os)* groove; → **chat**

gouvernable /guvɛʀnabl/ ADJ governable ◆ **difficilement ~** difficult to govern

gouvernail /guvɛʀnaj/ NM *(= pale)* rudder; *(= barre)* helm, tiller ◆ **~ de direction** rudder ◆ **~ de profondeur** elevator ◆ **tenir le ~** *(fig)* to be at the helm

gouvernance /guvɛʀnɑ̃s/ NF governance ◆ **~ d'entreprise** corporate governance

gouvernant, e[1] /guvɛʀnɑ̃, ɑ̃t/ ADJ *[parti, classe]* ruling *(épith)*, governing *(épith)* NMPL *(Pol)* ◆ **les ~s** the rulers, those in power ◆ **les gouvernés et les ~s** the citizens and those who govern them

gouvernante[2] /guvɛʀnɑ̃t/ NF *(= institutrice)* governess; *(= dame de compagnie)* housekeeper

gouverne /guvɛʀn/ NF 1 *(frm)* **pour ta ~** for your guidance 2 *(= pilotage d'un bateau)* steering 3 *(= surface d'une aile)* control surface ◆ **~ de profondeur** *(= dispositif)* elevator ◆ **~ latérale** aileron

gouverné /guvɛʀne/ NM *(gén pl)* citizen

gouvernement /guvɛʀnəmɑ̃/ NM *(= administration, régime)* government; *(= cabinet)* Cabinet, Government ◆ **former un ~** to set up *ou* form a government ◆ **il est au ~** he's a member of *ou* he's in the government ◆ **sous un ~ socialiste** under socialist rule *ou* government ◆ **ça a eu lieu sous le ~ de Thatcher** it happened during the Thatcher government *ou* during Thatcher's government ◆ **~ de cohabitation** cohabitation government ◆ **~ d'entreprise** corporate governance

gouvernemental, e (mpl **-aux**) /guvɛʀnəmɑ̃tal, o/ ADJ *[député]* of the governing party; *[organe, politique]* government *(épith)*, governmental *(épith)*; *[journal]* pro-government; *[troupes]* government *(épith)* ◆ **le parti ~** the governing *ou* ruling party, the party in office ◆ **l'équipe ~e** the government

gouverner /guvɛʀne/ ▸ conjug 1 ◂ VT 1 *(Pol)* to govern, to rule ◆ **le parti qui gouverne** the party in office, the governing *ou* ruling party ◆ **droit des peuples à se ~ (eux-mêmes)** right of peoples to self-government 2 *(littér) [+ passions]* to control ◆ **savoir ~ son cœur** to have control over one's heart ◆ **se laisser ~ par l'ambition/par qn** to let o.s. be ruled *ou* governed by ambition/by sb ◆ **il sait fort bien se ~** he is well able to control himself ◆ **l'intérêt gouverne le monde** self-interest rules the world 3 *(Naut)* to steer, to helm ◆ **~ vers tribord** to steer to(wards) starboard 4 *(Gram)* to govern, to take VI *(Naut)* to steer ◆ **le bateau gouverne bien/mal** the boat steers well/badly ◆ **~ sur son ancre/sa bouée** to steer towards one's anchor/one's buoy

gouverneur /guvɛʀnœʀ/ NM 1 *(Admin, Pol)* governor ◆ **le Gouverneur de la Banque de France** the Governor of the Bank of France ◆ **~ militaire** military governor ◆ **~ général** *(Can)* governor general 2 *(Hist = précepteur)* tutor

gouzi-gouzi * /guziguzi/ NM INV tickle ◆ **faire des ~ à qn** to tickle sb

goy /gɔj/ ADJ, NMF goy

goyave /gɔjav/ NF *(= fruit)* guava

goyavier /gɔjavje/ NM *(= arbre)* guava

GPAO /ʒepeao/ NF (abrév de **gestion de la production assistée par ordinateur**) → **gestion**

GPL /ʒepeɛl/ NM (abrév de **gaz de pétrole liquéfié**) LPG

GPS /ʒepeɛs/ NM (abrév de **global positioning system**) ◆ **(système) ~** GPS (system)

GQG /ʒekyʒe/ NM (abrév de **Grand Quartier Général**) GHQ

GR /ʒeɛʀ/ NM (abrév de **(sentier de) grande randonnée**) ◆ **emprunter un ~** to take an official hiking trail; → **randonnée**

Graal /gʀɑl/ NM Grail ◆ **la quête du ~** the quest for the Holy Grail

grabat /gʀaba/ NM pallet, mean bed

grabataire /gʀabatɛʀ/ ADJ bedridden NMF bedridden invalid

grabuge * /gʀabyʒ/ NM ◆ **il va y avoir du ~** there'll be ructions * *(Brit) ou* a ruckus * *(US) ou* a rumpus * ◆ **faire du ~** to create havoc

grâce /gʀɑs/ GRAMMAIRE ACTIVE 44.1 NF 1 *(= charme) [de personne, geste]* grace; *[de chose, paysage]* charm ◆ **plein de ~** graceful ◆ **visage sans ~** plain face ◆ **avec ~** *[danser]* gracefully; *[s'exprimer]* elegantly ◆ **faire des ~s** to put on airs (and graces)

2 *(= faveur)* favour *(Brit)*, favor *(US)* ◆ **demander une ~ à qn** to ask a favour of sb ◆ **accorder une ~ à qn** to grant sb a favour ◆ **trouver ~ auprès de** *ou* **aux yeux de qn** to find favour with sb ◆ **il nous a fait la ~ d'accepter** *(frm, hum)* he did us the honour of accepting ◆ **elle nous a fait la ~ de sa présence** *ou* **d'être présente** she graced *ou* honoured us with her presence ◆ **être en ~** to be in favour ◆ **rentrer en ~** to come back into favour ◆ **être dans les bonnes ~s de qn** to be in favour with sb, to be in sb's good graces *ou* good books * ◆ **chercher/gagner les bonnes ~s de qn** to seek/gain sb's favour ◆ **délai de ~** days of grace ◆ **donner à qn une semaine de ~** to give sb a week's grace

3 *(locutions)* **bonne/mauvaise ~** good/bad grace ◆ **faire qch de** *ou* **avec bonne/mauvaise ~** to do sth with (a) good/bad grace, to do sth willingly/grudgingly ◆ **il y a mis de la mauvaise ~** he did it very reluctantly ◆ **il a eu la bonne ~ de reconnaître ...** he had the good grace to admit ... ◆ **il aurait mauvaise ~ à refuser** it would be bad form *ou* in bad taste for him to refuse

4 *(= miséricorde)* mercy; *(Jur)* pardon ◆ **~ royale/présidentielle** royal/presidential pardon ◆ **demander** *ou* **crier ~** to beg *ou* cry for mercy ◆ **demander ~ pour qn** to appeal for clemency on sb's behalf ◆ **~ !** (have) mercy! ◆ **de ~, laissez-le dormir** for pity's sake *ou* for goodness' sake, let him sleep ◆ **je vous fais ~ des détails/du reste** I'll spare you the details/the rest ◆ **donner/recevoir le coup de ~** to give/receive the coup de grâce *ou* deathblow; → **droit**[3], **recours**

5 *(= reconnaissance)* **dire les ~s** to give thanks *(after a meal)*

◆ **grâce à** ◆ **~ à qn/qch** thanks to sb/sth ◆ **~ à Dieu !** thank God!, thank goodness!; → **action**[1], **jour, rendre**

6 *(Rel)* grace ◆ **à la ~ de Dieu !** it's in God's hands! ◆ **nous réussirons par la ~ de Dieu** with God's blessing we shall succeed ◆ **~ efficace/suffisante/vivifiante** efficacious/sufficient/life-giving grace; → **an, état**

7 *(= don, inspiration)* gift ◆ **avoir la ~** to have a gift ◆ **il a été touché par la ~** he has been inspired ◆ **c'est la ~ que nous lui souhaitons** that is what we wish for him

8 *(= déesse)* **les trois Grâces** the three Graces

9 *(= titre)* **Sa Grâce ...** *(homme)* His Grace ...; *(femme)* Her Grace ...

gracier /gʀasje/ ▸ conjug 7 ◂ VT to grant a pardon to, to pardon ◆ **il a été gracié par le président** he was granted a presidential pardon

gracieusement /gʀasjøzmɑ̃/ ADV *(= élégamment)* gracefully; *(= aimablement)* amiably, kindly; *(= gratuitement)* free of charge ◆ **ceci vous est ~ offert par la société Leblanc** Messrs Leblanc offer you this with their compliments, please accept this with the compliments of Messrs Leblanc ◆ **documents ~ prêtés par l'Institut Pasteur** documentation kindly loaned by the Pasteur Institute

gracieuseté /gʀasjøzte/ NF *(littér) (= amabilité)* amiability; *(= geste élégant)* graceful gesture; *(= cadeau)* free gift ◆ **je vous remercie de vos ~s** *(iro)* so kind of you to say so *(iro)*

gracieux, -ieuse /gʀasjø, jøz/ ADJ 1 *(= élégant) [gestes, silhouette, personne]* graceful 2 *(= aimable) [sourire, abord, personne]* amiable, kindly; *[enfant]* amiable ◆ **notre gracieuse souveraine** *(frm)* our gracious sovereign *(frm)* 3 *(frm = gratuit) [aide, service]* gratuitous *(frm)*; → **recours, titre**

gracile /gʀasil/ ADJ *[personne, corps, tige]* slender; *[cou]* slender, swanlike

gracilité /gʀasilite/ NF slenderness

Gracques /gʀak/ NMPL ◆ **les ~** the Gracchi

gradation /gʀadasjɔ̃/ NF gradation ◆ **il y a toute une ~ des réactions des victimes d'attentat** victims of bombings react in a variety of ways ◆ **il y a une ~ dans la difficulté des exercices** the exercises are graded

grade /gʀad/ NM 1 *(Admin, Mil)* rank ◆ **monter en ~** to be promoted ◆ **en prendre pour son ~** * to be hauled over the coals, to get a proper dressing-down * 2 *(= titre) (Univ)* degree ◆ **~ de licencié** (first) degree, bachelor's degree 3 *(Math)* grade 4 *[d'huile]* grade

gradé, e /gʀade/ NM,F *(Mil) (gén)* officer; *(= subalterne)* NCO, non-commissioned officer; *(Police)* officer, ≃ (police) sergeant *(Brit)*

gradient /gʀadjɑ̃/ NM gradient

gradin /gʀadɛ̃/ NM *(Théât)* tier; *[de stade]* step (of the terracing); *(Agr)* terrace ◆ **les ~s** *[de stade]* the terraces ◆ **dans les ~s** on the terraces ◆ **en ~s** terraced ◆ **la colline s'élevait/descendait en ~s** the hill went up/down in steps *ou* terraces

graduation /gʀadɥasjɔ̃/ NF *[d'instrument]* graduation

gradué, e /gʀadɥe/ (ptp de **graduer**) ADJ *[exercices]* graded; *[règle, thermomètre]* graduated ◆ **verre/pot ~** measuring glass/jug

graduel, -elle /gʀadɥɛl/ ADJ *[progression, amélioration, augmentation]* gradual; *[difficultés]* progressive NM *(Rel)* gradual

graduellement /gʀadɥɛlmɑ̃/ ADV gradually

graduer /gʀadɥe/ ▸ conjug 1 ◂ VT *[+ exercices]* to increase in difficulty; *[+ difficultés, efforts]* to step up *ou* increase gradually; *[+ règle, thermomètre]* to graduate

graffiter /gʀafite/ ▸ conjug 1 ◂ VT to write graffiti on

graffiteur, -euse /gʀafitœʀ, øz/ NM,F *(gén)* graffitist; *(= artiste)* graffiti artist

graffiti (pl **graffiti(s)**) /gʀafiti/ NM graffiti *(NonC)* ◆ **un ~** a piece of graffiti

graille ‡ /gʀɑj/ NF grub ‡, nosh ‡ *(Brit)*, chow ‡ *(US)* ◆ **à la ~ !** come and get it! *, grub's up! * *(Brit)*

grailler /gʀɑje/ ▸ conjug 1 ◂ VI 1 (‡ = *manger*) to nosh ‡ *(Brit)*, to chow down ‡ *(US)* 2 *[corneille]* to caw 3 *(= parler)* to speak in a throaty *ou* hoarse voice

graillon / gʀɑjɔ̃ / NM (péj = déchet) bit of burnt fat ◆ **ça sent le ~** there's a smell of burnt fat

graillonner * / gʀɑjɔne / ▸ conjug 1 ◂ VI (= tousser) to cough; (= parler) to speak in a throaty ou hoarse voice

grain / gʀɛ̃ / NM 1 [de blé, riz, maïs, sel] grain ◆ **le(s) ~(s)** (= céréales) (the) grain ◆ **~ d'orge** grain of barley, barleycorn ◆ **donner du ~ aux poules** to give grain to the chickens ◆ **alcool ou eau-de-vie de ~(s)** grain alcohol ◆ **le bon ~** (Rel) the good seed ◆ **cela leur a donné du ~ à moudre** (matière à réflexion) it gave them food for thought; (travail) it kept them occupied ou busy for a while ◆ **avoir du ~ à moudre** (= avoir ce qu'il faut) to have what it takes ◆ **mettre son ~ de sel** * to put ou stick one's oar in * (Brit), to put in one's two cents * (US); → **poulet, séparer**

2 [de café] bean ◆ **café en ~s** coffee beans, unground coffee ◆ **~ de raisin** grape ◆ **~ de cassis** blackcurrant ◆ **~ de poivre** peppercorn ◆ **poivre en ~s** whole pepper, peppercorns ◆ **moutarde en ~s** whole grain mustard

3 [de collier, chapelet] bead; (Méd = petite pilule) pellet

4 (= particule) [de sable, farine, pollen] grain; [de poussière] speck ◆ **~ de sable** (fig) blip *, glitch * ◆ **il suffit d'un ~ de sable pour tout bloquer** one blip * ou glitch * is enough to bring everything grinding to a halt

5 ◆ **un ~ de** (= un peu de) [+ fantaisie] a touch of; [+ bon sens] a grain ou an ounce of ◆ **il n'y a pas un ~ de vérité dans ce qu'il dit** there's not a grain ou scrap of truth in what he says ◆ **il a un (petit) ~** * he's a bit touched *, he's not quite all there * ◆ **il faut parfois un petit ~ de folie** it sometimes helps to be a bit eccentric

6 (= texture) [de peau] texture; (Photo) grain ◆ **à ~ fin** [bois, roche] fine-grained ◆ **à gros ~s** coarse-grained ◆ **travailler dans le sens du ~** to work with the grain

7 (= averse brusque) heavy shower; (Naut = bourrasque) squall ◆ **essuyer un ~** to run into a squall; → **veiller**

8 († † = poids) grain; (Can) grain (0.0647 gramme)

COMP **grain de beauté** mole, beauty spot
grain de plomb leadshot (NonC)

graine / gʀɛn / NF (Agr) seed ◆ **~s de radis** radish seeds ◆ **~s germées** sprouting seeds ◆ **~s pour oiseaux** birdseed (NonC) ◆ **monter en ~** [plante] to go ou run to seed, to bolt; (hum) [enfant] to shoot up ◆ **tu vois ce qu'a fait ton frère, prends-en de la ~** * you've seen what your brother has done so take a leaf out of his book * ◆ **c'est de la ~ de voleur** he has the makings of a thief ◆ **la petite ~** (hum) the precious seed (hum), sperm; → **casser, mauvais**

grainer / gʀene / ▸ conjug 1 ◂ VT, VI ⇒ **grener**

graineterie / gʀɛntʀi / NF (= commerce) seed trade; (= magasin) seed shop, seed merchant's (shop)

grainetier, -ière / gʀɛntje, jɛʀ / NM,F seed merchant; (= homme) seedsman

graissage / gʀɛsaʒ / NM [de machine] greasing, lubricating ◆ **faire faire un ~ complet de sa voiture** to take one's car in for a complete lubricating job

graisse / gʀɛs / NF 1 [d'animal, personne] fat; (laissée dans le récipient après cuisson) dripping (Brit), drippings (US); (= lubrifiant) grease ◆ **~(s) végétale(s)/animale(s)** animal/vegetable fat ◆ **prendre de la ~** [d'animal] to put on fat; → **bourrelet** 2 (Typo) weight

COMP **graisse de baleine** (whale) blubber
graisse de phoque seal blubber
graisse de porc lard

graisser / gʀese / ▸ conjug 1 ◂ VT (= lubrifier) (gén) to grease; [+ chaussures] to wax; (= salir) to get grease on, to make greasy; (= donner un aspect gras à) [+ cheveux, peau] to make greasy ◆ **cette lotion ne graisse pas** this lotion is non-greasy ◆ **~ la patte à qn** * to grease ou oil sb's palm * VI [cheveux] to get greasy

graisseur / gʀesœʀ / NM (= objet) lubricator ◆ **dispositif ~** lubricating ou greasing device ◆ **(pistolet) ~** grease gun

graisseux, -euse / gʀesø, øz / ADJ [main, objet] greasy; [papiers] grease-stained, greasy; [nourriture] greasy, fatty; [bourrelet] fatty, of fat; [tissu, tumeur] fatty

graminacée / gʀaminase / NF ⇒ **graminée**

graminée / gʀamine / NF ◆ **une ~** a grass ◆ **les ~s** grasses, graminae (SPÉC)

grammaire / gʀa(m)mɛʀ / NF (= science, livre) grammar ◆ **faute de ~** grammatical mistake ◆ **règle de ~** grammatical rule, rule of grammar ◆ **exercice/livre de ~** grammar exercise/book ◆ **~ des cas** case grammar ◆ **~ (de structure) syntagmatique** phrase structure grammar ◆ **~ de surface** surface grammar

grammairien, -ienne / gʀa(m)mɛʀjɛ̃, jɛn / NM,F grammarian

grammatical, e (mpl **-aux**) / gʀamatikal, o / ADJ (gén) grammatical ◆ **exercice ~** grammar exercise ◆ **phrase ~e** well-formed ou grammatical sentence; → **analyse**

grammaticalement / gʀamatikalmɑ̃ / ADV grammatically

grammaticalisation / gʀamatikalizasjɔ̃ / NF grammaticalization

grammaticalité / gʀamatikalite / NF grammaticality

gramme / gʀam / NM gram(me) ◆ **je n'ai pas pris/perdu un ~** (de mon poids) I haven't put on/lost an ounce ◆ **il n'a pas un ~ de jugeote** he hasn't an ounce of commonsense

gramophone ® † / gʀamɔfɔn / NM gramophone †

grand, e / gʀɑ̃, gʀɑ̃d / ADJ 1 (= de haute taille) [personne, verre] tall; [arbre, échelle] high, big, tall

2 (= plus âgé, adulte) **son ~ frère** his older ou elder ou big * brother ◆ **il a un petit garçon et deux ~es filles** he has a little boy and two older ou grown-up daughters ◆ **ils ont deux ~s enfants** they have two grown-up children ◆ **quand il sera ~** [d'enfant] when he grows up, when he's grown-up; [de chiot] when it's big, when it's fully grown ◆ **il est assez ~ pour savoir** he's big enough ou old enough to know ◆ **tu es ~/~e maintenant** you're a big boy/girl now

3 (en dimensions, gén) big, large; [hauteur, largeur] great; [bras, distance, voyage, enjambées] long; [avenue, marge] wide ◆ **aussi/plus ~ que nature** as large as/larger than life ◆ **ouvrir de ~s yeux** to open one's eyes wide ◆ **ouvrir la fenêtre/la bouche toute ~e** to open the window/one's mouth wide ◆ **l'amour avec un ~ A** love with a capital L

4 (en nombre, en quantité) [vitesse, poids, valeur, puissance] great; [nombre, quantité] large, great; [famille] large, big; [foule] large, great, big; [dépense] great; [fortune] great, large ◆ **la ~e majorité des gens** the great ou vast majority of people ◆ **une ~e partie de ce qu'il a** a great ou large proportion of what he has

5 (= intense, violent) [bruit, cri] loud; [froid] severe, intense; [chaleur] intense; [vent] strong, high; [effort, danger, plaisir, déception] great; [pauvreté] great, dire (épith); [soupir] deep, big ◆ **l'incendie a causé de ~s dégâts** the fire has caused extensive damage ou a great deal of damage ◆ **avec un ~ rire** with a loud ou big laugh ◆ **~ chagrin** deep ou great sorrow ◆ **à ma ~e surprise/honte** much to my surprise/shame, to my great surprise/shame

6 (= riche, puissant) [pays, firme, banquier, industriel] leading, big ◆ **les ~s trusts** the big trusts ◆ **un ~ personnage** an important person; → **train**

7 (= important) [aventure, progrès, intelligence] great; [différence, appétit, succès] great, big; [ville, travail] big ◆ **je t'annonce une ~e nouvelle !** I've got some great news! ◆ **le ~ moment approche** the big ou great moment is coming ◆ **c'est un ~ jour/honneur pour nous** this is a great day/honour for us

8 (= principal) main ◆ **c'est la ~e nouvelle du jour** it's the main news of the day ◆ **les ~s points de son discours** the main points of his speech ◆ **les ~s fleuves du globe** the major ou main ou great rivers of the world ◆ **la ~e difficulté consiste à ...** the main ou major difficulty lies in ...

9 (intensif) [travailleur] great, hard; [collectionneur] great, keen; [buveur] heavy, hard; [mangeur] big; [fumeur] heavy; [ami, rêveur] great, big; [menteur] big ◆ **c'est un ~ ennemi du bruit** he can't stand ou abide noise ◆ **un ~ amateur de musique** a great music lover ◆ **~ lâche/sot !** you big coward/fool! ◆ **~e jeunesse** extreme youth ◆ **un ~ mois/quart d'heure** a good month/quarter of an hour ◆ **rester un ~ moment** to stay a good while ◆ **un ~ kilomètre** a good kilometre ◆ **un ~ verre d'eau** a large glass of water ◆ **un ~ panier de champignons** a full basket of mushrooms ◆ **les ~s malades** the very ill ou sick ◆ **un ~ invalide** a seriously disabled person

10 (= remarquable) [champion, œuvre, savant, civilisation] great ◆ **un ~ vin/homme** a great wine/man ◆ **une ~e année** a vintage ou great year ◆ **le ~ Molière** the great Molière ◆ **c'est du ~ jazz** * it's jazz at its best ◆ **une ~e figure de l'Histoire** a major historical figure

11 (= de gala) [réception, dîner] grand ◆ **en ~e cérémonie** with great ceremony; → **apparat, pompe[2], tenue[2]**

12 (= noble) [âme] noble, great; [pensée, principe] high, lofty ◆ **se montrer ~ (et généreux)** to be big-hearted ou magnanimous

13 (= exagéré) **faire de ~es phrases** to trot out high-flown sentences ◆ **tous ces ~s discours** all these high-flown speeches ◆ **faire de ~s gestes** to wave one's arms about; → **cheval, mot**

14 (= beaucoup de) **cela te fera (le plus) ~ bien** it'll do you a great deal of ou the world of good ◆ **j'en pense le plus ~ bien** I think most highly of him ◆ **~ bien vous fasse !** much good may it do you! ◆ **il n'y a pas ~ danger** there's no great danger ◆ **cela lui fera ~ tort** it'll do him a lot of harm

ADV 1 (en taille) **ces sandales chaussent ~** these sandals are big-fitting (Brit) ou run large (US) ◆ **ce n'est pas une maquette, il l'a réalisé en ~** it's not a model, he made it full scale

2 (= largement) **ouvrir (en) ~** [+ porte] to open wide; [+ robinet] to turn full on ◆ **la fenêtre était ~(e) ouverte** the window was wide open ◆ **voir ~** to think big ◆ **il a vu trop ~** he was over-ambitious ◆ **dix bouteilles ? tu as vu ~ !** ten bottles? you don't do things by halves! ◆ **il fait toujours les choses en ~** he always does things on a large scale

NM 1 (Scol) older ou bigger boy, senior boy ou pupil ◆ **jeu pour petits et ~s** game for old and young alike ou for the young and the not-so-young ◆ **il va à l'école tout seul comme un ~** he goes to school on his own like a big boy

2 (terme d'affection) **mon ~** son, my lad (Brit)

3 (= personne puissante) **les ~s de ce monde** men in high places ◆ **les quatre Grands** (Pol) the Big Four ◆ **les cinq ~s de l'électronique** the five big ou major electronics companies ◆ **Pierre/Alexandre/Frédéric le Grand** Peter/Alexander/Frederick the Great

NF **grande** 1 *(Scol)* older *ou* bigger girl, senior girl *ou* pupil ◆ **elle parle comme une ~e** she talks like a big girl
2 *(terme d'affection)* **ma ~e** (my) dear
COMP **la grande Bleue** *ou* **bleue** the Med*, the Mediterranean
grand d'Espagne Spanish grandee
le grand huit † *[de fête foraine]* the scenic railway †
grand œuvre *(= réalisation très importante)* great work ◆ **le Grand Œuvre** *(Alchimie)* the Great Work
le Grand Orient the Grand Lodge of France
grande personne grown-up
la grande vie the good life ◆ **mener la ~e vie** to live in style, to live the good life

GRANDES ÉCOLES

The **grandes écoles** are competitive-entrance higher education establishments where engineering, business administration and other subjects are taught to a very high standard. The most prestigious include « l'École Polytechnique » (engineering), the three « Écoles normales supérieures » (humanities), l'« ENA » (the civil service college), and « HEC » (business administration).
Pupils prepare for entrance to the **grandes écoles** after their « baccalauréat » in two years of « classes préparatoires » (nicknamed « hypokhâgne » and « khâgne » for humanities and « hypotaupe » and « taupe » for science). → CLASSES PRÉPARATOIRES, CONCOURS, ÉCOLE NATIONALE D'ADMINISTRATION

grand-angle (pl **grands-angles**) /gʀɑ̃tɑ̃gl, gʀɑ̃zɑ̃gl/, **grand-angulaire** (pl **grands-angulaires**) /gʀɑ̃tɑ̃gylɛʀ, gʀɑ̃zɑ̃gylɛʀ/ NM wide-angle lens ◆ **faire une photo au ~** to take a picture with a wide-angle lens, to take a wide-angle shot

grand-chose /gʀɑ̃ʃoz/ PRON INDÉF ◆ **pas ~** not much ◆ **on ne sait pas ~ à son sujet** we don't know very much about him ◆ **cela ne vaut pas ~** it's not worth much, it's not up to much* *(Brit)*, it's no great shakes* ◆ **es-tu blessé ? – ce n'est pas ~** are you hurt? – it's nothing much ◆ **il n'y a plus ~ dans ce magasin** there isn't much *ou* there's nothing much left in this shop ◆ **il n'y a pas ~ à dire** there's not a lot to say, there's nothing much to say ◆ **il n'en sortira pas ~ de bon** not much good will come (out) of this, I can't see much good coming (out) of this ◆ **sans changer ~ au plan** without altering the plan much NMF INV *(péj)* ◆ **c'est un pas ~** he's a good-for-nothing

grand-croix (pl **grands-croix**) /gʀɑ̃kʀwa/ NM holder of the Grand Cross NF INV Grand Cross *(of the Légion d'honneur)*

grand-duc (pl **grands-ducs**) /gʀɑ̃dyk/ NM 1 *(= personne)* grand duke; → **tournée²** 2 *(= hibou)* eagle owl

grand-ducal, e (mpl **-aux**) /gʀɑ̃dykal, o/ ADJ *(= du grand-duc)* grand-ducal; *(= du grand-duché de Luxembourg)* of Luxembourg

grand-duché (pl **grands-duchés**) /gʀɑ̃dyʃe/ NM grand duchy ◆ **le ~ de Luxembourg** the grand duchy of Luxembourg

Grande-Bretagne /gʀɑ̃dbʀətaɲ/ NF ◆ **la ~** Great Britain

grande-duchesse (pl **grandes-duchesses**) /gʀɑ̃ddyʃɛs/ NF grand duchess

grandement /gʀɑ̃dmɑ̃/ ADV 1 *(= tout à fait)* **se tromper ~** to be greatly mistaken ◆ **avoir ~ raison/tort** to be absolutely right/wrong 2 *(= largement)* *[aider, contribuer]* a great deal, greatly ◆ **il a ~ le temps** he has plenty of time ◆ **il y en a ~ assez** there's plenty of it *ou* easily enough (of it) ◆ **être ~ logé** to have plenty of room *ou* ample room (in one's house) ◆ **nous ne sommes pas ~ logés** we haven't got (very) much room ◆ **je lui suis ~ reconnaissant** I'm deeply *ou* extremely grateful to him ◆ **il est ~ temps de partir** it's high time we went 3 *(= généreusement) [agir]* nobly ◆ **faire les choses ~** to do things lavishly *ou* in grand style

grandesse /gʀɑ̃dɛs/ NF Spanish grandeeship

grandeur /gʀɑ̃dœʀ/ NF 1 *(= dimension)* size ◆ **c'est de la ~ d'un crayon** it's the size of *ou* as big as a pencil ◆ **ils sont de la même ~** they are the same size ◆ **~ nature** *[statue]* life-size *(épith)*; *[expérience]* in real conditions ◆ **en vraie ~** *[maquette]* full-size *(épith)*, full-scale *(épith)*; → **haut, ordre¹**
2 *(= importance) [d'œuvre, sacrifice, amour]* greatness ◆ **avoir des idées de ~** to have delusions of grandeur; → **délire**
3 *(= dignité)* greatness; *(= magnanimité)* magnanimity ◆ **faire preuve de ~** to show magnanimity ◆ **la ~ humaine** the greatness of man ◆ **~ d'âme** generosity of spirit
4 *(= gloire)* greatness ◆ **~ et décadence de** rise and fall of ◆ **politique de ~** politics of national grandeur
5 *(Astron)* magnitude; *(Math)* ◆ **~ variable** variable magnitude ◆ **de première ~** *[étoile]* of first magnitude; *(fig)* of the first order
6 († = *titre*) **Sa Grandeur l'évêque de Lyon** (the) Lord Bishop of Lyons ◆ **oui, Votre Grandeur** yes, my Lord
NFPL *(= honneurs)* ◆ **~s** glory; → **folie**

Grand-Guignol /gʀɑ̃giɲɔl/ NM Grand Guignol ◆ **c'est du ~** *(fig)* it's all blood and thunder

grand-guignolesque (pl **grand-guignolesques**) /gʀɑ̃giɲɔlɛsk/ ADJ *[situation, événement, pièce de théâtre]* gruesome, blood-curdling

grandiloquence /gʀɑ̃dilɔkɑ̃s/ NF grandiloquence, bombast

grandiloquent, e /gʀɑ̃dilɔkɑ̃, ɑ̃t/ ADJ grandiloquent, bombastic

grandiose /gʀɑ̃djoz/ ADJ *[œuvre, spectacle, paysage]* imposing, grandiose ◆ **le ~ d'un paysage** the grandeur of a landscape

grandir /gʀɑ̃diʀ/ ► conjug 2 ◄ VI 1 *[plante, enfant]* to grow; *[ombre portée]* to grow (bigger) ◆ **il a grandi de 10 cm** he has grown 10 cm ◆ **je le trouve grandi** he has grown since I last saw him ◆ **en grandissant tu verras que …** as you grow up you'll see that … ◆ **il a grandi dans mon estime** he's gone up in my estimation, he has grown *ou* risen in my esteem ◆ **enfant grandi trop vite** lanky *ou* gangling child
2 *[sentiment, influence, foule]* to increase, to grow; *[bruit]* to grow (louder), to increase; *[firme]* to grow, to expand ◆ **l'obscurité grandissait** (the) darkness thickened, it grew darker and darker ◆ **son pouvoir va grandissant** his power grows ever greater *ou* constantly increases ◆ **~ en sagesse** to grow *ou* increase in wisdom
VT 1 *(= faire paraître grand) [microscope]* to magnify ◆ **~ les dangers/difficultés** to exaggerate the dangers/difficulties ◆ **ces chaussures te grandissent** those shoes make you (look) taller ◆ **il se grandit en se mettant sur la pointe des pieds** he made himself taller by standing on tiptoe
2 *(= rendre prestigieux)* **cette épreuve l'a grandi** this ordeal has made him grow in stature ◆ **il sort grandi de cette épreuve** he has come out of this ordeal with increased stature ◆ **la France n'en est pas sortie grandie** it did little for France's reputation

grandissant, e /gʀɑ̃disɑ̃, ɑ̃t/ ADJ *[foule, bruit, sentiment]* growing ◆ **nombre/pouvoir (sans cesse) ~** (ever-)growing *ou* (ever-)increasing number/power

grandissement † /gʀɑ̃dismɑ̃/ NM *(Opt)* magnification

grandissime /gʀɑ̃disim/ ADJ *(hum = très grand)* tremendous

grand-livre (pl **grands-livres**) /gʀɑ̃livʀ/ NM († *Comm*) ledger

grand-maman (pl **grands-mamans**) /gʀɑ̃mamɑ̃/ NF granny*, grandma

grand-mère (pl **grands-mères**) /gʀɑ̃mɛʀ/ NF *(= aïeule)* grandmother; (* = *vieille dame*) (old) granny*

grand-messe (pl **grands-messes**) /gʀɑ̃mɛs/ NF *(Rel)* high mass; *(Pol)* powwow*, ritual gathering ◆ **~ médiatique** media jamboree ◆ **la ~ cathodique** *ou* **du journal de 20 heures** the 8 o'clock TV news ritual

grand-oncle (pl **grands-oncles**) /gʀɑ̃tɔ̃kl, gʀɑ̃zɔ̃kl/ NM great-uncle

grand-papa (pl **grands-papas**) /gʀɑ̃papa/ NM grandpa, grandad*

grand-peine /gʀɑ̃pɛn/ **à grand-peine** LOC ADV with great difficulty

grand-père (pl **grands-pères**) /gʀɑ̃pɛʀ/ NM *(= aïeul)* grandfather; (* = *vieux monsieur*) old man ◆ **avance, ~ !*** *(péj)* get a move on, grandad!*

grand-route (pl **grand-routes**) /gʀɑ̃ʀut/ NF main road

grand-rue (pl **grand-rues**) /gʀɑ̃ʀy/ NF ◆ **la ~** the high street *(Brit)*, the main street *(US)*

grands-parents /gʀɑ̃paʀɑ̃/ NMPL grandparents

grand-tante (pl **grands-tantes**) /gʀɑ̃tɑ̃t/ NF great-aunt

grand-vergue (pl **grands-vergues**) /gʀɑ̃vɛʀg/ NF main yard

grand-voile (pl **grands-voiles**) /gʀɑ̃vwal/ NF mainsail

grange /gʀɑ̃ʒ/ NF barn

granit(e) /granit/ NM granite

granité, e /granite/ ADJ granite-like *(épith)* ◆ **papier ~** grained paper NM *(= tissu)* pebbleweave (cloth); *(= glace)* granita *(Italian water ice)*

graniteux, -euse /granitø, øz/ ADJ *(Minér)* granitic

granitique /granitik/ ADJ *(Minér)* granite *(épith)*, granitic

granivore /granivɔʀ/ ADJ grain-eating, granivorous *(SPÉC)* NM grain-eater, granivore *(SPÉC)*

granny smith /granismis/ NF INV Granny Smith (apple)

granulaire /granylɛʀ/ ADJ *(Sci)* granular

granulat /granyla/ NM aggregate

granulation /granylasjɔ̃/ NF 1 *(= grain)* grainy effect ◆ **~s** granular *ou* grainy surface ◆ **~s cytoplasmiques** cytoplasmic granules 2 *(Tech = action)* granulation 3 *(Photo)* graininess

granule /granyl/ NM granule; *(Pharm)* small pill ◆ **~ homéopathique** homeopathic pill

granulé, e /granyle/ (ptp de **granuler**) ADJ *[surface]* granular NM granule

granuler /granyle/ ► conjug 1 ◄ VT *[+ métal, poudre]* to granulate

granuleux, -euse /granylø, øz/ ADJ *(gén)* granular; *[peau]* grainy

grape(-)fruit (pl **grape(-)fruits**) /gʀɛpfʀut/ NM grapefruit

graphe /graf/ NM graph

graphème /grafɛm/ NM grapheme

grapheur /grafœr/ **NM** graphics application package, graphics software *(NonC)*

graphie /grafi/ **NF** written form ◆ **il y a plusieurs ~s pour ce mot** there are several written forms of this word *ou* several ways of spelling this word ◆ ~ **phonétique** phonetic spelling

graphique /grafik/ **ADJ** *(gén)* graphic; *(Ordin) [application, écran]* graphics *(épith)*; *[environnement]* graphic; *[interface]* graphical ◆ **l'industrie** ~ the computer graphics industry **NM** *(= courbe)* graph, chart ◆ ~ **en barres** *ou* **à colonnes** *ou* **à tuyaux d'orgue** bar chart *ou* graph ◆ ~ **à secteurs** pie chart

graphiquement /grafikmɑ̃/ **ADV** graphically

graphisme /grafism/ **NM** 1 *(= technique) (Design)* graphics *(sg)*; *(Art)* graphic arts 2 *(= style) [de peintre, dessinateur]* style of drawing 3 *(= écriture individuelle)* hand, handwriting; *(= alphabet)* script

graphiste /grafist/ **NMF** graphic designer

graphitage /grafitaʒ/ **NM** graphitization

graphite /grafit/ **NM** graphite

graphiter /grafite/ ▸ conjug 1 ◂ **VT** to graphitize ◆ **lubrifiant graphité** graphitic lubricant

graphiteux, -euse /grafitø, øz/ **ADJ** graphitic

graphologie /grafɔlɔʒi/ **NF** graphology

graphologique /grafɔlɔʒik/ **ADJ** of handwriting, graphological

graphologue /grafɔlɔg/ **NMF** graphologist

grappe /grap/ **NF** *[de fleurs]* cluster; *[de groseilles]* bunch ◆ ~ **de raisin** bunch of grapes ◆ **en** *ou* **par ~s** in clusters ◆ **~s humaines** clusters of people ◆ **les ~s de la cytise** the laburnum flowers

grappillage /grapijaʒ/ **NM** 1 *[de grains]* gathering; *[de fruits, fleurs]* picking, gathering; *(après la vendange)* gleaning 2 *[d'idées]* lifting; *[d'argent]* fiddling* ◆ **ses ~s se montaient à quelques centaines de francs** his pickings amounted to several hundred francs ◆ **pour limiter les ~s** to reduce fiddling*

grappiller /grapije/ ▸ conjug 1 ◂ **VI** *(après la vendange)* to glean ◆ **arrête de ~, prends la grappe** *(= picorer)* stop picking at it and take the whole bunch ◆ **elle ne mange pas, elle grappille** she doesn't eat, she just nibbles **VT** 1 *[+ grains]* to gather; *[+ fruits, fleurs]* to pick, to gather 2 *[+ connaissances, nouvelles]* to pick up; *[+ renseignements, informations]* to glean; *[+ idées]* to lift; *[+ objets]* to pick up (here and there) ◆ ~ **quelques sous** to fiddle* *ou* pick up a little extra on the side ◆ **réussir à ~ quelques voix/sièges** to manage to pick up a few votes/seats ◆ **il a beaucoup grappillé chez d'autres auteurs** *(péj)* he's lifted a lot from other authors

grappin /grapɛ̃/ **NM** *[de bateau]* grapnel; *[de grue]* grab *(Brit)*, drag *(US)* ◆ **mettre le ~ sur qn*** to grab sb, to collar sb* ◆ **elle lui a mis le ~ dessus*** *(pour l'épouser)* she's got her claws into him* ◆ **mettre le ~ sur qch*** to get one's claws on *ou* into sth*

gras, grasse /grɑ, grɑs/ **ADJ** 1 *[substance, aliment, bouillon]* fatty; *[huître]* fat ◆ **fromage ~** full fat cheese ◆ **crème grasse pour la peau** rich moisturizing cream; → **chou¹, corps, matière**

2 *(= gros) [personne, animal, visage, main]* fat; *[bébé]* podgy *(Brit)*, pudgy *(US)*; *[volaille]* plump ◆ **être ~ comme un chanoine** *ou* **un moine** †, **être ~ à lard** † to be as round as a barrel ◆ **être ~ du bide*** *(péj)* to have a bit of a belly* *ou* of a corporation* *(Brit)*; *(par excès de boisson)* to have a beer-gut* *ou* a beer-belly* ◆ **un ~ du bide*** *(péj)* a fat slob*‡; → **vache, veau**

3 *(= graisseux, huileux) [mains, cheveux, surface]* greasy; *[pavé, rocher]* slimy; *[boue, sol]* sticky, slimy; → **houille**

4 *(= épais) [trait, contour]* thick; → **caractère, crayon, plante¹**

5 *[toux]* loose, phlegmy; *[voix, rire]* throaty

6 *(= vulgaire) [mot, plaisanterie]* coarse, crude

7 *(= abondant) [pâturage]* rich, luxuriant; *[récompense]* fat* *(épith)* ◆ **la paye n'est pas grasse** the pay is rather meagre, it's not much of a salary ◆ **j'ai touché 50 €, ce n'est pas ~*** I earned €50, which is hardly a fortune ◆ **il n'y a pas ~ à manger*** there's not much to eat

8 *(locution)* **faire la grasse matinée** to have a lie in, to sleep in

NM 1 *(Culin)* fat; *[de baleine]* blubber; *(Théât)* greasepaint ◆ **j'ai les mains couvertes de ~** my hands are covered in grease

2 *(= partie charnue)* **le ~ de** *[de jambe, bras]* the fleshy part of

3 *(Typo)* **c'est imprimé en (caractères) ~** it's printed in bold (type)

4 *(* = profit)* profit

ADV 1 ◆ **manger ~** to eat fatty foods ◆ **faire ~** *(Rel)* to eat meat

2 ◆ **il tousse ~** he has a loose *ou* phlegmy cough ◆ **parler/rire ~*** to speak/laugh coarsely

gras-double (pl **gras-doubles**) /gradubl/ **NM** *(Culin)* tripe

grassement /grɑsmɑ̃/ **ADV** 1 *[rétribuer]* generously, handsomely ◆ **vivre ~** *(péj)* to live off the fat of the land ◆ ~ **payé** highly *ou* well paid 2 *[parler, rire]* coarsely

grasseyant, e /grasejɑ̃, ɑ̃t/ **ADJ** *[voix]* guttural

grasseyement /grasɛjmɑ̃/ **NM** guttural pronunciation

grasseyer /graseje/ ▸ conjug 1 ◂ **VI** to have a guttural pronunciation; *(Ling)* to use a fricative *ou* uvular (Parisian) R

grassouillet, -ette* /grɑsujɛ, ɛt/ **ADJ** podgy *(Brit)*, pudgy *(US)*, plump

gratifiant, e /gratifjɑ̃, jɑ̃t/ **ADJ** *[expérience, travail]* rewarding, gratifying

gratification /gratifikasjɔ̃/ **NF** 1 *(Admin = prime)* bonus ◆ ~ **de fin d'année** Christmas bonus *(Brit)* 2 *(Psych = satisfaction)* gratification

gratifier /gratifje/ ▸ conjug 7 ◂ **VT** ◆ ~ **qn de** *[+ récompense, avantage]* to present sb with; *[+ sourire, bonjour]* to favour *(Brit) ou* favor *(US) ou* grace sb with; *(iro) [+ amende]* to present sb with; *(iro) [+ punition]* to give sb ◆ **il nous gratifia d'un long sermon** he favoured *ou* honoured us with a long sermon ◆ **se sentir gratifié** *(Psych)* to feel gratified

gratin /gratɛ̃/ **NM** 1 *(Culin) (= plat)* cheese(-topped) dish, gratin; *(= croûte)* cheese topping, gratin ◆ ~ **de pommes de terre** potatoes au gratin ◆ **chou-fleur au ~** cauliflower cheese ◆ ~ **dauphinois** gratin Dauphinois 2 *(= haute société)* **le ~*** the upper crust*, the swells* *(US)* ◆ **tout le ~ de la ville était là** everybody who's anybody was there, all the nobs* *(Brit) ou* swells* *(US)* of the town were there

gratiné, e /gratine/ (ptp de **gratiner**) **ADJ** 1 *(Culin)* au gratin 2 *(* : intensif) [épreuve, amende]* (really) stiff; *[aventures, plaisanterie]* (really) wild ◆ **il m'a passé une engueulade ~e*‡** he gave me a heck of a telling-off*, he didn't half give me a telling-off* *(Brit)* ◆ **c'est un examen ~** it's a tough* *ou* stiff exam ◆ **comme film érotique, c'est plutôt ~** as erotic films go, it's pretty hot stuff* *ou* spicy ◆ **comme imbécile il est ~** he's a prize idiot **NF** **gratinée** French onion soup

gratiner /gratine/ ▸ conjug 1 ◂ **VT** *(Culin) [+ pommes de terre]* to cook au gratin **VI** *(= dorer)* to brown, to turn golden

gratis* /gratis/ **ADJ** free **ADV** free, for nothing

gratitude /gratityd/ **NF** gratitude

gratos*‡ /gratos/ **ADJ, ADV** ⇒ **gratis**

gratouiller* /gratuje/ ▸ conjug 1 ◂ **VT** 1 *(= démanger)* ~ **qn** to make sb itch 2 ◆ ~ **sa guitare** to strum on one's guitar

grattage /grataʒ/ **NM** 1 *[de surface] (avec un ongle, une pointe)* scratching; *(avec un outil)* scraping ◆ **j'ai gagné au ~** I won on the scratch cards 2 *(pour enlever) [de tache]* scratching off; *[d'inscription]* scratching out; *[de boue, papier peint]* scraping off ◆ **après un ~ à la toile émeri** after rubbing with emery cloth

gratte /grat/ **NF** 1 *(* = petit bénéfice illicite)* pickings ◆ **faire de la ~** to make a bit on the side* 2 *(*‡ = guitare)* guitar

gratte-ciel (pl **gratte-ciel(s)**) /gratsjɛl/ **NM** skyscraper

gratte-cul (pl **gratte-culs**) /gratky/ **NM** *(= baie)* rose hip

gratte-dos /gratdo/ **NM INV** backscratcher

grattement /gratmɑ̃/ **NM** scratching

gratte-papier (pl **gratte-papier(s)**) /gratpapje/ **NM** *(péj)* penpusher *(Brit)*, pencil pusher *(US)*

gratte-pieds /gratpje/ **NM INV** shoe-scraper

gratter /grate/ ▸ conjug 1 ◂ **VT** 1 *[+ surface] (avec un ongle, une pointe)* to scratch; *(avec un outil)* to scrape; *[+ guitare]* to strum; *[+ allumette]* to strike ◆ **gratte-moi le dos** scratch my back for me ◆ **pour gagner, il suffit de ~ le ticket** to win you just have to scratch the card

2 *(= enlever) [+ tache]* to scratch off; *[+ inscription]* to scratch out; *[+ boue, papier peint]* to scrape off ◆ **si on gratte un peu (le vernis) on se rend compte qu'il n'est pas très cultivé** if you scratch the surface you'll find he's not very educated

3 *(= irriter)* **ce drap me gratte** this sheet's really scratchy ◆ **ça (me) gratte** I've got an itch ◆ **la laine me gratte** wool makes me itch ◆ **il y a quelque chose qui me gratte la gorge** I've got a tickly throat, my throat's tickly ◆ **vin qui gratte la gorge** rough wine; → **poil**

4 *(* = grappiller)* ~ **quelques francs** to fiddle a few pounds* *(Brit)*, to make a bit on the side ◆ **il n'y a pas grand-chose à ~** there's not much to be made on that; → **fond**

5 * *(Sport = dépasser)* to overtake ◆ **on s'est fait ~ par nos concurrents** *(Écon)* we were overtaken by our competitors

VI 1 *[plume]* to scratch; *[drap]* to be scratchy ◆ **ça gratte !** it's really itchy!

2 *(* = économiser)* to scrimp and save ◆ **il gratte sur tout** he skimps on everything

3 *(* = travailler)* to slave away*, to slog away* *(Brit)*

4 *(* = écrire)* to scribble

5 *(= frapper)* ~ **à la porte** to scratch at the door

VPR **se gratter** to scratch (o.s.) ◆ **se ~ la tête** to scratch one's head ◆ **tu peux toujours te ~ !*‡** you can whistle for it!*

gratteur, -euse /gratœr, øz/ **NM,F** *[de guitare]* strummer ◆ ~ **de papier** *(péj)* penpusher *(Brit)*, pencil pusher *(US)*

grattoir /gratwar/ **NM** scraper

grattons /gratɔ̃/ **NMPL** *(Culin)* ≈ pork scratchings

grattouiller /gratuje/ **VT** ⇒ **gratouiller**

gratuiciel /gratɥisjɛl/ **NM** *(Can)* freeware

gratuit, e /gratɥi, ɥit/ **ADJ** 1 *(= non payant)* free ◆ **entrée ~e** admission free ◆ **appel ~ au ...** call free on ..., ring Freefone *(Brit)* ..., call toll-free on *(US)* ... ◆ **journal ~** free sheet ◆ **le premier exemplaire est ~** the first copy is free, no charge is made for the first copy ◆ **à titre ~** *(frm)* free of charge; → **crédit, ensei-**

gnement [2] *(= non motivé) [supposition, affirmation]* unwarranted; *[accusation]* unfounded, groundless; *[cruauté, insulte, violence]* gratuitous, wanton; *[geste]* gratuitous, unmotivated; *[meurtre]* motiveless, wanton ◆ **c'est une hypothèse purement ~e** it's pure speculation; → **acte** [3] *(littér = désintéressé)* disinterested

gratuité /gʀatɥite/ **NF** [1] *(= caractère non payant)* **grâce à la ~ de l'éducation/des soins médicaux** thanks to free education/medical care [2] *[de supposition, affirmation]* unwarranted nature; *[de cruauté, insulte]* wantonness; *[de geste]* gratuitousness, unmotivated nature [3] *(littér) [de geste]* disinterestedness

> ⚠ **gratuité** ne se traduit pas par **gratuity**, qui a le sens de 'pourboire'.

gratuitement /gʀatɥitmɑ̃/ **ADV** [1] *(= gratis) [entrer, participer, soigner]* free (of charge) [2] *(= sans raison) [détruire]* wantonly, gratuitously; *[agir]* gratuitously, without motivation ◆ **supposer ~ que ...** to make the unwarranted supposition that ...

gravats /gʀavɑ/ **NMPL** rubble

grave /gʀav/ **ADJ** [1] *(= solennel) [air, ton, personne, assemblée]* solemn, grave

[2] *(= important) [raison, opération, problème, avertissement, responsabilité]* serious ◆ **s'il n'en reste plus, ce n'est pas ~ !** if there's none left, it doesn't matter!

[3] *(= alarmant) [maladie, accident, nouvelle, blessure, menace]* serious; *[situation, danger]* serious, grave ◆ **l'heure est ~** it is a serious moment ◆ **il a de très ~s ennuis** he has very serious problems ◆ **c'est très ~ ce que vous m'annoncez là** what you've told me is most alarming ◆ **il n'y a rien de ~** it's nothing serious

[4] *(= bas) [note]* low; *[son, voix]* deep, low-pitched; → **accent**

[5] *(* : péj)* **il est vraiment ~** he's the pits* ◆ **t'es ~** you're a case*

NM *(Ling)* grave (accent); *(Mus)* low register ◆ **"grave-aigu"** *(Radio)* "bass-treble" ◆ **appareil qui vibre dans les ~s** *(Radio)* set that vibrates at the bass tones ◆ **les ~s et les aigus** *(Mus)* (the) low and high notes, the low and high registers

> ⚠ Attention à ne pas traduire automatiquement **grave** par le mot anglais **grave**, qui est d'un registre plus soutenu.

graveleux, -euse /gʀav(ə)lø, øz/ **ADJ** [1] *(= grivois)* smutty [2] *[terre]* gravelly; *[fruit]* gritty

gravelure /gʀavlyʀ/ **NF** smut *(NonC)*

gravement /gʀavmɑ̃/ **ADV** [1] *[parler, regarder]* gravely, solemnly [2] *(= de manière alarmante) [blesser, offenser]* seriously ◆ **être ~ compromis** to be seriously compromised ◆ **être ~ menacé** to be under a serious threat ◆ **être ~ coupable** to be seriously involved in an offence *ou* crime ◆ **être ~ malade** to be seriously ill

graver /gʀave/ ▸ conjug 1 ◂ **VT** [1] *[+ signe, inscription] (sur métal, papier)* to engrave; *(sur pierre, bois)* to carve, to engrave ◆ **~ à l'eau-forte** to etch ◆ **c'est à jamais gravé dans sa mémoire** it's imprinted *ou* engraved forever on his memory ◆ **c'est gravé sur son front** *(= évident)* it's written all over his face ◆ **être gravé dans le marbre** *(fig)* to be set in stone [2] *[+ médaille, monnaie]* to engrave [3] *[+ disque]* to cut; *[+ CD]* to burn [4] *(= imprimer)* to print ◆ **faire ~ des cartes de visite** to get some visiting cards printed

graveur, -euse /gʀavœʀ, øz/ **NM,F** *(sur pierre, métal, papier)* engraver; *(sur bois)* (wood) engraver, woodcutter ◆ **~ à l'eau-forte** etcher **NM** *(= machine) [de disque]* embossed groove recorder ◆ **~ de CD(-ROM)** CD burner ◆ **~ de DVD** DVD burner *ou* writer

gravide /gʀavid/ **ADJ** *[animal, utérus]* gravid *(SPÉC)* ◆ **truie ~** sow in pig

gravier /gʀavje/ **NM** *(= caillou)* (little) stone, bit of gravel; *(Géol = revêtement)* gravel *(NonC)* ◆ **allée de** *ou* **en ~** gravel *ou* gravelled path ◆ **recouvrir une allée de ~(s)** to gravel a path

gravière /gʀavjɛʀ/ **NF** gravel pit

gravillon /gʀavijɔ̃/ **NM** [1] *(= petit caillou)* bit of grit *ou* gravel [2] *(= revêtement)* **du ~, des ~s** gravel; *(sur une route)* gravel, loose chippings *(Brit)*

gravillonner /gʀavijɔne/ ▸ conjug 1 ◂ **VT** to gravel ◆ **~ une route** to gravel a road, to put loose chippings *(Brit)* on a road

gravimétrie /gʀavimetʀi/ **NF** gravimetry

gravimétrique /gʀavimetʀik/ **ADJ** gravimetric(al)

gravir /gʀaviʀ/ ▸ conjug 2 ◂ **VT** *[+ montagne]* to climb (up); *[+ escalier]* to climb ◆ **~ péniblement une côte** to struggle up a slope ◆ **~ les échelons de la hiérarchie** to climb the rungs of the (hierarchical) ladder

gravissime /gʀavisim/ **ADJ** extremely serious ◆ **ce n'est pas ~** it's not that serious

gravitation /gʀavitasjɔ̃/ **NF** gravitation

gravitationnel, -elle /gʀavitasjɔnɛl/ **ADJ** gravitational ◆ **la force gravitationnelle** the force of gravity

gravité /gʀavite/ **NF** [1] *[d'air, ton, personne]* gravity, solemnity; *[d'assemblée]* solemnity ◆ **plein de ~** very solemn [2] *[d'erreur, problème, maladie, situation, danger, moment]* seriousness, gravity; *[d'accident, blessure, menace]* seriousness ◆ **c'est un accident sans ~** it was a minor accident, it wasn't a serious accident ◆ **cela n'a** *ou* **ne présente aucun caractère de ~** it's not at all serious [3] *[de note]* lowness; *[de son, voix]* deepness [4] *(Phys, Rail)* gravity ◆ **les lois de la ~** the laws of gravity; → **centre, force**

graviter /gʀavite/ ▸ conjug 1 ◂ **VI** [1] *(= tourner) [astre]* to revolve *(autour de* round, about); *[personne]* to hover, to revolve *(autour de* round); ◆ **cette planète gravite autour du soleil** this planet revolves around *ou* orbits the sun ◆ **il gravite dans les milieux diplomatiques** he moves in diplomatic circles ◆ **les gens qui gravitent dans l'entourage du ministre** people in the minister's entourage ◆ **les pays qui gravitent dans l'orbite de cette grande puissance** the countries in the sphere of influence of this great power ◆ **les sociétés qui gravitent autour de cette banque** the companies that have links with this bank [2] *(= tendre vers)* **~ vers** *[astre]* to gravitate towards

gravure /gʀavyʀ/ **NF** [1] *[de signe, inscription, médaille, monnaie]* engraving [2] *[de disque]* cutting [3] *(= estampe)* engraving [4] *(= reproduction) (dans une revue)* plate; *(au mur)* print, engraving

COMP **gravure sur bois** *(= technique)* woodcutting, wood engraving; *(= dessin)* woodcut, wood engraving

gravure en creux intaglio engraving

gravure sur cuivre copperplate (engraving)

gravure directe hand-cutting

gravure à l'eau-forte etching

gravure sur métaux metal engraving

gravure de mode fashion plate ◆ **c'est une vraie ~ de mode** *(personne)* he *(ou* she) looks like a model

gravure sur pierre stone carving

gravure à la pointe sèche dry-point engraving

gravure en relief embossing

gravure en taille douce line-engraving

gré /gʀe/ **NM**

♦ **à mon/votre** *etc* **gré** *(goût)* to my/your *etc* liking *ou* taste; *(désir)* as I/you *etc* like *ou* please *ou* wish; *(choix)* as I/you *etc* like *ou* prefer *ou* please ◆ **c'est trop moderne, à mon ~** *(avis)* it's too modern for my liking *ou* to my mind ◆ **c'est à votre ~ ?** is it to your liking? *ou* taste? ◆ **agir** *ou* **(en) faire à son ~** to do as one likes *ou* pleases *ou* wishes ◆ **venez à votre ~ ce soir ou demain** come tonight or tomorrow, as you like *ou* prefer *ou* please

♦ **au gré de** ◆ **flottant au ~ de l'eau** drifting wherever the water carries (*ou* carried) it, drifting (along) on *ou* with the current ◆ **volant au ~ du vent** *[chevelure]* flying in the wind; *[plume, feuille]* carried along by the wind; *[planeur]* gliding wherever the wind carries (*ou* carried) it ◆ **au ~ des événements** *[décider, agir]* according to how *ou* the way things go *ou* develop ◆ **ballotté au ~ des événements** tossed about by events ◆ **il décorait sa chambre au ~ de sa fantaisie** he decorated his room as the fancy took him ◆ **son humeur change au ~ des saisons** his mood changes with *ou* according to the seasons ◆ **on a fait pour le mieux, au ~ des uns et des autres** we did our best to take everyone's wishes into account

♦ **bon gré mal gré** whether you (*ou* they *etc*) like it or not, willy-nilly

♦ **de gré à gré** by mutual agreement

♦ **contre le gré de qn** against sb's will

♦ **de gré ou de force** ◆ **il le fera de ~ ou de force** he'll do it whether he likes it or not, he'll do it willy-nilly

♦ **de bon gré** willingly

♦ **de mauvais gré** reluctantly, grudgingly

♦ **de son/ton** *etc* **plein gré** of one's/your *etc* own free will, of one's/your *etc* own accord

grèbe /gʀɛb/ **NM** grebe ◆ **~ huppé** great-crested grebe ◆ **~ castagneux** dabchick, little grebe

grec, grecque /gʀɛk/ **ADJ** *[île, personne, langue]* Greek; *[habit, architecture, vase]* Grecian, Greek; *[profil, traits]* Grecian; → **renvoyer** **NM** *(= langue)* Greek **NM,F** **Grec(que)** Greek **NF** **grecque** *(= décoration)* (Greek) fret ◆ **champignons à la grecque** *(Culin)* mushrooms à la grecque

Grèce /gʀɛs/ **NF** Greece

gréco- /gʀeko/ **PRÉF** Greek(-) ◆ **~catholique** Greek Catholic ◆ **~macédonien** Greek Macedonian ◆ **~turc** Greek-Turkish, greco-turkish

gréco-latin, e (mpl **gréco-latins**) /gʀekolatɛ̃, in/ **ADJ** Graeco-Latin *(Brit)*, Greco-Latin *(US)*

gréco-romain, e (mpl **gréco-romains**) /gʀekoʀɔmɛ̃, ɛn/ **ADJ** Graeco-Roman *(Brit)*, Greco-Roman *(US)*

gredin † /gʀədɛ̃/ **NM** *(= coquin)* scoundrel †, rascal

gréement /gʀemɑ̃/ **NM** *(Naut) (= équipement)* rigging; *(= disposition)* rig ◆ **le voilier a un ~ de cotre/ketch** the yacht is cutter-rigged/ketch-rigged ◆ **les vieux ~s** *(= voiliers)* old sailing ships; *(= grands voiliers)* tall ships

green /gʀin/ **NM** *(Golf)* green

gréer /gʀee/ ▸ conjug 1 ◂ **VT** *(Naut)* to rig

greffage /gʀefaʒ/ **NM** *(Bot)* grafting

greffe[1] /gʀɛf/ **NF** [1] *(Méd) [d'organe]* transplant; *[de tissu]* graft ◆ **~ du cœur/rein** heart/kidney transplant ◆ **on lui a fait une ~ de la cornée** he was given a corneal transplant ◆ **la ~ a pris** *(lit)* the graft has taken; *(fig)* things have turned out fine [2] *(Bot) (= action)* grafting; *(= pousse)* graft

greffe[2] /gʀɛf/ **NM** *(Jur)* Clerk's Office

greffé, e /gʀefe/ (ptp de **greffer**) **NM,F** ◆ **~ (du cœur)** *(récent)* heart transplant patient; *(ancien)* person who has had a heart transplant

greffer /gʀefe/ ▸ conjug 1 ◂ **VT** [1] *(Méd) [+ organe]* to transplant; *[+ tissu]* to graft ◆ **on lui a greffé un rein** he was given a kidney transplant [2]

(Bot) to graft VPR **se greffer** ◆ **se ~ sur** [problèmes] to come on top of

greffier, -ière /gʀefje, jɛʀ/ NM,F (Jur) clerk (of the court) NM († * = chat) malkin †

greffon /gʀefɔ̃/ NM 1 (Méd) (= organe) transplant, transplanted organ; (= tissu) graft ◆ **~ de rein** transplanted kidney 2 (Bot) graft

grégaire /gʀegɛʀ/ ADJ gregarious ◆ **instinct ~** (péj) herd instinct ◆ **avoir l'instinct ~** (péj) to go with the crowd, to be easily led; (= aimer la société) to like socialising, to be the sociable type

grégarisme /gʀegaʀism/ NM gregariousness

grège /gʀɛʒ/ ADJ [soie] raw; (couleur) dove-coloured, greyish-beige NM raw silk

grégeois /gʀeʒwa/ ADJ M → **feu¹**

grégorien, -ienne /gʀegɔʀjɛ̃, jɛn/ ADJ Gregorian NM ◆ **(chant) ~** Gregorian chant, plainsong

grêle¹ /gʀɛl/ ADJ [jambes, silhouette, tige] spindly; [personne] lanky; [son, voix] shrill; → **intestin¹**

grêle² /gʀɛl/ NF hail ◆ **averse de ~** hail storm ◆ **~ de coups/de pierres** hail ou shower of blows/stones

grêlé, e /gʀele/ (ptp de **grêler**) ADJ [visage] pockmarked; [région] damaged by hail

grêler /gʀele/ ▸ conjug 1 ◂ VB IMPERS ◆ **il grêle** it is hailing VT ◆ **la tempête a grêlé les vignes** the hail storm has damaged the vines

grêlon /gʀɛlɔ̃/ NM hailstone

grelot /gʀəlo/ NM (little spherical) bell ◆ **avoir les ~s** * to be shaking in one's shoes *

grelottant, e /gʀəlɔtɑ̃, ɑ̃t/ ADJ [personne] shivering

grelottement /gʀəlɔtmɑ̃/ NM (= tremblement) shivering; (= tintement) jingling

grelotter /gʀəlɔte/ ▸ conjug 1 ◂ VI 1 (= trembler) to shiver (de with); ◆ **~ de froid/de fièvre/ de peur** to shiver with cold/fever/fear 2 (= tinter) to jingle

greluche* /gʀəlyʃ/ NF (péj = fille) bird* (Brit), chick* (US)

Grenade /gʀənad/ N (= ville) Granada NF (= État) Grenada

grenade /gʀənad/ NF 1 (= fruit) pomegranate 2 (= explosif) grenade ◆ **~ à fusil/main** rifle/hand grenade ◆ **~ lacrymogène/fumigène** teargas/smoke grenade ◆ **~ sous-marine** depth charge 3 (= insigne) badge (on soldier's uniform etc)

grenadier /gʀənadje/ NM 1 (= arbre) pomegranate tree 2 (Mil) grenadier

grenadin¹ /gʀənadɛ̃/ NM 1 (= fleur) grenadin(e) 2 (Culin) **~ de veau** (small) veal medallion

grenadin², e¹ /gʀənadɛ̃, in/ ADJ Grenadian NM,F **Grenadin(e)** Grenadian

grenadine² /gʀənadin/ NF (= sirop) grenadine

grenaille /gʀənɑj/ NF ◆ **de la ~** (= projectiles) shot; (pour poules) middlings ◆ **~ de plomb** lead shot ◆ **~ de fer** iron filings

grenaison /gʀənɛzɔ̃/ NF seeding

grenat /gʀəna/ NM garnet ADJ INV dark red, garnet-coloured (Brit) ou -colored (US)

grené, e /gʀəne/ (ptp de **grener**) ADJ [cuir, peau] grainy; [dessin] stippled NM [de gravure, peau] grain

greneler /gʀɛnle/ ▸ conjug 4 ◂ VT [+ cuir, papier] to grain

grener /gʀəne/ ▸ conjug 5 ◂ VT [+ sel, sucre] to granulate, to grain; [+ métal, glace] to grain VI (Agr) [plante] to seed

grenier /gʀənje/ NM attic; (pour conserver le grain) loft ◆ **~ à blé** (lit) corn loft (Brit), wheat loft (US); [de pays] granary ◆ **~ à foin** hayloft

grenouillage /gʀənujaʒ/ NM (Pol péj) shady dealings, jiggery-pokery (Brit)

grenouille /gʀənuj/ NF frog ◆ **~ de bénitier** (péj) churchy old man (ou woman) (péj), Holy Joe* (Brit) (péj) ◆ **manger** ou **bouffer la ~** * to make off with the takings ◆ **avoir des ~s dans le ventre** * to have a rumbling stomach

grenouiller * /gʀənuje/ ▸ conjug 1 ◂ VI (péj) to be involved in shady dealings

grenouillère /gʀənujɛʀ/ NF (= pyjama) sleepsuit

grenu, e /gʀəny/ ADJ [peau] coarse-grained; [cuir, papier] grained; [roche] granular

grenure /gʀənyʀ/ NF graining

grès /gʀɛ/ NM 1 (Géol) sandstone 2 (Poterie) stoneware ◆ **cruche/pot de ~** stoneware pitcher/pot

grésil /gʀezil/ NM (fine) hail

grésillement /gʀezijmɑ̃/ NM 1 [de beurre, friture] sizzling, sputtering; [de poste de radio, téléphone] crackling 2 [de grillon] chirruping, chirping

grésiller¹ /gʀezije/ ▸ conjug 1 ◂ VI 1 [beurre, friture] to sizzle; [poste de radio, téléphone] to crackle 2 [grillon] to chirrup, to chirp

grésiller² /gʀezije/ ▸ conjug 1 ◂ VB IMPERS ◆ **il grésille** fine hail is falling, it's hailing

gressin /gʀesɛ̃/ NM breadstick

grève /gʀɛv/ NF 1 (= arrêt du travail) strike ◆ **se mettre en ~** to go on strike, to strike, to take strike ou industrial action ◆ **être en ~, faire ~** to be on strike, to be striking ◆ **usine en ~** striking factory ◆ **~ des cheminots/des transports** train/transport strike; → **briseur, droit³, piquet**

2 (= rivage) [de mer] shore, strand (littér); [de rivière] bank, strand (littér)

COMP **grève d'avertissement** warning strike
grève de la faim hunger strike ◆ **faire la ~ de la faim** to go (ou be) on hunger strike
grève générale general ou all-out strike
grève illimitée indefinite strike
grève de l'impôt non-payment of taxes
grève partielle partial strike
grève patronale lockout
grève perlée ≈ go-slow (Brit), slowdown (strike) (US) ◆ **faire une ~ perlée** ≈ to go slow (Brit), to slowdown (US)
grève de protestation protest strike
grève sauvage wildcat strike
grève de solidarité sympathy strike ◆ **faire une ~ de solidarité** to strike ou come out (Brit) in sympathy
grève surprise lightning strike
grève sur le tas sit-down strike
grève totale all-out strike
grève tournante strike by rota (Brit), staggered strike (US)
grève du zèle ≈ work-to-rule ◆ **faire la ~ du zèle** to work to rule

grever /gʀəve/ ▸ conjug 5 ◂ VT [+ budget] to put a strain on; [+ économie, pays] to burden ◆ **la hausse des prix grève sérieusement le budget des ménages** the rise in prices puts a serious strain on family budgets ◆ **grevé d'impôts** weighed down with ou crippled by taxes ◆ **maison grevée d'hypothèques** house mortgaged down to the last brick

gréviste /gʀevist/ ADJ [mouvement] strike (épith) NMF striker ◆ **les employés ~s** the striking employees ◆ **~ de la faim** hunger striker

gribiche /gʀibiʃ/ ADJ ◆ **sauce ~** vinaigrette sauce with chopped boiled eggs, gherkins, capers and herbs

gribouillage /gʀibujaʒ/ NM (= écriture) scrawl (NonC), scribble; (= dessin) doodle, doodling (NonC)

gribouille † /gʀibuj/ NM short-sighted idiot, rash fool ◆ **politique de ~** short-sighted policy

gribouiller /gʀibuje/ ▸ conjug 1 ◂ VT (= écrire) to scribble, to scrawl; (= dessiner) to scrawl VI (= dessiner) to doodle

gribouilleur, -euse /gʀibujœʀ, øz/ NM,F (péj) (= écrivain) scribbler; (= dessinateur) doodler

gribouillis /gʀibuji/ NM ⇒ **gribouillage**

grièche /gʀijɛʃ/ ADJ → **pie-grièche**

grief /gʀijɛf/ NM grievance ◆ **faire ~ à qn de qch** to hold sth against sb ◆ **ils me font ~ d'être parti** ou **de mon départ** they reproach me ou they hold it against me for having left

grièvement /gʀijɛvmɑ̃/ ADV ◆ **~ blessé** (very) seriously injured

griffade /gʀifad/ NF scratch

griffe /gʀif/ NF 1 [de mammifère, oiseau] claw ◆ **le chat fait ses ~s** the cat is sharpening its claws ◆ **sortir** ou **montrer/rentrer ses ~s** (lit, fig) to show/draw in one's claws ◆ **elle l'attendait, toutes ~s dehors** she was waiting, ready to pounce on him ◆ **tomber sous la ~/arracher qn des ~s d'un ennemi** to fall into/snatch sb from the clutches of an enemy ◆ **les ~s de la mort** the jaws of death ◆ **coup de ~** (lit) scratch; (fig) dig ◆ **donner un coup de ~ à qn** (lit) to scratch sb; (plus fort) to claw sb; (fig) to have a dig at sb 2 (= signature) signature; (= tampon) signature stamp; (= étiquette de couturier) maker's label (inside garment); (fig = empreinte) [d'auteur, peintre] stamp ◆ **l'employé a mis sa ~ sur le document** the clerk stamped his signature on the document 3 (Bijouterie) claw 4 [d'asperge] crown

griffé, e /gʀife/ ADJ [accessoire, vêtement] designer (épith), with a designer label ◆ **tous ses tailleurs sont ~s** all her suits have designer labels

griffer /gʀife/ ▸ conjug 1 ◂ VT 1 [chat] to scratch; (avec force) to claw; [ronces] to scratch ◆ **elle lui griffa le visage** she clawed ou scratched his face 2 (Haute Couture) to put one's name to

griffon /gʀifɔ̃/ NM (= chien) griffon; (= vautour) griffon vulture; (Myth) griffin

griffonnage /gʀifɔnaʒ/ NM (= écriture) scribble; (= dessin) hasty sketch

griffonner /gʀifɔne/ ▸ conjug 1 ◂ VT (= écrire) to scribble, to jot down; (= dessiner) to sketch hastily VI (= écrire) to scribble; (= dessiner) to sketch hastily

griffu, e /gʀify/ ADJ (lit, péj) ◆ **pattes** ou **mains ~es** claws

griffure /gʀifyʀ/ NF scratch

grignotage /gʀiɲɔtaʒ/ NM [de personne] snacking (NonC); [de salaires, espaces verts, majorité] (gradual) erosion, eroding, whittling away

grignotement /gʀiɲɔtmɑ̃/ NM [de souris] nibbling, gnawing

grignoter /gʀiɲɔte/ ▸ conjug 1 ◂ VT 1 [personne] to nibble (at); [souris] to nibble (at), to gnaw (at) 2 (= réduire) [+ salaires, espaces verts, libertés] to eat away (at), to erode gradually, to whittle away; [+ héritage] to eat away (at); (= obtenir) [+ avantage, droits] to win gradually ◆ **~ du terrain** to gradually gain ground ◆ **il a grignoté son adversaire** * he gradually made up on ou gained ground on his opponent ◆ **il n'y a rien à ~ dans cette affaire** there's nothing much to be gained in that business VI (= manger peu) to nibble (at one's food), to pick at one's food ◆ **~ entre les repas** to snack between meals

grigou * /gʀigu/ NM curmudgeon

grigri, gri-gri (pl **gris-gris**) /gʀigʀi/ NM (gén) charm; [d'indigène] grigri

gril /gʀil/ NM 1 *(Culin)* steak pan, grill pan ◆ **saint Laurent a subi le supplice du** ~ Saint Laurence was roasted alive ◆ **être sur le** ~* to be on tenterhooks, to be like a cat on hot bricks *(Brit)* ou on a hot tin roof *(US)* ◆ **faire cuire au** ~ to grill 2 *(Anat)* ~ **costal** rib cage

grill /gʀil/ NM → **grill-room**

grillade /gʀijad/ NF *(= viande)* grill; *(= morceau de porc)* pork steak ◆ ~ **d'agneau/de thon** grilled lamb/tuna

grillage[1] /gʀijaʒ/ NM 1 *[de pain, amandes]* toasting; *[de poisson, viande]* grilling; *[de café, châtaignes]* roasting 2 *(Tech) [de minerai]* roasting; *[de coton]* singeing

grillage[2] /gʀijaʒ/ NM *(= treillis métallique)* wire netting *(NonC)*; *(très fin)* wire mesh *(NonC)*; *(= clôture)* wire fencing *(NonC)* ◆ **entouré d'un** ~ surrounded by a wire fence

grillager /gʀijaʒe/ ▸ conjug 3 ◂ VT *(avec un treillis métallique)* to put wire netting on; *(très fin)* to put wire mesh on; *(= clôturer)* to put wire fencing around ◆ **à travers la fenêtre grillagée on voyait le jardin** through the wire mesh covering ou over the window we could see the garden ◆ **un enclos grillagé** an area fenced off with wire netting

grille /gʀij/ NF 1 *[de parc] (= clôture)* railings; *(= portail)* (metal) gate; *[de magasin]* shutter 2 *(= claire-voie) [de cellule, fenêtre]* bars; *[de comptoir, parloir]* grille; *[de château-fort]* portcullis; *[d'égout, trou]* (metal) grate, (metal) grating; *[de radiateur de voiture]* grille, grid; *[de poêle à charbon]* grate 3 *(= répartition) [de salaires, tarifs]* scale; *[de programmes de radio]* schedule; *[d'horaires]* grid, schedule 4 *(= codage)* (cipher ou code) grid ◆ ~ **de mots croisés** crossword puzzle (grid) ◆ ~ **de loto** lotto card ◆ **appliquer une** ~ **de lecture freudienne à un roman** to interpret a novel from a Freudian perspective 5 *(Élec)* grid 6 ~ **de départ** *[de course automobile]* starting grid

grillé, e* /gʀije/ ADJ *(= discrédité)* ◆ **tu es** ~ ! you're finished! *[espion]* his cover's been blown* ◆ **je suis** ~ **avec Gilles/chez cet éditeur** my name is mud* with Gilles/at that publisher's

grille-pain /gʀijpɛ̃/ NM INV toaster

griller /gʀije/ ▸ conjug 1 ◂ VT 1 *(Culin) [+ pain, amandes]* to toast; *[+ poisson, viande]* to grill; *[+ café, châtaignes]* to roast

2 *[+ visage, corps]* to burn ◆ **se** ~ **les pieds devant le feu** to toast one's feet in front of the fire ◆ **se** ~ **au soleil** to roast in the sun

3 *[+ plantes, cultures]* to scorch

4 *[+ fusible, lampe] (court-circuit)* to blow; *(trop de courant)* to burn out *[+ moteur]* to burn out ◆ **une ampoule grillée** a dud bulb

5 *(* = fumer)* ~ **une cigarette, en** ~ **une** to have a smoke*

6 *(* = dépasser)* ~ **qn à l'arrivée** to pip sb at the post* *(Brit)*, to beat sb (out) by a nose *(US)* ◆ **se faire** ~ to be outstripped

7 *(* = discréditer)* **elle m'a grillé auprès de lui** I've got no chance with him thanks to her

8 *(* = ne pas respecter)* ~ **un feu rouge** to go through a red light, to jump the lights* *(Brit)*, to run a stoplight *(US)* ◆ ~ **un arrêt** *[autobus]* to miss out ou go past a stop ◆ ~ **les étapes** to go too far too fast ◆ **ils ont grillé la politesse à leurs concurrents*** they pipped their competitors at the post* ◆ **se faire** ~ **la politesse*** to be pipped at the post*

9 *(Tech) [+ minerai]* to roast

VI 1 *(Culin)* **faire** ~ *[+ pain]* to toast; *[+ viande]* to grill; *[+ café]* to roast ◆ **on a mis les steaks à** ~ we've put the steaks on the grill

2 * **on grille ici !** *[personne]* we're ou it's roasting ou boiling in here!* ◆ **ils ont grillé dans l'incendie** they were roasted alive in the fire ◆ ~ **(d'impatience** ou **d'envie) de faire qch** to be burning ou itching to do sth ◆ ~ **de curiosité** to be burning with curiosity

grillon /gʀijɔ̃/ NM cricket

grimaçant, e /gʀimasɑ̃, ɑ̃t/ ADJ *[visage, bouche] (de douleur, de colère)* twisted, grimacing; *(sourire figé)* grinning unpleasantly ou sardonically

grimace /gʀimas/ NF 1 *(de douleur)* grimace; *(pour faire rire, effrayer)* grimace, (funny) face ◆ **l'enfant me fit une** ~ the child made a face at me ◆ **s'amuser à faire des ~s** to make ou pull (funny) faces, to grimace ◆ **il eut** ou **fit une** ~ **de dégoût/de douleur** he gave a grimace of disgust/pain, he grimaced with disgust/pain ◆ **avec une** ~ **de dégoût/de douleur** with a disgusted/pained expression ◆ **il eut** ou **fit une** ~ he pulled a wry face, he grimaced ◆ **il a fait la** ~ **quand il a appris la décision** he pulled a long face when he learned of the decision; → **apprendre, soupe**

2 *(= hypocrisies)* **~s** posturings ◆ **toutes leurs ~s me dégoûtent** I find their posturings ou hypocritical façade quite sickening

3 *(= faux pli)* pucker ◆ **faire une** ~ to pucker

grimacer /gʀimase/ ▸ conjug 3 ◂ VI 1 *(par contorsion)* ~ **(de douleur)** to grimace with pain, to wince ◆ ~ **(de dégoût)** to pull a wry face (in disgust) ◆ ~ **(sous l'effort)** to grimace ou screw one's face up (with the effort) ◆ **le soleil le faisait** ~ the sun made him screw his face up ◆ **à l'annonce de la nouvelle il grimaça** he pulled a wry face ou he grimaced when he heard the news 2 *(= sourire) [personne]* to grin unpleasantly ou sardonically; *[portrait]* to wear a fixed grin 3 *[vêtement]* to pucker VT *(littér)* ◆ ~ **un sourire** to force ou manage a smile

grimacier, -ière /gʀimasje, jɛʀ/ ADJ *(= affecté)* affected; *(= hypocrite)* hypocritical

grimage /gʀimaʒ/ NM *(Théât) (= action)* making up; *(= résultat)* (stage) make-up

grimer /gʀime/ ▸ conjug 1 ◂ VT *(Théât = maquiller)* to make up ◆ **on l'a grimé en vieille dame** he was made up as an old lady VPR **se grimer** to make (o.s.) up

grimoire /gʀimwaʀ/ NM 1 *(inintelligible)* piece of mumbo jumbo; *(illisible)* illegible scrawl *(NonC)*, unreadable scribble 2 *(= livre de magie)* **(vieux)** ~ book of magic spells

grimpant, e /gʀɛ̃pɑ̃, ɑ̃t/ ADJ ◆ **plante ~e** climbing plant, climber ◆ **rosier** ~ climbing rose, rambling rose

grimpe* /gʀɛ̃p/ NF rock-climbing

grimpée /gʀɛ̃pe/ NF *(= montée)* (steep) climb

grimper /gʀɛ̃pe/ ▸ conjug 1 ◂ VI 1 *[personne, animal]* to climb (up); *(avec difficulté)* to clamber up; *(dans la société)* to climb ◆ ~ **aux rideaux** *[chat]* to climb up the curtains ◆ **ça le fait** ~ **aux rideaux*** *(de colère)* it drives him up the wall*; *(sexuellement)* it makes him horny‡ ou randy *(Brit)** ◆ ~ **aux arbres** to climb trees ◆ ~ **à l'échelle** to climb (up) the ladder ◆ ~ **à la corde** to shin up ou climb a rope, to pull o.s. up a rope ◆ ~ **sur** ou **dans un arbre** to climb up ou into a tree ◆ ~ **le long de la gouttière** to shin up ou climb up the drain pipe ◆ ~ **dans un taxi*** to jump ou leap into a taxi ◆ **allez, grimpe !** *(dans une voiture)* come on, get in! ◆ **grimpé sur la table/le toit** having climbed ou clambered onto the table/roof

2 *[route, plante]* to climb ◆ **ça grimpe dur !** it's a hard ou stiff ou steep climb!

3 * *[fièvre]* to soar; *[prix]* to rocket, to soar ◆ **il grimpe dans les sondages** he's going up ou climbing in the polls

VT *[+ montagne, côte]* to climb (up), to go up ◆ ~ **l'escalier** to climb (up) the stairs ◆ ~ **un étage** to climb up a ou one floor

NM *(Athlétisme)* (rope-)climbing *(NonC)*

grimpereau (pl **grimpereaux**) /gʀɛ̃pʀo/ NM ◆ ~ **(des bois)** tree creeper ◆ ~ **(des jardins)** short-toed tree creeper

grimpette* /gʀɛ̃pɛt/ NF (steep little) climb

grimpeur, -euse /gʀɛ̃pœʀ, øz/ ADJ, NM ◆ **(oiseaux) ~s** climbing ou scansorial *(SPÉC)* birds, scansores *(SPÉC)* NM,F *(= varappeur)* (rock-)climber; *(= cycliste)* hill specialist, climber ◆ **c'est un bon/mauvais** ~ *(cycliste)* he's good/bad on hills, he's a good/bad climber

grinçant, e /gʀɛ̃sɑ̃, ɑ̃t/ ADJ *[comédie]* darkly humorous; *[charnière, essieux]* grating; *[porte]* creaking ◆ **ironie ~e** dark irony

grincement /gʀɛ̃smɑ̃/ NM *[d'objet métallique]* grating; *[de plancher, porte, ressort, sommier]* creaking; *[de freins]* squealing; *[de plume]* scratching; *[de craie]* squeaking ◆ **il ne l'a pas accepté sans ~s de dents** he accepted it only with much gnashing of teeth

grincer /gʀɛ̃se/ ▸ conjug 3 ◂ VI 1 *[objet métallique]* to grate; *[plancher, porte, ressort, sommier]* to creak; *[freins]* to squeal; *[plume]* to scratch; *[craie]* to squeak 2 ◆ ~ **des dents (de colère)** to grind ou gnash one's teeth (in anger) ◆ **ce bruit vous fait** ~ **les dents** that noise really sets your teeth on edge

grincheux, -euse /gʀɛ̃ʃø, øz/ ADJ *(= acariâtre)* grumpy ◆ **humeur grincheuse** grumpiness NM,F grumpy person, misery

gringalet /gʀɛ̃galɛ/ ADJ M *(péj = chétif)* puny NM *(péj)* ◆ **(petit)** ~ puny little thing, (little) runt

gringo /gʀiŋgo/ ADJ, NMF *(péj)* gringo

gringue* /gʀɛ̃g/ NM ◆ **faire du** ~ **à qn** to chat sb up

griot /gʀijo/ NM griot *(African musician and poet)*

griotte /gʀijɔt/ NF *(= cerise)* Morello cherry; *(Géol)* griotte

grip /gʀip/ NM *(= revêtement)* grip

grippage /gʀipaʒ/ NM *[de mécanisme]* jamming ◆ **pour éviter le** ~ **de l'économie** to prevent the economy seizing up

grippal, e (mpl **-aux**) /gʀipal, o/ ADJ flu *(épith)*, influenzal *(SPÉC)* ◆ **médicament pour état** ~ anti-flu drug

grippe /gʀip/ NF flu, influenza *(frm)* ◆ **avoir la** ~ to have (the) flu ◆ **il a une petite** ~ he's got a touch of flu ◆ ~ **intestinale** gastric flu ◆ ~ **aviaire,** ~ **du poulet** avian influenza, bird flu ◆ **prendre qn/qch en** ~ to take a sudden dislike to sb/sth

grippé, e /gʀipe/ ADJ *(Méd)* ◆ **il est** ~ he's got (the) flu ◆ **rentrer** ~ to go home with (the) flu ◆ **les ~s** people with ou suffering from flu

gripper /gʀipe/ ▸ conjug 1 ◂ VT *[+ mécanisme]* to jam VI *(= se bloquer) [moteur]* to jam, seize up; *(= se froncer) [tissu]* to bunch up VPR **se gripper** *[moteur]* to jam, seize up ◆ **le système judiciaire se grippe** the court system is seizing up

grippe-sou* (pl **grippe-sous**) /gʀipsu/ NM *(= avare)* penny-pincher*, skinflint

gris, e /gʀi, gʀiz/ ADJ 1 *[couleur, temps]* grey *(Brit)*, gray *(US)* ◆ ~ **acier/anthracite/ardoise/fer/perle/souris** steel/anthracite/slate/iron/pearl/squirrel grey ◆ **~-bleu/-vert** blue-/green-grey ◆ **cheval** ~ **pommelé** dapple-grey horse ◆ ~ **de poussière** grey with dust, dusty ◆ **aux cheveux** ~ grey-haired ◆ **il fait** ~ it's a grey ou dull day; → **ambre, éminence, matière** 2 *(= morne) [vie]* colourless *(Brit)*, colorless *(US)*, dull; *[pensées]* grey *(Brit)*, gray *(US)* 3 *(= éméché)* tipsy* 4 *(locutions)* **faire ~e mine** to pull a long face ◆ **faire ~e mine à qn** to give sb a cool reception NM 1 *(= couleur)* grey *(Brit)*, gray *(US)* 2 *(= tabac)* shag 3 *(Équitation)* grey *(Brit)* ou gray *(US)* (horse)

grisaille /gʀizɑj/ NF 1 *[de vie]* colourlessness *(Brit)*, colorlessness *(US)*, dullness; *[de ciel,* *temps, paysage]* greyness *(Brit)*, grayness *(US)* 2 *(Art)* grisaille ◆ **peindre qch en ~** to paint sth in grisaille

grisant, e /grizɑ̃, ɑ̃t/ ADJ *(= stimulant)* exhilarating; *(= enivrant)* intoxicating

grisâtre /grizɑtʀ/ ADJ greyish *(Brit)*, grayish *(US)*

grisbi /grizbi/ NM *(arg Crime)* loot*

grisé /grize/ NM grey *(Brit)* *ou* gray *(US)* tint ◆ **zone en ~** shaded area

griser /grize/ ► conjug 1 ◄ VT *[alcool]* to intoxicate, to make tipsy; *[air, vitesse, parfum]* to intoxicate ◆ **ce vin l'avait grisé** the wine had gone to his head *ou* made him tipsy* ◆ **l'air de la montagne grise** the mountain air goes to your head (like wine) ◆ **se laisser ~ par le succès/des promesses** to let success/promises go to one's head ◆ **se laisser ~ par l'ambition** to be carried away by ambition VPR **se griser** *[buveur]* to get tipsy* *(avec, de* on); ◆ **se ~ de** *[+ air, vitesse]* to get drunk on; *[+ émotion, paroles]* to allow o.s. to be intoxicated by *ou* carried away by

griserie /grizʀi/ NF *(lit, fig)* intoxication

grisette /grizɛt/ NF *(Hist)* grisette *(coquettish working girl)*

gris-gris /grigri/ NM INV ⇒ **grigri**

grison, -onne /grizɔ̃, ɔn/ ADJ of Graubünden NM *(= dialecte)* Romansh of Graubünden NM,F **Grison(ne)** native *ou* inhabitant of Graubünden NMPL **les Grisons** the Graubünden ◆ **canton des Grisons** canton of Graubünden ◆ **viande des Grisons** *(Culin) dried beef served in thin slices*

grisonnant, e /grizɔnɑ̃, ɑ̃t/ ADJ greying *(Brit)*, graying *(US)* ◆ **il avait les tempes ~es** he was greying *ou* going grey at the temples ◆ **la cinquantaine ~e, il ...** a greying fifty-year-old, he ...

grisonnement /grizɔnmɑ̃/ NM greying *(Brit)*, graying *(US)*

grisonner /grizɔne/ ► conjug 1 ◄ VI to be greying *(Brit)* *ou* graying *(US)*, to be going grey *(Brit)* *ou* gray *(US)*

grisou /grizu/ NM firedamp ◆ **coup de ~** firedamp explosion

grisoumètre /grizumɛtʀ/ NM firedamp detector

grive /griv/ NF thrush ◆ **~ musicienne** song thrush; → **faute**

grivèlerie /grivɛlʀi/ NF *(Jur)* offence of ordering food or drink in a restaurant and being unable to pay for it

griveton* /grivtɔ̃/ NM soldier

grivna /grivna/ NF grivna

grivois, e /grivwa, waz/ ADJ saucy

grivoiserie /grivwazʀi/ NF *(= mot)* saucy expression; *(= attitude)* sauciness; *(= histoire)* saucy story

grizzli, grizzly /grizli/ NM grizzly bear

grœnendael /grɔ(n)ɛndal/ NM Groenendael (sheepdog)

Groenland /grɔɛnlɑ̃d/ NM Greenland

groenlandais, e /grɔɛnlɑ̃dɛ, ɛz/ ADJ of *ou* from Greenland, Greenland *(épith)* NM,F **Groenlandais(e)** Greenlander

grog /grɔg/ NM ≈ (hot) toddy *(usually made with rum)*

groggy* /grɔgi/ ADJ INV *(Boxe)* groggy ◆ **être ~** *(d'émotion)* to be in a daze; *(de fatigue)* to be completely washed out

grognard /grɔɲaʀ/ NM *(Hist)* soldier of the old guard of Napoleon I

grognasse* /grɔɲas/ NF *(péj)* old bag*

grognasser* /grɔɲase/ ► conjug 1 ◄ VI to grumble *ou* moan on (and on)

grogne* /grɔɲ/ NF ◆ **la ~ des syndicats** the rumbling *ou* simmering discontent in the unions ◆ **face à la ~ sociale** faced with rumbling *ou* simmering social discontent ◆ **la ~ monte chez les étudiants** students are grumbling more and more *ou* are showing more and more signs of discontent

grognement /grɔɲmɑ̃/ NM *[de personne]* grunt; *[de cochon]* grunting (NonC), grunt; *[de sanglier]* snorting (NonC), snort; *[d'ours, chien]* growling (NonC), growl ◆ **il m'a répondu par un ~** he growled at me in reply

grogner /grɔɲe/ ► conjug 1 ◄ VI *[personne]* to grumble, to moan* *(contre* at); *[cochon]* to grunt; *[sanglier]* to snort; *[ours, chien]* to growl ◆ **les syndicats grognent** there are rumblings of discontent among the unions VT *[+ insultes]* to growl, to grunt

grognon, -onne /grɔɲɔ̃, ɔn/ ADJ *[air, expression, vieillard]* grumpy, gruff; *[attitude]* surly; *[enfant]* grouchy ◆ **elle est ~** *ou* **grognonne !, quelle ~(ne) !** what a grumbler! *ou* moaner!*

groin /grwɛ̃/ NM *[d'animal]* snout; *(péj) [de personne]* ugly *ou* hideous face

grolle* /grɔl/ NF shoe

grommeler /grɔm(ə)le/ ► conjug 4 ◄ VI *[personne]* to mutter (to o.s.), to grumble to o.s.; *[sanglier]* to snort VT *[+ insultes]* to mutter

grommellement /grɔmɛlmɑ̃/ NM muttering, indistinct grumbling

grondement /grɔ̃dmɑ̃/ NM *[de canon, train, orage]* rumbling (NonC); *[de torrent]* roar, roaring (NonC); *[de chien]* growl, growling (NonC); *[de foule]* (angry) muttering; *[de moteur]* roar ◆ **le ~ de la colère/de l'émeute** the rumbling of mounting anger/of the threatening riot ◆ **le train passa devant nous dans un ~ de tonnerre** the train thundered past us

gronder /grɔ̃de/ ► conjug 1 ◄ VT *(= réprimander) [+ enfant]* to tell off, to scold ◆ **je vais me faire ~ si je rentre tard** I'll get told off if I get in late ◆ **il faut que je vous gronde d'avoir fait ce cadeau** *(amicalement)* you're very naughty to have bought this present, I should scold you for buying this present VI 1 *[canon, train, orage]* to rumble; *[torrent, moteur]* to roar; *[chien]* to growl; *[foule]* to mutter (angrily) 2 *[émeute]* to be brewing ◆ **la colère gronde chez les infirmières** nursing staff are getting increasingly angry 3 *(littér = grommeler)* to mutter

gronderie /grɔ̃dʀi/ NF scolding

grondeur, -euse /grɔ̃dœʀ, øz/ ADJ *[ton, humeur, personne]* grumbling; *[vent, torrent]* rumbling ◆ **d'une voix grondeuse** in a grumbling voice

grondin /grɔ̃dɛ̃/ NM gurnard

groom /grum/ NM *(= employé)* bellboy, bellhop *(US)*; *[de porte]* door closer ◆ **je ne suis pas ton ~** I'm not your servant

gros, grosse¹ /gro, gros/

1 ADJECTIF	4 ADVERBE
2 NOM MASCULIN	5 COMPOSÉS
3 NOM FÉMININ	

1 - ADJECTIF

1 [dimension, gén] big, large; *[lèvres, corde]* thick; *[chaussures]* big, heavy; *[personne]* fat; *[ventre, bébé]* fat, big; *[pull, manteau]* thick, heavy ◆ **le ~ bout** the thick end ◆ **il pleut à grosses gouttes** it's raining heavily ◆ **c'est ~ comme une tête d'épingle/mon petit doigt** it's the size of *ou* it's no bigger than a pinhead/my little finger ◆ **des tomates grosses comme le poing** tomatoes as big as your fist ◆ **un mensonge ~ comme une maison*** a gigantic lie, a whopper* ◆ **je l'ai vu venir ~ comme une maison*** I could see it coming a mile off*

2 [= important] *[travail]* big; *[problème, ennui, erreur]* big, serious; *[somme]* large, substantial; *[entreprise]* big, large; *[soulagement, progrès]* great; *[dégâts]* extensive, serious; *(= violent) [averse]* heavy; *[fièvre]* high; *[rhume]* heavy, bad ◆ **une grosse affaire** a large business, a big concern ◆ **les grosses chaleurs** the height of summer, the hot season ◆ **les ~ consommateurs d'énergie** big energy consumers ◆ **un ~ mensonge** a terrible lie, a whopper* ◆ **c'est un ~ morceau*** *(= travail)* it's a big job; *(= livre)* it's a huge book; *(= obstacle)* it's a big hurdle (to clear) *ou* a big obstacle (to get over) ◆ **il a un ~ appétit** he has a big appetite ◆ **la grosse industrie** heavy industry ◆ **acheter par** *ou* **en grosses quantités** to buy in bulk, to bulk-buy *(Brit)*

3 [= houleux] *[mer]* heavy; *(Météo)* rough ◆ **la rivière est grosse** *(= gonflé)* the river is swollen

4 [= sonore] *[voix]* booming *(épith)*; *[soupir]* big, deep; → **rire**

5 [= riche et important] big ◆ **un ~ industriel/banquier** a big industrialist/banker

6 [intensif] **un ~ buveur** a heavy drinker ◆ **un ~ mangeur** a big eater ◆ **un ~ kilo/quart d'heure** a good kilo/quarter of an hour ◆ **tu es un ~ paresseux*** you're such a lazybones ◆ **~ nigaud !*** you big ninny!*

7 [= rude] *[drap, laine, vêtement]* coarse; *[traits du visage]* thick, heavy ◆ **le ~ travail** the heavy work ◆ **son ~ bon sens est réconfortant** his down-to-earth *ou* plain commonsense is a comfort ◆ **il aime les grosses plaisanteries** he likes obvious *ou* unsubtle *ou* inane jokes ◆ **oser nous dire ça, c'est vraiment un peu ~** how dare he say that to us, it's a bit thick* *ou* a bit much*

8 [† = enceinte] pregnant ◆ **grosse de 6 mois** 6 months' pregnant

9 [locutions] **avoir les yeux ~ de larmes** to have eyes filled *ou* brimming with tears ◆ **regard ~ de menaces** threatening *ou* menacing look, look full of menace ◆ **l'incident est ~ de conséquences** the incident is fraught with consequences ◆ **jouer ~ jeu** to play for big *ou* high stakes ◆ **faire les ~ yeux (à un enfant)** to glower (at a child) ◆ **faire la grosse voix*** to speak gruffly *ou* sternly ◆ **c'est une grosse tête*** he's brainy*, he's a brainbox* ◆ **avoir la grosse tête*** *(prétentieux)* to be big-headed ◆ **faire une grosse tête à qn*** to bash sb up*, to smash sb's face in* ◆ **il me disait des "Monsieur" ~ comme le bras** he was falling over himself to be polite to me and kept calling me "sir"

2 - NOM MASCULIN

1 [= personne corpulente] fat man ◆ **un petit ~*** a fat little man ◆ **mon ~*** old thing*; → **pêche²**

2 [= principal] **le ~ du travail est fait** the bulk of *ou* the main part of the work is done ◆ **le ~ des troupes** *(lit)* the main body of the army; *(fig)* the great majority ◆ **le ~ de l'orage est passé** the worst of the storm is over ◆ **faites le plus ~ d'abord** do the main things *ou* the essentials first

3 [= milieu] **au ~ de l'hiver** in the depths of winter ◆ **au ~ de l'été/de la saison** at the height of summer/of the season

4 [Comm] **le (commerce de) ~** the wholesale business ◆ **il fait le ~ et le détail** he deals in *ou* trades in both wholesale and retail ◆ **maison/prix/marché de ~** wholesale firm/prices/market

5 [locutions]

◆ **en gros** ◆ **c'est écrit en ~** it's written in big *ou* large letters ◆ **papetier en ~** wholesale stationer ◆ **commande en ~** bulk order ◆ **acheter/**

vendre en ~ to buy/sell wholesale; → **marchand** ◆ **évaluer en** ~ **la distance/le prix** to make a rough *ou* broad estimate of the distance/the price ◆ **dites-moi, en** ~, **ce qui s'est passé** tell me roughly *ou* broadly what happened

◆ **les gros** (= *personnes importantes*) the rich and powerful, the big fish *

3 - NOM FÉMININ

grosse (= *personne*) fat woman ◆ **ma grosse** * old girl *, old thing * (*Brit*) ◆ **c'est une bonne grosse** ⁑ (*péj*) she's a good-natured thing *; → aussi **grosse²**

4 - ADVERBE

◆ **écrire** ~ to write big, to write in large letters ◆ **il risque** ~ he's risking a lot *ou* a great deal ◆ **ça peut nous coûter** ~ it could cost us a lot *ou* a great deal ◆ **je donnerais** ~ **pour** ... I'd give a lot *ou* a great deal to ... ◆ **il y a** ~ **à parier que** ... it's a safe bet that ... ◆ **en avoir** ~ **sur le cœur** *ou* **sur la patate** ⁑ to be upset *ou* peeved *

5 - COMPOSÉS

gros bétail cattle
gros bonnet * bigwig *, big shot *
gros bras * muscleman ◆ **jouer les** ~ **bras** * to play *ou* act the he-man *
grosse caisse (*Mus*) big *ou* bass drum
grosse cavalerie * heavy stuff *
grosse-gorge ⁑ NF (*Can*) goitre
grosse légume * ⇒ **gros bonnet**
gros mot swearword ◆ **il dit des** ~ **mots** he uses bad language, he swears
gros œuvre (*Archit*) shell (*of a building*)
gros plan (*Photo*) close-up ◆ **une prise de vue en** ~ **plan** a shot in close-up, a close-up shot ◆ ~ **plan sur** ... (= *émission*) programme devoted to *ou* all about ...
gros poisson * ⇒ **gros bonnet**
(avion) gros porteur jumbo jet
gros rouge * rough (red) wine, (red) plonk * (*Brit*), Mountain Red (wine) (*US*)
gros sel cooking salt
gros temps rough weather ◆ **par** ~ **temps** in rough weather *ou* conditions; → **gibier, intestin¹, lot** *etc*

---

gros-bec (pl **gros-becs**) /gʀobɛk/ NM (= *oiseau*) hawfinch

gros-cul ⁑ (pl **gros-culs**) /gʀoky/ NM juggernaut (*Brit*), eighteen-wheeler * (*US*)

groseille /gʀozɛj/ NF ◆ ~ **(rouge)** red currant ◆ ~ **(blanche)** white currant ◆ ~ **à maquereau** gooseberry ADJ INV (cherry-)red

groseillier /gʀozeje/ NM currant bush ◆ ~ **rouge/blanc** red/white currant bush ◆ ~ **à maquereau** gooseberry bush

gros-grain (pl **gros-grains**) /gʀogʀɛ̃/ NM (= *tissu*) petersham

Gros-Jean /gʀoʒɑ̃/ NM INV ◆ **il s'est retrouvé** ~ **comme devant** †* he found himself back where he started *ou* back at square one (*Brit*)

grosse² /gʀos/ NF (*Jur*) engrossment; (*Comm*) gross

grossesse /gʀosɛs/ NF pregnancy ◆ ~ **nerveuse** false pregnancy, phantom pregnancy ◆ ~ **gémellaire/extra-utérine/à risque** twin/extrauterine/high-risk pregnancy; → **robe**

grosseur /gʀosœʀ/ NF 1 [*d'objet*] size; [*de fil, bâton*] thickness; [*de personne*] weight, fatness ◆ **être d'une** ~ **maladive** to be unhealthily fat ◆ **as-tu remarqué sa** ~ **?** have you noticed how fat he is? 2 (= *tumeur*) lump

grossier, -ière /gʀosje, jɛʀ/ ADJ 1 [*matière, tissu*] coarse; [*aliment*] unrefined; [*ornement, instrument*] crude 2 (= *sommaire*) [*travail*] superficially done, roughly done; [*imitation*] crude, poor; [*dessin*] rough; [*solution, réparation*] rough-and-ready; [*estimation*] rough ◆ **avoir une idée grossière des faits** to have a rough idea of the facts
3 (= *lourd*) [*manières*] unrefined, crude; [*esprit, être*] unrefined; [*traits du visage*] coarse, thick; [*ruse*] crude; [*plaisanterie*] unsubtle, inane; [*erreur*] stupid, gross (*épith*); [*ignorance*] crass (*épith*)
4 (= *bas, matériel*) [*plaisirs, jouissances*] base
5 (= *insolent*) [*personne*] rude
6 (= *vulgaire*) [*plaisanterie, geste, mots, propos*] coarse; [*personne*] coarse, uncouth ◆ **il s'est montré très** ~ **envers eux** he was very rude to them ◆ ~ **personnage !** uncouth individual! ◆ **il est** ~ **avec les femmes** he is coarse *ou* uncouth in his dealings with women

grossièrement /gʀosjɛʀmɑ̃/ ADV 1 (= *de manière sommaire*) [*exécuter, réparer, dessiner*] roughly, superficially; [*façonner, imiter*] crudely; [*hacher*] roughly, coarsely ◆ **pouvez-vous me dire** ~ **combien ça va coûter ?** can you tell me roughly how much that will cost? 2 (= *de manière vulgaire*) coarsely; (= *insolemment*) rudely 3 (= *lourdement*) **se tromper** ~ to be grossly mistaken, to make a gross error

grossièreté /gʀosjɛʀte/ NF 1 (= *insolence*) rudeness 2 (= *vulgarité*) [*de personne*] coarseness, uncouthness; [*de plaisanterie, geste*] coarseness ◆ **dire des** ~**s** to use coarse language ◆ **une** ~ a rude *ou* coarse remark 3 (= *rusticité*) [*de fabrication*] crudeness; [*de travail, exécution*] superficiality; [*d'étoffe*] coarseness 4 (*littér* = *manque de finesse*) [*de personne*] lack of refinement; [*de traits*] coarseness ◆ **la** ~ **de ses manières** his unrefined *ou* crude manners

grossir /gʀosiʀ/ ► conjug 2 ◄ VI [*personne*] (*signe de déficience*) to get fat(ter), to put on weight; (*signe de santé*) to put on weight; [*fruit*] to swell, to grow; [*rivière*] to swell; [*tumeur*] to swell, to get bigger; [*foule*] to grow (larger), to swell; [*somme, économies*] to grow, to get bigger; [*rumeur, nouvelle*] to spread; [*bruit*] to get louder, to grow (louder), to swell ◆ **l'avion grossissait dans le ciel** the plane grew larger *ou* bigger in the sky ◆ ~ **des cuisses/des hanches** to put on weight on the thighs/the hips ◆ **j'ai grossi de trois kilos** I've put on three kilos

VT 1 (= *faire paraître plus gros*) [+ *personne*] **ce genre de vêtement (vous) grossit** these sort of clothes make you look fatter
2 [*microscope*] to magnify; [*lentille, lunettes*] to enlarge, to magnify; [*imagination*] [+ *dangers, importance*] to magnify, to exaggerate
3 (= *exagérer volontairement*) [+ *fait, événement*] to exaggerate ◆ **ils ont grossi l'affaire à des fins politiques** they've exaggerated *ou* blown up the issue for political reasons
4 [+ *cours d'eau*] to swell; [+ *voix*] to raise
5 [+ *somme*] to increase, to add to; [+ *foule*] to swell ◆ ~ **les rangs/le nombre** *ou* **la liste de** to add to *ou* swell the ranks/the numbers of

grossissant, e /gʀosisɑ̃, ɑ̃t/ ADJ 1 [*lentille, verre*] magnifying, enlarging 2 [*foule, bruit*] swelling, growing

grossissement /gʀosismɑ̃/ NM 1 [*de tumeur*] swelling, enlarging 2 (= *pouvoir grossissant*) [*de microscope*] magnification, (magnifying) power ◆ ~ **de 200 fois** magnification *ou* magnifying power of 200 times ◆ **ceci peut être observé à un faible/fort** ~ this can be seen with a low-power/high-power lens 3 [*d'objet*] magnification, magnifying; (= *exagération*) [*de dangers*] magnification, exaggeration; [*de faits*] exaggeration

grossiste /gʀosist/ NMF wholesaler, wholesale dealer

grosso modo /gʀosomɔdo/ ADV (= *en gros*) more or less, roughly ◆ ~, **cela veut dire que** ... roughly speaking, it means that ... ◆ **dis-moi** ~ **de quoi il s'agit** tell me roughly what it's all about

grotesque /gʀɔtɛsk/ ADJ 1 (= *ridicule*) [*personnage, accoutrement, allure*] ludicrous, ridiculous; [*idée, histoire*] grotesque ◆ **c'est d'un** ~ **incroyable** it's absolutely ludicrous *ou* ridiculous 2 (*Art*) grotesque NM (*Littérat*) ◆ **le** ~ the grotesque NF (*Art*) grotesque

grotesquement /gʀɔtɛskəmɑ̃/ ADV grotesquely

grotte /gʀɔt/ NF (*naturelle*) cave; (*artificielle*) grotto ◆ ~ **préhistorique** prehistoric cave

grouillant, e /gʀujɑ̃, ɑ̃t/ ADJ [*foule, masse*] milling, swarming ◆ ~ **de** [+ *touristes, insectes*] swarming *ou* teeming *ou* crawling with; [+ *policiers*] bristling *ou* swarming with ◆ **boulevard/café** ~ **(de monde)** street/café swarming *ou* teeming *ou* crawling with people, bustling street/café

grouiller /gʀuje/ ► conjug 1 ◄ VI [*foule, touristes*] to mill about; [*café, rue*] to be swarming *ou* teeming *ou* bustling with people ◆ ~ **de** [+ *touristes, insectes*] to be swarming *ou* teeming *ou* crawling with VPR **se grouiller** * to get a move on * ◆ **grouille-toi ou on va rater le train !** get your skates on * *ou* get a move on * or we'll miss the train! ◆ **se** ~ **pour arriver à l'heure** to hurry so as not to be late

grouillot /gʀujo/ NM messenger (boy)

groupage /gʀupaʒ/ NM 1 (*Comm*) [*de colis*] bulking 2 (*Méd*) ~ **sanguin** blood grouping *ou* typing ◆ ~ **tissulaire** tissue typing

groupe /gʀup/ NM 1 (*Art, Écon, Math, Pol, Sociol*) group ◆ ~ **de communication/de distribution/industriel** communications/distribution/industrial group ◆ **le** ~ **de la majorité** the deputies *ou* MPs (*Brit*) *ou* Congressmen (*US*) of the majority party ◆ **psychologie de** ~ group psychology
2 [*de personnes*] group; [*de touristes*] party, group; [*de musiciens*] band, group ◆ ~ **de rock** rock group *ou* band ◆ **des** ~**s se formaient dans la rue** groups (of people) *ou* knots of people were forming in the street ◆ **par** ~**s de trois ou quatre** in groups of three or four, in threes or fours ◆ **travailler/marcher en** ~ to work/walk in *ou* as a group ◆ **travail/billet de** ~ group work/ticket
3 [*de club*] group ◆ **le** ~ **des Sept (pays les plus industrialisés)** the Group of Seven (most industrialized countries)
4 [*d'objets*] ~ **de maisons** cluster *ou* group of houses ◆ ~ **d'arbres** clump *ou* cluster *ou* group of trees
5 (*Ling*) group, cluster ◆ ~ **nominal/verbal** noun/verb phrase, nominal/verbal group ◆ ~ **consonantique** consonant cluster

COMP **groupe d'âge** age group
groupe d'aliments food group
groupe armé armed group
groupe de combat fighter group
groupe de discussion (*Internet*) discussion group
groupe électrogène generating set, generator
groupe hospitalier hospital complex
groupe d'intervention de la Gendarmerie nationale crack force of the Gendarmerie
groupe de mots word group, phrase
groupe parlementaire parliamentary group
groupe de presse (*gén*) publishing conglomerate; (*spécialisé dans la presse*) press group
groupe de pression pressure group, ginger group (*Brit*), special interest group (*US*)
groupe sanguin blood group
groupe de saut [*de parachutistes*] stick
groupe scolaire school complex
groupe de tête (*Sport*) (group of) leaders; (*Scol*) top pupils (in the class); (*Écon*) (group of)

leading firms
groupe tissulaire tissue type
groupe de travail working party

groupement /grupmɑ̃/ NM 1 (= action) [de personnes, objets, faits] grouping ♦ ~ **de mots par catégories** grouping words by categories 2 (= groupe) group; (= organisation) organization ♦ ~ **révolutionnaire** band of revolutionaries, revolutionary band ♦ ~ **tactique** (Mil) task force ♦ ~ **d'achats** (commercial) bulk-buying organization ♦ ~ **de gendarmerie** squad of Gendarmes ♦ ~ **professionnel** professional organization ♦ ~ **d'intérêt économique** economic interest group ♦ ~ **agricole d'exploitation en commun** farmers' economic interest group 3 (Chim) group

grouper /grupe/ ▸ conjug 1 ◂ VT 1 [+ personnes, objets, faits] to group (together); (Comm) [+ colis] to bulk; [+ efforts, ressources, moyens] to pool ♦ ~ **des colis par destination** to bulk parcels according to their destination ♦ **est-ce que je peux ~ mes achats ?** can I pay for everything together?
2 (Sport) [+ genoux] to tuck; → **saut**
VPR **se grouper** [foule] to gather; (= se coaliser) to form a group ♦ **groupez-vous par trois** get into threes ou into groups of three ♦ **restez groupés** keep together, stay in a group ♦ **les consommateurs doivent se ~ pour se défendre** consumers must band together to defend their interests ♦ **se ~ en associations** to form associations ♦ **on s'est groupé pour lui acheter un cadeau** we all got together ou chipped in* to buy him a present ♦ **se ~ autour d'un chef** (= se rallier) to rally round a leader ♦ **le village groupé autour de l'église** the village clustered round the church

groupie /grupi/ NMF [de chanteur] groupie; * [de parti] (party) faithful

groupuscule /grupyskyl/ NM (Pol péj) small group

grouse /gruz/ NF grouse

Grozny, Groznyï /grɔzni/ N Crozny

GRS /ʒeɛʀɛs/ NF abrév de **gymnastique rythmique et sportive**

gruau /gryo/ NM (= graine) hulled grain, groats ♦ **pain de ~** fine wheaten bread

grue /gry/ NF 1 (= engin) crane ♦ ~ **flottante** floating crane ♦ ~ **de levage** wrecking crane 2 (= oiseau) ~ **(cendrée)** crane ♦ ~ **couronnée** crowned crane; → **pied** 3 (‡ péj = prostituée) hooker‡ (péj), tart‡ (Brit) (péj)

gruge‡ /gryʒ/ NF (= escroquerie) ♦ **il y a eu de la ~** we ou they got ripped off*

gruger /gryʒe/ ▸ conjug 3 ◂ VT 1 (= escroquer) to swindle ♦ **se faire ~** to be swindled ♦ **il s'est fait ~ de 5 000 €** he was cheated out of €5,000 2 (* = agacer) to bug* ♦ **tu me gruges !** stop bugging me! 3 (Can) to nibble

grume /grym/ NF (= écorce) bark (left on timber) ♦ **bois de** ou **en ~** undressed timber, rough lumber (US)

grumeau (pl **grumeaux**) /grymo/ NM [de sel, sauce] lump ♦ **la sauce fait des ~x** the sauce is going lumpy ♦ **pâte pleine de ~x** lumpy dough

grumeler (se) /grym(ə)le/ ▸ conjug 4 ◂ VPR [sauce] to go lumpy; [lait] to curdle

grumeleux, -euse /grym(ə)lø, øz/ ADJ [sauce] lumpy; [lait] curdled; [fruit] gritty; [peau] bumpy, lumpy

grunge /grœnʒ/ ADJ [musique, mouvement] grunge (épith) NM grunge (music)

gruppetto /grupeto/ (pl **gruppetti** /grupeti/) NM (Mus) gruppetto, turn

gruter /gryte/ ▸ conjug 1 ◂ VT to crane ♦ ~ **un bateau hors de l'eau** to lift a boat out of the water with a crane

grutier, -ière /grytje, jɛʀ/ NM,F crane driver ou operator

gruyère /gryjɛʀ/ NM Gruyère (cheese) (Brit), Swiss (cheese) (US)

GSM /ʒeɛsɛm/ NM (abrév de **Global System for Mobile Communication**) GSM ♦ **réseau ~** GSM network

guacamole /gwakamɔle/ NM guacamole

Guadeloupe /gwadlup/ NF Guadeloupe

guadeloupéen, -enne /gwadlupeɛ̃, ɛn/ ADJ Guadelupian NM,F **Guadeloupéen(ne)** inhabitant ou native of Guadeloupe

Guam /gwam/ NM Guam

guano /gwano/ NM [d'oiseau] guano; [de poisson] manure

guarani /gwaʀani/ ADJ Guarani (épith) NM (= langue) Guarani; (= monnaie) guarani NMF **Guarani** Guarani

Guatemala /gwatemala/ NM Guatemala

guatémaltèque /gwatemaltɛk/ ADJ Guatemalan NMF **Guatémaltèque** Guatemalan

gué /ge/ NM ford ♦ **passer (une rivière) à ~** to ford a river

guéer /gee/ ▸ conjug 1 ◂ VT to ford

guéguerre* /gegɛʀ/ NF squabble ♦ **c'est la ~ entre les représentants** the representatives are squabbling amongst themselves

guelfe /gɛlf/ ADJ Guelphic NMF Guelph

guelte /gɛlt/ NF (Comm) commission

guenille /gənij/ NF (piece of) rag ♦ **~s** (old) rags ♦ **en ~s** in rags (and tatters)

guenon /gənɔ̃/ NF (= singe) female monkey; (péj = laideron) hag

guépard /gepaʀ/ NM cheetah

guêpe /gɛp/ NF wasp; → **fou, taille¹**

guêpier /gepje/ NM 1 (= oiseau) bee-eater 2 (= piège) trap; (= nid) wasp's nest ♦ **se fourrer dans un ~*** to land o.s. in the soup* ou in it* (Brit)

guêpière /gepjɛʀ/ NF basque

guère /gɛʀ/ ADV 1 (avec adj ou adv) (= pas très, pas beaucoup) hardly, scarcely ♦ **elle ne va ~ mieux** she's hardly any better ♦ **comment vas-tu, aujourd'hui ? – ~ mieux !** how are you feeling today? – much the same! ♦ **il n'est ~ poli** he's not very polite ♦ **le chef, ~ satisfait de cela, …** the boss, little ou hardly satisfied with that, … ♦ **il n'y a ~ plus de 2 km** there is barely ou scarcely more than 2 km to go ♦ **ça ne fera ~ moins de 25 €** it won't be (very) much less than €25
2 (avec vb) **ne … ~** (= pas beaucoup) not much ou really; (= pas souvent) hardly ou scarcely ever; (= pas longtemps) not (very) long ♦ **il n'a ~ d'argent/le temps** he has hardly any money/time ♦ **je n'aime ~ qu'on me questionne** I don't much like ou really care for being questioned ♦ **il n'en reste plus ~** there's hardly any left ♦ **cela ne te va ~** it doesn't really suit you ♦ **ce n'est plus ~ à la mode** it's hardly fashionable at all nowadays ♦ **il ne vient ~ nous voir** he hardly ou scarcely ever comes to see us ♦ **cela ne durera ~** it won't last (for) very long ♦ **il ne tardera ~** he won't be (very) long now ♦ **l'aimez-vous ? – ~** (frm) do you like it? – not (very) much ou not really ou not particularly
♦ **guère de** ♦ **il n'y a ~ de monde** there's hardly ou scarcely anybody there
♦ **guère que** ♦ **il n'y a ~ que lui qui …** he's about the only one who …, there's hardly ou scarcely anyone but he who …

guéret /geʀɛ/ NM tillage (NonC)

guéridon /geʀidɔ̃/ NM pedestal table

guérilla /geʀija/ NF guerrilla war ou warfare (NonC) ♦ ~ **urbaine** urban guerrilla warfare

guérillero, guérilléro /geʀijeʀo/ NM guerrilla

guérir /geʀiʀ/ ▸ conjug 2 ◂ VT (= soigner) [+ malade] to cure, to make better; [+ maladie] to cure; [+ membre, blessure] to heal ♦ **je ne peux pas le ~ de ses mauvaises habitudes** I can't cure ou break him of his bad habits
VI 1 (= aller mieux) [malade, maladie] to get better, to be cured; [blessure] to heal, to mend ♦ **sa main guérie était encore faible** his hand although healed was still weak ♦ **il est guéri (de son angine)** he is cured (of his throat infection) ♦ **dépenser de telles sommes, j'en suis guéri !** you won't catch me spending money like that again!, that's the last time I spend money like that!
2 [chagrin, passion] to heal
VPR **se guérir** [malade, maladie] to get better, to be cured ♦ **se ~ d'une habitude** to cure ou break o.s. of a habit ♦ **se ~ par les plantes** to cure o.s. by taking herbs, to cure o.s. with herbs ♦ **se ~ d'un amour malheureux** to get over ou recover from an unhappy love affair

guérison /geʀizɔ̃/ NF [de malade] recovery; [de maladie] curing (NonC); [de membre, plaie] healing (NonC) ♦ **sa ~ a été rapide** he made a rapid recovery ♦ ~ **par la foi** faith healing; → **voie**

guérissable /geʀisabl/ ADJ [malade, maladie] curable ♦ **sa jambe/blessure est ~** his leg/injury can be healed

guérisseur, -euse /geʀisœʀ, øz/ NM,F healer; (péj) quack (doctor) (péj)

guérite /geʀit/ NF 1 (Mil) sentry box 2 (sur chantier) workman's hut; (servant de bureau) site office

Guernesey /gɛʀn(ə)zɛ/ NF Guernsey

guernesiais, e /gɛʀnəzjɛ, ɛz/ ADJ of ou from Guernsey, Guernsey (épith) NM,F **Guernesiais(e)** inhabitant ou native of Guernsey

guerre /gɛʀ/ NF 1 (= conflit) war ♦ **de ~** [correspondant, criminel] war (épith) ♦ ~ **civile/sainte/atomique** civil/holy/atomic war ♦ ~ **de religion/de libération** war of religion/of liberation ♦ **la ~ scolaire** ongoing debate on church schooling versus state schooling ♦ **la Grande Guerre** the Great War (Brit), World War I ♦ **la Première Guerre mondiale** the First World War, World War I ♦ **la Seconde** ou **Deuxième Guerre mondiale** the Second World War, World War II ♦ **entre eux c'est la ~ (ouverte)** it's open war between them
2 (= technique) warfare ♦ **la ~ atomique/psychologique/chimique** atomic/psychological/chemical warfare
3 (loc) **de ~ lasse elle finit par accepter** she grew tired of resisting and finally accepted ♦ **à la ~ comme à la ~** we'll just have to make the best of things ♦ **c'est de bonne ~** that's fair enough ♦ **faire la ~ à** (Mil) to wage war on ou against ♦ **soldat qui a fait la ~** soldier who was in the war ♦ **ton chapeau a fait la ~*** your hat has been in the wars* (Brit) ou through the war (US) ♦ **elle lui fait la ~ pour qu'il s'habille mieux** she is constantly battling with him to get him to dress better ♦ **faire la ~ aux abus/à l'injustice** to wage war against ou on abuses/injustice ♦ **livrer une** ou **la ~ à** to wage war on ♦ ~ **des prix** price war
♦ **en guerre** (lit, fig) at war (avec, contre with, against); ♦ **dans les pays en ~** in the warring countries, in the countries at war ♦ **entrer en ~** to go to war (contre against); ♦ **partir en ~ contre** (Mil) to go to war against, to wage war on; (fig) to wage war on; → **entrer**
COMP **guerre bactériologique** bacteriological warfare
guerre biologique biological warfare
la guerre des Boers the Boer war
la guerre de Cent Ans the Hundred Years' War

guerre de conquête war of conquest
la guerre des Deux-Roses the Wars of the Roses
guerre éclair blitzkrieg, lightning war *(US)*
guerre économique economic warfare
guerre électronique electronic warfare
guerre d'embuscade guerrilla warfare
la guerre des étoiles Star Wars
guerre d'extermination war of extermination
guerre froide cold war
la guerre du Golfe the Gulf War
la guerre du Mexique the Mexican War
guerre mondiale world war
guerre de mouvement war of movement
guerre des nerfs war of nerves
guerre nucléaire nuclear war
guerre des ondes battle for the airwaves
guerre à outrance all-out war
guerre de position war of position
guerre presse-bouton push-button war
les guerres puniques the Punic Wars
la guerre de quarante the Second World War
la guerre de quatorze the 1914-18 war
la guerre de Sécession the American Civil War
guerre de succession war of succession
guerre totale total warfare, all-out war
guerre de tranchées trench warfare
la guerre de Trente Ans the Thirty Years War
la guerre de Troie the Trojan War
guerre d'usure war of attrition

guerrier, -ière /gɛʀje, jɛʀ/ ADJ *[nation, air]* warlike; *[danse, chants, exploits]* war *(épith)* NM,F warrior

guerroyer /gɛʀwaje/ ► conjug 8 ◄ VI *(littér)* to wage war *(contre* against, on)

guet /gɛ/ NM 1 ◆ **faire le ~** to be on (the) watch *ou* lookout ◆ **avoir l'œil au ~** *(littér)* to keep one's eyes open *ou* peeled* ◆ **avoir l'oreille au ~** *(littér)* to keep one's ears open 2 *(Hist = patrouille)* watch

guet-apens (pl **guets-apens**) /gɛtapɑ̃/ NM *(= embuscade)* ambush; *(fig)* trap ◆ **attirer qn dans un ~** *(lit)* to lure sb into an ambush; *(fig)* to lure sb into a trap ◆ **tomber dans un ~** *(lit)* to be caught in an ambush; *(fig)* to fall into a trap

guêtre /gɛtʀ/ NF gaiter; → **traîner**

guêtré, e /getʀe/ ADJ wearing gaiters *ou* spats

guetter /gete/ ► conjug 1 ◄ VT 1 *(= épier) [+ victime, ennemi]* to watch (intently); *[+ porte]* to watch 2 *(= attendre) [+ réaction, signal, occasion]* to watch out for, to be on the lookout for; *[+ personne]* to watch (out) for; *(hostilement)* to lie in wait for; *[+ proie]* to lie in wait for ◆ **~ le passage/l'arrivée de qn** to watch (out) for sb (to pass by)/(to come) ◆ **~ la sonnerie du téléphone** to be waiting for the telephone to ring ◆ **~ le pas de qn** to listen out for sb ◆ **ses fans guettent la sortie de son nouvel album** his fans are eagerly waiting for his new album 3 *(= menacer) [danger]* to threaten ◆ **la crise cardiaque/la faillite le guette** he's heading for a heart attack/bankruptcy ◆ **c'est le sort qui nous guette tous** it's the fate that's in store for all of us *ou* that's liable to befall all of us

guetteur /gɛtœʀ/ NM *(Mil, Naut)* lookout; *(Hist)* watch

gueulante‡ /gœlɑ̃t/ NF ◆ **pousser une** *ou* **sa ~** *(colère)* to kick up a stink*; *(douleur)* to give an almighty yell*

gueulard, e /gœlaʀ, aʀd/ ADJ 1 (‡ = *braillard) [personne]* loud-mouthed; *[air, musique]* noisy 2 (‡ = *criard) [couleur, vêtement]* gaudy, garish 3 (* = *gourmand)* **être ~** to love one's food NM,F 1 (‡ = *braillard)* loudmouth 2 (* = *gourmand)* **c'est un ~** he really loves his food NM *[de haut fourneau, chaudière]* throat

gueule /gœl/ NF 1 (‡ = *bouche)* **(ferme) ta ~ !** shut up!* ◆ **ta ~ !** *(= va te faire voir)* get stuffed!‡ ◆ **ça vous emporte** *ou* **brûle la ~** it takes the roof off your mouth ◆ **il dépense beaucoup d'argent pour la ~** he spends a lot on feeding his face* ◆ **s'en mettre plein la ~** to stuff o.s. *ou* one's face* ◆ **tu peux crever la ~ ouverte** you can go to hell for all I care‡ ◆ **il nous laisserait bien crever la ~ ouverte** he wouldn't give a damn what happened to us‡ ◆ **donner un coup de ~*** to shout one's head off* ◆ **il est connu pour ses coups de ~*** he's well known for being a loudmouth ◆ **un fort en ~, une grande ~** a loudmouth ◆ **bourré*** *ou* **rempli jusqu'à la ~** crammed to the gills‡, jam-packed; → **fin¹**
2 (* = *figure)* face ◆ **il a une belle ~** he's good-looking ◆ **il a une belle ~ de voyou** he looks the handsome hard guy ◆ **il a une bonne/sale ~** I like/I don't like the look of him ◆ **avoir une bonne/sale ~** *[aliment]* to look nice/horrible ◆ **avoir la ~ de l'emploi** to look the part ◆ **faire une ~ d'enterrement** to look really miserable ◆ **il a fait une sale ~ quand il a appris la nouvelle**‡ he didn't half pull a face when he heard the news* ◆ **bien fait pour sa ~ !**‡ serves him right!* ◆ **avoir de la ~** to look really nice ◆ **cette bagnole a de la ~** that's a great-looking car!*, that's some car!* ◆ **cette maison a une drôle de ~** that's a weird-looking house ◆ **les vêtements achetés en boutique ont plus de ~** boutique clothes look much nicer *ou* better ◆ **~ de raie**‡ fish-face‡ ◆ **~ d'empeigne**‡ *(péj)* shit-head*‡; → **casser, foutre, soûler**
◆ **faire la gueule**‡ *(= bouder)* to sulk ◆ **quand ils ont appris que je fumais mes parents ont fait la ~** my parents were not at all happy *ou* were really pissed off‡ when they found out I smoked ◆ **faire la ~ à qn** to be in a huff* with sb ◆ **arrête de me faire la ~ !** stop sulking! ◆ **qu'est-ce qu'il y a, tu me fais la ~ ?** what's the matter, aren't you speaking to me? ◆ **on s'est fait la ~ pendant trois jours** we didn't speak to each other for three days
3 *[d'animal]* mouth ◆ **se jeter** *ou* **se mettre dans la ~ du loup** to throw o.s. into the lion's jaws
4 *(= ouverture) [de four]* mouth; *[de canon]* muzzle
COMP **gueule de bois*** hangover ◆ **avoir la ~ de bois** to have a hangover, to be feeling the effects of the night before*
gueule cassée *war veteran with severe facial injuries*
gueule noire miner

gueule-de-loup (pl **gueules-de-loup**) /gœldəlu/ NF *(= plante)* snapdragon

gueulement‡ /gœlmɑ̃/ NM *(= cri)* bawl ◆ **pousser des ~s** *(douleur)* to yell one's head off*; *(colère)* to kick up a stink*

gueuler‡ /gœle/ ► conjug 1 ◄ VI 1 *[chien]* to bark like mad*; *[personne] (= crier)* to shout; *(= parler fort)* to bawl, to bellow; *(= chanter fort)* to bawl; *(= hurler de douleur)* to howl, to yell (one's head off*); *(= protester)* to kick up a stink* ◆ **~ après qn** to bawl sb out* ◆ **ça va ~** all hell will break loose‡, there'll be one hell of a row‡ 2 *[poste de radio]* to blast out, to blare out ◆ **faire ~ sa télé** to turn one's TV up full blast* VT *[+ ordres]* to bawl (out), to bellow (out); *[+ chanson]* to bawl

gueules /gœl/ NM *(Hér)* gules

gueuleton* /gœltɔ̃/ NM blow-out* *(Brit)*, chow-down‡ *(US)* ◆ **faire un ~** to have a blow-out* *(Brit) ou* a chow-down‡ *(US)*

gueuletonner* /gœltɔne/ ► conjug 1 ◄ VI to have a blow-out* *(Brit) ou* a chow-down‡ *(US)*

gueuse /gøz/ NF 1 († , *littér) (= mendiante)* beggar woman; *(= coquine)* rascally wench; → **courir** 2 *[de fonte]* pig 3 *(= bière)* **~(-lambic)** gueuse beer

gueux /gø/ NM († , *littér) (= mendiant)* beggar; *(= coquin)* rogue, villain

gugusse /gygys/ NM *(= clown)* ≈ Coco the clown; (* = *type)* guy*, bloke* *(Brit)*; (* = *personne ridicule)* twit*

gui /gi/ NM 1 *(= plante)* mistletoe 2 *(= espar de bateau)* boom

guibol(l)e* /gibɔl/ NF *(= jambe)* leg

guichet /giʃɛ/ NM 1 *(= comptoir individuel)* window ◆ **~(s)** *(= bureau) [de banque, poste]* counter; *[de théâtre]* box office, ticket office; *[de gare]* ticket office, booking office *(Brit)* ◆ **adressez-vous au ~ d'à côté** inquire at the next window ◆ **renseignez-vous au(x) ~(s)** *[de banque, poste]* go and ask at the counter; *[de théâtre, gare]* go and ask at the ticket office ◆ **"guichet fermé"** *(à la poste, à la banque)* "position closed" ◆ **on joue à ~s fermés** the performance is fully booked *ou* is booked out *(Brit)* ◆ **~ automatique (de banque)** cash dispenser, ATM 2 *[de porte, mur]* wicket, hatch; *(grillagé)* grille

guichetier, -ière /giʃ(ə)tje, jɛʀ/ NM,F *[de banque]* counter clerk

guidage /gidaʒ/ NM *(Min, Tech) (= mécanisme)* guides; *(= action)* guidance

guide /gid/ NM 1 *(= idée, sentiment)* guide ◆ **l'ambition est son seul ~** ambition is his only guide 2 *(= livre)* guide(book) ◆ **~ pratique/touristique/gastronomique** practical/tourist/restaurant guide ◆ **~ de voyage** travel guide 3 *(Tech = glissière)* guide ◆ **~ de courroie** belt-guide NMF *(= personne)* guide ◆ **~ (de montagne)** (mountain) guide ◆ **"n'oubliez pas le guide"** "please remember the guide" ◆ **"suivez le guide !"** "this way, please!" ◆ **~-conférencier** lecturing guide ◆ **~-interprète** tour guide and interpreter NFPL **guides** *(= rênes)* reins NF *(= éclaireuse)* ≈ (girl) guide *(Brit)*, girl scout *(US)*

guider /gide/ ► conjug 1 ◄ VT *(= conduire) [+ voyageur, embarcation, cheval]* to guide; *(moralement)* to guide ◆ **l'ambition le guide** he is guided by (his) ambition, ambition is his guide ◆ **organisme qui guide les étudiants durant leur première année** organization that provides guidance for first-year students ◆ **il m'a guidé dans mes recherches** he guided me through *ou* in my research ◆ **se laissant ~ par son instinct** letting himself be guided by (his) instinct, letting (his) instinct be his guide ◆ **se guidant sur les étoiles/leur exemple** guided by the stars/their example, using the stars/their example as a guide ◆ **missile guidé par infrarouge** heat-seeking missile ◆ **bombe guidée au** *ou* **par laser** laser-guided bomb; → **visite**

guidon /gidɔ̃/ NM 1 *[de vélo]* handlebars 2 *(= drapeau)* guidon 3 *[de mire]* foresight, bead

guigne¹ /giɲ/ NF *(= cerise) type of cherry* ◆ **il s'en soucie comme d'une ~** he doesn't care a fig about it

guigne²* /giɲ/ NF *(= malchance)* rotten luck* ◆ **avoir la ~** to be jinxed* ◆ **porter la ~ à qn** to put a jinx on sb* ◆ **quelle ~ !** what rotten luck!*

guigner /giɲe/ ► conjug 1 ◄ VT *[+ personne]* to eye surreptitiously; *[+ héritage, place]* to have one's eye on, to eye

guignol /giɲɔl/ NM 1 *(Théât) (= marionnette) popular French glove puppet*; *(= spectacle)* puppet show, ≈ Punch and Judy show ◆ **aller au ~** to go to a puppet show ◆ **c'est du ~ !** it's a real farce! 2 *(péj = personne)* clown ◆ **arrête de faire le ~ !** stop clowning about!, stop acting the clown!

guignolet /giɲɔlɛ/ NM cherry liqueur

guignon /giɲɔ̃/ NM ⇒ **guigne²**

guilde /gild/ NF *(Hist)* guild; *(Comm)* club

guili-guili * /giligili/ NM tickle tickle * ◆ **faire ~ à qn** to tickle sb

Guillaume /gijom/ NM William ◆ **~ le Roux** William Rufus ◆ **~ Tell** William Tell ◆ **~ d'Orange** William of Orange ◆ **~ le Conquérant** William the Conqueror

guillaume /gijom/ NM rabbet plane

guilledou /gij(ə)du/ NM → **courir**

guillemet /gijmɛ/ NM quotation mark, inverted comma *(Brit)* ◆ **ouvrez les ~s** quote, open quotation marks *ou* inverted commas *(Brit)* ◆ **fermez les ~s** unquote, close quotation marks *ou* inverted commas *(Brit)* ◆ **sa digne épouse, entre ~s** his noble spouse, quote unquote *ou* in inverted commas *(Brit)* ◆ **mettre un mot entre ~s** to put a word in quotation marks *ou* quotes *ou* inverted commas *(Brit)*

guillemot /gijmo/ NM guillemot

guilleret, -ette /gijʀɛ, ɛt/ ADJ [1] *(= enjoué) [personne, air]* perky, bright ◆ **être tout ~** to be full of beans * [2] *(= leste) [propos]* saucy

guilloché, e /gijɔʃe/ (ptp de **guillocher**) ADJ ornamented with guilloche

guillotine /gijɔtin/ NF guillotine; → **fenêtre**

guillotiner /gijɔtine/ ► conjug 1 ◄ VT to guillotine

guimauve /gimov/ NF *(= plante)* marsh mallow; *(= bonbon)* marshmallow ◆ **c'est de la ~** *(péj) (mou)* it's jelly; *(sentimental)* it's mush *, it's schmaltzy * ◆ **chanson (à la) ~** mushy * *ou* schmaltzy * *ou* soppy * *(Brit)* song

guimbarde /gɛ̃baʀd/ NF *(Mus)* Jew's harp ◆ **(vieille) ~** (* = *voiture*) jalopy, old banger * *(Brit)*, old crock * *(Brit)*

guimpe /gɛ̃p/ NF *(Rel)* wimple; *(= corsage)* chemisette *(Brit)*, dickey *(US)*

guincher * /gɛ̃ʃe/ ► conjug 1 ◄ VI *(= danser)* to dance

guindé, e /gɛ̃de/ (ptp de **guinder**) ADJ *[personne]* starchy; *[soirée, ambiance]* formal; *[style]* stilted ◆ **cette cravate fait un peu ~** that tie is a bit too formal ◆ **il est ~ dans ses vêtements** his clothes make him look very stiff and starchy

guinder /gɛ̃de/ ► conjug 1 ◄ VT [1] *[+ style]* to make stilted ◆ **~ qn** *[vêtements]* to make sb look stiff and starchy [2] *(= hisser) [+ mât, charge]* to raise VPR **se guinder** *[personne]* to become starchy; *[style]* to become stilted

Guinée /gine/ NF Guinea

Guinée-Bissau /ginebiso/ NF Guinea-Bissau

Guinée-Équatoriale /gineekwatɔʀjal/ NF Equatorial Guinea

guinéen, -enne /gineɛ̃, ɛn/ ADJ Guinean NM,F **Guinéen(ne)** native of Guinea, Guinean

guingois * /gɛ̃gwa/ ADV *(= de travers)* ◆ **de ~** askew, skew-whiff * *(Brit)* ◆ **le tableau est (tout) de ~** the picture is askew *ou* skew-whiff * *ou* lop-sided ◆ **il se tient tout de ~ sur sa chaise** he's sitting lop-sidedly *ou* skew-whiff * in his chair ◆ **marcher de ~** to walk lop-sidedly ◆ **tout va de ~** everything's going haywire *

guinguette /gɛ̃gɛt/ NF *open-air café or dance hall*

guipure /gipyʀ/ NF guipure

guirlande /giʀlɑ̃d/ NF *[de fleurs]* garland ◆ **~ de Noël** tinsel garland ◆ **~ de papier** paper chain ◆ **~ électrique** string of Christmas lights *ou* fairy lights *(Brit)*

guise /giz/ GRAMMAIRE ACTIVE 53.1 NF ◆ **n'en faire qu'à sa ~** to do as one pleases *ou* likes ◆ **à ta ~ !** as you wish! *ou* please! *ou* like!

◆ **en guise de** by way of ◆ **en ~ de remerciement** by way of thanks ◆ **en ~ de chapeau il portait un pot de fleurs** he was wearing a flowerpot by way of a hat *ou* for a hat

guitare /gitaʀ/ NF guitar ◆ **~ hawaïenne/électrique** Hawaiian/electric guitar ◆ **~ basse/acoustique** *ou* **sèche/classique** bass/acoustic/classical guitar ◆ **à la ~, Joe** on guitar, Joe

guitariste /gitaʀist/ NMF guitarist, guitar player

guitoune * /gitun/ NF tent

Guj(a)rât /gudʒ(a)ʀat/ NM Gujarat

Gulf Stream /gœlfstʀim/ NM Gulf Stream

guru /guʀu/ NM ⇒ **gourou**

gus * /gys/ NM *(= type)* guy *, bloke * *(Brit)*

gustatif, -ive /gystatif, iv/ ADJ relating to taste ◆ **aspect ~** flavour ◆ **profil ~** flavour profile; → **nerf, papille**

gustation /gystasjɔ̃/ NF gustation

guttural, e (mpl **-aux**) /gytyʀal, o/ ADJ *[langue, son, consonne]* guttural; *[voix]* guttural, throaty NF **gutturale** *(Phon)* guttural

Guyana /gɥijana/ NM Guyana

guyanais, e /gɥijanɛ, ɛz/ ADJ Guyanese NM,F **Guyanais(e)** Guyanese

Guyane /gɥijan/ NF Guiana ◆ **~ française** French Guiana ◆ **~ hollandaise** Dutch Guyana ◆ **~ britannique** (British) Guyana

guyot /gɥijo/ NF *(= fruit)* guyot pear; *(= volcan)* guyot

gym * /ʒim/ NF (abrév de **gymnastique**) *(gén)* gym; *(Scol)* PE ◆ **je vais à la ~** I go to the gym ◆ **faire de la ~** *(sport)* to do gym; *(chez soi)* to do exercises

gymkhana /ʒimkana/ NM rally ◆ **~ motocycliste** motorcycle scramble ◆ **il faut faire du ~ pour arriver à la fenêtre !** it's like an obstacle course to get to the window!

gymnase /ʒimnɑz/ NM *(Sport)* gymnasium, gym; *(Helv = lycée)* secondary school *(Brit)*, high school *(US)*

gymnaste /ʒimnast/ NMF gymnast

gymnastique /ʒimnastik/ NF [1] *(= sport)* gymnastics *(sg)*; *(Scol)* physical education, gymnastics *(sg)* ◆ **de ~** *[professeur, instrument]* physical education *(épith)*, PE *(épith)* ◆ **faire de la ~** *(sport)* to do gymnastics; *(chez soi)* to do exercises; → **pas**[1]

[2] *(fig)* gymnastics *(sg)* ◆ **~ intellectuelle** *ou* **de l'esprit** mental gymnastics *(sg)* ◆ **c'est toute une ~ pour attraper ce que l'on veut dans ce placard** it's a real juggling act *ou* you have to stand on your head to find what you want in this cupboard

COMP **gymnastique acrobatique** acrobatics *(sg)*

gymnastique aquatique aquaerobics *(sg)*

gymnastique artistique artistic gymnastics

gymnastique chinoise t'ai chi (ch'uan)

gymnastique corrective remedial gymnastics

gymnastique douce ≃ Callanetics ®

gymnastique oculaire eye exercises

gymnastique orthopédique orthopaedic *(Brit) ou* orthopedic *(US)* exercises

gymnastique respiratoire breathing exercises

gymnastique rythmique eurhythmics *(sg)*

gymnastique rythmique et sportive rhythmic gymnastics

gymnastique au sol floor gymnastics

gymnique /ʒimnik/ ADJ gymnastic NF gymnastics *(sg)*

gymnosperme /ʒimnospɛʀm/ ADJ gymnospermous NF gymnosperm ◆ **les ~s** gymnosperms, the Gymnospermae *(SPÉC)*

gynécée /ʒinese/ NM [1] *(Hist)* gynaeceum; *(fig)* den of females [2] *(Bot)* gynoecium, gynecium *(US)*

gynéco * /ʒineko/ ADJ abrév de **gynécologique** NMF abrév de **gynécologue** NF abrév de **gynécologie**

gynécologie /ʒinekɔlɔʒi/ NF gynaecology *(Brit)*, gynecology *(US)*

gynécologique /ʒinekɔlɔʒik/ ADJ gynaecological *(Brit)*, gynecological *(US)*

gynécologue /ʒinekɔlɔg/ NMF gynaecologist *(Brit)*, gynecologist *(US)* ◆ **~ obstétricien** obstetrician, ob-gyn * *(US)*

gypaète /ʒipaɛt/ NM bearded vulture, lammergeyer

gypse /ʒips/ NM gypsum

gypsophile /ʒipsɔfil/ NF gypsophila

gyrophare /ʒiʀofaʀ/ NM revolving *ou* flashing light *(on vehicle)*

gyroscope /ʒiʀɔskɔp/ NM gyroscope

gyrostat /ʒiʀɔsta/ NM gyrostat

Hh

H /aʃ/ **NM** *(= lettre)* H, h ◆ **h aspiré** aspirate h ◆ **h muet** silent *ou* mute h ◆ **(à l')heure H** (at) zero hour; → **bombe**

ha¹ /'a/ **EXCL** oh! ◆ ~, ~ ! *(= rire)* ha-ha!

ha² (abrév de **hectare**) ha

habeas corpus /abeaskɔʀpys/ **NM INV** ◆ **l'~** habeas corpus

habile /abil/ **ADJ** 1 *[mains, ouvrier, peintre, politicien]* skilful *(Brit)*, skillful *(US)*, skilled; *[écrivain]* clever ◆ **il est ~ de ses mains** he's good *ou* clever with his hands ◆ **être ~ à (faire) qch** to be clever *ou* skilful *ou* good at (doing) sth 2 *[film, intrigue, raisonnement, argument]* clever; *[manœuvre]* clever, deft ◆ **ce n'était pas bien ~ de sa part** that wasn't very clever of him ◆ **un ~ trucage vidéo** a clever video effect 3 *(Jur)* fit *(à* to)

habilement /abilmɑ̃/ **ADV** *[manier un instrument]* skilfully *(Brit)*, skillfully *(US)*; *[manœuvrer]* skilfully *(Brit)*, skillfully *(US)*, cleverly; *[profiter, répondre, dissimuler]* cleverly ◆ **il fit ~ remarquer que** … he cleverly pointed out that … ◆ **il gère ~ sa carrière** he manages his career with skill

habileté /abilte/ **NF** 1 *[d'ouvrier, peintre, politicien]* skill *(à faire* at doing); ◆ **~ manuelle** manual dexterity *ou* skill ◆ **son ~ à travailler le bois** his woodworking skills ◆ **faire preuve d'une grande ~ politique/technique** to show considerable political/technical skill 2 *[de tactique, démarche]* skilfulness *(Brit)*, skillfulness *(US)*, cleverness; *[de manœuvre]* cleverness, deftness 3 *(Jur)* ⇒ **habilité**

habilitation /abilitasjɔ̃/ **NF** *(Jur)* capacitation ◆ **~ (à diriger des recherches)** *(Univ)* authorization *ou* accreditation to supervise research

habilité /abilite/ **NF** *(Jur)* fitness

habiliter /abilite/ ► **conjug 1** ◄ **VT** *(Jur)* to capacitate; *(Univ)* to authorize, to accredit ◆ **être habilité à faire qch** *(Jur, Pol)* to be empowered to do sth; *(gén)* to be entitled *ou* authorized to do sth ◆ **représentant dûment habilité** duly authorized officer

habillage /abijaʒ/ **NM** 1 *[d'acteur, poupée]* dressing 2 *[de montre]* assembly; *[de bouteille]* labelling and sealing; *[de marchandise]* packaging and presentation; *[de machine]* casing; *[de chaudière]* lagging; *[de peaux]* dressing ◆ **~ intérieur** *[de voiture]* interior trim 3 *(= présentation)* **~ de bilan** window dressing *(of a balance sheet)* ◆ **ces contrats ne sont que l'~ juridique de primes occultes** these contracts are just a front for secret bonus payments ◆ **le nouvel ~ de la chaîne devrait plaire** *(TV)* the channel's new format *ou* new look should go down well

habillé, e /abije/ (ptp de **habiller**) **ADJ** 1 *(= chic) [robe]* smart, dressy; *[chaussures]* dress *(épith)*, smart ◆ **soirée ~e** formal occasion ◆ **trop ~** *[costume]* too dressy; *[personne]* overdressed 2 *(= vêtu) [personne]* dressed ◆ **chaudement ~** warmly dressed ◆ **bien/mal ~** well/badly dressed ◆ **~ de noir/d'un costume** dressed in *ou* wearing black/a suit ◆ **elle était ~e en Chanel** she was wearing Chanel clothes *ou* a Chanel outfit ◆ **se coucher tout ~** to go to bed fully dressed *ou* with all one's clothes on

habillement /abijmɑ̃/ **NM** *(= action)* dressing, clothing; *(= toilette, costume)* clothes, dress *(NonC)*, outfit; *(Mil = uniforme)* outfit; *(= profession)* clothing trade, rag trade * *(Brit)*, garment industry *(US)*

habiller /abije/ ► **conjug 1** ◄ **VT** 1 *[+ poupée, enfant] (= vêtir)* to dress *(de* in); *(= déguiser)* to dress up *(en* as); ◆ **cette robe vous habille bien** that dress really suits you *ou* looks good on you ◆ **un rien l'habille** she looks good in anything, she can wear anything

2 *(= fournir en vêtements)* to clothe; *(Mil) [+ recrues]* to provide with uniforms ◆ **Mlle Lenoir est habillée par Givenchy** *(Couture)* Miss Lenoir buys *ou* gets all her clothes from Givenchy's; *(dans un générique)* Miss Lenoir's wardrobe *ou* clothes by Givenchy

3 *(= recouvrir, envelopper) [+ mur, fauteuil, livre]* to cover *(de* with); *[+ bouteille]* to label and seal; *[+ marchandise]* to package; *[+ machine, radiateur]* to encase *(de* in); *[+ chaudière]* to lag *(de* with); ◆ **l'~ un fauteuil d'une housse** to put a loose cover on an armchair ◆ **tableau de bord habillé de bois** wooden dashboard ◆ **il faut ~ ce coin de la pièce** we must put something in *ou* do something with this corner of the room

4 *[+ arbre]* to trim (for planting)

5 *(Typo) [+ image]* to set the text around

6 *[+ montre]* to assemble; *[+ peaux, carcasse]* to dress

7 *(= enjoliver) [+ réalité, vérité]* to adorn ◆ **ils ont habillé le bilan** they did some financial window-dressing

VPR **s'habiller** 1 *(= mettre ses habits)* to dress (o.s.), to get dressed; *(= se déguiser)* to dress up *(en* as); ◆ **aider qn à s'~** to help sb on with their clothes, to help sb get dressed ◆ **s'~ chaudement** to dress warmly ◆ **elle s'habille trop jeune/vieux** she wears clothes that are too young/old for her ◆ **elle s'habille long/court** she wears long/short skirts, she wears her skirts long/short ◆ **s'~ en Arlequin** to dress up as Harlequin ◆ **faut-il s'~ pour la réception ?** do we have to dress (up) for the reception? ◆ **comment t'habilles-tu ce soir ?** what are you wearing tonight? ◆ **elle ne sait pas s'~** she has no clothes sense *ou* dress sense

2 *(Couture)* **s'~ chez un tailleur** to buy *ou* get one's clothes from a tailor ◆ **s'~ sur mesure** to have one's clothes made to measure

habilleur, -euse /abijœʀ, øz/ **NM** *(Tech) [de peaux]* dresser **NM,F** *(Ciné, Théât)* dresser

habit /abi/ **NM** 1 ◆ **~s** clothes ◆ **mettre/ôter ses ~s** to put on/take off one's clothes *ou* things ◆ **~s de travail/de deuil** working/mourning clothes ◆ **il portait ses ~s du dimanche** he was wearing his Sunday best *ou* Sunday clothes ◆ **il était encore en ~s de voyage** he was still in his travelling clothes *ou* in the clothes he'd worn for the journey; → **brosse**

2 *(= costume)* dress *(NonC)*, outfit ◆ **~ d'arlequin** Harlequin suit *ou* costume ◆ **l'~ ne fait pas le moine** *(Prov)* appearances are sometimes deceptive, one shouldn't judge by appearances

3 *(= jaquette)* morning coat; *(= queue-de-pie)* tail coat, tails ◆ **en ~ (de soirée)** wearing tails, in evening dress ◆ **l'~ est de rigueur** formal *ou* evening dress must be worn

4 *(Rel)* habit ◆ **prendre l'~** *[homme]* to take (holy) orders, to take the cloth; *[femme]* to take the veil ◆ **quitter l'~** *[homme]* to leave the priesthood; *[femme]* to leave the Church ◆ **lors de sa prise d'~** *[d'homme]* when he took (holy) orders *ou* the cloth; *[de femme]* when she took the veil

COMP **habit de cheval** riding habit
habit de cour court dress *(NonC)*
habit ecclésiastique clerical dress *(NonC)* ◆ **porter l'~ ecclésiastique** *(= être prêtre)* to be a cleric
habit de gala formal *ou* evening dress *(NonC)*
habit de lumière bullfighter's costume
habit militaire military dress *(NonC)*
habit religieux (monk's) habit
habit de soirée ⇒ **habit de gala**
habit vert *green coat of member of the Académie française*

habitabilité /abitabilite/ **NF** *[de maison]* habitability, fitness for habitation; *[de voiture, ascenseur]* capacity

habitable /abitabl/ **ADJ** (in)habitable ◆ **35 m² ~s** *ou* **de surface ~** 35 m² living space ◆ **la maison n'est pas encore ~** the house isn't fit to live in yet *ou* isn't habitable yet ◆ **~ début mai** ready for occupation in early May

habitacle /abitakl/ **NM** 1 *[de bateau]* binnacle; *[d'avion]* cockpit; *[de voiture]* passenger compartment *ou* cell; *[véhicule spatial]* cabin 2 *(Rel, littér)* dwelling place *(littér)*, abode *(littér)*

habitant, e /abitɑ̃, ɑ̃t/ NM,F 1 *[de maison]* occupant, occupier; *[de ville, pays]* inhabitant ◆ **ville de 3 millions d'~s** town of 3 million inhabitants ◆ **les ~s du village/du pays** the people who live in the village/country, the inhabitants of the village/country ◆ **être** *ou* **loger chez l'~** *[touristes]* to stay with local people in their own homes; *[soldats]* to be billeted on *ou* with the local population ◆ **les ~s des bois** *(littér)* the denizens *(littér)* of the wood 2 *(Can* * *= fermier)* farmer; *(péj = rustre)* country bumpkin

habitat /abita/ NM *[de plante, animal]* habitat; *(= conditions de logement)* housing *ou* living conditions; *(= mode de peuplement)* settlement ◆ **~ rural/sédentaire/dispersé** rural/fixed/scattered settlement ◆ **~ individuel/collectif** detached/group housing

habitation /abitasjɔ̃/ NF 1 *(= fait de résider)* living, dwelling *(littér)* ◆ **locaux à usage d'~** dwellings ◆ **conditions d'~** housing *ou* living conditions ◆ **impropre à l'~** unfit for human habitation, uninhabitable 2 *(= domicile)* residence, home, dwelling place *(littér)* ◆ **la caravane qui lui sert d'~** the caravan that serves as his home ◆ **changer d'~** to change one's (place of) residence 3 *(= bâtiment)* house ◆ **des ~s modernes** modern housing *ou* houses ◆ **groupe d'~s** housing development *ou* estate *(Brit)* ◆ **~ à loyer modéré** *(= appartement)* ≈ council flat *(Brit)*, public housing unit *(US)*; *(= immeuble)* ≈ (block of) council flats *(Brit)*, housing project *(US)*

habité, e /abite/ (ptp de **habiter**) ADJ *[château, maison]* lived-in, occupied; *[planète, région]* inhabited; *[vol, engin, station orbitale]* manned ◆ **cette maison est-elle ~e ?** does anyone live in this house?, is this house occupied?

habiter /abite/ ▸ conjug 1 ◂ VT 1 *[+ maison, appartement]* to live in, to occupy; *[+ ville, région]* to live in; *[+ planète]* to live on ◆ **cette région a longtemps été habitée par les Celtes** for a long time, this region was inhabited by the Celts 2 *(= obséder) [sentiment]* to haunt ◆ **habité d'idées sombres** haunted by gloomy thoughts ◆ **habité par la jalousie/la peur** filled with jealousy/fear, in the grip of jealousy/fear VI to live *(en, dans* in); ◆ **~ à la campagne/chez des amis/en ville** to live in the country/with friends/in town ◆ **il habite (au) 17 (de la) rue Leblanc** he lives at number 17 rue Leblanc

habitude /abityd/ NF 1 *(= accoutumance)* habit ◆ **avoir/prendre l'~ de faire qch** to be/get used to doing sth ◆ **avoir pour ~ de faire qch** to be in the habit of doing sth ◆ **prendre de mauvaises ~s** to pick up *ou* get into bad habits ◆ **perdre une ~** to get out of a habit ◆ **faire perdre une ~ à qn** to break sb of a habit ◆ **avoir une longue ~ de qch** to have long experience of sth ◆ **ce n'est pas dans ses ~s de faire cela** he doesn't usually do that, he doesn't make a habit of (doing) that ◆ **j'ai l'~ !** I'm used to it! ◆ **je n'ai pas l'~ de me répéter** I'm not in the habit of repeating myself ◆ **je n'ai pas l'~ de cette voiture/de ces méthodes** I'm not used to this car/to these methods ◆ **elle a une grande ~ des enfants** she's used to (dealing with) children ◆ **l'~ est une seconde nature** *(Prov)* habit is second nature ◆ **avoir ses ~s dans un restaurant** to be a regular customer *ou* an habitué at a restaurant ◆ **il a ses petites ~s** he has his own little ways *ou* his own little routine ◆ **par ~** out of habit, from force of habit ◆ **selon** *ou* **suivant** *ou* **comme à son ~** as he usually does, as is his wont *(frm)*; → **esclave, question**

◆ **d'habitude** usually, as a rule ◆ **c'est meilleur que d'~** it's better than usual ◆ **comme d'~** as usual

2 *(= coutume)* **~s** customs ◆ **les ~s d'un pays** the customs of a country ◆ **il a des ~s de bourgeois** he has a middle-class way of life

habitué, e /abitɥe/ (ptp de **habituer**) NM,F *[de maison, musée, bibliothèque]* regular visitor, habitué(e); *[de café, hôtel]* regular (customer), habitué(e) ◆ **les ~s du festival** *(= visiteurs)* regular visitors to the festival; *(= artistes)* regular performers at the festival ◆ **ce metteur en scène est un ~ du festival de Cannes** this director makes regular appearances at *ou* is regularly featured at the Cannes film festival ◆ **c'est un ~ des lieux** *(gén)* he knows his way round; *(= client)* he's a regular (customer) ◆ **c'est un ~ du chèque sans provision** *(hum)* he's a master of the rubber cheque* *(Brit)* *ou* check* *(US)* ◆ **c'est un ~ des podiums** *(Sport)* he knows what winning is all about

habituel, -elle /abitɥɛl/ ADJ *[comportement]* usual, customary, habitual; *[réjouissances, formule de politesse]* customary, usual; *[fournisseur]* usual ◆ **avec le sourire qui lui était ~** with his usual smile ◆ **c'est l'histoire habituelle** it's the usual story

habituellement /abitɥɛlmɑ̃/ ADV usually, generally, as a rule

habituer /abitɥe/ ▸ conjug 1 ◂ VT ◆ **~ qn à qch/à faire qch** *(= accoutumer)* to accustom sb to sth/to doing sth, to get sb used to sth/to doing sth; *(= apprendre)* to teach sb sth/to do sth ◆ **on m'a habitué à obéir** I've been taught to obey ◆ **être habitué à qch/à faire qch** to be used *ou* accustomed to sth/to doing sth VPR **s'habituer** ◆ **s'~ à qch/à faire qch** to get *ou* become *ou* grow used *ou* accustomed to sth/to doing sth ◆ **je ne m'y habituerai jamais** I'll never get used to it

hâblerie /'ɑblәʀi/ NF *(= manière d'être)* bragging, boasting; *(= propos)* boast, big talk* *(NonC)*

hâbleur, -euse /'ɑblœʀ, øz/ ADJ bragging, boasting, boastful NM,F braggart, boaster

Habsbourg /'apsbuʀ/ NMF Hapsburg

hachage /'aʃaʒ/ NM *(au couteau)* chopping; *(avec un appareil)* mincing *(Brit)*, grinding *(US)*

hache /'aʃ/ NF axe, ax *(US)* ◆ **~ d'armes** battle-axe ◆ **~ du bourreau** executioner's axe ◆ **~ de guerre** *(gén)* hatchet, axe; *[d'indien]* tomahawk ◆ **déterrer/enterrer la ~ de guerre** to take up/bury the hatchet ◆ **casser qch/tuer qn à coups de ~** *ou* **à la ~** to smash sth/kill sb with an axe ◆ **abattre un arbre à coups de ~** to chop a tree down ◆ **visage taillé à la ~** *ou* **à coups de ~** angular *ou* roughly-hewn face ◆ **ils ont taillé à la ~ dans le budget de l'éducation** they have slashed the education budget, they have made drastic cuts in the education budget ◆ **mettre la ~ dans les dépenses** *(Can)* to cut expenses drastically

haché, e /'aʃe/ (ptp de **hacher**) ADJ 1 *[viande]* minced *(Brit)*, ground *(US)* ◆ **bifteck ~** minced beef *ou* steak *(Brit)*, (beef *ou* steak) mince *(Brit)*, ground beef *(US)*, hamburger *(US)* 2 *(fig) [style]* jerky; *[phrases]* jerky, disjointed ◆ **le match était assez ~** the game proceeded in fits and starts ◆ **il a lu son discours d'une voix ~e** he stumbled his way through the speech NM mince *(Brit)*, minced meat *(Brit)*, ground beef *(US)*

hache-légumes /'aʃlegym/ NM INV vegetable-chopper

hachement /'aʃmɑ̃/ NM ⇒ **hachage**

hachémite /'aʃemit/ ADJ Hashemite NMF **Hachémite** Hashemite

hache-paille /'aʃpɑj/ NM INV chaff-cutter

hacher /'aʃe/ ▸ conjug 1 ◂ VT 1 *(= couper) (au couteau)* to chop; *(avec un appareil)* to mince *(Brit)*, to grind *(US)* ◆ **~ menu** to chop finely, to mince ◆ **il a été haché menu comme chair à pâté** they made mincemeat of him ◆ **je me ferais ~ menu plutôt que d'accepter** I'd die rather than accept 2 *(= entrecouper) [+ discours, phrases]* to break up; → **haché** 3 *(Art)* to hatch

hachette /'aʃɛt/ NF hatchet

hache-viande /'aʃvjɑ̃d/ NM INV (meat-)mincer *(Brit)*, grinder *(US)*

hachich /'aʃiʃ/ NM ⇒ **hachisch**

hachis /'aʃi/ NM *[de légumes]* chopped vegetables; *[de viande]* mince *(Brit)*, minced meat *(Brit)*, hamburger *(US)*, ground meat *(US)*; *(= farce)* forcemeat *(NonC)* ◆ **~ de porc** pork mince ◆ **~ Parmentier** ≈ shepherd's *ou* cottage pie *(Brit)*

hachisch /'aʃiʃ/ NM hashish

hachoir /'aʃwaʀ/ NM *(= couteau) [de viande]* chopper, cleaver; *[de légumes]* chopper; *(= planche)* chopping board; *(= appareil)* (meat-)mincer *(Brit)*, grinder *(US)*

hachure /'aʃyʀ/ NF *(Art)* hatching *(NonC)*, hachure; *(Cartographie)* hachure

hachurer /'aʃyʀe/ ▸ conjug 1 ◂ VT *(Art)* to hatch; *(Cartographie)* to hachure

hacienda /asjɛnda/ NF hacienda

hacker /akœʀ/ NM *(Ordin)* hacker

haddock /'adɔk/ NM smoked haddock

hadj /'adʒ/ NM hajj

Hadrien /adʀijɛ̃/ NM Hadrian

hadron /adʀɔ̃/ NM hadron

Haendel /'ɛndɛl/ NM Handel

hagard, e /'agaʀ, aʀd/ ADJ *[yeux]* wild; *[visage, air, gestes]* distraught, frantic, wild

hagiographe /aʒjɔgʀaf/ NMF hagiographer

hagiographie /aʒjɔgʀafi/ NF hagiography

hagiographique /aʒjɔgʀafik/ ADJ hagiographic(al)

haie /'ɛ/ NF 1 *(= clôture)* hedge ◆ **~ d'aubépines** hawthorn hedge ◆ **~ vive** quickset hedge 2 *(Sport = obstacle) [de coureur]* hurdle; *[de chevaux]* fence ◆ **course de ~s** *(coureur)* hurdles (race); *(chevaux)* steeplechase ◆ **110 mètres ~s** 110 metres hurdles 3 *(= rangée) [de spectateurs, policiers]* line, row ◆ **faire une ~ d'honneur** to form a guard of honour ◆ **faire la ~** to form a line

haïku /'ajku, 'aiku/ NM haiku

haillon /'ɑjɔ̃/ NM rag ◆ **en ~s** in rags *ou* tatters

haillonneux, -euse /'ɑjɔnø, øz/ ADJ *(littér)* in rags, in tatters

Hainaut /'ɛno/ NM ◆ **le ~** Hainaut, Hainault

haine /'ɛn/ NF hatred *(de, pour* of, for); ◆ **cris/regards de ~** cries/looks of hatred *ou* hate ◆ **incitation à la ~ raciale** incitement to racial hatred ◆ **prendre qn en ~** to take a violent dislike *ou* a strong aversion to sb ◆ **avoir de la ~ pour** to feel hatred for, to be filled with hate *ou* hatred for ◆ **par ~ de** out of *ou* through hatred of ◆ **avoir la ~** * to be full of hatred *ou* aggro* *(Brit)*

haineusement /'ɛnøzmɑ̃/ ADV *[dire, regarder]* with hatred

haineux, -euse /'ɛnø, øz/ ADJ *[propos, personne]* full of hatred ◆ **regard ~** look of hate *ou* hatred

haïr /ˈaiʀ/ ▸ conjug 10 ◂ VT to hate, to detest ◆ **elle me hait de l'avoir trompée** she hates me for having deceived her ◆ **je hais ses manières affectées** I can't stand *ou* I hate *ou* I loathe his affected ways ◆ **je hais d'être dérangé** I hate being *ou* to be disturbed VPR **se haïr** to hate *ou* detest each other ◆ **ils se haïssent cordialement** they cordially detest one another

haire /ˈɛʀ/ NF (= *chemise*) hair shirt

haïssable /ˈaisabl/ ADJ detestable, hateful

Haïti /aiti/ NM Haiti

haïtien, -ienne /aisjɛ̃, jɛn/ ADJ Haitian NM,F **Haïtien(ne)** Haitian

halage /ˈalaʒ/ NM *(Naut)* towing; *(Can)* timber hauling ◆ **chemin de ~** towpath ◆ **cheval de ~** towhorse

halal /ˈalal/ ADJ halal

hâle /ˈɑl/ NM (sun)tan

hâlé, e /ˈɑle/ (ptp de **hâler**) ADJ (sun)tanned

haleine /alɛn/ NF 1 (= *souffle*) breath; (= *respiration*) breathing *(NonC)* ◆ **avoir l'~ courte** to be short of breath *ou* short-winded ◆ **retenir son ~** to hold one's breath ◆ **être hors d'~** to be out of breath, to be breathless ◆ **perdre ~** to lose one's breath, to get out of breath ◆ **rire à perdre ~** to laugh until one's sides ache *ou* until one is out of breath ◆ **reprendre ~** *(lit)* to get one's breath back; *(fig)* to get one's breath back, to take a breather ◆ **d'une seule ~** *[dire]* in one breath, in the same breath; *[faire]* (all) at one go ◆ **il respirait d'une ~ régulière** his breathing was regular; → **courir**

2 (= *air expiré*) breath ◆ **avoir l'~ fraîche** to have fresh breath ◆ **avoir mauvaise ~** to have bad breath ◆ **j'ai senti à son ~ qu'il avait bu** I could smell drink on his breath, I could tell from his breath that he'd been drinking

3 *(locutions)* **tenir qn en ~** *(attention)* to hold sb spellbound *ou* breathless; *(incertitude)* to keep sb in suspense *ou* on tenterhooks ◆ **travail de longue ~** long-term job

haler /ˈale/ ▸ conjug 1 ◂ VT *[+ corde, ancre]* to haul in; *[+ bateau]* to tow

hâler /ˈɑle/ ▸ conjug 1 ◂ VT to (sun)tan

haletant, e /ˈal(ə)tɑ̃, ɑ̃t/ ADJ *[personne]* (= *essoufflé*) panting, gasping for breath *(attrib)*, out of breath *(attrib)*; (= *assoiffé, effrayé*) panting *(de* with); (= *curieux*) breathless *(de* with); *[animal]* panting; *[poitrine]* heaving; *[voix]* breathless; *[roman policier]* suspenseful ◆ **sa respiration était ~e** he was panting, his breath came in gasps

halètement /ˈalɛtmɑ̃/ NM *[de personne] (par manque d'air)* panting *(NonC)*, gasping for breath *(NonC)*; *(de soif, d'émotion)* panting *(NonC)*; *[de chien]* panting *(NonC)*; *[de moteur]* puffing *(NonC)*

haleter /ˈal(ə)te/ ▸ conjug 5 ◂ VI *[personne]* (= *manquer d'air)* to pant, to gasp for breath; *(de soif, d'émotion)* to pant *(de* with); *[chien]* to pant; *[moteur, locomotive]* to puff ◆ **son auditoire haletait** his audience listened with bated breath

haleur, -euse /ˈalœʀ, øz/ NM (= *remorqueur*) tug (boat) NM,F (= *personne*) (boat) hauler

halieutique /aljøtik/ ADJ halieutic(al) NF halieutics *(sg)*

hall /ˈol/ NM *[d'immeuble]* hall; *[d'hôtel]* foyer, lobby; *[de cinéma, théâtre]* foyer; *[de gare, lycée, université]* concourse ◆ **~ d'arrivée** *[d'aéroport]* arrivals lounge *ou* hall ◆ **~ des départs** *[d'aéroport]* departure lounge ◆ **~ d'entrée** entrance hall ◆ **~ d'accueil** reception hall ◆ **~ d'exposition** exhibition hall ◆ **c'est un vrai ~ de gare !** it's like Piccadilly Circus *(Brit) ou* Grand Central Station *(US)* (here)!

> ⚠ Attention à ne pas traduire automatiquement **hall** par le mot anglais **hall**, qui a des emplois spécifiques.

hallal /ˈalal/ ADJ halal

hallali /alali/ NM *(Chasse)* (= *mise à mort)* kill; (= *sonnerie)* mort ◆ **sonner l'~** *(lit)* to blow the mort; *(fig)* to go in for the kill

halle /ˈal/ NF 1 (= *marché*) (covered) market; (= *grande salle*) hall ◆ **~ au blé** corn exchange *ou* market ◆ **~ aux vins** wine market 2 *(Belg)* **~ de gymnastique** (= *gymnase*) gymnasium, gym NFPL **halles** (covered) market; *(alimentation en gros)* central food market; → **fort²**

hallebarde /ˈalbaʀd/ NF halberd ◆ **il pleut** *ou* **tombe des ~s*** it's bucketing (down)*, it's raining cats and dogs*

hallebardier /ˈalbaʀdje/ NM halberdier

hallier /ˈalje/ NM thicket, brush *(NonC)*, brushwood *(NonC)*

Halloween /alɔwin/ NF *(Can)* Hallowe'en

hallucinant, e /a(l)lysinɑ̃, ɑ̃t/ ADJ *[histoire, image, spectacle, ressemblance]* staggering*, incredible

hallucination /a(l)lysinasjɔ̃/ NF hallucination ◆ **~ collective** group hallucination ◆ **avoir des ~s** to hallucinate ◆ **tu as des ~s !*** you must be seeing things!

hallucinatoire /a(l)lysinatwaʀ/ ADJ hallucinatory

halluciné, e /a(l)lysine/ (ptp de **halluciner**) ADJ *[malade]* suffering from hallucinations; *[yeux, regard]* haunted NM,F *(Méd)* person suffering from hallucinations; (* = *fou, exalté*) lunatic*

halluciner /a(l)lysine/ ▸ conjug 1 ◂ VI *(Méd)* to hallucinate ◆ **j'hallucine !*** I must be seeing things!

hallucinogène /a(l)lysinɔʒɛn/ ADJ *[drogue]* hallucinogenic, mind-expanding; → **champignon** NM hallucinogen, hallucinant

halo /ˈalo/ NM *(Astron, Tech* = *auréole)* halo; *(Photo)* fogging, halation ◆ **~ de lumière** halo of light ◆ **~ de gloire** cloud of glory ◆ **~ de mystère** aura of mystery

halogène /alɔʒɛn/ ADJ *(gén)* halogenous; *[lampe]* halogen *(épith)* NM *(Chim)* halogen; (= *lampe*) halogen lamp

halte /ˈalt/ NF 1 (= *pause, repos*) stop, break; (= *répit*) pause ◆ **faire ~** to (make a) stop *(à* in) 2 (= *endroit*) stopping place; *(Rail)* halt 3 *(locutions)* **~ !** *(gén)* stop!; *(Mil)* halt! ◆ **"halte au feu !"** "no fires!" ◆ **~ aux essais nucléaires !** no more atomic tests! ◆ **dire ~ à un conflit** to call for a stop *ou* an end to a conflict ◆ **~-là !** *(Mil)* halt! who goes there?; *(fig)* just a moment!, hold on!

halte-garderie (pl **haltes-garderies**) /ˈalt(ə)gaʀdəʀi/ NF crèche, ≃ day nursery

haltère /altɛʀ/ NM 1 *(Sport) (à boules)* dumbbell; *(à disques)* barbell ◆ **faire des ~s** to do weight lifting; → **poids** 2 *[d'insecte]* halter(e), balancer

haltérophile /alteʀɔfil/ NMF weight lifter

haltérophilie /alteʀɔfili/ NF weight lifting ◆ **faire de l'~** to do weight lifting

hamac /ˈamak/ NM hammock ◆ **accrocher** *ou* **suspendre un ~** to sling a hammock

hamadryade /amadʀijad/ NF *(Myth)* hamadryad

hamamélis /amamelis/ NM witch hazel

Hambourg /ˈɑ̃buʀ/ N Hamburg

hamburger /ˈɑ̃buʀgœʀ/ NM hamburger

hameau (pl **hameaux**) /ˈamo/ NM hamlet

hameçon /amsɔ̃/ NM (fish) hook; → **mordre**

hammam /ˈamam/ NM (= *établissement)* hammam; *(dans complexe sportif)* steam room, hammam

hampe¹ /ˈɑ̃p/ NF *[de drapeau]* pole; *[de lance]* shaft; *[de lettre] (vers le bas)* downstroke; *(vers le haut)* upstroke; *(Bot)* scape

hampe² /ˈɑ̃p/ NF *[de cerf]* breast; *[de bœuf]* flank

hamster /ˈamstɛʀ/ NM hamster

han /ˈɑ̃/ EXCL oof! ◆ **il poussa un ~ et souleva la malle** he gave a grunt as he lifted the trunk

hanche /ˈɑ̃ʃ/ NF 1 *[de personne]* hip; *[de cheval]* haunch; *[d'insecte]* coxa ◆ **balancer** *ou* **rouler des ~s** to wiggle one's hips ◆ **les mains sur les ~s, il ...** arms akimbo *ou* with his hands on his hips, he ...; → **tour²** 2 *(Naut)* quarter

hand* /ˈɑ̃d/ NM abrév de **hand(-)ball**

hand(-)ball /ˈɑ̃dbal/ NM handball

handballeur, -euse /ˈɑ̃dbalœʀ, øz/ NM,F handball player

Händel /ˈɛndɛl/ NM ⇒ **Haendel**

handicap /ˈɑ̃dikap/ NM *(lit, fig)* handicap ◆ **avoir un sérieux ~** to be seriously handicapped *ou* disadvantaged *(sur qn* in relation to sb)

handicapant, e /ˈɑ̃dikapɑ̃, ɑ̃t/ ADJ *[maladie]* crippling, disabling ◆ **c'est assez ~** (= *gênant)* it's a bit of a handicap ◆ **la fiscalité ne doit pas être ~e pour la croissance** taxation mustn't handicap *ou* cramp economic growth

handicapé, e /ˈɑ̃dikape/ (ptp de **handicaper**) ADJ disabled, handicapped ◆ **très ~** severely handicapped NM,F disabled *ou* handicapped person ◆ **~ mental/physique** mentally/physically handicapped person ◆ **~ moteur** person with motor disability

handicaper /ˈɑ̃dikape/ ▸ conjug 1 ◂ VT *(lit, fig)* to handicap

handicapeur /ˈɑ̃dikapœʀ/ NM *(Courses)* handicapper

handisport /ˈɑ̃dispɔʀ/ ADJ *[tennis, basket-ball]* wheelchair *(épith)*; *[natation]* for the disabled

hangar /ˈɑ̃gaʀ/ NM *[de matériel, machines]* shed; *[de fourrage]* barn; *[de marchandises]* warehouse, shed; *[d'avions]* hangar ◆ **~ à bateaux** boathouse

hanneton /ˈan(ə)tɔ̃/ NM cockchafer, may bug *ou* beetle; → **piqué**

Hannibal /anibal/ NM Hannibal

Hanoi, Hanoï /anɔj/ N Hanoi

Hanovre /ˈanɔvʀ/ N Hanover

hanovrien, -ienne /ˈanɔvʀijɛ̃, jɛn/ ADJ Hanoverian NM,F **Hanovrien(ne)** Hanoverian

Hanse /ˈɑ̃s/ NF *(Hist)* ◆ **la ~** Hanse

hanséatique /ˈɑ̃seatik/ ADJ Hanseatic ◆ **la ligue ~** the Hanseatic League

hantavirus /ɑ̃tavirys/ NM hantavirus

hanter /ˈɑ̃te/ ▸ conjug 1 ◂ VT *[fantôme, personne, souvenir]* to haunt ◆ **~ les mauvais lieux** to haunt places of ill repute ◆ **maison hantée** haunted house ◆ **cette question hante les esprits** this question is preying on people's minds

hantise /ˈɑ̃tiz/ NF ◆ **avoir la ~ de la maladie** to be haunted by a fear of illness ◆ **vivre dans la ~ du chômage/de l'échec** to live in dread of unemployment/failure ◆ **c'est ma ~ !** I never stop worrying about it!

haoussa /ˈausa/ ADJ Hausa NM *(Ling)* Hausa NMF **Haoussa** Hausa ◆ **les Haoussas** the Hausa

happening /'ap(ə)niŋ/ **NM** *(Art, Théât)* happening

happer /'ape/ ► conjug 1 ◄ **VT** *(avec la gueule, le bec)* to snap up; *(avec la main)* to snatch, to grab ◆ **il le happa au passage** he grabbed him as he went past ◆ **il a eu le bras happé par une machine** he got his arm caught in a piece of machinery ◆ **être happé par une voiture** to be hit by a car ◆ **happé par l'abîme** dragged down into the abyss ◆ **ils ont été happés dans un engrenage d'emprunts** they got caught up in a spiral of debt

happy end (pl **happy ends**) /'apiɛnd/ **NM** happy ending

happy few /'apifju/ **NMPL** ◆ **les ~** the privileged *ou* select few

haptonomie /aptɔnɔmi/ **NF** *communication with a foetus through sensory stimulation*

hara-kiri (pl **hara-kiris**) /'arakiri/ **NM** hara-kiri, hari-kiri ◆ **(se) faire ~** to commit hara-kiri

harangue /'arɑ̃g/ **NF** harangue

haranguer /'arɑ̃ge/ ► conjug 1 ◄ **VT** to harangue, to hold forth to *ou* at

harangueur, -euse /'arɑ̃gœr, øz/ **NM,F** mob orator, haranguer *(frm)*

Harare /'arare/ **N** Harare

haras /'ara/ **NM** stud farm

harassant, e /'arasɑ̃, ɑ̃t/ **ADJ** exhausting

harassé, e /'arase/ (ptp de **harasser**) **ADJ** exhausted, worn out ◆ **~ de travail** overwhelmed with work

harassement /'arasmɑ̃/ **NM** exhaustion

> ⚠ **harassement** ne se traduit pas par le mot anglais **harassment**, qui a le sens de 'harcèlement'.

harasser /'arase/ ► conjug 1 ◄ **VT** to exhaust

> ⚠ **harasser** ne se traduit pas par **to harass**, qui a le sens de 'harceler'.

harcèlement /'arsɛlmɑ̃/ **NM** *[de personne]* ◆ **~ (psychologique** *ou* **moral)** harassment ◆ **~ sexuel/policier** sexual/police harassment ◆ **il se dit victime de ~ judiciaire** he says he is being subjected to legal harassment ◆ **il y a des milliers de plaintes pour ~ téléphonique** thousands of people report nuisance calls ◆ **opérations** *ou* **guerre de ~** *(Mil)* guerrilla warfare ◆ **il faut mener une guerre de ~ contre les dealers** we must keep hounding the drug dealers

harceler /'arsəle/ ► conjug 5 ◄ **VT** 1 *[+ personne] (de critiques, d'attaques)* to harass, to plague *(de* with); *(de questions, de réclamations)* to plague, to pester *(de* with); ◆ **~ qn pour obtenir qch** to pester sb for sth ◆ **elle a été harcelée de coups de téléphone anonymes** she has been plagued by anonymous phone calls 2 *(Mil) [+ ennemi]* to harass, to harry 3 *[+ animal]* to worry; *[+ gibier]* to hunt down, to harry

harceleur /'arsəlœr/ **NM** harasser; *(qui suit qn)* stalker

hard * /'ard/ **NM** 1 *(Mus)* hard rock 2 *(= pornographie)* hard porn * 3 *(Ordin)* hardware **ADJ** 1 *[film, revue]* porno *, hard-core *[scène]* hard-core 2 *(= difficile)* hard

harde /'ard/ **NF** *[de cerfs]* herd

hardes /'ard/ **NFPL** *(littér, péj) (= vieux habits)* old clothes, rags

hardeur, -euse /'ardœr, øz/ **NM,F** hard-porn actor

hardi, e /'ardi/ **ADJ** 1 *(= audacieux) [initiative, personne, comparaison, métaphore]* bold, daring 2 *(= provocant) [décolleté]* daring; *[fille]* bold, brazen; *[plaisanterie]* daring, audacious; † *[mensonge]* brazen, barefaced *(épith)* 3 *(locution)* **~ les gars !** go to it, lads! *(Brit)*, come on lads! *(Brit) ou* you guys! *(US)*

hardiesse /'ardjɛs/ **NF** 1 *(littér = audace)* boldness, daring ◆ **avoir la ~ de** to be bold *ou* daring enough to ◆ **montrer une grande ~** to show great boldness *ou* daring 2 *(= effronterie) [de personne]* audacity, effrontery, impudence; *[de livre, plaisanterie]* audacity ◆ **la ~ de son décolleté choqua tout le monde** everyone was shocked by her daring neckline 3 *(= originalité) [de style, tableau, conception]* boldness 4 *(= libertés)* **~s** *[de livre, pamphlet]* bold statements; *[de domestique, soupirant]* liberties ◆ **~s de langage/de style** bold language/turns of phrase

hardiment /'ardimɑ̃/ **ADV** 1 *(= audacieusement) [innover]* boldly, daringly ◆ **ne vous engagez pas trop ~** don't commit yourself rashly 2 *(= effrontément)* brazenly ◆ **elle le dévisagea ~** she stared at him brazenly

hard-top (pl **hard-tops**) /'ardtɔp/ **NM** hardtop

hardware /'ardwɛr/ **NM** hardware

harem /'arɛm/ **NM** harem ◆ **entouré d'un véritable ~** *(hum)* surrounded by a bevy of girls

hareng /'arɑ̃/ **NM** herring ◆ **~ saur** smoked herring, kipper, bloater; → **sec, serré**

harfang /'arfɑ̃/ **NM** snowy owl

hargne /'arɲ/ **NF** *(= colère)* spiteful anger; *(= ténacité)* fierce determination ◆ **j'étais dans une telle ~ !** I was so angry! *ou* mad! * ◆ **avec ~** *(= avec colère)* spitefully

hargneusement /'arɲøzmɑ̃/ **ADV** *[répondre]* bad-temperedly; *[aboyer]* ferociously

hargneux, -euse /'arɲø, øz/ **ADJ** 1 *[personne, caractère]* bad-tempered, cantankerous; *[animal]* vicious, fierce ◆ **un petit chien ~** a snappy little dog 2 *[sportif]* aggressive

haricot /'ariko/ **NM** 1 *(= légume)* bean ◆ **~ beurre** *type of yellow French bean,* wax bean *(US)* ◆ **~ blanc** haricot bean ◆ **~ d'Espagne** scarlet runner ◆ **~ grimpant** *ou* **à rame** runner bean ◆ **~ rouge** red kidney bean ◆ **~ vert** French bean ◆ **~ sec** dried bean ◆ **~s à écosser** fresh beans *(for shelling)*; → **courir, fin²** 2 *(Culin)* **~ de mouton** lamb and bean stew 3 *(= cuvette)* kidney tray

haridelle /'aridɛl/ **NF** *(péj = cheval)* nag, jade

harissa /'arisa, arisa/ **NF** harissa *(hot chilli sauce)*

harki /'arki/ **NM** *Algerian soldier loyal to the French during the Algerian War of Independence*

harle /'arl/ **NM** ◆ **~ bièvre** goosander ◆ **~ huppé** red-breasted merganser

harmonica /armɔnika/ **NM** harmonica, mouth organ

harmoniciste /armɔnisist/ **NMF** harmonica player

harmonie /armɔni/ **NF** *(Littérat, Mus, gén)* harmony; *(= section de l'orchestre)* wind section; *(= fanfare)* wind band ◆ **~s** *(Mus)* harmonies ◆ **~ imitative** *(Littérat)* onomatopoeia ◆ **être en ~ avec** to be in harmony *ou* in keeping with ◆ **vivre en bonne ~** to live together harmoniously *ou* in harmony; → **table**

harmonieusement /armɔnjøzmɑ̃/ **ADV** harmoniously

harmonieux, -ieuse /armɔnjø, jøz/ **ADJ** *(gén)* harmonious ◆ **couleurs harmonieuses** well-matched *ou* harmonizing colours ◆ **un couple ~** a well-matched couple

harmonique /armɔnik/ **ADJ** *(gén, Math, Mus)* harmonic **NM** *(Mus)* harmonic

harmonisation /armɔnizasjɔ̃/ **NF** *[de couleurs]* matching, harmonization; *[de politiques, règlements]* harmonization, standardization ◆ **~ vocalique** vowel harmony

harmoniser /armɔnize/ ► conjug 1 ◄ **VT** *[+ couleurs]* to match, to harmonize *(avec* with); *[+ politiques, règlements]* to harmonize, to standardize ◆ **il faut ~ nos règlements avec les normes européennes** we must bring our rules into line with European regulations ◆ **il faut ~ la notation** *(Univ)* we have to make sure that grading is done consistently **VPR** **s'harmoniser** *[couleurs]* to match, to harmonize *(avec* with); *[politiques]* to be harmonized *ou* standardized

harmoniste /armɔnist/ **NMF** *(Rel, Mus)* harmonist; *[d'orgue]* organ tuner

harmonium /armɔnjɔm/ **NM** harmonium

harnachement /'arnaʃmɑ̃/ **NM** 1 *(= action) [de cheval, bébé, cascadeur]* harnessing 2 *(= objets) [de cheval de trait]* harness; *[de cheval de monte]* tack, saddlery; * *[de campeur, photographe]* gear *

harnacher /'arnaʃe/ ► conjug 1 ◄ **VT** *[+ cheval de trait, alpiniste]* to harness; *[+ cheval de monte]* to put the bridle and saddle on ◆ **il était drôlement harnaché** * *(péj)* he was wearing the strangest gear * *ou* rig-out * *(Brit) ou* get-up * **VPR** **se harnacher** *[alpiniste, parachutiste]* to put one's harness on; * *[campeur]* to put one's gear on *, to rig o.s. out *

harnais /'arnɛ/, **harnois** †† /'arnwa/ **NM** *[de cheval de trait, bébé, alpiniste]* harness; *[de cheval de monte]* tack, saddlery ◆ **~ (de sécurité)** (safety) harness ◆ **~ d'engrenage** train of gear wheels

haro /'aro/ **EXCL** († † *Jur*) harrow!, haro! ◆ **crier ~ sur qn/qch** *(littér)* to inveigh *ou* rail against sb/sth ◆ **crier ~ sur le baudet** *(littér)* to make a hue and cry

harpagon /arpagɔ̃/ **NM** skinflint, Scrooge

harpe /'arp/ **NF** *(Mus)* harp ◆ **~ éolienne** aeolian *ou* wind harp ◆ **~ celtique/irlandaise** Celtic/Irish harp

harpie /'arpi/ **NF** *(Myth, péj)* harpy; *(= oiseau)* harpy eagle

harpiste /'arpist/ **NMF** harpist

harpon /'arpɔ̃/ **NM** *(Pêche)* harpoon; *(Constr)* toothing stone; → **fusil, pêche²**

harponnage /'arpɔnaʒ/, **harponnement** /'arpɔnmɑ̃/ **NM** harpooning

harponner /'arpɔne/ ► conjug 1 ◄ **VT** *[+ baleine]* to harpoon; * *[+ malfaiteur]* to collar *, to nab *; * *[+ passant, voisin]* to waylay, to buttonhole *

harponneur /'arpɔnœr/ **NM** harpooner

hasard /'azar/ **NM** 1 *(= événement fortuit)* **un ~ heureux/malheureux** a stroke *ou* piece of luck/bad luck, a stroke of good fortune/misfortune ◆ **quel ~ de vous rencontrer ici !** what a coincidence meeting you here!, fancy meeting you here! * ◆ **c'est un vrai** *ou* **pur ~ que je sois libre** it's quite by chance *ou* it's a pure coincidence that I'm free ◆ **par un curieux ~** by a curious coincidence ◆ **on l'a retrouvé par le plus grand des ~s** it was quite by chance *ou* it was a piece of sheer luck that they found him ◆ **les ~s de la vie/de la carrière** the ups and downs of life/one's career

2 *(= destin)* **le** ~ chance, fate, luck; *(Stat)* chance ◆ **les caprices du** ~ the whims of fate ◆ **le** ~ **fait bien les choses !** what a stroke of luck! ◆ **faire la part du** ~ *(événements futurs)* to allow for chance (to play its part); *(événements passés)* to admit that chance had a hand in it ◆ **le** ~ **a voulu qu'il soit absent** as luck would have it he wasn't there ◆ **c'est ça le** ~ **!** * that's the luck of the draw! * ◆ **c'est un fait du** ~ it's a matter of chance ◆ **les lois du** ~ the laws of fate; → **jeu**

3 *(= risques)* ~**s** hazards ◆ **les** ~**s de la guerre** the hazards of war

4 *(locutions)*

◆ **au hasard** *[aller]* aimlessly; *[agir]* haphazardly, in a haphazard way; *[tirer, choisir, prendre]* at random ◆ **j'ai répondu au** ~ I gave an answer off the top of my head * ◆ **voici des exemples au** ~ here are some random examples *ou* some examples taken at random ◆ **faire confiance** *ou* **s'en remettre au** ~ to trust to luck ◆ **il ne laisse jamais rien au** ~ he never leaves anything to chance ◆ **rien n'est laissé au** ~ nothing is left to chance ◆ **son succès ne doit rien au** ~ his success has nothing to do with luck ◆ **son choix ne doit rien au** ~ his choice was not fortuitous

◆ **au hasard de** ◆ **il a acheté ces livres au** ~ **des ventes/de ses voyages** he bought these books just as he happened to see them in the sales/on his trips

◆ **à tout hasard** *(= en cas de besoin)* just in case; *(= espérant trouver ce qu'on cherche)* (just) on the off chance ◆ **on avait emporté une tente à tout** ~ we had taken a tent just in case ◆ **je suis entré à tout** ~ I looked in on the off chance ◆ **à tout** ~ **est-ce que tu aurais ses coordonnées ?** Would you by any chance have his contact details?

◆ **par hasard** by chance, by accident ◆ **je passais par** ~ I happened to be passing by ◆ **tu n'aurais pas par** ~ **20 € à me prêter ?** you wouldn't by any chance have *ou* you wouldn't happen to have €20 to lend me? ◆ **voudrais-tu par** ~ **m'apprendre mon métier ?** you wouldn't be trying to teach me my job by any chance? ◆ **comme par** ~ **!** what a coincidence! ◆ **il est arrivé comme par** ~ **au moment où on débouchait les bouteilles** he turned up as if by chance as we were opening the bottles ◆ **comme par** ~**, il était absent** *(iro)* he just happened to be away *(iro)* ◆ **si par** ~ **tu le vois** if you happen to see him, if by chance you should see him

> ⚠ **hasard** se traduit par le mot anglais **hazard** uniquement au sens de 'risque'.

hasarder /'azaʀde/ ▸ conjug 1 ◂ VT *[+ vie, réputation]* to risk; *[+ remarque, hypothèse, démarche]* to hazard, to venture; *[+ argent]* to gamble, to risk VPR **se hasarder** ◆ **se** ~ **dans un endroit dangereux** to venture into a dangerous place ◆ **se** ~ **à faire** to risk doing, to venture to do ◆ **à votre place je ne m'y hasarderais pas** if I were you I wouldn't risk it

hasardeux, -euse /'azaʀdø, øz/ ADJ *[entreprise]* hazardous, risky; *[investissement]* risky; *[hypothèse]* dangerous, rash ◆ **il serait bien** ~ **de** it would be dangerous *ou* risky to

has been * /'azbin/ NM INV *(péj)* has-been *

hasch * /'aʃ/ NM hash *, pot *, grass *

haschich /'aʃiʃ/ NM ⇒ **hachisch**

hase /'ɑz/ NF doe *(female hare)*

hassidique /asidik/ ADJ Hassidic

hâte /'ɑt/ NF *(= empressement)* haste; *(= impatience)* impatience ◆ **à la** ~ hurriedly, hastily ◆ **en (grande** *ou* **toute)** ~ as fast as you *(ou we etc)* can, posthaste, with all possible speed ◆ **elle est montée/descendue en toute** ~ she hurried up/down the stairs ◆ **mettre de la** ~ **à faire qch** to do sth speedily *ou* in a hurry *ou* hurriedly ◆ **avoir** ~ **de faire** to be eager *ou* anxious to do ◆ **je n'ai qu'une** ~**, c'est d'avoir terminé ce travail** I can't wait to get this work finished ◆ **sans** ~ unhurriedly

hâter /'ɑte/ ▸ conjug 1 ◂ VT *[+ fin, développement]* to hasten; *[+ départ]* to bring forward, to hasten; *[+ fruit]* to bring on, to force ◆ ~ **le pas** to quicken *ou* hasten one's pace *ou* step VPR **se hâter** to hurry, to hasten ◆ **se** ~ **de faire** to hurry *ou* hasten *ou* make haste to do ◆ **hâtez-vous** hurry up ◆ **je me hâte de dire que** I hasten to say that ◆ **hâte-toi lentement** more haste, less speed *(Prov)* ◆ **ne nous hâtons pas de juger** let's not be in a hurry to judge *ou* too hasty in our judgments

hâtif, -ive /'ɑtif, iv/ ADJ *[développement]* precocious; *[fruit, saison]* early; *[travail]* hurried; *[décision, jugement]* hasty ◆ **ne tirons pas de conclusions hâtives** let's not rush to conclusions

hâtivement /'ɑtivmɑ̃/ ADV hurriedly, hastily ◆ **dire qch un peu/trop** ~ to say sth rather/too hastily

hauban /'obɑ̃/ NM *(Naut)* shroud; *[de pont]* stay ◆ **pont à** ~**s** cable-stayed bridge

haubaner /'obane/ ▸ conjug 1 ◂ VT *[+ mât]* to prop *ou* shore up with shrouds

haubert /'obɛʀ/ NM *(Hist)* coat of mail, hauberk

hausse /'os/ NF *[de prix, niveau, température]* rise, increase *(de* in); *(Bourse)* rise *(de* in); ◆ ~ **de salaire** (pay) rise *(Brit) ou* raise *(US)* ◆ **une** ~ **à la pompe** *(essence)* a rise in pump prices

◆ **à la hausse** ◆ **marché à la** ~ *(Bourse)* bull(ish) market ◆ **tendance à la** ~ bullish *ou* upward trend ◆ **revoir** *ou* **réviser à la** ~ *[+ prévisions, chiffres, objectif]* to revise upwards, to scale up

◆ **en hausse** ◆ **être en** ~ *[prix, bénéfices, chiffres, températures]* to be rising, to be on the increase; *[actions, marchandises]* to be going up (in price) ◆ **nos dépenses sont en** ~ **de 15%** our outgoings have increased *ou* risen by 15% ◆ **terminer en** ~ *[action, monnaie]* to close higher ◆ **l'indice a terminé en** ~ **de 25 points** the index closed up 25 points ◆ **le CAC 40 a clôturé la séance en** ~ the CAC 40 was strong at close of trading ◆ **sa cote est** *ou* **ses actions sont en** ~ *[de personne]* things are looking up for him, his popularity is increasing

haussement /'osmɑ̃/ NM ◆ ~ **d'épaules** shrug ◆ **il eut un** ~ **d'épaules** he shrugged (his shoulders) ◆ **elle eut un** ~ **des sourcils** she raised her eyebrows

hausser /'ose/ ▸ conjug 1 ◂ VT 1 *(= élever) [+ barre, niveau, sourcil, voix]* to raise; *[+ prix]* to raise, increase ◆ ~ **les épaules** to shrug (one's shoulders); → **ton²** 2 *[+ mur]* to heighten, to raise; *[+ maison]* to heighten, to make higher ◆ ~ **une maison d'un étage** to add another floor to a house VPR **se hausser** ◆ **se** ~ **sur la pointe des pieds** to stand up on tiptoe ◆ **se** ~ **au niveau de qn** to raise o.s. up to sb's level ◆ **se** ~ **du col** to show off

haussier, -ière /'osje, jɛʀ/ ADJ *(Bourse) [marché]* bullish, bull *(épith)*; *[prix, cours]* rising ◆ **tendance haussière** bullish trend NM *(Bourse)* bull

haussmannien, -ienne /osmanjɛ̃, jɛn/ ADJ *[immeuble, façade]* Haussmann *(épith)* *(in the style of the 1850s and 1860s when Paris was redeveloped by Baron Haussmann)*

haut, e /'o, 'ot/

1 ADJECTIF	4 NOM FÉMININ
2 NOM MASCULIN	5 ADVERBE
3 NOM MASCULIN PL	6 COMPOSÉS

1 - ADJECTIF

1 = de taille élevée *[mur, montagne]* high; *[herbe, arbre, édifice]* tall, high ◆ **une** ~**e silhouette** a tall figure ◆ **de** ~**e taille** tall ◆ **un chien** ~ **sur pattes** a long-legged dog ◆ **il a le front** ~ he has a high forehead ◆ ~ **comme trois pommes** * knee-high to a grasshopper * ◆ **un mur** ~ **de 3 mètres** a wall 3 metres high ◆ **pièce** ~**e de plafond** room with a high ceiling

2 = situé en altitude *[plafond, branche, nuage, plateau]* high ◆ **le soleil était déjà** ~ **dans le ciel** the sun was already high up in the sky ◆ **le plus** ~ **étage** the top floor ◆ **dans les plus** ~**es branches de l'arbre** in the topmost branches of the tree; → **montagne, ville**

3 = de niveau élevé *[prix, température, rendement]* high; *(Élec) [fréquence, voltage]* high ◆ **c'est (la) marée** ~**e, la mer est** ~**e** it's high tide, the tide is in ◆ **à marée** ~**e** at high tide ◆ **pendant les** ~**es eaux (du fleuve)** while the river is high, during high water

4 Mus = aigu *[note, ton]* high, high-pitched

5 = fort, bruyant **son mari est si gentil – jamais un mot plus** ~ **que l'autre !** her husband is so nice – never an angry word! ◆ **pousser** *ou* **jeter les** *ou* **des** ~**s cris** to make a terrible fuss; → **verbe, voix**

6 dans une hiérarchie = supérieur *(gén avant n) [qualité, rang, précision]* high; *[âme, pensée]* lofty, noble ◆ **avoir une** ~**e idée** *ou* **opinion de soi-même** to have a high *ou* an exalted opinion of o.s. ◆ **c'est du plus** ~ **comique** it's highly amusing *ou* comical, it's excruciatingly funny ◆ ~ **en couleur** *(= rougeaud)* with a high colour *ou* a ruddy complexion; *(= coloré, pittoresque)* colourful ◆ **athlète/cadre de** ~ **niveau** top athlete/executive ◆ **discussions au plus** ~ **niveau** top-level discussions ◆ ~**s faits** *(hum)* heroic deeds ◆ **les** ~**es cartes** the high cards, the picture cards ◆ **la** ~**e cuisine/couture/coiffure** haute cuisine/couture/coiffure ◆ **les** ~**es mathématiques** higher mathematics ◆ ~ **personnage** high-ranking person; → **lutte**

7 = ancien **dans la plus** ~**e antiquité** in earliest antiquity ◆ **le** ~ **Moyen Âge** the Early Middle Ages ◆ **le** ~ **Empire** the Early (Roman) Empire ◆ **le** ~ **allemand** Old High German

8 Géog **le Haut Rhin** the Upper Rhine ◆ **la Haute Normandie** Upper Normandy ◆ **la Haute-Égypte** Upper Egypt ◆ **les** ~**es terres** the highlands ◆ **le Haut Canada** *(Hist)* Upper Canada

2 - NOM MASCULIN

1 = hauteur **le mur a 3 mètres de** ~ the wall is 3 metres high ◆ **combien fait-il de** ~ **?** how high is it?

2 = partie haute *[d'arbre, colline, armoire]* top ◆ **au** ~ **de l'arbre** at the top of the tree, high up in the tree ◆ **la colonne est évasée dans le** ~ the column gets wider at the top ◆ **le** ~ **du visage** the top part of the face ◆ **"haut"** *(sur un colis)* "top", "this way up", "this side up" ◆ **tenir le** ~ **du pavé** *[personne]* to be the leading light; *[produit, entreprise]* to be a market leader

3 = vêtement top

4 expressions figées

◆ **au plus haut** ◆ **être au plus** ~ *(dans les sondages) [personne]* to be riding high; *[cote, popularité]* to be at its peak ◆ **le prix de l'or est au plus** ~ the price of gold has reached a peak *ou* maximum

◆ **de + haut** ◆ **voir les choses de** ~ *(= avec détachement)* to take a detached view of things ◆ **prendre qch de (très)** ~ *(= avec mépris)* to react (most) indignantly to sth ◆ **le prendre de** ~ **avec** *ou* **à l'égard de qn, prendre** *ou* **traiter qn de** ~ to look down on sb, to treat sb disdainfully; → **regarder, tomber¹**

◆ **de haut en bas** *[s'ouvrir]* from the top downwards ◆ **regarder qn de** ~ **en bas** to look sb up and down ◆ **frapper de** ~ **en bas** to strike downwards ◆ **couvert de graffitis de** ~ **en bas** covered in graffiti from top to bottom ◆ **ça se**

lit de ~ en bas it reads vertically (starting at the top) ◆ **lissez le papier peint de ~ en bas** smooth the wallpaper, starting at the top and working down; → **bas¹**

◆ **d'en haut** ◆ **les chambres d'en ~** the upstairs bedrooms ◆ **ceux** *ou* **les gens d'en ~** *(socialement)* people at the top ◆ **un signe d'en ~** *(Rel)* a sign from on high ◆ **vu d'en ~** seen from above ◆ **des ordres qui viennent d'en ~** orders from on high *ou* from above

◆ **du haut** ◆ **les pièces du ~** the upstairs rooms ◆ **les voisins du ~** the neighbours *ou* people upstairs ◆ **l'étagère/le tiroir du ~** the top shelf/drawer ◆ **les dents du ~** the top teeth

◆ **du haut de** ◆ **du ~ d'un arbre** from the top of a tree ◆ **tomber du ~ du 5ᵉ étage** to fall from the 5th floor ◆ **parler du ~ d'une tribune/d'un balcon** to speak from a platform/a balcony ◆ **il me dévisageait, du ~ de son mètre cinquante** *(hum)* he looked down on me, which was quite something as he was all of five feet tall ◆ **il me regarda du ~ de sa grandeur** he looked down his nose at me

◆ **du haut en bas** *[couvrir, fouiller]* from top to bottom ◆ **du ~ en bas de la hiérarchie/société** at all levels of the hierarchy/of society

◆ **en haut** *(= au sommet)* at the top; *(dans un immeuble)* upstairs ◆ **il habite en ~/tout en ~** he lives upstairs/right at the top ◆ **écris l'adresse en ~ à gauche** write the address in the top left-hand corner ◆ **manteau boutonné jusqu'en ~** coat buttoned right up *ou* (right) up to the top ◆ **les voleurs sont passés par en ~** the burglars came in from upstairs *ou* got in upstairs

◆ **en haut de** *[+ immeuble, escalier, côte, écran]* at the top of ◆ **en ~ de l'échelle sociale** high up the social ladder

3 - NOM MASCULIN PLURIEL

hauts

1 = périodes fastes **des ~s et des bas** ups and downs ◆ **il a connu des ~s et des bas** he's had his ups and downs ◆ **elle gagne plus ou moins sa vie, il y a des ~s et des bas** she makes a reasonable living but it's a bit up and down

2 Géog **les Hauts de Meuse/de Seine** the upper reaches of the Meuse/Seine

3 Naut topside

4 - NOM FÉMININ

haute ◆ **(les gens de) la ~e** * the upper crust*, the toffs‡ *(Brit)*, the swells †*

5 - ADVERBE

1 *[monter, sauter, voler]* high ◆ **mettez vos livres plus ~** put your books higher up ◆ **c'est lui qui saute le plus ~** he can jump the highest ◆ **~ les mains !** hands up!, stick 'em up!‡ ◆ **~ les cœurs !** take heart!

2 = fort *[parler]* loudly ◆ **lire/penser tout ~** to read/think aloud *ou* out loud ◆ **mettez la radio plus ~** turn up the radio ◆ **j'ose le dire bien ~** I'm not afraid of saying it out loud ◆ **parle plus ~ !** speak up! ◆ **il a déclaré ~ et fort que …** he stated very clearly that …

3 Mus = dans les aigus **monter ~** to hit the top notes ◆ **chanter trop ~** to sing sharp

4 sur le plan social **des gens ~ placés** people in high places ◆ **arriver très ~** to reach a high position ◆ **viser ~** to aim high

5 = en arrière, dans le temps **aussi ~ qu'on peut remonter** as far back as we can go ◆ **"voir plus haut"** "see above" ◆ **comme je l'ai dit plus ~** as I said above *ou* previously

6 - COMPOSÉS

haut commandement high command

le Haut Commissariat (de l'ONU) pour les réfugiés the UN High Commission for Refugees

Haute Cour high court *(for impeachment of French President or Ministers)*

haute école *(Équitation)* haute école

haut fourneau blast *ou* smelting furnace

haut lieu ◆ **un ~ lieu de la culture/musique** a Mecca for culture/music ◆ **en ~ lieu** in high places

haute trahison high treason

haut vol, haute volée ◆ **de ~ vol, de ~e volée** *[personne]* high-flying; *[opération, activité]* far-reaching ◆ **un industriel/athlète de ~e volée** a top-flight industrialist/athlete ◆ **un escroc de ~ vol** a big-time swindler ◆ **une escroquerie de ~ vol** a major swindle

---

hautain, e /'otɛ̃, ɛn/ ADJ *[personne]* haughty; *[air, manière]* haughty, lofty

hautainement /'otɛnmɑ̃/ ADV haughtily, loftily

hautbois /'obwɑ/ NM *(= instrument)* oboe

hautboïste /'obɔist/ NMF oboist, oboe player

haut-commissaire (pl **hauts-commissaires**) /'okɔmisɛʀ/ NM high commissioner (à for); ◆ **~ des Nations unies pour les réfugiés** United Nations High Commissioner for Refugees

haut-commissariat (pl **hauts-commissariats**) /'okɔmisaʀja/ NM *(= ministère)* high commission (à of); *(= grade)* high commissionership

haut-de-chausse(s) (pl **hauts-de-chausse(s)**) /'od(ə)ʃos/ NM *(Hist)* (knee) breeches, trunk hose

haut-de-forme (pl **hauts-de-forme**) /'od(ə)fɔʀm/ NM top hat

haute-contre (pl **hautes-contre**) /'otkɔ̃tʀ/ ADJ, NM counter tenor NF counter tenor, alto

haute-fidélité (pl **hautes-fidélités**) /'ofidelite/ ADJ *[chaîne, son]* high-fidelity NF high-fidelity

hautement /'otmɑ̃/ ADV *(= extrêmement)* highly; *(= ouvertement)* openly ◆ **~ qualifié** *[personnel]* highly qualified

hauteur /'otœʀ/ GRAMMAIRE ACTIVE 42.4, 43.4 NF 1 *(= élévation verticale) [de tour, montagne, astre, personne]* height; *[de châssis de voiture]* ground clearance ◆ **il se redressa de toute sa ~** he drew himself up to his full height ◆ **d'une ~ de 4 mètres** *(dimension)* 4 metres high; *(d'un point élevé)* from a height of 4 metres ◆ **~ maximum** *ou* **libre 3 mètres** *(sous pont)* headroom 3 metres ◆ **pièce de 3 mètres de ~ sous plafond** room whose ceiling height is 3 metres ◆ **tomber de toute sa ~** *[personne]* to fall headlong *ou* flat, to measure one's length *(Brit)*; *[armoire]* to come crashing down ◆ **perdre de la ~** to lose height ◆ **prendre de la ~** *(lit)* to climb, to gain height; *(fig)* to distance o.s. ◆ **~ de vues** ability to distance o.s.; → **saut**

2 *(Géom)* perpendicular height; *(ligne)* perpendicular; *(Astron)* altitude

3 *[de son]* pitch

4 *(= colline)* height, hill ◆ **gagner les ~s** to make for the heights *ou* hills ◆ **construit sur les ~s d'Alger** built on the hills of Algiers ◆ **il s'est réfugié dans les ~s de la ville** he hid in the hills above the city

5 *(= arrogance)* haughtiness, loftiness ◆ **parler avec ~** to speak haughtily *ou* loftily

6 *(= noblesse)* loftiness, nobility ◆ **la ~ de ses sentiments** his noble *ou* lofty sentiments, the loftiness *ou* nobility of his sentiments

7 *(locutions)*

◆ **à hauteur de** ◆ **à ~ d'appui** at chest height ◆ **à ~ des yeux** at eye level ◆ **à ~ d'homme** at the right height *ou* level for a man ◆ **nous vous rembourserons à ~ de 300 €** we will refund up to €300 ◆ **il est actionnaire à ~ de 34%** he has a 34% share in the company ◆ **les nouvelles technologies ont contribué à ~ de 15% à la croissance du PIB** new technologies have created a 15% increase in the GNP ◆ **ce concours a été financé à ~ de 100 000 € par des entreprises** this competition received corporate funding of €100,000 ◆ **le groupe britannique a annoncé son entrée à ~ de 9% dans le club de football** the British group has announced that it is to acquire a 9% stake in the football club

◆ **à la hauteur** ◆ **être à la ~ de la situation** to be equal to the situation ◆ **il s'est vraiment montré à la ~** he proved he was up to it* ◆ **je ne me sentais pas à la ~** I didn't feel up to it*, I didn't feel equal to the task

◆ **à la hauteur de** ◆ **arriver à la ~ de qn** to draw level with sb ◆ **la procession arrivait à sa ~** the procession was drawing level with him ◆ **nous habitons à la ~ de la mairie** we live up by the town hall ◆ **arriver à la ~ d'un cap** to come abreast of a cape ◆ **un accident à la ~ de Tours** an accident near Tours *ou* in the vicinity of *ou* neighbourhood of Tours ◆ **être à la ~ de** *[+ réputation]* to live up to ◆ **le résultat n'est pas à la ~ de nos espérances** the result does not come up to our expectations ◆ **nous n'avons pas été à la ~ de la tâche** we were not equal to the task

◆ **en hauteur** ◆ **les moulins étaient construits en ~** the windmills were built on high ground ◆ **j'aime bien être en ~ quand je conduis** I like being in a high driving position ◆ **j'ai mis le vase en ~** I put the vase high up ◆ **le siège est réglable en ~** the height of the seat can be adjusted

Haute-Volta /'otvɔlta/ NF Upper Volta

haut-fond (pl **hauts-fonds**) /'ofɔ̃/ NM shallow, shoal

Haut-Karabakh /'okaʀabak/ N Nagorno Karabakh

haut-le-cœur /'ol(ə)kœʀ/ NM INV ◆ **avoir un ~** to retch, to heave

haut-le-corps /'ol(ə)kɔʀ/ NM INV ◆ **avoir un ~** to start, to jump

haut-parleur (pl **haut-parleurs**) /'opaʀlœʀ/ NM (loud)speaker ◆ **~ aigu** tweeter ◆ **~ grave** woofer ◆ **une voiture ~** a loudspeaker car

haut-relief (pl **hauts-reliefs**) /'oʀəljɛf/ NM high relief

hauturier, -ière /'otyʀje, jɛʀ/ ADJ ◆ **navigation hauturière** ocean navigation ◆ **pêche hauturière** deep-sea fishing ◆ **pilote ~** deep-sea pilot

havage /'avaʒ/ NM (mechanical) cutting

havanais, e /'avanɛ, ɛz/ ADJ of *ou* from Havana NM,F **Havanais(e)** inhabitant *ou* native of Havana

havane /'avan/ NM *(= tabac)* Havana tobacco; *(= cigare)* Havana cigar ADJ INV *(couleur)* tobacco brown NF **Havane** ◆ **la Havane** Havana

hâve /'ɑv/ ADJ *(= émacié)* gaunt, haggard; *(= pâle)* wan

haveneau (pl **haveneaux**) /'av(ə)no/ NM shrimping net

haver /'ave/ ► conjug 1 ◄ VT *(Tech)* to cut *(mechanically)*

haveuse /'avøz/ NF coal cutter

havre /'avʀ/ NM († *ou littér*) haven ◆ **~ de paix** haven of peace

havresac /'ɑvʀəsak/ NM haversack, knapsack

Hawaï, Hawaii /awai/ N Hawaii ◆ **les îles ~** the Hawaiian Islands

hawaïen, -ïenne /awajɛ̃, jɛn/ ADJ Hawaiian NM *(= langue)* Hawaiian NM,F **Hawaïen(ne)** Hawaiian

Haye /'ɛ/ NF • **La ~** The Hague

hayon /'ɛjɔ̃/ NM *[de camion, charrette]* tailboard • **~ (arrière)** *[de voiture]* hatchback, tailgate • **modèle avec ~ arrière** hatchback (model) • **~ élévateur** *[de camion]* fork-lift

HCH /aʃseaʃ/ NF (abrév de **hormone de croissance humaine**) HCH

HCR /'aʃseɛʀ/ NM (abrév de **Haut Commissariat des Nations Unies pour les réfugiés**) UNHCR

HDML /aʃdeɛmɛl/ (abrév de **Handled Device Markup Language**) HDML

hé /'e/ EXCL *(pour appeler)* hey!; *(pour renforcer)* well • **~ ! ~ !** well, well!, ha-ha! • **~ non !** not a bit of it!

heaume /'om/ NM *(Hist)* helmet

heavy metal /evimetal/ NM *(Mus)* heavy metal

hebdo * /ɛbdo/ NM abrév de **hebdomadaire**

hebdomadaire /ɛbdɔmadɛʀ/ ADJ, NM weekly • **~ d'actualité** news weekly; → **repos**

hebdomadairement /ɛbdɔmadɛʀmɑ̃/ ADV weekly

hébergement /ebɛʀʒəmɑ̃/ NM 1 *(= lieu)* housing, accommodation; *(pendant un séjour)* accommodation • **le prix comprend l'~** the price includes accommodation • **~ d'urgence** emergency housing *ou* accommodation 2 *(= action d'héberger) [d'ami]* putting up; *[de réfugiés]* taking in; *[d'évadé]* harbouring; *[de site Web]* hosting → **centre**

héberger /ebɛʀʒe/ ▸ conjug 3 ◂ VT 1 *(= loger) [+ touristes]* to accommodate; *[+ ami]* to put up • **pouvez-vous nous ~ ?** can you put us up? • **il est hébergé par un ami** he's staying with a friend 2 *(= accueillir) [+ réfugiés]* to take in; *[+ évadé]* to harbour • **les sinistrés ont été hébergés chez des voisins** the victims were taken in *ou* given shelter by neighbours • **le musée va ~ une collection de meubles** the museum will house a collection of furniture 3 *(Internet) [+ site]* to host

hébergeur /ebɛʀʒœʀ/ NM *(Internet)* host

hébété, e /ebete/ (ptp de **hébéter**) ADJ 1 *(= étourdi) [regard, air, personne]* dazed • **être ~ de fatigue/de douleur** to be numbed with fatigue/pain • **~ par l'alcool** in a drunken stupor 2 *(* = stupide) [regard, air]* dumb*, vacant

hébétement /ebɛtmɑ̃/ NM stupor

hébéter /ebete/ ▸ conjug 6 ◂ VT *[alcool]* to stupefy, to besot *(Brit)*; *[lecture, télévision]* to daze, to numb; *[fatigue, douleur]* to numb

hébétude /ebetyd/ NF *(littér)* stupor; *(Méd)* hebetude

hébraïque /ebʀaik/ ADJ Hebrew *(épith)*, Hebraic

hébraïsant, e /ebʀaizɑ̃, ɑ̃t/ ADJ Hebraistical NM,F Hebraist, Hebrew scholar

hébraïser /ebʀaize/ ▸ conjug 1 ◂ VT to assimilate into Jewish culture

hébraïsme /ebʀaism/ NM Hebraism

hébraïste /ebʀaist/ NMF ⇒ **hébraïsant**

hébreu (pl **hébreux**) /ebʀø/ ADJ M Hebrew NM *(= langue)* Hebrew • **pour moi, c'est de l'~** * it's all Greek *ou* double Dutch *(Brit)* to me! * NM **Hébreu** Hebrew

Hébrides /ebʀid/ NFPL • **les (îles) ~** the Hebrides

HEC /'aʃese/ NF (abrév de **(École des) Hautes études commerciales**) *top French business school*; → **Grandes Écoles**

hécatombe /ekatɔ̃b/ NF *(= tuerie)* slaughter • **quelle ~ sur les routes ce week-end !** it was absolute carnage on the roads this week-end! • **ça a été l'~ en maths** everybody got disastrous results in the maths exam

hectare /ɛktaʀ/ NM hectare

hectique /ɛktik/ ADJ *(Méd)* hectic

hecto... /ɛkto/ PRÉF hecto...

hectogramme /ɛktɔgʀam/ NM hectogram(me)

hectolitre /ɛktɔlitʀ/ NM hectolitre • **3 millions d'~s** 300 million litres

hectomètre /ɛktɔmɛtʀ/ NM hectometre

hectométrique /ɛktɔmetʀik/ ADJ hectometre *(épith)*

hectopascal /ɛktopaskal/ NM millibar

Hector /'ɛktɔʀ/ NM Hector

hectowatt /ɛktowat/ NM hectowatt, 100 watts

Hécube /'ekyb/ NF Hecuba

hédonisme /edɔnism/ NM hedonism

hédoniste /edɔnist/ ADJ hedonist(ic) NMF hedonist

hégélianisme /egeljanism/ NM Hegelianism

hégélien, -ienne /egeljɛ̃, jɛn/ ADJ, NM,F Hegelian

hégémonie /eʒemɔni/ NF hegemony

hégémonique /eʒemɔnik/ ADJ hegemonic

hégémonisme /eʒemɔnism/ NM *[de pays]* hegemonism

hégire /eʒiʀ/ NF • **l'~** the Hegira

hein * /'ɛ̃/ EXCL *(de surprise, pour faire répéter)* eh?*, what? • **qu'est-ce que tu feras, ~ ?** what are you going to do (then), eh?* • **tu veux partir, ~, tu veux t'en aller ?** you want to go, is that it, you want to leave? • **ça suffit, ~ !** that's enough, OK?* *ou* all right?* • **~ que je te l'ai dit ?** didn't I tell you so?, I told you so, didn't I? • **arrête ~ !** stop it, will you!

hélas /elas/ EXCL alas! • **~ non !** I'm afraid not!, unfortunately not • **~ oui !** I'm afraid so!, yes, unfortunately • **mais ~, ils n'ont pas pu en profiter** but unfortunately *ou* sadly they couldn't take advantage of it

Hélène /elɛn/ NF Helen, Helena • **~ de Troie** Helen of Troy

héler /'ele/ ▸ conjug 6 ◂ VT *[+ navire, taxi]* to hail; *[+ personne]* to call, to hail

hélianthe /eljɑ̃t/ NM helianthus, sunflower

hélianthine /eljɑ̃tin/ NF helianthine, methyl orange

hélice /elis/ NF *(= dispositif)* propeller; *(Archit, Géom)* helix • **escalier en ~** spiral staircase • **~ double** double helix

hélico * /eliko/ NM (abrév de **hélicoptère**) chopper*, copter*

hélicoïdal, e (mpl **-aux**) /elikɔidal, o/ ADJ *(gén)* helical; *(Bot, Math)* helicoid

hélicoïde /elikɔid/ ADJ, NM helicoid

hélicon /elikɔ̃/ NM helicon

hélicoptère /elikɔptɛʀ/ NM helicopter • **~ d'attaque** attack helicopter • **~ de combat** helicopter gunship • **transporter en ~** to transport by helicopter, to helicopter • **amener/évacuer par ~** to take in/out by helicopter, to helicopter in/out • **plateforme pour ~s** helipad

héligare /eligaʀ/ NF heliport

héliographe /eljɔgʀaf/ NM heliograph

héliographie /eljɔgʀafi/ NF *(Astron, Typo)* heliography

héliogravure /eljogʀavyʀ/ NF heliogravure

héliomarin, e /eljomaʀɛ̃, in/ ADJ *[cure]* of sun and sea-air • **établissement ~** seaside sanatorium *(specializing in heliotherapy)*

héliostat /eljɔsta/ NM heliostat

héliotrope /eljɔtʀɔp/ NM *(= plante, pierre)* heliotrope

héliport /elipɔʀ/ NM heliport

héliportage /elipɔʀtaʒ/ NM helicopter transport

héliporté, e /elipɔʀte/ ADJ *[troupes]* helicopter-borne; *[évacuation, opération]* helicopter *(épith)*

héliski /eliski/ NM heli-skiing

hélitreuiller /elitʀœje/ ▸ conjug 1 ◂ VT to winch up into a helicopter

hélium /eljɔm/ NM helium

hélix /eliks/ NM *(= escargot, partie de l'oreille)* helix

hellène /elɛn/ ADJ Hellenic NMF **Hellène** Hellene

hellénique /elenik/ ADJ *(gén)* Greek; *(Antiq)* Hellenic

hellénisant, e /elenizɑ̃, ɑ̃t/ ADJ, NM,F • **(juif) ~** Hellenist, Hellenistic Jew • **(savant) ~** Hellenist, Hellenic scholar

hellénisation /elenizasjɔ̃/ NF Hellenization

helléniser /elenize/ ▸ conjug 1 ◂ VT to Hellenize

hellénisme /elenism/ NM Hellenism

helléniste /elenist/ NMF ⇒ **hellénisant**

hellénistique /elenistik/ ADJ Hellenistic

hello * /'ɛllo/ EXCL hello, hullo, hi*

Helsinki /ɛlzinki/ N Helsinki

helvète /ɛlvɛt/ ADJ Helvetian NMF **Helvète** Helvetian

Helvétie /ɛlvesi/ NF Helvetia

helvétique /ɛlvetik/ ADJ Swiss, Helvetian

helvétisme /ɛlvetism/ NM *(Ling)* Swiss idiom

hem /'ɛm/ EXCL (a)hem!, h'm!

hématie /emasi/ NF red (blood) corpuscle

hématite /ematit/ NF h(a)ematite

hématologie /ematɔlɔʒi/ NF haematology *(Brit)*, hematology *(US)*

hématologique /ematɔlɔʒik/ ADJ haematological *(Brit)*, hematological *(US)*

hématologiste /ematɔlɔʒist/, **hématologue** /ematɔlɔg/ NMF haematologist *(Brit)*, hematologist *(US)*

hématome /ematom/ NM bruise, haematoma *(Brit) (SPÉC)*, hematoma *(US) (SPÉC)*

hématopoïèse /ematopɔjɛz/ NF haematopoiesis, haematosis, haematogenesis

héméralope /emeʀalɔp/ ADJ night-blind, nyctalopic *(SPÉC)* NMF person suffering from night-blindness *ou* nyctalopia *(SPÉC)*

héméralopie /emeʀalɔpi/ NF night-blindness, nyctalopia *(SPÉC)*

hémicycle /emisikl/ NM semicircle, hemicycle; *(= salle)* amphitheatre • **l'~ (de l'Assemblée nationale)** the benches of the French National Assembly, ≃ the benches of the Commons *(Brit) ou* House of Representatives *(US)*

hémiplégie /emipleʒi/ NF paralysis of one side, hemiplegia *(SPÉC)*

hémiplégique /emipleʒik/ ADJ paralyzed on one side, hemiplegic *(SPÉC)* NMF person paralyzed on one side, hemiplegic *(SPÉC)*

hémisphère /emisfɛʀ/ NM *(gén, Anat, Géog)* hemisphere • **~ sud** *ou* **austral/nord** *ou* **boréal** southern/northern hemisphere

hémisphérique /emisfeʀik/ ADJ hemispheric(al)

hémistiche /emistiʃ/ NM hemistich

hémodialyse /emodjaliz/ NF haemodialysis *(Brit)*, hemodialysis *(US)* • **séance d'~** session of haemodialysis *(Brit) ou* hemodialysis *(US)* treatment

hémoglobine /emɔglɔbin/ NF haemoglobin (*Brit*), hemoglobin (*US*) ◆ **dans ce film, l'~ coule à flots*** this film is full of blood and gore

hémophile /emɔfil/ ADJ haemophilic (*Brit*), hemophilic (*US*) NMF haemophiliac (*Brit*), hemophiliac (*US*)

hémophilie /emɔfili/ NF haemophilia (*Brit*), hemophilia (*US*)

hémorragie /emɔʀaʒi/ NF 1 (*Méd*) bleeding (*NonC*), haemorrhage (*Brit*), hemorrhage (*US*) ◆ ~ **cérébrale** brain *ou* cerebral haemorrhage ◆ ~ **interne** internal bleeding (*NonC*) *ou* haemorrhage ◆ **il a eu** *ou* **a fait une ~ interne** he suffered internal bleeding 2 (*= fuite*) [*de capitaux*] massive outflow *ou* drain; [*de cadres, talents*] mass exodus (*de* of); ◆ **pour stopper l'~ financière** to stem the massive outflow of money ◆ **l'~ démographique** *ou* **de population** the population drain

hémorragique /emɔʀaʒik/ ADJ haemorrhagic (*Brit*), hemorrhagic (*US*)

hémorroïdal, e (mpl **-aux**) /emɔʀɔidal, o/ ADJ (*Méd*) haemorrhoidal (*Brit*), hemorrhoidal (*US*); (*Anat*) [*artère*] anorectal

hémorroïde /emɔʀɔid/ NF (*gén pl*) haemorrhoid (*Brit*), hemorrhoid (*US*), pile ◆ **avoir des ~s** to have haemorrhoids *ou* piles

hémostatique /emɔstatik/ ADJ, NM haemostatic (*Brit*), hemostatic (*US*); → **crayon**

henné /'ene/ NM henna ◆ **se faire un ~** to henna one's hair ◆ **cheveux teints au ~** hennaed hair

hennin /'enɛ̃/ NM (*Hist = bonnet*) hennin (*conical hat with veil*) ◆ ~ **à deux cornes** horned headdress

hennir /'eniʀ/ ► conjug 2 ◄ VI to neigh, to whinny; (*péj*) to bray

hennissement /'enismɑ̃/ NM [*de cheval*] neigh, whinny; (*péj*) [*de personne*] braying (*NonC*)

Henri /ɑ̃ʀi/ NM Henry

hep /'ɛp/ EXCL hey!

héparine /epaʀin/ NF heparin

hépatique /epatik/ ADJ (*Méd*) hepatic NMF person suffering from a liver complaint NF (*= plante*) liverwort, hepatic (*SPÉC*) ◆ **les ~s** the Hepaticae (*SPÉC*)

hépatite /epatit/ NF hepatitis ◆ ~ **virale** viral hepatitis ◆ ~ **A/B/C** hepatitis A/B/C ◆ ~ **chronique/aiguë** chronic/acute hepatitis

hépatologie /epatɔlɔʒi/ NF hepatology

heptaèdre /ɛptaɛdʀ(ə)/ NM heptahedron

heptagonal, e (mpl **-aux**) /ɛptagɔnal, o/ ADJ heptagonal

heptagone /ɛptagɔn/ NM heptagon

heptasyllabe /ɛptasi(l)lab/ ADJ heptasyllabic NM heptasyllable

heptathlon /ɛptatlɔ̃/ NM heptathlon

heptathlonien, -ienne /ɛptatlɔnjɛ̃, jɛn/ NM,F heptathlete

Héra /eʀa/ NF Hera

Héraclite /eʀaklit/ NM Heraclitus

héraldique /eʀaldik/ ADJ heraldic NF heraldry

héraldiste /eʀaldist/ NMF heraldist, expert on heraldry

héraut /'eʀo/ NM 1 (*Hist*) ~ (**d'armes**) herald 2 (*littér*) herald, harbinger (*littér*)

herbacé, e /ɛʀbase/ ADJ herbaceous

herbage /ɛʀbaʒ/ NM (*= herbe*) pasture, pasturage; (*= pré*) pasture

herbager, -ère /ɛʀbaʒe, ɛʀ/ ADJ [*paysage*] grassy; [*région*] with lot of grazing land NM,F grazier

herbe /ɛʀb/ NF 1 (*= plante*) grass (*NonC*); (*= espèce*) grass ◆ **arracher une ~** to pull up a blade of grass ◆ **terrain en ~** field under grass ◆ **~s folles** wild grasses ◆ **jardin envahi par les ~s** weed-infested garden, garden overrun with weeds ◆ **dans les hautes ~s** in the long *ou* tall grass ◆ **faire de l'~ pour les lapins** to cut grass for rabbits ◆ **couper l'~ sous le pied de qn** to cut the ground *ou* pull the rug out from under sb's feet; → **déjeuner, mauvais**

2 (*Culin, Méd*) herb ◆ **~s médicinales/aromatiques/potagères** medicinal/aromatic/pot herbs ◆ **omelette/porc aux ~s** omelette/pork with herbs; → **fin**[1]

3 (** = drogue*) grass*, pot*

4 ◆ **en ~** [*blé*] in the blade (*attrib*); [*écrivain, chimiste*] budding

COMP **herbe au chantre** sisymbrium, hedge mustard

herbe à chat *ou* **aux chats** catmint, catnip

herbes de Provence herbes de Provence, ≃ mixed herbs

⚠ **herbe** se traduit par le mot anglais **herb** uniquement au sens culinaire ou médical.

herbeux, -euse /ɛʀbø, øz/ ADJ grassy

herbicide /ɛʀbisid/ ADJ herbicidal NM weedkiller, herbicide

herbier /ɛʀbje/ NM (*= collection*) herbarium; (*= planches*) set of illustrations of plants; (*= banc d'algues*) seagrass bed

herbivore /ɛʀbivɔʀ/ ADJ herbivorous NM herbivore

herborisation /ɛʀbɔʀizasjɔ̃/ NF (*= action*) collection of plants

herboriser /ɛʀbɔʀize/ ► conjug 1 ◄ VI to collect plants, to botanize

herboriste /ɛʀbɔʀist/ NMF herbalist

herboristerie /ɛʀbɔʀistəʀi/ NF (*= commerce*) herb trade; (*= magasin*) herbalist('s shop)

herbu, e /ɛʀby/ ADJ grassy

Hercule /ɛʀkyl/ NM (*Myth*) Hercules ◆ **c'est un ~** he's a real Hercules ◆ **hercule de foire** strongman; → **travail**[1]

herculéen, -enne /ɛʀkyleɛ̃, ɛn/ ADJ Herculean

hercynien, -ienne /ɛʀsinjɛ̃, jɛn/ ADJ Hercynian

hère /'ɛʀ/ NM (*frm*) ◆ **pauvre ~** poor *ou* miserable wretch

héréditaire /eʀeditɛʀ/ ADJ hereditary ◆ **c'est ~** (*hum*) it runs in the family

héréditairement /eʀeditɛʀmɑ̃/ ADV hereditarily ◆ **caractère ~ transmissible d'une maladie** (*Méd*) hereditary nature of an illness

hérédité /eʀedite/ NF 1 (*Bio*) heredity (*NonC*) ◆ **il a une lourde ~** *ou* **une ~ chargée** his family has a history of illness ◆ **une ~ catholique/royaliste** (*culturelle*) a Catholic/Royalist heritage 2 (*Jur*) (*= droit*) right of inheritance; (*= caractère héréditaire*) hereditary nature

hérésiarque /eʀezjaʀk/ NM heresiarch

hérésie /eʀezi/ NF (*Rel*) heresy; (*fig*) sacrilege, heresy ◆ **servir du vin rouge avec le poisson est une véritable ~ !** (*hum*) it's absolute sacrilege to serve red wine with fish!

hérétique /eʀetik/ ADJ heretical NMF heretic

hérissé, e /'eʀise/ (ptp de **hérisser**) ADJ 1 (*= dressé*) [*poils, cheveux*] standing on end, bristling; [*barbe*] bristly 2 (*= garni*) **tête ~e de cheveux roux** head bristling with red hair ◆ **~ de poils** bristling with hairs ◆ **~ d'épines/de clous** spiked with thorns/nails ◆ **un poisson au corps ~ de piquants** a fish covered in spines ◆ **les routes sont ~es de pancartes** there are signs everywhere along the roads ◆ **cette traduction est ~e de difficultés** the translation is full of difficulties 3 (*= garni de pointes*) [*cactus, tige*] prickly

hérisser /'eʀise/ ► conjug 1 ◄ VT 1 [*animal*] **le chat hérisse ses poils** the cat bristles its coat *ou* makes its coat bristle ◆ **le porc-épic hérisse ses piquants** the porcupine bristles its spines *ou* makes its spines bristle ◆ **l'oiseau hérisse ses plumes** the bird ruffles its feathers

2 [*vent, froid*] **le vent hérisse ses cheveux** the wind makes his hair stand on end

3 (*= armer*) **~ une planche de clous** to spike a plank with nails ◆ **~ une muraille de créneaux** to top *ou* crown a wall with battlements

4 (*= garnir*) **des clous hérissent la planche** the plank is spiked with nails ◆ **les créneaux qui hérissent la muraille** the battlements crowning the wall ◆ **de nombreuses difficultés hérissent le texte** numerous difficulties are scattered through the text

5 (*= mettre en colère*) **~ qn** to put *ou* get sb's back up*, to make sb's hackles rise ◆ **il y a une chose qui me hérisse (les poils*), c'est le mensonge** there's one thing that gets my back up* and that's lying

VPR **se hérisser** 1 [*poils, cheveux*] to stand on end, to bristle ◆ **ses poils se sont hérissés quand il a entendu ça** his hackles rose when he heard that

2 [*animal*] to bristle ◆ **le chat se hérissa** the cat's fur stood on end *ou* bristled, the cat bristled

3 (*= se fâcher*) to bristle, to get one's back up* ◆ **il se hérisse facilement** it's easy to get his back up*

hérisson /'eʀisɔ̃/ NM 1 (*= animal*) hedgehog ◆ **~ de mer** sea urchin ◆ **c'est un vrai ~** (*péj*) he's very prickly 2 [*de ramoneur*] (chimney sweep's) brush, flue brush; (*= égouttoir*) draining rack (*for bottles*); (*= herse*) beater

héritage /eʀitaʒ/ NM 1 (*= action*) inheritance 2 [*d'argent, biens*] inheritance, legacy; [*de coutumes, système*] heritage, legacy ◆ **faire un ~** to come into an inheritance ◆ **laisser qch en ~ à qn** to leave sth to sb, to bequeath sth to sb ◆ **l'~ du passé** the heritage *ou* legacy of the past ◆ **un tel déficit est un lourd ~** a deficit like that is a heavy burden to inherit

hériter /eʀite/ ► conjug 1 ◄ VT, **hériter de** VT INDIR [*+ maison, tradition, culture, qualités*] to inherit; (*hum*) [*+ punition*] to get ◆ **~ d'une fortune** to come into *ou* inherit a fortune ◆ **~ de son oncle** to inherit *ou* come into one's uncle's property ◆ **il a hérité de la maison de son oncle** he inherited his uncle's house ◆ **qui hériterait ?** who would benefit from the will?, who would inherit? ◆ **impatient d'~, il ...** eager to come into *ou* to gain his inheritance, he ... ◆ **et maintenant un bateau ? ils ont hérité !** (*hum*) and now they've got a boat? they must have won the lottery *ou* the pools (*Brit*)! ◆ **il a hérité d'un vieux chapeau** he has fallen heir to *ou* he has inherited an old hat ◆ **il a hérité d'un rhume** he's picked up a cold ◆ **ils ont hérité d'une situation catastrophique** they inherited a disastrous situation

héritier /eʀitje/ NM heir ◆ **~ naturel** heir-at-law ◆ **~ testamentaire** legatee ◆ **~ légitime** legitimate heir ◆ **~ présomptif de la couronne** heir apparent (to the throne) ◆ **~ d'une grande fortune/d'une longue tradition** heir to a large fortune/a long tradition ◆ **elle lui a donné un ~** (*hum*) she gave him an heir *ou* a son and heir

héritière /eʀitjɛʀ/ NF heiress

hermaphrodisme /ɛʀmafʀɔdism/ NM hermaphroditism

hermaphrodite /ɛʀmafʀɔdit/ ADJ hermaphrodite, hermaphroditic(al) NM hermaphrodite

herméneutique /ɛʀmenøtik/ ADJ hermeneutic NF hermeneutics (*sg*)

Hermès /ɛʀmɛs/ NM Hermes

hermétique /ɛʀmetik/ ADJ [1] (*= étanche*) [*récipient*] (*à l'air*) airtight; (*à l'eau*) watertight ◆ **cela assure une fermeture ~ de la porte** this makes sure that the door closes tightly *ou* that the door is a tight fit [2] (*= impénétrable*) [*secret*] impenetrable ◆ **visage ~** closed *ou* impenetrable expression ◆ **être ~ à** to be impervious to ◆ **il est ~ à ce genre de peinture** this kind of painting is a closed book to him [3] (*= obscur*) [*écrivain, livre*] abstruse, obscure [4] (*Alchimie, Littérat*) Hermetic

hermétiquement /ɛʀmetikmɑ̃/ ADV [1] [*fermer, joindre*] tightly, hermetically ◆ **emballage ~ fermé** hermetically sealed package ◆ **pièce ~ close** sealed(-up) room [2] [*s'exprimer*] abstrusely, obscurely

hermétisme /ɛʀmetism/ NM (*péj = obscurité*) abstruseness, obscurity; (*Alchimie, Littérat*) hermetism

hermine /ɛʀmin/ NF [1] (*= animal*) (*brune*) stoat; (*blanche*) ermine [2] (*= fourrure, blason*) ermine

herminette /ɛʀminɛt/ NF adze

Hermione /ɛʀmjɔn/ NF Hermione

herniaire /ˈɛʀnjɛʀ/ ADJ hernial; → **bandage**

hernie /ˈɛʀni/ NF (*Méd*) hernia, rupture; [*de pneu*] bulge ◆ **~ discale** herniated (*SPÉC*) *ou* slipped disc ◆ **~ étranglée** strangulated hernia

héro * /eʀo/ NF (abrév de **héroïne 2**) heroin, smack*‡*

Hérode /eʀɔd/ NM Herod; → **vieux**

Hérodiade /eʀɔdjad/ NF Herodias

Hérodote /eʀɔdɔt/ NM Herodotus

héroïcomique /eʀɔikɔmik/ ADJ mock-heroic

héroïne[1] /eʀɔin/ NF (*= femme*) heroine

héroïne[2] /eʀɔin/ NF (*= drogue*) heroin

héroïnomane /eʀɔinɔman/ ADJ addicted to heroin, heroin-addicted (*épith*) NMF heroin addict

héroïnomanie /eʀɔinɔmani/ NF heroin addiction

héroïque /eʀɔik/ ADJ heroic ◆ **l'époque ~** the pioneering days ◆ **les temps ~s** the heroic age

héroïquement /eʀɔikmɑ̃/ ADV heroically

héroïsme /eʀɔism/ NM heroism ◆ **manger ça, c'est de l'~ !*** eating that is nothing short of heroic! *ou* of heroism!

héron /ˈeʀɔ̃/ NM heron ◆ **~ cendré** grey heron

héros /ˈeʀo/ NM hero ◆ **mourir en ~** to die the death of a hero *ou* a hero's death ◆ **ils ont été accueillis en ~** they were given a hero's welcome ◆ **~ national** national hero ◆ **~ de la Résistance** hero of the (French) Resistance ◆ **le ~ du jour** the hero of the day

herpès /ɛʀpɛs/ NM (*gén*) herpes ◆ **~ génital** genital herpes ◆ **avoir de l'~** (*autour de la bouche*) to have a cold sore

herpétique /ɛʀpetik/ ADJ herpetic

hersage /ˈɛʀsaʒ/ NM (*Agr*) harrowing

herse /ˈɛʀs/ NF (*Agr*) harrow; [*de château*] portcullis; (*Théât*) batten

herser /ˈɛʀse/ ▸ conjug 1 ◂ VT (*Agr*) to harrow

hertz /ɛʀts/ NM hertz

hertzien, -ienne /ɛʀtsjɛ̃, jɛn/ ADJ [*ondes*] Hertzian; [*chaîne, diffusion, télévision*] terrestrial ◆ **réseau ~** (TV) terrestrial network; (*Radio*) radio-relay network

hésitant, e /ezitɑ̃, ɑ̃t/ ADJ [*personne, début*] hesitant; [*caractère*] wavering, hesitant; [*voix, pas*] hesitant, faltering

hésitation /ezitasjɔ̃/ NF hesitation ◆ **marquer une ~** *ou* **un temps d'~** to hesitate ◆ **j'accepte sans ~** I accept without hesitation *ou* unhesitatingly ◆ **après bien des ~s** after much hesitation ◆ **il eut un moment d'~ et répondit ...** he hesitated for a moment and replied ..., after a moment's hesitation he replied ... ◆ **je n'ai plus d'~s** I shall hesitate no longer ◆ **ses ~s continuelles** his continual hesitations *ou* dithering

hésiter /ezite/ GRAMMAIRE ACTIVE 36.2 ▸ conjug 1 ◂ VI [1] (*= balancer*) to hesitate ◆ **tu y vas ? – j'hésite** are you going? – I'm in two minds about it *ou* I'm not sure ◆ **il n'y a pas à ~** you don't need to think twice about it ◆ **sans ~** without hesitating, unhesitatingly ◆ **~ à faire** to hesitate to do, to be unsure whether to do ◆ **j'hésite à vous déranger** I don't want to disturb you ◆ **il hésitait sur la route à prendre** he hesitated as to which road to take, he dithered over which road to take (*Brit*) ◆ **~ sur une date** to hesitate over a date ◆ **~ entre plusieurs possibilités** to hesitate *ou* waver between several possibilities
[2] (*= s'arrêter*) to hesitate ◆ **~ dans ses réponses** to be hesitant in one's replies ◆ **~ en récitant sa leçon** to recite one's lesson falteringly *ou* hesitantly ◆ **~ devant l'obstacle** to falter *ou* hesitate before an obstacle

Hespérides /ɛspeʀid/ NFPL ◆ **les ~** the Hesperides

hétaïre /etaiʀ/ NF (*= prostituée*) courtesan; (*Antiq*) hetaera

hétéro * /eteʀo/ ADJ, NMF (abrév de **hétérosexuel**) hetero * (*épith*), straight *

hétéroclite /eteʀɔklit/ ADJ (*= disparate*) [*ensemble, roman, bâtiment*] heterogeneous; [*objets*] sundry, ill-assorted ◆ **pièce meublée de façon ~** room filled with a miscellaneous *ou* an ill-assorted collection of furniture

hétérodoxe /eteʀɔdɔks/ ADJ heterodox

hétérodoxie /eteʀɔdɔksi/ NF heterodoxy

hétérogamie /eteʀɔgami/ NF heterogamy

hétérogène /eteʀɔʒɛn/ ADJ heterogeneous ◆ **c'est un groupe très ~** it's a very mixed *ou* heterogeneous group

hétérogénéité /eteʀɔʒeneite/ NF heterogeneousness

hétérosexualité /eteʀosɛksɥalite/ NF heterosexuality

hétérosexuel, -elle /eteʀosɛksɥɛl/ ADJ, NM,F heterosexual

hétérozygote /eteʀozigɔt/ ADJ heterozygous NMF heterozygote

hêtraie /ˈɛtʀɛ/ NF beech grove

hêtre /ˈɛtʀ/ NM (*= arbre*) beech (tree); (*= bois*) beech (wood) ◆ **~ pourpre/pleureur** copper/weeping beech

heu /ˈø/ EXCL (*doute*) h'm!, hem!; (*hésitation*) um!, er!

heur †† /œʀ/ NM good fortune ◆ **je n'ai pas eu l'~ de lui plaire** (*littér, iro*) I did not have the good fortune to please him, I was not fortunate enough to please him

heure /œʀ/
NOM FÉMININ

[1] = mesure de durée hour ◆ **les ~s passaient vite/lentement** the hours went by quickly/slowly ◆ **l'~ tourne** time passes ◆ **j'ai attendu une bonne ~/une petite ~** I waited (for) a good hour/just under an hour ◆ **j'ai attendu 2 ~s d'horloge** I waited 2 solid hours ◆ **il a parlé des ~s** he spoke for hours ◆ **~ (de cours)** (*Scol*) class, ≈ period (*Brit*) ◆ **j'ai deux ~s de français aujourd'hui** ≈ I've two periods of French today ◆ **pendant les ~s de classe/de bureau** during school/office *ou* business hours ◆ **gagner/coûter 15 € de l'~** to earn/cost €15 an hour *ou* per hour ◆ **1 ~/3 ~s de travail** 1 hour's/3 hours' work ◆ **cela représente 400 ~s de travail** *ou* **400 ~s-homme** it represents 400 hours of work *ou* 400 man-hours ◆ **il me faut 12 ~s-machine** I need 12 hours' computer time ◆ **faire beaucoup d'~s** to put in long hours ◆ **lutter pour la semaine de 30 ~s (de travail)** to campaign for a 30-hour (working) week ◆ **c'est à plus d'une ~ de Paris** it's more than an hour (away) from Paris *ou* more than an hour's run from Paris ◆ **c'est à 2 ~s de route** it's 2 hours (away) by road ◆ **il y a 2 ~s de route** *ou* **voiture/train** it's a 2-hour drive/train journey, it takes 2 hours by car/train (to get there) ◆ **24 ~s sur 24** round the clock, 24 hours a day ◆ **ce sera fait dans les 24 ~s/48 ~s** it'll be done within 24 hours/48 hours

◆ **à l'heure** ◆ **être payé à l'~** [*travail*] to be paid by the hour; [*personne*] to be paid by the hour, to get an hourly rate ◆ **faire du 100 (km) à l'~** to do 100 km an hour *ou* per hour; → **réception, supplémentaire**

[2] = division de la journée **savoir l'~** to know what time it is, to know the time ◆ **quelle ~ est-il ?** what time is it? ◆ **quelle ~ as-tu ?** what time do you make it? ◆ **avez-vous l'~ ?** have you got the time? ◆ **tu as vu l'~ (qu'il est) ?** do you realize what time it is? ◆ **il est 6 ~s/6 ~s 10/6 ~s moins 10/6 ~s et demie** it is 6 (o'clock)/10 past *ou* after (*US*) 6/10 to *ou* of (*US*) 6/half past *ou* after (*US*) 6 ◆ **10 ~s du matin/du soir** 10 (o'clock) in the morning/at night, 10 a.m./p.m. ◆ **à 16 ~s 30** at 4.30 p.m., at 16.30 (*Admin*) ◆ **il est 8 ~s passées** *ou* **sonnées** it's gone 8 ◆ **à 4 ~s pile** * *ou* **sonnant(es)** *ou* **tapant(es)** * *ou* **pétant(es)**‡ at exactly 4 (o'clock), at dead on 4 (o'clock) * (*Brit*), at 4 (o'clock) on the dot * ◆ **à 4 ~s juste(s)** at 4 sharp ◆ **je prendrai le train de 6 ~s** I'll take the 6 o'clock train ◆ **les bus passent à l'~/à l'~ et à la demie** the buses come on the hour/on the hour and on the half hour ◆ **à une ~ avancée (de la nuit)** late at night ◆ **jusqu'à une ~ avancée (de la nuit)** late *ou* well into the night ◆ **ils ont joué aux échecs jusqu'à pas** * *ou* **point** * (*hum*) **d'~** they played chess into the early hours ◆ **se coucher à pas * d'~** to stay up till all hours ◆ **demain, à la première ~** (*= très tôt*) tomorrow at first light

◆ **de la première heure** ◆ **il fut un partisan de la première ~ de De Gaulle** he was a follower of De Gaulle from the beginning

◆ **de la dernière** *ou* **onzième heure** ◆ **les ouvriers de la dernière** *ou* **onzième ~** people who turn up when the work is almost finished ◆ **collaborateur/candidat de la dernière ~** last-minute helper/candidate

◆ **de bonne heure** (*dans la journée*) early; (*dans la vie*) early in life; → **lever**[1]

◆ **d'heure en heure** with each passing hour, hour by hour ◆ **le pays entier suit le sauvetage d'~ en ~** the whole country is following every minute of the rescue operation ◆ **son inquiétude grandissait d'~ en ~** hour by hour *ou* as the hours went by he grew more (and more) anxious, he grew hourly more anxious

◆ **d'une heure à l'autre** (*= incessamment*) ◆ **nous l'attendons d'une ~ à l'autre** we are expecting him any time (now) ◆ **la situation évolue d'une ~ à l'autre** (*= rapidement*) the situation changes from one moment to the next

[3] = moment fixé time ◆ **c'est l'~ !** (*de rendre un devoir*) time's up! ◆ **c'est l'~ de rentrer/d'aller au lit !** it's time to go home!/for bed! ◆ **avant l'~** before time, ahead of time, early ◆ **un homme vieilli avant l'~** a man grown old before his time ◆ **un cubiste avant l'~** a cubist before the term was ever invented ◆ **après l'~** late ◆ **venez quand vous voulez, je n'ai pas d'~** come when you like, I have no fixed timetable *ou* schedule, come when you like, any time suits me ◆ **~ de Greenwich** Greenwich mean time ◆ **~ légale/locale** standard/local time ◆ **il est midi, ~ locale/~ de Paris** it's

noon, local time/Paris time ◆ **nous venons de passer à l'~ d'hiver** we have just put the clocks back ◆ **~ d'été, ~ avancée** *(Can)* daylight saving(s) time, (British) summer time *(Brit)* ◆ **passer à l'~ d'été** to go over *ou* change to summer time ◆ **l'~ militaire** the right *ou* exact time ◆ **l'~ c'est l'~, avant l'~ ce n'est pas l'~, après l'~ ce n'est plus l'~** * a minute late is a minute too late ◆ **il n'y a pas d'~ pour les braves** *(hum)* any time is a good time; → **laitier**

◆ **à l'heure** ◆ **arriver/être à l'~** *[personne, train]* to arrive/be on time ◆ **ma montre/l'horloge est toujours à l'~** my watch/the clock is always right *ou* keeps good time ◆ **ma montre n'est pas à l'~** my watch is wrong ◆ **mettre sa montre à l'~** to set *ou* put one's watch right; → **remettre**

4 [= moment] time, moment ◆ **je n'ai pas une ~ à moi** I haven't a moment to myself ◆ **l'~ est venue** *ou* **a sonné** *(frm)* the time has come ◆ **nous avons passé ensemble des ~s merveilleuses** we spent many happy hours together ◆ **à ~s fixes** at fixed times ◆ **~s d'ouverture/de fermeture** opening/closing times ◆ **elle fait ses courses pendant son ~ de table** she does her shopping during the *ou* her lunch hour ◆ **les problèmes de l'~** the problems of the moment ◆ **l'~ est grave** it is a grave moment ◆ **l'~ est à la concertation** it is now time for consultation and dialogue, dialogue is now the order of the day ◆ **l'~ n'est pas à la rigolade** * this is no time for laughing *ou* for jokes ◆ **"Paris à l'heure écossaise"** "Paris goes Scottish" ◆ **à l'époque, tout le monde vivait à l'~ américaine** at that time everybody wanted an American lifestyle

◆ **l'heure de** ◆ **l'~ du déjeuner** lunchtime, time for lunch ◆ **l'~ d'aller se coucher** bedtime, time for bed ◆ **l'~ du biberon** (baby's) feeding time ◆ **à l'~** *ou* **aux ~s des repas** at mealtime(s) ◆ **l'~ des mamans** *(en maternelle)* home time ◆ **l'~ de la sortie** *[d'écoliers, ouvriers]* time to go home ◆ **travailler/rester jusqu'à l'~ de la sortie** to work/stay until it is time to go home

◆ **à l'heure qu'il est, à cette heure** at this moment in time, at present ◆ **à l'~ qu'il est, nous ignorons encore ...** at present we still don't know ... ◆ **à l'~ qu'il est, il devrait être rentré** he should be home by now ◆ **selon les informations dont nous disposons à cette ~ ...** according to the latest information ...; → **creux, H**

◆ **à l'heure de** ◆ **à l'~ de notre mort** at the hour of our death ◆ **à l'~ de la mondialisation, il est important d'être compétitif** with the advent of globalization, it is important to be competitive ◆ **la France à l'~ de l'ordinateur** France in the computer age ◆ **il faut mettre nos universités à l'~ de l'Europe** our universities have got to start thinking in terms of Europe *ou* start thinking European

◆ **à l'heure actuelle** *(= en ce moment)* at the moment; *(= à notre époque)* at present ◆ **à l'~ actuelle, il se trouve à New York** he's in New York at the moment ◆ **il n'existe pas, à l'~ actuelle, de remède** at present there is no cure

◆ **à toute heure** at any time (of the day) ◆ **repas chauds à toute ~** hot meals all day ◆ **à toute ~ du jour et de la nuit** at every hour of the day and night

◆ **pour l'heure** for the time being ◆ **pour l'~, rien n'est décidé** nothing has been decided as yet *ou* for the time being

◆ **sur l'heure** *(littér)* at once ◆ **il décommanda sur l'~ tous ses rendez-vous** he immediately cancelled all his meetings

5 [locutions]

◆ *adjectif possessif* + **heure** ◆ **il est poète/aimable à ses ~s** he writes poetry/he can be quite pleasant when the fancy takes him *ou* when he's in the mood ◆ **ce doit être Paul - c'est son ~** it must be Paul - it's his (usual) time ◆ **votre ~ sera la mienne** name *ou* say a time ◆ **elle a eu son ~ de gloire/de célébrité** she has had her hour of glory/fame ◆ **il aura son ~** *(de gloire etc)* his hour *ou* time will come ◆ **il attend son ~** he is biding his time *ou* waiting for the right moment ◆ **son ~ viendra/est venue** *(de mourir)* his time will come/has come ◆ **sa dernière ~ a sonné** his time has come *ou* is up

◆ **à la bonne heure!** * *(= très bien)* that's fine!; *(iro)* that's a fine idea! *(iro)*

6 [Rel] **~s canoniales** canonical hours ◆ **Grandes/Petites ~s** night/daylight offices; → **livre[1]**

heureusement /øʀøzmɑ̃/ **ADV** 1 *(= par bonheur, tant mieux)* fortunately, luckily ◆ **~, il n'y avait personne** fortunately, there was no one there ◆ **~ pour lui !** fortunately *ou* luckily for him! ◆ **il est parti, ~ !, ~ qu'il est parti** * thank goodness he's gone 2 *(= judicieusement)* happily ◆ **mot ~ choisi** well *ou* felicitously *(frm)* chosen word ◆ **phrase ~ tournée** cleverly turned sentence 3 *(= favorablement)* successfully ◆ **l'entreprise fut ~ menée à terme** the task was successfully completed ◆ **tout s'est ~ terminé** it all turned out well in the end

heureux, -euse /øʀø, øz/ GRAMMAIRE ACTIVE 30, 38.1, 38.3, 51.1, 51.2, 52.4 **ADJ** 1 *(gén après n = rempli de bonheur) [personne, souvenir, vie]* happy ◆ **il a tout pour être ~** he has everything he needs to be happy *ou* to make him happy ◆ **ils vécurent ~** *(dans un conte)* they lived happily ever after ◆ **~ comme un poisson dans l'eau** *ou* **comme un roi** *ou* **comme un pape** happy as Larry * *(Brit)* *ou* a sandboy *(Brit)* *ou* a clam *(US)* ◆ **~ celui qui ... !** happy is he who ...! ◆ **~ les simples d'esprit** *(Bible)* blessed are the poor in spirit ◆ **ces jouets vont faire des ~ !** these toys will make some children very happy! ◆ **ne jette pas tes vieux livres, ça pourrait faire des ~** don't throw away your old books, some people might be glad of them *ou* glad to have them; → **bon[1]**

2 *(= satisfait)* happy, pleased ◆ **je suis très ~ d'apprendre la nouvelle** I am very glad *ou* happy *ou* pleased to hear the news ◆ **M. et Mme Durand sont ~ de vous annoncer ...** Mr and Mrs Durand are happy *ou* pleased to announce ... ◆ **je suis ~ de ce résultat** I am pleased *ou* happy with this result ◆ **je suis ~ de cette rencontre** I am pleased *ou* glad about this meeting ◆ **il sera trop ~ de vous aider** he'll be only too glad *ou* happy *ou* pleased to help you ◆ **~ de vous revoir** nice *ou* good *ou* pleased to see you again ◆ **alors, heureuse ?** *(hum)* how was it for you? *(hum)*

3 *(gén avant n = qui a de la chance) [personne]* fortunate, lucky ◆ **~ au jeu/en amour** lucky at cards/in love ◆ **~ au jeu, malheureux en amour** lucky at cards, unlucky in love ◆ **c'est ~ (pour lui) que** it is fortunate *ou* lucky (for him) that ◆ **il accepte de venir – c'est encore ~ !** he's willing to come – it's just as well! *ou* I should think so too! ◆ **encore ~ que je m'en sois souvenu !** it's just as well *ou* it's lucky *ou* it's a good thing that I remembered!; → **élu, main**

4 *(gén avant n = optimiste, agréable) [disposition, caractère]* happy, cheerful; → **nature**

5 *(= judicieux) [décision, choix]* fortunate, happy; *[formule, expression, effet, mélange]* happy, felicitous *(frm)* ◆ **un ~ mariage de styles** a successful combination of styles

6 *(= favorable) [présage]* propitious, happy; *[résultat, issue]* happy ◆ **par un ~ hasard** by a fortunate coincidence ◆ **attendre un ~ événement** to be expecting a happy event

heuristique /øʀistik/ **ADJ** heuristic **NF** heuristics *(sg)*

heurt /'œʀ/ **NM** 1 *(= choc) [de voitures]* collision; *[d'objets]* bump 2 *(= conflit)* clash ◆ **il y a eu des ~s entre la police et les manifestants** there were clashes between the police and the demonstrators ◆ **sans ~(s)** *[se passer]* smoothly ◆ **la réforme ne se fera pas sans ~s** the reform will not have a smooth passage ◆ **leur amitié ne va pas sans quelques ~s** their friendship has its ups and downs *ou* goes through occasional rough patches

heurté, e /'œʀte/ (ptp de **heurter**) **ADJ** *[style, jeu, carrière]* jerky, uneven; *[discours]* jerky, halting

heurter /'œʀte/ ▸ conjug 1 ◂ **VT** 1 *(= cogner) [+ objet]* to strike, to hit; *[+ personne]* to collide with; *[+ voiture]* to bump into; *(= bousculer)* to jostle ◆ **~ qch du coude/du pied** to strike *ou* hit sth with one's elbow/foot ◆ **la voiture a heurté un arbre** the car ran into *ou* struck a tree

2 *(= choquer) [+ personne, préjugés]* to offend; *[+ théorie, bon goût, bon sens, tradition]* to go against, to run counter to; *[+ amour-propre]* to upset; *[+ opinions]* to conflict *ou* clash with ◆ **~ qn de front** to clash head-on with sb

VI ◆ **~ à** to knock at *ou* on ◆ **~ contre qch** *[personne]* to stumble against sth; *[objet]* to knock *ou* bang against sth

VPR **se heurter** 1 *(= s'entrechoquer) [passants, voitures]* to collide (with each other); *[objets]* to hit one another ◆ **ses idées se heurtaient dans sa tête** his head was a jumble of ideas, ideas jostled about in his head

2 *(= s'opposer) [personnes, opinions, couleurs]* to clash (with each other)

3 *(= cogner contre)* **se ~ à** *ou* **contre qn/qch** to collide with sb/sth ◆ **se ~ à un refus** to meet with *ou* come up against a refusal ◆ **se ~ à un problème** to come up against a problem

heurtoir /'œʀtwaʀ/ **NM** *[de porte]* (door) knocker; *(Tech = butoir)* stop; *(Rail)* buffer

hévéa /evea/ **NM** hevea, rubber tree

hexadécimal, e (mpl **-aux**) /ɛgzadesimal, o/ **ADJ** hexadecimal

hexaèdre /ɛgzaɛdʀ/ **ADJ** hexahedral **NM** hexahedron

hexaédrique /ɛgzaedʀik/ **ADJ** hexahedral

hexagonal, e (mpl **-aux**) /ɛgzagɔnal, o/ **ADJ** 1 *(Géom)* hexagonal 2 *(= français) [politique, frontière]* national; *(péj) [conception]* chauvinistic

hexagone /ɛgzagɔn/ **NM** 1 *(Géom)* hexagon 2 ◆ **l'Hexagone** (metropolitan) France

hexamètre /ɛgzamɛtʀ/ **ADJ** hexameter *(épith)*, hexametric(al) **NM** hexameter

Hezbollah /ɛzbɔla/ **NM** ◆ **le ~** Hezbollah

HF (abrév de **haute fréquence**) HF, h.f.

hiatal, e (mpl **-aux**) /'jatal, o/ **ADJ** hiatal, hiatus *(épith)* ◆ **hernie ~e** hiatus hernia

hiatus /'jatys/ **NM** *(Anat, Ling)* hiatus; *(= incompatibilité)* gap, discrepancy *(entre* between)

hibernal, e (mpl **-aux**) /ibɛʀnal, o/ **ADJ** winter *(épith)*, hibernal *(frm)*

hibernation /ibɛʀnasjɔ̃/ **NF** hibernation ◆ **~ artificielle** *(Méd)* induced hypothermia

hiberner /ibɛʀne/ ▸ conjug 1 ◂ **VI** to hibernate

hibiscus /ibiskys/ **NM** hibiscus

hibou (pl **hiboux**) /'ibu/ **NM** owl ◆ **(vieux) ~** * *(péj)* crusty old bird * *ou* beggar * *ou* devil *

hic * /'ik/ **NM** ◆ **c'est là le ~** that's the snag *ou* the trouble ◆ **il y a un ~** there's a snag *ou* slight problem

hic et nunc /'ikɛtnɔ̃k/ **LOC ADV** immediately, at once, there and then

hickory /'ikɔʀi/ **NM** hickory

hidalgo /idalgo/ **NM** hidalgo ◆ **un bel ~** *(hum)* a dark dashing Spaniard *(ou* Italian *etc)*

hideur /'idœʀ/ NF (littér) hideousness (NonC)

hideusement /'idøzmɑ̃/ ADV hideously

hideux, -euse /'idø, øz/ ADJ hideous

hidjab /'idʒab/ NM hijab

hier /jɛʀ/ ADV yesterday ◆ ~ **(au) soir** yesterday evening, last night *ou* evening ◆ **toute la matinée d'~** all yesterday morning ◆ **toute la journée d'~** all day yesterday ◆ **il avait tout ~ pour se décider** he had all (day) yesterday to make up his mind ◆ **je m'en souviens comme si c'était ~** I remember it as if it was *ou* were yesterday; → **dater, naître**

hiérarchie /'jeʀaʀʃi/ NF hierarchy; *(= supérieurs)* superiors

hiérarchique /'jeʀaʀʃik/ ADJ hierarchic(al) ◆ **chef** *ou* **supérieur ~** superior, senior in rank *ou* in the hierarchy; → **voie**

hiérarchiquement /'jeʀaʀʃikmɑ̃/ ADV hierarchically

hiérarchisation /'jeʀaʀʃizasjɔ̃/ NF *(= action)* organization into a hierarchy; *(= organisation)* hierarchical organization ◆ **la ~ des tâches** the prioritization of tasks

hiérarchiser /'jeʀaʀʃize/ ▸ conjug 1 ◂ VT *[+ structure]* to organize into a hierarchy; *[+ tâches]* to prioritize ◆ **institution/société hiérarchisée** hierarchical institution/society ◆ **hiérarchisons ces questions** let's sort out these questions in order of priority

hiératique /'jeʀatik/ ADJ hieratic

hiératisme /'jeʀatism/ NM hieratic quality

hiéroglyphe /'jeʀɔglif/ NM hieroglyph(ic) ◆ **~s** *(= plusieurs symboles)* hieroglyph(ic)s; *(= système d'écriture, aussi péj)* hieroglyphics

hiéroglyphique /'jeʀɔglifik/ ADJ hieroglyphic(al)

hi-fi /'ifi/ ADJ INV, NF INV (abrév de **high fidelity**) hi-fi

high-tech /'ajtɛk/ ADJ INV, NM INV (abrév de **high technology**) hi-tech, high-tech

hi-han /'iɑ̃/ EXCL heehaw!

hi-hi /hihi/ EXCL *(rire)* tee-hee!, hee-hee!; *(pleurs)* boo hoo!, sniff-sniff!

hijab /'iʒab/ NM hijab

hilarant, e /ilaʀɑ̃, ɑ̃t/ ADJ *[film, scène, aventure]* hilarious, side-splitting; → **gaz**

hilare /ilaʀ/ ADJ *[visage, personne]* beaming ◆ **il était ~** he was beaming all over his face

hilarité /ilaʀite/ NF hilarity, mirth ◆ **provoquer** *ou* **déclencher l'~ générale** to cause great mirth

hile /'il/ NM *(Anat, Bot)* hilum

hilote /ilɔt/ NM ⇒ **ilote**

Himalaya /imalaja/ NM ◆ **l'~** the Himalayas ◆ **escalader un sommet de l'~** to climb one of the Himalayan peaks *ou* one of the peaks in the Himalayas

himalayen, -yenne /imalajɛ̃, jɛn/ ADJ Himalayan

hindi /indi/ NM Hindi

hindou, e /ɛ̃du/ ADJ *[coutumes, dialecte]* Hindu; † *[nationalité]* Indian NM,F **Hindou(e)** *(= croyant)* Hindu; *(† = citoyen)* Indian

hindouisme /ɛ̃duism/ NM Hinduism

hindouiste /ɛ̃duist/ ADJ, NMF Hindu

Hindoustan /ɛ̃dustɑ̃/ NM Hindustan

hindoustani /ɛ̃dustani/ NM Hindustani

hip /'ip/ EXCL ◆ ~ ~ ~ **hourra!** hip hip hurray! *ou* hurrah!

hip(-)hop /ipɔp/ NM *(Mus)* hip-hop

hippie /'ipi/ ADJ, NMF hippy

hippique /ipik/ ADJ horse *(épith)*, equestrian ◆ **chronique ~** racing news *(sg)* ◆ **le sport ~** equestrian sport

hippisme /ipism/ NM (horse) riding, equestrianism

hippo* /ipo/ NM (abrév de **hippopotame**) hippo*

hippocampe /ipɔkɑ̃p/ NM *(Anat, Myth)* hippocampus; *(= poisson)* sea horse

Hippocrate /ipɔkʀat/ NM Hippocrates; → **serment**

hippocratisme /ipɔkʀatism/ NM *(Méd)* *(= doctrine)* Hippocratism ◆ **~ digital** Hippocratic *ou* clubbed fingers

hippodrome /ipodʀom/ NM *(= champ de courses)* racecourse *(Brit)*, racetrack *(US)*; *(Antiq)* hippodrome

hippogriffe /ipogʀif/ NM hippogriff, hippogryph

Hippolyte /ipɔlit/ NM Hippolytus

hippomobile /ipomɔbil/ ADJ horse-drawn

hippophagique /ipɔfaʒik/ ADJ ◆ **boucherie ~** horse(meat) butcher's

hippopotame /ipɔpɔtam/ NM hippopotamus, hippo* ◆ **c'est un vrai ~*** he *(ou* she) is like an elephant* *ou* a hippo*

hippy (pl **hippies**) /'ipi/ ADJ, NMF ⇒ **hippie**

hirondelle /iʀɔ̃dɛl/ NF 1 *(= oiseau)* swallow ◆ **~ de fenêtre/de rivage** house/sand martin ◆ **~ de cheminée** barn swallow ◆ **~ de mer** tern ◆ **une ~ ne fait pas le printemps** *(Prov)* one swallow doesn't make a summer *(Prov)* → **nid** 2 *(† * = policier)* (bicycle-riding) policeman

Hiroshima /'iʀɔʃima/ N Hiroshima

hirsute /iʀsyt/ ADJ 1 *(= ébouriffé)* *[tête]* tousled; *[personne]* shaggy-haired; *[barbe]* shaggy ◆ **un individu ~** a shaggy-haired *ou* hirsute individual 2 *(Méd)* hirsute

hirsutisme /iʀsytism/ NM *(Méd)* hirsutism

hispanique /ispanik/ ADJ Hispanic

hispanisant, e /ispanizɑ̃, ɑ̃t/ NM,F *(= spécialiste)* hispanist; *(= étudiant)* Spanish scholar

hispanisme /ispanism/ NM hispanicism

hispaniste /ispanist/ NMF ⇒ **hispanisant**

hispanité /ispanite/ NF Spanish identity

hispano-américain, e (mpl **hispano-américains**) /ispanoameʀikɛ̃, ɛn/ ADJ Spanish-American NM *(= langue)* Latin American Spanish NM,F **Hispano-Américain(e)** Spanish-American, Hispanic *(US)*

hispano-arabe (mpl **hispano-arabes**) /ispanoaʀab/, **hispano-mauresque** (mpl **hispano-mauresques**) /ispanomɔʀɛsk/ ADJ Hispano-Moresque

hispanophone /ispanɔfɔn/ ADJ Spanish-speaking; *[littérature]* Spanish-language *(épith)*, in Spanish *(attrib)* NMF Spanish speaker

hisse /'is/ **oh hisse** LOC EXCL heave ho!

hisser /'ise/ ▸ conjug 1 ◂ VT *(Naut)* to hoist; *(= soulever)* *[+ objet]* to hoist, to haul up, to heave up; *[+ personne]* to haul up, to heave up ◆ **~ les couleurs** to run up *ou* hoist the colours ◆ **hissez les voiles !** up sails! ◆ **~ qn au pouvoir** to hoist sb into a position of power VPR **se hisser** to heave o.s. up, to haul o.s. up ◆ **se ~ sur un toit** to heave *ou* haul o.s. (up) onto a roof ◆ **se ~ sur la pointe des pieds** to stand up *ou* raise o.s. on tiptoe ◆ **se ~ à la première place** to work one's way up to first place

histamine /istamin/ NF histamine

histaminique /istaminik/ ADJ histaminic

histocompatibilité /istokɔ̃patibilite/ NF histocompatibility

histogramme /istɔgʀam/ NM histogram

histoire /istwaʀ/ NF 1 *(= science, événements)* **l'~** history ◆ **l'~ jugera** posterity will be the judge ◆ **laisser son nom dans l'~** to find one's place in history ◆ **tout cela, c'est de l'~ ancienne*** all that's ancient history* ◆ **~ naturelle** † natural history ◆ **l'~ de France** French history, the history of France ◆ **l'~ de l'art/de la littérature** art/literary history ◆ **l'~ des sciences** the history of science ◆ **l'Histoire sainte** Biblical *ou* sacred history ◆ **la petite ~** the footnotes of history ◆ **pour la petite ~** anecdotally

2 *(= déroulement de faits)* history ◆ **son ~ familiale** his family history ◆ **raconter l'~ de sa vie** to tell one's life story *ou* the story of one's life

3 *(Scol)* *(= leçon)* history (lesson); *(† = livre)* history book

4 *(= récit, conte)* story ◆ **c'est toute une ~** it's a long story ◆ **une ~ vraie** a true story ◆ **~ de pêche/de revenants** fishing/ghost story ◆ **~ d'amour** love story ◆ **~ drôle** funny story, joke ◆ **~ marseillaise** tall story *ou* tale, fisherman's tale *(Brit)* ◆ **~ à dormir debout** cock-and-bull story, tall story ◆ **~ de fous** shaggy-dog story ◆ **c'est une ~ de fous !** it's absolutely crazy! ◆ **qu'est-ce que c'est que cette ~ ?** what on earth is all this about?, just what is all this about? ◆ **le plus beau** *ou* **curieux de l'~ c'est que** the best part *ou* strangest part of it is that ◆ **l'~ veut qu'il ait dit …** the story goes that he said …

5 *(* = mensonge)* story, fib* ◆ **tout ça, ce sont des ~s** that's just a lot of fibs*, you've *(ou* they *etc)* made all that up ◆ **tu me racontes des ~s** you're pulling my leg, come off it!*

6 *(* = affaire, incident)* business ◆ **c'est une drôle d'~** it's a funny business ◆ **il vient de lui arriver une curieuse ~/une drôle d'~** something odd/funny has just happened to him ◆ **ils se sont disputés pour une ~ d'argent/de femme** they had a fight over money/about a woman ◆ **se mettre dans une sale ~, se mettre une sale ~ sur le dos** to get mixed up in some nasty business ◆ **sa nomination va faire toute une ~** his appointment will cause a lot of fuss *ou* a great to-do, there will be quite a fuss *ou* to-do over his appointment ◆ **c'est toujours la même ~ !** it's always the same old story! ◆ **ça, c'est une autre ~ !** that's (quite) another story! ◆ **j'ai pu avoir une place mais ça a été toute une ~** I managed to get a seat but it was a real struggle ◆ **sans ~s** *[personne]* ordinary; *[vie, enfance]* uneventful; *[se dérouler]* uneventfully

7 * *(= relation amoureuse)* (love) affair; *(= dispute)* falling-out ◆ **pourquoi ne se parlent-ils pas ? – il y a une ~ entre eux** why aren't they on speaking terms? – they fell out over something

8 *(= chichis)* fuss, to-do, carry-on* *(Brit)* ◆ **quelle ~ pour si peu !** what a to-do *ou* fuss *ou* carry-on* *(Brit)* over so little! ◆ **faire un tas d'~s** to make a whole lot of fuss *ou* a great to-do ◆ **au lit, et pas d'~s !** off to bed, and I don't want any fuss! ◆ **il fait ce qu'on lui demande sans faire d'~s** he does what he is told without (making) a fuss

9 *(* locutions)* ◆ **~ de faire** just to do ◆ **~ de prendre l'air** just for a breath of (fresh) air ◆ **~ de rire** just for a laugh*, just for fun ◆ **il a essayé, ~ de voir/de faire quelque chose** he had a go just to see what it was like/just for something to do

NFPL **histoires** * *(= ennuis)* trouble ◆ **faire** *ou* **chercher des ~s à qn** to make trouble for sb ◆ **cela ne peut lui attirer** *ou* **lui valoir que des ~s** that's bound to get him into trouble, that will cause him nothing but trouble ◆ **je ne**

veux pas d'~s avec la police/les voisins I don't want any trouble with the police/the neighbours

histologie /istɔlɔʒi/ NF histology

histologique /istɔlɔʒik/ ADJ histological

historicisme /istɔʀisism/ NM historicism

historicité /istɔʀisite/ NF historicity

historié, e /istɔʀje/ ADJ *(Art)* historiated

historien, -ienne /istɔʀjɛ̃, jɛn/ NM,F *(= savant)* historian; *(= étudiant)* history student, historian

historiette /istɔʀjɛt/ NF little story, anecdote

historiographe /istɔʀjɔgʀaf/ NMF historiographer

historiographie /istɔʀjɔgʀafi/ NF historiography

historiographique /istɔʀjɔgʀafik/ ADJ *[tradition, courant, connaissance]* historiographical

historique /istɔʀik/ ADJ 1 *[étude, vérité, roman, temps]* historical; *[personnage, événement, monument]* historic; *(= mémorable)* historic ◆ **c'est une journée ~ pour notre équipe** it's a red letter day *ou* a historic day for our team ◆ **le yen a atteint son record ~ hier** the yen reached a record *ou* an all-time high yesterday ◆ **l'action a battu son record ~ de baisse** the share price fell to a record *ou* all-time low ◆ **le fleuve a atteint son plus haut niveau ~** the river reached the highest level ever recorded 2 *(= tout premier) [chef de parti, opérateur]* very first NM history ◆ **faire l'~ de** *[+ problème, institution]* to trace the history of

historiquement /istɔʀikmɑ̃/ ADV historically

histrion /istʀijɔ̃/ NM 1 *(Hist Théât)* (wandering) minstrel, strolling player 2 *(péj = comédien)* ham (actor)

hit * /it/ NM hit *

hitlérien, -ienne /itleʀjɛ̃, jɛn/ ADJ, NM,F Hitlerian, Hitlerite

hitlérisme /itleʀism/ NM Hitlerism

hit-parade (pl **hit-parades**) /itpaʀad/ NM *(Mus)* ◆ **le ~** the charts ◆ **premier/bien placé au ~** number one/high up in the charts ◆ **être en tête du ~** to be at the top of the charts ◆ **figurer au ~ du chômage** *[pays]* to be in the list of countries with high unemployment ◆ **être bien placé au ~ des hommes politiques** to be one of the most popular politicians ◆ **il arrive en tête au ~ des acteurs les plus payés** he's at the top of the list of the most highly paid actors

hittite /itit/ ADJ Hittite NMF **Hittite** Hittite

HIV /aʃive/ NM (abrév de **human immunodeficiency virus**) HIV ◆ **virus ~** HIV virus

hiver /ivɛʀ/ NM winter ◆ **il fait un temps d'~** it's like winter, it's wintry weather ◆ **~ nucléaire** nuclear winter ◆ **à l'~ de sa vie** *(littér)* in the twilight of his (*ou* her) life

hivernage /ivɛʀnaʒ/ NM 1 *[de bateau, caravane, bétail]* wintering 2 *(Météo)* rainy season 3 *(= fourrage)* winter fodder

hivernal, e (mpl **-aux**) /ivɛʀnal, o/ ADJ *(lit = de l'hiver) [brouillard, pluies]* winter *(épith)*, hibernal *(frm)*; *(= comme en hiver) [atmosphère, température, temps]* wintry *(épith)* ◆ **en période ~e** in winter ◆ **il faisait une température ~e** it was as cold as (in) winter, it was like winter ◆ **station ~e** winter resort NF **hivernale** *(Alpinisme)* winter ascent

hivernant, e /ivɛʀnɑ̃, ɑ̃t/ NM,F winter visitor *ou* holiday-maker *(Brit)*

hiverner /ivɛʀne/ ► conjug 1 ◄ VI to winter VT *[+ bétail]* to winter; *[+ terre]* to plough before winter

HLA /aʃɛla/ ADJ (abrév de **human leucocyte antigens**) HLA ◆ **système ~** HLA system

HLM /aʃɛlɛm/ NM *ou* nf (abrév de **habitation à loyer modéré**) ◆ **cité ~** council housing estate *(Brit)*, public housing project *(US)*; → **habitation**

ho /o/ EXCL *(appel)* hey (there)!; *(surprise, indignation)* oh!

hobby (pl **hobbies**) /ɔbi/ NM hobby

hobereau (pl **hobereaux**) /ɔbʀo/ NM *(= oiseau)* hobby; *(péj = seigneur)* local (country) squire

hochement /ɔʃmɑ̃/ NM ◆ **~ de tête** *(affirmatif)* nod (of the head); *(négatif)* shake (of the head)

hochequeue /ɔʃkø/ NM wagtail

hocher /ɔʃe/ ► conjug 1 ◄ VT ◆ **~ la tête** *(affirmativement)* to nod (one's head); *(négativement)* to shake one's head

hochet /ɔʃɛ/ NM *[de bébé]* rattle; *(= chose futile)* toy

Hô Chi Minh-Ville /oʃiminvil/ N Ho Chi Minh City

hockey /ɔkɛ/ NM hockey ◆ **faire du ~** to play hockey ◆ **~ sur glace** ice hockey, hockey *(US)* ◆ **~ sur gazon** hockey *(Brit)*, field hockey *(US)*

hockeyeur, -euse /ɔkɛjœʀ, øz/ NM,F hockey player

Hodgkin /ɔdʒkin/ N *(Méd)* ◆ **maladie de ~** Hodgkin's disease

hoirie †† /waʀi/ NF inheritance; → **avancement**

holà /ɔla/ EXCL *(pour attirer l'attention)* hello!; *(pour protester)* hang on a minute! NM ◆ **mettre le ~ à qch** to put a stop *ou* an end to sth

holding /ɔldiŋ/ NM *ou* NF holding company

hold-up /ɔldœp/ NM INV hold-up ◆ **faire un ~** to stage a hold-up ◆ **condamné pour le ~ d'une banque** sentenced for having held up a bank *ou* for a bank hold-up

holisme /ɔlism/ NM holism

holiste /ɔlist/, **holistique** /ɔlistik/ ADJ holistic

hollandais, e /ɔ(l)lɑ̃dɛ, ɛz/ ADJ Dutch; → **sauce** NM 1 *(= langue)* Dutch 2 ◆ **Hollandais** Dutchman ◆ **les Hollandais** the Dutch NF **hollandaise** 1 *(= vache)* Friesian *(Brit)*, Holstein *(US)* 2 ◆ **Hollandaise** *(= femme)* Dutchwoman

Hollande /ɔ(l)lɑ̃d/ NF Holland

hollande /ɔ(l)lɑ̃d/ NF *(= toile)* holland; *(= porcelaine)* Dutch porcelain NM *(= fromage)* Dutch cheese; *(= papier)* Holland

Hollywood /ɔliwud/ N Hollywood

hollywoodien, -ienne /ɔliwudjɛ̃, jɛn/ ADJ Hollywood *(épith)*

holocauste /ɔlokost/ NM 1 *(Rel, fig = sacrifice)* sacrifice, holocaust, burnt offering ◆ **l'Holocauste** *(Hist)* the Holocaust 2 *(= victime)* sacrifice

holocène /ɔlɔsɛn/ ADJ Holocene NM ◆ **l'~** the Holocene (period)

hologramme /ɔlɔgʀam/ NM hologram

holographe /ɔlɔgʀaf/ ADJ holograph *(épith)*

holographie /ɔlɔgʀafi/ NF holography

holographique /ɔlɔgʀafik/ ADJ holographic(al)

holophrastique /ɔlɔfʀastik/ ADJ holophrastic

homard /ɔmaʀ/ NM lobster ◆ **~ à l'armoricaine/à l'américaine/thermidor** lobster à l'armoricaine/à l'américaine/thermidor

home /om/ NM ◆ **~ d'enfants** children's home COMP **home cinéma** *ou* **cinema** home cinema

homélie /ɔmeli/ NF homily

homéopathe /ɔmeɔpat/ NMF homoeopath(ist), homeopath(ist) ◆ **médecin ~** hom(o)eopathic doctor

homéopathie /ɔmeɔpati/ NF hom(o)eopathy ◆ **se soigner à l'~** to take hom(o)eopathic medicine

homéopathique /ɔmeɔpatik/ ADJ homoeopathic ◆ **à dose ~** *(hum)* in small doses

Homère /ɔmɛʀ/ NM Homer

homérique /ɔmeʀik/ ADJ Homeric; → **rire**

home-trainer (pl **home-trainers**) /omtʀɛnœʀ/ NM exercise bike

homicide /ɔmisid/ ADJ († , *littér*) homicidal NMF *(littér = criminel)* homicide *(littér)*, murderer *(ou* murderess) NM *(Jur = crime)* murder, homicide *(US)* ◆ **~ volontaire** murder, voluntary manslaughter, first-degree murder *(US)* ◆ **~ involontaire** *ou* **par imprudence** manslaughter, second-degree murder *(US)*

hominidé /ɔminide/ NM hominid ◆ **les ~s** the Hominidae

hominien /ɔminjɛ̃/ NM hominoid

hommage /ɔmaʒ/ NM 1 *(= marque d'estime)* tribute ◆ **rendre ~ à qn/au talent de qn** to pay homage *ou* tribute to sb/to sb's talent ◆ **rendre ~ à Dieu** to pay homage to God ◆ **rendre un dernier ~ à qn** to pay one's last respects to sb ◆ **recevoir l'~ d'un admirateur** to accept the tribute paid by an admirer ◆ **discours en ~ aux victimes de la guerre** speech paying homage *ou* tribute to the victims of the war
2 *(= don)* **acceptez ceci comme un ~** *ou* **en ~ de ma gratitude** please accept this as a mark *ou* token of my gratitude ◆ **faire ~ d'un livre** to give a presentation copy of a book ◆ **~ de l'éditeur** with the publisher's compliments
3 *(Hist)* homage ◆ **~ lige** liege homage
NMPL **hommages** *(frm)* *(= civilités)* respects ◆ **mes ~s, Madame** my humble respects, madam ◆ **présenter ses ~s à une dame** to pay one's respects to a lady ◆ **présentez mes ~s à votre femme** give my regards to your wife

hommasse /ɔmas/ ADJ mannish

homme /ɔm/ NM 1 *(= espèce)* **l'~** man, mankind ◆ **les premiers ~s** early man
2 *(= individu)* man ◆ **approche si tu es un ~ !** come on if you're man enough *ou* if you dare! ◆ **l'enfant devient ~** the child grows into *ou* becomes a man ◆ **vêtements d'~** men's clothes ◆ **montre/veste d'~** man's watch/jacket ◆ **métier d'~** male profession ◆ **rayon ~s** men's *ou* menswear department ◆ **voilà votre ~** *(que vous cherchez)* there's the man you're looking for; *(qu'il vous faut)* that's the man for you ◆ **je suis votre ~ !** I'm your man! ◆ **elle a rencontré l'~ de sa vie** she's found Mr Right ◆ **c'est l'~ de ma vie** he's the man of my life ◆ **c'est l'~ du jour** he's the man of the moment *ou* hour ◆ **c'est l'~ de la situation** he's the right man for the job ◆ **l'~ fort du régime** the strongman of the régime ◆ **heure-/journée-/mois-** *etc* **~** *(unité)* man-hour/-day/-month *etc*; → **abominable, âge, mémoire¹**
3 *(* = mari, compagnon)* man ◆ **son ~** her man * ◆ **voilà mon ~** here comes that man of mine *
4 *(locutions)* **parler d'~ à ~** to speak man to man, to have a man-to-man talk ◆ **il n'est pas ~ à mentir** he's not one to lie *ou* a man to lie ◆ **comme un seul ~** as one man ◆ **il a trouvé son ~** *(un égal)* he has found his match ◆ **un ~ à la mer !** *(Naut)* man overboard! ◆ **un ~ averti en vaut deux** *(Prov)* forewarned is forearmed *(Prov)* ◆ **l'~ propose, Dieu dispose** *(Prov)* man proposes, God disposes *(Prov)*
COMP **homme d'action** man of action
homme d'affaires businessman
homme d'armes †† man-at-arms †
homme de barre helmsman
homme de bien † good man
les hommes en blanc *(= psychiatres)* men in white coats; *(= médecins)* doctors
les hommes bleus *(du désert)* the Blue Men

homme des cavernes cave man
l'homme de Cro-Magnon Cro-Magnon man
homme d'Église man of the Church
homme d'équipage member of a ship's crew ◆ **navire avec 30 ~s d'équipage** ship with a crew of 30 (men)
homme d'esprit man of wit
homme d'État statesman
homme à femmes womanizer, ladies' man
homme au foyer househusband
homme de lettres man of letters
homme lige liege man
homme de loi man of law, lawyer
homme de main hired man, henchman
homme de ménage (male) domestic help
homme du monde man about town, socialite ◆ **c'est un parfait ~ du monde** he's a real gentleman
l'homme de Neandertal Neanderthal man
homme de paille man of straw *(used as a front)*
homme de peine workhand
homme de plume man of letters, writer
homme politique politician
homme de quart man *ou* sailor on watch
homme de robe †† legal man, lawyer
l'homme de la rue the man in the street
homme de science man of science
homme à tout faire odd-job man
homme de troupe *(Mil)* private

homme-grenouille (pl **hommes-grenouilles**) /ɔmgʀənuj/ NM frogman

homme-orchestre (pl **hommes-orchestres**) /ɔmɔʀkɛstʀ/ NM *(Mus, fig)* one-man band; ◆ **c'est l'~ de l'entreprise** he's the man who looks after everything in the company ◆ **c'est l'~ de la campagne du président** he's the man orchestrating the presidential campaign

homme-sandwich (pl **hommes-sandwichs**) /ɔmsɑ̃dwitʃ/ NM sandwich man

homo * /omo/ ADJ (abrév de **homosexuel**) gay NM gay man ◆ **les ~s** gay men

homocentre /ɔmɔsɑ̃tʀ/ NM common centre

homocentrique /ɔmɔsɑ̃tʀik/ ADJ homocentric

homogène /ɔmɔʒɛn/ ADJ *(gén)* homogeneous ◆ **pour obtenir une pâte ~** to obtain a mixture of an even consistency ◆ **c'est une classe ~** they are all about the same level *ou* standard in that class ◆ **texte peu ~** text that lacks consistency

homogénéisation /ɔmɔʒeneizasjɔ̃/ NF homogenization

homogénéiser /ɔmɔʒeneize/ ► conjug 1 ◄ VT to homogenize

homogénéité /ɔmɔʒeneite/ NF homogeneity, homogeneousness ◆ **manquer d'~** *[texte]* to lack consistency

homographe /ɔmɔgʀaf/ ADJ homographic NM homograph

homologation /ɔmɔlɔgasjɔ̃/ NF *(Sport)* ratification; *(Jur)* approval, sanction; *(Admin)* approval ◆ **~ de testament** probate of will

homologie /ɔmɔlɔʒi/ NF *(Sci)* homology; *(gén)* equivalence

homologue /ɔmɔlɔg/ ADJ *(Sci)* homologous; *(gén)* equivalent, homologous (de to) NM *(Chim)* homologue; *(= personne)* counterpart, opposite number ◆ **son ~ en Grande-Bretagne** his British counterpart, his opposite number in Britain

homologuer /ɔmɔlɔge/ ► conjug 1 ◄ VT *(Sport)* to ratify; *(Jur)* to approve, to sanction; *[+ testament]* to grant probate of *(Brit)*, to probate *(US)*; *(Admin)* *[+ appareil, établissement]* to approve ◆ **tarif homologué** approved *ou* sanctioned rate ◆ **record homologué** official record ◆ **le record n'a pas pu être homologué** the record could not be made official

homoncule /ɔmɔ̃kyl/ NM ⇒ **homuncule**

homonyme /ɔmɔnim/ ADJ homonymous NM *(Ling)* homonym; *(= personne)* namesake

homonymie /ɔmɔnimi/ NF homonymy

homonymique /ɔmɔnimik/ ADJ homonymic

homoparental, e, -aux /ɔmɔpaʀɑ̃tal, o/ ADJ *[famille]* same sex, homoparental

homoparentalité /ɔmɔpaʀɑ̃talite/ NF same-sex parenting, homoparentality

homophobe /ɔmɔfɔb/ ADJ *[personne]* homophobic NMF homophobe

homophobie /ɔmɔfɔbi/ NF homophobia

homophone /ɔmɔfɔn/ ADJ *(Ling)* homophonous; *(Mus)* homophonic NM homophone

homophonie /ɔmɔfɔni/ NF homophony

homosexualité /ɔmɔsɛksɥalite/ NF homosexuality

homosexuel, -elle /ɔmɔsɛksɥɛl/ ADJ, NM,F homosexual

homozygote /omozigɔt/ ADJ homozygous NMF homozygote

homuncule /ɔmɔ̃kyl/ NM homunculus

Honduras /'ɔ̃dyʀas/ NM ◆ **le ~** Honduras ◆ **le ~ britannique** British Honduras

hondurien, -ienne /'ɔ̃dyʀjɛ̃, jɛn/ ADJ Honduran NM,F **Hondurien(ne)** Honduran

Hongkong, Hong-Kong /'ɔ̃gkɔ̃g/ N Hong Kong

hongkongais, e /'ɔ̃gkɔ̃gɛ, ɛz/ ADJ Hongkongese NM,F **Hongkongais(e)** Hongkongese

hongre /'ɔ̃gʀ/ ADJ gelded NM gelding

Hongrie /'ɔ̃gʀi/ NF Hungary

hongrois, e /'ɔ̃gʀwa, waz/ ADJ Hungarian NM *(= langue)* Hungarian NM,F **Hongrois(e)** Hungarian

honnête /ɔnɛt/ ADJ 1 *(= intègre)* *[personne]* honest, decent; *[conduite]* decent; *[procédés, intentions]* honest ◆ **ce sont d'~s gens** they are decent people *ou* folk* ◆ **des procédés peu ~s** dishonest practices 2 *(† = vertueux)* *[femme]* respectable 3 *(= correct)* *[marché]* fair; *[prix, résultats]* reasonable, fair; *[repas]* reasonable ◆ **ce livre est ~** this book isn't bad ◆ **rester dans une ~ moyenne** to maintain a fair average ◆ **un vin ~** an honest little wine 4 *(= franc)* honest, frank ◆ **sois ~, tu aimerais bien le renvoyer** be honest, you'd love to sack him
COMP **honnête homme** *(Hist)* gentleman, man of breeding

honnêtement /ɔnɛtmɑ̃/ ADV 1 *(= avec intégrité)* *[agir]* fairly, decently; *[gérer]* honestly ◆ **gagner ~ sa vie** to make an honest living 2 *(= correctement)* reasonably ◆ **c'est ~ payé** it's reasonably paid, you get a fair *ou* reasonable wage for it ◆ **il s'en sort ~** he's managing fairly well *ou* reasonably well ◆ **il gagne ~ sa vie** he makes a decent living 3 *(= franchement)* honestly, frankly ◆ **il a ~ reconnu son erreur** he frankly admitted his error ◆ **~, vous le saviez bien !** come on, you knew! ◆ **~, qu'en penses-tu ?** be honest, what do you think?

honnêteté /ɔnɛtte/ NF 1 *(= intégrité)* *[de personne]* honesty, decency; *[de conduite]* decency; *[de procédés, intentions]* honesty ◆ **~ intellectuelle** intellectual honesty ◆ **avec une ~ scrupuleuse** with scrupulous honesty 2 *(= franchise)* honesty ◆ **en toute ~, je ne le crois pas** in all honesty *ou* to be perfectly frank, I don't believe it ◆ **il a l'~ de reconnaître que ...** he is honest enough to admit that ... 3 *(† = vertu)* *[de femme]* respectability

honneur /ɔnœʀ/ NM 1 *(= réputation)* honour *(Brit)*, honor *(US)* ◆ **l'~ est sauf** our *(ou* their *etc)* honour is intact *ou* safe ◆ **l'~ m'oblige à le faire** I am in honour bound to do it ◆ **mettre son *ou* un point d'~ à faire qch** to make it a point of honour to do sth ◆ **jurer *ou* déclarer sur l'~** to give one's word; *(par écrit)* to make a sworn statement ◆ **homme/femme d'~** man/woman of honour, man/woman with a sense of honour ◆ **bandit d'~** outlaw *(because of a blood feud)*; → **dette, manquer, parole** *etc*
2 *(= mérite)* credit ◆ **avec ~** creditably ◆ **il s'en est tiré* avec ~** he made quite a creditable job of it ◆ **c'est tout à son ~** it does him (great) credit *ou* is much to his credit ◆ **c'est à lui que revient l'~ d'avoir inventé ...** the credit is his for having invented ... ◆ **être l'~ de sa profession** to be a credit *ou* an honour to one's profession ◆ **cette décision vous fait ~** this decision does you credit *ou* is to your credit ◆ **c'est trop d'~ que vous me faites** you're giving me too much credit; → **tour²**
3 *(= privilège, faveur)* honour ◆ **faire (à qn) l'~ de venir** to do sb the honour of coming ◆ **me ferez-vous l'~ de danser avec moi ?** may I have the pleasure of this dance? ◆ **avoir l'~ de** to have the honour of ◆ **j'ai eu l'~ de recevoir sa visite** he honoured me with a visit ◆ **je suis ravi de vous rencontrer – tout l'~ est pour moi** delighted to meet you – the pleasure is (all) mine *ou* it is my pleasure ◆ **qui commence à jouer ? – à toi l'~** who is it to start? – it's you (to start) ◆ **j'ai l'~ de solliciter ...** *(formule épistolaire)* I am writing to ask ... ◆ **j'ai l'~ de vous informer que** I am writing to inform you that, I beg to inform you that *(frm)* ◆ **garde/invité *ou* hôte d'~** guard/guest of honour ◆ **président/membre d'~** honorary president/member; → **baroud, champ¹, citoyen** *etc*
4 *(Cartes)* honour
5 *(= titre)* **votre Honneur** Your Honour
6 *(locutions)* **~ aux vainqueurs !** hail the victors!, honour to the conquerors! ◆ **~ aux dames** ladies first ◆ **à toi *ou* vous l'~** after you ◆ **être à l'~** *[personne]* to have the place of honour; *[mode, style]* to be to the fore, to be much in evidence ◆ **être en ~** *[coutume]* to be the done thing; *[style, mode]* to be in favour ◆ **remettre en ~** to reintroduce ◆ **en l'~ de nos hôtes/de cet événement** in honour of our guests/of this event ◆ **à qui ai-je l'~ ?** to whom do I have the honour of speaking? ◆ **que me vaut l'~ de votre visite ?** to what do I owe the honour of your visit? ◆ **en quel ~ toutes ces fleurs ?*** *(iro)* what are all these flowers in aid of?* ◆ **en quel ~ t'appelle-t-il "mon bijou" ?** *(iro)* what gives him the right to call you "my love"? ◆ **faire ~ à** *[+ engagements, signature]* to honour; *[+ traite]* to honour, to meet; *[+ sa famille]* to be a credit *ou* an honour to; *[+ repas]* to do justice to ◆ **il a fini la partie pour l'~** he gallantly finished the game (for its own sake); → **bras**
NMPL **honneurs** *(= marques de distinction)* honours ◆ **aimer/mépriser les ~s** to be fond of/despise honours ◆ **couvert d'~s** covered in honours ◆ **avec tous les ~s dus à son rang** with all the honours due to his rank ◆ **~s militaires** military honours ◆ **se rendre avec les ~s de la guerre** *(Mil)* to be granted the honours of war; *(fig)* to suffer an honourable defeat ◆ **faire les ~s de la maison à qn** to (do the honours and) show sb round the house ◆ **avoir les ~s de la première page** to make the front page ◆ **avoir les ~s de la cimaise** to have one's works exhibited ◆ **rendre les derniers ~s à qn** to pay one's last respects to sb

honnir /'ɔniʀ/ ► conjug 2 ◄ VT *(frm)* to hold in contempt ◆ **honni soit qui mal y pense** honi soit qui mal y pense

honorabilité /ɔnɔʀabilite/ NF *[de personne, sentiments]* worthiness ◆ **soucieux d'~** anxious to be thought honourable

honorable /ɔnɔʀabl/ ADJ 1 *(= respectable)* *[personne, but, sentiment]* honourable *(Brit)*, honorable *(US)*, worthy ◆ **l'~ compagnie** this worthy company *(frm) (aussi hum)* ◆ **mon ~ collègue** *(frm, iro)* my honourable *ou* esteemed colleague *(frm) (aussi iro)* ◆ **à cet âge** ~ at this grand old age ◆ **une défaite** ~ an honourable defeat 2 *(= suffisant) [salaire, résultats]* decent, respectable; → **amende**

honorablement /ɔnɔʀabləmɑ̃/ ADV 1 *(= de façon respectable)* honourably *(Brit)*, honorably *(US)* ◆ **~ connu dans le quartier** known and respected in the district 2 *(= convenablement)* decently ◆ **il gagne ~ sa vie** he makes a decent living ◆ **l'équipe s'est comportée ~** *(Sport)* the team put up a decent *ou* creditable performance

honoraire /ɔnɔʀɛʀ/ ADJ *[membre, président]* honorary ◆ **professeur ~** professor emeritus, emeritus professor NMPL **honoraires** *[de médecin, avocat]* fees

honorer /ɔnɔʀe/ ► conjug 1 ◄ VT 1 *(= glorifier) [+ savant, Dieu]* to honour *(Brit)*, to honor *(US)* ◆ **~ la mémoire de qn** to honour the memory of sb
2 *(littér = estimer)* to hold in high regard *ou* esteem ◆ **je l'honore à l'égal de ...** I have the same regard *ou* esteem for him as I do for ... ◆ **mon honoré collègue** my esteemed *ou* respected colleague
3 *(= gratifier)* ~ **qn de qch** to honour sb with sth ◆ **il m'honorait de son amitié/de sa présence** he honoured me with his friendship/his presence ◆ **il ne m'a pas honoré d'un regard** *(iro)* he did not honour me with so much as a glance *(iro)*, he did not (even) deign to look at me ◆ **je suis très honoré** I am highly *ou* greatly honoured
4 *(= faire honneur à)* to do credit to, to be a credit to ◆ **cette franchise l'honore** this frankness does him credit ◆ **il honore sa profession/son pays** he's a credit *ou* an honour to his profession/country
5 *[+ chèque, signature, promesse, contrat]* to honour; *[+ traite]* to honour, to meet; *[+ médecin, notaire]* to settle one's account with ◆ **votre honorée du ...** † *(= lettre)* yours of the ...
6 *(† ou hum)* ~ **sa femme** to fulfil one's conjugal duties *(hum)*
VPR **s'honorer** ◆ **s'~ de** to pride o.s. (up)on, to take pride in

honorifique /ɔnɔʀifik/ ADJ *[fonction]* honorary, ceremonial *(US)* ◆ **à titre ~** on an honorary basis

honoris causa /ɔnɔʀiskoza/ ADJ ◆ **il a été nommé docteur ~** he has been awarded an honorary doctorate ◆ **docteur ~ de l'université de Harvard** honorary doctor of the University of Harvard

honte /'ɔ̃t/ NF 1 *(= déshonneur, humiliation)* disgrace, shame ◆ **couvrir qn de ~** to bring disgrace *ou* shame on sb, to disgrace sb ◆ **quelle ~** *ou* **c'est une ~ pour la famille !** what a disgrace to the family!, he brings shame upon the family! ◆ **faire** *ou* **être la ~ de la famille/profession** to be the disgrace of one's family/profession ◆ **~ à celui qui ...** *(littér)* shame upon him who ... *(littér)* ◆ **~ à toi !** shame on you! ◆ **il n'y a aucune ~ à être ...** there's no shame *ou* disgrace in being ... ◆ **c'est une ~ !** that's disgraceful! *ou* a disgrace ◆ **c'est la ~ !*** it's pathetic!* ◆ **j'avais la ~ !*** I felt so pathetic!*
2 *(= sentiment de confusion, gêne)* shame ◆ **à ma (grande) ~** to my (great) shame ◆ **sans ~** shamelessly ◆ **sans fausse ~** quite openly ◆ **avoir ~ (de qch/de faire)** to be *ou* feel ashamed (of sth/of doing) ◆ **tu devrais avoir ~ !** you should be ashamed (of yourself)! ◆ **pleurer/rougir de ~** to weep for/blush with shame ◆ **mourir de ~** to die of shame ◆ **elle n'a aucune ~** † she is utterly shameless, she has no shame ◆ **avoir toute ~ bue** *(frm)* to be beyond shame ◆ **tu me fais ~ !** you're an embarrassment!, you make me feel so ashamed! ◆ **faire ~ à qn de sa lenteur** to make sb (feel) ashamed of how slow they are ◆ **il leur fait ~ par sa rapidité** he's so fast he puts them to shame; → **court¹**

honteusement /'ɔ̃tøzmɑ̃/ ADV 1 *(= scandaleusement) (gén)* shamefully; *[exploiter]* shamelessly 2 *(= avec confusion) [cacher]* in shame

honteux, -euse /'ɔ̃tø, øz/ ADJ 1 *(= déshonorant)* shameful; *(= scandaleux)* disgraceful, shameful ◆ **c'est ~ !** it's a disgrace!, it's disgraceful! *ou* shameful! ◆ **il n'y a rien de ~ à cela** that's nothing to be ashamed of, there's nothing shameful about that; → **maladie** 2 *(= confus)* ashamed *(de* of); ◆ **d'un air ~** shamefacedly ◆ **bourgeois/nationaliste ~** *(= cachant ses opinions)* closet bourgeois/nationalist 3 *(Anat) [nerf, artère]* pudendal

hooligan /'uligan/ NM hooligan

hooliganisme /'uliganism/ NM hooliganism

hop /'ɔp/ EXCL ◆ **~ (là)!** *(pour faire sauter)* hup!; *(pour faire partir)* off you go!; *(après un geste maladroit)* (w)oops!

hopi /'ɔpi/ ADJ *[village, indien]* Hopi NMF **Hopi** Hopi ◆ **les Hopis** the Hopis, the Hopi Indians

hôpital (pl **-aux**) /ɔpital, o/ NM hospital ◆ **être à l'~** *[patient]* to be in hospital *(Brit)*, to be in the hospital *(US)*; *[médecin, visiteur]* to be at the hospital ◆ **aller à l'~** to go to hospital ◆ **entrer à l'~** to go into hospital ◆ **~ militaire/psychiatrique** military/psychiatric hospital ◆ **~ de jour** day *(Brit) ou* outpatient *(US)* hospital ◆ **~ pour enfants** children's hospital ◆ **l'~ public** *(institution)* state-run hospitals ◆ **c'est l'~ qui se moque de la charité** it's the pot calling the kettle black

hoquet /'ɔkɛ/ NM *[de personne]* hiccup ◆ **~s** *[de machine, véhicule]* spluttering *(NonC)* ◆ **avoir le ~** to have (the) hiccups ◆ **il a eu un ~ de dégoût/peur** he gulped with distaste/fear ◆ **malgré quelques ~s, les négociations continuent** *(= dysfonctionnements)* despite a few hiccups *ou* the occasional glitch*, the negotiations are continuing

hoqueter /'ɔk(ə)te/ ► conjug 4 ◄ VI *[personne] (= avoir le hoquet)* to hiccup; *(= pleurer)* to gasp; *[machine, véhicule]* to splutter

Horace /ɔʀas/ NM Horatio; *(= le poète)* Horace

horaire /ɔʀɛʀ/ ADJ 1 *[débit, salaire, moyenne, coût]* hourly ◆ **vitesse ~** speed per hour
2 *(Astron)* horary; → **décalage, fuseau, tranche**
NM 1 *[de personnel]* schedule, working hours; *[d'élèves]* timetable ◆ **quand on est directeur, on n'a pas d'~** when you are a manager, you don't have any set working hours ◆ **je ne suis tenu à aucun ~** I can keep my own hours, I'm not tied down to a fixed schedule ◆ **~s de travail/bureau** working/office hours ◆ **avoir des ~s flexibles** *ou* **variables** *ou* **à la carte** to have flexible working hours, to work flexitime *(Brit) ou* flextime *(US)*
2 *[de bus, train]* timetable; *[de bateau, vols]* schedule, timetable ◆ **~s de train** train times ◆ **le train est en avance/en retard sur l'~ prévu** the train is ahead of/behind schedule ◆ **il a 20 minutes de retard sur l'~ prévu** *[car, train]* it's running 20 minutes late; *[avion]* it's 20 minutes late *ou* behind schedule ◆ **l'~** *ou* **les ~s de diffusion** *(Radio, TV)* the broadcasting schedule ◆ **ce n'est pas un bon ~ de diffusion pour cette émission** it's not a good time-slot for this programme

horde /'ɔʀd/ NF horde

horion /'ɔʀjɔ̃/ NM *(† ou hum) (gén pl)* blow, punch ◆ **échanger des ~s avec la police** to exchange blows with the police

horizon /ɔʀizɔ̃/ NM 1 *(Astron, Art)* horizon ◆ **la ligne d'~** the horizon ◆ **~ artificiel** artificial horizon ◆ **un bateau sur** *ou* **à l'~** a boat on the horizon *ou* skyline ◆ **disparaître à l'~** to disappear below the horizon ◆ **personne à l'~ ? on y va !** nobody around *ou* in sight? – let's go then! ◆ **se pointer** *ou* **se profiler** *ou* **poindre à l'~** *(lit, fig)* to loom on the horizon
2 *(= paysage)* landscape, view ◆ **on découvre un vaste ~/un ~ de collines** you come upon a vast panorama/a hilly landscape ◆ **changer d'~** to have a change of scenery *ou* scene ◆ **ce village était tout son ~** this village was his whole world *ou* the only world he knew ◆ **voyager vers de nouveaux ~s** to make for new horizons ◆ **venir d'~s divers** to come *ou* hail *(frm)* from different backgrounds
3 *(= avenir, perspective)* horizon ◆ **ça lui a ouvert de nouveaux ~s** it opened (up) new horizons *ou* vistas for him ◆ **l'~ économique du pays** the country's economic prospects ◆ **faire des prévisions pour l'~ 2020** to make forecasts for (the year) 2020 ◆ **à l'~ 2020** by (the year) 2020; → **tour²**

horizontal, e (mpl **-aux**) /ɔʀizɔ̃tal, o/ ADJ *(gén, Écon)* horizontal ◆ **être en position ~e** to be lying down flat NF **horizontale** *(gén, Géom)* horizontal ◆ **placer qch à l'horizontale** to put sth horizontal *ou* in a horizontal position ◆ **tendez vos bras à l'horizontale** stretch your arms out in front of you

horizontalement /ɔʀizɔ̃talmɑ̃/ ADV *(gén)* horizontally; *(dans mots croisés)* across

horizontalité /ɔʀizɔ̃talite/ NF horizontality, horizontalness

horloge /ɔʀlɔʒ/ NF *(gén, Ordin)* clock ◆ **avec une régularité d'~** as regular as clockwork ◆ **avec la précision d'une ~** with clockwork precision ◆ **il est 2 heures à l'~** it's 2 o'clock by *ou* according to the clock ◆ **l'~ parlante** the speaking clock *(Brit)*, Time *(US)* ◆ **~ astronomique/atomique** astronomical/atomic clock ◆ **~ normande** *ou* **de parquet** grandfather clock ◆ **~ interne/biologique** internal/biological clock; → **heure**

horloger, -ère /ɔʀlɔʒe, ɛʀ/ ADJ *[industrie]* watch-making *(épith)*, clock-making *(épith)* NM,F *(gén)* watchmaker; *(spécialement d'horloges)* clockmaker ◆ **~ bijoutier** jeweller *(specializing in clocks and watches)* ◆ **le grand ~** *(littér)* the Creator

horlogerie /ɔʀlɔʒʀi/ NF *(= fabrication) (gén)* watch-making; *[d'horloges]* clock-making; *(= objets)* time-pieces; *(= magasin)* watchmaker's (shop), clockmaker's (shop); *(= technique, science)* horology ◆ **~ bijouterie** jeweller's shop *(specializing in clocks and watches)* ◆ **pièces d'~** clock components; → **mouvement**

hormis /'ɔʀmi/ PRÉP *(frm)* except for, apart from ◆ **personne ~ ses fils** nobody except for *ou* apart from his sons, nobody but *ou* save *(frm)* his sons

hormonal, e (mpl **-aux**) /ɔʀmɔnal, o/ ADJ *[traitement]* hormonal, hormone *(épith)*; *[contraception, déséquilibre]* hormonal

hormone /ɔʀmɔn/ NF hormone ◆ **~ de croissance/sexuelle** growth/sex hormone ◆ **poulet/veau aux ~s*** hormone-fed *ou* hormone-treated chicken/veal

hormonothérapie /ɔʀmɔnoteʀapi/ NF hormone therapy

horodaté, e /ɔʀɔdate/ ADJ *[stationnement]* pay and display *(épith)*; *[ticket]* stamped with the hour and date *(attrib)* ◆ **une télécopie ~e à 12h05** a fax sent at 12.05

horodateur /ɔʀɔdatœʀ/ NM *[de parking]* ticket machine, pay-and-display ticket machine *(Brit)*

horoscope /ɔʀɔskɔp/ NM horoscope ◆ **faire l'~ de qn** to cast *ou* do sb's horoscope ◆ **regarder/lire son ~** to consult/read one's horoscope *ou* stars*

horreur /ɔʀœʀ/ NF 1 (= *effroi, répulsion*) horror ◆ **il était devenu pour elle un objet d'~** he had become an object of horror to her ◆ **frappé** *ou* **saisi d'~** horror-stricken, horror-struck ◆ **vision d'~** horrific *ou* horrendous *ou* horrifying sight ◆ **l'~ d'agir/du risque qui le caractérise** the horror of acting/taking risks which is typical of him ◆ **son ~ de la lâcheté** his horror *ou* loathing of cowardice ◆ **je me suis aperçu avec ~ que ...** to my horror I realized that ...
2 (= *laideur*) [*de crime, guerre*] horror ◆ **l'esclavage dans toute son ~** slavery in all its horror
3 (= *chose*) **les ~s de la guerre** the horrors of war ◆ **c'est une ~** [*tableau*] it's hideous *ou* ghastly*; [*personne laide*] he's (*ou* she's) hideous; [*personne méchante*] he's (*ou* she's) ghastly* ◆ **ce film/travail est une ~** this film/piece of work is awful *ou* dreadful ◆ **quelle ~!** how dreadful! *ou* awful!; → **film, musée**
4 (* = *actes, propos*) **~s** dreadful *ou* terrible things ◆ **débiter des ~s sur qn** to say dreadful *ou* terrible things about sb
5 (*locutions*) **cet individu me fait ~** that fellow disgusts me ◆ **le mensonge me fait ~** I loathe *ou* detest lying, I have a horror of lying ◆ **la viande me fait ~** I can't stand *ou* bear meat, I loathe *ou* detest meat ◆ **avoir qch/qn en ~** to loathe *ou* detest sth/sb ◆ **j'ai ce genre de livre en ~** I loathe *ou* detest this type of book, I have a horror of this type of book ◆ **prendre qch/qn en ~** to come to loathe *ou* detest sth/sb ◆ **avoir ~ de qch/de faire qch** to loathe *ou* detest sth/doing sth

horrible /ɔʀibl/ ADJ (= *effrayant*) [*crime, accident, blessure*] horrible; (= *extrême*) [*chaleur, peur*] terrible, dreadful; (= *laid*) [*chapeau, personne, tableau*] horrible, hideous; (= *mauvais*) [*temps*] terrible, ghastly*, dreadful; [*travail*] terrible, dreadful; (= *méchant*) [*personne, propos*] horrible, awful ◆ **il a été ~ avec moi** he was horrible to me

horriblement /ɔʀibləmɑ̃/ ADV (= *de façon effrayante*) horribly; (= *extrêmement*) horribly, terribly, dreadfully

horrifiant, e /ɔʀifjɑ̃, jɑ̃t/ ADJ horrifying

horrifier /ɔʀifje/ ▸ conjug 7 ◂ VT to horrify ◆ **horrifié par la dépense** horrified at the expense

horrifique /ɔʀifik/ ADJ (*hum*) blood-curdling, horrific

horripilant, e /ɔʀipilɑ̃, ɑ̃t/ ADJ trying, exasperating

horripiler /ɔʀipile/ ▸ conjug 1 ◂ VT ◆ **~ qn** to try sb's patience, to exasperate sb

hors /'ɔʀ/ PRÉP (= *excepté*) except (for), apart from, save (*littér*), but ◆ **~ que** (*littér*) save that (*littér*) ◆ **Arles ~ les murs** the outer parts of Arles (*beyond the city walls*)
LOC PRÉP **hors de** 1 (*position*) outside, out of, away from; (*changement de lieu*) out of ◆ **vivre ~ de la ville** to live out of town *ou* outside the town ◆ **vivre ~ de son pays** to live away from *ou* outside one's own country ◆ **le choc l'a projeté ~ de la voiture** the impact threw him out of the car ◆ **il est plus agréable d'habiter ~ du centre** it is more pleasant to live away from *ou* outside the centre ◆ **vivre ~ de son temps/la réalité** to live in a different age/in a dream world ◆ **~ du temps** [*personnage, univers*] timeless ◆ **~ d'ici !** get out of here! ◆ **~ de l'Église, point de salut** (*Prov*) without the Church there is no salvation ◆ **~ de l'Europe, point de salut** (*hum*) without Europe there can be no salvation *ou* there is no hope
2 (*locutions*) **il est ~ d'affaire** he is out of the wood (*Brit*) *ou* woods (*US*), he's over the worst ◆ **mettre qn ~ d'état de nuire** to render sb harmless ◆ **être ~ de soi** to be beside o.s. (with anger) ◆ **cette remarque l'a mise ~ d'elle** she was beside herself when she heard the remark; → **atteinte², commun, portée²** *etc*
COMP **hors antenne** off the air
hors jeu [*joueur*] offside; [*ballon*] out of play; (*Tennis*) out (of play); (*fig*) out of the running ◆ **mettre qn ~ jeu** (*Sport*) to put sb offside; (*fig*) to put sb out of the running ◆ **se mettre ~ jeu** to rule *ou* put o.s. out of the running
hors ligne ⇒ **hors pair**
hors pair outstanding, unparalleled, matchless
hors tout ◆ **longueur/largeur ~ tout** overall length/width; → **circuit, course, service** *etc*

hors-bord /'ɔʀbɔʀ/ NM INV (= *moteur*) outboard motor; (= *bateau*) speedboat (*with outboard motor*)

hors-cote /'ɔʀkɔt/ NM INV over-the-counter market, unofficial market, off-board market (*US*)

hors-d'œuvre /'ɔʀdœvʀ/ NM INV (*Culin*) hors d'œuvre ◆ **~ variés** assorted cold meats and salads ◆ **son discours n'était qu'un ~** his speech was just a taste of things to come

hors-jeu /'ɔʀʒø/ NM INV offside ◆ **être en position de ~** to be offside; → **hors**

hors-la-loi /'ɔʀlalwa/ NMF INV outlaw

hors-piste /'ɔʀpist/ ADV, ADJ INV off-piste NM INV off-piste skiing ◆ **faire du ~** to ski off piste

hors-série /'ɔʀseʀi/ NM INV (= *magazine*) special edition

hors-texte /'ɔʀtɛkst/ NM INV (= *gravure*) plate

hortensia /ɔʀtɑ̃sja/ NM hydrangea

horticole /ɔʀtikɔl/ ADJ horticultural

horticulteur, -trice /ɔʀtikyltœʀ, tʀis/ NM,F horticulturist

horticulture /ɔʀtikyltyʀ/ NF horticulture

hortillonnage /ɔʀtijɔnaʒ/ NM (= *marais*) *marsh used for vegetable farming*

hosanna /oza(n)na/ NM hosanna

hospice /ɔspis/ NM 1 (= *hôpital*) home ◆ **~ de vieillards** old people's home ◆ **mourir à l'~** to die in the poorhouse 2 [*de monastère*] hospice

hospitalier, -ière /ɔspitalje, jɛʀ/ ADJ 1 [*service, personnel, médecine*] hospital (*épith*) ◆ **centre** *ou* **établissement ~** hospital 2 (= *accueillant*) hospitable NM,F 1 (= *religieux*) **(frère) ~, (sœur) hospitalière** hospitaller 2 (= *infirmier*) nurse ◆ **les ~s** hospital staff

hospitalisation /ɔspitalizasjɔ̃/ NF hospitalization ◆ **~ à domicile** home (medical) care

hospitaliser /ɔspitalize/ ▸ conjug 1 ◂ VT to hospitalize, to send to hospital ◆ **malade hospitalisé** in-patient ◆ **10% des malades hospitalisés** 10% of hospital patients *ou* cases ◆ **être hospitalisé** to be admitted to hospital, to be hospitalized ◆ **elle a été hospitalisée d'urgence** she was rushed to hospital

hospitalisme /ɔspitalism/ NM hospitalism

hospitalité /ɔspitalite/ NF hospitality ◆ **donner l'~ à qn** to give *ou* offer sb hospitality ◆ **avoir le sens de l'~** to be hospitable

hospitalo-universitaire (mpl **hospitalo-universitaires**) /ɔspitaloynivɛʀsitɛʀ/ ADJ ◆ **centre ~** teaching hospital

hostellerie † /ɔstɛlʀi/ NF hostelry †

hostie /ɔsti/ NF (*Rel*) host; (†† = *victime*) sacrificial victim

hostile /ɔstil/ ADJ hostile (*à* to)

hostilement /ɔstilmɑ̃/ ADV in a hostile way

hostilité /ɔstilite/ NF hostility (*à, envers* to, towards); ◆ **ouvrir/reprendre les ~s** to open/reopen hostilities

hosto* /ɔsto/ NM hospital

hot(-)dog (pl **hot(-)dogs**) /'ɔtdɔg/ NM hot dog

hôte /ot/ NM (= *maître de maison*) host; († = *aubergiste*) landlord, host; (*Bio*) host; (*Ordin*) host computer ◆ **les ~s du bois/du marais** (*littér*) the denizens (*littér*) of the wood/marsh; → **chambre, table** NMF (= *invité*) guest; (= *client*) patron; (= *locataire*) occupant ◆ **un ~ de marque** a distinguished guest ◆ **~ payant** paying guest

> ⚠ Au sens de 'invité', 'client' ou 'locataire', **hôte** ne se traduit pas par **host**.

hôtel /ɔtɛl/ NM hotel ◆ **vivre/coucher à l'~** to live/sleep in a hotel ◆ **aller** *ou* **descendre à l'~** to put up at a hotel; → **maître, rat**
COMP **hôtel des impôts** tax office
hôtel meublé (cheap) residential hotel
l'hôtel de la Monnaie ≈ the Mint
hôtel particulier town house, (private) mansion
hôtel de passe hotel used by prostitutes
hôtel de police police station
hôtel de tourisme tourist hotel
hôtel des ventes saleroom, salesroom (*US*)
hôtel de ville town hall

hôtel-Dieu (pl **hôtels-Dieu**) /ɔtɛldjø/ NM general hospital

hôtelier, -ière /ɔtalje, jɛʀ/ ADJ [*chaîne, complexe, industrie, profession*] hotel (*épith*); → **école** NM,F hotelier, hotel-keeper ◆ **~ restaurateur** hotel-and-restaurant owner

hôtellerie /ɔtɛlʀi/ NF (= *auberge*) inn, hostelry †; [*d'abbaye*] guest quarters, hospice †; (= *profession*) hotel business; (= *matière enseignée*) hotel management ◆ **~ de plein air** camping and caravanning

hôtel-restaurant (pl **hôtels-restaurants**) /ɔtɛlʀɛstɔʀɑ̃/ NM hotel (with public restaurant)

hôtesse /otɛs/ NF (= *maîtresse de maison*) hostess; († = *aubergiste*) landlady ◆ **~ (de l'air)** stewardess, air hostess (*Brit*), flight attendant ◆ **~ (d'accueil)** [*d'hôtel, bureau*] receptionist; [*d'exposition, colloque*] hostess ◆ **~ de caisse** checkout assistant

hotte /'ɔt/ NF (= *panier*) basket (*carried on the back*); [*de cheminée, laboratoire*] hood ◆ **~ aspirante** *ou* **filtrante** [*de cuisine*] extractor *ou* cooker (*Brit*) *ou* range (*US*) hood ◆ **la ~ du Père Noël** Santa Claus's sack

hottentot, e /'ɔtɑ̃to, ɔt/ ADJ Hottentot NM,F **Hottentot(e)** Hottentot

hou /'u/ EXCL boo!

houblon /'ublɔ̃/ NM (= *plante*) hop; (= *ingrédient de la bière*) hops

houblonnière /'ublɔnjɛʀ/ NF hopfield

houe /'u/ NF hoe

houille /'uj/ NF coal ◆ **~ blanche** hydroelectric power ◆ **~ grasse/maigre** bituminous/lean coal

houiller, -ère /'uje, jɛʀ/ ADJ [*bassin, industrie*] coal (*épith*); [*terrain*] coal-bearing NF **houillère** coalmine

houle /'ul/ NF swell ◆ **une forte ~** a heavy swell

houlette /'ulɛt/ NF [*de pâtre, évêque*] crook; [*de jardinier*] trowel, spud ◆ **sous la ~ de** under the leadership of

houleux, -euse /'ulø, øz/ ADJ [*mer*] stormy; [*séance*] stormy, turbulent; [*salle, foule*] tumultuous, turbulent

houp /'up/ EXCL ⇒ **hop**

houppe /'up/ NF *[de plumes, cheveux]* tuft; *[de fils]* tassel ◆ ~ **à poudrer** powder puff

houppelande /'uplɑ̃d/ NF (loose-fitting) greatcoat

houppette /'upɛt/ NF powder puff

hourra /'uʀa/ EXCL hurrah! ◆ **pousser des ~s** to cheer, to shout hurrah ◆ **salué par des ~s** greeted by cheers; → **hip**

house (music) /aus(mjuzik)/ NF house (music)

houspiller /'uspije/ ▸ conjug 1 ◂ VT (= *réprimander*) to scold, to tell off, to tick off* *(Brit)*; († = *malmener*) to hustle

housse /'us/ NF *(gén)* cover; *[de meubles] (pour protéger temporairement)* dust cover; *(pour recouvrir à neuf)* loose cover; *(en tissu élastique)* stretch cover ◆ ~ **de couette** quilt cover ◆ ~ **(penderie)** *[d'habits]* hanging wardrobe

houx /'u/ NM holly

hovercraft /ɔvœʀkʀaft/ NM hovercraft

hoverport /ɔvœʀpɔʀ/ NM hoverport

HS /aʃɛs/ ADJ INV 1 * (abrév de **hors service**) *[appareil]* kaput*, bust* *(attrib)*; *[personne] (par fatigue)* beat* *(attrib)*, shattered* *(attrib) (Brit)*; *(par maladie)* out of it* *(attrib)* 2 *(Tourisme)* (abrév de **haute saison**) → **saison** NF (abrév de **heure supplémentaire**) → **supplémentaire**

HT (abrév de **hors taxe(s)**) → **taxe**

HTML /aʃteemɛl/ NM (abrév de **hypertext markup language**) HTML

http /aʃtetepe/ NM (abrév de **hypertext transfer protocol**) http

huard, huart /'ɥaʀ/ NM *(Can = oiseau)* diver *(Brit)*, loon *(US)*

hub /'œb/ NM (= *dispositif informatique, aéroport*) hub

hublot /'yblo/ NM *[de bateau]* porthole; *[d'avion, machine à laver]* window ◆ **~s*** (= *lunettes*) specs*

huche /'yʃ/ NF (= *coffre*) chest; (= *pétrin*) dough *ou* kneading trough ◆ ~ **à pain** bread bin

hue /'y/ EXCL ◆ ~ **(cocotte)!** gee up! ◆ **ils tirent tous à ~ et à dia** they are all pulling in opposite directions

huée /'ɥe/ NF *(Chasse)* hallooing ◆ **~s** *(de dérision)* boos, booing *(NonC)* ◆ **sous les ~s de la foule** to the boos of the crowd ◆ **il est sorti de scène sous les ~s du public** he was booed off the stage

huer /'ɥe/ ▸ conjug 1 ◂ VT *(Chasse)* to hallo; *(par dérision)* to boo VI *[chouette]* to hoot

hugolien, -ienne /ygɔljɛ̃, jɛn/ ADJ of Victor Hugo

huguenot, e /'yg(ə)no, ɔt/ ADJ, NM,F Huguenot

Hugues /'yg/ NM Hugh ◆ ~ **Capet** Hugh *ou* Hughes Capet

huilage /ɥilaʒ/ NM oiling, lubrication

huile /ɥil/ NF 1 (= *liquide*) oil; (= *pétrole*) petroleum, crude (oil) ◆ **cuit à l'~** cooked in oil ◆ **sardines/thon à l'~** sardines/tuna in oil ◆ **vérifier le niveau d'~** *(d'une voiture)* to check the oil ◆ **jeter** *ou* **verser de l'~ sur le feu** to add fuel to the flames *ou* fire ◆ **mettre de l'~ dans les rouages** to oil the wheels ◆ **mer d'~** glassy sea; → **lampe, saint, tache**

2 (* = *notabilité*) bigwig*, big noise*, big shot* ◆ **les ~s** the top brass*

3 *(Peinture)* (= *tableau*) oil painting; (= *technique*) oil painting, oils ◆ **peint à l'~** painted in oils; → **peinture**

COMP **huile d'amandes douces** sweet almond oil

huile d'arachide groundnut *(Brit) ou* peanut *(US)* oil

huile de bain bath oil

huile de colza rapeseed *ou* colza oil

huile de coude* elbow grease*

huile essentielle essential oil

huile de foie de morue cod-liver oil

huile de friture cooking *ou* frying oil

huile de graissage lubricating oil

huile de lin linseed oil

huile de maïs corn oil

huile de noix walnut oil

huile d'olive olive oil

huile de paraffine liquid paraffin

huile de ricin castor oil

huile de sésame sesame oil

huile de soja soya oil

huile solaire (sun)tan oil

huile de table salad oil

huile de tournesol sunflower oil

huile végétale vegetable oil

huile de vidange *(gén)* lubricating oil; *(usagée)* waste oil

huile vierge virgin olive oil

huiler /ɥile/ ▸ conjug 1 ◂ VT *[+ machine, serrure]* to oil, to lubricate; *[+ récipient]* to oil ◆ **papier huilé** oil-paper ◆ **la mécanique est bien/parfaitement huilée** *(fig)* it's a well-oiled/perfectly smooth-running machine ◆ **équipe bien huilée** slick team

huilerie /ɥilʀi/ NF (= *usine*) oil factory; (= *commerce*) oil trade; (= *moulin*) oil-mill

huileux, -euse /ɥilø, øz/ ADJ *[liquide, matière]* oily; *[aspect, surface]* oily, greasy

huilier /ɥilje/ NM (oil and vinegar) cruet, oil and vinegar bottle

huis /ɥi/ NM †† door ◆ **à ~ clos** *(Jur)* in camera ◆ **ordonner le ~ clos** *(Jur)* to order proceedings to be held in camera ◆ **les négociations se poursuivent à ~ clos** the talks are continuing behind closed doors

huisserie /ɥisʀi/ NF *[de porte]* doorframe; *[de fenêtre]* window frame

huissier /ɥisje/ NM 1 (= *appariteur*) usher 2 *(Jur)* ~ **(de justice)** ≈ bailiff

HUISSIER

Although in some respects the role of **huissiers** is similar to that of bailiffs, their activities are not identical. The main function of a **huissier** is to carry out decisions made in the courts, for example evictions for non-payment of rent and seizure of goods following bankruptcy proceedings. Unlike bailiffs, **huissiers** can also be called upon to witness the signature of important documents, and to ensure that public competitions are judged fairly.

huit /'ɥi(t)/ ADJ INV eight; *pour autres loc voir* **six** NM INV eight; *(en patinage)* figure of eight; *(en aviron)* eight ◆ **lundi en ~** a week on *(Brit) ou* from *(US)* Monday, Monday week* *(Brit)*; → **grand** COMP **huit jours** (= *une semaine*) a week ◆ **dans ~ jours** in a week, in a week's time *(Brit)* ◆ **donner ses ~ jours à un domestique** † to give a servant a week's notice

huitain /'ɥitɛ̃/ NM (= *poème*) octet, octave

huitaine /'ɥitɛn/ NF eight or so, about eight ◆ **dans une ~ (de jours)** in a week or so ◆ **son cas a été remis à ~** *(Jur)* the hearing has been postponed *ou* deferred for one week ◆ **sans réponse sous ~** if no reply is received within seven days

huitante /'ɥitɑ̃t/ ADJ INV *(Helv)* eighty

huitième /'ɥitjɛm/ ADJ, NMF eighth ◆ **la ~ merveille du monde** the eighth wonder of the world; *pour autres loc voir* **sixième** NF *(Scol) penultimate class of primary school, fifth grade (US)* NMPL *(Sport)* ◆ **~s de finale** second round in a five-round knock-out competition ◆ **être en ~s de finale** to be in the last sixteen

huitièmement /'ɥitjɛmmɑ̃/ ADV eighthly

huître /ɥitʀ/ NF oyster ◆ ~ **perlière** pearl oyster ◆ **se (re)fermer comme une ~** to clam up

huit-reflets /'ɥiʀ(ə)flɛ/ NM INV silk top hat

huîtrier, -ière /ɥitʀije, ijɛʀ/ ADJ *[industrie]* oyster *(épith)* NM (= *oiseau*) oyster catcher NF **huîtrière** (= *banc*) oyster bed; (= *établissement*) oyster farm

hula-ho(o)p /'ulaɔp/ NM Hula Hoop ®

hulotte /'ylɔt/ NF tawny owl

hululement /'ylylmɑ̃/ NM hooting, screeching

hululer /'ylyle/ ▸ conjug 1 ◂ VI to hoot, to screech

hum /'œm/ EXCL hem!, h'm!

humain, e /ymɛ̃, ɛn/ ADJ *(gén)* human; (= *compatissant, compréhensif*) humane ◆ **justice/espèce/condition ~e** human justice/race/condition ◆ **il n'avait plus figure ~e** he was disfigured beyond recognition ◆ **se montrer ~** to show humanity, to act humanely *(envers* towards); ◆ **il s'est sauvé – c'est ~** he ran away – it's only human; → **respect, science, voix** *etc* NM 1 *(Philos)* **l'~** the human element 2 (= *être humain*) human (being) ◆ **les ~s** humans, human beings

humainement /ymɛnmɑ̃/ ADV (= *avec bonté*) humanely; (= *par l'homme*) humanly ◆ **ce n'est pas ~ possible** it's not humanly possible ◆ **~, on ne peut pas le renvoyer** it would be heartless to dismiss him ◆ **une situation ~ intolérable** an unbearable situation for people to be in ◆ **la restructuration a été ~ douloureuse** the human cost of the restructuring was high, the restructuring was painful in human terms

humanisation /ymanizasjɔ̃/ NF humanization ◆ **la priorité est à l'~ des prisons** making prisons more humane is a priority

humaniser /ymanize/ ▸ conjug 1 ◂ VT *[+ doctrine]* to humanize; *[+ conditions]* to make more humane, to humanize ◆ **il faut ~ les prisons** prison conditions must be made more humane VPR **s'humaniser** *[personne]* to become more human; *[architecture]* to become less forbidding *ou* impersonal

humanisme /ymanism/ NM humanism

humaniste /ymanist/ ADJ humanist, humanistic NMF humanist

humanitaire /ymanitɛʀ/ ADJ *[intervention, convoi]* humanitarian ◆ **aide/action ~** humanitarian aid/relief ◆ **association ~** humanit-arian (aid) organization

humanitarisme /ymanitaʀism/ NM *(péj)* unrealistic humanitarianism

humanitariste /ymanitaʀist/ ADJ *(péj)* unrealistically humanitarian NMF unrealistic humanitarian

humanité /ymanite/ NF 1 (= *le genre humain*) **l'~** humanity, mankind 2 (= *bonté*) humaneness, humanity ◆ **geste d'~** humane gesture 3 *(Philos, Rel)* humanity NFPL **humanités** († *Scol*) classics, humanities ◆ **faire ses ~s** to study *ou* read *(Brit)* classics

humanoïde /ymanɔid/ ADJ, NM humanoid

humble /œbl(ə)/ ADJ (= *modeste, pauvre*) humble; (= *obscur*) humble, lowly ◆ **d'~ naissance** of humble *ou* lowly birth *ou* origins ◆ **à mon ~ avis** in my humble opinion ◆ **"je suis votre humble serviteur"** † "I am your humble servant" †

humblement /œbləmɑ̃/ ADV humbly

humecter /ymɛkte/ ▸ conjug 1 ◂ VT *[+ linge, herbe]* to dampen; *[+ front]* to moisten, to dampen ◆ **la sueur humectait ses tempes** his brow was damp with sweat ◆ **l'herbe humectée de rosée** the dewy *ou* dew-damp grass ◆ **s'~ les lèvres** to moisten one's lips ◆ **ses yeux s'humectèrent** his eyes grew moist (with tears),

tears welled in his eyes ◆ **s'~ le gosier** * to wet one's whistle *

humer /yme/ ▸ conjug 1 ◂ **VT** *[+ plat]* to smell; *[+ air, parfum]* to inhale, to breathe in

humérus /ymeʀys/ **NM** humerus

humeur /ymœʀ/ **NF** 1 *(= disposition momentanée)* mood, humour ◆ **selon son ~** *ou* **l'~ du moment** according to the mood he was in ◆ **se sentir d'~ à travailler** to feel in the mood for working *ou* for work *ou* to work ◆ **de quelle ~ est-il aujourd'hui ?** what kind of mood is he in today? ◆ **mettre/être de bonne ~** to put/be in a good mood *ou* humour, to put/be in good spirits ◆ **travailler dans la bonne ~** to work contentedly ◆ **la bonne ~ régnait dans la maison** contentment reigned in the house ◆ **roman/film plein de bonne ~** good-humoured novel/film, novel/film full of good humour ◆ **être de mauvaise ~** to be in a bad mood ◆ **il est d'une ~ massacrante** *ou* **de chien** he's in a rotten * *ou* foul temper *ou* mood ◆ **~ noire** black mood; → **saute**

2 *(= tempérament)* temper, temperament ◆ **d'~ changeante** *ou* **inégale** moody ◆ **d'~ égale** even-tempered, equable *(frm)* ◆ **être d'~** *ou* **avoir l'~ batailleuse** to be fiery-tempered ◆ **être d'~ maussade** to be sullen, to be a sullen type ◆ **il y a incompatibilité d'~ entre eux** they are temperamentally unsuited *ou* incompatible

3 *(= irritation)* bad temper, ill humour ◆ **passer son ~ sur qn** to take out *ou* vent one's bad temper *ou* ill humour on sb ◆ **accès** *ou* **mouvement d'~** fit of (bad) temper *ou* ill humour ◆ **geste d'~** bad-tempered gesture ◆ **agir par ~** to act in a fit of (bad) temper *ou* ill humour ◆ **dire qch avec ~** to say sth ill-humouredly *ou* testily *(littér)*

4 *(Méd)* secretion ◆ **~ aqueuse/vitreuse** *ou* **vitrée de l'œil** aqueous/vitreous humour of the eye ◆ **les ~s** †† the humours †

humide /ymid/ **ADJ** *[mains, front, terre]* moist, damp; *[torchon, habits, mur, poudre, herbe]* damp; *[local, climat, région, chaleur]* humid; *(= plutôt froid)* damp; *[tunnel, cave]* dank, damp; *[saison, route]* wet ◆ **yeux ~s d'émotion** eyes moist with emotion ◆ **il lui lança un regard ~** he looked at her with moist eyes ◆ **temps lourd et ~** muggy weather ◆ **temps froid et ~** cold wet weather

humidificateur /ymidifikatœʀ/ **NM** *[d'air]* humidifier

humidification /ymidifikasjɔ̃/ **NF** humidification

humidifier /ymidifje/ ▸ conjug 7 ◂ **VT** *[+ air]* to humidify; *[+ terre]* to moisten; *[+ linge]* to moisten, to dampen

humidité /ymidite/ **NF** *[d'air, climat]* humidity; *(plutôt froide)* dampness; *[de sol, mur]* dampness; *[de tunnel, cave]* dankness, dampness ◆ **~ (atmosphérique)** humidity (of the atmosphere) ◆ **air saturé d'~** air saturated with moisture ◆ **dégâts causés par l'~** damage caused by (the) damp ◆ **traces d'~ sur le mur** traces of moisture *ou* of damp on the wall ◆ **taches d'~** damp patches, patches of damp ◆ **"craint l'humidité", "à protéger de l'humidité"** *(sur emballage)* "to be kept dry", "keep in a dry place"

humiliant, e /ymiljɑ̃, jɑ̃t/ **ADJ** humiliating

humiliation /ymiljasjɔ̃/ **NF** *(gén)* humiliation; *(Rel)* humbling *(NonC)*

humilier /ymilje/ ▸ conjug 7 ◂ **VT** *(= rabaisser)* to humiliate; (††, *Rel = rendre humble)* to humble ◆ **s'~ devant** to humble o.s. before

humilité /ymilite/ **NF** *(= modestie)* humility, humbleness ◆ **ton d'~** humble tone ◆ **en toute ~** with all humility

humoral, e (mpl **-aux**) /ymɔʀal, o/ **ADJ** humoral

humoriste /ymɔʀist/ **ADJ** *[écrivain]* humorous **NMF** humorist

humoristique /ymɔʀistik/ **ADJ** humorous; → **dessin**

humour /ymuʀ/ **NM** humour ◆ **~ noir** black humour ◆ **~ à froid** deadpan humour ◆ **l'~ anglais** *ou* **britannique** British humour ◆ **manquer d'~** to have no sense of humour ◆ **avoir de l'~/beaucoup d'~** to have a sense of humour/a good *ou* great sense of humour ◆ **faire de l'~** to try to be funny

humus /ymys/ **NM** humus

Hun /'œ̃/ **NM** *(Hist)* Hun

hune /'yn/ **NF** top ◆ **mât de ~** topmast ◆ **grande ~** maintop

hunier /'ynje/ **NM** topsail ◆ **grand ~** main topsail

huppe /'yp/ **NF** *(= oiseau)* hoopoe; *(= crête)* crest

huppé, e /'ype/ **ADJ** 1 *[oiseau]* crested 2 (* = *riche)* posh *, swanky *

hure /'yʀ/ **NF** *(= tête)* head; *(= pâté)* pork brawn ◆ **~ de sanglier** boar's head

hurlant, e /'yʀlɑ̃, ɑ̃t/ **ADJ** *[foule]* howling; *[enfant]* yelling; *[sirène]* wailing; *[couleurs]* clashing

hurlement /'yʀləmɑ̃/ **NM** 1 *[de loup, chien]* howl, howling *(NonC)*; *[de personne]* yell, howl ◆ **pousser des ~s** *(de rage)* to howl with rage; *(de douleur)* to howl with pain; *(de joie)* to whoop for *ou* with joy ◆ **des ~s de rire** screams *ou* gales of laughter 2 *[de vent]* howling *(NonC)*; *[de sirènes]* wailing *(NonC)*; *[de pneus, freins]* screeching *(NonC)*, screech, squealing *(NonC)*, squeal

hurler /'yʀle/ ▸ conjug 1 ◂ **VI** 1 *(= crier) [personne] (de peur)* to shriek, to scream; *(de douleur)* to scream, to yell (out), to howl; *(de rage)* to roar, to bellow; *[foule]* to roar, to yell *(de* with, in); ◆ **~ de rire** * to roar *ou* bellow with laughter ◆ **il hurlait comme si on l'égorgeait** he was screaming like a stuck pig ◆ **elle hurlait après les enfants** she was yelling at the children ◆ **cette réforme va faire ~ l'opposition** this reform will enrage the opposition ◆ **ça me fait ~ !** it makes my blood boil!

2 *(= vociférer)* to yell

3 *[chien, vent]* to howl; *[freins]* to screech, to squeal; *[sirène]* to wail; *[radio]* to blare ◆ **faire ~ sa télé** to have the TV on full blast * ◆ **~ à la lune** *ou* **à la mort** to bay at the moon ◆ **~ avec les loups** *(fig)* to follow the pack *ou* crowd

4 *[couleurs]* to clash ◆ **ce tableau jaune sur le mur vert, ça hurle !** that yellow picture really clashes with the green wall

VT *[+ injures, slogans]* to yell, to roar; *[+ ordres]* to bellow, to yell ◆ **il hurlait son désespoir** he gave vent to his despair ◆ **"jamais !" hurla-t-il** "never!" he cried

hurleur, -euse /'yʀlœʀ, øz/ **ADJ** *(= braillard) [personne]* yelling *(épith)* **NM** ◆ **(singe) ~** howler (monkey)

hurluberlu, e /yʀlybɛʀly/ **NM,F** crank

huron, -onne /'yʀɔ̃, ɔn/ **ADJ** Huron ◆ **le lac Huron** Lake Huron **NM** *(= langue)* Huron **NM,F** **Huron(ne)** Huron

hurrah /'uʀa, huʀa/ **EXCL** ⇒ **hourra**

husky (pl **huskies**) /'œski/ **NM** husky

hussard /'ysaʀ/ **NM** hussar

hussarde /'ysaʀd/ **à la hussarde LOC ADV** in a rough and ready way

hutte /'yt/ **NF** hut

hutu /'utu/ **ADJ** Hutu **NMF** **Hutu** Hutu ◆ **les Hutus** the Hutus

hyacinthe /jasɛ̃t/ **NF** *(= pierre)* hyacinth, jacinth; († *= fleur)* hyacinth

hybridation /ibʀidasjɔ̃/ **NF** hybridization

hybride /ibʀid/ **ADJ, NM** hybrid

hybrider /ibʀide/ ▸ conjug 1 ◂ **VT** to hybridize

hybridisme /ibʀidism/ **NM** hybridism

hydracide /idʀasid/ **NM** hydracid

hydratant, e /idʀatɑ̃, ɑ̃t/ **ADJ** moisturizing **NM** moisturizer

hydratation /idʀatasjɔ̃/ **NF** *(Chim, Méd)* hydration; *[de peau]* moisturizing

hydrate /idʀat/ **NM** hydrate ◆ **~ de carbone** carbohydrate

hydrater /idʀate/ ▸ conjug 1 ◂ **VT** *(gén)* to hydrate; *[+ peau]* to moisturize **VPR** **s'hydrater** *(Chim)* to hydrate; *(= boire)* to take lots of fluids

hydraulicien, -ienne /idʀolisjɛ̃, jɛn/ **NM,F** hydraulics specialist

hydraulique /idʀolik/ **ADJ** *[circuit, énergie, frein, presse, travaux]* hydraulic ◆ **station ~** waterworks *(sg)* **NF** hydraulics *(sg)*

hydravion /idʀavjɔ̃/ **NM** seaplane, hydroplane

hydre /idʀ(ə)/ **NF** 1 *(Myth)* **l'~ de Lerne** the Lernean Hydra ◆ **on voit resurgir l'~ du racisme** racism is rearing *ou* raising its ugly head again 2 *(= animal)* hydra ◆ **~ d'eau douce** freshwater hydra

hydrique /idʀik/ **ADJ** water *(épith)* ◆ **ressources ~s** water resources ◆ **diète ~** *(Méd)* liquid diet

hydrocarbure /idʀokaʀbyʀ/ **NM** hydrocarbon ◆ **~s saturés/insaturés** saturated/unsaturated hydrocarbons

hydrocéphale /idʀɔsefal/ **ADJ** hydrocephalic, hydrocephalous **NMF** person suffering from hydrocephalus

hydrocéphalie /idʀɔsefali/ **NF** hydrocephalus

hydrocortisone /idʀokɔʀtizɔn/ **NF** hydrocortisone

hydrocution /idʀɔkysjɔ̃/ **NF** *(Méd)* immersion syncope ◆ **il est mort d'~** he died of shock *(after jumping or falling into cold water)*

hydrodynamique /idʀodinamik/ **ADJ** hydrodynamic **NF** hydrodynamics *(sg)*

hydro(-)électricité /idʀoelɛktʀisite/ **NF** hydroelectricity

hydro(-)électrique /idʀoelɛktʀik/ **ADJ** hydroelectric

hydrofoil /idʀofɔjl/ **NM** hydrofoil *(boat)*

hydrofuge /idʀofyʒ/ **ADJ** *[peinture]* water-repellent

hydrogénation /idʀɔʒenasjɔ̃/ **NF** hydrogenation

hydrogène /idʀɔʒɛn/ **NM** hydrogen ◆ **~ lourd** heavy hydrogen; → **bombe**

hydrogéner /idʀɔʒene/ ▸ conjug 6 ◂ **VT** to hydrogenate, to hydrogenize

hydroglisseur /idʀoglisœʀ/ **NM** hydroplane, jet-foil

hydrographe /idʀɔgʀaf/ **NM** hydrographer

hydrographie /idʀɔgʀafi/ **NF** hydrography

hydrographique /idʀɔgʀafik/ **ADJ** hydrographic(al)

hydrologie /idʀɔlɔʒi/ **NF** hydrology

hydrologique /idʀɔlɔʒik/ **ADJ** hydrologic(al)

hydrologiste /idʀɔlɔʒist/, **hydrologue** /idʀɔlɔg/ **NMF** hydrologist

hydrolyse /idʀɔliz/ **NF** hydrolysis

hydrolyser /idʀɔlize/ ▸ conjug 1 ◂ **VT** to hydrolize

hydromassant, e /idʀomasɑ̃, ɑ̃t/ **ADJ** ◆ **bain ~** hydromassage bath

hydromel /idʀɔmɛl/ **NM** mead

hydromètre /idʀɔmɛtʀ/ **NM** *(Tech)* hydrometer

hydrométrie /idʀɔmetʀi/ **NF** hydrometry

hydrométrique /idʀɔmetʀik/ ADJ hydrometric(al)

hydrophile /idʀɔfil/ ADJ *[lentilles cornéennes]* hydrophilic; → **coton**

hydrophobe /idʀɔfɔb/ ADJ, NMF hydrophobic

hydrophobie /idʀɔfɔbi/ NF hydrophobia

hydropique /idʀɔpik/ ADJ dropsical, hydropic(al) NMF person suffering from dropsy

hydropisie /idʀɔpizi/ NF dropsy

hydroponique /idʀɔpɔnik/ ADJ hydroponic ◆ **culture** ~ hydroponics *(sg)*, hydroponic gardening *ou* farming

hydroptère /idʀɔptɛʀ/ NM hydrofoil *(boat)*

hydrosoluble /idʀosɔlybl/ ADJ water-soluble

hydrosphère /idʀɔsfɛʀ/ NF hydrosphere

hydrostatique /idʀɔstatik/ ADJ hydrostatic NF hydrostatics *(sg)*

hydrothérapie /idʀoteʀapi/ NF *(= traitement)* hydrotherapy; *(= science)* hydrotherapeutics *(sg)* ◆ **soins d'**~ hydrotherapy treatments, water cures

hydrothérapique /idʀoteʀapik/ ADJ *[traitement]* hydrotherapy *(épith)*; *[science]* hydrotherapeutic

hydroxyde /idʀɔksid/ NM hydroxide

hyène /jɛn/ NF hyena

hygiaphone ® /iʒjafɔn/ NM Hygiaphone ® *(grill for speaking through at ticket counters etc)*

hygiène /iʒjɛn/ NF hygiene; *(= science)* hygienics *(sg)*, hygiene; *(Scol)* health education ◆ **ça manque d'**~ it's not very hygienic ◆ ~ **corporelle** personal hygiene ◆ ~ **intime** *[de femme]* personal hygiene ◆ ~ **mentale/publique** mental/public health ◆ ~ **du travail** industrial hygiene ◆ ~ **alimentaire** food hygiene ◆ **pour une meilleure** ~ **de vie** for a healthier life ◆ **il suffit d'avoir de l'**~ you just need to be careful about hygiene ◆ **n'avoir aucune** ~ to have no sense of hygiene

hygiénique /iʒjenik/ ADJ hygienic ◆ **promenade** ~ constitutional (walk); → **papier, seau, serviette**

hygiéniste /iʒjenist/ NMF hygienist

hygromètre /igʀɔmɛtʀ/ NM hygrometer

hygrométrie /igʀɔmetʀi/ NF hygrometry

hygrométrique /igʀɔmetʀik/ ADJ hygrometric

hygroscope /igʀɔskɔp/ NM hygroscope

hymen /imɛn/ NM *(littér = mariage)* marriage; *(Anat)* hymen

hyménée /imene/ NM *(littér)* marriage

hyménoptère /imenɔptɛʀ/ NM hymenopteran ◆ **les ~s** Hymenoptera

hymne /imn/ NM hymn ◆ **son discours était un** ~ **à la liberté** his speech was a hymn to liberty ◆ ~ **national** national anthem

hypallage /ipa(l)laʒ/ NF hypallage

hyper * /ipɛʀ/ NM abrév de **hypermarché**

hyper(-)... /ipɛʀ/ PRÉF 1 *(gén)* hyper(-)... 2 *(* : + adj = très)* really ◆ **hyper sympa** * really *ou* dead * nice ◆ **hyper riche** mega * rich ◆ **hyper important** really *ou* very important

hyperacidité /ipɛʀasidite/ NF hyperacidity

hyperactif, -ive /ipɛʀaktif, iv/ ADJ hyperactive

hyperactivité /ipɛʀaktivite/ NF hyperactivity

hyperbare /ipɛʀbaʀ/ ADJ hyperbaric

hyperbole /ipɛʀbɔl/ NF *(Math)* hyperbola; *(Littérat)* hyperbole

hyperbolique /ipɛʀbɔlik/ ADJ *(Math, Littérat)* hyperbolic

hyperboréen, -enne /ipɛʀbɔʀeɛ̃, ɛn/ ADJ hyperborean

hypercholestérolémie /ipɛʀkɔlɛsteʀɔlemi/ NF hypercholesterolaemia *(Brit)*, hypercholesterolemia *(US)*

hypercorrect, e /ipɛʀkɔʀɛkt/ ADJ *(Ling)* hypercorrect

hypercorrection /ipɛʀkɔʀɛksjɔ̃/ NF *(Ling)* hypercorrection

hyperémotivité /ipɛʀemɔtivite/ NF excess emotionality

hyperespace /ipɛʀɛspas/ NM hyperspace

hyperesthésie /ipɛʀɛstezi/ NF hyperaesthesia *(Brit)*, hyperesthesia *(US)*

hyperfocal, e (mpl **-aux**) /ipɛʀfɔkal, o/ ADJ hyperfocal

hyperfréquence /ipɛʀfʀekɑ̃s/ NF very *ou* ultra high frequency

hyperglycémie /ipɛʀglisemi/ NF hyperglycaemia *(Brit)*, hyperglycemia *(US)*

hyperinflation /ipɛʀɛ̃flasjɔ̃/ NF hyperinflation

hyperlien /ipɛʀljɛ̃/ NM *(Ordin)* hyperlink

hypermarché /ipɛʀmaʀʃe/ NM hypermarket, superstore

hypermédia /ipɛʀmedja/ ADJ, NM hypermedia

hypermétrope /ipɛʀmetʀɔp/ ADJ long-sighted, far-sighted *(US)*, hypermetropic *(SPÉC)* NMF long-sighted *ou* far-sighted *(US) ou* hypermetropic *(SPÉC)* person

hypermétropie /ipɛʀmetʀɔpi/ NF long-sightedness, far-sightedness *(US)*, hypermetropia *(SPÉC)*

hypernerveux, -euse /ipɛʀnɛʀvø, øz/ ADJ very highly strung *(Brit)*, very high strung *(US)*

hypernervosité /ipɛʀnɛʀvozite/ NF extreme nervous tension

hyperonyme /ipeʀɔnim/ NM superordinate

hyperplasie /ipɛʀplazi/ NF hyperplasia

hyperpuissance /ipɛʀpɥisɑ̃s/ NF hyperpower

hyperréalisme /ipɛʀʀealism/ NM hyperrealism

hyperréaliste /ipɛʀʀealist/ ADJ, NMF hyperrealist

hypersécrétion /ipɛʀsekʀesjɔ̃/ NF hypersecretion

hypersensibilité /ipɛʀsɑ̃sibilite/ NF hypersensitivity, hypersensitiveness

hypersensible /ipɛʀsɑ̃sibl/ ADJ hypersensitive

hypersonique /ipɛʀsɔnik/ ADJ hypersonic

hypertendu, e /ipɛʀtɑ̃dy/ ADJ suffering from high blood pressure *ou* from hypertension *(SPÉC)* NM,F hypertensive

hypertension /ipɛʀtɑ̃sjɔ̃/ NF ◆ ~ **(artérielle)** high blood pressure, hypertension *(SPÉC)* ◆ **faire de l'**~ to suffer from *ou* have high blood pressure

hypertexte /ipɛʀtɛkst/ NM *(Ordin)* hypertext ◆ **lien** ~ hypertext link ◆ **navigation en (mode)** ~ browsing hypertext

hypertextuel, -elle /ipɛʀtɛkstyɛl/ ADJ hypertext

hyperthyroïdie /ipɛʀtiʀɔidi/ NF hyperthyroidism

hypertrophie /ipɛʀtʀɔfi/ NF *(Méd)* hypertrophy; *[de ville, secteur]* overdevelopment

hypertrophié, e /ipɛʀtʀɔfje/ ADJ *[muscle]* hypertrophied, abnormally enlarged; *[administration, bureaucratie, secteur]* overdeveloped, hypertrophied

hypertrophier /ipɛʀtʀɔfje/ ▸ conjug 7 ◂ VT to hypertrophy VPR **s'hypertrophier** *(Méd)* to hypertrophy; *[ville, secteur]* to become overdeveloped

hypertrophique /ipɛʀtʀɔfik/ ADJ hypertrophic

hypervitaminose /ipɛʀvitaminoz/ NF hypervitaminosis

hypnose /ipnoz/ NF hypnosis ◆ **sous** ~, **en état d'**~ under hypnosis

hypnotique /ipnɔtik/ ADJ *(lit)* hypnotic; *(fig)* hypnotic, mesmeric, mesmerizing

hypnotiser /ipnɔtize/ ▸ conjug 1 ◂ VT *(lit)* to hypnotize; *(fig)* to hypnotize, to mesmerize

hypnotiseur /ipnɔtizœʀ/ NM hypnotist

hypnotisme /ipnɔtism/ NM hypnotism

hypo... /ipɔ/ PRÉF hypo...

hypoallergénique /ipoalɛʀʒenik/, **hypoallergique** /ipoalɛʀʒik/ ADJ hypoallergenic

hypocagne /ipɔkaɲ/ NF ⇒ **hypokhâgne**

hypocalorique /ipokalɔʀik/ ADJ *[aliment, régime]* low-calorie *(épith)*

hypocentre /iposɑ̃tʀ/ NM hypocentre

hypocondriaque /ipɔkɔ̃dʀijak/ ADJ, NMF *(Méd)* hypochondriac

hypocondrie /ipɔkɔ̃dʀi/ NF hypochondria

hypocrisie /ipɔkʀizi/ NF hypocrisy

hypocrite /ipɔkʀit/ ADJ hypocritical NMF hypocrite

hypocritement /ipɔkʀitmɑ̃/ ADV hypocritically

hypodermique /ipɔdɛʀmik/ ADJ hypodermic

hypofertile /ipofɛʀtil/ ADJ *[personne]* suffering from low fertility

hypofertilité /ipofɛʀtilite/ NF *[de personne]* low fertility

hypogastre /ipɔgastʀ/ NM hypogastrium

hypogée[2] /ipɔʒe/ NM *(Archéol)* hypogeum

hypoglycémie /ipoglisemi/ NF hypoglycaemia *(Brit)*, hypoglycemia *(US)* ◆ **avoir** *ou* **faire une crise d'**~ to suffer an attack of hypoglycaemia

hypoglycémique /ipoglisemik/ ADJ hypoglycaemic *(Brit)*, hypoglycemic *(US)* ◆ **évanouissement/coma** ~ fainting fit/coma brought on by an attack of hypoglycaemia NMF person suffering from hypoglycaemia

hypokhâgne /ipɔkaɲ/ NF *first year of two-year preparatory course for the arts section of the École normale supérieure;* → GRANDES ÉCOLES, CLASSES PRÉPARATOIRES, CONCOURS

hyponyme /ipɔnim/ NM hyponym

hypophysaire /ipɔfizɛʀ/ ADJ pituitary, hypophyseal *(SPÉC)* ◆ **glande/hormone** ~ pituitary gland/hormone ◆ **nanisme d'origine** ~ dwarfism caused by pituitary growth hormone deficiency

hypophyse /ipɔfiz/ NF pituitary gland, hypophysis *(SPÉC)*

hyposodé, e /iposɔde/ ADJ low-salt *(épith)*, low in salt *(attrib)*

hypostase /ipɔstɑz/ NF *(Méd, Rel)* hypostasis

hypostyle /ipɔstil/ ADJ hypostyle

hypotaupe /ipotop/ NF *first year of two-year preparatory course for the science section of the Grandes Écoles*

hypotendu, e /ipotɑ̃dy/ ADJ suffering from low blood pressure *ou* from hypotension *(SPÉC)* NM,F hypotensive

hypotension /ipotɑ̃sjɔ̃/ NF low blood pressure, hypotension *(SPÉC)*

hypoténuse /ipɔtenyz/ NF hypotenuse

hypothalamus /ipɔtalamys/ NM hypothalamus

hypothécable /ipɔtekabl/ ADJ mortgageable

hypothécaire /ipɔtekɛʀ/ ADJ *(gén)* hypothecary; *[marché, prêt]* mortgage *(épith)* ◆ **garantie ~** mortgage security

hypothèque /ipɔtɛk/ NF 1 *(Jur)* mortgage ◆ **prendre une ~ sur l'avenir** to mortgage the future 2 *(= obstacle)* obstacle ◆ **lever l'~** *(Pol)* to take away the obstacle

hypothéquer /ipɔteke/ ► conjug 6 ◄ VT *[+ maison]* to mortgage; *[+ créance]* to secure (by mortgage); *[+ avenir]* to mortgage

hypothermie /ipɔtɛʀmi/ NF hypothermia

hypothèse /ipɔtɛz/ NF *(gén)* hypothesis, assumption; *(Sci)* hypothesis ◆ **émettre l'~ que** *(gén)* to suggest the possibility that; *(Sci)* to theorize that ◆ **prenons comme ~ que** let's assume *ou* suppose that ◆ **l'~ du suicide n'a pas été écartée** the possibility of suicide has not been ruled out ◆ **en toute ~** in any case *ou* event, no matter what happens ◆ **dans l'~ où** ... in the event that ... ◆ **dans l'~ de leur victoire** in the event of their winning, should they win, supposing they win ◆ **dans la meilleure/pire des ~s** at best/worst ◆ **je le pense mais ce n'est qu'une ~** I think so but it's only a hypothesis *ou* I'm just hypothesizing ◆ **en être réduit aux ~s** to be reduced to speculation *ou* guessing ◆ **~ d'école** purely hypothetical case ◆ **~ de travail** working hypothesis

hypothétique /ipɔtetik/ ADJ hypothetical ◆ **cas ~** *(Jur)* moot case

hypothétiquement /ipɔtetikmɑ̃/ ADV hypothetically

hypovitaminose /ipovitaminoz/ NF hypovitaminosis

hypoxie /ipɔksi/ NF hypoxia ◆ **entraînement en ~** *(Sport)* altitude training

hysope /izɔp/ NF hyssop

hystérectomie /isteʀɛktɔmi/ NF hysterectomy

hystérie /isteʀi/ NF *(Méd)* hysteria ◆ **~ collective** mass hysteria ◆ **c'était l'~ dans le public** the audience went wild *ou* crazy ◆ **faire *ou* avoir une crise d'~** *(Méd)* to have an attack of hysteria, to have a fit of hysterics; *(excitation)* to become hysterical

hystérique /isteʀik/ ADJ hysterical NMF *(Méd)* hysteric ◆ **c'est un ~** *(péj)* he tends to get hysterical

hystérographie /isteʀɔgʀafi/ NF hysterography

Hz (abrév de **hertz**) Hz

I

I, i /i/ NM (= *lettre*) I, i; → **droit², point¹**

IAD /iade/ NF (abrév de **insémination artificielle avec donneur**) DI ◆ **enfant né d'~ ou par ~** DI baby, baby conceived by DI

iambe /jɑ̃b/ NM (*Littérat*) (= *pied*) iambus, iambic; (= *vers, poème*) iambic

iambique /jɑ̃bik/ ADJ iambic

IAO /iao/ NF (abrév de **ingénierie assistée par ordinateur**) CAE

ibère /ibɛʀ/ ADJ Iberian NMF **Ibère** Iberian

ibérique /ibeʀik/ ADJ Iberian; → **péninsule** NMF **Ibérique** Iberian

ibid ADV (abrév de **ibidem**) ibid

ibidem /ibidɛm/ ADV ibidem

ibis /ibis/ NM ibis

Ibiza /ibiza/ NF Ibiza

Icare /ikaʀ/ NM Icarus

iceberg /ajsbɛʀg/ NM iceberg ◆ **la partie immergée ou cachée de l'~** (*lit*) the invisible part of the iceberg; (*fig*) the hidden aspects of the problem ◆ **la partie visible de l'~** (*lit, fig*) the tip of the iceberg

icelui /isəlɥi/, **icelle** /isɛl/ (mpl **iceux** /isø/) (fpl **icelles** /isɛl/) PRON (††, *hum, Jur*) ⇒ **celui-ci, celle-ci, ceux-ci, celles-ci**; → **celui**

ichtyologie /iktjɔlɔʒi/ NF ichthyology

ichtyologique /iktjɔlɔʒik/ ADJ ichthyologic(al)

ichtyologiste /iktjɔlɔʒist/ NMF ichthyologist

ichtyosaure /iktjozɔʀ/ NM ichthyosaur

ici /isi/ ADV 1 (*dans l'espace*) here ◆ **~ !** (*à un chien*) here! ◆ **loin/près d'~** far from/near here ◆ **il y a 10 km d'~ à Paris** it's 10 km from here to Paris ◆ **c'est à 10 minutes d'~** it's 10 minutes away (from here) ◆ **passez par ~** come this way ◆ **par ~ s'il vous plaît** this way please ◆ **par ~** (= *dans le coin*) around here ◆ **par ~, Mesdames, par ~ les belles laitues !** (*au marché*) this way, ladies, lovely lettuces this way! *ou* over here! ◆ **par ~ la sortie** this way out ◆ **~ même** on this very spot, in this very place ◆ **c'est ~ que ...** this is the place where ..., it is here that ... ◆ **~ on est un peu isolé** we're a bit cut off (out) here ◆ **le bus vient jusqu'~** the bus comes as far as this *ou* this far; → **soupe**

2 (*dans le temps*) **d'~ demain/la fin de la semaine** by tomorrow/the end of the week ◆ **d'~ peu** before (very) long, shortly ◆ **d'~ là** before then, in the meantime ◆ **jusqu'~** (up) until now; (*dans le passé*) (up) until then ◆ **d'~ (à ce) qu'il se retrouve en prison, ça ne va pas être long** it won't be long before he lands up in jail (again) ◆ **d'~ (à ce) qu'il accepte, ça risque de faire long** it might be (quite) some time before he says yes ◆ **le projet lui plaît, mais d'~ à ce qu'il accepte !** he likes the plan, but there's a difference between just liking it and actually agreeing to it! ◆ **d'~ à l'an 2050** by the year 2050

3 (*loc*) **ils sont d'~/ne sont pas d'~** they are/aren't local *ou* from around here ◆ **les gens d'~** the local people ◆ **je vois ça d'~ !*** I can just see that! ◆ **tu vois d'~ la situation/sa tête !*** you can (just) imagine the situation/the look on his face! ◆ **vous êtes ~ chez vous** please make yourself (quite) at home ◆ **~ présent** here present ◆ **"ici Chantal Barry"** (*au téléphone*) "Chantal Barry speaking *ou* here"; (*à la radio*) "this is Chantal Barry" ◆ **~ et là** here and there ◆ **~ comme ailleurs *ou* partout** here as anywhere else

ici-bas /isiba/ ADV (*Rel, hum*) here below ◆ **les choses d'~** things of this world *ou* of this life ◆ **la vie (d')~** life here below

icône /ikon/ NF (*Art, fig, Ordin*) icon ◆ **l'~ sportive de son pays** the sporting icon of his country

iconoclasme /ikɔnɔklasm/ NM iconoclasm

iconoclaste /ikɔnɔklast/ ADJ iconoclastic NMF iconoclast

iconographe /ikɔnɔgʀaf/ NMF (= *documentaliste*) picture researcher; (= *spécialiste de l'iconographie*) iconographer

iconographie /ikɔnɔgʀafi/ NF (= *étude*) iconography; (= *images*) illustrations ◆ **l'~ chrétienne du Moyen-Âge** Christian iconography in the Middle Ages ◆ **elle s'inspire de l'~ préraphaélite** she draws on Pre-Raphaelite imagery ◆ **l'~ de ce livre est somptueuse** the book is lavishly *ou* richly illustrated

iconographique /ikɔnɔgʀafik/ ADJ iconographic(al) ◆ **étude ~** [*d'icônes*] iconographic research; [*d'illustrations*] picture research ◆ **service ~** picture department; (*d'un journal*) picture desk ◆ **cahier ~** illustrated section, supplement of illustrations

ictère /iktɛʀ/ NM icterus

id (abrév de **idem**) id.

Idaho /idao/ NM Idaho

idéal, e (mpl **-als** *ou* **-aux**) /ideal, o/ ADJ (= *imaginaire, parfait*) ideal NM 1 (= *modèle, aspiration*) ideal; (= *valeurs morales*) ideals ◆ **il n'a pas d'~** he has no ideals 2 (= *le mieux*) **l'~ serait qu'elle l'épouse** the ideal thing would be for her to marry him, it would be ideal if she married him ◆ **ce n'est pas l'~** it's not ideal ◆ **dans l'~ c'est ce qu'il faudrait faire** ideally that's what we should do, in an ideal world that's what we'd do

idéalement /idealmɑ̃/ ADV ideally

idéalisation /idealizasjɔ̃/ NF idealization

idéaliser /idealize/ ► conjug 1 ◄ VT to idealize

idéalisme /idealism/ NM idealism

idéaliste /idealist/ ADJ (*gén*) idealistic; (*Philos*) idealist NMF idealist

idée /ide/ GRAMMAIRE ACTIVE 28, 33.2, 53.1, 53.3, 53.5

NF 1 (= *concept*) idea ◆ **l'~ de nombre/de beauté** the idea of number/of beauty ◆ **l'~ que les enfants se font du monde** the idea *ou* concept children have of the world ◆ **c'est lui qui a eu le premier l'~ d'un moteur à réaction** it was he who first thought of *ou* conceived the idea of the jet engine, he was the first to hit upon the idea of the jet engine

2 (= *pensée*) idea ◆ **il a eu l'~ *ou* l'~ lui est venue de faire** he had the idea *ou* hit upon the idea of doing ◆ **l'~ ne lui viendrait jamais de nous aider** it would never occur to him to help us, he would never think of helping us ◆ **ça m'a donné l'~ qu'il ne viendrait pas** that made me think that he wouldn't come ◆ **à l'~ de faire qch/de qch** at the idea *ou* thought of doing sth/of sth ◆ **tout est dans l'~ qu'on s'en fait** it's all in the mind ◆ **avoir une ~ derrière la tête** to have something at the back of one's mind ◆ **ça va lui remettre les ~s en place !** that'll teach him! ◆ **~ directrice** driving principle; → **changer, haut, ordre¹**

3 (= *illusion*) idea ◆ **tu te fais des ~s** you're imagining things ◆ **ne te fais pas des ~s** don't get ideas into your head ◆ **ça pourrait lui donner des ~s** it might give him ideas *ou* put ideas into his head ◆ **quelle ~ !** the (very) idea!, what an idea! ◆ **il a de ces ~s !** the ideas he has!, the things he thinks up!

4 (= *suggestion*) idea ◆ **quelle bonne ~ !** what a good idea! ◆ **quelques ~s pour votre jardin** a few ideas *ou* suggestions for your garden ◆ **de nouvelles ~s-vacances/-rangement** some new holiday/storage tips *ou* hints ◆ **~-cadeau** gift idea ◆ **~-recette** recipe idea

5 (= *vague notion*) idea ◆ **donner à qn/se faire une ~ des difficultés** to give sb/get an *ou* some idea of the difficulties ◆ **avez-vous une ~ *ou* la moindre ~ de l'heure/de son âge ?** have you got any idea of the time/of his age? ◆ **je n'en ai pas la moindre ~** I haven't the faintest *ou* least *ou* slightest idea ◆ **vous n'avez pas ~ de sa bêtise** you've no idea how stupid he is ◆ **on n'a pas ~ (de faire des choses pareilles) !*** it's incredible (doing things like that)! ◆ **j'ai (comme une) ~ qu'il n'acceptera pas** I (somehow) have an idea *ou* a feeling *ou* I have a sort

of feeling that he won't accept ◆ **j'ai mon ~** *ou* **ma petite ~ sur la question** I have my own ideas on the subject

6 *(= opinion)* **~s** ideas, views ◆ **~s politiques/religieuses** political/religious ideas *ou* views ◆ **avoir des ~s avancées** to have progressive ideas ◆ **ce n'est pas dans ses ~s** he doesn't hold with these views ◆ **avoir des ~s larges/étroites** to be broad-minded/narrow-minded ◆ **avoir les ~s courtes** *(péj)* to have limited ideas

7 *(= goût, conception personnelle)* ideas ◆ **juger selon** *ou* **à son ~** to judge in accordance with one's own ideas ◆ **agir selon** *ou* **à son ~** to act *ou* do as one sees fit ◆ **il n'en fait qu'à son ~** he just does as he likes ◆ **pour être décorateur il faut de l'~** *ou* **un peu d'~** to be a decorator you have to have some imagination *ou* a few ideas ◆ **il y a de l'~** * *(dessin, projet)* there's something in it; *(décoration intérieure)* it's got (a certain) something

8 *(= esprit)* **avoir dans l'~ que** to have an idea that, to have it in one's mind that ◆ **il a dans l'~ de partir au Mexique** he's thinking of going to Mexico ◆ **ça m'est sorti de l'~** it went clean * *ou* right out of my mind *ou* head ◆ **cela ne lui viendrait jamais à l'~** it would never occur to him *ou* enter his head ◆ **on ne m'ôtera pas de l'~ qu'il a menti** you won't get me to believe that he didn't lie ◆ **il s'est mis dans l'~ de …** he took *ou* got it into his head to …

COMP **idée fixe** idée fixe, obsession

idée de génie, idée lumineuse brilliant idea, brainwave

idées noires black *ou* gloomy thoughts ◆ **il a souvent des ~s noires** he suffers from depression

idée reçue generally accepted idea, received idea

idée-force (pl **idées-forces**) /idefɔʀs/ NF key idea

idem /idɛm/ ADV *(à l'écrit)* ditto; *(à l'oral)* likewise ◆ **il a mauvais caractère et son frère ~** * he's got a nasty temper, and his brother's the same ◆ **une bière – ~ pour moi** * a beer – same * for me

identifiable /idɑ̃tifjabl/ ADJ identifiable

identificateur, -trice /idɑ̃tifikatœʀ, tʀis/ ADJ identifying *(épith)*, identity *(épith)* NM 1 *(à la morgue)* morgue employee 2 *(Ling, Ordin)* identifier

identification /idɑ̃tifikasjɔ̃/ NF identification *(à, avec* with)

identifier /idɑ̃tifje/ ▸ conjug 7 ◂ VT 1 *(= reconnaître)* to identify 2 *(= assimiler)* **~ qch/qn à** *ou* **avec** *ou* **et** to identify sth/sb with VPR **s'identifier** ◆ **s'~ à** *(= se mettre dans la peau de) [+ personnage, héros]* to identify with; *(= être l'équivalent de)* to identify o.s. with, to become identified with

identique /idɑ̃tik/ ADJ identical *(à* to); ◆ **elle reste toujours ~ à elle-même** she never changes, she's always the same

◆ **à l'identique** ◆ **reproduire qch à l'~** to reproduce *ou* copy sth exactly ◆ **cette maison a été refaite** *ou* **reconstruite à l'~** the house was rebuilt exactly as it was ◆ **ils ont repris leur ancien slogan à l'~** they're using exactly the same slogan as before

identiquement /idɑ̃tikmɑ̃/ ADV identically

identitaire /idɑ̃titɛʀ/ ADJ ◆ **crise ~** *[d'individu]* identity crisis; *[de pays]* crisis surrounding issues of national *ou* ethnic identity ◆ **quête ~** search for identity ◆ **sentiment ~** sense of identity ◆ **les revendications ~s des multiples ethnies** the various ethnic groups' demands for recognition

identité /idɑ̃tite/ NF 1 *(Psych)* identity ◆ **~ culturelle** cultural identity 2 *(Admin)* identity ◆ **~ d'emprunt** assumed *ou* borrowed identity ◆ **vérification/papiers d'~** identity check/papers ◆ **l'Identité judiciaire** ≃ the Criminal Records Office; → **carte, pièce** 3 *(= similarité)* identity, similarity; *(= égalité)* identity ◆ **une ~ de goûts les rapprocha** (their) similar tastes brought them together ◆ **~ (remarquable)** *(Math)* identity

idéogramme /ideɔgʀam/ NM ideogram

idéographie /ideɔgʀafi/ NF ideography

idéographique /ideɔgʀafik/ ADJ ideographic(al)

idéologie /ideɔlɔʒi/ NF ideology

idéologique /ideɔlɔʒik/ ADJ ideological

idéologue /ideɔlɔg/ NMF ideologist

ides /id/ NFPL *(Antiq)* ides ◆ **les ~ de mars** the ides of March

idiolecte /idjɔlɛkt/ NM idiolect

idiomatique /idjɔmatik/ ADJ idiomatic ◆ **expression ~** idiom, idiomatic expression

idiome /idjom/ NM *(Ling)* idiom

idiosyncrasie /idjosɛ̃kʀazi/ NF idiosyncrasy

idiot, e /idjo, idjɔt/ ADJ *[action, personne, histoire, erreur]* idiotic, stupid; *[accident]* stupid; *(† : Méd)* idiotic ◆ **dis-le moi, je ne veux pas mourir ~** * tell me, I don't want to go to my grave without knowing *ou* I don't want to die in ignorance NM,F *(gén)* idiot, fool; *(† : Méd)* idiot ◆ **ne fais pas l'~** * *(= n'agis pas bêtement)* don't be an idiot *ou* a fool; *(= ne simule pas la bêtise)* stop acting stupid * ◆ **l'~ du village** the village idiot

idiotement /idjɔtmɑ̃/ ADV idiotically, stupidly, foolishly

idiotie /idjɔsi/ NF 1 *[d'action, personne]* idiocy, stupidity; *(Méd)* idiocy 2 *(= action)* idiotic *ou* stupid *ou* foolish thing to do; *(= parole)* idiotic *ou* stupid *ou* foolish thing to say; *(= livre, film)* trash *(NonC)*, rubbish *(NonC)* *(Brit)* ◆ **ne va pas voir cette ~** *ou* **de telles ~s** don't go and see such trash *ou* rubbish *(Brit)* ◆ **et ne dis/fais pas d'~s** and don't say/do anything stupid *ou* idiotic

idiotisme /idjɔtism/ NM idiom, idiomatic phrase

idoine /idwan/ ADJ *(Jur, hum = approprié)* appropriate, fitting

idolâtre /idɔlɑtʀ/ ADJ *(Rel)* idolatrous *(de* of); *(fig) [public, foule]* adulatory NM *(Rel)* idolater NF *(Rel)* idolatress

idolâtrer /idɔlɑtʀe/ ▸ conjug 1 ◂ VT to idolize

idolâtrie /idɔlɑtʀi/ NF *(Rel, fig)* idolatry

idole /idɔl/ NF *(= personne, = artiste, Rel)* idol ◆ **il est devenu l'~ des jeunes** he's become a teenage idol ◆ **la jeune ~ du club de Liverpool** Liverpool's young icon *ou* star ◆ **la communauté juive avait fait du président son ~** the Jewish community idolized the President

IDS /idees/ NF (abrév de **initiative de défense stratégique**) SDI

idylle /idil/ NF *(= poème)* idyll; *(= amour)* romance ◆ **ce n'est plus l'~ entre les patrons et les syndicats** the honeymoon is over between management and unions

idyllique /idilik/ ADJ idyllic

i.e. (abrév de **id est**) i.e.

if /if/ NM 1 *(= arbre)* yew (tree); *(= bois)* yew 2 *(= égouttoir à bouteilles)* draining rack

IFOP /ifɔp/ NM (abrév de **Institut français d'opinion publique**) *French public opinion research institute*

IGF /iʒeef/ NM (abrév de **impôt sur les grandes fortunes**) → **impôt**

igloo /iglu/ NM igloo

IGN /iʒeɛn/ NM (abrév de **Institut géographique national**) → **institut**

Ignace /iɲas/ NM Ignatius ◆ **saint ~ de Loyola** (St) Ignatius Loyola

igname /iɲam/ NF yam

ignare /iɲaʀ/ *(péj)* ADJ ignorant NMF ignoramus

igné, e /igne, iɲe/ ADJ 1 *(littér = ardent)* fiery 2 *(Géol)* igneous

ignifugation /iɲifygasjɔ̃/ NF fireproofing

ignifuge /iɲifyʒ/ ADJ *[produit]* fire-retardant NM fire-retardant material *ou* substance

ignifugé, e /iɲifyʒe/ (ptp de **ignifuger**) ADJ fireproof(ed)

ignifugeant, e /iɲifyʒɑ̃, ɑ̃t/ ADJ fire-retardant NM fire-retardant material *ou* substance

ignifuger /iɲifyʒe/ ▸ conjug 3 ◂ VT to fireproof

ignoble /iɲɔbl/ ADJ horrible, foul ◆ **c'est ~ !** it's disgusting! ◆ **il est ~ !, quel ~ individu !** he's disgusting *ou* horrible! ◆ **il a été ~ avec moi** he was horrible to me

> ⚠ Le mot anglais **ignoble** existe, mais il est d'un registre plus soutenu que **ignoble**.

ignoblement /iɲɔbləmɑ̃/ ADV disgracefully, shamefully ◆ **des trafiquants de tous genres exploitent ~ leur misère** traffickers of all sorts are involved in the disgraceful *ou* shameful exploitation of their misery

ignominie /iɲɔmini/ NF 1 *(= caractère)* ignominy; *(= acte)* ignominious *ou* disgraceful act ◆ **c'est une ~ !** it's a disgrace! 2 *(= déshonneur)* ignominy, disgrace

ignominieusement /iɲɔminjøzmɑ̃/ ADV ignominiously

ignominieux, -ieuse /iɲɔminjø, jøz/ ADJ ignominious

ignorance /iɲɔʀɑ̃s/ NF 1 *(= inculture)* ignorance ◆ **~ de** *(= méconnaissance)* ignorance of ◆ **tenir qn/être dans l'~ de qch** to keep sb/be in ignorance of sth *ou* in the dark about sth ◆ **dans l'~ des résultats** ignorant of the results ◆ **d'une ~ crasse** * pig ignorant ‡ 2 *(= lacune)* **de graves ~s en anglais/en matière juridique** serious gaps in his knowledge of English/of legal matters ◆ **cet ouvrage permet de dissiper des ~s** this book helps to dispel people's ignorance; → **pécher**

ignorant, e /iɲɔʀɑ̃, ɑ̃t/ ADJ *(= ne sachant rien)* ignorant *(en* about); ◆ **~ de** *(= ne connaissant pas)* ignorant *ou* unaware of ◆ **~ des usages, il …** ignorant *ou* unaware of the customs, he …, not knowing the customs, he … NM,F ignoramus ◆ **quel ~ tu fais !** what an ignoramus you are! ◆ **ne fais pas l'~** stop pretending you don't know ◆ **parler en ~** to speak from ignorance

ignoré, e /iɲɔʀe/ (ptp de **ignorer**) ADJ *[travaux, chercheurs, événement]* unknown ◆ **~ de tous** *(inconnu)* unknown to anybody; *(boudé)* ignored by all ◆ **vivre ~** to live in obscurity

ignorer /iɲɔʀe/ GRAMMAIRE ACTIVE 33.3, 43.1 ▸ conjug 1 ◂

VT 1 *(= ne pas connaître) [+ incident]* to be unaware of, not to know about *ou* of; *[+ fait, artiste]* not to know ◆ **j'ignore comment/si …** I don't know how/if … ◆ **vous n'ignorez certainement pas que/comment …** you (will) doubtless know that/how …, you're no doubt well aware that/how … ◆ **je l'ignore** I don't know ◆ **j'ignore la réponse** I don't know the answer ◆ **j'ignore tout de cette affaire** I don't know anything *ou* I know nothing about this business ◆ **je n'ignorais pas ces problèmes** I was (fully) aware of these problems, I was not unaware of these problems ◆ **j'ignore avoir dit cela** I am not aware of having said that; → **nul**

2 (= être indifférent à) [+ personne, remarque, avertissement] to ignore
3 (= être sans expérience de) [+ plaisir, guerre, souffrance] not to know, to have had no experience of ◆ **des gosses qui ignorent le savon** (*hum*) kids who have never seen (a cake of) soap *ou* who are unaware of the existence of soap ◆ **des joues qui ignorent le rasoir** cheeks that never see a razor
VPR s'ignorer 1 (= *se méconnaître*) **une tendresse qui s'ignore** an unconscious tenderness ◆ **c'est un poète qui s'ignore** he should have been a poet
2 (= *être indifférents l'un à l'autre*) to ignore each other

⚠ Au sens de 'ne pas connaître' ou 'ne pas savoir', **ignorer** ne se traduit pas par **to ignore**.

IGPN /iʒepeɛn/ **NF** (abrév de **Inspection générale de la police nationale**) → **inspection**
IGS /iʒeɛs/ **NF** (abrév de **Inspection générale des services**) → **inspection**
iguane /igwan/ **NM** iguana
iguanodon /igwanɔdɔ̃/ **NM** iguanodon
ikebana /ikebana/ **NM** ikebana
il /il/ **PRON PERS M** 1 (= *personne*) he; (= *bébé, animal*) it, he; (= *chose*) it; (= *bateau, nation*) she, it ◆ **~s** they ◆ **~ était journaliste** he was a journalist ◆ **prends ce fauteuil, ~ est plus confortable** have this chair – it's more comfortable ◆ **je me méfie de son chien, ~ mord** I don't trust his dog – it bites ◆ **l'insecte emmagasine la nourriture qu'~ trouve** the insect stores the food it finds ◆ **le Japon/le Canada a décidé qu'~ n'accepterait pas** Japan/Canada decided she *ou* they *ou* it wouldn't accept; → **avoir**
2 (*interrog emphatique*) **Paul est-~ rentré ?** is Paul back? ◆ **le courrier est-~ arrivé ?** has the mail come? ◆ **les enfants sont-~s bien couverts ?** are the children warmly wrapped up? ◆ **~ est si beau cet enfant/cet arbre** this child/tree is so beautiful ◆ **tu sais, ton oncle, ~ est arrivé** * your uncle has arrived you know
3 (*impers*) it ◆ **~ fait beau** it's a fine day ◆ **~ y a un enfant/trois enfants** there is a child/are three children ◆ **~ est vrai que ...** it is true that ... ◆ **~ faut que je le fasse** I've got to *ou* I must do it; → **fois**
île /il/ **NF** island, isle (*littér*) ◆ **~ corallienne** coral island ◆ **~ déserte** desert island ◆ **les îles** (= *Antilles*) the (French) West Indies ◆ **l'~ de Ré/Bréhat** the île de Ré/Bréhat ◆ **vivre dans une ~** to live on an island
COMP les îles Anglo-Normandes the Channel Islands
l'île de Beauté Corsica
les îles Britanniques the British Isles
l'île de la Cité the Île de la Cité
l'île du Diable Devil's Island
les îles Féroé the Faroe Islands
île flottante (*Culin*) île flottante, floating island
île de glace (*Géog*) ice island
les îles ioniennes the Ionian Islands
l'île de Man the Isle of Man
les îles Marshall the Marshall Islands
l'île Maurice Mauritius
l'île de Pâques Easter Island
les îles Scilly the Scilly Isles, the Scillies
les îles Shetland the Shetland Islands, Shetland
les îles de la Sonde the Sunda Islands
les îles Sorlingues ⇒ **les îles Scilly**
les îles Sous-le-Vent Leeward Islands
l'île de la Tortue Tortuga, La Tortue
l'île de Vancouver Vancouver Island
les îles du Vent the Windward Islands
les îles Vierges the Virgin Islands
l'île de Wight the Isle of Wight

Île-de-France /ildəfʀɑ̃s/ **NF** ◆ **l'~** the Île-de-France (*Paris and the surrounding departments*)
iléon /ileɔ̃/ **NM** ileum
Iliade /iljad/ **NF** ◆ **l'~** the Iliad
iliaque /iljak/ **ADJ** iliac ◆ **os ~** hip bone, innominate bone (*SPÉC*)
îlien, îlienne /iljɛ̃, iljɛn/ **ADJ** island (*épith*) **NM,F** islander
ilion /iljɔ̃/ **NM** ilium
illégal, e (mpl **-aux**) /i(l)legal, o/ **ADJ** illegal; (*Admin*) unlawful; [*organisation, société*] illegal, outlawed ◆ **c'est ~** it's illegal, it's against the law
illégalement /i(l)legalmɑ̃/ **ADV** illegally; (*Admin*) unlawfully
illégalité /i(l)legalite/ **NF** [*d'action*] illegality; (*Admin*) unlawfulness; (= *acte illégal*) illegality ◆ **vivre dans l'~** to live outside the law ◆ **se mettre dans l'~** to break the law ◆ **en toute ~** illegally
illégitime /i(l)leʒitim/ **ADJ** 1 [*enfant*] illegitimate 2 [*acte, gouvernement*] illegitimate, illicit 3 [*optimisme, colère, crainte, soupçon*] unwarranted, unfounded; [*prétention, revendication*] unjustified
illégitimement /i(l)leʒitimmɑ̃/ **ADV** illegitimately
illégitimité /i(l)leʒitimite/ **NF** illegitimacy
illettré, e /i(l)letʀe/ **ADJ, NM,F** illiterate ◆ **les ~s** illiterates, illiterate people
illettrisme /i(l)letʀism/ **NM** illiteracy ◆ **campagne contre l'~** literacy campaign
illicite /i(l)lisit/ **ADJ** illicit
illicitement /i(l)lisitmɑ̃/ **ADV** illicitly
illico * /i(l)liko/ **ADV** ◆ **~ (presto)** pronto *, PDQ *
illimité, e /i(l)limite/ **ADJ** [*moyen, domaine, ressource*] unlimited, limitless; [*confiance*] boundless, unbounded, limitless; [*congé, durée*] indefinite, unlimited
Illinois /ilinwa/ **NM** Illinois
illisibilité /i(l)lizibilite/ **NF** illegibility
illisible /i(l)lizibl/ **ADJ** (= *indéchiffrable*) illegible, unreadable; (= *mauvais*) unreadable
illogique /i(l)lɔʒik/ **ADJ** illogical
illogiquement /i(l)lɔʒikmɑ̃/ **ADV** illogically
illogisme /i(l)lɔʒism/ **NM** illogicality
illumination /i(l)lyminasjɔ̃/ **NF** 1 (= *éclairage*) lighting, illumination; (*avec des projecteurs*) floodlighting 2 (= *lumières*) **~s** illuminations, lights ◆ **les ~s de Noël** the Christmas lights *ou* illuminations 3 (= *inspiration*) flash of inspiration; (*Rel*) inspiration
illuminé, e /i(l)lymine/ (ptp de **illuminer**) **ADJ** (= *éclairé*) lit up (*attrib*), illuminated; (*avec des projecteurs*) floodlit ◆ **il est comme ~ de l'intérieur** he seems to have a kind of inner light **NM,F** (*péj* = *visionnaire*) visionary, crank (*péj*)
illuminer /i(l)lymine/ ► conjug 1 ◄ **VT** 1 (= *éclairer*) to light up, to illuminate; (*avec des projecteurs*) to floodlight 2 [*joie, foi, colère*] to light up; (*Rel*) [+ *prophète, âme*] to enlighten, to illuminate ◆ **le bonheur illuminait son visage** his face shone *ou* was aglow with happiness ◆ **un sourire illumina son visage** a smile lit up her face ◆ **ça va ~ ma journée** that will brighten up my day **VPR s'illuminer** [*visage, ciel*] to light up (*de* with); [*rue, vitrine*] to be lit up
illusion /i(l)lyzjɔ̃/ **NF** illusion ◆ **~ d'optique** optical illusion ◆ **ne te fais aucune ~** don't be under any illusion, don't delude *ou* kid * yourself ◆ **tu te fais des ~s** you're deluding *ou* kidding * yourself ◆ **ça lui donne l'~ de servir à quelque chose** *ou* **qu'il sert à quelque chose** it gives him the illusion *ou* it makes him feel that he's doing something useful ◆ **cet imposteur/ce stratagème ne fera pas ~ longtemps** this impostor/tactic won't delude *ou* fool people for long ◆ **il a perdu ses ~s** he's become disillusioned, he's lost his illusions; → **bercer**
illusionner /i(l)lyzjɔne/ ► conjug 1 ◄ **VPR s'illusionner** to delude o.s. (*sur qch* about sth); ◆ **s'~ sur qn** to delude o.s. *ou* be mistaken about sb **VT** (= *induire en erreur*) to delude
illusionnisme /i(l)lyzjɔnism/ **NM** conjuring
illusionniste /i(l)lyzjɔnist/ **NMF** conjurer, illusionist
illusoire /i(l)lyzwaʀ/ **ADJ** (= *trompeur*) unrealistic, illusory (*frm*) ◆ **il est ~ de croire à une fin rapide de la violence** it would be unrealistic to believe in a swift end to the violence ◆ **un règlement prochain de la crise paraît bien ~** there is no real prospect of a quick end to the crisis
illustrateur, -trice /i(l)lystʀatœʀ, tʀis/ **NM,F** illustrator ◆ **~ sonore** (*TV, Ciné*) music arranger
illustratif, -ive /i(l)lystʀatif, iv/ **ADJ** illustrative
illustration /i(l)lystʀasjɔ̃/ **NF** 1 (= *gravure, exemple*) illustration; (= *iconographie*) illustrations ◆ **à l'~ abondante** copiously illustrated 2 (= *action, technique*) illustration ◆ **l'~ par l'exemple** illustration by example
illustre /i(l)lystʀ/ **ADJ** illustrious, renowned ◆ **l'~ M. Pinot** (*frm, iro*) the illustrious Mr Pinot ◆ **un ~ inconnu** (*hum*) a person of obscure repute (*hum*)
illustré, e /i(l)lystʀe/ **ADJ** illustrated **NM** (= *journal*) comic
illustrer /i(l)lystʀe/ GRAMMAIRE ACTIVE 53.5 ► conjug 1 ◄ **VT** 1 (*avec images, notes*) to illustrate (*de* with); ◆ **ça illustre bien son caractère** that's a good example of what he's like 2 (*littér* = *rendre célèbre*) to bring fame to, to render illustrious (*littér*) **VPR s'illustrer** [*personne*] to win fame *ou* renown, to become famous (*par, dans* through)
illustrissime /i(l)lystʀisim/ **ADJ** (*hum ou* ††) most illustrious
ILM /iɛlɛm/ **NM** (abrév de **immeuble à loyer moyen** *ou* **modéré**) → **immeuble**
îlot /ilo/ **NM** 1 (= *île*) small island, islet 2 (= *petite zone*) island ◆ **~ de fraîcheur/de verdure** oasis *ou* island of coolness/of greenery ◆ **~ de résistance/prospérité** pocket of resistance/prosperity 3 (= *groupe d'habitations*) (housing) block 4 (*Comm*) gondola 5 (*dans une rue*) **~ directionnel** traffic island
îlotage /ilɔtaʒ/ **NM** community policing
ilote /ilɔt/ **NMF** (*Hist*) Helot; (*littér*) slave, serf
îlotier /ilɔtje/ **NM** ≈ community policeman
image /imaʒ/ **NF** 1 (= *dessin*) picture; (*Scol*) *picture given to pupils as a reward for good work* ◆ **les ~s d'un film** the frames of a film ◆ **l'~ et le son** (*Audiov*) picture and sound ◆ **l'~ est nette/floue** (*Ciné, TV*) the picture is clear/fuzzy ◆ **popularisé par l'~** popularized by the camera ◆ **en ~s** on film, in pictures ◆ **apparaître à l'~** (*TV*) to appear on screen; → **chasseur, livre¹, sage**
2 ◆ **~ de** (= *représentation*) picture of; (= *ressemblance*) image of ◆ **l'~ du père** the father figure ◆ **une ~ fidèle de la France** an accurate picture of France ◆ **ils présentent l'~ du bonheur** they are the picture of happiness ◆ **fait à l'~ de** made in the image of ◆ **Dieu créa l'homme à son ~** God created man in his own image ◆ **donner une ~ saisissante de la situation** to paint a vivid picture of the situation
3 (= *métaphore*) image ◆ **les ~s chez Blake** Blake's imagery ◆ **s'exprimer par ~s** to express o.s. in images

[4] (= *reflet*) (*gén*) reflection, image; (*Phys*) image ◆ **regarder son ~ dans l'eau** to gaze at one's reflection in the water ◆ **~ réelle/virtuelle** real/virtual image
[5] (= *vision mentale*) image, picture; (= *réputation*) image ◆ **~ visuelle/auditive** visual/auditory image ◆ **~ de soi** self-image ◆ **se faire une ~ fausse/idéalisée de qch** to have a false/an idealized picture of sth ◆ **le pays veut améliorer/soigner son ~ à l'étranger** the country wants to improve/enhance its image abroad
COMP **l'image animée** ◆ **les ~s animées** (*gén*) moving pictures; (*Ordin*) animated graphics
images d'archives library pictures
image d'Épinal *popular 18th/19th century print depicting idealized scenes of traditional French life;* (*fig*) idealized image ◆ **on est loin des ~s d'Épinal de millionnaires roulant dans de rutilantes voitures de sport** this is far from the idealized images of millionaires driving around in gleaming sports cars ◆ **cette réunion familiale était une touchante ~ d'Épinal** the family reunion was a touching scene of traditional family life
image fixe (*Ciné*) still (frame); (*Ordin*) still image
image de marque [*de produit*] brand image; [*de parti, firme, politicien*] public image
image pieuse holy picture
image radar radar image
image satellite satellite picture
image de synthèse computer-generated image *ou* picture ◆ **~s de synthèse** (*domaine*) computer graphics; (*animées*) computer animation

IMAGES D'ÉPINAL

Distinctive prints depicting a variety of scenes in a realistic but stereotypical manner were produced in the town of Épinal, in the Vosges, in the early nineteenth century. The prints became so popular that the term **image d'Épinal** has passed into the language and is now used to refer to any form of stereotypical representation.

imagé, e /imaʒe/ (ptp de **imager**) ADJ [*poème, texte*] full of imagery (*attrib*); (*euph*) [*langage*] colourful

imager /imaʒe/ ► conjug 3 ◄ VT [+ *style, langage*] to embellish with images

imagerie /imaʒʀi/ NF (*Hist* = *commerce*) coloured-print trade; (= *images, gravures*) prints ◆ **l'~ romantique** (*Littérat*) romantic imagery ◆ **l'~ médicale** medical imaging ◆ **~ par résonance magnétique/par ultrasons** magnetic resonance/ultrasound imaging

imagiciel /imaʒisjɛl/ NM graphics software

imagier /imaʒje/ NM (*Hist*) (= *peintre*) painter of popular pictures; (= *sculpteur*) sculptor of figurines; (= *imprimeur*) coloured-print maker; (= *vendeur*) print seller

imaginable /imaʒinabl/ ADJ conceivable, imaginable ◆ **difficilement ~** hard to imagine ◆ **un tel comportement n'était pas ~ il y a 50 ans** such behaviour was inconceivable 50 years ago; → **possible**

imaginaire /imaʒinɛʀ/ ADJ (= *fictif*) imaginary; [*monde*] make-believe, imaginary ◆ **ces persécutés/incompris ~s** these people who (falsely) believe they are *ou* believe themselves persecuted/misunderstood; → **malade, nombre** NM ◆ **l'~** the imagination ◆ **dans l'~ de Joyce** in Joyce's imaginative world *ou* universe

imaginatif, -ive /imaʒinatif, iv/ ADJ imaginative ◆ **c'est un grand ~** he has a vivid imagination

imagination /imaʒinasjɔ̃/ NF (= *faculté*) imagination; (= *chimère, rêve*) imagination (*NonC*), fancy ◆ **tout ce qu'il avait vécu en ~** everything he had experienced in his imagination ◆ **ce sont de pures ~s** that's sheer imagination, those are pure fancies ◆ **monstres sortis tout droit de son ~** monsters straight out of his imagination ◆ **avoir de l'~** to be imaginative, to have a good imagination ◆ **avoir trop d'~** to imagine things ◆ **une ~ débordante** a lively *ou* vivid imagination ◆ **avec un peu d'~ ...** with a little imagination ... ◆ **l'~ au pouvoir !** (*slogan*) power to the imagination!

imaginer /imaʒine/ GRAMMAIRE ACTIVE 33.2 ► conjug 1 ◄
VT [1] (= *se représenter, supposer*) to imagine ◆ **~ que** to imagine that ◆ **tu imagines la scène !** you can imagine *ou* picture the scene! ◆ **on imagine mal leurs conditions de travail** their working conditions are hard to imagine ◆ **je l'imaginais plus vieux** I imagined him to be older, I pictured him as being older ◆ **qu'allez-vous ~ là ?** what on earth are you thinking of? ◆ **et tu vas t'y opposer, j'imagine ?** (*ton de défi*) and I imagine *ou* suppose you're going to oppose it?
[2] (= *inventer*) [+ *système, plan*] to devise, to dream up ◆ **qu'est-il encore allé ~ ?*** now what has he dreamed up? *ou* thought up? ◆ **il a imaginé d'ouvrir un magasin** he has taken it into his head to open up a shop, he has dreamed up the idea of opening a shop
VPR **s'imaginer** [1] (= *se figurer*) to imagine ◆ **imagine-toi une île paradisiaque** imagine *ou* picture an island paradise ◆ **je me l'imaginais plus jeune** I imagined him to be younger, I pictured him as being younger ◆ **comme on peut se l'~ ...** as you can (well) imagine ... ◆ **imagine-toi que je n'ai pas que ça à faire !** look, I've got other things to do!
[2] (= *se voir*) to imagine o.s., to picture o.s. ◆ **s'~ à 60 ans/en vacances** to imagine *ou* picture o.s. at 60/on holiday
[3] (= *croire à tort que*) **s'~ que** to imagine *ou* think that ◆ **il s'imaginait pouvoir faire cela** he imagined *ou* thought he could do that ◆ **si tu t'imagines que je vais te laisser faire !** don't think I'm going to let you get away with that!

imago /imago/ NF (*Bio, Psych*) imago

imam /imam/ NM imam

IMAX /imaks/ NM IMAX

imbattable /ɛ̃batabl/ ADJ [*prix, personne, record*] unbeatable ◆ **il est ~ aux échecs** he is unbeatable at chess

imbécile /ɛ̃besil/ ADJ (= *stupide*) stupid, idiotic; († : *Méd*) imbecilic (*SPÉC*), idiotic NMF [1] (= *idiot*) idiot, imbecile ◆ **faire l'~*** to act *ou* play the fool ◆ **ne fais pas l'~*** (= *n'agis pas bêtement*) don't be an idiot* *ou* a fool; (= *ne simule pas la bêtise*) stop acting stupid* ◆ **le premier ~ venu te le dira** any fool will tell you ◆ **c'est un ~ heureux** he's living in a fool's paradise ◆ **les ~s heureux** the blissfully ignorant [2] († : *Méd*) imbecile, idiot

imbécillité /ɛ̃besilite/ NF [1] [*d'action, personne*] idiocy; († : *Méd*) imbecility, idiocy [2] (= *action*) idiotic *ou* stupid *ou* imbecile thing to do; (= *propos*) idiotic *ou* stupid *ou* imbecile thing to say; (= *film, livre*) trash (*NonC*), rubbish (*NonC*) (*Brit*) ◆ **tu racontes des ~s** you're talking nonsense *ou* rubbish (*Brit*) ◆ **ne va pas voir de telles ~s** don't go and see such trash *ou* rubbish (*Brit*)

imberbe /ɛ̃bɛʀb/ ADJ [*personne*] beardless, smooth-cheeked; [*visage*] beardless

imbiber /ɛ̃bibe/ ► conjug 1 ◄ VT (= *imprégner*) ◆ **~ un tampon/une compresse de** to soak *ou* moisten *ou* impregnate a pad/compress with ◆ **imbibé d'eau** [+ *chaussures, étoffe*] saturated (with water), soaked; [+ *terre*] saturated, waterlogged ◆ **gâteau imbibé de rhum** cake soaked in rum ◆ **être imbibé*** (= *ivre*) to be sloshed*; (= *alcoolique*) to be a lush* VPR **s'imbiber** ◆ **s'~ de** to become saturated *ou* soaked with

imbit(t)able** /ɛ̃bitabl/ ADJ [1] (= *difficile à comprendre*) fucking** hard to understand ◆ **cette équation est imbit(t)able** I don't understand this fucking** equation [2] (= *insupportable*) **il est imbit(t)able** he's a fucking pain in the arse** (*Brit*) *ou* ass** (*US*)

imbrication /ɛ̃bʀikasjɔ̃/ NF [*de problèmes, souvenirs, parcelles*] interweaving; [*de plaques, tuiles*] overlapping, imbrication (*SPÉC*)

imbriqué, e /ɛ̃bʀike/ (ptp de **imbriquer**) ADJ [*plaques, tuiles*] overlapping, imbricate(d) (*SPÉC*); [*problèmes*] interwoven, interlinked; [*récits, souvenirs*] interwoven; [*économies, politiques*] interlinked ◆ **les deux cultures sont étroitement ~es l'une dans l'autre** the two cultures are inextricably interlinked *ou* deeply enmeshed

imbriquer /ɛ̃bʀike/ ► conjug 1 ◄ VPR **s'imbriquer** [*problèmes, affaires*] to be linked *ou* interwoven; [*plaques*] to overlap (each other), to imbricate (*SPÉC*) ◆ **ça s'imbrique l'un dans l'autre** [*cubes*] they fit into each other; [*problèmes*] they are linked *ou* interwoven ◆ **ce nouveau problème est venu s'~ dans une situation déjà compliquée** this new problem has arisen to complicate an already complex situation VT [+ *cubes*] to fit into each other; [+ *plaques*] to overlap

imbroglio /ɛ̃bʀɔljo/ NM (*fig*) tangle, mess ◆ **un véritable ~ judiciaire** a real legal tangle *ou* mess ◆ **la situation tourne à l'~ politique** the situation has developed into a real political tangle *ou* mess

imbu, e /ɛ̃by/ ADJ ◆ **~ de lui-même** *ou* **de sa personne** full of himself, self-important ◆ **le mâle humain, ~ de supériorité** the human male, always so superior *ou* so full of himself ◆ **un peuple ~ de préjugés** a people steeped in prejudice

imbuvable /ɛ̃byvabl/ ADJ [1] [*boisson*] undrinkable [2] (= *mauvais*) * [*personne*] unbearable, insufferable; [*film, livre*] unbearably awful*

IMC /iɛmse/ NM (abrév de **indice de masse corporelle**) BMI

IME /iɛmə/ NM (abrév de **Institut monétaire européen**) EMI

imitable /imitabl/ ADJ imitable ◆ **facilement ~** easy to imitate, easily imitated

imitateur, -trice /imitatœʀ, tʀis/ ADJ imitative NM,F imitator; (*Théât*) [*de voix, personne*] impersonator; [*de bruits*] imitator

imitatif, -ive /imitatif, iv/ ADJ imitative

imitation /imitasjɔ̃/ NF [1] (= *reproduction*) [*de bruit*] imitation; (= *parodie*) [*de personnage célèbre*] imitation, impersonation; [*de voix, geste*] imitation, mimicry; (= *sketch*) impression, imitation, impersonation ◆ **avoir le don d'~** to have a gift for imitating people *ou* for mimicry ◆ **à l'~ de** in imitation of [2] [*de héros, style*] imitation, copying [3] (= *contrefaçon*) [*de document, signature*] forgery [4] (= *copie*) [*de bijou, fourrure*] imitation; [*de meuble, tableau*] copy, reproduction ◆ **c'est en ~ cuir** it's imitation leather [5] (*Mus*) imitation

imiter /imite/ ► conjug 1 ◄ VT [1] [+ *bruit*] to imitate; [+ *personnage célèbre*] to imitate, to impersonate, to take off* (*Brit*); [+ *voix, geste, accent*] to imitate, to mimic [2] (= *prendre pour modèle*) [+ *héros, style, écrivain*] to imitate, to copy [3] [+ *document, signature*] to forge [4] (= *faire comme*) **il se leva et tout le monde l'imita** he got up and everybody did likewise *ou* followed suit [5] (= *avoir l'aspect de*) [*matière, revêtement*] to look like ◆ **un lino qui imite le marbre** lino made to look like marble, marble-effect lino

immaculé, e /imakyle/ ADJ [*linge, surface*] spotless, immaculate; [*blancheur*] immaculate;

[réputation] spotless, unsullied, immaculate ◆ **d'un blanc** ~ spotlessly white ◆ **l'Immaculée Conception** *(Rel)* the Immaculate Conception

immanence /imanɑ̃s/ NF immanence

immanent, e /imanɑ̃, ɑ̃t/ ADJ immanent *(à* in) → **justice**

immangeable /ɛ̃mɑ̃ʒabl/ ADJ uneatable, inedible

immanquable /ɛ̃mɑ̃kabl/ ADJ *[cible, but]* impossible to miss *(attrib)* ◆ **c'était** ~ ! it had to happen!, it was bound to happen!, it was inevitable!

immanquablement /ɛ̃mɑ̃kabləmɑ̃/ ADV inevitably, without fail

immatérialité /i(m)mateʀjalite/ NF immateriality

immatériel, -elle /i(m)mateʀjɛl/ ADJ *[légèreté, minceur, plaisir]* ethereal; *(Philos)* immaterial

immatriculation /imatʀikylasjɔ̃/ NF *(gén)* registration *(à* with); *(Helv = inscription à l'université)* enrolment *(Brit)*, enrollment *(US)*, registration; → **numéro, plaque**

> **IMMATRICULATION**
>
> The last two digits on vehicle number plates in France refer to the code number of the département where they were registered (cars registered in the Dordogne bear the number 24, for example).

immatriculer /imatʀikyle/ ► conjug 1 ◄ VT *[+ véhicule, personne]* to register ◆ **faire** ~ *[+ véhicule]* to register ◆ **se faire** ~ to register *(à* with); ◆ **voiture immatriculée dans le Vaucluse** car with a Vaucluse registration number *(Brit)* ou with a Vaucluse license plate *(US)* ◆ **une voiture immatriculée CM 75** a car with CM 75 on its number plate *(Brit)* ou its license plate *(US)* ◆ **s'~ (à l'université)** *(Helv)* to enrol at university, to register (as a student)

immature /imatyʀ/ ADJ immature

immaturité /imatyʀite/ NF *(littér)* immaturity

immédiat, e /imedja, jat/ ADJ immediate; *[soulagement]* immediate, instant *(épith)* ◆ **en contact** ~ **avec le mur** in direct contact with the wall ◆ **dans l'avenir** ~ in the immediate future ◆ **la mort fut ~e** death was instantaneous NM ◆ **dans l'~** for the time being, for the moment

immédiatement /imedjatmɑ̃/ ADV immediately, at once, directly ◆ ~ **après** immediately after, straight after

immédiateté /imedjatte/ NF *(Philos)* immediacy

immémorial, e (mpl **-iaux**) /i(m)memɔʀjal, jo/ ADJ age-old ◆ **depuis des temps immémoriaux** *(littér)*, **de temps** ~ from time immemorial

immense /i(m)mɑ̃s/ ADJ 1 (= *très grand)* vast; *[personne]* huge; *[bonté, sagesse, chagrin]* great, tremendous; *[influence, avantage succès, talent]* huge, tremendous ◆ **l'~ majorité des électeurs** the vast majority of voters ◆ **dans l'~ majorité des cas** in the vast majority of cases 2 (= *talentueux)* **c'est un** ~ **acteur/écrivain** he's a great ou tremendous actor/writer

immensément /i(m)mɑ̃semɑ̃/ ADV immensely, tremendously

immensité /i(m)mɑ̃site/ NF *[d'océan, espace, horizon, désert]* immensity; *[de fortune, pays]* vastness ◆ **le regard perdu dans l'~** *(littér)* gazing into infinity

immergé, e /imɛʀʒe/ (ptp de **immerger**) ADJ *[terres]* submerged; *[plantes]* immerged; *[câble]* laid under water ◆ ~ **par 100 mètres de fond** lying 100 metres down ◆ **rochers ~s** submerged ou underwater rocks, rocks under water ◆ **la partie ~e de la balise** the part of the buoy which is under water ou which is submerged ◆ ~ **dans ses problèmes** engrossed in ou taken up with his own problems ◆ **économie ~e** black ou underground economy; → **iceberg**

immerger /imɛʀʒe/ ► conjug 3 ◄ VT *[+ objet]* to immerse, to submerge; *[+ fondations]* to build under water; *[+ déchets]* to dump at sea, to dispose of at sea; *[+ câble]* to lay under water; *[+ corps]* to bury at sea; *(Rel) [+ catéchumène]* to immerse VPR **s'immerger** *[sous-marin]* to dive, to submerge ◆ **s'~ dans un travail** to immerse o.s. in a piece of work

immérité, e /imeʀite/ ADJ undeserved, unmerited

immersion /imɛʀsjɔ̃/ NF 1 *[d'objet]* immersion, submersion; *[de fondations]* building under water; *[de déchets]* dumping ou disposal at sea; *[de câble]* laying under water; *[de corps]* burying at sea ◆ **baptême par** ~ baptism by immersion ◆ **par ~ totale dans la langue** by immersing oneself totally in the language 2 *[de sous-marin]* diving, submersion 3 *(Astron)* immersion, ingress

immettable /ɛ̃metabl/ ADJ *[vêtement]* unwearable

immeuble /imœbl/ NM 1 (= *bâtiment)* building; *(à usage d'habitation)* block of flats *(Brit)*, apartment building *(US)* 2 *(Jur)* real estate *(NonC)* ADJ *(Jur) [biens]* real, immovable

COMP **immeuble de bureaux** office block *(Brit)* ou building *(US)*
immeuble d'habitation residential block, apartment building *(US)*
immeuble à loyer moyen, immeuble à loyer modéré ≈ block of council flats *(Brit)*, low-rent building *(US)*
immeuble de rapport residential property (for renting), investment property
immeuble à usage locatif block of rented flats *(Brit)*, rental apartment building *(US)*; → **copropriété**

immigrant, e /imigʀɑ̃, ɑ̃t/ ADJ, NM,F immigrant

immigration /imigʀasjɔ̃/ NF immigration ◆ **(les services de) l'~** the immigration department ◆ ~ **clandestine** illegal immigration

immigré, e /imigʀe/ (ptp de **immigrer**) ADJ, NM,F immigrant ◆ ~ **de la deuxième génération** second-generation immigrant ◆ ~ **clandestin** illegal immigrant

immigrer /imigʀe/ ► conjug 1 ◄ VI to immigrate *(à, dans* into)

imminence /iminɑ̃s/ NF imminence

imminent, e /iminɑ̃, ɑ̃t/ ADJ imminent, impending *(épith)*

immiscer (s') /imise/ ► conjug 3 ◄ VPR ◆ **s'~ dans** to interfere in ou with

immixtion /imiksjɔ̃/ NF interference *(dans* in, with)

immobile /i(m)mɔbil/ ADJ 1 *[personne, eau, air, arbre]* motionless, still; *[visage]* immobile; *[pièce de machine]* fixed ◆ **regard** ~ fixed stare ◆ **rester** ~ to stay ou keep still ◆ **il était** ~ he wasn't moving 2 *(littér) [dogme]* immovable; *[institutions]* unchanging, permanent

> ⚠ Attention à ne pas traduire automatiquement **immobile** par le mot anglais **immobile**, qui est d'un registre plus soutenu.

immobilier, -ière /imɔbilje, jɛʀ/ ADJ *[vente, crise]* property *(épith)*; *[succession]* in real estate *(attrib)* ◆ **marché** ~ property market ◆ **biens ~s** real estate, real property *(Brit)* ◆ **la situation immobilière est satisfaisante** the property situation is satisfactory; → **agence, société** NM ◆ **l'~** (= *commerce)* the property business, the real-estate business; *(Jur)* (= *biens)* real estate immovables

immobilisation /imɔbilizasjɔ̃/ NF 1 *[de membre blessé, circulation]* immobilization; *[de centrale nucléaire]* shutdown ◆ **cela a entraîné l'~ totale de la circulation** that brought the traffic to a complete standstill, that brought about the complete immobilization of traffic ◆ **attendez l'~ complète du train/de l'appareil** wait until the train is completely stationary/ the aircraft has come to a complete standstill ou halt ou stop ◆ **la réparation nécessite l'~ de la voiture/l'avion** the car will have to be taken off the road/the plane will have to be grounded to be repaired 2 *(Jur) [de bien]* conversion into an immovable 3 *[de capitaux]* immobilization, tying up ◆ **~s** fixed assets 4 *(Sport)* hold

immobiliser /imɔbilize/ ► conjug 1 ◄ VT *[+ troupes, membre blessé]* to immobilize; *[+ circulation, affaires]* to bring to a standstill, to immobilize; *[+ machine, véhicule]* (= *stopper)* to stop, to bring to a halt ou standstill; (= *empêcher de fonctionner)* to immobilize; *(avec un sabot de Denver)* to clamp; *(Jur) [+ biens]* to convert into immovables; *[+ capitaux]* to immobilize, to tie up ◆ **ça l'immobilise à son domicile** it keeps him housebound ◆ **avions immobilisés par la neige** aeroplanes grounded by snow ◆ **la peur l'immobilisa** he was paralyzed with fear, he was rooted to the spot with fear VPR **s'immobiliser** *[personne]* to stop, to stand still; *[machine, véhicule, échanges commerciaux]* to come to a halt ou a standstill

immobilisme /imɔbilism/ NM *[de gouvernement, entreprise]* failure to act ◆ **faire de/être partisan de l'~** to try to maintain/support the status quo

immobiliste /imɔbilist/ ADJ *[politique]* designed to maintain the status quo ◆ **c'est un** ~ he is a supporter of the status quo, he is opposed to progress

immobilité /imɔbilite/ NF *[de personne, foule, eau, arbre]* stillness; *[de visage]* immobility; *[de regard]* fixedness; *[d'institutions]* unchanging nature, permanence ◆ **le médecin lui a ordonné l'~ complète** the doctor ordered him not to move (at all) ◆ ~ **forcée** forced immobility ◆ ~ **politique** lack of political change, political inertia

immodération /imɔdeʀasjɔ̃/ NF immoderation

immodéré, e /imɔdeʀe/ ADJ immoderate, inordinate

immodérément /imɔdeʀemɑ̃/ ADV immoderately, inordinately

immodeste /imɔdɛst/ ADJ immodest

immodestie /imɔdɛsti/ NF immodesty

immolation /imɔlasjɔ̃/ NF *(Rel)* immolation ◆ ~ **(par le feu)** (= *suicide)* self-immolation

immoler /imɔle/ ► conjug 1 ◄ VT (= *sacrifier)* to immolate *(littér)*, to sacrifice *(à* to); *(littér = massacrer)* to slay *(littér)* ◆ **il a été immolé sur l'autel des intérêts nationaux** he was sacrificed on the altar of national interest VPR **s'immoler** to sacrifice o.s. *(à* to); ◆ **s'~ par le feu** to set fire to o.s., to immolate o.s.

immonde /i(m)mɔ̃d/ ADJ *[taudis]* squalid; *[langage, action, personne]* base, vile; *[crime]* sordid, hideous; (* = *laid)* ugly, hideous; *(Rel)* unclean ◆ **il est** ~ ! he's disgusting!

immondices /i(m)mɔ̃dis/ NFPL (= *ordures)* refuse *(NonC)* ◆ **commettre/proférer des** ~ *(littér)* to do/say unspeakable things

immoral, e (mpl **-aux**) /i(m)mɔʀal, o/ ADJ immoral

immoralisme /i(m)mɔʀalism/ NM immoralism

immoraliste /i(m)mɔʀalist/ ADJ, NMF immoralist

immoralité /i(m)mɔʀalite/ NF immorality

immortaliser /imɔʀtalize/ ▸ conjug 1 ◂ VT to immortalize VPR **s'immortaliser** to win immortality, to win eternal fame (*par* thanks to)

immortalité /imɔʀtalite/ NF immortality

immortel, -elle /imɔʀtɛl/ ADJ immortal NM,F **Immortel(le)** *member of the Académie française* NF **immortelle** (*= fleur*) everlasting flower

immotivé, e /i(m)mɔtive/ ADJ *[action, crime]* unmotivated; *[réclamation, crainte]* groundless

immuabilité /imɥabilite/ NF ⇒ **immutabilité**

immuable /imɥabl/ ADJ unchanging ◆ **il est resté ~ dans ses convictions** he remained unchanged in his convictions ◆ **vêtu de son ~ complet à carreaux** wearing that eternal checked suit of his

immuablement /imɥabləmɑ̃/ ADV *[fonctionner, se passer]* immutably; *[triste, grognon]* perpetually ◆ **ciel ~ bleu** permanently *ou* perpetually blue sky

immun, e /imœ̃, yn/ ADJ immune ◆ **réponse/réaction ~e** immune response/reaction

immunisation /imynizasjɔ̃/ NF immunization

immuniser /imynize/ ▸ conjug 1 ◂ VT (*Méd*) to immunize (*contre* against); ◆ **je suis immunisé** (*fig*) it no longer has any effect on me ◆ **être immunisé contre les tentations** to be immune to temptation ◆ **ça l'immunisera contre le désir de recommencer** this'll stop him ever *ou* this'll cure him of ever wanting to do it again ◆ **il s'est immunisé contre leurs critiques** he's become immune *ou* impervious to their criticism

immunitaire /imynitɛʀ/ ADJ immune; *[défenses]* immunological; *[réactions]* immune

immunité /imynite/ NF (*Bio, Jur*) immunity ◆ **~ diplomatique/parlementaire** diplomatic/parliamentary immunity ◆ **~ fiscale** immunity from taxation, tax immunity ◆ **~ cellulaire** cell-mediated immunity; → **levée**[2]

immunodéficience /imynodefisjɑ̃s/ NF immunodeficiency; → **syndrome, virus**

immunodéficitaire /imynodefisitɛʀ/ ADJ immunodeficient

immunodépresseur /imynodepʀesœʀ/ ADJ, NM immunosuppressant, immunodepressant

immunodépressif, -ive /imynodepʀesif, iv/ ADJ immunosuppressive, immunodepressive

immunodéprimé, e /imynodepʀime/ ADJ immunosuppressed, immunocompromised

immunogène /imynɔʒɛn/ ADJ immunogenic

immunoglobuline /imynoglɔbylin/ NF immunoglobulin

immunologie /imynɔlɔʒi/ NF immunology

immunologique /imynɔlɔʒik/ ADJ immunological

immunologiste /imynɔlɔʒist/ NMF immunologist

immunostimulant, e /imynostimylɑ̃, ɑ̃t/ ADJ *[substance, traitement]* that stimulates the immune system NM immunostimulant

immunosuppresseur /imynosypʀesœʀ/ NM immunosuppressive drug, immunosuppressant (drug)

immunothérapie /imynoteʀapi/ NF immunotherapy

immutabilité /i(m)mytabilite/ NF immutability

impact /ɛ̃pakt/ NM 1 (*= heurt*) impact (*sur* on); ◆ **mur criblé d'~s de balles** (*= trace de heurt*) wall riddled with bullet holes; → **point**[1] 2 (*= effet*) impact (*sur* on); ◆ **l'argument a de l'~** the argument has some impact ◆ **étude d'~** (*Admin, Écon*) impact study

impacté, e /ɛ̃pakte/ ADJ (*Ordin*) *[système]* impacted

impacter /ɛ̃pakte/ ▸ conjug 1 ◂ VT INDIR ◆ **~ sur** *[+ résultats, situation]* to impact on, to have an impact on

impair, e /ɛ̃pɛʀ/ ADJ *[nombre]* odd, uneven; *[jour]* odd; *[page]* odd-numbered; *[vers]* irregular (*with uneven number of syllables*); *[organe]* unpaired ◆ **côté ~ d'une rue** *side of the street where the buildings have odd numbers* NM 1 (*= gaffe*) blunder, faux pas ◆ **commettre un ~** to (make a) blunder, to make a faux pas 2 (*Casino*) **miser sur l'~** to put one's money on the impair *ou* odd numbers ◆ **"impair et manque"** "impair et manque"

impala /impala/ NM impala

impalpable /ɛ̃palpabl/ ADJ (*= très fin*) *[cendre, poussière]* extremely fine; (*= immatériel*) *[barrière, frontière]* intangible, impalpable

impaludation /ɛ̃palydasjɔ̃/ NF infection with malaria

impaludé, e /ɛ̃palyde/ ADJ *[malade]* suffering from malaria; *[région]* malaria-infected

imparable /ɛ̃paʀabl/ ADJ 1 *[coup, tir]* unstoppable 2 *[argument, riposte]* unanswerable; *[logique]* unanswerable, implacable

impardonnable /ɛ̃paʀdɔnabl/ ADJ *[faute]* unforgivable, unpardonable ◆ **vous êtes ~ (d'avoir fait cela)** you cannot be forgiven (for doing that), it's unforgivable of you (to have done that)

imparfait, e /ɛ̃paʀfɛ, ɛt/ ADJ (*gén*) imperfect NM (*Ling*) imperfect tense ◆ **à l'~** in the imperfect (tense)

imparfaitement /ɛ̃paʀfɛtmɑ̃/ ADV imperfectly ◆ **connaître ~ qch** to have an imperfect knowledge of sth

impartial, e (mpl **-iaux**) /ɛ̃paʀsjal, jo/ ADJ impartial, unbiased, unprejudiced

impartialement /ɛ̃paʀsjalmɑ̃/ ADV impartially, without bias *ou* prejudice

impartialité /ɛ̃paʀsjalite/ NF impartiality ◆ **en toute ~** from a completely impartial standpoint ◆ **faire preuve d'~ dans ses jugements** to show impartiality in one's judgements

impartir /ɛ̃paʀtiʀ/ ▸ conjug 2 ◂ VT (*littér = attribuer à*) ◆ **~ des devoirs/une mission à qn** to assign duties/a mission to sb ◆ **~ des pouvoirs à** to invest powers in ◆ **~ un délai à** (*Jur*) to grant an extension to ◆ **dans les délais impartis** within the time allowed ◆ **le temps qui vous était imparti est écoulé** (*Jeux*) your time is up ◆ **les dons que Dieu nous a impartis** the gifts God has bestowed upon us *ou* has endowed us with *ou* has imparted to us

impasse /ɛ̃pɑs/ NF 1 (*= cul-de-sac*) dead end, cul-de-sac; (*sur panneau*) no through road 2 (*= situation sans issue*) impasse ◆ **être dans l'~** *[négociations]* to have reached an impasse, to have reached deadlock; *[personne]* to be at a dead end; *[relation]* to have reached a dead end ◆ **pour sortir les négociations de l'~** to break the deadlock in the negotiations ◆ **notre pays doit sortir de l'~** our country must get out of the rut it's in 3 (*Scol, Univ*) **j'ai fait 3 ~s en géographie** I skipped over *ou* missed out (*Brit*) 3 topics in my geography revision ◆ **faire l'~ sur qch** to choose to overlook sth 4 (*Cartes*) finesse ◆ **faire une ~** to (make a) finesse ◆ **faire l'~ au roi** to finesse against the king 5 (*Fin*) **~ budgétaire** budget deficit

impassibilité /ɛ̃pasibilite/ NF impassiveness, impassivity

impassible /ɛ̃pasibl/ ADJ impassive

impassiblement /ɛ̃pasibləmɑ̃/ ADV impassively

impatiemment /ɛ̃pasjamɑ̃/ ADV impatiently

impatience /ɛ̃pasjɑ̃s/ NF impatience ◆ **il était dans l'~ de la revoir** he was impatient to see her again, he couldn't wait to see her again ◆ **il répliqua avec ~ que ...** he replied impatiently that ... ◆ **avoir des ~s dans les jambes** † to have the fidgets*

impatiens /ɛ̃pasjɑ̃s/ NF (*= plante*) Busy Lizzie, impatiens (*SPÉC*)

impatient, e /ɛ̃pasjɑ̃, jɑ̃t/ ADJ *[personne, geste, attente]* impatient ◆ **~ de faire qch** eager *ou* keen to do sth ◆ **j'étais ~e de voir leur réaction** I was eager *ou* keen to see how they would react ◆ **je suis si ~ de te revoir** I just can't wait to see you again*, I'm really looking forward to seeing you again NF **impatiente** ⇒ **impatiens**

impatienter /ɛ̃pasjɑ̃te/ ▸ conjug 1 ◂ VT to irritate, to annoy VPR **s'impatienter** to grow *ou* get impatient, to lose patience (*contre qn* with sb; *contre ou de qch* at sth)

impavide /ɛ̃pavid/ ADJ (*littér*) unruffled, impassive, cool ◆ **~ devant le danger** cool *ou* unruffled in the face of danger

impayable* /ɛ̃pɛjabl/ ADJ (*= drôle*) priceless* ◆ **il est ~ !** he's priceless!*, he's a scream!*

impayé, e /ɛ̃peje/ ADJ unpaid NMPL **impayés** outstanding payments

impec* /ɛ̃pɛk/ ADJ abrév de **impeccable**

impeccable /ɛ̃pekabl/ ADJ 1 (*= parfait*) *[travail, style, technique, service]* impeccable, perfect, faultless; *[employé]* perfect; *[diction]* impeccable ◆ **parler un français ~** to speak impeccable French ◆ **(c'est) ~ !*** great!*, brilliant!* ◆ **ça va ? – ~ !** is it OK? – it's fine! 2 (*= net*) *[personne]* impeccable, impeccably dressed; *[coiffure]* impeccable, immaculate; *[appartement, voiture]* spotless, spotlessly clean, impeccable

impeccablement /ɛ̃pekabləmɑ̃/ ADV *[coiffé, habillé, maquillé, repassé]* impeccably, immaculately; *[rangé, coupé, entretenu]* beautifully ◆ **une robe ~ finie** a beautifully finished dress

impécunieux, -ieuse /ɛ̃pekynjø, jøz/ ADJ (*littér*) impecunious

impécuniosité /ɛ̃pekynjozite/ NF (*littér*) impecuniousness

impédance /ɛ̃pedɑ̃s/ NF (*Élec*) impedance

impedimenta /ɛ̃pedimɛ̃ta/ NMPL (*Mil, fig*) impedimenta

impénétrabilité /ɛ̃penetʀabilite/ NF 1 *[de forêt, secteur]* impenetrability 2 *[de mystère, desseins]* unfathomableness, impenetrability 3 *[de personnage, caractère]* inscrutability, impenetrability; *[de visage]* inscrutability, impenetrability

impénétrable /ɛ̃penetʀabl/ ADJ 1 (*= inaccessible*) *[forêt]* impenetrable (*à* to, by); ◆ **un secteur quasi ~ pour les Européens** a market sector almost impossible for Europeans to break into 2 (*= insondable*) *[mystère, desseins]* unfathomable, impenetrable; → **voie** 3 (*= énigmatique*) *[personnage, caractère, visage]* inscrutable, impenetrable; *[air]* inscrutable

impénitence /ɛ̃penitɑ̃s/ NF unrepentance, impenitence

impénitent, e /ɛ̃penitɑ̃, ɑ̃t/ ADJ unrepentant, impenitent ◆ **fumeur ~** unrepentant smoker

impensable /ɛ̃pɑ̃sabl/ GRAMMAIRE ACTIVE 39.2 ADJ *[événement hypothétique]* unthinkable; *[événement arrivé]* unbelievable

imper* /ɛ̃pɛʀ/ NM (abrév de **imperméable**) raincoat

impératif, -ive /ɛ̃peʀatif, iv/ ADJ (*= obligatoire, urgent*) *[besoin, consigne]* urgent, imperative; (*= impérieux*) *[geste, ton]* imperative, imperious, commanding; (*Jur*) *[loi]* mandatory ◆ **il est ~ de .../que ...** it is absolutely essential *ou* it is imperative to .../that ... **NM** 1 *(Ling)* imperative mood ◆ **à l'~** in the imperative (mood) 2 *(= prescription) [de fonction, charge]* requirement; *[de mode]* demand; *(= nécessité) [de situation]* necessity; *(Mil)* imperative ◆ **des ~s d'horaire nous obligent à ...** we are obliged by the demands *ou* constraints of our timetable to ... ◆ **~ catégorique** *(Philos)* categorical imperative; *(fig)* essential requirement

impérativement /ɛ̃peʀativmɑ̃/ **ADV** imperatively ◆ **je le veux ~ pour demain** it is imperative that I have it for tomorrow, I absolutely must have it for tomorrow

impératrice /ɛ̃peʀatʀis/ **NF** empress

imperceptibilité /ɛ̃pɛʀseptibilite/ **NF** imperceptibility

imperceptible /ɛ̃pɛʀseptibl/ **ADJ** 1 *(= non perceptible) [son, détail, nuance]* imperceptible *(à* to) 2 *(= à peine perceptible) [son, sourire]* faint, imperceptible; *[détail, changement, nuance]* minute, imperceptible

imperceptiblement /ɛ̃pɛʀseptibləmɑ̃/ **ADV** imperceptibly

imperfectible /ɛ̃pɛʀfɛktibl/ **ADJ** which cannot be perfected, unperfectible

imperfectif, -ive /ɛ̃pɛʀfɛktif, iv/ **ADJ** imperfective, continuous **NM** imperfective

imperfection /ɛ̃pɛʀfɛksjɔ̃/ **NF** *(= caractère imparfait)* imperfection; *(= défaut) [de personne, caractère]* shortcoming, imperfection, defect; *[d'ouvrage, dispositif, mécanisme]* imperfection, defect; *[de peau]* blemish

impérial, e (mpl **-iaux**) /ɛ̃peʀjal, o/ **ADJ** imperial **NF** **impériale** 1 *[d'autobus]* top *ou* upper deck ◆ **autobus à ~e** ≈ double-decker (bus) ◆ **monter à l'impériale** to go upstairs *ou* on top 2 *(= barbe)* imperial 3 *(Jeux)* **(série) ~e** royal flush

impérialement /ɛ̃peʀjalmɑ̃/ **ADV** imperially

impérialisme /ɛ̃peʀjalism/ **NM** imperialism

impérialiste /ɛ̃peʀjalist/ **ADJ** imperialist(ic) **NMF** imperialist

impérieusement /ɛ̃peʀjøzmɑ̃/ **ADV** imperiously ◆ **avoir ~ besoin de qch** to need sth urgently, to have urgent need of sth

impérieux, -ieuse /ɛ̃peʀjø, jøz/ **ADJ** *(= autoritaire) [personne, ton, caractère]* imperious; *(= pressant) [besoin, nécessité]* urgent, pressing; *[obligation]* pressing

impérissable /ɛ̃peʀisabl/ **ADJ** *[œuvre]* imperishable; *[souvenir, gloire]* undying *(épith)*, imperishable; *[monument, valeur]* permanent, lasting *(épith)*

impéritie /ɛ̃peʀisi/ **NF** *(littér = incompétence)* incompetence

imperium /ɛ̃peʀjɔm/ **NM** *(Hist)* imperium; *(fig)* dominion *(sur* over)

imperméabilisation /ɛ̃pɛʀmeabilizasjɔ̃/ **NF** waterproofing

imperméabiliser /ɛ̃pɛʀmeabilize/ ► conjug 1 ◄ **VT** to waterproof ◆ **tissu imperméabilisé** waterproofed material

imperméabilité /ɛ̃pɛʀmeabilite/ **NF** 1 *[de terrain]* impermeability; *[de tissu]* waterproof qualities, impermeability 2 *(littér = insensibilité)* **~ à** imperviousness to

imperméable /ɛ̃pɛʀmeabl/ **ADJ** 1 *[terrain, roches]* impermeable; *[revêtement, tissu]* waterproof; *[frontière]* impenetrable ◆ **~ à l'eau** waterproof ◆ **~ à l'air** airtight 2 *(= insensible)* **~ à** impervious to **NM** *(= manteau)* raincoat

impersonnalité /ɛ̃pɛʀsɔnalite/ **NF** impersonality; *(Ling)* impersonal form

impersonnel, -elle /ɛ̃pɛʀsɔnɛl/ **ADJ** *(gén, Ling)* impersonal **NM** *(Ling)* impersonal verb

impersonnellement /ɛ̃pɛʀsɔnɛlmɑ̃/ **ADV** impersonally

impertinemment /ɛ̃pɛʀtinamɑ̃/ **ADV** impertinently

impertinence /ɛ̃pɛʀtinɑ̃s/ **NF** *(= caractère)* impertinence; *(= propos)* impertinent remark, impertinence ◆ **répondre avec ~** to reply impertinently *ou* cheekily ◆ **arrête tes ~s !** that's enough impertinence!, that's enough of your impertinent remarks!

impertinent, e /ɛ̃pɛʀtinɑ̃, ɑ̃t/ **ADJ** impertinent, cheeky ◆ **c'est un petit ~ !** he's so impertinent!

imperturbabilité /ɛ̃pɛʀtyʀbabilite/ **NF** imperturbability

imperturbable /ɛ̃pɛʀtyʀbabl/ **ADJ** *[sang-froid, gaieté, sérieux]* unshakeable; *[personne, caractère]* imperturbable ◆ **rester ~** to remain unruffled

imperturbablement /ɛ̃pɛʀtyʀbabləmɑ̃/ **ADV** imperturbably ◆ **il écouta ~** he listened imperturbably *ou* unperturbed *ou* unruffled

impétigo /ɛ̃petigo/ **NM** impetigo

impétrant, e /ɛ̃petʀɑ̃, ɑ̃t/ **NM,F** *(Jur)* applicant; *(Univ)* recipient *(of a qualification)*

impétueusement /ɛ̃petɥøzmɑ̃/ **ADV** *(littér)* impetuously

impétueux, -euse /ɛ̃petɥø, øz/ **ADJ** *(littér = fougueux) [caractère, jeunesse]* impetuous, hotheaded; *[orateur]* fiery; *[rythme]* impetuous; *[torrent, vent]* raging

impétuosité /ɛ̃petɥozite/ **NF** *(littér) [de rythme, personne]* impetuousness, impetuosity ◆ **méfiez-vous de l'~ des torrents de montagne** beware of raging mountain streams

impie /ɛ̃pi/ **ADJ** *[acte, parole]* impious, ungodly, irreligious **NMF** ungodly *ou* irreligious person

impiété /ɛ̃pjete/ **NF** († *ou littér*) *(= caractère)* impiety, ungodliness, irreligiousness; *(= parole, acte)* impiety

impitoyable /ɛ̃pitwajabl/ **ADJ** merciless, ruthless *(envers* towards); ◆ **dans le monde** *ou* **l'univers ~ du show-biz** in the cutthroat world of showbiz

impitoyablement /ɛ̃pitwajabləmɑ̃/ **ADV** mercilessly, ruthlessly

implacabilité /ɛ̃plakabilite/ **NF** implacability

implacable /ɛ̃plakabl/ **ADJ** *(= impitoyable)* implacable

implacablement /ɛ̃plakabləmɑ̃/ **ADV** implacably, relentlessly

implant /ɛ̃plɑ̃/ **NM** *(Méd)* implant ◆ **~ capillaire** hair graft ◆ **~ dentaire** implant

implantation /ɛ̃plɑ̃tasjɔ̃/ **NF** 1 *[d'usage, mode]* introduction; *[d'immigrants]* settlement; *[d'usine, industrie]* setting up; *[d'idée, préjugé]* implantation 2 *(= présence)* **nous bénéficions d'une solide ~ à l'étranger** *[entreprise]* we have a number of offices abroad ◆ **nous avons su renforcer notre ~ locale** we have reinforced our presence locally ◆ **la forte ~ du parti dans la région** the party's strong presence in the region 3 *(Méd) [d'organe, prothèse, embryon]* implantation 4 *(= disposition) [de dents]* arrangement ◆ **l'~ des cheveux** the way the hair grows

implanter /ɛ̃plɑ̃te/ ► conjug 1 ◄ **VT** 1 *(= introduire) [+ usage, mode]* to introduce ◆ **~ un produit sur le marché** to establish a product on the market 2 *(= établir) [+ usine, industrie]* to set up, to establish; *[+ idée, préjugé]* to implant ◆ **une société implantée dans la région depuis plusieurs générations** a company that has been established in the area for generations ◆ **la gauche est fortement implantée ici** the left is well-established here 3 *(Méd) [+ organe, prothèse, embryon]* to implant **VPR** **s'implanter** *[usine, industrie]* to be set up *ou* established; *[immigrants]* to settle; *[parti politique]* to establish itself, to become established ◆ **le parti est solidement implanté dans cette région** the party is well-established in this region

implémentation /ɛ̃plemɑ̃tasjɔ̃/ **NF** *(Ordin)* implementation

implémenter /ɛ̃plemɑ̃te/ ► conjug 1 ◄ **VT** *(Ordin)* to implement

implication /ɛ̃plikasjɔ̃/ **NF** 1 *(= relation logique)* implication 2 **~ dans** *(= mise en cause)* implication in; *(= participation à)* implication *ou* involvement in **NFPL** **implications** *(= conséquences, répercussions)* implications

implicite /ɛ̃plisit/ **ADJ** *[condition, foi, volonté]* implicit ◆ **connaissance ~** *(Ling)* tacit knowledge

implicitement /ɛ̃plisitmɑ̃/ **ADV** implicitly

impliquer /ɛ̃plike/ ► conjug 1 ◄ **VT** 1 *(= supposer)* to imply *(que* that) 2 *(= nécessiter)* to entail, to involve 3 ◆ **~ qn dans** *(= mettre en cause)* to implicate sb in; *(= mêler à)* to implicate *ou* involve sb in **VPR** **s'impliquer** ◆ **s'~ dans son travail/un projet** to get involved in one's work/a project ◆ **s'~ beaucoup dans qch** to put a lot into sth, to get heavily *ou* deeply involved in sth

implorant, e /ɛ̃plɔʀɑ̃, ɑ̃t/ **ADJ** imploring, beseeching ◆ **il me regarda d'un air ~** he looked at me imploringly *ou* beseechingly

imploration /ɛ̃plɔʀasjɔ̃/ **NF** entreaty

implorer /ɛ̃plɔʀe/ ► conjug 1 ◄ **VT** *(= supplier) [+ personne, Dieu]* to implore, to beseech *(frm)*; *(= demander) [+ faveur, aide]* to implore ◆ **~ la clémence de qn** to beg sb for mercy ◆ **~ le pardon de qn** to beg sb's forgiveness ◆ **~ qn de faire** to implore *ou* beseech *ou* entreat sb to do

imploser /ɛ̃ploze/ ► conjug 1 ◄ **VI** to implode

implosif, -ive /ɛ̃plozif, iv/ **ADJ** implosive

implosion /ɛ̃plozjɔ̃/ **NF** implosion

impoli, e /ɛ̃pɔli/ **ADJ** impolite, rude *(envers* to)

impoliment /ɛ̃pɔlimɑ̃/ **ADV** impolitely, rudely

impolitesse /ɛ̃pɔlitɛs/ **NF** *(= attitude)* impoliteness, rudeness; *(= remarque)* impolite *ou* rude remark; *(= acte)* impolite thing to do, impolite action ◆ **répondre avec ~** to answer impolitely *ou* rudely ◆ **c'est une ~ de faire** it is impolite *ou* rude to do

impolitique /ɛ̃pɔlitik/ **ADJ** impolitic

impondérabilité /ɛ̃pɔ̃deʀabilite/ **NF** imponderability

impondérable /ɛ̃pɔ̃deʀabl/ **ADJ** imponderable **NM** imponderable, unknown (quantity) ◆ **le marché du cuivre est celui de l'~** the copper market is an unknown quantity *ou* an imponderable ◆ **les ~s de la météo** the vagaries of the weather, unforeseen weather conditions

impopulaire /ɛ̃pɔpylɛʀ/ **ADJ** unpopular *(auprès de* with)

impopularité /ɛ̃pɔpylaʀite/ **NF** unpopularity

import /ɛ̃pɔʀ/ **NM** (abrév de **importation**) import

importable /ɛ̃pɔʀtabl/ **ADJ** *(Écon)* importable; *[vêtement]* unwearable

importance /ɛ̃pɔʀtɑ̃s/ **NF** 1 *[de problème, affaire, personne]* importance; *[d'événement, fait]* importance, significance ◆ **avoir de l'~** *[de personne, question]* to be important, to be of importance ◆ **ça a beaucoup d'~ pour moi** it's very important to me, it matters a great deal to me ◆ **accorder** *ou* **attacher de l'~ à qch** to give *ou* lend importance to sth ◆ **accorder beaucoup/peu d'~ à qch** to attach a lot of/little importance to sth ◆ **sans ~** *[personne]* unimportant; *[problème, incident, détail]* unimportant, insignificant ◆ **c'est sans ~, ça n'a pas d'~** it doesn't matter, it's of no importance *ou* consequence

◆ **(et alors,) quelle ~ ?** (so) does it really matter? ◆ **de peu d'~** *[événement, fait]* of little importance; *[détail]* trifling, minor; *[retard]* slight ◆ **d'une certaine ~** *[problème, événement]* fairly *ou* rather important ◆ **de la plus haute ~, de (la) première ~** *[problème, affaire, document]* of paramount *ou* of the highest importance; *[événement]* momentous

2 *(= taille) [de somme, effectifs, entreprise]* size; *(= ampleur) [de dégâts, désastre, retard]* extent ◆ **d'une certaine ~** *[entreprise]* sizeable; *[dégâts]* considerable, extensive

3 *(loc)* **prendre de l'~** *[question]* to gain in importance, to become more important; *[firme]* to increase in size; *[personne]* to become more important ◆ **se donner de l'~** *(péj)* to act important *ou* in a self-important way ◆ **l'affaire est d'~** *(frm)* this is no trivial matter, this is a matter of some seriousness ◆ **tancer/rosser qn d'~** *(littér)* to give sb a thorough dressing-down/trouncing *(littér)*

important, e /ɛ̃pɔʀtɑ̃, ɑ̃t/ GRAMMAIRE ACTIVE 28.1, 53.1 53.6

ADJ 1 *[personnage, question, rôle]* important; *[événement, fait]* important, significant ◆ **peu ~** of no great importance, of little significance ◆ **rien d'~** nothing important *ou* of importance ◆ **quelqu'un d'~** somebody important

2 *(quantitativement) [somme]* large, considerable, substantial; *[différence]* big; *[retard]* considerable; *[dégâts]* extensive, considerable ◆ **la présence d'un ~ service d'ordre** the presence of a considerable number *ou* a large contingent of police

3 *(péj) [airs]* (self-)important; *[personnage]* self-important

NM ◆ **l'~ est de ...** the important thing is to ... ◆ **ce n'est pas le plus ~** that's not what's most important

NM,F *(péj)* ◆ **faire l'~(e)** to be self-important

> ⚠ Quand le mot **important** se réfère à une quantité, il ne se traduit pas par l'anglais **important**.

importateur, -trice /ɛ̃pɔʀtatœʀ, tʀis/ ADJ importing ◆ **pays ~ de blé** wheat-importing country NM,F importer

importation /ɛ̃pɔʀtasjɔ̃/ NF 1 *[de marchandises]* importing, importation ◆ **produits/articles d'~** imported products/items 2 *[d'animal, plante, maladie]* introduction ◆ **cette marque est d'~ récente** this brand is a recent import 3 *(= produit)* import

importer[1] /ɛ̃pɔʀte/ ► conjug 1 ◄ VT to import; *[+ coutumes, danses]* to import, to introduce *(de* from)

importer[2] /ɛ̃pɔʀte/ GRAMMAIRE ACTIVE 34.5 ► conjug 1 ◄ VI 1 *(= être important)* to matter ◆ **les conventions importent peu à ces gens-là** conventions don't matter much *ou* aren't very important *ou* matter little to those people ◆ **ce qui importe, c'est d'agir vite** the important thing is *ou* what matters is to act quickly ◆ **que lui importe le malheur des autres ?** what does he care about other people's unhappiness?, what does other people's unhappiness matter to him? ◆ **il importe de faire** *(frm)* it is important to do ◆ **il importe qu'elle connaisse les risques** *(frm)* it is important that she knows *ou* should know the risks

2 ◆ **peu importe** *ou* **qu'importe** *(littér)* **qu'il soit absent** what does it matter if he is absent?, it matters little that he is absent *(frm)* ◆ **peu importe le temps, nous sortirons** we'll go out whatever the weather *ou* no matter what the weather is like ◆ **peu m'importe** *(= je n'ai pas de préférence)* I don't mind; *(= je m'en moque)* I don't care ◆ **que m'importe !** what do I care?, I don't care! ◆ **achetez des pêches ou des poires, peu importe** buy peaches or pears – it doesn't matter which ◆ **quel fauteuil veux-tu ? – oh, n'importe** which chair will you have? – it doesn't matter *ou* I don't mind *ou* any one will do ◆ **il ne veut pas ? qu'importe !** doesn't he want to? what does it matter? *ou* it doesn't matter! ◆ **les maisons sont chères, n'importe, elles se vendent !** houses are expensive, but no matter *ou* but never mind, they still sell ◆ **qu'importe le flacon pourvu qu'on ait l'ivresse !** *(Prov)* never mind the bottle, let's just drink it!

3 ◆ **n'importe comment** anyhow ◆ **il a fait cela n'importe comment !** he did it any old how* *(Brit) ou* any which way* *(US)* ◆ **n'importe comment, il part ce soir** anyway, he's leaving tonight, he's leaving tonight in any case *ou* anyhow ◆ **n'importe lequel d'entre nous** any (one) of us ◆ **n'importe où** anywhere ◆ **attention, n'allez pas vous promener n'importe où** be careful, don't go walking just anywhere ◆ **n'importe quand** anytime ◆ **entrez dans n'importe quelle boutique** go into any shop ◆ **n'importe quel docteur vous dira la même chose** any doctor will tell you the same thing ◆ **venez à n'importe quelle heure** come (at) any time ◆ **il cherche un emploi, mais pas n'importe lequel** he's looking for a job, but not just any job ◆ **n'importe qui** anybody, anyone ◆ **ce n'est pas n'importe qui** he's not just anybody ◆ **n'importe quoi** anything ◆ **il fait/dit n'importe quoi !** he has no idea what he's doing!/saying! ◆ **(c'est) n'importe quoi !*** what nonsense! *ou* rubbish! *(Brit)* ◆ **il mange tout et n'importe quoi** he'll eat anything

import-export (pl **imports-exports**) /ɛ̃pɔʀɛkspɔʀ/ NM import-export ◆ **société d'~** import-export company ◆ **entreprise d'~ de vins** import-export company dealing in wine ◆ **faire de l'~** to be in the import-export business

importun, e /ɛ̃pɔʀtœ̃, yn/ ADJ *(frm) [curiosité, présence, pensée, plainte]* troublesome, importunate *(frm)*; *[arrivée, visite]* inopportune, ill-timed; *[personne]* importunate *(frm)* ◆ **je ne veux pas être ~** *(déranger)* I don't wish to disturb you *ou* to intrude; *(irriter)* I don't wish to be importunate *(frm) ou* a nuisance ◆ **se rendre ~ par** to make o.s. objectionable by NM,F *(= gêneur)* irksome individual; *(= visiteur)* intruder

importunément /ɛ̃pɔʀtynemɑ̃/ ADV *(frm) (= de façon irritante)* importunately *(frm)*; *(= à un mauvais moment)* inopportunely

importuner /ɛ̃pɔʀtyne/ ► conjug 1 ◄ VT *(frm) [personne]* to importune *(frm)*, to bother; *[insecte, bruit]* to trouble, to bother; *[interruptions, remarques]* to bother ◆ **je ne veux pas vous ~** I don't wish to put you to any trouble *ou* to bother you

importunité /ɛ̃pɔʀtynite/ NF *(frm) [de démarche, demande]* importunity *(frm)* ◆ **~s** *(= sollicitations)* importunities

imposable /ɛ̃pozabl/ ADJ *[personne, revenu]* taxable

imposant, e /ɛ̃pozɑ̃, ɑ̃t/ ADJ *(= majestueux) [personnage, stature]* imposing; *[allure]* stately; *(= impressionnant) [bâtiment]* imposing; *(= considérable) [majorité, mise en scène, foule]* imposing, impressive ◆ **une ~e matrone** *(= gros)* a woman with an imposing figure ◆ **la présence d'un ~ service d'ordre** the presence of an imposing number *ou* a large contingent of police

imposé, e /ɛ̃poze/ (ptp de **imposer**) ADJ 1 *(Fin) [personne, revenu]* taxable 2 *(= obligatoire) [exercices, figures]* compulsory ◆ **prix ~** set price ◆ **tarif ~** set rate NM *(Sport = exercice)* compulsory exercise NM,F *(= contribuable)* taxpayer

imposer /ɛ̃poze/ ► conjug 1 ◄ VT 1 *(= prescrire) [+ tâche, date]* to set; *[+ règle, conditions]* to impose, to lay down; *[+ punition, taxe]* to impose *(à* on); *[+ prix]* to set, to fix ◆ **~ ses idées/sa présence à qn** to impose *ou* force one's ideas/one's company on sb ◆ **~ des conditions à qch** to impose *ou* place conditions on sth ◆ **~ un travail/une date à qn** to set sb a piece of work/a date ◆ **~ un régime à qn** to put sb on a diet ◆ **la décision leur a été imposée par les événements** the decision was forced *ou* imposed (up)on them by events ◆ **il nous a imposé son candidat** he has imposed his candidate on us ◆ **on lui a imposé le silence** silence has been imposed upon him; → **loi**

2 *(= faire connaître)* **~ son nom** *[candidat]* to come to the fore; *[artiste]* to make o.s. known, to compel recognition; *[firme]* to establish itself, to become an established name ◆ **il impose/sa conduite impose le respect** he commands/his behaviour compels respect

3 *(Fin = taxer) [+ marchandise, revenu, salariés]* to tax ◆ **~ insuffisamment** to undertax

4 *(Typo)* to impose

5 *(Rel)* **~ les mains** to lay on hands

VT INDIR **en imposer en ~ à qn** to impress sb ◆ **il en impose** he's an imposing individual ◆ **sa présence en impose** he's an imposing presence ◆ **son intelligence en impose** he is a man of striking intelligence ◆ **ne vous en laissez pas ~ par ses grands airs** don't let yourself be overawed by his haughty manner

VPR **s'imposer** 1 *(= être nécessaire) [décision, action]* to be essential *ou* vital *ou* imperative ◆ **dans ce cas, le repos s'impose** in this case rest is essential *ou* vital *ou* imperative ◆ **c'est la solution qui s'impose** it's the obvious solution ◆ **ces mesures ne s'imposaient pas** these measures were unnecessary ◆ **quand on est à Paris une visite au Louvre s'impose** when in Paris, a visit to the Louvre is imperative *ou* is a must*

2 *(= se contraindre à)* **s'~ une tâche** to set o.s. a task ◆ **il s'est imposé un trop gros effort** he put himself under too much strain ◆ **s'~ de faire** to make it a rule to do

3 *(= montrer sa supériorité)* to assert o.s.; *(= avoir une personnalité forte)* to be assertive ◆ **impose-toi !** assert yourself! ◆ **s'~ par ses qualités** to stand out *ou* to compel recognition because of one's qualities ◆ **il s'est imposé dans sa branche** he has made a name for himself in his branch ◆ **il s'est imposé comme le seul susceptible d'avoir le prix** he emerged *ou* he established himself as the only one likely to get the prize ◆ **le skieur s'est imposé dans le slalom géant** the skier dominated the giant slalom event ◆ **le joueur canadien s'est imposé face au russe** the Canadian player outplayed the Russian

4 *(= imposer sa présence à)* **s'~ à qn** to impose (o.s.) upon sb ◆ **je ne voudrais pas m'~** I don't want to impose ◆ **le soleil s'imposera peu à peu sur tout le pays** gradually sunshine will spread across the whole country

imposition /ɛ̃pozisjɔ̃/ NF *(Fin)* taxation; *(Typo)* imposition ◆ **l'~ des mains** *(Rel)* the laying on of hands ◆ **double ~** *(Fin)* double taxation ◆ **~ à la source** PAYE system *(Brit)*, withholding tax system *(US)*

impossibilité /ɛ̃pɔsibilite/ GRAMMAIRE ACTIVE 43.4 NF impossibility ◆ **l'~ de réaliser ce plan** the impossibility of carrying out this plan ◆ **en cas d'~** should it prove impossible ◆ **y a-t-il ~ à ce qu'il vienne ?** is it impossible for him to come? ◆ **être dans l'~ de faire qch** to be unable to do sth ◆ **l'~ dans laquelle il se trouvait de ...** the fact that he was unable to ..., the fact that he found it impossible to ... ◆ **se heurter à des ~s** to come up against insuperable obstacles

impossible /ɛ̃pɔsibl/ GRAMMAIRE ACTIVE 39.3, 43.3, 53.1, 53.6

ADJ 1 (= *irréalisable, improbable*) impossible ◆ ~ **à faire** impossible to do ◆ **il est ~ de .../que ...** it is impossible to .../that ... ◆ **il est ~ qu'il soit déjà arrivé** he cannot possibly have arrived yet ◆ **il m'est ~ de le faire** it's impossible for me to do it, I can't possibly do it ◆ **pouvez-vous venir lundi ? – non, cela m'est ~** can you come on Monday? – no, I can't *ou* no, it's impossible ◆ **ce n'est pas ~, ça n'a rien d'~** (= *ça peut arriver*) it may well happen; (= *ça peut être le cas*) it may well be the case ◆ **est-ce qu'il va partir ? – ce n'est pas ~** is he going to leave? – he may well ◆ **~ n'est pas français** (*Prov*) there's no such word as "can't"; → **vaillant**

2 (= *pénible, difficile*) [*enfant, situation*] impossible ◆ **rendre l'existence ~ à qn** to make sb's life impossible *ou* a misery ◆ **elle a des horaires ~s** she has impossible *ou* terrible hours ◆ **il mène une vie ~** he leads an incredible life

3 (= *invraisemblable*) [*nom, titre*] ridiculous, impossible ◆ **se lever à des heures ~s** to get up at an impossible *ou* a ridiculous time *ou* hour ◆ **il lui arrive toujours des histoires ~s** impossible things are always happening to him

NM 1 ◆ **l'~** the impossible ◆ **demander/tenter l'~** to ask for/attempt the impossible ◆ **je ferai l'~ (pour venir)** I'll do my utmost (to come) ◆ **à l'~ nul n'est tenu** (*Prov*) no one can be expected to do the impossible

2 ◆ **par ~** by some miracle, by some remote chance ◆ **si par ~ je terminais premier ...** if by some miracle *ou* some remote chance I were to finish first ...

imposte /ɛ̃pɔst/ NF 1 (*Archit* = *moulure*) impost 2 (= *fenêtre*) fanlight (*Brit*), transom (window) (*US*)

imposteur /ɛ̃pɔstœʀ/ NM impostor

imposture /ɛ̃pɔstyʀ/ NF imposture, deception ◆ **c'est une ~ !** it's all a sham!

impôt /ɛ̃po/ NM (= *taxe*) tax ◆ **payer l'~** to pay tax *ou* taxes ◆ **les ~s** (*gén*) taxes; (= *service local*) the tax office; (= *service national*) the Inland Revenue (*Brit*), the Internal Revenue Service (*US*) ◆ **les ~s me réclament 10 000 €** the taxman* wants €10,000 from me ◆ **payer des ~s** to pay tax ◆ **je paye plus de 10 000 € d'~s** I pay more than €10,000 (in) tax ◆ **frapper d'un ~** to put a tax on ◆ **~ direct/indirect/déguisé** direct/indirect/hidden tax ◆ **~ retenu à la source** tax deducted at source ◆ **bénéfices avant ~** pre-tax profits ◆ **faire un bénéfice de 10 000 € avant ~** to make a profit of €10,000 before tax; → **assiette, déclaration, feuille** *etc*

COMP **impôt sur les bénéfices** tax on profits, ≃ corporation tax
impôt sur le chiffre d'affaires tax on turnover
impôt foncier ≃ land tax
impôt (de solidarité) sur la fortune, impôt sur les grandes fortunes † wealth tax
impôts locaux local taxes, ≃ council tax (*Brit*)
impôt sur les plus-values ≃ capital gains tax
impôt sur le revenu (des personnes physiques) income tax
impôt du sang († , *littér*) blood tribute
impôt sécheresse *tax levied to help farmers in case of drought*
impôt sur les sociétés corporate tax
impôt sur le transfert des capitaux capital transfer tax

IMPÔTS

The main forms of taxation in France are income tax (« l'impôt sur le revenu »), value-added tax on consumer goods (« TVA »), local taxes funding public amenities (« les impôts locaux », which include « la taxe d'habitation » and « la taxe foncière ») and two kinds of company tax (« la taxe professionnelle » and « l'impôt sur les sociétés »).

Income tax for a given year is payable the following year and is calculated from information supplied in the « déclaration d'impôts ». It can either be paid in three instalments (the first two, known as « tiers provisionnels », are estimates based on the previous year's tax, while the third makes up the actual tax due), or in monthly instalments (an option known as « mensualisation »). Late payment incurs a 10% penalty known as a « majoration ».

impotence /ɛ̃pɔtɑ̃s/ NF (*Méd*) infirmity; (*fig*) impotence

impotent, e /ɛ̃pɔtɑ̃, ɑ̃t/ ADJ disabled, crippled ◆ **l'accident l'a rendu ~** the accident has disabled *ou* crippled him NM,F disabled person, cripple

> ⚠ **impotent** ne se traduit pas par le mot anglais **impotent**, qui a le sens de 'impuissant'.

impraticable /ɛ̃pʀatikabl/ ADJ [*idée*] impracticable, unworkable; [*tâche*] impracticable; (*Sport*) [*terrain*] unfit for play, unplayable; [*route, piste*] impassable ◆ **~ pour les** *ou* **aux véhicules à moteur** unsuitable for motor vehicles

imprécateur, -trice /ɛ̃pʀekatœʀ, tʀis/ NM,F (*littér*) doomsayer, prophet of doom

imprécation /ɛ̃pʀekasjɔ̃/ NF imprecation, curse ◆ **se répandre en** *ou* **lancer des ~s contre** to inveigh against

imprécatoire /ɛ̃pʀekatwaʀ/ ADJ (*littér*) imprecatory (*littér*)

imprécis, e /ɛ̃pʀesi, iz/ ADJ 1 [*souvenir, idée*] vague; [*contours*] vague, indistinct ◆ **les causes du décès restent encore ~es** the cause of death remains unclear 2 [*estimation, plan, chiffre, résultat*] imprecise; [*tir*] inaccurate

imprécision /ɛ̃pʀesizjɔ̃/ NF 1 [*de souvenir, idée*] vagueness 2 [*d'estimation, plan, chiffre, résultat*] imprecision, lack of precision; [*de tir*] inaccuracy ◆ **ce texte comporte de nombreuses ~s** there are a number of inaccuracies in the text

imprégnation /ɛ̃pʀeɲasjɔ̃/ NF 1 [*de tissu, matière*] impregnation; [*de pièce, air*] permeation ◆ **taux d'~ alcoolique** blood alcohol level, level of alcohol in the blood 2 (= *assimilation*) [*d'esprit*] imbuing, impregnation ◆ **pour apprendre une langue, rien ne vaut une lente ~** to learn a language there's nothing like gradually immersing oneself in it

imprégner /ɛ̃pʀeɲe/ ► conjug 6 ◄ VT 1 [+ *tissu, matière*] (*de liquide*) to impregnate, to soak (*de* with); (*d'une odeur, de fumée*) to impregnate (*de* with); [+ *pièce, air*] to permeate, to fill (*de* with); ◆ **cette odeur imprégnait toute la rue** the smell filled the whole street ◆ **maison imprégnée de lumière** house flooded with light ◆ **un endroit imprégné d'histoire** a place steeped in history

2 [+ *esprit*] to imbue, to impregnate (*de* with); ◆ **l'amertume qui imprégnait ses paroles** the bitterness which pervaded his words ◆ **imprégné des préjugés de sa caste** imbued with *ou* steeped in the prejudices of his class

VPR **s'imprégner** ◆ **s'~ de** [*tissu, substance*] (*de liquide*) to become impregnated *ou* soaked with; (*d'une odeur, de fumée*) to become impregnated with; [*pièce, air*] to become permeated *ou* filled with; [*esprits, élèves*] to become imbued with, to absorb ◆ **séjourner à l'étranger pour s'~ de la langue étrangère** to live abroad to immerse o.s. in *ou* to absorb the foreign language ◆ **s'~ d'alcool** to soak up alcohol

imprenable /ɛ̃pʀənabl/ ADJ [*forteresse*] impregnable ◆ **vue ~** unrestricted view

impréparation /ɛ̃pʀepaʀasjɔ̃/ NF lack of preparation

imprésario /ɛ̃pʀesaʀjo/ NM [*d'acteur, chanteur*] manager; [*de troupe de théâtre, ballet*] impresario, manager

imprescriptibilité /ɛ̃pʀɛskʀiptibilite/ NF ◆ **l'~ des crimes contre l'humanité** *the non-applicability of statutory limitation to crimes against humanity*

imprescriptible /ɛ̃pʀɛskʀiptibl/ ADJ [*crime*] to which the statute of limitations does not apply; [*droit*] inalienable

impression /ɛ̃pʀesjɔ̃/ GRAMMAIRE ACTIVE 33.2, 45.4

NF 1 (= *sensation physique*) feeling, impression; (= *sentiment, réaction*) impression ◆ **se fier à sa première ~** to trust one's first impressions ◆ **ils échangèrent leurs ~s (de voyage)** they exchanged their impressions (of the trip) ◆ **quelles sont vos ~s sur la réunion ?** what was your impression *ou* what did you think of the meeting? ◆ **l'~ que j'ai de lui** my impression of him, the impression I have of him ◆ **ça m'a fait peu d'~/une grosse ~** that made little/a great impression upon me ◆ **ça m'a fait une drôle d'~ de la revoir** it was really strange seeing her again ◆ **faire bonne/mauvaise/forte ~** to make *ou* create a good/bad/strong impression ◆ **avoir l'~ que ...** to have a feeling that ..., to get *ou* have the impression that ... ◆ **j'ai comme l'~ qu'il ne me dit pas toute la vérité*** I have a feeling *ou* a hunch* that he's not telling me the whole truth ◆ **créer/donner une ~ de ...** to create/give an impression of ... ◆ **il ne me donne** *ou* **fait pas l'~ d'(être) un menteur** I don't get the impression that he's a liar, he doesn't give me the impression of being a liar ◆ **faire ~** [*film, orateur*] to make an impression, to have an impact

2 [*de livre, tissu, motif*] printing ◆ **~ en couleur** colour printing ◆ **~ laser** (= *action*) laser printing; (= *feuille imprimée*) laser print *ou* copy ◆ **"impression écran"** (*Ordin*) "print screen" ◆ **ce livre en est à sa 3ᵉ ~** this book is at its 3rd impression *ou* printing ◆ **le livre est à l'~** the book is being printed ◆ **l'~ de ce livre est soignée** this book is beautifully printed; → **faute**

3 (= *motif*) pattern ◆ **tissu à ~s florales** floral pattern(ed) fabric, fabric with a floral pattern

4 (*Peinture*) **(couche d')~** undercoat

impressionnabilité /ɛ̃pʀesjɔnabilite/ NF (= *émotivité*) impressionability, impressionableness

impressionnable /ɛ̃pʀesjɔnabl/ ADJ [*personne*] impressionable

impressionnant, e /ɛ̃pʀesjɔnɑ̃, ɑ̃t/ ADJ (= *imposant*) [*somme, spectacle, monument*] impressive; (= *bouleversant*) [*scène, accident*] upsetting ◆ **elle était ~e de calme** her calmness was impressive

impressionner /ɛ̃pʀesjɔne/ ► conjug 1 ◄ VT 1 (= *frapper*) to impress, to make an impression on; (= *bouleverser*) to overawe, to overwhelm ◆ **ne te laisse pas ~** don't let yourself be overawed ◆ **cela risque d'~ les enfants** this may be upsetting for children ◆ **tu ne m'impressionnes pas !** you don't scare me!, I'm not afraid of you! 2 (*Opt*) [+ *rétine*] to act on; (*Photo*) [+ *pellicule*] [*image, sujet*] to show up on; [*photographe*] to expose ◆ **la pellicule n'a pas été impressionnée** the film hasn't been exposed

impressionnisme /ɛ̃pʀesjɔnism/ NM impressionism

impressionniste /ɛ̃pʀesjɔnist/ ADJ impressionistic; *(Art, Mus)* impressionist NMF impressionist

imprévisibilité /ɛ̃pʀevizibilite/ NF unpredictability

imprévisible /ɛ̃pʀevizibl/ ADJ unforeseeable, unpredictable ◆ **elle est assez ~ dans ses réactions** her reactions are quite unpredictable

imprévoyance /ɛ̃pʀevwajɑ̃s/ NF *(= insouciance)* lack of foresight; *(en matière d'argent)* improvidence

imprévoyant, e /ɛ̃pʀevwajɑ̃, ɑ̃t/ ADJ *(= insouciant)* lacking (in) foresight; *(en matière d'argent)* improvident

imprévu, e /ɛ̃pʀevy/ ADJ *[événement, succès, réaction]* unforeseen, unexpected; *[courage, geste]* unexpected; *[dépenses]* unforeseen ◆ **de manière ~e** unexpectedly NM 1 ◆ **l'~** the unexpected, the unforeseen ◆ **j'aime l'~** I like the unexpected ◆ **un peu d'~** an element of surprise *ou* of the unexpected *ou* of the unforeseen ◆ **vacances pleines d'~** holidays full of surprises ◆ **en cas d'~** if anything unexpected *ou* unforeseen crops up ◆ **sauf ~** barring any unexpected *ou* unforeseen circumstances, unless anything unexpected *ou* unforeseen crops up 2 *(= incident)* unexpected *ou* unforeseen event ◆ **il y a un ~** something unexpected *ou* unforeseen has cropped up ◆ **tous ces ~s nous ont retardés** all these unexpected *ou* unforeseen events have delayed us

imprimable /ɛ̃pʀimabl/ ADJ printable

imprimant, e /ɛ̃pʀimɑ̃, ɑ̃t/ ADJ printing *(épith)* NF **imprimante** printer ◆ **~e matricielle/ligne par ligne/à jet d'encre** dot-matrix/line/ink-jet printer ◆ **~e à marguerite/laser/feuille à feuille** daisywheel/laser/sheet-fed printer

imprimatur /ɛ̃pʀimatyʀ/ NM INV imprimatur

imprimé, e /ɛ̃pʀime/ (ptp de **imprimer**) ADJ *[tissu, feuille]* printed NM 1 *(= formulaire)* printed form ◆ **"imprimés"** *(Poste)* "printed matter" ◆ **envoyer qch au tarif ~s** to send sth at the printed paper rate ◆ **catalogue/section des ~s** catalogue/department of printed books ◆ **~ publicitaire** advertising leaflet 2 *(= tissu)* **l'~** printed material *ou* fabrics, prints ◆ **~ à fleur** floral print (fabric *ou* material) ◆ **l'~ et l'uni** printed and plain fabrics *ou* material

imprimer /ɛ̃pʀime/ ▸ conjug 1 ◂ VT 1 *[+ livre, foulard, billets de banque, dessin]* to print 2 *(= apposer) [+ visa, cachet]* to stamp *(sur, dans* on, in) 3 *(= marquer) [+ rides, traces, marque]* to imprint *(dans* in, on); ◆ **une scène imprimée dans sa mémoire** a scene imprinted on his memory 4 *(= publier) [+ texte, ouvrage]* to publish; *[+ auteur]* to publish the work of ◆ **la joie de se voir imprimé** the joy of seeing o.s. *ou* one's work in print 5 *(= communiquer) [+ impulsion]* to transmit *(à* to); ◆ **la pédale imprime un mouvement à la roue** the movement of the pedal causes the wheel to turn ◆ **~ une direction à** to give a direction to 6 *[+ surface à peindre]* to prime VI * ◆ **je n'ai pas imprimé** *(= retenir)* it didn't sink in *ou* register

imprimerie /ɛ̃pʀimʀi/ NF *(= firme, usine)* printing works; *(= atelier)* printing house; *(= section)* printery; *(pour enfants)* printing outfit *ou* kit ◆ **l'~** *(= technique)* printing ◆ **l'Imprimerie nationale** ≈ HMSO *(Brit)*, the Government Printing Office *(US)* ◆ **écrire en caractères** *ou* **lettres d'~** to write in block capitals *ou* letters

imprimeur /ɛ̃pʀimœʀ/ NM printer ◆ **~-éditeur** printer and publisher ◆ **~-libraire** printer and bookseller

impro * /ɛ̃pʀo/ NF abrév de **improvisation**

improbabilité /ɛ̃pʀɔbabilite/ NF unlikelihood, improbability

improbable /ɛ̃pʀɔbabl/ ADJ unlikely, improbable

improbité /ɛ̃pʀɔbite/ NF *(littér)* lack of integrity

improductif, -ive /ɛ̃pʀɔdyktif, iv/ ADJ *[travail, terrain]* unproductive, non-productive; *[capitaux]* non-productive NM,F *inactive member of society*

improductivité /ɛ̃pʀɔdyktivite/ NF unproductiveness, lack of productivity

impromptu, e /ɛ̃pʀɔ̃pty/ ADJ *(= improvisé) [départ]* sudden *(épith)*; *[visite]* surprise *(épith)*; *[repas, exposé]* impromptu *(épith)* ◆ **faire un discours ~ sur un sujet** to speak off the cuff *ou* make an impromptu speech on a subject, to extemporize on a subject NM *(Littérat, Mus)* impromptu ADV *(= à l'improviste) [arriver]* impromptu; *(= sans préparation) [répondre]* off the cuff, impromptu ◆ **il arriva ~, un soir de juin** he arrived (quite) out of the blue one evening in June

imprononçable /ɛ̃pʀɔnɔ̃sabl/ ADJ unpronounceable

impropre /ɛ̃pʀɔpʀ/ ADJ 1 *[terme]* inappropriate 2 **~ à** *[outil, personne]* unsuitable for, unsuited to ◆ **eau ~ à la consommation** water unfit for (human) consumption

improprement /ɛ̃pʀɔpʀəmɑ̃/ ADV *[appeler, qualifier]* incorrectly, improperly

impropriété /ɛ̃pʀɔpʀijete/ NF *[de forme]* incorrectness, inaccuracy ◆ **~ (de langage)** (language) error, mistake

improuvable /ɛ̃pʀuvabl/ ADJ unprovable

improvisateur, -trice /ɛ̃pʀɔvizatœʀ, tʀis/ NM,F improviser

improvisation /ɛ̃pʀɔvizasjɔ̃/ NF improvisation ◆ **faire une ~** to improvise ◆ **~ collective** *(Jazz)* jam session ◆ **j'adore l'~** I love doing things on the spur of the moment

improvisé, e /ɛ̃pʀɔvize/ (ptp de **improviser**) ADJ *(= de fortune) [réforme, table]* improvised, makeshift; *[solution]* makeshift, ad hoc; *[cuisinier, infirmier]* acting, temporary; *[équipe]* scratch *(épith)*; *(= impromptu) [+ conférence de presse, piquenique, représentation]* impromptu, improvised; *[discours]* off-the-cuff *(épith)*, improvised; *[excuse]* improvised, invented ◆ **avec des moyens ~s** with whatever means are available *ou* to hand

improviser /ɛ̃pʀɔvize/ ▸ conjug 1 ◂ VT *[+ discours, réunion, pique-nique]* to improvise; *[+ excuse]* to improvise, to invent VI *[organisateur]* to improvise; *[musicien]* to extemporize, to improvise; *[acteur, orateur]* to improvise, to extemporize, to ad-lib * VPR **s'improviser** 1 *[secours, réunion]* to be improvised 2 ◆ **s'~ cuisinier/infirmière** to act as cook/nurse ◆ **on ne s'improvise pas menuisier, être menuisier, ça ne s'improvise pas** you don't just suddenly become a carpenter, you don't become a carpenter just like that

improviste /ɛ̃pʀɔvist/ **à l'improviste** LOC ADV unexpectedly, without warning ◆ **je lui ai fait une visite à l'~** I dropped in on him unexpectedly *ou* without warning ◆ **prendre qn à l'~** to catch sb unawares

imprudemment /ɛ̃pʀydamɑ̃/ ADV *[circuler, naviguer]* carelessly; *[parler]* unwisely, imprudently ◆ **un inconnu qu'il avait ~ suivi** a stranger whom he had foolishly *ou* imprudently *ou* unwisely followed

imprudence /ɛ̃pʀydɑ̃s/ NF 1 *[de conducteur, geste, action]* carelessness 2 *[de remarque]* imprudence, foolishness; *[de projet]* foolishness, foolhardiness ◆ **il a eu l'~ de mentionner ce projet** he was foolish *ou* unwise *ou* imprudent enough to mention the project ◆ **blessures par ~** *(Jur)* injuries through negligence; → **homicide** 3 *(= étourderie, maladresse)* **commettre une ~** to do something foolish *ou* imprudent ◆ **(ne fais) pas d'~s** don't do anything foolish

imprudent, e /ɛ̃pʀydɑ̃, ɑ̃t/ ADJ *[personne]* foolhardy; *[conducteur, geste, action]* careless; *[remarque]* unwise, ill-advised; *[projet, politique]* ill-advised ◆ **il est ~ de se baigner tout de suite après un repas** it's unwise to swim straight after a meal ◆ **je vous trouve bien ~ de ne pas porter de casque** I think it's rather unwise of you not to wear a helmet NM,F unwise person ◆ **c'est un ~** he's very foolhardy ◆ **les ~s !** the fools!

> ⚠ Le mot anglais **imprudent** existe, mais il est d'un registre plus soutenu que **imprudent**.

impubère /ɛ̃pybɛʀ/ ADJ pre-pubescent NMF *(Jur)* ≈ minor

impubliable /ɛ̃pyblijabl/ ADJ unpublishable

impudemment /ɛ̃pydamɑ̃/ ADV *(frm) (= effrontément)* impudently; *(= cyniquement)* brazenly, shamelessly

impudence /ɛ̃pydɑ̃s/ NF *(frm)* 1 *(= effronterie)* impudence; *(= cynisme)* brazenness, shamelessness ◆ **quelle ~ !** what impudence! ◆ **il a eu l'~ d'exiger des excuses !** he had the effrontery to demand an apology! 2 *(= acte)* impudent action; *(= parole)* impudent remark ◆ **je ne tolérerai pas ses ~s** I won't put up with *ou* tolerate his impudent behaviour *ou* his impudence

impudent, e /ɛ̃pydɑ̃, ɑ̃t/ *(frm)* ADJ *(= insolent)* impudent; *(= cynique)* brazen, shameless NM,F impudent person ◆ **petite ~e !** impudent little girl!

impudeur /ɛ̃pydœʀ/ NF immodesty, shamelessness

impudicité /ɛ̃pydisite/ NF immodesty, shamelessness

impudique /ɛ̃pydik/ ADJ *[personne]* immodest, shameless; *[regard, pose, décolleté]* immodest; *[propos]* shameless

impudiquement /ɛ̃pydikmɑ̃/ ADV immodestly, shamelessly

impuissance /ɛ̃pɥisɑ̃s/ NF 1 *(= faiblesse)* powerlessness, helplessness ◆ **~ à faire** powerlessness *ou* incapacity to do ◆ **réduire qn à l'~** to render sb powerless 2 *(sexuelle)* impotence

impuissant, e /ɛ̃pɥisɑ̃, ɑ̃t/ ADJ 1 *[personne]* powerless, helpless ◆ **~ à faire** powerless to do, incapable of doing 2 *(sexuellement)* impotent NM impotent man

impulser /ɛ̃pylse/ ▸ conjug 1 ◂ VT *(Écon) [+ secteur]* to boost, to stimulate; *[+ politique, mouvement revendicatif]* to boost, to give impetus to ◆ **il est là pour écouter, ~** he's there to listen and to get things moving *ou* to make things happen

impulsif, -ive /ɛ̃pylsif, iv/ ADJ impulsive NM,F impulsive person

impulsion /ɛ̃pylsjɔ̃/ NF 1 *(mécanique)* impulse; *(électrique)* impulse, pulse ◆ **radar à ~s** pulse (-modulated) radar ◆ **~s nerveuses** nerve impulses 2 *(= élan)* impetus ◆ **l'~ donnée à l'économie** the boost *ou* impetus given to the economy ◆ **sous l'~ de leurs chefs/des circonstances** spurred on by their leaders/by circumstances ◆ **réforme entreprise sous l'~ de l'Irlande** reform undertaken at Ireland's instigation ◆ **sous l'~ du ministre** at the minister's behest 3 *(= mouvement, instinct)* impulse ◆ **cédant à des ~s morbides** yielding to morbid impulses; → **achat**

impulsivité /ɛ̃pylsivite/ NF impulsiveness

impunément /ɛ̃pynemɑ̃/ ADV with impunity ◆ **on ne se moque pas ~ de lui** you can't make fun of him and (expect to) get away with it, one can't make fun of him with impunity

impuni, e /ɛ̃pyni/ ADJ unpunished

impunité /ɛ̃pynite/ NF impunity ◆ **en toute ~** with complete impunity ◆ **ils déplorent l'~ dont jouissent certains** they deplore the way people get off scot-free *ou* go unpunished

impur, e /ɛ̃pyʀ/ ADJ 1 *(= altéré) [liquide, air]* impure; *[race]* mixed; *(Rel) [animal]* unclean 2 *(= immoral) [geste, pensée, personne]* impure

impureté /ɛ̃pyʀte/ NF *(gén)* impurity ◆ **vivre dans l'~** to live in a state of impurity ◆ **~s** impurities

imputabilité /ɛ̃pytabilite/ NF *(Jur)* imputability

imputable /ɛ̃pytabl/ ADJ 1 *[faute, accident]* **~ à** attributable to, due to ◆ **plus d'un tiers des décès par accident de la route est ~ à l'alcool** more than a third of road deaths are attributable to *ou* due to alcohol ◆ **les 64 morts ~s aux activités de cette secte** the 64 deaths attributable to *ou* caused by the sect's activities 2 *(Fin)* **~ sur** chargeable to

imputation /ɛ̃pytasjɔ̃/ NF 1 *(= accusation)* imputation *(frm)*, charge 2 *(Fin)* **~ à** *ou* **sur** *[de somme]* charging to

imputer /ɛ̃pyte/ ▸ conjug 1 ◂ VT 1 *(= attribuer)* **~ à** to attribute to ◆ **les crimes imputés à Internet** the crimes attributed to the Internet ◆ **on ne peut ~ au gouvernement la responsabilité des inondations** the government cannot be blamed *ou* held responsible for the floods ◆ **les crimes de guerre imputés au régime de Belgrade** the war crimes of which Belgrade is *ou* stands accused 2 *(Fin)* **~ à** *ou* **sur** to charge to

imputrescibilité /ɛ̃pytʀesibilite/ NF rotproof nature, imputrescibility *(SPÉC)*

imputrescible /ɛ̃pytʀesibl/ ADJ rotproof, imputrescible *(SPÉC)*

in †* /in/ ADJ trendy*, in*

INA /ina/ NM (abrév de **Institut national de l'audiovisuel**) → **institut**

inabordable /inabɔʀdabl/ ADJ *[personne]* unapproachable; *[lieu]* inaccessible; *[prix]* prohibitive, exorbitant ◆ **les fruits sont ~s** fruit is terribly expensive

inabouti, e /inabuti/ ADJ *[projet, tentative]* abortive

inabrogeable /inabʀɔʒabl/ ADJ *(Jur)* unrepealable

in absentia /inapsɑ̃sja/ LOC ADV in absentia

in abstracto /inapstʀakto/ LOC ADV in the abstract

inaccentué, e /inaksɑ̃tɥe/ ADJ unstressed, unaccented

inacceptable /inakseptabl/ ADJ unacceptable ◆ **c'est ~** it's unacceptable

inaccessibilité /inaksesibilite/ NF inaccessibility

inaccessible /inaksesibl/ ADJ 1 *[montagne, personne, but]* inaccessible; *[endroit]* out-of-the-way *(épith)*, inaccessible; *[objet]* inaccessible, out of reach *(attrib)* 2 *[texte] (= obscur)* obscure; *(= incompréhensible)* incomprehensible *(à* to) 3 *(= insensible à)* **~ à** impervious to

inaccompli, e /inakɔ̃pli/ ADJ *(littér) [vœux]* unfulfilled; *[tâche]* unaccomplished

inaccomplissement /inakɔ̃plismɑ̃/ NM *(littér) [de vœux]* non-fulfilment; *[de tâche]* non-execution

inaccoutumé, e /inakutyme/ ADJ unusual ◆ **~ à** *(littér)* unaccustomed to, unused to

inachevé, e /inaʃ(ə)ve/ ADJ unfinished, uncompleted ◆ **une impression d'~** a feeling of incompleteness *ou* incompletion

inachèvement /inaʃɛvmɑ̃/ NM incompleteness, incompletion

inactif, -ive /inaktif, iv/ ADJ 1 *[vie, personne, capitaux, machine]* inactive, idle; *(Bourse) [marché]* slack; *[population]* non-working; *[volcan]* inactive, dormant 2 *(= inefficace) [remède]* ineffective, ineffectual NMPL ◆ **les ~s** the non-working *ou* inactive population, those not in active employment

inaction /inaksjɔ̃/ NF *(= oisiveté)* inactivity, idleness

inactivation /inaktivasjɔ̃/ NF *(Méd)* inactivation ◆ **~ virale** viral inactivation

inactiver /inaktive/ ▸ conjug 1 ◂ VT *[+ gène, hormone, virus]* to inactivate ◆ **produits inactivés** inactivated blood products ◆ **vaccin inactivé** inactivated vaccine

inactivité /inaktivite/ NF *(= non-activité)* inactivity ◆ **être en ~** *(Admin, Mil)* to be out of active service

inactuel, -elle /inaktɥɛl/ ADJ irrelevant to the present day

inadaptable /inadaptabl/ ADJ *[roman]* impossible to adapt

inadaptation /inadaptasjɔ̃/ NF maladjustment ◆ **~ à** failure to adjust to *ou* adapt to ◆ **~ d'un enfant à la vie scolaire** a child's inability to cope with school life

inadapté, e /inadapte/ ADJ *[personne, enfance]* maladjusted; *[outil, moyens]* unsuitable *(à* for); ◆ **~ à** not adapted *ou* adjusted to ◆ **un genre de vie complètement ~ à ses ressources** a way of life quite unsuited to his resources ◆ **enfant ~ (à la vie scolaire)** maladjusted child, child with (school) behavioural problems NM,F *(péj = adulte)* misfit; *(Admin, Psych)* maladjusted person ◆ **les ~s (sociaux)** (social) misfits

inadéquat, e /inadekwa(t), kwat/ ADJ inadequate ◆ **la réaction du gouvernement a été totalement ~e** the government's response was totally inadequate

inadéquation /inadekwasjɔ̃/ NF 1 *(= caractère inadéquat)* inadequacy ◆ **l'~ des systèmes de protection sociale** the inadequacy of social welfare systems 2 *(= décalage)* **l'~ entre l'offre et la demande** the fact that supply does not match demand ◆ **l'~ entre formation et emploi** the failure of training programmes to meet employers' needs

inadmissibilité /inadmisibilite/ NF *(Jur)* inadmissibility

inadmissible /inadmisibl/ ADJ 1 *[comportement, négligence]* inadmissible, intolerable; *[propos]* unacceptable; *[situation]* unacceptable, intolerable ◆ **il est ~ de .../que ...** it is unacceptable to .../that ... ◆ **c'est ~ !** this is totally unacceptable! 2 *(Jur) [témoignage, preuve]* inadmissible

inadvertance /inadvɛʀtɑ̃s/ NF oversight ◆ **par ~** inadvertently, by mistake

inaliénabilité /inaljenabilite/ NF inalienability

inaliénable /inaljenabl/ ADJ inalienable

inaltérabilité /inalteʀabilite/ NF 1 *[de métal, substance]* stability; *[de couleur] (au lavage)* fastness; *(à la lumière)* fade-resistance; *[de vernis, encre]* permanence ◆ **~ à l'air** stability in air, ability to resist exposure to the air ◆ **~ à la chaleur** heat-resistance, ability to withstand heat ◆ **l'~ du ciel** *(littér)* the unvarying blue(ness) of the sky 2 *[de sentiment]* unchanging *ou* unfailing *ou* unshakeable nature; *[de principes, espoirs]* steadfastness ◆ **l'~ de son calme** his unchanging *ou* unshakeable calm(ness)

inaltérable /inalteʀabl/ ADJ 1 *[métal, substance]* stable; *[couleur] (au lavage)* fast; *(à la lumière)* fade-resistant; *[vernis, encre]* permanent; *[ciel, cycle]* unchanging ◆ **~ à l'air** unaffected by exposure to the air ◆ **~ à la chaleur** heat-resistant 2 *[sentiments]* unchanging, unfailing, unshakeable; *[bonne santé]* unfailing; *[principes, espoir]* steadfast, unshakeable, unfailing ◆ **il a fait preuve d'une ~ patience** he was unfailingly patient ◆ **d'une humeur ~** even-tempered

inaltéré, e /inalteʀe/ ADJ unchanged, unaltered

inamical, e (mpl **-aux**) /inamikal, o/ ADJ unfriendly

inamovibilité /inamɔvibilite/ NF *(Jur) [de fonction]* permanence; *[de juge, fonctionnaire]* irremovability

inamovible /inamɔvibl/ ADJ 1 *(Jur) [juge, fonctionnaire]* irremovable; *[fonction, emploi]* from which one is irremovable 2 *(= fixe) [plaque, panneau, capuche]* fixed ◆ **cette partie est ~** this part is fixed *ou* cannot be removed 3 *(hum) [casquette, sourire]* eternal ◆ **il travaille toujours chez eux ? il est vraiment ~** is he still with them? – he's a permanent fixture *ou* he's part of the furniture *(hum)*

inanimé, e /inanime/ ADJ *[matière]* inanimate; *[personne, corps] (= évanoui)* unconscious, senseless; *(= mort)* lifeless; *(Ling)* inanimate ◆ **tomber ~** to fall senseless to the ground, to fall to the ground unconscious

inanité /inanite/ NF *[de conversation]* inanity; *[de querelle, efforts]* futility, pointlessness; *[d'espoirs]* vanity, futility ◆ **dire des ~s** to come out with a lot of inane comments

inanition /inanisjɔ̃/ NF exhaustion through lack of nourishment ◆ **tomber/mourir d'~** to faint with/die of hunger

inapaisable /inapezabl/ ADJ *(littér) [colère, chagrin, désir]* unappeasable; *[soif]* unquenchable

inapaisé, e /inapeze/ ADJ *(littér) [colère, chagrin, désir]* unappeased; *[soif]* unquenched

inaperçu, e /inapɛʀsy/ ADJ unnoticed ◆ **passer ~** to pass *ou* go unnoticed ◆ **le geste ne passa pas ~** the gesture did not go unnoticed *ou* unremarked

inapparent, e /inapaʀɑ̃, ɑt/ ADJ *[maladie]* with no visible symptoms; *[tumeur]* invisible; *[motif]* hidden

inappétence /inapetɑ̃s/ NF *(= manque d'appétit)* lack of appetite, inappetence *(frm)*; *(littér = manque de désir)* lack of desire, inappetence *(frm)*

inapplicable /inaplikabl/ ADJ *[loi]* unenforceable ◆ **dans ce cas, la règle est ~** in this case, the rule cannot be applied *ou* is inapplicable *(à* to)

inapplication /inaplikasjɔ̃/ NF 1 *[d'élève]* lack of application 2 *[de loi]* non-application, non-enforcement

inappliqué, e /inaplike/ ADJ *[méthode]* not applied *(attrib)*; *[loi, règlement, traité]* not enforced *(attrib)*

inappréciable /inapʀesjabl/ ADJ 1 *(= précieux) [aide, service]* invaluable; *[avantage, bonheur]* inestimable 2 *(= difficilement décelable) [nuance, différence]* inappreciable, imperceptible

inapproprié, e /inapʀɔpʀije/ ADJ *[terme, mesure, équipement]* inappropriate

inapte /inapt/ ADJ *(= incapable)* incapable ◆ **~ aux affaires/à certains travaux** unsuited to *ou* unfitted for business/certain kinds of work ◆ **un accident l'a rendu ~ au travail** an accident has made him unfit for work ◆ **~ à faire** incapable of doing ◆ **~ (au service)** *(Mil)* unfit (for military service)

inaptitude /inaptityd/ NF *(mentale)* inaptitude, incapacity; *(physique)* unfitness *(à qch* for sth; *à faire qch* for doing sth); ◆ **~ (au service)** *(Mil)* unfitness (for military service)

inarticulé, e /inaʀtikyle/ ADJ *[mots, cris]* inarticulate

inassimilable /inasimilabl/ ADJ *[notions, substance, immigrants]* that cannot be assimilated

inassimilé, e /inasimile/ ADJ *[notions, immigrants, substance]* unassimilated

inassouvi, e /inasuvi/ ADJ *[haine, colère, désir]* unappeased; *[faim]* unsatisfied, unappeased; *(lit, fig) [soif]* unquenched ◆ **vengeance ~e** unappeased desire for revenge, unsated lust for revenge *(littér)* ◆ **soif ~e de puissance** unappeased *ou* unquenched lust for power

inassouvissement /inasuvismɑ̃/ NM ◆ **l'~ de sa faim/son désir** *(action)* the failure to appease his hunger/quench his desire; *(résultat)* his unappeased hunger/desire

inattaquable /inatakabl/ ADJ *[poste, position]* unassailable; *[preuve]* irrefutable; *[argument]* unassailable, irrefutable; *[conduite, réputation]* irreproachable, unimpeachable; *[personne] (par sa qualité)* beyond reproach *(attrib)*; *(par sa position)* unassailable; *[métal]* corrosion-proof, rustproof

inatteignable /inateɲabl/ ADJ *[objet, idéal, objectif]* unattainable

inattendu, e /inatɑ̃dy/ ADJ *[événement, réaction]* unexpected, unforeseen; *[visiteur, remarque]* unexpected NM ◆ **l'~** the unexpected, the unforeseen ◆ **l'~ d'une remarque** the unexpectedness of a remark

inattentif, -ive /inatɑ̃tif, iv/ ADJ inattentive ◆ **~ à** *(= ne prêtant pas attention à)* inattentive to; *(= se souciant peu de) [dangers, détails matériels]* heedless of, unmindful of

inattention /inatɑ̃sjɔ̃/ NF 1 *(= distraction)* lack of attention, inattention ◆ **(instant d')~** moment's inattention, momentary lapse of concentration ◆ **(faute d')~** careless mistake 2 *(littér = manque d'intérêt)* ~ **à** *[+ convenances, détails matériels]* lack of concern for

inaudible /inodibl/ ADJ *(= non ou peu audible)* inaudible; *(péj = mauvais)* unbearable, unlistenable*

inaugural, e (mpl **-aux**) /inogyʀal, o/ ADJ *[séance, cérémonie]* inaugural; *[vol, voyage]* maiden *(épith)* ◆ **discours ~** *[de député]* maiden *ou* inaugural speech; *(lors d'une inauguration)* inaugural speech; *(lors d'un congrès)* opening *ou* inaugural speech

inauguration /inogyʀasjɔ̃/ NF 1 *(= action) [de monument, plaque]* unveiling; *[de route, bâtiment]* inauguration, opening; *[de manifestation, exposition]* opening ◆ **cérémonie/discours d'~** inaugural ceremony/lecture *ou* speech 2 *(= cérémonie) [de monument, plaque]* unveiling ceremony; *[de route, bâtiment, exposition]* opening ceremony

inaugurer /inogyʀe/ ▸ conjug 1 ◂ VT 1 *[+ monument, plaque]* to unveil; *[+ route, bâtiment]* to inaugurate, to open; *[+ manifestation, exposition]* to open ◆ ~ **les chrysanthèmes*** to be a mere figurehead 2 *(= commencer) [+ politique, période]* to inaugurate; *[+ procédé]* to pioneer ◆ **nous inaugurions une période de paix** we were entering a time of peace ◆ ~ **la saison** *[spectacle]* to open *ou* begin the season 3 *(= étrenner) [+ raquette, bureau, chapeau]* to christen*

inauthenticité /inotɑ̃tisite/ NF inauthenticity

inauthentique /inotɑ̃tik/ ADJ *[document, fait]* not authentic *(attrib)*; *(Philos) [existence]* unauthentic

inavouable /inavwabl/ ADJ *[procédé, motifs, mœurs]* shameful, too shameful to mention *(attrib)*; *[bénéfices]* undisclosable

inavoué, e /inavwe/ ADJ *[crime]* unconfessed; *[sentiments]* unavowed, unspoken

INC /iɛnse/ NM abrév de **Institut national de la consommation**

inca /ɛ̃ka/ ADJ Inca NMF **Inca** Inca

incalculable /ɛ̃kalkylabl/ ADJ *(gén)* incalculable ◆ **un nombre ~ de** countless numbers of, an incalculable number of

incandescence /ɛ̃kɑ̃desɑ̃s/ NF incandescence ◆ **en ~** white-hot, incandescent ◆ **porter qch à ~** to heat sth white-hot *ou* to incandescence; → **lampe, manchon**

incandescent, e /ɛ̃kɑ̃desɑ̃, ɑ̃t/ ADJ *[substance, filament]* incandescent, white-hot; *[lave]* glowing; *[métal]* white-hot

incantation /ɛ̃kɑ̃tasjɔ̃/ NF incantation

incantatoire /ɛ̃kɑ̃tatwaʀ/ ADJ incantatory; → **formule**

incapable /ɛ̃kapabl/ GRAMMAIRE ACTIVE 43.4

ADJ 1 *(= inapte)* incapable, incompetent, useless*

◆ **incapable de faire** *(incompétence, impossibilité morale)* incapable of doing; *(impossibilité physique)* unable to do, incapable of doing ◆ **j'étais ~ de bouger** I was unable to move, I couldn't move ◆ **elle est ~ de mentir** she's incapable of lying, she can't tell a lie

◆ **incapable de qch** ◆ ~ **d'amour** incapable of loving, unable to love ◆ ~ **de malhonnêteté** incapable of dishonesty *ou* of being dishonest ◆ ~ **du moindre effort** unable to make the least effort, incapable of making the least effort

2 *(Jur)* incapable, (legally) incompetent

NMF 1 *(= incompétent)* incompetent ◆ **c'est un ~** he's incapable, he's an incompetent

2 *(Jur)* incapable *ou* (legally) incompetent person

incapacitant, e /ɛ̃kapasitɑ̃, ɑ̃t/ ADJ incapacitating *(épith)* NM incapacitant

incapacité /ɛ̃kapasite/ NF 1 *(= incompétence)* incompetence, incapability 2 *(= impossibilité)* **~ de faire** incapacity *ou* inability to do ◆ **être dans l'~ de faire** to be unable to do, to be incapable of doing 3 *(= invalidité)* disablement, disability ◆ ~ **totale/partielle/permanente** total/partial/permanent disablement *ou* disability ◆ ~ **de travail** industrial disablement *ou* disability 4 *(Jur)* incapacity, (legal) incompetence ◆ ~ **de jouissance** incapacity *(by exclusion from a right)* ◆ ~ **d'exercice** incapacity *(by restriction of a right)* ◆ ~ **civile** civil incapacity

incarcération /ɛ̃kaʀseʀasjɔ̃/ NF incarceration, imprisonment

incarcérer /ɛ̃kaʀseʀe/ ▸ conjug 6 ◂ VT to incarcerate, to imprison ◆ **il y est incarcéré depuis deux ans** he has been incarcerated *ou* held there for the past two years

incarnat, e /ɛ̃kaʀna, at/ ADJ *[teint]* rosy, pink; *[teinture]* crimson NM *[de teint, joues]* rosy hue, rosiness; *[de tissu]* crimson tint

incarnation /ɛ̃kaʀnasjɔ̃/ NF 1 *(Myth, Rel)* incarnation 2 *(= image, personnification)* **être l'~ de** to be the incarnation *ou* embodiment of

incarné, e /ɛ̃kaʀne/ (ptp de **incarner**) ADJ 1 *(Rel)* incarnate 2 *(= personnifié)* incarnate, personified ◆ **c'est la méchanceté ~e** he is wickedness incarnate *ou* personified, he is the embodiment of wickedness 3 *[ongle]* ingrown

incarner /ɛ̃kaʀne/ ▸ conjug 1 ◂ VT 1 *(Rel)* to incarnate 2 *(= représenter) [personne]* to embody, to personify, to incarnate; *[œuvre]* to embody; *(Théât) [acteur]* to play VPR **s'incarner** 1 *(Rel)* **s'~ dans** to become *ou* be incarnate in 2 *(= être représenté par)* **s'~ dans** *ou* **en** to be embodied in ◆ **tous nos espoirs s'incarnent en vous** you embody all our hopes, you are the embodiment of all our hopes 3 *[ongle]* to become ingrown

incartade /ɛ̃kaʀtad/ NF 1 *(= écart de conduite)* prank, escapade ◆ **ils étaient punis à la moindre ~** they were punished for the slightest prank ◆ **faire une ~** to go on an escapade 2 *(Équitation = écart)* swerve ◆ **faire une ~** to shy

incassable /ɛ̃kasabl/ ADJ unbreakable

incendiaire /ɛ̃sɑ̃djɛʀ/ NMF fire-raiser, arsonist ADJ *[balle, bombe]* incendiary; *[discours, article]* inflammatory, incendiary; *[lettre d'amour, œillade]* passionate; → **blond**

incendie /ɛ̃sɑ̃di/ NM 1 *(= sinistre)* fire, blaze ◆ **un ~ s'est déclaré dans ...** a fire broke out in ...; → **assurance, foyer, pompe¹** 2 *(littér)* **l'~ du couchant** the blaze of the sunset, the fiery glow of the sunset ◆ **l'~ de la révolte/de la passion** the fire of revolt/of passion

COMP **incendie criminel** arson *(NonC)*, case of arson

incendie de forêt forest fire

incendie volontaire arson

incendié, e /ɛ̃sɑ̃dje/ (ptp de **incendier**) ADJ *[bâtiment, voiture]* gutted (by fire), burned-out; *[village]* destroyed by fire

incendier /ɛ̃sɑ̃dje/ ▸ conjug 7 ◂ VT 1 *(= mettre le feu à)* to set fire to, to set on fire, to set alight; *(= brûler complètement) [+ bâtiment]* to burn down; *[+ voiture]* to burn; *[+ ville, récolte, forêt]* to burn (to ashes) 2 *[+ imagination]* to fire; *[+ bouche, gorge]* to burn, to set on fire ◆ **la fièvre lui incendiait le visage** *(sensation)* fever made his face burn; *(apparence)* his cheeks were burning *ou* glowing with fever ◆ **le soleil incendie le couchant** *(littér)* the setting sun sets the sky ablaze 3 *(* = réprimander)* ~ **qn** to give sb a stiff telling-off* *ou* a rocket* *(Brit)* ◆ **tu vas te faire ~** you're in for it*, you'll get a rocket* *(Brit)* ◆ **elle l'a incendié du regard** she looked daggers at him, she shot him a baleful look

incertain, e /ɛ̃sɛʀtɛ̃, ɛn/ ADJ 1 *[personne]* uncertain, unsure *(de qch* about *ou* as to sth); ◆ ~ **de savoir la vérité, il ...** uncertain *ou* unsure as to whether he knew the truth, he ... ◆ **encore ~ sur la conduite à suivre** still undecided *ou* uncertain about which course to follow 2 *[démarche]* uncertain, hesitant 3 *[temps]* uncertain, unsettled; *[contour]* indistinct, blurred; *[lumière]* dim, vague 4 *[avenir]* uncertain; *[résultat, entreprise, origine]* uncertain, doubtful; *[date, durée]* uncertain, unspecified; *[fait]* uncertain, doubtful NM *(Fin)* ◆ **l'~** the exchange rate

incertitude /ɛ̃sɛʀtityd/ GRAMMAIRE ACTIVE 43.1

NF 1 *[de personne, résultat, fait]* uncertainty ◆ **être dans l'~** to be in a state of uncertainty, to feel uncertain ◆ **être dans l'~ sur ce qu'on doit faire** to be uncertain as to the best course to follow 2 *(Math, Phys)* uncertainty ◆ **principe d'~** uncertainty principle NFPL **incertitudes** *(= hésitations)* doubts, uncertainties; *(= impondérables) [d'avenir, entreprise]* uncertainties

incessamment /ɛ̃sesamɑ̃/ ADV *(= sans délai)* (very) shortly ◆ **il doit arriver ~** he'll be here (very) shortly ◆ ~ **sous peu** *(hum)* any second now

> ⚠ **incessamment** ne se traduit pas par **incessantly**, qui a le sens de 'sans arrêt'.

incessant, e /ɛ̃sesɑ̃, ɑ̃t/ ADJ *[efforts, activité]* ceaseless, incessant, unremitting; *[pluie, bruit, réclamations, coups de téléphone]* incessant, unceasing

incessibilité /ɛ̃sesibilite/ NF nontransferability

incessible /ɛ̃sesibl/ ADJ non-transferable

inceste /ɛ̃sɛst/ NM incest

incestueux, -euse /ɛ̃sɛstɥø, øz/ ADJ *[relations, personne]* incestuous; *[enfant]* born of incest NM,F *(Jur)* person guilty of incest

inchangé, e /ɛ̃ʃɑ̃ʒe/ ADJ unchanged, unaltered ◆ **la situation/son expression reste ~e** the situation/his expression remains unchanged *ou* the same *ou* unaltered

inchangeable /ɛ̃ʃɑ̃ʒabl/ ADJ unchangeable

inchantable /ɛ̃ʃɑ̃tabl/ ADJ unsingable

inchauffable /ɛ̃ʃofabl/ ADJ impossible to heat *(attrib)*

inchavirable /ɛ̃ʃaviʀabl/ ADJ uncapsizable, self-righting

inchoatif, -ive /ɛ̃kɔatif, iv/ ADJ inchoative, inceptive NM inceptive

incidemment /ɛ̃sidamɑ̃/ ADV *(gén)* in passing; *(= à propos)* by the way, incidentally

incidence /ɛ̃sidɑ̃s/ NF *(= conséquence)* effect; *(Écon, Phys)* incidence ◆ **avoir une ~ sur** to affect, to have an effect (up)on ◆ **cette réforme est sans ~ directe sur l'emploi** this reform will have no direct impact on employment; → **angle**

incident, e /ɛ̃sidɑ̃, ɑ̃t/ NM 1 *(gén)* incident ◆ **la vie n'est qu'une succession d'~s** life is just a series of minor incidents ◆ **~ imprévu** unexpected incident, unforeseen event ◆ **c'est un ~ sans gravité** *ou* **sans importance** this incident is of no importance ◆ **l'~ est clos** that's the end of the matter ◆ **voyage sans ~(s)** uneventful journey ◆ **se dérouler sans ~(s)** to go off without incident *ou* smoothly; 2 *(Jur)* point of law

ADJ *(frm, Jur = accessoire)* incidental; *(Phys)* incident ◆ **il a évoqué ce fait de façon ~e** he mentioned this fact in passing ◆ **je désirerais poser une question ~e** I'd like to ask a question in connection with this matter, I'd like to interpose a question

NF **incidente** *(Ling)* **(proposition) ~e** parenthesis, parenthetical clause

COMP **incident cardiaque** slight heart attack

incident diplomatique diplomatic incident

incident de frontière border incident

incident de paiement *(Fin)* default in payment, nonpayment

incident de parcours *(gén)* (minor *ou* slight) setback, hitch; *(santé)* (minor *ou* slight) setback

incident technique *(lit, hum)* technical hitch

incinérateur /ɛ̃sineʀatœʀ/ NM incinerator ◆ **~ à ordures** refuse incinerator

incinération /ɛ̃sineʀasjɔ̃/ NF *[d'ordures, cadavre]* incineration; *(au crématorium)* cremation ◆ **four d'~ d'ordures ménagères** incinerator for household waste; → **usine**

incinérer /ɛ̃sineʀe/ ▸ conjug 6 ◂ VT *[+ ordures, cadavre]* to incinerate; *(au crématorium)* to cremate ◆ **se faire ~** to be cremated

incipit /ɛ̃sipit/ NM INV incipit

incirconcis /ɛ̃siʀkɔ̃si, iz/ ADJ M uncircumcised NM uncircumcised male

incise /ɛ̃siz/ NF *(dans un discours)* aside; *(Mus)* phrase ◆ **(proposition) ~** *(Ling)* interpolated clause

inciser /ɛ̃size/ ▸ conjug 1 ◂ VT *[+ écorce, arbre]* to incise, to make an incision in; *[+ peau]* to incise; *[+ abcès]* to lance

incisif, -ive /ɛ̃sizif, iv/ ADJ *[ton, style, réponse]* cutting, incisive; *[regard]* piercing ◆ **il était très ~ dans ses questions** he was very incisive in his questioning, his questions were very incisive NF **incisive** *(= dent)* incisor ◆ **incisive supérieure/inférieure** upper/lower incisor

incision /ɛ̃sizjɔ̃/ NF 1 *(= action) [d'écorce, arbre]* incising; *[de peau]* incision; *[d'abcès]* lancing 2 *(= entaille)* incision ◆ **pratiquer une ~ dans** to make an incision in, to incise

incitateur, -trice /ɛ̃sitatœʀ, tʀis/ NM,F instigator

incitatif, -ive /ɛ̃sitatif, iv/ ADJ ◆ **mesure incitative** incentive (à to); ◆ **aide incitative** incentive aid ◆ **prix ~** attractive price

incitation /ɛ̃sitasjɔ̃/ NF *(au meurtre, à la révolte)* incitement (à to); *(à l'effort, au travail)* incentive (*à* to; *à faire* to do); *(à la débauche, à la violence)* incitement ◆ **~ à la haine raciale** incitement to racial hatred ◆ **~ financière/fiscale** financial/tax incentive

inciter /ɛ̃site/ ▸ conjug 1 ◂ **inciter à** VT INDIR ◆ **~ qn à faire qch** to encourage sb to do sth ◆ **cela m'incite à la méfiance** that prompts me to be on my guard, that puts me on my guard ◆ **cela les incite à la violence/la révolte** that incites them to violence/revolt ◆ **ça n'incite pas au travail** it doesn't (exactly) encourage one to work, it's no incentive to work

incivil, e /ɛ̃sivil/ ADJ *(frm)* uncivil, rude

incivilité /ɛ̃sivilite/ NF *(frm) [d'attitude, ton]* incivility, rudeness; *(= propos impoli)* uncivil *ou* rude remark ◆ **ce serait commettre une ~ que de ...** it would be uncivil to ...

incivisme /ɛ̃sivism/ NM lack of civic *ou* public spirit

inclassable /ɛ̃klɑsabl/ ADJ unclassifiable, uncategorizable

inclémence /ɛ̃klemɑ̃s/ NF inclemency

inclément, e /ɛ̃klemɑ̃, ɑ̃t/ ADJ inclement

inclinable /ɛ̃klinabl/ ADJ *[dossier de siège]* reclining; *[lampe]* adjustable; *[toit d'une voiture]* tilting

inclinaison /ɛ̃klinɛzɔ̃/ NF 1 *(= déclivité) [de plan, pente]* incline; *[de route, voie ferrée]* incline, gradient; *[de toit]* slope, slant, pitch; *[de barre, tuyau]* slope, slant ◆ **toit à faible/forte ~** gently-sloping/steeply-sloping roof 2 *(= aspect) [de mur]* lean; *[de mât, tour]* lean, tilt; *[de chapeau]* slant, tilt; *[d'appareil, tête]* tilt; *[de navire]* list ◆ **régler l'~ d'un siège** to adjust the angle of a seat 3 *(Géom) [de droite, surface]* angle; *(Astron)* inclination; → **angle** COMP **inclinaison magnétique** *(Phys)* magnetic declination

inclination /ɛ̃klinasjɔ̃/ NF 1 *(= penchant)* inclination ◆ **suivre son ~** to follow one's (own) inclination ◆ **son ~ naturelle au bonheur** his natural inclination *ou* tendency towards happiness ◆ **~s altruistes** altruistic tendencies ◆ **une certaine ~ à mentir** a certain inclination *ou* tendency *ou* propensity to tell lies ◆ **avoir de l'~ pour la littérature** to have a strong liking *ou* a penchant for literature ◆ **~ pour qn** † liking for sb 2 *(= mouvement)* **~ de (la) tête** *(= acquiescement)* nod; *(= salut)* inclination of the head ◆ **~ (du buste)** bow

incliné, e /ɛ̃kline/ (ptp de **incliner**) ADJ 1 *(= en pente raide) [toit]* steep, sloping 2 *(= penché) [tour, mur]* leaning; *[mât, table d'architecte]* at an angle, sloping; *[récipient, dossier de siège]* tilted; *(Géol)* inclined ◆ **orbite ~e à 51 degrés** orbit inclined at 51 degrees; → **plan¹** 3 *(= enclin)* **~ à** inclined to

incliner /ɛ̃kline/ ▸ conjug 1 ◂ VT 1 *(= pencher) [+ appareil, mât, bouteille, dossier de siège]* to tilt; *(littér = courber) [+ arbre]* to bend (over); *(= donner de l'inclinaison à) [+ toit, surface]* to slope ◆ **le vent incline le navire** the wind heels the boat over ◆ **~ la tête** *ou* **le front** *(pour saluer)* to give a slight bow, to incline one's head; *(pour acquiescer)* to nod (one's head), to incline one's head ◆ **~ la tête de côté** to tilt *ou* incline one's head on one side ◆ **~ le buste** *(saluer)* to bow, to give a bow ◆ **inclinez le corps plus en avant** lean *ou* bend forward more

2 *(littér)* **~ qn à l'indulgence** to encourage sb to be indulgent ◆ **ceci m'incline à penser que** that makes me inclined to think that, that leads me to believe that

VI 1 ◆ **~ à** *(= tendre à)* to tend towards; *(= pencher pour)* to be *ou* feel inclined towards ◆ **il incline à l'autoritarisme/à l'indulgence** he tends towards authoritarianism/indulgence, he tends to be authoritarian/indulgent ◆ **il inclinait à la clémence/sévérité** he felt inclined to be merciful/severe, he inclined towards clemency/severity ◆ **~ à penser/croire que ...** to be inclined to think/believe that ... ◆ **j'incline à accepter cette offre** I'm inclined to accept this offer

2 *(littér) [mur]* to lean; *[arbre]* to bend ◆ **la colline inclinait doucement vers la mer** the hill sloped gently (down) towards the sea

3 *(= modifier sa direction)* **~ vers** to veer (over) towards *ou* to

VPR **s'incliner** 1 *(= se courber)* to bow *(devant* before); ◆ **s'~ jusqu'à terre** to bow to the ground

2 *(= rendre hommage à)* **s'~ devant qn** *ou* **devant la supériorité de qn** to bow before sb's superiority ◆ **devant un tel homme, on ne peut que s'~** one can only bow (down) before such a man ◆ **il est venu s'~ devant la dépouille mortelle du président** he came to pay his last respects at the coffin of the president

3 *(= céder)* **s'~ devant l'autorité/la volonté de qn** to yield *ou* bow to sb's authority/wishes ◆ **s'~ devant un ordre** to accept an order ◆ **puisque vous me l'ordonnez, je n'ai plus qu'à m'~** since you order me to do it, I can only accept it and obey

4 *(= s'avouer battu)* to admit defeat, to give in ◆ **le boxeur s'inclina (devant son adversaire) à la 3ᵉ reprise** the boxer admitted defeat in the 3rd round ◆ **Marseille s'est incliné devant Saint-Étienne (par) 2 buts à 3** Marseilles lost to Saint-Étienne by 2 goals to 3

5 *[arbre]* to bend over; *[mur]* to lean; *[navire]* to heel (over); *[chemin, colline]* to slope; *[toit]* to be sloping ◆ **le soleil s'incline à l'horizon** the sun is sinking (down) towards the horizon

inclure /ɛ̃klyʀ/ ▸ conjug 35 ◂ VT 1 *(= insérer) [+ clause]* to insert *(dans* in); *[+ nom]* to include *(dans* in); *(= joindre à un envoi) [+ billet, chèque]* to enclose *(dans* in) 2 *(= contenir)* to include ◆ **ce récit en inclut un autre** this is a story within a story

inclus, e /ɛ̃kly, yz/ (ptp de **inclure**) ADJ 1 *(= joint à un envoi)* enclosed 2 *(= compris) [frais]* included ◆ **eux ~** including them ◆ **jusqu'au 10 mars ~** until 10 March inclusive, up to and including 10 March ◆ **jusqu'au 3ᵉ chapitre ~** up to and including the 3rd chapter ◆ **les frais sont ~ dans la note** the bill is inclusive of expenses, expenses are included in the bill 3 *(Math)* **~ dans** *[ensemble]* included in ◆ **A est ~ dans B** A is the subset of B 4 *(Bot) [étamines]* included 5 *(Méd)* ◆ **dent ~e** impacted tooth

inclusif, -ive /ɛ̃klyzif, iv/ ADJ *(Gram, Logique)* inclusive

inclusion /ɛ̃klyzjɔ̃/ NF 1 *(gén, Math)* inclusion *(dans* in) 2 *(Méd) [de dent]* impaction 3 *(= élément inclus)* inclusion ◆ **cette pierre présente des ~s de tourmaline** the stone contains streaks of tourmaline *ou* has tourmaline inclusions *(frm)* 4 *(= objet de décoration) ornament set in acrylic*

inclusivement /ɛ̃klyzivmɑ̃/ ADV ◆ **jusqu'au 16ᵉ siècle ~** up to and including the 16th century ◆ **jusqu'au 1ᵉʳ janvier ~** until 1 January inclusive, up to and including 1 January

incoercible /ɛ̃kɔɛʀsibl/ ADJ *[toux]* uncontrollable; *[besoin, désir, rire]* uncontrollable, irrepressible

incognito /ɛ̃kɔɲito/ ADV incognito NM ◆ **garder l'~, rester dans l'~** to remain incognito ◆ **l'~ lui plaisait** he liked being incognito ◆ **l'~ dont il s'entourait** the secrecy with which he surrounded himself

incohérence /ɛ̃kɔeʀɑ̃s/ NF 1 *(= caractère illogique) [de geste, propos, texte]* incoherence; *[de comportement, politique]* inconsistency 2 *(= propos, acte)* inconsistency

incohérent, e /ɛ̃kɔeʀɑ̃, ɑ̃t/ ADJ [1] *[geste, propos, texte]* incoherent; *[comportement, politique]* inconsistent [2] *(Phys) [lumière, vibration]* incoherent

incollable /ɛ̃kɔlabl/ ADJ [1] *(= qui ne colle pas)* **riz ~** non-stick rice [2] *(* = imbattable)* unbeatable ◆ **il est ~** *[candidat]* he's got all the answers, you can't catch him out* *(Brit)*

incolore /ɛ̃kɔlɔʀ/ ADJ *[liquide, style]* colourless; *[verre, vernis]* clear; *[cirage]* neutral ◆ **~, inodore et sans saveur** *[personne]* without an ounce of personality; *[film]* (totally) bland

incomber /ɛ̃kɔ̃be/ ▸ conjug 1 ◂ **incomber à** VT INDIR *(frm) [devoirs, responsabilité]* to be incumbent (up)on; *[frais, réparations, travail]* to be the responsibility of ◆ **il m'incombe de faire cela** *(gén)* it falls to me to do it, it is incumbent upon me to do it; *(responsabilité morale)* the onus is on me to do it ◆ **ces frais leur incombent entièrement** these costs are to be paid by them in full *ou* are entirely their responsibility

incombustibilité /ɛ̃kɔ̃bystibilite/ NF incombustibility

incombustible /ɛ̃kɔ̃bystibl/ ADJ incombustible

incommensurabilité /ɛ̃kɔmɑ̃syʀabilite/ NF incommensurability

incommensurable /ɛ̃kɔmɑ̃syʀabl/ ADJ [1] *(= immense) (gén)* immeasurable; *[bêtise, haine]* boundless [2] *(= sans commune mesure : Math, littér)* incommensurable *(avec* with)

incommensurablement /ɛ̃kɔmɑ̃syʀabləmɑ̃/ ADV immeasurably

incommodant, e /ɛ̃kɔmɔdɑ̃, ɑ̃t/ ADJ *[odeur]* unpleasant, offensive; *[bruit]* annoying, unpleasant; *[chaleur]* uncomfortable

incommode /ɛ̃kɔmɔd/ ADJ [1] *(= peu pratique) [pièce, appartement]* inconvenient; *[heure]* awkward, inconvenient; *[meuble, outil]* impractical [2] *(= inconfortable) [siège]* uncomfortable; *[position, situation]* awkward, uncomfortable

incommodément /ɛ̃kɔmɔdemɑ̃/ ADV *[installé, assis]* awkwardly, uncomfortably; *[logé]* inconveniently; *[situé]* inconveniently, awkwardly

incommoder /ɛ̃kɔmɔde/ ▸ conjug 1 ◂ VT ◆ **~ qn** *[bruit]* to disturb *ou* bother sb; *[odeur, chaleur]* to bother sb; *[comportement]* to make sb feel ill at ease *ou* uncomfortable ◆ **être incommodé par** to be bothered by ◆ **se sentir incommodé** to feel indisposed *ou* unwell

incommodité /ɛ̃kɔmɔdite/ NF [1] *[de pièce, appartement]* inconvenience; *[d'heure]* awkwardness; *[de système, outil]* impracticability, awkwardness [2] *[de position, situation]* awkwardness ◆ **l'~ des sièges** the fact that the seating is so uncomfortable, the uncomfortable seats [3] *(= inconvénient)* inconvenience

incommunicabilité /ɛ̃kɔmynikabilite/ NF incommunicability

incommunicable /ɛ̃kɔmynikabl/ ADJ incommunicable

incommutabilité /ɛ̃kɔmytabilite/ NF inalienability

incommutable /ɛ̃kɔmytabl/ ADJ inalienable

incomparable /ɛ̃kɔ̃paʀabl/ ADJ *(= remarquable)* incomparable, matchless; *(= dissemblable)* not comparable ◆ **est-ce plus confortable ? – c'est ~ !** is it more comfortable? – there's no comparison!

incomparablement /ɛ̃kɔ̃paʀabləmɑ̃/ ADV ◆ **~ plus/mieux** incomparably *ou* infinitely more/better ◆ **chanter ~** to sing exceptionally well

incompatibilité /ɛ̃kɔ̃patibilite/ NF *(gén, Sci)* incompatibility ◆ **~ d'humeur** *(Jur)* (mutual) incompatibility ◆ **il y a ~ d'humeur entre les membres de cette équipe** the members of this team are (temperamentally) incompatible ◆ **~ médicamenteuse** incompatibility of medications

incompatible /ɛ̃kɔ̃patibl/ ADJ incompatible *(avec* with)

incompétence /ɛ̃kɔ̃petɑ̃s/ NF *(= incapacité)* incompetence; *(= ignorance)* lack of knowledge; *(Jur)* incompetence ◆ **il reconnaît volontiers son ~ en musique** he freely admits to his lack of knowledge of music *ou* that he knows nothing about music ◆ **il a atteint son seuil d'~** he's reached his level of incompetence

incompétent, e /ɛ̃kɔ̃petɑ̃, ɑ̃t/ ADJ *(= incapable)* incompetent; *(= ignorant)* ignorant, inexpert; *(Jur)* incompetent ◆ **en ce qui concerne la musique je suis ~** as far as music goes I'm not competent *ou* I'm incompetent to judge NM,F incompetent

incomplet, -ète /ɛ̃kɔ̃plɛ, ɛt/ ADJ incomplete

incomplètement /ɛ̃kɔ̃plɛtmɑ̃/ ADV *[renseigné]* incompletely; *[rétabli, guéri]* not completely

incomplétude /ɛ̃kɔ̃pletyd/ NF *(littér = insatisfaction)* non-fulfilment

incompréhensibilité /ɛ̃kɔ̃pʀeɑ̃sibilite/ NF incomprehensibility

incompréhensible /ɛ̃kɔ̃pʀeɑ̃sibl/ ADJ *(gén)* incomprehensible

incompréhensif, -ive /ɛ̃kɔ̃pʀeɑ̃sif, iv/ ADJ unsympathetic ◆ **il s'est montré totalement ~** he (just) refused to understand, he was totally unsympathetic ◆ **des parents totalement ~s** parents who show a total lack of understanding

incompréhension /ɛ̃kɔ̃pʀeɑ̃sjɔ̃/ NF *(= méconnaissance)* lack of understanding *(envers* of); *(= refus de comprendre)* unwillingness to understand ◆ **leur ~ du texte** their failure to understand the text ◆ **cet article témoigne d'une ~ totale du problème** the article shows a total lack of understanding of the problem ◆ **~ mutuelle** mutual incomprehension

incompressibilité /ɛ̃kɔ̃pʀesibilite/ NF *(Phys)* incompressibility ◆ **l'~ du budget** the irreducibility of the budget

incompressible /ɛ̃kɔ̃pʀesibl/ ADJ *(Phys)* incompressible; *(Jur) [peine]* to be served in full ◆ **nos dépenses sont ~s** our expenses cannot be reduced *ou* cut down

incompris, e /ɛ̃kɔ̃pʀi, iz/ ADJ misunderstood NM ◆ **il fut un grand ~ à son époque** he was never understood by his contemporaries

inconcevable /ɛ̃kɔ̃s(ə)vabl/ GRAMMAIRE ACTIVE 43.3 ADJ *(gén)* inconceivable ◆ **avec un toupet ~** with unbelievable *ou* incredible nerve

inconcevablement /ɛ̃kɔ̃s(ə)vabləmɑ̃/ ADV inconceivably, incredibly

inconciliable /ɛ̃kɔ̃siljabl/ ADJ, NM irreconcilable, incompatible *(avec* with); ◆ **concilier l'~** to reconcile the irreconcilable

inconditionnalité /ɛ̃kɔ̃disjɔnalite/ NF unreservedness, whole-heartedness ◆ **l'~ de son soutien au gouvernement** his wholehearted *ou* unreserved support for the government

inconditionnel, -elle /ɛ̃kɔ̃disjɔnɛl/ ADJ [1] *(= sans condition) [acceptation, ordre, soumission]* unconditional ◆ **libération inconditionnelle** unconditional release [2] *(= absolu) [appui]* wholehearted, unconditional, unreserved; *[partisan, foi]* unquestioning NM,F *[d'homme politique, doctrine]* unquestioning *ou* ardent supporter; *[d'écrivain, chanteur]* ardent admirer ◆ **les ~s des sports d'hiver** winter sports enthusiasts *ou* fanatics ◆ **c'est un ~ de l'informatique** he absolutely loves computers

inconditionnellement /ɛ̃kɔ̃disjɔnɛlmɑ̃/ ADV *[soutenir, admirer]* whole-heartedly; *[accepter]* unconditionally, without conditions

inconduite /ɛ̃kɔ̃dɥit/ NF *(= débauche)* loose living *(NonC)*

inconfort /ɛ̃kɔ̃fɔʀ/ NM *[de logement]* lack of comfort, discomfort; *[de situation, position]* unpleasantness ◆ **l'~ lui importait peu** discomfort didn't matter to him in the least ◆ **vivre dans l'~** to live in uncomfortable surroundings

inconfortable /ɛ̃kɔ̃fɔʀtabl/ ADJ [1] *(= sans confort) [maison, meuble]* uncomfortable; *[position]* uncomfortable, awkward [2] *(= gênant) [situation]* awkward

inconfortablement /ɛ̃kɔ̃fɔʀtabləmɑ̃/ ADV uncomfortably

incongru, e /ɛ̃kɔ̃gʀy/ ADJ [1] *(= déplacé) [attitude, bruit]* unseemly; *[remarque]* incongruous, ill-placed, ill-chosen [2] *(= bizarre, inattendu) [objet]* incongruous; *[personnage]* outlandish; *[situation]* strange, weird

incongruité /ɛ̃kɔ̃gʀyite/ NF [1] *(= caractère déplacé)* impropriety, unseemliness; *[de propos]* incongruity, inappropriateness [2] *(= bizarrerie) [de situation]* strangeness [3] *(= propos)* unseemly *ou* ill-chosen *ou* ill-placed remark; *(= acte)* unseemly action, unseemly behaviour *(NonC)*

incongrûment /ɛ̃kɔ̃gʀymɑ̃/ ADV *[agir, parler]* in an unseemly way

inconnaissable /ɛ̃kɔnesabl/ ADJ unknowable NM ◆ **l'~** the unknowable

inconnu, e /ɛ̃kɔny/ ADJ *[destination, fait]* unknown; *[odeur, sensation]* new, unknown; *[ville, personne]* unknown, strange *(de* to); ◆ **son visage m'était ~** his face was new *ou* unfamiliar to me, I didn't know his face ◆ **une joie ~e l'envahit** he was seized with a strange joy *ou* a joy that was (quite) new to him ◆ **on se sent très seul en pays ~** one feels very lonely in a strange country *ou* in a foreign country *ou* in strange surroundings ◆ **s'en aller vers des contrées ~es** to set off in search of unknown *ou* unexplored *ou* uncharted lands ◆ **~ à cette adresse** not known at this address ◆ **il est ~ au bataillon*** no one's ever heard of him; → **père, soldat**

NM,F stranger, unknown person ◆ **pour moi, ce peintre-là, c'est un ~** I don't know this painter, this painter is unknown to me ◆ **le coupable n'était pas un ~ pour la police** the culprit was known *ou* was not unknown *ou* was no stranger to the police ◆ **ne parle pas à des ~s** don't talk to strangers; → **illustre**

NM ◆ **l'~** *(= ce qu'on ignore)* the unknown

NF **inconnue** *(= élément inconnu)* unknown factor *ou* quantity, unknown; *(Math)* unknown ◆ **dans cette entreprise, il y a beaucoup d'inconnues** there are lots of unknowns *ou* unknown factors in this venture ◆ **l'avenir du service reste la grande ~e** a big question mark hangs over the future of the department ◆ **son attitude demeure la grande ~e** it's anybody's guess what line he'll take

inconsciemment /ɛ̃kɔ̃sjamɑ̃/ ADV *(= involontairement)* unconsciously

inconscience /ɛ̃kɔ̃sjɑ̃s/ NF [1] *(physique)* unconsciousness ◆ **sombrer dans l'~** to lose consciousness, to sink into unconsciousness [2] *(morale)* thoughtlessness, recklessness, rashness ◆ **c'est de l'~ !** that's sheer madness! *ou* stupidity! [3] *[d'événements extérieurs]* unawareness

inconscient, e /ɛ̃kɔ̃sjɑ̃, jɑ̃t/ ADJ [1] *(= évanoui)* unconscious [2] *(= échappant à la conscience) [sentiment]* subconscious; *(= machinal) [mouvement]* unconscious, automatic [3] *(= irréfléchi) [décision, action, personne]* thoughtless, reckless, rash; *(* : = fou)* mad*, crazy [4]

◆ **inconscient de** *(= qui ne se rend pas compte de)* oblivious to, unaware of; *(= indifférent à)* oblivous to, heedless of ◆ **~es du danger, elles**

exploraient le camp oblivious to the danger, they explored the camp ◆ ~ **du piège, il ...** failing to notice the trap, he ... ◆ ~ **de l'effet produit, il continuait** he continued, oblivious to *ou* unaware of the effect he was having **NM** *(Psych)* ◆ **l'~** the subconscious, the unconscious ◆ **l'~ collectif** the collective unconscious **NM,F** reckless person ◆ **c'est un ~ !** he must be mad!

inconséquence /ɛ̃kɔ̃sekɑ̃s/ **NF** *(= manque de logique)* inconsistency, inconsequence *(NonC)*; *(= légèreté)* thoughtlessness *(NonC)*, fecklessness *(NonC)*

inconséquent, e /ɛ̃kɔ̃sekɑ̃, ɑ̃t/ **ADJ** *(= illogique) [comportement, personne]* inconsistent, inconsequent; *(= irréfléchi) [démarche, décision, personne]* thoughtless

inconsidéré, e /ɛ̃kɔ̃sideʀe/ **ADJ** *[action]* rash, reckless; *[promesse]* rash; *[démarche]* ill-considered; *[propos]* ill-considered, thoughtless ◆ **l'usage ~ d'engrais** the indiscriminate use of fertilizers ◆ **il fait des dépenses ~es** he's extravagant, he throws money around ◆ **prendre des risques ~s** to take unnecessary risks

inconsidérément /ɛ̃kɔ̃sideʀemɑ̃/ **ADV** thoughtlessly, rashly, without thinking

inconsistance /ɛ̃kɔ̃sistɑ̃s/ **NF** 1 *[de preuve, idée, espoir]* flimsiness; *[de politique, argumentation, intrigue, personnage]* flimsiness, weakness; *[de personne]* colourlessness *(Brit)*, colorlessness *(US)*; *[de caractère]* weakness 2 *[de crème]* runniness; *[de bouillie, soupe]* watery *ou* thin consistency

inconsistant, e /ɛ̃kɔ̃sistɑ̃, ɑ̃t/ **ADJ** 1 *[personne, programme, ouvrage]* insubstantial 2 *[crème]* runny; *[bouillie, soupe]* watery, thin

> ⚠ **inconsistant** ne se traduit pas par le mot anglais **inconsistent**, qui a le sens de 'inconstant'.

inconsolable /ɛ̃kɔ̃sɔlabl/ **ADJ** *[personne]* disconsolate, inconsolable; *[chagrin]* inconsolable

inconsolé, e /ɛ̃kɔ̃sɔle/ **ADJ** *[personne]* disconsolate; *[chagrin]* unconsoled

inconsommable /ɛ̃kɔ̃sɔmabl/ **ADJ** unfit for consumption *(attrib)*

inconstance /ɛ̃kɔ̃stɑ̃s/ **NF** 1 *(= instabilité)* fickleness 2 *(littér)* ~**s** *(dans le comportement)* inconsistencies; *(en amour)* infidelities, inconstancies *(frm)*

inconstant, e /ɛ̃kɔ̃stɑ̃, ɑ̃t/ **ADJ** fickle

inconstitutionnalité /ɛ̃kɔ̃stitysjɔnalite/ **NF** unconstitutionality

inconstitutionnel, -elle /ɛ̃kɔ̃stitysjɔnɛl/ **ADJ** unconstitutional

inconstructible /ɛ̃kɔ̃stʀyktibl/ **ADJ** *[zone, terrain]* unsuitable for (building) development

incontestabilité /ɛ̃kɔ̃tɛstabilite/ **NF** incontestability

incontestable /ɛ̃kɔ̃tɛstabl/ **GRAMMAIRE ACTIVE 42.1** **ADJ** *(= indiscutable)* unquestionable, indisputable ◆ **il a réussi, c'est ~** he's succeeded, there is no doubt about that, it's undeniable that he has succeeded ◆ **il est ~ qu'elle est la meilleure** she is incontestably *ou* indisputably *ou* unquestionably the best

incontestablement /ɛ̃kɔ̃tɛstabləmɑ̃/ **ADV** unquestionably, indisputably ◆ **la reconnaissance vocale est ~ la voie du futur** voice recognition is unquestionably *ou* indisputably the way forward ◆ **c'est prouvé ? – ~** has it been proved? – beyond any shadow of (a) doubt

> ⚠ Évitez de traduire **incontestablement** par **incontestably**, qui est d'un registre plus soutenu.

incontesté, e /ɛ̃kɔ̃tɛste/ **ADJ** *[autorité, principe, fait]* undisputed ◆ **le chef/maître ~** the undisputed chief/master ◆ **le gagnant ~** the undisputed *ou* outright winner

incontinence /ɛ̃kɔ̃tinɑ̃s/ **NF** *(Méd)* incontinence ◆ ~ **urinaire** incontinence, enuresis (SPÉC) ◆ ~ **nocturne** bedwetting, enuresis (SPÉC)

COMP **incontinence de langage** lack of restraint in speech
incontinence verbale verbal diarrhoea*, garrulousness

incontinent¹, e /ɛ̃kɔ̃tinɑ̃, ɑ̃t/ **ADJ** *(Méd) [personne]* incontinent, enuretic (SPÉC); *[vessie]* weak **NM,F** person suffering from incontinence *ou* enuresis (SPÉC)

incontinent² † /ɛ̃kɔ̃tinɑ̃/ **ADV** *(littér = sur-le-champ)* forthwith † *(littér)*

incontournable /ɛ̃kɔ̃tuʀnabl/ **ADJ** *[réalité, fait]* inescapable; *[date, délai]* imperative; *[argument, problème, artiste]* that can't be ignored; *[personnage, interlocuteur]* key *(épith)*; *[œuvre d'art]* major *(épith)* ◆ **c'est un livre ~** the book is essential reading ◆ **ce produit est désormais ~** this product has become indispensable ◆ **trois personnalités étaient invitées, dont l'~ Éliane Hotin** *(hum)* three celebrities were invited, including the inevitable Éliane Hotin

incontrôlable /ɛ̃kɔ̃tʀolabl/ **ADJ** 1 *(= non vérifiable)* unverifiable, unable to be checked 2 *(= irrépressible) [personne, colère]* uncontrollable

incontrôlé, e /ɛ̃kɔ̃tʀole/ **ADJ** 1 *(= non réprimé)* uncontrolled 2 *(= non vérifié) [nouvelle, information]* unverified

inconvenance /ɛ̃kɔ̃v(ə)nɑ̃s/ **NF** 1 *(= caractère)* impropriety, unseemliness 2 *(= acte)* impropriety, indecorous *ou* unseemly behaviour *(NonC)*; *(= remarque)* impropriety, indecorous *ou* unseemly language *(NonC)*

inconvenant, e /ɛ̃kɔ̃v(ə)nɑ̃, ɑ̃t/ **ADJ** *[comportement, parole]* improper, indecorous, unseemly; *[question]* improper; *[personne]* ill-mannered ◆ **il serait ~ d'insister** it wouldn't be right to keep asking

inconvénient /ɛ̃kɔ̃venjɑ̃/ **GRAMMAIRE ACTIVE 36.1, 36.2, 53.3, 53.4** **NM** 1 *(= désavantage) [de situation, plan]* disadvantage, drawback ◆ **les avantages et les ~s** the advantages and disadvantages, the pros and cons *(de of)*

2 ◆ ~**s** *(= conséquences fâcheuses) [de situation]* (unpleasant) consequences, drawbacks

3 *(= risque)* risk ◆ **n'y a-t-il pas d'~ à mettre ce plat en faïence au four ?** is it (really) safe to put this earthenware plate in the oven? ◆ **peut-on sans ~ prendre ces deux médicaments ensemble ?** can one safely take *ou* is there any danger in taking these two medicines together?

4 *(= obstacle)* drawback ◆ **l'~ c'est que je ne serai pas là** the snag *ou* the annoying thing *ou* the one drawback is that I won't be there ◆ **il n'y a qu'un ~, c'est le prix !** there's only one drawback and that's the price ◆ **pouvez-vous sans ~ vous libérer jeudi ?** would it be convenient for you to get away on Thursday?, will you be able to get away on Thursday without any difficulty? ◆ **voyez-vous un ~** *ou* **y a-t-il un ~ à ce que je parte ce soir ?** have you *ou* is there any objection to my leaving this evening? ◆ **si vous n'y voyez pas d'~ ...** if you have no objections ...

inconvertibilité /ɛ̃kɔ̃vɛʀtibilite/ **NF** *(Fin)* inconvertibility

inconvertible /ɛ̃kɔ̃vɛʀtibl/ **ADJ** *(Fin)* inconvertible

incoordination /ɛ̃kɔɔʀdinasjɔ̃/ **NF** *[d'idées, opération]* lack of coordination; *(Méd)* incoordination, lack of coordination

incorporable /ɛ̃kɔʀpɔʀabl/ **ADJ** incorporable *(dans in, into)*

incorporalité /ɛ̃kɔʀpɔʀalite/ **NF** incorporeality

incorporation /ɛ̃kɔʀpɔʀasjɔ̃/ **NF** 1 *(= mélange) [de substance, aliment]* mixing, blending 2 *(= réunion) [de territoire]* incorporation; *(= intégration) [de chapitre]* incorporation, insertion, integration 3 *(Mil) (= appel)* enlistment *(à into)*; *(= affectation)* posting; → **report, sursis** 4 *(Psych)* incorporation

incorporel, -elle /ɛ̃kɔʀpɔʀɛl/ **ADJ** *(= immatériel)* incorporeal; *(Fin)* intangible

incorporer /ɛ̃kɔʀpɔʀe/ ► conjug 1 ◄ **VT** 1 *(= mélanger) [+ substance, aliment]* to mix *(à, avec* with, into) to blend *(à, avec* with) 2 *(= intégrer) [+ territoire]* to incorporate *(dans, à* into); *[+ chapitre]* to incorporate *(dans* in, into) to insert *(dans* in); *[+ personne]* to incorporate, to integrate *(dans, à* into); ◆ **il a très bien su s'~ à notre groupe** he fitted into our group very well ◆ **appareil photo avec flash incorporé** camera with built-in flash 3 *(Mil = appeler)* to recruit ◆ ~ **qn dans** *(= affecter)* to enrol *ou* enlist sb into ◆ **on l'a incorporé dans l'infanterie** he was recruited *ou* drafted into the infantry

incorrect, e /ɛ̃kɔʀɛkt/ **ADJ** 1 *(= inadéquat) [terme]* incorrect; *[réglage, interprétation]* faulty; *[solution]* incorrect, wrong 2 *(= impoli) [paroles, manières]* improper, impolite; *[tenue]* incorrect, indecent; *[personne]* rude, impolite ◆ **il s'est montré très ~** he was very rude *ou* impolite; → **politiquement** 3 *(= déloyal) [personne, procédé]* shabby ◆ **être ~ avec qn** to treat sb shabbily

incorrectement /ɛ̃kɔʀɛktəmɑ̃/ **ADV** *[prononcer, parler]* incorrectly; *[interpréter]* wrongly; *[se conduire] (= impoliment)* discourteously, impolitely; *(= indélicatement)* shabbily

incorrection /ɛ̃kɔʀɛksjɔ̃/ **NF** 1 *(= impropriété) [de terme]* impropriety; *(= inconvenance) [de tenue, personne, langage]* impropriety, incorrectness; *(= déloyauté) [de procédés, concurrent]* dishonesty, underhand nature 2 *(= terme impropre)* impropriety; *(= action inconvenante)* incorrect *ou* improper *ou* impolite behaviour *(NonC)*; *(= remarque inconvenante)* impolite *ou* improper remark

incorrigible /ɛ̃kɔʀiʒibl/ **ADJ** *[enfant, distraction]* incorrigible ◆ **cet enfant est ~ !** this child is incorrigible!, this child will never learn! ◆ **être d'une ~ paresse** to be incorrigibly lazy

incorruptibilité /ɛ̃kɔʀyptibilite/ **NF** incorruptibility

incorruptible /ɛ̃kɔʀyptibl/ **ADJ** incorruptible **NMF** incorruptible person ◆ **c'est un ~** he's incorruptible

incrédule /ɛ̃kʀedyl/ **ADJ** 1 *(= sceptique)* incredulous ◆ **d'un air ~** incredulously 2 *(Rel)* unbelieving **NMF** *(Rel)* unbeliever, nonbeliever

incrédulité /ɛ̃kʀedylite/ **NF** 1 *(= scepticisme)* incredulity ◆ **avec ~** incredulously 2 *(Rel)* unbelief, lack of belief

incréé, e /ɛ̃kʀee/ **ADJ** uncreated

incrément /ɛ̃kʀemɑ̃/ **NM** *(Ordin)* increment

incrémentation /ɛ̃kʀemɑ̃tasjɔ̃/ **NF** *(Ordin)* incrementation

incrémenter /ɛ̃kʀemɑ̃te/ ► conjug 1 ◄ **VT** *(Ordin, Math)* to increment

incrémentiel, -elle /ɛ̃kʀemɑ̃sjɛl/ **ADJ** *(Ordin)* incremental

increvable /ɛ̃kʀəvabl/ **ADJ** 1 *[ballon]* which cannot be burst, unburstable; *[pneu]* unpuncturable, puncture-proof 2 * *(= infatigable) [animal, travailleur]* tireless; *(= indestructible) [moteur, chaussures]* indestructible

incriminer /ɛ̃kʀimine/ ► conjug 1 ◄ **VT** *(= mettre en cause) [+ personne]* to incriminate, to accuse; *[+ action, conduite]* to bring under attack; *[+ honnêteté, bonne foi]* to call into question ◆ **il cherche à m'~ dans cette affaire** he's trying to incriminate *ou* implicate me in this business ◆ **après avoir analysé la clause incriminée du contrat ...** after having analysed the offending clause *ou* the clause in question *ou* at issue in the contract ... ◆ **au moment des faits incriminés** at the time of the crime, when the crime was committed

incrochetable /ɛ̃kʀɔʃ(ə)tabl/ ADJ *[serrure]* burglar-proof, which cannot be picked

incroyable /ɛ̃kʀwajabl/ ADJ *(= invraisemblable)* incredible, unbelievable; *(= inouï)* incredible, amazing ◆ **~ mais vrai** incredible *ou* unbelievable but true ◆ **c'est ~ ce qu'il fait chaud** it's unbelievably *ou* incredibly hot ◆ **il est ~ d'arrogance** he's incredibly *ou* unbelievably arrogant ◆ **il est ~, ce type !*** that guy's unreal!* *ou* something else!* NM 1 ◆ **l'~** the unbelievable 2 *(Hist = dandy)* dandy

incroyablement /ɛ̃kʀwajabləmɑ̃/ ADV *(= étonnamment)* incredibly, unbelievably, amazingly

incroyance /ɛ̃kʀwajɑ̃s/ NF *(Rel)* unbelief ◆ **il affirme son ~** he declares himself to be a non-believer

incroyant, e /ɛ̃kʀwajɑ̃, ɑ̃t/ ADJ unbelieving NM,F unbeliever, non-believer

incrustation /ɛ̃kʀystasjɔ̃/ NF 1 *(Art) (= technique)* inlaying; *(= ornement)* inlay; *(dans un corsage, une nappe)* inset, insert ◆ **des ~s d'ivoire** inlaid ivory work, ivory inlays ◆ **table à ~s d'ivoire/d'ébène** table inlaid with ivory/ebony 2 *(TV)* superimposition, overlay 3 *(= croûte) (dans un récipient)* fur *(Brit)*, residue *(US)*; *(dans une chaudière)* scale; *(sur une roche)* incrustation ◆ **pour empêcher l'~** to prevent the formation of scale, to prevent furring *(Brit)*

incruste⁑ /ɛ̃kʀyst/ NF ◆ **taper l'~** to be a hanger-on* *(péj)* ◆ **c'est un champion de l'~** once he's made himself at home in a place it's impossible to get rid of him

incruster /ɛ̃kʀyste/ ▸ conjug 1 ◂ VT 1 *(Art)* **~ qch dans** *(= insérer)* to inlay sth into ◆ **~ qch de** *(= décorer)* to inlay sth with ◆ **incrusté de** inlaid with 2 *(TV) [+ nom, numéro]* to superimpose, to overlay 3 *[+ chaudière]* to coat with scale, to scale up; *[+ récipient]* to fur up *(Brit)*, to become coated with residue *(US)* VPR **s'incruster** 1 *[corps étranger, caillou]* **s'~ dans** to become embedded in ◆ **l'ivoire s'incruste dans l'ébène** *(travail de marqueterie)* the ivory is inlaid in ebony 2 *(* = ne plus partir) [invité]* to take root ◆ **il va s'~ chez nous** he'll get himself settled down in our house and we'll never move him ◆ **la crise s'incruste** the recession is deepening 3 *[radiateur, conduite]* to become incrusted *(de* with) to fur up *(Brit)* 4 *(TV) [nom, numéro]* to be superimposed

incubateur, -trice /ɛ̃kybatœʀ, tʀis/ ADJ incubating NM incubator ◆ **~ d'entreprises** business incubator

incubation /ɛ̃kybasjɔ̃/ NF *[d'œuf, maladie]* incubation ◆ **période d'~** incubation period ◆ **~ artificielle** artificial incubation ◆ **une ~ de 21 jours** 3 weeks' incubation, an incubation period of 3 weeks

incube /ɛ̃kyb/ NM incubus

incuber /ɛ̃kybe/ ▸ conjug 1 ◂ VT to hatch, to incubate

inculpation /ɛ̃kylpasjɔ̃/ NF *(= chef d'accusation)* charge *(de* of); *(† = mise en examen)* charging, indictment ◆ **sous l'~ de** on a charge of ◆ **notifier à qn son ~** to inform sb of the charge against him

inculpé, e /ɛ̃kylpe/ (ptp de **inculper**) NM,F ◆ **l'~** † the accused ◆ **les deux ~s** the two accused, the two men accused

inculper /ɛ̃kylpe/ ▸ conjug 1 ◂ VT to charge *(de* with) to accuse *(de* of)

inculquer /ɛ̃kylke/ ▸ conjug 1 ◂ **inculquer à** VT INDIR ◆ **~ qch à qn** *[+ principes, politesse, notions]* to inculcate sth in sb, to instil *(Brit) ou* instill *(US)* sth into sb

inculte /ɛ̃kylt/ ADJ *[terre]* uncultivated; *[esprit, personne]* uneducated; *[chevelure, barbe]* unkempt

incultivable /ɛ̃kyltivabl/ ADJ unfarmable, unworkable

inculture /ɛ̃kyltyʀ/ NF *[de personne]* ignorance ◆ **son ~ musicale** his ignorance of things musical *ou* about music ◆ **l'~ des traducteurs en matière d'histoire naturelle** translators' ignorance about nature ◆ **ils sont d'une ~ !** they're so ignorant! ◆ **la prétendue ~ américaine** the supposed ignorance of Americans, so-called ignorant Americans

incunable /ɛ̃kynabl/ ADJ incunabular NM incunabulum ◆ **les ~s** incunabula

incurabilité /ɛ̃kyʀabilite/ NF incurability, incurableness

incurable /ɛ̃kyʀabl/ ADJ 1 *(Méd)* incurable ◆ **les malades ~s** the incurably ill 2 *[bêtise, ignorance]* incurable *(épith)*, hopeless *(épith)* ◆ **son ~ optimisme** *(hum)* his incurable optimism NMF *(Méd)* incurable

incurablement /ɛ̃kyʀabləmɑ̃/ ADV *(Méd)* incurably; *(= incorrigiblement)* hopelessly, incurably

incurie /ɛ̃kyʀi/ NF *(frm = négligence)* negligence

incuriosité /ɛ̃kyʀjozite/ NF *(littér)* incuriosity

incursion /ɛ̃kyʀsjɔ̃/ NF *(Mil)* incursion, foray *(en, dans* into); *(fig)* foray ◆ **faire une ~ dans** to make an incursion *ou* a foray into

incurvé, e /ɛ̃kyʀve/ (ptp de **incurver**) ADJ curved

incurver /ɛ̃kyʀve/ ▸ conjug 1 ◂ VT *[+ pied de chaise, fer forgé]* to form *ou* bend into a curve, to curve VPR **s'incurver** 1 *[barre]* to bend, to curve; *[poutre]* to sag 2 *[ligne, profil, route]* to curve

indatable /ɛ̃databl/ ADJ undatable

Inde /ɛ̃d/ NF India ◆ **les ~s** the Indies ◆ **les ~s occidentales** *(†† = Antilles)* the West Indies ◆ **les ~s orientales** *(†† = Indonésie)* the East Indies; → **cochon**

indéboulonnable* /ɛ̃debulɔnabl/ ADJ *[personne]* unbudgeable*, impossible to budge ◆ **il est absolument ~** they just can't get rid of him*

indébrouillable /ɛ̃debʀujabl/ ADJ *[affaire]* almost impossible to sort out *(attrib)*

indécelable /ɛ̃des(ə)labl/ ADJ *[produit, poison]* undetectable; *[effet]* indiscernible; *[accident, erreur]* undetectable, indiscernible

indécemment /ɛ̃desamɑ̃/ ADV indecently

indécence /ɛ̃desɑ̃s/ NF 1 *(= impudicité) [de posture, tenue, geste]* indecency; *[de chanson]* obscenity 2 *[de luxe]* obscenity 3 *(= acte)* act of indecency, indecency; *(= propos)* obscenity

indécent, e /ɛ̃desɑ̃, ɑ̃t/ ADJ 1 *[posture, tenue, geste]* indecent; *[chanson]* obscene, dirty* ◆ **habille-toi, tu es ~ !** get dressed, you're indecent! *ou* you're not decent! 2 *[luxe]* obscene; *[succès]* disgusting ◆ **avoir une chance ~e** to be disgustingly lucky ◆ **il serait ~ de demander plus** it wouldn't be proper to ask for more

indéchiffrable /ɛ̃deʃifʀabl/ ADJ *(= impossible à déchiffrer) [code]* indecipherable; *(= illisible) [texte, partition]* indecipherable; *(= incompréhensible) [traité, énigme]* incomprehensible; *(= impénétrable) [personne, regard]* inscrutable

indéchirable /ɛ̃deʃiʀabl/ ADJ tear-proof

indécidable /ɛ̃desidabl/ ADJ *(Math)* undecidable

indécis, e /ɛ̃desi, iz/ ADJ 1 *[personne] (par nature)* indecisive; *(temporairement)* undecided ◆ **~ sur** *ou* **devant** *ou* **quant à** undecided *ou* uncertain about 2 *(= incertain) [temps, paix]* unsettled; *[bataille]* indecisive; *[problème]* undecided, unsettled; *[victoire]* undecided ◆ **le résultat est encore ~** the result is as yet undecided 3 *(= vague) [réponse, sourire]* vague; *[pensée]* undefined, vague; *[forme, contour]* indecisive, indistinct NM,F *(gén)* indecisive person; *(Sondages)* don't know; *(dans une élection)* floating voter

indécision /ɛ̃desizjɔ̃/ NF *(chronique)* indecisiveness; *(temporaire)* indecision, uncertainty *(sur* about); ◆ **je suis dans l'~ quant à nos projets pour l'été** I'm uncertain *ou* undecided about our plans for the summer

indéclinable /ɛ̃deklinabl/ ADJ indeclinable

indécodable /ɛ̃dekɔdabl/ ADJ *[texte, expression]* undecodable, that cannot be decoded

indécollable /ɛ̃dekɔlabl/ ADJ *[objet]* that won't come unstuck *ou* come off

indécomposable /ɛ̃dekɔ̃pozabl/ ADJ *(gén)* that cannot be broken down *(en* into)

indécrottable* /ɛ̃dekʀɔtabl/ ADJ *(= borné)* dumb*, hopelessly thick* *(Brit)* ◆ **c'est un paresseux ~** *(= incorrigible)* he's hopelessly lazy

indéfectibilité /ɛ̃defɛktibilite/ NF *(frm)* indestructibility

indéfectible /ɛ̃defɛktibl/ ADJ *[foi, confiance]* indestructible, unshakeable; *[soutien, attachement]* unfailing

indéfectiblement /ɛ̃defɛktibləmɑ̃/ ADV unfailingly

indéfendable /ɛ̃defɑ̃dabl/ GRAMMAIRE ACTIVE 53.3 ADJ *(lit, fig)* indefensible

indéfini, e /ɛ̃defini/ ADJ *(= vague) [sentiment]* undefined; *(= indéterminé) [quantité, durée]* indeterminate, indefinite; *(Ling)* indefinite

indéfiniment /ɛ̃definimɑ̃/ ADV indefinitely ◆ **je ne peux pas attendre ~** I can't wait forever

indéfinissable /ɛ̃definisabl/ ADJ *[mot, charme, saveur]* indefinable

indéformable /ɛ̃defɔʀmabl/ ADJ that will keep its shape

indéfrisable † /ɛ̃defʀizabl/ NF perm, permanent *(US)*

indélébile /ɛ̃delebil/ ADJ *(lit, fig)* indelible

indélicat, e /ɛ̃delika, at/ ADJ 1 *(= grossier)* indelicate, tactless 2 *(= malhonnête) [employé]* dishonest; *[procédé]* dishonest, underhand

indélicatement /ɛ̃delikatmɑ̃/ ADV 1 *(= grossièrement) [agir, parler]* indelicately, tactlessly 2 *(= malhonnêtement) [se conduire]* dishonestly

indélicatesse /ɛ̃delikatɛs/ NF 1 *(= impolitesse)* indelicacy, tactlessness *(NonC)*; *(= malhonnêteté)* dishonesty *(NonC)* 2 *(= acte malhonnête)* indiscretion ◆ **commettre des ~s** to commit indiscretions

indémaillable /ɛ̃demɑjabl/ ADJ run-resistant, run-proof, ladderproof *(Brit)* ◆ **en ~** *[vêtement]* in run-resistant *ou* run-proof material; *[jersey, bas]* run-resistant, run-proof

indemne /ɛ̃dɛmn/ ADJ *(= sain et sauf)* unharmed, unhurt, unscathed ◆ **il est sorti ~ de l'accident** he came out of the accident unharmed *ou* unscathed

indemnisable /ɛ̃dɛmnizabl/ ADJ *[personne]* entitled to compensation *(attrib)*; *[dommage]* indemnifiable

indemnisation /ɛ̃dɛmnizasjɔ̃/ NF *(= action)* indemnification; *(= somme)* indemnity, compensation ◆ **l'~ a été fixée à 250 €** the indemnity *ou* compensation was fixed at €250 ◆ **250 € d'~** €250 compensation

indemniser /ɛ̃dɛmnize/ ▸ conjug 1 ◂ VT *(= dédommager) (d'une perte)* to compensate *(de* for); *(de frais)* to indemnify, to reimburse *(de* for); ◆ **se faire ~** to get indemnification *ou* compensation, to get reimbursed ◆ **~ qn en argent** to pay sb compensation in cash ◆ **les victimes**

seront indemnisées the victims will get *ou* receive compensation ◆ **vous serez indemnisés de tous vos frais de déplacement** all your travelling expenses will be reimbursed

indemnitaire /ɛ̃dɛmnitɛʀ/ ADJ compensational, compensatory ◆ **régime ~ du personnel** *employees' allowance scheme*

indemnité /ɛ̃dɛmnite/ NF (= *dédommagement*) *[de perte]* compensation *(NonC)*, indemnity; *[de frais]* allowance

COMP **indemnité de chômage** unemployment benefit
indemnité compensatoire *(gén)* compensatory allowance; *(pour agriculteurs)* deficiency payment
indemnité de départ severance pay
indemnité de fonction *(gén Admin) allowance paid to a civil servant; (payée à un élu)* attendance allowance
indemnité de guerre war indemnity
indemnités journalières daily allowance *(of sickness benefit)*
indemnité (légale) de licenciement redundancy payment *ou* money
indemnité de logement housing allowance
indemnité parlementaire *député's salary*
indemnité de résidence weighting allowance
indemnité de rupture de contrat (contract) termination penalty
indemnité de transfert *(Ftbl) (pour le club)* transfer fee; *(pour le joueur)* signing-on fee
indemnité de transport travel allowance
indemnité de vie chère cost of living allowance

indémodable /ɛ̃demɔdabl/ ADJ *[vêtement, mobilier, livre]* classic, that will never go out of fashion

indémontrable /ɛ̃demɔ̃tʀabl/ ADJ indemonstrable, unprovable

indéniable /ɛ̃denjabl/ GRAMMAIRE ACTIVE 53.1, 53.6 ADJ undeniable, indisputable, unquestionable ◆ **vous avez grossi, c'est ~** there's no doubt that *ou* it's undeniable that you've put on weight

indéniablement /ɛ̃denjabləmɑ̃/ GRAMMAIRE ACTIVE 53.6 ADV undeniably, indisputably, unquestionably

indénombrable /ɛ̃denɔ̃bʀabl/ ADJ countless, innumerable

indentation /ɛ̃dɑ̃tasjɔ̃/ NF indentation

indépassable /ɛ̃depɑsabl/ ADJ *[limite]* impassable

indépendamment /ɛ̃depɑ̃damɑ̃/ ADV 1 (= *abstraction faite de*) ~ **de** irrespective *ou* regardless of 2 (= *outre*) ~ **de** apart from, over and above 3 (= *de façon indépendante*) independently *(de of)*

indépendance /ɛ̃depɑ̃dɑ̃s/ NF *(gén)* independence *(de, par rapport à from)*; ◆ ~ **d'esprit** independence of mind ◆ **guerre/proclamation d'~** war/proclamation of independence ◆ **à 15 ans, il voulait son ~** at 15, he wanted to be independent

indépendant, e /ɛ̃depɑ̃dɑ̃, ɑ̃t/ ADJ 1 *(gén, Pol)* independent *(de of)*; ◆ **pour des causes** *ou* **raisons ~es de notre volonté** for reasons beyond *ou* outside our control ◆ **de façon ~e** independently
2 (= *séparé*) *[bâtiment]* separate ◆ **"à louer : chambre indépendante"** "to let: self-contained room - own key"
3 *[travail]* freelance *(épith)* ◆ **travailleur ~** (*non salarié*) freelance worker, freelancer; *(qui est son propre patron)* self-employed worker

NM,F 1 (= *non salarié*) freelance worker, freelancer; (= *petit patron*) self-employed worker ◆ **travailler en ~** (= *être non salarié*) to work freelance; (= *être son propre patron*) to be self-employed
2 *(Pol)* independent

NF **indépendante** *(Gram)* independent clause

> ⚠ Quand l'adjectif **indépendant** qualifie un travail ou un logement, il ne se traduit pas par le mot anglais **independent**.

indépendantisme /ɛ̃depɑ̃dɑ̃tism/ NM separatism

indépendantiste /ɛ̃depɑ̃dɑ̃tist/ ADJ *[mouvement]* independence *(épith)*; *[organisation, forces]* separatist; *[parti]* separatist, independence *(épith)* ◆ **combattant ~** freedom fighter ◆ **le leader ~** the leader of the independence movement NMF member of an independence movement

indéracinable /ɛ̃deʀasinabl/ ADJ *[préjugé]* deep-rooted, deep-seated; *[sentiment]* ineradicable; *[optimisme]* unshakeable ◆ **il est ~** *(gén)* he's a permanent fixture; *[élu]* he can't be unseated

indéréglable /ɛ̃deʀeglabl/ ADJ foolproof, totally reliable

Indes /ɛ̃d/ NPL → **Inde**

indescriptible /ɛ̃dɛskʀiptibl/ ADJ indescribable

indésirable /ɛ̃deziʀabl/ ADJ *[personne, conséquence]* undesirable ◆ **effets ~s** *[de médicament]* side-effects NMF undesirable

indestructibilité /ɛ̃dɛstʀyktibilite/ NF indestructibility

indestructible /ɛ̃dɛstʀyktibl/ ADJ *[objet, bâtiment, matériau, sentiment]* indestructible; *[marque, impression]* indelible

indétectable /ɛ̃detɛktabl/ ADJ undetectable

indéterminable /ɛ̃detɛʀminabl/ ADJ indeterminable

indétermination /ɛ̃detɛʀminasjɔ̃/ NF 1 (= *imprécision*) vagueness 2 (= *irrésolution*) *(chronique)* indecisiveness; *(temporaire)* indecision, uncertainty 3 *(Math)* indetermination

indéterminé, e /ɛ̃detɛʀmine/ ADJ 1 (= *non précisé*) *[date, cause, nature]* unspecified; *[forme, longueur, quantité]* indeterminate ◆ **pour des raisons ~es** for reasons which were not specified ◆ **à une date encore ~e** at a date to be specified *ou* as yet unspecified *ou* as yet undecided 2 (= *imprécis*) *[impression, sentiment]* vague; *[contours, goût]* indeterminable, vague 3 (= *irrésolu*) undecided ◆ **je suis encore ~ sur ce que je vais faire** I'm still undecided *ou* uncertain about what I'm going to do 4 *(Math)* indeterminate

indétrônable /ɛ̃detʀonabl/ ADJ *(Pol)* unassailable, impossible to topple; *(Sport) [champion]* invincible

index /ɛ̃dɛks/ NM 1 (= *doigt*) forefinger, index finger 2 (= *repère*) *[d'instrument]* pointer; (= *aiguille*) *[de cadran]* needle, pointer 3 (= *liste alphabétique*) index; *(Ordin)* index 4 *(Rel)* **l'Index** the Index ◆ **mettre qn/qch à l'~** *(fig)* to blacklist sb/sth

indexation /ɛ̃dɛksasjɔ̃/ NF *(Écon)* indexing, indexation; *(Ordin)* indexing ◆ ~ **sur le coût de la vie** cost-of-living indexation *ou* adjustment

indexé, e /ɛ̃dɛkse/ ADJ *[prix]* indexed *(sur to)*; *[prêt]* index-linked ◆ **salaire ~ sur l'inflation** salary index-linked to inflation

indexer /ɛ̃dɛkse/ ► conjug 1 ◄ VT 1 *(Écon)* to index *(sur to)* 2 *[+ document, mot]* to index 3 *(Ordin)* to index

Indiana /ɛ̃djana/ NM Indiana

indianité /ɛ̃djanite/ NF Indian identity

indic * /ɛ̃dik/ NM (abrév de **indicateur**) *(arg Police)* grass *(arg)*, informer, (copper's) nark *(arg)* *(Brit)*, fink* *(US)*

indicateur, -trice /ɛ̃dikatœʀ, tʀis/ ADJ → **panneau, poteau**

NM,F ◆ ~ **(de police)** (police) informer

NM 1 (= *guide*) guide; (= *horaire*) timetable
2 *(Tech = compteur, cadran)* gauge, indicator
3 *(Chim)* ~ **(coloré)** (= *substance*) indicator
4 *(Ling)* ~ **(de sens)** (semantic) indicator

COMP **indicateur d'altitude** altimeter
indicateur boursier Stock Exchange indicator
indicateur des chemins de fer railway timetable
indicateur de conjoncture ⇒ **indicateur économique**
indicateur de direction *[de bateau]* direction finder; *[de voitures]* (direction) indicator
indicateur économique economic indicator
indicateur de niveau de carburant fuel *ou* petrol *(Brit)* gauge
indicateur de niveau d'eau water(-level) gauge
indicateur de pression pressure gauge
indicateur des rues street directory
indicateurs sociaux social indicators
indicateur de tendance *(Bourse)* economic indicator
indicateur de vitesse *[de voiture]* speedometer; *[d'avion]* airspeed indicator

indicatif, -ive /ɛ̃dikatif, iv/ GRAMMAIRE ACTIVE 54.1 ADJ 1 indicative *(de of)* 2 *(Ling)* indicative; → **titre** NM 1 *(Radio = mélodie)* theme *ou* signature tune 2 *(Télex)* answer-back code ◆ ~ **(d'appel)** *[de poste émetteur]* call sign ◆ ~ **téléphonique** code, dialling code *(Brit)* ◆ ~ **départemental** area code 3 *(Ling)* **l'~** the indicative ◆ **à l'~** in the indicative

indication /ɛ̃dikasjɔ̃/ NF 1 (= *renseignement*) piece of information, information *(NonC)* ◆ **qui vous a donné cette ~ ?** who gave you that (piece of) information?, who told you that?
2 (= *mention*) **quelle ~ porte la pancarte ?** what does the notice say?, what has the notice got on it? ◆ **sans ~ de date/de prix** with no indication of the date/of the price, without a date stamp/price label ◆ **les ~s du compteur** the reading on the meter
3 (= *notification*) *[de prix, danger, mode d'emploi]* indication ◆ **l'~ du virage dangereux a permis d'éviter les accidents** signposting the dangerous bend has prevented accidents ◆ **l'~ d'une date est impérative** a date stamp must be shown, the date must be indicated ◆ **l'~ de l'heure vous sera fournie ultérieurement** you will be given the time *ou* informed *ou* notified of the time later ◆ **rendre obligatoire l'~ des prix** to make it compulsory to mark *ou* show prices
4 (= *indice*) indication *(de of)*; ◆ **c'est une ~ suffisante de sa culpabilité** that's a good enough indication of his guilt
5 (= *directive*) instruction, direction ◆ **sauf ~ contraire** unless otherwise stated *ou* indicated ◆ **sur son ~** on his instruction

COMP **indication d'origine** *[de produit]* place of origin
indications scéniques stage directions
indications (thérapeutiques) *[de remède, traitement]* indications

indice /ɛ̃dis/ NM 1 (= *signe*) indication, sign ◆ **être l'~ de** to be an indication *ou* a sign of ◆ **il n'y avait pas le moindre ~ de leur passage** there was no sign *ou* evidence *ou* indication that they had been there
2 (= *élément d'information*) clue; *(Jur = preuve)* piece of evidence ◆ **rechercher des ~s du crime** to look for clues about the crime

3 (Math) suffix; (= degré de racine) index; (Bourse, Écon, Opt, Phys) index; [de fonctionnaire] rating, grading ◆ **"a"** ~ **2** (Math) a (suffix) two ◆ **l'~ Dow Jones/Footsie** the Dow Jones/Footsie index

COMP **indice du coût de la vie** cost of living index
indice de croissance growth index
indice d'écoute audience rating ◆ **avoir un excellent ~ d'écoute** to have a high rating, to get good ratings
l'indice INSEE ≈ the retail price index
indice d'octane octane rating
indice de pollution (atmosphérique) air quality index
indice de popularité popularity rating(s) **indice des prix** price index
indice (de protection) [de crème solaire] protection factor; (Phys)
indice de réfraction refractive index
indice de traitement (Admin) salary grading

indiciaire /ɛ̃disjɛʀ/ ADJ [traitement] grade-related ◆ **classement ~ d'un fonctionnaire** grading of a civil servant

indicible /ɛ̃disibl/ ADJ [joie, peur] inexpressible; [souffrance] unspeakable; [beauté] indescribable

indiciblement /ɛ̃disibləmɑ̃/ ADV inexpressibly, unspeakably

indiciel, -elle /ɛ̃disjɛl/ ADJ (Écon) indexed

indien, -ienne /ɛ̃djɛ̃, jɛn/ ADJ Indian; → **chanvre, file, océan** NM,F **Indien(ne)** (d'Inde) Indian; (d'Amérique) American Indian, Native American NF **indienne** 1 (Hist = tissu) printed calico 2 (= nage) overarm sidestroke ◆ **nager l'indienne** to swim sidestroke

indifféremment /ɛ̃difeʀamɑ̃/ ADV 1 (= sans faire de distinction) indiscriminately, equally ◆ **fonctionner ~ au gaz ou à l'électricité** to run on either gas or electricity, to run equally well on gas or electricity ◆ **manger de tout ~** to eat indiscriminately, to eat (just) anything ◆ **il lit ~ de la poésie et des romans policiers** he's equally happy to read poetry or detective novels 2 (littér = avec indifférence) indifferently

indifférence /ɛ̃difeʀɑ̃s/ NF 1 (= désintérêt) indifference (à l'égard de, pour to, towards) lack of concern (à l'égard de for); ◆ **avec ~** indifferently ◆ **il les a regardés se battre en feignant l'~** he watched them fight with an air of indifference ◆ **il a été renvoyé dans l'~ générale** nobody showed the slightest interest when he was dismissed ◆ **être d'une ~ totale** to be totally indifferent 2 (= froideur) indifference (envers to, towards)

indifférenciable /ɛ̃difeʀɑ̃sjabl/ ADJ indistinguishable

indifférenciation /ɛ̃difeʀɑ̃sjasjɔ̃/ NF lack of differentiation

indifférencié, e /ɛ̃difeʀɑ̃sje/ ADJ (Bio, Sci) undifferentiated

indifférent, e /ɛ̃difeʀɑ̃, ɑ̃t/ GRAMMAIRE ACTIVE 34.5

ADJ 1 (= peu intéressé) [spectateur] indifferent (à to, towards) unconcerned (à about); ◆ **ça le laisse ~** it doesn't touch him in the least, he is quite unconcerned about it ◆ **leur souffrance ne peut laisser personne ~** it's impossible to remain indifferent to ou to be unmoved by their suffering ◆ **son charme ne peut laisser personne ~** no-one is immune ou impervious to his charm

2 (= sans importance) indifferent ◆ **elle m'est/ne m'est pas ~e** I am/am not indifferent to her ◆ **son sort m'est ~** his fate is of no interest to me ou is a matter of indifference to me ◆ **il m'est ~ de partir ou de rester** it is indifferent ou immaterial to me ou it doesn't matter to me whether I go or stay ◆ **parler de choses ~es** to talk of this and that ◆ **"quartier indifférent"** (dans une annonce) "any area ou neighborhood (US)" ◆ **"âge indifférent"** "any age"

3 (Sci) indifferent

NM,F indifferent person

indifférer /ɛ̃difeʀe/ ► conjug 6 ◄ VT ◆ **ceci m'indiffère totalement** I'm quite indifferent to that, I couldn't care less about that

indigence /ɛ̃diʒɑ̃s/ NF 1 (= misère) poverty, destitution, indigence (frm) ◆ **tomber/être dans l'~** to become/be destitute ◆ **l'~ de moyens dont souffre le pays** the country's dire lack of resources 2 (= médiocrité) [de scénario] mediocrity ◆ **~ intellectuelle** intellectual poverty ◆ **l'~ du débat intellectuel dans ce pays** the low level of intellectual debate in this country ◆ **~ d'idées** dearth ou paucity of ideas

indigène /ɛ̃diʒɛn/ NMF (= autochtone) native; (hum, Helv = personne du pays) local ADJ 1 (= autochtone) [coutume] native; [population] native, indigenous; (= non importé) [animal, plante] indigenous, native 2 (= local) [main-d'œuvre, population] local

indigent, e /ɛ̃diʒɑ̃, ɑ̃t/ ADJ 1 (matériellement) [personne] destitute, poverty-stricken, indigent (frm) 2 (intellectuellement) [film, roman] poor; [imagination, spectacle, architecture] mediocre 3 [végétation] poor, sparse NM,F pauper ◆ **les ~s** the destitute, the poor, the indigent (frm)

indigeste /ɛ̃diʒɛst/ ADJ (lit, fig) indigestible, difficult to digest (attrib)

indigestion /ɛ̃diʒɛstjɔ̃/ NF 1 (Méd) attack of indigestion, indigestion (NonC) ◆ **il a eu une ~ de pâtisseries** he gave himself ou he got indigestion from eating too many cakes 2 (fig) **j'ai une ~ de films policiers** I've been OD'ing* on detective films ou I've been watching too many detective films ◆ **j'en ai une ~, de toutes ces histoires*** I'm sick (and tired) of all these complications*, I'm fed up with all these complications* ◆ **il nous répétait les mêmes conseils, jusqu'à l'~** he repeated the same advice to us ad nauseam

indignation /ɛ̃diɲasjɔ̃/ NF indignation ◆ **avec ~** indignantly ◆ **à ma grande ~** to my great indignation ◆ **devant l'~ générale, il changea d'avis** faced with a mood of general indignation, he changed his mind

indigne /ɛ̃diɲ/ ADJ 1 (= pas digne de) ~ **de** [+ amitié, confiance, personne] unworthy of, not worthy of ◆ **il est ~ de vivre** he doesn't deserve to live, he's not fit to live ◆ **ce livre est ~ de figurer dans ma bibliothèque** this book is not worthy of a place in my library ◆ **c'est ~ de vous** [travail, emploi] it's beneath you; [conduite, attitude] it's unworthy of you ◆ **empêcher les débats d'idées est ~ d'un démocrate** a democrat worthy of the name doesn't try to stifle intellectual debate 2 (= abject) [acte] shameful, disgraceful; [mère, époux] unworthy; [fils] ungrateful ◆ **il a eu une attitude ~** he behaved disgracefully ◆ **c'est un père ~** he's not fit to be a father

indigné, e /ɛ̃diɲe/ (ptp de **indigner**) ADJ indignant (par at)

indignement /ɛ̃diɲmɑ̃/ ADV shamefully

indigner /ɛ̃diɲe/ ► conjug 1 ◄ VT ◆ ~ **qn** to make sb indignant VPR **s'indigner** (= se fâcher) to become ou get indignant ou annoyed (de about, at; contre with, about, at); ◆ **s'~ que/de, être indigné que/de** (= être écœuré) to be indignant that/about ou at ◆ **je l'écoutais s'~ contre les spéculateurs** I listened to him waxing indignant ou going on* ou sounding off* indignantly about speculators ◆ **je m'indigne de penser/voir que ...** it makes me indignant ou it fills me with indignation ou it infuriates me to think/see that ...

indignité /ɛ̃diɲite/ NF 1 (= caractère) [de personne] unworthiness; [de conduite] baseness, shamefulness 2 (= acte) shameful act ◆ **c'est une ~ !** it's a disgrace!, it's shameful!

indigo /ɛ̃digo/ NM (= matière, couleur) indigo ADJ INV indigo (blue)

indigotier /ɛ̃digɔtje/ NM (= plante) indigo (plant)

indiqué, e /ɛ̃dike/ (ptp de **indiquer**) ADJ 1 (= conseillé) advisable ◆ **ce n'est pas très ~** it's not really advisable, it's really not the best thing to do

2 (= adéquat) **prenons ça, c'est tout ~** let's take that - it's just the thing ou it's just what we need ◆ **pour ce travail M. Legrand est tout ~** Mr Legrand is the obvious choice ou is just the man we need for that job ◆ **c'est le moyen ~** it's the best ou right way to do it ◆ **c'était un sujet tout ~** it was obviously an appropriate ou a suitable subject

3 (= prescrit) [médicament, traitement] appropriate ◆ **le traitement ~ dans ce cas est ...** the appropriate ou correct ou prescribed treatment in this case is ... ◆ **ce remède est particulièrement ~ dans les cas graves** this drug is particularly appropriate ou suitable for serious cases

indiquer /ɛ̃dike/ ► conjug 1 ◄ VT 1 (= désigner) to point out, to indicate ◆ **~ qch/qn du doigt** to point sth/sb out (à qn to sb) to point to sth/sb ◆ **~ qch de la main/de la tête** to indicate sth with one's hand/with a nod ◆ **il m'indiqua du regard le coupable** his glance ou look directed me towards the culprit ◆ **~ le chemin à qn** to give directions to sb, to show sb the way ◆ **~ la réception/les toilettes à qn** to direct sb to ou show sb the way to the reception desk/the toilets

2 (= montrer) [flèche, voyant, écriteau] to show, to indicate ◆ **~ l'heure** [montre] to give ou show ou tell the time ◆ **la petite aiguille indique les heures** the small hand shows ou marks the hours ◆ **l'horloge indiquait 2 heures** the clock said ou showed it was 2 o'clock ◆ **qu'indique la pancarte ?** what does the sign say?

3 (= recommander) [+ livre, hôtel, médecin] to recommend

4 (= dire) [personne] [+ heure, solution] to tell; [+ dangers, désavantages] to point out, to show ◆ **il m'indiqua le mode d'emploi/comment le réparer** he told me how to use it/how to fix it

5 (= fixer) [+ heure, date, rendez-vous] to give, to name ◆ **à l'heure indiquée, je ...** at the time indicated ou stated, I ..., at the agreed ou appointed time, I ... ◆ **à la date indiquée** on the given ou agreed day ◆ **au lieu indiqué** at the given ou agreed place

6 (= faire figurer) [étiquette, plan, cartographe] to show; [table, index] to give, to show ◆ **est-ce indiqué sur la facture/dans l'annuaire ?** is it given ou mentioned on the invoice/in the directory? ◆ **il a sommairement indiqué les fenêtres sur le plan** he quickly marked ou drew in the windows on the plan ◆ **quelques traits pour ~ les spectateurs/ombres** a few strokes to give an impression of spectators/shadows ◆ **quelques croquis pour ~ le jeu de scène** a few sketches to give a rough idea of the action

7 (= dénoter) to indicate, to point to ◆ **tout indique que les prix vont augmenter** everything indicates that prices are going to rise, everything points to a forthcoming rise in prices ◆ **cela indique une certaine négligence/hésitation de sa part** that shows ou points to a certain carelessness/hesitation on his part

indirect, e /ɛ̃diʀɛkt/ ADJ (gén) indirect; (Jur) [ligne, héritier] collateral ◆ **d'une manière ~e** in a roundabout ou an indirect way ◆ **apprendre**

qch de manière ~e to hear of sth in a roundabout way; → **discours, éclairage, impôt**

indirectement /ɛ̃dirɛktəmɑ̃/ ADV *(gén)* indirectly; *(= de façon détournée) [faire savoir, apprendre]* in a roundabout way

indiscernable /ɛ̃disɛrnabl/ ADJ indiscernible, imperceptible

indiscipline /ɛ̃disiplin/ NF *(= insubordination)* indiscipline, lack of discipline ◆ **faire preuve d'~** to behave in an undisciplined *ou* unruly manner

indiscipliné, e /ɛ̃disipline/ ADJ *[troupes, écolier]* undisciplined; *[cheveux]* unmanageable, unruly

indiscret, -ète /ɛ̃diskrɛ, ɛt/ ADJ 1 *(= trop curieux) [personne]* inquisitive; *[question]* indiscreet; *[regard, yeux]* inquisitive, prying ◆ **à l'abri des regards ~s/des oreilles indiscrètes** away from prying *ou* inquisitive eyes/from eavesdroppers ◆ **serait-ce ~ de vous demander ... ?** would it be indiscreet to ask you ...? ◆ **mettre des documents à l'abri des ~s** to put documents out of the reach of inquisitive people 2 *(= bavard) [personne]* indiscreet ◆ **ne confiez rien aux ~s** don't confide in people who can't keep secrets

indiscrètement /ɛ̃diskrɛtmɑ̃/ ADV *[demander]* inquisitively; *[regarder]* indiscreetly

indiscrétion /ɛ̃diskresjɔ̃/ NF 1 *(= curiosité) [de question]* indiscreetness, indiscretion; *[de personne, regard]* inquisitiveness ◆ **excusez mon ~, mais quel âge avez-vous ?** I hope you don't mind me *ou* my asking, but how old are you? ◆ **elle pousse l'~ jusqu'à lire mon courrier** she's so inquisitive she even reads my mail ◆ **sans ~, peut-on savoir si ... ?** without wanting to be *ou* without being indiscreet, may we ask whether ...? ◆ **sans ~, combien l'avez-vous payé ?** would you mind if I asked how much you paid for it?
2 *(= tendance à trop parler)* indiscretion ◆ **il est d'une telle ~ !** he's so indiscreet!
3 *(= parole)* indiscreet word *ou* remark, indiscretion; *(= action)* indiscreet act, indiscretion ◆ **commettre une ~** to commit an indiscretion ◆ **les ~s de la presse à scandale** tabloid revelations

indiscutable /ɛ̃diskytabl/ ADJ indisputable, unquestionable

indiscutablement /ɛ̃diskytabləmɑ̃/ GRAMMAIRE ACTIVE 53.6 ADV indisputably, unquestionably

indiscuté, e /ɛ̃diskyte/ ADJ undisputed

indispensable /ɛ̃dispɑ̃sabl/ GRAMMAIRE ACTIVE 37.1
ADJ essential ◆ **cette lecture est ~** it's essential reading ◆ **ces outils/précautions sont ~s** these tools/precautions are essential ◆ **ce collaborateur m'est ~** I'd be lost without this colleague ◆ **tu veux que je vienne ? – ce n'est pas ~** do you want me to come? – it's not necessary *ou* there's no need ◆ **il est ~ que/de faire** it is essential *ou* absolutely necessary *ou* vital that/to do ◆ **je crois qu'il est ~ qu'ils y aillent** I think it's vital *ou* essential that they (should) go ◆ **emporter les vêtements ~s (pour le voyage)** to take the clothes which are essential *ou* indispensable (for the journey) ◆ **prendre les précautions ~s** to take the necessary precautions ◆ **crédits/travaux ~s à la construction d'un bâtiment** funds/work essential *ou* vital for the construction of a building ◆ **l'eau est un élément ~ à la vie** water is essential to life ◆ **savoir se rendre ~** to make o.s. indispensable
NM ◆ **nous n'avions que l'~** we only had what was absolutely essential *ou* necessary *ou* indispensable ◆ **faire l'~ d'abord** to do what is essential *ou* absolutely necessary first ◆ **l'~ est de ...** it's absolutely necessary *ou* essential to ...

> ⚠ **indispensable** se traduit rarement par le mot anglais **indispensable**, qui est d'un registre plus soutenu.

indisponibilité /ɛ̃disponibilite/ NF unavailability

indisponible /ɛ̃disponibl/ ADJ *(gén)* not available *(attrib)*, unavailable; *(Jur)* unavailable

indisposé, e /ɛ̃dispoze/ (ptp de **indisposer**) ADJ *(= fatigué, malade)* indisposed, unwell; *(euph) [femme]* indisposed

indisposer /ɛ̃dispoze/ ▸ conjug 1 ◂ VT *(= mécontenter) [personne, remarque]* to antagonize ◆ **il a des allures qui m'indisposent** his way of behaving irritates me *ou* puts me off him* *(Brit)* ◆ **il indispose tout le monde (contre lui)** he antagonizes everybody ◆ **tout l'indispose !** he's never happy with anything! ◆ **cette scène trop violente risque d'~ les spectateurs** audiences are likely to find this very violent scene disturbing

indisposition /ɛ̃dispozisjɔ̃/ NF *(= malaise)* (slight) indisposition, upset; *(euph = règles)* period

indissociable /ɛ̃disɔsjabl/ ADJ *[éléments, problèmes]* indissociable *(de* from*)*; ◆ **être un élément ~ de qch** to be an integral part of sth

indissociablement /ɛ̃disɔsjabləmɑ̃/ ADV inextricably

indissolubilité /ɛ̃disɔlybilite/ NF indissolubility

indissoluble /ɛ̃disɔlybl/ ADJ indissoluble

indissolublement /ɛ̃disɔlybləmɑ̃/ ADV indissolubly ◆ **~ liés** indissolubly *ou* inextricably linked

indistinct, e /ɛ̃distɛ̃(kt), ɛkt/ ADJ *[forme, idée, souvenir]* indistinct, vague; *[rumeur, murmure]* indistinct, confused; *[lumière]* faint; *[couleurs]* vague ◆ **des voix ~es** a confused murmur of voices

indistinctement /ɛ̃distɛ̃ktəmɑ̃/ ADV 1 *(= confusément)* indistinctly, vaguely ◆ **des bruits provenaient ~ du jardin** I could hear confused noises coming from the garden 2 *(= ensemble)* indiscriminately ◆ **tuant ~ femmes et enfants** killing women and children indiscriminately *ou* without distinction 3 *(= indifféremment)* **cette cuisinière marche ~ au gaz ou à l'électricité** this cooker runs either on gas or on electricity *ou* runs equally well on gas or on electricity ◆ **il se méfie ~ de la gauche et de la droite** he has an equal mistrust of the left wing and the right wing

indium /ɛ̃djɔm/ NM indium

individu /ɛ̃dividy/ NM 1 *(= unité) (gén, Bio)* individual ◆ **le conflit entre l'~ et la société** the conflict between the individual and society 2 *(hum = corps)* **dans la partie la plus charnue de son ~** in the fleshiest part of his anatomy 3 *(péj = homme)* fellow, individual, character ◆ **un ~ l'aborda** someone came up to him ◆ **il aperçut un drôle d'~/un ~ louche** he noticed an odd-looking/a shady-looking character *ou* individual

individualisation /ɛ̃dividɥalizasjɔ̃/ NF individualization, personalization ◆ **~ des salaires** wage negotiation on an individual basis ◆ **~ de l'enseignement** tailoring education to suit individual *ou* particular needs ◆ **l'~ d'une peine** *(Jur) sentencing according to the characteristics of the offender*

individualisé, e /ɛ̃dividɥalize/ (ptp de **individualiser**) ADJ *[caractères, groupe]* distinctive; *[objet personnel, voiture]* personalized, customized; *[formation, programme]* individualized, personalized ◆ **groupe fortement ~** highly distinctive group, group with a distinctive identity ◆ **des solutions ~es selon les besoins** solutions which are tailored to suit individual *ou* particular requirements

individualiser /ɛ̃dividɥalize/ ▸ conjug 1 ◂ VT 1 *(= personnaliser) [+ objet personnel, voiture]* to personalize, to customize; *[+ solutions, horaire, enseignement]* to tailor to suit individual *ou* particular needs; *(Jur) [+ peine]* to match with the characteristics of the offender 2 *(= caractériser)* to individualize VPR **s'individualiser** *[personne]* to acquire an identity of one's own, to become more individual; *[groupe, région]* to acquire an identity of its own

individualisme /ɛ̃dividɥalism/ NM individualism

individualiste /ɛ̃dividɥalist/ ADJ individualistic NMF individualist

individualité /ɛ̃dividɥalite/ NF *(= caractère individuel)* individuality; *(= personne)* individual; *(= personnalité)* personality

individuation /ɛ̃dividɥasjɔ̃/ NF individuation

individuel, -elle /ɛ̃dividɥɛl/ ADJ 1 *(= propre à l'individu) (gén)* individual; *[responsabilité, défaut, contrôle, livret]* personal, individual; *[ordinateur]* personal; *[caractères]* distinctive, individual; *[maison]* detached ◆ **propriété individuelle** personal *ou* private property ◆ **liberté individuelle** personal freedom, freedom of the individual ◆ **chambre individuelle** *(dans un hôtel)* single room ◆ **voyager en ~** to travel alone ◆ **parler à titre ~** to speak in a personal capacity 2 *(= isolé) [fait]* individual, isolated; *[sachet]* individual ◆ **les cas ~s seront examinés** individual cases *ou* each individual case will be examined 3 *(Sport)* individual ◆ **épreuve individuelle** individual event

individuellement /ɛ̃dividɥɛlmɑ̃/ ADV individually

indivis, e /ɛ̃divi, iz/ ADJ *(Jur) [propriété, succession]* undivided, joint *(épith)*; *[propriétaires]* joint *(épith)* ◆ **par ~** *[posséder]* jointly

indivisaire /ɛ̃divizɛr/ NMF *(Jur)* tenant in common

indivisément /ɛ̃divizemɑ̃/ ADV *(Jur)* jointly

indivisibilité /ɛ̃divizibilite/ NF indivisibility

indivisible /ɛ̃divizibl/ ADJ indivisible

indivisiblement /ɛ̃divizibləmɑ̃/ ADV indivisibly

indivision /ɛ̃divizjɔ̃/ NF *(Jur)* joint possession *ou* ownership ◆ **propriété en ~** jointly-held property ◆ **posséder qch en ~** to own sth jointly

Indochine /ɛ̃dɔʃin/ NF Indo-China

indochinois, e /ɛ̃dɔʃinwa, waz/ ADJ Indo-Chinese NM,F **Indochinois(e)** Indo-Chinese

indocile /ɛ̃dɔsil/ ADJ *[enfant]* unruly; *[mémoire]* intractable

indocilité /ɛ̃dɔsilite/ NF *[d'enfant]* unruliness; *[de mémoire]* intractability

indo-européen, -enne /ɛ̃doøʀɔpeɛ̃, ɛn/ ADJ Indo-European NM *(= langue)* Indo-European NM,F **Indo-Européen(ne)** Indo-European

indolemment /ɛ̃dɔlamɑ̃/ ADV indolently

indolence /ɛ̃dɔlɑ̃s/ NF *[d'élève]* idleness, indolence; *[de pouvoirs publics]* apathy, lethargy; *[de geste, regard]* indolence, languidness

indolent, e /ɛ̃dɔlɑ̃, ɑ̃t/ ADJ *[élève]* idle, indolent; *[pouvoirs publics]* apathetic, lethargic; *[air, geste, regard]* indolent, languid

indolore /ɛ̃dɔlɔr/ ADJ painless

indomptable /ɛ̃dɔ̃(p)tabl/ ADJ *[animal, adversaire, peuple] (hum) [personne]* untameable; *[cheval]* untameable, which cannot be broken *ou* mastered; *[enfant]* unmanageable, uncontrollable; *[caractère, courage, volonté]* indomitable, invincible; *[passion, haine]* ungovernable, invincible, uncontrollable

indompté, e /ɛ̃dɔ̃(p)te/ **ADJ** *[enfant, animal, peuple]* untamed, wild; *[cheval]* unbroken, untamed; *[courage]* undaunted; *[énergie]* unharnessed, untamed; *[passion]* ungoverned, unsuppressed

Indonésie /ɛ̃dɔnezi/ **NF** Indonesia

indonésien, -ienne /ɛ̃dɔnezjɛ̃, jɛn/ **ADJ** Indonesian **NM** *(= langue)* Indonesian **NM,F** **Indonésien(ne)** Indonesian

indou, e /ɛ̃du/ **ADJ, NM,F** ⇒ **hindou**

in-douze /induz/ **ADJ INV, NM INV** duodecimo, twelvemo

indu, e /ɛ̃dy/ **ADJ** 1 *(= qui n'est pas dû) [somme, charges]* not owed, unowed; *[avantage]* unwarranted, unjustified 2 *(hum, littér = déraisonnable)* undue ◆ **sans optimisme ~** without undue optimism ◆ **à une heure ~e** at an *ou* some ungodly hour **NM** *(Fin)* unowed sum

indubitable /ɛ̃dybitabl/ **ADJ** *[preuve]* irrefutable ◆ **c'est ~** there is no doubt about it, it's beyond doubt, it's indubitable ◆ **il est ~ qu'il a tort** he's definitely wrong

indubitablement /ɛ̃dybitabləmɑ̃/ **ADV** *(= assurément)* undoubtedly, indubitably ◆ **vous vous êtes ~ trompé** you have definitely made a mistake

inductance /ɛ̃dyktɑ̃s/ **NF** inductance

inducteur, -trice /ɛ̃dyktœʀ, tʀis/ **ADJ** *(gén, Phys)* inductive **NM** *(Chim, Phys)* inductor

inductif, -ive /ɛ̃dyktif, iv/ **ADJ** *(gén Phys)* inductive

induction /ɛ̃dyksjɔ̃/ **NF** *(gén, Bio, Élec, Phys)* induction ◆ **raisonnement par ~** reasoning by induction ◆ **~ magnétique** magnetic induction

induire /ɛ̃dɥiʀ/ ► conjug 38 ◄ **VT** 1 ◆ **~ qn en erreur** to mislead sb, to lead sb astray 2 († *= inciter*) **~ qn à** *[+ péché, gourmandise]* to lead sb into ◆ **~ qn à faire** to induce sb to do 3 *(= inférer)* to infer, to induce (*de* from); ◆ **j'en induis que** I infer from this that 4 *(= occasionner)* to lead to, to result in 5 *(Élec)* to induce

induit, e /ɛ̃dɥi, it/ **ADJ** *(= résultant) [avantage, risque]* resulting; *[ventes]* related; *[effet induit]* side-effect ◆ **emplois ~s** *(Écon)* spinoff jobs **NM** *(Élec)* armature

indulgence /ɛ̃dylʒɑ̃s/ **NF** 1 *(= bienveillance) [de parent, critique, commentaire]* indulgence; *[de juge, examinateur]* leniency ◆ **une erreur qui a rencontré l'~ du jury** a mistake for which the jury made allowances *ou* which the jury was prepared to overlook *ou* be lenient about ◆ **il a demandé l'~ des jurés** he asked the jury to make allowances for *ou* to show leniency towards his client ◆ **faire preuve d'~ envers** *ou* **à l'égard de** *[parent]* to be indulgent with; *[juge, examinateur]* to be lenient with; *[critique]* to be kind to ◆ **avec ~** leniently ◆ **d'une ~ excessive** overindulgent ◆ **sans ~** *[juge, jugement]* stern; *[portrait, critique]* brutally frank; *[punir]* without leniency; *[critiquer]* with brutal frankness ◆ **regard plein d'~** indulgent look 2 *(Rel)* indulgence

indulgent, e /ɛ̃dylʒɑ̃, ɑ̃t/ **ADJ** indulgent; *[juge, examinateur]* lenient ◆ **se montrer ~** *[juge]* to show leniency; *[examinateur]* to be lenient ◆ **la critique s'est montrée ~e** the critics were kind ◆ **15, c'est une note trop ~e** 15 is (far) too generous a mark ◆ **sous le regard ~ de la police** under the benevolent eye of the police

indûment /ɛ̃dymɑ̃/ **ADV** *[protester]* unduly; *[détenir]* without due cause *ou* reason, wrongfully ◆ **s'ingérer ~ dans les affaires de qn** to interfere unnecessarily in sb's business

induration /ɛ̃dyʀasjɔ̃/ **NF** hardening, induration *(SPÉC)*

induré, e /ɛ̃dyʀe/ (ptp de **indurer**) **ADJ** indurate *(SPÉC)*, hardened

indurer /ɛ̃dyʀe/ ► conjug 1 ◄ **VT** to indurate *(SPÉC)*, to harden **VPR** **s'indurer** to indurate *(SPÉC)*, to become indurate *(SPÉC)*, to harden

Indus /ɛ̃dys/ **NM** ◆ **l'~** the Indus

industrialisation /ɛ̃dystʀijalizasjɔ̃/ **NF** industrialization

industrialisé, e /ɛ̃dystʀijalize/ (ptp de **industrialiser**) **ADJ** *[pays, monde]* industrialized ◆ **région fortement ~e** heavily industrialized area ◆ **région faiblement ~e** area without much industry *ou* with a low level of industry

industrialiser /ɛ̃dystʀijalize/ ► conjug 1 ◄ **VT** to industrialize **VPR** **s'industrialiser** to become industrialized

industrialisme /ɛ̃dystʀijalism/ **NM** industrialism

industrialiste /ɛ̃dystʀijalist/ **ADJ** *[politique]* which favours *ou* encourages industrialization

industrie /ɛ̃dystʀi/ **NF** 1 *(= activité, secteur, branche)* industry ◆ **~ légère/lourde** light/heavy industry ◆ **la grande ~** big industry ◆ **~ naissante** infant industry ◆ **doter un pays d'une ~** to provide a country with an industrial structure; → **ministère, pointe**

2 *(= entreprise)* industry, industrial concern ◆ **petites et moyennes ~s** small businesses; → **capitaine**

3 *(littér,* †*)* *(= ingéniosité)* ingenuity; *(= ruse)* cunning

4 *(= activité)* **il exerçait sa coupable ~** *(littér, hum)* he plied his evil trade; → **chevalier**

COMP **industrie aéronautique** aviation industry

industrie alimentaire food (processing) industry

industrie automobile car *ou* automobile *(US)* industry

industrie chimique chemical industry

l'industrie cinématographique *ou* **du cinéma** the film industry

l'industrie hôtelière the hotel industry

industries de la langue language industries

industries du livre book-related industries

industrie de *ou* **du luxe** luxury goods industry

industrie manufacturière manufacturing industry

l'industrie du multimédia the multimedia industry

industrie pharmaceutique pharmaceutical *ou* drug industry

industrie de précision precision tool industry

l'industrie du spectacle the entertainment business, show business

industrie de transformation processing industry

industriel, -elle /ɛ̃dystʀijɛl/ **ADJ** industrial ◆ **aliments ~s** factory feedstuffs ◆ **pain ~** factory-baked bread ◆ **équipement à usage ~** heavy-duty equipment ◆ **élevage ~** *(= système)* factory farming; *(= ferme)* factory farm; → **quantité, zone** **NM** *(= fabricant)* industrialist, manufacturer ◆ **les ~s du textile/de l'automobile** textile/car *ou* automobile *(US)* manufacturers

industriellement /ɛ̃dystʀijɛlmɑ̃/ **ADV** industrially ◆ **poulets élevés ~** factory-farmed chickens

industrieux, -ieuse /ɛ̃dystʀijø, ijøz/ **ADJ** *(littér = besogneux)* industrious

inébranlable /inebʀɑ̃labl/ **ADJ** 1 *[adversaire, interlocuteur]* steadfast, unwavering; *[personne, foi, résolution]* unshakeable, steadfast, unwavering; *[certitude]* unshakeable, unwavering; *[principes, conviction]* steadfast ◆ **il était ~ dans sa conviction que ...** he was steadfast *ou* unshakeable *ou* unwavering in his belief that ... 2 *[objet pesant]* solid; *[objet encastré]* immovable, solidly *ou* firmly fixed

inébranlablement /inebʀɑ̃labləmɑ̃/ **ADV** unshakeably

inécoutable /inekutabl/ **ADJ** *[musique]* unbearable

inécouté, e /inekute/ **ADJ** unheeded

inédit, e /inedi, it/ **ADJ** 1 *(= non publié) [texte, auteur]* (previously *ou* hitherto) unpublished ◆ **ce film est ~ en France** this film has never been released *ou* distributed in France 2 *(= nouveau) [méthode, trouvaille]* novel, new, original; *[spectacle]* new **NM** *(= texte)* (previously *ou* hitherto) unpublished material *(NonC) ou* work ◆ **c'est de l'~ !** *(hum)* that's never happened before!

inéducable /inedykabl/ **ADJ** ineducable

ineffable /inefabl/ **ADJ** ineffable

ineffaçable /inefasabl/ **ADJ** indelible, ineffaceable

inefficace /inefikas/ **ADJ** *[remède, mesure, traitement]* ineffective; *[employé, machine]* inefficient

inefficacement /inefikasmɑ̃/ **ADV** *(= sans succès)* ineffectively; *(= de manière incompétente)* inefficiently

inefficacité /inefikasite/ **NF** *[de remède, mesure]* ineffectiveness; *[de machine, employé]* inefficiency ◆ **d'une totale ~** *[remède, mesure]* totally ineffective; *[employé, machine]* totally inefficient

inégal, e (mpl **-aux**) /inegal, o/ **ADJ** 1 *(= différent)* unequal ◆ **d'~e grosseur** of unequal size ◆ **de force ~e** of unequal strength ◆ **les hommes sont inégaux** all men are not equal 2 *(= irrégulier) [sol, pas, mouvement]* uneven; *[pouls]* irregular, uneven; *[artiste, sportif]* erratic; *[œuvre, jeu]* uneven; *[étalement, répartition]* uneven; *[humeur, caractère]* uneven, changeable; *[conduite]* changeable ◆ **d'intérêt ~** of varying *ou* mixed interest ◆ **de qualité ~e** of varying quality 3 *(= disproportionné) [lutte, partage]* unequal

inégalable /inegalabl/ **ADJ** incomparable, matchless

inégalé, e /inegale/ **ADJ** *[record]* unequalled, unbeaten; *[charme, beauté]* unrivalled

inégalement /inegalmɑ̃/ **ADV** *(= différemment, injustement)* unequally; *(= irrégulièrement)* unevenly ◆ **livre ~ apprécié** book which met (*ou* meets) with varying approval

inégalitaire /inegalitɛʀ/ **ADJ** *[société, système]* unequal, inegalitarian *(frm)*; *[traitement, loi]* unequal

inégalité /inegalite/ **NF** 1 *(= différence) [de hauteurs, volumes]* difference (*de* between); *[de sommes, parts]* difference, disparity (*de* between); ◆ **~ des chances** inequality of opportunity ◆ **l'~ de l'offre et de la demande** the difference *ou* disparity between supply and demand ◆ **l'~ de traitement entre hommes et femmes** the unequal treatment of men and women ◆ **les ~s sociales** social inequalities ◆ **~s de revenus** disparities in income 2 *(Math)* inequality 3 *(= injustice)* inequality 4 *(= irrégularité) [de sol, pas, rythme, répartition]* unevenness; *[d'humeur, caractère]* unevenness, changeability ◆ **~s de terrain** unevenness of the ground, bumps in the ground ◆ **~s d'humeur** moodiness

inélégamment /inelegamɑ̃/ **ADV** inelegantly

inélégance /inelegɑ̃s/ **NF** 1 *[de geste, toilette, silhouette]* inelegance; *[d'allure]* inelegance, ungainliness 2 *[de procédé]* discourtesy

inélégant, e /inelegɑ̃, ɑ̃t/ **ADJ** 1 *(= disgracieux) [geste, toilette, silhouette]* inelegant; *[allure]* inelegant, ungainly 2 *(= indélicat) [procédé]* discourteous ◆ **c'était très ~ de sa part** it was very discourteous of him

inéligibilité /ineliʒibilite/ NF *(Pol)* ineligibility

inéligible /ineliʒibl/ ADJ *(Pol)* ineligible

inéluctabilité /inelyktabilite/ NF inescapability, ineluctability *(frm)*

inéluctable /inelyktabl/ GRAMMAIRE ACTIVE 53.4 ADJ, NM unavoidable ◆ **la catastrophe semblait ~** disaster seemed unavoidable ◆ **cette évolution est ~** this development is unavoidable ◆ **le caractère ~ du verdict** the inevitability of the verdict

inéluctablement /inelyktabləmɑ̃/ ADV inevitably, ineluctably *(frm)* ◆ **une crise financière, qui conduira ~ à des élections anticipées** a financial crisis which will inevitably lead to early elections

inemployable /inɑ̃plwajabl/ ADJ *[procédé]* unusable; *[personnel]* unemployable

inemployé, e /inɑ̃plwaje/ ADJ *(= inutilisé) [outil, argent]* unused; *[talent, capacités]* untapped; *(= gâché) [dévouement, énergie]* unchannelled, unused

inénarrable /inenaʀabl/ ADJ 1 *(= désopilant)* hilarious ◆ **son ~ mari** her incredible husband* 2 *(= incroyable) [péripéties, aventure]* incredible

inentamé, e /inɑ̃tame/ ADJ *[réserve d'essence, d'argent]* intact *(attrib)*; *[victuailles]* intact *(attrib)*, untouched; *[bouteille]* unopened; *[énergie, moral]* (as yet) intact *(attrib)*

inenvisageable /inɑ̃vizaʒabl/ ADJ unthinkable

inéprouvé, e /inepʀuve/ ADJ *[méthode, vertu, procédé]* untested, untried, not yet put to the test *(attrib)*; *[émotion]* not yet experienced *(attrib)*

inepte /inɛpt/ ADJ *[personne]* inept, useless*, hopeless*; *[histoire, raisonnement]* inept

ineptie /inɛpsi/ NF 1 *(= caractère)* ineptitude 2 *(= acte, propos)* ineptitude; *(= idée, œuvre)* nonsense *(NonC)*, rubbish *(Brit) (NonC)* ◆ **dire des ~s** to talk nonsense ◆ **ce qu'il a fait est une ~** what he did was utterly stupid

inépuisable /inepɥizabl/ ADJ inexhaustible ◆ **il est ~ sur ce sujet** he could talk for ever on that subject ◆ **source ~ de conflits** unending *ou* abiding source of conflict

inéquation /inekwasjɔ̃/ NF inequation

inéquitable /inekitabl/ ADJ inequitable

inerte /inɛʀt/ ADJ *(= immobile) [corps, membre]* lifeless, inert; *[visage]* expressionless; *(= sans réaction) [personne]* passive, inert; *[esprit, élève]* apathetic; *(Sci)* inert ◆ **ne reste pas ~ sur ta chaise** don't just sit there

inertie /inɛʀsi/ NF *[de personne]* inertia, passivity, apathy; *[de service administratif]* apathy, inertia; *[d'élève]* apathy; *(Phys)* inertia ◆ **navigation par ~** *[d'avion]* inertial guidance *ou* navigation; → **force**

inescompté, e /inɛskɔ̃te/ ADJ unexpected, unhoped-for

inespéré, e /inɛspeʀe/ ADJ unexpected, unhoped-for

inesthétique /inɛstetik/ ADJ *[pylône, usine, cicatrice]* unsightly; *[démarche, posture]* ungainly

inestimable /inɛstimabl/ ADJ *[aide]* inestimable, invaluable; *[valeur]* priceless, incalculable, inestimable; *[dommages]* incalculable

inévitable /inevitabl/ ADJ *[obstacle, accident]* unavoidable; *(= fatal) [résultat]* inevitable, inescapable; *(hum) [chapeau, cigare]* inevitable ◆ **c'était ~ !** it was inevitable!, it was bound to happen!, it had to happen! NM ◆ **l'~** the inevitable

inévitablement /inevitabləmɑ̃/ GRAMMAIRE ACTIVE 42.1 ADV inevitably

inexact, e /inɛgza(kt), akt/ GRAMMAIRE ACTIVE 53.6 ADJ 1 *(= faux) [renseignement, calcul, traduction, historien]* inaccurate ◆ **non, c'est ~** no, that's not correct *ou* that's wrong 2 *(= sans ponctualité)* unpunctual ◆ **être ~ à un rendez-vous** to be late for an appointment

inexactement /inɛgzaktəmɑ̃/ ADV *[traduire, relater]* inaccurately, incorrectly

inexactitude /inɛgzaktityd/ NF 1 *(= manque de précision)* inaccuracy 2 *(= erreur)* inaccuracy 3 *(= manque de ponctualité)* unpunctuality *(NonC)*

inexaucé, e /inɛgzose/ ADJ *[prière]* (as yet) unanswered; *[vœu]* (as yet) unfulfilled

inexcusable /inɛkskyzabl/ ADJ *[faute, action]* inexcusable, unforgivable ◆ **vous êtes ~ (d'avoir fait cela)** you had no excuse (for doing that)

inexécutable /inɛgzekytabl/ ADJ *[projet, travail]* impractical, impracticable; *[musique]* unplayable; *[ordre]* which cannot be carried out *ou* executed

inexécution /inɛgzekysjɔ̃/ NF *[de contrat, obligation]* nonfulfilment

inexercé, e /inɛgzɛʀse/ ADJ *[soldats]* inexperienced, untrained; *[oreille]* unpractised, untrained

inexistant, e /inɛgzistɑ̃, ɑ̃t/ ADJ nonexistent ◆ **quant à son mari, il est ~** *(péj)* as for her husband, he's a complete nonentity

inexistence /inɛgzistɑ̃s/ NF non-existence

inexorabilité /inɛgzɔʀabilite/ NF *[de destin, vieillesse]* inexorability; *[de juge, arrêt, loi]* inflexibility, inexorability *(littér)*

inexorable /inɛgzɔʀabl/ ADJ 1 *(= implacable) [destin, vieillesse]* inexorable ◆ **l'~ montée de la violence** *(= inévitable)* the inexorable rise of violence 2 *(= impitoyable) [arrêt, loi]* inflexible, inexorable *(littér)*; *[juge]* unyielding, inflexible, inexorable *(littér)* ◆ **il fut ~ à leurs prières** he was unmoved by their entreaties

inexorablement /inɛgzɔʀabləmɑ̃/ ADV inexorably

inexpérience /inɛkspeʀjɑ̃s/ NF inexperience, lack of experience

inexpérimenté, e /inɛkspeʀimɑ̃te/ ADJ *[personne]* inexperienced; *[mouvements, gestes]* inexpert; *[arme, produit]* untested

inexpiable /inɛkspjabl/ ADJ inexpiable

inexpié, e /inɛkspje/ ADJ unexpiated

inexplicable /inɛksplikabl(ə)/ ADJ, NM inexplicable

inexplicablement /inɛksplikabləmɑ̃/ ADV inexplicably

inexpliqué, e /inɛksplike/ ADJ unexplained

inexploitable /inɛksplwatabl/ ADJ *(gén)* unexploitable; *[filon]* unworkable

inexploité, e /inɛksplwate/ ADJ *(gén)* unexploited; *[talent, ressources]* untapped

inexplorable /inɛksplɔʀabl/ ADJ unexplorable

inexploré, e /inɛksplɔʀe/ ADJ unexplored

inexplosible /inɛksplozibl/ ADJ non-explosive

inexpressif, -ive /inɛkspʀesif, iv/ ADJ *[visage, regard]* expressionless, inexpressive, blank; *[style, mots]* inexpressive

inexpressivité /inɛkspʀesivite/ NF inexpressiveness, expressionlessness

inexprimable /inɛkspʀimabl/ ADJ, NM inexpressible

inexprimé, e /inɛkspʀime/ ADJ *[sentiment]* unexpressed; *[reproches, doutes]* unspoken

inexpugnable /inɛkspygnabl/ ADJ *[citadelle]* impregnable, unassailable

inextensible /inɛkstɑ̃sibl/ ADJ *[matériau]* that does not stretch, unstretchable; *[étoffe]* non-stretch

in extenso /inɛkstɛso/ LOC ADV *[écrire, publier, lire]* in full, in extenso *(frm)* LOC ADJ *[texte, discours]* full *(épith)*

inextinguible /inɛkstɛ̃gibl/ ADJ *(littér) [passion, feu]* inextinguishable; *[haine]* undying; *[besoin, soif]* unquenchable; *[rire]* uncontrollable

in extremis /inɛkstʀemis/ LOC ADV *[sauver, arriver]* at the last minute LOC ADJ *[sauvetage, succès]* last-minute *(épith)* ◆ **faire un mariage/testament ~** to marry/make a will on one's deathbed

inextricable /inɛkstʀikabl/ ADJ inextricable

inextricablement /inɛkstʀikabləmɑ̃/ ADV inextricably

infaillibilité /ɛ̃fajibilite/ NF *(gén, Rel)* infallibility

infaillible /ɛ̃fajibl/ ADJ *[méthode, remède, personne]* infallible; *[instinct]* unerring, infallible

infailliblement /ɛ̃fajibləmɑ̃/ ADV *(= à coup sûr)* inevitably, without fail; *(= sans erreur)* infallibly

infaisable /ɛ̃fəzabl/ ADJ impossible, impracticable, not feasible *(attrib)* ◆ **ce n'est pas ~** it's not impossible, it's (just about) feasible ◆ **pourquoi serait-ce ~ en France ?** why couldn't this be done in France?

infalsifiable /ɛ̃falsifjabl/ ADJ *[document]* impossible to forge

infamant, e /ɛ̃famɑ̃, ɑ̃t/ ADJ *[acte]* infamous, ignominious; *[accusation]* libellous; *[propos]* defamatory; *[terme]* derogatory ◆ **peine ~e** *(Jur)* sentence involving exile or deprivation of civil rights

infâme /ɛ̃fɑm/ ADJ *(gén)* vile, loathsome; *[métier, action, trahison]* unspeakable, vile, loathsome; *[traître]* infamous, vile; *[complaisance, servilité]* shameful, vile; *[entremetteur, spéculateur]* despicable; *[nourriture, odeur, taudis]* revolting, vile, disgusting

infamie /ɛ̃fami/ NF 1 *(= honte)* infamy ◆ **couvert d'~** disgraced 2 *(= caractère infâme) [de personne, acte]* infamy 3 *(= insulte)* vile abuse *(NonC)*; *(= action infâme)* infamous *ou* vile *ou* loathsome deed; *(= ragot)* slanderous gossip *(NonC)* ◆ **c'est une ~** it's absolutely scandalous, it's an absolute scandal ◆ **dire des ~s sur le compte de qn** to make slanderous remarks about sb

infant /ɛ̃fɑ̃/ NM infante

infante /ɛ̃fɑ̃t/ NF infanta

infanterie /ɛ̃fɑ̃tʀi/ NF infantry ◆ **avec une ~ de 2 000 hommes** with 2,000 foot, with an infantry of 2,000 men ◆ **~ légère/lourde *ou* de ligne** light/heavy infantry ◆ **~ de marine** marines ◆ **d'~** *[régiment]* infantry *(épith)*

infanticide /ɛ̃fɑ̃tisid/ ADJ infanticidal NMF *(= personne)* infanticide, child-killer NM *(= acte)* infanticide

infantile /ɛ̃fɑ̃til/ ADJ 1 *[maladie]* infantile; *[médecine, clinique]* child *(épith)*; → **mortalité** 2 *(= puéril)* infantile, childish, babyish

infantilisant, e /ɛ̃fɑ̃tilizɑ̃, ɑ̃t/ ADJ condescending

infantilisation /ɛ̃fɑ̃tilizasjɔ̃/ NF ◆ **l'~ des personnes âgées/du public** treating old people/the public like children

infantiliser /ɛ̃fɑ̃tilize/ ► conjug 1 ◄ VT to treat like a child (*ou* like children) ◆ **on fait tout pour ~ les détenus** prisoners are treated like children in all sorts of ways

infantilisme /ɛ̃fɑ̃tilism/ NM *(Méd, Psych)* infantilism; *(= puérilité)* infantile *ou* childish *ou* babyish behaviour ◆ **c'est de l'~ !** how childish!

infarctus /ɛ̃faʀktys/ **NM** *(Méd)* coronary, infarction *(SPÉC)*, infarct *(SPÉC)* ◆ **~ du myocarde** coronary thrombosis, myocardial infarction *(SPÉC)* ◆ **il a eu** *ou* **fait trois** ~ he has had three coronaries ◆ **j'ai failli avoir un ~ quand il me l'a dit** I nearly had a heart attack when he told me

infatigable /ɛ̃fatigabl/ **ADJ** *[personne]* indefatigable, tireless; *[zèle]* tireless

infatigablement /ɛ̃fatigabləmɑ̃/ **ADV** indefatigably, tirelessly, untiringly

infatuation /ɛ̃fatɥasjɔ̃/ **NF** *(frm = vanité)* self-conceit, self-importance

infatué, e /ɛ̃fatɥe/ (ptp de **s'infatuer**) **ADJ** *[air, personne]* conceited, vain ◆ **être ~ de son importance** to be full of one's own importance ◆ **être ~ de son physique** to be vain *ou* conceited about one's looks ◆ **~ de sa personne** *ou* **de lui-même** full of himself *ou* of self-conceit, self-important

infatuer (s') /ɛ̃fatɥe/ ▸ conjug 1 ◂ **VPR** ① *(= s'engouer de)* **s'~ de** *[+ personne, choses]* to become infatuated with ② *(= tirer vanité de)* **s'~ de son importance** to become full of one's own importance ◆ **s'~ de son physique** to become vain *ou* conceited about one's looks ◆ **s'~ (de soi-même)** to become full of o.s. *ou* of self-conceit

infécond, e /ɛ̃fekɔ̃, ɔ̃d/ **ADJ** *[terre, femme, animal]* barren, sterile, infertile; *[œuf]* infertile; *[esprit]* infertile, sterile

infécondité /ɛ̃fekɔ̃dite/ **NF** *[de terre, femme, animal]* barrenness, sterility, infertility; *[d'esprit]* infertility, sterility

infect, e /ɛ̃fɛkt/ **ADJ** *[goût, nourriture, vin, attitude]* revolting; *[conduite, personne]* obnoxious; *[temps]* filthy, foul, rotten; *[taudis, chambre]* squalid; *[livre, film] (= très mauvais)* rotten*, appalling; *(= scandaleux)* revolting ◆ **odeur ~e** stench, vile *ou* foul smell ◆ **il a été ~ avec moi** he was horrible to me

infectant, e /ɛ̃fɛktɑ̃, ɑt/ **ADJ** *(Méd) [agent]* infective; *[contact, piqûre]* causing infection

infecter /ɛ̃fɛkte/ ▸ conjug 1 ◂ **VT** *(gén) [+ atmosphère, eau]* to contaminate; *[+ personne, plaie, fichier]* to infect; *(fig littér)* to poison, to infect ◆ **cellules infectées par un virus** virus-infected cells **VPR** **s'infecter** *[plaie]* to become infected, to turn septic

infectieux, -ieuse /ɛ̃fɛksjø, jøz/ **ADJ** *(Méd)* infectious

infection /ɛ̃fɛksjɔ̃/ **NF** infection; *(= puanteur)* stench ◆ **~ généralisée** systemic infection ◆ **~ microbienne/virale** bacterial/viral infection ◆ **quelle ~ !, c'est une ~ !** what a stench! ◆ **~ sexuellement transmissible** sexually transmitted infection

infectiosité /ɛ̃fɛksjɔzite/ **NF** *[de produit, virus]* infectivity

inféodation /ɛ̃feɔdasjɔ̃/ **NF** *(Pol)* allegiance *(à* to); *(Hist)* infeudation, enfeoffment

inféoder /ɛ̃feɔde/ ▸ conjug 1 ◂ **VT** *(Hist)* to enfeoff **VPR** **s'inféoder** ◆ **s'~ à** to give one's allegiance to, to pledge allegiance *ou* o.s. to ◆ **être inféodé à** to be subservient to, to be the vassal of

inférence /ɛ̃ferɑ̃s/ **NF** inference

inférer /ɛ̃fere/ ▸ conjug 6 ◂ **VT** to infer, to gather *(de* from); ◆ **j'infère de ceci que ..., j'en infère que ...** I infer *ou* gather from this that ..., this leads me to conclude that ...

inférieur, e /ɛ̃ferjœr/ GRAMMAIRE ACTIVE 32.3

ADJ ① *(dans l'espace, gén)* lower; *[mâchoire, lèvre]* lower, bottom; *[planètes]* inferior ◆ **la partie ~e du tableau** the bottom part of the picture ◆ **le feu a pris dans les étages ~s** fire broke out on the lower floors ◆ **descendez à l'étage ~** go down to the next floor *ou* the floor below, go to the next floor down ◆ **le cours ~ d'un fleuve** the lower course *ou* stretches of a river

② *(dans une hiérarchie) [classes sociales, animaux, végétaux]* lower ◆ **à l'échelon ~** on the next rung down ◆ **d'un rang ~** of a lower rank, lower in rank

③ *[qualité]* inferior, poorer; *[vitesse]* lower; *[nombre]* smaller, lower; *[quantité]* smaller; *[intelligence, esprit]* inferior ◆ **forces ~es en nombre** forces inferior *ou* smaller in number(s)

④ ◆ **~ à** *[nombre]* less *ou* lower *ou* smaller than, below; *[somme]* smaller *ou* less than; *[production]* inferior to, less *ou* lower than ◆ **note ~e à 20** mark below 20 *ou* less than 20 ◆ **intelligence/qualité ~e à la moyenne** below average *ou* lower than average intelligence/quality ◆ **travail d'un niveau ~ à ...** work of a lower standard than ..., work below the standard of ... ◆ **roman/auteur ~ à un autre** novel/author inferior to another ◆ **tu ne lui es ~ en rien** you're in no way inferior to him ◆ **être hiérarchiquement ~ à qn** to be lower (down) than sb *ou* be below sb in the hierarchy ◆ **il est ~ à sa tâche** *(fig)* he isn't equal to his task, he isn't up to the job

NM,F inferior

> ⚠ Attention à ne pas traduire automatiquement **inférieur** par **inferior**, qui a des emplois spécifiques.

inférieurement /ɛ̃ferjœrmɑ̃/ **ADV** *(= moins bien)* less well ◆ **~ équipé** *[armée, laboratoire, bateau]* less well-equipped

inférioriser /ɛ̃ferjɔrize/ ▸ conjug 1 ◂ **VT** *(= sous-estimer)* to underestimate; *(= complexer)* to make feel inferior

infériorité /ɛ̃ferjɔrite/ **NF** inferiority ◆ **en état** *ou* **position d'~** in an inferior position, in a position of inferiority; → **comparatif, complexe**

infernal, e (mpl **-aux**) /ɛ̃fɛrnal, o/ **ADJ** ① *(= intolérable) [bruit, allure, chaleur, cadence]* infernal; *[enfant]* impossible ◆ **c'est ~ !** it's unbearable!, it's sheer hell! ◆ **les disputes/images se succèdent à un rythme ~** the arguments/images come thick and fast ② *(= satanique) [caractère, personne, complot]* diabolical, infernal, devilish ③ *(= effrayant) [vision, supplice]* diabolical; *[spirale, engrenage]* vicious ◆ **cycle ~** vicious circle; → **machine** ④ *(Myth) [divinité]* infernal

infertile /ɛ̃fɛrtil/ **ADJ** *(lit, fig)* infertile

infertilité /ɛ̃fɛrtilite/ **NF** *(lit, fig)* infertility

infestation /ɛ̃fɛstasjɔ̃/ **NF** *(Méd)* infestation

infester /ɛ̃fɛste/ ▸ conjug 1 ◂ **VT** *(gén)* to infest, to overrun; *(Méd)* to infest ◆ **infesté de moustiques** infested with mosquitoes, mosquito-infested *ou* -ridden ◆ **infesté de souris/pirates** infested with *ou* overrun with *ou* by mice/pirates

infibulation /ɛ̃fibylasjɔ̃/ **NF** infibulation

infichu, e* /ɛ̃fiʃy/ **ADJ** ◆ **~ de faire qch** totally incapable of doing sth ◆ **je suis ~ de me rappeler où je l'ai mis** I can't remember where the hell I put it*

infidèle /ɛ̃fidɛl/ **ADJ** ① *[ami]* unfaithful, disloyal *(à qn* to sb); *[époux]* unfaithful *(à qn* to sb); ◆ **être ~ à sa promesse** *(littér)* to be untrue to one's promise ② *[récit, traduction, traducteur]* unfaithful, inaccurate; *[mémoire]* unreliable ③ *(Rel)* infidel **NMF** *(Rel)* infidel

infidèlement /ɛ̃fidɛlmɑ̃/ **ADV** *[traduire, raconter]* unfaithfully, inaccurately

infidélité /ɛ̃fidelite/ **NF** ① *(= inconstance) [d'ami]* disloyalty, unfaithfulness; *[d'époux]* infidelity, unfaithfulness *(à* to); ◆ **~ à une promesse** *(littér)* being untrue to a promise *(littér)* ② *(= acte déloyal) [d'époux]* infidelity ◆ **elle lui pardonna ses ~s** she forgave him his infidelities ◆ **faire une ~ à qn** to be unfaithful to sb ◆ **il a fait bien des ~s à sa femme** he has been unfaithful *ou* guilty of infidelity to his wife on many occasions ◆ **faire des ~s à son boucher/éditeur** *(hum)* to be unfaithful to *ou* forsake one's butcher/publisher ③ *(= manque d'exactitude) [de description, historien]* inaccuracy; *[de mémoire]* unreliability ④ *(= erreur) [de description, traducteur]* inaccuracy ◆ **on trouve beaucoup d'~s dans cette traduction** we find many inaccuracies in this translation

infiltration /ɛ̃filtʀasjɔ̃/ **NF** ① *[de liquide]* percolation, infiltration; *(dans le sol)* seepage; *[d'hommes, idées]* infiltration ◆ **il y a une ~** *ou* **des ~s dans la cave** there are leaks in the cellar, water is leaking into the cellar ② *(Méd = accumulation dans un tissu)* infiltration; *(= piqûre)* injection ◆ **se faire faire des ~s** to have injections

infiltrer /ɛ̃filtʀe/ ▸ conjug 1 ◂ **VT** *(= noyauter) [+ groupe, réseau]* to infiltrate **VPR** **s'infiltrer** *[liquide]* to percolate (through), to seep in, to infiltrate; *[lumière]* to filter through; *[hommes, idées]* to infiltrate ◆ **s'~ dans** *[personne]* to infiltrate; *[idées]* to filter into, to infiltrate (into); *[liquide]* to percolate (through), to seep through, to infiltrate; *[lumière]* to filter into ◆ **s'~ dans un groupe/chez l'ennemi** to infiltrate a group/the enemy

infime /ɛ̃fim/ **ADJ** *(= minuscule)* tiny, minute, minuscule; *(= inférieur)* lowly, inferior ◆ **une ~ minorité** a tiny minority

in fine /infine/ **LOC ADV** ultimately

infini, e /ɛ̃fini/ **ADJ** ① *(Math, Philos, Rel)* infinite ② *(= sans limites) [espace]* infinite, boundless; *[patience, bonté]* infinite, unlimited, boundless; *[douleur]* immense; *[prudence, soin, bêtise]* infinite, immeasurable; *[quantité]* infinite, unlimited ◆ **avec d'~es précautions** with infinite *ou* endless precautions

③ *(= interminable) [luttes, propos]* interminable, never-ending ◆ **un temps ~ me parut s'écouler** an eternity seemed to pass

NM ◆ **l'~** *(Philos)* the infinite; *(Math, Photo)* infinity ◆ **faire la mise au point à** *ou* **sur l'~** *(Photo)* to focus to infinity ◆ **l'~ des cieux** heaven's immensity, the infinity of heaven

◆ **à l'infini** *[discourir]* ad infinitum, endlessly; *[multiplier]* to infinity; *[se diversifier, faire varier]* infinitely ◆ **les champs s'étendaient à l'~** the fields stretched away endlessly into the distance ◆ **droite prolongée à l'~** straight line tending towards infinity

infiniment /ɛ̃finimɑ̃/ **ADV** ① *(= immensément)* infinitely ② *(sens affaibli = beaucoup)* infinitely ◆ **~ long/grand** immensely *ou* infinitely long/large ◆ **je vous suis ~ reconnaissant** I am immensely *ou* extremely *ou* infinitely grateful (to you) ◆ **je regrette ~** I'm extremely sorry ◆ **ça me plaît ~** I like it immensely, there's nothing I like more ◆ **~ meilleur/plus intelligent** infinitely better/more intelligent ◆ **avec ~ de soin/de tendresse** with infinite *ou* with the utmost care/tenderness ③ ◆ **l'~ grand** the infinitely great ◆ **l'~ petit** the infinitesimal

infinité /ɛ̃finite/ **NF** *(littér)* infinity ◆ **une ~ de** *(= quantité infinie)* an infinite number of

infinitésimal, e (mpl **-aux**) /ɛ̃finitezimal, o/ **ADJ** *(gén, Math)* infinitesimal

infinitif, -ive /ɛ̃finitif, iv/ **ADJ, NM** infinitive ◆ **~ de narration** historic infinitive ◆ **à l'~** in the infinitive

infirmatif, -ive /ɛ̃firmatif, iv/ **ADJ** *(Jur)* invalidating ◆ **~ de** invalidating, annulling, quashing

infirmation /ɛ̃firmasjɔ̃/ **NF** *(Jur)* invalidation, annulment, quashing *(de* of)

infirme /ɛ̃firm/ **ADJ** *[personne]* crippled, disabled; *(avec l'âge)* infirm ◆ **l'accident l'avait**

rendu ~ the accident had left him crippled *ou* disabled ◆ **il est ~ du bras droit** he has a crippled *ou* disabled right arm ◆ **être ~ de naissance** to be disabled from birth, to be born disabled **NM,F** disabled person ◆ **les ~s** the disabled ◆ **~ mental/moteur** mentally/physically handicapped *ou* disabled person ◆ **~ du travail** industrially disabled person ◆ **~ de guerre** disabled veteran

infirmer /ɛ̃fiʀme/ ▸ conjug 1 ◂ **VT** *(= démentir)* to invalidate; *(Jur)* *[+ décision, jugement]* to invalidate, to annul, to quash ◆ **merci de confirmer ou ~ ce qui suit** please confirm or contradict the following

infirmerie /ɛ̃fiʀməʀi/ **NF** *(gén)* infirmary; *[d'école]* sickroom, infirmary, sick bay *(Brit)*; *(Univ)* health centre; *[de navire]* sick bay

infirmier, -ière /ɛ̃fiʀmje, jɛʀ/ **ADJ** nursing *(épith)* ◆ **personnel ~** nursing staff ◆ **élève ~** student nurse **NM** (male) nurse ◆ **~ en chef** charge nurse *(Brit)*, head nurse *(US)* **NF** **infirmière** *(gén)* nurse; *[d'internat]* matron *(Brit)*, nurse *(US)* ◆ **infirmière chef** (nursing) sister *(Brit)*, charge nurse *(Brit)*, head nurse *(US)* ◆ **infirmière diplômée** registered nurse ◆ **infirmière diplômée d'État** ≃ state registered nurse ◆ **infirmière-major** *(Mil)* matron ◆ **infirmière visiteuse** visiting nurse, ≃ district nurse *(Brit)*

infirmité /ɛ̃fiʀmite/ **NF** 1 *(= invalidité)* disability ◆ **~ motrice cérébrale** physical disability ◆ **les ~s de la vieillesse** the infirmities of old age 2 *(† = imperfection)* weakness, failing

infixe /ɛ̃fiks/ **NM** *(Ling)* infix

inflammable /ɛ̃flamabl/ **ADJ** inflammable, flammable

inflammation /ɛ̃flamasjɔ̃/ **NF** *(Méd)* inflammation

inflammatoire /ɛ̃flamatwaʀ/ **ADJ** *(Méd)* inflammatory

inflation /ɛ̃flasjɔ̃/ **NF** *(Écon)* inflation ◆ **croissance de 4% hors ~** 4% growth over and above inflation ◆ **une ~ de projets/candidatures** a marked increase in the number of projects/applications

inflationniste /ɛ̃flasjɔnist/ **ADJ** *[politique, économie]* inflationist; *[tendance, risque, pressions]* inflationary; *[craintes, menace]* of inflation **NMF** inflationist

infléchi, e /ɛ̃fleʃi/ (ptp de **infléchir**) **ADJ** *[voyelle]* inflected

infléchir /ɛ̃fleʃiʀ/ ▸ conjug 2 ◂ **VT** 1 *(lit)* *[+ rayon]* to inflect, to bend 2 *(fig)* *[+ politique]* *(légèrement)* to change *ou* shift the emphasis of; *(plus nettement)* to reorientate; *[+ tendance, stratégie, attitude]* to modify; *[+ position]* to soften; *[+ décision]* to affect ◆ **pour ~ la courbe du chômage** to bring down unemployment **VPR** **s'infléchir** 1 *[route]* to bend, to curve round; *[poutre]* to sag; *[courbe]* *(vers le bas)* to dip, to go down; *(vers le haut)* to climb, to go up 2 *[politique]* to shift, to change emphasis; *(= conjoncture)* to change ◆ **cette tendance s'infléchit** this trend is becoming less marked

infléchissement /ɛ̃fleʃismɑ̃/ **NM** *[de politique]* *(léger)* (slight) shift (*de* in); *(plus marqué)* reorientation; *[de stratégie, attitude]* shift (*de* in); *[de position]* softening ◆ **un net ~ des ventes** *(à la baisse)* a sharp drop *ou* fall in sales; *(à la hausse)* a sharp *ou* marked increase in sales

inflexibilité /ɛ̃flɛksibilite/ **NF** *[de caractère, personne]* inflexibility, rigidity; *[de volonté]* inflexibility; *[de règle]* inflexibility, rigidity

inflexible /ɛ̃flɛksibl/ **ADJ** *[caractère, personne]* inflexible, rigid, unyielding; *[volonté]* inflexible; *[règle]* inflexible, rigid ◆ **il demeura ~ dans sa résolution** he remained inflexible *ou* unyielding *ou* unbending in his resolve

inflexiblement /ɛ̃flɛksibləmɑ̃/ **ADV** inflexibly

inflexion /ɛ̃flɛksjɔ̃/ **NF** 1 *[de voix]* inflexion, modulation ◆ **~ vocalique** *(Ling)* vowel inflexion 2 *(Sci = déviation)* *[de rayon]* deflection; *[de courbe]* inflexion 3 *(fig)* *[de politique]* reorientation (*de* of)

infliger /ɛ̃fliʒe/ ▸ conjug 3 ◂ **VT** *[+ défaite, punition, supplice]* to inflict (*à* on); *[+ amende, tâche]* to impose (*à* on); *[+ affront]* to deliver (*à* to); ◆ **~ de lourdes pertes à l'ennemi** to inflict heavy losses on the enemy ◆ **~ sa présence à qn** to inflict one's presence *ou* o.s. on sb ◆ **~ un avertissement *ou* un blâme à qn** *(Scol)* to give sb an order mark *(Brit)* *ou* a bad mark *(Brit)* *ou* a demerit point *(US)* ◆ **~ un démenti à qn** to give sb the lie ◆ **il s'est infligé volontairement des blessures** he harmed himself deliberately

inflorescence /ɛ̃flɔʀesɑ̃s/ **NF** inflorescence

influençable /ɛ̃flyɑ̃sabl/ **ADJ** easily influenced

influence /ɛ̃flyɑ̃s/ **NF** influence (*sur* on, upon); ◆ **c'est quelqu'un qui a de l'~** he's a person of influence, he's an influential person ◆ **avoir beaucoup d'~ sur qn, jouir d'une grande ~ auprès de qn** to have *ou* carry a lot of influence with sb ◆ **avoir une ~ bénéfique/néfaste sur** *[climat, médicament]* to have a beneficial/harmful effect on ◆ **ces fréquentations ont une mauvaise ~ sur ses enfants** these friends are a bad influence on her children ◆ **sous l'~ de** under the influence of ◆ **être sous ~*** *(de l'alcool, d'une drogue)* to be under the influence*; *(de qn)* to be under somebody's control *ou* spell ◆ **zone/sphère d'~** zone/sphere of influence; → **trafic**

influencer /ɛ̃flyɑ̃se/ ▸ conjug 3 ◂ **VT** *(gén)* to influence; *(= agir sur)* to act upon ◆ **ne te laisse pas ~ par lui** don't let yourself be influenced by him, don't let him influence you

influent, e /ɛ̃flyɑ̃, ɑ̃t/ **ADJ** influential

influenza /ɛ̃flyɑ̃za/ **NF** influenza

influer /ɛ̃flye/ ▸ conjug 1 ◂ **influer sur VT INDIR** to influence, to have an influence on

influx /ɛ̃fly/ **NM** 1 *(Méd)* ~ **(nerveux)** (nerve) impulse 2 *(Astrol = fluide)* influence

info* /ɛ̃fo/ **NF** 1 (abrév de **information**) *(Presse, TV)* news item, piece of news; *(= renseignements)* info* *(NonC)* ◆ **les ~s** *(Presse, TV)* the news 2 (abrév de **informatique**) *(Ordin)* computing ◆ **il fait de l'~** *(en amateur)* he's into computing; *(professionnellement)* he's in computers

infobulle /ɛ̃fobyl/ **NF** *(Ordin)* tooltip

infographie ® /ɛ̃fɔgʀafi/ **NF** computer graphics

infographique /ɛ̃fɔgʀafik/ **ADJ** ◆ **document ~** computer graphic picture ◆ **création ~** computer graphics *(sg)*

infographiste /ɛ̃fɔgʀafist/ **NMF** computer graphics artist

in-folio /infɔljo/ **ADJ INV, NM INV** folio

infomercial (pl **infomerciaux**) /ɛ̃fomɛʀsjal, o/ **ADJ, NM** infomercial

infondé, e /ɛ̃fɔ̃de/ **ADJ** *[critique, crainte, accusation]* unfounded, groundless; *[demande]* unjustified; *[rumeurs]* unfounded ◆ **ces rumeurs ne sont peut-être pas totalement ~es** there may be some truth in these rumours, these rumours are perhaps not totally unfounded

informant, e /ɛ̃fɔʀmɑ̃, ɑ̃t/ **NM,F** informant

informateur, -trice /ɛ̃fɔʀmatœʀ, tʀis/ **NM,F** *(gén)* informant; *(Police)* informer; *(Presse)* inside source

informaticien, -ienne /ɛ̃fɔʀmatisjɛ̃, jɛn/ **NM,F** *(= spécialiste)* computer scientist; *(= analyste-programmeur)* computer analyst ◆ **elle est informaticienne** she's in computers

informatif, -ive /ɛ̃fɔʀmatif, iv/ **ADJ** *[brochure]* informative ◆ **campagne de publicité informative pour un produit** advertising campaign giving information on a product

information /ɛ̃fɔʀmasjɔ̃/ GRAMMAIRE ACTIVE 46.3

NF 1 *(= renseignement)* piece of information; *(Presse, TV = nouvelle)* news item, piece of news ◆ **voilà une ~ intéressante** here's an interesting piece of information *ou* some interesting information ◆ **recueillir des ~s sur** to gather information on ◆ **voici nos ~s** here *ou* this is the news ◆ **~s politiques** political news ◆ **~s télévisées** television news ◆ **écouter/regarder les ~s** to listen to/watch the news (bulletins) ◆ **c'était aux ~s de 10 heures** it was on the 10 o'clock news ◆ **nous recevons une ~ de dernière minute** we've just received some lastminute *ou* late news ◆ **bulletin/flash d'~s** news bulletin/flash ◆ **aller aux ~s** to (go and) find out

2 *(= diffusion de renseignements)* information ◆ **pour votre ~, sachez que ...** for your (own) information you should know that ... ◆ **pour l'~ des voyageurs** for the information of travellers ◆ **assurer l'~ du public en matière d'impôts** to ensure that the public is informed *ou* has information on the subject of taxation ◆ **réunion d'~** briefing ◆ **journal d'~** serious newspaper

3 *(Ordin, Sci)* **l'~** information ◆ **traitement de l'~** data processing, processing of information ◆ **théorie de l'~** information theory ◆ **~ génétique** genetic information

4 *(Jur)* **~ judiciaire** (judicial) inquiry ◆ **ouvrir une ~** to start an initial *ou* a preliminary investigation ◆ **~ contre X** inquiry against person *ou* persons unknown

informationnel, -elle /ɛ̃fɔʀmasjɔnɛl/ **ADJ** *[système]* informational ◆ **révolution informationnelle** information revolution ◆ **le contenu ~ du document est assez limité** the document is not particularly informative

informatique /ɛ̃fɔʀmatik/ **NF** *(= science)* computer science, computing; *(= techniques)* data processing ◆ **~ de bureau/de gestion** office/commercial computing ◆ **il est dans l'~** he's in computers ◆ **l'ère de l'~** the computer age ◆ **loi ~ et libertés** data protection law, ≃ Data Protection Act *(Brit)* **ADJ** computer *(épith)* ◆ **l'industrie ~** the computer *ou* computing industry

informatiquement /ɛ̃fɔʀmatikmɑ̃/ **ADV** *[détecter]* by means of the computer ◆ **traiter qch ~** to process sth using a computer

informatisation /ɛ̃fɔʀmatizasjɔ̃/ **NF** computerization

informatiser /ɛ̃fɔʀmatize/ ▸ conjug 1 ◂ **VT** to computerize **VPR** **s'informatiser** to become computerized

informe /ɛ̃fɔʀm/ **ADJ** *[masse, tas]* shapeless, formless; *[vêtement]* shapeless; *[visage, être]* misshapen, ill-shaped, ill-formed; *[projet]* rough, undefined

informé /ɛ̃fɔʀme/ **ADJ** *[personne]* well-informed ◆ **journaux/milieux bien ~s** well-informed newspapers/circles

◆ **tenir qn informé** to keep sb informed, to keep sb up-to-date ◆ **je suis tenu ~ par mes collaborateurs** my colleagues keep me up-to-date *ou* informed ◆ **il se tient ~ des dernières évolutions technologiques** he keeps up-to-date with the latest technological developments

NM → **jusque**

informel, -elle /ɛ̃fɔʀmɛl/ **ADJ** *(gén, Art)* informal ◆ **l'économie informelle** the informal *ou* unofficial economy

informer /ɛ̃fɔʀme/ ▸ conjug 1 ◂ **VT** 1 *(d'un fait)* to inform, to tell (*de* of, about); *(d'un problème)* to inform (*sur* about); ◆ **m'ayant informé de ce**

fait having informed *ou* told me of this fact, having acquainted me with this fact ◆ **nous vous informons que nos bureaux ouvrent à 8 heures** we are pleased to inform you that *ou* for your information our offices open at 8 a.m. ◆ **s'il vient, vous voudrez bien m'en ~** if he comes, please let me know *ou* inform me *ou* tell me ◆ **on vous a mal informé** *(faussement)* you've been misinformed *ou* wrongly informed; *(imparfaitement)* you've been badly informed *ou* ill-informed ◆ **nous ne sommes pas assez informés** we don't have enough information

[2] *(Philos)* **les concepts informent la matière** concepts impart *ou* give form to matter

VI *(Jur)* ◆ **~ sur un crime** to inquire into *ou* investigate a crime ◆ **~ contre X** to start inquiries against person *ou* persons unknown

VPR **s'informer** *(d'un fait)* to inquire, to find out, to ask (*de* about); *(dans une matière)* to inform o.s. (*sur* about); ◆ **informez-vous s'il est arrivé** find out *ou* ascertain whether he has arrived ◆ **où puis-je m'~ de l'heure/à ce sujet/si ... ?** where can I inquire *ou* find out *ou* ask about the time/about this matter/whether ...? ◆ **s'~ de la santé de qn** to ask after *ou* inquire after *ou* about sb's health

informulé, e /ɛ̃fɔʀmyle/ ADJ unformulated

inforoute /ɛ̃foʀut/ NF information superhighway

infortune /ɛ̃fɔʀtyn/ NF *(= revers)* misfortune; *(= adversité)* ill fortune, misfortune ◆ **~s conjugales** marital misfortunes ◆ **le récit de ses ~s** the tale of his woes *ou* misfortunes ◆ **compagnon/frère/sœur d'~** companion/brother/sister in misfortune

infortuné, e /ɛ̃fɔʀtyne/ ADJ *[personne]* hapless *(épith)*, ill-fated, wretched; *[démarche, décision]* ill-fated NM,F (poor) wretch

infoutu, e‡ /ɛ̃futy/ **infoutu de** LOC ADJ ◆ **~ de faire quoi que ce soit** damn* *ou* bloody *(Brit)*‡ incapable of doing anything ◆ **je suis ~ de m'en souvenir** I can't for the life of me remember*

infra /ɛ̃fʀa/ ADV ◆ **voir ~** see below

infraction /ɛ̃fʀaksjɔ̃/ NF *(= délit)* offence ◆ **~ à** *[+ loi, règlement, sécurité]* breach of ◆ **~ au code de la route** driving offence ◆ **être en ~** to be committing an offence, to be breaking *ou* in breach of the law ◆ **~ à la loi** breach *ou* violation *ou* infraction of the law ◆ **~ fiscale** breach of the tax code ◆ **toute ~ sera punie** all offenders will be prosecuted

infranchissable /ɛ̃fʀɑ̃ʃisabl/ ADJ *(lit)* impassable; *(fig)* insurmountable, insuperable

infrangible /ɛ̃fʀɑ̃ʒibl/ ADJ *(littér)* infrangible *(littér)*

infrarouge /ɛ̃fʀaʀuʒ/ ADJ, NM infrared ◆ **missile guidé par ~** heat-seeking missile

infrason /ɛ̃fʀasɔ̃/ NM infrasonic vibration

infrastructure /ɛ̃fʀastʀyktyʀ/ NF *(Constr)* substructure, understructure; *(Écon)* infrastructure; *(Aviation)* ground installations ◆ **~ routière/de transports** road/transport infrastructure

infréquentable /ɛ̃fʀekɑ̃tabl/ ADJ not to be associated with ◆ **ce sont des gens ~s** they're people you just don't associate with *ou* mix with

infroissable /ɛ̃fʀwasabl/ ADJ crease-resistant, non-crease *(épith)*

infructueux, -euse /ɛ̃fʀyktyø, øz/ ADJ *[tentative, effort, réunion]* fruitless, unsuccessful; *[démarche]* unsuccessful

infumable /ɛ̃fymabl/ ADJ unsmokable

infus, e /ɛ̃fy, yz/ ADJ *(littér)* innate, inborn (*à* in) → **science**

infuser /ɛ̃fyze/ ▸ conjug 1 ◂ VT *(littér)* *[+ idée, conviction]* to instil (*à* into); ◆ **~ un sang nouveau à qch/à qn** to infuse *ou* inject *ou* instil new life into sth/into sb VI ◆ **(faire) ~** *[+ tisane]* to infuse; *[+ thé]* to brew, to infuse, to steep *(US)* ◆ **laisser ~ le thé quelques minutes** leave the tea to brew *ou* infuse a few minutes ◆ **le thé est-il assez infusé ?** has the tea brewed *ou* infused (long) enough?

infusion /ɛ̃fyzjɔ̃/ NF [1] *(= tisane)* infusion, herb tea ◆ **~ de tilleul** lime tea ◆ **boire une ~** to drink some herb tea *ou* an infusion ◆ **la verveine se boit en ~** verbena is drunk as an infusion [2] *(= action)* infusion ◆ **préparé par ~** prepared by infusion

ingambe /ɛ̃gɑ̃b/ ADJ spry, nimble

ingénier (s') /ɛ̃ʒenje/ ▸ conjug 7 ◂ VPR ◆ **s'~ à faire** to strive (hard) to do, to try hard to do ◆ **dès que j'ai rangé, il s'ingénie à tout remettre en désordre** *(iro)* as soon as I've tidied things up, he goes out of his way *ou* he contrives to mess them up again

ingénierie /ɛ̃ʒeniʀi/ NF engineering ◆ **~ financière/informatique/génétique** financial/computer/genetic engineering ◆ **~ inverse** reverse engineering

ingénieriste /ɛ̃ʒeniʀist/ NMF engineer

ingénieur, e /ɛ̃ʒenjœʀ/ NM, F engineer ◆ **~ chimiste/électricien** chemical/electrical engineer ◆ **~ agronome** agronomist ◆ **~ des mines/en génie civil** mining/civil engineer ◆ **~ système** system(s) engineer ◆ **~ électronicien** electronic engineer ◆ **~ du son** sound engineer ◆ **~ des eaux et forêts** forestry expert ◆ **~ des travaux publics** construction *ou* civil engineer; → **conseil**

ingénieusement /ɛ̃ʒenjøzmɑ̃/ ADV ingeniously, cleverly

ingénieux, -ieuse /ɛ̃ʒenjø, jøz/ ADJ ingenious, clever

ingéniosité /ɛ̃ʒenjozite/ NF ingenuity, cleverness

ingénu, e /ɛ̃ʒeny/ ADJ ingenuous, artless, naïve NM,F ingenuous *ou* artless *ou* naïve person NF **ingénue** *(Théât)* ingénue ◆ **jouer les ~es** to play ingénue roles; *(fig)* to pretend to be all sweet and innocent

ingénuité /ɛ̃ʒenɥite/ NF ingenuousness, artlessness, naïvety

ingénument /ɛ̃ʒenymɑ̃/ ADV ingenuously, artlessly, naïvely

ingérable /ɛ̃ʒeʀabl/ ADJ unmanageable

ingérence /ɛ̃ʒeʀɑ̃s/ NF interference, interfering *(NonC)*, meddling *(NonC)* (*dans* in); ◆ **le devoir d'~** *(Pol)* the duty to interfere

ingérer /ɛ̃ʒeʀe/ ▸ conjug 6 ◂ VT to ingest VPR **s'ingérer** ◆ **s'~ dans** to interfere in *ou* with, to meddle in

ingestion /ɛ̃ʒɛstjɔ̃/ NF ingestion

ingouvernable /ɛ̃guvɛʀnabl/ ADJ *[pays, passion, sentiment]* ungovernable ◆ **dans la tempête, le voilier était ~** in the storm it was impossible to steer the yacht

ingrat, e /ɛ̃gʀa, at/ ADJ [1] *[personne]* ungrateful (*envers* to, towards) [2] *(fig)* *[tâche, métier, sujet]* thankless *(épith)*, unrewarding; *[sol]* infertile, difficult; *[visage]* unprepossessing, unattractive; *[contrée]* bleak, hostile; *[mémoire]* unreliable, treacherous; → **âge** NM,F ungrateful person ◆ **tu n'es qu'un ~ !** how ungrateful of you! ◆ **vous n'aurez pas affaire à un ~** I won't forget what you've done (for me)

ingratitude /ɛ̃gʀatityd/ NF ingratitude, ungratefulness (*envers* to, towards); ◆ **avec ~** ungratefully

ingrédient /ɛ̃gʀedjɑ̃/ NM *[de recette, produit]* ingredient; *[de situation, crise]* ingredient, component

inguérissable /ɛ̃geʀisabl/ ADJ *[maladie, malade, blessure, paresse]* incurable; *[chagrin, amour]* inconsolable

inguinal, e (mpl **-aux**) /ɛ̃gɥinal, o/ ADJ inguinal

ingurgitation /ɛ̃gyʀʒitasjɔ̃/ NF ingurgitation

ingurgiter /ɛ̃gyʀʒite/ ▸ conjug 1 ◂ VT *[+ nourriture]* to swallow; *[+ vin]* to gulp (down), to swill *(péj)*; *(fig)* to ingest ◆ **faire ~ de la nourriture/une boisson à qn** to make sb swallow food/a drink, to force food/a drink down sb ◆ **faire ~ aux téléspectateurs des émissions insipides** to feed television viewers a diet of dull programmes ◆ **faire ~ des connaissances à qn** to force facts down sb's throat ◆ **faire ~ des données à un ordinateur** to feed data into a computer

inhabile /inabil/ ADJ *(littér)* [1] *(= peu judicieux)* *[discours, politicien]* inept; *[manœuvre]* inept, clumsy [2] *(= gauche)* *[apprenti]* unskilful, clumsy; *[gestes, mains, dessin, travail]* clumsy, awkward [3] *(Jur)* incapable ◆ **~ à tester** incapable of making a will

inhabileté /inabilte/ NF *(littér)* [1] *[de politicien, discours]* ineptitude; *[de manœuvre]* ineptitude, clumsiness [2] *[d'apprenti]* unskilfulness; *[de gestes, mains, dessin, travail]* clumsiness, awkwardness

inhabilité /inabilite/ NF *(Jur)* incapacity (*à* to)

inhabitable /inabitabl/ ADJ uninhabitable

> ⚠ **inhabitable** ne se traduit pas par le mot anglais **inhabitable**, qui a le sens de 'habitable'.

inhabité, e /inabite/ ADJ *[région]* uninhabited; *[maison]* uninhabited, unoccupied ◆ **la maison a l'air ~(e)** it doesn't look as if anyone is living in the house

> ⚠ **inhabité** ne se traduit pas par **inhabited**, qui a le sens de 'habité'.

inhabituel, -elle /inabitɥɛl/ ADJ unusual, unaccustomed

inhabituellement /inabitɥɛlmɑ̃/ ADV unusually

inhalateur /inalatœʀ/ NM inhaler

inhalation /inalasjɔ̃/ NF inhalation ◆ **faire des ~s** *(Méd)* to use steam inhalations

inhaler /inale/ ▸ conjug 1 ◂ VT *(Méd)* to inhale; *(littér)* to inhale, to breathe (in)

inharmonieux, -ieuse /inaʀmɔnjø, jøz/ ADJ *(littér)* inharmonious

inhérence /ineʀɑ̃s/ NF *(Philos)* inherence

inhérent, e /ineʀɑ̃, ɑ̃t/ ADJ inherent (*à* in, to)

inhibé, e /inibe/ (ptp de **inhiber**) ADJ inhibited NM,F inhibited person

inhiber /inibe/ ▸ conjug 1 ◂ VT *(Physiol, Psych)* to inhibit

inhibiteur, -trice /inibitœʀ, tʀis/ ADJ inhibitory, inhibitive NM *(Chim, Méd)* inhibitor

inhibition /inibisjɔ̃/ NF *(Chim, Physiol, Psych)* inhibition

inhospitalier, -ière /inɔspitalje, jɛʀ/ ADJ inhospitable

inhumain, e /inymɛ̃, ɛn/ ADJ inhuman

inhumainement /inymɛnmɑ̃/ ADV *(littér)* inhumanly

inhumanité /inymanite/ NF *(littér)* inhumanity

inhumation /inymasjɔ̃/ NF burial, interment, inhumation *(frm)*

inhumer /inyme/ ▸ conjug 1 ◂ VT to bury, to inter *(frm)*; → **permis**

inimaginable /inimaʒinabl/ ADJ unthinkable; *(sens affaibli)* unimaginable, unbelievable NM ◆ **l'~ s'est produit** the unthinkable happened

inimitable /inimitabl/ ADJ inimitable

inimitié /inimitje/ NF enmity ◆ **avoir de l'~ pour** *ou* **contre qn** to have hostile feelings towards sb

ininflammable /inɛ̃flamabl/ ADJ nonflammable, noninflammable

inintelligence /inɛ̃teliʒɑ̃s/ NF *[de personne, esprit]* lack of intelligence, unintelligence ◆ **l'~ du problème** *(= incompréhension)* the failure to understand the problem, the lack of understanding of the problem

inintelligent, e /inɛ̃teliʒɑ̃, ɑ̃t/ ADJ unintelligent

inintelligibilité /inɛ̃teliʒibilite/ NF unintelligibility

inintelligible /inɛ̃teliʒibl/ ADJ unintelligible

inintelligiblement /inɛ̃teliʒibləmɑ̃/ ADV unintelligibly

inintéressant, e /inɛ̃teʀesɑ̃, ɑ̃t/ ADJ uninteresting

ininterrompu, e /inɛ̃teʀɔ̃py/ ADJ *[suite, ligne]* unbroken; *[file de voitures]* unbroken, steady *(épith)*, uninterrupted; *[flot, vacarme]* steady *(épith)*, uninterrupted, nonstop; *[hausse, baisse]* steady; *[effort, travail]* unremitting, continuous, steady *(épith)* ◆ **12 heures de sommeil ~** 12 hours' uninterrupted *ou* unbroken sleep ◆ **30 ans de succès ~** 30 years of continuous *ou* unbroken success ◆ **programme de musique ~e** programme of continuous music

inique /inik/ ADJ iniquitous

iniquité /inikite/ NF *(gén, Rel)* iniquity

initial, e (mpl **-iaux**) /inisjal, jo/ ADJ initial; → **vitesse** NF **initiale** initial ◆ **mettre ses ~es sur qch** to put one's initials on sth, to initial sth

initialement /inisjalmɑ̃/ ADV initially

initialisation /inisjalisasjɔ̃/ NF *(Ordin)* initialization

initialiser /inisjalize/ ▸ conjug 1 ◂ VT *(Ordin)* to initialize

initiateur, -trice /inisjatœʀ, tʀis/ ADJ innovatory NM,F *(= maître, précurseur)* initiator; *[de mode, technique]* innovator, pioneer; *[de projet, mouvement artistique]* initiator, originator

initiation /inisjasjɔ̃/ NF initiation *(à* into); ◆ **stage d'~ à l'informatique** introductory *ou* beginners' course in computing ◆ **~ à la linguistique** *(titre d'ouvrage)* introduction to linguistics; → **rite**

initiatique /inisjatik/ ADJ *[rite, cérémonie]* initiation *(épith)*, initiatory; *[roman, film]* rite(s)-of-passage *(épith)* ◆ **parcours** *ou* **voyage** *ou* **quête ~** initiatory voyage *ou* journey ◆ **épreuves ~s** initiation rites

initiative /inisjativ/ NF *(gén, Pol)* initiative ◆ **prendre l'~ d'une action/de faire qch** to take the initiative for an action/in doing sth ◆ **garder l'~** to keep the initiative ◆ **avoir de l'~** to have initiative ◆ **~ de paix** peace initiative ◆ **~ de défense stratégique** Strategic Defense Initiative ◆ **à** *ou* **sur l'~ de qn** on sb's initiative ◆ **à l'~ de la France ...** following France's initiative ... ◆ **conférence à l'~ des USA** conference initiated by the USA ◆ **de sa propre ~** on his own initiative; → **droit³, syndicat**

initié, e /inisje/ (ptp de **initier**) ADJ initiated ◆ **le lecteur ~/non ~** the initiated/uninitiated reader NM,F initiate ◆ **les ~s** the initiated *ou* initiates; → **délit**

initier /inisje/ ▸ conjug 7 ◂ VT 1 *[+ personne]* to initiate *(à* into); ◆ **~ qn aux joies de la voile** to introduce sb to the joys of sailing 2 *[+ enquête, dialogue, politique]* to initiate VPR **s'initier** to become initiated, to initiate o.s. *(à* into); ◆ **j'ai besoin d'un peu de temps pour m'~ à l'informatique** I need some time to get to know a bit about computers

injectable /ɛ̃ʒɛktabl/ ADJ injectable

injecté, e /ɛ̃ʒɛkte/ (ptp de **injecter**) ADJ *(Méd, Tech)* injected *(de* with); *[visage]* congested ◆ **yeux ~s de sang** bloodshot eyes

injecter /ɛ̃ʒɛkte/ ▸ conjug 1 ◂ VT *(Méd, Tech)* to inject ◆ **elle s'est injecté de l'insuline** she injected herself with insulin ◆ **~ des fonds dans une entreprise** to pump money into a project

injecteur, -trice /ɛ̃ʒɛktœʀ, tʀis/ ADJ injection *(épith)* NM injector

injection /ɛ̃ʒɛksjɔ̃/ NF *(gén)* injection; *(Méd : avec une poire)* douche ◆ **il s'est fait une ~ d'insuline** he injected himself with insulin ◆ **~ d'argent frais** injection of fresh money, new injection of money ◆ **à ~** *[seringue, tube]* injection *(épith)*; *[moteur, système]* fuel-injection *(épith)* ◆ **à ~ électronique/directe** *[moteur]* with electronic/direct fuel injection

injoignable /ɛ̃ʒwaɲabl/ ADJ impossible to contact

injonction /ɛ̃ʒɔ̃ksjɔ̃/ NF injunction, command, order ◆ **sur son ~** on his orders *ou* command ◆ **~ thérapeutique** *(Jur) probation order which stipulates that the offender complete a drug rehabilitation programme*

injouable /ɛ̃ʒwabl/ ADJ *[musique]* unplayable; *[pièce]* unperformable; *(Sport) [coup, match, terrain]* unplayable

injure /ɛ̃ʒyʀ/ NF 1 *(= insulte)* term of abuse ◆ **"salaud" est une ~** "bastard" is a term of abuse ◆ **une bordée d'~s** a stream of abuse *ou* insults ◆ **~ et diffamation** *(Jur)* libel 2 *(littér = affront)* **faire ~ à qn** to offend sb ◆ **il m'a fait l'~ de ne pas venir** he insulted me by not coming ◆ **ce serait lui faire ~ que de le croire si naïf** it would be insulting to him to think that he could be so naïve 3 *(littér = dommage)* **l'~ des ans** the ravages of time ◆ **l'~ du sort** the slings and arrows of fortune *(littér)*

> ⚠ **injure** se traduit rarement par **injury**, qui a le sens de 'blessure'.

injurier /ɛ̃ʒyʀje/ ▸ conjug 7 ◂ VT to abuse, to shout abuse at

> ⚠ **injurier** ne se traduit pas par **to injure**, qui a le sens de 'blesser'.

injurieux, -ieuse /ɛ̃ʒyʀjø, jøz/ ADJ *[termes, propos]* abusive, offensive; *[attitude, article]* insulting, offensive *(pour, à l'égard de* to)

injuste /ɛ̃ʒyst/ ADJ 1 *(= inéquitable)* unjust 2 *(= partial)* unfair *(avec, envers* to, towards); ◆ **ne sois pas ~ !** be fair!

injustement /ɛ̃ʒystəmɑ̃/ ADV *[accuser, punir]* unfairly ◆ **~ oublié** unjustly forgotten

injustice /ɛ̃ʒystis/ NF 1 *(= iniquité)* injustice; *(= partialité)* unfairness ◆ **il a éprouvé un sentiment d'~** he felt he had been treated unfairly ◆ **lutter contre l'~ sociale** to fight against social injustice 2 *(= acte)* injustice ◆ **réparer des ~s** to right wrongs ◆ **il a été victime d'une ~** he was unfairly treated

injustifiable /ɛ̃ʒystifjabl/ ADJ unjustifiable

injustifié, e /ɛ̃ʒystifje/ GRAMMAIRE ACTIVE 53.3 ADJ unjustified, unwarranted

inlandsis /inlɑ̃dsis/ NM *(glaciaire)* icecap

inlassable /ɛ̃lasabl/ ADJ *[personne]* tireless, untiring; *[zèle]* unflagging, tireless; *[patience]* inexhaustible

inlassablement /ɛ̃lasabləmɑ̃/ ADV *[continuer, poursuivre]* tirelessly ◆ **répéter qch ~** to never tire of repeating sth ◆ **revenir ~** to keep (on) coming back

inné, e /i(n)ne/ ADJ innate, inborn ◆ **idées ~es** innate ideas

innervant, e /inɛʀvɑ̃, ɑ̃t/ ADJ ◆ **gaz ~** nerve gas

innervation /inɛʀvasjɔ̃/ NF innervation

innerver /inɛʀve/ ▸ conjug 1 ◂ VT to innervate

innocemment /inɔsamɑ̃/ ADV innocently

innocence /inɔsɑ̃s/ NF *(gén)* innocence ◆ **l'~ de ces farces** the innocence *ou* harmlessness of these pranks ◆ **il l'a fait en toute ~** he did it in all innocence, he meant no harm (by it) ◆ **tu n'as tout de même pas l'~ de croire que ...** come on, you're not so naïve as to believe that ...

innocent, e /inɔsɑ̃, ɑ̃t/ GRAMMAIRE ACTIVE 45.2 ADJ *(gén, Jur, Rel)* innocent ◆ **être ~ de qch** to be innocent of sth ◆ **remarque/petite farce bien ~e** quite innocent *ou* harmless remark/little prank ◆ **il est vraiment ~ !** he is a real innocent! ◆ **~ comme l'enfant** *ou* **l'agneau qui vient de naître** as innocent as a new-born babe NM,F 1 *(Jur)* innocent person 2 *(= candide)* innocent (person); *(= niais)* simpleton ◆ **ne fais pas l'~** don't act *ou* play the innocent (with me) ◆ **quel ~ tu fais !** how innocent can you be?, how innocent you are! ◆ **l'~ du village** the village simpleton *ou* idiot ◆ **aux ~s les mains pleines** *(Prov)* fortune favours the innocent; → **massacre**

innocenter /inɔsɑ̃te/ ▸ conjug 1 ◂ VT *(Jur = disculper)* to clear, to prove innocent *(de* of); *(= excuser)* to excuse, to justify

innocuité /inɔkɥite/ NF *(frm)* innocuousness *(frm)*, harmlessness

innombrable /i(n)nɔ̃bʀabl/ ADJ *[détails, péripéties, variétés]* innumerable, countless; *[foule]* vast

innomé, e /i(n)nɔme/ ADJ ⇒ **innommé**

innommable /i(n)nɔmabl/ ADJ *[conduite, action]* unspeakable, loathsome, unmentionable; *[nourriture, ordures]* foul, vile

innommé, e /i(n)nɔme/ ADJ *(= non dénommé)* unnamed; *(= obscur, vague)* nameless

innovant, e /inɔvɑ̃, ɑ̃t/ ADJ innovative

innovateur, -trice /inɔvatœʀ, tʀis/ ADJ innovatory, innovative NM,F innovator

innovation /inɔvasjɔ̃/ NF innovation

innover /inɔve/ ▸ conjug 1 ◂ VI to innovate ◆ **~ en matière de mode/d'art** to break new ground *ou* innovate in the field of fashion/of art ◆ **ce peintre innove par rapport à ses prédécesseurs** this painter is breaking new ground compared with his predecessors

inobservable /inɔpsɛʀvabl/ ADJ unobservable

inobservance /inɔpsɛʀvɑ̃s/ NF *(littér)* inobservance, non-observance

inobservation /inɔpsɛʀvasjɔ̃/ NF *(littér, Jur)* non-observance, inobservance

inobservé, e /inɔpsɛʀve/ ADJ *(littér, Jur)* unobserved

inoccupation /inɔkypasjɔ̃/ NF *(littér)* inoccupation *(littér)*, inactivity

inoccupé, e /inɔkype/ ADJ 1 *(= vide) [appartement]* unoccupied, empty; *[siège, emplacement, poste]* vacant, unoccupied, empty 2 *(= oisif)* unoccupied, idle

in-octavo /inɔktavo/ ADJ INV, NM INV octavo

inoculable /inɔkylabl/ ADJ inoculable

inoculation /inɔkylasjɔ̃/ NF *(Méd) (volontaire)* inoculation; *(accidentelle)* infection ◆ **l'~ (accidentelle) d'un virus/d'une maladie dans l'organisme par blessure** the (accidental) infection of the organism by a virus/by disease as a result of an injury

inoculer /inɔkyle/ ► conjug 1 ◄ VT [1] *(Méd)* ~ **un virus/une maladie à qn** *(volontairement)* to inoculate sb with a virus/a disease; *(accidentellement)* to infect sb with a virus/a disease ◆ ~ **un malade** to inoculate a patient *(contre* against) [2] *(fig = communiquer)* ~ **une passion/son enthousiasme à qn** to infect *ou* imbue sb with a passion/one's enthusiasm ◆ ~ **un vice à qn** to pass on a vice to sb

inodore /inɔdɔʀ/ ADJ *[gaz]* odourless; *[fleur]* scentless; *(fig) [personne, film, livre]* insipid; → **incolore**

inoffensif, -ive /inɔfɑ̃sif, iv/ ADJ *[personne, plaisanterie]* inoffensive, harmless, innocuous; *[piqûre, animal, remède]* harmless, innocuous

inondable /inɔ̃dabl/ ADJ liable to flooding

inondation /inɔ̃dasjɔ̃/ NF [1] *(= débordement d'eaux)* flood ◆ **la fuite a provoqué une ~ dans la salle de bains** the leak flooded the bathroom [2] *(= afflux)* flood, deluge ◆ **une véritable ~ de produits allégés** a flood of low-fat products

inonder /inɔ̃de/ ► conjug 1 ◄ VT [1] *(= submerger) [+ prés, cave]* to flood ◆ **populations inondées** flood victims, victims of flooding ◆ **tu as inondé toute la cuisine** * you've flooded the whole kitchen

[2] *(= envahir) [+ marché]* to flood, to swamp, to inundate *(de* with); ◆ **la foule a inondé les rues** the crowd flooded onto the streets ◆ **nous sommes inondés de lettres** we have been inundated with letters, we have received a flood of letters ◆ **inondé de soleil** bathed in sunlight ◆ **inondé de lumière** flooded with light ◆ **la joie inonda son cœur** he was overcome with joy

[3] *(= tremper)* to soak, to drench ◆ **se faire ~ (par la pluie)** to get soaked *ou* drenched (by the rain) ◆ **je suis inondé** I'm soaked (through) *ou* drenched *ou* saturated * ◆ ~ **ses cheveux de parfum** to saturate one's hair with scent ◆ **la sueur/le sang inondait son visage** the sweat/blood was pouring *ou* streaming down his face ◆ **inondé de larmes** *[+ joues]* streaming with tears; *[+ yeux]* full of tears

inopérable /inɔpeʀabl/ ADJ inoperable

inopérant, e /inɔpeʀɑ̃, ɑ̃t/ ADJ ineffective ◆ **cet additif rend ~s les pots catalytiques** this additive makes catalytic converters ineffective *ou* stops catalytic converters working

inopiné, e /inɔpine/ ADJ *[rencontre]* unexpected ◆ **mort ~e** sudden death

inopinément /inɔpinemɑ̃/ ADV unexpectedly

inopportun, e /inɔpɔʀtœ̃, yn/ ADJ *[demande, remarque]* ill-timed, inopportune, untimely ◆ **le moment est** ~ it's not the right *ou* best moment, it's not the most opportune moment

inopportunément /inɔpɔʀtynemɑ̃/ ADV inopportunely

inopportunité /inɔpɔʀtynite/ NF *(littér)* inopportuneness, untimeliness

inopposabilité /inɔpozabilite/ NF *(Jur)* non-invocability

inopposable /inɔpozabl/ ADJ *(Jur)* non-invocable

inorganique /inɔʀganik/ ADJ inorganic

inorganisé, e /inɔʀganize/ ADJ *[compagnie, industrie]* unorganized; *[personne]* disorganized, unorganized; *(Sci)* unorganized

inoubliable /inublijabl/ ADJ unforgettable

inouï, e /inwi/ ADJ *[événement, circonstances]* unprecedented, unheard-of; *[nouvelle]* extraordinary, incredible; *[vitesse, audace, force]* incredible, unbelievable ◆ **c'est/il est ~ !** it's/he's incredible! *ou* unbelievable!

inox /inɔks/ ADJ, NM (abrév de **inoxydable**) stainless steel ◆ **couteau/évier (en)** ~ stainless steel knife/sink

inoxydable /inɔksidabl/ ADJ *[acier, alliage]* stainless; *[couteau]* stainless steel *(épith)* NM stainless steel

in petto /inpeto/ LOC ADV ◆ **quel idiot, se dit-il ~** "what a fool", he thought *ou* said to himself

INPI /iɛnpei/ NM (abrév de **Institut national de la propriété industrielle**) → **institut**

input /input/ NM *(Écon, Ordin)* input

inqualifiable /ɛ̃kalifjabl/ ADJ *[conduite, propos]* unspeakable ◆ **d'une ~ bassesse** unspeakably low

in-quarto /inkwaʀto/ ADJ INV, NM INV quarto

inquiet, inquiète /ɛ̃kje, ɛ̃kjɛt/ ADJ *[personne] (momentanément)* worried, anxious; *(par nature)* anxious; *[gestes]* uneasy; *[attente, regards]* uneasy, anxious; *[sommeil]* uneasy, troubled; *(littér) [curiosité, amour]* restless ◆ **je suis ~ de son absence** I'm worried at his absence, I'm worried *ou* anxious that he's not here ◆ **je suis ~ de ne pas le voir** I'm worried *ou* anxious at not seeing him ◆ **je suis ~ qu'il ne m'ait pas téléphoné** I'm worried that he hasn't phoned me ◆ **c'est un (éternel)** ~ he's a (perpetual) worrier

inquiétant, e /ɛ̃kjetɑ̃, ɑ̃t/ ADJ *[situation, tendance]* worrying; *[signe, expérience, phénomène]* disturbing, disquieting *(frm)*, unsettling; *[propos, personnage]* disturbing

inquiéter /ɛ̃kjete/ ► conjug 6 ◄ VT [1] *(= alarmer)* to worry ◆ **la santé de mon fils m'inquiète** I'm worried about my son's health, my son's health worries me ◆ **le champion commence à ~ son adversaire** the champion is starting to get his opponent worried ◆ **ils n'ont jamais pu ~ leurs adversaires** *(Sport)* they never presented a real threat to their opponents

[2] *(= harceler) [+ ville, pays]* to harass ◆ **l'amant de la victime ne fut pas inquiété (par la police)** the victim's lover wasn't troubled *ou* bothered by the police

VPR **s'inquiéter** *(= s'alarmer)* to worry ◆ **ne t'inquiète pas** don't worry ◆ **il n'y a pas de quoi s'~** there's nothing to worry about *ou* get worried about ◆ **t'inquiète !** ‡ *(= ça ne te regarde pas)* none of your business! ‡, mind your own business! ‡, keep your nose out of it! ‡

◆ **s'inquiéter de** *(= s'enquérir)* to inquire about; *(= se soucier)* to worry about, to trouble about, to bother about ◆ **s'~ de l'heure/de la santé de qn** to inquire what time it is/about sb's health ◆ **ne t'inquiète pas de ça, je m'en occupe** don't (you) trouble yourself *ou* worry *ou* bother about that - I'll see to it ◆ **sans s'~ des circonstances/conséquences** without worrying *ou* bothering about the circumstances/consequences ◆ **sans s'~ de savoir si ...** without bothering to find out if ...

◆ **s'inquiéter pour** ◆ **je ne m'inquiète pas pour elle, elle se débrouille toujours** I'm not worried about her, she always manages somehow

inquiétude /ɛ̃kjetyd/ NF anxiety; *(littér = agitation)* restlessness ◆ **donner de l'~** *ou* **des ~s à qn** to worry sb, to give sb cause for worry *ou* anxiety ◆ **avoir** *ou* **éprouver des ~s au sujet de** to feel anxious *ou* worried about, to feel some anxiety about ◆ **sujet d'~** cause for concern ◆ **soyez sans ~** have no fear ◆ **fou d'~** mad with worry

inquisiteur, -trice /ɛ̃kizitœʀ, tʀis/ ADJ inquisitive, prying NM inquisitor ◆ **le Grand Inquisiteur** *(Hist)* the Grand Inquisitor

inquisition /ɛ̃kizisjɔ̃/ NF [1] *(Hist)* **l'Inquisition** the Inquisition ◆ **la Sainte Inquisition** the Holy Office [2] *(péj = enquête)* inquisition

inquisitoire /ɛ̃kizitwaʀ/ ADJ *(Jur)* ◆ **procédure** ~ proceeding presided over by an interrogating judge

inquisitorial, e (mpl **-iaux**) /ɛ̃kizitɔʀjal, jo/ ADJ inquisitorial

INRA /inʀa/ NM (abrév de **Institut national de la recherche agronomique**) → **institut**

inracontable /ɛ̃ʀakɔ̃tabl/ ADJ *(= trop osé)* unrepeatable; *(= trop compliqué)* unrecountable

inratable * /ɛ̃ʀatabl/ ADJ ◆ **ce plat est** ~ you can't go wrong with this dish ◆ **cet examen est** ~ you'd have to be an idiot to make a mess * of this exam

INRI (abrév de **Iesus Nazarenus Rex Iudaeorum**) INRI

insaisissabilité /ɛ̃sezisabilite/ NF *(Jur)* non-distrainability

insaisissable /ɛ̃sezisabl/ ADJ *[fugitif, ennemi]* elusive; *[personnage]* enigmatic, elusive; *[nuance, différence]* imperceptible, indiscernible; *(Jur) [biens]* not liable to seizure, non-distrainable

insalissable /ɛ̃salisabl/ ADJ dirt-proof

insalubre /ɛ̃salybʀ/ ADJ *[climat]* insalubrious, unhealthy; *[logement, bâtiment]* unfit for habitation; *[profession]* unhealthy

insalubrité /ɛ̃salybʀite/ NF *[de climat]* insalubrity, unhealthiness; *[de logement, bâtiment]* insalubrity; *[de profession]* unhealthiness ◆ **l'immeuble a été démoli pour ~** the building was demolished because it was unfit for habitation

insanité /ɛ̃sanite/ NF *(= caractère)* insanity, madness; *(= acte)* insane act; *(= propos)* insane talk *(NonC)* ◆ **proférer des ~s** to talk insanely

insatiabilité /ɛ̃sasjabilite/ NF insatiability

insatiable /ɛ̃sasjabl/ ADJ insatiable

insatiablement /ɛ̃sasjabləmɑ̃/ ADV insatiably

insatisfaction /ɛ̃satisfaksjɔ̃/ NF dissatisfaction

insatisfaisant, e /ɛ̃satisfəzɑ̃, ɑ̃t/ ADJ unsatisfactory; *(sur devoir scolaire)* poor

insatisfait, e /ɛ̃satisfɛ, ɛt/ ADJ *[personne] (= non comblé)* unsatisfied; *(= mécontent)* dissatisfied *(de* with); *[désir, passion]* unsatisfied NM,F ◆ **c'est un éternel** ~ he's never satisfied, he's perpetually dissatisfied ◆ **les ~s** the malcontents

insaturé, e /ɛ̃satyʀe/ ADJ *(Chim)* unsaturated

inscriptible /ɛ̃skʀiptibl/ ADJ *(gén)* inscribable; *(Ordin)* writable

inscription /ɛ̃skʀipsjɔ̃/ NF [1] *(= texte)* inscription ◆ **mur couvert d'~s** *(graffiti)* wall covered in graffiti; *(anciennes)* wall covered in inscriptions

[2] *(= action)* **l'~ du texte n'est pas comprise dans le prix** engraving is not included in the price ◆ **l'~ d'une question à l'ordre du jour** putting an item on the agenda ◆ **cela a nécessité l'~ de nouvelles dépenses au budget** this meant the budget had to accommodate additional costs

[3] *(= immatriculation) (gén)* registration; *(Univ)* registration, enrolment *(Brit)*, enrollment *(US) (à* at); ◆ **l'~ à un parti/club** joining a party/club ◆ **l'~ des enfants à l'école est obligatoire** it is compulsory to enrol *ou* register children for school ◆ **il y a déjà 20 ~s pour la sortie de jeudi** 20 people have already signed up for Thursday's outing ◆ **les ~s (en faculté) seront closes le 30 octobre** the closing date for enrolment *ou* registration (at the university) is 30 October ◆ **dossier d'~** *(gén)* registration form; *(Univ)* admission form, ≃ UCAS form *(Brit)* ◆ **votre ~ sur la liste dépend**

de ... the inclusion of your name on the list depends on ... ◆ **faire son ~** *ou* **prendre ses ~s † en faculté** to register *ou* enrol at university ◆ **les ~s sont en baisse de 5%** enrolment is down by 5% ◆ **droits d'~** enrolment *ou* registration fees ◆ **~ électorale** registration on the electoral roll *(Brit)*, voter registration *(US)*

4 *(Math)* inscribing

COMP **inscription de faux** *(Jur)* challenge *(to validity of document)*

inscription hypothécaire mortgage registration

inscription maritime registration of sailors *(in France)* ◆ **l'Inscription maritime** *(= service)* the Register of Sailors

inscrire /ɛ̃skʀiʀ/ ▸ conjug 39 ◂ VT 1 *(= marquer)* *[+ nom, date]* to note down, to write down; *(Ftbl)* *[+ but]* to score, to notch up ◆ **~ des dépenses au budget** to list *ou* include expenses in the budget ◆ **~ une question à l'ordre du jour** to put *ou* place a question on the agenda ◆ **ce n'est pas inscrit à l'ordre du jour** it isn't (down) on the agenda ◆ **~ qch dans la pierre/le marbre** to inscribe *ou* engrave sth on stone/marble ◆ **c'est demeuré inscrit dans ma mémoire** it has remained inscribed *ou* etched on my memory ◆ **sa culpabilité est inscrite sur son visage** his guilt is written all over his face *ou* on his face ◆ **greffier, inscrivez (sous ma dictée)** clerk, take *ou* note this down ◆ **le temple est inscrit au patrimoine mondial de l'humanité** the temple is listed as a World Heritage site ◆ **son nom est** *ou* **il est inscrit sur la liste des gagnants** his name is (written) on the list of winners ◆ **il a inscrit une quatrième victoire à son palmarès** he has added a fourth victory to his record

2 *(= enrôler)* *[+ client]* to put down; *[+ soldat]* to enlist; *[+ étudiant]* to register, to enrol ◆ **~ qn sur une liste d'attente** to put sb down *ou* put sb's name down on a waiting list ◆ **je ne peux pas vous ~ avant le 3 août** I can't put you down for an appointment *ou* I can't give you an appointment before 3 August ◆ **(faire) ~ un enfant à l'école** to put a child *ou* child's name down for school, to enrol *ou* register a child for school ◆ **(faire) ~ qn à la cantine/pour une vaccination** to register sb at the canteen/for a vaccination

3 *(Math)* to inscribe

VPR **s'inscrire** 1 *(= apparaître)* **un message s'inscrivit sur l'écran** a message came up *ou* appeared on the screen ◆ **l'avion ennemi s'inscrivit dans le viseur** the enemy aircraft came up on the viewfinder ◆ **la tour s'inscrivait tout entière dans la fenêtre** the tower was framed in its entirety by the window

2 *(= s'enrôler) (gén)* to register; *(sur la liste électorale)* to put one's name down *(sur* on); *(à l'université)* to register, to enrol *(Brit)*, to enroll *(US)* *(à* at); *(à une épreuve sportive)* to put o.s. down, to put one's name down, to enter *(à* for); ◆ **s'~ à un parti/club** to join a party/club ◆ **je me suis inscrit pour des cours du soir** I've enrolled in *ou* for some evening classes ◆ **s'~ au registre du commerce** ≈ to register with the Chamber of Commerce *(for a trade licence)*

3 *(= s'insérer dans)* **ces réformes s'inscrivent dans le cadre de notre nouvelle politique** these reforms lie *ou* come *ou* fall within the scope *ou* framework of our new policy ◆ **cette décision s'inscrit dans le cadre de la lutte contre le chômage** this decision is part of the general struggle against unemployment ◆ **cette mesure s'inscrit dans un ensemble** the measure is part of a package

4 *(Écon)* **s'~ en hausse/en baisse** *[indice, résultat, dépenses]* to be up/down ◆ **l'indice de la Bourse s'inscrivait en baisse de 3 points à la clôture** the share index closed 3 points down

5 *(Math)* to be inscribed *(dans* in)

6 *(Jur)* **s'~ en faux** to lodge a challenge ◆ **je m'inscris en faux contre de telles assertions** I strongly deny such assertions

inscrit, e /ɛ̃skʀi, it/ (ptp de **inscrire**) ADJ 1 *[étudiant]* registered, enrolled; *[candidat, électeur]* registered 2 *(Math)* inscribed NM,F *(= membre)* registered member; *(= étudiant)* registered student; *(= concurrent)* (registered) entrant; *(= candidat)* registered candidate; *(= électeur)* registered elector ◆ **~ maritime** registered sailor

insécable /ɛ̃sekabl/ ADJ indivisible, undividable ◆ **espace ~** *(Typo)* hard space

insecte /ɛ̃sɛkt/ NM insect

insecticide /ɛ̃sɛktisid/ NM insecticide ADJ insecticide *(épith)*, insecticidal

insectivore /ɛ̃sɛktivɔʀ/ NM insectivore ◆ **~s** insectivores, Insectivorae *(SPÉC)* ADJ insectivorous

insécurité /ɛ̃sekyʀite/ NF 1 *(= dangers)* **~ urbaine** urban violence ◆ **une campagne contre l'~ routière** a road safety campaign ◆ **les problèmes d'~ alimentaire** food safety issues ◆ **cela provoque un sentiment d'~ dans la population** it makes people feel unsafe 2 *(= malaise)* insecurity ◆ **~ économique** economic insecurity ◆ **les jeunes en situation d'~** youngsters who feel insecure

INSEE /inse/ NM (abrév de **Institut national de la statistique et des études économiques**) → **institut**

inséminateur, -trice /ɛ̃seminatœʀ, tʀis/ ADJ inseminating *(épith)* NM,F inseminator

insémination /ɛ̃seminasjɔ̃/ NF insemination ◆ **~ artificielle** artificial insemination

inséminer /ɛ̃semine/ ▸ conjug 1 ◂ VT to inseminate

insensé, e /ɛ̃sɑ̃se/ ADJ 1 *(= fou)* *[projet, action, espoir]* insane; *[personne, propos]* insane, demented; *[guerre]* senseless, insane; *[risques, course, défi]* mad, insane ◆ **vouloir y aller seul, c'est ~ !** it's insane *ou* crazy to want to go alone! ◆ **cela demande un travail ~ !** it takes an incredible *ou* a ridiculous amount of work! 2 *(= bizarre)* *[architecture, arabesques]* weird, extravagant 3 *(= incroyable)* *[somme]* enormous, extravagant; *[embouteillage]* impossible; *[personne, soirée]* crazy NM ◆ **c'est un ~ !** he's demented! *ou* insane!, he's a madman!

insensibilisation /ɛ̃sɑ̃sibilizasjɔ̃/ NF anaesthetization *(Brit)*, anesthetization *(US)*

insensibiliser /ɛ̃sɑ̃sibilize/ ▸ conjug 1 ◂ VT to anaesthetize *(Brit)*, to anesthetize *(US)* ◆ **nous sommes insensibilisés aux atrocités de la guerre** *(fig)* we've become insensitive *ou* inured to the atrocities of war

insensibilité /ɛ̃sɑ̃sibilite/ NF *(morale)* insensitivity, insensibility; *(physique)* numbness ◆ **~ au froid/à la douleur/aux reproches** insensitivity *ou* insensibility to cold/pain/blame

insensible /ɛ̃sɑ̃sibl/ ADJ 1 *(moralement)* insensitive *(à* to); *(physiquement)* numb ◆ **il est ~ à la douleur/au froid** he doesn't feel pain/the cold ◆ **il est ~ à la poésie** he has no feeling for poetry, he doesn't respond to poetry ◆ **~ à la critique** impervious *ou* immune to criticism ◆ **il n'est pas resté ~ à son charme** he was not impervious to her charm 2 *(= imperceptible)* imperceptible

> ⚠ **insensible** se traduit rarement par le mot anglais **insensible**, qui a le sens de 'inconscient'.

insensiblement /ɛ̃sɑ̃sibləmɑ̃/ ADV imperceptibly

inséparable /ɛ̃sepaʀabl/ ADJ inseparable *(de* from); ◆ **ils sont ~s** they are inseparable NM ◆ **~s** *(= oiseaux)* lovebirds

inséparablement /ɛ̃sepaʀabləmɑ̃/ ADV inseparably

insérable /ɛ̃seʀabl/ ADJ insertable *(dans* into)

insérer /ɛ̃seʀe/ ▸ conjug 6 ◂ VT *[+ feuillet, clause, objet]* to insert *(dans* into; *entre* between); *[+ annonce]* to put, to insert *(dans* in); ◆ **ces séquences ont été insérées après coup** *(Ciné, TV)* these scenes were edited in afterwards VPR **s'insérer** 1 *(= faire partie de)* **s'~ dans** to fit into ◆ **ces changements s'insèrent dans le cadre d'une restructuration de notre entreprise** these changes come within *ou* lie within *ou* fit into our overall plan for restructuring the firm 2 *(= s'introduire dans)* **s'~ dans** to filter into ◆ **le rêve s'insère parfois dans la réalité** sometimes dreams invade reality 3 *(= être attaché)* to be inserted *ou* attached

INSERM /insɛʀm/ NM (abrév de **Institut national de la santé et de la recherche médicale**) ≈ MRC *(Brit)*, NIH *(US)*

insert /ɛ̃sɛʀ/ NM *(Ciné, Radio, TV)* insert, cut-in ◆ **film comportant en ~ des images d'archives** film with archive footage edited into it ◆ **~ (de cheminée)** enclosed (glass-fronted) roomheater

insertion /ɛ̃sɛʀsjɔ̃/ NF *(= action)* insertion, inserting; *(= résultat)* insertion ◆ **(mode d')~** *(Ordin)* insert (mode) ◆ **~ sociale** social integration ◆ **l'~ professionnelle des jeunes** the integration of young people into the world of work ◆ **logements d'~** *housing for the rehabilitation of homeless or destitute people;* → **revenu**

insidieusement /ɛ̃sidjøzmɑ̃/ ADV insidiously

insidieux, -ieuse /ɛ̃sidjø, jøz/ ADJ *[maladie, question]* insidious

insigne[1] /ɛ̃siɲ/ ADJ *(= éminent)* *[honneur]* distinguished; *[services]* notable, distinguished; *[faveur]* signal *(épith)*, notable; *(iro)* *[maladresse, mauvais goût]* remarkable

insigne[2] /ɛ̃siɲ/ NM *(= cocarde)* badge ◆ **l'~ de, les ~s de** *(frm = emblème)* the insignia of ◆ **portant les ~s de sa fonction** wearing the insignia of his office

insignifiance /ɛ̃siɲifjɑ̃s/ NF 1 *(= banalité)* *[de personne, visage, œuvre]* insignificance 2 *(= médiocrité)* *[d'affaire, somme, propos, détails]* insignificance, triviality; *[de dispute]* triviality

insignifiant, e /ɛ̃siɲifjɑ̃, jɑ̃t/ ADJ 1 *(= quelconque)* *[personne, visage, œuvre]* insignificant 2 *(= dérisoire)* *[affaire, somme, détail]* insignificant, trivial, trifling; *[propos]* insignificant, trivial; *[dispute]* trivial

insincère /ɛ̃sɛ̃sɛʀ/ ADJ *(littér)* insincere

insincérité /ɛ̃sɛ̃seʀite/ NF *(littér)* insincerity

insinuant, e /ɛ̃sinɥɑ̃, ɑ̃t/ ADJ *[façons, ton, personne]* ingratiating

insinuation /ɛ̃sinɥasjɔ̃/ NF insinuation, innuendo

insinuer /ɛ̃sinɥe/ ▸ conjug 1 ◂ VT to insinuate, to imply ◆ **que voulez-vous ~ ?** what are you insinuating? *ou* implying? *ou* suggesting? VPR **s'insinuer** ◆ **s'~ dans** *[personne]* to worm one's way into, to insinuate o.s. into; *[eau, odeur]* to seep *ou* creep into ◆ **l'humidité s'insinuait partout** the dampness was creeping in everywhere ◆ **les idées qui s'insinuent dans mon esprit** the ideas that steal *ou* creep into my mind ◆ **ces arrivistes s'insinuent partout** these opportunists worm their way in everywhere ◆ **s'~ dans les bonnes grâces de qn** to worm one's way into *ou* insinuate o.s. into sb's favour

insipide /ɛ̃sipid/ ADJ 1 *[plat, boisson]* insipid, tasteless 2 *(péj)* *[conversation, style]* insipid, vapid; *[écrivain, film, œuvre, vie]* insipid

insipidité /ɛ̃sipidite/ NF 1 *[de plat, boisson]* insipidity, tastelessness 2 *(péj)* *[de conversation,* *style]* insipidity, vapidity; *[d'écrivain, film, œuvre, vie]* insipidity

insistance /ɛ̃sistɑ̃s/ NF insistence *(sur qch* on sth; *à faire qch* on doing sth); ◆ **avec ~** *[répéter, regarder]* insistently

insistant, e /ɛ̃sistɑ̃, ɑ̃t/ ADJ insistent

insister /ɛ̃siste/ ▸ conjug 1 ◂ VI 1 ◆ **~ sur** *[+ sujet, détail]* to stress, to lay stress on; *[+ syllabe, note]* to accentuate, to emphasize, to stress ◆ **j'insiste beaucoup sur la ponctualité** I lay great stress upon punctuality ◆ **frottez en insistant (bien) sur les taches** rub hard, paying particular attention to stains ◆ **c'est une affaire louche, enfin n'insistons pas** it's a shady business – however let us not dwell on it *ou* don't let us keep on about it* ◆ **je préfère ne pas ~ là-dessus** I'd rather not dwell on it, I'd rather let the matter drop

2 *(= s'obstiner)* to be insistent *(auprès de* with) to insist ◆ **il insiste pour vous parler** he is insistent about wanting to talk to you ◆ **comme ça ne l'intéressait pas, je n'ai pas insisté** since it didn't interest him, I didn't push the matter *ou* I didn't insist ◆ **sonnez encore, insistez, elle est un peu sourde** ring again and keep (on) trying because she's a little deaf ◆ **j'insiste, c'est très important !** I assure you it's very important! ◆ **bon, je n'insiste pas, je m'en vais*** OK, I won't insist - I'll go

in situ /insity/ ADV in situ

insociable /ɛ̃sɔsjabl/ ADJ unsociable

insolation /ɛ̃sɔlasjɔ̃/ NF 1 *(= malaise)* sunstroke *(NonC)*, insolation *(SPÉC)* ◆ **attraper une ~** to get sunstroke ◆ **j'ai eu une ~** I had a touch of sunstroke 2 *(= ensoleillement)* (period of) sunshine ◆ **ces stations ont une ~ très faible** these resorts get very little sun(shine) ◆ **une ~ de 1 000 heures par an** 1,000 hours of sunshine a year 3 *(= exposition au soleil) [de personne]* exposure to the sun; *[de pellicule]* exposure (to the light), insolation *(SPÉC)*

insolemment /ɛ̃sɔlamɑ̃/ ADV 1 *(= effrontément) [parler, répondre]* insolently 2 *(= outrageusement)* unashamedly, blatantly, brazenly 3 *(littér = avec arrogance)* arrogantly

insolence /ɛ̃sɔlɑ̃s/ NF *(= impertinence)* insolence *(NonC)*; *(littér) (= morgue)* arrogance; *(= remarque)* insolent remark ◆ **répondre/rire avec ~** to reply/laugh insolently ◆ **il a eu l'~ de la contredire** he was insolent enough to contradict her, he had the temerity to contradict her ◆ **encore une ~ comme celle-ci et je te renvoie** one more insolent remark like that *ou* any more of your insolence and I'll send you out

insolent, e /ɛ̃sɔlɑ̃, ɑ̃t/ ADJ 1 *(= impertinent)* cheeky, impertinent ◆ **tu es un ~ !** you're being cheeky! 2 *(= inouï) [luxe]* unashamed ◆ **il a une chance ~e !** he has the luck of the devil! 3 *(littér = arrogant) [parvenu, vainqueur]* arrogant

insolite /ɛ̃sɔlit/ ADJ unusual, out of the ordinary *(attrib)* NM ◆ **aimer l'~** to like things which are out of the ordinary, to like unusual things

insolubilité /ɛ̃sɔlybilite/ NF insolubility

insoluble /ɛ̃sɔlybl/ ADJ insoluble

insolvabilité /ɛ̃sɔlvabilite/ NF insolvency

insolvable /ɛ̃sɔlvabl/ ADJ insolvent

insomniaque /ɛ̃sɔmnjak/ ADJ, NMF insomniac ◆ **c'est un ~, il est ~** he suffers from insomnia

insomnie /ɛ̃sɔmni/ NF insomnia *(NonC)* ◆ **nuit d'~** sleepless night ◆ **ses ~s** his (periods of) insomnia

insondable /ɛ̃sɔ̃dabl/ ADJ *[gouffre, mystère, douleur]* unfathomable; *[stupidité]* immense, unimaginable

insonore /ɛ̃sɔnɔʀ/ ADJ soundproof

insonorisation /ɛ̃sɔnɔʀizasjɔ̃/ NF soundproofing

insonoriser /ɛ̃sɔnɔʀize/ ▸ conjug 1 ◂ VT to soundproof ◆ **immeuble mal insonorisé** badly soundproofed building

insortable* /ɛ̃sɔʀtabl/ ADJ ◆ **tu es ~ !** I *(ou* we *etc)* can't take you anywhere!*

insouciance /ɛ̃susjɑ̃s/ NF *(= nonchalance)* unconcern, lack of concern; *(= manque de prévoyance)* heedless *ou* happy-go-lucky attitude ◆ **vivre dans l'~** to live a carefree life

insouciant, e /ɛ̃susjɑ̃, jɑ̃t/ ADJ *(= sans souci) [personne, vie, humeur]* carefree, happy-go-lucky; *[rire, paroles]* carefree; *(= imprévoyant)* heedless, happy-go-lucky ◆ **quel ~ (tu fais) !** you're such a heedless *ou* happy-go-lucky person! ◆ **~ du danger** heedless of (the) danger

insoucieux, -ieuse /ɛ̃susjø, jøz/ ADJ carefree ◆ **~ du lendemain** unconcerned about the future, not caring about what tomorrow may bring

insoumis, e /ɛ̃sumi, iz/ ADJ *[caractère, enfant]* rebellious, insubordinate; *[tribu, peuple, région]* undefeated, unsubdued ◆ **soldat ~** *(Mil)* draft-dodger NM *(Mil)* draft-dodger

insoumission /ɛ̃sumisjɔ̃/ NF insubordination, rebelliousness; *(Mil)* absence without leave

insoupçonnable /ɛ̃supsɔnabl/ ADJ *[personne]* above *ou* beyond suspicion *(attrib)*; *[cachette]* impossible to find; *[desseins]* unsuspected

insoupçonné, e /ɛ̃supsɔne/ ADJ unsuspected

insoutenable /ɛ̃sut(ə)nabl/ ADJ *[spectacle, douleur, chaleur, odeur]* unbearable; *[théorie]* untenable ◆ **d'une violence ~** unbearably violent

inspecter /ɛ̃spɛkte/ ▸ conjug 1 ◂ VT *(= contrôler)* to inspect; *(= scruter)* to inspect, to examine

inspecteur, -trice /ɛ̃spɛktœʀ, tʀis/ NM,F *(gén)* inspector ◆ **~ des finances** *auditor at the Treasury (with special responsibility for the inspection of public finances)* ◆ **~ des impôts** ≈ tax inspector ◆ **~ de police (judiciaire)** ≈ detective *(Brit)*, (police) lieutenant *(US)* ◆ **~ de police principal** detective chief inspector *(Brit)*, (police) lieutenant *(US)* ◆ **~ du travail** factory inspector ◆ **~ primaire** primary school inspector ◆ **~ d'Académie** chief education officer ◆ **~ pédagogique régional** ≈ inspector of schools *(Brit)*, accreditation officer *(US)* ◆ **~ général de l'instruction publique** ≈ chief inspector of schools ◆ **voilà l'~ des travaux finis !*** *(hum ou péj)* it's a bit late to start offering your advice!

inspection /ɛ̃spɛksjɔ̃/ NF 1 *(= examen)* inspection ◆ **faire l'~ de** to inspect ◆ **soumettre qch à une ~ en règle** to give sth a good *ou* thorough inspection *ou* going-over* 2 *(= inspectorat)* inspectorship; *(= inspecteurs)* inspectorate ◆ **~ académique** *(= service)* school inspectorate ◆ **~ (générale) des Finances** *department of the Treasury responsible for auditing public bodies* ◆ **~ du Travail** ≈ factory inspectorate ◆ **l'Inspection générale des services** *(Police)* the police monitoring service, ≈ the Police Complaints Board *(Brit)* ◆ **Inspection générale de la police nationale** police disciplinary body, ≈ Complaints and Discipline Branch *(Brit)*, Internal Affairs *(US)*

inspectorat /ɛ̃spɛktɔʀa/ NM inspectorship

inspirateur, -trice /ɛ̃spiʀatœʀ, tʀis/ ADJ *[idée, force]* inspiring; *(Anat)* inspiratory NM,F *(= animateur)* inspirer; *(= instigateur)* instigator ◆ **le poète et son inspiratrice** the poet and the woman who inspires *(ou* inspired) him

inspiration /ɛ̃spiʀasjɔ̃/ NF 1 *(divine, poétique)* inspiration ◆ **avoir de l'~** to have inspiration, to be inspired ◆ **selon l'~ du moment** according to the mood of the moment, as the mood takes me *(ou* you *etc)* ◆ **Julie fut une source d'~ pour lui** Julie was an inspiration to him 2 *(= idée)* inspiration, brainwave* ◆ **par une heureuse ~** thanks to a flash of inspiration ◆ **j'eus la bonne/mauvaise ~ de refuser** I had the bright/bad idea of refusing 3 *(= instigation)* instigation; *(= influence)* inspiration ◆ **sous l'~ de qn** at sb's instigation, prompted by sb ◆ **tableau d'~ religieuse** picture inspired by a religious subject ◆ **mouvement d'~ communiste** communist-inspired movement 4 *(= respiration)* inspiration

inspiré, e /ɛ̃spiʀe/ (ptp de **inspirer**) ADJ 1 *[poète, œuvre, air]* inspired ◆ **qu'est-ce que c'est que cet ~ ?** *(iro)* whoever's this cranky character? *ou* this weirdo?* *(péj)* 2 *(* = avisé)* **il serait bien ~ de partir** he'd be well advised *ou* he'd do well to leave ◆ **j'ai été bien/mal ~ de refuser** *ou* **quand j'ai refusé** I was truly inspired/ill inspired when I refused 3 ◆ **~ de** inspired by ◆ **mode ~e des années cinquante** style inspired by the Fifties

inspirer /ɛ̃spiʀe/ ▸ conjug 1 ◂ VT 1 *[+ poète, prophète]* to inspire ◆ **sa passion lui a inspiré ce poème** his passion inspired him to write this poem ◆ **cette idée ne m'inspire pas beaucoup*** I'm not very taken with that idea, I'm not all that keen on this idea* *(Brit)* ◆ **le sujet de dissertation ne m'a pas vraiment inspiré** I didn't find the essay subject very inspiring

2 *(= susciter) [+ acte, personne]* to inspire ◆ **~ un sentiment à qn** to inspire sb with a feeling ◆ **~ le respect à qn** to command sb's respect ◆ **sa santé m'inspire des inquiétudes** his health gives me cause for concern ◆ **il ne m'inspire pas confiance** he doesn't inspire me with confidence, I don't really trust him ◆ **cela ne m'inspire rien de bon** I don't like the sound *(ou* look) of it ◆ **toute l'opération était inspirée par un seul homme** the whole operation was inspired by one man ◆ **l'horreur qu'il m'inspire** the horror he fills me with ◆ **sa réaction était inspirée par la crainte** his reaction sprang from fear

3 *(= insuffler)* **~ de l'air dans qch** to breathe air into sth

VI *(= respirer)* to breathe in, to inspire *(SPÉC)*

VPR **s'inspirer** ◆ **s'~ d'un modèle** *[artiste]* to draw one's inspiration from a model, to be inspired by a model; *[mode, tableau, loi]* to be inspired by a model

instabilité /ɛ̃stabilite/ NF 1 *(gén, Sci)* instability; *[de meuble, échafaudage]* unsteadiness ◆ **l'~ du temps** the unsettled (nature of the) weather 2 *(Psych) [de personne, caractère]* (emotional) instability

instable /ɛ̃stabl/ ADJ 1 *(gén, Sci)* unstable; *[meuble, échafaudage]* unsteady; *[temps]* unsettled; → **équilibre** 2 *(Psych) [personne, caractère]* (emotionally) unstable

installateur /ɛ̃stalatœʀ/ NM fitter ◆ **~ en chauffage central** central heating installation engineer ◆ **~ de cuisine** kitchen fitter

installation /ɛ̃stalasjɔ̃/ NF 1 *(= mise en service, pose) [d'électricité, chauffage central, téléphone, eau courante]* installation, installing, putting in; *[d'applique]* putting in; *[de rideaux, étagère]* putting up; *[de tente]* putting up, pitching ◆ **l'~ du téléphone n'est pas gratuite** there's a charge for installing the telephone ◆ **ils s'occupent aussi de l'~ du mobilier** they also take care of moving the furniture in *ou* of installing the furniture ◆ **frais/travaux d'~** installation costs/work

2 *(= aménagement) [de pièce, appartement]* fitting out; *(= meubles)* living arrangements, setup* ◆ **ils ont une ~ provisoire** they have temporary living arrangements *ou* a temporary setup* ◆ **qu'est-ce que vous avez comme ~ ?** what kind of a setup* do you have?

3 *(= établissement) [d'artisan, commerçant]* setting up; *[de dentiste, médecin]* setting up one's practice; *[d'usine]* setting up ◆ **il lui fallait**

songer à l'~ de son fils he had to think about setting his son up

4 *(dans un logement)* settling; *(= emménagement)* settling in ◆ **il voulait fêter son** ~ he wanted to celebrate moving in ◆ **leur ~ terminée, ils ...** when they had finally settled in, they ... ◆ **ils sont en pleine** ~ they're moving in at the moment

5 *(= équipement) (gén pl)* fittings, installations; *(= usine)* plant *(NonC)* ◆ **l'~ téléphonique** the phone system ◆ **l'~ électrique est défectueuse** the wiring is faulty ◆ **~(s) sanitaire(s)/électrique(s)** sanitary/electrical fittings *ou* installations ◆ **~s sportives** sports facilities ◆ **les ~s industrielles d'une région** the industrial installations *ou* plant of a region ◆ **~s nucléaires** nuclear plant ◆ **~s portuaires** port facilities ◆ **le camping est doté de toutes les ~s nécessaires** the campsite has all the necessary facilities

6 *(Art)* installation

installé, e /ɛ̃stale/ (ptp de **installer**) ADJ *(= aménagé)* ◆ **bien/mal ~** *[appartement]* well/badly fitted out; *[atelier, cuisine]* well/badly equipped *ou* fitted out ◆ **ils sont très bien ~s** they have a comfortable *ou* nice home ◆ **c'est un homme ~** † he is well-established

installer /ɛ̃stale/ ► conjug 1 ◄ VT 1 *(= mettre en service) [+ électricité, téléphone, eau courante]* to put in; *[+ chauffage central]* to install, to put in; *[+ usine]* to set up ◆ **faire ~ le gaz/le téléphone** to have (the) gas/the telephone put in

2 *(= placer, poser) [+ rideaux, étagère]* to put up; *[+ applique]* to put in; *[+ tente]* to put up, to pitch ◆ **où va-t-on ~ le lit ?** where shall we put the bed?

3 *(= aménager) [+ pièce, appartement]* to furnish ◆ **ils ont très bien installé leur appartement** they've furnished their flat *(Brit) ou* apartment *(US)* very nicely ◆ **ils ont installé leur bureau dans le grenier** they've turned the attic into a study, they've made a study in the attic

4 *(= loger) [+ malade, jeune couple]* to get settled, to settle ◆ **ils installèrent leurs hôtes dans une aile du château** they put their guests in a wing of the château

5 *(= établir)* **il a installé son fils dentiste/à son compte** he set his son up as a dentist/in his own business

6 *(= nommer) [+ fonctionnaire, évêque]* to install ◆ **il a été officiellement installé dans ses fonctions** he has been officially installed in his post

7 *(Ordin)* to install

VPR **s'installer** 1 *(= s'établir) [artisan, commerçant]* to set up *(comme* as*)*; *[dentiste, médecin]* to set up practice ◆ **s'~ à son compte** to set up on one's own ◆ **ils se sont installés à la campagne/à Lyon** they've settled *ou* they've gone to live in the country/in Lyons

2 *(= se loger)* to settle; *(= emménager)* to settle in ◆ **laisse-leur le temps de s'~** give them time to settle in ◆ **pendant la guerre, ils s'étaient installés chez des amis** during the war they moved in *ou* lived with friends ◆ **s'~ dans une maison abandonnée** to move into an abandoned house ◆ **ils sont bien installés dans leur nouvelle maison** they're nicely settled in their new house

3 *(sur un siège, à un emplacement)* to sit down ◆ **s'~ commodément** to settle o.s. ◆ **s'~ par terre/dans un fauteuil** to sit down on the floor/in an armchair ◆ **installe-toi comme il faut** *(confortablement)* make yourself comfortable; *(= tiens-toi bien)* sit properly ◆ **installons-nous près de cet arbre** shall we sit by this tree? ◆ **partout où il va il s'installe comme chez lui** wherever he goes he makes himself at home ◆ **les forains se sont installés sur un terrain vague** they've set up the fair on a piece of wasteland ◆ **la fête s'est installée sur la place du marché** they've set up the fair in the marketplace

4 *[grève, maladie]* to take hold ◆ **s'~ dans** *[personne] [+ inertie]* to sink into; *[+ malhonnêteté]* to entangle o.s. in, to get involved in ◆ **le doute s'installa dans mon esprit** I began to have doubts ◆ **la peur s'était installée dans la ville** the town was gripped by fear

> ⚠ Attention à ne pas traduire automatiquement **installer** par **to install** ; l'anglais préfère employer un verbe à particule.

instamment /ɛ̃stamɑ̃/ ADV insistently, earnestly ◆ **il demande ~ au gouvernement de prendre une décision** he is urging the government to make a decision

instance /ɛ̃stɑ̃s/ NF 1 *(= autorité)* authority ◆ **les ~s internationales/communautaires** the international/EU authorities ◆ **la plus haute ~ judiciaire du pays** the country's highest judicial body *ou* legal authorities ◆ **les plus hautes ~s du parti** the party leadership ◆ **le conflit devra être tranché par l'~ supérieure** the dispute will have to be resolved by a higher authority ◆ **les ~s dirigeantes du football** football's governing bodies

2 *(Jur)* (legal) proceedings ◆ **introduire une ~** to institute (legal) proceedings ◆ **en seconde ~** on appeal; → **juge, tribunal**

3 *(= prière, insistance)* **demander qch avec ~** to ask for something with insistence, to make an earnest request for sth ◆ **~s** entreaties ◆ **sur** *ou* **devant les ~s de ses parents** in the face of his parents' entreaties

4 *(locutions)*

◆ **en + instance** *(= en cours)* ◆ **l'affaire est en ~** the matter is pending ◆ **être en ~ de divorce** to be waiting for a divorce ◆ **le train est en ~ de départ** the train is on the point of departure *ou* about to leave ◆ **courrier en ~** mail ready for posting *ou* due to be dispatched ◆ **en dernière ~** in the final analysis, ultimately

5 *(Psych)* agency

instant[1] /ɛ̃stɑ̃/ NM *(= moment)* moment, instant ◆ **des ~s de tendresse** tender moments, moments of tenderness ◆ **j'ai cru (pendant) un ~ que** I thought for a moment *ou* a second that ◆ **(attendez) un ~ !** wait a moment!, just a moment! ◆ **l'~ fatal** the final moment ◆ **je n'en doute pas un (seul) ~** I don't doubt it for a (single) moment ◆ **au même ~** at the (very) same moment *ou* instant ◆ **d'~ en ~** from moment to moment, every moment ◆ **dans un ~** in a moment *ou* minute ◆ **en un ~** in an instant, in no time (at all) ◆ **par ~s** at times

◆ **à l'instant** ◆ **je l'ai vu à l'~** I've just this instant *ou* minute *ou* second seen him ◆ **il faut le faire à l'~** we must do it this instant *ou* minute ◆ **on me l'apprend à l'~ (même)** I've just been told, I've just heard about it ◆ **à l'~ (présent)** at this very instant *ou* moment *ou* minute ◆ **à l'~ où je vous parle** as I'm speaking to you now, as I speak ◆ **à l'~ (même) où il sortit** just as he went out, (just) at the very moment *ou* instant he went out

◆ **à chaque instant, à tout instant** *(= d'un moment à l'autre)* at any moment *ou* minute; *(= tout le temps)* all the time, every minute

◆ **dans l'instant** *(= immédiatement)* there and then, immediately ◆ **il faut vivre dans l'~** *(= le présent)* you must live in the present (moment)

◆ **d'un instant à l'autre** any minute now ◆ **ça peut changer d'un ~ à l'autre** it can change from one minute to the next

◆ **de tous les instants** *[surveillance]* perpetual, constant; *[dévouement, attention]* constant

◆ **dès l'instant où/que** ◆ **dès l'~ où** *ou* **que vous êtes d'accord** *(puisque)* since you agree ◆ **dès l'~ où je l'ai vu** *(dès que)* as soon as I saw him, from the moment I saw him

◆ **pour l'instant** for the moment, for the time being

instant[2]**, e** /ɛ̃stɑ, ɑt/ ADJ *(littér = pressant)* insistent, pressing, earnest

instantané, e /ɛ̃stɑ̃tane/ ADJ *[lait, café, soupe]* instant *(épith)*; *[mort, réponse, effet]* instantaneous; *(littér = bref) [vision]* momentary NM *(Photo)* snapshot, snap*; *(fig)* snapshot

instantanéité /ɛ̃stɑ̃taneite/ NF instantaneousness, instantaneity ◆ **cela favorise l'~ de l'accès à l'information** that enables us to have instant access to information

instantanément /ɛ̃stɑ̃tanemɑ̃/ ADV instantaneously ◆ **pour préparer ~ un bon café** to make good coffee instantly

instar /ɛ̃staʀ/ **à l'instar de** LOC ADV *(frm) (= à l'exemple de)* following the example of, after the fashion of; *(= comme)* like

instauration /ɛ̃stɔʀasjɔ̃/ NF *[de pratique]* institution; *[de régime, dialogue]* establishment; *[de taxe]* introduction; *[d'état d'urgence]* imposition

instaurer /ɛ̃stɔʀe/ ► conjug 1 ◄ VT *[+ usage, pratique]* to institute; *[+ paix, régime, dialogue]* to establish; *[+ méthode, quotas, taxe]* to introduce; *[+ couvre-feu, état d'urgence]* to impose ◆ **la révolution a instauré la république** the revolution established the republic ◆ **le doute s'est instauré dans les esprits** people have begun to have doubts

instigateur, -trice /ɛ̃stigatœʀ, tʀis/ NM,F instigator

instigation /ɛ̃stigasjɔ̃/ NF instigation ◆ **à l'~ de qn** at sb's instigation

instillation /ɛ̃stilasjɔ̃/ NF instillation

instiller /ɛ̃stile/ ► conjug 1 ◄ VT *(littér, Méd)* to instil *(Brit)*, to instill *(US)* *(dans* in, into*)*; ◆ **il m'a instillé la passion du jeu** he instilled the love of gambling in *ou* into me

instinct /ɛ̃stɛ̃/ NM *(gén)* instinct ◆ **~ maternel** maternal instinct ◆ **~ de mort** *(Psych)* death wish ◆ **~ de vie** will to live ◆ **~ grégaire** gregarious *ou* herd instinct ◆ **~ de conservation** instinct of self-preservation ◆ **il a l'~ des affaires** he has an instinct for business ◆ **faire qch d'~** *ou* **par ~** *ou* **à l'~** to do sth instinctively ◆ **d'~, il comprit la situation** intuitively *ou* instinctively he understood the situation ◆ **mon ~ me dit que** (my) instinct tells me that ◆ **céder à ses (mauvais) ~s** to yield to one's (bad) instincts

instinctif, -ive /ɛ̃stɛ̃ktif, iv/ ADJ *(gén)* instinctive, instinctual ◆ **c'est un ~** he (always) acts on instinct

instinctivement /ɛ̃stɛ̃ktivmɑ̃/ ADV instinctively

instit * /ɛ̃stit/ NMF abrév de **instituteur, -trice**

instituer /ɛ̃stitɥe/ ► conjug 1 ◄ VT *[+ règle, pratique, organisation]* to institute; *[+ relations commerciales]* to establish; *[+ impôt]* to introduce; *[+ évêque]* to institute; *[+ héritier]* to appoint, to institute VPR **s'instituer** *[relations commerciales]* to start up, to be (*ou* become) established

institut /ɛ̃stity/ NM institute; *(Univ)* institute, school *(Brit)* ◆ **l'Institut (de France)** the Institut de France, ≃ the Royal Society *(Brit)* ◆ **membre de l'Institut** member of the Institut de France, ≃ Fellow of the Royal Society *(Brit)* ◆ **~ de beauté** beauty salon *ou* parlor *(US)* ◆ **~ de sondage** polling organization

COMP **Institut géographique national** *French geographical institute*, ≃ Ordnance Survey *(Brit)*, United States Geological Survey *(US)*, USGS *(US)*

Institut du Monde Arabe *Arab cultural centre in Paris*

Institut monétaire européen European Monetary Institute, EMI

Institut national de l'audiovisuel *library of radio and television archives*
Institut national de la consommation *consumer research organization,* ≃ Consumers' Association *(Brit)*, Consumer Product Safety Commission *(US)*
Institut national de la propriété industrielle ≃ Patent Office
Institut national de la recherche agronomique *national institute for agronomic research*
Institut national de la santé et de la recherche médicale *national institute for health and medical research,* ≃ Medical Research Council *(Brit)*, National Institute of Health *(US)*
Institut national de la statistique et des études économiques *French national institute of economic and statistical information*
Institut Pasteur Pasteur Institute
Institut universitaire de formation des maîtres *teacher training college*
Institut universitaire de technologie ≃ polytechnic *(Brit)*, technical school *ou* institute *(US)*; → **médico-légal**

instituteur, -trice /ɛ̃stitytœʀ, tʀis/ NM,F (primary school) teacher ◆ ~ **spécialisé** teacher in special school (for the handicapped) NF **institutrice** *(Hist = gouvernante)* governess

institution /ɛ̃stitysjɔ̃/ NF 1 *(= organisme, structure)* institution; *(= école)* private school ◆ **nos ~s sont menacées** our institutions are threatened ◆ **ce présentateur est devenu une véritable** ~ *(iro)* this TV presenter has become a national institution ◆ **la mendicité est ici une véritable ~ !** *(iro)* begging is a way of life here! 2 *(= instauration) [de pratique]* institution; *[de relations]* establishment; *[d'impôt]* introduction; *[d'évêque]* institution
COMP **institution d'héritier** *(Jur)* appointment of an heir
institution religieuse *(gén)* denominational school; *(catholique)* Catholic school, parochial school *(US)*

institutionnalisation /ɛ̃stitysjɔnalizasjɔ̃/ NF institutionalization

institutionnaliser /ɛ̃stitysjɔnalize/ ▸ conjug 1 ◂ VT to institutionalize VPR **s'institutionnaliser** to become institutionalized

institutionnel, -elle /ɛ̃stitysjɔnɛl/ ADJ institutional

institutrice /ɛ̃stitytʀis/ NF → **instituteur**

instructeur /ɛ̃stʀyktœʀ/ NM instructor ADJ ◆ **juge** *ou* **magistrat** ~ examining magistrate ◆ **capitaine/sergent** ~ drill captain/sergeant

instructif, -ive /ɛ̃stʀyktif, iv/ ADJ instructive

instruction /ɛ̃stʀyksjɔ̃/ NF 1 *(= enseignement)* education ◆ **l'~ que j'ai reçue** the teaching *ou* education I received ◆ **niveau d'~** academic standard ◆ ~ **civique** civics *(sg)* ◆ ~ **militaire** army training ◆ ~ **religieuse** religious instruction *ou* education *ou* studies ◆ **l'~ publique** state education
2 *(= culture)* education ◆ **avoir de l'~** to be well educated ◆ **être sans ~** to have no education
3 *(Jur) pre-trial investigation of a case* ◆ **ouvrir une ~** to initiate an investigation into a crime; → **juge**
4 *(Admin = circulaire)* directive ◆ ~ **ministérielle/préfectorale** ministerial/prefectural directive
5 *(Ordin)* instruction ◆ **~s d'entrée-sortie** input-output instructions
NFPL **instructions** *(= directives)* instructions; *(= mode d'emploi)* instructions, directions ◆ **~s de lavage** *(gén)* washing instructions; *(= étiquette)* care label ◆ **suivre les ~s données sur le paquet** to follow the instructions *ou* directions given on the packet ◆ **conformément/contrairement à vos ~s** in accordance with/contrary to your instructions

> ⚠ Au sens de 'éducation', 'culture', **instruction** ne se traduit généralement pas par le mot anglais **instruction**.

instruire /ɛ̃stʀɥiʀ/ ▸ conjug 38 ◂ VT 1 *(= former) (gén)* to teach, to educate; *[+ recrue]* to train ◆ ~ **qn dans l'art oratoire** to educate *ou* instruct sb in the art of oratory ◆ **c'est la vie qui m'a instruit** life has educated me, life has been my teacher ◆ ~ **qn par l'exemple** to teach *ou* educate sb by example ◆ **instruit par son exemple** having learnt from his example ◆ **ces émissions ne visent pas à ~ mais à divertir** these broadcasts are not intended to teach *ou* educate *ou* instruct but to entertain
2 *(= informer)* ~ **qn de qch** to inform *ou* advise sb of sth
3 *(Jur) [+ affaire, dossier]* to conduct an investigation into ◆ ~ **contre qn** to conduct investigations concerning sb
VPR **s'instruire** *(= apprendre)* to educate o.s. ◆ **c'est comme ça qu'on s'instruit !** *(hum)* that's how you learn! ◆ **on s'instruit à tout âge** *(hum)* it's never too late to learn ◆ **s'~ de qch** *(frm = se renseigner)* to obtain information about sth, to find out about sth ◆ **s'~ de qch auprès de qn** to obtain information *ou* find out from sb about sth

instruit, e /ɛ̃stʀɥi, it/ (ptp de **instruire**) ADJ educated ◆ **peu ~** uneducated

instrument /ɛ̃stʀymɑ̃/ NM 1 *(= objet)* instrument ◆ ~ **de musique/de chirurgie/de mesure/à vent** musical/surgical/measuring/wind instrument ◆ **~s aratoires** ploughing implements ◆ ~ **de travail** tool ◆ **les ~s de bord** *[d'un avion]* the controls ◆ **naviguer aux ~s** *(en avion)* to fly on instruments
2 *(= moyen)* **être l'~ de qn** to be sb's tool ◆ **le président fut l'~ de/servit d'~ à la répression** the president was the instrument *ou* tool of/served as an *ou* the instrument of repression ◆ **elle a été l'~ de cette vengeance** she was *ou* served as the instrument of this revenge ◆ **elle a été l'~ privilégié de sa réussite** she was the key *ou* principal instrument of his success ◆ **~s de paiement** means of payment ◆ **~s financiers** financial instruments

instrumental, e (mpl **-aux**) /ɛ̃stʀymɑ̃tal, o/ ADJ *(Ling, Mus)* instrumental NM *(Ling)* instrumental

instrumentalisation /ɛ̃stʀymɑ̃talizasjɔ̃/ NF *[de personne, événement]* exploitation ◆ **cette ~ politique de la religion** this use of religion for political ends ◆ **il craint que les biotechnologies ne conduisent à une ~ du corps humain** he fears that biotechnologies will lead to the human body being treated as a mere object

instrumentaliser /ɛ̃stʀymɑ̃talize/ ▸ conjug 1 ◂ VT *[+ chose, événement, personne]* to make use of, to exploit ◆ **toutes les nations instrumentalisent l'histoire** all countries use *ou* exploit history for their own ends ◆ **la société instrumentalise l'individu** society turns people into robots

instrumentation /ɛ̃stʀymɑ̃tasjɔ̃/ NF 1 *(Mus)* instrumentation, orchestration 2 *(Tech)* instrumentation

instrumenter /ɛ̃stʀymɑ̃te/ ▸ conjug 1 ◂ VI *(Jur)* to draw up a formal document VT 1 *(Mus)* to orchestrate 2 *(Tech)* to instrument

instrumentiste /ɛ̃stʀymɑ̃tist/ NMF 1 *(Mus)* instrumentalist 2 *(dans bloc opératoire)* theatre nurse

insu /ɛ̃sy/ **à l'insu de** LOC PRÉP 1 *(= en cachette de)* **à l'~ de qn** without sb's knowledge, without sb's knowing 2 *(= inconsciemment)* **à mon** *(ou* **ton** *etc)* **~** without my *ou* me *(ou* your *ou* you *etc)* knowing it ◆ **je souriais à mon ~** I was smiling without knowing it

insubmersible /ɛ̃sybmɛʀsibl/ ADJ insubmersible, unsinkable

insubordination /ɛ̃sybɔʀdinasjɔ̃/ NF *(gén)* insubordination, rebelliousness; *(Mil)* insubordination ◆ **pour fait d'~** for insubordination

insubordonné, e /ɛ̃sybɔʀdɔne/ ADJ *(gén)* insubordinate, rebellious; *(Mil)* insubordinate

insuccès /ɛ̃syksɛ/ NM failure

insuffisamment /ɛ̃syfizamɑ̃/ ADV *(en quantité)* insufficiently; *(en qualité, intensité, degré)* inadequately ◆ **tu dors ~** you're not getting adequate *ou* sufficient sleep ◆ **pièce ~ éclairée** room with insufficient *ou* inadequate lighting, poorly-lit room

insuffisance /ɛ̃syfizɑ̃s/ NF 1 *(= médiocrité)* inadequacy; *(= manque)* insufficiency, inadequacy ◆ **l'~ de nos ressources** the inadequacy of our resources, the shortfall in our resources, our inadequate *ou* insufficient resources ◆ **nous souffrons d'une grande ~ de moyens** we are suffering from a great inadequacy *ou* insufficiency *ou* shortage of means ◆ **une ~ de personnel** a shortage of staff 2 *(= faiblesses)* **~s** inadequacies ◆ **avoir des ~s en maths** to be weak in *ou* at maths ◆ **il y a des ~s dans son travail** his work is not entirely adequate 3 *(Méd)* **~(s) cardiaque(s)/thyroïdienne(s)** cardiac/thyroid insufficiency *(NonC)* ◆ ~ **rénale/respiratoire** kidney/respiratory failure

insuffisant, e /ɛ̃syfizɑ̃, ɑt/ ADJ 1 *(en quantité)* insufficient ◆ **ce qu'il nous donne est ~** what he gives us is insufficient *ou* not enough ◆ **nous travaillons avec un personnel ~** we have insufficient staff ◆ **nous sommes en nombre ~** there aren't enough of us 2 *(en qualité, intensité, degré)* inadequate; *(Scol : sur une copie)* poor NM *(Méd)* ◆ **les ~s cardiaques/respiratoires** people with cardiac/respiratory insufficiency ◆ **les ~s rénaux** people suffering from kidney failure

insufflateur /ɛ̃syflatœʀ/ NM *(Méd)* insufflator

insufflation /ɛ̃syflasjɔ̃/ NF *(Méd)* insufflation

insuffler /ɛ̃syfle/ ▸ conjug 1 ◂ VT 1 *(= inspirer, donner)* ~ **le courage/le désir à qn** to inspire sb with courage/with desire, to breathe courage/desire into sb ◆ ~ **la vie à** *(Rel)* to breathe life into 2 *(Méd) [+ air]* to blow, to insufflate *(SPÉC) (dans* into); ◆ **se faire ~** to be insufflated *(SPÉC)*

insulaire /ɛ̃sylɛʀ/ ADJ 1 *[administration, population]* island *(épith)* 2 *(péj) [conception, attitude]* insular NMF islander

insularité /ɛ̃sylaʀite/ NF insularity

insuline /ɛ̃sylin/ NF insulin

insulinodépendance /ɛ̃sylinɔdepɑ̃dɑ̃s/ NF insulin-dependent diabetes

insulinodépendant, e /ɛ̃sylinɔdepɑ̃dɑ̃, ɑt/ ADJ *[diabète, diabétique]* insulin-dependent

insultant, e /ɛ̃syltɑ̃, ɑt/ ADJ insulting *(pour* to)

insulte /ɛ̃sylt/ NF *(= grossièreté)* abuse *(NonC)*, insult; *(= affront)* insult ◆ **c'est me faire ~ que de ne pas me croire** *(frm)* you insult me by not believing me ◆ **c'est une ~** *ou* **c'est faire ~ à son intelligence** it's an insult *ou* affront to his intelligence

insulté, e /ɛ̃sylte/ (ptp de **insulter**) ADJ insulted NM *(en duel)* injured party

insulter /ɛ̃sylte/ ▸ conjug 1 ◂ VT *(= faire affront à)* to insult; *(= injurier)* to abuse, to insult VT INDIR **insulter à** *(littér)* to be an insult to VPR **s'insulter** to insult one another

insulteur /ɛ̃syltœʀ/ NM insulter

insupportable /ɛ̃sypɔʀtabl/ ADJ unbearable, intolerable; *[personne]* unbearable, insufferable *(frm)* ◆ **il est ~ d'orgueil** he's unbearably *ou* unsufferably *(frm)* proud

insupportablement /ɛ̃sypɔʀtabləmɑ̃/ ADV unbearably, intolerably

insupporter /ɛ̃sypɔʀte/ ▸ conjug 1 ◂ VT *(hum)* ◆ **cela m'insupporte/l'insupporte** I/he can't stand this

insurgé, e /ɛ̃syʀʒe/ (ptp de **s'insurger**) ADJ, NM,F rebel, insurgent

insurger (s') /ɛ̃syʀʒe/ ▸ conjug 3 ◂ VPR *(lit, fig)* to rebel, to rise up, to revolt (*contre* against)

insurmontable /ɛ̃syʀmɔ̃tabl/ ADJ 1 *(= infranchissable) [difficulté, obstacle]* insurmountable, insuperable 2 *(= irrépressible) [peur, dégoût]* unconquerable

insurpassable /ɛ̃syʀpɑsabl/ ADJ unsurpassable, unsurpassed

insurrection /ɛ̃syʀɛksjɔ̃/ NF *(lit)* insurrection, revolt, uprising; *(fig)* revolt ◆ **mouvement/foyer d'**~ movement/nucleus of revolt

insurrectionnel, -elle /ɛ̃syʀɛksjɔnɛl/ ADJ *[mouvement, gouvernement, force]* insurrectionary ◆ **climat** ~ atmosphere of open rebellion

intact, e /ɛ̃takt/ ADJ *[objet, réputation, argent]* intact *(attrib)* ◆ **le vase est arrivé** ~ the vase arrived intact *ou* in one piece ◆ **le mystère reste** ~ the mystery remains unsolved ◆ **son enthousiasme reste** ~ he's still as enthusiastic as ever

intaille /ɛ̃taj/ NF intaglio

intangibilité /ɛ̃tɑ̃ʒibilite/ NF inviolability

intangible /ɛ̃tɑ̃ʒibl/ ADJ 1 *(= impalpable)* intangible 2 *(= sacré)* inviolable

intarissable /ɛ̃taʀisabl/ ADJ *(lit, fig)* inexhaustible ◆ **il est** ~ he could talk for ever (*sur* about)

intarissablement /ɛ̃taʀisabləmɑ̃/ ADV inexhaustibly

intégrable /ɛ̃tegʀabl/ ADJ that can be integrated

intégral, e (mpl **-aux**) /ɛ̃tegʀal, o/ ADJ complete, full ◆ **le remboursement** ~ **de qch** the repayment in full of sth, the full *ou* complete repayment of sth ◆ **publier le texte** ~ **d'un discours** to publish the text of a speech in full *ou* the complete text of a speech ◆ **version** ~**e** *(Ciné)* uncut version ◆ **texte** ~ *(Presse)* unabridged version ◆ **"texte intégral"** "unabridged" ◆ **le nu** ~ complete *ou* total nudity ◆ **bronzage** ~ all-over suntan ◆ **casque** ~ full-face helmet; → **calcul** NF **intégrale** 1 *(Math)* integral 2 *(Mus)* *(= série)* complete series; *(= œuvre)* complete works ◆ **l'intégrale des symphonies de Sibelius** the complete symphonies of Sibelius 3 *(= outil)* single-purpose tool

intégralement /ɛ̃tegʀalmɑ̃/ ADV in full, fully ◆ **le concert sera retransmis** ~ the concert will be broadcast in full

intégralité /ɛ̃tegʀalite/ NF whole ◆ **l'**~ **de la somme** the whole of the sum, the whole *ou* entire *ou* full sum *ou* amount ◆ **la somme vous sera remboursée dans son** ~ the sum will be repaid to you in its entirety *ou* in toto *ou* in full ◆ **le match sera retransmis dans son** ~ the match will be broadcast in full ◆ **l'**~ **de mon salaire** the whole of my salary, my whole *ou* entire salary

intégrant, e /ɛ̃tegʀɑ̃, ɑ̃t/ ADJ → **partie**[2]

intégrateur, -trice /ɛ̃tegʀatœʀ, tʀis/ ADJ ◆ **le rôle** ~ **de l'école** the role of schools in integrating children into society NM **intégrateur** *(Ordin)* integrator

intégration /ɛ̃tegʀasjɔ̃/ NF *(gén)* integration (*à, dans* into); ◆ **politique d'**~ **des immigrés** policy favouring the integration of immigrants ◆ **après son** ~ **à Polytechnique** *(Univ)* after getting into *ou* being admitted to the École polytechnique ◆ ~ **à très grande échelle** *(Ordin)* very large-scale integration

intégrationniste /ɛ̃tegʀasjɔnist/ ADJ, NMF integrationist

intègre /ɛ̃tɛgʀ/ ADJ upright, honest

intégré, e /ɛ̃tegʀe/ (ptp de **intégrer**) ADJ 1 *[circuit, système]* integrated; *[lecteur CD-ROM]* built-in ◆ **cuisine** ~**e** fitted kitchen 2 *(= assimilé)* **populations bien** ~**es** well-assimilated populations

intégrer /ɛ̃tegʀe/ ▸ conjug 6 ◂ VT 1 *(Math)* to integrate 2 *(= assimiler) [+ idées, personne]* to integrate (*à, dans* into) 3 *(= entrer dans) [+ entreprise, club]* to join VI *(Univ)* ◆ ~ **à ...** to get into ... VPR **s'intégrer** to become integrated (*à, dans* into); ◆ **bien s'**~ **dans une société** to integrate well into a society ◆ **cette maison s'intègre mal dans le paysage** this house doesn't really fit into the surrounding countryside

intégrisme /ɛ̃tegʀism/ NM fundamentalism

intégriste /ɛ̃tegʀist/ ADJ, NMF fundamentalist

intégrité /ɛ̃tegʀite/ NF *(= totalité)* integrity; *(= honnêteté)* integrity, honesty, uprightness

intellect /ɛ̃telɛkt/ NM intellect

intellectualisation /ɛ̃telɛktɥalizasjɔ̃/ NF intellectualization

intellectualiser /ɛ̃telɛktɥalize/ ▸ conjug 1 ◂ VT to intellectualize

intellectualisme /ɛ̃telɛktɥalism/ NM intellectualism

intellectualiste /ɛ̃telɛktɥalist/ ADJ, NMF intellectualist

intellectualité /ɛ̃telɛktɥalite/ NF *(littér)* intellectuality

intellectuel, -elle /ɛ̃telɛktɥɛl/ ADJ *[facultés, effort, supériorité]* mental, intellectual; *[fatigue]* mental; *[personne, mouvement, œuvre, vie]* intellectual; *(péj)* highbrow *(péj)* ◆ **activité intellectuelle** mental *ou* intellectual activity ◆ **les milieux** ~**s** intellectual circles; → **quotient** NM,F intellectual; *(péj)* highbrow *(péj)* ◆ **les** ~**s de gauche** left-wing intellectuals

intellectuellement /ɛ̃telɛktɥɛlmɑ̃/ ADV intellectually ◆ **un enfant** ~ **très doué** an intellectually gifted child

intelligemment /ɛ̃teliʒamɑ̃/ ADV *[agir]* intelligently, cleverly ◆ **les gens consomment plus** ~ people are consuming more intelligently ◆ **c'est fait très** ~ it's very intelligently *ou* cleverly done

intelligence /ɛ̃teliʒɑ̃s/ NF 1 *(= facultés mentales)* intelligence ◆ **personne à l'**~ **vive** person with a sharp *ou* quick mind ◆ **faire preuve d'**~ to show intelligence ◆ **avoir l'**~ **de faire** to have the intelligence *ou* the wit to do, to be intelligent enough to do ◆ **travailler avec** ~**/sans** ~ to work intelligently/unintelligently ◆ **il met beaucoup d'**~ **dans ce qu'il fait** he applies great intelligence to what he does ◆ **c'est une** ~ **exceptionnelle** he has a great intellect *ou* mind *ou* brain, he is a person of exceptional intelligence ◆ **les grandes** ~**s** great minds *ou* intellects ◆ ~ **artificielle** artificial intelligence

2 *(= compréhension)* understanding ◆ **pour l'**~ **du texte** for a clear understanding of the text, in order to understand the text ◆ **avoir l'**~ **des affaires** to have a good grasp *ou* understanding of business matters, to have a good head for business

3 *(= complicité)* secret agreement ◆ **agir d'**~ **avec qn** to act in (secret) agreement with sb ◆ **signe/sourire d'**~ sign/smile of complicity ◆ **être d'**~ **avec qn** to have a (secret) understanding *ou* agreement with sb ◆ **vivre en bonne/mauvaise** ~ **avec qn** to be on good/bad terms with sb

NFPL **intelligences** *(= relations secrètes)* secret relations *ou* contacts ◆ **entretenir des** ~**s avec l'ennemi** to have secret dealings with the enemy

intelligent, e /ɛ̃teliʒɑ̃, ɑ̃t/ ADJ 1 *[personne]* intelligent, clever, bright; *[visage, front, regard, animal]* intelligent; *[choix, réponse]* intelligent, clever ◆ **supérieurement** ~ of superior intelligence ◆ **c'est** ~ **!** *(iro)* very clever! *(iro)* ◆ **son livre est** ~ his book shows intelligence ◆ **armes** ~**es** smart weapons ◆ **ce n'était pas très** ~ **de sa part !** that wasn't very clever of him! 2 *(Ordin)* intelligent ◆ **terminal** ~ intelligent terminal

intelligentsia /ɛ̃teliʒɛnsja/ NF ◆ **l'**~ the intelligentsia

intelligibilité /ɛ̃teliʒibilite/ NF intelligibility

intelligible /ɛ̃teliʒibl/ ADJ intelligible ◆ **à haute et** ~ **voix** loudly and clearly ◆ **s'exprimer de façon peu** ~ to express o.s. unintelligibly *ou* in an unintelligible way

intelligiblement /ɛ̃teliʒibləmɑ̃/ ADV intelligibly

intello* /ɛ̃telo/ ADJ, NMF *(péj)* highbrow *(péj)*, intellectual ◆ **c'est l'**~ **de la famille** he's the brains of the family ◆ **il est du genre** ~ **rive gauche** he's the arty* intellectual type

intempérance /ɛ̃tɑ̃peʀɑ̃s/ NF *(frm)* *(= gloutonnerie, ivrognerie)* intemperance *(frm)*; *(= luxure)* overindulgence ◆ **une telle** ~ **de langage** such excessive language

intempérant, e /ɛ̃tɑ̃peʀɑ̃, ɑ̃t/ ADJ *(frm)* *(= glouton, ivrogne)* intemperate; *(= luxurieux)* overindulgent

intempéries /ɛ̃tɑ̃peʀi/ NFPL bad weather ◆ **affronter les** ~ to brave the (bad) weather

intempestif, -ive /ɛ̃tɑ̃pɛstif, iv/ ADJ untimely ◆ **pas de zèle** ~ **!** no misplaced *ou* excessive zeal!

intempestivement /ɛ̃tɑ̃pɛstivmɑ̃/ ADV at an untimely moment

intemporalité /ɛ̃tɑ̃pɔʀalite/ NF *(littér)* *(= atemporalité)* timelessness; *(= immatérialité)* immateriality

intemporel, -elle /ɛ̃tɑ̃pɔʀɛl/ ADJ *(littér)* *(= atemporel)* timeless; *(= immatériel)* immaterial

intenable /ɛ̃t(ə)nabl/ ADJ *(= intolérable) [chaleur, situation]* intolerable, unbearable; *[personne]* unruly; *(= indéfendable) [position, théorie]* untenable

intendance /ɛ̃tɑ̃dɑ̃s/ NF *(Mil)* *(= service)* Supply Corps; *(= bureau)* Supplies office; *(Scol)* *(= métier)* school management, financial administration; *(= bureau)* bursar's office; *[de propriété]* *(= métier)* estate management; *(= bureau)* estate office; *(Hist = province)* intendancy ◆ **les problèmes d'**~ *(Mil)* the problems of supply; *(gén)* the day-to-day problems of running a house (*ou* a company *etc*) ◆ **l'**~ **suivra** *(fig)* all material support will be provided

intendant /ɛ̃tɑ̃dɑ̃/ NM 1 *(Scol)* bursar 2 *(Mil)* quartermaster; *(= régisseur)* steward 3 *(Hist)* intendant

intendante /ɛ̃tɑ̃dɑ̃t/ NF 1 *(Scol)* bursar; *(= régisseur)* stewardess 2 *(Rel)* Superior

intense /ɛ̃tɑ̃s/ ADJ 1 *[lumière, moment, joie, activité, réflexion, match, chagrin]* intense; *[froid, douleur]* severe, intense ◆ **une chemise d'un bleu** ~ a vivid blue shirt ◆ **ça demande un travail** ~ it requires really hard work 2 *[circulation]* dense, heavy

intensément /ɛ̃tɑ̃semɑ̃/ ADV intensely

intensif, -ive /ɛ̃tɑ̃sif, iv/ ADJ *(gén, Agr, Ling)* intensive; → **cours, culture** NM *(Ling)* intensive

intensification /ɛ̃tɑ̃sifikasjɔ̃/ NF intensification ◆ **l'~ du trafic aérien** the increase in air traffic

intensifier /ɛ̃tɑ̃sifje/ ▸ conjug 7 ◂ VT *[+ coopération, concurrence, production]* to intensify; *[+ lutte, effort]* to intensify, to step up VPR **s'intensifier** *[combats, bombardements]* to intensify; *[concurrence]* to intensify, to become keener ◆ **le froid va s'~** it's going to get colder

intensité /ɛ̃tɑ̃site/ NF 1 *[de lumière, moment, activité]* intensity; *[de froid, douleur]* severity, intensity ◆ **un moment d'une grande ~** a very intense moment ◆ **~ dramatique** dramatic intensity 2 *[de circulation]* density 3 *(Ling)* **accent d'~** stress accent 4 *(Élec) [de courant]* strength; *(Phys) [de force]* intensity

intensivement /ɛ̃tɑ̃sivmɑ̃/ ADV intensively

intenter /ɛ̃tɑ̃te/ ▸ conjug 1 ◂ VT ◆ **~ un procès contre** *ou* **à qn** to take sb to court, to start *ou* institute proceedings against sb ◆ **~ une action contre** *ou* **à qn** to bring an action against sb

intention /ɛ̃tɑ̃sjɔ̃/ GRAMMAIRE ACTIVE 35, 45.1, 45.4 NF *(gén)* intention ◆ **quelles sont vos ~s ?** what are your intentions?, what do you intend to do? ◆ **bonnes ~s** good intentions ◆ **agir dans une bonne ~** to act with good intentions ◆ **elle l'a fait sans mauvaise ~** she didn't mean any harm ◆ **c'est l'~ qui compte** it's the thought that counts ◆ **il n'entre** *ou* **n'est pas dans ses ~s de démissionner** it's not his intention to resign, he has no intention of resigning ◆ **à cette ~** with this intention, to this end ◆ **avoir l'~ de faire** to intend *ou* mean to do, to have the intention of doing ◆ **avec** *ou* **dans l'~ de faire** with the intention of doing, with a view to doing ◆ **avec** *ou* **dans l'~ de tuer** with intent to kill ◆ **~ de vote** *(Pol)* voting intention ◆ **déclaration d'~** *(Pol)* declaration of intent; → **enfer, procès**

◆ **à l'intention de qn** for sb ◆ **des stages de formation à l'~ des guides** training courses for guides ◆ **un site Web à l'~ des personnes âgées** a website (designed) for older people ◆ **une campagne d'information à l'~ des très jeunes** an information campaign directed towards very young people

intentionnalité /ɛ̃tɑ̃sjɔnalite/ NF intentionality

intentionné, e /ɛ̃tɑ̃sjɔne/ ADJ ◆ **bien ~** well-meaning, well-intentioned ◆ **mal ~** ill-intentioned

intentionnel, -elle /ɛ̃tɑ̃sjɔnɛl/ ADJ intentional, deliberate

intentionnellement /ɛ̃tɑ̃sjɔnɛlmɑ̃/ ADV intentionally, deliberately

inter[1] † /ɛ̃tɛʀ/ NM *(Téléc)* abrév de **interurbain**

inter[2] † /ɛ̃tɛʀ/ NM *(Sport)* ◆ **~ gauche/droit** inside-left/-right

inter(-)... /ɛ̃tɛʀ/ PRÉF inter... ◆ **inter(-)africain** inter-African ◆ **inter(-)américain** inter-American ◆ **inter(-)arabe** inter-Arab

interactif, -ive /ɛ̃tɛʀaktif, iv/ ADJ interactive

interaction /ɛ̃tɛʀaksjɔ̃/ NF interaction *(entre* between)

interactivement /ɛ̃tɛʀaktivmɑ̃/ ADV *(gén, Ordin)* interactively

interactivité /ɛ̃tɛʀaktivite/ NF interactivity

interagir /ɛ̃tɛʀaʒiʀ/ ▸ conjug 2 ◂ VI to interact *(avec* with)

interallemand, e /ɛ̃tɛʀalmɑ̃, ɑ̃d/ ADJ *[frontière, relations]* between West and East Germany

interallié, e /ɛ̃tɛʀalje/ ADJ inter-Allied

interarmées /ɛ̃tɛʀaʀme/ ADJ INV *(Mil)* interservice ◆ **forces ~ combinées** combined joint task forces ◆ **chef d'état-major ~** commander of joint task forces

interarmes /ɛ̃tɛʀaʀm/ ADJ INV *[opération]* combined-arms *(épith)*, interservice *(épith)*

interbancaire /ɛ̃tɛʀbɑ̃kɛʀ/ ADJ *[relations, marché]* interbank

intercalaire /ɛ̃tɛʀkalɛʀ/ ADJ ◆ **feuillet ~** inset, insert ◆ **fiche ~** divider ◆ **jour ~** intercalary day NM *(= feuillet)* inset, insert; *(= fiche)* divider

intercalation /ɛ̃tɛʀkalasjɔ̃/ NF *[de mot, exemple]* insertion, interpolation; *[de feuillet]* insertion; *[de jour d'année bissextile]* intercalation

intercaler /ɛ̃tɛʀkale/ ▸ conjug 1 ◂ VT *[+ mot, exemple]* to insert, to interpolate; *[+ feuille]* to insert; *[+ jour d'année bissextile]* to intercalate ◆ **~ quelques jours de repos dans un mois de stage** to fit a few days' rest into a month of training ◆ **on a intercalé dans le stage des visites d'usines** the training course was interspersed with *ou* broken by visits to factories VPR **s'intercaler** ◆ **s'~ entre** to come in between

intercéder /ɛ̃tɛʀsede/ ▸ conjug 6 ◂ VI to intercede *(en faveur de* on behalf of; *auprès de* with)

intercellulaire /ɛ̃tɛʀselylɛʀ/ ADJ intercellular

intercensitaire /ɛ̃tɛʀsɑ̃sitɛʀ/ ADJ intercensal

intercepter /ɛ̃tɛʀsɛpte/ ▸ conjug 1 ◂ VT 1 *[+ ballon, message, conversation téléphonique, personne]* to intercept 2 *[+ lumière, chaleur]* to cut *ou* block off

intercepteur /ɛ̃tɛʀsɛptœʀ/ NM interceptor (plane)

interception /ɛ̃tɛʀsɛpsjɔ̃/ NF *[de ballon, message, personne]* interception; *[de lumière, chaleur]* cutting *ou* blocking off ◆ **avion** *ou* **chasseur d'~** *(Mil)* interceptor(-plane)

intercesseur /ɛ̃tɛʀsesœʀ/ NM *(littér, Rel)* intercessor

intercession /ɛ̃tɛʀsesjɔ̃/ NF *(littér, Rel)* intercession

interchangeabilité /ɛ̃tɛʀʃɑ̃ʒabilite/ NF interchangeability

interchangeable /ɛ̃tɛʀʃɑ̃ʒabl/ ADJ interchangeable

interclasse /ɛ̃tɛʀklɑs/ NM *(Scol)* break *(between classes)*

interclubs /ɛ̃tɛʀklœb/ ADJ INV *[tournoi]* interclub

intercommunal, e (mpl **-aux**) /ɛ̃tɛʀkɔmynal, o/ ADJ *[décision, stade]* shared by several French communes, ≈ intervillage, intermunicipal

intercommunalité /ɛ̃tɛʀkɔmynalite/ NF intermunicipal links

intercommunautaire /ɛ̃tɛʀkɔmynotɛʀ/ ADJ intercommunity, intercommunal

intercommunication /ɛ̃tɛʀkɔmynikasjɔ̃/ NF intercommunication

interconnecter /ɛ̃tɛʀkɔnɛkte/ ▸ conjug 1 ◂ VT *(Élec)* to interconnect

interconnexion /ɛ̃tɛʀkɔnɛksjɔ̃/ NF interconnection

intercontinental, e (mpl **-aux**) /ɛ̃tɛʀkɔ̃tinɑ̃tal, o/ ADJ intercontinental

intercostal, e (mpl **-aux**) /ɛ̃tɛʀkɔstal, o/ ADJ intercostal NMPL intercostal muscles, intercostals

intercours /ɛ̃tɛʀkuʀ/ NM *(Scol)* break *(between classes)*

interculturel, -elle /ɛ̃tɛʀkyltyʀɛl/ ADJ cross-cultural, intercultural

interdépartemental, e (mpl **-aux**) /ɛ̃tɛʀdepaʀtəmɑ̃tal, o/ ADJ *shared by several French departments*

interdépendance /ɛ̃tɛʀdepɑ̃dɑ̃s/ NF interdependence

interdépendant, e /ɛ̃tɛʀdepɑ̃dɑ̃, ɑ̃t/ ADJ interdependent, mutually dependent

interdiction /ɛ̃tɛʀdiksjɔ̃/ NF 1 ◆ **~ de qch** *(= action)* banning of sth; *(= état)* ban on sth ◆ **à cause de l'~ faite aux fonctionnaires de cumuler plusieurs emplois** because civil servants are not allowed to hold several positions ◆ **l'~ de coller des affiches/de servir de l'alcool** the ban on the posting of bills/the serving of alcohol, the ban on posting bills/serving alcohol ◆ **"interdiction de coller des affiches"** "(post *ou* stick *(Brit)*) no bills", "billposting *ou* bill-sticking *(Brit)* prohibited" ◆ **"interdiction (formelle** *ou* **absolue) de fumer"** "(strictly) no smoking", "smoking (strictly) prohibited" ◆ **"interdiction de tourner à droite"** "no right turn" ◆ **"interdiction de stationner"** "no parking" ◆ **"interdiction de déposer des ordures"** "no dumping" ◆ **~ d'en parler à quiconque/de modifier quoi que ce soit** it is (strictly) forbidden to talk to anyone about it/to alter anything ◆ **malgré l'~ d'entrer** despite not being allowed to enter ◆ **renouveler à qn l'~ de faire** to reimpose a ban on sb's doing ◆ **~ lui a été faite de sortir** he has been forbidden to go out

2 *(= interdit)* ban ◆ **enfreindre/lever une ~** to break/lift a ban ◆ **il a garé sa voiture malgré le panneau d'~** he parked his car in spite of the no parking sign

3 *(= suspension) [de livre, film]* banning *(de* of) ban *(de* on); *[de fonctionnaire]* banning from office; *[de prêtre]* interdiction ◆ **~ légale** *(Jur) suspension of a convict's civic rights*

COMP **interdiction de séjour** *order denying former prisoner access to specified places* ◆ **~ bancaire** suspension of banking privileges ◆ **~ de chéquier** withdrawal of chequebook facilities

interdigital, e (mpl **-aux**) /ɛ̃tɛʀdiʒital, o/ ADJ interdigital

interdire /ɛ̃tɛʀdiʀ/ GRAMMAIRE ACTIVE 36.3, 37.4 ▸ conjug 37 ◂

VT 1 *(= prohiber)* to forbid; *[+ stationnement, circulation]* to prohibit, to ban ◆ **~ l'alcool/le tabac à qn** to forbid sb alcohol/tobacco, to forbid sb to drink/smoke ◆ **~ à qn de faire qch** to tell sb not to do sth, to forbid sb to do sth, to prohibit *(frm)* sb from doing sth ◆ **elle nous a interdit d'y aller seuls, elle a interdit que nous y allions seuls** she forbade us to go on our own ◆ **on a interdit les camions dans le centre de la ville** lorries have been barred from *ou* banned from *ou* prohibited in the centre of the town

2 *(= empêcher) [contretemps, difficulté]* to preclude, to prevent; *[obstacle physique]* to block ◆ **son état de santé lui interdit tout travail/effort** his state of health does not allow *ou* permit him to do any work/to make any effort ◆ **sa maladie ne lui interdit pas le travail** his illness does not prevent him from working ◆ **la gravité de la crise (nous) interdit tout espoir** the gravity of the crisis leaves us no hope *ou* precludes all hope ◆ **leur attitude interdit toute négociation** their attitude precludes *ou* prevents any possibility of negotiation ◆ **une porte blindée interdisait le passage** an armoured door blocked *ou* barred the way

3 *(= frapper d'interdiction) [+ fonctionnaire]* to bar from office; *[+ prêtre]* to suspend; *[+ film, réunion, journal]* to ban ◆ **on lui a interdit le club** *(fig)* he has been barred *ou* banned from the club ◆ **~ sa porte aux intrus** to bar one's door to intruders

4 († *= interloquer)* to dumbfound, to take aback, to disconcert

VPR **s'interdire** ◆ **s'~ toute remarque** to refrain *ou* abstain from making any remark ◆ **nous nous sommes interdit d'intervenir** we have not allowed ourselves to intervene, we have refrained from intervening ◆ **s'~ la boisson/les cigarettes** to abstain from drink *ou* drinking/smoking ◆ **il s'interdit d'y pen-**

ser he doesn't let himself think about it *ou* allow himself to think about it ◆ **il s'est interdit toute possibilité de revenir en arrière** he has (deliberately) denied himself *ou* not allowed himself any chance of going back on his decision

interdisciplinaire /ɛ̃tɛʀdisiplinɛʀ/ **ADJ** interdisciplinary

interdisciplinarité /ɛ̃tɛʀdisiplinaʀite/ **NF** interdisciplinarity

interdit¹, e /ɛ̃tɛʀdi, it/ GRAMMAIRE ACTIVE 37.4 ptp de **interdire**

ADJ (= *défendu*) *[film, livre]* banned ◆ **film ~ aux moins de 18 ans** ≈ 18 film *(Brit)*, NC-17 film *(US)* ◆ **film ~ aux moins de 13 ans** ≈ PG film, PG-13 film *(US)* ◆ **"passage/stationnement interdit"** "no entry/parking" ◆ **il est strictement ~ de ...** it is strictly forbidden *ou* prohibited to ... ◆ **(il est) ~ de fumer** no smoking, smoking (is) prohibited ◆ **être ~ bancaire** to have one's banking privileges suspended ◆ **être ~ de chéquier** to have chequebook facilities withdrawn ◆ **~ de vol** *[pilote]* grounded ◆ **~ de vente** *[produit]* banned ◆ **"il est interdit d'interdire"** *(slogan)* forbidding is forbidden; → **reproduction**

NM (= *interdiction*) *(gén)* ban; *(Rel)* interdict; *(social)* prohibition ◆ **~s alimentaires** *(Rel)* dietary restrictions ◆ **transgresser les ~s** to break taboos ◆ **frapper d'~** to ban ◆ **lever l'~** to lift the ban

COMP **interdit de séjour** *(Jur) person banned from entering specified areas; (fig)* persona non grata ◆ **la violence est ~e de séjour sur les terrains de sport** violence is unacceptable in sports grounds

interdit², e /ɛ̃tɛʀdi, it/ **ADJ** (= *stupéfait*) dumbfounded, taken aback *(attrib)*, disconcerted ◆ **la réponse le laissa ~** the answer took him aback, he was dumbfounded *ou* disconcerted by *ou* at the answer

interentreprises /ɛ̃tɛʀɑ̃tʀəpʀiz/ **ADJ** *[crédit, coopération]* inter-company *(Brit)*, inter-corporate *(US)*

intéressant, e /ɛ̃teʀesɑ̃, ɑ̃t/ GRAMMAIRE ACTIVE 53.6 **ADJ** 1 (= *captivant*) *[livre, détail, visage]* interesting ◆ **un conférencier peu ~** a boring speaker ◆ **il faut toujours qu'il cherche à se rendre ~** *ou* **qu'il fasse son ~** he always has to draw attention to himself ◆ **elle est dans une situation** *ou* **position ~e** † she is in the family way *

2 (= *avantageux*) *[offre, prix, affaire]* good ◆ **ce n'est pas très ~ pour nous** it's not really worth our while, it's not really worth it for us ◆ **ce serait (financièrement) plus ~ pour nous de prendre le train** we'd be better off taking the train, it would work out cheaper for us to take the train ◆ **c'est une personne ~e à connaître** he's someone worth knowing

> ⚠ Au sens de 'avantageux', **intéressant** ne se traduit pas par **interesting**.

intéressé, e /ɛ̃teʀese/ (ptp de **intéresser**) **ADJ** 1 (= *qui est en cause*) concerned, involved ◆ **les ~s, les parties ~es** the interested parties, the parties involved *ou* concerned ◆ **dans cette affaire, c'est lui le principal ou premier ~** in this matter, he's the one who's most concerned 2 (= *qui cherche son intérêt personnel*) *[personne]* self-seeking, self-interested; *[motif]* interested ◆ **visite ~e** visit motivated by self-interest ◆ **rendre un service ~** to do a good turn out of self-interest ◆ **ce que je vous propose, c'est très ~** my suggestion to you is strongly motivated by self-interest

intéressement /ɛ̃teʀesmɑ̃/ **NM** *(Écon : = système)* profit-sharing (scheme) ◆ **l'~ des travailleurs aux bénéfices de l entreprise** the workers' participation in *ou* sharing of the firm's profits

intéresser /ɛ̃teʀese/ ▸ conjug 1 ◂ VT 1 (= *captiver*) to interest ◆ **~ qn à qch** to interest sb in sth ◆ **cela m'intéresserait de faire** I would be interested to do *ou* in doing, it would interest me to do ◆ **ça ne m'intéresse pas** I'm not interested, it doesn't interest me ◆ **rien ne l'intéresse** he isn't interested *ou* he takes no interest in anything ◆ **le film l'a intéressé** he found the film interesting, the film interested him ◆ **ça pourrait vous ~** this might interest you *ou* be of interest to you ◆ **cette question n'intéresse pas (beaucoup) les jeunes** this matter is of no (great) interest to *ou* doesn't (greatly) interest young people ◆ **il ne sait pas ~ son public** he doesn't know how to interest his audience ◆ **continue, tu m'intéresses !** *(iro)* do go on - I find that very interesting *ou* I'm all ears! * ◆ **tes petites histoires n'intéressent personne** no one cares about your little problems

2 (= *concerner*) to affect, to concern ◆ **la nouvelle loi intéresse les petits commerçants** the new law affects *ou* concerns small shopkeepers

3 *(Comm, Fin)* **~ le personnel de l'usine aux bénéfices** to give the factory employees a share *ou* an interest in the profits, to operate a profit-sharing scheme in the factory ◆ **être intéressé dans une affaire** to have a stake *ou* a financial interest in a business

4 *(Jeux)* **~ une partie** to stake money on a game

VPR **s'intéresser** ◆ **s'~ à qch/qn** to be interested in sth/sb, to take an interest in sth/sb ◆ **il s'intéresse vivement/activement à cette affaire** he is taking a keen/an active interest in this matter ◆ **il ne s'intéresse pas à nos activités** he isn't interested in our activities ◆ **il mérite qu'on s'intéresse à lui** he deserves one's *ou* people's interest ◆ **il s'intéresse beaucoup à cette jeune fille** he is taking *ou* showing a great deal of interest in that girl

intérêt /ɛ̃teʀe/ GRAMMAIRE ACTIVE 28.1, 29.2 **NM** 1 (= *attention*) interest ◆ **écouter avec ~/(un) grand ~** to listen with interest/with great interest ◆ **prendre ~ à qch** to take an interest in sth ◆ **il a perdu tout ~ à son travail** he has lost all interest in his work

2 (= *bienveillance*) interest ◆ **porter/témoigner de l'~ à qn** to take/show an interest in sb

3 (= *originalité*) interest ◆ **film dénué d'~** *ou* **sans aucun ~** film devoid of interest ◆ **tout l'~ réside dans le dénouement** the most interesting part is the ending, what is most interesting is the ending

4 (= *importance*) significance, importance, relevance ◆ **l'~ des recherches spatiales** the significance *ou* importance *ou* relevance of space research ◆ **après quelques considérations sans ~** after a few unimportant *ou* minor considerations, after considerations of minor interest *ou* importance ◆ **c'est sans ~ pour la suite de l'histoire** it's of no relevance *ou* consequence *ou* importance for the rest of the story ◆ **une découverte du plus haut ~** a discovery of the greatest *ou* utmost importance *ou* significance *ou* relevance ◆ **la nouvelle a perdu beaucoup de son ~** the news has lost much of its significance *ou* interest ◆ **être déclaré d'~ public** to be officially recognized as being beneficial to the general public

5 (= *avantage*) interest ◆ **ce n'est pas (dans) leur ~ de le faire** it is not in their interest to do it ◆ **agir dans/contre son ~** to act in/against one's own interests ◆ **dans l'~ général** in the general interest ◆ **autorisation refusée dans l'~ du service** permission refused on administrative grounds *ou* for administrative reasons ◆ **il y trouve son ~** he finds it to his (own) advantage, he finds it worth his while ◆ **il sait où est son ~** he knows where his interest lies, he knows which side his bread is buttered

◆ **avoir + intérêt** ◆ **il a (tout) ~ à accepter** it's in his interest to accept, he'd be well advised to accept, he'd do well to accept ◆ **quel ~ aurait-il à faire cela ?** why would he want to do that? ◆ **tu aurais plutôt ~ à te taire !** * you'd be well advised *ou* you'd do very well to keep quiet! ◆ **y a-t-il un ~ quelconque à se réunir ?** is there any point at all in getting together? ◆ **est-ce qu'il faut que je lui en parle ? – (il) y a ~ !** * should I talk to him about it? – you'd better! ◆ **t'as pas ~ !** * you'd better not!

6 *(Fin)* interest ◆ **recevoir 7% d'~** to get 7% interest ◆ **prêt à ~ élevé** high-interest loan ◆ **prêter à** *ou* **avec ~** to lend at *ou* with interest ◆ **~s simples/composés** simple/compound interest ◆ **~s courus** accrued interest; → **taux**

7 (= *recherche d'avantage personnel*) self-interest ◆ **agir par ~** to act out of self-interest; → **mariage**

8 ◆ **~s** interest(s) ◆ **la défense de nos ~s** the defence of our interests ◆ **il a des ~s dans l'affaire** *(Écon, Fin)* he has a stake *ou* an interest *ou* a financial interest in the deal

interétatique /ɛ̃teʀetatik/ **ADJ** *[accord, coopération]* inter-state *(épith)*

interethnique /ɛ̃teʀɛtnik/ **ADJ** inter-ethnic

interface /ɛ̃tɛʀfas/ **NF** interface ◆ **~ utilisateur/graphique** user/graphical interface ◆ **servir d'~ entre** *(fig)* to liaise between, to act as an interface between

interfacer VT, s'interfacer VPR /ɛ̃tɛʀfase/ ▸ conjug 3 ◂ to interface *(avec* with)

interférence /ɛ̃tɛʀfeʀɑ̃s/ **NF** 1 *(Phys)* interference 2 *(fig)* (= *conjonction*) conjunction; (= *immixtion*) *[de problème]* intrusion *(dans* into); *[de personne, pays]* interference *(NonC)* *(dans* in); ◆ **l'~ des problèmes économiques et politiques** the conjunction of economic and political problems ◆ **l'~ des problèmes économiques dans la vie politique** the intrusion of economic problems into political life ◆ **il se produit des ~s entre les deux services** there's interference between the two services

interférent, e /ɛ̃tɛʀfeʀɑ̃, ɑ̃t/ **ADJ** *(Phys)* interfering

interférer /ɛ̃tɛʀfeʀe/ ▸ conjug 6 ◂ **VI** to interfere *(avec* with; *dans* in); ◆ **les deux procédures interfèrent** the two procedures interfere with each other

interférométrie /ɛ̃tɛʀfeʀɔmetʀi/ **NF** interferometry

interféron /ɛ̃tɛʀfeʀɔ̃/ **NM** interferon ◆ **~ humain** human interferon

interfluve /ɛ̃tɛʀflyv/ **NM** interfluve

intergalactique /ɛ̃tɛʀgalaktik/ **ADJ** intergalactic

intergénérationnel, -elle /ɛ̃tɛʀʒeneʀasjɔnɛl/ **ADJ** intergenerational ◆ **solidarité ~le** good relations between generations

intergouvernemental, e (mpl **-aux**) /ɛ̃tɛʀguvɛʀnəmɑ̃tal, o/ **ADJ** intergovernmental ◆ **Affaires ~es** *(au Québec)* Intergovernmental Affairs

intergroupe /ɛ̃tɛʀgʀup/ **NM** *(Pol)* *[de plusieurs partis]* joint committee; *[de deux partis]* bipartisan committee

intérieur, e /ɛ̃teʀjœʀ/ ADJ 1 *[paroi]* inner, interior, inside, internal; *[escalier]* internal; *[cour]* inner ◆ **mer ~e** inland sea ◆ **la poche ~e de son manteau** the inside pocket of his coat ◆ **angle/point ~ à un cercle** angle/point interior to a circle; → **conduite**

2 *[vie, monde, voix, sentiment]* inner; → **for**

3 *[politique, dette]* domestic, internal; *[marché]* home *(épith)*, domestic, internal; *[communication, réseau, navigation]* inland; *[vol]* domestic

◆ **le commerce** ~ domestic trade ◆ **les affaires ~es** internal *ou* domestic affairs

NM 1 *[de tiroir, piste, champ de course]* inside; *[de maison]* inside, interior ◆ **l'~ de la maison était lugubre** the house was gloomy inside, the inside *ou* the interior of the house was gloomy ◆ **l'~ de la ville** the inner town ◆ **écrin avec un ~ de satin** case with a satin lining ◆ **à l'~** inside ◆ **je vous attends à l'~** I'll wait for you inside ◆ **à l'~ de la ville** inside the town ◆ **à l'~ de l'entreprise** *[promotion, corruption]* within the company; *[stage, formation]* in-house ◆ **rester à l'~** *(gén)* to stay inside; *(de la maison)* to stay inside *ou* indoors ◆ **vêtement/veste d'~** indoor garment/jacket ◆ **chaussures d'~** indoor *ou* house shoes ◆ **fermé/vu de l'~** locked/viewed from the inside ◆ **scènes tournées en ~** *(Ciné)* interior scenes, interiors; → **femme**

2 *(fig)* **à l'~** *[de personne]* within ◆ **il paraissait calme, mais à l'~ les soucis le rongeaient** he appeared to be calm, but inwardly *ou* inside he was consumed with anxiety

3 *[de pays]* interior ◆ **l'~ (du pays) est montagneux** the country is mountainous inland ◆ **les villes de l'~** the inland cities *ou* towns ◆ **la côte est riante mais l'~ est sauvage** the coast is pleasant, but it's wild inland ◆ **en allant vers l'~** going inland ◆ **à l'~ de nos frontières** within *ou* inside our frontiers ◆ **les ennemis de l'~** the enemies within (the country) ◆ **le moral de l'~** *(Mil)* the country's morale; → **ministère, ministre**

4 *(= décor, mobilier)* interior ◆ **un ~ douillet** a cosy interior ◆ **tableau d'~** interior (painting) ◆ **~ cuir** *[de voiture]* leather trim

5 *(Ftbl)* **~ gauche/droit** inside-left/-right

intérieurement /ɛ̃teʀjœʀmɑ̃/ **ADV** inwardly ◆ **rire ~** to laugh inwardly *ou* to o.s.

intérim /ɛ̃teʀim/ **NM** 1 *(= période)* interim period ◆ **il prendra toutes les décisions dans** *ou* **pendant l'~** he will make all the decisions in the interim ◆ **il assure l'~ en l'absence du directeur** he deputizes for the manager in his absence *ou* in the interim ◆ **diriger une firme par ~** to be the interim manager of a company ◆ **président/ministre par ~** acting *ou* interim president/minister 2 *(= travail à temps partiel)* temporary work, temping ◆ **agence** *ou* **société d'~** temping agency ◆ **faire de l'~** to temp

intérimaire /ɛ̃teʀimɛʀ/ **ADJ** *[directeur, ministre]* acting *(épith)*, interim *(épith)*; *[secrétaire, personnel, fonctions]* temporary; *[mesure, solution]* interim *(épith)*, temporary; *(Pol) [gouvernement, chef de parti]* caretaker *(épith)* **NMF** temporary worker *(recruited from an employment agency)*; *(= secrétaire)* temporary secretary, temp, Kelly girl *(US)*; *(= fonctionnaire)* deputy; *(= médecin, prêtre)* stand-in, locum *(Brit)* ◆ **travailler comme ~** to temp

interindividuel, -elle /ɛ̃teʀɛ̃dividɥɛl/ **ADJ** interpersonal ◆ **psychologie interindividuelle** psychology of interpersonal relationships

intériorisation /ɛ̃teʀjɔʀizasjɔ̃/ **NF** *[de conflit, émotion]* internalization, interiorization; *(Ling) [de règles]* internalization

intérioriser /ɛ̃teʀjɔʀize/ ▸ conjug 1 ◂ **VT** *[+ conflit, émotion]* to internalize, to interiorize; *(Ling) [+ règles]* to internalize ◆ **son jeu est très intériorisé** his acting is very introspective

intériorité /ɛ̃teʀjɔʀite/ **NF** interiority

interjectif, -ive /ɛ̃tɛʀʒɛktif, iv/ **ADJ** interjectional

interjection /ɛ̃tɛʀʒɛksjɔ̃/ **NF** *(Ling)* interjection; *(Jur)* lodging of an appeal

interjeter /ɛ̃tɛʀʒəte/ ▸ conjug 4 ◂ **VT** *(Jur)* ◆ **~ appel** to lodge an appeal

interleukine /ɛ̃tɛʀløkin/ **NF** interleukin

interlignage /ɛ̃tɛʀliɲaʒ/ **NM** *(Typo)* interline spacing

interligne /ɛ̃tɛʀliɲ/ **NM** *(= espace)* space between the lines; *(= annotation)* insertion between the lines; *(Mus)* space ◆ **double ~** double spacing ◆ **écrire qch dans l'~** to write *ou* insert sth between the lines *ou* in the space between the lines ◆ **taper un texte en double ~** to type a text in double spacing **NF** *(Typo)* lead

interligner /ɛ̃tɛʀliɲe/ ▸ conjug 1 ◂ **VT** *(= espacer)* to space; *(= inscrire)* to write between the lines

interlocuteur, -trice /ɛ̃tɛʀlɔkytœʀ, tʀis/ **NM,F** interlocutor *(frm)* ◆ **mon ~** *(= la personne à qui je parlais)* the person I was speaking to, my interlocutor *(frm)* ◆ **quel est mon ~ chez vous ?** who is the person I should speak to at your end? ◆ **~ valable** *(Pol)* recognized negotiator *ou* representative ◆ **les syndicats sont les ~s privilégiés d'un gouvernement de gauche** the unions have a privileged relationship with a left-wing government ◆ **c'est mon ~ privilégié** he's the person I liaise with

interlope /ɛ̃tɛʀlɔp/ **ADJ** 1 *(= équivoque)* shady 2 *(= illégal)* illicit, unlawful ◆ **navire ~** *ship carrying illicit merchandise*

interloqué, e /ɛ̃tɛʀlɔke/ (ptp de **interloquer**) **ADJ** taken aback ◆ **il a eu l'air un peu ~** he looked rather taken aback ◆ **tout le monde s'est tu, ~** everybody fell into a stunned silence

interloquer /ɛ̃tɛʀlɔke/ ▸ conjug 1 ◂ **VT** to take aback

interlude /ɛ̃tɛʀlyd/ **NM** *(Mus, TV)* interlude

intermariage /ɛ̃tɛʀmaʀjaʒ/ **NM** intermarriage

intermède /ɛ̃tɛʀmɛd/ **NM** *(= interruption, Théât)* interlude

intermédiaire /ɛ̃tɛʀmedjɛʀ/ **ADJ** *[niveau, choix, position]* intermediate, middle *(épith)*, intermediary ◆ **couleur ~ entre** colour halfway between ◆ **trouver/choisir une solution ~** to find/choose a compromise ◆ **il n'y a pas de solution ~** there's no half-way house *ou* no compromise solution ◆ **une date ~ entre le 25 juillet et le 3 août** a date midway between 25 July and 3 August **NM** ◆ **sans ~** *[vendre, négocier]* directly ◆ **par l'~ de qn** through sb ◆ **par l'~ de la presse** through (the medium) of the press **NMF** *(= médiateur)* intermediary, mediator, go-between; *(Comm, Écon)* middleman

intermédiation /ɛ̃tɛʀmedjasjɔ̃/ **NF** *(Fin)* (financial) intermediation

intermezzo /ɛ̃tɛʀmɛdzo/ **NM** intermezzo

interminable /ɛ̃tɛʀminabl/ **ADJ** *[conversation, série]* endless, interminable, never-ending; *(hum) [jambes, mains]* extremely long

interminablement /ɛ̃tɛʀminabləmɑ̃/ **ADV** endlessly, interminably

interministériel, -elle /ɛ̃tɛʀministeʀjɛl/ **ADJ** interdepartmental

intermission /ɛ̃tɛʀmisjɔ̃/ **NF** *(Méd)* intermission

intermittence /ɛ̃tɛʀmitɑ̃s/ **NF** 1 ◆ **par ~** *[travailler]* in fits and starts, sporadically, intermittently; *[pleuvoir]* on and off, sporadically, intermittently ◆ **le bruit nous parvenait par ~** the noise reached our ears at (sporadic) intervals 2 *(Méd) (entre deux accès)* remission; *[de pouls, cœur]* irregularity 3 *(littér)* intermittence, intermittency

intermittent, e /ɛ̃tɛʀmitɑ̃, ɑ̃t/ **ADJ** *[fièvre, lumière]* intermittent; *[douleur]* sporadic, intermittent; *[travail, bruit]* sporadic, periodic; *[pouls]* irregular, intermittent; *[fontaine, source]* intermittent ◆ **pluies ~es sur le nord** scattered showers in the north **NM,F** contract worker ◆ **les ~s du spectacle** *workers in the entertainment industry without steady employment*

intermoléculaire /ɛ̃tɛʀmɔlekylɛʀ/ **ADJ** intermolecular

intermusculaire /ɛ̃tɛʀmyskylɛʀ/ **ADJ** intermuscular

internat /ɛ̃tɛʀna/ **NM** 1 *(Scol) (= établissement)* boarding school; *(= système)* boarding; *(= élèves)* boarders; → **maître** 2 *(Méd) (= concours)* entrance examination (for hospital work); *(= stage)* hospital training *(as a doctor)*, period *ou* time as a houseman *(Brit) ou* an intern *(US)*, internship *(US)*

international, e (mpl **-aux**) /ɛ̃tɛʀnasjɔnal, o/ **ADJ** international **NM,F** *(Ftbl, Tennis etc)* international player; *(Athlétisme)* international athlete **NM** *(Écon)* ◆ **le tiers du chiffre d'affaires est réalisé à l'~** a third of all sales are on the international market **NF** **Internationale** *(= association)* International; *(= hymne)* Internationale ◆ **l'Internationale ouvrière** the International Workingmen's Association **NMPL** **internationaux** *(Sport)* internationals ◆ **les internationaux de France (de tennis)** the French Open

internationalement /ɛ̃tɛʀnasjɔnalmɑ̃/ **ADV** internationally

internationalisation /ɛ̃tɛʀnasjɔnalizasjɔ̃/ **NF** internationalization

internationaliser /ɛ̃tɛʀnasjɔnalize/ ▸ conjug 1 ◂ **VT** to internationalize

internationalisme /ɛ̃tɛʀnasjɔnalism/ **NM** internationalism

internationaliste /ɛ̃tɛʀnasjɔnalist/ **NMF** internationalist

internationalité /ɛ̃tɛʀnasjɔnalite/ **NF** internationality

internaute /ɛ̃tɛʀnot/ **NMF** net surfer, Internet user

interne /ɛ̃tɛʀn/ **ADJ** *[partie, politique, organe, hémorragie]* internal; *[oreille]* inner; *[angle]* interior ◆ **médecine ~** internal medicine **NMF** 1 *(Scol)* boarder ◆ **être ~** to be at boarding school 2 *(Méd)* **~ (des hôpitaux)** house doctor *(Brit)*, houseman *(Brit)*, intern *(US)* ◆ **~ en médecine** house physician *(Brit)*, intern *(US)* ◆ **~ en chirurgie** house surgeon *(Brit)*, intern in surgery *(US)* 3 ◆ **travail réalisé en ~** work carried out in-house

interné, e /ɛ̃tɛʀne/ (ptp de **interner**) **NM,F** *(Pol)* internee; *(Méd)* inmate (of a mental hospital)

internement /ɛ̃tɛʀnəmɑ̃/ **NM** *(Pol)* internment; *(Méd)* confinement (to a mental hospital) ◆ **~ abusif** wrongful confinement

interner /ɛ̃tɛʀne/ ▸ conjug 1 ◂ **VT** *(Pol)* to intern ◆ **~ qn (dans un hôpital psychiatrique)** *(Méd)* to confine sb to a mental hospital, to institutionalize sb *(US)* ◆ **on devrait l'~** he ought to be locked up *ou* certified *, he's certifiable

Internet /ɛ̃tɛʀnɛt/ **NM** ◆ **(l')~** (the) Internet ◆ **sur ~** on (the) Internet

interocéanique /ɛ̃teʀɔseanik/ **ADJ** interoceanic

interopérabilité /ɛ̃teʀɔpeʀabilite/ **NF** *(Ordin, Mil)* interoperability

interopérable /ɛ̃teʀɔpeʀabl/ **ADJ** *(Ordin, Mil)* interoperable

interosseux, -euse /ɛ̃teʀɔsø, øz/ **ADJ** interosseous

interparlementaire /ɛ̃tɛʀpaʀləmɑ̃tɛʀ/ **ADJ** interparliamentary

interpellateur, -trice /ɛ̃tɛʀpelatœʀ, tʀis/ **NM,F** 1 *(Pol)* interpellator, questioner 2 *(dans un débat)* questioner; *(= perturbateur)* heckler

interpellation /ɛ̃tɛʀpelasjɔ̃/ **NF** 1 *(= appel)* hailing *(NonC)* 2 *(dans un débat)* questioning; *(perturbatrice)* heckling *(NonC)*; *(Pol)* interpellation, questioning *(NonC)* 3 *(Police)* **il y a eu**

une dizaine d'~s about ten people were taken in for questioning

interpeller /ɛ̃tɛʀpəle/ ▸ conjug 1 ◂ VT 1 *(= appeler)* to call out to, to shout out to, to hail; *(impoliment)* to shout at ◆ **les automobilistes se sont interpellés grossièrement** the motorists shouted insults at each other 2 *(au cours d'un débat)* to question; *(en chahutant)* to heckle; *(Pol)* to interpellate, to question 3 *(Police)* to take in for questioning 4 *(= concerner) [de problème, situation]* to concern, to be of concern to ◆ **ça m'interpelle (quelque part)** *(hum)* I can relate to that*

interpénétration /ɛ̃tɛʀpenetʀasjɔ̃/ NF interpenetration

interpénétrer (s') /ɛ̃tɛʀpenetʀe/ ▸ conjug 6 ◂ VPR to interpenetrate

interpersonnel, -elle /ɛ̃tɛʀpɛʀsɔnɛl/ ADJ interpersonal

interphone /ɛ̃tɛʀfɔn/ NM intercom, interphone; *[d'immeuble]* entry phone

interplanétaire /ɛ̃tɛʀplanetɛʀ/ ADJ interplanetary

Interpol /ɛ̃tɛʀpɔl/ NM (abrév de **International Criminal Police Organization**) Interpol

interpolation /ɛ̃tɛʀpɔlasjɔ̃/ NF interpolation

interpoler /ɛ̃tɛʀpɔle/ ▸ conjug 1 ◂ VT to interpolate

interposé, e /ɛ̃tɛʀpoze/ (ptp de **interposer**) ADJ ◆ **par personne ~e** through an intermediary *ou* a third party ◆ **par service ~** through another department ◆ **par journaux ~s** through the press

interposer /ɛ̃tɛʀpoze/ ▸ conjug 1 ◂ VT *(= intercaler)* to interpose *(entre* between) VPR **s'interposer** *[personne]* to intervene, to interpose o.s. *(frm) (dans* in); ◆ **elle s'interposa entre le père et le fils** she intervened between father and son

interposition /ɛ̃tɛʀpozisjɔ̃/ NF 1 *(= intercalation)* interposition 2 *(= médiation)* intervention ◆ **force d'~** *(Pol)* intervention force 3 *(Jur) fraudulent use of a third party's identity*

interprétable /ɛ̃tɛʀpʀetabl/ ADJ interpretable

interprétariat /ɛ̃tɛʀpʀetaʀja/ NM interpreting ◆ **école d'~** interpreting school

interprétatif, -ive /ɛ̃tɛʀpʀetatif, iv/ ADJ *(gén)* interpretative ◆ **émettre des réserves interprétatives sur un texte de loi** *(Jur)* to express reservations about the possible interpretations of a bill ◆ **ce texte requiert un gros travail ~** this text needs a lot of interpreting ◆ **délire ~** *(Méd)* delusions of reference, referential delusion ◆ **le délire ~ de certains critiques** *(hum)* the tendency of some critics to go overboard in their interpretations

interprétation /ɛ̃tɛʀpʀetasjɔ̃/ NF 1 *(Théât, Ciné)* performance; *(Mus)* interpretation, rendering ◆ **son ~ de Macbeth** his Macbeth; → **prix** 2 *(= explication)* interpretation ◆ **donner une ~ fausse de qch** to give a misleading interpretation of sth ◆ **l'~ des rêves** the interpretation of dreams ◆ **c'est une erreur d'~** it's a misinterpretation 3 *(= métier d'interprète)* interpreting ◆ **~ simultanée** simultaneous translation

interprète /ɛ̃tɛʀpʀɛt/ NMF 1 *(= traducteur)* interpreter ◆ **~ de conférence** conference interpreter ◆ **faire l'~, servir d'~** to act as an interpreter

2 *[de musique]* performer; *[de chanson]* singer; *(Théât)* performer ◆ **les ~s par ordre d'entrée en scène ...** the cast in order of appearance ... ◆ **l'un des plus grands ~s de Shakespeare** one of the greatest Shakespearean actors ◆ **l'~ de Phèdre** the actress playing the part of Phèdre ◆ **Paul était l'~ de cette sonate** Paul played this sonata ◆ **Paul était l'~ de cette chanson** Paul was the singer of *ou* sang this song

3 *(= porte-parole)* **servir d'~ à qn/aux idées de qn** to act *ou* serve as a spokesman for sb/for sb's ideas ◆ **je me ferai votre ~ auprès du ministre** I'll speak to the minister on your behalf

4 *(= exégète) [de texte]* interpreter; *[de rêves, signes]* interpreter

interpréter /ɛ̃tɛʀpʀete/ GRAMMAIRE ACTIVE 53.6 ▸ conjug 6 ◂ VT 1 *[+ musique]* to perform, to play; *[+ chanson]* to sing; *[+ rôle]* to play ◆ **il interprète superbement Hamlet** his (performance of) Hamlet is excellent ◆ **je vais maintenant vous ~ un nocturne de Chopin** I'm now going to play one of Chopin's nocturnes for you 2 *(= comprendre)* to interpret ◆ **comment ~ son silence ?** how should one interpret his silence?, what does his silence mean? ◆ **il a mal interprété mes paroles** he misinterpreted my words ◆ **son attitude peut s'~ de plusieurs façons** there are several ways of understanding his position 3 *(= traduire)* to interpret 4 *(Ordin)* to interpret ◆ **langage interprété** interpreted language

interpréteur /ɛ̃tɛʀpʀetœʀ/ NM *(Ordin)* interpreter

interprofession /ɛ̃tɛʀpʀɔfesjɔ̃/ NF *(Écon)* joint-trade organization

interprofessionnel, -elle /ɛ̃tɛʀpʀɔfesjɔnɛl/ ADJ *[réunion]* interprofessional; → **salaire**

interracial, e (mpl **-iaux**) /ɛ̃tɛʀʀasjal, jo/ ADJ interracial

interrégional, e (mpl **-aux**) /ɛ̃tɛʀʀeʒjɔnal, o/ ADJ interregional

interrègne /ɛ̃tɛʀʀɛɲ/ NM interregnum

interreligieux, -euse /ɛ̃tɛʀʀəliʒjø, øz/ ADJ *[relations, dialogue]* interfaith

interro* /ɛ̃teʀo/ NF (abrév de **interrogation**) *(Scol)* test

interrogateur, -trice /ɛ̃teʀɔgatœʀ, tʀis/ ADJ *[air, regard, ton]* questioning *(épith)*, inquiring *(épith)* ◆ **d'un air *ou* ton ~** questioningly, inquiringly NM,F (oral) examiner NM *(Téléc)* ◆ **~ à distance** remote access facility

interrogatif, -ive /ɛ̃teʀɔgatif, iv/ ADJ *[air, regard]* questioning *(épith)*, inquiring *(épith)*; *(Ling)* interrogative NM interrogative ◆ **mettre à l'~** to put into the interrogative NF **interrogative** interrogative clause

interrogation /ɛ̃teʀɔgasjɔ̃/ NF 1 *(= interrogatoire)* questioning; *(serrée, prolongée)* interrogation 2 *[d'élève]* testing, examination ◆ **~ (écrite)** short (written) test *(Brit)*, quiz *(US)* ◆ **~ (orale)** oral (test) 3 *(= question)* question ◆ **~ directe/indirecte** *(Gram)* direct/indirect question ◆ **les sourcils levés, en signe d'~** his eyebrows raised questioningly *ou* inquiringly ◆ **les yeux pleins d'une ~ muette** his eyes silently questioning; → **point**[1] 4 *(= réflexions)* **~s** questioning ◆ **ces ~s continuelles sur la destinée humaine** this continual questioning about human destiny 5 *(Ordin, Téléc)* **système d'~ à distance** remote access system

interrogatoire /ɛ̃teʀɔgatwaʀ/ NM *(Police)* questioning; *(au tribunal)* cross-examination, cross-questioning *(NonC)*; *(= compte rendu)* statement; *(fig = série de questions)* cross-examination, interrogation ◆ **subir un ~ en règle** to undergo a thorough *ou* detailed interrogation ◆ **pendant l'~, elle s'est évanouie** while being cross-examined, she fainted

interrogeable /ɛ̃teʀɔʒabl/ ADJ ◆ **répondeur ~ à distance** answering machine with a remote access facility ◆ **compte en banque ~ par Minitel** *bank account that can be accessed by Minitel*

interroger /ɛ̃teʀɔʒe/ ▸ conjug 3 ◂ VT 1 *(= questionner)* to question; *(pour obtenir un renseignement)* to ask; *(Police)* to interview, to question; *(de manière serrée, prolongée)* to interrogate *(sur* about); *(sondage)* to poll ◆ **15% des personnes interrogées** 15% of the people polled *ou* asked ◆ **~ qn du regard** to give sb a questioning *ou* an inquiring look, to look questioningly *ou* inquiringly at sb

2 *(Scol, Univ)* **~ un élève** to test *ou* examine a pupil (orally) ◆ **~ par écrit les élèves** to give the pupils a written test ◆ **elle a été interrogée sur un sujet difficile** she was examined *ou* questioned on a difficult subject

3 *(= examiner) [+ ciel, conscience]* to examine; *[+ mémoire]* to search

4 *[+ base de données]* to search ◆ **~ son répondeur** to check calls on one's answering machine

VPR **s'interroger** *(= se poser des questions) (sur un problème)* to wonder *(sur* about); ◆ **s'~ sur la conduite à tenir** to wonder what course to follow

interrompre /ɛ̃teʀɔ̃pʀ/ ▸ conjug 41 ◂ VT 1 *(= arrêter) [+ voyage, circuit électrique]* to break, to interrupt; *[+ conversation] (gén)* to interrupt, to break off; *(pour s'interposer)* to break into, to cut into; *[+ études]* to break off, to interrupt; *[+ émission]* to interrupt; *[+ négociations, traitement médical]* to break off ◆ **il a interrompu la conversation pour téléphoner** he broke off *ou* interrupted his conversation to telephone ◆ **elle a interrompu sa carrière pour voyager** she took a career break *ou* she interrupted her career to travel ◆ **le match a été interrompu par la pluie** the match was stopped by rain ◆ **sans ~ sa lecture** without looking up (from his *ou* her book) ◆ **~ une grossesse** *(Méd)* to terminate a pregnancy

2 *(= couper la parole à, déranger)* **~ qn** to interrupt sb ◆ **je ne veux pas qu'on m'interrompe (dans mon travail)** I don't want to be interrupted (in my work) ◆ **je ne veux pas ~ mais ...** I don't want to cut in *ou* interrupt but ...

VPR **s'interrompre** *[personne, conversation]* to break off ◆ **nos émissions s'interrompront à 23h50** *(TV)* we will be going off the air *ou* closing down *(Brit)* at 11.50 pm

interrupteur, -trice /ɛ̃teʀyptœʀ, tʀis/ NM *(Élec)* switch NM,F interrupter

interruption /ɛ̃teʀypsjɔ̃/ NF *(= action)* interruption *(de* of); *(= état)* break *(de* in) interruption *(de* of, in); *[de négociations]* breaking off *(de* of); ◆ **une ~ de deux heures** a break *ou* an interruption of two hours ◆ **~ (volontaire) de grossesse** termination (of pregnancy) ◆ **~ thérapeutique de grossesse** *termination of pregnancy for medical reasons* ◆ **il y a eu une ~ de courant** there has been a power cut ◆ **après l'~ des hostilités** after hostilities had ceased ◆ **sans ~** *[parler]* without a break *ou* an interruption, uninterruptedly, continuously; *[pleuvoir]* without stopping, without a break, continuously ◆ **"ouvert sans interruption de 9h à 19h"** "open all day from 9 am to 7 pm" ◆ **réélu sans ~ jusqu'en 1998** reelected to hold office until 1998 ◆ **un moment d'~** a moment's break

intersaison /ɛ̃tɛʀsɛzɔ̃/ NF *(Sport)* close season; *(Tourisme)* low season ◆ **à *ou* pendant l'~** *(Sport)* during the close season; *(Tourisme)* out of season

interscolaire /ɛ̃tɛʀskɔlɛʀ/ ADJ inter-schools

intersection /ɛ̃tɛʀsɛksjɔ̃/ NF *[de lignes]* intersection; *[de routes]* intersection, junction; → **point**[1]

intersession /ɛ̃tɛʀsesjɔ̃/ NF *(Pol)* recess

intersexualité /ɛ̃tɛʀsɛksɥalite/ NF intersexuality

intersexuel, -elle /ɛ̃tɛʀsɛksɥɛl/ ADJ intersexual

intersidéral, e (mpl **-aux**) /ɛ̃tɛʀsideʀal, o/ ADJ interstellar

interstellaire /ɛ̃tɛʀsteləʀ/ ADJ interstellar

interstice /ɛ̃tɛʀstis/ NM *(gén)* crack, chink, interstice; *[de volet, cageot]* slit ◆ **à travers les ~s des rideaux** through the cracks *ou* chinks in the curtains

interstitiel, -ielle /ɛ̃tɛʀstisjɛl/ ADJ *(Anat, Méd)* interstitial

intersubjectif, -ive /ɛ̃tɛʀsybʒɛktif, iv/ ADJ intersubjective

intersubjectivité /ɛ̃tɛʀsybʒɛktivite/ NF intersubjectivity

intersyndical, e (mpl **-aux**) /ɛ̃tɛʀsɛ̃dikal, o/ ADJ interunion NF **intersyndicale** inter-union association, trade union group *(Brit)*

intertitre /ɛ̃tɛʀtitʀ/ NM *(Presse)* subheading; *(Ciné)* title

intertropical, e (mpl **-aux**) /ɛ̃tɛʀtʀɔpikal, o/ ADJ intertropical

interurbain, e /ɛ̃tɛʀyʀbɛ̃, ɛn/ ADJ 1 *[relations]* interurban 2 *(Téléc)* long-distance NM ◆ **l'~** the long-distance telephone service, the trunk call service *(Brit)*

intervalle /ɛ̃tɛʀval/ NM 1 *(= espace)* space, distance; *(entre 2 mots, 2 lignes)* space; *(= temps)* interval; *(Mus)* interval; *(Math)* interval ◆ **~ fermé/ouvert** closed/open interval 2 *(locutions)* **c'est arrivé à 2 jours/mois d'~** it happened after a space *ou* an interval of 2 days/months ◆ **ils sont nés à 3 mois d'~** they were born 3 months apart ◆ **à ~s réguliers/rapprochés** at regular/close intervals ◆ **à ~s de 5 mètres, à 5 mètres d'~** 5 metres apart ◆ **par ~s** at intervals ◆ **dans l'~** *(temporel)* in the meantime, meanwhile; *(spatial)* in between

intervenant, e /ɛ̃tɛʀvənɑ̃, ɑ̃t/ NM,F *(Jur)* intervener; *(= conférencier)* contributor; *(Écon)* participant ◆ **~ extérieur** outside contributor

intervenir /ɛ̃tɛʀvəniʀ/ ▸ conjug 22 ◂ VI 1 *(= entrer en action)* to intervene; *(= contribuer)* to play a part ◆ **puis-je ~ ?** *(dans une discussion)* may I interrupt?, can I say something (here)? ◆ **~ auprès de qn pour** to intercede *ou* intervene with sb (in order) to ◆ **il est intervenu en notre faveur** he interceded *ou* intervened on our behalf ◆ **~ militairement** to intervene militarily ◆ **on a dû faire ~ l'armée, l'armée a dû ~** the army had to intervene, the army had to be brought in *ou* called in ◆ **les pompiers n'ont pas pu ~** the firemen were unable to help

2 *(Méd)* to operate

3 *(= survenir) [fait, événement]* to take place, to occur; *[accord]* to be reached, to be entered into; *[décision, mesure]* to be taken; *[élément nouveau]* to arise, to come up ◆ **cette mesure intervient au moment où …** this measure is being taken *ou* comes at a time when …

4 *(Jur)* to intervene

intervention /ɛ̃tɛʀvɑ̃sjɔ̃/ NF 1 *(gén, Jur)* intervention; *(= discours)* speech ◆ **cela a nécessité l'~ de la police** the police had to be brought in *ou* to intervene ◆ **son ~ en notre faveur** his intercession *ou* intervention on our behalf ◆ **~ armée** armed intervention ◆ **plusieurs ~s aériennes** several air strikes; → **force** 2 *(Écon, Pol)* **~ de l'État** state intervention ◆ **politique d'~** policy of intervention, interventionist policy ◆ **prix d'~** intervention price ◆ **beurre d'~** (EU) subsidized butter 3 *(Méd)* operation ◆ **~ chirurgicale** surgical operation

interventionnisme /ɛ̃tɛʀvɑ̃sjɔnism/ NM interventionism

interventionniste /ɛ̃tɛʀvɑ̃sjɔnist/ ADJ, NMF interventionist

interversion /ɛ̃tɛʀvɛʀsjɔ̃/ NF inversion ◆ **~ des rôles** reversal *ou* inversion of roles

intervertir /ɛ̃tɛʀvɛʀtiʀ/ ▸ conjug 2 ◂ VT to invert *ou* reverse the order of, to invert ◆ **~ les rôles** to reverse *ou* invert roles

interview /ɛ̃tɛʀvju/ NF *(Presse, TV)* interview

interviewé, e /ɛ̃tɛʀvjuve/ (ptp de **interviewer**) NM,F *(Presse, TV)* interviewee

interviewer[1] /ɛ̃tɛʀvjuve/ ▸ conjug 1 ◂ VT *(Presse, TV)* to interview

interviewer[2] /ɛ̃tɛʀvjuvœʀ/ NMF *(= journaliste)* interviewer

intervocalique /ɛ̃tɛʀvɔkalik/ ADJ intervocalic

intestat /ɛ̃tɛsta/ ADJ *(Jur)* ◆ **mourir ~** to die intestate NMF intestate

intestin[1] /ɛ̃tɛstɛ̃/ NM intestine ◆ **~s** intestines, bowels ◆ **~ grêle** small intestine ◆ **gros ~** large intestine ◆ **avoir l'~ fragile** *ou* **les ~s fragiles** to have an irritable bowel, to have irritable bowel syndrome

intestin[2], **e** /ɛ̃tɛstɛ̃, in/ ADJ *[lutte, rivalité]* internecine, internal ◆ **querelles ~es** internecine quarrels *ou* strife, infighting

intestinal, e (mpl **-aux**) /ɛ̃tɛstinal, o/ ADJ intestinal; → **grippe**

Intifada /intifada/ NF ◆ **l'~** the Intifada

intimation /ɛ̃timasjɔ̃/ NF *(Jur) (= assignation)* summons *(sg) (before an appeal court)*; *(= signification)* notification

intime /ɛ̃tim/ ADJ 1 *(= privé) [hygiène, confidences]* personal; *[vie, chagrin]* private; *[confidences, secret]* close; *[cérémonie, mariage]* quiet; *[atmosphère]* cosy ◆ **dîner ~** *(entre amis)* dinner with (old) friends; *(entre amoureux)* romantic dinner 2 *(= étroit) [relation, rapport]* intimate; *[union]* close; *[ami]* close, intimate ◆ **être ~ avec qn** to be intimate with *ou* close to sb ◆ **avoir des relations** *ou* **rapports ~s avec qn** to be on intimate terms with sb ◆ **un mélange ~** a subtle mixture 3 *(= profond) [nature, structure]* innermost; *[sens, sentiment, conviction]* deep ◆ **j'ai l'~ conviction que** I'm absolutely convinced that NMF close friend ◆ **seuls les ~s sont restés dîner** only close friends stayed to dinner ◆ **je m'appelle Jonathan, Jo pour les ~s*** *(hum)* my name's Jonathan but my friends call me Jo

intimé, e /ɛ̃time/ (ptp de **intimer**) NM,F *(Jur)* respondent, appellee

intimement /ɛ̃timmɑ̃/ ADV *[connaître, lié]* intimately ◆ **~ persuadé** *ou* **convaincu** deeply *ou* firmly convinced ◆ **être ~ mêlé à qch** to be closely involved in sth

intimer /ɛ̃time/ ▸ conjug 1 ◂ VT 1 ◆ **~ à qn (l'ordre) de faire** to order sb to do 2 *(Jur) (= assigner)* to summon *(before an appeal court)*; *(= signifier)* to notify

intimidable /ɛ̃timidabl/ ADJ easily intimidated

intimidant, e /ɛ̃timidɑ̃, ɑ̃t/ ADJ intimidating

intimidateur, -trice /ɛ̃timidatœʀ, tʀis/ ADJ intimidating

intimidation /ɛ̃timidasjɔ̃/ NF intimidation ◆ **manœuvre/moyens d'~** device/means of intimidation ◆ **on l'a fait parler en usant d'~** they scared *ou* frightened him into talking

intimider /ɛ̃timide/ ▸ conjug 1 ◂ VT to intimidate ◆ **ne te laisse pas ~ par lui** don't let him intimidate you, don't let yourself be intimidated by him

intimisme /ɛ̃timism/ NM *(Art, Littérat)* intimism *(SPÉC)*

intimiste /ɛ̃timist/ ADJ, NMF *(Art, Littérat)* intimist *(SPÉC)* ◆ **un roman/film ~** *a novel/film focusing on the private world of people's feelings and relationships* ◆ **un peintre ~** a painter who specializes in interior scenes

intimité /ɛ̃timite/ NF 1 *(= vie privée)* privacy ◆ **dans l'~ c'est un homme très simple** in private life, he's a man of simple tastes ◆ **nous serons dans l'~** there will only be a few of us *ou* a few close friends and relatives ◆ **se marier dans l'~** to have a quiet wedding ◆ **la cérémonie a eu lieu dans la plus stricte ~** the ceremony took place in the strictest privacy ◆ **pénétrer dans l'~ de qn** to be admitted into sb's private life 2 *(= familiarité)* intimacy ◆ **dans l'~ conjugale** in the intimacy of one's married life ◆ **vivre dans l'~ de qn** to be on very intimate terms with sb 3 *(= confort) [d'atmosphère, salon]* cosiness, intimacy 4 *(littér = profondeur)* depths ◆ **dans l'~ de sa conscience** in the depths of *ou* innermost recesses of one's conscience

intitulé /ɛ̃tityle/ NM *[de livre, loi, jugement]* title; *[de chapitre]* heading, title; *[de sujet de dissertation]* wording; *[de compte en banque] (= type de compte)* type; *(= coordonnées)* name, address and account number

intituler /ɛ̃tityle/ ▸ conjug 1 ◂ VT to entitle, to call VPR **s'intituler** *[livre, chapitre]* to be entitled *ou* called; *[personne]* to call o.s., to give o.s. the title of

intolérable /ɛ̃toleʀabl/ GRAMMAIRE ACTIVE 34.3 ADJ *(gén)* intolerable, unbearable; *[douleur]* unbearable

intolérablement /ɛ̃toleʀabləmɑ̃/ ADV intolerably

intolérance /ɛ̃toleʀɑ̃s/ NF 1 *(gén)* intolerance 2 *(Méd)* **~ à un médicament, ~ médicamenteuse** inability to tolerate a drug

intolérant, e /ɛ̃toleʀɑ̃, ɑ̃t/ ADJ intolerant

intonation /ɛ̃tɔnasjɔ̃/ NF *(Ling, Mus)* intonation ◆ **voix aux ~s douces** soft-toned voice

intouchabilité /ɛ̃tuʃabilite/ NF untouchability

intouchable /ɛ̃tuʃabl/ ADJ, NMF untouchable

intox(e)* /ɛ̃tɔks/ NF (abrév de **intoxication**) *(Pol)* brainwashing, propaganda; *(= désinformation)* disinformation ◆ **c'est de l'~(e) !** it's pure propaganda! ◆ **il nous fait de l'~(e) pour avoir un magnétoscope** he's trying to brainwash us into getting (him) a video recorder

intoxication /ɛ̃tɔksikasjɔ̃/ NF 1 *(= empoisonnement)* poisoning *(NonC)* ◆ **~ alimentaire/au plomb** food/lead poisoning *(NonC)* ◆ **~ médicamenteuse** drug intoxication 2 *(Pol)* brainwashing, indoctrination

intoxiqué, e /ɛ̃tɔksike/ (ptp de **intoxiquer**) NM,F 1 *(= empoisonné)* **quarante enfants ont été très gravement ~s** forty children suffered very serious poisoning ◆ **~ par le plomb** suffering from lead poisoning 2 *(par la drogue)* addict 3 *(= fanatique)* addict ◆ **les ~s du rugby/de la science-fiction** rugby/sci-fi addicts

intoxiquer /ɛ̃tɔksike/ ▸ conjug 1 ◂ VT 1 *(= empoisonner) [fumée, pollution]* to poison 2 *(= corrompre)* to brainwash, to indoctrinate ◆ **intoxiqué par la publicité** brainwashed by advertisements VPR **s'intoxiquer** to be poisoned

> ⚠ **intoxiquer** se traduit rarement par **intoxicate**, qui a le sens de 'enivrer'.

intracellulaire /ɛ̃tʀaselylɛʀ/ ADJ intracellular

intracommunautaire /ɛ̃tʀakɔmynotɛʀ/ ADJ *(Pol)* intra-Community *(épith)* ◆ **50% du commerce de l'UE est ~** 50% of EU trade is conducted between member states of the Community

intradermique /ɛ̃tʀadɛʀmik/ ADJ intradermal, intradermic, intracutaneous

intradermo(-)réaction /ɛ̃tʀadɛʀmoʀeaksjɔ̃/ NF INV skin test

intraduisible /ɛ̃tʀadɥizibl/ ADJ 1 *[texte]* untranslatable 2 *(= inexprimable) [sentiment, idée]* inexpressible ◆ **il eut une intonation ~** his intonation was impossible to reproduce

intraitable /ɛ̃tʀɛtabl/ ADJ uncompromising, inflexible ◆ **il est ~ sur la discipline** he's a stickler for discipline, he's uncompromising *ou* inflexible about discipline

intra-muros /ɛ̃tʀamyʀos/ ADV ◆ **habiter ~** to live inside the town ◆ **Paris ~** inner Paris

intramusculaire /ɛ̃tʀamyskylɛʀ/ ADJ intramuscular NF intramuscular injection

Intranet, intranet /ɛ̃tʀanɛt/ NM intranet

intransigeance /ɛ̃tʀɑ̃ziʒɑ̃s/ NF intransigence ◆ **faire preuve d'~** to be uncompromising *ou* intransigent

intransigeant, e /ɛ̃tʀɑ̃ziʒɑ̃, ɑ̃t/ ADJ *[personne, attitude]* uncompromising, intransigent; *[morale]* uncompromising ◆ **se montrer ~** *ou* **adopter une ligne de conduite ~e envers qn** to take a hard line with sb

intransitif, -ive /ɛ̃tʀɑ̃zitif, iv/ ADJ, NM intransitive

intransitivement /ɛ̃tʀɑ̃zitivmɑ̃/ ADV intransitively

intransitivité /ɛ̃tʀɑ̃zitivite/ NF intransitivity, intransitiveness

intransmissibilité /ɛ̃tʀɑ̃smisibilite/ NF intransmissibility; *(Jur)* untransferability, nontransferability

intransmissible /ɛ̃tʀɑ̃smisibl/ ADJ intransmissible; *(Jur)* untransferable, nontransferable

intransportable /ɛ̃tʀɑ̃spɔʀtabl/ ADJ *[objet]* untransportable; *[malade]* who is unfit *ou* unable to travel

intrant /ɛ̃tʀɑ̃/ NM *(Écon)* input

intra-utérin, e (mpl **intra-utérins**) /ɛ̃tʀayteʀɛ̃, in/ ADJ intra-uterine ◆ **vie ~e** life in the womb, intra-uterine life *(SPÉC)*

intraveineux, -euse /ɛ̃tʀavɛnø, øz/ ADJ intravenous NF **intraveineuse** intravenous injection

intrépide /ɛ̃tʀepid/ ADJ (= *courageux*) intrepid, dauntless, bold; (= *résolu*) dauntless; *[bavard]* unashamed; *[menteur]* barefaced *(épith)*, unashamed

intrépidement /ɛ̃tʀepidmɑ̃/ ADV intrepidly, dauntlessly, boldly

intrépidité /ɛ̃tʀepidite/ NF intrepidity, dauntlessness, boldness ◆ **avec ~** intrepidly, dauntlessly, boldly

intrication /ɛ̃tʀikasjɔ̃/ NF intrication, intricacy

intrigant, e /ɛ̃tʀigɑ̃, ɑ̃t/ ADJ scheming NM,F schemer, intriguer

intrigue /ɛ̃tʀig/ NF (= *manœuvre*) intrigue, scheme; *(Ciné, Littérat, Théât)* plot ◆ **~ amoureuse** *ou* **sentimentale** (= *liaison*) (love) affair

intriguer /ɛ̃tʀige/ ► conjug 1 ◄ VT to intrigue, to puzzle VI to scheme, to intrigue

intrinsèque /ɛ̃tʀɛ̃sɛk/ ADJ intrinsic

intrinsèquement /ɛ̃tʀɛ̃sɛkmɑ̃/ ADV intrinsically; *[lié]* inextricably ◆ **des moyens ~ mauvais** means that are intrinsically evil

intriquer (s') /ɛ̃tʀike/ ► conjug 1 ◄ VPR *(souvent ptp)* *[facteurs]* to be interlinked *(dans* with); ◆ **les deux phénomènes sont étroitement intriqués** the two phenomena are closely interlinked

introducteur, -trice /ɛ̃tʀɔdyktœʀ, tʀis/ NM,F (= *initiateur*) initiator *(à* to)

introductif, -ive /ɛ̃tʀɔdyktif, iv/ ADJ 1 *(gén)* *[chapitre]* introductory, opening *(épith)*; *[discours]* opening *(épith)* 2 *(Jur)* **réquisitoire ~** opening speech for the prosecution

introduction /ɛ̃tʀɔdyksjɔ̃/ GRAMMAIRE ACTIVE 53.1 NF 1 (= *présentation*) introduction ◆ **paroles/chapitre d'~** introductory words/chapter ◆ **en (guise d')~** by way of introduction ◆ **~, développement et conclusion** *[de dissertation, exposé]* introduction, exposition, conclusion 2 (= *recommandation*) introduction ◆ **lettre/mot d'~** letter/note of introduction 3 *[d'objet]* insertion, introduction; *[de liquide]* introduction; *[de visiteur]* admission, introduction 4 (= *lancement*) *[de mode, idée]* launching ◆ **~ en Bourse** stock market listing *ou* flotation 5 *(Jur)* *[d'instance]* institution 6 *(Rugby)* put-in

introduire /ɛ̃tʀɔdɥiʀ/ ► conjug 38 ◄ VT 1 (= *faire entrer*) *[+ objet]* to place *(dans* in) to insert, to introduce *(dans* into); *[+ liquide]* to introduce *(dans* into); *[+ visiteur]* to show in ◆ **il introduisit sa clé dans la serrure** he put his key in the lock, he inserted his key into the lock ◆ **on m'introduisit dans le salon/auprès de la maîtresse de maison** I was shown into *ou* ushered into the lounge/shown in *ou* ushered in to see the mistress of the house ◆ **~ la balle en mêlée** *(Rugby)* to put the ball into the scrum

2 (= *lancer*) *[+ mode]* to launch, to introduce; *[+ idées nouvelles]* to bring in, to introduce; *(Ling)* *[+ mot]* to introduce *(dans* into); ◆ **~ un produit sur le marché** *(Écon)* to launch a product on the market ◆ **~ des valeurs en Bourse** to list *ou* float shares on the stock market

3 (= *présenter*) *[+ ami, protégé]* to introduce ◆ **il m'a introduit auprès du directeur/dans le groupe** he introduced me to the manager/to the group

4 *(Jur)* *[+ instance]* to institute

VPR **s'introduire** 1 (= *pénétrer*) **s'~ dans un groupe** to work one's way into a group, to be *ou* get o.s. admitted *ou* accepted into a group ◆ **s'~ chez qn par effraction** to break into sb's home ◆ **s'~ dans une pièce** to get into *ou* enter a room ◆ **l'eau/la fumée s'introduisait partout** the water/smoke was getting in everywhere ◆ **le doute s'introduisit dans son esprit** he began to have doubts

2 (= *être adopté*) *[usage, mode, idée]* to be introduced *(dans* into)

introduit, e /ɛ̃tʀɔdɥi, it/ (ptp de **introduire**) ADJ *(frm)* ◆ **être bien ~ dans un milieu** to be well connected in a certain milieu ◆ **bien ~ auprès du ministre** on good terms with the minister

intromission /ɛ̃tʀɔmisjɔ̃/ NF intromission

intronisation /ɛ̃tʀɔnizasjɔ̃/ NF *[de roi, pape]* enthronement ◆ **discours d'~** *(hum)* *[de président]* acceptance speech

introniser /ɛ̃tʀɔnize/ ► conjug 1 ◄ VT *[+ roi, pape]* to enthrone; *(hum)* *[+ président]* to set up ◆ **il a été intronisé (comme) chef du parti** he was set up as leader of the party

introspectif, -ive /ɛ̃tʀɔspɛktif, iv/ ADJ introspective

introspection /ɛ̃tʀɔspɛksjɔ̃/ NF introspection

introuvable /ɛ̃tʀuvabl/ ADJ which *(ou* who) cannot be found ◆ **ma clé est ~** I can't find my key anywhere, my key is nowhere to be found ◆ **l'évadé demeure toujours ~** the escaped prisoner has still not been found *ou* discovered, the whereabouts of the escaped prisoner remain unknown ◆ **ces meubles sont ~s aujourd'hui** furniture like this is unobtainable *ou* just cannot be found these days ◆ **l'accord reste ~ entre les deux pays** the two countries are still unable to reach an agreement

introversion /ɛ̃tʀɔvɛʀsjɔ̃/ NF introversion

introverti, e /ɛ̃tʀɔvɛʀti/ ADJ introverted NM,F introvert

intrus, e /ɛ̃tʀy, yz/ NM,F intruder ◆ **cherchez l'~** *(jeu)* find the odd one out ADJ intruding, intrusive

intrusion /ɛ̃tʀyzjɔ̃/ NF *(gén, Géol)* intrusion ◆ **~ dans les affaires de qn** interference *ou* intrusion in sb's affairs ◆ **roches d'~** intrusive rocks

intubation /ɛ̃tybasjɔ̃/ NF *(Méd)* intubation

intuber /ɛ̃tybe/ ► conjug 1 ◄ VT *(Méd)* to intubate

intuitif, -ive /ɛ̃tɥitif, iv/ ADJ intuitive NM,F intuitive person ◆ **c'est un ~** he's very intuitive

intuition /ɛ̃tɥisjɔ̃/ NF intuition ◆ **avoir de l'~** to have intuition ◆ **l'~ féminine** feminine intuition ◆ **mon ~ me dit que ...** I feel instinctively that ... ◆ **j'avais l'~ que ce rôle était fait pour elle** I had a feeling that this role was made for her ◆ **Newton a eu l'~ de la loi de la gravité en regardant tomber une pomme de son arbre** Newton intuited the law of gravity when he saw an apple fall off a tree

intuitivement /ɛ̃tɥitivmɑ̃/ ADV intuitively

intumescence /ɛ̃tymesɑ̃s/ NF intumescence

intumescent, e /ɛ̃tymesɑ̃, ɑ̃t/ ADJ intumescent

inuit, e /inɥit/ ADJ INV Inuit NMF **Inuit** Inuit

inusable /inyzabl/ ADJ *[vêtement]* hard-wearing

inusité, e /inyzite/ ADJ *[mot]* uncommon, not in common use *(attrib)*; *[méthode]* no longer in use ◆ **ce mot est pratiquement ~** this word is practically never used

inusuel, -elle /inyzɥɛl/ ADJ *(littér)* unusual

in utero /inyteʀo/ ADJ, ADV in utero

inutile /inytil/ ADJ 1 (= *qui ne sert pas*) *[objet]* useless; *[effort, parole, démarche]* pointless ◆ **connaissances ~s** useless knowledge ◆ **sa voiture lui est ~ maintenant** his car is (of) no use *ou* is no good *ou* is useless to him now ◆ **~ d'insister !** it's useless *ou* no use *ou* no good insisting!, there's no point *ou* it's pointless (insisting)! ◆ **je me sens ~** I feel so useless ◆ **vous voulez de l'aide ? – non, c'est ~** do you want some help? – no, there's no need 2 (= *superflu*) *[paroles, crainte, travail, effort, dépense]* needless; *[bagages]* unnecessary ◆ **évitez toute fatigue ~** avoid tiring yourself unnecessarily ◆ **~ de vous dire que je ne suis pas resté** needless to say I didn't stay, I hardly need tell you I didn't stay; → **bouche**

inutilement /inytilmɑ̃/ ADV unnecessarily, needlessly

inutilisable /inytilizabl/ ADJ unusable

inutilisé, e /inytilize/ ADJ unused

inutilité /inytilite/ NF *[d'objet]* uselessness; *[d'effort, paroles, travail, démarche]* pointlessness

invaincu, e /ɛ̃vɛ̃ky/ ADJ *(gén)* unconquered, unvanquished, undefeated; *(Sport)* unbeaten, undefeated

invalidant, e /ɛ̃validɑ̃, ɑ̃t/ ADJ *[maladie]* incapacitating, disabling

invalidation /ɛ̃validasjɔ̃/ NF *[de contrat, élection]* invalidation; *[de député]* removal (from office)

invalide /ɛ̃valid/ NMF disabled person ◆ **grand ~ civil** severely disabled person ◆ **(grand) ~ de guerre** (severely) disabled ex-serviceman ◆ **~ du travail** industrially disabled person ◆ **l'hôtel des Invalides, les Invalides** the Invalides ADJ *(Méd)* disabled; *(Jur)* invalid

invalider /ɛ̃valide/ ► conjug 1 ◄ VT *(Jur)* to invalidate; *[+ député]* to remove from office; *[+ élection]* to invalidate; *(Méd)* to disable

invalidité /ɛ̃validite/ NF disablement, disability; → **assurance**

invariabilité /ɛ̃vaʀjabilite/ NF invariability

invariable /ɛ̃vaʀjabl/ ADJ *(gén, Ling)* invariable; *(littér)* unvarying

invariablement /ɛ̃vaʀjabləmɑ̃/ ADV invariably

invariance /ɛ̃vaʀjɑ̃s/ NF invariance, invariancy

invariant, e /ɛ̃vaʀjɑ̃, jɑ̃t/ ADJ, NM invariant

invasif, -ive /ɛ̃vazif, iv/ ADJ *(Méd) [cancer, tumeur, traitement]* invasive ◆ **chirurgie non invasive** non-invasive surgery

invasion /ɛ̃vazjɔ̃/ NF invasion ◆ **c'est l'~ !** it's an invasion!

invective /ɛ̃vɛktiv/ NF invective ◆ **~s** abuse, invectives ◆ **se répandre en ~s contre qn** to let loose a torrent *ou* stream of abuse against sb

invectiver /ɛ̃vɛktive/ ▸ conjug 1 ◂ VT to hurl *ou* shout abuse at ◆ **ils se sont violemment invectivés** they hurled *ou* shouted violent abuse at each other VI to inveigh, to rail *(contre* against)

invendable /ɛ̃vɑ̃dabl/ ADJ *(gén)* unsaleable; *(Comm)* unmarketable

invendu, e /ɛ̃vɑ̃dy/ ADJ unsold NM *(= objet)* unsold item; *(= magazine)* unsold copy ◆ **ce magasin brade ses ~s** this shop is selling off its unsold stock

inventaire /ɛ̃vɑ̃tɛʀ/ NM 1 *(gén, Jur)* inventory ◆ **faire un ~** to make an inventory; → **bénéfice** 2 *(Comm) (= liste)* stocklist *(Brit)*, inventory *(US)*; *(= opération)* stocktaking *(Brit)*, inventory *(US)* ◆ **faire un ~** *(Comm)* to take stock, to do the stocktaking *(Brit) ou* inventory *(US)* ◆ **"fermé pour cause d'inventaire"** "closed for stocktaking *(Brit) ou* inventory *(US)*" 3 *[de monuments, souvenirs]* survey ◆ **faire l'~ de** to assess, to make an assessment of

inventer /ɛ̃vɑ̃te/ ▸ conjug 1 ◂ VT 1 *(= créer, découvrir) (gén)* to invent; *[+ moyen, procédé]* to devise ◆ **il n'a pas inventé la poudre** *ou* **le fil à couper le beurre** *ou* **l'eau chaude** he'll never set the world *ou* the Thames *(Brit)* on fire, he's no bright spark*

2 *(= imaginer, trouver) [+ jeu]* to think up, to make up; *[+ mot]* to make up; *[+ excuse, histoire fausse]* to invent, to make *ou* think up ◆ **c'est lui qui a inventé le mot** he coined the word ◆ **il ne sait plus quoi ~ pour échapper à l'école** he doesn't know what to think up *ou* dream up next to get out of school ◆ **ils avaient inventé de faire entrer les lapins dans le salon** they had the bright idea of bringing the rabbits into the drawing room ◆ **je n'invente rien** I'm not making anything up, I'm not inventing a thing ◆ **qu'est-ce que tu vas ~ là !** whatever can you be thinking of!; → **pièce**

3 *(Jur) [+ trésor]* to find

VPR **s'inventer** ◆ **ce sont des choses qui ne s'inventent pas** those are things people just don't make up ◆ **s'~ une famille** to invent a family for o.s. ◆ **tu t'inventes des histoires !** you're imagining things!

inventeur, -trice /ɛ̃vɑ̃tœʀ, tʀis/ NM,F inventor; *(Jur)* finder

inventif, -ive /ɛ̃vɑ̃tif, iv/ ADJ *[esprit, solution, cuisine]* inventive; *[personne]* resourceful, inventive

invention /ɛ̃vɑ̃sjɔ̃/ NF *(gén, péj)* invention; *(= ingéniosité)* inventiveness, spirit of invention; *(Jur) [de trésor]* finding ◆ **cette excuse est une pure** *ou* **de la pure ~** that excuse is a pure invention *ou* fabrication ◆ **l'histoire est de son ~** the story was made up *ou* invented by him *ou* was his own invention ◆ **un cocktail de mon ~** a cocktail of my own creation; → **brevet**

inventivité /ɛ̃vɑ̃tivite/ NF *[d'esprit, solution, cuisine]* inventiveness; *[de personne]* resourcefulness, inventiveness

inventorier /ɛ̃vɑ̃tɔʀje/ ▸ conjug 7 ◂ VT *(gén, Jur)* to make an inventory of; *(Comm)* to make a stocklist of

invérifiable /ɛ̃veʀifjabl/ ADJ *(gén)* unverifiable; *[chiffres]* that cannot be checked

inverse /ɛ̃vɛʀs/ ADJ *(gén)* opposite; *(Logique, Math)* inverse ◆ **arriver en sens ~** to arrive from the opposite direction ◆ **l'image apparaît en sens ~ dans le miroir** the image is reversed in the mirror ◆ **dans l'ordre ~** in (the) reverse order ◆ **dans le sens ~ des aiguilles d'une montre** counterclockwise, anticlockwise *(Brit)* NM ◆ **l'~** *(gén)* the opposite, the reverse; *(Philos)* the converse ◆ **tu as fait l'~ de ce que je t'ai dit** you did the opposite to *ou* of what I told you ◆ **t'a-t-il attaqué ou l'~ ?** did he attack you or vice versa?, did he attack you or was it the other way round? ◆ **à l'~** conversely ◆ **cela va à l'~ de nos prévisions** that goes contrary to our plans ◆ **à l'~ de sa sœur, il est très timide** unlike his sister, he is very shy

inversé, e /ɛ̃vɛʀse/ (ptp de **inverser**) ADJ *[image]* reversed; *[relief]* inverted

inversement /ɛ̃vɛʀsəmɑ̃/ ADV *(gén)* conversely; *(Math)* inversely ◆ **~ proportionnel à** inversely proportional to ◆ **... et/ou ~** ... and/or vice versa

inverser /ɛ̃vɛʀse/ ▸ conjug 1 ◂ VT *[+ ordre]* to reverse, to invert; *[+ courant électrique]* to reverse; *[+ rôles]* to reverse

inverseur /ɛ̃vɛʀsœʀ/ NM *(Élec, Tech)* reverser ◆ **~ de poussée** *(Aéronautique)* thrust reverser

inversible /ɛ̃vɛʀsibl/ ADJ *(Photo)* ◆ **film ~** reversal film

inversion /ɛ̃vɛʀsjɔ̃/ NF 1 *(gén, Anat, Ling)* inversion; *(Élec)* reversal ◆ **~ thermique** *(Météo)* temperature inversion ◆ **~ de poussée** *(Aéronautique)* thrust reversal ◆ **~ du sucre** *(Chim)* inversion of sucrose 2 *(Psych)* homosexuality, inversion *(SPÉC)*

invertébré, e /ɛ̃vɛʀtebʀe/ ADJ, NM invertebrate ◆ **~s** invertebrates, Invertebrata *(SPÉC)*

inverti, e /ɛ̃vɛʀti/ (ptp de **invertir**) ADJ *(Chim)* ◆ **sucre ~** invert sugar NM,F † homosexual, invert †

invertir † /ɛ̃vɛʀtiʀ/ ▸ conjug 2 ◂ VT to invert

investigateur, -trice /ɛ̃vɛstigatœʀ, tʀis/ ADJ *[technique]* investigative; *[esprit]* inquiring *(épith)*; *[regard]* searching *(épith)*, scrutinizing *(épith)* NM,F investigator

investigation /ɛ̃vɛstigasjɔ̃/ NF *(gén)* investigation; *(Méd)* examination ◆ **~s** *(gén, Police)* investigations ◆ **la police poursuit ses ~s** the police are continuing their investigations ◆ **champ d'~** *[de chercheur]* field of research ◆ **journalisme d'~** investigative journalism

investiguer /ɛ̃vɛstige/ ▸ conjug 1 ◂ VT INDIR ◆ **~ sur qch** to investigate sth

investir /ɛ̃vɛstiʀ/ ▸ conjug 2 ◂ VT 1 *(Fin) [+ capital]* to invest *(dans* in) 2 *[+ fonctionnaire]* to induct; *[+ évêque]* to invest ◆ **~ qn de pouvoirs/droits** to invest *ou* vest sb with powers/rights, to vest powers/rights in sb ◆ **~ qn de sa confiance** to place one's trust in sb 3 *(Mil) [+ ville]* to surround, to besiege; *(Police)* to surround, to cordon off VPR **s'investir** ◆ **s'~ dans son travail/une relation** to put a lot into one's work/a relationship ◆ **s'~ beaucoup pour faire qch** to put a lot of effort into doing sth

investissement /ɛ̃vɛstismɑ̃/ NM *(Écon, Méd, Psych)* investment; *(Mil)* investing; *(= efforts)* contribution

investisseur, -euse /ɛ̃vɛstisœʀ, øz/ ADJ investing *(épith)* NM investor ◆ **~s institutionnels** institutional investors

investiture /ɛ̃vɛstityʀ/ NF *[de candidat]* nomination; *[d'évêché]* investiture ◆ **recevoir l'~ de son parti** *(gén)* to be endorsed by one's party; *(Pol US)* to be nominated by one's party ◆ **discours d'~** inaugural speech

invétéré, e /ɛ̃veteʀe/ ADJ *[fumeur, joueur]* inveterate, confirmed; *[menteur]* out-and-out, downright; *[habitude]* inveterate, deep-rooted

invincibilité /ɛ̃vɛ̃sibilite/ NF *[d'adversaire, nation]* invincibility

invincible /ɛ̃vɛ̃sibl/ ADJ *[adversaire, nation]* invincible, unconquerable; *[courage]* invincible, indomitable; *[charme]* irresistible; *[difficultés]* insurmountable, insuperable; *[argument]* invincible, unassailable

invinciblement /ɛ̃vɛ̃sibləmɑ̃/ ADV invincibly

inviolabilité /ɛ̃vjɔlabilite/ NF *[de droit]* inviolability; *[de serrure]* impregnability; *[de parlementaire, diplomate]* immunity

inviolable /ɛ̃vjɔlabl/ ADJ *[droit]* inviolable; *[serrure]* impregnable, burglar-proof; *[parlementaire, diplomate]* immune

inviolé, e /ɛ̃vjɔle/ ADJ *(gén)* unviolated, inviolate *(frm)*; *[tombe]* intact; *[paysage, île]* unspoilt

invisibilité /ɛ̃vizibilite/ NF invisibility

invisible /ɛ̃vizibl/ ADJ *(= impossible à voir)* invisible; *(= minuscule)* barely visible *(à* to); *(Écon)* invisible ◆ **~ à l'œil nu** invisible to the naked eye ◆ **la maison était ~ derrière les arbres** the house was invisible *ou* couldn't be seen behind the trees ◆ **danger ~** unseen *ou* hidden danger ◆ **il est ~ pour l'instant** he can't be seen *ou* he's unavailable at the moment ◆ **il est ~ depuis deux mois** he hasn't been seen (around) for two months NM ◆ **l'~** the invisible ◆ **~s** *(Écon)* invisibles

invisiblement /ɛ̃viziblәmɑ̃/ ADV invisibly

invitant, e /ɛ̃vitɑ̃, ɑ̃t/ ADJ *(littér)* inviting ◆ **puissance ~e** *(Pol)* host country

invitation /ɛ̃vitasjɔ̃/ GRAMMAIRE ACTIVE 52.1, 52.4 NF invitation *(à* to); ◆ **carte** *ou* **carton d'~** invitation card ◆ **lettre d'~** letter of invitation ◆ **"sur invitation (uniquement)"** "by invitation only" ◆ **~ à dîner** invitation to dinner ◆ **faire une ~ à qn** to invite sb, to extend an invitation to sb ◆ **venir sans ~** to come uninvited *ou* without (an) invitation ◆ **à** *ou* **sur son ~** at his invitation ◆ **une ~ à déserter** an (open) invitation to desert ◆ **cet événement est une ~ à réfléchir sur le sens de la vie** this event leads us to reflect on the meaning of life ◆ **ses tableaux sont une ~ au voyage** his paintings make us dream of faraway places

invite /ɛ̃vit/ NF *(littér)* invitation ◆ **à son ~** at his invitation

invité, e /ɛ̃vite/ (ptp de **inviter**) NM,F guest ◆ **~ de marque** distinguished guest ◆ **~ d'honneur** guest of honour

inviter /ɛ̃vite/ GRAMMAIRE ACTIVE 52.1, 52.4 ▸ conjug 1 ◂ VT 1 *(= convier)* to invite, to ask *(à* to); ◆ **~ qn chez soi/à dîner** to invite *ou* ask sb to one's house/to *ou* for dinner ◆ **elle ne l'a pas invité à entrer/monter** she didn't invite *ou* ask him (to come) in/up ◆ **il s'est invité** he invited himself ◆ **c'est moi qui invite** it's my treat, it's on me* 2 *(= engager)* ◆ **à** to invite to ◆ **~ qn à démissionner** to invite sb to resign ◆ **il l'invita de la main à s'approcher** he beckoned *ou* motioned (to) her to come nearer ◆ **ceci invite à croire que ...** this induces *ou* leads us to believe that ..., this suggests that ... ◆ **la chaleur invitait au repos** the heat tempted one to rest

in vitro /invitʀo/ LOC ADJ, LOC ADV in vitro

invivable /ɛ̃vivabl/ ADJ *(gén)* unbearable; *[personne]* unbearable, obnoxious

in vivo /invivo/ LOC ADJ, LOC ADV in vivo

invocation /ɛ̃vɔkasjɔ̃/ NF invocation *(à* to)

invocatoire /ɛ̃vɔkatwaʀ/ ADJ *(littér)* invocatory *(littér)*

involontaire /ɛ̃vɔlɔ̃tɛʀ/ ADJ *[sourire, mouvement]* involuntary; *[peine, insulte]* unintentional, unwitting; *[témoin, complice]* unwitting

involontairement /ɛ̃vɔlɔ̃tɛʀmɑ̃/ ADV *[sourire]* involuntarily; *[bousculer qn]* unintentionally, unwittingly ◆ **l'accident dont je fus (bien) ~ le témoin** the accident to *ou* of which I was an *ou* the unintentional witness

involutif, -ive /ɛ̃vɔlytif, iv/ ADJ *(Bio, Math)* involute ◆ **(processus)** ~ *(Méd)* involution

involution /ɛ̃vɔlysjɔ̃/ NF *(Bio, Méd, Math)* involution ◆ ~ **utérine** *(Méd)* involution of the uterus

invoquer /ɛ̃vɔke/ ▸ conjug 1 ◂ VT 1 *(= alléguer)* *[+ argument]* to put forward; *[+ témoignage]* to call upon; *[+ excuse]* to put forward; *[+ ignorance]* to plead; *[+ loi, texte]* to cite, to refer to ◆ **il a invoqué sa jeunesse** he said he'd done it because he was young ◆ **les raisons invoquées** the reasons put forward 2 *(= appeler à l'aide)* *[+ Dieu]* to invoke, to call upon ◆ ~ **le secours de qn** to call upon sb for help ◆ ~ **la clémence de qn** to beg sb *ou* appeal to sb for clemency

invraisemblable /ɛ̃vʀɛsɑ̃blabl/ ADJ 1 *(= peu plausible)* *[histoire, nouvelle]* unlikely, improbable; *[argument]* implausible 2 *(= inimaginable)* *[insolence, habit]* incredible ◆ **aussi ~ que cela paraisse** incredible though it may seem ◆ **c'est ~ !** it's incredible!

invraisemblablement /ɛ̃vʀɛsɑ̃blabləmɑ̃/ ADV incredibly

invraisemblance /ɛ̃vʀɛsɑ̃blɑ̃s/ NF *[de fait, nouvelle]* unlikelihood (NonC), unlikeliness (NonC), improbability; *[d'argument]* implausibility ◆ **plein d'~s** full of improbabilities *ou* implausibilities

invulnérabilité /ɛ̃vylneʀabilite/ NF invulnerability

invulnérable /ɛ̃vylneʀabl/ ADJ *(lit)* invulnerable ◆ ~ **à** *(fig)* *[+ maladie]* immune to; *[+ attaque]* invulnerable to, impervious to

iode /jɔd/ NM iodine ◆ **faites le plein d'~ !** get some healthy sea air! → **phare, teinture**

iodé, e /jɔde/ ADJ *[air, sel]* iodized ◆ **les huîtres ont un goût** ~ oysters really taste of the sea

ioder /jɔde/ ▸ conjug 1 ◂ VT to iodize

iodler /jɔdle/ ▸ conjug 1 ◂ VI ⇒ **jodler**

iodoforme /jɔdɔfɔʀm/ NM iodoform

iodure /jɔdyʀ/ NM iodide

ion /jɔ̃/ NM ion

ionien, -ienne /jɔnjɛ̃, jɛn/ ADJ Ionian NM *(= langue)* Ionic NMPL **Ioniens** Ionians

ionique /jɔnik/ ADJ *(Archit)* Ionic; *(Sci)* ionic NM *(Archit)* ◆ **l'**~ the Ionic

ionisant, e /jɔnizɑ̃, ɑ̃t/ ADJ ionizing

ionisation /jɔnizasjɔ̃/ NF ionization

ioniser /jɔnize/ ▸ conjug 1 ◂ VT to ionize

ionosphère /jɔnɔsfɛʀ/ NF ionosphere

iota /jɔta/ NM iota ◆ **je n'y ai pas changé un** ~ I didn't change it one iota, I didn't change one *ou* an iota of it ◆ **il n'a pas bougé d'un** ~ he didn't move an inch, he didn't budge

iourte /juʀt/ NF ⇒ **yourte**

Iowa /ajɔwa/ NM Iowa

ipéca /ipeka/ NM ipecacuanha, ipecac *(US)*

ipomée /ipɔme/ NF ipomoea

IPR /ipeɛʀ/ NM (abrév de **inspecteur pédagogique régional**) → **inspecteur**

ipso facto /ipsofakto/ LOC ADV ipso facto

IRA /iʀa/ NF (abrév de **Irish Republican Army**) IRA

Irak /iʀak/ NM Iraq, Irak

irakien, -ienne /iʀakjɛ̃, jɛn/ ADJ Iraqi NM,F **Irakien(ne)** Iraqi

Iran /iʀɑ̃/ NM Iran

iranien, -ienne /iʀanjɛ̃, jɛn/ ADJ Iranian NM,F **Iranien(ne)** Iranian

Iraq /iʀak/ NM ⇒ **Irak**

iraqien, -ienne /iʀakjɛ̃, jɛn/ ADJ, NM,F ⇒ **irakien**

irascibilité /iʀasibilite/ NF short- *ou* quick-temperedness, irascibility

irascible /iʀasibl/ ADJ short- *ou* quick-tempered, irascible

ire /iʀ/ NF *(littér)* ire *(littér)*

iridacée /iʀidase/ NF iridaceous plant ◆ **les ~s** iridaceous plants, the Iridaceae *(SPÉC)*

iridié, e /iʀidje/ ADJ iridic; → **platine**[1]

iridium /iʀidjɔm/ NM iridium

iris /iʀis/ NM 1 *(Anat, Photo)* iris 2 *(= plante)* iris ◆ ~ **jaune/des marais** yellow/water flag

irisation /iʀizasjɔ̃/ NF iridescence, irisation

irisé, e /iʀize/ (ptp de **iriser**) ADJ iridescent

iriser /iʀize/ ▸ conjug 1 ◂ VT to make iridescent VPR **s'iriser** to become iridescent

irlandais, e /iʀlɑ̃dɛ, ɛz/ ADJ Irish NM 1 *(Ling)* Irish 2 ◆ **Irlandais** Irishman ◆ **les Irlandais** the Irish ◆ **les Irlandais du Nord** the Northern Irish NF **Irlandaise** Irishwoman

Irlande /iʀlɑ̃d/ NF *(= pays)* Ireland; *(= État)* Irish Republic, Republic of Ireland ◆ **l'~ du Nord** Northern Ireland, Ulster ◆ **de l'~ du Nord** Northern Irish ◆ ~ **du Sud** Southern Ireland

IRM /iɛʀɛm/ NF (abrév de **imagerie par résonance magnétique**) MRI ◆ **on m'a fait une** ~ I had an MRI scan

Iroise /iʀwaz/ N ◆ **la mer d'~** the Iroise ◆ **le pays d'~** the Iroise region *(in Western Brittany)*

ironie /iʀɔni/ NF *(lit, fig)* irony ◆ **par une curieuse ~ du sort** by a strange irony of fate ◆ ~ **grinçante** bitter irony ◆ **il sait manier l'~** he is a master of irony ◆ **je le dis sans ~** I mean what I say ◆ ~ **de l'histoire...** ironically enough...

ironique /iʀɔnik/ ADJ ironic

ironiquement /iʀɔnikmɑ̃/ ADV ironically

ironiser /iʀɔnize/ ▸ conjug 1 ◂ VI to be ironic(al) *(sur* about); ◆ **ce n'est pas la peine d'~** there's no need to be ironic(al) (about it)

ironiste /iʀɔnist/ NMF ironist

iroquois, e /iʀɔkwa, waz/ ADJ *[peuplade]* Iroquoian; *(Hist)* Iroquois NM 1 *(Ling)* Iroquoian 2 *(= coiffure)* Mohican (haircut) *(Brit)*, Mohawk *(US)* NM,F **Iroquois(e)** Iroquoian, Iroquois

IRPP /iɛʀpepe/ NM (abrév de **impôt sur le revenu des personnes physiques**) → **impôt**

irradiant, e /iʀadjɑ̃, jɑ̃t/ ADJ *[douleur]* radiant

irradiation /iʀadjasjɔ̃/ NF *(= action)* irradiation; *(= halo)* irradiation; *(= rayons)* radiation, irradiation; *(Méd)* radiation

irradier /iʀadje/ ▸ conjug 7 ◂ VT *(Phys)* to irradiate ◆ **les personnes irradiées** the people who were irradiated *ou* exposed to radiation ◆ **combustible irradié** spent (nuclear) fuel, irradiated fuel ◆ **un sourire irradiait son visage** a smile lit up his face VI *[lumière]* to radiate, to irradiate; *[douleur]* to radiate; *(fig)* to radiate

irraisonné, e /iʀɛzɔne/ ADJ irrational

irrationalisme /iʀasjɔnalism/ NM irrationalism

irrationalité /iʀasjɔnalite/ NF irrationality

irrationnel, -elle /iʀasjɔnɛl/ ADJ *(gén, Math)* irrational NM ◆ **l'~** the irrational

irrationnellement /iʀasjɔnɛlmɑ̃/ ADV irrationally

irrattrapable /iʀatʀapabl/ ADJ *[bévue]* irretrievable

irréalisable /iʀealizabl/ ADJ *(gén)* unrealizable, unachievable; *[projet]* impracticable, unworkable ◆ **c'est ~** it's not feasible, it's unworkable

irréalisé, e /iʀealize/ ADJ *(littér)* unrealized, unachieved

irréalisme /iʀealism/ NM lack of realism, unrealism

irréaliste /iʀealist/ ADJ unrealistic

irréalité /iʀealite/ NF unreality

irrecevabilité /iʀəs(ə)vabilite/ NF 1 *[d'argument, demande]* unacceptability 2 *(Jur)* inadmissibility

irrecevable /iʀəs(ə)vabl/ ADJ 1 *(= inacceptable)* *[argument, demande]* unacceptable 2 *(Jur)* inadmissible ◆ **témoignage** ~ inadmissible evidence ◆ **leur plainte a été jugée** ~ their claim was declared inadmissible

irréconciliable /iʀekɔ̃siljabl/ ADJ irreconcilable *(avec* with)

irrécouvrable /iʀekuvʀabl/ ADJ irrecoverable

irrécupérable /iʀekypeʀabl/ ADJ *(gén)* irretrievable; *[créance]* irrecoverable; *[ferraille, meubles]* unreclaimable; *[voiture]* beyond repair *(attrib)* ◆ **il est ~** *[personne]* he's beyond redemption

irrécusable /iʀekyzabl/ ADJ *[témoin, juge]* unimpeachable; *[témoignage, preuve]* incontestable, indisputable

irrédentisme /iʀedɑ̃tism/ NM irredentism

irrédentiste /iʀedɑ̃tist/ ADJ, NMF irredentist

irréductibilité /iʀedyktibilite/ NF 1 *[de fait, élément]* irreducibility 2 *(= caractère invincible)* *[d'obstacle]* insurmountability, invincibility; *[de volonté]* implacability 3 *(Chim, Math, Méd)* irreducibility

irréductible /iʀedyktibl/ ADJ 1 *(= qui ne peut être réduit)* *[fait, élément]* irreducible 2 *(= invincible)* *[obstacle]* insurmountable, invincible; *[opposition, ennemi]* implacable; *[volonté]* unwavering ◆ **les ~s du parti** the hard core of the party 3 *(Chim, Math, Méd)* irreducible

irréductiblement /iʀedyktibləmɑ̃/ ADV implacably ◆ **être ~ opposé à une politique** to be implacably opposed to a policy

irréel, -elle /iʀeɛl/ ADJ unreal NM ◆ **l'~** the unreal ◆ **(mode)** ~ *(Ling)* mood expressing unreal condition ◆ **l'~ du présent/passé** the hypothetical present/past

irréfléchi, e /iʀefleʃi/ ADJ *[geste, paroles, action]* thoughtless, unconsidered; *[personne]* impulsive; *[courage, audace]* reckless, impetuous

irréflexion /iʀeflɛksjɔ̃/ NF thoughtlessness

irréfutabilité /iʀefytabilite/ NF irrefutability

irréfutable /iʀefytabl/ ADJ *[preuve, logique]* irrefutable; *[signe]* undeniable ◆ **de façon ~** irrefutably

irréfutablement /iʀefytabləmɑ̃/ ADV irrefutably

irréfuté, e /iʀefyte/ ADJ unrefuted

irrégularité /iʀegylaʀite/ NF 1 *(= asymétrie)* *[de façade, traits, forme]* irregularity; *[d'écriture]* irregularity, unevenness ◆ **les ~s du terrain** the unevenness of the ground ◆ **les ~s de ses traits** his irregular features 2 *(= variabilité)* *[de développement, horaire, pouls, respiration]* irregularity; *[de rythme, courant, vitesse]* variation; *[de sommeil, vent]* fitfulness; *[de service, visites, intervalles]* irregularity 3 *(= inégalité)* *[de travail, effort, qualité, résultats]* unevenness; *[d'élève, athlète]* erratic performance 4 *(= illégalité)* irregularity ◆ **des ~s ont été commises lors du scrutin** irregularities occurred during the ballot 5 *(Ling)* *[de verbe, pluriel]* irregularity

irrégulier, -ière /iʀegylje, jɛʀ/ ADJ 1 (= *asymétrique*) [*façade, traits, forme*] irregular; [*écriture*] irregular, uneven; [*terrain*] irregular, uneven
2 (= *variable*) [*développement, horaire*] irregular; [*rythme, courant, vitesse*] irregular, varying (*épith*); [*sommeil, pouls, respiration*] irregular, fitful; [*service, visites, intervalles*] irregular; [*vent*] fitful
3 (= *inégal*) [*travail, effort, qualité, résultats*] uneven; [*élève, athlète*] erratic
4 (= *illégal*) [*opération, situation, procédure*] irregular; [*détention*] illegal; [*agent, homme d'affaires*] dubious ◆ **absence irrégulière** (*Jur*) unauthorized absence ◆ **étranger en situation irrégulière** foreign national whose papers are not in order ◆ **pour éviter de vous mettre en situation irrégulière** to avoid being in breach of the regulations ◆ **il était en séjour** ~ he was in the country illegally
5 (*Ling*) [*verbe, pluriel*] irregular
6 (*Mil*) irregular
NM (*Mil : gén pl*) irregular

irrégulièrement /iʀegyljɛʀmɑ̃/ ADV (*gén*) irregularly; (= *sporadiquement*) sporadically; (= *illégalement*) illegally ◆ **il ne paie son loyer que très** ~ he only pays his rent at very irregular intervals ◆ **ceux entrés** ~ **dans le pays** those who came into the country illegally

irréligieux, -ieuse /iʀeliʒjø, jøz/ ADJ irreligious

irréligion /iʀeliʒjɔ̃/ NF irreligiousness, irreligion

irrémédiable /iʀemedjabl/ ADJ 1 (= *irréparable*) [*dommage, perte*] irreparable ◆ **essayer d'éviter l'**~ to try to avoid doing anything that can't be undone 2 (= *incurable*) [*mal, vice*] incurable, irremediable 3 (= *irréversible*) [*changement, tendance*] irreversible ◆ **l'**~ **montée du chômage** the inexorable rise of unemployment

irrémédiablement /iʀemedjabləmɑ̃/ ADV irreparably, irremediably

irrémissible /iʀemisibl/ ADJ (*littér*) irremissible

irrémissiblement /iʀemisibləmɑ̃/ ADV (*littér*) irremissibly

irremplaçable /iʀɑ̃plasabl/ ADJ irreplaceable ◆ **nul** *ou* **personne n'est** ~ (*Prov*) everyone is replaceable

irréparable /iʀepaʀabl/ ADJ 1 (= *hors d'état*) [*objet*] irreparable, unmendable, beyond repair (*attrib*) ◆ **la voiture est** ~ the car is beyond repair *ou* is a write-off 2 (= *irrémédiable*) [*dommage, perte, impair*] irreparable ◆ **pour éviter l'**~ to avoid doing something that can't be undone

irrépréhensible /iʀepʀeɑ̃sibl/ ADJ (*littér*) irreprehensible

irrépressible /iʀepʀesibl/ ADJ irrepressible

irréprochable /iʀepʀɔʃabl/ ADJ [*technique, travail*] perfect, impeccable; [*alibi*] perfect; [*moralité, conduite, vie*] irreproachable, beyond reproach (*attrib*); [*tenue*] impeccable, faultless ◆ **c'est une mère** ~ she's the perfect mother

irréprochablement /iʀepʀɔʃabləmɑ̃/ ADV ◆ ~ **pur/propre** impeccably pure/clean

irrésistible /iʀezistibl/ ADJ [*personne, charme, plaisir, force*] irresistible; [*besoin, désir, preuve, logique*] compelling ◆ **il est (d'un comique)** ~ **!** (*amusant*) he's hilarious!

irrésistiblement /iʀezistibləmɑ̃/ ADV irresistibly

irrésolu, e /iʀezɔly/ ADJ [*personne*] irresolute, indecisive; [*problème*] unresolved, unsolved

irrésolution /iʀezɔlysjɔ̃/ NF irresolution, irresoluteness, indecisiveness

irrespect /iʀɛspɛ/ NM disrespect (*envers, de* for)

irrespectueusement /iʀɛspɛktɥøzmɑ̃/ ADV disrespectfully

irrespectueux, -euse /iʀɛspɛktɥø, øz/ ADJ disrespectful (*envers* to, towards)

irrespirable /iʀɛspiʀabl/ ADJ 1 [*air*] (= *pénible à respirer*) unbreathable; (= *dangereux*) unsafe, unhealthy 2 [*ambiance*] oppressive, stifling

irresponsabilité /iʀɛspɔ̃sabilite/ NF irresponsibility

irresponsable /iʀɛspɔ̃sabl/ ADJ irresponsible (*de* for); ◆ **c'est un** ~ **!** he's (totally) irresponsible! ◆ **notre pays est entre les mains d'~s** this country is in irresponsible hands

irrétrécissable /iʀetʀesisabl/ ADJ (*sur étiquette, publicité*) unshrinkable, nonshrink

irrévérence /iʀeveʀɑ̃s/ NF (= *caractère*) irreverence; (= *propos*) irreverent word; (= *acte*) irreverent act

irrévérencieusement /iʀeveʀɑ̃sjøzmɑ̃/ ADV irreverently

irrévérencieux, -ieuse /iʀeveʀɑ̃sjø, jøz/ ADJ irreverent (*envers, à l'égard de* towards)

irréversibilité /iʀevɛʀsibilite/ NF irreversibility

irréversible /iʀevɛʀsibl/ ADJ irreversible

irréversiblement /iʀevɛʀsibləmɑ̃/ ADV irreversibly

irrévocabilité /iʀevɔkabilite/ NF (*littér, Jur*) irrevocability

irrévocable /iʀevɔkabl/ ADJ [*décision, choix, juge*] irrevocable; [*temps, passé*] beyond *ou* past recall (*attrib*), irrevocable ◆ **l'**~ the irrevocable

irrévocablement /iʀevɔkabləmɑ̃/ ADV irrevocably

irrigable /iʀigabl/ ADJ irrigable

irrigation /iʀigasjɔ̃/ NF (*Agr, Méd*) irrigation

irriguer /iʀige/ ► conjug 1 ◄ VT (*Agr, Méd*) to irrigate

irritabilité /iʀitabilite/ NF irritability

irritable /iʀitabl/ ADJ irritable

irritant, e /iʀitɑ̃, ɑ̃t/ ADJ (= *agaçant*) irritating, annoying, irksome; (*Méd*) irritant NM irritant

irritation /iʀitasjɔ̃/ NF (= *colère*) irritation, annoyance; (*Méd*) irritation

irrité, e /iʀite/ (ptp de **irriter**) ADJ [*gorge, yeux*] irritated; [*geste, regard*] irritated, annoyed, angry ◆ **être** ~ **contre qn** to be annoyed *ou* angry with sb

irriter /iʀite/ ► conjug 1 ◄ VT 1 (= *agacer*) to irritate, to annoy, to irk 2 (= *enflammer*) [+ *œil, peau, blessure*] to make inflamed, to irritate ◆ **il avait la gorge irritée par la fumée** the smoke irritated his throat 3 (*littér* = *aviver*) [+ *désir, curiosité*] to arouse VPR **s'irriter** 1 (= *s'agacer*) **s'**~ **de qch/contre qn** to get annoyed *ou* angry at sth/with sb, to feel irritated at sth/with sb 2 [*œil, peau, blessure*] to become inflamed *ou* irritated

irruption /iʀypsjɔ̃/ NF (= *entrée subite ou hostile*) irruption (*NonC*); [*de nouvelles technologies, doctrine*] sudden emergence ◆ **pour empêcher l'**~ **des manifestants dans le bâtiment** to prevent the demonstrators from storming the building *ou* bursting into the building ◆ **faire** ~ **(chez qn)** to burst in (on sb) ◆ **les eaux firent** ~ **dans les bas quartiers** the waters swept into *ou* flooded the low-lying parts of the town ◆ **ils ont fait** ~ **dans le monde musical en 1996** they burst onto the music scene in 1996

Isaac /izak/ NM Isaac

Isabelle /izabɛl/ NF Isabel ◆ ~ **la Catholique** Isabella the Catholic

isabelle /izabɛl/ ADJ INV light-tan NM light-tan horse

Isaïe /isai/ NM Isaiah ◆ **(le livre d')~** (the Book of) Isaiah

isard /izaʀ/ NM izard

isba /izba/ NF isba

ISBN /iɛsbeɛn/ ADJ, NM (abrév de **International Standard Book Number**) ISBN

ischémie /iskemi/ NF ischaemia (*Brit*), ischemia (*US*)

ischion /iskjɔ̃/ NM ischium

Iseu(l)t /isø/ NF Isolde; → **Tristan**

ISF /iɛsɛf/ NM (abrév de **impôt de solidarité sur la fortune**) → **impôt**

Isis /izis/ NF Isis

Islam /islam/ NM ◆ **l'**~ Islam

Islamabad /islamabad/ N Islamabad

islamique /islamik/ ADJ Islamic ◆ **la République** ~ **de ...** the Islamic Republic of ...

islamisation /islamizasjɔ̃/ NF Islamization

islamiser /islamize/ ► conjug 1 ◄ VT to Islamize

islamisme /islamism/ NM Islamism

islamiste /islamist/ ADJ Islamic NMF Islamist

islamophobe /islamɔfɔb/ ADJ Islamophobic

islamophobie /islamɔfɔbi/ NF Islamophobia

islandais, e /islɑ̃dɛ, ɛz/ ADJ Icelandic NM (= *langue*) Icelandic NM,F **Islandais(e)** Icelander

Islande /islɑ̃d/ NF Iceland

ISO /izo/ NM INV (abrév de **International Standardization Organization**) ◆ **degré/norme/certification** ~ ISO rating/standard/certification

isobare /izɔbaʀ/ ADJ isobaric NF isobar

isocèle /izɔsɛl/ ADJ isosceles

isochrone /izɔkʀɔn/, **isochronique** /izɔkʀɔnik/ ADJ isochronal, isochronous

isoglosse /izɔglɔs/ ADJ isoglossal, isoglottic NF isogloss

isolable /izɔlabl/ ADJ isolable ◆ **difficilement** ~ difficult to isolate

isolant, e /izɔlɑ̃, ɑ̃t/ ADJ (*Constr, Élec*) insulating; (= *insonorisant*) soundproofing, sound-insulating; (*Ling*) isolating NM insulator, insulating material ◆ ~ **thermique/électrique** heat/electrical insulator ◆ ~ **phonique** soundproofing material

isolat /izɔla/ NM (*Bio, Chim, Ling*) isolate

isolateur, -trice /izɔlatœʀ, tʀis/ ADJ [*écran, gaine*] insulating NM (= *support*) insulator

isolation /izɔlasjɔ̃/ NF (*Élec*) insulation ◆ ~ **phonique** *ou* **acoustique** soundproofing, sound insulation ◆ ~ **thermique** thermal *ou* heat insulation ◆ ~ **de diodes** diode isolation

> ⚠ Attention à ne pas traduire automatiquement **isolation** par le mot anglais **isolation**.

isolationnisme /izɔlasjɔnism/ NM isolationism

isolationniste /izɔlasjɔnist/ ADJ, NMF isolationist

isolé, e /izɔle/ ADJ [*cas, personne, protestation, acte*] isolated; [*incident*] isolated, one-off; [*lieu*] isolated, remote; [*philosophe, tireur, anarchiste*] lone (*épith*); (*Élec*) insulated ◆ **se sentir** ~ to feel isolated ◆ **vivre** ~ to live in isolation ◆ **phrase ~e de son contexte** sentence taken out of context ◆ **quelques voix ~es se sont élevées pour dénoncer ...** a few lone voices have been raised in protest against ... NM,F (= *personne délaissée*) lonely person; (= *personne qui agit seule*) loner ◆ **le problème des ~s** the problem of the lonely *ou* isolated ◆ **seuls quelques ~s l'ont encouragé** only a few isolated individuals encouraged him ◆ **ce dissident n'est plus un ~** this dissident is no longer out on his own

isolement /izɔlmɑ̃/ **NM** [1] (= *solitude*) isolation ◆ **leur pays tente de sortir de son ~** their country is trying to break out of its isolation [2] (*Élec*) [*de câble*] insulation

isolément /izɔlemɑ̃/ **ADV** in isolation, individually ◆ **chaque élément pris ~** each element considered separately *ou* individually *ou* in isolation

isoler /izɔle/ ▸ conjug 1 ◂ **VT** [1] (= *éloigner*) [+ *prisonnier*] to place in solitary confinement; [+ *malade*] to isolate (*de* from); [+ *lieu*] to cut off (*de* from) to isolate ◆ **hameau isolé par l'inondation/la neige** village cut off by floods/snow [2] (*contre le froid, Élec*) to insulate; (*contre le bruit*) to soundproof, to insulate [3] (*Bio, Chim*) to isolate **VPR** **s'isoler** (*dans un coin, pour travailler*) to isolate o.s. ◆ **s'~ du reste du monde** to cut o.s. off *ou* isolate o.s. from the rest of the world ◆ **pourrait-on s'~ quelques instants ?** could we go somewhere quiet for a few minutes?

> ⚠ Au sens de 'protéger contre quelque chose', **isoler** ne se traduit pas par **to isolate**.

isoloir /izɔlwaʀ/ **NM** polling booth

isomère /izɔmɛʀ/ **ADJ** isomeric **NM** isomer

isométrique /izɔmetʀik/ **ADJ** (*Math, Sci*) isometric

isomorphe /izɔmɔʀf/ **ADJ** (*Chim*) isomorphic, isomorphous; (*Math, Ling*) isomorphic

isomorphisme /izɔmɔʀfism/ **NM** isomorphism

Isorel ® /izɔʀɛl/ **NM** hardboard

isotherme /izɔtɛʀm/ **ADJ** isothermal (*SPÉC*) ◆ **sac ~** cool *ou* insulated bag ◆ **caisse ~** ice box ◆ **camion ~** refrigerated lorry (*Brit*) *ou* truck (*US*) **NF** isotherm

isotope /izɔtɔp/ **ADJ** isotopic **NM** isotope

isotrope /izɔtʀɔp/ **ADJ** isotropic, isotropous

Israël /isʀaɛl/ **NM** Israel ◆ **l'État d'~** the state of Israel

israélien, -ienne /isʀaeljɛ̃, jɛn/ **ADJ** Israeli **NM,F** **Israélien(ne)** Israeli

israélite /isʀaelit/ **ADJ** Jewish **NM** (*gén*) Jew; (*Hist*) Israelite **NF** Jewess; (*Hist*) Israelite

ISSN /iɛsesɛn/ **ADJ, NM** (abrév de **International Standard Serial Number**) ISSN

issu, e[1] /isy/ **issu de LOC ADJ** [+ *parents*] born of ◆ **être ~ de** (= *résulter de*) to stem from; (= *être né de*) [+ *parents*] to be born of; [+ *milieu familial*] to be born into; → **cousin**[1]

issue[2] /isy/ **NF** [1] (= *sortie*) exit; [*d'eau, vapeur*] outlet ◆ **voie sans ~** (*lit, fig*) dead end; (*panneau*) "no through road" ◆ **~ de secours** (*lit*) emergency exit; (*fig*) fallback option ◆ **il a su se ménager une ~** he has managed to leave himself a way out [2] (= *solution*) way out, solution ◆ **la seule ~ possible** the only way out ◆ **la situation est sans ~** there is no way the situation can be resolved ◆ **un avenir sans ~** a future without prospects ◆ **ils n'ont pas d'autre ~ que la soumission** *ou* **que de se soumettre** their only option is to give in [3] (= *fin*) outcome ◆ **heureuse ~** happy outcome ◆ **~ fatale** fatal outcome ◆ **à l'~ de** at the end of

> ⚠ Attention à ne pas traduire automatiquement **issue** par le mot anglais **issue**, qui n'a pas le sens de 'sortie', ni de 'solution'.

IST /iɛste/ **N** (abrév de **infection sexuellement transmissible**) STI

Istanbul /istɑ̃bul/ **N** Istanbul

isthme /ism/ **NM** (*Anat, Géog*) isthmus ◆ **l'~ de Corinthe/de Panama/de Suez** the Isthmus of Corinth/of Panama/of Suez

isthmique /ismik/ **ADJ** isthmian

Istrie /istʀi/ **NF** Istria

italianisant, e /italjanizɑ̃, ɑ̃t/ **ADJ** [*œuvre*] Italianate; [*artiste*] Italianizing (*épith*) **NM,F** (*Univ*) Italianist; (= *artiste*) Italianizer

italianisme /italjanism/ **NM** Italianism

Italie /itali/ **NF** Italy

italien, -ienne /italjɛ̃, jɛn/ **ADJ** Italian **NM** (*Ling*) Italian **NM,F** **Italien(ne)** Italian **LOC ADJ** **à l'italienne** [*cuisine, mobilier, situation politique*] Italian-style; [*théâtre*] with a proscenium; (*Ordin*) [*format*] landscape (*épith*) ◆ **la comédie à l'italienne** the commedia dell'arte

italique /italik/ **NM** [1] (*Typo*) italics ◆ **mettre un mot en ~** to put a word in italics, to italicize a word [2] (*Hist, Ling*) Italic **ADJ** (*Typo*) italic; (*Hist, Ling*) Italic

item /itɛm/ **ADV** (*Comm*) ditto **NM** (*Ling, Psych*) item

itératif, -ive /iteʀatif, iv/ **ADJ** (*gén, Gram, Ordin*) iterative; (*Jur*) reiterated, repeated

itération /iteʀasjɔ̃/ **NF** iteration

Ithaque /itak/ **NF** Ithaca

itinéraire /itineʀɛʀ/ **NM** (= *chemin*) route, itinerary; (*Alpinisme*) route ◆ **son ~ philosophique/religieux** his philosophical/religious path ◆ **~ bis** *ou* **de délestage** alternative route ◆ **faire** *ou* **tracer un ~** to map out a route *ou* an itinerary

itinérant, e /itineʀɑ̃, ɑ̃t/ **ADJ** itinerant, travelling ◆ **vacances ~es** (*en voiture*) touring holiday (*Brit*) *ou* vacation (*US*); (*à pied*) rambling holiday (*Brit*) *ou* vacation (*US*) ◆ **ambassadeur ~** roving ambassador ◆ **troupe ~e** (band of) strolling players ◆ **exposition ~e** travelling exhibition ◆ **bibliothèque ~e** mobile library, bookmobile (*US*)

itou* † /itu/ **ADV** likewise ◆ **et moi ~ !** (and) me too! *

IUFM /iyɛfɛm/ **NM** (abrév de **Institut universitaire de formation des maîtres**) → **institut**

IUP /iype/ **NM** (abrév de **Institut universitaire professionnalisé**) → **institut**

IUT /iyte/ **NM** (abrév de **Institut universitaire de technologie**) → **institut**

Ivan /ivɑ̃/ **NM** Ivan ◆ **~ le Terrible** Ivan the Terrible

IVG /iveʒe/ **NF** (abrév de **interruption volontaire de grossesse**) → **interruption**

ivoire /ivwaʀ/ **NM** [1] [*d'éléphant*] (= *matière, objet*) ivory ◆ **en** *ou* **d'~** ivory (*épith*) ◆ **~ végétal** vegetable ivory, ivory nut; → **côte, tour**[1] [2] [*de dent*] dentine

ivoirien, -ienne /ivwaʀjɛ̃, jɛn/ **ADJ** of *ou* from Côte d'Ivoire **NM,F** **Ivoirien(ne)** inhabitant *ou* native of Côte d'Ivoire

ivraie /ivʀɛ/ **NF** rye grass; → **séparer**

ivre /ivʀ/ **ADJ** drunk ◆ **~ mort** dead *ou* blind drunk ◆ **légèrement ~** slightly drunk, tipsy ◆ **complètement ~** blind drunk*, completely drunk ◆ **~ de joie/rage** wild with joy/rage, beside o.s. with joy/rage ◆ **~ de vengeance** thirsting for revenge

ivresse /ivʀɛs/ **NF** (= *ébriété*) drunkenness, intoxication ◆ **dans l'~ du combat/de la victoire** in the exhilaration of the fight/of victory ◆ **l'~ du plaisir** the (wild) ecstasy of pleasure ◆ **l'~ de la vitesse** the thrill *ou* exhilaration of speed ◆ **avec ~** rapturously, ecstatically ◆ **instants/heures d'~** moments/hours of rapture *ou* (wild) ecstasy ◆ **~ chimique** drug dependence ◆ **~ des profondeurs** (*Méd*) staggers; → **état**

ivrogne /ivʀɔɲ/ **NMF** drunkard; → **serment** **ADJ** drunken (*épith*)

ivrognerie /ivʀɔɲʀi/ **NF** drunkenness

Jj

J¹, j /ʒi/ NM (= lettre) J, j; → **jour**

J² (abrév de **Joule**) J

j' /ʒ/ → **je**

jabot /ʒabo/ NM [1] [d'oiseau] crop [2] (Habillement) jabot

jacassement /ʒakasmɑ̃/ NM [de pie] chatter (NonC); (péj) [de personnes] jabber(ing) (NonC), chatter(ing) (NonC)

jacasser /ʒakase/ ▸ conjug 1 ◂ VI [pie] to chatter; (péj) [personne] to jabber, to chatter

jachère /ʒaʃɛʀ/ NF fallow (NonC); (= procédé) practice of fallowing land ◆ **laisser une terre en** ~ to leave a piece of land fallow, to let a piece of land lie fallow ◆ **rester en** ~ to lie fallow

jacinthe /ʒasɛ̃t/ NF hyacinth ◆ ~ **sauvage** ou **des bois** bluebell

jack /(d)ʒak/ NM (= fiche mâle) jack (plug)

jackpot /(d)ʒakpɔt/ NM (= combinaison) jackpot; (= machine) slot machine ◆ **gagner** ou **ramasser** ou **toucher le** ~ * to hit the jackpot ◆ **c'est le** ~ **assuré !** * you're (ou we're etc) going to make a mint! *

Jacob /ʒakɔb/ NM Jacob; → **échelle**

jacobin, e /ʒakɔbɛ̃, in/ ADJ [1] (Hist) Jacobinic(al) [2] (fig) [État, conception] centralized; [personne] in favour of a centralized government ◆ **la France ~e** France's centralized system NM (Hist) ◆ **Jacobin** Jacobin

jacobinisme /ʒakɔbinism/ NM Jacobinism ◆ **le** ~ **français** French centralism

jacobite /ʒakɔbit/ NM Jacobite

jacquard /ʒakaʀ/ ADJ [pull] Jacquard NM (= métier) Jacquard loom; (= tissu) Jacquard (weave)

jacquerie /ʒakʀi/ NF jacquerie

Jacques /ʒak/ NM James ◆ **faire le** ~ † * to play ou act the fool, to fool about; → **maître**

jacquet /ʒakɛ/ NM backgammon

Jacquot /ʒako/ NM (= prénom de perroquet) Polly

jactance /ʒaktɑ̃s/ NF [1] (* = bavardage) chat ◆ **il a de la** ~ **!** he's got the gift of the gab! * [2] (littér = vanité) conceit

jacter * /ʒakte/ ▸ conjug 1 ◂ VI to jabber, to gas *; (arg Police) to talk, to sing *

jacuzzi ® /ʒakyzi/ NM Jacuzzi ®

jade /ʒad/ NM (= pierre) jade; (= objet) jade object ou ornament ◆ **de** ~ jade (épith)

jadis /ʒadis/ ADV in times past, formerly, long ago ◆ **mes amis de** ~ my friends of long ago ou of old ◆ ~ **on se promenait dans ces jardins** in olden days ou long ago people used to walk in these gardens ADJ ◆ **au temps** ~ in days of old, in days gone by, once upon a time ◆ **du temps** ~ of times gone by, of yesteryear

jaguar /ʒagwaʀ/ NM (= animal) jaguar

jaillir /ʒajiʀ/ ▸ conjug 2 ◂ VI [1] [liquide, sang] (par à-coups) to spurt out; (abondamment) to gush forth; [larmes] to flow; [geyser] to spout up, to gush forth; [vapeur, source] to gush forth; [flammes] to shoot up, to spurt out; [étincelles] to fly out; [lumière] to flash on (de from, out of); ◆ **faire** ~ **des étincelles** to make sparks fly ◆ **un éclair jaillit dans l'obscurité** a flash of lightning split the darkness, lightning flashed in the darkness

[2] (= apparaître, s'élancer) [personne] to spring out; [voiture] to shoot out ◆ **des soldats jaillirent de tous côtés** soldiers sprang out ou leapt out from all sides ◆ **le train jaillit du tunnel** the train shot ou burst out of the tunnel ◆ **des montagnes jaillissaient au-dessus de la plaine** mountains towered above the plain ◆ **des tours qui jaillissent de terre** soaring tower blocks ◆ **des monstres jaillis de son imagination** monsters sprung from his imagination

[3] [cris, rires, réponses] to burst forth ou out

[4] [idée] to spring up; [vérité, solution] to spring (de from)

jaillissant, e /ʒajisɑ̃, ɑ̃t/ ADJ [eau] spurting, gushing

jaillissement /ʒajismɑ̃/ NM [de liquide, vapeur] spurt, gush; [d'idées] outpouring

jais /ʒɛ/ NM (Minér) jet ◆ **de** ou **en** ~ [perles, bijou] jet (épith) ◆ **cheveux de** ~ jet-black hair; → **noir**

Jakarta /dʒakaʀta/ N Jakarta

jalon /ʒalɔ̃/ NM [1] (= piquet) ranging-pole; [d'arpenteur] (surveyor's) staff [2] (= point de référence) landmark, milestone ◆ **planter** ou **poser les premiers ~s de qch** to prepare the ground for sth, to pave the way for sth ◆ **il commence à poser des ~s** he's beginning to prepare the ground

jalonnement /ʒalɔnmɑ̃/ NM [de route] marking out

jalonner /ʒalɔne/ ▸ conjug 1 ◂ VT [1] (= déterminer le tracé de) [+ route, chemin de fer] to mark out ou off [2] (= border, s'espacer sur) to line, to stretch along ◆ **des champs de fleurs jalonnent la route** fields of flowers line the road [3] (= marquer) [+ vie] to punctuate ◆ **carrière jalonnée de succès/d'obstacles** career punctuated with successes/with obstacles

jalousement /ʒaluzmɑ̃/ ADV jealously ◆ **ils défendent** ~ **leur autonomie** they jealously guard their autonomy

jalouser /ʒaluze/ ▸ conjug 1 ◂ VT to be jealous of ◆ **il est jalousé par tous ses collègues** all his colleagues envy him VPR **se jalouser** to be jealous of one another ◆ **les deux entreprises se concurrencent et se jalousent** the two companies are competitors and there is fierce rivalry between them

jalousie /ʒaluzi/ NF [1] (entre amants) jealousy; (= envie) jealousy, envy ◆ **~s mesquines** petty jealousies ◆ **être malade de** ~, **crever de** ~ * [amant] to be mad ou sick with jealousy; [envieux] to be green with envy ◆ **c'est la** ~ **qui te fait parler** you're only saying that because you're jealous [2] (= persienne) slatted blind, jalousie

jaloux, -ouse /ʒalu, uz/ ADJ [1] (en amour) jealous ◆ ~ **comme un tigre** madly jealous ◆ **observer qn d'un œil** ~ to keep a jealous eye on sb, to watch sb jealously ◆ **c'est un** ~ he's the jealous type, he's a jealous man [2] (= envieux) jealous, envious ◆ ~ **de qn/de la réussite de qn** jealous of sb/of sb's success ◆ **faire des** ~ to make people jealous [3] (littér = désireux de) ~ **de** intent upon, eager for ◆ ~ **de perfection** eager for perfection ◆ **il est très** ~ **de son indépendance/ses privilèges** (= qui tient à) he jealously guards his independence/his privileges

jamaïcain, e, jamaïquain, e /ʒamaikɛ̃, ɛn/ ADJ Jamaican NM,F **Jamaïcain(e), Jamaïquain(e)** Jamaican

Jamaïque /ʒamaik/ NF Jamaica

jamais /ʒamɛ/ GRAMMAIRE ACTIVE 39.3 ADV [1] (avec ne = à aucun moment) never, not ever ◆ **il n'a** ~ **avoué** he never confessed ◆ **n'a-t-il** ~ **avoué ?** did he never confess?, didn't he ever confess? ◆ **il n'a** ~ **autant travaillé** he's never worked as hard (before), he's never done so much work (before) ◆ ~ **je n'ai vu un homme si égoïste** I've never met ou seen such a selfish man (before), never (before) have I met ou seen such a selfish man ◆ ~ **mère ne fut plus heureuse** there was never a happier mother ◆ **il n'est** ~ **trop tard** it's never too late ◆ **on ne l'a** ~ **encore entendu se plaindre** he's never yet been heard to complain ◆ **ne dites** ~ **plus cela !** never say that again!, don't you ever say that again! ◆ **il ne lui a** ~ **plus écrit** he's never ou he hasn't (ever) written to her since ◆ **il partit pour ne** ~ **plus revenir** he left never to return ◆ **nous sommes restés deux ans sans** ~ **recevoir de nouvelles** we were ou went two years without ever hearing any news, for two years we never (once) heard any news ◆ **je n'ai**

~ de ma vie vu un chien aussi laid never in my life have I *ou* I have never in my life seen such an ugly dog ◆ **~ au grand ~ on ne me reprendra à le faire** you'll never ever catch me doing it again ◆ **~ de la vie je n'y retournerai** I shall never in my life go back there, I shall never ever go back there ◆ **accepterez-vous ? – ~ de la vie !** will you accept? – never! *ou* not on your life! * ◆ **~ plus !, plus ~ !** never again! ◆ **c'est ce que vous avez dit – ~ !** that's what you said – never! *ou* I never did! * ◆ **presque ~** hardly *ou* scarcely ever, practically never ◆ **c'est maintenant ou ~, c'est le moment ou ~** it's now or never ◆ **c'est le moment ou ~ d'acheter** now is the time to buy, if ever there was a time to buy it's now ◆ **une symphonie ~ jouée/terminée** an unplayed/unfinished symphony ◆ **il ne faut ~ dire ~** never say never ◆ **~ deux sans trois !** *(choses agréables)* good things come *ou* happen in threes!; *(malheurs)* bad things come *ou* happen in threes! ◆ **alors, ~ on ne dit "merci" ?** * didn't anyone ever teach you to say "thank you"? ◆ **y'a ~ penalty !** * no way was that a penalty! *; → **mieux, savoir**

2 *(sans ne : intensif)* **elle est belle comme ~** she's more beautiful than ever ◆ **il travaille comme ~ (il n'a travaillé)** he's working harder than ever, he's working as he's never worked before

3 *(sans ne = un jour, une fois)* ever ◆ **a-t-il ~ avoué ?** did he ever confess? ◆ **si ~ vous passez par Londres venez nous voir** if ever you're passing *ou* if ever you should pass through London come and see us ◆ **si ~ j'avais un poste pour vous je vous préviendrais** if ever I had *ou* if I ever had a job for you I'd let you know ◆ **si ~ tu rates le train, reviens** if by (any) chance you miss *ou* if you (should) happen to miss the train, come back ◆ **si ~ tu recommences, gare !** don't you ever do that again or you'll be in trouble! ◆ **il désespère d'avoir ~ de l'avancement** he despairs of ever getting promotion *ou* of ever being promoted ◆ **avez-vous ~ vu ça ?** have you ever seen *ou* did you ever see such a thing? ◆ **c'est le plus grand que j'aie ~ vu** it's the biggest one I've ever seen ◆ **de telles inondations, c'est du ~ vu** we've never seen such floods

4 *(avec que : intensif)* **je n'ai ~ fait que mon devoir** I've always just done my duty ◆ **il n'a ~ fait que critiquer (les autres)** he's never done anything but criticize (others) ◆ **ça ne fait ~ que deux heures qu'il est parti** it's no more than two hours since he left ◆ **ce n'est ~ qu'un enfant** he is only a child (after all)

5 *(avec comparatif)* ever ◆ **les œufs sont plus chers que ~** eggs are more expensive than ever (before) ◆ **c'est pire que ~** it's worse than ever

6 *(locutions)*

◆ **à jamais** for good, for ever ◆ **leur amitié est à ~ compromise** their friendship will never be the same again

◆ **à tout jamais, pour jamais** for ever (and ever), for evermore ◆ **je renonce à tout ~ à le lui faire comprendre** I've given up ever trying to make him understand it

jambage /ʒɑ̃baʒ/ NM 1 *[de lettre]* downstroke, descender 2 *(Archit)* jamb

jambe /ʒɑ̃b/ NF 1 *(Anat, Habillement, Zool)* leg ◆ **fille aux longues ~s** *ou* **toute en ~s** girl with long legs, long-legged *ou* leggy * girl ◆ **remonte ta ~ (de pantalon)** roll up your trouser leg ◆ **~ de bois/artificielle/articulée** *(Méd)* wooden/artificial/articulated leg

2 *(locutions)* **avoir les ~s comme du coton** *ou* **en coton** to have legs like jelly *ou* cotton wool *(Brit)* ◆ **n'avoir plus de ~s, en avoir plein les ~s** * to be worn out *ou* on one's knees * ◆ **avoir 20 km dans les ~s** to have walked 20 km ◆ **je n'ai plus mes ~s de vingt ans !** I'm not as quick on my feet as I used to be! ◆ **la peur/l'impatience lui donnait des ~s** fear/impatience lent new strength to his legs *ou* lent him speed ◆ **ça me fait une belle ~ !** *(iro)* a fat lot of good that does me! * ◆ **se mettre en ~s** *(Sport)* to warm up, to limber up ◆ **mise en ~s** warming-up exercises ◆ **tirer** *ou* **traîner la ~** *(par fatigue)* to drag one's feet, to trudge along; *(= boiter)* to limp along ◆ **elle ne peut plus (se) tenir sur ses ~s** her legs are giving way under her, she can hardly stand ◆ **prendre ses ~s à son cou** to take to one's heels ◆ **traiter qn/qch par-dessous** *ou* **par-dessus la ~** * to treat sb/deal with sth in a casual *ou* an offhand manner ◆ **faire qch par-dessous** *ou* **par-dessus la ~** * to do sth carelessly *ou* in a slipshod way ◆ **il m'a tenu la ~ pendant des heures** * he kept me hanging about talking for hours * ◆ **tirer dans les ~s de qn** * to make life difficult for sb ◆ **il s'est jeté dans nos ~s** * he got under our feet ◆ **elle est toujours dans mes ~s** * she's always getting in my way, she's always under my feet ◆ **j'en ai eu les ~s coupées !** it knocked me sideways * *ou* for six * *ou* for a loop * *(US)* ◆ **il est reparti sur une ~** * *(= ivre)* he could hardly stand up *ou* he was legless * when he left ◆ **c'est un cautère** *ou* **un emplâtre sur une ~ de bois** it's no use at all; → **dégourdir, partie²**

3 *(Tech) [de compas]* leg; *(= étai)* prop, stay ◆ **~ de force** *(pour poteau)* strut; *(dans voiture)* torque rod

jambette /ʒɑ̃bɛt/ NF *(Can = croc-en-jambe)* ◆ **faire une ~ à qqn** to trip sb up

jambier, -ière¹ /ʒɑ̃bje, jɛʀ/ ADJ, NM ◆ **(muscle) ~** leg muscle

jambière² /ʒɑ̃bjɛʀ/ NF *(gén)* legging, gaiter; *(Sport)* pad; *[d'armure]* greave ◆ **~s (en laine)** legwarmers

jambon /ʒɑ̃bɔ̃/ NM 1 *(Culin)* ham ◆ **~ blanc** *ou* **cuit** *ou* **de Paris** boiled *ou* cooked ham ◆ **~ cru** *ou* **de pays** cured ham ◆ **~ de Parme/d'York** Parma/York ham ◆ **~ à l'os** ham on the bone ◆ **~ au torchon** top-quality cooked ham ◆ **un ~-beurre** * a ham sandwich *(made from baguette)* 2 *(* péj = cuisse)* thigh

jambonneau (pl **jambonneaux**) /ʒɑ̃bɔno/ NM knuckle of ham

jamboree /ʒɑ̃bɔʀe/ NM *(Scoutisme)* jamboree

janissaire /ʒanisɛʀ/ NM janissary

jansénisme /ʒɑ̃senism/ NM Jansenism; *(fig)* austere code of morals

janséniste /ʒɑ̃senist/ ADJ, NMF Jansenist

jante /ʒɑ̃t/ NF *[de bicyclette, voiture]* rim ◆ **~s (en) alu/en alliage (léger)** aluminium *(Brit)* *ou* aluminum *(US)*/alloy wheels

Janus /ʒanys/ NM Janus ◆ **c'est un ~** he's two-faced

janvier /ʒɑ̃vje/ NM January; *pour autres loc voir* **septembre**

Japon /ʒapɔ̃/ NM Japan

japonais, e /ʒapɔnɛ, ɛz/ ADJ Japanese NM *(= langue)* Japanese NM,F **Japonais(e)** Japanese

japonaiserie /ʒapɔnɛzʀi/ NF Japanese curio

japonisant, e /ʒapɔnizɑ̃, ɑ̃t/ ADJ *[décor, style]* Japanese-inspired NM,F expert on Japan

jappement /ʒapmɑ̃/ NM yap, yelp

japper /ʒape/ ► conjug 1 ◄ VI to yap, to yelp

jaquette /ʒakɛt/ NF 1 *[d'homme]* morning coat; *[de femme]* jacket; *(Helv = cardigan)* cardigan ◆ **il est de la ~ (flottante)** †* he's one of them *, he's a poof* *(Brit)* *ou* a fag* *(US)* 2 *[de livre]* (dust) jacket, (dust) cover; *[de cassette vidéo]* (plastic) cover 3 *[de dent]* crown

jardin /ʒaʀdɛ̃/ NM garden, yard *(US)* ◆ **rester au** *ou* **dans le ~** to stay in the garden *ou* yard *(US)* ◆ **faire le ~** to do the gardening ◆ **siège/table de ~** garden seat/table ◆ **c'est mon ~ secret** *(fig)* those are my private secrets; → **côté, cultiver, pierre**

COMP **jardin d'acclimatation** zoological garden(s)

jardin d'agrément ornamental *ou* pleasure garden

jardin anglais *ou* **à l'anglaise** landscaped garden

jardin botanique botanical garden(s)

jardin de curé *small enclosed garden*

jardin d'enfants kindergarten

jardin à la française formal garden

le jardin des Hespérides the garden of Hesperides

jardin d'hiver *[de château]* winter garden; *[de maison]* conservatory

jardin japonais Japanese garden

le jardin des Oliviers *(Bible)* the Garden of Gethsemane

jardins ouvriers *small plots of land rented out for gardening*, allotments *(Brit)*

jardin potager vegetable *ou* kitchen garden

jardin public (public) park, public gardens

jardin de rapport † market garden

jardins suspendus terraced gardens, hanging gardens ◆ **les ~s suspendus de Babylone** the hanging gardens of Babylon

jardin zoologique ⇒ **jardin d'acclimatation**

jardinage /ʒaʀdinaʒ/ NM *(gén)* gardening; *(Sylviculture)* selective harvesting, selection ◆ **faire du ~** to garden, to do some gardening

jardiner /ʒaʀdine/ ► conjug 1 ◄ VI to garden, to do some gardening VT *[+ forêt]* to manage

jardinerie /ʒaʀdinʀi/ NF garden centre

jardinet /ʒaʀdinɛ/ NM small garden ◆ **les ~s des pavillons de banlieue** the small gardens *ou* the little patches of garden round suburban houses

jardinier, -ière /ʒaʀdinje, jɛʀ/ ADJ garden *(épith)* ◆ **culture jardinière** horticulture ◆ **plantes jardinières** garden plants NM,F gardener NF **jardinière** 1 *(= caisse à fleurs)* window box; *(d'intérieur)* jardinière 2 *(Culin)* **jardinière (de légumes)** mixed vegetables, jardinière 3 *(Scol)* **jardinière d'enfants** kindergarten teacher

jargon /ʒaʀgɔ̃/ NM 1 *(= baragouin)* gibberish *(NonC)*, double Dutch * *(NonC)* *(Brit)* 2 *(= langue professionnelle)* jargon *(NonC)*, lingo * *(NonC)* ◆ **~ administratif** officialese *(NonC)*, official jargon ◆ **~ informatique** computerese * *(NonC)* ◆ **~ journalistique** journalese *(NonC)* ◆ **~ médical** medical jargon ◆ **~ de métier** trade jargon *ou* slang ◆ **~ du palais** *(Jur)* legal jargon, legalese *(NonC)*

jargonner /ʒaʀgɔne/ ► conjug 1 ◄ VI *(= utiliser un jargon)* to talk in *ou* use jargon; *(péj)* to talk gibberish

Jarnac /ʒaʀnak/ N ◆ **coup de ~** stab in the back

jarre /ʒaʀ/ NF (earthenware) jar

jarret /ʒaʀɛ/ NM 1 *(Anat) [d'homme]* back of the knee, ham; *[d'animal]* hock ◆ **avoir des ~s d'acier** to have strong legs 2 *(Culin)* **~ de veau** knuckle *ou* shin of veal, veal shank *(US)*

jarretelle /ʒaʀtɛl/ NF suspender *(Brit)*, garter *(US)*

jarretière /ʒaʀtjɛʀ/ NF garter; → **ordre¹**

jars /ʒaʀ/ NM gander

jaser /ʒaze/ ► conjug 1 ◄ VI 1 *[enfant]* to chatter, to prattle; *[personne]* to chat away, to chat on *; *[oiseau]* to chatter, to twitter; *[jet d'eau, ruisseau]* to babble, to sing ◆ **on entend ~ la pie/le geai** you can hear the magpie/the jay chattering 2 *(arg Police)* to talk, to sing* ◆ **essayer de faire ~ qn** to try to make sb talk 3 *(= médire)* to gossip ◆ **cela va faire ~ les gens** that'll set tongues wagging, that'll set people talking *ou* gossiping

jasette * /ʒazɛt/ NF (*Can*) ◆ **faire un brin de ~** to have a chat *ou* a natter* (*Brit*) ◆ **avoir de la ~** to have the gift of the gab*

jaseur, -euse /ʒɑzœʀ, øz/ ADJ [*enfant*] chattering (*épith*), prattling (*épith*); [*oiseau*] chattering (*épith*), twittering (*épith*); [*ruisseau, jet d'eau*] babbling (*épith*), singing (*épith*); [*personne*] (= *médisant*) gossipy, tittle-tattling (*épith*) (*Brit*) NM 1 (= *bavard*) gasbag*, chatterbox; (= *médisant*) gossip, tittle-tattle 2 (= *oiseau*) waxwing

jasmin /ʒasmɛ̃/ NM (= *arbuste*) jasmine ◆ **(essence de) ~** (= *parfum*) jasmine (perfume)

jaspe /ʒasp/ NM (= *pierre*) jasper; (= *objet*) jasper ornament ◆ **~ sanguin** bloodstone

jaspé, e /ʒaspe/ ADJ mottled, marbled

jaspiner ⁑ /ʒaspine/ ► conjug 1 ◄ VI to chatter, to natter* (*Brit*)

jatte /ʒat/ NF (shallow) bowl, basin

jauge /ʒoʒ/ NF 1 (= *instrument*) gauge ◆ **~ d'essence** petrol gauge ◆ **~ (de niveau) d'huile** (oil) dipstick 2 (= *capacité*) [*de réservoir*] capacity; [*de navire*] tonnage, burden; [*de tricot*] tension 3 (*Agr*) trench ◆ **mettre en ~** ≈ to heel in

jauger /ʒoʒe/ ► conjug 3 ◄ VT 1 [+ *réservoir*] to gauge the capacity of; [+ *navire*] to measure the tonnage of 2 [+ *personne*] to size up ◆ **il le jaugea du regard** he looked him up and down ◆ **~ qn d'un coup d'œil** to size sb up at a glance VI to have a capacity of ◆ **navire qui jauge 500 tonneaux** ship with a tonnage of 500, ship of 500 tonnes *ou* tons burden

jaunasse * /ʒonas/ ADJ (*péj*) yellowish, dirty yellow (*épith*)

jaunâtre /ʒonɑtʀ/ ADJ [*lumière, couleur*] yellowish; [*teint*] sallow, yellowish

jaune /ʒon/ ADJ [*couleur, dents*] yellow; (*littér*) [*blés*] golden ◆ **il a le teint ~** (*mauvaise mine*) he looks yellow *ou* sallow; (*basané*) he has a sallow complexion ◆ **~ d'or** golden yellow ◆ **~ moutarde** mustard yellow ◆ **~ comme un citron** *ou* **un coing** as yellow as a lemon; → **corps, fièvre, nain, péril** NM 1 (= *couleur*) yellow 2 (*Culin*) **~ (d'œuf)** (egg) yolk 3 (* = *pastis*) **un (petit) ~** a (small glass of) pastis NMF 1 (⁑: *injurieux*) **Jaune** Asian; (= *Chinois*) Chink⁑ (*injurieux*); (= *Japonais*) Jap⁑ (*injurieux*), Nip⁑ (*injurieux*) 2 (*péj* = *non-gréviste*) scab⁑, blackleg (*Brit*)

jaunet, -ette /ʒonɛ, ɛt/ ADJ slightly yellow, yellowish NM †† gold coin

jaunir /ʒoniʀ/ ► conjug 2 ◄ VT [+ *feuillage, vêtements*] to turn yellow ◆ **doigts jaunis par la nicotine** nicotine-stained fingers, fingers stained yellow with nicotine ◆ **photos jaunies** yellowed photos VI to yellow, to turn *ou* become yellow

jaunissant, e /ʒonisɑ̃, ɑt/ ADJ (*littér*) [*papier, feuillage*] yellowing; [*blé*] ripening, yellowing (*littér*)

jaunisse /ʒonis/ NF (*Méd*) jaundice ◆ **en faire une ~** * (*de dépit*) to be pretty miffed*; (*de jalousie*) to be *ou* turn green with envy ◆ **tu ne vas pas nous en faire une ~ !*** you're not going to get all huffy*, are you?

jaunissement /ʒonismɑ̃/ NM yellowing

Java /ʒava/ NF Java

java /ʒava/ NF (= *danse*) popular waltz ◆ **faire la ~** ⁑ to live it up*, to have a rave-up⁑ (*Brit*) ◆ **ils ont fait une de ces ~s** they had a really wild time* *ou* a real rave-up⁑ (*Brit*)

javanais, e /ʒavanɛ, ɛz/ ADJ Javanese NM 1 (= *langue*) Javanese; (= *argot*) *slang formed by adding av before each vowel of a word*; (= *charabia*) gibberish, double Dutch* (*Brit*) 2 (*Ordin*) **Java** Java NM,F **Javanais(e)** Javanese

Javel /ʒavɛl/ NF ◆ **(eau de) ~** bleach

javeline /ʒavlin/ NF javelin

javelle /ʒavɛl/ NF [*de céréales*] swath ◆ **mettre en ~s** to lay in swaths

javellisation /ʒavelizasjɔ̃/ NF chlorination

javelliser /ʒavelize/ ► conjug 1 ◄ VT to chlorinate ◆ **cette eau est trop javellisée** there's too much chlorine in this water ◆ **eau très javellisée** heavily chlorinated water

javelot /ʒavlo/ NM (*Mil, Sport*) javelin; → **lancement**

jazz /dʒɑz/ NM jazz ◆ **la musique (de) ~** jazz (music)

jazzman /dʒɑzman/ (pl **jazzmen** /dʒɑzmɛn/) NM jazzman, jazz musician

jazzy /dʒɑzi/ ADJ INV [*musique*] jazz-style (*épith*), jazzy; [*musicien*] jazz-style (*épith*) ◆ **une version ~ de leur chanson** a jazz version of their song

J.-C. (abrév de **Jésus-Christ**) ◆ **en (l'an) 300 av./apr. ~** in (the year) 300 BC/AD

je, j' /ʒ(ə)/ PRON PERS I NM ◆ **le ~** (*Ling*) the I-form, the 1st person singular; (*Philos*) the I

Jean /ʒɑ̃/ NM John ◆ **(saint) ~-Baptiste** (St) John the Baptist ◆ **(saint) ~ de la Croix** St John of the Cross ◆ **~ sans Terre** John Lackland ◆ **c'est ~ qui rit et ~ qui pleure** one minute he's laughing, the next minute he's crying

jean /dʒin/ NM (= *tissu*) denim; (= *vêtement*) (pair of) jeans, (pair of) denims ◆ **~ (de *ou* en) velours** cord(uroy) jeans ◆ **blouson en ~ vert** green denim jacket ◆ **être en ~(s)** to be wearing jeans

jean-foutre * /ʒɑ̃futʀ/ NM INV (*péj*) jackass (*péj*)

Jeanne /ʒan/ NF Jane, Joan, Jean ◆ **~ d'Arc** Joan of Arc ◆ **coiffure à la ~ d'Arc** page boy (haircut)

jeannette /ʒanɛt/ NF 1 ◆ **(croix à la) ~** gold cross (*worn around neck*) 2 (= *planche à repasser*) sleeve-board 3 (*Scoutisme*) Brownie (Guide)

Jeannot /ʒano/ NM Johnny ◆ **~ lapin** bunny (rabbit), Mr Rabbit

Jeep ® /(d)ʒip/ NF Jeep ®

Jéhovah /ʒeova/ NM Jehovah; → **témoin**

jéjunum /ʒeʒynɔm/ NM jejunum

je-m'en-fichisme * /ʒ(ə)mɑ̃fiʃism/ NM (I-)couldn't-care-less attitude*

je-m'en-fichiste * (pl **je-m'en-fichistes**) /ʒ(ə)mɑ̃fiʃist/ ADJ couldn't-care-less* (*épith*) ◆ **il est trop ~** he really just couldn't care less* NMF couldn't-care-less type*

je-m'en-foutisme ⁑ /ʒ(ə)mɑ̃futism/ NM (I-)couldn't-give-a-damn attitude⁑

je-m'en-foutiste ⁑ (pl **je-m'en-foutistes**) /ʒ(ə)mɑ̃futist/ ADJ (I-)couldn't-give-a-damn⁑ (*épith*) NMF (I-)couldn't-give-a-damn type⁑

je-ne-sais-quoi, je ne sais quoi /ʒən(ə)sɛkwa/ NM INV (certain) something ◆ **elle a un ~ qui attire** there's (a certain) something about her that's very attractive, she has a certain je-ne-sais-quoi *ou* a certain indefinable charm ◆ **cette journée avait un ~ d'inhabituel** there was something unusual about today

jenny /ʒeni/ NF spinning jenny

jérémiades * /ʒeʀemjad/ NFPL moaning, whining

Jérémie /ʒeʀemi/ NM (= *prophète*) Jeremiah

Jéricho /ʒeʀiko/ N Jericho

jéroboam /ʒeʀɔbɔam/ NM 1 (= *bouteille*) jeroboam (*bottle containing 3 litres*) 2 (*Bible*) **Jéroboam** Jeroboam

jerricane, jerrycan /(d)ʒeʀikan/ NM jerry can

Jersey /ʒɛʀzɛ/ NF Jersey

jersey /ʒɛʀzɛ/ NM 1 (= *vêtement*) jersey top (*ou* garment *etc*), sweater, jumper (*Brit*) 2 (= *tissu*) jersey (cloth) ◆ **~ de laine/de soie** jersey wool/silk ◆ **point de ~** stocking stitch ◆ **tricoter un pull en ~** to knit a jumper in stocking stitch

jersiais, e /ʒɛʀzjɛ, jɛz/ ADJ Jersey (*épith*), of *ou* from Jersey ◆ **race ~e** (*Agr*) Jersey breed ◆ **(vache) ~e** Jersey (cow) NM,F **Jersiais(e)** inhabitant *ou* native of Jersey

Jérusalem /ʒeʀyzalɛm/ N Jerusalem ◆ **la ~ nouvelle/céleste** the New/Heavenly Jerusalem

jésuite /ʒezɥit/ ADJ, NM (*Rel, péj*) Jesuit

jésuitique /ʒezɥitik/ ADJ (*Rel, péj*) Jesuitical

jésuitisme /ʒezɥitism/ NM (*Rel, péj*) Jesuitism, Jesuitry

jésus /ʒezy/ NM 1 ◆ **Jésus** (*prénom*) Jesus ◆ **le petit Jésus** the baby *ou* infant Jesus ◆ **Jésus-Christ** Jesus Christ ◆ **en 300 avant/après Jésus-Christ** in 300 BC/AD ◆ **doux Jésus !*** sweet Jesus!⁑ 2 (= *statue*) statue of the infant Jesus 3 (= *terme d'affection*) **mon ~** (my) darling 4 (= *saucisson*) *kind of pork sausage* 5 ◆ **(papier) ~** super royal (printing paper) ◆ **(papier) petit ~** super royal (writing paper)

jet¹ /ʒɛ/ NM 1 (= *jaillissement*) [*d'eau, gaz, flamme*] jet; [*de sang*] spurt, gush; [*de salive*] stream; [*de pompe*] flow ◆ **~ de lumière** beam of light

2 [*de pierre, grenade*] (= *action*) throwing; (= *résultat*) throw ◆ **à un ~ de pierre** a stone's throw away ◆ **un ~ de 60 mètres au disque** a 60-metre discus throw ◆ **il a gagné par ~ de l'éponge au troisième round** (*Boxe*) he won because his opponent's corner threw in the towel in the third round; → **arme**

3 (*locutions*) **premier ~** [*de lettre, livre*] first *ou* rough draft; [*de dessin*] first *ou* rough sketch ◆ **du premier ~** at the first attempt ◆ **écrire d'un (seul) ~** to write in one go ◆ **à ~ continu** in a continuous *ou* an endless stream

4 (*Tech* = *coulage*) casting ◆ **couler une pièce d'un seul ~** to produce a piece in a single casting

5 (*Bot* = *pousse*) main shoot; (= *rameau*) branch

COMP **jet d'eau** (= *fontaine*) fountain; (= *gerbe*) spray; (*au bout d'un tuyau*) nozzle; (*Archit*) weathering

jet à la mer (*Naut*) jettison(ing)

jet² /dʒɛt/ NM (= *avion*) jet

jetable /ʒ(ə)tabl/ ADJ [*briquet, mouchoir, rasoir, seringue, lentilles, appareil-photo*] disposable ◆ **c'est l'ère du salarié ~** these days employees are seen as expendable NM (= *appareil-photo*) disposable camera; (= *briquet*) disposable lighter

jeté, e¹ /ʒ(ə)te/ ADJ (⁑ = *fou*) mad*, crazy* NM 1 (*Danse*) **~ (simple)** jeté ◆ **~ battu** grand jeté 2 (*Sport*) jerk 3 (*Tricot*) **~ (simple)** make one ◆ **faire un ~** to drop a stitch

COMP **jeté de canapé** throw

jeté de lit bedspread

jeté de table table runner

jetée² /ʒ(ə)te/ NF jetty; (*grande*) pier ◆ **~ flottante** floating bridge

jeter /ʒ(ə)te/ ► conjug 4 ◄ VT 1 (= *lancer*) to throw; (*avec force*) to fling, to hurl, to sling; [+ *dés*] to throw ◆ **~ qch à qn** (*pour qu'il l'attrape*) to throw sth to sb; (*agressivement*) to throw *ou* fling *ou* hurl sth at sb ◆ **~ qn/qch à l'eau** (*de la rive*) to throw sb/sth into the water; (*d'un bateau*) to throw sb/sth overboard ◆ **le navire a été jeté à la côte** (*Naut*) the ship was driven towards the coast ◆ **elle lui a jeté son cadeau à la figure** *ou* **à la tête** she threw *ou* hurled his present at him ◆ **~ à la mer** *ou* **par-dessus bord** (*Naut*) [+ *personne*] to throw overboard; [+ *objet*] to throw overboard, to jettison ◆ **~ bas** (*littér*) [+ *statue, gouvernement*] to topple ◆ **~ qn à terre** *ou* **à bas** [*cheval*] to throw sb ◆ **il a jeté son camion contre un arbre** he crashed his truck *ou* lorry (*Brit*) into a tree, his truck *ou* lorry (*Brit*) careered into a tree ◆ **~ dehors** *ou* **à la porte**

[+ visiteur] to throw out, to chuck out⁑ *(Brit)*; *[+ employé]* to fire, to sack *(Brit)* ◆ ~ **qn en prison** to throw *ou* cast sb into prison ◆ ~ **qch par la fenêtre** to throw sth out of the window ◆ ~ **sa cigarette/un papier par terre** to throw one's cigarette/a piece of paper on the ground ◆ **il a jeté sa serviette/son sac par terre** he threw down his towel/his bag ◆ **les gens qui jettent leurs papiers par terre** people who drop litter ◆ **il a jeté son agresseur par** *ou* **à terre** he threw his attacker to the ground ◆ **n'en jetez plus (la cour est pleine) !*** *(après compliments)* don't! *ou* stop it! you're embarrassing me!; *(après injures etc)* cut it out!*, pack it in!* *(Brit)*; → **ancre, bébé, dévolu rue¹** *etc*

[2] *(= mettre au rebut)* *[+ papiers, objets]* to throw away *ou* out; *(Cartes)* to discard ◆ ~ **qch au panier/à la poubelle/au feu** to throw sth into the wastepaper basket/in the dustbin/in *ou* on the fire ◆ **jette l'eau sale dans l'évier** pour *ou* tip the dirty water down the sink ◆ **il n'y a rien à ~*** *(hum)* it *(ou he etc)* can't be faulted ◆ **se faire ~**⁑ *(d'une réunion, entreprise)* to get thrown out, to get chucked⁑ out *(Brit)* *(de* of); *(lors d'une requête, déclaration d'amour)* to be sent packing*; → **bon¹**

[3] *(= construire)* *[+ pont]* to throw *(sur* over, across); *[+ fondations]* to lay ◆ ~ **les bases d'une nouvelle Europe** *(fig)* to lay the foundations of a new Europe ◆ **jetez la passerelle !** *(Naut)* set up the gangway!

[4] *(= émettre)* *[+ lueur]* to give out, to cast, to shed; *[+ ombre]* to cast; *[+ son]* to let out, to give out; *[+ cri]* to utter, to let out ◆ **il en jette, dans son smoking !**⁑ he's a knockout* *ou* he looks a million dollars* in his dinner jacket! ◆ **ce nouveau tapis dans le salon, ça en jette**⁑ the new carpet in the sitting room looks really great* ◆ **elle (en) jette, cette voiture !*** that's some car!*; → **feu¹**

[5] *(= mettre rapidement)* ~ **des vêtements dans un sac** to sling *ou* throw some clothes into a bag ◆ **va ~ cette carte à la boîte** go and pop* this card into the postbox ◆ ~ **une veste sur ses épaules** to slip a jacket over *ou* round one's shoulders ◆ ~ **une idée sur le papier** to jot down an idea

[6] *(= plonger)* to plunge, to throw ◆ ~ **qn dans le désespoir** to plunge sb into despair ◆ ~ **qn dans l'embarras** to throw sb into confusion ◆ **il a jeté son pays dans la guerre** he plunged his country into war

[7] *(= répandre)* to cast ◆ ~ **l'effroi chez/parmi** to sow alarm and confusion in/among ◆ ~ **le trouble dans les esprits** *(= perturber)* to disturb *ou* trouble people; *(= rendre perplexe)* to sow confusion in people's minds ◆ **sa remarque a jeté un froid** his remark put a damper on things *ou* cast a chill over the company; → **discrédit, sort**

[8] *(= dire)* to say *(à* to); ◆ **"dépêche-toi !", me jeta-t-il en passant** "hurry up!", he called out to me as he went by ◆ ~ **des remarques dans la conversation** to throw in *ou* toss in remarks ◆ ~ **des insultes/menaces** to hurl insults/threats ◆ **je lui ai jeté la vérité/l'accusation à la figure** *ou* **à la tête** I hurled *ou* flung the truth/accusation at him ◆ **il lui jeta à la tête qu'il n'était qu'un imbécile** he told him to his face that he was nothing but a fool ◆ **il nous jette à la tête ses relations/ses diplômes** he's always trying to impress us with *ou* always harping on* to us about the important people he knows/all the qualifications he's got

[9] *(mouvement du corps)* ~ **les épaules/la tête en avant** to throw *ou* thrust one's shoulders/one's head forward ◆ ~ **les bras autour du cou de qn** to throw *ou* fling one's arms round sb's neck ◆ **elle lui jeta un regard plein de mépris** she cast a withering look at him, she looked *ou* glanced witheringly at him; → **œil**

VPR se jeter [1] *(= s'élancer)* **se ~ par la fenêtre/du douzième étage** to throw o.s. out of the window/from the twelfth floor ◆ **se ~ à l'eau** *(lit)* to launch o.s. *ou* plunge into the water; *(fig)* to take the plunge ◆ **se ~ à la tête de qn** to throw o.s. at sb ◆ **se ~ dans les bras/aux pieds de qn** to throw o.s. into sb's arms/at sb's feet ◆ **sa voiture s'est jetée contre un arbre** his car crashed into a tree ◆ **un chien s'est jeté sous mes roues** a dog rushed out under the wheels of my car ◆ **il s'est jeté sous un train** he threw himself under *ou* in front of a train ◆ **se ~ sur qn** to rush at sb ◆ **se ~ sur sa proie** to swoop down *ou* pounce on one's prey ◆ **il se jeta sur la nourriture comme un affamé** he fell (up)on the food like a starving man ◆ **se ~ sur** *[+ lit]* to throw *ou* fling o.s. onto; *[+ téléphone]* to rush to; *[+ journal, roman]* to pounce on; *[+ occasion, solution]* to jump at ◆ **se ~ dans la politique/les affaires** to launch o.s. into politics/business; → **corps, cou, genou**

[2] *(= se déverser)* *[de rivière]* to flow *(dans* into); ◆ **le Rhône se jette dans la Méditerranée** the Rhone flows into the Mediterranean

[3] *(= se lancer)* *[+ pierres, ballon]* to throw *ou* hurl at each other ◆ **ils se jetèrent des injures à la tête** they hurled insults at each other

[4] *(⁑ = boire)* **on va s'en ~ un (derrière la cravate)** we'll have a quick one* ◆ **on va s'en ~ un dernier** we'll have one for the road*

[5] *(sens passif)* **ça se jette** it's disposable, you can throw it away (once you've used it)

jeteur /ʒ(ə)tœʀ/ **NM** ◆ ~ **de sort** wizard

jeteuse /ʒ(ə)tøz/ **NF** ◆ ~ **de sort** witch

jeton /ʒ(ə)tɔ̃/ **NM** [1] *(= pièce)* *(gén)* token; *(Jeux)* counter; *(Roulette)* chip ◆ ~ **de téléphone** telephone token ◆ ~ **(de présence)** *(= argent)* director's fees; *(= objet)* token ◆ **toucher ses ~s** *(= somme)* to draw one's fees; → **faux²** [2] *⁑ (= coup)* bang; *(= marque)* dent ◆ **ma voiture a pris un ~** my car was dented ◆ **avoir les ~s** to have the jitters* *ou* the willies⁑ ◆ **ça lui a fichu les ~s** it gave him the jitters* *ou* the willies⁑

jet-set (pl **jet-sets**) /dʒɛtsɛt/ **NM** *ou* **NF**, **jet-society** /dʒɛtsɔsajti/ **NF** jet set ◆ **membre de la ~** jet setter

jet-ski /dʒɛtski/ **NM** jet-ski

jeu (pl **jeux**) /ʒø/ **NM** [1] *(= amusement, divertissement)* **le ~** play ◆ **l'enfant s'éduque par le ~** the child learns through play ◆ **le ~ du soleil sur l'eau** *(fig)* the play of the sunlight on the water ◆ **c'est un ~ d'enfant** it's child's play, it's a snap* *(US)* ◆ **il s'est fait un ~ de résoudre ce problème** he made light work of the problem ◆ **par ~** for fun ◆ **il critiquait tout, comme par ~** he criticized everything as if it was some kind of game

[2] *(gén avec règles)* game ◆ ~ **d'intérieur/de plein air** indoor/outdoor game ◆ ~ **d'adresse** game of skill ◆ ~ **de cartes** card game ◆ **le ~ d'échecs/de quilles** the game of chess/of skittles ◆ ~ **à 13/15** *(Rugby)* rugby league/union ◆ **le ~ de la vérité** the truth game ◆ **quel ~ de cons !**⁑ how bloody⁑ *(Brit)* *ou* goddam⁑ *(US)* stupid! ◆ **c'est le ~** it's fair (play) ◆ **ce n'est pas de** *ou* **du ~*** that's not (playing) fair ◆ **ce n'est qu'un ~** it's just a game ◆ **ce n'est qu'un ~ de l'esprit** it's just a mental exercise ◆ **le ~ n'en vaut pas la chandelle** the game is not worth the candle ◆ **~x de main(s), ~x de vilain(s) !** *(Prov)* stop fooling around or it will end in tears!; → **jouer**

[3] *(Sport = partie)* game ◆ **il mène (par) 5 ~x à 2** *(Tennis)* he leads (by) 5 games to 2 ◆ **"jeu, set, et match"** "game, set and match" ◆ **la pluie a ralenti le ~** the rain slowed down play (in the game) ◆ **faire ~ égal avec qn** to be evenly matched

[4] *(Sport = terrain)* ~ **de boules** *(sur sol nu)* *area where boules is played*; *(sur gazon)* bowling green ◆ ~ **de quilles** skittle alley ◆ **la balle est sortie du ~** the ball has gone out of play; → **hors**

[5] *(Casino)* gambling ◆ **il a perdu toute sa fortune au ~** he has gambled away his entire fortune, he lost his fortune (at) gambling ◆ **"faites vos jeux"** "place your bets" ◆ **les ~x sont faits** *(Casino)* les jeux sont faits; *(fig)* the die is cast ◆ **~x de tirage** lotteries, draws ◆ **~x de grattage** scratch-card games; → **heureux**

[6] *(= ensemble des pions, boîte)* game, set ◆ ~ **d'échecs/de boules/de quilles** chess/bowls/skittle set ◆ ~ **de 52 cartes** pack *ou* deck *(US)* of 52 cards

[7] *(= série complète)* *[de clés, aiguilles]* set ◆ ~ **de caractères** *(Ordin)* character set ◆ ~ **d'orgue(s)** organ stop

[8] *(= cartes)* hand ◆ **il laisse voir son ~** he shows his hand ◆ **je n'ai jamais de ~** I never have a good hand ◆ **le grand ~** *(aux tarots)* the major arcana ◆ **sortir le grand ~** *(fig)* to pull out all the stops ◆ **il a beau ~ de protester maintenant** it's easy for him to complain now; → **cacher**

[9] *(= façon de jouer)* *(Sport)* game; *(Mus)* technique, (manner of) playing; *(Ciné, Théât)* acting ◆ **il a un ~ rapide/lent/efficace** *(Sport)* he plays a fast/a slow/an effective game ◆ **pratiquer un ~ ouvert** *(Rugby)* to keep the game open ◆ **elle a un ~ saccadé/dur** *(Mus)* she plays jerkily/harshly, her playing is jerky/harsh

[10] *(= fonctionnement)* *(Admin, Pol etc)* working, interaction, interplay; *(Tech)* play ◆ **le ~ des pistons** the play of the pistons ◆ **le ~ des alliances/des institutions** the interplay of alliances/of institutions ◆ **le marché est régulé par le ~ de l'offre et de la demande** the market is regulated by (the interplay between) supply and demand ◆ **fausser le ~ de la concurrence** to restrict *ou* hamper the free play of competition

[11] *(= stratégie, manège)* game ◆ **j'ai compris son petit ~ !** I know his little game *ou* what he's up to! ◆ **à quel ~ joues-tu ?** what are you playing at? ◆ **c'est un ~ de dupes** it's a fool's *ou* mug's* *(Brit)* game ◆ **entrer** *ou* **marcher dans le ~ de qn** to go *ou* play along with sb, to play sb's game ◆ **faire** *ou* **jouer le ~ de qn** to play into sb's hands ◆ **je vois clair** *ou* **je lis dans son ~** I know his little game, I know what he's playing at *ou* what he's up to ◆ **il s'est piqué** *ou* **pris au ~** he really got into it*, he got hooked* ◆ **il a été pris à son propre ~** he was caught out at his own game; → **bascule, double**

[12] *(= espace)* **donner du ~ à qch** to loosen sth up a bit ◆ **la vis a pris du ~** the screw has worked loose ◆ **la porte ne ferme pas bien, il y a du ~** the door isn't a tight fit

LOC ADV en jeu [1] *(Sport)* in play ◆ **mettre** *ou* **remettre en ~** to throw in ◆ **mise en ~** *(Tennis)* serve; *(Hockey)* bully-off; *(sur glace)* face-off ◆ **remise en ~** throw-in

[2] *(= en action)* **les forces en ~** the forces at work ◆ **entrer/mettre en ~** to come/bring into play ◆ **mise en ~** *[de facteur, élément]* bringing into play; *[de mécanisme]* activation, bringing into operation

[3] *(= en cause)* **être en ~** to be at stake ◆ **les intérêts/les sommes en ~ sont considérables** there are considerable interests/sums of money at stake ◆ **il mettra tout en ~ pour nous aider** he'll risk everything *ou* stake his all to help us

COMP jeu d'arcade arcade video game
jeu blanc *(Tennis)* love game
jeux du cirque *(Hist)* circus games
jeu pour console console game
jeu de construction building *ou* construction set
jeu décisif *(Tennis)* tie-break, tiebreaker
jeux d'eau fountains

jeu d'écritures *(Comm)* dummy entry
jeu électronique electronic game
jeu d'entreprise business *ou* management game
jeu de hasard game of chance
jeu de jambes *(Sport)* footwork, leg movement
jeux de lumière *(artificiels)* lighting effects; *(naturels)* play of light *(NonC)*
jeu de mains *[de pianiste]* playing, technique
jeu de massacre *(à la foire)* Aunt Sally; *(fig)* wholesale massacre *ou* slaughter
jeu de mots play on words *(NonC)*, pun
jeu de l'oie ≃ snakes and ladders
Jeux olympiques Olympic games, Olympics ◆ **les Jeux olympiques d'hiver** the Winter Olympics ◆ **Jeux olympiques handisports** *ou* **pour handicapés** Paralympics
jeu de patience puzzle
jeux de physionomie facial expressions
jeu de piste treasure hunt
jeu radiophonique radio game
jeu de rôles role play
jeu de scène *(Théât)* stage business *(NonC)*
jeu des sept erreurs (game of) spot the difference
jeu de société *(charades, portrait etc)* parlour game; *(Monopoly, Scrabble etc)* board game
jeux du stade *(Hist)* (ancient) Olympic games
jeu de stratégie game of strategy
jeu télévisé television game; *(avec questions)* (television) quiz
jeu vidéo video game
jeu virtuel computer game ◆ **le ~ virtuel** (computer) gaming

jeu-concours (pl **jeux-concours**) /ʒøkɔ̃kuʀ/ NM *(Presse, Radio, TV)* competition; *(avec questions)* quiz

jeudi /ʒødi/ NM Thursday ◆ **le ~ de l'Ascension** Ascension Day; → **saint;** *pour autres loc voir* **samedi**

jeun /ʒœ̃/ **à jeun** LOC ADV ◆ **être à ~** *(= n'avoir rien mangé)* to have eaten nothing; *(= n'avoir rien bu)* to have drunk nothing; *(= ne pas être ivre)* to be sober ◆ **boire à ~** to drink on an empty stomach ◆ **à prendre à ~** *(Méd)* to be taken on an empty stomach ◆ **venez à ~** don't eat or drink anything before you come

jeune /ʒœn/ ADJ 1 *(en années)* young ◆ **homme ~** young man ◆ **~ chien** young dog ◆ **mes ~s années** the years of my youth ◆ **dans mon ~ âge** *ou* **temps** in my youth, when I was young ◆ **vu son ~ âge** in view of his youth ◆ **il n'est plus tout** *ou* **très ~** he's not as young as he used to be, he's not in his first youth ◆ **il est plus ~ que moi de cinq ans** he's five years younger than me, he's five years my junior ◆ **ils font ~(s)** they look young ◆ **il fait plus ~ que son âge** he doesn't look his age, he looks younger than he is ◆ **cette coiffure la fait paraître plus ~** that hairstyle makes her look younger

2 *(après nom) [apparence, visage]* youthful; *[couleur, vêtement]* young, which makes one look young ◆ **soyez/restez ~s !** be/stay young! *ou* youthful! ◆ **être ~ d'allure** to be young-looking, to be youthful in appearance ◆ **être ~ de caractère** *ou* **d'esprit** *(puéril)* to have a childish outlook, to be immature; *(dynamique)* to have a young *ou* youthful outlook ◆ **être ~ de cœur** to be young at heart ◆ **être ~ de corps** to have a youthful figure

3 *(= récent) [industrie, science, vin]* young

4 *(= inexpérimenté)* raw, inexperienced, green* ◆ **il est encore bien ~** he's still very inexperienced ◆ **être ~ dans le métier** to be new *ou* a newcomer to the trade

5 *(= cadet)* junior ◆ **mon ~ frère** my younger brother ◆ **mon plus ~ frère** my youngest brother ◆ **Durand ~** Durand junior

6 *(* = insuffisant)* short, skimpy ◆ **ça fait ~, c'est un peu ~** *[temps]* it's cutting it a bit short *ou* fine; *[argent]* that's not much; *[tissu]* it's not (going to be) enough; *[boisson, nourriture]* there's not enough to go round

NM 1 *(= personne)* youngster, youth, young man ◆ **un petit ~** a young lad ◆ **les ~s de maintenant** *ou* **d'aujourd'hui** young people *ou* the young *ou* the youth of today ◆ **club** *ou* **maison de ~s** youth club

◆ **donner un coup de jeune à** * *[+ bâtiment, local]* to give a face-lift to, to freshen up; *[+ émission]* to give a new look to ◆ **ils ont donné un coup de ~ au cinéma australien** they've breathed new life into Australian cinema ◆ **cette relation lui a donné un coup de ~** this relationship gave him a new lease of life

2 *(= animal)* young animal

NF girl ◆ **une petite ~** a young girl

ADV ◆ **s'habiller ~** to dress young for one's age ◆ **se coiffer ~** to have a young *ou* modern hairstyle

COMP **jeune femme** young woman
jeune fille girl
jeune garçon boy, young lad*
jeune génération younger generation
jeunes gens *(gén)* young people; *(= garçons)* boys
jeune homme young man
jeune loup *(gén)* go-getter; *(= politicien)* young Turk
jeune marié bridegroom ◆ **les ~s mariés** the newlyweds ◆ **un couple de ~s mariés** a couple of newlyweds
jeune mariée bride
jeune premier *(Ciné,Théât)* romantic male lead ◆ **il a un physique** *ou* **une tête de ~ premier** he has film-star looks ◆ **il veut encore jouer les ~s premiers** he still thinks he can play young roles
jeune première *(Ciné, Théât)* romantic female lead

jeûne /ʒøn/ NM fast ◆ **rompre le ~** to break one's fast ◆ **jour de ~** fast day ◆ **faire un ~ de trois jours** to fast for three days ◆ **le Jeûne fédéral** *(Helv) Swiss holiday weekend at the end of September*

jeûner /ʒøne/ ► conjug 1 ◄ VI *(gén)* to go without food; *(Rel)* to fast ◆ **faire ~ un malade** to make a sick person go without food ◆ **laisser ~ ses enfants** to let one's children go hungry

jeunesse /ʒœnɛs/ NF 1 *(= période)* youth ◆ **la ~ du monde** *(littér)* the dawn of the world ◆ **en pleine ~** in the prime of youth ◆ **dans ma ~** in my youth, in my younger days ◆ **folie/erreur/péché de ~** youthful prank/mistake/indiscretion ◆ **je n'ai pas eu de ~** I didn't have much of a childhood ◆ **en raison de son extrême ~** owing to his extreme youth ◆ **il n'est plus de la première ~** he's not as young as he was *ou* as he used to be, he's not in the first flush of youth ◆ **il faut que ~ se passe** *(Prov)* youth must have its fling; → **œuvre**

2 *(= qualité)* youth, youthfulness ◆ **~ de cœur** youthfulness of heart ◆ **la ~ de son visage/de son corps** his youthful face/ figure ◆ **avoir un air de ~** to have a youthful look ◆ **il a une grande ~ d'esprit** he has a very young outlook

3 *(= personnes jeunes)* youth, young people ◆ **la ~ dorée** the young jet set ◆ **la ~ ouvrière** (the) young workers ◆ **la ~ étudiante/des écoles** young people at university/at school ◆ **livres pour la ~** books for the young *ou* for young people ◆ **la ~ est partie devant** † the young ones *ou* the young people have gone on ahead ◆ **si ~ savait, si vieillesse pouvait** *(Prov)* if youth but knew, if old age but could; → **auberge, voyage**

4 († * = *jeune fille)* (young) girl

5 *(gén pl = groupe)* youth ◆ **les ~s communistes** the Communist Youth Movement

jeunet, -ette * /ʒœnɛ, ɛt/ ADJ *(péj)* rather young ◆ **il est un peu ~ pour lire ce roman** he's rather young *ou* he's a bit on the young side to be reading this novel

jeûneur, -euse /ʒønœʀ, øz/ NM,F person who fasts *ou* is fasting

jeunisme /ʒœnism/ NM *(en faveur des jeunes)* ageism, cult of youth; *(contre les jeunes)* discrimination against young people ◆ **faire du ~** to discriminate in favour of (*ou* against) young people

jeuniste /ʒœnist/ ADJ *(en faveur des jeunes)* pro-youth; *(contre les jeunes)* anti-youth

jeunot, -otte * /ʒœno, ɔt/ ADJ ⇒ **jeunet** NM young fellow*

jf 1 (abrév de **jeune fille**) → **jeune** 2 (abrév de **jeune femme**) → **jeune**

jh (abrév de **jeune homme**) → **jeune**

jihad /ʒi(j)ad/ NM ⇒ **djihad**

jiu-jitsu /ʒjyʒitsy/ NM jujitsu, jiujitsu

JO /ʒio/ NMPL (abrév de **Jeux olympiques**) Olympics NM (abrév de **Journal officiel**) → **journal**

joaillerie /ʒɔajʀi/ NF 1 *(= travail)* jewellery *(Brit) ou* jewelry *(US)* making; *(= commerce)* jewellery *(Brit) ou* jewelry *(US)* trade ◆ **travailler dans la ~** to work in jewellery *ou* in the jewel trade 2 *(= marchandise)* jewellery *(Brit)*, jewelry *(US)* 3 *(= magasin)* jeweller's *(Brit) ou* jeweler's *(US)* (shop)

joaillier, -ière /ʒɔaje, jɛʀ/ NM,F jeweller

Job /ʒɔb/ NM *(Rel)* Job; → **pauvre**

job /dʒɔb/ NM *(* = travail)* job ◆ **il a trouvé un petit ~ pour l'été** he's found a summer job NF *(Can)* job

jobard, e * /ʒɔbaʀ, aʀd/ ADJ gullible NM,F *(= dupe)* sucker*, mug* *(Brit)*

jobarderie * /ʒɔbaʀd(ə)ʀi/, **jobardise** * /ʒɔbaʀdiz/ NF gullibility

jobiste /(d)ʒɔbist/ NMF *(Belg) student who does part-time jobs*

jockey /ʒɔkɛ/ NM jockey; → **régime**[1]

Joconde /ʒɔkɔ̃d/ NF ◆ **la ~** the Mona Lisa

jocrisse † /ʒɔkʀis/ NM *(= niais)* simpleton

jodhpur(s) /dʒɔdpyʀ/ NM(PL) jodhpurs

jodler /jɔdle/ ► conjug 1 ◄ VI to yodel

joggeur, -euse /dʒɔgœʀ, øz/ NM,F jogger

jogging /dʒɔgiŋ/ NM 1 *(= sport)* jogging ◆ **faire du ~** to go jogging ◆ **il faisait son ~ dans le parc** he was jogging in the park ◆ **je fais mon ~ tous les jours** I go for a jog *ou* I go jogging every day 2 *(= survêtement)* jogging suit, sweatsuit *(surtout US)*

> ⚠ Au sens de 'survêtement', **jogging** ne se traduit pas par le mot anglais **jogging**.

joie /ʒwa/ GRAMMAIRE ACTIVE 51.1

NF 1 *(= sentiment)* joy; *(sens diminué)* pleasure ◆ **à ma grande ~** to my great joy *ou* delight ◆ **fou** *ou* **ivre de ~** wild with joy ◆ **la nouvelle le mit au comble de la ~** he was overjoyed at hearing the news *ou* to hear the news ◆ **accueillir la nouvelle avec une ~ bruyante** to greet the news with great shouts of joy ◆ **ses enfants sont sa plus grande ~** his children are his greatest delight *ou* joy ◆ **c'était une ~ de le regarder** it was a joy *ou* delight to look at him, he was a joy to look at ◆ **quand aurons-nous la ~ de vous revoir ?** when shall we have the pleasure of seeing you again? ◆ **il accepta avec ~** he accepted with delight ◆ **sauter** *ou* **bondir de ~** to jump for joy ◆ **on travaille dans la ~ et la bonne humeur ici** *(souvent iro)* it's a real joy to work here; → **cœur, feu**[1]**, fille**

2 *(locutions)* **~ de vivre** joie de vivre, joy of life ◆ **être plein de ~ de vivre** to be full of joie de vivre *ou* the joys of life ◆ **cela le mit en ~** he

was overjoyed ◆ **ce livre a fait la ~ de tous** this book has delighted *ou* has given great pleasure to everyone ◆ **le clown tomba pour la plus grande ~ des enfants** the clown fell over to the (great) delight of the children ◆ **il se faisait une telle ~ d'y aller** he was so looking forward to going ◆ **je me ferai une ~ de le faire** I shall be delighted *ou* only too pleased to do it ◆ **c'est pas la ~ !*** it's no fun!

NFPL **joies** ◆ **les ~s de la vie** the joys of life ◆ **les ~s du monde** *ou* **de la terre** (*Rel*) worldly *ou* earthly pleasures *ou* joys ◆ **les ~s du mariage** the joys of marriage ◆ **encore une panne, ce sont les ~s de la voiture !** (*iro*) another breakdown, that's one of the joys *ou* delights of motoring! (*iro*)

joignable /ʒwaɲabl/ ADJ ◆ **être difficilement ~** to be difficult to reach *ou* contact ◆ **il est ~ à tous moments** he can be reached at any time

joindre /ʒwɛ̃dʀ/ GRAMMAIRE ACTIVE 52.2 ▸ conjug 49 ◂

VT 1 (= *mettre ensemble*) to join, to put together ◆ **~ deux tables/planches** to put two tables/planks together ◆ **~ un bout de ficelle à un autre** to join one piece of string to another ◆ **~ les mains** to put *ou* bring one's hands together, to clasp one's hands ◆ **~ les talons/les pieds** to put one's heels/one's feet together ◆ **les mains jointes** with his (*ou* her *etc*) hands together

2 (= *relier*) to join, to link ◆ **une digue/un câble joint l'île au continent** a dyke/a cable links the island with the mainland

3 (= *unir*) [+ *efforts*] to combine, to join ◆ **~ l'utile à l'agréable** to combine business with pleasure ◆ **elle joint l'intelligence à la beauté** she combines intelligence and beauty ◆ **~ le geste à la parole** to act in accordance with what one says, to match one's action to one's words ◆ **~ les deux bouts*** to make (both) ends meet

4 (= *ajouter*) to add, to attach (*à* to); (= *inclure*) [+ *timbre, chèque*] to enclose (*à* with); ◆ **les avantages joints à ce poste** the advantages attached to this post, the fringe benefits of this post ◆ **carte jointe à un bouquet/cadeau** card attached to a bouquet/a gift ◆ **pièce jointe** [*de lettre*] enclosure; (*Ordin*) attachment ◆ **envoyer qch en pièce jointe** to send sth as an attachment

5 (= *contacter*) [+ *personne*] to get in touch with, to contact ◆ **essayez de le ~ par téléphone** try to get in touch with *ou* try to get hold of *ou* try to contact him by telephone

VI [*fenêtre, porte*] to shut, to close ◆ **ces fenêtres joignent mal** these windows don't shut *ou* close properly ◆ **est-ce que ça joint bien ?** [*planches*] does it make a good join?, does it join well?

VPR **se joindre** 1 (= *s'unir à*) **se ~ à** to join ◆ **se ~ à la procession** to join the procession ◆ **se ~ à la foule** to mingle *ou* mix with the crowd ◆ **voulez-vous vous ~ à nous ?** would you like to join us? ◆ **se ~ à la discussion** to join in the discussion ◆ **mon mari se joint à moi pour vous exprimer notre sympathie** my husband and I wish to express our sympathy, my husband joins me in offering our sympathy (*frm*)

2 [*mains*] to join

joint¹ /ʒwɛ̃/ NM 1 (*Anat, Géol, Tech*) (= *assemblage, articulation*) joint; (= *ligne de jonction*) join; (*en ciment*) pointing ◆ **~ de cardan** cardan joint ◆ **~ de culasse** cylinder head gasket ◆ **~ d'étanchéité** seal ◆ **~ de robinet** washer 2 (*locutions*) **faire le ~*** (*en provisions*) to last *ou* hold out; (*en argent*) to bridge the gap (*jusqu'à* until); ◆ **chercher/trouver le ~*** to look (around) for/find the answer

joint²* /ʒwɛ̃/ NM (*Drogue*) joint*, spliff* ◆ **se faire** *ou* **se rouler un ~** to roll (o.s.) a joint* *ou* a spliff*

jointé, e /ʒwɛ̃te/ ADJ ◆ **cheval court-~/long-~** short-/long-pasterned horse, horse with short/long pasterns

jointif, -ive /ʒwɛ̃tif, iv/ ADJ joined, contiguous; [*planches*] butt-jointed ◆ **(cloison) jointive** butt-jointed partition

jointoyer /ʒwɛ̃twaje/ ▸ conjug 8 ◂ VT [+ *mur*] to point ◆ **des murs de pierre grossièrement jointoyés** stone walls with rather crudely-finished pointing

jointure /ʒwɛ̃tyʀ/ NF 1 (*Anat*) joint ◆ **~ du genou** knee joint ◆ **à la ~ du poignet** at the wrist (joint) ◆ **faire craquer ses ~s** to crack one's knuckles ◆ **à la ~ de deux os** at the joint between two bones ◆ **~s** [*de cheval*] fetlock-joints 2 (*Tech*) (= *assemblage*) joint; (= *ligne de jonction*) join

joint-venture, joint venture (pl **joint(-)ventures**) /dʒɔjntvɛntʃœʀ/ NF joint venture

jojo* /ʒoʒo/ ADJ [*personne, objet*] ◆ **il est pas ~** he's (*ou* it's) not much to look at NM ◆ **affreux ~** (= *enfant*) little horror; (= *adulte*) nasty piece of work*

jojoba /ʒɔʒɔba/ NM jojoba ◆ **huile de ~** jojoba oil

joker /(d)ʒɔkɛʀ/ NM 1 (*Cartes*) joker ◆ **jouer** *ou* **sortir** *ou* **utiliser son ~** (*lit*) to play one's joker; (*fig*) to play one's trump card 2 (*Ordin*) **(caractère) ~** wild card

joli, e /ʒɔli/ ADJ 1 [*enfant, femme*] pretty, attractive, nice; [*objet*] pretty, nice; [*chanson, pensée, promenade, appartement*] nice ◆ **d'ici, la vue est très ~e** you get a very nice view from here ◆ **~ comme un cœur** (as) pretty as a picture ◆ **il est ~ garçon** he's quite good-looking

2 (* = *non négligeable*) [*revenu, profit*] nice (*épith*), good, handsome (*épith*); [*résultat*] good ◆ **ça fait une ~e somme** it's quite a tidy sum ◆ **il a une ~e situation** he has a good position

3 (*iro*) **embarquez tout ce ~ monde !** take this nasty bunch *ou* crew* away! ◆ **un ~ coco*** *ou* **monsieur** a nasty character, a nasty piece of work*

4 (*locutions*) **tout ça c'est bien ~ mais...** that's all very well *ou* fine but ... ◆ **vous avez fait du ~ !** (*iro*) you've made a fine mess of things! ◆ **tu as encore menti, c'est du ~ !** (*iro*) you've lied again – shame on you!* ◆ **faire le ~ cœur** to play the ladykiller ◆ **ce n'était pas ~ à voir** it wasn't a pretty sight ◆ **elle est ~e, votre idée !** (*iro*) that's a great idea! (*iro*) ◆ **c'est ~ de dire du mal des gens !** (*iro*) that's nice, spreading nasty gossip about people! (*iro*) ◆ **c'est pas ~-~ !*** (*laid*) it's not a pretty sight*; (*méchant*) that wasn't very nice*

joliesse /ʒɔljɛs/ NF (*littér*) [*de personne*] prettiness; [*de gestes*] grace

joliment /ʒɔlimɑ̃/ ADV 1 (= *élégamment*) [*décoré, habillé*] nicely ◆ **il l'a ~ arrangé !** (*iro*) he sorted him out nicely *ou* good and proper!* 2 (* = *très, beaucoup*) really ◆ **il était ~ content/en retard** he was really glad/late

Jonas /ʒɔnas/ NM Jonah, Jonas

jonc /ʒɔ̃/ NM 1 (= *plante*) rush, bulrush; (= *canne*) cane, rattan ◆ **corbeille** *ou* **panier de ~** rush basket 2 [*de voiture*] trim 3 ◆ **~ (d'or)** (= *bracelet*) (plain gold) bangle; (= *bague*) (plain gold) ring

jonchée /ʒɔ̃ʃe/ NF swath ◆ **des ~s de feuilles mortes couvraient la pelouse** dead leaves lay in drifts on *ou* lay scattered *ou* strewn over the lawn

joncher /ʒɔ̃ʃe/ ▸ conjug 1 ◂ VT [*papiers*] to litter, to be strewn over; [*cadavres, détritus, fleurs*] to be strewn over ◆ **jonché de** littered *ou* strewn with

jonchets /ʒɔ̃ʃɛ/ NMPL jackstraws, spillikins

jonction /ʒɔ̃ksjɔ̃/ NF (= *action*) joining, junction; (= *état*) junction; (*Élec*) junction ◆ **à la ~ des deux routes** at the junction of the two roads, where the two roads meet ◆ **opérer une ~** (*Mil*) to effect a junction, to link up ◆ **point de ~** junction, meeting point ◆ **~ d'instance** (*Jur*) joinder

jongler /ʒɔ̃gle/ ▸ conjug 1 ◂ VI (*lit*) to juggle (*avec* with); ◆ **~ avec** [+ *dates, emplois du temps, chiffres*] to juggle (with); [+ *difficultés*] to juggle with

jonglerie /ʒɔ̃gləʀi/ NF juggling

jongleur, -euse /ʒɔ̃glœʀ, øz/ NM,F 1 (*gén*) juggler 2 (*Hist*) jongleur

jonque /ʒɔ̃k/ NF (*Naut*) junk

jonquille /ʒɔ̃kij/ NF daffodil, jonquil ADJ INV daffodil yellow

Jordanie /ʒɔʀdani/ NF Jordan

jordanien, -ienne /ʒɔʀdanjɛ̃, jɛn/ ADJ Jordanian NM,F **Jordanien(ne)** Jordanian

Joseph /ʒozɛf/ NM Joseph

Josué /ʒɔzɥe/ NM Joshua

jouabilité /ʒuabilite/ NF [*de jeu vidéo*] playability

jouable /ʒwabl/ ADJ playable ◆ **ce sera difficile, mais c'est ~** [*projet*] it'll be difficult, but it's worth a try *ou* a go

jouasse* /ʒwas/ ADJ pleased as Punch*, chuffed* (*Brit*) ◆ **il n'était pas ~ !** he wasn't too thrilled!

joue /ʒu/ NF 1 (*Anat*) cheek ◆ **~ contre ~** cheek to cheek ◆ **tendre la ~** to offer one's cheek ◆ **présenter** *ou* **tendre l'autre ~** to turn the other cheek ◆ **~ de bœuf** (*Culin*) ox cheek 2 (*Mil*) **en ~ !** take aim! ◆ **coucher** *ou* **mettre une cible/qn en ~** to aim at *ou* take aim at a target/sb ◆ **coucher** *ou* **mettre en ~ un fusil** to take aim with a rifle, to aim a rifle ◆ **tenir qn en ~** to keep one's gun trained on sb 3 (*Naut*) **~s d'un navire** bows of a ship

jouer /ʒwe/

▸ conjug 1 ◂

1 VERBE INTRANSITIF	3 VERBE TRANSITIF
2 VERBE TRANSITIF INDIRECT	4 VERBE PRONOMINAL

1 – VERBE INTRANSITIF

1 = s'amuser to play (*avec* with); ◆ **arrête, je ne joue plus** stop it, I'm not playing any more ◆ **faire qch pour ~** to do sth for fun ◆ **elle jouait avec son crayon/son collier** (= *manipuler*) she was toying *ou* fiddling with her pencil/her necklace ◆ **~ avec les sentiments de qn** to play *ou* trifle with sb's feelings ◆ **~ avec sa vie/sa santé** (= *mettre en danger*) to gamble with one's life/one's health ◆ **~ avec le feu** (*lit, fig*) to play with fire ◆ **on ne joue pas avec ces choses-là** (*fig*) matters like these are not to be treated lightly; → **cour**

◆ **jouer à** ◆ **~ à la poupée** to play with one's dolls ◆ **~ au golf/au ping-pong/aux cartes/aux échecs** to play golf/table tennis/cards/chess ◆ **~ aux soldats/aux cow-boys et aux Indiens** to play (at) soldiers/(at) cowboys and Indians ◆ **~ au docteur (et au malade)** to play (at) doctors and nurses ◆ **~ à qui sautera le plus loin** to see who can jump the furthest ◆ **~ au chat et à la souris (avec qn)** to play cat and mouse with sb ◆ **~ au héros/à l'aristocrate** (*fig*) to play the hero/the aristocrat ◆ **à quoi joues-tu ?** (*fig*) what are you playing at? ◆ **n'essaie pas de ~ au plus fin** *ou* **malin avec moi** don't try to outsmart me ◆ **~ au con*** to mess about*, to arse around** (*Brit*); → **bille**

2 = pratiquer un jeu, un sport **il joue bien/mal (au tennis)** he is a good/poor (tennis) player, he plays (tennis) well/badly ◆ **il a vraiment bien joué** he played an excellent game, he played really well ◆ **~ contre qn/une équipe** to play (against) sb/a team ◆ **à qui de ~ ?** whose go *ou* turn is it? ◆ **à vous (*ou* moi *etc*) de**

~ ! (*lit, fig*) your (*ou* my *etc*) go! *ou* turn!; (*Échecs*) your (*ou* my *etc*) move! ◆ **bien joué !** (*lit*) well played!; (*fig*) well done! ◆ ~ **petit bras** (*Tennis*) to play underarm ◆ ~ **serré** to play (it) tight, to play a close game ◆ ~ **perdant/gagnant** to play a losing/winning game

3 Mus to play ◆ **l'orchestre joue ce soir à l'opéra** the orchestra is playing at the opera this evening ◆ **ce pianiste joue bien/mal** this pianist plays well/badly

4 pour de l'argent (*Casino*) to gamble ◆ ~ **pair/impair** to play (on) the even/odd numbers ◆ ~ **aux courses** to bet on the horses ◆ ~ **à la** *ou* **en Bourse** to speculate *ou* gamble on the Stock Exchange

5 Ciné, Théât, TV to act ◆ **il joue dans "Hamlet"** he's acting *ou* he's in "Hamlet" ◆ **il joue au théâtre des Mathurins** he's playing *ou* acting at the théâtre des Mathurins ◆ **elle joue très bien/mal** she is a very good/bad *ou* poor actress, she acts very well/badly ◆ **elle a très bien joué Juliette** she gave an excellent performance as Juliet ◆ **la troupe va ~ à Avignon** the company is going to perform in Avignon; → **guichet**

6 locutions

◆ **jouer sur** ◆ ~ **sur les mots** to play with words ◆ **ils ont joué sur votre inquiétude** (= *spéculer sur*) they took advantage of the fact that you were worried ◆ ~ **sur l'effet de surprise** to use the element of surprise ◆ **il joue sur la fibre nationaliste** he is playing on nationalist feeling *ou* exploiting nationalist sentiment ◆ **il a réussi en jouant sur les différences de législations** he succeeded by exploiting differences in legislation ◆ **en jouant sur la qualité du papier, on peut réduire le coût de fabrication** you can reduce manufacturing costs by changing the quality of the paper; → **velours**

7 = fonctionner to work ◆ **la clé joue dans la serrure** the key turns in the lock ◆ **la clé joue mal dans la serrure** the key doesn't fit (in) the lock very well ◆ **faire ~ un ressort** to activate *ou* trigger a spring ◆ **la barque jouait sur son ancre** the boat bobbed about at anchor

8 = joindre mal [*pièce, cheville*] to fit loosely, to be loose; (= *travailler*) [*bois*] to warp

9 = bouger [*soleil, lumière*] to play ◆ **la lumière jouait au plafond** the light played *ou* danced on the ceiling

10 = intervenir, s'appliquer to apply (*pour* to); ◆ **l'âge ne joue pas** age doesn't come into it *ou* is of no consequence ◆ **cet argument joue à plein** this argument is entirely applicable ◆ **cette augmentation joue pour tout le monde** this rise applies to *ou* covers everybody ◆ **l'augmentation joue depuis le début de l'année** the rise has been operative from *ou* since the beginning of the year ◆ **ses relations ont joué pour beaucoup dans la décision** his connections counted for a lot in the decision ◆ **cet élément a joué en ma faveur/contre moi** this factor worked in my favour/against me ◆ **le temps joue contre lui** time is against him *ou* is not on his side ◆ **faire ~** [*+ clause de sauvegarde*] to invoke ◆ **les distributeurs font ~ la concurrence** the distributors are playing the competitors off against each other ◆ **il a fait ~ ses appuis politiques pour obtenir ce poste** he made use of his political connections to get this post

2 - VERBE TRANSITIF INDIRECT

jouer de

1 Mus ~ **d'un instrument/du piano/de la guitare** to play an instrument/the piano/the guitar

2 = manier to make use of, to use ◆ ~ **de l'éventail** to play with one's fan ◆ **ils durent ~ du couteau/du revolver pour s'enfuir** they had to use knives/revolvers to get away ◆ **ils jouent trop facilement du couteau** they are too quick with their knives, they use knives too readily ◆ ~ **de la fourchette** (*hum*) to dig in*, to tuck in* (*Brit*) ◆ ~ **des jambes*** *ou* **des flûtes*** (= *se servir de*) to leg it*, to hare off* ◆ ~ **des coudes pour arriver au buffet/pour entrer** to elbow one's way to the buffet/one's way in; → **prunelle**

3 = utiliser to use, to make use of ◆ **il sait ~ de l'espace et des couleurs** he knows how to use *ou* how to make use of space and colour ◆ ~ **de son influence/charme pour obtenir qch** to use *ou* make use of one's influence/charm to get sth ◆ **il joue de sa maladie pour ne rien faire** he plays on his illness to get out of doing anything

4 = être victime de ~ **de malheur** *ou* **de malchance** to be dogged by ill luck

3 - VERBE TRANSITIF

1 Ciné, Théât [*+ rôle*] to play, to act; [*+ pièce, film*] to put on, to show ◆ **on joue "Macbeth" ce soir** "Macbeth" is on *ou* is being played this evening ◆ **elle joue toujours les soubrettes** she always has the maid's part ◆ ~ **la fille de l'air** (*fig*) to vanish into thin air ◆ **qu'est-ce que tu nous joues, là ?** (*hum : reproche*) what are you playing at?; → **comédie, rôle**

2 = simuler ~ **les héros/les victimes** to play the hero/the victim ◆ ~ **la surprise/le désespoir** to pretend to be surprised/in despair, to affect *ou* feign surprise/despair ◆ ~ **un double jeu** to play a double game

3 locutions

◆ **jouer + tour(s) à qn** ◆ **jouer un mauvais tour à qn** to play a (dirty) trick on sb ◆ **mes yeux me jouent des tours** my eyes are playing tricks on me ◆ **cela te jouera un mauvais** *ou* **vilain tour** you'll get your comeuppance*, you'll be sorry for it

4 Mus [*+ concerto, valse*] to play ◆ **il va ~ du Bach** he is going to play (some) Bach ◆ **il joue très mal Chopin** he plays Chopin very badly

5 Jeux, Sport [*+ partie d'échecs, de tennis*] to play; [*+ carte*] to play; [*+ pion*] to play, to move ◆ **il est interdit de ~ le ballon à la main** (*Ftbl*) it is forbidden to handle the ball ◆ **il préfère ~ le ballon à la main** (*Rugby*) he prefers to run the ball ◆ **jouez le ballon plutôt que l'adversaire** play the ball, not your opponent ◆ ~ **un coup facile/difficile** (*Sport*) to play an easy/a difficult shot; (*Échecs*) to make an easy/a difficult move ◆ ~ **la montre** (*fig*) to play for time, to kill the clock (*US*) ◆ **il faut ~ le jeu** you've got to play the game ◆ **ils ont refusé de ~ le jeu** they refused to play ball* *ou* to play the game ◆ ~ **franc jeu** to play fair; → **atout**

6 = mettre en jeu (*Casino*) [*+ argent*] to stake, to wager; (*Courses*) [*+ argent*] to bet, to stake (*sur* on); [*+ cheval*] to back, to bet on; (*fig*) [*+ fortune, possessions, réputation*] to wager ◆ ~ **gros jeu** *ou* **un jeu d'enfer** to play for high stakes ◆ **il ne joue que des petites sommes** he only places small bets *ou* plays for small stakes ◆ **il a joué et perdu une fortune** he gambled away a fortune ◆ ~ **son mandat/son ministère sur qch** (*Pol*) to stake one's re-election prospects/one's ministerial position on sth ◆ **dans cette histoire, il joue sa tête/sa réputation** (*fig*) he's risking his neck/his reputation in this affair ◆ **rien n'est encore joué** (= *décidé*) nothing is settled *ou* decided yet, there's still everything to play for; → **gros, tout, va-tout**

7 Bourse ~ **les financières/les pétrolières** (= *investir dans*) to speculate in financials/oil

8 frm = tromper [*+ personne*] to deceive, to dupe

9 = opter pour ~ **la prudence/la sécurité** to be cautious/play safe; → **carte**

4 - VERBE PRONOMINAL

se jouer

1 mutuellement **ils se jouent des tours** they're playing tricks on each other

2 = être joué **ce jeu se joue à quatre** this is a game for four people, you need four people to play this game ◆ **la pièce se joue au théâtre des Mathurins** the play is on at the théâtre des Mathurins ◆ **le drame s'est joué très rapidement** (*fig*) the tragedy happened very quickly

3 = être décidé **tout va se ~ demain** everything will be settled *ou* decided tomorrow ◆ **l'avenir de l'entreprise va se ~ sur cette décision** the future of the company hinges *ou* depends on this decision ◆ **c'est l'avenir de l'entreprise qui se joue** the future of the company is at stake ◆ **son sort se joue en ce moment** his fate is hanging in the balance at the moment

4 locutions

◆ **se jouer de** (*frm*)
(= *tromper*) ◆ **se ~ de qn** to deceive sb, to dupe sb ◆ **se ~ des lois/de la justice** (= *se moquer de*) to scoff at the law/at justice
(= *triompher facilement de*) ◆ **se ~ des difficultés** to make light of the difficulties

◆ **se la jouer*** to show off ◆ **depuis qu'il a eu sa promotion, il se la joue** getting that promotion has really gone to his head*

---

jouet /ʒwɛ/ NM 1 [*d'enfant*] toy 2 (= *victime*) plaything ◆ **il n'était qu'un ~ entre leurs mains** he was just a plaything in their hands ◆ **être le ~ des vagues/des événements/de rivalités politiques** to be at the mercy of the waves/of events/of rivalries between political parties ◆ **être le ~ d'une hallucination** to be the victim of a hallucination

joueur, joueuse /ʒwœʀ, ʒwøz/ ADJ [*enfant, animal*] playful ◆ **il a un tempérament ~, il est très ~** [*enfant, animal*] he loves to play, he's very playful; [*parieur*] he loves to gamble, he's a keen gambler NM,F (*Échecs, Mus, Sport*) player; (*Jeux*) gambler ◆ ~ **de cricket** cricketer ◆ ~ **de golf** golfer ◆ ~ **de cornemuse** (bag)piper ◆ ~ **de cartes** card player ◆ **être beau/mauvais ~** to be a good/bad loser ◆ **sois beau ~ !** be a sport! ◆ **il faut être beau ~** it's important to be a good loser

joufflu, e /ʒufly/ ADJ [*personne*] chubby-cheeked, round-faced; [*visage*] chubby

joug /ʒu/ NM 1 (*Agr, fig*) yoke ◆ **tomber sous le ~ de** to come under the yoke of ◆ **mettre sous le ~** to yoke, to put under the yoke 2 [*de balance*] beam 3 (*Antiq*) yoke

jouir /ʒwiʀ/ ► conjug 2 ◄ VT INDIR **jouir de** 1 (*frm*) [*+ autorité, réputation, liberté*] to enjoy; (*Jur*) [*+ bien*] to enjoy the use of ◆ ~ **de toutes ses facultés** to be in full possession of one's faculties ◆ **la région jouit d'un bon climat** the region has *ou* enjoys a good climate ◆ **cette pièce jouit d'une superbe vue** the room has a magnificent view 2 (= *savourer*) [*+ vie*] to enjoy ◆ **il jouissait de leur embarras évident** he delighted in *ou* enjoyed their obvious embarrassment VI 1 (* : *plaisir sexuel*) to have an orgasm, to come* ◆ **ça me fait ~ de les voir s'empoigner** I get a (real) kick out of seeing them at each other's throats* 2 (* : *douleur*) to suffer agonies ◆ **on va ~ !** we're going to have a hell of a time!*, we aren't half going to have fun!*

jouissance /ʒwisɑ̃s/ NF 1 (= *volupté*) pleasure, enjoyment, delight; (*sensuelle*) sensual pleasure; (= *orgasme*) orgasm, climax ◆ **cela lui a procuré une vive ~** (*frm*) this afforded him intense pleasure 2 (*Jur* = *usage*) use, possession; [*de propriété, bien*] use, enjoyment ◆ **avoir la ~ de certains droits** to enjoy certain rights

jouisseur, -euse /ʒwisœʀ, øz/ ADJ sensual NM,F sensualist

jouissif, -ive* /ʒwisif, iv/ ADJ fun ◆ **c'est ~** it's fun ◆ **c'est un mélange ~ de hip-hop et de rock** it's a fun mix of hip-hop and rock

joujou (pl **joujoux**) /ʒuʒu/ **NM** *(langage enfantin)* toy; (* = *revolver*) gun ◆ **cette voiture est son nouveau ~** this car is his new toy ◆ **faire ~ avec** to play with ◆ **il ne faut pas faire ~ avec ça** *(fig)* that's not a toy

joule /ʒul/ **NM** joule

jour /ʒuʀ/

1 NOM MASCULIN 3 COMPOSÉS
2 NOM MASCULIN PLURIEL

1 - NOM MASCULIN

1 [= espace de temps] day ◆ **dans deux ~s** in two days' time, in two days ◆ **c'était il y a deux ~s** it was two days ago ◆ **(à prendre) trois fois par ~** (to be taken) three times a day ◆ **des poussins d'un ~** day-old chicks ◆ **d'un ~** *(fig)* *[célébrité, joie]* short-lived, fleeting ◆ **c'est à deux ~s de marche/de voiture de ...** it's a two-day walk/drive from ... ◆ **faire 30 ~s (de prison)** to do 30 days (in jail)* ◆ **les ~s se suivent et ne se ressemblent pas** *(Prov)* time goes by and every day is different, the days go by and each is different from the last ◆ **pas un ~ ne se passe sans qu'il y ait une agression** not a day passes without there being a mugging ◆ **sept ~s sur sept** seven days a week; → **compter, huit, quinze**

◆ **au jour le jour** *[existence, gestion]* day-to-day *(épith)* ◆ **taux d'intérêt** *ou* **loyer de l'argent au ~ le ~** *(Fin)* call-money rate ◆ **vivre au ~ le ~** (= *sans soucis*) to live from day to day; (= *pauvrement*) to live from hand to mouth ◆ **il gère la situation au ~ le ~** he's dealing with the situation on a day-by-day basis

◆ **de jour en jour** day by day, from day to day

◆ **du jour au lendemain** overnight ◆ **ça ne se fera pas du ~ au lendemain** it won't happen overnight

◆ **d'un jour à l'autre** (= *incessamment*) ◆ **on l'attend d'un ~ à l'autre** he's expected any day (now) ◆ **il change d'avis d'un ~ à l'autre** (= *très rapidement*) he changes his mind from one day to the next

◆ **jour après jour** day after day, day in day out

◆ **jour par jour** day by day

2 [= époque précise] day ◆ **quel ~ sommes-nous ?** what day is it today? ◆ **ce ~-là** that day ◆ **le ~ de Noël/de Pâques** Christmas/Easter Day ◆ **par un ~ de pluie/de vent** on a rainy/windy day ◆ **le ~ précédent** *ou* **d'avant** the day before, the previous day ◆ **le ~ suivant** *ou* **d'après** the day after, the next day, the following day ◆ **l'autre ~** the other day ◆ **un ~ il lui écrivit** one day he wrote to her ◆ **un beau ~** *(passé)* one (fine) day; *(futur)* one of these (fine) days, one (fine) day ◆ **le grand ~ approche** the big day *ou* D-day is drawing nearer ◆ **le ~ où tu sauras conduire, tu m'emmèneras** you can take me there the day you learn to drive ◆ **un ~ viendra où ...** a day will come when ... ◆ **le ~ n'est pas loin où ...** the day is not far off when ... ◆ **premier ~** *[de vacances, mois etc]* first day; *[d'exposition]* opening *ou* first day ◆ **enveloppe premier ~** *(Philat)* first day cover ◆ **ils s'aiment comme au premier ~** they're still as much in love as ever ◆ **dès le premier ~** from day one, from the outset *ou* beginning ◆ **être dans un bon/mauvais ~** to be in a good/bad mood ◆ **il est dans (un de) ses bons ~s/ses mauvais ~s** he's having a good spell/a bad spell, it's one of his good/his bad days ◆ **décidément c'est mon ~ !** *(iro)* I'm having a real day of it today!, really it's just not my day today! ◆ **il y a des ~s avec et des ~s sans** there are good days and bad days ◆ **ce n'est vraiment pas le ~ !** you've (*ou* we've etc) picked the wrong day! ◆ **prendre ~ avec qn** to fix a day with sb, to make a date with sb; → **autre**

◆ **à jour** ◆ **être/mettre/tenir à ~** *[+ liste, comptes, notes]* to be/bring/keep up to date ◆ **remettre à ~ un catalogue** to update a catalogue, to bring a catalogue up to date ◆ **ce tarif n'est plus à ~** this price list is out of date ◆ **se mettre à ~ dans son travail** to catch up with one's work ◆ **mise à ~** (= *action*) updating; (= *résultat*) update ◆ **la mise à ~ d'un compte/d'un dossier** the updating of an account/of a file ◆ **la mise à ~ d'un dictionnaire** the revision *ou* updating of a dictionary ◆ **programme de mise à ~** *(Ordin)* update routine ◆ **il est/n'est pas à ~ de sa cotisation** he's up to date with/behind with his subscription

◆ **à ce jour** to date ◆ **il n'existe à ce ~ aucun traitement efficace** no effective treatment has been found to date *ou* up to now

◆ **au jour d'aujourd'hui** in this day and age

◆ **du jour** ◆ **un œuf du ~** a new-laid egg, a freshly-laid egg ◆ **les nouvelles du ~** the news of the day, the day's news ◆ **le héros du ~** the hero of the day *ou* hour ◆ **l'homme du ~** the man of the moment ◆ **la mode du ~** the fashion of the day ◆ **il a remis ces vieilles chansons au goût du ~** he's done modern versions of these old songs; → **cours, ordre**[1], **plat**[2]

◆ **du jour où ...** from the day that ... ◆ **du ~ où sa femme l'a quitté, il s'est mis à boire** he started drinking the day his wife left him

◆ **jour pour jour** ◆ **il y a deux ans ~ pour ~** two years ago to the day

◆ **tous les jours** every day ◆ **cela arrive tous les ~s** it happens every day, it's an everyday occurrence ◆ **tous les deux ~s** every other day, every two days ◆ **tous les ~s que (le bon) Dieu fait** every blessed day ◆ **de tous les ~s** everyday *(épith)*, ordinary ◆ **dans la vie de tous les ~s** in everyday life ◆ **mon manteau de tous les ~s** my everyday *ou* ordinary coat

◆ **un de ces jours** one of these (fine) days ◆ **à un de ces ~s !** see you again sometime!, be seeing you!*

◆ **un jour ou l'autre** sometime or other, sooner or later

3 [= lumière] day(light) ◆ **il fait ~** it's daylight ◆ **demain, il fera ~ à 7 h** tomorrow it'll be *ou* it'll get light at 7 ◆ **un faible ~ filtrait à travers les volets** a faint light filtered through the shutters ◆ **le ~ entra à flots** daylight streamed *ou* flooded in ◆ **le ~ tombe** *ou* **baisse** it's getting dark ◆ **avoir le ~ dans les yeux** to have the light in one's eyes ◆ **tes deux enfants, c'est le ~ et la nuit** your two children are as different as night and day *ou* chalk and cheese *(Brit)* ◆ **ça va mieux avec le nouveau produit ? – c'est le ~ et la nuit !** is it better with this new product? – there's absolutely no comparison!

4 [= période où le soleil éclaire] day(time) ◆ **de ~ comme de nuit** night and day ◆ **je fais ça le ~** I do it during the day *ou* in the daytime ◆ **se lever avant le ~** to get up *ou* rise before dawn *ou* daybreak ◆ **à la Sainte Luce, les ~s augmentent** *ou* **croissent du saut d'une puce** *(Prov)* Lucy light, the shortest day and the longest night *(Prov)* → **grand, lumière, plein**

◆ **au petit jour** at dawn *ou* daybreak

◆ **de jour** *[crème, équipe, service]* day *(épith)* ◆ **hôpital de ~** *(pour traitement)* outpatient clinic; *(Psych)* day hospital; *(pour activités)* day-care centre ◆ **être de ~** to be on day duty ◆ **il travaille de ~, cette semaine** he's on day shifts *ou* he's working days this week ◆ **voyager de ~** to travel by day

◆ **jour et nuit** night and day ◆ **ils ont travaillé ~ et nuit pour préparer le bateau** they worked day and night *ou* night and day *ou* round the clock to get the boat ready

5 [fig = éclairage] light ◆ **montrer/présenter/voir qch sous un ~ favorable/flatteur** to show/present/see sth in a favourable/flattering light ◆ **jeter un ~ nouveau sur** to throw (a) new light on ◆ **se présenter sous un ~ favorable** *[projet]* to look promising *ou* hopeful; *[personne]* to show o.s. to advantage *ou* in a favourable light ◆ **nous voyons le problème sous un autre ~** we can see the problem in a different light ◆ **nous le voyons maintenant sous son véritable ~** now we see him in his true colours *ou* see what he is really like ◆ **mettre au ~** (= *révéler*) to bring to light ◆ **se faire ~** (= *apparaître*) to become clear, to come out ◆ **la vérité se fit ~ dans mon esprit** the truth dawned on me *ou* became clear to me; → **faux**[2], **grand**

6 [= symbole de de la naissance] **donner le ~ à** to give birth to, to bring into the world ◆ **voir le ~** *[enfant]* to be born, to come into the world; *[projet]* to see the light, to come into being

7 [= ouverture] *[de mur]* gap, chink; *[de haie]* gap ◆ **clôture à ~** openwork fence

8 [Couture] **~ simple** openwork, drawn-threadwork ◆ **drap à ~s** sheet with an openwork border ◆ **faire des ~s dans un drap/dans un mouchoir** to hemstitch a sheet/a handkerchief

2 - NOM MASCULIN PLURIEL

jours

1 [= période] time, days ◆ **la fuite des ~s** the swift passage of time ◆ **il faut attendre des ~s meilleurs** we must wait for better times *ou* days ◆ **nous avons connu des ~s difficiles** we've been through hard times ◆ **nous gardons cela pour les mauvais ~s** we're keeping that for a rainy day *ou* for hard times ◆ **aux beaux ~s** in (the) summertime ◆ **il y a encore de beaux ~s pour les escrocs** there are good times ahead for crooks ◆ **ces vedettes ont fait les beaux ~s de Broadway** these stars made Broadway what it was ◆ **comme aux plus beaux ~s de la dictature** *(iro)* just like in the good old days of the dictatorship *(iro)* ◆ **du Moyen Âge à nos ~s** from the Middle Ages right up until today

◆ **ces jours-ci** *(passé)* ◆ **il a fait très beau ces ~s-ci** the weather's been very fine lately *ou* these last few days ◆ **elle doit arriver ces ~s-ci** *(futur)* she'll be here any day now ◆ **ceux qui veulent prendre l'avion ces ~s-ci** *(présent)* people wanting to fly now *ou* at this time

◆ **de nos jours** these days, nowadays, in this day and age

2 [= vie] days, life ◆ **jusqu'à la fin de mes ~s** until I die ◆ **finir ses ~s à l'hôpital** to end one's days in hospital ◆ **attenter à/mettre fin à ses ~s** to make an attempt on/put an end to one's life ◆ **nous gardons cela pour nos vieux ~s** we're keeping that for our old age ◆ **sur ses vieux ~s, il était devenu sourd** he had gone deaf in his old age; → **couler**

3 - COMPOSÉS

le jour de l'An New Year's Day
jour d'arrêt *(Mil)* day of detention ◆ **donner huit ~s d'arrêt** to give a week's detention
jour de congé day off, holiday
jour de deuil day of mourning
jour férié public holiday
jour de fête feastday, holiday
le jour J D-day
jour de maladie day off sick
jour mobile discretionary holiday *(granted by company, boss etc)*
le jour des Morts All Souls' Day
jour ouvrable weekday, working day
jour ouvré working day
jour des prix † *(Scol)* prize (giving) day
jour de réception *(Admin)* day of opening (to the public); *[de dame du monde]* at home day ◆ **le ~ de réception du directeur est le lundi** the director is available to see people on Mondays
jour de repos *[de salarié]* day off ◆ **après deux**

~s de repos, il est reparti after taking a two-day break, he set off again
le jour des Rois Epiphany, Twelfth Night
le jour du Seigneur Sunday, the Sabbath †
jour de sortie *[de domestique]* day off, day out; *[d'élève]* day out
jour de travail working day

Jourdain /ʒuʀdɛ̃/ NM (= *fleuve*) ◆ **le** ~ the (river) Jordan

journal (pl **-aux**) /ʒuʀnal, o/ NM 1 *(Presse)* (news)paper; (= *magazine*) magazine; (= *bulletin*) journal ◆ **je suis passé au** ~ (= *bureaux*) I dropped by at the office *ou* paper ◆ **dans** *ou* **sur le** ~ in the (news)paper ◆ ~ **local** local paper ◆ **grand** ~ national paper *ou* daily ◆ ~ **du matin/du soir** morning/evening paper; → **papier**

2 *(TV, Radio)* news (bulletin) ◆ **le ~ de 20 h** the 8 o'clock news

3 (= *recueil*) diary, journal ◆ **tenir un** *ou* **son** ~ **intime** to keep a private *ou* personal diary

COMP **journal de bord** *[de bateau]* (ship's) log, log book; *[d'avion]* flight log; *(fig)* record ◆ **tenir un ~ de bord** to keep a log
journal électronique electronic newspaper
journal d'enfants *ou* **pour enfants** children's paper
journal interne in-house newsletter
journal littéraire literary journal
journal lumineux electronic noticeboard
journal de mode fashion magazine
le Journal officiel (de la République française) *official bulletin giving details of laws and official announcements*, ≃ the Gazette *(Brit)*, The Congressional Record *(US)*
journal parlé *(Radio)* radio news
journal sportif sports magazine
journal télévisé television news

JOURNAUX

The main French national daily newspapers are *Le Monde* (centre-left), *Libération* (centre-left) and *Le Figaro* (right). *Le Canard enchaîné* is an influential satirical weekly famous for uncovering political scandals. There is also a thriving regional press, with prominent newspapers published in all the major provincial cities. The best-selling newspaper in the country, *Ouest-France*, is a regional paper. Although some newspapers are tabloid format, the British and American « tabloid » press has no real equivalent in France.

journaleux * /ʒuʀnalø/ NM *(péj)* hack (journalist) *(péj)*, journo *

journalier, -ière /ʒuʀnalje, jɛʀ/ ADJ (= *de chaque jour*) *[travail, trajet, production, pratique]* daily *(épith)*; (= *banal*) *[existence]* everyday *(épith)* ◆ **c'est** ~ it happens every day; → **indemnité**
NM *(Agr)* day labourer

journalisme /ʒuʀnalism/ NM (= *métier, style*) journalism ◆ **faire du** ~ to be in journalism, to be a journalist ◆ ~ **d'investigation** investigative journalism

journaliste /ʒuʀnalist/ NMF journalist ◆ ~ **sportif/parlementaire** sports/parliamentary correspondent ◆ ~ **d'investigation** investigative journalist ◆ ~ **de radio/de télévision** radio/television reporter *ou* journalist ◆ ~ **de (la) presse écrite** newspaper *ou* print journalist

journalistique /ʒuʀnalistik/ ADJ journalistic ◆ **style** ~ journalistic style; *(péj)* journalese

journée /ʒuʀne/ NF 1 (= *jour*) day ◆ **dans** *ou* **pendant la** ~ during the day, in the daytime ◆ **dans la ~ d'hier** yesterday, in the course of yesterday ◆ **passer sa ~/toute sa ~ à faire qch** to spend the day/one's entire day doing sth ◆ **passer des ~s entières à rêver** to daydream for days on end ◆ **une ~ d'action dans les transports publics** (= *grève*) a day of action organized by the public transport unions

2 *[d'ouvrier]* ~ **(de travail)** day's work ◆ ~ **(de salaire)** day's wages *ou* pay ◆ **faire de dures ~s** to put in a heavy day's work ◆ **faire des ~s chez les autres** † to work as a domestic help *ou* daily help *(Brit)* ◆ **il se fait de bonnes ~s** he gets a good daily wage ◆ **travailler/être payé à la** ~ to work/be paid by the day ◆ **faire la ~ continue** *[bureau, magasin]* to remain open over lunch *ou* all day; *[personne]* to work over lunch ◆ ~ **de 8 heures** 8-hour day ◆ ~ **de repos** day off, rest day

3 (= *événement*) day ◆ **~s d'émeute** days of rioting ◆ **la ~ a été chaude, ce fut une chaude** ~ *(Mil)* it was a hard struggle *ou* a stiff fight ◆ ~ **d'études** *(Pol)* seminar

4 (= *distance*) **à trois ~s de voyage/de marche** three days' journey/walk away ◆ **voyager à petites ~s** † to travel in short *ou* easy stages

journellement /ʒuʀnɛlmɑ̃/ ADV (= *quotidiennement*) daily, every day; (= *souvent*) all the time ◆ **on est ~ confronté à la violence** we are confronted with violence every day

joute /ʒut/ NF 1 *(au Moyen-Âge)* joust, tilt ◆ **~s nautiques** water jousting 2 (= *combat verbal*) ◆ **~s politiques/électorales** political/pre-election sparring *ou* jousting ◆ ~ **oratoire** *ou* **verbale** (= *compétition*) debate; *(entre avocats, députés)* verbal jousting *ou* sparring *(NonC)* ◆ ~ **d'esprit** battle of wits

jouter /ʒute/ ► conjug 1 ◄ VI *(Hist)* to joust, to tilt; *(fig, frm)* to joust *(contre* against) to spar *(contre* with)

jouteur /ʒutœʀ/ NM jouster, tilter

jouvence /ʒuvɑ̃s/ NF ◆ **Fontaine de Jouvence** Fountain of Youth ◆ **eau de** ~ waters of youth; → **bain**

jouvenceau (pl **jouvenceaux**) /ʒuvɑ̃so/ NM (††, *hum*) stripling †, youth

jouvencelle /ʒuvɑ̃sɛl/ NF (††, *hum*) damsel † *(hum)*

jouxter /ʒukste/ ► conjug 1 ◄ VT to adjoin, to be next to

jovial, e (mpl **-iaux** *ou* **jovials**) /ʒɔvjal, jo/ ADJ jovial, jolly ◆ **d'humeur ~e** in a jovial mood

jovialement /ʒɔvjalmɑ̃/ ADV jovially

jovialité /ʒɔvjalite/ NF joviality, jollity

jovien, -ienne /ʒɔvjɛ̃, jɛn/ ADJ Jovian

joyau (pl **joyaux**) /ʒwajo/ NM *(lit, fig)* gem, jewel ◆ **les ~x de la couronne** the crown jewels ◆ ~ **de l'art gothique** jewel *ou* masterpiece of Gothic art

joyeusement /ʒwajøzmɑ̃/ ADV *[célébrer]* merrily, joyfully; *[accepter]* gladly; *[crier]* joyfully ◆ **ils reprirent ~ le travail** they cheerfully went back to work

joyeusetés /ʒwajøzte/ NFPL *(littér ou iro)* ◆ **ce sont les ~ de la vie en couple** these are just some of the joys *ou* pleasures of living together

joyeux, -euse /ʒwajø, øz/ GRAMMAIRE ACTIVE 50.2, 50.3 ADJ 1 *[personne, groupe]* cheerful, merry, joyous; *[repas]* cheerful; *[cris]* merry, joyful; *[musique]* joyful, joyous; *[visage]* cheerful, joyful; *[nouvelle]* joyful ◆ **c'est un ~ luron** *ou* **drille** he's a jolly fellow ◆ **être en joyeuse compagnie** to be in merry company *ou* with a merry group ◆ **mener joyeuse vie** to lead a merry life ◆ **être d'humeur joyeuse** to be in a joyful mood ◆ **ils étaient partis ~** they had set out merrily *ou* in a merry group ◆ **il était tout ~ à l'idée de partir** he was overjoyed *ou* (quite) delighted at the idea of going ◆ **c'est ~ !** * *(iro)* great! * *(iro)*, brilliant! * *(iro)* ◆ **ce n'est pas ~ !** * *[film]* it's not very funny; *[histoire triste]* it's no joke! ◆ **le défilé progressait dans un ~ désordre** the procession went along in an atmosphere of cheerful chaos

2 *(dans les souhaits)* **joyeuses fêtes !** Happy Christmas! *(ou* New Year)!; *(sur carte)* Season's Greetings; → **anniversaire, Noël**

JT /ʒite/ NM (abrév de **journal télévisé**) → **journal**

jubé /ʒybe/ NM (= *clôture*) jube, rood-screen; (= *galerie*) jube, rood-loft

jubilaire /ʒybilɛʀ/ ADJ *(Rel)* jubilee *(épith)*

jubilation /ʒybilasjɔ̃/ NF jubilation, exultation

jubilatoire /ʒybilatwaʀ/ ADJ *[spectacle, livre, expérience, humour]* exhilarating ◆ **il observait leur dispute avec un enthousiasme quasi** ~ he felt something akin to jubilation as he watched them quarrel

jubilé /ʒybile/ NM jubilee

jubiler * /ʒybile/ ► conjug 1 ◄ VI to be jubilant, to gloat *(péj)*

jucher VT, **se jucher** VPR /ʒyʃe/ ► conjug 1 ◄ to perch *(sur* on, upon); ◆ **juchée sur les épaules de son père** perched on her father's shoulders ◆ **juchée sur des talons aiguilles** teetering on stiletto heels

Juda /ʒyda/ NM Judah

judaïque /ʒydaik/ ADJ *[loi]* Judaic; *[religion]* Jewish

judaïsme /ʒydaism/ NM Judaism

judas /ʒyda/ NM 1 *[de porte]* spyhole 2 *(Bible)* **Judas** Judas

Judée /ʒyde/ NF Judaea, Judea

judéité /ʒydeite/ NF Jewishness

judéo-allemand, e /ʒydeoalmɑ̃, ɑ̃d/ ADJ German-Jewish

judéo-arabe /ʒydeoaʀab/ ADJ, NMF Judeo-Arab, Judaeo-Arab *(Brit)*

judéo-catholique /ʒydeokatɔlik/ ADJ Jewish-Catholic

judéo-chrétien, -ienne /ʒydeokʀetjɛ̃, jɛn/ ADJ, NM,F Judeo-Christian, Judaeo-Christian *(Brit)*

judéo-christianisme /ʒydeokʀistjanism/ NM Judeo-Christianity, Judaeo-Christianity *(Brit)*

judiciaire /ʒydisjɛʀ/ ADJ judicial ◆ **l'autorité** ~ (= *concept*) the judiciary; (= *tribunal*) judicial authority ◆ **pouvoir** ~ judicial power ◆ **poursuites ~s** judicial *ou* legal proceedings ◆ **vente** ~ sale by order of the court ◆ **enquête** ~ judicial inquiry ◆ **actes ~s** judicial documents ◆ **procédure** ~ legal procedure ◆ **cette affaire n'a pas eu de suites ~s** there were no legal repercussions to this affair ◆ **de source ~ française, on apprend que ...** from a French legal source we have learned that ...; → **casier, erreur, police¹** *etc* NM ◆ **le** ~ the judiciary

judiciairement /ʒydisjɛʀmɑ̃/ ADV judicially

judiciarisation /ʒydisjaʀizasjɔ̃/ NF ◆ **la ~ croissante de notre société** *(législation)* the fact that our society is producing more and more legislation; *(litiges)* the fact that our society is becoming ever more litigious ◆ **la ~ de la relation médecin-patient** the increasingly litigious nature of doctor-patient relationships

judiciariser /ʒydisjaʀize/ ► conjug 1 ◄ VT *[+ question]* to legislate on VPR **se judiciariser** ◆ **notre société se judiciarise de plus en plus** (= *légifère*) our society is producing more and more legislation; *(litiges)* our society is becoming ever more litigious

judicieusement /ʒydisjøzmɑ̃/ ADV judiciously, wisely ◆ **avec quelques vins ~ choisis** with a few well-chosen wines

judicieux, -ieuse /ʒydisjø, jøz/ ADJ *[choix, idée, remarque]* wise, judicious; *[conseils]* wise, sound ◆ **faire un emploi ~ de son temps** to use one's time wisely, to make judicious use of one's time ◆ **son utilisation judicieuse du flashback** his clever use of flashback ◆ **il serait plus ~ de ...** it would be wiser to ... ◆ **ce choix s'est**

révélé peu ~ it proved (to be) an unfortunate choice, it was an unwise choice

judo /ʒydo/ NM judo ◆ **faire du** ~ to do judo

judoka /ʒydɔka/ NMF judoka

juge /ʒyʒ/ NMF (*Jur, Rel, Sport, fig*) judge ◆ **oui, Monsieur le Juge** yes, your Honour ◆ **(madame)/(monsieur) le** ~ **Ledoux** Mrs/Mr Justice Ledoux ◆ **prendre qn pour** ~ to ask sb to be (the) judge ◆ **être bon/mauvais** ~ to be a good/bad judge (*en matière de* of); ◆ **être à la fois** ~ **et partie** to be both judge and judged ◆ **je te laisse** ~ you can see for yourself ◆ **je vous fais** ~ **(de tout ceci)** I'll let you be the judge (of all this) ◆ **se faire** ~ **de ses propres actes/de qch** to be the judge of one's own actions/of sth ◆ **il est seul** ~ **en la matière** he is the only one who can judge ◆ **aller devant le** ~ to go before the judge ◆ **le livre des Juges** (*Bible*) the Book of Judges

COMP **juge aux affaires matrimoniales** divorce court judge
juge de l'application des peines *judge responsible for overseeing the terms and conditions of a prisoner's sentence*
juge d'arrivée (*Sport*) finishing judge
juge constitutionnel ≈ constitutional judge
juge consulaire *judge in a commercial court*
juge des *ou* **pour enfants** children's judge, ≈ juvenile court judge
juge de filet (*Tennis*) net cord judge
juge d'instance justice of the peace, magistrate
juge d'instruction examining *ou* investigating magistrate
juge de ligne (*Tennis*) (*gén*) line judge, linesman; (*pour ligne de fond*) foot-fault judge
juge de paix † ⇒ **juge d'instance** ◆ **cette épreuve sera le** ~ **de paix** (*fig*) this test will be the determining factor *ou* will determine the outcome
juge de proximité ≈ lay judge
juge de touche (*Rugby*) touch judge, linesman; (*Ftbl*) linesman

jugé /ʒyʒe/ **au jugé** LOC ADV (*lit, fig*) by guesswork ◆ **tirer au** ~ to fire blind ◆ **faire qch au** ~ to do sth by guesswork

jugeable /ʒyʒabl/ ADJ (*Jur*) subject to judgment in court ◆ **difficilement** ~ (*= évaluable*) difficult to judge

juge-arbitre (pl **juges-arbitres**) /ʒyʒaʀbitʀ/ NM referee

jugement /ʒyʒmɑ̃/ NM [1] (*Jur = décision, verdict*) [*d'affaire criminelle*] sentence; [*d'affaire civile*] decision, award ◆ **prononcer** *ou* **rendre un** ~ to pass sentence ◆ **passer en** ~ [*personne*] to stand trial; [*affaire*] to come to court ◆ **faire passer qn en** ~ to put sb on trial ◆ ~ **par défaut** judgment by default ◆ ~ **déclaratoire** declaratory judgment ◆ **détention sans** ~ detention without trial

[2] (*= opinion*) judgment, opinion ◆ ~ **de valeur** value judgment ◆ **exprimer/formuler un** ~ to express/formulate an opinion ◆ **porter un** ~ **(sur)** to pass judgment (on) ◆ **s'en remettre au** ~ **de qn** to defer to sb's judgment ◆ **j'ai peur de son** ~ I'm afraid of what he'll think (of me)

[3] (*= discernement*) judgment ◆ **avoir du/manquer de** ~ to have/lack (good) judgment ◆ **on peut faire confiance à son** ~ you can trust his judgment ◆ **il a une grande sûreté de** ~ he has very sound judgment

[4] (*Rel*) judgment ◆ **le** ~ **de Dieu** Divine Judgment; (*Hist*) the Ordeal ◆ **le Jugement dernier** the Last Judgment ◆ **le jour du Jugement dernier** Judgment Day, Doomsday ◆ **le** ~ **de Salomon** the judgment of Solomon

jugeote * /ʒyʒɔt/ NF common sense, gumption * (*Brit*) ◆ **manquer de** ~ to lack common sense ◆ **il n'a pas deux sous de** ~ he hasn't got an ounce of common sense, he's got no gumption * (*Brit*) ◆ **(aie) un peu de** ~ **!** use your head! *ou* loaf! *, wise up! ⁑ (*surtout US*)

juger[1] /ʒyʒe/ ► conjug 3 ◄ VT [1] (*Jur*) [+ *affaire*] to judge, to try; [+ *accusé*] to try ◆ ~ **un différend** to arbitrate in a dispute ◆ **le tribunal jugera** the court will decide ◆ **être jugé pour meurtre** to be tried for murder ◆ **le jury a jugé qu'il n'était pas coupable** the jury found him not guilty ◆ **l'affaire doit se** ~ **à l'automne** the case is to come before the court *ou* is to be heard in the autumn ◆ **l'histoire jugera** history will judge

[2] (*= décider, statuer*) to judge, to decide ◆ **à vous de** ~ **(ce qu'il faut faire/si c'est nécessaire)** it's up to you to decide *ou* to judge (what must be done/whether *ou* if it's necessary)

[3] (*= apprécier*) [+ *livre, film, personne, situation*] to judge ◆ ~ **qn d'après les résultats** to judge sb on his results ◆ **il ne faut pas** ~ **d'après les apparences** you must not judge from *ou* go by appearances ◆ ~ **qch/qn à sa juste valeur** to judge sth/sb at its/his real value ◆ ~ **bien/mal les gens** to be a good/bad judge of character ◆ **jugez combien j'étais surpris** *ou* **si ma surprise était grande** imagine how surprised I was *ou* what a surprise I got

[4] (*= estimer*) ~ **qch/qn ridicule** to consider *ou* find *ou* think sth/sb ridiculous ◆ ~ **que** to think *ou* consider that ◆ **pourquoi est-ce que vous me jugez mal ?** why do you think badly of me?, why do you have such a low opinion of me? ◆ **si vous le jugez bon** if you see fit, if you think it's a good idea *ou* it's advisable ◆ ~ **bon/malhonnête de faire qch** to consider it a good thing *ou* advisable/dishonest to do sth ◆ **il se jugea perdu** he thought *ou* considered himself lost ◆ **il se juge capable de le faire** he thinks *ou* reckons he is capable of doing it ◆ **je n'ai pas jugé utile de le prévenir** I didn't think it was worth telling him (about it)

VT INDIR **juger de** to appreciate, to judge ◆ **si j'en juge par mon expérience** judging by *ou* if I (can) judge by my experience ◆ **à en** ~ **par ...** judging by ..., to judge by ... ◆ **à en** ~ **par ce résultat, il ...** if this result is any indication *ou* anything to go by, he ... ◆ **lui seul peut** ~ **de l'urgence** only he can appreciate the urgency, only he can tell how urgent it is ◆ **autant que je puisse en** ~ as far as I can judge ◆ **jugez de ma surprise !** imagine my surprise!

juger[2] /ʒyʒe/ NM ⇒ **jugé**

jugulaire /ʒygylɛʀ/ ADJ [*veines, glandes*] jugular ◆ **il est** ~ ~ (†, *hum*) he's a stickler for the rules NF [1] (*Mil*) chin strap [2] (*Anat*) jugular vein

juguler /ʒygyle/ ► conjug 1 ◄ VT [+ *maladie*] to arrest, to halt; [+ *envie, désirs*] to suppress, to repress; [+ *inflation*] to curb, to stamp out; [+ *révolte*] to put down, to quell, to repress

juif, juive /ʒɥif, ʒɥiv/ ADJ Jewish NM Jew NF **juive** Jew, Jewish woman

juillet /ʒɥijɛ/ NM July ◆ **la révolution/monarchie de Juillet** the July revolution/monarchy; *pour autres loc voir* **septembre** *et* **quatorze**

Le Quatorze Juillet

Bastille Day, commemorating the fall of the Bastille in 1789, is the most important day of national celebration in France. The festivities actually begin on 13 July, with dances (« bals ») organized in the streets of large towns. On the day itself there is a large military parade in Paris in the morning, and firework displays take place throughout France in the evening.

juilletiste /ʒɥijetist/ NMF July holiday-maker (*Brit*) *ou* vacationer (*US*)

juin /ʒɥɛ̃/ NM June; *pour autres loc voir* **septembre**

juive /ʒɥiv/ ADJ F, NF → **juif**

juiverie † /ʒɥivʀi/ NF (*injurieux*) ◆ **la** ~ the Jews, the Jewish people

jujube /ʒyʒyb/ NM (*= fruit, pâte*) jujube

jujubier /ʒyʒybje/ NM jujube (tree)

juke-box (pl **juke-boxes**) /ʒykbɔks/ NM jukebox

julep /ʒylɛp/ NM julep

jules /ʒyl/ NM [1] († * *= amoureux*) boyfriend, guy *, bloke * (*Brit*); (⁑ *= proxénète*) pimp, ponce ⁑ (*Brit*) [2] († * *= vase de nuit*) chamber pot, jerry ⁑ (*Brit*) [3] ◆ **Jules** Julius ◆ **Jules César** Julius Caesar

julien, -ienne /ʒyljɛ̃, jɛn/ ADJ (*Astron*) Julian NF **julienne** [1] (*Culin*) [*de légumes*] julienne; [2] (*= poisson*) ling [3] (*= plante*) rocket

jumbo-jet (pl **jumbo-jets**) /dʒœmbodʒɛt/ NM jumbo jet

jumeau, -elle[1] (mpl **jumeaux**) /ʒymo, ɛl/ ADJ [*frère, sœur*] twin ◆ **c'est mon frère** ~ he's my twin (brother) ◆ **fruits ~x** double fruits ◆ **maison jumelle** semi-detached house (*Brit*), duplex (*US*) ◆ **muscles ~x** gastrocnemius (*sg*) ◆ **les deux dogmes ~x de l'internationalisme** the twin dogmas of internationalism ◆ **le journal est partagé en deux cahiers ~x de 24 pages chacun** the newspaper is divided into two equal sections of 24 pages each NM,F [1] (*= personne*) twin ◆ **vrais/faux ~x** identical/fraternal twins [2] (*= sosie*) double ◆ **c'est mon ~/ma jumelle** he's/she's my double ◆ **j'aimerais trouver le** ~ **de ce vase** I'd like to find the partner to this vase NM (*Culin*) clod of beef

jumelage /ʒym(ə)laʒ/ NM twinning

jumelé, e /ʒym(ə)le/ (ptp de **jumeler**) ADJ [*colonnes, vergues, mât*] twin ◆ **roues ~es** double wheels ◆ **billets ~s** (*Loterie*) double series ticket ◆ **villes ~es** twin towns ◆ **être** ~ **avec** [*ville*] to be twinned with ◆ **pari** ~ (*Courses*) dual forecast (*for first and second place in the same race*)

jumeler /ʒym(ə)le/ ► conjug 4 ◄ VT [+ *villes*] to twin; [+ *efforts*] to join; [+ *mâts, poutres*] to double up, to fish (*SPÉC*)

jumelle[2] /ʒymɛl/ NF [1] (*Opt*) **(paire de) ~s** (pair of) binoculars ◆ **~s de spectacle** *ou* **théâtre** opera glasses ◆ ~ **marine** binoculars ◆ **observer qch à la** ~ to look at sth through binoculars [2] [*de mât*] fish ◆ ~ **de ressort** (*Aut*) shackle; → aussi **jumeau**

jument /ʒymɑ̃/ NF mare

jumping /dʒœmpiŋ/ NM (*gén*) jumping; (*= concours équestre*) show jumping

jungle /ʒœ̃gl/ NF (*lit, fig*) jungle ◆ ~ **urbaine** urban jungle; → **loi**

junior /ʒynjɔʀ/ ADJ junior ◆ **Dupont** ~ Dupont junior ◆ **équipe** ~ junior team ◆ **mode** ~ young *ou* junior fashion ◆ ~ **entreprise** *student organization that obtains contract work from businesses whose activities are related to the students' field of study* NMF junior

junk bond (pl **junk bonds**) /(d)ʒœnkbɔ̃d/ NM junk bond

junkie * /dʒœnki/ ADJ, NMF junkie *

Junon /ʒynɔ̃/ NF Juno

junte /ʒœ̃t/ NF junta

jupe /ʒyp/ NF (*Habillement, Tech*) skirt ◆ ~ **plissée/droite** pleated/straight skirt ◆ **~s** skirts ◆ **il est toujours dans les ~s de sa mère** he's still tied to his mother's apron strings ◆ **il est toujours dans mes ~s** he's always under my feet COMP **jupe portefeuille** wrap-around skirt

jupe-culotte (pl **jupes-culottes**) /ʒypkylɔt/ NF culottes, divided skirt

jupette /ʒypɛt/ NF (short) skirt

Jupiter /ʒypitɛʀ/ NM (*Myth*) Jupiter, Jove; (*Astron*) Jupiter; → **cuisse**

jupon /ʒypɔ̃/ NM [1] *(Habillement)* petticoat, underskirt ◆ **il est toujours dans les ~s de sa mère** he's always clinging to his mother's skirts [2] *(† = femme)* bit of skirt* ◆ **aimer le ~** to love anything in a skirt

juponné, e /ʒypɔne/ ADJ *[robe]* with an underskirt

Jura /ʒyʀa/ NM ◆ **le ~** *(= montagne, région)* the Jura

jurassien, -ienne /ʒyʀasjɛ̃, jɛn/ ADJ of *ou* from the Jura, Jura *(épith)* NM,F **Jurassien(ne)** inhabitant *ou* native of the Jura

jurassique /ʒyʀasik/ ADJ Jurassic NM ◆ **le ~** the Jurassic

juré, e /ʒyʀe/ (ptp de **jurer**) ADJ *(= qui a prêté serment)* sworn ◆ **ennemi ~** sworn enemy ◆ **promis ? – ~, craché !*** do you promise? – cross my heart (and hope to die)! NM juror, juryman ◆ **premier ~** foreman of the jury ◆ **Mesdames et Messieurs les ~s apprécieront** the members of the jury will bear that in mind ◆ **être convoqué comme ~** to be called for jury service *ou* duty NF **jurée** juror, jurywoman

jurer /ʒyʀe/ ► conjug 1 ◄ VT [1] *(= promettre)* to swear, to vow ◆ **~ fidélité/obéissance/amitié à qn** to swear *ou* pledge loyalty/obedience/friendship to sb ◆ **~ la perte de qn** to swear to ruin sb *ou* bring about sb's downfall ◆ **je jure que je me vengerai** I swear *ou* vow I'll get my revenge ◆ **faire ~ à qn de garder le secret** to swear *ou* pledge sb to secrecy ◆ **jure-moi que tu reviendras** swear (to me) you'll come back ◆ **~ sur la Bible/sur la croix/devant Dieu** to swear on the Bible/on the cross/to God ◆ **~ sur la tête de ses enfants** *ou* **de sa mère** to swear by all that one holds dear *ou* sacred, to swear on one's children's *ou* one's mother's life ◆ **il jurait ses grands dieux qu'il n'avait rien fait** he swore blind* *ou* by all the gods † that he hadn't done anything ◆ **je vous jure que ce n'est pas facile** I can tell you *ou* assure you that it isn't easy ◆ **ah ! je vous jure !** honestly! ◆ **il faut de la patience, je vous jure, pour la supporter !** I swear you need a lot of patience to put up with her, you need a lot of patience to put up with her, I can tell you

[2] *(admiration)* **on ne jure plus que par lui/par ce nouveau remède** everyone swears by him/by this new medicine

VT INDIR **jurer de** to swear to ◆ **j'en jurerais** I could swear to it, I'd swear to it ◆ **il ne faut ~ de rien** *(Prov)* you never can tell

VI [1] *(= pester)* to swear, to curse ◆ **~ après** *ou* **contre qch/qn** to swear *ou* curse at sth/sb ◆ **~ comme un charretier** to swear like a trooper

[2] *[couleurs]* to clash *(avec* with); *[propos]* to jar *(avec* with)

VPR **se jurer** [1] *(à soi-même)* to vow to o.s., to promise o.s. ◆ **il se jura bien que c'était la dernière fois** he vowed it was the last time

[2] *(réciproquement)* to pledge (to) each other, to swear, to vow ◆ **ils se sont juré un amour éternel** they pledged *ou* vowed *ou* swore eternal love

juridiction /ʒyʀidiksjɔ̃/ NF [1] *(= compétence)* jurisdiction ◆ **hors de/sous sa ~** beyond/within his jurisdiction ◆ **exercer sa ~** to exercise one's jurisdiction ◆ **tombant sous la ~ de** falling *ou* coming within the jurisdiction of [2] *(= tribunal)* court(s) of law

juridictionnel, -elle /ʒyʀidiksjɔnɛl/ ADJ jurisdictional ◆ **pouvoir ~** power of jurisdiction ◆ **fonctions juridictionnelles** judicial powers ◆ **aide juridictionnelle** ≃ legal aid

juridique /ʒyʀidik/ ADJ legal, juridical ◆ **études ~s** law *ou* legal studies

juridiquement /ʒyʀidikmɑ̃/ ADV juridically, legally ◆ **c'est ~ impossible** it's not legally possible

juridisme /ʒyʀidism/ NM legalism

jurisconsulte /ʒyʀiskɔ̃sylt/ NM jurisconsult

jurisprudence /ʒyʀispʀydɑ̃s/ NF *(= source de droit)* ≃ case law, jurisprudence; *(= décisions)* (judicial) precedents ◆ **faire ~** to set a precedent ◆ **cas qui fait ~** test case

jurisprudentiel, -ielle /ʒyʀispʀydɑ̃sjɛl/ ADJ jurisprudential ◆ **décision jurisprudentielle** *decision taken by a court that sets a legal precedent* ◆ **précédent ~** legal *ou* judicial precedent ◆ **le droit ~** case law

juriste /ʒyʀist/ NMF *(= auteur, légiste)* jurist ◆ **~ d'entreprise** corporate lawyer

juron /ʒyʀɔ̃/ NM swearword ◆ **dire des ~s** to swear

jury /ʒyʀi/ NM [1] *(Jur)* jury ◆ **~ populaire** *civilian jury* ◆ **président du ~** foreman of the jury ◆ **membre du ~** member of the jury, juror [2] *(Art, Sport)* panel of judges; *(Scol)* board of examiners, jury ◆ **~ de thèse** PhD examining board *ou* committee *(US)*

jus /ʒy/ NM [1] *(= liquide)* juice ◆ **~ de fruit** fruit juice ◆ **~ de raisin** grape juice ◆ **~ de viande** juice(s) from the meat, ≃ gravy ◆ **plein de ~** juicy ◆ **~ de la treille*** juice of the vine *(hum)*, wine; → **cuire, mijoter**

[2] *(* = café)* coffee ◆ **c'est un ~ infâme** it's a foul brew* ◆ **au ~ !** coffee's ready!, coffee's up!* ◆ **~ de chaussette** *(péj)* dishwater *(fig)*

[3] *(* = courant)* juice* ◆ **prendre le ~** *ou* **un coup de ~** to get a shock

[4] *(* locutions)* **jeter/tomber au ~** *ou* **dans le ~** to throw/fall into the water *ou* drink* ◆ **au ~ !** *(en poussant qn)* into the water with him!, in he goes!; *(en y allant)* here I come! ◆ **ça valait le ~ !** it was priceless!* ◆ **il a laissé le bâtiment dans son ~** he left the building in its original state

[5] *(arg Mil)* **soldat de 1er ~** ≃ lance corporal *(Brit)* ◆ **soldat de 2e ~** ≃ private ◆ **c'est du huit au ~** only a week to go (to the end of military service)

[6] *(= lavis)* colourwash *(Brit)*, colorwash *(US)*

jusant /ʒyzɑ̃/ NM ebb tide

jusqu'au-boutisme /ʒyskobutism/ NM *(= politique)* hard-line policy; *(= attitude)* extremist attitude

jusqu'au-boutiste (pl **jusqu'au-boutistes**) /ʒyskobutist/ NMF extremist, hard-liner ◆ **c'est un ~** he takes things to the bitter end, he always goes the whole hog* ADJ *[attitude]* hardline *(épith)*; *[théorie]* extremist

jusque /ʒysk(ə)/ PRÉP [1] *(lieu)* **jusqu'à la, jusqu'au** to, as far as, (right) up to, all the way to ◆ **j'ai couru jusqu'à la maison/l'école** I ran all the *ou* right the way home/to school ◆ **j'ai marché jusqu'au village** I walked to *ou* as far as the village ◆ **ils sont montés jusqu'à 2 000 mètres** they climbed up to 2,000 metres ◆ **il s'est avancé jusqu'au bord du précipice** he walked (right) up to the edge of the precipice ◆ **il a rampé jusqu'à nous** he crawled up to us ◆ **il avait de la neige jusqu'aux genoux** he had snow up to his knees, he was knee-deep in snow ◆ **la nouvelle est venue jusqu'à moi** the news has reached me ◆ **il menace d'aller jusqu'au ministre** he's threatening to take it to the minister

[2] *(temps)* **jusqu'à, jusqu'en** until, till, up to ◆ **jusqu'en mai** until May ◆ **jusqu'à samedi** until Saturday ◆ **du matin jusqu'au soir** from morning till night ◆ **jusqu'à cinq ans il vécut à la campagne** he lived in the country until *ou* up to the age of five ◆ **les enfants restent dans cette école jusqu'à (l'âge de) dix ans** (the) children stay at this school until they are ten *ou* until the age of ten ◆ **marchez jusqu'à ce que vous arriviez à la mairie** walk until you reach the town hall, walk as far as the town hall ◆ **rester jusqu'au bout** *ou* **à la fin** to stay till *ou* to the end ◆ **de la Révolution jusqu'à nos jours** from the Revolution (up) to the present day

[3] *(limite)* **jusqu'à 20 kg** up to 20 kg, not exceeding 20 kg ◆ **véhicule transportant jusqu'à 15 personnes** vehicle which can carry up to *ou* as many as 15 people ◆ **pousser l'indulgence jusqu'à la faiblesse** to carry indulgence to the point of weakness ◆ **aller jusqu'à dire/faire qch** to go so far as to say/do sth ◆ **j'irai jusqu'à 100** I'll go as far as *ou* up to 100 ◆ **je n'irais pas jusqu'à faire ça** I wouldn't go so far as to do that

[4] *(= y compris)* even ◆ **il a mangé jusqu'aux arêtes** he ate everything including *ou* even the bones, he ate the lot *(Brit)* – bones and all *(Brit)* ◆ **ils ont regardé ~ sous le lit** they even looked under the bed ◆ **tous jusqu'au dernier l'ont critiqué** every single *ou* last one of them criticized him

[5] *(avec prép ou adv)* **accompagner qn ~ chez lui** to take *ou* accompany sb (right) home ◆ **veux-tu aller ~ chez le boucher pour moi ?** would you go (along) to the butcher's for me? ◆ **jusqu'où ?** how far? ◆ **jusqu'à quand ?** until when?, how long for? ◆ **jusqu'à quand restez-vous ?** how long *ou* till when are you staying?, when are you staying till? ◆ **jusqu'ici** *(temps présent)* so far, until now; *(au passé)* until then; *(lieu)* up to *ou* as far as here ◆ **~-là** *(temps)* until then; *(lieu)* up to there ◆ **j'en ai ~-là !** I'm sick and tired of it!, I've had about as much as I can take! *ou* I've had it up to here! ◆ **jusqu'alors, ~s alors** until then ◆ **jusqu'à maintenant, jusqu'à présent** until now, so far ◆ **~ (très) tard** until (very) late ◆ **~ vers 9 heures** until about 9 o'clock; → **mettre**

[6] *(locutions)* **jusqu'au bout** to the (very) end ◆ **jusqu'à concurrence de 25 €** to the amount of €25 ◆ **vrai jusqu'à un certain point** true up to a certain point ◆ **jusqu'au fond** to the (very) bottom ◆ **elle a été touchée jusqu'au fond du cœur** she was deeply touched ◆ **jusqu'à nouvel ordre** *(Admin)* until further notice ◆ **jusqu'à plus ample informé** until further information is available, pending further information ◆ **tu vois jusqu'à quel point tu t'es trompé** you see how wrong you were ◆ **jusqu'au moment où** until, till ◆ **jusqu'à la gauche*** totally

ADV ◆ **~(s) et y compris** up to and including ◆ **jusqu'à** *(= même)* even ◆ **j'ai vu jusqu'à des enfants tirer sur des soldats** I even saw children shooting at soldiers ◆ **il n'est pas jusqu'au paysage qui n'ait changé** the very landscape *ou* even the landscape has changed

LOC CONJ **jusqu'à ce que, jusqu'à tant que** until ◆ **sonnez jusqu'à ce que l'on vienne ouvrir** ring until someone answers the door ◆ **il faudra le lui répéter jusqu'à ce** *ou* **jusqu'à tant qu'il ait compris** you'll have to keep on telling him until he understands

jusques /ʒysk(ə)/ ADV, CONJ, PRÉP *(littér)* ⇒ **jusque**

jusquiame /ʒyskjam/ NF henbane

justaucorps /ʒystokɔʀ/ NM *(Hist)* jerkin; *[de gymnaste]* leotard

juste /ʒyst/ GRAMMAIRE ACTIVE 53.3, 53.6

ADJ [1] *(= équitable) [personne, notation]* just, fair; *[sentence, guerre, cause]* just ◆ **être ~ pour** *ou* **envers** *ou* **à l'égard de qn** to be fair to sb ◆ **c'est un homme ~** he is a just man ◆ **il faut être ~** one must be fair ◆ **pour être ~ envers lui** in fairness to him, to be fair to him ◆ **ce n'est pas ~ !** it isn't fair! ◆ **il n'est pas ~ de l'accuser** it is unfair to accuse him ◆ **c'est un ~ retour des choses** it's poetic justice ◆ **il finira par se faire renvoyer, et ce ne sera qu'un ~ retour des choses** he'll end up getting the sack, and it'll serve him right

[2] *(= légitime) [revendication, vengeance, fierté]* just; *[colère]* righteous, justifiable ◆ **la ~ récompense de son travail** the just reward for his work

♦ **à juste titre** justly, rightly ♦ **il en est fier, et à ~ titre** he's proud of it and rightly *ou* understandably so

3 *(= exact) [addition, réponse, heure]* right, exact ♦ **à l'heure** ~ right on time, dead on time* ♦ **à 6 heures ~s** on the stroke of 6, at 6 o'clock sharp* ♦ **apprécier qch à son ~ prix** *ou* **à sa ~ valeur** to appreciate the true worth of sth ♦ **le ~ milieu** the happy medium, the golden mean; *(Pol)* the middle course *ou* way ♦ **le mot ~** the right word, the mot juste

4 *(= pertinent, vrai) [idée, raisonnement]* sound; *[remarque, expression]* apt ♦ **il a dit des choses très ~s** he made some pertinent points, he said some very sound things ♦ **très ~ !** good point!, quite right! ♦ **c'est ~** that's right, that's a fair point

5 *(= précis, sûr) [appareil, montre]* accurate; *[esprit]* sound; *[balance]* accurate, true; *[oreille]* good

6 *(Mus) [note]* right, true; *[voix]* true; *[instrument]* in tune *(attrib)*, well-tuned ♦ **il a une voix ~** he has a true voice, he sings in tune ♦ **quinte ~** perfect fifth

7 *(= trop court, étroit) [vêtement, chaussure]* tight; *[longueur, hauteur]* on the short side ♦ **1 kg pour six, c'est un peu ~** 1 kg for six people, is barely enough *ou* is a bit on the short *ou* skimpy side ♦ **trois heures pour faire cette traduction, c'est ~** three hours to do that translation is barely enough ♦ **elle n'a pas raté son train mais c'était ~** she didn't miss her train but it was a close thing ♦ **mon salaire est trop ~** my salary is inadequate, I don't earn enough ♦ **je suis un peu ~ actuellement*** I'm a bit strapped for cash* *ou* things are a bit tight at the moment ♦ **ses notes sont trop ~s** *[d'élève]* his marks aren't good enough ♦ **il est un peu ~ (intellectuellement)*** he's not very bright

8 *(excl)* ~ **ciel !** † heavens (above)! ♦ ~ **Dieu !** † almighty God!, ye Gods!

ADV 1 *(= avec précision) [compter, viser]* accurately; *[raisonner]* soundly; *[deviner]* rightly, correctly; *[chanter]* in tune ♦ **tomber** ~ *(= deviner)* to hit the nail on the head, to be (exactly) right; *[calculs]* to come out right ♦ **division qui tombe** ~ division which works out exactly ♦ ~ **à temps** *[arriver]* just in time ♦ **travailler en ~ à temps** *(Écon)* to use the just-in-time system *ou* techniques

2 *(= exactement)* just, exactly ♦ ~ **au-dessus** just above ♦ ~ **au coin** just on *ou* round the corner ♦ **il a dit ~ ce qu'il fallait** he said exactly *ou* just what was needed ♦ **c'est ~ le contraire** it's exactly *ou* just the opposite ♦ ~ **au moment où j'entrais** (just) at the very moment when I was coming in ♦ **j'arrive ~** I've only just arrived ♦ **je suis arrivé ~ quand/comme il sortait** I arrived just when/as he was leaving ♦ **j'ai ~ assez** I have just enough ♦ **3 kg** ~ 3 kg exactly

3 *(= seulement)* only, just ♦ **j'ai ~ à passer un coup de téléphone** I only *ou* just have to make a telephone call ♦ **il est parti il y a ~ un moment** he left just *ou* only a moment ago

4 *(= pas assez)* **(un peu)** ~ *[compter, prévoir]* not quite enough, too little ♦ **il est arrivé un peu ~** *ou* **bien ~** he cut it a bit too close *ou* fine* *(Brit)*, he arrived at the last minute ♦ **il a mesuré trop ~** he didn't allow quite enough

5 *(locutions)* **que veut-il au ~ ?** what exactly does he want? *ou* is he after?*, what does he actually want? ♦ **au plus ~ prix** at the lowest *ou* minimum price ♦ **calculer au plus ~** to work things out to the minimum ♦ **comme de ~ il pleuvait !** and of course it was raining!

♦ **tout juste** *(= seulement)* only just; *(= à peine)* hardly, barely; *(= exactement)* exactly ♦ **c'est tout ~ s'il ne m'a pas frappé** he came this close to hitting me ♦ **son livre vaut tout ~ la peine qu'on le lise** his book is barely worth reading ♦ **c'est tout ~ passable** it's just *ou* barely passable

NM *(Rel)* just man ♦ **les ~s** *(gén)* the just; *(Rel)* the righteous ♦ **avoir la conscience du ~** to have a clear *ou* an untroubled conscience; → **dormir**

justement /ʒystəmɑ̃/ ADV 1 *(= précisément)* exactly, just, precisely ♦ **il ne sera pas long, ~, il arrive** he won't be long, in fact he's just coming ♦ **on parlait ~ de vous** we were just talking about you ♦ ~**, j'allais le dire** actually, that's what I was going to say 2 *(= à plus forte raison)* **puisque vous me l'interdisez ... eh bien, ~ je le lui dirai** since you say I mustn't ... just for that I'll tell him ♦ **tu n'étais pas obligé d'accepter – si, ~ !** you didn't have to accept – that's the problem, I did have to! 3 *(= avec justesse) [remarquer]* rightly; *[raisonner]* soundly ♦ **comme l'a rappelé fort ~ Paul** as Paul has quite rightly pointed out 4 *(= à juste titre)* justly ♦ ~ **puni** justly punished ♦ ~ **inquiet/fier** justifiably anxious/proud

justesse /ʒystɛs/ NF 1 *(= exactitude) [d'appareil, montre, balance, tir]* accuracy, precision; *[de calcul]* accuracy, correctness; *[de réponse, comparaison, observation]* exactness; *[de coup d'œil, oreille]* accuracy

2 *[de note, voix, instrument]* accuracy

3 *(= pertinence) [d'idée, raisonnement]* soundness; *[de remarque, expression]* aptness, appropriateness ♦ **on est frappé par la ~ de son esprit** one is struck by the soundness of his judgment *ou* by how sound his judgment is

LOC ADV **de justesse** just, barely ♦ **gagner de ~** to win by a narrow margin ♦ **rattraper qn/qch de ~** to catch sb/sth just in time ♦ **j'ai évité l'accident de ~** I barely *ou* only just avoided having an accident ♦ **il s'en est tiré de ~** he got out of it by the skin of his teeth ♦ **il a eu son examen de ~** he only just passed his exam, he scraped through his exam

justice /ʒystis/ NF 1 *(= équité)* fairness, justice ♦ **en bonne** *ou* **toute ~** in all fairness ♦ **on lui doit cette ~ que ...** it must be said in fairness to him that ... ♦ **ce n'est que ~ qu'il soit récompensé** it's only fair that he should have his reward ♦ **il a la ~ pour lui** justice is on his side ♦ **traiter qn avec ~** to treat sb justly *ou* fairly ♦ ~ **sociale** social justice

2 *(= fait de juger)* justice ♦ **exercer/rendre la ~** to exercise/dispense justice ♦ **passer en ~** to stand trial ♦ **décision de ~** judicial decision ♦ **aller en ~** to go to court ♦ **traîner qn en ~** to drag sb before the courts ♦ **demander/obtenir ~** to demand/obtain justice ♦ ~ **de paix** † court of first instance ♦ ~ **immanente** *(Rel, Philos)* immanent justice ♦ **sans le vouloir, il s'est puni lui-même, il y a une sorte de ~ immanente** *(fig)* there's a sort of poetic justice in the fact that, without meaning to, he punished himself; → **déni, palais, traduire** *etc*

3 *(= loi)* **la ~** the law ♦ **la ~ le recherche** he is wanted by the law ♦ **il a eu des démêlés avec la ~** he's had a brush *ou* he's had dealings with the law ♦ **la ~ de notre pays** the law of our country ♦ **c'est du ressort de la ~ militaire** it comes under military law

4 *(locutions)* **faire ~ de qch** *(= récuser qch)* to refute sth; *(= réfuter qch)* to disprove sth ♦ **il a pu faire ~ des accusations** he was able to refute the accusations ♦ **se faire ~** *(= se venger)* to take the law into one's own hands, to take (one's) revenge; *(= se suicider)* to take one's own life ♦ **rendre ~ à qn** to do sb justice, to do justice to sb ♦ **il faut lui rendre cette ~ qu'il n'a jamais cherché à nier** he's never tried to deny it, we must grant *ou* give him that, in fairness to him it must be said that he's never tried to deny it ♦ **on n'a jamais rendu ~ à son talent** his talent has never had fair *ou* due recognition

justiciable /ʒystisjabl/ ADJ 1 *(Jur)* **criminel ~ de la cour d'assises** criminal subject to trial in a criminal court 2 *(= responsable)* **l'homme politique est ~ de l'opinion publique** politicians are accountable to the public *ou* are publicly accountable 3 *(= qui nécessite)* **situation ~ de mesures énergiques** situation where strong measures are indicated *ou* required, situation requiring strong measures NMF *(Jur)* person subject to trial ♦ **les ~s** those to be tried

justicier, -ière /ʒystisje, jɛʀ/ NM,F 1 *(gén)* upholder of the law, dispenser of justice; *(dans les westerns)* lawman ♦ **il veut jouer au ~** he wants to take the law into his own hands 2 († † *: Jur)* dispenser of justice

justifiable /ʒystifjabl/ ADJ justifiable ♦ **cela n'est pas ~** that is unjustifiable, that can't be justified

justificateur, -trice /ʒystifikatœʀ, tʀis/ ADJ *[raison, action]* justificatory, justifying

justificatif, -ive /ʒystifikatif, iv/ ADJ *[démarche, document]* supporting, justificatory ♦ **pièce justificative** *(officielle)* written proof; *(= reçu)* receipt NM *(= pièce officielle)* written proof; *(= reçu)* receipt ♦ ~ **de domicile** proof of address

justification /ʒystifikasjɔ̃/ NF 1 *(= explication)* justification ♦ **cette mesure ne trouve guère de ~ économique** there is no economic justification for this measure ♦ **fournir des ~s** to give some justification 2 *(= preuve)* proof 3 *(Typo)* justification

justifier /ʒystifje/ ► conjug 7 ◄ VT 1 *(= légitimer) [+ personne, attitude, action]* to justify ♦ **rien ne justifie cette colère** such anger is quite unjustified

2 *(= donner raison) [+ opinion]* to justify, to bear out, to vindicate; *[+ espoir, inquiétude]* to justify ♦ **ça justifie mon point de vue** it bears out *ou* vindicates my opinion ♦ ~ **qn d'une erreur** to clear sb of having made a mistake ♦ **craintes parfaitement justifiées** perfectly justified fears

3 *(= prouver)* to prove, to justify ♦ **pouvez-vous ~ ce que vous affirmez ?** can you justify *ou* prove your assertions?

4 *(Typo)* to justify ♦ ~ **à droite/gauche** to justify right/left, to right(-)/left(-)justify

VT INDIR **justifier de** to prove ♦ ~ **de son identité** to prove one's identity ♦ ~ **de son domicile** to show proof of one's address ♦ **cette quittance justifie du paiement** this receipt is evidence *ou* proof of payment

VPR **se justifier** to justify o.s. ♦ **se ~ d'une accusation** to clear o.s. of an accusation

jute /ʒyt/ NM jute; → **toile**

juter /ʒyte/ ► conjug 1 ◄ VI *[fruit]* to be juicy, to drip with juice ♦ **pipe qui jute*** dribbling pipe

juteux, -euse /ʒytø, øz/ ADJ 1 *[fruit]* juicy 2 * *[affaire, contrat, marché]* lucrative; *[bénéfices]* juicy NM *(arg Mil = adjudant)* adjutant

Juvénal /ʒyvenal/ NM Juvenal

juvénile /ʒyvenil/ ADJ 1 *[criminalité, délinquance]* juvenile; *[violence]* juvenile, youth *(épith)* 2 *[ardeur, enthousiasme, passion]* youthful; *[allure]* young, youthful NM *(Zool)* juvenile

juvénilité /ʒyvenilite/ NF *(littér)* youthfulness

juxtalinéaire /ʒykstalineɛʀ/ ADJ ♦ **traduction ~** line by line translation

juxtaposer /ʒykstapoze/ ► conjug 1 ◄ VT to juxtapose, to place side by side ♦ **propositions juxtaposées** juxtaposed clauses

juxtaposition /ʒykstapozisjɔ̃/ NF juxtaposition

Kk

K[1], k[1] /kɑ/ NM (= lettre) K, k; (Ordin) K ◆ **K 7** (= cassette) cassette, tape

K[2] (abrév de **Kelvin**) K

k[2] (abrév de **kilo**) k

kabbale /kabal/ NF ⇒ **cabale**

kabbaliste /kabalist/ NMF ⇒ **cabaliste**

kabbalistique /kabalistik/ ADJ ⇒ **cabalistique**

Kaboul /kabul/ N Kabul

kabuki /kabuki/ NM Kabuki

Kabul /kabul/ N ⇒ **Kaboul**

kabyle /kabil/ ADJ Kabyle NM (= langue) Kabyle NMF **Kabyle** Kabyle

Kabylie /kabili/ NF Kabylia ◆ **Grande/Petite** ~ Great/Lesser Kabylia

kafkaïen, -ïenne /kafkajɛ̃, jɛn/ ADJ [univers] Kafkaesque

kaiser /kezɛʀ, kajzɛʀ/ NM Kaiser

kakatoès /kakatɔɛs/ NM ⇒ **cacatoès**

kaki /kaki/ ADJ INV khaki, olive drab (US) NM INV (= couleur) khaki, olive drab (US) NM (= fruit) persimmon, sharon fruit

kalachnikov /kalaʃnikɔf/ NF Kalashnikov

Kalahari /kalaari/ N ◆ **désert du** ~ Kalahari Desert

kaléidoscope /kaleidɔskɔp/ NM kaleidoscope

kaléidoscopique /kaleidɔskɔpik/ ADJ kaleidoscopic

kamikaze /kamikaz/ ADJ (lit, fig) ◆ **opération** ~ kamikaze *ou* suicide mission ◆ **être** ~* [*personne*] to have a death wish ◆ **ce serait ~ !** it would be suicidal *ou* suicide! NM kamikaze

Kampala /kɑ̃pala/ N Kampala

Kampuchea /kɑ̃putʃea/ NM ◆ ~ **(démocratique)** (Democratic) Kampuchea

kampuchéen, -enne /kɑ̃putʃeɛ̃, ɛn/ ADJ Kampuchean NM,F **Kampuchéen(ne)** Kampuchean

kanak, e /kanak/ ADJ, NM,F ⇒ **canaque**

kangourou /kɑ̃guʀu/ NM kangaroo ◆ **sac** *ou* **poche** ~ baby carrier; → **slip**

Kansas /kɑ̃sas/ NM Kansas

kantien, -ienne /kɑ̃sjɛ̃, jɛn/ ADJ Kantian

kantisme /kɑ̃tism/ NM Kantianism

kaolin /kaɔlɛ̃/ NM kaolin(e)

kapo /kapo/ NM kapo, capo

kapok /kapɔk/ NM kapok

kapokier /kapɔkje/ NM kapok tree, silk cotton tree

Kaposi /kapozi/ N ◆ **(maladie** *ou* **sarcome** *ou* **syndrome de)** ~ Kaposi's sarcoma ◆ **il a un (début de)** ~ he is suffering from (the early stages of) Kaposi's sarcoma

kappa /kapa/ NM kappa

kaput* /kaput/ ADJ [*personne*] shattered*, bushed*, dead(-beat)*; [*machine*] kaput*

karaoké, karaoke /kaʀaɔke/ NM karaoke ◆ **bar (à)** ~ karaoke bar ◆ **faire un** ~ (= *chanter une chanson*) to sing a karaoke song; (= *aller dans un bar*) to go to a karaoke bar

karaté /kaʀate/ NM karate

karatéka /kaʀateka/ NMF karateka

Karcher ® /kaʀʃɛʀ/ NM high-pressure water cleaner

karité /kaʀite/ NM shea(-tree) ◆ **beurre de** ~ shea butter

karma /kaʀma/ NM karma

karstique /kaʀstik/ ADJ karstic

kart /kaʀt/ NM go-cart, kart

karting /kaʀtiŋ/ NM go-carting, karting ◆ **faire du** ~ to go-cart, to go karting

kascher /kaʃɛʀ/ ADJ kosher

Katanga /katɑ̃ga/ NM Katanga

katangais, e /katɑ̃gɛ, ɛz/ ADJ Katangese NM,F Katangese

Katmandou /katmɑ̃du/ N Katmandu

kawa* /kawa/ NM (= *café*) (cup of) coffee

kayak /kajak/ NM [*d'esquimau*] kayak; [*de sportif*] canoe, kayak; (= *sport*) canoeing ◆ **faire du** ~ to go canoeing

kayakiste /kajakist/ NMF kayaker

kazakh /kazak/ ADJ kazakh NM (= *langue*) Kazakh NMF **Kazakh** Kazakh

Kazakhstan /kazakstɑ̃/ N Kazakhstan

kebab /kebab/ NM kebab

kéfié, keffieh /kefje/ NM keffiyeh, kaffiyeh, kufiyah

kelvin /kɛlvin/ NM kelvin

kendo /kɛndo/ NM kendo

Kenya /kenja/ NM Kenya ◆ **le mont** ~ Mount Kenya

kényan, -ane /kenjɑ̃, jan/ ADJ Kenyan NM,F **Kényan(e)** Kenyan

képi /kepi/ NM kepi

kératine /keʀatin/ NF keratin

kératite /keʀatit/ NF keratitis

kératose /keʀatoz/ NF keratosis

Kerguelen /kɛʀgelɛn/ NFPL ◆ **les (îles)** ~ the Kerguelen (Islands)

kermesse /kɛʀmɛs/ NF (= *fête populaire*) fair; (= *fête de charité*) bazaar, charity fête ◆ ~ **paroissiale** church fête *ou* bazaar

kérosène /keʀozɛn/ NM [*d'avion*] aviation fuel, kerosene (*US*); [*de jet*] (jet) fuel; [*de fusée*] (rocket) fuel

ketch /kɛtʃ/ NM ketch

ketchup /kɛtʃœp/ NM ketchup, catsup (*US*)

keuf** /kœf/ NM cop*

keum** /kœm/ NM guy*

kevlar ® /kɛvlaʀ/ NM kevlar ®

keynésianisme /kenezjanism/ NM Keynesianism, Keynesian economics (*sg*)

keynésien, -ienne /kenezjɛ̃, jɛn/ ADJ Keynesian

kF /kaɛf/ NM (abrév de **kilofranc**) ≈ K* ◆ **il gagne 240** ~ ≈ he earns 24 K*

kg (abrév de **kilogramme**) kg

KGB /kaʒebe/ NM (abrév de **Komitet Gosudarstvennoy Bezopasnosti**) KGB

khâgne /kaɲ/ NF *second year of a two-year preparatory course for the arts section of the École Normale Supérieure*; → CLASSES PRÉPARATOIRES, GRANDES ÉCOLES

khâgneux, -euse /kaɲø, øz/ NM,F *student in khâgne*

khalife /kalif/ NM ⇒ **calife**

khan /kɑ̃/ NM khan

Khartoum /kaʀtum/ N Khartoum

khat /kat/ NM k(h)at

khédive /kediv/ NM khedive

khi /ki/ NM chi

khmer, -ère /kmɛʀ/ ADJ Khmer NM (*Ling*) Khmer NM **Khmer** Khmer ◆ **les Khmers rouges** the Khmer Rouge

khôl /kol/ NM kohl

kibboutz /kibuts/ NM INV kibbutz

kick /kik/ NM kick-start(er) ◆ **démarrer au** ~ [*personne*] to kick-start one's motorbike ◆ **la moto (se) démarre au** ~ you have to kick-start the motorbike

kickboxing /kikbɔksiŋ/ NM kickboxing

kidnapper /kidnape/ ► conjug 1 ◄ VT to kidnap, to abduct

kidnappeur, -euse /kidnapœʀ, øz/ NM,F kidnapper, abductor

kidnapping /kidnapiŋ/ NM kidnapping, abduction

Kiev /kjev/ N Kiev

kif[1] /kif/ NM (*= hachisch*) kif, kef ◆ **c'est le ~ !*** (*= super*) it's great *ou* cool*!

kif[2]* /kif/ NM ◆ **c'est du ~** it's all the same, it makes no odds* (*Brit*)

kif(f)ant, e* /kifɑ̃, ɑ̃t/ ADJ ◆ **c'est ~!** it's great!

kif(f)er* /kife/ ▸ conjug 1 ◂ VI ◆ **ça me fait ~** it turns me on* VT ◆ **~ qch** to get a kick out of sth* ◆ **je peux pas le ~** I can't stand him

kif-kif* /kifkif/ ADJ INV ◆ **c'est ~ (bourricot)** it's all the same, it makes no odds* (*Brit*)

Kigali /kigali/ N Kigali

kiki* /kiki/ NM 1 (*= cou*) **serrer le ~ à qn** [*personne*] to throttle sb, to grab sb by the throat; [*cravate, encolure*] to choke sb; → **partir**[1] 2 (*hum, langage enfantin = pénis*) willie* (*Brit*), peter* (*US*)

kikouyou, kikuyu /kikuju/ ADJ Kikuyu NMF **Kikouyou** Kikuyu ◆ **les Kikouyous** the Kikuyu

kil* /kil/ NM ◆ **~ de rouge** bottle of cheap (red) wine *ou* plonk* (*Brit*)

Kilimandjaro /kilimɑ̃dʒaʀo/ NM ◆ **le ~** Mount Kilimanjaro

kilo /kilo/ NM kilo ◆ **en faire des ~s*** to go over the top*

kilo... /kilo/ PRÉF kilo...

kilobar /kilɔbaʀ/ NM kilobar

kilocalorie /kilokalɔʀi/ NF kilocalorie

kilocycle /kilosikl/ NM kilocycle

kilofranc /kilofʀɑ̃/ NM thousand francs

kilogramme /kilɔgʀam/ NM kilogramme

kilohertz /kiloɛʀts/ NM kilohertz

kilojoule /kilɔʒul/ NM kilojoule

kilométrage /kilɔmetʀaʒ/ NM 1 [*de voiture, distance*] ≈ mileage ◆ **voiture en** *ou* **à ~ illimité** car with unlimited mileage 2 [*de route*] ≈ marking with milestones

kilomètre /kilɔmɛtʀ/ NM 1 (*= distance*) kilometre (*Brit*), kilometer (*US*) ◆ **200 ~s à l'heure** *ou* **~s-heure** 200 kilometres an hour *ou* per hour ◆ **bouffer du ~*** ≈ to eat up the miles* ◆ **~-passager** passenger kilometre, ≈ passenger mile ◆ **~ lancé** (*Ski*) speed-record trial ◆ **d'ici à ce qu'il ne vienne pas, il n'y a pas des ~s*** I wouldn't be surprised if he didn't turn up 2 (*grande quantité*) **des ~s de** [+ *pellicule*] rolls and rolls of; [+ *tissu*] yards and yards of ◆ **ils produisent des émissions au ~** they churn out one programme after another

kilométrer /kilɔmetʀe/ ▸ conjug 6 ◂ VT [+ *route*] ≈ to mark with milestones

kilométrique /kilɔmetʀik/ ADJ ◆ **distance ~** distance in kilometres (*Brit*) *ou* kilometer (*US*) ◆ **borne ~** ≈ milestone ◆ **indemnité ~** ≈ mileage allowance ◆ **tarif ~** rate per kilometre

kilo-octet (pl **kilo-octets**) /kilookte/ NM kilobyte

kilotonne /kilotɔn/ NF kiloton

kilowatt /kilowat/ NM kilowatt

kilowattheure /kilowatœʀ/ NM kilowatt-hour

kilt /kilt/ NM kilt; (*pour femme*) pleated *ou* kilted skirt

kimono /kimɔno/ NM kimono; → **manche**[1]

kinase /kinɑz/ NF kinase

kiné(si)* /kine(zi)/ NMF (abrév de **kinésithérapeute**) physio*

kinésithérapeute /kineziteʀapøt/ NMF physiotherapist (*Brit*), physical therapist (*US*)

kinésithérapie /kineziteʀapi/ NF physiotherapy (*Brit*), physical therapy (*US*)

kinesthésique /kinɛstezik/ ADJ kinaesthetic

Kingston /kiŋstɔn/ N Kingston

Kingstown /kiŋstaun/ N Kingstown

Kinshasa /kinʃasa/ N Kinshasa

kiosque /kjɔsk/ NM 1 (*= étal*) kiosk, stall ◆ **~ à journaux** newsstand, newspaper kiosk ◆ **en vente en ~** on sale at newsstands 2 (*Internet*) kiosk; (*Téléc*) ◆ **~ télématique**® *information service provided by Minitel* 3 [*de jardin*] pavilion, summerhouse ◆ **~ à musique** bandstand 4 [*de sous-marin*] conning tower; [*de bateau*] wheelhouse

kiosquier, -ière /kjɔskje, jɛʀ/ NM,F newspaper seller (*at kiosk*)

kippa /kipa/ NF kippa

kir /kiʀ/ NM kir (*white wine with blackcurrant liqueur*) ◆ **~ royal** kir royal (*champagne with blackcurrant liqueur*)

kirghiz /kiʀgiz/ ADJ Kirghiz NM (*= langue*) Kirghiz NMF **Kirghiz(e)** Kirghiz

Kirghizistan /kiʀgizistɑ̃/, **Kirghizstan** /kiʀgistɑ̃/ NM Kirghizia

Kiribati /kiʀibati/ N Kiribati

kirsch /kiʀʃ/ NM kirsch

kit /kit/ NM kit ◆ **en ~** in kit form ◆ **~ mains libres** *ou* **piéton** (*pour téléphone mobile*) hands-free kit ◆ **~ de connexion** connection kit

kit(s)ch /kitʃ/ ADJ INV, NM kitsch

kitchenette /kitʃ(ə)nɛt/ NF kitchenette

kitesurf /kaitsœʀf/ NM kitesurfing

kiwi /kiwi/ NM 1 (*= oiseau*) kiwi 2 (*= arbre*) kiwi tree; (*= fruit*) kiwi (fruit), Chinese gooseberry

klaxon® /klaksɔn/ NM horn ◆ **coup de ~** (*fort*) hoot; (*léger*) toot ◆ **donner des coups de ~** to hoot (one's horn), to sound one's horn

klaxonner /klaksɔne/ ▸ conjug 1 ◂ VI (*gén*) to hoot (one's horn), to sound one's horn; (*doucement*) to toot (the horn) ◆ **klaxonne, il ne t'a pas vu** hoot your horn *ou* give him a toot, he hasn't seen you VT ◆ **~ qn** (*gén*) to hoot at sb; (*doucement*) to give sb a toot

kleb(s)* /klɛp(s)/ NM ⇒ **clebs**

Kleenex® /klinɛks/ NM tissue, paper hanky, Kleenex®

kleptomane /klɛptɔman/ ADJ, NMF kleptomaniac

kleptomanie /klɛptɔmani/ NF kleptomania

km (abrév de **kilomètre(s)**) km

km/h (abrév de **kilomètres/heure**) km/h, kph, ≈ mph

knickerbockers /knikɛʀbɔkɛʀs, nikœʀbɔkœʀ/ NMPL knickerbockers

knock-out /nɔkaut/ ADJ (*Boxe, **) knocked out, out for the count* ◆ **mettre qn ~** to knock sb out ◆ **il est complètement ~** he's out cold* NM knockout

knout /knut/ NM knout

Ko (abrév de **kilo-octet**) kb

K.-O., KO /kao/ (abrév de **knock out**) NM (*Boxe*) KO ◆ **perdre par ~** to be knocked out ◆ **gagner par ~** to win by a knockout ◆ **mettre ~** to KO*, to knock out ◆ **il a été mis ~ au 5e round** he was knocked out in round 5 ◆ **être ~** to be out for the count ◆ **être K.-O debout** [*boxeur*] to be punch-drunk; (*vaincu*) to be knocked for six*; (*stupéfait*) to be stunned ADJ (** = fatigué*) shattered*, knackered*

koala /kɔala/ NM koala (bear)

kola /kɔla/ NM ⇒ **cola**

kolkhoze /kɔlkoz/ NM kolkhoz

kolkhozien, -ienne /kɔlkozjɛ̃, jɛn/ ADJ, NM,F kolkhozian

kommandantur /kɔmɑ̃dɑ̃tuʀ/ NF German military command

kopeck /kɔpɛk/ NM kopeck ◆ **je n'ai plus un ~** †* I haven't got a penny left

korrigan, e /kɔʀigɑ̃, an/ NM,F Breton goblin

kosovar /kosovaʀ/ ADJ Kosovar NMF **Kosovar** Kosovar

Kosovo /kosovo/ NM Kosovo

kouglof /kuglɔf/ NM kugelhopf (*kind of bun*)

koulak /kulak/ NM kulak

Koweït /kɔwɛt/ NM Kuwait

koweïtien, -ienne /kɔwɛtjɛ̃, jɛn/ ADJ Kuwaiti NM,F **Koweïtien(ne)** Kuwaiti

krach /kʀak/ NM (*Bourse*) crash ◆ **~ boursier** stock market crash

kraft /kʀaft/ NM → **papier**

Kremlin /kʀɛmlɛ̃/ NM ◆ **le ~** the Kremlin

krill /kʀil/ NM krill

krypton /kʀiptɔ̃/ NM krypton

ksi /ksi/ NM xi

Kuala Lumpur /kwalalumpuʀ/ N Kuala Lumpur

Ku Klux Klan /kyklyksklɑ̃/ NM Ku Klux Klan

kummel /kymɛl/ NM kümmel

kumquat /kɔmkwat/ NM kumquat

kung-fu /kuŋfu/ NM INV (*= art*) kung fu; (*= personne*) person who practises *ou* does kung fu

kurde /kyʀd/ ADJ Kurdish NM (*= langue*) Kurdish NMF **Kurde** Kurd

Kurdistan /kyʀdistɑ̃/ NM Kurdistan

kW (abrév de **kilowatt**) kW

K-way® /kawɛ/ NM (lightweight nylon) cagoule

kWh (abrév de **kilowattheure**) kWh

Kyoto /kjɔto/ N Kyoto

kyrie (eleison) /kiʀje(eleisɔn)/ NM INV (*Rel, Mus*) Kyrie (eleison)

kyrielle /kiʀjɛl/ NF [*d'injures, réclamations*] string, stream; [*de personnes, enfants*] crowd, stream; [*d'objets*] pile

kyste /kist/ NM cyst ◆ **~ de l'ovaire** *ou* **ovarien** ovarian cyst

kystique /kistik/ ADJ cystic

L l

L, l' /ɛl/ **NM** *(= lettre)* L, l

l² (abrév de **litre(s)**) l

l' /l/ → **le¹, le²**

la¹ /la/ → **le¹, le²**

la² /la/ **NM INV** *(Mus)* A; *(en chantant la gamme)* lah ◆ **donner le** ~ *(lit)* to give an A; *(fig)* to set the tone *ou* the fashion

là /la/

1 ADVERBE	3 LOC ADVERBIALE
2 LOC ADVERBIALE	4 EXCLAMATION

1 - ADVERBE

1 [par opposition à ici] there ◆ ~, **on s'occupera bien de vous** you will be well looked after there ◆ **je le vois** ~, **sur la table** I can see it (over) there, on the table ◆ **c'est** ~ **que** *ou* **c'est** ~ **où je suis né** that's where I was born; → **çà, fait¹**

2 [= ici] here, there ◆ **ne restez pas** ~ **au froid** don't stand here *ou* there in the cold ◆ **n'ayez pas peur, je suis** ~ don't be afraid, I'm here ◆ **qui est** ~ **?** who's there? ◆ **c'est** ~ **! je reconnais le portail !** there it is! *ou* here we are! I recognize the gate! ◆ **M. Roche n'est pas** ~ Mr Roche isn't here *ou* in ◆ **je suis** ~ **pour ça !** that's what I'm here for! ◆ **ce monument est** ~ **pour nous rappeler que** ... this monument is here *ou* exists to remind us that ... ◆ **c'est** ~ **qu'il est tombé** that's *ou* this is where he fell ◆ ~ **où tu es/d'où tu viens** where you are/come from ◆ **déjà** ~ **?** (are you) here already? ◆ **qu'est-ce que tu fais** ~ **?** *(lit)* what are you doing here?; *(fig)* what are you up to? ◆ **la crise est** ~ **et bien** ~ there really is a crisis; → **fait¹**

3 [dans le temps] then, at this *ou* that moment ◆ **c'est** ~ **qu'il comprit qu'il était en danger** that was when he realized *ou* it was then that he realized he was in danger ◆ **ce qu'il propose** ~ **n'est pas bête** what he's just suggested isn't a bad idea; → **ici, jusque**

4 [= dans cette situation] **tout cela pour en arriver** *ou* **en venir** ~ **!** all that effort just for this! ◆ **il faut s'en tenir** *ou* **en rester** ~ we'll have to leave it at that *ou* stop there ◆ **les choses en sont** ~ that's how things stand at the moment, that's the state of play at present ◆ **ils en sont** ~ *(lit)* that's how far they've got, that's the stage they've reached; *(péj)* that's how low they've sunk ◆ **ils n'en sont pas encore** ~ they haven't got that far yet *ou* reached that stage yet; *(péj)* they haven't reached that stage yet *ou* come to that yet ◆ **j'en étais** ~ **de mes réflexions quand** ... such was my state of mind when ... ◆ **c'est bien** ~ **qu'on voit les paresseux !** that's where *ou* when you see who the lazy ones are! ◆ **il a été courageux** ~ **où d'autres auraient eu peur** he was courageous where others would have been afraid; → **loin**

5 [intensif] **n'allez pas croire** ~ **que** ... don't get the idea that ..., don't go thinking that ... ◆ **qu'est-ce que tu me racontes** ~ **?** what (on earth) are you saying to me?

6 [= en cela, dans cela] **c'est** ~ **où** *ou* **que nous ne sommes plus d'accord** that's where I take issue *ou* start to disagree with you ◆ ~, **ils exagèrent !** now they're really going too far! ◆ **je ne vois** ~ **rien d'étonnant** I don't see anything surprising in *ou* about that ◆ **il y a** ~ **quelque chose d'inquiétant** there's something worrying about that ◆ **tout est** ~ that's the whole question ◆ **c'est** ~ **qu'est la difficulté,** ~ **est la difficulté** that's where the difficulty lies ◆ **il y a** ~ **une contradiction** there's a contradiction in that; → **question**

7 [avec trait d'union]

◆ **ce** *ou* **cette ...-là** that ... ◆ **ce jour-**~ that day ◆ **cet homme-**~ **est détesté par tout le monde** everybody hates that man ◆ **c'est à ce point-**~ **?** it's as bad as that, is it? ◆ **en ce temps-**~ in those days

◆ **ces ...-là** those ... ◆ **ces gens-**~ those people; → **ce¹**

◆ **celui-là, celle-là** *(= objet, personne)* that one ◆ **je veux celui-**~ I want that one ◆ **celui-/celle-**~ **alors !** *(irritation)* oh, that man/woman!; *(surprise)* how does he/she do it! ◆ **il est marrant*, celui-**~ **!** that guy's such a laugh!

◆ **ceux-là, celles-là** *(= objets)* those ◆ **certains le croient, Luc est de ceux-**~ *(= personnes)* some people, including Luc, believe it ◆ **celles-**~, **elles ne risquent rien** THEY're not in any danger; → aussi **celui**

2 - LOCUTION ADVERBIALE

de là

1 [dans l'espace] **il est allé à Paris, et de** ~ **à Londres** he went to Paris, and from there to London *ou* and then (from there) on to London ◆ **c'est à 3 km de** ~ it's 3 km away (from there)

2 [dans le temps] **à partir de** ~ from then on, after that ◆ **à quelques jours de** ~ a few days later *ou* after(wards)

3 [conséquence] **il n'a pas travaillé, de** ~ **son échec** he didn't work, hence his failure *ou* which explains why he failed ◆ **de** ~ **vient que nous ne le voyons plus** that's why we no longer see him ◆ **de** ~ **à dire qu'il ment, il n'y a qu'un pas** there isn't much difference between saying that and saying he's lying, that's tantamount to saying he's a liar ◆ **oui, mais de** ~ **à prétendre qu'il a tout fait seul !** there's a big difference between saying that and claiming that he did it all himself!

3 - LOCUTION ADVERBIALE

par là

1 [dans l'espace] **quelque part par** ~ *(= de ce côté)* somewhere around there *ou* near there ◆ **passez par** ~ *(= par cet endroit)* go that way ◆ **c'est par ici ou par** ~ **?** is it this way or that way?

2 [* = environ] **il doit avoir 20 ans, par** ~ he must be about 20, he must be 20 or so

3 [locutions] **que veux-tu dire par** ~ **?** what do you mean by that? ◆ **si tu (y) vas par** ~ **...** if that's what you're saying ...; → **entendre, passer**

4 - EXCLAMATION

◆ **fiche-moi la paix,** ~ **!*** leave me alone, will you! * ◆ **hé** ~ **!** *(appel)* hey!; *(surprise)* good grief! ◆ **là, là, du calme !** now, now, calm down! ◆ **il est entré dans une rage, mais** ~, **une de ces rages !** he flew into a rage, and what a rage! ◆ **alors** ~ *ou* **oh** ~, **ça ne m'étonne pas** (oh) now, that doesn't surprise me

◆ **oh là là (là là)!** *(surprise)* oh my goodness!; *(consternation)* oh dear! (oh dear!) ◆ **oh là là !, ce que j'ai froid !** God*, I'm so cold! ◆ **oh là là ! quel désastre !** oh dear! *ou* oh no! what a disaster!

---

là-bas /laba/ **ADV** (over) there, yonder ◆ ~ **aux USA** over in the USA ◆ ~ **dans le nord** up (there) in the north ◆ ~ **dans la plaine** down there in the plain ◆ **Serge a réapparu, tout** ~ Serge reappeared way over there

labbe /lab/ **NM** skua ◆ ~ **parasite** Arctic skua

label /labɛl/ **NM** label ◆ ~ **d'origine** label of origin ◆ ~ **de qualité** *(lit)* quality label; *(fig)* guarantee of quality ◆ ~ **rouge** *quality label for meat* ◆ ~ **politique** political label ◆ **l'association a accordé son** ~ **à 80 projets** the association has given its seal of approval to 80 projects ◆ **ils ont sorti un album sous un** ~ **indépendant** they've brought out an album on an independent label

labelliser /labelize/ ► conjug 1 ◄ **VT** *[+ produit]* to label, to put a label on; *[+ projet]* to give one's seal of approval to

labeur /labœʀ/ **NM** *(littér)* labour, toil *(NonC)* ◆ **c'est un dur** ~ it's hard work

labial, e (mpl **-iaux**) /labjal, jo/ ADJ *[consonne]* labial; *[muscle]* lip *(épith)*, labial *(SPÉC)* NF **labiale** labial

labialisation /labjalizasjɔ̃/ NF *[de consonne]* labialization; *[de voyelle]* labialization, rounding

labialiser /labjalize/ ► conjug 1 ◄ VT *[+ consonne]* to labialize; *[+ voyelle]* to labialize, to round

labié, e /labje/ ADJ labiate NF labiate ◆ **les ~es** labiates, Labiatae *(SPÉC)*

labiodental, e (mpl **-aux**) /labjodɑ̃tal, o/ ADJ, NF labiodental

labo * /labo/ NM (abrév de **laboratoire**) lab * ◆ **~ photo** photo lab

laborantin, e /labɔʀɑ̃tɛ̃, in/ NM,F laboratory *ou* lab * assistant

laboratoire /labɔʀatwaʀ/ NM *(gén)* laboratory ◆ **~ spatial/de recherches** space/research laboratory ◆ **~ d'analyses (médicales)** (medical) analysis laboratory ◆ **~ (de) photo** photo laboratory ◆ **~ de langue(s)** language laboratory ◆ **~ d'essai** *(lit)* testing laboratory; *(fig)* testing ground ◆ **simulation/essais en ~** laboratory simulation/trials ◆ **produit en ~** produced in a laboratory *ou* under laboratory conditions

laborieusement /labɔʀjøzmɑ̃/ ADV laboriously, with much effort ◆ **gagner ~ sa vie** to struggle to earn a living, to earn a living by the sweat of one's brow

laborieux, -ieuse /labɔʀjø, jøz/ ADJ 1 *(= pénible)* laborious, painstaking; *[entreprise, négociations, recherches]* laborious; *[style, récit]* laboured, laborious; *[digestion]* heavy ◆ **il s'exprimait dans un français ~** his French was very laboured ◆ **il a enfin fini, ça a été ~ !** he's finished at last, it was hard going! 2 *(= travailleur)* hard-working, industrious ◆ **les classes laborieuses** the working *ou* labouring classes ◆ **une vie laborieuse** a life of toil *ou* hard work

labour /labuʀ/ NM 1 *(avec une charrue)* ploughing *(Brit)*, plowing *(US)*; *(avec une bêche)* digging (over); → **cheval** 2 *(= champ)* ploughed *(Brit) ou* plowed *(US)* field

labourable /labuʀabl/ ADJ *(avec une charrue)* ploughable *(Brit)*, plowable *(US)*; *(avec une bêche)* soft enough for digging ◆ **terres ~s** arable land

labourage /labuʀaʒ/ NM *(avec une charrue)* ploughing *(Brit)*, plowing *(US)*; *(avec une bêche)* digging (over)

labourer /labuʀe/ ► conjug 1 ◄ VT 1 *(avec une charrue)* to plough *(Brit)*, to plow *(US)*; *(avec une bêche)* to dig (over) ◆ **terre qui se laboure bien** land which ploughs well *ou* is easy to plough ◆ **~ le fond** *(Naut) [navire]* to scrape *ou* graze the bottom; *[ancre]* to drag ◆ **terrain labouré par les sabots des chevaux** ground churned *ou* ploughed up by the horses' hooves 2 ◆ **la balle lui avait labouré la jambe** the bullet had ripped into *ou* gashed his leg ◆ **labouré de rides** lined *ou* furrowed with wrinkles ◆ **ce corset me laboure les côtes** this corset is digging into my sides ◆ **se ~ le visage/les mains** to tear at one's face/one's hands ◆ **le chat lui a labouré le visage** the cat scratched his face really badly

laboureur /labuʀœʀ/ NM ploughman *(Brit)*, plowman *(US)*; *(Hist)* husbandman

Labrador /labʀadɔʀ/ NM *(Géog)* Labrador

labrador /labʀadɔʀ/ NM *(= chien)* Labrador (retriever)

labradorite /labʀadɔʀit/ NF *(Minér)* labradorite

labrit /labʀi/ NM Pyrenean sheepdog

labyrinthe /labiʀɛ̃t/ NM *(lit, fig)* maze, labyrinth; *(Anat)* labyrinth

labyrinthique /labiʀɛ̃tik/ ADJ labyrinthine

lac /lak/ NM lake ◆ **~ de montagne** mountain lake ◆ **le ~ Léman** *ou* **de Genève** Lake Geneva ◆ **le ~ Majeur** Lake Maggiore ◆ **les ~s écossais** the Scottish lochs ◆ **les Grands Lacs** the Great Lakes ◆ **être (tombé) dans le ~** * *(fig)* to have fallen through, to have come to nothing

laçage /lasaʒ/ NM lacing(-up)

lacanien, -ienne /lakanjɛ̃, jɛn/ ADJ *(Psych)* Lacanian

Lacédémone /lasedemɔn/ N Lacedaemonia

lacédémonien, -ienne /lasedemɔnjɛ̃, jɛn/ ADJ Lacedaemonian NM,F **Lacédémonien(ne)** Lacedaemonian

lacement /lasmɑ̃/ NM ⇒ **laçage**

lacer /lase/ ► conjug 3 ◄ VT *[+ chaussure]* to tie; *[+ corset]* to lace up; *(Naut) [+ voile]* to lace ◆ **lace tes chaussures** *ou* **tes lacets** do up *ou* tie your shoelaces ◆ **ça se lace (par) devant** it laces up at the front

lacération /laseʀasjɔ̃/ NF *[de vêtement, affiche]* ripping up, tearing up; *[de corps, visage]* laceration; *[de tableau]* slashing

lacérer /laseʀe/ ► conjug 6 ◄ VT *[+ affiche, papier, vêtement]* to tear *ou* rip up, to tear to shreds; *[+ tableau]* to slash; *[+ corps, visage]* to lacerate ◆ **il avait été lacéré de coups de couteau** he had been slashed with a knife

lacet /lasɛ/ NM 1 *[de chaussure]* (shoe)lace; *[de botte]* (boot)lace; *[de corset]* lace ◆ **chaussures à ~s** lace-ups, lace-up shoes ◆ **faire** *ou* **nouer ses ~s** to do up *ou* tie one's laces 2 *[de route]* (sharp) bend, twist ◆ **en ~(s)** winding, twisty ◆ **la route fait des ~s** *ou* **monte en ~s** the road twists *ou* winds steeply upwards 3 *(= piège)* snare ◆ **prendre des lièvres au ~** to trap *ou* snare hares 4 *(Couture)* braid

lâchage * /lɑʃaʒ/ NM *(= abandon)* desertion ◆ **écœuré par le ~ de ses amis** disgusted at the way his friends had deserted him *ou* run out on him ◆ **ils dénoncent le ~ du pays par l'ONU** they're denouncing the UN's abandonment of the country

lâche /lɑʃ/ ADJ 1 *[corde, ressort]* slack; *[nœud]* loose; *[vêtement]* loose(-fitting); *[tissu]* loosely-woven, open-weave *(épith)* 2 *[discipline, morale]* lax; *[règlement, canevas]* loose 3 *(littér) [style, expression]* loose, woolly ◆ **dans ce roman, l'intrigue est un peu ~** the novel has quite a loose plot 4 *[personne, fuite, attitude]* cowardly; *[attentat]* vile, despicable; *[procédé]* low ◆ **se montrer ~** to be a coward ◆ **c'est assez ~ de sa part d'avoir fait ça** it was pretty cowardly of him to do that 5 *(littér = faible)* weak, feeble NMF coward

lâchement /lɑʃmɑ̃/ ADV 1 *(= sans courage)* in a cowardly way ◆ **il a ~ refusé** like a coward, he refused ◆ **il a été ~ assassiné** he was killed in the most cowardly way 2 *[nouer]* loosely

lâcher /lɑʃe/ ► conjug 1 ◄ VT 1 *[+ ceinture]* to loosen, to let out, to slacken ◆ **~ la taille d'une jupe** to let a skirt out at the waist ◆ **~ du fil** *(Pêche)* to let out some line

2 *[+ main, proie]* to let go of; *[+ bombes]* to drop, to release; *[+ pigeon, ballon]* to release; *[+ chien de garde]* to unleash, to set loose; *[+ frein]* to release, to let out; *[+ amarres]* to cast off; *(Chasse) [+ chien, faucon]* to slip ◆ **lâche-moi !** let go (of me)! ◆ **attention ! tu vas ~ le verre** careful, you're going to drop the glass! ◆ **le professeur nous a lâchés à 4 heures** * the teacher let us go *ou* let us out at 4 ◆ **~ un chien sur qn** to set a dog on sb ◆ **s'il veut acheter ce tableau, il va falloir qu'il les lâche** * *ou* **qu'il lâche ses sous** * if he wants this picture, he'll have to part with the cash * ◆ **il les lâche difficilement** * he hates to part with his money

3 *[+ bêtise, juron]* to come out with; *[+ pet]* to let out; † *[+ coup de fusil]* to fire ◆ **~ quelques mots** to say a few words ◆ **voilà le grand mot lâché !** there's the fatal word! ◆ **~ un coup de poing à qn** † to deal *ou* fetch *(Brit)* sb a blow with one's fist

4 *(* = abandonner) [+ époux]* to leave, to walk out on; *[+ amant]* to jilt, to drop, to chuck ‡ *(Brit)*; *[+ ami]* to drop; *[+ études, métier]* to give up, to pack in * *(Brit)*, to chuck in * *(Brit)*; *[+ avantage]* to give up ◆ **il a tout lâché pour la rejoindre à New York** he gave everything up and followed her to New York ◆ **~ le peloton** to leave the rest of the field behind, to build up a good lead (over the rest of the pack) ◆ **ne pas ~ qn** *[poursuivant, créancier]* to stick to sb; *[importun, représentant]* not to leave sb alone; *[mal de tête]* not to let up on sb *, not to leave sb ◆ **il nous a lâchés en plein milieu du travail** he walked out on us right in the middle of the work ◆ **il ne m'a pas lâché d'une semelle** he stuck close all the time, he stuck to me like a leech ◆ **la communauté internationale nous a lâchés** the international community has abandoned us ◆ **ma voiture m'a lâché** my car gave up on me * ◆ **une bonne occasion, ça ne se lâche pas** *ou* **il ne faut pas la ~** you don't miss *ou* pass up * an opportunity like that

5 *(locutions)* **~ prise** *(lit)* to let go; *(fig)* to loosen one's grip ◆ **~ pied** to fall back, to give way ◆ **~ la bride** *ou* **les rênes à un cheval** to give a horse its head ◆ **~ la bride à qn** *(fig)* to give sb more of a free rein ◆ **tu me lâches !** * leave me alone! ◆ **lâche-moi les baskets !** * *ou* **la grappe !** * get off my back! *, get off my case! * *(US)* ◆ **il les lâche avec des élastiques** ‡ he's as stingy as hell ‡, he's a tight-fisted so-and-so *; → **lest**

VI *[corde]* to break, to give way; *[frein]* to fail

VPR **se lâcher** * *(= faire ce qu'on veut)* to let o.s. go *; *(= parler franchement)* to speak one's mind

NM ◆ **~ de ballons** balloon release

lâcheté /lɑʃte/ NF 1 *(= couardise)* cowardice, cowardliness; *(= bassesse)* lowness ◆ **par ~** through *ou* out of cowardice ◆ **je trouve ça d'une ~ !** that's so cowardly! 2 *(= acte)* cowardly act, act of cowardice 3 *(littér = faiblesse)* weakness, feebleness

lâcheur, -euse * /lɑʃœʀ, øz/ NM,F unreliable *ou* fickle so-and-so * ◆ **alors, tu n'es pas venu, ~ !** so you didn't come then – you're a dead loss! * *ou* you old so-and-so! * ◆ **c'est une lâcheuse, ta sœur !** your sister's so unreliable! *

lacis /lasi/ NM *[de ruelles]* maze; *[de veines]* network; *[de soie]* web

laconique /lakɔnik/ ADJ *[personne, réponse]* laconic; *[style]* terse

laconiquement /lakɔnikmɑ̃/ ADV laconically, tersely

laconisme /lakɔnism/ NM terseness

lacrymal, e (mpl **-aux**) /lakʀimal, o/ ADJ lacrimal *(SPÉC)*, lachrymal *(SPÉC)*, tear *(épith)*

lacrymogène /lakʀimɔʒɛn/ ADJ → **gaz, grenade**

lacs /lɑ/ NMPL († †, *littér*) snare ◆ **~ d'amour** lover's *ou* love knot

lactaire /laktɛʀ/ ADJ *(Anat)* lacteal NM *(= champignon)* milk cap

lactalbumine /laktalbymin/ NF lactalbumin

lactase /laktɑz/ NF lactase

lactation /laktasjɔ̃/ NF lactation

lacté, e /lakte/ ADJ *[sécrétion]* milky, lacteal *(SPÉC)*; *[couleur, suc]* milky; *[régime]* milk *(épith)*; → **voie**

lactifère /laktifɛʀ/ ADJ lactiferous

lactique /laktik/ ADJ lactic

lactogène /laktɔʒɛn/ ADJ lactogenic

lactose /laktoz/ NM lactose

lactosérum /laktoseʀɔm/ NM whey

lacunaire /lakynɛʀ/ ADJ 1 *[informations, documentation, récit, caractère]* incomplete ◆ **il a des connaissances ~s** there are gaps in his knowledge 2 *(Bio) [tissu]* lacunary, lacunal

lacune /lakyn/ NF 1 *[de texte, mémoire, connaissances]* gap; *[de manuscrit]* lacuna; *[de loi]* gap, loophole ◆ **les ~s du système éducatif** the shortcomings of the education system ◆ **elle a de grosses ~s en histoire** there are big gaps in her knowledge of history ◆ **il y a de sérieuses ~s dans ce livre** this book has some serious deficiencies *ou* leaves out *ou* overlooks some serious points 2 *(Anat, Bot)* lacuna

lacustre /lakystʀ/ ADJ lake *(épith)*, lakeside *(épith)* ◆ **cité ~** lakeside village (on piles)

lad /lad/ NM *(Équitation)* stable-boy, stable-lad

là-dedans /lad(ə)dɑ̃/ ADV *(lit)* inside, in there ◆ **il y a du vrai ~** there's some truth in that ◆ **il n'a rien à voir ~** it's nothing to do with him ◆ **il a voulu mettre de l'argent ~** he wanted to put some money into it ◆ **quand il s'est embarqué ~** when he got involved in that *ou* in it ◆ **(il) y en a ~ !*** *(admiratif)* you see, I'm (*ou* he's *etc*) not just a pretty face! ◆ **et nous, ~, qu'est-ce qu'on devient ?*** and where do we fit into all this?

là-dessous /lad(ə)su/ ADV underneath, under there, under that ◆ **il y a quelque chose ~** *(fig)* there's something odd about it *ou* that, there's more to it than meets the eye

là-dessus /lad(ə)sy/ ADV *(= sur cet objet)* on that, on there; *(= sur ces mots)* at that point, thereupon *(frm)*; *(= à ce sujet)* about that, on that point ◆ **~, il sortit** with that, he left ◆ **vous pouvez compter ~** you can count on that ◆ **il n'y a aucun doute ~** there's no doubt about it

ladite /ladit/ ADJ → **ledit**

ladre /ladʀ/ *(littér)* ADJ *(= avare)* mean, miserly NMF miser

ladrerie /ladʀəʀi/ NF 1 *(littér = avarice)* meanness, miserliness 2 *(Hist = hôpital)* leper-house

lady /ledi/ NF *(= titre)* ◆ **Lady** Lady ◆ **c'est une vraie ~** she's a real lady

lagon /lagɔ̃/ NM lagoon

lagopède /lagɔpɛd/ NM ◆ **~ d'Écosse** (red) grouse ◆ **~ blanc** willow grouse ◆ **~ des Alpes** ptarmigan

Lagos /lagos/ N Lagos

lagunaire /lagynɛʀ/ ADJ lagoon *(épith)*, of a lagoon

lagune /lagyn/ NF lagoon

là-haut /lao/ ADV *(gén)* up there; *(= dessus)* up on top; *(= à l'étage)* upstairs; *(= au ciel)* on high, in heaven above ◆ **tout ~, au sommet de la montagne** way up there, at the top of the mountain ◆ **~ dans les nuages** above in the clouds

lai¹ /lɛ/ NM *(Poésie)* lay

lai², e¹ /lɛ/ ADJ *(Rel)* lay ◆ **frère ~** lay brother

laïc /laik/ ADJ, NM ⇒ **laïque**

laîche /lɛʃ/ NF sedge

laïcisation /laisizasjɔ̃/ NF secularization, laicization

laïciser /laisize/ ► conjug 1 ◄ VT *[+ institutions]* to secularize, to laicize

laïcité /laisite/ NF *(= caractère)* secularity; *(Pol = système)* secularism

laid, e /lɛ, lɛd/ ADJ 1 *(physiquement) [personne, visage, animal, meuble, dessin]* ugly; *[ville, région]* ugly, unattractive; *[bâtiment]* ugly, unsightly ◆ **~ comme un singe** *ou* **un pou** *ou* **un crapaud** *ou* **les sept péchés capitaux** *ou* **à faire peur** as ugly as sin ◆ **il est très ~ de visage** he's got a terribly ugly face 2 *(moralement) [action]* despicable, low; *[vice]* ugly, loathsome ◆ **c'est ~, ce que tu as fait** that was a nasty *ou* disgusting thing to do

laidement /lɛdmɑ̃/ ADV *(= sans beauté)* in an ugly way; *(littér = bassement)* despicably

laideron /lɛdʀɔ̃/ NM ugly girl *ou* woman ◆ **c'est un vrai ~** she's a real ugly duckling

laideur /lɛdœʀ/ NF 1 *(physique) [de personne, visage, animal, meuble, dessin]* ugliness; *[de ville, région]* ugliness, unattractiveness; *[de bâtiment]* ugliness, unsightliness ◆ **c'est d'une ~ !** it's so ugly! 2 *(morale) [d'action]* lowness, meanness ◆ **la guerre/l'égoïsme dans toute sa ~** the full horror of war/of selfishness, war/selfishness in all its ugliness ◆ **les ~s de la vie** the ugly side of life ◆ **les ~s de la guerre** the ugliness of war

laie² /lɛ/ NF *(= sanglier)* wild sow

laie³ /lɛ/ NF *(= sentier)* forest track *ou* path

lainage /lɛnaʒ/ NM 1 *(= vêtement)* woollen *ou* woolen *(US)* garment, woolly* ◆ **la production des ~s** the manufacture of woollens *ou* of woollen goods 2 *(= étoffe)* woollen material *ou* fabric ◆ **beau ~** fine quality woollen material

laine /lɛn/ NF wool ◆ **de ~** *[vêtement, moquette]* wool, woollen ◆ **tapis de haute ~** deep *ou* thick pile wool carpet ◆ **il faut mettre une petite ~*** *(= vêtement)* you'll need a sweater ◆ **il ne faut pas te laisser tondre** *ou* **manger la ~ sur le dos** you shouldn't let people walk all over you; → **bas²**

COMP **laine d'acier** steel wool
laine à matelas flock
laine peignée *[de pantalon, veston]* worsted wool; *[de pull]* combed wool
laine de roche rockwool
laine à tricoter knitting wool
laine de verre glass wool
laine vierge new *ou* virgin wool

laineux, -euse /lɛnø, øz/ ADJ *[tissu, plante]* woolly

lainier, -ière /lɛnje, jɛʀ/ ADJ *[industrie]* wool(len) *(épith)* NM,F *(= marchand)* wool merchant; *(= ouvrier)* wool worker

laïque /laik/ ADJ *[tribunal]* lay, civil; *[vie]* secular; *[habit]* ordinary; *[collège]* non-religious, secular ◆ **l'enseignement** *ou* **l'école ~** *(gén)* secular education; *(en France)* state education NM layman ◆ **les ~s** laymen, the laity NF laywoman

laisse /lɛs/ NF 1 *(= attache)* leash, lead ◆ **tenir en ~** *[+ chien]* to keep on a leash *ou* lead; *(fig) [+ personne]* to keep a tight rein on, to keep in check 2 *(Géog)* foreshore ◆ **~ de mer** tide mark ◆ **~ de haute/basse mer** high-/low-water mark 3 *(Poésie)* laisse

laissé-pour-compte, laissée-pour-compte (mpl **laissés-pour-compte**) /lesepuʀkɔ̃t/ ADJ 1 *(Comm) (= refusé)* rejected, returned; *(= invendu)* unsold, left over 2 *[personne]* rejected; *[chose]* rejected, discarded NM 1 *(Comm) (refusé)* reject; *(invendu)* unsold article ◆ **brader les laissés-pour-compte** to sell off old *ou* leftover stock cheaply 2 *(= personne)* **les laissés-pour-compte de la société** society's rejects ◆ **les laissés-pour-compte de la mondialisation/du progrès** those left behind by globalization/progress

laisser /lese/ GRAMMAIRE ACTIVE 36.3 ► conjug 1 ◄

VT 1 *(= abandonner) [+ place, fortune, personne, objet]* to leave ◆ **~ sa clé au voisin** to leave one's key with the neighbour, to leave the neighbour one's key ◆ **laisse-lui du gâteau** leave him some cake, leave some cake for him ◆ **il m'a laissé ce vase pour 25 €** he let me have this vase for €25 ◆ **laissez, je vais le faire/c'est moi qui paie** leave that, I'll do it/I'm paying ◆ **laisse-moi le temps d'y réfléchir** give me time to think about it ◆ **laisse-moi devant la banque** drop *ou* leave me at the bank ◆ **il a laissé un bras dans l'accident** he lost an arm in the accident ◆ **il y a laissé sa vie** it cost him his life ◆ **elle l'a laissé de meilleure humeur** she left him in a better mood ◆ **au revoir, je vous laisse** good-bye, I must leave you ◆ **laisse-moi !** leave me alone! ◆ **je l'ai laissé à son travail** *(accompagné)* I dropped him off at work; *(pour ne plus le déranger)* I left him to get on with his work

2 *(= faire demeurer) [+ trace, regrets, goût]* to leave ◆ **~ qn indifférent/dans le doute** to leave sb unmoved/in doubt ◆ **~ qn debout** to keep sb standing (up) ◆ **on lui a laissé ses illusions, on l'a laissé à ses illusions** we didn't disillusion him ◆ **elle m'a laissé une bonne impression** she made a good impression on me ◆ **on l'a laissé dans l'erreur** we didn't tell him that he was mistaken ◆ **il vaut mieux le ~ dans l'ignorance de nos projets** it is best to leave him in the dark *ou* not to tell him about our plans ◆ **~ un enfant à ses parents** *(gén)* to leave a child with his parents; *(Jur)* to leave a child in the custody of his parents ◆ **vous laissez le village sur votre droite** you go past the village on your right ◆ **~ la vie à qn** to spare sb's life

3 *(locutions)* **~ la porte ouverte** *(lit, fig)* to leave the door open ◆ **~ le meilleur pour la fin** to leave the best till last ◆ **je te laisse à penser combien il était content** you can imagine *ou* I don't need to tell you how pleased he was; → **champ¹, désirer, plan¹**

4 *(littér = manquer)* **il n'a pas laissé de me le dire** he didn't fail to tell me, he could not refrain from telling me ◆ **cela n'a pas laissé de me surprendre** I couldn't fail to be surprised by *ou* at that ◆ **cela ne laisse pas d'être vrai** it is true nonetheless

VB AUX ◆ **~ (qn) faire qch** to let sb do sth ◆ **laisse-le partir** let him go ◆ **laisse-le monter/descendre** let him come *ou* go up/down ◆ **laissez-moi rire !** *(iro)* don't make me laugh! ◆ **~ voir** *(= révéler)* to show, to reveal ◆ **il a laissé voir sa déception** he couldn't help showing his disappointment ◆ **~ voir ses sentiments** to let one's feelings show ◆ **il n'en a rien laissé voir** he showed no sign of it, he gave no inkling of it ◆ **laisse-le faire** *(sans l'aider)* let him do it himself; *(à sa manière)* let him do it his own way; *(ce qui lui plaît)* let him do as he likes *ou* wants ◆ **il faut ~ faire le temps** we must let things take their course ◆ **laisse faire !** never mind!, don't bother! ◆ **j'ai été attaqué dans la rue et les gens ont laissé faire** I was attacked in the street and people did nothing *ou* people just stood by ◆ **on ne va pas le ~ faire sans réagir !** we're not going to let him get away with that!; → **courir, penser, tomber¹**

VPR **se laisser** ◆ **se ~ persuader/exploiter/duper** to let o.s. be persuaded/exploited/fooled ◆ **il ne faut pas se ~ décourager/abattre** you mustn't let yourself become *ou* allow yourself to become discouraged/downhearted ◆ **je me suis laissé surprendre par la pluie** I got caught in the rain ◆ **ce petit vin se laisse boire*** this wine goes down well *ou* nicely ◆ **se ~ aller** to let o.s. go ◆ **se ~ aller à mentir** to stoop to telling lies ◆ **je me suis laissé faire** I let myself be persuaded, I let myself be talked into it ◆ **je n'ai pas l'intention de me ~ faire** I'm not going to let myself be pushed around ◆ **laisse-toi faire !** *(à qn que l'on soigne)* come on, it won't hurt (you)!; *(à qn que l'on habille)* let me do it; *(en offrant une liqueur etc)* go on, be a devil!* ◆ **laisse-toi faire, je vais te peigner** just let me comb your hair, keep still while I comb your hair ◆ **et tu t'es laissé faire sans protester ?** and you just let them do it without saying anything?; → **conter, dire, vivre¹**

laisser-aller /leseale/ NM INV *(gén)* casualness, carelessness; *[de travail, langage, vêtements]* sloppiness, carelessness ◆ **il y a beaucoup de ~**

dans ce service things are very lax in this department, this department is very slack

laisser-faire /lesefɛʀ/ NM INV *(Écon)* laissez-faire (policy *ou* economics *(sg)*), non-interventionism

laissez-passer /lesepɑse/ NM INV *(gén)* pass; *(Douane)* transire

lait /lɛ/ NM 1 *(animal)* milk ◆ **~ de vache/de chèvre/d'ânesse** cow's/goat's/ass's milk ◆ **~ concentré sucré/non sucré** condensed/evaporated milk ◆ **~ écrémé** skimmed milk ◆ **~ entier** whole *ou* full cream *(Brit)* milk ◆ **~ cru** unpasteurized milk ◆ **mettre qn au ~** to put sb on a milk diet ◆ **boire du (petit) ~** *(fig)* to lap it up ◆ **cela se boit comme du petit ~** you don't notice you're drinking it ◆ **frère/sœur de ~** foster brother/sister; → **café, chocolat, cochon, dent**

2 *(végétal)* milk ◆ **~ d'amande/de coco/de soja** almond/coconut/soy(a) milk

3 *(Cosmétique)* lotion ◆ **~ de beauté** beauty lotion ◆ **~ démaquillant** cleansing milk ◆ **~ solaire** sun lotion

COMP **lait caillé** curds
lait de chaux lime water
lait de croissance vitamin-enriched milk *(for babies and young children)*
lait fraise strawberry-flavoured milk
lait maternel mother's milk, breast milk
lait maternisé formula, baby milk *(Brit)*
lait en poudre dried *ou* powdered milk
lait de poule *(Culin)* eggflip, eggnog
lait végétal latex

laitage /lɛtaʒ/ NM (= *produit laitier*) dairy product

laitance /lɛtɑ̃s/ NF soft roe

laiterie /lɛtʀi/ NF (= *usine, magasin*) dairy; (= *industrie*) dairy industry

laiteux, -euse /lɛtø, øz/ ADJ *[couleur, liquide, peau, huître]* milky; *[teint]* milky(-white), creamy; *[lumière]* pearly; *[chair]* creamy

laitier, -ière /letje, jɛʀ/ ADJ *[industrie, produit]* dairy *(épith)*; *[production, vache]* milk *(épith)*, dairy *(épith)* NM 1 (= *livreur*) milkman; (= *vendeur*) dairyman ◆ **à l'heure du ~** at the crack of dawn, in the early hours 2 (= *scorie*) slag NF **laitière** (= *vendeuse*) dairywoman; (= *livreuse*) milkwoman; (= *vache*) dairy *ou* milk cow ◆ **une bonne laitière** a good milker

laiton /lɛtɔ̃/ NM (= *alliage*) brass; (= *fil*) brass wire

laitue /lety/ NF lettuce ◆ **~ de mer** sea lettuce

laïus * /lajys/ NM INV (= *discours*) long-winded speech; (= *verbiage*) verbiage *(NonC)*, padding *(NonC)* ◆ **faire un ~** to hold forth at great length, to give a long-winded speech

laïusser * /lajyse/ ▸ conjug 1 ◂ VI to expatiate, to hold forth, to spout * *(sur* on)

lama /lama/ NM 1 (= *animal*) llama; 2 (= *moine*) lama

lamaïsme /lamaism/ NM Lamaism

lamaïste /lamaist/ ADJ, NM,F Lamaist

lamantin /lamɑ̃tɛ̃/ NM manatee

lamarckien, -ienne /lamaʀkjɛ̃, jɛn/ ADJ *(Bio)* Lamarckian

lamaserie /lamazʀi/ NF lamasery

lambada /lɑ̃bada/ NF lambada

lambda /lɑ̃bda/ NM (= *lettre*) lambda ADJ INV (= *quelconque*) *[spectateur, lecteur]* average ◆ **le citoyen ~** the average citizen, the man in the street

lambeau (pl **lambeaux**) /lɑ̃bo/ NM *[de papier, tissu]* scrap ◆ **~x de chair** strips of flesh ◆ **en ~x** *[vêtements]* in tatters *ou* rags, tattered; *[affiche]* in tatters, tattered ◆ **mettre en ~x** to tear to shreds *ou* bits ◆ **tomber** *ou* **partir en ~x** to fall to pieces *ou* bits ◆ **~x de conversation** scraps of conversation ◆ **~x du passé** fragments *ou* remnants of the past

lambic(k) /lɑ̃bik/ NM *kind of strong Belgian beer;* → **gueuse**

lambin, e * /lɑ̃bɛ̃, in/ ADJ slow ◆ **que tu es ~ !** you're such a dawdler! *ou* slowcoach * *(Brit) ou* slowpoke! * *(US)* NM,F dawdler *, slowcoach * *(Brit)*, slowpoke * *(US)*

lambiner * /lɑ̃bine/ ▸ conjug 1 ◂ VI to dawdle

lambourde /lɑ̃buʀd/ NF *(pour parquet)* backing strip *(on joists)*; *(pour solive)* wall-plate

lambrequin /lɑ̃bʀəkɛ̃/ NM *[de fenêtre]* pelmet, lambrequin; *[de ciel de lit]* valance; (= *ornement*) lambrequin ◆ **~s** *(Hér)* lambrequin, mantling

lambris /lɑ̃bʀi/ NM *(en bois)* panelling *(NonC)*, wainscoting *(NonC)*; *(en marbre)* marble wall panels ◆ **sous les ~ dorés des ministères** *(fig)* in the corridors of power

lambrisser /lɑ̃bʀise/ ▸ conjug 1 ◂ VT *(avec du bois)* to panel, to wainscot; *(avec du marbre)* to panel ◆ **lambrissé de pin** pine-panelled

lame /lam/ NF 1 *[de métal, verre]* strip; *[de bois]* strip, lath; *(Aut) [de ressort]* leaf; *[de store]* slat; *(pour microscope)* slide 2 *[de couteau, tondeuse, scie]* blade ◆ **visage en ~ de couteau** hatchet face 3 *(fig)* (= *épée*) sword ◆ **une bonne** *ou* **fine ~** (= *escrimeur*) good swordsman (*ou* swordswoman) 4 (= *vague*) wave 5 (= *partie de la langue*) blade

COMP **lame de fond** *(lit)* ground swell *(NonC)*; *(fig)* tidal wave ◆ **c'est une véritable ~ de fond qui l'a porté au pouvoir** he came to power following a landslide victory
lame de parquet floorboard, strip of parquet flooring
lame de rasoir razor blade

lamé, e /lame/ ADJ lamé *(épith)* ◆ **robe ~e (d')or** gold lamé dress NM lamé

lamelle /lamɛl/ NF *(de métal, plastique)* (small) strip; *[de persiennes]* slat; *[de champignon]* gill; *(pour microscope)* coverglass ◆ **~ de mica** mica flake ◆ **couper en ~s** *[+ légumes]* to cut into thin strips *ou* slices

lamellé-collé (pl **lamellés-collés**) /lamelekɔle/ NM glued laminated timber

lamellibranche /lamelibʀɑ̃ʃ/ NM bivalve, lamellibranch ◆ **les ~s** lamellibranchia

lamentable /lamɑ̃tabl/ ADJ 1 (= *mauvais*) *[conditions, résultat, état, comportement]* appalling, lamentable, awful; *[concurrent, spectacle]* appalling, awful ◆ **cette émission est ~ !** what a pathetic * programme! 2 (= *tragique*) *[sort]* miserable, pitiful; *[histoire]* dreadful, appalling

lamentablement /lamɑ̃tabləmɑ̃/ ADV *[échouer]* miserably, lamentably ◆ **il se traînait ~ dans la maison** he was moping around the house

lamentation /lamɑ̃tasjɔ̃/ NF (= *cri de désolation*) lamentation, wailing *(NonC)*; *(péj* = *jérémiades)* moaning *(NonC)* ◆ **le livre des Lamentations** *(Bible)* (the Book of) Lamentations; → **mur**

lamenter (se) /lamɑ̃te/ ▸ conjug 1 ◂ VPR to moan, to lament ◆ **se ~ sur qch** to moan over sth, to bemoan sth ◆ **se ~ sur son sort** to bemoan *ou* bewail *ou* lament one's fate ◆ **arrête de te ~ sur ton propre sort** stop feeling sorry for yourself ◆ **il se lamente d'avoir échoué** he is bemoaning his failure

lamento /lamento/ NM lament

laminage /laminaʒ/ NM *(Tech)* lamination

laminaire /laminɛʀ/ NF (= *algue*) laminaria

laminer /lamine/ ▸ conjug 1 ◂ VT 1 *[+ métal]* to laminate ◆ **laminé à chaud/à froid** hot-/cold-rolled 2 (= *détruire*) **ses marges bénéficiaires ont été laminées par les hausses de prix** his profit margins have been eaten away *ou* eroded by price rises ◆ **les petites formations politiques ont été laminées aux dernières élections** small political groupings were practically wiped out in the last election ◆ **ils les ont laminés** * *[équipe]* they wiped the floor with them *

lamineur, -euse /laminœʀ, øz/ ADJ M ◆ **cylindre ~** roller NM,F rolling mill operator

laminoir /laminwaʀ/ NM rolling mill ◆ **passer au ~** *(fig)* to steamroller

lampadaire /lɑ̃padɛʀ/ NM *[d'intérieur]* standard lamp; *[de rue]* street lamp ◆ **(pied de) ~** *[d'intérieur]* lamp standard; *[de rue]* lamppost

lampant /lɑ̃pɑ̃/ ADJ M → **pétrole**

lamparo /lɑ̃paʀo/ NM lamp ◆ **pêche au ~** fishing by lamplight *(in the Mediterranean)*

lampe /lɑ̃p/ NF lamp, light; (= *ampoule*) bulb; *(Radio)* valve ◆ **éclairé par une ~** lit by lamplight; → **mettre**

COMP **lampe à acétylène** acetylene lamp *(Brit) ou* torch *(US)*
lampe à alcool spirit lamp
lampe à arc arc light *ou* lamp
lampe d'architecte Anglepoise lamp ®
lampe Berger ® Berger lamp ®
lampe à bronzer sun lamp
lampe de bureau desk lamp *ou* light
lampe de chevet bedside lamp *ou* light
lampe électrique flashlight, torch *(Brit)*
lampe à huile oil lamp
lampe à incandescence incandescent lamp
lampe de lecture reading lamp
lampe de mineur (miner's) safety lamp
lampe au néon neon light
lampe à pétrole paraffin *(Brit) ou* kerosene *(US) ou* oil lamp
lampe pigeon (small) oil *ou* paraffin *(Brit) ou* kerosene *(US)* lamp
lampe de poche flashlight, torch *(Brit)*
lampe à sodium sodium light
lampe solaire sun lamp
lampe à souder *(lit)* blowtorch, blowlamp *(Brit)*; *(arg Mil)* machine gun
lampe de table table lamp
lampe témoin *(gén)* warning light; *[de magnétoscope etc]* (indicator) light
lampe à ultraviolets ultraviolet lamp; → **halogène**

lampée * /lɑ̃pe/ NF gulp, swig * ◆ **boire qch à grandes ~s** to gulp *ou* swig * sth down

lamper * † /lɑ̃pe/ ▸ conjug 1 ◂ VT to gulp down, to swig (down) *

lampe-tempête (pl **lampes-tempête**) /lɑ̃ptɑ̃pɛt/ NF storm lantern, hurricane lamp

lampion /lɑ̃pjɔ̃/ NM Chinese lantern; → **air³**

lampiste /lɑ̃pist/ NM *(lit)* light (maintenance) man; (*, *hum* = *subalterne)* underling, dogsbody * *(Brit)* ◆ **c'est toujours la faute du ~** * it's always the underling who gets the blame

lamproie /lɑ̃pʀwa/ NF ◆ **~ (de mer)** lamprey ◆ **~ de rivière** river lamprey, lampern

Lancastre /lɑ̃kastʀ(ə)/ N Lancaster

lance /lɑ̃s/ NF 1 (= *arme*) spear; *[de tournoi]* lance ◆ **frapper qn d'un coup de ~** to hit sb with one's lance; → **fer, rompre** 2 (= *tuyau*) **~ (à eau)** hose ◆ **~ d'arrosage** garden hose ◆ **~ d'incendie** fire hose

lance-bombes /lɑ̃sbɔ̃b/ NM INV bomb launcher

lancée /lɑ̃se/ NF ◆ **être sur sa ~** to have got started ◆ **continuer sur sa ~** to keep going ◆ **il a encore travaillé trois heures sur sa ~** once he was under way *ou* he'd got going he worked for another three hours ◆ **je peux encore courir deux kilomètres sur ma ~** now I'm in my stride I can run another two kilometres ◆ **je ne voulais pas t'interrompre sur ta ~** I didn't want to interrupt you in full flow

lance-engins /lɑ̃sɑ̃ʒɛ̃/ NM INV missile launcher ◆ **sous-marin nucléaire ~** nuclear missile submarine

lance-flammes /lɑ̃sflɑm/ NM INV flamethrower

lance-fusées /lɑ̃sfyze/ NM INV *(Mil)* rocket launcher; *[de fusée éclairante]* flare gun

lance-grenades /lɑ̃sgʀənad/ NM INV grenade launcher ◆ **fusil** ~ shoulder-held grenade launcher

lancement /lɑ̃smɑ̃/ NM 1 *[d'entreprise]* launching, starting up; *[de campagne]* launching; *[de fusée]* launching, launch; *[de processus]* starting (off); *[de produit]* launching; *[d'emprunt]* issuing, floating ◆ **lors du ~ du nouveau produit** when the new product was launched ◆ **fenêtre** *ou* **créneau de ~** launch window 2 *(Sport)* throwing ◆ **~ du disque/javelot/marteau** throwing the discus/javelin/hammer, discus/javelin/hammer throwing ◆ **~ du poids** putting the shot, shot put

lance-missiles /lɑ̃smisil/ NM INV missile launcher ◆ **sous-marin ~** ballistic missile submarine

lancéolé, e /lɑ̃seɔle/ ADJ *(Bot)* lanceolate; *(Archit)* lanceted

lance-pierre (pl **lance-pierres**) /lɑ̃spjɛʀ/ NM catapult ◆ **manger avec un ~** * to grab a quick bite (to eat) * ◆ **payer qn avec un ~** * to pay sb peanuts *

lancer¹ /lɑ̃se/ ▸ conjug 3 ◂ VT 1 *(= jeter) (gén)* to throw; *(violemment)* to hurl, to fling; *(Sport) [+ disque, marteau, javelot]* to throw ◆ **~ qch à qn** *(pour qu'il l'attrape)* to throw sth to sb, to throw sb sth; *(agressivement)* to throw sth at sb ◆ **lance-moi mes clés** throw me my keys ◆ **~ une balle/son chapeau en l'air** to throw *ou* toss a ball/one's hat into the air *ou* up in the air ◆ **~ sa ligne** *(Pêche)* to cast one's line ◆ **il lança sa voiture dans la foule** he drove his car straight at the crowd ◆ **~ son chien contre qn** to set one's dog on sb ◆ **~ ses hommes contre l'ennemi/à l'assaut** *(Mil)* to launch one's men against the enemy/into the assault ◆ **lance ta jambe en avant** kick your leg up ◆ **~ un coup de poing** to throw a punch, to lash out with one's fist ◆ **~ un coup de pied** to kick out, to lash out with one's foot ◆ **~ le poids** *(Sport)* to put the shot ◆ **il lance à 15 mètres** he can throw 15 metres ◆ **~ un pont sur une rivière** *(fig)* to throw a bridge across a river ◆ **la cathédrale lance sa flèche de pierre vers le ciel** the stone spire of the cathedral thrusts up into the sky

2 *(= projeter) [+ flèche, obus]* to fire; *[+ bombe]* to drop; *[+ torpille]* to fire, to launch; *[+ fumée]* to send up *ou* out; *[+ flammes, lave]* to throw out ◆ **~ des éclairs** *[bijoux]* to sparkle ◆ **ses yeux lançaient des éclairs** *(de colère)* his eyes blazed *ou* flashed with anger; → **étincelle**

3 *(= émettre) [+ accusations]* to level, to hurl; *[+ menaces, injures]* to hurl; *[+ avertissement, proclamation, mandat d'arrêt]* to issue, to put out; *[+ théorie]* to put forward, to advance; *[+ appel]* to launch; *[+ SOS, signal]* to send out; *[+ fausse nouvelle, rumeur]* to put out; *[+ invitation]* to send off ◆ **~ un cri** to cry out ◆ **~ une plaisanterie** to crack a joke ◆ **elle lui lança un coup d'œil furieux** she flashed *ou* darted a furious glance at him ◆ **"je refuse" lança-t-il fièrement** "I refuse," he retorted proudly ◆ **"salut" me lança-t-il du fond de la salle** "hello," he called out to me from the far end of the room

4 *(= faire démarrer) [+ fusée, satellite, navire]* to launch; *[+ affaire, entreprise]* to launch, to start up; *[+ attaque, campagne électorale]* to launch; *[+ processus]* to start (off); *[+ emprunt]* to issue, to float; *[+ projet]* to launch; *(Ordin) [+ programme, recherche]* to start ◆ **~ une application** to launch an application ◆ **~ une impression** to print ◆ **~ une souscription** to start a fund ◆ **~ une discussion** to get a discussion going, to start a discussion ◆ **c'est lui qui a lancé l'idée du voyage** he's the one who came up with the idea of the trip ◆ **on a lancé quelques idées** we floated a few ideas ◆ **il a lancé son parti dans une aventure dangereuse** he has launched his party into *ou* set his party off on a dangerous venture ◆ **ne le lancez pas sur son sujet favori** don't set him off on *ou* don't let him get launched on his pet subject ◆ **une fois lancé, on ne peut plus l'arrêter !** once he gets the bit between his teeth *ou* once he gets warmed up there's no stopping him!

5 *(= faire connaître ou adopter) [+ vedette]* to launch; *[+ produit]* to launch, to bring out ◆ **~ une nouvelle mode** to launch *ou* start a new fashion ◆ **~ qn dans la politique/les affaires/le monde** to launch sb into politics/in business/in society ◆ **c'est ce film qui l'a lancé** it was this film that launched his career ◆ **il est lancé maintenant** he has made a name for himself *ou* has made his mark now

6 *(= donner de l'élan) [+ moteur]* to open up; *[+ voiture]* to get up to speed; *[+ balançoire]* to set going ◆ **~ un cheval** to give a horse its head ◆ **~ le balancier d'une horloge** to set the pendulum in a clock going ◆ **la moto était lancée à 140 quand elle l'a heurté** the motorbike had reached *ou* had got up to a speed of 140 km/h when it hit him ◆ **une fois lancée, la voiture ...** once the car gets up speed *ou* builds up speed, it ...

7 *(= faire mal à)* **ça me lance (dans le bras** *etc***)** I've got shooting pains (in my arm *etc*)

VPR **se lancer** 1 *(mutuellement) [+ balle]* to throw to each other; *[+ injures, accusations]* to hurl at each other, to exchange ◆ **ils n'arrêtent pas de se ~ des plaisanteries** they're always cracking jokes together

2 *(= sauter)* to leap, to jump; *(= se précipiter)* to dash, to rush ◆ **se ~ dans le vide** to leap *ou* jump into space ◆ **il faut sauter, n'hésite pas, lance-toi !** you've got to jump, don't hesitate, just do it! *ou* let yourself go! ◆ **se ~ contre un obstacle** to dash *ou* rush at an obstacle ◆ **se ~ en avant** to dash *ou* rush *ou* run forward ◆ **se ~ à l'assaut** to leap to the attack ◆ **se ~ à l'assaut d'une forteresse** to launch an attack on a fortress ◆ **chaque week-end, des milliers de voitures se lancent sur les routes** thousands of cars take to *ou* pour onto the roads every weekend

3 *(= s'engager)* **se ~ à la recherche de qn/qch** to go off in search of sb/sth ◆ **il s'est lancé à la recherche d'un emploi** he started looking for a job ◆ **l'entreprise se lance sur le marché** the company is entering the market ◆ **il construit un bateau – dis donc, il se lance !** * he's building a boat – wow, he's aiming high! *ou* he's thinking big! * ◆ **elle n'attend que toi ! vas-y, lance-toi !** * it's you she wants! go for it! * ◆ **se ~ dans** *[+ aventure]* to embark on, to set off on; *[+ discussion]* to launch into, to embark on; *[+ dépenses]* to embark on, to take on; *[+ métier]* to go into, to take up; *[+ travaux, grève]* to embark on, to start; *[+ passe-temps]* to take up; *[+ bataille]* to pitch into ◆ **se ~ dans la politique/les affaires** to go into politics/business ◆ **se ~ dans la course au pouvoir/à l'audience** to enter the race for power/the ratings battle ◆ **ils se sont lancés dans des opérations financières hasardeuses** they got involved in some risky financial deals ◆ **se ~ dans la lecture d'un roman** to set about *ou* begin reading a novel ◆ **se ~ dans la production/fabrication de qch** to start producing/manufacturing sth

4 *(* = se faire une réputation)* **il cherche à se ~** he's trying to make a name for himself

lancer² /lɑ̃se/ NM 1 *(Sport)* throw ◆ **il a droit à trois ~s** he is allowed three attempts *ou* throws ◆ **~ annulé** no throw ◆ **~ franc** *(Basket)* free throw, charity toss *(US)* ◆ **~ de corde** *(Alpinisme)* lassoing *(NonC)*, lasso ◆ **le ~ du disque/du javelot/du marteau** the discus/javelin/hammer ◆ **le ~ du poids** putting the shot, the shot put 2 *(Pêche)* **(pêche au) ~** casting ◆ **~ léger** spinning ◆ **~ lourd** bait-casting

lance-roquettes /lɑ̃sʀɔkɛt/ NM INV rocket launcher

lance-satellites /lɑ̃satelit/ NM INV satellite launcher

lance-torpilles /lɑ̃stɔʀpij/ NM INV torpedo tube

lancette /lɑ̃sɛt/ NF *(Archit, Méd)* lancet

lanceur, -euse /lɑ̃sœʀ, øz/ NM,F 1 *[de disque, javelot, marteau, pierres]* thrower; *(Cricket)* bowler; *(Base-ball)* pitcher ◆ **~ de poids** shot putter ◆ **~ de couteau** *(au cirque)* knife thrower ◆ **~ de pierre** stone-thrower 2 ◆ **~ de mode** trendsetter ◆ **le ~ du produit** the company which launched the product NM *(Espace, Mil)* launcher ◆ **~ d'engins/de satellites** missile/satellite launcher

lancier /lɑ̃sje/ NM *(Mil)* lancer ◆ **les ~s** *(= danse)* the lancers

lancinant, e /lɑ̃sinɑ̃, ɑ̃t/ ADJ 1 *[douleur]* shooting *(épith)*, piercing *(épith)* 2 *(= obsédant) [souvenir]* haunting; *[musique]* insistent, monotonous; *[problème, question]* nagging ◆ **ce que tu peux être ~ à toujours réclamer** * you are a real pain * *ou* you get on my nerves the way you're always asking for things

lanciner /lɑ̃sine/ ▸ conjug 1 ◂ VI to throb VT *[pensée]* to obsess, to haunt, to plague ◆ **il nous a lancinés pendant trois jours pour aller au cirque** * *[enfant]* he tormented *ou* plagued us *ou* he went on at us * for three days about going to the circus

lançon /lɑ̃sɔ̃/ NM sand-eel

landais, e /lɑ̃dɛ, ɛz/ ADJ of *ou* from the Landes region

landau /lɑ̃do/ NM *(= voiture d'enfant)* pram *(Brit)*, baby carriage *(US)*; *(= carrosse)* landau

lande /lɑ̃d/ NF moor, heath NFPL **Landes** ◆ **les Landes** the Landes (region) *(south-west France)*

Landern(e)au /lɑ̃dɛʀno/ NM *(hum)* ◆ **dans le ~ littéraire/universitaire** in the literary/academic fraternity

landgrave /lɑ̃dgʀav/ NM *(Hist)* landgrave

langage /lɑ̃gaʒ/ NM 1 *(Ling, gén)* language ◆ **le ~ de l'amour/des fleurs** the language of love/of flowers ◆ **en ~ administratif/technique** in administrative/technical language ◆ **je n'aime pas que l'on me tienne ce ~** I don't like being spoken to like that ◆ **il m'a tenu un drôle de ~** he said some odd things to me ◆ **quel ~ me tenez-vous là ?** what do you mean by that? ◆ **il m'a parlé avec** *ou* **il m'a tenu le ~ de la raison** he spoke to me with the voice of reason ◆ **tenir un double ~** to use double talk ◆ **il a dû changer de ~** he had to change his tune

2 *(Ordin)* language ◆ **~ évolué/naturel** high-level/natural language ◆ **~ de haut/bas niveau** high-/low-level language ◆ **~ de programmation** programming language

COMP **le langage des animaux** the language of animals
langage argotique slang
langage chiffré cipher, code (language)
langage courant everyday language
langage enfantin childish *ou* children's language; *[de bébé]* baby talk
langage intérieur *(Philos)* inner language
langage machine *(Ordin)* machine language
langage parlé spoken language, speech
langage populaire popular speech

langagier, -ière /lɑ̃gaʒje, jɛʀ/ ADJ linguistic, of language *(épith)* NM,F *(Can)* linguist

lange /lɑ̃ʒ/ NM (baby's) flannel blanket ◆ **~s** swaddling clothes ◆ **dans les ~s** *(fig)* in (its) infancy

langer /lɑ̃ʒe/ ▸ conjug 3 ◂ VT ◆ **~ un bébé** *(= lui mettre une couche)* to change a baby, to change the nappy *(Brit)* *ou* diaper *(US)*; *(= l'emmailloter)* to wrap a baby in swaddling clothes ◆ **table/matelas à** ~ changing table/mat

langoureusement /lɑ̃guʀøzmɑ̃/ ADV languorously

langoureux, -euse /lɑ̃guʀø, øz/ ADJ languorous

langouste /lɑ̃gust/ NF spiny *ou* rock lobster, crayfish, crawfish; *(Culin)* lobster

langoustier /lɑ̃gustje/ NM *(= filet)* crayfish net; *(= bateau)* fishing boat *(for crayfish)*

langoustine /lɑ̃gustin/ NF langoustine, Dublin bay prawn

langue /lɑ̃g/ NF 1 *(Anat)* tongue ◆ ~ **de bœuf/veau** ox/veal tongue ◆ **avoir la** ~ **blanche** *ou* **chargée** *ou* **pâteuse** to have a coated *ou* furred tongue ◆ **tirer la** ~ *(au médecin)* to stick out *ou* put out one's tongue *(à qn* for sb); *(par impolitesse)* to stick out *ou* put out one's tongue *(à qn* at sb); *(= être dans le besoin)* to have a rough time of it*; *(* = être frustré)* to be green with envy ◆ **il tirait la** ~* *(= avoir soif)* his tongue was hanging out*, he was dying of thirst* ◆ **coup de** ~ lick ◆ **le chien lui a donné un coup de** ~ the dog licked him

2 *(= organe de la parole)* tongue ◆ **avoir la** ~ **déliée** *ou* **bien pendue** to be a bit of a gossip, to have a ready tongue ◆ **avoir la** ~ **bien affilée** to have a quick *ou* sharp tongue ◆ **avoir la** ~ **fourchue** *(hum)* to speak with a forked tongue ◆ **il a la** ~ **trop longue, il ne sait pas tenir sa** ~ he can't hold his tongue, he doesn't know when to hold his tongue ◆ **il n'a pas la** ~ **dans sa poche** he's never at a loss for words ◆ **tu as avalé** *ou* **perdu ta** ~ **?** has the cat got your tongue?, have you lost your tongue? ◆ **tu as retrouvé ta** ~ **?** so we're talking again, are we? ◆ **délier** *ou* **dénouer la** ~ **à qn** to loosen sb's tongue ◆ **donner sa** ~ **au chat** to give in *ou* up ◆ **j'ai le mot sur (le bout de) la** ~ the word is on the tip of my tongue ◆ **il faut tourner sept fois sa** ~ **dans sa bouche avant de parler** you should count to ten before you say anything ◆ **prendre** ~ **avec qn** † to make contact with sb ◆ **les** ~**s vont aller bon train** *(hum)* tongues will start wagging *ou* will wag

3 *(= personne)* **mauvaise** *ou* **méchante** ~ spiteful *ou* malicious gossip ◆ **je ne voudrais pas être mauvaise** ~ **mais ...** I don't want to tittle-tattle *ou* to spread scandal but ... ◆ **les bonnes** ~**s diront que ...** *(iro)* worthy *ou* upright folk will say that ...

4 *(Ling)* language, tongue *(frm)* ◆ **la** ~ **française/anglaise** the French/English language ◆ **les gens de** ~ **anglaise/française** English-speaking/French-speaking people ◆ ~ **maternelle** mother tongue ◆ ~ **mère** parent language ◆ ~ **vivante/morte/étrangère** living/dead/foreign language ◆ **j'ai choisi allemand en** ~ **vivante I/II** I'm taking German as my first/second foreign language ◆ ~ **officielle** official language ◆ ~ **écrite/parlée** written/spoken language ◆ ~ **source** *ou* **de départ/cible** *ou* **d'arrivée** *(en traduction)* source/target language ◆ ~ **vernaculaire** vernacular (language) ◆ **la** ~ **de Shakespeare** *(gén)* Shakespearian language, the language of Shakespeare; *(= l'anglais)* English, the language of Shakespeare ◆ **il parle une** ~ **très pure** his use of the language is very pure, his spoken language is very pure ◆ **nous ne parlons pas la même** ~ *(lit, fig)* we don't speak the same language

5 *(Géog)* ~ **glaciaire** spur of ice ◆ ~ **de terre** strip *ou* spit of land

COMP **la langue du barreau** legal parlance, the language of the courts

langue de bois *(péj)* waffle*, cant

la langue diplomatique the language of diplomacy

langue de feu tongue of fire

la langue journalistique journalistic language, journalese *(péj)*

langue d'oc langue d'oc

langue d'oïl langue d'oïl

langue populaire *(idiome)* popular language; *(usage)* popular speech

langue de serpent *(= plante)* adder's tongue, ophioglossum *(SPÉC)*

langue de spécialité specialist language

langue de travail working language

langue verte slang

langue de vipère spiteful gossip ◆ **elle a une** ~ **de vipère** she's got a vicious *ou* venomous tongue

langue-de-bœuf (pl **langues-de-bœuf**) /lɑ̃gdəbœf/ NF *(= champignon)* beefsteak fungus

langue-de-chat (pl **langues-de-chat**) /lɑ̃gdəʃa/ NF (flat) finger biscuit, langue de chat

languette /lɑ̃gɛt/ NF *[de bois, cuir]* tongue; *[de papier]* (narrow) strip; *[d'orgue]* languet(te), languid; *[d'instrument à vent]* metal reed; *[de balance]* pointer

langueur /lɑ̃gœʀ/ NF *[de personne]* languidness, languor; *[de style]* languidness ◆ **regard plein de** ~ languid *ou* languishing look; → **maladie**

languide /lɑ̃gid/ ADJ *(littér)* languid, languishing

languir /lɑ̃giʀ/ ► conjug 2 ◄ VI 1 *(= dépérir)* to languish ◆ ~ **dans l'oisiveté/d'ennui** to languish in idleness/in boredom ◆ **(se)** ~ **d'amour pour qn** to be languishing with love for sb 2 *[conversation, intrigue]* to flag; *[affaires]* to be slack 3 *(littér = désirer)* ~ **après qn/qch** to languish for *ou* pine for sb/sth 4 *(= attendre)* to wait, to hang around* ◆ **je ne languirai pas longtemps ici** I'm not going to hang around here for long* ◆ **faire** ~ **qn** to keep sb waiting ◆ **ne nous fais pas** ~**, raconte !** don't keep us in suspense, tell us about it!

languissamment /lɑ̃gisamɑ̃/ ADV *(littér)* languidly

languissant, e /lɑ̃gisɑ̃, ɑt/ ADJ *[personne]* languid, listless; *[regard]* languishing *(épith)*; *[conversation, industrie]* flagging *(épith)*; *[récit, action]* dull; *[activité économique]* slack

lanière /lanjɛʀ/ NF *[de cuir]* thong, strap; *[d'étoffe]* strip; *[de fouet]* lash; *[d'appareil photo]* strap ◆ **sandales à** ~**s** strappy sandals ◆ **découper qch en** ~**s** *(Culin)* to cut sth into strips

lanoline /lanɔlin/ NF lanolin

lansquenet /lɑ̃skənɛ/ NM *(Cartes, Hist)* lansquenet

lanterne /lɑ̃tɛʀn/ NF *(gén)* lantern; *(électrique)* lamp, light; *(Hist = réverbère)* street lamp; *(Archit)* lantern ◆ **allumer ses** ~**s** † *(en voiture)* to switch on one's (side)lights ◆ **éclairer la** ~ **de qn** *(fig)* to enlighten sb ◆ **les aristocrates à la** ~ **!** string up the aristocracy!; → **vessie**

COMP **lanterne d'Aristote** Aristotle's lantern

lanterne arrière † *[de voiture]* rear light

lanterne de bicyclette bicycle lamp

lanterne magique magic lantern

lanterne de projection slide projector

lanterne rouge *[de convoi]* rear *ou* tail light; *[de maison close]* red light ◆ **être la** ~ **rouge** *(fig = être le dernier)* to lag behind

lanterne sourde dark lantern

lanterne vénitienne paper lantern, Chinese lantern

lanterneau (pl **lanterneaux**) /lɑ̃tɛʀno/ NM *[de coupole]* lantern; *[d'escalier, atelier]* skylight

lanterner /lɑ̃tɛʀne/ ► conjug 1 ◄ VI *(= traîner)* to dawdle ◆ **sans** ~ straight away ◆ **faire** ~ **qn** to keep sb waiting around *ou* hanging about *(Brit)*

lanternon /lɑ̃tɛʀnɔ̃/ NM ⇒ **lanterneau**

lanthane /lɑ̃tan/ NM lanthanum

Laos /laɔs/ NM Laos

laotien, -ienne /laɔsjɛ̃, jɛn/ ADJ Laotian NM *(= langue)* Laotian NM,F **Laotien(ne)** Laotian

Lao-Tseu /laɔtsø/ NM Lao-tze

La Palice /lapalis/ N ◆ **c'est une vérité de** ~ it's stating the obvious, it's a truism ◆ **avant d'être en panne, cette machine marchait –** ~ **n'aurait pas dit mieux !** *(hum)* this machine worked before it broke down – well, that's very observant of you! *(hum)*

lapalissade /lapalisad/ NF statement of the obvious ◆ **c'est une** ~ **de dire que ...** it's stating the obvious to say that ...

laparoscopie /lapaʀɔskɔpi/ NF laparoscopy

laparotomie /lapaʀɔtɔmi/ NF laparotomy

La Paz /lapaz/ N La Paz

lapement /lapmɑ̃/ NM *(= bruit, action)* lapping *(NonC)*; *(= gorgée)* lap

laper /lape/ ► conjug 1 ◄ VT to lap up VI to lap

lapereau (pl **lapereaux**) /lapʀo/ NM young rabbit

lapidaire /lapidɛʀ/ ADJ 1 *[musée, inscription]* lapidary 2 *(= concis) [style, formule]* terse NM *(= artisan)* lapidary

lapidation /lapidasjɔ̃/ NF stoning

lapider /lapide/ ► conjug 1 ◄ VT *(= tuer)* to stone (to death); *(= attaquer)* to stone, to throw *ou* hurl stones at

lapin /lapɛ̃/ NM *(= animal)* rabbit; *(= fourrure)* rabbit(skin) ◆ **manteau en** ~ rabbitskin coat ◆ ~ **domestique/de garenne** domestic/wild rabbit ◆ **on s'est fait tirer comme des** ~**s** they were taking potshots at us ◆ **mon petit** ~ *(terme d'affection)* my lamb, my sweetheart ◆ **coup du** ~* rabbit punch; *(dans un accident de voiture)* whiplash ◆ **faire le coup du** ~ **à qn*** to give sb a rabbit punch ◆ **poser un** ~ **à qn*** to stand sb up*; → **chaud, courir**

lapine /lapin/ NF (doe) rabbit ◆ **c'est une vraie** ~ *(péj)* she has one baby after another

lapiner /lapine/ ► conjug 1 ◄ VI to litter, to give birth ◆ **elle n'arrête pas de** ~ *(péj) [femme]* she churns out babies one after another *(péj)*

lapinière /lapinjɛʀ/ NF rabbit hutch

lapis(-lazuli) /lapis(lazyli)/ NM INV lapis lazuli

lapon, e /lapɔ̃, ɔn/ ADJ Lapp, Lappish NM *(= langue)* Lapp, Lappish NM,F **Lapon(e)** Lapp, Laplander

Laponie /lapɔni/ NF Lapland

laps /laps/ NM ◆ ~ **de temps** *(gén)* period of time ◆ **au bout d'un certain** ~ **de temps** *(écoulé)* after a certain period *ou* length of time

lapsus /lapsys/ NM *(parlé)* slip of the tongue; *(écrit)* slip of the pen ◆ ~ **révélateur** Freudian slip ◆ **faire un** ~ to make a slip of the tongue (*ou* of the pen)

laquage /lakaʒ/ NM *[de support]* lacquering

laquais /lakɛ/ NM *(= domestique)* lackey, footman; *(péj = personne servile)* lackey *(péj)*, flunkey *(péj)*

laque /lak/ NF *(= produit brut)* lac, shellac; *(= vernis)* lacquer; *(pour les cheveux)* hairspray, (hair) lacquer; *(pour les ongles)* nail varnish ◆ ~ **(brillante)** *(= peinture)* gloss paint NM *ou* NF *(de Chine)* lacquer NM *(= objet d'art)* piece of lacquerware

laqué, e /lake/ (ptp de **laquer**) ADJ *[cheveux]* lacquered; *[ongles]* painted; *[peinture]* gloss *(épith)* ◆ **meubles (en)** ~ **blanc** furniture with a white gloss finish ◆ **murs** ~**s (de) blanc** walls painted in white gloss ◆ **ses ongles** ~**s de rouge** her red fingernails; → **canard**

laquelle /lakɛl/ → **lequel**

laquer /lake/ ► conjug 1 ◄ VT *[+ support]* to lacquer ◆ **se** ~ **les cheveux** to put hairspray *ou* lacquer on one's hair

larbin* /laʀbɛ̃/ NM *(péj)* servant, flunkey *(péj)* ◆ **je ne suis pas ton ~ !** I'm not your slave!

larcin /laʀsɛ̃/ NM *(littér)* *(= vol)* theft; *(= butin)* spoils, booty ◆ **dissimuler son ~** to hide one's spoils *ou* what one has stolen

lard /laʀ/ NM *(= gras)* fat *(of pig)*; *(= viande)* bacon ◆ **~ fumé** ≈ smoked bacon ◆ **~ maigre, petit ~** ≈ streaky bacon *(usually diced or in strips)* ◆ **(se) faire du ~*** to lie back *ou* sit around doing nothing ◆ **un gros ~*** *(fig)* a fat lump* ◆ **on ne sait jamais avec lui si c'est du ~ ou du cochon*** you never know where you are with him*; → **rentrer, tête**

larder /laʀde/ ► conjug 1 ◄ VT *[+ viande]* to lard ◆ **~ qn de coups de couteau** to hack at sb with a knife ◆ **texte lardé de citations** text larded *ou* crammed with quotations

lardoire /laʀdwaʀ/ NM *(Culin)* larding-needle, larding-pin; *(* = épée)* sword, steel

lardon /laʀdɔ̃/ NM 1 *(= tranche de lard)* lardon ◆ **(petits) ~s** *(cubes)* diced bacon 2 *(* = enfant)* kid*

lares /laʀ/ NMPL, ADJ PL ◆ **(dieux) ~** lares

largage /laʀgaʒ/ NM *[d'amarres]* casting off; *[d'étage de fusée]* jettisoning; *[de module, satellite]* release; *[de parachutiste, bombe, vivres, tracts]* dropping ◆ **zone de ~** drop zone ◆ **opération de ~** drop

large /laʀʒ/ ADJ 1 *[rue, fleuve, lit, couloir, ouverture]* wide; *[lame, dos, visage, main, nez, front]* broad; *[jupe]* full; *[chemise]* loose-fitting; *[pantalon]* baggy ◆ **à cet endroit, le fleuve est le plus ~** at this point the river is at its widest ◆ **~ de 3 mètres** 3 metres wide ◆ **chapeau à ~s bords** broad-brimmed *ou* wide-brimmed hat ◆ **décrire un ~ cercle** to describe a big *ou* wide circle ◆ **ouvrir une ~ bouche** to open one's mouth wide ◆ **d'un geste ~** with a broad *ou* sweeping gesture ◆ **avec un ~ sourire** with a broad smile ◆ **ce veston est trop ~** this jacket is too big across the shoulders ◆ **être ~ d'épaules** *[de personne]* to be broad-shouldered; *[de vêtement]* to be big across the shoulders ◆ **être ~ de dos/de hanches** *[de personne]* to have a broad back/wide hips; *[de vêtement]* to be big across the back/the hips

2 *(= important)* *[concession, amnistie]* broad, wide; *[pouvoirs, diffusion]* wide, extensive; *[soutien]* extensive; *[choix, gamme]* wide ◆ **une ~ majorité** a big majority ◆ **retransmettre de ~s extraits d'un match** to show extensive extracts of a match ◆ **destiné à un ~ public** designed for a wide audience ◆ **faire une ~ part à qch** to give great weight to sth ◆ **dans une ~ mesure** to a great *ou* large extent ◆ **il a une ~ part de responsabilité dans l'affaire** he must take a large share of the responsibility in this matter ◆ **au sens ~ du terme** in the broad sense of the term

3 *(= généreux)* *[personne]* generous ◆ **une vie ~** a life of ease

4 *(= tolérant)* *[conscience]* accommodating ◆ **~s vues** liberal views ◆ **il est ~ d'idées** *ou* **d'esprit, il a les idées ~s** *ou* **l'esprit ~** he's very broad-minded

ADV ◆ **voir ~** to think big ◆ **prends un peu plus d'argent, il vaut mieux prévoir ~** take a bit more money, it's better to allow a bit extra ◆ **calculer/mesurer ~** to be generous *ou* allow a bit extra in one's calculations/measurements ◆ **prendre un virage ~** *(Aut)* to take a bend wide ◆ **s'habiller ~** to wear loose-fitting styles ◆ **cette marque taille** *ou* **habille ~** the sizes in this brand tend to be on the large side ◆ **chausser ~** to be wide-fitting; → **mener**

NM 1 *(= largeur)* **une avenue de 8 mètres de ~** an avenue 8 metres wide *ou* 8 metres in width ◆ **acheter une moquette en 2 mètres de ~** to buy a carpet in 2 metre widths ◆ **cela se fait en 2 mètres et 4 mètres de ~** that comes in 2-metre and 4-metre widths ◆ **être au ~** *(= avoir de la place)* to have plenty of room *ou* space; *(† = avoir de l'argent)* to be well-provided for, to have plenty of money; → **long**

2 *(Naut)* **le ~** the open sea ◆ **le grand ~** the high seas ◆ **se diriger vers/gagner le ~** to head for/reach the open sea ◆ **au ~ de Calais** off Calais ◆ **se tenir au ~ de qch** *(fig)* to stay clear of sth ◆ **prendre le ~*** *(fig)* to clear off*, to make o.s. scarce, to hop it* *(Brit)* ◆ **ils ont pris le ~ avec les bijoux*** they made off with the jewels; → **appel, vent**

> ⚠ Attention à ne pas traduire automatiquement **large** par le mot anglais **large**, qui a le sens de 'grand'.

largement /laʀʒəmɑ̃/ ADV 1 *(= amplement)* *[écarter]* widely ◆ **~ espacés** *[arbres, maisons]* widely spaced, wide apart ◆ **fenêtre ~ ouverte** wide open window ◆ **robe ~ décolletée** dress with a very open *ou* very scooped neckline

2 *(= sur une grande échelle)* *[répandre, diffuser]* widely ◆ **amnistie ~ accordée** wide *ou* widely extended amnesty ◆ **idée ~ répandue** widespread *ou* widely held view ◆ **bénéficier de pouvoirs ~ étendus** to hold greatly increased powers

3 *(= de loin, de beaucoup)* greatly ◆ **ce succès dépasse ~ nos prévisions** this success greatly exceeds our expectations *ou* is far beyond our expectations ◆ **ce problème dépasse ~ ses compétences** this problem is altogether beyond *ou* is way beyond* his capabilities ◆ **vous débordez ~ le sujet** you are going well beyond the limits of the subject ◆ **elle vaut ~ son frère** she's every bit as *ou* at least as good as her brother ◆ **~ battu** *(Pol, Sport)* heavily defeated

4 *(= grandement)* **vous avez ~ le temps** you have ample time *ou* plenty of time ◆ **c'est ~ suffisant** that's plenty, that's more than enough ◆ **cela me suffit ~** that's plenty *ou* ample *ou* more than enough for me ◆ **il est ~ temps de commencer** it's high time we started ◆ **j'ai été ~ récompensé de ma patience** my patience has been amply rewarded ◆ **ça vaut ~ la peine/la visite** it's well worth the trouble/the visit ◆ **ce film est ~ inspiré de mon livre** this film is, to a great extent, inspired by my book

5 *(= généreusement)* *[payer, donner]* generously ◆ **ils nous ont servis/indemnisés ~** they gave us generous *ou* ample helpings/compensation ◆ **vivre ~** to live handsomely

6 *(= au moins)* easily, at least ◆ **il gagne ~ 7 000 € par mois** he earns easily *ou* at least €7,000 a month ◆ **tu as mis trois heures pour le faire ? – oh oui, ~** you took three hours to do it? – yes, easily *ou* at least ◆ **il a ~ 50 ans** he is well past 50, he is well into his fifties ◆ **c'est à 5 minutes/5 km d'ici, ~** it's a good 5 minutes/5 km from here

largesse /laʀʒɛs/ NF 1 *(= caractère)* generosity ◆ **avec ~** generously 2 *(= dons)* **~s** liberalities ◆ **faire des ~s** to make generous gifts

largeur /laʀʒœʀ/ NF 1 *[de rue, fleuve, lit, couloir, ouverture]* width; *[de lame, dos, visage, main, nez, front]* breadth; *[de voie ferrée]* gauge ◆ **sur toute la ~** right across, all the way across ◆ **dans le sens de la ~** widthways, widthwise ◆ **quelle est la ~ de la fenêtre ?** how wide is the window? ◆ **tissu en grande/petite ~** double-width/single-width material 2 *[d'idées]* broadness ◆ **~ d'esprit** broad-mindedness ◆ **~ de vues** broadness of outlook 3 *(* : locutions)* **dans les grandes ~s** with a vengeance, well and truly ◆ **il s'est trompé dans les grandes ~s** he's slipped up with a vengeance, he's boobed this time, and how!* ◆ **cette fois on les a eus dans les grandes ~s** we had them well and truly this time*, we didn't half put one over on them this time* *(Brit)*

largo /laʀgo/ ADV, NM largo

largue /laʀg/ ADJ *[cordage]* slack; *[vent]* quartering NM *(= vent)* quartering wind ◆ **adopter l'allure du grand ~** to start to sail off the wind *ou* to sail large

largué, e /laʀge/ (ptp de **larguer**) ADJ ◆ **être ~*** to be all at sea ◆ **être un peu ~** to be a bit lost

larguer /laʀge/ ► conjug 1 ◄ VT 1 *(Naut)* *[+ cordage]* to loose, to release; *[+ voile]* to let out, to unfurl; *[+ amarres]* to cast off, to slip 2 *[+ parachutiste, bombe, vivres, tracts]* to drop; *[+ carburant, étage de fusée]* to jettison; *[+ cabine spatiale, module, satellite]* to release 3 *(* = se débarrasser de)* *[+ ami]* to drop, to dump*; *[+ amant]* to dump*, to ditch*; *[+ collaborateur]* to drop, to get rid of, to dump*; *[+ emploi]* to quit*; *[+ objet]* to chuck out*, to get rid of; *[+ principes]* to jettison, to ditch* ◆ **il s'est fait ~** he was dumped

larigot /laʀigo/ NM → **tire-larigot**

larme /laʀm/ NF 1 *(Physiol)* tear ◆ **en ~s** in tears ◆ **~s de joie/de rage** tears of joy/of rage ◆ **verser des ~s sur qch/qn** to shed tears over sth/sb ◆ **avec des ~s dans la voix** with tears in his voice, with a tearful voice ◆ **avoir les ~s aux yeux** to have tears in one's eyes ◆ **ça lui a fait venir les ~s aux yeux** it brought tears to his eyes ◆ **elle a la ~ facile** she is easily moved to tears ◆ **y aller de sa (petite) ~*** to shed a tear, to have a little cry ◆ **avoir toujours la ~ à l'œil** to be a real cry-baby; → **fondre, rire, vallée** etc 2 *(* = goutte)* *[de vin]* drop

COMP **larmes de crocodile** crocodile tears
larmes de sang tears of blood

larmier /laʀmje/ NM *(Archit)* dripstone; *[de cerf]* tearpit; *[de cheval]* temple

larmoiement /laʀmwamɑ̃/ NM 1 *(= pleurnicherie)* whimpering *(NonC)*, snivelling *(NonC)* 2 *(Physiol)* watering (of the eyes)

larmoyant, e /laʀmwajɑ̃, ɑ̃t/ ADJ 1 *[yeux]* *(gén)* tearful; *(= toujours humides)* watery; *[personne]* in tears *(attrib)* ◆ **d'une voix ~e, d'un ton ~** in a tearful voice *ou* tearfully 2 *(péj)* *[récit]* maudlin; *[scène]* tear-jerking ◆ **comédie ~e** *(Théât)* sentimental comedy ◆ **c'est un de ces mélos ~s** it's a real tear-jerker

larmoyer /laʀmwaje/ ► conjug 8 ◄ VI 1 *(= pleurnicher)* to whimper, to snivel 2 *[yeux]* to water, to run

larron /laʀɔ̃/ NM *(†, Bible)* thief ◆ **s'entendre comme ~s en foire** to be as thick as thieves; → **occasion, troisième**

larsen /laʀsɛn/ NM ◆ **(effet) Larsen** interference ◆ **il y a du ~ dans les micros** there's interference in the mikes*

larvaire /laʀvɛʀ/ ADJ *(lit)* larval; *(fig)* embryonic

larve /laʀv/ NF *(gén)* larva; *(= asticot)* grub ◆ **~ (humaine)** *(péj)* worm

larvé, e /laʀve/ ADJ *[crise, conflit]* dormant, latent; *[racisme]* latent; *(Méd)* *[fièvre, maladie]* larvate *(SPÉC)*

laryngé, e /laʀɛ̃ʒe/ ADJ laryngeal

laryngectomie /laʀɛ̃ʒɛktɔmi/ NF laryngectomy

laryngien, -ienne /laʀɛ̃ʒjɛ̃, jɛn/ ADJ ⇒ **laryngé**

laryngite /laʀɛ̃ʒit/ NF laryngitis *(NonC)*

laryngologie /laʀɛ̃gɔlɔʒi/ NF laryngology

laryngologiste /laʀɛ̃gɔlɔʒist/, **laryngologue** /laʀɛ̃gɔlɔg/ NMF throat specialist, laryngologist

laryngoscope /laʀɛ̃gɔskɔp/ NM laryngoscope

laryngoscopie /laʀɛ̃gɔskɔpi/ NF laryngoscopy

laryngotomie /laʀɛ̃gɔtɔmi/ NF laryngotomy

larynx /laʀɛ̃ks/ NM larynx, voice-box

las¹, lasse /lɑ, lɑs/ ADJ *(frm)* weary, tired ◆ **~ de qn/de faire qch/de vivre** tired *ou* weary of sb/of doing sth/of life; → **guerre**

las² †† /lɑs/ EXCL alas!

lasagne /lazaɲ/ NF lasagna

lascar †* /laskaʀ/ NM *(= type louche)* character; *(= malin)* rogue; *(hum = enfant)* terror ◆ **drôle de ~** *(louche)* shady character*; *(malin)* real rogue, smart customer* ◆ **je vous aurai, mes ~s !** *(à des adultes)* I'll get you yet, you old rogues!*; *(à des enfants)* I'll get you yet, you little *ou* young rascals!*

lascif, -ive /lasif, iv/ ADJ lascivious

lascivement /lasivmɑ̃/ ADV lasciviously

lasciveté /lasivte/, **lascivité** /lasivite/ NF lasciviousness

laser /lazɛʀ/ NM laser ◆ **~ de puissance** power laser ◆ **disque/rayon ~** laser disk/beam ◆ **au ~** *[nettoyer, détruire]* using a laser ◆ **opération au ~** laser operation

laserdisc /lazɛʀdisk/ NM laser disk

lassant, e /lɑsɑ̃, ɑt/ ADJ *(frm)* wearisome, tiresome

lasser /lɑse/ ▸ conjug 1 ◂ VT *[+ auditeur, lecteur]* to weary, to tire ◆ **~ la patience/bonté de qn** to exhaust sb's patience/goodwill, to stretch sb's patience/goodwill too far ◆ **je suis lassée de ses mensonges** I'm tired of his lies ◆ **sourire lassé** weary smile ◆ **lassé de tout** weary of everything VPR **se lasser** ◆ **se ~ de qch/de faire qch** to (grow) weary of sth/of doing sth, to tire *ou* grow tired of sth/of doing sth ◆ **parler sans se ~** to speak without tiring *ou* flagging ◆ **on écoute 5 minutes, et puis on se lasse** you listen for 5 minutes and then you get tired of it

lassitude /lɑsityd/ NF weariness *(NonC)*, lassitude *(NonC) (frm)* ◆ **avec ~** wearily

lasso /laso/ NM lasso ◆ **prendre au ~** to lasso

lasure /lazyʀ/ NF tint, stain

lasuré, e /lazyʀe/ ADJ tinted, stained

latence /latɑ̃s/ NF latency ◆ **temps de ~** *(gén)* latent period; *(Comm)* lead time ◆ **période de ~** latency period

latent, e /latɑ̃, ɑt/ ADJ *(gén)* latent ◆ **à l'état ~** latent, in the latent state

latéral, e (mpl **-aux**) /lateʀal, o/ ADJ side *(épith)*, lateral *(frm)* NF **latérale** *(Phon)* lateral (consonant)

latéralement /lateʀalmɑ̃/ ADV *(gén)* laterally; *[être situé]* on the side; *[arriver, souffler]* from the side; *[diviser]* sideways

latéralité /lateʀalite/ NF laterality

latérite /lateʀit/ NF laterite

latex /latɛks/ NM INV latex; *(euph = préservatif)* condom, rubber*

latifundiaire /latifɔ̃djɛʀ/ ADJ ◆ **propriétaire ~** owner of a latifundium ◆ **propriété ~** latifundium

latifundium /latifɔ̃djɔm/ (pl **latifundia** /latifɔ̃dja/) NM latifundium

latin, e /latɛ̃, in/ ADJ Latin ◆ **langues ~es** romance *ou* Latin languages; → **Amérique, quartier, voile¹** NM *(= langue)* Latin ◆ **~ vulgaire** vulgar Latin ◆ **~ de cuisine** *(péj)* dog Latin ◆ **j'y ou j'en perds mon ~** I can't make head nor tail of it; → **bas¹** NM,F **Latin(e)** Latin ◆ **les Latins** the Latin people, Latins

latinisation /latinizasjɔ̃/ NF latinization

latiniser /latinize/ ▸ conjug 1 ◂ VTI to latinize

latinisme /latinism/ NM latinism

latiniste /latinist/ NMF *(= spécialiste)* latinist, Latin scholar; *(= enseignant)* Latin teacher; *(= étudiant)* Latin student

latinité /latinite/ NF *(Ling = caractère)* latinity ◆ **la ~** *(= civilisation)* the Latin world

latino * /latino/ ADJ, NMF Latino

latino-américain, e (mpl **latino-américains**) /latinoameʀikɛ̃, ɛn/ ADJ Latin-American, Hispanic NM,F **Latino-Américain(e)** Latin-American, Hispanic

latitude /latityd/ NF 1 *(Astron, Géog)* latitude ◆ **Paris est à 48° de ~ Nord** Paris is situated at latitude 48° north 2 *(= pouvoir, liberté)* latitude, scope ◆ **avoir toute ~ pour faire qch** to have a free hand *ou* have carte blanche to do sth ◆ **laisser/donner toute ~ à qn** to allow/give sb full scope *ou* a free hand ◆ **on a une certaine ~** we have some leeway *ou* latitude *ou* some freedom of movement NFPL **latitudes** latitudes ◆ **sous toutes les ~s** in all latitudes, in all parts of the world ◆ **sous nos ~s** in our part of the world

latitudinaire /latitydinɛʀ/ ADJ, NMF *(littér)* latitudinarian

latomies /latɔmi/ NFPL latomies

lato sensu /latosɛ̃sy/ LOC ADV in the broader sense of the word

latrines /latʀin/ NFPL latrines

lattage /lataʒ/ NM lathing

latte /lat/ NF *(gén)* lath; *[de plancher]* board; *[de fauteuil, sommier]* slat ◆ **~s** * *(Ski)* boards* ◆ **donner un coup de ~ à qn** * to wack sb*

latté, e /late/ (ptp de **latter**) ADJ lathed NM blockboard

latter /late/ ▸ conjug 1 ◂ VT to lath

lattis /lati/ NM lathing *(NonC)*, lathwork *(NonC)*

laudanum /lodanɔm/ NM laudanum

laudateur, -trice /lodatœʀ, tʀis/ NM,F *(littér)* adulator, laudator *(frm)*

laudatif, -ive /lodatif, iv/ ADJ laudatory ◆ **parler de qn en termes ~s** to speak highly of sb, to be full of praise for sb ◆ **il a été très ~ envers son collaborateur** he was full of praise for his colleague

lauréat, e /lɔʀea, at/ ADJ (prize-)winning NM,F (prize-)winner, award winner ◆ **les ~s du prix Nobel** the Nobel prize-winners

Laurent /lɔʀɑ̃/ NM Lawrence, Laurence ◆ **~ le Magnifique** Lorenzo the Magnificent

laurier /lɔʀje/ NM *(Culin)* ◆ **~ (commun)** bay-tree, (sweet) bay ◆ **feuille de ~** bay leaf ◆ **mettre du ~** to put in some bay leaves NMPL **lauriers** laurels ◆ **s'endormir** *ou* **se reposer sur ses ~s** to rest on one's laurels ◆ **être couvert de ~s** to be showered with praise

laurier-cerise (pl **lauriers-cerises**) /lɔʀjesəʀiz/ NM cherry laurel

laurier-rose (pl **lauriers-roses**) /lɔʀjeʀoz/ NM oleander, rosebay

laurier-sauce (pl **lauriers-sauce**) /lɔʀjesos/ NM (sweet) bay, bay-tree

laurier-tin (pl **lauriers-tins**) /lɔʀjetɛ̃/ NM laurustinus

lavable /lavabl/ ADJ washable ◆ **~ en machine** machine-washable ◆ **papier peint ~ (et lessivable)** washable wallpaper

lavabo /lavabo/ NM washbasin, bathroom sink *(US)* NMPL **lavabos** *(euph)* **les ~s** the toilets, the loo* *(Brit)*

lavage /lavaʒ/ NM 1 *[de plaie]* bathing, cleaning; *[de corps, cheveux]* washing ◆ **~ d'intestin** intestinal wash ◆ **on lui a fait un ~ d'estomac** he had his stomach pumped

2 *(= action) [de mur, vêtement, voiture]* washing *(NonC)*; *(= opération)* wash ◆ **après le ~ vient le rinçage** after the wash comes the rinse ◆ **pour un meilleur ~, utilisez ...** for a better wash, use ... ◆ **"lavage à la main"** "hand wash only" ◆ **"lavage en machine"** "machine wash" ◆ **le ~ des sols à la brosse/à l'éponge** scrubbing/sponging (down) floors ◆ **on a dû faire trois ~s** it had to be washed three times, it had to have three washes ◆ **le ~ de la vaisselle** dishwashing, washing-up *(Brit)* ◆ **ça a rétréci/c'est parti au ~** it shrunk/came out in the wash ◆ **ton chemisier est au ~** your blouse is in the wash; → **froid, température**

3 *(Tech) [de gaz, charbon, laine]* washing

COMP **lavage de cerveau** brainwashing ◆ **on lui a fait subir un ~ de cerveau** he was brainwashed

lavallière /lavaljɛʀ/ NF floppy necktie, lavallière

lavande /lavɑ̃d/ NF lavender ◆ **(eau de) ~** lavender water ADJ INV ◆ **(bleu) ~** lavender (blue)

lavandière /lavɑ̃djɛʀ/ NF *(= laveuse)* washerwoman; *(= oiseau)* wagtail

lavandin /lavɑ̃dɛ̃/ NM hybrid lavender

lavant, e /lavɑ̃, ɑt/ ADJ cleansing ◆ **machine à laver ~e-séchante** washer-drier

lavaret /lavaʀɛ/ NM *(= poisson)* pollan

lavasse * /lavas/ NF dishwater* ◆ **ce café, c'est de la ~** *ou* **une vraie ~** this coffee tastes like dishwater*

lave /lav/ NF lava *(NonC)*

lavé, e /lave/ (ptp de **laver**) ADJ *[couleur]* watery, washy, washed-out; *[ciel]* pale, colourless *(Brit)*, colorless *(US)*; *[yeux]* pale ◆ **dessin ~** *(Art)* wash drawing

lave-auto (pl **lave-autos**) /lavoto/ NM *(Can)* car wash

lave-glace (pl **lave-glaces**) /lavglas/ NM windscreen *(Brit) ou* windshield *(US)* washer, screen wash(er) *(Brit)*

lave-linge /lavlɛ̃ʒ/ NM INV washing machine ◆ **~ séchant** washer-dryer

lave-mains /lavmɛ̃/ NM INV (small) washbasin *(Brit) ou* washbowl *(US)*

lavement /lavmɑ̃/ NM *(Méd)* enema ◆ **~ baryté** barium enema ◆ **le ~ des pieds** *(Bible)* the washing of the feet

laver /lave/ ▸ conjug 1 ◂ VT 1 *(gén)* to wash; *[+ mur]* to wash (down); *[+ plaie]* to bathe, to cleanse; *[+ tache]* to wash out *ou* off; *[+ intestin]* to wash out ◆ **~ avec une brosse** to scrub (down) ◆ **~ avec une éponge** to wash with a sponge, to sponge (down) ◆ **~ au jet** to hose down ◆ **~ à grande eau** *[+ sol]* to wash down; *[+ trottoir, pont de navire]* to sluice down; *[+ légume]* to wash *ou* rinse thoroughly ◆ **~ la vaisselle** to do *ou* wash the dishes, to wash up *(Brit)*, to do the washing-up *(Brit)* ◆ **il faut ~ son linge sale en famille** it doesn't do to wash one's dirty linen in public ◆ **~ la tête à qn** *(fig)* to haul sb over the coals, to give sb a dressing down*; → **machine**

2 *(en emploi absolu) [personne]* to do the washing ◆ **ce savon lave bien** this soap washes well

3 *[+ affront, injure]* to avenge; *[+ péchés, honte]* to cleanse, to wash away ◆ **~ qn d'une accusation/d'un soupçon** to clear sb of an accusation/of suspicion

4 *(Art) [+ couleur]* to dilute; *[+ dessin]* to wash

VPR **se laver** 1 *[personne]* to wash, to have a wash ◆ **se ~ la figure/les mains** to wash one's face/one's hands ◆ **se ~ les dents** to clean *ou* brush one's teeth ◆ **se ~ dans un lavabo/une baignoire** to have a stand-up wash/a bath, to wash (o.s.) at the basin/in the bath

2 *[vêtement, tissu]* **ça se lave en machine** it's machine-washable ◆ **ça se lave à la main** it has to be hand-washed ◆ **ce tissu se lave bien** this material washes well ◆ **le cuir ne se lave pas** leather isn't washable

3 ◆ **se ~ de** *[+ accusation]* to clear o.s. of; *[+ affront]* to avenge o.s. of ◆ **je m'en lave les mains** *(fig)* I wash my hands of it

laverie /lavʀi/ **NF** 1 *(pour linge)* laundry ◆ **~ (automatique)** Launderette ® *(Brit)*, Laundromat ® *(US)* 2 *(industrielle)* washing *ou* preparation plant

lavette /lavɛt/ **NF** 1 *(= chiffon)* dish cloth; *(= brosse)* dish mop; *(Belg, Helv = gant de toilette)* (face) flannel *(Brit)*, washcloth *(US)* 2 *(péj = homme)* wimp *, drip *

laveur /lavœʀ/ **NM** *(= personne)* washer ◆ **~ de carreaux** *ou* **de vitres** window cleaner ◆ **~ de voitures** car cleaner; → **raton**

laveuse /lavøz/ **NF** *(= personne)* ◆ **~ (de linge)** washerwoman; *(Can = lave-linge)* washing machine

lave-vaisselle /lavvɛsɛl/ **NM INV** dishwasher

lavis /lavi/ **NM** *(= procédé)* washing ◆ **(dessin au) ~** wash drawing ◆ **colorier au ~** to wash-paint

lavoir /lavwaʀ/ **NM** *(découvert)* washing-place; *(= édifice)* wash house; *(= bac)* washtub; *(Tech) (= machine)* washer; *(= atelier)* washing plant

lavure /lavyʀ/ **NF** *[de minerai]* washing ◆ **~s** washings

Lawrence /lɔʀɑ̃s/ **N** ◆ **~ d'Arabie** Lawrence of Arabia

laxatif, -ive /laksatif, iv/ **ADJ, NM** laxative

laxisme /laksism/ **NM** *(= indulgence)* laxness, laxity ◆ **le gouvernement est accusé de ~ à l'égard des syndicats** the government is accused of being too soft *ou* lax with the trade unions ◆ **après des années de ~ budgétaire** after years of poor budget management

laxiste /laksist/ **ADJ** *[personne, attitude, interprétation, politique, justice]* lax **NMF** 1 *(indulgent)* lax person 2 *(Rel)* latitudinarian

layette /lɛjɛt/ **NF** baby clothes, layette ◆ **rayon ~** *[de magasin]* babywear department ◆ **couleurs ~** baby *ou* pastel colours ◆ **bleu/rose ~** baby blue/pink

layon /lɛjɔ̃/ **NM** (forest) track *ou* trail

Lazare /lazaʀ/ **NM** Lazarus

lazaret /lazaʀɛ/ **NM** lazaret

lazulite /lazylit/ **NF** lazulite

lazzi /la(d)zi/ **NM** gibe ◆ **être l'objet des ~(s) de la foule** to be gibed at *ou* heckled by the crowd

LCD /ɛlsede/ **ADJ, NM** (abrév de **liquid crystal display**) *(Ordin) [écran]* LCD

le[1] /lə/, **la** /la/ (pl **les** /le/) **ART DÉF** *(contraction avec à, de : au, aux, du, des)* 1 *(détermination)* the ◆ **le propriétaire de la voiture** the owner of the car ◆ **la femme de l'épicier** the grocer's wife ◆ **les parcs de la ville** the town parks, the parks in the town ◆ **je suis inquiète, les enfants sont en retard** I'm worried because the children are late ◆ **le thé/le café que je viens d'acheter** the tea/the coffee I have just bought ◆ **allons à la gare ensemble** let's go to the station together ◆ **il n'a pas le droit/l'intention de le faire** he has no right to do it/no intention of doing it ◆ **il n'a pas eu la patience/l'intelligence d'attendre** he didn't have the patience/the sense to wait ◆ **il a choisi le tableau le plus original de l'exposition** he chose the most original picture in the exhibition ◆ **le plus petit des deux frères est le plus solide** the smaller of the two brothers is the more robust *ou* the stronger ◆ **le Paris de Balzac** Balzac's Paris ◆ **l'Angleterre que j'ai connue** the England (that) I knew

2 *(dans le temps)* the *(souvent omis)* ◆ **venez le dimanche de Pâques** come on Easter Sunday ◆ **l'hiver dernier/prochain** last/next winter ◆ **l'hiver 1998** the winter of 1998 ◆ **le premier/dernier lundi du mois** the first/last Monday of *ou* in the month ◆ **il ne travaille pas le samedi** he doesn't work on Saturdays *ou* on a Saturday ◆ **elle travaille le matin** she works mornings *ou* in the morning ◆ **vers les cinq heures** at about five o'clock ◆ **il est parti le 5 mai** *(à l'oral)* he left on the 5th of May *ou* on May the 5th; *(à l'écrit, dans une lettre)* he left on 5 May ◆ **il n'a pas dormi de la nuit** he didn't sleep a wink all night

3 *(distribution)* a, an ◆ **8 € le mètre/le kg/le litre/la pièce** €8 a metre/a kg/a litre/each *ou* a piece ◆ **60 km à l'heure** 60 km an *ou* per hour ◆ **deux fois la semaine/l'an** twice a week/a year

4 *(fraction)* a, an ◆ **le tiers/quart** a third/quarter ◆ **j'en ai fait à peine la moitié/le dixième** I have barely done (a) half/a tenth of it

5 *(dans les généralisations, les abstractions : gén non traduit)* **le hibou vole surtout la nuit** owls fly *ou* the owl flies mainly at night ◆ **l'enfant n'aime pas** *ou* **les enfants n'aiment pas l'obscurité** children don't like the dark ◆ **le thé et le café sont chers** tea and coffee are expensive ◆ **j'aime la musique/la poésie/la danse** I like music/poetry/dancing ◆ **le beau/grotesque** the beautiful/grotesque ◆ **les riches** the rich ◆ **aller au concert/au restaurant** to go to a concert/out for a meal

6 *(possession : gén adj poss, parfois art indéf)* **elle ouvrit les yeux/la bouche** she opened her eyes/her mouth ◆ **elle est sortie le manteau sur le bras** she went out with her coat over her arm ◆ **la tête baissée, elle pleurait** she hung her head and wept ◆ **assis les jambes pendantes** sitting with one's legs dangling ◆ **j'ai mal à la main droite/au pied** I've got a pain in my right hand/in my foot, my right hand/my foot hurts ◆ **il a la jambe cassée** he's got a broken leg ◆ **croisez les bras** fold your arms ◆ **il a l'air fatigué/le regard malin** he has a tired look/a mischievous look ◆ **il a les cheveux noirs/le cœur brisé** he has black hair/a broken heart ◆ **il a l'air hypocrite** he looks like a hypocrite

7 *(valeur démonstrative)* **il ne faut pas agir de la sorte** you must not do that kind of thing *ou* things like that ◆ **que pensez-vous de la pièce/de l'incident ?** what do you think of the play/of the incident? ◆ **faites attention, les enfants !** be careful children! ◆ **oh le beau chien !** what a lovely dog!, look at that lovely dog!

le[2] /l(ə)/, **la** /la/ (pl **les** /le/) **PRON M,F,PL** 1 *(= homme)* him; *(= femme, bateau)* her; *(= animal, bébé)* it, him, her; *(= chose)* it ◆ **les** them ◆ **je ne le/la/les connais pas** I don't know him/her/them ◆ **regarde-le/-la/-les** look at him *ou* it/her *ou* it/them ◆ **cette écharpe est à vous, je l'ai trouvée par terre** this scarf is yours, I found it on the floor ◆ **voulez-vous ces fraises ? je les ai apportées pour vous** would you like these strawberries? I brought them for you ◆ **le Canada demande aux USA de le soutenir** Canada is asking the USA for its support

2 *(emphatique)* **il faut le féliciter ce garçon !** this boy deserves congratulations! ◆ **cette femme-là, je la déteste** I can't bear that woman ◆ **cela vous le savez aussi bien que moi** you know that as well as I do ◆ **vous l'êtes, beau** you really do look nice; → **copier, voici, voilà**

3 *(neutre : souvent non traduit)* **vous savez qu'il est malade ? – je l'ai entendu dire** did you know he was ill? – I had heard ◆ **elle n'est pas heureuse, mais elle ne l'a jamais été et elle ne le sera jamais** she is not happy but she never has been and never will be ◆ **pourquoi il n'est pas venu ? – demande-le-lui/je me le demande** why hasn't he come? – ask him/I wonder ◆ **il était ministre, il ne l'est plus** he used to be a minister but he isn't any longer ◆ **il sera puni comme il le mérite** he'll be punished as he deserves

lé /le/ **NM** *[d'étoffe]* width; *[de papier peint]* length, strip

LEA /ɛləa/ **NM** (abrév de **langues étrangères appliquées**) modern languages

leader /lidœʀ/ **NM** *(Pol, Écon, Sport)* leader; *(Presse)* leader, leading article ◆ **produit ~** *(Comm)* leader, leading product ◆ **~ d'opinion** opinion former, person who shapes public opinion ◆ **cette entreprise est ~ sur son marché** this company is the market leader ◆ **notre société est en position de ~ dans son secteur** our company holds a leading *ou* lead position in its sector

leadership /lidœʀʃip/ **NM** *[de parti]* leadership; *[d'entreprise]* leading position; *(= dirigeants)* leaders ◆ **ils ont perdu leur ~ technologique** they've lost their leading position in the field of technology ◆ **ils ont pris le ~ dans ce secteur** they have taken the lead in this sector

leasing /liziŋ/ **NM** leasing ◆ **acheter qch en ~** to buy sth leasehold

léchage /leʃaʒ/ **NM** *(gén)* licking ◆ **~ (de bottes)** * bootlicking *

lèche** /lɛʃ/ **NF** bootlicking * ◆ **faire de la ~** to be a bootlicker * ◆ **faire de la ~ à qn** to suck up to sb**, to lick sb's boots *

lèche-botte * (pl **lèche-bottes**) /lɛʃbɔt/ **NMF** bootlicker *

lèche-cul** (pl **lèche-culs**) /lɛʃky/ **NMF** arse-licker** *(Brit)*, ass-kisser** *(US)*, brown nose** *(US)*

lèchefrite /lɛʃfʀit/ **NF** dripping-pan *(Brit)*, broiler *(US)*

lécher /leʃe/ ▸ conjug 6 ◂ **VT** 1 *(gén)* to lick; *[+ assiette]* to lick clean ◆ **se ~ les doigts** to lick one's fingers ◆ **s'en ~ les doigts/babines** *(fig)* to lick one's lips/chops ◆ **~ la confiture d'une tartine** to lick the jam off a slice of bread ◆ **~ les bottes de qn** * to suck up to sb**, to lick sb's boots * ◆ **~ le cul à** *ou* **de qn**** to lick sb's arse** *(Brit)*, to kiss sb's ass** *(US)* ◆ **~ les vitrines** * to go window-shopping; → **ours** 2 *[flammes]* to lick; *[vagues]* to wash against, to lap against 3 *(* = fignoler)* to polish up ◆ **article bien léché** polished *ou* finely honed article ◆ **trop léché** overdone *(attrib)*, overpolished

lécheur, -euse * /leʃœʀ, øz/ **NM,F** ◆ **~ (de bottes)** bootlicker * ◆ **il est du genre ~** he's the bootlicking type *, he's always sucking up to someone**

lèche-vitrines /lɛʃvitʀin/ **NM INV** window-shopping ◆ **faire du ~** to go window-shopping

lécithine /lesitin/ **NF** lecithin

leçon /l(ə)sɔ̃/ **NF** 1 *(Scol) (= cours)* lesson, class; *(à apprendre)* homework *(NonC)* ◆ **~ de danse/de français/de piano** dancing/French/piano lesson ◆ **~s particulières** private lessons *ou* tuition *(Brit)* ◆ **faire la ~** to teach ◆ **elle a bien appris sa ~** *(lit)* she's learnt her homework well; *(hum)* she's learnt her script *ou* lines well

2 *(= conseil)* (piece of) advice ◆ **suivre les ~s de qn** to heed sb's advice, to take a lesson from sb ◆ **je n'ai pas de ~ à recevoir de toi** I don't need your advice ◆ **faire la ~ à qn** *(= l'endoctriner)* to tell sb what to do; *(= le réprimander)* to give sb a lecture ◆ **donner des ~s de morale à qn** to preach at sb ◆ **je n'ai pas besoin de tes ~s de morale** I don't need lessons from you

3 *(= enseignement) [de fable, parabole]* lesson ◆ **les ~s de l'expérience** the lessons of experience *ou* that experience teaches ◆ **que cela te serve de ~** let that be a lesson to you ◆ **cela m'a servi de ~** that taught me a lesson ◆ **nous avons tiré la ~ de notre échec** we learnt (a lesson) from our failure ◆ **maintenant que notre plan a échoué, il faut en tirer la ~** now that our plan has failed we should learn from it ◆ **cela lui donnera une ~** that'll teach him a lesson

4 *[de manuscrit, texte]* reading

lecteur, -trice /lɛktœʀ, tʀis/ **NM,F** 1 *(gén)* reader • **c'est un grand ~ de poésie** he reads a lot of poetry • **le nombre de ~s de ce journal a doublé** the readership of this paper has doubled • **~-correcteur** proofreader; → **avis** 2 *(Univ)* (foreign language) assistant, (foreign) teaching assistant *(US)* **NM** 1 *(Audiov)* ~ **de cassettes** cassette deck *ou* player • ~ **de disques compacts** *ou* ~ **de CD audio** CD player, compact disc player • ~ **de DVD** DVD player • ~ **de vidéodisque** videodisc player • ~ **de son** (reading) head 2 *(Ordin)* ~ **de cartes à puce** smart-card reader • ~ **de disquettes/de CD-ROM** disk/CD-ROM drive • ~ **MP3** MP3 player • ~ **optique** optical character reader, optical scanner 3 ~ **de cartes** *(= lampe dans voiture)* map-light

lecteur-enregistreur /lɛktœʀɑ̃ʀəʒistʀœʀ/ **NM** • ~ **de DVD** DVD player/recorder

lectorat /lɛktɔʀa/ **NM** 1 *(Univ)* (teaching) assistantship 2 *[de magazine]* readership

lecture /lɛktyʀ/ **NF** 1 *[de carte, texte]* reading; *(= interprétation)* reading, interpretation • **la ~ de Proust est difficile** reading Proust is difficult, Proust is difficult to read • **aimer la ~** to like reading • **d'une ~ facile** easy to read, very readable • **ce livre est d'une ~ agréable** this book makes pleasant reading • **la ~ à haute voix** reading aloud • **faire la ~ à qn** to read to sb • **donner** *ou* **faire ~ de qch** *(frm)* to read sth out *(à qn* to sb); • **faire une ~ marxiste de Balzac** to read Balzac from a Marxist perspective • ~ **à vue** *(Mus)* sight-reading • **méthode de ~** reading method • ~ **rapide** speed reading • **nous n'avons pas la même ~ des événements** we have a different interpretation of the events; → **cabinet, livre**[1]

2 *(= livre)* reading *(NonC)*, book • **c'est une ~ à recommander** it's recommended reading *ou* it's a book to be recommended • **apportez-moi de la ~** bring me something to read • **~s pour la jeunesse** books for children • **quelles sont vos ~s favorites ?** what do you like reading best? • **enrichi par ses ~s** enriched by his reading *ou* by what he has read • **il a de mauvaises ~s** he reads the wrong things

3 *[de projet de loi]* reading • **examiner un projet en première ~** to give a bill its first reading • **le projet a été accepté en seconde ~** the bill passed its second reading

4 *(Audiov) [de CD, cassette] (= bouton)* play • **pendant la ~ de la cassette** while the tape is playing

5 *[de disque dur, CD-ROM]* reading • ~ **optique** *(= procédé)* optical character recognition; *(= action)* optical scanning • **procédé/tête de ~-écriture** read-write cycle/head • **en ~ seule** read-only; → **tête**

Léda /leda/ **NF** *(Myth)* Leda

ledit /lədi/, **ladite** /ladit/ (pl **lesdit(e)s** /ledi(t)/) **ADJ** *(frm)* the aforementioned *(frm)*, the aforesaid *(frm)*, the said *(frm)*

légal, e (mpl **-aux**) /legal, o/ **ADJ** *[âge, dispositions, formalité, statut, base]* legal; *[armes, moyens]* legal, lawful • **cours ~ d'une monnaie** official rate of exchange of a currency • **monnaie ~e** legal tender, official currency • **la durée ~e du temps de travail** maximum working hours • **recourir aux moyens légaux contre qn** to take legal action against sb • **cette entreprise n'a pas d'existence ~e** this company has no legal existence; → **fête, heure, médecine, vitrine**

légalement /legalmɑ̃/ **ADV** legally • **des personnes ~ installées en France** people living legally in France

légalisation /legalizasjɔ̃/ **NF** 1 *(= action)* legalization 2 *(= certification)* authentication

légaliser /legalize/ ► conjug 1 ◄ **VT** 1 *(= rendre légal)* to legalize 2 *(= certifier)* to authenticate

légalisme /legalism/ **NM** legalism

légaliste /legalist/ **ADJ** legalist(ic) **NMF** legalist

légalité /legalite/ **NF** *[de régime, acte]* legality, lawfulness • **rester dans/sortir de la ~** *(= loi)* to remain *ou* keep within/breach the law • **en toute ~** quite legally

légat /lega/ **NM** • ~ **(du Pape)** (papal) legate

légataire /legatɛʀ/ **NMF** legatee, devisee • ~ **universel** sole legatee

légation /legasjɔ̃/ **NF** *(Diplomatie)* legation

légendaire /leʒɑ̃dɛʀ/ **ADJ** legendary

légende /leʒɑ̃d/ **NF** 1 *(= histoire, mythe)* legend • **entrer dans la ~** to go down in legend, to become legendary • **entrer vivant dans la ~** to become a legend in one's own lifetime • **de ~** *[personnage, film, pays]* legendary 2 *(= inscription) [de médaille]* legend; *[de dessin]* caption; *[de liste, carte]* key • **"sans légende"** *[dessin]* "no caption" 3 *(péj = mensonge)* tall story

légender /leʒɑ̃de/ ► conjug 1 ◄ **VT** to caption

léger, -ère /leʒe, ɛʀ/ **ADJ** 1 *(= de faible poids) [objet, gaz]* light • **arme/industrie légère** light weapon/industry • **construction légère** light *ou* flimsy *(péj)* construction • ~ **comme une plume** as light as a feather • **se sentir ~ (comme un oiseau)** to feel as light as a bird • **je me sens plus ~** *(après un régime, après m'être débarrassé)* I feel pounds lighter; *(= soulagé)* that's a weight off my mind • **je me sens plus ~ de 20 €** *(hum)* I feel €20 poorer • **faire qch l'esprit ~** to do sth with a light heart • **il partit d'un pas ~** he walked away with a spring in his step • **avec une grâce légère** with easy grace; → **main, poids, sommeil**

2 *(= délicat) [parfum, tissu, style]* light

3 *(= non gras) [repas, sauce]* light • **cuisine légère** low-fat cooking

4 *(= faible) [brise]* gentle, slight; *[bruit]* faint; *[couche]* thin, light; *[thé]* weak; *[coup, vin, maquillage]* light; *[alcool]* not very strong; *[blessure]* slight, minor; *[châtiment, tabac]* mild; *[accent]* slight, faint; *[augmentation]* slight • **une légère pointe d'ironie** a touch of irony • **il y a un ~ mieux** there's been a slight improvement • **soprano/ténor ~** light soprano/tenor • **il a été condamné à une peine légère** he was given a light sentence • **deux bouteilles de vin pour sept, c'est un peu ~** * two bottles of wine for seven people isn't very much *ou* isn't really enough; → **blessé**

5 *(= superficiel) [personne]* thoughtless; *[preuve, argument]* lightweight, flimsy; *[jugement, propos]* thoughtless, flippant, careless • **se montrer ~ dans ses actions** to act thoughtlessly • **pour une thèse, c'est un peu ~** it's rather lightweight *ou* a bit on the flimsy side for a thesis

6 *(= frivole) [personne, caractère, humeur]* fickle; *[propos, plaisanterie]* ribald, broad; *[comédie, livre, film]* light • **femme légère** *ou* **de mœurs légères** loose woman, woman of easy virtue; → **cuisse, musique**

ADV • **voyager ~** to travel light • **manger ~** *(non gras)* to eat low-fat foods, to avoid fatty foods; *(peu)* to eat lightly • **s'habiller ~** to wear light clothes

LOC ADV **à la légère** *[parler, agir]* rashly, thoughtlessly, without giving the matter proper consideration • **il prend toujours tout à la légère** he never takes anything seriously, he's very casual about everything

légèrement /leʒɛʀmɑ̃/ **ADV** 1 *[habillé, armé, maquillé] [poser]* lightly • **il a mangé ~** he ate a light meal • **s'habiller ~** to wear light clothes 2 *[courir]* lightly, nimbly 3 *[blesser, bouger]* slightly; *[parfumé]* lightly • ~ **plus grand** slightly bigger • ~ **surpris** mildly *ou* slightly surprised • **il boite/louche ~** he has a slight limp/squint 4 *[agir]* rashly, thoughtlessly, without thinking (properly) • **parler ~ de la mort** to speak flippantly *ou* lightly of death, to speak of death in an offhand *ou* a flippant way

légèreté /leʒɛʀte/ **NF** 1 *[d'objet, tissu, style, repas, sauce]* lightness 2 *[de démarche]* lightness, nimbleness • ~ **de main** light-handedness • **avec une ~ d'oiseau** with bird-like grace • **danser avec ~** to dance lightly *ou* with a light step 3 *[de punition, coup]* lightness, mildness; *[de tabac]* mildness; *[de thé]* weakness; *[de vin]* lightness 4 *(= superficialité) [de conduite, personne, propos]* thoughtlessness; *[de preuves, argument]* flimsiness • **faire preuve de ~** to speak *(ou* behave) rashly *ou* thoughtlessly 5 *(= frivolité) [de personne]* fickleness, flightiness; *[de propos]* flippancy; *[de plaisanterie]* ribaldry

légiférer /leʒifeʀe/ ► conjug 6 ◄ **VI** *(Jur)* to legislate, to make legislation

légion /leʒjɔ̃/ **NF** *(Hist, fig)* legion • ~ **de gendarmerie** corps of gendarmes • **la Légion (étrangère)** the Foreign Legion • **Légion d'honneur** Legion of Honour • **ils sont ~** they are legion *(frm)*, there are any number of them • **les volontaires ne sont pas ~** volunteers are few and far between

> **LÉGION D'HONNEUR**
>
> Created by Napoléon Bonaparte in 1802, the **Légion d'honneur** is a prestigious order awarded for either civil or military merit. The order is divided into five ranks or « classes »: « chevalier », « officier », « commandeur », « grand officier » and « grand-croix » (given here in ascending order). Full regalia worn on official occasions consists of medals and sashes, but on less formal occasions these are replaced by a discreet red ribbon or rosette (according to rank) worn on the lapel.

légionnaire /leʒjɔnɛʀ/ **NM** *(Hist)* legionary; *[de Légion étrangère]* legionnaire; → **maladie** **NMF** *[de Légion d'honneur]* holder of the Legion of Honour

législateur, -trice /leʒislatœʀ, tʀis/ **NM,F** *(= personne)* legislator, lawmaker • **le ~ a prévu ce cas** *(= la loi)* the law makes provision for this case

législatif, -ive /leʒislatif, iv/ **ADJ** legislative • **les (élections) législatives** the legislative elections ≈ the general election *(Brit)*, the Congressional elections *(US)*; → **ÉLECTIONS** **NM** legislature

législation /leʒislasjɔ̃/ **NF** legislation • ~ **fiscale** fiscal *ou* tax legislation, tax laws • ~ **du travail** labour laws, industrial *ou* job legislation

législature /leʒislatyʀ/ **NF** *(Parl) (= durée)* term (of office); *(= corps)* legislature

légiste /leʒist/ **NM** jurist; → **médecin**

légitimation /leʒitimasjɔ̃/ **NF** *[d'enfant]* legitimization; *[de pouvoir]* recognition, legitimation; *(littér) [d'action, conduite]* legitimation

légitime /leʒitim/ **ADJ** 1 *(= légal) [droits, gouvernement]* legitimate, lawful; *[union, femme]* lawful; *[enfant]* legitimate; *[héritier]* legitimate, rightful • **la ~ défense** self-defence • **j'étais en état de ~ défense** I was acting in self-defence 2 *(= juste) [excuse, intérêt]* legitimate; *[colère]* justifiable, justified; *[revendication]* legitimate, rightful; *[récompense]* just, legitimate • **rien de plus ~ que ...** nothing could be more justified than ... **NF** • **ma ~** †* the missus*, the wife*

légitimement /leʒitimmɑ̃/ **ADV** 1 *(Jur)* legitimately 2 *[penser, espérer, attendre, se demander]* reasonably ◆ **on pouvait ~ penser que...** one might reasonably think that ...

légitimer /leʒitime/ ► conjug 1 ◄ VT *[+ enfant]* to legitimate, to legitimize; *[+ conduite, action]* to legitimate, to legitimize, to justify; *[+ titre]* to recognize; *[+ pouvoir]* to recognize, to legitimate

légitimisme /leʒitimism/ NM *(Hist)* legitimism

légitimiste /leʒitimist/ NMF, ADJ *(Hist)* legitimist

légitimité /leʒitimite/ NF *(gén)* legitimacy

Le Greco /ləgʀeko/ NM El Greco

legs /lɛg/ NM *(Jur)* legacy, bequest; *(fig)* legacy ◆ **faire un ~ à qn** to leave sb a legacy ◆ **~ (de biens immobiliers)** devise ◆ **~ (de biens mobiliers)** legacy ◆ **~ (à titre) universel** general legacy

léguer /lege/ ► conjug 6 ◄ VT *(Jur)* to bequeath; *[+ tradition, vertu, tare]* to hand down *ou* on, to pass on ◆ **~ qch à qn par testament** to bequeath sth to sb (in one's will) ◆ **la mauvaise gestion qu'on nous a léguée** the bad management that we inherited

légume /legym/ NM *(lit, fig)* vegetable ◆ **~s secs** pulses ◆ **~s verts** green vegetables, greens*; → **bouillon** NF *(= personne importante)* ◆ **grosse ~** * bigwig*, big shot*

légumier, -ière /legymje, jɛʀ/ ADJ vegetable *(épith)* NM 1 *(= agriculteur)* market gardener; *(Belg = commerçant)* greengrocer 2 *(= plat)* vegetable dish

légumineuse /legyminøz/ NF legume, leguminous plant ◆ **les ~s** legumes, Leguminosae *(SPÉC)*

leitmotiv /lɛtmɔtiv, lajtmɔtif/ NM *(lit, fig)* leitmotiv, leitmotif

Léman /lemɑ̃/ NM ◆ **le (lac) ~** Lake Geneva

lemmatisation /lematizasjɔ̃/ NF lemmatization

lemmatiser /lematize/ ► conjug 1 ◄ VT to lemmatize

lemme /lɛm/ NM lemma

lemming /lemiŋ/ NM lemming

lémur /lemyʀ/ NM lemur

lémure /lemyʀ/ NM *(Antiq)* lemur ◆ **~s** lemures

lémurien /lemyʀjɛ̃/ NM lemur

lendemain /lɑ̃dmɛ̃/ NM 1 *(= jour suivant)* **le ~** the next *ou* following day, the day after ◆ **le ~ de son arrivée/du mariage** the day after he arrived/after the marriage, the day following his arrival/the marriage ◆ **le ~ matin/soir** the next *ou* following morning/evening ◆ **~ de fête** day after a holiday ◆ **au ~ de la guerre** just after the war ◆ **au ~ de la défaite/de son mariage** soon after *ou* in the days following the defeat/his marriage ◆ **le ~ a été difficile** *(gén)* it was the morning after the night before; *(= gueule de bois)* I had a hangover ◆ **ils vont connaître des ~s difficiles** they're in for a tough time → **jour, remettre**

2 *(= avenir)* **le ~** tomorrow, the future ◆ **penser au ~** to think of tomorrow *ou* the future ◆ **bonheur/succès sans ~** short-lived happiness/success

NMPL **lendemains** *(= conséquences)* consequences, repercussions; *(= perspectives)* prospects, future ◆ **cette affaire a eu de fâcheux ~s** this business had unfortunate consequences *ou* repercussions ◆ **des ~s qui chantent** a brighter *ou* better future ◆ **ça nous promet de beaux ~s** the future looks very promising for us ◆ **on peut s'attendre à des ~s qui déchantent** we can expect bad days *ou* hard times ahead

lénifiant, e /lenifjɑ̃, jɑ̃t/ ADJ 1 *(= apaisant) [médicament]* soothing 2 *[propos, discours]* mollifying, soothing; *(péj = amollissant) [atmosphère]* languid, enervating; *[climat]* enervating, draining *(attrib)*

lénifier /lenifje/ ► conjug 7 ◄ VT *(= apaiser)* to soothe; *(péj = amollir)* to enervate

Lénine /lenin/ NM Lenin

léninisme /leninism/ NM Leninism

léniniste /leninist/ ADJ, NMF Leninist

lénitif, -ive /lenitif, iv/ ADJ, NM lenitive

lent, e[1] /lɑ̃, lɑ̃t/ ADJ *(gén)* slow; *[poison]* slow, slow-acting; *[mort]* slow, lingering; *[croissance]* sluggish, slow ◆ **à l'esprit ~** slow-witted, dim-witted ◆ **marcher d'un pas ~** to walk at a slow pace *ou* slowly ◆ **"véhicules lents"** "slow-moving vehicles", "crawler lane" *(Brit)* ◆ **elle est ~e à manger** she's a slow eater, she eats slowly ◆ **il est ~ à comprendre** he is slow to understand *ou* slow on the uptake* ◆ **nous avons été trop ~s à réagir** we were too slow to act ◆ **les résultats ont été ~s à venir** the results were slow to appear

lente[2] /lɑ̃t/ NF *(= œuf de pou)* nit

lentement /lɑ̃tmɑ̃/ ADV slowly ◆ **progresser ~** to make slow progress ◆ **~ mais sûrement** slowly but surely ◆ **qui va ~ va sûrement** *(Prov)* slow and steady wins the race *(Prov)*

lenteur /lɑ̃tœʀ/ NF slowness ◆ **avec ~** slowly ◆ **~ d'esprit** slow-wittedness ◆ **la ~ de la construction** the slow progress of the building work ◆ **des retards dus à des ~s administratives** delays due to slow *ou* cumbersome administrative procedures

lentigo /lɑ̃tigo/ NM lentigo

lentille /lɑ̃tij/ NF 1 *(= plante, graine)* lentil ◆ **~s d'eau** duckweed 2 *(Opt)* lens ◆ **~s (cornéennes ou de contact) dures/souples/jetables** hard/soft/disposable contact lenses ◆ **~ micro-cornéenne** microcorneal lens

> ⚠ **lentille** se traduit par le mot anglais **lentil** uniquement au sens culinaire et botanique.

lentisque /lɑ̃tisk/ NM mastic tree

Léonard /leɔnaʀ/ NM Leonard ◆ **~ de Vinci** Leonardo da Vinci

léonin, e /leɔnɛ̃, in/ ADJ *(= de lion)* leonine; *[rime]* Leonine; *(= injuste) [contrat, partage]* one-sided

léopard /leɔpaʀ/ NM leopard ◆ **manteau de ~** leopardskin coat ◆ **tenue ~** *(Mil)* camouflage (uniform)

LEP /lɛp/ NM (abrév de **lycée d'enseignement professionnel**) → **lycée**

lépidoptère /lepidɔptɛʀ/ ADJ lepidopterous NM lepidopteran, lepidopterous insect ◆ **les ~s** Lepidoptera

lépiote /lepjɔt/ NF parasol mushroom

lèpre /lɛpʀ/ NF *(Méd)* leprosy; *(fig = mal)* scourge, plague ◆ **mur rongé de ~** flaking *ou* peeling wall

lépreux, -euse /lepʀø, øz/ ADJ *(lit)* leprous, suffering from leprosy; *[mur]* flaking, peeling; *[quartier, maison]* rundown NM,F *(lit, fig)* leper

léproserie /lepʀozʀi/ NF leper-house

lequel /ləkɛl/, **laquelle** /lakɛl/ (pl **lesquel(le)s** /lekɛl/) *(contraction avec à, de : auquel, auxquels, auxquelles, duquel, desquels, desquelles)* PRON 1 *(relatif, personne : sujet)* who; *(personne : objet)* whom; *(chose)* which ◆ **j'ai écrit au directeur de la banque, ~ n'a jamais répondu** I wrote to the bank manager, who has never answered ◆ **la patience avec laquelle il écoute** the patience with which he listens ◆ **le règlement d'après ~ ...** the ruling whereby ... ◆ **la femme à laquelle j'ai acheté mon chien** the woman from whom I bought my dog, the woman (who *ou* that) I bought my dog from ◆ **c'est un problème auquel je n'avais pas pensé** that's a problem I hadn't thought of *ou* which hadn't occurred to me ◆ **le pont sur ~ vous êtes passé** the bridge you came over *ou* over which you came ◆ **le docteur/le traitement sans ~ elle serait morte** the doctor without whom/the treatment without which she would have died ◆ **cette société sur laquelle on dit tant de mal** this society about which so much ill is spoken ◆ **la plupart desquels** *(personnes)* most of whom; *(choses)* most of which ◆ **les gens chez lesquels j'ai logé** the people at whose house I stayed, the people I stayed with; → **importer**[2]

2 *(interrogatif)* which ◆ **~ des deux acteurs préférez-vous ?** which of the two actors do you prefer? ◆ **dans ~ de ces hôtels avez-vous logé ?** in which of these hotels did you stay? ◆ **laquelle des sonates de Mozart avez-vous entendue ?** which of Mozart's sonatas *ou* which Mozart sonata did you hear? ◆ **laquelle des chambres est la sienne ?** which is his room?, which of the rooms is his? ◆ **je ne sais à laquelle des vendeuses m'adresser** I don't know which saleswoman I should speak to ◆ **devinez lesquels de ces tableaux elle aimerait avoir** guess which of these pictures she would like to have ◆ **donnez-moi un melon/deux melons – ~ ?/lesquels ?** give me one melon/two melons – which one?/which ones? ◆ **va voir ma sœur – laquelle ?** go and see my sister – which one?

ADJ ◆ **son état pourrait empirer, auquel cas je reviendrais** his condition could worsen, in which case I would come back ◆ **il écrivit au ministre, ~ ministre ne répondit jamais** *(littér, iro)* he wrote to the minister but the latter *ou* the said minister never replied

lerch(e)* /lɛʀʃ/ ADV ◆ **pas ~(e)** not much ◆ **il n'y en a pas ~(e)** there's not much of it

lérot /leʀo/ NM lerot, garden dormouse

les /le/ → **le**[1], **le**[2]

lesbianisme /lɛsbjanism/ NM lesbianism

lesbien, -ienne /lɛsbjɛ̃, jɛn/ ADJ lesbian NF **lesbienne** lesbian

lesdites /ledit/, **lesdits** /ledi/ ADJ → **ledit**

lèse-majesté /lɛzmaʒɛste/ NF lese-majesty; → **crime**

léser /leze/ ► conjug 6 ◄ VT 1 *(Jur = frustrer) [+ personne]* to wrong; *[+ intérêts]* to damage ◆ **je ne voudrais ~ personne** I don't want to cheat anyone ◆ **la partie lésée** the injured party ◆ **~ les droits de qn** to infringe on sb's rights ◆ **ils s'estiment lésés par cette réforme** they feel that they were the losers in this reform ◆ **il s'est senti lésé par rapport à son frère** he felt that his brother got a better deal than him, he felt he did less well out of it than his brother ◆ **je me sens lésé quelque part** I somehow feel that I got a raw deal 2 *(Méd = blesser) [+ organe]* to injure

lésiner /lezine/ ► conjug 1 ◄ VI to skimp *(sur qch* on sth); ◆ **ne pas ~ sur les moyens** *(gén)* to use all the means at one's disposal; *(pour mariage, repas)* to push the boat out*, to pull out all the stops*

lésinerie /lezinʀi/ NF stinginess *(NonC)*

lésion /lezjɔ̃/ NF *(Jur, Méd)* lesion ◆ **~s internes** internal injuries

lésionnel, -elle /lezjɔnɛl/ ADJ *[trouble]* caused by a lesion; *[syndrome]* of a lesion

Lesotho /lezɔto/ NM Lesotho

lesquels, lesquelles /lekɛl/ → **lequel**

lessivable /lesivabl/ ADJ *[papier peint]* washable

lessivage /lesivaʒ/ NM *(gén)* washing; *(Chim, Géol)* leaching

lessive /lesiv/ NF 1 *(= produit) (en poudre)* washing powder *(Brit)*, (powdered) laundry detergent (US); *(liquide)* liquid detergent; *(Tech = soude)* lye 2 *(= lavage)* washing *(NonC)* ◆ **le jeudi est mon jour de ~** Thursday is washday for me ◆ **faire la ~** to do the washing ◆ **faire quatre ~s par semaine** to do four washes a week ◆ **mettre une chemise à la ~** to put a shirt in the wash *ou* in the laundry ◆ **la grande ~** *(fig)* the big cleanup 3 *(= linge)* washing *(NonC)* ◆ **porter sa ~ à la blanchisserie** to take one's washing to the laundry

lessiver /lesive/ ▸ conjug 1 ◂ VT 1 *[+ mur, plancher, linge]* to wash 2 *(Chim, Géol)* to leach 3 *(* = battre) (au jeu)* to clean out*; *[+ adversaire]* to lick* 4 *(* = fatiguer)* to tire out, to exhaust ◆ **être lessivé** to be dead-beat* *ou* all-in* *ou* tired out

lessiveuse /lesivøz/ NF boiler *(for washing laundry)*

lessiviel /lesivjel/ ADJ M ◆ **produit ~** detergent product

lessivier /lesivje/ NM *(= fabricant)* detergent manufacturer

lest /lɛst/ NM *(Naut, Aviat)* ballast ◆ **sur son ~** in ballast ◆ **garnir un bateau de ~** to ballast a ship ◆ **jeter** *ou* **lâcher du ~** *(lit)* to dump ballast; *(fig)* to make concessions

lestage /lɛstaʒ/ NM ballasting

leste /lɛst/ ADJ 1 *[personne, animal]* nimble, agile; *[démarche]* light, nimble; → **main** 2 *(= grivois) [plaisanterie]* risqué 3 *(= cavalier) [ton, réponse]* offhand

lestement /lɛstəmɑ̃/ ADV 1 *(= souplement)* with great agility, nimbly 2 *(= cavalièrement) [traiter]* offhandedly

lester /lɛste/ ▸ conjug 1 ◂ VT 1 *(= garnir de lest)* to ballast 2 *(* = remplir) [+ portefeuille, poches]* to fill, to cram ◆ **~ son estomac, se ~ (l'estomac)** to fill one's stomach ◆ **lesté d'un repas copieux** weighed down with a heavy meal

let /lɛt/ NM *(Tennis)* let ◆ **balle ~** let ball ◆ **jouer une balle ~, faire un ~** to play a let

létal, e (mpl **-aux**) /letal, o/ ADJ *[dose, gène]* lethal

léthargie /letaʀʒi/ NF *(= apathie, Méd)* lethargy ◆ **tomber en ~** to fall into a state of lethargy

léthargique /letaʀʒik/ ADJ lethargic ◆ **état ~** lethargic state, state of lethargy

lette /lɛt/ NM *(Ling)* Latvian, Lett, Lettish

letton, -on(n)e /letɔ̃, ɔn/ ADJ Latvian NM *(= langue)* Latvian NM,F **Letton(ne)** Latvian

Lettonie /letɔni/ NF Latvia

lettrage /letʀaʒ/ NM lettering

lettre /lɛtʀ/ GRAMMAIRE ACTIVE 48.1

NF 1 *(= caractère)* letter ◆ **mot de six ~s** six-letter word, word of six letters ◆ **écrire un nom en toutes ~s** to write out a name in full ◆ **écrivez la somme en (toutes) ~s** write out the sum in full ◆ **c'est en toutes ~s dans les journaux** it's there in black and white *ou* it's there for all to read in the newspapers ◆ **c'est en grosses ~s dans les journaux** it's made headlines ◆ **c'est écrit en toutes ~s sur sa figure** it's written all over his face ◆ **c'est à écrire en ~s d'or** it's a momentous event, it's something to celebrate ◆ **inscrit** *ou* **gravé en ~s de feu** written in letters of fire ◆ **cette lutte est écrite en ~s de sang** this bloody struggle will remain branded *ou* engraved on people's memories; → **cinq, majuscule, minuscule**

2 *(= missive)* letter ◆ **~s** *(= courrier)* letters, mail, post ◆ **faire une ~** to write a letter *(à* to*)*; ◆ **jeter** *ou* **mettre une ~ à la boîte** *ou* **à la poste** to post *ou* mail (US) a letter ◆ **y avait-il des ~s aujourd'hui ?** were there any letters today?, was there any mail *ou* post today? ◆ **écris-lui donc une petite ~** write him a note, drop him a line* ◆ **~ d'injures** abusive letter ◆ **~ de condoléances/de félicitations/de réclamations/of complaint** letter of condolence/of congratulations/of complaint ◆ **~ d'amour/d'affaires** love/business letter ◆ **~ de rupture** letter ending a relationship, Dear John letter ◆ **"lettre suit"** "letter follows"

3 *(= sens strict)* **prendre qch au pied de la ~** to take sth literally ◆ **suivre la ~ de la loi** to follow the letter of the law ◆ **exécuter des ordres à la ~** to carry out orders to the letter

4 *(locutions)* **rester ~ morte** *[remarque, avis, protestation]* to go unheeded ◆ **devenir ~ morte** *[loi, traité]* to become a dead letter ◆ **c'est passé comme une ~ à la poste*** it went off smoothly *ou* without a hitch ◆ **Anne Lemoine, cette féministe (bien) avant la ~** Anne Lemoine, a feminist (long) before the term existed *ou* had been coined

NFPL **lettres** 1 *(= littérature)* **les (belles) ~s** literature ◆ **femme/homme/gens de ~s** woman/man/men of letters ◆ **le monde des ~s** the literary world ◆ **avoir des ~s** to be well-read

2 *(Scol, Univ) (gén)* arts (subjects); *(= français)* French literature and language ◆ **il est très fort en ~s** he's very good at arts subjects *ou* at the arts ◆ **il fait des ~s** he's doing an arts degree ◆ **professeur de ~s** teacher of French, French teacher *(in France)* ◆ **~s classiques** classics *(sg)* ◆ **~s modernes** *(= section)* French department, department of French (language and literature); *(= discipline)* French (language and literature); → **faculté, licence**

COMP **lettre d'accompagnement** covering *(Brit) ou* cover *(US)* letter
lettre de cachet *(Hist)* lettre de cachet
lettre de change bill of exchange
lettre de château thank-you letter
lettre circulaire circular
lettres de créance credentials
lettre de crédit letter of credit
lettre exprès express letter
lettre d'intention letter of intent
lettres de noblesse *(lit)* letters patent of nobility ◆ **donner ses ~s de noblesse à** *(fig)* to lend credibility to ◆ **gagner ses ~s de noblesse** *(fig)* to win acclaim, to establish one's pedigree
lettre ouverte *(Presse)* open letter
lettres patentes letters (of) patent, letters patent of nobility
lettre de rappel reminder
lettre de recommandation letter of recommendation, reference
lettre de service notification of command
lettres supérieures *(Scol) first year of two-year preparatory course for the arts section of the École normale supérieure*
lettre de voiture consignment note, waybill; → **motivation, recommandé, relance**

lettré, e /letʀe/ ADJ well-read NM,F man *(ou* woman) of letters

lettrine /letʀin/ NF 1 *[de dictionnaire]* headline 2 *[de chapitre]* dropped initial

leu /lø/ NM → **queue**

leucémie /løsemi/ NF leukaemia *(Brit)*, leukemia *(US)*

leucémique /løsemik/ ADJ leukaemic *(Brit)*, leukemic *(US)* NMF leukaemia *(Brit) ou* leukemia *(US)* sufferer

leucocytaire /løkositɛʀ/ ADJ leucocytic, leukocytic *(US)*

leucocyte /løkɔsit/ NM leucocyte, leukocyte *(US)* ◆ **~ mononucléaire** monocyte ◆ **~ polynucléaire** polymorphonuclear leucocyte

leucorrhée /løkɔʀe/ NF leucorrhoea

leucotomie /løkɔtɔmi/ NF leucotomy

leur /lœʀ/ PRON PERS them ◆ **je le ~ ai dit** I told them ◆ **il ~ est facile de le faire** it is easy for them to do it ◆ **elle ~ serra la main** she shook their hand, she shook them by the hand ◆ **je ~ en ai donné** I gave them some, I gave some to them

ADJ POSS 1 *(gén)* their ◆ **~ jardin est une vraie forêt vierge** their garden is a real jungle ◆ **~ maladroite de sœur** that clumsy sister of theirs ◆ **ils ont passé tout ~ dimanche à travailler** they spent all Sunday working

2 *(littér)* theirs, their own ◆ **un ~ cousin** a cousin of theirs ◆ **ils ont fait ~s ces idées** they made these ideas their own ◆ **ces terres qui étaient ~s** these estates of theirs *ou* which were theirs

PRON POSS ◆ **le ~, la ~, les ~s** theirs ◆ **ces sacs sont les ~s** these bags are theirs, these are their bags ◆ **ils sont partis dans une voiture qui n'était pas la ~** they left in a car which wasn't theirs *ou* their own ◆ **à la (bonne) ~ !** their good health!, here's to them!; *pour autres loc voir* **sien**

NM 1 *(= énergie, volonté)* **ils y ont mis du ~** they pulled their weight, they did their bit*; → aussi **sien**

2 ◆ **les ~s** *(= famille)* their family, their (own) folks*; *(= partisans)* their own people ◆ **nous étions des ~s** we were with them ◆ **l'un des ~s** one of their people

leurre /lœʀ/ NM *(= illusion)* delusion, illusion; *(= duperie)* deception; *(= piège)* trap, snare; *(Fauconnerie, Pêche)* lure; *(Chasse, Mil)* decoy

leurrer /lœʀe/ ▸ conjug 1 ◂ VT *(gén)* to deceive, to delude; *(Fauconnerie, Pêche)* to lure ◆ **ils nous ont leurrés par des promesses fallacieuses** they deluded us with false promises ◆ **ils se sont laissé ~** they let themselves be taken in *ou* deceived ◆ **ne vous leurrez pas** don't delude yourself ◆ **ne nous leurrons pas sur leurs intentions** we should not delude ourselves about their intentions

levage /ləvaʒ/ NM *[de charge]* lifting; *[de pâte, pain]* rising, raising; → **appareil**

levain /ləvɛ̃/ NM leaven ◆ **sans ~** unleavened ◆ **pain au ~** leavened bread ◆ **~ de haine/de vengeance** seeds of hate/of vengeance

levant /ləvɑ̃/ ADJ ◆ **soleil ~** rising sun ◆ **au soleil ~** at sunrise NM 1 *(= est)* east ◆ **du ~ au couchant** from east to west ◆ **les chambres sont au ~** the bedrooms face east 2 *(= l'Orient)* **le Levant** the Levant

levantin, -ine † /ləvɑ̃tɛ̃, in/ ADJ Levantine NM,F **Levantin(e)** Levantine

levé[1] /l(ə)ve/ NM *(= plan)* survey ◆ **~ de terrain** land survey

levé[2]**, e**[1] /l(ə)ve/ (ptp de **lever**) ADJ *(= sorti du lit)* ◆ **être ~** to be up ◆ **sitôt ~** as soon as he is up ◆ **il n'est pas encore ~** he isn't up yet ◆ **toujours le premier ~** always the first up; → **pierre** NM *(Mus)* up-beat

levée[2] /l(ə)ve/ NF 1 *[de blocus, siège]* raising; *[de séance]* closing; *[d'interdiction, punition]* lifting ◆ **ils ont voté la ~ de son immunité parlementaire** they voted to take away *ou* to withdraw his parliamentary immunity

2 *(Poste)* collection ◆ **la ~ du matin est faite** the morning collection has been made, the morning post has gone *(Brit)* ◆ **dernière ~ à 19 heures** last collection (at) 7 p.m.

3 *(Cartes)* trick ◆ **faire une ~** to take a trick

4 *[d'impôts]* levying; *[d'armée]* raising, levying

5 *(= remblai)* levee

COMP **levée de boucliers** *(fig)* general outcry, hue and cry
levée du corps ◆ **la ~ du corps aura lieu à 10 heures** the funeral will start from the house at 10 o'clock
levée d'écrou release (from prison)
levée de jugement transcript (of a verdict)
levée en masse mass conscription
levée des scellés removal of the seals
levée de terre levee

lever[1] /l(ə)ve/ ► conjug 5 ◄ VT 1 *(= soulever, hausser) [+ poids, objet]* to lift; *[+ main, bras, vitre]* to raise; *(à la manivelle)* to wind up; *[+ tête]* to raise, to lift up ◆ **levez la main** *ou* **le doigt** *(en classe)* put your hand up ◆ **lève ton coude, je veux prendre le papier** lift *ou* raise your elbow, I want to take the paper away ◆ **lève les pieds quand tu marches** pick your feet up when you walk ◆ ~ **les yeux** to lift up *ou* raise one's eyes, to look up *(de* from); ◆ ~ **les yeux sur qn** *(= le regarder)* to look at sb; *(† = vouloir l'épouser)* to set one's heart on marrying sb ◆ ~ **le visage vers qn** to look up at sb ◆ ~ **un regard suppliant/éploré vers qn** to look up imploringly/tearfully at sb

2 *(= faire cesser, supprimer) [+ blocus]* to raise; *[+ séance, audience]* to close; *[+ obstacle, difficulté]* to remove; *[+ interdiction, sanction, restriction]* to lift; *[+ ambiguïté]* to clear up; *[+ immunité parlementaire]* to withdraw, to take away ◆ ~ **les scellés** to remove the seals ◆ **cela a levé tous ses scrupules** that has removed all his scruples ◆ **on lève la séance ?*** shall we call it a day?, shall we break up? *(US)*

3 *(Fin, Jur) [+ option]* to exercise, to take up

4 *(= ramasser) [+ impôts]* to levy; *[+ armée]* to raise, to levy; *[+ fonds]* to raise; *(Cartes) [+ pli]* to take; *[facteur] [+ lettres]* to collect

5 *(Chasse) [+ lapin]* to start; *[+ perdrix]* to flush; *[+ femme]* to pick up*; → **lièvre**

6 *(= établir) [+ plan]* to draw (up); *[+ carte]* to draw

7 *(= sortir du lit) [+ enfant, malade]* to get up ◆ **le matin, pour le faire ~, il faut se fâcher** in the morning, you have to get angry before he'll get up *ou* to get him out of bed

8 *(= prélever) [+ morceau de viande]* to take off, to remove ◆ ~ **les filets d'un poisson** to fillet a fish

9 *(locutions)* ~ **l'ancre** *(Naut)* to weigh anchor; *(* = s'en aller)* to make tracks* ◆ ~ **les bras au ciel** to throw one's arms up in the air ◆ ~ **les yeux au ciel** to raise one's eyes heavenwards ◆ ~ **le camp** *(lit)* to strike *ou* break camp; *(fig = partir)* to clear off* ◆ ~ **le siège** *(lit)* to lift *ou* raise the siege; *(fig = partir)* to clear off* ◆ **il lève bien le coude*** he enjoys a drink, he drinks a fair bit* ◆ ~ **la patte** *[chien] (pour uriner)* to cock *ou* lift its leg; *(pour dire bonjour)* to give a paw ◆ ~ **le pied** *(= disparaître)* to vanish; *(= ralentir)* to slow down ◆ **entre Paris et Lyon, il n'a pas levé le pied** he didn't take his foot off the accelerator between Paris and Lyons ◆ ~ **la main sur qn** to raise one's hand to sb ◆ ~ **le rideau** *(Théât)* to raise the curtain ◆ ~ **le voile** to reveal the truth *(sur* about); ◆ ~ **le masque** to unmask o.s. ◆ ~ **son verre à la santé de qn** to raise one's glass to sb, to drink (to) sb's health; → **main, pied**

VI 1 *[plante, blé]* to come up

2 *(Culin)* to rise ◆ **faire ~ la pâte** leave the dough to rise

VPR **se lever** 1 *[rideau, main]* to go up ◆ **toutes les mains se levèrent** every hand went up

2 *(= se mettre debout)* to stand up, to get up ◆ **se ~ de table/de sa chaise** to get down from the table/get up from one's chair ◆ **le maître les fit se ~** the teacher made them stand up *ou* get up ◆ **levez-vous !** stand up!

3 *(= sortir du lit)* to get up ◆ **se ~ tôt** to get up early, to rise early ◆ **le convalescent commence à se ~** the convalescent is beginning to walk about ◆ **ce matin, il s'est levé du pied gauche** he got out of bed on the wrong side this morning ◆ **se ~ sur son séant** to sit up ◆ **il faut se ~ de bonne heure pour le convaincre !*** you've got your work cut out for you if you want to persuade him

4 *[soleil, lune]* to rise; *[jour]* to break ◆ **le soleil n'était pas encore levé** the sun had not yet risen *ou* was not yet up

5 *(Météo) [vent]* to get up, to rise; *[brume]* to lift, to clear; *[mer]* to swell ◆ **le temps se lève, ça se lève** the weather *ou* it is clearing

6 *(= se révolter)* to rise up

lever[2] /ləve/ NM 1 ◆ ~ **de soleil** sunrise, sun-up* *(US)* ◆ **le ~ du jour** daybreak, dawn ◆ **il partit dès le ~ du jour** he left at daybreak *ou* dawn 2 *(au réveil)* **prenez trois comprimés au ~** take three tablets when you get up ◆ **au ~, à son ~** *(présent)* when he gets up; *(passé)* when he got up ◆ **le ~ du roi** the levee of the king 3 *(Théât)* **le ~ du rideau** *(= action de monter le rideau)* the raising of the curtain; *(= commencement d'une pièce)* curtain up ◆ **un ~ de rideau** *(= pièce, match)* a curtain-raiser ◆ **en ~ de rideau, nous avons ...** as a curtain-raiser *ou* to start with, we have ... 4 ⇒ **levé**[1]

lève-tard /lɛvtaʀ/ NMF INV late riser

lève-tôt /lɛvto/ NMF INV early riser

lève-vitre (pl **lève-vitres**) /lɛvvitʀ/ NM (window) winder ◆ ~ **électrique** electric window

Léviathan /levjatɑ̃/ NM *(Bible)* Leviathan

levier /ləvje/ NM lever ◆ ~ **de commande** control lever ◆ ~ **de changement de vitesse** gear lever *(Brit)*, gearshift *(US)*, stick shift* *(US)* ◆ ~ **de frein** handbrake (lever) ◆ **faire ~ sur qch** to lever sth up *(ou off etc)* ◆ **être aux ~s (de commande)** *(fig)* to be in control *ou* command ◆ **l'argent est un puissant ~** money is a powerful lever

lévitation /levitasjɔ̃/ NF levitation ◆ **être en ~** to be levitating

lévite /levit/ NM Levite

Lévitique /levitik/ NM ◆ **le ~** Leviticus

levraut /ləvʀo/ NM leveret

lèvre /lɛvʀ/ NF 1 *[de bouche]* lip ◆ **le sourire aux ~s** with a smile on one's lips ◆ **la cigarette aux ~s** with a cigarette between one's lips ◆ **son nom est sur toutes les ~s** his name is on everyone's lips ◆ **j'ai les ~s scellées** *(fig)* my lips are sealed; → **bout, pincer, rouge** *etc* 2 *[de plaie]* edge; *[de vulve]* lip, labium *(SPÉC)* ◆ **petites/grandes ~s** labia minora/majora *(SPÉC)* 3 *(Géog) [de faille]* side ◆ ~ **soulevée/abaissée** upthrow/downthrow side

levrette /ləvʀɛt/ NF *(= femelle)* greyhound bitch; *(= variété de lévrier)* Italian greyhound ◆ **en ~** *(= position sexuelle)* doggie-style, doggie-fashion

lévrier /levʀije/ NM greyhound ◆ **courses de ~s** greyhound racing ◆ ~ **afghan** Afghan (hound) ◆ ~ **irlandais** Irish wolfhound ◆ ~ **italien** Italian greyhound

levure /l(ə)vyʀ/ NF *(= ferment)* yeast ◆ ~ **de bière** brewers' yeast ◆ ~ **de boulanger** *ou* **de boulangerie** baker's yeast ◆ ~ **chimique** baking powder

lexème /lɛksɛm/ NM lexeme

lexical, e (mpl **-aux**) /lɛksikal, o/ ADJ lexical

lexicalisation /lɛksikalizasjɔ̃/ NF lexicalization

lexicalisé, e /lɛksikalize/ ADJ lexicalized

lexicaliser /lɛksikalize/ ► conjug 1 ◄ VT to lexicalize VPR **se lexicaliser** to become lexicalized

lexicographe /lɛksikɔgʀaf/ NMF lexicographer

lexicographie /lɛksikɔgʀafi/ NF lexicography

lexicographique /lɛksikɔgʀafik/ ADJ lexicographical

lexicologie /lɛksikɔlɔʒi/ NF lexicology

lexicologique /lɛksikɔlɔʒik/ ADJ lexicological

lexicologue /lɛksikɔlɔg/ NMF lexicologist

lexie /lɛksi/ NF lexical item

lexique /lɛksik/ NM 1 *(= glossaire)* glossary; *(d'une langue ancienne)* lexicon 2 *(= mots d'une langue)* lexicon, lexis *(SPÉC)*; *(= mots d'une personne)* vocabulary, lexicon

lézard /lezaʀ/ NM *(= animal)* lizard; *(= peau)* lizardskin ◆ ~ **vert/des murailles** green/wall lizard ◆ **sac/gants en ~** lizardskin bag/gloves ◆ **faire le ~ (au soleil)*** to bask in the sun ◆ **y a pas de ~ !*** no problem!*, no prob!*

lézarde /lezaʀd/ NF *(= fissure)* crack

lézarder[1]* /lezaʀde/ ► conjug 1 ◄ VI to bask in the sun

lézarder[2] VT, **se lézarder** VPR /lezaʀde/ ► conjug 1 ◄ *(= craquer)* to crack

Lhassa /lasa/ N Lhasa, Lassa

liaison /ljɛzɔ̃/ NF 1 *(= fréquentation)* ~ **(amoureuse)** (love) affair, liaison ◆ **avoir/rompre une ~** to have/break off an affair *ou* a love affair

2 *(= contact)* **assurer la ~ entre les différents services** to liaise between the different departments ◆ **avoir des ~s avec** *(péj)* to have links *ou* dealings with ◆ **j'espère que nous allons rester en ~** I hope that we shall remain in contact *ou* in touch ◆ **entrer/être en ~ étroite avec qn** to get/be in close contact with sb ◆ **travailler en ~ étroite avec qn** to work closely with *ou* in close collaboration with sb ◆ **en ~ (étroite) avec nos partenaires, nous avons décidé de ...** in (close) collaboration with *ou* after (close) consultation with our partners, we have decided to ... ◆ **se tenir en ~ avec l'état-major** to keep in contact with headquarters, to liaise with headquarters ◆ **officier** *ou* **agent de ~** liaison officer

3 *(Radio, Téléc)* ~ **radio** radio contact ◆ **les ~s téléphoniques avec le Japon** telephone links with Japan ◆ ~ **par satellite/câble** satellite/cable link ◆ **je suis en ~ avec notre envoyé spécial à Moscou** I have our special correspondent on the line from Moscow ◆ ~ **de transmission** *(Ordin)* data link

4 *(= rapport, enchaînement)* connection ◆ **manque de ~ entre deux idées** lack of connection between two ideas ◆ **il n'y a aucune ~ entre les deux idées/événements** the two ideas/events are unconnected

5 *(Gram, Phon)* liaison ◆ **consonne de ~** linking consonant ◆ **mot** *ou* **terme de ~** link-word ◆ **faire la ~** to make a liaison

6 *(Transport)* link ◆ ~ **aérienne/routière/ferroviaire/maritime** air/road/rail/sea link

7 *(Culin) (= action)* thickening, liaison; *(= ingrédients)* liaison

8 *(Mus) (même hauteur)* tie; *(hauteurs différentes)* slur

9 *(Chim)* bond

10 *(Constr) (= action)* bonding; *(= mortier)* bond

liane /ljan/ NF creeper, liana

liant, liante /ljɑ̃, ljɑ̃t/ ADJ sociable NM 1 *(littér : en société)* sociable disposition ◆ **il a du ~** he has a sociable disposition *ou* nature, he is sociable 2 *(Métal = souplesse)* flexibility 3 *(= substance)* binder

liard /ljaʀ/ NM *(Hist)* farthing ◆ **je n'ai pas un ~ †** I haven't (got) a farthing †

lias /ljɑs/ NM *(Géol)* Lias

liasique /ljɑzik/ ADJ *(Géol)* Liassic

liasse /ljas/ NF *[de billets]* wad; *[de papiers]* bundle ◆ **mettre des billets en ~s** to make (up) wads of notes

Liban /libɑ̃/ NM ◆ **(le) ~** (the) Lebanon

libanais, e /libanɛ, ɛz/ ADJ Lebanese NM,F **Libanais(e)** Lebanese

libanisation /libanizasjɔ̃/ NF *(Pol)* ◆ **la ~ du pays** the fragmentation of the country

libation /libasjɔ̃/ NF *(Antiq)* libation ◆ **faire de copieuses ~s** *(fig)* to indulge in great libations *(hum)*

libelle /libɛl/ NM (= *satire*) lampoon ◆ **faire des ~s contre qn** to lampoon sb

libellé /libele/ NM (*gén*) wording; (*Fin*) description, particulars

libeller /libele/ ▸ conjug 1 ◂ VT [*+ acte*] to draw up; [*+ chèque*] to make out (*à l'ordre de* to); [*+ lettre, demande, réclamation*] to word ◆ **sa lettre était ainsi libellée** so went his letter, his letter was worded thus

libelliste /libelist/ NM (*littér*) lampoonist

libellule /libelyl/ NF dragonfly

liber /libɛʀ/ NM (*Bot*) phloem

libérable /libeʀabl/ ADJ [*militaire*] dischargeable ◆ **permission ~** leave in hand (*allowing early discharge*)

libéral, e (mpl **-aux**) /libeʀal, o/ ADJ 1 (*Pol*) Liberal 2 (*Écon*) [*économie, modèle*] free-market (*épith*) ◆ **travailler en ~** [*médecin*] to have a private practice; [*chauffeur de taxi*] to work for oneself; → **profession** 3 (= *tolérant*) liberal, open-minded NM,F (*Pol*) Liberal

libéralement /libeʀalmɑ̃/ ADV liberally

libéralisation /libeʀalizasjɔ̃/ NF (*gén*) liberalization ◆ **la ~ du commerce** trade liberalization, the easing of restrictions on trade ◆ **~ de l'avortement** liberalization of the abortion laws

libéraliser /libeʀalize/ ▸ conjug 1 ◂ VT (*gén*) to liberalize ◆ **~ la vente des seringues** to lift restrictions on the sale of syringes

libéralisme /libeʀalism/ NM (*gén*) liberalism ◆ **être partisan du ~ économique** to be a supporter of economic liberalism *ou* of free enterprise

libéralité /libeʀalite/ NF (*littér*) (= *générosité*) liberality; (*gén pl* = *don*) generous gift, liberality (*frm*) ◆ **vivre des ~s d'un ami** to live off a friend's generosity

libérateur, -trice /libeʀatœʀ, tʀis/ ADJ ◆ **guerre/croisade libératrice** war/crusade of liberation ◆ **rire ~** liberating laugh ◆ **expérience libératrice** liberating experience NM,F liberator

libération /libeʀasjɔ̃/ NF 1 [*de prisonnier, otage*] release; [*de soldat*] discharge; [*de pays, peuple, ville*] freeing, liberation ◆ **front/mouvement de ~** liberation front/movement ◆ **la Libération** (*Hist*) the Liberation ◆ **~ anticipée** early release ◆ **~ conditionnelle** release on parole ◆ **la ~ de la femme** Women's Liberation ◆ **~ sexuelle** sexual liberation 2 (*Fin*) **~ de capital** paying up of capital, payment in full of capital ◆ **~ des prix** price deregulation 3 (*Sci*) [*d'énergie, électrons*] release; → **vitesse**

libératoire /libeʀatwaʀ/ ADJ (*Fin*) ◆ **paiement ~** payment in full discharge ◆ **prélèvement ~** levy at source (*on share dividends*)

libéré, e /libeʀe/ (ptp de **libérer**) ADJ liberated

libérer /libeʀe/ ▸ conjug 6 ◂ VT 1 [*+ prisonnier*] to discharge, to release (*de* from); [*+ otage*] to release, to set free; [*+ soldat*] to discharge (*de* from); [*+ élèves, employés*] to let go; [*+ pays, peuple, ville*] to free, to liberate ◆ **être libéré sur parole** (*Jur*) to be released on parole; → **caution**

2 [*+ esprit, personne*] (*de soucis*) to free (*de* from); (*d'inhibition*) to liberate (*de* from); ◆ **~ qn de** [*+ liens*] to release *ou* free sb from; [*+ promesse*] to release sb from; [*+ dette*] to free sb from ◆ **ça m'a libéré de lui dire ce que je pensais** it was a relief to tell him what I was thinking

3 [*+ appartement*] to move out of, to vacate; [*+ étagère*] to clear; [*+ tiroir*] to empty ◆ **nous libérerons la salle à 11 heures** we'll clear the room at 11 o'clock ◆ **~ le passage** to free *ou* unblock the way ◆ **ça a libéré trois postes** it made three jobs available

4 (*Tech*) [*+ levier, cran d'arrêt*] to release; (*Écon*) [*+ échanges commerciaux*] to ease restrictions on; [*+ prix*] to decontrol; (*Méd*) [*+ intestin*] to unblock

5 (= *soulager*) **~ son cœur/sa conscience** to unburden one's heart/one's conscience ◆ **~ ses instincts** to give free rein to one's instincts

6 (*Sci*) [*+ énergie, électrons, hormones*] to release; [*+ gaz*] to release, to give off

VPR **se libérer** 1 [*personne*] (*de ses liens*) to free o.s. (*de* from); (*d'une promesse*) to release o.s. (*de* from); (*d'une dette*) to clear o.s. (*de* of); ◆ **se ~ d'un rendez-vous** to get out of a meeting ◆ **désolé, jeudi je ne peux pas me ~** I'm sorry, I'm not free on Thursday ◆ **je n'ai pas pu me ~ plus tôt** I couldn't get away any earlier ◆ **se ~ du joug de l'oppresseur** (= *s'affranchir*) to free o.s. from the yoke of one's oppressor

2 [*appartement*] to become vacant; [*place assise*] to become available; [*poste*] to become vacant *ou* available

Libéria /libeʀja/ NM Liberia

libérien, -ienne /libeʀjɛ̃, jɛn/ ADJ Liberian NM,F **Libérien(ne)** Liberian

libériste /libeʀist/ NMF (= *sportif*) hang-glider ADJ hang-gliding

libéro /libeʀo/ NM (*Ftbl*) libero (*SPÉC*), ≈ sweeper

libertaire /libɛʀtɛʀ/ ADJ, NMF libertarian

liberté /libɛʀte/ NF 1 (*gén, Jur*) freedom, liberty ◆ **rendre la ~ à un prisonnier** to free *ou* release a prisoner, to set a prisoner free ◆ **elle a quitté son mari et repris sa ~** she has left her husband and regained her freedom *ou* her independence ◆ **sans la ~ de critiquer/de choisir aucune opinion n'a de valeur** without the freedom to criticize/to choose any opinion is valueless ◆ **avoir toute ~ pour agir** to have full liberty *ou* freedom *ou* scope to act ◆ **donner à qn toute ~ d'action** to give sb complete freedom of action, to give sb a free hand ◆ **agir en toute *ou* pleine ~** to act with complete freedom, to act quite freely

2 (*locutions*) **laisser en ~** to allow to remain at liberty ◆ **mise en ~** [*de prisonnier*] discharge, release ◆ **être en ~** to be free ◆ **animaux en ~** animals in the wild *ou* natural state ◆ **les animaux sont en ~ dans le parc** the animals roam free in the park ◆ **le voleur est encore en ~** the thief is still at large ◆ **remettre en ~** [*+ animal*] to set free (again); [*+ otage, prisonnier*] to release, to set free

3 (*gén, Pol* = *indépendance*) freedom ◆ **~ de la presse/d'opinion/de conscience** freedom of the press/of thought/of conscience ◆ **~ individuelle** personal freedom ◆ **~ d'information/d'expression** freedom of information/of expression ◆ **~ religieuse *ou* de culte** religious freedom, freedom of worship ◆ **vive la ~ !** long live freedom! ◆ **~, égalité, fraternité** liberty, equality, fraternity ◆ **la Statue de la Liberté** the Statue of Liberty

4 (= *loisir*) **heures/moments de ~** free hours/moments ◆ **ils ont droit à deux jours de ~ par semaine** they are allowed two free days a week *ou* two days off each week ◆ **son travail ne lui laisse pas beaucoup de ~** his work doesn't leave him much free time

5 (= *absence de retenue, de contrainte*) **~ d'esprit/de jugement** independence of mind/of judgment ◆ **~ de langage/de mœurs** freedom of language/of morals ◆ **la ~ de ton du ministre a étonné** the fact that the minister expressed himself so openly *ou* freely surprised people ◆ **la ~ de ton de l'émission a choqué** the frank approach of the programme shocked people ◆ **s'exprimer avec (grande) ~** to express o.s. (very) freely ◆ **prendre la ~ de faire** to take the liberty of doing ◆ **prendre *ou* se permettre des ~s avec** [*+ personne, texte, grammaire, règlement*] to take liberties with

6 (= *droit*) **la ~ du travail** the right *ou* freedom to work ◆ **~ d'association/de réunion** right of association/to meet *ou* hold meetings ◆ **~s individuelles** individual freedoms *ou* liberties ◆ **~s syndicales** union rights ◆ **~s civiles** civil liberties ◆ **~s des villes** (*Hist*) borough franchises

COMP **liberté conditionnelle** parole ◆ **être mis en ~ conditionnelle** to be granted parole, to be released on parole ◆ **mise en ~ conditionnelle** release on parole

liberté provisoire temporary release ◆ **être mis en ~ provisoire** to be released temporarily

liberté surveillée release on probation ◆ **être mis en ~ surveillée** to be put on probation

libertin, e /libɛʀtɛ̃, in/ ADJ (= *dissolu*) [*personne*] libertine, dissolute; (= *grivois*) [*roman*] licentious; (*Hist* = *irréligieux*) [*philosophe*] libertine NM,F (*littér* = *dévergondé*) libertine NM (*Hist* = *libre-penseur*) libertine, freethinker

libertinage /libɛʀtinaʒ/ NM (= *débauche*) [*de personne*] debauchery, dissoluteness; (= *grivoiserie*) [*de roman*] licentiousness; (*Hist* = *impiété*) libertine outlook *ou* philosophy

liberty ® /libɛʀti/ NM INV Liberty fabric ®

libidinal, e (mpl **-aux**) /libidinal, o/ ADJ libidinal

libidineux, -euse /libidinø, øz/ ADJ (*littér, hum*) libidinous, lustful

libido /libido/ NF libido

libraire /libʀɛʀ/ NMF bookseller ◆ **~-éditeur** publisher and bookseller ◆ **en vente chez votre ~** available in all good bookshops

librairie /libʀeʀi/ NF 1 (= *magasin*) bookshop (*Brit*), bookstore (*US*) ◆ **~ d'art/de livres anciens** art/antiquarian bookshop ◆ **~-papeterie** bookseller's and stationer's ◆ **ça ne se vend plus en ~** it's no longer in the bookshops, the bookshops no longer sell it ◆ **ce livre va bientôt paraître en ~** this book will soon be on sale (in the shops) *ou* will soon be available 2 ◆ **la ~** (= *activité*) bookselling (*NonC*); (= *corporation*) the book trade

⚠ **librairie** ne se traduit pas par **library**, qui a le sens de 'bibliothèque'.

libre /libʀ/ GRAMMAIRE ACTIVE 52.3

ADJ 1 (= *sans contrainte*) [*personne, presse, commerce, prix*] free; (*Sport*) [*figure, programme*] free ◆ **garder l'esprit *ou* la tête ~** to keep a clear mind ◆ **être ~ comme l'air** to be as free as a bird ◆ **être/rester ~** (*non marié*) to be/remain unattached ◆ **il n'est plus ~ (de lui-même)** he is no longer a free agent ◆ **être ~ de ses mouvements** to be free to do what one pleases ◆ **avoir la ~ disposition de ses biens** to have free disposal of one's property ◆ **la ~ circulation des personnes** the free movement of people ◆ **le monde ~** (*Pol*) the free world; → **vente**

2 ◆ **~ de** free from ◆ **~ de tout engagement/préjugé** free from any commitment/all prejudice ◆ **~ de faire qch** free to do sth ◆ **à vous de poser vos conditions** you are free to *ou* it's (entirely) up to you to state your conditions ◆ **vous êtes parfaitement ~ de refuser l'invitation** you're quite free *ou* at liberty to refuse the invitation

3 (= *non occupé*) [*passage, voie*] clear; [*taxi*] for hire; [*personne, place*] free; [*salle*] free, available; [*toilettes,*] vacant ◆ **poste ~** vacancy, vacant position ◆ **"libre de suite"** (*appartement à louer*) "available immediately"; (*appartement à vendre*) "with immediate vacant possession" ◆ **la ligne n'est pas ~** (*Téléc*) the line *ou* number is busy *ou* engaged (*Brit*) ◆ **ça ne sonne pas ~** (*Téléc*) I'm getting an engaged tone (*Brit*),

there's a busy signal *(US)* ◆ **est-ce que cette place est ~ ?** is this seat free? *ou* empty? ◆ **heure ~** *ou* **de ~** * free hour; *(Scol)* free period ◆ **avoir du temps ~** *ou* **de ~** * to have some spare *ou* free time ◆ **avoir des journées ~s** to have some free days ◆ **êtes-vous ~ ce soir ?** are you free this evening? ◆ **vous ne pouvez pas voir M. Durand, il n'est pas ~ aujourd'hui** you can't see Mr Durand, he's not free *ou* available today ◆ **le jeudi est son jour ~** Thursday is his free day *ou* his day off ◆ **je vais essayer de me rendre ~ pour demain** I'll try to keep tomorrow free; → **air[1], champ[1]**

[4] *(Scol = non étatisé)* *[enseignement]* private and Roman Catholic ◆ **école ~** private *ou* independent Roman Catholic school; → ÉDUCATION NATIONALE

[5] *(= autorisé, non payant)* *[entrée, accès]* free; → **auditeur, entrée**

[6] *(= non entravé)* *[mouvement, respiration]* free; *[traduction, improvisation, adaptation]* free; *[pignon, engrenage]* disengaged ◆ **robe qui laisse le cou ~** dress which leaves the neck bare *ou* which shows the neck ◆ **robe qui laisse la taille ~** dress which is not tight-fitting round the waist *ou* which fits loosely at the waist ◆ **avoir les cheveux ~s** to have one's hair loose ◆ **le sujet de la dissertation est ~** the subject of this essay is left open; → **main, roue, vers[2]**

[7] *(= sans retenue)* *[personne]* free *ou* open in one's behaviour; *[plaisanteries]* broad ◆ **tenir des propos assez ~s sur la politique du gouvernement** to be fairly plain-spoken *ou* make fairly candid remarks about the policies of the government ◆ **être très ~ avec qn** to be very free with sb ◆ **donner ~ cours à sa colère/son indignation** to give free rein *ou* vent to one's anger/one's indignation

COMP **libre arbitre** free will ◆ **avoir son ~ arbitre** to have free will

libre concurrence, libre entreprise free enterprise ◆ **un partisan de la ~ entreprise** *ou* **concurrence** a free-marketeer, a supporter of the free-market economy *ou* of free enterprise

libre pensée freethinking

libre penseur, -euse freethinker

libre-échange (pl **libres-échanges**) /libʀeʃɑ̃ʒ/ NM free trade

libre-échangisme /libʀeʃɑ̃ʒism/ NM (doctrine of) free trade

libre-échangiste (pl **libres-échangistes**) /libʀeʃɑ̃ʒist/ ADJ free-market *(épith)*, free-trade *(épith)* NMF free-trader

librement /libʀəmɑ̃/ ADV *[agir]* freely ◆ **~ adapté d'une pièce de Molière** freely adapted from a play by Molière

libre-service (pl **libres-services**) /libʀəsɛʀvis/ NM *(= restaurant)* self-service restaurant; *(= magasin)* self-service store ◆ **ce magasin propose un fax et une photocopieuse en ~** the shop provides self-service fax and photocopying facilities

librettiste /libʀetist/ NMF librettist

libretto † /libʀeto/ (pl **librettos** *ou* **libretti** /libʀeti/) NM libretto

Libreville /libʀəvil/ N Libreville

Libye /libi/ NF Libya

libyen, -enne /libjɛ̃, ɛn/ ADJ Libyan NM,F **Libyen(ne)** Libyan

lice /lis/ NF *(Hist)* lists ◆ **entrer en ~** *(fig)* to enter the lists ◆ **les candidats encore en ~** candidates still in contention

licence /lisɑ̃s/ NF [1] *(Univ)* ≃ (bachelor's) degree ◆ **~ ès lettres** Arts degree, ≃ BA ◆ **~ ès sciences** Science degree, ≃ BSc ◆ **faire une ~ d'anglais** to do a degree in English; → DIPLÔMES

[2] *(= autorisation)* permit; *(Comm, Jur)* licence *(Brit)*, license *(US)*; *(Sport)* membership card ◆ **un produit sous ~** a licensed product ◆ **fabriqué sous ~ française** manufactured under French licence ◆ **~ d'exploitation** *[de logiciel, réseau]* licence; *[de ligne aérienne]* operating permit ◆ **~ d'exportation** export licence

[3] *(littér = liberté)* **~ (des mœurs)** licentiousness *(NonC)* ◆ **avoir toute** *ou* **pleine ~ pour faire qch** to have a free hand to do sth ◆ **prendre des ~s avec qn** to take liberties with sb ◆ **~ poétique** *(Littérat)* poetic licence ◆ **une ~ orthographique** an accepted alternative spelling

⚠ Au sens de 'diplôme', **licence** ne se traduit pas par le mot anglais **licence.**

licencié, e /lisɑ̃sje/ ADJ *(Univ)* ◆ **professeur ~** graduate teacher ◆ **elle est ~e** she is a graduate NM,F [1] *(Univ)* **~ ès lettres/ès sciences/en droit** arts/science/law graduate, ≃ Bachelor of Arts/of Science/of Law [2] *(Sport)* member [3] *(Jur)* licensee

licenciement /lisɑ̃simɑ̃/ NM *(pour raisons économiques)* redundancy; *(pour faute professionnelle)* dismissal ◆ **il y a eu des centaines de ~s pour raisons économiques** hundreds of people were laid off *ou* made redundant *(Brit)*, there were hundreds of redundancies ◆ **~ abusif** unfair dismissal ◆ **~ collectif** mass redundancy *ou* lay-offs *ou* redundancies *(Brit)* ◆ **~ sec** compulsory redundancy *(without any compensation)* ◆ **lettre de ~** letter of dismissal, pink slip * *(US)*; → **indemnité**

licencier /lisɑ̃sje/ ▸ conjug 7 ◂ VT *(pour raisons économiques)* to lay off, to make redundant *(Brit)*; *(pour faute)* to dismiss ◆ **on licencie beaucoup dans ce secteur** there are a lot of redundancies in this sector

licencieusement /lisɑ̃sjøzmɑ̃/ ADV licentiously

licencieux, -ieuse /lisɑ̃sjø, jøz/ ADJ *(littér)* licentious

lichen /likɛn/ NM *(Bot, Méd)* lichen

licher * /liʃe/ ▸ conjug 1 ◂ VT *(= boire)* to drink; *(= lécher)* to lick

lichette * /liʃɛt/ NF [1] *(= morceau)* **~ de pain/de fromage** tiny piece of bread/of cheese ◆ **tu en veux une ~ ?** do you want a bit? ◆ **il n'en restait qu'une ~** there was only a (tiny) taste left [2] *(Belg = attache)* loop

licite /lisit/ ADJ lawful, licit

licitement /lisitmɑ̃/ ADV lawfully, licitly

licol † /likɔl/ NM halter

licorne /likɔʀn/ NF unicorn ◆ **~ de mer** narwhal, sea unicorn

licou /liku/ NM halter

licteur /liktœʀ/ NM lictor

lie /li/ NF *[de vin]* sediment, lees ◆ **la ~ (de la société)** *(péj)* the dregs of society; → **boire**

COMP **lie-de-vin, lie de vin** ADJ INV wine(-coloured)

lié, e /lje/ (ptp de **lier**) ADJ [1] *[personne]* **être très ~ à** *ou* **avec qn** to be very close to sb ◆ **ils sont très ~s** they're very close [2] *(Mus)* **note ~e** tied note ◆ **morphème ~** *(Ling)* bound morpheme

Liechtenstein /liʃtɛnʃtajn/ NM Liechtenstein

liechtensteinois, e /liʃtɛnʃtajnwa, waz/ ADJ of Liechtenstein NM,F **Liechtensteinois(e)** inhabitant *ou* native of Liechtenstein

lied (pl **lieder** *ou* **lieds**) /lid, lidœʀ/ NM lied

liège /ljɛʒ/ NM cork ◆ **de** *ou* **en ~** cork *(épith)*; → **bout**

liégeois, e /ljeʒwa, waz/ ADJ of *ou* from Liège ◆ **café/chocolat ~** coffee/chocolate sundae NM,F **Liégeois(e)** inhabitant *ou* native of Liège

lien /ljɛ̃/ NM [1] *(= attache)* bond ◆ **le prisonnier se libéra de ses ~s** the prisoner freed himself from his bonds ◆ **de solides ~s de cuir** strong leather straps

[2] *(= corrélation)* link, connection ◆ **il y a un ~ entre les deux événements** there's a link *ou* connection between the two events ◆ **il n'y a aucun ~ entre les deux affaires** the two cases are not connected in any way ◆ **servir de ~ entre deux personnes** to act as a link between two people ◆ **idées sans ~** unconnected *ou* unrelated ideas

[3] *(= relation)* tie ◆ **~s familiaux** *ou* **de parenté** family ties ◆ **avoir un ~ de parenté avec qn** to be related to sb ◆ **~s de sang** blood ties ◆ **~s d'amitié** bonds of friendship ◆ **~ affectif** emotional bond ◆ **un ~ très fort l'attache à son pays** he has a very strong attachment to his country ◆ **le ~ qui les unit** the bond that unites them ◆ **quels sont vos ~s ?** what's your relationship? ◆ **~s du mariage** marriage bonds *ou* ties ◆ **le ~ social** social cohesion ◆ **les ~s financiers/économiques entre ces deux entreprises** the financial/economic links between these two companies

[4] *(Internet)* link ◆ **~ hypertexte** hypertext link

lier /lje/ ▸ conjug 7 ◂ VT [1] *(= attacher)* *[+ mains, pieds]* to bind, to tie up; *[+ fleurs, bottes de paille]* to tie up ◆ **elle lui a lié les pieds et les mains** she bound him hand and foot ◆ **~ de la paille en bottes** to bind *ou* tie straw into bales ◆ **~ qn à un arbre/une chaise** to tie sb to a tree/a chair ◆ **~ qch avec une ficelle** to tie sth with a piece of string; → **fou, pied**

[2] *(= relier)* *[+ mots, phrases]* to link up, to join up ◆ **~ la cause à l'effet** to link cause to effect ◆ **tous ces événements sont étroitement liés** all these events are closely linked *ou* connected ◆ **cette maison est liée à tout un passé** there is a whole history attached to this house ◆ **tout est lié** everything links up *ou* ties up ◆ **~ les notes** *(Mus)* to slur the notes ◆ **~ un passage** to play a passage legato

[3] *(= unir)* *[+ personnes]* to bind, to unite ◆ **l'amitié qui nous lie à elle** the friendship which binds us to her ◆ **l'amitié qui les lie** the friendship which unites them ◆ **un goût/mépris commun pour le théâtre les liait** they were united by a common liking/scorn for the theatre

[4] *[contrat]* to bind ◆ **~ qn par un serment/une promesse** to bind sb with an oath/a promise

[5] *(Culin)* *[+ sauce]* to thicken ◆ **~ des pierres avec du mortier** *(Constr)* to bind stones with mortar

[6] *(locutions)* **~ amitié/conversation** to strike up a friendship/conversation ◆ **~ la langue à qn** † to make sb tongue-tied

VPR **se lier** to make friends *(avec qn* with sb); ◆ **se ~ d'amitié avec qn** to strike up a friendship with sb ◆ **il ne se lie pas facilement** he doesn't make friends easily ◆ **se ~ par un serment** to bind o.s. by an oath

lierre /ljɛʀ/ NM ivy ◆ **~ terrestre** ground ivy

liesse /ljɛs/ NF *(littér = joie)* jubilation ◆ **en ~** jubilant

lieu[1] (pl **lieux**) /ljø/ GRAMMAIRE ACTIVE 42.2, 44.2

NM [1] *(gén = endroit)* place; *[d'événement]* scene ◆ **adverbe de ~** adverb of place ◆ **~ de pèlerinage/résidence/retraite** place of pilgrimage/residence/retreat ◆ **sur le ~ de travail** in the workplace ◆ **le club est devenu un ~ de vie important dans le quartier** the club has become a major centre of social activity in the area ◆ **il faut maintenir la personne âgée dans son ~ de vie habituel** old people should be allowed to stay in their usual environment ◆ **en quelque ~ qu'il soit** wherever he may be, wherever he is ◆ **en tous ~x** everywhere ◆ **en aucun ~ du monde** nowhere in the world ◆ **cela varie avec le ~** it varies from place to place ◆ **en ~ sûr** in a safe place; → **haut, nom**

[2] *(avec notion temporelle)* **en premier/second ~** in the first/second place, firstly/second-

ly ♦ **en dernier** ~ lastly, finally ♦ **ce n'est pas le ~ d'en parler** this isn't the place to speak about it ♦ **en son** ~ in due course; → **temps**[1]

3 *(locutions)* **signer en ~ et place de qn** to sign on behalf of sb

♦ **au lieu de/que** instead of ♦ **tu devrais téléphoner au ~ d'écrire** you should telephone instead of writing ♦ **il devrait se réjouir, au ~ de cela, il se plaint** he should be glad, instead of which he complains *ou* but instead he complains ♦ **au ~ que nous partions** instead of (us) leaving

♦ **avoir lieu** *(= se produire)* to take place, to occur ♦ **avoir ~ d'être inquiet/de se plaindre** to have (good) grounds for being worried/for complaining, to have (good) reason to be worried/to complain ♦ **vos craintes/critiques n'ont pas ~ d'être** your fears/criticisms are groundless

♦ **il y a lieu** ♦ **il y a ~ d'être inquiet** there is cause for anxiety *ou* good reason to be anxious ♦ **il y a tout ~ de s'étonner** we have every reason to be surprised

♦ **s'il y a lieu** if the need arises ♦ **vous appellerez le médecin, s'il y a** ~ send for the doctor if necessary *ou* if the need arises

♦ **donner lieu à** *[débat, critiques]* to give rise to ♦ **ce centenaire a donné ~ à de nombreuses manifestations** the centenary was an opportunity for many different events ♦ **ces chiffres donneront ~ à diverses interprétations** these figures will be interpreted in various ways

♦ **tenir lieu de** to be a substitute for ♦ **ces quelques réformes ne peuvent tenir ~ de programme politique** this handful of reforms cannot be a substitute for a proper political programme ♦ **elle lui a tenu ~ de mère** she took the place of his mother ♦ **ce vieux manteau tient ~ de couverture** this old overcoat serves as a blanket

NMPL **lieux** (= *locaux)* premises ♦ **quitter** *ou* **vider les ~x** *(gén)* to get out, to leave; *(Admin)* to vacate the premises ♦ **se rendre sur les ~x du crime** to go to the scene of the crime ♦ **être sur les ~x de l'accident** to be at *ou* on the scene of the accident ♦ **notre envoyé est sur les ~x** our special correspondent is on the spot *ou* at the scene; → **état**

COMP **lieux d'aisances** († *ou hum*) lavatory *(Brit)*, comfort station *(US)*
lieu commun commonplace
lieu de débauche († *ou hum*) den of iniquity
lieu géométrique *(Math, fig)* locus
lieu de mémoire ≃ heritage site
lieu de naissance *(gén)* birthplace; *(Admin)* place of birth
lieu de passage *(entre régions)* crossing point; *(entre villes)* stopping-off place; *(dans un bâtiment)* place where people are constantly coming and going
lieu de perdition den of iniquity
lieu de promenade place *ou* spot for walking
lieu public public place
lieu de rendez-vous meeting place ♦ **c'est le ~ de rendez-vous de tous les amateurs de jazz** it's a mecca for jazz enthusiasts
les Lieux saints the Holy Places
lieu de vacances *(gén)* place *ou* spot for one's holidays *(Brit) ou* vacation *(US)*; *(= ville)* holiday *(Brit) ou* vacation *(US)* resort ♦ **je l'ai appelé sur son ~ de vacances** I phoned him at the place where he was spending his holiday

lieu[2] /ljø/ NM (= *poisson)* ♦ **~ jaune** pollack, pollock ♦ **~ noir** coley

lieu-dit (pl **lieux-dits**) /ljødi/ NM locality ♦ **au ~ le Bouc étourdi** at the place known as the Bouc étourdi

lieue /ljø/ NF *(Hist)* league ♦ **j'étais à mille ~s de penser à vous** you were far from my mind ♦ **j'étais à cent** *ou* **mille ~s de penser qu'il viendrait** it never occurred to me *ou* I never dreamt for a moment that he'd come ♦ **il sent son marin d'une** ~ you can tell he's a sailor a mile off*, the fact that he's a sailor sticks out a mile ♦ **à vingt ~s à la ronde** for miles around; → **botte**[1]

lieuse /ljøz/ NF *(Agr)* binder

lieutenant /ljøt(ə)nɑ̃/ NM *(armée de terre)* lieutenant *(Brit)*, first lieutenant *(US)*; *(armée de l'air)* flying officer *(Brit)*, first lieutenant *(US)*; *(marine marchande)* (first) mate, first officer; *(gén = second)* lieutenant, second in command ♦ **oui mon ~ !** yes sir! ♦ **l'un de ses ~s** *(fig)* one of his right-hand men COMP **lieutenant de vaisseau** *(marine nationale)* lieutenant

lieutenant-colonel (pl **lieutenants-colonels**) /ljøt(ə)nɑ̃kɔlɔnɛl/ NM *(armée de terre)* lieutenant colonel; *(armée de l'air)* wing commander *(Brit)*, lieutenant colonel *(US)*

lièvre /ljɛvʀ/ NM (= *animal)* hare; *(Sport)* pacemaker ♦ **courir** *ou* **chasser deux/plusieurs ~s à la fois** *(fig)* to try to do two/several things at once ♦ **vous avez levé** *ou* **soulevé un** ~ *(fig)* you've hit on a problem there

lift /lift/ NM topspin

lifter /lifte/ ► conjug 1 ◄ VT 1 *(Sport)* to put topspin on ♦ **balle liftée** ball with topspin ♦ **elle a un jeu très lifté** she uses a lot of topspin 2 *[+ personne, bâtiment, image de marque]* to give a face-lift to VI to put topspin on the ball

liftier, -ière /liftje, jɛʀ/ NM,F lift *(Brit) ou* elevator *(US)* attendant

lifting /liftiŋ/ NM *(lit, fig)* face-lift ♦ **se faire faire un** ~ to have a face-lift

ligament /ligamɑ̃/ NM ligament

ligamentaire /ligamɑ̃tɛʀ/ ADJ ligamentary ♦ **lésion** ~ ligament injury

ligature /ligatyʀ/ NF 1 *(Méd)* (= *opération)* ligation *(SPÉC)*, tying; (= *lien)* ligature ♦ **~ des trompes** tubal ligation *(SPÉC)*, tying of the Fallopian tubes 2 *(Agr)* (= *opération)* tying up; (= *lien)* tie 3 *(Typo)* ligature 4 *(Mus)* ligature, tie

ligaturer /ligatyʀe/ ► conjug 1 ◄ VT *(Méd)* to ligature, to tie up; *(Agr)* to tie up ♦ **se faire ~ les trompes** to have one's Fallopian tubes tied, to have one's tubes tied *

lige /liʒ/ ADJ liege ♦ **homme** ~ *(Hist)* liegeman ♦ **être l'homme ~ de qn** *(fig)* to be sb's henchman

light /lajt/ ADJ INV *(gén)* light; *[boisson, chocolat]* diet *(épith)*, low-calorie *(épith)* ♦ **c'est la version ~ de l'ancienne secte** it's the 'lite' version of the old sect

lignage /liɲaʒ/ NM 1 (= *extraction)* lineage ♦ **de haut** ~ of noble lineage 2 *(Typo)* linage, lineage

ligne[1] /liɲ/

GRAMMAIRE ACTIVE 54.4, 54.5, 54.7

1 NOM FÉMININ 2 COMPOSÉS

1 - NOM FÉMININ

1 = trait, limite line ♦ **~ brisée/courbe** broken/curved line ♦ **~ pointillée** dotted line ♦ **~ droite** *(gén)* straight line; (= *route)* stretch of straight road ♦ **la dernière ~ droite avant l'arrivée** *(lit, fig)* the final *ou* home straight ♦ **courir en ~ droite** to run in a straight line ♦ **la route coupe la forêt en ~ droite** the road cuts right *ou* straight through the forest ♦ **ça fait 4 km en ~ droite** it's 4 km as the crow flies ♦ **il arrive en droite ~ de son Texas natal** he has come straight from his native Texas ♦ **~ de départ/d'arrivée** starting/finishing line ♦ **la ~ de fracture au sein de la majorité** the rift dividing the majority ♦ **la ~ des 10/22 mètres** *(Rugby)* the 10/22 metre line ♦ **les ~s de la main** the lines of the hand ♦ **~ de vie/de cœur** life/love line ♦ **la ~ des collines dans le lointain** the line of hills in the distance ♦ **passer la ~ (de l'équateur)** to cross the line; → **juge**

2 = contour, silhouette *[de meuble, voiture]* line(s); *[de personne]* figure ♦ **avoir la** ~ to have a slim figure ♦ **garder/perdre la** ~ to keep/lose one's figure ♦ **elle mange peu pour garder la** ~ she doesn't eat much because she's watching her figure ♦ **la ~ lancée par les dernières collections** the look launched by the most recent collections ♦ **voiture aux ~s aérodynamiques** streamlined car, car built on aerodynamic lines

3 = règle, orientation line ♦ **~ de conduite/d'action** line of conduct/of action ♦ **~ politique** political line ♦ **la ~ du parti** the party line ♦ **les grandes ~s d'un programme** the broad lines *ou* outline of a programme ♦ **l'objectif a été fixé dans ses grandes ~s** the objective has been established in broad outline ♦ **à propos de ce problème, les deux présidents sont sur la même** ~ (= *ils sont d'accord)* the two presidents are in agreement *ou* are of one mind with regard to this problem ♦ **ce projet s'inscrit dans la droite ~ de la politique européenne** this project is fully *ou* directly in line with European policy ♦ **son livre est dans la droite ~ du roman américain** his book is in the direct tradition of the American novel

4 = suite de personnes, de choses line; (= *rangée)* row; *(Mil)* line; *[de cocaïne]* line ♦ **une ~ d'arbres le long de l'horizon** a line *ou* row of trees on the horizon ♦ **la ~ d'avants** *ou* **des avants/d'arrières** *ou* **des arrières** *(Ftbl)* the forwards/backs ♦ **la première/deuxième/troisième ~ (de mêlée)** *(Rugby)* the front/second/back row (of the scrum) ♦ **un première** ~ a man in the front row ♦ **en première** ~ *(Mil, fig)* on the front line; → **hors**

♦ **en ligne**
(= *alignés)* ♦ **enfants placés en** ~ children in a line *ou* lined up ♦ **coureurs en ~ pour le départ** runners lined up for the start *ou* on the starting line ♦ **mettre des personnes en** ~ to line people up, to get people lined up ♦ **se mettre en** ~ to line up, to get lined up, to get into line; → **cylindre**
♦ **monter en** ~ *(Mil)* to go off to war *ou* to fight
(= *en accord)* ♦ **ces résultats sont en ~ avec les prévisions** these results are in line *ou* on target with projections ♦ **pour le chiffre de ventes, nous sommes en** ~ our sales figures are on target; → **6**

5 Transport, Rail line ♦ **~ d'autobus** (= *service)* bus service; (= *parcours)* bus route ♦ **~ aérienne** (= *compagnie)* airline; (= *service)* (air) service, air link; (= *trajet)* (air) route ♦ **~ maritime** shipping line ♦ **~ de chemin de fer/de métro** railway *(Brit) ou* railroad *(US)*/underground *(Brit) ou* subway *(US)* line ♦ **les grandes ~s** *(Rail)* (= *voies)* main lines; (= *services)* main-line services ♦ **~s intérieures/internationales** (= *vols)* domestic/international flights ♦ **nous espérons vous revoir prochainement sur nos ~s** we look forward to seeing you on board again soon, we hope that you will fly with us again soon ♦ **la ~ d'autobus passe dans notre rue** the bus (route) goes along our street ♦ **quelle ~ faut-il prendre ?** which train *(ou* bus) should I take? ♦ **il faut prendre la ~ 12** *(en autobus)* you have to take the number 12 bus; → **avion, grand, pilote**

6 Élec, Téléc, Ordin line; (= *câbles)* wires; *(TV : composant l'image)* line ♦ **la ~ est occupée** the line is engaged *(Brit) ou* busy *(US)* ♦ **la ~ a été coupée** we've been cut off ♦ **la ~ passe dans notre jardin** the wires go through our garden ♦ **~ d'alimentation** *(Élec)* feeder

♦ **en ligne** *(Téléc)* ♦ **être en** ~ to be connected ♦ **vous êtes en** ~ you're connected *ou* through

now, I am connecting you now ◆ **je suis encore en** ~ I'm still holding ◆ **M. Lebrun est en** ~ *(= il est occupé)* Mr Lebrun's line is engaged *(Brit) ou* busy *(US)*; *(= il veut vous parler)* I have Mr Lebrun on the line for you
(Ordin) on-line ◆ **services/réseaux en** ~ on-line services/networks

7 = texte écrit line ◆ **écrire quelques ~s** to write a few lines ◆ **donner 100 ~s à faire à un élève** to give a pupil 100 lines to do ◆ **je vous envoie ces quelques ~s** I'm sending you these few lines *ou* this short note; → **lire**[1]

◆ **à la ligne** ◆ **"à la ligne"** "new paragraph", "new line" ◆ **aller à la** ~ to start on the next line, to begin a new paragraph ◆ **rédacteur payé à la** ~ editor paid by the line ◆ **tirer à la** ~ to pad out an article

◆ **en ligne de compte** ◆ **entrer en ~ de compte** to be taken into account *ou* consideration ◆ **prendre** *ou* **faire entrer en ~ de compte** to take into account *ou* consideration ◆ **votre vie privée n'entre pas en ~ de compte** your private life doesn't come *ou* enter into it

◆ **sur toute la ligne** from start to finish ◆ **il m'a menti sur toute la** ~ he lied to me from start to finish *ou* from beginning to end ◆ **c'est une réussite sur toute la** ~ it's a success throughout

8 Comm ~ **de produits** (product) line ◆ **notre nouvelle ~ de maquillage** our new range of make-up

9 Pêche (fishing) line

10 = série de générations ~ **directe/collatérale** direct/collateral line ◆ **descendre en ~ directe** *ou* **en droite ~ de ...** to be a direct descendant of ...

11 Belg = raie dans les cheveux parting

2 – COMPOSÉS

ligne de ballon mort *(Rugby)* dead-ball line
ligne blanche *(sur route)* white line ◆ **franchir la ~ blanche** *(lit)* to cross the white line; *(fig)* to overstep the mark
ligne de but *(Ftbl)* goal line, *(Rugby)* try line
ligne continue *(sur route)* solid line
ligne de côté *(Tennis)* sideline, tramline *(Brit)*
ligne de crédit credit line, line of credit
ligne de crête *(gén)* ridge; *(= ligne de partage des eaux)* watershed
ligne de défense *(gén, Mil)* line of defence *(Brit) ou* defense *(US)* ◆ **la ~ de défense irlandaise** *(Sport)* the Irish defenders *ou* defence *(Brit) ou* defense *(US)*
ligne de démarcation *(gén)* boundary; *(Mil)* line of demarcation, demarcation line
ligne directrice *(Géom)* directrix; *(fig)* guiding line
ligne discontinue *(sur route)* broken line
ligne d'eau *(Natation)* lane
ligne d'essai *(Rugby)* try line
ligne de faille fault line
ligne de faîte ⇒ **ligne de crête**
ligne de feu line of fire
ligne de flottaison water line ◆ **~ de flottaison en charge** load line, Plimsoll line
ligne de fond *(Pêche)* ledger line; *(Basket)* end line ◆ **~ de fond (de court)** *(Tennis)* baseline
lignes de force *(Phys)* lines of force; *[de discours, politique]* main themes
ligne de front *(Mil)* frontline
ligne à haute tension high-voltage line
ligne d'horizon skyline
ligne jaune *(sur route)* ⇒ **ligne blanche**
ligne médiane *(gén, Tennis)* centre line; *(Ftbl, Rugby etc)* halfway line
ligne de mire line of sight ◆ **avoir qn dans sa ~ de mire** to have sb in one's sights ◆ **être dans la ~ de mire de qn** to be in sb's sights
ligne de partage des eaux watershed, height of land *(US)*
ligne de service *(Tennis)* service line
ligne supplémentaire *(Mus)* ledger line
ligne de tir ⇒ **ligne de feu**
ligne de touche *(gén)* sideline; *(Ftbl, Rugby)* touchline; *(Basket)* boundary line
ligne de visée line of sight

ligne[2] /liɲ/ NF *(Can)* line *(3,175 mm)*

lignée /liɲe/ NF *(= postérité)* descendants; *(= race, famille)* line, lineage ◆ **laisser une nombreuse** ~ to leave a lot of descendants ◆ **le dernier d'une longue ~** the last of a long line ◆ **de bonne ~ irlandaise** of good Irish stock *ou* lineage ◆ **dans la ~ des grands romanciers** in the tradition of the great novelists

ligneux, -euse /liɲø, øz/ ADJ woody, ligneous *(SPÉC)*

lignifier (se) /liɲifje/ ▸ conjug 7 ◂ VPR to lignify

lignite /liɲit/ NM lignite, brown coal

ligoter /ligɔte/ ▸ conjug 1 ◂ VT *[+ personne]* to bind hand and foot ◆ **~ qn à un arbre** to tie sb to a tree

ligue /lig/ NF league ◆ **la Ligue des droits de l'homme** the League of Human Rights ◆ **la Ligue arabe** the Arab League ◆ **la (Sainte) Ligue** *(Rel)* the Catholic Holy League

liguer /lige/ ▸ conjug 1 ◂ VT to unite *(contre* against); ◆ **être ligué avec** to be in league with
VPR **se liguer** to league, to form a league *(contre* against); ◆ **tout se ligue contre moi** everything is in league *ou* is conspiring against me

ligueur, -euse /ligœʀ, øz/ NM,F member of a league

ligure /ligyʀ/ *(Hist)* ADJ Ligurian NM *(Ling)* Ligurian NMF **Ligure** Ligurian

Ligurie /ligyʀi/ NF Liguria

lilas /lilɑ/ NM, ADJ INV lilac

liliacée /liljase/ NF liliaceous plant ◆ **les ~s** liliaceous plants, the Liliaceae *(SPÉC)*

lilliputien, -ienne /lilipysjɛ̃, jɛn/ ADJ Lilliputian NM,F **Lilliputien(ne)** Lilliputian

Lilongwe /lilɔ̃gwe/ N Lilongwe

Lima /lima/ N Lima

limace /limas/ NF *(= animal)* slug; († * = *chemise)* shirt ◆ **quelle ~ !** *(= personne)* what a sluggard! *ou* slowcoach! *(Brit)** *ou* slowpoke *(US)**; *(= train)* this train is just crawling along!, what a dreadfully slow train!

limaçon /limasɔ̃/ NM (†† = *escargot)* snail; *(Anat)* cochlea

limage /limaʒ/ NM filing

limaille /limɑj/ NF filings ◆ **~ de fer** iron filings

limande /limɑ̃d/ NF *(= poisson)* dab ◆ **~-sole** lemon sole ◆ **fausse ~** flatfish; → **plat**[1]

limbe /lɛ̃b/ NM *(Astron, Bot, Math)* limb NMPL **limbes** *(Rel)* limbo ◆ **dans les ~s** *(Rel)* in limbo ◆ **c'est encore dans les ~s** *[de projet, science]* it's still very much in limbo, it's still up in the air

limbique /lɛ̃bik/ ADJ *[système]* limbic

lime /lim/ NF 1 *(= outil)* file ◆ **~ douce** smooth file ◆ **~ à ongles** nail file, fingernail file *(US)* ◆ **donner un coup de ~ à qch** to run a file over sth 2 *(= mollusque)* lima 3 *(= fruit)* lime; *(= arbre)* lime (tree)

limer /lime/ ▸ conjug 1 ◂ VT *[+ ongles]* to file; *[+ métal]* to file (down); *[+ aspérité]* to file off ◆ **le prisonnier avait limé un barreau** the prisoner had filed through a bar

limier /limje/ NM *(= chien)* bloodhound; *(fig)* sleuth, detective ◆ **c'est un fin ~** he's a really good sleuth

liminaire /liminɛʀ/ ADJ *[discours, note]* introductory

limitatif, -ive /limitatif, iv/ ADJ restrictive ◆ **liste limitative/non limitative** closed/open list

limitation /limitasjɔ̃/ NF limitation, restriction ◆ **~ des prix/des naissances** price/birth control ◆ **un accord sur la ~ des armements** an agreement on arms limitation *ou* control ◆ **sans ~ de durée** without a *ou* with no time limit ◆ **une ~ de vitesse (à 60 km/h)** a (60 km/h) speed limit ◆ **l'introduction de ~s de vitesse** the introduction of speed restrictions *ou* limits ◆ **~ de la circulation automobile** traffic restrictions

limite /limit/ NF 1 *[de pays, jardin]* boundary ◆ **la rivière marque la ~ du parc** the river marks the boundary of the park
2 *[de pouvoir, période]* limit ◆ **~ d'âge/de poids** age/weight limit ◆ **il connaît ses ~s** he knows his limits ◆ **ma patience a des ~s !** there's a limit to my patience! ◆ **la tolérance a des ~s !** tolerance has its limits! ◆ **la bêtise a des ~s !** you can only be so stupid! ◆ **sa joie ne connaissait pas de ~s** his joy knew no bounds ◆ **sa colère ne connaît pas de ~s** his anger knows no limits ◆ **ce crime atteint les ~s de l'horreur** this crime is too horrible to imagine ◆ **il franchit** *ou* **dépasse les ~s !** he's going a bit too far! ◆ **sans ~(s)** *[patience]* infinite; *[pouvoir]* limitless; *[joie, confiance]* boundless ◆ **son ambition est sans** ~ his ambition knows no bounds *ou* limits
3 *(Math)* limit
4 *(locutions)* **tu peux t'inscrire jusqu'à demain dernière** ~ you have until tomorrow to register ◆ **avant la ~** *(Boxe)* inside *ou* within the distance

◆ **à la + limite** ◆ **à la ~ on croirait qu'il le fait exprès** you'd almost think he's doing it on purpose ◆ **à la ~, j'accepterais ces conditions, mais pas plus** if pushed *ou* if absolutely necessary, I'd accept those conditions, but no more ◆ **à la ~ tout roman est réaliste** ultimately *ou* at a pinch you could say any novel is realistic ◆ **c'est à la ~ de l'insolence** it borders *ou* verges on insolence ◆ **jusqu'à la dernière ~** *[rester, résister]* to the bitter end, till the end; *[se battre]* to the death ◆ **jusqu'à la ~ de ses forces** to the point of exhaustion ◆ **aller** *ou* **tenir jusqu'à la ~** *(Boxe)* to go the distance

◆ **dans + limite(s)** ◆ **dans une certaine ~** up to a point, to a certain extent *ou* degree ◆ **"dans la limite des stocks disponibles"** "while stocks last" ◆ **dans les ~s du possible/du sujet** within the limits of what is possible/of the subject ◆ **l'entrée est gratuite dans la ~ des places disponibles** admission is free subject to availability ◆ **dans les ~s de mes moyens** *(aptitude)* within my capabilities; *(argent)* within my means

ADJ 1 *(= extrême)* **cas ~** borderline case ◆ **prix ~** upper price limit ◆ **cours ~** *(Bourse)* limit price ◆ **vitesse/âge ~** maximum speed/age ◆ **hauteur/longueur/charge ~** maximum height/length/load ◆ **heure ~** deadline
2 (* = *juste)* **elle a réussi son examen/à attraper la balle, mais c'était ~** she passed her exam/managed to catch the ball – but only just ◆ **ils ne se sont pas injuriés/battus, mais c'était ~** they didn't actually insult each other/come to blows but they came fairly close ◆ **sa remarque était vraiment ~** she was pushing it with that remark * ◆ **l'acoustique était ~** the acoustics were OK but only just, the acoustics were OK but not brilliant

ADV (* = *presque)* ◆ **c'est ~ raciste** it's borderline racist

COMP **limite d'élasticité** elastic limit
limite de rupture breaking point

limité, e /limite/ ADJ *[durée, choix, portée]* limited; *[nombre]* limited, restricted ◆ **je n'ai qu'une**

confiance ~e en ce remède I only trust this treatment so far ◆ **il est un peu ~*** *(intellectuellement)* he's not very bright ◆ **comme romancier, il est un peu ~** as a novelist, he's a bit limited; → **société, tirage**

limiter /limite/ ▸ conjug 1 ◂ VT 1 *(= restreindre)* *[+ dépenses, pouvoirs, temps]* to limit, to restrict *(à* to); ◆ **ils ont dû liquider leur affaire pour ~ les dégâts** they had to sell up the business to cut *ou* minimize their losses ◆ **on a réussi à ~ les dégâts en marquant deux buts** we managed to limit the damage by scoring two goals ◆ **nous limiterons notre étude à quelques cas généraux** we'll limit *ou* restrict our study to a few general cases ◆ **la vitesse est limitée à 50 km/h** the speed limit is 50 km/h

2 *(= délimiter)* *[frontière, montagnes]* to border ◆ **les collines qui limitent l'horizon** the hills which bound the horizon

VPR **se limiter** 1 *[personne]* **se ~ à** *[+ remarque]* to confine o.s. to; *[+ consommation]* to limit o.s. to ◆ **je me limite à cinq cigarettes par jour** I only allow myself five cigarettes a day, I limit *ou* restrict myself to five cigarettes a day ◆ **il faut savoir se ~** you have to know when to stop

2 *[connaissance, sanctions]* **se ~ à** to be limited to

limitrophe /limitʀɔf/ ADJ *[département]* bordering, adjoining; *[population]* border *(épith)* ◆ **provinces ~s de la France** *(françaises)* border provinces of France; *(étrangères)* provinces bordering on France

limnée /limne/ NF great pond snail

limogeage /limɔʒaʒ/ NM dismissal

limoger /limɔʒe/ ▸ conjug 3 ◂ VT to dismiss

limon /limɔ̃/ NM 1 *(Géog)* alluvium; *(gén)* silt 2 *[d'attelage]* shaft; *(Constr)* string-board

limonade /limɔnad/ NF 1 *(gazeuse)* (fizzy) lemonade *(Brit)*, Seven-Up ® *(US)*, Sprite ® *(US)* 2 († *= citronnade*) (home-made) lemonade *ou* lemon drink

limonadier, -ière /limɔnadje, jɛʀ/ NM,F 1 *(= fabricant)* soft drinks manufacturer 2 († *= commerçant)* café owner 3 *(= tire-bouchon)* waiter's corkscrew

limoneux, -euse /limɔnø, øz/ ADJ silt-laden, silty

limousin, e¹ /limuzɛ̃, in/ ADJ of *ou* from Limousin NM 1 *(= dialecte)* Limousin dialect 2 *(= région)* Limousin NM,F **Limousin(e)** inhabitant *ou* native of Limousin

limousine² /limuzin/ NF 1 *(= voiture)* limousine 2 († *= pèlerine*) cloak

limpide /lɛ̃pid/ ADJ *[eau, air, ciel regard]* clear, limpid; *[explication]* clear, crystal-clear *(attrib)*; *[style]* lucid, limpid; *[affaire]* clear, straightforward; *(iro)* straightforward ◆ **tu as compris ? – c'était ~ !** *(iro)* do you get it? – it was crystal-clear! *(iro)* *ou* as clear as mud!

limpidité /lɛ̃pidite/ NF *[d'eau, ciel, ciel, regard]* clearness, limpidity; *[d'explication]* clarity, lucidity; *[de style]* lucidity, limpidity; *[d'affaire]* clarity, straightforwardness

lin /lɛ̃/ NM *(= plante, fibre)* flax; *(= tissu)* linen; → **huile, toile**

linceul /lɛ̃sœl/ NM *(lit, fig)* shroud

lindane /lɛ̃dan/ NM lindane

linéaire /lineɛʀ/ ADJ linear NM *(= rayonnage)* shelf space

linéairement /lineɛʀmɑ̃/ ADV linearly

linéaments /lineamɑ̃/ NMPL *(littér)* 1 *[de visage]* lineaments *(littér)*, features; *[de forme]* lines, outline 2 *(= ébauche)* outline

linéarité /lineaʀite/ NF linearity

linge /lɛ̃ʒ/ NM 1 *(= draps, serviettes)* linen; *(= sous-vêtements)* underwear ◆ **le gros ~** household linen ◆ **le petit ~** small items of linen ◆ **il y avait du beau ~ à leur mariage** *(fig)* all the right people were at their wedding 2 *(= lessive)* **le ~** the washing ◆ **laver/étendre le** *ou* **son ~** to wash/hang out the *ou* one's washing; → **laver** 3 *(= morceau de tissu)* cloth ◆ **essuyer qch avec un ~** to wipe sth with a cloth ◆ **blanc** *ou* **pâle comme un ~** as white as a sheet 4 *(Helv = serviette de toilette)* towel

COMP **linges d'autel** altar cloths

linge de corps underwear

linge de maison household linen

linge de table table linen

linge de toilette bathroom linen

lingère /lɛ̃ʒɛʀ/ NF *(= personne)* linen maid; *(= meuble)* linen cupboard *ou* closet

lingerie /lɛ̃ʒʀi/ NF 1 *(= local)* linen room 2 *(= sous-vêtements féminins)* (women's) underwear ◆ **~ fine** lingerie ◆ **rayon ~** lingerie department

lingette /lɛ̃ʒɛt/ NF towelette

lingot /lɛ̃go/ NM *[de métal]* ingot; *(Typo)* slug ◆ **~ d'or** gold ingot

lingua franca /liŋgwafʀɑka/ NF lingua franca

lingual, e (pl **-aux**) /lɛ̃gwal, o/ ADJ lingual

lingue /lɛ̃g/ NF *(= poisson)* ling

linguiste /lɛ̃gɥist/ NMF linguist

linguistique /lɛ̃gɥistik/ NF linguistics *(sg)* ADJ *(gén)* linguistic; *[barrière, politique]* language *(épith)* ◆ **communauté ~** speech community

linguistiquement /lɛ̃gɥistikmɑ̃/ ADV linguistically

liniment /linimɑ̃/ NM liniment

linnéen, -enne /lineɛ̃, ɛn/ ADJ Linn(a)ean

lino* /lino/ NM (abrév de **linoléum**) lino

linoléique /linɔleik/ ADJ ◆ **acide ~** linoleic acid

linoléum /linɔleɔm/ NM linoleum

linon /linɔ̃/ NM *(= tissu)* lawn

linotte /linɔt/ NF linnet; → **tête**

linotype ® /linɔtip/ NF Linotype ®

linteau (pl **linteaux**) /lɛ̃to/ NM lintel

lion /ljɔ̃/ NM 1 *(= animal)* lion ◆ **~ de mer** sea lion ◆ **tu as mangé** *ou* **bouffé*** **du ~ !** you're full of beans!*; → **fosse, part** 2 *(Astron)* **le Lion** Leo, the Lion ◆ **il est Lion, il est du (signe du) Lion** he's (a) Leo

lionceau (pl **lionceaux**) /ljɔ̃so/ NM lion cub

lionne /ljɔn/ NF lioness

lipase /lipɑz/ NF lipase

lipide /lipid/ NM lipid

lipidique /lipidik/ ADJ lipid *(épith)*

lipo(-)aspiration /lipoaspiʀasjɔ̃/ NF liposuction

liposoluble /liposɔlybl/ ADJ fat-soluble

liposome /lipozom/ NM liposome

liposuccion /liposy(k)sjɔ̃/ NF liposuction

lippe /lip/ NF *(littér)* (fleshy) lower lip ◆ **faire la ~** *(= bouder)* to sulk; *(= faire la moue)* to pout; *(= faire la grimace)* to make *ou* pull a face

lippu, e /lipy/ ADJ thick-lipped

liquéfaction /likefaksjɔ̃/ NF *(Chim)* liquefaction

liquéfiable /likefjabl/ ADJ liquefiable

liquéfiant, e /likefjɑ̃, jɑt/ ADJ *(Chim)* liquefying; *[atmosphère, chaleur]* draining *(attrib)*, exhausting

liquéfier /likefje/ ▸ conjug 7 ◂ VT 1 *(Chim)* to liquefy ◆ **gaz naturel liquéfié** liquefied natural gas 2 *(* = amollir)* to drain, to exhaust ◆ **je suis liquéfié*** I'm dead beat* *ou* dog-tired*

VPR **se liquéfier** 1 *(lit)* to liquefy 2 * *(= avoir peur, être ému)* to turn to jelly; *(= avoir chaud)* to be melting

liquette* /likɛt/ NF *(= chemise d'homme)* shirt ◆ **(chemisier)** ~ (woman's) shirt

liqueur /likœʀ/ NF *(= boisson)* liqueur; († † *= liquide)* liquid ◆ **~ titrée/de Fehling** *(Pharm)* standard/Fehling's solution

liquidateur, -trice /likidatœʀ, tʀis/ NM,F *(Jur)* ≈ liquidator, receiver ◆ **~ judiciaire** *ou* **de faillite** ≈ official liquidator ◆ **placer une entreprise entre les mains d'un ~** to put a company into the hands of a receiver *ou* into receivership *(Brit)*

liquidatif, -ive /likidatif, iv/ ADJ ◆ **valeur liquidative** market price *ou* value

liquidation /likidasjɔ̃/ NF 1 *(= règlement légal)* *[de dettes, compte]* settlement, payment; *[de société]* liquidation; *[de biens, stock]* selling off, liquidation; *[de succession]* settlement; *[de problème]* elimination ◆ **~ judiciaire** compulsory liquidation ◆ **~ (judiciaire) personnelle** personal bankruptcy ◆ **mettre une société en ~** to put a company into liquidation *ou* receivership, to liquidate a company ◆ **afin de procéder à la ~ de votre retraite** in order to commence payment of your pension ◆ **"50% de rabais jusqu'à liquidation du stock"** "stock clearance, 50% discount"; → **bilan** 2 *(= vente)* selling (off), sale 3 (* *= meurtre)* liquidation, elimination 4 *(Bourse)* **~ de fin de mois** (monthly) settlement

liquide /likid/ ADJ *[corps, son]* liquid ◆ **la sauce/peinture est trop ~** the sauce/paint is too runny *ou* too thin ◆ **argent ~** cash NM 1 *(= substance)* liquid ◆ **~ de frein** brake fluid ◆ **~ de refroidissement** coolant ◆ **~ vaisselle*** washing-up liquid *(Brit)*, (liquid) dish soap *(US)* ◆ **~ amniotique/céphalorachidien** amniotic/cerebrospinal fluid 2 *(= argent)* cash ◆ **je n'ai pas beaucoup de ~** I haven't much ready money *ou* ready cash ◆ **payer** *ou* **régler en ~** to pay (in) cash ◆ **être payé en ~** to be paid cash in hand NF *(Ling)* liquid

liquider /likide/ ▸ conjug 1 ◂ VT 1 *(Fin, Jur)* *[+ succession, dettes]* to settle, to pay; *[+ compte]* to settle, to clear; *[+ société]* to liquidate, to wind up; *[+ biens, stock]* to liquidate, to sell off 2 *(= vendre)* to sell (off) 3 (* *= tuer)* to liquidate, to eliminate 4 * *(= régler)* *[+ problème]* to get rid of; *(= finir)* to finish off ◆ **c'est liquidé maintenant** it is all finished *ou* over now

liquidité /likidite/ NF *(Chim, Jur)* liquidity ◆ **~s** liquid assets

liquoreux, -euse /likɔʀø, øz/ ADJ *[vin]* syrupy

lire¹ /liʀ/ ▸ conjug 43 ◂ VT 1 *(= déchiffrer)* to read; *[+ message enregistré]* to listen to ◆ **il sait ~ l'heure** he can *ou* knows how to tell the time ◆ **à sept ans, il ne lit pas encore** *ou* **il ne sait pas encore ~** he's seven and he still can't read ◆ **~ sur les lèvres** to lip-read ◆ **~ ses notes avant un cours** to read over *ou* read through *ou* go over one's notes before a lecture ◆ **~ un discours/un rapport devant une assemblée** to read (out) a speech/a report at a meeting ◆ **il l'a lu dans le journal** he read (about) it in the paper ◆ **chaque soir, elle lit des histoires à ses enfants** every night she reads stories to her children ◆ **à le ~, on croirait que ...** from what he writes *ou* from reading what he writes one would think that ... ◆ **là où il y a 634, ~** *ou* **lisez 643** *(erratum)* for 634 read 643 ◆ **ce roman se lit bien** *ou* **se laisse ~** the novel is very readable ◆ **ce roman se lit facilement/très vite** the novel makes easy/quick reading ◆ **ce roman mérite d'être lu** *ou* **est à ~** the novel is worth reading ◆ **~ entre les lignes** to read between the lines ◆ **je lis en lui à livre ouvert** I can read him like an open book; → **aussi lu**

2 *(= deviner)* to read ◆ **~ dans le cœur de qn** to see into sb's heart ◆ **la peur se lisait** *ou* **on**

lisait la peur sur son visage/dans ses yeux you could see *ou* read fear in his face/in his eyes, fear showed on his face/in his eyes ◆ **~ l'avenir dans les lignes de la main de qn** to read in sb's palm ◆ **elle m'a lu les lignes de la main** she read my palm, she did a palm-reading for me ◆ **~ l'avenir dans le marc de café** ≃ to read (the future in) tea leaves ◆ **~ dans le jeu de qn** to see through sb, to see what sb is up to

3 *(formule de lettre)* **nous espérons vous ~ bientôt** we hope to hear from you soon ◆ **à bientôt de vous ~** hoping to hear from you soon

4 *(= interpréter)* *[+ statistiques, événement]* to read, to interpret

lire² /liʀ/ **NF** lira

lirette /liʀɛt/ **NF** rag rug

lis /lis/ **NM** lily ◆ **blanc comme un ~, d'une blancheur de ~** lily-white; → **fleur**

Lisbonne /lisbɔn/ **N** Lisbon

liseré /liz(ə)ʀe/, **liséré** /lizeʀe/ **NM** *(= bordure)* border, edging ◆ **un ~ de ciel bleu** a strip of blue sky

liserer /liz(ə)ʀe/ ▸ conjug 5 ◂, **lisérer** /lizeʀe/ ▸ conjug 6 ◂ **VT** to edge with ribbon

liseron /lizʀɔ̃/ **NM** bindweed, convolvulus

liseur, -euse /lizœʀ, øz/ **NM,F** reader **NF liseuse** *(= couvre-livre)* book jacket; *(= vêtement)* bed jacket

lisibilité /lizibilite/ **NF** *[d'écriture]* legibility; *[de livre]* readability ◆ **d'une parfaite ~** perfectly legible ◆ **le manque de ~ des textes officiels** the fact that official documents are so difficult to read ◆ **ils se plaignent d'une mauvaise ~ de l'action gouvernementale** they're complaining that the government's policy lacks clarity

lisible /lizibl/ **ADJ** *[écriture]* legible; *[livre]* readable, worth reading ◆ **une carte peu ~** a map that is difficult to read ◆ **ce livre est ~ à plusieurs niveaux** the book can be read on several levels ◆ **leur stratégie est peu ~** their strategy lacks clarity

lisiblement /lizibləmɑ̃/ **ADV** legibly

lisier /lizje/ **NM** liquid manure

lisière /lizjɛʀ/ **NF** 1 *[de bois, village]* edge ◆ **à la ~ de la** *ou* **en ~ de forêt** on the edge of the forest ◆ **ils sont à la ~ de la légalité** they're only just within the law 2 *[d'étoffe]* selvage

lissage /lisaʒ/ **NM** smoothing

lisse¹ /lis/ **ADJ** *[peau, surface]* smooth; *[cheveux]* sleek, smooth; *[pneu]* bald; *(Anat)* *[muscle]* smooth

lisse² /lis/ **NF** *(Naut)* *(= rambarde)* handrail; *(de la coque)* ribband

lisser /lise/ ▸ conjug 1 ◂ **VT** *[+ cheveux]* to smooth (down); *[+ moustache]* to smooth, to stroke; *[+ papier, drap froissé]* to smooth out; *[+ vêtement]* to smooth (out) ◆ **l'oiseau lisse ses plumes** *ou* **se lisse les plumes** the bird is preening itself *ou* its feathers ◆ **fromage blanc lissé** creamy fromage blanc

listage /listaʒ/ **NM** *(= action)* listing; *(= liste)* list; *(Ordin)* print-out

liste¹ /list/ GRAMMAIRE ACTIVE 54.5

NF 1 *(gén)* list ◆ **faire** *ou* **dresser une ~** to make a list, to draw up a list ◆ **faire la ~ de** to make out *ou* draw up a list of, to list ◆ **faites-moi la ~ des absents** make me out a list of people who are absent ◆ **~ des courses** shopping list ◆ **~ nominative des élèves** class roll *ou* list

2 *(Pol)* *[de candidats]* (list of) candidates ◆ **être inscrit sur les ~s électorales** to be on the electoral roll, to be registered to vote ◆ **la ~ de la gauche** the list of left-wing candidates ◆ **~ unique** *(commune)* joint list (of candidates); *(sans choix)* single list (of candidates) ◆ **leurs partis présentent une ~ commune** their parties are putting forward a joint list (of candidates); → **scrutin**

COMP liste d'attente waiting list

liste civile civil list

liste de contrôle ⇒ **liste de vérification**

liste de diffusion *(Ordin)* distribution list

liste d'envoi mailing list

liste de mariage wedding list

liste noire blacklist; *(pour élimination)* hit list

liste de publipostage mailing list

liste rouge *(Téléc)* **demander à être sur (la) ~ rouge** (to ask) to go ex-directory *(Brit)* *ou* unlisted *(US)* ◆ **il est sur ~ rouge** he's ex-directory *(Brit)*, he's unlisted *(US)*

liste de vérification check list

liste² /list/ **NF** *[de cheval]* list

listel (pl **listels** *ou* **-eaux**) /listɛl, o/ **NM** *(Archit)* listel, fillet; *[de monnaie]* rim

lister /liste/ ▸ conjug 1 ◂ **VT** to list

listeria /listeʀja/ **NF INV** listeria

listériose /listeʀjoz/ **NF** listeriosis

listing /listiŋ/ **NM** ⇒ **listage**

lit /li/ **NM** 1 *(= meuble)* bed; *(= structure)* bedstead, bed ◆ **~ d'une personne** *ou* **à une place** single bed ◆ **~ de deux personnes** *ou* **à deux places** double bed ◆ **~ de fer/de bois** iron/wooden bedstead ◆ **~ d'hôpital/d'hôtel** hospital/hotel bed ◆ **hôpital de 250 ~s** hospital with 250 beds ◆ **aller** *ou* **se mettre au ~** to go to bed ◆ **garder le ~** to stay in bed ◆ **mettre un enfant au ~** to put a child to bed ◆ **être/lire au ~** to be/read in bed ◆ **faire le ~** to make the bed ◆ **faire le ~ de** *(fig)* *(= renforcer)* to bolster; *(= préparer le terrain pour)* to pave the way for ◆ **comme on fait son ~, on se couche** *(Prov)* you've made your bed, now you must lie on it ◆ **faire ~ à part** to sleep in separate beds ◆ **le ~ n'avait pas été défait** the bed had not been slept in ◆ **au ~ les enfants !** bedtime *ou* off to bed children! ◆ **arracher** *ou* **sortir** *ou* **tirer qn du ~** to drag *ou* haul sb out of bed ◆ **tu es tombé du ~ ce matin !** you're up bright and early!; → **saut**

2 *(Jur = mariage)* **enfants du premier/deuxième ~** children of the first/second marriage ◆ **enfants d'un autre ~** children of a previous marriage

3 *[de rivière]* bed ◆ **les pluies ont fait sortir le fleuve de son ~** the river has burst *ou* overflowed its banks because of the rains

4 *(= couche, épaisseur)* bed, layer ◆ **~ d'argile** bed *ou* layer of clay ◆ **~ de cendres** *ou* **de braises** bed of hot ashes ◆ **~ de salade** *(Culin)* bed of lettuce

5 *(Naut)* *[de vent, marée, courant]* set

COMP lit à baldaquin canopied fourposter bed

lit bateau cabin bed

lit breton box bed

lit de camp campbed

lit clos box bed

lit à colonnes fourposter bed

lit conjugal marriage bed

lit de douleur bed of pain

lit d'enfant cot

lit gigogne pullout *ou* stowaway bed

lits jumeaux twin beds

lit de justice bed of justice

lit de mort deathbed

lit nuptial wedding-bed

lit de parade ◆ **sur un ~ de parade** lying in state

lit pliant folding bed

lit en portefeuille apple-pie bed

lit de repos couch

lit de sangle trestle bed

lits superposés bunk beds

litanie /litani/ **NF** *(Rel, fig péj)* litany

lit-cage (pl **lits-cages**) /likaʒ/ **NM** (folding metal) bed

litchi /litʃi/ **NM** lychee, litchi

liteau /lito/ **NM** *(pour toiture)* batten; *(pour tablette)* bracket; *(dans tissu)* stripe

litée /lite/ **NF** *(= jeunes animaux)* litter

literie /litʀi/ **NF** bedding

lithiase /litjɑz/ **NF** lithiasis

lithiné, e /litine/ **ADJ** ◆ **eau ~e** lithia water **NMPL lithinés** lithium salts

lithium /litjɔm/ **NM** lithium

litho* /lito/ **NF** (abrév de **lithographie**) litho

lithographe /litɔgʀaf/ **NMF** lithographer

lithographie /litɔgʀafi/ **NF** *(= technique)* lithography; *(= image)* lithograph

lithographier /litɔgʀafje/ ▸ conjug 7 ◂ **VT** to lithograph

lithographique /litɔgʀafik/ **ADJ** lithographic

lithosphère /litɔsfɛʀ/ **NF** lithosphere

lithotritie /litɔtʀisi/ **NF** lithotripsy

lithuanien, -ienne /litɥanjɛ̃, jɛn/ **ADJ, NM,F** ⇒ **lituanien, -ienne**

litière /litjɛʀ/ **NF** *(= couche de paille)* litter *(NonC)*; *(pour cheval)* bedding; *(Hist = palanquin)* litter ◆ **il s'était fait une ~ avec de la paille** he had made himself a bed of straw ◆ **~ pour chats** cat litter *(Brit)*, Kitty Litter ® *(US)* ◆ **faire ~ de qch** *(littér)* to scorn *ou* spurn sth

litige /litiʒ/ **NM** *(gén)* dispute; *(Jur)* lawsuit ◆ **être en ~** *(gén)* to be in dispute *(avec* with); *(Jur)* to be at law *ou* in litigation ◆ **les parties en ~** the litigants, the disputants *(US)* ◆ **point/objet de ~** point/object of contention ◆ **l'objet du ~** *(fig)* the matter at issue ◆ **l'objet du ~ est l'organisation du débat entre les deux candidats** the matter at issue is how the discussion between the two candidates should be organized

litigieux, -ieuse /litiʒjø, jøz/ **ADJ** *[point, question]* contentious; *[article, document]* controversial; *[facture, frontière]* disputed ◆ **cas ~** contentious issue

litorne /litɔʀn/ **NF** fieldfare

litote /litɔt/ **NF** *(gén)* understatement; *(Littérat)* litotes *(SPÉC)*

litre /litʀ/ **NM** *(= mesure)* litre *(Brit)*, liter *(US)*; *(= récipient)* litre *(Brit)* *ou* liter *(US)* bottle

litron* /litʀɔ̃/ **NM** ◆ **~ (de vin)** litre *(Brit)* *ou* liter *(US)* of wine

littéraire /liteʀɛʀ/ **ADJ** *(gén)* literary; *[souffrance, passion]* affected ◆ **faire des études ~s** to study literature **NMF** *(par don, goût)* literary person; *(= étudiant)* arts student; *(= enseignant)* arts teacher, teacher of arts subjects

littérairement /liteʀɛʀmɑ̃/ **ADV** in literary terms

littéral, e (mpl **-aux**) /liteʀal, o/ **ADJ** *(littér, Math)* literal ◆ **arabe ~** written Arabic

littéralement /liteʀalmɑ̃/ **ADV** *(lit, fig)* literally

littéralité /liteʀalite/ **NF** literality, literalness

littérateur /liteʀatœʀ/ **NM** man of letters; *(péj = écrivain)* literary hack

littérature /liteʀatyʀ/ **NF** 1 *(= art)* literature; *(= profession)* writing ◆ **faire de la ~** to go in for writing, to write ◆ **tout cela, c'est de la ~** *(péj)* it's of trifling importance ◆ **écrire de la ~ alimentaire** to write potboilers ◆ **~ de colportage** chapbooks 2 *(= ensemble d'ouvrages, bibliographie)* literature ◆ **il existe une abondante ~ sur ce sujet** there's a wealth of literature *ou* material on this subject 3 *(= manuel)* history of literature

littoral, e (mpl **-aux**) /litɔʀal, o/ ADJ coastal, littoral (*SPÉC*); → **cordon** NM coast, littoral (*SPÉC*)

Lituanie /litɥani/ NF Lithuania

lituanien, -ienne /litɥanjɛ̃, jɛn/ ADJ Lithuanian NM (= *langue*) Lithuanian NM,F **Lituanien(ne)** Lithuanian

liturgie /lityʀʒi/ NF liturgy

liturgique /lityʀʒik/ ADJ liturgical

livarde /livaʀd/ NF sprit

livarot /livaʀo/ NM Livarot (*creamy Normandy cheese*)

livide /livid/ ADJ 1 (= *pâle*) (*par maladie*) pallid; (*de peur*) white 2 (*littér* = *bleuâtre*) livid

lividité /lividite/ NF lividness

living /liviŋ/, **living-room** (pl **living-rooms** /liviŋʀum/) NM (= *pièce*) living room; (= *meuble*) unit

Livourne /livuʀn/ N Leghorn, Livorno

livrable /livʀabl/ ADJ which can be delivered ◆ **cet article est ~ dans les 10 jours/à domicile** this article will be delivered within 10 days/can be delivered to your home

livraison /livʀɛzɔ̃/ GRAMMAIRE ACTIVE 47.2, 47.3, 47.4 NF 1 [*de marchandise*] delivery ◆ **"livraison à domicile"** "we deliver", "home deliveries" ◆ **"payable à la livraison"** "payable on delivery", "cash on delivery", "COD" ◆ **la ~ à domicile est comprise dans le prix** the price includes (the cost of) delivery ◆ **faire une ~** to make a delivery ◆ **faire la ~ de qch** to deliver sth ◆ **prendre ~ de qch** to take *ou* receive delivery of sth 2 [*de revue*] part, instalment

livre¹ /livʀ/ NM 1 (= *ouvrage*) book ◆ **le ~** (= *commerce*) the book industry, the book trade (*Brit*) ◆ **~ de géographie** geography book ◆ **~ du maître/de l'élève** teacher's/pupil's textbook ◆ **il a toujours le nez dans les ~s, il vit dans les ~s** he's always got his nose in a book ◆ **je ne connais l'Australie que par les ~s** I only know Australia through *ou* from books ◆ **ça n'arrive que dans les ~s** it only happens in books ◆ **écrire/faire un ~ sur** to write/do a book on; → **parler**

2 (= *volume*) book ◆ **le ~ 2 *ou* le second ~ de la Genèse** book 2 of Genesis, the second book of Genesis

COMP **livre audio** audiobook
livre blanc (*gén*) official report; [*de gouvernement*] white paper
livre de bord [*de bateau*] logbook
livre de caisse (*Comptabilité*) cashbook
livre de chevet bedside book
livre de classe schoolbook, textbook
les livres de commerce (*Comptabilité*) the books, the accounts
livre de comptes account(s) book
livre de cuisine cookbook, cookery book (*Brit*)
livre électronique e-book
livre d'enfant children's book
livre d'heures book of hours
livre d'images picture book
livre journal (*Comptabilité*) daybook
livre de lecture reader, reading book
livre de messe missal
livre d'or visitors' book
livre de poche paperback
livre de prières prayer book
livre scolaire ⇒ **livre de classe**

livre² /livʀ/ NF 1 (= *poids*) half a kilo, ≈ pound; (*Can*) pound 2 (= *monnaie*) pound; (*Hist française*) livre ◆ **~ sterling** pound sterling ◆ **~ égyptienne** Egyptian pound ◆ **~ irlandaise** Irish pound, punt ◆ **ce chapeau coûte 6 ~s** this hat costs £6

livre-cassette (pl **livres-cassettes**) /livʀkasɛt/ NM audiobook (*on tape*)

livrée /livʀe/ NF 1 (= *uniforme*) livery ◆ **en ~** in livery (*attrib*), liveried 2 [*d'animal, oiseau*] markings

livre-jeu (pl **livres-jeux**) /livʀʒø/ NM activity book

livrer /livʀe/ ▸ conjug 1 ◂ VT 1 [+ *commande, marchandises*] to deliver ◆ **se faire ~ qch** to have sth delivered ◆ **~ qn** to deliver sb's order ◆ **je serai livré demain, ils me livreront demain** they'll do the delivery tomorrow ◆ **nous livrons à domicile** we do home deliveries

2 (= *abandonner : à la police, à l'ennemi*) to hand over (*à* to); ◆ **~ qn à la mort** to send sb to their death ◆ **~ qn au bourreau** to deliver sb up *ou* hand sb over to the executioner ◆ **le pays a été livré au pillage/à l'anarchie** the country was given over to pillage/to anarchy ◆ **être livré à soi-même** to be left to o.s. *ou* to one's own devices

3 (= *confier*) [+ *informations*] to supply ◆ **il m'a livré un peu de lui-même** he opened up to me a little ◆ **~ ses secrets** [*personne*] to tell one's secrets ◆ **cette statue n'a pas fini de ~ ses secrets** this statue still holds secrets

VPR **se livrer** 1 (= *se rendre*) to give o.s. up, to surrender (*à* to); ◆ **se ~ à la police** to give o.s. up to the police

2 (= *se confier*) to open up ◆ **se ~ à un ami** to confide in a friend, to open up to a friend ◆ **il ne se livre pas facilement** he doesn't open up easily

3 (= *s'abandonner à*) **se ~ à** [+ *destin*] to abandon o.s. to; [+ *plaisir, excès, douleur*] to give o.s. over to ◆ **elle s'est livrée à son amant** she gave herself to her lover

4 (= *faire, se consacrer à*) **se ~ à** [+ *exercice, analyse, expérience*] to do; [+ *jeu*] to play; [+ *sport*] to practise; [+ *recherches*] to do, to engage in, to carry out; [+ *enquête*] to hold, to set up ◆ **se ~ à l'étude** to study, to devote o.s. to study ◆ **pendant dix ans il s'est livré à des activités politiques** he was involved in political activity for ten years ◆ **se ~ à des pratiques délictueuses** to indulge in illegal practices

livresque /livʀɛsk/ ADJ [*connaissances*] acquired from books, academic ◆ **j'ai une culture ~ assez limitée** I'm not very well-read ◆ **enseignement purement ~** purely theoretical *ou* academic training

livret /livʀɛ/ NM 1 (*Mus*) **~ (d'opéra)** (opera) libretto 2 († = *petit livre*) booklet; (= *catalogue*) catalogue; → **compte** 3 (*Helv* = *table de multiplication*) times tables

COMP **livret de caisse d'épargne** (= *carnet*) (savings) bankbook; (= *compte*) savings account
livret de famille official family record book (*containing registration of births and deaths in a family*)
livret matricule (*Mil*) army file
livret militaire military record
livret scolaire (= *carnet*) (school) report book; (= *appréciation*) (school) report

livreur /livʀœʀ/ NM delivery man (*ou* boy)

livreuse /livʀøz/ NF delivery woman (*ou* girl)

Ljubljana /ljubljana/ N Ljubljana

lob /lɔb/ NM (*Tennis*) lob ◆ **faire un ~** to hit a lob

lobby (pl **lobbies**) /lɔbi/ NM (*Pol*) lobby

lobbying /lɔbiiŋ/, **lobbyisme** /lɔbiism/ NM lobbying

lobbyiste /lɔbiist/ NMF lobbyist

lobe /lɔb/ NM 1 (*Anat, Bot*) lobe ◆ **~ de l'oreille** earlobe 2 (*Archit*) foil

lobé, e /lɔbe/ (ptp de **lober**) ADJ (*Bot*) lobed; (*Archit*) foiled

lobectomie /lɔbɛktɔmi/ NF lobectomy

lobélie /lɔbeli/ NF lobelia

lober /lɔbe/ ▸ conjug 1 ◂ VI (*Tennis*) to lob VT (*Ftbl, Tennis*) to lob (over)

lobotomie /lɔbɔtɔmi/ NF lobotomy

lobotomiser /lɔbɔtɔmize/ ▸ conjug 1 ◂ VT to perform a lobotomy on

lobule /lɔbyl/ NM lobule

local, e (mpl **-aux**) /lɔkal, o/ ADJ local ◆ **averses ~es** scattered *ou* local showers, rain in places; → **anesthésie, couleur, impôt** NM (= *salle*) premises ◆ **~ (à usage) commercial** commercial premises ◆ **~ d'habitation** domestic premises, private (dwelling) house ◆ **~ professionnel** business premises ◆ **le club cherche un ~** the club is looking for premises *ou* for a place in which to meet ◆ **il a un ~ au fond de la cour qui lui sert d'atelier** he's got a place at the far end of the yard which he uses as a workshop

NMPL **locaux** (= *bureaux*) offices, premises ◆ **dans les locaux de la police** on police premises ◆ **les locaux de la société sont au deuxième étage** the company's offices *ou* premises are on the second floor

localement /lɔkalmɑ̃/ ADV (= *ici*) locally; (= *par endroits*) in places

localisable /lɔkalizabl/ ADJ localizable ◆ **facilement ~** easy to localize

localisation /lɔkalizasjɔ̃/ NF (= *repérage*) localization; (= *emplacement*) location ◆ **système de ~ par satellite** satellite locating system ◆ **la ~ des investissements est libre** investors are free to invest wherever they wish

localisé, e /lɔkalize/ (ptp de **localiser**) ADJ [*conflit, douleur*] localized; [*gymnastique, musculation*] concentrating on one part of the body ◆ **le cancer est resté très ~** the cancer remained very localized ◆ **la production est très ~e** production is highly localized

localiser /lɔkalize/ ▸ conjug 1 ◂ VT 1 (= *circonscrire*) (*gén*) to localize; [+ *épidémie, incendie*] to confine ◆ **l'épidémie s'est localisée dans cette région** the epidemic was confined to this area 2 (= *repérer*) to locate

localité /lɔkalite/ NF (= *ville*) town; (= *village*) village

locataire /lɔkatɛʀ/ NMF (*gén*) tenant; (*habitant avec le propriétaire*) lodger, roomer (*US*) ◆ **les ~s de mon terrain** the people who rent land from me, the tenants of my land ◆ **nous sommes ~s de nos bureaux** we rent our office space ◆ **avoir/prendre des ~s** to have/take in tenants ◆ **l'ancien/le nouveau ~ de Matignon** the former/present French Prime Minister

locatif, -ive /lɔkatif, iv/ ADJ 1 [*valeur, secteur*] rental ◆ **local à usage ~** premises for letting (*Brit*) *ou* rent (*US*) ◆ **risques ~s** tenant's risks ◆ **réparations locatives** repairs incumbent upon the tenant ◆ **marché ~** rental *ou* letting market ◆ **immeuble ~** block of rented flats; → **charge** 2 (*Gram*) **préposition locative** preposition of place NM (*Gram*) locative (case) ◆ **au ~** in the locative

location /lɔkasjɔ̃/ NF 1 (*par le locataire*) [*de maison, terrain*] renting; [*de matériel, voiture*] renting, hire (*Brit*), hiring (*Brit*) ◆ **prendre en ~** [+ *maison*] to rent; [+ *voiture, matériel*] to rent, to hire (*Brit*) ◆ **c'est pour un achat ou pour une ~ ?** is it to buy or to rent?

2 (*par le propriétaire*) [*de maison, terrain*] renting (out), letting (*Brit*); [*de matériel, véhicule*] renting, hiring (out) (*Brit*) ◆ **mettre en ~** [+ *maison*] to rent out, to let (*Brit*); [+ *véhicule*] rent, to hire out (*Brit*) ◆ **~ de voitures** (*écriteau*) "car rental", "cars for hire" (*Brit*), "car-hire" (*Brit*); (*métier*) car rental, car hiring (*Brit*) ◆ **"location de voitures sans chauffeur"** "self-drive car rental *ou* hire (*Brit*)" ◆ **c'est pour une vente ou pour une ~ ?** is it to sell or to rent? *ou* to let? (*Brit*) ◆ **nous ne faisons pas de ~ de matériel** we don't rent out *ou* hire out (*Brit*) equipment

3 (= *bail*) lease ◆ **contrat de ~** lease

4 (= *logement*) rented accommodation (*NonC*) ◆ **il a trois ~s dans la région** he has got three properties (for letting) in the area ◆ **il a pris une ~ pour un mois** he has taken *ou* rented a house *ou* a flat for a month ◆ **être/habiter en ~** to be/live in rented accommodation

5 (= *réservation*) [*de spectacle*] reservation, booking (*Brit*) ◆ **bureau de ~** (advance) booking office; (*Théât*) box office, booking office ◆ **la ~ des places se fait quinze jours à l'avance** seats must be reserved *ou* booked two weeks in advance

COMP **location avec option d'achat** leasing, lease-option agreement

location saisonnière holiday let (*Brit*), vacation *ou* summer rental (*US*)

location-gérance (pl **locations-gérances**) /lɔkasjɔ̃ʒeʀɑ̃s/ NF ≈ management agreement ◆ **être en ~** [*entreprise*] to be run by a manager

location-vente (pl **locations-ventes**) /lɔkasjɔ̃vɑ̃t/ NF hire purchase (*Brit*), instalment (*Brit*) *ou* installment (*US*) plan ◆ **acheter un ordinateur en ~** to buy a computer on instalments

loch /lɔk/ NM 1 (*Naut* = *appareil*) log 2 (= *lac*) loch

loche /lɔʃ/ NF 1 (= *poisson*) ~ **(de rivière)** loach ◆ ~ **de mer** rockling 2 (= *limace*) grey slug

loci /lɔki/ pl de **locus**

lockout, lock-out /lɔkaut/ NM INV lockout

loco * /lɔko/ NF (abrév de **locomotive**) loco *

locomoteur, -trice[1] /lɔkɔmɔtœʀ, tʀis/ ADJ locomotive ◆ **ataxie locomotrice** locomotor ataxia

locomotion /lɔkɔmosjɔ̃/ NF locomotion; → **moyen**[2]

locomotive /lɔkɔmɔtiv/ NF 1 (*Rail*) locomotive, engine ◆ ~ **haut le pied** light engine (*Brit*), wildcat (*US*) 2 (= *entreprise, secteur, région*) driving force, powerhouse; (= *coureur*) pacesetter, pacemaker ◆ **les exportations sont les ~s de la croissance** exports are the driving force behind economic growth ◆ **cet élève est la ~ de la classe** this pupil sets the standard for the rest of the class

locomotrice[2] /lɔkɔmɔtʀis/ NF motive *ou* motor unit

locus /lɔkys/ (pl **locus** *ou* **loci** /lɔki/) NM (*Bio*) locus

locuste /lɔkyst/ NF locust

locuteur, -trice /lɔkytœʀ, tʀis/ NM,F (*Ling*) speaker ◆ ~ **natif** native speaker

locution /lɔkysjɔ̃/ NF phrase, locution (*SPÉC*) ◆ ~ **figée** set phrase, idiom ◆ ~ **verbale/adverbiale/prépositive** verbal/adverbial/prepositional phrase

loden /lɔdɛn/ NM (= *tissu*) loden; (= *manteau*) loden coat

lœss /løs/ NM loess

lof /lɔf/ NM (*Naut*) windward side ◆ **aller** *ou* **venir au ~** to luff ◆ **virer ~ pour ~** to wear (ship)

lofer /lɔfe/ ▸ conjug 1 ◂ VI (*Naut*) to luff

loft /lɔft/ NM loft (*converted living space*)

log /lɔg/ NM (abrév de **logarithme**) log

logarithme /lɔgaʀitm/ NM logarithm

logarithmique /lɔgaʀitmik/ ADJ logarithmic

loge /lɔʒ/ NF 1 [*de concierge, francs-maçons*] lodge; † [*de bûcheron*] hut ◆ **la Grande Loge de France** the Grand Lodge of France 2 (*Théât*) [*d'artiste*] dressing room; [*de spectateur*] box ◆ **premières ~s** boxes in the dress *ou* grand (*Brit*) circle ◆ **être aux premières ~s** (*fig*) to have a ringside seat, to have a front seat ◆ **secondes ~s** boxes in the upper circle 3 (= *salle de préparation*) (individual) exam room 4 (*Archit*) loggia 5 (*Bot*) loculus ◆ **les ~s** loculi

logé, e /lɔʒe/ (ptp de **loger**) ADJ ◆ **être ~, nourri, blanchi** to have board and lodging *ou* room and board (*US*) and one's laundry done ◆ **être bien ~** to be comfortably housed ◆ **les personnes mal ~es** people in inadequate housing, people who are poorly housed ◆ **je suis mal ~** I'm not really comfortable where I live ◆ **être ~ à la même enseigne** to be in the same boat ◆ **on n'est pas tous ~s à la même enseigne** we don't all get treated in the same way

logeable /lɔʒabl/ ADJ (= *habitable*) habitable, fit to live in (*attrib*); (= *spacieux, bien conçu*) roomy

logement /lɔʒmɑ̃/ NM 1 (= *hébergement*) housing ◆ **le ~ était un gros problème en 1950** housing was a big problem in 1950 ◆ **trouver un ~ provisoire chez des amis** to find temporary accommodation with friends 2 (= *appartement*) accommodation (*NonC*), flat (*Brit*), apartment (*US*) ◆ ~**s collectifs** apartment buildings (*US*), blocks of flats (*Brit*) ◆ ~**s sociaux** ≈ council houses (*ou* flats) (*Brit*), local authority housing (*NonC*) (*Brit*), housing projects (*US*) ◆ **il a réussi à trouver un ~** he managed to find somewhere to live; → **fonction** 3 (*Mil*) [*de troupes*] (*à la caserne*) quartering; (*chez l'habitant*) billeting ◆ ~**s** (*à la caserne*) quarters; (*chez l'habitant*) billet 4 (*Tech*) [*de machine, moteur*] housing

loger /lɔʒe/ ▸ conjug 3 ◂ VI 1 [*personne*] to live (*dans* in; *chez* with, at); ◆ ~ **à l'hôtel/rue Lepic** to live in a hotel/in rue Lepic ◆ ~ **chez l'habitant** [*militaire*] to be billeted on the local inhabitants; [*touriste*] to stay with the local inhabitants

2 [*meuble, objet*] to belong, to go

VT 1 [+ *amis*] to put up; [+ *clients, élèves*] to accommodate; [+ *objet*] to put; [+ *soldats*] (*chez l'habitant*) to billet ◆ **on va ~ les malles dans le grenier** we're going to put *ou* store the trunks in the loft

2 (= *contenir*) to accommodate ◆ **hôtel qui peut ~ 500 personnes** hotel which can accommodate 500 people ◆ **salle qui loge beaucoup de monde** room which can hold *ou* accommodate a lot of people

3 (= *envoyer*) ~ **une balle dans** to lodge a bullet in ◆ **il s'est logé une balle dans la tête** he shot himself in the head, he put a bullet through his head

VPR **se loger** 1 (= *habiter*) (*gén*) to find a house (*ou* flat *etc*), to find somewhere to live, to find accommodation; [*touristes*] to find accommodation, to find somewhere to stay ◆ **il n'a pas trouvé à se ~** he hasn't found anywhere to live *ou* any accommodation ◆ **il a trouvé à se ~ chez un ami** a friend put him up

2 (= *tenir*) **crois-tu qu'on va tous pouvoir se ~ dans la voiture ?** do you think we'll all be able to fit into the car?

3 **se ~ dans/entre** [*objet, balle*] to lodge itself in/between ◆ **le ballon alla se ~ entre les barreaux de la fenêtre** the ball lodged itself *ou* got stuck between the bars of the window ◆ **le chat est allé se ~ sur l'armoire** the cat sought refuge on top of the cupboard ◆ **où est-il allé se ~ ?** [*objet tombé*] where has it gone and hidden itself?, where has it got to? ◆ **la haine se logea dans son cœur** hatred filled his heart

logeur /lɔʒœʀ/ NM landlord (*who lets furnished rooms*)

logeuse /lɔʒøz/ NF landlady

loggia /lɔdʒja/ NF (*Archit*) loggia; (= *balcon*) small balcony

logiciel, -ielle /lɔʒisjɛl/ ADJ software NM piece of software, software program *ou* package ◆ ~ **intégré** integrated software (*NonC*) ◆ ~ **d'application** application software (*NonC*) *ou* program ◆ ~ **contributif** shareware (*NonC*) ◆ ~ **gratuit** *ou* **public** freeware (*NonC*) ◆ ~ **espion** (piece of) spyware ◆ ~ **de navigation** browser ◆ ~ **néfaste** piece of malware

logicien, -ienne /lɔʒisjɛ̃, jɛn/ NM,F logician

logique /lɔʒik/ GRAMMAIRE ACTIVE 53.4

NF 1 (= *rationalité*) logic ◆ **en toute ~** logically ◆ **cela manque un peu de ~** that's rather unreasonable ◆ **c'est dans la ~ des choses** it's in the nature of things

2 (= *façon de raisonner*) logic ◆ ~ **déductive** deductive reasoning

3 (= *processus*) **le pays est entré dans une ~ de guerre** the country has embarked on a course that will inevitably lead to war ◆ **ces négociations s'inscrivent dans une ~ de paix** these negotiations are part of the peace process ◆ **cet accord répond à une ~ de marché** this agreement is in keeping with market principles *ou* practice ◆ **les chaînes publiques vont entrer dans une ~ de rentabilité** state-owned channels are going to start putting emphasis on profitability

4 (= *science*) **la ~** logic

ADJ 1 (= *conforme à la logique*) logical; → **analyse**

2 (= *conforme au bon sens*) sensible ◆ **il ne serait pas ~ de refuser** it wouldn't make sense to refuse

3 (= *normal*) **c'est toujours moi qui fais tout, ce n'est pas ~ !** * I'm the one who does everything, it's not fair! ◆ **il n'est pas ~ que toute la banlieue soit obligée d'aller au cinéma à Paris** people from the suburbs shouldn't have to go into Paris to go to the cinema

4 (= *cohérent*) **tu n'es pas ~** you're not thinking straight ◆ **sois ~ avec toi-même** don't contradict yourself ◆ **sa candidature s'inscrit dans la suite ~ des choses** it is quite understandable that he should become a candidate

COMP **logique formelle** formal logic

logique moderne (*Math*) modern logic

logique pure ⇒ **logique formelle**

> ⚠ Au sens de 'normal', l'adjectif **logique** ne se traduit pas par **logical**.

logiquement /lɔʒikmɑ̃/ GRAMMAIRE ACTIVE 53.4 ADV (= *rationnellement*) logically ◆ ~, **il devrait faire beau** (= *normalement*) the weather should be good

logis /lɔʒi/ NM (*littér*) dwelling, abode (*littér*) ◆ **rentrer au ~** to return to one's abode (*littér*) ◆ **le ~ paternel** the paternal home; → **corps, fée, fou, maréchal**

logisticien, -ienne /lɔʒistisjɛ̃, jɛn/ NM,F logistician

logistique /lɔʒistik/ ADJ logistic NF logistics

logithèque /lɔʒitɛk/ NF software library

logo /lɔgo/ NM logo

logomachie /lɔgɔmaʃi/ NF (= *verbiage*) verbosity

logomachique /lɔgɔmaʃik/ ADJ verbose

logorrhée /lɔgɔʀe/ NF logorrhoea (*Brit*), logorrhea (*US*)

logotype /lɔgɔtip/ NM ⇒ **logo**

loguer (se) /lɔge/ VPR (*Ordin*) to log on

loi /lwa/ NF 1 (= *concept, justice*) **la ~** the law ◆ **la ~ du plus fort** the law of the strongest ◆ **c'est la ~ de la jungle** it's the law of the jungle ◆ **la ~ naturelle** *ou* **de la nature** natural law ◆ **dicter** *ou* **imposer sa ~** to lay down the law ◆ **subir la ~ de qn** (*frm*) to be ruled by sb ◆ **se faire une ~ de faire qch** (*frm*) to make a point *ou* rule of doing sth, to make it a rule to do sth ◆ **avoir la ~ pour soi** to have the law on one's side ◆ **il n'a pas la ~ chez lui !** * he's not master in his own house! ◆ **tu ne feras pas la ~ ici !** * you're not going to lay down the law here! ◆ **ce qu'il dit fait ~** his word is law, what he says goes ◆ **c'est la ~ et les prophètes** it's taken as gospel ◆ **tomber sous le coup de la ~** [*activité, acte*] to be an offence *ou* a criminal offence ♦ **être hors la** ~ to be outlawed ♦ **mettre** *ou* **déclarer hors la** ~ to outlaw; → **force, nom**

2 *(= décret)* law, act ♦ **la** ~ **sur l'égalité des chances** the Equal Opportunities Act ♦ **voter une** ~ to pass a law *ou* an act ♦ **les ~s de la République** the laws of the Republic

3 *(= vérité d'expérience)* law ♦ **la** ~ **de la chute des corps** the law of gravity ♦ **la** ~ **de Faraday** Faraday's law ♦ **la** ~ **de l'offre et de la demande** the law of supply and demand ♦ **la** ~ **des grands nombres** the law of large numbers ♦ **trois trains ont déraillé ce mois-ci, c'est la** ~ **des séries** three trains have been derailed this month – disasters always seem to happen in a row *ou* it's one disaster after another

4 *(= code humain)* **les ~s de la mode** the dictates of fashion ♦ **les ~s de l'honneur** the code of honour ♦ **les ~s de l'hospitalité** the laws of hospitality ♦ **la** ~ **du milieu** the law of the underworld ♦ **la** ~ **du silence** the law of silence ♦ **les ~s de l'étiquette** the rules of etiquette

COMP **loi de finances** Finance Act
loi informatique et liberté data protection act
loi martiale martial law
loi d'orientation blueprint law
loi salique Salic law
loi du talion *(Hist)* lex talionis ♦ **appliquer la** ~ **du talion** *(fig)* to demand an eye for an eye

loi-cadre (pl **lois-cadres**) /lwakadʀ/ NF framework law

loin /lwɛ̃/ ADV 1 *(en distance)* far, a long way ♦ **est-ce** ~ ? is it far? ♦ **ce n'est pas très** ~ it's not very far ♦ **plus** ~ further, farther ♦ **moins** ~ not so far ♦ **la gare n'est pas** ~ **du tout** the station is no distance at all *ou* isn't far at all ♦ **vous nous gênez, mettez-vous plus** ~ you're in our way, go and stand *(ou* sit) somewhere else ♦ **il est** ~ **derrière/devant** he's a long way behind/in front, he's far behind/ahead ♦ **être** ~ *(Helv = parti, absent)* to be away ♦ **foutre**‡ **qch** ~ *(Helv)* to throw sth out

2 *(dans le temps)* **le temps est** ~ **où cette banlieue était un village** it's a long time since this suburb was a village ♦ **c'est** ~ **tout cela !, comme c'est** ~ **!** *(passé)* that was a long time ago!, what a long time ago that was!; *(futur)* that's a long way in the future!, that's (still) a long way off! ♦ **l'été n'est plus** ~ **maintenant** summer's not far off now, summer's just around the corner ♦ **Noël est encore** ~ Christmas is still a long way off ♦ ~ **dans le passé** in the remote past, a long time ago ♦ **voir** *ou* **prévoir** ~ to be farsighted, to see a long way *ou* far ahead ♦ **ne pas voir plus** ~ **que le bout de son nez** to see no further than the end of one's nose ♦ **d'aussi** ~ **que je me rappelle** for as long as I can remember ♦ **en remontant** ~ **dans le temps** if you go back a long way in time ♦ **en remontant plus** ~ **encore dans le passé** by looking even further back into the past

3 *(locutions)*

♦ **loin de** *(en distance)* far from, a long way from, far away from; *(dans le temps)* a long way off from ♦ ~ **de là** *(lieu)* far from there; *(fig)* far from it ♦ **c'est assez** ~ **d'ici** it's quite a long way from here ♦ **non** ~ **de là** not far from there ♦ **leur maison est** ~ **de toute civilisation** their house is a long way from civilization ♦ ~ **des yeux,** ~ **du cœur** *(Prov)* out of sight, out of mind *(Prov)* ♦ **il y a** ~ **de la coupe aux lèvres** *(Prov)* there's many a slip 'twixt cup and lip *(Prov)* ♦ **on est encore** ~ **de la vérité/d'un accord** we're still a long way from the truth/from reaching an agreement ♦ **il leur doit pas** ~ **de 200** € he owes them little short of *ou* not far off €200 ♦ **il ne doit pas y avoir** ~ **de 5 km d'ici à la gare** it can't be much less than 5 km from here to the station ♦ **il n'est pas** ~ **de 10 heures** it's getting on for 10 o'clock ♦ **il n'y a pas** ~ **de 5 ans qu'ils sont partis** it's not far off 5 years since they left ♦ **on est** ~ **du compte** we're far short of the target ♦ **être très** ~ **du sujet** to be way off the subject ♦ ~ **de moi/de lui la pensée de vous blâmer !** far be it from me/from him to blame you! ♦ ~ **de moi** *ou* **de nous !** *(littér, hum)* begone! *(littér) (aussi hum)* ♦ **elle est** ~ **d'être certaine de réussir** she is far from being certain of success, she is by no means assured of success ♦ **ceci est** ~ **de lui plaire** he's far from pleased with this ♦ **c'est très** ~ **de ce que nous attendions de lui** this is not at all what we expected of him ♦ **ils ne sont pas** ~ **de le croire coupable** they almost believe him to be guilty

♦ **au loin** in the distance, far off ♦ **partir au** ~ to go a long way away

♦ **de** + **loin** ♦ **de** ~ *(dans l'espace)* from a distance; *(dans une comparaison)* by far ♦ **de très** ~ from a great distance, from afar *(littér)* ♦ **il voit mal de** ~ he can't see distant objects clearly ♦ **d'aussi** ~ *ou* **du plus** ~ **qu'elle le vit, elle courut vers lui** she saw him in the distance and she ran towards him ♦ **suivre de** ~ **les événements** to follow events from a distance ♦ **le directeur voit ces problèmes de très** ~ the manager is very detached from these issues ♦ **il est de** ~ **le meilleur** he is by far the best, he is far and away the best

♦ **de loin en loin** *(= parfois)* every now and then, every now and again ♦ **de** ~ **en** ~ **brillaient quelques lumières** a few lights shone here and there

♦ **aller** + **loin** *(lit)* to go a long way, to go far (afield) ♦ **nous n'avons pas** ~ **à aller** we don't have far to go ♦ **aussi** ~ **que vous alliez, vous ne trouverez pas d'aussi beaux jardins** however far you go *ou* wherever you go, you won't find such lovely gardens ♦ **il est doué, il ira** ~ he's very gifted, he'll go far (in life) ♦ **tu vas trop** ~ **!** you're going too far! ♦ **on ne va pas** ~ **avec 20** € €20 doesn't go very far ♦ **j'irais même plus** ~ I would go even further

♦ **mener loin** ♦ **cette affaire peut mener (très)** ~ this matter could have far-reaching consequences *ou* repercussions

♦ **il n'y a pas loin** ♦ **d'ici à l'accuser de vol il n'y a pas** ~ it's tantamount to an accusation of theft, it's practically an accusation of theft

lointain, e /lwɛ̃tɛ̃, ɛn/ ADJ 1 *(dans l'espace) [région]* faraway, distant, remote; *[musique, horizons, exil]* distant ♦ **contrées ~es** *(littér)* far-off lands *(littér)* 2 *(dans le temps) [ancêtre, passé]* distant, remote; *[avenir]* distant ♦ **les jours ~s** far-off days 3 *(= vague) [parent, rapport]* remote, distant; *[regard]* faraway; *[cause]* indirect, distant; *[ressemblance]* remote NM 1 ♦ **au** ~**, dans le** ~ in the distance 2 *(Peinture)* background

lointainement /lwɛ̃tɛnmɑ̃/ ADV *(= vaguement)* remotely, vaguely

loi-programme (pl **lois-programmes**) /lwapʀɔgʀam/ NF *act providing framework for government programme*

loir /lwaʀ/ NM dormouse; → **dormir**

Loire /lwaʀ/ NF ♦ **la** ~ *(= fleuve, département)* the Loire

loisible /lwazibl/ ADJ *(frm)* ♦ **s'il vous est** ~ **de vous libérer quelques instants** if you could possibly spare a few moments ♦ **il vous est tout à fait** ~ **de refuser** you are perfectly at liberty to refuse

loisir /lwaziʀ/ NM 1 *(gén pl = temps libre)* leisure *(NonC)*, spare time *(NonC)* ♦ **pendant mes heures de** ~ in my spare *ou* free time, in my leisure hours *ou* time ♦ **que faites-vous pendant vos ~s ?** what do you do in your spare *ou* free time?

2 *(= activités)* **~s** leisure *ou* spare-time activities ♦ **quels sont vos ~s préférés ?** what are your favourite leisure activities?, what do you like doing best in your spare *ou* free time? ♦ **équipements de ~s** recreational *ou* leisure facilities ♦ **la société de ~s** the leisure society; → **base, parc**

3 *(locutions frm)* **avoir (tout) le** ~ **de faire qch** to have leisure *(frm) ou* time to do sth ♦ **je n'ai pas eu le** ~ **de vous écrire** I have not had the leisure *ou* time to write to you ♦ **(tout) à** ~ *(en prenant son temps)* at leisure; *(autant que l'on veut)* at will, at one's pleasure *(frm)*, as much as one likes ♦ **donner** *ou* **laisser à qn le** ~ **de faire** to allow sb (the opportunity) to do

lolita * /lɔlita/ NF nymphet

lolo /lolo/ NM 1 *(langage enfantin = lait)* milk 2 *(*‡ *= sein)* tit‡, boob‡

lombaire /lɔ̃bɛʀ/ ADJ lumbar; → **ponction** NF lumbar vertebra

lombalgie /lɔ̃balʒi/ NF lumbago

lombard, e /lɔ̃baʀ, aʀd/ ADJ Lombard NM *(= dialecte)* Lombard dialect NM,F **Lombard(e)** Lombard

Lombardie /lɔ̃baʀdi/ NF Lombardy

lombes /lɔ̃b/ NMPL loins

lombric /lɔ̃bʀik/ NM earthworm

Lomé /lɔme/ N Lomé

lompe /lɔ̃p/ NM ⇒ **lump**

londonien, -ienne /lɔ̃dɔnjɛ̃, jɛn/ ADJ London *(épith)*, of London NM,F **Londonien(ne)** Londoner

Londres /lɔ̃dʀ/ N London

long, longue /lɔ̃, lɔ̃g/ ADJ 1 *(dans l'espace) [cheveux, liste, robe]* long ♦ **un pont** ~ **de 30 mètres** a 30-metre bridge, a bridge 30 metres long ♦ **2 cm plus ~/trop** ~ 2 cm longer/too long ♦ **plus ~/trop** ~ **de 2 cm** longer/too long by 2 cm; → **chaise, culotte**

2 *(dans le temps) [carrière, série, tradition, voyage]* long; *[amitié, habitude]* long-standing ♦ **il est mort des suites d'une longue maladie** he died after a long illness ♦ **version longue** *(Ciné)* uncut version ♦ **lait longue conservation** longlife milk ♦ **il écouta (pendant) un** ~ **moment le bruit** he listened to the noise for a long while ♦ **l'attente fut longue** there was a long *ou* lengthy wait, I *(ou* they *etc)* waited a long time ♦ **les heures lui paraissaient longues** the hours seemed long to him *ou* seemed to drag by ♦ **faire de longues phrases** to produce long-winded sentences ♦ **avoir une longue habitude de qch/de faire qch** to be long accustomed to sth/to doing sth ♦ **cinq heures, c'est** ~ five hours is a long time ♦ **ne sois pas trop** ~ don't be too long ♦ **nous pouvons vous avoir ce livre, mais ce sera** ~ we can get you the book, but it will take some time *ou* a long time ♦ **vin** ~ **en bouche** wine which lingers long on the palate

3 *(+ infinitif)* **ce travail est** ~ **à faire** this work takes a long time ♦ **il fut** ~ **à se mettre en route/à s'habiller** he took a long time *ou* it took him a long time to get started/to get dressed ♦ **la réponse était longue à venir** the reply was a long time coming

4 *(Culin) [sauce]* thin

5 *(locutions)* **au** ~ **cours** *[voyage]* ocean *(épith)*; *[navigation]* deep-sea *(épith)*, ocean *(épith)*; *[capitaine]* seagoing *(épith)*, ocean-going *(épith)* ♦ **faire** ~ **feu** *(lit, fig)* to fizzle out ♦ **ce pot de confiture n'a pas fait** ~ **feu** that jar of jam didn't last long ♦ **il n'a pas fait** ~ **feu à la tête du service** he didn't last long as head of department ♦ **préparé de longue main** prepared well *ou* long beforehand, prepared well in advance ♦ **il est** ~ **comme un jour sans pain** he's a real beanpole *(Brit) ou* string bean *(US)*; → **date, échéance, haleine, terme**

ADV ♦ **s'habiller** ~ to wear long clothes ♦ **s'habiller trop** ~ to wear clothes that are too long ♦ **en savoir ~/trop ~/plus** ~ to know a lot/too much/more *(sur* about); ♦ **en dire** ~ *[attitude]*

to speak volumes; *[images]* to be eloquent ◆ **regard qui en dit ~** meaningful *ou* eloquent look, look that speaks volumes ◆ **cela en dit ~ sur ses intentions** that tells us a good deal *ou* speaks volumes about his intentions ◆ **son silence en dit ~** his silence speaks for itself *ou* speaks volumes *ou* tells its own story

NM [1] ◆ **un bateau de 7 mètres de ~** a boat 7 metres long ◆ **en ~** lengthways, lengthwise

[2] *(= vêtements)* **le ~** long skirts (*ou* dresses) ◆ **la mode est au ~ cette année** hemlines are down this year

[3] *(loc)* **tomber de tout son ~** to fall sprawling (onto the ground), to fall headlong ◆ **étendu de tout son ~** spread out at full length ◆ **(tout) le ~ du fleuve/de la route** (all) along the river/the road ◆ **tout le ~ du jour/de la nuit** all *ou* the whole day/night long ◆ **tout au ~ de sa carrière/son récit** throughout his career/his story ◆ **l'eau coule le ~ du caniveau** the water flows down *ou* along the gutter ◆ **grimper le ~ d'un mât** to climb up a mast ◆ **tout du ~** *(dans le temps)* the whole time, all along ◆ **tirer un trait tout du ~ (de la page)** to draw a line right down the page ◆ **tout au ~ du parcours** all along the route, the whole way ◆ **de ~ en large** back and forth, to and fro, up and down ◆ **en ~ et en large** in great detail, at great length ◆ **je lui ai expliqué en ~, en large et en travers*** I explained it to him over and over again ◆ **écrire qch au ~** to write sth in full

NF **longue** *(Ling = voyelle)* long vowel; *(Poésie = syllabe)* long syllable; *(Mus = note)* long note ◆ **avoir une longue à carreaux** *(Cartes)* to have a long suit of diamonds

LOC ADV **à la longue** ◆ **à la longue, il s'est calmé** in the end he calmed down ◆ **à la longue, ça a fini par coûter cher** in the long run *ou* in the end it turned out very expensive ◆ **à la longue ça s'arrangera/ça s'usera** it will sort itself out/it will wear out in time *ou* eventually

longanimité /lɔ̃ganimite/ NF *(littér)* forbearance

long-courrier (pl **long-courriers**) /lɔ̃kurje/ ADJ *[navire]* ocean-going *(épith)*; *[vol, avion]* long-haul *(épith)*, long-distance *(épith)* NM *(= navire)* ocean liner, ocean-going ship; *(= avion)* long-haul *ou* long-distance aircraft

longe /lɔ̃ʒ/ NF [1] *(pour attacher)* tether; *(pour mener)* lead [2] *(Boucherie)* loin

longer /lɔ̃ʒe/ ▸ conjug 3 ◂ VT [1] *[bois]* to border; *[mur, sentier, voie ferrée]* to border, to run along(side) ◆ **la voie ferrée longe la nationale** the railway line runs along(side) the main road [2] *[personne]* to go along, to walk along *ou* alongside; *[voiture, train]* to go *ou* pass along *ou* alongside ◆ **naviguer en longeant la côte** to sail along *ou* hug the coast ◆ **~ les murs pour ne pas se faire voir** to keep close to the walls to stay out of sight

longeron /lɔ̃ʒʀɔ̃/ NM [1] *[de pont]* (central) girder [2] *[de châssis]* side frame; *[de fuselage]* longeron; *[d'aile]* spar

longévité /lɔ̃ʒevite/ NF *(= longue vie)* longevity; *(Sociol = durée de vie)* life expectancy ◆ **il attribue sa ~ à la pratique de la bicyclette** he attributes his long life *ou* longevity to cycling ◆ **tables de ~** life-expectancy tables

longiligne /lɔ̃ʒiliɲ/ ADJ *[objet, forme]* slender; *[personne]* tall and slender ◆ **sa silhouette ~** her willowy figure

longitude /lɔ̃ʒityd/ NF longitude ◆ **à** *ou* **par 50° de ~ ouest/est** at 50° longitude west/east

longitudinal, e (mpl **-aux**) /lɔ̃ʒitydinal, o/ ADJ *[section, coupe]* longitudinal; *[vallée, poutre, rainure]* running lengthways ◆ **moteur ~** front-to-back engine

longitudinalement /lɔ̃ʒitydinalmɑ̃/ ADV longitudinally, lengthways

longtemps /lɔ̃tɑ̃/ ADV (for) a long time; *(dans phrase nég ou interrog)* (for) long ◆ **pendant ~** (for) a long time, (for) long ◆ **absent pendant ~** absent (for) a long time ◆ **pendant ~ ils ne sont pas sortis** for a long time *ou* a long while they didn't go out ◆ **avant ~** *(= sous peu)* before long ◆ **pas avant ~** not for a long time ◆ **~ avant/après** long before/after ◆ **on ne le verra pas de ~** we won't see him for a long time *ou* for ages ◆ **il ne reviendra pas d'ici ~** he won't be back for a long time *ou* for ages* yet ◆ **il vivra encore ~** he'll live (for) a long time yet ◆ **il n'en a plus pour ~** *(pour finir)* it won't be long before he's finished; *(avant de mourir)* he hasn't got long ◆ **y a-t-il ~ à attendre ?** is there long to wait?, is there a long wait?, will it take long? ◆ **je n'en ai pas pour ~** I won't be long, it won't take me long ◆ **il a mis** *ou* **été* ~, ça lui a pris ~** it took him a long time, he was a long time over it *ou* doing it ◆ **il arrivera dans ~ ?** will it be long before he gets here? ◆ **rester assez ~ quelque part** *(trop)* to stay somewhere (for) quite *ou* rather a long time *ou* (for) quite a while; *(suffisamment)* to stay somewhere long enough ◆ **tu es resté si ~ !** you stayed so long! *ou* (for) such a long time! ◆ **tu peux le garder aussi ~ que tu veux** you can keep it as long as you want ◆ **il y a** *ou* **cela fait** *ou* **voilà ~ qu'il habite ici** he has been living here (for) a long time ◆ **c'était il y a ~/il n'y a pas ~** that was a long time ago/not long ago ◆ **il y a** *ou* **cela fait** *ou* **voilà ~ que j'ai fini** I finished a long time ago *ou* ages ago ◆ **ça fait ~ qu'il n'est plus venu** it's (been) a long time now since he came, he hasn't come for a long time ◆ **il a cassé un carreau ! – ça faisait ~ !*** *(iro)* he's broken a window! – not again!

◆ **depuis longtemps** ◆ **il habite ici depuis ~** he has been living here (for) a long time ◆ **il n'était pas là depuis ~ quand je suis arrivé** he hadn't been here (for) long when I arrived ◆ **je n'y mangeais plus depuis ~** I had given up eating there long before then ◆ **j'ai fini depuis ~** I finished a long time ago *ou* long ago

longue /lɔ̃g/ ADJ F, NF → **long**

longuement /lɔ̃gmɑ̃/ ADV *(= longtemps) [regarder, parler, hésiter]* for a long time; *(= en détail) [expliquer, étudier, raconter, interroger]* at length ◆ **plus ~** for longer; *(= en plus grand détail)* at greater length ◆ **le plan avait été ~ médité** the plan had been pondered over at length ◆ **elle a ~ insisté sur le fait que…** she strongly emphasized the fact that … ◆ **il m'a ~ remercié** he thanked me profusely ◆ **j'ai écrit ~ sur le sujet** I wrote at length on the subject ◆ **je t'écrirai plus ~ plus tard** I'll write to you more fully later

longuet, -ette* /lɔ̃gɛ, ɛt/ ADJ *[film, discours]* a bit long *(attrib)*, a bit on the long side* *(attrib)* ◆ **tu as été ~ !** you took your time! ◆ **il est ~ à manger** he's a bit of a slow eater NM *(= gressin)* bread stick

longueur /lɔ̃gœʀ/ NF [1] *(= espace)* length ◆ **mesures/unités de ~** measures/units of length, linear measures/units ◆ **la pièce fait trois mètres de** *ou* **en ~** the room is three metres in length *ou* three metres long ◆ **la plage s'étend sur une ~ de 7 km** the beach stretches for 7 km ◆ **dans le sens de la ~** lengthways, lengthwise ◆ **s'étirer en ~** to stretch out lengthways ◆ **pièce tout en ~** long, narrow room ◆ **~ d'onde** *(lit, fig)* wavelength ◆ **nous ne sommes pas sur la même ~ d'onde** *(fig)* we're not on the same wavelength

[2] *(= durée)* length ◆ **à ~ de journée/de semaine/d'année** all day/week/year long ◆ **à ~ de temps** all the time ◆ **traîner** *ou* **tirer en ~** to drag on ◆ **tirer les choses en ~** to drag things out ◆ **attente qui tire** *ou* **traîne en ~** long-drawn-out wait

[3] *(Courses, Natation)* length ◆ **faire des ~s** *[nageur]* to do lengths ◆ **l'emporter de plusieurs ~s** to win by several lengths ◆ **avoir une ~ d'avance (sur qn)** *(lit)* to be one length ahead (of sb); *(fig)* to be ahead (of sb) ◆ **prendre deux ~s d'avance** to go into a two-length lead ◆ **~ de corde** *(Alpinisme)* *(= passage)* pitch; *(= distance)* rope-length

[4] *(= remplissage)* **~s** overlong passages ◆ **ce film/livre a des ~s** parts of this film/book are overlong *ou* seem to drag on

longue-vue (pl **longues-vues**) /lɔ̃gvy/ NF telescope

loofa(h) /lufa/ NM *(= plante)* luffa, dishcloth gourd; *(= éponge)* loofa(h), luffa *(US)*

look* /luk/ NM *(= style, allure) [de personne]* look, image; *[de chose]* look, style ◆ **soigner son ~** to pay great attention to one's look *ou* one's image ◆ **il a un ~ d'enfer** he looks dead cool*

looké, e* /luke/ ADJ *[produit]* sexy*, well-packaged ◆ **la pochette de l'album est ~e sixties** the album cover has got a very sixties look ◆ **je veux pas être ~ impeccable** I don't want to look too well-groomed

looping /lupiŋ/ NM looping the loop *(NonC)* ◆ **faire des ~s** to loop the loop

looser /luzœʀ/ NM ⇒ **loser**

lope** /lɔp/, **lopette**** /lɔpɛt/ NF *(péj)* queer** *(péj)*, fag** *(péj)* *(surtout US)*

lopin /lɔpɛ̃/ NM ◆ **~ (de terre)** patch of land, plot (of land)

loquace /lɔkas/ ADJ talkative, loquacious *(frm)*

loquacité /lɔkasite/ NF talkativeness, loquacity *(frm)*

loque /lɔk/ NF [1] *(= vêtements)* **~s** rags (and tatters) ◆ **être en ~s** to be in rags ◆ **vêtu de ~s** dressed in rags ◆ **tomber en ~s** to be falling to bits [2] *(péj = personne)* **~ (humaine)** wreck ◆ **je suis une vraie ~ ce matin** I feel a wreck *ou* like a wet rag this morning

loquet /lɔkɛ/ NM latch

loqueteau (pl **loqueteaux**) /lɔk(ə)to/ NM (small) latch, catch

loqueteux, -euse /lɔk(ə)tø, øz/ ADJ *[personne]* ragged, (dressed) in rags *ou* in tatters; *[vêtement, livre]* tattered, ragged NM,F pauper

lordose /lɔʀdoz/ NF hollow-back *(NonC)*, lordosis *(SPÉC)*

lorgner* /lɔʀɲe/ ▸ conjug 1 ◂ VT *[+ objet]* to peer at, to eye; *[+ personne] (gén)* to eye; *(avec concupiscence)* to ogle, to eye up* *(Brit)*; *[+ poste, décoration, héritage, pays]* to have one's eye on ◆ **~ qch du coin de l'œil** to look *ou* peer at sth out of the corner of one's eye, to cast sidelong glances at sth VI ◆ **~ sur** *[+ journal, copie]* to sneak a look at; *[+ entreprise, marché]* to have one's eye on; *[+ personne]* to ogle, to eye up* *(Brit)* ◆ **ils lorgnent vers l'Amérique pour y trouver des modèles économiques** they are looking towards *ou* to America for economic models

lorgnette /lɔʀɲɛt/ NF opera glasses ◆ **regarder** *ou* **voir les choses par le petit bout de la ~** *(fig)* to take a very limited *ou* narrow view of things

lorgnon /lɔʀɲɔ̃/ NM *(= face-à-main)* lorgnette; *(= pince-nez)* pince-nez

lori /lɔʀi/ NM *(= oiseau)* lory

loriot /lɔʀjo/ NM ◆ **~ (jaune)** golden oriole

lorrain, e /lɔʀɛ̃, ɛn/ ADJ of *ou* from Lorraine; → **quiche** NM *(= dialecte)* Lorraine dialect NM,F **Lorrain(e)** inhabitant *ou* native of Lorraine NF **Lorraine** *(= région)* Lorraine

lors /lɔʀ/ ADV ◆ **~ de** *(= au moment de)* at the time of; *(= durant)* during ◆ **~ de sa mort** at the time of his death ◆ **elle a annoncé sa démission ~ de la réunion** she announced her resignation during the meeting ◆ **~ même que** even though *ou* if ◆ **pour** ~ for the time being, for the moment; → **dès**

lorsque /lɔʀsk(ə)/ CONJ when ◆ **lorsqu'il entra/entrera** when *ou* as he came/comes in

losange /lɔzɑ̃ʒ/ NM diamond, lozenge ◆ **en forme de** ~ diamond-shaped ◆ **dallage en ~s** diamond tiling

losangé, e /lɔzɑ̃ʒe/ ADJ *[morceau]* diamond-shaped; *[dessin, tissu]* with a diamond pattern

loser * /luzœʀ/ NM *(péj)* loser *

lot /lo/ NM 1 *(Loterie)* prize ◆ **le gros** ~ the first prize, the jackpot ◆ ~ **de consolation** consolation prize 2 *(= portion)* share ◆ ~ **(de terre)** plot (of land) ◆ **chaque jour apporte son ~ de surprises/mauvaises nouvelles** every day brings its share of surprises/bad news 3 *[de tablettes de chocolat, cassettes]* pack; *[de livres, chiffons]* batch; *[de draps, vaisselle]* set; *[aux enchères]* lot; *(Ordin)* batch ◆ **vendu par ~s de cinq** sold in packs of five ◆ **dans le ~, il n'y avait que deux candidats valables** in the whole batch there were only two worthwhile applicants ◆ **se détacher du** ~ *[personne, produit]* to stand out 4 *(fig, littér = destin)* lot *(littér)*, fate ◆ ~ **commun** common fate *ou* lot *ou* destiny ◆ ~ **quotidien** daily *ou* everyday lot

loterie /lɔtʀi/ NF 1 *(= jeu)* lottery; *(dans une kermesse)* raffle ◆ **mettre qch en** ~ to put sth up to be raffled ◆ **la Loterie nationale** the French national lottery *ou* sweepstake ◆ **jouer à la** ~ to buy tickets for the raffle *ou* lottery ◆ **gagner à la** ~ to win on the raffle *ou* lottery 2 *(= hasard)* lottery ◆ **c'est une vraie** ~ it's (all) the luck of the draw ◆ **la vie est une** ~ life is a game of chance, life is a lottery

Loth /lɔt/ NM Lot

loti, e /lɔti/ (ptp de **lotir**) ADJ ◆ **être bien/mal** ~ to be well-/badly off ◆ **il n'est guère mieux** ~ **(que nous)** he's scarcely any better off (than we are) ◆ **on est bien** ~ **avec un chef comme lui !** *(iro)* with a boss like him who could ask for more? *(iro)*

lotion /losjɔ̃/ NF lotion ◆ ~ **capillaire** hair lotion ◆ ~ **après rasage** after-shave lotion ◆ ~ **avant rasage** preshave lotion

lotionner /losjɔne/ ► conjug 1 ◄ VT to apply (a) lotion to

lotir /lɔtiʀ/ ► conjug 2 ◄ VT 1 *[+ terrain]* *(= diviser)* to divide into plots; *(= vendre)* to sell by lots ◆ **terrains à** ~ plots for sale 2 *(Jur)* *[+ succession]* to divide up, to share out ◆ ~ **qn de qch** to allot sth to sb, to provide sb with sth

lotissement /lɔtismɑ̃/ NM 1 *(= terrains à bâtir)* housing estate *ou* site; *(= terrains bâtis)* (housing) development *ou* estate; *(= parcelle)* plot, lot 2 *[de terrain]* *(= division)* division; *(= vente)* sale (by lots) 3 *(Jur)* *[de succession]* sharing out

loto /loto/ NM *(= jeu de société)* lotto; *(= matériel)* lotto set; *(= loterie à numéros)* national lottery ◆ **le** ~ **sportif** ≈ the pools ◆ **gagner au** ~ to win the Lottery

lotte /lɔt/ NF *(de rivière)* burbot; *(de mer)* angler(fish), devilfish, monkfish; *(Culin)* monkfish

lotus /lɔtys/ NM lotus ◆ **être/se mettre en position du** ~ to be/sit in the lotus position

louable /lwabl/ ADJ 1 *[efforts]* praiseworthy, commendable, laudable 2 *[maison]* rentable ◆ **bureau difficilement** ~ **à cause de sa situation** office that is hard to let *(Brit)* *ou* rent *(US)* because of its location

louage /lwaʒ/ NM hiring ◆ **(contrat de)** ~ rental contract ◆ ~ **de services** work contract

louange /lwɑ̃ʒ/ NF praise ◆ **il méprise les ~s** he despises praise ◆ **chanter les ~s de qn** to sing sb's praises ◆ **faire un discours à la** ~ **de qn** to make a speech in praise of sb ◆ **je dois dire, à sa ~, que ...** I must say, to his credit *ou* in his praise, that ...

louanger /lwɑ̃ʒe/ ► conjug 3 ◄ VT *(littér)* to praise, to extol, to laud *(littér)*

louangeur, -euse /lwɑ̃ʒœʀ, øz/ ADJ *(littér)* laudatory, laudative

loubard, e * /lubaʀ, aʀd/ NM,F hooligan, yob * *(Brit)*

louche[1] /luʃ/ ADJ *[affaire, manœuvre, milieu, passé]* shady; *[individu]* shifty, shady, dubious; *[histoire]* dubious, fishy *; *[bar, hôtel]* seedy; *[conduite, acte]* dubious, suspicious, shady; *[réaction, attitude]* dubious, suspicious ◆ **j'ai entendu du bruit, c'est** ~ I heard a noise, that's funny *ou* odd ◆ **il y a du** ~ **dans cette affaire** this business is a bit shady *ou* fishy * *ou* isn't quite above board

louche[2] /luʃ/ NF *(= ustensile)* ladle; *(= quantité)* ladleful ◆ **serrer la** ~ **à qn** * to shake hands with sb, to shake sb's hand ◆ **il y en a environ 3 000, à la** ~ * there are about 3,000 of them, roughly

loucher /luʃe/ ► conjug 1 ◄ VI *(Méd)* to squint, to have a squint ◆ ~ **sur** * *[+ objet]* to eye; *[+ personne]* to ogle, to eye up * *(Brit)*; *[+ poste, héritage]* to have one's eye on ◆ **ils louchent vers l'Europe pour y trouver des modèles économiques** they are looking towards *ou* to Europe for economic models

louer[1] /lwe/ ► conjug 1 ◄ VT to praise ◆ ~ **qn de** *ou* **pour qch** to praise sb for sth ◆ **on ne peut que le** ~ **d'avoir agi ainsi** he deserves only praise *ou* one can only praise him for acting in that way ◆ **louons le Seigneur !** *(Rel)* (let us) praise the Lord! ◆ **Dieu soit loué !** *(fig)* thank God! ◆ **loué soit le fax !** thank God for fax machines! VPR **se louer** ◆ **se** ~ **de** *[+ employé, appareil]* to be very happy *ou* pleased with; *[+ action, mesure]* to congratulate o.s. on ◆ **se** ~ **d'avoir fait qch** to congratulate o.s. on *ou* for having done sth ◆ **n'avoir qu'à se** ~ **de** *[+ employé, appareil]* to have nothing but praise for ◆ **nous n'avons qu'à nous** ~ **de ses services** we have nothing but praise for the service he gives, we have every cause for satisfaction with his services

louer[2] /lwe/ ► conjug 1 ◄ VT 1 *[propriétaire]* *[+ maison, chambre]* to rent out, to let (out) *(Brit)*; *[+ voiture, tente, téléviseur]* to rent (out), to hire out *(Brit)* ◆ ~ **ses services à qn** to work for sb 2 *[locataire]* *[+ maison, chambre]* to rent; *[+ voiture, tente]* to rent, to hire *(Brit)*; *[+ place]* to reserve, to book *(Brit)* ◆ **ils ont loué une maison au bord de la mer** they rented a house by the sea ◆ **à** ~ *[appartement, bureau]* to let *(Brit)*, for rent *(US)*; *[véhicule]* for hire *(Brit)*, for rent *(US)* ◆ **cette maison doit se** ~ **cher** that house must be expensive to rent ◆ ~ **les services de qn** to hire sb

loueur, -euse /lwœʀ, øz/ NM,F *(= entreprise)* rental *ou* hire *(Brit)* company ◆ ~ **de bateaux/de gîtes** *(= personne)* person who rents *ou* hires *(Brit)* out boats/who rents holiday homes

loufiat * /lufja/ NM waiter

loufoque * /lufɔk/ ADJ *[personne, humour, film]* zany * ◆ **comédie** ~ screwball * comedy

loufoquerie * /lufɔkʀi/ NF zaniness *

Louis /lwi/ NM Louis

louis /lwi/ NM ◆ ~ **(d'or)** (gold) louis

louise-bonne (pl **louises-bonnes**) /lwizbɔn/ NF louise-bonne pear

Louisiane /lwizjan/ NF Louisiana

louis-philippard, e /lwifilipaʀ, aʀd/ ADJ *(péj)* of *ou* relating to the reign of Louis Philippe

loukoum /lukum/ NM Turkish delight *(NonC)* ◆ **un** ~ a piece of Turkish delight

loulou[1] /lulu/ NM *(= chien)* spitz ◆ ~ **de Poméranie** Pomeranian dog, Pom *

loulou[2] *, **loulout(t)e** * /lulu, lulut/ NM,F 1 *(terme affectueux)* darling; *(péj)* fishy customer *, seedy character 2 ⇒ **loubard, e**

loup /lu/ NM 1 *(= carnassier)* wolf ◆ **mon (gros** *ou* **petit)** ~ * (my) pet * *ou* love ◆ **le grand méchant** ~ the big bad wolf ◆ **les ~s ne se mangent pas** *ou* **ne se dévorent pas entre eux** *(Prov)* there is honour among thieves *(Prov)* ◆ **l'homme est un** ~ **pour l'homme** brother will turn on brother ◆ **quand on parle du** ~ **(on en voit la queue)** *(Prov)* talk *ou* speak of the devil ◆ **enfermer** *ou* **mettre le** ~ **dans la bergerie** to set the fox to mind the geese ◆ **crier au** ~ to cry wolf ◆ **voir le** ~ *(hum)* to lose one's virginity; → **gueule, hurler, jeune** *etc* 2 *(= poisson)* bass 3 *(= masque)* (eye) mask 4 *(= malfaçon)* flaw COMP **loup de mer** * *(= marin)* old salt *, old seadog *; *(= vêtement)* (short-sleeved) jersey

loup-cervier (pl **loups-cerviers**) /lusɛʀvje/ NM lynx

loupe /lup/ NF 1 *(Opt)* magnifying glass ◆ **examiner** *ou* **regarder qch à la** ~ *(lit)* to look at sth with *ou* through a magnifying glass; *(fig)* to go through sth with a fine-tooth comb, to look into *ou* examine sth in great detail 2 *(Méd)* wen 3 *[d'arbre]* burr ◆ **table en** ~ **de noyer** table in burr walnut

loupé * /lupe/ (ptp de **louper**) NM *(= échec)* failure; *(= défaut)* defect, flaw

louper * /lupe/ ► conjug 1 ◄ VT 1 *[+ occasion, train, balle, personne]* to miss ◆ **loupé !** missed! ◆ **il n'en loupe pas une !** *(iro)* he's forever putting his big foot in it! * ◆ **la prochaine fois, je ne te louperai pas !** I'll get you next time!

2 *[+ travail, gâteau]* to mess up *, to make a mess of; *[+ examen]* to flunk * ◆ ~ **son entrée** to fluff * *ou* bungle one's entrance ◆ **il a loupé son coup/son suicide** he bungled *ou* botched * it/his suicide attempt

VI ◆ **je t'ai dit qu'il ferait une erreur, ça n'a pas loupé !** I told you that he'd make a mistake and sure enough he did! ◆ **ça va tout faire** ~ that'll muck everything up *

VPR **se louper** * 1 *(= rater son suicide)* to bungle one's suicide attempt ◆ **tu ne t'es pas loupée !** *(accident)* that's a nasty cut *(ou* bruise *etc)*!

2 *(= ne pas se rencontrer)* **nous nous sommes loupés de peu** we just missed each other

loup-garou (pl **loups-garous**) /lugaʀu/ NM werewolf ◆ **le** ~ **va te manger !** the Bogeyman will get you!

loupiot, -iotte * /lupjo, jɔt/ NM,F kid *

loupiote * /lupjɔt/ NF *(= lampe)* (small) light

lourd, e[1] /luʀ, luʀd/ ADJ 1 *(= de poids élevé)* *[objet, vêtement]* heavy; *[armement, artillerie, industrie, métal]* heavy *(épith)* ◆ **terrain** ~ heavy *ou* soft ground ◆ **c'est trop** ~ **à porter** it's too heavy to carry; → **eau, franc**[2]

2 *(= désagréablement pesant)* *[silence, sommeil]* heavy, deep; *[chagrin]* deep; *[parfum, odeur]* heavy, strong; *[aliment, vin]* heavy; *[repas]* heavy, big ◆ **yeux ~s de sommeil/fatigue** eyes heavy with sleep/tiredness ◆ **il avait les paupières ~es** his eyelids were *ou* felt heavy ◆ **c'est** ~ **(à digérer)** it's heavy (on the stomach *ou* the digestion) ◆ **se sentir** ~**, avoir l'estomac** ~ to feel bloated ◆ **j'ai** *ou* **je me sens les jambes ~es** my legs feel heavy ◆ **j'ai** *ou* **je me sens la tête ~e** my head feels fuzzy, I feel a bit headachy * ◆ **il a un** ~ **passé** he's a man with a past; → **hérédité**

3 *[ciel, nuage]* heavy; *[temps, chaleur]* sultry, close ◆ **il fait** ~ the weather is close, it's sultry

4 *(= massif, gauche)* *[construction]* inelegant; *[mouvement, style]* heavy, ponderous; *[plaisanterie]* unsubtle; *[compliment]* clumsy ◆ **marcher d'un pas** ~ to tread heavily, to walk with a heavy step ◆ **avoir une démarche ~e** to walk awkwardly ◆ **cet oiseau a un vol assez** ~ this

bird is quite clumsy in the air ◆ **il est un peu ~*** *(= bête)* he's a bit slow; *(d'un plaisantin)* his jokes are a bit heavy

5 *(= important) [dettes, impôts, tâche, responsabilité, charge]* heavy, weighty; *[pertes]* heavy, severe, serious; *[faute]* serious, grave; *[chirurgie]* extensive ◆ **les tendances ~es du marché** the broad *ou* main trends in the market ◆ **de ~es présomptions pèsent sur lui** suspicion falls heavily on him ◆ **les cas les plus ~s sont gardés à l'hôpital** the most serious *ou* severe cases are kept in hospital

6 *(= difficile à gérer) [dispositif]* unwieldy ◆ **35 enfants par classe, c'est trop ~** 35 children per class is too much ◆ **trois enfants à élever, c'est ~/trop ~ (pour elle)** bringing up three children is a lot/too much (for her)

7 *(= chargé)* **le silence était ~ de menaces** there was a threatening *ou* an ominous silence ◆ **décision ~e de conséquences** decision fraught with consequences ◆ **cette défaite est ~e de signification** this defeat is extremely *ou* highly significant ◆ **cette démarche est ~e de dangers** this approach is fraught with danger ◆ **un geste ~ de symboles** a highly symbolic gesture

ADV * ◆ **il n'y a pas ~ de pain** there isn't much bread ◆ **du bon sens, il n'en a pas ~ !** he hasn't got much common sense ◆ **il n'en sait/n'en fait pas ~** he doesn't know/do much ◆ **il ne gagne pas ~** he doesn't earn much ◆ **ça ne fait pas ~** it doesn't amount to much; → **peser**

lourdaud, e* /luʀdo, od/ ADJ oafish, clumsy NM,F oaf

lourde²* /luʀd/ NF *(= porte)* door

lourdement /luʀdəmɑ̃/ ADV *(gén)* heavily ◆ **marcher ~** to walk with a heavy tread ◆ **se tromper ~** to be sadly mistaken, to make a big mistake ◆ **insister ~ sur qch/pour faire qch** to insist strenuously on sth/on doing sth ◆ **s'endetter ~** to get heavily into debt

lourder* /luʀde/ ► conjug 1 ◄ VT to kick out*, to boot out* ◆ **se faire ~** to get kicked out* *ou* booted out*

lourdeur /luʀdœʀ/ NF 1 *(= pesanteur) [d'objet, fardeau]* heaviness, weight; *[de bureaucratie, infrastructure]* cumbersomeness; *[de tâche, responsabilité]* weight; *(Bourse) [de marché]* slackness, sluggishness ◆ **les ~s administratives/bureaucratiques** administrative/bureaucratic red tape 2 *[d'édifice]* heaviness, massiveness; *[de démarche]* heaviness; *[de style, forme]* heaviness, ponderousness ◆ **~ d'esprit** dull-wittedness, slow-wittedness ◆ **s'exprimer avec ~** to express o.s. clumsily *ou* ponderously ◆ **avoir des ~s de tête** to have a fuzzy* head, to feel headachy* ◆ **avoir des ~s d'estomac** to have indigestion, to feel a bit bloated ◆ **j'ai des ~s dans les jambes** my legs feel heavy ◆ **cette traduction comporte des ~s** this translation is a bit heavy *ou* awkward in places 3 *[de temps]* sultriness, closeness

lourdingue* /luʀdɛ̃g/ ADJ *[plaisanterie]* predictable; *[personne]* oafish, clumsy; *[construction]* hefty-looking*; *[phrase]* laboured *(Brit)*, labored *(US)*, clumsy

loustic* /lustik/ NM *(= enfant)* kid*; *(= taquin)* villain* *(hum)*; *(= type)* (funny) guy* *ou* chap* *(Brit)* ◆ **faire le ~** to play the fool, to act the goat* *(Brit)* ◆ **un drôle de ~** *(= type)* an oddball*, an oddbod* *(Brit)*; *(= enfant)* a little villain* *(hum) ou* rascal

loutre /lutʀ/ NF *(= animal)* otter; *(= fourrure)* otter-skin ◆ **~ de mer** sea otter

louve /luv/ NF she-wolf

louveteau (pl **louveteaux**) /luv(ə)to/ NM *(= animal)* (wolf) cub; *(Scoutisme)* cub (scout)

louvoiement /luvwamɑ̃/ NM 1 *(Naut)* tacking *(NonC)* 2 *(= tergiversations)* hedging *(NonC)*, dithering, shilly-shallying* *(Brit)* ◆ **assez de ~s** stop beating about the bush

louvoyer /luvwaje/ ► conjug 8 ◄ VI 1 *(Naut)* to tack ◆ **~ au plus près** to beat to windward ◆ **~ entre les écueils** *(fig)* to tread a delicate path ◆ **il doit ~ entre les tendances différentes de son parti** he has to tread a delicate path *ou* steer a delicate course between the different political currents in his party 2 *(= tergiverser)* to hedge, to dither, to shilly-shally* *(Brit)*

Louvre /luvʀ/ NM ◆ **le (Musée du) ~** the Louvre (museum) ◆ **l'École du ~** the Ecole du Louvre *(training college for museum curators and guides based at the Louvre)*

Louxor /luksɔʀ/ N Luxor

lover /lɔve/ ► conjug 1 ◄ VT to coil VPR **se lover** *[serpent]* to coil up; *[personne]* to curl up

loxodromie /lɔksɔdʀɔmi/ NF *(Naut)* loxodromics *(sg)*, loxodromy

loyal, e (mpl **-aux**) /lwajal, o/ ADJ 1 *(= fidèle) [sujet, ami]* loyal, faithful, trusty ◆ **après 50 ans de bons et loyaux services** after 50 years of good and faithful service 2 *(= honnête) [personne, procédé]* fair, honest; *[conduite]* upright, fair; *[jeu]* fair, straight* ◆ **se battre à la ~e*** to fight cleanly

loyalement /lwajalmɑ̃/ ADV *[agir]* fairly, honestly; *[servir]* loyally, faithfully; *[se battre]* cleanly ◆ **accepter ~ une défaite** to take a defeat sportingly *ou* in good part *(Brit)*

loyalisme /lwajalism/ NM loyalty

loyaliste /lwajalist/ ADJ 1 *(= fidèle)* loyal 2 *(Pol)* loyalist, Loyalist NMF 1 *(= fidèle)* loyal supporter 2 *(Pol)* loyalist, Loyalist

loyauté /lwajote/ NF 1 *(= fidélité)* loyalty, faithfulness 2 *(= honnêteté)* honesty, fairness; *[de conduite]* fairness, uprightness ◆ **avec ~** fairly, honestly

loyer /lwaje/ NM rent ◆ **~ commercial** office rent ◆ **~ de l'argent** rate of interest, interest rate

LP /ɛlpe/ NM (abrév de **lycée professionnel**) → **lycée**

LSD /ɛlɛsde/ NM (abrév de **Lysergsäure Diethylamid**) LSD

lu, e /ly/ (ptp de **lire**) ADJ ◆ **~ et approuvé** read and approved ◆ **elle est très ~e en Europe** she is widely read in Europe

Luanda /luɑ̃nda/ N Luanda

lubie /lybi/ NF *(= centre d'intérêt, passe-temps)* fad; *(= idée)* hare-brained idea; *(= mode)* craze, fad ◆ **encore une de ses ~s !** another of his hare-brained *ou* mad ideas! ◆ **il lui a pris la ~ de ne plus manger de pain** he has taken it into his head not to eat bread any more

lubricité /lybʀisite/ NF *[de personne]* lustfulness, lechery; *[de propos, conduite]* lewdness

lubrifiant, e /lybʀifjɑ̃, jɑ̃t/ ADJ lubricating NM lubricant

lubrification /lybʀifikasjɔ̃/ NF lubrication

lubrifier /lybʀifje/ ► conjug 7 ◄ VT to lubricate

lubrique /lybʀik/ ADJ *[personne]* lustful, lecherous; *[propos]* lewd, libidinous; *[danse]* lewd; *[amour]* lustful, carnal ◆ **regarder qch d'un œil ~** to gaze at sth with a lustful eye

Luc /lyk/ NM Luke

lucarne /lykaʀn/ NF *[de toit]* skylight; *(en saillie)* dormer window ◆ **envoyer la balle dans la ~** *(Ftbl)* to send the ball into the top corner of the net ◆ **la petite ~, les étranges ~s** *(= télévision)* the small screen

lucide /lysid/ ADJ 1 *(= conscient) [malade, vieillard]* lucid; *[accidenté]* conscious 2 *(= perspicace) [personne]* lucid, clear-headed; *[esprit, analyse, raisonnement]* lucid, clear ◆ **il a une vision plus ~ des choses** he has a clearer view of things ◆ **le témoin le plus ~ de son temps** the most clear-sighted *ou* perceptive observer of the times he lived in ◆ **juger qch d'un œil ~** to judge sth with a lucid *ou* clear eye

lucidement /lysidmɑ̃/ ADV lucidly, clearly

lucidité /lysidite/ NF 1 *[de malade, vieillard]* lucidity; *[d'accidenté]* consciousness ◆ **il a des moments de ~** he has moments of lucidity, he has lucid moments *ou* intervals ◆ **il a toute sa ~** he still has the use of his faculties, he's still quite lucid 2 *(= perspicacité) [de personne]* lucidity, clear-headedness; *[d'esprit, analyse, raisonnement]* lucidity, clearness ◆ **il a analysé la situation avec ~** he gave a very clear-headed analysis of the situation

Lucifer /lysifɛʀ/ NM Lucifer

luciole /lysjɔl/ NF firefly

lucratif, -ive /lykʀatif, iv/ ADJ *[activité, marché, trafic, entreprise]* lucrative, profitable; *[emploi]* lucrative, well-paid ◆ **association à but ~/non ~** profit-making/non-profit-making *ou* not-for-profit *(US)* organization

lucrativement /lykʀativmɑ̃/ ADV lucratively

lucre /lykʀ/ NM *(péj)* lucre *(péj)*

Lucrèce /lykʀɛs/ NM Lucretius NF Lucretia

ludiciel /lydisjɛl/ NM computer game ◆ **~s** computer games, game software *(NonC)*

ludion /lydjɔ̃/ NM Cartesian diver

ludique /lydik/ ADJ playful ◆ **activité ~** *(Scol)* play activity; *(de loisir)* recreational activity ◆ **l'informatique ~** computer games ◆ **il veut une émission plus ~** he wants the programme to be more entertaining ◆ **nous avons donné une dimension ~ aux exercices** we've made the exercises more like games

ludo-éducatif, -ive (mpl **ludo-éducatifs**) /lydoedykatif, iv/ ADJ *[programme, logiciel]* edutainment *(épith)*

ludothèque /lydɔtɛk/ NF games library

luette /lɥɛt/ NF uvula *(SPÉC)*

lueur /lɥœʀ/ NF 1 *[de flamme]* glimmer *(NonC)*; *[d'étoile, lune, lampe]* (faint) light; *[de braises]* glow *(NonC)* ◆ **à la ~ d'une bougie** by candlelight ◆ **les ~s de la ville** the city lights ◆ **les premières ~s de l'aube/du jour** the first light of dawn/of day ◆ **les ~s du couchant** the glow of sunset- 2 *[de désir, colère]* gleam; *[d'intelligence]* glimmer ◆ **il avait une ~ malicieuse dans le regard** he had a mischievous gleam *ou* glint in his eye ◆ **pas la moindre ~ d'espoir** not the faintest glimmer of hope 3 *(gén hum = connaissances)* **il a quelques ~s sur le sujet** he knows a bit about the subject ◆ **peux-tu apporter quelques ~s sur le fonctionnement de cette machine ?** can you shed some light on the working of this machine?

luffa /lufa/ NM ⇒ **loofa(h)**

luge /lyʒ/ NF toboggan, sledge *(Brit)*, sled *(US)* ◆ **faire de la ~** to toboggan, to sledge *(Brit)*, to sled *(US)*

luger /lyʒe/ ► conjug 3 ◄ VI to toboggan, to sledge *(Brit)*, to sled *(US)*

lugeur, -euse /lyʒœʀ, øz/ NM,F tobogganist

lugubre /lygybʀ/ ADJ *[pensée, ambiance, récit]* gloomy, dismal, lugubrious *(littér)*; *[paysage]* dreary, dismal; *[maison]* gloomy; *[musique, cri]* mournful ◆ **d'un ton ~** in a funereal voice

lugubrement /lygybʀəmɑ̃/ ADV gloomily, dismally, lugubriously

lui /lɥi/ PRON PERS *(objet indirect, homme)* him; *(femme)* her; *(animal, bébé)* it, him, her; *(bateau, nation)* her, it; *(insecte, chose)* it ◆ **je le ~ ai dit** *(à un homme)* I told him; *(à une femme)* I told her ◆ **tu ~ as donné de l'eau ?** *(à un animal)* have you given it (*ou* him *ou* her) some water?; *(à une plante)* have you watered it? ◆ **je ne le ~ ai jamais caché** I have never kept it from him (*ou* her) ◆ **il ~ est facile de le faire** it's easy for him (*ou* her) to do it ◆ **je ne ~ connais pas de défauts** he's (*ou* she's) got no faults that I know of ◆ **je ~ ai entendu dire que** I heard him (*ou* her) say that ◆ **le bateau est plus propre depuis qu'on ~ a donné un coup de peinture** the boat is cleaner now they've given her (*ou* it) a coat of paint

PRON M 1 (*fonction objet, personne*) him; (*animal*) him, her, it; (*chose*) it; (*pays, bateau*) her, it ◆ **elle n'admire que ~** she only admires him ◆ **à ~, elle n'a pas dit un mot** she never said a word to him ◆ **~, le revoir ? jamais !** see him again? never! ◆ **c'est ~, je le reconnais** it's him, I recognize him ◆ **je l'ai bien vu, ~ !** I saw him all right!*, I definitely saw him! ◆ **si j'étais ~, j'accepterais** if I were him *ou* he (*frm*) I would accept; → aussi **même, non, seul**

2 (*sujet, gén emphatique, personne*) he; (*chose*) it; (*animal*) it, he, she ◆ **elle est vendeuse, ~ est maçon** she's a saleswoman and he's a bricklayer ◆ **~, furieux, a refusé** furious, he refused ◆ **le Japon, ~, serait d'accord** Japan, for its *ou* her part, would agree ◆ **l'enfant, ~, avait bien vu les bonbons** the child had seen the sweets all right ◆ **qu'est-ce qu'ils ont dit ? – ~, rien** what did they say? – he said nothing ◆ **elle est venue mais pas ~** she came but not him *ou* but he didn't ◆ **mon frère et ~ sont partis ensemble** my brother and he went off together ◆ **~ parti, j'ai pu travailler** with him gone *ou* after he had gone I was able to work ◆ **~(, il) n'aurait jamais fait ça, il n'aurait jamais fait ça, ~** he would never have done that ◆ **est-ce qu'il le sait, ~ ?, est-ce que ~(, il) le sait ?** does he know about it? ◆ **~, se marier ? jamais !** him get married? that'll be the day!

3 (*emphatique avec qui, que*) **c'est ~ que nous avions invité** it's *ou* it was him we had invited ◆ **c'est à ~ que je veux parler** it's him I want to speak to, I want to speak to him ◆ **il y a un hibou dans le bois, c'est ~ que j'ai entendu** there is an owl in the wood – that's what I heard ◆ **c'est ~ qui me l'a dit** he told me himself, it was he who told me ◆ **c'est ~ qui le dit !** that's his story!, that's what he says! ◆ **ce fut ~ qui le premier découvrit ...** (*frm*) it was he who first discovered ... ◆ **chasse le chien, c'est ~ qui m'a mordu** chase that dog away – it's the one that bit me ◆ **de tous les arbres, c'est ~ qui a le bois le plus dur** of all the trees it's this one that has the hardest wood ◆ **ils ont trois chats, et ~ qui ne voulait pas d'animaux !** they have three cats and to think that he didn't want any animals!

4 (*dans des comparaisons : sujet*) he, him; (*objet*) him ◆ **elle est plus mince que ~** she is slimmer than he is *ou* than him ◆ **j'ai mangé plus/moins que ~** I ate more/less than he did *ou* than him ◆ **ne fais pas comme ~** don't do as he does *ou* did, don't do the same as he did ◆ **je ne la connais pas aussi bien que ~** (*que je le connais*) I don't know her as well as (I know) him; (*qu'il la connaît*) I don't know her as well as he does

lui-même /lɥimɛm/ PRON → **même**

luire /lɥiʀ/ ► conjug 38 ◄ VI [*métal*] to shine, to gleam; [*surface mouillée*] to glisten; [*reflet intermittent*] to glint; [*étoile*] to twinkle; (*en scintillant*) to glimmer, to shimmer; (*en rougeoyant*) to glow ◆ **l'herbe/l'étang luisait au soleil du matin** the grass/the pond glistened in the morning sunlight ◆ **yeux qui luisent de colère/d'envie** eyes gleaming with anger/with desire ◆ **le lac luisait sous la lune** the lake shimmered *ou* glimmered in the moonlight ◆ **l'espoir luit encore** there is still a glimmer of hope

luisant, e /lɥizɑ̃, ɑ̃t/ ADJ [*métal*] gleaming, shining; [*surface mouillée*] glistening; (*reflet intermittent*) glinting; (*en scintillant*) glimmering, shimmering; (*en rougeoyant*) glowing ◆ **front ~ de sueur** forehead gleaming *ou* glistening with sweat ◆ **vêtements ~s d'usure** clothes shiny with wear ◆ **yeux ~s de fièvre** eyes bright with fever; → **ver** NM [*d'étoffe*] sheen; [*de pelage*] gloss

lumbago /lɔ̃bago/ NM lumbago

lumière /lymjɛʀ/ NF 1 (*gén, Phys*) light ◆ **la ~ du jour** daylight ◆ **la ~ du soleil l'éblouit** he was dazzled by the sunlight ◆ **à la ~ artificielle/électrique** by artificial/electric light ◆ **la ~ entrait à flots dans la pièce** daylight streamed into the room ◆ **il n'y a pas beaucoup/ça ne donne guère de ~** there isn't/it doesn't give much light ◆ **donne-nous de la ~** switch *ou* put the light on, will you? ◆ **il y a de la ~ dans sa chambre** there's a light on in his room ◆ **Il dit "que la lumière soit" et la ~ fut** (*Bible*) He said "let there be light" and there was light ◆ **les ~s de la ville** (*gén*) the lights of the town; (*plus grande*) the city lights; → **effet, habit, siècle**

2 (*= connaissance*) light ◆ **avoir/acquérir quelque ~ sur qch** to have/gain some knowledge of sth, to have/gain some insight into sth ◆ **avoir des ~s sur une question** to have some ideas *ou* some knowledge on a question, to know something about a question ◆ **aidez-nous de vos ~s** give us the benefit of your wisdom *ou* insight

3 (*= personne*) light ◆ **il fut une des ~s de son siècle** he was one of the (shining) lights of his age ◆ **le pauvre garçon, ce n'est pas une ~** the poor boy, he's no Einstein* *ou* no genius

4 (*Tech*) [*de machine à vapeur*] port; [*de canon*] sight ◆ **~ d'admission/d'échappement** (*dans moteur*) inlet/exhaust port *ou* valve

5 (*locutions*) **faire (toute) la ~ sur qch** to get right to the bottom of sth ◆ **il faut que toute la ~ soit faite sur cette affaire** we must get to the bottom of this business ◆ **entrevoir la ~ au bout du tunnel** to see the light at the end of the tunnel ◆ **jeter une nouvelle ~ sur qch** to throw *ou* shed new light on sth

◆ **à la lumière de** ◆ **à la ~ des étoiles** by the light of the stars, by starlight ◆ **à la ~ des récents événements** in the light of recent events

◆ **mettre qch en lumière** to bring sth to light

COMP **lumière blanche** white light
lumière cendrée (*Astron*) earth-light, earthshine
lumière noire black light
lumière stroboscopique strobe lighting
lumière de Wood ⇒ **lumière noire**

lumignon /lymiɲɔ̃/ NM (*= lampe*) (small) light; (*= bougie*) candle-end

luminaire /lyminɛʀ/ NM (*gén*) light, lamp; (*= cierge*) candle ◆ **magasin de ~s** lighting shop

luminescence /luminesɑ̃s/ NF luminescence

luminescent, e /lyminesɑ̃, ɑ̃t/ ADJ (*littér*) luminescent

lumineusement /lyminøzmɑ̃/ ADV [*expliquer*] lucidly, clearly ◆ **son explication était ~ claire** his explanation was crystal clear

lumineux, -euse /lyminø, øz/ ADJ 1 [*corps, intensité, cadran, aiguille*] luminous; [*fontaine, enseigne*] illuminated; [*rayon, faisceau*] of light ◆ **onde/source lumineuse** light wave/source; → **flèche¹, panneau** 2 [*teint, regard*] radiant; [*ciel, couleur*] luminous; [*pièce, appartement*] bright, light 3 (*littér = pur, transparent*) luminous (*littér*), lucid; (*iro*) [*exposé*] limpid, brilliant ◆ **j'ai compris, c'est ~** I understand, it's as clear as daylight *ou* it's crystal clear; → **idée**

luminosité /lyminozite/ NF 1 [*de teint, regard*] radiance; [*de ciel, couleur*] luminosity ◆ **il y a beaucoup de ~** there's lots of light, it's very bright 2 (*Photo, Sci*) luminosity

lump /lœp/ NM lumpfish, lumpsucker; → **œuf**

lumpenprolétariat /lumpɛnpʀoletaʀja/ NM lumpenproletariat

lunaire¹ /lynɛʀ/ ADJ [*année, cycle, paysage, sol*] lunar; [*roche*] moon (*épith*); [*visage*] moonlike

lunaire² /lynɛʀ/ NF (*Bot*) honesty

lunaison /lynɛzɔ̃/ NF lunar month

lunapark /lynapaʀk/ NM (fun)fair

lunatique /lynatik/ ADJ moody

lunch (pl **lunch(e)s**) /lœntʃ/ NM buffet

lundi /lœdi/ NM Monday ◆ **le ~ de Pâques/de Pentecôte** Easter/Whit Monday ◆ **ça va ? – (ça va) comme un ~** how are you? – I've got the Monday blues* *ou* I'm already longing for the weekend; *pour autres loc voir* **samedi**

lune /lyn/ NF 1 (*Astron*) moon ◆ **pleine/nouvelle ~** full/new moon ◆ **nuit sans ~** moonless night ◆ **~ rousse** April moon; → **clair, croissant¹** 2 (* *= derrière*) bottom*, backside* 3 (*locutions*) **~ de miel** (*lit, fig*) honeymoon ◆ **être dans la ~** to have one's head in the clouds, to be in a dream ◆ **tomber de la ~** to have dropped in from another planet ◆ **demander** *ou* **vouloir la ~** to ask *ou* cry for the moon ◆ **il décrocherait la ~ pour elle** he'd move heaven and earth to please her ◆ **promettre la ~** to promise the moon *ou* the earth ◆ **elle veut lui faire voir la ~ en plein midi** she's trying to pull the wool over his eyes ◆ **il y a (bien) des ~s** † many moons ago; → **face, vieux**

luné, e * /lyne/ ADJ ◆ **être bien/mal ~** to be in a good/bad mood ◆ **comment est-elle ~e ce matin ?** what sort of (a) mood is she in this morning?

lunetier, -ière /lyn(ə)tje, jɛʀ/ ADJ [*industrie*] spectacle (*épith*) NM,F (*= vendeur*) optician; (*= fabricant*) spectacle *ou* eyeglasses (*US*) manufacturer

lunette /lynɛt/ NF 1 (*Astron = télescope*) telescope; [*de fusil*] sight(s) 2 (*Archit*) lunette NFPL **lunettes** (*correctives*) glasses, eyeglasses (*US*), spectacles †; (*de protection*) goggles, glasses ◆ **mets tes ~s !** (*lit, fig*) put your glasses *ou* specs* on! ◆ **un intello* à ~s** a bespectacled intellectual

COMP **lunette d'approche** telescope
lunette arrière [*de voiture*] rear window
lunette astronomique astronomical telescope
lunette (des cabinets) toilet rim
lunettes de glacier snow goggles
lunette méridienne meridian circle
lunettes de natation swimming goggles
lunettes noires dark glasses
lunettes de plongée swimming *ou* diving goggles
lunettes de ski ski goggles
lunettes de soleil sunglasses
lunettes de vue prescription *ou* corrective glasses

lunetterie /lynɛtʀi/ NF spectacle trade

lunule /lynyl/ NF [*d'ongle*] half-moon, lunula (*SPÉC*); (*Math*) lune

lupanar /lypanaʀ/ NM (*littér*) brothel

lupin /lypɛ̃/ NM lupin

lupus /lypys/ NM lupus

lurette /lyʀɛt/ NF ◆ **il y a belle ~ de cela*** that was ages ago *ou* donkey's years* (*Brit*) ago ◆ **il y a belle ~ que je ne fume plus*** I stopped smoking ages ago, it's ages since I stopped smoking

lurex /lyʀɛks/ NM lurex

luron* /lyʀɔ̃/ NM ◆ **(joyeux** *ou* **gai) ~** likely lad ◆ **c'est un (sacré) ~ †** he's a great one for the girls*, he's quite a lad*

luronne* /lyʀɔn/ **NF** ◆ **(gaie)** ~ (lively) lass* ◆ **c'est une (sacrée)** ~ † she's a great one for the men*, she's quite a lass*

Lusaka /lusaka/ **N** Lusaka

lusitanien, -ienne /lyzitanjɛ̃, jɛn/ **ADJ** Lusitanian **NM,F** **Lusitanien(ne)** Lusitanian

lusophone /lyzɔfɔn/ **ADJ** Portuguese-speaking **NMF** Portuguese speaker

lusophonie /lyzɔfɔni/ **NF** ◆ **la** ~ the Portuguese-speaking world

lustrage /lystʀaʒ/ **NM** *(Tech) [d'étoffe, peaux, fourrures]* lustring; *[de glace]* shining

lustral, e (mpl **-aux**) /lystʀal, o/ **ADJ** *(littér)* lustral *(littér)*

lustrant /lystʀɑ̃/ **ADJ M, NM** ◆ **(produit)** ~ polish

lustre /lystʀ/ **NM** 1 *[d'objet, peaux, vernis]* shine, lustre *(Brit)*, luster *(US)*; *[de personne, cérémonie]* lustre ◆ **redonner du ~ à une institution** to restore the prestige of an institution 2 *(= luminaire)* centre light *(with several bulbs)*; *(très élaboré)* chandelier 3 *(littér = 5 ans)* lustrum *(littér)* ◆ **depuis des ~s** for ages, for aeons

lustré, e /lystʀe/ (ptp de **lustrer**) **ADJ** *[cheveux, fourrure, poil]* glossy; *[manche usée]* shiny

lustrer /lystʀe/ ▸ conjug 1 ◂ **VT** *(Tech) [+ étoffe, peaux, fourrures]* to lustre; *[+ glace]* to shine; *(gén = faire briller)* to shine, to put a shine on; *(par l'usure)* to make shiny ◆ **le chat lustre son poil** the cat is licking its fur ◆ **la pluie lustrait le feuillage** the rain put a sheen on the leaves ◆ **ce tissu se lustre facilement** this fabric gets shiny very quickly

lustrerie /lystʀəʀi/ **NF** lighting (appliance) trade

lustrine /lystʀin/ **NF** lustre *(fabric)*

Lutèce /lytɛs/ **N** Lutetia

lutétium /lytesjɔm/ **NM** lutetium

luth /lyt/ **NM** lute

Luther /lytɛʀ/ **NM** Luther

luthéranisme /lyteʀanism/ **NM** Lutheranism

luthérien, -ienne /lyteʀjɛ̃, jɛn/ **ADJ** Lutheran **NM,F** **Luthérien(ne)** Lutheran

luthier, -ière /lytje, jɛʀ/ **NM,F** (stringed-)instrument maker

luthiste /lytist/ **NMF** lutenist, lutanist

lutin, e /lytɛ̃, in/ **ADJ** impish, mischievous **NM** *(= farfadet) (gentil)* imp, sprite; *(méchant)* goblin; *(irlandais)* leprechaun ◆ **(petit)** ~ *(= enfant)* (little) imp

lutiner /lytine/ ▸ conjug 1 ◂ **VT** to fondle, to tickle

lutrin /lytʀɛ̃/ **NM** *(sur pied)* lectern; *(sur table)* book-rest

lutte /lyt/ **NF** 1 *(gén = combat)* struggle, fight *(contre* against); ◆ **~s politiques** political struggles ◆ **~ antipollution/contre l'alcoolisme** fight against pollution/against alcoholism ◆ **~ contre le crime** crime prevention ◆ **~ antidrogue** battle *ou* fight against drugs ◆ **~ pour la vie** *(Bio, fig)* struggle for existence *ou* survival ◆ **~ entre le bien et le mal** conflict *ou* struggle between good and evil ◆ **~ de l'honneur et de l'intérêt** conflict between honour and self-interest ◆ **aimer la** ~ to enjoy a struggle ◆ **engager/abandonner la** ~ to take up/give up the struggle *ou* fight ◆ **nous sommes engagés dans une ~ inégale** we're fighting an uneven battle, it's an unequal struggle ◆ **après plusieurs années de** ~ after several years of struggling ◆ **gagner** *ou* **conquérir qch de haute** ~ to win sth after a brave fight *ou* struggle

2 *(locutions)* **entrer/être en ~ (contre qn)** to enter into/be in conflict (with sb) ◆ **en ~ ouverte contre sa famille** in open conflict with his family ◆ **travailleurs en** ~ *(en grève)* striking workers ◆ **le pays en** ~ *(Mil)* the country at war ◆ **les partis en** ~ *(Pol)* the opposing parties

3 *(Sport)* wrestling ◆ **~ libre/gréco-romaine** all-in/Greco-Roman *ou* Graeco-Roman *(Brit)* wrestling ◆ **faire de la** ~ to wrestle

COMP **lutte armée** armed struggle ◆ **en ~ armée** in armed conflict

lutte des classes class struggle *ou* war

lutte d'influence(s) struggle for influence

lutte d'intérêts conflict *ou* clash of interests

lutter /lyte/ ▸ conjug 1 ◂ **VI** 1 *(= se battre)* to struggle, to fight ◆ **~ contre un adversaire** to struggle *ou* fight against an opponent ◆ **~ contre le vent** to fight against *ou* battle with the wind ◆ **~ contre l'ignorance/un incendie** to fight ignorance/a fire ◆ **~ contre l'adversité/le sommeil** to fight off adversity/sleep ◆ **~ contre la mort** to fight *ou* struggle for one's life ◆ **~ pour ses droits/la liberté** to fight for one's rights/freedom ◆ **~ avec sa conscience** to struggle *ou* wrestle with one's conscience ◆ **les deux navires luttaient de vitesse** the two ships were racing each other 2 *(Sport)* to wrestle

lutteur, -euse /lytœʀ, øz/ **NM,F** *(Sport)* wrestler; *(fig)* fighter

lux /lyks/ **NM** lux

luxation /lyksasjɔ̃/ **NF** dislocation, luxation *(SPÉC)*

luxe /lyks/ **NM** 1 *(= richesse)* luxury; *[de maison, objet]* luxuriousness, sumptuousness ◆ **vivre dans le** ~ to live in (the lap of) luxury ◆ **de** ~ *[produits]* de luxe *(épith)*; *[voiture, appartement]* luxury *(épith)* ◆ **modèle (de) grand** ~ de luxe model ◆ **boutique de** ~ shop selling luxury goods ◆ **deux salles de bains, c'est le** *ou* **du ~ !** two bathrooms, it's the height of luxury! *ou* what luxury! ◆ **je me suis acheté un nouveau manteau, ce n'était pas du** ~ I bought myself a new coat, I badly needed one ◆ **j'ai lavé la cuisine, ce n'était pas du ~ !** I washed the kitchen floor, it badly needed it

2 *(= plaisir coûteux)* luxury ◆ **son seul ~ : sa chaîne hi-fi** his only luxury *ou* indulgence was his stereo system ◆ **il s'est offert** *ou* **payé le ~ d'aller au casino** he allowed himself the indulgence *ou* luxury of a trip to the casino ◆ **je ne peux pas me payer** *ou* **m'offrir le ~ d'être malade/d'aller au restaurant** I can't afford the luxury of being ill/eating out

3 *(= profusion) [de détails]* wealth, host; *[de précautions]* host ◆ **il nous l'a décrit avec un ~ de précisions** he described it to us in great *ou* lavish detail

Luxembourg /lyksɑ̃buʀ/ **NM** ◆ **(le grand-duché de)** ~ (the Grand Duchy of) Luxembourg ◆ **le palais du** ~ *(Pol) the seat of the French Senate*

luxembourgeois, e /lyksɑ̃buʀʒwa, waz/ **ADJ** of *ou* from Luxembourg **NM,F** **Luxembourgeois(e)** inhabitant *ou* native of Luxembourg

luxer /lykse/ ▸ conjug 1 ◂ **VT** to dislocate, to luxate *(SPÉC)* ◆ **se ~ un membre** to dislocate a limb ◆ **avoir l'épaule luxée** to have a dislocated shoulder

luxueusement /lyksɥøzmɑ̃/ **ADV** luxuriously

luxueux, -euse /lyksɥø, øz/ **ADJ** luxurious

luxure /lyksyʀ/ **NF** lust

luxuriance /lyksyʀjɑ̃s/ **NF** luxuriance

luxuriant, e /lyksyʀjɑ̃, jɑ̃t/ **ADJ** *[végétation]* luxuriant, lush; *[imagination]* fertile, luxuriant *(littér)*

luxurieux, -ieuse /lyksyʀjø, jøz/ **ADJ** lustful, lascivious

luzerne /lyzɛʀn/ **NF** *(cultivée)* lucerne, alfalfa; *(sauvage)* medick *(Brit)*, medic *(US)*

lycanthropie /likɑ̃tʀɔpi/ **NF** lycanthropy

lycée /lise/ **NM** lycée, ≃ secondary school, high school *(US)* ◆ **~ (technique et) professionnel,** ~ **d'enseignement professionnel** † *secondary school for vocational training*

LYCÉE

Lycées are state secondary schools where pupils study for their « baccalauréat » after leaving the « collège ». The **lycée** covers the school years known as « seconde » (15-16 year-olds), « première » (16-17 year-olds) and « terminale » (up to leaving age at 18). The term **lycée professionnel** refers to a **lycée** which provides vocational training as well as the more traditional core subjects. → BACCALAURÉAT, COLLÈGE, ÉDUCATION NATIONALE

lycéen, -enne /liseɛ̃, ɛn/ **ADJ** *[journal, manifestation]* (secondary school *ou* high school *(US)*) students' *(épith)* ◆ **le mouvement** ~ the (secondary school) students' protest movement **NM** secondary school *ou* high-school *(US)* boy *ou* student ◆ **lorsque j'étais** ~ when I was at secondary school *ou* in high school *(US)* ◆ **quelques ~s étaient attablés à la terrasse** some boys from the secondary school were sitting at a table outside the café ◆ **les ~s sont en grève** secondary school students are on strike **NF** **lycéenne** secondary school *ou* high-school *(US)* girl *ou* student

lychee /litʃi/ **NM** ⇒ **litchi**

Lycra ® /likʀa/ **NM** Lycra ® ◆ **en** ~ Lycra *(épith)*

lymphatique /lɛ̃fatik/ **ADJ** *(Bio)* lymphatic; *(péj)* lethargic, sluggish, lymphatic *(frm)*

lymphe /lɛ̃f/ **NF** lymph

lymphocyte /lɛ̃fɔsit/ **NM** lymphocyte ◆ **~ T4** T4 lymphocyte

lymphoïde /lɛ̃fɔid/ **ADJ** lymphoid

lymphome /lɛ̃fom/ **NM** *(Méd)* lymphoma

lynchage /lɛ̃ʃaʒ/ **NM** *(= exécution, pendaison)* lynching; *(= coups)* beating ◆ **il a fait l'objet d'un ~ médiatique** he was torn to pieces by the media

lyncher /lɛ̃ʃe/ ▸ conjug 1 ◂ **VT** *(= tuer, pendre)* to lynch; *(= malmener)* to beat up ◆ **je vais me faire ~ si je rentre en retard*** they'll lynch *ou* kill me if I come home late

lynx /lɛ̃ks/ **NM** lynx; → **œil**

Lyon /ljɔ̃/ **N** Lyon(s)

lyonnais, e /ljɔnɛ, ɛz/ **ADJ** of *ou* from Lyon(s) **NM** *(= région)* ◆ **le Lyonnais** the Lyon(s) region **NM,F** **Lyonnais(e)** inhabitant *ou* native of Lyon(s)

lyophile /ljɔfil/ **ADJ** lyophilic

lyophilisation /ljɔfilizasjɔ̃/ **NF** freeze-drying, lyophilization (SPEC)

lyophiliser /ljɔfilize/ ▸ conjug 1 ◂ **VT** to freeze-dry, to lyophilize *(SPÉC)* ◆ **café lyophilisé** freeze-dried coffee

lyre /liʀ/ **NF** lyre

lyrique /liʀik/ **ADJ** 1 *(Poésie)* lyric 2 *(Mus, Théât) [ouvrage, représentation, répertoire]* operatic; *[saison]* opera *(épith)*; *[ténor, soprano]* lyric, operatic ◆ **l'art** ~ opera ◆ **artiste** ~ opera singer ◆ **théâtre** *ou* **scène** ~ opera house ◆ **comédie/tragédie** ~ comic/tragic opera ◆ **spectacle** ~ opera; → **envolée** 3 *(= exalté) [film, style]* lyrical ◆ **il a été ~ sur le sujet** he waxed lyrical on the topic **NM** 1 *(Mus, Théât)* **le** ~ opera 2 *(= poète)* lyric poet

lyriquement /liʀikmɑ̃/ **ADV** lyrically

lyrisme /liʀism/ **NM** *(Littérat, Poésie)* lyricism ◆ **s'exprimer avec ~ sur** *(= exaltation)* to wax lyrical about, to enthuse over ◆ **film plein de** ~ lyrical film

lys /lis/ **NM** ⇒ **lis**

lysergique /lizɛʀʒik/ **ADJ** ◆ **acide ~ diéthylamide** lysergic acid diethylamide

lytique /litik/ **ADJ** lytic ◆ **cocktail** ~ lethal cocktail

Mm

M, m¹ /ɛm/ **NM** *(= lettre)* M, m ◆ **M6** *private television channel broadcasting mainly serials and music programmes*

m² (abrév de **mètre**) m ◆ **m²** (abrév de **mètre carré**) m², sq. m. ◆ **m³** (abrév de **mètre cube**) m³, cu. m.

M. (abrév de **Monsieur**) Mr ◆ ~ **Dupond** Mr Dupond

m' /m/ → **me**

MA /ɛma/ **NMF** (abrév de **maître auxiliaire**) → **maître**

ma /ma/ **ADJ POSS** → **mon**

Maastricht /mastʀiʃt/ **N** ◆ **le traité/les accords de** ~ the Maastricht Treaty/agreement ◆ **répondre aux critères de** ~ to meet the Maastricht criteria (for economic and monetary union)

maastrichtien, -ienne /mastʀiʃtjɛ̃, jɛn/ **ADJ** Maastricht *(épith)* **NM,F** **Maastrichtien(ne)** inhabitant *ou* native of Maastricht

maboul, e * † /mabul/ **ADJ** crazy * **NM,F** loony *, crackpot *

mac ‡ /mak/ **NM** *(= souteneur)* pimp

macabre /makɑbʀ/ **ADJ** *[histoire, découverte]* macabre, gruesome; *[goûts, humour]* macabre, ghoulish; → **danse**

macadam /makadam/ **NM** *[de pierres]* macadam; *[de goudron]* tarmac(adam) ® *(Brit)*, blacktop *(US)* ◆ **sur le** ~ *[de rue]* on the road; *[d'aéroport]* on the tarmac ◆ **sur le ~ parisien** on the streets of Paris

macadamia /makadamja/ **NM** ◆ **noix de** ~ macadamia nut

macadamisage /makadamizaʒ/ **NM, macadamisation** /makadamizasjɔ̃/ **NF** *(= empierrement)* macadamization, macadamizing; *(= goudronnage)* tarmacking

macadamiser /makadamize/ ▸ conjug 1 ◂ **VT** *(= empierrer)* to macadamize; *(= goudronner)* to tarmac ◆ **chaussée** *ou* **route macadamisée** macadamized *ou* tarmac road

macaque /makak/ **NM** *(= singe)* macaque ◆ ~ **rhésus** rhesus monkey ◆ **qui est ce (vieux) ~ ?** * *(péj)* who's that ugly (old) ape? ‡

macareux /makaʀø/ **NM** ◆ ~ **(moine)** puffin

macaron /makaʀɔ̃/ **NM** 1 *(Culin)* macaroon 2 *(= insigne)* (round) badge; *(= autocollant)* (round) sticker; *(* = décoration)* medal, gong * ◆ ~ **publicitaire** publicity badge; *(sur voiture)* advertising sticker 3 *(Coiffure)* **~s** coils, earphones *

macaroni /makaʀɔni/ **NM** 1 *(Culin)* piece of macaroni ◆ **~s** macaroni ◆ **~(s) au gratin** macaroni cheese *(Brit)*, macaroni and cheese *(US)* 2 *(injurieux)* ~, **mangeur de ~s** *‡ *(= Italien)* Eyeti(e) ‡ *(injurieux)*

macaronique /makaʀɔnik/ **ADJ** *(Poésie)* macaronic

maccarthysme /makkaʀtism/ **NM** McCarthyism

maccarthyste /makkaʀtist/ **ADJ, NMF** McCarthyist

macchabée ‡ /makabe/ **NM** stiff ‡, corpse

macédoine /masedwan/ **NF** 1 *(Culin)* ~ **de légumes** diced mixed vegetables, macedoine (of vegetables) ◆ ~ **de fruits** *(gén)* fruit salad; *(en boîte)* fruit cocktail 2 *(Géog)* **Macédoine** Macedonia

macédonien, -ienne /masedɔnjɛ̃, jɛn/ **ADJ** Macedonian **NM,F** **Macédonien(ne)** Macedonian

macération /maseʀasjɔ̃/ **NF** 1 *(= procédé)* maceration, soaking; *(= liquide)* marinade ◆ **pendant leur ~ dans le vinaigre** while they are soaking in vinegar ◆ **arroser la viande avec le cognac de** ~ baste the meat with the brandy in which it has been marinated 2 *(Rel = mortification)* mortification, scourging (of the flesh) ◆ **s'infliger des ~s** to scourge one's body *ou* flesh

macérer /masere/ ▸ conjug 6 ◂ **VT** 1 *(Culin)* to macerate, to soak ◆ **cerises macérées dans l'eau de vie** cherries macerated in brandy 2 *(Rel)* ~ **sa chair** *(= mortifier)* to mortify one's *ou* the flesh **VI** 1 *(Culin)* **faire** *ou* **laisser** ~ to macerate, to soak 2 *(péj)* ~ **dans son ignorance** to wallow in one's ignorance ◆ **laisser ~ qn (dans son jus)** * *(= le faire attendre)* to let sb stew in his own juice *

macfarlane /makfaʀlan/ **NM** *(= manteau)* Inverness cape

Mach /mak/ **NM** Mach ◆ **voler à ~ 2** to fly at Mach 2 ◆ **nombre de** ~ Mach (number)

machaon /makaɔ̃/ **NM** swallowtail butterfly

mâche /mɑʃ/ **NF** corn salad, lambs' lettuce

mâchefer /mɑʃfɛʀ/ **NM** clinker *(NonC)*, cinders

mâcher /mɑʃe/ ▸ conjug 1 ◂ **VT** *[personne]* to chew; *(avec bruit)* to munch; *[animal]* to chomp; *(Tech) (= couper en déchirant)* to chew up ◆ **il faut lui ~ tout le travail** you have to do half his work for him *ou* to spoon-feed him * ◆ **il ne mâche pas ses mots** he doesn't mince his words; → **papier**

machette /maʃɛt/ **NF** machete

Machiavel /makjavel/ **NM** Machiavelli

machiavélique /makjavelik/ **ADJ** Machiavellian

machiavélisme /makjavelism/ **NM** Machiavell(ian)ism

mâchicoulis /mɑʃikuli/ **NM** machicolation ◆ **à** ~ machicolated

machin * /maʃɛ̃/ **NM** 1 *(= chose) (dont le nom échappe)* what-d'you-call-it *, thingummyjig * *(Brit)*, thingamajig * *(US)*, whatsit * *(Brit)*; *(qu'on n'a jamais vu avant)* thing, contraption; *(qu'on ne prend pas la peine de nommer)* thing ◆ **passe-moi ton ~** give me your thingy * ◆ **les antibiotiques ! il faut te méfier de ces ~s-là** antibiotics! you should beware of those things ◆ **espèce de vieux ~ !** *(péj)* doddering old fool! * 2 *(= personne)* **Machin (chouette), Machin (chose)** what's-his-name *, what-d'you-call-him *, thingumabob ‡ ◆ **hé ! Machin !** hey (you), what's-your-name! * ◆ **le père/la mère Machin** Mr/Mrs what's-his-/her-name *; → aussi **Machine**

machinal, e (mpl **-aux**) /maʃinal, o/ **ADJ** *(= automatique)* mechanical, automatic; *(= instinctif)* automatic, unconscious

machinalement /maʃinalmɑ̃/ **ADV** *(= automatiquement)* mechanically, automatically; *(= instinctivement)* unconsciously ◆ **il regarda ~ sa montre** he looked at his watch without thinking ◆ **j'ai fait ça ~** I did it automatically *ou* without thinking

machination /maʃinasjɔ̃/ **NF** *(= complot)* plot, conspiracy; *(= coup monté)* put-up job *, frame-up * ◆ **je suis victime d'une ~** I've been framed * ◆ **être victime d'une ~ politique** to be a victim of a political conspiracy *ou* of political machinations

Machine * /maʃin/ **NF** *(= personne)* what's-her-name *, what-d'you-call-her * ◆ **hé ! ~ !** hey! (you) – what's-your-name! *; → aussi **machin**

machine /maʃin/ **NF** 1 *(Tech)* machine; *(= locomotive)* engine, locomotive; *(= avion)* plane, machine; *(* = bicyclette, moto)* bike *, machine; *(= ordinateur)* machine ◆ **il n'est qu'une ~ à penser** he's nothing more than a sort of thinking machine ◆ **la ~ est usée/fatiguée** *(= corps)* the old body is wearing out/getting tired; → **salle**

2 *(= lave-linge)* (washing) machine; *(= lessive)* washing ◆ **faire une ~/trois ~s** to do a load of washing/three loads of washing ◆ **ça va en ~** it's machine-washable ◆ **laver/passer qch en** *ou* **à la ~** to wash/put sth in the (washing) machine

3 (= structure) machine; (= processus) machinery ◆ **la ~ politique/parlementaire** the political/parliamentary machine ◆ **la ~ de l'État** the machinery of state ◆ **la ~ humaine** the human body ◆ **la ~ administrative** the bureaucratic machine ou machinery ◆ **une grosse ~ hollywoodienne** (= film) a Hollywood blockbuster*

4 [de navire] engine ◆ **faire ~ arrière** (lit) to go astern; (fig) to back-pedal; → **salle**

LOC ADV **à la machine** ◆ **faire qch à la ~** to machine sth, to do sth on a machine ◆ **fait à la ~** machine-made, done ou made on a machine ◆ **cousu/tricoté à la ~** machine-sewn/-knitted; → **taper**

COMP **machine à adresser** addressing machine
machine à affranchir franking machine
machine agricole agricultural machine
machine à café coffee machine
machine à calculer calculating machine
machine à coudre sewing machine
machine à écrire typewriter
machine de guerre machine of war, instrument of warfare
machine infernale † time bomb, (explosive) device
machine à laver washing machine
machine à laver séchante washer-dryer
machine à laver la vaisselle dishwasher
machine simple simple machine
machine à sous (de jeu) slot machine, one-armed bandit (Brit), fruit machine (Brit); (= distributeur automatique) slot ou vending machine
machine à timbrer ⇒ **machine à affranchir**
machine à tisser power loom
machine à ou de traitement de texte word processor
machine à tricoter knitting machine
machine à vapeur steam engine
machine volante flying machine

machine-outil (pl **machines-outils**) /maʃinuti/ NF machine tool

machiner /maʃine/ ► conjug 1 ◄ VT [+ trahison] to plot; [+ complot] to hatch ◆ **tout était machiné d'avance** the whole thing was fixed beforehand ou was prearranged, it was all a put-up job* ◆ **c'est lui qui a tout machiné** he engineered the whole thing ◆ **qu'est-ce qu'il est en train de ~ ?** what's he cooking up?* ou hatching?*

machinerie /maʃinʀi/ NF 1 (= équipement) machinery, plant (NonC) 2 (= salle) (Naut) engine room; (= atelier) machine room

machinisme /maʃinism/ NM mechanization

machiniste /maʃinist/ NMF (Théât) scene shifter, stagehand; (Ciné) grip; (Transport) driver ◆ **"faire signe au machiniste"** ≈ request stop

machisme /ma(t)ʃism/ NM (= sexisme) male chauvinism

machiste /ma(t)ʃist/ ADJ (male) chauvinist

macho* /matʃo/ ADJ [comportement] macho, male chauvinist (épith) ◆ **il est (un peu) ~** he's a (bit of a) male chauvinist* NM (d'apparence physique) macho man; (sexiste) male chauvinist ◆ **sale ~ !** male chauvinist pig!*

mâchoire /mɑʃwaʀ/ NF (Anat, Tech) jaw ◆ **~s de frein** brake shoes; → **bâiller**

mâchonnement /mɑʃɔnmɑ̃/ NM chewing; (Méd) bruxism (SPÉC)

mâchonner /mɑʃɔne/ ► conjug 1 ◄ VT [personne] to chew (at); [cheval] to munch ◆ **~ son crayon** to chew ou bite one's pencil

mâchouiller* /mɑʃuje/ ► conjug 1 ◄ VT to chew (away) at ou on

mâchurer /mɑʃyʀe/ ► conjug 1 ◄ VT 1 (= salir) [+ papier, habit] to stain (black); [+ visage] to blacken; (Typo) to mackle, to blur 2 (Tech = écraser) to dent 3 (= mâcher) to chew

macle[1] /makl/ NF (= plante) water chestnut

macle[2] /makl/ NF (= cristal) twin, macle; (Hér) mascle

maclé, e /makle/ ADJ [cristal] twinned, hemitrope

maçon /masɔ̃/ NM 1 (gén) builder; (qui travaille la pierre) (stone) mason; (qui pose les briques) bricklayer ◆ **ouvrier** ou **compagnon ~** builder's mate (Brit) ou helper (US) 2 ⇒ **franc-maçon**

maçonnage /masɔnaʒ/ NM 1 (= travail) building; (en briques) bricklaying 2 (= ouvrage) (en pierres) masonry, stonework; (en briques) brickwork; (= revêtement) facing

maçonne /masɔn/ ADJ F → **abeille, fourmi**

maçonner /masɔne/ ► conjug 1 ◄ VT (= construire) to build; (= consolider) to build up; (= revêtir) to face; (= boucher) (avec briques) to brick up; (avec pierres) to block up (with stone) ◆ **la partie maçonnée** the part made of bricks, the brickwork

maçonnerie /masɔnʀi/ NF 1 (= ouvrage) [de pierres] masonry, stonework; [de briques] brickwork ◆ **~ de béton** concrete ◆ **~ en blocage** ou **de moellons** rubble work 2 (= travail) building; (avec briques) bricklaying ◆ **entrepreneur/entreprise de ~** building contractor/firm ◆ **grosse ~** erection of the superstructure ◆ **petite ~** finishing and interior building 3 ⇒ **franc-maçonnerie**

maçonnique /masɔnik/ ADJ masonic, Masonic

macoute /makut/ ADJ (terme d'Haïti) [groupe, prison] Macoute ◆ **(tonton) ~** Macoute, member of the Tonton Macoute(s)

macramé /makʀame/ NM macramé ◆ **en ~** macramé (épith)

macre /makʀ/ NF ⇒ **macle**[1]

macreuse /makʀøz/ NF 1 (= viande) shoulder of beef 2 (= oiseau) scoter

macro /makʀo/ PRÉF (dans les composés à trait d'union, le préfixe reste invariable) ◆ **~(-)** macro(-) NF (Ordin) macro (instruction)

macrobiotique /makʀɔbjɔtik/ ADJ macrobiotic NF macrobiotics (sg)

macrocéphale /makʀosefal/ ADJ macrocephalic

macrocosme /makʀɔkɔsm/ NM macrocosm

macro-économie /makʀoekɔnɔmi/ NF macroeconomics (sg)

macro-économique /makʀoekɔnɔmik/ ADJ macroeconomic

macrographie /makʀɔgʀafi/ NF macrography

macro-instruction /makʀoɛ̃stʀyksjɔ̃/ NF macro instruction

macromoléculaire /makʀomɔlekylɛʀ/ ADJ macromolecular

macromolécule /makʀomɔlekyl/ NF macromolecule

macrophage /makʀɔfaʒ/ ADJ macrophagic NM macrophage

macrophotographie /makʀofɔtɔgʀafi/ NF macrophotography

macroscopique /makʀɔskɔpik/ ADJ macroscopic

macrostructure /makʀostʀyktyʀ/ NF macrostructure

maculage /makylaʒ/ NM 1 (gén) maculation 2 (Typo) (= action) offsetting; (= tache) offset, set-off

macule /makyl/ NF 1 [d'encre] smudge 2 (Astron, Méd) macula

maculer /makyle/ ► conjug 1 ◄ VT 1 (= salir) to stain (de with); ◆ **chemise maculée de boue/sang** shirt spattered ou covered with mud/blood 2 (d'encre) to smudge, to mackle (SPÉC)

Madagascar /madagaskaʀ/ N Madagascar ◆ **République démocratique de ~** Malagasy Republic

Madame /madam/ (pl **Mesdames** /medam/) NF 1 (s'adressant à qn) **bonjour ~** (gén) good morning; (nom connu) good morning, Mrs X; (frm) good morning, Madam ◆ **bonjour Mesdames** good morning ◆ **~, vous avez oublié quelque chose** excuse me ou Madam (frm) you've forgotten something ◆ **Mesdames** (devant un auditoire) ladies ◆ **Mesdames, Mesdemoiselles, Messieurs** ladies and gentlemen ◆ **~ la Présidente** [de société, assemblée] Madam Chairman; [de gouvernement] Madam President ◆ **oui, ~ la Générale/la Marquise** yes Mrs X/Madam ◆ **~ !** (Scol) please Mrs X!, please Miss! ◆ **et pour (vous) ~ ?** (au restaurant) and for (you) madam? ◆ **~ est servie** (frm) dinner is served (Madam) ◆ **~ n'est pas contente !** (iro) her ladyship ou Madam isn't pleased! (iro)

2 (parlant de qn) **~ X est malade** Mrs X is ill ◆ **~ votre mère** † your dear ou good mother ◆ **~ est sortie** (frm) Madam ou the mistress is not at home ◆ **je vais le dire à ~** (parlant à un visiteur) I'll inform Madam (frm) ou Mrs X; (parlant à un autre employé de maison) I'll tell Mrs X ou the missus* † ◆ **~ dit que c'est à elle** the lady says it belongs to her ◆ **~ la Présidente** (en adresse) Madam Chairman ◆ **veuillez vous occuper de ~** please attend to this lady('s requirements)

3 (sur une enveloppe) **~ X** Mrs X ◆ **~ veuve X** (Admin) Mrs X, widow of the late John etc X ◆ **Mesdames X** the Mrs X ◆ **Mesdames X et Y** Mrs X and Mrs Y ◆ **Monsieur X et ~** Mr and Mrs X ◆ **~ la Maréchale X** Mrs X ◆ **~ la Marquise de X** the Marchioness of X ◆ **Mesdames les employées de la comptabilité** (the ladies on) the staff of the accounts department

4 (en-tête de lettre) Dear Madam ◆ **Chère ~** Dear Mrs X ◆ **~, Mademoiselle, Monsieur** (Admin) Dear Sir or Madam ◆ **~ la Maréchale/Présidente/Duchesse** Dear Madam

5 (Hist) Madame (title given to female members of the French royal family)

6 (sans majuscule, pl madames : souvent péj) lady ◆ **jouer à la madame** to play the fine lady, to put on airs and graces ◆ **toutes ces (belles) madames** all these fine ladies ◆ **c'est une petite madame maintenant** she's quite a (grown-up) young lady now

made in /mɛdin/ LOC ADJ (Comm) made in ◆ **la machine est ~ Germany** the machine is German-made ou made in Germany ◆ **le prestige du ~ France** the prestige of French brand names ◆ **des habitudes ~ USA** typically American habits

Madeleine /madlɛn/ NF Magdalen(e), Madel(e)ine; → **pleurer**

madeleine /madlɛn/ NF (Culin) madeleine ◆ **c'est la ~ de Proust** (fig) it brings back a flood of memories

Madelon /madlɔ̃/ NF ◆ **la ~** old French song popular during World War I

Mademoiselle /madmwazɛl/ (pl **Mesdemoiselles** /medmwazɛl/) NF 1 (s'adressant à qn) **bonjour ~** (gén) good morning; (nom connu : frm) good morning, Miss X ◆ **bonjour Mesdemoiselles** good morning ladies; (jeunes filles) good morning young ladies ◆ **~, vous avez oublié quelque chose** excuse me miss, you've forgotten something ◆ **et pour vous ~ ?** (au restaurant) and for the young lady?, and for you, miss? ◆ **Mesdemoiselles** (devant un auditoire) ladies ◆ **~ n'est pas contente !** her ladyship isn't pleased!

2 (parlant de qn) **~ X est malade** Miss X is ill ◆ **~ votre sœur** † your dear sister ◆ **~ est sortie**

(frm) the young lady (of the house) is out • **je vais le dire à** ~ I shall tell Miss X • ~ **dit que c'est à elle** the young lady says it's hers
3 *(sur une enveloppe)* ~ **X** Miss X • **Mesdemoiselles X** the Misses X • **Mesdemoiselles X et Y** Miss X and Miss Y
4 *(en-tête de lettre)* Dear Madam • **Chère** ~ Dear Miss X
5 *(Hist)* Mademoiselle *(title given to the nieces of the French King)*

madère /madɛʀ/ NM Madeira (wine); → **sauce** NF **Madère** • **(l'île de) Madère** Madeira

madériser (se) /madeʀize/ ▸ conjug 1 ◂ VPR *[eau-de-vie, vin]* to maderize

Madone /madɔn/ NF 1 *(Art, Rel)* Madonna 2 *(= beauté)* **madone** beautiful woman, Madonna-like woman • **elle a un visage de madone** she has the face of a Madonna

madras /madʀas/ NM *(= étoffe)* madras (cotton); *(= foulard)* (madras) scarf N **Madras** Madras

madré, e /madʀe/ ADJ 1 *(littér = malin)* crafty, wily, sly • **c'est une petite ~e !** *(hum)* she's a crafty *ou* fly* *(Brit)* one! *(hum)* 2 *[bois]* whorled

madrépore /madʀepɔʀ/ NM madrepore • **les ~s** madrepores, Madrepora *(SPÉC)*

Madrid /madʀid/ N Madrid

madrier /madʀije/ NM *(Constr)* beam

madrigal (pl **-aux**) /madʀigal, o/ NM *(Littérat, Mus)* madrigal; († = *propos galant)* compliment

madrilène /madʀilɛn/ ADJ of *ou* from Madrid NMF **Madrilène** inhabitant *ou* native of Madrid

maelström, maelstrom /malstʀɔm/ NM *(lit, fig)* maelstrom

maestria /maɛstʀija/ NF (masterly) skill, mastery *(à faire qch* in doing sth); • **avec** ~ brilliantly, with consummate skill

maestro /maɛstʀo/ NM *(Mus)* maestro

mafflu, e /mafly/ ADJ *(littér) [visage, joues]* round, full; *[personne]* chubby(-cheeked *ou* -faced)

maf(f)ia /mafja/ NF 1 • **la Maf(f)ia** the Maf(f)ia 2 *[de bandits, trafiquants]* gang, ring • **c'est une vraie maf(f)ia !** what a bunch* *ou* shower*̣ *(Brit)* of crooks! • **maf(f)ia d'anciens élèves** old boy network

maf(f)ieux, -ieuse /mafjø, jøz/ ADJ Mafia *(épith)* • **pratiques maf(f)ieuses** Mafia-like practices NM,F maf(f)ioso

maf(f)ioso /mafjozo/ (pl **maf(f)iosi** /mafjozi/) NM maf(f)ioso

magasin /magazɛ̃/ NM 1 *(= boutique)* shop, store; *(= entrepôt)* warehouse • **grand** ~ department store • **faire** *ou* **courir les ~s** to go shopping, to go (a)round *ou* do* the shops • **nous ne l'avons pas en** ~ we haven't got it in stock; → **chaîne**
2 *[de fusil, appareil-photo]* magazine
COMP **magasin des accessoires** *(Théât)* prop room
magasin d'alimentation grocery store
magasin d'armes armoury
magasin (d'articles) de sport sports shop *(Brit)*, sporting goods store *(US)*
magasin de confection (ready-to-wear) dress shop *ou* tailor's, clothing store *(US)*
magasin des décors *(Théât)* scene dock
magasins généraux *(Comm, Jur)* bonded warehouse
magasin à grande surface supermarket, hypermarket *(Brit)*
magasin d'habillement *(Mil)* quartermaster's stores
magasin à succursales (multiples) chain store
magasin d'usine factory shop *ou* outlet
magasin de vivres *(Mil)* quartermaster's stores

magasinage /magazinaʒ/ NM 1 *(Comm)* warehousing • **frais de** ~ storage costs 2 *(Can)* shopping • **faire son** ~ to do one's shopping

magasiner /magazine/ ▸ conjug 1 ◂ VI *(Can)* to go shopping

magasinier /magazinje/ NM *[d'usine]* storekeeper, storeman; *[d'entrepôt]* warehouseman

magazine /magazin/ NM 1 *(Presse)* magazine • ~ **de luxe** glossy* (magazine) 2 *(TV, Radio)* magazine (programme *(Brit)* *ou* program *(US)*) • ~ **féminin/pour les jeunes** women's/children's programme • ~ **d'actualités** news magazine • ~ **d'information** current affairs programme

magdalénien, -ienne /magdalenjɛ̃, jɛn/ ADJ Magdalenian NM • **le Magdalénien** the Magdalenian

mage /maʒ/ NM *(Antiq, fig)* magus; *(= devin, astrologue)* witch • **les (trois) Rois ~s** *(Rel)* the Magi, the (Three) Wise Men, the Three Kings

Magellan /maʒelɑ̃/ NM Magellan • **le détroit de** ~ the Strait of Magellan • **les nuages de** ~ the Magellanic Clouds

magenta /maʒɛ̃ta/ ADJ INV, NM magenta

Maghreb /magʀɛb/ NM • **le** ~ the Maghreb, North Africa

maghrébin, e /magʀebɛ̃, in/ ADJ of *ou* from the Maghreb *ou* North Africa NM,F **Maghrébin(e)** North African

magicien, -ienne /maʒisjɛ̃, jɛn/ NM,F *(= illusionniste)* magician, conjuror; *(= sorcier)* magician; *(= sorcière)* enchantress; *(fig)* wizard, magician • **c'est un** ~ **du verbe** *ou* **des mots** he's a wizard *ou* magician with words

magie /maʒi/ NF magic • ~ **blanche/noire** white/black magic • **la** ~ **du verbe** the magic of words • **comme par** ~ like magic, (as if) by magic • **c'est de la** ~ it's (like) magic • **faire de la** ~ *[prestidigitateur]* to perform *ou* do magic tricks

Maginot /maʒino/ NM • **la ligne** ~ the Maginot Line

magique /maʒik/ ADJ *[mot, baguette, pouvoir]* magic; *(= enchanteur) [spectacle]* magical; → **lanterne**

magiquement /maʒikmɑ̃/ ADV magically • **le portail s'ouvrit** ~ the gate opened as if by magic

magister † /maʒistɛʀ/ NM (village) schoolmaster; *(péj)* pedant

magistère /maʒistɛʀ/ NM 1 *(Univ) diploma taken over 3 years after completing 2 years at university, usually in vocational subjects,* ≃ master's degree 2 *(Rel)* magisterium 3 *(Alchimie)* magistery

magistral, e (mpl **-aux**) /maʒistʀal, o/ ADJ 1 *[œuvre]* masterly, brilliant; *[réussite, démonstration]* brilliant; *[adresse]* masterly • **elle est ~e dans le rôle de Phèdre** she's brilliant as Phèdre • **son interprétation du concerto fut ~e** he gave a brilliant performance of the concerto • **de façon ~e** brilliantly • **ça a été une leçon ~e de football** it was a brilliant demonstration of how to play football 2 *[ton]* authoritative, masterful • **cours** ~ *(Univ)* lecture • **enseignement** ~ lecturing 3 *(intensif) [victoire, réussite]* magnificent 4 *(Pharm)* magistral 5 *(Tech)* **ligne ~e** magistral line

magistralement /maʒistʀalmɑ̃/ ADV brilliantly • **réussir** ~ **qch** to make a brilliant job of sth • **le film est** ~ **interprété** the film is beautifully acted

magistrat, e /maʒistʀa, at/ NM,F *(Jur) (gén)* magistrate; *(= juge)* judge • ~ **du parquet** public prosecutor *(Brit)*, prosecuting *ou* district attorney *(US)* • ~ **du siège** judge • ~ **municipal** town councillor • **c'est le premier** ~ **de France/du département** he holds the highest public office in France/the department • ~ **militaire** judge advocate

magistrature /maʒistʀatyʀ/ NF 1 *(Jur)* magistracy, magistrature • **la** ~ **assise** *ou* **du siège** the judges, the bench • **la** ~ **debout** *ou* **du parquet** the state prosecutors • **entrer dans la** ~ to be appointed a judge *(ou* a state prosecutor) 2 *(Admin, Pol)* public office • **la** ~ **suprême** the supreme *ou* highest office

magma /magma/ NM *(Chim, Géol)* magma; *(= mélange)* jumble, muddle

magmatique /magmatik/ ADJ magmatic

magnanime /maɲanim/ ADJ magnanimous • **se montrer** ~ to show magnanimity

magnanimement /maɲanimmɑ̃/ ADV magnanimously

magnanimité /maɲanimite/ NF magnanimity

magnat /magna/ NM tycoon, magnate • ~ **de la presse/de la télévision** press/television baron *ou* lord *ou* tycoon • ~ **de l'audiovisuel** broadcasting tycoon • ~ **du pétrole** oil tycoon *ou* magnate

magner (se)*̣ /maɲe/ ▸ conjug 1 ◂ VPR to get a move on*, to hurry up • **on a intérêt à se** ~ we'd better get cracking* • **magne-toi (le train** *ou* **le popotin) !** get a move on!*, get moving!* • **magne-toi le cul !*̣*** shift your arse!*̣ *(Brit)* *ou* ass!*̣ *(US)*

magnésie /maɲezi/ NF magnesia

magnésien, -ienne /maɲezjɛ̃, jɛn/ ADJ *[roche, magma]* magnesian • **déficit** ~ magnesium deficiency

magnésium /maɲezjɔm/ NM magnesium; → **éclair**

magnétique /maɲetik/ ADJ *(Phys, fig)* magnetic; → **bande¹**

magnétisable /maɲetizabl/ ADJ 1 *(Phys)* magnetizable 2 *(= sujet à l'hypnose)* hypnotizable

magnétisation /maɲetizasjɔ̃/ NF 1 *(Phys)* magnetization 2 *(= hypnose)* mesmerization, hypnotization

magnétiser /maɲetize/ ▸ conjug 1 ◂ VT 1 *(Phys)* to magnetize 2 *(= hypnotiser)* to mesmerize, to hypnotize

magnétiseur, -euse /maɲetizœʀ, øz/ NM,F *(= hypnotiseur)* hypnotizer; *(= guérisseur)* magnetic healer

magnétisme /maɲetism/ NM *(= charme, Phys)* magnetism; *(= hypnotisme)* hypnotism, mesmerism • ~ **terrestre** terrestrial magnetism • **le** ~ **d'un grand homme** the magnetism *ou* charisma of a great man

magnétite /maɲetit/ NF lodestone, magnetite

magnéto¹* /maɲeto/ NM abrév de **magnétophone**

magnéto² /maɲeto/ NF *(Élec)* magneto

magnétocassette /maɲetokasɛt/ NM cassette player *ou* recorder

magnétoélectrique /maɲetoelɛktʀik/ ADJ magnetoelectric

magnétophone /maɲetɔfɔn/ NM tape recorder • ~ **à cassette(s)** cassette recorder • **enregistré au** ~ (tape-)recorded, taped

magnétoscope /maɲetɔskɔp/ NM *(= appareil)* video (tape *ou* cassette) recorder, VCR • **enregistrer au** ~ to video(-tape)

magnétoscoper /maɲetɔskɔpe/ ▸ conjug 1 ◂ VT to video(-tape)

magnificence /maɲifisɑ̃s/ NF *(littér)* 1 *(= faste)* magnificence, splendour 2 *(= prodigalité)* munificence *(littér)*, lavishness

magnifier /maɲifje/ ▸ conjug 7 ◂ VT (*littér*) (= *louer*) to magnify (*littér*), to glorify; (= *idéaliser*) to idealize

magnifique /maɲifik/ ADJ magnificent ◆ ~ ! fantastic!, great! * ◆ **il a été ~ hier soir !** he was magnificent *ou* fantastic last night! ◆ **Soliman/Laurent le Magnifique** Suleiman/ Lorenzo the Magnificent

magnifiquement /maɲifikmɑ̃/ ADV magnificently

magnitude /maɲityd/ NF (*Astron, Géol*) magnitude ◆ **séisme de ~ 7 sur l'échelle de Richter** earthquake measuring 7 *ou* of magnitude 7 on the Richter scale

magnolia /maɲɔlja/ NM magnolia

magnum /magnɔm/ NM magnum

magot /mago/ NM [1] (= *singe*) Barbary ape, magot [2] (= *figurine*) magot [3] * (= *somme d'argent*) pile (of money) *, packet *; (= *argent volé*) loot; (= *économies*) savings, nest egg ◆ **ils ont amassé un joli ~** (*gén*) they've made a nice little pile * *ou* packet *; (*économies*) they've got a tidy sum put by *ou* a nice little nest egg ◆ **où ont-ils caché le ~ ?** where did they stash * the loot?

magouillage * /maguja3/ NM, **magouille** * /maguj/ NF (*péj*) scheming (*péj*) ◆ **c'est le roi de la magouille** he's a born schemer ◆ **ça sent la magouille** there's some funny business * going on ◆ **magouillage électoral** pre-election scheming ◆ **magouilles politiques** political skulduggery ◆ **magouilles financières** financial wheeling and dealing * (*NonC*), sharp practice * (*NonC*) (*Brit*) ◆ **c'était une sombre magouille** it was a very shady deal

magouiller * /maguje/ ▸ conjug 1 ◂ VI (*péj*) to wheel and deal * ◆ **il a dû ~ pour avoir le permis de construire** he had to do a bit of wheeling and dealing * to get planning permission VT ◆ **qu'est-ce qu'il magouille ?** what's he up to? *

magouilleur, -euse * /magujœr, øz/ ADJ (*péj*) crafty * NM,F (*péj*) schemer (*péj*), crafty operator * (*Brit*)

magret /magrɛ/ NM ◆ ~ **(de canard)** fillet of duck, duck breast

magyar, e /magjar/ ADJ Magyar NM,F **Magyar(e)** Magyar

mahara(d)jah /maara(d)ʒa/ NM Maharajah

maharani /ma(a)rani/, **maharané** /maarane/ NF Maharanee

mahatma /maatma/ NM mahatma

mah-jong (pl **mah-jongs**) /maʒɔ̃g/ NM mah-jong(g)

Mahomet /maɔmɛt/ NM Mahomet, Mohammed

mahométan, -ane † /maɔmetɑ̃, an/ ADJ Mahometan, Mohammedan

mahométisme † /maɔmetism/ NM Mohammedanism

mahonia /maɔnja/ NM mahonia

mahorais, e /maɔrɛ, ɛz/ ADJ of *ou* from Mayotte NM,F **Mahorais(e)** inhabitant *ou* native of Mayotte

mahous * /maus/ ADJ ⇒ **maous**

mai /mɛ/ NM May ◆ **le joli mois de ~** the merry month of May; *pour autres loc voir* **septembre** *et* **premier**

MAI 68

Widespread unrest in 1968, both in French industry and among students, resulted in huge demonstrations in May and culminated in a general strike. The events were perceived both as a challenge to the established order and a utopian cry for freedom, though the government was not in fact overthrown and order soon returned. The term « soixante-huitard(e) » literally means a person who participated in the events, but used as an adjective it also refers to the kind of anarchistic and utopian ideals expressed by many of the demonstrators. These ideals are also effectively summed up in their best-known slogan, « sous les pavés, la plage » (literally, « under the paving stones there's a beach »).

maie /mɛ/ NF (= *huche*) bread box; (*pour pétrir*) dough trough

maïeuticien /majøtisjɛ̃/ NM male midwife

maïeutique /majøtik/ NF maieutics (*sg*)

maigre /mɛgr/ ADJ [1] [*personne*] thin, skinny (*péj*); [*animal*] thin, scraggy; [*visage, joue*] thin, lean; [*membres*] thin, scrawny (*péj*), skinny (*péj*) ◆ **~ comme un clou** *ou* **un coucou** * as thin as a rake *ou* a lath (*Brit*) *ou* a rail (*US*)

[2] (*Culin : après n*) [*bouillon*] clear; [*viande*] lean; [*fromage*] low-fat

[3] (*Rel*) **repas ~** meal without meat ◆ **faire ~ (le vendredi)** (*gén*) to abstain from meat (on Fridays); (= *manger du poisson*) to eat fish (on Fridays) ◆ **le vendredi est un jour ~** people don't eat meat on Fridays

[4] (= *peu important*) [*profit, revenu*] meagre, small, slim; [*ration, salaire*] meagre, poor; [*ressources, moyens, budget*] meagre, scanty; [*résultat*] poor; [*exposé, conclusion*] sketchy, skimpy, slight; [*espoir, chance*] slim, slight; [*public*] sparse ◆ **comme dîner, c'est un peu ~** it's a bit of a skimpy *ou* meagre dinner, it's not much of a dinner ◆ **c'est une ~ consolation** it's small consolation, it's cold comfort

[5] (= *peu épais*) [*végétation*] thin, sparse; [*récolte, terre*] poor ◆ **un ~ filet d'eau** a thin trickle of water ◆ **avoir le cheveu ~** (*hum*) to be a bit thin on top

[6] (*Typo*) **caractère ~** light-faced letter

NMF ◆ **grand/petit ~** tall/small thin person ◆ **les gros et les ~s** fat people and thin people ◆ **c'est une fausse ~** she looks deceptively thin

NM [1] (*Culin*) (= *viande*) lean meat; (= *jus*) thin gravy

[2] (*Typo*) light face ◆ **en ~** in light face

[3] (= *poisson*) meagre

maigrelet, -ette /mɛgrəlɛ, ɛt/ ADJ thin, scrawny, skinny ◆ **gamin ~** skinny little kid * NM ◆ **un petit ~** a skinny little chap *ou* fellow *ou* man

maigreur /mɛgrœr/ NF [1] [*de personne*] thinness, leanness; [*d'animal*] thinness, scrawniness, scragginess; [*de membre*] thinness, scrawniness, skinniness ◆ **il est d'une ~ !** he's so thin! *ou* skinny! ◆ **d'une ~ excessive** *ou* **extrême** extremely thin, emaciated [2] [*de végétation*] thinness, sparseness; [*de sol*] poverty; [*de profit*] meagreness, smallness, scantiness; [*de salaire*] meagreness, poorness; [*de réponse, exposé*] sketchiness, poverty; [*de preuve, sujet, auditoire*] thinness

maigrichon, -onne * /mɛgriʃɔ̃, ɔn/, **maigriot, -iotte** * /mɛgrijo, ijɔt/ ADJ ⇒ **maigrelet**

maigrir /mɛgrir/ ▸ conjug 2 ◂ VI to grow *ou* get thinner, to lose weight ◆ **je l'ai trouvé maigri** I thought he had got thinner *ou* he was thinner *ou* he had lost weight ◆ **il a maigri de visage** his face has got thinner ◆ **il a maigri de 5 kg** he has lost 5 kg ◆ **régime pour ~** reducing *ou* slimming (*Brit*) diet ◆ **se faire ~** to diet (to lose weight), to slim (*Brit*) ◆ **faire ~ qn** to make sb lose weight VT [1] ◆ **~ qn** [*vêtement*] to make sb look slim(mer); [*maladie, régime*] to make sb lose weight [2] (*Tech*) [+ *pièce de bois*] to thin

mail[1] /maj/ NM [1] (= *promenade*) mall †, tree-lined walk [2] (†† = *jeu, terrain*) (pall-)mall; (= *maillet*) mall

mail[2] /mɛl/ NM (= *courrier*) e-mail

mailing /meliŋ/ NM mailing ◆ **faire un ~** to do a mailing *ou* a mailshot (*Brit*)

maillage /mɑjaʒ/ NM [1] (*Pêche*) [*de filet*] meshing [2] (= *quadrillage*) **un système ferroviaire au ~ très lâche** a very loose railway network ◆ **le ~ complet du territoire avec des centres de soins** the creation of a network of clinics throughout the country ◆ **le ~ de la région par l'entreprise est insuffisant** the company has not set up enough outlets in the region

maillant /mɑjɑ̃/ ADJ M ◆ **filet ~** gill net

maille /mɑj/ NF [1] (*Couture*) stitch ◆ **~ qui a filé** [*de tissu, tricot*] stitch which has run ◆ **~ filée** [*de bas*] run, ladder (*Brit*) ◆ **~ (à l')endroit** plain (stitch) ◆ **~ (à l')envers** purl (stitch) ◆ **une ~ à l'endroit, une ~ à l'envers** knit one, purl one ◆ **tissu à fines ~s** fine-knit material ◆ **la ~** (= *tissu*) knitwear; (= *secteur économique*) the knitwear industry [2] [*de filet*] mesh ◆ **passer entre** *ou* **à travers les ~s (du filet)** (*lit, fig*) to slip through the net ◆ **à larges/fines ~s** wide/ fine mesh (*épith*) [3] [*d'armure, grillage*] link; → **cotte** [4] (*locutions*) **avoir ~ à partir avec qn** to get into trouble with sb, to have a brush with sb

maillé, e /maje/ (ptp de **mailler**) ADJ [1] [*organisation*] network-based ◆ **réseau ~ dense** *ou* closely-knit network ◆ **au niveau transports en commun, la région est maintenant ~e** the area now has an integrated public transport network [2] [*oiseau*] speckled; [*poisson*] netted

maillechort /mɑjʃɔr/ NM nickel silver

mailler /mɑje/ ▸ conjug 1 ◂ VT [1] (*Naut*) [+ *chaîne*] to shackle; [+ *filet*] to mesh [2] [+ *région*] to create a network in [3] (*Helv* = *tordre*) to twist ◆ **se ~ de rire** to be doubled up *ou* bent double with laughter

maillet /majɛ/ NM mallet

mailloche /majɔʃ/ NF [1] (= *outil*) beetle, maul [2] (*Mus*) bass drumstick

maillon /mɑjɔ̃/ NM [1] (*lit, fig* = *anneau*) link ◆ **il n'est qu'un ~ de la chaîne** he's just one link in the chain ◆ **c'est le ~ faible** it's the weak link (in the chain) [2] (= *petite maille*) small stitch

maillot /majo/ NM [1] (*gén*) vest (*Brit*), undershirt (*US*); [*de danseur*] leotard; [*de footballeur*] (football) shirt *ou* jersey; [*de coureur, basketteur*] singlet ◆ **s'épiler** *ou* **se faire le ~** to do one's bikini line ◆ **~ jaune** (*Cyclisme*) yellow jersey (*worn by the leading cyclist in the Tour de France*) ◆ **il est ~ jaune** he's the leader in the Tour (de France) [2] [*de bébé*] swaddling clothes (*Hist*), baby's wrap ◆ **enfant** *ou* **bébé au ~** † babe in arms

COMP **maillot de bain** [*d'homme*] swimming *ou* bathing (*Brit*) trunks; [*de femme*] swimming *ou* bathing (*Brit*) costume, swimsuit ◆ **~ de bain une pièce/deux pièces** one-piece/two-piece swimsuit

maillot de corps vest (*Brit*), undershirt (*US*)

main / mɛ̃ /

1 NOM FÉMININ 3 COMPOSÉS
2 ADVERBE

1 - NOM FÉMININ

1 [Anat] hand ◆ **donner la ~ à qn, tenir la ~ à** *ou* **de qn** to hold sb's hand ◆ **donne-moi la ~ pour traverser** give me your hand *ou* let me hold your hand to cross the street ◆ **ils se tenaient (par) la ~** *ou* **se donnaient la ~** they were holding hands ◆ **tu es aussi maladroit que moi, on peut se donner la ~** *(fig)* you're as clumsy as me, we're two of a kind ◆ **il entra le chapeau à la ~** he came in with his hat in his hand ◆ **il me salua de la ~** he waved to me ◆ **il me fit adieu de la ~** he waved goodbye to me ◆ **il m'a pris le plateau des ~s** he took the tray from me ◆ **prendre qch des** *ou* **à deux ~s/de la ~ gauche** to take sth with both hands/with one's left hand ◆ **à ~ droite/gauche** on the right-/left-hand side ◆ **applaudir/signer des deux ~s** *(avec enthousiasme)* to applaud/sign enthusiastically ◆ **il y a ~ !** *(Ftbl)* hands!, hand ball! ◆ **regarde, sans les ~s !** look, no hands! ◆ **les ~s en l'air !, haut les ~s !** hands up!, stick 'em up! * ◆ **j'en mettrais ma ~ au feu** *ou* **ma ~ à couper** I'd stake my life on it ◆ **passer la ~ dans le dos à qn** *(fig)* to butter sb up * ◆ **ils se passaient la ~ dans le dos** they were patting one another on the back ◆ **la ~ sur le cœur** *(hum) [déclarer, protester]* hand on heart ◆ **il va prendre ma ~ sur la figure !** * he's going to get a smack in the face! ◆ **il lui a mis la ~ aux fesses** * *ou* **au panier** * *ou* **au cul** ** he groped her behind * ◆ **prendre qn par la ~** *(lit, fig)* to take sb by the hand ◆ **tu n'as qu'à te prendre par la ~ si tu veux que ça soit terminé plus vite** you'll just have to sort things out yourself if you want it finished more quickly ◆ **prends-toi par la ~ si tu n'es pas content** do it yourself if you're not happy ◆ **mettre la ~ à la poche** *(= payer)* to put one's hand in one's pocket

◆ **de la main à la main** *[payer, verser]* directly *(without receipt)*

◆ **de main en main** *[passer, circuler]* from hand to hand ◆ **cette moto a passé de ~ en ~ depuis cinq ans** this motorbike has had a number of owners in the past five years

◆ **en main** ◆ **il se promenait, micro en ~** he walked around holding the microphone *ou* with the microphone in his hand ◆ **ce livre est en ~** *(= non disponible)* this book is in use *ou* is out; → **clé, montre**[1]

◆ **(la) main dans la main** *(contact physique, collaboration)* hand in hand; *(complicité)* hand in glove

◆ **les mains dans les poches** *(lit)* with one's hands in one's pockets; *(= sans rien préparer)* unprepared

◆ **la main dans le sac** ◆ **on l'a pris la ~ dans le sac** he was caught red-handed *ou* in the act

◆ **sous la main** ◆ **avoir tout sous la ~** to have everything to hand *ou* at hand *ou* handy ◆ **j'ai pris ce qui m'est tombé sous la ~** I took whatever came to hand ◆ **ce papier m'est tombé sous la ~** I came across this paper

2 [= instrument de l'action, du choix] hand ◆ **être adroit/maladroit de ses ~s** to be clever/clumsy with one's hands ◆ **il ne sait rien faire de ses ~s** he's no good *ou* he's useless with his hands ◆ **d'une ~ experte** with an expert hand ◆ **dans cette affaire, on a cru voir la ~ de la CIA** the CIA was believed to have had a hand in *ou* some involvement in this affair ◆ **mettre la dernière ~ à qch** to put the finishing touches to sth ◆ **il a eu la ~ heureuse : il a choisi le numéro gagnant** he was lucky - he picked the winning number ◆ **en engageant cet assistant, on a vraiment eu la ~ heureuse** when we took on that assistant we really picked a winner ◆ **avoir la ~ légère** *(pour toucher, masser)* to have a light touch; *(pour diriger)* to be lenient ◆ **tu as eu la ~ légère avec le sel** you didn't put enough salt in ◆ **il a la ~ leste** he's free *ou* quick with his hands ◆ **laisser les ~s libres à qn** to give sb a free hand *ou* rein ◆ **avoir les ~s liées** to have one's hands tied ◆ **ce boucher a toujours la ~ lourde** this butcher always gives *ou* cuts you more than you ask for ◆ **le juge a eu la ~ lourde** the judge gave him *(ou her etc)* a stiff sentence ◆ **j'ai eu la ~ lourde avec le sel** I overdid the salt ◆ **mettre la ~ à la pâte** to lend a hand, to muck in * ◆ **il n'y va pas de ~ morte** he doesn't pull his punches ◆ **avoir la ~ verte** to have green fingers *(Brit)*, to have a green thumb *(US)*; → **plein, quatre**

◆ **à la main** ◆ **fait à la ~** *(gén)* handmade; *[artisanat]* handmade, handcrafted ◆ **écrit à la ~** handwritten ◆ **cousu à la ~** hand-sewn, hand-stitched

◆ **à main armée** ◆ **vol/attaque à ~ armée** armed robbery/attack

◆ **à main levée** *[vote] [voter]* on *ou* by a show of hands; *[dessin] [dessiner]* freehand

◆ **à mains nues** *[boxer]* without gloves; *[combattre]* with one's bare fists *ou* hands; *[combat]* bare-knuckle, bare-fisted

◆ **à sa (***ou* **ma** *etc***) main** ◆ **il faudrait être à sa ~ pour réparer ce robinet** you'd have to be able to get at this tap properly to mend it ◆ **je ne suis pas à ma ~** I can't get a proper hold *ou* grip

◆ **de la main de** ◆ **dessin de la ~ de Cézanne** drawing by Cézanne ◆ **c'était (écrit) de sa ~** it was in his hand(writing) ◆ **une lettre signée de sa ~** a personally signed letter, a letter signed in his own hand

◆ **de main de maître** masterfully, expertly

◆ **en sous main** → **sous-main**

3 [= symbole d'autorité, d'aide, de possession] hand ◆ **la ~ de Dieu/du destin** the hand of God/of fate ◆ **il lui faut une ~ ferme** he needs a firm hand ◆ **une ~ de fer dans un gant de velours** an iron hand in a velvet glove ◆ **avoir la haute ~ sur qch** to have supreme control of sth ◆ **trouver une ~ secourable** to find a helping hand ◆ **donner la ~ à qn** *(= l'aider)* to give sb a hand ◆ **se donner la ~** *(= s'aider)* to give one another a helping hand ◆ **tomber aux** *ou* **dans les ~s de l'ennemi** to fall into the hands of the enemy *ou* into enemy hands ◆ **dans** *ou* **entre des ~s étrangères** in foreign hands ◆ **être en (de) bonnes ~s** to be in good hands ◆ **en ~s sûres** in safe hands ◆ **en ~ tierce** *(Fin)* in escrow ◆ **les ~s vides** empty-handed ◆ **faire ~ basse sur qch** *(gén)* to help o.s. to sth; *(et prendre la fuite)* to run off *ou* make off with sth ◆ **ils font ~ basse sur nos plus beaux hôtels** they're buying up all our best hotels ◆ **mettre la ~ sur** *[+ objet, livre]* to lay (one's) hands on; *[+ coupable]* to lay hands on, to collar * ◆ **je ne peux pas mettre la ~ sur mon passeport** I can't lay my hands on my passport ◆ **si vous portez la ~ sur elle, je …** if you lay a hand on her, I'll …; → **opération, prêter, tendre**[1]

◆ **coup de main** * *(= aide)* (helping) hand, help ◆ **donne-moi un coup de ~** give me a hand; → 4

◆ **de première/seconde main** *[information, témoignage]* firsthand/secondhand ◆ **acheter une voiture de première ~** *(Comm)* to buy a car secondhand *(which has only had one previous owner)* ◆ **il a obtenu ces renseignements de seconde ~** he got this information secondhand ◆ **travailler sur des ouvrages de seconde ~** *[chercheur]* to work from secondary sources

◆ **en main** *(= sous contrôle)* ◆ **avoir une voiture bien en ~** to have the feel of a car ◆ **avoir la situation (bien) en ~** to have the situation (well) in hand *ou* (well) under control ◆ **prendre qn/qch en ~** to take sb/sth in hand ◆ **il lui a fallu deux heures pour prendre en ~ sa nouvelle voiture** it took him a couple of hours to get used to *ou* to get the feel of his new car ◆ **la prise en ~ de l'organisation par des professionnels** the takeover of the organization by professionals

◆ **en mains propres** ◆ **il me l'a remis en ~s propres** he handed *ou* gave it to me personally

◆ **entre les mains de** ◆ **être entre les ~s de qn** to be in sb's hands ◆ **la décision est entre ses ~s** the decision is in his hands *ou* lies with him ◆ **je l'ai mis entre les ~s d'un bon entraîneur** I put him in the hands of a good coach ◆ **ce livre n'est pas à mettre entre toutes les ~s** this book is not suitable for the general public

4 [= manière, habileté] **se faire la ~** to get one's hand in ◆ **garder la ~** to keep one's hand in ◆ **perdre la ~** to lose one's touch ◆ **on reconnaît la ~ de l'artiste/de l'auteur** it is easy to recognize the artist's/the writer's touch

◆ **coup de main** *(= habileté)* knack ◆ **avoir le coup de ~ (pour faire qch)** to have the knack (of doing sth) ◆ **j'ai dû m'y reprendre à plusieurs fois avant d'avoir le coup de ~** I had to try several times before getting the hang of it *ou* the knack ◆ **pour la mayonnaise, tout est dans le coup de ~** there's a knack to making mayonnaise

(= attaque) raid; → **homme**

5 [† = permission d'épouser] **demander/obtenir la ~ d'une jeune fille** to ask for/win a girl's hand (in marriage) ◆ **accorder la ~ de sa fille à qn** to give sb one's daughter's hand in marriage

6 [Cartes] hand ◆ **avoir la ~** *(= jouer le premier)* to lead; *(= distribuer les cartes)* to deal ◆ **perdre la ~** to lose the lead ◆ **passer la ~ à qn** *(lit)* to lead to sb ◆ **à 65 ans, il est temps qu'il passe la ~** *(= qu'il se retire)* at 65 it's time he made way for someone else *ou* stood down ◆ **la ~ passe !** *(Casino)* next deal! ◆ **faire la ~, être à la ~** *(Casino)* to have the deal

7 [Couture] **première ~** head seamstress; → **petit**

8 [quantité de papier] ≃ quire *(25 sheets)*

9 [Imprim] bulk

10 [par analogie de forme] *[de bananes]* hand, bunch

2 - ADVERBE

◆ **entièrement fait ~** *(gén)* entirely handmade; *(artisanat)* entirely handmade *ou* handcrafted ◆ **cousu ~** *(lit)* hand-sewn, hand-stitched ◆ **c'est du cousu ~** * *(de qualité)* it's first-rate *ou* top-quality stuff

3 - COMPOSÉS

la main chaude *(Jeux)* hot cockles

main courante *(= câble)* handrail; *(Comm)* rough book, daybook ◆ **faire établir une ~ courante** *(Police)* to notify the police of a complaint

main de Fatma hand of Fatima

mains libres *[fonction, kit, téléphone]* hands-free

main de ressort *[de véhicule]* dumb iron

---

mainate / mɛnat / **NM** myna(h) bird

main-d'œuvre (pl **mains-d'œuvre**) / mɛ̃dœvʀ / **NF** *(= travail)* labour *(Brit)*, labor *(US)*, manpower; *(= personnes)* workforce, labour *(Brit)* *ou* labor *(US)* force ◆ **embaucher de la ~** to hire workers ◆ **~ qualifiée** skilled labour ◆ **la ~ locale disponible** the local available workforce *ou* labour force ◆ **industries de ~** labour-intensive industries ◆ **il m'a compté deux heures de ~** he charged me two hours' labour

main(-)forte / mɛ̃fɔʀt / **NF INV** → **prêter**

mainlevée / mɛ̃l(ə)ve / **NF** *(Jur)* withdrawal ◆ **~ d'hypothèque** *(Fin)* release of mortgage

mainmise /mɛ̃miz/ **NF** *(= prise de contrôle)* takeover; *(= emprise)* grip; *(autoritaire)* stranglehold ◆ **la ~ de l'Église sur l'éducation** the Church's stranglehold on education ◆ **avoir la ~ sur** to have a grip *ou* a stranglehold on

maint, mainte /mɛ̃, mɛ̃t/ **ADJ** *(frm)* (a great *ou* good) many (+ *npl*), many a (+ *nsg*) ◆ **~ exemple** many an example ◆ **~s exemples** many *ou* numerous examples ◆ **à ~es reprises, (~es et) ~es fois** time and (time) again, many a time ◆ **en ~ endroit** in many places ◆ **en ~es occasions** on numerous *ou* many occasions

maintenance /mɛ̃t(ə)nɑ̃s/ **NF** maintenance, servicing ◆ **contrat de ~** maintenance *ou* service contract ◆ **assurer la ~ d'une machine** to service a machine

maintenant /mɛ̃t(ə)nɑ̃/ GRAMMAIRE ACTIVE 53.2
ADV 1 *(= en ce moment)* now ◆ **que fait-il ~ ?** what's he doing now? ◆ **il doit être arrivé ~** he must have arrived by now ◆ **~ qu'il est grand** now that he's bigger ◆ **à toi ~** it's your turn now; ◆ **plus ~** not any longer → **dès, jusque, partir¹**

2 *(= à ce moment)* now, by now ◆ **ils devaient ~ chercher à se nourrir** they now had to try and find something to eat ◆ **ils étaient ~ très fatigués** by now they were very tired ◆ **ils marchaient ~ depuis deux heures** (by) now they had been walking for two hours

3 *(= actuellement)* today, nowadays ◆ **les jeunes de ~** young people nowadays *ou* today

4 *(= ceci dit)* now (then) ◆ **~ ce que j'en dis, c'est pour ton bien** now (then) what I say is for your own good ◆ **il y a un cadavre, certes, ~, y a-t-il un crime ?** we're agreed there's a corpse, now the question is, is there a crime?

5 *(= à partir de ce moment)* from now on ◆ **il l'ignorait ? ~ il le saura** he didn't know that? he will now *ou* from now on

maintenir /mɛ̃t(ə)niʀ/ ▸ conjug 22 ◂ **VT** 1 *(= soutenir, contenir)* [+ *édifice*] to hold *ou* keep up, to support; [+ *cheville, os*] to give support to, to support ◆ **~ qch fixe/en équilibre** to keep *ou* hold sth in position/balanced ◆ **les oreillers le maintiennent assis** the pillows keep him in a sitting position *ou* keep him sitting up ◆ **~ la tête hors de l'eau** to keep one's head above water ◆ **~ les prix** to keep prices steady *ou* in check

2 *(= garder) (gén)* to keep; [+ *statu quo, tradition*] to maintain, to preserve, to uphold; [+ *décision*] to maintain, to stand by, to uphold; [+ *candidature*] to maintain ◆ **~ qn en vie** to keep sb alive ◆ **~ des troupes en Europe** to keep troops in Europe ◆ **~ l'ordre/la paix** to keep *ou* maintain law and order/the peace ◆ **~ qn en poste** to keep sb on, to keep sb at *ou* in his job ◆ **pour ~ les personnes âgées à leur domicile** to enable old people to go on living in their own homes

3 *(= affirmer)* to maintain ◆ **je l'ai dit et je le maintiens !** I've said it and I'm sticking to it! *ou* I'm standing by it! ◆ **~ que ...** to maintain *ou* hold that ...

VPR **se maintenir** [*temps*] to stay fair, to hold; [*amélioration*] to persist; [*préjugé*] to live on, to persist, to remain; [*malade*] to be doing well ◆ **se ~ en bonne santé** to keep in good health, to manage to keep well ◆ **les prix se maintiennent** prices are keeping *ou* holding steady ◆ **cet élève devrait se ~ dans la moyenne** this pupil should be able to keep up with the middle of the class ◆ **comment ça va ? – ça se maintient*** how are you doing? – not so bad* ◆ **se ~ en équilibre sur un pied/sur une poutre** to balance on one foot/on a beam ◆ **se ~ au pouvoir** to remain in power ◆ **le candidat s'est maintenu au deuxième tour** *(Pol)* the candidate stayed through to the second round

maintien /mɛ̃tjɛ̃/ **NM** 1 *(= sauvegarde)* [*de tradition*] preservation, upholding, maintenance ◆ **assurer le ~ de** [+ *tradition*] to maintain, to preserve, to uphold ◆ **le ~ de troupes/de l'ordre** the maintenance of troops/of law and order ◆ **ils veulent le ~ du pouvoir d'achat** they want to keep *ou* maintain their purchasing power ◆ **qu'est-ce qui a pu justifier le ~ de sa décision/candidature ?** what(ever) were his reasons for standing by his decision/for maintaining his candidature? ◆ **ils souhaitent le ~ des personnes âgées à domicile** they want old people to be looked after *ou* cared for in their own homes

2 *(= soutien)* support ◆ **ce soutien-gorge assure un bon ~ de la poitrine** this bra gives firm support

3 *(= posture)* bearing, deportment ◆ **leçon de ~** lesson in deportment ◆ **professeur de ~** teacher of deportment

maire /mɛʀ/ **NM** mayor ◆ **passer devant (monsieur) le ~** *(hum)* to tie the knot*, to get married; → **adjoint, écharpe**

> **MAIRE**
>
> Each French commune has its **maire**, elected by the « conseil municipal » (or, in Paris, Lyons and Marseille, by the « conseil d'arrondissement »). The « maire » is responsible for organizing council meetings and ensuring that the decisions of the « conseil municipal » are carried out. He or she has a wide range of administrative duties as the chief civic representative of the « commune », including maintaining public order through the municipal police. As a representative of the State, he or she is empowered to perform marriages (which take place in the « salle des mariages » at the « mairie ») and is responsible for keeping the local register of births, marriages and deaths.
>
> The **maire** is assisted in his or her functions by one or several « adjoints » (deputies). Note that a « député-maire » is not a deputy mayor but a **maire** who is also a member of parliament. → CONSEIL, COMMUNE, DÉPUTÉ

mairesse † /mɛʀɛs/ **NF** mayoress

mairie /meʀi/ **NF** *(= bâtiment)* town hall, city hall; *(= administration)* town council, municipal corporation; *(= charge)* mayoralty, office of mayor ◆ **la ~ a décidé que ...** the (town) council has decided that ... ◆ **projet financé par la Mairie de Paris** project funded by the City of Paris ◆ **~ d'arrondissement** *town hall of an arrondissement*; → **secrétaire**; → MAIRE

mais¹ /mɛ/ GRAMMAIRE ACTIVE 53.3
CONJ 1 *(objection, restriction, opposition)* but ◆ **ce n'est pas bleu ~ (bien) mauve** it isn't blue, it's (definitely) mauve ◆ **non seulement il boit ~ (encore *ou* en outre) il bat sa femme** not only does he drink but on top of that *ou* even worse he beats his wife ◆ **il est peut-être le patron ~ tu as quand même des droits** he may be the boss but you've still got your rights ◆ **il est parti ? ~ tu m'avais promis qu'il m'attendrait !** he has left? but you promised he'd wait for me!

2 *(renforcement)* **je n'ai rien mangé hier, ~ vraiment rien** I ate nothing at all yesterday, absolutely nothing ◆ **tu me crois ? – ~ oui *ou* bien sûr *ou* certainement** do you believe me? – (but) of course *ou* of course I do ◆ **~ je te jure que c'est vrai !** but I swear it's true! ◆ **~ si, je veux bien !** but of course I agree!, sure, I agree! ◆ **~ ne te fais pas de soucis !** don't you worry! ◆ **je vous dérange ? – ~ pas du tout** am I disturbing you? – not at all ◆ **je croyais qu'il serait content, ~ pas du tout !** I thought he'd be happy – but no!

3 *(transition, surprise)* **~ qu'arriva-t-il ?** but what happened (then)? ◆ **~ alors qu'est-ce qui est arrivé ?** well then *ou* for goodness' sake what happened? ◆ **~ dites-moi, c'est intéressant tout ça !** well, well *ou* well now that's all very interesting! ◆ **~ j'y pense, vous n'avez pas déjeuné** by the way I've just thought, you haven't had any lunch ◆ **~, vous pleurez** good Lord *ou* good gracious, you're crying ◆ **~ enfin, tant pis !** well, too bad!

4 *(protestation, indignation)* **ah ~ ! il verra de quel bois je me chauffe !** I can tell you he'll soon see what I have to say about it! ◆ **non ~ (des fois) !*** *ou* **(alors) !*** hey look here!*, for goodness sake!* ◆ **non ~ (des fois)* tu me prends pour un imbécile ?** I ask you!* *ou* come off it!*, do you think I'm a complete idiot? ◆ **~ enfin, tu vas te taire ?** look here, are you going to *ou* will you shut up?*

NM *(sg)* objection, snag; *(pl)* buts ◆ **je ne veux pas de ~** I don't want any buts ◆ **il n'y a pas de ~ qui tienne** there's no but about it ◆ **il y a un ~** there's one snag *ou* objection ◆ **il va y avoir des si et des ~** there are sure to be some ifs and buts

mais² † /mɛ/ **ADV** *(littér)* ◆ **il n'en pouvait ~** *(impuissant)* he could do nothing about it; *(épuisé)* he was exhausted *ou* worn out

maïs /mais/ **NM** *(gén)* maize *(Brit)*, Indian corn *(Brit)*, corn *(US)*; *(en conserve)* sweet corn ◆ **~ en épi** corn on the cob ◆ **papier ~** corn paper *(used for rolling cigarettes)*; → **farine**

maison /mɛzɔ̃/ **NF** 1 *(= bâtiment)* house; *(= immeuble)* building; *(locatif)* block of flats *(Brit)*, apartment building *(US)* ◆ **~ individuelle** house *(as opposed to apartment)* ◆ **la ~ individuelle** *(secteur)* private housing

2 *(= logement, foyer)* home ◆ **être/rester à la ~** to be/stay at home *ou* in ◆ **rentrer à la ~** to go (back) home ◆ **quitter la ~** to leave home ◆ **tenir la ~ de qn** to keep house for sb ◆ **les dépenses de la ~** household expenses ◆ **fait à la ~** home-made ◆ **c'est la ~ du bon Dieu** their door is always open; ◆ **remettre de l'ordre dans la ~** *(fig)* to put one's house in order → **linge, maître, train**

3 *(= famille, maisonnée)* family ◆ **quelqu'un de la ~ m'a dit ...** someone in the family told me ... ◆ **un ami de la ~** a friend of the family ◆ **il n'est pas heureux à la ~** he doesn't have a happy home life *ou* family life ◆ **nous sommes 7 à la ~** there are 7 of us at home

4 *(= entreprise)* firm, company; *(= magasin de vente) (grand)* store; *(petit)* shop ◆ **il est dans la ~ depuis 15 ans, il a 15 ans de ~** he's been *ou* he has worked with the firm for 15 years ◆ **la ~ n'est pas responsable de ...** the company *ou* management accepts no responsibility for ... ◆ **c'est offert par la ~** it's on the house ◆ **la ~ ne fait pas crédit** no credit (given) ◆ **la grande ~** *(arg Police)* the police force

5 *(= famille royale)* House ◆ **la ~ de Hanovre/de Bourbon** the House of Hanover/of Bourbon

6 *(= place de domestiques, domesticité)* household ◆ **la ~ du Roi/du président de la République** the Royal/Presidential Household ◆ **~ civile/militaire** civil/military household ◆ **gens** † *ou* **employés de ~** servants, domestic staff

7 *(Astrol)* house, mansion; *(Rel)* house

ADJ INV 1 [*gâteau, confiture*] home-made; [*personne*] (* = *formé sur place*) trained by the firm; (* = *travaillant exclusivement pour l'entreprise*) in-house *(épith)* ◆ **pâté ~** *(au restaurant)* pâté maison, chef's own pâté ◆ **est-ce que c'est fait ~ ?** do you make it yourself?

2 (* : *intensif*) first-rate ◆ **il y a eu une bagarre (quelque chose de) ~** there was an almighty* *ou* a stand-up fight ◆ **il avait une bosse ~ sur la tête** he had one hell of a bump on his head* ◆ **il s'est fait engueuler* quelque chose (de) ~ !** he got one hell of a talking to!*

COMP **maison d'arrêt** prison
la Maison Blanche the White House
maison bourgeoise large impressive house
maison de campagne house in the country

maison centrale prison, (state) penitentiary *(US)*
maison close brothel
maison de commerce (commercial) firm
maison de correction † *(Jur)* reformatory †
maison de couture couture house
maison de la culture (community) arts centre
la Maison de Dieu ⇒ **la Maison du Seigneur**
maison de disques record company
maison d'édition publishing house
maison d'éducation surveillée ≃ approved school *(Brit)*, reform school *(US)*
maison familiale *[de famille]* family home; *(= centre de formation) training centre for young apprentices; (= lieu de vacances)* holiday *(Brit) ou* vacation *(US)* centre *(for low-income families)*
maison de fous* *(lit, fig)* ≃ madhouse
maison de gros wholesaler's
maison de jeu gambling *ou* gaming club
maison des jeunes et de la culture ≃ community arts centre, youth club and arts centre
maison de maître mansion
maison mère *(= société)* parent company; *(Rel)* mother house
maison de passe *hotel used as a brothel*
maison de poupée doll's house
maison de la presse ≃ newsagent's *(Brit)*, newsdealer *(US)*
maison de rapport block of flats for letting *(Brit)*, rental apartment building *(US)*
maison de redressement † reformatory †
maison religieuse convent
maison de rendez-vous † *house used by lovers as a discreet meeting-place*
maison de repos convalescent home
maison de retraite old people's home
maison de santé *(= clinique)* nursing home; *(= asile)* mental home
la Maison du Seigneur the House of God
maison de titres securities firm *ou* house
maison de tolérance ⇒ **maison close**

maisonnée /mezɔne/ **NF** household, family

maisonnette /mɛzɔnɛt/ **NF** small house

maistrance /mɛstʀɑ̃s/ **NF** petty officers

maître, maîtresse /mɛtʀ, mɛtʀɛs/ **ADJ** 1 *(= principal) [branche]* main; *[qualité]* chief, main, major; *[atout, carte]* master *(épith)*; *(Ordin) [document, ordinateur]* master *(épith)* ◆ **c'est une œuvre maîtresse** it's a major work ◆ **c'est la pièce maîtresse de la collection** it's the major *ou* main *ou* principal piece in the collection ◆ **poutre maîtresse** main beam ◆ **position maîtresse** major *ou* key position ◆ **idée maîtresse** principal *ou* governing idea ◆ **c'est le ~ mot** it's the key word *ou* THE word ◆ **en mode ~-esclave** *(Ordin)* in master-slave mode; → **pièce**

2 *(avant n : intensif)* **un ~ filou** *ou* **fripon** an arrant *ou* out-and-out rascal ◆ **c'est une maîtresse femme** she's a very capable woman

NM 1 *(gén)* master; *(Art)* master; *(Pol = dirigeant)* ruler ◆ **parler/agir en ~** to speak/act authoritatively ◆ **ils se sont installés en ~s dans ce pays** they have set themselves up as the ruling power in the country, they have taken command of the country ◆ **d'un ton de ~** in an authoritative *ou* a masterful tone ◆ **je vais t'apprendre qui est le ~ ici !** I'll teach you who's the boss* round here! *ou* who's in charge round here! ◆ **la main/l'œil du ~** the hand/the eye of the master ◆ **le ~ de céans** the master of the house ◆ **le ~/la maîtresse des lieux** the master/the mistress *ou* lady of the house ◆ **seul ~ à bord après Dieu** *(Naut)* sole master on board under God ◆ **les ~s du monde** the masters of the world ◆ **grand ~** *(Échecs)* grandmaster; *(Franc-maçonnerie)* Grand Master ◆ **le grand ~ des études celtiques** *(fig)* the greatest authority on Celtic studies; → **chauffeur, toile**

2 *(Scol)* **~ (d'école)** teacher, (school)master ◆ **~ de piano/d'anglais** piano/English teacher

3 *(= artisan)* **~ charpentier/maçon** master carpenter/builder

4 *(= titre)* **Maître** *term of address given to lawyers, artists, professors etc; (Art)* maestro; *(dans la marine)* petty officer ◆ **mon cher Maître** Dear Mr *ou* Professor *etc* X ◆ **Maître X** *(Jur)* Mr X

5 *(locutions)* **coup de ~** masterstroke ◆ **être ~ à cœur** *(Cartes)* to have *ou* hold the master *ou* best heart ◆ **le roi de cœur est ~** the king of hearts is master, the king is the master *ou* best heart ◆ **être ~ chez soi** to be master in one's own home ◆ **être son (propre) ~** to be one's own master ◆ **être ~ de refuser/faire** to be free to refuse/do ◆ **rester ~ de soi** to retain *ou* keep one's self-control ◆ **être ~ de soi** to be in control *ou* have control of o.s. ◆ **être/rester ~ de la situation** to be/remain in control of the situation, to have/keep the situation under control ◆ **être/rester ~ de son véhicule** to be/remain in control of one's vehicle ◆ **être ~ de sa destinée** to be the master of one's fate ◆ **être/rester ~ du pays** to be/remain in control *ou* command of the country ◆ **être ~ d'un secret** to be in possession of a secret ◆ **être ~ de son sujet** to have a mastery of one's subject ◆ **se rendre ~ de** *[+ ville, pays]* to gain control *ou* possession of; *[+ personne, animal, incendie, situation]* to bring *ou* get under control ◆ **il est passé ~ dans l'art de mentir** he's a past master in the art of lying

NF maîtresse 1 *(= amante)* mistress

2 *(Scol)* **maîtresse (d'école)** teacher, (school) mistress ◆ **maîtresse !** (please) Miss!

3 *(locutions)* **être/rester/se rendre/passer maîtresse (de)** → **nm 5**

COMP maître d'armes fencing master
maître artisan *(gén)* master craftsman; *(= boulanger)* master baker
maître assistant † *(Univ)* ≃ (senior) lecturer *(Brit)*, assistant professor *(US)*
maître auxiliaire non-certified teacher
maître/maîtresse de ballet ballet master/mistress
maître de cérémonies master of ceremonies
maître chanteur *(= escroc)* blackmailer; *(Mus)* Meistersinger, mastersinger
maître de chapelle choirmaster, precentor
maître de conférences NMF *(Univ)* ≃ (senior) lecturer *(Brit)*, assistant professor *(US)*
maître d'équipage boatswain
maître d'hôtel *[de maison]* butler; *[d'hôtel, restaurant]* head waiter, maître (d'hôtel) *(US)*; *(Naut)* chief steward ◆ **pommes de terre ~ d'hôtel** *(Culin)* maître d'hôtel potatoes
maître/maîtresse d'internat house master/mistress
maître Jacques jack-of-all-trades
maître de maison host
maîtresse de maison housewife; *(= hôtesse)* hostess
maître nageur swimming teacher *ou* instructor
maître d'œuvre *(Constr)* project manager
maître d'ouvrage *(Constr)* owner; *(dans le public)* contracting authority ◆ **la mairie est ~ d'ouvrage de ce projet** the town council has contracted the project
maître à penser intellectual guide *ou* leader
maître queux *(Culin)* chef
maître des requêtes *(Admin)* **NMF** counsel of the Conseil d'État
maître titulaire permanent teacher *(in primary school)*

maître-autel (pl **maîtres-autels**) /mɛtʀotɛl/ **NM** *(Rel)* high altar

maître-chien (pl **maîtres-chiens**) /mɛtʀəʃjɛ̃/ **NM** dog handler

maîtrisable /metʀizabl/ **ADJ** 1 *(= contrôlable)* controllable ◆ **l'incendie était difficilement ~** the fire was hard to control ◆ **la crise/la situation est difficilement ~** the crisis/the situation is getting out of hand 2 *[langue, technique]* which can be mastered

maîtrise /metʀiz/ **NF** 1 *(= sang-froid)* **~ (de soi)** self-control, self-command, self-possession

2 *(= contrôle) [de domaine]* mastery, command, control; *[de budget]* control ◆ **sa ~ du français** his command of the French language ◆ **avoir la ~ de la mer** *(Mil)* to have command *ou* control *ou* mastery of the sea(s), to control the sea ◆ **avoir la ~ d'un marché** to control *ou* have control of a market ◆ **avoir la ~ de l'atome** to have mastered the atom ◆ **pour une plus grande ~ des dépenses de santé** to ensure better control of health expenditure

3 *(= habileté)* skill, mastery, expertise ◆ **faire** *ou* **exécuter qch avec ~** to do sth with skill *ou* skilfully

4 *(dans une usine)* supervisory staff; → **agent**

5 *(Rel) (= école)* choir school; *(= groupe)* choir

6 *(Univ) research degree,* ≃ master's degree ◆ **~ de conférences** ≃ senior lectureship; → **DIPLÔMES**

COMP maîtrise d'œuvre *(= action)* project management; *(= personnes)* project managers ◆ **ce cabinet d'architectes assurera la ~ d'œuvre** this firm of architects will manage the project
maîtrise d'ouvrage contracting; *(= commanditaire)* owner; *(dans le public)* contracting authority ◆ **le ministère de la Culture assure la ~ d'ouvrage du projet** the Ministry of Culture is the contracting authority for the project

maîtriser /metʀize/ ► conjug 1 ◄ **VT** 1 *(= soumettre) [+ cheval, feu, foule, forcené]* to control, to bring under control; *[+ adversaire]* to overcome, to overpower; *[+ émeute, révolte]* to suppress, to bring under control; *[+ problème, difficulté]* to master, to overcome; *[+ inflation]* to curb ◆ **nous maîtrisons la situation** the situation is under control 2 *[+ langue, technique]* to master ◆ **il ne maîtrise pas du tout cette langue** he has no command of the language, he has a very poor grasp of the language 3 *(= contenir) [+ émotion, geste, passion]* to control, to master; *[+ larmes, rire]* to force back, to control ◆ **il ne peut plus ~ ses nerfs** he can no longer control *ou* contain his temper **VPR se maîtriser** to control o.s. ◆ **elle ne sait pas se ~** she has no self-control

maïzena ® /maizena/ **NF** cornflour *(Brit)*, cornstarch *(US)*

majesté /maʒɛste/ **NF** 1 *(= dignité)* majesty; *(= splendeur)* majesty, grandeur ◆ **la ~ divine** divine majesty ◆ **de** *ou* **en ~** *(Art)* in majesty, enthroned; → **lèse-majesté, pluriel** 2 ◆ **Votre Majesté** Your Majesty ◆ **Sa Majesté** *(= roi)* His Majesty; *(= reine)* Her Majesty

majestueusement /maʒɛstɥøzmɑ̃/ **ADV** majestically

majestueux, -euse /maʒɛstɥø, øz/ **ADJ** *(= solennel) [personne, démarche]* majestic, stately; *(= imposant) [taille]* imposing, impressive; *(= beau) [fleuve, paysage]* majestic, magnificent

majeur, e /maʒœʀ/ **ADJ** 1 *[problème, crise] (= très important)* major; *(= le plus important)* main, major, greatest ◆ **ils ont rencontré une difficulté ~e** they came up against a major *ou* serious difficulty ◆ **c'est son œuvre ~e** it's his magnum opus *ou* his greatest work ◆ **c'est une œuvre ~e de la littérature irlandaise** it's one of the major *ou* greatest works of Irish literature ◆ **sa préoccupation ~e** his major *ou* main *ou* prime concern ◆ **pour des raisons ~es** for reasons of the greatest importance ◆ **en ~e partie** for the most part ◆ **la ~e partie de ...** the greater *ou* major part of ..., the bulk of ... ◆ **la ~e partie des gens sont restés** most of *ou* the majority of the people have stayed on; → **cas**

[2] *(Jur)* of age *(attrib)* ◆ **il sera ~ en l'an 2005** he will come of age in the year 2005 ◆ **il n'est pas encore ~** he's still under age ◆ **il est ~ et vacciné** *(hum)* he's old enough to look after himself ◆ **les électeurs sont ~s** *(= responsables)* voters are responsible adults

[3] *(Mus)* *[intervalle, mode]* major ◆ **en sol ~** in G major

[4] *(Logique)* *[terme, prémisse]* major

[5] *(Rel)* **ordres ~s** major orders ◆ **causes ~es** causae majores

[6] *(Cartes)* **tierce/quarte ~e** tierce/quart major

NM,F person who has come of *ou* who is of age, person who has attained his *(ou her)* majority, major *(SPÉC)*

NM middle finger

NF **majeure** [1] *(Logique)* major premise

[2] *(Univ = matière)* main subject *(Brit)*, major *(US)*

[3] *(Écon)* major company

majolique /maʒɔlik/ NF majolica, maiolica

major /maʒɔʀ/ NM [1] *(Mil = sous-officier)* ≈ warrant officer; *(Helv = commandant)* major ◆ **(médecin) ~** medical officer, MO ◆ **~ général** *(Mil)* ≈ deputy chief of staff *(Brit)*, major general *(US)*; *(Naut)* ≈ rear admiral [2] *(Univ)* **être ~ de promotion** ≈ to be *ou* come first in one's year NF *(Écon)* major company ADJ INV → **état-major, infirmier, sergent¹, tambour**

majoration /maʒɔʀasjɔ̃/ NF *(= hausse)* rise, increase *(de* in); *(= supplément)* surcharge, additional charge; *(= surestimation)* overvaluation, overestimation ◆ **~ sur une facture** surcharge on a bill ◆ **~ pour retard de paiement** surcharge *ou* additional charge for late payment; → IMPÔTS

majordome /maʒɔʀdɔm/ NM butler, majordomo

majorer /maʒɔʀe/ ► conjug 1 ◄ VT [1] *(= accroître)* *[+ impôt, prix]* to increase, to raise, to put up *(de* by); *[+ facture]* to increase, to put a surcharge on; *[+ risque]* to increase [2] *(= surestimer)* to overestimate [3] *(= accorder trop d'importance à)* to lend *ou* give too much importance to

majorette /maʒɔʀɛt/ NF (drum) majorette

majoritaire /maʒɔʀitɛʀ/ ADJ *[actionnaire, groupe, motion]* majority *(épith)* ◆ **vote ~** majority vote ◆ **les femmes sont ~s dans cette profession** women are in the majority in this profession ◆ **les socialistes sont ~s dans le pays** the socialists are the majority *ou* largest party in the country ◆ **ils sont ~s à l'assemblée** they are the majority party *ou* in the majority in Parliament ◆ **dans ce vote, nous serons sûrement ~s** we shall certainly have a majority on this vote; → **scrutin** NMF *(Pol)* member of the majority party

majoritairement /maʒɔʀitɛʀmɑ̃/ ADV *[choisir, voter]* by a majority ◆ **le lectorat est ~ féminin** the readership is predominantly female, the majority of the readers are women ◆ **les enseignants sont ~ favorables aux réformes** the majority of teachers are in favour of the reforms ◆ **il est celui que, ~, les Français soutiennent** he is the one who most French people support ◆ **le groupe contrôle ~ notre société** *(Fin)* the group has a majority holding in our company

majorité /maʒɔʀite/ NF [1] *(électorale)* majority ◆ **~ absolue/relative/simple** absolute/relative/simple majority ◆ **~ qualifiée** *ou* **renforcée** qualified majority ◆ **élu à une ~ de ...** elected by a majority of ... ◆ **avoir la ~** to have the majority

[2] *(= parti majoritaire)* government, party in power ◆ **député de la ~** member of the governing party *ou* of the party in power, ≈ government backbencher *(Brit)*, majority party Representative *(US)* ◆ **la ~ et l'opposition** the majority party *ou* the government *(Brit)* and the opposition

[3] *(= majeure partie)* majority ◆ **ils détiennent la ~ du capital de l'entreprise** they have a majority holding in the company ◆ **il y a des mécontents, mais ce n'est pas la ~** there are some dissatisfied people, but they're not in the majority ◆ **la ~ silencieuse** the silent majority ◆ **être en ~** to be in (the) majority ◆ **la ~ est d'accord** the majority agree ◆ **les hommes dans leur grande ~** the great majority of mankind ◆ **dans la ~ des cas** in the majority of cases, in most cases ◆ **groupe composé en ~ de ...** group mainly *ou* mostly composed of ... ◆ **les enseignants sont en ~ des femmes** teachers are, in the majority, women

[4] *(Jur)* **atteindre sa ~** to come of age, to reach one's majority ◆ **jusqu'à sa ~** until he comes of age *ou* reaches his majority ◆ **~ pénale** legal majority ◆ **atteindre la ~ civile** to reach voting age

Majorque /maʒɔʀk/ NF Majorca

majorquin, e /maʒɔʀkɛ̃, in/ ADJ Majorcan NM,F **Majorquin(e)** Majorcan

majuscule /maʒyskyl/ ADJ capital; *(Typo)* upper case ◆ **A ~** capital A NF ◆ **(lettre) ~** capital letter; *(Typo)* upper case letter ◆ **en ~s d'imprimerie** in block *ou* capital letters ◆ **écrivez votre nom en ~s (d'imprimerie)** please print your name in block letters ◆ **mettre une ~ à qch** *(gén)* to write sth with a capital; *(Typo)* to capitalize sth

makaire /makɛʀ/ NM *(= poisson)* marlin

making of /meikiŋɔf/ NM ◆ **le ~ de son film** the documentary about how his film was made

mal¹ /mal/

1 ADVERBE 2 ADJECTIF INVARIABLE

1 - ADVERBE

Lorsque **mal** est suivi d'un participe passé adjectif (ex : **mal logé/loti/connu/aimé/vécu**) chercher aussi sous l'adjectif ou le verbe concerné.

[1] = de façon défectueuse *[entretenu, organisé, réparé]* badly, poorly ◆ **ce travail est ~ fait, c'est du travail ~ fait** this is poor *ou* shoddy work, this work is badly done ◆ **c'est ~ fait !** *(Helv = dommage)* it's a pity! ◆ **il se nourrit ~** he doesn't eat properly ◆ **il travaille ~** he doesn't do his work properly, his work isn't good ◆ **cette porte ferme ~** this door doesn't shut properly ◆ **j'ai ~ dormi** I didn't sleep well, I slept badly ◆ **il parle ~ l'anglais** his English isn't good *ou* is poor ◆ **nous sommes ~ nourris/logés à l'hôtel** the food/accommodation is poor *ou* bad at the hotel ◆ **tout va ~** everything's going wrong; → **tomber¹**

♦ **de mal en pis** from bad to worse ◆ **son entreprise va de ~ en pis** things are going from bad to worse in his company

[2] = de façon peu judicieuse ou opportune **~ choisi/inspiré** ill-chosen/-advised ◆ **cette annonce tombe au plus ~** this announcement couldn't have come at a worse moment

[3] = avec difficulté with difficulty ◆ **il respire ~** he has difficulty in breathing, he can't breathe properly ◆ **ils vivent très ~ avec un seul salaire** they have difficulty living on *ou* off just one income ◆ **on s'explique** *ou* **comprend ~ pourquoi** it is not easy *ou* it is difficult to understand why ◆ **nous voyons très ~ comment ...** we fail to see how ...

[4] = de façon répréhensible *[se conduire]* badly, wrongly ◆ **il ne pensait pas ~ faire, il ne pensait pas à ~** he didn't think he was doing the wrong thing *ou* doing wrong ◆ **il ne pense qu'à ~ faire** he's always up to no good, he's always thinking up some nasty trick ◆ **tu trouves ça ~ qu'il y soit allé ?** do you think it was wrong of him to go?; → **juger¹, porter, sentir, trouver** *etc*

[5] locutions

♦ **pas mal** *(= assez bien)* not badly, rather well ◆ **on est pas ~ (assis) dans ces fauteuils** these armchairs are quite comfortable ◆ **il ne s'est pas trop ~ débrouillé** he managed quite well ◆ **vous (ne) vous en êtes pas ~ tirés** you haven't done *ou* come off badly, you've done rather well ◆ **vous (ne) feriez pas ~ de le surveiller** you would be well-advised to keep *ou* it wouldn't be a bad thing if you kept an eye on him ◆ **ça va ? – pas ~** how are you? – not (too) bad *ou* pretty good

(= très, beaucoup) *[déçu, surpris]* quite, rather ◆ **on a pas ~ travaillé aujourd'hui** we've done quite a lot of work today, we've worked pretty hard today ◆ **il est pas ~ fatigué** he's rather *ou* pretty tired ◆ **il a pas ~ vieilli** he's aged quite a bit *ou* quite a lot ◆ **elle a pas ~ grossi** she's put on quite a bit *ou* quite a lot of weight

♦ **pas mal de** *(= beaucoup)* quite a lot of ◆ **il y a pas ~ de temps qu'il est parti** it's quite a time since he left, he's been away for quite a time ◆ **pas ~ de gens pensent que ...** quite a lot of people think that ...

2 - ADJECTIF INVARIABLE

[1] = contraire à la morale wrong, bad ◆ **c'est ~ de mentir/de voler** it is bad *ou* wrong to lie/to steal ◆ **(pour elle) il ne peut rien faire de ~** *(iro)* (in her eyes) he can do no wrong ◆ **c'est ~ à lui** *(frm)* **ou de sa part de dire cela** it's bad *ou* wrong of him to say this

[2] = malade ill ◆ **j'ai été ~ toute la matinée** I felt ill all morning ◆ **il est très ~ ce soir** he's very ill *ou* not at all well tonight ◆ **le malade est au plus ~** the patient's condition couldn't be worse ◆ **je me sens ~ quand il fait trop chaud** the heat doesn't agree with me ◆ **elle s'est sentie ~** she felt faint ◆ **il est ~ dans sa tête** he's not a happy person

♦ **mal en point** *[personne, voiture]* in a bad *ou* sorry state, in a bad way; *[secteur économique, parti]* in a bad way

[3] = mal à l'aise uncomfortable ◆ **vous devez être ~ sur ce banc** you can't be comfortable on that seat, that seat can't be comfortable *ou* must be uncomfortable; → **aise, peau**

[4] = en mauvais termes **être ~ avec qn** to be on bad terms with sb, to be in sb's bad books* ◆ **les deux cousins sont au plus ~** the two cousins are at daggers drawn ◆ **se mettre ~ avec qn** to get on the wrong side of sb, to get into sb's bad books*

[5] locutions

♦ **pas mal** *(= assez bien)* not bad, quite *ou* fairly good ◆ **il n'est pas ~ dans le rôle** he's not bad *ou* quite good in that role ◆ **c'est pas ~ (du tout)** it's not bad (at all)

(= assez beau) *[personne]* quite good-looking, not bad; *[maison]* quite nice, not bad ◆ **tu n'es pas ~ sur cette photo** that's quite a good picture of you

mal² /mal/ (pl **maux**)

1 NOM MASCULIN 2 COMPOSÉS

1 - NOM MASCULIN

[1] Philos: opposé au bien **le ~** evil ◆ **le conflit entre le bien et le ~** the conflict between good and evil ◆ **distinguer le bien du ~** to tell right from wrong, to know the difference between right and wrong ◆ **faire le ~ pour le ~** to do *ou* commit evil for its own sake *ou* for evil's sake ◆ **rendre le ~ pour le ~** to return evil for evil

2 = souffrance morale, peine sorrow pain ◆ **le ~ du siècle** (= *fléau*) the scourge of the age; (*littér* = *mélancolie*) world-weariness ◆ **des paroles qui font du ~** words that hurt, hurtful words

3 = dommage harm ◆ **excusez-moi - il n'y a pas de ~** I'm sorry - no harm done ◆ **il n'y a pas grand ~** there's no real harm done ◆ **il n'y a pas de ~ à (faire) ça/à ce qu'il fasse** there's no harm in (doing) that/in his *ou* him doing ◆ **~ lui en a pris !** he's had cause to regret it! ◆ **~ m'en a pris de sortir** going out was a grave mistake (on my part) ◆ **ces médicaments, ça fait plus de ~ que de bien** these medicines do more harm than good ◆ **ça fait du ~ au commerce** it's not good for business ◆ **vouloir du ~ à qn** to wish sb ill *ou* harm, to be ill-disposed towards sb ◆ **je ne lui veux pas de ~** *ou* **aucun ~** I don't wish him any harm; → **peur**

◆ **mettre à mal** [+ *personne, relations*] to harm; [+ *principe, politique, processus, système, réputation*] to harm, to damage

4 = travail pénible, difficulté difficulty ◆ **on n'a rien sans ~** you get nothing without (some) effort ◆ **faire qch sans trop de ~/non sans ~** to do sth without undue difficulty/not without difficulty ◆ **j'ai obtenu son accord/le document, mais non sans ~ !** I got him to agree/I got the document, but it wasn't easy! ◆ **il a dû prendre son ~ en patience** (= *attendre*) he had to put up with the delay; (= *supporter*) he had to grin and bear it

◆ **avoir du mal (à faire qch)** to have trouble *ou* difficulty (doing sth) ◆ **je n'ai eu aucun ~ à l'imaginer** I had no difficulty imagining it ◆ **j'ai du ~** (*elliptiquement*) it's hard for me, I find it hard *ou* difficult

◆ **donner du mal à qn** to give sb trouble ◆ **ce travail/cet enfant m'a donné du ~/bien du ~** this work/this child gave me some trouble/a lot of trouble ◆ **se donner du ~** to go to a lot of trouble

◆ **se donner du mal pour faire qch** to take trouble *ou* pains over sth, to go to great pains to do sth ◆ **ne vous donnez pas ce ~** don't bother ◆ **se donner un ~ de chien pour faire qch** * to bend over backwards *ou* go to great lengths to do sth

5 = ce qui est mauvais evil, ill ◆ **c'est un ~ nécessaire** it's a necessary evil ◆ **accuser qn de tous les maux** to accuse sb of all the evils in the world ◆ **les maux dont souffre notre société** the ills *ou* evils afflicting our society ◆ **penser/dire du ~ de qn/qch** to think/speak ill of sb/sth ◆ **sans penser** *ou* **songer à ~** without meaning any harm ◆ **aux grands maux les grands remèdes** (*Prov*) desperate times call for desperate measures; → **moindre**

6 = douleur physique pain, ache; (= *maladie*) illness, disease, sickness ◆ **le ~ s'aggrave** (*lit*) the disease is getting worse, he (*ou* she *etc*) is getting worse; (*fig*) the situation is deteriorating, things are getting worse ◆ **faire du ~ à qn** to harm *ou* hurt sb ◆ **ne leur faites pas de ~ !** don't harm *ou* hurt them! ◆ **il ne ferait pas de ~ à une mouche** he wouldn't hurt *ou* harm a fly ◆ **prendre ~** † to be taken ill, to feel unwell ◆ **~ de tête** headache ◆ **des maux d'estomac** stomach pains

◆ **avoir mal** ◆ **je me suis cogné - tu as ~ ?/très ~ ?** I bumped myself - does it hurt?/really hurt? ◆ **où avez-vous ~ ?** where does it hurt?, where is the pain? ◆ **avoir ~ partout** to be aching all over ◆ **avoir ~ au cœur** to feel nauseous *ou* sick (*Brit*) ◆ **ils ont souvent ~ au cœur en voiture** they often get carsick ◆ **avoir ~ à la gorge** to have a sore throat ◆ **avoir ~ à la tête** to have a headache *ou* a bad head* ◆ **avoir ~ aux dents/aux oreilles** to have toothache/earache ◆ **j'ai ~ au pied** my foot hurts ◆ **j'ai ~ au dos/à l'estomac** I've got backache/stomach ache, I've got a pain in my back/stomach, my back/stomach hurts

◆ **faire mal** (*physiquement*) to hurt; (*psychologiquement*) to be hurtful ◆ **des critiques qui font ~** hurtful criticism ◆ **500 € de réparations, ça fait ~ !*** €500 in repairs, that hurts! ◆ **ça va faire ~ !*** (*confrontation, match*) it's going to be tough! ◆ **le jour où le fisc s'occupera de lui, ça va faire ~ !*** the day the taxman catches up with him, he'll be in real trouble! ◆ **ils sortent un nouvel album, ça va faire ~ !*** they're bringing out a new album, it's going to be a big hit!

◆ **faire mal à** to hurt ◆ **tu m'as fait ~ !** you hurt me! ◆ **mon coude me fait ~** my elbow hurts ◆ **ces chaussures me font ~ (au pied)** these shoes hurt *ou* pinch (my feet) ◆ **il s'est fait ~ en tombant** he hurt himself when he fell ◆ **se faire ~ au genou** to hurt one's knee ◆ **ça me fait ~ au cœur** (= *ça me rend malade*) it makes me feel sick; (= *ça me fait pitié, ça me fait de la peine*) it breaks my heart; (= *ça me révolte*) it makes me sick, it's sickening ◆ **ça me ferait ~ (au ventre** *ou* **aux seins) !*** it would make me sick!, it would really piss me off!**

◆ **en mal de** (= *en manque de*) [+ *argent, idées*] short of; [+ *tendresse, amour*] yearning for ◆ **journaliste en ~ de copie** journalist short of copy ◆ **être en ~ d'inspiration** to be lacking in inspiration, to have no inspiration ◆ **association en ~ de publicité/reconnaissance** organization craving publicity/recognition

2 - COMPOSÉS

mal de l'air airsickness
mal blanc † whitlow
mal de l'espace space sickness
mal des grands ensembles sick building syndrome
le mal joli (†, *hum*) the pains of (giving) birth
mal de mer seasickness ◆ **avoir le ~ de mer** to be seasick
mal des montagnes mountain sickness ◆ **avoir le ~ des montagnes** to have mountain sickness
le mal du pays homesickness ◆ **avoir le ~ du pays** to feel homesick
mal de la route carsickness
mal des transports travel *ou* motion (*US*) sickness ◆ **pilule contre le ~ des transports** travel-sickness pill, anti-motion-sickness pill (*US*)
mal de vivre profound discontentment

Malabar /malabaʀ/ **NM** ◆ **le ~, la côte de ~** the Malabar (Coast)

malabar * /malabaʀ/ **NM** muscle man*, hefty fellow*

Malabo /malabo/ **N** Malabo

Malachie /malaʃi/ **NM** (*Bible*) Malachi

malachite /malaʃit/ **NF** malachite

malade /malad/ **ADJ** 1 (= *atteint*) [*personne*] ill, unwell (*attrib*), sick (*surtout US*); [*organe, plante*] diseased; [*dent, poitrine*] bad; [*jambe, bras*] bad, gammy* (*Brit*) (*épith*) ◆ **être bien/gravement/sérieusement ~** to be really/gravely/seriously ill ◆ **être ~ du cœur, avoir le cœur ~** to have heart trouble *ou* a bad heart *ou* a heart condition ◆ **être ~ des reins** to have kidney trouble ◆ **tomber ~** to fall ill *ou* sick ◆ **se faire porter ~** to report *ou* go sick ◆ **faire le ~** to feign *ou* sham illness ◆ **j'ai été ~** (*gén*) I was ill; (= *j'ai vomi*) I was sick ◆ **je me sens (un peu) ~** I feel (a bit) peculiar*, I don't feel very well ◆ **être ~ comme un chien*** *ou* **une bête*** (*gén*) to be dreadfully ill; (*euph* = *vomir*) to be as sick as a dog* ◆ **être ~ à crever**‡ to be dreadfully ill, to feel like death (warmed up (*Brit*) *ou* warmed over (*US*))*

2 (= *fou*) mad ◆ **tu n'es pas (un peu) ~ ?*** are you out of your mind? ◆ **tu es complètement ~ !*** you need your head examining!* ◆ **être ~ d'inquiétude** to be sick *ou* ill with worry ◆ **être ~ de jalousie** to be mad *ou* sick with jealousy ◆ **rien que d'y penser j'en suis ~*, ça me rend ~ rien que d'y penser*** the very thought of it makes me sick *ou* ill

3 (= *en mauvais état*) [*objet, pays*] in a sorry state ◆ **l'entreprise étant ~, ils durent licencier** as the business was failing, they had to lay people off ◆ **le gouvernement est trop ~ pour durer jusqu'aux élections** the government is too shaky to last till the elections ◆ **notre économie est bien ~** our economy is in bad shape *ou* a bad way

NMF 1 (*Méd*) (*gén*) invalid, sick person; (*d'un médecin*) patient ◆ **grand ~** seriously ill person ◆ **faux ~** malingerer ◆ **~ imaginaire** hypochondriac ◆ **~ mental** mentally sick *ou* ill person ◆ **les ~s** the sick ◆ **les grands ~s** the seriously *ou* critically ill ◆ **le médecin et ses ~s** the doctor and his patients

2 (* = *fanatique*) **un ~ de la moto** a (motor) bike freak‡ *ou* fanatic ◆ **un ~ de la vitesse** a speed merchant* (*Brit*) *ou* demon* (*US*)

3 (* = *fou*) maniac* ◆ **il conduit comme un ~** he drives like a maniac* *ou* madman* ◆ **elle frappait comme une ~** she was knocking like mad* *ou* like a mad woman ◆ **on a bossé comme des ~s** we worked like crazy*

maladie /maladi/ **NF** 1 (*Méd*) illness, disease; [*de plante, vin*] disease ◆ **~ bénigne** minor *ou* slight illness, minor complaint ◆ **~ grave** serious illness ◆ **~ de cœur/foie** heart/liver complaint *ou* disease ◆ **ces enfants ont eu une ~ après l'autre** these children have had one sickness *ou* illness after another ◆ **le cancer est la ~ du siècle** cancer is the disease of this century ◆ **il a fait une petite ~*** he's been slightly ill, he's had a minor illness ◆ **elle est en ~*** she's off sick* ◆ **en longue ~** (off) on extended sick leave ◆ **il en a fait une ~*** (*fig*) he got into a terrible state about it, he had a fit* ◆ **tu ne vas pas en faire une ~ !*** don't you get in (such) a state over it!, don't make a song and dance about it!* ◆ **mes rosiers ont la ~*** my rose bushes are in a bad way*

2 ◆ **la ~** illness, ill health ◆ **la ~ et la famine dans le monde** disease and famine in the world; → **assurance**

3 **la ~** (= *maladie de Carré*) distemper

4 (* = *obsession*) mania ◆ **avoir la ~ de la vitesse** to be a speed maniac ◆ **quelle ~ as-tu de toujours intervenir !** what a mania you have for interfering! ◆ **c'est une ~ chez lui** it's a mania with him

COMP **la maladie bleue** the blue disease, cyanosis
maladie honteuse † ⇒ **maladie vénérienne**
maladie infantile childhood *ou* infantile disease *ou* complaint
maladie de langueur wasting disease
maladie du légionnaire legionnaires' disease
maladie mentale mental illness
maladie mortelle fatal illness *ou* disease
maladie de peau skin disease *ou* complaint
maladie professionnelle occupational disease
maladie sexuellement transmissible sexually transmitted disease, STD
la maladie du sommeil sleeping sickness
maladie du travail ⇒ **maladie professionnelle**
maladie tropicale tropical disease
maladie vénérienne venereal disease, VD; → **Alzheimer, Carré, Hodgkin**

maladif, -ive /maladif, iv/ **ADJ** 1 [*personne*] sickly, weak; [*air, pâleur*] sickly, unhealthy 2 [*obsession, peur*] pathological ◆ **il est d'une timidité maladive** he's pathologically shy ◆ **il faut qu'il mente, c'est ~ chez lui** he's a pathological liar

maladivement /maladivmɑ̃/ **ADV** [*pâle, maigre*] unhealthily; [*anxieux, timide*] pathologically

maladrerie † /maladʀəʀi/ NF lazaret †, lazar house †

maladresse /maladʀɛs/ NF 1 (= *gaucherie*) [*de personne, geste, expression*] clumsiness, awkwardness; [*d'ouvrage, style, intervention*] clumsiness 2 (= *indélicatesse*) [*de personne, remarque*] clumsiness, tactlessness ◆ **quelle ~ !** how tactless! 3 (= *bévue*) blunder, gaffe ◆ **~s de style** awkward *ou* clumsy turns of phrase

maladroit, e /maladʀwa, wat/ ADJ 1 (= *malhabile*) [*personne, geste, expression*] clumsy, awkward; [*ouvrage, style, dessin, intervention, mensonge*] clumsy ◆ **il est vraiment ~ de ses mains** he's really useless with his hands 2 (= *indélicat*) [*personne, remarque*] clumsy, tactless ◆ **ce serait ~ de lui en parler** it would be tactless *ou* ill-considered to mention it to him NM,F (= *malhabile*) clumsy person *ou* oaf *; (= *qui fait tout tomber*) butterfingers *; (= *indélicat*) tactless person, blunderer * ◆ **quel ~ je fais !** how clumsy of me!

maladroitement /maladʀwatmɑ̃/ ADV [*marcher, dessiner*] clumsily, awkwardly; [*agir*] clumsily ◆ **il a tenté ~ de se justifier** he made a clumsy attempt to justify himself

malaga /malaga/ NM (= *vin*) Malaga (wine); (= *raisin*) Malaga grape

mal-aimé, e (mpl **mal-aimés**) /maleme/ NM,F unpopular figure ◆ **il est devenu le ~ de la presse** he has become the man the press love to hate, he has become an unpopular figure with the press

malais, e[1] /malɛ, ɛz/ ADJ Malay(an) NM (= *langue*) Malay NM,F **Malais(e)** Malay(an)

malaise[2] /malɛz/ NM 1 (*gén*) feeling of general discomfort *ou* ill-being; (*Méd*) feeling of sickness *ou* faintness, malaise (*frm*) ◆ **~ cardiaque** mild heart attack ◆ **être pris d'un ~, avoir un ~** to feel faint *ou* dizzy, to come over faint *ou* dizzy 2 (= *trouble*) uneasiness ◆ **éprouver un ~** to feel uneasy ◆ **le ~ étudiant/politique** student/political unrest ◆ **~ économique/social** economic/social malaise

malaisé, e /maleze/ ADJ difficult

malaisément /malezemɑ̃/ ADV with difficulty

Malaisie /malɛzi/ NF Malaysia

malaisien, -ienne /malɛzjɛ̃, jɛn/ ADJ Malaysian NM,F **Malaisien(ne)** Malaysian

malandrin † /malɑ̃dʀɛ̃/ NM (*littér*) brigand (*littér*), bandit

malappris, e /malapʀi, iz/ ADJ ill-mannered, boorish NM ill-mannered lout, boor, yob * (*Brit*)

malard /malaʀ/ NM drake; (*sauvage*) mallard

malaria /malaʀja/ NF malaria (*NonC*)

malavisé, e /malavize/ ADJ [*personne, remarque*] ill-advised, injudicious, unwise

Malawi /malawi/ NM Malawi

malawien, -ienne /malawjɛ̃, jɛn/ ADJ Malawian NM,F **Malawien(ne)** Malawian

malaxage /malaksaʒ/ NM 1 [*d'argile, pâte*] kneading; [*de muscle*] massaging; [*de beurre*] creaming 2 (= *mélange*) blending, mixing

malaxer /malakse/ ► conjug 1 ◄ VT 1 [+ *argile, pâte*] to knead; [+ *muscle*] to massage; [+ *beurre*] to cream 2 (= *mélanger*) to blend, to mix

malaxeur /malaksœʀ/ ADJ M mixing NM mixer

mal-bouffe *, **malbouffe** * /malbuf/ NF ◆ **la ~** junk food

malchance /malʃɑ̃s/ NF (= *déveine*) bad *ou* ill luck, misfortune; (= *mésaventure*) misfortune, mishap ◆ **il a eu beaucoup de ~** he's had a lot of bad luck ◆ **j'ai eu la ~ de ...** I had the misfortune to ..., I was unlucky enough to ... ◆ **par ~** unfortunately, as ill luck would have it ◆ **il a joué de ~** (*gén*) he was out of luck; (*de manière répétée*) he had one bit of bad luck after another

malchanceux, -euse /malʃɑ̃sø, øz/ ADJ unlucky

malcommode /malkɔmɔd/ ADJ [*objet, vêtement*] impractical, unsuitable; [*horaire*] awkward, inconvenient; [*outil, meuble*] inconvenient, impractical ◆ **ça m'est vraiment très ~** it's really most inconvenient for me, it really doesn't suit me at all

Maldives /maldiv/ NFPL ◆ **les ~** the Maldives

maldonne /maldɔn/ NF (*Cartes*) misdeal ◆ **faire (une) ~** to misdeal, to deal the cards wrongly ◆ **il y a ~** (*lit*) there's been a misdeal, the cards have been dealt wrongly; (*fig*) there's been a mistake somewhere

Malé /male/ N Malé

mâle /mɑl/ ADJ 1 (*Bio, Tech*) male 2 (= *viril*) [*voix, courage*] manly; [*style, peinture*] virile, strong, forceful NM male ◆ **titre de noblesse transmis par les ~s** noble title handed down through the male line ◆ **c'est un ~ ou une femelle ?** is it a he or a she? *, is it a male or a female? ◆ **c'est un beau ~** * (*hum*) he's a real hunk *, he's a fine specimen (of manhood) (*hum*) ◆ **(éléphant) ~** bull (elephant) ◆ **(lapin) ~** buck (rabbit) ◆ **(moineau) ~** cock (sparrow) ◆ **(ours) ~** he-bear ◆ **souris ~** male mouse

malédiction /malediksjɔ̃/ NF (*Rel* = *imprécation, adversité*) curse, malediction (*littér*) ◆ **la ~ divine** the curse of God ◆ **n'écoute pas les ~s de cette vieille folle** don't listen to the curses of that old fool ◆ **la ~ pèse sur nous** a curse is hanging over us, we're under a curse ◆ **appeler la ~ sur qn** to call down curses upon sb EXCL († †, *hum*) curse it! *, damn! * ◆ **~ ! j'ai perdu la clé** curse it! * I've lost the key

maléfice /malefis/ NM evil spell

maléfique /malefik/ ADJ [*étoile*] unlucky; [*charme, signe, pouvoir*] evil, baleful ◆ **les puissances ~s** the forces of evil

malemort /malmɔʀ/ NF († †, *littér*) cruel death ◆ **mourir de ~** to die a cruel *ou* violent death

malencontreusement /malɑ̃kɔ̃tʀøzmɑ̃/ ADV [*arriver*] at the wrong moment, inopportunely, inconveniently; [*faire tomber*] inadvertently ◆ **faire ~ remarquer que ...** to make the unfortunate remark that ...

malencontreux, -euse /malɑ̃kɔ̃tʀø, øz/ ADJ 1 (= *malheureux*) [*erreur, incident*] unfortunate; [*geste*] awkward; [*remarque*] awkward, unfortunate; [*décision*] unwise, unfortunate 2 (= *déplacé*) [*allusion*] inopportune 3 (= *à contretemps*) [*événement*] untimely

malentendant, e /malɑ̃tɑ̃dɑ̃, ɑ̃t/ NM,F person who is hard of hearing ◆ **les ~s** hearing-impaired people, people who are hard of hearing

malentendu /malɑ̃tɑ̃dy/ NM misunderstanding

mal-être /malɛtʀ/ NM INV [*de personne*] malaise, disquiet, ill-being (*US*); [*de groupe social*] malaise

malfaçon /malfasɔ̃/ NF fault, defect (*due to bad workmanship*)

malfaisant, e /malfəzɑ̃, ɑ̃t/ ADJ [*personne*] evil, wicked, harmful; [*influence*] evil, harmful; [*animal, théories*] harmful

malfaiteur /malfɛtœʀ/ NM (*gén*) criminal; (= *gangster*) gangster; (= *voleur*) burglar, thief ◆ **dangereux ~** dangerous criminal

malformation /malfɔʀmasjɔ̃/ NF malformation

malfrat /malfʀa/ NM (= *escroc*) crook; (= *bandit*) thug, gangster

malgache /malgaʃ/ ADJ Malagasy, Madagascan NM (= *langue*) Malagasy NMF **Malgache** Malagasy, Madagascan

malgracieux, -ieuse /malgʀasjø, jøz/ ADJ (*littér*) [*silhouette*] ungainly, clumsy; † [*caractère*] loutish, boorish

malgré /malgʀe/ PRÉP (= *en dépit de*) in spite of, despite ◆ **~ son père/l'opposition de son père, il devint avocat** despite his *ou* in spite of his father/his father's objections he became a barrister ◆ **~ son intelligence, il n'a pas réussi** in spite of *ou* for all *ou* notwithstanding (*frm*) his undoubted intelligence he hasn't succeeded ◆ **j'ai signé ce contrat ~ moi** (*en hésitant*) I signed the contract reluctantly *ou* against my better judgment; (*contraint et forcé*) I signed the contract against my will ◆ **j'ai fait cela presque ~ moi** I did it almost in spite of myself ◆ **il est devenu célèbre/un sex-symbol ~ lui** he became a reluctant celebrity/sex-symbol, he became famous/a sex-symbol in spite of himself

◆ **malgré tout** (= *en dépit de tout*) in spite of everything, despite everything; (*concession* = *quand même*) all the same, even so, after all ◆ **~ tout, c'est dangereux** all the same *ou* after all it's dangerous ◆ **il a continué ~ tout** he went on in spite of *ou* despite everything ◆ **je le ferai ~ tout** I'll do it all the same *ou* come what may

◆ **malgré que** (* = *bien que*) in spite of the fact that, despite the fact that, although

malhabile /malabil/ ADJ clumsy, awkward ◆ **~ à (faire) qch** unskilful *ou* bad at (doing) sth

malheur /malœʀ/ NM 1 (= *événement pénible*) misfortune; (= *événement très grave*) calamity; (= *épreuve*) ordeal, hardship; (= *accident*) accident, mishap ◆ **il a supporté ses ~s sans se plaindre** he suffered his misfortunes without complaint ◆ **cette famille a eu beaucoup de ~s** this family has had a lot of misfortune ◆ **un ~ est si vite arrivé** accidents *ou* mishaps happen so easily ◆ **en cas de ~** in case anything should go wrong ◆ **cela a été le grand ~ de sa vie** it was the great tragedy of his life ◆ **ce n'est pas un gros ~ !, c'est un petit ~ !** it's not such a calamity! *ou* tragedy! *ou* disaster! ◆ **un ~ n'arrive jamais seul** (*Prov*) troubles never come singly it never rains but it pours (*Prov*) ◆ **à quelque chose ~ est bon** (*Prov*) every cloud has a silver lining (*Prov*) it's an ill wind that blows nobody any good (*Prov*)

2 ◆ **le ~** (= *l'adversité*) adversity; (= *la malchance*) ill luck, misfortune ◆ **dans son ~** amongst all his misfortune ◆ **ils ont eu le ~ de perdre leur mère** they had the misfortune to lose their mother ◆ **nos voisins sont dans le ~** our neighbours are going through hard times ◆ **le ~ des uns fait le bonheur des autres** (*Prov*) it's an ill wind that blows nobody any good (*Prov*) ◆ **le ~ a voulu qu'un policier le voie** as ill luck would have it a policeman saw him ◆ **c'est dans le ~ qu'on connaît ses amis** (*Prov*) a friend in need is a friend indeed (*Prov*) it's in times of trouble that you know who your real friends are

3 (*locutions*) **~ !** oh, lord! *, hell! * ◆ **le ~ c'est que ..., il n'y a qu'un ~, c'est que ...** the trouble *ou* snag is that ... ◆ **son ~, c'est qu'il boit** his trouble is that he drinks ◆ **le ~ dans tout cela, c'est qu'elle a perdu tout son argent** the sad thing about it *ou* the tragedy is that she lost all her money ◆ **faire le ~ de ses parents** to bring sorrow to one's parents, to cause one's parents nothing but unhappiness ◆ **faire un ~** (= *avoir un gros succès*) [*spectacle*] to be a big hit; [*artiste, joueur*] to make a great hit, to be all the rage ◆ **s'il continue à m'ennuyer, je fais un ~** * if he carries on annoying me I'll do something I'll regret ◆ **quel ~ qu'il ne soit pas venu** what a shame *ou* pity he didn't come ◆ **il a eu le ~ de dire que cela ne lui plaisait pas** he made the big mistake of saying he didn't like it ◆ **pour son ~** for his sins ◆ **ne parle pas de ~ !** God forbid!

♦ **de malheur*** *(= maudit)* wretched ♦ **cette pluie de ~ a tout gâché** this wretched rain has spoilt everything
♦ **malheur à** ♦ **~ à l'homme** *ou* **à celui par qui le scandale arrive** *(Bible)* woe to that man by whom the offence cometh ♦ **~ à (celui) qui ...** † woe betide him who ... ♦ **~ à toi si tu y touches !** woe betide you if you touch it!
♦ **par malheur** unfortunately, as ill luck would have it

malheureusement /maløʀøzmɑ̃/ GRAMMAIRE ACTIVE 29.3, 39.2, 47.4, 52.5, 52.6 ADV unfortunately

malheureux, -euse /maløʀø, øz/ ADJ 1 *(= infortuné)* unfortunate ♦ **les malheureuses victimes des bombardements** the unfortunate *ou* hapless *(frm)* victims of the bombings
2 *(= regrettable, fâcheux) [résultat, jour, geste]* unfortunate ♦ **pour un mot ~** because of an unfortunate remark ♦ **c'est bien ~ qu'il ne puisse pas venir** it's very unfortunate *ou* it's a great shame *ou* it's a great pity that he can't come ♦ **si c'est pas ~ d'entendre ça !*** it makes you sick to hear that!* ♦ **ah te voilà enfin, c'est pas ~ !*** oh, there you are at last and about time too!*
3 *(= triste, qui souffre) [enfant, vie]* unhappy, miserable ♦ **on a été très ~ pendant la guerre** we had a miserable life during the war ♦ **il était très ~ de ne pouvoir nous aider** he was most distressed *ou* upset at not being able to help us ♦ **prendre un air ~** to look unhappy *ou* distressed ♦ **rendre qn ~** to make sb unhappy ♦ **être ~ comme les pierres** to be wretchedly unhappy *ou* utterly wretched
4 *(après n = malchanceux) [candidat]* unsuccessful, unlucky; *[tentative]* unsuccessful; *[expérience]* unfortunate ♦ **il prit une initiative malheureuse** he took an unfortunate step ♦ **Leblanc, héros ~ de ce championnat** Leblanc, the heroic loser of the championship ♦ **être ~ au jeu/en amour** to be unlucky at gambling/in love ♦ **amour ~** unhappy love affair; → **heureux, main**
5 *(* : avant n = insignifiant)* wretched, miserable ♦ **toute une histoire pour un ~ billet de 20 €/pour une malheureuse erreur** such a to-do for a wretched *ou* measly* *ou* mouldy* 20-euro note/for a miserable mistake ♦ **il y avait deux ou trois ~ spectateurs** there was a miserable handful of spectators ♦ **sans même un ~ coup de fil** without so much as a phone call
NM,F *(= infortuné)* poor wretch *ou* soul *ou* devil*; *(= indigent)* needy person ♦ **il a tout perdu ? le ~ !** did he lose everything? the poor man! ♦ **un ~ de plus** another poor devil* ♦ **ne fais pas cela, ~ !** don't do that, you fool! ♦ **aider les ~** *(indigents)* to help the needy *ou* those who are badly off ♦ **la malheureuse a agonisé pendant des heures** the poor woman suffered for hours before she died

malhonnête /malɔnɛt/ ADJ 1 *(= déloyal)* dishonest; *(= crapuleux)* crooked 2 *(† = indécent)* rude NMF *(= personne déloyale)* dishonest person; *(= escroc)* crook

malhonnêtement /malɔnɛtmɑ̃/ ADV dishonestly

malhonnêteté /malɔnɛtte/ NF 1 *(= improbité)* dishonesty, crookedness ♦ **faire des ~s** to carry on dishonest *ou* crooked dealings 2 *(† = manque de politesse)* rudeness ♦ **dire des ~s** to make rude remarks, to say rude things

Mali /mali/ NM Mali

malice /malis/ NF 1 *(= espièglerie)* mischievousness ♦ **réponse pleine de ~** mischievous reply ♦ **... dit-il non sans ~** ... he said somewhat mischievously ♦ **boîte/sac à ~** box/bag of tricks 2 *(= méchanceté)* malice, spite ♦ **par ~** out of malice *ou* spite ♦ **elle a dit ça sans ~** she meant no harm by it ♦ **il est sans ~** he is quite guileless ♦ **il n'y voit ou entend pas ~** he means no harm by it

malicieusement /malisjøzmɑ̃/ ADV mischievously

malicieux, -ieuse /malisjø, jøz/ ADJ *[personne, remarque]* mischievous; *[sourire]* mischievous, impish ♦ **notre oncle est très ~** our uncle is a great tease ♦ **petit ~ !** little imp *ou* monkey!

> ⚠ Évitez de traduire **malicieux** par **malicious**, qui a le sens de 'malveillant'.

malien, -enne /maljɛ̃, ɛn/ ADJ of *ou* from Mali, Malian NM,F **Malien(ne)** Malian

maligne /maliɲ/ ADJ F, NF → **malin**

malignité /maliɲite/ NF 1 *(= malveillance)* malice, spite 2 *(Méd)* malignancy

malin, maligne *ou* **maline*** /malɛ̃, maliɲ, malin/ ADJ 1 *(= intelligent) [personne, air]* smart, shrewd, cunning ♦ **sourire ~** cunning *ou* knowing *ou* crafty smile ♦ **il est ~ comme un singe** *[adulte]* he's a crafty old devil*; *[enfant]* he's a crafty little devil* ♦ **bien ~ qui le dira !** who can tell! ♦ **il n'est pas bien ~** he isn't very bright *ou* clever ♦ **c'est ~ !** *(iro)* oh, very clever! *(iro)* ♦ **si tu te crois ~ de faire ça !** I suppose you think that's clever?; → **jouer**
2 *(† * = difficile)* **ce n'est pourtant pas bien ~** but it isn't so difficult *ou* tricky ♦ **ce n'est pas plus ~ que ça** it's as easy *ou* simple as that, that's all there is to it
3 *(= mauvais) [influence]* malignant, baleful, malicious ♦ **prendre un ~ plaisir à faire qch** to take (a) malicious pleasure in doing sth ♦ **l'esprit ~** the devil
4 *(Méd)* malignant
NM,F ♦ **c'est un (petit) ~** he's a crafty one, he knows a thing or two, there are no flies on him *(Brit)* ♦ **gros ~ !** *(iro)* you're a bright one! *(iro)* ♦ **ne fais pas ton** *ou* **le ~** * don't try to show off ♦ **à ~, ~ et demi** there's always someone cleverer than you
NM ♦ **le Malin** the Devil

malingre /malɛ̃gʀ/ ADJ *[personne]* sickly, puny; *[corps]* puny

malinois /malinwa/ NM police dog, ≃ German Shepherd, Alsatian *(Brit)*

malintentionné, e /malɛ̃tɑ̃sjɔne/ ADJ ill-intentioned, malicious, spiteful *(envers* towards)

malle /mal/ NF 1 *(= valise)* trunk ♦ **faire sa ~** *ou* **ses ~s** to pack one's trunk ♦ **ils se sont fait la ~*** they've cleared off*, they've done a bunk* *(Brit)* *ou* a runner* *(Brit)* ♦ **on a intérêt à se faire la ~*** we'd better make ourselves scarce*, we'd better scarper* *(Brit)* 2 *[de voiture]* **~ (arrière)** boot *(Brit)*, trunk *(US)* 3 *(Hist)* **la Malle des Indes** the Indian Mail

malléabilité /maleabilite/ NF malleability

malléable /maleabl/ ADJ malleable

malle-poste (pl **malles-poste**) /malpɔst/ NF *(Hist = diligence)* mail coach

mallette /malɛt/ NF 1 *(= valise)* (small) suitcase; *(= porte-documents)* briefcase, attaché case ♦ **~ de voyage** overnight case, grip 2 *(Belg = cartable)* schoolbag, satchel

mal-logé, e /mallɔʒe/ NM,F *person living in substandard housing*

mal-logement /mallɔʒmɑ̃/ NM poor housing

malmener /malməne/ ► conjug 5 ◄ VT *(= brutaliser) [+ personne]* to manhandle, to handle roughly; *(Mil, Sport) [+ adversaire]* to give a rough time *ou* handling to ♦ **être malmené par la critique** to be given a rough ride by the critics

malnutrition /malnytʀisjɔ̃/ NF malnutrition

malodorant, e /malɔdɔʀɑ̃, ɑ̃t/ ADJ *[personne, pièce]* foul-smelling, malodorous *(frm)*, smelly; *[haleine]* bad, foul *(Brit)*

malotru, e /malɔtʀy/ NM,F lout, yob* *(Brit)*

malouin, e /malwɛ̃, in/ ADJ of *ou* from Saint-Malo NM,F **Malouin(e)** inhabitant *ou* native of Saint-Malo NFPL **Malouines** ♦ **les (îles) Malouines** the Falkland Islands, the Falklands

mal-pensant, e (mpl **mal-pensants**) /malpɑ̃sɑ̃, ɑ̃t/ ADJ malicious NM,F malicious person

malpoli, e /malpɔli/ ADJ impolite, discourteous

malpropre /malpʀɔpʀ/ ADJ 1 *(= sale) [personne, objet]* dirty; *[travail]* slovenly 2 *(= indécent) [allusion, histoire]* smutty, dirty, unsavoury 3 *(= indélicat) [conduite, personne, action]* unsavoury, dishonest, despicable NMF *(hum)* swine ♦ **se faire chasser comme un ~*** to be thrown *ou* kicked* out

malproprement /malpʀɔpʀəmɑ̃/ ADV in a dirty way ♦ **manger ~** to be a messy eater

malpropreté /malpʀɔpʀəte/ NF 1 ♦ **la ~** dirtiness, griminess 2 *(= acte)* despicable trick; *(= parole)* low *ou* unsavoury remark

malsain, e /malsɛ̃, ɛn/ ADJ 1 *[climat, logement]* unhealthy; *[travail]* hazardous to one's health 2 *[influence, littérature, curiosité]* unhealthy, unwholesome; *[esprit, mentalité]* nasty, unhealthy ♦ **il a une relation ~e avec l'argent** he has an unhealthy relationship with money ♦ **c'est un film ~** it's a pretty sick film ♦ **le climat ~ qui règne dans certaines entreprises** the unsavoury *ou* unwholesome atmosphere in some companies ♦ **l'atmosphère devient ~e au bureau** things are getting a bit unpleasant at work ♦ **tous ces monopoles, c'est ~ pour l'économie** all these monopolies are bad for the economy ♦ **sauvons-nous, ça devient ~** *(dangereux)* let's get out of here, things are looking a bit dangerous *ou* dodgy* *(Brit)* ♦ **c'est quelqu'un de ~** he's an unsavoury character

malséant, e /malseɑ̃, ɑ̃t/ ADJ *(littér)* unseemly, unbecoming, improper

malsonnant, e /malsɔnɑ̃, ɑ̃t/ ADJ *(littér) [propos]* offensive

malt /malt/ NM malt ♦ **whisky pur ~** malt (whisky)

maltage /maltaʒ/ NM malting

maltais, e /maltɛ, ɛz/ ADJ Maltese ♦ **(orange) ~e** *type of juicy orange* NM *(= langue)* Maltese NM,F **Maltais(e)** Maltese

maltase /maltɑz/ NF maltase

Malte /malt/ NF Malta

malter /malte/ ► conjug 1 ◄ VT to malt

malthusianisme /maltyzjanism/ NM Malthusianism ♦ **~ économique** Malthusian economics *(sg)*

malthusien, -ienne /maltyzjɛ̃, jɛn/ ADJ *(Écon, Sociol)* Malthusian NM,F Malthusian

maltose /maltoz/ NM maltose, malt sugar

maltraitance /maltʀɛtɑ̃s/ NF ♦ **~ d'enfants** *ou* **à enfants** ill-treatment of children; *(sexuelle)* child abuse

maltraitant, e /maltʀɛtɑ̃, ɑ̃t/ ADJ *[famille, parent]* abusive

maltraiter /maltʀete/ ► conjug 1 ◄ VT 1 *(= brutaliser)* to manhandle, to handle roughly, to ill-treat; *[+ enfant]* to abuse 2 *(= mal user de) [+ langue, grammaire]* to misuse 3 *(= critiquer) [+ œuvre, auteur]* to give a rough ride to

malus /malys/ NM (car insurance) surcharge

malveillance /malvɛjɑ̃s/ NF *(= méchanceté)* spite, malevolence; *(= désobligeance)* ill will *(pour, envers* towards) ♦ **avoir agi sans ~** *(Jur)* to have acted without malicious intent ♦ **acte de ~** spiteful *ou* malevolent action ♦ **propos dus à**

la ~ publique spiteful *ou* malicious public rumour ◆ **regarder qn avec ~** to look at sb malevolently ◆ **je dis cela sans ~ à son égard** I say that without wishing to be spiteful to him ◆ **c'est par pure ~ qu'il a agi ainsi** he did that out of sheer spite *ou* malevolence

malveillant, e /malvɛjɑ̃, ɑ̃t/ ADJ *[personne, regard, remarque]* malevolent, malicious, spiteful

malvenu, e /malvəny/ ADJ *(= déplacé)* out of place *(attrib)*, out-of-place *(épith)*; *(= mal développé)* malformed; → **venu**

malversation /malvɛʀsasjɔ̃/ NF *(gén pl)* embezzlement *(NonC)*, misappropriation of funds

mal-vivre /malvivʀ/ NM INV malaise

malvoisie /malvwazi/ NM *(= vin)* malmsey (wine); *(= cépage)* malvasia

malvoyant, e /malvwajɑ̃, ɑ̃t/ NM,F person who is partially sighted ◆ **les ~s** the partially sighted

maman /mamɑ̃/ NF mother, mum* *(Brit)*, mummy* *(Brit)*, mom* *(US)*, mommy* *(US)* ◆ **les ~s qui viennent chercher leurs enfants** mums* *(Brit) ou* moms* *(US)* coming to pick their kids up; → **futur**

mambo /mɑ̃(m)bo/ NM mambo

mamelle /mamɛl/ NF 1 *[d'animal]* teat; *(= pis)* udder, dug 2 † *[de femme]* breast; *(péj)* tit*; *[d'homme]* breast ◆ **à la ~** at the breast

mamelon /mam(ə)lɔ̃/ NM 1 *(Anat)* nipple 2 *(Géog)* knoll, hillock

mamelu, e /mam(ə)ly/ ADJ *(péj ou hum)* big-breasted, well-endowed *(hum)*

mamel(o)uk /mamluk/ NM Mameluke

mamie¹ /mami/ NF *(langage enfantin = grand-mère)* granny*, gran*

mamie² ††, **m'amie** /mami/ NF ⇒ **ma mie**; → **mie²**

mammaire /mamɛʀ/ ADJ *[glande]* mammary

mammectomie /mamɛktɔmi/ NF mastectomy

mammifère /mamifɛʀ/ NM mammal ◆ **les ~s** mammals ADJ mammalian

mammographie /mamɔgʀafi/ NF mammography

Mammon /mamɔ̃/ NM Mammon

mammouth /mamut/ NM mammoth

mammy /mami/ NF ⇒ **mamie¹**

mamours* /mamuʀ/ NMPL *(hum)* ◆ **faire des ~ à qn** to caress *ou* fondle sb ◆ **se faire des ~** to bill and coo

mam'selle*, **mam'zelle*** /mamzɛl/ NF abrév de **mademoiselle**

Man /mɑ̃/ NF ◆ **l'île de ~** the Isle of Man

manade /manad/ NF *(en Provence) [de taureaux]* herd of bulls; *[de chevaux]* herd of horses

management /manaʒmɑ̃, manadʒmɛnt/ NM management

manager¹ /manadʒɛʀ/ NM *(Écon, Sport)* manager; *(Théât)* agent

manager² /mana(d)ʒe/ ▸ conjug 3 ◂ VT to manage

managérial, e (mpl **-iaux**) /manaʒeʀjal, jo/ ADJ *[pratique]* managerial ◆ **équipe ~e** management team

Managua /managwa/ N Managua

Manama /manama/ N Manama

manant /manɑ̃/ NM 1 († , *littér*) churl † 2 *(Hist) (= villageois)* yokel; *(= vilain)* villein

Manche /mɑ̃ʃ/ NF ◆ **la ~** *(= mer)* the English Channel; *(= département français)* the Manche; *(= région d'Espagne)* la Mancha ◆ **des deux côtés/de l'autre côté de la ~** on both sides of/across the Channel

manche¹ /mɑ̃ʃ/ NF 1 *(Habillement)* sleeve ◆ **à ~s courtes/longues** short-/long-sleeved ◆ **sans ~s** sleeveless ◆ **se mettre en ~s** to roll up one's sleeves ◆ **avoir qn dans sa ~** † to be well in with sb* ◆ **relever** *ou* **retrousser ses ~s** *(lit, fig)* to roll up one's sleeves ◆ **faire la ~*** *[mendiant]* to beg; *[artiste]* to perform in the streets, to busk *(Brit)*; → **chemise, effet, paire²**
2 *(= partie) (gén, Pol, Sport)* round; *(Bridge)* game; *(Tennis)* set ◆ **~ décisive** tiebreak(er) ◆ **on a gagné la première ~** *(fig)* we've won the first round in the battle
3 *[de ballon]* neck
COMP **manche à air** *(Aviation)* wind sock
manche ballon puff sleeve
manche à crevés slashed sleeve
manche gigot leg-of-mutton sleeve
manche kimono kimono *ou* loose sleeve
manche montée set-in sleeve
manche raglan raglan sleeve
manche trois-quarts three-quarter sleeve
manche à vent airshaft

manche² /mɑ̃ʃ/ NM 1 *(gén)* handle; *(long)* shaft; *(Mus)* neck ◆ **être du côté du ~*** to be on the winning side ◆ **se mettre du côté du ~*** to side with the winner ◆ **jeter le ~ après la cognée** to throw in one's hand ◆ **il ne faut pas jeter le ~ après la cognée !** don't give up so easily!; → **branler**
2 (* = *incapable*) clumsy fool *ou* oaf, clot *(Brit)* ◆ **conduire comme un ~** to be a hopeless *ou* rotten* driver ◆ **tu t'y prends comme un ~ !** you're making a real mess* *ou* a hash* of it!
COMP **manche à balai** *(gén)* broomstick, broomshaft *(Brit)*; *(= manette de contrôle)* joystick
manche à gigot leg-of-mutton holder
manche de gigot knuckle (of a leg-of-mutton)

mancheron¹ /mɑ̃ʃʀɔ̃/ NM *[de vêtement]* short sleeve

mancheron² /mɑ̃ʃʀɔ̃/ NM *[de charrue]* handle

manchette /mɑ̃ʃɛt/ NF 1 *[de chemise]* cuff; *(protectrice)* oversleeve 2 *(Presse = titre)* headline ◆ **mettre en ~** to headline, to put in headlines 3 *(= note)* marginal note ◆ **en ~** in the margin 4 *(= coup)* forearm blow

manchon /mɑ̃ʃɔ̃/ NM 1 *(Habillement) (pour les mains)* muff; *(= guêtre)* snow gaiter; → **chien** 2 *(Tech) [de tuyau]* coupler ◆ **~ à incandescence** incandescent (gas) mantle 3 *(Culin)* wing ◆ **~s de canard** duck wings

manchot, e /mɑ̃ʃo, ɔt/ ADJ *(d'un bras)* one-armed; *(des deux bras)* armless; *(d'une main)* one-handed; *(des deux mains)* with no hands, handless ◆ **être ~ du bras droit/gauche** to have the use of only one's left/right arm ◆ **il n'est pas ~ !*** *(adroit)* he's clever *ou* he's no fool with his hands!; *(courageux)* he's no lazybones!* NM,F *(d'un bras)* one-armed person; *(des deux bras)* person with no arms NM *(= oiseau)* penguin ◆ **~ royal/empereur** king/emperor penguin

mandala /mɑ̃dala/ NM mandala

mandale* /mɑ̃dal/ NF biff*, cuff, clout *(Brit)*

mandant, e /mɑ̃dɑ̃, ɑ̃t/ NM,F *(Jur)* principal ◆ **je parle au nom de mes ~s** *(frm : Pol)* I speak on behalf of my constituents

mandarin /mɑ̃daʀɛ̃/ NM *(Hist, péj)* mandarin; *(= langue)* Mandarin (Chinese); *(= canard)* mandarin duck

mandarinal, e (mpl **-aux**) /mɑ̃daʀinal, o/ ADJ mandarin

mandarinat /mɑ̃daʀina/ NM *(Hist)* mandarinate; *(péj)* academic establishment *(péj)*

mandarine /mɑ̃daʀin/ NF mandarin (orange), tangerine ADJ INV tangerine

mandarinier /mɑ̃daʀinje/ NM mandarin (orange) tree

mandat /mɑ̃da/ NM 1 *(gén, Pol)* mandate ◆ **donner à qn ~ de faire** to mandate sb to do, to give sb a mandate to do ◆ **obtenir le renouvellement de son ~** to be re-elected, to have one's mandate renewed ◆ **la durée du ~ présidentiel** the president's term of office ◆ **territoires sous ~** mandated territories, territories under mandate 2 **~ (postal)** money order, postal order *(Brit)* 3 *(Jur = procuration)* power of attorney, proxy; *(Police)* warrant
COMP **mandat d'amener** ≃ summons
mandat d'arrêt *(Jur)* ≃ warrant for arrest
mandat de comparution ≃ summons (to appear), subpoena
mandat de dépôt ≃ committal order ◆ **placer qn sous ~ de dépôt** ≃ to place sb under a committal order
mandat d'expulsion eviction order
mandat international *(Fin)* international money order
mandat de perquisition search warrant

mandataire /mɑ̃datɛʀ/ NMF *(Jur)* proxy, attorney; *(= représentant)* representative ◆ **je ne suis que son ~** I'm only acting as a proxy for him ◆ **~ aux Halles** (sales) agent (at the Halles)

mandat-carte (pl **mandats-cartes**) /mɑ̃dakaʀt/ NM money *ou* postal *(Brit)* order *(in postcard form)*

mandatement /mɑ̃datmɑ̃/ NM 1 *[de somme]* payment (by money order) 2 *[de personne]* appointment, commissioning

mandater /mɑ̃date/ ▸ conjug 1 ◂ VT 1 *(= donner pouvoir à) [+ personne]* to appoint, to commission; *(Pol) [+ député]* to give a mandate to, to elect 2 *(Fin)* **~ une somme** *(= écrire)* to write out a money order for a sum; *(= payer)* to pay a sum by money order

mandat-lettre (pl **mandats-lettres**) /mɑ̃dalɛtʀ/ NM money *ou* postal *(Brit)* order *(with space for correspondence)*

mandchou, e /mɑ̃tʃu/ ADJ Manchu(rian) NM *(= langue)* Manchu NM,F **Mandchou(e)** Manchu

Mandchourie /mɑ̃tʃuʀi/ NF Manchuria

mandement /mɑ̃dmɑ̃/ NM 1 *(Rel)* pastoral 2 *(Hist = ordre)* mandate, command; *(Jur = convocation)* subpoena

mander /mɑ̃de/ ▸ conjug 1 ◂ VT 1 †† *(= ordonner)* to command; *(= convoquer)* to summon 2 *(littér = dire par lettre)* **~ qch à qn** to send *ou* convey the news of sth to sb, to inform sb of sth

mandibule /mɑ̃dibyl/ NF mandible ◆ **jouer des ~s*** to nosh* *(Brit)*, to chow down* *(US)*

mandoline /mɑ̃dɔlin/ NF mandolin(e)

mandragore /mɑ̃dʀagɔʀ/ NF mandrake

mandrill /mɑ̃dʀil/ NM mandrill

mandrin /mɑ̃dʀɛ̃/ NM *(pour serrer)* chuck; *(pour percer, emboutir)* punch; *(pour élargir, égaliser des trous)* drift; *[de tour]* mandrel

manducation /mɑ̃dykasjɔ̃/ NF manducation

manécanterie /manekɑ̃tʀi/ NF (parish) choir school

manège /manɛʒ/ NM 1 *[de fête foraine]* fairground attraction ◆ **~ (de chevaux de bois)** merry-go-round, roundabout *(Brit)*, carousel *(US)*; → **tour²** 2 *(Équitation = piste, salle)* ring, school ◆ **~ couvert** indoor school ◆ **faire du ~** to do exercises in the indoor school 3 *(péj) (= agissements)* game, ploy ◆ **j'ai deviné son petit ~** I guessed what he was up to, I saw through his little game

mânes /man/ NMPL *(Antiq Rel)* manes ◆ **les ~ de ses ancêtres** *(littér)* the shades of his ancestors *(littér)*

maneton /man(ə)tɔ̃/ NM *[de moteur]* clankpin

manette /manɛt/ NF lever ◆ ~ **des gaz** throttle lever ◆ ~ **de jeux** joystick ◆ **être aux** ~**s*** to be in charge; → **fond**

manga /mɑ̃ga/ NF manga

manganate /mɑ̃ganat/ NM manganate

manganèse /mɑ̃ganɛz/ NM manganese

mangeable /mɑ̃ʒabl/ ADJ edible

mangeaille /mɑ̃ʒɑj/ NF *(péj)* *(= nourriture mauvaise)* pigswill, disgusting food; *(= grande quantité de nourriture)* mounds of food ◆ **il nous venait des odeurs de** ~ we were met by an unappetizing smell of food (cooking)

mange-disques /mɑ̃ʒdisk/ NM INV slot-in record player *(for singles)*

mangeoire /mɑ̃ʒwaʀ/ NF *(gén)* trough, manger; *[d'oiseaux]* feeding dish

mangeotter* /mɑ̃ʒɔte/ ▸ conjug 1 ◂ VT to nibble

manger /mɑ̃ʒe/ ▸ conjug 3 ◂ VT 1 *(gén)* to eat; *[+ soupe]* to drink, to eat ◆ ~ **dans une assiette/dans un bol** to eat off *ou* from a plate/out of a bowl ◆ **il mange peu** he doesn't eat much ◆ **il ne mange pas** *ou* **rien en ce moment** he's off his food at present, he is not eating at all at present ◆ **ils ont mangé tout ce qu'elle avait (à la maison)** they ate her out of house and home ◆ **il a mangé tout ce qui restait** he has eaten (up) all that was left ◆ **ils leur ont fait** *ou* **donné à** ~ **un excellent poisson** they served *ou* gave them some excellent fish (to eat) ◆ **faire** ~ **qn** to feed sb ◆ **faire** ~ **qch à qn** to give sb sth to eat, to make sb eat sth ◆ **donner à** ~ **à un bébé/un animal** to feed a baby/an animal ◆ ~ **goulûment** to wolf down one's food, to eat greedily ◆ ~ **salement** to be a messy eater ◆ ~ **comme un cochon*** to eat like a pig* ◆ **finis de** ~ **!, mange !** eat up! ◆ **on mange bien/mal ici** the food is good/bad here ◆ **les enfants ne mangent pas à leur faim à l'école** the children don't get *ou* are not given enough to eat at school

2 *(= faire un repas)* ~ **dehors** *ou* **au restaurant** to eat out, to have a meal out ◆ **c'est l'heure de** ~ *(midi)* it's lunchtime; *(soir)* it's dinnertime ◆ **inviter qn à** ~ to invite sb for a meal ◆ **boire en mangeant** to drink with one's meal ◆ ~ **sur le pouce** to have a (quick) snack, to snatch a bite (to eat); → **carte**

3 *(fig)* ~ **qn des yeux** to gaze hungrily at sb, to devour sb with one's eyes ◆ ~ **qn de baisers** to smother sb with kisses ◆ **allez le voir, il ne vous mangera pas** go and see him, he won't eat you ◆ **il va te** ~ **tout cru** he'll have you for breakfast, he'll swallow you whole ◆ **se faire** ~ **par les moustiques** to get eaten alive *ou* bitten to death by mosquitoes

4 *(= ronger)* to eat (away) ◆ **mangé par les mites** *ou* **aux mites** moth-eaten ◆ **la grille (de fer) est mangée par la rouille** the (iron) railing is eaten away with *ou* by rust

5 *(= faire disparaître, consommer)* **toutes ces activités lui mangent son temps** all these activities take up his time ◆ ~ **ses mots** to swallow one's words ◆ **les grosses entreprises mangent les petites** the big firms swallow up the smaller ones ◆ **une barbe touffue lui mangeait le visage** his face was half hidden under a bushy beard ◆ **des yeux énormes lui mangeaient le visage** his face seemed to be just two great eyes

6 *(= dilapider) [+ fortune, capital, économies]* to go through, to squander ◆ **l'entreprise mange de l'argent** the business is eating money ◆ **dans cette affaire il mange de l'argent** he's spending more than he earns *ou* his outgoings are more than his income in this business

7 *(locutions)* ~ **la consigne** *ou* **la commission** to forget one's errand ◆ ~ **comme un oiseau** to eat like a bird ◆ ~ **le morceau**‡ *(= parler)* to spill the beans‡, to talk, to come clean* ◆ ~ **son pain blanc le premier** to have it easy at the start ◆ **je ne mange pas de ce pain-là !** I'm having nothing to do with that!, I'm not stooping to anything like that! ◆ **ça ne mange pas de pain !** it doesn't cost much!, you won't have to do much! ◆ ~ **son blé en herbe** to spend one's money in advance *ou* before one gets it, to eat one's seed corn *(US)* ◆ ~ **à tous les râteliers** to cash in* on all sides ◆ ~ **la soupe sur la tête de qn*** to tower over sb; → **laine, sang, vache** *etc*

VPR **se manger** 1 *[aliment]* **cela se mange ?** can you eat it?, is it edible? ◆ **ce plat se mange très chaud** this dish should be eaten piping hot

2 (‡ *= se heurter à*) **se** ~ **une porte (dans la figure)** to bash* into a door ◆ **je me suis mangé le trottoir** I banged my foot on the kerb

NM food ◆ **préparer le** ~ **des enfants*** to get the children's food *ou* meal ready ◆ **"ici on peut apporter son manger"*** "customers may consume their own food on the premises" ◆ **à prendre après** ~ to be taken after meals ◆ **je rentrerai avant** ~ I'll be back before lunch *(ou* dinner); → **perdre**

mange-tout /mɑ̃ʒtu/ NM INV ◆ **(pois)** ~ mangetout peas ◆ **(haricots)** ~ string beans

mangeur, -euse /mɑ̃ʒœʀ, øz/ NM,F eater ◆ **être gros** *ou* **grand/petit** ~ to be a big/small eater ◆ **c'est un gros** ~ **de pain** he eats a lot of bread, he's a big bread-eater* ◆ ~ **d'hommes** man-eater

manglier /mɑ̃glije/ NM mangrove tree

mangoustan /mɑ̃gustɑ̃/ NM mangosteen

mangouste /mɑ̃gust/ NF *(= animal)* mongoose; *(= fruit)* mangosteen

mangrove /mɑ̃gʀɔv/ NF mangrove swamp

mangue /mɑ̃g/ NF mango

manguier /mɑ̃gje/ NM mango(tree)

maniabilité /manjabilite/ NF *[d'objet]* handiness, manageability; *[de voiture]* driveability; *[d'avion, bateau]* manoeuvrability ◆ **appareil d'une grande** ~ implement which is very easy to handle, very handy implement ◆ **c'est un véhicule d'une étonnante** ~ this vehicle is incredibly easy to handle *ou* drive

maniable /manjabl/ ADJ 1 *[objet, taille]* handy, manageable, easy to handle *(attrib)*; *[véhicule]* easy to handle *ou* drive *(attrib)*; *[avion, bateau]* easy to manoeuvre *(attrib)* ◆ **peu** ~ *[objet]* awkward, cumbersome; *[véhicule]* difficult to handle 2 *(= influençable) [électeur]* easily swayed *ou* influenced *(attrib)* 3 *(= accommodant) [personne, caractère]* accommodating, amenable 4 *(Naut) [temps]* good; *[vent]* moderate

maniaco-dépressif, -ive (mpl **maniaco-dépressifs**) /manjakodepʀesif, iv/ ADJ, NM,F manic-depressive

maniaque /manjak/ ADJ *[personne]* finicky, fussy, pernickety ◆ **faire qch avec un soin** ~ to do sth with almost fanatical *ou* obsessive care NMF 1 *(= fou)* maniac, lunatic ◆ ~ **sexuel** sex maniac 2 *(= fanatique)* fanatic, enthusiast ◆ **quel** ~ **tu fais !** *(= méticuleux)* you're so fussy! ◆ **c'est un** ~ **de la propreté** he's fanatical about cleanliness, cleanliness is an obsession with him ◆ **c'est un** ~ **de l'exactitude** he's fanatical about punctuality, he's a stickler for punctuality ◆ **c'est un** ~ **de la voile** he's sailing mad* *ou* a sailing fanatic

maniaquerie /manjakʀi/ NF fussiness ◆ **il est d'une** ~ **!** he's so fussy!

manichéen, -enne /manikeɛ̃, ɛn/ ADJ, NM,F Manich(a)ean

manichéisme /manikeism/ NM *(Philos)* Manich(a)eism; *(péj)* over-simplification ◆ **il fait du** ~ *(fig)* he sees everything in black and white, everything is either good or bad to him

manichéiste /manikeist/ ADJ, NMF ⇒ **manichéen, -enne**

manie /mani/ NF 1 *(= habitude)* odd habit ◆ **elle est pleine de (petites)** ~**s** she's got all sorts of funny little ways *ou* habits ◆ **avoir ses petites** ~**s** to have one's little ways ◆ **mais quelle** ~ **tu as de te manger les ongles !** you've got a terrible habit of biting your nails! ◆ **elle a la** ~ **de tout nettoyer** she's a compulsive *ou* obsessive cleaner 2 *(= obsession)* mania ◆ ~ **de la persécution** *(Méd)* persecution mania *ou* complex

maniement /manimɑ̃/ NM 1 *(= manipulation)* handling ◆ **d'un** ~ **difficile** difficult to handle ◆ **ils apprennent le** ~ **du logiciel** they are learning how to use the software ◆ **le** ~ **de cet objet est pénible** this object is difficult to handle ◆ **il possède à fond le** ~ **de la langue** he has a very good mastery of the language 2 *(Mil)* ~ **d'armes** arms drill *(Brit)*, manual of arms *(US)*

manier /manje/ ▸ conjug 7 ◂ VT 1 *[+ objet, explosifs, armes, outil]* to handle; *[+ pâte]* to knead; *[+ logiciel]* to use ◆ ~ **l'aviron** to pull *ou* ply *(littér)* the oars ◆ ~ **de grosses sommes d'argent** to handle large sums of money ◆ **cheval/voiture facile à** ~ horse/car which is easy to handle ◆ **il sait** ~ **le pinceau, il manie le pinceau avec adresse** he knows how to handle a brush, he's a painter of some skill ◆ **savoir** ~ **la plume** to be a good writer ◆ **savoir** ~ **l'ironie** to make good use of irony ◆ **il manie très bien le français** he has good mastery of French, he speaks fluent French ◆ **ces chiffres doivent être maniés avec prudence** these figures must be used with caution 2 *[+ personne, foule]* to handle VPR **se manier** ⇒ **se magner**

manière /manjɛʀ/ NF 1 *(= façon)* way ◆ **sa** ~ **d'agir/de parler** the way he behaves/speaks ◆ **il le fera à sa** ~ he'll do it (in) his own way ◆ ~ **de vivre** way of life ◆ ~ **de voir (les choses)** outlook (on things) ◆ **c'est sa** ~ **d'être habituelle** that's just the way he is, that's just how he usually is ◆ **ce n'est pas la bonne** ~ **de s'y prendre** this is not the right *ou* best way to go about it ◆ **d'une** ~ **efficace** in an efficient way ◆ **de quelle** ~ **as-tu fait cela ?** how did you do that? ◆ **à la** ~ **d'un singe** like a monkey, as a monkey would do

2 *(= savoir-faire)* **avec les animaux/les enfants, il a la** ~ he's good with animals/children ◆ **c'est un Matisse dernière** ~ *(Art = style)* it's a late Matisse *ou* an example of Matisse's later work ◆ **dans la** ~ **classique** in the classical style ◆ **à la** ~ **de Racine** in the style of Racine ◆ **robe/examen nouvelle** ~ new-style *ou* new-look dress/exam ◆ **démocrate/directeur nouvelle** ~ new-style democrat/director

3 *(Gram)* **adverbe/complément de** ~ adverb/adjunct of manner

4 *(locutions)* **employer la** ~ **forte, user de la** ~ **forte** to use strong-arm methods *ou* tactics ◆ **il l'a giflé de belle** ~ **!** he gave him a sound *ou* good slap! ◆ **en** ~ **d'excuse** by way of (an) excuse ◆ **d'une** ~ **générale** generally speaking, as a general rule ◆ **de toute(s)** ~**(s)** in any case, at any rate, anyway ◆ **de cette** ~ (in) this way ◆ **de telle** ~ **que ...** in such a way that ... ◆ **d'une** ~ **ou d'une autre** somehow or other ◆ **d'une certaine** ~ in a way, in some ways ◆ **en quelque** ~ *(frm)* in a certain way ◆ **en aucune** ~, **d'aucune** ~ in no way, under no circumstances ◆ **je n'accepterai en aucune** ~ I shall not agree on any account ◆ **de** ~ **à faire** so as to do ◆ **de** ~ **(à ce) que nous arrivions à l'heure, de** ~ **à arriver à l'heure** so that we get there on time

5 († *= genre*) kind ◆ **une** ~ **de pastiche** a kind of pastiche ◆ **quelle** ~ **d'homme est-ce ?** what kind *ou* sort of a man is he?, what manner of man is he? †

NFPL **manières** manners ◆ **avoir de bonnes/mauvaises ~s** to have good/bad manners ◆ **apprendre les belles ~s** to learn good manners ◆ **il n'a pas de ~s, il est sans ~s** he has no manners ◆ **ce ne sont pas des ~s !** that's no way to behave! ◆ **en voilà des ~s !** what a way to behave! ◆ **je n'aime pas ces ~s !** I don't like this kind of behaviour! ◆ **faire des ~s** *(minauderies)* to be affected, to put on airs; *(chichis)* to make a fuss ◆ **ne fais pas de ~s avec nous** you needn't stand on ceremony with us

maniéré, e /manjeʀe/ ADJ 1 *(péj = affecté) [personne, style, voix]* affected 2 *(Art) [genre]* mannered ◆ **les tableaux très ~s de ce peintre** the mannered style of this painter's work

maniérisme /manjeʀism/ NM *(Art)* mannerism

maniériste /manjeʀist/ ADJ mannerist(ic) NMF mannerist

manieur, -ieuse /manjœʀ, jøz/ NM,F ◆ **~ d'argent** *ou* **de fonds** big businessman

manif* /manif/ NF (abrév de **manifestation**) demo*

manifestant, e /manifɛstɑ̃, ɑ̃t/ NM,F demonstrator, protester

manifestation /manifɛstasjɔ̃/ NF 1 *(Pol)* demonstration 2 *(= expression) [d'opinion, sentiment]* expression; *[de maladie] (= apparition)* appearance; *(= symptômes)* outward sign *ou* symptom ◆ **~ de mauvaise humeur** show of bad temper ◆ **~ de joie** demonstration *ou* expression of joy ◆ **accueillir qn avec de grandes ~s d'amitié** to greet sb with great demonstrations of friendship 3 *[de Dieu] (= vérité)* revelation 4 *(= réunion, fête)* event ◆ **~ artistique/culturelle/sportive** artistic/cultural/sporting event ◆ **le maire assistait à cette sympathique ~** the mayor was present at this happy gathering *ou* on this happy occasion

> ⚠ Au sens politique, et au sens de 'réunion' en général, **manifestation** ne se traduit pas par le mot anglais **manifestation**.

manifeste /manifɛst/ ADJ *[vérité, injustice]* manifest, obvious, evident; *[sentiment, différence]* obvious, evident ◆ **erreur ~** glaring error ◆ **il est ~ que ...** it is quite obvious *ou* evident that ... NM *(Littérat, Pol)* manifesto; *(= document de bord)* manifest

manifestement /manifɛstəmɑ̃/ ADV obviously, manifestly *(frm)* ◆ **~, ça n'a servi à rien** it was obviously a waste of time ◆ **il est ~ ivre** he's obviously drunk ◆ **c'est fini ? – ~** is it finished? – apparently

manifester /manifɛste/ ▸ conjug 1 ◂ VT *[+ opinion, intention, sentiment]* to show, to indicate; *[+ courage]* to show, to demonstrate ◆ **il m'a manifesté son désir de venir** he indicated to me that he wanted to come ◆ **par ce geste, la France tient à nous ~ son amitié** *(frm)* France intends this gesture as a demonstration *ou* an indication of her friendship towards us

VI *(Pol)* to demonstrate, to hold a demonstration

VPR **se manifester** 1 *(= se révéler) [émotion]* to express itself; *[difficultés]* to emerge, to arise; *[phénomène]* to be apparent ◆ **sa frustration se manifeste par des crises de colère** his frustration expresses *ou* manifests itself in angry outbursts ◆ **cette maladie se manifeste par des boutons** the appearance of a rash is the first symptom of this disease *ou* indicates the onset of this disease ◆ **la crise se manifeste par l'effondrement des marchés** the crisis is reflected in the collapse of the markets ◆ **la violence se manifeste à différents niveaux de la société** violence occurs at various levels of society ◆ **Dieu s'est manifesté aux hommes** God revealed himself to mankind

2 *(= se présenter) [personne]* to appear, to turn up; *(par écrit, par téléphone)* to get in touch *ou* contact; *[bénévole, candidat, témoin]* to come forward

3 *(= intervenir) [élève]* to participate (in class) ◆ **il n'a pas eu l'occasion de se ~ dans le débat** he didn't get a chance to make himself heard in the discussion ◆ **il s'est manifesté par une déclaration fracassante** he came to public notice *ou* he attracted attention with a sensational statement

manigance /manigɑ̃s/ NF *(gén pl)* scheme, trick, ploy ◆ **encore une de ses ~s** another of his little schemes *ou* tricks *ou* ploys

manigancer /manigɑ̃se/ ▸ conjug 3 ◂ VT to plot, to devise ◆ **qu'est-ce qu'il manigance maintenant ?** what's he up to now?, what's his latest little scheme? ◆ **c'est lui qui a tout manigancé** he set the whole thing up*, he engineered it all

manille¹ /manij/ NM Manila cigar N **Manille** Manila

manille² /manij/ NF 1 *(Cartes) (= jeu)* manille; *(= dix)* ten 2 *(Tech)* shackle

manillon /manijɔ̃/ NM ace *(in game of manille)*

manioc /manjɔk/ NM manioc, cassava

manip* /manip/ NF abrév de **manipulation**

manipulateur, -trice /manipylatœʀ, tʀis/ ADJ 1 *(péj) [personne]* manipulative 2 *(Tech)* **bras ~** manipulator arm NM,F 1 *(= technicien)* technician ◆ **~ de laboratoire** laboratory technician ◆ **~ radio** radiographer 2 *(péj)* manipulator 3 *(= prestidigitateur)* conjurer NM *(Téléc)* key

manipulation /manipylasjɔ̃/ NF 1 *(= maniement)* handling ◆ **ces produits chimiques sont d'une ~ délicate** these chemicals should be handled with great care, great care should be taken in handling these chemicals 2 *(Sci)* experiment ◆ **obtenu par ~ génétique** genetically engineered ◆ **les ~s génétiques posent des problèmes éthiques** genetic engineering poses ethical problems 3 *(péj)* manipulation *(NonC)* ◆ **il y a eu des ~s électorales** there's been some vote-rigging 4 *(= prestidigitation)* sleight of hand 5 *(Méd) [d'os]* manipulation

manipule /manipyl/ NM *(Antiq, Rel)* maniple

manipuler /manipyle/ ▸ conjug 1 ◂ VT 1 *[+ objet, produit]* to handle 2 *(péj) [+ électeurs, presse, information]* to manipulate; *[+ statistiques]* to massage, to doctor ◆ **~ une élection** to rig an election ◆ **~ les écritures** to rig *ou* fiddle* *(Brit)* the accounts, to cook the books* *(Brit)*

manique /manik/ NF *[d'ouvrier]* protective glove; *[de cuisinier]* oven glove

Manitoba /manitɔba/ NM Manitoba

manitou /manitu/ NM 1 ◆ **grand ~** * big shot*, big noise* *(Brit)* ◆ **le grand ~ de l'entreprise** the big boss* in the company 2 *(Rel)* manitou

manivelle /manivɛl/ NF *(gén)* handle; *(Aut) (pour changer une roue)* wheel crank; *(pour démarrer)* crank, starting handle ◆ **faire partir à la ~** to crank(-start); → **retour, tour²**

manne /man/ NF 1 *(Rel)* **la ~** manna ◆ **recevoir la ~ (céleste)** *(la bonne parole)* to receive the word from on high 2 *(= aubaine)* godsend, manna ◆ **ça a été pour nous une ~ (providentielle** *ou* **céleste)** that was a godsend for us, it was heaven-sent 3 *(Bot)* manna 4 *(= panier)* large wicker basket

mannequin /mankɛ̃/ NM 1 *(= personne)* model, mannequin † ◆ **être ~ chez ...** to model for ...; → **défilé, taille¹** 2 *(= objet) [de couturière]* (tailor's) dummy, mannequin; *[de vitrine]* model, dummy; *[de peintre]* model; *(= pantin)* stuffed dummy 3 *(= panier)* small (gardener's) basket

manœuvrabilité /manœvʀabilite/ NF manoeuvrability

manœuvrable /manœvʀabl/ ADJ manoeuvrable, easy to handle

manœuvre /manœvʀ/ NF 1 *(= opération)* manoeuvre *(Brit)*, maneuver *(US)*, operation ◆ **~ (d'aiguillage)** *(Rail)* shunting *(NonC) (Brit)*, switching *(NonC) (US)* ◆ **diriger/surveiller la ~** to control/supervise the operation *ou* manoeuvre ◆ **faire une ~** *(en voiture, en bateau)* to do a manoeuvre ◆ **je ne sais pas faire les ~s** *(en voiture)* I'm not good at parking *(ou* reversing *etc)* ◆ **les ~s sont difficiles par gros temps** *(Naut)* it's difficult to manoeuvre (the boat) in bad weather ◆ **il voulait se garer mais il a manqué sa ~** he tried to park but he got the angle wrong ◆ **fausse ~** *(lit)* mistake; *(fig)* wrong *ou* false move ◆ **une fausse ~ et il perd les élections** if he puts one foot wrong *ou* makes one wrong move he'll lose the election ◆ **faire la ~** *(Rail)* to shunt

2 *(Mil)* manoeuvre *(Brit)*, maneuver *(US)* ◆ **champ** *ou* **terrain de ~s** parade ground ◆ **~ d'encerclement** encircling movement ◆ **les grandes ~s de printemps** spring army manoeuvres *ou* exercises ◆ **être en ~s, faire des ~s** to be on manoeuvres

3 *(= agissements, combinaison)* manoeuvre *(Brit)*, maneuver *(US)*; *(= machination, intrigue)* manoeuvring, ploy ◆ **il a toute liberté de ~** he has complete freedom of manoeuvre ◆ **~ de diversion** diversionary tactic ◆ **~s électorales** vote-catching ploys ◆ **~s frauduleuses** fraudulent schemes *ou* devices ◆ **~ d'obstruction** obstructive move ◆ **~ boursière** stock-market manipulation ◆ **les grandes ~s politiques** intense political manoeuvring

4 *(Naut)* **~s dormantes/courantes** *(= cordages)* standing/running rigging

NM *(gén)* labourer; *(en usine)* unskilled worker ◆ **c'est un travail de ~** it's unskilled labour *ou* work ◆ **~ agricole** farm labourer *ou* hand

manœuvrer /manœvʀe/ ▸ conjug 1 ◂ VT 1 *[+ véhicule]* to manoeuvre *(Brit)*, to maneuver *(US)*; *[+ machine]* to operate, to work 2 *(= manipuler) [+ personne]* to manipulate ◆ **il se laisse ~ par sa femme** he allows himself to be manipulated by his wife VI *(gén)* to manoeuvre ◆ **il a manœuvré habilement** *(fig)* he moved *ou* manoeuvred skilfully

manœuvrier, -ière /manœvʀije, ijɛʀ/ ADJ manoeuvring NM,F *(Mil)* tactician; *(Pol)* manoeuvrer

manoir /manwaʀ/ NM manor *ou* country house

manomètre /manɔmɛtʀ/ NM gauge, manometer

manométrique /manɔmetʀik/ ADJ manometric

manouche* /manuʃ/ NMF gipsy

manouvrier, -ière † /manuvʀije, ijɛʀ/ NM,F (casual) labourer

manquant, e /mɑ̃kɑ̃, ɑ̃t/ ADJ missing; → **chaînon** NM,F missing one

manque /mɑ̃k/ NM 1 ◆ **~ de** *(= pénurie) [+ nourriture, argent]* lack of, shortage of, want of; *(= faiblesse) [+ intelligence, goût]* lack of, want of ◆ **son ~ de sérieux au travail** his unreliability at work ◆ **par ~ de** through lack *ou* shortage of, for want of ◆ **quel ~ de chance !** *ou* **de pot !*** *ou* **de bol !*** what bad *ou* hard luck! ◆ **~ à gagner** loss of earnings ◆ **cela représente un sérieux ~ à gagner pour les cultivateurs** that means a serious loss of income *ou* a serious drop in earnings for the farmers ◆ **c'est un ~ de respect** it shows a lack of respect *(pour, à l'égard de* for) it's disrespectful *(pour, à l'égard de* to)

2 *(= vide)* gap, emptiness; *(Drogue)* withdrawal ◆ **je ressens comme un grand ~** it's as if there were a great emptiness inside me ◆ **un ~ que rien ne saurait combler** a gap which nothing could fill ◆ **symptômes de ~** with-

drawal symptoms ◆ **en (état de)** ~, **être en état de** ~ to be experiencing withdrawal symptoms

◆ **en manque de** ◆ **des hôpitaux en ~ de moyens** cash-starved hospitals ◆ **des enfants en ~ d'amour** children deprived of affection ◆ **il était en ~ d'inspiration** he had run out of inspiration

3 *(dans un tissu)* flaw ◆ **il faut faire un raccord (de peinture), il y a des ~s** we'll have to touch up the paintwork, there are bare patches

4 *(Roulette)* manque

NMPL **manques** *(= défauts) [de roman]* faults, flaws; *[de personne]* failings, shortcomings; *[de mémoire, connaissances]* gaps

LOC ADJ **à la manque** (*, *péj*) *[chanteur]* crummy*, second-rate ◆ **lui et ses idées à la ~** him and his half-baked* *ou* crummy* ideas

manqué, e /mɑ̃ke/ (ptp de **manquer**) ADJ 1 *[essai]* failed, abortive, missed; *[photo]* spoilt; *[vie]* wasted; *(Tech) [pièce]* faulty ◆ **occasion ~e** lost *ou* wasted opportunity ◆ **roman ~** flawed novel ◆ **c'est un écrivain ~** *(vocation ratée)* he should have been a writer; → **garçon, rendez-vous** 2 *(Culin)* **(gâteau) ~** ≈ sponge cake

manquement /mɑ̃kmɑ̃/ NM *(frm)* ◆ **~ à** *[+ discipline, règle]* breach of ◆ **~ au devoir** dereliction of duty ◆ **au moindre ~** at the slightest lapse ◆ **~ (à des obligations contractuelles)** *(Jur)* default ◆ **~ à une obligation de sécurité ou de prudence** ≈ negligence

manquer /mɑ̃ke/ GRAMMAIRE ACTIVE 37.1

► conjug 1 ◄

VT 1 *(= ne pas atteindre, saisir ou rencontrer) [+ but, occasion, personne, train]* to miss ◆ **la gare est sur la place, tu ne peux pas la ~** the station's right on the square, you can't miss it ◆ **~ une marche** to miss a step ◆ **il l'a manqué qn de peu** *(en lui tirant dessus)* he missed him by a fraction, he just missed him; *(à un rendez-vous)* he just missed him ◆ **je l'ai manqué de 5 minutes** I missed him by 5 minutes ◆ **c'est un film/une pièce à ne pas ~** this film/play is a must*, it's a film/play that's not to be missed ◆ **il ne faut pas ~ ça !** it's not to be missed! ◆ **il n'en manque jamais une !*** *(iro)* he puts his foot in it every time!* ◆ **vous n'avez rien manqué (en ne venant pas)** you didn't miss anything (by not coming) ◆ **je ne le manquerai pas** *(= je vais lui donner une leçon)* I won't let him get away with it; → **coche**

2 *(= ne pas réussir) [+ photo, gâteau]* to spoil, to make a mess of*, to botch*; *[+ examen]* to fail ◆ **il a manqué sa vie** he has wasted his life; → **coup**

3 *(= être absent de) (involontairement)* to be absent from, to miss; *(volontairement)* to miss, to skip ◆ **~ l'école** to be absent from *ou* miss school ◆ **il a manqué deux réunions** he missed two meetings

VI 1 *(= faire défaut)* to be lacking ◆ **l'argent/la nourriture vint à ~** money/food ran out *ou* ran short ◆ **les occasions ne manquent pas (de faire)** there is no shortage of *ou* there are endless opportunities (to do) ◆ **ici, les chats c'est pas ça qui manque*** there's no shortage of cats round here ◆ **les mots manquent pour décrire ...** no words can describe ... ◆ **ce qui lui manque, c'est l'imagination** what he lacks *ou* what he hasn't got is (the) imagination ◆ **les mots me manquent pour exprimer ...** I can't find the words to express ... ◆ **le temps me manque pour raconter la suite** I don't have (the) time to tell you the rest of the story ◆ **j'irais bien, ce n'est pas l'envie qui me** *ou* **m'en manque** I would like to go, it's not that I don't want to ◆ **le pied lui manqua** his foot slipped, he missed his footing ◆ **la voix lui manqua** words failed him, he stood speechless ◆ **un carreau manquait à la fenêtre** there was a pane missing in *ou* from the window ◆ **qu'est-ce qui manque à ton bonheur ?** *(hum)* is there something not to your liking?, what are you unhappy about? ◆ **il lui manque toujours dix-neuf sous pour faire un franc** *(hum)* he doesn't have two pennies to rub together

2 *(= être absent)* to be absent; *(= avoir disparu)* to be missing *(à* from); ◆ **il a souvent manqué l'an dernier** *(Scol)* he was often absent last year, he missed a lot of school last year ◆ **~ à l'appel** *(lit)* to be absent from roll call; *(fig)* to be missing ◆ **il ne manque pas un bouton de guêtre** *(fig)* everything's in apple-pie order, there's not a thing out of place

3 *(= échouer) [expérience]* to fail

4 *(= être dans le besoin)* **il a toujours peur de ~** he's always afraid of being hard up*

5 *(= se dérober)* **le sol a manqué sous ses pieds** the ground gave (way) beneath his feet

6 *(avec infin = faillir)* **il a manqué mourir** he nearly *ou* almost died ◆ **elle a manqué (de) se faire écraser** she nearly *ou* almost got run over

VT INDIR **manquer à** 1 *(= être regretté)* **il nous manque, sa présence nous manque** we miss him ◆ **la campagne me manque** I miss the country

2 *(= ne pas respecter)* **~ à ses promesses** to go back on one's promises, to fail to keep one's word ◆ **~ à tous les usages** to flout every convention ◆ **il manque à tous ses devoirs** he neglects all his duties ◆ **~ à son honneur/devoir** to fail in one's honour/duty ◆ **~ à qn** † *(= être impoli)* to be disrespectful to sb

VT INDIR **manquer de** 1 *(= être dépourvu de) [+ intelligence, générosité]* to lack; *[+ argent, main-d'œuvre]* to be short of, to lack ◆ **ils ne manquent de rien** they want for nothing, they don't want for anything, they lack nothing ◆ **le pays ne manque pas d'un certain charme** the country is not without a certain charm ◆ **on manque d'air ici** there's no air in here, it's stuffy in here ◆ **tu ne manques pas d'audace !** *ou* **d'air !*** *ou* **de culot !*** you've got a *ou* some nerve!* ◆ **nous manquons de personnel** we're short-staffed, we're short of staff

2 *(formules négatives)* **ne manquez pas de le remercier pour moi** don't forget to thank him for me, be sure to thank him for me ◆ **je ne manquerai pas de le lui dire** I'll be sure to tell him ◆ **nous ne manquerons pas de vous en informer** we shall inform you without fail ◆ **il n'a pas manqué de le lui dire** he made sure he told him ◆ **remerciez-la – je n'y manquerai pas** thank her – I won't forget ◆ **on ne peut ~ d'être frappé par ...** one cannot fail to marvel at ..., one cannot help but be struck by ... ◆ **ça ne va pas ~ (d'arriver)*** it's bound to happen ◆ **j'avais prévu qu'il se fâcherait, et ça n'a pas manqué !** I knew he'd be angry and sure enough he was!

VB IMPERS ◆ **il manque un pied à la chaise** there's a leg missing from the chair ◆ **il (nous) manque dix personnes/deux chaises** *(= elles ont disparu)* there are ten people/two chairs missing; *(= on en a besoin)* we are ten people/two chairs short, we are short of ten people/two chairs ◆ **il ne manquera pas de gens pour dire ...** there'll be no shortage of people who say ... ◆ **il ne lui manque que de savoir danser** the only thing he can't do is dance ◆ **il ne lui manque que la parole** *(en parlant d'un animal)* if only he could talk ◆ **il ne manquait plus que ça** that's all we needed, that's the last straw* ◆ **il ne manquerait plus que ça !** that really would be the end!* ◆ **il ne manquerait plus qu'il parte sans elle !** it really would be the end* if he went off without her!

VPR **se manquer** 1 *(= rater son suicide)* to fail *(in one's attempt to commit suicide)* ◆ **cette fois-ci, il ne s'est pas manqué** he made a good job of it this time

2 *(à un rendez-vous)* to miss each other ◆ **ils se sont manqués à la gare** they missed each other at the station

mansarde /mɑ̃saʀd/ NF *(= pièce)* attic, garret

mansardé, e /mɑ̃saʀde/ ADJ *[chambre, étage]* attic *(épith)* ◆ **la chambre est ~e** the room has a sloping ceiling, it's an attic room

mansuétude /mɑ̃sɥetyd/ NF leniency, indulgence

mante /mɑ̃t/ NF 1 *(= insecte)* mantis; *(= poisson)* manta (ray) ◆ **~ religieuse** *(lit)* praying mantis; *(fig)* man-eater *(hum)* 2 († *= manteau)* (woman's) mantle, cloak

manteau (pl **manteaux**) /mɑ̃to/ NM 1 *(Habillement)* coat ◆ **~ de pluie** raincoat ◆ **~ trois-quarts** three-quarter-length coat ◆ **sous le ~** *(fig)* clandestinely, on the sly 2 *(littér) [de neige]* mantle, blanket; *[d'ombre, hypocrisie]* cloak ◆ **sous le ~ de la nuit** under (the) cover of darkness 3 *[de mollusque]* mantle 4 *(Hér)* mantle, mantling 5 *(Géol)* mantle

COMP **manteau d'Arlequin** proscenium arch
manteau de cheminée mantelpiece

mantelet /mɑ̃t(ə)lɛ/ NM *(Habillement)* short cape, mantelet; *(Naut)* deadlight

mantille /mɑ̃tij/ NF mantilla

mantisse /mɑ̃tis/ NF mantissa

Mantoue /mɑ̃tu/ N Mantua

mantra /mɑ̃tʀa/ NM mantra

manucure /manykyʀ/ NMF *(= personne)* manicurist NM *ou* NF *(= soins)* manicure

manucurer /manykyʀe/ ► conjug 1 ◄ VT to manicure ◆ **se faire ~** to have a manicure

manuel, -elle /manɥɛl/ ADJ manual ◆ **passer en ~** to switch to manual; → **travail¹, travailleur** NM,F *(= travailleur)* manual worker ◆ **c'est/ce n'est pas un ~** *(qui a du sens pratique)* he's good/he's not very good with his hands NM *(= livre)* manual, handbook ◆ **~ de lecture** reader ◆ **~ scolaire** textbook ◆ **~ d'entretien** service manual ◆ **~ d'utilisation/de l'utilisateur** instruction/user's manual

manuellement /manɥɛlmɑ̃/ ADV *[fabriquer]* by hand, manually; *[fonctionner]* manually ◆ **être bon ~** to be good with one's hands

manufacture /manyfaktyʀ/ NF 1 *(= usine)* factory ◆ **~ d'armes/de porcelaine/de tabac** munitions/porcelain/tobacco factory ◆ **~ de tapisserie** tapestry workshop 2 *(= fabrication)* manufacture

manufacturer /manyfaktyʀe/ ► conjug 1 ◄ VT to manufacture; → **produit**

manufacturier, -ière /manyfaktyʀje, jɛʀ/ ADJ manufacturing *(épith)* NM † factory owner

manu militari /manymilitaʀi/ LOC ADV by (main) force

manuscrit, e /manyskʀi, it/ ADJ *(= écrit à la main)* handwritten ◆ **pages ~es** manuscript pages NM manuscript; *(dactylographié)* manuscript, typescript ◆ **les ~s de la mer Morte** the Dead Sea Scrolls

manutention /manytɑ̃sjɔ̃/ NF *(= opération)* handling; *(= local)* storehouse ◆ **frais de ~** handling charges ◆ **~ portuaire** dock work

manutentionnaire /manytɑ̃sjɔnɛʀ/ NMF packer

manutentionner /manytɑ̃sjɔne/ ► conjug 1 ◄ VT to handle, to pack

Mao (Tsé-toung) /mao(tsetuŋ)/ NM Mao (Tse Tung)

maoïsme /maɔism/ NM Maoism

maoïste /maɔist/ ADJ, NMF Maoist

maori, e /maɔʀi/ ADJ Maori NM *(= langue)* Maori NM,F **Maori(e)** Maori

maous, -ousse* /maus/ ADJ huge

Mao Zedong /maozedɔŋ/ NM Mao Zedong

mappemonde /mapmɔ̃d/ NF (= *carte*) map of the world (*in two hemispheres*); (= *sphère*) globe

Maputo /maputo/ N Maputo

maquer * /make/ ► conjug 1 ◄ VT (= *prostituer*) to be a pimp for VPR **se maquer** ◆ **se ~ avec qn** to (go and) live with sb, to shack up with sb * (*péj*) ◆ **il est déjà maqué** he's already got a woman

maquereau[1] (pl **maquereaux**) /makʀo/ NM (= *poisson*) mackerel; → **groseille**

maquereau[2] * (pl **maquereaux**) /makʀo/ NM (= *proxénète*) pimp, ponce * (*Brit*)

maquerelle * /makʀɛl/ NF ◆ **(mère)** ~ madam *

maquette /makɛt/ NF 1 (*à échelle réduite*) [*d'objet, bâtiment*] (scale) model; [*de décor, œuvre d'art*] model 2 (*grandeur nature*) (*Ind*) mock-up, model; (= *livre*) dummy 3 (*Peinture* = *carton*) sketch 4 (*Typo*) (= *conception graphique*) design; (= *mise en page*) layout; (= *couverture*) artwork

maquettiste /maketist/ NMF [*de modèles réduits*] model maker; [*de livre*] dummy maker

maquignon /makiɲɔ̃/ NM (*lit*) horse dealer; (*péj*) shady *ou* crooked dealer

maquignonnage /makiɲɔnaʒ/ NM (*lit*) horse dealing; (*péj*) underhand dealings, sharp practice (*Brit*)

maquignonner /makiɲɔne/ ► conjug 1 ◄ VT (*péj*) [+ *animal*] to sell by shady methods; [+ *affaire*] to rig, to fiddle

maquillage /makijaʒ/ NM 1 (= *crème, fard*) make-up ◆ **passer du temps à son** ~ to spend a long time putting on one's make-up *ou* making up ◆ **produits de** ~ make-up 2 (*péj*) [*de voiture*] disguising, doing over *; [*de document, vérité, faits*] faking, doctoring; [*de chiffres, résultats*] massaging, fiddling * (*Brit*)

maquiller /makije/ ► conjug 1 ◄ VT 1 [+ *visage, personne*] to make up ◆ **très maquillé** heavily made-up 2 [+ *document, vérité, faits*] to fake, to doctor; [+ *résultats, chiffres*] to massage, to fiddle * (*Brit*); [+ *voiture*] to do over *, to disguise ◆ **meurtre maquillé en accident** murder made to look like an accident VPR **se maquiller** to make up, to put on one's make-up ◆ **elle est trop jeune pour se** ~ she is too young to use make-up ◆ **se ~ les yeux** to put eye make-up on

maquilleur /makijœʀ/ NM make-up artist, make-up man

maquilleuse /makijøz/ NF make-up artist, make-up girl

maquis /maki/ NM 1 (*Géog*) scrub, bush ◆ **le ~ corse** the Corsican scrub ◆ **prendre le** ~ to take to the bush 2 (= *labyrinthe*) tangle, maze ◆ **le ~ de la procédure** the jungle of legal procedure 3 (= *résistance*) resistance movement; (*Deuxième Guerre mondiale*) maquis ◆ **prendre le** ~ to take to the maquis, to go underground

maquisard /makizaʀ/ NM maquis, member of the Resistance

marabout /maʀabu/ NM 1 (= *oiseau*) marabou(t) 2 (*Rel*) marabout; (= *envoûteur*) witch doctor

maraca /maʀaka/ NF maraca

maraîchage /maʀɛʃaʒ/ NM market gardening (*Brit*), truck farming (*US*) ◆ **~ sous verre** glasshouse cultivation

maraîcher, -ère /maʀeʃe, ɛʀ/ NM,F market gardener (*Brit*), truck farmer (*US*) ADJ ◆ **culture maraîchère** market gardening (*NonC*) (*Brit*), truck farming (*NonC*) (*US*) ◆ **produits ~s** market garden produce (*NonC*), truck (*NonC*) (*US*) ◆ **jardin** ~ market garden (*Brit*), truck farm (*US*)

marais /maʀɛ/ NM 1 (= *terrain*) marsh, swamp ◆ **~ salant** (*gén*) salt marsh; (*exploité*) saltern; → **gaz** 2 ◆ **le Marais** *historic area in the centre of Paris that contains the old Jewish quarter and fashionable bars and galleries*

marasme /maʀasm/ NM 1 (*Écon, Pol*) stagnation, slump ◆ **les affaires sont en plein** ~ business is completely stagnant, there is a complete slump in business 2 (= *accablement*) dejection, depression 3 (*Méd*) marasmus

marasquin /maʀaskɛ̃/ NM maraschino

marathon /maʀatɔ̃/ NM (*Sport, fig*) marathon ◆ **~ de danse** dance marathon ◆ **faire/courir un** ~ to do/run a marathon ◆ **visite-/négociations-**~ marathon visit/talks

marathonien, -ienne /maʀatɔnjɛ̃, jɛn/ NM,F marathon runner

marâtre /maʀɑtʀ/ NF (= *mauvaise mère*) cruel *ou* unnatural mother; (†† = *belle-mère*) stepmother

maraud, e[1] †† /maʀo, od/ NM,F rascal, rogue

maraudage /maʀodaʒ/ NM pilfering, thieving (*of poultry, crops etc*)

maraude[2] /maʀod/ NF 1 (= *vol*) thieving, pilfering (*of poultry, crops etc*), pillaging (*from farms, orchards*) 2 (*locutions*) **taxi en** ~ cruising *ou* prowling taxi, taxi cruising *ou* prowling for fares ◆ **vagabond en** ~ tramp on the prowl

marauder /maʀode/ ► conjug 1 ◄ VI [*personne*] to thieve, to pilfer; [*taxi*] to cruise *ou* prowl for fares

maraudeur, -euse /maʀodœʀ, øz/ NM,F (= *voleur*) prowler; (= *soldat*) marauder ADJ ◆ **oiseau** ~ thieving bird

marbre /maʀbʀ/ NM 1 (*Géol*) marble ◆ **de** *ou* **en** ~ marble ◆ **~ de Carrare** Carrara marble ◆ **peindre un mur en faux** ~ to marble a wall ◆ **rester de ~, garder un visage de** ~ (*fig*) to remain stony-faced *ou* impassive ◆ **ça l'a laissé de** ~ it left him cold ◆ **avoir un cœur de** ~ to have a heart of stone ◆ **passer une voiture au** ~ to check a car for structural damage; → **froid** 2 (= *surface*) marble top; (= *statue*) marble (statue) 3 (*Typo*) stone, bed ◆ **être sur le** ~ [*journal*] to be put to bed, to be on the stone; [*livre*] to be at *ou* in press ◆ **rester sur le** ~ to be excess copy

marbré, e /maʀbʀe/ (ptp de **marbrer**) ADJ [*papier, cuir*] marbled; [*peau*] mottled, blotchy; [*fromage*] veined ◆ **(gâteau)** ~ marble cake

marbrer /maʀbʀe/ ► conjug 1 ◄ VT [+ *papier, cuir*] to marble; [+ *bois, surface*] to vein, to mottle

marbrerie /maʀbʀəʀi/ NF (= *atelier*) marble mason's workshop *ou* yard; (= *industrie*) marble industry ◆ **travailler dans la** ~ to be a marble mason; (*funéraire*) to be a monumental mason

marbrier, -ière /maʀbʀije, ijɛʀ/ ADJ [*industrie*] marble (*épith*) NM (*funéraire*) monumental mason NF **marbrière** marble quarry

marbrure /maʀbʀyʀ/ NF 1 [*de papier, cuir*] marbling 2 [*de peau*] **~s** (*par le froid*) blotches, mottling; (*par un coup*) marks; [*de bois, surface*] veins, mottling

Marc /maʀk/ NM Mark ◆ **~ Aurèle** Marcus Aurelius ◆ **~-Antoine** Mark Antony

marc[1] /maʀ/ NM (= *poids, monnaie*) mark ◆ **au ~ le franc** (*Jur*) pro rata, proportionally

marc[2] /maʀ/ NM [*de raisin, pomme*] marc ◆ **~ (de café)** (coffee) grounds *ou* dregs ◆ **(eau de vie de)** ~ marc brandy; → **lire**[1]

marcassin /maʀkasɛ̃/ NM young wild boar

marcassite /maʀkasit/ NF marcasite

marcel * /maʀsɛl/ NM (= *maillot*) vest (*Brit*), undershirt (*US*)

marchand, e /maʀʃɑ̃, ɑ̃d/ ADJ [*valeur*] market (*épith*); [*prix*] trade (*épith*); [*rue*] shopping (*épith*) ◆ **navire** ~ merchant ship ◆ **secteur ~/non ~** market sector/non-market sector; → **galerie, marine**[2]

NM,F 1 (= *boutiquier*) shopkeeper, tradesman (*ou* tradeswoman); (*sur un marché*) stallholder; [*de vins, fruits, charbon, grains*] merchant; [*de meubles, bestiaux, cycles*] dealer ◆ **~ au détail** retailer ◆ **~ en gros** wholesaler ◆ **la ~e de chaussures me l'a dit** the woman in the shoe shop *ou* the shoe shop owner told me ◆ **jouer au ~** (*ou* **à la ~e**) to play shop (*Brit*) *ou* store (*US*)

2 (= *boutique*) shop, store ◆ **rapporte-le chez le** ~ take it back to the shop

COMP **marchand ambulant** hawker, door-to-door salesman, pedlar (*Brit*), peddler (*US*)
marchande d'amour (*hum*) lady of pleasure (*hum*)
marchand d'art art dealer
marchand de biens property agent
marchand de canons (*péj*) arms dealer
marchand de couleurs hardware dealer, ironmonger (*Brit*)
marchand d'esclaves slave trader
marchand de frites (= *boutique*) chip shop (*Brit*), chippy * (*Brit*)
marchand de fromages cheese vendor *ou* seller, cheesemonger (*Brit*)
marchand de fruits fruit merchant *ou* vendor *ou* seller, fruiterer (*Brit*)
marchand de glaces ice cream vendor
marchand d'illusions purveyor of illusions
marchand de journaux newsagent (*Brit*), newsdealer (*US*)
marchand de légumes greengrocer (*Brit*), produce dealer (*US*)
marchand de marrons chestnut seller
marchand de meubles furniture dealer
marchand de poissons fish merchant, fishmonger (*Brit*), fish vendor *ou* seller (*US*)
marchand des quatre saisons street merchant (selling fresh fruit and vegetables), costermonger (*Brit*)
marchand de rêves dream-merchant
marchand de sable (*fig*) sandman ◆ **le ~ de sable est passé** it's bedtime, the sandman is coming
marchand de sommeil (*péj*) slum landlord, slumlord * (*US*)
marchand de soupe (*péj* = *restaurateur*) low-grade restaurant owner, profiteering café owner; (*Scol*) money-grubbing *ou* profit-minded headmaster (of a private school)
marchand de tableaux art dealer
marchand de tapis carpet dealer ◆ **c'est un vrai ~ de tapis** (*péj*) he drives a really hard bargain, he haggles over everything ◆ **des discussions de ~ de tapis** endless haggling
les marchands du Temple (*Bible*) the moneychangers in the Temple
marchand de vin wine merchant, vintner

marchandage /maʀʃɑ̃daʒ/ NM 1 (*au marché*) bargaining, haggling; (*péj : aux élections*) bargaining ◆ **je viens si tu promets de m'aider – mais qu'est-ce-que c'est que ce ~ ?** I'll come if you promise to help me – what's this, blackmail? 2 (*Jur*) **le** ~ *subcontracting of labour*

marchander /maʀʃɑ̃de/ ► conjug 1 ◄ VT 1 [+ *objet*] to haggle over, to bargain over ◆ **savoir** ~ to know how to haggle ◆ **il a l'habitude de** ~ he is used to haggling *ou* bargaining ◆ **~ son soutien électoral** to use one's political support as a bargaining chip 2 (*fig*) **il ne marchande pas sa peine** he spares no pains, he grudges no effort ◆ **il ne m'a pas marchandé ses compliments** he wasn't sparing of his compliments 3 (*Jur*) to subcontract

marchandeur, -euse /maʀʃɑ̃dœʀ, øz/ NM,F 1 [*d'objet, prix*] haggler 2 (*Jur*) subcontractor (of labour)

marchandisage /maʀʃɑ̃dizaʒ/ NM merchandizing

marchandisation /maʀʃɑ̃dizasjɔ̃/ **NF** ◆ **nous sommes contre la ~ de la culture** we do not want to see culture treated as a commodity

marchandise /maʀʃɑ̃diz/ **GRAMMAIRE ACTIVE 47.3** **NF** 1 (= *article, unité*) commodity ◆ **~s** goods, merchandise (*NonC*), wares † ◆ **~s en gros/au détail** wholesale/retail goods ◆ **il a de la bonne ~** he has *ou* sells good stuff 2 (= *cargaison, stock*) **la ~** the goods, the merchandise ◆ **la ~ est dans l'entrepôt** the goods are *ou* the merchandise is in the warehouse ◆ **faire valoir** *ou* **vanter la ~** * to show o.s. off *ou* to show off one's wares to advantage, to make the most of o.s. *ou* one's wares ◆ **elle étale la ~**‡ she displays her charms (*hum*), she shows you *ou* she flaunts all she's got *

marchante /maʀʃɑ̃t/ **ADJ F** → **aile**

marche¹ /maʀʃ/ **NF** 1 (= *action, Sport*) walking ◆ **il fait de la ~** he goes in for walking, he does quite a bit of walking ◆ **poursuivre sa ~** to walk on ◆ **chaussures de ~** walking shoes

2 (= *démarche*) walk, step, gait; (= *allure, rythme*) pace, step ◆ **une ~ pesante** a heavy step *ou* gait ◆ **régler sa ~ sur celle de qn** to adjust one's pace *ou* step to sb else's

3 (= *trajet*) walk ◆ **faire une longue ~** to go for a long walk ◆ **la Longue Marche** (*Hist*) the Long March ◆ **le village est à deux heures/à dix km de ~ d'ici** the village is a two-hour walk/a 10-km walk from here ◆ **une ~ de 10 km** a 10-km walk

4 (= *mouvement, Mil, Pol*) march ◆ **air/chanson de ~** marching tune/song ◆ **fermer la ~** to bring up the rear ◆ **ouvrir la ~** (*lit, fig*) to lead the way ◆ **faire ~ sur** to march upon ◆ **~ victorieuse sur la ville** victorious march on the town ◆ **en avant, ~ !** quick march!, forward march!; → **ordre¹**

5 (= *fonctionnement*) [*de train, voiture*] running; [*de machine*] running, working; [*de navire*] sailing; [*d'étoile*] course; [*d'horloge*] working; [*d'usine, établissement*] running, working, functioning ◆ **dans le sens de la ~** facing the engine ◆ **dans le sens contraire de la ~** with one's back to the engine ◆ **en (bon) état de ~** in (good) working order ◆ **régler la ~ d'une horloge** to adjust the workings *ou* movement of a clock ◆ **assurer la bonne ~ d'un service** to ensure the smooth running of a service ◆ **~ – arrêt** (*Tech*) on – off

6 (= *développement*) [*de maladie*] progress; [*d'affaire, événements, opérations*] course; [*d'histoire, temps, progrès*] march ◆ **la ~ de l'intrigue** the unfolding *ou* development of the plot

7 (*locutions*)

◆ **en marche** ◆ **armée en ~** marching army ◆ **être en ~** [*personnes, soldats*] to be on the move; [*moteur*] to be running; [*machine*] to be (turned) on ◆ **ne montez pas dans un véhicule en ~** do not board a moving vehicle ◆ **j'ai pris le bus en ~** I jumped onto the bus while it was moving ◆ **se mettre en ~** [*personne*] to make a move, to get moving; [*machine*] to start ◆ **mettre en ~** [*+ moteur, voiture*] to start (up); [*+ machine*] to put on, to turn on, to set going; [*+ pendule*] to start (going) ◆ **lire les instructions avant la mise en ~ de l'appareil** read the instructions before starting the machine ◆ **remettre en ~** [*+ usine, machine*] to restart

8 (*Mus*) march ◆ **~ funèbre/militaire/nuptiale** funeral *ou* dead/military/wedding march

COMP **marche arrière** reverse ◆ **entrer/sortir en ~ arrière** to reverse in/out, to back in/out ◆ **faire ~ arrière** (*lit*) to reverse; (*fig*) to backpedal, to backtrack

marche avant forward ◆ **en ~ avant** in forward gear

marche forcée (*Mil*) forced march ◆ **se rendre vers un lieu à ~(s) forcée(s)** to get to a place by forced marches ◆ **la privatisation à ~ forcée des entreprises** the accelerated privatization of companies ◆ **ils avancent à ~ forcée sur la voie de la démocratisation** they're on the fast track to democracy ◆ **l'entreprise se modernise à ~ forcée** the company is undergoing a rapid modernization programme

marche à suivre (= *procédure*) (correct) procedure (*pour* for); (= *mode d'emploi*) directions (for use)

marche² /maʀʃ/ **NF** [*de véhicule*] step; [*d'escalier*] step, stair ◆ **manquer une ~** to miss a step ◆ **attention à la ~** mind (*Brit*) *ou* watch (*US*) the step ◆ **sur les ~s** (*de l'escalier*) on the stairs; (*de l'escalier extérieur, de l'escabeau*) on the steps ◆ **~ palière** last step before the landing, ≃ top step ◆ **~ dansante** winder

marche³ /maʀʃ/ **NF** (*gén pl : Géog, Hist*) march ◆ **les ~s** the Marches

marché /maʀʃe/ **NM** 1 (= *lieu*) market; (= *ville*) trading centre ◆ **~ aux bestiaux/aux fleurs/aux poissons** cattle/flower/fish market ◆ **~ couvert/en plein air** covered/open-air market ◆ **aller au ~, aller faire le ~** to go to (the) market ◆ **aller faire son ~** to go to the market; (*plus gén*) to go shopping ◆ **le choix est vaste, il faut faire son ~** (*fig*) there is a vast choice available, you have to shop around ◆ **faire les ~s** [*marchand, acheteur*] to go round *ou* do the markets ◆ **boucher qui fait les ~s** butcher who has a market stall ◆ **vendre/acheter au ~** *ou* **sur les ~s** to buy/sell at the market ◆ **Lyon, le grand ~ des soieries** Lyons, the great trading centre for silk goods

2 (*Comm, Écon* = *débouchés, opérations*) market ◆ **~ monétaire** money market ◆ **~ libre** open market ◆ **le ~ libre de Rotterdam** (*Pétrole*) the Rotterdam spot market ◆ **le ~ unique européen** the single European market ◆ **~ gris** grey market ◆ **acquérir** *ou* **trouver de nouveaux ~s (pour)** to find new markets (for) ◆ **lancer/offrir qch sur le ~** to launch/put sth on the market ◆ **le ~ de l'immobilier** the real estate market ◆ **le ~ du travail** the labour market ◆ **il n'y a pas de ~ pour ces produits** there is no market for these goods; → **analyse, étude**

3 (= *transaction, contrat*) bargain, transaction, deal ◆ **faire un ~ avantageux** to make *ou* strike a good bargain ◆ **un ~ de dupes** a fool's bargain *ou* deal ◆ **conclure** *ou* **passer un ~ avec qn** to make a deal with sb ◆ **~ conclu !** it's a deal! ◆ **~ ferme** firm deal ◆ **~ de gré à gré** mutual agreement, private contract ◆ **~ public** procurement contract ◆ **mettre le ~ en main à qn** to give sb an ultimatum

4 (*Bourse*) market ◆ **le ~ est animé** the market is lively ◆ **~ des valeurs/des actions** securities/share market ◆ **~ des changes** *ou* **des devises** foreign exchange market ◆ **~ financier** financial market ◆ **~ obligataire** bond market ◆ **~ au comptant/à terme** *ou* **à règlement mensuel** spot *ou* cash/forward market ◆ **~ à terme d'instruments financiers, ~ à terme international de France** *French financial futures market*, ≃ LIFFE (*Brit*) ◆ **second ~** ≃ unlisted securities market

5 (*locutions*)

◆ **bon marché** [*acheter*] cheap; [*produit*] cheap, inexpensive

◆ **meilleur marché** ◆ **c'est meilleur ~** it's better value, it's cheaper

COMP **Marché commun** (*Hist*) Common Market

marché d'intérêt national *wholesale market for perishable food and horticultural products*

marché international du disque et de l'édition musicale *music industry trade fair*

marché noir black market ◆ **faire du ~ noir** to buy and sell on the black market

marché aux puces flea market

marché-gare (pl **marchés-gares**) /maʀʃegaʀ/ **NM** *wholesale market to which goods are transported by rail*

marchepied /maʀʃəpje/ **NM** [*de train*] step; [*de voiture*] running board; (*fig*) stepping stone ◆ **servir de ~ à qn** to be sb's stepping stone

marcher /maʀʃe/ ▸ **conjug 1** ◂ **VI** 1 (*gén*) to walk; [*soldats*] to march ◆ **~ à grandes enjambées** *ou* **à grands pas** to stride (along) ◆ **il marche en boitant** he walks with a limp ◆ **~ en canard** to walk like a duck ◆ **~ sur les mains/à quatre pattes** to walk on one's hands/on all fours ◆ **on marche sur la tête !** * it's crazy!, there's no rhyme or reason to it! ◆ **venez, on va ~ un peu** come on, let's have a walk *ou* let's go for a walk ◆ **il marchait sans but** he walked *ou* wandered (along) aimlessly ◆ **~ sur des œufs** (*fig*) to act with caution ◆ **faire ~ un bébé** to get a baby to walk, to help a baby walk ◆ **c'est marche ou crève !**‡ it's sink or swim!; → **pas¹**

2 (= *mettre le pied sur, dans*) **~ dans une flaque d'eau** to step in a puddle ◆ **défense de ~ sur les pelouses** keep off the grass ◆ **~ sur les pieds de qn/sur sa robe** (*lit*) to stand *ou* tread on sb's toes/on one's dress ◆ **ne te laisse pas ~ sur les pieds** (*fig*) don't let anyone tread on your toes *ou* take advantage of you ◆ **~ sur qn** (*fig*) to walk all over sb; → **brisées, côté, trace** *etc*

3 (= *progresser*) **~ à la conquête de la gloire/vers le succès** to be on the road to fame/to success, to step out *ou* stride towards fame/success ◆ **~ au supplice** to walk to one's death *ou* to the stake ◆ **~ au combat** to march into battle ◆ **~ sur une ville/un adversaire** (*Mil*) to advance on *ou* march against a town/an enemy

4 (= *obéir*) to toe the line; (* = *consentir*) to agree, to play * ◆ **il marche à tous les coups** * (= *croire naïvement*) he is taken in *ou* falls for it * every time ◆ **on lui raconte n'importe quoi et il marche** you can tell him anything and he'll swallow it * ◆ **il n'a pas voulu ~ dans la combine** he didn't want to be involved in the affair ◆ **faire ~ qn** (= *taquiner*) to pull sb's leg; (= *tromper*) to take sb for a ride *, to lead sb up the garden path * ◆ **il sait faire ~ sa grand-mère** he knows how to get round his grandmother ◆ **son père saura le faire ~ (droit)** his father will soon have him toeing the line

5 (*avec véhicule*) **le train a/nous avons bien marché jusqu'à Lyon** the train/we made good time as far as Lyon ◆ **nous marchions à 100 à l'heure** we were doing a hundred

6 (= *fonctionner*) [*appareil*] to work; [*ruse*] to work, to come off; [*usine*] to work (well); [*affaires, études*] to go (well); [*train*] to run ◆ **faire ~** [*+ appareil*] to work, to operate; [*+ entreprise*] to run ◆ **ça fait ~ les affaires** it's good for business ◆ **ça marche à l'électricité** it works by *ou* on electricity ◆ **est-ce que le métro marche aujourd'hui ?** is the underground running today? ◆ **ces deux opérations marchent ensemble** these two procedures go *ou* work together ◆ **les affaires marchent mal** things are going badly, business is bad ◆ **son restaurant marche bien** his restaurant does good business *ou* does a brisk trade ◆ **le film a bien marché en Europe** the film was a big success in Europe ◆ **il marche au whisky** * whisky keeps him going ◆ **les études, ça marche ?** * how's studying going? ◆ **rien ne marche** nothing's going right, nothing's working ◆ **ça marche !** (*dans un restaurant*) coming up!; (= *c'est d'accord*) great!, OK! * ◆ **ça marche pour 8 h/lundi** 8 o'clock/Monday is fine; → **roulette**

marcheur, -euse /maʀʃœʀ, øz/ **ADJ** [*oiseau*] flightless **NM,F** (*gén*) walker; (= *manifestant*) marcher **NF** **marcheuse** (= *figurante*) walk-on

Marco Polo /maʀkopolo/ **NM** Marco Polo

marcottage /maʀkɔtaʒ/ **NM** [*de végétaux*] layering

marcotte /maʀkɔt/ **NF** [*de plante*] layer, runner

marcotter /maʀkɔte/ ► conjug 1 ◄ VT [+ plantes] to layer

mardi /maʀdi/ NM Tuesday ◆ **Mardi gras** Shrove *ou* Pancake* (*Brit*) Tuesday, Mardi Gras ◆ **elle se croit à ~ gras !** (*hum*) she's dressed up like a dog's dinner!; *pour autres loc voir* **samedi**

mare /maʀ/ NF [1] (*= étang*) pond ◆ **~ aux canards** duck pond; → **pavé** [2] (*= flaque*) pool ◆ **~ de sang/d'huile** pool of blood/of oil

marécage /maʀekaʒ/ NM (*Géog*) marsh, swamp, bog; (*péj*) quagmire

marécageux, -euse /maʀekaʒø, øz/ ADJ [*terrain*] marshy, swampy, boggy; [*plante*] marsh (*épith*) ◆ **c'est très ~ par ici** the ground is very marshy *ou* boggy in this area

maréchal (pl **-aux**) /maʀeʃal, o/ NM (*armée française*) marshal; (*armée britannique*) field marshal ◆ **~ de camp** (*Hist*) brigadier ◆ **Maréchal de France** Marshal of France ◆ **~ des logis** ≈ sergeant ◆ **~ des logis-chef** ≈ battery *ou* squadron sergeant-major; → **bâton**

maréchalat /maʀeʃala/ NM rank of marshal, marshalcy

maréchale /maʀeʃal/ NF marshal's wife; → **Madame**

maréchalerie /maʀeʃalʀi/ NF (*= atelier*) smithy, blacksmith's (shop); (*= métier*) blacksmith's trade

maréchal-ferrant /maʀeʃalfeʀɑ̃/ (pl **maréchaux-ferrants** /maʀeʃofeʀɑ̃/) NM blacksmith, farrier

maréchaussée /maʀeʃose/ NF (*hum*) ◆ **la ~** the police (force); (*Hist*) the mounted constabulary

marée /maʀe/ NF [1] (*lit*) tide ◆ **~ montante/descendante** flood *ou* rising/ebb tide ◆ **à (la) ~ montante/descendante** when the tide comes in/goes out, when the tide is rising/ebbing *ou* falling ◆ **(à) ~ haute** (at) high tide *ou* water ◆ **(à) ~ basse** (at) low tide *ou* water ◆ **grande ~** spring tide ◆ **faible** *ou* **petite ~** neap tide ◆ **~ noire** oil slick ◆ **ça sent la ~** it smells of the sea [2] (*fig*) [*produits*] flood; [*de touristes*] flood, influx ◆ **~ humaine** great flood *ou* influx of people [3] (*Comm*) **la ~** (*= poissons de mer*) the fresh catch, the fresh (sea) fish

marelle /maʀɛl/ NF (*= jeu*) hopscotch; (*= dessin*) (drawing of a) hopscotch game ◆ **jouer à la ~** to play hopscotch

marémoteur, -trice /maʀemɔtœʀ, tʀis/ ADJ (*Élec*) [*énergie*] tidal ◆ **usine marémotrice** tidal power station

marengo /maʀɛ̃go/ ADJ INV (*Culin*) ◆ **poulet/veau (à la) ~** chicken/veal marengo NM *black flecked cloth*

marennes /maʀɛn/ NF Marennes oyster

mareyage /maʀɛjaʒ/ NM fish trade

mareyeur, -euse /maʀɛjœʀ, øz/ NM,F wholesale fish merchant

margarine /maʀgaʀin/ NF margarine, marge* (*Brit*), oleo* (*US*)

marge /maʀʒ/ NF [1] [*de feuille*] margin [2] (*= latitude*) **il y a de la ~** (*du temps*) there's time to spare; (*de l'espace*) there's plenty of room; (*de l'argent*) there's enough (money) left over ◆ **c'est une taille 42, j'ai de la ~ !** it's size 14, it's easily big enough for me ◆ **donner de la ~ à qn** (*temps*) to give sb a reasonable margin of time; (*latitude*) to give sb some leeway *ou* latitude *ou* scope

◆ **en marge** ◆ **faire des annotations en ~** to make notes in the margin ◆ **ceux qui sont en ~, les exclus de la société** people on the margins of society, the socially excluded ◆ **dans son parti, il est toujours resté en ~** he's always been on the sidelines of the party

◆ **en marge de** ◆ **vivre en ~ de la société** to live on the fringe of society ◆ **vivre en ~ du monde** to live cut off from the world ◆ **la Suisse reste en ~ de l'intégration européenne** Switzerland remains on the sidelines of European integration ◆ **activités en ~ du festival** fringe activities ◆ **ils ne veulent pas rester en ~ du débat** they don't want to be left on the sidelines of the debate ◆ **en ~ de cette affaire, on peut aussi signaler que …** in addition, one might also point out that …

COMP **marge (bénéficiaire)** (profit) margin, mark-up
marge brute gross margin
marge brute d'autofinancement cash flow
marge commerciale gross margin *ou* profit, trading margin
marge continentale (*Géog*) continental terrace
marge d'erreur margin of error
marge de garantie (*Fin*) margin
marge de liberté *ou* **de manœuvre** room for *ou* to manoeuvre, leeway ◆ **ça ne nous laisse pas une grande ~ de manœuvre** it doesn't leave us much room for manoeuvre
marge de sécurité safety margin
marge de tolérance tolerance

margelle /maʀʒɛl/ NF [*de puits*] edge, coping (*SPÉC*)

marger /maʀʒe/ ► conjug 3 ◄ VT [*+ machine à écrire, feuille*] to set the margins on; (*Typo*) to feed (in)

margeur /maʀʒœʀ/ NM [*de machine à écrire*] margin stop

marginal, e (mpl **-aux**) /maʀʒinal, o/ ADJ [1] (*= secondaire*) [*phénomène*] marginal, minor; [*activité, rôle*] marginal, peripheral ◆ **ces réactions/critiques restent ~es** only a minority of people have these reactions/make these criticisms ◆ **l'évasion fiscale reste ~e** tax evasion is still relatively rare *ou* uncommon [2] (*Écon, Fin, Stat*) [*coût, taux*] marginal [3] (*= non conformiste*) unconventional ◆ **groupe ~** fringe *ou* marginal group ◆ **l'accroissement d'une population ~e** the increase in the number of people living on the fringes *ou* margins of society ◆ **les partis politiques plus marginaux** the more marginal political parties [4] (*= sur le bord*) **notes ~es** marginal notes, marginalia (*pl*) NM,F (*= déshérité*) dropout; (*= non-conformiste*) unconventional figure

marginalement /maʀʒinalmɑ̃/ ADV marginally ◆ **cela n'influence le chiffre d'affaires que très ~** this has only a marginal impact on turnover

marginalisation /maʀʒinalizasjɔ̃/ NF marginalization ◆ **pour éviter la ~ sociale** to prevent people from being marginalized in society *ou* from becoming marginalized

marginaliser /maʀʒinalize/ ► conjug 1 ◄ VT to marginalize, to edge out ◆ **il n'a pas l'intention de se laisser ~** he has no intention of being marginalized *ou* of being sidelined *ou* of being left out in the cold ◆ **ils se sentent de plus en plus marginalisés** they feel more and more marginalized VPR **se marginaliser** [*personne, pays, parti*] to become marginalized

marginalité /maʀʒinalite/ NF marginality ◆ **vivre/tomber dans la ~** to live as/become a dropout

margis /maʀʒi/ NM (abrév de **maréchal des logis**) (*arg Mil*) sarge (*arg*)

margoulette* /maʀgulɛt/ NF ◆ **se casser la ~** to fall flat on one's face

margoulin /maʀgulɛ̃/ NM (*péj*) swindler, shark (*fig*)

margrave /maʀgʀav/ NM (*Hist*) margrave

marguerite /maʀgəʀit/ NF [1] (*Bot*) (*cultivée*) marguerite; (*des champs*) daisy; → **effeuiller** [2] [*de machine à écrire*] daisywheel

marguillier /maʀgije/ NM (*Hist*) churchwarden

mari /maʀi/ NM husband ◆ **son petit ~** her hubby*

mariable /maʀjabl/ ADJ marriageable

mariage /maʀjaʒ/ GRAMMAIRE ACTIVE 51.3

NM [1] (*= institution, union*) marriage; (*Rel*) matrimony ◆ **50 ans de ~** 50 years of married life *ou* of marriage ◆ **ils ont fêté leurs 20 ans de ~** they celebrated their 20th (wedding) anniversary ◆ **au début de leur ~** when they were first married, at the beginning of their marriage ◆ **son ~ avec son cousin** her marriage to her cousin ◆ **on parle de ~ entre eux** there is talk of their getting married ◆ **il avait un enfant d'un premier ~** he had a child from his first marriage ◆ **il l'a demandée en ~** he asked if he could marry her ◆ **promettre/donner qn en ~ à** to promise/give sb in marriage to ◆ **elle lui a apporté beaucoup d'argent en ~** she brought him a lot of money when she married him ◆ **faire un riche ~** to marry into money ◆ **hors ~** [*cohabitation*] outside of marriage; [*naissance, né*] out of wedlock; [*relations sexuelles*] extramarital; → **acte, demande**

[2] (*= cérémonie*) wedding ◆ **grand ~** society wedding ◆ **cadeau/faire-part/messe de ~** wedding present/invitation/service; → **corbeille, liste**[1]; → **MAIRE**

[3] [*de couleurs, parfums, matières*] marriage, blend; [*d'entreprises*] merger, amalgamation ◆ **c'est le ~ de la carpe et du lapin** (*couple*) they make an odd couple; (*associés*) they are strange *ou* unlikely bedfellows

[4] (*Cartes*) **avoir le ~ à cœur** to have *ou* hold (the) king and queen of hearts ◆ **faire des ~s** to collect kings and queens

COMP **mariage d'amour** love match ◆ **faire un ~ d'amour** to marry for love, to make a love match
mariage d'argent marriage for money, money match
mariage blanc (*non consommé*) unconsummated marriage; (*de convenance*) marriage of convenience
mariage en blanc white wedding
mariage civil civil wedding, registry (office) wedding (*Brit*)
mariage de convenance marriage of convenience
mariage à l'essai trial marriage
mariage d'intérêt marriage for money (*and other advantages*); (*entre entreprises*) merger ◆ **faire un ~ d'intérêt** to marry for money
mariage mixte mixed marriage
mariage politique political alliance
mariage de raison marriage of convenience
mariage religieux church wedding

marial, e (mpl **marials**) /maʀjal/ ADJ (*Rel*) [*culte*] Marian

Marianne /maʀjan/ NF (*Pol*) Marianne (*symbol of the French Republic*)

MARIANNE

Marianne is an allegorical figure representing a woman wearing a « bonnet phrygien » (a red woollen conical hat worn by commoners under the « Ancien Régime »). The name **Marianne** was used at the end of the 18th century to refer to the French Republic, and statues and busts began to appear around fifty years later. All « mairies » have a bust of **Marianne** on public view, and she also appears on postage stamps. **Marianne**'s face changes from time to time, Catherine Deneuve and Laetitia Casta both having been used as models in recent years.

Mariannes /maʀjan/ NFPL ◆ **les (îles) ~, l'archipel des ~** the Mariana Islands ◆ **les ~-du-Nord** the Northern Mariana Islands

Marie /maʀi/ NF Mary ◆ ~ **Stuart** Mary Stuart, Mary Queen of Scots

marié, e /maʀje/ (ptp de **marier**) ADJ married ◆ **non** ~ unmarried, single NM (bride) groom ◆ **les** ~**s** *(jour du mariage)* the bride and (bride) groom; *(après le mariage)* the newly-weds; → **jeune, nouveau** NF **mariée** bride ◆ **trouver** *ou* **se plaindre que la** ~**e est trop belle** *(fig)* to object that everything's too good to be true ◆ **couronne/robe/voile de** ~**e** wedding head-dress/dress/veil; → **jeune**

marie-couche-toi-là †* /maʀikuʃtwala/ NF INV *(péj)* slut, tart* *(Brit)*

Marie-Galante /maʀigalɑ̃t/ NF Marie Galante

marie-jeanne /maʀiʒan/ NF INV *(arg Drogue)* Mary Jane *(arg)*, pot *(arg)*

marie-louise (pl **maries-louises**) /maʀilwiz/ NF *[d'assiette]* inner surface; *[d'encadrement]* inner frame

marier /maʀje/ GRAMMAIRE ACTIVE 51.3 ▸ conjug 7 ◂ VT 1 *[maire, prêtre]* to marry ◆ **il a marié sa fille à un homme d'affaires** he married his daughter to a businessman ◆ **il a fini par** ~ **sa fille** he finally got his daughter married, he finally married off his daughter ◆ **demain, je marie mon frère** *(hum)* tomorrow I see my brother (get) married ◆ **nous sommes mariés depuis 15 ans** we have been married for 15 years ◆ **il a encore deux filles à** ~ he still has two unmarried daughters, he still has two daughters to marry off ◆ **fille (bonne) à** ~ daughter of marriageable age, marriageable daughter ◆ **on n'est pas mariés avec lui !** * *(fig)* we don't owe him anything!

2 *[+ couleurs, goûts, parfums, styles]* to blend, to harmonize; *[+ entreprises]* to merge, to amalgamate

VPR **se marier** 1 *[personne]* to get married ◆ **se** ~ **à** *ou* **avec qn** to marry sb, to get married to sb ◆ **se** ~ **à la mairie/à l'église** to get married at a registry office/in church ◆ **se** ~ **de la main gauche** † to live as man and wife

2 *[couleurs, goûts, parfums, styles]* to blend, to harmonize ◆ **le beige se marie très bien avec le noir** beige goes very well with black

marie-salope (pl **maries-salopes**) /maʀisalɔp/ NF 1 *(= péniche)* hopper (barge) 2 (* *péj* = *souillon)* slut

marieur, -ieuse /maʀjœʀ, jøz/ NM,F matchmaker

marigot /maʀigo/ NM backwater, cutoff, oxbow lake

marihuana, marijuana /maʀiʀwana/ NF marijuana

marimba /maʀimba/ NM marimba

marin, e¹ /maʀɛ̃, in/ ADJ *[air]* sea; *[carte]* maritime, navigational; *[faune, flore]* marine, sea ◆ **bateau (très)** ~ seaworthy ship ◆ **missile** ~ sea-based missile ◆ **sciences** ~**es** marine science ◆ **costume** ~ sailor suit; → **mille², pied** *etc* NM sailor ◆ **(simple)** ~ *(grade)* ordinary seaman ◆ ~ **pêcheur** fisherman ◆ ~ **d'eau douce** landlubber ◆ **un peuple de** ~**s** a seafaring nation, a nation of seafarers ◆ **béret/tricot de** ~ sailor's hat/jersey; → **fusilier**

marina /maʀina/ NF marina

marinade /maʀinad/ NF 1 *(Culin)* marinade ◆ ~ **de viande** meat in (a) marinade, marinaded meat 2 *(Can)* ~**s** pickles

marine² /maʀin/ NF 1 *(= flotte, administration)* navy ◆ **terme de** ~ nautical term ◆ **au temps de la** ~ **à voiles** in the days of sailing ships ◆ ~ **(de guerre)** navy ◆ ~ **marchande** merchant navy; → **lieutenant, officier¹** 2 *(= tableau)* seascape NM *(= soldat) (britannique)* Royal Marine; *(américain)* US Marine ◆ **les** ~**s** the Marines ADJ INV *(couleur)* navy (blue); → **bleu**

mariner /maʀine/ ▸ conjug 1 ◂ VT *(Culin)* to marinade, to marinate; *(dans la saumure)* to pickle ◆ **harengs marinés** pickled herrings VI 1 *(Culin)* **(faire)** ~ to marinade, to marinate 2 (* = *attendre)* to hang about* ◆ ~ **en prison** to stew* in prison ◆ **faire** *ou* **laisser** ~ **qn** *(à un rendez-vous)* to keep sb waiting *ou* hanging about*; *(pour une décision)* to let sb stew* (for a bit)

maringouin /maʀɛ̃gwɛ̃/ NM *(Can)* mosquito

marinier /maʀinje/ NM bargee *(Brit)*, bargeman *(US)*; → **officier¹**

marinière /maʀinjɛʀ/ NF *(Habillement)* over-blouse, smock; → **moule²**

mariol(le) * /maʀjɔl/ NM ◆ **c'est un** ~**(le)** *(malin)* he's a crafty *ou* sly one; *(qui plaisante)* he's a bit of a joker *ou* a waster*; *(incompétent)* he's a bungling idiot* ◆ **(ne) fais pas le** ~**(le)** stop trying to be clever *ou* smart*, stop showing off

marionnette /maʀjɔnɛt/ NF *(lit, fig = pantin)* puppet ◆ ~**s** *(= spectacle)* puppet show ◆ ~ **à fils** marionette ◆ ~ **à doigt/à gaine** finger/glove puppet ◆ **faire les** ~**s** to move one's hands *(to amuse a baby)*; → **montreur, théâtre**

marionnettiste /maʀjɔnetist/ NMF puppeteer, puppet-master (*ou* -mistress)

mariste /maʀist/ NMF Marist ◆ **frère/sœur** ~ Marist brother/sister

marital, e (mpl **-aux**) /maʀital, o/ ADJ *(Jur)* ◆ **autorisation** ~**e** husband's permission *ou* authorization ◆ **la vie** ~**e** living together, cohabitation

maritalement /maʀitalmɑ̃/ ADV ◆ **vivre** ~ to live as husband and wife, to cohabit

maritime /maʀitim/ ADJ 1 *[climat]* maritime; *[ville]* seaboard, coastal, seaside; *[province]* seaboard, coastal, maritime; → **gare¹, pin, port¹** 2 *[navigation]* maritime; *[commerce, agence]* shipping; *[droit]* shipping, maritime; *[assurance]* marine ◆ **une grande puissance** ~ *(Pol)* a great sea power ◆ **affecté à la navigation** ~ sea-going; → **arsenal**

maritorne † /maʀitɔʀn/ NF *(= souillon)* slut, slattern

marivaudage /maʀivodaʒ/ NM *(littér = badinage)* light-hearted gallantries; *(Littérat)* sophisticated banter in the style of Marivaux

marivauder /maʀivode/ ▸ conjug 1 ◂ VI *(littér)* to engage in lively sophisticated banter; († : *Littérat)* to write in the style of Marivaux

marjolaine /maʀʒɔlɛn/ NF marjoram

mark /maʀk/ NM *(Fin)* mark ◆ **le deutsche** ~ the Deutsche mark ◆ **le** ~ **allemand/finlandais** the German/Finnish mark

marketing /maʀketiŋ/ NM marketing ◆ ~ **direct** direct marketing ◆ ~ **téléphonique** telemarketing, telephone sales ◆ ~ **politique** political marketing

marlin /maʀlɛ̃/ NM marlin

marlou * /maʀlu/ NM *(= souteneur)* pimp; *(= voyou)* wide boy* *(Brit)*, punk* *(US)*

marmaille * /maʀmɑj/ NF gang *ou* horde of kids* *ou* brats* *(péj)* ◆ **toute la** ~ **était là** the whole brood was there

marmelade /maʀməlad/ NF *(Culin)* stewed fruit, compote ◆ ~ **de pommes/poires** stewed apples/pears, compote of apples/pears ◆ ~ **d'oranges** (orange) marmalade

◆ **en marmelade** *[légumes, fruits] (= cuits)* cooked to a mush; *(= crus)* reduced to a pulp ◆ **avoir le nez en** ~ to have one's nose reduced to a pulp ◆ **réduire qn en** ~ to smash sb to pulp, to reduce sb to a pulp

marmite /maʀmit/ NF *(Culin)* (cooking) pot; *(arg Mil)* heavy shell ◆ **une** ~ **de soupe** a pot of soup; → **bouillir, nez**

COMP **marmite (de géants)** *(Géog)* pothole

marmite norvégienne ≃ haybox

marmiton /maʀmitɔ̃/ NM kitchen boy

marmonnement /maʀmɔnmɑ̃/ NM mumbling, muttering

marmonner /maʀmɔne/ ▸ conjug 1 ◂ VTI to mumble, to mutter ◆ ~ **dans sa barbe** to mutter into one's beard, to mutter to o.s.

marmoréen, -éenne /maʀmɔʀeɛ̃, eɛn/ ADJ *(littér)* marble *(épith)*, marmoreal *(littér)*

marmot * /maʀmo/ NM kid*, brat* *(péj)*; → **croquer**

marmotte /maʀmɔt/ NF *(= animal)* marmot; *(fig)* sleepyhead, dormouse; *(= cerise) type of bigarreau cherry*; → **dormir**

marmottement /maʀmɔtmɑ̃/ NM mumbling, muttering

marmotter /maʀmɔte/ ▸ conjug 1 ◂ VTI to mumble, to mutter ◆ **qu'est-ce que tu as à** ~ **?** * what are you mumbling (on) about? *ou* muttering about?

marmouset /maʀmuzɛ/ NM *(Sculp)* quaint *ou* grotesque figure; *(= singe)* marmoset

marnage¹ /maʀnaʒ/ NM *(Agr)* marling

marnage² /maʀnaʒ/ NM *(Naut)* tidal range

marne /maʀn/ NF *(Géol)* marl, calcareous clay

marner /maʀne/ ▸ conjug 1 ◂ VT *(Agr)* to marl VI (* = *travailler dur)* to slog* ◆ **faire** ~ **qn** to make sb slog*

marneux, -euse /maʀnø, øz/ ADJ marly

marnière /maʀnjɛʀ/ NF marlpit

Maroc /maʀɔk/ NM Morocco

marocain, e /maʀɔkɛ̃, ɛn/ ADJ Moroccan NM,F **Marocain(e)** Moroccan

maronite /maʀɔnit/ ADJ, NMF Maronite

maronner * /maʀɔne/ ▸ conjug 1 ◂ VI 1 *(= grommeler)* to grouse*, to moan* 2 ◆ **faire** ~ **qn** *(= faire attendre qn)* keep sb hanging about*

maroquin /maʀɔkɛ̃/ NM 1 *(= cuir)* morocco (leather) ◆ **relié en** ~ morocco-bound 2 *(Pol)* (minister's) portfolio ◆ **obtenir un** ~ to be made a minister

maroquinerie /maʀɔkinʀi/ NF *(= boutique)* leather goods shop; *(= atelier)* tannery; *(= métier)* fine leather craft; *(= préparation)* tanning ◆ **(articles de)** ~ fancy *ou* fine leather goods ◆ **il travaille dans la** ~ *[artisan]* he does leatherwork; *[commerçant]* he sells leather goods

maroquinier /maʀɔkinje/ NM *(= marchand)* dealer in fine leather goods; *(= fabricant)* leather worker *ou* craftsman

marotte /maʀɔt/ NF 1 *(= dada)* hobby, craze ◆ **c'est sa** ~ **!** it's his pet craze! ◆ **encore une de ses** ~**s** another one of his daft ideas* ◆ **le voilà lancé sur sa** ~ **!** there he goes on his pet subject! 2 *(Hist = poupée)* fool's bauble; *(Coiffure, Habillement = tête)* milliner's *ou* hairdresser's dummy head

maroufler /maʀufle/ ▸ conjug 1 ◂ VT *[+ toile]* to mount

marquage /maʀkaʒ/ NM 1 *[de linge, marchandises]* marking; *[d'animal]* branding; *[d'arbre]* blazing 2 *(sur la chaussée)* road-marking 3 *(Sport) [de joueur]* marking ◆ ~ **à la culotte** close marking 4 *(Sci)* labelling ◆ ~ **radioactif** radioactive tracing

marquant, e /maʀkɑ̃, ɑ̃t/ ADJ *[personnage, événement, rôle]* outstanding, striking; *[souvenir]* vivid ◆ **le fait le plus** ~ the most significant *ou* striking fact ◆ **c'est l'un des aspects les plus** ~**s de son œuvre** it is one of the most striking aspects of his work

marque /maʀk/ NF 1 *(= repère, trace)* mark; *(= signe) (lit, fig)* mark, sign; *(= preuve)* token; *(= marque-page)* bookmark; *[de linge]* name tab ◆ **~s de doigts** fingermarks, fingerprints ◆ **~s de pas** footmarks, footprints ◆ **~s d'une blessure/de coups/de fatigue** marks of a wound/of blows/of fatigue ◆ **il porte encore les ~s de son accident** he still bears the scars from his accident ◆ **faites une ~ au crayon devant chaque nom** put a pencil mark beside each name, tick each name ◆ **~ de confiance/de respect** sign *ou* token *ou* mark of confidence/of respect ◆ **porter la ~ du pluriel** to be in the plural (form)
2 *(= estampille) [d'or, argent]* hallmark; *[de meubles, œuvre d'art]* mark; *[de viande, œufs]* stamp ◆ **la ~ du génie** the hallmark *ou* stamp of genius
3 *[de nourriture, produits chimiques]* brand; *[d'automobiles, produits manufacturés]* make ◆ **~ de fabrique** *ou* **de fabrication** *ou* **du fabricant** trademark, trade name, brand name ◆ **~ d'origine** maker's mark ◆ **~ déposée** registered trademark *ou* trade name *ou* brand name ◆ **une grande ~ de vin/de voiture** a well-known brand of wine/make of car ◆ **produits de ~** high-class products ◆ **personnage de ~** distinguished person, VIP ◆ **visiteur de ~** important *ou* distinguished visitor; → **image**
4 *(= insigne) [de fonction, grade]* badge ◆ **les ~s de sa fonction** *(frm)* the insignia *ou* regalia of his office
5 *(= décompte de points)* **la ~** the score ◆ **tenir la ~** to keep (the) score ◆ **mener à la ~** to lead on the scoresheet, to be ahead on goals, to be in the lead ◆ **ouvrir la ~** to open the scoring
6 *(Sport = empreinte)* marker ◆ **à vos ~s ! prêts ! partez !** *(athlètes)* on your marks! get set! go!; *(enfants)* ready, steady, go! *(Brit)*, ready, set, go! *(US)* ◆ **~ !** *(Rugby)* mark! ◆ **prendre ses ~s** *(lit)* to place one's marker *(for one's run-up)*; *(fig)* to get one's bearings ◆ **il cherche encore ses ~s** *(fig)* he's trying to find his bearings

marqué, e /maʀke/ (ptp de **marquer**) ADJ 1 *(= accentué)* marked, pronounced; *(Ling)* marked 2 *(= signalé)* **le prix ~** the price on the label ◆ **au prix ~** at the labelled price, at the price shown on the label ◆ **c'est un homme ~** *(fig)* he's a marked man ◆ **il est très ~ politiquement** his political leanings are very obvious

marque-page (pl **marque-pages**) /maʀk(ə)paʒ/ NM bookmark

marquer /maʀke/ ▸ conjug 1 ◂ VT 1 *(par un signe distinctif) [+ objet personnel]* to mark *(au nom de qn* with sb's name); *[+ animal, criminel]* to brand; *[+ arbre]* to blaze; *[+ marchandise]* to label, to stamp
2 *(= indiquer) [+ limite, position]* to mark; *(sur une carte) [+ village, accident de terrain]* to mark, to show, to indicate; *[thermomètre]* to show, to register; *[balance]* to register; *[isotope radioactif]* to trace ◆ **~ sa page (avec un signet)** to mark one's page (with a bookmark) ◆ **marquez la longueur voulue d'un trait de crayon** mark off the length required with a pencil ◆ **l'animal marque son territoire** the animal marks its territory ◆ **j'ai marqué ce jour-là d'une pierre blanche/noire** I'll remember it as a red-letter day/black day ◆ **marquez d'une croix l'emplacement du véhicule** mark the position of the vehicle with a cross ◆ **la pendule marque 6 heures** the clock shows *ou* says 6 o'clock ◆ **des pinces marquent la taille** *(Couture)* darts emphasize the waist(line) ◆ **robe qui marque la taille** dress which shows off the waistline ◆ **cela marque (bien) que le pays veut la paix** that definitely indicates *ou* shows that the country wants peace, that's a clear sign that the country wants peace
3 *[+ événement]* to mark ◆ **un bombardement a marqué la reprise des hostilités** a bomb attack marked the renewal *ou* resumption of hostilities ◆ **des réjouissances populaires ont marqué la prise de pouvoir par la junte** the junta's takeover was marked by public celebrations ◆ **pour ~ cette journée on a distribué ...** to mark *ou* commemorate this day they distributed ...
4 *(= écrire) [+ nom, rendez-vous, renseignement]* to write down, to note down, to make a note of ◆ **~ les points** *ou* **les résultats** to keep *ou* note the score ◆ **on l'a marqué absent** he was marked absent ◆ **j'ai marqué 3 heures sur mon agenda** I've got 3 o'clock (noted) down in my diary ◆ **il a marqué qu'il fallait prévenir les élèves** he noted down that the pupils should be told, he made a note to tell the pupils ◆ **c'est marqué en bas de la feuille** it's written at the bottom of the sheet ◆ **qu'y a-t-il de marqué ?** what does it say?, what's written (on it)?
5 *(= endommager) [+ glace, bois]* to mark; *(= affecter) [+ personne]* to mark ◆ **~ son époque** *(influencer)* to put one's mark *ou* stamp on one's time ◆ **la souffrance l'a marqué** suffering has left its mark on him ◆ **il est marqué par la vie** life has left its mark on him ◆ **visage marqué par la maladie** face marked by illness ◆ **visage marqué par la petite vérole** face pitted *ou* scarred with smallpox ◆ **la déception se marquait sur son visage** disappointment showed in his face *ou* was written all over his face
6 *(= manifester, montrer) [+ désapprobation, fidélité, intérêt]* to show
7 *(Sport) [+ joueur]* to mark; *[+ but, essai]* to score ◆ **~ qn de très près** *ou* **à la culotte** *(Sport)* to mark sb very closely *ou* tightly; *(fig)* to keep close tabs on sb
8 *(locutions)* **~ le coup** * *(= fêter un événement)* to mark the occasion; *(= accuser le coup)* to react ◆ **j'ai risqué une allusion, mais il n'a pas marqué le coup** * I made an allusion to it but he showed no reaction ◆ **~ un point/des points (sur qn)** to score a point/several points (against sb) ◆ **~ la mesure** to keep the beat ◆ **~ le pas** *(lit)* to beat *ou* mark time; *(fig)* to mark time ◆ **~ un temps d'arrêt** to pause momentarily
VI 1 *[événement, personnalité]* to stand out, to be outstanding; *[coup]* to reach home, to tell ◆ **cet incident a marqué dans sa vie** that particular incident stood out in *ou* had a great impact on his life
2 *[crayon]* to write; *[tampon]* to stamp ◆ **ne pose pas le verre sur ce meuble, ça marque** don't put the glass down on that piece of furniture, it will leave a mark

marqueté, e /maʀkəte/ ADJ *[bois]* inlaid

marqueterie /maʀkɛtʀi/ NF *(= technique)* marquetry; *(= objet)* marquetry, inlaid work; *(fig)* mosaic ◆ **table en ~** inlaid *ou* marquetry table

marqueur, -euse /maʀkœʀ, øz/ NM,F 1 *(Sport, Jeux) [de points]* score-keeper, scorer; *(= buteur)* scorer; *[de joueur]* marker 2 *[de bétail]* brander
NM 1 *(= stylo)* felt-tip pen; *(indélébile)* marker pen 2 *(Méd = substance radioactive)* tracer ◆ **~ génétique** genetic marker 3 *(= tableau)* scoreboard 4 *(Ling)* marker ◆ **~ syntagmatique** phrase marker NF **marqueuse** *(Comm = appareil)* (price) labeller

marquis /maʀki/ NM marquis, marquess ◆ **petit ~** *(péj)* lordling

marquisat /maʀkiza/ NM marquisate

marquise /maʀkiz/ NF 1 *(= noble)* marchioness; → **Madame** 2 *(= auvent)* glass canopy *ou* awning; *(= tente de jardin)* marquee *(Brit)*, garden tent *(US)* 3 ◆ **les (îles) Marquises** the Marquesas Islands 4 *(Culin)* **~ au chocolat** chocolate charlotte 5 *(= siège)* marquise 6 *(= bague)* marquise

marraine /maʀɛn/ NF *[d'enfant]* godmother; *[de navire]* christener, namer; *(dans un club)* sponsor, proposer ◆ **~ de guerre** *soldier's wartime (woman) penfriend*

Marrakech /maʀakɛʃ/ N Marrakech, Marrakesh

marrant, e * /maʀɑ̃, ɑ̃t/ ADJ 1 *(= amusant)* funny ◆ **c'est un ~, il est ~** he's a scream * *ou* a great laugh * ◆ **ce n'est pas ~** it's not funny, it's no joke ◆ **il n'est pas ~** *(ennuyeux, triste)* he's pretty dreary *, he's not much fun; *(sévère)* he's pretty grim *; *(empoisonnant)* he's a pain in the neck * ◆ **tu es ~ toi ! comment vais-je faire sans voiture ?** *(iro)* don't make me laugh! what am I going to do without a car? 2 *(= étrange)* funny, odd

marre ⁑ /maʀ/ ADV ◆ **en avoir ~** to be fed up * *ou* cheesed off ⁑ *(Brit) (de* with) to be sick * *(de* of); ◆ **j'en ai ~ de toi** I've just about had enough of you *, I am fed up with you * ◆ **c'est ~ !, il y en a ~ !** that's enough!

marrer (se) ⁑ /maʀe/ ▸ conjug 1 ◂ VPR to laugh, to have a good laugh * ◆ **on s'est (bien) marré !** *(= on a ri)* we had a good laugh! *; *(= on s'est bien amusés)* we had a great time!; *(iro)* that was a barrel of laughs! ◆ **il se marrait comme un fou** he was in fits * (of laughter) *ou* kinks ⁑ *(Brit)* ◆ **on ne se marre pas tous les jours au boulot !** work isn't always fun and games * *ou* a laugh a minute ◆ **faire ~ qn** to make sb laugh ◆ **tu me fais ~ avec ta démocratie !** you make me laugh with all your talk about democracy!

marri, e † /maʀi/ ADJ *(littér = triste)* sad, doleful *(de* about); *(= désolé)* sorry, grieved † *(de* about)

marron[1] /maʀɔ̃/ NM 1 *(= fruit)* chestnut ◆ **~ d'Inde** horse chestnut ◆ **~s chauds** roast chestnuts ◆ **~ glacé** marron glacé ◆ **tirer les ~s du feu** *(= être le bénéficiaire)* to reap the benefits; *(= être la victime)* to be a cat's paw; → **purée** 2 *(= couleur)* brown 3 *(⁑ = coup)* blow, thump, cuff, clout *(Brit)* ◆ **tu veux un ~ ?** do you want a cuff *ou* a thick ear * *(Brit)*? ADJ INV 1 *(= couleur)* brown 2 *(⁑ = trompé)* **être ~** to be had *

marron[2]**, -onne** /maʀɔ̃, ɔn/ ADJ *(= sans titres)* ◆ **médecin ~** quack, unqualified doctor ◆ **notaire/avocat ~** *(= sans scrupule)* crooked notary/lawyer ◆ **esclave ~** *(Hist)* runaway *ou* fugitive slave

marronnier /maʀɔnje/ NM 1 *(= arbre)* chestnut (tree) ◆ **~ (d'Inde)** horse chestnut tree 2 *(arg Presse)* chestnut *(arg)*

Mars /maʀs/ NM *(Astron, Myth)* Mars; → **champ**[1]

mars /maʀs/ NM *(= mois)* March ◆ **arriver** *ou* **venir** *ou* **tomber comme ~ en carême** to come *ou* happen as sure as night follows day; *pour loc voir* **septembre**

marseillais, e /maʀsɛjɛ, ɛz/ ADJ of *ou* from Marseilles; → **histoire** NM,F **Marseillais(e)** inhabitant *ou* native of Marseilles NF **Marseillaise** ◆ **la Marseillaise** the Marseillaise *(French national anthem)*

Marseille /maʀsɛj/ N Marseilles

Marshall /maʀʃal/ N ◆ **les îles ~** the Marshall Islands

marsouin /maʀswɛ̃/ NM *(= animal)* porpoise; *(† : Mil)* marine

marsupial, e (mpl **-iaux**) /maʀsypjal, jo/ ADJ, NM marsupial ◆ **poche ~e** marsupium

marte /maʀt/ NF ⇒ **martre**

marteau (pl **marteaux**) /maʀto/ NM 1 *(Menuiserie, Mus, Sport)* hammer; *[d'enchères, médecin]* hammer; *[de président, juge]* gavel; *[d'horloge]* striker; *[de porte]* knocker; *[de forgeron]* (sledge) hammer ◆ **il l'a cassé à coups de ~** he broke it with a hammer ◆ **donner un coup de ~ sur qch** to hit sth with a hammer ◆ **enfoncer qch à coups de ~** to hammer sth in, to drive sth in with a hammer ◆ **passer**

sous le ~ du commissaire-priseur to be put up for auction, to go under the (auctioneer's) hammer ◆ **entre le ~ et l'enclume** *(fig)* between the devil and the deep blue sea ◆ **être ~*** to be nuts* *ou* bats* *ou* cracked*; → **faucille, requin** [2] *(Anat)* hammer, malleus *(SPÉC)*

COMP **marteau pneumatique** pneumatic drill

marteau-perforateur (pl **marteaux-perforateurs**) /maʀtopɛʀfɔʀatœʀ/ NM hammer drill

marteau-pilon (pl **marteaux-pilons**) /maʀtopilɔ̃/ NM power hammer

marteau-piolet (pl **marteaux-piolets**) /maʀtopjɔlɛ/ NM piton hammer

marteau-piqueur (pl **marteaux-piqueurs**) /maʀtopikœʀ/ NM pneumatic drill

martel /maʀtɛl/ NM ◆ **se mettre ~ en tête** to worry o.s. sick, to get all worked up*

martelage /maʀtəlaʒ/ NM *(Métal)* hammering, planishing

martelé, e /maʀtəle/ (ptp de **marteler**) ADJ ◆ **cuivre ~** planished *ou* beaten copper ◆ **notes ~es** *(Mus)* martelé notes

martèlement /maʀtɛlmɑ̃/ NM *[de bruit, obus]* hammering, pounding; *[de pas]* pounding, clanking; *[de mots]* hammering out, rapping out

marteler /maʀtəle/ ▸ conjug 5 ◂ VT *[marteau, obus, coups de poings]* to hammer, to pound; *[+ objet d'art]* to planish, to beat; *[+ thème, message]* to drum out ◆ **~ ses mots** to hammer out *ou* rap out one's words ◆ **ce bruit qui me martèle la tête** that noise hammering *ou* pounding through my head ◆ **ses pas martelaient le sol gelé** his footsteps were pounding on the frozen ground

martellement /maʀtɛlmɑ̃/ NM ⇒ **martèlement**

martial, e (mpl **-iaux**) /maʀsjal, jo/ ADJ *(hum, littér) [peuple, discours]* martial, warlike, soldierlike; *[allure]* soldierly, martial ◆ **arts martiaux** martial arts; → **cour, loi**

martialement /maʀsjalmɑ̃/ ADV *(hum, littér)* martially, in a soldierly manner

martien, -ienne /maʀsjɛ̃, jɛn/ ADJ, NM,F Martian

martinet /maʀtinɛ/ NM [1] *(= fouet)* small whip *(used on children)*, strap [2] *(= oiseau)* swift [3] *(= marteau)* tilt hammer

martingale /maʀtɛ̃gal/ NF *(Habillement)* half belt; *(Équitation)* martingale; *(Roulette) (= combinaison)* winning formula; *(= mise double)* doubling-up

martiniquais, e /maʀtinikɛ, ɛz/ ADJ of *ou* from Martinique NM,F **Martiniquais(e)** inhabitant *ou* native of Martinique

Martinique /maʀtinik/ NF Martinique

martin-pêcheur (pl **martins-pêcheurs**) /maʀtɛ̃pɛʃœʀ/ NM kingfisher

martre /maʀtʀ/ NF marten ◆ **~ zibeline** sable

martyr, e[1] /maʀtiʀ/ ADJ *[soldats, peuple]* martyred ◆ **enfant ~** battered child NM,F martyr *(d'une cause* to a cause); ◆ **ne prends pas ces airs de ~ !** stop acting the martyr!, it's no use putting on that martyred look! ◆ **c'est le ~ de la classe** he's always being bullied by the rest of the class

martyre[2] /maʀtiʀ/ NM *(Rel)* martyrdom; *(fig = souffrance)* martyrdom, agony ◆ **le ~ de ce peuple** the martyrdom *ou* suffering of this people ◆ **sa vie fut un long ~** his life was one long agony ◆ **cette longue attente est un ~** it's agony waiting so long ◆ **mettre au ~** to torture

martyriser /maʀtiʀize/ ▸ conjug 1 ◂ VT [1] *(= faire souffrir) [+ personne, animal]* to torture; *[+ élève]* to bully; *[+ enfant, bébé]* to batter [2] *(Rel)* to martyr

martyrologe /maʀtiʀɔlɔʒ/ NM list of martyrs, martyrology

marxien, -ienne /maʀksjɛ̃, jɛn/ ADJ Marxian

marxisant, e /maʀksizɑ̃, ɑ̃t/ ADJ leaning towards Marxism

marxisme /maʀksism/ NM Marxism ◆ **~-léninisme** Marxism-Leninism

marxiste /maʀksist/ ADJ, NMF Marxist ◆ **~-léniniste** Marxist-Leninist

maryland /maʀilɑ̃(d)/ NM [1] *(= tabac) type of Virginia tobacco,* ≃ virginia [2] *(= État)* **le Maryland** Maryland

mas /mɑ(s)/ NM mas *(house or farm in Provence)*

mascara /maskaʀa/ NM mascara

mascarade /maskaʀad/ NF [1] *(péj = tromperie)* farce, masquerade ◆ **ce procès est une ~** this trial is a farce [2] *(= réjouissance, déguisement)* masquerade

Mascareignes /maskaʀɛɲ/ NFPL ◆ **l'archipel des ~** the Mascarene Islands

mascaret /maskaʀɛ/ NM (tidal) bore

mascarpone /maskaʀpɔn/ NM Mascarpone

Mascate /maskat/ N Muscat

mascotte /maskɔt/ NF mascot

masculin, e /maskylɛ̃, in/ ADJ *[hormone, population, sexe]* male; *[mode]* men's; *(péj = hommasse) [femme, silhouette]* mannish, masculine; *(Gram)* masculine ◆ **voix ~e** *[d'homme]* male voice; *[de femme]* masculine voice; *(virile)* manly voice ◆ **l'équipe ~e** *(Sport)* the men's team; → **rime** NM *(Gram)* masculine ◆ **"fer" est (du) ~** "fer" is masculine

masculiniser /maskylinize/ ▸ conjug 1 ◂ VT [1] ◆ **~ qn** to make sb look mannish *ou* masculine [2] *(Bio)* to make masculine

masculinité /maskylinite/ NF masculinity; *(= virilité)* manliness; *[de femme]* mannishness ◆ **taux de ~** *(Démographie)* male population rate

Maseru /mazeʀu/ N Maseru

maskinongé /maskinɔ̃ʒe/ NM *(Can = brochet)* muskellunge, muskie* *(Can)*, maskinonge

maso* /mazo/ (abrév de **masochiste**) ADJ masochistic ◆ **il est complètement ~ !** *(fig)* he's a glutton for punishment! NMF masochist

masochisme /mazɔʃism/ NM masochism

masochiste /mazɔʃist/ ADJ masochistic NMF masochist

masquant, e /maskɑ̃, ɑ̃t/ ADJ ◆ **produit ~** masking drug

masque /mask/ NM [1] *(= objet, Méd, Ordin)* mask ◆ **~ de saisie** data entry form ◆ **effet de ~** *(Phys)* masking effect; → **bas[1]**

[2] *(= expression du visage)* mask-like expression ◆ **dès que je lui ai dit ça, ça été le ~*** when I told him his face froze

[3] *(= cosmétique)* **~ (de beauté)** face pack ◆ **~ nettoyant** cleansing mask ◆ **se faire un ~** to put on a face pack *ou* mask

[4] *(= apparence)* mask, façade, front ◆ **ce n'est qu'un ~** it's just a mask *ou* front *ou* façade ◆ **sous** *ou* **derrière le ~ de la respectabilité** beneath the façade of respectability ◆ **lever** *ou* **jeter le ~** to unmask o.s., to reveal o.s. in one's true colours ◆ **arracher son ~ à qn** to unmask sb

[5] *(Hist = personne déguisée)* mask, masker

COMP **masque antipollution** anti-pollution mask
masque de carnaval carnival mask
masque chirurgical *ou* **de chirurgien** surgical mask
masque funéraire funeral mask
masque à gaz gas mask
masque de grossesse chloasma
masque mortuaire death mask
masque à oxygène oxygen mask
masque de plongée diving mask

masqué, e /maske/ (ptp de **masquer**) ADJ *[bandit]* masked; *[personne déguisée]* wearing *ou* in a mask ◆ **s'avancer ~** *(fig)* to hide one's hand ◆ **virage ~** blind corner *ou* bend; → **bal**

masquer /maske/ ▸ conjug 1 ◂ VT *(lit, fig = cacher) (gén)* to hide, to mask, to conceal *(à qn* from sb); *[+ lumière]* to screen, to shade; *[+ vue]* to block out; *(Mil) [+ troupes]* to screen, to mask ◆ **ça masque le goût** it masks the flavour ◆ **ces questions secondaires ont masqué l'essentiel** these questions of secondary importance masked *ou* obscured the essential point ◆ **avec un mépris à peine masqué** with barely concealed contempt VPR **se masquer** [1] *(= mettre un masque)* to put on a mask [2] *(= se cacher) [sentiment]* to be hidden; *[personne]* to hide, to conceal o.s. *(derrière* behind)

Massachusetts /masaʃysɛts/ NM ◆ **le ~** Massachusetts

massacrante /masakʀɑ̃t/ ADJ F → **humeur**

massacre /masakʀ/ NM [1] *(= tuerie) [de personnes]* slaughter *(NonC)*, massacre; *[d'animaux]* slaughter *(NonC)* ◆ **ce fut un véritable ~** it was sheer butchery ◆ **échapper au ~** to escape the massacre *ou* slaughter ◆ **envoyer des soldats au ~** to send soldiers to the slaughter ◆ **le ~ des bébés phoques** seal cull(ing) ◆ **~ écologique** ecological disaster ◆ **le ~ des innocents** *(Bible)* the massacre of the innocents ◆ **le Massacre de la Saint-Barthélemy** the Saint Bartholomew's Day Massacre ◆ **je vais faire un ~ !*** I'm going to kill somebody!; → **jeu**

[2] * **quel ~ !, c'est un vrai ~ !** *(= sabotage)* it's a complete mess!; *(= défaite sportive)* what a massacre!* ◆ **arrête le ~ !** stop before you do any more damage!

[3] *(* = succès)* **faire un ~** *[spectacle, chanteur]* to be a roaring success*

[4] *(Chasse)* stag's head *ou* antlers

massacrer /masakʀe/ ▸ conjug 1 ◂ VT [1] *(= tuer) [+ personnes]* to slaughter, to massacre; *[+ animaux]* to slaughter, to butcher ◆ **se ~** to massacre *ou* slaughter one another [2] *(* = saboter) [+ opéra, pièce]* to murder, to botch up; *[+ travail]* to make a mess *ou* hash* of; *(= mal découper, scier) [+ viande, planche]* to hack to bits, to make a mess of [3] *(* = vaincre) [+ adversaire]* to massacre, to slaughter, to make mincemeat of* ◆ **il s'est fait ~ par son adversaire** he was massacred by his opponent, his opponent made mincemeat of him* [4] *(* = éreinter) [+ œuvre, auteur]* to slam*, to tear to pieces, to slate* *(Brit)*

massacreur, -euse* /masakʀœʀ, øz/ NM,F *(= saboteur)* bungler, botcher; *(= tueur)* slaughterer, butcher

massage /masaʒ/ NM massage ◆ **~ facial** facial *ou* face massage ◆ **~ thaïlandais** Thai massage ◆ **faire un ~ à qn** to give sb a massage ◆ **faire un ~ cardiaque à qn** to give sb cardiac *ou* heart massage ◆ **salon de ~** massage parlour

masse /mas/ NF [1] *(= volume, Phys)* mass; *(= forme)* massive shape *ou* bulk ◆ **~ d'eau** *[de lac]* body *ou* expanse of water; *[de chute]* mass of water ◆ **~ de nuages** bank of clouds ◆ **~ d'air** *(Météo)* air mass ◆ **~ musculaire** muscle mass ◆ **la ~ de l'édifice** the massive structure of the building ◆ **pris** *ou* **taillé dans la ~** carved from the block ◆ **s'écrouler** *ou* **tomber comme une ~** to slump down *ou* fall in a heap

[2] *(= foule)* **les ~s (laborieuses)** the (working) masses, the toiling masses ◆ **les ~s populaires** the masses ◆ **les ~s paysannes** the agricultural work force; † the peasantry ◆ **la (grande)**

~ **des lecteurs** the (great) majority of readers ◆ **ça plaît à la** ~ *ou* **aux ~s** it appeals to the masses ◆ **éducation/psychologie des ~s** mass education/psychology, education/psychology of the masses ◆ **culture/manifestation/tourisme/production de** ~ mass culture/demonstration/tourism/production; → **fondre, noyer**[2]

3 *(= quantité)* quantity ◆ **la** ~ **d'informations est telle que ...** there is so much information that ... ◆ **la grande** ~ **des jeunes** the majority of young people

◆ **une masse de, des masses de** *(= beaucoup de)* masses of, loads of * ◆ **des ~s de touristes** crowds *ou* masses of tourists ◆ **cela représente une** ~ **de travail énorme** it represents an enormous amount *ou* quantity of work

◆ **pas des masses** * ◆ **des gens comme lui, je n'en connais pas des ~s** * I don't know many people like him ◆ **tu as aimé ce film ? – pas des ~s !** * did you like that film? – not all that much! ◆ **il n'y en a pas des ~s** * *[d'eau, argent]* there isn't much; *[de chaises, spectateurs]* there aren't many

◆ **en masse** *[exécutions, production]* mass *(épith)* ◆ **arrivée en** ~ mass influx ◆ **il y a eu des démissions/licenciements en** ~ there have been mass resignations/redundancies ◆ **fabriquer** *ou* **produire en** ~ to mass-produce ◆ **acheter/vendre en** ~ to buy/sell in bulk ◆ **manifester/protester en** ~ to hold a mass demonstration/protest ◆ **venir en** ~ to come en masse ◆ **ils sont venus en** ~ **à son concert** people flocked to his concert, people came in droves to his concert ◆ **il en a en** ~ he has masses *ou* lots *ou* loads *

4 *(Élec)* earth *(Brit)*, ground *(US)* ◆ **mettre à la** ~ to earth *(Brit)*, to ground *(US)* ◆ **faire** ~ to act as an earth *(Brit) ou* a ground *(US)* ◆ **être à la** ~ * *(fou)* to be nuts ‡ *ou* crazy *; *(fatigué)* to be out of it *

5 *(= argent) (Mil)* fund; *(Prison)* prisoner's earnings ◆ ~ **monétaire** money supply ◆ ~ **salariale** wage bill ◆ ~ **active** *(Jur)* assets ◆ ~ **passive** liabilities

6 *(= maillet)* sledgehammer; *[d'huissier]* mace ◆ ~ **d'armes** mace ◆ **ça a été le coup de** ~ **!** *(fig) (choc émotif)* it was quite a blow!; *(prix excessif)* it cost a bomb! *

massé /mase/ NM *(Billard)* massé (shot) ◆ **faire un** ~ to play a massé shot

masselotte /mas(ə)lɔt/ NF *[de voiture]* lead (for wheel balancing); *(en fonderie)* feeder

massepain /maspɛ̃/ NM marzipan

masser[1] /mase/ ▸ conjug 1 ◂ VT 1 *(= grouper) [+ gens]* to assemble, to bring *ou* gather together; *[+ choses]* to put *ou* gather together; *[+ troupes]* to mass ◆ **les cheveux massés en (un) chignon/derrière la tête** her hair gathered in a chignon/at the back of the head 2 *(Art)* to group VPR **se masser** *[foule]* to mass, to gather, to assemble

masser[2] /mase/ ▸ conjug 1 ◂ VT 1 *(= frotter) [+ personne]* to massage ◆ **se faire** ~ to have a massage, to be massaged ◆ **masse-moi le dos !** massage *ou* rub my back! 2 *(Billard)* ~ **la bille** to play a massé shot

massette /masɛt/ NF 1 *(= outil)* sledgehammer 2 *(= plante)* bulrush, reed mace

masseur /masœʀ/ NM *(= personne)* masseur; *(= machine)* massager ◆ ~**-kinésithérapeute** physiotherapist

masseuse /masøz/ NF masseuse

massicot /masiko/ NM *(Typo)* guillotine; *(Chim)* massicot

massicoter /masikɔte/ ▸ conjug 1 ◂ VT *[+ papier]* to guillotine

massif, -ive /masif, iv/ ADJ 1 *(d'aspect) [meuble, bâtiment, porte]* massive, solid, heavy; *[personne]* sturdily built; *[visage]* large, heavy ◆ **front** ~ massive forehead ◆ **homme de carrure massive** big strong man 2 *(= pur)* **or/argent/chêne** ~ solid gold/silver/oak 3 *(= important) [afflux, bombardements, dose, vote]* massive 4 *(= de nombreuses personnes) [arrestations, licenciements, exode, manifestation]* mass *(épith)* ◆ **armes de destruction massive** weapons of mass destruction ◆ **l'arrivée massive des réfugiés** the mass *ou* massive influx of refugees 5 *(Ling)* **terme** ~ mass noun NM 1 *(Géog)* ~ **(montagneux)** massif ◆ **le Massif central** the Massif Central 2 *(Bot) [de fleurs]* clump, bank; *[d'arbres]* clump 3 *(Archit)* pillar

massique /masik/ ADJ *[volume]* mass *(épith)* ◆ **puissance** ~ power-weight ratio ◆ **activité** ~ specific activity

massivement /masivmɑ̃/ ADV *[démissionner, partir]* en masse; *[voter, réduire]* massively; *[rejeter]* overwhelmingly; *[investir]* heavily ◆ **le pays importe** ~ **les céréales** the country imports huge quantities of cereals ◆ **les Parisiens ont** ~ **approuvé le projet** an overwhelming majority of Parisians are in favour of the project ◆ **la Banque centrale a dû intervenir** ~ **pour soutenir le yen** the Central Bank had to intervene heavily to support the yen

mass(-)media /masmedja/ NMPL mass media

massue /masy/ NF club, bludgeon ◆ ~ **de gymnastique** (Indian) club ◆ **coup de** ~ *(lit)* blow with a club *(ou* bludgeon) ◆ **ça a été le coup de** ~ **!** * *(très cher)* it cost a bomb! *; *(choc émotif)* it was quite a blow!; → **argument**

mastaba /mastaba/ NM mastaba(h) *(Egyptian burial chamber)*

mastectomie /mastɛktɔmi/ NF mastectomy

mastère /mastɛʀ/ NM *diploma awarded by a grande école or university for a year's advanced study or research*

mastic /mastik/ NM 1 *[de vitrier]* putty; *[de menuisier]* filler, mastic 2 *(Bot)* mastic 3 *(Typo) [de caractères, pages]* (faulty) transposition ADJ INV putty-coloured ◆ **imperméable (couleur)** ~ light-coloured *ou* off-white raincoat

masticage /mastikaʒ/ NM *[de vitre]* puttying; *[de fissure]* filling

masticateur, -trice /mastikatœʀ, tʀis/ ADJ chewing *(épith)*, masticatory

mastication /mastikasjɔ̃/ NF chewing, mastication

masticatoire /mastikatwaʀ/ ADJ chewing, masticatory NM masticatory

mastiff /mastif/ NM mastiff

mastiquer[1] /mastike/ ▸ conjug 1 ◂ VT *(= mâcher)* to chew, to masticate

mastiquer[2] /mastike/ ▸ conjug 1 ◂ VT *(avec du mastic) [+ vitre]* to putty, to apply putty to; *[+ fissure]* to fill, to apply filler to ◆ **couteau à** ~ putty knife

mastoc * /mastɔk/ ADJ INV *[personne]* hefty *, strapping *(épith)*; *[chose]* large and cumbersome ◆ **c'est un (type)** ~ he's a big hefty guy * *ou* bloke * *(Brit)*, he's a great strapping fellow * ◆ **une statue** ~ a great hulking statue

mastodonte /mastɔdɔ̃t/ NM 1 *(= animal)* mastodon 2 *(hum) (= personne)* colossus, mountain of a man *(ou* woman); *(= animal)* monster; *(= véhicule)* great bus *(hum) ou* tank *(hum)*; *(= camion)* huge vehicle, juggernaut *(Brit)*; *(= firme)* mammoth company

mastoïde /mastɔid/ NF *(= os)* mastoid

mastroquet * † /mastʀɔkɛ/ NM *(= bar)* pub, bar; *(= tenancier)* publican

masturbation /mastyʀbasjɔ̃/ NF masturbation ◆ **c'est de la** ~ **intellectuelle** *(péj)* it's mental masturbation

masturber VT, **se masturber** VPR /mastyʀbe/ ▸ conjug 1 ◂ to masturbate

m'as-tu-vu * /matyvy/ NMF INV *(pl inv)* show-off *, swank * ◆ **il est du genre** ~ he's a real show-off * ADJ INV *[mobilier, style]* showy

masure /mɑzyʀ/ NF tumbledown *ou* dilapidated house, hovel *(péj)*

mat[1] /mat/ ADJ INV *(Échecs)* ◆ **être** ~ to be in checkmate ◆ **(tu es)** ~ **!** checkmate! ◆ **faire** ~ to checkmate ◆ **il a fait** ~ **en 12 coups** he got checkmate in 12 moves ◆ **tu m'as fait** ~ **en 10 coups** you've (check)mated me in 10 moves NM checkmate; → **échec**[2]

mat[2]**, e** /mat/ ADJ *(= sans éclat) [métal]* mat(t), dull; *[couleur]* mat(t), dull, flat; *[peinture, papier, photo]* mat(t) ◆ **bruit** ~ dull noise, thud ◆ **avoir la peau ~e** *ou* **le teint** ~ to have a dark complexion

mat' * /mat/ NM (abrév de **matin**) morning ◆ **à deux/six heures du** ~ at two/six in the morning

mât /mɑ/ NM 1 *(Naut)* mast ◆ **grand** ~ mainmast 2 *(= pylône, poteau)* pole, post; *(= hampe)* flagpole; *(Sport)* climbing pole

COMP **mât d'artimon** mizzenmast
mât de charge derrick, cargo boom
mât de cocagne greasy pole
mât de hune topmast
mât de misaine foremast
mât de perroquet topgallant mast

matador /matadɔʀ/ NM matador, bullfighter

mataf /mataf/ NM *(arg Marine)* sailor

matage /mataʒ/ NM *[de dorure, verre]* matting; *[de soudure]* caulking

matamore /matamɔʀ/ NM *(= fanfaron)* braggart ◆ **jouer les ~s** to swagger

match /matʃ/ NM *(Sport)* match, game *(US)* ◆ ~ **aller** first-leg match ◆ ~ **avancé/en retard** *match that has been brought forward/delayed* ◆ ~ **retour** return match, second-leg match ◆ ~ **amical** friendly (match) ◆ ~ **nul** tie, draw ◆ **ils ont fait** ~ **nul** they tied, they drew ◆ **ils ont fait** ~ **nul 0 à 0/2 à 2** it was a nil-nil/2-all *(Brit)* draw, they drew nil-nil/2-all *(Brit)*, they tied at zero all/2-all *(US)* ◆ ~ **à l'extérieur** *ou* **sur terrain adverse** away match ◆ ~ **à domicile** *ou* **sur son propre terrain** home match ◆ **faire un** ~ **de tennis/volley-ball** to play a tennis/volleyball match; → **disputer**

maté /mate/ NM maté

matelas /mat(ə)lɑ/ NM 1 *[de lit]* mattress ◆ ~ **de laine/à ressorts** wool/(interior-)sprung mattress ◆ ~ **de** *ou* **en mousse** foam mattress ◆ ~ **d'eau** water bed ◆ ~ **pneumatique** *(= lit)* air bed; *(de plage)* Lilo ® *(Brit)*, air mattress *(US)* ◆ ~ **d'air** *(Constr)* air space *ou* cavity ◆ **dormir sur un** ~ **de feuilles mortes** to sleep on a carpet of dead leaves; → **toile** 2 *(= réserve) [de devises]* reserve, cushion ◆ **pour préserver son petit** ~ **de voix** *(Pol)* to preserve his small majority ◆ **j'ai un** ~ **de sécurité** I have something to fall back on ◆ ~ **(de billets)** * wad of notes ◆ **il a un joli petit** ~ * he's got a tidy sum put by *

matelassé, e /mat(ə)lase/ (ptp de **matelasser**) ADJ *[veste, jupe, manteau]* quilted, padded; *[doublure]* padded NM quilting

matelasser /mat(ə)lase/ ▸ conjug 1 ◂ VT *[+ meuble, porte]* to pad, to upholster; *[+ tissu]* to quilt; *[+ vêtement] (= rembourrer)* to pad; *(= doubler)* to line; *(avec tissu matelassé)* to quilt

matelassier, -ière /mat(ə)lasje, jɛʀ/ NM,F mattress maker

matelassure /mat(ə)lasyʀ/ NF *(= rembourrage)* padding; *(= doublure)* quilting, lining

matelot /mat(ə)lo/ NM 1 *(gén = marin)* sailor, seaman; *(dans la marine de guerre)* ordinary rating *(Brit)*, seaman recruit *(US)* ◆ ~ **de première/deuxième/troisième classe** leading/

able/ordinary seaman ◆ ~ **breveté** able rating *(Brit)*, seaman apprentice *(US)* 2 *(= navire)* ~ **d'avant/d'arrière** (next) ship ahead/astern

matelote /mat(ə)lɔt/ NF 1 *(= plat)* matelote; *(= sauce)* matelote sauce *(made with wine)* ◆ ~ **d'anguille** eels stewed in wine sauce 2 *(= danse)* hornpipe

mater[1] /mate/ ▸ conjug 1 ◂ VT 1 *[+ rebelles]* to bring to heel, to subdue; *[+ terroristes]* to bring ou get under control; *[+ enfant]* to take in hand; *[+ révolution]* to put down, to quell, to suppress; *[+ incendie]* to bring under control, to check ◆ **je vais les ~ !** I'll show them who's boss! 2 *(Échecs)* to put in checkmate, to checkmate, to mate

mater[2] ‡ /mate/ ▸ conjug 1 ◂ VT *(= regarder)* to eye up*, to ogle; *(= épier)* to spy on ◆ **mate si le prof arrive !** keep an eye out for the teacher coming!

mater[3] /mate/ ▸ conjug 1 ◂ VT 1 *(= marteler)* *[+ métal]* to caulk 2 ⇒ **matir**

mater[4] ‡ /matɛʀ/ NF mum* *(Brit)*, mom* *(US)* ◆ **ma** ~ my old woman* ou mum‡ *(Brit)* ou mom* *(US)*

mâter /mate/ ▸ conjug 1 ◂ VT *(Naut)* to mast

matérialisation /mateʀjalizasjɔ̃/ NF *[de projet, promesse, doute]* materialization; *(Phys)* mass energy conversion; *(Spiritisme)* materialization

matérialiser /mateʀjalize/ ▸ conjug 1 ◂ VT 1 *(= concrétiser)* *[+ projet]* to bring about, to carry out; *[+ promesse, doute]* to realize; *(= symboliser)* *[+ vertu, vice]* to embody; *(Philos)* to materialize 2 *(= signaliser)* *[+ frontière]* to mark ◆ ~ **au sol un passage clouté** to mark a pedestrian crossing ◆ **"chaussée non matérialisée"** "unmarked road" VPR **se matérialiser** to materialize

matérialisme /mateʀjalism/ NM materialism

matérialiste /mateʀjalist/ ADJ materialistic NMF materialist

matérialité /mateʀjalite/ NF materiality

matériau (pl **matériaux**) /mateʀjo/ NM *(Constr)* material; *(= documents)* material *(NonC)* ◆ ~**x de récupération** waste material ◆ ~**x de construction** building materials; → **résistance**

matériel, -elle /mateʀjɛl/ ADJ 1 *[monde, preuve, bien-être, confort]* material ◆ **être** ~ material ou physical being ◆ **dégâts ~s** material damage ◆ **j'ai la preuve matérielle de son crime** I have tangible ou material proof of his crime ◆ **je suis dans l'impossibilité matérielle de le faire** it's materially impossible for me to do it ◆ **je n'ai pas le temps ~ de le faire** I simply don't have the time to do it

2 *[plaisirs, biens, préoccupations]* worldly

3 *(= financier)* *[gêne, problèmes]* financial; *(= pratique)* *[organisation, obstacles]* practical ◆ **aide matérielle** material aid ◆ **de nombreux avantages ~s** a large number of material advantages ◆ **sa vie matérielle est assurée** his material needs are provided for, he is provided for materially

NM *(Agr, Mil)* equipment *(NonC)*, materials; *(Tech)* equipment *(NonC)*, plant *(NonC)*; *(= attirail)* gear *(NonC)*, kit *(NonC)*; *(= données)* material *(NonC)* ◆ **le** ~ *(Ordin)* the hardware ◆ ~ **de camping/d'enregistrement/de jardinage** camping/recording/gardening equipment ◆ ~ **de bureau/d'imprimerie/de laboratoire** office/printing/laboratory equipment ◆ ~ **de pêche** fishing tackle ◆ ~ **pédagogique** teaching equipment ou aids

COMP **matériel d'exploitation** plant *(NonC)*
matériel génétique genetic material
matériel de guerre weaponry *(NonC)*
matériel humain human material, labour force
matériel roulant *(Rail)* rolling stock
matériel scolaire *(= livres, cahiers)* school (reading ou writing) materials; *(= pupitres, projecteurs)* school equipment

matériellement /mateʀjɛlmɑ̃/ ADV 1 *(= physiquement)* *[se concrétiser, exister]* physically ◆ **c'est ~ possible** it can be done, it's feasible ◆ **c'est ~ impossible** it cannot be done, it's physically impossible 2 *(= financièrement)* *[aider]* financially

maternage /matɛʀnaʒ/ NM *(= dorlotement)* mothering, babying*, cosseting; *(fait de mâcher le travail)* spoonfeeding

maternant, e /matɛʀnɑ̃, ɑ̃t/ ADJ motherly

maternel, -elle /matɛʀnɛl/ ADJ 1 *(= d'une mère)* *[instinct, amour]* maternal, motherly; *(= comme d'une mère)* *[geste, soin]* motherly; *[lait]* mother's *(épith)* 2 *(= de la mère)* of the mother, maternal ◆ **du côté** ~ *(Généalogie)* on one's mother's side, on the maternal side ◆ **c'est mon grand-père** ~ he's my grandfather on my mother's side, he's my maternal grandfather ◆ **écoute les conseils ~s !** listen to your mother's advice! ◆ **la protection maternelle et infantile** *(Admin)* ≃ mother and infant welfare; → **allaitement, lait, langue** NF **maternelle** ◆ **(école) maternelle** nursery school ◆ **il est en** ou **à la maternelle** he's at nursery school

materner /matɛʀne/ ▸ conjug 1 ◂ VT *(= dorloter)* to mother, to baby*, to cosset; *(= mâcher le travail à)* to spoonfeed ◆ **se faire** ~ *(gén)* to be babied*; *[employé]* to be spoonfed

maternisé /matɛʀnize/ ADJ M → **lait**

maternité /matɛʀnite/ NF 1 *(= bâtiment)* maternity hospital ou home 2 *(Bio)* pregnancy ◆ **fatiguée par plusieurs ~s** exhausted by several pregnancies ou from having had several babies 3 *(= état de mère)* motherhood, maternity ◆ **la ~ l'a mûrie** motherhood ou being a mother has made her more mature; → **allocation, congé** 4 *(Art)* painting of mother and child (ou children)

mateur, -euse ‡ /matœʀ, øz/ NM,F ogler

math /mat/ NFPL → **math(s)**

mathématicien, -ienne /matematisjɛ̃, jɛn/ NM,F mathematician

mathématique /matematik/ ADJ *[problème, méthode, précision, rigueur]* mathematical ◆ **c'est ~ !*** *(sûr)* it's bound to happen!, it's a dead cert!‡ *(Brit)*; *(logique)* it's logical! NF ◆ ~ mathematics *(sg)* NFPL **mathématiques** mathematics *(sg)* ◆ ~**s modernes/pures** modern/pure maths *(Brit)* ou math *(US)* ◆ ~**s supérieures/spéciales** *first/second year advanced maths class preparing for the Grandes Écoles*

mathématiquement /matematikmɑ̃/ ADV *(Math, fig)* mathematically ◆ ~**, il n'a aucune chance** logically he hasn't a hope

mathématiser /matematize/ ▸ conjug 1 ◂ VT to express mathematically

matheux, -euse* /matø, øz/ NM,F *(= spécialiste)* mathematician, maths *(Brit)* ou math *(US)* specialist; *(= étudiant)* maths *(Brit)* ou math *(US)* student ◆ **c'est la matheuse de la famille** she's the mathematician ou maths expert in the family

Mathieu /matjø/ NM Matthew

math(s)* /mat/ NFPL (abrév de **mathématiques**) maths* *(Brit)*, math* *(US)* ◆ **être en ~ sup/spé** *to be in the first/second year advanced maths class preparing for the Grandes Écoles*

Mathusalem /matyzalɛm/ NM Methuselah ◆ **ça date de ~*** *[situation]* it goes back a long way; *[objet]* it's as old as the hills

matière /matjɛʀ/ NF 1 *(Philos, Phys)* **la** ~ matter ◆ **la ~ vivante** living matter

2 *(= substances)* matter *(NonC)*, material ◆ ~ **combustible/inflammable** combustible/inflammable material ◆ ~ **organique** organic matter ◆ ~ **précieuse** precious substance ◆ ~**s (fécales)** faeces *(Brit)*, feces *(US)* ◆ **le transport de ~s dangereuses** the transport of hazardous materials

3 *(= fond, sujet)* material, matter; *(Scol)* subject ◆ **cela lui a fourni la ~ de son dernier livre** that gave him the material for his latest book ◆ **il est bon dans toutes les ~s** *(Scol)* he is good at all subjects ◆ **il est très ignorant en la ~** he is completely ignorant on the subject, it's a matter ou subject he knows nothing about ◆ **en la ~, il faudrait demander à un spécialiste** it's better to ask a specialist about that kind of thing ◆ ~ **principale** *(Univ)* main subject *(Brit)*, major *(US)* ◆ ~ **secondaire** *(Univ)* subsidiary *(Brit)*, second subject *(Brit)*, minor *(US)* ◆ **entrée en** ~ introduction; → **option, table**

4 *(locutions)* **en ~ poétique/commerciale** where ou as far as poetry/commerce is concerned ◆ **en ~ d'art/de jardinage** as regards art/gardening ◆ **donner ~ à plaisanter** to give cause for laughter ◆ **il y a là ~ à réflexion** this is a matter for serious thought ◆ **ça lui a donné ~ à réflexion** it gave him food for thought ◆ **il n'y a pas là ~ à rire** this is no laughing matter ◆ **il n'y a pas là ~ à se réjouir** this is no matter for rejoicing

COMP **matière(s) grasse(s)** fat content, fat ◆ **yaourt à 15% de ~ grasse** yoghurt with 15% fat content
matière grise *(lit, fig)* grey *(Brit)* ou gray *(US)* matter ◆ **faire travailler sa ~ grise** to use one's grey matter
matière imposable object of taxation
matière noire *(Astron)* dark matter
matière plastique plastic ◆ **en ~ plastique** plastic *(épith)*
matière première raw material

MATIF /matif/ NM (abrév de **marché à terme d'instruments financiers** ou **marché à terme international de France**) ≃ LIFFE *(Brit)*

matifiant, e /matifjɑ̃, ɑ̃t/ ADJ matifying

matifier /matifje/ ▸ conjug 7 ◂ VT *[fond de teint, crème]* to matify

Matignon /matiɲɔ̃/ NM ◆ **(l'hôtel)** ~ the Hotel Matignon *(the offices of the Prime Minister of the French Republic)* ◆ **les accords** ~ the Matignon Agreements *(which laid down workers' rights)*

matin /matɛ̃/ NM 1 *(= partie de journée)* morning ◆ **par un ~ de juin** on a June morning, one June morning ◆ **le 10 au ~, le ~ du 10** on the morning of the 10th ◆ **2h du** ~ 2 a.m., 2 in the morning ◆ **je suis du** ~ *(actif dès le matin)* I'm a morning person; *(de l'équipe du matin)* I'm on ou I work mornings ◆ **du ~ au soir** from morning till night, morning noon and night ◆ **je ne travaille que le** ~ I only work mornings* ou in the morning ◆ **à prendre ~ midi et soir** *(Méd)* to be taken three times a day ◆ **jusqu'au** ~ until morning ◆ **de bon** ou **de grand** ~ early in the morning ◆ **au petit** ~ in the small ou early hours ◆ **nous avons parlé jusqu'au petit ~** we talked into the small ou early hours; → **quatre**

2 *(littér)* **au ~ de sa vie** in the morning of one's life

ADV † ◆ **partir/se lever** ~ to leave/get up very early ou at daybreak

mâtin /mɑtɛ̃/ NM 1 *(† = coquin)* cunning devil*, sly dog* 2 *(= chien)* *(de garde)* (big) watchdog; *(de chasse)* hound EXCL † by Jove!, my word!

matinal, e (mpl **-aux**) /matinal, o/ ADJ *[tâches, toilette]* morning *(épith)* ◆ **gelée ~e** early morning frost ◆ **heure ~e** early hour ◆ **être** ~ to be an early riser, to get up early ◆ **il est bien ~ aujourd'hui** he's up early today

mâtine /mɑtin/ NF hussy

mâtiné, e /mɑtine/ (ptp de **mâtiner**) ADJ *[animal]* crossbred ◆ **chien ~** mongrel (dog) ◆ **~ de** *[+ animal]* crossed with; *(fig)* mixed with ◆ **il parle un français ~ d'espagnol** he speaks a mixture of French and Spanish ◆ **un libéralisme ~ de socialisme** liberalism mixed with socialism ◆ **il est ~ cochon d'Inde**** *(injurieux)* he's a half-breed *(pej)*

matinée /matine/ NF 1 *(= matin)* morning ◆ **je le verrai demain dans la ~** I'll see him sometime (in the course of) tomorrow morning ◆ **en début/en fin de ~** at the beginning/at the end of the morning ◆ **après une ~ de chasse** after a morning's hunting; → **gras** 2 *(Ciné, Théât)* matinée, afternoon performance ◆ **j'irai en ~** I'll go to the matinée (performance) ◆ **~ dansante** tea dance ◆ **~ enfantine** children's matinée

mâtiner /mɑtine/ ▸ conjug 1 ◂ VT *[+ chien]* to cross

matines /matin/ NFPL matins

matir /matiʀ/ ▸ conjug 2 ◂ VT *[+ verre, argent]* to mat(t), to dull

matité /matite/ NF *[de peinture, teint]* mat(t) aspect; *[de son]* dullness ◆ **~ pulmonaire** *(Méd)* flatness

matois, e /matwa, waz/ ADJ *(littér = rusé)* wily, sly, crafty ◆ **c'est un(e) ~(e)** he's (*ou* she's) a sly *ou* a crafty one

maton, -onne /matɔ̃, ɔn/ NM,F *(arg Prison)* screw *(arg)*

matos* /matos/ NM equipment *(NonC)*, gear *(NonC)*

matou /matu/ NM tomcat, tom

matraquage /matʀakaʒ/ NM 1 *(par la police)* beating (up) *(with a truncheon)* 2 *(Presse, Radio)* plugging ◆ **le ~ publicitaire** media hype* *ou* overkill ◆ **le ~ idéologique** ideological brainwashing

matraque /matʀak/ NF *[de police]* baton, truncheon *(Brit)*, billy (club) *(US)*; *[de malfaiteur]* club, cosh *(Brit)* ◆ **coup de ~** *(lit)* blow from *ou* with a baton *ou* club ◆ **ça a été le coup de ~*** *(fig) (cher)* it cost a bomb*; *(inattendu)* it was a bolt from the blue

matraquer /matʀake/ ▸ conjug 1 ◂ VT 1 *[police]* to beat up *(with a truncheon)*; *[malfaiteur]* to club, to cosh *(Brit)* 2 *(* = escroquer)* **~ le client** to fleece* *ou* soak** *(US)* customers ◆ **se faire ~*** to get ripped off* *ou* fleeced* *ou* done* 3 *(Presse, Radio) [+ chanson, produit, publicité]* to plug, to hype*; *[+ public]* to bombard (*de* with)

matraqueur /matʀakœʀ/ NM *(arg Sport)* dirty player; *(= policier, malfaiteur)* dirty worker

matriarcal, e (mpl **-aux**) /matʀijaʀkal, o/ ADJ matriarchal

matriarcat /matʀijaʀka/ NM matriarchy

matricaire /matʀikɛʀ/ NF mayweed

matrice /matʀis/ NF 1 *(= utérus)* womb 2 *(Tech)* mould, die; *(Ordin, Typo)* matrix; *[de disque]* matrix 3 *(Ling, Math)* matrix ◆ **~ réelle/complexe** matrix of real/complex numbers 4 *(Admin)* register ◆ **~ cadastrale** cadastre ◆ **~ du rôle des contributions** ≃ original of register of taxes

matricide /matʀisid/ ADJ matricidal NMF, NM matricide

matriciel, -ielle /matʀisjɛl/ ADJ *(Math)* matrix *(épith)*, done with a matrix; *(Admin)* pertaining to assessment of taxes ◆ **loyer ~** rent assessment *(to serve as basis for calculation of rates or taxes)* ◆ **imprimante matricielle** dot-matrix printer

matricule /matʀikyl/ NM *(Mil)* regimental number; *(Admin)* administrative *ou* official *ou* reference number ◆ **dépêche-toi, sinon ça va barder** *ou* **mal aller pour ton ~ !*** hurry up or your number'll be up!* *ou* you'll really get yourself bawled out!** NF roll, register ADJ ◆ **numéro ~** → nm ◆ **registre ~** → nf → **livret**

matrilinéaire /matʀilineɛʀ/ ADJ matrilineal

matrimonial, e (mpl **-iaux**) /matʀimɔnjal, jo/ ADJ matrimonial, marriage *(épith)*; → **agence, régime**[1]

matrone /matʀɔn/ NF *(péj) (= mère de famille)* matronly woman; *(= grosse femme)* stout woman; *(Antiq) wife of a Roman citizen*

Matthieu /matjø/ NM Matthew

matu* /maty/ NF *(Helv Scol)* abrév de **maturité**

maturation /matyʀasjɔ̃/ NF *(Bot, Méd)* maturation; *[de fromage]* maturing, ripening; *[d'idée, projet]* gestation

mature /matyʀ/ ADJ mature

mâture /mɑtyʀ/ NF masts ◆ **dans la ~** aloft

maturité /matyʀite/ NF 1 *(gén)* maturity ◆ **arriver** *ou* **parvenir à ~** *[fruit]* to become ripe; *[plante]* to reach maturity; *[idée]* to come to maturity; *[technique]* to be perfected; *[entreprise, service]* to be fully operational; *[sportif]* to be at one's best ◆ **manquer de ~** to be immature ◆ **il manque de ~ politique** he's politically immature ◆ **un homme en pleine ~** a man in his prime *ou* at the height of his powers ◆ **~ d'esprit** maturity of mind ◆ **il fait preuve d'une grande ~** he's very mature ◆ **cet enfant a gagné en ~** this child has matured 2 *(Helv = baccalauréat) secondary school examination giving university entrance qualification*, ≃ A-levels *(Brit)*, high school diploma *(US)*

maudire /modiʀ/ ▸ conjug 2 ◂ VT to curse

maudit, e /modi, it/ (ptp de **maudire**) ADJ 1 *(* : avant n)* blasted*, damned** ◆ **quel ~ temps !** what lousy* *ou* filthy weather! 2 *(après n : littér = réprouvé)* (ac)cursed *(by God, society)* ◆ **poète/écrivain ~** *(Littérat)* accursed poet/writer 3 *(littér)* **~e soit la guerre !, la guerre soit ~e !** cursed be the war! ◆ **~ soit le jour où ...** cursed be the day on which ..., a curse *ou* a plague on the day on which ... ◆ **soyez ~ !** curse you!, a plague on you! NM,F damned soul ◆ **les ~s** the damned NM ◆ **le Maudit** the Devil

maugréer /mogʀee/ ▸ conjug 1 ◂ VI to grouse, to grumble (*contre* about, at)

maul /mol/ NM *(Rugby)* maul ◆ **faire un ~** to maul

maure, mauresque /mɔʀ, mɔʀɛsk/ ADJ Moorish NM **Maure** Moor NF **Mauresque** Moorish woman

Maurice /mɔʀis/ NM Maurice, Morris; → **île**

mauricien, -ienne /mɔʀisjɛ̃, jɛn/ ADJ Mauritian NM,F **Mauricien(ne)** Mauritian

Mauritanie /mɔʀitani/ NF Mauritania

mauritanien, -ienne /mɔʀitanjɛ̃, jɛn/ ADJ Mauritanian NM,F **Mauritanien(ne)** Mauritanian

mausolée /mozɔle/ NM mausoleum

maussade /mosad/ ADJ *[personne]* glum; *[ciel, temps, paysage]* gloomy, sullen; *[conjoncture]* bleak; *[marché]* sluggish ◆ **d'un air ~** sullenly, morosely ◆ **être d'humeur ~** to be sullen

maussaderie /mosadʀi/ NF sullenness, glumness, moroseness

mauvais, e /mɔvɛ, ɛz/ ADJ 1 *(= défectueux) [appareil, instrument]* bad, faulty; *[marchandise]* inferior, shoddy, bad; *[route]* bad, in bad repair; *[santé, vue, digestion, mémoire, roman, film]* poor, bad ◆ **elle a de ~ yeux** her eyes are *ou* her eyesight is bad ◆ **~e excuse** poor *ou* lame *ou* feeble excuse ◆ **un ~ contact** *(Élec)* a faulty connection ◆ **la balle est ~e** *(Tennis)* the ball is out ◆ **son français est bien ~** his French is very bad *ou* poor

2 *(= inefficace, incapable) [père, élève, acteur, ouvrier]* poor, bad ◆ **il est ~ en géographie** he's bad *ou* weak at geography ◆ **les ~ ouvriers ont toujours de ~ outils** *(Prov)* a bad workman always blames his tools *(Prov)*

3 *(= erroné) [méthode, moyens, direction, date]* wrong ◆ **tu as fait le ~ choix** you made the wrong choice ◆ **il roulait sur le ~ côté de la route** he was driving on the wrong side of the road ◆ **c'est un (très) ~ calcul de sa part** he's (badly) misjudged it *ou* things ◆ **il ne serait pas ~ de se renseigner** *ou* **que nous nous renseignions** it wouldn't be a bad idea *ou* it would be no bad thing if we found out more about this

4 *(= inapproprié) [jour, heure]* awkward, bad, inconvenient ◆ **il a choisi un ~ moment** he picked an awkward *ou* a bad time ◆ **il a choisi le ~ moment** he picked the wrong time

5 *(= dangereux, nuisible) [maladie, blessure]* nasty, bad ◆ **il a fait une ~e grippe/rougeole** he's had a bad *ou* nasty attack *ou* bout of flu/measles ◆ **la mer est ~e** the sea is rough ◆ **c'est ~ pour la santé** it's bad for your health ◆ **il est ~ de se baigner en eau froide** it's not good for you *ou* it's not a good idea to bathe in cold water ◆ **vous jugez ~ qu'il sorte le soir ?** do you think it's a bad thing for him to go out at night?

6 *(= défavorable) [rapport, critique]* unfavourable, bad; *(Scol) [bulletin, note]* bad

7 *(= désagréable) [temps]* bad, unpleasant, nasty; *[nourriture, repas]* bad, poor; *[odeur]* bad, unpleasant, offensive; *(= pénible) [nouvelle, rêve]* bad ◆ **ce n'est pas ~ !** it's not bad!, it's quite good! ◆ **il fait ~ aujourd'hui** the weather's bad today ◆ **la soupe a un ~ goût** the soup has an unpleasant *ou* a nasty taste, the soup tastes nasty ◆ **ce n'est qu'un ~ moment à passer** it's just a bad spell *ou* patch you've got to get through; → **caractère, gré, volonté**

8 *(= immoral, nuisible) [instincts, action, fréquentations, lectures]* bad ◆ **il n'a pas un ~ fond** he's not bad at heart; → **génie**

9 *(= méchant) [sourire, regard]* nasty, malicious, spiteful; *[personne, joie]* malicious, spiteful ◆ **être ~ comme la gale*** to be a nasty piece of work *(fig)* ◆ **ce n'est pas un ~ garçon** he's not a bad boy ◆ **ce n'est pas un ~ bougre*** *ou* **le ~ type*** *ou* **le ~ cheval*** he's not a bad guy* ◆ **il est vraiment ~ aujourd'hui** he's in an evil *ou* a foul mood today

10 *(locutions)* **quand on l'a renvoyé, il l'a trouvée** *ou* **eue ~e*** he was really angry when he got the sack* ◆ **il fait ~ le contredire** it is not advisable to contradict him

NM 1 *(= partie)* **enlève le ~ et mange le reste** cut out the bad part and eat the rest ◆ **la presse ne montre que le ~** the press only shows the bad side (of things)

2 *(= personnes)* **les ~** the wicked; → **bon**[1]

COMP **mauvais coucheur** awkward customer

mauvais coup ◆ **recevoir un ~ coup** to get a nasty blow ◆ **un ~ coup porté à nos institutions** a blow to *ou* an attack on our institutions ◆ **faire un ~ coup** to play a mean *ou* dirty trick (*à qn* on sb)

mauvaise graine ◆ **c'est de la ~e graine** he's (*ou* she's *ou* they're) a bad lot *(Brit) ou* seed *(US)*

mauvaise herbe weed ◆ **enlever** *ou* **arracher les ~es herbes du jardin** to weed the garden ◆ **la ~e herbe, ça pousse !** *(hum)* kids grow like weeds! *(hum)*

mauvais lieu place of ill repute

mauvais œil ◆ **avoir le ~ œil** to have the evil eye

mauvais pas ◆ **tirer qn/se sortir d'un ~ pas** to get sb out of/get out of a tight spot *ou* corner

mauvais plaisant hoaxer

mauvaise plaisanterie rotten trick

mauvaise saison rainy season

mauvais sort misfortune, ill fate

mauvais sujet bad lot *(Brit) ou* seed *(US)*

mauvaise tête ◆ **c'est une ~e tête** he's headstrong ◆ **faire la** *ou* **sa ~e tête** *(= bouder)* to sulk; *(= être difficile)* to be awkward *ou* difficult **mauvais traitement** ill treatment ◆ **subir de ~ traitements** to be ill-treated ◆ **~ traitements à enfants** child abuse, child battering ◆ **faire subir des ~ traitements à** to ill-treat; → **passe**[1]

mauve /mov/ ADJ, NM *(= couleur)* mauve NF *(= plante)* mallow

mauviette /movjɛt/ NF *(péj)* wimp *, weakling

mauvis /movi/ NM redwing

maux /mo/ NPL → **mal**[2]

max* /maks/ (abrév de **maximum**) ADV max* ◆ **à 8 heures ~** at 8 o'clock at the latest NM *(= condamnation)* ◆ **il a pris le ~, ils lui ont filé le ~** they threw the book at him *

◆ **un max** *[dépenser]* a hell of a lot * ◆ **ça coûte un ~** it costs a packet * ◆ **il se fait un ~ de fric** he makes loads * *ou* pots * *(Brit)* of money ◆ **il m'agace un ~** he drives me up the wall *

maxi /maksi/ PRÉF ◆ **~...** maxi ... ◆ **~-jupe** maxi-skirt ◆ **~-bouteille/-paquet** giant-size bottle/packet ADJ INV 1 *(* = maximum)* maximum 2 *(= long)* **manteau/jupe ~** maxi-coat/-skirt ◆ **la mode ~** the maxi-length fashion NM *(= mode)* maxi ◆ **elle s'habille en ~** she wears maxis ◆ **la mode est au ~** maxis are in (fashion) ADV *(* = maximum)* (at the) maximum, at the most

maxillaire /maksilɛʀ/ ADJ maxillary ◆ **os ~** jawbone NM jawbone, maxilla *(SPÉC)* ◆ **~ supérieur/inférieur** upper/lower maxilla *(SPÉC) ou* jawbone

maxima /maksima/ → **appel, maximum**

maximal, e (mpl **-aux**) /maksimal, o/ ADJ maximum, maximal ◆ **il a été condamné à la peine ~e** he was given the maximum sentence ◆ **la température ~e a été de 33 degrés** the top *ou* maximum temperature was 33°C, there was a high of 33°C

maximalisme /maksimalism/ NM *[de personne]* extremist attitude, extremism

maximaliste /maksimalist/ ADJ maximalist

maxime /maksim/ NF maxim

maximisation /maksimizasjɔ̃/ NF maximization

maximiser /maksimize/ ► conjug 1 ◄ VT to maximize

maximum (pl **maximum(s)** *ou* **maxima**) /maksimɔm, maksima/ ADJ maximum ◆ **la température ~** the maximum *ou* highest temperature ◆ **dans un délai ~ de dix jours** within ten days at the latest

NM maximum; *(Jur)* maximum sentence ◆ **faire le** *ou* **son ~** to do one's level best *ou* one's utmost *(pour* to*)*; ◆ **atteindre son ~** *[production]* to reach its maximum, to reach an all-time high; *[valeur]* to reach its highest *ou* maximum point

◆ **au maximum** at the maximum, at the most ◆ **ça vous coûtera 800 € au ~** it will cost you €800 at the most ◆ **sa radio était au ~** his radio was on full ◆ **au ~ de ses capacités** *ou* **possibilités** *[employé, sportif]* stretched to one's limits; *[usine, chaîne hi-fi]* at maximum *ou* full capacity

◆ **un maximum** * *(= beaucoup)* ◆ **il y a un ~ de frais sur un bateau** boats cost a fortune to run ◆ **il m'a fait payer un ~** he charged me a fortune ◆ **ça consomme un ~, ces voitures** these cars are real gas guzzlers *, these cars are really heavy on petrol *(Brit)*

ADV at the maximum, at the most ◆ **à six heures ~** at six o'clock at the latest ◆ **j'en ai pour 2 heures ~** I'll be 2 hours maximum *ou* at the most

maya /maja/ ADJ Mayan NM *(= langue)* Maya(n) NMF **Maya** Maya(n)

mayday /mɛde/ NM *(Naut)* Mayday

mayo* /majo/ NF (abrév de **mayonnaise**) mayo

mayonnaise /majɔnɛz/ NF mayonnaise ◆ **poisson/œufs (à la) ~** fish/eggs (with *ou* in) mayonnaise ◆ **la ~ n'a pas pris** *(lit)* the mayonnaise didn't thicken; *(fig)* the mix was all wrong ◆ **la ~ prend** *(lit)* the mayonnaise is thickening; *(fig)* things are looking good ◆ **faire monter la ~** *(fig)* to stir things *ou* it up *

Mayotte /majɔt/ NF Mayotte

mazagran /mazagʀɑ̃/ NM pottery goblet *(for coffee)*

mazette † /mazɛt/ EXCL *(admiration, étonnement)* my!, my goodness! NF *(= incapable)* nonentity

mazout /mazut/ NM heating *ou* domestic oil ◆ **chaudière/poêle à ~** oil-fired boiler/stove ◆ **chauffage central au ~** oil-fired central heating

mazouté, e /mazute/ ADJ *[mer, plage]* oil-polluted *(épith)*, polluted with oil *(attrib)*; *[oiseaux]* oil-covered *(épith)*, covered in oil *(attrib)*

mazurka /mazyʀka/ NF maz(o)urka

Mbabane /mbaban/ N Mbabane

MCJ /ɛmseʒi/ NF (abrév de **maladie de Creutzfeldt-Jakob**) CJD

MD ® /ɛmde/ NM (abrév de **MiniDisc**) MD

Me (abrév de **Maître**) *barrister's title* ◆ **~ Marlon** ≈ Mr *(ou* Mrs*)* Marlon QC *(Brit)*

me, m' /m(ə)/ PRON PERS 1 *(objet direct ou indirect)* me ◆ **~ voyez-vous ?** can you see me? ◆ **elle m'attend** she is waiting for me ◆ **il ~ l'a dit** he told me (it), he told me about it ◆ **il m'en a parlé** he spoke to me about it ◆ **il ~ l'a donné** he gave it to me, he gave it me * *(Brit)* ◆ **va ~ fermer cette porte !** *(intensif)* shut the door, would you! 2 *(réfléchi)* myself ◆ **je ne ~ vois pas dans ce rôle-là** I can't see myself in that part ◆ **je ~ regardais dans le miroir** I was looking at myself in the mirror

mea-culpa /meakylpa/ NM INV ◆ **faire son ~** *(lit)* to say one's mea culpa ◆ **j'ai fait mon mea culpa** *(fig)* I admitted I was wrong ◆ **mea culpa !** my fault!, my mistake!

méandre /meɑ̃dʀ/ NM *(Art, Géog)* meander; *[de politique]* twists and turns; *[d'intrigue]* ins and outs ◆ **les ~s de sa pensée** the twists and turns *ou* ins and outs *ou* complexities of his thought ◆ **se perdre dans les ~s administratifs/juridiques** to get lost in the maze of the administrative/legal system

méat /mea/ NM 1 *(Anat)* meatus 2 *(Bot)* lacuna

mec** /mɛk/ NM 1 *(= homme)* guy *, bloke * *(Brit)* ◆ **ça va les ~s ?** how's it going guys? * ◆ **ça c'est un ~ !** he's a real man! ◆ **c'est des histoires de ~s** it's man talk * 2 *(= compagnon)* **son ~** her man *

mécanicien, -ienne /mekanisjɛ̃, jɛn/ ADJ *[civilisation]* mechanistic NM,F 1 *(pour voitures)* (garage *ou* motor) mechanic ◆ **ouvrier ~** garage hand ◆ **c'est un bon ~** he's a good mechanic, he's good with cars *ou* with machines ◆ **ingénieur ~** mechanical engineer 2 *(dans avion, bateau)* engineer ◆ **~ navigant, ~ de bord** *(dans avion)* flight engineer; → **officier**[1] 3 *(= chauffeur de train)* train *ou* engine driver *(Brit)*, engineer *(US)* 4 **~ dentiste** dental technician *ou* mechanic *(Brit)*

mécanique /mekanik/ ADJ 1 *(gén)* mechanical; *[tapis]* machine-made; *[jouet]* clockwork, wind-up *(épith)* ◆ **les industries ~s** mechanical engineering industries ◆ **avoir des ennuis ~s** to have engine trouble ◆ **sports ~s** motor sports ◆ **énergie ~** mechanical energy ◆ **lois ~s** laws of mechanics; → **escalier, piano**[1], **rasoir**

2 *(= automatique) [hausse, effets]* automatic

3 *(= machinal) [geste, réflexe]* mechanical

NF 1 *(= science des machines)* (mechanical) engineering; *(= science du mouvement)* mechanics *(sg)* ◆ **il fait de la ~ (sur sa voiture)** he's tinkering with his car ◆ **la ~, ça le connaît** * he knows what he's doing in mechanics ◆ **~ céleste/ondulatoire** celestial/wave mechanics ◆ **~ hydraulique** hydraulics *(sg)* ◆ **~ des fluides/quantique** quantum/fluid mechanics

2 *(= mécanisme)* **la ~ d'une horloge** the mechanism of a clock ◆ **cette voiture, c'est de la** *ou* **une belle ~** this car is a fine piece of engineering ◆ **la ~ est rouillée** *ou* **usée** * *(= corps)* the old bones * aren't what they used to be

mécaniquement /mekanikmɑ̃/ ADV 1 *(= automatiquement)* automatically ◆ **cela entraîne ~ une hausse de l'inflation** it automatically leads to a rise in inflation 2 *(= par des machines)* mechanically ◆ **objet fait ~** machine-made object

mécanisation /mekanizasjɔ̃/ NF mechanization

mécaniser /mekanize/ ► conjug 1 ◄ VT to mechanize

mécanisme /mekanism/ NM mechanism ◆ **les ~s économiques/politiques** economic/political mechanisms ◆ **~s psychologiques/biologiques** psychological/biological workings *ou* mechanisms ◆ **le ~ de change(s)** the exchange rate mechanism ◆ **le ~ d'une action** the mechanics of an action

mécaniste /mekanist/ ADJ mechanistic

mécano* /mekano/ NM (abrév de **mécanicien**) mechanic, grease monkey * *(US)*

Meccano ® /mekano/ NM Meccano ®

mécénat /mesena/ NM *(Art)* patronage ◆ **~ d'entreprise** corporate sponsorship

mécène /mesɛn/ NM 1 sponsor; *(Hist)* patron (of the arts) ◆ **il a trouvé un ~** he has found a sponsor ◆ **le ~ du festival** the sponsor of the festival 2 ◆ **Mécène** *(Antiq)* Maecenas

méchamment /meʃamɑ̃/ ADV 1 *(= cruellement) [rire, agir]* spitefully, nastily, wickedly 2 *(* = très)* fantastically *, terrifically * ◆ **~ bon** fantastically * *ou* bloody ** *(Brit)* good ◆ **~ abîmé** really badly damaged ◆ **il a été ~ surpris** he got one hell * *ou* heck * of a surprise ◆ **ils se sont ~ disputés** they had a blazing row *(surtout Brit) ou* a terrible argument ◆ **on est ~ en retard** we're terribly late

méchanceté /meʃɑ̃ste/ NF 1 *(= caractère) [de personne, action]* nastiness, spitefulness, wickedness ◆ **faire qch par ~** to do sth out of spite ◆ **soit dit sans ~, il n'est pas à la hauteur** I don't want to be nasty, but he's not up to it 2 *(= action)* mean *ou* nasty action; *(= parole)* mean *ou* nasty remark ◆ **~ gratuite** unwarranted piece of unkindness *ou* spitefulness ◆ **dire des ~s à qn** to say nasty things to sb

méchant, e /meʃɑ̃, ɑ̃t/ ADJ 1 *(= malveillant) [personne]* nasty, malicious; *[enfant]* naughty; *[intention]* malicious ◆ **devenir ~** to turn *ou* get nasty ◆ **arrête, tu es ~** stop it, you're being horrid *ou* nasty ◆ **il n'est pas ~, ce n'est pas un ~ homme** he's not such a bad fellow; → **chien**

2 *(= dangereux, désagréable)* **ce n'est pas bien ~** * *[blessure, difficulté, dispute]* it's nothing to worry about; *[examen]* it's not too difficult ◆ **impliqué dans une ~e affaire de pots de vin** mixed up in an unsavoury bribery scandal ◆ **de ~e humeur** in a foul *ou* rotten mood

3 *(avant n) († = médiocre, insignifiant)* miserable, mediocre ◆ **~ vers/poète** poor *ou* second-rate verse/poet ◆ **un ~ morceau de fromage** one miserable *ou* sorry-looking bit of cheese ◆ **que de bruit pour une ~e clé perdue !** what a fuss over one stupid lost key!

4 *(avant n) (* intensif)* **il a une ~e bosse au front** he's got a nasty lump on his forehead ◆ **un ~ cigare** a great big cigar* ◆ **il a une ~e moto** he's got a fantastic* motorbike

NM,F ◆ **tais-toi, ~!** be quiet you naughty boy! ◆ **les ~s** *(gén)* the wicked; *(dans un film)* the baddies*, the bad guys* ◆ **faire le ~*** to be difficult, to be nasty

mèche /mɛʃ/ NF 1 *[de bougie, briquet, lampe]* wick; *[de bombe, mine]* fuse; *[de canon]* match ◆ **~ fusante** safety fuse 2 *[de cheveux]* tuft of hair, lock; *(sur le front)* forelock, lock of hair ◆ **~ postiche, fausse ~** hairpiece ◆ **~s folles** straggling locks *ou* wisps of hair ◆ **~ rebelle** stray lock (of hair) ◆ **se faire faire des ~s** to have highlights *ou* streaks put in (one's hair), to have one's hair streaked 3 *(Méd)* pack, dressing; *[de fouet]* lash; *[de perceuse]* bit 4 *(Naut)* main piece 5 *[de métier à filer]* rove 6 *(locutions)* **il a éventé** *ou* **vendu la ~** he gave the game away*, he let the cat out of the bag* ◆ **allumer la ~** to light the fuse *(fig)* ◆ **être de ~ avec qn*** to be in cahoots with sb* ◆ **un employé de la banque devait être de ~** a bank employee must have been in on it*

mécher /meʃe/ ▸ conjug 6 ◂ VT *(Tech)* to sulphurize; *(Méd)* to pack

méchoui /meʃwi/ NM *(= repas)* barbecue of a whole roast sheep

mécompte /mekɔ̃t/ NM *(frm)* 1 *(= désillusion : gén pl)* disappointment 2 *(= erreur de calcul)* miscalculation, miscount

méconium /mekɔnjɔm/ NM meconium

méconnaissable /mekɔnɛsabl/ ADJ *(= impossible à reconnaître)* unrecognizable; *(= difficile à reconnaître)* hardly recognizable

méconnaissance /mekɔnɛsɑ̃s/ NF *(= ignorance)* lack of knowledge (*de* about) ignorance (*de* of); *(littér = mauvais jugement)* lack of comprehension, misappreciation (*de* of); *(= refus de reconnaître)* refusal to take into consideration ◆ **il fait preuve d'une ~ totale de la situation** he knows absolutely nothing about the situation

méconnaître /mekɔnɛtʀ/ ▸ conjug 57 ◂ VT *(frm)* 1 *(= ignorer) [+ faits]* to be unaware of ◆ **je ne méconnais pas que ...** I am fully *ou* quite aware that ... 2 *(= mésestimer) [+ situation, problème, personne]* to misjudge; *[+ mérites, talent]* to underrate 3 *(= ne pas tenir compte de) [+ lois, devoirs]* to ignore

méconnu, e /mekɔny/ (ptp de **méconnaître**) ADJ 1 *(= peu connu)* little-known ◆ **des textes largement ~s** little-known writings ◆ **les films les plus ~s de Godard** Godard's least-known films ◆ **ce sport est largement ~ en France** this sport is largely unknown in France 2 *(= non reconnu) [talent, génie]* unrecognized ◆ **son œuvre est injustement ~e en France** his work has been unjustly ignored *ou* neglected in France

mécontent, e /mekɔ̃tɑ̃, ɑ̃t/ ADJ *(= insatisfait)* discontented, displeased, dissatisfied (*de* with); *(= contrarié)* annoyed (*de* with, at); ◆ **il a l'air très ~** he looks very annoyed *ou* displeased ◆ **il n'est pas ~ de cela** he is not altogether dissatisfied *ou* displeased with it NM,F malcontent, grumbler* ◆ **les ~s** *(Pol)* the malcontents ◆ **cette décision va faire des ~s** this decision is going to make some people very unhappy

mécontentement /mekɔ̃tɑ̃tmɑ̃/ NM *(Pol)* discontent; *(= déplaisir)* dissatisfaction, displeasure; *(= irritation)* annoyance ◆ **exprimer** *ou* **manifester son ~** to express one's dissatisfaction ◆ **motif** *ou* **sujet de ~** cause for dissatisfaction ◆ **provoquer un vif ~** to cause considerable discontent (*chez* among)

mécontenter /mekɔ̃tɑ̃te/ ▸ conjug 1 ◂ VT *[personne, décision]* to displease, to annoy

Mecque /mɛk/ NF ◆ **La ~** *(lit)* Mecca ◆ **ces îles sont la ~ des surfers** these islands are a Mecca for surfers

mécréant, e /mekʀeɑ̃, ɑ̃t/ NM,F 1 *(† ou hum = non-croyant)* non-believer ◆ **tu n'es qu'un ~** you're just a heathen 2 *(† péj = bandit)* scoundrel, miscreant †

médaillable /medajabl/ ADJ *[sportif]* likely to win a medal ◆ **les ~s des Jeux olympiques** the potential medal-winners at the Olympic Games

médaille /medaj/ GRAMMAIRE ACTIVE 53.3 NF 1 *(= pièce, décoration)* medal; *(† * = tache)* stain, mark ◆ **~ militaire** military decoration ◆ **~ pieuse** medal *(of a saint etc)* ◆ **~ du travail** long-service medal *(in industry etc)* ◆ **elle est ~ d'argent** she's got a silver medal, she's a silver medallist; → **profil, revers** 2 *(= insigne d'identité) [d'employé]* badge; *[de chien]* identification disc, name tag; *[de volaille]* guarantee tag

médaillé, e /medaje/ (ptp de **médailler**) ADJ *(Admin, Mil)* decorated *(with a medal)*; *(Sport)* holding a medal NM,F medal-holder ◆ **il est** *ou* **c'est un ~ olympique** he is an Olympic medallist, he is the holder of an Olympic medal

médailler /medaje/ ▸ conjug 1 ◂ VT *(Admin, Sport)* to award a medal to; *(Mil)* to decorate, to award a medal to ◆ **se ~ †*** *(= se tacher)* to get a stain *ou* mark on one's clothing

médaillon /medajɔ̃/ NM *(Art)* medallion; *(= bijou)* locket; *(Culin)* medaillon

mède /mɛd/ ADJ of Media NMF **Mède** Mede

médecin /med(ə)sɛ̃/ NM doctor, physician *(frm)* ◆ **femme ~** woman doctor ◆ **~ de l'âme** confessor ◆ **~ de bord** *(Naut)* ship's doctor ◆ **~ de campagne** country doctor ◆ **~-chef** head doctor ◆ **~-conseil** *doctor who decides whether certain forms of medical treatment should be reimbursed by the Sécurité sociale* ◆ **~ de famille** family practitioner *ou* doctor ◆ **~ des hôpitaux** ≈ consultant, physician *ou* doctor *(Brit)* with a hospital appointment ◆ **~ légiste** forensic scientist *ou* pathologist, expert in forensic medicine, medical examiner *(US)* ◆ **~ généraliste** *ou* **de ~e générale** general practitioner, GP *(Brit)*, family practitioner *(US)* ◆ **~ militaire** army medical officer ◆ **~ scolaire** school doctor, schools medical officer *(Brit Admin)* ◆ **~ du sport** sports doctor ◆ **~ traitant** attending physician ◆ **votre ~ traitant** your (usual *ou* family) doctor ◆ **quel est votre ~ référent ?** who's your G.P. *(Brit) ou* your family doctor *(US)*? ◆ **~ du travail** company doctor ◆ **~ de ville** doctor *(working in a town)*

médecine /med(ə)sin/ NF 1 *(= science)* medicine ◆ **~ alternative** *ou* **parallèle** alternative *ou* complementary medicine ◆ **~ douce** *ou* **naturelle** natural medicine ◆ **~ générale** general medicine ◆ **~ hospitalière** *medicine practised in hospitals* ◆ **~ infantile** paediatrics *(sg) (Brit)*, pediatrics *(US)* ◆ **~ légale** forensic medicine *ou* science ◆ **~ libérale** *medicine as practised by doctors in private practice* ◆ **~ opératoire** surgery ◆ **~ préventive** preventive medicine ◆ **~ du travail** occupational *ou* industrial medicine ◆ **~ du sport** sports medicine ◆ **~ spécialisée** specialized branches of medicine ◆ **~ de ville** *medicine as practised in general practices in towns* ◆ **~ d'urgence** emergency medicine ◆ **faire des études de ~, faire (sa) ~** to study *ou* do medicine ◆ **pratiquer une ~ révolutionnaire** to practise a revolutionary type of medicine ◆ **il exerçait la ~ dans un petit village** he had a (medical) practice *ou* he was a doctor in a small village; → **docteur, étudiant, faculté** 2 *(† = médicament)* medicine

medecine-ball (pl **medecine-balls**) /medsinbol/ NM medicine ball

média /medja/ NM medium ◆ **les ~s** the media ◆ **dans les ~s** in the media

médial, e (mpl **-aux**) /medjal, o/ ADJ medial NF **médiale** median

médian, e /medjɑ̃, jan/ ADJ *(Math, Stat)* median; *(Ling)* medial NF **médiane** *(Math, Stat)* median; *(Ling)* medial sound, mid vowel; → **ligne**[1]

médiante /medjɑ̃t/ NF *(Mus)* mediant

médiat, e /medja, jat/ ADJ mediate

médiateur, -trice /medjatœʀ, tʀis/ ADJ *(gén, Pol)* mediatory, mediating; *(relations sociales)* arbitrating NM,F *(gén)* mediator; *(entre partenaires sociaux)* arbitrator; *(Pol)* ≈ Ombudsman, Parliamentary Commissioner *(Brit)* ◆ **~ chimique** *(Méd)* transmitter substance ◆ **jouer le rôle de ~, servir de ~** to act as a mediator NF **médiatrice** *(Géom)* median

médiathèque /medjatɛk/ NF multimedia library

médiatico- /medjatiko/ PRÉF ◆ **c'est un événement ~politique** it's both a media and a political event ◆ **une affaire ~judiciaire** a legal case with a lot of media hype ◆ **groupe ~financier** media and finance group ◆ **dans le monde ~littéraire** in the world of the media and publishing

médiation /medjasjɔ̃/ NF 1 *(gén, Philos, Pol)* mediation; *(entre partenaires sociaux)* arbitration ◆ **offrir sa ~ dans un conflit** *(Pol)* to offer to mediate in a conflict; *(conflits sociaux)* to offer to arbitrate *ou* intervene in a dispute ◆ **tenter une ~ entre deux parties** to attempt to mediate between two parties 2 *(Logique)* mediate inference

médiatique /medjatik/ ADJ *[image, couverture, battage]* media *(épith)* ◆ **c'est quelqu'un de très ~** he comes across really well in the media, he's very media-friendly ◆ **sport très ~** sport that lends itself to media coverage ◆ **ce fut une rencontre très ~** this meeting got a lot of media attention

médiatisation /medjatizasjɔ̃/ NF 1 *(= diffusion par les médias)* media coverage ◆ **la ~ à outrance de ces jeunes chanteurs** the excessive media coverage given to these young singers 2 *(Hist, Philos)* mediatization

médiatiser /medjatize/ ▸ conjug 1 ◂ VT 1 *(= diffuser par les médias)* to give media coverage to ◆ **cet événement a été très médiatisé** the event was given a lot of (media) coverage 2 *(Hist, Philos)* to mediatize

médiator /medjatɔʀ/ NM plectrum

médiatrice /medjatʀis/ ADJ F, NF → **médiateur**

médical, e (mpl **-aux**) /medikal, o/ ADJ medical ◆ **délégué** *ou* **visiteur ~** medical representative *ou* rep*; → **examen, visite**

médicalement /medikalmɑ̃/ ADV medically ◆ **suicide ~ assisté** medically-assisted suicide; → **procréation**

médicalisation /medikalizasjɔ̃/ NF 1 *[de région, population]* provision of medical care for 2 *[de problème, grossesse]* medicalization

médicaliser /medikalize/ ▸ conjug 1 ◂ VT 1 *[+ région, population]* to provide with medical care ◆ **c'est une population peu médicalisée** these people have little access to medical care ◆ **la distribution médicalisée de la drogue** the distribution of drugs under medical supervision ◆ **ils sont traités en milieu médicalisé** they receive treatment in a medical environment ◆ **résidence** *ou* **maison de retraite médicalisée** nursing home ◆ **ils prônent la maîtrise médicalisée des dépenses de santé** they want health expenditure to be supervised by medical professionals ◆ **avion/hélicoptère médicalisé** hospital plane/helicopter 2 *[+ problème, grossesse]* to medicalize

médicament /medikamɑ̃/ NM medicine, drug ◆ **prendre des ~s** to take medicines *ou* medication ◆ **~ de confort** ≈ pain-relieving medicine

médicamenteux, -euse /medikamɑ̃tø, øz/ ADJ *[plante, substance]* medicinal; *[traitement, intoxication, prescription]* drug *(épith)* ◆ **produits ~** medicines ◆ **associations médicamenteuses** medicines used in combination

médicastre † /medikastʀ/ NM *(hum)* charlatan, quack

médication /medikasjɔ̃/ NF (medical) treatment, medication

médicinal, e (mpl **-aux**) /medisinal, o/ ADJ *[plante, substance]* medicinal

medicine-ball (pl **medicine-balls**) /medisinbol/ NM medicine ball

médico- /mediko/ PRÉF *(dans les mots composés à trait d'union, le préfixe reste invariable)* ◆ **~social** *[mesure, structure]* for health care and social welfare ◆ **centre** *ou* **institut ~éducatif** *ou* **~pédagogique** special school *(for physically or mentally handicapped children)* ◆ **examen ~psychologique** medical and psychological examination ◆ **centre ~psychologique** *psychiatric clinic mainly dealing with prisoners, people who have attempted suicide and drug addicts*

médico-chirurgical, e (mpl **-aux**) /medikoʃiʀyʀʒikal, o/ ADJ ◆ **centre ~** clinic *(with a surgical unit)* ◆ **personnel/matériel ~** medical and surgical staff/equipment

médico-légal, e (mpl **-aux**) /medikolegal, o/ ADJ *[expert]* forensic ◆ **certificat** *ou* **rapport ~** forensic report ◆ **expertise ~e** forensic analysis *ou* examination ◆ **institut ~** mortuary *(where autopsies and forensic examinations are carried out)*, medico-legal institute *(US)*

médiéval, e (mpl **-aux**) /medjeval, o/ ADJ medieval

médiéviste /medjevist/ NMF medievalist

médina /medina/ NF medina

Médine /medin/ N Medina

médiocre /medjɔkʀ/ ADJ *[travail, roman, élève]* mediocre, second-rate; *(sur copie d'élève)* poor; *[intelligence, qualité]* poor, mediocre, inferior; *[résultats, situation économique]* poor; *[revenu, salaire]* meagre, poor; *[vie, existence]* mediocre ◆ **il a une situation ~** he holds some second-rate position ◆ **il a montré un intérêt ~ pour ce projet** he showed little or no interest in the project ◆ **génie incompris par les esprits ~s** genius misunderstood by those with small minds NMF nonentity, second-rater *

médiocrement /medjɔkʀəmɑ̃/ ADV *[intéressé, intelligent]* not very, not particularly ◆ **gagner ~ sa vie** to earn a poor living ◆ **~ satisfait** barely satisfied, not very well satisfied ◆ **c'est un roman ~ réussi** it's not a particularly good novel ◆ **il joue ~ du piano** he plays the piano indifferently, he's not very good at (playing) the piano

médiocrité /medjɔkʀite/ NF *[de travail]* poor quality, mediocrity; *[d'élève, homme politique]* mediocrity; *[de copie d'élève]* poor standard; *[de revenu, salaire]* meagreness, poorness; *[d'intelligence]* mediocrity, inferiority; *[de vie]* mediocrity ◆ **étant donné la ~ de ses revenus** given the slimness of his resources, seeing how slight *ou* slim his resources are ◆ **cet homme est une (vraie) ~** this man is a complete mediocrity

médique /medik/ ADJ *(Antiq)* Median

médire /mediʀ/ ▸ conjug 37 ◂ VI ◆ **~ de qn** to speak ill of sb; *(à tort)* to malign sb ◆ **elle est toujours en train de ~** she's always running people down *ou* saying nasty things about people ◆ **je ne voudrais pas ~ mais ...** I don't want to tittle-tattle *ou* to gossip, but ...

médisance /medizɑ̃s/ NF 1 *(= diffamation)* malicious gossip *(NonC)* ◆ **être en butte à la ~** to be made a target of malicious gossip 2 *(= propos)* piece of scandal ◆ **~s** scandal *(NonC)*, gossip *(NonC)* ◆ **ce sont des ~s !** that's just scandal! *ou* malicious gossip! ◆ **arrête de dire des ~s** stop spreading scandal *ou* gossip

médisant, e /medizɑ̃, ɑ̃t/ ADJ *[paroles]* slanderous; *[personne]* malicious ◆ **les gens sont ~s** people say nasty things ◆ **ne soyons pas ~s** let's not be nasty ◆ **sans vouloir être ~, il faut reconnaître que ...** I don't want to sound nasty, but we have to admit that ... NM,F scandalmonger, slanderer

méditatif, -ive /meditatif, iv/ ADJ *[caractère]* meditative, thoughtful; *[air]* musing, thoughtful

méditation /meditasjɔ̃/ NF *(= pensée)* meditation; *(= recueillement)* meditation *(NonC)* ◆ **après de longues ~s sur le sujet** after giving the subject much *ou* deep thought, after lengthy meditation on the subject ◆ **il était plongé dans la ~** *ou* **une profonde ~** he was sunk in deep thought, he was deep in thought

méditer /medite/ ▸ conjug 1 ◂ VT *[+ pensée]* to meditate on, to ponder (over); *[+ livre, projet, vengeance]* to meditate ◆ **~ de faire qch** to contemplate doing sth, to plan to do sth VI to meditate ◆ **~ sur qch** to ponder *ou* muse over sth

Méditerranée /mediteʀane/ NF ◆ **la (mer) ~** the Mediterranean (Sea)

méditerranéen, -enne /mediteʀaneɛ̃, ɛn/ ADJ Mediterranean NM,F **Méditerranéen(ne)** *(gén)* inhabitant *ou* native of a Mediterranean country; *(en France)* (French) Southerner

médium /medjɔm/ NM 1 *(= spirite, moyen de communication)* medium 2 *(Mus)* middle register 3 *(Logique)* middle term 2 *(= bois)* MDF

médiumnique /medjɔmnik/ ADJ *[dons, pouvoir]* of a medium

médiumnité /medjɔmnite/ NF powers of a medium, mediumship

médius /medjys/ NM middle finger

médoc /medɔk/ NM 1 *(= vin)* Médoc (wine) ◆ **le Médoc** *(= région)* the Médoc 2 *(* = médicament)* med *

médullaire /medylɛʀ/ ADJ medullary

méduse /medyz/ NF 1 *(= animal)* jellyfish 2 *(Myth)* **Méduse** Medusa

méduser /medyze/ ▸ conjug 1 ◂ VT *(gén pass)* to dumbfound, to stupefy ◆ **je suis resté médusé** I was dumbfounded

meeting /mitiŋ/ NM *(Pol, Sport)* meeting ◆ **~ aérien** *ou* **d'aviation** air show *ou* display ◆ **~ d'athlétisme** athletics meeting

méfait /mefɛ/ NM 1 *(= ravages)* **~s** *[de temps]* ravages; *[de passion, épidémie]* ravages, damaging effects ◆ **les ~s de l'alcoolisme/de la drogue/du soleil** the damaging *ou* ill effects of alcohol/of drugs/of the sun 2 *(= acte)* wrongdoing; *(hum)* misdeed

méfiance /mefjɑ̃s/ NF distrust, mistrust, suspicion ◆ **avoir de la ~ envers qn** to mistrust *ou* distrust sb ◆ **apaiser/éveiller la ~ de qn** to allay/arouse sb's suspicion(s) ◆ **regarder qn/qch avec ~** to look at sb/sth suspiciously ◆ **être sans ~** *(= avoir confiance)* to be completely trusting; *(= ne rien soupçonner)* to be quite unsuspecting ◆ **ce projet paraît peu sérieux, ~ !** this project doesn't seem very worthwhile, we'd better be careful!

méfiant, e /mefjɑ̃, jɑ̃t/ ADJ *[personne]* distrustful, mistrustful, suspicious ◆ **air** *ou* **regard ~** distrustful *ou* mistrustful *ou* suspicious look, look of distrust *ou* mistrust *ou* suspicion

méfier (se) /mefje/ ▸ conjug 7 ◂ VPR 1 *(= ne pas avoir confiance)* **se ~ de qn/des conseils de qn** to mistrust *ou* distrust sb/sb's advice ◆ **je me méfie de lui** I mistrust him, I don't trust him, I'm suspicious of him ◆ **méfiez-vous de lui, il faut vous ~ de lui** don't trust him, beware of him ◆ **je ne me méfie pas assez de mes réactions** I should be more wary of my reactions ◆ **méfiez-vous des imitations** *ou* **des contrefaçons** beware of imitations ◆ **se ~ de qn/qch comme de la peste** to be highly suspicious of sb/sth 2 *(= faire attention)* **se ~ de qch** to be careful about sth ◆ **il faut vous ~** you must be careful *ou* watch out ◆ **méfie-toi de cette marche** watch *ou* mind *(Brit)* the step, look out for the step * ◆ **méfie-toi, tu vas tomber** look out * *ou* be careful or you'll fall

méforme /mefɔʀm/ NF *(Sport)* lack of fitness ◆ **traverser une période de ~** to be (temporarily) off form ◆ **être en ~** to be off form

méga /mega/ PRÉF 1 *(Sci)* mega ◆ **~watt** megawatt ◆ **~volt** megavolt 2 *(* : intensif)* **~-concert** mega-concert ◆ **~-entreprise** huge *ou* enormous company, mega-company ◆ **~-dissertation** essay and a half * ◆ **un ~-cigare à la bouche** a whopping great * *ou* humungous * *(US)* cigar in his mouth NM (abrév de **mégaoctet**) *(Ordin)* megabyte

mégabit /megabit/ NM megabyte

mégacycle /megasikl/ NM megacycle

mégahertz /megaɛʀts/ NM megahertz

mégalithe /megalit/ NM megalith

mégalithique /megalitik/ ADJ megalithic

mégalo * /megalo/ ADJ, NMF (abrév de **mégalomaniaque, mégalomane**) *[personne]* megalomaniac; *[projet]* self-indulgent ◆ **il est complètement ~, c'est un ~** he thinks he's God

mégalomane /megalɔman/ ADJ *[personne]* megalomaniac; *[projet]* self-indulgent NMF megalomaniac

mégalomaniaque /megalɔmanjak/ ADJ *(Méd)* megalomaniac; *[projet]* self-indulgent ◆ **délire ~** *(Méd)* megalomaniac delusion

mégalomanie /megalɔmani/ NF megalomania

mégalopole /megalɔpɔl/ NF megalopolis

mégaoctet /megaɔktɛ/ NM megabyte

mégaphone † /megafɔn/ NM *(= porte-voix)* megaphone

mégapole /megapɔl/ NF ⇒ **mégalopole**

mégarde /megaʀd/ **par mégarde** LOC ADV *(= accidentellement)* accidentally, by accident; *(= par erreur)* by mistake, inadvertently; *(= par négligence)* accidentally ◆ **un livre que j'avais emporté par ~** a book that I had accidentally *ou* inadvertently taken away with me

mégastore /megastɔʀ/ NM megastore

mégatonne /megatɔn/ NF megaton

mégawatt /megawat/ NM megawatt

mégère /meʒɛʀ/ NF *(péj = femme)* shrew

mégisserie /meʒisʀi/ NF *(= lieu)* tawery

mégissier /meʒisje/ NM tawer

mégot * /mego/ NM *[de cigarette]* cigarette butt *ou* end, fag end * *(Brit)*; *[de cigare]* stub, butt

mégotage * /megɔtaʒ/ NM cheeseparing *ou* miserly attitude

mégoter * /megɔte/ ▸ conjug 1 ◂ VI to skimp ◆ **le patron mégote sur des détails et dépense des fortunes en repas d'affaires** the boss skimps over small items and spends a fortune on business lunches ◆ **pour marier leur fille ils n'ont pas mégoté** they spared no expense for their daughter's wedding

méharée /meaʀe/ NF camel safari ◆ **j'ai fait une ~ dans le Sahara** I went on a camel safari across the Sahara

méhari /meaʀi/ NM dromedary, mehari

méhariste /meaʀist/ NM camel rider; *(Hist) soldier in the French Camel corps*

meilleur, e /mɛjœʀ/ ADJ 1 *(compar de bon)* better ◆ **il est ~ que moi** *(plus charitable)* he's a better person than I am; *(plus doué)* he's better than I am *(en* at); ◆ **avoir ~ goût** *[aliment]* to taste better ◆ **ce gâteau est (bien) ~ avec du rhum** this cake tastes *ou* is (much) better with rum ◆ **il est ~ chanteur que compositeur** he makes a better singer than (a) composer, he is better at singing than (at) composing ◆ **de ~e qualité** of better *ou* higher quality ◆ **~ marché** cheaper ◆ **être en ~e santé** to be better, to be in better health ◆ **faire un ~ temps au deuxième tour** *(Sport)* to put up *ou* do a better time on the second lap ◆ **il a ~ temps de rester chez lui** *(Helv ou vieilli)* he'd be better off staying at home ◆ **partir de ~e heure** † to leave earlier ◆ **prendre (une) ~e tournure** to take a turn for the better ◆ **~s vœux** best wishes ◆ **ce sera pour des jours/des temps ~s** that will be for better days/happier times ◆ **il n'y a rien de ~** there's nothing better, there's nothing to beat it

2 *(superl de bon)* **le ~ des deux** the better of the two ◆ **la ~e de toutes** the best of all ◆ **c'est le ~ des hommes, c'est le ~ homme du monde** he is the best of men, he's the best man in the world ◆ **les ~s spécialistes** the best *ou* top specialists ◆ **son ~ ami** his best *ou* closest friend ◆ **servir les ~s mets/vins** to serve the best *ou* finest dishes/wines ◆ **information tirée des ~es sources** information from the most reliable sources ◆ **tissu de la ~e qualité** best quality material ◆ **le ~ marché** the cheapest ◆ **acheter au ~ prix** to buy at the lowest price

ADV ◆ **il fait ~ qu'hier** it's better *ou* nicer (weather) than yesterday ◆ **sentir ~** to smell better *ou* nicer

NM,F *(= personne)* ◆ **le ~, la ~e** the best one ◆ **ce sont toujours les ~s qui partent les premiers** the best people always die young ◆ **que le ~ gagne** may the best man win; → **raison**

NM *(= partie, chose)* ◆ **le ~** the best ◆ **il a choisi le ~** he took the best (one) ◆ **pour le ~ et pour le pire** for better or for worse ◆ **donner le ~ de soi-même** to give of one's best ◆ **passer le ~ de sa vie à faire ...** to spend the best days *ou* years of one's life doing ... ◆ **prendre le ~ sur qn** *(Sport)* to get the better of sb ◆ **garder** *ou* **réserver le ~ pour la fin** to keep the best till last ◆ **et le ~ dans tout ça, c'est qu'il avait raison !** and the best bit about it all was that he was right!

NF **meilleure** * ◆ **ça alors, c'est la ~e!** that's the best one yet! ◆ **j'en passe et des ~es** and that's not all ◆ **tu connais la ~e ? il n'est même pas venu !** haven't you heard the best (bit) though? he didn't even come!

méiose /mejoz/ NF meiosis

meistre /mɛstʀ/ NM ⇒ **mestre**

méjuger /meʒyʒe/ ▸ conjug 3 ◂ *(littér)* VT to misjudge VT INDIR **méjuger de** to underrate, to underestimate VPR **se méjuger** to underestimate o.s.

Mékong /mekɔ̃g/ NM Mekong

mél /mɛl/ NM e-mail

mélamine /melamin/ NF melamine

mélaminé, e /melamine/ ADJ melamine-coated

mélancolie /melɑ̃kɔli/ NF melancholy, gloom; *(Méd)* melancholia ◆ **elle avait des accès de ~** she suffered from bouts of melancholy; → **engendrer**

mélancolique /melɑ̃kɔlik/ ADJ *[personne, paysage, musique]* melancholy; *(Méd)* melancholic

mélancoliquement /melɑ̃kɔlikmɑ̃/ ADV with a melancholy air, melancholically

Mélanésie /melanezi/ NF Melanesia

mélanésien, -ienne /melanezjɛ̃, jɛn/ ADJ Melanesian NM *(= langue)* Melanesian NM,F **Mélanésien(ne)** Melanesian

mélange /melɑ̃ʒ/ NM 1 *(= opération) [de produits]* mixing; *[de vins, tabacs]* blending ◆ **faire un ~ de** *[+ substances]* to make a mixture of; *[+ idées]* to mix up ◆ **quand on boit il ne faut pas faire de ~s** you shouldn't mix your drinks 2 *(= résultat)* mixture; *[de vins, tabacs, cafés]* blend ◆ **~ détonant** *ou* **explosif** *(lit)* explosive mixture; *(fig)* explosive combination *ou* mixture ◆ **~ réfrigérant** freezing mixture ◆ **~ pauvre/riche** *(= carburant)* weak/rich mixture ◆ **joie sans ~** unalloyed *ou* unadulterated joy ◆ **sans ~ de ...** *(littér)* free from ..., unadulterated by ... ◆ **~s** *(Littérat)* miscellanies, miscellany

mélanger /melɑ̃ʒe/ ▸ conjug 3 ◂ VT 1 *(gén)* to mix; *[+ couleurs, vins, parfums, tabacs]* to blend; *[+ cartes]* to shuffle ◆ **mélangez le beurre et la farine** mix the butter and flour together ◆ **un public très mélangé** a very varied *ou* mixed audience

2 *(= confondre) [+ dates, idées]* to mix (up), to muddle up *(surtout Brit)*, to confuse ◆ **tu mélanges tout !** you're getting it all mixed up! *ou* muddled up! *(surtout Brit)* ◆ **il ne faut pas ~ les torchons et les serviettes** *(fig)* we *(ou* you *etc)* must sort out the sheep from the goats

3 *(= mettre en désordre) [+ documents]* to mix up, to muddle up

VPR **se mélanger** 1 *[produits, personnes]* to mix; *[vins]* to mix, to blend

2 *(en désordre)* **les dates se mélangent dans ma tête** I'm confused about the dates, I've got the dates mixed up *ou* in a muddle ◆ **se ~ les pieds** * *ou* **les pédales** * *ou* **les pinceaux** * *ou* **les crayons** * to get mixed up *ou* into a muddle *(surtout Brit)*

mélangeur /melɑ̃ʒœʀ/ NM *(= appareil)* mixer; *(= robinet)* mixer tap *(Brit)*, mixing faucet *(US)*; *(Ciné, Radio)* mixer

mélanine /melanin/ NF melanin

mélanocyte /melanɔsit/ NM melanocyte

mélanome /melanom/ NM melanoma

mélasse /melas/ NF 1 *(Culin)* treacle *(Brit)*, molasses *(US)* 2 *(*, péj) (= boue)* muck; *(= brouillard)* murk ◆ **quelle ~ !** *(= problèmes, confusion)* what a mess! ◆ **être dans la ~** *(= avoir des ennuis)* to be in the soup *, to be in a sticky situation *; *(= être dans la misère)* to be down and out, to be on one's beam ends * *(Brit)*

mélatonine /melatɔnin/ NF melatonin

Melba /mɛlba/ ADJ INV Melba ◆ **pêche/ananas ~** peach/pineapple Melba

mêlé, e[1] /mele/ (ptp de **mêler**) ADJ *[sentiments]* mixed, mingled; *[couleurs, tons]* mingled; *[monde, société]* mixed

mêlée[2] /mele/ NF 1 *(= bataille)* mêlée; *(hum)* fray, kerfuffle * *(Brit)* ◆ **~ générale** free-for-all ◆ **la ~ devint générale** it developed into a free-for-all, scuffles broke out all round *ou* on all sides ◆ **se jeter dans la ~** *(lit, fig)* to plunge into the fray ◆ **rester au-dessus de** *ou* **à l'écart de la ~** *(fig)* to stay *ou* keep aloof, to keep out of the fray 2 *(Rugby)* scrum, scrummage ◆ **faire une ~** to go into a scrum ◆ **~ ordonnée** set scrum ◆ **~ ouverte** *ou* **spontanée** ruck, loose scrum ◆ **dans la ~ ouverte** in the loose

mêler /mele/ ▸ conjug 1 ◂ VT 1 *(= unir, mettre ensemble) [+ substances]* to mingle, to mix together; *[+ races]* to mix; *[animaux]* to cross; *(Culin = mélanger)* to mix, to blend; *(= joindre, allier)* to combine, to mingle ◆ **les deux fleuves mêlent leurs eaux** the two rivers mingle their waters ◆ **elles mêlèrent leurs larmes/leurs soupirs** their tears/their sighs mingled ◆ **vin mêlé d'eau** wine mixed with water

2 *(= mettre en désordre, embrouiller) [+ papiers, dossiers]* to muddle (up), to mix up; *(= battre) [+ cartes]* to shuffle ◆ **~ la réalité et le rêve** to confuse reality and dream

3 *(= associer)* **~ à** *ou* **avec** to mix *ou* mingle with ◆ **~ la douceur à la fermeté** to combine gentleness with firmness ◆ **~ du feuillage à un bouquet** to put some greenery in with a bouquet ◆ **récit mêlé de détails comiques** story interspersed with comic(al) details ◆ **joie mêlée de remords** pleasure mixed with *ou* tinged with remorse

4 *(= impliquer)* **~ qn à** *[+ affaire suspecte]* to involve sb in, to get sb mixed up *ou* involved in; *[+ action, négociations]* to involve sb in ◆ **j'y ai été mêlé contre mon gré** I was dragged into it against my will, I got mixed up *ou* involved in it against my will ◆ **il a été mêlé au scandale/à une affaire d'espionnage** he got mixed up in *ou* got involved in the scandal/in a spy scandal ◆ **~ qn à la conversation** to bring *ou* draw sb into the conversation

VPR **se mêler** 1 *(= se mélanger) [odeurs, voix]* to mingle; *[cultures, races]* to mix

2 ◆ **se ~ à** *(= se joindre à)* to join; *(= s'associer à)* to mix with; *[cris, sentiments]* to mingle with ◆ **il se mêla à la foule** he joined the crowd, he mingled with the crowd ◆ **se ~ à une querelle** to get mixed up *ou* involved in a quarrel ◆ **il ne se mêle jamais aux autres enfants** he never mixes with other children ◆ **il se mêlait à toutes les manifestations** he got involved *ou* took part in all the demonstrations ◆ **des rires se mêlaient aux applaudissements** there was laughter mingled with the applause ◆ **se ~ à la conversation** to join in the conversation

3 ◆ **se ~ de** *(= s'impliquer dans)* to get mixed up *ou* involved in; *(= s'ingérer dans)* to meddle with, to interfere with ◆ **je ne veux pas me ~ de politique** I don't want to get mixed up in *ou* involved in politics ◆ **se ~ des affaires des autres** to meddle *ou* interfere in other people's business *ou* affairs ◆ **mêle-toi de ce qui te regarde !** *ou* **de tes affaires !** *ou* **de tes oignons !** * mind your own business! ◆ **de quoi je me mêle !** * *(iro)* what business is it of yours?, what's it got to do with you? ◆ **si le mauvais temps s'en mêle, nous n'y arriverons jamais** if the weather turns against us, we'll never make it ◆ **quand la politique/l'amour s'en mêle ...** when politics/love comes into it ... ◆ **se ~ de faire qch** to take it upon o.s. to do sth, to make it one's business to do sth ◆ **voilà qu'il se mêle de nous donner des conseils !** who is he to give us advice!, look at him butting in with his advice! ◆ **ne vous mêlez pas d'intervenir !** don't you take it into your head to interfere!, just you keep out of it!

mélèze /melɛz/ NM larch

mélilot /melilo/ NM melilot, sweet clover

méli-mélo * (pl **mélis-mélos**) /melimelo/ NM *[de situation]* mess, muddle *(surtout Brit)*; *[d'objets]* jumble ◆ **cette affaire est un véritable ~ !** what a terrible mess *ou* muddle this business is! ◆ **~ de poissons/de légumes** *(Culin)* assortment of fish/of vegetables

mélioratif, -ive /meljɔʀatif, iv/ ADJ meliorative NM meliorative term

mélisse /melis/ NF *(= plante)* (lemon) balm

mellifère /melifɛʀ/ ADJ melliferous

mélo * /melo/ ADJ (abrév de **mélodramatique**) *[film, roman]* soppy *, sentimental ◆ **feuilleton ~** *(Presse)* sentimental serial; *(TV)* soap (opera) NM abrév de **mélodrame**

mélodie /melɔdi/ NF 1 *(= motif, chanson)* melody, tune ◆ **les ~s de Debussy** Debussy's melodies *ou* songs ◆ **une petite ~ entendue à la radio** a little tune heard on the radio 2 *(= qualité)* melodiousness

mélodieusement /melɔdjøzmɑ̃/ ADV melodiously, tunefully

mélodieux, -ieuse /melɔdjø, jøz/ ADJ melodious, tuneful

mélodique /melɔdik/ ADJ melodic

mélodiste /melɔdist/ NMF melodist ◆ **c'est un excellent ~** he composes fine melodies, he's a very good melodist

mélodramatique /melɔdʀamatik/ ADJ *(Littérat, péj)* melodramatic

mélodrame /melɔdʀam/ NM *(Littérat, péj)* melodrama

mélomane /melɔman/ ADJ music-loving *(épith)*, keen on music *(attrib)* NMF music lover

melon /m(ə)lɔ̃/ NM 1 (= *fruit*) melon ◆ **~ (cantaloup)** cantaloup(e) ◆ **choper le ~*** (= *la grosse tête*) to get bigheaded* ◆ **il a le ~* depuis qu'il a eu sa promotion** that promotion has really gone to his head* 2 ◆ **(chapeau) ~** bowler (hat) *(Brit)*, derby (hat) *(US)*

COMP **melon d'eau** watermelon
melon d'Espagne ≈ honeydew melon

mélopée /melɔpe/ NF 1 *(gén = chant monotone)* monotonous chant, threnody *(littér)* 2 *(Hist Mus)* recitative

membrane /mɑ̃bʀan/ NF *(gén)* membrane; *[de haut-parleur]* diaphragm ◆ **~ cellulaire** *(Bio)* plasma *ou* cell membrane

membraneux, -euse /mɑ̃bʀanø, øz/ ADJ membran(e)ous

membre /mɑ̃bʀ/ NM 1 (= *partie du corps*) limb ◆ **~ inférieur/supérieur** lower/upper limb ◆ **~ antérieur/postérieur** fore/hind limb ◆ **~ (viril)** male member *ou* organ

2 *[de famille, groupe, société savante]* member; *[d'académie]* fellow ◆ **~ fondateur** founder member ◆ **~ actif/perpétuel** active/life member ◆ **~ permanent du Conseil de sécurité** permanent member of the Security Council ◆ **un ~ de la société/du public** a member of society/of the public ◆ **les ~s du gouvernement** the members of the government ◆ **être ~ de** to be a member of ◆ **devenir ~ d'un club** to become a member of a club, to join a club ◆ **ce club a 300 ~s** this club has a membership of 300 *ou* has 300 members ◆ **pays/États ~s (de l'Union européenne)** member countries/states (of the European union)

3 *(Math)* member ◆ **premier/second ~** left-hand/right-hand member

4 *(Ling)* **~ de phrase** (sentence) member

5 *(Archit)* member

6 *(Naut)* timber, rib

membré, e /mɑ̃bʀe/ ADJ limbed ◆ **bien/mal ~** strong-/weak-limbed ◆ **bien ~*** *[homme]* well-hung*

membru, e /mɑ̃bʀy/ ADJ *(littér)* strong-limbed

membrure /mɑ̃bʀyʀ/ NF *(Anat)* limbs, build; *(Naut)* rib; *(collectif)* frame ◆ **homme à la ~ puissante** strong-limbed *ou* powerfully built man

mémé* /meme/ NF *(langage enfantin = grand-mère)* gran(ny)*, grandma; (= *vieille dame*) old lady; *(péj)* old granny* *(péj)* ADJ INV ◆ **ça fait ~** it looks dowdy ◆ **tu fais ~ avec cette robe** that dress makes you look like an old lady *ou* makes you look dowdy

même /mɛm/ GRAMMAIRE ACTIVE 32.4, 53.5

ADJ 1 *(avant n = identique)* same, identical ◆ **des bijoux de ~ valeur** jewels of equal *ou* of the same value ◆ **ils ont la ~ taille/la ~ couleur, ils sont de ~ taille/de ~ couleur** they are the same size/the same colour ◆ **j'ai exactement la ~ robe qu'hier** I am wearing the very same dress I wore yesterday *ou* exactly the same dress as yesterday ◆ **nous sommes du ~ avis** we are of the same mind *ou* opinion, we agree ◆ **ils ont la ~ voiture que nous** they have the same car as we have *ou* as us* ◆ **que vous veniez ou non, c'est la ~ chose** it makes no difference *ou* odds *(Brit)* whether you come or not ◆ **c'est toujours la ~ chose !** it's always the same (old story)! ◆ **c'est la ~ chose** (= *c'est équivalent*) it amounts to the same (thing), it's six of one and half a dozen of the other* ◆ **arriver en ~ temps (que)** to arrive at the same time (as) ◆ **en ~ temps qu'il le faisait, l'autre s'approchait** as *ou* while he was doing it the other drew nearer

2 *(après n ou pron = exact, personnifié)* very, actual ◆ **ce sont ses paroles ~s** those are his very *ou* actual words ◆ **il est la générosité/gentillesse ~** he is generosity/kindness itself, he is the (very) soul of generosity/kindness ◆ **il est la méchanceté/bêtise ~** he's wickedness/stupidity itself ◆ **la grande maison, celle-là ~ que vous avez visitée** the big house, the very one you visited *ou* precisely the one you visited

3 ◆ **moi-~** myself ◆ **toi-~** yourself ◆ **lui-~** himself ◆ **elle-~** herself ◆ **nous-~s** ourselves ◆ **vous-~** yourself ◆ **vous-~s** yourselves ◆ **eux-** *ou* **elles-~s** themselves ◆ **un autre soi-~** another self ◆ **on est soi-~ conscient de ses propres erreurs** one is aware (oneself) of one's own mistakes ◆ **nous devons y aller nous-~s** we must go ourselves ◆ **s'apitoyer sur soi-~** to feel sorry for oneself ◆ **tu n'as aucune confiance en toi-~** you have no confidence in yourself ◆ **c'est lui-~ qui l'a dit, il l'a dit lui-~** he said it himself, he himself said it ◆ **au plus profond d'eux-~s/de nous-~s** in their/our heart of hearts ◆ **elle fait ses habits elle-~** she makes her own clothes, she makes her clothes herself ◆ **c'est ce que je me dis en** *ou* **à moi-~** that's what I tell myself (inwardly), that's what I think to myself ◆ **elle se disait en elle-~ que ...** she thought to herself that ..., she thought privately *ou* inwardly that ... ◆ **faire qch de soi-~** to do sth on one's own initiative *ou* off one's own bat* *(Brit)* ◆ **faire qch (par) soi-~** to do sth (by) oneself

PRON INDÉF *(avec le, la, les)* ◆ **ce n'est pas le ~** it's not the same (one) ◆ **la réaction n'a pas été la ~ qu'à Paris** the reaction was not the same as in Paris ◆ **elle est bien toujours la ~ !** she's just the same as ever! ◆ **ce sont toujours les ~s qui se font prendre** it's always the same ones who catch it* ◆ **c'est le ~ que j'ai revu plus tard** it was the same man that I saw later on ◆ **les ~s, trois heures plus tard** *(aussi hum)* same scene, three hours later; → **pareil, revenir**

ADV 1 *(gén)* even ◆ **ils sont tous sortis, ~ les enfants** they are all out, even the children ◆ **il n'a ~ pas** *ou* **pas ~ de quoi écrire** he hasn't even got anything to write with ◆ **il est intéressant et ~ amusant** he's interesting and amusing too *ou* besides ◆ **elle ne me parle ~ plus** she no longer even speaks to me, she doesn't even speak to me anymore ◆ **~ lui ne sait pas** even he doesn't know ◆ **personne ne sait, ~ pas lui** nobody knows, not even him ◆ **~ si** even if, even though ◆ **c'est vrai, ~ que je peux le prouver !*** it's true, and what's more I can prove it!

2 (= *précisément*) **aujourd'hui ~** this very day ◆ **ici ~** in this very place, on this very spot ◆ **c'est celui-là ~ qui ...** he's the very one who ... ◆ **c'est cela ~** that's just *ou* exactly it

3 *(locutions)*

◆ **à même** ◆ **boire à ~ la bouteille** to drink (straight) from the bottle ◆ **coucher à ~ le sol** to lie on the bare ground ◆ **à ~ la peau** next to the skin ◆ **être à ~ de faire** to be able *ou* to be in a position to do ◆ **je ne suis pas à ~ de juger** I'm in no position to judge

◆ **de même** ◆ **il fera de ~** he'll do the same, he'll do likewise, he'll follow suit ◆ **vous le détestez ? moi de ~** you hate him? so do I *ou* I do too *ou* me too *ou* same here* ◆ **de ~ qu'il nous a dit que ...** just as he told us that ... ◆ **il en est** *ou* **il en va de ~ pour moi** it's the same for me, same here*

◆ **quand même, tout de même** (= *en dépit de cela*) all the same, even so; (= *vraiment*) really ◆ **tout de ~ !, quand ~ !** *(indignation)* honestly! ◆ **quel crétin quand ~ !** really, what an idiot! ◆ **merci quand ~** *(lit, hum)* thanks all the same *ou* just the same ◆ **c'est tout de ~** *ou* **quand ~ agaçant** (= *cependant*) all the same it is annoying; (= *vraiment*) it's really annoying ◆ **elle m'agace ! – elle est gentille tout de ~** she annoys me! – but she's quite nice really ◆ **tout de ~** *ou* **quand ~, il aurait pu nous prévenir !** well, he might have warned us! ◆ **il exagère tout de ~ !** really, he's going too far! ◆ **il a tout de ~ réussi à s'échapper** he managed to escape all the same ◆ **c'est tout de ~ étonnant** it's quite surprising ◆ **je lui ai interdit de le faire, mais il l'a fait quand ~** I told him not to do it, but he did it anyway

mêmement /mɛmmɑ̃/ ADV *(frm)* likewise

mémento /memɛ̃to/ NM (= *agenda*) appointments book *ou* diary *(Brit)*, engagement diary *(Brit) ou* calendar *(US)*; *(Scol = aide-mémoire)* summary ◆ **~ des vivants/des morts** *(Rel)* prayers for the living/the dead

mémère* /memɛʀ/ NF *(langage enfantin = grand-mère)* granny*, grandma; *(péj = vieille dame)* old dear* ◆ **le petit chien à sa ~** *(hum)* mummy's little doggy *(hum)* ◆ **elle fait ~ avec ce chapeau** she looks like an old granny in that hat*

mémo* /memo/ NM (abrév de **mémorandum**) memo

mémoire[1] /memwaʀ/ NF 1 *(Psych, Sci)* memory ◆ **citer de ~** to quote from memory ◆ **de ~ d'homme** in living memory ◆ **de ~ de Parisien, on n'avait jamais vu ça !** no one could remember such a thing happening in Paris before ◆ **pour ~** *(gén)* as a matter of interest; *(Comm)* for the record ◆ **~ associative/collective** associative/collective memory ◆ **~ auditive/visuelle/olfactive** aural/visual/olfactory memory; → **effort, rafraîchir, trou**

2 *(locutions)* **avoir de la ~/une très bonne ~** to have a good memory/a very good memory ◆ **si j'ai bonne ~** if I remember right *ou* rightly, if my memory serves me right ◆ **il n'a pas de ~, il n'a aucune ~** he can never remember anything ◆ **avoir la ~ courte** to have a short memory ◆ **avoir une ~ d'éléphant** to have a memory like an elephant('s) ◆ **perdre la ~** to lose one's memory ◆ **avoir la ~ des noms** to have a good memory for names ◆ **je n'ai pas la ~ des dates/visages** I have no memory for dates/faces, I can never remember dates/faces ◆ **garder qch en ~** to remember sth ◆ **j'ai gardé (la) ~ de cette conversation** *(frm)* I remember *ou* recall this conversation ◆ **chercher un nom dans sa ~** to try to recall a name, to rack one's brains to remember a name ◆ **ça y est, ça me revient en ~** I remember now, it's coming back to me now ◆ **il me l'a remis en ~** he reminded me of it, he brought it back to me ◆ **son nom restera (gravé) dans notre ~** his name will remain (engraved) in our memories ◆ **nous avons un devoir de ~** it is our duty to remember

3 (= *réputation*) memory, good name; (= *renommée*) memory, fame, renown ◆ **soldat de glorieuse ~** soldier of blessed memory ◆ **de sinistre ~** of evil memory, remembered with fear *ou* horror; *(hum)* fearful, ghastly ◆ **salir la ~ de qn** to sully the memory of sb ◆ **à la ~ de** in memory of, to the memory of

4 *(Ordin)* memory ◆ **~ cache/externe** cache/external storage ◆ **~ vive** RAM, random access memory ◆ **~ morte** ROM, read-only memory ◆ **~ volatile** volatile memory ◆ **~ de masse, ~ auxiliaire** mass memory *ou* storage ◆ **~ centrale** *ou* **principale** main memory ◆ **avoir 24 Mo de ~ centrale** to have 24 Mb of main

memory ◆ ~ **tampon** buffer memory ◆ **capacité de** ~ storage capacity, memory size ◆ **mettre qch en** ~ to store sth ◆ **mise en** ~ storage

mémoire[2] /memwaʀ/ NM (= *requête*) memorandum; (= *rapport*) report; (= *exposé*) paper, dissertation (*Brit*); (= *facture*) bill; (*Jur*) statement of case ◆ ~ **de maîtrise** (*Univ*) *dissertation done for research degree* ≃ master's thesis; → DIPLÔMES NMPL **mémoires** (= *souvenirs*) memoirs ◆ **tu écris tes ~s ?** (*hum*) are you writing your life story? (*hum*)

mémorable /memɔʀabl/ ADJ memorable, unforgettable

mémorandum /memɔʀɑ̃dɔm/ NM (*Pol*) memorandum; (*Comm*) order sheet, memorandum; (= *carnet*) notebook, memo book

mémorial (pl **-iaux**) /memɔʀjal, jo/ NM (*Archit*) memorial ◆ **Mémorial** (*Littérat*) Chronicles

mémorialiste /memɔʀjalist/ NMF writer of memoirs

mémorisation /memɔʀizasjɔ̃/ NF memorization, memorizing; (*Ordin*) storage

mémoriser /memɔʀize/ ▸ conjug 1 ◂ VT to memorize, to commit to memory; (*Ordin*) to store

menaçant, e /mənasɑ̃, ɑ̃t/ ADJ [*geste, paroles, foule, orage, regard*] threatening, menacing; [*nuages*] ominous, threatening; [*ciel*] lowering (*épith*), threatening, menacing ◆ **sa voix se fit ~e** his voice took on a threatening *ou* menacing tone ◆ **elle se fit ~e** she started to make *ou* issue threats

menace /mənas/ NF 1 (= *intimidation*) threat ◆ **c'est une ~ ?** is that a threat?, are you threatening me? ◆ **il eut un geste de** ~ he made a threatening gesture ◆ **il eut des paroles de** ~ he made some threats ◆ **malgré les ~s de représailles** despite the threat of reprisals ◆ **il y a des ~s de grève** there's a threat of strike action ◆ **signer sous la** ~ to sign under duress ◆ **sous la ~ de** under (the) threat of ◆ **sous la ~ d'un couteau/d'un pistolet** at knife-point/gunpoint

2 (= *danger*) threat ◆ **la ~ nucléaire** the nuclear threat ◆ ~ **d'épidémie** threat of an epidemic ◆ **être sous la ~ d'une expulsion/de sanctions** to be threatened with *ou* be under threat of expulsion/of sanctions

3 (*Jur*) **~s** intimidation, threats ◆ **recevoir des ~s de mort** to receive death threats *ou* threats on one's life

menacer /mənase/ ▸ conjug 3 ◂ VT 1 (= *faire peur à*) to threaten, to menace (*gén pass*) ◆ ~ **qn de mort/d'un revolver** to threaten sb with death/with a gun ◆ ~ **qn du poing/de sa canne** to shake one's fist/one's stick at sb ◆ ~ **de faire qch** to threaten to do sth

2 (= *mettre en danger*) [*+ équilibre, projet*] to jeopardize ◆ **ses jours sont menacés** his life is threatened *ou* in danger ◆ **la guerre menaçait le pays** the country was threatened *ou* menaced by *ou* with war ◆ **espèces menacées** threatened *ou* endangered species ◆ **le processus de paix est menacé** the peace process is in jeopardy ◆ **être menacé de disparition** [*espèce*] to be threatened by extinction, to be in danger of extinction; [*culture, parti, revue, institution, profession*] to be in danger of disappearing ◆ **le théâtre est menacé de fermeture** the theatre is threatened with closure

3 (= *risquer de survenir*) [*chômage, grève, guerre*] to loom large ◆ **la pluie menace** it looks like rain, it's threatening to rain ◆ **l'orage menace (d'éclater)** the storm is about to break *ou* is threatening to break ◆ **chaise qui menace de se casser** chair which is showing signs of *ou* looks like breaking (*Brit*) *ou* looks like it will break ◆ **pluie/discours qui menace de durer** rain/speech which threatens to last some time ◆ **la maison menace ruine** the house is in danger of falling down

ménage /menaʒ/ NM 1 (= *entretien d'une maison*) housekeeping; (= *nettoyage*) housework ◆ **les soins du** ~ the housework, the household duties ◆ **s'occuper de** *ou* **tenir son** ~ to look after one's house, to keep house ◆ **faire du** ~ to do some housework *ou* cleaning ◆ **faire le** ~ (= *nettoyer*) to do the housework; (= *remettre en ordre*) to put one's house in order; (= *licencier*) to get rid of the deadwood ◆ **faire le ~ à fond** *ou* **en grand** to clean the house from top to bottom, to do the housework thoroughly ◆ **faire le** *ou* **du ~ dans ses archives/ses tiroirs** to sort out *ou* tidy one's files/one's drawers ◆ **faire du ~ dans sa vie** to sort one's life out ◆ **faire des ~s** to work as a cleaner ◆ **le grand** ~ (*Can*) the spring-cleaning; → **femme**

2 (= *couple, communauté familiale*) married couple, household; (*Écon*) household ◆ ~ **sans enfant** childless couple ◆ ~ **à trois** ménage à trois ◆ **jeune/vieux** ~ young/old couple ◆ **cela ne va pas dans le** ~ their marriage is a bit shaky *ou* isn't really working ◆ **être heureux/malheureux en** ~ to have a happy/an unhappy married life ◆ **se mettre en ~ avec qn** to set up house with sb, to move in with sb ◆ **querelles de** ~ domestic quarrels *ou* rows ◆ **faire bon/mauvais ~ avec qn** to get on well/badly with sb, to hit it off/not hit it off with sb* ◆ **notre chat et la perruche font très bon** ~ our cat and the budgie are good friends ◆ **bêtise et lâcheté font bon** ~ stupidity and cowardice go hand in hand ◆ **économie et culture font rarement bon** ~ economics and culture are rarely compatible; → **paix, scène**

3 († = *ordinaire*) **de** ~ [*chocolat*] for ordinary *ou* everyday consumption; [*pain*] homemade

ménagement /menaʒmɑ̃/ NM (= *douceur*) care; (= *attention*) attention ◆ **~s** (= *égards*) consideration ◆ **traiter qn avec** ~ to treat sb considerately *ou* tactfully ◆ **il lui annonça la nouvelle avec** ~ he broke the news to her gently *ou* cautiously ◆ **elle a besoin de ~ car elle est encore très faible** she needs care and attention as she's still very weak

◆ **sans ménagement(s)** ◆ **traiter qn sans ~(s)** to show no consideration towards sb; (*avec brutalité*) to manhandle sb ◆ **il les a congédiés sans ~(s)** he dismissed them without further ado *ou* with scant ceremony ◆ **la police les a expulsés sans ~(s)** they were forcibly evicted by the police ◆ **annoncer qch sans ~(s) à qn** to break the news of sth bluntly to sb, to tell sb sth bluntly

ménager[1], -ère /menaʒe, ɛʀ/ ADJ [*ustensiles, appareils*] household (*épith*), domestic (*épith*) ◆ **travaux ~s, tâches ménagères** housework, domestic chores ◆ **collège d'enseignement** ~ † school of domestic science; → **art, eau, ordure** NF **ménagère** 1 (= *femme d'intérieur*) housewife 2 (= *couverts*) canteen (of cutlery)

ménager[2] /menaʒe/ ▸ conjug 3 ◂ VT 1 (= *traiter avec prudence*) [*+ personne puissante, adversaire*] to handle carefully, to treat tactfully *ou* considerately; [*+ sentiments*] to spare, to show consideration for ◆ **elle est très sensible, il faut la** ~ she's very sensitive, you must treat her gently ◆ ~ **les deux parties** to keep both parties happy ◆ **afin de ~ les susceptibilités** so as not to offend people's sensibilities ◆ ~ **la chèvre et le chou** (= *rester neutre*) to sit on the fence; (= *être conciliant*) to keep both parties sweet*

2 (= *utiliser avec économie ou modération*) [*+ appareil*] to go easy on; [*+ réserves*] to use carefully *ou* sparingly; [*+ vêtement*] to treat with care; [*+ argent, temps*] to use carefully, to economize; [*+ expressions*] to moderate, to tone down ◆ **c'est un homme qui ménage ses paroles** he's a man of few words ◆ ~ **ses forces** to save *ou* conserve one's strength ◆ ~ **sa santé** to take great care of one's health, to look after o.s. ◆ **il n'a pas ménagé ses efforts** he spared no effort ◆ **nous n'avons rien ménagé pour vous plaire** we've spared no pains to please you ◆ **il ne lui a pas ménagé les louanges** he heaped praise on him

3 (= *préparer*) [*+ entretien, rencontre*] to arrange, to organize, to bring about; [*+ transition*] to contrive, to bring about ◆ ~ **l'avenir** to prepare for the future ◆ **il nous ménage une surprise** he's got a surprise in store for us ◆ **il sait ~ ses effets** [*orateur*] he knows how to make the most of his effects

4 (= *disposer, pratiquer*) [*+ porte, fenêtre*] to put in; [*+ chemin*] to cut ◆ ~ **un espace entre** to make a space between ◆ ~ **une place pour** to make room for

VPR **se ménager** 1 (= *ne pas abuser de ses forces*) to take it easy ◆ **il faut** *ou* **vous devriez vous ~ un peu** you should take things easy, you should try not to overtax yourself ◆ **l'athlète se ménage pour la finale** the athlete is conserving his energy *ou* is saving himself for the final

2 (= *se réserver*) **se ~ du temps pour se reposer** to set time aside to rest ◆ **se ~ une marge de manœuvre** to leave o.s. room for manoeuvre ◆ **se ~ un passage** to clear a path for o.s. ◆ **se ~ une revanche** to plan one's revenge

ménagerie /menaʒʀi/ NF (*lit*) menagerie; (* *fig*) zoo

menchevik /mɛnʃevik/ NMF Menshevik (*épith*)

mendélévium /mɛ̃delevjɔm/ NM mendelevium

mendiant, e /mɑ̃djɑ̃, jɑ̃t/ NM,F beggar; → **frère, ordre[1]** NM (= *pâtisserie*) mixed dried fruit(s) and nuts (*on a chocolate base*) ≃ florentine ◆ **des ~s** (= *fruits et noix*) dried fruit and nuts

mendicité /mɑ̃disite/ NF begging ◆ **arrêter qn pour** ~ to arrest sb for begging ◆ **être réduit à la** ~ to be reduced to beggary *ou* begging

mendier /mɑ̃dje/ ▸ conjug 7 ◂ VT [*+ argent, nourriture, caresse, emploi*] to beg for ◆ ~ **qch à qn** to beg sb for sth ◆ ~ **des compliments** to fish for compliments VI to beg

mendigot * /mɑ̃digo/ NM (*péj*) beggar

mendigoter * /mɑ̃digɔte/ ▸ conjug 1 ◂ VTI to beg ◆ **toujours à ~ (quelque chose)** always begging (for something)

meneau (pl **meneaux**) /məno/ NM (*horizontal*) transom; (*vertical*) mullion; → **fenêtre**

menée /məne/ NF 1 (*Vénerie*) stag's track (*in flight*) 2 (*Helv* = *amas de neige*) snowdrift NFPL **menées** (= *machinations*) intrigues, manoeuvres, machinations ◆ **déjouer les ~s de qn** to foil sb's manoeuvres *ou* little game* ◆ **~s subversives** subversive activities

mener /m(ə)ne/ ▸ conjug 5 ◂ VT 1 (= *conduire*) [*+ personne*] to take, to lead; (*en voiture*) to drive, to take (*à* to; *dans* into); ◆ ~ **un enfant à l'école/chez le médecin** to take a child to school/to see the doctor ◆ ~ **la voiture au garage** to take the car to the garage ◆ **mène ton ami à sa chambre** show *ou* take *ou* see your friend to his room ◆ ~ **promener le chien** to take the dog for a walk ◆ ~ **qn en bateau*** to take sb for a ride*, to lead sb up the garden path*, to have sb on* ◆ **il a bien su ~ sa barque** he's managed his career very effectively

2 [*véhicule, personne*] to take; [*route*] to lead, to take; [*profession, action*] to lead, to get (*à* to; *dans* into); ◆ **c'est le chemin qui mène à la mer** this is the path (leading) to the sea ◆ **le car vous mène à Chartres en deux heures** the bus will take *ou* get you to Chartres in two hours ◆ **cette route vous mène à Chartres** this road will take you to Chartres, you'll get to Chartres on this road ◆ **où mène ce chemin ?** where does this path go *ou* lead (to)? ◆ **où tout cela va-t-il nous ~ ?** where's all this going to get us?, where does all this lead us? ◆ **cela ne (nous) mène à rien** this won't get us

anywhere, this will get us nowhere ◆ **le journalisme mène à tout** all roads are open to you in journalism ◆ **de telles infractions pourraient le ~ loin** offences such as these could get him into trouble *ou* into deep water ◆ **~ qn à faire qch** to lead sb to do qch; → **chemin**

3 *(= commander) [+ personne, cortège]* to lead; *[+ pays]* to run, to rule; *[+ entreprise]* to manage, to run; *[+ navire]* to command ◆ **il sait ~ les hommes** he knows how to lead men, he is a good leader ◆ **~ qn par le bout du nez** to lead sb by the nose ◆ **il est mené par le bout du nez par sa femme** his wife has got him on a string ◆ **elle se laisse ~ par son frère** she lets herself be led by her brother ◆ **l'argent mène le monde** money rules the world, money makes the world go round ◆ **~ le jeu** *ou* **la danse** to call the tune, to say what goes* ◆ **~ les débats** to chair the discussion

4 *(gén, Sport = être en tête)* to lead; *(emploi absolu)* to lead, to be in the lead ◆ **il mène (par) 3 jeux à 1** *(Tennis)* he's leading (by) 3 games to 1 ◆ **la France mène (l'Écosse par 2 buts à 1)** France is in the lead *ou* is leading (by 2 goals to 1 against Scotland)

5 *(= orienter) [+ vie]* to lead, to live; *[+ négociations, lutte, conversation]* to carry on; *[+ enquête]* to carry out, to conduct; *[+ affaires]* to manage, to run; *[+ carrière]* to handle, to manage ◆ **~ les choses rondement** to manage things efficiently ◆ **~ qch à bien** *ou* **à bonne fin** *ou* **à terme** to see sth through, to carry sth through to a successful conclusion ◆ **il mène deux affaires de front** he runs *ou* manages two businesses at once ◆ **~ la vie dure à qn** to rule sb with an iron hand, to keep a firm hand on sb ◆ **il n'en menait pas large** his heart was in his boots; → **barque, train** *etc*

6 *(Math)* **~ une parallèle à une droite** to draw a line parallel to a straight line

ménestrel /menɛstʀɛl/ **NM** minstrel

ménétrier /menetʀije/ **NM** fiddler

meneur, -euse /mənœʀ, øz/ **NM,F** *(= chef)* (ring) leader; *(= agitateur)* agitator ◆ **~ d'hommes** born leader ◆ **~ de jeu** *[de spectacles, variétés]* master of ceremonies, compere *(Brit)*, emcee *(US)*; *[de jeux-concours]* quizmaster; *(Sport)* team leader ◆ **meneuse de revue** *(Music-hall)* captain *(of chorus girls)*

menhir /meniʀ/ **NM** menhir, standing stone

méninge /menɛ̃ʒ/ **NF** *(Méd)* meninx ◆ **~s** meninges ◆ **se creuser les ~s*** to rack one's brains ◆ **tu ne t'es pas fatigué les ~s !*** you didn't strain* *ou* overtax yourself!

méningé, e /menɛ̃ʒe/ **ADJ** meningeal

méningite /menɛ̃ʒit/ **NF** meningitis *(NonC)* ◆ **faire une ~** to have meningitis ◆ **ce n'est pas lui qui attrapera une ~ !*** he's not one to strain himself!*

ménisque /menisk/ **NM** *(Anat, Opt, Phys)* meniscus; *(Bijouterie)* crescent-shaped jewel

ménopause /menopoz/ **NF** menopause ◆ **troubles de la ~** menopausal problems

ménopausée /menopoze/ **ADJ F** post-menopausal **NF** post-menopausal woman, woman past the menopause

ménopausique /menopozik/ **ADJ** *[troubles]* menopausal

menotte /mənɔt/ **NF** *(langage enfantin)* little *ou* tiny hand, handy *(langage enfantin)* **NFPL menottes** handcuffs ◆ **il est parti, ~s aux poignets** he left handcuffed *ou* in handcuffs ◆ **mettre** *ou* **passer les ~s à qn** to handcuff sb

mensonge /mɑ̃sɔ̃ʒ/ **NM** 1 *(= contre-vérité)* lie ◆ **faire** *ou* **dire un ~** to tell a lie ◆ **~ par omission** lie by omission ◆ **pieux ~** white lie ◆ **c'est vrai, ce ~ ?** *(hum)* are you sure you're not fibbing? ◆ **tout ça, c'est des ~s*** it's all a pack of lies; → **détecteur** 2 ◆ **le ~** lying, untruthfulness ◆ **je hais le ~** I hate lies *ou* untruthfulness ◆ **il vit dans le ~** he's living a lie 3 *(littér = illusion)* illusion

mensonger, -ère /mɑ̃sɔ̃ʒe, ɛʀ/ **ADJ** *(= faux) [rapport, nouvelle]* untrue, false; *[promesse]* deceitful, false; *(littér = trompeur) [bonheur]* illusory, delusive, deceptive

mensongèrement /mɑ̃sɔ̃ʒɛʀmɑ̃/ **ADV** untruthfully, falsely ◆ **témoigner ~** to give a false statement

menstruation /mɑ̃stʀyasjɔ̃/ **NF** menstruation

menstruel, -elle /mɑ̃stʀyɛl/ **ADJ** menstrual

menstrues /mɑ̃stʀy/ **NFPL** menses

mensualisation /mɑ̃sɥalizasjɔ̃/ **NF** *[de salaires, impôts, factures]* monthly payment ◆ **effectuer la ~ des salaires** to put workers on monthly salaries, to pay salaries monthly ◆ **la ~ de l'impôt** the monthly payment of tax; → **IMPÔTS**

mensualiser /mɑ̃sɥalize/ ▸ **conjug 1** ◂ **VT** *[+ salaires, employés, impôts, factures]* to pay on a monthly basis ◆ **être mensualisé** *[salaire]* to be paid monthly *ou* on a monthly basis; *[employé]* to be on a monthly salary; *[contribuable]* to pay income tax monthly

mensualité /mɑ̃sɥalite/ **NF** *(= traite)* monthly payment *ou* instalment; *(= salaire)* monthly salary ◆ **payer par ~s** to pay monthly *ou* in monthly instalments

mensuel, -elle /mɑ̃sɥɛl/ **ADJ** monthly **NM** *(Presse)* monthly (magazine)

mensuellement /mɑ̃sɥɛlmɑ̃/ **ADV** monthly, every month

mensuration /mɑ̃syʀasjɔ̃/ **NF** *(= mesure, calcul)* mensuration ◆ **~s** *(= mesures)* measurements ◆ **quelles sont ses ~s ?** *[de femme]* what are her measurements *ou* vital statistics* *(hum)*?

mental, e (mpl **-aux**) /mɑ̃tal, o/ **ADJ** *[maladie, âge, processus]* mental; → **calcul, malade** **NM** *(= état d'esprit)* ◆ **le ~** the mental state

mentalement /mɑ̃talmɑ̃/ **ADV** mentally ◆ **calculer qch ~** to calculate sth *ou* work sth out in one's head ◆ **c'est quelqu'un de très solide ~** mentally he's very strong

mentalité /mɑ̃talite/ **NF** mentality ◆ **les ~s ont changé** people think differently now, (people's) attitudes have changed ◆ **quelle ~ !, jolie ~ !** *(iro)* what an attitude! ◆ **avoir une sale ~*** to be a nasty piece of work*

menterie † /mɑ̃tʀi/ **NF** *(= mensonge)* untruth, falsehood ◆ **ce sont des ~s** *(hum)* it's all a pack of lies

menteur, -euse /mɑ̃tœʀ, øz/ **ADJ** *[proverbe]* fallacious, false; *[enfant]* untruthful, lying ◆ **il est très ~** he's an awful liar, he's always lying **NM,F** liar, fibber* ◆ **sale ~ !*** you dirty liar! **NM** *(Cartes)* cheat

menthe /mɑ̃t/ **NF** 1 *(= plante)* mint ◆ **~ poivrée** peppermint ◆ **~ verte** spearmint, garden mint ◆ **à la** *ou* **de ~** mint *(épith)*; → **alcool, pastille, thé** 2 *(= boisson fraîche)* peppermint cordial; *(= infusion)* mint tea ◆ **une ~ à l'eau** a glass of peppermint cordial; → **diabolo**

menthol /mɑ̃tɔl/ **NM** menthol

mentholé, e /mɑ̃tɔle/ **ADJ** mentholated, menthol *(épith)*

mention /mɑ̃sjɔ̃/ **NF** 1 *(= note brève)* mention ◆ **faire ~ de** to mention, to make mention of ◆ **il n'y a pas ~ de son nom dans la liste** his name is not on the list ◆ **faire l'objet d'une ~** to be mentioned

2 *(= annotation)* note, comment ◆ **le paquet est revenu avec la ~ "adresse inconnue"** the parcel was returned marked "address unknown" ◆ **"rayer la mention inutile"** *(Admin)* "delete as appropriate"

3 *(Scol, Univ)* grade ◆ **~ très honorable** *[de doctorat]* (with) distinction ◆ **être reçu avec ~** to pass with distinction *ou* honours ◆ **être reçu sans ~** to get a pass ◆ **~ passable** ≈ pass, pass mark *(Brit)*, passing grade *(US)*, (grade) C ◆ **~ assez bien** *(Scol)* ≈ (grade) B; *(Univ)* ≈ lower second class honours *(Brit)*, (grade) B *(US)* ◆ **~ bien** *(Scol)* ≈ B+ *ou* A-; *(Univ)* ≈ upper second class honours *(Brit)*, cum laude *(US)* ◆ **~ très bien** *(Scol)* ≈ A *ou* A+ ; *(Univ)* ≈ first class honours *(Brit)*, magna cum laude *(US)* ◆ **son film a obtenu une ~ spéciale lors du dernier festival** his film received a special award at the last festival

> ⚠ Au sens de 'annotation' ou pour un examen, **mention** ne se traduit pas par le mot anglais **mention**.

mentionner /mɑ̃sjɔne/ GRAMMAIRE ACTIVE 53.2 ▸ **conjug 1** ◂ **VT** to mention ◆ **la personne mentionnée ci-dessus** the above-mentioned person ◆ **l'île n'est pas mentionnée sur la carte** the island doesn't appear on the map

mentir /mɑ̃tiʀ/ ▸ **conjug 16** ◂ **VI** 1 *[personne]* to lie *(à qn* to sb; *sur* about); *[photo, apparences]* to be deceptive ◆ **tu mens !** you're a liar!, you're lying! ◆ **~ effrontément** to lie boldly, to be a barefaced liar ◆ **je t'ai menti** I lied to you, I told you a lie ◆ **sans ~** (quite) honestly ◆ **il ment comme il respire** *ou* **comme un arracheur de dents** he's a compulsive liar, he lies in *ou* through his teeth* ◆ **a beau ~ qui vient de loin** *(Prov)* long ways long lies *(Prov)* ◆ **ne me fais pas ~ !** don't prove me wrong! ◆ **faire ~ le proverbe** to give the lie to the proverb, to disprove the proverb

2 *(littér)* ◆ **~ à** *(= manquer à)* to betray; *(= démentir)* to belie ◆ **il ment à sa réputation** he belies *ou* does not live up to his reputation ◆ **vous en avez menti** († *ou hum*) you told an untruth

VPR se mentir *[personnes]* to lie to each other ◆ **se ~ à soi-même** to fool o.s. ◆ **il se ment à lui-même** he's not being honest with himself, he's fooling himself

menton /mɑ̃tɔ̃/ **NM** *(= partie du visage)* chin ◆ **~ en galoche** protruding *ou* jutting chin ◆ **~ fuyant** receding chin, weak chin ◆ **double/triple ~** double/triple chin

mentonnière /mɑ̃tɔnjɛʀ/ **NF** *[de chapeau]* (chin) strap; *(Hist) [de casque]* chin piece; *(Mus)* chin rest; *(Méd)* chin bandage

mentor /mɛ̃tɔʀ/ **NM** *(frm)* mentor

menu[1] /məny/ **NM** 1 *(= repas)* meal; *(= carte)* menu ◆ **faites votre ~ à l'avance** plan your meal in advance ◆ **quel est le** *ou* **qu'y a-t-il au ~ ?** what's on the menu? ◆ **vous prenez le ~ (à prix fixe) ou la carte ?** are you having the set menu or the à la carte (menu)? ◆ **~ du jour** today's menu ◆ **~ dégustation** tasting menu ◆ **~ touristique** set menu ◆ **~ gastronomique** gourmet menu ◆ **~ enfant** children's menu 2 *(= programme)* **quel est le ~ de la réunion ?*** what's the agenda for the meeting? ◆ **au ~ du festival** in the festival programme *(Brit)* *ou* program *(US)* ◆ **au ~ de l'émission, il y a …** lined up (for you) on the programme *(Brit)* *ou* program *(US)* is … ◆ **au ~ de son voyage officiel, il …** during his official visit, he … 3 *(Ordin)* menu ◆ **~ déroulant** pull-down menu

menu[2], e /məny/ **ADJ** 1 *(= fin) [doigt, tige, taille]* slender, slim; *[personne]* slim, slight; *[pied]* slender; *[herbe]* fine; *[écriture]* small, tiny; *[voix]* thin ◆ **en ~s morceaux** in tiny pieces

2 *(= peu important) [difficultés, incidents, préoccupations]* minor, petty, trifling ◆ **dire/raconter dans les ~s détails** to tell/relate in minute detail ◆ **~s frais** incidental *ou* minor expenses ◆ **~ fretin** *(lit, fig)* small fry ◆ **~s larcins** pilferage, pilfering ◆ **~e monnaie** small *ou* loose change ◆ **~ peuple** humble folk ◆ **Menus Plaisirs** *(Hist)* (royal) entertainment *(NonC)* ◆ **se**

réserver de l'argent pour ses ~s plaisirs to keep some money by for (one's) amusements ◆ **~s propos** small talk (NonC)

3 *(locutions)* **par le ~** in detail ◆ **raconter qch par le ~** to relate sth in great detail ◆ **on fit par le ~ la liste des fournitures** they made a detailed list of the supplies

ADV *[couper, hacher, piler]* fine(ly) ◆ **écrire ~** to write small

menuet /mənɥɛ/ NM minuet

menuiserie /mənɥizʀi/ NF 1 *(= métier)* joinery; *(pour le bâtiment)* carpentry ◆ **~ d'art** cabinetwork ◆ **spécialiste en ~ métallique** specialist in metal fittings *(for doors, windows etc)* ◆ **faire de la ~** *(passe-temps)* to do woodwork *ou* carpentry *ou* joinery 2 *(= atelier)* joiner's workshop 3 *(= ouvrage)* woodwork (NonC), joinery (NonC), carpentry (NonC)

menuisier /mənɥizje/ NM *[de meubles]* joiner; *[de bâtiment]* carpenter ◆ **~ d'art** cabinet-maker

Méphistophélès /mefistɔfelɛs/ NM Mephistopheles

méphistophélique /mefistɔfelik/ ADJ Mephistophelean

méphitique /mefitik/ ADJ noxious, noisome †, mephitic

méphitisme /mefitism/ NM sulphurous (air) pollution

méplat /mepla/ NM *(Anat, Archit)* plane

méprendre (se) /mepʀɑ̃dʀ/ ► conjug 58 ◄ VPR *(littér)* to make a mistake, to be mistaken *(sur* about); ◆ **se ~ sur qn** to misjudge sb, to be mistaken about sb ◆ **se ~ sur qch** to make a mistake about sth, to misunderstand sth ◆ **ils se ressemblent tellement que c'est à s'y ~** *ou* **qu'on pourrait s'y ~** they are so alike that you can't tell them apart *ou* that it's difficult to tell which is which

mépris /mepʀi/ NM 1 *(= mésestime)* contempt, scorn ◆ **avoir** *ou* **éprouver du ~ pour qn** to despise sb, to feel contempt for sb ◆ **sourire/regard de ~** scornful *ou* contemptuous smile/look ◆ **avec ~** contemptuously, scornfully, with contempt *ou* scorn 2 *(= indifférence)* ◆ **~ de** *ou* **pour** *[+ argent, gens, honneurs, danger]* contempt for, disregard for ◆ **avoir le ~ des conventions/traditions** to have no regard for conventions/traditions ◆ **au ~ du danger/des lois/de l'opinion publique** regardless *ou* in defiance of danger/the law/public opinion ◆ **au ~ de leur (propre) vie** without giving a single thought to *ou* without thought for their own lives

méprisable /mepʀizabl/ ADJ contemptible, despicable

méprisant, e /mepʀizɑ̃, ɑ̃t/ ADJ contemptuous, scornful; *(= hautain)* disdainful

méprise /mepʀiz/ NF *(= erreur)* mistake, error; *(= malentendu)* misunderstanding ◆ **par ~** by mistake

mépriser /mepʀize/ ► conjug 1 ◄ VT *[+ personne]* to despise, to look down on; *[+ danger, conseil, offre]* to scorn, to spurn; *[+ vice, faiblesse]* to scorn, to despise ◆ **~ les conventions** to scorn *ou* spurn convention

mer /mɛʀ/ NF 1 *(= océan)* sea ◆ **~ fermée** *ou* **intérieure** inland *ou* landlocked sea ◆ **~ de glace** glacier ◆ **~ de sable** sea of sand ◆ **naviguer sur une ~ d'huile** to sail on a glassy sea *ou* on a sea as calm as a millpond ◆ **aller à la ~** to go to the seaside ◆ **il a navigué sur toutes les ~s** he has sailed the seven seas ◆ **vent/port de ~** sea breeze/harbour ◆ **gens de ~** sailors, seafarers, seafaring men ◆ **coup de ~** heavy swell; → **bras, mal²**

2 *(= marée)* tide ◆ **la ~ est haute** *ou* **pleine/basse** the tide is high *ou* in/low *ou* out ◆ **c'est la haute** *ou* **pleine/basse ~** it is high/low tide

3 *(locutions)* **en ~** at sea ◆ **en haute** *ou* **pleine ~** out at sea, on the open sea ◆ **prendre la ~** *[personne, bateau]* to put out to sea ◆ **mettre une embarcation à la ~** to launch a boat ◆ **bateau qui tient bien la ~** good seagoing boat ◆ **aller/voyager par ~** to go/travel by sea ◆ **ce n'est pas la ~ à boire !** * it's no big deal! ◆ **j'avalerais** *ou* **boirais la ~ et les poissons** I could drink gallons (and gallons)

COMP **la mer des Antilles** the Caribbean (Sea)
la mer d'Aral the Aral Sea
la mer d'Azov the Sea of Azov
la mer des Caraïbes the Caribbean (Sea)
la mer Caspienne the Caspian Sea
la mer de Chine the China Sea
la mer Égée the Aegean Sea
la mer Icarienne the Icarian Sea
la mer Ionienne the Ionian Sea
la mer d'Irlande the Irish Sea
la mer d'Iroise the Iroise Sea
la mer de Marmara the Sea of Marmara
la mer Morte the Dead Sea
la mer Noire the Black Sea
la mer du Nord the North Sea
la mer d'Oman the sea of Oman
la mer Rouge the Red Sea
la mer des Sargasses the Sargasso Sea
les mers du Sud the South Seas
la mer Tyrrhénienne the Tyrrhenian Sea

mercanti /mɛʀkɑ̃ti/ NM *(péj)* profiteer; *(= marchand oriental ou africain)* bazaar merchant

mercantile /mɛʀkɑ̃til/ ADJ *(péj)* mercenary, venal

mercantilisme /mɛʀkɑ̃tilism/ NM *(péj)* mercenary *ou* venal attitude; *(Écon, Hist)* mercantile system, mercantilism

mercantiliste /mɛʀkɑ̃tilist/ ADJ, NM mercantilist

mercatique /mɛʀkatik/ NF marketing

mercenaire /mɛʀsənɛʀ/ ADJ *[soldat]* mercenary, hired; *(péj) [attitude, personne]* mercenary NM *(Mil)* mercenary ◆ **tous ces ~s qui se vendent au plus offrant** *(péj)* all these mercenary individuals who sell themselves to the highest bidder

mercerie /mɛʀsəʀi/ NF *(= boutique)* haberdasher's shop *(Brit)*, notions store *(US)*; *(= articles)* haberdashery *(Brit)*, notions *(US)*, dry goods *(US)*; *(= profession)* haberdashery *(Brit) ou* notions (US) (trade)

mercerisé /mɛʀsəʀize/ ADJ ◆ **coton ~** mercerized cotton

merchandising /mɛʀʃɑ̃dajziŋ, mɛʀʃɑ̃diziŋ/ NM merchandising

merci /mɛʀsi/ GRAMMAIRE ACTIVE 48.1, 49, 52.4

EXCL 1 *(pour remercier)* thank you ◆ **~ bien** thank you, many thanks ◆ **~ beaucoup** thank you very much, thanks a lot * ◆ **~ mille fois** thank you (ever) so much ◆ **~ de** *ou* **pour votre carte** thank you for your card ◆ **~ d'avoir répondu** thank you for replying ◆ **sans même me dire ~** without even thanking me, without even saying thank you ◆ **~ du compliment !** *(iro)* thanks for the compliment! ◆ **~ mon chien !** * *(iro)* thank you too! *(iro)*, don't bother saying thank you! *(iro)*; → **dieu**

2 *(pour accepter)* **du lait ? – (oui) ~** some milk? – (yes) please

3 *(pour refuser)* **Cognac ? – (non) ~** Cognac? – no thank you ◆ **y retourner ? ~ (bien) !** go back there? no thank you!

NM thank-you ◆ **je n'ai pas eu un ~** I didn't get *ou* hear a word of thanks ◆ **nous vous devons/nous devons vous dire un grand ~ pour ...** we owe you/we must say a big thank-you for ... ◆ **et encore un grand ~ pour votre cadeau** and once again thank you so much *ou* many thanks for your present ◆ **mille ~s** many thanks

NF *(= pitié)* mercy ◆ **crier/implorer ~** to cry/beg for mercy

♦ **sans merci** *[concurrence]* merciless, ruthless; *[guerre, lutte]* ruthless *[combattre]* ruthlessly

♦ **à merci** ◆ **exploitable à ~** liable to be ruthlessly exploited, open to ruthless exploitation ◆ **réduire à ~** to force into submission

♦ **à la merci de** ◆ **à la ~ de qn** at sb's mercy ◆ **tout le monde est à la ~ d'une erreur** anyone can make a mistake ◆ **nous sommes toujours à la ~ d'un accident** accidents can happen at any time

mercier, -ière /mɛʀsje, jɛʀ/ NM,F haberdasher *(Brit)*, notions dealer *(US)*

mercredi /mɛʀkʀədi/ NM Wednesday ◆ **~ des Cendres** Ash Wednesday; *pour autres loc voir* **samedi** EXCL * sugar! *, shoot! * *(US)*

mercure /mɛʀkyʀ/ NM 1 *(Chim)* mercury 2 *(Astron, Myth)* **Mercure** Mercury

mercuriale /mɛʀkyʀjal/ NF 1 *(littér = reproche)* reprimand, rebuke 2 *(= plante)* mercury 3 *(= tableaux de prix)* market price list

mercurochrome ® /mɛʀkyʀokʀom/ NM Mercurochrome ®

merde /mɛʀd/ NF ** 1 *(= excrément)* shit**; *(= étron)* turd** ◆ **une ~ de chien** some dog shit**, a dog turd**

2 *(= livre, film)* crap** ◆ **son dernier bouquin est de la vraie** *ou* **une vraie ~** his latest book is a load of crap** ◆ **quelle voiture de ~ !** what a fucking awful car!**, what a shitty car!** ◆ **quel boulot de ~ !** what a crap** *ou* shitty** job!

3 *(= ennuis)* **quelle ~ !** shit!** ◆ **la moto est en panne, quelle ~** *ou* **c'est la ~ !** the bike's broken down, what a bummer!‡ ◆ **on est dans la ~** we're really in the shit**, we're in one hell of a mess‡ ◆ **ils sont venus pour foutre** la ~** they came to cause trouble ◆ **il a mis** *ou* **foutu** la ~ dans mes affaires** he messed up * my things ◆ **mettre** *ou* **foutre** qn dans la ~** to land sb in the shit** ◆ **il ne m'arrive que des ~s** I've had one goddam‡ problem after another

4 *(locutions)* **je te dis ~ !** *(insulte)* you can go to hell!‡; *(bonne chance)* good luck!, break a leg! * ◆ **tu le veux, oui ou ~ ?** for Christ's sake *ou* for God's sake, do you want it or not?‡ ◆ **tu as de la ~ dans les yeux !** are you blind or what? * ◆ **il ne se prend pas pour de la** *ou* **une ~** he thinks the sun shines out of his arse** *(Brit) ou* ass** *(US)*, he thinks his shit doesn't stink** *(US)*

EXCL ‡ *(impatience, contrariété)* hell!‡, shit!**; *(indignation, surprise)* shit!**, bloody hell!‡ *(Brit)* ◆ **~ alors !** damn‡!

merder** /mɛʀde/ ► conjug 1 ◄ VI *[personne]* to cock up‡, to fuck up** ◆ **t'arrives à le réparer ? – non, ça merde** can you fix it? – no, it's knackered‡ ◆ **le projet a merdé du début à la fin** the project was a bloody** *(Brit) ou* goddam‡ *(US)* mess *ou* shambles from start to finish ◆ **j'ai merdé en anglais/à l'écrit** I fucked up** my English exam/the written paper

merdeux, -euse** /mɛʀdø, øz/ ADJ shitty** ◆ **il se sent ~** he feels shitty** NM,F squirt‡, twerp *

merdier** /mɛʀdje/ NM *(= situation)* fuck-up**, muck-up *; *(= désordre)* shambles *(sg)* ◆ **être dans un beau ~** to be really in the shit**, to be up shit creek (without a paddle)** ◆ **c'est le ~ dans ses dossiers** his files are an absolute shambles

merdique‡ /mɛʀdik/ ADJ *[film, discours, idée]* pathetic, moronic, crappy** ◆ **c'était ~, cette soirée** that party was the pits‡ *ou* was bloody awful** *(Brit)*

merdouille‡ /mɛʀduj/ NF ⇒ **merde**

merdouiller* /mɛʀduje/ ▸ conjug 1 ◂ **VI** ⇒ **merder**

mère /mɛʀ/ **NF** 1 *(= génitrice)* mother ◆ **elle est ~ de quatre enfants** she is a *ou* the mother of four (children) ◆ **tu es une ~ pour moi** *(fig hum)* you are like a mother to me ◆ **la France, ~ des arts** *(littér)* France, mother of the arts ◆ **frères par la ~** half-brothers (on the mother's side) ◆ **devenir ~** to become a mother; → **Madame, reine**

2 *(= femme)* **la ~ Morand*** *(péj)* old mother Morand, old Ma Morand *(péj)* ◆ **allons la petite ~, dépêchez-vous !*** come on missis, hurry up!* ◆ **ma petite ~** *(affectueux : à une enfant, un animal)* my little pet *ou* love ◆ **bonjour, ~ Martin** *(dial)* good day to you, Mrs Martin

3 *(Rel)* mother ◆ **(la) Mère Catherine** Mother Catherine ◆ **oui, ma ~** yes, Mother

4 *(Tech = moule)* mould

5 *(apposition : après n) (= cellule, compagnie)* parent ◆ **fichier ~** *(Ordin)* mother file ◆ **langue ~** *(Ling)* mother tongue *ou* language; → **carte, maison**

COMP **Mère abbesse** mother abbess
mère d'accueil ⇒ **mère porteuse**
mère biologique natural *ou* biological mother
mère de famille mother, housewife
mère génétique ⇒ **mère biologique**
mère patrie motherland
mère porteuse surrogate mother
mère poule* mother hen ◆ **c'est une vraie ~ poule*, elle est très ~ poule*** she's a real mother hen
mère de substitution ⇒ **mère porteuse**
Mère supérieure Mother Superior
mère de vinaigre mother of vinegar

mère-grand † (pl **mères-grand**) /mɛʀgʀɑ̃/ **NF** grandma

merguez /mɛʀgɛz/ **NF** merguez sausage *(spicy sausage from North Africa)*

mergule /mɛʀgyl/ **NM** ◆ **~ (nain)** little auk

méridien, -ienne /meʀidjɛ̃, jɛn/ **ADJ** *(Sci)* meridian; *(littér)* meridian *(littér)*, midday *(épith)*
NM *(Astron, Géog)* meridian ◆ **~ d'origine** prime meridian ◆ **le ~ de Greenwich** the Greenwich meridian **NF** **méridienne** 1 *(Astron)* meridian line; *(Géodésie)* line of triangulation points 2 *(= fauteuil)* meridienne 3 *(littér = sieste)* siesta

méridional, e (mpl **-aux**) /meʀidjɔnal, o/ **ADJ** *(= du Sud)* southern; *(= du sud de la France)* Southern (French) **NM,F** **Méridional(e)** *(= du Sud)* Southerner; *(= du sud de la France)* Southern Frenchman (*ou* Frenchwoman), Southerner

meringue /məʀɛ̃g/ **NF** meringue

meringuer /məʀɛ̃ge/ ▸ conjug 1 ◂ **VT** *(gén ptp)* to coat *ou* cover with meringue ◆ **tarte au citron meringuée** lemon meringue pie

mérinos /meʀinos/ **NM** merino; → **pisser**

merise /məʀiz/ **NF** wild cherry

merisier /məʀizje/ **NM** *(= arbre)* wild cherry (tree); *(= bois)* cherry (wood)

méritant, e /meʀitɑ̃, ɑ̃t/ **ADJ** deserving

mérite /meʀit/ **NM** 1 *(= vertu intrinsèque)* merit; *(= respect accordé)* credit ◆ **le ~ de cet homme est grand** he is a man of great merit ◆ **il n'en a que plus de ~** he deserves all the more credit, it's all the more to his credit ◆ **il n'y a aucun ~ à cela** there's no merit in that ◆ **tout le ~ lui revient** all the credit is due to him, he deserves all the credit ◆ **il a le grand ~ d'avoir réussi** it's greatly to his credit that *ou* his great merit is that he succeeded ◆ **il a au moins le ~ d'être franc** at least he's frank ◆ **cette explication a la ~ de la clarté** this explanation has the virtue of being clear ◆ **elle a bien du ~ de le supporter** she deserves a lot of credit for putting up with him

2 *(= valeur)* merit, worth; *(= qualité)* quality ◆ **salaire au ~** merit pay ◆ **promotion au ~** promotion on merit ◆ **de grand ~** of great worth *ou* merit ◆ **ce n'est pas sans ~** it's not without merit ◆ **si nombreux que soient ses ~s** however many qualities he may have ◆ **son geste n'a eu d'autre ~ que ...** the only good point about *ou* merit in what he did was that ...

3 *(= décoration)* **l'ordre national du Mérite** the national order of merit *(French decoration)*

4 *(Rel)* **~(s) du Christ** merits of Christ

mériter /meʀite/ ▸ conjug 1 ◂ **VT** 1 *[+ louange, châtiment]* to deserve, to merit ◆ **il mérite la prison** he deserves to go to prison ◆ **tu mériterais qu'on t'en fasse autant** you deserve (to get) the same treatment ◆ **~ l'estime de qn** to be worthy of *ou* deserve *ou* merit sb's esteem ◆ **tu n'as que ce que tu mérites** you've got what you deserved, it serves you right ◆ **un repos bien mérité** a well-deserved rest ◆ **on a les amis qu'on mérite** you have the friends you deserve ◆ **ça se mérite !** you have to earn it!

2 *(= valoir)* to merit, to deserve, to be worth; *(= exiger)* to call for, to require ◆ **le fait mérite d'être noté** the fact is worth noting, the fact is worthy of note ◆ **ceci mérite réflexion** *ou* **qu'on y réfléchisse** *(exiger)* this calls for *ou* requires careful thought; *(valoir)* this merits *ou* deserves careful thought ◆ **ça lui a mérité le respect de tous** this earned him everyone's respect

3 ◆ **il a bien mérité de la patrie** *(frm)* he deserves well of his country; *(hum)* he deserves a medal for that

méritocratie /meʀitɔkʀasi/ **NF** meritocracy

méritocratique /meʀitɔkʀatik/ **ADJ** meritocratic

méritoire /meʀitwaʀ/ **ADJ** praiseworthy, meritorious *(frm)*

merlan /mɛʀlɑ̃/ **NM** 1 *(= poisson)* whiting 2 *(† * = coiffeur)* barber, hairdresser 3 *(Boucherie)* ≈ topside *(Brit)*, top round *(US)*

merle /mɛʀl/ **NM** 1 *(= oiseau européen)* blackbird ◆ **~ à plastron** ring ouzel 2 *(= oiseau américain)* (American) robin

merlette /mɛʀlɛt/ **NF** female blackbird

merlin /mɛʀlɛ̃/ **NM** 1 *[de bûcheron]* axe; *(Boucherie)* cleaver 2 *(Naut)* marline

merlu /mɛʀly/ **NM** hake

merluche /mɛʀlyʃ/ **NF** 1 *(Culin)* dried cod, stockfish 2 ⇒ **merlu**

merluchon /mɛʀlyʃɔ̃/ **NM** small hake

mérou /meʀu/ **NM** grouper

mérovingien, -ienne /meʀɔvɛ̃ʒjɛ̃, jɛn/ **ADJ** Merovingian **NM,F** **Mérovingien(ne)** Merovingian

merveille /mɛʀvɛj/ **NF** 1 *(= chose exceptionnelle)* marvel, wonder ◆ **les ~s de la technique moderne** the wonders *ou* marvels of modern technology ◆ **cette montre est une ~ de précision** this watch is a marvel of precision ◆ **les ~s de la nature** the wonders of nature ◆ **cette machine est une (petite) ~** this machine is a (little) marvel ◆ **regarde ma bague – quelle ~ !** look at my ring – it's beautiful! ◆ **faire ~** *ou* **des ~s** to work wonders ◆ **c'est ~ que vous soyez vivant** it's a wonder *ou* a marvel that you are alive ◆ **on en dit ~** *ou* **des ~s** people say it's marvellous; → **huitième, sept**

2 *(Culin)* fritter

LOC ADV **à merveille** perfectly, wonderfully, marvellously ◆ **cela te va à ~** it suits you perfectly *ou* to perfection ◆ **se porter à ~** to be in excellent health, to be in the best of health ◆ **ça s'est passé à ~** it went off like a dream *ou* without a single hitch ◆ **ça tombe à ~** this comes at an ideal moment *ou* just at the right time

merveilleusement /mɛʀvɛjøzmɑ̃/ **ADV** *[propre]* wonderfully, amazingly; *[interpréter]* brilliantly ◆ **elle joue ~ bien au tennis** she's a brilliant tennis player ◆ **la maison est ~ située** the house is in a marvellous position ◆ **l'endroit se prête ~ à ce genre de festival** the place is wonderful for this kind of festival

merveilleux, -euse /mɛʀvɛjø, øz/ **ADJ** 1 *(= magnifique) [paysage, bijoux]* wonderful 2 *(= sensationnel) [nouvelle, événement heureux, personne]* wonderful, fantastic ◆ **il est ~ de dévouement** he's wonderfully devoted 3 *(après n = surnaturel)* magic **NM** ◆ **le ~** the supernatural; *(Art, Littérat)* the fantastic element **NF** **merveilleuse** *(Hist)* fine lady, belle

mes /me/ **ADJ POSS** → **mon**

mésalliance /mezaljɑ̃s/ **NF** misalliance, marriage beneath one's station † ◆ **faire une ~** to marry beneath o.s. *ou* one's station †

mésallier (se) /mezalje/ ▸ conjug 7 ◂ **VPR** to marry beneath o.s. *ou* one's station †

mésange /mezɑ̃ʒ/ **NF** tit(mouse) ◆ **~ bleue** blue tit ◆ **~ charbonnière** great tit ◆ **~ huppée** crested tit ◆ **~ à longue queue** long-tailed tit ◆ **~ noire** coal tit

mésaventure /mezavɑ̃tyʀ/ **NF** misadventure ◆ **il a connu bien des ~s** he's had many misadventures ◆ **après la récente ~ survenue à notre navigateur** after our navigator's recent misadventure *ou* accident

mescaline /mɛskalin/ **NF** mescaline

mesclun /mɛsklœ̃/ **NM** mixed green salad

Mesdames /medam/ **NFPL** → **Madame**

Mesdemoiselles /medmwazɛl/ **NFPL** → **Mademoiselle**

mésencéphale /mezɑ̃sefal/ **NM** midbrain, mesencephalon *(SPÉC)*

mésentente /mezɑ̃tɑ̃t/ **NF** *(= désaccord profond)* dissension, disagreement; *(= incompréhension)* misunderstanding ◆ **la ~ règne dans leur famille** there is constant disagreement in their family ◆ **il y a eu (une) ~ entre les deux joueurs** *(Sport)* the two players misread each other ◆ **faire le ménage est une source de ~ conjugale** housework is a source of marital strife ◆ **~ sexuelle** sexual incompatibility

mésentère /mezɑ̃tɛʀ/ **NM** mesentery

mésestime /mezɛstim/ **NF** *(littér) [de personne]* low regard, low esteem ◆ **tenir qn en ~** to have little regard for sb, to hold sb in low esteem

mésestimer /mezɛstime/ ▸ conjug 1 ◂ **VT** *(littér = sous-estimer) [+ difficulté, adversaire]* to underestimate, to underrate; *[+ opinion]* to set little store by, to have little regard for; *[+ personne]* to have little regard for, to hold in low esteem

mésintelligence /mezɛ̃teliʒɑ̃s/ **NF** disagreement *(entre* between) dissension, discord

mesmérisme /mɛsmeʀism/ **NM** mesmerism

mésoderme /mezɔdɛʀm/ **NM** mesoderm, mesoblast

mésolithique /mezɔlitik/ **ADJ** Mesolithic **NM** ◆ **le ~** the Mesolithic

méson /mezɔ̃/ **NM** meson

Mésopotamie /mezɔpɔtami/ **NF** Mesopotamia

mésopotamien, -ienne /mezɔpɔtamjɛ̃, jɛn/ **ADJ** Mesopotamian **NM,F** **Mésopotamien(ne)** Mesopotamian

mésothérapie /mezoteʀapi/ **NF** mesotherapy

mésozoïque /mezɔzɔik/ **ADJ** Mesozoic **NM** ◆ **le ~** the Mesozoic (era)

mesquin, e /mɛskɛ̃, in/ **ADJ** *(= avare)* stingy, mean *(Brit)*; *(= vil)* mean, petty ◆ **c'est un es-**

prit ~ he is a mean-minded *ou* small-minded *ou* petty person ◆ **le repas faisait un peu** ~ the meal was a bit stingy

mesquinement /mɛskinmɑ̃/ ADV *[agir]* meanly, pettily

mesquinerie /mɛskinʀi/ NF *(= bassesse)* meanness, pettiness; *(= avarice)* stinginess, meanness; *(= procédé)* mean *ou* petty trick

mess /mɛs/ NM *(Mil)* mess

message /mesaʒ/ GRAMMAIRE ACTIVE 54.3 NM message ◆ ~ **chiffré** coded message ◆ ~ **d'erreur** *(Ordin)* error message ◆ ~ **publicitaire** *ou* **commercial** commercial, advertisement ◆ **film/chanson à** ~ film/song with a message ◆ **dans ce livre, l'auteur essaie de faire passer un** ~ the author tries to put a message across in this book ◆ **j'espère que le** ~ **est passé** I hope they've (*ou* he's *etc*) got the message ◆ **j'ai compris le** ~ **!** I got the message!

messager, -ère /mesaʒe, ɛʀ/ NM,F messenger ◆ ~ **de bonheur/du printemps** *(littér)* harbinger of glad tidings/of spring *(littér)* ◆ ~ **de malheur** bearer of bad tidings *ou* news NM *(= appareil)* ◆ ~ **(de poche)** pager

messagerie /mesaʒʀi/ NF 1 *(Transport)* **(service de) ~s** parcel service ◆ **~s aériennes/maritimes** *(= entreprise)* air freight/shipping company ◆ ~ **s de presse** press distribution service ◆ **les ~s royales** *(Hist)* the royal mail-coach service 2 *(Ordin, Téléc)* ~ **électronique** electronic mail, e-mail ◆ ~ **instantanée** instant messaging ◆ ~ **vocale** *(Internet)* voice mail; → **rose**

messe /mɛs/ NF *(Mus, Rel)* mass ◆ **aller à la** ~ to go to mass ◆ **célébrer la** ~ to celebrate mass ◆ **entendre la** ~ to hear *ou* attend mass ◆ **la** ~ **est dite** *(fig)* the die is cast; → **livre**[1]

COMP **messe basse** *(Rel)* low mass ◆ **~s basses** *(péj)* muttering, muttered conversation *ou* talk ◆ **finissez vos ~s basses** stop muttering *ou* whispering together
messe chantée sung mass
messe de minuit midnight mass
messe des morts mass for the dead
messe noire black mass

Messeigneurs /mesɛɲœʀ/ NMPL → **Monseigneur**

messeoir †† /meswaʀ/ ▸ conjug 26 ◂ VI *(littér)* *(moralement)* to be unseemly *(littér)* *(à* for) to ill befit *(littér)*; *(pour l'allure)* to ill become *(littér)*, to be unbecoming *(littér)* *(à* to); ◆ **avec un air qui ne lui messied pas** with a look that is not unbecoming to him ◆ **il vous messiérait de le faire** it would be unseemly for you to do it, it would ill become you to do it

messianique /mesjanik/ ADJ messianic

messianisme /mesjanism/ NM *(Rel, fig)* messianism ◆ **la tendance au ~ de certains révolutionnaires** the messianic tendencies of certain revolutionaries

messidor /mesidɔʀ/ NM Messidor *(tenth month in the French Republican Calendar)*

messie /mesi/ NM messiah ◆ **le Messie** the Messiah ◆ **ils l'ont accueilli comme le Messie** they welcomed him like a saviour *ou* the Messiah; → **attendre**

Messieurs /mesjø/ NMPL → **Monsieur**

messire †† /mesiʀ/ NM *(= noble)* my lord; *(= bourgeois)* Master ◆ **oui** ~ yes my lord, yes sir ◆ ~ **Jean** my lord John, master John

mestrance /mɛstʀɑ̃s/ NF ⇒ **maistrance**

mestre /mɛstʀ/ NM *(Naut)* mainmast

mesurable /məzyʀabl/ ADJ *[grandeur, quantité]* measurable ◆ **difficilement** ~ *[grandeur, quantité]* hard to measure; *[conséquences, impact]* difficult to assess

mesure /m(ə)zyʀ/ GRAMMAIRE ACTIVE 43.4, 53.6 NF 1 *(= évaluation, dimension)* measurement ◆ **appareil de** ~ measuring instrument *ou* device ◆ **système de** ~ system of measurement ◆ **prendre les ~s de qch** to take the measurements of sth; → **poids**

2 *(= taille)* **la ~ de ses forces/sentiments** the measure of his strength/feelings ◆ **monde/ville à la ~ de l'homme** world/town on a human scale ◆ **il est à ma** ~ *[de travail]* it's within my capabilities, I am able to do it; *[d'adversaire]* he's a match for me ◆ **trouver un adversaire à sa** ~ to find one's match ◆ **le résultat n'est pas à la ~ de nos espérances** the result is not up to our expectations ◆ **prendre la (juste** *ou* **pleine) ~ de qn/qch** to size sb/sth up, to get the measure of sb/sth ◆ **donner (toute) sa** ~ *ou* **sa pleine** ~ to show one's worth, to show what one is capable of *ou* made of ◆ **elle a donné toute la ~ de son talent** she showed the (full) extent of her talent

3 *(= unité, récipient, quantité)* measure ◆ ~ **de capacité** *(pour liquides)* liquid measure; *(pour poudre, grains)* dry measure ◆ ~ **de superficie/volume** square/cubic measure ◆ ~ **de longueur** measure of length ◆ ~ **graduée** measuring jug ◆ **donne-lui deux ~s d'avoine** give it two measures of oats ◆ **faire bonne** ~ to give good measure ◆ **pour faire bonne** ~ *(fig)* for good measure

4 *(= quantité souhaitable)* **la juste** *ou* **bonne** ~ the happy medium ◆ **la ~ est comble** that's the limit ◆ **dépasser** *ou* **excéder** *ou* **passer la** ~ to overstep the mark, to go too far ◆ **boire outre** ~ to drink immoderately *ou* to excess ◆ **cela ne me gêne pas outre** ~ that doesn't bother me overmuch, I'm not too bothered

5 *(= modération)* moderation ◆ **il n'a pas le sens de la** ~ he has no sense of moderation ◆ **avec** ~ with *ou* in moderation ◆ **il a beaucoup de** ~ he's very moderate ◆ **se dépenser sans** ~ *(= se dévouer)* to give one's all; *(= se fatiguer)* to overtax one's strength *ou* o.s.

6 *(= disposition, moyen)* measure, step ◆ **~s d'hygiène** health *ou* hygiene measures ◆ **par ~ d'hygiène** in the interest of hygiene ◆ **~s sociales** social measures ◆ **~s de soutien à l'économie** measures to bolster the economy ◆ **~s de rétorsion** reprisals, retaliatory measures ◆ **prendre des ~s d'urgence** to take emergency action *ou* measures ◆ **il faut prendre les ~s nécessaires pour ...** the necessary measures *ou* steps must be taken to ... ◆ **par ~ de restriction** as a restrictive measure

7 *(Mus)* *(= cadence)* time, tempo; *(= division)* bar; *(Poésie)* metre ◆ **en** ~ in time *ou* tempo ◆ ~ **composée/simple/à deux temps/à quatre temps** compound/simple/duple/common *ou* four-four time ◆ **être/ne pas être en** ~ to be in/out of time ◆ **jouer quelques ~s** to play a few bars ◆ **deux ~s pour rien** two bars for nothing; → **battre**

8 *(Habillement)* measure, measurement ◆ **prendre les ~s de qn** to take sb's measurements ◆ **ce costume est-il bien à ma ~ ?** *ou* **à mes ~s ?** is this suit my size?, will this suit fit me? ◆ **costume fait à la** ~ made-to-measure suit

9 *(Escrime)* (fencing) measure

10 *(locutions)*

◆ **sur mesure** ◆ **acheter** *ou* **s'habiller sur** ~ to have one's clothes made to measure ◆ **costume fait sur** ~ made-to-measure suit ◆ **c'est du sur** ~ *(lit)* it's made to measure, it's tailor-made; *(fig)* it's tailor-made ◆ **j'ai un emploi du temps/un patron sur** ~ my schedule/boss suits me down to the ground ◆ **c'est un rôle/emploi (fait) sur** ~ it's a role/job that was tailor-made for me (*ou* him *etc*)

◆ **dans + mesure** ◆ **dans la ~ de mes forces** *ou* **capacités** as far as *ou* insofar as I am able, to the best of my ability ◆ **dans la ~ de mes moyens** as far as my circumstances permit, as far as I am able ◆ **dans la ~ du possible** as far as possible ◆ **dans la ~ où** inasmuch as, insofar as ◆ **dans une certaine** ~ to some *ou* to a certain extent ◆ **dans une large** ~ to a large extent, to a great extent ◆ **dans une moindre** ~ to a lesser extent

◆ **être en mesure de faire qch** to be able to do sth; *(= avoir le droit)* to be in a position to do sth

◆ **au fur et à mesure** ◆ **il les pliait et me les passait au fur et à** ~ he folded them and handed them to me one by one *ou* as he went along ◆ **tu devrais ranger tes dossiers au fur et à** ~ you should put your files in order as you go along

◆ **(au fur et) à mesure que** as ◆ **(au fur et) à ~ que le temps passe** as time goes by

◆ **hors de mesure** out of proportion *(avec* with)

mesuré, e /məzyʀe/ (ptp de **mesurer**) ADJ *[ton]* steady; *[pas]* measured; *[personne, attitude, propos]* moderate ◆ **il est ~ dans ses paroles/ses actions** he is moderate *ou* temperate in his language/his actions

mesurer /məzyʀe/ ▸ conjug 1 ◂ VT 1 *[+ chose]* to measure; *[+ personne]* to take the measurements of, to measure (up); *(par le calcul)* *[+ distance, pression, volume]* to calculate; *[+ longueur à couper]* to measure off *ou* out ◆ **il a mesuré 3 cl d'acide** he measured out 3 cl of acid ◆ **il m'a mesuré 3 mètres de tissu** he measured me off *ou* out 3 metres of fabric ◆ ~ **les autres à son aune** to judge others by one's own standards

2 *(= évaluer, juger)* *[+ risque, efficacité]* to assess, to weigh up; *[+ valeur d'une personne]* to assess, to rate ◆ **vous n'avez pas mesuré la portée de vos actes !** you did not weigh up *ou* consider the consequences of your actions! ◆ **on n'a pas encore mesuré l'étendue des dégâts** the extent of the damage has not yet been assessed ◆ ~ **les efforts aux** *ou* **d'après les résultats (obtenus)** to gauge *ou* assess the effort expended by *ou* according to the results (obtained) ◆ ~ **ses forces avec qn** to pit o.s. against sb, to measure one's strength with sb ◆ ~ **qn du regard** to look sb up and down

3 *(= avoir pour taille)* to measure ◆ **cette pièce mesure 3 mètres sur 10** this room measures 3 metres by 10 ◆ **il mesure 1 mètre 80** *[personne]* he's 1 metre 80 tall; *[objet]* it's 1 metre 80 long *ou* high, it measures 1 metre 80

4 *(avec parcimonie)* to limit ◆ **elle leur mesure la nourriture** she rations them on food, she limits their food ◆ **le temps nous est mesuré** our time is limited, we have only a limited amount of time

5 *(avec modération)* ~ **ses paroles** *(= savoir rester poli)* to moderate one's language; *(= être prudent)* to weigh one's words

6 *(= proportionner)* to match *(à, sur* to) to gear *(à, sur* to); ◆ ~ **le travail aux forces de qn** to match *ou* gear the work to sb's strength ◆ ~ **le châtiment à l'offense** to make the punishment fit the crime, to match the punishment to the crime; → **brebis**

VPR **se mesurer** ◆ **se ~ à** *ou* **avec** *[+ personne]* to pit o.s. against; *[+ difficulté]* to confront, to tackle ◆ **se ~ des yeux** to weigh *ou* size each other up

mesureur /məzyʀœʀ/ NM *(= personne)* measurer; *(= appareil)* gauge, measure ADJ M ◆ **verre** ~ measuring cup (*ou* glass *ou* jug)

mésuser /mezyze/ ▸ conjug 1 ◂ **mésuser de** VT INDIR *(littér)* *(gén)* to misuse ◆ ~ **de son pouvoir** to abuse one's power

métabolique /metabɔlik/ ADJ metabolic

métaboliser /metabɔlize/ ▸ conjug 1 ◂ VT *(Physiol)* to metabolize

métabolisme /metabɔlism/ NM metabolism

métacarpe /metakaʀp/ NM metacarpus

métacarpien, -ienne /metakaʀpjɛ̃, jɛn/ ADJ metacarpal NMPL **métacarpiens** metacarpals, metacarpal bones

métairie /meteʀi/ NF smallholding, farm *(held on a métayage agreement)*

métal (pl **-aux**) /metal, o/ NM 1 *(gén, Chim, Fin, Min)* metal ◆ **~ blanc** white metal ◆ **le ~ jaune** *(Fin)* gold ◆ **les métaux précieux** precious metals ◆ **en ~ argenté/doré** *[couverts]* silver-/gold-plated 2 *(littér = matière)* metal *(littér)*, stuff

métalangage /metalɑ̃gaʒ/ NM, **métalangue** /metalɑ̃g/ NF metalanguage

métalinguistique /metalɛ̃gɥistik/ ADJ metalinguistic NF metalinguistics *(sg)*

métallifère /metalifɛʀ/ ADJ metalliferous *(SPÉC)*, metal-bearing *(épith)*

métallique /metalik/ ADJ 1 *(gén, Chim)* metallic; *[voix, couleur]* metallic; *[objet] (= en métal)* metal *(épith)*; *(= qui ressemble au métal)* metallic ◆ **bruit** *ou* **son ~** *[de clés]* jangle, clank; *[d'épée]* clash 2 *(Fin)* → **encaisse, monnaie**

métallisation /metalizasjɔ̃/ NF *[de métal]* plating; *[de miroir]* silvering

métallisé, e /metalize/ (ptp de **métalliser**) ADJ *[bleu, gris]* metallic; *[peinture, couleur]* metallic, with a metallic finish; *[miroir]* silvered; *[papier]* metallic, metallized

métalliser /metalize/ ► conjug 1 ◄ VT 1 *(= couvrir) [+ surface]* to plate, to metallize; *[+ miroir]* to silver 2 *(= donner un aspect métallique à)* to give a metallic finish to

métallo * /metalo/ NM (abrév de **métallurgiste**) steelworker, metalworker

métallographie /metalɔgʀafi/ NF metallography

métallographique /metalɔgʀafik/ ADJ metallographic

métalloïde /metalɔid/ NM metalloid

métalloplastique /metaloplastik/ ADJ copper asbestos *(épith)*

métallurgie /metalyʀʒi/ NF *(= industrie)* metallurgical industry; *(= technique, travail)* metallurgy

métallurgique /metalyʀʒik/ ADJ metallurgic

métallurgiste /metalyʀʒist/ NM ◆ **(ouvrier) ~** steelworker, metalworker ◆ **(industriel) ~** metallurgist

métamorphique /metamɔʀfik/ ADJ metamorphic, metamorphous

métamorphiser /metamɔʀfize/ ► conjug 1 ◄ VT *(Géol)* to metamorphose

métamorphisme /metamɔʀfism/ NM metamorphism

métamorphose /metamɔʀfoz/ NF *(Bio, Myth)* metamorphosis; *(fig)* (complete) transformation, metamorphosis

métamorphoser /metamɔʀfoze/ ► conjug 1 ◄ VT *(Myth, fig)* to transform, to metamorphose *(gén pass) (en* into); ◆ **son succès l'a métamorphosé** his success has (completely) transformed him *ou* has made a new man of him VPR **se métamorphoser** *(Bio)* to be metamorphosed; *(Myth, fig)* to be transformed *(en* into)

métaphore /metafɔʀ/ NF metaphor ◆ **par ~** metaphorically

métaphorique /metafɔʀik/ ADJ metaphorical

métaphoriquement /metafɔʀikmɑ̃/ ADV metaphorically

métaphysicien, -ienne /metafizisjɛ̃, jɛn/ ADJ metaphysical NM,F metaphysician, metaphysicist

métaphysique /metafizik/ ADJ *(Philos)* metaphysical; *[amour]* spiritual; *(péj) [argument]* abstruse, obscure NF *(Philos)* metaphysics *(sg)*

métaphysiquement /metafizikmɑ̃/ ADV metaphysically

métapsychique /metapsiʃik/ ADJ psychic ◆ **recherches ~s** psychic(al) research

métapsychologie /metapsikɔlɔʒi/ NF parapsychology, metapsychology

métastase /metastɑz/ NF metastasis ◆ **former des ~s** to metastasize ◆ **il a des ~s** he's got secondaries *ou* secondary cancer *ou* metastases *(SPÉC)*

métastaser /metastaze/ ► conjug 1 ◄ VI to metastasize

métatarse /metataʀs/ NM metatarsus

métatarsien, -ienne /metataʀsjɛ̃, jɛn/ ADJ metatarsal NMPL **métatarsiens** metatarsals, metatarsal bones

métathèse /metatɛz/ NF metathesis

métayage /metɛjaʒ/ NM métayage system *(where farmer pays rent in kind)*, sharecropping *(US)*

métayer /meteje/ NM (tenant) farmer *(paying rent in kind)*, sharecropper (tenant) *(US)*

métayère /metɛjɛʀ/ NF *(= épouse)* farmer's *ou* sharecropper's *(US)* wife; *(= paysanne)* (woman) farmer *ou* sharecropper *(US)*

métazoaire /metazɔɛʀ/ NM metazoan ◆ **les ~s** metazoans, Metazoa *(SPÉC)*

méteil /metɛj/ NM *mixed crop of wheat and rye*

métempsycose /metɑ̃psikoz/ NF metempsychosis, transmigration of the soul

météo /meteo/ ADJ abrév de **météorologique** NF 1 *(= science, service)* ⇒ **météorologie** 2 *(= bulletin)* (weather) forecast, weather report ◆ **la ~ est bonne/mauvaise** the weather forecast is good/bad ◆ **la ~ marine** the shipping forecast ◆ **présentateur (de la) ~** weather forecaster, weatherman *

météore /meteɔʀ/ NM *(lit)* meteor ◆ **passer comme un ~** *(fig)* to have a brief but brilliant career

météorique /meteɔʀik/ ADJ *(Astron)* meteoric

météorisme /meteɔʀism/ NM *(Méd)* meteorism

météorite /meteɔʀit/ NM *ou* NF meteorite

météorologie /meteɔʀɔlɔʒi/ NF *(Sci)* meteorology ◆ **la ~ nationale** *(= services)* the meteorological office, ≃ the Met Office * *(Brit)*, the Weather Bureau *(US)*

météorologique /meteɔʀɔlɔʒik/ ADJ *[phénomène, observation]* meteorological; *[conditions, carte, prévisions, station]* weather *(épith)*; → **bulletin**

météorologiquement /meteɔʀɔlɔʒikmɑ̃/ ADV meteorologically

météorologiste /meteɔʀɔlɔʒist/, **météorologue** /meteɔʀɔlɔg/ NMF meteorologist

métèque /metɛk/ NMF 1 *(*, injurieux)* Mediterranean, wop ** *(injurieux)* 2 *(Hist)* metic

méthadone /metadɔn/ NF methadone

méthane /metan/ NM methane

méthanier /metanje/ NM (liquefied) gas carrier *ou* tanker

méthanol /metanɔl/ NM methanol

méthode /metɔd/ NF 1 *(= moyen)* method ◆ **de nouvelles ~s d'enseignement du français** new methods of *ou* for teaching French, new teaching methods for French ◆ **la ~ douce** the softly-softly approach ◆ **avoir une bonne ~ de travail** to have a good way *ou* method of working ◆ **avoir sa ~ pour faire qch** to have one's own way of *ou* method for *ou* of doing sth ◆ **elle n'a pas vraiment la ~ avec les enfants** she doesn't really know how to handle children, she's not very good with children ◆ **service des ~s** process planning department

2 *(= ordre)* **il a beaucoup de ~** he's very methodical, he's a man of method ◆ **il n'a aucune ~** he's not in the least methodical, he has no (idea of) method ◆ **faire qch avec/sans ~** to do sth methodically *ou* in a methodical way/unmethodically

3 *(= livre)* manual, tutor ◆ **~ de piano** piano manual *ou* tutor ◆ **~ de latin** Latin primer

méthodique /metɔdik/ ADJ methodical

méthodiquement /metɔdikmɑ̃/ ADV methodically

méthodisme /metɔdism/ NM Methodism

méthodiste /metɔdist/ ADJ, NMF Methodist

méthodologie /metɔdɔlɔʒi/ NF methodology

méthodologique /metɔdɔlɔʒik/ ADJ methodological

méthyle /metil/ NM methyl

méthylène /metilɛn/ NM *(Comm)* methyl alcohol; *(Chim)* methylene; → **bleu**

méthylique /metilik/ ADJ methyl

méticuleusement /metikyløzmɑ̃/ ADV meticulously

méticuleux, -euse /metikylø, øz/ ADJ *[soin]* meticulous, scrupulous; *[personne]* meticulous ◆ **d'une propreté méticuleuse** *[endroit, objets]* spotlessly *ou* scrupulously clean

méticulosité /metikylozite/ NF meticulousness

métier /metje/ NM 1 *(= travail)* job; *(Admin)* occupation; *(commercial)* trade; *(artisanal)* craft; *(intellectuel)* profession ◆ **~ manuel** manual job ◆ **donner un ~ à son fils** to have one's son learn a trade ◆ **enseigner son ~ à son fils** to teach one's son one's trade ◆ **il a fait tous les ~s** he's tried his hand at everything, he's done all sorts of jobs ◆ **après tout ils font leur ~** they are only doing their job (after all) ◆ **les ~s du livre/de la communication** the publishing/communications industry ◆ **prendre le ~ des armes** to become a soldier, to join the army ◆ **les ~s de bouche** catering and allied trades; → **corps, gâcher**

2 *(= technique)* (acquired) skill; *(= expérience)* experience ◆ **avoir du ~** to have practical experience ◆ **manquer de ~** to be lacking in practical experience ◆ **avoir deux ans de ~** to have two years' experience, to have been in the job *(ou* trade *ou* profession) for two years

3 *(locutions)* **homme de ~** expert, professional, specialist ◆ **il est plombier de son ~** he is a plumber by trade ◆ **le plus vieux ~ du monde** *(euph)* the oldest profession (in the world) ◆ **il est du ~** he is in the trade ◆ **il connaît son ~** he knows his job, he's good at his job ◆ **je connais mon ~ !** I know what I'm doing! ◆ **tu ne vas pas m'apprendre mon ~ !** you're not going to teach me my job! ◆ **ce n'est pas mon ~** it's not my job ◆ **c'est le ~ qui rentre** * *(hum)* it's just learning the hard way ◆ **chacun son ~ (et les vaches seront bien gardées)** you should stick to what you know

4 *(= machine)* loom ◆ **~ à tisser** (weaving) loom ◆ **~ à filer** spinning frame ◆ **~ à broder** embroidery frame ◆ **remettre qch sur le ~** *(littér)* to make some improvements to sth ◆ **vingt fois sur le ~ remettez votre ouvrage** you should keep going back to your work and improving it

métis, -isse /metis/ ADJ *[personne]* mixed-race *(épith)*, of mixed race *(attrib)*; *[animal]* crossbred; *[chien]* crossbred, mongrel; *[plante]* hybrid; *[tissu, toile]* made of cotton and linen NM,F *(= personne)* person of mixed race; *(= animal)* crossbreed; *(= chien)* crossbreed, mongrel; *(= plante)* hybrid NM ◆ **toile/drap de ~** linen-cotton mix *ou* blend fabric/sheet

métissage /metisaʒ/ NM *[d'animaux]* crossbreeding, crossing; *[de plantes]* crossing; *[de* *musiques, genres]* mixing ♦ **cette population est le produit d'un** ~ these people are of mixed origins ♦ **le** ~ **culturel** *ou* **de cultures** the mixing of cultures

métisser /metise/ ▸ conjug 1 ◂ VT *[+ plantes, animaux]* to crossbreed, to cross ♦ **c'est une population très métissée** it's a very mixed population ♦ **une culture métissée** an ethnically diverse culture ♦ **une musique métissée** a musical style that draws from many cultural sources

métonymie /metɔnimi/ NF metonymy

métonymique /metɔnimik/ ADJ metonymical

métrage /metʀaʒ/ NM [1] *(Couture)* length ♦ **grand/petit** ~ long/short length ♦ **quel** ~ **vous faut-il ?** how many yards *ou* metres do you need? [2] *(= mesure)* measurement, measuring (in metres) ♦ **procéder au** ~ **de qch** to measure sth out [3] *(Ciné)* footage, length ♦ **court** ~ short (film), one-reeler *(US)* ♦ **(film) long** ~ feature(-length) film ♦ **moyen** ~ medium-length film

métré /metʀe/ NM *(= métier)* quantity surveying; *(= mesure)* measurement; *(= devis)* bill of quantities

mètre /mɛtʀ/ NM [1] *(Math)* metre *(Brit)*, meter *(US)* ♦ ~ **carré/cube** square/cubic metre ♦ **vendre qch au** ~ **linéaire** to sell sth by the metre [2] *(= instrument)* (metre *(Brit)* *ou* meter *(US)*) rule ♦ ~ **étalon** standard metre ♦ ~ **pliant** folding rule ♦ ~ **à ruban** tape measure, measuring tape [3] *(Athlétisme)* **le 100/400** ~**s** the 100/400 metres *(Brit)* *ou* meters *(US)*, the 100-/400-metre *(Brit)* *ou* -meter *(US)* race [4] *(Ftbl, Rugby)* **les 22/50** ~**s** the 22 metre *(Brit)* *ou* meter *(US)*/halfway line [5] *(Littérat)* metre *(Brit)*, meter *(US)*

métrer /metʀe/ ▸ conjug 6 ◂ VT to measure (in metres); *[vérificateur]* to survey

métreur, -euse /metʀœʀ, øz/ NM,F ♦ ~ **(vérificateur)** quantity surveyor NF **métreuse** *(Ciné)* footage counter

métrique /metʀik/ ADJ *(Littérat)* metrical, metric; *(Mus)* metrical; *(Math)* *[système, tonne]* metric ♦ **géométrie** ~ metrical geometry NF *(Littérat)* metrics *(sg)*; *(Math)* metric theory

métro /metʀo/ NM *(= système)* underground *(Brit)*, subway *(US)*; *(= station)* *(gén)* underground *(Brit)* *ou* subway *(US)* station; *(à Paris)* metro station ♦ ~ **aérien** elevated railway, el* *(US)* ♦ **le** ~ **de Paris** the Paris metro ♦ **le** ~ **de Londres** the London underground, the tube ♦ **j'irai en** ~ I'll go by underground ♦ **le premier** ~ the first *ou* milk train ♦ **le dernier** ~ the last train ♦ **c'est** ~**, boulot, dodo*** it's the same old routine day in day out, it's work work work ♦ **il a toujours un** ~ **de retard*** he's always one step behind NMF (* *: terme des îles) person from metropolitan France*

métrologie /metʀɔlɔʒi/ NF metrology

métrologique /metʀɔlɔʒik/ ADJ metrological

métrologiste /metʀɔlɔʒist/ NMF metrologist

métronome /metʀɔnɔm/ NM metronome ♦ **avec la régularité d'un** ~ with clockwork regularity, like clockwork

métronomique /metʀɔnɔmik/ ADJ *[mouvement]* metronomic ♦ **avec une régularité** ~ with clockwork *ou* metronomic regularity

métropole /metʀɔpɔl/ NF [1] *(= ville)* metropolis ♦ ~ **régionale** large regional centre ♦ **la Métropole** (metropolitan) France ♦ **quand est prévu votre retour en** ~ **?** when do you go back home? *ou* back to the home country? ♦ **en** ~ **comme à l'étranger** at home and abroad [2] *(Rel)* metropolis

métropolitain, e /metʀɔpɔlitɛ̃, ɛn/ ADJ *(Admin, Rel)* metropolitan ♦ **la France** ~**e** metropolitan France ♦ **troupes** ~**es** home troops NM [1] *(Rel)* metropolitan [2] († = *métro)* underground *(Brit)*, subway *(US)*

métrosexuel, -elle /metʀosɛksɥɛl/ ADJ, NM, F metrosexual

mets /mɛ/ NM *(Culin)* dish

mettable /metabl/ ADJ *(gén nég)* wearable, decent ♦ **ça n'est pas** ~ this is not fit to wear *ou* to be worn ♦ **je n'ai rien de** ~ I've got nothing (decent) to wear *ou* nothing that's wearable ♦ **ce costume est encore** ~ you can still wear that suit, that suit is still decent *ou* wearable

metteur /metœʀ/ NM ♦ ~ **en œuvre** *(Bijouterie)* mounter ♦ ~ **en ondes** *(Radio)* producer ♦ ~ **en pages** *(Typo)* layout *ou* make-up artist ♦ ~ **au point** *(Tech)* adjuster ♦ ~ **en scène** *(Théât, Ciné)* director

mettre /mɛtʀ/

▸ conjug 56 ◂

1 VERBE TRANSITIF 2 VERBE PRONOMINAL

1 - VERBE TRANSITIF

Lorsque **mettre** s'emploie dans des expressions telles que **mettre qch en place, mettre qn au pas/au régime** etc, cherchez sous le nom.

[1] [= placer] to put (*dans* in, into; *sur* on); *(fig = classer)* to rank, to rate ♦ ~ **une assiette/carte sur une autre** to put one *ou* a plate/card on top of another ♦ **où mets-tu tes verres ?** where do you keep your glasses?, where are your glasses kept? ♦ **elle lui mit la main sur l'épaule** she put *ou* laid her hand on his shoulder ♦ **elle met son travail avant sa famille** she puts her work before her family ♦ **je mets Molière parmi les plus grands écrivains** I rank *ou* rate Molière among the greatest writers ♦ ~ **qch debout** to stand sth up ♦ ~ **qn sur son séant/sur ses pieds** to sit/stand sb up ♦ ~ **qch à** *ou* **par terre** to put sth down (on the ground) ♦ ~ **qch à l'ombre/au frais** to put sth in the shade/in a cool place ♦ ~ **qch à plat** to lay sth down (flat) ♦ ~ **qch droit** to put *ou* set sth straight *ou* to rights, to straighten sth out *ou* up ♦ ~ **qn au** *ou* **dans le train** to put sb on the train ♦ **mettez-moi à la gare, s'il vous plaît*** take me to *ou* drop me at the station please ♦ **elle a mis la tête à la fenêtre** she put *ou* stuck her head out of the window ♦ **mettez les mains en l'air** put your hands up, put your hands in the air ♦ **mets le chat dehors** put the cat out

♦ **mettre qch à** + *infinitif* ♦ ~ **qch à cuire/à chauffer** to put sth on to cook/heat ♦ ~ **du linge à sécher** *(à l'intérieur)* to put *ou* hang washing up to dry; *(à l'extérieur)* to put *ou* hang washing out to dry

[2] [= ajouter] ~ **du sucre dans son thé** to put sugar in one's tea ♦ ~ **une pièce à un drap** to put a patch in *ou* on a sheet, to patch a sheet ♦ ~ **une idée dans la tête de qn** to put an idea into sb's head ♦ **ne mets pas d'encre sur la nappe** don't get ink on the tablecloth

[3] [= placer dans une situation] ~ **un enfant à l'école** to send a child to school ♦ ~ **qn au régime** to put sb on a diet ♦ ~ **qn dans la nécessité** *ou* **l'obligation de faire** to oblige *ou* compel sb to do ♦ ~ **au désespoir** to throw into despair ♦ **cela m'a mis dans une situation difficile** that has put me in *ou* got me into a difficult position ♦ **on l'a mis* à la manutention/aux réclamations** he was put in the packing/complaints department ♦ ~ **qn au pas** to bring sb into line, to make sb toe the line

[4] [= revêtir] *[+ vêtements, lunettes]* to put on ♦ ~ **une robe/du maquillage** to put on a dress/some make-up ♦ **depuis qu'il fait chaud je ne mets plus mon gilet** since it has got warmer I've stopped wearing my cardigan ♦ **elle n'a plus rien à** ~ **sur elle** she's got nothing (left) to wear ♦ **mets-lui son chapeau et on sort** put his hat on (for him) and we'll go ♦ **il avait mis un manteau** he was wearing a coat, he had a coat on ♦ **elle avait mis du bleu** she was wearing blue, she was dressed in blue

[5] [= consacrer] **j'ai mis 2 heures à le faire** I took 2 hours to do it *ou* 2 hours over it, I spent 2 hours on *ou* over it *ou* 2 hours doing it ♦ **le train met 3 heures** it takes 3 hours by train, the train takes 3 hours ♦ ~ **toute son énergie à faire** to put all one's effort *ou* energy into doing ♦ ~ **tous ses espoirs dans** to pin all one's hopes on ♦ ~ **beaucoup de soin à faire** to take great care in doing, to take great pains to do ♦ ~ **de l'ardeur à faire qch** to do sth eagerly *ou* with great eagerness ♦ **il y a mis le temps !** he's taken his time (about it)!, he's taken an age *ou* long enough!; → **cœur**

[6] [= faire fonctionner] ~ **la radio/le chauffage** to put *ou* switch *ou* turn the radio/the heating on ♦ ~ **les informations** to put *ou* turn the news on ♦ ~ **le réveil (à 7 heures)** to set the alarm (for 7 o'clock) ♦ ~ **le réveil à l'heure** to put the alarm clock right ♦ ~ **le verrou** to bolt *ou* lock the door ♦ **mets France Inter/la 2e chaîne** put on France Inter/channel 2 ♦ ~ **une machine en route** to start up a machine

[7] [= installer] *[+ eau]* to lay on; *[+ placards]* to put in, to build, to install; *[+ étagères]* to put up *ou* in, to build; *[+ moquette]* to fit, to lay; *[+ rideaux]* to put up ♦ ~ **du papier peint** to hang some wallpaper ♦ ~ **de la peinture** to put on a coat of paint

[8] [= écrire] ~ **en anglais/au pluriel** to put into English/the plural ♦ ~ **à l'infinitif/au futur** to put in(to) the infinitive/the future tense ♦ ~ **des vers en musique** to set verse to music ♦ ~ **sa signature (à)** to put *ou* append one's signature (to) ♦ ~ **un mot à qn*** to drop a line to sb ♦ **mettez bien clairement que ...** put (down) quite clearly that ... ♦ **il met qu'il est bien arrivé** he says in his letter *ou* writes that he arrived safely

[9] [= dépenser] ~ **de l'argent sur un cheval** to put money on a horse ♦ ~ **de l'argent dans une affaire** to put money into a business ♦ **combien avez-vous mis pour cette table ?** how much did you pay for that table? ♦ ~ **de l'argent sur son compte** to put money into one's account ♦ **je suis prêt à** ~ **100 (euro)** I'm willing to give *ou* I don't mind giving €100 ♦ **si on veut du beau il faut y** ~ **le prix** if you want something nice you have to pay the price *ou* pay for it; → **caisse**

[10] [= lancer] ~ **la balle dans le filet** to put the ball into the net ♦ ~ **une balle à la peau de qn*** to put a bullet in sb* ♦ ~ **son poing dans** *ou* **sur la figure de qn** to punch sb in the face, to give sb a punch in the face

[11] [= supposer] **mettons que je me suis** *ou* **sois trompé** let's say *ou* (just) suppose *ou* assume I've got it wrong ♦ **nous arriverons vers 10 heures, mettons, et après ?** say we arrive about 10 o'clock, then what?, we'll arrive about 10 o'clock, say, then what?

[12] [locutions] ~ **les bouts** *ou* **les voiles***, **les** ~‡ to clear off*, to beat it*, to scarper‡ *(Brit)* ♦ **qu'est-ce qu'ils nous ont mis !*** *(bagarre, match)* they gave us a real hammering!* ♦ **va te faire** ~ **!****fuck off!**, bugger off!** *(Brit)*

2 - VERBE PRONOMINAL

se mettre

[1] [= se placer] *[d'objet]* to go ♦ **mets-toi là** *(debout)* (go and) stand there; *(assis)* (go and) sit there ♦ **se** ~ **au piano/dans un fauteuil** to sit down at the piano/in an armchair ♦ **se** ~ **au chaud/à l'ombre** to come *ou* go into the warmth/into the shade ♦ **elle ne savait plus où se** ~ *(fig)* she didn't know where to look, she didn't know where to put herself *ou* what to do with herself ♦ **il s'est mis dans une situation délicate** he's

put himself in *ou* got himself into an awkward situation ◆ **se ~ autour (de)** to gather round ◆ **ces verres se mettent dans le placard** these glasses go in the cupboard ◆ **l'infection s'y est mise** it has become infected ◆ **les vers s'y sont mis** the maggots have got at it ◆ **il y a un bout de métal qui s'est mis dans l'engrenage** a piece of metal has got caught in the works; → **poil, rang, table, vert**

2 [Météo] **se ~ au froid/au chaud/à la pluie** to turn cold/warm/wet ◆ **on dirait que ça se met à la pluie** it looks like rain, it looks as though it's turning to rain

3 [= s'habiller] **se ~ en robe/en short, se ~ une robe/un short** to put on a dress/a pair of shorts ◆ **se ~ en bras de chemise** to take off one's jacket ◆ **se ~ nu** to strip (off *ou* naked), to take (all) one's clothes off ◆ **comment je me mets ?** what (sort of thing) should I wear? ◆ **elle s'était mise très simplement** she was dressed very simply ◆ **elle s'était mise en robe du soir** she was wearing *ou* she had on an evening dress ◆ **se ~ une veste/du maquillage** to put on a jacket/some make-up ◆ **elle n'a plus rien à se ~** she's got nothing (left) to wear

4 [= s'ajouter] **se ~ une idée dans la tête** to get an idea into one's head ◆ **il s'est mis de l'encre sur les doigts** he's got ink on his fingers ◆ **il s'en est mis partout** he's covered in it, he's got it all over him

5 [= commencer]

♦ **se mettre à** + *nom* ◆ **se ~ au régime** to go on a diet ◆ **se ~ au travail** to set to work, to get down to work, to set about one's work ◆ **se ~ à une traduction** to start *ou* set about (doing) a translation ◆ **se ~ à la peinture** to take up painting, to take to painting ◆ **se ~ au latin** to take up Latin ◆ **il s'est bien mis à l'anglais** he's really taken to English

♦ **se mettre à** + *infinitif* ◆ **se ~ à rire/à manger** to start laughing/eating, to start *ou* begin to laugh/eat ◆ **se ~ à traduire** to start to translate, to start translating, to set about translating ◆ **se ~ à boire** to take to drink *ou* the bottle* ◆ **voilà qu'il se met à pleuvoir !** and now it's beginning *ou* starting to rain!, and now it's coming on to *(Brit)* rain!

♦ **s'y mettre** ◆ **il est temps de s'y ~** it's (high) time we got down to it *ou* got on with it ◆ **qu'est-ce que tu es énervant quand tu t'y mets !*** you can be a real pain when you get going!* *ou* once you get started!*

6 [= se grouper] **ils se sont mis à plusieurs/deux pour pousser la voiture** several of them/the two of them joined forces to push the car ◆ **se ~ avec qn** *(= faire équipe)* to team up with sb; *(= prendre parti)* to side with sb; *(* : en ménage)* to move in with sb*, to shack up‡ *(péj)* with sb ◆ **se ~ bien/mal avec qn** to get on the right/wrong side of sb; → **partie²**

7 [locutions] **on s'en est mis jusque-là** *ou* **plein la lampe*** we had a real blow-out‡ ◆ **qu'est-ce qu'ils se sont mis !*** *(bagarre)* they really laid into each other!* *ou* had a go at each other!*, they didn't half *(Brit)* lay into each other!* *ou* have a go at each other!*

meublant, e /mœblɑ̃, ɑ̃t/ ADJ → **meuble**

meuble /mœbl/ NM 1 *(= objet)* piece of furniture ◆ **les ~s** the furniture *(NonC)* ◆ **~ de rangement** cupboard, storage unit ◆ **~ hi-fi** hi-fi unit ◆ **faire la liste des ~s** to make a list *ou* an inventory of the furniture, to list each item of furniture ◆ **nous sommes dans nos ~s** we have our own home ◆ **il fait partie des ~s** *(péj, hum)* he's part of the furniture; → **sauver** 2 *(= ameublement)* **le ~** furniture 3 *(Jur)* movable ◆ **~s meublants** furniture, movables ◆ **en fait de ~s possession vaut titre** possession is nine tenths *ou* points of the law 4 *(Hér)* charge ADJ *[terre, sol]* loose, soft; *[roche]* soft, crumbly; → **bien**

meublé, e /mœble/ (ptp de **meubler**) ADJ furnished ◆ **non ~** unfurnished NM *(= pièce)* furnished room; *(= appartement)* furnished apartment *ou* flat *(Brit)* ◆ **être** *ou* **habiter en ~** to be *ou* live in furnished accommodation

meubler /mœble/ ► conjug 1 ◄ VT *[+ pièce, appartement]* to furnish *(de* with); *[+ pensée, mémoire, loisirs]* to fill *(de* with); *[+ dissertation]* to fill out, to pad out *(de* with); ◆ **~ la conversation** to keep the conversation going ◆ **une table et une chaise meublaient la pièce** the room was furnished with a table and a chair ◆ **étoffe/papier qui meuble bien** decorative *ou* effective material/paper VPR **se meubler** to buy *ou* get (some) furniture, to furnish one's home ◆ **ils se sont meublés dans ce magasin/pour pas cher** they got *ou* bought their furniture from this shop/for a very reasonable price

meuf‡ /mœf/ NF *(= femme)* woman ◆ **sa ~** his girlfriend

meuglement /møgləmɑ̃/ NM mooing *(NonC)*, lowing † *(NonC)*

meugler /møgle/ ► conjug 1 ◄ VI to moo, to low †

meuh /mø/ EXCL, NM moo ◆ **faire ~** to moo

meulage /mølaʒ/ NM grinding

meule¹ /møl/ NF 1 *(à moudre)* millstone; *(à polir)* buff wheel; *(Dentisterie)* wheel ◆ **~ (à aiguiser)** grindstone ◆ **~ courante** *ou* **traînante** upper (mill)stone 2 *(Culin)* **~ (de gruyère)** round of gruyère 3 *(‡ = motocyclette)* bike, hog‡ *(US)*

meule² /møl/ NF *(Agr)* stack, rick; *(= champignonnière)* mushroom bed ◆ **~ de foin** haystack, hayrick ◆ **~ de paille** stack *ou* rick of straw ◆ **mettre en ~s** to stack, to rick

meuler /møle/ ► conjug 1 ◄ VT *(Tech, Dentisterie)* to grind down

meuleuse /møløz/ NF grinder

meulière /møljɛʀ/ NF ◆ **(pierre) ~** millstone, buhrstone

meunerie /mønʀi/ NF *(= industrie)* flour trade; *(= métier)* milling

meunier, -ière /mønje, jɛʀ/ ADJ milling NM miller NF **meunière** miller's wife ◆ **sole/truite meunière** *(Culin)* sole/trout meunière

meurette /mœʀɛt/ NF red wine sauce ◆ **œufs en ~** eggs in red wine sauce

meurtre /mœʀtʀ/ NM murder ◆ **au ~ !** murder! ◆ **crier au ~** *(fig)* to scream blue murder

meurtrier, -ière /mœʀtʀije, ijɛʀ/ ADJ *[attentat, combat, affrontements]* bloody; *[épidémie]* fatal; *[intention, fureur]* murderous; *[arme]* deadly, lethal; † *[personne]* murderous ◆ **week-end ~** weekend of carnage on the roads ◆ **cette route est meurtrière** this road is lethal *ou* a death-trap ◆ **c'est le séisme le plus ~ depuis 1995** it's the worst *ou* deadliest earthquake since 1995 ◆ **le bombardement a été particulièrement ~** the bombing claimed very many lives ◆ **être saisi par une folie meurtrière** to be possessed by murderous rage NM murderer NF **meurtrière** 1 *(= criminelle)* murderess 2 *(Archit)* arrow slit, loophole

meurtrir /mœʀtʀiʀ/ ► conjug 2 ◄ VT 1 *[+ chair, fruit]* to bruise ◆ **être meurtri** *[personne]* to be covered in bruises, to be black and blue all over ◆ **il est encore meurtri par son échec** he's still smarting from his defeat 2 *(littér) [+ personne, âme]* to wound ◆ **un pays meurtri par la guerre** a country ravaged by war

meurtrissure /mœʀtʀisyʀ/ NF 1 *[de chair, fruit]* bruise 2 *(littér) [d'âme]* scar, bruise ◆ **les ~s laissées par la vie/le chagrin** the scars *ou* bruises left by life/sorrow

meute /møt/ NF *(Chasse, péj)* pack ◆ **lâcher la ~ sur** to set the pack on ◆ **une ~ de journalistes** a pack of journalists

mévente /mevɑ̃t/ NF *(Écon)* slump *ou* drop in sales; *(† = vente à perte)* selling at a loss ◆ **une période de ~** a slump, a period of poor sales

mexicain, e /mɛksikɛ̃, ɛn/ ADJ Mexican NM,F **Mexicain(e)** Mexican

Mexico /mɛksiko/ N Mexico City

Mexique /mɛksik/ NM ◆ **le ~** Mexico

mézigue‡ /mezig/ PRON PERS me, yours truly* ◆ **c'est pour ~** it's for yours truly*

mezzanine /mɛdzanin/ NF *(Archit) (= étage)* mezzanine (floor); *(= fenêtre)* mezzanine window; *(Théât)* mezzanine

mezza-voce /mɛdzavɔtʃe/ ADV *(Mus)* mezza voce; *(littér)* in an undertone

mezzo /mɛdzo/ NM mezzo (voice) NF mezzo

mezzo-soprano (pl **mezzo-sopranos**) /mɛdzosɔpʀano/ NM mezzo-soprano (voice) NF mezzo-soprano

mezzo-tinto /mɛdzotinto/ NM INV mezzotint

MF 1 (abrév de **modulation de fréquence**) FM 2 (abrév de **millions de francs**) → **million**

mg (abrév de **milligramme**) mg

Mgr (abrév de **Monseigneur**) Mgr

mi /mi/ NM *(Mus)* E; *(en chantant la gamme)* mi, me

mi- /mi/ PRÉF *(le préfixe reste invariable dans les mots composés à trait d'union)* half, mid- ◆ **la ~janvier** the middle of January, midJanuary ◆ **à ~cuisson ajoutez le vin** add the wine half way through cooking ◆ **pièce ~salle à manger ~salon** living-dining room, dining-cum-living room *(Brit)* ◆ **~riant ~pleurant** half-laughing half-crying, halfway between laughing and crying

MIAGE /mjaʒ/ NF (abrév de **maîtrise d'informatique appliquée à la gestion des entreprises**) *master's degree in business data processing*

miam-miam* /mjammjam/ EXCL *(langage enfantin)* yum-yum!*, yummy!* ◆ **faire ~** to eat

miaou /mjau/ EXCL, NM miaow ◆ **faire ~** to miaow

miasme /mjasm/ NM *(gén pl)* miasma ◆ **~s** putrid fumes, miasmas

miaulement /mjolmɑ̃/ NM mewing, meowing

miauler /mjole/ ► conjug 1 ◄ VI to mew, to meow

mi-bas /miba/ NM INV *(pour homme)* knee-length sock; *(pour femme)* pop sock *(Brit)*, knee-high *(US)*

mi-blanc /miblɑ̃/ NM *(Helv = pain)* white bread containing a little bran

mica /mika/ NM *(= roche)* mica; *(pour vitre, isolant)* Muscovy glass, white mica

mi-carême /mikaʀɛm/ NF ◆ **la ~** the third Thursday in Lent

micaschiste /mikaʃist/ NM mica-schist

miche /miʃ/ NF *[de pain]* round loaf, cob loaf *(Brit)* NFPL **miches ‡** *(= fesses)* bum* *(Brit)*, butt‡ *(surtout US)*

Michel-Ange /mikɛlɑ̃ʒ/ NM Michelangelo

micheline /miʃlin/ NF railcar

mi-chemin /miʃ(ə)mɛ̃/ **à mi-chemin** LOC ADV ◆ **je l'ai rencontré à ~** I met him halfway there ◆ **la poste est à ~** the post office is halfway there, the post office is halfway *ou* midway between the two ◆ **à ~ de la gare** halfway to the station ◆ **ces reportages sont à ~ de la fiction et du réel** these reports are a mixture of fiction and truth *ou* are half fiction half truth ◆ **à ~ entre ...** *(lit, fig)* halfway *ou* midway between ...

micheton † /miʃtɔ̃/ NM *(arg Crime)* punter* *(Brit)*, John‡ *(US)*

Michigan /miʃigɑ̃/ NM Michigan ◆ **le lac** ~ Lake Michigan

mi-clos, e /miklo, kloz/ ADJ half-closed ◆ **les yeux** ~ with half-closed eyes, with one's eyes half-closed

micmac* /mikmak/ NM *(péj) (= intrigue)* funny business*; *(= confusion)* mix-up ◆ **je devine leur petit** ~ I can guess their little game* *ou* what they're playing at* ◆ **tu parles d'un ~ pour aller jusqu'à chez elle !** it's such a hassle getting to her place!

micocoulier /mikɔkulje/ NM nettle tree, European hackberry

mi-combat /mikɔ̃ba/ **à mi-combat** LOC ADV halfway through the match

mi-corps /mikɔʀ/ **à mi-corps** LOC ADV up to *ou* down to the waist ◆ **plongé à ~ dans l'eau glacée** waist-deep in the icy water

mi-côte /mikot/ **à mi-côte** LOC ADV halfway up *(ou* down) the hill

mi-course /mikuʀs/ **à mi-course** LOC ADV *(Sport)* halfway through the race, at the halfway mark

micro /mikʀo/ NM 1 (abrév de **microphone**) microphone, mike*; *(Radio, TV)* ◆ **dites-le au** ~ *ou* **devant le** ~ say it in front of the mike* ◆ **parlez dans le** ~ speak into the microphone ◆ **ils l'ont dit au** ~ *(dans un aéroport, une gare)* they announced it over the intercom *ou* PA system ◆ **il était au ~ de France Inter** he was on France Inter 2 abrév de **micro-ordinateur** NF abrév de **micro-informatique**

micro... /mikʀo/ PRÉF micro... ◆ **microcurie** microcurie ◆ **microséisme** microseism

microalgue /mikʀoalg/ NF microalga

microampère /mikʀoɑ̃pɛʀ/ NM microamp

microbalance /mikʀobalɑ̃s/ NF microbalance

microbe /mikʀɔb/ NM 1 *(Méd)* germ, bug*, microbe *(SPÉC)* 2 *(* péj)* pipsqueak*, little runt‡ *(péj)*

microbien, -ienne /mikʀɔbjɛ̃, jɛn/ ADJ *[culture]* microbial, microbic; *[infection]* bacterial ◆ **maladie microbienne** bacterial disease

microbille, micro-bille (pl **micro-billes**) /mikʀobij/ NF *[d'abrasif]* micro-granule, microparticle

microbiologie /mikʀobjɔlɔʒi/ NF microbiology

microbiologique /mikʀobjɔlɔʒik/ ADJ microbiological

microbiologiste /mikʀobjɔlɔʒist/ NMF microbiologist

microbrasserie /mikʀobʀasʀi/ NF microbrewery

microcassette /mikʀokasɛt/ NF microcassette

microcéphale /mikʀosefal/ ADJ, NMF microcephalic

microchirurgie /mikʀoʃiʀyʀʒi/ NF microsurgery

microcircuit /mikʀosiʀkɥi/ NM microcircuit

microclimat /mikʀoklima/ NM microclimate

microcoque /mikʀɔkɔk/ NM micrococcus

microcosme /mikʀɔkɔsm/ NM microcosm

microcosmique /mikʀɔkɔsmik/ ADJ microcosmic

microcoupure /mikʀokupyʀ/ NF *(Ordin)* power dip

micro-cravate (pl **micros-cravates**) /mikʀokʀavat/ NM clip-on microphone *ou* mike*

microcrédit /mikʀokʀedi/ NM microcredit

microculture /mikʀokyltyʀ/ NF *(Bio)* microculture

microéconomie /mikʀoekɔnɔmi/ NF microeconomics *(sg)*

microéconomique /mikʀoekɔnɔmik/ ADJ microeconomic

microédition /mikʀoedisjɔ̃/ NF desktop publishing, DTP

microélectronique /mikʀoelɛktʀɔnik/ NF microelectronics *(sg)*

micro-entreprise (pl **micro-entreprises**) /mikʀoɑ̃tʀəpʀiz/ NF micro-business

microfibre /mikʀofibʀ/ NF microfibre ◆ **tissu/fil** ~ microfibre fabric/thread ◆ **en ~s** microfibre *(épith)*

microfiche /mikʀofiʃ/ NF microfiche

microfilm /mikʀofilm/ NM microfilm

microgramme /mikʀogʀam/ NM microgram

micrographie /mikʀɔgʀafi/ NF micrography

microgravité /mikʀogʀavite/ NF microgravity

micro-informatique /mikʀoɛ̃fɔʀmatik/ NF microcomputing

micromécanique /mikʀomekanik/ NF micromechanics *(sg)*

microméteorite /mikʀometeɔʀit/ NF micrometeorite

micromètre /mikʀɔmɛtʀ/ NM micrometer

micrométrie /mikʀɔmetʀi/ NF micrometry

micron /mikʀɔ̃/ NM micron

Micronésie /mikʀonezi/ NF Micronesia

micronésien, -ienne /mikʀɔnezjɛ̃, jɛn/ ADJ Micronesian NM,F **Micronésien(ne)** Micronesian

micro-onde (pl **micro-ondes**) /mikʀoɔ̃d/ NF microwave NM ◆ **(four à) ~s** microwave (oven)

micro-ordinateur (pl **micro-ordinateurs**) /mikʀoɔʀdinatœʀ/ NM microcomputer

micro-organisme (pl **micro-organismes**) /mikʀoɔʀganism/ NM microorganism

microphone /mikʀɔfɔn/ NM microphone

microphotographie /mikʀofɔtɔgʀafi/ NF *(= procédé)* photomicrography; *(= image)* photomicrograph

microphysique /mikʀofizik/ NF microphysics *(sg)*

microprocesseur /mikʀopʀɔsesœʀ/ NM microprocessor

microprogramme /mikʀopʀɔgʀam/ NM microprogram, applet

microscope /mikʀɔskɔp/ NM microscope ◆ **examiner qch au** ~ *(lit)* to examine sth *ou* look at sth under a microscope; *(fig)* to put sth under the microscope ◆ ~ **électronique** electron microscope ◆ ~ **(électronique) à balayage (par transmission)** scanning electron microscope

microscopie /mikʀɔskɔpi/ NF microscopy

microscopique /mikʀɔskɔpik/ ADJ microscopic

microseconde /mikʀos(ə)gɔ̃d/ NF microsecond

microsillon /mikʀosijɔ̃/ NM *(= sillon)* microgroove ◆ **(disque)** ~ LP, microgroove record

microsonde /mikʀosɔ̃d/ NF microprobe

microstructure /mikʀostʀyktyʀ/ NF microstructure

micro-trottoir (pl **micros-trottoirs**) /mikʀotʀɔtwaʀ/ NM ◆ **faire un** ~ to interview people in the street, to do a vox pop* *(Brit)*

miction /miksjɔ̃/ NF micturition

mi-cuisse(s) /mikɥis/ **à mi-cuisses** LOC ADV ◆ **ses bottes lui arrivaient à ~s** his boots came up to his thighs *ou* over his knees ◆ **l'eau leur arrivait à ~s** they were thigh-deep in water, they were up to their thighs in water

MIDEM /midɛm/ NM (abrév de **marché international du disque et de l'édition musicale**) → **marché**

midi /midi/ NM 1 *(= heure)* midday, 12 (o'clock), noon ◆ ~ **dix** 10 past 12 ◆ **de ~ à 2 heures** from 12 *ou* (12) noon to 2 ◆ **entre ~ et 2 heures** between 12 *ou* (12) noon and 2 ◆ **hier à** ~ yesterday at 12 o'clock *ou* at noon *ou* at midday; → **chacun, chercher, coup**

2 *(= période du déjeuner)* lunchtime, lunch hour; *(= mi-journée)* midday, middle of the day ◆ **à/pendant** ~ at/during lunchtime, at/during the lunch hour ◆ **demain** ~ tomorrow lunchtime ◆ **tous les ~s** every lunchtime *ou* lunch hour ◆ **que faire ce** ~ ? what shall we do at lunchtime? *ou* midday?, what shall we do this lunch hour? ◆ **le repas de** ~ the midday meal, lunch ◆ **qu'est-ce que tu as eu à ~ ?** what did you have for lunch? ◆ **à ~ on va au restaurant** we're going to a restaurant for lunch ◆ **en plein** ~ *(= à l'heure du déjeuner)* (right) in the middle of the day, at midday; *(= en plein zénith)* at the height of noon, at high noon ◆ **ça s'est passé en plein** ~ it happened right in the middle of the day; → **démon**

3 *(Géog = sud)* south ◆ **exposé au** *ou* **en plein** ~ facing due south ◆ **le ~ de la France, le Midi** the South of France, the Midi; → **accent**

ADJ INV *[chaîne hi-fi, slip, jupe]* midi

midinette /midinɛt/ NF *(= jeune fille)* young girl; *(† = vendeuse)* shopgirl *(in the dress industry)*; *(† = ouvrière)* dressmaker's apprentice ◆ **elle a des goûts de** ~ *(péj)* she has the tastes of a sixteen-year-old schoolgirl

mi-distance /midistɑ̃s/ **à mi-distance (entre)** LOC PRÉP halfway *ou* midway (between) ◆ **à ~ de Vienne et de Prague** halfway *ou* midway between Vienna and Prague

mie[1] /mi/ NF soft part *(of bread)*; *(Culin)* bread with crusts removed ◆ **il a mangé la croûte et laissé la** ~ he's eaten the crust and left the soft part *ou* the inside (of the bread) ◆ **faire une farce avec de la ~ de pain** to make stuffing with fresh white breadcrumbs; → **pain**

mie[2] †† /mi/ NF *(littér = bien-aimée)* lady-love †, beloved *(littér)*

miel /mjɛl/ NM honey ◆ **bonbon/boisson au** ~ honey sweet *(Brit) ou* candy *(US)*/drink ◆ **être tout** ~ *[personne]* to be all sweetness and light ◆ ~ **rosat** rose honey ◆ **faire son ~ de qch** *(fig)* to turn sth to one's advantage; → **gâteau, lune**

EXCL *(euph *)* sugar!*

miellat /mjela/ NM honeydew

miellé, e[1] /mjele/ ADJ *(littér)* honeyed

mielleusement /mjeløzmɑ̃/ ADV *(péj)* unctuously

mielleux, -euse /mjelø, øz/ ADJ *(péj) [personne]* unctuous, syrupy, smooth-tongued; *[paroles]* honeyed, smooth; *[ton]* honeyed, sugary; *[sourire]* sugary, sickly sweet; *(† ou littér) [saveur]* sickly sweet

mien, mienne /mjɛ̃, mjɛn/ PRON POSS ◆ **le ~, la mienne, les ~s, les miennes** mine ◆ **ce sac n'est pas le** ~ this bag is not mine, this is not my bag ◆ **ton prix/ton jour sera le** ~ name your price/the day ◆ **vos fils sont sages comparés aux ~s** your sons are well-behaved compared to mine *ou* my own NMPL **miens** ◆ **les ~s** *(= ma famille)* my family, my (own) folks*; *(= mon peuple)* my people ADJ POSS *(† ou littér)* ◆ **un ~ cousin** a cousin of mine ◆ **je fais miennes vos observations** I agree wholeheartedly (with you); → **sien**

miette /mjɛt/ NF *[de pain, gâteau]* crumb ◆ **~s de crabe/de thon** *(Culin)* flaked crab/tuna ◆ **il ne perdait pas une ~ de la conversation/du spectacle** he didn't miss a scrap of the conversation/the show ◆ **les ~s de sa fortune** the remnants of his fortune ◆ **je n'en prendrai qu'une** ~ I'll just have a tiny bit *ou* a sliver ◆ **il**

n'en a pas laissé une ~ *(repas)* he didn't leave a scrap; *(fortune)* he didn't leave a penny *(Brit)* *ou* one red cent *(US)*

♦ **en miettes** *[gâteau]* in pieces; *[bonheur]* in pieces *ou* shreds; *[pays, union]* fragmented ♦ **leur voiture est en ~s** there's nothing left of their car, their car was totaled* *(US)* ♦ **mettre** *ou* **réduire qch en ~s** to break *ou* smash sth to bits *ou* to smithereens

mieux /mjø/ (compar, superl de **bien**) ADV 1 *(gén)* better ♦ **aller** *ou* **se porter** ~ to be better ♦ **il ne s'est jamais** ~ **porté** he's never been *ou* felt better in his life ♦ **plus il s'entraîne,** ~ **il joue** the more he practises the better he plays ♦ **elle joue** ~ **que lui** she plays better than he does ♦ **c'est (un peu/beaucoup)** ~ **expliqué** it's (slightly/much) better explained ♦ **il n'écrit pas** ~ **qu'il ne parle** he writes no better than he speaks ♦ **s'attendre à** ~ to expect better ♦ **espérer** ~ to hope for better (things) ♦ **il peut faire** ~ he can do *ou* is capable of better ♦ **tu ferais** ~ **de te taire** you'd better shut up*; → **reculer, tant, valoir** *etc*

2 ♦ **le** ~, **la** ~, **les** ~ *(de plusieurs)* (the) best; *(de deux)* (the) better ♦ **je passe par les rues les** ~ **éclairées** I take the better lit streets ♦ **c'est ici qu'il dort le** ~ he sleeps best here, this is where he sleeps best ♦ **tout va le** ~ **du monde** everything's going beautifully ♦ **tout est pour le** ~ **dans le meilleur des mondes** everything is for the best in the best of all possible worlds ♦ **une école des** ~ **conçues/équipées** one of the best planned/best equipped schools ♦ **un dîner des** ~ **réussis** a most *ou* highly successful dinner ♦ **j'ai fait le** ~ *ou* **du** ~ **que j'ai pu** I did my (level *ou* very) best, I did the best I could ♦ **des deux, elle est la** ~ **habillée** she is the better dressed of the two

3 *(locutions)* ~ **que jamais** better than ever ♦ ~ **vaut trop de travail que pas assez** too much work is better than not enough ♦ ~ **vaut tard que jamais** *(Prov)* better late than never *(Prov)* ♦ ~ **vaut prévenir que guérir** *(Prov)* prevention is better than cure *(Prov)*

♦ **au mieux** *(gén)* at best ♦ **en mettant les choses au** ~ at (the very) best ♦ **tout se passe au** ~ **avec nos collègues** we get on extremely well with our colleagues ♦ **utiliser au** ~ **les ressources/le temps** to make best use of (one's) resources/time ♦ **pour apprécier au** ~ **les charmes de la ville** to best appreciate *ou* enjoy the charms of the town ♦ **il sera là au** ~ **à midi** he'll be there by midday at the earliest ♦ **faites au** ~ do what you think best *ou* whatever is best ♦ **être au** ~ **avec qn** to be on the best of terms with sb ♦ **acheter/vendre au** ~ *(Fin)* to buy/sell at the best price

♦ **au mieux de** ♦ **au** ~ **de sa forme** in peak condition ♦ **au** ~ **de nos intérêts** in our best interests

♦ **de mieux en mieux** ♦ **il va de** ~ **en** ~ he's getting better and better ♦ **de** ~ **en** ~ **! maintenant il s'est mis à boire** *(iro)* that's great *ou* terrific *(iro)*, now he has taken to the bottle*

♦ **à qui mieux mieux** *(gén)* each one more so than the other; *[crier]* each one louder than the other; *[frapper]* each one harder than the other

ADJ INV 1 *(= plus satisfaisant)* better ♦ **le** ~, **la** ~, **les** ~ *(de plusieurs)* (the) best; *(de deux)* (the) better ♦ **c'est la** ~ **de nos secrétaires** * *(de toutes)* she is the best of our secretaries, she's our best secretary; *(de deux)* she's the better of our secretaries ♦ **il est** ~ **qu'à son arrivée** he's improved since he (first) came, he's better than when he (first) came ♦ **c'est beaucoup** ~ **ainsi** it's (much) better this way ♦ **le** ~ **serait de** ... the best (thing *ou* plan) would be to ... ♦ **c'est ce qu'il pourrait faire de** ~ it's the best thing he could do

2 *(= en meilleure santé)* better; *(= plus à l'aise)* better, more comfortable ♦ **le** ~, **la** ~, **les** ~ (the) best, (the) most comfortable ♦ **être** ~**/le** ~ **du monde** to be better/in perfect health ♦ **je le trouve** ~ **aujourd'hui** I think he is looking better *ou* he seems better today ♦ **ils seraient** ~ **à la campagne qu'à la ville** they would be better (off) in the country than in (the) town ♦ **c'est à l'ombre qu'elle sera le** ~ she'll be more comfortable in the shade; → **sentir**

3 *(= plus beau)* better looking, more attractive ♦ **le** ~, **la** ~, **les** ~ *(de plusieurs)* (the) best looking, (the) most attractive; *(de deux)* (the) better looking, (the) more attractive ♦ **elle est** ~ **les cheveux longs** she looks better with her hair long *ou* with long hair, long hair suits her better ♦ **c'est avec les cheveux courts qu'elle est le** ~ she looks best with her hair short *ou* with short hair, short hair suits her best ♦ **il est** ~ **que son frère** he's better looking than his brother

4 *(loc)* **c'est ce qui se fait de** ~ it's the best there is *ou* one can get ♦ **tu n'as rien de** ~ **à faire que (de) traîner dans les rues ?** haven't you got anything better to do than hang around the streets? ♦ **ce n'est pas mal, mais il y a** ~ it's not bad, but I've seen better; → **changer, faute**

♦ **en mieux** ♦ **c'est son frère, en** ~ he's (just) like his brother only better looking ♦ **ça rappelle son premier film, mais en** ~ it's like his first film, only better

♦ **qui mieux est** even better, better still

NM 1 *(= ce qui est préférable)* **le** ~ best ♦ **le** ~ **serait d'accepter** the best thing to do would be to accept ♦ **j'ai fait pour le** ~ I did what I thought best ♦ **tout allait pour le** ~ **avant qu'il n'arrive** everything was perfectly fine before he came ♦ **le** ~ **est l'ennemi du bien** *(Prov)* (it's better to) let well alone ♦ **partez tout de suite, c'est le** ~ it's best (that) you leave immediately, the best thing would be for you to leave immediately

2 *(avec adj poss)* **faire de son** ~ to do one's (level *ou* very) best, to do the best one can ♦ **aider qn de son** ~ to do one's best to help sb, to help sb the best one can *ou* to the best of one's ability ♦ **j'ai essayé de répondre de mon** ~ **aux questions** I tried to answer the questions to the best of my ability

3 *(= amélioration, progrès)* improvement ♦ **il y a un** ~ *ou* **du** ~ there's (been) some improvement

mieux-disant (pl **mieux-disants**) /mjødizɑ̃/ NM best offer ♦ **le choix s'est fait sur le** ~ **culturel** the choice was based on a view of what was, culturally, the best offer ♦ **c'est le** ~ **social qui devrait guider le choix du gouvernement** the government should choose the option that is most socially beneficial

mieux-être /mjøzɛtʀ/ NM INV *(gén)* greater welfare; *(matériel)* improved standard of living ♦ **ils ressentent un** ~ **psychologique** they feel better in themselves

mieux-vivre /mjøvivʀ/ NM INV improved standard of living

mièvre /mjɛvʀ/ ADJ *[paroles, musique, roman]* soppy; *[tableau]* pretty-pretty*; *[sourire]* mawkish; *[charme]* vapid ♦ **elle est un peu** ~ she's a bit colourless *(Brit)* *ou* colorless *(US)* *ou* insipid

mièvrerie /mjɛvʀəʀi/ NF *[de paroles, musique]* sentimentality, soppiness; *[de tableau]* pretty-prettiness*; *[de sourire]* mawkishness; *[de charme]* vapidity; *[de personne]* colourlessness *(Brit)*, colorlessness *(US)*, insipidness; *(= propos)* insipid *ou* sentimental talk *(NonC)* ♦ **il faut éviter de tomber dans la** ~ we must avoid getting all sentimental ♦ **ses chansons sont d'une** ~ **affligeante** his songs are incredibly soppy

mi-figue mi-raisin /mifigmiʀɛzɛ̃/ ADJ INV *[sourire]* wry; *[remarque]* half-humorous, wry ♦ **on leur fit un accueil** ~ they received a mixed reception

mignard, e /miɲaʀ, aʀd/ ADJ *[style]* mannered, precious; *[décor]* pretty-pretty*, overornate; *[musique]* pretty-pretty*, overdelicate; *[manières]* precious, dainty, simpering *(péj)*

mignardise /miɲaʀdiz/ NF 1 *[de tableau, poème, style]* preciousness; *[de décor]* ornateness; *[de manières]* preciousness *(péj)*, daintiness, affectation *(péj)* 2 *(= fleur)* **de la** ~, **des œillets** ~ pinks 3 *(Culin)* ♦ ~**s** petits fours

mignon, -onne /miɲɔ̃, ɔn/ ADJ *(= joli)* *[enfant]* sweet, cute; *[femme]* sweet(-looking), pretty; *[homme]* cute; *[bras, pied, geste]* dainty, cute; *(= gentil, aimable)* nice, sweet ♦ **donne-le-moi, tu seras mignonne*** give it to me, there's a dear* *ou* love* *(Brit)*, be a dear* and give it to me ♦ **c'est** ~ **chez vous** you've got a nice little place; → **péché** NM,F (little) darling, poppet* *(Brit)*, cutie* *(US)* ♦ **mon** ~, **ma mignonne** sweetheart, pet* NM 1 *(Hist = favori)* minion 2 *(Boucherie)* **(filet)** ~ fillet *(Brit)* *ou* filet *(US)* mignon

mignonnet, -ette /miɲɔnɛ, ɛt/ ADJ *[enfant, objet]* sweet, cute* ♦ **c'est** ~ **chez eux** they've got a cute little place* NF **mignonnette** 1 *(= bouteille)* miniature 2 *(= œillet)* wild pink; *(= saxifrage)* Pyrenean saxifrage 3 *(= poivre)* coarse-ground pepper 4 *(= gravier)* fine gravel

migraine /migʀɛn/ NF *(gén)* headache; *(Méd)* migraine ♦ **j'ai la** ~ I've got a bad headache, my head aches

migraineux, -euse /migʀɛnø, øz/ ADJ migrainous NM,F person suffering from migraine

migrant, e /migʀɑ̃, ɑt/ ADJ, NM,F migrant

migrateur, -trice /migʀatœʀ, tʀis/ ADJ migratory NM migrant, migratory bird

migration /migʀasjɔ̃/ NF *(gén)* migration; *(Rel)* transmigration ♦ **oiseau en** ~ migrating bird

migratoire /migʀatwaʀ/ ADJ migratory

migrer /migʀe/ ▸ conjug 1 ◂ VI to migrate *(vers* to)

mi-hauteur /mihotœʀ/ **à mi-hauteur** LOC ADV halfway up *(ou* down) ♦ **des carreaux s'élevaient à** ~ **du mur** the lower half of the wall was covered with tiles

mi-jambe(s) /miʒɑ̃b/ **à mi-jambe(s)** LOC ADV up *(ou* down) to the knees ♦ **l'eau leur arrivait à** ~**s** they were knee-deep in water, they were up to their knees in water

mijaurée /miʒɔʀe/ NF pretentious *ou* affected woman *ou* girl ♦ **faire la** ~ to give o.s. airs (and graces) ♦ **regarde-moi cette** ~ **!** just look at her with her airs and graces! ♦ **petite** ~ **!** little madam!

mijoter /miʒɔte/ ▸ conjug 1 ◂ VT 1 *(= cuire)* *[+ plat, soupe]* to simmer; *(= préparer avec soin)* to cook *ou* prepare lovingly ♦ **plat mijoté** dish which has been slow-cooked *ou* simmered ♦ **il lui mijote des petits plats** he cooks (up) *ou* concocts tempting *ou* tasty dishes for her 2 (* = *tramer*) to cook up* ♦ ~ **un complot** to hatch a plot ♦ **il mijote un mauvais coup** he's cooking up* *ou* plotting some mischief ♦ **qu'est-ce qu'il peut bien** ~ **?** what's he up to?*, what's he cooking up?* ♦ **il se mijote quelque chose** something's brewing *ou* cooking* VI *[plat, soupe]* to simmer; *[complot]* to be brewing ♦ **laissez** *ou* **faites** ~ **20 mn** (leave to) simmer for 20 mins ♦ **laisser qn** ~ **(dans son jus)** * to leave sb to stew*, to let sb stew in his own juice*

mijoteuse ® /miʒɔtøz/ NF slow cooker

mikado /mikado/ NM *(= jeu)* jackstraws *(sg)*, spillikins *(sg)* ♦ **jouer au** ~ to play jackstraws, to have a game of jackstraws

mil[1] /mil/ NM *(dans une date)* a *ou* one thousand

mil[2] /mij, mil/ NM ⇒ **millet**

milady /miledi/ NF (titled English) lady ♦ **oui** ~ yes my lady

milan /milɑ̃/ **NM** (= *oiseau*) kite

milanais, e /milanɛ, ɛz/ **ADJ** Milanese ◆ **escalope (à la) ~e** escalope milanaise **NM,F** **Milanais(e)** Milanese

mildiou /mildju/ **NM** (*Agr*) mildew

mile /majl/ **NM** mile (1 609 *m*)

milice /milis/ **NF** [1] (= *corps paramilitaire*) militia ◆ **la Milice** (*Hist de France*) the Milice (*collaborationist militia during the German occupation*) [2] (*Belg*) (= *armée*) army; (= *service militaire*) military service

milicien /milisjɛ̃/ **NM** (*gén*) militiaman; (*Belg*) conscript (*Brit*), draftee (*US*)

milicienne /milisjɛn/ **NF** woman serving in the militia

milieu (pl **milieux**) /miljø/ **NM** [1] (= *centre*) middle ◆ **casser/couper/scier qch en son ~** *ou* **par le ~** to break/cut/saw sth down *ou* through the middle ◆ **le bouton/la porte du ~** the middle *ou* centre knob/door ◆ **je prends celui du ~** I'll take the one in the middle *ou* the middle one ◆ **tenir le ~ de la chaussée** to keep to the middle of the road ◆ **~ de terrain** (*Ftbl*) midfield player ◆ **le ~ du terrain** (*Ftbl*) the midfield ◆ **il est venu vers le ~ de l'après-midi/la matinée** he came towards the middle of the afternoon/the morning, he came about mid-afternoon/mid-morning ◆ **vers/depuis le ~ du 15e siècle** towards/since the mid-15th century, towards/since the mid-1400s; → **empire**

[2] (= *état intermédiaire*) middle course *ou* way ◆ **il n'y a pas de ~ (entre)** there is no middle course *ou* way (between) ◆ **avec lui, il n'y a pas de ~** there's no in-between with him ◆ **le juste ~** the happy medium, the golden mean ◆ **un juste ~** a happy medium ◆ **il est innocent ou coupable, il n'y a pas de ~** he is either innocent or guilty, he can't be both ◆ **tenir le ~** to steer a middle course

[3] (*Bio, Géog*) environment; (*Chim, Phys*) medium ◆ **~ physique/géographique/humain** physical/geographical/human environment ◆ **~ de culture** culture medium ◆ **les animaux dans leur ~ naturel** animals in their natural surroundings *ou* environment *ou* habitat

[4] (= *entourage social, moral*) milieu, environment; (= *groupe restreint*) set, circle; (= *provenance*) background ◆ **le ~ familial** (*gén*) the family circle; (*Sociol*) the home *ou* family background, the home environment ◆ **s'adapter à un nouveau ~** to adapt to a different milieu *ou* environment ◆ **il ne se sent pas dans son ~** he feels out of place, he doesn't feel at home ◆ **elle se sent** *ou* **est dans son ~ chez nous** she feels (quite) at home with us ◆ **de quel ~ sort-il ?** what is his (social) background? ◆ **les ~x littéraires/financiers** literary/financial circles ◆ **dans les ~x autorisés/bien informés** in official/well-informed circles ◆ **c'est un ~ très fermé** it is a very closed circle *ou* exclusive set

[5] (*Crime*) **le ~** the underworld ◆ **les gens du ~** (people of) the underworld ◆ **membre du ~** gangster, mobster

[6] (*locutions*)

◆ **au milieu** in the middle

◆ **au milieu de** (= *au centre de*) in the middle of; (= *parmi*) amid, among, in the midst of, amidst (*littér*) ◆ **il est là au ~ de ce groupe** he's over there in the middle of that group ◆ **au ~ de toutes ces difficultés/aventures** in the middle *ou* midst of *ou* amidst all these difficulties/adventures ◆ **au ~ de son affolement** in the middle *ou* midst of his panic ◆ **elle n'est heureuse qu'au ~ de sa famille/de ses enfants** she's only happy when she's among *ou* surrounded by her family/her children *ou* with her family/her children around her ◆ **au ~ de la journée** in the middle of the day ◆ **au ~ de la nuit** in the middle of the night ◆ **comment travailler au ~ de ce vacarme ?** how can anyone work in this din? ◆ **au ~ de la descente** halfway down (the hill) ◆ **au ~ de la page** in the middle of the page, halfway down the page ◆ **au ~/en plein ~ de l'hiver** in mid-winter/the depth of winter ◆ **au ~ de l'été** in mid-summer, at the height of summer ◆ **au beau ~ de, en plein ~ de** right *ou* bang* *ou* slap bang* in the middle of, in the very middle of ◆ **il est parti au beau ~ de la réception** he left right in the middle of the party

militaire /militɛʀ/ **ADJ** military, army (*épith*); → **attaché, service** **NM** serviceman, soldier ◆ **il est ~** he's in the forces *ou* services, he's a soldier ◆ **~ de carrière** professional *ou* career soldier ◆ **les ~s sont au pouvoir** the army *ou* the military are in power

militairement /militɛʀmɑ̃/ **ADV** militarily ◆ **la ville a été occupée ~** the town was occupied by the army ◆ **occuper ~ une ville** to occupy a town

militant, e /militɑ̃, ɑt/ **ADJ, NM,F** activist, militant ◆ **~ de base** rank and file *ou* grassroots militant ◆ **~ pour les droits de l'homme** human rights activist *ou* campaigner

militantisme /militɑ̃tism/ **NM** (political) activism, militancy

militarisation /militaʀizasjɔ̃/ **NF** militarization

militariser /militaʀize/ ▸ conjug 1 ◂ **VT** to militarize **VPR** **se militariser** to become militarized

militarisme /militaʀism/ **NM** militarism

militariste /militaʀist/ **ADJ** militaristic **NMF** militarist

militer /milite/ ▸ conjug 1 ◂ **VI** [1] [*personne*] to be a militant *ou* an activist ◆ **il milite au parti communiste** he is a communist party militant, he is a militant in the communist party ◆ **~ pour les droits de l'homme** to campaign for human rights [2] [*arguments, raisons*] **~ en faveur de** *ou* **pour** to militate in favour of, to argue for ◆ **~ contre** to militate *ou* tell against

milk-shake (pl **milk-shakes**) /milkʃɛk/ **NM** milk shake

millage /milaʒ/ **NM** (*Can*) mileage

mille[1] /mil/ **ADJ INV** [1] (= *nombre*) a *ou* one thousand ◆ **~ un** a *ou* one thousand and one ◆ **trois ~** three thousand ◆ **deux ~ neuf cents** two thousand nine hundred ◆ **page ~** page one thousand ◆ **l'an ~** (*dans les dates*) the year one thousand

[2] (= *nombreux*) **~ regrets** I'm terribly sorry ◆ **je lui ai dit ~ fois** I've told him a thousand times ◆ **tu as ~ fois raison** you're absolutely right ◆ **c'est ~ fois trop grand** it's far too big ◆ **~ excuses** *ou* **pardons** I'm (*ou* we're) terribly sorry ◆ **le vase s'est cassé/était en ~ morceaux** the vase smashed into smithereens/was in smithereens

[3] (*locutions*) **~ et un problèmes/exemples** a thousand and one problems/examples ◆ **dans un décor des Mille et Une Nuits** in a setting like something from the Arabian Nights ◆ **je vous le donne en ~*** you'll never guess ◆ **~ sabords !*** (*hum*) blistering barnacles!*

NM INV [1] (= *chiffre*) a *ou* one thousand ◆ **cinq pour ~ d'alcool** five parts of alcohol to a thousand ◆ **cinq enfants sur ~** five children out of *ou* in every thousand ◆ **vendre qch au ~** to sell sth by the thousand ◆ **deux ~ de boulons** two thousand bolts ◆ **l'ouvrage en est à son centième ~** the book has sold 100,000 copies; → **gagner**

[2] [*de cible*] bull's-eye, bull (*Brit*) ◆ **mettre** *ou* **taper (en plein) dans le ~** (*lit*) to hit the bull's-eye *ou* bull (*Brit*); (*fig*) to score a bull's-eye, to be bang on target* ◆ **tu as mis dans le ~ en lui faisant ce cadeau** you were bang on target* with the present you gave him

mille[2] /mil/ **NM** [1] ◆ **~ (marin)** nautical mile [2] (*Can*) mile (1 609 *m*)

millefeuille /milfœj/ **NM** (*Culin*) mille feuilles, ≃ cream *ou* vanilla slice (*Brit*), napoleon (*US*)

millénaire /milenɛʀ/ **ADJ** (*lit*) thousand-year-old (*épith*), millenial; (= *très vieux*) ancient, very old ◆ **monument ~** thousand-year-old monument ◆ **des rites plusieurs fois ~s** rites several thousand years old, age-old rites **NM** (= *période*) millennium, a thousand years; (= *anniversaire*) thousandth anniversary, millennium ◆ **nous entrons dans le troisième ~** we're beginning the third millenium

millénarisme /milenaʀism/ **NM** millenarianism

millénariste /milenaʀist/ **ADJ, NMF** millenarian

millénium /milenjɔm/ **NM** millennium

mille-pattes /milpat/ **NM INV** centipede, millipede

millepertuis, mille-pertuis /milpɛʀtɥi/ **NM** St.-John's-wort

mille-raies /milʀɛ/ **NM INV** (= *tissu*) finely-striped material ◆ **velours ~** needlecord

millésime /milezim/ **NM** (= *date, Admin, Fin*) year, date; [*de vin*] year, vintage ◆ **vin d'un bon ~** vintage wine ◆ **quel est le ~ de ce vin ?** what is the vintage *ou* year of this wine?

millésimé, e /milezime/ **ADJ** vintage ◆ **bouteille ~e** bottle of vintage wine ◆ **un bordeaux ~** a vintage Bordeaux ◆ **un champagne ~ 1990** a 1990 champagne ◆ **la version ~e 2002 du dictionnaire** the 2002 edition of the dictionary

millet /mijɛ/ **NM** (*Agr*) millet ◆ **donner des grains de ~ aux oiseaux** to give the birds some millet *ou* (bird)seed

milli... /mili/ **PRÉF** milli... ◆ **millirem** millirem

milliaire /miljɛʀ/ **ADJ** (*Antiq*) milliary ◆ **borne ~** milliary column

milliampère /miliɑ̃pɛʀ/ **NM** milliamp

milliard /miljaʀ/ **NM** billion, thousand million ◆ **un ~ de personnes** a billion *ou* a thousand million people ◆ **2 ~s d'euros** 2 billion euros, 2 thousand million euros ◆ **des ~s de** billions of, thousands of millions of

milliardaire /miljaʀdɛʀ/ **NMF** multimillionaire **ADJ** ◆ **il est ~** he's worth millions, he's a multimillionaire ◆ **une société plusieurs fois ~ en dollars** a company worth (many) billions of dollars

milliardième /miljaʀdjɛm/ **ADJ, NM** thousand millionth, billionth

millibar /milibaʀ/ **NM** millibar

millième /miljɛm/ **ADJ, NM** thousandth ◆ **c'est la ~ fois que je te le dis !** I've told you a thousand times! ◆ **la ~ (représentation)** (*Théât*) the thousandth performance

millier /milje/ **NM** (= *mille*) thousand; (= *environ*) a thousand or so, about a thousand ◆ **par ~s** in (their) thousands, by the thousand ◆ **il y en a des ~s** there are thousands (of them)

milligramme /miligʀam/ **NM** milligram(me)

millilitre /mililitʀ/ **NM** millilitre (*Brit*), milliliter (*US*)

millimétré, e /milimetʀe/ **ADJ** [1] [*papier*] graduated (*in millimetres*) [2] (= *précis*) [*passe, tir, réglage*] perfectly judged; [*organisation*] meticulous ◆ **un spectacle ~** a perfectly choreographed spectacle

millimètre /milimɛtʀ/ **NM** millimetre (*Brit*), millimeter (*US*)

millimétrique /milimetʀik/ ADJ *(Sci)* millimetric • **avec une précision** ~ *(fig)* with absolute precision

million /miljɔ̃/ NM million • **2 ~s de francs** 2 million francs • **être riche à ~s** to be a millionaire, to have millions, to be worth millions • **ça a coûté des ~s** it cost millions

millionième /miljɔnjɛm/ ADJ, NMF millionth

millionnaire /miljɔnɛʀ/ NMF millionaire ADJ • **la société est** ~ the company is worth millions *ou* worth a fortune • **il est plusieurs fois** ~ he's a millionaire several times over • **un ~ en dollars** a dollar millionaire

milliseconde /milis(ə)gɔ̃d/ NF millisecond

millivolt /milivɔlt/ NM millivolt

mi-long, mi-longue /milɔ̃, milɔ̃g/ ADJ *[manteau, jupe]* calf-length *(épith)*; *[manche]* elbow-length *(épith)*; *[cheveux]* shoulder-length *(épith)*

milord †* /milɔʀ/ NM (= *noble anglais*) lord, nobleman; (= *riche étranger*) immensely rich foreigner • **oui ~ !** yes my lord!

mi-lourd /miluʀ/ NM, ADJ *(Boxe)* light heavyweight

mime /mim/ NM 1 (= *personne*) *(Théât)* mime artist, mime; (= *imitateur*) mimic 2 *(Théât = art, action)* mime, miming • **il fait du** ~ he's a mime (artist) • **(spectacle de)** ~ mime show

mimer /mime/ ▸ conjug 1 ◂ VT *(Théât)* to mime; (= *singer*) to mimic, to imitate; (*pour ridiculiser*) to take off

mimétique /mimetik/ ADJ mimetic

mimétisme /mimetism/ NM *(Bio)* (protective) mimicry; *(fig)* unconscious imitation, mimetism • **il croisa les bras, par ~ avec son frère** he folded his arms, unconsciously imitating *ou* in unconscious imitation of his brother

mimi* /mimi/ NM 1 *(langage enfantin)* (= *chat*) pussy(cat), puss*; (= *baiser*) little kiss; (= *câlin*) cuddle • **faire des ~s à qn** to kiss and cuddle sb 2 *(terme affectueux)* **mon** ~ darling, sweetie* ADJ INV (= *mignon*) cute, lovely

mimique /mimik/ NF 1 (= *grimace comique*) comical expression, funny face • **ce singe a de drôles de ~s !** this monkey makes such funny faces! • **il eut une ~ de dégoût** he grimaced in disgust 2 (= *signes, gestes*) gesticulations; *[de sourds-muets]* sign language *(NonC)* • **il eut une ~ expressive pour dire qu'il avait faim** his gestures *ou* gesticulations made it quite clear that he was hungry

mimodrame /mimɔdʀam/ NM *(Théât)* mime show

mimolette /mimɔlɛt/ NF *type of Dutch cheese*

mi-mollet /mimɔlɛ/ **à mi-mollet** LOC ADV • **(arrivant à)** ~ *[jupe]* calf-length, below-the-knee *(épith)* • **j'avais de l'eau jusqu'à** ~ the water came up to just below my knees

mimosa /mimoza/ NM mimosa; → **œuf**

mi-moyen /mimwajɛ̃/ NM, ADJ *(Boxe)* welterweight

MIN /min/ NM (abrév de **marché d'intérêt national**) → **marché**

min. 1 (abrév de **minimum**) min 2 (abrév de **minute**) min

minable /minabl/ ADJ (= *décrépit*) *[lieu, aspect, personne]* shabby(-looking), seedy(-looking); (= *médiocre*) *[devoir, film, personne]* hopeless*, useless*, pathetic*; *[salaire, vie]* miserable, wretched; *[voyou]* wretched; *[complot]* shoddy • **habillé de façon** ~ shabbily dressed NMF *(péj)* loser*, dead loss* • **(espèce de)** ~ **!** you're so pathetic!* • **une bande de ~s** a pathetic *ou* useless bunch*

minablement /minabləmɑ̃/ ADV 1 (= *médiocrement*) hopelessly*, uselessly*, pathetically* 2 *[habillé]* shabbily

minage /minaʒ/ NM *[de pont, tranchée]* mining

minaret /minaʀɛ/ NM minaret

minauder /minode/ ▸ conjug 1 ◂ VI to simper, to put on simpering airs • **oh oui, dit-elle en minaudant** oh yes, she simpered • **je n'aime pas sa façon de** ~ I don't like her (silly) simpering ways

minauderie /minodʀi/ NF • **~s** simpering (airs) • **faire des ~s** to put on simpering airs, to simper

minaudier, -ière /minodje, jɛʀ/ ADJ affected, simpering *(épith)*

mince /mɛ̃s/ ADJ 1 (= *peu épais*) thin; (= *svelte, élancé*) slim, slender • **tranche** ~ thin slice • **elle est ~ comme un fil** she's (as) thin as a rake • **~ comme une feuille de papier à cigarette** *ou* **comme une pelure d'oignon** paper-thin, wafer-thin • **avoir la taille** ~ to be slim *ou* slender
2 (= *faible, insignifiant*) *[profit]* slender; *[salaire]* meagre *(Brit)*, meager *(US)*, small; *[prétexte]* lame, weak; *[preuve, chances]* slim, slender; *[excuse]* lame; *[connaissances, rôle, mérite]* slight, small • **l'intérêt du film est bien** ~ the film is decidedly lacking in interest *ou* is of very little interest • **ce n'est pas une ~ affaire** it's quite a job *ou* business, it's no easy task • **l'espoir de les retrouver est bien** ~ there is very little hope of finding them • **il n'y sera pas non plus – ~ consolation !** he won't be there either – that's not much of a consolation! • **ce n'est pas une ~ victoire** *ou* **un ~ exploit** it's no mean feat • **c'est un peu ~ comme réponse*** that's not much of an answer
ADV *[couper]* thinly, in thin slices
EXCL • **~ (alors) !*** *(contrariété)* drat (it)!*, blow (it)!* *(Brit)*, darn (it)!* *(US)*; *(surprise)* you don't say!; *(admiration)* wow!*

minceur /mɛ̃sœʀ/ NF 1 (= *finesse*) thinness; (= *gracilité*) slimness, slenderness • **cuisine** ~ cuisine minceur • **régime** ~ slimming diet • **produits** ~ slimming products 2 (= *insignifiance*) **la ~ des preuves** the slimness *ou* the insufficiency of the evidence

mincir /mɛ̃siʀ/ ▸ conjug 2 ◂ VI to get slimmer, to get thinner VT *[vêtement]* • **cette robe te mincit** this dress makes you look slimmer

mine[1] /min/ NF 1 (= *physionomie*) expression, look • **... dit-il, la ~ réjouie** ... he said with a cheerful *ou* delighted expression on his face • **elle est arrivée, la ~ boudeuse** she arrived, looking sulky *ou* with a sulky expression on her face • **ne fais pas cette ~-là** stop making *ou* pulling that face • **faire triste ~ à qn** to give sb a cool reception; → **gris**
2 (= *allure*) exterior, appearance • **tu as la ~ de quelqu'un qui n'a rien compris** you look as if you haven't understood a single thing • **il cachait sous sa ~ modeste un orgueil sans pareil** his modest exterior concealed an overweening pride • **votre rôti a bonne** ~ your roast looks good *ou* appetizing • **tu as bonne ~ maintenant !** *(iro)* now you look (like) an utter *ou* a right* idiot!; → **payer**
3 (= *teint*) **avoir bonne** ~ to look well • **il a mauvaise** ~ he doesn't look well, he looks unwell *ou* poorly • **avoir une sale** ~ to look awful* *ou* dreadful • **avoir une ~ de papier mâché** to look washed out • **il a meilleure ~ qu'hier** he looks better than (he did) yesterday • **tu as une ~ superbe** you look terrific
4 *(locutions)* **faire ~ de faire qch** to pretend to do sth • **j'ai fait ~ de le croire** I acted as if I believed it • **j'ai fait ~ de lui donner une gifle** I made as if to slap him • **il n'a même pas fait ~ de résister** he didn't even put up a token resistance, he didn't even offer a show of resistance
♦ **mine de rien*** • **il est venu nous demander comment ça marchait, ~ de rien*** he came and asked us with a casual air *ou* all casually* how things were going • **~ de rien, tu sais qu'il n'est pas bête*** though you wouldn't think it to look at him he's no dummy* you know • **~ de rien, ça fait deux heures qu'on attend/ça nous a coûté 200 €** you wouldn't think it but we've been waiting for two hours/it cost us €200
NFPL **mines** *[de personne]* simpering airs; *[de bébé]* expressions • **faire des ~s** to put on simpering airs, to simper • **il fait ses petites ~s** *[de bébé]* he makes (funny) little faces

mine[2] /min/ NF 1 (= *gisement*) deposit, mine; *(exploité)* mine • **~ d'or** *(lit, fig)* gold mine • **région de ~s** mining area *ou* district • **~ à ciel ouvert** opencast mine • **la nationalisation des ~s** *(gén)* the nationalization of the mining industry; *(charbon)* the nationalization of coal *ou* of the coalmining industry • **~ de charbon** *(gén)* coalmine; *(puits)* pit, mine; *(entreprise)* colliery • **descendre dans la** ~ to go down the mine *ou* pit • **travailler à la** ~ to work in the mines, to be a miner; → **carreau, galerie, puits**
2 (= *source*) *[de renseignements]* mine • **une ~ inépuisable de documents** an inexhaustible source of documents • **cette bibliothèque est une (vraie)** ~ this library is a treasure trove
3 • **~ (de crayon)** (pencil) lead • **crayon à ~ dure/tendre** hard/soft pencil, pencil with a hard/soft lead • **~ de plomb** black lead, graphite
4 *(Mil)* (= *galerie*) gallery, sap, mine; (= *explosif*) mine • **~ dormante/flottante** unexploded/floating mine • **~ terrestre** landmine; → **champ[1], détecteur**
NFPL **Mines** • **les Mines** *(Admin)* ≈ the (National) Mining and Geological service • **l'École des Mines** ≈ the (National) School of Mining Engineering • **ingénieur des Mines** (state qualified) mining engineer • **le service des Mines** *the French government vehicle testing service*

miner /mine/ ▸ conjug 1 ◂ VT 1 (= *garnir d'explosifs*) to mine • **ce pont est miné** this bridge has been mined 2 (= *ronger*) *[+ falaise, fondations]* to undermine, to erode, to eat away; *[+ société, autorité, santé]* to undermine; *[+ force]* to sap, to undermine • **la maladie l'a miné** his illness has left him drained (of energy) *ou* has sapped his strength • **miné par le chagrin/l'inquiétude** worn down by grief/anxiety • **miné par la jalousie** eaten up *ou* consumed with jealousy • **tout ça le mine** all this is eating into him • **c'est un sujet/terrain miné** *(fig)* it's a highly sensitive subject/area

minerai /minʀɛ/ NM ore • **~ de fer/cuivre** iron/copper ore

minéral, e (mpl **-aux**) /mineʀal, o/ ADJ *[huile, sel, règne]* mineral; *[chimie]* inorganic; *[paysage]* stony; → **chimie, eau** NM mineral

minéralier /mineʀalje/ NM ore tanker

minéralisation /mineʀalizasjɔ̃/ NF mineralization

minéralisé, e /mineʀalize/ (ptp de **minéraliser**) ADJ *[eau]* mineralized • **peu/moyennement ~e** with a low/medium mineral content

minéraliser /mineʀalize/ ▸ conjug 1 ◂ VT to mineralize

minéralogie /mineʀalɔʒi/ NF mineralogy

minéralogique /mineʀalɔʒik/ ADJ 1 **numéro ~** *[de véhicule]* registration *(Brit)* *ou* license *(US)* number; → **plaque** 2 *(Géol)* mineralogical

minéralogiste /mineʀalɔʒist/ NMF mineralogist

minerve /minɛʀv/ NF 1 *(Méd)* (surgical) collar 2 *(Typo)* platen machine 3 *(Myth)* **Minerve** Minerva

minestrone /minɛstʀɔn/ NM minestrone

minet, -ette /minɛ, ɛt/ NM,F *(langage enfantin = chat)* puss*, pussy (cat), kitty (cat) *(surtout US)* ◆ **mon ~, ma minette** *(terme affectif)* (my) pet*, sweetie(-pie)* NM *(péj = jeune élégant)* pretty boy*, young trendy* *(Brit)* NF **minette** *(* = jeune fille)* (cute) chick*

mineur[1], e /minœʀ/ ADJ 1 *(Jur)* minor ◆ **enfant ~** young person who is under age, minor ◆ **être ~** to be under age, to be a minor 2 *(= peu important) [soucis, œuvre, artiste]* minor; → **Asie** 3 *(Mus) [gamme, intervalle, mode]* minor ◆ **en do ~** in C minor 4 *(Logique) [terme, proposition]* minor NM,F *(Jur)* minor, young person under 18 (years of age) ◆ **"établissement interdit aux mineurs"** "no person under 18 allowed on the premises" ◆ **le film est interdit aux ~s de moins de 12 ans** the film is unsuitable for children under 12; → **détournement** NM *(Mus)* minor ◆ **en ~** in a minor key NF **mineure** 1 *(Logique)* minor premise 2 *(Univ = matière)* subsidiary *(Brit)*, second subject *(Brit)*, minor *(US)*

mineur[2] /minœʀ/ NM 1 *(= ouvrier)* miner; *[de houille]* (coal) miner ◆ **~ de fond** pitface *ou* underground worker, miner at the pitface ◆ **village de ~s** mining village 2 *(Mil)* sapper *(who lays mines)*

mini /mini/ ADJ INV 1 *(Mode)* **la mode ~** the fashion for minis 2 *(= très petit)* **c'est ~ chez eux*** they've got a minute *ou* tiny (little) place ◆ **~ budget, budget ~** shoestring budget NM INV *(Mode)* ◆ **elle s'habille (en) ~** she wears minis ◆ **la mode est au ~** minis are in (fashion)

mini- /mini/ PRÉF mini ◆ **~conférence de presse** mini press-conference

miniature /minjatyʀ/ NF 1 *(gén)* miniature ◆ **en ~** in miniature ◆ **cette région, c'est la France en ~** this region is a miniature France *ou* France in miniature 2 *(Art)* miniature 3 *(* = nabot)* (little) shrimp* *ou* tich* *(Brit)*, tiddler* *(Brit)* ◆ **tu as vu cette ~ ?** did you see that little shrimp?* ADJ miniature ◆ **train/jeu d'échecs ~** miniature train/chess set

miniaturisation /minjatyʀizasjɔ̃/ NF miniaturization

miniaturiser /minjatyʀize/ ► conjug 1 ◄ VT to miniaturize ◆ **transistor miniaturisé** miniaturized transistor ◆ **les ordinateurs se miniaturisent** computers are becoming smaller and smaller

miniaturiste /minjatyʀist/ NMF miniaturist

minibar /minibaʀ/ NM *(= réfrigérateur)* minibar; *(= chariot)* refreshments trolley *(Brit) ou* cart

minibombe /minibɔ̃b/ NF bomblet

minibus /minibys/ NM minibus

minicam /minikam/ NF minicam

minicassette /minikasɛt/ NF minicassette

minichaîne /miniʃɛn/ NF mini (music) system

MiniDisc ® /minidisk/ NM MiniDisc ®

minidosée /minidoze/ ADJ F ◆ **pilule ~** mini-pill

minier, -ière /minje, jɛʀ/ ADJ mining

minigolf /minigɔlf/ NM *(= jeu)* mini-golf, crazy-golf; *(= lieu)* mini-golf *ou* crazy-golf course

minijupe /miniʒyp/ NF miniskirt

minima /minima/ → **minimum**

minimal, e (mpl **-aux**) /minimal, o/ ADJ minimum, minimal ◆ **les logements doivent répondre à des normes ~es de sécurité** housing must meet minimum safety requirements ◆ **art ~** minimal art

minimalisme /minimalism/ NM minimalism

minimaliste /minimalist/ ADJ, NMF minimalist

minime /minim/ ADJ *[dégât, rôle, différence]* minimal; *[salaire, somme]* modest, paltry *(pej)* ◆ **le plus ~ changement** the slightest change ◆ **le plus ~ écart de température** the tiniest difference in temperature ◆ **les progrès sont très ~s** very minimal progress has been made NMF 1 *(Sport)* junior (13-15 years) 2 *(Rel)* Minim

mini-message /minimesaʒ/ NM (pl **mini-messages**) text message

minimisation /minimizasjɔ̃/ NF minimization

minimiser /minimize/ ► conjug 1 ◄ VT *[+ risque, rôle]* to minimize; *[+ incident, importance]* to play down

minimum /minimɔm/ (f **minimum**) (pl **minimum(s)** *ou* **minima**) ADJ minimum ◆ **vitesse/âge ~** minimum speed/age ◆ **la température ~ a été de 6° C** the minimum temperature was 6° C, there was a low of 6° C today ◆ **assurer un service ~** *(Transport)* to run a reduced service ◆ **programme ~** *(TV)* restricted service; → **revenu, salaire**

NM 1 minimum; *(Jur)* minimum sentence ◆ **dans le ~ de temps** in the shortest time possible ◆ **il faut un ~ de temps/d'intelligence pour le faire** you need a minimum amount of time/a modicum of intelligence to be able to do it ◆ **il faut quand même travailler un ~** you still have to do a minimum (amount) of work ◆ **ils ont fait le ~ syndical** they did no more than they had to ◆ **avec un ~ d'efforts il aurait réussi** with a minimum of effort he would have succeeded ◆ **il n'a pris que le ~ de précautions** he took only minimum *ou* minimal precautions ◆ **c'est vraiment le ~ que tu puisses faire** it's the very least you can do ◆ **la production a atteint son ~** production has sunk to its lowest level (yet) *ou* an all-time low ◆ **avoir tout juste le ~ vital** *(salaire)* to earn barely a living wage; *(subsistance)* to be *ou* live at subsistence level ◆ **il faut rester le ~ (de temps) au soleil** you must stay in the sun as little as possible

◆ **au minimum** at least, at a minimum ◆ **ça coûte au ~ 15 €** it costs at least €15 *ou* a minimum of €15 ◆ **dépenses réduites au ~** expenditure cut (down) to the minimum

2 *(Admin)* ~ **vieillesse** basic old age pension ◆ **les minima sociaux** basic welfare benefits ◆ **dépenses réduites à un ~** expenditure cut (down) to a minimum

ADV at least, at a minimum ◆ **ça dure quinze jours ~** it lasts at least fifteen days

mini-ordinateur (pl **mini-ordinateurs**) /miniɔʀdinatœʀ/ NM minicomputer

minipilule /minipilyl/ NF minipill

ministère /ministɛʀ/ NM 1 *(= département)* ministry, department *(US)* ◆ **employé de ~** government employee ◆ **~ de l'Agriculture/de l'Éducation (nationale)** ministry *ou* department *(US)* of Agriculture/of Education; → aussi **comp**

2 *(= cabinet)* government, cabinet ◆ **sous le ~ (de) Pompidou** under the premiership of Pompidou, under Pompidou's government ◆ **le premier ~ Poincaré** Poincaré's first government ◆ **former un ~** to form a government *ou* a cabinet ◆ **~ de coalition** coalition government

3 *(Jur)* **le ~ public** *(= partie)* the Prosecution; *(= service)* the public prosecutor's office ◆ **par ~ d'huissier** served by a bailiff

4 *(Rel)* ministry ◆ **exercer son ~ à la campagne** to have a country parish

5 *(littér = entremise)* agency ◆ **proposer son ~ à qn** to offer to act for sb

COMP **ministère des Affaires étrangères** Ministry of Foreign Affairs, Foreign Office *(Brit)*, Department of State *(US)*, State Department *(US)*

ministère des Affaires européennes Ministry of European Affairs

ministère des Affaires sociales Social Services Ministry

ministère des Anciens Combattants *Ministry responsible for ex-servicemen,* ≃ Veterans Administration *(US)*

ministère du Budget Ministry of Finance, ≃ Treasury *(Brit)*, Treasury Department *(US)*

ministère du Commerce Ministry of Trade, Department of Trade and Industry *(Brit)*, Department of Commerce *(US)*

ministère du Commerce extérieur Ministry of Foreign Trade, Board of Trade *(Brit)*

ministère de la Culture Ministry for the Arts

ministère de la Défense nationale Ministry of Defence *(Brit)*, Department of Defense *(US)*

ministère des Départements et Territoires d'outre-mer *Ministry for French overseas territories*

ministère de l'Économie et des Finances Ministry of Finance, ≃ Treasury *(Brit)*, Treasury Department *(US)*

ministère de l'Environnement Ministry of the Environment, ≃ Department of the Environment *(Brit)*, Environmental Protection Agency *(US)*

ministère de l'Industrie ≃ Department of Trade and Industry *(Brit)*, Department of Commerce *(US)*

ministère de l'Intérieur Ministry of the Interior, ≃ Home Office *(Brit)*

ministère de la Jeunesse et des Sports Ministry of Sport

ministère de la Justice Ministry of Justice, Lord Chancellor's Office *(Brit)*, Department of Justice *(US)*

ministère de la Santé Ministry of Health, ≃ Department of Health and Social Security *(Brit)*, Department of Health and Human Services *(US)*

ministère des Transports Ministry of Transport *(Brit)*, Department of Transportation *(US)*

ministère du Travail Ministry of Employment *(Brit)*, Department of Labor *(US)*

ministériel, -elle /ministeʀjɛl/ ADJ *[document, solidarité]* ministerial; *[crise, remaniement]* cabinet *(épith)* ◆ **département ~** ministry, department *(surtout US)* ◆ **accéder à une fonction ministérielle** to become a minister ◆ **équipe ministérielle** cabinet; → **arrêté, officier[1]**

ministrable /ministʀabl/ ADJ, NMF ◆ **il fait partie des ~s** he's one of those in line for a ministerial post ◆ **il y a plusieurs premiers ~s** there are several possible candidates for the premiership

ministre /ministʀ/ NMF 1 *[de gouvernement]* minister *(Brit)*, secretary *(surtout US)* ◆ **pourriez-vous nous dire Monsieur** (*ou* **Madame**) **le ~ ...** could you tell us Minister ... *(Brit)*, could you tell us Mr (*ou* Madam) Secretary *(US)* ... ◆ **Premier ~** Prime Minister, Premier ◆ **Madame/Monsieur le Premier ~** Prime Minister ◆ **les ~s** the members of the cabinet ◆ **~ de l'Agriculture/de l'Éducation (nationale)** minister *(Brit) ou* secretary *(surtout US)* of Agriculture/of Education, Agriculture/Education minister *(Brit) ou* secretary *(surtout US)* ◆ **~ délégué** minister of state *(à* for; *auprès de* reporting to), ≃ junior minister *(Brit)*, undersecretary *(US)* ◆ **~ d'État** *(sans portefeuille)* minister without portfolio; *(de haut rang)* senior minister ◆ **~ sans portefeuille** minister without portfolio; → aussi **nm**; → **bureau, conseil, papier**

2 *(= envoyé, ambassadeur)* envoy ◆ **~ plénipotentiaire** (minister) plenipotentiary *(Brit)*, ambassador plenipotentiary *(US)*

NM 1 *(Rel) (protestant)* minister, clergyman; *(catholique)* priest ◆ **~ du culte** minister of religion ◆ **~ de Dieu** minister of God

2 *(littér = représentant)* agent

COMP **ministre des Affaires étrangères** Minister of Foreign Affairs, Foreign Secretary *(Brit)*, ≈ Secretary of State *(US)*
ministre des Affaires européennes Minister of European Affairs
ministre des Affaires sociales Social Services Minister
ministre du Budget Finance Minister *ou* Secretary, ≈ Chancellor of the Exchequer *(Brit)*, Secretary of the Treasury *(US)*
ministre du Commerce Minister of Trade *(Brit)*, Secretary of Commerce *(US)*
ministre de la Culture ≈ Minister for Arts
ministre de la Défense nationale Defence Minister *(Brit)*, Defense Secretary *(US)*
ministre des Départements et Territoires d'outre-mer *Minister for French overseas territories*
ministre de l'Économie et des Finances Finance Minister *ou* Secretary, ≈ Chancellor of the Exchequer *(Brit)*, Secretary of the Treasury *(US)*
ministre de l'Environnement ≈ Minister of the Environment *(Brit)*, Director of the Environmental Protection Agency *(US)*
ministre de l'Industrie Secretary of State for Trade and Industry *(Brit)*, Secretary of Commerce *(US)*
ministre de l'Intérieur Minister of the Interior, Home Secretary *(Brit)*, Secretary of the Interior *(US)*
ministre de la Jeunesse et des Sports Sports Minister
ministre de la Justice Minister of Justice, ≈ Lord Chancellor *(Brit)*, Attorney General *(US)*
ministre de la Santé (et de la Sécurité sociale) ≈ Minister of Health and Social Security *(Brit)*, Secretary of Health and Human Services *(US)*
ministre des Transports Minister of Transport *(Brit)*, Transportation Secretary *(US)*
ministre du Travail Minister of Employment, Labor Secretary *(US)*

Minitel ® /minitɛl/ NM Minitel ® ◆ **obtenir un renseignement par (le) ~** to get information on Minitel ®

MINITEL

The **Minitel** has been widely used in French businesses and households for many years, and despite the growing importance of the Internet it remains a familiar feature of daily life. **Minitel** is a public-access information system consisting of a small terminal with a built-in modem, screen and keyboard. Users key in the access code for the service they require, and pay for the time spent linked to the server as part of their regular telephone bill. The term « Minitel rose » refers to sex chatlines available on **Minitel**

minitéliste /minitelist/ NMF Minitel user

minium /minjɔm/ NM *(Chim)* red lead, minium; *(Peinture)* red lead paint

minivague /minivag/ NF soft perm ◆ **se faire faire une ~** to have a soft perm

Minnesota /minezɔta/ NM Minnesota

minois /minwa/ NM *(= visage)* little face ◆ **son joli ~** her pretty little face

minoration /minɔʀasjɔ̃/ NF *(= réduction)* cut, reduction *(de* in*)*; ◆ **ce projet n'entraîne pas une ~ de leur influence** their influence will not be reduced as a result of this project

minorer /minɔʀe/ ► conjug 1 ◄ VT 1 *[+ taux, impôts]* to cut, to reduce *(de* by*)*; ◆ **ces tarifs seront minorés de 40%** these rates will be cut *ou* reduced by 40% 2 *[+ incident]* to play down (the importance of); *[+ importance]* to play down; *[+ rôle]* to reduce, to minimize

minoritaire /minɔʀitɛʀ/ ADJ minority *(épith)* ◆ **groupe ~** minority group ◆ **ils sont ~s** they are a minority, they are in a *ou* in the minority ◆ **ils sont ~s au Parlement** they have a minority in Parliament NMF member of a minority party *(ou* group *etc)* ◆ **les ~s** the minority (party)

minorité /minɔʀite/ NF 1 *(= âge) (gén)* minority; *(Jur)* minority, (legal) infancy, nonage ◆ **pendant sa ~** while he is *(ou* was) under age, during his minority *ou* infancy *(Jur)* ◆ **~ pénale** ≈ legal infancy 2 *(= groupe)* minority (group) ◆ **~ ethnique/nationale** racial *ou* ethnic/national minority ◆ **~ agissante/opprimée** active/oppressed minority ◆ **~ de blocage** *(Écon)* blocking minority 3 ◆ **~ de** minority of ◆ **dans la ~ des cas** in the minority of cases ◆ **je m'adresse à une ~ d'auditeurs** I'm addressing a minority of listeners
◆ **en minorité** ◆ **être en ~** to be in a *ou* in the minority, to be a minority ◆ **le gouvernement a été mis en ~ sur la question du budget** the government was defeated on the budget

Minorque /minɔʀk/ NF Minorca

minorquin, e /minɔʀkɛ̃, in/ ADJ Minorcan NM,F **Minorquin(e)** Minorcan

Minos /minɔs/ NM Minos

Minotaure /minɔtɔʀ/ NM Minotaur

minoterie /minɔtʀi/ NF *(= industrie)* flour-milling (industry); *(= usine)* (flour-)mill

minotier /minɔtje/ NM miller

minou /minu/ NM 1 *(langage enfantin = chat)* pussy(cat), puss* 2 *(terme d'affection)* **mon ~** sweetie(-pie)*, (my) pet* 3 (** = *sexe de femme)* pussy**

minuit /minɥi/ NM midnight, twelve (o'clock) (at night) ◆ **à ~** at (twelve) midnight, at twelve (o'clock) (at night) ◆ **~ vingt** twenty past twelve *ou* midnight ◆ **il est ~, l'heure du crime** *(hum)* it's midnight, the witching hour ◆ **de ~** *[soleil, messe]* midnight *(épith)* ◆ **bain de ~** midnight *ou* moonlight swim

minus * /minys/ NMF *(péj)* dead loss*, washout* ◆ **viens ici, ~ !** come over here, you wimp!* ◆ **~ habens** moron

minuscule /minyskyl/ ADJ 1 *(= très petit)* minute, tiny, minuscule 2 *(Écriture)* small; *(Typo)* lower case ◆ **h ~** small h NF small letter; *(Typo)* lower case letter

minutage /minytaʒ/ NM (strict *ou* precise) timing

minute /minyt/ NF 1 *(= division de l'heure, d'un degré)* minute; *(= moment)* minute, moment ◆ **une ~ de silence** a minute's silence, a minute of silence ◆ **la ~ de vérité** the moment of truth ◆ **je n'ai pas une ~ à moi/à perdre** I don't have a minute *ou* moment to myself/to lose ◆ **une ~ d'inattention a suffi** a moment's inattention was enough ◆ **~ (papillon) !*** hey, just a minute!*, hold *ou* hang on (a minute)!* ◆ **une ~, j'arrive !** just a second *ou* a minute, I'm coming! ◆ **attendez une petite ~** can you wait just a *ou* half a minute? ◆ **une (petite) ~ ! je n'ai jamais dit ça !** hang on a minute! I never said that! ◆ **elle va arriver d'une ~ à l'autre** she'll be here any minute now ◆ **en (l'espace de) cinq ~s, c'était fait** it was done in five minutes
◆ **à la minute** ◆ **on me l'a apporté à la ~** it has just this instant *ou* moment been brought to me ◆ **avec toi, il faut toujours tout faire à la ~** you always have to have things done there and then *ou* on the spot ◆ **réparations à la ~** on-the-spot repairs, repairs while you wait ◆ **elle arrive toujours à la ~ (près)** she's always there on the dot*, she always arrives to the minute *ou* right on time* ◆ **on n'est pas à la ~ près** there's no rush
2 *(en apposition)* **steak** *ou* **entrecôte ~** minute steak ◆ **"talons minute"** "shoes repaired while you wait", "heel bar" *(Brit)*
3 *(Jur) [de contrat]* original draft ◆ **les ~s de la réunion** the minutes of the meeting ◆ **rédiger les ~s de qch** to minute sth

minuter /minyte/ ► conjug 1 ◄ VT 1 *(= chronométrer, limiter)* to time; *(= organiser)* to time (carefully *ou* to the last minute) ◆ **dans son emploi du temps tout est minuté** everything's worked out *ou* timed down to the last second in his timetable ◆ **mon temps est minuté** I've got an extremely tight schedule 2 *(Jur)* to draw up, to draft

minuterie /minytʀi/ NF *[de lumière]* time switch; *[d'horloge]* regulator; *[de four]* timer; *[de bombe]* timing device, timer ◆ **allumer la ~** to switch on the (automatic) light *(on stairs, in passage etc)*

minuteur /minytœʀ/ NM *[de cafetière, four]* timer

minutie /minysi/ NF 1 *[de personne, travail]* meticulousness ◆ **j'ai été frappé par la ~ de son inspection** I was amazed by the detail of his inspection, I was amazed how detailed his inspection was ◆ **l'horlogerie demande beaucoup de ~** clock-making requires a great deal of precision ◆ **avec ~** *(= avec soin)* meticulously; *(= dans le détail)* in minute detail 2 *(= détails)* **~s** *(péj)* trifles, trifling details, minutiae

minutieusement /minysjøzmɑ̃/ ADV *(= avec soin)* meticulously; *(= dans le détail)* in minute detail

minutieux, -ieuse /minysjø, jøz/ ADJ *[personne, soin, analyse]* meticulous; *[description, inspection]* minute; *[dessin]* minutely detailed ◆ **il s'agit d'un travail ~** it's a job that demands painstaking attention to detail ◆ **c'est une opération minutieuse** it's an extremely delicate operation ◆ **il est très ~** he is very meticulous

miocène /mjɔsɛn/ ADJ Miocene NM ◆ **le Miocène** the Miocene

mioche * /mjɔʃ/ NMF *(= gosse)* kid*, nipper* *(Brit)*; *(péj)* brat* ◆ **sale ~ !** dirty *ou* horrible little brat!*

mi-pente /mipɑ̃t/ **à mi-pente** LOC ADV halfway up *ou* down the hill

mirabelle /miʀabɛl/ NF *(= prune)* cherry plum; *(= alcool)* plum brandy

mirabellier /miʀabelje/ NM cherry-plum tree

miracle /miʀɑkl/ NM 1 *(lit, fig)* miracle ◆ **~ économique** economic miracle ◆ **son œuvre est un ~ d'équilibre** his work is a miracle *ou* marvel of balance ◆ **cela tient** *ou* **relève du ~** it's a miracle ◆ **faire** *ou* **accomplir des ~s** *(lit)* to work *ou* do *ou* accomplish miracles; *(fig)* to work wonders *ou* miracles ◆ **c'est ~ qu'il résiste dans ces conditions** it's a wonder *ou* a miracle he manages to cope in these conditions ◆ **il faudrait une ~ pour qu'il soit élu** nothing short of a miracle will get him elected, it'll take a miracle for him to get elected ◆ **par ~** miraculously, by a *ou* by some miracle ◆ **comme par ~ !** *(iro)* surprise, surprise! ◆ **~ ! il est revenu !** amazing! he's come back!; → **crier**
2 *(Hist, Littérat)* miracle (play)
ADJ INV ◆ **remède/solution ~** miracle cure/solution ◆ **potion ~** magic potion ◆ **il n'y a pas de recette ~** there's no miracle solution ◆ **médicament ~** wonder *ou* miracle drug

miraculé, e /miʀakyle/ ADJ, NM,F ◆ **(malade) ~** (person) who has been miraculously cured *ou* who has been cured by a miracle ◆ **les trois ~s de la route** the three (people) who miraculously *ou* who by some miracle survived the accident ◆ **voilà le ~ !** *(hum)* here comes the miraculous survivor!

miraculeusement /miʀakyløzmɑ̃/ ADV miraculously

miraculeux, -euse /miʀakylø, øz/ ADJ *[guérison, victoire, source]* miraculous; *[progrès, réussite]* wonderful ◆ **traitement** *ou* **remède** ~ miracle cure ◆ **ça n'a rien de** ~ there's nothing so miraculous *ou* extraordinary about that ◆ **il n'y a pas de solution miraculeuse** there is no miracle solution; → **pêche²**

mirador /miʀadɔʀ/ NM *(Mil)* watchtower, mirador; *(pour l'observation d'animaux)* raised (observation) hide; *(Archit)* belvedere, mirador

mirage /miʀaʒ/ NM 1 *(lit, fig)* mirage ◆ **c'est un ~ !** *(hum)* you *(ou* I *etc)* must be seeing things! 2 *[d'œufs]* candling

miraud, e* /miʀo, od/ ADJ *(= myope)* short-sighted ◆ **tu es ~ !** you need glasses! ◆ **il est complètement** ~ he's as blind as a bat

mire /miʀ/ NF *(TV)* test card; *(Arpentage)* surveyor's rod ◆ **prendre sa** ~ *(= viser)* to take aim ◆ **point de** ~ *(lit)* target; *(fig)* focal point; → **cran, ligne¹**

mire-œufs /miʀø/ NM INV light *(for candling eggs)*

mirer /miʀe/ ▸ conjug 1 ◂ VT 1 *[+ œufs]* to candle 2 *(littér)* to mirror VPR **se mirer** *(littér)* *[personne]* to gaze at o.s. *ou* at one's reflection *(in the mirror, water etc)*; *[chose]* to be mirrored *ou* reflected *(in the water etc)*

mirettes* /miʀɛt/ NFPL eyes, peepers* *(hum)* ◆ **ils en ont pris plein les** ~ they were completely dazzled by it

mirifique /miʀifik/ ADJ *(hum)* *[contrat]* extremely lucrative; *[salaire]* huge; *[promesses]* extravagant; *[offre]* fantastic ◆ **des projets ~s** *(= irréalistes)* harebrained schemes

mirliton /miʀlitɔ̃/ NM *(Mus)* reed pipe; *[de carnaval]* party whistle; → **vers²**

mirmidon /miʀmidɔ̃/ NM ⇒ **myrmidon**

mirobolant, e* /miʀɔbɔlɑ̃, ɑ̃t/ ADJ *(hum)* *[contrat, salaire]* extravagant; *[résultats]* brilliant

miroir /miʀwaʀ/ NM *(lit)* mirror; *(fig)* mirror, reflection ◆ **le ~ des eaux** *(littér)* the glassy waters ◆ **un roman n'est jamais le ~ de la réalité** a novel is never a true reflection of reality *ou* never really mirrors reality ◆ **écriture/image en** ~ mirror writing/image
COMP **miroir aux alouettes** *(lit)* decoy; *(fig)* lure
miroir de courtoisie *[de voiture]* vanity mirror
miroir déformant distorting mirror
miroir d'eau ornamental pond
miroir grossissant magnifying mirror

miroitant, e /miʀwatɑ̃, ɑ̃t/ ADJ *[eau, lac]* sparkling, shimmering; *[étoffe]* shimmering; *[collier, vitres]* sparkling; *[métal]* gleaming

miroitement /miʀwatmɑ̃/ NM *(= étincellement)* sparkling (NonC), gleaming (NonC); *(= chatoiement)* shimmering (NonC)

miroiter /miʀwate/ ▸ conjug 1 ◂ VI *(= étinceler)* to sparkle, to gleam; *(= chatoyer)* to shimmer ◆ **il lui fit ~ les avantages qu'elle aurait à accepter ce poste** he painted in glowing colours what she stood to gain from taking the job ◆ **ils ont fait ~ la perspective d'une baisse des cotisations** they held out the possibility of a cut in contributions

miroiterie /miʀwatʀi/ NF 1 *(= commerce)* mirror trade; *(= industrie)* mirror industry 2 *(= usine)* mirror factory

miroitier, -ière /miʀwatje, jɛʀ/ NM,F *(= vendeur)* mirror dealer; *(= fabricant)* mirror manufacturer; *(= artisan)* mirror cutter, silverer

mironton* /miʀɔ̃tɔ̃/, **miroton** /miʀɔtɔ̃/ NM ◆ **(bœuf) miroton** boiled beef in onion sauce

mis, e¹ † /mi, miz/ (ptp de **mettre**) ADJ *(= vêtu)* attired †, clad ◆ **bien** ~ nicely turned out

misaine /mizɛn/ NF ◆ **(voile de)** ~ foresail; → **mât**

misanthrope /mizɑ̃tʀɔp/ ADJ *[attitude]* misanthropic ◆ **il est devenu très** ~ he's come to dislike everyone *ou* to hate society, he's turned into a real misanthropist NMF misanthropist, misanthrope

misanthropie /mizɑ̃tʀɔpi/ NF misanthropy

misanthropique /mizɑ̃tʀɔpik/ ADJ *(frm)* misanthropic, misanthropical

miscellanées /miselane/ NFPL miscellanea

mise² /miz/ NF 1 *(= enjeu)* stake, ante; *(Comm)* outlay ◆ **récupérer sa** ~ to recoup one's outlay ◆ **gagner 100 € pour une ~ de 10 €** to make €100 on an outlay of €10 ◆ **remporter la** ~ *(fig)* to carry the day; → **sauver** 2 *(= habillement)* attire, clothing ◆ **avoir une ~ débraillée** to be untidily dressed ◆ **juger qn sur** *ou* **à sa** ~ to judge sb by his clothes *ou* by what he wears ◆ **soigner sa** ~ to take pride in one's appearance 3 ◆ **être de** ~ †† *(Fin)* to be in circulation, to be legal currency; *(fig)* to be acceptable ◆ **ces propos ne sont pas de** ~ those remarks are out of place 4 *(= action de mettre)* putting, setting; → **boîte, bouteille** *etc* COMP **mise en plis** *(Coiffure)* set ◆ **se faire faire une ~ en plis** to have a set, to have one's hair set; *(pour autres expressions voir sous le second terme)*

miser /mize/ ▸ conjug 1 ◂ VT 1 *(= parier)* *[+ argent]* to stake, to bet *(sur* on); ◆ ~ **sur un cheval** to bet on a horse, to put money on a horse ◆ ~ **à 8 contre 1** to bet at odds of 8 to 1, to take 8 to 1 ◆ **il a misé sur le mauvais cheval** *(fig)* he backed the wrong horse; → **tableau** 2 *(* = compter sur)* ~ **sur** to bank on, to count on 3 *(Helv)* *(= vendre)* to sell by auction; *(= acheter)* to buy by auction ◆ ~ **sur qn** to overbid sb

misérabilisme /mizeʀabilism/ NM miserabilism, tendency to dwell on the sordid side of life

misérabiliste /mizeʀabilist/ ADJ *[personne, livre, film]* dwelling on the sordid side of life ◆ **ils contestent l'image ~ qu'on donne de leur région** they reject the bleak picture that is generally painted of their region

misérable /mizeʀabl/ ADJ 1 *(= pauvre)* *[famille, personne]* destitute, poverty-stricken; *[région]* impoverished, poverty-stricken; *[logement]* seedy, mean, dingy; *[vêtements]* shabby ◆ **d'aspect** ~ shabby-looking, seedy-looking 2 *(= pitoyable)* *[existence, conditions]* miserable, wretched, pitiful; *[personne, famille]* pitiful, wretched 3 *(= sans valeur, minable)* *[somme d'argent]* paltry, miserable ◆ **un salaire** ~ a pittance, a miserable salary ◆ **ne te mets pas en colère pour 5 ~s euros** don't get all worked up about a measly* 5 euros 4 *(††, littér = méprisable)* vile †, base †, contemptible NMF *(†, littér)* *(= méchant)* wretch, scoundrel; *(= pauvre)* poor wretch ◆ **petit ~ !** you (little) rascal! *ou* wretch!

misérablement /mizeʀabləmɑ̃/ ADV *(= pitoyablement)* miserably, wretchedly; *(= pauvrement)* in great *ou* wretched poverty

misère /mizɛʀ/ NF 1 *(= pauvreté)* (extreme) poverty, destitution *(frm)* ◆ **la ~ en gants blancs** *ou* **dorée** genteel poverty ◆ **être dans la** ~ to be destitute *ou* poverty-stricken ◆ **vivre dans la** ~ to live in poverty ◆ **tomber dans la** ~ to fall on hard *ou* bad times, to become destitute ◆ **traitement** *ou* **salaire de** ~ starvation wage ◆ ~ **noire** utter destitution ◆ **réduire qn à la** ~ to make sb destitute, to reduce sb to a state of (dire) poverty ◆ **crier** *ou* **pleurer** ~ *(pour ne pas payer)* to plead poverty ◆ **il est venu chez nous crier** *ou* **pleurer** ~ *(pour obtenir de l'argent)* he came to us begging for money, he came to us with a sob story* about having no money
2 *(= carence)* ~ **culturelle** lack of culture ◆ ~ **sexuelle** sexual deprivation ◆ ~ **physiologique** *(Méd)* malnutrition
3 *(= malheur)* **~s** woes, miseries, misfortunes ◆ **petites ~s*** *(= ennuis)* little troubles ◆ **faire des ~s à qn*** to be nasty to sb ◆ **les ~s de la guerre** the miseries of war ◆ **c'est une ~ de la voir s'anémier** it's pitiful *ou* wretched to see her growing weaker ◆ **quelle ~ !** what a wretched shame! ◆ ~ **!, ~ de moi !** *(†, hum)* woe is me! † *(hum)* ◆ **la ~ de l'homme** *(Rel)* man's wretchedness
4 *(= somme négligeable)* **il l'a eu pour une** ~ he got it for a song* *ou* for next to nothing ◆ **c'est une ~ pour eux** that's nothing *ou* a trifle to them
5 *(= plante)* tradescantia, wandering Jew

miserere, miséréré /mizeʀeʀe/ NM *(= psaume, chant)* Miserere

miséreux, -euse /mizeʀø, øz/ ADJ *[existence, ville]* poverty-stricken; *[population, famille]* destitute NM,F destitute person ◆ **les** ~ the destitute

miséricorde /mizeʀikɔʀd/ NF 1 *(= pitié)* mercy, forgiveness ◆ **la ~ divine** divine mercy; → **péché** 2 *[de stalle]* misericord EXCL † mercy me! †, mercy on us! †

miséricordieux, -ieuse /mizeʀikɔʀdjø, jøz/ ADJ merciful, forgiving

miso /mizo/ NM miso

misogyne /mizɔʒin/ ADJ misogynous NMF misogynist, woman-hater

misogynie /mizɔʒini/ NF misogyny

miss /mis/ NF 1 *[de concours de beauté]* beauty queen ◆ **Miss France** Miss France 2 *(† = nurse)* (English *ou* American) governess 3 *(= vieille demoiselle)* ~ **anglaise** elderly English spinster

missel /misɛl/ NM missal

missile /misil/ NM missile ◆ ~ **antichar/antiaérien** antitank/antiaircraft missile ◆ ~ **antimissile** antimissile missile ◆ ~ **nucléaire/balistique** nuclear/ballistic missile ◆ ~ **sol-sol/sol-air** *etc* ground-to-ground/ground-(to)-air *etc* missile ◆ ~ **de moyenne portée** *ou* **de portée intermédiaire** intermediate-range weapon *ou* missile ◆ ~ **tactique/de croisière** tactical/cruise missile ◆ ~ **de courte/longue portée** short-/long-range missile ◆ ~ **à tête chercheuse** homing missile

mission /misjɔ̃/ NF 1 *(= charge, tâche)* *(gén, Rel)* mission; *(Pol)* mission, assignment; *[d'intérimaire]* brief, assignment ◆ ~ **lui fut donnée de ...** he was commissioned to ... ◆ **partir/être en** ~ *(Admin, Mil)* to go/be on an assignment; *[de prêtre]* to go/be on a mission ◆ ~ **accomplie** mission accomplished ◆ ~ **de reconnaissance** *(Mil)* reconnaissance (mission), recce* *(Brit)* ◆ ~ **diplomatique/scientifique/d'information** diplomatic/scientific/fact-finding mission ◆ ~ **impossible** *(lit)* impossible task; *(hum)* mission impossible; → **chargé, ordre²** 2 *(= but, vocation)* task, mission ◆ **la ~ de la littérature** the task of literature ◆ **il s'est donné pour ~ de faire cela** he set himself the task of doing it, he has made it his mission (in life) to do it 3 *(Rel)* *(= bâtiment)* mission (station); *(= groupe)* mission

missionnaire /misjɔnɛʀ/ ADJ, NMF missionary

Mississippi /misisipi/ NM Mississippi

missive /misiv/ ADJ F *(Jur)* ◆ **(lettre)** ~ document *(in the form of a letter, postcard or telegram)* NF *(hum = lettre)* missive

Missouri /misuʀi/ NM Missouri

mistigri /mistigʀi/ NM 1 *(† * = chat)* malkin † 2 *(Cartes)* jack of clubs ◆ **repasser** *ou* **refiler* le ~ à qn** *(fig)* to leave sb holding the baby

mistoufle †† * /mistufl/ NF ◆ **être dans la** ~ to have hit hard *ou* bad times, to be on one's beam ends* *(Brit)*

mistral /mistʀal/ NM mistral *(cold, dry wind that blows in the Rhône Valley and the South of France)*

mitage /mitaʒ/ NM ◆ **le ~ des campagnes** intensive building of houses in the countryside

mitaine /mitɛn/ NF (fingerless) mitten *ou* mitt

mitan /mitɑ̃/ NM (†† *ou dial*) middle, centre ◆ **dans le ~ de** in the middle of

mitard /mitaʀ/ NM *(arg Crime)* solitary* ◆ **il a fait 15 jours de ~** he did 2 weeks (in) solitary*

mite /mit/ NF clothes moth ◆ **mangé aux ~s** moth-eaten ◆ **~ du fromage** cheese mite ◆ **avoir la ~ à l'œil** †* to have sleep in one's eyes

mité, e /mite/ (ptp de **se miter**) ADJ moth-eaten

mi-temps /mitɑ̃/ NF INV *(Sport) (= période)* half; *(= repos)* half-time ◆ **à la ~** at half-time ◆ **première/seconde ~** first/second half ◆ **l'arbitre a sifflé la ~** the referee blew (the whistle) for half-time ◆ **la troisième ~** *(hum)* the post-match celebrations NM ◆ **(travail à) ~** part-time work ◆ **~ thérapeutique** *part-time working hours granted for medical reasons* ◆ **à ~** part-time ◆ **travailler à ~** to work part-time, to do part-time work ◆ **elle est serveuse à ~** she's a part-time waitress

miter (se) /mite/ ► conjug 1 ◄ VPR to be *ou* become moth-eaten ◆ **pour éviter que les vêtements se mitent** to stop the moths getting at the clothes

miteux, -euse /mitø, øz/ ADJ *[lieu]* seedy, grotty* *(Brit)*; *[vêtement]* shabby, tatty*, grotty* *(Brit)*; *[personne]* shabby(-looking), seedy(-looking) NM,F seedy(-looking) character

Mithridate /mitʀidat/ NM Mithridates

mithridatisation /mitʀidatizasjɔ̃/ NF, **mithridatisme** /mitʀidatism/ NM mithridatism

mithridatiser /mitʀidatize/ ► conjug 1 ◄ VT ◆ **~ qn** to mithridatize sb *(SPÉC)*, *to make sb immune to a poison by administering small doses in gradually increasing amounts* ◆ **mithridatisé** immunized

mitigation /mitigasjɔ̃/ NF *(Jur)* mitigation

mitigé, e /mitiʒe/ (ptp de **mitiger**) ADJ *[accueil, enthousiasme]* lukewarm, half-hearted ◆ **sentiments ~s** mixed feelings ◆ **joie ~e de regrets** joy mixed *ou* mingled with regret ◆ **ils ont eu un succès ~** they weren't particularly successful ◆ **les réactions ont été très ~es** we've had some very mixed reactions ◆ **le bilan est ~** things haven't turned out as well as they might have

mitiger † /mitiʒe/ ► conjug 3 ◄ VT to mitigate

mitigeur /mitiʒœʀ/ NM mixer tap *(Brit) ou* faucet *(US)* ◆ **~ thermostatique** temperature control tap *(Brit) ou* faucet *(US)*

mitochondrie /mitɔkɔ̃dʀi/ NF mitochondrion

mitonner /mitɔne/ ► conjug 1 ◄ VT 1 *(Culin) (à feu doux)* to simmer, to cook slowly; *(avec soin)* to prepare *ou* cook with loving care ◆ **elle (lui) mitonne des petits plats** she cooks (up) *ou* concocts tasty dishes (for him) 2 * *[+ affaire]* to cook up quietly*; *[+ personne]* to cosset VI to simmer, to cook slowly

mitose /mitoz/ NF mitosis ◆ **se reproduire par ~** to replicate ◆ **reproduction par ~** replication

mitoyen, -yenne /mitwajɛ̃, jɛn/ ADJ *[bâtiments, jardins]* adjoining ◆ **mur ~** party wall ◆ **cloison mitoyenne** partition wall ◆ **maisons mitoyennes** *(deux)* semi-detached houses *(Brit)*, duplex houses *(US)*; *(plus de deux)* terraced houses *(Brit)*, town houses *(US)* ◆ **notre jardin est ~ avec le leur** our garden adjoins theirs

mitoyenneté /mitwajɛnte/ NF *[de mur]* common ownership ◆ **la ~ des maisons** the (existence of a) party wall between the houses

mitraillade /mitʀɑjad/ NF 1 *(= coups de feu)* (volley of) shots; *(= échauffourée)* exchange of shots 2 ⇒ **mitraillage**

mitraillage /mitʀɑjaʒ/ NM machine-gunning ◆ **~ au sol** strafing

mitraille /mitʀɑj/ NF 1 († *Mil*) *(= projectiles)* grapeshot; *(= décharge)* volley of shots, hail of bullets ◆ **fuir sous la ~** to flee under a hail of bullets 2 (* *= petite monnaie)* loose *ou* small change

mitrailler /mitʀɑje/ ► conjug 1 ◄ VT 1 *(Mil)* to machine-gun ◆ **~ au sol** to strafe ◆ **~ qn de cailloux/grains de riz** to pelt sb with stones/grains of rice 2 (* *= photographier) [+ monument]* to take shot after shot of ◆ **les touristes mitraillaient la cathédrale** the tourists' cameras were clicking away madly at the cathedral ◆ **être mitraillé par les photographes** to be mobbed *ou* besieged by the photographers 3 ◆ **~ qn de questions** to bombard sb with questions, to fire questions at sb

mitraillette /mitʀɑjɛt/ NF submachine gun ◆ **tirer à la ~** to shoot *ou* fire with a submachine gun

mitrailleur /mitʀɑjœʀ/ NM *(au sol)* machine gunner; *(dans avion)* air gunner

mitrailleuse /mitʀɑjøz/ NF machine gun

mitral, e (mpl **-aux**) /mitʀal, o/ ADJ *(Anat)* mitral

mitre /mitʀ/ NF 1 *(Rel)* mitre ◆ **recevoir** *ou* **coiffer la ~** to be appointed bishop, to be mitred 2 *[de cheminée]* cowl

mitré, e /mitʀe/ ADJ mitred; → **abbé**

mitron /mitʀɔ̃/ NM 1 *(= boulanger)* baker's boy; *(= pâtissier)* pastrycook's boy 2 *[de cheminée]* chimney top

mi-vitesse /mivitɛs/ **à mi-vitesse** LOC ADV at half speed

mi-voix /mivwa/ **à mi-voix** LOC ADV *[parler]* in a low *ou* hushed voice; *[lire]* in a low voice; *[chantonner]* softly

mixage /miksaʒ/ NM 1 *(Ciné, Radio)* (sound) mixing 2 *(= mélange)* mix

mixer[1] /mikse/ ► conjug 1 ◄ VT *(Ciné, Radio)* to mix; *(Culin)* to blend

mixer[2], **mixeur** /miksœʀ/ NM *(Culin)* blender, liquidizer *(Brit)*

mixité /miksite/ NF *(de sexes, gén)* mixing of the sexes; *(Scol)* coeducation ◆ **il faut une plus grande ~ sociale/de l'habitat dans nos villes** we need a greater social mix/more variety of housing in our towns

mixte /mikst/ ADJ 1 *(= des deux sexes) [équipe]* mixed; *[classe, école, enseignement]* mixed, coeducational, coed*; *(= de races différentes) [couple, mariage]* mixed; → **double** 2 *(= d'éléments divers) [économie, train]* mixed *(épith)*; *[équipe]* combined *(épith)*; *[tribunal, commission]* joint; *[rôle]* dual *(épith)*; *(Chim, Géog) [roche, végétation]* mixed ◆ **outil à usage ~** dual-purpose tool ◆ **peau ~** combination skin ◆ **navire** *ou* **cargo ~** cargo-passenger ship *ou* vessel ◆ **cuisinière ~** combined gas and electric stove *ou* cooker *(Brit)* ◆ **l'opéra-bouffe est un genre ~** comic opera is a mixture of genres ◆ **mode de scrutin ~** mixed electoral *ou* voting system ◆ **le local est à usage ~** the premises can be used for either business or residential purposes ◆ **une solution ~** a hybrid solution

mixtion /mikstjɔ̃/ NF *(= action)* blending, compounding; *(= médicament)* mixture

mixture /mikstyʀ/ NF *(Chim, Pharm)* mixture; *(Culin)* mixture, concoction; *(péj)* concoction

MJC /ɛmʒise/ NF (abrév de **maison des jeunes et de la culture**) → **maison**

ml (abrév de **millilitre**) ml

MLF /ɛmɛlɛf/ NM (abrév de **Mouvement de libération de la femme**) Women's Liberation Movement, Women's Lib*

Mlle (abrév de **Mademoiselle**) ◆ **~ Martin** Miss Martin

Mlles (abrév de **Mesdemoiselles**) → **Mademoiselle**

mm (abrév de **millimètre**) mm

MM. (abrév de **Messieurs**) Messrs

Mme (abrév de **Madame**) Mrs ◆ **~ Martin** Mrs Martin

Mmes (abrév de **Mesdames**) → **Madame**

MMS /ɛmɛmɛs/ NM (abrév de **multimedia messaging service**) MMS

mn (abrév de **minute**) min

mnémotechnique /mnemotɛknik/ ADJ mnemonic NF mnemonics, mnemotechnics

Mo (abrév de **mégaoctet**) Mb, MB

mob * /mɔb/ NF abrév de **mobylette**

mobile /mɔbil/ ADJ 1 *[pièce, objet] (= qui bouge)* moving; *(= qui peut bouger)* movable; *[feuillets de cahier, calendrier]* loose; → **échelle, fête** 2 *[main-d'œuvre, population]* mobile 3 *[reflet]* changing; *[traits]* mobile, animated; *[regard, yeux]* mobile, darting *(épith)* 4 *[troupes]* mobile ◆ **boxeur très ~** boxer who is very quick on his feet, nimble-footed boxer ◆ **avec la voiture on est très ~** you can really get around *ou* about with a car, having a car makes you very mobile; → **garde**[1], **garde**[2] NM 1 *(= impulsion)* motive *(de* for); ◆ **quel était le ~ de son action ?** what was the motive for *ou* what prompted his action? ◆ **chercher le ~ du crime** to look for the motive for the crime 2 *(Art, Jeux)* mobile 3 *(Phys)* moving object *ou* body 4 ◆ **(téléphone) ~** mobile phone COMP **mobile(-)home** mobile home

mobilier, -ière /mɔbilje, jɛʀ/ ADJ *(Jur) [propriété, bien]* movable, personal; *[valeurs]* transferable ◆ **saisie/vente mobilière** seizure/sale of personal *ou* movable property ◆ **contribution** *ou* **cote mobilière** † property tax NM 1 *(= ameublement)* furniture ◆ **le ~ du salon** the lounge furniture ◆ **nous avons un ~ Louis XV** our furniture is Louis XV, our house is furnished in Louis XV (style) ◆ **il fait partie du ~** *(hum)* he's part of the furniture *(hum)* ◆ **~ de bureau** office furniture ◆ **~ urbain** street furniture ◆ **le Mobilier national** state-owned furniture *(used to furnish buildings of the state)* 2 *(Jur)* personal *ou* movable property

mobilisable /mɔbilizabl/ ADJ *[citoyen]* who can be called up *ou* mobilized; *[énergie, ressources]* that can be mobilized; *[capitaux]* mobilizable ◆ **il n'est pas ~** *(Mil)* he cannot be called up

mobilisateur, -trice /mɔbilizatœʀ, tʀis/ ADJ ◆ **c'est un slogan ~** it's a slogan which will stir people into action ◆ **c'est un thème très ~ chez les étudiants** it's an issue that students feel strongly about ◆ **il faut définir de nouveaux objectifs ~s** new objectives capable of attracting people's support must be defined

mobilisation /mɔbilizasjɔ̃/ NF 1 *(Mil) [de citoyens]* mobilization, calling up; *[de troupes, ressources, syndicats]* mobilization ◆ **~ générale/partielle** general/partial mobilization ◆ **il y a eu une forte ~ des électeurs** there was a big turnout at the polls ◆ **grâce à la forte ~ des écologistes au second tour** because so many Greens turned out for the second ballot ◆ **il appelle à la ~ de tous contre le racisme** he's calling on everybody to join forces and fight racism ◆ **les syndicats appellent à une ~ générale** the unions are calling for widespread industrial action 2 *(Fin) [de fonds]* mobilization of realty, raising ◆ **~ d'actif** conversion into movable property, mobilization of realty *(US)*

mobiliser /mɔbilize/ ▸ conjug 1 ◂ VT 1 *(= faire appel à) [+ citoyens]* to call up, to mobilize; *[+ troupes, ressources, adhérents, opinion publique]* to mobilize; *[+ fonds]* to raise, to mobilize ◆ **les (soldats) mobilisés** the mobilized troops ◆ **ce projet a mobilisé les énergies de 600 personnes** the project mobilized 600 people ◆ **cette nouvelle a mobilisé les esprits** the news has alerted people to the issue ◆ **tout le monde était mobilisé pour l'aider** everyone rallied round to help her

2 *(Méd = faire bouger) [+ articulation, muscle]* to mobilize

VPR **se mobiliser** *[personnes]* to join forces (and take action) *(contre* against); ◆ **il faut se ~ contre le chômage/pour la sauvegarde de nos droits** we must join forces and fight unemployment/to protect our rights ◆ **ils se sont mobilisés autour du Premier ministre** they rallied around the Prime Minister

mobilité /mɔbilite/ NF *(gén)* mobility ◆ **~ géographique/professionnelle/sociale** geographic/professional/social mobility ◆ **~ sociale ascendante** upward (social) mobility ◆ **"mobilité géographique totale"** *(sur CV)* "willing to relocate" ◆ **la ~ de son regard** his darting eyes ◆ **la voiture nous permet une plus grande ~** having the car means we can get around more easily *ou* makes us more mobile

mobinaute /mɔbinot/ NMF mobile Internet user

Möbius /møbjys/ NM *(Math)* ◆ **bande** *ou* **ruban de ~** Möbius strip *ou* band

Mobylette ® /mɔbilɛt/ NF moped

mocassin /mɔkasɛ̃/ NM *(gén)* moccasin, loafer; *(indien)* moccasin

moche* /mɔʃ/ ADJ 1 *(= laid)* ugly ◆ **~ comme un pou** as ugly as sin 2 *(= mauvais, méchant)* rotten*, nasty ◆ **tu es ~ avec elle** you're rotten* to her ◆ **c'est ~ ce qu'il a fait** that was a nasty thing he did ◆ **c'est ~ ce qui lui arrive** it's awful what's happening to him

mocheté* /mɔʃte/ NF 1 *(= laideur)* ugliness 2 *(= personne)* fright; *(= objet, bâtiment)* eyesore ◆ **c'est une vraie ~ !** she's as ugly as sin!

modal, e (mpl **-aux**) /mɔdal, o/ ADJ modal NM *(= verbe)* modal (verb)

modalité /mɔdalite/ NF 1 *(= forme)* form, mode; *(= méthode)* method ◆ **~ d'application de la loi** mode of enforcement of the law ◆ **~s de financement** methods of funding ◆ **~s de remboursement** terms of repayment ◆ **~s de paiement** methods *ou* modes of payment ◆ **~s de mise en œuvre** *(Jur)* details of implementation ◆ **~s de contrôle** *(Scol)* methods of assessment 2 *(Ling, Mus, Philos)* modality ◆ **adverbe de ~** modal adverb 3 *(Jur = condition)* clause

mode[1] /mɔd/ NF 1 *(= tendance)* fashion; *(péj)* fad*, craze ◆ **la ~ des années 60** Sixties' fashions ◆ **la ~ automne-hiver de cette année** this year's autumn and winter fashions ◆ **c'est la dernière ~** it's the very latest thing *ou* fashion ◆ **suivre la ~** to follow fashion, to keep up with the fashions ◆ **une de ces nouvelles ~s** *(péj)* one of these new fads* *ou* crazes ◆ **passer de ~** *[vêtement]* to go out of fashion; *[pratique]* to become outdated ◆ **c'est passé de ~** *[vêtement]* it's gone out of fashion; *[pratique]* it's outdated ◆ **c'est la ~ des talons hauts** high heels are in fashion *ou* are in* ◆ **marchande de ~s** †† milliner

◆ **à la mode** fashionable, in fashion ◆ **femme très à la ~** very fashionable woman ◆ **les jupes courtes sont très à la ~** short skirts are very much in fashion *ou* are really in* *ou* are all the rage* ◆ **être habillé très à la ~** *(gén)* to be very fashionably dressed; *[de jeunes]* to be very trendily* dressed ◆ **habillé à la dernière ~** dressed in the latest fashion *ou* style ◆ **mettre qch à la ~** to make sth fashionable, to bring sth into fashion ◆ **revenir à la ~** to come back into fashion *ou* vogue, to come back (in)*

2 *(= industrie)* **la ~** the fashion industry *ou* business ◆ **travailler dans la ~** to work *ou* be in the fashion world *ou* industry *ou* business ◆ **journal/présentation/rédactrice de ~** fashion magazine/show/editor; → **gravure**

3 † *(= mœurs)* custom; *(= goût, style)* style, fashion ◆ **selon la ~ de l'époque** according to the custom of the day ◆ **(habillé) à l'ancienne ~** (dressed) in the old style ◆ **cousin à la ~ de Bretagne** *(hum)* distant cousin, cousin six times removed *(hum)* ◆ **oncle** *ou* **neveu à la ~ de Bretagne** *(Jur, hum)* first cousin once removed ◆ **à la ~ du 18e siècle** in the style of *ou* after the fashion of the 18th century, in 18th century style; → **bœuf, tripe**

ADJ INV *[coiffure]* fashionable ◆ **tissu ~** fashion fabric ◆ **coloris ~** fashion *ou* fashionable colours ◆ **c'est très ~** it's very fashionable

mode[2] /mɔd/ NM 1 *(= méthode)* form, mode, method; *(= genre)* way ◆ **quel est le ~ d'action de ce médicament ?** how does this medicine work? ◆ **~ de gouvernement/de transport** mode of government/of transport ◆ **~ de scrutin** voting system ◆ **~ de pensée/de vie** way of thinking/of life ◆ **~ de paiement** method *ou* mode of payment ◆ **~ d'emploi** *(gén)* directions for use; *(= document)* instructions leaflet ◆ **~ de cuisson** *(gén)* cooking method; *(sur boîte, paquet)* cooking instructions ◆ **~ de calcul/fonctionnement** way of calculating/working ◆ **~ de production** mode *ou* method of production ◆ **~ de gestion** management method

2 *(Gram, Ling)* mood; *(Mus, Philos)* mode ◆ **au ~ subjonctif** in the subjunctive mood

3 *(Ordin)* mode ◆ **~ synchrone/asynchrone** synchronous/asynchronous mode ◆ **~ interactif/émulation/natif** interactive/emulation/native mode ◆ **fonctionner en ~ local** to operate in local mode ◆ **~ texte** text mode

modelage /mɔd(ə)laʒ/ NM *(= activité)* modelling; *(= ouvrage)* model

modelé /mɔd(ə)le/ NM *[de sculpture, corps]* contours; *(Géog)* relief

modèle /mɔdɛl/ NM 1 *(Comm)* model; *(Mode)* design, style ◆ **nous avons tous nos ~s en vitrine** our full range is *ou* all our models are in the window ◆ **petit/grand ~** small/large version *ou* model ◆ **voulez-vous le petit ou le grand ~ ?** *(boîte)* do you want the small or the big size (box)? ◆ **il a le ~ 5 portes** *(voiture)* he has the 5-door hatchback model *ou* version ◆ **Chanel présente ses ~s d'automne** Chanel presents its autumn models *ou* styles

2 *(à reproduire, à imiter)* pattern, model; *(Scol = corrigé)* fair copy ◆ **fabriquer qch d'après le ~** to make sth from the model *ou* pattern ◆ **faire qch sur le ~ de ...** to model sth on ..., to make sth on the pattern *ou* model of ... ◆ **~ de conjugaison/déclinaison** conjugation/declension pattern ◆ **son courage devrait nous servir de ~** his courage should be a model *ou* an example to us ◆ **c'est un ~ du genre** it's a model of the genre

3 *(= personne exemplaire)* model, example ◆ **~ de vertu** paragon of virtue ◆ **c'est le ~ du bon élève/ouvrier** he's a model pupil/workman, he's the epitome of the good pupil/workman ◆ **elle est un ~ de loyauté** she is a model of *ou* the very model of loyalty ◆ **il restera pour nous un ~** he will remain an example to us ◆ **prendre qn pour ~** to model *ou* pattern o.s. upon sb ◆ **il rejette le ~ paternel** he rejects everything his father stands for

4 *(Art)* model ◆ **dessiner/peindre d'après ~** to draw/paint from a model *ou* from life

ADJ *(= parfait) [conduite, ouvrier, mari, usine]* model *(épith)*; *(= de référence) [appartement]* show *(épith)* ◆ **petite fille ~** perfect little girl

COMP **modèle courant** standard *ou* production model

modèle déposé registered design

modèle économique *(Écon)* economic model; *(= paquet géant)* economy-size pack; *(= voiture)* economy model

modèle réduit small-scale model ◆ **~ réduit au 1/100** model on the scale (of) 1 to 100 ◆ **~ réduit d'avion, avion ~ réduit** model plane, scale model of a plane ◆ **monter des ~s réduits d'avions/de bateaux** to build model aircraft/ships

modèle de série ⇒ **modèle courant**

modeler /mɔd(ə)le/ ▸ conjug 5 ◂ VT 1 *(= façonner) [+ statue, poterie, glaise]* to model; *[+ corps]* to shape; *[+ chevelure]* to style; *[+ intelligence, caractère]* to shape, to mould *(Brit)*, to mold *(US)* ◆ **le relief a été modelé par la glaciation** the ground *ou* the terrain was moulded *ou* shaped by glaciation ◆ **cuisse bien modelée** shapely thigh; → **pâte** 2 *(= conformer)* **~ ses attitudes/réactions sur** to model one's attitudes/reactions on ◆ **se ~ sur qn/qch** to model *ou* pattern o.s. (up)on sb/sth

modeleur, -euse /mɔd(ə)lœʀ, øz/ NM,F 1 *(= sculpteur)* modeller; 2 *(= ouvrier)* pattern maker

modélisation /mɔdelizasjɔ̃/ NF modelling ◆ **~ par** *ou* **sur ordinateur** computer modelling

modéliser /mɔdelize/ ▸ conjug 1 ◂ VT to model

modélisme /mɔdelism/ NM model-making

modéliste /mɔdelist/ NMF 1 *[de mode]* (dress) designer 2 *[de maquettes]* model maker

modem /mɔdɛm/ NM (abrév de **modulateur-démodulateur**) modem ◆ **~ courte/longue distance** limited-distance/long-haul modem ◆ **transmettre des données par ~** to transmit data via *ou* by modem

modérateur, -trice /mɔdeʀatœʀ, tʀis/ ADJ *[rôle, effet, action, influence]* moderating *(épith)* ◆ **il est considéré comme un élément ~ de l'extrême-droite** he is said to have a moderating influence on the far right; → **ticket** NM *(Tech)* regulator; *(Nucl Phys)* moderator ◆ **jouer le rôle de ~** *(fig)* to have a moderating influence, to play a moderating role

modération /mɔdeʀasjɔ̃/ NF 1 *(= retenue)* moderation, restraint ◆ **avec ~** *[réagir]* with restraint; *[utiliser]* sparingly ◆ **à consommer avec ~** to be taken in moderation ◆ **faire preuve de ~ dans ses propos** to take a moderate line 2 *(= diminution) [d'inflation, impôt, vitesse]* reduction *(de* in); *(Jur) [de peine]* mitigation

modéré, e /mɔdeʀe/ (ptp de **modérer**) ADJ moderate ◆ **il a tenu des propos très ~s** he took a very moderate line ◆ **d'un optimisme ~** cautiously *ou* guardedly optimistic ◆ **prix ~s** moderate *ou* reasonable prices; → **habitation** NM,F ◆ **les ~s** *(Pol)* the moderates

modérément /mɔdeʀemɑ̃/ ADV *[boire, manger]* in moderation; *[augmenter, progresser]* slightly; *[satisfait, enthousiaste]* moderately ◆ **je n'apprécie que ~ ses plaisanteries** I don't find his jokes very funny ◆ **il se montre ~ optimiste** he's cautiously *ou* guardedly optimistic

modérer /mɔdeʀe/ ▸ conjug 6 ◂ VT *[+ colère, passion]* to restrain; *[+ ambitions, exigences]* to moderate; *[+ dépenses, désir, appétit]* to curb; *[+ vitesse]* to reduce; *[+ impact négatif]* to reduce, to limit ◆ **modérez vos propos !** tone down your remarks! *ou* language! VPR **se modérer** *(= s'apaiser)* to calm down, to control o.s.; *(= montrer de la mesure)* to restrain o.s.

moderne /mɔdɛʀn/ ADJ *(gén)* modern; *[cuisine, équipement]* up-to-date, modern; *(opposé à classique) [études]* modern ◆ **le héros ~** the modern-day hero ◆ **la femme ~** the woman of today, today's woman ◆ **à l'époque ~** in modern times; → **confort, lettre** NM 1 ◆ **le ~** *(= style)* modern style; *(= meubles)* modern furniture

♦ **aimer le** ~ to like modern furniture *ou* the contemporary style of furniture ♦ **meublé en** ~ with modern furniture, furnished in contemporary style 2 *(= personne)* modern painter *(ou novelist etc)*; → **ancien**

modernisateur, -trice /mɔdɛʀnizatœʀ, tʀis/ ADJ modernizing NM,F modernizer

modernisation /mɔdɛʀnizasjɔ̃/ NF modernization ♦ **des efforts de ~ ont été faits dans notre entreprise** steps have been taken towards modernizing our company

moderniser /mɔdɛʀnize/ ► conjug 1 ◄ VT to modernize, to bring up to date VPR **se moderniser** to modernize, to be modernized

modernisme /mɔdɛʀnism/ NM modernism

moderniste /mɔdɛʀnist/ NMF modernist ADJ modernistic

modernité /mɔdɛʀnite/ NF modernity ♦ **ce texte est d'une ~ surprenante** this text is amazingly modern ♦ **la ~ des pièces de Shakespeare** the modernity of *ou* the contemporary relevance of Shakespeare's plays

modern style /mɔdɛʀnstil/ ADJ INV, NM ≈ Art Nouveau

modeste /mɔdɛst/ ADJ 1 *(= humble) [personne, attitude, air]* modest ♦ **faire le ~** to put on *ou* make a show of modesty ♦ **tu fais le ~** you're just being modest 2 *(= simple) [vie, appartement, tenue, revenu]* modest ♦ **c'est un cadeau bien ~** it's a very modest gift, it's not much of a present ♦ **un train de vie ~** an unpretentious *ou* a modest way of life ♦ **je ne suis qu'un ~ employé** I'm just an ordinary employee ♦ **être d'un milieu** *ou* **d'origine ~** to have *ou* come from a modest *ou* humble background ♦ **il est ~ dans ses ambitions** his ambitions are modest, he has modest ambitions 3 *(† ou littér = pudique)* modest

modestement /mɔdɛstəmɑ̃/ ADV 1 *(= avec modestie)* modestly ♦ **j'ai très ~ contribué au débat** I made a very modest contribution to the discussion ♦ **il a commencé ~ sa carrière comme simple courtier** he began his career as a humble insurance broker ♦ **le chiffre d'affaires a progressé plus ~ cette année** increase in turnover has been more modest this year 2 *(= simplement)* **ils sont vêtus très ~** they are dressed simply ♦ **elle vit ~ dans une petite ville de province** she lives very simply in a small country town

modestie /mɔdɛsti/ NF *(= absence de vanité)* modesty; *(= réserve, effacement)* self-effacement; *(littér = pudeur)* modesty ♦ **en toute ~** with all due modesty ♦ **fausse ~** false modesty

modicité /mɔdisite/ NF *[de prix, salaire]* lowness; *[de retraite, bourse]* smallness ♦ **malgré la ~ des sommes en jeu** in spite of the small sums involved

modif * /mɔdif/ NF (abrév de **modification**)

modifiable /mɔdifjabl/ ADJ modifiable ♦ **les dates du billet ne sont pas ~s** the dates on the ticket cannot be changed ♦ **ce billet est-il ~ ?** can this ticket be changed?

modificateur, -trice /mɔdifikatœʀ, tʀis/ ADJ modifying, modificatory NM modifier

modificatif, -ive /mɔdifikatif, iv/ ADJ ♦ **décision modificative de budget** decision to alter a budget ♦ **permis (de construire) ~** planning permission *(for alterations)*

modification /mɔdifikasjɔ̃/ NF *[comportement]* change, alteration; *[de règles, statut]* change, alteration ♦ **apporter des ~s à** *[+ statut, règles]* to change, to alter; *[+ constitution]* to alter, to modify; *[+ texte]* to make alterations to

modifier /mɔdifje/ ► conjug 7 ◄ VT *[+ statut, règles]* to change, to alter; *[+ constitution, comportement]* to alter, to modify; *(Gram)* to modify, to alter VPR **se modifier** *[comportement, situation]* to change, to alter; *[habitudes]* to change

modique /mɔdik/ ADJ *[salaire, prix]* modest ♦ **pour la ~ somme de** for the modest sum of ♦ **il ne recevait qu'une pension ~** he received only a modest *ou* meagre pension

modiste /mɔdist/ NF milliner

modulable /mɔdylabl/ ADJ *[tarif, mesure, siège, espace, salle]* adjustable; *[horaire]* flexible; *[prêt]* adjustable, flexible *[technologie, réseau informatique]* scalable

modulaire /mɔdylɛʀ/ ADJ modular

modulateur, -trice /mɔdylatœʀ, tʀis/ ADJ modulating *(épith)* NM *(Élec, Radio)* modulator ♦ **~-dé~** modulator-demodulator

modulation /mɔdylasjɔ̃/ NF *(Ling, Mus, Radio)* modulation; *[de tarif, mesure]* adjustment ♦ **~ de fréquence** frequency modulation ♦ **poste à ~ de fréquence** VHF *ou* FM radio ♦ **écouter une émission sur** *ou* **en ~ de fréquence** to listen to a programme on VHF *ou* on FM

module /mɔdyl/ NM *(= étalon, Archit, Espace, Ordin)* module; *(Math, Phys)* modulus; *(Univ)* module, unit; *(= éléments d'un ensemble)* unit ♦ **~ lunaire** lunar module, mooncraft ♦ **acheter une cuisine par ~s** to buy a kitchen in separate units ♦ **~ d'extension** *(Ordin)* extension module

moduler /mɔdyle/ ► conjug 1 ◄ VT *[+ voix]* to modulate, to inflect; *[+ tarif, mesure]* to adjust; *(Mus, Radio)* to modulate ♦ **~ les peines en fonction des délits** to make the punishment fit the crime VI *(Mus)* to modulate

modus operandi /mɔdysɔpeʀɑ̃di/ NM modus operandi ♦ **trouver un ~ avec qn** to work out a modus operandi with sb

modus vivendi /mɔdysvivɛ̃di/ NM INV modus vivendi, working arrangement ♦ **trouver un ~ avec qn** to reach *ou* find a modus vivendi with sb

moelle /mwal/ NF *(Anat)* marrow, medulla *(SPÉC)*; *(Bot)* pith; *(fig)* pith, core ♦ **~ osseuse** bone marrow ♦ **~ épinière** spinal cord ♦ **~ (de bœuf)** *(Culin)* beef marrow ♦ **être transi jusqu'à la ~ (des os)** to be frozen to the marrow ♦ **pourri** * *ou* **corrompu jusqu'à la ~** rotten to the core, rotten through and through; → **os, substantifique**

moelleux, -euse /mwalø, øz/ ADJ *[tapis, lit]* soft; *[couleur, son]* mellow; *[viande]* tender; *[gâteau]* moist ♦ **vin ~** sweet wine NM 1 *[de tapis, lit, veste]* softness; *[de vin]* mellowness 2 *(= gâteau)* **~ au chocolat** rich chocolate cake

moellon /mwalɔ̃/ NM *(Constr)* rubble stone

mœurs /mœʀ(s)/ NFPL 1 *(= morale)* morals ♦ **il a des ~ particulières** *(euph)* he has certain tendencies *(euph)* ♦ **contraire aux bonnes ~** contrary to accepted standards of (good) behaviour ♦ **femme de ~ légères** *ou* **faciles** woman of easy virtue ♦ **femme de mauvaises ~** loose woman ♦ **affaire** *ou* **histoire de ~** *(Jur, Presse)* sex case ♦ **la police des ~, les Mœurs** * the vice squad; → **attentat, certificat, outrage**

2 *(= coutumes, habitudes) [de peuple, époque]* customs, habits, mores *(frm)*; *[d'abeilles, fourmis]* habits ♦ **c'est (entré) dans les ~** it's (become) normal practice, it's (become) a standard *ou* an everyday feature of life ♦ **les ~ politiques/littéraires de notre siècle** the political/literary practices *ou* usages of our century ♦ **avoir des ~ simples/aristocratiques** to lead a simple/an aristocratic life, to have a simple/an aristocratic life style; → **autre**

3 *(= manières)* manners, ways; *(Littérat)* manners ♦ **ils ont de drôles de ~** they have some peculiar ways *ou* manners ♦ **quelles ~ !, drôles de ~ !** what a way to behave! *ou* carry on!, what manners!; → **comédie, peinture**

Mogadiscio /mogadiʃjo/ N Mogadishu

mohair /mɔɛʀ/ NM mohair ♦ **laine ~** mohair

Mohammed /mɔamɛd/ NM Mohammed

Mohican /mɔikɑ̃/ NM Mohican

moi /mwa/ PRON PERS 1 *(objet direct ou indirect)* me ♦ **aide-~** help me ♦ **donne-~ ton livre** give me your book, give your book to me ♦ **donne-le-~** give it to me ♦ **si vous étiez ~, que feriez-vous ?** if you were me *ou* in my shoes what would you do? ♦ **il nous a regardés ma femme et ~** he looked at my wife and me ♦ **écoute-~ ça !** * just listen to that! ♦ **il n'obéit qu'à ~** he only obeys me, I'm the only one he obeys ♦ **~, elle me déteste** she hates me; → aussi **même, non**

2 *(sujet)* I *(emphatique)*, I myself *(emphatique)*, me ♦ **qui a fait cela ? – (c'est) ~/(ce n'est) pas ~** who did this? – I did/I didn't *ou* me*/not me* ♦ **~, le saluer ? jamais !** me, say hallo to him? never! ♦ **mon mari et ~ (nous) refusons** my husband and I refuse ♦ **~ malade, que ferez-vous ?** when I'm ill what will you do?, what will you do with me ill? ♦ **et ~ de rire de plus belle !** and so I (just) laughed all the more! ♦ **je ne l'ai pas vu, ~** I didn't see him myself, I myself didn't see him ♦ **~, je ne suis pas d'accord** (for my part) I don't agree

3 *(emphatique avec qui, que)* **c'est ~ qui vous le dis !** you can take it from me!, I'm telling you! ♦ **merci – c'est ~ (qui vous remercie)** thank you – thank YOU ♦ **~ qui vous parle, je l'ai vu** I saw him personally *ou* with my own eyes ♦ **c'est ~ qu'elle veut voir** it's me she wants to see ♦ **~ que le théâtre passionne, je n'ai jamais vu cette pièce** even I, with all my great love for the theatre, have never seen this play ♦ **et ~ qui avais espéré gagner !** and to think that I had hoped to win!

♦ **à moi!** *(= au secours)* help (me)!; *(dans un jeu)* my turn!; *(passe au rugby etc)* over here!

4 *(dans comparaisons)* I, me ♦ **il est plus grand que ~** he is taller than I (am) *ou* than me ♦ **il mange plus/moins que ~** he eats more/less than I (do) *ou* than me ♦ **fais comme ~** do as I do, do like me*, do the same as me ♦ **il l'aime plus que ~** *(plus qu'il ne m'aime)* he loves her more than (he loves) me; *(plus que je ne l'aime)* he loves her more than I do

NM ♦ **le ~** the self, the ego ♦ **notre vrai ~** our true self ♦ **son ~ profond** his (*ou* her *ou* one's) inner self

moignon /mwaɲɔ̃/ NM stump ♦ **il n'avait plus qu'un ~ de bras** he had just the *ou* a stump of an arm left

moi-même /mwamɛm/ PRON → **autre, même**

moindre /mwɛ̃dʀ/ ADJ 1 *(compar) (= moins grand)* less, lesser; *(= inférieur)* lower, poorer ♦ **les dégâts sont bien** *ou* **beaucoup ~s** the damage is much less ♦ **à ~ coût** at a lower cost ♦ **de ~ qualité, de qualité ~** of lower *ou* poorer quality ♦ **enfant de ~ intelligence** child of lower intelligence ♦ **c'est un inconvénient ~** it's less of a drawback ♦ **c'est un ~ mal** it's the lesser evil

2 *(superl)* **le ~, la ~, les ~s** the slightest; *(de deux)* the lesser ♦ **le ~ bruit/doute/risque** the slightest noise/doubt/risk ♦ **la ~ chance/idée** the slightest *ou* remotest chance/idea ♦ **jusqu'au ~ détail** down to the smallest detail ♦ **au ~ signe de fatigue, il faut arrêter** at the least sign of tiredness, you must stop ♦ **sans se faire le ~ souci** without worrying in the slightest ♦ **il n'a pas fait le ~ commentaire** he didn't make a single comment ♦ **la loi du ~ effort** the line of least resistance *ou* effort ♦ **de deux maux il faut choisir le ~** you must choose the lesser of two evils ♦ **certains spécialistes et non des ~s disent que ...** some specialists and important ones at that say that ... ♦ **c'est un de nos problèmes et non le ~** *ou* **des ~s** it is by no means the least of our problems

◆ **le/la moindre de** ◆ **c'est la ~ de mes difficultés** that's the least of my difficulties ◆ **merci – c'est la ~ des choses** *ou (Helv)* **la ~ !** thank you – it's a pleasure! *ou* you're welcome! *ou* not at all! ◆ **remerciez-le de m'avoir aidé – c'était la ~ des choses** *ou (Helv)* **la ~** thank him for helping me – it was the least he could do ◆ **la ~ des politesses veut que ...** common politeness *ou* courtesy demands that ... ◆ **ce n'est pas la ~ de ses qualités** it's not the least of his qualities

moindrement /mwɛ̃dʀəmɑ̃/ **ADV** *(littér : avec nég)* ◆ **il n'était pas le ~ surpris** he was not in the least surprised, he was not surprised in the slightest ◆ **sans l'avoir le ~ voulu** without having in any way wanted this

moine /mwan/ **NM** 1 *(Rel)* monk, friar ◆ **~ bouddhiste** Buddhist monk; → **habit** 2 *(= phoque)* monk seal; *(= macareux)* puffin 3 *(Hist = chauffe-lit)* bedwarmer

moineau **(pl moineaux)** /mwano/ **NM** *(= oiseau)* sparrow ◆ **~ domestique** house sparrow ◆ **sale** *ou* **vilain ~** († , *péj*) dirty dog *(péj)* ◆ **manger comme un ~, avoir un appétit de ~** to eat like a bird

moinillon /mwanijɔ̃/ **NM** young monk; *(hum)* little monk *(hum)*

moins /mwɛ̃/

1 ADVERBE (EMPLOI COMPARATIF)
2 ADVERBE (EMPLOI SUPERLATIF)
3 PRÉPOSITION
4 NOM MASCULIN
5 COMPOSÉS

1 - ADVERBE (EMPLOI COMPARATIF)

1 *(gén)*

◆ **moins... (que)** less ... (than)
(+ adjectif) ◆ **rien n'est ~ sûr, (il n'y a) rien de ~ sûr** nothing is less certain ◆ **non ~ célèbre/idiot** no less famous/silly

> Notez que l'anglais a souvent recours à d'autres formes, en particulier **not as** ou **not so ... as**.

◆ **il est ~ intelligent qu'elle** he's not as *ou* so intelligent as her *ou* as she is, he's less intelligent than her *ou* than she is ◆ **c'est ~ grand que je ne croyais** it's not as big as I thought (it was) ◆ **il ressemble à son père, en ~ grand** he looks like his father only he's not as tall, he's a smaller version of his father ◆ **c'est le même genre de livre, en ~ bien** it's the same kind of book, only *ou* but not as *ou* so good ◆ **il est non ~ évident que ...** it is equally *ou* just as clear that ... ◆ **c'est deux fois ~ grand/large** it's half as big/wide
(+ adverbe) ◆ **beaucoup/un peu ~** much/a little less ◆ **tellement ~** so much less ◆ **encore ~** even less ◆ **trois fois ~** three times less
(+ verbe) ◆ **exiger/donner ~** to demand/give less ◆ **je gagne (un peu) ~ que lui** I earn (a little) less than him *ou* than he does ◆ **il travaille ~ que vous** he works less than you (do) ◆ **il a fait ~ froid qu'hier** it's been less cold than yesterday ◆ **nous sortons ~ (souvent)** we don't go out so often *ou* so much, we go out less often ◆ **il tousse ~ qu'avant** he coughs less than he used to

> Notez que là encore l'anglais a souvent recours à d'autres formes que **less**, en particulier **not as** ou **not so ... as**.

◆ **j'aime ~ la campagne en hiver (qu'en été)** I don't like the countryside as *ou* so much in winter (as in summer), I like the countryside less in winter (than insummer) ◆ **cela coûtait deux/trois fois ~** it was half/one-third the price

2 locutions

◆ **moins de (... que)** *(avec nom non comptable)* less (... than), not so much (... as); *(avec nom comptable)* fewer (... than), not so many (... as) ◆ **je mange ~ de pain (qu'avant)** I eat less bread (than I used to), I don't eat so much bread (as I used to) ◆ **j'ai perdu ~ d'argent/de poids que je ne croyais** I've lost less money/weight that I thought I had, I haven't lost as much money/weight as I thought I had ◆ **mange ~ de bonbons** eat fewer sweets, don't eat so many sweets ◆ **il y aura ~ de monde demain** there'll be fewer people tomorrow, there won't be so many people tomorrow ◆ **il a eu ~ de mal que nous à trouver une place** he had less trouble than we did *ou* than us finding a seat ◆ **ils publient ~ d'essais que de romans** they publish fewer essays than novels

◆ **moins de** + *nombre* ◆ **les ~ de 25 ans** the under-25s ◆ **nous l'avons fait en ~ de cinq minutes** we did it in less than *ou* in under five minutes ◆ **il y a ~ de deux ans qu'il vit ici** he's been living here (for) less than two years ◆ **il devrait y avoir ~ de 100 personnes** there should be under 100 people *ou* fewer *ou* less than 100 people ◆ **il y avait beaucoup ~ de 100 personnes** there were well under 100 people ◆ **il est ~ de minuit** it is not yet midnight ◆ **il était un peu ~ de 6 heures** it was a little before 6 o'clock ◆ **vous ne pouvez pas lui donner ~ de 15 €** you can't give him less than €15 ◆ **vous ne trouverez rien à ~ de 15 €** you won't find anything under €15 *ou* for less than €15 ◆ **la frontière est à ~ de 3 km** the border is less than 3 km away

◆ **en moins de rien, en moins de deux*** in next to no time

◆ **moins ..., moins ...** ◆ **~ je mange, ~ j'ai d'appétit** the less I eat, the less hungry I feel ◆ **~ il y a de clients, ~ j'ai de travail** the fewer customers I have, the less work I have to do

◆ **moins ..., plus .../mieux ...** ◆ **~ je fume, plus je mange/mieux je me porte** the less I smoke, the more I eat/the better I feel ◆ **~ j'ai de coups de fil, mieux je travaille** the fewer phone calls I get, the better I work

◆ **moins que rien** ◆ **cela m'a coûté ~ que rien** it cost me next to nothing ◆ **je l'ai eu pour ~ que rien** I got it for next to nothing ◆ **ne me remerciez pas, c'est ~ que rien** don't thank me, it's nothing at all; → composés

◆ **à moins** ◆ **vous ne l'obtiendrez pas à ~** you won't get it for less ◆ **il est ravi/fatigué – on le serait à ~** he's delighted/tired – as well he might (be) *ou* that's hardly surprising

◆ **à moins de** + *infinitif* unless ◆ **à ~ de faire une bêtise, il devrait gagner** unless he does something silly he should win ◆ **vous ne trouverez plus de billet, à ~ de payer 10 fois le prix** you won't get a ticket unless you're prepared to pay 10 times the price MAIS **à ~ d'un accident/d'un désastre, ça devrait marcher** barring accidents/disasters, it should work ◆ **à ~ d'une blessure, il jouera dans le prochain match** barring injury, he'll play in the next match

◆ **à moins que** + *subjonctif* unless ◆ **à ~ qu'il ne vienne** unless he comes ◆ **l'entreprise devra fermer, à ~ qu'on ne trouve un repreneur** the company will have to close unless a buyer is found

◆ **de moins** ◆ **il gagne 100 € de ~ qu'elle** he earns €100 less than she does ◆ **vous avez cinq ans de ~ qu'elle** you're five years younger than her *ou* than she is ◆ **ah, si j'avais 20 ans de ~ ...** ah, if only I were 20 years younger ... ◆ **avec 5 kilos de ~, je me sentirais mieux** I'd feel better if I was 5 kilos lighter

◆ **de moins de** ◆ **les enfants de ~ de quatre ans voyagent gratuitement** children under four (years of age) travel free ◆ **les entreprises de ~ de 50 salariés** companies with less than 50 employees

◆ **de moins en moins** less and less ◆ **c'est de ~ en ~ utile** it's less and less useful ◆ **il entend de ~ en ~ bien** his hearing is getting worse and worse ◆ **il a de ~ en ~ de clients** he has fewer and fewer clients ◆ **j'ai de ~ en ~ de temps libre** I've got less and less free time ◆ **je supporte de ~ en ~ ces conditions de travail** I find these working conditions harder and harder to put up with

◆ **en moins** ◆ **il y a trois verres en ~** there are three glasses missing ◆ **ça me fera du travail en ~ !** that'll be less work for me! ◆ **c'est la même voiture, le toit ouvrant en ~** it's the same car minus the sunroof *ou* except it hasn't got a sunroof

◆ **pas moins (de/que)** ◆ **un crapaud ne mange pas ~ de 400 insectes chaque jour** a toad eats no less than 400 insects a day ◆ **pas ~ de 40 km les sépare de la ville la plus proche** the nearest town is no less than 40 km away ◆ **gravement malade, il n'en continue pas ~ d'écrire** despite being seriously ill, he still continues to write ◆ **la situation n'en comporte pas ~ de nombreux risques** the situation is still very risky for all that ◆ **je suis tolérante mais je n'en suis pas ~ choquée par leur attitude** I'm tolerant but that doesn't mean I'm not shocked by their behaviour ◆ **le résultat n'en demeure pas ~ surprenant** the result is none the less surprising for that ◆ **il n'en reste pas ~ que ...** the fact remains that ..., even so ... ◆ **il n'en est pas ~ vrai que ...** it is no less true that ...; → **penser**

2 - ADVERBE (EMPLOI SUPERLATIF)

◆ **le** *ou* **la** *ou* **les moins** + *adjectif ou adverbe (de plusieurs)* the least; *(de deux)* the less ◆ **c'est le ~ doué de mes élèves** he's the least gifted of my pupils ◆ **c'est le ~ doué des deux** he's the less gifted of the two ◆ **ce sont les fleurs les ~ chères** they are the least expensive *ou* the cheapest flowers

◆ *verbe* + **le moins** (the) least ◆ **c'est celle que j'aime le ~** it's the one I like (the) least ◆ **l'émission que je regarde le ~ (souvent)** the programme I watch (the) least often ◆ **de nous tous, c'est lui qui a bu le ~ (d'alcool)** of all of us, he was the one who drank the least (alcohol) ◆ **c'est bien le ~ qu'on puisse faire** it's the least one can do ◆ **ce qui me dérangerait le ~** what would be least inconvenient for me MAIS **c'est le ~ qu'on puisse dire!** that's putting it mildly! ◆ **ce qui lui déplairait le ~** what he would prefer

◆ **le moins (...) possible** ◆ **je lui parle le ~ possible** I talk to him as little as possible ◆ **je prends le métro/des médicaments le ~ souvent possible** I take the underground/medicine as little as possible ◆ **afin de payer le ~ d'impôts possible** in order to pay as little tax as possible ◆ **j'y resterai le ~ longtemps** *ou* **de temps possible** I won't stay there any longer than I have to ◆ **pour que les choses se passent le ~ mal possible** so that things go as smoothly as possible

3 - PRÉPOSITION

1 soustraction **6 ~ 2 font 4** 6 minus 2 equals 4, 2 from 6 makes 4 ◆ **j'ai retrouvé mon sac, ~ le portefeuille** I found my bag, minus the wallet ◆ **nous avons roulé sept heures, ~ l'arrêt pour déjeuner** we drove for seven hours not counting the stop for lunch

2 heure to ◆ **il est 4 heures ~ 5 (minutes)** it's 5 (minutes) to 4 ◆ **nous avons le temps, il n'est que ~ 10*** we've got plenty of time, it's only 10 to* ◆ **il s'en est tiré, mais il était ~ cinq*** *ou* **~ une*** *(fig)* he got out of it but it was a close shave* *ou* a near thing*

3 nombre négatif, température below ◆ **il fait ~ 5°** it's 5° below freezing *ou* minus 5° ◆ **dix puissance ~ sept** *(Math)* ten to the power (of) minus seven

4 - NOM MASCULIN

1 Math **(signe)** ~ minus sign

2 locutions

◆ **à tout le moins** *(frm)* to say the least, at the very least

◆ **au moins** at least ◆ **elle a payé cette robe au ~ 500 €** she paid at least €500 for that dress ◆ **600 au ~** at least 600, 600 at the least ◆ **la moitié au ~** at least half ◆ **la moitié au ~ du personnel/des candidats** at least half (of) the staff/the candidates ◆ **ça fait au ~ dix jours qu'il est parti** it's at least ten days since he left ◆ **vous en avez au ~ entendu parler** you must at least have heard about it ◆ **tout au ~** at (the very) least

◆ **du moins** *(restriction)* at least ◆ **il ne pleuvra pas, du ~ c'est ce qu'annonce la radio** it's not going to rain, at least that's what it says on the radio ◆ **laissez-le sortir, du ~ s'il** *ou* **si du ~ il ne fait pas froid** let him go out, as long as it isn't cold MAIS **j'arriverai vers 4 heures, du ~ si l'avion n'a pas de retard** I'll be there around 4 o'clock – if the plane's on time, that is

◆ **pour le moins** *(avec adjectif ou verbe)* to say the least *(évaluation d'une quantité)* at the very least ◆ **sa décision est pour le ~ bizarre** his decision is odd to say the least ◆ **ils étaient 2 000, pour le ~** there were 2,000 of them at the very least

5 - COMPOSÉS

moins que rien * NMF *(péj = minable)* complete loser*, schlemiel* *(US)* ◆ **on les traite comme des ~ que rien** they're treated like scum

moins-perçu (pl **moins-perçus**) /mwɛ̃pɛʀsy/ NM amount not drawn, short payment

moins-value (pl **moins-values**) /mwɛ̃valy/ NF *(Comm)* depreciation, capital loss ◆ **~ de recettes fiscales** taxation shortfall

moirage /mwaʀaʒ/ NM *(= procédé)* watering; *(= reflet)* watered effect

moire /mwaʀ/ NF *(= tissu)* moiré; *(= soie)* watered *ou* moiré silk; *(= procédé)* watering

moiré, e /mwaʀe/ (ptp de **moirer**) ADJ *[papier peint, tissu]* moiré; *[soie]* watered, moiré; *[papier]* marbled; *(fig)* shimmering NM *(Tech)* moiré, water; *(littér) [de lac]* shimmering ripples

moirer /mwaʀe/ ▸ conjug 1 ◂ VT *(Tech)* to water ◆ **la lune moirait l'étang de reflets argentés** *(littér)* the moon cast a shimmering silvery light over the pool

moirure /mwaʀyʀ/ NF *(Tech)* moiré; *(littér)* shimmering ripples

mois /mwa/ NM 1 *(= période)* month ◆ **le ~ de Marie** the month of Mary ◆ **manger les huîtres les ~ en R** to eat oysters when there is an R in the month ◆ **au ~ de janvier** in (the month of) January ◆ **dans un ~** in a month('s time) ◆ **le 10 de ce ~** the 10th of this month ◆ **au ~** *[payer, louer]* monthly, by the month ◆ **50 € par ~** €50 a *ou* per month ◆ **billet à 3 ~** *(Comm)* bill at 3 months ◆ **un bébé de 6 ~** a 6-month-old baby ◆ **tous les 4 ~** every 4 months ◆ **devoir 3 ~ de loyer** to owe 3 months' rent; → **tout** 2 *(= salaire)* monthly pay, monthly salary ◆ **toucher son ~** * to draw one's pay *ou* salary for the month *ou* one's month's pay *ou* salary ◆ **~ double** extra month's pay *(as end-of-year bonus)* ◆ **treizième/quatorzième ~** one month's/two months' extra pay; → **fin²**

Moïse /mɔiz/ NM *(Bible)* Moses

moisi, e /mwazi/ (ptp de **moisir**) ADJ mouldy, moldy *(US)*, mildewed NM mould *(NonC)*, mold *(US)* *(NonC)*, mildew *(NonC)* ◆ **odeur de ~** musty *ou* fusty smell ◆ **goût de ~** musty taste ◆ **ça sent le ~** it smells musty *ou* fusty

moisir /mwaziʀ/ ▸ conjug 2 ◂ VT to make mouldy *ou* moldy *(US)* VI 1 *(= se gâter)* to go mouldy *ou* moldy *(US)*, to mould, to mold *(US)* 2 *[personne] (dans une prison, une entreprise)* to rot; *(= attendre)* to hang around ◆ **on ne va pas ~ ici jusqu'à la nuit !** * we're not going to hang around here till night-time! * ◆ **il ne faut pas laisser ~ votre argent** you shouldn't let your money gather dust

moisissure /mwazisyʀ/ NF *(gén)* mould *(NonC)*, mold *(US)* *(NonC)*; *(par l'humidité)* mould *(NonC)*, mold *(US)* *(NonC)*, mildew *(NonC)* ◆ **enlever les ~s sur un fromage** to scrape the mould off a piece of cheese

moisson /mwasɔ̃/ NF 1 *(Agr)* *(= saison, travail)* harvest; *(= récolte)* harvest ◆ **à l'époque de la ~** at harvest time ◆ **rentrer la ~** to bring in the harvest ◆ **faire la ~** to harvest, to reap 2 *[de données]* wealth, crop ◆ **faire une abondante ~ de renseignements/souvenirs** to gather *ou* amass a wealth of information/memories ◆ **les Français ont récolté une belle ~ de médailles** the French have picked up a good crop of medals

moissonner /mwasɔne/ ▸ conjug 1 ◂ VT *[+ céréale]* to harvest, to reap; *[+ champ]* to reap; *[+ récompenses]* to carry off, to reap; *[+ renseignements]* to gather, to garner ◆ **il a commencé à ~** he's started harvesting *ou* the harvest ◆ **notre pays moissonne les médailles** our country is winning one medal after the other

moissonneur, -euse /mwasɔnœʀ, øz/ NM,F harvester, reaper † *(littér)* NF **moissonneuse** *(= machine)* harvester

moissonneuse-batteuse(-lieuse) (pl **moissonneuses-batteuses(-lieuses)**) /mwasɔnøzbatøz(ljøz)/ NF combine harvester

moissonneuse-lieuse (pl **moissonneuses-lieuses**) /mwasɔnøzljøz/ NF self-binder

moite /mwat/ ADJ *[peau, mains]* sweaty, clammy; *[atmosphère]* sticky, muggy; *[chaleur]* sticky ◆ **il a le front ~ de sueur** his forehead is damp with sweat

moiteur /mwatœʀ/ NF *[de peau, mains]* sweatiness; *[d'atmosphère]* stickiness, mugginess

moitié /mwatje/ NF 1 *(= partie)* half ◆ **partager qch en deux ~s** to halve sth, to divide sth in half *ou* into (two) halves ◆ **quelle est la ~ de 40 ?** what is half of 40? ◆ **donne-m'en la ~** give me half (of it) ◆ **faire la ~ du chemin avec qn** to go halfway *ou* half of the way with sb ◆ **je veux bien faire la ~ du chemin** *(dans une négociation)* I'm prepared to meet you halfway ◆ **la ~ des habitants a été sauvée** *ou* **ont été sauvés** half (of) the inhabitants were rescued ◆ **la ~ du temps** half the time ◆ **il en faut ~ plus/moins** you need half as much again/half (of) that ◆ **~ anglais, ~ français** half-English, half-French

2 *(= milieu)* halfway mark, half ◆ **parvenu à la ~ du trajet** having completed half the journey, having reached halfway *ou* the halfway mark ◆ **parvenu à la ~ de sa vie, il ...** halfway through his life, he ..., when he reached the middle of his life, he ... ◆ **arrivé à la ~ du travail** having done half the work *ou* got halfway through the work

3 *(hum = époux, épouse)* **ma ~** my better half* *(hum)* ◆ **ma tendre ~** my ever-loving wife *(ou* husband) *(hum)*

4 *(locutions)*

◆ **moitié moitié** ◆ **on a partagé le pain ~ ~** we halved *ou* shared the bread between us ◆ **ils ont partagé** *ou* **fait ~ ~** they went halves *ou* fifty-fifty* *ou* Dutch* ◆ **ça a marché ? – ~ ~** * how did it go? – so-so*

◆ **à moitié** half ◆ **il a fait le travail à ~** he has (only) half done the work ◆ **il a mis la table à ~** he's half set the table ◆ **il ne fait jamais rien à ~** he never does things by halves ◆ **à ~ plein/mûr** half-full/-ripe ◆ **à ~ chemin** (at) halfway, at the halfway mark ◆ **à ~ prix** (at) half-price

◆ **de moitié** by half ◆ **réduire de ~** *[+ trajet, production, coût]* to cut *ou* reduce by half, to halve ◆ **plus grand de ~** half as big again, bigger by half ◆ **être/se mettre de ~ dans une entreprise** to have half shares/go halves in a business

◆ **par moitié** in two, in half ◆ **diviser qch par ~** to divide sth in two *ou* in half

◆ **pour moitié** ◆ **il est pour ~ dans cette faillite** he is half responsible *ou* half to blame for this bankruptcy

moka /mɔka/ NM *(= gâteau à la crème)* cream cake, cream gâteau; *(= gâteau au café)* mocha *ou* coffee cake, mocha *ou* coffee gâteau; *(= café)* mocha coffee

mol /mɔl/ ADJ M → **mou¹**

molaire¹ /mɔlɛʀ/ NF *(= dent)* molar

molaire² /mɔlɛʀ/ ADJ *(Chim)* molar

molasse /mɔlas/ NF ⇒ **mollasse²**

moldave /mɔldav/ ADJ Moldavian NMF **Moldave** Moldavian

Moldavie /mɔldavi/ NF Moldavia

mole /mɔl/ NF *(Chim)* mole, mol

môle¹ /mol/ NM *(= digue)* breakwater, mole; *(= quai)* pier, jetty

môle² /mol/ NF *(= poisson)* sunfish

moléculaire /mɔlekylɛʀ/ ADJ molecular

molécule /mɔlekyl/ NF molecule

moleskine /mɔlɛskin/ NF imitation leather, leatherette ®

molester /mɔlɛste/ ▸ conjug 1 ◂ VT to manhandle, to rough up ◆ **molesté par la foule** mauled by the crowd

moleté, e /mɔlte/ ADJ *[roue, vis]* knurled

molette /mɔlɛt/ NF 1 *(Tech)* toothed wheel; *(pour couper)* cutting wheel 2 *[de briquet]* striker wheel; *[de clé]* adjusting screw; *[d'éperon]* rowel ◆ **~ de mise au point** *[de jumelles]* focussing wheel; → **clé**

moliéresque /mɔljeʀɛsk/ ADJ in the style of Molière

mollah /mɔ(l)la/ NM mulla(h)

mollard‡ /mɔlaʀ/ NM *(= crachat)* gob of spit‡

mollasse¹ * /mɔlas/ *(péj)* ADJ *(= léthargique)* sluggish, lethargic; *(= flasque)* flabby, flaccid ◆ **une grande fille ~** a great lump* of a girl

mollasse² /mɔlas/ NF *(Géol)* molasse

mollasserie /mɔlasʀi/ NF sluggishness, lethargy

mollasson, -onne * /mɔlasɔ̃, ɔn/ *(péj)* ADJ sluggish, lethargic NM,F great lump*

molle /mɔl/ ADJ F → **mou¹**

mollement /mɔlmɑ̃/ ADV *(= doucement)* *[tomber]* softly; *[couler]* gently, sluggishly; *(= paresseusement)* *[travailler]* half-heartedly, unenthusiastically; *(= faiblement)* *[réagir, protester]* feebly, weakly ◆ **il s'est défendu assez ~** he didn't defend himself very vigorously ◆ **la journée avait commencé ~** the day had got off to a sluggish start ◆ **les jours s'écoulaient ~** one day turned into the next, the days drifted by

mollesse /mɔlɛs/ NF 1 *(au toucher)* *[de substance, oreiller]* softness; *[de poignée de main]* limpness, flabbiness

2 *(à la vue)* *[de contours, lignes]* softness; *[de relief]* softness, gentleness; *[de traits du visage]* flabbi-

ness, sagginess; *(Peinture) [de dessin, traits]* lifelessness, weakness

3 *(= manque d'énergie) [de geste]* lifelessness, feebleness; *[de protestations, opposition]* weakness, feebleness; *[de style]* vagueness, woolliness *(Brit)*; *(Mus) [d'exécution]* lifelessness, dullness; *[de personne] (= indolence)* sluggishness, lethargy; *(= manque d'autorité)* spinelessness; *(= grande indulgence)* laxness; *[marché]* sluggishness ◆ **la ~ des réformes** the fact that the reforms are not farreaching enough ◆ **la ~ de la police face aux manifestants** the feebleness of the police's response to the demonstrators ◆ **accusé de ~ dans la répression des attentats** accused of lacking determination in the fight against terrorism

mollet¹, -ette /mɔlɛ, ɛt/ ADJ soft; → **œuf**

mollet² /mɔlɛ/ NM *(Anat)* calf ◆ **~s de coq** *(fig)* wiry legs

molletière /mɔltjɛʀ/ ADJ, NF ◆ **(bande) ~** puttee

molleton /mɔltɔ̃/ NM *(= tissu)* cotton fleece, swansdown; *(pour table)* felting

molletonner /mɔltɔne/ ▸ conjug 1 ◂ VT to put a warm lining in ◆ **anorak molletonné** quilted anorak, anorak with a warm lining

mollir /mɔliʀ/ ▸ conjug 2 ◂ VI 1 *(= fléchir) [sol]* to give (way), to yield; *[ennemi]* to yield, to give way, to give ground; *[père, créancier]* to come round, to relent; *[courage, personne]* to flag ◆ **sa plaidoirie a fait ~ les jurés** his speech for the defence softened the jury's attitude *ou* made the jury relent ◆ **ce n'est pas le moment de ~ !*** you (*ou* we *etc*) mustn't slacken now! ◆ **il a senti ses jambes/genoux ~ sous lui** he felt his legs/knees give way beneath him 2 *[substance]* to soften, to go soft 3 *[vent]* to abate, to die down

mollo‡ /mɔlo/ ADV ◆ **(vas-y) ~!** take it easy!*, (go) easy!*, easy does it!*

mollusque /mɔlysk/ NM *(= animal)* mollusc, mollusk *(US)*; *(* péj = personne)* great lump*

molosse /mɔlɔs/ NM *(littér, hum)* big (ferocious) dog, huge hound

Molotov /mɔlɔtɔf/ NM → **cocktail**

Moluques /mɔlyk/ NFPL ◆ **les ~** the Moluccas, the Molucca Islands

molybdène /mɔlibdɛn/ NM molybdenum

môme /mom/ NMF *(* = enfant)* kid*; *(péj)* brat*; *(‡ = fille)* bird‡ *(Brit)*, chick* *(US)* ◆ **belle ~**‡ nice-looking girl, cute chick* *(US)* ◆ **quels sales ~s !**‡ horrible little brats!*

moment /mɔmɑ̃/ NM 1 *(= court instant)* moment ◆ **il réfléchit pendant un ~** he thought for a moment ◆ **c'est l'affaire d'un ~** it won't take a minute *ou* moment, it'll only take a minute ◆ **je n'en ai que pour un petit ~** it won't take me long, it'll only take me a moment ◆ **ça ne dure qu'un ~** it doesn't last long, it (only) lasts a minute ◆ **un ~ de silence** a moment of silence, a moment's silence ◆ **j'ai eu un ~ de panique** I had a moment's panic, for a moment I panicked ◆ **dans un ~ de colère** in a moment of anger, in a momentary fit of anger ◆ **dans un ~** in a little while, in a moment ◆ **un ~, il arrive !** just a moment *ou* a minute *ou* a mo'* *(Brit)*, he's coming!

2 *(= période)* time ◆ **à quel ~ est-ce arrivé ?** at what point in time *ou* when exactly did this occur? ◆ **connaître/passer de bons ~s** to have/spend (some) happy times ◆ **les ~s que nous avons passés ensemble** the times we spent together ◆ **il a passé un mauvais** *ou* **sale ~*** he went through *ou* had a difficult time, he had a rough time ◆ **je n'ai pas un ~ à moi** I haven't got a moment to myself ◆ **le ~ présent** the present time ◆ **à ses ~s perdus** in his spare time ◆ **les grands ~s de l'histoire** the great moments of history ◆ **il a ses bons et ses mauvais ~s** he has his good times and his bad (times) ◆ **il est dans un de ses mauvais ~s** it's one of his off *ou* bad spells, he's having one of his off *ou* bad spells ◆ **la célébrité/le succès du ~** the celebrity/the success of the moment *ou* day ◆ **n'attends pas le dernier ~ pour réviser ta leçon** don't wait till the last minute to do your revision

3 *(= long instant)* while ◆ **je ne l'ai pas vu depuis un (bon) ~** I haven't seen him for a (good) while *ou* for quite a time *ou* while ◆ **j'en ai pour un petit ~** it'll take me some time *ou* quite a while

4 *(= occasion)* **il faut profiter du ~** you must take advantage of *ou* seize the opportunity ◆ **ce n'est pas le ~** this is not the right moment ◆ **tu arrives au bon ~** you've come just at the right time ◆ **c'était le ~ de réagir** it was time to react ◆ **le ~ psychologique** the psychological moment; → **jamais**

5 *(Tech)* moment; *(Phys)* momentum

6 *(locutions)*

◆ **le moment venu** ◆ **il se prépare afin de savoir quoi dire le ~ venu** he's getting ready so that he'll know what to say when the time comes ◆ **le ~ venu ils s'élancèrent** when the time came they hurled themselves forward

◆ **à ce moment-là** *(temps)* at that point *ou* time; *(circonstance)* in that case, if that's the case, if that's so

◆ **à aucun moment** ◆ **à aucun ~ je n'ai dit que ...** I never at any time said that ..., at no point did I say that ...

◆ **au moment de** ◆ **au ~ de l'accident** at the time of the accident, when the accident happened ◆ **au ~ de partir** just as I (*ou* he *etc*) was about to leave, just as I (*ou* he *etc*) was on the point of leaving

◆ **au moment où** ◆ **au ~ où elle entrait, lui sortait** as she was going in he was coming out ◆ **au ~ où il s'y attendait le moins** (at a time) when he was least expecting it ◆ **au ~ où je te parle, ils sont au musée** right now, they're at the museum

◆ **à un moment donné** ◆ **à un ~ donné il cesse d'écouter** at a certain point he stops listening ◆ **à un ~ donné, il faut savoir dire non** there comes a time when you have to say no

◆ **à tout moment, à tous moments** ◆ **des voitures arrivaient à tout ~** *ou* **à tous ~s** cars were constantly *ou* continually arriving, cars kept on arriving ◆ **il peut arriver à tout ~** he may arrive (at) any time (now) *ou* any moment (now)

◆ **d'un moment à l'autre** *[changer]* from one moment to the next ◆ **on l'attend d'un ~ à l'autre** he is expected any moment now *ou* (at) any time now

◆ **du moment où** *ou* **que** *(dans le temps)* since, seeing that; *(= pourvu que)* as long as ◆ **je m'en fiche, du ~ que c'est fait** I don't care, as long as it's done

◆ **dès le moment que** *ou* **où** as soon as, from the moment *ou* time when

◆ **en ce moment** *(= maintenant)* at the moment, at present, just now; *(= ces temps-ci)* currently, presently

◆ **par moments** now and then, at times, every now and again

◆ **pour le moment** for the time being *ou* the moment, at present

◆ **sur le moment** at the time

momentané, e /mɔmɑ̃tane/ ADJ *[absence, gêne, crise, arrêt, interruption]* momentary *(épith)*; *[espoir, effort]* short-lived, brief

momentanément /mɔmɑ̃tanemɑ̃/ ADV 1 *(= provisoirement)* for a short while, momentarily ◆ **il est privé de ce droit, au moins ~** this right has been taken away from him, at least for the time being ◆ **certains se retrouvent ~ sans contrat** some people find themselves temporarily without a contract ◆ **la signature de l'accord est ~ suspendue** the signing of the agreement has been postponed for the moment 2 *(= en ce moment)* at the moment, at present ◆ **je suis ~ absent, merci de laisser un message** *(sur répondeur)* I'm not here at the moment, please leave a message

mômeries* /momʀi/ NFPL childish behaviour ◆ **arrête tes ~ !** don't be so childish!

momie /mɔmi/ NF mummy ◆ **ne reste pas là comme une ~*** don't stand there like a stuffed dummy*

momification /mɔmifikasjɔ̃/ NF mummification

momifier /mɔmifje/ ▸ conjug 7 ◂ VT to mummify VPR **se momifier** *[esprit]* to atrophy, to fossilize

mon /mɔ̃/, **ma** /ma/ (pl **mes** /me/) ADJ POSS 1 *(possession, relation)* my, my own *(emphatique)* ◆ **~ fils et ma fille** my son and (my) daughter ◆ **j'ai ~ idée là-dessus** I have my own ideas *ou* views about that; *pour autres loc voir* **son¹** 2 *(valeur affective, ironique, intensive)* **alors voilà ~ type/~ François qui se met à m'injurier*** and then the fellow/our François starts bawling insults at me ◆ **voilà ~ mal de tête qui me reprend** that's my headache back again ◆ **on a changé ~ Paris** they've changed the Paris I knew *ou* what I think of as Paris ◆ **j'ai eu ~ lundi*** I got Monday off; → **son¹** 3 *(dans termes d'adresse)* my ◆ **~ cher ami** my dear friend ◆ **~ cher Monsieur** my dear Sir ◆ **oui ~ père/ma sœur/ma mère** *(Rel)* yes Father/Sister/Mother ◆ **mes (bien chers) frères** *(Rel)* my (dear) brethren

monacal, e (mpl **-aux**) /mɔnakal, o/ ADJ *(lit, fig)* monastic

monachisme /mɔnaʃism/ NM monachism

Monaco /mɔnako/ NM ◆ **(la principauté de) ~** (the principality of) Monaco

monade /mɔnad/ NF monad

monarchie /mɔnaʀʃi/ NF monarchy ◆ **~ absolue/constitutionnelle/parlementaire** absolute/constitutional/parliamentary monarchy ◆ **la ~ de Juillet** *(Hist)* the July Monarchy

monarchique /mɔnaʀʃik/ ADJ monarchic, monarchial

monarchisme /mɔnaʀʃism/ NM monarchism

monarchiste /mɔnaʀʃist/ ADJ, NMF monarchist

monarque /mɔnaʀk/ NM monarch ◆ **~ absolu** absolute monarch ◆ **~ de droit divin** monarch *ou* king by divine right

monastère /mɔnastɛʀ/ NM monastery

monastique /mɔnastik/ ADJ monastic

monceau (pl **monceaux**) /mɔ̃so/ NM ◆ **un ~ de** *[+ objets]* a heap *ou* pile of; *[+ erreurs]* a heap *ou* load* of ◆ **des ~x de** heaps *ou* piles of

mondain, e /mɔ̃dɛ̃, ɛn/ ADJ 1 *[réunion, vie]* society *(épith)* ◆ **plaisirs ~s** pleasures of society ◆ **alcoolisme ~** *alcoholism brought about by social drinking* ◆ **mener une vie ~e** to be a socialite ◆ **goût pour la vie ~e** taste for society life *ou* the high life ◆ **leurs obligations ~es** their social obligations ◆ **ils sont très ~s** they are great socialites, they like moving in fashionable society *ou* circles ◆ **ce festival est l'événement ~ de l'année** the festival is the society event of the year ◆ **c'est un peu trop ~ (à mon goût)** it's a bit too posh* (for my taste); → **soirée**

2 *(= qui traite de la haute société)* **chronique ~e** society gossip column ◆ **journaliste** *ou* **chroniqueur ~** society writer ◆ **journal d'actualité ~e** society paper; → **carnet**

3 *[politesse, ton]* refined, urbane, sophisticated ◆ **il a été très ~ avec moi** he treated me with studied politeness *ou* courtesy

4 *(Philos)* mundane; *(Rel)* worldly, earthly

5 *(ancienn̄t)* **la police** *ou* **brigade ~e, la Mondaine** * *(des mœurs)* ≈ the vice squad; *(des stupéfiants)* ≈ the drugs squad

NM socialite

NF **mondaine** *(= femme)* society woman, socialite

mondanité /mɔ̃danite/ NF 1 *(= goût)* taste for *ou* love of society life; *(= habitude, connaissance des usages)* savoir-faire 2 *(Rel)* worldliness NFPL **mondanités** *(= divertissements, soirées)* society life; *(= politesses, propos)* polite small talk; *(Presse = chronique)* society gossip column ◆ **je n'aime pas trop les ~s** I'm not much of a socialite ◆ **toutes ces ~s me fatiguent** I'm exhausted by this social whirl *ou* round

monde /mɔ̃d/ NM 1 *(= univers, terre)* world ◆ **dans le ~ entier, de par le ~** all over the world, the world over, throughout the world ◆ **le ~ entier s'indigna** the whole world was outraged ◆ **le ~ des vivants** the land of the living ◆ **il se moque** * *ou* **se fout**‡ **du ~** he's got a nerve * *ou* cheek * *(Brit)*, he's got a damn‡ *ou* bloody*‡ *(Brit)* nerve ◆ **venir au ~** to be born, to come into the world ◆ **mettre un enfant au ~** to bring a child into the world ◆ **si je suis encore de ce ~** if I'm still here *ou* in the land of the living ◆ **depuis qu'il est de ce ~** since he was born ◆ **elle n'est plus de ce ~** she is no longer with us, she has departed this life ◆ **rêver à un ~ meilleur** to dream of a better world ◆ **où va le ~ ?** whatever is the world coming to? ◆ **dans ce (bas) ~** here below, in this world ◆ **l'Ancien/le Nouveau Monde** the Old/the New World; → **depuis, unique**

2 *(= ensemble, groupement spécifique)* world ◆ **le ~ végétal/animal** the vegetable/animal world ◆ **le ~ des affaires/du théâtre** the world of business/of (the) theatre, the business/the theatre world ◆ **le ~ chrétien/communiste** the Christian/communist world

3 *(= domaine)* world, realm ◆ **le ~ de l'illusion/du rêve** the realm of illusion/of dreams ◆ **le ~ de la folie** the world *ou* realm of madness ◆ **elle vit dans son ~** *ou* **dans un ~ à elle** she lives in a world of her own

4 *(= gens)* **j'entends du ~ à côté** I can hear people in the next room ◆ **est-ce qu'il y a du ~ ?** *(= qn est-il présent ?)* is there anybody there?; *(= y a-t-il foule ?)* are there many people there?, are there a lot of people there? ◆ **il y a du ~** *(= ce n'est pas vide)* there are some people there; *(= il y a foule)* there's quite a crowd ◆ **il n'y a pas grand ~** there aren't very many (people) here ◆ **il y a beaucoup de ~** there's a real crowd, there are a lot of people ◆ **il y avait un ~ !** *ou* **un ~ fou !** * there were crowds!, the place was packed! ◆ **ils voient beaucoup de ~** they have a busy social life ◆ **ils reçoivent beaucoup de ~** they entertain a lot, they do a lot of entertaining ◆ **ce week-end nous avons du ~** we have people coming *ou* visitors this weekend ◆ **il y avait du beau ~ au vernissage** there were lots of celebrities at the opening ◆ **il y a du ~ au balcon !**‡ she's very well-endowed! * ◆ **elle est venue avec tout son petit ~** she came with her entire brood ◆ **tout ce petit ~ s'est bien amusé ?** and did everyone have a nice time?, did we all enjoy ourselves? ◆ **il connaît son ~** he knows the people he deals with ◆ **je n'ai pas encore tout mon ~** my group *ou* lot * *(Brit)* aren't all here yet; → **Monsieur, tout**

5 *(Rel)* **le ~** the world ◆ **les plaisirs du ~** worldly pleasures, the pleasures of the world

6 *(= milieu social)* set, circle ◆ **le (grand** *ou* **beau) ~** *(= la bonne société)* (high) society ◆ **embarquez**‡ **tout ce beau ~** *(péj)* cart this lot * away ◆ **aller dans le ~** to mix with high society ◆ **appartenir au meilleur ~** to move in the best circles ◆ **il n'est pas de notre ~** he is from a different set, he's not one of our set *ou* crowd * ◆ **nous ne sommes pas du même ~** we don't move in *ou* belong to the same circles (of society) ◆ **cela ne se fait pas dans le ~** that isn't done in the best circles *ou* in polite society ◆ **homme/femme/gens du ~** society man/woman/people ◆ **se conduire en parfait homme du ~** to be a perfect gentleman

7 *(locutions)* **l'autre ~** *(Rel)* the next world ◆ **envoyer** *ou* **expédier qn dans l'autre ~** to send sb to meet his (*ou* her) maker ◆ **c'est le ~ à l'envers !** *ou* **renversé !** whatever next! ◆ **comme le ~ est petit !** it's a small world! ◆ **se faire (tout) un ~ de qch** to get worked up about sth ◆ **se faire un ~ de rien** to make a mountain out of a molehill, to make a fuss over nothing ◆ **se faire un ~ de tout** to make a fuss over everything, to make everything into a great issue ◆ **c'est un ~ !** * it's (just) not right!, it's (just) not on! * *(Brit)* ◆ **il y a un ~ entre ces deux personnes/conceptions** these two people/concepts are worlds apart, there's a world of difference between these two people/concepts

◆ **au monde, du monde** *(intensif)* in the world, on earth ◆ **produit parmi les meilleurs au** *ou* **du ~** product which is among the best in the world *ou* among the world's best ◆ **au demeurant, le meilleur homme du** *ou* **au ~** *(littér)* otherwise, the finest man alive ◆ **tout s'est passé le mieux du ~** everything went (off) perfectly *ou* like a dream * ◆ **pas le moins du ~ !** not at all!, not in the least! ◆ **il n'était pas le moins du ~ anxieux** he was not the slightest *ou* least bit worried, he wasn't worried in the slightest *ou* in the least, he wasn't the least bit worried ◆ **sans se préoccuper le moins du ~ de ses adversaires** without giving a single thought *ou* the least thought to his opponents ◆ **je ne m'en séparerais pour rien au ~, je ne m'en séparerais pas pour tout l'or du ~** I wouldn't part with it for anything (in the world) *ou* for all the world *ou* for all the tea in China ◆ **nul au ~ ne peut ...** nobody in the world can ... ◆ **j'en pense tout le bien du ~** I have the highest opinion of him (*ou* her *ou* it)

◆ **le bout du monde** ◆ **ce village, c'est le bout du ~** that village is in the middle of nowhere *ou* at the back of beyond * ◆ **il irait au bout du ~ pour elle** he would go to the ends of the earth for her ◆ **ce n'est pas le bout du ~ !** *(fig)* it won't kill you! ◆ **si tu as 5 € à payer, c'est le bout du ~** * at the (very) worst it might cost you €5

monder /mɔ̃de/ ▸ conjug 1 ◂ VT *[+ orge]* to hull; *[+ amandes]* to blanch

mondial, e (mpl **-iaux**) /mɔ̃djal, jo/ ADJ *[guerre, population, production]* world *(épith)*; *[épidémie, tendance, réseau, crise]* world *(épith)*, world-wide ◆ **une célébrité ~e** a world-famous personality *ou* celebrity NM ◆ **le Mondial** the World Cup

mondialement /mɔ̃djalmɑ̃/ ADV throughout the world, the (whole) world over ◆ **il est ~ connu** he's known the (whole) world over *ou* throughout the world, he's world-famous

mondialisation /mɔ̃djalizasjɔ̃/ NF *[d'échanges, économie, marchés]* globalization ◆ **pour éviter la ~ du conflit** to prevent the conflict from spreading throughout the world *ou* worldwide

mondialiser /mɔ̃djalize/ ▸ conjug 1 ◂ VT *[+ activité, capitaux]* to globalize VPR **se mondialiser** *[économie, offre]* to become globalized ◆ **l'entreprise s'est mondialisée** the company has extended its operations worldwide *ou* globalized its operations ◆ **ce phénomène se mondialise** this is becoming a world-wide phenomenon ◆ **dans une économie de plus en plus mondialisée** in an increasingly globalized economy

mondialisme /mɔ̃djalism/ NM internationalism

mondialiste /mɔ̃djalist/ ADJ, NMF internationalist

mond(i)ovision /mɔ̃d(j)ɔvizjɔ̃/ NF worldwide (satellite) television broadcast ◆ **retransmis en mond(i)ovision** broadcast (by satellite) worldwide

monégasque /mɔnegask/ ADJ Monegasque, Monacan NMF **Monégasque** Monegasque, Monacan

monème /mɔnɛm/ NM moneme

MONEP /mɔnɛp/ NM (abrév de **Marché des options négociables de Paris**) *(Fin)* ◆ **le ~** *the traded-options exchange in the Paris stock market*

monétaire /monetɛʀ/ ADJ *[crise, valeur, unité, système, politique, stabilité]* monetary ◆ **le marché ~** the money market ◆ **les dirigeants ~s internationaux** the international monetary authorities; → **circulation, masse, union**

monétarisme /mɔnetaʀism/ NM monetarism

monétariste /mɔnetaʀist/ ADJ, NMF monetarist

monétique /mɔnetik/ NF electronic banking (services)

monétiser /mɔnetize/ ▸ conjug 1 ◂ VT to monetize

mongol, e /mɔ̃gɔl/ ADJ Mongol, Mongolian ◆ **République populaire ~e** Mongolian People's Republic NM *(= langue)* Mongolian NM,F **Mongol(e)** *(gén)* Mongol, Mongoloid; *(= habitant ou originaire de la Mongolie)* Mongolian

Mongolie /mɔ̃gɔli/ NF Mongolia ◆ **République populaire de ~** People's Republic of Mongolia ◆ **~-Intérieure** Inner Mongolia ◆ **~-Extérieure** Outer Mongolia

mongolien, -ienne † /mɔ̃gɔljɛ̃, jɛn/ *(Méd)* ADJ with Down's syndrome *(attrib)*, Down's syndrome *(épith)* NM,F *(= enfant)* Down's syndrome baby (*ou* boy *ou* girl); *(= adulte)* person with Down's syndrome

mongolique /mɔ̃gɔlik/ ADJ *(Géog)* Mongol(ic), Mongolian

mongolisme † /mɔ̃gɔlism/ NM Down's syndrome, mongolism †

monisme /mɔnism/ NM monism

moniste /mɔnist/ ADJ monistic NMF monist

moniteur /mɔnitœʀ/ NM 1 *(Sport)* instructor, coach; *[de colonie de vacances]* supervisor *(Brit)*, (camp) counselor *(US)* ◆ **~ de ski** skiing instructor ◆ **~ d'auto-école** driving instructor 2 *(= appareil)* monitor ◆ **~ cardiaque** heart-rate monitor 3 *(Univ)* graduate assistant

monitorage /mɔnitɔʀaʒ/ NM ⇒ **monitoring**

monitorat /mɔnitɔʀa/ NM *(= formation)* training to be an instructor; *(= fonction)* instructorship ◆ **il prépare son ~ de ski** he's training to be a ski instructor

monitoring /mɔnitɔʀiŋ/ NM *(gén)* monitoring

monitrice /mɔnitʀis/ NF *(Sport)* instructress; *[de colonie de vacances]* supervisor *(Brit)*, (camp) counselor *(US)*; *(Univ)* graduate assistant

monnaie /mɔnɛ/ NF 1 *(= espèces, devises)* currency ◆ **~ forte/faible** strong/weak currency ◆ **~ d'or/d'argent** gold/silver currency ◆ **~ décimale** decimal coinage *ou* currency ◆ **la ~ américaine** *(Bourse)* the American dollar ◆ **la ~ allemande** the German mark; → **battre, faux²**

2 *(= pièce, médaille)* coin ◆ **une ~ d'or** a gold coin ◆ **émettre/retirer une ~** to issue/ withdraw a coin

3 *(= appoint)* change; *(= petites pièces)* (loose) change ◆ **petite** *ou* **menue ~** small change ◆ **vous n'avez pas de ~ ?** *(pour payer)* don't you have (the) change? *ou* any change? ◆ **auriez-vous de la ~ ?, pourriez-vous me faire de la ~ ?** could you give me some change? ◆ **faire de la ~** to get (some) change ◆ **faire la ~ de 50 €** to get change for *ou* to change a 50-euro note *ou*

50 euros ◆ **faire** *ou* **donner à qn la ~ de 10** € to change €10 for sb, to give sb change for €10 ◆ **elle m'a rendu la ~ sur 10** € she gave me the change out of *ou* from €10 ◆ **passez** *ou* **envoyez la ~ !***, **par ici la ~ !*** let's have the money!, cough up* everyone!

4 *(= bâtiment)* **la Monnaie, l'hôtel des ~s** the Mint

5 *(locutions)* **c'est ~ courante** *[faits, événements]* it's common *ou* widespread, it's a common *ou* an everyday occurrence; *[actions, pratiques]* it's common practice ◆ **donner** *ou* **rendre à qn la ~ de sa pièce** to pay sb back in the same *ou* in his own coin, to repay sb in kind ◆ **à l'école, les billes servent de ~ d'échange** at school, marbles are used as money *ou* as a currency ◆ **otages qui servent de ~ d'échange** hostages who are used as bargaining chips *ou* counters ◆ **payer qn en ~ de singe** to fob sb off with empty promises

COMP **monnaie de banque** ⇒ **monnaie scripturale**
monnaie divisionnaire fractional currency
monnaie électronique plastic money
monnaie fiduciaire fiduciary currency, paper money
monnaie légale legal tender
monnaie métallique coin *(NonC)*
monnaie de papier paper money
monnaie plastique plastic money
monnaie scripturale representative *ou* bank money
monnaie unique *(Europe)* single currency

monnaie-du-pape (pl **monnaies-du-pape**) /mɔnɛdypap/ NF *(= plante)* honesty

monnayable /mɔnɛjabl/ ADJ *[terres, titres]* convertible into cash; *[diplôme]* marketable ◆ **c'est un diplôme facilement ~** you can easily get a job with that qualification

monnayer /mɔneje/ ▸ conjug 8 ◂ VT *[+ terres, titres]* to convert into cash ◆ **~ son talent/ses capacités** to make money from one's talents/one's abilities ◆ **~ son silence/soutien** to sell one's silence/support ◆ **ce genre de service, ça se monnaie** you have to pay to get that kind of help ◆ **dans ce pays, tout se monnaie** in that country, you can get whatever you want as long as you're willing to pay for it

monnayeur /mɔnɛjœʀ/ NM *(= machine) (pour fabriquer la monnaie)* minting machine; *(pour changer)* (automatic) change maker; *(système à pièces)* coin-operated device

mono* /mɔno/ NMF (abrév de **moniteur**) *[Sport]* instructor; *[de colonie de vacances]* supervisor *(Brit)*, (camp) counselor *(US)* NM abrév de **monoski** NF (abrév de **monophonie**) ◆ **en ~** in mono ADJ INV (abrév de **monophonique**) *[disque, électrophone]* mono

monoacide /mɔnoasid/ ADJ mon(o)acid

monobasique /mɔnobazik/ ADJ monobasic

monobloc /mɔnoblɔk/ ADJ INV cast in one piece *(attrib)*

monocaméral (pl **-aux**) /mɔnokameʀal, o/ ADJ M unicameral

monocamérisme /mɔnokameʀism/ NM unicameralism

monochromatique /mɔnɔkʀɔmatik/ ADJ monochromatic

monochrome /mɔnokʀom/ ADJ monochrome, monochromatic

monocle /mɔnɔkl/ NM monocle, eyeglass

monoclonal, e (mpl **-aux**) /mɔnoklonal, o/ ADJ monoclonal

monocoque /mɔnɔkɔk/ ADJ *[voiture, avion]* monocoque; *[yacht]* monohull, single-hull ◆ **voilier ~** monohull NM *(= voilier)* monohull

monocorde /mɔnɔkɔʀd/ ADJ *[instrument]* with a single chord; *[voix, timbre, discours]* monotonous ◆ **sur un ton ~** in a monotonous voice NM monochord

monocorps /mɔnɔkɔʀ/ ADJ *[voiture]* monobox, with a one-box design

monocratie /mɔnɔkʀasi/ NF monocracy

monoculture /mɔnokyltyʀ/ NF single-crop farming, monoculture

monocycle /mɔnosikl/ NM monocycle, unicycle

monocylindre /mɔnosilɛ̃dʀ/ NM single-cylinder engine

monocyte /mɔnɔsit/ NM monocyte

monodie /mɔnɔdi/ NF monody

monogame /mɔnɔgam/ ADJ monogamous ◆ **union ~** *[d'animaux]* pair-bonding NMF monogamist

monogamie /mɔnɔgami/ NF monogamy

monogamique /mɔnɔgamik/ ADJ monogamistic

monogramme /mɔnɔgʀam/ NM monogram

monographie /mɔnɔgʀafi/ NF monograph

monoï /mɔnɔj/ NM INV monoï *(perfumed oil made from coconut and Tahitian flowers)*

monokini /mɔnɔkini/ NM topless swimsuit, monokini ◆ **faire du ~** to go topless

monolingue /mɔnɔlɛ̃g/ ADJ monolingual

monolinguisme /mɔnɔlɛ̃gɥism/ NM monolingualism

monolithe /mɔnɔlit/ NM monolith ADJ monolithic

monolithique /mɔnɔlitik/ ADJ *(lit, fig)* monolithic

monolithisme /mɔnɔlitism/ NM *(Archit, Constr)* monolithism

monologue /mɔnɔlɔg/ NM monologue ◆ **~ intérieur** interior monologue

monologuer /mɔnɔlɔge/ ▸ conjug 1 ◂ VI to soliloquize ◆ **il monologue pendant des heures** *(péj)* he talks away *ou* holds forth for hours

monomane /mɔnɔman/, **monomaniaque** /mɔnɔmanjak/ ADJ, NMF monomaniac

monomanie /mɔnɔmani/ NF monomania

monôme /mɔnom/ NM *(Math)* monomial; *(arg Scol)* students' rag procession

monomère /mɔnɔmɛʀ/ ADJ monomeric NM monomer

monométallisme /mɔnometalism/ NM monometallism

monomoteur, -trice /mɔnɔmɔtœʀ, tʀis/ ADJ single-engined NM single-engined aircraft

mononucléaire /mɔnonykleɛʀ/ ADJ *(Bio)* mononuclear NM mononuclear (cell), mononucleate

mononucléose /mɔnonykleoz/ NF mononucleosis ◆ **~ infectieuse** infectious mononucleosis *(SPÉC)*, glandular fever *(Brit)*

monopalme /mɔnɔpalm/ NM monofin

monoparental, e (mpl **-aux**) /mɔnɔpaʀɑ̃tal, o/ ADJ ◆ **famille ~e** single-parent *ou* lone-parent *ou* one-parent family ◆ **foyer ~** single-parent *ou* lone-parent *ou* one-parent household

monophasé, e /mɔnofaze/ ADJ single-phase *(épith)* NM single-phase current

monophonie /mɔnɔfɔni/ NF monaural *ou* monophonic reproduction

monophonique /mɔnɔfɔnik/ ADJ monaural, monophonic

monoplace /mɔnoplas/ ADJ single-seater *(épith)*, one-seater *(épith)* NMF *(= voiture, avion)* single-seater, one-seater

monoplan /mɔnoplɑ̃/ NM monoplane

monoplégie /mɔnɔpleʒi/ NF monoplegia

monopole /mɔnɔpɔl/ NM *(Écon, fig)* monopoly ◆ **avoir le ~ de** *(Écon)* to have the monopoly of; *[+ vérité, savoir]* to have a monopoly on ◆ **avoir un ~ sur** to have a monopoly in ◆ **être en situation de ~** to have a monopoly, to be in a monopoly position ◆ **~ d'achat** monopsony, buyer's monopoly ◆ **~ d'État** state *ou* public monopoly ◆ **~ fiscal** tax monopoly

monopolisateur, -trice /mɔnɔpɔlizatœʀ, tʀis/ NM,F monopolizer

monopolisation /mɔnɔpɔlizasjɔ̃/ NF monopolization

monopoliser /mɔnɔpɔlize/ ▸ conjug 1 ◂ VT *(lit, fig)* to monopolize ◆ **il a monopolisé la parole toute la soirée** he monopolized the conversation all evening, he didn't let anybody get a word in all evening

monopoliste /mɔnɔpɔlist/, **monopolistique** /mɔnɔpɔlistik/ ADJ monopolistic

Monopoly ® /mɔnɔpɔli/ NM Monopoly ® ◆ **jouer au ~** to play Monopoly ◆ **c'est un vaste jeu de ~** *(fig)* it's one great big Monopoly game

monoposte /mɔnɔpɔst/ ADJ *(Ordin) [version, licence]* single-user

monorail /mɔnoʀaj/ NM *(= voie)* monorail; *(= voiture)* monorail coach

monosémique /mɔnɔsemik/ ADJ monosemic

monoski /mɔnoski/ NM monoski ◆ **faire du ~** to go monoskiing

monospace /mɔnɔspas/ NM people carrier *(Brit)*, minivan *(US)*

monosyllabe /mɔnosi(l)lab/ NM *(lit, fig)* monosyllable ◆ **répondre par ~s** to reply in monosyllables

monosyllabique /mɔnosi(l)labik/ ADJ monosyllabic

monosyllabisme /mɔnosil(l)abism/ NM monosyllabism

monothéique /mɔnɔteik/ ADJ monotheistic

monothéisme /mɔnɔteism/ NM monotheism

monothéiste /mɔnɔteist/ ADJ monotheistic NMF monotheist

monothérapie /mɔnɔteʀapi/ NF *(Méd)* monotherapy, single-drug treatment

monotone /mɔnɔtɔn/ ADJ *[son, voix, paysage, tâche]* monotonous; *[spectacle, style, discours]* monotonous, dull, dreary; *[existence, vie]* monotonous, humdrum, dull; *(Math)* monotone

monotonie /mɔnɔtɔni/ NF *[de son, voix, paysage, tâche]* monotony; *[de discours, spectacle, vie]* monotony, dullness

monotype /mɔnɔtip/ NM *(Art)* monotype; *(Naut)* one-design sailboat

monovalent, e /mɔnɔvalɑ̃, ɑ̃t/ ADJ *(Chim)* monovalent, univalent

monoxyde /mɔnɔksid/ NM monoxide ◆ **~ de carbone** carbon monoxide ◆ **~ d'azote** nitric oxide

monozygote /mɔnozigɔt/ ADJ monozygotic

Monrovia /mɔ̃ʀɔvja/ N Monrovia

Monseigneur /mɔ̃sɛɲœʀ/ (pl **Messeigneurs** /mesɛɲœʀ/) NM 1 *(formule d'adresse, à archevêque, duc)* Your Grace; *(à cardinal)* Your Eminence; *(à évêque)* Your Grace, Your Lordship, My Lord (Bishop); *(à prince)* Your (Royal) Highness 2 *(à la troisième personne, à archevêque, duc)* His Grace; *(à cardinal)* His Eminence; *(à évêque)* His Lordship; *(à prince)* His (Royal) Highness

Monsieur /məsjø/ (pl **Messieurs** /mesjø/) NM 1 *(s'adressant à qn)* **bonjour ~** *(gén)* good morning; *(nom connu)* good morning Mr X; *(nom inconnu)* good morning, good morning, sir *(frm)*

◆ **bonjour Messieurs** good morning (gentlemen) ◆ **(bonjour) Messieurs Dames*** morning all *ou* everyone* ◆ ~, **vous avez oublié quelque chose** excuse me, you've forgotten something ◆ **et pour (vous) ~/Messieurs ?** *(au restaurant)* and for you, sir/gentlemen? ◆ **Messieurs** *(devant un auditoire)* gentlemen ◆ **Messieurs et chers collègues** gentlemen ◆ ~ **le Président** *[de gouvernement]* Mr President; *[d'entreprise]* Mr Chairman ◆ **oui, ~ le juge** ≈ yes, Your Honour *ou* My Lord *ou* Your Worship ◆ ~ **l'abbé** Father ◆ ~ **le curé** Father ◆ ~ **le ministre** Minister ◆ ~ **le duc** Your Grace ◆ ~ **le comte (***ou* **baron** *etc***)** Your Lordship, my Lord ◆ ~ **devrait prendre son parapluie** *(frm)* I suggest you take your umbrella, sir *(frm)* ◆ ~ **est servi** *(frm)* dinner is served, sir *(frm)* ◆ ~ **n'est pas content ?** *(iro)* is something not to Your Honour's *(iro) ou* Your Lordship's *(iro)* liking? ◆ **mon bon** *ou* **pauvre** ~* my dear sir; → **Madame**

2 *(parlant de qn)* ~ **X est malade** Mr X is ill ◆ ~ **votre fils** († *ou iro*) your dear son ◆ ~ **est sorti** *(frm)* Mr X *ou* the Master (of the house) is not at home ◆ ~ **dit que c'est à lui** the gentleman says it's his ◆ ~ **le Président** the President, the Chairman ◆ ~ **le juge X** ≈ (His Honour) Judge X ◆ ~ **le duc de X** (His Grace) the Duke of X ◆ ~ **l'abbé (X)** Father X ◆ ~ **le curé** the parish priest ◆ ~ **le curé X** Father X ◆ ~ **loyal** *(Cirque)* ringmaster

3 *(sur une enveloppe)* ~ **John X** Mr John X, John X Esq; *(à un enfant)* Master John X ◆ **Messieurs Dupont** Messrs Dupont and Dupont ◆ **Messieurs J. et P. Dupont** Messrs J and P Dupont ◆ **Messieurs Dupont et fils** Messrs Dupont and Son ◆ **Messieurs X et Y** Messrs X and Y; → **Madame**

4 *(en-tête de lettre)* ~ *(gén)* Dear Sir; *(personne connue)* Dear Mr X ◆ **cher** ~ Dear Mr X ◆ ~ **et cher collègue** My dear Sir, Dear Mr X ◆ ~ **le Président** *[de gouvernement]* Dear Mr President; *[d'entreprise]* Dear Mr Chairman

5 *(Hist = parent du roi)* Monsieur

6 *(sans majuscule)* gentleman; *(= personnage important)* great man ◆ **ces messieurs désirent ?** what would you like, gentlemen? ◆ **maintenant il se prend pour un monsieur** he thinks he's quite the gentleman now, he fancies himself as a (proper) gentleman now *(Brit)* ◆ **les beaux messieurs** the well-to-do *ou* smart *(Brit)* gentlemen ◆ **c'est un grand monsieur** he's a great man ◆ **un méchant monsieur** *(langage enfantin)* a nasty man

7 *(= représentant)* ~ **Tout-le-monde** the man in the street, the average man ◆ ~ **Muscle** Muscleman ◆ ~ **Météo** *(= responsable)* the weatherman

monstre /mɔ̃stʀ/ **NM** 1 *(par la difformité)* freak (of nature), monster; *(par la taille)* monster ◆ ~ **de foire** fairground freak

2 *(Myth)* monster ◆ ~ **sacré** *(fig)* giant ◆ **un sacré du théâtre** a legendary figure in the theatre ◆ **un ~ sacré du cinéma** a screen giant *ou* legend

3 *(péj = méchant)* monster, brute ◆ **c'est un ~ (de laideur)** he is monstrously *ou* hideously ugly ◆ **c'est un ~ (de méchanceté)** he's a wicked *ou* an absolute monster ◆ **quel ~ d'égoïsme !/d'orgueil !** what fiendish *ou* monstrous egoism!/pride! ◆ **être un ~ froid** to be pitiless

4 (* : *affectueux*) **petit ~ !** you little monster! * *ou* horror! *

ADJ * *[rabais]* gigantic, colossal, mammoth; *[manifestation, foule, embouteillage]* massive ◆ **succès** ~ runaway *ou* raving * success ◆ **elle a un culot** ~ she's got a hell of a nerve * ◆ **il gagne un argent** ~ he earns a vast amount of money ◆ **faire une publicité ~ à qch** to launch a massive publicity campaign for sth ◆ **j'ai un travail** ~ I've got loads * of work to do *ou* a horrendous amount of work to do ◆ **un dîner** ~ a colossal dinner, a whacking * great dinner *(Brit)*

monstrueusement /mɔ̃stʀyøzmɑ̃/ **ADV** *[laid]* monstrously, hideously; *[intelligent]* prodigiously, stupendously; *[riche]* enormously ◆ **il est ~ gros** he's massively overweight

monstrueux, -euse /mɔ̃stʀyø, øz/ **ADJ** *(= difforme) [bête]* monstrous; *[personne]* freakish; *[bâtiment]* hideous; *(= abominable) [guerre, massacre]* horrendous; *[crime]* heinous, monstrous; *(* = gigantesque) [erreur, bruit]* horrendous; *[appétit]* terrific, huge ◆ **faire du chantage, c'est ~ !** blackmail! it's monstrous!

monstruosité /mɔ̃stʀyozite/ **NF** 1 *[de crime]* monstrousness, monstrosity 2 *(= acte)* monstrous act, monstrosity; *(= propos)* monstrous remark ◆ **dire des ~s** to say monstrous *ou* horrendous things 3 *(= laideur)* hideousness

mont /mɔ̃/ **NM** 1 *(= montagne) (littér)* mountain ◆ **le ~ X** *(avec un nom propre)* Mount X ◆ **par ~s et par vaux** *(littér)* up hill and down dale ◆ **être toujours par ~s et par vaux*** to be always on the move *; → **promettre** 2 *(Voyance) [de main]* mount

COMP **les monts d'Auvergne** the mountains of Auvergne, the Auvergne mountains
le mont Blanc Mont Blanc
le mont Carmel Mount Carmel
le mont des Oliviers the Mount of Olives
le mont Sinaï Mount Sinaï
mont de Vénus *(Anat)* mons veneris

montage /mɔ̃taʒ/ **NM** 1 *(= assemblage) [d'appareil, montre]* assembly; *[de bijou]* mounting, setting; *[de manche]* setting in; *[de tente]* pitching, putting up ◆ **le ~ d'une opération publicitaire** the mounting *ou* organization of an advertising campaign ◆ ~ **financier** financial set-up *ou* arrangement ◆ **il faut décider du ~ financier de l'opération** we must decide how the operation is to be funded ◆ **le ~ juridique adopté pour l'entreprise** the legal arrangements for setting up the company; → **chaîne**

2 *(Ciné = opération)* editing ◆ ~ **final** final cut *ou* edit ◆ ~ **réalisé par** edited *ou* editing by ◆ ~ **photographique** photomontage ◆ ~ **audiovisuel** slide show with sound ◆ ~ **vidéo** *(= film)* video(-tape) ◆ **table/salle de ~** cutting table/room ◆ **le film est en cours de ~** the film is being cut *ou* edited ◆ **cette scène a disparu au ~** this scene ended up on the cutting room floor *ou* was edited out

3 *(Élec)* wiring (up); *[de radio etc]* assembly ◆ ~ **en parallèle/en série** connection in parallel/in series

4 *(Typo)* paste-up

montagnard, e /mɔ̃taɲaʀ, aʀd/ **ADJ** mountain *(épith)*, highland *(épith)*; *(Hist Pol)* Mountain *(épith)* **NM,F** 1 *(Géog)* mountain dweller ◆ **~s** mountain people *ou* dwellers 2 *(Hist Pol)* **Montagnard(e)** Montagnard

montagne /mɔ̃taɲ/ **NF** 1 *(= sommet)* mountain ◆ **la ~** *(= région montagneuse)* the mountains ◆ **vivre à** *ou* **habiter la ~** to live in the mountains ◆ **faire de la ~** *(en randonnée)* to go mountain-hiking; *(en escalade)* to go mountain-climbing *ou* mountaineering ◆ **haute/moyenne/basse ~** high/medium/low mountains ◆ **plantes des ~s** mountain plants; → **chaîne, guide**

2 *(intensif)* **une ~ de** a mountain of, masses * *ou* mountains of ◆ **une ~ de travail l'attendait** a mountain of work was waiting for him, there was masses * of work waiting for him ◆ **recevoir une ~ de lettres/cadeaux** to receive a whole stack of *ou* a (great) mountain of letters/presents

3 *(locutions)* **se faire une ~ de** *ou* **d'un rien** to make a mountain out of a molehill ◆ **il se fait une ~ de cet examen** he's getting really worked up about this exam, he's blown this exam out of all proportion ◆ **il n'y a que les ~s qui ne se rencontrent pas** *(Prov)* there are none so distant that fate cannot bring them together ◆ **déplacer** *ou* **soulever des ~s** to move mountains ◆ **c'est la ~ qui accouche d'une souris** after all that it's a bit of an anticlimax ◆ **c'est gros comme une ~*** it's obvious, it's plain for all to see

4 *(Hist Pol)* **la Montagne** the Mountain

COMP **montagnes russes** roller-coaster, big dipper, scenic railway
montagne à vaches low hills ◆ **nous faisons de la ~ à vaches mais pas d'escalade** *(hum)* we only go hill walking, not rock climbing

montagneux, -euse /mɔ̃taɲø, øz/ **ADJ** *(Géog)* mountainous; *(= accidenté)* hilly

Montana /mɔ̃tana/ **NM** Montana

montant, e /mɔ̃tɑ̃, ɑt/ **ADJ** *[mouvement]* upward, rising; *[bateau]* (travelling) upstream; *[col]* high; *[robe, corsage]* highnecked; *[chemin]* uphill ◆ **train ~** up train ◆ **voie ~e** up line ◆ **une star ~e de la chanson française** a rising star in French pop music; → **chaussure, colonne, garde**[1]

NM 1 *[d'échelle]* upright; *[de lit]* post; *[de porte]* jamb; *[d'échafaudage]* pole ◆ **les ~s de la fenêtre** the uprights of the window frame ◆ ~ **(de but)** *(Ftbl)* (goal) post

2 *(= somme)* (sum) total, total amount ◆ **le ~ s'élevait à** the total added up to, the total (amount) came to *ou* was ◆ **chèque d'un ~ de 50 €** cheque for the sum of €50 ◆ **emprunt d'un ~ d'un million d'euros** loan of one million euros ◆ **~s compensatoires en matière agricole** *(Europe)* farming subsidies ◆ **~s compensatoires monétaires** monetary compensation amounts ◆ ~ **dû/forfaitaire** *(Fin, Jur)* outstanding/flat-rate amount ◆ ~ **nominal** *(Fin, Jur)* par value ◆ ~ **net d'une succession** *(Jur)* residuary estate

3 *(Équitation)* cheek-strap

mont-blanc (pl **monts-blancs**) /mɔ̃blɑ̃/ **NM** *(Culin)* chestnut cream dessert *(topped with cream)*

mont-de-piété (pl **monts-de-piété**) /mɔ̃d(ə)pjete/ **NM** (state-owned) pawnshop *ou* pawnbroker's ◆ **mettre qch au ~** to pawn sth

monte /mɔ̃t/ **NF** 1 *(Équitation)* horsemanship 2 *(= accouplement)* **station/service de ~** stud farm/service ◆ **mener une jument à la ~** to take a mare to be covered

monté, e /mɔ̃te/ (ptp de **monter**) **ADJ** 1 *(= équipé, pourvu)* equipped ◆ **être bien/mal ~ en qch** to be well/ill equipped with sth 2 (*: *physiquement)* **il est bien ~** he's well hung* *ou* well endowed *

monte-charge (pl **monte-charges**) /mɔ̃tʃaʀʒ/ **NM** hoist, goods lift *(Brit)*, service elevator *(US)*

montée /mɔ̃te/ **NF** 1 *(= escalade)* climb, climbing ◆ **la ~ de la côte** the ascent of the hill, the climb up the hill, climbing *ou* going up the hill ◆ **la ~ de l'escalier** climbing the stairs ◆ **c'est une ~ difficile** it's a hard *ou* difficult climb ◆ **en escalade, la ~ est plus facile que la descente** when you're climbing, going up is easier than coming down ◆ **la côte était si raide qu'on a fait la ~ à pied** the hill was so steep that we walked up *ou* we went up on foot

2 *(= ascension) [de ballon, avion]* ascent ◆ **pendant la ~ de l'ascenseur** while the lift is *(ou* was) going up

3 *[d'eaux, sève]* rise; *[de lait]* inflow ◆ **la soudaine ~ des prix/de la température** the sudden rise in prices/in (the) temperature

4 *(= augmentation) [de chômage, homme politique]* rise; *[d'hostilités]* escalation; *[de colère]* increase ◆ **la ~ des tensions raciales** rise in racial

tension, increasing racial tension ◆ **la ~ des périls en Europe** the growing danger of war in Europe

5 *(= côte, pente)* hill, uphill slope ◆ **la maison était en haut de la ~** the house stood at the top of the hill *ou* rise ◆ **une petite ~ mène à leur maison** there is a little slope leading up to their house

monte-en-l'air* † /mɔ̃tɑ̃lɛʀ/ **NM INV** *(= voleur)* cat burglar

monténégrin, e /mɔ̃tenegʀɛ̃, in/ **ADJ** Montenegrin, from Montenegro **NM,F** **Monténégrin(e)** Montenegrin

Monténégro /mɔ̃tenegʀo/ **NM** Montenegro

monte-plats /mɔ̃tpla/ **NM INV** service lift *(Brit)*, dumbwaiter

monter[1] /mɔ̃te/ ► conjug 1 ◄ **VI** *(avec auxiliaire être)* 1 *(gén)* to go up *(à* to; *dans* into); *[oiseau]* to fly up; *[avion]* to climb ◆ **~ à pied/à bicyclette/en voiture** to walk/cycle/drive up ◆ **~ en courant/en titubant** to run/stagger up ◆ **~ en train/par l'ascenseur** to go up by train/in the lift ◆ **~ dans** *ou* **à sa chambre** to go up(stairs) to one's room ◆ **il est monté en courant jusqu'au grenier** he ran up to the attic ◆ **monte me voir** come up and see me ◆ **monte le prévenir** go up and tell him ◆ **faites-le ~** *(visiteur)* ask him to come up ◆ **~ aux arbres** to climb trees ◆ **~ à Paris** *(en voyage)* to go up to Paris; *(pour travailler)* to go to work in Paris; *(pour s'installer)* to move to Paris

2 ◆ **~ sur** *[+ table, rocher, toit]* to climb (up) on *ou* onto ◆ **monté sur une chaise, il accrochait un tableau** he was standing on a chair hanging a picture ◆ **~ sur un arbre/une échelle** to climb up a tree/a ladder ◆ **~ sur une colline** to go up *ou* climb up *ou* walk up a hill ◆ **~ sur une bicyclette** to get on a bicycle ◆ **monté sur un cheval gris** riding *ou* on a grey horse ◆ **~ sur le trône** *(fig)* to come to *ou* ascend the throne

3 *(Transport)* **~ en voiture** to get into a car ◆ **~ dans un train/un avion** to get on *ou* into a train/an aircraft, to board a train/an aircraft ◆ **beaucoup de voyageurs sont montés à Lyon** a lot of people got on at Lyon ◆ **~ à bord (d'un navire)** to go on board *ou* aboard (a ship) ◆ **~ à bicyclette** *(= faire du vélo)* to ride a bicycle ◆ **~ à cheval** *(= se mettre en selle)* to get on *ou* mount a horse; *(= faire de l'équitation)* to ride, to go riding ◆ **je n'ai jamais monté** I've never been on a horse ◆ **elle monte bien** she's a good horsewoman, she rides well

4 *(= progresser) (dans une hiérarchie)* to rise, to go up; *[vedette]* to be on the way up ◆ **c'est l'artiste qui monte** he's the up-and-coming artist ◆ **c'est l'homme qui monte** he's on the way up; → **grade**

5 *[eau, vêtements]* **~ à** *ou* **jusqu'à** to come up to ◆ **robe qui monte jusqu'au cou** high-necked dress ◆ **la vase lui montait jusqu'aux genoux** the mud came right up to his knees, he was knee-deep in the mud

6 *(= s'élever) [colline, route]* to go up, to rise; *[soleil, flamme, brouillard]* to rise ◆ **~ en pente douce** to slope gently upwards, to rise gently ◆ **le chemin monte en lacets** the path winds *ou* twists upwards ◆ **jusqu'où monte le téléphérique ?** where does the cable car go up to? ◆ **notre maison monte très lentement** building is progressing very slowly on our house, our house is going up very slowly ◆ **un bruit/une odeur montait de la cave** there was a noise/a smell coming from the cellar, a noise was drifting up/a smell was wafting up from the cellar

7 *(= hausser de niveau) [mer, marée]* to come in; *[fleuve]* to rise; *[prix, température, baromètre]* to rise, to go up; *(Mus) [voix, note]* to go up ◆ **le lait monte** *(sur le feu)* the milk's about to boil over; *(dans le sein)* the milk is coming in ◆ **~ dans l'estime de qn** to go up *ou* rise in sb's estimation ◆ **ça a fait ~ les prix** it sent *ou* put *ou* pushed prices up ◆ **la colère/la tension monte** tempers are/tension is rising ◆ **le ton monte** *(colère)* the discussion is getting heated, voices are being raised; *(animation)* the conversation is getting noisier ◆ **le tricot monte vite avec cette laine*** this wool knits up quickly ◆ **la voiture peut ~ jusqu'à 250 km/h** the car can do up to 250 km/h, the car can reach speeds of up to 250 km/h ◆ **ce tableau peut ~ jusqu'à 5 000 €** this painting could fetch up to €5,000 ◆ **les blancs montent/n'arrivent pas à ~** *(Culin)* the egg whites are going stiff/won't whip up *ou* won't go stiff; → **flèche**[1], **neige**

8 *(exprimant des émotions)* **elle sentait la colère/peur ~ en elle** she could feel (the) anger/fear well up inside her ◆ **les larmes lui montaient aux yeux** tears were welling up in her eyes, tears filled her eyes ◆ **ça lui a fait ~ les larmes aux yeux** it brought tears to his eyes ◆ **le vin lui monte à la tête** wine goes to his head ◆ **le succès lui monte à la tête** success is going to his head; → **moutarde, rouge**

9 *(Agr) [plante]* to bolt, to go to seed ◆ **la salade est (toute) montée** the lettuce has bolted *ou* has gone to seed; → **graine**

10 *(Cartes)* to play a higher card ◆ **il est monté à cœur** he played a higher heart

VT *(avec auxiliaire avoir)* 1 *(= gravir)* to go up ◆ **~ l'escalier** *ou* **les marches précipitamment** to rush upstairs *ou* up the steps ◆ **~ l'escalier** *ou* **les marches quatre à quatre** to go upstairs *ou* up the steps four at a time ◆ **~ une côte** *(en marchant)* to walk *ou* go *ou* come up a hill; *(en courant)* to run up a hill ◆ **~ la gamme** *(Mus)* to go up the scale

2 *(= porter) [+ valise, meuble]* to take *ou* carry *ou* bring up ◆ **montez-lui son petit déjeuner** take his breakfast up to him ◆ **faire ~ ses valises** to have one's luggage brought *ou* taken *ou* sent up

3 ◆ **~ un cheval** to ride a horse ◆ **ce cheval n'a jamais été monté** this horse has never been ridden

4 *(= augmenter)* **~ le son** to turn the sound *ou* volume up

5 *(= exciter)* **~ qn contre qn** to set sb against sb ◆ **être monté contre qn** to be dead set against sb ◆ **~ la tête** *ou* **le bourrichon*** **à qn** to get sb worked up ◆ **quelqu'un lui a monté la tête contre moi** someone has set him against me

6 *(= couvrir) [+ animal]* to cover, to serve

7 ◆ **~ la garde** *(Mil)* to mount guard, to go on guard; *[chien]* to be on guard ◆ **"je monte la garde !"** *(sur un écriteau)* "beware of the dog"

VPR **se monter** 1 ◆ **se ~ à** *[prix, frais]* to come to, to amount to; *[dette]* to amount to

2 ◆ **se ~ la tête** *ou* **le bourrichon*** to get (all) worked up *ou* het up* ◆ **il se monte la tête pour un rien** he gets het up* *ou* worked up over nothing

monter[2] /mɔ̃te/ ► conjug 1 ◄ **VT** *(avec auxiliaire avoir)* 1 *(= assembler) [+ machine]* to assemble; *[+ tente]* to pitch, to put up; *[+ film]* to edit, to cut; *[+ robe]* to assemble, to sew together ◆ **~ des mailles** to cast on stitches ◆ **~ en parallèle/en série** *(Élec, Radio)* to connect in parallel/in series

2 *(= organiser) [+ pièce de théâtre]* to put on, to stage; *[+ opération, campagne publicitaire]* to mount, to organize, to set up; *[+ affaire]* to set up; *[+ canular]* to play; *[+ complot]* to hatch ◆ **~ un coup** to plan a job ◆ **~ le coup à qn**‡ to take sb for a ride‡ ◆ **~ une histoire pour déshonorer qn** to cook up* *ou* invent a scandal to ruin sb's good name ◆ **c'est une histoire montée de toutes pièces** it's a complete fabrication

3 († *= pourvoir, équiper)* to equip ◆ **~ son ménage** *ou* **sa maison** to set up house ◆ **se ~ en linge** to equip o.s. with linen ◆ **se ~** to get o.s. (well) set up

4 *(= fixer) [+ diamant, perle]* to set, to mount; *[+ pneu]* to put on ◆ **~ qch en épingle** to blow sth up out of all proportion, to make a thing of sth* ◆ **faire ~ un diamant en bague** to have a ring made with a diamond

monteur, -euse /mɔ̃tœʀ, øz/ **NM,F** 1 *(= ouvrier)* fitter 2 *[de films]* (film) editor 3 *(Typo)* paste-up artist

Montevideo /mɔ̃tevideo/ **N** Montevideo

montgolfière /mɔ̃gɔlfjɛʀ/ **NF** hot-air balloon ◆ **voyage en ~** hot-air balloon trip

monticule /mɔ̃tikyl/ **NM** *(= colline)* hillock, mound; *(= tas)* mound, heap

montmartrois, e /mɔ̃maʀtʀwa, waz/ **ADJ** of *ou* from Montmartre **NM,F** **Montmartrois(e)** inhabitant *ou* native of Montmartre

montmorency /mɔ̃mɔʀɑ̃si/ **NF INV** morello cherry

montrable /mɔ̃tʀabl/ **ADJ** *[personne]* fit to be seen *(attrib)*; *[objet]* which can be shown ◆ **tu es tout à fait ~** you're quite presentable

montre[1] /mɔ̃tʀ/ **NF** 1 *(gén)* watch ◆ **~ analogique** analogue watch ◆ **~-bracelet** wrist watch ◆ **~ digitale** *ou* **à affichage numérique** digital watch ◆ **~ de gousset** fob watch ◆ **~ de plongée** diver's watch ◆ **~ de précision** precision watch ◆ **~ à quartz** quartz watch ◆ **~ à remontoir** stem-winder, stem-winding watch ◆ **~ à répétition** repeating *ou* repeater watch

2 *(locutions)* **il est 2 heures à ma ~** it is 2 o'clock by my watch ◆ **j'ai mis 2 heures ~ en main** it took me exactly *ou* precisely 2 hours, it took me 2 hours exactly by the clock ◆ **course** *ou* **épreuve contre la ~** *(Sport)* race against the clock, time-trial; *(fig)* race against time *ou* the clock ◆ **ils sont engagés dans une course contre la ~** *(fig)* they are in a race against time ◆ **le contre la ~ individuel/par équipe** *(Sport)* individual/team time-trial ◆ **jouer la ~** *(fig)* to play for time; → **chaîne, sens**

montre[2] /mɔ̃tʀ/ **NF** 1 ◆ **faire ~ de** *[+ courage, ingéniosité, détermination, qualités]* to show, to display 2 *(littér = ostentation)* **pour la ~** for show, for the sake of appearances 3 († *Comm = en vitrine)* display, show ◆ **publication interdite à la ~** publication banned from public display ◆ **en ~** on display *ou* show

Montréal /mɔ̃ʀeal/ **N** Montreal

montréalais, e /mɔ̃ʀealɛ, ɛz/ **ADJ** of *ou* from Montreal **NM,F** **Montréalais(e)** Montrealer

montrer /mɔ̃tʀe/ GRAMMAIRE ACTIVE 53.4 ► conjug 1 ◄

VT 1 *(gén)* to show *(à* to); *(par un geste)* to point to; *(= faire remarquer) [+ détail, personne, faute]* to point out *(à* to); *(avec ostentation)* to show off, to display *(à* to); ◆ **je vais vous ~ le jardin** *(= faire visiter)* I'll show you (round) the garden ◆ **~ un enfant au docteur** to let the doctor see a child ◆ **l'aiguille montre le nord** the needle points north ◆ **~ ses fesses*** *ou* **son cul***** *(= se déculotter)* to show one's bare bottom *ou* arse*** *(Brit) ou* ass*** *(US)*; *(= se déshabiller)* to bare all, to strip naked ◆ **je l'ai ici – montre !** I've got it here – show me!

2 *(= laisser voir)* to show ◆ **jupe qui montre le genou** skirt which leaves the knee uncovered *ou* bare ◆ **elle montrait ses jambes en s'asseyant** she showed her legs as she sat down ◆ **elle montre ses charmes** *(hum)* she's showing off *ou* displaying her charms *(hum)*

3 *(= mettre en évidence)* to show, to prove ◆ **il a montré que l'histoire était fausse** he has shown *ou* proved the story to be false *ou* that the story was false ◆ **l'avenir montrera qui avait raison** the future will show *ou* prove who was right ◆ **~ la complexité d'un problème** to show how complex a problem is, to demonstrate the complexity of a problem ◆ **l'auteur montre un pays en décadence** the

author shows *ou* depicts a country in decline ◆ **ce qui montre bien que j'avais raison** which just goes to show that I was right

4 *(= manifester)* *[+ humeur, courage]* to show, to display; *[+ surprise]* to show ◆ **son visage montra de l'étonnement** his face registered (his) surprise

5 *(= apprendre)* ~ **à qn à faire** *ou* **comment faire qch** to show sb how *ou* the way to do sth

VPR se montrer 1 *[personne]* to appear, to show o.s.; *[chose]* to appear ◆ **elle ne s'est pas montrée au dîner** she didn't appear at dinner ◆ **il n'aime pas se ~ avec elle** he doesn't like to be seen with her ◆ **j'y vais juste pour me ~** I'm going there just to put in an appearance ◆ **montre-toi voir si la robe te va** let's have a look at you in that dress ◆ **il ne se montre pas beaucoup dans les réunions** he doesn't go to many meetings ◆ **ton père devrait se ~ davantage** *(fig)* your father should assert himself more *ou* show his authority more ◆ **sa lâcheté s'est montrée au grand jour** his cowardice was plain for all to see

2 *(= s'avérer)* *[personne]* to show o.s. (to be), to prove (o.s.) (to be); *[chose]* to prove (to be) ◆ **se ~ digne de sa famille** to show o.s. (to be) *ou* prove o.s. worthy of one's family ◆ **il s'est montré très désagréable** he was very unpleasant, he behaved very unpleasantly ◆ **il s'est montré intraitable** he was *ou* he showed himself quite unrelenting ◆ **il faudrait se ~ plus prudent** we should be more careful ◆ **le traitement s'est montré efficace** the treatment proved (to be) effective ◆ **se ~ d'une lâcheté révoltante** to show *ou* display despicable cowardice ◆ **si les circonstances se montrent favorables** if conditions prove (to be) *ou* turn out to be favourable ◆ **il faut se ~ ferme** you must appear firm, you must show firmness

montreur, -euse /mɔ̃tʀœʀ, øz/ **NM,F** ◆ ~ **de marionnettes** puppet master (*ou* mistress), puppeteer ◆ ~ **d'ours** bear leader

montueux, -euse /mɔ̃tɥø, øz/ **ADJ** *(littér)* (very) hilly

monture /mɔ̃tyʀ/ **NF** 1 *(= cheval)* mount; → **voyager** 2 *(Tech)* mounting; *[de lunettes]* frame; *[de bijou, bague]* setting *[d'appareil photo]* mount ◆ **lunettes à ~ d'écaille/de métal** horn-/metal-rimmed glasses

monument /mɔnymɑ̃/ **NM** 1 *(= statue, ouvrage commémoratif)* monument, memorial ◆ ~ **(funéraire)** monument ◆ ~ **aux morts** war memorial

2 *(= bâtiment, château)* monument, building ◆ ~ **historique** ancient monument, historic building ◆ **la maison est classée ~ historique** the house is listed *(Brit)* *ou* is a listed building *(Brit)*, the house is on the historical register *(US)* ◆ ~ **public** public building ◆ **visiter les ~s de Paris** to go sight-seeing in Paris, to see the sights of Paris

3 *(= œuvre majeure)* monument ◆ **c'est un ~ de la littérature française** it's one of the monuments *ou* great masterpieces of French literature ◆ **ce buffet est un ~, on ne peut pas le soulever** this sideboard is so huge, we can't shift it* ◆ **c'est un ~ de bêtise !*** what colossal *ou* monumental stupidity!

monumental, e (mpl **-aux**) /mɔnymɑ̃tal, o/ **ADJ** 1 *[taille, erreur]* monumental, colossal; *[œuvre]* monumental ◆ **d'une bêtise ~e** incredibly *ou* unbelievably stupid 2 *(Archit)* monumental

monumentalité /mɔnymɑ̃talite/ **NF** monumentality

moquer /mɔke/ ▸ conjug 1 ◂ **VT** († *ou littér*) to mock ◆ **j'ai été moqué** I was laughed at *ou* mocked

VPR se moquer de 1 *(= ridiculiser)* to make fun of, to poke fun at ◆ **on va se ~ de toi** people will laugh at you *ou* make fun of you (*ou* him *etc*), you'll make yourself a laughing stock ◆ **tu riais – oui, mais je ne me moquais pas** († *ou frm*) you were laughing – yes but I wasn't laughing at you *ou* making fun of you ◆ **vous vous moquez, j'espère** I trust that you are not in earnest *(frm)*

2 *(= tromper)* **vous vous moquez du monde** *ou* **des gens !** you've got a nerve! ◆ **je n'aime pas qu'on se moque de moi !** I don't like being made a fool of ◆ **le réparateur s'est vraiment moqué de nous** the repairman really took us for a ride* ◆ **de qui se moque-t-on ?** who are they trying to kid?* ◆ **du champagne ? ils ne se sont pas moqués de vous !*** champagne? they really treat you right!*

3 *(= mépriser)* *[+ conseils, autorité]* to scorn ◆ **il se moque bien de nous maintenant qu'il est riche** he looks down on us *ou* looks down his nose at us now that he's rich

4 *(= être indifférent)* **je m'en moque** I don't care ◆ **je m'en moque pas mal*** I couldn't care less* ◆ **je me moque de ne pas être cru** *ou* **qu'on ne me croie pas** I don't care if nobody believes me; → **an, chemise, tiers**

moquerie /mɔkʀi/ **NF** 1 *(= caractère)* mockery, mocking 2 *(= quolibet, sarcasme)* mockery *(NonC)*, jibe ◆ **en butte aux ~s continuelles de sa sœur** the target of constant mockery from his sister *ou* of his sister's constant mockery

moquette /mɔkɛt/ **NF** 1 *(= tapis)* (wall-to-wall) carpet, fitted carpet *(Brit)* ◆ **faire poser une ~** *ou* **de la ~** to have a wall-to-wall *ou* a fitted *(Brit)* carpet laid ◆ ~ **murale** fabric wall covering 2 *(= étoffe)* moquette

moquetter /mɔkete/ ▸ conjug 1 ◂ **VT** to carpet (wall-to-wall) ◆ **chambre moquettée** bedroom with wall-to-wall *ou* (a) fitted *(Brit)* carpet

moqueur, -euse /mɔkœʀ, øz/ **ADJ** 1 *[remarque, sourire]* mocking ◆ **il est très ~** he's always making fun of people 2 ◆ **(oiseau) ~** mocking bird

moraine /mɔʀɛn/ **NF** moraine

morainique /mɔʀenik/ **ADJ** morainic, morainal

moral, e¹ (mpl **-aux**) /mɔʀal, o/ **ADJ** 1 *(= éthique)* *[ordre, valeurs, problème]* moral ◆ **j'ai pris l'engagement ~ de le faire** I'm morally committed to doing it ◆ **avoir l'obligation ~e de faire** to be under a moral obligation *ou* be morally obliged to do ◆ **conscience ~e** moral conscience ◆ **n'avoir aucun sens ~** to be totally amoral, to have no sense of right and wrong

2 *(= honnête, vertueux)* *[personne, œuvre]* moral; *[conduite]* ethical, moral ◆ **ce n'est pas très ~ de faire cela** it's not very moral *ou* ethical to do that

3 *(= mental, psychologique)* *[autorité, crise, préjudice, force, courage, soutien, victoire]* moral; *[douleur]* mental ◆ **il a fait preuve d'une grande force ~e** he showed great moral fibre; → **personne**

NM 1 *(= état d'esprit)* morale ◆ **les troupes ont bon/mauvais ~** the morale of the troops is high/low ◆ **avoir le ~, avoir (un) bon ~, avoir un ~ d'acier** to be in good spirits ◆ **tu vas garder ses enfants ? tu as le ~ !*** you're going to babysit for him? that's brave of you! ◆ **il a mauvais ~, il n'a pas le ~** he is in low *ou* poor spirits ◆ **avoir le ~ à zéro*** to be (feeling) down in the dumps* ◆ **son ~ est (tombé) très bas** his morale is very low *ou* is at a low ebb, he's in very low spirits ◆ **le ~ est atteint** it has shaken *ou* undermined his morale *ou* his confidence ◆ **garder le ~** to keep one's spirits up ◆ **remonter le ~ de qn** to cheer sb up ◆ **il faut remonter le ~ de l'équipe** we need to boost the team's morale

2 ◆ **au ~ comme au physique** mentally as well as physically ◆ **au ~ il est irréprochable** morally he is beyond reproach

morale² /mɔʀal/ **NF** 1 *(= doctrine)* moral doctrine *ou* code, ethic *(Philos)*; *(= mœurs)* morals; *(= valeurs traditionnelles)* morality, moral standards, ethic *(Philos)* ◆ **la ~** *(Philos)* moral philosophy, ethics ◆ **action conforme à la ~** act in keeping with morality *ou* moral standards ◆ **c'est contraire à la ~** it's immoral ◆ **faire la ~ à qn** to lecture sb, to preach at sb ◆ **avoir une ~ relâchée** to have loose morals ◆ ~ **protestante** Protestant ethic 2 *[de fable]* moral ◆ **la ~ de cette histoire** the moral of this story

moralement /mɔʀalmɑ̃/ **ADV** 1 *(= selon l'éthique)* morally 2 *(= psychologiquement)* **soutenir qn ~** to give moral support to sb ◆ **physiquement et ~** physically and mentally

moralisant, e /mɔʀalizɑ̃, ɑt/ **ADJ** moralizing

moralisateur, -trice /mɔʀalizatœʀ, tʀis/ **ADJ** *[discours, ton]* moralizing, sententious *(frm)*; *[histoire]* edifying, elevating **NM,F** moralizer

moralisation /mɔʀalizasjɔ̃/ **NF** raising of moral standards (*de* in)

moraliser /mɔʀalize/ ▸ conjug 1 ◂ **VI** to moralize, to sermonize *(péj)* (*sur* about) **VT** 1 *(= sermonner)* ~ **qn** to preach at sb, to lecture sb 2 *(= rendre plus moral)* *[+ société]* to moralize, to improve the morals of; *[+ vie politique, profession]* to make more ethical

moralisme /mɔʀalism/ **NM** moralism

moraliste /mɔʀalist/ **ADJ** moralistic **NMF** moralist

moralité /mɔʀalite/ **NF** 1 *(= mœurs)* morals, morality, moral standards ◆ **d'une ~ douteuse** *[personne]* of doubtful morals; *[film]* of dubious morality ◆ **d'une haute ~** *[personne]* of high moral standards; *[discours]* of a high moral tone ◆ **la ~ publique** public morality ◆ **il n'a aucune ~** he has no sense of right or wrong, he's totally amoral; → **témoin** 2 *(= valeur)* *[d'attitude, action]* morality 3 *(= enseignement)* *[de fable]* moral ◆ ~ **: il ne faut jamais mentir !** the moral is: never tell lies! ◆ ~**, j'ai eu une indigestion*** the result was (that) I had indigestion 4 *(Littérat)* morality play

morasse /mɔʀas/ **NF** *(Typo)* final *ou* foundry proof

moratoire¹ /mɔʀatwaʀ/ **ADJ** moratory ◆ **intérêts ~s** interest on arrears

moratoire² /mɔʀatwaʀ/, **moratorium** † /mɔʀatɔʀjɔm/ **NM** *(Jur)* moratorium (*sur* on)

morave /mɔʀav/ **ADJ** Moravian **NMF Morave** Moravian

Moravie /mɔʀavi/ **NF** Moravia

morbide /mɔʀbid/ **ADJ** *(gén, Méd)* morbid

morbidité /mɔʀbidite/ **NF** morbidity

morbier /mɔʀbje/ **NM** 1 *(= fromage)* cow's milk cheese from the Jura 2 *(Helv = comtoise)* grandfather clock

morbleu /mɔʀblø/ **EXCL** (††, *hum*) zounds! †, gadzooks! †

morceau (pl **morceaux**) /mɔʀso/ **NM** 1 *(comestible)* *[de pain]* piece, bit; *[de sucre]* lump; *[de viande]* *(à table)* piece, bit; *(chez le boucher)* piece, cut ◆ ~ **de choix** choice morsel *ou* piece ◆ **c'était un ~ de roi** it was fit for a king ◆ **manger un ~** to have a bite (to eat) *ou* a snack ◆ **manger** *ou* **lâcher** *ou* **cracher le ~** * *(fig)* *(= dénoncer)* to spill the beans*; *(= avouer)* to come clean* ◆ **il a emporté le ~*** *(= il a gagné)* he carried it off; → **bas¹, sucre**

2 *(= fragment)* *(gén)* piece; *[de bois]* piece, lump; *[de fer]* lump; *[de ficelle]* bit, piece; *[de terre]* piece, patch, plot; *[de tissu]* piece

◆ **en morceaux** in pieces ◆ **couper en ~x** to cut into pieces ◆ **mettre qch en ~x** to pull sth to bits *ou* pieces ◆ **tomber en ~x** *[gâteau]* to crumble to bits; *[empire, relation]* to crumble, to fall apart

[3] *(Littérat, Mus) (= œuvre)* piece; *(= extrait)* passage, excerpt ◆ **(recueil de) ~x choisis** (collection of) selected passages *ou* extracts ◆ **un beau ~ d'éloquence** a fine piece of eloquence ◆ **c'est un ~ d'anthologie** it's a classic ◆ **~ de bravoure** *(Littérat)* purple passage; *(Mus)* bravura passage ◆ **~ de concours** competition piece ◆ **~ pour piano/violon** piece for piano/violin

[4] *(* = personne, objet)* **c'est un sacré ~** he (*ou* it *etc*) is a hell of a size* ◆ **beau ~** *(= femme)* nice bit of stuff* *(Brit)*, nice-looking woman

morceler /mɔʀsəle/ ▸ conjug 4 ◂ VT *[+ domaine, terrain]* to parcel out, to divide up; *[+ héritage]* to divide up; *[+ troupes, territoire]* to divide up, to split up ◆ **opposition morcelée** *(Pol)* divided opposition

morcellement /mɔʀsɛlmɑ̃/ NM [1] *(= action) [de domaine, terrain]* parcelling (out), dividing (up); *[d'héritage]* division, dividing (up); *[de troupes, territoire]* division, dividing (up), splitting (up) [2] *(= résultat)* division

mordant, e /mɔʀdɑ̃, ɑ̃t/ ADJ [1] *(= caustique) [ton, réplique]* cutting, scathing, mordant, caustic; *[pamphlet]* scathing, cutting; *[polémiste, critique]* scathing ◆ **avec une ironie ~e** with caustic *ou* biting *ou* mordant irony [2] *[froid]* biting *(épith)* NM [1] *(= dynamisme) [de personne]* spirit, drive; *[de troupe, équipe]* spirit, keenness; *[de style, écrit]* bite, punch ◆ **discours plein de ~** speech full of bite *ou* punch [2] *[de scie]* bite [3] *(Tech) (= substance)* mordant [4] *(Mus)* mordent

mordicus* /mɔʀdikys/ ADV *[défendre, soutenir, affirmer]* obstinately, stubbornly

mordillage /mɔʀdijaʒ/, **mordillement** /mɔʀdijmɑ̃/ NM nibble, nibbling *(NonC)*

mordiller /mɔʀdije/ ▸ conjug 1 ◂ VT to nibble at ◆ **il lui mordillait l'oreille** he nibbled her ear

mordoré, e /mɔʀdɔʀe/ ADJ, NM (lustrous) bronze ◆ **les tons ~s de l'automne** the rich bronze tints *ou* the browns and golds of autumn

mordorure /mɔʀdɔʀyʀ/ NF *(littér)* bronze ◆ **les ~s de l'étoffe** the bronze lustre of the cloth

mordre /mɔʀdʀ/ ▸ conjug 41 ◂ VT [1] *[animal, personne]* to bite ◆ **~ qn à la main** to bite sb's hand ◆ **un chien l'a mordu à la jambe, il s'est fait ~ à la jambe par un chien** a dog bit him on the leg, he was bitten on the leg by a dog ◆ **~ une pomme (à belles dents)** to bite into an apple ◆ **~ un petit bout de qch** to bite off a small piece of sth, to take a small bite (out) of sth ◆ **le chien l'a mordu jusqu'au sang** the dog bit him and drew blood ◆ **approche, je ne mords pas** come closer, I won't bite you ◆ **~ la poussière** to bite the dust ◆ **faire ~ la poussière à qn** to make sb bite the dust

[2] *[lime, vis]* to bite into; *[acide]* to bite (into), to eat into; *[froid]* to bite, to nip ◆ **les crampons mordaient la glace** the crampons gripped the ice *ou* bit into the ice ◆ **l'inquiétude/la jalousie lui mordait le cœur** worry/jealousy was eating at *ou* gnawing at his heart

[3] *(= toucher)* **la balle a mordu la ligne** the ball (just) touched the line ◆ **~ la ligne de départ** to be touching the starting line ◆ **~ la ligne blanche** *(en voiture)* to go over *ou* cross the white line

VT INDIR **mordre sur** *(= empiéter sur) [+ vacances]* to overlap into, to eat into; *[+ espace]* to overlap into, to encroach onto; *(= corroder)* to bite into ◆ **ça va ~ sur l'autre semaine** that will go over into *ou* overlap into *ou* cut into the following week ◆ **~ sur la marge** to go over into the margin ◆ **ils mordent sur notre clientèle** they're eating into *ou* cutting into our customer base ◆ **il a mordu sur la ligne blanche** *(en voiture)* he went over *ou* crossed the white line

VI [1] ◆ **~ dans** *[+ fruit]* to bite into ◆ **~ dans le sable** *[ancre]* to grip *ou* hold the sand

[2] *(Pêche, fig)* to bite ◆ **~ (à l'hameçon** *ou* **à l'appât)** *(lit)* to bite, to rise (to the bait); *(fig)* to rise to the bait ◆ **ça mord aujourd'hui ?** are the fish biting *ou* rising today? ◆ **il a mordu au latin/aux maths*** he's taken to Latin/to maths

[3] *(Gravure)* to bite; *[étoffe]* to take the dye; *[teinture]* to take

[4] *(Tech)* **l'engrenage ne mord plus** the gear won't mesh any more

VPR **se mordre** ◆ **se ~ la joue** to bite the inside of one's mouth ◆ **se ~ la langue** *(lit)* to bite one's tongue; *(fig) (= se retenir)* to hold one's tongue; *(= se repentir)* to bite one's tongue ◆ **maintenant il s'en mord les doigts** he could kick himself now* ◆ **tu t'en mordras les doigts** you'll live to regret it, you'll rue the day ◆ **se ~ la queue** *[chien]* to chase its tail; *(*fig)* to chase one's tail

mordu, e /mɔʀdy/ (ptp de **mordre**) ADJ [1] *(* = amoureux)* smitten ◆ **il est vraiment ~** he's really smitten with her, he's crazy* about her [2] *(* = fanatique)* **~ de football/jazz** crazy* *ou* mad* about *ou* mad keen* on *(Brit)* football/jazz NM,F *(* = fanatique)* enthusiast, buff*, fan ◆ **~ de la voile/de musique** sailing/music enthusiast *ou* buff* ◆ **~ d'informatique** computer buff* *ou* freak* ◆ **c'est un ~ de football** he's a great football fan *ou* buff*

more /mɔʀ/, **moresque** /mɔʀɛsk/ ADJ, NMF ⇒ **maure, mauresque**

morfal, e* (mpl **morfals**) /mɔʀfal/ NM,F greedy guts*, pig*

morfler* /mɔʀfle/ ▸ conjug 1 ◂ VI *(= souffrir)* to have a hard time of it; *(= se faire battre)* to catch it*, to cop it* *(Brit)* ◆ **j'ai une rage de dents, qu'est-ce que je morfle !** I've got a toothache, it's agony!* *ou* it's killing me!* ◆ **ça va ~ !** there's going to be trouble!

morfondre (se) /mɔʀfɔ̃dʀ/ ▸ conjug 41 ◂ VPR *(tristement)* to mope; *(nerveusement)* to fret ◆ **il se morfondait en attendant le résultat** he waited fretfully for the result ◆ **les enfants qui se morfondent dans les orphelinats** children languishing in orphanages

morfondu, e /mɔʀfɔ̃dy/ (ptp de **morfondre**) ADJ *(littér)* dejected, crestfallen

morganatique /mɔʀganatik/ ADJ morganatic

morgue¹ /mɔʀg/ NF *(littér = orgueil)* pride, haughtiness ◆ **il me répondit plein de ~ que ...** he answered me haughtily that ...

morgue² /mɔʀg/ NF *(Police)* morgue; *[d'hôpital]* mortuary

moribond, e /mɔʀibɔ̃, ɔ̃d/ ADJ *[personne]* dying; *[économie, marché, institution]* moribund NM,F dying man (*ou* woman) ◆ **les ~s** the dying

moricaud, e** /mɔʀiko, od/ *(injurieux)* ADJ dark(-skinned) NM,F darkie** *(injurieux)*

morigéner /mɔʀiʒene/ ▸ conjug 6 ◂ VT *(littér)* to take to task, to reprimand ◆ **il faut le ~** he will have to be taken to task (over it) *ou* reprimanded (for it)

morille /mɔʀij/ NF morel

morillon /mɔʀijɔ̃/ NM [1] *(= canard)* tufted duck [2] *(= raisin) kind of black grape* [3] *(= pierre)* small rough emerald

mormon, e /mɔʀmɔ̃, ɔn/ ADJ, NM,F Mormon

mormonisme /mɔʀmɔnism/ NM Mormonism

morne¹ /mɔʀn/ ADJ *[personne, visage]* doleful, glum; *[temps]* gloomy, dismal, dull; *[silence]* mournful, gloomy, dismal; *[conversation, vie, paysage, ville]* dismal, dreary, dull ◆ **d'un ton ~** gloomily ◆ **passer un après-midi ~** to spend a dreary *ou* dismal afternoon

morne² /mɔʀn/ NM *(aux Antilles etc = colline)* hill

mornifle* /mɔʀnifl/ NF slap, clout* *(Brit)* ◆ **donner** *ou* **filer** *ou* **flanquer une ~ à qn** to box sb's ears, to give sb a clip round the ear *(Brit)*

Moroni /mɔʀɔni/ N Moroni

morose /mɔʀoz/ ADJ *[humeur, personne, ton]* sullen, morose; *[marché, Bourse, journée]* sluggish, dull; → **délectation**

morosité /mɔʀozite/ NF *[de personne]* sullenness, moroseness; *[de temps]* dullness; *[de marché, économie]* sluggishness ◆ **climat de ~ économique/sociale** gloomy *ou* depressed economic/social climate

morphe /mɔʀf/ NM morph

Morphée /mɔʀfe/ NM Morpheus; → **bras**

morphème /mɔʀfɛm/ NM morpheme ◆ **~ libre/lié** free/bound morpheme

morphine /mɔʀfin/ NF morphine ◆ **~-base** morphine base

morphinique /mɔʀfinik/ ADJ *[médicament, substance]* morphinated, containing morphine

morphinisme /mɔʀfinism/ NM morphinism

morphinomane /mɔʀfinɔman/ ADJ addicted to morphine NMF morphine addict

morphinomanie /mɔʀfinɔmani/ NF morphine addiction, morphinomania

morphologie /mɔʀfɔlɔʒi/ NF morphology

morphologique /mɔʀfɔlɔʒik/ ADJ morphological

morphologiquement /mɔʀfɔlɔʒikmɑ̃/ ADV morphologically

morphophonologie /mɔʀfɔfɔnɔlɔʒi/ NF morphophonology

morphosyntaxe /mɔʀfosɛ̃taks/ NF morphosyntax

morphosyntaxique /mɔʀfosɛ̃taksik/ ADJ morphosyntactical

morpion /mɔʀpjɔ̃/ NM [1] *(Jeux)* ≈ noughts and crosses *(Brit)*, tic tac toe *(US)* [2] *(* = pou du pubis)* crab* [3] *(*, péj = gamin)* brat*

mors /mɔʀ/ NM [1] *(Équitation)* bit ◆ **prendre le ~ aux dents** *[cheval]* to take the bit between its teeth; *(= agir)* to take the bit between one's teeth; *(= s'emporter)* to fly off the handle*, to blow one's top* *ou* stack* *(US)*; *(= prendre l'initiative)* to take the matter into one's own hands [2] *(Tech)* jaw; *(Reliure)* joint

morse¹ /mɔʀs/ NM *(= animal)* walrus

morse² /mɔʀs/ NM *(= code)* Morse (code)

morsure /mɔʀsyʀ/ NF bite ◆ **~ de chien** dog bite ◆ **~ de serpent** snakebite ◆ **les ~s du vent/du froid** *(littér)* the biting wind/cold

mort¹ /mɔʀ/ NF [1] *(lit)* death ◆ **~ clinique/cérébrale** clinical/brain death ◆ **~ naturelle** natural death ◆ **~ subite du nourrisson** cot *(Brit)* *ou* crib *(US)* death, sudden infant death syndrome ◆ **~ volontaire** suicide ◆ **tu veux ma ~ ?*** do you want to kill me or what?* ◆ **trouver la ~ dans un accident** to die *ou* be killed in an accident ◆ **souhaiter la ~** to long for death, to long to die ◆ **souhaiter la ~ de qn** to wish death upon sb *(littér)*, to wish sb (were) dead ◆ **donner la ~ (à qn)** to kill (sb) ◆ **se donner la ~** to take one's own life, to kill o.s. ◆ **périr** *ou* **mourir de ~ violente/accidentelle** to die a violent/an accidental death ◆ **mourir dans son sommeil, c'est une belle ~** dying in one's sleep is a good way to go ◆ **à la ~ de sa mère** on the death of his mother, when his mother died ◆ **il a vu la ~ de près** he has come close to death, he has looked death in the face ◆ **il n'y a pas eu ~ d'homme** no one was killed, there was no loss of life ◆ **il n'y a pas ~ d'homme !** *(fig)* it's not the end of the world! ◆ **la petite ~**

(littér) orgasm, petite mort *(littér)* ◆ **ça coûte 30 €, ce n'est pas la ~ !*** it's only 30 euros, it won't kill you *(ou* me *etc)*! *; → **hurler, pâle**

2 *(fig)* death, end ◆ **c'est la ~ de ses espoirs** that puts an end to *ou* is the end of his hopes, that puts paid to his hopes *(Brit)* ◆ **le supermarché sera la ~ du petit commerce** supermarkets will spell the end *ou* the death of small businesses ◆ **cet enfant sera ma ~ !*** this child will be the death of me! *

3 *(locutions)* **~ au tyran !, à ~ le tyran !** down with the tyrant!, death to the tyrant! ◆ **~ aux vaches !**‡ down with the cops! * *ou* pigs!‡ **souffrir mille ~s** to suffer agonies, to be in agony ◆ **la ~ dans l'âme** with a heavy *ou* an aching heart, grieving inwardly ◆ **il avait la ~ dans l'âme** his heart ached

◆ **à mort** ◆ **lutte à ~** fight to the death ◆ **détester qn à ~** to hate sb to death ◆ **blessé à ~** *(dans un combat)* mortally wounded; *(dans un accident)* fatally injured ◆ **frapper qn à ~** to strike sb dead ◆ **mettre à ~** *[+ personne]* to deliver the death blow to; *[+ taureau]* to put to death ◆ **mise à ~** *[de taureau]* kill ◆ **nous sommes fâchés à ~** we're at daggers drawn (with each other) ◆ **en vouloir à qn à ~** to be bitterly resentful of sb ◆ **il m'en veut à ~** he hates me (for it) ◆ **défendre qch à ~** *(fig)* to defend sth to the bitter end ◆ **freiner à ~*** to jam on the brakes *ou* the anchors * *(Brit)* ◆ **s'ennuyer à ~** to be bored to death ◆ **visser qch à ~*** to screw sth right home, to screw sth tight

◆ **de mort** ◆ **silence de ~** deathly *ou* deathlike hush ◆ **d'une pâleur de ~** deathly *ou* deadly pale ◆ **engin de ~** lethal *ou* deadly weapon

mort², e /mɔʀ, mɔʀt/ **GRAMMAIRE ACTIVE 51.4** ptp de **mourir**

ADJ 1 *[être animé, arbre, feuille]* dead ◆ **il est ~ depuis deux ans** he's been dead (for) two years, he died 2 years ago ◆ **on l'a laissé pour ~** he was left for dead ◆ **il est ~ et bien ~** he's dead and gone ◆ **il est ~ et enterré** he's dead and buried ◆ **ramenez-les ~s ou vifs** bring them back dead or alive ◆ **~ au champ d'honneur** *(Mil)* killed in action ◆ **il était comme ~** he looked (as though he were) dead ◆ **tu es un homme ~ !*** you're a dead man! *

2 *(fig)* **je suis ~ (de fatigue) !** I'm dead (tired)! *ou* dead beat! *, I'm all in! * *(Brit)* ◆ **il était ~ de peur** *ou* **plus ~ que vif** he was frightened to death *ou* scared stiff * ◆ **ils étaient ~s de rire** they were doubled up with laughter; → **ivre**

3 *(= inerte, sans vie) [chair, peau, rivière]* dead; *[pied, doigt]* dead, numb; *[yeux]* lifeless, dull; *(Fin) [marché]* dead ◆ **la ville est ~e le dimanche** the town is dead on a Sunday ◆ **opération ville ~e** *decision to close shops and businesses for a short period in protest, mourning etc;* → **poids, point¹, temps¹**

4 *(= qui n'existe plus) [civilisation]* extinct, dead; *[langue]* dead ◆ **leur vieille amitié est ~e** their old friendship is dead ◆ **le passé est bien ~** the past is over and done with *ou* is dead and gone

5 *(* = usé, fini) [pile, radio, moteur]* dead

NM 1 *(= personne)* dead man ◆ **les ~s** the dead ◆ **les ~s de la guerre** those *ou* the men killed in the war, the war dead ◆ **il y a eu un ~** one person was killed, there was one death ◆ **il y a eu de nombreux ~s** many (people) were killed, there were many deaths ◆ **l'accident a fait cinq ~s** five (people) were killed in the accident ◆ **jour** *ou* **fête des ~s** All Souls' Day ◆ **office/messe/prière des ~s** office/mass/prayer for the dead ◆ **c'est un ~ vivant/un ~ en sursis** he's more dead than alive/living on borrowed time ◆ **faire le ~** *(lit)* to pretend to be dead, to sham death; *(fig = ne pas se manifester)* to lie low ◆ **la place du ~** *(Aut)* the (front) seat next to the driver; → **monument, tête**

2 *(Cartes)* dummy ◆ **être le ~** to be dummy

NF **morte** dead woman

mortadelle /mɔʀtadɛl/ **NF** mortadella

mortaise /mɔʀtɛz/ **NF** mortise

mortaiser /mɔʀteze/ ► conjug 1 ◄ **VT** to mortise

mortalité /mɔʀtalite/ **NF** mortality, death rate ◆ **~ infantile** infant mortality ◆ **régression de la ~** fall in the death rate

mort-aux-rats /mɔʀ(t)oʀa/ **NF INV** rat poison

morte-eau (pl **mortes-eaux**) /mɔʀto/ **NF** neap tide

mortel, -elle /mɔʀtɛl/ **ADJ** 1 *(= qui périt)* mortal; → **dépouille**

2 *(= entraînant la mort) [chute, maladie]* fatal; *[blessure, plaie]* fatal, lethal; *[poison]* deadly, lethal ◆ **danger ~** mortal danger ◆ **coup ~** *(lit)* lethal *ou* fatal blow; *(fig)* death-blow, mortal blow ◆ **cela a porté un coup ~ au parti** this dealt the death-blow to the party ◆ **cette révélation lui serait mortelle** such a discovery would kill him *ou* would be fatal to him

3 *(= intense) [frayeur]* mortal; *[pâleur, silence]* deadly, deathly; *[ennemi]* mortal, deadly; *[haine]* deadly ◆ **il fait un froid ~** it's deathly cold, it's as cold as death ◆ **cette attente mortelle se prolongeait** this deadly wait dragged on ◆ **allons, ce n'est pas ~ !*** come on, it's not all that bad! *ou* it won't kill you!

4 *(* = ennuyeux) [livre, soirée]* deadly *, deadly boring *ou* dull ◆ **il est ~** he's a deadly * *ou* crashing * bore

5 ‡ *(= excellent)* fabulous; *(= mauvais)* terrible

NM,F *(littér, hum)* mortal ◆ **simple ~** mere mortal ◆ **heureux ~ !*** lucky fellow! * *ou* chap! * *(Brit)* ◆ **nous autres pauvres ~s** *(hum)* we lesser mortals; → **commun**

mortellement /mɔʀtɛlmɑ̃/ **ADV** 1 *[blesser] (dans un combat)* mortally; *(dans un accident)* fatally ◆ **il a été ~ atteint d'une balle de fusil** he was shot and fatally wounded ◆ **elle a été ~ poignardée** she was stabbed to death 2 *(fig) [offenser, vexer]* mortally, deeply ◆ **~ ennuyeux** deadly boring *ou* dull

morte-saison (pl **mortes-saisons**), **morte saison** /mɔʀt(ə)sɛzɔ̃/ **NF** off-season, slack season ◆ **à la ~** in *ou* during the off-season

mortier /mɔʀtje/ **NM** *(Constr, Culin, Mil, Pharm)* mortar; *(= toque)* cap *(worn by certain French judges)* ◆ **attaque au ~** mortar attack

mortifère /mɔʀtifɛʀ/ **ADJ** *(hum) [ambiance, discours]* deadly *

mortifiant, e /mɔʀtifjɑ̃, jɑ̃t/ **ADJ** *[paroles]* hurtful; *[expérience]* mortifying; *[échec]* humiliating

mortification /mɔʀtifikasjɔ̃/ **NF** mortification

mortifier /mɔʀtifje/ ► conjug 7 ◄ **VT** *(Rel)* to mortify; *(= vexer)* to mortify

mortinatalité /mɔʀtinatalite/ **NF** incidence of stillbirths

mort-né, mort-née (mpl **mort-nés**, fpl **mort-nées**) /mɔʀne/ **ADJ** *[enfant]* stillborn; *[projet]* abortive, stillborn

mortuaire /mɔʀtɥɛʀ/ **ADJ** *[chapelle]* mortuary *(épith)*; *[rites]* mortuary *(épith)*, funeral *(épith)*; *[cérémonie]* funeral *(épith)* ◆ **salon ~** *(Can)* funeral home *ou* parlor *(US, Can)* ◆ **la chambre ~** the death chamber ◆ **la maison ~** the house of the departed *ou* deceased; → **couronne, drap, masque**

morue /mɔʀy/ **NF** 1 *(= poisson)* cod ◆ **~ fraîche/séchée/salée** fresh/dried/salted cod ◆ **~ verte** undried salted cod; → **brandade, huile** 2 *(‡ = prostituée)* whore, tart‡

morutier, -ière /mɔʀytje, jɛʀ/ **ADJ** cod-fishing *(épith)* **NM** *(= pêcheur)* cod-fisherman; *(= bateau)* cod-fishing boat

morve /mɔʀv/ **NF** snot‡, (nasal) mucus; *(= maladie du cheval)* glanders *(sg)*

morveux, -euse /mɔʀvø, øz/ **ADJ** 1 *[enfant]* snotty(-nosed)‡ ◆ **qui se sent ~, qu'il se mouche** *(Prov)* if the cap *ou* shoe *(US)* fits, wear it *(Prov)* 2 *[cheval]* glandered **NM,F** ‡ *(= enfant)* nasty little brat *; *(= adulte)* jerk‡

mosaïque¹ /mɔzaik/ **NF** *(Art, Bot)* mosaic; *[de champs]* chequered pattern, patchwork; *[d'idées, peuples]* medley ◆ **de** *ou* **en ~** mosaic

mosaïque² /mɔzaik/ **ADJ** *(Bible)* Mosaic(al), of Moses

Moscou /mɔsku/ **N** Moscow

moscovite /mɔskɔvit/ **ADJ** of *ou* from Moscow, Moscow *(épith)*, Muscovite **NMF** **Moscovite** Muscovite

Moselle /mozɛl/ **NF** Moselle

mosquée /mɔske/ **NF** mosque

mot /mo/ **GRAMMAIRE ACTIVE 48.1**

NM 1 *(gén)* word ◆ **le ~ (d')orange** the word "orange" ◆ **ce ne sont que des ~s** it's just (so many) empty words, it's just talk ◆ **je n'en crois pas un (traître) ~** I don't believe a (single) word of it ◆ **paresseux, c'est bien le ~ !** lazybones is the right word to describe him! ◆ **ça alors, c'est bien le ~ !** you've said it!, you never spoke *ou* said a truer word! ◆ **de grands ~s** high-flown *ou* fancy words ◆ **tout de suite les grands ~s !** you start straight in with these high-sounding words! ◆ **voilà le grand ~ lâché !** you've come out with it at last! ◆ **génie, c'est un bien grand ~ !** genius, that's a big word! ◆ **à ces ~s** at this *ou* that ◆ **sur ces ~s** with this *ou* that, so saying, with these words ◆ **à ~s couverts** in veiled terms ◆ **en d'autres ~s** in other words ◆ **en un ~** in a word ◆ **en un ~ comme en cent** in a nutshell, in brief ◆ **faire du ~ à ~, traduire ~ à ~** to translate word for word ◆ **c'est du ~ à ~** it's a word for word rendering *ou* translation ◆ **rapporter une conversation ~ pour ~** to give a word for word *ou* a verbatim report of a conversation ◆ **il n'a pas eu de ~s assez durs pour condamner les attentats** he condemned the attacks in the strongest possible terms

2 *(= message)* word; *(= courte lettre)* note, line ◆ **je vais lui en toucher un ~** I'll have a word with him about it, I'll mention it to him ◆ **glisser un ~ à qn** *ou* **dans l'oreille de qn** to have a word in sb's ear ◆ **se donner** *ou* **se passer le ~** to send *ou* pass the word round, to pass the word on ◆ **mettez-lui un petit ~** drop him a line *ou* note, write him a note ◆ **il ne m'a même pas dit un ~ de remerciement** he didn't even thank me

3 *(= expression frappante)* saying ◆ **~s célèbres/historiques** famous/historic sayings ◆ **bon ~** witticism, witty remark ◆ **il aime faire des bons ~s** he likes to make witty remarks

4 *(Ordin)* word ◆ **~ machine** machine word

5 *(locutions)* **avoir des ~s avec qn** to have words with sb ◆ **avoir toujours le ~ pour rire** to be a born joker ◆ **le ~ de l'énigme** the key to the mystery ◆ **avoir le ~ de la fin** *ou* **le dernier ~** to have the last word ◆ **c'est votre dernier ~ ?** *(gén)* is that your last word in the matter?; *(dans négociations)* is that your final offer? ◆ **je n'ai pas dit mon dernier ~** you *(ou* they *etc)* haven't heard the last of me ◆ **sans ~ dire** without saying a *ou* one word ◆ **vous n'avez qu'un ~ à dire et je le ferai** (you have only to) say the word and I'll do it ◆ **j'estime avoir mon ~ à dire dans cette affaire** I think I'm entitled to have my say in this matter ◆ **je vais lui dire deux ~s** I'll give him a piece of my mind ◆ **prendre qn au ~** to take sb at his word ◆ **il n'en connaît** *ou* **n'en sait pas le premier ~** he doesn't know the first thing about it ◆ **il ne sait pas le premier ~ de sa leçon** he doesn't know a word of his lesson ◆ **il ne sait pas un (traître) ~ d'allemand** he doesn't know a (single) word of German ◆ **je n'ai pas pu lui tirer un ~** I couldn't get a word out of him ◆ **il lui a dit le ~ de Cambronne** ≈ he said a four-letter word to him ◆ **pas un ~ à qui que ce soit** mum's the word, don't breathe a word

of this to anyone ◆ **il n'a jamais un ~ plus haut que l'autre** he's very even-tempered ◆ **j'ai dû dire un ~ de travers** I must have said something wrong ◆ **au bas** ~ at the very least, at the lowest estimate ◆ **qui ne dit ~ consent** *(Prov)* silence gives consent

COMP **mot apparenté** *(Ling)* cognate
mot d'auteur revealing *ou* witty remark from the author
mot composé compound
mots croisés crossword (puzzle) ◆ **faire des ~s croisés** to do crosswords ◆ **faire les ~s croisés** *(d'un journal)* to do the crossword (puzzle)
mot d'emprunt loan word
mot d'enfant child's (funny) remark
mot d'esprit witticism, witty remark
mot d'excuse *(gén)* letter of apology; *(Scol) (gén)* (absence) note; *(pour maladie)* sick note
mots fléchés crossword (puzzle) *(with clues given inside the boxes)*
mot d'ordre watchword, slogan
mot de passe password
mot souche root-word

motard, -arde /mɔtaʀ, aʀd/ NM,F motorcyclist, biker* NM *(Police)* motorcycle policeman *ou* cop*; *(de la gendarmerie, de l'armée)* motorcyclist ◆ **les ~s de l'escorte présidentielle** the president's motorcycle escort, the president's motorcade

mot-clé (pl **mots-clés**), **mot clé** /mokle/ NM keyword

motel /mɔtɛl/ NM motel

motet /mɔtɛ/ NM motet, anthem

moteur[1] /mɔtœʀ/ NM 1 *(Tech)* engine; *(électrique)* motor ◆ ~ **atmosphérique** atmospheric engine ◆ ~ **à combustion interne**, ~ **à explosion** internal combustion engine ◆ ~ **à 2/4 temps** 2-/4-stroke engine ◆ **à** ~ power-driven, motor *(épith)* ◆ ~ **!** *(Ciné)* action! ◆ ~ **de recherche** *(Ordin)* search engine; → **frein** 2 *(= force)* mover, mainspring ◆ **le grand ~ de l'univers** *(littér)* the prime mover of the universe ◆ **être le ~ de qch** to be the mainspring of sth, to be the driving force behind sth

moteur[2], -trice /mɔtœʀ, tʀis/ ADJ 1 *(Anat)* *[muscle, nerf, troubles]* motor *(épith)* 2 *(Rail)* **engin** ~ power unit ◆ **force motrice** *(lit, fig)* driving force; → **arbre, roue** NF **motrice** *(Rail)* power unit

motif /mɔtif/ NM 1 *(= raison)* motive *(de* for) grounds *(de* for); *(= but)* purpose *(de* of); ◆ **quel est le ~ de votre visite ?** what is the motive for *ou* the purpose of your visit? ◆ **quel ~ as-tu de te plaindre ?** what grounds have you got for complaining? ◆ **il a de bons ~s pour le faire** he has good grounds for doing it ◆ **fréquenter une jeune fille pour le bon** ~ († *ou hum)* to court a girl with honourable intentions ◆ **faire qch sans** ~ to have no motive for doing sth ◆ **colère sans** ~ groundless *ou* irrational anger ◆ ~ **d'inquiétude** cause for concern ◆ **donner des ~s de satisfaction à qn** to give sb grounds *ou* cause for satisfaction
2 *(= ornement)* motif, design, pattern; *(Peinture, Mus)* motif ◆ **tissu à ~s** patterned material ◆ **papier peint à ~ de fleurs** floral wallpaper, wallpaper with a floral design *ou* motif
3 *(Jur) [de jugement]* grounds *(de* for)

motion /mosjɔ̃/ NF *(Jur, Pol)* motion COMP **motion de censure** censure motion ◆ **déposer une ~ de censure** to table a censure motion ◆ **voter la ~ de censure** to pass a vote of no confidence *ou* of censure

motivant, e /mɔtivɑ̃, ɑ̃t/ ADJ *[travail]* rewarding, satisfying ◆ **rémunération ~e** attractive salary

motivation /mɔtivasjɔ̃/ NF 1 *(= justification)* motivation *(de* for); ◆ **quelles sont ses ~s ?** *(raisons personnelles)* what are his motives? *(pour* for); ◆ **lettre de** ~ covering letter, letter in support of one's application 2 *(= dynamisme)* motivation

motivé, e /mɔtive/ (ptp de **motiver**) ADJ 1 *[action] (= expliqué)* reasoned, justified; *(= légitime)* well-founded, motivated ◆ **non** ~ unexplained, unjustified ◆ **absence ~e** *(Scol)* legitimate *ou* genuine absence ◆ **refus** ~ justified refusal 2 *[personne]* motivated ◆ **non** ~ unmotivated

motiver /mɔtive/ ► conjug 1 ◄ VT 1 *(= justifier, expliquer) [+ action, attitude, réclamation]* to justify, to account for ◆ **il a motivé sa conduite en disant que ...** he justified his behaviour by saying that ... ◆ **rien ne peut ~ une telle conduite** nothing can justify *ou* warrant such behaviour 2 *(= fournir un motif à) [+ refus, intervention, jugement]* to motivate, to found; *(Psych)* to motivate 3 *(= pousser à agir) [personne, salaire]* to motivate

moto /moto/ NF (abrév de **motocyclette**) 1 *(= véhicule)* motorbike, motorcycle, bike* ◆ **je viendrai à** *ou* **en** ~ I'll come by bike* *ou* on my bike* ◆ ~ **de course** racing motorcycle ◆ ~ **de route** (standard) motorbike ◆ ~ **de trial** trail bike *(Brit)*, dirt bike *(US)* 2 *(= activité)* motorcycling, biking*

motocross, moto-cross /motokʀɔs/ NM INV *(= sport)* motocross, scrambling; *(= épreuve)* motocross race, scramble

moto-crottes* (pl **motos-crottes**) /motokʀɔt/ NF motorbike pooper scooper

motoculteur /mɔtɔkyltœʀ/ NM (motorized) cultivator

motocycle /mɔtɔsikl/ NM *(Admin)* motor bicycle

motocyclette /mɔtɔsiklɛt/ NF motorcycle, motorbike

motocyclisme /mɔtɔsiklism/ NM motorcycle racing

motocycliste /mɔtɔsiklist/ NMF motorcyclist ADJ *[course]* motorcycle *(épith)* ◆ **le sport** ~ motorcycle racing

motomarine /mɔtɔmaʀin/ NF jetski

motonautique /motonotik/ ADJ ◆ **sport** ~ speedboat *ou* motorboat racing

motonautisme /motonotism/ NM speedboat *ou* motorboat racing

motoneige /motonɛʒ/ NF snow-bike, skidoo ® *(Can)*

motoneigiste /motonɛʒist/ NMF snow-bike *ou* skidoo *(Can)* rider

motopompe /motopɔ̃p/ NF motor-pump, power-driven pump

motorisation /mɔtɔʀizasjɔ̃/ NF motorization; *(= type de moteur)* engine type

motorisé, e /mɔtɔʀize/ ADJ 1 *[mécanisme]* motorized, motor-driven; *(Mil) [compagnie, patrouille]* motorized, mechanized ◆ **la circulation ~e** motor traffic ◆ **sports ~s** motor sports; → **deux-roues** 2 ◆ **être** ~* *(= posséder un véhicule)* to have a car; *(= être en voiture)* to have transport *(Brit) ou* transportation *(US)*, to be car-borne* ◆ **tu es ~ ? sinon je te ramène** have you got transport? if not I'll drop you home ◆ **les voyageurs non ~s** passengers without cars, foot passengers

motoriser /mɔtɔʀize/ ► conjug 1 ◄ VT to motorize

motoriste /mɔtɔʀist/ NM *(= mécanicien)* car *ou* auto *(US)* mechanic; *(= constructeur)* engine manufacturer

mot-outil (pl **mots-outils**) /mouti/ NM grammatical word

motrice /mɔtʀis/ ADJ, NF → **moteur[2]**

motricité /mɔtʀisite/ NF motivity

motte /mɔt/ NF 1 *(Agr)* ~ **(de terre)** lump of earth, clod (of earth) ◆ ~ **de gazon** turf, sod ◆ **en** ~ *[plante]* balled 2 *(Culin)* ~ **de beurre** lump *ou* block of butter ◆ **acheter du beurre en** *ou* **à la** ~ to buy butter loose

motus* /mɔtys/ EXCL ◆ ~ **(et bouche cousue)!** mum's the word!*, keep it under your hat!, don't breathe a word!

mot-valise (pl **mots-valises**) /movaliz/ NM portmanteau word

mou[1], molle /mu, mɔl/ (m: devant voyelle ou h muet **mol** /mɔl/) ADJ 1 *(au toucher) [substance, oreiller]* soft; *[tige, tissu]* limp; *[chair, visage]* flabby ◆ **ce melon est tout** ~ this melon has gone all soft *ou* mushy ◆ **ajouter le beurre** ~ add the softened butter; → **chapeau, ventre**
2 *[traits du visage]* weak, slack
3 *(à l'oreille)* **bruit** ~ muffled noise, soft thud ◆ **voix aux inflexions molles** gently lilting voice
4 *(= sans énergie) [geste, poignée de main]* limp, lifeless; *[protestations, opposition]* weak, feeble; *[style]* feeble, dull; *(Mus) [exécution]* dull, lifeless; *[croissance, reprise économique, marché]* sluggish; *[dictature]* benign ◆ **personne molle** *(apathique)* lethargic *ou* sluggish person; *(sans autorité)* spineless character; *(trop indulgent)* lax *ou* soft person ◆ **j'ai les jambes molles** my legs feel weak *ou* like jelly *(Brit)* ◆ **dépêche-toi, c'est ~ tout ça !** you're so slow, hurry up! ◆ **il est ~ comme une chiffe** *ou* **chique** he's spineless ◆ **qu'est-ce qu'il est ~ !** he's so hopeless! ◆ **il est un peu ~ du genou*** he hasn't got much get-up-and-go*
5 *[temps]* muggy; *[tiédeur]* languid
NM 1 *[de corde]* **avoir du** ~ to be slack *ou* loose ◆ **donner du** ~ to give some slack, to loosen ◆ **il y a du ~ dans la pédale de frein** the brakes are soft *ou* spongy ◆ **donne un peu de ~ pour que je puisse faire un nœud** let the rope out a bit *ou* give a bit of play on the rope so that I can make a knot ◆ **donner** *ou* **laisser du ~ à qn** *(fig)* to give sb some leeway
2 *(= personne)* spineless character

mou[2] /mu/ NM *(Boucherie)* lights, lungs ◆ **bourrer le ~ à qn**‡ to take sb in, to have sb on* *(Brit)*

mouais /mwɛ/ EXCL yeah*

mouchard, e /muʃaʀ, aʀd/ NM,F (*: *Scol)* sneak* NM 1 *(arg Police)* informer, grass* *(Brit)*, fink‡ *(US)* 2 *(Tech = enregistreur) [d'avion, train]* black box; *[de camion]* tachograph; *[de veilleur de nuit]* control clock; *(Mil)* spy plane; *[de porte]* spyhole

mouchardage* /muʃaʀdaʒ/ NM *(Scol)* sneaking*; *(arg Police)* informing, grassing* *(Brit)*, ratting* *(US)* ◆ **il y a eu des ~s auprès de la direction** someone's been sneaking to the management

moucharder* /muʃaʀde/ ► conjug 1 ◄ VT *(Scol)* to sneak on*, to split on* *(Brit)*; *(arg Police)* to inform on, to grass on* *(Brit)*, to rat on* *(US)*

mouche /muʃ/ NF 1 *(= insecte, appât)* fly ◆ **quelle ~ t'a piqué ?** what's bitten you?*, what's got into you? ◆ **il faut toujours qu'il fasse la ~ du coche** he's always fussing around as if he's indispensable ◆ **mourir/ tomber comme des ~s** to die (off)/fall like flies ◆ **prendre la** ~ to get into *ou* go into a huff*, to get huffy* ◆ **on ne prend pas les ~s avec du vinaigre** *(Prov)* you have to be nice if you want something; → **voler[1], fin[1], mal[2]**
2 *(Escrime)* button ◆ **faire** ~ *(Tir)* to score a *ou* hit the bull's-eye; *(fig)* to score, to hit home; → **poids**
3 *(en taffetas)* patch, beauty spot; *(= touffe de poils sous la lèvre)* short goatee
NFPL **mouches** *(Opt)* specks, spots
COMP **mouche bleue** ⇒ **mouche de la viande**
mouche d'escadre *(Naut)* advice boat
mouche à feu *(Can)* firefly

mouche à merde* dung fly
mouche à miel honey bee
mouche tsé-tsé tsetse fly
mouche à vers blowfly
mouche verte greenbottle
mouche de la viande bluebottle
mouche du vinaigre fruit fly

moucher /muʃe/ ▸ conjug 1 ◂ VT 1 ◆ ~ **(le nez de) qn** to blow sb's nose ◆ **mouche ton nez** blow your nose ◆ **il mouche du sang** there are traces of blood (in his handkerchief) when he blows his nose 2 (* = *remettre à sa place*) ~ **qn** to put sb in his place ◆ **se faire** ~ to get put in one's place 3 [+ *chandelle*] to snuff (out) VPR **se moucher** to blow one's nose ◆ **il ne se mouche pas du coude*** *ou* **du pied*** (= *il est prétentieux*) he thinks he's it* *ou* the cat's whiskers* (*Brit*) *ou* meow (*US*); (= *il ne se refuse rien*) he doesn't deny himself anything

moucheron /muʃʀɔ̃/ NM (= *insecte*) midge, gnat; (* = *enfant*) kid*, nipper* (*Brit*)

moucheté, e /muʃ(ə)te/ (ptp de **moucheter**) ADJ [*œuf*] speckled; [*poisson*] spotted; [*laine*] flecked; → **fleuret**

moucheter /muʃ(ə)te/ ▸ conjug 4 ◂ VT 1 (= *tacheter*) to fleck (*de* with) 2 [+ *fleuret*] to put a button on; → **fleuret**

mouchetis /muʃ(ə)ti/ NM (*Constr*) pebble dash (*Brit*), rock dash (*US*)

mouchette /muʃɛt/ NF (*Archit*) [*de larmier*] lip; [*de fenêtrage*] outer fillet NFPL **mouchettes** (*Hist*) snuffers

moucheture /muʃ(ə)tyʀ/ NF (*sur les habits*) speck, spot, fleck; (*sur un animal*) spot, patch ◆ ~**s d'hermine** (*Hér*) ermine tips

mouchoir /muʃwaʀ/ NM (*de poche, en tissu*) handkerchief, hanky*; († : *autour du cou*) neckerchief ◆ ~ **(en papier)** tissue, paper handkerchief ◆ **jardin grand comme un** ~ **de poche** garden as big as *ou* the size of *ou* no bigger than a pocket handkerchief ◆ **cette pièce est grande comme un** ~ **de poche** this room's tiny, there isn't room to swing a cat in here (*Brit*) ◆ **ils sont arrivés dans un** ~ it was a close finish ◆ **les deux candidats se tiennent dans un** ~ the two candidates are neck and neck; → **nœud**

moudjahiddin /mudʒa(j)idin/ NMPL mujahedin, mujahedeen

moudre /mudʀ/ ▸ conjug 47 ◂ VT [+ *blé*] to mill, to grind; [+ *café, poivre*] to grind; († : *Mus*) [+ *air*] to grind out ◆ ~ **qn de coups** † to thrash sb, to give sb a drubbing; → **grain, moulu**

moue /mu/ NF pout ◆ **faire la** ~ (*gén*) to pull a face; [*enfant gâté*] to pout ◆ **faire une** ~ **de dédain/de dégoût** to give a disdainful pout/a pout of disgust ◆ **il eut une** ~ **dubitative** he looked doubtful

mouette /mwɛt/ NF (sea) gull ◆ ~ **rieuse** black-headed gull ◆ ~ **tridactyle** kittiwake

mou(f)fette /mufɛt/ NF skunk

moufle /mufl/ NF (= *gant*) mitt, mitten; (*pour plats chauds*) oven glove NM *ou* NF (*Tech*) (= *poulie*) pulley block; [*de four*] muffle

mouflet, -ette* /muflɛ, ɛt/ NM,F brat* (*péj*), kid*

mouflon /muflɔ̃/ NM mouf(f)lon (*mountain sheep*)

mouf(e)ter* /mufte/ ▸ conjug 1 ou 4 ◂ VI to blink ◆ **il n'a pas mouf(e)té** he didn't bat an eyelid

mouillage /mujaʒ/ NM 1 (*Naut* = *action*) [*de navire*] anchoring, mooring; [*d'ancre*] casting; [*de mine*] laying ◆ **au** ~ (lying) at anchor 2 (= *abri, rade*) anchorage, moorage 3 (*Tech*) [*de cuir, linge*] moistening, damping; [*de vin, lait*] watering(-down)

mouillé, e /muje/ (ptp de **mouiller**) ADJ 1 [*herbe, vêtement, personne*] wet; [*regard*] watery, tearful; [*voix*] tearful ◆ **tout** ~ all wet ◆ **il pèse 50 kilos tout** ~ (*hum*) he weighs 50 kilos soaking wet *ou* with his socks on (*Brit*) (*hum*) ◆ **tu sens le chien** ~ you smell like a wet dog ◆ **ne marche pas dans le** ~ don't tread in the wet patch; → **poule**[1] 2 (*Ling*) **l** ~ palatalized l, palatal l

mouillement /mujmɑ̃/ NM (*Ling*) palatalization

mouiller /muje/ ▸ conjug 1 ◂ VT 1 (*pour humidifier*) [+ *linge, sol*] to dampen; (*accidentellement*) [+ *vêtement, livre*] to get *ou* make wet ◆ ~ **son doigt pour tourner la page** to moisten one's finger to turn the page ◆ ~ **sa chemise** *ou* **son maillot*** (*fig*) to put in some hard work *ou* graft* (*Brit*)

2 [*pluie*] [+ *route*] to make wet ◆ **se faire** ~ to get wet

3 (*Culin*) [+ *vin, lait*] to water (down); [+ *viande*] to moisten (*with stock ou wine etc*)

4 (*Naut*) [+ *mine*] to lay; [+ *sonde*] to heave ◆ ~ **l'ancre** to cast *ou* drop anchor

5 (* = *compromettre*) [+ *personne*] to drag (*dans* into) to mix up (*dans* in); ◆ **plusieurs personnes ont été mouillées dans l'histoire** several people were mixed up in the affair

6 (*Ling*) to palatalize

VI 1 (*Naut*) to lie *ou* be at anchor ◆ **ils mouillèrent 3 jours à Papeete** they anchored *ou* they lay at anchor at Papeete for 3 days

2 (* = *avoir peur*) to be scared out of one's mind, to be scared shitless**

3 (* : *sexuellement*) to be wet

VPR **se mouiller** 1 (= *se tremper*) (*accidentellement*) to get o.s. wet; (*pour un bain rapide*) to have a quick dip ◆ **se** ~ **les pieds** (*sans faire exprès*) to get one's feet wet; (*exprès*) to dabble one's feet in the water, to have a little paddle

2 [*yeux*] to fill *ou* brim with tears

3 * (= *prendre des risques*) to get one's feet wet, to commit o.s.; (= *se compromettre*) to get mixed up *ou* involved (*dans* in)

mouillette /mujɛt/ NF finger of bread, soldier* (*Brit*)

mouilleur /mujœʀ/ NM 1 [*de timbres*] (stamp) sponge 2 (*Naut*) [*d'ancre*] tumbler ◆ ~ **de mines** minelayer

mouillure /mujyʀ/ NF 1 (= *trace*) wet mark 2 (*Ling*) palatalization

mouise* /mwiz/ NF ◆ **être dans la** ~ (*misère*) to be flat broke*, to be on one's beam-ends* (*Brit*); (*ennuis*) to be up the creek* ◆ **c'est lui qui m'a sorti de la** ~ he got me out of a hole*

moujik /muʒik/ NM mujik, muzhik

moujingue* /muʒɛ̃g/ NMF brat* (*péj*), kid*

moukère †* /mukɛʀ/ NF woman, female

moulage[1] /mulaʒ/ NM 1 (= *fabrication*) [*de briques, pain*] moulding (*Brit*), molding (*US*); [*de caractères d'imprimerie*] casting; [*de statue, buste*] casting ◆ **le** ~ **d'un bas-relief** making *ou* taking a cast of a bas-relief 2 (= *reproduction*) cast ◆ **prendre un** ~ **de** to take a cast of ◆ **sur la cheminée il y avait le** ~ **en plâtre d'une statue** there was a plaster figure on the mantelpiece ◆ **ce n'est qu'un** ~ it's only a copy ◆ **les enfants ont fait des** ~**s en plâtre** the children have been making plaster models

moulage[2] /mulaʒ/ NM [*de grain*] milling, grinding

moulant, e /mulɑ̃, ɑt/ ADJ [*robe*] figure-hugging; [*pantalon, pull*] tight(-fitting)

moule[1] /mul/ NM 1 (*pour objet fabriqué*) mould (*Brit*), mold (*US*); (*Typo*) matrix ◆ **le** ~ **est cassé** *ou* **on a cassé le** ~ (*fig*) they broke the mould ◆ **il n'a jamais pu sortir du** ~ **étroit de son éducation** he has never been able to free himself from *ou* break out of the straitjacket of his strict upbringing ◆ **fait sur** *ou* **coulé dans le même** ~ (*lit, fig*) cast in the same mould ◆ **être fait au** ~ (= *être beau*) to be shapely ◆ **se couler** *ou* **se fondre** *ou* **entrer dans le** *ou* **un** ~ to conform to the *ou* a norm ◆ **il refuse d'entrer dans le** ~ **de l'école** he refuses to fit into the school mould

2 (*Culin*) (*pour gâteaux*) tin (*Brit*), pan (*US*); (*pour aspic*) mould (*Brit*), mold (*US*)

COMP **moule à beurre** butter print
moule à briques brick mould
moule à cake loaf tin
moule à gâteaux cake tin (*Brit*), cake pan (*US*)
moule à gaufres waffle-iron
moule à manqué (deep) sandwich tin (*Brit*), deep cake pan (*US*)
moule à pisé clay mould
moule à soufflé soufflé dish
moule à tarte pie plate, flan dish

moule[2] /mul/ NF 1 (= *coquillage*) mussel ◆ ~**s marinières** moules marinières (*mussels cooked in their own juice with white wine and shallots*) 2 (* = *idiot*) idiot, twit* 3 (** = *sexe féminin*) cunt**

mouler /mule/ ▸ conjug 1 ◂ VT 1 (= *couler*) [+ *briques, pain*] to mould (*Brit*), to mold (*US*); [+ *caractères d'imprimerie*] to cast; [+ *statue, buste*] to cast ◆ ~ **un buste en plâtre** to cast a bust in plaster ◆ **fromage blanc moulé à la louche** ≈ farmhouse fromage frais ◆ **selles moulées** (*Méd*) solid stools

2 (= *prendre l'empreinte de*) [+ *bas-relief, buste*] to make *ou* take a cast of ◆ ~ **en plâtre/en cire** [+ *visage, buste*] to make a plaster/wax cast of

3 [+ *lettre, mot*] to shape *ou* form with care

4 (= *calquer sur*) ~ **son style/sa conduite sur** to model one's style/one's conduct on

5 [+ *cuisses, hanches*] to hug, to fit closely round ◆ **une robe qui moule** a figure-hugging dress ◆ **pantalon qui moule** tight (fitting) trousers ◆ **une robe qui lui moulait les hanches** a dress which clung to *ou* around her hips ◆ **son corps se moulait au sien** her body pressed closely against his

mouleur /mulœʀ/ NM caster, moulder (*Brit*), molder (*US*)

moulin /mulɛ̃/ NM 1 (= *instrument, bâtiment*) mill ◆ ~ **à eau** water mill ◆ ~ **à vent** windmill ◆ ~ **à café/poivre** coffee/pepper mill ◆ ~ **à légumes** vegetable mill ◆ ~ **à paroles** chatterbox ◆ ~ **à prières** prayer wheel ◆ **on y entre comme dans un** ~ anyone can just walk right in 2 (* = *moteur*) engine

mouliner /muline/ ▸ conjug 1 ◂ VT 1 (*Culin*) to put through a vegetable mill; (*Pêche*) to reel in 2 (* : *Ordin*) to process, to crunch* 3 [+ *soie*] to throw VI [*cycliste*] to pedal rapidly (*without any effort*)

moulinet /mulinɛ/ NM (*Pêche*) reel; (*Tech*) winch; (*Escrime*) flourish; (*Danse*) moulinet ◆ **faire des** ~**s avec une canne** to twirl *ou* whirl a walking stick ◆ **faire des** ~**s avec les bras** to whirl one's arms about *ou* round

moulinette ® /mulinɛt/ NF vegetable mill ◆ **passer qch à la** ~ (*Culin*) to put sth through the vegetable mill; (*fig*) to subject sth to close scrutiny; (* : *Ordin*) to process *ou* crunch* sth

moult /mult/ ADV (†† *ou hum*) (= *beaucoup*) many; (= *très*) very ◆ ~ **gens** many people, many a person ◆ ~ **fois** oft(en)times (*hum*), many a time

moulu, e /muly/ (ptp de **moudre**) ADJ 1 [*café, poivre*] ground (*épith*) 2 († = *meurtri*) bruised, black and blue ◆ ~ **(de fatigue)*** dead-beat*, worn-out, all-in*

moulure /mulyʀ/ NF (*gén*) moulding (*Brit*), molding (*US*); (*sur porte*) beading

moulurer /mulyʀe/ ▸ conjug 1 ◂ VT to decorate with mouldings (*Brit*) *ou* moldings (*US*) ◆ **machine à** ~ moulding (*Brit*) *ou* molding (*US*) machine ◆ **panneau mouluré** moulded (*Brit*) *ou* molded (*US*) panel

moumoute * /mumut/ NF 1 *(hum)* *(= perruque)* wig; *(= postiche)* *(pour hommes)* hairpiece, toupee; *(pour femmes)* hairpiece 2 *(= veste)* fleece-lined *ou* fleecy jacket

mouquère †* /mukɛʀ/ NF ⇒ **moukère**

mourant, e /muʀɑ̃, ɑ̃t/ ADJ *[personne, feu, jour]* dying; *[voix]* faint; *[regard]* languishing NM,F ◆ **un ~** a dying man ◆ **une ~e** a dying woman ◆ **les ~s** the dying

mourir /muʀiʀ/ ► conjug 19 ◄ VI 1 *[être animé, plante]* to die ◆ **~ dans son lit** to die in one's bed ◆ **~ de sa belle mort** to die a natural death ◆ **~ avant l'âge** to die young *ou* before one's time ◆ **~ à la peine** *ou* **à la tâche** to die in harness *(fig)* ◆ **~ assassiné** to be murdered ◆ **~ empoisonné** *(crime)* to be poisoned (and die); *(accident)* to die of poisoning ◆ **~ en héros** to die a hero's death ◆ **il est mort très jeune** he died very young, he was very young when he died ◆ **faire ~ qn** to kill sb ◆ **cet enfant me fera ~** this child will be the death of me ◆ **c'est une simple piqûre, tu n'en mourras pas !** it's only a little injection, it won't kill you! ◆ **je l'aime à (en) ~** I love him more than life itself ◆ **s'ennuyer à ~** to be bored to death *ou* to tears ◆ **ennuyeux à ~** deadly boring ◆ **elle est belle à ~** she's heart-stoppingly beautiful, she's drop-dead gorgeous* ◆ **triste à ~** deadly dull ◆ **il attend que le patron meure pour prendre sa place** he's waiting for his boss to die so that he can step into his shoes ◆ **on ne meurt qu'une fois** *(Prov)* you only die once *(Prov)* ◆ **plus bête que lui, tu meurs !*** you can't possibly be more stupid than he is!, he's as stupid as they come!*

2 *[civilisation, empire, coutume]* to die out; *[bruit]* to die away; *[jour]* to fade, to die; *[feu]* to die out, to die down ◆ **la vague vint ~ à ses pieds** the wave died away at his feet ◆ **le ballon vint ~ à ses pieds** the ball came to rest at his feet

3 *(suivi d'un complément)* **~ de vieillesse/chagrin** to die of old age/grief ◆ **~ d'une maladie/d'une blessure** to die of a disease/from a wound ◆ **~ de froid** *(lit)* to die of exposure ◆ **on meurt de froid ici** *(fig)* it's freezing *ou* perishing *(Brit)* cold in here ◆ **je meurs de sommeil** I'm dead on my feet ◆ **~ de faim** *(lit)* to starve to death, to die of hunger; *(fig = avoir faim)* to be starving *ou* famished *ou* ravenous ◆ **faire ~ qn de faim** to starve sb to death ◆ **~ de soif** *(lit)* to die of thirst; *(fig = avoir soif)* to be parched ◆ **il me fera ~ d'inquiétude** he'll drive me to my death with worry ◆ **~ de honte** to die of shame ◆ **~** *ou* **être mort de peur** to be frightened *ou* scared to death ◆ **il me fera ~ de peur** he'll frighten the life out of me ◆ **~ d'ennui** to be bored to death *ou* to tears ◆ **il meurt d'envie de le faire** he's dying to do it ◆ **faire ~ qn d'impatience** to keep sb on tenterhooks ◆ **faire ~ qn à petit feu** *(lit)* to kill sb slowly *ou* by inches; *(fig)* to torment the life out of sb ◆ **(se) ~ d'amour pour qn** *(littér)* to pine for sb

VPR **se mourir** *(littér)* to be dying

mouroir /muʀwaʀ/ NM *(péj : pour vieillards)* old people's home ◆ **le camp/l'hôpital est devenu un ~** the camp/the hospital has become a place for people to die

mouron /muʀɔ̃/ NM 1 *(= plante)* pimpernel ◆ **~ rouge** scarlet pimpernel ◆ **~ blanc** *ou* **des oiseaux** chickweed 2 *(locutions)* **se faire du ~*** to worry o.s. sick* ◆ **arrête de te faire du ~ (pour lui)*** stop worrying *ou* fretting (about him)

mouscaille * /muskaj/ NF ◆ **être dans la ~** *(misère)* to be down and out, to be stony broke*, to be on one's beam-ends* *(Brit)*; *(ennuis)* to be up the creek*

mousquet /muskɛ/ NM musket

mousquetaire /muskətɛʀ/ NM musketeer ◆ **col/poignet ~** mousquetaire collar/cuff

mousqueton /muskətɔ̃/ NM *(= boucle)* snap hook, clasp; *(= fusil)* carbine; *(Alpinisme)* crab, karabiner ◆ **coup de ~** musket shot

moussaillon * /musajɔ̃/ NM ship's boy ◆ **par ici ~ !** over here, (my) boy!

moussaka /musaka/ NF moussaka

moussant, e /musɑ̃, ɑ̃t/ ADJ *[savon, crème à raser]* foaming, lathering; → **bain**

mousse[1] /mus/ NF 1 *(= plante)* moss; → **pierre, vert**

2 *(= écume)* *[de bière, eau, café, lait]* froth; *[de savon]* lather; *[de champagne]* bubbles ◆ **la ~ sur le verre de bière** the head on the beer

3 *(* = bière)* pint*

4 *(Culin)* mousse ◆ **~ au chocolat** chocolate mousse ◆ **~ d'avocat** avocado mousse

5 *(= caoutchouc)* foam rubber ◆ **matelas en ~** foam rubber mattress ◆ **balle (en) ~** rubber ball ◆ **collant/bas ~** *(= nylon)* stretch tights *(Brit)* *ou* pantyhose *(US)*/stockings ◆ **~ de caoutchouc** foam rubber

6 **se faire de la ~** †* to worry o.s. sick*, to get all het up* ◆ **ne te fais pas de ~*, tout ira bien** don't worry *ou* don't get so het up*, everything'll be alright

COMP **mousse carbonique** (fire-fighting) foam
mousse coiffante styling mousse
mousse de nylon *(= tissu)* stretch nylon; *(pour rembourrer)* foam
mousse de platine platinum sponge
mousse à raser shaving foam; → **point**[2]

mousse[2] /mus/ NM ship's boy

mousseline /muslin/ NF 1 *(= coton)* muslin; *(= soie, tergal)* chiffon ◆ **verre ~** muslin glass 2 *(Culin = mousse)* mousseline; → **pomme, sauce**

mousser /muse/ ► conjug 1 ◄ VI 1 *[bière, eau]* to froth; *[champagne]* to bubble, to sparkle; *[détergent]* to foam, to lather; *[savon, shampooing, crème à raser]* to lather ◆ **faire ~** *[+ savon, détergent]* to lather up 2 ◆ **faire ~ qn*** *(vanter)* to boost sb*, to puff sb up* *(US)*; *(mettre en colère)* to make sb mad* *ou* wild* ◆ **se faire ~*** to blow one's own trumpet, to sing one's own praises *(auprès de to)*; *(auprès d'un supérieur)* to sell o.s. hard* *(auprès de to)*

mousseron /musʀɔ̃/ NM meadow mushroom

mousseux, -euse /musø, øz/ ADJ *[vin]* sparkling *(épith)*; *[bière, chocolat]* frothy ◆ **eau mousseuse** soapy water NM sparkling wine

mousson /musɔ̃/ NF monsoon

moussu, e /musy/ ADJ *[sol, arbre]* mossy; *[banc]* moss-covered

moustache /mustaʃ/ NF *[d'homme]* moustache, mustache *(US)* ◆ **~s** *[d'animal]* whiskers ◆ **porter la ~** *ou* **des ~s** to have *ou* wear a moustache ◆ **avoir de la ~** *[de femme]* to have a moustache, to have hair on one's upper lip ◆ **il s'était fait une ~ blanche en buvant le lait** he had a white moustache from drinking the milk ◆ **~ en brosse** toothbrush moustache ◆ **~ en croc** *ou* **en guidon de vélo*** handlebar moustache ◆ **~ (à la) gauloise** walrus moustache

moustachu, e /mustaʃy/ ADJ with a moustache, moustached ◆ **c'est un ~** he has a moustache ◆ **elle est un peu ~e** she's got a bit of a moustache

moustérien, -ienne /musteʀjɛ̃, jɛn/ ADJ Mousterian NM ◆ **le Moustérien** the Mousterian

moustiquaire /mustikɛʀ/ NF *(= rideau)* mosquito net; *[de fenêtre, porte]* mosquito screen

moustique /mustik/ NM *(= insecte)* mosquito; *(* = enfant)* (little) kid*, tich* *(Brit)*, nipper* *(Brit)*

moût /mu/ NM *[de raisin]* must; *[de bière]* wort

moutard * /mutaʀ/ NM brat* *(péj)*, kid*

moutarde /mutaʀd/ NF mustard ◆ **~ blanche** white mustard ◆ **~ (extra-)forte** English mustard, hot mustard *(US)* ◆ **~ à l'estragon** *ou* **aux aromates** French mustard ◆ **~ à l'ancienne** grain mustard ◆ **~ de Dijon** Dijon mustard ◆ **graines de ~** mustard seeds ◆ **la ~ me monta au nez** I flared up, I lost my temper ◆ **il sentit la ~ lui monter au nez** he felt his temper flaring, he felt he was going to flare up ADJ INV ◆ **(jaune) ~** mustard(-yellow); → **gaz, sauce**

moutardier /mutaʀdje/ NM *(= pot)* mustard pot; *(= fabricant)* mustard maker *ou* manufacturer ◆ **il se croit le premier ~ du pape** † he thinks he's the bee's knees *(Brit)* *ou* the cat's whiskers *(Brit)* *ou* the cat's meow *(US)*

mouton, -onne /mutɔ̃, ɔn/ ADJ sheeplike

NM 1 *(= animal)* sheep; *(= peau)* sheepskin ◆ **doublé de ~** lined with sheepskin ◆ **relié en ~** bound in sheepskin, sheepskin-bound ◆ **manteau en ~ doré** Persian lamb coat ◆ **mais revenons** *ou* **retournons à nos ~s** *(fig)* but let's get back to the subject, but to get back to the subject ◆ **compter les ~s** *(pour s'endormir)* to count sheep

2 *(= viande)* mutton ◆ **côte de ~** mutton chop

3 *(* = personne)* *(grégaire, crédule)* sheep; *(doux, passif)* sheep, lamb ◆ **c'est un ~** *(grégaire)* he's easily led, he goes with the crowd; *(doux)* he's as gentle as a lamb ◆ **il m'a suivi comme un ~** he followed me like a lamb ◆ **ils se comportent comme des ~s de Panurge** they behave like sheep

4 *(arg Police : dans une prison)* stool pigeon *(arg)*, grass *(Brit)* *(arg)*

5 *(Constr)* ram, monkey

NMPL **moutons** *(sur la mer)* white horses *(Brit)*, white caps *(US)*; *(sur le plancher)* (bits of) fluff; *(dans le ciel)* fluffy *ou* fleecy clouds

COMP **mouton à cinq pattes** rare bird, rara avis *(littér)*
mouton à laine sheep reared for wool
mouton retourné sheepskin
mouton à viande sheep reared for meat

MOUTONS DE PANURGE

The expression **moutons de Panurge** is an allusion to a famous scene in Rabelais' « Pantagruel », in which Pantagruel throws a sheep into the sea and the rest of the flock throw themselves in after it. The term **mouton de Panurge** is used metaphorically to refer to any person who blindly follows the herd.

moutonnant, e /mutɔnɑ̃, ɑ̃t/ ADJ *[mer]* flecked with white horses *(Brit)* *ou* with white caps *(US)*; *(littér)* *[collines]* rolling *(épith)*

moutonné, e /mutɔne/ (ptp de **moutonner**) ADJ *[ciel]* flecked with fleecy *ou* fluffy clouds

moutonnement /mutɔnmɑ̃/ NM ◆ **contempler le ~ de la mer** to look at the white horses *(Brit)* *ou* white caps *(US)* on the sea ◆ **le ~ des collines** *(littér)* the rolling hills

moutonner /mutɔne/ ► conjug 1 ◄ VI *[mer]* to be flecked with white horses *(Brit)* *ou* white caps *(US)*; *(littér)* *[collines]* to roll; *[ciel]* to be flecked with fleecy *ou* fluffy clouds

moutonneux, -euse /mutɔnø, øz/ ADJ *[mer]* flecked with white horses *(Brit)* *ou* with white caps *(US)*; *[ciel]* flecked with fleecy *ou* fluffy clouds

moutonnier, -ière /mutɔnje, jɛʀ/ ADJ *[réflexe, personne]* sheep-like ◆ **ils ont un comportement ~** they behave like sheep

mouture /mutyʀ/ NF 1 *(= action)* *[de blé]* milling, grinding; *[de café]* grinding 2 *(= résultat)* **une ~ fine** *[de café]* finely ground coffee ◆ **c'est la première ~** *[d'article, rapport]* it's the first draft • **c'est la 3e ~ du même livre** *(péj)* it's the 3rd rehash of the same book

mouvance /muvɑ̃s/ **NF** 1 *(= domaine d'influence)* sphere of influence • **entraîner qn dans sa ~** to draw sb into one's sphere of influence • **il n'appartient pas à la ~ présidentielle** *(Pol)* he's not at the same end of the political spectrum as the president • **au sein de la ~ écologiste** among the different ecological parties 2 *(gén péj) [de pensée, situation]* ever-changing nature • **la ~ politique/sociale** the ever-changing political/social scene • **une culture en perpétuelle ~** an ever-changing culture 3 *(Hist)* subinfeudation; *(Philos)* mobility

mouvant, e /muvɑ̃, ɑ̃t/ **ADJ** *[situation]* unsettled, fluid; *[ombre, flamme]* moving, changing; *[pensée, univers]* changing; *[frontières]* shifting; *[terrain]* unsteady, shifting • **être sur un** *ou* **en terrain ~** *(fig)* to be on shaky *ou* uncertain ground; → **sable**[1]

mouvement /muvmɑ̃/ **NM** 1 *(= geste)* movement, motion • **~s de gymnastique** (physical) exercises • **il a des ~s très lents** he is very slow in his movements • **il approuva d'un ~ de tête** he nodded his approval, he gave a nod of approval • **elle refusa d'un ~ de tête** she shook her head in refusal, she refused with a shake of her head • **elle eut un ~ de recul** she started back • **le ~ des lèvres** the movement of the lips • **faire un ~** to move, to make a move • **elle ne pouvait plus faire le moindre ~** she could no longer move at all • **rester sans ~** to remain motionless; → **faux**[2], **temps**[1]

2 *(= impulsion, réaction)* **dans un ~ de colère/d'indignation** in a fit *ou* a burst of anger /of indignation • **les ~s de l'âme** the impulses of the soul • **des ~s dans l'auditoire** a stir in the audience • **discours accueilli avec des ~s divers** speech which got a mixed reception • **son premier ~ fut de refuser** his first impulse was to refuse • **agir de son propre ~** to act of one's own accord • **avoir un bon ~** to make a nice *ou* kind gesture • **allons, un bon ~ !** come on, just a small gesture! • **dans un bon ~** on a kindly impulse

3 *(= activité) [de ville, entreprise]* activity, bustle • **une rue pleine de ~** a busy *ou* lively street • **il aime le ~** *(= il est dynamique)* he likes to be on the go; *(= il aime l'animation)* he likes the bustle of the city • **il n'y a pas beaucoup de ~ le dimanche** not much happens on Sundays

4 *(= déplacement)* movement • **suivre le ~** to follow the crowd • **presser le ~** *(lit, fig)* to step up the pace • **~ de balancier** *(lit, fig)* swing of the pendulum, pendulum swing • **le ~ perpétuel** perpetual motion • **~ de foule** movement in the crowd • **~s de population** *(Sociol)* shifts in population • **d'importants ~s de troupes à la frontière** large-scale troop movements at *ou* along the frontier • **~ de repli** *(Mil)* withdrawal • **~ tournant** (out)flanking movement • **~ de marchandises/de capitaux** *ou* **de fonds** movement of goods/of capital • **les ~s monétaires internationaux** fluctuations on the world money markets • **~ d'un compte** *(Banque)* account activity, turnover in an account • **~ de personnel** changes in staff *ou* personnel

♦ **en mouvement** • **être sans cesse en ~** to be constantly on the move *ou* on the go • **mettre qch en ~** to set sth in motion, to set sth going • **se mettre en ~** to set off, to get going; → **guerre**

5 *(Philos, Pol etc = évolution)* **le ~ des idées** the evolution of ideas • **le parti du ~** the party in favour of change, the party of progress • **être dans le ~** to keep up-to-date • **un ~ d'opinion se dessine en faveur de ...** one can detect a trend of opinion in favour of ... • **le ~ des prix** price trends • **~ de baisse/de hausse (sur les ventes)** downward/upward movement *ou* trend (in sales)

6 *(= rythme) [de phrase]* rhythm; *[de tragédie]* movement, action; *[de mélodie]* tempo

7 *(Pol, Sociol = groupe, action)* movement • **~ politique** political movement • **le ~ ouvrier/étudiant** the labour/student movement • **Mouvement de libération de la femme** Women's Liberation Movement, Women's Lib * • **~(s) de grève** strike *ou* industrial action *(NonC)* • **~ de protestation** *ou* **de contestation** protest movement

8 *(Mus)* movement

9 *(Tech = mécanisme)* movement • **par un ~ d'horlogerie** by clockwork • **fermeture à ~ d'horlogerie** time lock

10 *(= ligne, courbe) [de sculpture]* contours; *[de draperie, étoffe]* drape; *[de collines]* undulations, rise and fall *(NonC)* • **~ de terrain** undulation

mouvementé, e /muvmɑ̃te/ **ADJ** *[vie, poursuite, récit]* eventful; *[séance]* turbulent, stormy; *[terrain]* rough • **j'ai eu une journée assez ~e** I've had quite a hectic day

mouvoir /muvwaʀ/ ▸ conjug 27 ◂ **VT** *(gén ptp)* 1 *[+ machine]* to drive, to power; *[+ bras, levier]* to move • **il se leva comme mû par un ressort** he sprang up as if propelled by a spring *ou* like a Jack-in-the-box 2 *[motif, sentiment]* to drive, to prompt **VPR** **se mouvoir** to move • **faire (se) ~** *[+ partie du corps]* to move; *[+ robot] (gén)* to move; *[source d'énergie]* to drive, to power

moyen[1]**, -yenne**[1] /mwajɛ̃, jɛn/ **ADJ** 1 *(= ni grand ni petit, modéré) [taille]* medium, average; *[ville, maison]* medium-sized; *[prix]* moderate • **les moyennes entreprises** medium-sized companies • **un produit de qualité moyenne** a product of average *ou* medium quality; → **cours, onde, poids**

2 *(= intermédiaire) [cadre, classe, revenu]* middle • **la solution moyenne** the middle-of-the-road solution • **il doit exister une voie moyenne entre liberté totale et discipline** there must be a middle way between complete freedom and discipline • **une voiture de gamme moyenne** *(Écon)* a mid-range *ou* middle-of-the-range car; → aussi **cours**

3 *(= du type courant)* average • **le Français/le lecteur ~** the average Frenchman/reader

4 *(= ni bon ni mauvais) [résultats, intelligence, équipe]* average; *(Scol : sur copie d'élève)* fair, average • **nous avons eu un temps ~** we had mixed weather, the weather was so-so * • **il est ~ en géographie** he is average at geography • **son devoir est très ~** his essay is pretty poor * • **comment as-tu trouvé le spectacle ? – très ~** what did you think of the show? – pretty average

5 *(d'après des calculs) [température, âge]* average, mean; *[prix, durée, densité, vitesse]* average • **le revenu ~ par tête d'habitant** the average per capita income • **la consommation moyenne annuelle de chocolat** the average annual consumption of chocolate

6 *(Géog)* **le cours ~ du fleuve** the middle reaches of the river • **les régions de la Loire moyenne** the middle regions of the Loire

7 *(Ling)* **voyelle moyenne** mid *ou* central vowel

moyen[2] /mwajɛ̃/ GRAMMAIRE ACTIVE 44.1

NM 1 *(= procédé, manière)* means, way • **il y a toujours un ~** there's always a way, there are ways and means • **par quel ~ allez-vous le convaincre ?** how will you manage to convince him? • **connaissez-vous un bon ~ pour ... ?** do you know a good way to ...? • **c'est le meilleur ~ de rater ton examen** it's the best way to fail your exam • **c'est l'unique ~ de s'en sortir** it's the only way out, it's the only way we can get out of it • **tous les ~s lui sont bons** *(péj)* he'll stop at nothing *ou* he'll do anything to get what he wants • **quand on veut réussir tous les ~s sont bons** anything goes when one wants to succeed • **tous les ~s seront mis en œuvre pour réussir** we shall use all possible means to succeed • **se débrouiller avec les ~s du bord** to get by as best one can, to make do and mend • **employer les grands ~s** to resort to *ou* take drastic *ou* extreme measures • **trouver le ~ de faire qch** *(lit)* to find some means *ou* way of doing sth • **il a trouvé (le) ~ de se perdre** *(fig hum)* he managed *ou* contrived *(frm)* to get lost • **il trouve toujours (un) ~ de me mettre en colère** he always manages to make me angry • **nous avons les ~s de vous faire parler !** we have ways of making you talk! • **adverbe de ~** *(Gram)* adverb of means

♦ **au moyen de, par le moyen de** by means of, using • **au ~ d'un parachute** by means of *ou* using a parachute • **enlevez la rouille au ~ d'une brosse métallique** remove the rust with a wire brush

♦ **par tous les moyens** *(gén)* by all possible means; *(même malhonnêtes)* by fair means or foul, by hook or by crook • **essayer par tous les ~s** to try every possible means • **j'ai essayé par tous les ~s de le convaincre** I've done everything to try and convince him

2 *(= possibilité)* **est-ce qu'il y a ~ de lui parler ?** is it possible to speak to him? • **voyons s'il y a ~ de trouver les fonds** let's see if it's possible to get *ou* if there's some way of getting the funding • **le ~ de dire autre chose !** what else could I say? • **le ~ de lui refuser !** how could I possibly refuse? • **il n'y a pas ~ de sortir par ce temps** you can't go out in this weather • **pas ~ d'avoir une réponse claire !** there's no way you can get a clear answer! • **pas ~ de savoir ce qu'ils se sont dit** there's no (way of) knowing what they said to each other • **non, il n'y a pas ~ !** no, nothing doing!*, no, no chance!* • **il n'y a plus ~ de lui parler** you can't talk to him any more • **il n'y a jamais ~ qu'il fasse son lit** you'll never get him to make his bed, he'll never make his bed

NMPL **moyens** 1 *(= capacités intellectuelles, physiques)* **il a de grands ~s (intellectuels)** he has great powers of intellect *ou* intellectual powers • **ça lui a enlevé** *ou* **fait perdre tous ses ~s** it left him completely at a loss, it completely threw him * • **il était en pleine possession de ses ~s** *ou* **en possession de tous ses ~s** *(gén)* his powers were at their peak; *[personne âgée]* he was in full possession of his faculties • **c'est au-dessus de ses ~s** it's beyond him, it's beyond his abilities *ou* capabilities • **par ses propres ~s** *[réussir]* all by oneself, on one's own • **ils ont dû rentrer par leurs propres ~s** they had to make their own way home, they had to go home under their own steam * *(Brit)*

2 *(= ressources financières)* means • **il a les ~s** he has the means, he can afford it • **avoir de gros/petits ~s** to have a large/small income, to be well/badly off • **c'est dans mes ~s** I can afford it • **il vit au-dessus de ses ~s** he lives beyond his means • **il n'a pas les ~s de s'acheter une voiture** he can't afford to buy a car • **c'est au-dessus de ses ~s** he can't afford it, it's beyond his means

COMP **moyen d'action** means of action
moyen anglais Middle English
moyens audiovisuels audiovisual aids
moyen de communication means of communication
moyen de défense means of defence
moyen d'existence means of existence
moyen d'expression means of expression
moyen de locomotion means of transport
moyen de paiement method *ou* means of payment
moyen de pression means of (applying) pressure • **nous n'avons aucun ~ de pression sur lui** we have no means of putting pressure on him *ou* no hold on him

moyen de production means of production **moyen de transport** means *ou* mode of transport

Moyen Âge, Moyen-Âge /mwajɛnɑʒ/ **NM** ◆ **le** ~ the Middle Ages ◆ **le haut** ~ the early Middle Ages ◆ **au** ~ in the Middle Ages

moyenâgeux, -euse /mwajɛnɑʒø, øz/ **ADJ** *[ville, costumes]* medieval; *(péj) [pratiques, théorie]* antiquated, outdated

moyen-courrier (pl **moyens-courriers**) /mwajɛ̃kuʀje/ **ADJ** *[vol]* medium-haul **NM** *(= avion)* medium-haul aircraft

moyennant /mwajɛnɑ̃/ **PRÉP** *[+ argent]* for; *[+ service]* in return for; *[+ travail, effort]* with ◆ ~ **finance(s)** for a fee *ou* a consideration ◆ ~ **quoi** in return for which, in consideration of which

moyenne² /mwajɛn/ **NF** 1 *(gén)* average ◆ **au-dessus/au-dessous de la** ~ above/below average ◆ **faites la** ~ **de ces chiffres** work out the average of these figures ◆ **la** ~ **d'âge/des températures** the average *ou* mean age/temperature ◆ **la** ~ **des gens pense que ...** most people *ou* the broad mass of people think that ... ◆ ~ **géométrique/arithmétique** *(Math)* geometric/arithmetic mean ◆ **le taux de natalité y est inférieur à la** ~ **nationale** the birthrate there is lower than the national average

2 *(Scol)* **avoir la** ~ *(à un devoir)* to get fifty per cent, to get half marks *(Brit)*; *(à un examen)* to get a pass *ou* a pass mark *(Brit)* ◆ ~ **générale (de l'année)** average (for the year) ◆ **améliorer** *ou* **remonter sa** ~ to improve one's marks *ou* grades ◆ **la** ~ **de la classe est de 9 sur 20** the class average is 9 out of 20 ◆ **cet élève est dans la** ~**/la bonne** ~ this pupil is about/above average

3 *(= vitesse)* average speed ◆ **faire du 100 de** ~ to average 100 km/h, to drive at an average speed of 100 km/h

LOC ADV **en moyenne** on average ◆ **l'usine produit en** ~ **500 voitures par jour** the factory turns out 500 cars a day on average, the factory averages 500 cars a day

moyennement /mwajɛnmɑ̃/ **ADV** 1 *(= médiocrement)* **c'est** ~ **bon** it's pretty average ◆ **c'est** ~ **intéressant/drôle** it's not that interesting/funny ◆ **il est** ~ **apprécié** he's not liked that much ◆ **c'est très** ~ **payé** it's poorly paid ◆ **je ne suis que** ~ **convaincu** I'm only half convinced ◆ **j'ai réussi** ~ **en anglais** I didn't do that well in English ◆ **j'aime** ~ **ça** I don't like it that much, I'm not that keen on it *(Brit)* ◆ **ça va ?** – ~ * how are things? – so-so * *ou* could be worse * 2 *(= dans la moyenne) [radioactif, sucré]* moderately ◆ ~ **intelligent** of average intelligence

Moyen-Orient /mwajɛnɔʀjɑ̃/ **NM** ◆ **le** ~ the Middle East ◆ **au** ~ in the Middle East ◆ **les pays/villes du** ~ Middle Eastern countries/cities

moyen-oriental, e (mpl **moyen-orientaux**) /mwajɛ̃ɔʀjɑ̃tal, o/ **ADJ** Middle Eastern

moyeu (pl **moyeux**) /mwajø/ **NM** *[de roue]* hub; *[d'hélice]* boss

mozambicain, e /mɔzɑ̃bikɛ̃, ɛn/ **ADJ** Mozambican **NM,F** **Mozambicain(e)** Mozambican

Mozambique /mɔzɑ̃bik/ **NM** Mozambique

Mozart /mɔzaʀ/ **NM** Mozart

mozartien, -ienne /mɔzaʀtjɛ̃, jɛn/ **ADJ** Mozartian, of Mozart

mozzarella /mɔdzaʀela/ **NF** mozzarella

mp3 /ɛmpetʀwa/ **NM** *(Mus, Ordin)* MP3 ◆ **lecteur** ~ MP3 player

MRAP /mʀap/ **NM** (abrév de **mouvement contre le racisme, l'antisémitisme et pour l'amitié des peuples**) *French anti-racist and peace movement*

MST /ɛmɛste/ **NF** 1 (abrév de **maladie sexuellement transmissible**) STD 2 (abrév de **maîtrise de sciences et techniques**) *master's degree in science and technology*

mu /my/ **NM** mu

mû, mue¹ /my/ ptp de **mouvoir**

mucilage /mysilaʒ/ **NM** mucilage

mucosité /mykozite/ **NF** *(gén pl)* mucus *(NonC)*

mucoviscidose /mykovisidoz/ **NF** cystic fibrosis, mucoviscidosis *(SPÉC)*

mucus /mykys/ **NM** mucus *(NonC)*

mue² /my/ **NF** 1 *(= transformation) [d'oiseau]* moulting *(Brit)*, molting *(US)*; *[de serpent]* sloughing; *[de mammifère]* shedding, moulting *(Brit)*, molting *(US)*; *[de cerf]* casting; *[de voix]* breaking *(Brit)*, changing *(US)* ◆ **la** ~ **(de la voix) intervient vers 14 ans** the voice breaks *(Brit) ou* changes *(US)* at about 14 years of age 2 *(= époque)* moulting *etc* season 3 *(= peau, plumes) [de serpent]* slough; *[de mammifère]* moulted *ou* shed hair; *[d'oiseau]* moulted *ou* shed feathers 4 *(Agr = cage)* coop

muer /mɥe/ ▸ conjug 1 ◂ **VI** *[oiseau]* to moult *(Brit)*, to molt *(US)*; *[serpent]* to slough (its skin), to shed its skin; *[mammifère]* to moult *(Brit)*, to molt *(US)*, to shed hair *(ou skin etc)*; *[cerf]* to cast its antlers ◆ **sa voix mue, il mue** his voice is breaking *(Brit) ou* changing *(US)* **VT** *(littér)* ◆ ~ **qch en** to transform *ou* change *ou* turn sth into **VPR** **se muer** *(littér)* **se** ~ **en** to transform *ou* change *ou* turn into ◆ **il s'est mué en défenseur acharné de notre cause** he's turned into a fervent supporter of our cause

muesli /mysli/ **NM** muesli

muet, muette /mɥɛ, mɥɛt/ **ADJ** 1 *(Méd)* dumb 2 *(= silencieux) [colère, prière, personne]* silent, mute; *(littér) [forêt]* silent ◆ ~ **de colère/surprise** speechless with anger/surprise ◆ ~ **de peur** dumb with fear ◆ **le code est** ~ **à ce sujet** the law is silent on this matter ◆ ~ **comme une tombe** (as) silent as the grave ◆ **rester** ~ *[témoin, rapport]* to remain silent *(sur* on); ◆ **il est resté** ~ **comme une carpe** he never opened his mouth ◆ **en rester** ~ **(d'étonnement)** to stand speechless, to be struck dumb (with astonishment)

3 *(Ciné, Théât) [film, cinéma]* silent; *[rôle]* non-speaking *(épith)*; *[scène]* with no dialogue ◆ **carte muette** *(au restaurant)* menu without prices *(given to guests)*

4 *(Ling)* mute, silent

5 *(Scol, Géog) [carte, clavier de machine à écrire]* blank ◆ **clavier** ~ *(Mus)* dummy keyboard

NM 1 *(= infirme)* mute, dumb man

2 *(Ciné)* **le** ~ the silent cinema *ou* screen

NF **muette** mute, dumb woman ◆ **la grande Muette** *(Mil)* the army

muezzin /mɥɛdzin/ **NM** muezzin

mufle /myfl/ **NM** 1 *[de bovin]* muffle; *[de chien, lion]* muzzle 2 *(* = goujat)* boor, lout ◆ **ce qu'il est** ~ **alors !** he's such a lout *ou* yob*‡* *(Brit)*!

muflerie /myfləʀi/ **NF** boorishness *(NonC)*, loutishness *(NonC)*

muflier /myflije/ **NM** antirrhinum, snapdragon

mufti /myfti/ **NM** *(Rel)* mufti

muge /myʒ/ **NM** grey mullet

mugir /myʒiʀ/ ▸ conjug 2 ◂ **VI** 1 *[vache]* to low, to moo; *[bœuf]* to bellow 2 *(littér) [vent]* to howl; *[mer]* to roar; *[sirène]* to wail

mugissement /myʒismɑ̃/ **NM** 1 *[de vache]* lowing, mooing; *[de bœuf]* bellowing 2 *(littér) [de vent]* howling; *[de mer]* roaring; *[de sirène]* wailing

muguet /mygɛ/ **NM** 1 *(= plante)* lily of the valley 2 *(Méd)* thrush

mulâtre, mulâtresse /mylɑtʀ, mylɑtʀɛs/ **NM,F**, **mulâtre** **ADJ INV** mulatto

mule /myl/ **NF** 1 *(= animal)* (female) mule; → **tête, têtu** 2 *(= pantoufle)* mule ◆ **la** ~ **du pape** the Pope's slipper 3 *(arg Drogue)* mule *(arg)*

mulet /mylɛ/ **NM** 1 *(= animal)* (male) mule; *(= poisson)* mullet 2 *(arg = voiture)* spare *ou* replacement car

muletier, -ière /myl(ə)tje, jɛʀ/ **ADJ** ◆ **sentier** *ou* **chemin** ~ mule track **NM,F** mule-driver, muleteer

mullah /myla/ **NM** ⇒ **mollah**

mulot /mylo/ **NM** field mouse

multi(-) /mylti/ **PRÉF** multi(-) ◆ ~**-usage** multipurpose

multicarte /myltikaʀt/ **ADJ** → **représentant**

multicellulaire /myltiselylɛʀ/ **ADJ** multicellular

multicolore /myltikɔlɔʀ/ **ADJ** multicoloured *(Brit)*, many-coloured *(US)*

multiconfessionnel, -elle /myltikɔ̃fesjɔnɛl/ **ADJ** *[association, État]* multi-denominational

multicoque /myltikɔk/ **ADJ, NM** ◆ **(voilier)** ~ multihull

multicouche /myltikuʃ/ **ADJ** *[revêtement]* multilayered ◆ **objectif** ~ *(Photo)* lens with multiple coatings

multicritères, multi-critères /myltikʀitɛʀ/ **ADJ** *(Ordin) [recherche]* multicriteria *(épith)*

multiculturalisme /myltikyltyʀalism/ **NM** multiculturalism

multiculturel, -elle /myltikyltyʀɛl/ **ADJ** multicultural

multidiffusion /myltidifyzjɔ̃/ **NF** *(Audiov)* repeat broadcasting ◆ **le film passera en** ~ the film will be broadcast several times, there will be several repeats *ou* repeat broadcasts of the film

multidimensionnel, -elle /myltidimɑ̃sjɔnɛl/ **ADJ** multidimensional

multidisciplinaire /myltidisiplinɛʀ/ **ADJ** multidisciplinary

multiethnique, multi-ethnique /myltiɛtnik/ **ADJ** multi-ethnic

multifactoriel, -elle /myltifaktɔʀjɛl/ **ADJ** multifactorial

multifenêtre /myltifənɛtʀ/ **ADJ** *(Ordin)* multiwindow *(épith)*

multiflore /myltiflɔʀ/ **ADJ** multiflora

multifonction /myltifɔ̃ksjɔ̃/ **ADJ** *(gén)* multifunction *(épith)*; *(Ordin)* multiprocessing *(épith)*, multitask(ing) *(épith)*

multiforme /myltifɔʀm/ **ADJ** *[apparence]* multiform; *[problème]* many-sided

multigrade /myltigʀad/ **ADJ** ◆ **huile** ~ multigrade oil

multilatéral, e (mpl **-aux**) /myltilateʀal, o/ **ADJ** multilateral

multilatéralisme /myltilateʀalism/ **NM** *(Écon)* multilateralism

multilingue /myltilɛ̃g/ **ADJ** multilingual

multilinguisme /myltilɛ̃gɥism/ **NM** multilingualism

multimédia /myltimedja/ **ADJ** multimedia **NM** ◆ **le** ~ multimedia

multimédiathèque /myltimedjatɛk/ **NF** multimedia library

multimédiatique /myltimedjatik/ **ADJ** multimedia *(épith)*

multimilliardaire /myltimiljaʀdɛʀ/, **multimillionnaire** /myltimiljɔnɛʀ/ **ADJ, NMF** multimillionaire

multinational, e (mpl **-aux**) /myltinasjɔnal, o/ ADJ multinational NF **multinationale** multinational (company)

multiniveaux /myltinivo/ ADJ multilevel

multipare /myltipaʀ/ ADJ multiparous NF (= *femme*) multipara; (= *animal*) multiparous animal

multipartenariat /myltipaʀtənaʀja/ NM *having several sexual partners*

multipartisme /myltipaʀtism/ NM (*Pol*) multiparty system

multipartite /myltipaʀtit/ ADJ (*Pol*) multiparty (*épith*)

multiple /myltipl/ ADJ 1 (= *nombreux*) numerous, multiple, many; [*fracture, blessures, grossesses, naissances, partenaires*] multiple ◆ **dans de ~s cas** in numerous *ou* many instances ◆ **en de ~s occasions** on numerous *ou* many occasions ◆ **pour des raisons ~s** *ou* **de ~s raisons** for many different reasons ◆ **à de ~s reprises** time and again, repeatedly ◆ **à têtes ~s** [*missile*] multiple-warhead; [*outil*] with (a range of) attachments ◆ **outil à usages ~s** multi-purpose tool ◆ **choix ~** multiple choice ◆ **la xénophobie revêt des formes ~s** xenophobia comes in many different guises *ou* forms ◆ **c'est une évolution aux causes ~s** there are many different reasons behind this development; → **magasin, prise²**

2 (= *varié*) [*activités, aspects*] many, multifarious, manifold

3 (= *complexe*) [*pensée, problème, homme*] many-sided, multifaceted; [*monde*] complex, mixed

4 (*Math*) **100 est ~ de 10** 100 is a multiple of 10

NM multiple ◆ **plus petit commun ~** lowest common multiple

⚠ Attention à ne pas traduire automatiquement **multiple** par le mot anglais **multiple**, qui est d'un registre plus soutenu.

multiplex /myltiplɛks/ ADJ, NM (*Téléc*) multiplex ◆ **émission (réalisée) en ~** multiplex programme

multiplexage /myltiplɛksaʒ/ NM (*Téléc*) multiplexing

multiplexe /myltiplɛks/ NM (*Ciné*) multiplex (cinema), multiscreen cinema

multiplexeur /myltiplɛksœʀ/ NM (*Téléc*) multiplexer

multipliable /myltiplijabl/ ADJ multipli(c)able

multiplicande /myltiplikɑ̃d/ NM multiplicand

multiplicateur, -trice /myltiplikatœʀ, tʀis/ ADJ multiplying ◆ **effet ~** multiplier effect NM multiplier

multiplicatif, -ive /myltiplikatif, iv/ ADJ (*Math*) multiplying; (*Gram*) multiplicative

multiplication /myltiplikasjɔ̃/ NF 1 (= *prolifération*) proliferation ◆ **devant la ~ des accidents** with the increasing number of accidents ◆ **ils demandent la ~ des contrôles** they are asking for more checks *ou* for an increase in the number of checks ◆ **on observe la ~ des faillites d'entreprises** there has been an increase in the number of bankruptcies ◆ **la ~ des pains** (*Bible*) the miracle of the loaves and fishes 2 (*Bio, Bot, Math*) multiplication ◆ **faire une ~** (*Math*) to do a multiplication 3 (*Tech*) gear ratio

multiplicité /myltiplisite/ NF multiplicity

multiplier /myltiplije/ ▸ conjug 7 ◂ VT 1 (*Math*) to multiply (*par* by); ◆ **les prix ont été multipliés par deux/trois** prices have doubled/tripled, prices have increased twofold/threefold

2 (= *répéter*) **~ les attaques/avertissements** to make repeated attacks/warnings ◆ **nous multiplions les initiatives pour aider les sans-abri** we are bringing in more schemes to help the homeless ◆ **les universités multiplient les contacts avec les entreprises** universities are having more and more contact with businesses ◆ **les autorités multiplient les appels au calme** the authorities are issuing repeated appeals for calm ◆ **je pourrais ~ les exemples** I could give you hundreds of examples ◆ **malgré nos efforts multipliés** in spite of our increased efforts

VPR **se multiplier** 1 [*incidents, attaques, difficultés*] to increase ◆ **les rumeurs se multiplient sur son éventuelle démission** there is increasing speculation about his possible resignation ◆ **les licenciements se multiplient dans ce secteur** redundancies are on the increase in this sector ◆ **les parcs à thème se multiplient en France** the number of theme parks in France is on the increase ◆ **les réunions se multiplient** there are more and more meetings

2 (= *se reproduire*) [*animaux*] to multiply; → **croître**

3 (= *se donner à fond*) [*personne*] to do one's utmost, to give of one's best (*pour faire* in order to do)

⚠ Au sens de 'répéter', **multiplier** ne se traduit pas par **to multiply**.

multipoint(s) /myltipwɛ̃/ ADJ INV [*serrure*] multipoint ◆ **injection ~(s)** (*dans moteur*) multipoint fuel injection

multipolaire /myltipɔlɛʀ/ ADJ (*Tech, fig*) multipolar

multiposte /myltipɔst/ ADJ → **configuration**

multiprise /myltipʀiz/ NF adaptor

multiprocesseur /myltipʀɔsesœʀ/ NM multiprocessor

multiprogrammation /myltipʀɔgʀamasjɔ̃/ NF multiprogramming

multipropriété /myltipʀɔpʀijete/ NF timesharing ◆ **acheter un appartement en ~** to buy a timeshare in a flat (*Brit*) *ou* apartment (*US*)

multiracial, e (mpl **-iaux**) /myltiʀasjal, jo/ ADJ multiracial

multirécidive /myltiʀesidiv/ NF repeat offending

multirécidiviste /myltiʀesidivist/ (*Jur*) ADJ [*personne*] who has committed several criminal offences NMF persistent offender

multirésistant, e /myltiʀezistɑ̃, ɑ̃t/ ADJ (*Bio*) [*microbe, souche*] multi-resistant

multirisque(s) /myltiʀisk/ ADJ ◆ **assurance ~(s)** ≈ comprehensive insurance ◆ **contrat ~s habitation** comprehensive home insurance policy

multisalle(s) /myltisal/ ADJ ◆ **(cinéma** *ou* **complexe) ~(s)** multiplex (cinema), multiscreen cinema (complex)

multistandard /myltistɑ̃daʀ/ ADJ [*téléviseur, magnétoscope*] multistandard

multitâche /myltitaʃ/ ADJ (*Ordin*) multitask(ing) (*épith*)

multithérapie /myltiteʀapi/ NF combination therapy

multitraitement /myltitʀɛtmɑ̃/ NM (*Ordin*) multiprocessing

multitude /myltityd/ NF 1 (= *grand nombre*) **(toute) une ~ de** [+ *personnes*] a multitude of, a vast number of; [+ *objets, idées*] a vast number of ◆ **une ~ de gens** a multitude *ou* a throng of people 2 (= *ensemble, masse*) mass ◆ **on pouvait voir d'en haut la ~ des champs** from the air you could see the mass of fields 3 († *ou littér* = *foule de gens*) **la ~** the multitude, the throng

mumuse* /mymyz/ NF ◆ **faire ~** to play (*avec* with); ◆ **alors, on fait ~ ?** are you having a nice time then?

Munich /mynik/ N Munich

munichois, e /mynikwa, waz/ ADJ of *ou* from Munich, Munich (*épith*) ◆ **bière ~e** Munich beer NM,F **Munichois(e)** inhabitant *ou* native of Munich ◆ **les Munichois** (*Pol*) the men of Munich

municipal, e (mpl **-aux**) /mynisipal, o/ ADJ [*élection, taxe, bibliothèque*] municipal; [*employé*] council (*épith*); [*conseil, conseiller*] local, town (*épith*), borough (*épith*); → **arrêté** NFPL **municipales** ◆ **les ~es** the local *ou* council elections

municipalité /mynisipalite/ NF 1 (= *ville*) town 2 (= *conseil*) town council, municipality (*Admin*)

munificence /mynifisɑ̃s/ NF (*littér*) munificence

munificent, e /mynifisɑ̃, ɑ̃t/ ADJ (*littér*) munificent

munir /myniʀ/ ▸ conjug 2 ◂ VT ◆ **~ un objet de** to provide *ou* fit an object with ◆ **~ une machine de** to equip *ou* fit a machine with ◆ **~ un bâtiment de** to equip *ou* fit out a building with ◆ **~ qn de** to provide *ou* supply *ou* equip sb with ◆ **canne munie d'un bout ferré** walking stick with an iron tip ◆ **muni de ces conseils** armed with this advice ◆ **muni d'un bon dictionnaire** equipped with a good dictionary ◆ **muni des sacrements de l'Église** fortified with the rites of the Church VPR **se munir** ◆ **se ~ de** [+ *papiers*] to provide o.s. with; [+ *imperméable*] to take; [+ *argent, nourriture*] to take a supply of ◆ **se ~ de courage** to pluck up one's courage ◆ **munissez-vous de votre passeport** take your passport (with you)

munitions /mynisjɔ̃/ NFPL 1 (*Mil, Chasse*) ammunition (*NonC*), munitions 2 († = *ressources*) supplies

munster /mœ̃stɛʀ/ NM Munster (cheese)

muon /myɔ̃/ NM muon

muphti /myfti/ NM ⇒ **mufti**

muqueux, -euse /mykø, øz/ ADJ mucous NF **muqueuse** mucous membrane

mur /myʀ/ NM 1 (*Constr*) wall ◆ **leur jardin est entouré d'un ~** their garden is walled *ou* is surrounded by a wall ◆ **une maison aux ~s de brique** a brick house ◆ **~ d'appui** parapet ◆ **mettre/pendre qch au ~** to put/hang sth on the wall ◆ **sauter** *ou* **faire le ~*** to go over the wall ◆ **on va droit dans le ~** (*fig*) we're heading straight for disaster ◆ **ils n'ont laissé que les (quatre) ~s** they left nothing but the bare walls ◆ **rester entre quatre ~s** [*prisonnier*] to stay within the confines of one's cell; (*chez soi*) to stay indoors *ou* inside ◆ **l'ennemi est dans nos ~s** the enemy is within our gates ◆ **M. X est dans nos ~s aujourd'hui** we have Mr X with us today ◆ **maintenant que nous sommes dans nos ~s** now (that) we're in our new house (*ou flat etc*), now we have our own four walls ◆ **être propriétaire des ~s** (*Jur*) to own the premises ◆ **les ~s ont des oreilles !** walls have ears! ◆ **faire le ~** (*Sport*) to make a wall ◆ **faire du ~** (*Tennis*) to practise against a wall

2 (= *obstacle*) (*Ski*) wall; [*de feu, pluie*] wall; [*de silence, hostilité*] barrier, wall ◆ **il y a un ~ entre nous** there is a barrier between us ◆ **se heurter à** *ou* **se trouver devant un ~** to come up against a stone *ou* a brick wall ◆ **se heurter à un ~ d'incompréhension** to come up against a wall of incomprehension ◆ **être** *ou* **avoir le dos au ~** to have one's back to the wall ◆ **on parle à un ~** it's like talking to a brick wall; → **pied**

3 **~ du son/de la chaleur** sound/heat barrier ◆ **passer** *ou* **franchir le ~ du son** to break the sound barrier

COMP **mur artificiel** ⇒ **mur d'escalade**
le mur de l'Atlantique *(Mil, Pol)* the Atlantic Wall
le mur de Berlin the Berlin Wall
mur d'escalade climbing wall
le mur d'Hadrien Hadrian's Wall
le mur des Lamentations the Wailing Wall
mur pare-feu *(Internet)* firewall

mûr, e[1] /myʀ/ ADJ 1 *[fruit, projet]* ripe; *[toile, tissu]* worn ◆ **fruit pas ~/trop ~** unripe/overripe fruit 2 *[personne] (= sensé)* mature; *(= âgé)* middle-aged ◆ **une femme assez ~e** a woman of mature years ◆ **il est ~ pour le mariage** he is ready for marriage ◆ **leur pays est-il ~ pour la démocratie ?** is their country ripe for democracy? 3 *(* = ivre)* tight*, plastered* 4 ◆ **après ~e réflexion** after much thought, on mature reflection

murage /myʀaʒ/ NM *[d'ouverture]* walling up, bricking up, blocking up

muraille /myʀɑj/ NF (high) wall ◆ **la Grande Muraille de Chine** the Great Wall of China ◆ **~ de glace/roche** wall of ice/rock, ice/rock barrier ◆ **couleur (de) ~** (stone) grey

mural, e (mpl **-aux**) /myʀal, o/ ADJ *(gén)* wall *(épith)*; *(Art)* mural; *[télévision, panneau]* wall-mounted ◆ **peinture** *ou* **fresque ~e** mural (painting) ◆ **revêtement ~** wall-covering ◆ **papier (peint) ~** wallpaper

mûre[2] /myʀ/ NF *(gén)* blackberry; *[de mûrier blanc]* mulberry

mûrement /myʀmɑ̃/ ADV ◆ **~ réfléchi** *[décision]* carefully thought out ◆ **après avoir ~ réfléchi** *ou* **délibéré** after much *ou* considerable thought, after careful consideration

murène /myʀɛn/ NF moray (eel)

murer /myʀe/ ► conjug 1 ◄ VT 1 *[+ ouverture]* to wall up, to brick up, to block up; *[+ lieu, ville]* to wall (in) 2 *[+ personne] (lit)* to wall in, to wall up; *(fig)* to isolate VPR **se murer** *(chez soi)* to shut o.s. away ◆ **se ~ dans sa douleur/son silence** to immure o.s. in one's grief/in silence ◆ **il est muré dans la solitude** he has shut himself away

muret /myʀɛ/ NM, **murette** /myʀɛt/ NF low wall

murex /myʀɛks/ NM murex

mûrier /myʀje/ NM *(cultivé)* blackberry bush; *(sauvage)* blackberry bush, bramble (bush) ◆ **~ blanc** (white) mulberry tree

mûrir /myʀiʀ/ ► conjug 2 ◄ VI *[fruit]* to ripen; *[idée]* to mature, to develop; *[personne]* to mature; *[abcès, bouton]* to come to a head ◆ **faire ~** *[+ fruit]* to ripen ◆ **il a beaucoup mûri** he has matured a lot, he has become much more mature VT *[+ fruit]* to ripen; *[+ idée, projet]* to nurture; *[+ personne]* to (make) mature

mûrissage /myʀisaʒ/ NM *[de fruits]* ripening

mûrissant, e /myʀisɑ̃, ɑ̃t/ ADJ *[fruit]* ripening; *[personne]* of mature years

mûrissement /myʀismɑ̃/ NM *[de fruit]* ripening; *[d'idée]* maturing, development; *[de projet]* nurturing

mûrisserie /myʀisʀi/ NF *[de bananes]* ripening room

murmure /myʀmyʀ/ NM 1 *(= chuchotement) [de personne]* murmur; *[de ruisseau]* murmur(ing), babble; *[de vent]* murmur(ing) ◆ **~ vésiculaire** *(Méd)* vesicular murmur 2 *(= commentaire)* murmur ◆ **~ d'approbation/de protestation** murmur of approval/of protest ◆ **obéir sans ~** to obey without a murmur ◆ **~s** *(= protestations)* murmurings, mutterings; *(= objections)* objections; *(= rumeurs)* rumours *(Brit)*, rumors *(US)*

murmurer /myʀmyʀe/ ► conjug 1 ◄ VT *(= parler bas)* to murmur ◆ **ils se murmuraient des mots tendres** they were whispering sweet nothings to each other ◆ **on murmure que ..., certains murmurent que ...** *(rumeurs)* it's whispered that ..., rumour has it that ..., it is rumoured that ... ◆ **la situation va s'aggraver, murmurent les spécialistes** there are rumours among the experts that the situation is going to get worse ◆ **de mauvaises langues murmurent que ...** malicious tongues are putting (it) about that ... VI 1 *(= chuchoter) [personne, vent]* to murmur; *[ruisseau]* to murmur, to babble 2 *(= protester)* to mutter, to complain *(contre* about); ◆ **il a consenti sans ~** he agreed without a murmur (of protest)

musaraigne /myzaʀɛɲ/ NF shrew

musarder /myzaʀde/ ► conjug 1 ◄ VI *(littér) (en se promenant)* to dawdle (along); *(en perdant son temps)* to idle (about)

musc /mysk/ NM musk

muscade /myskad/ NF 1 *(Culin)* nutmeg; → **noix** 2 *[de prestidigitateur]* (conjurer's) ball ◆ **passez ~ !** hey presto!

muscadet /myskadɛ/ NM muscadet (wine)

muscadier /myskadje/ NM nutmeg (tree)

muscadin /myskadɛ̃/ NM *(Hist = élégant)* fop, coxcomb †, popinjay †

muscari /myskaʀi/ NM grape hyacinth

muscat /myska/ NM *(= raisin)* muscat grape; *(= vin)* muscat(el)

muscle /myskl/ NM muscle ◆ **~ cardiaque** heart *ou* cardiac muscle ◆ **~s lisses/striés** smooth/striated muscles ◆ **il est tout en ~** he's all muscle ◆ **il a des ~s ou du ~** * he's muscular *ou* beefy* *ou* brawny ◆ **pour gagner** *ou* **prendre du ~** to build up your muscles

musclé, e /myskle/ (ptp de **muscler**) ADJ 1 *[corps, membre, personne]* muscular ◆ **elle est très ~e des jambes** she's got very muscular legs, her legs are very muscular 2 *(= autoritaire) [régime, appariteur]* strong-arm *(épith)*; *[interrogatoire]* brutal, violent; *[discours]* forceful ◆ **méthodes ~es** strong-arm tactics ◆ **une intervention ~e de la police** a forceful intervention by the police ◆ **l'OTAN a lancé un avertissement ~ au dictateur** NATO has sent a strong warning to the dictator 3 *(* = difficile)* **un problème ~** a stinker* of a problem, a knotty problem

muscler /myskle/ ► conjug 1 ◄ VT 1 *[+ corps, membre, personne]* to develop the muscles of 2 *[+ économie, industrie, projet, défense, équipe]* to strengthen VPR **se muscler** *[personne]* to develop one's muscles ◆ **pour que vos jambes se musclent** to develop your leg muscles

muscu* /mysky/ NF (abrév de **musculation**) ◆ **faire de la ~** to do body building

musculaire /myskylɛʀ/ ADJ *[effort, force, puissance]* muscular; *[cellule, douleur, fibre, masse]* muscle *(épith)* ◆ **une déchirure ~** a torn muscle

musculation /myskylasjɔ̃/ NF body building ◆ **exercices de ~** muscle-development exercises ◆ **salle de ~** weights room ◆ **faire de la ~** to do body building

musculature /myskylatyʀ/ NF muscle structure, musculature *(SPÉC)* ◆ **il a une ~ imposante** he has an impressive set of muscles

musculeux, -euse /myskylø, øz/ ADJ *[corps, membre, femme]* muscular; *[homme]* muscular, brawny

muse /myz/ NF *(Littérat, Myth)* Muse ◆ **les (neuf) ~s** the Muses ◆ **cultiver** *ou* **taquiner la ~** *(hum)* to court the Muse *(hum)*

muséal (mpl **muséaux**) /myseal, o/ ADJ museum *(épith)*

museau (pl **museaux**) /myzo/ NM 1 *[de chien]* muzzle; *[de bovin]* muffle; *[de porc]* snout; *[de souris]* nose 2 *(Culin)* brawn *(Brit)*, headcheese *(US)* 3 * *(= visage)* face, snout*; *(= bouche)* mouth ◆ **elle a un joli petit ~** she's got a pretty little face ◆ **essuie ton ~** wipe your mouth

musée /myze/ NM *(art, peinture)* art gallery; *(technique, scientifique)* museum ◆ **le ~ des Offices** the Uffizi (gallery) ◆ **~ de cire** waxworks *(sg)*, wax museum ◆ **Nîmes est une ville-~** Nîmes is a historical town, Nîmes is a town of great historical interest ◆ **~ des horreurs** *(hum)* junkshop *(hum)* ◆ **il ferait bien dans un ~ des horreurs** he should be in a chamber of horrors ◆ **objet** *ou* **pièce de ~** *(lit, fig)* museum piece

museler /myz(ə)le/ ► conjug 4 ◄ VT *[+ animal]* to muzzle; *[+ personne, liberté, presse]* to muzzle, to gag

muselière /myzəljɛʀ/ NF muzzle ◆ **mettre une ~ à** to muzzle

musellement /myzɛlmɑ̃/ NM *[d'animal]* muzzling; *[de personne, liberté, presse]* muzzling, gagging

muséographie /myzeɔgʀafi/ NF museography

muséographique /myzeɔgʀafik/ ADJ *[atelier, programme, projet]* museum *(épith)*

muséologie /myzeɔlɔʒi/ NF museology

muser /myze/ ► conjug 1 ◄ VI *(† ou littér) (en se promenant)* to dawdle (along); *(en perdant son temps)* to idle (about)

musette /myzɛt/ NF 1 *(= sac) [d'ouvrier]* lunchbag; †† *[d'écolier]* satchel; *[de soldat]* haversack; *[de cheval]* nosebag ◆ **avec cinq médailles dans sa ~, il ...** with five medals under his belt, he ... 2 *(Mus = instrument, air)* musette 3 *(= animal)* common shrew NM *(= bal)* popular dance *(to the accordion)* ◆ **le ~** *(= genre)* accordion music ADJ INV *[genre, style]* musette; *[orchestre]* accordion *(épith)*; → **bal**

muséum /myzeɔm/ NM ◆ **~ (d'histoire naturelle)** (natural history) museum

musical, e (mpl **-aux**) /myzikal, o/ ADJ *[chaîne, critique, programmation]* music *(épith)*; *[directeur]* musical, music *(épith)* ◆ **l'œuvre ~e de Debussy** Debussy's musical works *ou* compositions ◆ **avoir l'oreille ~e** to have a good ear for music ◆ **spectacle ~** *(gén)* music show; *(= comédie)* musical; → **comédie**

musicalement /myzikalmɑ̃/ ADV musically

musicalité /myzikalite/ NF musicality, musical quality

music-hall (pl **music-halls**) /myzikol/ NM *(= spectacle)* music hall; *(= salle)* variety theatre, music hall ◆ **faire du ~** to be in *ou* do variety ◆ **spectacle/numéro de ~** variety show/turn *ou* act *ou* number

musicien, -ienne /myzisjɛ̃, jɛn/ ADJ musical NM,F musician

musicographe /myzikɔgʀaf/ NMF musicographer

musicographie /myzikɔgʀafi/ NF musicography

musicologie /myzikɔlɔʒi/ NF musicology

musicologique /myzikɔlɔʒik/ ADJ musicological

musicologue /myzikɔlɔg/ NMF musicologist

musicothérapie /myzikoteʀapi/ NF music therapy

musique /myzik/ NF 1 *(= art, harmonie, notations)* music; *[morceau]* piece of music ◆ **~ folklorique/militaire/sacrée** folk/military/sacred music ◆ **~ pour piano** piano music ◆ **elle fait de la ~** she does music, she plays an instrument ◆ **si on faisait de la ~** let's make some music ◆ **mettre un poème en ~** to set a poem to music ◆ **déjeuner en ~** to lunch against a background of music ◆ **travailler en ~** to work to music ◆ **je n'aime pas travailler**

en ~ I don't like working with music playing ◆ **elle nous chante maintenant "Manhattan", sur une ~ de Georges Leblanc** she's now going to sing "Manhattan" for us, music by Georges Leblanc ◆ **qui a écrit la ~ du film ?** who wrote the film score? *ou* the soundtrack? ◆ **il compose beaucoup de ~s de film** he composes a lot of film music ◆ **la ~ adoucit les mœurs** music has a civilizing influence, music soothes the savage breast ◆ **c'est toujours la même ~** * it's always the same old song *ou* tune ◆ **tu veux toujours aller plus vite que la ~** you always want to do things too quickly; → **boîte, connaître, papier**

2 *(= orchestre, fanfare)* band ◆ **~ militaire** military band ◆ **marcher** *ou* **aller ~ en tête** *(Mil)* to march with the band leading; → **chef¹**

COMP **musique d'ambiance** background *ou* ambient music
musique d'ascenseur *(péj)* Muzak ®, elevator *ou* lift *(Brit)* music
musique de ballet ballet music
musique de chambre chamber music
musique classique classical music
musique concrète concrete music, musique concrète
musique de fond *(gén)* background music; *[de film]* incidental music
musique légère light music
musique noire black music
musique pop pop music
musique de scène incidental music
musique de supermarché ⇒ **musique d'ascenseur**

musiquette /myziket/ NF *(péj)* bland music

musli /mysli/ NM ⇒ **muesli**

musoir /myzwaʀ/ NM *(Naut)* pierhead

musqué, e /myske/ ADJ *[odeur, goût]* musky ◆ **bœuf ~** musk ox ◆ **rose ~e** musk rose; → **rat**

mussolinien, -ienne /mysɔlinjɛ̃, jɛn/ ADJ *(lit)* Mussolini *(épith)*; *(péj) [architecture]* Mussolini-style ◆ **l'Italie mussolinienne** Italy under the rule of Mussolini

must * /mœst/ NM *(film, livre etc)* ◆ **c'est un ~** it's a must *

mustang /mystɑ̃g/ NM mustang

musulman, e /myzylmɑ̃, an/ ADJ, NM,F Moslem, Muslim

mutabilité /mytabilite/ NF *(Bio, Jur)* mutability

mutagène /mytaʒɛn/ ADJ mutagenic

mutant, e /mytɑ̃, ɑ̃t/ ADJ, NM,F mutant

mutation /mytasjɔ̃/ NF 1 *(= transfert) [d'employé]* transfer 2 *(= changement) (gén)* transformation; *(Bio)* mutation ◆ **société en ~** changing society ◆ **entreprise en pleine ~** company undergoing massive changes 3 *(Jur)* transfer; *(Mus)* mutation ◆ **~ consonantique/vocalique/phonétique** *(Ling)* consonant/vowel/sound shift

mutatis mutandis /mytatismytɑ̃dis/ LOC ADV mutatis mutandis, allowing for a few minor variations

muter /myte/ ► conjug 1 ◄ VT *(Admin)* to transfer ◆ **il a été muté à Caen/au service informatique** he has been transferred to Caen/to the computer department VI to mutate

mutilant, e /mytilɑ̃, ɑ̃t/ ADJ *[opération]* mutilating, mutilative

mutilateur, -trice /mytilatœʀ, tʀis/ *(littér)* ADJ mutilating, mutilative NM,F mutilator

mutilation /mytilasjɔ̃/ NF *[de corps]* mutilation, maiming; *[de texte, statue, arbre]* mutilation ◆ **~ volontaire** self-inflicted injury ◆ **~ sexuelle** sexual mutilation

mutilé, e /mytile/ (ptp de **mutiler**) NM,F *(= infirme)* cripple, disabled person ◆ **les (grands) ~s** the (badly *ou* severely) disabled ◆ **~ de la face** disfigured person ◆ **~ de guerre** disabled ex-serviceman ◆ **~ du travail** disabled worker

mutiler /mytile/ ► conjug 1 ◄ VT *[+ personne]* to mutilate, to maim; *[+ statue, tableau, arbre, texte]* to mutilate; *[+ paysage]* to disfigure ◆ **être mutilé des deux jambes** to have lost both legs ◆ **se ~ (volontairement)** to mutilate o.s.

mutin, e /mytɛ̃, in/ ADJ *(= espiègle)* mischievous, impish NM *(= révolté)* rebel; *(Mil, Naut)* mutineer

mutiné, e /mytine/ (ptp de **se mutiner**) ADJ *[marin, soldat]* mutinous NM *(Mil, Naut)* mutineer; *(gén)* rebel

mutiner (se) /mytine/ ► conjug 1 ◄ VPR *(Mil, Naut)* to mutiny; *(gén)* to rebel, to revolt

mutinerie /mytinʀi/ NF *(Mil, Naut)* mutiny; *(gén)* rebellion, revolt

mutisme /mytism/ NM 1 *(= silence)* silence ◆ **elle s'enferma dans un ~ total** she withdrew into total silence ◆ **la presse observe un ~ total** the press is maintaining a complete silence *ou* blackout on the subject 2 *(Psych)* mutism

mutité /mytite/ NF *(Méd)* muteness

mutualisme /mytɥalism/ NM mutual (benefit) insurance system

mutualiste /mytɥalist/ ADJ mutualistic ◆ **société (d'assurances) ~** mutual benefit society, mutual (benefit) insurance company, ≃ Friendly Society *(Brit)* NMF mutualist

mutualité /mytɥalite/ NF *(= système d'entraide)* mutual (benefit) insurance system ◆ **la ~ française** *(= compagnies)* French mutual insurance companies

mutuel, -elle /mytɥɛl/ ADJ *(= réciproque)* mutual; → **pari** NF **mutuelle** mutual benefit society, mutual (benefit) insurance company ≃ Friendly Society *(Brit)* ◆ **prendre une mutuelle** * to take out (supplementary) private health insurance ◆ **payer sa cotisation à la mutuelle** ≃ to pay one's insurance premium *(for back-up health cover)*

MUTUELLE

In addition to standard health cover provided by the « Sécurité sociale », many French people contribute to complementary insurance schemes run by mutual benefit organizations known as **mutuelles**, often linked to specific professions. The **mutuelle** reimburses some or all of the medical expenses that cannot be met by the « Sécurité sociale ». → **SÉCURITÉ SOCIALE**

mutuellement /mytɥɛlmɑ̃/ ADV *[s'accuser, se renforcer]* one another, each other ◆ **~ ressenti** mutually felt ◆ **s'aider ~** to give each other mutual help, to help one another ◆ **ces options s'excluent ~** these options are mutually exclusive

MW NM (abrév de **mégawatt**) MW

Myanmar /mijanmaʀ/ NM Myanmar

mycélium /miseljɔm/ NM mycelium

Mycènes /misɛn/ N Mycenae

mycénien, -ienne /misenjɛ̃, jɛn/ ADJ Mycenaean

mycologie /mikɔlɔʒi/ NF mycology

mycologique /mikɔlɔʒik/ ADJ mycologic(al)

mycologue /mikɔlɔg/ NMF mycologist

mycorhize /mikɔʀiz/ NM myco(r)rhiza

mycose /mikoz/ NF fungal infection, mycosis *(SPÉC)* ◆ **la ~ du pied** athlete's foot ◆ **~ vaginale** vaginal thrush

mycosique /mikɔsik/ ADJ mycotic

myéline /mjelin/ NF myelin

myélite /mjelit/ NF myelitis

mygale /migal/ NF trap-door spider

myocarde /mjɔkaʀd/ NM myocardium; → **infarctus**

myopathe /mjɔpat/ ADJ suffering from myopathy, ≃ suffering from muscular dystrophy NMF person suffering from myopathy, ≃ person suffering from muscular dystrophy

myopathie /mjɔpati/ NF myopathy, ≃ muscular dystrophy

myope /mjɔp/ ADJ short-sighted, near-sighted *(US)*, myopic *(SPÉC)* ◆ **tu es ~ ou quoi ?** * are you blind? ◆ **~ comme une taupe** * (as) blind as a bat * NMF short-sighted *ou* near-sighted *(US)* person, myope *(SPÉC)*

myopie /mjɔpi/ NF short-sightedness, near-sightedness *(US)*, myopia *(SPÉC)*

myosotis /mjɔzɔtis/ NM forget-me-not

myriade /miʀjad/ NF myriad

myriapode /miʀjapɔd/ NM myriapods ◆ **les ~s** Myriapoda *(SPÉC)*

myrmidon /miʀmidɔ̃/ NM († *péj = nabot*) pipsqueak *

myrrhe /miʀ/ NF myrrh

myrte /miʀt/ NM myrtle

myrtille /miʀtij/ NF whortleberry, bilberry *(Brit)*, blueberry *(US)*

mystère /mistɛʀ/ NM 1 *(= énigme, dissimulation)* mystery ◆ **pas tant de ~(s) !** don't be so mysterious! *ou* secretive! ◆ **faire (un) ~ de** to make a mystery out of ◆ **elle en fait grand ~** she makes a big mystery of it ◆ **il restera un ~ pour moi** he'll always be a mystery *ou* a closed book to me ◆ **~ et boule de gomme !** * who knows!, search me! * ◆ **ce n'est un ~ pour personne** it's no secret ◆ **il faut travailler beaucoup, il n'y a pas de ~ !** * you just have to work hard, there's no two ways about it! * ◆ **le ~ de la Trinité/de l'Incarnation** *(Rel)* the mystery of the Trinity/of the Incarnation 2 *(Littérat)* mystery (play) 3 ® *(= glace) ice-cream with a meringue centre, decorated with chopped hazelnuts*

mystérieusement /misteʀjøzmɑ̃/ ADV mysteriously

mystérieux, -ieuse /misteʀjø, jøz/ ADJ *(= secret, bizarre)* mysterious; *(= cachottier)* secretive

mysticisme /mistisism/ NM mysticism

mystificateur, -trice /mistifikatœʀ, tʀis/ ADJ ◆ **j'ai reçu un coup de fil ~** I had a phone call which was a hoax ◆ **tenir des propos ~s à qn** to say things to trick sb NM,F *(= farceur)* hoaxer, practical joker

mystification /mistifikasjɔ̃/ NF *(= farce)* hoax, practical joke; *(péj = mythe)* myth

mystifier /mistifje/ ► conjug 7 ◄ VT to fool, to deceive

mystique /mistik/ ADJ mystic(al) NMF *(= personne)* mystic NF *(= science, pratiques)* mysticism; *(péj = vénération)* blind belief *(de* in*)*; ◆ **avoir la ~ du travail** to have a blind belief in work

mystiquement /mistikmɑ̃/ ADV mystically

mythe /mit/ NM *(gén)* myth

mythifier /mitifje/ ► conjug 7 ◄ VT *(surtout au ptp)* *[+ passé, personne]* to mythologize, to mythicize

mythique / mitik / ADJ mythical

mytho* / mito / ADJ, NMF abrév de **mythomane**

mythologie / mitɔlɔʒi / NF mythology

mythologique / mitɔlɔʒik / ADJ mythological

mythomane / mitɔman / ADJ, NMF (*Psych*) mythomaniac; (*= menteur*) compulsive liar ◆ **elle est un peu** ~ she has a tendency to embroider the truth ◆ **il est complètement** ~ he makes up the most incredible stories

mythomanie / mitɔmani / NF mythomania

mytiliculteur, -trice / mitilikyltœʀ, tʀis / NM,F mussel breeder

mytiliculture / mitilikyltyʀ / NF mussel breeding

myxomatose / miksomatoz / NF myxomatosis

Nn

N¹, n /ɛn/ **NM** (= *lettre*) N, n; *(Math)* n

N² (abrév de **Nord**) N

n' /n/ → **ne**

na /na/ **EXCL** *(langage enfantin)* so there! ◆ **je n'en veux pas, ~ !** I don't want any, so there!

nabab /nabab/ **NM** *(Hist, † ou littér)* nabob

nabi /nabi/ **NM** *(Art)* Nabi

nabot, e /nabo, ɔt/ **NM,F** *(péj)* dwarf, midget

nabuchodonosor /nabykɔdɔnɔzɔʀ/ **NM** (= *bouteille*) nebuchadnezzar ◆ **Nabuchodonosor** Nebuchadnezzar

nacelle /nasɛl/ **NF** *[de ballon, montgolfière, dirigeable]* gondola; *[de landau]* carriage; *[d'engin spatial]* pod; *[d'ouvrier]* cradle; *(littér = bateau)* skiff

nacre /nakʀ/ **NF** mother-of-pearl

nacré, e /nakʀe/ (ptp de **nacrer**) **ADJ** pearly, nacreous *(littér)*; *[vernis à ongles]* pearly

nacrer /nakʀe/ ▸ conjug 1 ◂ **VT** (= *iriser*) to cast a pearly sheen over; *[+ fausse perle]* to give a pearly gloss to

nadir /nadiʀ/ **NM** nadir

nævus /nevys/ (pl **nævi** /nevi/) **NM** naevus

Nagasaki /nagazaki/ **N** Nagasaki

nage /naʒ/ **NF** 1 (= *activité*) swimming; (= *manière*) stroke, style of swimming ◆ **~ sur le dos** backstroke ◆ **~ en eau vive** white-water swimming ◆ **~ indienne** sidestroke ◆ **faire un 100 m ~ libre** to swim a 100 m (in) freestyle ◆ **~ sous-marine** underwater swimming, skin diving ◆ **~ de vitesse** speed stroke ◆ **~ synchronisée** synchronized swimming

2 ◆ **se sauver à la ~** to swim away *ou* off ◆ **gagner la rive/traverser une rivière à la ~** to swim to the bank/across a river ◆ **homard/écrevisses à la ~** *(Culin)* lobster/crayfish (cooked) in a court-bouillon

3 ◆ **en ~** pouring with sweat, bathed in sweat ◆ **cela m'a mis en ~** it made me sweat, it brought me out in a sweat ◆ **ne te mets pas en ~** don't get yourself in a lather*

4 *(Naut)* **~ à couple/en pointe** rowing two abreast/in staggered pairs; → **banc, chef¹**

nageoire /naʒwaʀ/ **NF** *[de poisson]* fin; *[de phoque, dauphin]* flipper ◆ **~ anale/dorsale/ventrale** anal/dorsal/ventral fin ◆ **~ caudale** *[de poisson]* caudal fin; *[de baleine]* tail flukes

nager /naʒe/ ▸ conjug 3 ◂ **VI** 1 *[personne, poisson]* to swim; *[objet]* to float ◆ **elle nage bien** she's a good swimmer ◆ **~ comme un fer à repasser*/un poisson*** to swim like a brick/a fish ◆ **la viande nage dans la graisse** the meat is swimming in fat ◆ **tes manches nagent dans la soupe** your sleeves are dipping in the soup ◆ **on nageait dans le sang** the place was swimming in blood, the place was awash with blood; → **apprendre, savoir**

2 *(fig)* **il nage dans le bonheur** he is overjoyed, his joy knows no bounds ◆ **~ dans l'opulence** to be rolling in money* ◆ **il nage dans ses vêtements** his clothes are miles too big for him ◆ **on nage dans l'absurdité/le grotesque dans ce film** this film is totally absurd/ridiculous ◆ **en allemand, je nage complètement*** I'm completely at sea* *ou* lost in German

3 *(Naut)* to row ◆ **~ à couple/en pointe** to row two abreast/in staggered pairs

VT to swim ◆ **~ la brasse/le 100 mètres** to swim breast-stroke/the 100 metres

nageur, -euse /naʒœʀ, øz/ **NM,F** swimmer; (= *rameur*) rower ◆ **~ de combat** naval frogman

Nagorny(ï)-Karabakh /nagɔʀni(i)kaʀabak/, **Nagorno-Karabakh** /nagɔʀnokaʀabak/ **NM** Nagorno-Karabakh

naguère /nageʀ/ **ADV** *(frm)* 1 (= *il y a peu de temps*) not long ago, recently 2 (= *autrefois*) formerly ◆ **la rivière, qui ~ zigzaguait librement ...** the river, which in the past meandered freely *ou* which used to meander freely ...

naïade /najad/ **NF** *[= divinité, plante]* naiad; *(hum, littér)* nymph

naïf, naïve /naif, naiv/ **GRAMMAIRE ACTIVE 53.1**

ADJ 1 (= *ingénu*) innocent, naïve ◆ **d'un air ~** innocently 2 (= *crédule*) *[personne]* naïve, gullible; *[foi]* naïve 3 *(Art) [peintre, art]* naïve **NM,F** gullible fool, innocent ◆ **vous me prenez pour un ~** you must think I'm a gullible fool *ou* a complete innocent **NM** *(Art)* naïve painter

nain, e /nɛ̃, nɛn/ **ADJ** dwarfish, dwarf *(épith)* ◆ **chêne/haricot ~** dwarf oak/runner bean ◆ **poule ~e** bantam (hen) ◆ **rosier ~** miniature rose (bush) **NM,F** dwarf ◆ **le ~ jaune** *(Cartes)* pope Joan ◆ **~ de jardin** garden gnome **NF naine** *(Astron)* dwarf ◆ **~e blanche/rouge** white/red dwarf

Nairobi /neʀobi/ **N** Nairobi

naissain /nɛsɛ̃/ **NM** (= *larves d'huîtres*) spat

naissance /nɛsɑ̃s/ **GRAMMAIRE ACTIVE 51.1** **NF** 1 *[de personne, animal]* birth ◆ **à la ~** at birth ◆ **il est aveugle/muet/sourd de ~** he has been blind/dumb/deaf from birth, he was born blind/dumb/deaf ◆ **français de ~** French by birth ◆ **chez lui, c'est de ~*** he was born like that ◆ **nouvelle ~** new arrival *ou* baby ◆ **~ double** birth of twins ◆ **~ multiple** multiple birth; → **contrôle, extrait, limitation** *etc*

2 *(frm = origine, famille)* birth ◆ **de ~ obscure/illustre** of obscure/illustrious birth ◆ **de haute** *ou* **bonne ~** of noble *ou* high birth ◆ **peu importe sa ~** no matter what his birth *ou* parentage (is)

3 (= *point de départ*) *[de rivière]* source; *[de langue, ongles]* root; *[de cou, colonne]* base ◆ **à la ~ des cheveux** at the roots of the hair ◆ **la ~ des seins** the top of the cleavage

4 *(littér = commencement) [de printemps, monde, idée, amour]* dawn, birth ◆ **la ~ du jour** daybreak ◆ **la ~ du cinéma** the birth *ou* advent of cinema

5 *(locutions)* **prendre ~** *[projet, idée]* to originate, to take form *ou* shape; *[soupçon, sentiment]* to arise (*dans* in); ◆ **donner ~ à** *[+ enfant]* to give birth to; *[+ rumeurs, sentiment]* to give rise to

naissant, e /nɛsɑ̃, ɑ̃t/ **ADJ** *[calvitie]* incipient; *[passion]* burgeoning; *[industrie, marché, démocratie, talent]* burgeoning, budding; *[capitalisme]* burgeoning, nascent *(frm)* ◆ **une barbe ~e** the beginnings of a beard ◆ **(à l'état) ~** *(Chim)* nascent

naître /nɛtʀ/ ▸ conjug 59 ◂ **VI** 1 *[personne, animal]* to be born ◆ **quand l'enfant doit-il ~ ?** when is the baby due? ◆ **il vient tout juste de ~** he has only just been born, he is just newly born ◆ **il est né** *ou* **il naquit** *(frm)* **le 4** he was born on the 4th ◆ **l'homme naît libre** man is born free ◆ **l'enfant qui naît aveugle/infirme** the child who is born blind/disabled ◆ **l'enfant qui va ~, l'enfant à ~** the unborn child ◆ **l'enfant qui vient de ~** the newborn child ◆ **en naissant** at birth ◆ **prématuré né à 7 mois** baby born prematurely at 7 months, premature baby born at 7 months ◆ **né sous le signe du Verseau** born under (the sign of) Aquarius ◆ **enfant né de père inconnu** child of an unknown father ◆ **être né de parents français** to be of French parentage, to be born of French parents ◆ **être né d'une mère anglaise** to be born of an English mother ◆ **un sauveur nous est né** *(Bible)* a saviour is born to us ◆ **être né coiffé** *(Méd)* to be born with a caul ◆ **être né coiffé** *ou* **sous une bonne étoile** *(fig)* to be born lucky *ou* under a lucky star ◆ **il n'est pas né d'hier** *ou* **de la dernière pluie** *ou* **de la dernière couvée** *(fig)* he wasn't born yesterday, he is not as green as he looks ◆ **je l'ai vu ~ !** *(fig)* I've known him since he was born *ou* since he was a baby ◆ **le pays qui l'a vu ~** the land of his birth, his native country; → aussi **né**

2 (= *apparaître*) *[sentiment, craintes]* to arise, to be born; *[idée, projet]* to be born; *[ville, industrie]* to spring up; *[jour]* to break; *[difficultés]* to arise; *[fleur, plante]* to burst forth ◆ **la rivière naît au**

pied de ces collines the river has its source *ou* rises at the foot of these hills ◆ **je vis ~ un sourire sur son visage** I saw the beginnings of a smile on his face, I saw a smile creep over his face ◆ **faire ~** *[+ industrie, difficultés]* to create; *[+ soupçons, désir]* to arouse

3 *(= résulter de)* **~ de** to spring from, to arise from ◆ **la haine née de ces querelles** the hatred arising from *ou* which sprang from these quarrels ◆ **de cette rencontre naquit le mouvement qui ...** from this meeting sprang the movement which ...

4 *(= être destiné à)* **il était né pour commander/pour la magistrature** he was born to command/to be a judge ◆ **ils sont nés l'un pour l'autre** they were made for each other ◆ **il est né poète** he is a born *ou* natural poet

5 *(littér = s'éveiller à)* **~ à l'amour/la poésie** to awaken to love/poetry

VB IMPERS ◆ **il naît plus de garçons que de filles** there are more boys born than girls ◆ **il vous est né un fils** *(littér)* a son has been born to you *(littér)*; → aussi **né**

naïvement /naivmɑ̃/ ADV *(= ingénument)* innocently, naïvely; *(= avec crédulité)* naïvely

naïveté /naivte/ NF 1 *(= ingénuité) [de personne]* innocence, naivety; *[de réponse, gaieté]* naivety 2 *(= crédulité) [de personne]* naivety, gullibility; *[de foi]* naivety ◆ **il a eu la ~ de ...** he was naïve enough to ... ◆ **d'une grande ~** very naïve ◆ **tu est d'une ~ !** you're so naïve!

naja /naʒa/ NM cobra

Namibie /namibi/ NF Namibia

namibien, -ienne /namibjɛ̃, jɛn/ ADJ Namibian NM,F **Namibien(ne)** Namibian

nana * /nana/ NF *(= femme)* woman; *(= petite amie)* girlfriend

nanan * /nanɑ̃/ NM ◆ **c'est du ~** *(agréable)* it's really nice; *(facile)* it's a walkover* *ou* a doddle* *(Brit)* *ou* a cakewalk* *(US)*; *(succulent)* it's scrumptious*

nanar * /nanaʀ/ NM *(péj) (= objet invendable)* piece of junk ◆ **~ des années 30** *(= film démodé)* second-rate film from the 1930s

nandrolone /nɑ̃dʀɔlɔn/ NF nandrolone

nanifier /nanifje/ ▸ conjug 7 ◂ VT *[+ arbre]* to dwarf

nanisme /nanism/ NM dwarfism, nanism *(SPÉC)*

nankin /nɑ̃kɛ̃/ NM *(= tissu)* nankeen

nanomètre /nanɔmɛtʀ/ NM nanometre *(Brit)*, nanometer *(US)*

nanoscience /nanosjɑ̃s/ NF nanoscience.

nanoseconde /nanos(ə)gɔ̃d/ NF nanosecond

nanotechnologie /nanotɛknɔlɔʒi/ NF nanotechnology

nantais, e /nɑ̃tɛ, ɛz/ ADJ of *ou* from Nantes NM,F **Nantais(e)** inhabitant *ou* native of Nantes

nanti, e /nɑ̃ti/ (ptp de **nantir**) ADJ rich, affluent, well-to-do ◆ **les ~s** the rich, the affluent, the well-to-do

nantir /nɑ̃tiʀ/ ▸ conjug 2 ◂ VT (†, *Jur) [+ créancier]* to secure ◆ **~ qn de** *(fig, littér = munir)* to provide *ou* equip sb with ◆ **nanti de** equipped with VPR **se nantir** (†, *Jur)* to secure o.s. ◆ **se ~ de** *(fig, littér)* to provide o.s. with, to equip o.s. with

nantissement /nɑ̃tismɑ̃/ NM *(Jur)* security

napalm /napalm/ NM napalm

naphtaline /naftalin/ NF *(= antimite)* mothballs ◆ **sa théorie sent la ~** his theory is straight out of the ark

naphte /naft/ NM naphtha

napoléon /napɔleɔ̃/ NM *(Fin)* napoleon ◆ **Napoléon** *(Hist)* Napoleon NF *(= cerise) type of bigaroon cherry*

napoléonien, -ienne /napɔleɔnjɛ̃, jɛn/ ADJ Napoleonic

napolitain, e /napɔlitɛ̃, ɛn/ ADJ Neapolitan NM,F **Napolitain(e)** Neapolitan

nappage /napaʒ/ NM *(Culin)* topping

nappe /nap/ NF 1 *[de table]* tablecloth ◆ **mettre la ~** to put the tablecloth on 2 *(= couche)* layer, sheet ◆ **~ de gaz** layer of gas ◆ **~ d'eau** sheet *ou* expanse of water 3 *(Géom)* nappe 4 *(= bande de textile)* lap

COMP **nappe d'autel** altar cloth

nappe de brouillard blanket *ou* layer of fog ◆ **des ~s de brouillard** fog patches

nappe de charriage nappe

nappe de feu sheet of flame

nappe de mazout, **nappe de pétrole** oil slick

nappe phréatique ground water

napper /nape/ ▸ conjug 1 ◂ VT *(Culin)* to top *(de* with); ◆ **nappé de chocolat** topped with chocolate, with a chocolate topping

napperon /napʀɔ̃/ NM doily, tablemat; *(pour vase, lampe)* mat

narcisse /naʀsis/ NM *(= plante)* narcissus ◆ **Narcisse** *(Myth)* Narcissus ◆ **c'est un vrai Narcisse** he's terribly vain

narcissique /naʀsisik/ ADJ narcissistic, vain NMF narcissist

narcissisme /naʀsisism/ NM narcissism, vanity

narco- /naʀko/ PRÉF narco- ◆ **~analyse** narcoanalysis ◆ **~terroriste** narco-terrorist

narcodollars /naʀkodɔlaʀ/ NMPL drug(s) money *(usually in dollars)* ◆ **3 millions de ~** 3 million dollars' worth of drug(s) money

narcose /naʀkoz/ NF narcosis

narcotique /naʀkɔtik/ ADJ, NM narcotic

narcotrafic /naʀkotʀafik/ NM drug trafficking

narcotrafiquant, e /naʀkotʀafikɑ̃, ɑ̃t/ NM,F drug trafficker

narghileh /naʀgile/ NM hookah, nargileh, narghile

narguer /naʀge/ ▸ conjug 1 ◂ VT *[+ danger, traditions]* to flout, to thumb one's nose at; *[+ personne]* to deride, to scoff at ◆ **il nous nargue avec son argent** we're not good enough for him now he's got all that money

narguilé /naʀgile/ NM ⇒ **narghileh**

narine /naʀin/ NF nostril

narquois, e /naʀkwa, waz/ ADJ *(= railleur)* derisive, sardonic, mocking

narquoisement /naʀkwazmɑ̃/ ADV derisively, sardonically, mockingly

narrateur, -trice /naʀatœʀ, tʀis/ NM,F narrator

narratif, -ive /naʀatif, iv/ ADJ narrative

narration /naʀasjɔ̃/ NF 1 *(= action)* narration; → **infinitif, présent**¹ 2 *(= récit)* narrative, account; *(Scol = rédaction)* essay, composition; *(Rhétorique)* narration

narrer /naʀe/ ▸ conjug 1 ◂ VT *(frm)* to narrate, to relate

narthex /naʀtɛks/ NM narthex

narval /naʀval/ NM narwhal

NASA, Nasa /naza/ NF (abrév de **National Aeronautics and Space Administration**) NASA

nasal, e (mpl **-aux**) /nazal, o/ ADJ nasal; → **fosse** NF **nasale** nasal

nasalisation /nazalizasjɔ̃/ NF nasalization

nasaliser /nazalize/ ▸ conjug 1 ◂ VT to nasalize

nasalité /nazalite/ NF nasality

nase ⁑ /nɑz/ ADJ 1 *(= hors d'usage)* bust* *(attrib)*, kaput* *(attrib)* ◆ **ma télé est ~** my TV's conked out⁑ *ou* is bust* ◆ **je suis ~** *(exténué)* I'm exhausted *ou* knackered⁑ *(Brit)*; *(psychologiquement)* I'm out of it* 2 *(= fou)* cracked* *(attrib)*, touched* *(attrib)* 3 *(= nul) [projet]* useless; *[personne]* hopeless*; *(= stupide)* stupid, daft* *(Brit)* NMF *(= personne nulle)* moron* NM *(= nez)* conk*, hooter⁑ *(Brit)*

naseau (pl **naseaux**) /nazo/ NM *[de cheval, bœuf]* nostril

nasillard, e /nazijaʀ, aʀd/ ADJ *[voix]* nasal; *[gramophone]* whiny, tinny; *[instrument]* tinny

nasillement /nazijmɑ̃/ NM *[de voix]* (nasal) twang; *[de microphone, gramophone]* whine; *[d'instrument]* tinny sound; *[de canard]* quack

nasiller /nazije/ ▸ conjug 1 ◂ VT to say *(ou* sing *ou* intone) with a (nasal) twang VI *[personne]* to have a (nasal) twang, to speak with a nasal voice; *[instrument]* to give a tinny *ou* twangy sound; *[microphone, gramophone]* to whine; *[canard]* to quack

nasique /nazik/ NM *(= singe)* proboscis monkey

Nassau /naso/ N Nassau

nasse /nɑs/ NF *(pour oiseaux)* hoop net; *(Pêche)* fish trap, creel ◆ **être pris dans la ~** *(fig)* to be caught in the net

Natal /natal/ NM *(Géog)* Natal

natal, e (mpl **natals**) /natal/ ADJ native ◆ **ma maison ~e** the house where I was born ◆ **ma terre ~e** my native soil

nataliste /natalist/ ADJ *[politique, argument]* pro-birth, which supports a rising birth rate

natalité /natalite/ NF ◆ **(taux de) ~** birth rate

natation /natasjɔ̃/ NF swimming ◆ **~ artistique** *ou* **synchronisée** synchronized swimming ◆ **faire de la ~** to go swimming, to swim

natatoire /natatwaʀ/ ADJ swimming *(épith)*; → **vessie**

Natel ® /natel/ NM *(Helv) (= téléphone portable)* mobile

natif, -ive /natif, iv/ ADJ, NM,F *(gén)* native ◆ **~ de Nice** native of Nice ◆ **locuteur ~** native speaker ◆ **les ~s du Lion** people born under the sign of Leo

nation /nasjɔ̃/ NF *(= pays, peuple)* nation ◆ **les Nations Unies** the United Nations; → **société**

national, e (mpl **-aux**) /nasjɔnal, o/ ADJ *(gén)* national; *[économie, monnaie]* domestic ◆ **au plan ~ et international** at home and abroad, at the national and international level ◆ **entreprise ~e** state-owned company ◆ **grève ~e** nationwide *ou* national strike ◆ **obsèques ~es** state funeral ◆ **route ~e** ≈ A *ou* trunk road *(Brit)*, state highway *(US)*; → **assemblée, éducation, fête** NMPL **nationaux** *(= citoyens)* nationals NF **nationale** *(= route)* A *ou* trunk road *(Brit)*, state highway *(US)*

> ⚠ Attention à ne pas traduire automatiquement **national** par le mot anglais **national**.

nationalement /nasjɔnalmɑ̃/ ADV nationally

nationalisable /nasjɔnalizabl/ ADJ targetted for nationalization

nationalisation /nasjɔnalizasjɔ̃/ NF nationalization

nationaliser /nasjɔnalize/ ▸ conjug 1 ◂ VT to nationalize ◆ **(entreprises) nationalisées** nationalized companies

nationalisme /nasjɔnalism/ NM nationalism

nationaliste /nasjɔnalist/ ADJ, NMF nationalist

nationalité /nasjɔnalite/ NF nationality ◆ **les personnes de ~ française** French citizens ◆ **il a la double ~ française et suisse** he has dual French and Swiss *ou* French/Swiss nationality

national-socialisme /nasjɔnalsɔsjalism/ NM National Socialism

national-socialiste /nasjɔnalsɔsjalist/ (mpl **nationaux-socialistes**) ADJ, NMF National Socialist

nativisme /nativism/ NM *(Philos)* nativism

nativiste /nativist/ ADJ *(Philos)* nativistic

nativité /nativite/ NF nativity; *(Art)* (painting of the) nativity, nativity scene

natte /nat/ NF (= *tresse*) plait *(Brit)*, braid *(US)*; (= *paillasse*) mat, matting *(NonC)* ◆ **se faire des ~s** to plait *(Brit)* ou braid *(US)* one's hair, to put one's hair in plaits *(Brit)* ou braids *(US)* ◆ **~s africaines** corn rows

natter /nate/ ▸ conjug 1 ◂ VT *[+ cheveux, laine]* to plait *(Brit)*, to braid *(US)*

naturalisation /natyʀalizasjɔ̃/ NF 1 *[de personne, espèce, mot]* naturalization 2 *[d'animaux morts]* stuffing; *[de plantes]* preserving

naturalisé, e /natyʀalize/ (ptp de **naturaliser**) ADJ naturalized ◆ **Français ~** naturalized Frenchman ◆ **il est ~ français** he's a naturalized Frenchman, he has French citizenship NM,F naturalized citizen

naturaliser /natyʀalize/ ▸ conjug 1 ◂ VT 1 *[+ personne, espèce, mot]* to naturalize ◆ **se faire ~ français** to be granted French citizenship, to become a naturalized Frenchman 2 *[+ animal]* to stuff; *[+ plante]* to preserve *(with glycerine)*

naturalisme /natyʀalism/ NM naturalism

naturaliste /natyʀalist/ ADJ naturalistic NMF *(Littérat, Sci)* naturalist; (= *empailleur*) taxidermist; *(pour les plantes)* flower-preserver

nature /natyʀ/ NF 1 (= *monde physique*) **la ~** nature ◆ **la ~ a horreur du vide** nature abhors a vacuum ◆ **laisser agir la ~** to let nature take its course, to leave it to nature ◆ **la ~ fait bien les choses** nature is a wonderful thing ◆ **crimes contre ~** unnatural crimes ◆ **goûts contre ~** depraved tastes; → **force**

2 (= *campagne*) countryside ◆ **il aime la ~, les fleurs, les bêtes** he loves the countryside, flowers and animals ◆ **perdu dans la ~, en pleine ~** in the middle of nowhere ◆ **lâcher qn dans la ~** * to send sb off without any directions; *(pour commettre un crime)* to let sb loose ◆ **disparaître** ou **s'évanouir dans la ~** * *[personne]* to vanish into thin air; → **retour**

3 (= *caractère*) *[de personne, substance, sentiment]* nature ◆ **la ~ humaine** human nature ◆ **c'est une** ou **il est d'une ~ arrogante** he has an ou he is of an arrogant nature ◆ **il est arrogant de** ou **par ~** he is naturally arrogant ou arrogant by nature ◆ **ce n'est pas dans sa ~** it is not (in) his nature *(d'être* to be); ◆ **c'est/ce n'est pas de ~ à arranger les choses** it's liable to/not likely to make things easier ◆ **il n'est pas de ~ à accepter** he's not the sort of person who would agree ◆ **il a une heureuse ~** he has a happy disposition ou a sunny temperament ◆ **tu es une petite ~ !** you're so delicate!, you've got a delicate constitution! ◆ **quelle petite ~ tu fais !** *(péj)* what a weakling you are! ◆ **c'est dans la ~ des choses** it's in the nature of things; → **habitude**

4 (= *sorte*) nature, kind, sort ◆ **de toute(s) ~(s)** of all kinds, of every kind

5 *(Art)* **peindre d'après ~** to paint from life ◆ **plus grand que ~** larger than life ◆ **~ morte** still life; → **grandeur**

6 *(Fin)* **en ~** *[payer] [don]* in kind

ADJ INV 1 (= *sans adjonction*) *[café]* black; *[eau, crêpe, omelette]* plain; *[thé]* without milk; *[yaourt]* natural, plain; *[salade]* without dressing ◆ **riz ~** (plain) boiled rice ◆ **boire le whisky ~** to drink whisky neat ou straight ◆ **manger les fraises ~** to eat strawberries without anything on them

2 * *[personne]* (= *sans artifice*) natural, unaffected ◆ **il est très ~ !** (= *spontané*) he's very spontaneous!

> ⚠ Au sens de 'campagne', **nature** ne se traduit pas par le mot anglais **nature**.

naturel, -elle /natyʀɛl/ ADJ 1 *[caractère, frontière, produit, phénomène]* natural; *[besoins, fonction]* bodily *(épith)*; *[soie, laine]* pure ◆ **aliments/produits ~s** natural ou organic foods/products

2 (= *inné*) natural ◆ **son intelligence naturelle** his natural intelligence, his native wit ◆ **elle a un talent ~ pour le piano** playing the piano comes naturally to her, she has a natural talent for the piano

3 (= *normal, habituel*) natural ◆ **avec sa voix naturelle** in his normal voice ◆ **c'est un geste ~ chez lui** it's a natural thing for him to do ◆ **votre indignation est bien naturelle** your indignation is quite ou very natural ou quite understandable ◆ **je vous remercie ! – c'est (tout) ~** thank you! – don't mention it ou you're welcome ◆ **ne me remerciez pas, c'est bien** ou **tout ~** don't thank me, anybody would have done the same ou it was the obvious thing to do ◆ **il trouve ça tout ~** he finds it the most natural thing in the world ou perfectly normal ◆ **il trouve tout ~ de ...** he thinks nothing of ...

4 (= *simple, spontané*) *[voix, style, personne]* natural, unaffected ◆ **elle sait rester très naturelle** she manages to stay very natural ◆ **il est très ~ sur les photos** he always looks very natural in photos

5 *(Mus)* natural

6 *(Math)* **(nombre entier) ~** natural number

NM 1 (= *caractère*) nature, disposition ◆ **être d'un** ou **avoir un bon ~** to have a happy ou sunny nature ou disposition ◆ **il est d'un ~ optimiste/méfiant** he is an optimistic/wary kind of person; → **chasser**

2 (= *absence d'affectation*) naturalness ◆ **avec (beaucoup de) ~** (completely) naturally ◆ **il manque de ~** he's not very natural, he has a rather self-conscious manner

3 ◆ **au ~** (= *sans assaisonnement*) *[thon]* in brine; *[salade, asperges]* without any dressing (ou seasoning) ◆ **pêches au ~** peaches in natural fruit juice ◆ **elle est mieux en photo qu'au ~** (= *en réalité*) she's better in photos than in real life

naturellement /natyʀɛlmɑ̃/ ADV 1 (= *sans artifice, avec aisance*) naturally 2 (= *bien sûr*) naturally, of course

naturisme /natyʀism/ NM (= *nudisme*) naturism; *(Philos)* naturism; *(Méd)* naturopathy

naturiste /natyʀist/ ADJ, NMF (= *nudiste*) naturist; *(Philos)* naturist; *(Méd)* naturopath

naturopathe /natyʀɔpat/ NMF naturopath

naturopathie /natyʀɔpati/ NF naturopathy, naturopathic medicine

naufrage /nofʀaʒ/ NM 1 *[de bateau]* wreck, wrecking ◆ **le ~ du Titanic** the sinking of the Titanic ◆ **ils ont trouvé la mort dans un ~** they drowned in a shipwreck ◆ **ces rochers ont causé bien des ~s** many ships have been wrecked on these rocks ◆ **faire ~** *[bateau]* to be wrecked; *[personne]* to be shipwrecked 2 (= *déchéance*) *[d'ambitions, réputation]* ruin, ruination; *[de projet, pays]* foundering, ruination; *[d'entreprise]* collapse ◆ **sauver du ~** *[+ personne]* to save from disaster; *[+ argent, biens]* to salvage (from the wreckage); *[+ entreprise]* to save from collapse

naufragé, e /nofʀaʒe/ ADJ *[marin]* shipwrecked; *[bateau]* wrecked NM,F shipwrecked person; *(sur une île)* castaway ◆ **les ~s de la croissance économique** the casualties of economic growth

naufrageur, -euse /nofʀaʒœʀ, øz/ NM,F *(lit, fig)* wrecker

Nauru /nauʀu/ N Nauru

nauséabond, e /nozeabɔ̃, ɔ̃d/ ADJ *[odeur]* putrid, nauseating, foul; *[effluves, fumées]* foul-smelling; *[cloaque]* stinking; *(fig)* nauseating, sickening

nausée /noze/ NF (= *sensation*) nausea *(NonC)*; (= *haut-le-cœur*) bout of nausea ◆ **avoir la ~** to feel sick ou nauseous ou queasy ◆ **avoir des ~s** to have bouts of nausea ◆ **ça me donne la ~** *(lit, fig)* it makes me (feel) sick, it nauseates me

nauséeux, -euse /nozeø, øz/ ADJ *[personne]* nauseous, queasy; *[odeur, goût]* nauseating, nauseous ◆ **état ~** nausea

nautile /notil/ NM (= *animal*) nautilus

nautique /notik/ ADJ *[science, mille]* nautical ◆ **fête/ballet ~** water festival/ballet ◆ **club ~** watersports club ◆ **loisirs ~s** water-based recreational activities ◆ **salon ~** boat show; → **ski, sport**

nautisme /notism/ NM water sport(s)

navajo /navaxo/ ADJ Navajo, Navaho NMF **Navajo** Navajo, Navaho ◆ **les Navajos** the Navajo(s) ou Navaho(s), the Navajo ou Navaho Indians

naval, e (mpl **navals**) /naval/ ADJ *[combat, base]* naval; *[industrie]* shipbuilding ◆ **école ~e** naval college; → **chantier, construction, force**

navarin /navaʀɛ̃/ NM navarin, ≃ mutton stew

navarrais, e /navaʀɛ, ɛz/ ADJ Navarrian NM,F **Navarrais(e)** Navarrian

Navarre /navaʀ/ NF Navarre

navel /navɛl/ NF navel orange

navet /navɛ/ NM 1 (= *légume*) turnip ◆ **~ fourrager** fodder beet; → **sang** 2 *(péj* = *film)* rubbishy ou third-rate film ◆ **quel ~ !** what a load of trash ou rubbish! *(Brit)*

navette[1] /navɛt/ NF 1 *[de métier à tisser]* shuttle; (= *aiguille*) netting ou meshing needle ◆ **~ volante** flying shuttle 2 (= *service de transport*) shuttle (service) ◆ **~ diplomatique** diplomatic shuttle ◆ **faire la ~ entre** *[banlieusard, homme d'affaires]* to commute between; *[véhicule]* to operate a shuttle (service) between; *[bateau]* to ply between; *[projet de loi, circulaire]* to be sent backwards and forwards between ◆ **elle fait la ~ entre la cuisine et la chambre** she comes and goes between the kitchen and the bedroom ◆ **faire faire la ~ à qn/qch** to have sb/sth going back and forth *(entre* between) 3 *(Espace)* **~ spatiale** space shuttle 4 *(à encens)* incense holder

navette[2] /navɛt/ NF (= *plante*) rape

navetteur, -euse /navɛtœʀ, øz/ NM,F *(Belg)* commuter

navigabilité /navigabilite/ NF *[de rivière]* navigability; *[de bateau]* seaworthiness; *[d'avion]* airworthiness

navigable /navigabl/ ADJ *[rivière]* navigable

navigant, e /navigɑ̃, ɑ̃t/ ADJ, NM ◆ **le personnel ~, les ~s** *(dans avion)* flying personnel; *(dans bateau)* seagoing personnel

navigateur, -trice /navigatœʀ, tʀis/ NM,F (= *marin*) sailor; (= *personne chargée d'un itinéraire*) navigator ◆ **~ solitaire** single-handed sailor ou yachtsman NM *(Internet)* browser

navigation /navigasjɔ̃/ NF 1 (= *trafic maritime*) (sea) traffic *(NonC)*; (= *pilotage*) navigation *(NonC)*, sailing *(NonC)* ◆ **les récifs rendent la ~ dangereuse** the reefs make sailing ou navigation dangerous ◆ **canal ouvert/fermé** ou **interdit à la ~** canal open/closed to shipping ou ships ◆ **~ côtière/intérieure** coastal/inland navigation ◆ **~ de plaisance** (pleasure) sailing ◆ **~ à voiles** sailing, yachting ◆ **compagnie de ~** shipping company ◆ **terme de ~** nautical term [2] (= *trafic aérien*) (air) traffic (*NonC*); (= *pilotage*) navigation (*NonC*), flying (*NonC*) ◆ ~ **aérienne/spatiale** aerial/space navigation [3] (*Ordin*) ~ **sur Internet** browsing the Internet ◆ ~ **hypertexte** browsing hypertext ◆ **logiciel de** ~ browser

naviguer /navige/ ► conjug 1 ◄ **VI** [1] (= *voyager*) [*bateau, passager, marin*] to sail; [*avion, passager, pilote*] to fly ◆ ~ **à la voile** to sail ◆ **ce bateau n'a jamais navigué** this ship has never been to sea *ou* has never sailed ◆ **bateau en état de** ~ seaworthy ship ◆ ~ **à 24 000 pieds** to fly at an altitude of 24,000 feet

[2] (= *piloter*) [*marin, pilote*] to navigate ◆ ~ **au compas/aux instruments/à l'estime** to navigate by (the) compass/by instruments/by dead reckoning ◆ ~ **à travers Detroit** (*en voiture*) to find *ou* negotiate one's way through Detroit ◆ ~ **entre les obstacles** to negotiate one's way between obstacles

[3] (*Ordin*) ~ **sur Internet** to surf *ou* browse the Internet

[4] (*fig*) **pour réussir ici, il faut savoir** ~* to succeed here you need to know how to get around *ou* you need to know the ropes ◆ **c'est un type qui a beaucoup navigué*** he's a man who's been around a lot *ou* who's knocked about quite a bit* ◆ **le gouvernement doit** ~ **entre les écueils** the government must tread a delicate path ◆ **le dossier a navigué de bureau en bureau** the file found its way from office to office, the file went the rounds of the offices

navire /naviʀ/ **NM** (= *bateau*) ship; (*Jur*) vessel ◆ ~ **amiral** flagship ◆ ~**-citerne** tanker ◆ ~ **marchand** *ou* **de commerce** merchant ship, merchantman ◆ ~ **jumeau** sister ship ◆ ~ **de guerre** warship

navire-école (pl **navires-écoles**) /naviʀekɔl/ **NM** training ship

navire-hôpital (pl **navires-hôpitaux**) /naviʀɔpital, o/ **NM** hospital ship

navire-usine (pl **navires-usines**) /naviʀyzin/ **NM** factory ship

navrant, e /navʀɑ̃, ɑ̃t/ **ADJ** (= *attristant*) [*spectacle, conduite, nouvelle*] distressing, upsetting; (= *regrettable*) [*contretemps, malentendu*] unfortunate, regrettable ◆ **tu es** ~ **!** you're hopeless! ◆ **un spectacle** ~ **de bêtise** a depressingly silly show ◆ **ce film est d'une médiocrité** ~**e** this film is terribly mediocre ◆ **il n'écoute personne, c'est** ~ he won't listen to anybody, it's a shame

navré, e /navʀe/ **GRAMMAIRE ACTIVE 45.3** (ptp de **navrer**) **ADJ** sorry (*de* to); ◆ **je suis (vraiment)** ~ I'm (so *ou* terribly) sorry ◆ ~ **de vous décevoir mais ...** sorry to disappoint you but ... ◆ **avoir l'air** ~ (*pour s'excuser, compatir*) to look sorry; (*d'une nouvelle*) to look distressed *ou* upset ◆ **d'un ton** ~ (*exprimant la tristesse*) in a distressed *ou* an upset voice; (*pour s'excuser*) in an apologetic tone, apologetically; (*pour compatir*) in a sympathetic tone

navrer /navʀe/ ► conjug 1 ◄ **VT** [1] (= *consterner*) [*spectacle, conduite, nouvelle*] to distress, to upset [2] (= *contrarier*) [*contretemps, malentendu*] to annoy

nazaréen, -enne /nazaʀeɛ̃, ɛn/ **ADJ** Nazarene **NM,F** **Nazaréen(ne)** Nazarene

Nazareth /nazaʀɛt/ **N** Nazareth

naze* /nɑz/ **ADJ** ⇒ **nase***

nazi, e /nazi/ **ADJ, NM,F** Nazi

nazisme /nazism/ **NM** Nazism

N.B., NB /ɛnbe/ **NM** (abrév de **nota bene**) NB

N.-D. (abrév de **Notre-Dame**) → **notre**

N'Djamena /nʒamena/ **N** Ndjamena

NDLR (abrév de **note de la rédaction**) → **note**

NdT (abrév de **note du traducteur**) translator's note

ne /nə/ **ADV NÉG** [1] (*valeur négative, avec négation avant ou après*) **il n'a rien dit** he didn't say anything, he said nothing ◆ **elle** ~ **nous a pas vus** she didn't *ou* did not see us, she hasn't *ou* has not seen us ◆ **personne** *ou* **nul** (*frm*) **n'a compris** nobody *ou* no one understood ◆ **il n'y a aucun mal à ça** there's no harm *ou* there's nothing wrong in that ◆ **il n'est pas du tout** *ou* **nullement idiot** he's no fool, he's by no means stupid ◆ **je** ~ **le ferai jamais** I'll never do it ◆ **je n'ai pas d'argent** I haven't got *ou* I don't have any money, I have no money ◆ **il** ~ **sait plus ce qu'il dit** he no longer knows what he's saying, he doesn't know what he's saying any more ◆ **plus rien** ~ **l'intéresse, rien** ~ **l'intéresse plus** nothing interests him any more, he's not interested in anything any more ◆ ~ **me dérangez pas** don't *ou* do not disturb me ◆ **je** ~ **connais ni son fils ni sa fille** I know neither his son nor his daughter, I don't know (either) his son or his daughter ◆ **je n'ai pas du tout** *ou* **aucunement l'intention de refuser** I have not the slightest *ou* least intention of refusing ◆ **je n'ai guère le temps** I scarcely *ou* hardly have the time ◆ **il** ~ **sait pas parler** he can't *ou* cannot speak ◆ **pas un seul** ~ **savait sa leçon** not (a single) one (of them) knew his lesson

[2] (*valeur négative, sans autre négation : littér*) **il** ~ **cesse de se plaindre** he's always *ou* constantly complaining, he doesn't stop *ou* never stops complaining ◆ **je** ~ **sais qui a eu cette idée** I don't know who had that idea ◆ **elle** ~ **peut jouer du violon sans qu'un voisin (**~**) proteste** she can't play her violin without some neighbour objecting ◆ **il n'a que faire de vos conseils** he has no use for your advice, he's not interested in your advice ◆ **que n'a-t-il songé à me prévenir** if only he had thought to warn me ◆ **n'était la situation internationale, il serait parti** had it not been for *ou* were it not for the international situation he would have left ◆ **il n'est de paysage qui** ~ **soit maintenant gâché** not a patch of countryside remains unspoilt, there is no unspoilt countryside left ◆ **il n'est de jour qu'elle** ~ **se plaigne** not a day goes by but she complains (about something) *ou* without her complaining ◆ **cela fait des années que je n'ai été au cinéma** it's years since I (last) went to the cinema, I haven't been to the cinema for years ◆ **il a vieilli depuis que je** ~ **l'ai vu** he has aged since I (last) saw him ◆ **si je** ~ **me trompe** if I'm not mistaken; → **cure**[1], **empêcher, importer**[2]

[3] ◆ ~ **... que** only ◆ **elle n'a confiance qu'en nous** she trusts only us, she only has confidence in us ◆ **c'est mauvais de** ~ **manger que des conserves** it's bad to eat only canned foods *ou* nothing but canned foods ◆ **il n'a que trop d'assurance** he's only too self-assured ◆ **il n'a d'autre idée en tête que de se lancer dans la politique** his (one and) only thought is to go into politics ◆ **il n'y a que lui pour dire des choses pareilles !** only he *ou* nobody but he would say such things! ◆ **il n'y a pas que vous qui le dites !** you're not the only one who says so! ◆ **et il n'y a pas que ça !** and that's not all!; → **demander**

[4] (*explétif sans valeur nég, gén omis dans la langue parlée*) **je crains** *ou* **j'ai peur qu'il** ~ **vienne** I am afraid *ou* I fear (that) he is coming *ou* (that) he will come ◆ **je** ~ **doute pas/je** ~ **nie pas qu'il** ~ **soit compétent** I don't doubt/deny that he's competent ◆ **empêche que les enfants** ~ **touchent aux animaux** stop the children touching *ou* prevent the children from touching the animals ◆ **mangez avant que la viande** ~ **refroidisse** do eat before the meat gets cold ◆ **j'irai la voir avant qu'il/à moins qu'il** ~ **pleuve** I shall go and see her before/unless it rains ◆ **il est parti avant que je** ~ **l'aie remercié** he left before I'd thanked him ◆ **il est parti sans que je** ~ **l'aie remercié** he left without my having thanked him ◆ **peu s'en faut qu'il n'ait oublié la réunion** he all but *ou* he very nearly forgot the meeting ◆ **il est plus/moins malin qu'on** ~ **pense** he's more cunning than/not as cunning as you (might) think

né, e /ne/ (ptp de **naître**) **ADJ** ◆ **orateur-/acteur-**~ born orator/actor ◆ **bien/mal** ~ of noble *ou* high/humble *ou* low birth ◆ **Paul est son premier-/dernier-**~ Paul is her first-/last-born *ou* her first/last child ◆ **Mme Durand,** ~**e Dupont** Mrs Durand née Dupont; → aussi **naître**

néandertalien, -ienne /neɑ̃dɛʀtaljɛ̃, jɛn/ **ADJ** Neanderthal (*épith*) **NM** Neanderthal man

néanmoins /neɑ̃mwɛ̃/ **ADV** (= *pourtant*) nevertheless, yet ◆ **il était malade, il est** ~ **venu** he was ill, (and) nevertheless *ou* (and) yet he came ◆ **c'est incroyable mais** ~ **vrai** it's incredible but nonetheless true *ou* but it's true nevertheless ◆ **il est agressif et** ~ **patient** he is aggressive yet patient, he is aggressive but nevertheless patient

néant /neɑ̃/ **NM** ◆ **le** ~ nothingness (*NonC*) ◆ **le** ~ **de la vie/de l'homme** the emptiness of life/man ◆ **replonger dans le** ~ to sink back into oblivion ◆ **et après c'est le** ~ then there's a total blank ◆ **signes particuliers :** ~ distinguishing marks: none ◆ **sortir/surgir du** ~ to appear/spring up out of nowhere; → **réduire**

Nébraska /nebʀaska/ **NM** Nebraska

nébuleuse[1] /nebyløz/ **NF** (*Astron*) nebula; (*fig*) loose conglomeration ◆ **c'est encore à l'état de** ~ (*fig*) it's still very vague

nébuleusement /nebyløzmɑ̃/ **ADV** nebulously, vaguely

nébuleux, -euse[2] /nebylø, øz/ **ADJ** [*ciel*] cloudy, overcast; [*écrivain*] nebulous, obscure; [*projet, idée, discours*] nebulous, vague, woolly (*Brit*), wooly (*US*)

nébuliseur /nebylizœʀ/ **NM** nebulizer

nébulosité /nebylozite/ **NF** [*de ciel*] cloud covering, nebulosity (*SPÉC*); [*de discours*] obscureness, vagueness, woolliness (*Brit*), wooliness (*US*)

nécessaire /nesesɛʀ/ **GRAMMAIRE ACTIVE 37.2, 37.3, 44.2**

ADJ [1] (*gén, Math, Philos*) necessary ◆ **est-ce (bien)** ~ **?** is it (really) necessary? ◆ **ce n'est pas** ~ it's not necessary ◆ **il est** ~ **de le faire ou qu'on le fasse** it needs to be done ◆ **il n'est pas** ~ **que tu le fasses** you don't need *ou* have to (do it), it's not (really) necessary (for you to do it) ◆ **l'eau est** ~ **à la vie** *ou* **pour vivre/aux hommes** water is a necessity of life/a human necessity ◆ **une alimentation variée apporte à l'organisme tout ce qui lui est** ~ **en vitamines** a varied diet provides the body with everything it needs as regards vitamins ◆ **cette attitude lui est** ~ **pour réussir** it's necessary for him to have this attitude if he wants to be successful ◆ **c'est une condition** ~ it's a necessary condition ◆ **le temps** ~ **pour maquiller une star** the time it takes to make up a star ◆ **a-t-il les moyens financiers** ~**s ?** does he have the necessary funds? ◆ **faire les démarches** ~**s** to take the necessary *ou* requisite steps ◆ **nous ferons la grève si** ~ we'll go on strike if necessary

[2] [*personne*] needed ◆ **se sentir** ~ to feel needed

NM [1] (= *l'indispensable*) **as-tu emporté le** ~ **?** have you got all *ou* everything you need? ◆ **tout le** ~ **pour préparer et réussir votre voyage** everything you need to prepare for and make a success of your trip ◆ **il peut faire froid, prenez le** ~ it may be cold so take the right things *ou* gear * ◆ **emporter le strict** ~ to take only what's absolutely necessary ◆ **il faut d'abord penser au** ~ one must first consider the essentials ◆ **manquer du** ~ to lack the (basic) necessities of life ◆ **j'ai fait le** ~ I've seen to it ◆ **je vais faire le** ~ I'll see to it

2 *(Philos)* **le** ~ the necessary

COMP **nécessaire à couture** (pocket) sewing kit

nécessaire à ongles manicure set

nécessaire à ouvrage ⇒ **nécessaire à couture**

nécessaire de toilette travel pack (of toiletries)

nécessaire de voyage overnight bag, grip

nécessairement /nesesɛʀmɑ̃/ ADV necessarily ◆ **dois-je** ~ **m'en aller ?** is it (really) necessary for me to go?, do I (really) have to go? ◆ **passeras-tu par Londres ? – oui, ~/non, pas** ~ will you go via London? – yes, it's unavoidable *ou* you have to/no, not necessarily ◆ **il devra** ~ **s'y faire** he will (just) have to get used to it ◆ **il ne m'a pas** ~ **vu** I can't be sure (that) he saw me ◆ **il y a** ~ **une raison** there must be a reason ◆ **ce n'est pas** ~ **faux** it isn't necessarily wrong ◆ **causes et effets sont liés** ~ *(Philos)* causes and effects are necessarily linked *ou* are of necessity linked

nécessité /nesesite/ NF 1 *(= obligation)* necessity ◆ **c'est une** ~ **absolue** it's an absolute necessity ◆ **sévère sans** ~ unnecessarily severe ◆ **il souligne la** ~ **d'un débat** he emphasizes the need *ou* necessity for a debate ◆ **je n'en vois pas la** ~ I don't see the need for it ◆ **se trouver** *ou* **être dans la** ~ **de faire qch** to have no choice *ou* alternative but to do sth ◆ **mettre qn dans la** ~ **de faire** to make it necessary for sb to do ◆ **la** ~ **où nous nous trouvons de faire cela** the fact that we have no choice *ou* alternative but to do that ◆ **état de** ~ *(Jur)* necessity

2 *(Philos)* **la** ~ necessity ◆ **la** ~ **de mourir** the inevitability of death

3 *(†† = pauvreté)* destitution ◆ **être dans la** ~ to be in need, to be poverty-stricken

4 *(locutions)* **je l'ai fait par** ~ I did it because I had to *ou* because I had no choice ◆ **de première** ~ absolutely essential ◆ **articles de première** ~ bare necessities *ou* essentials ◆ **faire de** ~ **vertu** to make a virtue of necessity ◆ ~ **fait loi** *(Prov)* necessity knows no law *(Prov)*

NFPL **nécessités** ◆ **les ~s de la vie** the necessities *ou* essentials of life ◆ **les ~s du service** the demands *ou* requirements of the job ◆ **~s financières** (financial) liabilities

nécessiter /nesesite/ ▸ conjug 1 ◂ VT *(= requérir)* to require, to call for, to necessitate ◆ **l'intervention nécessite plusieurs jours d'hospitalisation** the operation means *ou* involves a hospital stay of several days ◆ **la maison nécessite de gros travaux** the house needs a lot of work (done on it) *ou* is in need of a lot of renovation

nécessiteux, -euse *(frm)* /nesesitø, øz/ ADJ needy, necessitous *(frm)* NM,F needy person ◆ **les** ~ the needy, the poor

nec plus ultra /nɛkplysyltʀa/ NM ◆ **c'est le** ~ it's the last word *(de* in)

nécrologie /nekʀɔlɔʒi/ NF *(= liste)* obituary column; *(= notice biographique)* obituary

> ⚠ Attention à ne pas traduire automatiquement **nécrologie** par le mot anglais **necrology**, qui est d'un registre plus soutenu.

nécrologique /nekʀɔlɔʒik/ ADJ obituary *(épith)*

nécromancie /nekʀɔmɑ̃si/ NF necromancy

nécromancien, -ienne /nekʀɔmɑ̃sjɛ̃, jɛn/ NM,F necromancer

nécrophage /nekʀɔfaʒ/ ADJ necrophagous

nécrophile /nekʀɔfil/ ADJ necrophilic NM,F necrophiliac

nécrophilie /nekʀɔfili/ NF necrophilia

nécropole /nekʀɔpɔl/ NF necropolis

nécrose /nekʀoz/ NF necrosis

nécroser VT, **se nécroser** VPR /nekʀoze/ ▸ conjug 1 ◂ to necrose, to necrotize

nectar /nɛktaʀ/ NM nectar

nectarine /nɛktaʀin/ NF nectarine

néerlandais, e /neɛʀlɑ̃dɛ, ɛz/ ADJ Dutch, of the Netherlands NM 1 *(= langue)* Dutch 2 ◆ **Néerlandais** Dutchman ◆ **les Néerlandais** the Dutch NF **Néerlandaise** Dutchwoman

néerlandophone /neɛʀlɑ̃dɔfɔn/ ADJ Dutch-speaking NM,F Dutch speaker

nef /nɛf/ NF 1 *(Archit)* nave ◆ ~ **latérale** side aisle 2 *(†† ou littér = bateau)* vessel, ship

néfaste /nefast/ ADJ *(= nuisible)* harmful *(à* to); *(= funeste)* ill-fated, unlucky ◆ **cela lui fut** ~ it had disastrous consequences for him

nèfle /nɛfl/ NF medlar ◆ **des ~s !*** nothing doing! *, not likely! *

néflier /neflije/ NM medlar (tree)

négateur, -trice /negatœʀ, tʀis/ *(littér)* ADJ given to denying, contradictory NM,F denier

négatif, -ive /negatif, iv/ ADJ *[attitude, réponse]* negative; *[quantité, nombre]* negative, minus *(épith)* ◆ **particule négative** negative particle NM *(Photo, Ling)* negative ◆ **au** ~ in the negative ADV ◆ **vous êtes prêts ? –** ~ ! * are you ready? – negative! * NF **négative** ◆ **répondre par la négative** to reply in the negative ◆ **dans la négative** if not

négation /negasjɔ̃/ NF *(gén)* negation; *(Ling)* negative ◆ **double** ~ double negative

négationnisme /negasjɔnism/ NM revisionism *(denying the existence of the Nazi gas chambers)*

négationniste /negasjɔnist/ ADJ, NMF revisionist *(denying the existence of the Nazi gas chambers)*

négativement /negativmɑ̃/ ADV *[réagir]* negatively ◆ **répondre** ~ to reply in the negative ◆ **juger qch/qn** ~ to be critical of sth/sb

négativisme /negativism/ NM negativism, negativity

négativité /negativite/ NF *(Phys)* negativity; *[d'attitude]* negativeness, negativity

négaton † /negatɔ̃/ NM negatron

négligé, e /neglige/ (ptp de **négliger**) ADJ *[épouse, ami]* neglected; *[personne, tenue]* slovenly, sloppy; *[ongles]* uncared-for, neglected; *[travail]* slapdash, careless; *[style]* slipshod; *[occasion]* missed *(épith)* NM *(= laisser-aller)* slovenliness; *(= déshabillé)* négligé ◆ **il était en** ~ he was casually dressed *ou* wearing casual clothes ◆ **le** ~ **de sa tenue** the slovenliness of his dress

négligeable /negliʒabl/ ADJ *(gén)* negligible; *[détail]* unimportant, trivial, trifling; *[adversaire]* insignificant ◆ **qui n'est pas ~, non** ~ *[facteur, élément]* not inconsiderable; *[adversaire, aide, offre]* by no means insignificant; *[détail, rôle, nombre]* not insignificant ◆ **une quantité non** ~ an appreciable amount

négligemment /negliʒamɑ̃/ ADV *(= sans soin)* carelessly, negligently, in a slovenly way; *(= nonchalamment)* casually

négligence /negliʒɑ̃s/ NF *(= manque de soin)* negligence, slovenliness; *(= faute, erreur)* omission, act of negligence; *(Jur)* criminal negligence ◆ **il est d'une (telle)** ~ **!** he's so careless! ◆ **c'est une** ~ **de ma part** it's an oversight *ou* a careless mistake on my part ◆ **par** ~ out of carelessness ◆ ~ **(de style)** stylistic blunder, carelessness *(NonC)* of style ◆ **faire preuve de** ~ to be negligent

négligent, e /negliʒɑ̃, ɑt/ ADJ *(= sans soin)* negligent, careless; *(= nonchalant)* casual

négliger /negliʒe/ ▸ conjug 3 ◂ VT *(gén)* to neglect; *[+ style, tenue]* to be careless about; *[+ conseil]* to pay no attention *ou* no heed to, to disregard; *[+ occasion]* to miss; *[+ rhume, plaie]* to ignore ◆ **il néglige ses amis** he neglects his friends ◆ **ce n'est pas à** ~ *(offre)* it's not to be sneezed at; *(difficulté)* it mustn't be overlooked ◆ **ne rien ~ (pour)** to do everything possible (to)

◆ **négliger de faire** to fail to do ◆ **certains services négligent de répondre aux lettres de la clientèle** some departments fail to reply to customers' letters

VPR **se négliger** *(santé)* to neglect o.s., not to look after o.s.; *(tenue)* to neglect one's appearance, not to bother with one's appearance

négoce /negɔs/ NM 1 *(Écon)* trade ◆ **le** ~ **international** international trade *ou* trading ◆ **faire du** ~ to be in business ◆ **faire du** ~ **avec un pays** to trade with a country ◆ **il fait le** ~ **de** he trades *ou* deals in 2 *(† = boutique, affaire)* business ◆ **dans mon** ~ in my trade *ou* business ◆ **il tenait un** ~ **de fruits et légumes** he sold fruit and vegetables, he had a greengrocery business *(surtout Brit)*

négociabilité /negɔsjabilite/ NF negotiability

négociable /negɔsjabl/ ADJ negotiable

négociant, e /negɔsjɑ̃, jɑt/ NM,F merchant ◆ ~ **en gros** wholesaler ◆ ~ **en vin(s)** wine merchant

négociateur, -trice /negɔsjatœʀ, tʀis/ NM,F negotiator

négociation /negɔsjasjɔ̃/ NF *(Comm, Pol)* negotiation ◆ **engager** *ou* **entamer des ~s** to enter into negotiations ◆ **~s commerciales** trade talks ◆ **~s salariales/bilatérales** wage/bilateral negotiations *ou* talks ◆ **le contrat est actuellement en** ~ the contract is currently under negotiation

négocier /negɔsje/ ▸ conjug 7 ◂ VI 1 *(gén)* to negotiate 2 *(†† : Comm)* to trade VT to negotiate ◆ ~ **un virage** to negotiate a bend

nègre /nɛgʀ/ NM 1 *(†, injurieux = personne)* Negro ◆ **travailler comme un** ~ to work like a slave, to slave away 2 *(péj = écrivain)* ghost (writer) 3 *(Culin)* ~ **en chemise** chocolate and cream dessert ADJ *(†, injurieux)* Negro *(épith)*; → **art**

négresse /negʀɛs/ NF *(†, injurieux)* Negress

négrier, -ière /negʀije, ijɛʀ/ ADJ slave *(épith)* ◆ **(bateau)** ~ slave ship ◆ **(capitaine)** ~ slave-ship captain NM *(= marchand d'esclaves)* slave trader; *(fig péj = patron)* slave driver *

négrillon ** /negʀijɔ̃/ NM *(injurieux)* piccaninny ** *(injurieux)*

négrillonne ** /negʀijɔn/ NF *(injurieux)* piccaninny ** *(injurieux)*

négritude /negʀityd/ NF negritude

négro ** /negʀo/ NM *(injurieux)* nigger ** *(injurieux)*

négro-africain, e (mpl **négro-africains**) /negʀoafʀikɛ̃, ɛn/ ADJ *[littérature]* of Sub-Saharan Africa and the African diaspora; *[population]* of Sub-Saharan Africa

négroïde /negʀɔid/ ADJ Negroid

negro-spiritual (pl **negro-spirituals**) /negʀospiʀitɥɔl/ NM Negro spiritual

Néguev /negɛv/ NM ◆ **le désert du** ~ the Negev desert

négus /negys/ NM *(= titre)* Negus

neige /nɛʒ/ NF 1 *(Météo)* snow; *(arg Drogue = cocaïne)* snow *(arg)* ◆ **le temps est à la** ~ it looks like (it's going to) snow ◆ **aller à la** ~ * to go to the ski resorts, to go on a skiing holiday ◆ **cheveux/teint de** ~ snow-white hair/complexion [2] (*Culin*) **battre** *ou* **faire monter des blancs en** ~ to whisk *ou* beat (up) egg whites to form stiff peaks ◆ **blancs** *ou* **œufs battus en** ~ stiffly beaten egg whites

COMP **neige artificielle** artificial snow
neige carbonique dry ice
neiges éternelles eternal *ou* everlasting snow(s)
neige fondue (= *pluie*) sleet; (*par terre*) slush
neige fraîche fresh snow, newly fallen snow
neige poudreuse powder snow
neige de printemps spring snow; → **bonhomme, boule, train** *etc*

neiger /neʒe/ ► conjug 3 ◄ VB IMPERS to snow ◆ **il neige** it's snowing

neigeux, -euse /nɛʒø, øz/ ADJ [*sommet*] snow-covered, snow-clad; [*temps, aspect*] snowy

nem /nɛm/ NM (Vietnamese) small spring roll

nématode /nematɔd/ NM nematode (worm) ◆ **les ~s** nematodes, Nematoda (*SPÉC*)

Némésis /nemezis/ NF Nemesis

néné* /nene/ NM boob*, tit*

nénette* /nenɛt/ NF (= *jeune femme*) chick*, bird* (*Brit*); → **casser vpr 3**

nenni /neni/ ADV († † *ou régional* = *non*) nay

nénuphar /nenyfaʀ/ NM water lily

néo- /neo/ PRÉF neo- ◆ **~libéral/-gaulliste** neo-conservative/-Gaullist

néo-calédonien, -ienne /neokaledɔnjɛ̃, jɛn/ ADJ New Caledonian NM,F **Néo-Calédonien(ne)** New Caledonian

néo-canadien, -ienne /neokanadjɛ̃, jɛn/ ADJ New Canadian NM,F **Néo-Canadien(ne)** New Canadian

néocapitalisme /neokapitalism/ NM neocapitalism

néocapitaliste /neokapitalist/ ADJ neocapitalist

néoclassicisme /neoklasisism/ NM neoclassicism

néoclassique /neoklasik/ ADJ neoclassical

néocolonialisme /neokɔlɔnjalism/ NM neocolonialism

néocolonialiste /neokɔlɔnjalist/ ADJ neocolonialist

néocortex /neokɔʀtɛks/ NM neocortex, isocortex

néodarwinisme /neodaʀwinism/ NM neo-Darwinism

néo-écossais, e /neoekɔsɛ, ɛz/ ADJ, NM,F Nova Scotian

néofascisme, néo-fascisme (pl **néo-fascismes**) /neofaʃism/ NM neofascism

néofasciste, néo-fasciste (pl **néo-fascistes**) /neofaʃist/ ADJ, NMF neofascist

néogothique /neogɔtik/ ADJ, NM neogothic

néo-libéralisme /neolibeʀalism/ NM neoliberalism

néolithique /neɔlitik/ ADJ, NM neolithic

néologie /neɔlɔʒi/ NF neology

néologique /neɔlɔʒik/ ADJ neological

néologisme /neɔlɔʒism/ NM neologism

néon /neɔ̃/ NM (= *gaz*) neon; (= *éclairage*) neon lighting (*NonC*)

néonatal, e (mpl **néonatals**) /neonatal/ ADJ neonatal

néonatologie /neonatɔlɔʒi/, **néonatalogie** /neonatalɔʒi/ NF neonatology

néonazi, e /neonazi/ ADJ, NM,F neo-Nazi

néonazisme /neonazism/ NM neo-Nazism

néophyte /neɔfit/ ADJ neophytic NMF (*Rel*) neophyte; (*fig*) novice, neophyte (*frm*)

néoplasique /neɔplazik/ ADJ neoplastic

néoplasme /neɔplasm/ NM neoplasm

néoplatonicien, -ienne /neoplatɔnisjɛ̃, jɛn/ ADJ neoplatonic NM,F neoplatonist

néoplatonisme /neoplatɔnism/ NM Neo-Platonism

néopositivisme /neopozitivism/ NM logical positivism

néopositiviste /neopozitivist/ ADJ, NMF logical positivist

néoprène /neɔpʀɛn/ NM ◆ **colle au** ~ neoprene glue

néoréalisme /neoʀealism/ NM neorealism

néoréaliste /neoʀealist/ ADJ neorealist

néo-zélandais, e /neozelɑ̃dɛ, ɛz/ ADJ New Zealand (*épith*) NM,F **Néo-Zélandais(e)** New Zealander

Népal /nepal/ NM Nepal

népalais, e /nepalɛ, ɛz/ ADJ Nepalese, Nepali NM (= *langue*) Nepalese, Nepali NM,F **Népalais(e)** Nepalese, Nepali

népérien, -ienne /nepeʀjɛ̃, jɛn/ ADJ Nap(i)erian ◆ **logarithmes ~s** natural *ou* Nap(i)erian logarithms

néphrétique /nefʀetik/ ADJ, NMF nephritic; → **colique**

néphrite /nefʀit/ NF [1] (*Méd*) nephritis ◆ **avoir une** ~ to have nephritis [2] (= *jade*) nephrite

néphrologie /nefʀɔlɔʒi/ NF nephrology

néphrologue /nefʀɔlɔg/ NMF nephrologist, kidney specialist

népotisme /nepɔtism/ NM nepotism

Neptune /nɛptyn/ NM, NF (*Astron, Myth*) Neptune

neptunium /nɛptynjɔm/ NM neptunium

néréide /neʀeid/ NF (= *divinité, ver marin*) nereid

nerf /nɛʀ/ NM [1] (*Anat*) nerve

[2] (*locutions*) **avoir les ~s malades** to suffer from nerves ◆ **avoir les ~s fragiles** to be highly strung ◆ **avoir les ~s à vif** to be very edgy *ou* nervy (*Brit*), to be on edge ◆ **avoir les ~s en boule*** *ou* **en pelote*** to be very tensed up *ou* tense *ou* edgy ◆ **avoir les ~s à toute épreuve** *ou* **des ~s d'acier** to have nerves of steel ◆ **avoir ses ~s** to have an attack *ou* a fit of nerves, to have a temperamental outburst ◆ **être sur les ~s** to be all keyed up* ◆ **vivre sur les ~s** to live on one's nerves ◆ **porter** *ou* **taper*** **sur les ~s de qn** to get on sb's nerves ◆ **passer ses ~s sur qn** to take it out on sb ◆ **ça me met les ~s à vif** that gets on my nerves ◆ **ça va te calmer les ~s** that will calm *ou* settle your nerves ◆ **ses ~s ont été ébranlés** that shook him ◆ **ses ~s ont craqué*** *ou* **lâché*** he went to pieces *ou* cracked up*; → **bout, crise, fleur**

[3] (= *vigueur*) **allons du** ~ ! *ou* **un peu de** ~ ! come on, buck up! * *ou* show some spirit! ◆ **son style a du** ~ he has a vigorous style ◆ **c'est une voiture qui a du** ~ it's a responsive car ◆ **dépêche-toi, ça manque de** ~ **tout ça !** come on, get a move on, let's have some life about you! ◆ **l'argent est le** ~ **de la guerre** money is the sinews of war

[4] (* = *tendon*) nerve ◆ **~s** [*de viande*] gristle (*NonC*)

[5] (*Reliure*) cord

COMP **nerf de bœuf** † cosh (*Brit*), ≃ blackjack (*US*)
nerf gustatif gustatory nerve
nerf moteur motor nerve
nerf optique optic nerve
nerf pneumogastrique vagus
nerf sensitif sensory nerve
nerf vague vagus

Néron /neʀɔ̃/ NM Nero

nerprun /nɛʀpʀœ̃/ NM buckthorn

nerveusement /nɛʀvøzmɑ̃/ ADV (= *d'une manière excitée*) nervously, tensely; (= *de façon irritable*) irritably, touchily; (= *avec vigueur*) energetically, vigorously ◆ **ébranlé** ~ shaken, with shaken nerves

nerveux, -euse /nɛʀvø, øz/ ADJ [1] (*Méd*) [*tension, dépression, fatigue, système*] nervous; (*Anat*) [*cellule, centre, tissu*] nerve (*épith*) ◆ **pourquoi pleures-tu ? – c'est** ~ **!** why are you crying? – it's my nerves!; → **grossesse, système** [2] (= *agité*) [*personne, animal, rire*] nervous, tense; (= *irritable*) irritable; (*Écon*) [*marché*] nervous, jittery ◆ **ça me rend** ~ (= *anxieux*) it makes me nervous; (= *excité, tendu*) it puts me on edge [3] (= *vigoureux*) [*corps*] energetic, vigorous; [*cheval*] spirited, skittish; [*moteur, voiture*] responsive; [*style*] energetic, vigorous ◆ **il n'est pas très** ~ (*dans ce qu'il fait*) he doesn't go about things with much energy [4] (= *sec*) [*personne, main*] wiry; [*viande*] gristly NM,F ◆ **c'est un grand** ~ he's very highly strung (*Brit*) *ou* high-strung (*US*)

nervi /nɛʀvi/ NM (*gén pl*) bully boy, hatchet man

nervosité /nɛʀvozite/ NF [1] (= *agitation*) (*permanente*) nervousness, excitability; (*passagère*) nervousness, agitation, tension; (*Écon*) [*de marché*] nervousness, jumpiness, jitteriness ◆ **dans un état de grande** ~ in a highly nervous state, in a state of great agitation [2] (= *irritabilité*) (*permanente*) irritability; (*passagère*) irritability, touchiness [3] [*de moteur*] responsiveness ◆ **manque de** ~ sluggishness

nervure /nɛʀvyʀ/ NF [*de plante, animal*] nervure, vein; [*de voûte, pièce métallique*] rib; (*Typo*) raised band

nervuré, e /nɛʀvyʀe/ ADJ [*feuille*] veined, nervate (*SPÉC*); [*aile*] veined; [*couvercle, voûte*] ribbed

Nescafé ® /nɛskafe/ NM Nescafé ®, instant coffee

n'est-ce pas /nɛspɑ/ ADV [1] (*appelant l'acquiescement*) isn't it?, doesn't he? *etc* (*selon le verbe qui précède*) ◆ **il est fort,** ~ **?** he's strong, isn't he? ◆ **c'est bon,** ~ **?** it's nice, isn't it? *ou* don't you think? ◆ **il n'est pas trop tard,** ~ **?** it's not too late, is it? ◆ **tu iras,** ~ **?** you will go, won't you? [2] (*intensif*) ~ **que c'est bon/difficile ?** it's nice/difficult, isn't it? ◆ **eux,** ~**, ils peuvent se le permettre** of course they can afford it ◆ **le problème,** ~**, c'est qu'il s'en fiche** he doesn't care - that's the problem, isn't it?

Net /nɛt/ NM (abrév de **Internet**) ◆ **le** ~ the Net

net[1]**, nette** /nɛt/ ADJ [1] (= *propre : après nom*) [*surface, ongles, mains*] clean; [*intérieur, travail, copie*] neat, tidy ◆ **elle est toujours très nette (dans sa tenue)** she's always neatly dressed *ou* turned out, she's always very neat and tidy ◆ **avoir la conscience nette** to have a clear conscience

◆ **au net** ◆ **mettre au** ~ [*rapport, devoir*] to copy out, to make a neat *ou* fair copy of; [*plan, travail*] to tidy up ◆ **mise au** ~ copying out, tidying up

[2] (*Comm, Fin : après nom*) [*bénéfice, prix, poids*] net ◆ ~ **de** free of ◆ **emprunt** ~ **de tout impôt** tax-free loan ◆ **revenu** ~ disposable income

[3] (= *clair, précis : après nom*) [*idée, explication, esprit*] clear; (= *sans équivoque*) [*réponse*] straight, clear, plain; [*refus*] flat (*épith*); [*situation, position*] clear-cut ◆ **je serai** ~ **avec vous** I shall be (quite) candid *ou* frank with you ◆ **son attitude dans cette affaire n'est pas très nette** his attitude in this matter is a bit dubious ◆ **ce type n'est pas très** ~* (*bizarre*) that guy's slightly odd *ou* strange*; (*fou*) that guy's slightly mad*

[4] (= *marqué, évident*) [*différence, amélioration*] marked, distinct, sharp; [*distinction*] marked, sharp, clear(-cut); [*avantage*] clear ◆ **il y a une très nette odeur** *ou* **une odeur très nette de brûlé** there's a distinct *ou* a very definite smell

of burning ◆ **il est très ~ qu'il n'a aucune intention de venir** it's quite clear *ou* obvious that he doesn't intend to come

5 *(= distinct : après nom) [dessin, écriture]* clear; *[ligne, contour, image]* sharp; *[voix, son]* clear, distinct; *[cassure, coupure]* clean ◆ **j'ai un souvenir très ~ de sa visite** I remember his visit very clearly, I have a very clear *ou* vivid memory of his visit

ADV 1 *(= brusquement) [s'arrêter]* dead ◆ **se casser ~** to snap (in two), to break clean through ◆ **il a été tué ~** he was killed outright *ou* instantly

2 *(= franchement) [refuser]* flatly, point-blank ◆ **il (m')a dit tout ~ que ...** he made it quite clear (to me) that ..., he told me frankly *ou* bluntly that ... ◆ **parlons ~** let's be frank ◆ **je vous le dis tout ~** I'm telling you *ou* I'm giving it to you straight*, I'm telling you bluntly *ou* frankly ◆ **pour vous *ou* à parler ~** to be blunt *ou* frank with you

3 *(Comm)* net ◆ **il reste 40 € ~** there remains €40 net ◆ **cela pèse 2 kg ~** it weighs 2 kg net

NM *(Écon)* ◆ **le ~** net profit

net² /nɛt/ ADJ INV *(Tennis)* net *(épith)* NM net shot

nettement /nɛtmɑ̃/ ADV 1 *(= sans ambiguïté) [expliquer, répondre]* clearly ◆ **il refusa ~** he flatly refused, he refused point-blank ◆ **je lui ai dit ~ ce que j'en pensais** I told him bluntly *ou* frankly what I thought of it ◆ **il a ~ pris position contre nous** he has clearly *ou* quite obviously taken up a stance against us

2 *(= distinctement) [apercevoir, entendre, se souvenir]* clearly, distinctly; *[se détacher, apparaître]* clearly, distinctly, sharply

3 *(= incontestablement) [s'améliorer, se différencier]* markedly, distinctly; *[mériter]* definitely ◆ **j'aurais ~ préféré ne pas venir** I would have definitely *ou* distinctly preferred not to come ◆ **ça va ~ mieux** things are decidedly *ou* distinctly better ◆ **~ meilleur/plus grand** markedly *ou* distinctly better/bigger ◆ **coûter ~ moins cher** to cost much less *ou* a great deal less ◆ **ils sont ~ moins nombreux** there are far fewer of them ◆ **arriver ~ en avance** to arrive far too early

netteté /nɛtte/ NF 1 *(= propreté) [de tenue, travail]* neatness 2 *(= clarté) [d'explication, expression, esprit, idées]* clearness, clarity 3 *(= caractère distinct) [de dessin, écriture]* clearness; *[de contour, image]* sharpness, clarity, clearness; *[de souvenir, voix, son]* clearness, clarity; *[de cassure]* cleanness

nettoiement /netwamɑ̃/ NM *[de rues]* cleaning; *(Agr) [de terre]* clearing ◆ **service du ~** refuse disposal *ou* collection service

nettoyable /netwajabl/ ADJ ◆ **facilement/difficilement ~** easy/difficult to clean ◆ **~ à sec** dry-cleanable

nettoyage /netwajaʒ/ NM *(gén)* cleaning; *[de plage, rue, rivière]* cleaning (up); *[d'écurie, cage, réfrigérateur]* cleaning (out); *(Mil, Police)* cleaning up *ou* out ◆ **faire le ~ par le vide*** to throw everything out ◆ **~ de printemps** spring-cleaning ◆ **~ à sec** dry cleaning ◆ **un ~ complet** a thorough cleanup ◆ **~ de peau** skin cleansing ◆ **opération de ~** *(Mil)* mopping-up operation ◆ **entreprise/produit de ~** cleaning firm/agent ◆ **ils ont fait du ~ dans cette entreprise** *(fig)* they've got rid of the deadwood in this company; → **ethnique**

nettoyant, e /netwajɑ̃, ɑ̃t/ ADJ cleaning *(épith)* NM cleaner

nettoyer /netwaje/ ▸ conjug 8 ◂ VT 1 *(gén) [+ objet]* to clean; *[+ plaie]* to cleanse, to clean; *[+ jardin]* to clear; *[+ canal, rue, plage]* to clean (up); *[+ écurie, cage, réfrigérateur]* to clean (out) ◆ **~ au chiffon *ou* avec un chiffon** to dust ◆ **~ au balai** to sweep (out) ◆ **~ à l'eau/avec du savon** to wash in water/with soap ◆ **~ à la brosse** to brush (out) ◆ **~ à l'éponge** to sponge (down) ◆ **~ à sec** to dry-clean ◆ **nettoyez-vous les mains au robinet** wash your hands under the tap, give your hands a rinse under the tap ◆ **~ son assiette** to clean one's plate ◆ **le chien avait nettoyé le réfrigérateur*** the dog had cleaned out *ou* emptied the fridge ◆ **l'orage a nettoyé le ciel** the storm has cleared away the clouds

2 * *[+ personne] (= tuer)* to kill, to finish off*; *(= ruiner)* to clean out; *(= fatiguer)* to wear out ◆ **il a été nettoyé en une semaine par la grippe** the flu finished him off* *ou* did for him* in a week ◆ **~ son compte en banque** to clear one's bank account ◆ **se faire ~ au jeu** to be cleaned out at gambling

3 *(Mil, Police)* to clean out *ou* up

nettoyeur, -euse /netwajœʀ, øz/ NM,F cleaner

Neuchâtel /nøʃatɛl/ N Neuchâtel ◆ **le lac de ~** Neuchâtel Lake

neuf¹ /nœf/ ADJ INV, NM INV *(= chiffre)* nine; → **preuve**; *pour loc voir* **six**

neuf², neuve /nœf, nœv/ ADJ *(gén)* new; *[vision, esprit, pensée]* fresh, new; *[pays]* young, new ◆ **quelque chose de ~** something new ◆ **regarder qch avec un œil ~** to look at sth with new eyes *ou* a fresh eye ◆ **être ~ dans le métier/en affaires** to be new to the trade/to business ◆ **à l'état ~, comme ~** as good as new, as new ◆ **c'est tout ~** *[objet]* it's brand new ◆ **son bonheur tout ~** *(littér)* his new-found happiness; → **flambant, peau**

NM new ◆ **il y a du ~** something new has turned up, there's been a new development ◆ **quoi de/rien de ~ ?** what's/nothing new? ◆ **faire du ~** *(politique)* to introduce new *ou* fresh ideas; *(artisanat)* to make new things ◆ **être vêtu *ou* habillé de ~** to be wearing new clothes, to have new clothes on ◆ **son appartement est meublé de ~** all the furniture in his flat is new ◆ **remettre *ou* refaire à ~** to do up like new *ou* as good as new ◆ **remise à ~** restoration ◆ **repeindre un appartement à ~** to redecorate a flat ◆ **on ne peut pas faire du ~ avec du vieux** you can't make new things out of old

neuneu * /nønø/ NM *(= idiot)* dummy*

neurasthénie /nøʀasteni/ NF *(gén)* depression; *(Méd)* neurasthenia *(SPÉC)* ◆ **faire de la ~** to be depressed, to be suffering from depression

neurasthénique /nøʀastenik/ ADJ depressed, depressive; *(Méd)* neurasthenic *(SPÉC)* NMF depressed person, depressive; *(Méd)* neurasthenic *(SPÉC)*

neuro... /nøʀɔ/ PRÉF neuro...

neurobiologie /nøʀobjɔlɔʒi/ NF neurobiology

neurobiologiste /nøʀobjɔlɔʒist/ NMF neurobiologist

neurochimie /nøʀoʃimi/ NF neurochemistry

neurochirurgical, e (mpl **-aux**) /nøʀoʃiʀyʀʒikal, o/ ADJ neurosurgical

neurochirurgie /nøʀoʃiʀyʀʒi/ NF neurosurgery

neurochirurgien, -ienne /nøʀoʃiʀyʀʒjɛ̃, jɛn/ NM,F neurosurgeon

neurodégénératif, -ive /nøʀodeʒeneʀatif, iv/ ADJ *[maladie, affection]* neurodegenerative

neuroendocrinien, -ienne /nøʀoɑ̃dɔkʀinjɛ̃, jɛn/ ADJ neuroendocrine

neuroleptique /nøʀɔlɛptik/ ADJ, NM neuroleptic

neurologie /nøʀɔlɔʒi/ NF neurology

neurologique /nøʀɔlɔʒik/ ADJ neurological

neurologiste /nøʀɔlɔʒist/, **neurologue** /nøʀɔlɔg/ NMF neurologist

neuromédiateur /nøʀomedjatœʀ/ NM neurotransmitter

neuromusculaire /nøʀomyskylɛʀ/ ADJ neuromuscular

neuronal, e (mpl **-aux**) /nøʀɔnal, o/ ADJ *(Méd)* neuronal; *(Ordin)* neural ◆ **réseau ~** neural network ◆ **ordinateur ~** neurocomputer, neural computer

neurone /nøʀɔn/ NM neuron

neuropathie /nøʀopati/ NF neuropathy

neuropathologie /nøʀopatɔlɔʒi/ NF neuropathology

neurophysiologie /nøʀofizjɔlɔʒi/ NF neurophysiology

neurophysiologique /nøʀofizjɔlɔʒik/ ADJ neurophysiological

neurophysiologiste /nøʀofizjɔlɔʒist/ NMF neurophysiologist

neuropsychiatre /nøʀopsikjatʀ/ NMF neuropsychiatrist

neuropsychiatrie /nøʀopsikjatʀi/ NF neuropsychiatry

neuropsychiatrique /nøʀopsikjatʀik/ ADJ neuropsychiatric

neuropsychologie /nøʀopsikɔlɔʒi/ NF neuropsychology

neuropsychologue /nøʀopsikɔlɔg/ NMF neuropsychologist

neurosciences /nøʀosjɑ̃s/ NFPL neuroscience

neurotoxine /nøʀotɔksin/ NF neurotoxin

neurotransmetteur /nøʀotʀɑ̃smetœʀ/ NM neurotransmitter

neurovégétatif, -ive, neuro-végétatif, -ive (mpl **neuro-végétatifs**) /nøʀoveʒetatif, iv/ ADJ neurovegetative

neutralisation /nøtʀalizasjɔ̃/ NF neutralization

neutraliser /nøtʀalize/ ▸ conjug 1 ◂ VT *(Mil, Pol, Sci)* to neutralize; *[+ gardien, agresseur]* to overpower ◆ **la voie de gauche est neutralisée** *(sur autoroute)* the left-hand lane is closed to traffic ◆ **les poubelles sont neutralisées** the bins have been sealed VPR **se neutraliser** ◆ **les deux influences/produits se neutralisent** the two influences/products cancel each other out

neutralisme /nøtʀalism/ NM neutralism

neutraliste /nøtʀalist/ ADJ, NMF neutralist

neutralité /nøtʀalite/ NF neutrality ◆ **rester dans la ~** to remain neutral ◆ **~ bienveillante** benevolent neutrality

neutre /nøtʀ/ ADJ 1 *(gén)* neutral ◆ **rester ~** *(dans un conflit)* to remain neutral, not to take sides *(dans* in) 2 *[genre grammatical, animal]* neuter NM *(= genre grammatical)* neuter; *(= nom)* neuter noun; *(Élec)* neutral; *(= animal)* neuter (animal) ◆ **les ~s** *(= pays)* the neutral nations

neutrino /nøtʀino/ NM neutrino

neutron /nøtʀɔ̃/ NM neutron; → **bombe**

neutronique /nøtʀɔnik/ ADJ neutron *(épith)*

neuvaine /nœvɛn/ NF novena ◆ **faire une ~** to make a novena

neuvième /nœvjɛm/ ADJ, NMF ninth; *pour loc voir* **sixième**

neuvièmement /nœvjɛmmɑ̃/ ADV ninthly, in the ninth place; *pour loc voir* **sixièmement**

Nevada /nevada/ NM Nevada

ne varietur /nevaʀjetyʀ/ LOC ADJ *[édition]* definitive LOC ADV without any variation

névé /neve/ NM névé, firn

neveu (pl **neveux**) /n(ə)vø/ NM nephew; (††, *littér = descendant*) descendant ◆ **un peu, mon ~ !*** you bet!*, of course!, and how!*

névralgie /nevʀalʒi/ NF neuralgia *(NonC)* ◆ ~ **dentaire** dental neuralgia ◆ **avoir des ~s** to suffer from neuralgia

névralgique /nevʀalʒik/ ADJ neuralgic ◆ **centre** *ou* **point** ~ *(Méd)* nerve centre; *(fig)* *(= point sensible)* sensitive spot; *(= point capital)* nerve centre ◆ **question** ~ sensitive issue

névrite /nevʀit/ NF neuritis *(NonC)*

névritique /nevʀitik/ ADJ neuritic

névropathe /nevʀɔpat/ ADJ neuropathic, neurotic NMF neuropath, neurotic

névropathie /nevʀɔpati/ NF neuropathy

névrose /nevʀoz/ NF neurosis ◆ ~ **obsessionnelle** obsessional neurosis ◆ ~ **phobique** phobia

névrosé, e /nevʀoze/ ADJ, NM,F neurotic

névrotique /nevʀɔtik/ ADJ neurotic

New Delhi /njudɛli/ N New Delhi

New Hampshire /njuɑ̃pʃœʀ/ NM New Hampshire

New Jersey /njuʒɛʀze/ NM New Jersey

new-look * /njuluk/ ADJ, NM INV new look

Newton /njutɔn/ NM *(= savant)* Newton ◆ **newton** *(= unité)* newton

newtonien, -ienne /njutɔnjɛ̃, jɛn/ ADJ Newtonian

New York /njujɔʀk/ N *(= ville)* New York NM ◆ **l'État de** ~ New York State

new-yorkais, e /njujɔʀkɛ, ɛz/ ADJ New-York *(épith)*, of *ou* from New York NM,F **New-Yorkais(e)** New Yorker

nez /ne/ NM [1] *(= organe)* nose ◆ **avoir le ~ grec/aquilin** to have a Grecian/an aquiline nose ◆ ~ **épaté** *ou* **écrasé** *ou* **aplati** flat nose ◆ ~ **en trompette** turned-up nose ◆ ~ **en pied de marmite** bulbous turned-up nose ◆ **ton ~ remue, tu mens** I can tell by looking at you that you're lying ◆ **parler du** ~ to talk through one's nose ◆ **cela se voit comme le ~ au milieu de la figure** *ou* **du visage** it's as plain as the nose on your face, it sticks out a mile ◆ **cela sent le brûlé à plein** ~ there's a strong smell of burning ◆ **le bureau sentait la fumée à plein** ~ the office reeked of cigarette smoke

[2] *(= visage, face)* **le ~ en l'air** *ou* **au vent** with one's nose in the air ◆ **où est mon sac ? – tu as le ~ dessus !** *ou* **sous ton ~ !** where's my bag? – (right) under your nose! ◆ **baisser/lever le** ~ to bow/raise one's head ◆ **le ~ dans son assiette** with his head bent over his plate ◆ **il ne lève jamais le ~ de ses livres** he's always got his nose in a book, he's a real bookworm * ◆ **il ne lève jamais le ~ de son travail** he never looks up from his work ◆ **mettre le** ~ *ou* **son ~ à la fenêtre/au bureau** to show one's face at the window/at the office ◆ **je n'ai pas mis le ~ dehors hier** I didn't put my nose outside the door yesterday ◆ **il fait un temps à ne pas mettre le ~ dehors** it's weather you wouldn't put a dog out in ◆ **rire/fermer la porte au ~ de qn** to laugh/shut the door in sb's face ◆ **elle m'a raccroché au** ~ *(au téléphone, couper la communication)* she hung up on me; *(avec colère)* she slammed the phone down on me ◆ **faire qch au ~ et à la barbe de qn** to do sth under sb's very nose ◆ **regarder qn sous le** ~ to stare sb in the face ◆ **sous son** ~ (right) under his nose, under his (very) nose ◆ **se trouver ~ à ~ avec qn** to find o.s. face to face with sb ◆ **faire un (drôle de)** ~ to pull a (funny) face

[3] *(= flair)* **il a du** ~ he has good instincts ◆ **en affaires, il a du** ~ *ou* **le ~ fin** he has a flair for business ◆ **j'ai eu le ~ creux de m'en aller** * I had a hunch that I should leave; → **vue**[2]

[4] *[d'avion, bateau]* nose ◆ **sur le** ~ *[bateau]* down at the bows; → **piquer**

[5] *(= créateur de parfums, Œnol)* nose

[6] *(locutions)* **avoir qn dans le** ~ * to have it in for sb *, to have something against sb ◆ **il m'a dans le** ~ * he's got it in for me *, he's got something against me ◆ **avoir un verre** *ou* **un coup dans le** ~ * to have had a drop too much * ◆ **se manger** *ou* **se bouffer le** ~ * to be at each others' throats ◆ **mettre** *ou* **fourrer** * **le** *ou* **son ~ dans qch** to poke *ou* stick * one's nose into sth, to nose *ou* pry into sth ◆ **l'affaire lui est passée sous le** ~ * the bargain slipped through his fingers ◆ **je vais lui mettre le ~ dans sa crotte**‡ *ou* **son caca**‡ *ou* **sa merde**** I'll rub his (*ou* her) nose in it * ◆ **montrer (le bout de)** *ou* **pointer son** ~ *(= se manifester)* to make an appearance, to show up ◆ **il a montré** *ou* **pointé le bout de son ~ à la porte et il a disparu** he popped his head round the door *ou* he just showed his face then disappeared ◆ **aujourd'hui, le soleil montre le bout de son** ~ today the sun has peeped through; → **casser, doigt, mener**

NF /ɛnɛf/ [1] (abrév de **norme française**) **avoir le label** ~ to have the mark of the approved French standard of manufacture, ≃ to have the Kite mark *(Brit)* [2] (abrév de **nouveau(x) franc(s)**) → **franc**[2]

ni /ni/ CONJ *(après la négation)* nor, or ◆ **il ne boit ~ ne fume** he doesn't drink or smoke, he neither drinks nor smokes ◆ **il ne pouvait (~) parler ~ entendre** he could neither speak nor hear, he couldn't speak or hear ◆ **personne ne l'a (jamais) aidé ~ (même) encouragé** nobody (ever) helped or (even) encouraged him ◆ **je ne veux ~ ne peux accepter** I neither wish to nor can accept, I don't wish to accept, nor can I ◆ **il ne veut pas, ~ moi non plus** he doesn't want to and neither do I *ou* and nor do I

◆ **ni ... ni ...** neither ... nor ... ◆ ~ **lui ~ moi** neither he nor I, neither of us, neither him nor me * ◆ ~ **l'un ~ l'autre** neither one nor the other, neither of them ◆ ~ **d'un côté ~ de l'autre** on neither one side nor the other, on neither side ◆ **il n'a dit ~ oui ~ non** he didn't say either yes or no ◆ ~ **vu ~ connu (je t'embrouille)** * no one'll be any the wiser * ◆ **il n'est ~ plus bête ~ plus paresseux qu'un autre** he is neither more stupid nor any lazier than anyone else, he's no more stupid and no lazier than anyone else

◆ **ni plus ni moins** ◆ **elle est secrétaire, ~ plus ~ moins** she's just a secretary, no more no less

niable /njabl/ ADJ deniable ◆ **cela n'est pas** ~ that's undeniable, you can't deny that

Niagara /njagaʀa/ NM ◆ **le** ~ the Niagara (river); → **chute**

niais, niaise /njɛ, njɛz/ ADJ *[personne, air]* silly; *[rire, sourire, style, livre, film]* silly, inane NM,F simpleton ◆ **pauvre ~ !** poor fool!

niaisement /njɛzmɑ̃/ ADV *[rire]* inanely

niaiserie /njɛzʀi/ NF [1] *(= bêtise)* silliness [2] *(= action)* foolish *ou* inane behaviour *(NonC)*; *(= parole)* foolish *ou* inane talk *(NonC)* ◆ **dire des ~s** to talk rubbish *ou* twaddle *(Brit)* *ou* nonsense ◆ **ils regardent des ~s à la télé** they're watching some rubbish on TV

niaiseux, -euse /njɛzø, øz/ *(Can)* ADJ stupid, idiotic NM,F idiot

Niamey /njamɛ/ N Niamey

niaque * /njak/ NF determination (to succeed) ◆ **elle a la** ~ she's really determined (to succeed)

Nicaragua /nikaʀagwa/ NM Nicaragua

nicaraguayen, -enne /nikaʀagwajɛ̃, jɛn/ ADJ Nicaraguan NM,F **Nicaraguayen(ne)** Nicaraguan

niche /niʃ/ NF [1] *(= alcôve)* niche, recess [2] *[de chien]* kennel ◆ **à la ~ !** *(à un chien)* (into your) kennel!; *(hum : à une personne)* scram!‡, make yourself scarce! * [3] († *= farce*) trick, hoax ◆ **faire des ~s à qn** to play tricks on sb [4] *(Comm, Écol)* niche

nichée /niʃe/ NF *[d'oiseaux]* brood ◆ ~ **de chiens** litter of puppies ◆ ~ **de pinsons** nest *ou* brood of chaffinches ◆ **l'instituteur et toute sa ~ (d'enfants)** * the teacher and all his charges

nicher /niʃe/ ► conjug 1 ◄ VI *[oiseau]* to nest; * *[personne]* to hang out * VPR **se nicher** *[oiseau]* to nest; *(littér = se blottir)* *[village, maison]* to nestle *(dans* in); (* *= se cacher)* *[personne]* to stick * *ou* put o.s.; *[objet]* to lodge itself ◆ **où la vertu va-t-elle se ~ !** *(hum)* of all the unlikely places to find such virtue! ◆ **les cerises nichées dans les feuilles** the cherries nestling among the leaves

nichon‡ /niʃɔ̃/ NM tit**, boob‡

nickel /nikɛl/ NM nickel ADJ * *(= propre)* spotless; *(= irréprochable)* perfect ◆ **chez eux, c'est** ~ their home is always spick and span

nickelage /niklaʒ/ NM nickel-plating

nickelé, e /nikle/ ADJ nickelled, nickel-plated ◆ **acier** ~ nickel-plated steel

nickeler /nikle/ ► conjug 4 ◄ VT to nickel-plate

niçois, e /niswa, waz/ ADJ of *ou* from Nice; → **salade** NM,F **Niçois(e)** inhabitant *ou* native of Nice ◆ **à la ~e** *(Culin)* with tomatoes and garlic *(attrib)*

Nicolas /nikɔla/ NM Nicholas

Nicosie /nikɔzi/ N Nicosia

nicotine /nikɔtin/ NF nicotine

nid /ni/ NM [1] *[d'animal, oiseau]* nest ◆ ~ **d'oiseau/de guêpes** bird's/wasps' nest [2] *(= abri, foyer)* cosy little nest; *(= repaire)* den ◆ **trouver le ~ vide** to find the bird has *ou* the birds have flown, to find the nest empty ◆ **surprendre qn au ~, trouver l'oiseau au** ~ to find *ou* catch sb at home *ou* in

COMP **nid(s) d'abeilles** *(= point)* honeycomb stitch; *(= tissu)* waffle cloth ◆ **radiateur en ~(s) d'abeilles** cellular radiator

nid d'aigle *(lit, fig)* eyrie

nid d'amoureux love nest

nid d'ange ≃ (baby) nest

nid de brigands robbers' den

nids d'hirondelles *(Culin)* birds' nest ◆ **potage aux ~s d'hirondelles** birds' nest soup

nid de mitrailleuses nest of machine guns

nid de pie *(Naut)* crow's-nest

nid de poule pothole

nid à poussière dust trap

nid de résistance *(Mil)* pocket of resistance

nid de vipères *(lit, fig)* nest of vipers

nidation /nidasjɔ̃/ NF nidation, implantation

nidification /nidifikasjɔ̃/ NF nesting

nidifier /nidifje/ ► conjug 7 ◄ VI to nest

nièce /njɛs/ NF niece

nielle /njɛl/ NF *(Agr)* *(= plante)* corncockle ◆ ~ **(du blé)** *(= maladie)* blight NM *(= incrustation)* niello

nieller /njele/ ► conjug 1 ◄ VT *(Agr)* to blight; *(Tech)* to niello

niellure /njelyʀ/ NF *(Agr)* blight; *(Tech)* niello

n-ième, nième /ɛnjɛm/ ADJ *(Math)* nth; (* *fig)* nth, umpteenth ◆ **x à la ~ puissance** x to the power (of) n, x to the nth power ◆ **je te le dis pour la ~ fois** I'm telling you for the nth *ou* umpteenth time

nier /nje/ ► conjug 7 ◄ VT *(gén)* to deny; *(Jur = désavouer)* *[+ dette, fait]* to repudiate ◆ **il nie l'avoir fait** he denies having done it ◆ ~ **l'évidence** to deny the obvious ◆ **je ne (le) nie pas** I'm not denying it, I don't deny it ◆ **on ne peut ~ que** one cannot deny that ◆ **l'accusé nia** the accused denied the charges

niet‡ /njɛt/ EXCL no way!, nothing doing! *

nietzschéen, -enne /nitʃeɛ̃, ɛn/ ADJ, NM,F Nietzschean

nigaud, e /nigo, od/ ADJ silly, simple NM,F simpleton ◆ **grand** *ou* **gros ~ !** big silly!, big ninny! *, silly billy! * *(Brit)*

nigauderie /nigodʀi/ NF *(= caractère)* silliness, simpleness; *(= action)* silly thing to do

Niger /niʒɛʀ/ NM ◆ **le ~** (the) Niger

Nigéria, Nigeria /niʒeʀja/ NM Nigeria

nigérian, e /niʒeʀjɑ̃, an/ ADJ Nigerian NM,F **Nigérian(e)** Nigerian

nigérien, -ienne /niʒeʀjɛ̃, jɛn/ ADJ of *ou* from Niger NM,F **Nigérien(ne)** inhabitant *ou* native of Niger

night-club (pl **night-clubs**) /najtklœb/ NM nightclub

nihilisme /niilism/ NM nihilism

nihiliste /niilist(ə)/ ADJ nihilistic NMF nihilist

Nikkei /nikej/ NM *(Bourse)* ◆ **l'indice ~, le ~** the Nikkei (index)

Nil /nil/ NM ◆ **le ~** the Nile ◆ **le ~ Blanc/Bleu** the White/Blue Nile

nilotique /nilɔtik/ ADJ of *ou* from the Nile, Nile *(épith)*

nimbe /nɛ̃b/ NM *(Rel, fig)* nimbus, halo

nimber /nɛ̃be/ ▸ conjug 1 ◂ VT *(= auréoler)* to halo ◆ **nimbé de lumière** radiant *ou* suffused with light

nimbostratus /nɛ̃bostʀatys/ NM nimbostratus

nimbus /nɛ̃bys/ NM *(= nuage)* nimbus

n'importe /nɛ̃pɔʀt(ə)/ → **importer²**

ninas /ninas/ NM small cigar

niobium /njɔbjɔm/ NM niobium

niôle * /njol/ NF ⇒ **gnôle**

nippe * /nip/ NF (old) thing * *ou* rag * ◆ **~s** togs *, gear * ◆ **de vieilles ~s** old togs *, old clothes

nipper * /nipe/ ▸ conjug 1 ◂ VT *(= habiller)* to deck out, to tog out * *(Brit)* ◆ **bien/mal nippé** in a nice/an awful getup * *ou* rig-out * *(Brit)* VPR **se nipper** to get decked out, to get togged up * *(Brit)*

nippon, e *ou* **-onne** /nipɔ̃, ɔn/ ADJ Japanese NM,F **Nippon(e), Nippon(ne)** Japanese NM *(= pays)* ◆ **Nippon** Japan

nique /nik/ NF ◆ **faire la ~ à qn** to thumb one's nose at sb, to cock a snook at sb *(Brit)*

niquedouille * /nik(ə)duj/ ADJ, NM,F ⇒ **nigaud**

niquer *** /nike/ ▸ conjug 1 ◂ VT *(sexuellement)* to fuck ***, to screw ***; *(= abîmer) [+ machine, ordinateur]* to fuck up ***, to bugger up ** *(Brit)*, to knacker ** *(Brit)* ◆ **se faire ~** *(fig)* to get screwed ***

nirvana /niʀvana/ NM nirvana

nitouche /nituʃ/ NF → **saint**

nitrate /nitʀat/ NM nitrate ◆ **~ d'argent** silver nitrate

nitreux, -euse /nitʀø, øz/ ADJ nitrous

nitrifier /nitʀifje/ ▸ conjug 1 ◂ VT to nitrify

nitrique /nitʀik/ ADJ nitric

nitrite /nitʀit/ NM nitrite

nitro... /nitʀo/ PRÉF nitro... ◆ **nitrosamine** nitrosamine

nitrobenzène /nitʀobɛ̃zɛn/ NM nitrobenzene

nitroglycérine /nitʀogliseʀin/ NF nitroglycerine

nival, e (mpl **-aux**) /nival, o/ ADJ nival

niveau (pl **niveaux**) /nivo/ GRAMMAIRE ACTIVE 32.3

NM 1 *[d'huile, eau]* level; *[de bâtiment]* level, floor ◆ **le ~ de l'eau** the water level ◆ **cent mètres au-dessus du ~ de la mer** a hundred metres above sea level → **courbe, passage**

◆ **au niveau de** ◆ **au ~ de l'eau/du sol** at water/ground level ◆ **l'eau est arrivée au ~ du quai** the water has risen to the level of the embankment ◆ **la neige m'arrivait au ~ des genoux** the snow came up to my knees *ou* was knee-deep ◆ **une tache au ~ du coude** a mark at the elbow ◆ **serré au ~ de la taille** tight at the waist ◆ **il avait une cicatrice sur la joue au ~ de la bouche** he had a scar on his cheek about level with his mouth ◆ **il s'arrêta au ~ du village** he stopped once he got to the village

◆ **de niveau (avec), au même niveau (que)** level (with) ◆ **le plancher n'est pas de ~** the floor isn't level ◆ **les deux pièces ne sont pas de ~** the two rooms are not on a level ◆ **mettre qch de** *ou* **à ~** to make sth level ◆ **les deux vases sont au même ~** the two vases are level *ou* at the same height

2 *(Scol) [de connaissances, études]* standard ◆ **le ~ des études en France** the standard of French education ◆ **le ~ d'instruction baisse** educational standards are falling ◆ **cet élève est d'un bon ~** this pupil keeps up a good level of attainment *ou* a good standard ◆ **son anglais est d'un bon ~** his English is of a good standard ◆ **il est/il n'est pas au ~** he is/he isn't up to standard ◆ **ils ne sont pas du même ~** they're not (of) the same standard, they're not on a par *ou* on the same level ◆ **les cours ne sont pas à son ~** the classes aren't up to his standard ◆ **remettre à ~** to bring up to standard ◆ **cours** *ou* **stage de remise à ~** refresher course

3 *(= degré)* level ◆ **le ~ intellectuel de la classe moyenne** the intellectual level of the middle class ◆ **le franc a atteint son ~ le plus haut/bas depuis 3 ans** the franc has reached its highest/lowest point for 3 years ◆ **la production littéraire a atteint son ~ le plus bas** literary production has reached its lowest ebb *ou* level ◆ **à tous les ~x** at all levels ◆ **le directeur envisage une remise à ~ des salaires** the director is considering bringing salaries into line with standard rates *ou* upgrading salaries to standard rates ◆ **cela exige un haut ~ de concentration** it demands a high level *ou* degree of concentration ◆ **athlète/cadre de haut ~** top athlete/executive ◆ **des candidats (ayant le) ~ licence** candidates at degree level

◆ **au + niveau** ◆ **au ~ de l'usine/des gouvernements** at factory/government level ◆ **au ~ européen** at the European level ◆ **négociations au plus haut ~** top-level negotiations ◆ **il faut se mettre au ~ des enfants** you have to put yourself on the same level as the children

4 *(Constr = instrument)* level; *(= jauge dans voiture)* gauge

COMP **niveau de base** *(Géog)* base level
niveau à bulle (d'air) spirit level
niveau d'eau water level
niveau d'énergie energy level
niveau hydrostatique water table
niveau de langue register
niveau à lunette dumpy level
niveau de maçon plumb level
niveau social social standing *ou* rank
niveau de vie standard of living, living standards

nivelage /niv(ə)laʒ/ NM *[de surface]* levelling; *[de fortunes, conditions sociales]* levelling out, evening out

niveler /niv(ə)le/ ▸ conjug 4 ◂ VT 1 *(= égaliser) [+ surface]* to level; *[+ fortunes, conditions sociales]* to level *ou* even out ◆ **l'érosion nivelle les montagnes** erosion wears down *ou* wears away the mountains ◆ **sommets nivelés** mountain tops worn down *ou* worn away by erosion ◆ **~ par le bas/le haut** to level down/up 2 *(= mesurer avec un niveau)* to measure with a spirit level, to level

niveleur, -euse /niv(ə)lœʀ, øz/ ADJ *[doctrine, morale]* egalitarian NM *(Hist)* Leveller NF **niveleuse** *(Constr)* grader

nivellement /nivɛlmɑ̃/ NM 1 *[de surface]* levelling; *[de fortunes, conditions sociales]* levelling out, evening out ◆ **~ par le bas/par le haut** levelling down/up 2 *(= mesure)* surveying

nivoglaciaire /nivoglasjɛʀ/ ADJ snow and ice *(épith)*

nivopluvial, e (mpl **-iaux**) /nivoplyvjal, jo/ ADJ snow and rain *(épith)*

nivôse /nivoz/ NM Nivôse *(fourth month of French Republican calendar)*

NN (abrév de **nouvelles normes**) *revised standard of hotel classification*

nô /no/ NM No(h) ◆ **le théâtre ~** the No(h) theatre

Nobel /nɔbɛl/ NM ◆ **le (prix) ~** the Nobel prize

nobélisable /nɔbelizabl/ ADJ potential Nobel prize-winning *(épith)* NMF potential Nobel prize-winner

nobélisé, e /nɔbelize/ ADJ *[personne]* Nobel prize-winning

nobélium /nɔbeljɔm/ NM nobelium

nobiliaire /nɔbiljɛʀ/ ADJ nobiliary NM *(= livre)* peerage list

noble /nɔbl/ ADJ 1 *(= de haute naissance)* noble 2 *(= généreux, digne) [ton, attitude]* noble, dignified; *[cause]* noble, worthy ◆ **âme/cœur ~** noble spirit/heart ◆ **le ~ art (de la boxe)** the noble art (of boxing) 3 *(= supérieur) [matière, métal, vin]* noble NM 1 *(= personne)* nobleman ◆ **les ~s** the nobility 2 *(= monnaie)* noble NF noblewoman

noblement /nɔbləmɑ̃/ ADV *(= généreusement)* nobly; *(= dignement)* with dignity

noblesse /nɔblɛs/ NF 1 *(= générosité, dignité)* nobleness, nobility ◆ **~ d'esprit/de cœur** nobleness *ou* nobility of spirit/heart 2 *(= caste)* **la (haute) ~** the nobility ◆ **la ~ d'épée** the old nobility *ou* aristocracy ◆ **la ~ de robe** the noblesse de robe ◆ **la ~ de cour** the courtiers, the nobility at court ◆ **la petite ~** the minor nobility, the gentry *(Brit)* ◆ **~ terrienne** landed gentry ◆ **~ oblige** noblesse oblige

nobliau (pl **nobliaux**) /nɔblijo/ NM *(péj)* one of the lesser nobility, petty noble

noce /nɔs/ NF 1 *(= cérémonie)* wedding; *(= cortège, participants)* wedding party ◆ **~s** *(frm)* wedding, nuptials *(frm)* ◆ **être de la ~** to be a member of the wedding party, to be among the wedding guests ◆ **être de ~** to be invited to a wedding ◆ **aller à la ~ de qn** to go to sb's wedding ◆ **repas/robe/nuit de ~(s)** wedding banquet/dress/night ◆ **~s d'argent/d'or/de diamant** silver/golden/diamond wedding ◆ **les ~s de Cana** *(Bible)* the wedding *ou* marriage feast at Cana ◆ **il l'avait épousée en premières/secondes ~s** she was his first/second wife; → **convoler, voyage** 2 *(locutions)* **faire la ~** * to live it up *, to have a wild time ◆ **je n'étais pas à la ~** * I wasn't exactly enjoying myself, I was having a pretty uncomfortable time

noceur, -euse * /nɔsœʀ, øz/ NM,F fast liver, reveller ◆ **il est assez ~** he likes to live it up *

nocif, -ive /nɔsif, iv/ ADJ harmful ◆ **~ pour la couche d'ozone** harmful to the ozone layer

nocivité /nɔsivite/ NF harmfulness

noctambule /nɔktɑ̃byl/ ADJ, NMF ◆ **il est ~, c'est un ~** *(= noceur)* he's a night reveller; *(= qui veille la nuit)* he's a night bird *ou* night owl; *(†† = somnambule)* he's a noctambulist †

noctambulisme /nɔktɑ̃bylism/ NM (= *débauche*) night-time revelling, night revels; (= *habitudes nocturnes*) nocturnal habits; († † = *somnambulisme*) noctambulism †

nocturne /nɔktyʀn/ ADJ [*animal*] nocturnal; [*visite, sortie*] night (*épith*) ◆ **la vie ~ à Paris** Parisian nightlife ◆ **équipement de vision ~** night-vision equipment; → **tapage** NM [1] (= *oiseau*) night hunter [2] (*Rel*) nocturn [3] (*Mus*) nocturne; (*Peinture*) nocturne, night scene NF evening fixture; [*de magasin*] late night opening ◆ **réunion en ~** evening meeting ◆ **la rencontre sera jouée en ~** (*Sport*) the game will be played under floodlights ◆ **le magasin est ouvert en ~ le vendredi** the shop is open *ou* opens late on Fridays

nodal, e (mpl **-aux**) /nɔdal, o/ ADJ (*Phys, Ling*) nodal

nodosité /nɔdozite/ NF (= *corps dur*) node, nodule; (= *état*) knottiness, nodosity (*SPÉC*)

nodule /nɔdyl/ NM nodule ◆ **~ polymétallique** polymetallic nodule

Noé /nɔe/ NM Noah

Noël /nɔɛl/ GRAMMAIRE ACTIVE 50.2 NM [1] (= *fête*) Christmas; (= *chant*) (Christmas) carol ◆ **à la ~** at Christmas (time) ◆ **que faites-vous pour (la) ~ ?** what are you doing for *ou* at Christmas? ◆ **joyeux ~ !** merry *ou* happy Christmas! ◆ **~ au balcon, Pâques au tison** a warm Christmas means a cold Easter; → **bûche, sapin, veille** [2] (= *cadeau*) **noël** Christmas present ◆ **que veux-tu pour ton (petit) noël ?** what would you like for Christmas?

nœud /nø/ NM [1] (*gén : pour attacher*) knot; (*ornemental : de ruban*) bow ◆ **faire/défaire un ~** to make *ou* tie/untie *ou* undo a knot *ou* bow ◆ **la fillette avait des ~s dans les cheveux** (*rubans*) the little girl had bows *ou* ribbons in her hair; (*cheveux emmêlés*) the little girl's hair was all tangled ◆ **fais un ~ à ton mouchoir !** tie *ou* make a knot in your hanky! ◆ **avoir un ~ dans la gorge** to have a lump in one's throat ◆ **il y a un ~ !*** there's a hitch! *ou* snag! ◆ **les ~s d'un serpent** the coils of a snake ◆ **~ de perles/de diamants** pearl/diamond knot; → **corde**

[2] (= *vitesse sur l'eau*) knot; → **filer**

[3] (= *protubérance*) [*de planche, canne*] knot; [*de branche, tige*] knot, node

[4] (*fig*) **le ~ de** [*de problème, débat*] the crux *ou* nub of ◆ **le ~ de l'intrigue** (*Littérat, Théât*) the crux of the plot

[5] (*littér* = *lien*) bond ◆ **le (saint) ~ du mariage** the bonds of (holy) wedlock ◆ **les ~s de l'amitié** the bonds *ou* ties of friendship

[6] (*Astron, Élec, Géog, Ling, Phys, Tech*) node

[7] (*‡* = *pénis*) cock*‡, dick*‡, prick*‡

[8] (*‡* = *crétin*) ninny‡ ◆ **il est nœud-nœud** he's a real ninny*

COMP **nœud autoroutier** interchange
nœud de chaise bowline
nœud coulant slipknot, running knot
nœud de cravate tie knot ◆ **faire son nœud de cravate** to knot one's tie
nœud ferroviaire (= *endroit*) rail junction
nœud gordien Gordian knot ◆ **couper** *ou* **trancher le nœud gordien** to cut the Gordian knot
nœud pap*, nœud papillon bow tie
nœud plat reef knot
nœud routier (= *endroit*) crossroad(s)
nœud de vache granny knot
nœud de vipères (*lit, fig*) nest of vipers
nœud vital nerve centre

noir, e /nwaʀ/ ADJ [1] (= *couleur*) black; [*yeux*] dark; [*fumée, mer, ciel, nuage*] black, dark ◆ **~ de coups** black and blue ◆ **~ comme du jais/de l'encre** jet/ink(y) black, black as jet/ink ◆ **~ comme du cirage** as black as soot ◆ **~ comme l'ébène** jet-black ◆ **mets-moi ça ~ sur blanc** put it down in black and white for me ◆ **je l'ai vu/c'est écrit ~ sur blanc** I saw it/it is (written down) in black and white ◆ **les murs étaient ~s de crasse/suie** the walls were black with dirt/soot ◆ **avoir les mains ~es/les ongles ~s** to have dirty *ou* grubby hands/dirty *ou* grubby fingernails; → **beurre, chemise, marée**

[2] [*personne, race*] black

[3] (* = *bronzé*) black

[4] (= *obscur*) dark ◆ **il faisait ~ comme dans un four*** it was pitch dark ◆ **la rue était ~e de monde** the street was teeming *ou* swarming with people; → **boîte, chambre, nuit**

[5] (*fig*) [*désespoir*] deep; [*humeur, pressentiment, colère*] black; [*idée*] gloomy, sombre (*Brit*), somber (*US*); [*jour, année*] dark ◆ **faire un tableau assez ~ de la situation** to paint a rather black *ou* gloomy picture of the situation ◆ **le jeudi ~** (*Hist*) black Thursday ◆ **plongé dans le plus ~ désespoir** *ou* **le désespoir le plus ~** plunged in the depths of despair ◆ **être dans la misère ~e** to be in utter *ou* abject poverty; → **bête, humour, liste[1]** *etc*

[6] (= *hostile, mauvais*) [*âme, ingratitude, trahison, regard*] black ◆ **regarder qn d'un œil ~** to give sb a black look ◆ **il se trame un ~ complot** some dark plot is being hatched ◆ **nourrir de ~s desseins** to be plotting dark deeds; → **magie, messe**

[7] (= *policier*) **roman ~** thriller ◆ **film ~** film noir

[8] (* = *ivre*) drunk, sloshed‡, tight*

NM [1] (= *couleur*) black ◆ **photo/télévision en ~ et blanc** black and white photo/television ◆ **film en ~ et blanc** black and white film ◆ **le ~ et blanc** (*Photo*) black and white *ou* monochrome photography ◆ **le ~** (*Casino*) black ◆ **le ~ de ses cheveux accentuait sa pâleur** her dark *ou* black hair accentuated her pallor, the blackness of her hair accentuated her pallor ◆ **la mer était d'un ~ d'encre** the sea was inky black ◆ **peindre les choses en ~** (*fig*) to paint things black, to paint a black picture ◆ **voir les choses en ~** to take a black view of things ◆ **il voit tout en ~** he sees the black side of everything; → **broyer, pousser**

[2] (= *matière*) **elle avait du ~ sur le menton** she had a black mark *ou* smudge on her chin ◆ **se mettre du ~ aux yeux** to put black eyeliner on ◆ **~ de fumée** lampblack ◆ **~ animal** bone charcoal

[3] (*Habillement*) **elle ne porte jamais de ~, elle n'est jamais en ~** she never wears black ◆ **elle est en ~** she is in *ou* is wearing black; (*en deuil*) she is in mourning

[4] (= *obscurité*) dark, darkness ◆ **avoir peur du ~** to be afraid of the dark ◆ **dans le ~** (*lit*) in the dark *ou* darkness; (*fig*) in the dark ◆ **nous sommes dans le ~ le plus complet** we're completely in the dark

[5] (* = *café*) **(petit) ~** (cup of) black coffee

NM,F **Noir(e)** black (person) ◆ **les Noirs d'Amérique** American blacks, African Americans

NF **noire** (*Mus*) crotchet (*Brit*), quarter note (*US*)

LOC ADV **au noir** (= *illégalement*) **acheter/vendre au ~** to buy/sell on the black market ◆ **travailler au ~** (*gén*) to work on the side; (*deuxième emploi*) to moonlight; [*clandestin*] to work illegally ◆ **le travail au ~** (*gén*) working on the side; (= *deuxième emploi*) moonlighting ◆ **il se fait payer au ~** he gets paid cash in hand ◆ **embaucher qn au ~** to hire sb without declaring him

noirâtre /nwaʀɑtʀ/ ADJ blackish

noiraud, e /nwaʀo, od/ ADJ dark, swarthy NM,F dark *ou* swarthy person

noirceur /nwaʀsœʀ/ NF (*littér*) [1] (= *couleur noire*) blackness; [*de fumée, mer, ciel, nuage, temps, nuit*] blackness, darkness [2] (= *perfidie*) [*d'âme, ingratitude, trahison, dessein, regard*] blackness [3] (= *acte perfide*) black *ou* evil deed

noircir /nwaʀsiʀ/ ► conjug 2 ◄ VT [1] (= *salir*) [*fumée*] to blacken; [*encre, charbon*] to dirty ◆ **les murs noircis par la crasse** walls black with dirt ◆ **~ du papier** (*fig*) to write page after page [2] (= *colorer*) to blacken; (*à la cire, à la peinture*) to darken [3] (= *dénigrer*) [+ *réputation*] to blacken ◆ **~ qn** to blacken sb's reputation *ou* name [4] (= *assombrir*) **~ le tableau** *ou* **la réalité** to paint a black picture of the situation VI [*fruit, légume*] to go black, to discolour (*Brit*), to discolor (*US*); [*ciel*] to darken, to grow black *ou* dark; [*couleur*] to darken VPR **se noircir** [1] [*ciel*] to darken, to grow black *ou* dark; [*temps*] to turn stormy; [*couleur, bois*] to darken [2] († ‡ = *s'enivrer*) to get plastered‡

noircissement /nwaʀsismɑ̃/ NM [1] (= *salissure*) (*par la fumée*) blackening; (*par l'encre, le charbon*) dirtying [2] (= *coloration*) blackening; (*à la cire, à la peinture*) darkening; [*de fruit, légume*] blackening, discolouring (*Brit*), discoloring (*US*); [*de ciel*] darkening ◆ **pour éviter le ~ de l'avocat** to stop the avocado discolouring

noircissure /nwaʀsisyʀ/ NF black smudge

noise /nwaz/ NF ◆ **chercher ~** *ou* **des ~s à qn** to try to pick a quarrel with sb

noisetier /nwaz(ə)tje/ NM hazel tree

noisette /nwazɛt/ NF (= *fruit*) hazel(nut); (= *café*) *espresso coffee with a drop of milk* ◆ **~ de beurre** (= *morceau*) knob of butter ◆ **~ d'agneau** (*Culin*) noisette of lamb ADJ INV [*couleur, yeux*] hazel ◆ **beurre ~** browned butter; → **pomme**

noix /nwa/ NF (= *fruit*) walnut; (‡ = *idiot*) nut*; (*Culin*) [*de côtelette*] eye ◆ **à la ~*** pathetic*, crummy‡; → **brou, coquille, gîte[1]**

COMP **noix de beurre** knob of butter
noix de (coquille) Saint-Jacques scallops (with roe removed)
noix du Brésil Brazil nut
noix de cajou cashew nut
noix de coco coconut
noix de galle oak apple, oak-gall
noix (de) muscade nutmeg
noix de pacane pecan nut
noix pâtissière cushion of veal
noix de pécan pecan nut
noix de veau cushion of veal
noix vomique nux vomica

nolens volens /nɔlɛ̃svɔlɛ̃s/ ADV (*frm*) willingly or unwillingly

noliser /nɔlize/ ► conjug 1 ◄ VT to charter ◆ **avion nolisé** charter plane

nom /nɔ̃/ NM [1] (= *nom propre*) name ◆ **~ de fille/de garçon** girl's/boy's name ◆ **vos ~ et prénom ?** your surname and first name, please? ◆ **Henri le troisième du ~** Henry III ◆ **un homme du ~ de Dupont** *ou* **qui a (pour) ~ Dupont** a man called Dupont, a man by the name of Dupont ◆ **il porte le ~ de sa mère** he has his mother's surname ◆ **il ne connaît pas ses élèves par leur ~** he doesn't know his pupils by name *ou* by their names ◆ **je le connais de ~** I know him by name ◆ **il écrit sous le ~ de Martin Suard** he writes under the name of Martin Suard ◆ **c'est un ~** *ou* **ce n'est qu'un ~ pour moi !** he *ou* it is just a name to me! ◆ **je n'arrive pas à mettre un ~ sur son visage** I can't put a name to his (*ou* her) face ◆ **~ à coucher dehors*** (*péj*) unpronounceable *ou* impossible-sounding name ◆ **~ à charnière** *ou* **à rallonge** *ou* **à tiroirs** (*péj*) double-barrelled name; → **faux[2], petit, répondre**

[2] (= *désignation*) name ◆ **quel est le ~ de cet arbre ?** what is the name of this tree?, what's this tree called? ◆ **c'est une sorte de fascisme qui n'ose pas dire son ~** it's fascism of a kind hiding under *ou* behind another name ◆ **c'est du dirigisme qui n'ose pas dire son ~** it's covert *ou* disguised state control ◆ **comme son**

~ **l'indique** as is indicated by its name, as the name indicates ◆ **il appelle les choses par leur** ~ he's not afraid to call a spade a spade ◆ **les beaux ~s de justice, de liberté** these fine-sounding words of justice and liberty ◆ **il n'est spécialiste que de** ~ he is only nominally a specialist, he is a specialist in name only ◆ **crime sans** ~ unspeakable crime ◆ **ce qu'il a fait n'a pas de** ~ what he did was unspeakable

3 *(= célébrité)* name; *(= noblesse)* name ◆ **se faire un** ~ to make a name for o.s. ◆ **laisser un** ~ to make one's mark ◆ **c'est un (grand)** ~ **dans l'histoire** he's one of the great names of history

4 *(Gram)* noun; → **complément**

5 *(locutions)* **en mon/votre** ~ in my/your name ◆ **il a parlé au** ~ **de tous les employés** he spoke for all *ou* on behalf of all the employees ◆ **au** ~ **de la loi, ouvrez** open up in the name of the law ◆ **au** ~ **de quoi vous permettez-vous ... ?** whatever gives you the right to ...? ◆ **au** ~ **du Père, du Fils ...** in the name of the Father and of the Son ... ◆ **au** ~ **du ciel !** in heaven's name! ◆ **au** ~ **de ce que vous avez de plus cher** in the name of everything you hold most dear ◆ ~ **de Dieu !**‡ God damn it!‡, bloody hell!‡ *(Brit)* ◆ ~ **de** ~ **!** *ou* **d'un chien !** *ou* **d'une pipe !** *ou* **d'un petit bonhomme !*** heck!*, blimey!* *(Brit)* ◆ **donner à qn des ~s d'oiseaux** to call sb names ◆ **traiter qn de tous les ~s** to call sb everything under the sun

COMP **nom de baptême** Christian name, given name *(US)*
nom de chose concrete noun
nom commercial (company) name
nom commun common noun
nom composé compound (word *ou* noun)
nom déposé (registered) trade name
nom d'emprunt *(gén)* alias, assumed name; *[d'écrivain]* pen name, nom de plume ◆ **se présenter sous un** ~ **d'emprunt** to use an assumed name *ou* an alias
nom de famille surname
nom de femme mariée married name
nom de guerre nom de guerre
nom de jeune fille maiden name
nom de lieu place name
nom de marque trade name
nom de plume nom de plume, pen name
nom propre proper noun
nom de rue street name
nom de scène *ou* **de théâtre** stage name

nomade /nɔmad/ ADJ *[peuple, vie]* nomadic; *[animal, oiseau]* migratory NMF *(Ethnol)* nomad; *(= gitan)* traveller

nomadisme /nɔmadism/ NM nomadism

no man's land /nomanslɑd/ NM no-man's-land

nombrable /nɔ̃bʀabl/ ADJ countable, numerable ◆ **difficilement** ~ difficult to count

nombre /nɔ̃bʀ/ NM 1 *(Ling, Sci)* number ◆ **loi des grands ~s** law of large numbers ◆ **les Nombres** *(Bible)* (the Book of) Numbers ◆ **~s rationnels/réels** rational/real numbers ◆ **s'accorder en** ~ *(Gram)* to agree in number

2 *(= quantité)* number ◆ **le** ~ **des victimes** the number of victims ◆ **un certain/grand** ~ **de** a certain/great number of ◆ **dans (un) bon** ~ **de pays** in a good *ou* great many countries ◆ **je lui ai dit** ~ **de fois que ...** I've told him many *ou* a number of times that ... ◆ **depuis** ~ **d'années** for many years, for a number of years ◆ **les gagnants sont au** ~ **de 3** there are 3 winners, the winners are 3 in number ◆ **être supérieur en** ~ to be superior in numbers ◆ **être en** ~ **suffisant** to be in sufficient number(s) *ou* sufficient in number ◆ **ils sont en** ~ **égal** their numbers are equal *ou* even, they are equal in number ◆ **des ennemis sans** ~ innumerable *ou* countless enemies

3 *(= masse)* numbers ◆ **être/venir en** ~ to be/come in large numbers ◆ **faire** ~ to make up the number(s) ◆ **être submergé par le** ~, **succomber sous le** ~ to be overcome by sheer weight of *ou* force of numbers ◆ **il y en avait dans le** ~ **qui riaient** there were some among them who were laughing ◆ **ça ne se verra pas dans le** ~ it won't be seen among all the rest *ou* when they're all together ◆ **pour le plus grand** ~ for the great majority (of people) ◆ **le plus grand** ~ **d'entre eux** the great majority, most of them

4 *(= parmi)* **je le compte au** ~ **de mes amis** I count him as *ou* consider him one of my friends, I number him among my friends ◆ **il n'est plus du** ~ **des vivants** he is no longer of this world ◆ **est-il du** ~ **des reçus ?** is he among those who passed?

COMP **nombre aléatoire** random number
nombre atomique atomic number
nombre complexe complex number
nombre entier whole number, integer
nombre imaginaire imaginary number
nombre d'or golden section
nombre parfait perfect number
nombre premier prime number; → **Mach**

nombrer /nɔ̃bʀe/ ► conjug 1 ◄ VT († *ou littér*) to number †, to count

nombreux, -euse /nɔ̃bʀø, øz/ ADJ 1 *(= en grand nombre)* **être** ~ *[exemples, visiteurs]* to be numerous; *[accidents]* to be numerous *ou* frequent ◆ **les cambriolages sont très** ~ **dans ce quartier** there are a great many burglaries in that area ◆ ~ **sont ceux qui souhaiteraient travailler davantage** there are many people who would like to work more hours ◆ ~ **furent ceux qui ...** there were many who ... ◆ **les gens étaient venus** ~ a lot of people *ou* a great many people had come ◆ **venez** ~ **!** all welcome! ◆ **certains, et ils sont** ~ certain people, and there are quite a few of them ◆ **peu** ~ few ◆ **le public était moins/plus** ~ **hier** there was a smaller/bigger audience yesterday, the audience was smaller/bigger yesterday ◆ **nous ne sommes pas si** ~ there aren't so many of us ◆ **les visiteurs arrivaient sans cesse plus** ~ *ou* **de plus en plus** ~ visitors came in ever-increasing numbers ◆ **ils étaient plus** ~ **que nous** they outnumbered us, there were more of them than of us

2 *(= le grand nombre de)* numerous, many ◆ **parmi les nombreuses personnalités** amongst the numerous *ou* many personalities

3 *(= un grand nombre de)* **de** ~ *[accidents, exemples]* many, numerous

4 *(= important) [foule, assistance, collection]* large

nombril /nɔ̃bʀi(l)/ NM *[de personne]* navel, belly button* ◆ **il se prend pour le** ~ **du monde*** he thinks he's the cat's whiskers* ◆ **se regarder le** ~* to contemplate one's navel

nombrilisme* /nɔ̃bʀilism/ NM *(péj)* navel-gazing ◆ **faire du** ~ to contemplate one's navel

nombriliste* /nɔ̃bʀilist/ ADJ, NMF ◆ **être** ~ to spend one's time contemplating one's navel

nomenclature /nɔmɑ̃klatyʀ/ NF *(gén = liste)* list; *(Ling, Sci)* nomenclature; *[de dictionnaire]* word list

nomenklatura /nɔmɛnklatuʀa/ NF *(Pol)* nomenklatura, elite

nominal, e (mpl **-aux**) /nɔminal, o/ ADJ 1 *(gén)* nominal; *(Ling) [groupe, phrase]* nominal, noun *(épith)* ◆ **liste ~e** list of names ◆ **procéder à l'appel** ~ to call the register *ou* the roll, to do the roll call ◆ **expression ~e** nominal expression ◆ **syntagme** ~ noun phrase 2 *(= sans réalité) [autorité, pouvoir]* nominal 3 *(Écon, Fin) [salaire]* nominal; → **valeur** 4 *(Tech) [puissance, vitesse]* rated NM *(Ling)* pronoun

nominalement /nɔminalmɑ̃/ ADV *(gén, Ling)* nominally ◆ **appeler qn** ~ to call sb by name

nominalisation /nɔminalizasjɔ̃/ NF nominalization

nominaliser /nɔminalize/ ► conjug 1 ◄ VT to nominalize

nominalisme /nɔminalism/ NM nominalism

nominaliste /nɔminalist/ ADJ, NMF nominalist

nominatif, -ive /nɔminatif, iv/ ADJ *(Fin) [titre, action]* registered ◆ **état** ~ *(Comm)* list of items ◆ **liste nominative** list of names ◆ **carte nominative** nontransferable card ◆ **l'invitation n'est pas nominative** the invitation doesn't specify a name NM *(Ling)* nominative

nomination /nɔminasjɔ̃/ NF 1 *(= promotion)* appointment, nomination *(à* to); *(= titre, acte)* appointment *ou* nomination papers ◆ **obtenir sa** ~ to be nominated *ou* appointed *(au poste de* to the post of); ◆ **le film a reçu 6 ~s aux Oscars** the film has received 6 Oscar nominations 2 *(Ling, Philos)* naming

nominativement /nɔminativmɑ̃/ ADV by name

nominé, e /nɔmine/ ADJ *[film, acteur, auteur]* nominated ◆ **être** ~ **à qch** to be nominated *ou* shortlisted for sth

nommément /nɔmemɑ̃/ ADV 1 *(= par son nom)* by name 2 *(= spécialement)* notably, especially, particularly

nommer /nɔme/ ► conjug 1 ◄ VT 1 *(= promouvoir) [+ fonctionnaire]* to appoint; *[+ candidat]* to nominate ◆ ~ **qn à un poste** to appoint *ou* nominate sb to a post ◆ ~ **qn son héritier** to name sb (as) one's heir ◆ **il a été nommé gérant/ministre** he was appointed *ou* made manager/minister

2 *(= appeler) [+ personne]* to call, to name; *(= dénommer) [+ découverte, produit]* to name, to give a name to ◆ **ils l'ont nommé Richard** they called *ou* named him Richard ◆ **un homme nommé Martin** a man named *ou* called *ou* by the name of Martin ◆ **le nommé Martin** the man named *ou* called Martin ◆ **ce que nous nommons le bonheur** what we call happiness; → **point¹**

3 *(= citer) [+ fleuves, batailles, auteurs, complices]* to name ◆ **M. Sartin, pour ne pas le** ~, ... *(hum)* without mentioning any names, Mr Sartin ... ◆ **quelqu'un que je ne nommerai pas** somebody who shall remain nameless

VPR **se nommer** 1 *(= s'appeler)* to be called ◆ **comment se nomme-t-il ?** what is he called?, what is his name? ◆ **il se nomme Paul** he's called Paul, his name is Paul

2 *(= se présenter)* to introduce o.s. ◆ **il se leva et se nomma** he stood up and gave his name

non /nɔ̃/

1 ADVERBE	3 PRÉFIXE
2 NOM MASCULIN INV	4 COMPOSÉS

1 - ADVERBE

1 réponse négative no ◆ **le connaissez-vous ?** – ~ do you know him? – no (I don't) ◆ **est-elle chez elle ?** – ~ is she at home? – no (she isn't *ou* she's not) ◆ **je vais ouvrir la fenêtre** – ~, **il y aura des courants d'air** I'll open the window – no (don't), it'll make a draught ◆ **il n'a pas encore dit** ~ **!** he hasn't said no yet!, he hasn't refused yet! ◆ **je ne dis pas** ~ *(= ce n'est pas de refus)* I wouldn't say no; *(= je n'en disconviens pas)* I don't disagree ◆ **ah ça** ~ **!** certainly *ou* definitely not!, no way!* ◆ ~ **et** ~ **!** no, no, no!, absolutely not! ◆ **que** ~ **!** I should say not!, definitely not! ◆ ~ **merci !** no thank you! ◆ **certes** ~ **!** most certainly *ou* definitely not! ◆ **vous n'y allez pas ?** – **mais** ~ **!** *ou* **bien sûr que** ~ **!** aren't you going? – of course not! *ou* I should

think not! ◆ **répondre (par) ~ à toutes les questions** to answer no *ou* answer in the negative to all the questions ◆ **faire ~ de la tête** to shake one's head

2 remplaçant une proposition not ◆ **est-ce que c'est nécessaire ? – je pense** *ou* **crois que** ~ is that necessary? – I don't think so *ou* I don't think it is *ou* I think not *(frm)* ◆ **je crains que** ~ I'm afraid not, I fear not *(frm)* ◆ **il nous quitte ? – j'espère que** ~ is he leaving us? – I hope not *ou* I hope he isn't ◆ **je le crois – moi** ~ I believe him – well I don't *ou* not me* ◆ **il l'aime bien, moi** ~ he likes him but I don't ◆ **dire/répondre que** ~ to say/answer it isn't (*ou* it won't *etc*) ◆ **j'ai demandé si elle était venue, lui dit que** ~ I asked if she had come – he says not *ou* he says no *ou* he says she hadn't ◆ **ah ~ ?** really?, no? ◆ **partez-vous ou ~ ?** are you going or not?, are you going or aren't you? ◆ **il se demandait s'il irait ou** ~ he wondered whether to go or not ◆ **erreur ou ~/qu'il l'ait voulu ou ~ le mal est fait** mistake or no mistake/whether he meant it or not the damage is done; → **signe**

3 frm = pas not ◆ **c'est par paresse et ~ par prudence que ...** it is through laziness and not caution that ... ◆ **je veux bien de leur aide mais ~ de leur argent** I'm willing to accept their help but not their money *ou* but I want none of their money ◆ **c'est votre avis ~ le mien** it's your opinion not mine

◆ **non que** + *subjonctif* not that ... ◆ ~ **qu'il soit stupide, mais ...** not that he's stupid, but ...

4 exprimant l'impatience, l'indignation **tu vas cesser de pleurer ~ ?** will you stop crying?, just stop that crying(, will you?) ◆ ~ **par exemple !** for goodness sake!, good gracious! ◆ ~ **mais alors !***, ~ **mais (des fois) !*** for goodness sake!*, honestly! ◆ ~ **mais (des fois)*, tu me prends pour qui ?** look here* *ou* for God's sake‡ what do you take me for? ◆ ~ **mais je rêve !*** I don't believe this!

5 exprimant le doute no? ◆ **il me l'a dit lui-même – ~ ?** he told me so himself – no *ou* really? ◆ **c'est bon, ~ ?** it's good, isn't it?

6 locutions

◆ **non** + *adverbe ou conjonction ou préposition* not ◆ ~ **loin d'ici, il y a ...** not far from here there's ... ◆ **c'est une expérience ~ moins intéressante** it's an experience that is no less interesting ◆ **il est ~ moins vrai/évident que ...** it is nonetheless true/obvious that ... ◆ **un homme ~ pas érudit mais instruit** a man who is not erudite but well-informed ◆ ~ **pas que j'aie peur, mais ...** not that I'm afraid, but ... ◆ **il l'a fait ~ sans raison/~ sans mal** he did it not without reason/difficulty ◆ **il y est allé ~ sans protester** he went, but not without protest *ou* protesting; → **seulement**

◆ **non plus** ◆ **il a continué ~ plus en voiture mais en train** he continued on his way, no longer by car but by train ◆ **il parle ~ plus en médecin mais en ami** he is talking now not as a doctor but as a friend ◆ **ils sont désormais associés, et ~ plus rivaux** they're no longer rivals *ou* they're not rivals any more but associates ◆ **il n'a pas hésité, ~ plus qu'eux d'ailleurs** he didn't hesitate any more than they did

◆ *pronom personnel* + **non plus** ◆ **il ne l'a pas vu ni moi ~ plus** he didn't see him and neither did I *ou* and I didn't either ◆ **nous ne l'avons pas vu – nous ~ plus** we didn't see him – neither did we *ou* we didn't either ◆ **nous ~ plus nous ne l'avons pas vu** we didn't see him either ◆ **il n'a pas compris lui ~ plus** he didn't understand either

2 - NOM MASCULIN INV

no ◆ **répondre par un ~ catégorique** to reply with a categorical no ◆ **il y a eu 30 ~** there were 30 votes against *ou* 30 noes; → **oui**

3 - PRÉFIXE

Nouns starting with **non** are usually hyphenated, eg **non-agression**, adjectives are usually not, eg **non spécialisé**.

◆ **non** + *adjectif ou participe*

Pour ce type de composés (ex : **non coupable, non négligeable, non polluant**, etc), cherchez ci-dessous, en entrée ou sous l'adjectif concerné.

non-, un- ◆ ~ **ferreux/gazeux** non-ferrous/-gaseous ◆ ~ **vérifié** unverified ◆ ~ **spécialisé** unspecialized, non-specialized ◆ **les objets ~ réclamés** unclaimed items ◆ **toutes les places ~ réservées** all the unreserved seats, all seats not reserved ◆ **les travaux ~ terminés** the unfinished work

◆ **non-** + *nom* ◆ **la ~-reconnaissance de qch** the fact that sth is unrecognized ◆ **en cas de ~-réponse** if there is no reply ◆ **le ~-respect de cette règle entraînerait la rupture du contrat** non-observance of this rule will result in breach of contract

4 - COMPOSÉS

non accompli, e ADJ *(Ling)* continuous
non aligné, e ADJ nonaligned
non arrondi, e ADJ *(Phon)* spread
non belligérant, e ADJ, NM,F nonbelligerent
non combattant, e ADJ, NM,F noncombatant
non conformiste ADJ, NM,F nonconformist
non dénombrable ADJ *(Ling)* uncountable
non directif, -ive ADJ *[entretien, questionnaire]* with no leading questions; *[thérapie]* nondirective
non engagé, e ADJ *[artiste]* with no political commitment; *[pays]* neutral, nonaligned
non existant, e ADJ nonexistent
non figuratif, -ive ADJ nonrepresentational
non lucratif, -ive ADJ ◆ **à but ~ lucratif** non-profit-making
non marqué, e ADJ *(Ling)* unmarked
non voisé, e ADJ *(Phon)* unvoiced, voiceless

non-activité /nɔnaktivite/ NF inactivity

nonagénaire /nɔnaʒenɛʀ/ ADJ, NMF nonagenarian, ninety-year-old

non-agression /nɔnagʀesjɔ̃/ NF non-aggression

non-alignement /nɔnaliɲmɑ̃/ NM nonalignment

nonante /nɔnɑ̃t/ ADJ *(Belg, Helv)* ninety

nonantième /nɔnɑ̃tjɛm/ ADJ *(Belg, Helv)* ninetieth

non-appartenance /nɔnapaʀtənɑ̃s/ NF *(à un parti, un organisme)* non-membership ◆ **sa ~ à l'ethnie dominante** the fact that he did not belong to the dominant ethnic group

non-assistance /nɔnasistɑ̃s/ NF *(Jur)* ◆ ~ **à personne en danger** failure to assist a person in danger

non-belligérance /nɔ̃beliʒeʀɑ̃s/ NF nonbelligerence

nonce /nɔ̃s/ NM nuncio ◆ ~ **apostolique** apostolic nuncio

nonchalamment /nɔ̃ʃalamɑ̃/ ADV nonchalantly

nonchalance /nɔ̃ʃalɑ̃s/ NF nonchalance

nonchalant, e /nɔ̃ʃalɑ̃, ɑ̃t/ ADJ nonchalant

nonciature /nɔ̃sjatyʀ/ NF nunciature

non-communication /nɔ̃kɔmynikasjɔ̃/ NF 1 *[de document, information]* non-disclosure 2 *(dans une entreprise, un couple)* non-communication, lack of communication

non-comparution /nɔ̃kɔ̃paʀysjɔ̃/ NF *(Jur)* nonappearance

non-conciliation /nɔ̃kɔ̃siljasjɔ̃/ NF refusal to settle out of court

non-concurrence /nɔ̃kɔ̃kyʀɑ̃s/ NF lack of competition ◆ **clause de ~** non-competition clause, non-compete clause *(surtout US)*

non-conformisme /nɔ̃kɔ̃fɔʀmism/ NM nonconformism

non-conformité /nɔ̃kɔ̃fɔʀmite/ NF nonconformity

non-contradiction /nɔ̃kɔ̃tʀadiksjɔ̃/ NF ◆ **principe de ~** law of noncontradiction

non-croyant, e /nɔ̃kʀwajɑ̃, ɑ̃t/ NM,F unbeliever, non-believer

non-cumul /nɔ̃kymyl/ NM *(Jur)* ◆ **il y a ~ de peines** sentences run concurrently ◆ **le principe du ~ des fonctions** the rule prohibiting anyone from holding more than one post at a time

non-dénonciation /nɔ̃denɔ̃sjasjɔ̃/ NF *[de crime, sévices]* failure to report ◆ **il a été poursuivi pour ~ de malfaiteur** he was prosecuted for failing to report an offence

non-discrimination /nɔ̃diskʀiminasjɔ̃/ NF nondiscrimination

non-dit /nɔ̃di/ NM ◆ **cette dispute a fait ressortir tous les ~s** in the quarrel unspoken resentments surfaced ◆ **ces ~s qui se transmettent de génération en génération** these things that remain unmentioned from generation to generation ◆ **dix émissions sur les mensonges et les ~s familiaux** ten programmes on family secrets and lies

non-droit /nɔ̃dʀwa/ NM ◆ **zone de ~** ≈ no-go area*, *urban area where law and order have broken down* ◆ **État de ~** *state in which human and civil rights are not respected*

non-engagement /nɔnɑ̃gaʒmɑ̃/ NM non-involvement

non-être /nɔnɛtʀ/ NM *(Philos)* non-being

non-événement /nɔnevɛnmɑ̃/ NM nonevent

non-exécution /nɔnɛgzekysjɔ̃/ NF *[de contrat]* non-completion

non-existence /nɔnɛgzistɑ̃s/ NF nonexistence

non-fumeur, -euse /nɔ̃fymœʀ, øz/ ADJ nosmoking *(épith)*; *[compartiment]* nonsmoking *(épith)* NM,F non-smoker ◆ **(compartiment) ~s** non-smoking compartment *(Brit) ou* car *(US)*, non-smoker ◆ **place fumeur ou ~ ?** *(en train, en avion)* smoking or nonsmoking?

non-ingérence /nɔnɛ̃ʒeʀɑ̃s/ NF noninterference

non(-)initié, e /nɔninisje/ ADJ *[lecteur]* lay; *[observateur]* uninformed NM,F lay person ◆ **pour les ~s** for the uninitiated

non(-)inscrit, e /nɔnɛ̃skʀi, it/ *(Pol)* ADJ independent NM,F independent (member)

non-intervention /nɔnɛ̃tɛʀvɑ̃sjɔ̃/ NF nonintervention

non(-)interventionniste /nɔnɛ̃tɛʀvɑ̃sjɔnist/ ADJ, NMF noninterventionist

non-jouissance /nɔ̃ʒwisɑ̃s/ NF *(Jur)* nonenjoyment

non-lieu (pl **non-lieux**) /nɔ̃ljø/ NM *(Jur)* ◆ **(arrêt ou ordonnance de) ~** dismissal of a charge ◆ **bénéficier d'un ~** to be discharged *ou* have one's case dismissed for lack of evidence ◆ **rendre une ordonnance de ~** to dismiss a case for lack of evidence, to direct a nonsuit

non-moi /nɔ̃mwa/ NM INV *(Philos)* nonego

nonne /nɔn/ NF (††, *hum*) nun

nonnette /nɔnɛt/ NF *(Culin)* spiced bun *(made of pain d'épice)*

nonobstant /nɔnɔpstɑ̃/ PRÉP († ou *Jur = malgré*) notwithstanding, despite, in spite of ADV († = *néanmoins*) notwithstanding †, nevertheless

non-paiement /nɔ̃pɛmɑ̃/ NM nonpayment

nonpareil, -eille †† /nɔ̃paʀɛj/ ADJ nonpareil, peerless

non-partant /nɔ̃paʀtɑ̃/ NM (*Sport*) non-runner

non-parution /nɔ̃paʀysjɔ̃/ NF failure to appear *ou* be published

non-pratiquant, e /nɔ̃pʀatikɑ̃, ɑt/ NM,F (*Rel, gén*) person who does not practise his *ou* her religion; (= *chrétien*) non-churchgoer

non-prolifération /nɔ̃pʀɔlifeʀasjɔ̃/ NF nonproliferation

non-recevoir /nɔ̃ʀ(ə)səvwaʀ/ NM INV (*Jur*) demurrer, objection; (*fig*) blunt refusal ♦ **il m'a opposé une fin de ~** he turned down my request point-blank

non-résident, e /nɔ̃ʀezidɑ̃, ɑt/ NM,F nonresident

non-respect /nɔ̃ʀɛspɛ/ NM [*de droit, engagement, règle*] failure to respect ♦ **en cas de ~ des délais ...** if the deadlines are not met *ou* observed ...

non-retour /nɔ̃ʀətuʀ/ NM no return; → **point¹**

non-rétroactivité /nɔ̃ʀetʀoaktivite/ NF (*Jur*) nonretroactivity

non-salarié, e /nɔ̃salaʀje/ NM,F self-employed person

non-sens /nɔ̃sɑ̃s/ NM INV (= *absurdité*) (piece of) nonsense; (= *erreur de traduction*) meaningless word (*ou* phrase *etc*)

non-signataire /nɔ̃siɲatɛʀ/ NMF non-signatory

non-spécialiste /nɔ̃spesjalist/ NMF nonspecialist

non-stop /nɔnstɔp/ ADJ INV, ADV non-stop

non(-)syndiqué, e /nɔ̃sɛ̃dike/ ADJ nonunion(ized) NM,F nonunion member, nonmember (of a *ou* the union)

non-valeur /nɔ̃valœʀ/ NF 1 (*Jur*) unproductiveness; (*Fin*) bad debt; (*fig*) nonproductive asset, wasted asset 2 (*péj = personne*) nonentity

non-violence /nɔ̃vjɔlɑ̃s/ NF nonviolence

non(-)violent, e /nɔ̃vjɔlɑ̃, ɑt/ ADJ nonviolent NM,F advocate *ou* supporter of nonviolence

non(-)voyant, e /nɔ̃vwajɑ̃, ɑt/ NM,F visually handicapped *ou* impaired person ADJ visually handicapped *ou* impaired

noosphère /noosfɛʀ/ NF noosphere

noradrénaline /nɔʀadʀenalin/ NF noradrenalin(e) (*Brit*), norepinephrine (*US*)

nord /nɔʀ/ NM INV 1 (= *point cardinal*) north ♦ **~ géographique/magnétique** true/magnetic north ♦ **le vent du ~** the north wind ♦ **un vent du ~** (*gén*) a north(erly) wind; (*Naut*) a northerly ♦ **le vent tourne/est au ~** the wind is veering north(wards) *ou* towards the north/is blowing from the north ♦ **regarder vers le ~** *ou* **dans la direction du ~** to look north(wards) *ou* towards the north ♦ **au ~** (*situation*) in the north; (*direction*) to the north, north(wards) ♦ **au ~ de** north of, to the north of ♦ **la maison est (exposée) au ~/en plein ~** the house faces (the) north *ou* northwards/due north; → **perdre**

2 (= *région*) north ♦ **pays/peuples du ~** northern countries/peoples, countries/peoples of the north ♦ **l'Europe/l'Italie/la Bourgogne du ~** Northern Europe/Italy/Burgundy ♦ **la mer du Nord** the North Sea ♦ **le ~ de la France, le Nord** the North (of France) ♦ **les gens du Nord** (*dans un pays*) Northerners ♦ **le Grand Nord** the far North

ADJ INV [*région, partie*] northern (*épith*); [*entrée, paroi*] north (*épith*); [*versant, côte*] north(ern) (*épith*); [*côté*] north(ward) (*épith*); [*direction*] northward (*épith*), northerly (*Mét*); → **hémisphère, latitude, pôle**

nord-africain, e (mpl **nord-africains**) /nɔʀafʀikɛ̃, ɛn/ ADJ North African NM,F **Nord-Africain(e)** North African

nord-américain, e (mpl **nord-américains**) /nɔʀameʀikɛ̃, ɛn/ ADJ North American NM,F **Nord-Américain(e)** North American

nord-coréen, -enne (mpl **nord-coréens**) /nɔʀkɔʀeɛ̃, ɛn/ ADJ North Korean NM,F **Nord-Coréen(ne)** North Korean

nord-est /nɔʀɛst/ ADJ INV, NM northeast

Nordeste /nɔʀdeste/ NM Nordeste

nordique /nɔʀdik/ ADJ [*pays, race*] Nordic; [*langues*] Scandinavian, Nordic; → **ski** NMF **Nordique** Nordic

nordiste /nɔʀdist/ (*Hist US*) ADJ Northern, Yankee NMF **Nordiste** Northerner, Yankee

nord-nord-est /nɔʀnɔʀɛst/ ADJ INV, NM north-northeast

nord-nord-ouest /nɔʀnɔʀwɛst/ ADJ INV, NM north-northwest

nord-ouest /nɔʀwɛst/ ADJ INV, NM northwest

nord-vietnamien, -ienne (mpl **nord-vietnamiens**) /nɔʀvjɛtnamjɛ̃, jɛn/ ADJ North Vietnamese NM,F **Nord-Vietnamien(ne)** North Vietnamese

noria /nɔʀja/ NF noria, bucket waterwheel ♦ **une ~ d'hélicoptères transportait les blessés vers les hôpitaux** a fleet of helicopters shuttled *ou* ferried the wounded to the hospitals

normal, e (mpl **-aux**) /nɔʀmal, o/ ADJ 1 (= *habituel*) normal, usual ♦ **de dimension ~e** normal-sized, standard-sized ♦ **c'est une chose très ~e, ça n'a rien que de très ~** that's quite usual *ou* normal ♦ **rien à signaler, tout est ~** nothing to report, everything is fine ♦ **il n'est pas ~** he's not normal, there's something wrong with him

2 (= *correct, logique*) **c'est ~ !** it's (quite) natural! ♦ **ce n'est pas ~** (= *bizarre*) there must be something wrong; (= *ce n'est pas juste*) that's not right ♦ **ce n'est pas ~ qu'ils aient droit aux soins gratuits** it's not right that they get free treatment, it's outrageous that they get free treatment; → **état, temps¹**

NF **normale** 1 ♦ **s'écarter de la ~e** to diverge from the norm ♦ **revenir à la ~e** to return to normality, to get back to normal ♦ **au-dessus de la ~e** above average ♦ **température voisine des ~es saisonnières** temperature close to the seasonal average

2 (*Math*) normal (*à* to)

3 ♦ **Normale (sup)** (abrév de **École normale supérieure**) → **école**

> ⚠ Au sens de 'correct', 'logique', **normal** ne se traduit pas par le mot anglais **normal**.

normalement /nɔʀmalmɑ̃/ ADV 1 (= *d'une manière normale*) [*se dérouler, fonctionner*] normally 2 (= *si tout va bien*) **~, il devrait être là demain** he should be here tomorrow ♦ **tu pourras venir ? – ~, oui** will you be able to come? – yes, I should think so 3 (= *d'habitude*) usually, generally ♦ **~ il vient le jeudi** he usually *ou* generally comes on a Thursday

> ⚠ **normalement** se traduit par **normally** uniquement au sens de 'd'une manière normale'.

normalien, -ienne /nɔʀmaljɛ̃, jɛn/ NM,F (= *futur professeur*) *student at the École normale supérieure*; (= *diplômé*) *graduate of the École normale supérieure*; (*ancienn = futur instituteur*) *student at teacher training college*

normalisateur, -trice /nɔʀmalizatœʀ, tʀis/ ADJ [*effet*] normalizing ♦ **une conception normalisatrice de l'éducation** a rigidly conventional approach to education

normalisation /nɔʀmalizasjɔ̃/ NF 1 (= *régularisation*) [*de situation, relations*] normalization ♦ **on espère une ~ des relations diplomatiques** we are hoping diplomatic relations will be back to normal soon 2 (= *standardisation*) [*de produit*] standardization

> ⚠ Au sens de 'standardisation', **normalisation** ne se traduit pas par le mot anglais **normalization**.

normaliser /nɔʀmalize/ ► conjug 1 ◄ VT 1 (= *régulariser*) [+ *situation, relations*] to normalize 2 (= *standardiser*) [+ *produit*] to standardize ♦ **taille normalisée** standard size VPR **se normaliser** 1 (= *revenir à la normale*) to get back to normal; (= *devenir normal*) to normalize 2 (= *devenir standard*) to be standardized

normalité /nɔʀmalite/ NF normality

normand, e /nɔʀmɑ̃, ɑd/ ADJ (= *de Normandie*) Norman; (*Hist = scandinave*) Norse; → **armoire, trou** NM **Normand** (= *de Normandie*) Norman; (*Hist = Scandinave*) Norseman, Northman; → **réponse** NF **Normande** (= *de Normandie*) Norman; (*Hist = Scandinave*) Norsewoman

Normandie /nɔʀmɑ̃di/ NF Normandy

normatif, -ive /nɔʀmatif, iv/ ADJ prescriptive, normative

norme /nɔʀm/ NF (*Math, gén*) norm; (*Tech*) standard ♦ **~s de fabrication** manufacturing standards, standards of manufacture ♦ **mettre qch aux ~s de sécurité** to ensure that sth complies with safety standards ♦ **ce produit n'est pas conforme aux ~s françaises** this product doesn't conform to French standards ♦ **tant que ça reste dans la ~** as long as it's kept within limits ♦ **pourvu que vous restiez dans la ~** provided you don't overdo it *ou* you don't overstep the limits ♦ **hors ~(s)** [*personnage*] unconventional; [*carrière*] unusual ♦ **c'est une voiture hors ~(s)** it's no ordinary car

normé, e /nɔʀme/ ADJ (*Math*) normed

normographe /nɔʀmɔgʀaf/ NM stencil

nor(r)ois, e /nɔʀwa, waz/ ADJ, NM Old Norse

Norvège /nɔʀvɛʒ/ NF Norway ♦ **la mer de ~** the Norwegian sea

norvégien, -ienne /nɔʀveʒjɛ̃, jɛn/ ADJ Norwegian; → **marmite, omelette** NM (= *langue*) Norwegian NM,F **Norvégien(ne)** Norwegian

nos /no/ ADJ POSS → **notre**

nosocomial, e (mpl **-iaux**) /nozɔkɔmjal, jo/ ADJ nosocomial (*SPÉC*) ♦ **les infections ~es** hospital-acquired infections

nostalgie /nɔstalʒi/ NF nostalgia ♦ **avoir** *ou* **garder la ~ de ...** to feel nostalgic for ... ♦ **avoir la ~ du pays natal** to be homesick

nostalgique /nɔstalʒik/ ADJ nostalgic NMF ♦ **les ~s des années 60** those who feel nostalgic for the 1960s ♦ **les ~s de la monarchie** those who look back nostalgically to the monarchy

nota (bene) /nɔta (bene)/ NM INV nota bene

notabilité /nɔtabilite/ NF notability

notable /nɔtabl/ ADJ [*fait*] notable, noteworthy; [*changement, progrès*] notable NM notable, worthy

notablement /nɔtabləmɑ̃/ ADV notably

notaire /nɔtɛʀ/ NM notary (public); *(en Grande-Bretagne)* ≃ solicitor (Brit)

notamment /nɔtamɑ̃/ ADV *(= entre autres)* among others; *(= plus particulièrement)* particularly, in particular, notably ◆ **elle a ~ publié une histoire de l'aviation** among other books she has written a history of flying ◆ **les constructeurs automobiles français, ~ Renault** French car manufacturers, particularly Renault

notarial, e (mpl **-iaux**) /nɔtaʀjal, jo/ ADJ ◆ **étude ~e** office of a notary (public); *(en Grande-Bretagne)* ≃ solicitor's office

notariat /nɔtaʀja/ NM profession of (a) notary (public); *(en Grande-Bretagne)* ≃ profession of a solicitor

notarié, e /nɔtaʀje/ ADJ drawn up by a notary (public), notarized (SPÉC); *(en Grande-Bretagne)* ≃ drawn up by a solicitor

notation /nɔtasjɔ̃/ NF 1 *(= symboles, système)* notation 2 *(= touche, note)* *[de couleurs]* touch; *[de sons]* variation ◆ **une ~ intéressante** *(Littérat)* an interesting touch *ou* variation 3 *(= transcription)* *[de sentiment, geste, son]* expression 4 *(= jugement)* *[de devoir]* marking (Brit), grading (US); *[d'employé]* assessment ◆ **agence de ~ (financière)** *(Fin)* (credit) rating agency

note /nɔt/ NF 1 *(= remarque, communication)* note ◆ **~ diplomatique/officielle** diplomatic/official note ◆ **prendre des ~s** to take notes ◆ **prendre (bonne) ~ de qch** to take (good) note of sth ◆ **prendre qch en ~** to make a note of sth, to write sth down; *(hâtivement)* to jot sth down ◆ **relire ses ~s** to read over one's notes ◆ **remarque en ~** marginal comment, note in the margin ◆ **c'est écrit en ~** it's written in the margin

2 *(= appréciation chiffrée)* mark (Brit), grade (US) ◆ **mettre une ~ à** *[+ dissertation]* to mark (Brit), to grade (US); *[+ élève]* to give a mark to (Brit), to grade (US); *[+ employé]* to assess ◆ **avoir de bonnes/mauvaises ~s** to have good/bad marks *ou* grades ◆ **avoir une bonne/mauvaise ~ à un devoir/en histoire** to get a good/bad mark for a homework exercise/for *ou* in history ◆ **c'est une mauvaise ~ pour lui** *(fig)* it's a black mark against him

3 *(= compte)* *[de gaz, blanchisserie]* bill, account; *[de restaurant, hôtel]* bill, check (US) ◆ **demander/présenter/régler la ~** *(à l'hôtel)* to ask for/present/settle the bill ◆ **vous me donnerez la ~, s'il vous plaît** *(au restaurant)* may I have the bill *ou* check (US) please?, I'd like my bill ◆ **je vais vous faire la ~** I'll make out the bill ◆ **mettez-le sur ma ~** put it on my bill *ou* check (US) ◆ **~ de frais** *(= bulletin)* claim form (for expenses); *(= argent dépensé)* expenses ◆ **~ d'honoraires** (doctor's *ou* lawyer's) account

4 *(Mus, fig)* note ◆ **donner la ~** *(Mus)* to give the key; *(fig)* to set the tone ◆ **la ~ juste** the right note ◆ **c'est tout à fait dans la ~** it fits in perfectly with the rest ◆ **ses paroles étaient tout à fait dans la ~/n'étaient pas dans la ~** his words struck exactly the right note/struck the wrong note (altogether) ◆ **ce n'est pas dans la ~** it doesn't strike the right note at all; → **faux²**

5 *(= trace, touche)* note, touch ◆ **mettre une ~ triste** *ou* **de tristesse dans qch** to lend a touch *ou* note of sadness to sth ◆ **une ~ d'anxiété/de fierté perçait sous ses paroles** a note of anxiety/pride was discernible in his words ◆ **une ~ de santal** *[de parfum]* a hint of sandalwood

COMP **note de l'auteur** author's note
note en bas de page footnote
note de conjoncture economic outlook report
note d'information memorandum
note marginale marginal note, note in the margin
note de passage *(Mus)* passing note
note de la rédaction editor's note
note de service memorandum
note du traducteur translator's note

> ⚠ Dans un contexte scolaire et au sens de 'facture', **note** ne se traduit pas par le mot anglais **note**.

noter /nɔte/ ► conjug 1 ◄ VT 1 *(= inscrire)* *[+ adresse, rendez-vous]* to write down, to note down, to make a note of; *[+ idées]* to jot down, to write down, to note down; *(Mus)* *[+ air]* to write down, to take down ◆ **si vous pouviez le ~ quelque part** could you make a note of it *ou* write it down somewhere? ◆ **notez que nous serons absents** note that we'll be away

2 *(= remarquer)* *[+ faute, progrès]* to notice ◆ **notez la précision du bas-relief** note the fine bas relief work ◆ **on note une certaine amélioration** there has been some improvement, some improvement has been noted ◆ **notez (bien) que je n'ai rien dit, je n'ai rien dit, notez-le** *ou* **notez (bien)** note that I didn't say anything, mark you, I didn't say anything ◆ **il faut ~ qu'il a des excuses** admittedly he has an excuse, he has an excuse mind you *ou* mark you (Brit) ◆ **ceci est à ~** *ou* **mérite d'être noté** this is worth noting *ou* making a note of

3 *(= cocher, souligner)* *[+ citation, passage]* to mark

4 *(= juger)* *[+ devoir]* to mark, to grade (US); *[+ élève]* to give a mark to, to grade (US); *[+ employé]* to assess ◆ **~ sur 10/20** to mark out of 10/20 ◆ **devoir bien/mal noté** homework with a good/bad mark *ou* grade ◆ **employé bien/mal noté** highly/poorly rated employee, employee with a good/bad record ◆ **elle note sévèrement/large** she is a strict/lenient marker

notice /nɔtis/ NF *(= préface, résumé)* note; *(= mode d'emploi)* instructions ◆ **~ biographique/bibliographique** biographical/bibliographical note ◆ **~ explicative** *ou* **d'emploi** directions for use, explanatory leaflet ◆ **~ technique** specification sheet, specifications ◆ **~ nécrologique** obituary

notificatif, -ive /nɔtifikatif, iv/ ADJ notifying ◆ **lettre notificative** letter of notification

notification /nɔtifikasjɔ̃/ NF *(Admin)* notification ◆ **~ vous a été envoyée de vous présenter** notification has been sent to you to present yourself ◆ **recevoir ~ de** to be notified of, to receive notification of ◆ **~ d'actes** *(Jur)* service of documents

notifier /nɔtifje/ ► conjug 7 ◄ VT to notify ◆ **~ qch à qn** to notify sb of sth, to notify sth to sb ◆ **on lui a notifié que ...** he was notified that ..., he received notice that ... ◆ **~ une citation à qn** to serve a summons *ou* a writ on sb ◆ **il s'est vu ~ son licenciement** he received notice of his dismissal

notion /nosjɔ̃/ NF 1 *(= conscience)* notion ◆ **je n'ai pas la moindre ~ de** I haven't the faintest notion of ◆ **perdre la ~ du temps** *ou* **de l'heure** to lose track of the time 2 *(= connaissances)* **~s** notion, elementary knowledge ◆ **avoir quelques ~s de grammaire** to have some knowledge of grammar, to have a smattering of grammar ◆ **~s d'algèbre/d'histoire** *(titre)* algebra/history primer

notionnel, -elle /nosjɔnɛl/ ADJ notional

notoire /nɔtwaʀ/ ADJ *[criminel, méchanceté]* notorious; *[fait, vérité]* well-known, acknowledged *(épith)* ◆ **il est ~ que** it is common *ou* public knowledge that, it's an acknowledged fact that

notoirement /nɔtwaʀmɑ̃/ ADV *[insuffisant]* manifestly; *[malhonnête]* notoriously ◆ **c'est ~ reconnu** it's generally recognized, it's well known

notoriété /nɔtɔʀjete/ NF *[de fait]* notoriety; *(= renommée)* fame ◆ **c'est de ~ publique** that's common *ou* public knowledge

notre (pl **nos**) /nɔtʀ, no/ ADJ POSS 1 *(possession, relation)* our; *(emphatique)* our own ◆ **~ fils et ~ fille** our son and daughter ◆ **nous avons tous laissé ~ manteau et ~ chapeau au vestiaire** we have all left our coats and hats in the cloakroom ◆ **~ bonne ville de Tours est en fête** our fine city of Tours is celebrating; *pour autres loc voir* **son¹**

2 *(valeur affective, ironique, intensive)* **et comment va ~ malade aujourd'hui ?** and how's the *ou* our patient today? ◆ **~ héros décide alors ...** and so our hero decides ... ◆ **~ homme a filé sans demander son reste** the fellow *ou* chap (Brit) has run off without asking for his due ◆ **voilà ~ bon Martin !** here's good old Martin! ◆ **~ maître** *(dial)* the master; → **son¹**

3 *(représentant la généralité des hommes)* **~ planète** our planet ◆ **~ corps/esprit** our bodies/minds ◆ **~ maître à tous** our master, the master of us all ◆ **Notre Seigneur/Père** Our Lord/Father ◆ **Notre-Dame** Our Lady; *(église)* Notre Dame, Our Lady ◆ **Notre-Dame de Paris** *(cathédrale)* Notre Dame of Paris ◆ **Notre-Dame de Chartres/Lourdes** Our Lady of Chartres/Lourdes ◆ **le Notre Père** the Lord's Prayer, Our Father

4 *(de majesté, dans un discours etc = mon, ma, mes)* our ◆ **car tel est ~ bon plaisir** for such is our wish, for so it pleases us ◆ **dans cet exposé ~ intention est de ...** in this essay we intend to ...

nôtre /notʀ/ PRON POSS ◆ **le ~, la ~, les ~s** ours ◆ **cette voiture n'est pas la ~** this car is not ours, this is not our car ◆ **leurs enfants sont sortis avec les ~s** their children are out with ours ◆ **à la (bonne) ~ !** our good health!, here's to us!; *pour autres loc voir* **sien** NM 1 ◆ **nous y mettrons du ~** we'll do our bit*; → aussi **sien** 2 ◆ **les ~s** *(= famille)* our family, our folks*; *(= partisans)* our own people ◆ **j'espère que vous serez des ~s ce soir** I hope you will join our party *ou* join us tonight ◆ **il est des ~s** he's one of us ADJ POSS *(littér)* ours, our own ◆ **ces idées ne sont plus exclusivement ~s** these ideas are no longer ours alone *ou* exclusively ◆ **ces principes, nous les avons faits ~s** we have made these principles our own

Nouakchott /nwakʃɔt/ N Nouakchott

nouba* /nuba/ NF ◆ **faire la ~** to live it up*, to have a rave-up* (Brit)

nouer /nwe/ ► conjug 1 ◄ VT 1 *(= faire un nœud avec)* *[+ ficelle]* to tie, to knot; *[+ lacets, foulard, ceinture]* to tie; *[+ cravate]* to knot, to fasten ◆ **~ les bras autour de la taille de qn** to put one's arms round sb's waist ◆ **l'émotion lui nouait la gorge** his throat was tight with emotion ◆ **avoir la gorge nouée (par l'émotion)** to have a lump in one's throat ◆ **j'ai l'estomac noué** my stomach is in knots

2 *(= entourer d'une ficelle)* *[+ bouquet, paquet]* to tie up, to do up; *[+ cheveux]* to tie up *ou* back

3 *(= former)* *[+ complot]* to hatch; *[+ alliance]* to make, to form; *[+ relations]* to strike up; *[+ amitié]* to form, to build up ◆ **~ conversation avec qn** to start (up) *ou* strike up a conversation with sb

4 *(Tissage)* **~ la chaîne/la trame** to splice the warp/weft

5 *(Littérat)* *[+ action, intrigue]* to build up

VI *(Bot)* to set

VPR **se nouer** 1 *(= s'unir)* *[mains]* to join together ◆ **sa gorge se noua** a lump came to his throat

2 *(= se former)* *[complot]* to be hatched; *[alliance]* to be made, to be formed; *[amitié]* to be formed, to build up; *[conversation]* to start, to be started

3 *(pièce de théâtre)* **c'est là où l'intrigue se noue** it's at that point that the plot takes shape *ou* develops

noueux, -euse /nwø, øz/ ADJ *[branche]* knotty, gnarled; *[main]* gnarled; *[vieillard]* wizened

nougat /nuga/ NM *(Culin)* nougat ◆ **~s*** *(= pieds)* feet ◆ **c'est du ~*** it's dead easy*, it's a cinch* *ou* a piece of cake* ◆ **c'est pas du ~*** it's not so easy

nougatine /nugatin/ NF nougatine

nouille /nuj/ NF 1 *(Culin)* piece *ou* bit of pasta ◆ **~s** *(gén)* pasta; *(en rubans)* noodles ◆ **~s chinoises** Chinese noodles ◆ **style ~** *(Art)* Art Nouveau 2 * *(= imbécile)* idiot, noodle* *(Brit)*; *(= mollasson)* big lump* ◆ **ce que c'est ~*** how idiotic (it is)

noumène /numɛn/ NM noumenon

nounou* /nunu/ NF nanny

nounours /nunuʀs/ NM teddy (bear)

nourri, e /nuʀi/ (ptp de **nourrir**) ADJ *[fusillade]* heavy; *[applaudissements]* hearty, prolonged; *[conversation]* lively; *[style]* rich ◆ **tirs ~s** heavy *ou* sustained gunfire

nourrice /nuʀis/ NF 1 *(= gardienne)* childminder, nanny; *(qui allaite)* wet nurse ◆ **~ sèche** † dry nurse ◆ **~ agréée** registered childminder ◆ **mettre un enfant en ~** to put a child in the care of a nurse *ou* out to nurse *(Brit)* ◆ **prendre un enfant en ~** to act as nurse to a child; → **épingle** 2 *(= bidon)* jerry can *(Brit)*, can *(US)* 3 *(= abeille)* nurse bee

nourricier, -ière /nuʀisje, jɛʀ/ ADJ *(Anat)* *[canal, artère]* nutrient; *(Bot)* *[suc, sève]* nutritive; *(† = adoptif)* *[mère, père]* foster *(épith)* ◆ **la terre nourricière** *(littér)* the nourishing earth NM *(† = père adoptif)* foster father ◆ **les ~s** the foster parents

nourrir /nuʀiʀ/ ▸ conjug 2 ◂ VT 1 *(= alimenter)* *[+ animal, personne]* to feed; *[+ feu]* to stoke; *[+ récit, devoir]* to fill out; *[+ cuir, peau]* to nourish ◆ **~ au biberon** to bottle-feed ◆ **~ au sein** to breast-feed, to nurse ◆ **~ à la cuiller** to spoon-feed ◆ **~ un oiseau au grain** to feed a bird (on) seed ◆ **les régions qui nourrissent la capitale** the areas which provide food for the capital *ou* provide the capital with food ◆ **bien/mal nourri** well-/poorly-fed; → **logé**

2 *(= faire vivre)* *[+ famille, pays]* to feed, to provide for ◆ **cette entreprise nourrit 10 000 ouvriers** this firm provides work for 10,000 workers ◆ **ce métier ne nourrit pas son homme** this job doesn't give a man a living wage

3 *(= caresser)* *[+ désir, espoir, illusion]* to have, to cherish; *[+ haine, rancune]* to feel; *[+ vengeance]* to harbour *(Brit)* *ou* harbor *(US)* thoughts of ◆ **~ le projet de faire qch** to plan to do sth

4 *(littér = former)* **être nourri dans les bons principes** to be nurtured on good principles ◆ **la lecture nourrit l'esprit** reading improves the mind

VI to be nourishing

VPR **se nourrir** to eat ◆ **se ~ de** *[+ aliments]* to feed (o.s.) on, to eat; *[+ illusions]* to feed on, to live on ◆ **il se nourrit de romans** *(fig)* novels are his staple diet

nourrissant, e /nuʀisɑ̃, ɑt/ ADJ *[aliment]* nourishing, nutritious; *[crème, cosmétique]* nourishing *(épith)*

nourrisson /nuʀisɔ̃/ NM (unweaned) infant, nursling *(littér)*

nourriture /nuʀityʀ/ NF 1 *(= aliments, fig)* food ◆ **assurer la ~ de qn** to provide sb's meals *ou* sb with food 2 *(= alimentation)* food ◆ **il lui faut une ~ saine** he needs a healthy diet ◆ **il ne supporte aucune ~ solide** he can't take solids ◆ **~ pour animaux** *(de compagnie)* pet food; *(de ferme)* animal feed ◆ **la lecture est une bonne ~ pour l'esprit** reading is good nourishment for the mind

nous /nu/ PRON PERS 1 *(sujet)* we ◆ **~ vous écrirons** we'll write to you ◆ **~ avons bien ri tous les deux** the two of us had a good laugh, we both had a good laugh ◆ **eux ont accepté, ~ non** *ou* **pas** ~ they accepted but we didn't, they accepted but not us* ◆ **c'est enfin ~, ~ voilà enfin** here we are at last ◆ **qui l'a vu ? – ~/pas ~** who saw him? – we did/we didn't *ou* us/not us* ◆ **~, accepter ? jamais !** us accept that? never!, you expect us to accept that?, never!; → aussi **même**

2 *(objet)* us ◆ **aide-~** help us, give us a hand ◆ **donne-~ ton livre** give us your book, give your book to us ◆ **si vous étiez ~ que feriez-vous ?** if you were us *ou* if you were in our shoes what would you do? ◆ **donne-le-~** give it to us, give us it ◆ **écoutez-~** listen to us ◆ **il n'obéit qu'à ~** we are the only ones he obeys, he obeys only us

3 *(insistance, sujet)* we, we ourselves; *(objet)* us ◆ **~, ~ le connaissons bien – mais ~ aussi** we know him well ourselves – but so do we *ou* we do too ◆ **pourquoi ne le ferait-il pas ?, ~ l'avons bien fait, ~** why shouldn't he do it?, we did it (all right) ◆ **alors ~, restons pour compte ?** and what about us, are we to be left out? ◆ **~, elle ~ déteste** she hates us ◆ **elle ~ connaît bien, ~** she knows us all right

4 *(emphatique avec qui, que, sujet)* we; *(objet)* us ◆ **c'est ~ qui sommes fautifs** we are the culprits, we are the ones to blame ◆ **merci – c'est ~ qui vous remercions** thank you – it's we who should thank you ◆ **et ~ (tous) qui vous parlons l'avons vu** we (all) saw him personally ◆ **est-ce ~ qui devons vous le dire ?** do we have to tell you?, are we the ones to have to tell you? ◆ **et ~ qui n'avions pas le sou !** and there were we without a penny!, and to think we didn't have a penny! ◆ **~ que le théâtre passionne, ~ n'avons jamais vu cette pièce** great theatre lovers that we are we've still never seen that play, even we with our great love for the theatre have never seen that play ◆ **il ~ dit cela à ~ qui l'avons tant aidé** and that's what he says to us who have helped him so much ◆ **c'est ~ qu'elle veut voir** it's us she wants to see

5 *(avec prép)* us ◆ **à ~ cinq, ~ devrions pouvoir soulever ça** between the five of us we should be able to lift that ◆ **cette maison est à ~** this house belongs to us *ou* is ours ◆ **~ avons une maison à ~** we have a house of our own, we have our own house ◆ **avec/sans ~** with/without us ◆ **c'est à ~ de décider** it's up to us *ou* for us to decide ◆ **elle l'a appris par ~** she heard about it through *ou* from us ◆ **un élève à ~** one of our pupils ◆ **l'un de ~** *ou* **d'entre ~ doit le savoir** one of us must know (it) ◆ **nos enfants à ~** our children ◆ **l'idée vient de ~** the idea comes from us *ou* is ours ◆ **elle veut une photo de ~ tous** she wants a photo of us all *ou* of all of us

6 *(dans comparaisons)* we, us ◆ **il est aussi fort que ~** he is as strong as we are *ou* as us ◆ **il mange plus/moins que ~** he eats more/less than we do *ou* than us ◆ **faites comme ~** do as we do, do the same as us ◆ **il vous connaît aussi bien que ~** *(aussi bien que nous vous connaissons)* he knows you as well as we do *ou* as us; *(aussi bien qu'il nous connaît)* he knows you as well as (he knows) us

7 *(avec vpr)* **~ ~ sommes bien amusés** we had a good time, we thoroughly enjoyed ourselves ◆ **(lui et moi) ~ ~ connaissons depuis le lycée** we have known each other since we were at school ◆ **~ ~ détestons** we hate (the sight of) each other ◆ **asseyons-~ donc** let's sit down, shall we sit down? ◆ **~ ~ écrirons** we'll write to each other

8 *(pl de majesté, dans discours etc = moi)* we ◆ **~, préfet des Yvelines, décidons que** we, (the) prefect of the Yvelines, decide that ◆ **dans cet exposé, ~ essaierons d'expliquer** in this paper, we shall try to explain

NM ◆ **le ~ de majesté** the royal we

nous-même (pl **nous-mêmes**) /numɛm/ PRON → **même**

nouveau, nouvelle[1] /nuvo, nuvɛl/ GRAMMAIRE ACTIVE 48.1, 48.2 (devant nm commençant par une voyelle ou h muet **nouvel**, mpl **nouveaux**)

ADJ 1 *(gén après nom = qui apparaît pour la première fois)* new ◆ **pommes de terre nouvelles** new potatoes ◆ **vin ~** new wine ◆ **carottes nouvelles** spring carrots ◆ **la mode nouvelle** the latest fashion ◆ **la mode nouvelle du printemps** the new spring fashions ◆ **un sentiment si ~ pour moi** such a new feeling for me ◆ **montrez-moi le chemin, je suis ~ ici** show me the way, I'm new here ◆ **ce rôle est ~ pour lui** this is a new role for him ◆ **tout ~ tout beau*** (just) wait till the novelty wears off; → **art, quoi**

2 *(après nom = original)* *[idée]* novel, new, original; *[style]* new, original; *(= moderne)* *[méthode]* new, up-to-date, new-fangled *(péj)* ◆ **le dernier de ses romans, et le plus ~** his latest and most original novel ◆ **présenter qch sous un jour ~** to present sth in a new light ◆ **c'est tout ~, ce projet** this project is brand-new ◆ **il n'y a rien de/ce n'est pas ~ !** there's/it's nothing new!

3 *(= inexpérimenté)* new *(en, dans* to); ◆ **il est ~ en affaires** he's new to business

4 *(avant nom = qui succède)* new ◆ **le ~ président** the new president, the newly-elected president ◆ **le nouvel élu** the newly-elected representative ◆ **nous avons un ~ président/une nouvelle voiture** we have a new president/car ◆ **avez-vous lu son ~ livre ?** have you read his new *ou* latest book? ◆ **un ~ Napoléon** a second Napoleon ◆ **les ~x philosophes** the new philosophers ◆ **les ~x pauvres** the new poor ◆ **les ~x parents** today's parents, the parents of today ◆ **il y a eu un ~ tremblement de terre** there has been a further *ou* another earthquake ◆ **je ferai un nouvel essai** I'll make another *ou* a new *ou* a fresh attempt ◆ **il y eut un ~ silence** there was another silence ◆ **c'est la nouvelle mode maintenant** it's the new fashion now; → **jusque**

5 *(= qui s'ajoute)* new, fresh ◆ **c'est là une nouvelle preuve que** it's fresh proof *ou* further proof that ◆ **avec une ardeur/énergie nouvelle** with renewed ardour/energy

NM 1 *(= homme)* new man; *(Scol)* new boy

2 *(= nouveauté)* **y a-t-il du ~ à ce sujet ?** is there anything new on this? ◆ **il y a du ~ dans cette affaire** there has been a fresh *ou* new *ou* further development in this business ◆ **le public veut sans cesse du ~** the public always wants something new ◆ **il n'y a rien de ~ sous le soleil** there's nothing new under the sun

3 *(= encore)* **de ~** again ◆ **faire qch de ~** to do sth again, to repeat sth ◆ **à ~** *(= d'une manière différente)* anew, afresh, again; *(= encore une fois)* again ◆ **nous examinerons la question à ~** we'll examine the question anew *ou* afresh *ou* again

NF **nouvelle** *(= femme)* new woman *ou* girl; *(Scol)* new girl; → aussi **nouvelle**[2]

COMP **Nouvel An, Nouvelle Année** New Year ◆ **pour le/au Nouvel An** for/at New Year ◆ **le Nouvel An juif/chinois** the Jewish/Chinese New Year

nouvelle cuisine nouvelle cuisine

nouvelle lune new moon

nouveaux mariés newlyweds, newly married couple

Nouveau Monde New World

nouveaux pays industrialisés newly industrialized countries

nouveau riche nouveau riche

le nouveau roman *(Littérat)* the nouveau roman
le Nouveau Testament the New Testament
Nouvelle Vague *(Ciné)* New Wave, Nouvelle Vague
nouveau venu, nouvelle venue NM,F newcomer (*à, dans* to)

Nouveau-Brunswick /nuvobʀœsvik/ NM New Brunswick

Nouveau-Mexique /nuvomeksik/ NM New Mexico

nouveau-né, nouveau-née (mpl **nouveau-nés**, fpl **nouveau-nées**) /nuvone/ ADJ newborn NM,F (= *enfant*) newborn child; (= *dernière création*) newest *ou* latest model ◆ **les ~s de notre gamme de jouets** the newest *ou* latest additions to our range of toys

nouveauté /nuvote/ NF 1 (= *objet*) new thing *ou* article ◆ **les ~s du mois** (= *disques*) the month's new releases; (= *livres*) the month's new titles ◆ **les ~s du salon** (= *machines, voitures*) the new models on display at the show ◆ **la grande ~ de cet automne** the latest thing this autumn 2 *(Habillement)* **~s de printemps** new spring fashions ◆ **le commerce de la ~** † the fashion trade ◆ **magasin de ~s** † draper's shop *(Brit)*, fabric store *(US)* 3 (= *caractère nouveau*) novelty, newness; (= *originalité*) novelty; (= *chose*) new thing, something new ◆ **il n'aime pas la ~** he hates anything new *ou* new ideas, he hates change ◆ **il travaille ? c'est une ~ !** he's working? that's new! ◆ **il boit – ce n'est pas une ~ !** he's drinking too much – that's nothing new!

nouvel /nuvɛl/ ADJ M → **nouveau**

nouvelle² /nuvɛl/ NF 1 (= *écho*) news *(NonC)* ◆ **une ~** a piece of news ◆ **une bonne/mauvaise ~** some good/bad news ◆ **la ~ de cet événement nous a surpris** we were surprised by the news of this event ◆ **ce n'est pas une ~ !** that's not news!, that's nothing new! ◆ **vous connaissez la ~ ?** have you heard the news? ◆ **première ~ !** that's the first I've heard about it!, it's news to me!; → **faux²**
2 ◆ **~s** news *(NonC)* ◆ **quelles ~s ?*** what's new?, what's been happening? ◆ **aller aux ~s** to go and find out what is happening ◆ **voici les dernières ~s concernant l'accident** here is the latest news of the accident, here is an up-to-the-minute report on the accident ◆ **aux dernières ~s, il était à Paris** the last I (*ou* we *etc*) heard (of him) he was in Paris ◆ **avez-vous de ses ~s ?** *(de sa propre main)* have you heard from him?, have you had any news from him?; (= *par un tiers*) have you heard anything about *ou* of him?, have you had any news of him? ◆ **j'irai prendre de ses ~s** I'll go and see how he's doing *ou* how he's getting along *ou* on *(Brit)* ◆ **il a fait prendre de mes ~s (par qn)** he asked for news of me (from sb) ◆ **il ne donne plus de ses ~s** you never hear from him any more ◆ **je suis sans ~s (de lui) depuis huit jours** I haven't heard anything (of him) for a week, I've had no news (of him) for a week ◆ **pas de ~s, bonnes ~s** no news is good news ◆ **il aura** *ou* **entendra de mes ~s !*** I'll give him a piece of my mind!, I'll give him what for!* ◆ **goûtez mon vin, vous m'en direz des ~s*** taste my wine, I'm sure you'll like it
3 *(Presse, Radio, TV)* **les ~s** the news *(NonC)* ◆ **écouter/entendre les ~s** to listen to/hear the news ◆ **voici les ~s** here is the news ◆ **les ~s sont bonnes** the news is good
4 (= *court récit*) short story

Nouvelle-Angleterre /nuvɛlɑ̃glətɛʀ/ NF New England

Nouvelle-Calédonie /nuvɛlkaledɔni/ NF New Caledonia

Nouvelle-Écosse /nuvɛlekɔs/ NF Nova Scotia

Nouvelle-Guinée /nuvɛlgine/ NF New Guinea

nouvellement /nuvɛlmɑ̃/ ADV newly

Nouvelle-Orléans /nuvɛlɔʀleɑ̃/ NF New Orleans

Nouvelles-Galles du Sud /nuvɛlgaldysyd/ NF New South Wales

Nouvelles-Hébrides /nuvɛlzebʀid/ NFPL ◆ **les ~** the New Hebrides

Nouvelle-Zélande /nuvɛlzelɑ̃d/ NF New Zealand

nouvelliste /nuvelist/ NMF short story writer, writer of short stories

nova /nɔva/ (pl **novæ** /nɔve/) NF nova

novateur, -trice /nɔvatœʀ, tʀis/ ADJ innovatory, innovative NM,F innovator

novation /nɔvasjɔ̃/ NF 1 *(frm* = *nouveauté)* innovation 2 *(Jur)* novation

novélisation, novellisation /nɔvelizasjɔ̃/ NF novelization

novembre /nɔvɑ̃bʀ/ NM November; *pour autres loc voir* **septembre** *et* **onze**

novice /nɔvis/ ADJ inexperienced (*dans* in) green* (*dans* at) NMF (= *débutant*) novice, beginner, greenhorn*; *(Rel)* novice, probationer ◆ **être ~ en affaires** to be a novice in business matters

noviciat /nɔvisja/ NM (= *bâtiment, période*) noviciate, novitiate ◆ **de ~** *(Rel)* probationary

Novocaïne ® /nɔvɔkain/ NF Novocaine ®

noyade /nwajad/ NF drowning; (= *événement*) drowning accident, death by drowning ◆ **il y a eu de nombreuses ~s à cet endroit** many people have drowned *ou* there have been many deaths by drowning at this spot ◆ **sauver qn de la ~** to save sb from drowning

noyau (pl **noyaux**) /nwajo/ NM 1 *[de fruit]* stone, pit; *(Astron, Bio, Phys)* nucleus; *(Géol)* core; *(Ling)* kernel, nucleus; *(Ordin)* kernel; *(Art)* centre, core; *(Élec)* core *(of induction coil etc)*; *(Constr)* newel ◆ **enlevez les ~x** remove the stones (from the fruit), pit the fruit 2 (= *groupe humain*) nucleus; (= *groupe de fidèles*) small circle; (= *groupe de manifestants, d'opposants*) small group ◆ **~ de résistance** hard core *ou* pocket of resistance ◆ **~ dur** *(Écon)* hard core shareholders; *[de groupe]* (= *irréductibles*) hard core; (= *éléments essentiels*) kernel ◆ **le ~ familial** the family unit

noyautage /nwajotaʒ/ NM *(Pol)* infiltration

noyauter /nwajote/ ► conjug 1 ◄ VT *(Pol)* to infiltrate

noyé, e /nwaje/ (ptp de **noyer²**) ADJ ◆ **être ~** (= *ne pas comprendre*) to be out of one's depth, to be all at sea (*en* in) NM,F drowned person ◆ **il y a eu beaucoup de ~s ici** a lot of people have drowned here

noyer¹ /nwaje/ NM (= *arbre*) walnut (tree); (= *bois*) walnut

noyer² /nwaje/ ► conjug 8 ◄ VT 1 *(gén)* *[+ personne, animal, flamme]* to drown; *[+ moteur]* to flood ◆ **la crue a noyé les champs** the high water has flooded *ou* drowned *ou* swamped the fields ◆ **il avait les yeux noyés de larmes** his eyes were brimming *ou* swimming with tears ◆ **ils ont noyé la révolte dans le sang** they quelled the revolt with much bloodshed ◆ **~ la poudre** *(Mil)* to wet the powder ◆ **~ son chagrin dans l'alcool** to drown one's sorrows ◆ **~ le poisson** *(fig)* to evade the issue, to duck *ou* sidestep the question ◆ **qui veut ~ son chien l'accuse de la rage** *(Prov)* give a dog a bad name and hang him *(Prov)*
2 *(gén pass* = *perdre)* **~ qn sous un déluge d'explications** to swamp sb with explanations ◆ **quelques bonnes idées noyées dans des détails inutiles** a few good ideas lost in *ou* buried in *ou* swamped by a mass of irrelevant detail ◆ **être noyé dans l'obscurité/la brume** to be shrouded in darkness/mist ◆ **être noyé dans la foule** to be lost in the crowd ◆ **noyé dans la masse, ce détail architectural était passé inaperçu** this architectural detail went unnoticed because it was surrounded by so many other features ◆ **cette dépense ne se verra pas, noyée dans la masse** this expense won't be noticed when it's lumped *ou* put together with the rest ◆ **ses paroles furent noyées par** *ou* **dans le vacarme** his words were drowned in the din
3 *(Culin)* *[+ alcool, vin]* to water down; *[+ sauce]* to thin too much, to make too thin
4 *(Tech)* *[+ clou]* to drive right in; *[+ pilier]* to embed ◆ **noyé dans la masse** embedded
5 (= *effacer*) *[+ contours, couleur]* to blur
VPR **se noyer** 1 *(lit)* *(accidentellement)* to drown; *(volontairement)* to drown o.s. ◆ **une personne qui se noie** a drowning person ◆ **il s'est noyé** *(accidentellement)* he drowned *ou* was drowned; *(volontairement)* he drowned himself
2 *(fig)* **se ~ dans un raisonnement** to become tangled up *ou* bogged down in an argument ◆ **se ~ dans les détails** to get bogged down in details ◆ **se ~ dans la foule/dans la nuit** to disappear into the crowd/the night ◆ **se ~ dans un verre d'eau** to make a mountain out of a molehill, to make heavy weather of the simplest thing ◆ **se ~ l'estomac** to overfill one's stomach *(by drinking too much liquid)*

NPI /ɛnpei/ NMPL (abrév de **nouveaux pays industrialisés**) NIC

N.-S. J.-C. abrév de **Notre-Seigneur Jésus-Christ**

NU NFPL (abrév de **Nations Unies**) UN

nu¹, e¹ /ny/ ADJ 1 *[personne]* naked, nude; *[torse, membres]* naked; *[crâne]* bald ◆ **~-pieds, (les) pieds ~s** barefoot, with bare feet ◆ **aller pieds ~s** *ou* **~-pieds** to go barefoot(ed) ◆ **~-tête, (la) tête ~e** bareheaded ◆ **~-jambes, (les) jambes ~es** barelegged, with bare legs ◆ **(les) bras ~s** barearmed, with bare arms ◆ **(le) torse ~, ~ jusqu'à la ceinture** stripped to the waist, naked from the waist up ◆ **à moitié** *ou* **à demi ~** half-naked ◆ **il est ~ comme un ver** *ou* **comme la main** he is as naked as the day he was born ◆ **tout ~** stark naked ◆ **ne reste pas tout ~ !** put something on! ◆ **se mettre ~** to strip (off), to take one's clothes off ◆ **se montrer ~ à l'écran** to appear in the nude on the screen ◆ **poser ~** to pose nude; → **épée, main, œil**
2 *[mur, chambre]* bare; *[arbre, pays, plaine]* bare, naked; *[style]* plain; *[vérité]* plain, naked; *[fil électrique]* bare
3 *[mollusque, souris]* naked
4 *(locutions)* **mettre à ~** *[+ fil électrique]* to strip; *[+ erreurs, vices]* to expose, to lay bare ◆ **mettre son cœur à ~** to lay bare one's heart *ou* soul
NM *(Peinture, Photo)* nude ◆ **album de ~s** album of nude photographs ◆ **le ~ intégral** full frontal nudity

nu² /ny/ NM INV (= *lettre grecque*) nu

nuage /nɥaʒ/ NM *(lit, fig)* cloud ◆ **~ de grêle/de pluie** hail/rain cloud ◆ **~ de fumée/de tulle/de poussière/de sauterelles** cloud of smoke/tulle/dust/locusts ◆ **~ radioactif** radioactive cloud ◆ **~ de points** *(Math)* scatter of points ◆ **il y a des ~s noirs à l'horizon** *(lit, fig)* there are dark clouds on the horizon ◆ **le ciel se couvre de ~s/est couvert de ~s** the sky is clouding over/has clouded over ◆ **juste un ~ (de lait)** just a drop (of milk) ◆ **il est (perdu) dans les ~s, il vit sur son petit ~** he's got his head in the clouds ◆ **sans ~s** *[ciel]* cloudless; *[bonheur]* unmarred, unclouded ◆ **une amitié qui n'est pas sans ~s** a friendship which is not entirely untroubled *ou* quarrelfree; → **Magellan**

nuageux, -euse /nɥaʒø, øz/ ADJ ① *[temps]* cloudy; *[ciel]* cloudy, overcast; *[zone, bande]* cloud *(épith)* ◆ **système ~** cloud system ◆ **couche nuageuse** layer of cloud ② *(= vague)* nebulous, hazy

nuance /nɥɑ̃s/ NF ① *[de couleur]* shade, hue; *(Littérat, Mus)* nuance ◆ **~ de sens** shade of meaning, nuance ◆ **~ de style** nuance of style ◆ **~ politique** shade of political opinion ◆ **de toutes les ~s politiques** of all shades of political opinion
② *(= différence)* slight difference ◆ **il y a une ~ entre mentir et se taire** there's a slight difference between lying and keeping quiet ◆ **je ne lui ai pas dit non, je lui ai dit peut-être, ~ !** I didn't say no to him, I said perhaps, and there's a difference between the two! ◆ **tu vois** *ou* **saisis la ~ ?** do you see the difference?
③ *(= subtilité, variation)* **apporter des ~s à une affirmation** to qualify a statement ◆ **faire ressortir les ~s** to bring out the finer *ou* subtler points ◆ **tout en ~s** *[esprit, discours, personne]* very subtle, full of nuances ◆ **sans ~** *[discours]* unsubtle, cut and dried; *[esprit, personne]* unsubtle
④ *(= petit élément)* touch, hint ◆ **avec une ~ de tristesse** with a touch *ou* a hint *ou* a slight note of sadness

nuancé, e /nɥɑ̃se/ (ptp de **nuancer**) ADJ *[opinion]* qualified; *[attitude, réponse]* balanced; *(Mus)* nuanced ◆ **il dresse un portrait** *ou* **un tableau ~ de cette époque** he gives a well-balanced account of the period ◆ **ironie ~e d'amertume** irony with a tinge *ou* a note *ou* a hint of bitterness

nuancer /nɥɑ̃se/ ► conjug 3 ◄ VT *[+ tableau, couleur]* to shade; *[+ opinion]* to qualify; *(Mus)* to nuance

nuancier /nɥɑ̃sje/ NM colour *(Brit)* *ou* color *(US)* chart

Nubie /nybi/ NF Nubia

nubien, -ienne /nybjɛ̃, jɛn/ ADJ *[personne]* Nubian; *[région]* of Nubia NM,F **Nubien(ne)** Nubian

nubile /nybil/ ADJ nubile

nubilité /nybilite/ NF nubility

nubuck /nybyk/ NM nubuck ◆ **en ~** nubuck *(épith)*

nucléaire /nykleɛʀ/ ADJ nuclear NM ◆ **le ~** *(= énergie)* nuclear energy; *(= technologie)* nuclear technology

nucléarisation /nykleaʀizasjɔ̃/ NF *[de pays]* nuclearization, equipping with nuclear weapons

nucléariser /nykleaʀize/ ► conjug 1 ◄ VT *[+ pays]* *(en armes)* to equip with nuclear weapons; *(en énergie)* to equip with nuclear energy

nucléé, e /nyklee/ ADJ nucleate(d)

nucléide /nykleid/ NM nuclide

nucléine /nyklein/ NF nuclein

nucléique /nykleik/ ADJ nucleic

nucléon /nykleɔ̃/ NM nucleon

nucléosynthèse /nykleosɛ̃tɛz/ NF nucleosynthesis

nucléotide /nykleɔtid/ NM nucleotide

nudisme /nydism/ NM nudism ◆ **faire du ~** to practise nudism

nudiste /nydist/ ADJ, NMF nudist ◆ **plage/camp de ~s** nudist beach/camp

nudité /nydite/ NF *[de personne]* nakedness, nudity; *[de mur]* bareness; *(Art)* nude ◆ **la laideur des gens s'étale dans toute sa ~** people are exposed in all their ugliness, people's ugliness is laid bare for all to see

nue² /ny/ NF ① († † *ou littér*) **~(s)** *(= nuage)* clouds ◆ **la ~, les ~s** *(= ciel)* the skies ② ◆ **porter** *ou* **mettre qn aux ~s** to praise sb to the skies ◆ **tomber des ~s** to be completely taken aback *ou* flabbergasted ◆ **je suis tombé des ~s** you could have knocked me down with a feather, I was completely taken aback

nuée /nɥe/ NF ① *(littér = nuage)* thick cloud ◆ **~s d'orage** storm clouds ◆ **~ ardente** nuée ardente, glowing cloud ② *(= multitude) [d'insectes]* cloud, horde; *[de flèches]* cloud; *[de photographes, spectateurs, ennemis]* horde, host ◆ **comme une ~ de sauterelles** *(fig)* like a plague *ou* swarm of locusts

nue-propriété /nypʀɔpʀijete/ NF ownership without usufruct ◆ **avoir un bien en ~** to have property without usufruct

nuer /nɥe/ ► conjug 1 ◄ VT *(littér)* *[+ couleurs]* to blend *ou* match the different shades of

nuire /nɥiʀ/ ► conjug 38 ◄ VT INDIR **nuire à** *(= desservir)* *[+ personne]* to harm, to injure; *[+ santé, réputation]* to damage, to harm; *[+ action]* to prejudice ◆ **sa laideur lui nuit beaucoup** his ugliness is very much against him *ou* is a great disadvantage to him ◆ **il a voulu le faire mais ça va lui ~** he wanted to do it, but it will go against him *ou* it will do him harm ◆ **chercher à ~ à qn** to try to harm sb, to try to do *ou* run sb down ◆ **cela risque de ~ à nos projets** there's a risk that it will spoil our plans ◆ **un petit whisky, ça peut pas ~ !*** a little glass of whisky won't hurt you! *ou* won't do you any harm! VPR **se nuire** *(à soi-même)* to do o.s. a lot of harm; *(l'un l'autre)* to work against each other's interests, to harm each other

nuisance /nɥizɑ̃s/ NF *(gén pl)* (environmental) pollution *(NonC)* *ou* nuisance *(NonC)* ◆ **les ~s (sonores)** noise pollution

nuisette /nɥizɛt/ NF very short nightdress *ou* nightie*

nuisible /nɥizibl/ ADJ *[climat, temps]* harmful, injurious *(à* to); *[influence, gaz]* harmful, noxious *(à* to); ◆ **animaux ~s** vermin, pests ◆ **insectes ~s** pests ◆ **~ à la santé** harmful *ou* injurious to (the) health

nuit /nɥi/ NF ① *(= obscurité)* darkness, night ◆ **il fait ~** it's dark ◆ **il fait ~ à 5 heures** it gets dark at 5 o'clock ◆ **il fait ~ noire** it's pitch dark *ou* black ◆ **une ~ d'encre** a pitch dark *ou* black night ◆ **la ~ tombe** it's getting dark, night is falling ◆ **à la ~ tombante** at nightfall, at dusk ◆ **pris ou surpris par la ~** overtaken by darkness *ou* night ◆ **rentrer avant la ~/à la ~** to come home before dark/in the dark ◆ **la ~ polaire** the polar night *ou* darkness ◆ **la ~ tous les chats sont gris** *(Prov)* everyone looks the same *ou* all cats are grey in the dark
② *(= espace de temps)* night ◆ **cette ~** *(passée)* last night; *(qui vient)* tonight ◆ **j'ai passé la ~ chez eux** I spent the night at their house ◆ **dans la ~ de jeudi** during Thursday night ◆ **dans la ~ de jeudi à vendredi** during the night of Thursday to Friday ◆ **souhaiter (une) bonne ~ à qn** to wish sb goodnight ◆ **~ blanche** *ou* **sans sommeil** sleepless night ◆ **~ d'amour** night of love ◆ **leur bébé fait ses ~s*** their baby sleeps right through the night ◆ **~ et jour** night and day ◆ **au milieu de la ~, en pleine ~** in the middle of the night, at dead of night ◆ **elle part cette ~** *ou* **dans la ~** she's leaving tonight ◆ **ouvert la ~** open at night ◆ **sortir/travailler la ~** to go out/work at night ◆ **la ~ porte conseil** *(Prov)* it's best to sleep on it ◆ **de ~** *[service, travail, garde, infirmière]* night *(épith)* ◆ **elle est de ~ cette semaine** she's on nights *ou* she's working nights this week ◆ **voyager de ~** to travel by night ◆ **conduire de ~ ne me gêne pas** I don't mind night-driving *ou* driving at night
③ *(littér)* darkness ◆ **dans la ~ de ses souvenirs** in the darkness of his memories ◆ **ça se perd dans la ~ des temps** it's lost in the mists of time ◆ **ça remonte à la ~ des temps** that goes back to the dawn of time, that's as old as the hills ◆ **la ~ du tombeau/de la mort** the darkness of the grave/of death

COMP **nuit américaine** day for night
nuit bleue night of bombings
nuit d'hôtel night spent in a hotel room, overnight stay in a hotel ◆ **payer sa ~ d'hôtel** to pay one's hotel bill
la Nuit des longs couteaux *(Hist)* the Night of the Long Knives
nuit de noces wedding night
nuit de Noël Christmas Eve
la nuit des Rois Twelfth Night

nuitamment /nɥitamɑ̃/ ADV *(frm)* by night

nuitée /nɥite/ NF *(Tourisme)* night ◆ **trois ~s** three nights (in a hotel room)

Nuku'alofa /nukualɔfa/ N Nuku'alofa

nul, nulle /nyl/ ADJ INDÉF ① *(devant nom = aucun)* no ◆ **il n'avait ~ besoin/nulle envie de sortir** he had no need/no desire to go out at all ◆ **~ doute qu'elle ne l'ait vu** there is no doubt (whatsoever) that she saw him ◆ **~ autre que lui (n'aurait pu le faire)** no one (else) but he (could have done it) ◆ **sans ~ doute/nulle exception** without any doubt/any exception
② *(après nom)* *(= proche de zéro)* *[résultat, différence, risque]* nil *(attrib)*; *(= invalidé)* *[testament, élection, bulletin de vote]* null and void *(attrib)*; *(= inexistant)* *[récolte]* non-existent ◆ **pour toute valeur non nulle de x** *(Math)* where x is not equal to zero ◆ **~ et non avenu** *(Jur)* invalid, null and void ◆ **rendre ~** *(Jur, fig)* to annul, to nullify ◆ **nombre ~/non-~** zero/non-zero number
③ *(Sport)* **le résultat** *ou* **le score est ~** *(pour l'instant)* there's no score; *(en fin de match)* *(= 0 à 0)* the match has ended in a nil draw; *(= 2 à 2 etc)* the match has ended in a draw; → **match**
④ *(= qui ne vaut rien)* *[film, livre, personne]* useless, hopeless; *[intelligence]* nil; *[travail]* worthless, useless ◆ **être ~ en géographie** to be hopeless *ou* useless at geography ◆ **il est ~ pour** *ou* **dans tout ce qui est manuel** he's hopeless *ou* useless at anything manual ◆ **ce devoir est ~** this piece of work is worth nothing *ou* doesn't deserve any marks ◆ **c'est ~ de lui avoir dit ça*** it was really stupid to tell him that
NM,F * idiot
PRON INDÉF *(sujet sg = personne, aucun)* no one ◆ **~ n'est censé ignorer la loi** ignorance of the law is no excuse ◆ **~ d'entre vous n'ignore que ...** none of you is ignorant of the fact that ... ◆ **afin que ~ n'en ignore** *(frm)* so that nobody is left in ignorance ◆ **à ~ autre pareil** peerless, unrivalled ◆ **~ n'est prophète en son pays** *(Prov)* no man is a prophet in his own country *(Prov)* → **impossible**
LOC ADV **nulle part** nowhere ◆ **il ne l'a trouvé nulle part** he couldn't find it anywhere ◆ **je n'ai nulle part où aller** I've got nowhere to go ◆ **nulle part ailleurs** nowhere else

nullard, e* /nylaʀ, aʀd/ ADJ hopeless, useless *(en* at) NM,F numskull ◆ **c'est un ~** he's a complete numskull, he's a dead loss*

nullement /nylmɑ̃/ ADV not at all, not in the least ◆ **il n'a ~ l'intention de ...** he has no intention whatsoever *ou* he hasn't got the slightest intention of ... ◆ **cela n'implique ~ que ...** this doesn't in any way *ou* by any means imply that ...

nullipare /nylipaʀ/ ADJ nulliparous NF nullipara

nullité /nylite/ NF ① *(Jur)* nullity ◆ **frapper de ~** to render void; → **entacher** ② *(= médiocrité)* *[d'employé]* incompetence; *[d'élève]* uselessness ◆ **ce film est d'une ~ affligeante** the film is absolutely dreadful ③ *(= futilité)* *[de raisonnement, objection]* invalidity ④ *(= personne)* nonentity, wash-out*

nûment /nymɑ̃/ ADV (littér) (= sans fard) plainly, frankly; (= crûment) bluntly ◆ **dire (tout) ~ que** … to say (quite) frankly that …

numéraire /nymeʀɛʀ/ ADJ ◆ **pierres ~s** milestones ◆ **espèces ~s** legal tender ou currency ◆ **valeur** ~ face value NM specie (SPÉC), cash ◆ **paiement en** ~ cash payment, payment in specie (SPÉC)

numéral, e (mpl **-aux**) /nymeʀal, o/ ADJ, NM numeral

numérateur /nymeʀatœʀ/ NM numerator

numération /nymeʀasjɔ̃/ NF (= comptage) numeration; (= code) notation ◆ ~ **globulaire** (Méd) blood count ◆ ~ **binaire** (Math, Ordin) binary notation

numérique /nymeʀik/ ADJ 1 (= relatif aux nombres) numerical 2 (= digital) digital NM ◆ **le** ~ digital technology

numériquement /nymeʀikmɑ̃/ ADV 1 (= en nombre) numerically ◆ ~ **inférieur** numerically inferior 2 (= de façon numérique) digitally ◆ **enregistré** ~ digitally recorded

Numéris ® /nymeʀis/ NM ◆ **(réseau)** ~ Numeris (network) (France Télécom's digital communications system) ◆ **données** ~ data transmitted on the Numeris network

numérisation /nymeʀizasjɔ̃/ NF digitization

numériser /nymeʀize/ ▸ conjug 1 ◂ VT to digitize

numériseur /nymeʀizœʀ/ NM digitizer

numéro /nymeʀo/ GRAMMAIRE ACTIVE 54 NM 1 (gén, Aut, Phys) number ◆ **j'habite au** ~ **6** I live at number 6 ◆ ~ **atomique** atomic number ◆ ~ **d'ordre** number, queue ticket (Brit) ◆ ~ **minéralogique** ou **d'immatriculation** ou **de police** registration (Brit) ou license (US) number, car number ◆ ~ **d'immatriculation à la Sécurité sociale** National Insurance number (Brit), Social Security number (US) ◆ ~ **(de téléphone),** ~ **d'appel** (tele)phone number ◆ ~ **vert** ® ou **d'appel gratuit** Freefone ® (Brit) ou toll-free (US) number ◆ ~ **de fax** fax number ◆ ~ **de compte** account number ◆ ~ **de série** serial number ◆ ~ **postal** (Helv) post code (Brit), zip code (US) ◆ **faire** ou **composer un** ~ to dial a number ◆ **pour eux, je ne suis qu'un** ~ I'm just a ou another number to them ◆ **notre ennemi/problème** ~ **un** our number one enemy/problem ◆ **le** ~ **un/deux du textile** the number one/two textile producer ou manufacturer ◆ **le** ~ **un/deux du parti** the party's leader/deputy leader ou number two ◆ **le bon/mauvais** ~ (lit) the right/wrong number ◆ **tirer le bon** ~ (dans une loterie) to draw the lucky number; (fig) to strike lucky ◆ **tirer le mauvais** ~ (fig) to draw the short straw ◆ ~ **gagnant** winning number

2 (Presse) issue, number ◆ **le** ~ **du jour** the day's issue ◆ **vieux** ~ back number, back issue ◆ ~ **spécial** special issue ◆ ~ **zéro** dummy issue; → **suite**

3 (= spectacle) [de chant, danse] number; [de cirque, music-hall] act, turn, number ◆ **il nous a fait son** ~ **habituel** ou **son petit** ~ (fig) he gave us ou put on his usual (little) act

4 (= personne) **quel** ~ **!*, c'est un drôle de** ~ **!*, c'est un sacré** ~ **!*** what a character!

numérologie /nymeʀɔlɔʒi/ NF numerology

numérologue /nymeʀɔlɔg/ NMF numerologist

numérotage /nymeʀɔtaʒ/ NM numbering, numeration

numérotation /nymeʀɔtasjɔ̃/ NF numbering, numeration ◆ ~ **téléphonique** telephone number system ◆ ~ **à 10 chiffres** (Téléc) 10-digit dialling (Brit) ou dialing (US)

numéroter /nymeʀɔte/ ▸ conjug 1 ◂ VT to number ◆ **si tu continues, tu as intérêt à** ~ **tes abattis !*** if you go on like this you'll get what's coming to you! *

numerus clausus /nymeʀysklozys/ NM restricted intake

numide /nymid/ ADJ Numidian NMF **Numide** Numidian

Numidie /nymidi/ NF Numidia

numismate /nymismat/ NMF numismatist

numismatique /nymismatik/ ADJ numismatic NF numismatics (sg), numismatology

Nunavut /nunavut/ NM Nunavut

nunuche* /nynyʃ/ ADJ (gén) silly NMF ninny*

nu-pieds /nypje/ NM (= sandale) beach sandal, flip-flop (Brit) ADV barefoot

nu-propriétaire, nue-propriétaire (mpl **nus-propriétaires**) /nypʀɔpʀijetɛʀ/ NM,F (Jur) owner without usufruct

nuptial, e (mpl **-iaux**) /nypsjal, jo/ ADJ [bénédiction, messe] nuptial (littér); [robe, marche, anneau, cérémonie] wedding (épith); [lit, chambre] bridal, nuptial (littér); (en parlant d'un comportement animal) nuptial

nuptialité /nypsjalite/ NF ◆ **(taux de)** ~ marriage rate

nuque /nyk/ NF nape of the neck ◆ **tué d'une balle dans la** ~ killed by a bullet in the back of the neck

Nuremberg /nyʀɛbɛʀ/ N Nuremberg ◆ **le procès de** ~ (Hist) the Nuremberg trials

nurse /nœʀs/ NF nanny, (children's) nurse †

> ⚠ **nurse** se traduit rarement par le mot anglais **nurse**, qui dans ce sens est vieilli.

nursery (pl **nurserys** ou **nurseries**) /nœʀsəʀi/ NF [de maison, maternité] nursery

nutriment /nytʀimɑ̃/ NM nutriment

nutritif, -ive /nytʀitif, iv/ ADJ (= nourrissant) nourishing, nutritious; (Méd) [besoins, fonction, appareil] nutritive ◆ **qualité** ou **valeur nutritive** food value, nutritional value

nutrition /nytʀisjɔ̃/ NF nutrition

nutritionnel, -elle /nytʀisjɔnɛl/ ADJ nutritional

nutritionniste /nytʀisjɔnist/ NMF nutritionist

Nyasaland, Nyassaland /njasalɑ̃d/ NM Nyasaland

nyctalope /niktalɔp/ ADJ day-blind, hemeralopic (SPÉC) ◆ **les chats sont ~s** cats see well in the dark NMF day-blind ou hemeralopic (SPÉC) person

nyctalopie /niktalɔpi/ NF day blindness, hemeralopia (SPÉC)

nylon ® /nilɔ̃/ NM nylon ◆ **bas (de)** ~ nylons, nylon stockings

nymphe /nɛ̃f/ NF (Myth, fig) nymph; (= insecte) nymph, pupa ◆ **~s** (Anat) nymphae, labia minora

nymphéa /nɛ̃fea/ NM white water lily

nymphette /nɛ̃fɛt/ NF nymphet

nymphomane /nɛ̃fɔman/ ADJ, NF nymphomaniac

nymphomanie /nɛ̃fɔmani/ NF nymphomania

Oo

O¹, o /o/ **NM** *(= lettre)* O, o

O² (abrév de **Ouest**) W

ô /o/ **EXCL** oh!, O!

OAS /oaɛs/ **NF** (abrév de **Organisation de l'armée secrète)** OAS *(illegal military organization supporting French rule in Algeria in the 60s)*

oasis /ɔazis/ **NF** *(lit)* oasis; *(fig)* oasis, haven ◆ ~ **de paix** haven of peace

obédience /ɔbedjɑ̃s/ **NF** 1 *(= appartenance)* **d'~ communiste** of Communist allegiance ◆ **de même ~ religieuse** of the same religious persuasion ◆ **musulman de stricte ~** strict *ou* devout Muslim ◆ **socialiste de stricte ~** staunch socialist 2 *(Rel, littér = obéissance)* obedience

obéir /ɔbeiʀ/ ▸ conjug 2 ◂ **obéir à VT INDIR** 1 *[+ personne]* to obey; *[+ ordre]* to obey, to comply with; *[+ loi, principe, règle]* to obey; *[+ critère]* to meet ◆ **il sait se faire ~ de ses élèves** he knows how to command obedience from his pupils *ou* how to make his pupils obey him ◆ **on lui obéit au doigt et à l'œil** he commands strict obedience ◆ **obéissez !** do as you're told! ◆ **je lui ai dit de le faire mais il n'a pas obéi** I told him to do it but he took no notice *ou* didn't obey (me) ◆ **ici, il faut ~** you have to toe the line *ou* obey orders here

2 *(fig) [+ conscience, mode]* to follow (the dictates of) ◆ **~ à une impulsion** to act on an impulse ◆ **obéissant à un sentiment de pitié** prompted *ou* moved by a feeling of pity ◆ **~ à ses instincts** to submit to *ou* obey one's instincts ◆ **son comportement n'obéit à aucune logique** his behaviour is completely illogical ◆ **l'orthographe obéit à des règles complexes** spelling is governed by *ou* follows complex rules

3 *[voilier, moteur, monture]* to respond to ◆ **le cheval obéit au mors** the horse responds to the bit ◆ **le moteur/voilier obéit bien** the engine/boat responds well

obéissance /ɔbeisɑ̃s/ **NF** *[d'animal, personne]* obedience (à to)

obéissant, e /ɔbeisɑ̃, ɑ̃t/ **ADJ** obedient (à to, towards)

obélisque /ɔbelisk/ **NM** *(= monument)* obelisk

obérer /ɔbeʀe/ ▸ conjug 6 ◂ **VT** *(frm) [+ bilan, budget]* to be a burden on; *[+ avenir, situation]* to compromise, to be a threat to

obèse /ɔbɛz/ **ADJ** obese **NMF** obese person

obésité /ɔbezite/ **NF** obesity

obituaire /ɔbitɥɛʀ/ **ADJ, NM** ◆ **(registre) ~** record of memorial services

objectal, e (mpl **-aux**) /ɔbʒɛktal, o/ **ADJ** *(Psych)* object *(épith)* ◆ **libido/lien ~** object libido/relationship

objecter /ɔbʒɛkte/ ▸ conjug 1 ◂ **VT** 1 *(à une idée ou une opinion)* **~ un argument à une théorie** to put forward an argument against a theory ◆ **il m'objecta une très bonne raison, à savoir que ...** against that he argued convincingly that ..., he gave me *ou* he put forward a very sound reason against (doing) that, namely that ... ◆ **~ que ...** to object that ... ◆ **il m'objecta que ...** he objected to me that ..., the objection he mentioned *ou* raised to me was that ... ◆ **que puis-je lui ~ ?** what can I say to him? ◆ **je n'ai rien à ~** I have no objection (to make) ◆ **elle a toujours quelque chose à ~** she always has some objection or other (to make), she always raises some objection or other

2 *(à une demande)* **il objecta le manque de temps/la fatigue pour ne pas y aller** he pleaded lack of time/tiredness to save himself going ◆ **il m'a objecté mon manque d'expérience/le manque de place** he objected on the grounds of my lack of experience/on the grounds that there was not enough space, he objected that I lacked experience/that there was not enough space

objecteur /ɔbʒɛktœʀ/ **NM** ◆ **~ de conscience** conscientious objector

objectif, -ive /ɔbʒɛktif, iv/ **ADJ** 1 *[article, jugement, observateur]* objective, unbiased 2 *(Ling, Philos)* objective; *(Méd) [symptôme]* objective **NM** 1 *(= but)* objective, purpose; *(Mil = cible)* objective, target ◆ **~ de vente** sales target 2 *[de télescope, lunette]* objective, object glass, lens; *[de caméra]* lens, objective ◆ **~ traité** coated lens ◆ **braquer son ~ sur** to train one's camera on

objection /ɔbʒɛksjɔ̃/ **GRAMMAIRE ACTIVE 28.1, 36.2, 38.1, 38.3** **NF** objection ◆ **faire une ~** to raise *ou* make an objection, to object ◆ **si vous n'y voyez pas d'~** if you've no objection (to that) ◆ **la proposition n'a soulevé aucune ~** there were no objections to the proposal ◆ **~ !** *(Jur)* objection! ◆ **~ de conscience** conscientious objection

objectivement /ɔbʒɛktivmɑ̃/ **ADV** objectively

objectiver /ɔbʒɛktive/ ▸ conjug 1 ◂ **VT** to objectivize

objectivisme /ɔbʒɛktivism/ **NM** objectivism

objectivité /ɔbʒɛktivite/ **NF** objectivity ◆ **juger en toute ~** to judge with complete objectivity

objet /ɔbʒɛ/ **NM** 1 *(= chose)* object ◆ **~ décoratif/inanimé/usuel** decorative/inanimate/household object ◆ **emporter quelques ~s de première nécessité** to take a few basic essentials *ou* a few essential items *ou* things ◆ **il collectionne toutes sortes d'~s** he collects all sorts of things

2 *(= sujet) [de méditation, rêve, désir]* object; *[de discussion, recherches, science]* subject ◆ **l'~ de la psychologie est le comportement humain** psychology is the study of human behaviour

3 *(= cible) [de mépris, convoitise]* object ◆ **un ~ de raillerie/d'admiration** an object of fun/of admiration ◆ **femme-/homme-~** woman/man as a sex object ◆ **~ sexuel** sex object

4 ◆ **faire** *ou* **être l'~ de** *[+ discussion, recherches]* to be the subject of; *[+ surveillance, enquête]* to be subjected to; *[+ pressions]* to be subjected to, to be under; *[+ soins]* to be given ◆ **le malade fit** *ou* **fut l'~ d'un dévouement de tous les instants** the patient was given every care and attention ◆ **faire l'~ d'une attention particulière** to receive particular attention ◆ **les marchandises faisant l'~ de cette facture** goods covered by this invoice

5 *(= but) [de visite, réunion, démarche]* object, purpose ◆ **cette enquête a rempli son ~** the investigation has achieved its purpose *ou* object *ou* objective ◆ **craintes sans ~** unfounded *ou* groundless fears ◆ **votre plainte est dès lors sans ~** you therefore have no grounds for complaint

6 *(Ling, Philos, Ordin)* object ◆ **~ mathématique** mathematical object; → **complément**

COMP **l'objet aimé** the object of one's affection

objet d'art objet d'art

objet social *[d'une entreprise]* business

objets de toilette toilet requisites *ou* articles

objets trouvés lost property (office) *(Brit)*, lost and found *(US)*

objets de valeur valuables

objet volant non identifié unidentified flying object

objurgations /ɔbʒyʀgasjɔ̃/ **NFPL** *(littér) (= exhortations)* objurgations *(frm)*; *(= prières)* pleas, entreaties

oblat, e /ɔbla, at/ **NM,F** oblate

oblation /ɔblasjɔ̃/ **NF** oblation

obligataire /ɔbligatɛʀ/ **ADJ** *[marché]* bond *(épith)* ◆ **emprunt ~** bond issue **NMF** bond *ou* debenture holder

obligation /ɔbligasjɔ̃/ **NF** 1 *(= contrainte)* obligation ◆ **il faudrait les inviter – ce n'est pas une ~** we should invite them – we don't have to ◆ **avoir l'~ de faire** to be under an obligation to do, to be obliged to do ◆ **il se fait une ~ de cette visite/de lui rendre visite** he feels (himself) obliged *ou* he feels he is under an obligation to make this visit/to visit him

◆ **être** *ou* **se trouver dans l'~ de faire** to be obliged to do ◆ **sans ~ d'achat** with no *ou* without obligation to buy ◆ **c'est sans ~ de votre part** there's no obligation on your part, you're under no obligation; → **réserve**
2 ◆ **~s** *(= devoirs)* obligations, duties; *(= engagements)* commitments ◆ **~s sociales/professionnelles** social/professional obligations ◆ **~s de citoyen/de chrétien** one's obligations *ou* responsibilities *ou* duties as a citizen/Christian ◆ **être dégagé des ~s militaires** to have completed one's military service ◆ **~s familiales** family commitments *ou* responsibilities ◆ **avoir des ~s envers une autre entreprise** to have a commitment to another firm ◆ **remplir ses ~s vis-à-vis d'un autre pays** *(Pol)* to discharge one's commitments towards another country
3 *(littér = reconnaissance)* **~(s)** obligation ◆ **avoir de l'~ à qn** to be under an obligation to sb
4 *(Jur)* obligation; *(= dette)* obligation ◆ **faire face à ses ~s (financières)** to meet one's liabilities ◆ **~ légale** legal obligation ◆ **~ alimentaire** maintenance obligation ◆ **l'~ scolaire** *legal obligation to provide an education for children* ◆ **contracter une ~ envers qn** to contract an obligation towards sb
5 *(Fin = titre)* bond, debenture ◆ **~ d'État** government bond ◆ **~s convertibles/à taux fixe/à taux variable** convertible/fixed-rate/variable-rate bonds

obligatoire /ɔbligatwaʀ/ GRAMMAIRE ACTIVE 37.1 ADJ 1 *(= à caractère d'obligation)* compulsory, obligatory ◆ **la scolarité est ~ jusqu'à 16 ans** schooling is compulsory until 16 ◆ **réservation ~** *(dans un train, pour un spectacle)* reservations *ou* bookings *(Brit)* required 2 *(= inévitable)* inevitable ◆ **il est arrivé en retard ? – c'était ~ !** he arrived late? – that goes without saying! ◆ **c'était ~ qu'il rate son examen** it was a foregone conclusion that he would fail the exam

obligatoirement /ɔbligatwaʀmɑ̃/ ADV 1 *(= nécessairement)* necessarily ◆ **les candidats doivent ~ passer une visite médicale** applicants are required to *ou* must have a medical examination ◆ **la réunion se tiendra ~ ici** the meeting will have to be held here ◆ **pas ~** not necessarily 2 *(= inévitablement)* inevitably ◆ **il aura ~ des ennuis s'il continue comme ça** he's bound to *ou* he'll be bound to make trouble for himself if he carries on like that

obligé, e /ɔbliʒe/ GRAMMAIRE ACTIVE 37.1, 37.3, 45.4 ptp de **obliger**
ADJ 1 *(= inévitable)* *[conséquence]* inevitable ◆ **c'est ~ !** it's inevitable! ◆ **c'était ~ !** it had to happen!, it was sure *ou* bound to happen!
2 *(= indispensable)* necessary, required ◆ **le parcours ~ pour devenir ministre** the career path a would-be minister needs to follow ◆ **ce port est le point de passage ~ pour les livraisons vers l'Europe** all deliveries to Europe have to go through *ou* via this port ◆ **apprendre la langue d'un pays est un passage ~ pour comprendre sa civilisation** learning the language of a country is a prerequisite to understanding *ou* is essential if you want to understand its civilization
3 *(frm = redevable)* **être ~ à qn** to be (most) obliged to sb, to be indebted to sb *(de qch* for sth; *d'avoir fait* for having done, for doing)
NM,F 1 *(Jur)* obligee, debtor ◆ **le principal ~** the principal obligee
2 *(frm)* **être l'~ de qn** to be under an obligation to sb

> ⚠ **obligé** se traduit par **obliged** uniquement au sens de 'redevable'.

obligeamment /ɔbliʒamɑ̃/ ADV obligingly

obligeance /ɔbliʒɑ̃s/ NF ◆ **ayez l'~ de vous taire pendant que je parle** have the goodness *ou* be good enough to keep quiet while I'm speaking ◆ **il a eu l'~ de me reconduire en voiture** he was obliging *ou* kind enough to drive me back ◆ **nous connaissons tous son ~** we all know how obliging he is

obligeant, e /ɔbliʒɑ̃, ɑ̃t/ ADJ *[offre]* kind, helpful; *[personne, parole]* kind, obliging, helpful

obliger /ɔbliʒe/ ► conjug 3 ◄ VT 1 *(= forcer)* **~ qn à faire** *[circonstances, agresseur]* to force sb to do, to make sb do; *[règlement, autorités]* to require sb to do, to make it compulsory for sb to do; *[principes moraux]* to oblige *ou* obligate *(US)* sb to do ◆ **le règlement vous y oblige** you are required to by the regulations ◆ **mes principes m'y obligent** my principles compel me to do it ◆ **l'honneur m'y oblige** I'm honour bound to do it ◆ **quand le temps l'y oblige, il travaille dans sa chambre** if the weather makes it necessary, he works in his room ◆ **ses parents l'obligent à travailler dur** his parents make him work hard ◆ **rien ne l'oblige à partir** there's no reason why he should leave ◆ **le manque d'argent l'a obligé à emprunter** lack of money forced him to borrow ◆ **tu vas m'~ à me mettre en colère** you're going to make me lose my temper ◆ **je suis obligé de vous laisser** I have to *ou* I must leave you ◆ **il va accepter ? – il est bien obligé !** is he going to agree? – he'll have to! *ou* he has no choice *ou* alternative! ◆ **tu n'es pas obligé de me croire** you don't have to believe me
2 *(locutions)* **crise économique/compétitivité oblige** in view of the economic crisis/the need to be competitive ◆ **tradition oblige** as is the tradition ◆ **campagne électorale oblige** because of the electoral campaign; → **noblesse**
3 *(Jur)* to bind
4 *(= rendre service à)* to oblige ◆ **vous m'obligeriez en acceptant** *ou* **si vous acceptiez** I would be delighted if you would agree ◆ **je vous serais très obligé de bien vouloir ...** *(formule de politesse)* I would be very grateful if you would ... ◆ **nous vous serions obligés de bien vouloir nous répondre dans les plus brefs délais** we would be grateful if you could reply as soon as possible ◆ **entre voisins, il faut bien s'~** neighbours have to help each other

> ⚠ Attention à ne pas traduire automatiquement **obliger** par **to oblige**, qui est d'un registre plus soutenu.

oblique /ɔblik/ ADJ *(gén, Ling, Math)* oblique ◆ **regard ~** sidelong *ou* side glance ◆ **(muscle) ~** oblique muscle ◆ **en ~** obliquely ◆ **il a traversé la rue en ~** he crossed the street diagonally NF *(Math)* oblique line

obliquement /ɔblikmɑ̃/ ADV *[planter, fixer]* at an angle; *[se diriger]* obliquely ◆ **regarder qn ~** to look sideways *ou* sidelong at sb, to give sb a sidelong look *ou* glance

obliquer /ɔblike/ ► conjug 1 ◄ VI ◆ **obliquez juste avant l'église** turn off just before the church ◆ **~ à droite** to turn off *ou* bear right ◆ **obliquez en direction de la ferme** *(à travers champs)* cut across towards the farm; *(sur un sentier)* turn off towards the farm

obliquité /ɔblik(ɥ)ite/ NF *[de rayon]* *(Math)* obliqueness, obliquity; *(Astron)* obliquity

oblitérateur /ɔbliteʀatœʀ/ NM canceller

oblitération /ɔbliteʀasjɔ̃/ NF 1 *[de timbre]* cancelling, cancellation; *[de billet]* stamping ◆ **cachet d'~** postmark 2 *(† ou littér)* *[de souvenir]* obliteration 3 *(Méd)* *[d'artère]* obstruction

oblitérer /ɔbliteʀe/ ► conjug 6 ◄ VT 1 *[+ timbre]* to cancel ◆ **il faut ~ son billet** tickets must be stamped 2 *(† ou littér = effacer)* *[+ souvenir]* to obliterate 3 *(Méd)* *[+ artère]* to obstruct

oblong, -ongue /ɔblɔ̃, ɔ̃g/ ADJ oblong

obnubiler /ɔbnybile/ ► conjug 1 ◄ VT to obsess ◆ **se laisser ~ par** to become obsessed by ◆ **elle est obnubilée par l'idée que ...** she's obsessed with the idea that ...

obole /ɔbɔl/ NF 1 *(= contribution)* offering ◆ **verser** *ou* **apporter son ~ à qch** to make one's small (financial) contribution to sth 2 *(= monnaie française)* obole; *(= monnaie grecque)* obol

obscène /ɔpsɛn/ ADJ *[film, propos, geste]* obscene ◆ **il est si riche que c'en est ~ !*** he's obscenely *ou* disgustingly rich!

obscénité /ɔpsenite/ NF 1 *(= caractère)* obscenity 2 *(= propos, écrit)* obscenity ◆ **dire des ~s** to make obscene remarks

obscur, e /ɔpskyʀ/ ADJ 1 *(= sombre)* *[nuit, ruelle, pièce]* dark; → **salle** 2 *(= incompréhensible)* *[texte, passage]* obscure 3 *(= mystérieux)* obscure ◆ **pour des raisons ~es** for some obscure reason ◆ **forces ~es** dark forces 4 *(= vague)* *[malaise]* vague; *[pressentiment, sentiment]* vague, dim 5 *(= méconnu)* *[œuvre, auteur]* obscure; *(= humble)* *[vie, situation, besogne]* humble ◆ **des gens ~s** humble folk ◆ **de naissance ~e** of obscure *ou* humble birth

> ⚠ Au sens de "sombre", **obscur** ne se traduit pas par le mot anglais **obscure**.

obscurantisme /ɔpskyʀɑ̃tism/ NM obscurantism

obscurantiste /ɔpskyʀɑ̃tist/ ADJ, NMF obscurantist

obscurcir /ɔpskyʀsiʀ/ ► conjug 2 ◄ VT 1 *(= assombrir)* to darken ◆ **ce tapis obscurcit la pièce** this carpet makes the room look dark *ou* darkens the room ◆ **des nuages obscurcissaient le ciel** the sky was dark with clouds 2 *(= compliquer)* to obscure ◆ **ce critique aime ~ les choses les plus simples** this critic likes to obscure *ou* cloud the simplest issues ◆ **cela obscurcit encore plus l'énigme** that deepens the mystery even further 3 *(= troubler)* **le vin obscurcit les idées** wine makes it difficult to think straight VPR **s'obscurcir** 1 *[ciel]* to darken, to grow dark; *[regard]* to darken ◆ **tout d'un coup le temps s'obscurcit** suddenly the sky grew dark *ou* darkened ◆ **son horizon politique s'obscurcit** his political future is looking less and less bright 2 *[style]* to become obscure; *[esprit]* to become confused; *[vue]* to grow dim

obscurcissement /ɔpskyʀsismɑ̃/ NM *[de ciel]* darkening; *[d'esprit]* confusing; *[de vue]* dimming

obscurément /ɔpskyʀemɑ̃/ ADV obscurely ◆ **il sentait ~ que ...** he felt in an obscure way *ou* a vague (sort of) way that ..., he felt obscurely that ...

obscurité /ɔpskyʀite/ NF 1 *[de nuit]* darkness ◆ **dans l'~** in the dark, in darkness ◆ **la maison fut soudain plongée dans l'~** the house was suddenly plunged into darkness ◆ **il a laissé cet aspect du problème dans l'~** he cast no light *ou* didn't enlighten us on that aspect of the problem 2 *[de texte]* obscurity 3 *[de vie, situation, besogne, œuvre, auteur]* obscurity ◆ **vivre/travailler dans l'~** to live/work in obscurity 4 *(littér = passage peu clair)* obscure passage

obsédant, e /ɔpsedɑ̃, ɑ̃t/ ADJ *[musique, souvenir]* haunting, obsessive; *[question, idée]* obsessive

obsédé, e /ɔpsede/ (ptp de **obséder**) NM,F obsessive ◆ **~ (sexuel)** sex maniac ◆ **c'est un ~ de propreté** he's obsessed with cleanliness ◆ **les ~s du caméscope** *(hum)* camcorder freaks *

obséder /ɔpsede/ ► conjug 6 ◄ VT 1 *(= obnubiler)* to haunt; *(maladivement)* to obsess ◆ **cette tragédie, dont la mémoire douloureuse continue d'~ les esprits** this tragedy which continues to haunt people's memories ◆ **le remords l'obsédait** he was racked *ou* consumed by remorse ◆ **être obsédé par** *[+ souvenir, peur]* to be haunted by; *(maladivement)* to be obsessed by; *[+ idée, problème, mort, image, sexe]* to be obsessed with *ou* by ◆ **il est obsédé** *(sexuellement)* he's obsessed (with sex), he's got a one-track mind* 2 *(littér = importuner)* to pester ◆ ~ **qn de ses assiduités** to pester *ou* importune sb with one's attentions

obsèques /ɔpsɛk/ NFPL funeral ◆ ~ **civiles/religieuses/nationales** civil/religious/state funeral

obséquieusement /ɔpsekjøzmɑ̃/ ADV obsequiously

obséquieux, -ieuse /ɔpsekjø, jøz/ ADJ obsequious

obséquiosité /ɔpsekjozite/ NF obsequiousness

observable /ɔpsɛʀvabl/ ADJ observable ◆ **ce phénomène est difficilement** ~ this phenomenon is not easy to observe

observance /ɔpsɛʀvɑ̃s/ NF observance ◆ **de stricte** ~ devout

observateur, -trice /ɔpsɛʀvatœʀ, tʀis/ ADJ *[personne, regard]* observant NM,F observer ◆ **avoir des talents d'~** to have a talent for observation ◆ ~ **des Nations Unies** United Nations *ou* UN observer

observation /ɔpsɛʀvasjɔ̃/ NF 1 *(= obéissance) [de règle]* observance
2 *(= examen, surveillance)* observation ◆ **être/mettre en** ~ *(Méd)* to be/put under observation ◆ ~ **aérienne** *(Mil)* aerial observation ◆ **technique/instrument d'~** observation technique/instrument ◆ **round/set d'~** *(Sport)* first round/set *(in which one plays a guarded or a wait-and-see game)*; → **poste², satellite**
3 *(= chose observée)* observation ◆ **il consignait ses ~s dans son carnet** he noted down his observations *ou* what he had observed in his notebook
4 *(= remarque)* observation, remark; *(= objection)* remark; *(= reproche)* reproof; *(Scol)* warning ◆ **il fit quelques ~s judicieuses** he made one or two judicious remarks *ou* observations ◆ **je lui en fis l'~** I pointed it out to him ◆ **ce film appelle quelques ~s** this film calls for some comment ◆ **pas d'~s je vous prie** no remarks *ou* comments please ◆ **faire une ~ à qn** to reprove sb ◆ **~s** *(Scol)* teacher's comments

observatoire /ɔpsɛʀvatwaʀ/ NM 1 *(Astron)* observatory 2 *(Mil = lieu)* observation *ou* look-out post ◆ ~ **économique** economic research institute

observer /ɔpsɛʀve/ ► conjug 1 ◄ VT 1 *(= regarder) (gén)* to watch; *(Sci) [+ phénomène, réaction]* to observe; *(au microscope)* to examine ◆ **se sentant observée, elle se retourna** feeling she was being watched she turned round ◆ **il ne dit pas grand-chose mais il observe** he doesn't say much but he observes what goes on around him *ou* he watches keenly what goes on around him
2 *(= contrôler)* ~ **ses manières** to be mindful of *ou* watch one's manners
3 *(= remarquer)* to notice, to observe ◆ **elle n'observe jamais rien** she never notices anything ◆ **faire ~ que** to point out *ou* remark *ou* observe that ◆ **faire ~ un détail à qn** to point out a detail to sb, to bring a detail to sb's attention ◆ **je vous ferai ~ qu'il est interdit de fumer ici** please note that you're not allowed to smoke here, can I point out that smoking is forbidden here?
4 *(= dire)* to observe, to remark ◆ **vous êtes en retard, observa-t-il** you're late, he observed *ou* remarked
5 *(= respecter) [+ règlement]* to observe, to abide by; *[+ fête, jeûne]* to keep, to observe; *[+ coutume, trêve, neutralité]* to observe ◆ ~ **une minute de silence** to observe a minute's silence ◆ **faire ~ un règlement** to enforce a rule
6 *(littér) [+ attitude, maintien]* to keep (up), to maintain
VPR **s'observer** 1 *(réciproque)* to observe *ou* watch each other
2 *(réfléchi = surveiller sa tenue, son langage)* to keep a check on o.s., to be careful of one's behaviour ◆ **il ne s'observe pas assez en public** he's not careful enough of his behaviour in public
3 *(passif = se manifester)* to be observed

obsession /ɔpsesjɔ̃/ NF obsession ◆ **il avait l'~ de la mort/l'argent** he had an obsession with death/money, he was obsessed by death/money ◆ **je veux aller à Londres – c'est une ~ !/ça tourne à l'~ !** I want to go to London – you're obsessed!/it's becoming an obsession!

obsessionnel, -elle /ɔpsesjɔnɛl/ ADJ obsessional, obsessive; → **névrose** NM,F obsessive

obsidienne /ɔpsidjɛn/ NF obsidian, volcanic glass

obsolescence /ɔpsɔlesɑ̃s/ NF *(Tech, littér)* obsolescence

obsolescent, e /ɔpsɔlesɑ̃, ɑ̃t/ ADJ *(Tech, littér)* obsolescent

obsolète /ɔpsɔlɛt/ ADJ obsolete

obstacle /ɔpstakl/ NM *(gén)* obstacle; *(Hippisme)* fence; *(Équitation)* jump, fence ◆ ~ **technique/juridique** technical/legal barrier *ou* obstacle ◆ **faire ~ à la lumière** to block (out) *ou* obstruct the light ◆ **faire ~ à un projet** to hinder a project, to put obstacles *ou* an obstacle in the way of a project ◆ **tourner l'~** *(Équitation)* to go round *ou* outside the jump; *(fig)* to get round the obstacle *ou* difficulty ◆ **progresser sans rencontrer d'~s** *(lit, fig)* to make progress without meeting any obstacles ◆ **dans ce métier, son âge n'est pas un ~** his age is no impediment *ou* obstacle in this job ◆ **je ne vois pas d'~ à sa venue** *ou* **à ce qu'il vienne** I don't see any reason why he shouldn't come ◆ **si vous n'y voyez pas d'~** if that's all right with you; → **course, refuser**

obstétrical, e (mpl **-aux**) /ɔpstetʀikal, o/ ADJ obstetric(al)

obstétricien, -ienne /ɔpstetʀisjɛ̃, jɛn/ NM,F obstetrician

obstétrique /ɔpstetʀik/ ADJ obstetric(al) NF obstetrics *(sg)*

obstination /ɔpstinasjɔ̃/ NF *[de personne, caractère]* obstinacy, stubbornness ◆ ~ **à faire** obstinate *ou* stubborn determination to do ◆ **son ~ à refuser** his persistent refusal

obstiné, e /ɔpstine/ (ptp de **s'obstiner**) ADJ *[personne, caractère]* obstinate, stubborn; *[efforts, résistance, travail, demandes]* obstinate, persistent; *[refus, silence]* stubborn; *[brouillard, pluie, malchance]* persistent; *[toux]* persistent, stubborn

obstinément /ɔpstinemɑ̃/ ADV stubbornly, obstinately ◆ **le téléphone reste ~ muet** the telephone stubbornly refuses to ring

obstiner (s') /ɔpstine/ ► conjug 1 ◄ VPR to insist, to dig one's heels in ◆ **s'~ sur un problème** to keep working *ou* labour away stubbornly at a problem ◆ **s'~ dans une opinion** to cling stubbornly *ou* doggedly to an opinion ◆ **s'~ dans son refus (de faire qch)** to refuse categorically *ou* absolutely (to do sth) ◆ **s'~ à faire** to persist in doing ◆ **s'~ au silence** to remain obstinately silent, to maintain an obstinate *ou* a stubborn silence ◆ **j'ai dit non mais il s'obstine !** I said no but he insists!

obstruction /ɔpstʀyksjɔ̃/ NF 1 *(= blocage)* obstruction, blockage; *(Méd)* obstruction 2 *(= tactique)* obstruction ◆ **faire de l'~** *(Pol)* to obstruct (the passage of) legislation; *(gén)* to use obstructive tactics, to be obstructive; *(Ftbl)* to obstruct ◆ **faire de l'~ parlementaire** to filibuster

obstructionnisme /ɔpstʀyksjɔnism/ NM obstructionism, filibustering

obstructionniste /ɔpstʀyksjɔnist/ ADJ obstructionist, filibustering *(épith)* NMF obstructionist, filibuster, filibusterer

obstruer /ɔpstʀye/ ► conjug 1 ◄ VT *[+ passage, circulation, artère]* to obstruct, to block ◆ ~ **la vue/le passage** to block *ou* obstruct the view/the way VPR **s'obstruer** *[passage]* to get blocked up; *[artère]* to become blocked

obtempérer /ɔptɑ̃peʀe/ ► conjug 6 ◄ **obtempérer à** VT INDIR to obey, to comply with ◆ **il refusa d'~** he refused to comply *ou* obey ◆ **refus d'~** refusal to comply

obtenir /ɔptəniʀ/ ► conjug 22 ◄ VT 1 *(= réussir à avoir)* to get, to obtain; *[+ récompense]* to receive, to get; *[+ prix]* to be awarded, to get ◆ ~ **satisfaction** to get *ou* obtain satisfaction ◆ ~ **la main de qn** to win sb's hand ◆ **je peux vous ~ ce livre rapidement** I can get you this book quite quickly ◆ **il m'a fait ~** *ou* **il m'a obtenu de l'avancement** he got promotion for me, he got me promoted ◆ **il obtint de lui parler** he was (finally) allowed to speak to him ◆ **elle a obtenu qu'il paie** she got him to pay, she managed to make him pay ◆ **j'ai obtenu de lui qu'il ne dise rien** I got him to agree not to say anything
2 *(= parvenir à) [+ résultat, total]* to get ◆ **cette couleur s'obtient par un mélange** you get this colour by mixing ◆ **en additionnant ces quantités, on obtient 2 000** when you add these amounts together you get 2,000 ◆ ~ **un corps à l'état gazeux** to get a substance in the gaseous state

> ⚠ Attention à ne pas traduire automatiquement **obtenir** par **to obtain**, qui est d'un usage moins courant que 'to get'.

obtention /ɔptɑ̃sjɔ̃/ NF *[de permission, explication, diplôme]* obtaining; *[de résultat, température]* achieving ◆ **pour l'~ du visa** to obtain the visa ◆ **les délais d'~ de la carte de séjour** the time it takes to obtain a resident's permit ◆ **mélangez le tout jusqu'à (l')~ d'une pâte onctueuse** *(Culin)* mix everything together until the mixture is smooth

obturateur, -trice /ɔptyʀatœʀ, tʀis/ ADJ *(Tech) [plaque]* obturating; *[membrane, muscle]* obturator *(épith)* NM 1 *(Photo)* shutter ◆ ~ **à secteur** rotary shutter ◆ ~ **à rideau** focal plane shutter ◆ ~ **à tambour** *ou* **à boisseaux** drum shutter 2 *(Tech)* obturator; *[de fusil]* gas check

obturation /ɔptyʀasjɔ̃/ NF *[de conduit, ouverture]* closing (up), sealing; *[de fuite]* sealing; *[de dent]* filling ◆ **faire une ~ (dentaire)** to fill a tooth, to do a filling ◆ **vitesse d'~** *(Photo)* shutter speed

obturer /ɔptyʀe/ ► conjug 1 ◄ VT *[+ conduit, ouverture]* to close (up), to seal; *[+ fuite]* to seal *ou* block off; *[+ dent]* to fill

obtus, e /ɔpty, yz/ ADJ *(Math) [angle]* obtuse; *(fig = stupide)* dull-witted, obtuse

obus /ɔby/ NM shell ◆ ~ **explosif** high-explosive shell ◆ ~ **fumigène** smoke bomb ◆ ~ **incendiaire** incendiary *ou* fire bomb ◆ ~ **de mortier** mortar shell ◆ ~ **perforant** armour-piercing shell; → **éclat, trou**

obusier /ɔbyzje/ NM howitzer ◆ ~ **de campagne** field howitzer

obvier /ɔbvje/ ► conjug 7 ◄ **obvier à** VT INDIR *(littér) [+ danger, mal]* to take precautions against, to obviate *(frm)*; *[+ inconvénient]* to overcome, to obviate *(frm)*

OC (abrév de **ondes courtes**) SW

oc /ɔk/ NM → **langue**

> **LANGUE D'OC, LANGUE D'OÏL**
>
> The terms **langue d'oc** (also called « occitan ») and **langue d'oïl** broadly refer to the local languages and dialects spoken in the southern and northern half of France respectively. « Oc » and « oïl » mean « yes » in southern and northern dialects respectively.

ocarina /ɔkaʀina/ NM ocarina

occase * /ɔkɑz/ NF (abrév de **occasion**) **1** *(= article usagé)* secondhand buy; *(= achat avantageux)* bargain, snip* *(Brit)* ◆ **d'~** *[livres, vêtements]* secondhand, used *(US)*, pre-owned *(US)*; *[acheter, vendre]* secondhand **2** *(= conjoncture favorable)* (lucky) chance

occasion /ɔkazjɔ̃/ NF **1** *(= circonstance)* occasion ◆ **à cette ~** on this occasion ◆ **à cette ~, il a lancé un appel à l'OTAN** on this occasion he appealed to NATO ◆ **dans/pour les grandes ~s** on/for important *ou* special occasions ◆ **la bouteille/la robe des grandes ~s** the bottle put by/the dress kept for special *ou* great occasions ◆ **pour l'~** for the occasion ◆ **je l'ai rencontré à plusieurs ~s** I've met him several times ◆ **l'~ fait le larron** *(Prov)* opportunity makes the thief *(Prov)* ◆ **cela a été l'~ d'une grande discussion** this led to a lengthy discussion

◆ **à l'occasion** sometimes, on occasions ◆ **à l'~ venez dîner** come and have dinner some time ◆ **à l'~ de son anniversaire** on the occasion of his birthday, on his birthday ◆ **à l'~ du cinquantième anniversaire de l'OTAN** on NATO's 50th anniversary

◆ **par la même occasion** at the same time ◆ **j'irai à Paris et, par la même ~, je leur rendrai visite** I'll go to Paris, and visit them while I'm there

2 *(= conjoncture favorable)* opportunity, chance ◆ **avoir l'~ de faire** to have the opportunity to do ◆ **profiter de l'~ pour faire qch** to take the opportunity to do sth ◆ **sauter sur*** *ou* **saisir l'~** to jump at *ou* seize the opportunity *ou* chance ◆ **il a laissé échapper** *ou* **passer l'~** he let slip the opportunity ◆ **manquer** *ou* **rater*** *ou* **perdre une ~ de faire** to miss an opportunity to do ◆ **tu as manqué** *ou* **raté* une belle** *ou* **bonne ~ de te taire** *(iro)* you'd have done better to have kept quiet, why couldn't you keep your mouth shut? ◆ **c'est l'~ rêvée !** it's a heaven-sent opportunity! ◆ **c'est l'~ rêvée de faire** it's an ideal opportunity to do ◆ **c'est l'~ ou jamais !** it's now or never! ◆ **c'est l'~ ou jamais d'observer cette comète** it's a once-in-a-lifetime chance *ou* opportunity to see this comet ◆ **si l'~ se présente** if the opportunity arises, should the opportunity *ou* occasion arise ◆ **à la première ~** at the earliest *ou* first opportunity

3 *(= objet d'occasion)* secondhand buy; *(= acquisition avantageuse)* bargain ◆ **(le marché de) l'~** the secondhand market ◆ **faire le neuf et l'~** to deal in new and secondhand goods

4 *(locutions)*

◆ **d'occasion** *(= accidentel) [amitié, rencontre]* casual; *(= pas neuf)* secondhand; *[voiture]* secondhand, used *(US)*, pre-owned *(US)*; *[acheter, vendre]* secondhand

> ⚠ Au sens de 'acquisition avantageuse', **occasion** ne se traduit pas par le mot anglais **occasion**.

occasionnel, -elle /ɔkazjɔnɛl/ ADJ **1** *(= non régulier)* occasional; *[travaux, emploi]* casual **2** *(= fortuit) [incident, rencontre]* chance *(épith)* **3** *(Philos)* occasional

occasionnellement /ɔkazjɔnɛlmɑ̃/ ADV occasionally, from time to time

occasionner /ɔkazjɔne/ ▸ conjug 1 ◂ VT *[+ frais, dérangement]* to cause, to occasion *(frm)*; *[+ accident]* to cause, to bring about ◆ **en espérant ne pas vous ~ trop de dérangement** hoping not to put you to *ou* to cause you too much trouble ◆ **cet accident va m'~ beaucoup de frais** this accident is going to involve me in *ou* to cause me a great deal of expense

occident /ɔksidɑ̃/ NM *(littér = ouest)* west ◆ **l'Occident** the West, the Occident *(littér)*; → **empire**

> ⚠ **Occident** se traduit rarement par le mot anglais **Occident**, qui est d'un registre plus soutenu que 'West'.

occidental, e (mpl **-aux**) /ɔksidɑ̃tal, o/ ADJ *(littér = d'ouest)* western; *(Pol) [pays, peuple]* Western, Occidental *(littér)*; → **Inde** NM,F **Occidental(e)** Westerner, Occidental *(littér)* ◆ **les Occidentaux** *(gén)* Westerners; *(Pol)* the West, western countries

occidentalisation /ɔksidɑ̃talizasjɔ̃/ NF westernization

occidentaliser /ɔksidɑ̃talize/ ▸ conjug 1 ◂ VT to westernize VPR **s'occidentaliser** to become westernized

occipital, e (mpl **-aux**) /ɔksipital, o/ ADJ occipital ◆ **trou ~** occipital foramen, foramen magnum NM occipital (bone)

occiput /ɔksipyt/ NM back of the head, occiput *(SPÉC)*

occire /ɔksiʀ/ VT († † *ou hum*) to slay

occitan, e /ɔksitɑ̃, an/ ADJ, NM Occitan NM,F **Occitan(e)** Occitan

Occitanie /ɔksitani/ NF *region in France where Occitan is spoken*

occitaniste /ɔksitanist/ NMF specialist in Occitan

occlure /ɔklyʀ/ ▸ conjug 35 ◂ VT *(Chim, Méd)* to occlude

occlusif, -ive /ɔklyzif, iv/ ADJ *(gén)* occlusive; *(Ling)* occlusive, plosive ◆ **(consonne) occlusive** occlusive, stop (consonant)

occlusion /ɔklyzjɔ̃/ NF *(Ling, Méd, Météo, Tech)* occlusion ◆ **~ intestinale** intestinal blockage, obstruction of the bowels *ou* intestines, ileus *(SPÉC)*

occultation /ɔkyltasjɔ̃/ NF *(Astron)* occultation; *(fig)* overshadowing, eclipse ◆ **l'~ du problème du chômage pendant la campagne électorale** the temporary eclipse of the issue of unemployment during the election campaign

occulte /ɔkylt/ ADJ **1** *(= surnaturel)* supernatural, occult; → **science** **2** *(= secret) [+ financement, fonds]* secret, covert; *[+ commission, prime]* hidden; *[+ pouvoir, rôle]* secret, hidden

> ⚠ **occulte** se traduit par **occult** uniquement au sens de 'surnaturel'.

occulter /ɔkylte/ ▸ conjug 1 ◂ VT *(Astron, Tech)* to occult ◆ **n'essayez pas d'~ le problème** don't try to hide the problem ◆ **cela ne doit pas ~ les dures réalités de la situation sur le terrain** this should not blind us to the harsh realities of the situation ◆ **ses musiques de film ont souvent été occultées par ses chansons à succès** his film scores have often been overshadowed by his hit songs ◆ **ces questions capitales, longtemps occultées, devront faire l'objet d'un débat national** we need a national debate on the key issues, which have long been lost sight of *ou* neglected

occultisme /ɔkyltism/ NM occultism

occultiste /ɔkyltist/ ADJ, NMF occultist

occupant, e /ɔkypɑ̃, ɑ̃t/ ADJ *(Pol) [autorité, puissance]* occupying ◆ **l'armée ~e** the army of occupation, the occupying army NM,F *[de maison]* occupant, occupier; *[de place, compartiment, voiture]* occupant ◆ **le premier ~** *(gén, Jur)* the first occupier NM ◆ **l'~, les ~s** the occupying forces

occupation /ɔkypasjɔ̃/ NF **1** *(Mil, Pol)* occupation ◆ **les forces/l'armée d'~** the forces/the army of occupation, the occupying forces/army ◆ **pendant l'Occupation** *(Hist)* during the Occupation ◆ **grève avec ~ d'usine** sit-in, sit-down strike **2** *(Jur) [de logement]* occupancy, occupation **3** *(= passe-temps)* occupation; *(= emploi)* occupation, job ◆ **vaquer à ses ~s** to go about one's business, to attend to one's affairs ◆ **une ~ fixe/temporaire** a permanent/temporary job *ou* occupation ◆ **les enfants, ça donne de l'~** having children certainly keeps you busy

occupé, e /ɔkype/ GRAMMAIRE ACTIVE 54.5 (ptp de **occuper**) ADJ **1** *(= non disponible, affairé)* busy ◆ **je suis très ~ en ce moment** I'm very busy at the moment ◆ **il ne peut pas vous recevoir, il est ~** he can't see you, he's busy **2** *[ligne téléphonique]* engaged *(Brit) (attrib)*, busy *(US) (attrib)*; *[toilettes]* occupied, engaged *(Brit) (attrib)*; *[places, sièges]* taken *(attrib)* ◆ **ça sonne ~*** it's engaged *(Brit) ou* busy *(US)* ◆ **c'est ~ ?** *(place)* is this seat taken? **3** *(Mil, Pol) [zone, usine]* occupied

occuper /ɔkype/ ▸ conjug 1 ◂ VT **1** *[+ endroit, appartement]* to occupy; *[+ place, surface]* to occupy, to take up ◆ **le bureau occupait le coin de la pièce** the desk stood in the corner of the room ◆ **leurs bureaux occupent tout l'étage** their offices take up *ou* occupy the whole floor ◆ **le piano occupe très peu/trop de place** the piano takes up very little/too much room ◆ **l'appartement qu'ils occupent est trop exigu** their present flat is *ou* the flat they're in now is too small

2 *[+ moment, période] (= prendre)* to occupy, to fill, to take up; *(= faire passer)* to occupy, to spend, to employ ◆ **cette besogne occupait le reste de la journée** this task took (up) the rest of the day ◆ **la lecture occupe une trop petite part de mon temps** I don't spend enough time reading ◆ **la lecture occupe une très grande part de mon temps** I spend a lot of my time reading ◆ **comment ~ ses loisirs ?** how can one fill one's free time? ◆ **ça occupe** it's something to do, it fills the time

3 *[+ poste, fonction]* to hold, to occupy; *[+ rang]* to hold, to have

4 *(= absorber) [+ personne, enfant]* to occupy, to keep occupied *ou* busy; *(= employer) [+ main d'œuvre]* to employ ◆ **mon travail m'occupe beaucoup** my work keeps me very busy ◆ **laisse-le faire, ça l'occupe !** let him get on with it, it keeps him busy! *ou* occupied! ◆ **la ganterie occupait naguère un millier d'ouvriers dans cette région** the glove industry used to employ to about a thousand workers in this area ◆ **le sujet qui nous occupe aujourd'hui** the matter which concerns us today

5 *(Mil, Pol) (= envahir)* to occupy; *(= être maître de)* to occupy ◆ **ils ont occupé tout le pays/l'immeuble** they occupied the whole country/the whole building ◆ **les forces qui occupaient le pays** the forces occupying the country ◆ **grâce à son nouveau produit, l'entreprise occupe le terrain** thanks to its new product the company has been able to take a prominent position in the market ◆ **il veut ~ le terrain médiatique** he wants to hog* the media limelight ◆ **ils occupent le terrain de l'informatique** they've cornered a significant share of the computer market

VPR **s'occuper** **1** ◆ **s'~ de qch** *(= se charger de)* to deal with sth, to take care *ou* charge of sth; *(= être chargé de)* to be in charge of sth, to be dealing with *ou* taking care of sth; *(= s'intéresser à)* to take an interest in sth, to interest o.s. in sth ◆ **je vais m'~ de ce problème** I'll deal with *ou* take care of this problem ◆ **c'est lui qui s'occupe de cette affaire** he's the one responsible for this, he's the one who's dealing with this ◆ **il s'occupe de vous trouver un emploi** he'll see about finding you a job ◆ **je vais m'~ de rassembler les documents nécessaires** I'll get to work and collect the documents we need, I'll undertake to get the necessary documents together ◆ **il s'occupe un peu de politique** he takes a bit of an interest *ou* he dabbles a bit in politics ◆ **je m'occupe de tout** I'll see to everything, I'll take care of everything ◆ **je m'occuperai des boissons** I'll organize *ou* look after the drinks ◆ **il veut s'~ de trop de choses à la fois** he tries to take on *ou* to do too many things at once ◆ **ne t'occupe pas de ça, c'est leur problème** don't worry about it, that's their problem ◆ **occupe-toi de tes affaires** * *ou* **oignons** * mind your own business ◆ **t'occupe (pas) !*** none of your business! * mind your own business!

2 ◆ **s'~ de** *(= se charger de)* *[+ enfants, malades]* to take care of sb, to look after sb; *[+ client]* to attend to sb; *(= être responsable de)* *[+ enfants, malades]* to be in charge of sb, to look after sb ◆ **je vais m'~ des enfants** I'll take care of *ou* I'll look after the children ◆ **qui s'occupe des malades ?** who is in charge of *ou* looks after the patients? ◆ **je m'occupe de vous tout de suite** I'll be with you in a moment ◆ **est-ce qu'on s'occupe de vous Madame ?** are you being attended to *ou* served?

3 *(= s'affairer)* to occupy o.s., to keep o.s. busy ◆ **s'~ à faire qch/à qch** to busy o.s. doing sth/with sth ◆ **il a trouvé à s'~** he has found something to do *ou* to occupy his time ◆ **il y a de quoi s'~** there is plenty to do ◆ **je ne sais pas à quoi m'~** I don't know what to do with myself ◆ **s'~ l'esprit** to keep one's mind occupied

occurrence /ɔkyʀɑ̃s/ **NF** 1 *(frm)* instance, case ◆ **en cette/toute autre** ~ in this/in any other instance ◆ **en l'~** to be specific ◆ **un même sport, en l'~ le football, peut être très différent en deux endroits de la planète** the same sport, football to be specific, can be very different in two parts of the world ◆ **en pareille** ~ in such circumstances, in such a case ◆ **suivant** *ou* **selon l'~** *(frm)* according to the circumstances 2 *(Ling)* occurrence, token

OCDE /ɔsedeə/ **NF** (abrév de **Organisation de coopération et de développement économique**) OECD

océan /ɔseɑ̃/ **NM** 1 *(lit)* ocean ◆ **l'Océan** *(= Atlantique)* the Atlantic (Ocean) ◆ **un ~ de verdure/de sable** a sea of greenery/of sand ◆ **l'~ Antarctique** *ou* **Austral** the Antarctic (Ocean) ◆ **l'~ Arctique** the Arctic (Ocean) ◆ **l'~ Atlantique** the Atlantic (Ocean) ◆ **l'~ glacial** the polar sea ◆ **l'~ Indien** the Indian Ocean ◆ **l'~ Pacifique** the Pacific (Ocean) 2 *(Myth)* **Océan** Oceanus

océanarium /ɔseanaʀjɔm/ **NM** oceanarium

océane /ɔsean/ **ADJ F** 1 *(littér)* *[vague, tempête]* ocean *(épith)*; *[fureur, senteur]* of the sea *ou* ocean ◆ **l'(autoroute)** ~ *the motorway that links Paris to Brittany* 2 *(Culin)* *[salade, paella]* seafood *(épith)*

Océanie /ɔseani/ **NF** ◆ **l'~** Oceania, the South Sea Islands

océanien, -ienne /ɔseanjɛ̃, jɛn/ **ADJ** Oceanian, Oceanic **NM,F** ◆ **Océanien(ne)** South Sea Islander, Oceanian

océanique /ɔseanik/ **ADJ** oceanic

océanographe /ɔseanɔgʀaf/ **NMF** oceanographer

océanographie /ɔseanɔgʀafi/ **NF** oceanography

océanographique /ɔseanɔgʀafik/ **ADJ** oceanographic

océanologie /ɔseanɔlɔʒi/ **NF** oceanology

océanologique /ɔseanɔlɔʒik/ **ADJ** oceanological

océanologue /ɔseanɔlɔg/ **NMF** oceanologist

ocelle /ɔsɛl/ **NM** ocellus

ocellé, e /ɔsele, ɔselle/ **ADJ** ocellate(d)

ocelot /ɔs(ə)lo/ **NM** *(= animal)* ocelot; *(= fourrure)* ocelot fur

ocre /ɔkʀ/ **NMF, ADJ INV** ochre

ocré, e /ɔkʀe/ **ADJ** ochred

octaèdre /ɔktaɛdʀ/ **ADJ** octahedral **NM** octahedron

octaédrique /ɔktaedʀik/ **ADJ** octahedral

octal, e (pl **-aux**) /ɔktal, o/ **ADJ** octal ◆ **système** ~ octal notation

octane /ɔktan/ **NM** octane; → **indice**

octante /ɔktɑ̃t/ **ADJ INV** *(dial)* eighty

octave /ɔktav/ **NF** 1 *(Mus)* octave ◆ **monter à l'~** to go an octave higher 2 *(Escrime, Rel)* octave

octet /ɔktɛ/ **NM** byte

octobre /ɔktɔbʀ/ **NM** October; *pour loc voir* **septembre**

octogénaire /ɔktɔʒenɛʀ/ **ADJ, NMF** octogenarian

octogonal, e (mpl **-aux**) /ɔktɔgɔnal, o/ **ADJ** octagonal, eight-sided

octogone /ɔktɔgɔn/ **NM** octagon

octopode /ɔktɔpɔd/ **ADJ** octopod **NM** octopod ◆ **les ~s** octopods, Octopoda *(SPÉC)*

octosyllabe /ɔktosi(l)lab/ **ADJ** octosyllabic **NM** octosyllable

octosyllabique /ɔktosi(l)labik/ **ADJ** octosyllabic

octroi /ɔktʀwa/ **NM** 1 *[de charte, permission, délai, augmentation]* granting; *[de faveur, pardon]* bestowing, granting ◆ **l'~ d'une bourse n'est pas automatique** grants are not given automatically 2 *(Hist)* octroi, city toll

octroyer /ɔktʀwaje/ ▸ conjug 8 ◂ **VT** *(frm)* *[+ charte, permission, délai, augmentation]* to grant *(à* to); *[+ bourse]* to give *(à* to); *[+ faveur, pardon]* to bestow *(à* on, upon) to grant *(à* to) **VPR** **s'octroyer** *[+ droit, pouvoirs]* to claim; *(Sport)* *[+ médaille, place]* to claim, win ◆ **s'~ une augmentation** to give o.s. a pay rise ◆ **je vais m'~ quelques jours de congé** I'm going to allow myself a few days off

octuor /ɔktɥɔʀ/ **NM** *(Mus)* octet

octuple /ɔktypl/ **ADJ** *[quantité, rangée, nombre]* octuple ◆ **une quantité ~ de l'autre** a quantity eight times (as great as) the other **NM** *(Math)* octuple ◆ **je l'ai payé l'~ (de l'autre)** I paid eight times as much (as the other) for it

oculaire /ɔkylɛʀ/ **ADJ** *(Anat)* ocular; → **globe, témoin** **NM** *(Opt)* eyepiece, ocular *(SPÉC)*

oculiste /ɔkylist/ **NMF** eye specialist, oculist, eye doctor *(US)*

odalisque /ɔdalisk/ **NF** odalisque

ode /ɔd/ **NF** ode

odeur /ɔdœʀ/ **NF** 1 *(gén : bonne ou mauvaise)* smell; *[de fleur, parfum]* fragrance, scent ◆ **sans ~** odourless *(Brit)*, odorless *(US)*, which has no smell ◆ **mauvaise ~** bad *ou* unpleasant smell ◆ **produit qui combat les (mauvaises) ~s** air freshener ◆ **~ suave/délicieuse** sweet/delicious smell *ou* scent ◆ **à l'~ fétide** evil-smelling, foul-smelling ◆ **~ de brûlé/de gaz** smell of burning/of gas ◆ **~ de renfermé** musty *ou* fusty smell ◆ **avoir une bonne/une mauvaise ~** to smell nice/bad; → **argent**

2 *(locutions)* **ne pas être en ~ de sainteté auprès de qn** to be in sb's bad books, to be out of favour with sb, to be in bad odour with sb ◆ **mourir en ~ de sainteté** *(Rel)* to die in the odour of sanctity

> ⚠ Attention à ne pas traduire automatiquement **odeur** par **odour**, qui a des emplois spécifiques et est d'un registre plus soutenu.

odieusement /ɔdjøzmɑ̃/ **ADV** odiously

odieux, -ieuse /ɔdjø, jøz/ **ADJ** 1 *(= infâme)* *[personne, conduite, caractère, tâche]* horrible; *[crime, chantage, accusation]* appalling ◆ **tu as été ~ avec elle** you were horrible to her ◆ **c'est ~ ce que tu viens de dire !** that's a horrible thing to say! ◆ **tu es ~ !** you're horrible! 2 *(= insupportable)* **la vie m'est odieuse** life is unbearable to me ◆ **cette femme m'est odieuse** I can't bear that woman, I can't stand that woman

odontologie /ɔdɔ̃tɔlɔʒi/ **NF** odontology

odontologique /ɔdɔ̃tɔlɔʒik/ **ADJ** odontological

odontologiste /ɔdɔ̃tɔlɔʒist/ **NMF** odontologist

odorant, e /ɔdɔʀɑ̃, ɑ̃t/ **ADJ** *(gén)* scented; *(plus agréable)* fragrant, sweet-smelling; *[herbes, essences]* aromatic; *[substance, molécule]* odorous

odorat /ɔdɔʀa/ **NM** (sense of) smell ◆ **avoir l'~ fin** to have a keen sense of smell

odoriférant, e /ɔdɔʀifeʀɑ̃, ɑ̃t/ **ADJ** sweet-smelling, fragrant, odoriferous *(littér)*

odyssée /ɔdise/ **NF** odyssey

OEA /ɔəa/ **NF** (abrév de **Organisation des États américains**) OAS

œcuménique /ekymenik/ **ADJ** (o)ecumenical; → **concile**

œcuménisme /ekymenism/ **NM** (o)ecumenicalism, (o)ecumenism

œcuméniste /ekymenist/ **ADJ, NMF** (o)ecumenist

œdémateux, -euse /edematø, øz/ **ADJ** oedematous, oedematose

œdème /edɛm/ **NM** oedema ◆ **~ du poumon** pulmonary oedema

œdipien, -ienne /edipjɛ̃, jɛn/ **ADJ** oedipal, oedipean

œil /œj/ (pluriel **yeux**)

1 NOM MASCULIN	2 COMPOSÉS

1 - NOM MASCULIN

1 Anat eye ◆ **il a les yeux bleus** he has blue eyes, his eyes are blue ◆ **aux yeux bleus** blue-eyed, with blue eyes ◆ **yeux de biche** doe eyes ◆ **aux yeux de biche** doe-eyed *(épith)* ◆ **yeux en boutons de bottines** button eyes ◆ **elle se fait les yeux** she's putting her eye make-up on ◆ **elle a les yeux faits, elle s'est fait les yeux** she's wearing eye make-up ◆ **avoir un ~ au beurre noir** * *ou* **un ~ poché** * to have a black eye *ou* a shiner * ◆ **avoir les yeux battus** to have dark *ou* black rings under one's eyes ◆ **avoir un ~ qui dit zut** * *ou* **merde** * **à l'autre, avoir les yeux qui se croisent (les bras)** *, **avoir un ~ à Paris, l'autre à Pontoise** * to be cross-eyed * *ou* boss-eyed *, to have a squint ◆ **les yeux lui sortaient de la tête, il avait les yeux hors de la tête** his eyes were (nearly) popping out of his head, his eyes were out on stalks * *(Brit)* ◆ **je vois mal de cet ~** I don't see well with this eye ◆ **je l'ai vu de mes (propres) yeux, je l'ai vu, de mes yeux vu** I saw it with my own eyes ◆ **regarde-moi dans les yeux** look me in the eye ◆ **j'ai le soleil dans les yeux** the sun is in my eyes, I've got the sun in my eyes ◆ **la casquette sur l'~** with his cap cocked over one eye ◆ **faire qch pour les beaux yeux**

de qn to do sth just for sb *ou* just to please sb ◆ **il n'a pas les yeux en face des trous** * (*= il est endormi*) he's half asleep; (*= il n'arrive pas à réfléchir*) he's not thinking straight ◆ **il a les yeux plus grands** *ou* **gros que le ventre** (*gloutonnerie*) his eyes are bigger than his belly *ou* stomach; (*ambition*) he has bitten off more than he can chew ◆ **œil pour œil, dent pour dent** (*Prov*) an eye for an eye, a tooth for a tooth (*Prov*) → **fermer, gros**

◆ **à l'œil nu** [*visible, identifiable, invisible*] to the naked eye ◆ **on peut observer cette comète à l'~ nu** the comet is visible to the naked eye

◆ **les yeux dans les yeux** ◆ **se regarder les yeux dans les yeux** to gaze into each other's eyes ◆ **je lui ai dit/répliqué les yeux dans les yeux** ... I looked him straight in the eye and said/replied ... ◆ **ils en ont discuté les yeux dans les yeux** (*franchement*) they spoke very frankly with each other

2 = regard **attirer** *ou* **tirer l'~ de qn** to catch sb's eye ◆ **publicité qui attire l'~** eye-catching advertisement ◆ **être agréable à l'~** to be easy on the eye ◆ **n'avoir d'yeux que pour qn/qch** to have one's attention focussed on sb/sth ◆ **il n'a d'yeux que pour elle** he only has eyes for her ◆ **jeter un ~** * **à** *ou* **sur qn/qch** to have a look* at sb/sth ◆ **cela s'est passé devant nos yeux** it happened in front of *ou* before *ou* under our very eyes; → **chercher, couver, dévorer, suivre**

◆ **aux yeux de** (*= en étant vu de*) ◆ **faire qch aux yeux de tous** to do sth in full view of everyone ◆ **aux yeux de l'opinion publique** in the eyes of the public

◆ **les yeux fermés** (*= sans regarder*) with one's eyes closed *ou* shut; (*= avec confiance*) with complete confidence ◆ **j'irais les yeux fermés** I could get there with my eyes closed

◆ **sous l'œil** *ou* **les yeux (de)** ◆ **vous avez l'article sous les yeux** you have the article there before you *ou* right in front of you *ou* your eyes ◆ **sous l'~ (vigilant/inquiet) de** under the (watchful/anxious) eye *ou* gaze of ◆ **ils jouaient sous l'~ de leur mère** they played under the watchful eye of their mother *ou* with their mother looking on ◆ **sous l'~ des caméras** in front of the cameras

3 = faculté de voir **avoir de bons/mauvais yeux** to have good/bad eyes *ou* eyesight ◆ **il n'a plus ses yeux de vingt ans** his eyes aren't what they used to be ◆ **avoir un ~** *ou* **des yeux de lynx** (*= avoir une très bonne vue*) to have eyes like a hawk; (*fig*) to be eagle-eyed ◆ **avoir des yeux de chat** (*= voir dans le noir*) to have good night vision ◆ **il faudrait avoir des yeux derrière la tête** you need eyes in the back of your head

4 = expression look ◆ **il a l'~ taquin/méchant** he has a twinkle/a malicious look in his eye ◆ **elle a l'~ vif** she has a lively look about her *ou* a lively expression ◆ **il le regardait l'~ mauvais** *ou* **d'un ~ mauvais** he fixed him with a threatening stare *ou* look, he looked *ou* stared at him threateningly ◆ **faire des yeux de velours à qn, faire les yeux doux à qn** to make sheep's eyes at sb ◆ **faire de l'~ à qn** * to make eyes at sb, to give sb the eye* ◆ **faire** *ou* **ouvrir des yeux ronds, ouvrir de grands yeux** to stare wide-eyed ◆ **il me regardait avec des yeux comme des soucoupes** he looked at me with eyes like saucers ◆ **regarder qn avec des yeux de merlan frit** * *ou* **de crapaud mort d'amour** * to look at sb like a lovesick puppy ◆ **faire des yeux de merlan frit** * (*surprise*) to gawp*

5 = attention, observation **il a l'~** * he has sharp *ou* keen eyes ◆ **avoir l'~ à tout** to keep an eye on everything ◆ **avoir l'~ américain** to have a quick eye ◆ **avoir l'~ du spécialiste/du maître** to have a trained/an expert eye, to have the eye of a specialist/of an expert ◆ **cacher qch aux yeux de qn** to hide sth from sb's eyes ◆ **il n'a pas les yeux dans sa poche** he doesn't miss a thing ◆ **garder un ~ sur qn/qch** to keep an eye on sb/sth ◆ **être tout yeux** * to be all eyes*; → **compas, ouvrir**

◆ **à l'œil** (*= sous surveillance*) ◆ **avoir** *ou* **tenir qn à l'~** to keep an eye on sb ◆ **je vous ai à l'~ !** I've got my eye on you!

6 = jugement **voir** *ou* **regarder qch d'un bon/d'un mauvais ~** to look on *ou* view sth favourably/unfavourably, to view sth in a favourable/in an unfavourable light ◆ **considérer qch d'un ~ critique** to consider sth with a critical eye, to look at sth critically ◆ **il ne voit pas cela du même ~ qu'elle** he doesn't take the same view as she does ◆ **il voit cela avec les yeux de la foi** he sees it through the eyes of a believer

◆ **à mes yeux** in my opinion *ou* eyes

7 locutions **coûter/payer les yeux de la tête** (*= très cher*) to cost/pay the earth *ou* a (small) fortune ◆ **à l'~** * (*= gratuitement*) for nothing, for free* ◆ **mon ~ !**‡ (*= je n'y crois pas*) my eye!*, my foot!*; (*= je ne le ferai pas*) nothing doing!*, not likely!*

◆ **coup d'œil** (*= regard rapide*) glance, quick look; (*= vue*) view ◆ **d'ici, le coup d'~ est joli** there's a lovely view from here ◆ **ça vaut le coup d'~** it's worth seeing ◆ **au** *ou* **du premier coup d'~** at first glance ◆ **avoir le coup d'~ pour** (*fig*) to have an eye for ◆ **jeter** *ou* **lancer un coup d'~ à qn** to glance at sb, to look quickly at sb ◆ **jeter un coup d'~ à** [*+ texte, objet*] to glance at, to take *ou* have (*Brit*) a glance *ou* quick look at ◆ **allons jeter un coup d'~** let's go and take *ou* have (*Brit*) a look

8 = trou, boucle [*d'aiguille, marteau*] eye; [*de filin*] eye, loop

9 Typo [*de caractère*] (pl **œils**) face

10 Bot = bourgeon bud; [*de pomme de terre*] eye

11 Culin **les yeux du bouillon** the globules *ou* droplets of fat in the stock

2 - COMPOSÉS

l'œil du cyclone (*Météo*) the eye of the cyclone *ou* hurricane; (*fig*) the eye of the storm
œil électronique electric eye
œil de verre glass eye

œil-de-bœuf (pl **œils-de-bœuf**) /œjdəbœf/ NM bull's-eye (window), œil-de-bœuf

œil-de-chat (pl **œils-de-chat**) /œjdəʃa/ NM (*Minér*) cat's eye

œil-de-perdrix (pl **œils-de-perdrix**) /œjdəpɛʀdʀi/ NM (*= cor au pied*) soft corn

œil-de-pie (pl **œils-de-pie**) /œjdəpi/ NM (*Naut*) eyelet

œil-de-tigre (pl **œils-de-tigre**) /œjdətigʀ/ NM (*Minér*) tiger's-eye, tigereye

œillade /œjad/ NF wink ◆ **faire des ~s à qn** to make eyes at sb, to give sb the eye* ◆ **jeter** *ou* **décocher une ~ à qn** to wink at sb, to give sb a wink

œillère /œjɛʀ/ NF (*Méd*) eyebath, eyecup NFPL **œillères** [*de cheval*] blinkers ◆ **avoir des œillères** (*fig, péj*) to wear blinkers, to be blinkered

œillet /œjɛ/ NM 1 (*= fleur*) carnation ◆ **~ d'Inde** French marigold ◆ **~ mignardise** pink ◆ **~ de poète** sweet william 2 (*= petit trou*) eyelet; (*= bordure*) grommet

œilleton /œjtɔ̃/ NM [*de télescope*] eyepiece; [*de porte*] spyhole; (*Bot*) bud

œillette /œjɛt/ NF (*= pavot*) oil poppy; (*= huile*) poppy(seed) oil

œnologie /enɔlɔʒi/ NF oenology

œnologique /enɔlɔʒik/ ADJ oenological

œnologue /enɔlɔg/ NMF oenologist, wine expert

œsophage /ezɔfaʒ/ NM oesophagus (*Brit*), esophagus (*US*)

œsophagien, -ienne /ezɔfaʒjɛ̃, jɛn/, **œsophagique** /ezɔfaʒik/ ADJ oesophageal (*Brit*), esophageal (*US*)

œstradiol /ɛstʀadjɔl/ NM oestradiol (*Brit*), estradiol (*US*)

œstral, e (mpl **-aux**) /ɛstʀal, o/ ADJ ◆ **cycle ~** oestrous (*Brit*) *ou* estrous (*US*) cycle

œstrogène /ɛstʀɔʒɛn/ NM oestrogen (*Brit*), estrogen (*US*)

œstrus /ɛstʀys/ NM oestrus (*Brit*), estrus (*US*)

œuf (pl **œufs**) /œf, ø/ NM 1 (*Bio, Culin*) egg ◆ **~ du jour/frais** new-laid (*Brit*) *ou* freshly-lain (*US*)/fresh egg ◆ **~ de caille/de poule** quail's/hen's egg ◆ **~s de poisson** (*dans l'eau*) spawn; (*utilisés en cuisine*) fish roe ◆ **en (forme d')~** egg-shaped; → **blanc, jaune**

2 (* *= idiot*) **quel ~ ce type !** what a blockhead* this fellow is!

3 (*= télécabine*) (egg-shaped) cablecar

4 (*locutions*) **étouffer** *ou* **écraser** *ou* **détruire qch dans l'~** to nip sth in the bud ◆ **mettre tous ses ~s dans le même panier** to put all one's eggs in one basket ◆ **c'est comme l'~ de Colomb (, il fallait y penser) !** it's simple when you know how!, it's easy once you think of it! ◆ **c'est l'~ et la poule** it's a chicken and egg situation ◆ **il est à peine sorti de l'~** * he's still wet behind the ears* ◆ **va te faire cuire un ~ !**‡ (go and) take a running jump!*, get stuffed!‡; → **marcher, omelette**

COMP **œufs brouillés** scrambled eggs
œuf en chocolat chocolate egg
œuf à la coque (soft-)boiled egg
œuf dur hard-boiled egg
œuf en gelée egg in aspic *ou* jelly
œufs au lait ≈ egg custard
œufs de lump lumpfish roe
œufs mimosa eggs mimosa (*hors d'oeuvre made with chopped egg yolks*)
œuf (au) miroir ⇒ **œuf sur le plat**
œuf mollet soft-boiled egg
œufs à la neige œufs à la neige, floating islands
œuf de Pâques Easter egg
œuf de pigeon (*lit*) pigeon's egg; (* *= bosse*) bump (on the head) ◆ **gros comme un ~ de pigeon** the size of a pigeon's egg
œuf sur le plat *ou* **au plat** fried egg
œuf poché poached egg
œuf à repriser darning egg

œuvre /œvʀ/ NF 1 (*= livre, tableau, film*) work; (*= ensemble d'une production artistique*) works ◆ **c'est une ~ de jeunesse** it's an early work ◆ **toute l'~ de Picasso** Picasso's entire oeuvre ◆ **les ~s complètes/choisies de Victor Hugo** the complete/selected works of Victor Hugo ◆ **l'~ romanesque de Balzac** the novels of Balzac

2 (*= tâche*) undertaking, task; (*= travail achevé*) work (*NonC*) ◆ **ce sera une ~ de longue haleine** it will be a long-term task *ou* undertaking ◆ **admirant leur ~** admiring their work ◆ **la satisfaction de l'~ accomplie** the satisfaction of a job well done ◆ **ce beau gâchis, c'est l'~ des enfants** this fine mess is the children's doing *ou* work ◆ **ces formations sont l'~ du vent et de l'eau** these formations are the work of wind and water; → **maître, pied**

3 (*= acte*) **~(s)** deed, work ◆ **être jugé selon ses ~s** to be judged by one's works *ou* deeds ◆ **enceinte de ses ~s** (*frm, hum*) with child by him, bearing his child ◆ **(bonnes) ~s** good *ou* charitable works ◆ **faire ~ pie** (*littér*) to do a pious deed ◆ **aide-le, ce sera une bonne ~** help him, that will be a kind act *ou* an act of kindness; → **fils**

4 (*= organisation*) **~ (de bienfaisance** *ou* **de charité)** charitable organization, charity ◆ **les ~s** charity, charities

5 (locutions) **être/se mettre à l'~** to be at/get down to work ◆ **voir qn à l'~** (lit) to see sb at work; (iro) to see sb in action ◆ **faire ~ utile** to do something worthwhile ou useful ◆ **faire ~ de pionnier/médiateur** to act as a pioneer/mediator ◆ **la mort avait fait son ~** death had (already) claimed its own ◆ **le feu avait fait son ~** the fire had wrought its havoc ou had done its work ◆ **faire ~ durable** to create a work of lasting significance ou importance ◆ **mettre en ~** [+ moyens] to implement, to make use of ◆ **il avait tout mis en ~ pour éviter la dévaluation/pour les aider** he had done everything possible ou had taken all possible steps to avoid devaluation/to help them ◆ **la mise en ~ d'importants moyens** the implementation ou the bringing into play of considerable resources ◆ **à l'~ on ou c'est à l'~ qu'on connaît l'ouvrier** (Prov) a man is judged ou known by his works ou by the work he does

NM 1 (littér) **l'~ gravé/sculpté de Picasso** the etchings/sculptures of Picasso

2 (Constr) **second ~** finishings; → **grand, gros**

COMP **œuvre d'art** (lit, fig) work of art

œuvres mortes (Naut) upper works, topsides

œuvres sociales (Jur) company benefit scheme (Brit) ou plan (US)

œuvres vives (Naut) quickwork; (fig, littér) vitals

œuvrer /œvʀe/ ► conjug 1 ◄ VI (littér ou hum) to work (à, pour for) ◆ **~ aux côtés de qn** to work side by side with sb

off /ɔf/ ADJ INV [concert, festival] fringe, alternative; → **voix**

offensant, e /ɔfɑ̃sɑ̃, ɑ̃t/ ADJ insulting, offensive

offense /ɔfɑ̃s/ NF 1 (frm = affront) insult ◆ **faire ~ à** to offend, to insult ◆ **il n'y a pas d'~** * (hum) no offence taken ◆ **soit dit sans ~** (frm) no offence (intended ou meant) 2 (Rel = péché) transgression, trespass, offence ◆ **pardonnez-nous nos ~s** forgive us our trespasses ◆ **~ à ou envers** [+ chef d'État] libel against; [+ Dieu] offence against

offensé, e /ɔfɑ̃se/ (ptp de **offenser**) ADJ offended NM,F offended ou injured party

offenser /ɔfɑ̃se/ ► conjug 1 ◄ VT 1 [+ personne] to offend, to give offence to ◆ **je n'ai pas voulu vous ~** I didn't mean to offend you ou to give offence ◆ **~ Dieu** to offend God, to trespass against God 2 (littér) [+ sentiments] to offend, to insult; [+ souvenir] to insult; [+ personne, bon goût] to offend; [+ règles, principes] to offend against VPR **s'offenser** to take offence (de qch at sth)

offenseur /ɔfɑ̃sœʀ/ NM offender

offensif, -ive /ɔfɑ̃sif, iv/ ADJ (Mil) offensive ◆ **il sont très ~s, ils ont un jeu très ~** (Sport) they play an attacking game

offensive /ɔfɑ̃siv/ NF offensive ◆ **prendre l'~** to take the offensive ◆ **passer à l'~** to go on the offensive ◆ **lancer une ~** to launch an offensive (contre against); ◆ **l'~ de l'hiver/du froid** the onslaught of winter/of the cold ◆ **~ diplomatique/de paix** diplomatic/peace offensive ◆ **~ commerciale de grande envergure** large-scale commercial offensive

offertoire /ɔfɛʀtwaʀ/ NM (Rel) offertory

office /ɔfis/ NM 1 (littér = tâche) duties, office; (Hist) charge, office; (Admin) office ◆ **remplir l'~ de directeur/chauffeur** to hold the office ou post of manager/chauffeur ◆ **~ ministériel** ministerial office ◆ **le bourreau a fait ou rempli son ~** the executioner carried out his duties

2 (= usage) **faire ~ de** to act ou serve as ◆ **faire ~ de chauffeur** to act as (a) chauffeur ◆ **remplir son ~** [appareil, loi] to serve its purpose, to fulfil its function, to do its job *

3 (= bureau) office, bureau ◆ **~ national/départemental** national/regional office ◆ **~ du tourisme** tourist information (centre), tourist office ◆ **Office national des forêts** ≈ Forest Commission (Brit), Forestry Service (US); → **musée**

4 (Rel) (= messe) (church) service; (= prières) prayers ◆ **l'~ (divin)** the (divine) office ◆ **l'~ des morts** the office ou service for the dead ◆ **aller à/manquer l'~** to go to/miss church ou the church service

5 (locutions)

◆ **d'office** ◆ **être nommé/mis à la retraite d'~** to be appointed/retired automatically ou as a matter of course ◆ **faire qch d'~** (Admin) to do sth automatically; (gén) to do sth as a matter of course ou automatically ◆ **avocat/expert (commis) d'~** officially appointed lawyer/expert

6 (littér = service) office ◆ **bons ~s** (Pol) good offices ◆ **Monsieur bons ~s** * mediator

NM (= pièce de rangement) pantry; (= lieu de repas des domestiques) servants' hall

L'OFFICE DE LA LANGUE FRANÇAISE

The **Office de la langue française** is a government body set up by the National Assembly of Quebec in 1977. It plays an important role in defending the Francophone identity of Quebec by promoting the use of French in the workplace, in business and in government. The OLF is also responsible for decision-making on points of usage and terminology, and produces regular bulletins setting out its recommendations. → **QUÉBEC, RÉVOLUTION TRANQUILLE**

officialisation /ɔfisjalizasjɔ̃/ NF officializing, officialization

officialiser /ɔfisjalize/ ► conjug 1 ◄ VT to make official, to officialize

officiant, e /ɔfisjɑ̃, jɑ̃t/ ADJ officiating NM ◆ **(prêtre) ~** officiant, officiating priest NF ◆ **(sœur) ~e** officiating sister

officiel, -elle /ɔfisjɛl/ ADJ (gén) official ◆ **(c'est) ~ !** * it's no joke!, it's for sure! * ◆ **rendre ~** to make official ou public ◆ **à titre ~** officially; → **journal** NM,F official ◆ **les ~s de la course** the race officials

officiellement /ɔfisjɛlmɑ̃/ ADV officially

officier[1] /ɔfisje/ NM officer ◆ **~ subalterne/supérieur/général** junior/field/general officer ◆ **~ de garde** duty officer ◆ **~ de marine** naval officer ◆ **~ marinier** petty officer ◆ **~ mécanicien** engineer officer ◆ **~ d'ordonnance** aide-de-camp ◆ **~ de paix** (police) inspector (Brit), (police) lieutenant (US) ◆ **~ de police** senior police officer ◆ **~ de police judiciaire** official empowered to make arrests and act as a policeman ◆ **~ de semaine** ≈ orderly officer ◆ **~ de l'état civil** (mayor considered in his capacity as) registrar ◆ **~/grand ~ de la Légion d'honneur** Officer/Grand Officer of the Legion of Honour ◆ **~ ministériel** member of the legal profession ◆ **~ technicien** technical officer; → **col**

officier[2] /ɔfisje/ ► conjug 7 ◄ VI (Rel, hum) to officiate

officieusement /ɔfisjøzmɑ̃/ ADV unofficially

officieux, -ieuse /ɔfisjø, jøz/ ADJ unofficial ◆ **à titre ~** unofficially, in an unofficial capacity

⚠ **officieux** ne se traduit pas par **officious**, qui a le sens de 'trop zélé'.

officinal, e (mpl **-aux**) /ɔfisinal, o/ ADJ [plante] medicinal

officine /ɔfisin/ NF [de pharmacie] dispensary; (Admin, Jur = pharmacie) pharmacy; (péj = repaire) headquarters, agency

offrande /ɔfʀɑ̃d/ NF (= don) offering ◆ **l'~** (Rel = cérémonie) the offertory ◆ **apporter qch en ~** to bring sth as a gift ou an offering

offrant /ɔfʀɑ̃/ NM (Jur, Fin) ◆ **au plus ~** to the highest bidder ◆ **"au plus offrant"** (petites annonces) "highest offer secures sale"

offre /ɔfʀ/ GRAMMAIRE ACTIVE 46.5

NF 1 (gén) offer; (aux enchères) bid; (Admin = soumission) tender ◆ **il m'a fait une ~** (pour un prix, un emploi) he made me an offer ◆ **~ spéciale** (Comm) special offer, special (US) ◆ **~s de paix** (Pol) peace overtures; → **appel**

2 (Écon) supply ◆ **l'~ et la demande** supply and demand ◆ **théorie de l'~** supply-side economics

COMP **offre d'emploi** job ad * ◆ **as-tu regardé les ~s d'emploi ?** have you checked the job ads * ou situations vacant column? (Brit) ◆ **il y avait plusieurs ~s d'emploi pour des ingénieurs** there were several jobs advertised for engineers, there were several advertisements ou ads * for engineering jobs

offre publique d'achat takeover bid, tender offer (US)

offre publique d'échange public offer of exchange

offre publique de vente offer for sale

offre(s) de service (frm) offer of service

⚠ Au sens économique, **offre** ne se traduit pas par **offer**.

offreur, -euse /ɔfʀœʀ, øz/ NM,F offerer, offeror

offrir /ɔfʀiʀ/ GRAMMAIRE ACTIVE 30 ► conjug 18 ◄

VT 1 (= donner) to give (à to); (= acheter) to buy (à for); ◆ **c'est pour ~ ?** is it for a present ou a gift? ◆ **la joie d'~** the joy of giving ◆ **il lui a offert un bracelet** he gave her a bracelet, he presented her with a bracelet ◆ **il s'est fait ~ une voiture** he was given a car ◆ **il nous a offert à boire** (chez lui) he gave us a drink; (au café) he bought ou stood (Brit) us a drink ◆ **c'est moi qui offre !** [+ tournée] it's my round!, this is on me!; [+ repas] I'm paying!, this is on me!

2 (= proposer) [+ aide, marchandise, excuse] to offer; [+ sacrifice] to offer up; [+ choix, possibilité] to offer, to give; [+ démission] to tender, to offer ◆ **~ l'hospitalité à qn** to offer sb hospitality ◆ **il m'offrit un fauteuil** he offered me a chair ◆ **~ son bras à qn** to offer sb one's arm ◆ **~ ses services à qn** to offer sb one's services ◆ **~ de faire** to offer to do ◆ **combien m'en offrez-vous ?** how much will you give me for it? ou will you offer for it? ◆ **~ sa vie pour une cause** to offer up one's life to a cause

3 (= présenter) [+ spectacle, image] to present, to offer; [+ vue] to offer ◆ **~ son corps aux regards** to reveal ou expose one's body to the world at large ◆ **~ sa poitrine aux balles** to proffer (frm) ou present one's chest to the bullets ◆ **le paysage n'offrait rien de particulier** the countryside had no particular features ◆ **ces ruines n'offrent guère d'intérêt** these ruins are of little interest

4 (= apporter) [+ avantage, inconvénient] to offer, to present; [+ exemple, explication] to provide, to afford (frm); [+ analogie] to offer, to have; [+ échappatoire] to offer ◆ **~ de la résistance** [coffre-fort] to resist, to offer resistance; [personne] to put up ou offer resistance (à to)

VPR **s'offrir** 1 (= se présenter) **s'~ aux regards** [personne] to expose ou reveal o.s. to the public gaze; [spectacle] to present itself to the gaze, to meet ou greet our (ou your etc) eyes ◆ **la première idée qui s'est offerte à mon esprit** the first idea that occurred to me ou that came into my mind ◆ **il a saisi l'occasion qui s'offrait à lui** he seized the opportunity presented to him ◆ **il s'est offert aux coups** he let the blows rain down on him, he submitted to the blows

2 (sexuellement) to offer o.s.

3 ◆ **s'~ à** *ou* **pour faire qch** to offer *ou* volunteer to do sth ◆ **s'~ comme guide** to volunteer to act as a guide
4 *(= se payer) [+ repas, vacances]* to treat o.s. to; *[+ disque]* to buy o.s., to treat o.s. to; → **luxe**

⚠ Quand on parle d'un cadeau, **offrir** ne se traduit pas par **to offer**.

offset /ɔfset/ NM, ADJ INV *(Typo)* offset ◆ **journal tiré en ~** offset (litho-)printed newspaper NF INV offset (printing) machine

offshore /ɔfʃɔʀ/ ADJ INV *[plateforme, exploitation, pétrole]* offshore; *(Fin) [fonds]* offshore NM INV *(Sport) (= bateau)* powerboat; *(= activité)* powerboat racing ◆ **faire du ~** to go powerboat racing

offusquer /ɔfyske/ ▸ conjug 1 ◂ VT to offend ◆ **ses manières offusquent beaucoup de gens** his manners offend many people VPR **s'offusquer** to take offence *ou* umbrage *(de* at) to be offended *(de* at, by)

oflag /ɔflag/ NM oflag

ogival, e (mpl **-aux**) /ɔʒival, o/ ADJ *[voûte]* rib *(épith)*, ogival *(SPÉC)*; *[arc]* pointed, ogival *(SPÉC)*; *[architecture, art]* gothic

ogive /ɔʒiv/ NF 1 *(Archit)* diagonal rib ◆ **arc d'~s** pointed *ou* equilateral arch ◆ **arc en ~** lancet arch; → **croisée²**, **voûte** 2 *(Mil) [de missile]* nose cone ◆ **~ nucléaire** nuclear warhead

OGM /ɔʒeɛm/ NM (abrév de **organisme génétiquement modifié**) *(Bio)* GMO

ogre /ɔgʀ/ NM ogre ◆ **manger comme un ~, être un vrai ~** to eat like a horse

ogresse /ɔgʀɛs/ NF ogress ◆ **elle a un appétit d'~** she's got an appetite like a horse

oh /o/ EXCL oh! ◆ **pousser des ~** to exclaim

ohé /ɔe/ EXCL hey (there)! ◆ **~ du bateau !** ahoy (there)!, hey (there)!, hullo (there)!

Ohio /ɔjo/ NM Ohio

ohm /om/ NM ohm

ohmmètre /ommɛtʀ/ NM ohmmeter

oïdium /ɔidjɔm/ NM powdery mildew

oie /wa/ NF *(= oiseau)* goose; *(péj = niaise)* silly goose ◆ **~ cendrée** greylag goose ◆ **~ sauvage** wild goose ◆ **~ des neiges** snow goose ◆ **~ blanche** *(péj)* innocent young thing; → **caca, jeu, patte-d'oie** *etc*

oignon /ɔɲɔ̃/ NM 1 *(= légume)* onion ◆ **petits ~s** pickling onions ◆ **aux petits ~s** *(Culin)* with (pickling) onions ◆ **soigner qn aux petits ~s*** *(fig)* to treat sb like a king *(ou* queen) ◆ **c'était aux petits ~s*** *(fig)* it was first-rate ◆ **ce n'est pas** *ou* **ce ne sont pas mes ~s*** it's none of my business, it's nothing to do with me ◆ **mêle-toi** *ou* **occupe-toi de tes ~s*** mind your own business; → **pelure, rang** 2 *(= bulbe de fleur)* bulb 3 *(Méd)* bunion 4 *(= montre)* turnip watch

oïl /ɔjl/ NM → **langue**

oindre /wɛ̃dʀ/ ▸ conjug 49 ◂ VT to anoint

oint, ointe /wɛ̃, wɛ̃t/ (ptp de **oindre**) ADJ, NM,F anointed ◆ **l'~ du Seigneur** the Lord's anointed

oiseau (pl **oiseaux**) /wazo/ NM bird ◆ **être comme l'~ sur la branche** to be here today and gone tomorrow ◆ **trouver** *ou* **dénicher l'~ rare** to find the man *(ou* woman) in a million ◆ **les ~x s'étaient envolés** *(fig)* the birds had flown ◆ **drôle d'~** *(= personne)* odd customer, oddball* ◆ **un ~ de passage** a bird of passage ◆ **le petit ~ va sortir !** *(hum)* watch the birdie!; → **appétit, cervelle, vol¹**

COMP **oiseaux de basse-cour** poultry
oiseau chanteur songbird
oiseau des îles exotic bird
oiseau de malheur, oiseau de mauvais augure *(fig)* bird of ill omen
oiseau migrateur migratory bird, migrant
oiseau moqueur mocking bird
oiseau de nuit *(lit)* night-bird, bird of the night; *(fig)* night owl, night-bird
oiseau de paradis bird of paradise
oiseau de proie bird of prey

oiseau-lyre (pl **oiseaux-lyres**) /wazoliʀ/ NM lyrebird

oiseau-mouche (pl **oiseaux-mouches**) /wazomuʃ/ NM hummingbird

oiseleur /waz(ə)lœʀ/ NM bird-catcher

oiselier, -ière /wazəlje, jɛʀ/ NM,F bird-seller

oisellerie /wazɛlʀi/ NF *(= magasin)* birdshop; *(= commerce)* bird-selling

oiseux, -euse /wazø, øz/ ADJ *[dispute, digression, commentaire]* pointless; *[propos]* idle *(épith)*, pointless; *[question]* trivial, trifling

oisif, -ive /wazif, iv/ ADJ idle ◆ **une vie oisive** a life of leisure, an idle life NM,F man *(ou* woman) of leisure ◆ **les ~s** *(gén)* the idle; *(Écon = non-actifs)* those not in active employment

oisillon /wazijɔ̃/ NM young bird, fledgling

oisivement /wazivmɑ̃/ ADV idly ◆ **vivre ~** to live a life of leisure *ou* idleness

oisiveté /wazivte/ NF idleness ◆ **heures d'~** leisure time ◆ **~ forcée** forced idleness *ou* inactivity ◆ **l'~ est (la) mère de tous les vices** *(Prov)* the devil finds work for idle hands *(Prov)*

oison /wazɔ̃/ NM gosling

OIT /ɔite/ NF (abrév de **Organisation internationale du travail**) ILO

OK* /oke/ EXCL, ADJ INV OK*, okay* ◆ **~, d'accord !*** OK, fine!*

okapi /ɔkapi/ NM okapi

Oklahoma /ɔklaɔma/ NM Oklahoma

okoumé /ɔkume/ NM gaboon (mahogany)

ola /ɔla/ NF *(Sport)* Mexican wave

olé /ɔle/ EXCL olé! ADJ INV **olé olé*** *(= excentrique) [tenue]* crazy, over the top* *(Brit)*; *(= osé) [film, livre, chanson]* risqué, near the knuckle* *(attrib)*; *[tenue]* risqué, daring ◆ **elle est un peu ~ ~** *(d'allure)* she's a bit over the top* *(Brit) ou* outrageous; *(de mœurs)* she leads quite a wild life

oléacée /ɔlease/ NF member of the Oleaceae family ◆ **~s** Oleaceae

oléagineux, -euse /ɔleaʒinø, øz/ ADJ oil-producing, oleaginous *(SPÉC)* ◆ **graines oléagineuses** oilseeds ◆ **fruits ~** nuts, oleaginous fruits *(SPÉC)* NM oil-producing *ou* oleaginous *(SPÉC)* plant

oléfine /ɔlefin/ NF olefine, alkene

oléiculteur, -trice /ɔleikyltœʀ, tʀis/ NM olive grower

oléiculture /ɔleikyltyʀ/ NF olive growing

oléifère /ɔleifɛʀ/ ADJ oil-producing, oleiferous *(SPÉC)*

oléine /ɔlein/ NF olein, triolein

oléoduc /ɔleɔdyk/ NM oil pipeline

oléoprotéagineux /ɔleopʀɔteaʒinø/ NM *(Agr)* oilseed

oléum /ɔleɔm/ NM oleum

OLF /ɔɛlɛf/ NM (abrév de **Office de la Langue Française**) → **office**

olfactif, -ive /ɔlfaktif, iv/ ADJ olfactory

olfaction /ɔlfaksjɔ̃/ NF olfaction

olibrius /ɔlibʀijys/ NM *(péj)* (queer) customer* *ou* fellow*

olifant /ɔlifɑ̃/ NM (ivory) horn

oligarchie /ɔligaʀʃi/ NF oligarchy

oligarchique /ɔligaʀʃik/ ADJ oligarchic

oligarque /ɔligaʀk/ NM oligarch

oligocène /ɔligɔsɛn/ ADJ oligocene NM ◆ **l'~** the Oligocene

oligoélément /ɔligoelemɑ̃/ NM trace element

oligopole /ɔligɔpɔl/ NM oligopoly

olivaie /ɔlivɛ/ NF ⇒ **oliveraie**

olivâtre /ɔlivɑtʀ/ ADJ *(gén)* olive-greenish; *[teint]* sallow

olive /ɔliv/ NF 1 *(= fruit)* olive ◆ **~ noire/verte** black/green olive; → **huile** 2 *(= ornement)* bead *ou* pearl moulding; *(= interrupteur)* switch 3 *(Anat)* olivary body 4 *(= coquillage)* olive(-shell) ADJ INV olive(-green)

oliveraie /ɔlivʀɛ/ NF olive grove

olivette /ɔlivɛt/ NF plum tomato

olivier /ɔlivje/ NM *(= arbre)* olive tree; *(= bois)* olive (wood); → **jardin, mont, rameau**

olivine /ɔlivin/ NF olivine

olographe /ɔlɔgʀaf/ ADJ → **testament**

OLP /ɔɛlpe/ NF (abrév de **Organisation de libération de la Palestine**) PLO

Olympe¹ /ɔlɛ̃p/ NM ◆ **l'~** *(= mont)* Mount Olympus

Olympe² /ɔlɛ̃p/ NF *(Myth)* Olympia

olympiade /ɔlɛ̃pjad/ NF Olympiad

Olympie /ɔlɛ̃pi/ N Olympia

olympien, -ienne /ɔlɛ̃pjɛ̃, jɛn/ ADJ *[dieux]* Olympic; *[calme]* Olympian ◆ **air ~** air of Olympian aloofness

olympique /ɔlɛ̃pik/ ADJ Olympic ◆ **il est dans une forme ~** he's in great shape *ou* top form *(Brit)*; → **jeu, piscine**

olympisme /ɔlɛ̃pism/ NM *(= organisation)* organization of the Olympic games; *(= principe)* Olympic spirit

OM (abrév de **ondes moyennes**) MW

Oman /ɔman/ NM ◆ **(le Sultanat d')~** (the Sultanate of) Oman

omanais, e /ɔmanɛ, ɛz/ ADJ Omani NM,F **Omanais(e)** Omani

ombelle /ɔ̃bɛl/ NF umbel ◆ **en ~** umbellate *(SPÉC)*, parasol-shaped

ombellifère /ɔ̃belifɛʀ/ ADJ umbelliferous NF umbellifer ◆ **~s** Umbelliferae *(SPÉC)*

ombilic /ɔ̃bilik/ NM 1 *(= nombril)* umbilicus, navel 2 *(= plante)* navelwort 3 *(Bot)* hilum; *(= renflement) [de bouclier]* boss; *(Math)* umbilic

ombilical, e (mpl **-aux**) /ɔ̃bilikal, o/ ADJ *(Anat)* umbilical; *(Sci, Tech)* navel-like; → **cordon**

omble /ɔ̃bl(ə)/ NM char(r) fish ◆ **~(-)chevalier** arctic char(r)

ombrage /ɔ̃bʀaʒ/ NM 1 *(= ombre)* shade ◆ **sous les ~s (du parc)** *(= feuillage)* in the shade of the trees (in the park), in the leafy shade (of the park) 2 *(locutions)* **prendre ~ de qch** *(frm)* to take umbrage *ou* offence at sth ◆ **porter ~ à qn** † *(aussi littér)*, **causer** *ou* **donner de l'~ à qn** to offend sb

ombragé, e /ɔ̃bʀaʒe/ (ptp de **ombrager**) ADJ shaded, shady

ombrager /ɔ̃bʀaʒe/ ▸ conjug 3 ◂ VT *[arbres]* to shade ◆ **une mèche ombrageait son front** *(fig littér)* a lock of hair shaded his brow

ombrageux, -euse /ɔ̃bʀaʒø, øz/ ADJ 1 *[personne]* touchy, quick to take offence *(attrib)*, easily offended; *[caractère]* touchy, prickly 2 *[âne, cheval]* skittish, nervous

ombre¹ /ɔ̃bʀ/ NF 1 *(lit)* shade *(NonC)*; *(= ombre portée)* shadow; *(littér = obscurité)* darkness ◆ **25° à l'~** 25° in the shade ◆ **dans l'~ de l'arbre/du vestibule** in the shade of the tree/of the hall ◆ **ces arbres font de l'~** these trees give (us) shade ◆ **ôte-toi de là, tu me fais de l'~** get out of my light, move - you're in my light ◆ **places sans ~/pleines d'~** shadeless/shady squares

◆ **tapi dans l'~** crouching in the darkness *ou* in the shadows; → **théâtre**
2 *(= forme vague)* shadow, shadowy figure *ou* shape
3 *(= anonymat)* obscurity; *(= secret, incertitude)* dark ◆ **laisser une question dans l'~** to leave a question unresolved, to deliberately ignore a question ◆ **tramer quelque chose dans l'~** to plot something in the dark ◆ **travailler dans l'~** to work behind the scenes ◆ **sortir de l'~** *[auteur]* to emerge from one's obscurity; *[terroriste]* to come out into the open ◆ **rester dans l'~** *[artiste]* to remain in obscurity; *[meneur]* to keep in the background; *[détail]* to be still obscure, to remain unclear ◆ **c'est un homme de l'~** he works in the background
4 *(= soupçon)* **une ~ de moustache** a hint *ou* suspicion of a moustache ◆ **il n'y a pas** *ou* **ça ne fait pas l'~ d'un doute** there's not the (slightest) shadow of a doubt ◆ **sans l'~ d'un doute** beyond *ou* without the shadow of a doubt ◆ **tu n'as pas l'~ d'une chance** you haven't got a ghost of a chance ◆ **sans l'~ d'une hésitation** without a moment's hesitation ◆ **une ~ de tristesse passa sur son visage** a look of sadness darkened his face ◆ **il y avait dans sa voix l'~ d'un reproche** there was a hint of reproach in his voice
5 *(= fantôme)* shade; → **royaume**
6 *(locutions)* **à l'~ de** *(= tout près de)* in the shadow of, close beside; *(= à l'abri de)* in the shade of ◆ **vivre dans l'~ de qn** to live in the shadow of sb ◆ **être l'~ de qn** to be sb's (little) shadow ◆ **faire de l'~ à qn** *(fig)* to overshadow sb ◆ **mettre qn à l'~** * to put sb behind bars, to lock sb up ◆ **il y a une ~ au tableau** there's a fly in the ointment ◆ **seule ~ au tableau : il ne parle pas grec** the only snag *ou* problem is that he doesn't speak Greek ◆ **n'être plus que l'~ de soi-même** to be a (mere) shadow of one's former self ◆ **jeter une ~ sur qch** to cast a shadow over sth ◆ **il tire plus vite que son ~** *(hum)* he's the fastest draw in the West; → **peur, proie, suivre**
COMP **ombres chinoises** *(improvisées)* shadowgraph; *(= spectacle)* shadow show *ou* pantomime
ombre méridienne noonday shadow
ombre à paupières eye shadow
ombre portée shadow

ombre² /ɔ̃bʀ/ NM *(= poisson)* grayling

ombre³ /ɔ̃bʀ/ NF *(= terre, couleur)* umber ◆ **terre d'~** umber

ombrelle /ɔ̃bʀɛl/ NF *(= parasol)* parasol, sunshade; *[de méduse]* umbrella

ombrer /ɔ̃bʀe/ ▸ conjug 1 ◂ VT *[+ dessin]* to shade ◆ **~ ses paupières** to put on eye shadow

ombreux, -euse /ɔ̃bʀø, øz/ ADJ *(littér)* *[pièce, forêt]* shady

Ombrie /ɔ̃bʀi/ NF Umbria

ombrien, -ienne /ɔ̃bʀijɛ̃, ijɛn/ ADJ Umbrian

ombudsman /ɔmbydsman/ NM *(Can)* ombudsman

OMC /oɛmse/ NF (abrév de **Organisation mondiale du commerce**) WTO

oméga /ɔmega/ NM omega; → **alpha**

omelette /ɔmlɛt/ NF omelette ◆ **~ aux champignons/au fromage** mushroom/cheese omelette ◆ **~ baveuse** runny omelette ◆ **~ norvégienne** baked Alaska ◆ **on ne fait pas d'~ sans casser des œufs** *(Prov)* you can't make an omelette without breaking eggs *(Prov)*

omerta /ɔmɛʀta/ NF code of silence, omerta

omettre /ɔmɛtʀ/ ▸ conjug 56 ◂ VT to leave out, to omit ◆ **~ de faire qch** to fail *ou* omit *ou* neglect to do sth

OMI /oɛmi/ NF (abrév de **Organisation maritime internationale**) IMO

omicron /ɔmikʀɔn/ NM omicron

omission /ɔmisjɔ̃/ NF *(= action)* omission; *(= chose oubliée)* omission, oversight ◆ **pécher par ~** to sin by omission

OMM /oɛmɛm/ NF (abrév de **Organisation météorologique mondiale**) WMO

omnibus /ɔmnibys/ NM ◆ **(train) ~** slow *ou* local train; *(Hist = bus)* omnibus ◆ **le train est ~ jusqu'à Paris** the train stops at every station before *ou* until Paris; → **barre**

omnidirectionnel, -elle /ɔmnidiʀɛksjɔnɛl/ ADJ omnidirectional

omnipotence /ɔmnipɔtɑ̃s/ NF omnipotence

omnipotent, e /ɔmnipɔtɑ̃, ɑ̃t/ ADJ omnipotent, all-powerful

omnipraticien, -ienne /ɔmnipʀatisjɛ̃, jɛn/ NM,F general practitioner

omniprésence /ɔmnipʀezɑ̃s/ NF omnipresence

omniprésent, e /ɔmnipʀezɑ̃, ɑ̃t/ ADJ omnipresent ◆ **son influence est ~e** his influence is felt everywhere

omniscience /ɔmnisjɑ̃s/ NF omniscience

omniscient, e /ɔmnisjɑ̃, jɑ̃t/ ADJ omniscient

omnisports /ɔmnispɔʀ/ ADJ INV *[terrain]* general-purpose *(épith)* ◆ **association ~** (general) sports club ◆ **salle ~** games hall ◆ **palais ~** sports centre

omnium /ɔmnjɔm/ NM 1 *(Cyclisme)* prime; *(Courses)* open handicap 2 *(Comm)* corporation

omnivore /ɔmnivɔʀ/ ADJ omnivorous NM omnivorous creature, omnivore *(SPÉC)*

omoplate /ɔmɔplat/ NF shoulder blade, scapula *(SPÉC)*

OMS /oɛmɛs/ NF (abrév de **Organisation mondiale de la santé**) WHO

OMT /oɛmte/ NF (abrév de **Organisation mondiale du tourisme**) WTO

on /ɔ̃/ PRON 1 *(indétermination : souvent traduit par passif)* **~ les interrogea sans témoins** they were questioned without (any) witnesses ◆ **~ va encore augmenter l'essence** (the price of) petrol's going up again, they are putting up the price of petrol again ◆ **~ demande jeune fille** *(annonce)* young girl wanted *ou* required ◆ **~ ne nous a pas demandé notre avis** nobody asked our opinion, our opinion wasn't asked ◆ **~ ne devrait pas poser des questions si ambiguës** you *ou* one shouldn't ask such ambiguous questions ◆ **dans cet hôtel, ~ n'accepte pas les chiens** dogs aren't allowed in this hotel ◆ **~ prétend que ...** they say that ..., it is said that ... ◆ **~ se précipita sur les places vides** there was a rush for the empty seats ◆ **~ n'est jamais si bien servi que par soi-même** *(Prov)* a job is never so well done as when you do it yourself; → **dire**
2 *(= quelqu'un)* someone, anyone ◆ **~ a déposé ce paquet pendant que vous étiez sorti** someone left this parcel *ou* this parcel was left while you were out ◆ **qu'est-ce que je dis si ~ demande à vous parler ?** what shall I say if someone *ou* anyone asks to speak to you? ◆ **~ vous demande au téléphone** you're wanted on the phone, there's someone on the phone for you ◆ **~ frappa à la porte** there was a knock at the door ◆ **est-ce qu'~ est venu réparer la porte ?** has anyone *ou* someone been to repair the door? ◆ **~ peut très bien aimer la pluie** some people may well like the rain ◆ **je n'admets pas qu'~** *ou* **que l'~ ne sache pas nager** I can't understand how (some) people can't swim
3 *(indéf = celui qui parle)* you, one *(frm)*, we ◆ **~ ne dort pas par cette chaleur** you (*ou* one *(frm)*) can't sleep in this heat ◆ **est-ce qu'~ est censé s'habiller pour le dîner ?** is one *(frm)* *ou* are we expected to dress for dinner? ◆ **~ aimerait être sûr que ...** one *ou* we would like to be sure that ... ◆ **de nos fenêtres, ~ voit les collines** from our windows you (*ou* we) can see the hills ◆ **~ a trop chaud ici** it's too hot here ◆ **quand ~ est inquiet rien ne peut vous** *ou* **nous distraire** when you are (*ou* one is) worried nothing can take your (*ou* one's) mind off it ◆ **~ comprend difficilement pourquoi** it is difficult to understand why ◆ **~ ne pense jamais à tout** you can't think of everything ◆ **~ ne lui donnerait pas 70 ans** you wouldn't think she was 70 ◆ **~ ne dirait pas que ...** you wouldn't think that ...
4 *(éloignement dans temps, espace)* they, people ◆ **autrefois, ~ se préoccupait peu de l'hygiène** years ago, they (*ou* people) didn't worry about hygiene ◆ **en Chine ~ mange avec des baguettes** in China they eat with chopsticks ◆ **dans aucun pays ~ ne semble pouvoir arrêter l'inflation** it doesn't seem as if inflation can be stopped in any country, no country seems (to be) able to stop inflation
5 *(* = nous)* we ◆ **~ a décidé tous les trois de partir chacun de son côté** the three of us decided to go (each) our separate ways ◆ **chez nous ~ mange beaucoup de pain** we eat a lot of bread in our family ◆ **lui et moi ~ n'est pas d'accord** we don't see eye to eye, him and me * ◆ **nous, ~ a amené notre chien** we've brought along the dog ◆ **nous, ~ a tous réclamé une augmentation** we all (of us) demanded a rise ◆ **~ fait ce qu'~ peut** *ou* **de son mieux** you can only do your best ◆ **il faut bien qu'~ vive** a guy's (*ou* a girl's) got to eat * ◆ **dans ce chapitre ~ essaiera de prouver ...** in this chapter we *(frm)* shall attempt to prove ...
6 *(gén langue parlée : familiarité, reproche etc)* **~ est bien sage aujourd'hui !** aren't we a good boy (*ou* girl) today!, we are a good boy (*ou* girl) today! ◆ **alors, ~ ne dit plus bonjour aux amis !** don't we say hello to our friends any more? ◆ **alors, ~ est content ?** well, are you pleased? ◆ **~ n'a pas un sou mais ~ s'achète une voiture !** *(iro)* he hasn't (*ou* they haven't *etc*) a penny to his (*ou* their *etc*) name but he goes and buys (*ou* they go and buy *etc*) a car! ◆ **~ parle, ~ parle et puis ~ finit par dire des sottises** talk, talk, talk and it's all nonsense in the end
7 *(intensif)* **c'est ~ ne peut plus beau/ridicule** it couldn't be lovelier/more ridiculous ◆ **je suis ~ ne peut plus heureux de vous voir** I couldn't be more delighted to see you, I'm absolutely delighted to see you; → **pouvoir¹**

onagre¹ /ɔnagʀ/ NM *(= âne, machine de guerre)* onager

onagre² /ɔnagʀ/ NF *(= plante)* evening primrose

onanisme /ɔnanism/ NM onanism

once¹ /ɔ̃s/ NF *(= mesure)* ounce ◆ **il n'a pas une ~ de bon sens** he hasn't an ounce of common sense

once² /ɔ̃s/ NF *(= animal)* ounce, snow leopard

oncial, e (mpl **-iaux**) /ɔ̃sjal, jo/ ADJ uncial NF **onciale** uncial

oncle /ɔ̃kl/ NM uncle ◆ **~ d'Amérique** *(fig)* rich uncle ◆ **l'Oncle Sam** Uncle Sam ◆ **l'Oncle Tom** Uncle Tom

oncogène /ɔ̃kɔʒɛn/ ADJ oncogenic, oncogenous NM oncogene

oncologie /ɔ̃kɔlɔʒi/ NF oncology

oncologiste /ɔ̃kɔlɔʒist/, **oncologue** /ɔ̃kɔlɔg/ NMF oncologist

oncques †† /ɔ̃k/ ADV never

onction /ɔ̃ksjɔ̃/ NF *(Rel, fig)* unction ◆ **~ des malades** anointing of the sick

onctueusement /ɔ̃ktɥøzmɑ̃/ ADV *[couler]* unctuously; *[parler]* with unction, suavely

onctueux, -euse /ɔ̃ktɥø, øz/ ADJ *[crème]* smooth, creamy, unctuous; *[manières, voix]* unctuous, smooth

onctuosité /ɔ̃ktɥozite/ NF unctuousness, smoothness, creaminess

onde /ɔ̃d/ NF 1 *(gén, Phys)* wave ◆ **~s hertziennes/radioélectriques/sonores** Hertzian/radio/sound waves ◆ **~s courtes** short waves ◆ **petites ~s, ~s moyennes** medium waves ◆ **grandes ~s** long waves ◆ **transmettre sur ~s courtes/petites ~s/grandes ~s** to broadcast on short/medium/long wave ◆ **~ de choc** *(lit, fig)* shock wave; → **longueur** 2 *(locutions)* **sur les ~s et dans la presse** on the radio and in the press ◆ **nous espérons vous retrouver sur nos ~s demain à 6 heures** we hope you'll join us again on the air tomorrow at 6 o'clock ◆ **il passe sur les ~s demain** he's going on the air tomorrow ◆ **mise en ~** *(Radio)* production ◆ **mettre en ~s** *[+ pièce, récit]* to produce for the radio ◆ **par ordre d'entrée en ~s** in order of appearance 3 *(littér = lac, mer)* **l'~** the waters ◆ **l'~ amère** the briny deep *(littér)*

ondé, e¹ /ɔ̃de/ ADJ *(littér)* *[tissu]* watered; *[cheveux]* wavy

ondée² /ɔ̃de/ NF shower *(of rain)*

ondin, e /ɔ̃dɛ̃, in/ NM,F water sprite

on-dit /ɔ̃di/ NM INV rumour, hearsay *(NonC)* ◆ **ce ne sont que des ~** it's only hearsay

ondoiement /ɔ̃dwamɑ̃/ NM 1 *(littér)* *[de blés, surface moirée]* undulation 2 *(Rel)* provisional baptism

ondoyant, e /ɔ̃dwajɑ̃, ɑ̃t/ ADJ 1 *[eaux, blés]* undulating; *[flamme]* wavering; *[reflet]* shimmering; *[démarche]* swaying, supple 2 († *ou littér*) *[caractère, personne]* unstable, changeable

ondoyer /ɔ̃dwaje/ ► conjug 8 ◄ VI *[blés]* to undulate, to ripple; *[drapeau]* to wave, to ripple VT *(Rel)* to baptize *(in an emergency)*

ondulant, e /ɔ̃dylɑ̃, ɑ̃t/ ADJ 1 *[démarche]* swaying, supple; *[ligne, profil, surface]* undulating 2 *(Méd)* *[pouls]* uneven

ondulation /ɔ̃dylasjɔ̃/ NF *[de vagues, blés, terrain]* undulation ◆ **~s** *[de sol]* undulations; *[de cheveux]* waves

ondulatoire /ɔ̃dylatwaʀ/ ADJ *(Phys)* undulatory, wave *(épith)*; → **mécanique**

ondulé, e /ɔ̃dyle/ (ptp de **onduler**) ADJ *[surface]* undulating; *[chevelure]* wavy; *[carton, tôle]* corrugated

onduler /ɔ̃dyle/ ► conjug 1 ◄ VI *(gén)* to undulate; *[drapeau]* to ripple, to wave; *[route]* to snake up and down, to undulate; *[cheveux]* to be wavy, to wave VT † *[+ cheveux]* to wave

onduleur /ɔ̃dylœʀ/ NM *(Élec)* inverter

onduleux, -euse /ɔ̃dylø, øz/ ADJ *[courbe, ligne]* wavy; *[plaine]* undulating; *[silhouette, démarche]* sinuous, swaying, supple

onéreux, -euse /ɔneʀø, øz/ ADJ expensive, costly; → **titre**

ONF /ɔɛnɛf/ NM (abrév de **Office national des forêts**) → **office**

ONG /ɔɛnʒe/ NF (abrév de **organisation non gouvernementale**) NGO

ongle /ɔ̃gl/ NM *[de personne]* (finger)nail; *[d'animal]* claw ◆ **~ de pied** toenail ◆ **porter** *ou* **avoir les ~s longs** to have long nails ◆ **avoir les ~s en deuil** * to have dirty (finger)nails ◆ **se faire les ~s** to do one's nails ◆ **avoir les ~s faits** to be wearing nail varnish *(Brit)* *ou* nail polish, to have painted nails; → **bout, incarné, payer**

onglée /ɔ̃gle/ NF ◆ **j'avais l'~** my fingers were numb with cold

onglet /ɔ̃glɛ/ NM 1 *[de tranche de livre]* *(dépassant)* tab; *(en creux)* thumb index ◆ **dictionnaire à ~s** dictionary with a thumb index 2 *[de lame de canif]* (thumbnail) groove 3 *(Menuiserie)* mitre *(Brit)*, miter *(US)* ◆ **boîte à ~s** mitre *(Brit)* *ou* miter *(US)* box 4 *(Math)* ungula; *(Bot)* unguis; *(Reliure)* guard 5 *(Boucherie)* *prime cut of beef* 6 *(Ordin)* thumbnail

onglier /ɔ̃glije/ NM manicure set

onguent /ɔ̃gɑ̃/ NM 1 *(Pharm)* ointment, salve 2 († = *parfum*) unguent

ongulé, e /ɔ̃gyle/ ADJ hoofed, ungulate *(SPÉC)* NM hoofed *ou* ungulate *(SPÉC)* animal ◆ **~s** ungulata

onirique /ɔniʀik/ ADJ *(Art, Littérat)* dreamlike, dream *(attrib)*, oneiric *(frm)*

onirisme /ɔniʀism/ NM *(Psych)* hallucinosis; *(Littérat)* fantasizing ◆ **la demi-brume portait à l'~** the mist created a dreamy atmosphere

onomasiologie /ɔnɔmazjɔlɔʒi/ NF onomasiology

onomastique /ɔnɔmastik/ ADJ onomastic NF onomastics *(sg)*

onomatopée /ɔnɔmatɔpe/ NF onomatopoeia

onomatopéique /ɔnɔmatɔpeik/ ADJ onomatopoeic

ontarien, -ienne /ɔ̃taʀjɛ̃, jɛn/ ADJ Ontarian NM,F **Ontarien(ne)** Ontarian

Ontario /ɔ̃taʀjo/ NM Ontario ◆ **le lac ~** Lake Ontario

ontogenèse /ɔ̃tɔʒənɛz/ ADJ ontogeny, ontogenesis

ontogénétique /ɔ̃tɔʒenetik/ ADJ ontogenetic, ontogenic

ontogénie /ɔ̃tɔʒeni/ NF ⇒ **ontogenèse**

ontogénique /ɔ̃tɔʒenik/ ADJ ⇒ **ontogénétique**

ontologie /ɔ̃tɔlɔʒi/ NF ontology

ontologique /ɔ̃tɔlɔʒik/ ADJ ontological

ONU /ɔny/ NF (abrév de **Organisation des Nations Unies**) UNO ◆ **l'~** the UN, (the) UNO

onusien, -ienne /ɔnyzjɛ̃, jɛn/ ADJ UN *(épith)* NM,F UN official

onyx /ɔniks/ NM onyx

onze /'ɔ̃z/ ADJ INV eleven ◆ **le ~ novembre** Armistice Day; *pour autres loc voir* **six** NM INV *(Ftbl)* ◆ **le ~ de France** the French eleven *ou* team; *pour autres loc voir* **six**

onzième /'ɔ̃zjɛm/ ADJ, NMF eleventh ◆ **les ouvriers de la ~ heure** *(péj)* last-minute helpers, people who turn up when the work is practically finished; *pour autres loc voir* **sixième**

onzièmement /'ɔ̃zjɛmmɑ̃/ ADV in the eleventh place; *pour loc voir* **sixièmement**

oocyte /ɔɔsit/ NM oocyte

oolithe /ɔɔlit/ NM oolite

oolithique /ɔɔlitik/ ADJ oolitic

OPA /ɔpea/ NF (abrév de **offre publique d'achat**) *(Fin)* takeover bid *(Brit)*, tender offer *(US)* ◆ **faire une ~ sur** *(lit, fig)* to take over

opacifiant /ɔpasifjɑ̃/ NM *(Méd)* contrast medium

opacification /ɔpasifikasjɔ̃/ NF opacification

opacifier /ɔpasifje/ ► conjug 7 ◄ VT to make opaque

opacité /ɔpasite/ NF 1 *(Phys)* *[de verre, corps]* opacity 2 *[de brouillard, nuit]* impenetrability 3 *[de mot, personnage, texte]* opaqueness, lack of clarity

opale /ɔpal/ NF opal

opalescence /ɔpalesɑ̃s/ NF opalescence

opalescent, e /ɔpalesɑ̃, ɑ̃t/ ADJ opalescent

opalin, e¹ /ɔpalɛ̃, in/ ADJ opaline

opaline² /ɔpalin/ NF opaline

opaque /ɔpak/ ADJ 1 *[verre, corps]* opaque (*à* to); ◆ **collants ~s** opaque tights 2 *[brouillard, nuit, forêt]* impenetrable 3 *[mot, personnage]* opaque

op' art /ɔpaʀt/ NM op art

op. cit. (abrév de **opere citato**) op. cit.

OPE /ɔpeə/ NF (abrév de **offre publique d'échange**) → **offre**

opéable /ɔpeabl/ ADJ liable to be taken over *(attrib)* NF firm liable to be taken over

open /ɔpɛn/ ADJ INV, NM open ◆ **(tournoi) ~** open (tournament)

OPEP /ɔpɛp/ NF (abrév de **Organisation des pays exportateurs de pétrole**) OPEC

opéra /ɔpeʀa/ NM 1 (= *œuvre, genre, spectacle*) opera; (= *édifice*) opera house ◆ **~ bouffe** opéra bouffe, comic opera ◆ **~ rock** rock opera ◆ **~ ballet** opéra ballet 2 *(Culin)* coffee and chocolate gâteau

opérable /ɔpeʀabl/ ADJ operable ◆ **le malade est-il ~ ?** can the patient be operated on? ◆ **ce cancer n'est plus ~** this cancer is too far advanced for an operation *ou* to be operable

opéra-comique (pl **opéras-comiques**) /ɔpeʀakɔmik/ NM light opera, opéra comique

opérande /ɔpeʀɑ̃d/ NM *(Math, Ordin)* operand

opérant, e /ɔpeʀɑ̃, ɑ̃t/ ADJ (= *efficace*) effective

opérateur, -trice /ɔpeʀatœʀ, tʀis/ NM,F 1 *(sur machine, téléphone, radio)* operator ◆ **~ (de prise de vues)** cameraman ◆ **~ de saisie** keyboard operator, keyboarder 2 *(Bourse)* dealer, trader, operator NM 1 *(Math, Ordin)* operator ◆ **~ booléen** Boolean operator 2 *[de calculateur]* processing unit 3 *(Bourse, Fin)* operator 4 *(Téléc)* telecommunication company ◆ **~ (de téléphone mobile)** network provider

opération /ɔpeʀasjɔ̃/ NF 1 *(Méd)* operation ◆ **~ à cœur ouvert** open-heart surgery *(NonC)* ◆ **salle/table d'~** operating theatre *(Brit)* *ou* room *(US)*/table ◆ **faire** *ou* **pratiquer une ~** to operate, to perform an operation ◆ **subir une ~ (chirurgicale)** to have *ou* undergo surgery, to have an operation

2 *(Math)* operation ◆ **les ~s fondamentales** the fundamental operations ◆ **ça peut se résoudre en 2 ou 3 ~s** that can be solved in 2 or 3 calculations *ou* operations ◆ **tu as fini tes ~s ?** *(Scol)* have you done your sums?

3 *(Mil, gén)* operation ◆ **~ de police/de sauvetage** police/rescue operation ◆ **"opération Tango"** *(nom de code)* "operation Tango" ◆ **~ mains propres** anti-corruption operation; → **théâtre**

4 *(Comm)* (= *campagne*) campaign, drive; (= *action*) operation ◆ **~ promotionnelle** promotional campaign ◆ **"opération baisse des prix"** "cut-price sale" ◆ **~ escargot** go-slow *(Brit)*, slow-down *(US)*

5 (= *tractation*) *(Comm)* deal; *(Bourse)* deal, transaction, operation ◆ **~ bancaire** *ou* **de banque** banking operation *ou* transaction ◆ **~ financière/commerciale/immobilière** financial/commercial/property deal ◆ **~s de Bourse** stock-exchange transactions ◆ **notre équipe a réalisé une bonne ~** *(en affaires)* our team got a good deal; *(en sport)* our team did a really good job

6 *(Tech, gén)* process, operation ◆ **les diverses ~s de la fabrication du papier** the different operations *ou* processes in the making of paper ◆ **l'~ de la digestion** the operation of the digestive system ◆ **les ~s de la raison** the processes of thought ◆ **par l'~ du Saint-Esprit** *(Rel)* through the workings of the Holy Spirit; *(hum)* by magic

opérationnalité /ɔpeʀasjɔnalite/ NF ◆ **pour une ~ immédiate des nouvelles recrues** so that new starts can immediately become effective workers

opérationnel, -elle /ɔpeʀasjɔnɛl/ ADJ operational

opératoire /ɔpeʀatwaʀ/ ADJ *(Méd) [méthodes, techniques]* operating; *[maladie, commotion, dépression]* post-operative; → **bloc**

opercule /ɔpɛʀkyl/ NM *[de plante, animal]* operculum; *(= couvercle)* protective cap *ou* cover; *[de pot de crème, carton de lait]* seal

opéré, e /ɔpeʀe/ (ptp de **opérer**) NM,F *(Méd)* patient *(who has undergone an operation)*

opérer /ɔpeʀe/ ▸ conjug 6 ◂ VT 1 *(Méd) [+ malade, organe]* to operate on *(de* for); *[+ tumeur]* to remove ◆ **on l'a opéré d'une tumeur** he had an operation for a tumour *ou* to remove a tumour ◆ ~ **qn de l'appendicite** to operate on sb for appendicitis, to take sb's appendix out ◆ **se faire** ~ to have an operation, to have surgery ◆ **se faire** ~ **des amygdales** to have one's tonsils removed *ou* out* ◆ **il faut** ~ we'll have to operate

2 *(= exécuter) [+ transformation, réforme]* to carry out, to implement; *[+ choix, distinction, transition]* to make ◆ **la Bourse a opéré un redressement spectaculaire** the stock exchange made a spectacular recovery ◆ **cette méthode a opéré des miracles** this method has worked wonders ◆ ~ **un retrait/transfert** to make a withdrawal/transfer ◆ **ce traitement a opéré sur lui un changement remarquable** this treatment has brought about an amazing change in him ◆ **un changement considérable s'était opéré** a major change had taken place *ou* occurred

VI *(= agir) [remède]* to act, to work, to take effect; *[charme]* to work; *(= procéder) [photographe, technicien]* to proceed ◆ **comment faut-il** ~ **pour nettoyer le moteur ?** how does one go about *ou* what's the procedure for cleaning the engine? ◆ **opérons en douceur** let's go about it gently ◆ **les cambrioleurs qui opèrent dans cette région** the burglars who work this area

> ⚠ **opérer qn** ne se traduit pas par **to operate sb.**

opérette /ɔpeʀɛt/ NF operetta, light opera ◆ **paysage/village d'~** chocolate-box landscape/village ◆ **général/bandit d'~** caricature of a general/bandit

Ophélie /ɔfeli/ NF Ophelia

ophidien /ɔfidjɛ̃/ NM ophidian ◆ **~s** Ophidia

ophrys /ɔfʀis/ NM *ou* NF ophrys

ophtalmie /ɔftalmi/ NF ophthalmia ◆ ~ **des neiges** snow blindness

ophtalmique /ɔftalmik/ ADJ ophthalmic

ophtalmo* /ɔftalmo/ NMF abrév de **ophtalmologiste**

ophtalmologie /ɔftalmɔlɔʒi/ NF ophthalmology

ophtalmologique /ɔftalmɔlɔʒik/ ADJ ophthalmological

ophtalmologiste /ɔftalmɔlɔʒist/, **ophtalmologue** /ɔftalmɔlɔg/ NMF ophthalmologist

ophtalmoscope /ɔftalmɔskɔp/ NM ophthalmoscope

ophtalmoscopie /ɔftalmɔskɔpi/ NF ophthalmoscopy

opiacé, e /ɔpjase/ ADJ *[médicament, substance]* opiate, opium-containing ◆ **odeur ~e** smell of *ou* like opium NM opiate

opimes /ɔpim/ ADJ PL *(hum, littér)* ◆ **dépouilles ~** rich booty *ou* spoils

opinel ® /ɔpinɛl/ NM (wooden-handled) penknife

opiner /ɔpine/ ▸ conjug 1 ◂ VI *(littér = se prononcer)* ◆ ~ **pour/contre qch** to come out in favour of/against sth, to pronounce o.s. in favour of/against sth ◆ ~ **de la tête** *(= acquiescer)* to nod one's agreement, to nod assent ◆ ~ **du bonnet** *ou* **du chef** *(hum)* to nod (in agreement) ◆ ~ **à qch** *(Jur)* to give one's consent to sth

opiniâtre /ɔpinjɑtʀ/ ADJ 1 *(= entêté) [personne, caractère]* stubborn, obstinate 2 *(= acharné) [efforts, haine]* unrelenting, persistent; *[résistance, lutte, toux]* stubborn, persistent; *[fièvre]* persistent

opiniâtrement /ɔpinjɑtʀəmɑ̃/ ADV *(= avec entêtement)* stubbornly; *(= avec acharnement)* persistently

opiniâtreté /ɔpinjɑtʀəte/ NF *(= entêtement)* stubbornness; *(= acharnement)* persistence

opinion /ɔpinjɔ̃/ GRAMMAIRE ACTIVE 33, 39.1, 41, 53.1, 53.3 NF 1 *(= jugement, conviction, idée)* opinion *(sur* on, about); ◆ **~s politiques/religieuses** political/religious beliefs *ou* convictions ◆ **avoir une ~/des ~s** to have an opinion *ou* a point of view/(definite) opinions *ou* views *ou* points of view ◆ **être sans** ~ to have no opinion ◆ **se faire une** ~ to form an opinion *(sur* on) to make up one's mind *(sur* about); ◆ **mon ~ est faite sur son compte** I've made up my mind about him ◆ **c'est une affaire d'~** it's a matter of opinion ◆ **j'ai la même** ~ I am of the same opinion, I hold the same view ◆ **être de l'~ du dernier qui a parlé** to agree with whoever spoke last ◆ **avoir bonne/mauvaise ~ de qn/de soi** to have a good/bad opinion of sb/of o.s. ◆ **j'ai piètre ~ de lui** I've a very low *ou* poor opinion of him ◆ **~s toutes faites** cut-and-dried opinions, uncritical opinions

2 *(= manière générale de penser)* **l'~ publique** public opinion ◆ **l'~ ouvrière** working-class opinion ◆ **l'~ française** French public opinion ◆ **informer/alerter l'~** to inform/alert the public ◆ **braver l'~** to defy public opinion ◆ **l'~ est unanime/divisée** opinion is unanimous/divided ◆ **il se moque de l'~ des autres** he doesn't care what (other) people think ◆ **avoir l'~ pour soi** to have public opinion on one's side; → **presse**

3 *(dans les sondages)* **le nombre d'~s favorables** those who agreed *ou* said yes ◆ **les "sans opinion"** the "don't knows"

opiomane /ɔpjɔman/ NMF opium addict

opiomanie /ɔpjɔmani/ NF opium addiction

opium /ɔpjɔm/ NM opium ◆ **l'~ du peuple** *(fig)* the opium of the people

opossum /ɔpɔsɔm/ NM opossum

opportun, e /ɔpɔʀtœ̃, yn/ ADJ *[démarche, visite, remarque]* timely, opportune ◆ **il n'avait pas jugé ~ d'avertir la police** he didn't see fit to alert the police ◆ **le président avait alors jugé ~ de briser un tabou** the president had then decided that the time had come to break a taboo ◆ **il serait ~ de faire** it would be appropriate *ou* advisable to do ◆ **nous le ferons en temps** ~ we shall do it at the appropriate *ou* right time ◆ **je donnerai plus de détails au moment** ~ I'll give more details when the time is right ◆ **prendre au moment ~ les mesures nécessaires** to take the necessary action at the right time

opportunément /ɔpɔʀtynemɑ̃/ ADV opportunely ◆ **il est arrivé** ~ his arrival was timely *ou* opportune, he arrived opportunely *ou* just at the right time

opportunisme /ɔpɔʀtynism/ NM opportunism

opportuniste /ɔpɔʀtynist/ ADJ *[personne]* opportunist; *[maladie, infection]* opportunistic NMF opportunist

opportunité /ɔpɔʀtynite/ NF 1 *[de mesure, démarche] (qui vient au bon moment)* timeliness; *(qui est approprié)* appropriateness ◆ **ils ont contesté l'~ de cette intervention** they said they thought the intervention had been ill-judged 2 *(= occasion)* opportunity

opposabilité /ɔpozabilite/ NF *(Jur)* opposability

opposable /ɔpozabl/ ADJ *(Jur)* opposable *(à* to)

opposant, e /ɔpozɑ̃, ɑt/ NM,F opponent *(à* of) ADJ 1 *[minorité] (Jur) [partie]* opposing *(épith)* 2 *(Anat) [muscle]* opponent

opposé, e /ɔpoze/ (ptp de **opposer**) ADJ 1 *[rive, direction]* opposite; *[parti, équipe]* opposing *(épith)* ◆ **venant en sens** ~ coming in the opposite *ou* other direction ◆ **la maison ~e à la nôtre** the house opposite *ou* facing ours ◆ **l'équipe ~e à la nôtre** the team playing against ours

2 *(= contraire) [intérêts, forces]* conflicting, opposing; *[opinions]* conflicting; *[caractères]* opposite; *[couleurs, styles]* contrasting; *(Math) [nombres, angles]* opposite ◆ ~ **à** conflicting *ou* contrasting with, opposed to ◆ **opinions totalement ~es** totally conflicting *ou* opposed opinions, opinions totally at variance ◆ **ils sont d'un avis** ~ *(au nôtre)* they are of a different *ou* the opposite opinion; *(l'un à l'autre)* they disagree, they are at odds ◆ **angles ~s par le sommet** *(Math)* vertically opposite angles; → **diamétralement**

3 *(= hostile à)* ~ **à** opposed to, against ◆ **je suis ~ à la publicité/à ce mariage** I'm opposed to *ou* I'm against advertising/this marriage ◆ **je ne serais pas ~ à cette solution** I wouldn't be against this solution

NM 1 *(= contraire)* **l'~** the opposite, the reverse ◆ **il fait tout l'~ de ce qu'on lui dit** he does the opposite *ou* the reverse of what he is told ◆ **à l'~, il serait faux de dire ...** on the other hand *ou* conversely it would be wrong to say ... ◆ **ils sont vraiment à l'~ l'un de l'autre** they are totally unalike ◆ **à l'~ de Paul, je pense que ...** contrary to *ou* unlike Paul, I think that ...

2 *(= direction)* **à l'~** *(= dans l'autre direction)* the other *ou* opposite way *(de* from); *(= de l'autre côté)* on the other *ou* opposite side *(de* from)

opposer /ɔpoze/ GRAMMAIRE ACTIVE 39.3, 41 ▸ conjug 1 ◂

VT 1 *[+ équipes, boxeurs]* to bring together; *[+ rivaux, pays]* to bring into conflict; *[+ idées, personnages, couleurs]* to contrast *(à* with); *[+ objets, meubles]* to place opposite each other ◆ **le match opposant l'équipe de Lyon et** *ou* **à celle de Caen** the Lyons v Caen game ◆ **on m'a opposé à un finaliste olympique** they made me compete against an Olympic finalist ◆ **des questions d'intérêts les ont opposés/les opposent** matters of personal interest have brought them into conflict/divide them ◆ **quel orateur peut-on ~ à Cicéron ?** what orator compares with Cicero?

2 *(= utiliser comme défense contre)* ~ **à qn/qch** *[+ armée, tactique]* to set against sb/sth ◆ ~ **son refus le plus net** to give an absolute refusal *(à* to); ◆ ~ **de véhémentes protestations à une accusation** to protest vehemently at an accusation ◆ **opposant son calme à leurs insultes** setting his calmness against their insults ◆ **il nous opposa une résistance farouche** he put up a fierce resistance to us ◆ **il n'y a rien à ~ à cela** there's nothing you can say *(ou* do) against that, there's no answer to that ◆ ~ **la force à la force** to match strength with strength

3 *(= objecter) [+ raisons]* to put forward *(à* to); ◆ **que va-t-il ~ à notre proposition/nous ?** what objections will he make *ou* raise to our proposal/to us? ◆ **il nous opposa que cela coûtait cher** he objected that it was expensive

VPR **s'opposer** 1 *[équipes, boxeurs]* to confront each other, to meet; *[rivaux, partis]* to clash *(à* with); *[opinions, théories]* to conflict; *[couleurs, styles]* to contrast *(à* with); *[immeubles]* to face each other ◆ **haut s'oppose à bas** high is the opposite of low ◆ **il s'est opposé à plus fort**

que lui *(dans un combat)* he took on *ou* he pitted himself against someone *ou* an opponent who was stronger than him

2 *(= se dresser contre)* **s'~ à** *[+ parents]* to rebel against; *[+ mesure, mariage, progrès]* to oppose ◆ **je m'oppose à lui en tout** I am opposed to him in everything ◆ **rien ne s'oppose à leur bonheur** nothing stands in the way of their happiness ◆ **je m'oppose formellement à ce que vous y alliez** I am strongly opposed to *ou* I am strongly against your going there ◆ **ma conscience s'y oppose** it goes against my conscience ◆ **sa religion s'y oppose** it is against his religion, his religion doesn't allow it ◆ **votre état de santé s'oppose à tout excès** your state of health makes any excess extremely inadvisable

opposite /ɔpozit/ **NM** *(frm)* ◆ **à l'~** on the other *ou* opposite side *(de* from)

opposition /ɔpozisjɔ̃/ GRAMMAIRE ACTIVE 32.1

NF 1 *(= résistance)* opposition *(à* to); ◆ **faire de l'~ systématique (à tout ce qu'on propose)** to oppose systematically (everything that is put forward) ◆ **loi passée sans ~** *(Jur, Pol)* law passed unopposed

2 *(= conflit, contraste) (gén)* opposition; *[d'idées, intérêts]* conflict; *[de couleurs, styles, caractères]* contrast ◆ **l'~ des deux partis en cette circonstance ...** *(divergence de vue)* the opposition between the two parties on that occasion ...; *(affrontement)* the clash *ou* confrontation between the two parties on that occasion ... ◆ **l'~ du gris et du noir a permis de ...** contrasting grey with *ou* and black has made it possible to ... ◆ **mettre deux styles/théories en ~** to oppose *ou* contrast two styles/theories

3 *(Pol)* **l'~** the opposition ◆ **les partis de l'~** the opposition parties ◆ **les élus de l'~** the members of the opposition parties, opposition MPs *(Brit)* ◆ **l'~ parlementaire** the parliamentary opposition, the opposition in parliament

4 *(locutions)* **en ~ avec** *(contraste, divergence)* in opposition to, at variance with; *(résistance, rébellion)* in conflict with; *(situation dans l'espace)* in opposition to ◆ **agir en ~ avec ses principes** to act contrary to one's principles ◆ **nous sommes en ~ sur ce point** we differ on this point ◆ **ceci est en ~ avec les faits** this conflicts with the facts ◆ **les deux planètes sont en ~** *(Astron)* the two planets are in opposition ◆ **faire** *ou* **mettre ~ à** *[+ loi, décision]* to oppose; *[+ chèque]* to stop ◆ **par ~** in contrast ◆ **par ~ à** as opposed to, in contrast with

COMP **opposition à mariage** *(Jur)* objection to a marriage

opposition à paiement *(Jur) objection by unpaid creditor to payment being made to debtor*

oppositionnel, -elle /ɔpozisjɔnɛl/ **ADJ** oppositional **NM,F** oppositionist

oppressant, e /ɔpʀesɑ̃, ɑ̃t/ **ADJ** *[temps, souvenirs, ambiance, chaleur]* oppressive

oppresser /ɔpʀese/ ► conjug 1 ◄ **VT** *[chaleur, ambiance, souvenirs]* to oppress; *[poids, vêtement serré]* to suffocate; *[remords, angoisse]* to oppress, to weigh heavily on, to weigh down ◆ **avoir une respiration oppressée** to have difficulty with one's breathing ◆ **se sentir oppressé** to feel suffocated

oppresseur /ɔpʀesœʀ/ **NM** oppressor **ADJ M** oppressive

oppressif, -ive /ɔpʀesif, iv/ **ADJ** oppressive

oppression /ɔpʀesjɔ̃/ **NF** *(= asservissement)* oppression; *(= gêne, malaise)* feeling of suffocation *ou* oppression

opprimé, e /ɔpʀime/ (ptp de **opprimer**) **ADJ** oppressed **NM,F** ◆ **les ~s** the oppressed

opprimer /ɔpʀime/ ► conjug 1 ◄ **VT** 1 *[+ peuple]* to oppress; *[+ opinion, liberté]* to suppress, to stifle 2 *(= oppresser) [chaleur]* to suffocate, to oppress

opprobre /ɔpʀɔbʀ/ **NM** *(littér = honte)* opprobrium *(littér)*, obloquy *(littér)*, disgrace ◆ **accabler** *ou* **couvrir qn d'~** to cover sb with opprobrium ◆ **jeter l'~ sur** to heap opprobrium on ◆ **être l'~ de la famille** to be a source of shame to the family ◆ **vivre dans l'~** to live in infamy

optatif, -ive /ɔptatif, iv/ **ADJ, NM** optative

opter /ɔpte/ ► conjug 1 ◄ **VI** *(= choisir)* ◆ **~ pour** *[+ carrière, solution, nationalité]* to opt for, to choose ◆ **~ entre** to choose *ou* decide between

opticien, -ienne /ɔptisjɛ̃, jɛn/ **NM,F** (dispensing) optician

optimal, e (mpl **-aux**) /ɔptimal, o/ **ADJ** optimal, optimum *(épith)*

optimalisation /ɔptimalizasjɔ̃/ **NF** ⇒ **optimisation**

optimisation /ɔptimizasjɔ̃/ **NF** optimization

optimiser /ɔptimize/ ► conjug 1 ◄ **VT** to optimize

optimisme /ɔptimism/ **NM** optimism ◆ **pêcher par excès d'~** to be overoptimistic ◆ **faire preuve d'~** to be optimistic

optimiste /ɔptimist/ **ADJ** optimistic ◆ **il est ~ de nature** he's a born optimist, he always looks on the bright side **NMF** optimist

optimum (pl **optimums** *ou* **optima**) /ɔptimɔm, a/ **NM** optimum **ADJ** optimum *(épith)*, optimal

option /ɔpsjɔ̃/ **NF** *(= choix)* option, choice; *(Comm, Jur)* option; *(= accessoire auto)* optional extra ◆ **(matière à) ~** *(Scol)* optional subject *(Brit)*, option *(Brit)*, elective ◆ **texte à ~** optional text ◆ **avec ~ mathématique(s)** *(Scol)* with a mathematical option, with optional mathematics ◆ **prendre une ~ sur** *(Fin)* to take (out) an option on ◆ **grâce à cette victoire, il a pris une ~ sur le championnat** with this victory he now has a chance of winning the championship ◆ **l'~ zéro** *(Pol)* the zero option ◆ **climatisation en ~** *(Aut)* optional air-conditioning, air-conditioning available as an optional extra

COMP **option d'achat** *(Fin)* option to buy, call

option de vente *(Fin)* option to sell, put

optionnel, -elle /ɔpsjɔnɛl/ **ADJ** optional ◆ **matière ~le** optional subject *(Brit)*, option *(Brit)*, elective *(US)*

optique /ɔptik/ **ADJ** *[verre, disque]* optical; *[nerf]* optic; → **angle, fibre, télégraphie** **NF** 1 *(= science, technique, commerce)* optics *(sg)* ◆ **~ médicale/photographique** medical/photographic optics ◆ **instrument d'~** optical instrument; → **illusion** 2 *(= lentilles, miroirs) [de caméra, microscope]* optics *(sg)* 3 *(= manière de voir)* perspective ◆ **il faut situer ses arguments dans une ~ sociologique** we must place his arguments in a sociological perspective ◆ **voir qch avec** *ou* **dans une certaine ~** to look at sth from a certain angle *ou* viewpoint ◆ **j'ai une tout autre ~ que la sienne** my way of looking at things is quite different from his, I have a completely different perspective from his

optoélectronique /ɔptoelɛktʀɔnik/ **ADJ** optoelectronic **NF** optoelectronics *(sg)*

opulence /ɔpylɑ̃s/ **NF** 1 *(= richesse) [de province, région, pays]* wealthiness, richness; *[de prairie]* richness; *[de personne]* wealth; *[de luxe, vie]* opulence ◆ **vivre dans l'~** to live an opulent life ◆ **nager dans l'~** to live in the lap of luxury ◆ **il est né dans l'~** he was born into a life of opulence 2 *(= ampleur)* **~ des formes** richness *ou* fullness of form ◆ **l'~ de sa poitrine** the ampleness of her bosom

opulent, e /ɔpylɑ̃, ɑ̃t/ **ADJ** 1 *(= riche) [province, pays, personne]* wealthy, rich; *[prairie]* rich; *[luxe, vie]* opulent 2 *(= abondant) [formes]* full; *[poitrine]* ample, generous ◆ **une chevelure ~e** *(= abondant)* a mane of hair

opus /ɔpys/ **NM** opus

opuscule /ɔpyskyl/ **NM** *(= brochure)* opuscule

OPV /ɔpeve/ **NF** (abrév de **offre publique de vente**) → **offre**

or[1] /ɔʀ/ **NM** 1 *(= métal)* gold; *(= dorure)* gilt, gilding, gold ◆ **~ gris/jaune/rouge** white/yellow/red gold ◆ **~ fin/massif** fine/solid gold ◆ **en lettres d'~** in gilt *ou* gold lettering ◆ **ses cheveux d'~** his golden hair ◆ **les blés d'~** the golden cornfields ◆ **les ~s des coupoles/de l'automne** the golden tints of the cupolas/of autumn ◆ **peinture/franc ~** gold paint/franc; → **cœur, cousu, étalon², lingot** *etc*

2 *(locutions)* **c'est de l'~ en barre** *(commerce, investissement)* it's a rock-solid investment, it's as safe as houses *(Brit)* ◆ **pour (tout) l'~ du monde** for all the money in the world, for all the tea in China

◆ **en or** *[objet]* gold; *[occasion]* golden *(épith)*; *[mari, enfant, sujet]* marvellous, wonderful ◆ **bijoux en ~ massif** solid gold jewellery, jewellery in solid gold ◆ **c'est une affaire en ~** *(achat)* it's a real bargain; *(commerce, magasin)* it's a gold mine ◆ **ils font des affaires en ~** *(ponctuellement)* they're making money hand over fist, they're raking it in *

COMP **or blanc** *(= métal)* white gold; *(= neige)* snow

or bleu *(= eau)* water

or noir *(= pétrole)* oil, black gold

or vert *(= agriculture)* agricultural wealth

or[2] /ɔʀ/ **CONJ** 1 *(mise en relief)* **~, ce jour-là, le soleil brillait** now, on that particular day, the sun was shining ◆ **il m'a téléphoné hier, ~ j'avais pensé à lui le matin même** he phoned me yesterday, and it just so happened that I'd been thinking about him that very morning 2 *(opposition)* and yet, but ◆ **nous l'attendions, ~ il n'est pas venu** we waited for him and yet *ou* but he didn't come 3 *(dans un syllogisme : non traduit)* **tous les chats ont quatre pattes ; ~ mon chien a quatre pattes ; donc mon chien est un chat** all cats have four legs; my dog has four legs; therefore my dog is a cat 4 († *ou frm*) **~ donc** thus, therefore

oracle /ɔʀɑkl/ **NM** *(gén)* oracle ◆ **rendre un ~** to pronounce an oracle ◆ **l'~ de la famille** *(hum)* the oracle of the family ◆ **il parlait en ~** *ou* **comme un ~** he talked like an oracle

orage /ɔʀaʒ/ **NM** 1 *(= tempête)* thunderstorm, (electric) storm ◆ **pluie/temps d'~** thundery *ou* stormy shower/weather ◆ **vent d'~** stormy wind ◆ **il va y avoir de l'~** *ou* **un ~** there's going to be a (thunder)storm 2 *(= dispute)* upset ◆ **laisser passer l'~** to let the storm blow over ◆ **elle sentait venir l'~** she could sense the storm brewing 3 *(littér = tumulte)* **les ~s de la vie** the turmoils of life ◆ **les ~s des passions** the tumult *ou* storm of the passions 4 *(locutions)* **il y a de l'~ dans l'air** *(lit)* there is a (thunder)storm brewing; *(fig)* there is trouble *ou* a storm brewing ◆ **le temps est à l'~** there's thunder in the air, the weather is thundery

COMP **orage de chaleur** summer storm

orage magnétique magnetic storm

orageusement /ɔʀaʒøzmɑ̃/ **ADV** *(fig)* tempestuously

orageux, -euse /ɔʀaʒø, øz/ **ADJ** 1 *(lit) [ciel]* stormy, lowering *(épith)*; *[région, saison]* stormy; *[pluie, chaleur, atmosphère]* thundery ◆ **temps ~** thundery weather 2 *(fig = mouvementé) [époque, vie, adolescence, discussion]* turbulent, stormy

oraison /ɔʀɛzɔ̃/ **NF** orison *(frm)*, prayer ◆ **~ funèbre** funeral oration

oral, e (mpl **-aux**) /ɔʀal, o/ **ADJ** *[tradition, littérature, épreuve]* oral; *[confession, déposition]* verbal, oral; *(Ling, Méd, Psych)* oral; → **stade, voie** **NM** *(Scol)* oral (examination) ◆ **il est meilleur à l'~**

qu'à l'écrit his oral work is better than his written work

oralement /ɔʀalmɑ̃/ ADV *[transmettre]* orally, by word of mouth; *[conclure un accord, confesser]* verbally, orally; *(Méd, Scol)* orally

oralité /ɔʀalite/ NF oral character

orange /ɔʀɑ̃ʒ/ NF (= *fruit*) orange ◆ **je t'apporterai des ~s** *(hum)* I'll come and visit you in prison *(ou* in hospital) NM (= *couleur*) orange ◆ **l'~** (= *feu de signalisation*) amber *(Brit)*, yellow *(US)* ◆ **le feu était à l'~** the lights were on amber *(Brit)*, the light was yellow *(US)* ◆ **passer à l'~** to go through on amber *(Brit) ou* when the lights are (on) amber *(Brit)*, to go through a yellow light *(US) ou* when the light is yellow *(US)* ADJ INV orange; *[feu de signalisation]* amber *(Brit)*, yellow *(US)*

COMP **orange amère** bitter orange
orange douce sweet orange
orange sanguine blood orange

> ⚠ Quand il qualifie la couleur d'un feu de signalisation, **orange** ne se traduit pas par le mot anglais **orange**.

orangé, e /ɔʀɑ̃ʒe/ ADJ orangey, orange-coloured NM orangey colour ◆ **l'~ de ces rideaux** the orangey shade of these curtains

orangeade /ɔʀɑ̃ʒad/ NF orange squash

oranger /ɔʀɑ̃ʒe/ NM orange tree; → **fleur**

orangeraie /ɔʀɑ̃ʒʀɛ/ NF orange grove

orangerie /ɔʀɑ̃ʒʀi/ NF (= *serre*) orangery

orangette /ɔʀɑ̃ʒɛt/ NF (= *fruit*) Seville orange, bitter orange; (= *friandise*) *strip of orange covered with chocolate*

orangiste /ɔʀɑ̃ʒist/ *(Hist, Pol)* ADJ ◆ **défilé ~** Orange parade *ou* march NM Orangeman NF Orangewoman

orang-outan(g) (pl **orangs-outan(g)s**) /ɔʀɑ̃utɑ̃/ NM orang-outang

orateur, -trice /ɔʀatœʀ, tʀis/ NM,F *(gén)* speaker; (= *homme politique, tribun*) orator, speaker; *(Can)* Speaker (of House of Commons)

oratoire /ɔʀatwaʀ/ ADJ *[art, morceau]* oratorical, of oratory; *[ton, style]* oratorical ◆ **il a des talents ~s** he's a very good speaker; → **joute, précaution** NM (= *chapelle*) oratory, small chapel; *(au bord du chemin)* (wayside) shrine

oratorio /ɔʀatɔʀjo/ NM oratorio

orbe[1] /ɔʀb/ NM *(littér = globe)* orb; *(Astron)* (= *surface*) plane of orbit; (= *orbite*) orbit

orbe[2] /ɔʀb/ ADJ *(Constr)* ◆ **mur ~** blind wall

orbital, e (mpl **-aux**) /ɔʀbital, o/ ADJ orbital

orbite /ɔʀbit/ NF 1 *(Anat)* (eye-)socket, orbit *(SPÉC)* ◆ **aux yeux enfoncés dans les ~s** with sunken eyes 2 *(Astron, Phys)* orbit ◆ **mettre ou placer sur** *ou* **en ~** to put *ou* place in(to) orbit ◆ **la mise en** *ou* **sur ~ d'un satellite** putting a satellite into orbit ◆ **être sur** *ou* **en ~** *[satellite]* to be in orbit ◆ **satellite en ~ à 900 km de la Terre** satellite orbiting 900 km above the earth 3 (= *sphère d'influence*) sphere of influence, orbit ◆ **être/entrer dans l'~ de** to be in/enter the sphere of influence of ◆ **vivre dans l'~ de** to live in the sphere of influence of ◆ **attirer qn dans son ~** to draw sb into one's orbit 4 *(locutions)* **mettre** *ou* **placer sur ~** *[+ auteur, projet, produit]* to launch ◆ **être sur ~** *[auteur, produit, méthode, projet]* to be successfully launched

orbiter /ɔʀbite/ ▸ conjug 1 ◂ VI *[satellite]* to orbit ◆ **~ autour de la terre** to orbit (around) the earth

orbiteur /ɔʀbitœʀ/ NM orbiter

Orcades /ɔʀkad/ NFPL ◆ **les ~** Orkney, the Orkneys, the Orkney Islands

orchestral, e (mpl **-aux**) /ɔʀkɛstʀal, o/ ADJ orchestral

orchestrateur, -trice /ɔʀkɛstʀatœʀ, tʀis/ NM,F orchestrator

orchestration /ɔʀkɛstʀasjɔ̃/ NF 1 *(Mus)* (= *composition*) orchestration; (= *adaptation*) orchestration, scoring 2 (= *organisation*) *[de manifestation, propagande, campagne de presse]* organization, orchestration

orchestre /ɔʀkɛstʀ/ NM 1 (= *musiciens*) *[de musique classique, bal]* orchestra; *[de jazz, danse]* band ◆ **grand ~** full orchestra; → **chef**[1] 2 *(Ciné, Théât)* (= *emplacement*) stalls *(Brit)*, orchestra (section) *(US)*; (= *fauteuil*) seat in the (orchestra) stalls *(Brit)*, seat in the orchestra (section) *(US)* ◆ **l'~ applaudissait** applause came from the stalls *(Brit) ou* orchestra (section) *(US)*; → **fauteuil, fosse**

COMP **orchestre de chambre** chamber orchestra
orchestre à cordes string orchestra
orchestre de cuivres brass band
orchestre de danse dance band
orchestre de jazz jazz band
orchestre symphonique symphony orchestra

orchestrer /ɔʀkɛstʀe/ ▸ conjug 1 ◂ VT 1 *(Mus)* (= *composer*) to orchestrate; (= *adapter*) to orchestrate, to score 2 (= *organiser*) *[+ campagne, manifestation, propagande]* to organize, to orchestrate ◆ **une campagne savamment orchestrée** a well-orchestrated *ou* well-organized campaign

orchidée /ɔʀkide/ NF orchid

orchite /ɔʀkit/ NF orchitis

ordalie /ɔʀdali/ NF *(Hist)* ordeal

ordi* /ɔʀdi/ NM computer

ordinaire /ɔʀdinɛʀ/ ADJ 1 (= *habituel*) ordinary, normal; *(Jur) [session]* ordinary ◆ **avec sa maladresse ~** with his customary *ou* usual clumsiness ◆ **personnage/fait peu ~** unusual character/fact ◆ **avec un courage pas*** *ou* **peu ~** with incredible *ou* extraordinary courage ◆ **ça alors, c'est pas ~ !*** that's (really) unusual! *ou* out of the ordinary!

2 (= *courant*) *[vin]* ordinary; *[vêtement]* ordinary, everyday *(épith)*; *[service de table]* everyday *(épith)*; *[qualité]* standard; *[essence]* two-star *(Brit)*, 2-star *(Brit)*, regular *(US)* ◆ **croissant ~** *croissant made with margarine instead of butter*

3 *(péj = commun) [personne, manières]* common; *[conversation]* ordinary, run-of-the-mill ◆ **un vin très ~** a very indifferent wine ◆ **mener une existence très ~** to lead a humdrum existence

NM 1 (= *la banalité*) **l'~** the ordinary ◆ **ça sort de l'~** that's out of the ordinary ◆ **cet homme-là sort de l'~** he's one of a kind

2 (= *nourriture*) **l'~** ordinary *ou* everyday fare

3 *(locutions) (littér)* **à l'~** usually, ordinarily ◆ **comme à l'~** as usual ◆ **d'~** ordinarily, usually ◆ **il fait plus chaud que d'~** *ou* **qu'à l'~** it's warmer than usual ◆ **(comme) à son/mon ~** in his/my usual way, as was his/my wont *(littér) (aussi hum)*

COMP **l'ordinaire de la messe** the ordinary of the Mass

ordinairement /ɔʀdinɛʀmɑ̃/ ADV ordinarily, usually

ordinal, e (mpl **-aux**) /ɔʀdinal, o/ ADJ ordinal NM ordinal number

ordinateur /ɔʀdinatœʀ/ NM computer ◆ **~ individuel** *ou* **personnel** personal computer ◆ **~ familial** home computer ◆ **~ de bureau** desktop (computer) ◆ **~ de bord** onboard computer ◆ **~ central** mainframe computer ◆ **mettre sur ~** *[+ données]* to enter into a computer; *[+ système]* to computerize, to put onto a computer ◆ **l'ensemble du système est géré par ~** the entire system is managed by computer *ou* is computerized ◆ **simulation sur** *ou* **par ~** computer simulation

ordination /ɔʀdinasjɔ̃/ NF *(Rel)* ordination

ordinogramme /ɔʀdinɔgʀam/ NM flow chart *ou* sheet

ordonnance /ɔʀdɔnɑ̃s/ NF 1 *(Méd)* prescription ◆ **préparer une ~** to make up a prescription ◆ **ce médicament n'est délivré** *ou* **vendu que sur ~** this medicine is only available on prescription ◆ **médicament vendu** *ou* **délivré sans ~** over-the-counter medicine 2 *(Jur = arrêté) [de gouvernement]* order, edict; *[de juge]* (judge's) order, ruling ◆ **par ~ du 2-2-92** in the edict of 2/2/92 ◆ **rendre une ~** to give a ruling 3 (= *disposition*) *[de poème, phrase, tableau]* organization, layout; *[de bâtiment]* plan, layout; *[de cérémonie]* organization; *[de repas]* order NM *ou* NF *(Mil)* 1 (= *subalterne*) orderly, batman *(Brit)* 2 ◆ **d'~** *[revolver, tunique]* regulation *(épith)*; → **officier**[1]

COMP **ordonnance de paiement** authorization of payment
ordonnance de police police regulation
ordonnance royale royal decree *ou* edict

ordonnancement /ɔʀdɔnɑ̃smɑ̃/ NM 1 *(Fin)* order to pay 2 (= *disposition*) *[de phrase, tableau]* organization, layout; *[de cérémonie]* organization

ordonnancer /ɔʀdɔnɑ̃se/ ▸ conjug 3 ◂ VT 1 *(Fin)* *[+ dépense]* to authorize 2 (= *agencer*) *[+ phrase, tableau]* to put together; *[+ cérémonie]* to organize

ordonnancier /ɔʀdɔnɑ̃sje/ NM (= *liasse d'ordonnances*) book of prescription forms; (= *registre*) register of prescriptions

ordonnateur, -trice /ɔʀdɔnatœʀ, tʀis/ NM,F 1 *[de fête, cérémonie]* organizer, arranger ◆ **~ des pompes funèbres** funeral director *(in charge of events at the funeral itself)* 2 *(Fin)* official with power to authorize expenditure

ordonné, e /ɔʀdɔne/ (ptp de **ordonner**) ADJ 1 (= *méthodique*) *[enfant]* tidy; *[employé]* methodical 2 (= *bien arrangé*) *[maison]* orderly, tidy; *[vie]* (well-)ordered, orderly; *[idées, discours]* well-ordered; → **charité** 3 *(Math)* ordered ◆ **couple ~** ordered pair NF **ordonnée** *(Math)* ordinate, Y-coordinate ◆ **axe des ~es** Y-axis

ordonner /ɔʀdɔne/ ▸ conjug 1 ◂ VT 1 (= *arranger*) *[+ espace, idées, éléments]* to arrange, to organize; *[+ discours, texte]* to organize; *(Math) [+ polynôme]* to arrange in order ◆ **il avait ordonné sa vie de telle façon que ...** he had arranged *ou* organized his life in such a way that ...

2 (= *commander*) *(Méd) [+ traitement, médicament]* to prescribe; *(Jur) [+ huis-clos, enquête]* to order ◆ **~ à qn de faire qch** to order sb to do sth, to give sb orders to do sth ◆ **il nous ordonna le silence** he ordered us to be quiet ◆ **ils ordonnèrent la fermeture des cafés** they ordered the closure of the cafés ◆ **ce qui m'a été ordonné** what I've been ordered to do ◆ **je vais ~ que cela soit fait immédiatement** I'm going to order that it be done immediately

3 *(Rel) [+ prêtre]* to ordain ◆ **être ordonné prêtre** to be ordained priest

VPR **s'ordonner** *[idées, faits]* to organize themselves ◆ **les idées s'ordonnaient dans sa tête** the ideas began to organize themselves *ou* sort themselves out in his head

ordre[1] /ɔʀdʀ/ NM 1 (= *succession régulière*) order ◆ **l'~ des mots** *(Ling)* word order ◆ **par ~ alphabétique** in alphabetical order ◆ **par ~ d'ancienneté/de mérite** in order of seniority/of merit ◆ **alignez-vous par ~ de grandeur** line up in order of height *ou* size ◆ **par ~ d'importance** in order of importance ◆ **dans l'~** in order ◆ **dans le bon ~** in the right order ◆ **par ~** *ou* **dans l'~ d'entrée en scène** in order of appearance ◆ **~ de départ/d'arrivée** *(Sport)* order (of competitors) at the starting/finishing line *ou* post ◆ ~ **des descendants** *ou* **héritiers** *(Jur)* order of descent ◆ **le nouvel ~ mondial** the new world order

◆ **en + ordre** ◆ **en ~ de bataille/de marche** *(Mil)* in battle/marching order ◆ **se replier en bon ~** to retreat in good order ◆ **en ~ dispersé** *(Mil)* in extended order; *(fig)* without a common line *ou* plan of action; → **numéro, procéder**

2 *(Archit, Bio = catégorie)* order ◆ **l'~ ionique/dorique** the Ionic/Doric order

3 *(= nature, catégorie)* **dans le même ~ d'idées** similarly ◆ **dans un autre ~ d'idées** in a different *ou* another connection ◆ **pour des motifs d'~ personnel/différent** for reasons of a personal/different nature ◆ **c'est dans l'~ des choses** it's in the nature *ou* order of things ◆ **une affaire/un chiffre du même ~** a matter/a figure of the same nature *ou* order ◆ **un chiffre de l'~ de 2 millions** a figure in the region of *ou* of the order of 2 million ◆ **avec une somme de cet ~** with a sum of this order ◆ **donnez-nous un ~ de grandeur** *(prix)* give us a rough estimate *ou* a rough idea ◆ **un chiffre de** *ou* **dans cet ~ de grandeur** a figure in that region ◆ **de premier/deuxième/troisième ~** first-/second-/third-rate ◆ **de dernier ~** third-rate, very inferior ◆ **considérations d'~ pratique/général** considerations of a practical/general nature

4 *(= légalité)* **l'~** order ◆ **l'~ établi** the established order ◆ **l'~ public** law and order ◆ **le maintien de l'~ (public)** the maintenance of law and order *ou* of public order ◆ **quand tout fut rentré dans l'~** when order had been restored, when all was back to order ◆ **le parti de l'~** the party of law and order ◆ **un partisan de l'~** a supporter of law and order; → **force, rappeler, service**

5 *(= méthode, bonne organisation) [de personne, chambre]* tidiness, neatness, orderliness ◆ **avoir de l'~** *(rangements)* to be tidy *ou* orderly; *(travail)* to have method, to be systematic *ou* methodical ◆ **manquer d'~, n'avoir pas d'~** to be untidy *ou* disorderly, to have no method, to be unsystematic *ou* unmethodical ◆ **travailler avec ~ et méthode** to work in an orderly *ou* a methodical *ou* systematic way ◆ **mettre bon ~ à qch** to put sth to rights, to sort out sth ◆ **un homme d'~** a man of order ◆ **(re)mettre de l'~ dans** *[+ affaires]* to set *ou* put in order, to tidy up; *[+ papiers, bureau]* to tidy (up), to clear up

◆ **en ordre** *[tiroir, maison, bureau]* tidy, orderly; *[comptes]* in order ◆ **tenir en ~** *[+ chambre]* to keep tidy; *[+ comptes]* to keep in order ◆ **(re)mettre en ~** *[+ affaires]* to set *ou* put in order, to tidy up; *[+ papiers, bureau]* to tidy (up), to clear up ◆ **ils travaillent à une remise en ~ de l'économie** they are trying to sort out the economy ◆ **la remise en ~ du pays** restoring the country to order ◆ **défiler en ~** to go past in an orderly manner

◆ **en ordre de marche** *[machine]* in (full) working order

6 *(= association, congrégation)* order; *[de profession libérale]* ≃ professional association ◆ **~ de chevalerie** order of knighthood ◆ **~ monastique** monastic order ◆ **~ mendiant** mendicant order ◆ **l'~ de la jarretière/du mérite** the Order of the Garter/of Merit ◆ **les ~s** *(Rel)* (holy) orders ◆ **les ~s majeurs/mineurs** *(Rel)* major/minor orders ◆ **entrer dans les ~s** *(Rel)* to take (holy) orders, to go into the Church ◆ **l'~ des architectes** the association of architects ◆ **l'~ des avocats** ≃ the Bar, the Bar Association *(US)* ◆ **l'~ des médecins** the medical association, ≃ the British Medical Association *(Brit)*, the American Medical Association *(US)* ◆ **l'~ des pharmaciens** the pharmaceutical association; → **radier**

COMP **ordre du jour** *[de conférence, réunion]* agenda ◆ **"autres questions à l'ordre du jour"** *(en fin de programme)* "any other business" ◆ **l'~ du jour de l'assemblée** *(Admin)* the business before the meeting ◆ **passons à l'~ du jour** let's turn to the business of the day ◆ **inscrit à l'~ du jour** on the agenda ◆ **être à l'~ du jour** *(lit)* to be on the agenda; *(fig = être d'actualité)* to be (very) topical ◆ **ce n'est pas à l'~ du jour** *(fig)* it's not on the agenda

ordre² /ɔʀdʀ/ NM 1 *(= commandement, directive)* *(gén)* order; *(Mil)* order, command ◆ **donner (l')~ de** to give an order *ou* the order to, to give orders to ◆ **par ~** *ou* **sur les ~s du ministre** by order of the minister, on the orders of the minister ◆ **j'ai reçu des ~s formels** I have formal instructions ◆ **j'ai reçu l'~ de ...** I've been given orders to ... ◆ **je n'ai d'~ à recevoir de personne** I don't take orders from anyone ◆ **être aux ~s de qn** to be at sb's disposal ◆ **je suis à vos ~s** *(formule de politesse)* I am at your service ◆ **dis donc, je ne suis pas à tes ~s !** you can't give me orders!, I don't take orders from you!, I'm not at your beck and call! ◆ **à vos ~s !** *(Mil)* yes sir! ◆ **être/combattre sous les ~s de qn** to be/fight under sb's command ◆ **j'ai agi sur ~** I was (just) following orders; → **désir, jusque, mot**

2 *(Comm, Fin)* order ◆ **à l'~ de** payable to, to the order of ◆ **chèque à mon ~** cheque made out to me ◆ **passer un ~** *(de Bourse)* to put in an order; → **billet, chèque, citer**

COMP **ordre d'achat** buying order
ordre d'appel *(Mil)* call-up papers *(Brit)*, draft notice *(US)*
ordre de Bourse stock exchange order
ordre de grève strike call
ordre du jour *(Mil)* order of the day ◆ **citer qn à l'~ du jour** to mention sb in dispatches
ordre au mieux *(Fin)* order at best
ordre de mission *(Mil)* orders *(for a mission)*
ordre de prélèvement automatique direct debit instruction
ordre de route *(Mil)* marching orders
ordre de vente sale order
ordre de virement transfer order

ordré, e /ɔʀdʀe/ ADJ *(Helv = ordonné) [personne]* tidy

ordure /ɔʀdyʀ/ NF 1 *(= saleté)* dirt *(NonC)*, filth *(NonC)* ◆ **les chiens qui font leurs ~s sur le trottoir** dogs that foul the pavement

2 *(péj)* **ce film est une ~** this film is pure filth ◆ **ce type est une belle ~**‡ that guy's a real bastard‡

3 *(littér = abjection)* mire *(littér)* ◆ **il aime à se vautrer dans l'~** he likes to wallow in filth

NFPL **ordures** 1 *(= détritus)* refuse *(NonC)*, rubbish *(NonC) (Brit)*, garbage *(NonC) (US)* ◆ **~s ménagères** household refuse ◆ **l'enlèvement** *ou* **le ramassage des ~s** refuse *ou* rubbish *(Brit)* *ou* garbage *(US)* collection ◆ **jeter** *ou* **mettre qch aux ~s** to throw *ou* put sth into the dustbin *(Brit)* *ou* rubbish bin *(Brit)* *ou* garbage can *(US)* ◆ **c'est juste bon à mettre aux ~s** it's fit for the dustbin *ou* rubbish bin *(Brit)*, it belongs in the garbage can *(US)*; → **boîte**

2 *(= grossièretés)* obscenities, filth ◆ **dire des ~s** to utter obscenities, to talk filth ◆ **écrire des ~s** to write filth

ordurier, -ière /ɔʀdyʀje, jɛʀ/ ADJ filthy

orée /ɔʀe/ NF *(littér) [de bois]* edge ◆ **à l'~ de l'an 2000** at the beginning of the year 2000

Oregon /ɔʀegɔ̃/ NM Oregon

oreillard /ɔʀɛjaʀ/ NM *(gén)* long-eared animal; *(= chauve-souris)* long-eared bat

oreille /ɔʀɛj/ NF 1 *(Anat)* ear ◆ **l'~ moyenne/interne** the middle/inner ear ◆ **l'~ externe** the outer *ou* external ear, the auricle *(SPÉC)* ◆ **~s décollées** protruding *ou* sticking-out ears ◆ **~s en feuille de chou** big flappy ears ◆ **~s en chou-fleur** cauliflower ears ◆ **le béret sur l'~** his beret cocked over one ear *ou* tilted to one side ◆ **animal aux longues ~s** *(fig)* long-eared animal ◆ **aux ~s pointues** with pointed ears ◆ **l'~ basse** *(fig)* crestfallen, (with) one's tail between one's legs ◆ **c'est l'avocat qui montre le bout de l'~** it's the lawyer coming out in him, it's the lawyer in him showing through ◆ **tirer les ~s à qn** *(lit)* to pull *ou* tweak sb's ears; *(fig)* to give sb a (good) telling off*, to tell sb off* ◆ **se faire tirer l'~** *(fig)* to take *ou* need a lot of persuading; → **boucher¹, boucle, dresser, puce,** *etc*

2 *(= ouïe)* hearing, ear ◆ **avoir l'~ fine** to have keen *ou* acute hearing, to have a sharp ear ◆ **avoir de l'~** to have a good ear (for music) ◆ **il n'a pas d'~** he has no ear for music; → **casser, écorcher, écouter**

3 *(comme organe de communication)* ear ◆ **écouter de toutes ses ~s, être tout ~s** to be all ears ◆ **n'écouter que d'une ~, écouter d'une ~ distraite** to only half listen, to listen with (only) one ear ◆ **ouvre bien tes ~s** listen carefully ◆ **dire qch à l'~ de qn, dire qch à qn dans le creux** *ou* **tuyau de l'~** to have a word in sb's ear about sth ◆ **il pédalait, casque sur les ~s** he was pedalling along with his headphones on ◆ **les ~s ont dû lui tinter** *ou* **siffler** *(hum)* his ears must have been burning ◆ **ce n'est pas tombé dans l'~ d'un sourd** it didn't fall on deaf ears ◆ **ça entre par une ~ et ça (res)sort par l'autre*** it goes in one ear and out the other ◆ **il y a toujours des ~s qui traînent** there's always someone listening ◆ **avoir l'~ de qn** to have sb's ear ◆ **porter qch/venir aux ~s de qn** to let sth be/come to be known to sb, to bring sth/come to sb's attention; → **bouche, prêter, rebattre**

4 *[d'écrou, fauteuil]* wing; *[de soupière]* handle; *[de casquette]* earflap

oreille-de-mer (pl **oreilles-de-mer**) /ɔʀɛjdəmɛʀ/ NF *(= coquillage)* ear shell, abalone

oreiller /ɔʀeje/ NM pillow ◆ **se réconcilier sur l'~** to make it up in bed; → **confidence, taie**

oreillette /ɔʀɛjɛt/ NF 1 *[de cœur]* auricle ◆ **orifice de l'~** atrium 2 *[de casquette]* earflap 3 *(= écouteur)* earphone; *[de téléphone portable, baladeur]* earpiece; → **fauteuil**

oreillon /ɔʀɛjɔ̃/ NM *[d'abricot]* (apricot) half
NMPL **oreillons** *(Méd)* **les ~s** (the) mumps

Orénoque /ɔʀenɔk/ NM Orinoco

ores /ɔʀ/ **d'ores et déjà** LOC ADV already

Oreste /ɔʀɛst/ NM Orestes

orfèvre /ɔʀfɛvʀ/ NM silversmith, goldsmith ◆ **il est ~ en la matière** *(fig)* he's an expert (on the subject)

orfèvrerie /ɔʀfɛvʀəʀi/ NF *(= art, commerce)* silversmith's *(ou* goldsmith's) trade; *(= magasin)* silversmith's *(ou* goldsmith's) shop; *(= ouvrage)* (silver) plate, (gold) plate

orfraie /ɔʀfʀɛ/ NF white-tailed eagle

organdi /ɔʀgɑ̃di/ NM organdie

organe /ɔʀgan/ NM 1 *(Anat, Physiol)* organ ◆ **~s des sens/sexuels** sense/sex(ual) organs ◆ **~s génitaux** genitals; → **fonction, greffe¹** 2 *(fig)* *(= véhicule, instrument)* instrument, organ; *(= institution, organisme)* organ ◆ **le juge est l'~ de la loi** the judge is the instrument of the law ◆ **la parole est l'~ de la pensée** speech is the medium *ou* vehicle of thought ◆ **un des ~s du gouvernement** one of the organs of government 3 *(= porte-parole)* representative, spokesman; *(= journal)* mouthpiece, organ 4 *(† ou littér = voix)* voice ◆ **avoir un bel ~** to have a beautiful voice

COMP **organes de commande** controls
organe de presse newspaper
organes de transmission transmission system

organigramme /ɔʀganigʀam/ NM *(= tableau hiérarchique, structurel)* organization chart; *(= tableau des opérations de synchronisation, Ordin)* flow chart *ou* diagram

organique /ɔʀganik/ ADJ *(Chim, Jur, Méd)* organic; → **chimie**

organiquement /ɔʀganikmɑ̃/ ADV organically

organisateur, -trice /ɔʀganizatœʀ, tʀis/ ADJ *[faculté, puissance]* organizing *(épith)* NM,F organizer ◆ **~-conseil** management consultant ◆ **~ de voyages** tour operator

organisation /ɔʀganizasjɔ̃/ NF 1 *(= préparation) [de voyage, fête, réunion]* organization, arranging; *[de campagne]* organization; *[de pétition]* organization, getting up; *[de service, coopérative]* organization, setting up; *(= agencement) [d'emploi du temps, travail]* organization, setting out; *[de journée]* organization ◆ **~ scientifique du travail** scientific management ◆ **il a l'esprit d'~** he's good at organizing things ◆ **il manque d'~** he's not very organized

2 *(= structure) [de service, armée, parti]* organization; *[de texte]* organization, layout ◆ **une ~ sociale encore primitive** a still rather basic social structure ◆ **l'~ infiniment complexe du corps humain** the infinitely complex organization of the human body

3 *(= association, organisme)* organization ◆ **~ non gouvernementale** non-governmental organization ◆ **~ humanitaire** humanitarian organization ◆ **~ syndicale** trade(s) union *(Brit)*, labor union *(US)*

COMP **Organisation de coopération et de développement économique** Organization for Economic Cooperation and Development

Organisation des États américains Organization of American States

Organisation internationale du travail International Labour Organization

Organisation de libération de la Palestine Palestine Liberation Organization

Organisation maritime internationale International Maritime Organization

Organisation météorologique mondiale World Meteorological Organization

Organisation mondiale du commerce World Trade Organization

Organisation mondiale de la santé World Health Organization

Organisation mondiale du tourisme World Tourism Organization

Organisation des Nations Unies United Nations Organization

Organisation des pays exportateurs de pétrole Organization of Petroleum Exporting Countries

Organisation des territoires de l'Asie du Sud-Est South-East Asia Treaty Organization

Organisation du Traité de l'Atlantique Nord North Atlantic Treaty Organization

Organisation de l'unité africaine Organization of African Unity

organisationnel, -elle /ɔʀganizasjɔnɛl/ ADJ *[problème, moyens]* organizational

organisé, e /ɔʀganize/ (ptp de **organiser**) ADJ organized ◆ **personne bien ~e** well-organized person; → **voyage**

organiser /ɔʀganize/ GRAMMAIRE ACTIVE 52.2 ► conjug 1 ◄

VT 1 *(= mettre sur pied) [+ voyage, réunion]* to organize, to arrange; *[+ campagne]* to organize; *[+ pétition]* to organize, to get up; *[+ service, coopérative]* to organize, to set up ◆ **j'organise une petite fête** I'm having a little party

2 *(= structurer) [+ travail, opérations, armée, parti, journée]* to organize; *[+ emploi du temps]* to organize, to set out

VPR **s'organiser** 1 *(= se regrouper) [personne, entreprise]* to organize o.s. *(ou* itself), to get (o.s. *ou* itself) organized

2 *(= agencer son temps)* to organize o.s. ◆ **il ne sait pas s'~** he doesn't know how to organize himself, he can't get (himself) organized ◆ **je m'organiserai en fonction de toi** I'll just fit in with you, I'll fit *ou* arrange my plans round yours

3 *(= s'articuler)* **s'~ autour d'un thème** *[ouvrage, histoire]* to be organized around a theme

organiseur /ɔʀganizœʀ/ NM (personal) organizer ◆ **~ électronique** electronic organizer

organisme /ɔʀganism/ NM 1 *(= organes, corps)* body, organism *(SPÉC)* ◆ **les besoins/fonctions de l'~** the needs/functions of the body *ou* organism, bodily needs/functions ◆ **~ génétiquement modifié** genetically modified organism 2 *(= individu)* organism ◆ **une nation est un ~ vivant** a nation is a living organism 3 *(= institution, bureaux)* body, organization ◆ **~ de crédit** credit company *ou* institution ◆ **~ de recherche** research body *ou* organization ◆ **~ de formation** training institution *ou* body ◆ **les ~s sociaux** social welfare bodies

⚠ Au sens de 'institution', **organisme** ne se traduit pas par le mot anglais **organism**.

organiste /ɔʀganist/ NMF organist

orgasme /ɔʀgasm/ NM orgasm, climax

orgasmique /ɔʀgasmik/, **orgastique** /ɔʀgastik/ ADJ orgasmic, climactic(al)

orge /ɔʀʒ/ NF, NM barley ◆ **~ perlé** pearl barley; → **sucre**

orgeat /ɔʀʒa/ NM orgeat; → **sirop**

orgelet /ɔʀʒəlɛ/ NM *(Méd)* sty(e)

orgiaque /ɔʀʒjak/ ADJ orgiastic

orgie /ɔʀʒi/ NF 1 *(Hist) (= repas)* orgy; *(= beuverie)* drinking orgy ◆ **faire une ~** to have an orgy ◆ **faire des ~s de gâteaux** to gorge o.s. on cakes 2 *(fig)* **~ de** profusion of ◆ **~ de fleurs** profusion of flowers ◆ **~ de couleurs** riot of colour

orgue /ɔʀg/ NM organ ◆ **tenir l'~** to play the organ ◆ **~ de chœur/de cinéma/électrique/portatif** choir/theatre/electric/portable organ ◆ **~ de Barbarie** barrel organ, hurdy-gurdy; → **point¹** NFPL **orgues** 1 *(Mus)* organ ◆ **les grandes ~s** the great organ ◆ **les petites ~s** the small pipe organ 2 *(Géol)* **~s basaltiques** basalt columns 3 *(Mil)* **~s de Staline** rocket launcher *(mounted on a truck)*

orgueil /ɔʀgœj/ NM 1 *(= arrogance)* pride, arrogance; *(= amour-propre)* pride ◆ **gonflé d'~** puffed up *ou* bursting with pride ◆ **~ démesuré** overweening pride *ou* arrogance ◆ **il a l'~ de son rang** he has all the arrogance associated with his rank ◆ **avec l'~ légitime du vainqueur** with the victor's legitimate pride ◆ **par ~ il ne l'a pas fait** he was too proud to do it, it was his pride that stopped him doing it ◆ **le péché d'~** the sin of pride

2 *(locutions)* **ce tableau, ~ de la collection** this picture, pride of the collection ◆ **l'~ de se voir confier les clés lui fit oublier sa colère** his pride at being entrusted with the keys made him forget his anger ◆ **avoir l'~ de qch, tirer ~ de qch** to take pride in sth, to pride o.s. on sth ◆ **mettre son ~ à faire qch** to take pride in doing sth

orgueilleusement /ɔʀgøjøzmɑ̃/ ADV proudly, arrogantly

orgueilleux, -euse /ɔʀgøjø, øz/ ADJ *(défaut)* proud, arrogant; *(qualité)* proud ◆ **~ comme un paon** as proud as a peacock NM,F (very) proud person

oriel /ɔʀjɛl/ NM oriel window

orient /ɔʀjɑ̃/ NM 1 *(littér = est)* orient *(littér)*, east ◆ **l'Orient** *(= Moyen-Orient)* the Middle East; *(= Extrême-Orient)* the Far East ◆ **les pays d'Orient** the countries of the Orient *(littér)*, the oriental countries 2 *[de perle]* orient 3 → **grand**

orientable /ɔʀjɑ̃tabl/ ADJ *[bras d'une machine]* swivelling, rotating; *[lampe, antenne, lamelles de store]* adjustable

oriental, e (mpl **-aux**) /ɔʀjɑ̃tal, o/ ADJ *(= de l'Orient)* oriental; *(= de l'est) [partie, côte, frontière, extrémité]* eastern; *(= du Maghreb)* North African; → **Inde** NM **Oriental** Oriental NF **Orientale** Oriental woman

orientaliser (s') /ɔʀjɑ̃talize/ ► conjug 1 ◄ VPR *[quartier]* to take on an oriental character; *(influence maghrébine)* to take on a North African character; *[personne]* to become orientalized

orientalisme /ɔʀjɑ̃talism/ NM orientalism

orientaliste /ɔʀjɑ̃talist/ NMF, ADJ orientalist

orientation /ɔʀjɑ̃tasjɔ̃/ NF 1 *(= position) [de maison]* aspect; *[de phare, antenne]* direction ◆ **l'~ du jardin au sud** the garden's southern aspect *ou* the fact that the garden faces south

2 *[de carte]* orientating, orientation; *(Math) [de droite]* orientating, orientation

3 *[de touristes, voyageurs, recherches, enquête]* directing ◆ **en ville, j'ai des problèmes d'~** I have problems finding my way around town; → **course, sens, table**

4 *(Scol)* **l'~ professionnelle** careers advice *ou* guidance *(Brit)* ◆ **l'~ scolaire** advice *ou* guidance *(Brit)* on courses ◆ **ils lui suggèrent une ~ vers un lycée professionnel/vers les sciences** they're suggesting he should go to a technical college/he should specialize in science ◆ **il veut changer d'~** he wants to change courses; → **centre, conseiller², cycle¹**

5 *(= tendance, Bourse)* trend; *[de magazine]* leanings, (political) tendencies ◆ **l'~ générale de notre enquête/de ses recherches** the general direction *ou* orientation of our inquiry/of his research ◆ **~ à la hausse** upward trend, upturn ◆ **~ à la baisse** downward trend, downturn

6 *(= ajustement)* adjustment

orienté, e /ɔʀjɑ̃te/ (ptp de **orienter**) ADJ 1 *(= disposé)* **~ à l'est/au sud** *[maison]* facing east/south, with an eastern/a southern aspect; *[antenne]* directed *ou* turned towards the east/the south ◆ **bien/mal ~** *[maison]* well/badly positioned; *[antenne]* properly/badly directed 2 *(= tendancieux) [article]* biased ◆ **question ~e** leading question 3 *(= marqué) [plan, carte]* orientated; *(Math) [droite, vecteur]* oriented 4 *(Bourse)* **bien/mal ~** *[marché]* rising/falling ◆ **valeurs bien ~es** shares which are rising 5 *(Ordin)* **~ objet** *[langage, méthode]* object-oriented

orienter /ɔʀjɑ̃te/ ► conjug 1 ◄ VT 1 *(= disposer) [+ maison]* to position; *[+ lampe, phare, rétroviseur]* to adjust; *[+ miroir, bras de machine]* to position, to adjust; *[+ antenne]* to direct, to adjust ◆ **~ un poste de radio pour améliorer la réception** to move a radio to get better reception ◆ **~ qch vers qch** to turn sth towards sth ◆ **~ une maison vers le** *ou* **au sud** to build a house facing south ◆ **~ une antenne vers le** *ou* **au nord** to turn *ou* direct an aerial towards the north ◆ **la lampe peut s'~ dans toutes les positions** the lamp is fully adjustable

2 *(= guider) [+ touristes, voyageurs]* to direct, to orient *(vers* to); *[+ enquête, recherches]* to direct *(vers* towards); ◆ **~ un élève** to advise a pupil on what courses to follow *ou* on what subjects to specialize in ◆ **elle a été mal orientée** she was put on the wrong courses ◆ **il a été orienté vers les sciences/vers un lycée professionnel** he was steered towards science subjects/towards technical college ◆ **le patient a été orienté vers un service de cardiologie** the patient was referred to a cardiology unit ◆ **~ la conversation vers un sujet** to turn the conversation towards a subject

3 (= marquer) [+ carte] to orientate; (Math) [+ droite] to orient
4 (Naut) [+ voiles] to trim
VPR **s'orienter** 1 (= se repérer) to find one's bearings
2 (= se diriger vers) **s'~ vers** (lit) to turn towards; [goûts] to turn towards; [chercheur, parti, société] to move towards ◆ **s'~ vers les sciences** [étudiant] to specialize in science ◆ **il s'est orienté vers un lycée professionnel** he decided to go to a technical college
3 (Bourse) **le marché s'oriente à la hausse/à la baisse** the market is on a rising/a falling trend, the market is trending upward/downward (US)

orienteur, -euse /ɔʀjɑ̃tœʀ, øz/ NM,F (Scol) careers adviser NM (Tech) orientator

orifice /ɔʀifis/ NM [de caverne, digue] opening, orifice, aperture; [de puits, gouffre, four, tuyau] opening, mouth; (Anat) orifice; (Phon) cavity ◆ **~ d'admission/d'échappement (des gaz)** intake/exhaust port

oriflamme /ɔʀiflɑm/ NF (= bannière) banner, standard; (Hist) oriflamme

origami /ɔʀigami/ NM origami

origan /ɔʀigɑ̃/ NM oregano

originaire /ɔʀiʒinɛʀ/ ADJ 1 ◆ **~ de** (= natif de) [famille, personne] originating from; (= provenant de) [plante, coutume, mets] native to ◆ **il est ~ de** he is a native of, he was born in 2 (= originel) [titulaire, propriétaire] original, first; [vice, défaut] innate, inherent

originairement /ɔʀiʒinɛʀmɑ̃/ ADV originally, at first

original, e (mpl **-aux**) /ɔʀiʒinal, o/ ADJ 1 (= premier, originel) original ◆ **édition ~e** original *ou* first edition; → **bande¹, version** 2 (= neuf, personnel) [idée, décor] original, novel; [artiste, talent, style, œuvre] original ◆ **cela n'a rien d'~** there's nothing original about that 3 (péj = bizarre) eccentric, odd NM,F (péj) (= excentrique) eccentric; (= fantaisiste) clown*, joker* ◆ **c'est un ~** he's a (real) character *ou* a bit of an eccentric NM [d'ouvrage, tableau] original; [de document] original (copy); [de texte dactylographié] top copy, original (US) ◆ **l'~ de ce personnage** the model for *ou* the original of this character

> ⚠ Au sens de 'bizarre', **original** ne se traduit pas par le mot anglais **original**.

originalement /ɔʀiʒinalmɑ̃/ ADV (= de façon personnelle) originally, in an original way; (= originellement) originally

originalité /ɔʀiʒinalite/ NF 1 (= nouveauté) [d'idée, décor] originality, novelty; [d'artiste, talent, œuvre] originality ◆ **d'une grande ~** very original 2 (= caractéristique originale) original aspect *ou* feature 3 (= excentricité) eccentricity

origine /ɔʀiʒin/ GRAMMAIRE ACTIVE 44.2 NF origin; (= commencement) origin, beginning ◆ **les ~s de la vie** the origins of life ◆ **tirer son ~ de, avoir son ~ dans** to have one's (*ou* its) origins in, to originate in ◆ **avoir pour ~** to be caused by ◆ **quelle est l'~ de sa fortune ?** where did his fortune come from?, how did he make his fortune? ◆ **"l'Automobile, des origines à nos jours"** (titre d'ouvrage) "the Motor Car, from its Origins to the Present Day" ◆ **elle a de lointaines ~s bretonnes** she has distant Breton roots ◆ **dès l'~** at *ou* from the outset, at *ou* from the very beginning
◆ **d'origine** [nationalité, région de production] of origin; [langue, pays d'une personne] native ◆ **d'~ française/noble** of French/noble origin *ou* extraction ◆ **être d'~ paysanne/ouvrière** to come from peasant stock/a working-class background ◆ **produit d'~ animale** product of animal origin ◆ **mot d'~ française** word of French origin ◆ **coutume d'~ ancienne** long-standing custom, custom of long standing ◆ **les pneus sont d'~** it still has its original tyres, the tyres are the original ones; → **méridien**
◆ **à l'origine** originally, to begin with ◆ **être à l'~ de** (gén) to be the cause of; [+ proposition, initiative, projet, attentat] to be behind

originel, -elle /ɔʀiʒinɛl/ ADJ [innocence, pureté, beauté] original, primeval; [état, sens] original; → **péché**

originellement /ɔʀiʒinɛlmɑ̃/ ADV (= primitivement) originally; (= dès le début) from the (very) beginning, from the outset

orignal (pl **-aux**) /ɔʀiɲal, o/ NM moose, Canadian elk

Orion /ɔʀjɔ̃/ NM Orion ◆ **le Baudrier d'~** Orion's Belt ◆ **la constellation d'~** the constellation (of) Orion

oripeaux /ɔʀipo/ NMPL (= haillons) rags; (= guenilles clinquantes) showy *ou* flashy rags

ORL /ɔɛʀɛl/ NF (abrév de **oto-rhino-laryngologie**) ENT NMF (abrév de **oto-rhino-laryngologiste**) ENT doctor *ou* specialist

orléaniste /ɔʀleanist/ ADJ, NMF Orleanist

Orlon ® /ɔʀlɔ̃/ NM Orlon ®

orme /ɔʀm/ NM elm

ormeau (pl **ormeaux**) /ɔʀmo/ NM 1 (= arbre) (young) elm; 2 (= coquillage) ormer, abalone, ear shell

Ormuz /ɔʀmuz/ N Hormuz, Ormuz ◆ **le détroit d'~** the Strait of Hormuz *ou* Ormuz

orné, e /ɔʀne/ (ptp de **orner**) ADJ [style] ornate, florid ◆ **lettres ~es** illuminated letters

ornement /ɔʀnəmɑ̃/ NM (gén) ornament; (Archit, Art) embellishment, adornment; (Mus) grace note(s), ornament ◆ **sans ~(s)** [élégance, toilette, style] plain, unadorned ◆ **d'~** [arbre, jardin] ornamental ◆ **~s de style** ornaments of style ◆ **~s sacerdotaux** vestments

ornemental, e (mpl **-aux**) /ɔʀnəmɑ̃tal, o/ ADJ [style, plante] ornamental; [motif] decorative

ornementation /ɔʀnəmɑ̃tasjɔ̃/ NF ornamentation

ornementer /ɔʀnəmɑ̃te/ ► conjug 1 ◄ VT to ornament

orner /ɔʀne/ ► conjug 1 ◄ VT 1 (= décorer) [+ chambre, vêtement] to decorate (de with); (= embellir) [+ discours, récit] to embellish (de with); ◆ **~ une rue de drapeaux** to deck out a street with flags ◆ **sa robe était ornée d'un galon** her dress was trimmed with braid ◆ **livre orné de dessins** book illustrated with drawings ◆ **~ la vérité** (littér) to adorn *ou* embellish the truth ◆ **~ son esprit** (littér) to enrich one's mind 2 (= servir d'ornement à) to adorn, to decorate, to embellish ◆ **la fleur qui ornait sa boutonnière** the flower which adorned *ou* decorated his buttonhole ◆ **les sculptures qui ornaient la façade** the sculptures which adorned *ou* decorated *ou* embellished the façade

ornière /ɔʀnjɛʀ/ NF (lit) rut ◆ **il est sorti de l'~ maintenant** (fig) he's out of the wood(s) now ◆ **retomber dans l'~** to go back to one's old ways

ornithologie /ɔʀnitɔlɔʒi/ NF ornithology; (= hobby) birdwatching

ornithologique /ɔʀnitɔlɔʒik/ ADJ ornithological

ornithologue /ɔʀnitɔlɔg/ NMF ornithologist

ornithorynque /ɔʀnitɔʀɛ̃k/ NM duck-billed platypus

orogenèse /ɔʀoʒenɛz/ NF (= processus) orogenesis; (= période) orogeny

orogénie /ɔʀoʒeni/ NF orogeny

orogénique /ɔʀoʒenik/ ADJ orogenic, orogenetic

orographie /ɔʀɔgʀafi/ NF or(e)ography

orographique /ɔʀɔgʀafik/ ADJ or(e)ographic(al)

oronge /ɔʀɔ̃ʒ/ NF agaric ◆ **~ vraie** imperial mushroom ◆ **fausse ~** fly agaric

orpaillage /ɔʀpajaʒ/ NM gold washing

orpailleur /ɔʀpajœʀ/ NM gold washer

Orphée /ɔʀfe/ NM Orpheus

orphelin, e /ɔʀfəlɛ̃, in/ ADJ orphan(ed) ◆ **être ~ de père/de mère** to be fatherless/motherless, to have lost one's father/mother NM,F orphan; → **veuf**

orphelinat /ɔʀfəlina/ NM (= lieu) orphanage; (= orphelins) children of the orphanage

orphéon /ɔʀfeɔ̃/ NM (= fanfare) (village *ou* town) band

orphie /ɔʀfi/ NF garfish

orphique /ɔʀfik/ ADJ Orphic

orphisme /ɔʀfism/ NM Orphism

orpiment /ɔʀpimɑ̃/ NM orpiment

orpin /ɔʀpɛ̃/ NM stonecrop

orque /ɔʀk/ NF killer whale

ORSEC /ɔʀsɛk/ NF (abrév de **Organisation des secours**) → **plan¹**

orteil /ɔʀtɛj/ NM toe ◆ **gros/petit ~** big/little toe

ORTF † /ɔɛʀteɛf/ NF (abrév de **Office de radiodiffusion-télévision française**) former French broadcasting service

orthocentre /ɔʀtosɑ̃tʀ/ NM orthocentre

orthodontie /ɔʀtɔdɔ̃ti/ NF orthodontics (sg), dental orthopaedics (sg) (Brit) *ou* orthopedics (sg) (US)

orthodontique /ɔʀtɔdɔ̃tik/ ADJ orthodontic

orthodontiste /ɔʀtɔdɔ̃tist/ NMF orthodontist

orthodoxe /ɔʀtɔdɔks/ ADJ 1 (Rel, gén) Orthodox; → **église** 2 (en emploi négatif) **peu ~, pas très ~** [méthode, pratiques] rather unorthodox, not very orthodox NMF (Rel) Orthodox; (Pol) one who follows the orthodox (party) line ◆ **les ~s grecs/russes** the Greek/Russian Orthodox

orthodoxie /ɔʀtɔdɔksi/ NF orthodoxy

orthodromie /ɔʀtɔdʀɔmi/ NF orthodromy

orthogenèse /ɔʀtoʒenɛz/ NF orthogenesis

orthogénie /ɔʀtoʒeni/ NF family planning ◆ **centre d'~** family planning *ou* birth control centre

orthogonal, e (mpl **-aux**) /ɔʀtɔgɔnal, o/ ADJ orthogonal

orthographe /ɔʀtɔgʀaf/ NF (gén) spelling, orthography (SPÉC); (= forme écrite correcte) spelling; (= système) spelling (system) ◆ **réforme de l'~** spelling reform, reform of the spelling system ◆ **quelle est l'~ de votre nom ?** how do you spell your name?, how is your name spelt? ◆ **ce mot a deux ~s** this word has two different spellings *ou* can be spelt in two (different) ways ◆ **il a une bonne ~** he's good at spelling, he's a good speller ◆ **~ d'usage** spelling ◆ **~ d'accord** spelling of grammatical agreements; → **faute**

orthographier /ɔʀtɔgʀafje/ ► conjug 7 ◄ VT to spell (in writing) ◆ **mal orthographié** incorrectly *ou* wrongly spelt

orthographique /ɔʀtɔgʀafik/ ADJ spelling (épith), orthographical ◆ **signe ~** orthographical sign

orthonormé, e /ɔʀtonɔʀme/ ADJ orthonormal

orthopédie /ɔʀtɔpedi/ NF orthopaedics (sg) (Brit), orthopedics (sg) (US)

orthopédique /ɔʀtɔpedik/ ADJ orthopaedic (Brit), orthopedic (US) ◆ **chaussures ~s** orthopaedic shoes

orthopédiste /ɔʀtɔpedist/ **NMF** *(= médecin)* orthopaedic *(Brit) ou* orthopedic *(US)* specialist, orthopaedist *(Brit)*, orthopedist *(US)*; *(= fabricant)* maker of orthopaedic *(Brit) ou* orthopedic *(US)* devices ◆ **chirurgien ~** orthopaedic *(Brit) ou* orthopedic *(US)* surgeon

orthophonie /ɔʀtɔfɔni/ **NF** *(= traitement)* speech therapy; *(= prononciation correcte)* correct pronunciation

orthophoniste /ɔʀtɔfɔnist/ **NMF** speech therapist

orthoptère /ɔʀtɔptɛʀ/ **ADJ** orthopterous, orthopteran **NM** orthopteran, orthopteron

orthoptiste /ɔʀtɔptist/ **NMF** orthoptist

ortie /ɔʀti/ **NF** (stinging) nettle ◆ **~ blanche** white dead-nettle ◆ **jeter qch aux ~s** to throw sth out of the window ◆ **jeter la soutane** *ou* **le froc aux ~s** to leave the priesthood; → **piqûre**

ortolan /ɔʀtɔlɑ̃/ **NM** ortolan (bunting) ◆ **à l'époque, je ne me nourrissais pas d'~s** those were lean days for me

orvet /ɔʀvɛ/ **NM** slow worm

oryx /ɔʀiks/ **NM** oryx

OS /oɛs/ **NM** (abrév de **ouvrier spécialisé**) → **ouvrier**

os (pl **os**) /ɔs, o/ **NM** 1 *(Anat)* bone ◆ **avoir de petits/gros ~** to be small-boned/big-boned ◆ **viande avec ~** meat on the bone ◆ **viande sans ~** boned *ou* boneless meat, meat off the bone ◆ **fait en ~** made of bone ◆ **jetons/manche en ~** bone counters/handle ◆ **à manche en ~** bone-handled

2 *(locutions)* **c'est un paquet** *ou* **sac d'~** he's a bag of bones, he's (all) skin and bone(s) ◆ **mouillé** *ou* **trempé jusqu'aux ~** soaked to the skin, wet through ◆ **donner** *ou* **jeter un ~ à ronger à qn** to give sb something to keep him occupied *ou* quiet ◆ **il ne fera pas de vieux ~** *(= il ne vivra pas longtemps)* he won't last *ou* live long ◆ **il n'a pas fait de vieux ~ dans cette entreprise** he didn't last long in that firm ◆ **il est pourri jusqu'à l'~** * he's rotten to the core ◆ **ils t'ont eu** *ou* **possédé jusqu'à l'~** * they had you good and proper* ◆ **l'avoir dans l'~** ⁑ *(= être roulé)* to be had* ◆ **il y a un ~** * there's a snag *ou* hitch ◆ **tomber sur un ~** * *(obstacle temporaire)* to come across *ou* hit* a snag; *(impasse)* to be stymied; *(échec)* to come unstuck; → **chair, rompre**

COMP **os à moelle** marrowbone

os de seiche cuttlebone

oscar /ɔskaʀ/ **NM** *(Ciné)* Oscar; *(autres domaines)* prize, award *(de* for); ◆ **l'~ du meilleur film/scénario** the Oscar for best film/screenplay

oscarisé, e /ɔskaʀize/ **ADJ** *(Ciné)* Oscar-winning

oscillateur /ɔsilatœʀ/ **NM** *(Phys)* oscillator

oscillation /ɔsilasjɔ̃/ **NF** *(Élec, Phys)* oscillation; *[de pendule]* swinging *(NonC)*, oscillation; *[de navire]* rocking *(NonC)*; *[de température, cours, taux, opinion]* fluctuation, variation *(de* in); ◆ **les ~s de son esprit** his (mental) fluctuations

oscillatoire /ɔsilatwaʀ/ **ADJ** *(Sci)* oscillatory; *[mouvement]* swinging, oscillatory *(SPÉC)*

osciller /ɔsile/ ▸ conjug 1 ◂ **VI** *(Sci)* to oscillate; *[pendule]* to swing, to oscillate; *[navire]* to rock ◆ **le vent fit ~ la flamme/la statue** the wind made the flame flicker/made the statue rock ◆ **sa tête oscillait de droite à gauche** his head rocked from side to side ◆ **il oscillait sur ses pieds** he rocked on his feet ◆ **~ entre** *(fig) [personne]* to waver *ou* oscillate between; *[prix, température]* to fluctuate *ou* vary between

oscillogramme /ɔsilɔgʀam/ **NM** oscillogram

oscillographe /ɔsilɔgʀaf/ **NM** oscillograph

oscilloscope /ɔsilɔskɔp/ **NM** oscilloscope

osé, e /oze/ (ptp de **oser**) **ADJ** *[tentative, démarche, toilette]* bold, daring; *[sujet, plaisanterie]* risqué, daring

Osée /oze/ **NM** Hosea

oseille /ozɛj/ **NF** 1 *(= plante)* sorrel 2 *(⁑ = argent)* dough⁑, bread⁑, dosh⁑ *(surtout Brit)* ◆ **avoir de l'~** to be in the money*, to have plenty of dough⁑ *ou* dosh⁑ *(surtout Brit)*

oser /oze/ ▸ conjug 1 ◂ **VT** 1 to dare ◆ **~ faire qch** to dare (to) do sth ◆ **~ qch** *(littér)* to dare sth ◆ **il faut ~ !** one must take risks! ◆ **(il) fallait ~ !** * he's *(ou* they've, *etc.)* certainly got a nerve! ◆ **il n'osait (pas) bouger** he did not dare (to) move ◆ **je voudrais bien mais je n'ose pas** I'd like to but I don't dare *ou* I daren't ◆ **ose le répéter !** I dare you to repeat it! ◆ **approche si tu l'oses !** come over here if you dare! ◆ **il a osé m'insulter** he dared *ou* presumed to insult me ◆ **comment osez-vous !** how dare you! ◆ **on n'ose pas faire la lessive le dimanche** *(Helv)* you're not allowed to do washing on Sundays ◆ **est-ce que j'ose entrer ?** *(Helv)* can I come in?

2 *(locutions)* **si j'ose dire** if I may say so, if I may make *(Brit) ou* be *(US)* so bold † *(aussi hum)* ◆ **si j'ose m'exprimer ainsi** if I can put it that way, if you'll pardon the expression ◆ **j'ose espérer** *ou* **croire que ...** I hope that ... ◆ **j'ose l'espérer** I should hope so ◆ **je n'ose y croire** I daren't believe it ◆ **j'oserais même dire que ...** I'd even venture to *ou* go as far as to say that ...

oseraie /ozʀɛ/ **NF** osier plantation

osier /ozje/ **NM** *(= arbre)* willow, osier; *(= fibres)* wicker *(NonC)* ◆ **corbeille en ~** wicker(work) basket ◆ **fauteuil en ~** wicker(work) chair, basket chair; → **brin**

Osiris /oziʀis/ **NM** Osiris

Oslo /ɔslo/ **N** Oslo

osmium /ɔsmjɔm/ **NM** osmium

osmonde /ɔsmɔ̃d/ **NF** osmund

osmose /ɔsmoz/ **NF** *(lit, fig)* osmosis ◆ **~ inverse** reverse osmosis ◆ **vivre en ~ avec** to live in harmony with

osmotique /ɔsmɔtik/ **ADJ** osmotic

ossature /ɔsatyʀ/ **NF** *[de corps]* frame, skeletal structure *(SPÉC)*; *[de tête, visage]* bone structure; *[d'appareil, immeuble]* framework; *[de voûte]* frame(work); *[de société, discours]* framework, structure ◆ **à ~ grêle/robuste** slender-/heavy-framed

osselet /ɔslɛ/ **NM** 1 *(= jeu)* **~s** knucklebones, jacks 2 *(Anat) [d'oreille]* ossicle

ossements /ɔsmɑ̃/ **NMPL** *(= squelettes)* bones

osseux, -euse /ɔsø, øz/ **ADJ** 1 *(Anat) [tissu]* bone *(épith)*, osseous *(SPÉC)*; *[charpente, carapace]* bony; *(Bio) [poisson]* bony; *(Méd) [greffe]* bone *(épith)*; *[maladie]* bone *(épith)*, of the bones 2 *(= maigre) [main, visage]* bony

ossification /ɔsifikasjɔ̃/ **NF** *(Méd)* ossification

ossifier **VT**, **s'ossifier** **VPR** /ɔsifje/ ▸ conjug 7 ◂ *(lit, fig)* to ossify

ossu, e /ɔsy/ **ADJ** *(littér)* large-boned

ossuaire /ɔsɥɛʀ/ **NM** *(= lieu)* ossuary

ostéite /ɔsteit/ **NF** osteitis

ostensible /ɔstɑ̃sibl/ **ADJ** conspicuous ◆ **de façon ~** conspicuously ◆ **signes religieux ~s** visible religious symbols

> ⚠ **ostensible** ne se traduit pas par le mot anglais **ostensible**, qui a le sens de 'prétendu'.

ostensiblement /ɔstɑ̃sibləmɑ̃/ **ADV** conspicuously

ostensoir /ɔstɑ̃swaʀ/ **NM** monstrance

ostentation /ɔstɑ̃tasjɔ̃/ **NF** ostentation ◆ **il détestait toute ~** he hated any kind of ostentation ◆ **agir avec ~** to act with ostentation *ou* ostentatiously ◆ **un style résolument dépourvu d'~** a style that is totally without pretentiousness ◆ **élégance sans ~** quiet elegance ◆ **faire qch sans ~** to do sth without ostentation *ou* unostentatiously ◆ **faire ~ de qch** *(littér)* to make a display *ou* show of sth, to parade sth

ostentatoire /ɔstɑ̃tatwaʀ/ **ADJ** *(littér)* ostentatious ◆ **port ~ de signes religieux** wearing of visible religious symbols

ostéoblaste /ɔsteɔblast/ **NM** osteoblast

ostéogenèse /ɔsteɔʒənɛz/, **ostéogénie** /ɔsteɔʒeni/ **NF** osteogenesis

ostéologie /ɔsteɔlɔʒi/ **NF** osteology

ostéomalacie /ɔsteomalasi/ **NF** osteomalacia

ostéomyélite /ɔsteomjelit/ **NF** osteomyelitis

ostéopathe /ɔsteɔpat/ **NMF** osteopath

ostéopathie /ɔsteɔpati/ **NF** *(= maladie)* bone disease; *(= pratique)* osteopathy

ostéophyte /ɔsteɔfit/ **NM** osteophyte

ostéoplastie /ɔsteɔplasti/ **NF** osteoplasty

ostéoporose /ɔsteɔpɔʀoz/ **NF** osteoporosis

ostéosarcome /ɔsteosaʀkom/ **NM** osteosarcoma

ostéotomie /ɔsteɔtɔmi/ **NF** osteotomy

ostraciser /ɔstʀasize/ ▸ conjug 1 ◂ **VT** to ostracize

ostracisme /ɔstʀasism/ **NM** ostracism ◆ **être frappé d'~** to be ostracized ◆ **leur ~ m'était indifférent** being ostracized by them didn't bother me

ostréicole /ɔstʀeikɔl/ **ADJ** *[production]* oyster *(épith)*; *[techniques]* oyster-farming *(épith)*

ostréiculteur, -trice /ɔstʀeikyltœʀ, tʀis/ **NM,F** oyster-farmer, ostreiculturist *(SPÉC)*

ostréiculture /ɔstʀeikyltyʀ/ **NF** oyster-farming, ostreiculture *(SPÉC)*

ostrogot(h), e /ɔstʀɔgo, gɔt/ **ADJ** Ostrogothic **NM,F** **Ostrogot(h)(e)** Ostrogoth **NM** († *ou hum) (= mal élevé)* barbarian; *(= original, olibrius)* odd fish* *ou* fellow

otage /ɔtaʒ/ **NM** hostage ◆ **prendre qn en** *ou* **comme ~** to take sb hostage ◆ **être pris** *ou* **retenu en ~** to be held hostage ◆ **la prise d'~s** the hostage-taking incident ◆ **le gouvernement s'élève contre les prises d'~s** the government condemns hostage-taking *ou* the taking *ou* seizure of hostages

OTAN /ɔtɑ̃/ **NF** (abrév de **Organisation du Traité de l'Atlantique Nord**) NATO

otarie /ɔtaʀi/ **NF** sea-lion

OTASE /ɔtaz/ **NF** (abrév de **Organisation des territoires de l'Asie du Sud-Est**) SEATO

ôter /ote/ ▸ conjug 1 ◂ **VT** 1 *(= enlever) [+ ornement]* to take away, to remove *(de* from); *[+ lunettes, vêtement]* to take off, to remove; *[+ arêtes, épine]* to take out *(de* of) to remove *(de* from); *[+ tache]* to take out *(de* of) to remove *(de* from) to lift *(de* from); *[+ hésitation, scrupule]* to remove, to take away; *[+ remords]* to relieve ◆ **ôte les assiettes (de la table)** clear the table, clear the dishes off the table ◆ **un produit qui ôte l'acidité (à une** *ou* **d'une substance)** a product which removes the acidity (from a substance) ◆ **ôte tes mains de la porte !** take your hands off the door! ◆ **ôte tes pieds de là !** get your feet off there! ◆ **cela lui a ôté un gros poids** that took a great weight off his chest *ou* lifted a great weight from his chest ◆ **on lui ôta ses menottes** they took his handcuffs off, they unhandcuffed him

2 *(= retrancher) [+ somme]* to take away; *[+ paragraphe]* to remove, to cut out *(de* from); ◆ **~ un nom d'une liste** to remove a name from a list,

to take a name off a list ◆ **5 ôté de 8 égale 3** 5 (taken away) from 8 equals *ou* leaves 3
[3] *(= prendre)* ~ **qch à qn** to take sth (away) from sb ◆ ~ **un enfant à sa mère** to take a child (away) from its mother ◆ ~ **à qn ses illusions** to rid *ou* deprive sb of his illusions ◆ ~ **à qn ses forces/son courage** to deprive sb of his strength/his courage ◆ **ça lui ôtera toute envie de recommencer** that will stop him wanting to do it again, that will rid him of any desire to do it again ◆ **ôte-lui le couteau (des mains)** take the knife (away) from him, take the knife out of *ou* from his hands ◆ **on ne m'ôtera pas de l'idée que …** I can't get it out of my mind *ou* head that … ◆ **il faut absolument lui ~ cette idée de la tête** we must get this idea out of his head; → **pain**
VPR **s'ôter** ◆ **ôtez-vous de là** move yourself!, get out of there! ◆ **ôtez-vous de la lumière, ôte-toi de mon soleil** *(hum)* get out of my light ◆ **ôte-toi de là (que je m'y mette) !*** *(hum)* (get) out of the way (and give me some room)!, move *ou* shift* out of the way (and give me some room)! ◆ **je ne peux pas m'~ ça de l'idée** I can't get it out of my mind *ou* head ◆ **comment est-ce que ça s'ôte ?** how do you remove it? *ou* take it off? ◆ **s'~ la vie** to take one's (own) life

otite /ɔtit/ NF ear infection, otitis (SPÉC) ◆ ~ **moyenne/interne** otitis media/interna

oto-rhino (pl **oto-rhinos**) /ɔtoʀino/ NMF ⇒ **oto-rhino-laryngologiste**

oto-rhino-laryngologie /ɔtoʀinolaʀɛ̃gɔlɔʒi/ NF oto(rhino)laryngology

oto-rhino-laryngologiste (pl **oto-rhino-laryngologistes**) /ɔtoʀinolaʀɛ̃gɔlɔʒist/ NMF ear, nose and throat specialist, oto(rhino) laryngologist

otoscope /ɔtɔskɔp/ NM otoscope

Ottawa /ɔtawa/ N Ottawa

ottoman, e /ɔtɔmɑ̃, an/ ADJ Ottoman NM [1] *(= personne)* **Ottoman** Ottoman [2] *(= tissu)* ottoman NF **ottomane** [1] *(= personne)* **Ottomane** Ottoman woman [2] *(= canapé)* ottoman

ou /u/ CONJ [1] *(alternative)* or ◆ **est-ce qu'il doit venir aujourd'hui ~ demain ?** is he coming today or tomorrow? ◆ **il faut qu'il vienne aujourd'hui ~ demain** he must come (either) today or tomorrow ◆ **avec ~ sans sucre ?** with or without sugar? ◆ **que vous alliez chez cet épicier ~ chez l'autre, c'est le même prix** it's the same price whether you go to this grocer or (to) the other one ◆ **un kilo de plus ~ de moins, cela ne se sent pas** one kilo more or less doesn't show up ◆ **que vous le vouliez ~ non** whether you like it or not ◆ **jolie ~ non, elle plaît** (whether she's) pretty or not, she's attractive ◆ **est-ce qu'elle veut se lever ~ préfère-t-elle attendre demain ?** does she want to get up or does she prefer to wait until tomorrow? ◆ **il nous faut 3 pièces, ~ plutôt/~ même 4** we need 3 rooms, or preferably/or even 4 ◆ **apportez-moi une bière, ~ plutôt non, un café** bring me a beer, or rather a coffee ◆ ~ **pour mieux dire** or rather, or I should say
[2] *(approximation)* or ◆ **à 5 ~ 6 km d'ici** 5 or 6 km from here ◆ **ils étaient 10 ~ 12** there were (some) 10 or 12 of them
[3] *(avec exclusion)* **donne-moi ça ~ je me fâche** give me that or I'll get cross ◆ **il faut qu'il travaille ~ (bien) il échouera à son examen** he'll have to work or (else) *ou* otherwise he'll fail his exam
◆ **ou (bien) … ou (bien)** either … or ◆ ~ **il est malade ~ (bien) il est fou** he's either sick or mad, either he's sick or (else) he's mad ◆ ~ **(bien) tu m'attends ~ (bien) alors tu pars à pied** either you wait for me or (else) you'll have to walk, you (can) either wait for me or (else) go on foot

où /u/ PRON [1] *(situation, direction)* where ◆ **l'endroit ~ je vais/je suis** the place where I'm going/I am, the place I'm going to/I'm in ◆ **l'endroit idéal ~ s'établir** the ideal place to settle ◆ **je cherche un endroit ~ m'asseoir** I'm looking for a place to sit down *ou* for somewhere to sit ◆ **la ville ~ j'habite** the town I live in *ou* where I live ◆ **le mur ~ il est accoudé** the wall he's leaning against ◆ **le tiroir ~ tu as rangé le livre** the drawer you put the book in *ou* where you put the book ◆ **le tiroir ~ tu a pris le livre** the drawer you took the book from ◆ **le livre ~ il a trouvé ce renseignement** the book where *ou* in which he found this piece of information ◆ **le livre ~ il a copié ceci** the book he copied this from *ou* from which he copied this ◆ **le chemin par ~ il est passé** the road he went along *ou* he took ◆ **le village par ~ il est passé** the village he went through ◆ **l'endroit d'~ je viens** the place I've come from ◆ **la pièce d'~ il sort** the room he's come out of ◆ **la crevasse d'~ on l'a retiré** the crevasse they pulled him out of ◆ **une chambre d'~ s'échappent des gémissements** a room from which moans are coming ◆ **l'endroit jusqu'~ ils ont grimpé** the place (where) they have climbed to *ou* to which they've climbed; → **là, partout**
[2] *(antécédent abstrait : institution, groupe, état, condition)* **la famille ~ il est entré** the family he has become part of, the family he has joined ◆ **la famille/la firme d'~ il sort** the family/firm he comes *ou* has come from ◆ **la ville d'~ il vient** *(origine)* the town he comes from ◆ **l'école ~ il est inscrit** the school where *ou* in which he is enrolled ◆ **les mathématiques, domaine ~ je ne suis guère compétent** mathematics, an area in which I have little skill ◆ **dans l'état ~ il est** in the state he's in *ou* in which he is ◆ **l'obligation ~ il se trouve de partir** the fact that he finds himself obliged to leave ◆ **dans l'embarras ~ j'étais** in my embarrassment ◆ **les conditions ~ ils travaillent** the conditions they work in *ou* in which they work ◆ **la rêverie ~ il est plongé/d'~ je l'ai tiré** the daydream he's in/from which I roused him ◆ **les extrêmes ~ il s'égare** the extremes into which he is straying ◆ **le but ~ tout homme tend** the goal towards which all men strive ◆ **la mélancolie ~ il se complaît** the melancholy in which he wallows ◆ **au rythme/train ~ ça va** at the speed/rate it's going ◆ **au prix ~ c'est** at the price it is ◆ **au tarif ~ ils font payer ça** at the rate they charge for it ◆ **à l'allure ~ ils vont** at the rate they're going ◆ **voilà ~ nous en sommes** that's the position to date *ou* so far, that's where we're at*; → **prix, train** *(et pour autres constructions voir verbes appropriés)*
[3] *(temporel)* **le siècle ~ se passe cette histoire** the century in which this story takes place ◆ **le jour ~ je l'ai rencontré** the day (when *ou* on which) I met him ◆ **l'époque ~ on n'avait rien à manger** the time when we had nothing to eat ◆ **à l'instant ~ il est arrivé** the moment he arrived ◆ **mais là ~ je me suis fâché, c'est quand il a recommencé** but what (finally) made me explode was when he started doing it again; → **moment**
ADV REL [1] *(situation, direction)* where ◆ **j'irai ~ il veut** I'll go where *ou* wherever he wants ◆ **s'établir ~ l'on veut** to settle where one likes ◆ **je ne sais pas d'~ il vient** I don't know where he comes from ◆ **on ne peut pas passer par ~ on veut** you can't just go where you like ◆ **d'~ je suis on voit la mer** you can see the sea from where I am
◆ **où que** ◆ ~ **que l'on aille/soit** wherever one goes/is ◆ **d'~ que l'on vienne** wherever one comes from ◆ **par ~ que l'on passe** wherever one goes
[2] *(abstrait)* ~ **cela devient grave, c'est lorsqu'il prétend que …** where it gets serious is when he claims that … ◆ **savoir ~ s'arrêter** to know where *ou* when to stop ◆ **d'~ l'on peut conclure que …** from which one may conclude that … ◆ **d'~ son silence/ma méfiance** hence his silence/my wariness ◆ **"où l'on voit que …"** *(titre de chapitre)* "in which the reader sees *ou* learns that …" ◆ ~ **il y a de la gêne, il n'y a pas de plaisir** *(Prov)* comfort comes first, there's no sense in being uncomfortable; *(reproche)* talk about making yourself at home!, some people think only of their own comfort
ADV INTERROG [1] *(situation, direction)* where ◆ ~ **vas-tu/es-tu/l'as-tu mis ?** where are you going/are you/did you put it? ◆ **d'~ viens-tu ?** where have you come from? ◆ **par ~ y aller ?** which way should we (*ou* I *etc*) go? ◆ ~ **aller ?** where should I (*ou* he *etc*) go? ◆ ~ **ça ?*** where's that?
[2] *(abstrait)* ~ **en étais-je ?** where was I?, where had I got to? ◆ ~ **en êtes-vous ?** where are you up to? ◆ ~ **allons-nous ?** where are we going? ◆ **d'~ vient cette attitude ?** what's the reason for this attitude? ◆ **d'~ vient qu'il n'a pas répondu ?** how come he hasn't replied?*, what's the reason for his not having replied? ◆ **d'~ le tenez-vous ?** where did you hear that? ◆ ~ **voulez-vous en venir ?** what are you leading up to? *ou* getting at?

OUA /ɔya/ NF (abrév de **Organisation de l'unité africaine**) OAU

Ouagadougou /wagadugu/ N Ouagadougou

ouah /ʼwa/ EXCL (* *joie*) wow!*, ooh!* ◆ **ouah, ouah !** *(aboiement)* woof! woof!

ouailles /waj/ NFPL *(Rel, hum)* flock ◆ **l'une de ses ~** one of his flock

ouais * /ʼwe/ EXCL *(= oui)* yeah*, yep*; *(sceptique)* oh yeah?*

ouananiche /wananiʃ/ NM *(Can)* fresh water salmon

ouaouaron * /wawaʀɔ̃/ NM *(Can)* bullfrog

ouate /(ʼ)wat/ NF [1] *(pour pansement)* cotton wool *(Brit)*, cotton *(US)* [2] *(pour rembourrage)* padding, wadding ◆ **doublé d'~** quilted
COMP **ouate hydrophile** cotton wool *(Brit)*, absorbent cotton *(US)*
ouate thermogène Thermogene ®

ouaté, e /ʼwate/ (ptp de **ouater**) ADJ [1] *[pansement]* cotton-wool *(épith) (Brit)*, cotton *(épith) (US)*; † *[vêtement]* quilted [2] *[univers]* safe and comfortable ◆ **le confort ~ de l'appartement de mes parents** the comfort and safety of my parents' flat ◆ **dans cette atmosphère ~e, elle se retranche du monde** in this safe cocoon she takes refuge from the world

ouater /ʼwate/ ► conjug 1 ◄ VT *[+ manteau, couverture]* to quilt ◆ **les collines ouatées de neige** the hills covered *ou* blanketed in snow

ouatine /watin/ NF wadding, padding

ouatiner /watine/ ► conjug 1 ◄ VT to quilt ◆ **veste ouatinée** quilted jacket

oubli /ubli/ NM [1] *(= omission)* oversight ◆ **il s'agit d'un simple ~** it was just an oversight ◆ **il y a des ~s dans ce récit** there are gaps *ou* things missed out in this account ◆ **l'~ de cette date a eu des conséquences graves** the fact the date was forgotten has had serious repercussions ◆ **j'ai réparé mon ~** I made up for having forgotten [2] *(= trou de mémoire)* **ses ~s répétés m'inquiètent** his constant lapses of memory worry me, his constant forgetfulness worries me [3] ◆ **l'~** oblivion, forgetfulness ◆ **l'~ de soi(-même)** self-effacement, selflessness ◆ **tirer qch de l'~** to bring sth out of oblivion ◆ **tomber dans l'~** to sink into oblivion ◆ **le temps apporte l'~** memories fade with the passage of time

oublié, e /ublije/ NM,F (ptp de **oublier**) forgotten person ◆ **c'est un peu l'~ parmi les grands**

chanteurs among the great singers he tends to be overlooked ◆ **les ~s de l'Histoire** those who have been left out of the history books, those who have been forgotten by history

oublier /ublije/ GRAMMAIRE ACTIVE 53.1 ▸ conjug 7 ◂

VT [1] *(= ne pas se souvenir de)* to forget; *(= ne plus penser à) [+ soucis, chagrin, client, visiteur]* to forget (about) ◆ ~ **de faire qch** to forget to do sth ◆ ~ **pourquoi** to forget why ◆ **ça s'oublie facilement** it's easily forgotten ◆ **j'ai oublié qui je dois prévenir** I can't remember who (it is) *ou* I've forgotten who (it is) I should warn ◆ **j'ai complètement oublié l'heure** I completely forgot about the time ◆ **j'ai oublié si j'ai bien éteint le gaz** I forget *ou* I can't remember if I turned off the gas ◆ **n'oublie pas que nous sortons ce soir** remember *ou* don't forget we're going out tonight ◆ **boire pour** ~ to drink to forget ◆ **ah oui, j'oubliais, il faut que tu rappelles ton frère** oh, yes, I almost forgot, you should phone your brother ◆ **il oubliera avec le temps** he'll forget in time, time will help him forget ◆ **oublions le passé** let's forget about the past, let's let bygones be bygones ◆ **c'est oublié, n'y pensons plus** it's all forgotten now, let's not think about it any more ◆ **j'avais complètement oublié sa présence** I had completely forgotten that he was there ◆ **sa gentillesse fait** ~ **sa laideur** the fact he's so nice makes you forget how ugly he is ◆ **il essaie de se faire** ~ he's trying to keep out of the limelight ◆ **mourir oublié** to die forgotten

[2] *(= laisser) [+ chose]* to forget, to leave behind; *[+ fautes d'orthographe]* to miss; *(= omettre) [+ virgule, phrase]* to leave out ◆ **j'ai oublié mon parapluie dans le train** I left my umbrella on the train ◆ **j'ai oublié mon parapluie** I forgot my umbrella, I left my umbrella behind ◆ **tu as oublié (de laver) une vitre** you've missed a pane ◆ **un jour tu oublieras ta tête !** *(hum)* you'll forget your head one of these days!

[3] *(= négliger) [+ famille, devoir, travail, promesse]* to forget, to neglect ◆ ~ **les règles de la politesse** to forget *ou* neglect the rules of etiquette ◆ **n'oubliez pas le guide !** don't forget (to tip) the guide! ◆ **il ne faut pas** ~ **que c'est un pays pauvre** we must not lose sight of the fact *ou* forget that it's a poor country ◆ ~ **qn dans son testament** to forget (to include) sb in one's will ◆ **il ne vous oublie pas** he hasn't forgotten (about) you ◆ **on l'a oublié sur la liste** he's been left off the list

VPR **s'oublier** [1] *(= ne pas être retenu)* to be forgotten ◆ **quelqu'un comme ça ne s'oublie pas facilement** someone like that is not easily forgotten ◆ **il ne s'est pas oublié (dans le partage)** *(iro)* he didn't forget himself (in the share-out)

[2] *(littér = manquer d'égards)* **vous vous oubliez !** you're forgetting yourself!

[3] *(euph = faire ses besoins)* **le chat s'est oublié sur la moquette** the cat had an accident on the carpet

oubliettes /ublijɛt/ NFPL oubliettes ◆ **jeter** *ou* **mettre aux** ~ *[+ projet]* to shelve ◆ **tomber dans les ~ (de l'histoire)** *[déclaration, procès]* to sink into oblivion ◆ **ce livre/projet est tombé aux** ~ this book/plan has been forgotten

oublieux, -ieuse /ublijø, ijøz/ ADJ *(frm)* deliberately forgetful ◆ ~ **de** *[+ bienfaits]* quick to forget; *[+ obligations, devoirs]* neglectful of

oued /wɛd/ NM wadi

ouest /wɛst/ NM INV [1] *(= point cardinal)* west ◆ **le vent d'**~ the west wind ◆ **un vent d'**~ a west(erly) wind, a westerly *(SPÉC)* ◆ **le vent tourne/est à l'**~ the wind is veering west(wards) *ou* towards the west/is blowing from the west ◆ **regarder vers l'**~ *ou* **dans la direction de l'**~ to look west(wards) *ou* towards the west ◆ **à l'**~ *(situation)* in the west; *(direction)* to the west, west(wards) ◆ **le soleil se couche à l'**~ the sun sets in the west ◆ **à l'**~ **de** west of, to the west of ◆ **la maison est (exposée) à l'~/exposée plein** ~ the house faces (the) west *ou* westwards/due west, the house looks west(wards)/due west ◆ **il est à l'**~ * *(= il ne sait plus quoi faire)* he's totally out of it* ◆ **l'Europe/la Bourgogne de l'**~ Western Europe/Burgundy; → **Allemagne**

[2] *(= régions occidentales)* west ◆ **l'Ouest** *(Pol)* the West ◆ **l'**~ **de la France, l'Ouest** the West of France ◆ **les rapports entre l'Est et l'Ouest** East-West relations, relations between the East and the West

ADJ INV *[région, partie]* western; *[entrée, paroi]* west; *[versant, côte]* west(ern); *[côté]* west(ward); *[direction]* westward, westerly; → **longitude**

ouest-allemand, e /wɛstalmɑ̃, ɑd/ *(Hist)* ADJ West German NM,F **Ouest-Allemand(e)** West German

ouest-nord-ouest /wɛstnɔʀwɛst/ ADJ INV, NM west-northwest

ouest-sud-ouest /wɛstsydwɛst/ ADJ INV, NM west-southwest

ouf /'uf/ EXCL, NM phew, whew ◆ **pousser un** ~ **de soulagement** to breathe *ou* give a sigh of relief ◆ **ils ont dû repartir sans avoir le temps de dire** ~ * they had to leave again before they had time to catch their breath *ou* before they knew where they were

Ouganda /ugɑ̃da/ NM Uganda

ougandais, e /ugɑ̃dɛ, ɛz/ ADJ Ugandan NM,F **Ougandais(e)** Ugandan

ougrien, -ienne /ugʀijɛ̃, ijɛn/ ADJ, NM,F → **finno-ougrien**

oui /'wi/ ADV [1] *(réponse affirmative)* yes ◆ **le connaissez-vous ?** – ~ do you know him? – yes (I do) ◆ **est-elle chez elle ?** – ~ is she at home? – yes (she is) ◆ **vous avez aimé le film ?** – ~ **et non** did you like the film? – yes and no *ou* I did and I didn't ◆ **je vais ouvrir la fenêtre** – ~, **cela fera un peu d'air** I'll open the window – yes (do), we could do with some fresh air ◆ **il n'a pas encore dit** ~ he hasn't said yes yet, he hasn't agreed *ou* accepted (as) yet ◆ **dire** ~ *(pendant le mariage)* to say "I do" ◆ **il ne dit ni** ~ **ni non** he's not saying either yes or no ◆ **ah, ça** ~ **!** you can say that again!*, and how!* ◆ **que** ~ **!** I should say so!, rather! *(Brit)* ◆ **certes** ~ **!** (yes) most definitely *ou* certainly!, yes indeed! ◆ **vous en voulez ?** – **mais** ~ *ou* **bien sûr que** ~ *ou* ~, **bien sûr** do you want some? – of course (I do) *ou* I most certainly do ◆ ~, **mais il y a un obstacle** yes but there is a difficulty ◆ **eh bien** ~, **j'avoue** all right (then), I confess ◆ **contraception** ~, **avortement non** *(slogan)* yes to contraception, no to abortion, contraception – yes, abortion – no ◆ **répondre (par)** ~ **à toutes les questions** to answer yes *ou* answer in the affirmative to all the questions ◆ **répondez par** ~ **ou par non** answer yes or no ◆ **faire** ~ **de la tête, faire signe que** ~ to nod (one's head) ◆ **ah** ~ **?** really?, yes? ◆ ~**-da** (†, *hum*) yes indeed, absolutely ◆ ~, **capitaine** *(Naut)* aye aye sir

[2] *(remplaçant une proposition)* **est-il chez lui ?/est-ce qu'il travaille ?** – **je pense** *ou* **je crois que** ~ is he at home?/is he working? – (yes) I think so *ou* I believe he is ◆ **il nous quitte ?** – **je crains bien/j'espère que** ~ is he leaving us? – I am afraid so *ou* I am afraid he is/I hope so *ou* I hope he is ◆ **est-ce qu'elle sort souvent ?** – **j'ai l'impression que** ~ does she often go out? – I have an idea *ou* the impression that she does ◆ **tu as aimé ce film ?** – **moi** ~ did you like the film? – I did ◆ **j'ai demandé si elle était venue, lui dit que** ~ I asked if she had been and he says she has

[3] *(intensif)* **je suis surprise,** ~ **très surprise** I'm surprised – indeed very surprised ◆ **c'est un escroc,** ~, **un escroc** he's a rogue, an absolute rogue ◆ ~ **vraiment, il a répondu ça ?** did he really answer that? ◆ **tu vas cesser de pleurer,** ~ **?** have you quite finished crying?, will you stop crying? ◆ ~ **(évidemment), c'est toujours facile de critiquer** of course it's always easy to criticize ◆ **c'est bon,** ~ **?** isn't that good? ◆ **il va accepter,** ~ **ou non ?** is he or isn't he going to accept? ◆ **tu te presses,** ~ **ou non ?** will you please hurry up?, will you hurry up? ◆ **tu te décides** ~ **ou merde !**‡ make up your mind for Christ's sake!‡

NM INV yes, aye ◆ **il y a eu 30** ~ there were 30 votes for, there were 30 ayes ◆ **j'aimerais un** ~ **plus ferme** I should prefer a more definite yes ◆ **pleurer pour un** ~ **(ou) pour un non** to cry over the slightest thing

ouï-dire /'widiʀ/ NM INV hearsay *(NonC)* ◆ **par** ~ by hearsay

ouïe[1] /'uj/ EXCL ⇒ **ouille**

ouïe[2] /wi/ NF hearing *(NonC)* ◆ **avoir l'**~ **fine** to have sharp hearing, to have a keen sense of hearing ◆ **être tout** ~ to be all ears

ouïes /wi/ NFPL *[de poisson]* gills; *[d'instrument de musique]* sound holes

ouille /'uj/ EXCL ouch!

ouïr /wiʀ/ ▸ conjug 10 ◂ VT (††, *littér, hum*) to hear; *(Jur) [+ témoins]* to hear ◆ **j'ai ouï dire à mon père que ...** I've heard my father say that ... ◆ **j'ai ouï dire que ...** it has come to my ears that ..., I've heard it said that ... ◆ **oyez !** *(hum)* hark! († *ou hum*), hear ye! († *ou hum*) ◆ **oyez, oyez, braves** *ou* **bonnes gens !** oyez! oyez! oyez!

ouistiti /'wistiti/ NM *(= animal)* marmoset ◆ **un drôle de** ~ * *(= type)* an oddball*

oukase /ukaz/ NM *(Hist, fig)* ukase

Oulan-Bator /ulanbatɔʀ/ N Ulan Bator

ouléma /ulema/ NM ⇒ **uléma**

ouragan /uʀagɑ̃/ NM [1] *(Météo)* hurricane [2] *(fig)* storm ◆ **cet homme est un véritable** ~ he's like a whirlwind, he's a human tornado ◆ **ce livre va déchaîner un** ~ this book is going to create an uproar ◆ **arriver comme un** ~ to arrive like a whirlwind

Oural /uʀal/ NM *(= fleuve)* ◆ **l'**~ the Ural ◆ **l'**~, **les monts** ~ the Urals, the Ural Mountains

ouralo-altaïque /uʀalɔaltaik/ ADJ, NM Ural-Altaic

ourdir /uʀdiʀ/ ▸ conjug 2 ◂ VT [1] *[+ tissu]* to warp [2] *(littér) [+ complot]* to hatch; *[+ intrigue]* to weave

ourdou /uʀdu/ ADJ INV, NM Urdu

ourlé, e /uʀle/ (ptp de **ourler**) ADJ hemmed ◆ **oreilles délicatement ~es** delicately rimmed ears ◆ **lèvres bien ~es** well-defined lips

ourler /uʀle/ ▸ conjug 1 ◂ VT *(Couture)* to hem ◆ ~ **de** *(fig littér)* to fringe with

ourlet /uʀlɛ/ NM [1] *(Couture)* hem ◆ **faux** ~ false hem ◆ **faire un** ~ **à** to hem [2] *(Tech)* hem [3] *[d'oreille]* rim, helix *(SPÉC)*

ours /uʀs/ NM [1] *(= animal)* bear ◆ **être** *ou* **tourner comme un** ~ **en cage** to pace up and down like a caged animal; → **fosse, montreur, vendre** [2] *(= jouet)* ~ **(en peluche)** teddy bear [3] *(péj = misanthrope)* (old) bear ◆ **vivre comme un** ~ to be at odds with the world ◆ **elle est un peu** ~ she's a bit of a bear *ou* a gruff individual [4] *(arg Presse)* ≈ credits *(for written publication)* [5] *(‡ = règles)* **avoir ses** ~ to have one's period

COMP **ours blanc** polar bear
ours brun brown bear
ours mal léché *(péj)* uncouth fellow
ours marin fur seal
ours polaire ⇒ **ours blanc**
ours savant trained *ou* performing bear

ourse /uʀs/ NF [1] *(= animal)* she-bear [2] *(Astron)* **la Petite Ourse** the Little Bear, Ursa Minor, the Little Dipper *(US)* ◆ **la Grande Ourse** the

Great Bear, Ursa Major, the Plough *(Brit)*, the Big Dipper *(US)*

oursin /uʀsɛ̃/ NM sea urchin

ourson /uʀsɔ̃/ NM bear cub

oust(e)* /'ust/ EXCL buzz off!*, hop it!* *(Brit)* ◆ **allez, ~e ! dehors !** go on, out with you! *ou* out you go!

out /'aut/ ADJ INV *[personne]* out of touch* *(attrib)*; *(Tennis)* out

outarde /utaʀd/ NF bustard; *(Can = bernache)* Canada goose

outil /uti/ NM *(lit, fig)* tool; *(agricole, de jardin)* implement, tool ◆ **~ de travail** tool ◆ **~ pédagogique** teaching aid ◆ **~ de programmation** programming tool ◆ **~ de production/gestion** production/management tool ◆ **il maîtrise bien l'~ informatique** he's good with computers ◆ **nous avons tous les ~s en main** we have the right tools in hand; → **mauvais**

outillage /utijaʒ/ NM *[de mécanicien, bricoleur]* (set of) tools; *[de fermier, jardinier]* implements, equipment *(NonC)*; *[d'atelier, usine]* equipment *(NonC)*

outiller /utije/ ► conjug 1 ◄ VT *[+ ouvrier]* to supply *ou* provide with tools, to equip, to kit out *(Brit)*, to outfit *(US)*; *[+ atelier]* to fit out, to equip ◆ **je suis bien/mal outillé pour ce genre de travail** I'm well-/badly-equipped for this kind of work ◆ **pour ce travail, il faudra qu'on s'outille** to do this job, we'll have to equip ourselves *ou* kit ourselves out *(Brit)* properly ◆ **les ouvriers s'outillent à leurs frais** the workers buy their own tools

outilleur /utijœʀ/ NM tool-maker

outplacement /autplesmɛnt/ NM outplacement ◆ **cabinet d'~** outplacement consultancy firm

outrage /utʀaʒ/ NM insult ◆ **accabler qn d'~s** to heap insults on sb ◆ **faire ~ à** *[+ réputation, mémoire]* to dishonour *(Brit)*, to dishonor *(US)*; *[+ pudeur]* to outrage, to be an outrage to ◆ **faire subir les derniers ~s à une femme** *(euph †)* to ravish *ou* violate a woman ◆ **les ~s du temps** *(littér)* the ravages of time

COMP **outrage à agent** insulting behaviour *(to police officer)*
outrage aux bonnes mœurs outrage *ou* affront to public decency
outrage à magistrat contempt of court
outrage à la pudeur gross indecency
outrage public à la pudeur indecent exposure *(NonC)*

outragé, e /utʀaʒe/ (ptp de **outrager**) ADJ *[air, personne]* gravely offended

outrageant, e /utʀaʒɑ̃, ɑ̃t/ ADJ offensive

outrager /utʀaʒe/ ► conjug 3 ◄ VT *(littér)* *[+ personne]* to offend gravely; *[+ mœurs, morale]* to outrage; *[+ bon sens, raison]* to insult

outrageusement /utʀaʒøzmɑ̃/ ADV *(= excessivement)* outrageously, excessively

outrageux, -euse /utʀaʒø, øz/ ADJ *(= excessif)* outrageous, excessive ◆ **de manière outrageuse** outrageously, excessively

outrance /utʀɑ̃s/ NF 1 *(= caractère)* extravagance ◆ **pousser le raffinement jusqu'à l'~** to take refinement to extremes *ou* to excess ◆ **choqué par l'~ de ses propos** shocked by the outrageousness of his remarks 2 *(= excès)* excess ◆ **il y a des ~s dans ce roman** there are some extravagant passages in this novel ◆ **ses ~s de langage** his outrageous language

◆ **à outrance** *[urbanisation, automatisation]* excessive; *[raffiné]* excessively, to excess ◆ **spécialisé à ~** over-specialized ◆ **cette affaire a été médiatisée à ~** this affair has been hyped up* by the media *ou* has been the subject of intense media hype*

outrancier, -ière /utʀɑ̃sje, jɛʀ/ ADJ *[personne, propos]* extreme ◆ **son caractère ~** the extreme nature of his character, the extremeness of his character

outre¹ /utʀ/ NF goatskin, wine *ou* water skin ◆ **gonflé** *ou* **plein comme une ~** full to bursting

outre² /utʀ/ GRAMMAIRE ACTIVE 53.5 PRÉP *(= en plus de)* as well as, besides ◆ **~ sa cargaison, le bateau transportait des passagers** besides *ou* as well as its cargo the boat was carrying passengers ◆ **~ son salaire, il a des pourboires** on top of *ou* in addition to his salary, he gets tips ◆ **~ le fait que** as well as *ou* besides the fact that

◆ **en ~** moreover, besides, further(more)

◆ **outre mesure** to excess, overmuch, inordinately ◆ **manger/boire ~ mesure** to eat/drink to excess *ou* immoderately ◆ **cela ne lui plaît pas ~ mesure** he doesn't like that too much, he's not overkeen on that *(Brit)* ◆ **ma décision ne l'a pas étonné/inquiété ~ mesure** he wasn't unduly *ou* overly surprised at/worried by my decision

◆ **outre que** ◆ **~ qu'il a le temps, il a les capacités pour le faire** not only does he have the time but he also has the ability to do it, apart from having the time *ou* besides having the time he also has the ability to do it

◆ **passer outre** to carry on regardless ◆ **passer ~ à un ordre** to disregard an order, to carry on regardless of an order

outré, e /utʀe/ (ptp de **outrer**) ADJ 1 *(littér = exagéré)* *[éloges, flatterie]* excessive, exaggerated, overdone *(attrib)*; *[description]* exaggerated, extravagant, overdone *(attrib)* 2 *(= indigné)* outraged *(de, par* at, by)

outre-Atlantique /utʀatlɑ̃tik/ ADV across the Atlantic, in the United States ◆ **les films d'~** American films

outrecuidance /utʀəkɥidɑ̃s/ NF 1 *(littér = présomption)* presumptuousness ◆ **parler avec ~** to speak presumptuously 2 *(= effronterie)* impertinence ◆ **répondre à qn avec ~** to answer sb impertinently ◆ **~s** impudence *(NonC)*, impertinences

outrecuidant, e /utʀəkɥidɑ̃, ɑ̃t/ ADJ 1 *(= présomptueux)* presumptuous 2 *(= effronté)* *[attitude, réponse]* impertinent

outre-Manche /utʀəmɑ̃ʃ/ ADV across the Channel, in Britain ◆ **nos voisins d'~** our British neighbours

outremer /utʀəmɛʀ/ NM *(= pierre)* lapis lazuli; *(= couleur)* ultramarine ADJ INV ultramarine

outre-mer /utʀəmɛʀ/ ADV overseas NM overseas territories ◆ **l'~ français** France's overseas departments and territories

outrepassé /utʀəpɑse/ (ptp de **outrepasser**) ADJ → **arc**

outrepasser /utʀəpɑse/ ► conjug 1 ◄ VT *[+ droits]* to go beyond; *[+ pouvoir, ordres]* to exceed; *[+ limites]* to go beyond, to overstep

outre-Pyrénées /utʀəpiʀene/ ADV in Spain ◆ **d'~** Spanish

outrer /utʀe/ ► conjug 1 ◄ VT 1 *(littér = exagérer)* to exaggerate ◆ **cet acteur outre son jeu** this actor overacts 2 *(= indigner)* to outrage ◆ **votre ingratitude m'a outré** your ingratitude has outraged me, I am outraged at *ou* by your ingratitude

outre-Rhin /utʀəʀɛ̃/ ADV across the Rhine ◆ **d'~** *(= allemand)* German

outre-tombe /utʀətɔ̃b/ ADV beyond the grave ◆ **d'une voix d'~** in a lugubrious voice

outsider /autsajdœʀ/ NM *(Sport, fig)* outsider

outsourcer /autsuʀse/ ► conjug 3 ◄ VT to outsource

ouvert, e /uvɛʀ, ɛʀt/ (ptp de **ouvrir**) ADJ 1 *[porte, magasin, valise, lieu, espace]* open; *[voiture]* open, unlocked; *[voyelle, syllabe]* open; *[angle]* wide; *[série, ensemble]* open-ended; *[robinet]* on, running; *[col, chemise]* open, undone *(attrib)* ◆ **la bouche ~e** *[dormir]* with one's mouth open; *[rester]* open-mouthed ◆ **entrez, c'est ~ !** come in, the door isn't locked! *ou* the door's open! ◆ **~ au public** open to the public ◆ **bibliothèque ~e à tous** library open to all members of the public ◆ **le magasin restera ~ pendant les travaux** the shop will remain open (for business) during the alterations ◆ **nous sommes ~s jusqu'à Noël** we're open till Christmas ◆ **~ à la circulation** open to traffic ◆ **le col du Simplon est ~** the Simplon pass is open (to traffic) ◆ **~ à la navigation** open to ships *ou* for sailing ◆ **une rose trop ~e** a rose which is too (far) open ◆ **elle est partie en laissant le robinet/le gaz ~** she went away leaving the tap *ou* the water on *ou* running/the gas on; → **bras, ciel** *etc*

2 *(= commencé)* open ◆ **la chasse/pêche est ~e** the shooting season/fishing season is open; → **pari**

3 *(= percé, incisé)* *[plaie]* open ◆ **il a le crâne/le bras ~** he has a gaping wound in his head/in his arm; → **cœur, fracture**

4 *[débat, compétition sportive]* open ◆ **la question reste ~e** the question remains open ◆ **une partie très ~e** an open-ended game ◆ **pratiquer un jeu ~** to play an open game

5 *(= déclaré, non dissimulé)* *[guerre, conflit, crise, haine]* open ◆ **de façon ~e** openly, overtly

6 *(= communicatif, franc)* *[personne, caractère]* open, frank; *[visage, physionomie]* open; *(= éveillé, accessible)* *[intelligence, milieu, marché]* open ◆ **à l'esprit ~** open-minded ◆ **je suis ~ à toute discussion/négociation** I'm open to discussion/negotiation

ouvertement /uvɛʀtəmɑ̃/ ADV *[dire, avouer]* openly; *[agir]* openly, overtly

ouverture /uvɛʀtyʀ/ NF 1 *(= action)* *[de porte, fenêtre, bouteille, parapluie, huîtres, compte bancaire]* opening; *[de porte fermée à clé, verrou]* unlocking; *[de frontière, passage, chaussée]* opening up; *[de robinet]* turning on ◆ **à ~ facile** easy to open ◆ **l'~ de la porte est automatique** the door opens *ou* is operated automatically ◆ **les documents nécessaires à l'~ d'un compte bancaire** the papers required to open a bank account

2 *(Écon)* *[de marché]* opening ◆ **pour obtenir l'~ des marchés nippons** to open up Japanese markets ◆ **ils ont mis en place une politique d'~ économique** they have established a policy of economic openness ◆ **procéder à une ~ de capital** *(Fin)* to float shares

3 *(Comm)* opening ◆ **jours d'~** days of opening ◆ **heures d'~** *[de magasin]* opening hours, hours of business *ou* of opening; *[de musée]* opening hours, hours of opening ◆ **le client était là dès l'~** the customer was there as soon as the shop opened ◆ **"ouverture de 10 h à 15 h"** "open from 10 till 3" ◆ **à l'heure d'~, à l'~** at opening time

4 *(= commencement)* *[de colloque]* opening ◆ **cérémonie/discours/match d'~** opening ceremony/speech/match ◆ **en ~ du festival** to open the festival ◆ **avant l'~ officielle de la campagne électorale** before the official opening of the electoral campaign ◆ **après une ~ en hausse** *(Bourse)* after a strong opening ◆ **ils réclament l'~ immédiate de négociations** they want to open talks immediately ◆ **il a demandé l'~ d'une enquête** he has requested an enquiry ◆ **faire l'~** *(Chasse)* to go on *ou* be at the first shoot ◆ **c'est demain l'~ de la chasse** tomorrow sees the opening of *ou* is the first day of the shooting season

5 *(= trou, passage, issue)* opening; *[de puits]* mouth, opening ◆ **toutes les ~s sont gardées** all the openings *ou* all means of access (*ou* exit) are guarded, all the access points (*ou* exit

points) are guarded ◆ **il y a de petites ~s sur le couvercle** there are little holes in the lid

6 (= opportunité) opening ◆ **il y a peut-être une ~ dans notre filiale suisse** there may be an opening in our Swiss subsidiary ◆ **je crois que j'ai une ~ avec lui** *(pour relation amoureuse)* I think I'm in with a chance with him

7 *(= proposition)* overture ◆ **faire des ~s à qn** to make overtures to sb ◆ **faire des ~s de paix/conciliation** to make peace/conciliatory overtures

8 *(= tolérance)* ~ **d'esprit, esprit d'~** open-mindedness ◆ **il a une grande ~ d'esprit** he is extremely open-minded

9 *(= rapprochement, relation)* **l'absence d'~ sur le monde de certaines universités** the inward-looking attitude of some universities ◆ **leur manque d'~ sur le monde menace leur communauté** their reluctance to embrace other cultures poses a threat to their community ◆ **l'~ (politique)** the opening up of the political spectrum ◆ **être partisan de l'~ au centre** *(Pol)* to be in favour of an alliance with the centre ◆ **ils multiplient les signes d'~ en direction des Verts** they are showing more and more signs of being open to an alliance with the Green party ◆ **adopter une politique de plus grande ~ avec l'Est** to develop a more open relationship with the East

10 *(Mus)* overture

11 *(Math)* *[d'angle]* magnitude; *[de compas]* degree of opening; *(Photo)* aperture

12 *(Cartes)* opening ◆ **avoir l'~** *(Échecs)* to have the first *ou* opening move

13 *(Ftbl)* through-ball; *(Rugby)* pass *(by the stand-off half to the three-quarter backs)* ◆ **faire une ~** *(Ftbl)* to hit *ou* play a through-ball; *(Rugby)* to pass the ball to the three-quarter backs; → **demi²**

ouvrable /uvʀabl/ ADJ ◆ **jour ~** weekday, working day ◆ **heures ~s** business hours

ouvrage /uvʀaʒ/ NM 1 *(= travail)* work *(NonC)* ◆ **se mettre à l'~** to set to *ou* get (down) to *ou* start work ◆ **l'~ du temps/du hasard** *(littér)* the work of time/of chance; → **cœur**

2 *(= objet produit)* piece of work; *(Couture)* work *(NonC)* ◆ ~ **d'orfèvrerie** piece of goldwork ◆ ~ **à l'aiguille** (piece of) needlework; → **boîte, corbeille, panier**

3 *(= œuvre)* work; *(= volume)* book ◆ ~ **collectif** *book to which several authors have contributed* ◆ **ce dictionnaire est un ~ collectif** this dictionary was written by a team of editors; → **référence**

4 *(Constr)* work

NF *(† ou hum = travail)* ◆ **de la belle ~** a nice piece of work

COMP **ouvrage d'art** *(Génie Civil)* structure *(bridge or tunnel etc)*

ouvrage avancé *(Mil)* outwork

ouvrage de dames *(† ou hum)* fancy work *(NonC)*

ouvrage défensif *(Mil)* defences, defence work(s)

ouvrage de maçonnerie masonry work

ouvrage militaire fortification

ouvragé, e /uvʀaʒe/ ADJ *[meuble, bois]* (finely) carved; *[napperon]* (finely) embroidered; *[signature]* elaborate; *[métal, bijou]* finely worked

ouvrant, e /uvʀɑ̃, ɑ̃t/ ADJ *[panneau]* which opens *(attrib)*; → **toit**

ouvré, e /uvʀe/ ADJ 1 *(Tech, littér)* *[meuble, bois]* (finely) carved; *[napperon]* (finely) embroidered; *[métal, bijou]* finely worked 2 *(Admin)* **jour ~** working day

ouvre-boîte (pl **ouvre-boîtes**) /uvʀəbwat/ NM can-opener, tin-opener *(Brit)*

ouvre-bouteille (pl **ouvre-bouteilles**) /uvʀəbutɛj/ NM bottle opener

ouvre-huître (pl **ouvre-huîtres**) /uvʀ(ə)ɥitʀ/ NM oyster knife

ouvreur, -euse /uvʀœʀ, øz/ NM,F *(Cartes)* opener; *(Ski)* forerunner NM *[de cinéma, théâtre]* usher NF **ouvreuse** *[de cinéma, théâtre]* usherette

ouvrier, -ière /uvʀije, ijɛʀ/ ADJ *[enfance, éducation, quartier]* working-class *(épith)*; *[conflit, agitation, législation]* industrial *(épith)*, labour *(épith)*; *[questions, mouvement]* labour *(épith)* ◆ **association ouvrière** workers' *ou* working men's association; → **cité, classe, syndicat**

NM *(gén, Pol, Sociol)* worker; *(= membre du personnel)* workman ◆ **les revendications des ~s** the workers' claims ◆ **il a 15 ~s** he has 15 workmen, he has 15 men working for him ◆ **des mains d'~** workman's hands ◆ **150 ~s ont été mis en chômage technique** 150 men *ou* workers have been laid off ◆ **l'~ de cette réforme** *(fig)* the author of this reform; → **mauvais, œuvre**

NF **ouvrière** 1 *(gén, Admin)* female worker ◆ **ouvrière (d'usine)** female factory worker *ou* factory hand; *(jeune)* factory girl, young factory hand ◆ **les ouvrières sortaient de l'usine** the women *ou* girls were coming out of the factory

2 **(abeille) ouvrière** worker (bee)

COMP **ouvrier agricole** agricultural labourer, farm worker, farmhand

ouvrier de chantier labourer

ouvrier à façon pieceworker, jobber

ouvrier hautement qualifié highly-skilled worker

ouvrier à la journée day labourer

ouvrier qualifié skilled workman

ouvrier spécialisé unskilled *ou* semiskilled worker

ouvrier d'usine factory worker *ou* hand

ouvriérisme /uvʀijeʀism/ NM worker control, worker power

ouvriériste /uvʀijeʀist/ ADJ *[doctrine, attitude]* in favour of giving power to the workers NMF supporter of control by the workers

ouvrir /uvʀiʀ/ ► conjug 18 ◄ VT 1 *[+ porte, fenêtre, bouteille, huître]* to open; *[+ verrou, porte fermée à clé]* to unlock; *(par effraction)* *[+ porte, coffre]* to break open ◆ ~ **la porte toute grande/le portail tout grand** to open the door/the gate wide ◆ **il a ouvert brusquement la porte** he opened the door abruptly, he threw *ou* flung the door open ◆ ~ **sa porte** *ou* **sa maison à qn** to throw open one's doors *ou* one's house to sb ◆ **ils ouvrent leur maison au public tous les étés** they open up their house to the public every summer, they throw their house open to the public every summer; → **parenthèse**; → aussi **porte**

2 *[+ bouche, yeux, paupières]* to open ◆ ~ **le bec, l'~**‡, ~ **la** *ou* **sa gueule**‡ *(fig)* to open one's mouth *ou* trap‡ ◆ ~ **l'œil** *(fig)* to keep one's eyes open *(fig)* ◆ ~ **les yeux** *(lit)* to open one's eyes ◆ **ce voyage en Asie m'a ouvert les yeux** that trip through Asia opened my eyes *ou* was an eye-opener (to me) ◆ **ouvre l'œil, et le bon !*** keep your eyes peeled!* ◆ ~ **les oreilles** to pin back one's ears* ◆ **elle m'a ouvert son cœur** she opened her heart to me ◆ **ça m'a ouvert l'appétit** that whetted my appetite ◆ **ce séjour à l'étranger lui a ouvert l'esprit** that time he spent abroad has widened his horizons; → aussi **œil**

3 *(= déplier, déployer)* *[+ journal, couteau, livre]* to open; *[+ parapluie]* to open, to put up; *[+ éventail, bras, ailes, main]* to open (out); *[+ manteau, veste]* to undo, to unfasten, to open; *[+ lit, drap]* to turn down; *[+ couture]* to iron flat ◆ **ouvrez les rangs !** *(Mil)* dress! ◆ ~ **ses rangs à qn** *(fig)* to welcome sb among one's ranks

4 *(= faire un trou dans)* *[+ chaussée, mur]* to open up; *[+ membre, ventre]* to open up, to cut open ◆ **les rochers lui ont ouvert la jambe** he cut his leg open on the rocks ◆ **le médecin pense qu'il faudra ~*** the doctor thinks that they will have to open him *(ou her etc)* up*

5 *(= faire, construire)* *[+ porte, passage]* to open up, to make; *[+ autoroute]* to build; *(fig)* *[+ horizons, perspectives]* to open up ◆ **il a fallu ~ une porte dans ce mur** a doorway had to be made in this wall ◆ ~ **un passage dans le roc à la dynamite** to open up *ou* blast a passage in the rock with dynamite ◆ **ils lui ont ouvert un passage** *ou* **le passage dans la foule** they made way for him through the crowd ◆ **s'~ un passage à travers la forêt** to open up *ou* cut a path for o.s. through the forest ◆ **cette autoroute a été ouverte pour desservir la nouvelle banlieue** this motorway has been built to serve the new suburb

6 *(= rendre accessible)* *[+ chemin, passage]* to open; *[+ route, col, frontière]* to open (up) ◆ **le chasse-neige a ouvert la route** the snowplough opened up the road ◆ ~ **le jeu** *(Sport)* to open up the game ◆ ~ **la voie (à qn)** *(fig)* to lead the way (for sb) ◆ **le pays a ouvert son marché aux produits étrangers** the country has opened up its market to foreign products ◆ **l'entreprise a ouvert son capital à de nouveaux actionnaires** the country has opened up its capital to new shareholders ◆ **l'ordinateur à l'école ouvre de nouvelles perspectives aux enseignants** having computers in the classroom opens up new possibilities for teachers; → **horizon**

7 *(= créer, commencer à exploiter)* *[+ restaurant, théâtre, magasin, usine]* to open; *[+ école, succursale]* to open (up)

8 *(= commencer, mettre en train)* *[+ période, négociations]* to begin; *[+ débat, dialogue, enquête]* to begin, to open ◆ ~ **le feu** to open fire

9 *(Ordin)* *[+ fichier, boîte de dialogue]* to open

10 *(Ski)* ~ **la piste** to open the piste *ou* run ◆ ~ **la marque à la 16e minute du jeu** *(Ftbl)* to open the scoring after 16 minutes of play ◆ **il ouvre toujours sur un joueur faible** *(Ftbl, Rugby)* he always passes to a weak player ◆ ~ **le jeu** *(Cartes)* to open play ◆ **il a ouvert à pique** *(Cartes)* he opened on *ou* with spades; → **bal, hostilité**

11 *[+ compte bancaire]* to open; *[+ emprunt]* to take out

12 *(= être au début de)* *[+ liste, œuvre]* to head; *[+ procession]* to lead; → **marche¹**

13 *(= faire fonctionner)* *[+ électricité, gaz, radio, télévision]* to turn on, to switch on, to put on; *[+ eau, robinet]* to turn on; *[+ vanne]* to open

VI 1 *(= ouvrir la porte)* **on a frappé, va ~ !** there's someone at the door, go and open it! ◆ **ouvrez, au nom de la loi !** open up, in the name of the law! ◆ **n'ouvre à personne !** don't open the door to anybody! ◆ **fais-toi ~ par le gardien** ask *ou* get the caretaker to let you in

2 *[fenêtre, porte]* to open ◆ **cette fenêtre ouvre sur la cour** this window opens (out) onto the yard ◆ **la porte de derrière n'ouvre pas** the back door doesn't open

3 *[magasin]* to open ◆ **le boulanger ouvre de 7 heures à 19 heures** the baker is open *ou* opens from 7 am till 7 pm

4 *(= commencer)* to open

VPR **s'ouvrir** 1 *(gén)* to open; *[fleur]* to open (out); *[esprit]* to open out ◆ **robe qui s'ouvre par devant** dress that undoes *ou* unfastens at the front ◆ **sa robe s'est ouverte** her dress came undone *ou* unfastened ◆ **la fenêtre s'ouvre sur une cour** the window opens (out) onto a courtyard ◆ **la foule s'ouvrit pour le laisser passer** the crowd parted to let him through ◆ **la porte s'ouvrit violemment** the door flew open *ou* was flung open *ou* was thrown open ◆ **la porte/boîte a dû s'~** the door/box must have come open

2 *(= commencer)* *[récit, séance, exposition]* to open *(par* with*)*; ◆ **la séance s'ouvrit par un chahut** the meeting opened in uproar

3 *(= se présenter)* **un chemin poussiéreux s'ouvrit devant eux** a dusty path opened in front of *ou* before them ◆ **la vie qui s'ouvre devant elle est pleine d'embûches** the life which is opening in front of *ou* before her is full of pitfalls

4 *(= béer)* to open (up) ◆ **la terre s'ouvrit devant eux** the ground opened up before them ◆ **le gouffre s'ouvrait à leurs pieds** the chasm lay open *ou* gaped at their feet

5 *(= se blesser)* to cut open ◆ **elle s'est ouvert les veines** she slashed *ou* cut her wrists ◆ **il s'ouvrit la jambe en tombant sur une faux** he cut his leg open when he fell onto a scythe

6 *(= devenir accessible, communiquer)* **s'~ à** *[+ amour, art, problèmes économiques]* to open one's mind to, to become aware of ◆ **son esprit s'est ouvert aux souffrances d'autrui** he became aware of the suffering of others ◆ **pays qui s'ouvre sur le monde extérieur** country which is opening up to the outside world

7 *(= se confier)* **s'~ à qn de** to open one's heart to sb about ◆ **il s'en est ouvert à son confesseur** he opened his heart to his confessor about it

ouvroir /uvʀwaʀ/ NM *[de couvent]* workroom; *[de paroisse]* sewing room

ouzbek /uzbɛk/ ADJ Uzbek NM *(= langue)* Uzbek NMF **Ouzbek** Uzbek

Ouzbékistan /uzbekistɑ̃/ NM Uzbekistan

ovaire /ɔvɛʀ/ NM ovary

ovale /ɔval/ ADJ *[table, surface]* oval; *[volume]* egg-shaped; → **ballon¹** NM oval ◆ **l'~ du visage** the oval of the face ◆ **en ~** oval (-shaped)

ovalie /ɔvali/ NF *(journalistique)* ◆ **l'~** the world of rugby

ovariectomie /ɔvaʀjɛktɔmi/ NF ovariectomy, oophorectomy

ovarien, -ienne /ɔvaʀjɛ̃, jɛn/ ADJ ovarian

ovariotomie /ɔvaʀjɔtɔmi/ NF ovariotomy

ovarite /ɔvaʀit/ NF ovaritis, oophoritis

ovation /ɔvasjɔ̃/ NF ovation ◆ **faire une ~ à qn** to give sb an ovation ◆ **ils se levèrent pour lui faire une ~** they gave him a standing ovation ◆ **sous les ~s du public** to the rapturous applause of the audience (*ou* crowd *etc*)

ovationner /ɔvasjɔne/ ▸ conjug 1 ◂ VT ◆ **~ qn** to give sb an ovation

ove /ɔv/ NM *(Archit)* ovum

ové, e /ɔve/ ADJ egg-shaped

overdose /ɔvœʀdoz/ NF *(Méd)* (drug) overdose; * *[de musique, informations]* overdose ◆ **c'est l'~ !*** I've had enough!

overdrive /ɔvœʀdʀajv/ NM overdrive

Ovide /ɔvid/ NM Ovid

oviducte /ɔvidykt/ NM oviduct

ovin, e /ɔvɛ̃, in/ ADJ *[viande, élevage]* sheep *(épith)* ◆ **la race ~e limousine** the sheep of Limousin NMPL ◆ **les ~s** sheep

ovipare /ɔvipaʀ/ ADJ oviparous NM oviparous animal ◆ **~s** ovipara

ovni /ɔvni/ NM (abrév de **objet volant non identifié**) UFO ◆ **c'est un véritable ~** *(fig)* it's like something from another planet

ovocyte /ɔvɔsit/ NM oocyte

ovoïde /ɔvɔid/ ADJ egg-shaped, ovoid *(SPÉC)*

ovovivipare /ovovivipaʀ/ ADJ ovoviviparous

ovulaire /ɔvylɛʀ/ ADJ ovular

ovulation /ɔvylasjɔ̃/ NF ovulation

ovulatoire /ɔvylatwaʀ/ ADJ ovulatory

ovule /ɔvyl/ NM *(Physiol)* ovum; *(Bot)* ovule; *(Pharm)* pessary

ovuler /ɔvyle/ ▸ conjug 1 ◂ VI to ovulate

oxacide /ɔksasid/ NM oxyacid, oxygen acid

oxalique /ɔksalik/ ADJ ◆ **acide ~** oxalic acid

Oxford /ɔksfɔʀd/ N Oxford

oxford /ɔksfɔʀ(d)/ NM *(= tissu)* oxford

oxfordien, -ienne /ɔksfɔʀdjɛ̃, jɛn/ ADJ Oxonian NM,F **Oxfordien(ne)** Oxonian

oxhydrique /ɔksidʀik/ ADJ oxyhydrogen *(épith)*

oxonien, -ienne /ɔksɔnjɛ̃, jɛn/ ADJ Oxonian NM,F **Oxonien(ne)** Oxonian

oxyacétylénique /ɔksiasetilenik/ ADJ oxyacetylene *(épith)*

oxydable /ɔksidabl/ ADJ liable to rust, oxidizable *(SPÉC)*

oxydant, e /ɔksidɑ̃, ɑt/ ADJ oxidizing NM oxidizer, oxidizing agent

oxydase /ɔksidɑz/ NF oxidase

oxydation /ɔksidasjɔ̃/ NF oxid(iz)ation

oxyde /ɔksid/ NM oxide ◆ **~ de carbone** carbon monoxide ◆ **~ de plomb** lead oxide *ou* monoxide ◆ **~ de cuivre/de fer** copper/iron oxide

oxyder /ɔkside/ ▸ conjug 1 ◂ VT to oxidize VPR **s'oxyder** to become oxidized

oxydoréduction /ɔksidɔʀedyksjɔ̃/ NF oxidation-reduction

oxygénateur /ɔksiʒenatœʀ/ NM *[d'aquarium]* oxygenator

oxygénation /ɔksiʒenasjɔ̃/ NF oxygenation

oxygène /ɔksiʒɛn/ NM oxygen ◆ **il est allé chercher un bol d'~ à la campagne** he's gone to the countryside to get some fresh air into his lungs ◆ **ce week-end fut pour moi une bouffée d'~** that weekend did me a power of good * *ou* really lifted my spirits ◆ **apporter un peu** *ou* **une bouffée d'~ à l'économie** to give the economy a shot in the arm; → **ballon¹**

⚠ **oxygène** se traduit par le mot anglais **oxygen** uniquement au sens chimique.

oxygéner /ɔksiʒene/ ▸ conjug 6 ◂ VT *(Chim)* to oxygenate; *[+ cheveux]* to peroxide, to bleach ◆ **s'~ (les poumons)*** to get some fresh air (into one's lungs) ◆ **elle est allée au concert pour s'~ la tête*** *ou* **l'esprit** she went to the concert to take her mind off things; → **blond, eau**

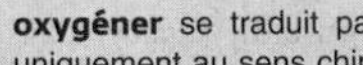

⚠ **oxygéner** se traduit par **to oxygenate** uniquement au sens chimique.

oxyhémoglobine /ɔksiemɔglɔbin/ NF oxyhaemoglobin

oxymore /ɔksimɔʀ/, **oxymoron** /ɔksimɔʀɔ̃/ NM oxymoron

oxyure /ɔksjyʀ/ NM pinworm, threadworm

oyat /ɔja/ NM beachgrass

oyez /ɔje/ → **ouïr**

ozone /ozon/ NM ozone ◆ **la couche d'~** the ozone layer ◆ **"préserve la couche d'ozone"** *(sur emballage)* "ozone-friendly"

ozonisation /ozonizasjɔ̃/ NF ozonization

ozoniser /ozonize/ ▸ conjug 1 ◂ VT to ozonize

P, p[1] /pe/ NM (= *lettre*) P, p

p[2] (abrév de **page**) p

PAC /pak/ NF (abrév de **politique agricole commune**) CAP

PACA /paka/ NF (abrév de **Provence-Alpes-Côte d'Azur**) *region in southern France*

pacage /pakaʒ/ NM pasture, grazing (land) (*NonC*)

pacager /pakaʒe/ ► conjug 3 ◄ VT to pasture, to graze VI to graze

pacane /pakan/ NF ◆ **(noix de)** ~ pecan (nut)

pacemaker /pesmekœʀ/ NM pacemaker

pacha /paʃa/ NM pasha ◆ **mener une vie de ~, faire le** ~ (= *vivre richement*) to live like a lord; (= *se prélasser*) to live a life of ease

pachyderme /paʃidɛʀm/ NM 1 (*SPÉC*) pachyderm (*SPÉC*); (= *éléphant*) elephant 2 (*péj, hum* = *personne*) elephant ◆ **de** ~ [*allure, démarche*] elephantine, heavy

pacificateur, -trice /pasifikatœʀ, tʀis/ ADJ [*action, discours*] placatory, pacifying ◆ **les vertus pacificatrices de la musique** the soothing qualities of music NM,F (= *personne*) peacemaker

pacification /pasifikasjɔ̃/ NF pacification

pacifier /pasifje/ ► conjug 7 ◄ VT [+ *pays*] to pacify, to bring peace to; [+ *esprits*] to pacify ◆ **il rêve d'un monde pacifié** he dreams of a world at peace

pacifique /pasifik/ ADJ 1 [*coexistence, manifestation, règlement, intention, solution*] peaceful; [*humeur*] peaceable; [*personne, peuple*] peace-loving, peaceable ◆ **utilisé à des fins ~s** used for peaceful purposes 2 (*Géog*) Pacific NM (*Géog*) ◆ **le Pacifique** the Pacific ◆ **les îles du Pacifique** the Pacific Islands

pacifiquement /pasifikmɑ̃/ ADV peacefully

pacifisme /pasifism/ NM pacifism

pacifiste /pasifist/ NMF pacifist ADJ [*doctrine*] pacifistic, pacifist ◆ **manifestation** ~ peace march *ou* demonstration

pack /pak/ NM 1 (*Rugby*) pack 2 (*Comm*) pack ◆ ~ **de bière/yaourts** pack of beer/yoghurts 3 (= *banquise*) pack ice

package /paka(d)ʒ, pakɛdʒ/ NM (*Écon, Ordin*) package ◆ ~ **(tour)** (*Tourisme*) package holiday

packageur /paka(d)ʒœʀ/ NM packager

packaging /paka(d)ʒiŋ/ NM packaging

pacotille /pakɔtij/ NF 1 (*de mauvaise qualité*) cheap junk* *ou* trash*; (*clinquant*) showy stuff ◆ **c'est de la** ~ it's junk*, it's cheap rubbish (*Brit*) ◆ **meubles/bijoux de** ~ cheap furniture/jewellery 2 (*Hist*) *goods carried free of freightage*

PACS /paks/ NM (abrév de **pacte civil de solidarité**) *contract for people in long-term relationship*

pacsé, e /pakse/ ADJ ◆ **ils sont ~s** they've signed a PACS contract

pacser (se) /pakse/ VPR to sign a PACS contract

pacson⁎ /paksɔ̃/ NM packet

pacte /pakt/ NM pact, treaty ◆ ~ **d'alliance** treaty of alliance ◆ ~ **de non-agression** non-aggression pact ◆ **le ~ de Varsovie** the Warsaw Pact ◆ **faire** *ou* **conclure** *ou* **signer un ~ avec qn** to sign a pact *ou* treaty with sb ◆ **il a signé un ~ avec le diable** he made a pact with the devil

pactiser /paktize/ ► conjug 1 ◄ VI (*péj* = *se liguer*) to make a deal (*avec* with); ◆ ~ **avec l'ennemi** to collude with the enemy ◆ ~ **avec le diable** to make a pact with the devil ◆ ~ **avec le racisme/le nazisme** to condone racism/Nazism

pactole /paktɔl/ NM (= *source de richesse*) gold mine; (* = *argent*) fortune ◆ **un bon** ~ a tidy sum* *ou* packet* ◆ **un petit** ~ a tidy little sum*, a small fortune ◆ **le Pactole** (*Géog*) the Pactolus

paddock /padɔk/ NM 1 [*de champ de courses*] paddock 2 (⁎ = *lit*) bed ◆ **aller au** ~ to hit the sack* *ou* the hay*, to turn in*

Padoue /padu/ N Padua

paella /paela/ NF paella

PAF /paf/ NM (abrév de **paysage audiovisuel français**) → **paysage** NF (abrév de **police de l'air et des frontières**) → **police**[1]

paf /paf/ EXCL (*chute*) bam!; (*gifle*) slap!, wham! ADJ INV (⁎ = *ivre*) drunk, tight* (*Brit*) ◆ **complètement** ~ plastered⁎

pagaie /pagɛ/ NF paddle

pagaille, pagaïe /pagaj/ NF 1 (= *objets en désordre*) mess, shambles (*NonC*); (= *cohue, manque d'organisation*) chaos (*NonC*) ◆ **quelle ~ dans cette pièce !** what a mess this room is! ◆ **c'est la ~ sur les routes/dans le gouvernement** there is (complete) chaos on the roads/in the government ◆ **il a mis** *ou* **semé la ~ dans mes affaires/dans la réunion** he has messed up all my things/the meeting 2 (= *beaucoup*) **il y en a en** ~* there are loads* *ou* masses of them

paganiser /paganize/ ► conjug 1 ◄ VT to paganize, to heathenize

paganisme /paganism/ NM paganism, heathenism

pagaye /pagaj/ NF ⇒ **pagaille**

pagayer /pageje/ ► conjug 8 ◄ VI to paddle

pagayeur, -euse /pagɛjœʀ, øz/ NM,F paddler

page[1] /paʒ/ NF (= *feuillet*) page; (*fig* = *passage*) passage, page; (= *événement*) page, chapter, episode ◆ **(à la)** ~ **35** on page 35 ◆ **une pleine ~ de publicité** a full-page ad ◆ **belle/fausse** ~ (*Typo*) right-hand/left-hand page ◆ ~ **suivante/précédente** (*Ordin*) page down/up ◆ ~ **d'accueil/de démarrage/de recherche** (*Internet*) home/start-up/search page ◆ **une ~ d'écriture** a page of writing ◆ **les plus belles ~s de Corneille** the finest passages of Corneille ◆ **une ~ glorieuse/nouvelle de l'histoire de France** a glorious chapter/new page in the history of France ◆ **tourner la** ~ (*lit, fig*) to turn the page ◆ **une ~ est tournée** a page has been turned; → **garde**[1]

◆ **en page** ◆ **mettre en** ~ (*Typo*) to lay out, to make up (into pages) ◆ **mise en** ~ (*Typo*) layout, make-up; (*Ordin*) layout

◆ **à la page** * (= *à la mode*) ◆ **être à la** ~ to be with it* ◆ **ne plus être à la** ~ to be out of touch ◆ **se mettre à la** ~ [*institution*] to bring itself up to date ◆ **j'essaie de me mettre à la** ~ I try to keep in touch with what's going on

COMP **page blanche** blank page ◆ **l'angoisse de l'écrivain devant la ~ blanche** writer's block ◆ **les ~s blanches** [*d'annuaire*] the phone book, the white pages

les pages jaunes (de l'annuaire) the Yellow pages ®

page de publicité (*Radio, TV*) commercial break, commercials

page de titre title page

page[2] /paʒ/ NM (*Hist*) page (boy)

page[3]⁎ /paʒ/ NM bed ◆ **se mettre au** ~ to turn in*, to hit the sack* *ou* the hay*

page-écran (pl **pages-écrans**) /paʒekʀɑ̃/ NF (*Ordin*) screenful

pageot⁎ /paʒo/ NM ⇒ **page**[3]

pageoter (se)⁎ /paʒɔte/ ► conjug 1 ◄ VPR to turn in*, to hit the sack* *ou* the hay*

pagination /paʒinasjɔ̃/ NF (*gén* = *numérotation*) pagination; (*Ordin*) paging; (*Presse* = *nombre de pages*) pagination, page count ◆ **erreur de** ~ pagination error

paginer /paʒine/ ► conjug 1 ◄ VT (*gén*) to paginate; (*Ordin*) to page ◆ **livre non paginé** book without page numbers ◆ **mémoire paginée** expanded memory

pagne /paɲ/ NM (*en tissu*) loincloth; (*en paille*) grass skirt

pagode /pagɔd/ NF pagoda ◆ **manche ~** pagoda sleeve

paie /pɛ/ NF *[de militaire]* pay; *[d'ouvrier]* pay, wages ◆ **jour de ~** payday ◆ **bulletin** *ou* **feuille de ~** payslip ◆ **toucher sa ~** to be paid, to get one's wages ◆ **il travaille à la ~** *ou* **au service ~** he works in the wages department ◆ **il y a** *ou* **ça fait une ~ que nous ne nous sommes pas vus*** it's been ages since we last saw each other, we haven't seen each other for ages *ou* yonks‡ *(Brit)*

paiement /pɛmɑ̃/ NM payment *(de* for); ◆ **faire un ~** to make a payment ◆ **~ à la commande** payment *ou* cash with order ◆ **~ à la livraison** cash on delivery ◆ **~ comptant** payment in full ◆ **~ échelonné** payment by *ou* in instalments ◆ **~ en liquide** cash payment ◆ **~ par chèque/d'avance** payment by cheque/in advance ◆ **~ électronique** electronic payment ◆ **~ sécurisé** secure payment → **facilité**

païen, païenne /pajɛ̃, pajɛn/ ADJ, NM,F pagan, heathen

paierie /pɛʀi/ NF ◆ **~ (générale)** local office of the treasury *(paying salaries, state bills etc)*

paillage /pɑjaʒ/ NM *(Agr)* mulching

paillard, e* /pajaʀ, aʀd/ ADJ *[personne]* bawdy, coarse; *[histoire]* bawdy, lewd, dirty ◆ **chanson ~e** bawdy song

paillardise /pajaʀdiz/ NF *(= débauche)* bawdiness; *(= plaisanterie)* dirty *ou* lewd joke *(ou* story *ou* remark *etc)*

paillasse[1] /pajas/ NF 1 *(= matelas)* straw mattress 2 *[d'évier]* draining board, drainboard *(US)*; *[de laboratoire]* (tiled) work surface 3 († = *prostituée)* trollop † 4 *(* : locutions)* **crever la ~ à qn** to do sb in* ◆ **se crever la ~ à faire qch** to slog one's guts out doing sth

paillasse[2] /pajas/ NM *(= clown)* clown

paillasson /pajasɔ̃/ NM *[de porte]* doormat; *(péj = personne)* doormat *(fig) (Agr)* matting; → **clé**

paille /pɑj/ NF 1 *(= tige coupée)* straw; *(pour boire)* (drinking) straw ◆ **chapeau/panier de ~** straw hat/basket ◆ **botte de ~** bale of straw ◆ **boire avec une ~** to drink through a straw
2 *(locutions)* **être sur la ~** to be penniless ◆ **mettre qn sur la ~** to reduce sb to poverty ◆ **mourir sur la ~** to die penniless *ou* in poverty ◆ **voir la ~ dans l'œil du prochain (mais pas la poutre dans le sien)** to see the mote in one's neighbour's *ou* one's brother's eye (but not the beam in one's own) ◆ **c'est la ~ et la poutre** it's the pot calling the kettle black ◆ **deux millions de francs ? une ~ !*** two million francs? that's peanuts!*; → **court[1], feu[1], homme**
3 *(Tech = défaut)* flaw
ADJ INV ◆ **jaune ~** straw-coloured *(Brit) ou* -colored *(US)*
COMP **paille de fer** steel wool
paille de riz rice straw ◆ **balai en ~ de riz** straw broom

pailler /pɑje/ ▸ conjug 1 ◂ VT *[+ chaise]* to put a straw bottom in; *[+ arbre, fraisier]* to mulch ◆ **chaise paillée** straw-bottomed chair

pailleté, e /pɑj(ə)te/ (ptp de **pailleter**) ADJ *[robe]* sequined ◆ **yeux noisette ~s d'or** hazel eyes speckled with gold

pailleter /pɑj(ə)te/ ▸ conjug 4 ◂ VT *(gén)* to spangle; *[+ robe]* to sew sequins on

paillette /pɑjɛt/ NF 1 *(Habillement)* sequin, spangle ◆ **corsage à ~s** sequined blouse, blouse with sequins on it ◆ **des émissions ~s** glitzy* TV shows 2 *[d'or]* speck; *[de mica, lessive]* flake ◆ **savon en ~s** soapflakes 3 *(Méd)* ~ **de sperme** sperm straw 4 *[de maquillage]* **~s** glitter *(NonC)*

paillis /pɑji/ NM mulch

paillon /pɑjɔ̃/ NM *[de bouteille]* straw case *ou* wrapping; *[de métal]* small strip

paillote /pɑjɔt/ NF straw hut

pain /pɛ̃/ NM 1 *(= substance)* bread *(NonC)* ◆ **du gros ~** bread sold by weight ◆ **du ~ frais/dur/rassis** fresh/dry/stale bread ◆ **~ de ménage/de boulanger** home-made/baker's bread ◆ **le ~ et le vin** *(Rel)* the bread and wine ◆ **notre ~ quotidien** *(Rel)* our daily bread ◆ **mettre qn au ~ sec** to put sb on dry bread ◆ **je vais au ~*** I'm going to get the bread
2 *(= miche)* loaf ◆ **un ~ (de 2 livres)** a (2-lb) loaf ◆ **un ~ long/rond** a long/round loaf ◆ **deux ~s** two loaves (of bread) ◆ **gros ~** large (crusty) loaf
3 *(en forme de pain) [de cire]* bar; *[de savon]* bar, cake ◆ **~ de poisson/de légumes** *etc (Culin)* fish/vegetable *etc* loaf ◆ **~ de glace** block of ice ◆ **le liquide s'est pris en ~ (dans le congélateur)** the liquid has frozen into a block of ice (in the deep-freeze) ◆ **~ dermatologique** hypoallergenic cleansing bar
4 *(*‡ = coup)* punch, sock* ◆ **se prendre un ~** to get punched *ou* socked one* ◆ **mettre un ~ à qn** to punch *ou* sock sb one*
5 *(locutions)* **on a du ~ sur la planche*** *(beaucoup à faire)* we've got a lot to do, we've got a lot on our plate *(Brit)*; *(travail difficile)* we have our work cut out (for us) ◆ **il reste du ~ sur la planche** there's still a lot to do *ou* to be done ◆ **ôter** *ou* **retirer le ~ de la bouche de qn** to take the bread out of sb's mouth ◆ **ôter** *ou* **faire passer le goût du ~ à qn*** to do sb in*; → **bouchée[2], manger, petit** *etc*
COMP **pain azyme** unleavened bread
pain bénit consecrated bread ◆ **c'est ~ bénit** *(fig)* it's a godsend
pain bis brown bread
pain brioché brioche bread; *(= miche)* brioche loaf
pain brûlé ADJ INV deep golden brown
pain à cacheter bar of sealing wax, sealing wafer
pain de campagne farmhouse bread; *(= miche)* farmhouse loaf
pain au chocolat pain au chocolat, chocolate croissant
pain complet wholewheat *ou* wholemeal *(Brit)* bread; *(= miche)* wholewheat *ou* wholemeal *(Brit)* loaf
pain d'épice(s) *cake made with honey, rye, aniseed, etc,* ≃ gingerbread
pain de Gênes sponge cake
pain grillé toast
pain de gruau ⇒ **pain viennois**
pain au lait *kind of sweet bun*
pain au levain leavened bread
pain de mie sandwich bread; *(= miche)* sandwich loaf
pain parisien *long loaf of bread*
pain perdu French toast
pain pita pitta *ou* pita bread
pain de plastic stick of gelignite
pain polaire polar bread *(type of soft flatbread)*
pain aux raisins ≃ Danish pastry *(with raisins)*
pain de seigle rye bread; *(= miche)* rye loaf
pain de son bran bread; *(= miche)* bran loaf
pain de sucre sugar loaf ◆ **montagne en ~ de sucre** sugar-loaf mountain ◆ **tête en ~ de sucre** egg-shaped head
pain suédois ⇒ **pain polaire**
pain viennois Vienna bread; *(= miche)* Vienna loaf

pair[1] /pɛʀ/ NM 1 *(= dignitaire)* peer 2 *(= égaux)* **~s** peers; → **hors** 3 *(Fin)* par ◆ **valeur remboursée au ~** stock repayable at par ◆ **cours au ~** par rate 4 *(locutions)*
◆ **au pair** ◆ **travailler/être au ~** to work as/be an au pair ◆ **jeune fille au ~** au pair (girl) ◆ **jeune homme au ~** (male) au pair
◆ **de pair** ◆ **aller** *ou* **marcher de ~** to go hand in hand ◆ **aller de ~ avec** to go hand in hand with

pair[2], e[1] /pɛʀ/ ADJ *[nombre]* even ◆ **le côté ~ de la rue** the side of the street with even numbers ◆ **jours ~s** even dates ◆ **jouer ~** to bet on the even numbers

paire[2] /pɛʀ/ NF 1 *[de ciseaux, lunettes, tenailles, chaussures]* pair; *[de bœufs]* yoke; *[de pistolets, pigeons]* brace; *(Cartes)* pair ◆ **ils forment une ~ d'amis** the two of them are great friends ◆ **une belle ~ d'escrocs** a real pair of crooks ◆ **avoir une bonne ~ de joues** to be chubby-cheeked 2 *(locutions)* **les deux font la ~** they're two of a kind ◆ **ils font la ~ ces deux-là !*** they're a right pair!* ◆ **c'est une autre ~ de manches*** that's another kettle of fish, that's another story ◆ **se faire la ~**‡ to clear off‡, to beat it‡

pairesse /pɛʀɛs/ NF peeress

pairie /peʀi/ NF peerage

paisible /pezibl/ ADJ 1 *[personne, caractère]* quiet; *[vie, quartier, village, retraite]* peaceful, quiet ◆ **dormir d'un sommeil ~** to be sleeping peacefully 2 *(Jur)* quiet, peaceable

paisiblement /pezibləmɑ̃/ ADV peacefully

paître /pɛtʀ/ ▸ conjug 57 ◂ VI to graze ◆ **le pâturage où ils font ~ leur troupeau** the pasture where they graze their herd ◆ **envoyer ~ qn**‡ to send sb packing* VT *[+ herbe]* to graze on; *[+ feuilles, fruits]* to feed on ◆ **~ l'herbe d'un pré** to graze in a meadow

paix /pɛ/ NF 1 *(Mil, Pol)* peace ◆ **~ armée** armed peace ◆ **~ séparée** separate peace agreement ◆ **demander la ~** to sue for peace ◆ **signer la ~** to sign a peace treaty ◆ **en temps de ~** in peacetime ◆ **traité/pourparlers de ~** peace treaty/talks ◆ **soldats de la ~** peacekeeping force ◆ **Mouvement pour la ~** Peace Movement ◆ **si tu veux la ~, prépare la guerre** *(Prov)* if you wish to have peace, prepare for war
2 *(= état d'accord)* peace ◆ **~ sociale** social peace ◆ **pour rétablir la ~ sociale au sein de l'entreprise** to re-establish peaceful relations within the company ◆ **ramener la ~ entre ...** to make peace between ... ◆ **il a fait la ~ avec son frère** he has made his peace with his brother, he and his brother have made up *ou* made it up *(Brit)* ◆ **être pour la ~ des ménages** *(hum)* to believe in domestic harmony; → **baiser[1], gardien, juge**
3 *(= tranquillité)* peace, quiet; *(= silence)* stillness, peacefulness ◆ **tout le monde est sorti, quelle ~ dans la maison !** how peaceful *ou* quiet it is in the house now everyone has gone out! ◆ **est-ce qu'on pourrait avoir la ~ ?** could we have a bit of peace and quiet?
4 *(= calme intérieur)* peace ◆ **la ~ de l'âme** inner peace ◆ **allez** *ou* **partez en ~** *(Rel)* go in peace ◆ **~ à sa mémoire** *ou* **à son âme** *ou* **à ses cendres** *(hum)* God rest his soul ◆ **~ sur la terre aux hommes de bonne volonté** *(Bible)* peace on Earth and good will to all men ◆ **avoir la conscience en ~, être en ~ avec sa conscience** to have a clear *ou* an easy conscience, to be at peace with one's conscience ◆ **qu'il repose en ~** may he rest in peace ◆ **laisser qn en ~, laisser la ~ à qn** to leave sb alone *ou* in peace ◆ **fous-moi**‡ *ou* **fiche-moi* la ~ !** stop pestering me!, clear off!‡ ◆ **la ~ !** shut up!*, quiet!

Pakistan /pakistɑ̃/ NM Pakistan

pakistanais, e /pakistanɛ, ɛz/ ADJ Pakistani
NM,F **Pakistanais(e)** Pakistani

PAL /pal/ NM (abrév de **Phase Alternative Line**) PAL

pal (pl **pals**) /pal/ NM *(Héraldique)* pale; *(= pieu)* stake ◆ **le (supplice du) ~** torture by impalement

palabrer /palabʀe/ ▸ conjug 1 ◂ VI (= *bavarder*) to talk *ou* chat away; (= *parlementer*) to argue endlessly ◆ **je n'ai pas envie de l'entendre ~ pendant des heures** I don't want to listen to him going on *ou* waffling on* (*Brit*) for hours ◆ **assez palabré, il faut agir** that's enough talk, let's have some action

palabres /palabʀ/ NFPL never-ending discussions

palace /palas/ NM luxury hotel ◆ **ils habitent un vrai ~** their house is (like) a palace

paladin /paladɛ̃/ NM paladin

palais /palɛ/ NM 1 (= *édifice*) palace; → **révolution** 2 (*Jur*) **le Palais** the law courts ◆ **en argot du Palais, en termes de Palais** in legal parlance ◆ **les gens du Palais** lawyers 3 (*Anat*) palate ◆ **~ dur/mou** hard/soft palate ◆ **avoir le ~ desséché** to be parched, to be dying of thirst ◆ **avoir le ~ fin** to have a discerning palate ◆ **~ fendu** (*Méd*) cleft palate; → **flatter, voile²**

COMP **le palais Brongniart** *the Paris Stock Exchange*
le palais de Buckingham Buckingham Palace
palais des congrès convention centre
le palais de l'Élysée the Élysée Palace
palais des expositions exhibition centre
Palais de justice law courts
le palais du Luxembourg *the seat of the French Senate*
le palais des Nations the Palais des Nations
Palais des sports sports stadium

Palais-Bourbon /palebuʀbɔ̃/ NM ◆ **le ~** (the seat of) the French National Assembly

palan /palɑ̃/ NM hoist

palangre /palɑ̃gʀ/ NF (*Pêche*) long-line ◆ **la pêche à la ~** long-lining

palanque /palɑ̃k/ NF stockade

palanquée /palɑ̃ke/ NF **une palanquée** *ou* **des palanquées de** * loads of *

palanquin /palɑ̃kɛ̃/ NM palanquin, palankeen

palatal, e (mpl **-aux**) /palatal, o/ ADJ (*Ling*) [*consonne*] palatal (*épith*); [*voyelle*] front (*épith*); (*Anat*) palatal NF **palatale** (= *consonne*) palatal consonant; (= *voyelle*) front vowel

palatalisation /palatalizasjɔ̃/ NF palatalization

palataliser /palatalize/ ▸ conjug 1 ◂ VT to palatalize

palatin, e /palatɛ̃, in/ ADJ 1 (*Hist*) Palatine ◆ **le comte/l'électeur ~** the count/the elector Palatine ◆ **princesse Palatine** Princess Palatine 2 (*Géog*) **le (mont) Palatin** the Palatine Hill 3 (*Anat*) palatine NM (*Hist*) Palatine; (*Anat*) palatine

Palatinat /palatina/ NM ◆ **le ~** the Palatinate

pale /pal/ NF [*d'hélice, rame*] blade; [*de roue, écluse*] paddle

pâle /pɑl/ ADJ 1 [*teint, personne*] pale; (= *maladif*) pallid, pale ◆ **~ comme un linge** as white as a sheet ◆ **~ comme la mort** deathly pale *ou* white ◆ **~ de peur** white with fear ◆ **~ de colère** pale *ou* white *ou* livid with anger ◆ **se faire porter ~*** to report *ou* go* sick; → **visage** 2 [*lueur*] pale, weak; [*couleur, soleil, ciel*] pale 3 [*style*] weak; [*imitation*] pale, poor; [*sourire*] faint, wan ◆ **un ~ crétin** (*péj*) a downright *ou* an utter fool

palefrenier, -ière /palfʀənje, jɛʀ/ NM,F groom; (*Hist*) [*d'auberge*] ostler

palefroi /palfʀwa/ NM (*Hist*) palfrey

paléoanthropologie /paleoɑ̃tʀɔpɔlɔʒi/ NF palaeoanthropology (*Brit*), paleoanthropology (*US*)

paléoanthropologue /paleoɑ̃tʀɔpɔlɔg/ NMF palaeoanthropologist (*Brit*), paleoanthropologist (*US*)

paléobotanique /paleobɔtanik/ NF palaeobotany (*Brit*), paleobotany (*US*)

paléobotaniste /paleobɔtanist/ NMF palaeobotanist (*Brit*), paleobotanist (*US*)

paléochrétien, -ienne /paleokʀetjɛ̃, jɛn/ ADJ early Christian

paléographe /paleɔgʀaf/ NMF palaeographer (*Brit*), paleographer (*US*)

paléographie /paleɔgʀafi/ NF palaeography (*Brit*), paleography (*US*)

paléographique /paleɔgʀafik/ ADJ palaeographic(al) (*Brit*), paleographic(al) (*US*)

paléolithique /paleɔlitik/ ADJ Palaeolithic (*Brit*), Paleolithic (*US*) NM ◆ **le ~** the Palaeolithic (*Brit*) *ou* Paleolithic (*US*) (age)

paléomagnétisme /paleomaɲetism/ NM palaeomagnetism (*Brit*), paleomagnetism (*US*)

paléontologie /paleɔ̃tɔlɔʒi/ NF palaeontology (*Brit*), paleontology (*US*)

paléontologique /paleɔ̃tɔlɔʒik/ ADJ palaeontologic(al) (*Brit*), paleontologic(al) (*US*)

paléontologiste /paleɔ̃tɔlɔʒist/, **paléontologue** /paleɔ̃tɔlɔg/ NMF palaeontologist (*Brit*), paleontologist (*US*)

paléozoïque /paleozɔik/ ADJ Palaeozoic (*Brit*), Paleozoic (*US*) NM ◆ **le ~** the Palaeozoic (*Brit*) *ou* Paleozoic (*US*) (age)

Palerme /palɛʀm/ N Palermo

paleron /palʀɔ̃/ NM (*Boucherie*) chuck (steak)

Palestine /palɛstin/ NF Palestine

palestinien, -ienne /palɛstinjɛ̃, jɛn/ ADJ Palestinian NM,F **Palestinien(ne)** Palestinian

palet /palɛ/ NM (*gén*) (metal *ou* stone) disc; [*de hockey*] puck

paletot /palto/ NM (thick) cardigan ◆ **il m'est tombé** *ou* **m'a sauté sur le ~*** he jumped on me

palette /palɛt/ NF 1 (*Peinture : lit, fig*) palette 2 [*de produits, services*] range ◆ **~ graphique/d'outils** (*Ordin*) graphics/tool palette 3 (*Boucherie*) shoulder 4 (= *aube de roue*) paddle; (= *battoir à linge*) beetle; (*Manutention, Constr*) pallet

palétuvier /paletyvje/ NM mangrove

pâleur /pɑlœʀ/ NF [*de teint*] paleness; (*maladive*) pallor, paleness; [*de couleur, ciel*] paleness

pâlichon, -onne* /pɑliʃɔ̃, ɔn/ ADJ [*personne*] (a bit) pale *ou* peaky* (*Brit*) *ou* peaked* (*US*); [*soleil*] watery

palier /palje/ NM 1 [*d'escalier*] landing ◆ **être voisins de ~, habiter sur le même ~** to live on the same landing ◆ **~ de repos** half landing 2 (= *étape*) stage; [*de graphique*] plateau ◆ **les prix ont atteint un nouveau ~** prices have found a *ou* risen to a new level ◆ **procéder par ~s** to proceed in stages 3 [*de route, voie*] level, flat ◆ **voler en ~** [*avion*] to fly level 4 (*Tech*) bearing ◆ **~ de butée** thrust bearing

palière /paljɛʀ/ ADJ F → **marche², porte**

palimpseste /palɛ̃psɛst/ NM palimpsest

palindrome /palɛ̃dʀom/ NM palindrome

palinodie /palinɔdi/ NF (*Littérat*) palinode ◆ **~s** (*fig*) recantations

pâlir /pɑliʀ/ ▸ conjug 2 ◂ VI 1 [*personne*] to turn *ou* go pale; [*lumière, étoiles*] to grow dim; [*ciel*] to grow pale; [*couleur, encre*] to fade ◆ **~ de colère** to go *ou* turn pale *ou* white with anger ◆ **~ de crainte** to turn pale *ou* white with fear, to blench (with fear) ◆ **faire ~ qn d'envie** *ou* **de jalousie** to make sb green with envy 2 (*littér*) [*souvenir*] to fade (away), to dim; [*gloire*] to dim, to fade VT (*littér*) [+ *ciel*] to turn pale ◆ **encre pâlie par le soleil** ink faded by the sun

palissade /palisad/ NF [*de pieux*] fence; [*de planches*] boarding; (*Mil*) stockade

palissandre /palisɑ̃dʀ/ NM rosewood

pâlissant, e /pɑlisɑ̃, ɑ̃t/ ADJ [*teinte, lumière*] wan, fading

palladium /paladjɔm/ NM (*Chim, fig*) palladium

Pallas Athena /palasatena/ NF Pallas Athena

palliatif, -ive /paljatif, iv/ ADJ (*Méd*) palliative ◆ **soins ~s** palliative care NM (*Méd*) palliative (*à* to, for); (= *mesure*) palliative, stopgap measure; (= *réparation sommaire*) makeshift repair

pallier /palje/ ▸ conjug 7 ◂ VT [+ *difficulté*] to overcome, to get round; [+ *manque*] to offset, to compensate for, to make up for; (*littér*) [+ *défaut*] to disguise, to palliate (*littér*) VT INDIR **pallier à** (*usage critiqué*) [+ *difficulté, manque*] ⇒ **pallier**

palmarès /palmaʀɛs/ NM 1 (= *classement*) [*de lauréats, cinéastes*] (list of) prizewinners *ou* award winners; [*de sportifs*] (list of) medal winners; [*de chansons*] charts, hit parade ◆ **le ~ des universités françaises** (the list of) the top French universities ◆ **le ~ des émissions les plus écoutées** (the list of) the most popular programmes ◆ **cette voiture est** *ou* **figure au ~ des meilleures ventes** this car is among the best-selling models *ou* is a best-seller ◆ **la Grèce figure au ~ des pays les plus visités** Greece is one of the most visited countries in the world
2 (= *liste de victoires, de titres etc*) record *ou* list of achievements ◆ **il a de nombreuses victoires à son ~** he has a number of victories to his credit *ou* under his belt ◆ **c'est un titre qu'il n'a pas encore à son ~** this is a title that he can't yet call his own

palme /palm/ NF 1 (*Archit, Bot*) palm leaf; (= *symbole*) palm ◆ **vin/huile de ~** palm wine/oil 2 (= *distinction*) prize ◆ **la ~ revient à ...** the prize goes to ... ◆ **disputer la ~ à qn** to compete with sb ◆ **remporter la ~** to win, to be the winner ◆ **pour ce qui est des bêtises, il remporte la ~** when it comes to being silly he wins hands down ◆ **la Palme d'or** (*Ciné*) the Palme d'or ◆ **la ~ du martyre** the crown of martyrdom ◆ **décoration avec ~** (*Mil*) ≈ decoration with a bar ◆ **~s académiques** *decoration for services to education in France* 3 [*de nageur*] flipper

palmé, e /palme/ ADJ [*feuille*] palmate (SPÉC); [*patte*] webbed; [*oiseau*] webfooted, palmate (SPÉC) ◆ **avoir les pieds ~s** to have webbed feet ◆ **il les a ~es*** (*hum*) he's bone-idle*

palmer¹ /palmɛʀ/ NM (*Tech*) micrometer

palmer² /palme/ ▸ conjug 1 ◂ VI to kick (*when wearing flippers*) ◆ **j'ai dû ~ fort contre le courant** I had to kick hard because of the current

palmeraie /palməʀɛ/ NF palm grove

palmier /palmje/ NM 1 (= *plante*) palm tree ◆ **~-dattier** date palm 2 (= *gâteau*) *heart-shaped biscuit made of flaky pastry*

palmipède /palmipɛd/ NM palmiped (SPÉC) ADJ webfooted

palmiste /palmist/ ADJ M → **chou¹**

palombe /palɔ̃b/ NF woodpigeon, ringdove

palonnier /palɔnje/ NM [*d'avion*] rudder bar; [*de voiture*] compensator; [*de cheval*] swingletree; (*en ski nautique*) handle; [*d'appareil de levage*] crosspiece

palot* /palo/ NM (= *baiser*) kiss

pâlot, -otte* /pɑlo, ɔt/ ADJ [*personne*] (a bit) pale *ou* peaky* (*Brit*) *ou* peaked* (*US*)

palourde /paluʀd/ NF clam

palpable /palpabl/ ADJ (*lit, fig*) palpable ◆ **il rend ~ l'atmosphère du Paris des années 20**

he vividly evokes the atmosphere of 1920s Paris

palpation /palpasjɔ̃/ NF palpation

palper /palpe/ ▸ conjug 1 ◂ VT 1 [+ objet] to feel, to finger; (Méd) to palpate 2 * [+ argent] (= recevoir) to get; (= gagner) to make ◆ **qu'est-ce qu'il a dû ~ (comme argent) !** he must have made a fortune ou a mint! *

palpeur /palpœʀ/ NM [de chaleur, lumière] sensor

palpitant, e /palpitɑ̃, ɑ̃t/ ADJ 1 (= passionnant) [livre, moment] thrilling, exciting; [vie] exciting ◆ **d'un intérêt ~, ~ d'intérêt** terribly exciting, thrilling ◆ **être ~ d'émotion** to be quivering with emotion 2 [chair] quivering (épith), wobbly; [blessure] throbbing (épith) NM †* (= cœur) ticker *

palpitation /palpitasjɔ̃/ NF [de cœur] racing (NonC); [de paupières] fluttering (NonC); [de lumière, flamme] quivering (NonC) ◆ **avoir des ~s** (Méd) to have palpitations ◆ **ça m'a donné des ~s** (fig) it gave me quite a turn

palpiter /palpite/ ▸ conjug 1 ◂ VI [cœur] (= battre) to beat; (= battre rapidement) to race; [paupières] to flutter; [chair] to quiver; [blessure] to throb; [narines, lumière, flamme] to quiver

paltoquet /paltɔkɛ/ NM (littér : péj) (= rustre) boor; (= freluquet) pompous fool

palu * /paly/ NM abrév de **paludisme**

paluche * /palyʃ/ NF (= main) hand, paw * ◆ **serrer la ~ à qn** to shake hands with sb, to shake sb's hand

paludéen, -enne /palydeɛ̃, ɛn/ ADJ (Méd) malarial

paludisme /palydism/ NM paludism (SPÉC), malaria

palustre /palystʀ/ ADJ paludal ◆ **plante ~** marsh plant

pâmer (se) /pɑme/ ▸ conjug 1 ◂ VPR (littér) to swoon † ◆ **se ~ ou être pâmé devant qch** (fig) to swoon ou be in raptures ou be ecstatic over sth ◆ **se ~ d'admiration/d'amour** to be overcome with admiration/with love ◆ **se ~ de rire** to be convulsed with laughter

pâmoison /pɑmwazɔ̃/ NF (littér, hum) swoon † ◆ **tomber en ~** (lit) to swoon † ◆ **tomber en ~ devant un tableau** (fig) to swoon over ou go into raptures over a painting

pampa /pɑ̃pa/ NF pampas (pl)

pamphlet /pɑ̃flɛ/ NM satirical tract, lampoon

pamphlétaire /pɑ̃fletɛʀ/ NMF lampoonist

pampille /pɑ̃pij/ NF [de lustre] pendant

pamplemousse /pɑ̃pləmus/ NM grapefruit

pamplemoussier /pɑ̃pləmusje/ NM grapefruit tree

pampre /pɑ̃pʀ/ NM (littér) vine branch

Pan /pɑ̃/ NM Pan; → **flûte**

pan[1] /pɑ̃/ NM 1 (= morceau) piece; [d'habit] tail; (= face, côté) side, face; [de toit] side; [de nappe] overhanging part; [de lumière] patch 2 [d'économie, industrie] area; [de société] section ◆ **un ~ de ma vie/de l'histoire de France** a chapter in ou of my life/in the history of France

COMP **pan de chemise** shirt-tail ◆ **se promener en ~s de chemise** to wander about in (one's) shirt-tails ou with just one's shirt on
pan de ciel patch of sky
pan coupé cut-off corner (of room) ◆ **maison en ~ coupé** house with a slanting ou cut-off corner ◆ **mur en ~ coupé** wall with a cut-off corner
pan de mur (section of) wall
pan de rideau curtain

pan[2] /pɑ̃/ EXCL [de coup de feu] bang!; [de gifle] slap!, whack! ◆ **je vais te faire ~ ~ (les fesses)** (langage enfantin) you'll get your bottom smacked

panacée /panase/ NF panacea, cure-all

panachage /panaʃaʒ/ NM 1 (Pol) voting for candidates from different parties instead of for the set list of one party 2 (= mélange) [de couleurs] combination; [de programmes, plats] selection

panache /panaʃ/ NM 1 (= plumet) plume, panache ◆ **~ de fumée** plume of smoke 2 (= brio) [de personne] panache ◆ **avoir du ~** to have panache ◆ **personnage sans ~** lacklustre individual ◆ **victoire sans ~** unimpressive victory

panaché, e /panaʃe/ (ptp de **panacher**) ADJ 1 [fleur, feuilles] variegated, many-coloured (Brit) ou -colored (US) ◆ **pétunias blancs ~s de rouge** white petunias with splashes of red ou with red stripes 2 [foule, assortiment] motley; [glace] two- ou mixed-flavour (Brit) ou -flavor (US) (épith); [salade] mixed ◆ **bière ~e** shandy NM (= boisson) shandy

panacher /panaʃe/ ▸ conjug 1 ◂ VT (= mélanger) [+ couleurs, fleurs] to put together; [+ genres] to mix, to combine; [+ plantes] to cross; [+ biscuits, bonbons] to make an assortment ou a selection of; (= varier) [+ programmes, exercices] to vary ◆ **dois-je prendre l'un des menus ou puis-je ~ (les plats) ?** do I have to take a set menu or can I make my own selection (of courses)? ◆ **~ une liste électorale** to vote for candidates from different parties instead of for the set list of one party

panachure /panaʃyʀ/ NF (gén pl) motley colours (Brit) ou colors (US)

panade /panad/ NF bread soup ◆ **être dans la ~** * (= avoir des ennuis) to be in the soup *, to be in a sticky situation; (= avoir des ennuis d'argent) to be strapped for cash * (Brit), to be down to one's last dollar (US)

panafricain, e /panafʀikɛ̃, ɛn/ ADJ Pan-African

panafricanisme /panafʀikanism/ NM Pan-Africanism

panais /panɛ/ NM parsnip

panama /panama/ NM 1 (Géog) **le Panama** Panama 2 (= chapeau) Panama hat

Paname * /panam/ N Paris

panaméen, -enne /panameɛ̃, ɛn/ ADJ Panamanian NM,F **Panaméen(ne)** Panamanian

panaméricain, e /panameʀikɛ̃, ɛn/ ADJ Pan-American ◆ **route ~e** Pan-American Highway

panaméricanisme /panameʀikanism/ NM Pan-Americanism

panamien, -ienne /panamjɛ̃, jɛn/ ADJ ⇒ **panaméen**

panarabe /panaʀab/ ADJ Pan-Arab(ic)

panarabisme /panaʀabism/ NM Pan-Arabism

panard * /panaʀ/ NM foot ◆ **c'est le ~ !** it's magic! * ou ace * (Brit)!

panaris /panaʀi/ NM whitlow

pan-bagnat (pl **pans-bagnats**) /pɑ̃baɲa/ NM sandwich (with tomatoes, lettuce, hard-boiled eggs, tuna and anchovies, seasoned with olive oil)

pancarte /pɑ̃kaʀt/ NF (gén) sign, notice; (sur route) (road)sign; [de manifestant] placard

pancréas /pɑ̃kʀeas/ NM pancreas

pancréatique /pɑ̃kʀeatik/ ADJ pancreatic

panda /pɑ̃da/ NM panda ◆ **grand ~** giant panda

pandémie /pɑ̃demi/ NF pandemic (disease) ◆ **la ~ de sida** the Aids pandemic

pandémonium /pɑ̃demɔnjɔm/ NM (littér) pandemonium ◆ **le Pandémonium** Pandemonium

pandit /pɑ̃di(t)/ NM pandit, pundit

Pandore /pɑ̃dɔʀ/ NF (Myth) Pandora

pandore * † /pɑ̃dɔʀ/ NM (= gendarme) cop *, gendarme

panégyrique /paneʒiʀik/ NM (frm) panegyric ◆ **faire le ~ de qn** to extol sb's merits ◆ **quel ~ il a fait de son chef !** what a tribute he paid to his boss!

panégyriste /paneʒiʀist/ NMF panegyrist

panel /panɛl/ NM (= jury) panel; (= échantillon) sample group

paner /pane/ ▸ conjug 1 ◂ VT to coat with breadcrumbs ◆ **pané** [escalope] coated with breadcrumbs, breaded

panetière /pan(ə)tjɛʀ/ NF breadbin (Brit), breadbox (US)

paneuropéen, -enne /panøʀɔpeɛ̃, ɛn/ ADJ Pan-European

pangermanisme /pɑ̃ʒɛʀmanism/ NM Pan-Germanism

pangermaniste /pɑ̃ʒɛʀmanist/ ADJ Pan-German(ic) NMF Pan-German

panhellénique /panelenik/ ADJ Panhellenic

panhellénisme /panelenism/ NM Panhellenism

panier /panje/ NM 1 (gén, Sport) basket; (= contenu) basket(ful) ◆ **ils sont tous à mettre dans le même ~** (fig) there's not much to choose between them, they are all much of a muchness (Brit) ◆ **ne les mets pas tous dans le même ~** (fig) don't lump them all together ◆ **mettre ou jeter qch au ~** to throw sth out ◆ **réussir ou marquer un ~** (Basket) to score ou make a basket; → **anse, dessus, œuf**

2 (Photo : pour diapositives) magazine ◆ **~ circulaire** rotary magazine

3 (= vêtement) pannier ◆ **robe à ~s** dress with panniers

COMP **panier à bouteilles** bottle-carrier
panier de crabes (fig) **c'est un ~ de crabes** they're always fighting among themselves, they're always at each other's throats
panier à frites chip basket (Brit), fry basket (US)
panier à linge linen basket
le panier de la ménagère (Écon) the housewife's shopping basket
panier de monnaies (Fin) basket of currencies
panier à ouvrage workbasket
panier percé (fig) spendthrift
panier à provisions shopping basket
panier à salade (Culin) salad shaker ou basket; (* = camion) police van, Black Maria * (Brit), paddy waggon * (US)

panière /panjɛʀ/ NF large basket

panier-repas (pl **paniers-repas**) /panjeʀəpa/ NM lunch ou dinner ou picnic basket, packed lunch

panifiable /panifjabl/ ADJ (suitable for) breadmaking (épith)

panification /panifikasjɔ̃/ NF bread-making

panifier /panifje/ ▸ conjug 7 ◂ VT to make bread from

panini /panini/ NM panini

paniquant, e /panikɑ̃, ɑ̃t/ ADJ scary *

paniquard * /panikaʀ/ NM (péj) coward, yellow belly *

panique /panik/ NF panic ◆ **pris de ~** panic-stricken ◆ **un mouvement de ~ a saisi ou s'est emparé de la foule** a wave of panic swept through the crowd ◆ **cela a provoqué un mouvement de ~ parmi la population** it caused panic among ou sent a wave of panic through the population ◆ **il y a eu un début de ~ chez les investisseurs** investors were beginning to panic ou were showing signs of panic ◆ **pas de ~ !** * don't panic!, there's no need to panic! ◆ **c'était la ~ (générale)** * it was panic all round ou panic stations * (Brit); → **semer, vent** ADJ ◆ **terreur ou peur ~** panic

paniquer * /panike/ ▸ conjug 1 ◂ VT ◆ **~ qn** to put the wind up sb *, to give sb a scare ◆ **il a**

essayé de me ~ he tried to put the wind up me* VI **se paniquer** VPR to panic, to get the wind up* ◆ **commencer à** ~ *ou* **à se** ~ to get panicky ◆ **il n'a pas paniqué, il ne s'est pas paniqué** he didn't panic, he kept his head ◆ **être paniqué** to be in a panic ◆ **être paniqué à l'idée de faire qch** to be scared stiff at the idea of doing sth

panislamique /panislamik/ ADJ Panislamic

panislamisme /panislamism/ NM Panislamism

panne[1] /pan/ NF 1 (= *incident*) breakdown ◆ ~ **de courant** *ou* **d'électricité** power *ou* electrical failure ◆ ~ **de secteur** local mains failure ◆ ~ **de moteur** *[d'avion, voiture]* engine failure ◆ **tolérant aux ~s** *(Ordin)* fault-tolerant ◆ **il n'a pas trouvé la** ~ he couldn't find the fault *ou* problem ◆ **il m'a fait le coup de la** ~ *(hum)* he tried on the old trick about the car breaking down ◆ **avoir une** ~ **d'oreiller** *(hum)* to oversleep ◆ **il a eu une** ~ *(sexuellement)* he couldn't rise to the occasion *(hum)*

◆ **en panne** *[machine]* out of order; *[voiture]* broken-down ◆ **être** *ou* **tomber en** ~ *[machine]* to break down ◆ **je suis tombé en** ~ **(de voiture)** my car has broken down ◆ **je suis tombé en** ~ **sèche** *ou* **en** ~ **d'essence** I have run out of petrol *(Brit) ou* gas *(US)* ◆ **je suis en** ~ **de réfrigérateur** my refrigerator is broken ◆ **mettre en** ~ *(Naut)* to bring to, to heave to ◆ **le candidat est resté en** ~ (= *ne savait pas quoi dire)* the candidate was at a loss for words ◆ **les travaux sont en** ~ work has come to a halt ◆ **ce projet est en** ~ work is at a standstill *ou* has come to a halt on this project ◆ **laisser qn en** ~ to leave sb in the lurch, to let sb down ◆ **je suis en** ~ **de cigarettes/d'idées/d'inspiration** I've run out of *ou* I'm out of cigarettes/of ideas/of inspiration ◆ **rester en** ~ **devant une difficulté** to be stumped* (by a problem)

2 *(Théât* = *rôle mineur)* bit part

panne[2] /pan/ NF 1 (= *graisse)* fat 2 (= *étoffe)* panne 3 (= *poutre)* purlin 4 *[de marteau]* peen; *[de piolet]* adz(e)

panneau (pl **panneaux**) /pano/ NM *(Art, Couture, Menuiserie)* panel; (= *écriteau)* sign, notice; *(Constr)* prefabricated section; *(Basket)* backboard ◆ **les ~x qui ornent la salle** the panelling round the room ◆ **à ~x** panelled ◆ **tomber** *ou* **donner dans le** ~* to fall *ou* walk (right) into the trap, to fall for it*

COMP **panneau d'affichage** *(pour résultats etc)* notice board *(Brit)*, bulletin board *(US)*; *(pour publicité)* billboard, hoarding *(Brit)*
panneau d'écoutille *(Naut)* hatch cover
panneaux électoraux *notice boards for election posters*
panneau indicateur signpost
panneau lumineux electronic display (sign) board; *[de stade]* electronic scoreboard
panneau de particules chipboard *(NonC)*
panneau publicitaire billboard, hoarding *(Brit)*
panneau de signalisation roadsign, traffic sign
panneau solaire solar panel
panneau de stop stop sign
panneau vitré glass panel

panonceau (pl **panonceaux**) /panɔ̃so/ NM (= *plaque de médecin)* plaque; (= *écriteau publicitaire)* sign

panoplie /panɔpli/ NF 1 (= *jouet)* outfit ◆ ~ **d'Indien** Red Indian outfit ◆ ~ **d'armes** *(sur un mur)* display of weapons; *[de gangster, policier]* armoury *(Brit)*, armory *(US)* ◆ **il a sorti toute sa** ~ *(hum* = *instruments)* he brought out all his equipment ◆ **il a la** ~ **du parfait explorateur** he has everything the best-equipped explorer could require 2 (= *gamme) [d'arguments, médicaments, sanctions, services]* range; *[de mesures]* package, range

panorama /panɔʀama/ NM *(lit)* panorama ◆ **l'émission dresse un** ~ **complet de l'histoire du 20e siècle** the programme gives a comprehensive overview of the history of the 20th century ◆ **le** ~ **politique a complètement changé** the political landscape has been transformed

panoramique /panɔʀamik/ ADJ *[vue, appareil-photo, photo]* panoramic; *[restaurant]* with a panoramic view; *[carrosserie]* with panoramic *ou* wraparound windows; *[car, voiture]* with wraparound windscreen ◆ **ascenseur** ~ glass lift *(Brit) ou* elevator *(US)* ◆ **écran** ~ *(Ciné)* wide *ou* panoramic screen ◆ **wagon** ~ observation car NM *(Ciné, TV)* panoramic shot

panosse /panɔs/ NF *(Helv)* floorcloth ◆ **passer la** ~ to mop the floor

panse /pɑ̃s/ NF *[de ruminant]* paunch; * *[de personne]* paunch, belly*; *[de bouteille]* belly ◆ **s'en mettre plein la** ~* to stuff o.s.* *ou* one's face* ◆ **j'ai la** ~ **bien remplie*** I'm full to bursting* ◆ **manger à s'en faire crever** *ou* **éclater la** ~* to eat until one's fit to burst, to stuff o.s.* *ou* one's face* ◆ **je pourrais manger des cerises à m'en faire crever la** ~* I could eat cherries till they come out of my ears*

pansement /pɑ̃smɑ̃/ NM *(Méd) [de plaie, membre]* dressing; (= *bandage)* bandage; (= *sparadrap)* plaster *(Brit)*, Band Aid ® ◆ **faire un** ~ *(gén)* to dress a wound; *(sur une dent)* to put in a temporary filling ◆ **refaire un** ~ to put a clean dressing on a wound ◆ **(tout) couvert de ~s** (all) bandaged up ◆ ~ **adhésif** sticking plaster *(Brit)*, Band Aid ®

panser /pɑ̃se/ ▸ conjug 1 ◂ VT 1 *(Méd) [+ plaie]* to dress; *[+ bras, jambe]* to put a dressing on; *(avec un bandage)* to bandage; *(avec du sparadrap)* to put a plaster *(Brit) ou* a Band Aid ® on; *[+ blessé]* to dress the wounds of ◆ ~ **ses blessures** *ou* **ses plaies** *(fig)* to lick one's wounds ◆ ~ **les blessures de l'histoire** to heal the wounds of history ◆ **le temps panse les blessures (du cœur)** time is a great healer 2 *[+ cheval]* to groom

panseur, -euse /pɑ̃sœʀ, øz/ NM,F wound care nurse

panslavisme /pɑ̃slavism/ NM Pan-Slavism

panslaviste /pɑ̃slavist/ ADJ Pan-Slav(onic) NMF Pan-Slavist

pansu, e /pɑ̃sy/ ADJ *[personne]* potbellied, paunchy; *[vase]* potbellied

pantacourt /pɑ̃takuʀ/ NM (pair of) pedalpushers

pantagruélique /pɑ̃tagʀyelik/ ADJ pantagruelian

pantalon /pɑ̃talɔ̃/ NM 1 *(Habillement)* (pair of) trousers, (pair of) pants *(US)*; († = *sous-vêtement)* knickers ◆ **un** ~ **neuf** a new pair of trousers *ou* pants *(US)*, new trousers *ou* pants *(US)* ◆ **10 ~s** 10 pairs of trousers *ou* pants *(US)* ◆ ~ **cigarette** straight(-leg) *ou* cigarette trousers *ou* pants *(US)* ◆ ~ **de** *ou* **en flanelle** flannels ◆ ~ **de golf** plus fours ◆ ~ **de pyjama** pyjama *ou* pajama *(US)* bottoms ◆ ~ **de ski** ski pants; → **corsaire, porter** 2 *(Théât)* **Pantalon** Pantaloon

pantalonnade /pɑ̃talɔnad/ NF *(Théât)* slapstick comedy, knockabout farce *(Brit)*; *(péj)* tomfoolery *(NonC)*

pantelant, e /pɑ̃t(ə)lɑ̃, ɑ̃t/ ADJ *[personne]* gasping for breath *(attrib)*, panting; *[gorge]* heaving; *[cadavre, animal]* twitching

panthéisme /pɑ̃teism/ NM pantheism

panthéiste /pɑ̃teist/ ADJ pantheistic NMF pantheist

panthéon /pɑ̃teɔ̃/ NM 1 (= *bâtiment)* pantheon ◆ **le Panthéon** the Pantheon 2 (= *divinités, personnages célèbres)* pantheon ◆ **le** ~ **grec/romain** the Greek/Roman pantheon ◆ **le** ~ **littéraire** the literary pantheon, the great names of literature ◆ **ce film est entré au** ~ **du cinéma** this film has become a classic

panthéoniser /pɑ̃teonize/ ▸ conjug 1 ◂ VT *[+ personne]* to elevate to the Hall of Fame

panthère /pɑ̃tɛʀ/ NF 1 (= *félin)* panther ◆ ~ **noire** black panther ◆ **sa femme est une vraie** ~ his wife is a real hellcat* 2 *(Hist US)* **Panthères noires** Black Panthers

pantin /pɑ̃tɛ̃/ NM (= *jouet)* jumping jack; *(péj* = *personne)* puppet

pantographe /pɑ̃tɔgʀaf/ NM pantograph

pantois, e /pɑ̃twa, az/ ADJ stunned ◆ **j'en suis resté** ~ I was stunned

pantomime /pɑ̃tɔmim/ NF (= *art)* mime *(NonC)*; (= *spectacle)* mime show; *(fig)* scene, fuss *(NonC)* ◆ **il nous a fait la** ~ **pour avoir un vélo** he made a great fuss about having a bike

pantouflage /pɑ̃tuflaʒ/ NM *(arg Admin) [de fonctionnaire]* leaving the civil service to work in the private sector

pantouflard, e* /pɑ̃tuflaʀ, aʀd/ ADJ *[personne, caractère]* stay-at-home *(épith)*; *[vie]* quiet, uneventful, humdrum NM,F stay-at-home

pantoufle /pɑ̃tufl/ NF slipper ◆ **il était en ~s** he was in his slippers

pantoufler /pɑ̃tufle/ ▸ conjug 1 ◂ VI 1 *(arg Admin) [fonctionnaire]* to leave the civil service to work in the private sector 2 (* = *paresser)* to laze *ou* lounge around (at home)

panty (pl **panties**) /pɑ̃ti/ NM (= *gaine)* panty girdle

panure /panyʀ/ NF breadcrumbs

Panurge /panyʀʒ/ NM → **mouton**

PAO /peao/ NF (abrév de **publication assistée par ordinateur**) DTP

paon /pɑ̃/ NM peacock ◆ **faire le** ~ to strut about (like a peacock) ◆ **fier** *ou* **vaniteux comme un** ~ proud as a peacock; → **parer[1]**

paonne /pan/ NF peahen

PAP /pap/ NM (abrév de **prêt aidé d'accession à la propriété**) → **prêt[2]**

papa /papa/ NM *(gén)* dad; *(langage enfantin)* daddy; *(langage de bébé)* dada ◆ ~**-poule** doting father ◆ **la musique/les voitures de** ~* old-fashioned music/cars ◆ **c'est vraiment l'usine de** ~ **!*** this factory is really antiquated! *ou* behind the times! ◆ **conduire à la** ~* to potter along *(Brit)*, to drive at a snail's pace ◆ **alors** ~, **tu avances ?*** come on grandad, get a move on!* ◆ **fils (ou fille) à** ~ *(péj)* rich kid* ◆ **jouer au** ~ **et à la maman** to play mummies *(Brit) ou* mommies *(US)* and daddies, to play house ◆ **il préfère rester chez ~-maman*** he prefers to stay with his Mum and Dad; → **gâteau**

papal, e (mpl **-aux**) /papal, o/ ADJ papal

paparazzi /papaʀadzi/ NMPL *(péj)* paparazzi

papauté /papote/ NF papacy

papavérine /papaveʀin/ NF papaverine

papaye /papaj/ NF pawpaw, papaya

papayer /papaje/ NM pawpaw *ou* papaya (tree)

pape /pap/ NM pope; *[d'école littéraire etc]* leading light ◆ **le** ~ **Jean XXIII** Pope John XXIII ◆ **du** ~ papal

papé /pape/ NM ⇒ **papet**

Papeete /papet/ N Papeete

papelard[1]* /paplaʀ/ NM (= *feuille)* (bit of) paper; (= *article de journal)* article; (= *journal)* paper ◆ **~s** (= *papiers d'identité)* papers

papelard[2], e /paplaʀ, aʀd/ ADJ *(littér)* suave

paperasse /papʀas/ NF *(péj)* ◆ **~(s)** *(= documents)* papers, bumf* *(Brit)*; *(à remplir)* forms ◆ **j'ai des ~s ou de la ~ à faire** I've got some paperwork to do

paperasserie /papʀasʀi/ NF *(péj : = travail)* paperwork ◆ **~ administrative** red tape

paperassier, -ière /papʀasje, jɛʀ/ *(péj)* ADJ *[personne]* fond of paperwork; *[administration]* cluttered with red tape, obsessed with form filling NM,F *(= bureaucrate)* penpusher *(Brit)*, pencilpusher *(US)* ◆ **quel ~ !** he's forever poring over his papers!

papesse /papɛs/ NF female pope; *[d'école littéraire etc]* leading light ◆ **la ~ Jeanne** Pope Joan

papet /pape/ NM *(terme du Sud) (= grand-père)* grandpa*; *(= vieil homme)* old man

papeterie /papetʀi/ NF *(= magasin)* stationer's (shop); *(= fourniture)* stationery; *(= fabrique)* paper mill; *(= fabrication)* paper-making industry; *(= commerce)* stationery trade

papetier, -ière /pap(ə)tje, jɛʀ/ NM,F *(= vendeur)* stationer; *(= fabricant)* paper-maker ◆ **~-libraire** stationer and bookseller

papi /papi/ NM *(langage enfantin)* grandad*, grandpa*; *(* = vieil homme)* old man

papier /papje/ NM 1 *(= matière)* paper ◆ **morceau/bout de ~** piece/bit ou slip of paper ◆ **de ou en ~** paper *(épith)* ◆ **mets-moi cela sur ~** *(pour ne pas oublier)* write that down for me; *(pour confirmation écrite)* let me have that in writing ◆ **sur le ~** *(= en projet, théoriquement)* on paper ◆ **jeter une idée sur le ~** to jot down an idea; → **noircir, pâte**

2 *(= feuille écrite)* paper; *(= feuille blanche)* sheet ou piece of paper; *(Presse = article)* article ◆ **~s personnels** personal papers ◆ **être/ne pas être dans les petits ~s de qn** to be in sb's good/bad books ◆ **un ~ à signer/à remplir** a form to be signed/filled in ◆ **faire un ~ sur qn** *(Presse)* to do an article ou a story on sb ◆ **rayez cela de vos ~s !** *(fig)* you can forget about that!

3 *(= emballage)* paper; *[de bonbon]* paper, wrapper

4 ◆ **~s (d'identité)** (identity) papers ◆ **vos ~s, s'il vous plaît !** could I see your identity papers, please?; *(automobiliste)* may I see your driving licence *(Brit)* ou driver's license *(US)*, please? ◆ **ses ~s ne sont pas en règle** his papers are not in order

COMP **papier alu***, **papier aluminium** aluminium *(Brit)* ou aluminum *(US)* foil, tinfoil
papier d'argent silver foil ou paper, tinfoil
papier d'Arménie incense paper
papier bible bible paper, India paper
papier (de) brouillon rough paper
papier buvard blotting paper
papier cadeau gift wrap, wrapping paper
papier calque tracing paper
papier carbone carbon paper
papier chiffon rag paper
papier à cigarettes cigarette paper
papier collant † sticky tape
papier collé *(Art)* (paper) collage
papier en continu *(Ordin)* continuous stationery
papier couché art paper
papier crépon crêpe paper
papier cul* bogpaper* *(Brit)*, TP* *(US)*
papier à dessin drawing paper
papier doré gold paper
papier d'emballage *(gén)* wrapping paper; *(brun, kraft)* brown paper
papier à en-tête headed notepaper
papier d'étain tinfoil, silver paper
papier glacé glazed paper
papiers gras *(= ordures)* litter, rubbish
papier hygiénique toilet paper
papier journal newspaper
papier kraft ® brown wrapping paper
papier à lettres writing paper, notepaper
papier libre plain unheaded paper ◆ **envoyez votre réponse sur ~ libre à ...** send your answer on a sheet of paper to ...
papier mâché papier-mâché ◆ **mine de ~ mâché** pasty complexion
papier machine typing paper
papiers militaires army papers
papier millimétré graph paper
papier ministre ≃ foolscap paper ◆ **écrit sur ~ ministre** written on official paper
papier à musique manuscript *(Brit)* ou music *(US)* paper
papier paraffiné *(gén)* wax paper; *(Culin)* greaseproof *(Brit)* ou wax *(US)* paper
papier peint wallpaper
papier pelure India paper
papier sensible *(Photo)* bromide paper
papier de soie tissue paper
papier sulfurisé ⇒ **papier paraffiné**
papier timbré stamped paper
papier toilette toilet paper
papier de tournesol litmus paper
papier de verre glasspaper, sandpaper

papier-émeri (pl **papiers-émeri**) /papjeem(ə)ʀi/ NM emery paper

papier-filtre (pl **papiers-filtres**) /papjefiltʀ/ NM filter paper

papier-monnaie (pl **papiers-monnaies**) /papjemɔnɛ/ NM paper money

papille /papij/ NF papilla ◆ **~s gustatives** taste buds

papillon /papijɔ̃/ NM 1 *(= insecte)* butterfly; *(= personne volage)* fickle person ◆ **(brasse) ~** *(= nage)* butterfly (stroke) ◆ **~ de nuit** moth; → **minute, nœud** 2 *(Tech = écrou)* wing ou butterfly nut 3 *(* = contravention)* (parking) ticket; *(= autocollant)* sticker

papillonner /papijɔne/ ▸ conjug 1 ◂ VI 1 *(= voltiger)* to flit about ou around *(entre* between) 2 *(entre activités diverses)* to switch back and forth, to chop and change *(Brit) (entre* between); ◆ **~ d'un sujet/d'un homme à l'autre** to flit from one subject/one man to another ◆ **~ autour d'une femme** to hover round a woman

papillote /papijɔt/ NF *(= bigoudi)* curlpaper; *[de bonbon]* (sweet *(Brit)* ou candy *(US)*) wrapper, (sweet *(Brit)* ou candy *(US)*) paper; *[de gigot]* frill; *(= papier beurré)* buttered paper; *(= papier aluminium)* tinfoil ◆ **poisson en ~** fish cooked in a parcel ou en papillotte ◆ **tu peux en faire des ~s** * you can just chuck it in the bin

papillotement /papijɔtmɑ̃/ NM 1 *[de lumière, étoiles]* twinkling *(NonC)*; *[de reflets]* sparkling *(NonC)* 2 *[de paupières]* fluttering *(NonC)*; *[d' yeux]* blinking *(NonC)*

papilloter /papijɔte/ ▸ conjug 1 ◂ VI 1 *[lumière, étoiles]* to twinkle; *[reflets]* to sparkle 2 *[paupières]* to flutter; *[yeux]* to blink

papisme /papism/ NM papism, popery

papiste /papist/ NMF papist

papivore /papivɔʀ/ NMF avid reader

papotage /papɔtaʒ/ NM *(= action)* chattering *(NonC)*; *(= propos)* (idle) chatter *(NonC)*

papoter /papɔte/ ▸ conjug 1 ◂ VI to chatter, to have a natter* *(Brit)*

papou, e /papu/ ADJ Papuan NM *(= langue)* Papuan NM,F **Papou(e)** Papuan

papouan-néo-guinéen, -enne /papwɑ̃neɔgineɛ̃, ɛn/ ADJ Papua-New-Guinean, (of) Papua New Guinea NM,F **Papouan-Néo-Guinéen(ne)** Papua-New-Guinean

Papouasie-Nouvelle-Guinée /papwazinuvɛlgine/ NF Papua New Guinea

papouille* /papuj/ NF tickling *(NonC)* ◆ **faire des ~s à qn** to tickle sb

papounet /papunɛ/ NM *(langage enfantin)* granddad*

paprika /papʀika/ NM paprika

papule /papyl/ NF papule, papula

papy /papi/ NM ⇒ **papi**

papy-boom /papibum/ NM *population boom among the over 50s*

papyrus /papiʀys/ NM papyrus

paqson* /paksɔ̃/ NM ⇒ **pacson**

pâque /pɑk/ NF ◆ **la ~** Passover; → aussi **Pâques**

paquebot /pak(ə)bo/ NM (ocean) liner

pâquerette /pɑkʀɛt/ NF daisy

Pâques /pɑk/ NM Easter ◆ **le lundi/la semaine de ~** Easter Monday/week ◆ **à ~ ou à la Trinité** *(fig)* some fine day *(iro)* ◆ **faire ~ avant les Rameaux** † to become pregnant before marriage ◆ **l'île de ~** Easter Island; → **dimanche, œuf** NFPL ◆ **bonnes ou joyeuses ~ !** Happy Easter! ◆ **faire ses ~** to go to Easter mass (and take communion)

paquet /pakɛ/ NM 1 *(pour emballer etc) [de café, biscuits, pâtes, riz, farine, lessive]* packet *(Brit)*, package *(US)*; *[de cigarettes]* packet, pack *(US)*; *[de bonbons, sucre]* bag, packet; *[de cartes à jouer]* pack *(Brit)*, deck *(surtout US)*; *[de linge]* bundle ◆ **il fume deux ~s par jour** he smokes forty a day, he smokes two packs a day *(US)* ◆ **porter qn comme un ~ de linge sale** to carry sb like a sack of potatoes ◆ **c'est un vrai ~ de nerfs** *(fig)* he's a bag ou bundle of nerves ◆ **c'est un vrai ~ d'os** he's a bag of bones

2 *(= colis)* parcel, package ◆ **mettre en ~** to parcel up, to package up ◆ **faire un ~** to make up a parcel ou package

3 *(= tas)* **~ de** *[+ neige]* pile ou mass of; *[+ boue]* lump of; *[+ billets]* wad of

4 *(Rugby)* **~ (d'avants)** pack (of forwards)

5 *(Naut)* **~ de mer** big wave

6 *(* = argent)* **ça coûte un ~** it costs a small fortune ou a packet* *(Brit)* ◆ **il a touché un bon ~** he got a tidy sum* ◆ **ils lui ont donné un bon petit ~ pour qu'il se taise** they gave him a tidy little sum* to keep him quiet

7 *(locutions)* **faire son ~ ou ses ~s** to pack one's bags ◆ **lâcher son ~ à qn** † to tell sb a few home truths ◆ **mettre le ~** *(argent)* to spare no expense; *(efforts, moyens)* to pull out all the stops; → **risquer**

paquetage /pak(ə)taʒ/ NM *(Mil)* pack, kit ◆ **faire son ~** to get one's pack ou kit ready

paquet-cadeau (pl **paquets-cadeaux**) /pakɛkado/ NM giftwrapped parcel ◆ **pouvez-vous me faire un ~ ?** could you giftwrap it for me?

paquet-poste (pl **paquets-poste**) /pakɛpɔst/ NM mailing box

par[1] /paʀ/

PRÉPOSITION

GRAMMAIRE ACTIVE 44.1

Lorsque **par** s'emploie dans des expressions telles que **par cœur, par terre, par principe, passer par, un par un**, etc, cherchez sous l'autre mot.

1 agent, cause **le carreau a été cassé ~ l'orage/~ un enfant** the pane was broken by the storm/by a child ◆ **accablé ~ le désespoir** overwhelmed with despair ◆ **elle nous a fait porter des fraises ~ son fils** she got her son to bring us some strawberries, she had her son bring us some strawberries ◆ **il a appris la nouvelle ~ le journal/~ un ami** he learned the news from the paper/from ou through a friend ◆ **elle veut tout faire ~ elle-même** she wants to do everything (for) herself ◆ **la découverte de la pénicilline ~ Fleming** Fleming's discovery of penicillin, the discovery of penicillin by Fleming

2 manière, moyen ~ **le train** by rail *ou* train ◆ ~ **route** by road ◆ ~ **la poste** by post *ou* mail, through the post ◆ **communiquer ~ fax/Internet** to communicate by *ou* via fax/the Internet ◆ **la porte ferme ~ un verrou** the gate is locked with a bolt *ou* by means of a bolt ◆ **obtenir qch ~ la force/la persuasion/la ruse** to obtain sth by force/with persuasion/by *ou* through cunning ◆ **arriver ~ l'intelligence/le travail** to succeed through intelligence/hard work ◆ **ils se ressemblent ~ leur sens de l'humour** they are alike in their sense of humour ◆ **ils diffèrent ~ bien des côtés** they are different *ou* they differ in many ways *ou* aspects ◆ **il descend des Bourbons ~ sa mère** he is descended from the Bourbons through his mother *ou* on his mother's side

3 raison, motif : généralement sans article ~ **pure bêtise** through *ou* out of sheer stupidity ◆ ~ **habitude** by *ou* out of *ou* from (sheer) habit ◆ **faire qch ~ plaisir/pitié** to do sth for pleasure/out of pity ◆ ~ **souci d'exactitude** for the sake of accuracy, out of a concern for accuracy ◆ ~ **manque de temps** owing to lack of time ◆ **la ville est célèbre ~ ses musées** the city is famous for its museums

4 lieu, direction (*= en empruntant ce chemin*) by (way of); (*= en traversant*) through, across; (*suivi d'un nom propre*) via; (*= en longeant*) along ◆ **il est sorti ~ la fenêtre** he went out by *ou* through the window ◆ **il est venu ~ le chemin le plus court** he took the shortest route ◆ **nous sommes venus ~ la côte/~ Lyon/~ l'Espagne** we came along the coast/via Lyons/via *ou* through Spain ◆ **se promener ~ les rues/les champs** to walk through the streets/through *ou* across the fields ◆ ~ **tout le pays** throughout *ou* all over the country ◆ **sortez ~ ici/là** go out this/that way ◆ ~ **où sont-ils entrés ?** which way *ou* how did they get in? ◆ ~ **où est-il venu ?** which way did he come? ◆ **la rumeur s'était répandue ~ la ville** the rumour had spread through the town ◆ **l'épave repose ~ 20 mètres de fond** the wreck is lying 20 metres down ◆ ~ **10° de latitude sud** at a latitude of 10° south ◆ **arriver ~ le nord/la gauche/le haut** *ou* **en haut** to arrive from the north/the left/the top

5 distribution, mesure **gagner tant ~ semaine/mois** to earn so much a *ou* per week/month ◆ ~ **an** a *ou* per year ◆ **rendement de 10% ~ an** yield of 10% per annum ◆ **trois fois ~ jour/semaine/mois** three times a day/a week/a month ◆ **marcher deux ~ deux/trois ~ trois** to walk two by two *ou* in twos/three by three *ou* in threes ◆ **six étudiants ~ appartement** six students to a flat *ou* per flat ◆ **ils déduisent 5 € ~ enfant** they take off €5 for each child *ou* per child ◆ ~ **poignées/charretées** in handfuls/cartloads, by the handful/cartload

6 = pendant ~ **une belle nuit d'été** on a beautiful summer('s) night ◆ **il partit ~ une pluvieuse journée de mars** he left on a rainy March day ◆ **ne restez pas dehors ~ ce froid/cette chaleur** (*en parlant du climat, de la température*) don't stay out in this cold/this heat ◆ **évitez cette route ~ temps de pluie/de brouillard** avoid that road in wet weather *ou* when it's wet/in fog *ou* when it's foggy ◆ **sortir ~ moins 10°** to go out when it's minus 10°

7 dans des exclamations, des serments by ◆ ~ **tous les dieux du ciel** in heaven's name, by heaven ◆ ~ **tout ce que j'ai de plus cher, je vous promets que ...** I promise you by all that I hold most dear that ...

8 locutions

◆ **commencer/finir** *etc* **par** to start/end with ◆ **on a commencé ~ des huîtres** we started with oysters, we had oysters to start ◆ **la fête se termina ~ un feu d'artifice** the party ended with a fireworks display ◆ **on a clôturé la séance ~ des élections** elections brought the meeting to a close, the meeting closed with elections ◆ **il a fini ~ tout avouer** he finally confessed everything, he ended up confessing everything ◆ **il finit ~ m'agacer avec ses plaisanteries !** his jokes are starting to get on my nerves!

◆ **de par** (*frm = à travers*) ◆ **il voyageait de ~ le monde** he travelled throughout *ou* all over the world ◆ **il y a de ~ le monde des milliers de gens qui pensent que ...** thousands of people the world over *ou* throughout the world think that ...

(*= à cause de*) because of ◆ **de ~ son milieu et son éducation, il ...** because of *ou* by virtue of his background and upbringing, he ... ◆ **de ~ la nature même de ses activités** by the very nature of his activities

(*= par l'autorité de, au nom de*) ◆ **de ~ le roi** by order of the king, in the name of the king ◆ **de ~ la loi** by law, legally

par[2] /paʀ/ NM (*Golf*) par

para * /paʀa/ NM (abrév de **parachutiste**) para *

parabellum /paʀabelɔm/ NM parabellum, big automatic pistol

parabole /paʀabɔl/ NF (*Math*) parabola; (*Rel*) parable; (*TV*) dish aerial, satellite dish, dish antenna (*US*)

parabolique /paʀabɔlik/ ADJ parabolic ◆ **antenne ~** satellite dish, dish aerial, dish antenna (*US*); → **ski** NM (*= radiateur*) electric fire

paracentèse /paʀasɛ̃tɛz/ NF paracentesis

paracétamol /paʀasetamɔl/ NM paracetamol

parachèvement /paʀaʃɛvmɑ̃/ NM perfection, perfecting

parachever /paʀaʃ(ə)ve/ ▸ conjug 5 ◂ VT to perfect, to put the finishing touches to

parachutage /paʀaʃytaʒ/ NM [*de soldats, vivres*] parachuting, dropping *ou* landing by parachute ◆ **ils n'ont pas apprécié le ~ d'un ministre dans leur département** they didn't like the way a minister was suddenly landed on them ◆ **tout le monde parle de son ~ à la tête du service** everybody is talking about the way he's suddenly been appointed head of department

parachute /paʀaʃyt/ NM parachute ◆ ~ **ventral/dorsal/de secours** lap-pack/back(-pack)/reserve parachute ◆ **descendre en ~** to parachute down ◆ **faire du ~ ascensionnel** (*tiré par une voiture*) to go parascending; (*tiré par un bateau*) to go parasailing ◆ ~ **doré** *ou* **en or** (*= indemnités*) golden parachute

parachuter /paʀaʃyte/ ▸ conjug 1 ◂ VT 1 (*Mil, Sport*) to parachute, to drop by parachute 2 (* *= désigner*) ~ **qn à un poste** to pitchfork sb into a job ◆ ~ **un candidat dans une circonscription** (*Pol*) to bring in *ou* field a candidate from outside a constituency ◆ **ils nous ont parachuté un nouveau directeur de Paris** a new manager from Paris has suddenly been landed on us *

parachutisme /paʀaʃytism/ NM parachuting ◆ ~ **ascensionnel** (*par voiture*) parascending; (*par bateau*) parasailing ◆ **faire du ~** to go parachuting ◆ **faire du ~ en chute libre** to skydive, to go skydiving

parachutiste /paʀaʃytist/ NMF (*Sport*) parachutist; (*Mil*) paratrooper ◆ **nos unités de ~s** our paratroops ADJ [*unité*] paratrooper (*épith*)

parade /paʀad/ NF 1 (*= ostentation*) show, ostentation ◆ **faire ~ de** [*+ érudition*] to parade, to display, to show off; [*+ relations*] to boast about, to brag about ◆ **de ~** [*uniforme, épée*] ceremonial ◆ **afficher une générosité de ~** (*péj*) to make an outward show *ou* display of generosity ◆ **ce n'est que de la ~** it's just done for show

2 (*= spectacle*) parade ◆ ~ **militaire/foraine** military/circus parade ◆ **les troupes s'avancèrent comme à la ~** the troops moved forward as if they were (still) on the parade ground *ou* on parade ◆ ~ **nuptiale** (*Zool*) mating *ou* courtship display ◆ **comme à la ~** (*= avec facilité*) with panache

3 (*Équitation*) pulling up

4 (*Escrime*) parry, parade; (*Boxe*) parry; (*Ftbl*) dummy; (*fig*) answer; (*orale*) riposte, rejoinder ◆ **il faut trouver la (bonne) ~** we must find the (right) answer ◆ **nous n'avons pas encore trouvé la ~ contre cette maladie** we still haven't found a way to counter this disease

parader /paʀade/ ▸ conjug 1 ◂ VI (*péj*) to strut about, to show off; (*Mil*) to parade

paradigmatique /paʀadigmatik/ ADJ paradigmatic NF paradigmatics (*sg*)

paradigme /paʀadigm/ NM paradigm

paradis /paʀadi/ NM 1 paradise, heaven ◆ **le Paradis terrestre** (*Bible*) the Garden of Eden; (*fig*) heaven on earth ◆ **aller au** *ou* **en ~** to go to heaven ◆ **c'est le ~ des enfants/chasseurs ici** it's a children's/hunters' paradise here ◆ **il s'est cru au ~** (*fig*) he was over the moon, he was in (seventh) heaven ◆ ~ **fiscal** tax haven; → **emporter, oiseau** 2 † **le ~** (*Théât*) the gallery, the gods * (*Brit*)

paradisiaque /paʀadizjak/ ADJ heavenly ◆ **une vision ~** a vision of paradise ◆ **c'est ~ ici** it's paradise here

paradisier /paʀadizje/ NM bird of paradise

paradoxal, e (mpl **-aux**) /paʀadɔksal, o/ GRAMMAIRE ACTIVE 53.3 ADJ paradoxical ◆ **il est assez ~ de ...** it doesn't make sense to ..., it's somewhat illogical to ...; → **sommeil**

paradoxalement /paʀadɔksalmɑ̃/ ADV paradoxically

paradoxe /paʀadɔks/ NM paradox

parafe /paʀaf/ NM ⇒ **paraphe**

parafer /paʀafe/ ▸ conjug 1 ◂ VT ⇒ **parapher**

parafeur /paʀafœʀ/ NM ⇒ **parapheur**

paraffinage /paʀafinaʒ/ NM paraffining

paraffine /paʀafin/ NF (*gén : solide*) paraffin wax; (*Chim*) paraffin

paraffiner /paʀafine/ ▸ conjug 1 ◂ VT to paraffin(e); → **papier**

parafiscal, e (mpl **-aux**) /paʀafiskal, o/ ADJ ◆ **taxe ~e** special tax (*road-fund tax, stamp duty etc*)

parages /paʀaʒ/ NMPL 1 ◆ **dans les ~** (*= dans la région*) in the area, in the vicinity; (** = pas très loin*) round about ◆ **est-ce que Sylvie est dans les ~ ?** * is Sylvie about? ◆ **dans ces ~** in these parts ◆ **dans les ~ de** near, round about, in the vicinity of 2 (*Naut*) waters, region

paragraphe /paʀagʀaf/ NM paragraph; (*Typo*) section (mark)

paragrêle /paʀagʀɛl/ ADJ anti-hail (*épith*)

Paraguay /paʀagwɛ/ NM Paraguay

paraguayen, -enne /paʀagwajɛ̃, ɛn/ ADJ Paraguayan NM,F **Paraguayen(ne)** Paraguayan

paraître /paʀɛtʀ/ ▸ conjug 57 ◂ VI 1 (*= se montrer*) (*gén*) to appear; [*personne*] to appear, to make one's appearance ◆ ~ **en scène/à** *ou* **sur l'écran/au balcon** to appear on stage/on the screen/on the balcony ◆ **il n'a pas paru de la journée** he hasn't appeared all day ◆ **il n'a pas paru à la réunion** he didn't appear *ou* turn up at the meeting ◆ ~ **en public** to appear in public, to make a public appearance ◆ **un sourire parut sur ses lèvres** a smile appeared on his lips

2 (*Presse*) to appear, to be published, to come out ◆ **faire ~ qch** [*éditeur*] to bring sth out, to publish sth; [*auteur*] to have sth published ◆ **"vient de paraître"** "just out", "just published" ◆ **"à paraître"** "forthcoming"

3 (= *briller*) to be noticed ◆ **chercher à ~** to show off ◆ **le désir de ~** the desire to be noticed *ou* to show off

4 (= *être visible*) to show (through) ◆ **laisser ~ ses sentiments/son irritation** to let one's feelings/one's annoyance show

5 (= *sembler*) to look, to seem, to appear ◆ **elle paraît heureuse** she seems (to be) happy ◆ **cela me paraît être une erreur** it looks like a mistake to me ◆ **elle paraissait l'aimer** she seemed *ou* appeared to love him ◆ **il paraît 20 ans** (= *il est plus jeune*) he looks (at least) 20; (= *il est plus âgé*) he only looks 20 ◆ **le voyage a paru long** the journey seemed long ◆ **cette robe la fait ~ plus grande** that dress makes her look taller

VB IMPERS 1 (= *il semble*) **il me paraît difficile qu'elle puisse venir** it seems to me that it will be difficult for her to come ◆ **il ne lui paraît pas essentiel qu'elle sache** he doesn't think it essential for her to know ◆ **il lui paraissait impossible de refuser** he didn't see how he could refuse ◆ **il paraîtrait ridicule de s'offenser** it would seem stupid to take offence

2 (= *le bruit court*) **il va se marier, paraît-il** *ou* **à ce qu'il paraît** apparently he's getting married, he's getting married apparently ◆ **il paraît** *ou* **il paraîtrait qu'on va construire une autoroute** apparently *ou* it seems they're going to build a motorway ◆ **il paraît que oui** so it seems *ou* appears, apparently so ◆ **il paraît que non** apparently not

3 (*avec nég*) **il n'y paraîtra bientôt plus** (*tache, cicatrice*) there will soon be no trace of it left; (*maladie*) soon no one will ever know you've had it ◆ **sans qu'il n'y paraisse rien** without anything being obvious, without letting anything show ◆ **sans qu'il y paraisse, elle a obtenu ce qu'elle voulait** she got what she wanted without appearing to

NM ◆ **le ~** appearance(s)

paralangage /paralɑ̃gaʒ/ NM paralanguage

paralittérature /paraliteratyr/ NF marginal literature

parallactique /paralaktik/ ADJ parallactic

parallaxe /paralaks/ NF parallax

parallèle /paralɛl/ ADJ 1 (*Géom, Math*) parallel (*à* to) → **barre**

2 (= *comparable*) parallel, similar; [*enquêtes*] parallel ◆ **mener une action ~** to take similar action, to act on *ou* along the same lines ◆ **les deux institutions ont suivi une évolution ~** the two institutions have developed in parallel

3 (= *non officiel*) [*marché, cours, police, économie*] unofficial; [*énergie, société, médecine*] alternative; [*diplomatie*] parallel, unofficial

4 (= *indépendant*) [*univers*] parallel; (*Ordin*) [*machine, traitement*] parallel ◆ **nous menons des vies ~s** (*dans un couple*) we lead (two) separate lives ◆ **nous avons développé des activités ~s** we've developed some activities in parallel

NF (*Math*) parallel (line) ◆ **monté en ~** (*Élec*) wired (up) in parallel

NM (*Géog, fig*) parallel ◆ **établir un ~ entre deux textes** to draw a parallel between two texts

◆ **en parallèle** ◆ **faire** *ou* **mettre en ~** [+ *choses opposées*] to compare; [+ *choses semblables*] to draw a parallel between ◆ **avancer en ~** [*projets*] to move along at the same pace ◆ **une exposition était organisée en ~ à sa visite** an exhibition was mounted to coincide with his visit ◆ **elle suit des cours en ~ à son travail** she's doing a course at the same time as working

parallèlement /paralɛlmɑ̃/ ADV (*lit*) parallel (*à* to); (*fig*) (= *ensemble*) in parallel; (= *en même temps*) at the same time; (= *similairement*) in the same way

parallélépipède /paralelepipɛd/ NM parallelepiped

parallélépipédique /paralelepipedik/ ADJ parallelepipedal, parallelepipedic

parallélisme /paralelism/ NM (*lit, fig*) parallelism; [*de voiture*] wheel alignment ◆ **faire vérifier le ~ de ses roues** to have one's wheels aligned

parallélogramme /paralelɔgram/ NM parallelogram

paralympiques /paralɛ̃pik/ ADJ, NMPL ◆ **les Jeux ~, les Paralympiques** the Paralympics

paralysant, e /paralizɑ̃, ɑ̃t/ ADJ paralyzing

paralysé, e /paralize/ (ptp de **paralyser**) ADJ paralyzed ◆ **rester ~** to be left paralyzed ◆ **il est ~ des jambes** his legs are paralyzed NM,F paralytic

paralyser /paralize/ ▸ conjug 1 ◂ VT (*Méd, fig*) to paralyze ◆ **paralysé par le brouillard** [*aéroport*] fogbound ◆ **paralysé par la neige** snowbound ◆ **paralysé par la grève** [*gare*] strikebound; [*hôpital*] crippled by a strike ◆ **le trafic a été complètement paralysé** the traffic was at a complete halt *ou* standstill

paralysie /paralizi/ NF (*Méd, fig*) paralysis; (*Bible*) palsy ◆ **~ infantile** infantile paralysis ◆ **~ générale (progressive)** general paralysis of the insane ◆ **être frappé de ~** to be struck down with paralysis

paralytique /paralitik/ ADJ, NMF paralytic

paramécie /paramesi/ NF paramecium

paramédical, e (mpl **-aux**) /paramedikal, o/ ADJ paramedical ◆ **le personnel ~** the paramedics, the paramedical staff

paramétrage /parametraʒ/ NM [*de logiciel*] parametering

paramètre /paramɛtr/ NM parameter

paramétrer /parametre/ ▸ conjug 1 ◂ VT to define, to parametrize; [+ *logiciel*] to set the parameters of

paramilitaire /paramilitɛr/ ADJ paramilitary

parangon /parɑ̃gɔ̃/ NM paragon ◆ **~ de vertu** paragon of virtue

parano * /parano/ ADJ, NMF abrév de **paranoïaque** NF abrév de **paranoïa**

paranoïa /paranɔja/ NF paranoia

paranoïaque /paranɔjak/ ADJ, NMF paranoiac, paranoid

paranoïde /paranɔid/ ADJ paranoid

paranormal, e (mpl **-aux**) /paranɔrmal, o/ ADJ paranormal ◆ **le ~** the paranormal

parapente /parapɑ̃t/ NM (= *engin*) paraglider ◆ **le ~** (= *sport*) paragliding ◆ **faire du ~** to go paragliding ◆ **~ à ski** paraskiing, parapenting

parapentiste /parapɑ̃tist/ NMF paraglider ◆ **~ à ski** paraskier

parapet /parapɛ/ NM parapet

parapharmaceutique /parafarmasøtik/ ADJ [*produit*] parapharmaceutical

parapharmacie /parafarmasi/ NF personal hygiene products (*sold in pharmacies*)

paraphe /paraf/ NM (= *trait*) paraph, flourish; (= *initiales*) initials; (*littér* = *signature*) signature

parapher /parafe/ ▸ conjug 1 ◂ VT (*Admin*) to initial; (*littér* = *signer*) to sign

parapheur /parafœr/ NM signature book

paraphrase /parafraz/ NF paraphrase ◆ **faire de la ~** to paraphrase

paraphraser /parafraze/ ▸ conjug 1 ◂ VT to paraphrase

paraphrastique /parafrastik/ ADJ paraphrastic

paraplégie /parapleʒi/ NF paraplegia

paraplégique /parapleʒik/ ADJ, NMF paraplegic

parapluie /paraplɥi/ NM umbrella ◆ **~ atomique** *ou* **nucléaire** nuclear shield *ou* umbrella ◆ **ouvrir le ~** (*fig*) to take cover (*from criticism*)

parapsychique /parapsiʃik/ ADJ parapsychological

parapsychologie /parapsikɔlɔʒi/ NF parapsychology

parapsychologue /parapsikɔlɔg/ NMF parapsychologist

parapublic, -ique /parapyblik/ ADJ (= *semi-public*) semi-public

parascolaire /paraskɔlɛr/ ADJ extracurricular ◆ **l'édition ~, le ~** educational publishing (*excluding textbooks*)

parasismique /parasismik/ ADJ earthquake-resistant

parasitage /parazitaʒ/ NM [*de discussion, situation*] interference (*de* in, with)

parasitaire /parazitɛr/ ADJ 1 [*maladie, affection*] parasitic 2 [*activités*] parasitic(al)

parasite /parazit/ NM parasite; (*péj* = *personne*) parasite, sponger *, scrounger * NMPL **parasites** (= *électricité statique*) atmospherics, static; (*Radio, TV*) interference ADJ parasitic(al) ◆ **bruits ~s** (*Radio, TV*) interference; (*électricité statique*) atmospherics, static

parasiter /parazite/ ▸ conjug 1 ◂ VT [+ *plante, animal*] to live as a parasite on; (*Radio, TV*) to cause interference on; (*fig*) to interfere with, to get in the way of

parasitique /parazitik/ ADJ parasitic(al)

parasitisme /parazitism/ NM parasitism

parasitose /parazitoz/ NF parasitosis

parasol /parasɔl/ NM [*de plage*] beach umbrella, parasol; [*de café, terrasse*] sunshade, parasol; († = *ombrelle*) parasol, sunshade; → **pin**

parasympathique /parasɛ̃patik/ ADJ parasympathetic

parataxe /parataks/ NF parataxis

parathyroïde /paratirɔid/ NF parathyroid (gland)

paratonnerre /paratɔnɛr/ NM lightning conductor

paratyphique /paratifik/ ADJ paratyphoid

paratyphoïde /paratifɔid/ NF paratyphoid fever

paravent /paravɑ̃/ NM folding screen *ou* partition; (*fig*) screen

parbleu †† /parblø/ EXCL by Jove! * †

parc /park/ NM 1 (= *jardin public*) park; [*de château*] grounds; (*Mil* = *entrepôt*) depot

2 (*Écon* = *ensemble*) stock ◆ **~ automobile** [*de pays*] number of vehicles on the road; [*d'entreprise*] fleet ◆ **~ immobilier/locatif** housing/rental stock ◆ **~ ferroviaire** rolling stock ◆ **~ nucléaire** nuclear installations ◆ **le ~ français des ordinateurs individuels** the total number of personal computers owned in France ◆ **la ville dispose d'un ~ hôtelier de 7 000 chambres** the town has a total of 7,000 hotel rooms

3 (*Helv* = *stationnement*) → **place**

COMP **parc à l'anglaise** landscaped garden
parc animalier safari park
parc d'attractions amusement park
parc à bébé playpen
parc à bestiaux cattle pen *ou* enclosure
parc des expositions exhibition centre
parc à la française formal (French) garden
parc à huîtres oyster bed
parc industriel industrial estate (*Brit*) *ou* park
parc de loisirs leisure park

parc à moules mussel bed
parc à moutons sheep pen, sheepfold
parc national national park
parc naturel nature reserve
parc récréatif amusement park
parc régional country park
parc scientifique science park
parc de stationnement car park *(Brit)*, parking lot *(US)*
parc à thème theme park
parc zoologique zoological gardens

parcage /paʀkaʒ/ NM *[de moutons]* penning; *[de voitures]* parking

parcellaire /paʀselɛʀ/ ADJ (= *fragmentaire) [informations, vision]* incomplete; *[témoignage]* incomplete, fragmentary; *[travail]* fragmented

parcelle /paʀsɛl/ NF fragment, particle, bit; *(sur un cadastre)* parcel *(of land)* ◆ ~ **de terre** plot of land ◆ ~ **de vérité/bon sens** grain of truth/commonsense ◆ **il n'y a pas la moindre ~ de vérité dans ce que tu dis** there's not a grain *ou* scrap of truth in what you say ◆ **une ~ de bonheur/gloire** a bit of happiness/fame

parcellisation /paʀselizasjɔ̃/ NF *[de tâche]* breakdown into individual operations; *[de terrain]* dividing up, division

parcelliser /paʀselize/ ▸ conjug 1 ◂ VT *[+ tâche]* to break down into individual operations; *[+ terrain]* to divide up

parce que /paʀs(ə)kə/ CONJ because ◆ **Robert, de mauvaise humeur ~ fatigué, répondit ...** Robert, who was in a bad mood because he was tired, replied ... ◆ **pourquoi n'y vas-tu pas ? – ~ !** why aren't you going? – because!

parchemin /paʀʃəmɛ̃/ NM parchment; *(hum : Univ)* diploma, degree

parcheminé, e /paʀʃəmine/ (ptp de **parcheminer**) ADJ *[peau]* wrinkled; *[visage]* wizened

parcheminer /paʀʃəmine/ ▸ conjug 1 ◂ VT to give a parchment finish to VPR **se parcheminer** to wrinkle up

parcimonie /paʀsimɔni/ NF parsimony ◆ **avec ~** sparingly

parcimonieusement /paʀsimɔnjøzmɑ̃/ ADV parsimoniously, sparingly

parcimonieux, -ieuse /paʀsimɔnjø, jøz/ ADJ *[personne]* parsimonious; *[distribution]* miserly, ungenerous

par-ci par-là /paʀsipaʀla/ ADV *(espace)* here and there; *(temps)* now and then, from time to time ◆ **elle mangeait un yaourt par-ci, une pomme par-là** she'd eat the odd yoghurt or apple ◆ **avec lui, c'est toujours ma maison par-ci, ma voiture par-là** with him it's always my house this, my car that ◆ **il m'agace avec ses bien sûr par-ci, bien sûr par-là** he gets on my nerves saying "of course" all the time

parcmètre /paʀkmɛtʀ/, **parcomètre** /paʀkɔmɛtʀ/ NM (parking) meter

parcotrain /paʀkotʀɛ̃/ NM train users' car park *(Brit) ou* parking lot *(US)*

parcourir /paʀkuʀiʀ/ ▸ conjug 11 ◂ VT 1 *[+ trajet, distance]* to cover, to travel; *[+ lieu]* to go all over; *[+ pays]* to travel up and down ◆ **ils ont parcouru toute la région en un mois** they travelled the length and breadth of the region *ou* they covered the whole region in a month ◆ ~ **la ville à la recherche de qch** to search for sth all over (the) town, to scour the town for sth ◆ **leurs navires parcourent les mers** their ships sail all over ◆ **un frisson parcourut tout son corps** a shiver ran through his body ◆ **le ruisseau parcourt toute la vallée** the stream runs along *ou* through the whole valley *ou* right along the valley ◆ **l'obus parcourut le ciel** the shell flew through *ou* across the sky

2 (= *regarder rapidement) [+ lettre, livre]* to glance *ou* skim through ◆ **il parcourut la foule des yeux** he cast *ou* ran his eye over the crowd

parcours /paʀkuʀ/ NM 1 (= *distance)* distance; (= *trajet)* journey; (= *itinéraire)* route; *[de fleuve]* course ◆ **le prix du ~** the fare

2 *(Sport)* course ◆ **sur un ~ difficile** over a difficult course ◆ ~ **de golf** (= *terrain)* golf course; (= *partie, trajet)* round of golf ◆ **faire** *ou* **accomplir un ~ sans faute** *(Équitation)* to have a clear round; *(dans un jeu télévisé)* to get all the answers right ◆ **jusqu'à présent, il a réussi un ~ sans faute** *(dans sa carrière etc)* up to now, he hasn't put a foot wrong; → **accident, incident**

3 (= *activités, progression)* **son ~ politique/scolaire** his political/school career ◆ **son ~ professionnel** his career path ◆ **son ~ d'écrivain n'a pas toujours été facile** making a career as a writer has not always been easy for him

COMP **parcours du combattant** *(Mil)* assault course; *(fig)* obstacle course ◆ **faire le ~ du combattant** *(Mil)* to go round an assault course
parcours de santé fitness trail
parcours Vita ® *(Helv)* fitness trail

par-delà /paʀdəla/ PRÉP *[+ dans l'espace]* beyond; *[+ dans le temps]* across ◆ ~ **les montagnes/les mers** beyond the mountains/the seas ◆ ~ **le temps/les années** across time/the years ◆ ~ **les querelles, la solidarité demeure** there is a feeling of solidarity which goes beyond the quarrels

par-derrière /paʀdɛʀjɛʀ/ PRÉP (round) behind, round the back of ADV *[passer]* round the back; *[attaquer, emboutir]* from behind, from the rear; *[être endommagé]* at the back *ou* rear; *[se boutonner]* at the back ◆ **dire du mal de qn ~** to speak ill of sb behind their back

par-dessous /paʀd(ə)su/ PRÉP, ADV under(neath); → **jambe**

pardessus /paʀdəsy/ NM overcoat

par-dessus /paʀd(ə)sy/ PRÉP over (the top of) ◆ **il a mis un pull-over ~ sa chemise** he has put a pullover over *ou* on top of his shirt ◆ **sauter ~ une barrière/un mur** to jump over a barrier/a wall ◆ ~ **tout** above all ◆ **en avoir ~ la tête*** to be fed up to the back teeth* ◆ **j'en ai ~ la tête de toutes ces histoires** I'm sick and tired* of *ou* I'm fed up to the back teeth* with all this ◆ ~ **le marché** on top of all that ◆ ~ **bord** overboard; → **jambe** ADV over (the top)

par-devant /paʀd(ə)vɑ̃/ PRÉP *(Jur)* ◆ ~ **notaire** in the presence of *ou* before a lawyer ADV *[passer]* round the front; *[attaquer, emboutir]* from the front; *[être abîmé, se boutonner]* at the front ◆ **il te fait des compliments ~ puis dit du mal de toi par-derrière** he pays you compliments to your face but says nasty things about you behind your back

par-devers /paʀdəvɛʀ/ PRÉP *(Jur)* before ◆ ~ **soi** *(frm)* (= *en sa possession)* in one's possession

pardi † /paʀdi/ EXCL by Jove!* †

pardieu †† /paʀdjø/ EXCL by Jove!* †

pardon /paʀdɔ̃/ NM 1 *(pour s'excuser)* **demander ~ à qn d'avoir fait qch** to apologize to sb for doing *ou* having done sth ◆ **demande ~ !** say you're sorry! ◆ **(je vous demande) ~** (I'm) sorry, excuse me ◆ **c'est Maud – ~ ?** it's Maud – (I beg your) pardon? *ou* (I'm) sorry? ◆ **t'es débile* – ~ ?** you're a moron* – I beg your pardon? ◆ ~ **Monsieur, avez-vous l'heure ?** excuse me, have you got the time? ◆ **tu n'y es pas allé – (je te demande bien) ~, j'y suis allé ce matin** you didn't go – oh yes I did, I went this morning

2 (= *grâce)* forgiveness, pardon *(frm) (Jur)*

3 *(Rel) (en Bretagne)* pardon *(religious festival)* ◆ **le Grand ~, le jour du Pardon** (= *fête juive)* the Day of Atonement

4 (* : *intensif)* **et puis ~ ! il travaille dur** he works hard, I'm telling you *ou* I can tell you! ◆ **je suis peut-être un imbécile mais alors lui, ~ !** maybe I'm stupid but he's even worse! *ou* he takes the biscuit!* *(Brit) ou* cake!* *(US)* ◆ **j'ai une belle voiture mais alors celle de mon frère, ~ !** I've got a nice car but wow*, you should see my brother's! ◆ **elle a un œil au beurre noir, ~ !** she's got one hell of a black eye!*, she's got a real shiner!*

pardonnable /paʀdɔnabl/ ADJ forgivable, excusable ◆ **il l'a oublié mais c'est ~** he can be forgiven for forgetting it, he has forgotten it but you have to forgive *ou* excuse him ◆ **une erreur pareille, ce n'est pas ~** there's no excuse for making a mistake like that

pardonner /paʀdɔne/ GRAMMAIRE ACTIVE 45.1 ▸ conjug 1 ◂

VT *[+ péché]* to forgive, to pardon; *[+ indiscrétion]* to forgive, to excuse ◆ ~ **(à) qn** to forgive sb ◆ ~ **qch à qn/à qn d'avoir fait qch** to forgive sb for sth/for doing sth ◆ **pour se faire ~ son erreur** so as to be forgiven for his mistake ◆ **pardonnez-moi de vous avoir dérangé** I'm sorry to have disturbed you, excuse me for disturbing you ◆ **vous êtes tout pardonné** I'll let you off, you're forgiven ◆ **on lui pardonne tout** he gets away with everything ◆ **je ne me le pardonnerai jamais** I'll never forgive myself ◆ **ce genre d'erreur ne se pardonne pas** this is an unforgivable *ou* inexcusable mistake ◆ **pardonnez-moi, mais je crois que ...** excuse me but I think that ... ◆ **pardonnez-leur car ils ne savent pas ce qu'ils font** *(Bible)* forgive them, for they know not what they do; → **faute**

VI to forgive ◆ **il faut savoir ~** you have to forgive and forget ◆ **c'est une erreur qui ne pardonne pas** it's a fatal mistake ◆ **c'est une maladie qui ne pardonne pas** it's an illness that's always fatal

⚠ Attention à ne pas traduire automatiquement **pardonner** par **to pardon**, qui est d'un registre plus soutenu.

paré, e /paʀe/ (ptp de **parer²**) ADJ (= *prêt)* ready, all set; (= *préparé)* prepared ◆ **être ~ contre le froid** to be prepared for the cold weather

pare-avalanches /paʀavalɑ̃ʃ/ NM INV avalanche barrier

pare-balles /paʀbal/ ADJ INV bulletproof NM INV bullet shield

pare-boue /paʀbu/ NM INV mud flap

pare-brise NM INV, **parebrise** NM /paʀbʀiz/ windscreen *(Brit)*, windshield *(US)*

pare-chocs /paʀʃɔk/ NM INV bumper *(Brit)*, fender *(US)* ◆ **avancer ~ contre ~** to be bumper to bumper

pare-éclats /paʀekla/ ADJ INV ◆ **gilet ~** flak jacket NM INV *(Mil)* traverse

pare-étincelles /paʀetɛ̃sɛl/ NM INV fireguard

pare-feu /paʀfø/ NM INV *[de forêt]* firebreak, fire line; *[de foyer]* fireguard; *(Ordin)* firewall

parégorique /paʀegɔʀik/ ADJ, NM paregoric; → **élixir**

pareil, -eille /paʀɛj/ GRAMMAIRE ACTIVE 32.4

ADJ 1 (= *identique)* the same, similar, alike *(attrib)* ◆ **il n'y en a pas deux ~s** no two are the same *ou* alike ◆ ~ **que, ~ à** the same as, similar to, just like ◆ **comment va-t-elle ? – c'est toujours ~** how is she? – (she's) just the same (as ever) *ou* there's no change (in her) ◆ **c'est toujours ~, il ne peut pas être à l'heure** it's always the same, he's never on time ◆ **il est ~ à lui-même** he doesn't change, he's the same as ever ◆ **tu as vu son sac ? j'en ai un ~/presque ~** have you seen her bag? I've got one the same *ou* one just like it/one very similar *ou* almost identical ◆ **à nul autre** ~ *(littér)* peerless *(littér)*, unrivalled, unmatched ◆ **l'an dernier à pareille époque** this time last year

2 *(= tel)* such (a) ◆ **je n'ai jamais entendu ~ discours** *ou* **un discours** ~ I've never heard such a speech *ou* a speech like it ◆ **en ~ cas** in such a case ◆ **en pareille occasion** on such an occasion ◆ **à pareille heure, il devrait être debout** he ought to be up at this hour ◆ **se coucher à une heure pareille !** what a time to be going to bed!

NM,F ◆ **nos ~s** *(= nos semblables)* our fellow men; *(= nos égaux)* our equals *ou* peers ◆ **je ne retrouverai jamais son** ~ *(chose)* I'll never find another one like it; *(employé)* I'll never find another one like him *ou* to match him ◆ **ne pas avoir son** ~ **(ou sa pareille)** to be second to none ◆ **il n'a pas son ~ pour faire la mayonnaise** no-one makes mayonnaise as well as he does ◆ **vous et vos ~s** you and your kind, people like you ◆ **sans** ~ unparalleled, unequalled ◆ **c'est du ~ au même*** it doesn't make the slightest difference, it comes to the same thing, it makes no odds; → **rendre**

ADV * *[s'habiller]* the same, in the same way, alike ◆ **faire** ~ to do the same thing *(que* as)

pareillement /paʀɛjmɑ̃/ GRAMMAIRE ACTIVE 53.5 ADV *(= de la même manière) [s'habiller]* in the same way *(à* as); *(= également)* likewise, also, equally ◆ **cela m'a ~ surpris** it surprised me also *ou* too ◆ **~ heureux** equally happy ◆ **mon père va bien et ma mère** ~ my father is well and so is my mother *ou* and my mother too ◆ **à vous ~ !** the same to you!

parement /paʀmɑ̃/ NM *(Constr, Couture)* facing

parenchyme /paʀɑ̃ʃim/ NM parenchyma

parent, e /paʀɑ̃, ɑ̃t/ ADJ related NM,F 1 *(= personne apparentée)* relative, relation ◆ **être ~ de qn** to be related to *ou* a relative of sb ◆ **nous sommes ~s par alliance/par ma mère** we are related by marriage/on my mother's side ◆ **~s en ligne directe** blood relations ◆ **~s proches** close relations *ou* relatives ◆ **~s et amis** friends and relations *ou* relatives ◆ **nous ne sommes pas ~s** we aren't related ◆ **~ pauvre** *(fig)* poor relation *(de* to) 2 *(= père ou mère)* parent ◆ **~ isolé** *ou* **unique** single *ou* lone parent NMPL **parents** *(= père et mère)* parents; *(littér = ancêtres)* ancestors, forefathers ◆ **les devoirs des ~s** parental duties ◆ **accompagné de l'un de ses ~s** accompanied by one parent *ou* one of his parents ◆ **nos premiers ~s** our first parents, Adam and Eve

parental, e (mpl **-aux**) /paʀɑ̃tal, o/ ADJ parental ◆ **retrait d'autorité ~e** loss of parental rights ◆ **participation ~e** parental involvement

parenté /paʀɑ̃te/ NF *(= rapport)* relationship, kinship; *(= ensemble des parents)* relations, relatives ◆ **degré de** ~ degree of relationship ◆ **ils se sont découvert une lointaine** ~ they found out they were distantly related ◆ **ces deux langues n'ont aucune** ~ these two languages are not in any way related *ou* have no common roots; → **lien**

parenthèse /paʀɑ̃tɛz/ NF *(= digression)* parenthesis, digression; *(= signe)* parenthesis, bracket *(Brit)* ◆ **ouvrir/fermer la** ~ *(lit)* to open/close the parentheses *ou* brackets *(Brit)* ◆ **ouvrir une** ~ *(fig)* to digress, to make a digression ◆ **je me permets d'ouvrir une ~ pour dire ...** may I interrupt *ou* digress for a moment to say ... ◆ **je ferme la** ~ *(fig)* ... (but) to get back to the subject ... ◆ **mettre qch entre ~s** to put sth in *ou* between parentheses *ou* brackets *(Brit)* ◆ **entre ~s** *(lit)* in parentheses *ou* brackets *(Brit)*; *(fig)* incidentally, in parenthesis ◆ **il vaut mieux mettre cet aspect entre ~s** it would be better to leave that aspect aside ◆ **entre ~s, ce qu'il dit est faux** by the way, what he says is wrong ◆ **par** ~ incidentally, in passing ◆ **soit dit par ~, elle aurait mieux fait de rester** it could *ou* let it be said incidentally *ou* in passing that she would have done better to stay

parenthétisation /paʀɑ̃tetizasjɔ̃/ NF parenthesizing, bracketing *(Brit)*

paréo /paʀeo/ NM pareo

parer[1] /paʀe/ ▸ conjug 1 ◂ VT 1 *(= orner) [+ chose]* to adorn, to bedeck; *[+ personne]* to adorn, to deck out *(de* with); ◆ **robe richement parée** richly trimmed *ou* ornamented dress ◆ **~ qn de toutes les vertus** *(fig)* to attribute every virtue to sb 2 *(= préparer) [+ viande]* to dress, to trim; *[+ cuir]* to dress VPR **se parer** *(littér = se faire beau)* to put on all one's finery ◆ **se ~ de** *[+ bijoux]* to adorn o.s. with; *[+ robe]* to attire o.s. in; *(péj) [+ faux titre]* to assume, to invest o.s. with ◆ **se ~ des plumes du paon** *(fig)* to take all the credit (for o.s.)

parer[2] /paʀe/ ▸ conjug 1 ◂ VT *(= se protéger de) [+ coup]* to stave off, to fend off; *(Boxe, Escrime)* to parry; *(Ftbl) [+ tir]* to deflect; *(fig) [+ attaque]* to stave off, to parry VT INDIR **parer à** 1 *(= remédier) [+ inconvénient]* to deal with, to remedy, to overcome; *[+ danger]* to ward off 2 *(= pourvoir à) [+ éventualité]* to prepare for, to be prepared for ◆ **~ au plus pressé** to attend to the most urgent things first ◆ **il faut ~ au plus pressé** first things first ◆ **paré à virer !** *(Naut)* about ship! ◆ **paré ? alors on s'en va !** ready? off we go!

pare-soleil /paʀsɔlɛj/ NM INV *[de voiture]* sun visor; *(Archit)* sun screen; *[d'appareil photo]* sun hood

paresse /paʀɛs/ NF *[de personne]* laziness, idleness; *(= péché)* sloth ◆ **~ intellectuelle** *ou* **d'esprit** intellectual laziness ◆ **il est enclin à la** ~ he tends to be lazy ◆ **c'est une solution de** ~ it's the lazy way out ◆ **~ intestinale** *(Méd)* sluggishness of the digestive system

paresser /paʀese/ ▸ conjug 1 ◂ VI to laze about *ou* around ◆ **~ au lit** to laze in bed

paresseusement /paʀesøzmɑ̃/ ADV *(= avec indolence)* lazily; *(= avec lenteur)* sluggishly, slowly

paresseux, -euse /paʀesø, øz/ ADJ *[personne]* lazy, idle; *[allure, pose]* lazy; *[esprit]* slow; *[fleuve]* lazy, sluggish ◆ **~ comme une couleuvre*** *ou* **un loir*** *ou* **un lézard*** thoroughly lazy, bone-idle* *(Brit)* ◆ **il est ~ pour se lever** he's not very good at getting up NM,F lazy *ou* idle person, lazybones* NM *(= animal)* sloth

parfaire /paʀfɛʀ/ ▸ conjug 60 ◂ VT *[+ travail]* to perfect, to bring to perfection; *[+ connaissances]* to perfect, to round off; *[+ décor, impression]* to complete, to put the finishing touches to; *[+ somme]* to make up

parfait, e /paʀfɛ, ɛt/ (ptp de **parfaire**) ADJ 1 *(= impeccable) [travail, condition, exemple, crime]* perfect; *[exécution, raisonnement]* perfect, flawless; *[manières]* perfect, faultless; → **filer**

2 *(= absolu) [bonne foi, tranquillité]* complete, total, perfect; *[ressemblance]* perfect ◆ **il a été d'une discrétion ~e** *ou* **~ de discrétion** *(frm)* he has shown absolute discretion, he has been the soul of discretion ◆ **dans la plus ~e ignorance** in total *ou* utter *ou* complete ignorance ◆ **en ~ accord avec** in perfect *ou* total agreement with ◆ **en ~e harmonie** in perfect harmony

3 *(= accompli, achevé) [élève, employé]* perfect; *(péj) [crétin, crapule]* utter, perfect ◆ **le type même du ~ mari** the epitome of the perfect husband ◆ **~ homme du monde** perfect gentleman

4 *(= à son plein développement) [fleur, insecte]* perfect; → **accord, gaz, nombre**

5 *(= très bon)* **(c'est) ~ !** (that's) perfect! *ou* excellent! *ou* great!*; *(iro)* (that's) marvellous! *ou* great!* ◆ **vous refusez ? (voilà qui est) ~, vous l'aurez voulu !** you won't? (that's) fine – it's up to you! ◆ **vous avez été ~ !** you were fantastic!

NM 1 *(Culin)* parfait ◆ **~ au café** coffee parfait 2 *(Ling)* perfect

parfaitement /paʀfɛtmɑ̃/ ADV 1 *(= très bien) [connaître]* perfectly ◆ **je comprends** ~ I quite understand, I understand perfectly

2 *(= tout à fait) [heureux, clair, exact]* perfectly, quite; *[hermétique, étanche]* completely; *[idiot]* utterly, absolutely, perfectly ◆ **cela m'est ~ égal** it makes absolutely no difference to me, it's all the same to me ◆ **vous avez ~ le droit de le garder** you have a perfect right to keep it, you're perfectly entitled to keep it

3 *(= certainement)* (most) certainly ◆ **tu as fait ce tableau tout seul ? – ~ !** you did this picture all on your own? – I (most) certainly did! *ou* I did indeed! ◆ **tu ne vas pas partir sans moi ! – ~ !** you're not going to leave without me! – oh yes *ou* indeed I am! ◆ **je refuse d'obéir, ~, et j'en suis fier** yes, I'm refusing to obey, and I'm proud of it

parfois /paʀfwa/ ADV *(= dans certains cas)* sometimes; *(= de temps en temps)* sometimes, occasionally, at times ◆ **~ je lis, ~ je sors** sometimes I (may) read *ou* I'll read, other times I (may) go out *ou* I'll go out ◆ **il y a ~ du brouillard en hiver** occasionally *ou* sometimes there's fog in winter

parfum /paʀfœ̃/ NM 1 *(= substance)* perfume, scent, fragrance 2 *(= odeur) [de fleur, herbe]* scent; *[de tabac, vin, café]* aroma; *[de glace]* flavour *(Brit)*, flavor *(US)*; *[de savon]* scent, fragrance; *[de fruit]* smell; *(littér) [de louanges, vertu]* odour *(Brit)*, odor *(US)* ◆ **ceci a un ~ de scandale/d'hérésie** that has a whiff of scandal/of heresy about it 3 *(locutions)* **être au ~*** to be in the know* ◆ **mettre qn au ~*** to put sb in the picture*, to give sb the lowdown*

parfumé, e /paʀfyme/ (ptp de **parfumer**) ADJ *[papier à lettres, savon]* scented; *[air, fleur]* fragrant, sweet-smelling; *[vin, fruit]* fragrant; *[huile]* aromatic; *[bougie]* perfumed, scented ◆ **elle est trop ~e** she's wearing too much scent ◆ **~ au citron** *[glace]* lemon-flavour(ed) *(Brit)*, lemon-flavor(ed) *(US)*; *[savon]* lemon-scented

parfumer /paʀfyme/ ▸ conjug 1 ◂ VT *[+ pièce, air] [fleurs]* to perfume, to scent; *[café, tabac]* to fill with its aroma; *[+ mouchoir]* to put scent *ou* perfume on; *(Culin)* to flavour *(Brit)*, to flavor *(US)* *(à* with); ◆ **pour ~ votre linge** to make your linen smell nice ◆ **vous voulez que je vous parfume ?** would you like to try some perfume? VPR **se parfumer** to use *ou* wear perfume *ou* scent ◆ **elle se parfuma rapidement** she quickly put *ou* dabbed some perfume *ou* scent on

parfumerie /paʀfymʀi/ NF *(= usine, industrie)* perfumery; *(= boutique)* perfume shop; *(= rayon)* perfumery (department); *(= produits)* perfumery, perfumes, fragrances

parfumeur, -euse /paʀfymœʀ, øz/ NM,F perfumer

pari /paʀi/ NM bet, wager; *(Sport)* bet; *(= activité)* betting ◆ **faire/tenir un** ~ to make *ou* lay/take up a bet ◆ **~ mutuel (urbain)** ≈ tote, parimutuel ◆ **les ~s sont ouverts** *(fig)* there's no knowing, it's anyone's guess* ◆ **c'est un ~ sur l'avenir** it's a gamble on the future ◆ **je tiens le ~ !** you're on! ◆ **il avait dit qu'il arriverait premier : ~ tenu !** he said he would come first and so he did! *ou* and he managed it! *ou* and he pulled it off!

PMU

The **PMU** (« pari mutuel urbain ») is a government-regulated network of horse-racing betting counters run from bars displaying the **PMU** sign. Punters buy fixed-price tickets predicting winners or finishing positions. The traditional bet is a triple forecast (« tiercé »), although other multiple forecasts (« quarté », « quarté + », « quinté » etc) are also popular.

paria /paʀja/ NM (social) outcast, pariah; *(en Inde)* Pariah

parier /paʀje/ ▸ conjug 7 ◂ VT 1 *(= gager)* to bet, to wager ◆ **je (te) parie que c'est lui/tout ce que tu veux** I bet you it's him/anything you like ◆ **tu ne le feras pas – qu'est-ce que tu paries ?** you won't do it – what do you bet? *ou* do you want to bet? ◆ **il y a gros à ~ qu'elle ...** the odds are (that) she ..., ten to one she ... ◆ **je l'aurais parié** I might have known ◆ **tu as faim, je parie** I bet you're hungry 2 *(Courses) [+ argent]* to bet, to lay, to stake ◆ **~ 20 € sur le favori** to bet *ou* lay €20 on the favourite ◆ **~ sur un cheval** to bet on a horse, to back a horse ◆ **~ gros sur un cheval** to bet heavily on *ou* lay a big bet on a horse ◆ **~ aux courses** to bet on the races

pariétal, e (mpl **-aux**) /paʀjetal, o/ ADJ *(Anat)* parietal; *(Art)* wall *(épith)* NM parietal bone

parieur, -ieuse /paʀjœʀ, jøz/ NM,F punter, better

parigot, e * /paʀigo, ɔt/ ADJ Parisian NM,F **Parigot(e)** Parisian

Paris /paʀi/ N Paris

Pâris /paʀis/ NM *(Myth)* Paris

paris-brest (pl **paris-brests**) /paʀibʀɛst/ NM *choux pastry ring filled with praline-flavoured cream*

parisianisme /paʀizjanism/ NM *(= habitude)* Parisian habit; *(= façon de parler)* Parisian way of speaking; *(= importance donnée à Paris)* Paris bias ◆ **faire du ~** to focus excessively on Paris

parisien, -ienne /paʀizjɛ̃, jɛn/ ADJ *(gén)* Paris *(épith)*, of Paris; *[société, goûts, ambiance]* Parisian ◆ **le Bassin ~** the Paris basin ◆ **la région parisienne** the Paris region *ou* area, the region *ou* area around Paris ◆ **la vie parisienne** Paris *ou* Parisian life, life in Paris; → **pain** NM,F **Parisien(ne)** Parisian NM *(= pain) long loaf of bread*

paritaire /paʀitɛʀ/ ADJ *[commission]* joint *(épith)*, with equal representation of both sides; *[représentation]* equal

paritarisme /paʀitaʀism/ NM *(Écon)* (theory of) co-management

parité /paʀite/ NF parity ◆ **la ~ des changes** exchange parity ◆ **réclamer la ~ des *ou* entre les salaires** to demand equal pay ◆ **elles réclament la ~ hommes-femmes** they are demanding equality between men and women

parjure /paʀʒyʀ/ ADJ *[personne]* disloyal; *[serment]* false NM *(= violation de serment)* betrayal NMF traitor

parjurer (se) /paʀʒyʀe/ ▸ conjug 1 ◂ VPR to betray one's oath *ou* promise

parka /paʀka/ NF parka

parking /paʀkiŋ/ NM car park *(Brit)*, parking lot *(US)* ◆ **~ souterrain/à étages** underground/multistorey car park *(Brit) ou* parking lot *(US)* ◆ **"parking gratuit"** "free parking", "free car park" *(Brit)* ◆ **~ payant** = pay and display car park *(Brit) ou* parking lot *(US)* ◆ **~ sauvage** *area used illegally for parking* ADJ *(péj)* dead-end *(épith)*, which leads nowhere *(attrib)* ◆ **section-~** dead-end department ◆ **stage-~** dead-end training course, training course which leads nowhere

Parkinson /paʀkinsɔn/ NM ◆ **la maladie de ~** Parkinson's disease

parkinsonien, -ienne /paʀkinsɔnjɛ̃, jɛn/ ADJ associated with Parkinson's disease NM,F patient suffering from Parkinson's disease

parlant, e /paʀlɑ̃, ɑ̃t/ ADJ 1 *[comparaison, description]* graphic, vivid; *[exemple]* eloquent; *[geste, regard]* eloquent, meaningful ◆ **les chiffres sont ~s/très ~s** the figures speak for themselves/speak volumes ◆ **un schéma est souvent plus ~ qu'un texte** a diagram often conveys more than written text 2 *(= doué de parole)* speaking *(épith)*, talking *(épith)* ◆ **il n'est pas très ~** he's not very talkative; → **cinéma** ADV ◆ **scientifiquement/économiquement** *etc* **~** scientifically/economically *etc* speaking

parlé, e /paʀle/ (ptp de **parler**) ADJ *[langue]* spoken; → **chaîne, journal** NM *(Théât)* spoken part

parlement /paʀləmɑ̃/ NM parliament ◆ **le Parlement européen** the European Parliament

parlementaire /paʀləmɑ̃tɛʀ/ ADJ *(Pol)* parliamentary NMF 1 *(Pol)* member of Parliament; *(aux USA)* member of Congress; *(Hist Brit = partisan)* Parliamentarian 2 *(= négociateur)* negotiator, mediator

parlementairement /paʀləmɑ̃tɛʀmɑ̃/ ADV parliamentarily

parlementarisme /paʀləmɑ̃taʀism/ NM parliamentarism

parlementer /paʀləmɑ̃te/ ▸ conjug 1 ◂ VI *(= négocier)* to negotiate, to parley †; *(* = discuter)* to argue things over ◆ **~ avec qn** *(hum = palabrer)* to argue endlessly with sb

parler /paʀle/

▸ conjug 1 ◂

GRAMMAIRE ACTIVE 46.2, 53.2

1 VERBE INTRANSITIF	4 VERBE TRANSITIF
2 VERBE TRANSITIF INDIRECT	5 VERBE PRONOMINAL
3 VERBE TRANSITIF INDIRECT	6 NOM MASCULIN

1 – VERBE INTRANSITIF

1 faculté physique to talk, to speak ◆ **il a commencé à ~ à 2 ans** he started talking when he was 2 ◆ **votre perroquet parle ?** can your parrot talk? ◆ **~ du nez** to talk through one's nose ◆ **~ distinctement** to speak distinctly ◆ **je n'aime pas sa façon de ~** I don't like the way he talks *ou* speaks ◆ **parlez plus fort !** speak up!, speak louder!; → **dent, façon**

2 = exprimer sa pensée to speak; *(= bavarder)* to talk ◆ **~ franc/crûment** to speak frankly/bluntly ◆ **~ bien/mal** to be a good/not to be a (very) good speaker ◆ **~ d'or** to speak words of wisdom ◆ **~ avec les mains** to speak with one's hands ◆ **~ comme un livre** *(péj)* to talk like a book ◆ **~ par paraboles *ou* par énigmes** to talk *ou* speak in riddles ◆ **il aime s'écouter ~** he likes the sound of his own voice ◆ **parlons peu mais parlons bien** let's get straight to the point ◆ **~ pour qn** to speak for sb ◆ **parle pour toi !** *(iro)* speak for yourself! ◆ **c'est à vous de ~** *(Cartes)* it's your bid ◆ **au lieu de ~ en l'air, renseigne-toi/agis** don't just talk about it, find out/do something ◆ **plutôt que de ~ en l'air, allons lui demander** instead of talking (wildly) let's go and ask him ◆ **~ à tort et à travers** to blether, to talk drivel *, to talk through one's hat ◆ **~ pour ne rien dire** to talk for the sake of talking ◆ **voilà qui est (bien) parlé !** hear hear!, well said! ◆ **mais je parle, je parle, et toi, comment vas-tu ?** but that's enough about me – how are you (doing)?

3 fig ~ **par gestes** to use sign language ◆ **faire ~ la poudre** *(= se battre)* to start a gunfight; *(= faire la guerre)* to resort to war ◆ **le devoir a parlé** I *(ou* he *etc)* heard the call of duty, duty called ◆ **son cœur a parlé** he heeded the call of his heart

4 = révéler les faits to talk ◆ **faire ~** *[+ suspect]* to make talk, to loosen the tongue of; *[+ introverti, timide]* to draw out ◆ **les chiffres/faits parlent d'eux-mêmes** the figures/facts speak for themselves

5 locutions **vous n'avez qu'à ~** just say the word, you've only to say the word ◆ **ne m'en parlez pas !** you're telling me! *, I don't need telling! * ◆ **n'en parlons plus !** let's forget (about) it, let's not mention it again ◆ **sans ~ de ...** not to mention ..., to say nothing of ..., let alone ... ◆ **tu as été dédommagé, non ? – parlons-en !** *(= ça ne change rien)* you've been compensated, haven't you? – some good *ou* a lot of use that is (to me)! *; *(= pas du tout)* you've been compensated, haven't you? – not likely! * *ou* you must be joking! * ◆ **tu parles (Charles) ! *, vous parlez ! *** *(= bien sûr)* you're telling me! *, you bet! *; *(iro)* no chance! *, you must be joking! * ◆ **tu parles *ou* vous parlez d'une brute !** talk about a brute! ◆ **leur proposition, tu parles si on s'en fiche ! *** a fat lot we think of their idea! * ◆ **tu parles si ça nous aide/si c'est pratique ! *** *(iro)* a fat lot of help/use that is! * ◆ **tu peux ~ ! *** you can talk! *

2 – VERBE TRANSITIF INDIRECT

parler à

1 = converser ~ **à qn** to talk *ou* speak to sb ◆ **il faut que je lui parle** I must talk to him *ou* have a word with him ◆ **nous ne nous parlons pas** we're not on speaking terms ◆ **moi qui vous parle** I myself ◆ **trouver à qui ~** *(fig)* to meet one's match ◆ **c'est ~ à un mur** it's like talking to a (brick) wall

2 fig ~ **aux yeux/à l'imagination** to appeal to the eye/the imagination ◆ **~ au cœur** to speak to the heart ◆ **ce tableau/cette œuvre me parle** this painting/this work really speaks to me ◆ **ses romans/sculptures ne me parlent pas du tout** his novels/sculptures don't do anything for me

3 – VERBE TRANSITIF INDIRECT

parler de

1 = s'entretenir ~ **de qch/qn** to talk about sth/sb ◆ **~ de la pluie et du beau temps, ~ de choses et d'autres** *(fig)* to talk about the weather *(fig)*, to talk of this and that ◆ **faire ~ de soi** to get o.s. talked about ◆ **~ mal de qn** to speak ill of sb ◆ **on parle beaucoup de lui comme ministre** he's being talked about *ou* spoken of as a possible *ou* future minister, he's tipped as a likely minister ◆ **on ne parle que de ça** it's the only topic of conversation, it's the only thing *ou* that's all people are talking about ◆ **tout le monde en parle** everybody's talking about it ◆ **toute la ville en parle** it's the talk of the town ◆ **il n'en parle jamais** he never mentions it *ou* refers to it *ou* talks about it ◆ **nous recevons un immense acteur, je veux ~ bien sûr de Jean Lattu** we'll be welcoming a great actor, I am, of course, referring to Jean Lattu ◆ **et je ne parle pas de ...** not to mention ..., to say nothing of ... ◆ **de quoi ça parle, ton livre ? – ça parle de bateaux** what is your book about? – it's about ships; → **loup**

2 pour informer ◆ **~ de qch à qn** to tell sb about sth ◆ **parlez-nous de vos vacances/projets** tell us about your holidays/plans ◆ **on m'avait parlé d'une vieille maison** I had been told about an old house ◆ **je lui parlerai de cette affaire** I'll speak to him *ou* I'll have a word with him about this business ◆ **il a parlé de moi au patron** *(= soutenir)* he put in a word for

me with the boss ◆ **on m'a beaucoup parlé de vous** I've heard a lot about you

3 [pour annoncer une intention] ~ **de faire qch** to talk of doing sth ◆ **elle a parlé d'aller voir un docteur** she has talked of going to see a doctor ◆ **on parle de construire une route** they're talking of building a road, there's talk of a road being built *ou* of building a road

4 [= évoquer] **le jardin lui parlait de son enfance** the garden brought back memories of his childhood (to him) ◆ **tout ici me parle de toi** everything here reminds me of you

4 - VERBE TRANSITIF

1 *[+ langue]* to speak ◆ ~ **(l')anglais** to speak English

2 ◆ ~ **politique/affaires** to talk politics/business ◆ ~ **boutique*** to talk shop ◆ **si nous parlions finances ?** *(hum)* how about talking cash?*

5 - VERBE PRONOMINAL

se parler

1 [à soi-même] to talk to o.s.; *(les uns aux autres)* to talk to each other *ou* one another ◆ **depuis cette querelle, ils ne se parlent plus** they haven't been on speaking terms since that argument

2 [= être parlé] **ce dialecte ne se parle plus** this dialect is no longer spoken, nobody speaks this dialect any more

6 - NOM MASCULIN

1 [= manière de parler] speech ◆ **le ~ vrai** straight talking ◆ **le ~ de tous les jours** everyday speech, common parlance ◆ **il a un ~ vulgaire** he has a coarse way of speaking; → **franc¹**

2 [= langue régionale] dialect

parleur /paʀlœʀ/ **NM** ◆ **beau ~** smooth *ou* glib talker

parloir /paʀlwaʀ/ **NM** *[d'école, prison]* visiting room; *[de couvent]* parlour *(Brit)*, parlor *(US)*

parlot(t)e* /paʀlɔt/ **NF** chitchat* *(NonC)* ◆ **toutes ces parlot(t)es ne mènent à rien** all this chitchat* is a waste of time ◆ **c'est de la parlot(t)e tout ça** it's all *ou* just talk

Parme /paʀm/ **N** *(= ville)* Parma **NM** ◆ **(jambon de) ~** Parma ham **ADJ** *(= couleur)* ◆ **parme** violet

Parmentier /paʀmɑ̃tje/ **N** → **hachis**

parmesan, e /paʀməzɑ̃, an/ **ADJ** Parmesan, of *ou* from Parma **NM,F Parmesan(e)** inhabitant *ou* native of Parma **NM** *(= fromage)* Parmesan (cheese)

parmi /paʀmi/ **PRÉP** among(st) ◆ **~ la foule** among *ou* in the crowd ◆ **venez ici ~ nous** come over here with us ◆ **je passerai ~ vous distribuer les questionnaires** I'll come round and give you each a questionnaire ◆ **c'est un cas ~ d'autres** it's one case among many, it's one of many cases ◆ **qui ~ vous en a entendu parler ?** have any of you heard of it? ◆ **personne ~ nous/eux/les victimes** none of us/them/the victims **ADV** *(Helv = mutuellement)* * each other ◆ **on s'invite ~** we have each other to dinner

Parnasse /paʀnɑs/ **NM** Parnassus ◆ **le Mont ~** (Mount) Parnassus

parnassien, -ienne /paʀnasjɛ̃, jɛn/ **ADJ, NM,F** Parnassian **NM** *(= papillon)* apollo

parodie /paʀɔdi/ **NF** parody ◆ **une ~ de procès/de démocratie/d'élection** a travesty of a trial/of democracy/of an election

parodier /paʀɔdje/ ▸ conjug 7 ◂ **VT** to parody

parodique /paʀɔdik/ **ADJ** *[style]* parodic(al)

parodiste /paʀɔdist/ **NMF** parodist

paroi /paʀwa/ **NF** *(gén, Anat, Bot)* wall; *[de récipient]* (inside) surface, (inner) wall; *[de véhicule, baignoire]* side; *(= cloison)* partition ◆ **~ rocheuse** rock face

paroisse /paʀwas/ **NF** parish

paroissial, e (mpl **-iaux**) /paʀwasjal, jo/ **ADJ** parish *(épith)* ◆ **église ~e** parish church ◆ **salle ~e** church hall ◆ **à l'échelon ~** at the parochial *ou* parish level

paroissien, -ienne /paʀwasjɛ̃, jɛn/ **NM,F** parishioner **NM** *(= missel)* prayer book, missal

parole /paʀɔl/ **NF** 1 *(= mot)* word ◆ **comprenez-vous le sens de ses ~s ?** can you understand (the meaning of) what he says? ◆ **assez de ~s, des actes !** that's enough talking, now it's time to act! ◆ **il n'a pas dit une ~ de la soirée** he didn't say a word *ou* open his mouth all evening ◆ **les ~s s'envolent, les écrits restent** *(Prov)* verba volant, scripta manent *(Prov)* ◆ **voilà une bonne ~ !** *(hum)* that's what I like to hear! ◆ **la ~ de Dieu, la bonne ~** the word of God ◆ **porter** *ou* **prêcher la bonne ~** *(lit)* to preach *ou* spread the word of God; *(fig)* to spread the (good) word ◆ **toutes ces belles ~s n'ont convaincu personne** all these fine(-sounding) words failed to convince anybody ◆ ~ **célèbre** famous words *ou* saying ◆ **prononcer une ~ historique** to make a historic remark ◆ **ce sont des ~s en l'air** it's just idle talk ◆ **il est surtout courageux en ~s** he's brave enough when it's just a matter of words *ou* talking about it ◆ **tout cela est bien joli en ~s mais ...** it sounds fair enough but ...; → **boire, moulin, payer**

2 *(= texte)* ~s *[de chanson]* words, lyrics ◆ **histoire sans ~s** wordless cartoon ◆ **"sans paroles"** *(légende)* "no caption"

3 *(= promesse)* word ◆ **tenir ~** to keep one's word ◆ **il a tenu ~** he kept his word, he was as good as his word ◆ **c'est un homme de ~, il est de ~, il n'a qu'une ~** he's a man of his word, his word is his bond ◆ **il n'a aucune ~** you (just) can't trust a word he says ◆ **je l'ai cru sur ~** I took his word for it ◆ **(je vous donne** *ou* **vous avez ma) ~ d'honneur !** I give you *ou* you have my word (of honour)! ◆ ~ **de scout/marin** *etc* scout's/sailor's *etc* honour ◆ **manquer à sa ~** to fail to keep one's word, to go back on one's word ◆ **ma ~ !*** (upon) my word! ◆ **tu es fou ma ~ !*** heavens - you're mad! ◆ **prisonnier sur ~** prisoner on parole

4 *(= faculté d'expression)* speech ◆ **doué de ~** capable of speech ◆ **avoir la ~ facile** to find it easy to talk, to have the gift of the gab* ◆ **avoir le don de la ~** to be a gifted speaker ◆ **la ~ est d'argent, le silence est d'or** *(Prov)* speech is silver, silence is golden *(Prov)* ◆ **perdre/retrouver la ~** to lose/recover one's speech; *(fig)* to lose/find one's tongue* ◆ **il n'a jamais droit à la ~** he's never allowed to get a word in edgeways; → **manquer**

5 *(Ling)* speech, parole *(SPÉC)* ◆ **acte de ~** speech act

6 *(Cartes)* ~ **!** (I) pass!

7 *(dans un débat, une discussion)* **droit de ~** right to speak ◆ **temps de ~** speaking time ◆ **puis-je avoir la ~ ?** may I say something? ◆ **vous avez la ~** *(gén)* it's your turn to speak; *(au parlement etc)* you have the floor ◆ **je vous rends la ~** back *ou* over to you ◆ **qui veut la ~ ?** who wants to speak? ◆ **laissez-moi la ~** let me speak ◆ **la ~ est à M. Duval** it's Mr Duval's turn to speak ◆ **passer** *ou* **céder la ~ à qn** to hand over to sb ◆ **demander la ~** to ask to be allowed to speak ◆ **prendre la ~** to speak ◆ **je voudrais prendre la ~ pour dire ...** *(gén)* I'd like to say ...; *(au parlement etc)* I'd like to take the floor to say ... ◆ **pour empêcher la prise de ~ des extrémistes** to prevent extremists from voicing their opinions

parolier, -ière /paʀɔlje, jɛʀ/ **NM,F** lyric writer

paronyme /paʀɔnim/ **NM** paronym

paronymie /paʀɔnimi/ **NF** paronymy

paronymique /paʀɔnimik/ **ADJ** paronymic

parotide /paʀɔtid/ **NF** ◆ **(glande) ~** parotid gland

paroxysme /paʀɔksism/ **NM** *[de maladie]* crisis (point), paroxysm *(SPÉC)*; *[de crise, sensation, sentiment]* paroxysm, height ◆ **être au ~ de la joie/colère** to be beside o.s. with joy/anger ◆ **le bruit était à son ~** the noise was at its loudest *ou* height ◆ **son désespoir était à son ~** he was in the depths of despair ◆ **l'incendie/la douleur avait atteint son ~** the fire/the pain was at its height *ou* at its fiercest ◆ **la crise avait atteint son ~** the crisis had reached a head *ou* climax

paroxystique /paʀɔksistik/ **ADJ** *(Méd)* paroxysmal; *(= extrême) [émotion, pression]* intense; *[situation, état]* extreme ◆ **au moment le plus ~ de la pièce** at the very climax *ou* climactic moment of the play

parpaillot, e /paʀpajo, ɔt/ **NM,F** *(Hist, péj)* Protestant

parpaing /paʀpɛ̃/ **NM** *(= pierre pleine)* perpend, parpen *(US)*; *(aggloméré)* breeze-block

Parque /paʀk/ **NF** *(Myth)* ◆ **la ~** Fate ◆ **les ~s** the Fates, the Parcae

parquer /paʀke/ ▸ conjug 1 ◂ **VT** *[+ voiture, artillerie]* to park; *[+ moutons, bétail]* to pen (in *ou* up); *[+ huîtres, moules]* to put in a bed (*ou* beds); *(péj) [+ personnes]* to pack in ◆ **on les parquait dans des réserves** they were herded into reservations ◆ **les réfugiés étaient parqués comme des bestiaux** the refugees were cooped up *ou* penned in like animals **VPR se parquer** * *(en voiture)* to park

parquet /paʀkɛ/ **NM** 1 *(= plancher) (gén)* wooden floor; *(à chevrons etc)* parquet (floor) ◆ **les lattes du ~** the floorboards ◆ ~ **flottant** floating floor 2 *(Jur)* **le ~** the public prosecutor's department *ou* office 3 *(Bourse)* **le ~** *(= enceinte)* the (dealing *ou* trading) floor; *(= agents)* the stock exchange *ou* market

parqueter /paʀkəte/ ▸ conjug 4 ◂ **VT** to lay a wooden *ou* parquet floor in ◆ **pièce parquetée** room with a wooden *ou* parquet floor

parrain /paʀɛ̃/ **NM** 1 *(Rel)* godfather ◆ **accepter d'être le ~ d'un enfant** to agree to be a child's godfather *ou* to stand godfather to a child 2 *[de navire]* namer, christener 3 *(qui introduit dans un cercle, un club)* proposer; *(qui aide financièrement)* sponsor; *[d'entreprise, initiative]* promoter; *[d'œuvre, fondation]* patron ◆ **un ~ de la Mafia** a godfather in the Mafia

parrainage /paʀɛnaʒ/ **NM** 1 *(= introduction dans un cercle, un club)* proposing (for membership) 2 *(= aide financière)* sponsorship; *[d'entreprise, initiative]* promoting; *(= appui moral) [d'œuvre, fondation]* patronage ◆ ~ **publicitaire** advertising sponsorship 3 *[de navire]* naming, christening

parrainer /paʀene/ ▸ conjug 1 ◂ **VT** 1 *(= introduire : dans un cercle, un club)* to propose (for membership) ◆ **se faire ~ par qn** to be proposed by sb 2 *(= aider financièrement)* to sponsor; *[+ entreprise, initiative]* to promote; *(= patronner) [+ œuvre, fondation, association]* to be the patron of

parraineur /paʀɛnœʀ/ **NM** sponsor

parricide /paʀisid/ **ADJ** parricidal **NMF** parricide **NM** *(= crime)* parricide

parsec /paʀsɛk/ **NM** parsec

parsemer /paʀsəme/ ▸ conjug 5 ◂ **VT** 1 *(= répandre)* ~ **de** to sprinkle with, to strew with *(littér)* ◆ ~ **le sol de fleurs** to scatter flowers over the ground, to strew the ground with flowers *(littér)* ◆ ~ **un tissu de paillettes d'or** to sew gold sequins all over a piece of material ◆ ~ **un**

texte de citations to scatter quotations through a text [2] *(= être répandu sur)* to be scattered *ou* sprinkled over ◆ **les feuilles qui parsèment le gazon** the leaves which are scattered *ou* which lie scattered over the lawn ◆ **ciel parsemé d'étoiles** star-studded sky, sky sprinkled *ou* strewn *ou* studded with stars ◆ **champ parsemé de fleurs** field dotted with flowers ◆ **parsemé de difficultés/fautes** riddled with difficulties/mistakes

parsi, e /paʀsi/ ADJ Parsee NM *(= langue)* Parsee NM,F **Parsi(e)** Parsee

part /paʀ/
NOM FÉMININ

GRAMMAIRE ACTIVE 53.5

[1] dans un partage share; *(= portion)* portion; *(= tranche)* slice ◆ **sa ~ d'héritage/de soucis** his share of the inheritance/of worries ◆ **faire huit ~s dans un gâteau** to cut a cake into eight (slices) ◆ **c'est 2 € la ~ de gâteau** it's €2 a slice ◆ **vouloir sa ~ du gâteau** *(fig)* to want one's slice *ou* share of the cake ◆ **la ~ du lion** the lion's share ◆ **la ~ du pauvre** *(repas) portion kept for a poor visitor; (fig)* the crumbs ◆ **~ à deux !** share and share alike! ◆ **chacun paie sa ~** everyone pays his share, everyone chips in *

◆ **faire la part belle à qn** to give sb more than his (*ou* her) due

◆ **faire la part de qch** ◆ **faire la ~ de la fatigue/du hasard** to take tiredness/chance into account, to allow for *ou* make allowances for tiredness/chance ◆ **il faut faire la ~ du vrai et du faux dans ce qu'elle dit** you can't believe everything she says ◆ **faire la ~ des choses** to make allowances ◆ **faire la ~ du feu** *(fig)* to cut one's losses

[2] = participation part ◆ **~ patronale/salariale** *(Sécurité sociale)* employer's/worker's contribution ◆ **le hasard n'a eu aucune ~ dans leur rencontre** chance had nothing to do with *ou* played no part in their meeting ◆ **il a pris une ~ importante dans l'élaboration du projet** he played an important part in the development of the project

◆ **à part entière** ◆ **membre/citoyen à ~ entière** full member/citizen ◆ **Français à ~ entière** person with full French citizenship, fully-fledged French citizen ◆ **artiste à ~ entière** artist in his (*ou* her) own right ◆ **l'Europe sera le partenaire à ~ entière des USA** Europe will be a fully-committed partner for the USA

◆ **avoir part à** *(littér)* to have a share in

◆ **faire part de qch à qn** to announce sth to sb, to inform sb of sth, to let sb know *ou* tell sb about sth ◆ **il m'a fait ~ de son inquiétude** he told me how worried he was

◆ **prendre part à** *[+ travail]* to take part in, to join in, to collaborate in; *[+ frais]* to share in, to contribute to; *[+ manifestation]* to join in, to take part in ◆ **prendre ~ à un débat** to participate in *ou* take part in a debate ◆ **"prenez part au développement de votre ville !"** "help to develop your town!" ◆ **je prends ~ à vos soucis** I share (in) your worries

[3] = partie part ◆ **c'est une toute petite ~ de sa fortune** it's only a tiny fraction *ou* part of his fortune ◆ **~ de marché** *(Écon)* market share

◆ **pour une part** partly ◆ **cela explique pour une ~ l'ambiance qui règne ici** this partly explains the atmosphere here ◆ **pour une ~, son attitude s'explique par sa timidité** to some extent, one can put his attitude down to shyness

◆ **pour une bonne** *ou* **large part** largely, to a great extent

◆ **pour une petite part** in a small way

[4] Fin ≃ share *(giving right to participate in profits but not running of firm); (Impôts)* ≃ tax unit ◆ **~ de fondateur** founder's share ◆ **~ d'intérêt** *ou* **sociale** partner's *ou* partnership share

[5] expressions figées

◆ **à part** *(= de côté)* aside, on one side; *(= séparément)* separately, on its (*ou* their) own; *(= excepté)* except for, apart from, aside from *(surtout US)*; *(Théât = en aparté)* aside ◆ **nous mettrons ces livres à ~ pour vous** we'll put these books aside *ou* on one side for you ◆ **prendre qn à ~** to take sb aside ◆ **étudier chaque problème à ~** to study each problem separately *ou* on its own ◆ **à ~ vous, je ne connais personne ici** apart from *ou* aside from *ou* except for you I don't know anyone here ◆ **à ~ cela** apart *ou* aside from that, otherwise ◆ **plaisanterie à ~** joking apart *ou* aside
(= exceptionnel) special, extraordinary ◆ **un cas/une place à ~** a special case/place ◆ **c'est un homme à ~** he's in a class of his own ◆ **il est vraiment à ~** there aren't many like him around; → **bande²**, **chambre**

◆ **à part soi (***ou* **moi** *etc***)** *(littér)* ◆ **garder qch à ~ soi** to keep sth to o.s. ◆ **je pensais à ~ moi que ...** I thought to myself that ...

◆ **autre part** somewhere else, elsewhere ◆ **il ne veut plus habiter autre ~** he doesn't want to live anywhere else

◆ **d'autre part** *(= de plus)* moreover; *(= par ailleurs)* on the other hand ◆ **il est beau, et d'autre ~ il est riche** he's handsome, and what's more he's rich ◆ **il n'est pas très doué, d'autre ~ il est travailleur** *(= en revanche)* he's not very talented, but on the other hand he's very hard-working ◆ **d'une ~ ..., d'autre ~ ...** on the one hand ..., on the other hand ...

◆ **de la part de** *(provenance)* from; *(= au nom de)* on behalf of ◆ **je viens de la ~ de Guy** *(il m'a envoyé)* I've been sent by Guy; *(comme porte-parole)* I've come *ou* I'm here on behalf of Guy ◆ **de la ~ de qui venez-vous ?** who sent you? ◆ **cela demande un peu de bon sens de la ~ de l'utilisateur** it requires a little commonsense on the part of the user *ou* from the user ◆ **cela m'étonne de sa ~** I'm surprised at that (coming) from him ◆ **dites-lui bonjour de ma ~** give him my regards ◆ **c'est gentil de sa ~** that's nice of him ◆ **c'est de la ~ de qui ?** *(Téléc)* who's calling? *ou* speaking?

◆ **de part en part** right through

◆ **de part et d'autre** on both sides, on either side

◆ **de toute(s) part(s)** from all sides *ou* quarters

◆ **en bonne/mauvaise part** ◆ **prendre qch en bonne ~** to take sth in good part ◆ **prendre qch en mauvaise ~** to take sth amiss, to take offence at sth

◆ **pour ma (***ou* **ta** *etc***) part** as for me (*ou* you *etc*), for my (*ou* your *etc*) part ◆ **pour ma ~ je pense que ...** I for one think that ...; → **nul, quelque**

partage /paʀtaʒ/ NM [1] *(= fractionnement, division) [de terrain, surface]* dividing up, division; *[de gâteau]* cutting; *(Math) [de nombre]* factorizing ◆ **faire le ~ de qch** to divide sth up ◆ **le ~ du pays en deux camps** the division of the country into two camps ◆ **~ de temps** *(Ordin)* time sharing ◆ **~ de fichiers** file-sharing ◆ **~ du travail** job sharing; → **ligne¹**

[2] *(= distribution) [de butin, héritage]* sharing out ◆ **procéder au ~ de qch** to share sth out ◆ **le ~ n'est pas juste** the way it's shared out isn't fair, it isn't fairly shared out ◆ **j'ai été oublié dans le ~** I've been left out (in the share-out) ◆ **quel a été le ~ des voix entre les candidats ?** how were the votes divided among the candidates? ◆ **en cas de ~ des voix** *(Pol)* in the event of a tie in the voting

[3] *(= participation)* sharing ◆ **l'enquête a conclu au ~ des responsabilités** the inquiry came to the conclusion that the responsibility was shared ◆ **le ~ du pouvoir avec nos adversaires** the sharing of power with our opponents ◆ **fidélité sans ~** *(fig)* undivided loyalty ◆ **un pouvoir sans ~** absolute power ◆ **régner sans ~** to rule supreme

[4] *(= part)* share ◆ **donner/recevoir qch en ~** to give/receive sth in a will ◆ **la maison lui échut en ~** the house came to him in the will ◆ **le bon sens qu'il a reçu en ~** the common sense with which he has been endowed

partagé, e /paʀtaʒe/ (ptp de **partager**) ADJ [1] *(= divisé) [avis, opinion]* divided ◆ **les experts sont très ~s sur la question** the experts are divided on the question ◆ **~ entre l'amour et la haine** torn between love and hatred [2] *(littér = doté)* endowed ◆ **il est bien/mal ~ par le sort** fate has been/has not been kind to him [3] *(Ordin)* **logiciel ~** shareware; → **temps¹**

partageable /paʀtaʒabl/ ADJ divisible, which can be shared out *ou* divided up ◆ **frais ~s entre tous** costs that are shared by all ◆ **votre gaieté est difficilement ~** it is difficult to share (in) your happiness

partager /paʀtaʒe/ GRAMMAIRE ACTIVE 38.1, 40.1
► conjug 3 ◄

VT [1] *(= fractionner) [+ terrain, feuille, gâteau]* to divide up ◆ **~ en deux/en deux bouts/par moitié** to divide sth in two/into two pieces *ou* bits/in half

[2] *(= distribuer, répartir) [+ butin, gâteau]* to share (out); *[+ frais]* to share ◆ **il partage son temps entre son travail et sa famille** he divides his time between his work and his family ◆ **il partage son affection entre plusieurs personnes** several people have to share his affections

[3] *(= avoir une part de, avoir en commun) [+ héritage, gâteau, appartement, sort]* to share *(avec* with); ◆ **voulez-vous ~ notre repas ?** will you share our meal? ◆ **~ le lit de qn** to share sb's bed ◆ **il n'aime pas ~** he doesn't like sharing ◆ **les torts sont partagés** both (*ou* all) parties are at fault, there is fault on both (*ou* all) sides

[4] *(= s'associer à) [+ sentiments, bonheur, goûts]* to share (in); *[+ opinion, idée]* to share, to agree with ◆ **je partage votre douleur/surprise** I share your sorrow/surprise ◆ **amour partagé** mutual love ◆ **c'est une opinion largement partagée** it is an opinion that is widely shared

[5] *(= diviser)* to divide ◆ **ce débat partage le monde scientifique** th scientific community is divided over this issue

[6] *(frm = douer)* to endow ◆ **la nature l'a bien partagé** nature has been generous to him

VPR **se partager** [1] *(= se fractionner)* to be divided ◆ **ça peut facilement se ~ en trois/en trois morceaux** it can easily be divided (up) *ou* cut in three/into three pieces *ou* bits ◆ **se ~ entre diverses tendances** *[vote]* to be divided between different groups ◆ **pour lui, le monde se partage en deux** for him, there are two kinds of people ◆ **à l'endroit où les branches se partagent** where the branches fork *ou* divide ◆ **le reste des voix s'est partagé entre les autres candidats** the remaining votes are distributed *ou* shared among the other candidates ◆ **le pouvoir ne se partage pas** power is not something which can be shared ◆ **il se partage entre son travail et son jardin** he divides his time between his work and his garden

[2] *(= se distribuer)* **ils se sont partagé le gâteau** *(lit)* they shared the cake between them *ou* among themselves; *(fig)* they shared it out ◆ **ils se sont partagé le butin** they shared the booty between them ◆ **nous nous sommes partagé le travail** we shared the work between us ◆ **les trois candidats se sont partagé les suffrages** the votes were divided among the three candidates ◆ **se ~ les faveurs du public** to be equally popular

partageur, -euse¹ /paʀtaʒœʀ, øz/ ADJ ready *ou* willing to share ◆ **il n'est pas ~** he doesn't like sharing

partageux, -euse² † /paʀtaʒø, øz/ NM,F distributionist

partance /paʀtɑ̃s/ **en partance** LOC ADV *[train]* due to leave; *[avion]* outward bound; *[bateau]* sailing *(attrib)*, outward bound ◆ **en ~ pour Londres** *[train, avion]* for London, London *(épith)*; *[bateau]* bound *ou* sailing for London *(attrib)*; *[passager]* (bound) for London *(attrib)*

partant¹, e /paʀtɑ̃, ɑ̃t/ GRAMMAIRE ACTIVE 38.1 NM,F 1 *(= coureur)* starter; *(= cheval)* runner ◆ **tous ~s** all horses running ◆ **non-~** non-runner 2 *(= personne)* person leaving, departing traveller *(ou* visitor *etc)* ◆ **les ~s et les arrivants** the departures and arrivals ADJ ◆ **je suis ~** count me in ◆ **il est toujours ~ pour un bon repas** * he's always ready for a good meal ◆ **si c'est comme ça, je ne suis plus ~** if that's how it is (you can) count me out

partant² /paʀtɑ̃/ CONJ *(littér)* hence, therefore, consequently

partenaire /paʀtənɛʀ/ NMF partner ◆ **les ~s sociaux** ≃ unions and management, management and labour ◆ **il était son ~ dans le film** he played opposite her in the film ◆ **~ sexuel** sexual partner

partenarial, e (pl **-iaux**) /paʀtənaʀjal, jo/ ADJ *[accord]* partnership, joint; *[négociations]* joint

partenariat /paʀtənaʀja/ NM partnership

parterre /paʀtɛʀ/ NM 1 *(= plate-bande)* border, (flower)bed; *(* = plancher)* floor 2 *(Théât)* *(= emplacement)* stalls *(Brit)*, orchestra *(US)*; *(= public)* (audience in the) stalls *(Brit) ou* orchestra *(US)*

Parthe /paʀt/ NM Parthian; → **flèche¹**

parthénogenèse /paʀtenoʒenɛz/ NF parthenogenesis

parthénogénétique /paʀtenoʒenetik/ ADJ parthenogenetic

parthénogénétiquement /paʀtenoʒenetikmɑ̃/ ADV parthenogenetically

Parthénon /paʀtenɔ̃/ NM ◆ **le ~** the Parthenon

parti¹ /paʀti/ NM 1 *(= groupe : gén, Pol)* party ◆ **le ~ des mécontents** the malcontents ◆ **le ~ de la défaite** the defeatists ◆ **le ~ (communiste)** the Communist party

2 *(= solution)* option, course of action ◆ **hésiter entre deux ~s** to wonder which of two courses *ou* which course to follow ◆ **prendre un ~** to come to *ou* make a decision, to make up one's mind ◆ **prendre le ~ de faire qch** to make up one's mind to do sth, to decide *ou* resolve to do sth ◆ **mon ~ est pris** my mind is made up ◆ **crois-tu que c'est le meilleur ~ (à prendre) ?** do you think that's the best course (to take)? *ou* the best idea? ◆ **prendre le ~ de qn, prendre ~ pour qn** *(= se mettre du côté de qn)* to side with sb, to take sb's side; *(= donner raison à qn)* to stand up for sb ◆ **prendre ~ (dans une affaire)** *(= se rallier)* to take sides (on an issue); *(= dire ce qu'on pense)* to take a stand (on an issue) ◆ **prendre son ~ de qch** to come to terms with sth, to reconcile o.s. to sth ◆ **il faut bien en prendre son ~** you just have to come to terms with it *ou* put up with it

3 *(= personne à marier)* match ◆ **beau** *ou* **bon** *ou* **riche ~** good match

4 *(locutions)* **tirer ~ de** *[+ situation, occasion, information]* to take advantage of, to turn to (good) account; *[+ outil, ressources]* to put to (good) use; *[+ victoire]* to take advantage of ◆ **tirer le meilleur ~ possible d'une situation** to turn a situation to best account, to get the most one can out of a situation ◆ **il sait tirer ~ de tout** *(situation)* he can turn anything to his advantage, he can make capital out of anything; *(objets)* he can put everything to good use ◆ **faire un mauvais ~ à qn** to beat sb up

COMP **parti pris** *(= préjugé)* prejudice, bias ◆ **je crois, sans ~ pris ...** I think without bias (on my part) ... *ou* being quite objective about it ... ◆ **juger sans ~ pris** to take an unbiased *ou* objective view ◆ **il est de ~ pris** he's prejudiced *ou* biased ◆ **éviter le ~ pris** to avoid being prejudiced *ou* biased ◆ **~ pris théorique** *(= choix)* theoretical perspective *ou* standpoint ◆ **~ pris artistique/esthétique** artistic/aesthetic choice

PARTIS POLITIQUES FRANÇAIS

Among the many active right-wing political parties in France, the most prominent include the Gaullist RPR (« le Rassemblement pour la République »), the UDF (« l'Union pour la démocratie française », a more recent movement founded by Valéry Giscard d'Estaing), and the extreme right-wing Front national (FN). On the left, the Parti socialiste (PS) is the most influential party, though the Parti communiste français (PCF) continues to draw a significant number of votes. Of the numerous ecological parties, Les Verts is the most prominent. → **COMMUNISTE, ÉLECTIONS**

parti², e¹ /paʀti/ (ptp de **partir¹**) ADJ 1 *(* = ivre)* tipsy, tight * ◆ **il est bien ~** he's had a few *, he's well away * *(Brit)* 2 *(Hér)* party

partial, e (mpl **-iaux**) /paʀsjal, jo/ ADJ biased, prejudiced, partial ◆ **être ~ envers qn** to be biased *ou* prejudiced against sb

partialement /paʀsjalmɑ̃/ ADV in a biased way ◆ **juger qch ~** to take a biased view of sth

partialité /paʀsjalite/ NF ◆ **~ (envers** *ou* **contre qn)** bias (against sb) ◆ **faire preuve de ~ envers** *ou* **contre qn** to be unfair to sb, to be biased against sb, to show bias against sb ◆ **se montrer d'une regrettable ~** to be dreadfully biased

participant, e /paʀtisipɑ̃, ɑ̃t/ ADJ participating NM,F *(à un concours, une course)* entrant *(à* in); *(à un débat, un projet)* participant, person taking part *(à* in); *(à une association)* member *(à* of); *(à une cérémonie, un complot)* person taking part *(à* in); ◆ **les ~s aux bénéfices** those sharing in the profits ◆ **les ~s à la manifestation/au concours** those taking part in the demonstration/in the competition

participatif, -ive /paʀtisipatif, iv/ ADJ ◆ **gestion participative** participative management ◆ **prêt ~** participating capital loan ◆ **titre ~** non-voting share *(in a public sector company)*

participation /paʀtisipasjɔ̃/ NF 1 *(= action)* **~ à** *[+ concours, colloque, cérémonie, entreprise]* taking part in, participation in; *[+ spectacle]* appearance in; *[+ aventure, complot, escroquerie]* involvement in ◆ **la réunion aura lieu sans leur ~** the meeting will take place without their taking part *ou* without them ◆ **peu importe l'habileté : c'est la ~ qui compte** skill doesn't really matter: what counts is taking part *ou* joining in ◆ **il s'est assuré la ~ de deux équilibristes** he has arranged for two tightrope walkers to appear ◆ **c'est la ~ de Marie Vincent qui va attirer les spectateurs** it's Marie Vincent who'll draw the crowds, it's the fact that Marie Vincent is appearing *ou* performing that will draw the crowds ◆ **ce soir, grand gala avec la ~ de plusieurs vedettes** tonight, grand gala with several star appearances ◆ **avec la ~ de Deneuve** *(Ciné)* with guest appearance by Deneuve, with (special) guest star Deneuve ◆ **~ électorale** turnout at the polls *(Brit)*, voter turnout *(US)* ◆ **fort/faible taux de ~ électorale** high/low turnout at the polls; → **participer**

2 *(Écon = détention d'actions)* interest ◆ **prise de ~s** acquisition of holdings ◆ **prendre une ~ majoritaire dans une entreprise** to acquire a majority interest in a firm ◆ **la ~ (ouvrière)** worker participation ◆ **~ aux bénéfices** profit-sharing ◆ **~ du personnel à la marche d'une entreprise** staff participation *ou* involvement in the running of a firm ◆ **~s croisées** cross holdings

3 *(financière)* contribution ◆ **~ aux frais : 10 €** contribution towards costs: €10 ◆ **nous demandons une petite ~ (de 5 €)** we request a small donation (of €5)

participe /paʀtisip/ NM participle ◆ **~ passé/présent** past/present participle

participer /paʀtisipe/ ► conjug 1 ◄ VT INDIR **participer à** 1 *(= prendre part à)* *[+ concours, colloque, cérémonie]* to take part in ◆ **je compte ~ au concours/à l'épreuve de fond** I intend to take part in *ou* enter the competition/the long-distance event ◆ **peu d'électeurs ont participé au scrutin** there was a low turnout at the polls, there was a low voter turnout *(US)*

2 *(= prendre une part active à)* *[+ entreprise, discussion, jeu]* to participate in, to take part in, to join in; *[+ spectacle]* *[artiste]* to appear in; *[+ aventure, complot, escroquerie]* to take part in, to be involved in ◆ **l'important n'est pas de gagner mais de ~** the important thing is not winning but taking part ◆ **~ à la joie/au chagrin de qn** to share sb's joy/sorrow ◆ **ils ont participé à l'allégresse générale** they joined in the general happy mood ◆ **on demande aux élèves de ~ davantage pendant le cours** pupils are asked to participate more *ou* take a more active part in class

3 *(= payer sa part de)* *[+ frais, dépenses]* to share in, to contribute to ◆ **~ (financièrement) à** *[+ entreprise, projet]* to make a (financial) contribution to

4 *(= avoir part à)* *[+ profits, pertes, succès]* to share (in)

VT INDIR **participer de** *(littér = tenir de)* to partake of *(frm)*, to have something of the nature of

participial, e (mpl **-iaux**) /paʀtisipjal, jo/ ADJ participial NF **participiale** participial phrase *ou* clause

particularisation /paʀtikylaʀizasjɔ̃/ NF particularization

particulariser /paʀtikylaʀize/ ► conjug 1 ◄ VT to particularize VPR **se particulariser** to be distinguished *ou* characterized *(par* by)

particularisme /paʀtikylaʀism/ NM 1 *(Pol = attitude)* sense of identity ◆ **~(s)** *(= particularité)* specific (local) character *(NonC)*, specific characteristic(s) ◆ **~s régionaux** *(Pol, Sociol)* regional idiosyncrasies 2 *(Rel)* particularism

particularité /paʀtikylaʀite/ NF 1 *(= caractéristique)* *[d'individu, caractère, religion]* particularity, (distinctive) characteristic; *[de texte, paysage]* (distinctive) characteristic *ou* feature; *[d'appareil, modèle]* (distinctive) feature ◆ **ces modèles ont en commun la ~ d'être ...** these models all have the distinctive feature of being ..., these models are all distinguished by being ... ◆ **cet animal présente la ~ d'être herbivore** a distinctive feature *ou* characteristic of this animal is that it is herbivorous 2 *(†, littér = détail)* particular 3 *(littér = unicité)* particularity

particule /paʀtikyl/ NF *(Ling, Phys)* particle ◆ **~ (nobiliaire)** nobiliary particle ◆ **nom à ~** *name with a de usually belonging to a noble family,* ≃ name with a handle ◆ **il a un nom à ~** he has a handle to his name

particulier, -ière /paʀtikylje, jɛʀ/ GRAMMAIRE ACTIVE 53.1

ADJ 1 (= *spécifique*) [*aspect, point, exemple*] particular, specific; [*trait, style, manière de parler*] characteristic, distinctive ◆ **dans ce cas** ~ in this particular case ◆ **il n'avait pas d'aptitudes particulières** he had no particular *ou* special aptitudes ◆ **cette habitude lui est particulière** this habit is peculiar to him ◆ **signes ~s** (*gén*) distinctive signs; (*sur un passeport*) distinguishing marks

2 (= *spécial*) exceptional, special, particular ◆ **la situation est un peu particulière** the situation is rather exceptional ◆ **ce que j'ai à dire est un peu** ~ what I have to say is slightly unusual ◆ **cela constitue un cas** ~ this is a special *ou* an unusual *ou* an exceptional case ◆ **rien de ~ à signaler** nothing unusual to report ◆ **je l'ai préparé avec un soin tout** ~ I prepared it with very special care *ou* with particular care

3 (= *étrange*) [*mœurs*] peculiar, odd; [*goût, odeur*] strange, odd ◆ **il a toujours été un peu** ~ he has always been a bit peculiar *ou* odd

4 (= *privé*) [*voiture, secrétaire, conversation, intérêt*] private ◆ **l'entreprise a son service ~ de livraison** the company has its own delivery service ◆ **intervenir à titre** ~ to intervene in a private capacity; → **hôtel, leçon**

NM 1 (= *personne*) person; (*Admin, Comm*) private individual ◆ **comme un simple** ~ like any ordinary person ◆ **vente/location de ~ à ~** (*petites annonces*) private sale/let (*Brit*) *ou* rental (*US*) ◆ **"particulier vend"** (*petite annonce*) "for sale privately", "for private sale"

2 (* = *individu*) individual, character ◆ **un drôle de** ~ an odd individual *ou* character

3 (= *chose*) **le** ~ the particular ◆ **du général au** ~ from the general to the particular

◆ **en particulier** (= *en privé*) [*parler*] in private; (= *séparément*) [*examiner*] separately; (= *surtout*) in particular, particularly, especially; (= *entre autres choses*) in particular

particulièrement /partikyljɛrmɑ̃/ ADV particularly, especially, specially ◆ ~ **bon/évolué** particularly *ou* specially good/well-developed ◆ **je ne le connais pas** ~ I don't know him very *ou* particularly well ◆ **il aime tous les arts et tout ~ la peinture** he enjoys all the arts, especially *ou* specially painting ◆ ~ **difficile** particularly difficult ◆ ~ **drôle** exceptionally funny ◆ **je voudrais plus ~ vous faire remarquer ce détail** I'd particularly like to draw your attention to this detail ◆ **voulez-vous du café ? – je n'y tiens pas** ~ would you like a coffee? – not particularly *ou* specially

partie² /parti/ NF 1 (= *portion, fraction*) part; (= *quantité*) part, amount ◆ **diviser qch en trois ~s** to divide sth into three parts ◆ **il y a des ~s amusantes dans le film** the film is funny in parts, the film has its funny moments ◆ **il ne possède qu'une ~ du terrain** he only owns part of the land ◆ **~s communes/privatives** (*Constr*) common/privately-owned parts ◆ **une petite ~ de l'argent** a small part *ou* amount of the money ◆ **une grande *ou* bonne ~ du travail** a large *ou* good part of *ou* a good deal of the work ◆ **la majeure *ou* plus grande ~ du temps/du pays** most of *ou* the greater *ou* the best part of the time/of the country ◆ **la majeure ~ des gens** the majority of people, most people ◆ **la plus grande ~ de ce que l'on vous a dit** most of what you were told ◆ **tout ou ~ de** all or part of ◆ **le film sera diffusé en première ~ de soirée** (*TV*) the film will be shown early on in the evening

◆ **faire partie + de** [*+ ensemble, obligations, risques*] to be part of; [*+ club, association*] to belong to, to be a member of; [*+ catégorie, famille*] to belong to; [*+ élus, gagnants*] to be among, to be one of ◆ **la rivière fait ~ du domaine** the river is part of the estate ◆ **les villes faisant ~ de ma circonscription** the towns that make up my constituency ◆ **elle fait ~ de notre groupe** she belongs to our group, she's one of our group ◆ **faire ~ intégrante de** to be an integral part of, to be part and parcel of

◆ **en + partie** ◆ **en** ~ partly, in part ◆ **en grande *ou* majeure** ~ largely, mainly ◆ **cela s'explique, en grande ~, par ...** this can be explained, for the most part, by ..., this can largely be explained by ...

2 (= *spécialité*) field, subject ◆ **moi qui suis de la** ~ knowing the field *ou* subject as I do ◆ **il n'est pas dans *ou* de la** ~ it's not his line *ou* field ◆ **quand on lui parle électricité, il est dans sa** ~ when it comes to electricity, he knows what he's talking about ◆ **demande à ton frère, c'est sa** ~ *ou* **il est de la** ~ ask your brother – it's his field *ou* his line

3 (*Cartes, Sport*) game; (*Golf*) round; (= *lutte*) struggle, fight ◆ **faisons une ~ de ...** let's have a game of ... ◆ **on a fait une bonne** ~ we had a good game ◆ **abandonner la** ~ (*fig*) to give up the fight ◆ **la ~ est délicate** it's a tricky situation *ou* business ◆ **la ~ n'est pas égale** (*lit, fig*) it's an uneven contest

4 (*Jur*) [*de contrat*] party; [*de procès*] litigant; (*Mil* = *adversaire*) opponent ◆ **la ~ adverse** the opposing party ◆ **les ~s en présence** the parties ◆ **les ~s belligérantes** the warring factions ◆ **avoir affaire à forte** ~ to have a strong *ou* tough opponent to contend with ◆ **être ~ prenante dans une négociation** to be a party to a negotiation ◆ **prise à** ~ (*Jur*) *action against a judge*; → **juge**

5 (*Mus*) part

6 († , *euph*) **~s sexuelles *ou* génitales** private parts ◆ **~s viriles** male organs ◆ **les ~s*** the privates*

7 (*locutions*) **avoir la ~ belle** to be sitting pretty* ◆ **se mettre de la** ~ to join in ◆ **je veux être de la** ~ I don't want to miss this, I want to be in on this* ◆ **avoir ~ liée (avec qn)** (*littér*) to be hand in glove (with sb) ◆ **ce n'est que ~ remise** it will be for another time, we'll take a raincheck* (*US*) ◆ **prendre qn à** ~ (= *apostropher*) to take sb to task; (= *malmener*) to set on sb ◆ **comptabilité en ~ simple/double** single-/double-entry book-keeping

COMP **partie de campagne** day *ou* outing in the country

partie carrée wife-swapping party

partie de chasse shooting party *ou* expedition

partie civile (*Jur*) *private party associating in a court action with public prosecutor* ◆ **se porter *ou* se constituer ~ civile** *to associate in a court action with the public prosecutor* ◆ **constitution de ~ civile** *independent action for damages*

partie du discours (*Ling*) part of speech

partie fine orgy

partie de jambes en l'air‡ **tout ce qui l'intéresse, c'est une ~ de jambes en l'air** all he's interested in is getting his leg over‡

partie de pêche fishing party *ou* trip

partie de plaisir (*fig*) **ce n'est pas une ~ de plaisir !** it's no picnic!*, it's not my idea of fun!

partiel, -elle /parsjɛl/ ADJ (*gén*) partial ◆ **paiement** ~ part payment ◆ **les (élections) partielles** by(e)-elections; → **temps¹** NM (*Univ*) class (*Brit*) *ou* mid-term (*US*) exam

partiellement /parsjɛlmɑ̃/ ADV partially, partly

partir¹ /partir/ ▸ conjug 16 ◂ VI 1 (= *quitter un lieu*) to go, to leave; (= *se mettre en route*) to leave, to set off, to set out; (= *s'éloigner*) to go away *ou* off; (= *disparaître*) to go ◆ **pars, tu vas être en retard** go *ou* off you go, you're going to be late ◆ **pars, tu m'embêtes** go away, you're annoying me ◆ **es-tu prêt à ~ ?** are you ready to go? ◆ **allez, je pars** I'm off now ◆ **il est parti sans laisser d'adresse** he left without leaving an address ◆ **nos voisins sont partis il y a six mois** our neighbours left six months ago ◆ **depuis que mon pauvre mari est parti** (*euph* = *mourir*) since my poor husband passed on *ou* away ◆ **ma lettre ne partira pas ce soir** my letter won't go this evening ◆ **quand partez-vous (pour Paris) ?** when are you going (to Paris)? *ou* leaving (for Paris)?, when are you off (to Paris)?* ◆ ~ **pour le bureau** to leave *ou* set off for the office ◆ **elle est partie de Nice à 9 heures** she left Nice *ou* set off from Nice at 9 o'clock ◆ **sa femme est partie de la maison** his wife has left home ◆ **sa femme est partie avec un autre** his wife has gone off with another man ◆ **le mauvais temps a fait ~ les touristes** the bad weather has driven the tourists away ◆ **j'espère que je ne vous fais pas** ~ I hope I'm not chasing you away ◆ **fais ~ le chat de ma chaise** get the cat off my chair ◆ **ceux-là, quand ils viennent bavarder, c'est dur de les faire** ~ when that lot come round for a chat, it's hard to get rid of them* ◆ ~, **c'est mourir un peu** to leave is to die a little

2 (= *aller*) to go ◆ **il est parti en Irlande** (*il y est encore*) he has gone to Ireland; (*il en est revenu*) he went to Ireland ◆ **il est parti dans sa chambre/acheter du pain** he has gone to his room/to buy some bread ◆ ~ **faire des courses/se promener** to go (out) shopping/for a walk ◆ **pars devant acheter les billets** go on ahead and buy the tickets ◆ ~ **à la chasse/à la pêche** to go shooting/fishing ◆ ~ **en vacances/en voyage** to go on holiday/on a trip ◆ ~ **à pied** to set off on foot ◆ **tu pars en avion ou en voiture ?** are you flying or driving?, are you going by plane or (by) car? ◆ ~ **à la guerre/au front** to go (off) to the war/to the front

3 (= *démarrer*) [*moteur*] to start; [*avion*] to take off; [*train*] to leave; [*coureur*] to be off; [*plante*] to take ◆ **la voiture partit sous son nez** the car started up *ou* drove off and left him standing ◆ **il partit en courant** he ran *ou* dashed off ◆ **il partit en trombe *ou* comme une flèche** he was off *ou* set off like a shot ◆ **attention, le train va** ~ look out, the train's leaving ◆ **l'avion va ~ dans quelques minutes** the plane is taking off in a few minutes ◆ **ce cheval est bien/mal parti** that horse got off to a good/bad start ◆ ~ **gagnant** to begin as if one is sure of success ◆ **les voilà partis !** they're off! ◆ **c'est parti (mon kiki) !*** here we go!* ◆ **faire ~ une voiture/un moteur** to start (up) a car/an engine; → **marque**

4 (= *être lancé*) [*fusée*] to go off *ou* up; [*coup de feu*] to go off; [*bouchon*] to pop *ou* shoot out ◆ **le coup est parti tout seul** the gun went off on its own ◆ **le coup ne partit pas** the gun didn't go off, the gun misfired ◆ **le bouchon est parti au plafond** the cork shot up to *ou* hit the ceiling ◆ **les cris qui partaient de la foule** the shouts *ou* cries (coming *ou* that came) from the crowd ◆ **le pétard n'a pas voulu** ~ the banger wouldn't go off ◆ **le mot partit malgré lui** the word came out *ou* slipped out before he could stop it ◆ **le ballon partit comme un boulet de canon** the ball shot off like a bullet ◆ **faire** ~ [*+ fusée*] to launch; [*+ pétard*] to set off, to light

5 (= *être engagé*) ~ **sur une idée fausse/une mauvaise piste** to start off with the wrong idea/on the wrong track ◆ ~ **bien/mal** to get off to a good/bad start, to start (off) well/badly ◆ **le pays est mal parti** the country is in a bad way *ou* in a mess *ou* in a sorry state ◆ **nous sommes mal partis pour arriver à l'heure** it seems unlikely we'll arrive on time now ◆ **son affaire est bien partie** his business has got off to a good start ◆ **il est bien parti pour gagner** he seems all set to win ◆ ~ **dans des digressions sans fin** to wander off *ou* launch into endless digressions ◆ **quand ils sont partis à discuter, il y en a pour des heures*** once they're off* *ou* launched on one of their discussions, they'll be at it for hours* ◆ ~ **à rire*** *ou* **d'un éclat de rire** to burst out laughing ◆ **il est (bien) parti pour parler deux heures** the

way he's going, he'll be talking for *ou* he looks all set to talk for two hours ◆ **la pluie est partie pour (durer) toute la journée** the rain has set in for the day ◆ **on est parti pour ne pas déjeuner** at this rate *ou* the way things are going, we won't get any lunch

6 *(= commencer)* ~ **de** *[contrat, vacances]* to begin on, to run from; *[course, excursion]* to start *ou* leave from ◆ **l'autoroute part de Lille** the motorway starts at Lille ◆ **un chemin qui part de l'église** a path going from *ou* leaving the church ◆ **les branches qui partent du tronc** the branches going out from the trunk ◆ **c'est le troisième en partant de la droite** it's (the) third from the right ◆ **cet industriel est parti de rien** *ou* **de zéro** this industrialist started from scratch *ou* from *ou* with nothing ◆ **cette rumeur est partie de rien** this rumour grew up out of nothing ◆ **notre analyse part de cette constatation** our analysis is based on this observation *ou* takes this observation as its starting point ◆ **partons de l'hypothèse que ...** let's assume that ... ◆ **si tu pars du principe que tu as toujours raison/qu'ils ne peuvent pas gagner** if you start off by assuming that you're always right/that they can't win ◆ **en partant de ce principe, rien n'est digne d'intérêt** on that basis, nothing's worthy of interest ◆ **en partant de là, on peut faire n'importe quoi** looking at things that way, one can do anything

7 *(= provenir)* ~ **de** to come from ◆ **ces mots partent/ça part du cœur** these words come/it comes (straight) from the heart ◆ **cela part d'un bon sentiment/d'un bon naturel** that comes from his (*ou* her *etc*) kindness/good nature

8 *(= disparaître) [tache]* to go, to come out; *[crochet, bouton]* to come off; *[douleur]* to go; *[rougeurs, boutons]* to go, to clear up; *[odeur]* to go, to clear ◆ **la tache est partie au lavage** the stain has come out in the wash *ou* has washed out ◆ **toute la couleur est partie** all the colour has gone *ou* faded ◆ **faire** ~ *[+ tache]* to remove; *[+ odeur]* to clear, to get rid of

LOC PRÉP **à partir de** from ◆ **à** ~ **d'aujourd'hui** (as) from today, from today onwards ◆ **à** ~ **de 4 heures** from 4 o'clock on(wards) ◆ **à** ~ **de maintenant** from now on ◆ **à** ~ **de ce moment-là** from then on ◆ **à** ~ **du moment où ...** *(= dès que)* as soon as ...; *(= pourvu que)* so *ou* as long as ... ◆ **à** ~ **d'ici le pays est plat** from here on(wards) the land is flat ◆ **c'est le troisième à** ~ **de la gauche** it's the third (along) from the left ◆ **lire à** ~ **de la page 5** to start reading at page 5 ◆ **allez jusqu'à la poste et, à** ~ **de là, c'est tout droit** go as far as the post office and after that it's straight ahead ◆ **pantalons à** ~ **de 45 €** trousers from €45 (upwards) ◆ **à** ~ **de ces 3 couleurs vous pouvez obtenir toutes les nuances** with *ou* from these 3 colours you can get any shade ◆ **c'est fait à** ~ **de produits chimiques** it's made from chemicals

partir² /paʀtiʀ/ VT → **maille**

partisan, e /paʀtizɑ̃, an/ ADJ 1 *(= partial)* partisan 2 ◆ **être** ~ **de qch/de faire qch** to be in favour *(Brit)* *ou* favor *(US)* of sth/of doing sth ◆ **être** ~ **du moindre effort** to be a believer in (taking) the line of least resistance NM,F *[de personne, thèse, régime]* supporter; *[d'action]* supporter, advocate, proponent; *[de doctrine, réforme]* partisan, supporter, advocate; *(Mil)* partisan ◆ **c'est un** ~ **de la fermeté** he's an advocate of *ou* a believer in firm measures, he supports *ou* advocates firm measures

partita /paʀtita/ NF *(Mus)* partita

partitif, -ive /paʀtitif, iv/ ADJ partitive NM partitive (article)

partition /paʀtisjɔ̃/ NF 1 *(Mus)* score ◆ **grande** ~ full score 2 *(frm, gén Pol = division)* partition 3 *(Ordin)* partition

partouse* /paʀtuz/ NF orgy

partouser* /paʀtuze/ ► conjug 1 ◄ VI to have an orgy *ou* orgies

partout /paʀtu/ ADV everywhere, everyplace *(US)* ◆ ~ **où** everywhere (that), wherever ◆ **avoir mal** ~ to ache all over ◆ **tu as mis des papiers** ~ you've put papers all over the place ◆ **2/15** ~ *(Sport)* 2/15 all ◆ **40** ~ *(Tennis)* deuce

partouze* /paʀtuz/ NF ⇒ **partouse**

parturiente /paʀtyʀjɑ̃t/ ADJ F, NF parturient

parturition /paʀtyʀisjɔ̃/ NF parturition

parure /paʀyʀ/ NF 1 *(= toilette)* costume, finery *(NonC)*; *(= bijoux)* jewels; *(= sous-vêtements)* set of lingerie; *(littér)* finery, livery *(littér)* ◆ ~ **de table/de lit** set of table/bed linen ◆ ~ **de berceau** cot *(Brit)* *ou* crib *(US)* set ◆ ~ **de diamants** set of diamond jewellery ◆ **les arbres ont revêtu leur** ~ **de feuilles** *(littér)* the trees have put on their leafy finery *(littér)* 2 *(= déchet)* trimming

parution /paʀysjɔ̃/ NF publication ◆ **dès sa** ~, **ce roman a eu beaucoup de succès** this novel was a huge success as soon as it came out

parvenir /paʀvəniʀ/ ► conjug 22 ◄ VT INDIR **parvenir à** 1 *(= arriver) [+ sommet]* to get to, to reach; *[+ honneurs]* to achieve; *[+ état, âge]* to reach ◆ ~ **aux oreilles de qn** to reach sb's ears ◆ **ma lettre lui est parvenue** my letter reached him, he got my letter ◆ **ses ordres nous sont parvenus** his orders reached us ◆ **faire** ~ **qch à qn** to send sth to sb ◆ ~ **à ses fins** to achieve one's ends, to get what one wants ◆ **sa renommée est parvenue jusqu'à notre époque** *ou* **nous** his renown survives to this day 2 *(= réussir)* ~ **à faire qch** to manage to do sth, to succeed in doing sth ◆ **il y est parvenu** he managed it ◆ **il n'y parvient pas tout seul** he can't manage on his own VI *(péj = faire fortune)* to succeed *ou* get on in life, to arrive

parvenu, e /paʀvəny/ (ptp de **parvenir**) ADJ upstart ADJ, NM,F *(péj)* parvenu, upstart

parvis /paʀvi/ NM square *(in front of church or public building)*

pas¹ /pɑ/ NM 1 *(gén)* step; *(= bruit)* footstep; *(= trace)* footprint ◆ **faire un** ~ **en arrière/en avant, reculer/avancer d'un** ~ to step back/forward, to take a step *ou* a pace back/forward ◆ **(il fait) un** ~ **en avant et deux en arrière** *(fig)* (he takes) one step forward and two steps back ◆ **il reconnut son** ~ **dans le couloir** he recognized the sound of her footsteps in the corridor ◆ **revenir** *ou* **retourner sur ses** ~ to retrace one's steps ◆ **je vais là où me conduisent mes** ~ I am going where my steps take me ◆ **avancer à petits** ~ *(lit, fig)* to inch forward, to inch one's way along ◆ **faire de grands** ~**/de petits** ~ to take long strides/short steps ◆ **la politique des petits** ~ the policy of taking things one step at a time ◆ **marcher à grands** ~ to stride along ◆ **à** ~ **mesurés** *ou* **comptés** with measured steps ◆ ~ **à** ~ *(lit, fig)* step by step ◆ **à chaque** ~ *(lit, fig)* at every step ◆ **il ne peut pas faire un** ~ **sans elle/sans la rencontrer** he can't go anywhere without her/without meeting her ◆ **ne le quittez pas d'un** ~ follow him wherever he goes ◆ **arriver sur les** ~ **de qn** to arrive just after sb, to follow close on sb's heels ◆ **marcher sur les** ~ **de qn** to follow in sb's footsteps ◆ **faire ses premiers** ~ to start walking *ou* to walk

2 *(= distance)* pace ◆ **à 20** ~ at 20 paces ◆ **c'est à deux** ~ **d'ici** it's only a minute away, it's just a stone's throw from here

3 *(= vitesse)* pace; *(Mil)* step; *[de cheval]* walk ◆ **aller** *ou* **marcher d'un bon** ~ to walk at a good *ou* brisk pace ◆ **marcher d'un** ~ **lent** to walk slowly ◆ **changer de** ~ to change step ◆ **allonger** *ou* **hâter** *ou* **presser le** ~ to hurry on, to quicken one's step *ou* pace ◆ **ralentir le** ~ to slow down ◆ **marcher au** ~ to march ◆ **se mettre au** ~ to get in step ◆ **mettre son cheval au** ~ to walk one's horse ◆ **rouler** *ou* **aller au** ~ *(en voiture)* to crawl along, to go at a walking pace ◆ **"roulez au pas"** "dead slow" ◆ **au** ~ **cadencé** in quick time ◆ **au** ~ **de charge** at the double ◆ **au** ~ **de course** at a run ◆ **au** ~ **de gymnastique** at a jog trot ◆ **au** ~ **redoublé** in double time, double-quick

4 *(= démarche)* tread ◆ **d'un** ~ **lourd** *ou* **pesant** with a heavy tread ◆ ~ **d'éléphant** heavy tread

5 *(Danse)* step ◆ ~ **de danse/valse** dance/waltz step; → **esquisser**

6 *(Géog = passage) [de montagne]* pass; *[de mer]* strait

7 *[de vis, écrou]* thread; *[d'hélice]* pitch

8 *(locutions)* **faire un grand** ~ **en avant** to take a big step *ou* a great leap forward ◆ **la science avance à grands** ~**/à** ~ **de géant** science is taking great/gigantic steps forward ◆ **il progresse à** ~ **de géant** he's coming on in leaps and bounds ◆ **faire le(s) premier(s)** ~ to take the initiative, to make the first move ◆ **il n'y a que le premier** ~ **qui coûte** the first step is the hardest ◆ **à** ~ **de loup, à** ~ **feutrés** stealthily ◆ **d'un** ~ **léger** *(= avec insouciance)* airily, blithely; *(= joyeusement)* with a spring in one's step ◆ **entrer/sortir d'un** ~ **léger** *(= agilement)* to pad in/out ◆ **j'y vais de ce** ~ I'll go straightaway *(Brit)* *ou* at once ◆ **mettre qn au** ~ to bring sb to heel, to make sb toe the line ◆ **avoir le** ~ **sur qn** to rank before *ou* above sb ◆ **prendre le** ~ **sur** *[+ considérations, préoccupations]* to override; *[+ théorie, méthode]* to supplant; *[+ personne]* to steal a lead over ◆ **franchir** *ou* **sauter le** ~ to take the plunge ◆ **du mensonge à la calomnie il n'y a qu'un** ~ it's a short *ou* small step from lies to slander; → **céder, cent¹, faux²**

COMP **pas battu** *(Danse)* pas battu

le pas de Calais *(= détroit)* the Straits of Dover

pas de clerc *(littér)* blunder

pas de deux *(Danse)* pas de deux

pas de l'oie *(Mil)* goose-step ◆ **faire le** ~ **de l'oie** to goose-step

le pas de la porte the doorstep ◆ **sur le** ~ **de la porte** on the doorstep, in the doorway

pas de tir *[de champ de tir]* shooting range; *(Espace)* launching pad

pas de vis thread

pas² /pɑ/ ADV 1 *(avec ne : formant nég verbale)* not ◆ **je ne vais** ~ **à l'école** *(aujourd'hui)* I'm not *ou* I am not going to school; *(habituellement)* I don't *ou* I do not go to school ◆ **ce n'est** ~ **vrai, c'est** ~ **vrai*** it isn't *ou* it's not *ou* it is not true ◆ **je ne suis** ~**/il n'est** ~ **allé à l'école** I/he didn't *ou* did not go to school ◆ **je ne trouve** ~ **mon sac** I can't *ou* cannot find my bag ◆ **je ne la vois** ~ I can't *ou* cannot see her ◆ **je ne prends** ~**/je ne veux** ~ **de pain** I won't have/I don't want any bread ◆ **ils n'ont** ~ **de voiture/d'enfants** they don't have *ou* haven't got a car/any children, they have no car/children ◆ **il m'a dit de (ne)** ~ **le faire** he told me not to do it ◆ **ça me serait insupportable de ne** ~ **le voir, ne** ~ **le voir me serait insupportable** it would be unbearable not to see him, not to see him would be unbearable ◆ **je pense qu'il ne viendra** ~ I don't think he'll come ◆ **ce n'est** ~ **sans peine que je l'ai convaincu** it was not without (some) difficulty that I convinced him ◆ **non** ~ *ou* **ce n'est** ~ **qu'il soit bête** (it's) not that he's a fool ◆ **ce n'est** ~ **que je refuse** it's not that I refuse ◆ **il n'y a** ~ **que ça** it's not just that ◆ **il n'y a** ~ **que lui** he's not the only one ◆ **je n'en sais** ~ **plus que vous** I don't know any more about it than you (do) ◆ **il n'y avait** ~ **plus de 20 personnes** there were no more than 20 people there ◆ **il n'est** ~ **plus/moins intelligent que vous** he is no more/no less intelligent than you ◆ **ne me parle** ~ **sur ce ton** don't speak to me like that, do NOT speak to me like that

2 *(indiquant ou renforçant opposition)* **elle travaille, (mais) lui** ~ she works, but he doesn't ◆ **il aime ça,** ~ **toi ?** he likes it, don't you? ◆ **ils**

sont quatre et non ~ trois there are four of them, not three ◆ **vient-il ou (ne vient-il) ~ ?** is he coming or not?, is he coming or isn't he? ◆ **leur maison est chauffée, la nôtre ~** their house is heated but ours isn't *ou* is not

3 *(dans réponses négatives)* not ◆ **~ de sucre, merci !** no sugar, thanks! ◆ **~ du tout** not at all, not a bit ◆ **il t'a remercié, au moins ? – ~ du tout** *ou* **absolument ~** he did at least thank you? – he certainly didn't *ou* did not ◆ **~ encore** not yet ◆ **tu as aimé le film ? – ~ plus que ça** did you like the film? – it was so-so* ◆ **~ tellement***, **~ tant que ça** not (all) that much, not so very much ◆ **~ des masses*** not a lot*, not an awful lot* ◆ **qui l'a prévenu ? – ~ moi/elle** *etc* who told him? – not me/her *etc ou* I didn't/she didn't *etc*

4 *(devant adj, n, dans excl : *)* **ce sont des gens ~ fiers** they're not proud people ◆ **il est dans une situation ~ banale** *ou* **~ ordinaire** he's in an unusual situation ◆ **~ un n'est venu** not one *ou* none (of them) came ◆ **~ possible !** no!, you don't say!* ◆ **~ de chance*** hard *ou* bad luck*!, too bad* ◆ **~ vrai ?*** isn't that so?, (isn't that) right? ◆ **tu es content ? eh bien ~ moi !** are you satisfied? well I'm not! ◆ **tu es content, ~ vrai ? !*** you're pleased, aren't you? *ou* admit it ◆ **t'es ~ un peu fou ?*** you must be *ou* you're crazy!* ◆ **~ d'histoires** *ou* **de blagues, il faut absolument que j'arrive à l'heure** no nonsense now, I absolutely must be on time ◆ **(c'est) ~ bête, cette idée !** that's not a bad idea (at all)! ◆ **si c'est ~ malheureux !*** *ou* **honteux !*** isn't that disgraceful! ◆ **tu viendras, ~ ?*** you're coming, aren't you?, you'll come, won't you? ◆ **~ de ça !** we'll have none of that! ◆ **ah non, ~ ça !** oh no, anything but that! ◆ **ah non, ~ lui !** oh no, not him!; → **falloir, fou**

COMP **pas grand-chose** *(péj)* NMF INV good-for-nothing

Pascal /paskal/ NM *(Ordin)* Pascal

pascal[1]**, e** (mpl **-aux**) /paskal, o/ ADJ *[agneau]* paschal; *[messe]* Easter

pascal[2] (pl **pascals**) /paskal/ NM *(Phys)* pascal; *(† * = billet)* 500 franc note

pascalien, -ienne /paskaljɛ̃, jɛn/ ADJ of Pascal

pas-de-porte /padpɔʀt/ NM INV *(= argent)* ≈ key money *(for shop, flat etc)*

pashmina /paʃmina/ NM pashmina

pasionaria /pasjɔnaʀja/ NF passionate (female) militant ◆ **Marie Dupont, la ~ de la libération des femmes** Marie Dupont, the ardent champion of women's liberation

paso doble /pasodɔbl/ NM paso doble

passable /pasabl/ ADJ passable, tolerable; *(sur copie d'élève)* fair ◆ **mention ~** *(Univ)* ≈ pass-(mark) ◆ **à peine ~** barely passable, not so good

passablement /pasabləmɑ̃/ ADV *(= moyennement) [jouer, travailler]* tolerably *ou* reasonably well; *(= assez) [irritant, long]* rather, fairly, pretty*; *(= beaucoup)* quite a lot *ou* a bit* ◆ **il faut ~ de courage pour ...** it requires a fair amount of courage to ...

passade /pasad/ NF passing fancy, whim, fad; *(amoureuse)* brief affair

passage /pasaʒ/ NM 1 *(= venue)* **guetter le ~ du facteur** to watch for the postman to come by, to be on the look-out for the postman ◆ **attendre le ~ de l'autobus** to wait for the bus to come ◆ **agrandir une voie pour permettre le ~ de gros camions** to widen a road to allow heavy vehicles to use it *ou* to allow heavy vehicles through ◆ **observer le ~ des oiseaux dans le ciel** to watch the birds fly by *ou* over ◆ **pour empêcher le ~ de l'air sous la porte** to stop draughts (coming in) under the door ◆ **lors de votre ~ à la douane** when you go *ou* pass through customs ◆ **lors d'un récent ~ à Paris** when I *(ou he etc)* was in *ou* visiting Paris recently, on a recent trip to Paris ◆ **la navette d'autobus fait quatre ~s par jour** the shuttle bus runs four times a day ◆ **prochain ~ de notre représentant le 8 mai** our representative will be in the area again on 8 May ◆ **"passage interdit"** "no entry", "no thoroughfare" ◆ **"passage de troupeaux"** "cattle crossing" ◆ **livrer ~** to make way ◆ **livrer ~ à qn** to let sb pass, to make way for sb ◆ **il y a beaucoup de ~ l'été** a lot of people come through here in the summer ◆ **lors de son ~ au gouvernement** during his time in the government

◆ **de passage** ◆ **il est de ~ à Paris** he is in *ou* passing through Paris at the moment ◆ **amours/amants de ~** casual affairs/lovers ◆ **les commerçants travaillent avec les clients de ~** the shopkeepers cater for passing trade; → **lieu**[1]

◆ **au passage** ◆ **il a saisi le panier au ~** he picked up the basket as he went past ◆ **ils l'ont, au ~, délesté de son portefeuille** in passing they relieved him of his wallet ◆ **il a rappelé au ~ que ce sont les socialistes qui ont proposé cette réforme** he recalled in passing that it was the Socialists who proposed this reform ◆ **il oublia, au ~, de prévenir le maire** incidentally he forgot to inform the mayor

2 *(= transfert)* **le ~ de l'état solide à l'état gazeux** the change from the solid to the gaseous state ◆ **le ~ de l'enfance à l'adolescence** the transition *ou* passage from childhood to adolescence ◆ **le ~ du jour à la nuit** the change from day to night ◆ **le ~ du grade de capitaine à celui de commandant** promotion from captain to major ◆ **le ~ de l'alcool dans le sang** the entry of alcohol into the bloodstream ◆ **son ~ en classe supérieure est problématique** there are problems about his moving up *ou* promotion *(US)* to the next class *(Brit) ou* grade *(US)* ◆ **pour réussir le ~ à l'euro** to make a smooth transition to the euro, to make the changeover to the euro successful ◆ **le ~ à l'heure d'été** changing to summer time; → **examen**

3 *(= lieu)* passage; *(= chemin)* way, passage; *(= itinéraire)* route; *(= rue)* passage(way), alley-(way) ◆ **un ~ dangereux sur la falaise** a dangerous section of the cliff ◆ **il faut trouver un ~ dans ces broussailles** we must find a way through this undergrowth ◆ **on a mis des barrières sur le ~ de la procession** barriers have been put up along the route of the procession ◆ **on se retourne sur son ~** people turn round and look when he goes past ◆ **l'ouragan dévasta tout sur son ~** the hurricane demolished everything in its path ◆ **barrer le ~ à qn** to block sb's way ◆ **laisser le ~ à qn** to let sb pass *ou* past ◆ **va plus loin, tu gênes le ~** move along, you're in the way ◆ **ne laissez pas vos valises dans le ~** don't leave your cases in the way ◆ **le ~ du Nord-Ouest** the North-West Passage; → **frayer**

4 *(en bateau)* **payer son ~** to pay for one's passage, to pay one's fare

5 *(= fragment) [de livre, symphonie]* passage

6 *(= traversée) [de rivière, limite, montagnes]* crossing ◆ **le ~ de la ligne** *(Naut)* crossing the Line

7 *(= moment)* **ça a été un ~ difficile dans sa vie** it was a difficult period in his life ◆ **~s nuageux** cloudy spells

COMP **passage à l'acte** acting out ◆ **ce qui a déclenché le ~ à l'acte** *(crime, suicide)* what pushed him to carry out the murder *(ou* suicide)

passage clouté pedestrian crossing, ≈ zebra crossing *(Brit)*, crosswalk *(US)*

passage à niveau level crossing *(Brit)*, grade crossing *(US)*

passage (pour) piétons pedestrian walkway

passage protégé *(sur route)* priority *ou* right of way *(over secondary roads)*

passage souterrain *(gén)* underground *ou* subterranean passage; *(pour piétons)* underpass, subway *(Brit)*

passage à tabac beating up

passage à vide *(= baisse de forme, mauvaises performances) [d'équipe, entreprise, économie]* bad patch ◆ **j'ai toujours un petit ~ à vide vers 16 h** I always start to flag around 4 o'clock ◆ **j'ai eu un ~ à vide pendant l'examen** my mind went blank during the exam

passager, -ère /pasaʒe, ɛʀ/ ADJ 1 *(= de courte durée) [malaise]* passing *(épith)*, brief; *[inconvénient]* temporary; *[bonheur, beauté]* passing *(épith)*, transient, ephemeral ◆ **j'ai eu un malaise ~** I felt faint for a few minutes ◆ **pluies passagères** intermittent *ou* occasional showers 2 *[rue]* busy NM,F passenger ◆ **~ clandestin** stowaway

passagèrement /pasaʒɛʀmɑ̃/ ADV for a short time, temporarily ◆ **il était revenu ~ au gouvernement** he returned to the government for a short time, he made a brief return to the government ◆ **ce sera une assez belle journée, ~ nuageuse** it will be quite a fine day, cloudy at times

passant, e /pasɑ̃, ɑ̃t/ ADJ *[rue]* busy; → **bande**[1] NM,F passer-by NM *[de ceinture]* loop

passation /pasasjɔ̃/ NF *[de contrat]* signing; *(Comm) [d'écriture]* entry ◆ **~ de pouvoirs** handing over of office *ou* power, transfer of power

passavant /pasavɑ̃/ NM 1 *(Comm, Jur)* transire, carnet 2 *(Naut)* catwalk

passe[1] /pas/ NF 1 *(Sport)* pass ◆ **faire une ~** to pass *(à* to); ◆ **~ en retrait/en avant** back/forward pass ◆ **~ croisée** *(Ftbl)* cross ◆ **faire une ~ croisée à qn** to cross to sb

2 *(= situation)* **être dans une bonne ~** *[personne, économie, équipe]* to be doing well ◆ **être dans** *ou* **traverser une mauvaise ~** *[personne, économie, entreprise, monnaie]* to be going through a bad patch ◆ **est-ce qu'il va sortir de cette mauvaise ~ ?** will he manage to pull through?; → **mot**

◆ **être en passe de faire qch** to be on one's *ou* the way to doing sth ◆ **il est en ~ de réussir** he is poised to succeed ◆ **c'est un rêve en ~ de devenir réalité** it's a dream that is about to become a reality ◆ **cette ville est en ~ de devenir le centre de la mode européenne** this city is poised to become the centre of European fashion ◆ **cette espèce est en ~ de disparaître** this species is on the way to extinction *ou* is dying out

3 *[de magnétiseur, prestidigitateur]* pass

4 *(Roulette)* passe

5 *(= chenal)* pass, channel

6 *[de prostituée]* **c'est 50 € la ~** it is 50 euros a time ◆ **faire 20 ~s par jour** to have 20 clients *ou* customers a day; → **hôtel, maison**

7 *(Imprim)* **(main de) ~** surplus paper ◆ **exemplaire de ~** over, surplus copy

COMP **passe d'armes** *(fig)* heated exchange

passe de caisse *(Comm) sum allowed for cashier's errors*

passe[2] * /pas/ NM abrév de **passe-partout**

passé, e /pase/ (ptp de **passer**) ADJ 1 *(= dernier)* last ◆ **c'est arrivé le mois ~/l'année ~e** it happened last month/last year ◆ **au cours des semaines/années ~es** over these last *ou* the past (few) weeks/years

2 *(= révolu) [action, conduite]* past ◆ **songeant à sa gloire ~e/ses angoisses ~es** thinking of his past *ou* former glory/distress ◆ **regrettant sa jeunesse/sa beauté ~e** yearning for her vanished youth/beauty ◆ **si l'on se penche sur les événements ~s** if one looks back over past events ◆ **cette époque est ~e maintenant** that era is now over ◆ **ce qui est ~ est ~** what's done is done, that's all in the past (now) ◆ **il a 60 ans ~s** he's over 60 ◆ **où sont mes années**

~es ? where has my life gone? ◆ **il se rappelait le temps ~** he was thinking back to days *ou* times gone by

3 *(= fané) [couleur, fleur]* faded ◆ **tissu ~** material that has lost its colour, faded material

4 *(= plus de)* **il est 8 heures ~es** it's past *ou* gone *(Brit)* 8 o'clock ◆ **il est rentré à 9 heures ~es** it was past *ou* gone *(Brit)* 9 o'clock when he got back ◆ **ça fait une heure ~e que je t'attends** I've been waiting for you for more than *ou* over an hour

NM 1 ◆ **le ~** the past ◆ **il faut oublier le ~** we should forget the past ◆ **c'est du ~, n'en parlons plus** it's (all) in the past now, let's not say any more about it ◆ **il est revenu nous voir comme par le ~** he came back to see us as he used to in the past ◆ **il a eu plusieurs condamnations dans le ~** he had several previous convictions

2 *(= vie écoulée)* past ◆ **pays fier de son ~** country proud of its past ◆ **bandit au ~ chargé** gangster with a past ◆ **son ~ m'est inconnu** I know nothing of his past

3 *(Gram)* past tense ◆ **les temps du ~** the past tenses ◆ **mettez cette phrase au ~** put this sentence into the past (tense) ◆ **~ antérieur** past anterior ◆ **~ composé** perfect ◆ **~ simple** past historic, preterite

PRÉP after ◆ **~ 6 heures on ne sert plus les clients** after 6 o'clock we stop serving ◆ **~ cette maison, on quitte le village** after this house, you are out of the village

passe-crassane (pl **passe-crassanes**) /paskʀasan/ **NF** *type of winter pear*

passe-droit (pl **passe-droits**) /pasdʀwa/ **NM** (undeserved) privilege, favour *(Brit)*, favor *(US)* ◆ **il a obtenu un ~** he got preferential treatment

passéisme /paseism/ **NM** *(péj)* attachment to the past

passéiste /paseist/ **ADJ** *(péj)* backward-looking **NMF** *(péj)* devotee of the past

passe-lacet (pl **passe-lacets**) /paslasɛ/ **NM** bodkin; → **raide**

passement /pasmɑ̃/ **NM** braid *(NonC)*

passementer /pasmɑ̃te/ ► **conjug 1** ◄ **VT** to braid

passementerie /pasmɑ̃tʀi/ **NF** *(= objets)* soft furnishings; *(= commerce)* soft furnishings, sale of soft furnishings ◆ **rayon de ~** department selling soft furnishings

passementier, -ière /pasmɑ̃tje, jɛʀ/ **ADJ** ◆ **industrie passementière** soft furnishings industry **NM,F** *(= fabricant)* manufacturer of soft furnishings; *(= vendeur)* salesman (*ou* -woman) specializing in soft furnishings

passe-montagne (pl **passe-montagnes**) /pasmɔ̃taɲ/ **NM** balaclava

passe-muraille /pasmyʀaj/ **ADJ** *[personne, tenue]* unremarkable **NM INV** unremarkable person

passe-partout /paspaʀtu/ **ADJ INV** *[tenue]* for all occasions, all-purpose *(épith)*; *[formule]* all-purpose *(épith)*, catch-all *(épith)* **NM INV** 1 *(= clé)* master *ou* skeleton key 2 *(= encadrement)* passe-partout 3 *(= scie)* crosscut saw

passe-passe /paspas/ **NM INV** ◆ **tour de ~** *[de magicien]* conjuring trick; *(fig)* trick, sleight of hand ◆ **faire des tours de ~** to perform conjuring tricks ◆ **par un tour de ~ financier** by a financial sleight of hand

passe-plat (pl **passe-plats**) /paspla/ **NM** serving hatch

passepoil /paspwal/ **NM** piping *(NonC)*

passepoilé, e /paspwale/ **ADJ** piped

passeport /paspɔʀ/ **NM** passport ◆ **demander ses ~s** *[ambassadeur]* to withdraw one's credentials ◆ **ce diplôme est un ~ pour l'emploi** this degree is a passport to a job

passer /pase/

► **conjug 1** ◄

GRAMMAIRE ACTIVE 54.1, 54.2, 54.4

1 VERBE INTRANSITIF 3 VERBE PRONOMINAL
2 VERBE TRANSITIF

Lorsque **passer** s'emploie dans des locutions figurées telles que **passer sous le nez de qn, passer sur le ventre/le corps à qn** etc, cherchez sous le nom.

1 - VERBE INTRANSITIF

avec auxiliaire être

1 gén to pass, to go *ou* come past ◆ **~ en courant** to run past ◆ **~ à pas lents** to go slowly past ◆ **le train va bientôt ~** the train will be coming past *ou* by soon ◆ **où passe la route ?** where does the road go? ◆ **faire ~ les piétons** to let the pedestrians cross; → **bouche, main**

◆ **passer** + *préposition ou adverbe* ◆ **~ sous/sur/devant/derrière** *etc* to go under/over/in front of/behind *etc* ◆ **la route passe à Vierzon** the road goes through Vierzon ◆ **la Seine passe à Paris** the Seine flows through Paris ◆ **les poissons sont passés au travers du filet** the fish slipped through the net ◆ **les camions ne passent pas dans notre rue** lorries don't come along *ou* down our street ◆ **il passait dans la rue avec son chien/en voiture** he was walking down the street with his dog/driving down the street ◆ **le fil passe dans ce tuyau** the wire goes down *ou* through this pipe ◆ **une lueur cruelle passa dans son regard** a cruel gleam came into his eyes ◆ **l'autobus lui est passé dessus, il est passé sous l'autobus** he was run over by the bus ◆ **~ devant la maison de qn** to go past *ou* to pass sb's house ◆ **je passe devant vous pour vous montrer le chemin** I'll go in front to show you the way ◆ **passez donc devant** you go first ◆ **la voie ferrée passe le long du fleuve** the railway line runs alongside the river ◆ **la balle/flèche n'est pas passée loin** the bullet/arrow didn't miss by much ◆ **pour y aller, je passe par Amiens** I go *ou* pass through Amiens to get there, I go there via Amiens ◆ **je passe par la gare, je peux vous déposer** I'm going by the station, I can drop you off ◆ **par où êtes-vous passé ?** which way did you go? *ou* come? ◆ **le chien est trop gros pour ~ par le trou** the dog is too big to get through the hole ◆ **ça fait du bien par où ça passe !** * that's just what the doctor ordered! * ◆ **l'air passe sous la porte** there's a draught from under the door ◆ **~ sous les fenêtres de qn** to go past *ou* to pass sb's window ◆ **le confort, ça passe après** comfort is less important *ou* comes second ◆ **le travail passe avant tout/avant les loisirs** work comes first/before leisure ◆ **~ devant Monsieur le maire** to get married *ou* hitched * ◆ **~ devant un jury** to go before a jury ◆ **ma famille passe en premier** my family comes first ◆ **une idée m'est passée par la tête** an idea occurred to me ◆ **elle dit tout ce qui lui passe par la tête** she says whatever comes into her head

◆ **passer sur** *[+ faute]* to pass over, to overlook; *[+ détail inutile ou scabreux]* to pass over ◆ **je veux bien ~ sur cette erreur** I'm willing to pass over *ou* overlook this mistake ◆ **je passe sur les détails** I shall pass over *ou* leave out *ou* skip the details

◆ **en passant** *(= sur le chemin)* ◆ **j'irai le voir en passant** I'll call in to see him *ou* I'll call in and see him on my way

◆ **il m'a glissé quelques remarques en passant** *(dans la conversation)* he said a few words to me in passing; → **dire**

◆ **en passant par** ◆ **il aime tous les sports, du football à la boxe en passant par le golf** *(dans une énumération)* he likes all sports, from football to golf to boxing

2 = faire une halte rapide ~ **au** *ou* **par le bureau/chez un ami** to call in at *ou* drop in at *ou* drop by the office/a friend's ◆ **je ne fais que ~** *(chez qn)* I'm not stopping *, I can't stay long; *(dans une ville)* I'm just passing through ◆ **~ à la visite médicale** to go for a medical ◆ **~ à la douane** to go through customs, to clear customs ◆ **le facteur est passé** the postman has been ◆ **à quelle heure passe le laitier ?** what time does the milkman come? ◆ **le releveur du gaz passera demain** the gasman will call tomorrow

◆ **passer** + *infinitif* ◆ **~ chercher** *ou* **prendre qn** to call for sb, to go *ou* come and pick sb up ◆ **je passerai prendre ce colis demain** I'll come and pick the parcel up tomorrow ◆ **~ voir qn** *ou* **rendre visite à qn** to call (in) on sb ◆ **le médecin passera te voir ce soir** the doctor will come and see you this evening ◆ **puis-je ~ te voir en vitesse ?** can I pop round (to see you)?

3 = changer de lieu, d'attitude, d'état to go ◆ **~ d'une pièce dans une autre** to go from one room to another ◆ **si nous passions au salon ?** shall we go into *ou* through to the sitting room? ◆ **~ à table** to sit down to eat ◆ **il est passé en Belgique** he went over to Belgium ◆ **~ à l'ennemi/l'opposition** to go over *ou* defect to the enemy/the opposition ◆ **la photo passa de main en main** the photo was passed *ou* handed round ◆ **~ d'un extrême à l'autre** to go from one extreme to the other ◆ **~ de l'état solide à l'état liquide** to go *ou* change from the solid to the liquid state ◆ **~ du rire aux larmes** to switch from laughter to tears ◆ **~ à un ton plus sévère** to take a harsher tone ◆ **~ dans les mœurs/les habitudes** to become the custom/the habit ◆ **~ dans la langue** to pass *ou* come into the language ◆ **~ en proverbe** to become proverbial ◆ **son argent de poche passe en bonbons** *ou* **dans les bonbons** all his pocket money goes on sweets ◆ **l'alcool passe dans le sang** alcohol enters the bloodstream ◆ **le reste des légumes est passé dans le potage** the left-over vegetables went into the soup

4 = changer de vitesse ~ **en première/marche arrière** to go into first/reverse ◆ **~ en seconde/quatrième** to go *ou* change into second/fourth ◆ **les vitesses passent mal** the gears are stiff

5 = franchir un obstacle *[véhicule]* to get through; *[cheval, sauteur]* to get over; *(Alpinisme)* to get up ◆ **ça passe ?** *(en manœuvrant en voiture)* can I make it?, have I got enough room?

6 = s'écouler : temps to go by, to pass ◆ **comme le temps passe (vite) !** how time flies! ◆ **ça fait ~ le temps** it passes the time

7 = s'écouler : liquide to go *ou* come through, to seep through; *[café]* to go through; *(= circuler) [courant électrique]* to get through

8 = être digéré, avalé to go down ◆ **mon déjeuner ne passe pas** my lunch won't go down ◆ **prendre un cachet pour faire ~ le déjeuner** to take a tablet to help one's lunch down ◆ **prends de l'eau pour faire ~ le gâteau** have some water to wash down the cake

9 = être accepté *[demande, proposition]* to pass ◆ **je ne pense pas que ce projet de loi passera** I don't think this bill will be passed *ou* will go through ◆ **cette plaisanterie ne passe pas dans certains milieux** that joke doesn't go down well *ou* isn't appreciated in some circles ◆ **il y a des plaisanteries/erreurs qui passent dans certaines circonstances mais pas dans d'autres** there are certain jokes/mistakes which are all right in some circumstances but not in others ◆ **le gouvernement se demande comment faire ~ les hausses de prix** the government is wondering how to get the price

increases through ◆ **il est passé de justesse à l'examen** he only just scraped through *ou* passed the exam ◆ **il est passé dans la classe supérieure** he's moved up to the next class *(Brit)*, he's passed *ou* been promoted to the next grade *(US)* ◆ **l'équipe est passée en 2e division** *(progrès)* the team were promoted to *ou* have moved up to the second division; *(recul)* the team have been relegated to *ou* have moved down to the second division ◆ **ça passe ou ça casse** it's make or break (time)

10 [= devenir] to become ◆ **~ directeur/président** to become *ou* be appointed director/chairman

11 [= être montré] *(Ciné)* *[film]* to be showing, to be on; *(TV)* *[émission]* to be on; *[personne]* to be on, to appear ◆ **~ à la radio/à la télé** * to be on the radio/on TV

12 [= être présenté] *(Jur, Parl)* to come up ◆ **le projet de loi va ~ devant la Chambre** the bill will come *ou* be put before Parliament ◆ **il est passé devant le conseil de discipline de l'école** he came up *ou* was brought up before the school disciplinary committee

13 [= dépasser] **le panier est trop petit, la queue du chat passe** the basket is too small – the cat's tail is sticking out ◆ **son manteau est trop court, la robe passe** her coat is too short – her dress shows underneath ◆ **ne laisse pas ~ ton bras par la portière** don't put your arm out of the window

14 [= disparaître] *[douleur]* to pass, to wear off; *(lit, fig)* *[orage]* to blow over, to die down; *[beauté, couleur]* to fade; *[colère]* to die down; *[mode]* to die out; *(= mourir)* *[personne]* to pass on *ou* away ◆ **la jeunesse passe (vite)** you're old before you know it ◆ **faire ~ à qn le goût** *ou* **l'envie de faire** to cure sb of doing ◆ **cela fera ~ votre rhume** that will get you over your cold *ou* get rid of your cold for you ◆ **le plus dur est passé** the worst is over now ◆ **il était très amoureux, mais ça lui a passé** he was very much in love but he got over it ◆ **il voulait être pompier mais ça lui a passé** he wanted to be a fireman but he grew out of it ◆ **ça lui passera (avant que ça me reprenne) !*** *[sentiment]* he'll get over it!; *[habitude]* he'll grow out of it!

15 [Cartes] to pass

16 [locutions] **qu'il soit menteur, passe (encore), mais voleur c'est plus grave** he may be a liar, that's one thing, but a thief, that's more serious ◆ **passe pour cette erreur, mais si tu recommences ...** we'll forget about it this time, but if you make the same mistake again ... ◆ **passons** let's say no more (about it)

~ par *[+ intermédiaire]* to go through; *[+ expérience]* to go through, to undergo ◆ **pour lui parler, j'ai dû ~ par sa secrétaire** I had to go through *ou* via his secretary *ou* I had to see his secretary before I could speak to him ◆ **pour téléphoner, il faut ~ par le standard** you have to go through the switchboard to make a call ◆ **~ par de dures épreuves** to go through some very trying times ◆ **il est passé par des moments difficiles** he's been through some hard times ◆ **~ par l'université/un lycée technique** to go through university/technical college ◆ **elle est passée par toutes les couleurs de l'arc-en-ciel** *(gêne)* she blushed to the roots of her hair; *(peur)* she turned pale ◆ **nous sommes tous passés par là** we've all been through that, that's happened to all of us

◆ **en passer par** ◆ **il faudra bien en ~ par là** there's no way round it ◆ **il a bien fallu en ~ par là** it had to come to that (in the end) ◆ **il faudra bien en ~ par ce qu'il demande** we'll have to give him what he wants, we'll have to comply with *ou* give in to his request

◆ **passer pour** ◆ **je ne voudrais pas ~ pour un imbécile** I wouldn't like to be taken for a fool ◆ **il pourrait ~ pour un Allemand** you could take him for a German, he could pass for *ou* as a German ◆ **auprès de ses amis, il passait pour un séducteur** he was regarded by his friends as (being) a ladies' man ◆ **il passe pour un intellectuel** he passes for an intellectual ◆ **il passe pour intelligent** he's thought of as intelligent, he's supposed to be intelligent ◆ **il passe pour beau auprès de certaines femmes** some women think *ou* find him good-looking, he's considered good-looking by some women ◆ **il passe pour un escroc** people say he's a crook ◆ **cela passe pour vrai** it's thought to be true ◆ **se faire ~ pour** to pass o.s. off as ◆ **il s'est fait ~ pour son patron** he passed himself off as his boss ◆ **il s'est fait ~ pour fou pour se faire réformer** he pretended to be mad so he could be declared unfit for service ◆ **faire ~ qn pour** to make sb out to be ◆ **tu veux me faire ~ pour un idiot !** do you want to make me look stupid?

◆ **y passer** * ◆ **on a eu la grippe, tout le monde y est passé** we've had the flu – everybody got it *ou* nobody escaped it ◆ **si tu conduis comme ça, on va tous y ~** if you go on driving like that, we've all had it* ◆ **toute sa fortune y est passée** he spent all his fortune on it, his whole fortune went on it ◆ **si elle veut une promotion, il faudra bien qu'elle y passe** *(sexuellement)* if she wants to be promoted, she'll have to sleep with the boss

◆ **laisser passer** *[+ air, lumière]* to let in; *[+ personne, procession]* to let through *ou* past; *[+ erreur]* to overlook, to miss; *[+ occasion]* to let slip, to miss ◆ **il faut laisser ~ le temps** give it time ◆ **s'écarter pour laisser ~ qn** to move back to let sb (get) through *ou* past ◆ **nous ne pouvons pas laisser ~ cette affaire sans protester** we cannot let this matter pass without a protest, we can't let this matter rest there – we must protest

2 – VERBE TRANSITIF

[avec auxiliaire avoir]

1 [= franchir] *[+ rivière, frontière, seuil]* to cross; *[+ porte]* to go through; *[+ haie]* to jump *ou* get over ◆ **~ une rivière à la nage/en bac** to swim across/take the ferry across a river

2 [= se soumettre à] *[+ examen]* to sit, to take ◆ **~ son permis (de conduire)** to take one's driving test ◆ **~ une visite médicale** to have a medical (examination) ◆ **~ un examen avec succès** to pass an exam

3 [= utiliser] *[+ temps, vacances]* to spend ◆ **~ sa vie à faire** to spend one's life doing ◆ **(faire qch) pour ~ le temps** (to do sth) to while away *ou* pass the time ◆ **j'ai passé la soirée chez Luc** I spent the evening at Luc's (place); → **mauvais**

4 [= assouvir] **~ sa colère/sa mauvaise humeur sur qn** to take one's anger/one's bad mood out on sb ◆ **~ son envie de chocolat** to satisfy one's craving for chocolate

5 [= omettre] *[+ mot, ligne]* to leave out, to miss out *(Brit)* ◆ **~ son tour** to miss one's turn ◆ **et j'en passe !** and that's not all! ◆ **j'en passe, et des meilleures !** and that's not all – I could go on!, and that's the least of them!; → **silence**

6 [= permettre] **~ une faute à qn** to overlook sb's mistake ◆ **~ un caprice à qn** to humour sb, to indulge sb's whim ◆ **on lui passe tout** *[+ bêtises]* he gets away with anything; *[+ désirs]* he gets everything he wants ◆ **passez-moi l'expression** (if you'll) pardon the expression

7 [= transmettre] *[+ consigne, message, maladie]* to pass on; *(Sport)* *[+ ballon]* to pass ◆ **~ qch à qn** to give *ou* hand sth to sb ◆ **tu (le) fais ~** pass *ou* hand it round ◆ **~ une affaire/un travail à qn** to hand a matter/a job over to sb ◆ **passe-moi une cigarette** pass *ou* give me a cigarette ◆ **passez-moi du feu** give me a light ◆ **il m'a passé un livre** he's lent me a book ◆ **je suis fatigué, je vous passe le volant** I'm tired, you take the wheel *ou* you drive ◆ **je vous passe M. Duroy** *(au téléphone)* *[standard]* I'm putting you through to Mr Duroy; *(= je lui passe l'appareil)* here's Mr Duroy ◆ **passe-lui un coup de fil** phone *ou* call *ou* ring *(Brit)* him, give him a ring *(Brit)* ◆ **passez-moi tous vos paquets** give me *ou* let me have all your parcels

8 [Douane] **~ la douane** to go through customs ◆ **après avoir passé la douane, je ...** once I'd been through *ou* cleared Customs, I ... ◆ **~ des marchandises en transit** to carry goods in transit ◆ **~ qch en fraude** to smuggle sth (in *ou* out *ou* through *etc*) ◆ **~ des faux billets** to pass forged notes

9 [= enfiler] *[+ pull]* to slip on; *[+ robe]* to slip into ◆ **~ une bague au doigt de qn** to slip a ring on sb's finger ◆ **~ un lacet dans qch** to thread a lace through sth ◆ **~ la corde au cou de qn** to put the rope round sb's neck

10 [= mettre] **~ la tête à la porte** to poke one's head round the door ◆ **~ la main/tête à travers les barreaux** to stick one's hand/head through the bars

11 [= dépasser] *[+ gare, maison]* to pass, to go past ◆ **~ le poteau** to pass the post, to cross the finishing line ◆ **~ les limites** *ou* **les bornes** to go too far ◆ **tu as passé l'âge (de ces jeux)** you're too old (for these games) ◆ **il ne passera pas la nuit/la semaine** he won't last the night/the week, he won't see the night/the week out; → **cap**[1]

12 [Culin] *[+ thé, lait]* to strain; † *[+ café]* to pour the water on ◆ **~ la soupe** *(à la passoire)* to strain the soup; *(au mixer)* to blend the soup, to put the soup through the blender

13 [+ vitesse] **~ la seconde/la troisième** to go *ou* change (up *ou* down) into second/third (gear)

14 [= montrer, faire écouter] *[+ film, diapositives]* to show; *[+ disque]* to put on, to play ◆ **qu'est-ce qu'ils passent au cinéma ?** what's on *ou* showing at the cinema?

15 [Comm] *[+ écriture]* to enter; *[+ commande]* to place; *[+ accord]* to reach, to come to; *[+ contrat]* to sign ◆ **~ un marché** to do a deal; → **profit**

16 [= faire subir une action] **~ une pièce à l'aspirateur** to vacuum *ou* hoover ® *(Brit)* a room, to go over a room with the vacuum cleaner ◆ **~ la cuisine à la serpillière, ~ la serpillière dans la cuisine** to wash (down) the kitchen floor ◆ **~ le balai/l'aspirateur/le chiffon dans une pièce** to sweep/vacuum *ou* hoover ® *(Brit)*/dust a room ◆ **passe le chiffon dans le salon** dust the sitting room, give the sitting room a dust ◆ **~ une couche de peinture sur qch** to give sth a coat of paint ◆ **~ un mur à la chaux** to whitewash a wall ◆ **~ qch sous le robinet** to rinse *ou* run sth under the tap ◆ **elle lui passa la main dans les cheveux** she ran her hand through his hair ◆ **passe-toi de l'eau sur le visage** give your face a (quick) wash ◆ **qu'est-ce qu'il lui a passé (comme savon) !*** he gave him a really rough time!*, he really laid into him!*; → **arme, éponge, menotte, revue, tabac**

3 – VERBE PRONOMINAL

se passer

1 [= avoir lieu] to take place; *(= arriver)* to happen ◆ **la scène se passe à Paris** *(Théât)* the scene takes place in Paris ◆ **qu'est-ce qui s'est passé ?** what happened? ◆ **que se passe-t-il ?, qu'est-ce qu'il se passe ?** what's going on?, what's happening? ◆ **ça ne s'est pas passé comme je l'espérais** it didn't work out as I'd hoped ◆ **tout s'est bien passé** everything went off smoothly ◆ **ça s'est mal passé** it turned out badly, it went off badly ◆ **je ne sais pas ce qui se passe en lui** I don't know what's the matter with him *ou* what's come over him *ou* what's got into him ◆ **ça ne se passera pas comme ça !** I won't stand for that!, I won't let it rest at that!

2 [= s'écouler] to pass; *(= finir)* to pass, to be over ◆ **il ne se passe pas un seul jour sans qu'il ne pleuve** not a day goes by *ou* passes without it

raining ◆ **il faut attendre que ça se passe** you'll have to wait till it's over *ou* it passes

3 (= s'appliquer, se mettre à soi-même) **elle s'est passé de la crème solaire sur les épaules** *[+ produit]* she put some sun cream on her shoulders ◆ **il se passa un mouchoir sur le front** he wiped his forehead with a handkerchief ◆ **se ~ les mains à l'eau** to rinse one's hands

4 (= s'accorder) **il faut bien se ~ quelques fantaisies** you've got to allow yourself a few *ou* indulge in a few extravagances

5 (se transmettre) *[+ ballon, plat]* to pass to each other; *[+ notes de cours, livre]* to give to each other

6 (locutions)

◆ **se passer de** *[+ chose]* to do without; *[+ personne]* to manage without ◆ **s'il n'y en a plus, je m'en passerai** if there isn't any more, I'll do without ◆ **je peux me ~ de ta présence** I can manage without you around ◆ **nous nous voyons dans l'obligation de nous ~ de vos services** we find ourselves obliged to dispense with your services ◆ **je me passe de tes conseils !** I can do without your advice! ◆ **la citation se passe de commentaires** the quotation needs no comment *ou* speaks for itself

◆ **se passer de** + *infinitif* ◆ **on peut se ~ d'aller au théâtre** we can do without going to the theatre ◆ **je me passerais bien d'y aller !** I could do without having to go! ◆ **il se passerait de manger plutôt que de faire la cuisine** he'd go without eating *ou* without food rather than cook ◆ **tu pourrais te ~ de fumer** *(iro)* you could refrain from smoking

passereau (pl **passereaux**) /pasʀo/ **NM** *(Orn)* passerine; *(† = moineau)* sparrow

passerelle /pasʀɛl/ **NF** *(= pont)* footbridge; *(= pont supérieur d'un bateau)* bridge; *(= voie d'accès)* gangway; *(fig)* bridge; *(Ordin)* gateway ◆ **(classe) ~** *(Scol)* reorientation class *(facilitating change of course at school)* ◆ **jeter** *ou* **lancer des ~s entre** to build bridges between

passerose, passe-rose (pl **passe(-)roses**) /pasʀoz/ **NF** hollyhock

passe-temps /pastɑ̃/ **NM INV** pastime, hobby ◆ **c'est un ~ national** it's a national pastime

passe-thé /paste/ **NM INV** tea strainer

passette /pasɛt/ **NF** tea strainer

passeur /pasœʀ/ **NM** *[de rivière]* ferryman, boatman; *[de frontière]* smuggler *(of drugs, refugees etc)*

passe-vue (pl **passe-vues**) /pasvy/ **NM** slide changer

passible /pasibl/ **ADJ** ◆ **~ d'une amende/peine** *[personne]* liable to a fine/penalty; *[délit]* punishable by a fine/penalty ◆ **~ d'un impôt** liable for tax ◆ **~ de droits** *(Comm)* liable to duty

passif, -ive /pasif, iv/ **ADJ** passive ◆ **rester ~ devant une situation** to remain passive in the face of a situation; → **défense**[1] **NM** 1 *(Ling)* passive ◆ **au ~** in the passive (voice) 2 *(Fin)* liabilities ◆ **le ~ d'une succession** the liabilities on an estate ◆ **au ~ de ce gouvernement, plus de 3 millions de chômeurs** the fact that there are over 3 million unemployed is a black mark against the government ◆ **ces problèmes sont à mettre au ~ de la nouvelle équipe** these problems reflect badly on the new team

passiflore /pasiflɔʀ/ **NF** passionflower, passiflora *(SPÉC)*

passing-shot (pl **passing-shots**) /pasiŋʃɔt/ **NM** passing shot ◆ **faire un ~** to play a passing shot

passion /pasjɔ̃/ **NF** 1 *(= goût)* passion ◆ **avoir la ~ du jeu/des voitures** to have a passion for gambling/for cars ◆ **le tennis est sa ~** *ou* **est une ~ chez lui** he is mad* *ou* crazy* about tennis, his one passion is tennis

2 *(= amour)* passion ◆ **déclarer sa ~** to declare one's love ◆ **aimer à la** *ou* **avec ~** to love passionately

3 *(= émotion, colère)* passion ◆ **emporté par la ~** carried away by passion ◆ **discuter avec ~/sans ~** to argue passionately *ou* heatedly/dispassionately *ou* coolly ◆ **débat sans ~** lifeless debate ◆ **œuvre pleine de ~** work full of passion

4 *(Mus, Rel)* **Passion** Passion ◆ **le dimanche de la Passion** Passion Sunday ◆ **le jour de la Passion** the day of the Passion ◆ **la semaine de la Passion** Passion week ◆ **la Passion selon saint Matthieu** *(Rel)* the Passion according to St Matthew; *(Mus)* the St Matthew Passion; → **fruit**[1]

passionaria /pasjɔnaʀja/ **NF** ⇒ **pasionaria**

passionnant, e /pasjɔnɑ̃, ɑt/ **ADJ** *[personne]* fascinating; *[livre, film]* gripping, fascinating; *[métier, match]* exciting

passionné, e /pasjɔne/ (ptp de **passionner**) **ADJ** 1 *(= exalté) [personne, tempérament, haine]* passionate; *[description, orateur, jugement]* impassioned ◆ **débat ~** heated *ou* impassioned debate 2 *(= enthousiaste) [amateur, photographe]* keen ◆ **être ~ de** *ou* **pour qch** to have a passion for sth **NM,F** 1 *(= personne exaltée)* passionate person 2 *(= amateur)* enthusiast ◆ **c'est un ~ de jazz** he's a jazz enthusiast ◆ **c'est un ~ de voyages** he loves travelling

passionnel, -elle /pasjɔnɛl/ **ADJ** *[débat, relation, sentiment]* passionate ◆ **les négociations se sont déroulées dans un climat ~** the atmosphere at the talks was heated; → **crime**

passionnément /pasjɔnemɑ̃/ **ADV** *[aimer]* passionately ◆ **~ amoureux de** madly *ou* passionately in love with ◆ **s'intéresser ~ à qch** to have a passionate interest in sth ◆ **écrivain, il l'est ~** he writes with a passion

passionner /pasjɔne/ ▸ conjug 1 ◂ **VT** *[+ personne] [mystère, match]* to fascinate, to grip; *[livre, sujet]* to fascinate; *[sport, science]* to be a passion with; *[+ débat]* to inflame ◆ **ce film/roman m'a passionné** I found that film/novel fascinating ◆ **la musique le passionne** music is his passion, he has a passion for music ◆ **j'ai un métier qui me passionne** I have a fascinating job **VPR** **se passionner** ◆ **se ~ pour** *[+ livre, mystère]* to be fascinated by; *[+ sport, science]* to have a passion for, to be mad keen on*; *[+ métier]* to be fascinated by

passivation /pasivasjɔ̃/ **NF** *(Ling)* putting in the passive (voice); *(Tech)* passivation; *(Chim)* making passive

passivement /pasivmɑ̃/ **ADV** passively ◆ **ils ont assisté, ~, au lynchage** they were passive spectators at the lynching

passivité /pasivite/ **NF** passivity, passiveness

passoire /paswaʀ/ **NF** *(gén)* sieve; *[de thé]* strainer; *[de légumes]* colander ◆ **être une (vraie) ~** *(fig)* to be like a sieve ◆ **quelle ~ ce gardien de but !** what a useless goalkeeper – he lets everything in! ◆ **avoir la tête** *ou* **la mémoire comme une ~** to have a memory like a sieve ◆ **troué comme une ~** riddled with *ou* full of holes

pastel /pastɛl/ **NM** *(= plante)* woad, pastel; *(= teinture bleue)* pastel; *(= bâtonnet de couleur)* pastel (crayon); *(= œuvre)* pastel ◆ **au ~** in pastels **ADJ INV** *[tons]* pastel ◆ **un bleu/vert ~** a pastel blue/green

pastelliste /pastelist/ **NMF** pastellist

pastenague /pastənag/ **NF** stingray

pastèque /pastɛk/ **NF** watermelon

pasteur /pastœʀ/ **NM** 1 *(Rel = prêtre)* minister, pastor, preacher *(US)* 2 *(littér, Rel = berger)* shepherd ◆ **le Bon Pasteur** the Good Shepherd

pasteurien, -ienne /pastœʀjɛ̃, jɛn/ **ADJ** of Pasteur ◆ **la méthode pasteurienne** Pasteur's method **NM,F** scientist of the Pasteur Institute

pasteurisation /pastœʀizasjɔ̃/ **NF** pasteurization

pasteuriser /pastœʀize/ ▸ conjug 1 ◂ **VT** to pasteurize

pastiche /pastiʃ/ **NM** *(= imitation)* pastiche

pasticher /pastiʃe/ ▸ conjug 1 ◂ **VT** to do *(ou write etc)* a pastiche of

pasticheur, -euse /pastiʃœʀ, øz/ **NM,F** *(gén)* imitator; *(= auteur)* author of pastiches

pastille /pastij/ **NF** *[de médicament, sucre]* pastille, lozenge; *[d'encens, couleur]* block; *[de papier, tissu]* disc ◆ **~s de menthe** mints ◆ **~s pour la toux** cough drops *ou* lozenges *ou* pastilles *(Brit)* ◆ **~s pour la gorge** throat lozenges *ou* pastilles *(Brit)* ◆ **~ de silicium** silicon chip

pastis /pastis/ **NM** *(= boisson)* pastis; *(* dial = ennui)* fix* ◆ **être dans le ~** to be in a fix* *ou* a jam*

pastoral, e (mpl **-aux**) /pastɔʀal, o/ **ADJ** *(gén)* pastoral **NF** **pastorale** *(Littérat, Peinture, Rel)* pastoral; *(Mus)* pastorale

pastorat /pastɔʀa/ **NM** pastorate

pastorien, -ienne /pastɔʀjɛ̃, jɛn/ **ADJ, NM,F** ⇒ **pasteurien**

pastoureau (pl **pastoureaux**) /pastuʀo/ **NM** *(littér)* shepherd boy

pastourelle /pastuʀɛl/ **NF** *(littér)* shepherd girl; *(Mus)* pastourelle

pat /pat/ **ADJ INV** stalemate(d) **NM** ◆ **le ~** stalemate ◆ **faire ~** to end in (a) stalemate ◆ **faire qn ~** to stalemate sb

patachon /pataʃɔ̃/ **NM** → **vie**

patagon, -onne /patagɔ̃, ɔn/ **ADJ** Patagonian **NM,F** **Patagon(ne)** Patagonian

Patagonie /patagɔni/ **NF** Patagonia

patagonien, -ienne /patagɔnjɛ̃, jɛn/ **ADJ** Patagonian **NM,F** **Patagonien(ne)** Patagonian

pataphysique /patafizik/ **NF** pataphysics *(sg)*

patapouf /patapuf/ **EXCL** *(langage enfantin)* whoops! ◆ **faire ~** to tumble (down) **NMF** * fatty* ◆ **un gros ~** a big fat lump*

pataquès /patakɛs/ **NM** 1 *(= faute de liaison)* mistaken elision; *(= faute de langage)* malapropism 2 *(péj) (= discours)* incoherent jumble; *(= confusion)* muddle ◆ **il a fait un ~** *(discours)* his speech was an incoherent jumble; *(confusion)* he got things really confused, he muddled things up *(surtout Brit)*

patata * /patata/ **EXCL** → **patati**

patate /patat/ **NF** 1 **~ (douce)** sweet potato 2 *(* = pomme de terre)* potato, spud* *(surtout Brit)* 3 *(* = imbécile)* chump*, clot* 4 *(* = coup de poing)* punch ◆ **il s'est reçu une ~ en pleine figure** he got smacked in the mouth*, he got punched in the face; → **gros** 5 *(* = argent)* 10,000 francs

patati /patati/ **EXCL** **et patati et patata** * and so on and so forth

patatras /patatʀa/ **EXCL** crash!

pataud, e /pato, od/ **ADJ** clumsy, lumpish *(Brit)* **NM,F** lump **NM** *(= chien)* pup(py) *(with large paws)*

pataugas ® /patogas/ **NM** hiking boot

pataugeoire /patoʒwaʀ/ **NF** paddling pool

patauger /patoʒe/ ▸ conjug 3 ◂ **VI** 1 *(= marcher) (avec effort)* to wade about; *(avec plaisir)* to paddle, to splash about ◆ **on a dû ~ dans la boue pour y aller** we had to squelch through the mud to get there 2 *(dans un discours)* to get bogged down; *(dans une matière)* to flounder ◆ **le projet patauge** the project is getting nowhere

patch /patʃ/ NM *(Méd = timbre)* (skin) patch

patchouli /patʃuli/ NM patchouli

patchwork /patʃwœʀk/ NM patchwork ◆ **en ~** patchwork *(épith)*

pâte /pɑt/ NF 1 *(Culin) (à tarte)* pastry; *(à gâteaux)* mixture; *(à pain)* dough; *(à frire)* batter ◆ **il est de la ~ dont sont faits les héros** he's the stuff heroes are made of; → **bon¹, coq¹, main**

2 *[de fromage]* cheese ◆ **(fromage à) ~ dure/molle/cuite/fermentée** hard/soft/cooked/fermented cheese

3 ◆ **~s (alimentaires)** pasta; *(dans la soupe)* noodles

4 *(gén) (= substance)* paste; *(= crème)* cream

5 *(Art)* paste

COMP **pâte d'amandes** almond paste, marzipan
pâte brisée shortcrust *(Brit) ou* pie crust *(US)* pastry
pâte à choux choux pastry
pâte à crêpes pancake *(Brit) ou* crepe batter
pâte dentifrice toothpaste
pâte feuilletée puff *ou* flaky *(Brit)* pastry
pâte à frire batter
pâte de fruits fruit jelly ◆ **une framboise en ~ de fruit** a raspberry fruit jelly
pâte à modeler modelling clay, Plasticine ®
pâte molle *(péj)* milksop, spineless individual
pâte à pain (bread) dough
pâte à papier wood pulp
pâtes pectorales cough drops *ou* pastilles *(Brit)*
pâte sablée sablé *(Brit) ou* sugar crust *(US)* pastry
pâte à sel salt dough
pâte de verre molten glass ◆ **bijoux en ~ de verre** paste jewellery

pâté /pɑte/ NM 1 *(Culin)* pâté ◆ **~ en croûte** ≃ pork pie ◆ **petit ~** meat patty, small pork pie ◆ **~ de campagne** pâté de campagne, farmhouse pâté ◆ **~ de foie** liver pâté ◆ **~ impérial** spring roll *(Brit)*, egg roll *(US)* 2 *(= tache d'encre)* (ink) blot 3 ◆ **~ de maisons** block *(of houses)* 4 ◆ **~ (de sable)** sandpie

pâtée /pɑte/ NF 1 *[de volaille]* mash *(NonC)*, feed *(NonC)*; *[de porcs]* swill *(NonC)* ◆ **~ pour chiens** dog food 2 *(* = punition, défaite)* hiding* ◆ **recevoir la** *ou* **une ~** to get a hiding* ◆ **donner la** *ou* **une ~ à qn** to give sb a hiding*

patelin¹* /patlɛ̃/ NM village ◆ **~ paumé** *(péj)* godforsaken place*

patelin², e /patlɛ̃, in/ ADJ *(littér péj)* bland, smooth, ingratiating

patelinerie /patlinʀi/ NF *(littér péj)* blandness *(NonC)*, smoothness *(NonC)*

patelle /patɛl/ NF *(= coquillage)* limpet; *(= vase)* patera

patène /patɛn/ NF paten

patenôtre /pat(ə)notʀ(ə)/ NF († , *péj*) *(= prière)* paternoster, orison † *(littér)*; *(= marmonnement)* gibberish *(NonC)*

patent, e¹ /patɑ̃, ɑ̃t/ ADJ obvious, manifest, patent *(frm)* ◆ **il est ~ que ...** it is patently obvious that ...; → **lettre**

patentable /patɑ̃tabl/ ADJ *(Comm)* liable to trading dues, subject to a (trading) licence

patente² /patɑ̃t/ NF *(Comm)* trading dues *ou* licence; *(Naut)* bill of health

patenté, e /patɑ̃te/ ADJ *(Comm)* licensed; *(hum = attitré)* established, officially recognized ◆ **c'est un menteur ~** he's a thoroughgoing liar

pater /patɛʀ/ NM INV 1 (*‡ = père*) old man*, pater* † *(Brit)* 2 *(Rel)* **Pater** pater, paternoster 3 *(Antiq, fig)* ~ **familias** paterfamilias

patère /patɛʀ/ NF *(= portemanteau)* (hat- *ou* coat-)peg; *[de rideau]* curtain hook; *(= vase, rosace)* patera

paternalisme /patɛʀnalism/ NM paternalism

paternaliste /patɛʀnalist/ ADJ paternalistic

paterne /patɛʀn/ ADJ *(littér)* bland

paternel, -elle /patɛʀnɛl/ ADJ 1 *[autorité, descendance]* paternal; *[famille]* on one's father's side ◆ **la maison ~le** his *(ou* her *etc)* father's home ◆ **du côté ~** on one's father's side ◆ **ma grand-mère paternelle** my grandmother on my father's side, my paternal grandmother ◆ **quitter le domicile ~** to leave one's father's house ◆ **demander l'autorisation paternelle** to ask for one's father's permission ◆ **elle a repris l'entreprise paternelle** she took over her father's company ◆ **l'amour ~** fatherly *ou* paternal love 2 *(= bienveillant) [personne, regard, conseil]* fatherly NM (*‡ = père*) old man*

paternité /patɛʀnite/ NF 1 *(Jur)* paternity, fatherhood ◆ **attribution de ~** paternity ◆ **action en recherche de ~** paternity suit ◆ **jugement en constatation de ~** paternity order 2 *[de roman]* paternity, authorship; *[d'invention, théorie]* paternity ◆ **il s'attribue la ~ de cette découverte** he claims to be the one who made the discovery

pâteux, -euse /pɑtø, øz/ ADJ *(gén)* pasty; *[pain]* doughy; *[encre]* thick; *[langue]* coated, furred *(Brit)*; *[voix]* thick; *[style]* fuzzy, woolly *(Brit)* ◆ **avoir la bouche pâteuse** to have a coated tongue

pathétique /patetik/ ADJ 1 *(= émouvant)* moving ◆ **c'est une scène très ~** it's a very moving scene 2 *(= lamentable) [tentative, personne]* pathetic 3 *(Anat)* pathetic NM ◆ **le ~** pathos

> ⚠ Au sens de 'émouvant', **pathétique** ne se traduit pas par le mot anglais **pathetic**.

pathétisme /patetism/ NM *(littér)* pathos

pathogène /patɔʒɛn/ ADJ pathogenic

pathologie /patɔlɔʒi/ NF pathology

pathologique /patɔlɔʒik/ ADJ pathological ◆ **c'est un cas ~*** he's *(ou* she's) sick*

pathologiquement /patɔlɔʒikmɑ̃/ ADV pathologically

pathologiste /patɔlɔʒist/ NMF pathologist

pathos /patos/ NM (overdone) pathos, emotionalism

patibulaire /patibylɛʀ/ ADJ *[personnage]* sinister-looking ◆ **avoir une mine** *ou* **un air ~** to look sinister, to be sinister-looking

patiemment /pasjamɑ̃/ ADV patiently

patience¹ /pasjɑ̃s/ NF 1 *(gén)* patience ◆ **souffrir avec ~** to bear one's sufferings with patience *ou* patiently ◆ **perdre ~** to lose (one's) patience ◆ **prendre** *ou* **s'armer de ~** to be patient, to have patience ◆ **il faut avoir une ~ d'ange pour le supporter** it takes the patience of a saint *ou* of Job to put up with him ◆ **je suis à bout de ~** I'm at the end of my patience, my patience is exhausted ◆ **ma ~ a des limites !** there are limits to my patience!; → **mal²**

2 *(Cartes) (= jeu)* patience *(Brit) (NonC)*, solitaire *(US) (NonC)*; *(= partie)* game of patience *(Brit) ou* solitaire *(US)* ◆ **faire des ~s** to play patience *(Brit) ou* solitaire *(US)*

3 *(locutions)* **~, j'arrive !** wait a minute! *ou* hang on!*, I'm coming ◆ **~, il est bientôt l'heure** be patient – it's almost time ◆ **encore un peu de ~** not long now – hold on ◆ **~, j'aurai ma revanche** I'll get even in the end

patience² /pasjɑ̃s/ NF *(= plante)* (patience) dock

patient, e /pasjɑ̃, jɑ̃t/ ADJ patient NM,F *(Méd)* patient

patienter /pasjɑ̃te/ ► conjug 1 ◄ VI to wait ◆ **faites-le ~** *(pour un rendez-vous)* ask him to wait, have him wait; *(au téléphone)* ask him to hold ◆ **si vous voulez ~ un instant** could you wait *ou* bear with me a moment? ◆ **lisez ce journal, ça vous fera ~** read this paper to fill in *ou* pass the time ◆ **pour ~, il regardait les tableaux** to fill in *ou* pass the time, he looked at the paintings

patin /patɛ̃/ NM 1 *[de patineur]* skate; *[de luge]* runner; *[de rail]* base; *(pour le parquet)* cloth pad *(used as slippers on polished wood floors)* ◆ **~ (de frein)** brake block ◆ **~s à glace** ice-skates ◆ **~s à roulettes** roller skates ◆ **~s en ligne** rollerblades, in-line skates ◆ **faire du ~ à glace** to go ice-skating ◆ **faire du ~ à roulettes** to go roller-skating ◆ **faire du ~ en ligne** to go rollerblading 2 (*‡ = baiser*) French kiss ◆ **rouler un ~ à qn** to give sb a French kiss

patinage¹ /patinaʒ/ NM 1 *(Sport)* skating ◆ **~ artistique** figure skating ◆ **~ à roulettes** roller-skating ◆ **~ de vitesse** speed skating; 2 *(Aut) [de roue]* spinning; *[d'embrayage]* slipping

patinage² /patinaʒ/ NM *(Tech)* patination

patine /patin/ NF *(= dépôt naturel, vert-de-gris)* patina; *(= coloration, vernis)* sheen ◆ **la ~ du temps** the patina of age ◆ **la table a pris une certaine ~ avec le temps** the table has acquired a patina with age

patiner¹ /patine/ ► conjug 1 ◄ VI 1 *(Sport)* to skate 2 *[roue]* to spin; *[embrayage]* to slip ◆ **la voiture patina sur la chaussée verglacée** the car skidded on the icy road ◆ **faire ~ l'embrayage** to slip the clutch ◆ **ça patine sur la route** the roads are very slippery 3 *[négociations]* to be at a virtual standstill, to be making no headway; *[projet]* to be making no headway

patiner² /patine/ ► conjug 1 ◄ VT *(= vieillir) [+ bois, bronze, meuble]* to patinate, to give a patina to ◆ **des meubles patinés (par les siècles)** furniture that has acquired a patina (over the centuries)

patinette /patinɛt/ NF scooter ◆ **~ à pédale** pedal scooter ◆ **faire de la ~** to ride a scooter

patineur, -euse /patinœʀ, øz/ NM,F skater

patinoire /patinwaʀ/ NF skating rink, ice rink ◆ **cette route est une vraie ~** this road is like an ice rink

patio /pasjo/ NM patio

pâtir /pɑtiʀ/ ► conjug 2 ◄ VI *(littér)* to suffer *(de* because of, on account of)

pâtisserie /pɑtisʀi/ NF 1 *(= magasin)* cake shop, patisserie; *(= gâteau)* cake; *(avec pâte à tarte)* pastry ◆ **~ industrielle** *(= gâteaux)* factory-baked cakes; *(= usine)* bakery, cake factory 2 ◆ **la ~** *(= art ménager)* cake-making, pastry-making, baking; *(= métier, commerce)* ≃ confectionery ◆ **apprendre la ~** *(comme métier)* to learn to be a pastrycook, ≃ to learn confectionery ◆ **faire de la ~** *(en amateur)* to make cakes ◆ **moule/ustensiles à ~** pastry dish/utensils; → **rouleau** 3 *(= stuc)* fancy (plaster) moulding

pâtissier, -ière /pɑtisje, jɛʀ/ NM,F *(de métier)* pastrycook, ≃ confectioner ◆ **~-glacier** confectioner and ice-cream maker ◆ **~-chocolatier** confectioner and chocolate maker ◆ **il est bon ~** he makes good cakes; → **crème**

pâtisson /pɑtisɔ̃/ NM custard marrow *(Brit) ou* squash *(US)*

patois, e /patwa, waz/ ADJ patois *(épith)*, dialectal, dialect *(épith)* NM patois, (provincial) dialect ◆ **parler (en) ~** to speak (in) patois

patoisant, e /patwazɑ̃, ɑ̃t/ ADJ patois-speaking, dialect-speaking NM,F patois *ou* dialect speaker

patoiser /patwaze/ ▸ conjug 1 ◂ VI to speak (in) dialect *ou* patois

patraque* /patʀak/ ADJ peaky* *(Brit)*, off-colour *(Brit) (attrib)*, peaked* *(US)* ◆ **être/se sentir ~** to be/feel off-colour* *(Brit) ou* peaked* *(US)*

pâtre /pɑtʀ/ NM *(littér)* shepherd

patriarcal, e (mpl **-aux**) /patʀijaʀkal, o/ ADJ patriarchal

patriarcat /patʀijaʀka/ NM *(Rel)* patriarchate; *(Sociol)* patriarchy, patriarchate

patriarche /patʀijaʀʃ/ NM patriarch

patricien, -ienne /patʀisjɛ̃, jɛn/ ADJ, NM,F patrician

patrie /patʀi/ NF *[de personne] (= pays)* homeland, native country *ou* land; *(= région)* native region; *(= ville)* native town ◆ **mourir pour la ~** to die for one's country ◆ **c'est ma seconde ~** it's my adoptive country ◆ **Florence, la ~ de l'art** Florence, cradle of the arts ◆ **la France, ~ des droits de l'homme** France, the birthplace of human rights; → **mère**

patrimoine /patʀimwan/ NM 1 *(gén)* inheritance, patrimony *(frm)*; *(= bien commun)* heritage, patrimony *(frm)* ◆ **~ héréditaire** *ou* **génétique** genetic inheritance ◆ **~ culturel/national/naturel** cultural/national/natural heritage ◆ **site inscrit au ~ mondial de l'Unesco** Unesco World Heritage Site

2 *(Jur)* patrimony; *(Fin = biens)* property ◆ **~ immobilier** *[de ville]* public buildings; *[de personne]* residential property ◆ **~ social** *(= logements)* public housing

JOURNÉES DU PATRIMOINE

The term **les Journées du patrimoine** refers to an annual cultural event held throughout France, during which state properties are opened to the public for the weekend. The rare opportunity to visit the inside of such prestigious institutions as ministries and the Élysée Palace has made the **Journées du patrimoine** extremely popular.

patrimonial, e (mpl **-iaux**) /patʀimɔnjal, jo/ ADJ *(d'un pays)* relating to its national *(ou* cultural*)* heritage; *(d'un particulier)* relating to personal assets ◆ **déclaration de situation ~e** statement of net personal assets *(made by a politician when taking up office)* ◆ **le droit ~** inheritance law, law of succession ◆ **intérêts patrimoniaux** proprietary interests

patriote /patʀijɔt/ ADJ patriotic NMF *(gén)* patriot ◆ **les ~s** *(Hist)* the Patriots

patriotique /patʀijɔtik/ ADJ patriotic

patriotiquement /patʀijɔtikmɑ̃/ ADV patriotically

patriotisme /patʀijɔtism/ NM patriotism

patron¹ /patʀɔ̃/ NM 1 *(= propriétaire)* owner, boss; *(= gérant)* manager, boss; *(= employeur)* employer ◆ **le ~ est là ?** is the boss in? ◆ **le ~ de l'usine** the factory owner *ou* manager ◆ **le ~ du restaurant** the restaurant owner ◆ **il est ~ d'hôtel** he's a hotel proprietor ◆ **c'est le grand ~*** he's *(ou* she's*)* the big boss* ◆ **un petit ~** a boss of a small company ◆ **~ boulanger/boucher** master baker/butcher ◆ **le ~ des ~s** *(= représentant)* the head of the employers' union

2 *(Hist, Rel = protecteur)* patron ◆ **saint ~** patron saint

3 *(* = mari)* **le ~** her *(ou* my *ou* your*)* old man*

4 *(Hôpital)* ≈ senior consultant *(of teaching hospital)*

COMP **patron (pêcheur)** *(Naut)* skipper
patron d'industrie captain of industry
patron de presse press baron *ou* tycoon *ou* magnate
patron de thèse *(Univ)* supervisor *(of a doctoral thesis)*

patron² /patʀɔ̃/ NM *(Couture)* pattern; *(= pochoir)* stencil ◆ **~ de robe** dress pattern ◆ **(taille) demi-~/~/grand ~** small/medium/large (size)

patronage /patʀɔnaʒ/ NM 1 *(= protection)* patronage ◆ **sous le (haut) ~ de** under the patronage of 2 *(= organisation)* youth club; *(Rel)* youth fellowship ◆ **film/spectacle de ~** *(péj)* childish film/show

patronal, e (mpl **-aux**) /patʀɔnal, o/ ADJ 1 *[charges, responsabilité, cotisation, syndicat, organisation, fédération]* employers' 2 *(Rel) [fête]* patronal

patronat /patʀɔna/ NM ◆ **le ~** the employers

patronne /patʀɔn/ NF 1 *(= propriétaire)* owner, boss; *(= gérante)* manager, boss; *(= employeur)* employer 2 *(* = épouse)* **la ~** the *ou* his *(ou* my *ou* your*)* missus* *(Brit)*, his *(ou* my *ou* your*)* old lady* 3 *(= sainte)* patron saint

patronner /patʀɔne/ ▸ conjug 1 ◂ VT *[+ association, personne, projet, candidature]* to support; *(financièrement)* to sponsor ◆ **négociations de paix patronnées par l'ONU** peace talks sponsored by the UN

patronnesse /patʀɔnɛs/ NF → **dame**

patronyme /patʀɔnim/ NM patronymic

patronymique /patʀɔnimik/ ADJ patronymic

patrouille /patʀuj/ NF patrol ◆ **partir** *ou* **aller en/être de ~** to go/be on patrol ◆ **~ de reconnaissance/de chasse** reconnaissance/fighter patrol

patrouiller /patʀuje/ ▸ conjug 1 ◂ VI to patrol, to be on patrol ◆ **~ dans les rues** to patrol the streets

patrouilleur /patʀujœʀ/ NM *(= soldat)* soldier on patrol (duty), patroller; *(= bateau)* patrol boat; *(= avion)* patrol *ou* scout plane

patte¹ /pat/ NF 1 *(= jambe d'animal)* leg; *(= pied) [de chat, chien]* paw; *[d'oiseau]* foot ◆ **~s de devant** forelegs, forefeet ◆ **~s de derrière** hindlegs, hind feet ◆ **coup de ~** *(fig)* cutting remark ◆ **donner un coup de ~ à qch** *[animal]* to hit sth with its paw ◆ **le chien tendit la ~** the dog put its paw out *ou* gave a paw ◆ **faire ~ de velours** *[de chat]* to draw in *ou* sheathe its claws; *[de personne]* to be all sweetness and light ◆ **ça ne va** *ou* **ne marche que sur trois ~s** *[affaire, projet]* it limps along; *[relation amoureuse]* it struggles along; → **bas¹, mouton**

2 *(* = jambe)* leg ◆ **nous avons 50 km dans les ~s** we've walked 50 km ◆ **à ~s** on foot ◆ **nous y sommes allés à ~s** we walked *ou* hoofed* it ◆ **bas** *ou* **court sur ~s** *[personne]* short-legged; *[table, véhicule]* low ◆ **il est toujours dans mes ~s** he's always under my feet ◆ **tirer** *ou* **traîner la ~** to hobble along ◆ **avoir une ~ folle** to have a gammy* *(Brit) ou* a game* *(US)* leg

3 *(* = main)* hand, paw* ◆ **s'il me tombe sous la ~, gare à lui !** if I get my hands on him he'd better look out! ◆ **tomber dans les/se tirer des ~s de qn** to fall into/get out of sb's clutches ◆ **montrer ~ blanche** to show one's credentials

4 *(= style) [d'auteur, peintre]* style, touch ◆ **elle a un bon coup de ~** she has a nice style *ou* touch

5 *[d'ancre]* palm, fluke; *(= languette) [de poche]* flap; *[de vêtement]* strap; *(sur l'épaule)* epaulette; *[de portefeuille]* tongue; *[de chaussure]* tongue

6 *(= favoris)* **~s (de lapin)** sideburns; → **fil, graisser, quatre** *etc*

COMP **pantalon (à) pattes d'éléphant** *ou* **pattes d'ef*** bell-bottom *ou* flared trousers, bell-bottoms, flares
patte à glace mirror clamp
patte(s) de mouche spidery scrawl ◆ **faire des ~s de mouche** to write (in) a spidery scrawl

patte² /pat/ NF *(Helv = chiffon)* rag ◆ **~ à poussière** duster *(Brit)*, dustcloth *(US)* ◆ **~ à relaver** tea *ou* dish towel

patte-d'oie (pl **pattes-d'oie**) /patdwa/ NF *(= rides)* crow's-foot; *(= carrefour)* branching crossroads *ou* junction

pattemouille /patmuj/ NF damp cloth *(for ironing)*

pâturage /pɑtyʀaʒ/ NM *(= lieu)* pasture; *(= action)* grazing, pasturage; *(= droits)* grazing rights

pâture /pɑtyʀ/ NF 1 *(= nourriture)* food ◆ **donner qn en ~ aux fauves** *(lit, fig)* to throw sb to the lions ◆ **il fait sa ~ de romans noirs** he is an avid reader of detective stories, detective stories form his usual reading matter ◆ **les dessins animés qu'on donne en ~ à nos enfants** the cartoons served up to our children ◆ **donner une nouvelle en ~ aux journalistes** to feed a story to journalists 2 *(= pâturage)* pasture

pâturer /pɑtyʀe/ ▸ conjug 1 ◂ VI to graze VT ◆ **~ l'herbe** to graze

paturon /patyʀɔ̃/ NM pastern

Paul /pɔl/ NM Paul

paulinien, -ienne /polinjɛ̃, jɛn/ ADJ of Saint Paul, Pauline

paulownia /polɔnja/ NM paulownia

paume /pom/ NF *[de main]* palm ◆ **jeu de ~** *(= sport)* real *ou* royal tennis; *(= lieu)* real-tennis *ou* royal-tennis court ◆ **jouer à la ~** to play real *ou* royal tennis

paumé, e* /pome/ (ptp de **paumer**) ADJ 1 *(dans un lieu)* lost; *(dans un milieu inconnu)* bewildered; *(dans une explication)* lost, at sea* ◆ **habiter un bled** *ou* **trou ~** *(isolé)* to live in a godforsaken place *ou* hole*, to live in the middle of nowhere; *(sans attrait)* to live in a real dump *ou* godforsaken hole* 2 *(= socialement inadapté)* **la jeunesse ~e d'aujourd'hui** the young dropouts* of today ◆ **il est complètement ~** he's totally lost, he hasn't got a clue where he's going in life NM,F *(= marginal)* misfit ◆ **un pauvre ~** a poor bum*

paumelle /pomɛl/ NF *(= gond)* split hinge; *(Naut)* palm

paumer* /pome/ ▸ conjug 1 ◂ VT 1 *(= perdre)* to lose 2 *(= prendre)* **se faire ~** *[criminel]* to get nabbed* VPR **se paumer** to get lost

paupérisation /popeʀizasjɔ̃/ NF pauperization, impoverishment

paupériser /popeʀize/ ▸ conjug 1 ◂ VT to pauperize, to impoverish

paupérisme /popeʀism/ NM pauperism

paupière /popjɛʀ/ NF eyelid ◆ **il écoutait, les ~s closes** he was listening with his eyes closed ◆ **battre** *ou* **cligner des ~s** to flutter one's eyelashes

paupiette /popjɛt/ NF ◆ **~ de veau** veal olive

pause /poz/ NF *(= arrêt)* break; *(en parlant)* pause; *(Mus)* pause; *(Sport)* half-time ◆ **faire une ~** to have a break, to break off ◆ **marquer une ~** *[orateur]* to pause; *[négociations]* to break off momentarily ◆ **ils ont marqué une ~ dans la diversification** they have stopped diversifying for the time being, they have put their diversification programme on hold ◆ **ça fait sept ans que je fais ce métier, j'ai besoin de marquer une ~** I've been doing this job for seven years now, I need (to take) a break ◆ **~-café/-thé/-déjeuner** coffee/tea/lunch break ◆ **la ~ de midi** the midday break ◆ **~ publicitaire** commercial break ◆ **faire une ~-cigarette** to stop for a cigarette

pauser /poze/ ▸ conjug 1 ◂ VI ◆ **laissez ~ la permanente/le masque 20 minutes** leave the perm in/the face-pack on for 20 minutes ◆ **faire ~ qn** † to keep sb waiting

pauvre /povʀ/ ADJ 1 *[personne, pays, sol, minerai, gisement]* poor; *[végétation]* sparse, poor; *[style]* weak; *[mélange de carburant]* weak; *[mobilier, vêtements]* cheap-looking; *[nourriture, salaire]* meagre (Brit), meager (US), poor ◆ **minerai ~ en cuivre** ore with a low copper content, ore poor in copper ◆ **air ~ en oxygène** air low in oxygen ◆ **pays ~ en ressources/hommes** country short of *ou* lacking resources/men ◆ **nourriture ~ en calcium** *(par manque)* diet lacking in calcium; *(par ordonnance)* low-calcium diet ◆ **un village ~ en distractions** a village which is lacking in *ou* short of amusements ◆ **~ comme Job** as poor as a church mouse ◆ **les couches ~s de la population** the poorer *ou* deprived sections of the population ◆ **je suis ~ en vaisselle** I don't have much crockery; → **rime**

2 *(avant n = piètre) [excuse, argument]* weak, pathetic; *[devoir]* poor; *[orateur]* weak, bad ◆ **de ~s chances de succès** only a slim *ou* slender chance of success ◆ **il esquissa un ~ sourire** he smiled weakly *ou* gave a weak smile

3 *(avant n)* poor ◆ **~ type !** * *(= malheureux)* poor guy! * *ou* chap! * *(Brit)*; *(= crétin)* stupid bastard! *✻ ◆ **c'est un ~ type** * *(mal adapté)* he's a sad case; *(minable)* he's a dead loss *; *(salaud)* he's a swine ✻ ◆ **pourquoi une fille comme elle épouserait-elle un ~ type comme moi ?** why would a girl like that marry a nobody * like me? ◆ **~ con !** *✻ you stupid bastard! *✻ *ou* sod! *✻ *(Brit)* ◆ **tu es bien naïve ma ~ fille !** poor dear, you're so naïve! ◆ **c'est une ~ fille** she's a sad case ◆ **~ hère** *(littér, hum)* down-and-out ◆ **~ d'esprit** *(= simple d'esprit)* half-wit ◆ **les ~s d'esprit** *(Rel)* the poor in spirit ◆ **comme disait mon ~ mari** as my poor (dear) husband used to say ◆ **~ de moi !** *(hum)* poor (little) me! ◆ **~ petit !** poor (little) thing! ◆ **mon ~ ami** my dear friend ◆ **tu es complètement fou, mon ~ vieux !** you must be crazy, mate! * *(Brit) ou* man! * ◆ **elle me faisait pitié avec son ~ petit air** I felt sorry for her, she looked so wretched *ou* miserable

NMF 1 *(= personne pauvre)* poor man *ou* woman, pauper † ◆ **les ~s** the poor ◆ **ce pays compte encore beaucoup de ~s** there's still a lot of poverty *ou* there are still many poor people in this country ◆ **le caviar du ~** the poor man's caviar

2 *(marquant dédain ou commisération)* **mon** *(ou* **ma) ~, si tu voyais comment ça se passe ...** but my dear fellow *(ou girl etc) ou* friend, if you saw what goes on ... ◆ **le ~, il a dû en voir !** * the poor guy * *ou* chap * *(Brit)*, he must have had a hard time of it! ◆ **les ~s !** the poor things!

pauvrement /povʀəmɑ̃/ ADV *[meublé, éclairé] [vivre]* poorly; *[vêtu]* poorly, shabbily

pauvresse † /povʀɛs/ NF poor woman *ou* wretch

pauvret, -ette /povʀɛ, ɛt/ NM,F poor (little) thing

pauvreté /povʀəte/ NF *[de personne]* poverty; *[de mobilier]* cheapness; *[de langage]* weakness, poorness; *[de sol]* poverty, poorness ◆ **la ~ des moyens disponibles** the dearth of available resources, the inadequacy of the available resources ◆ **la ~ de leur vocabulaire** the poverty of their vocabulary ◆ **~ n'est pas vice** *(Prov)* poverty is not a vice, there is no shame in being poor; → **vœu**

pavage /pavaʒ/ NM *(avec des pavés)* cobbling; *(avec des dalles)* paving ◆ **refaire le ~ d'une rue** to recobble *(ou* repave) a street

pavane /pavan/ NF pavane

pavaner (se) /pavane/ ▸ conjug 1 ◂ VPR to strut about ◆ **se ~ comme un dindon** to strut about like a turkey-cock

pavé /pave/ NM 1 *[de chaussée, cour]* cobblestone ◆ **déraper sur le ~** *ou* **les ~s** to skid on the cobbles ◆ **être sur le ~** *(sans domicile)* to be on the streets, to be homeless; *(sans emploi)* to be out of a job ◆ **mettre** *ou* **jeter qn sur le ~** *(domicile)* to turn *ou* throw sb out (onto the streets); *(emploi)* to give sb the sack *, to throw sb out ◆ **j'ai l'impression d'avoir un ~ sur l'estomac** * I feel as if I've got a lead weight in my stomach ◆ **c'est l'histoire du ~ de l'ours** it's another example of misguided zeal ◆ **lancer** *ou* **jeter un ~ dans la mare** *(fig)* to set the cat among the pigeons ◆ **ça a fait l'effet d'un ~ dans la mare** that really set the cat among the pigeons; → **battre, brûler, haut**

2 (* = *livre épais)* massive *ou* hefty * tome

3 *(Culin) (= viande) thickly-cut steak* ◆ **~ au chocolat** *(= gâteau)* chocolate slab cake

4 *(Presse)* **~ publicitaire** (large) display advertisement

5 *(Ordin)* **~ numérique** numeric keypad

pavement /pavmɑ̃/ NM ornamental tiling

paver /pave/ ▸ conjug 1 ◂ VT *(avec des pavés)* to cobble; *(avec des dalles)* to pave ◆ **cour pavée** cobbled (ou paved) yard; → **enfer**

paveur /pavœʀ/ NM paver

pavillon /pavijɔ̃/ NM 1 *(= villa)* house; *(= loge de gardien)* lodge; *(= section d'hôpital)* ward, pavilion; *(= corps de bâtiment)* wing, pavilion; *[de jardin]* pavilion; *[de club de golf]* clubhouse 2 *(Naut)* flag ◆ **sous ~ panaméen** under the Panamanian flag; → **baisser, battre** 3 *(Mus) [d'instrument]* bell; *[de phonographe]* horn 4 *[d'oreille]* pavilion, pinna

COMP **pavillon de banlieue** suburban house, house in the suburbs
pavillon de chasse hunting lodge
pavillon de complaisance flag of convenience
pavillon de détresse distress flag
pavillon de guerre war flag
pavillon noir Jolly Roger
pavillon de quarantaine yellow flag
pavillon à tête de mort skull and crossbones
pavillon de verdure leafy arbour *ou* bower

pavillonnaire /pavijɔnɛʀ/ ADJ ◆ **lotissement ~** private housing estate ◆ **banlieue ~** residential suburb *(consisting of houses rather than apartment blocks)*

Pavlov /pavlɔv/ N Pavlov ◆ **le chien de ~** Pavlov's dog ◆ **réflexe de ~** Pavlovian response *ou* reaction

pavlovien, -ienne /pavlɔvjɛ̃, jɛn/ ADJ Pavlovian

pavois /pavwa/ NM *(Naut = bordage)* bulwark; *(Hist = bouclier)* shield ◆ **hisser le grand ~** to dress over all *ou* full ◆ **hisser le petit ~** to dress with masthead flags ◆ **hisser qn sur le ~** to carry sb shoulder-high

pavoiser /pavwaze/ ▸ conjug 1 ◂ VT *[+ navire]* to dress; *[+ monument]* to deck with flags VI to put out flags; *(fig, Sport) [supporters]* to rejoice, to wave the banners, to exult ◆ **toute la ville a pavoisé** there were flags out all over the town ◆ **il pavoise maintenant qu'on lui a donné raison publiquement** he's rejoicing openly now that he has been publicly acknowledged to be in the right ◆ **il n'y a pas de quoi ~ !** it's nothing to write home about! *ou* to get excited about!

pavot /pavo/ NM poppy

payable /pɛjabl/ ADJ payable ◆ **~ en 3 fois** *[somme]* payable in 3 instalments; *[objet]* that can be paid for in 3 instalments ◆ **l'impôt est ~ par tous** taxes must be paid by everyone ◆ **billet ~ à vue** *(Fin)* bill payable at sight ◆ **chèque ~ à** cheque payable to ◆ **appareil ~ à crédit** piece of equipment which can be paid for on credit

payant, e /pɛjɑ̃, ɑ̃t/ ADJ *[spectateur]* paying; *[billet, place]* which one must pay for, not free *(attrib)*; *[spectacle]* with an admission charge; *(= rentable) [affaire]* profitable; *[politique, conduite, effort]* which pays off ◆ **"entrée payante"** "admission fee payable" ◆ **c'est ~ ?** do you have to pay (to get in)?

paye /pɛj/ NF ⇒ **paie**

payement /pɛjmɑ̃/ NM ⇒ **paiement**

payer /peje/ ▸ conjug 8 ◂ VT 1 *[+ somme, cotisation, intérêt]* to pay; *[+ facture, dette]* to pay, to settle ◆ **~ comptant** to pay cash ◆ **~ rubis sur l'ongle** † to pay cash on the nail ◆ **c'est lui qui paie** he's paying ◆ **qui paie ses dettes s'enrichit** *(Prov)* the rich man is the one who pays his debts

2 *[+ employé]* to pay; *[+ tueur]* to hire; *[+ entrepreneur]* to pay, to settle up with ◆ **être payé par chèque/en espèces/en nature/à l'heure** to be paid by cheque/in cash/in kind/by the hour ◆ **être payé à la pièce** to be on piecework ◆ **~ qn de** *ou* **en paroles/promesses** to fob sb off with (empty) words/promises ◆ **je ne suis pas payé pour ça** * that's not what I'm paid for ◆ **il est payé pour le savoir !** *(fig)* he should know!

3 *[+ travail, service, maison, marchandise]* to pay for ◆ **je l'ai payé de ma poche** I paid for it out of my own pocket ◆ **les réparations ne sont pas encore payées** the repairs haven't been paid for yet ◆ **il m'a fait ~ 5 €** he charged me €5 *(pour* for); ◆ **~ le déplacement de qn** to pay sb's travelling expenses ◆ **~ la casse** to pay for the damage ◆ **~ les pots cassés** *(fig)* to pick up the pieces ◆ **travail bien/mal payé** well-paid/badly-paid work; → **addition, congé**

4 (* = *offrir)* **~ qch à qn** to buy sth for sb ◆ **c'est moi qui paie (à boire)** the drinks are on me *, have this one on me * ◆ **~ des vacances/un voyage à qn** to pay for sb to go on holiday/on a trip ◆ **~ à boire à qn** to stand *ou* buy sb a drink ◆ **sa mère lui a payé une voiture** his mother bought him a car

5 *(= récompenser)* to reward ◆ **le succès le paie de tous ses efforts** his success makes all his efforts worthwhile *ou* rewards him for all his efforts ◆ **il l'aimait et elle le payait de retour** he loved her and she returned his love

6 *(= expier) [+ faute, crime]* to pay for ◆ **~ qch de cinq ans de prison** to get five years in jail for sth ◆ **il l'a payé de sa vie/santé** it cost him his life/health ◆ **il a payé cher son imprudence** he paid dearly for his rashness, his rashness cost him dear(ly) ◆ **il me le paiera !** *(en menace)* he'll pay for this!, I'll make him pay for this!

VI 1 *[effort, tactique]* to pay off; *[métier]* to be well-paid ◆ **le crime ne paie pas** crime doesn't pay ◆ **~ pour qn** *(lit)* to pay for sb; *(fig)* to take the blame instead of sb, to carry the can for sb *

2 *(locutions)* **~ d'audace** to take a gamble *ou* a risk ◆ **~ de sa personne** to make sacrifices ◆ **pour que notre association fonctionne, il faut que chacun paie de sa personne** in order for our association to work, everyone must pull their weight *ou* make a real effort ◆ **ce poisson ne paie pas de mine** this fish doesn't look very appetizing ◆ **l'hôtel ne paie pas de mine** the hotel isn't much to look at

VPR **se payer** 1 ◆ **tout se paie** *(lit)* everything must be paid for; *(fig)* everything has its price ◆ **payez-vous et rendez-moi la monnaie** take what I owe you and give me the change

2 (* = *s'offrir) [+ objet]* to buy o.s., to treat o.s. to ◆ **on va se ~ un bon dîner/le restaurant** we're going to treat ourselves to a slap-up * meal/to a meal out ◆ **se ~ une pinte de bon sang** † to have a good laugh * ◆ **se ~ la tête de**

qn (= *ridiculiser*) to make fun of sb, to take the mickey out of sb* (*Brit*); (= *tromper*) to take sb for a ride*, to have sb on* (*Brit*) ◆ **se ~ une bonne grippe** to get a bad dose of the flu ◆ **il s'est payé un arbre/le trottoir/un piéton** he wrapped his car round a tree/ran into the kerb/mowed a pedestrian down ◆ **j'ai glissé et je me suis payé la chaise** I slipped and banged *ou* crashed into the chair ◆ **ils s'en sont drôlement payé, ils s'en sont payé une bonne tranche** they had (themselves) a good time *ou* a whale of a time* ◆ **se ~ qn**⁑ (*physiquement*) to knock the living daylights out of sb*; (*verbalement*) to give sb what for*; → **luxe**

3 (= *se contenter*) **on ne peut plus se ~ de mots** it's time we stopped all the talking and took some action ◆ **dans la lutte contre le chômage, il ne s'agit pas de se ~ de mots** fine words are not enough in the battle against unemployment

payeur, -euse /pɛjœʀ, øz/ ADJ ◆ **organisme/service ~** claims department/office ◆ **établissement ~** [*de chèque*] paying bank NM,F payer; (*Mil, Naut*) paymaster ◆ **mauvais ~** bad debtor; → **conseilleur**

pays[1] /pei/ NM 1 (= *contrée, habitants*) country ◆ **des ~ lointains** far-off countries *ou* lands ◆ **les ~ membres de l'Union européenne** the countries which are members of *ou* the member countries of the European Union ◆ **la France est le ~ du vin** France is the land of wine; → **mal[2]**

2 (= *région*) region ◆ **un ~ de légumes, d'élevage et de lait** a vegetable-growing, cattle-breeding and dairy region ◆ **c'est le ~ de la tomate** it's tomato-growing country ◆ **le ~ de Colette/Yeats** Colette/Yeats country ◆ **nous sommes en plein ~ du vin** we're in the heart of the wine country ◆ **revenir au ~** to go back home ◆ **il est du ~** he's from these parts *ou* this area ◆ **les gens du ~** the local people, the locals ◆ **vin de *ou* du ~** locally-produced *ou* local wine, vin de pays (*Brit*) ◆ **melons/pêches de *ou* du ~** local(ly)-grown melons/peaches; → **jambon**

3 († = *village*) village

4 (*locutions*) **le ~ des fées** fairyland ◆ **le ~ des rêves *ou* des songes** the land of dreams, dreamland ◆ **je veux voir du ~** I want to travel around ◆ **il a vu du ~** he's been round a bit *ou* seen the world ◆ **se comporter comme en ~ conquis** to lord it over everyone, to act all high and mighty ◆ **être en ~ de connaissance** (*dans une réunion*) to be among friends *ou* familiar faces; (*sur un sujet, dans un lieu*) to be on home ground *ou* on familiar territory

COMP **pays d'accueil** [*de conférences, jeux*] host country; [*de réfugiés*] country of refuge
le Pays basque the Basque Country
pays de cocagne land of plenty, land of milk and honey
pays développé developed country *ou* nation
le pays de Galles Wales
pays industrialisé industrialized country *ou* nation ◆ **nouveaux ~ industrialisés** newly industrialized countries
les pays les moins avancés the less developed countries
le pays du Soleil Levant the Land of the Rising Sun
pays en voie de développement developing country
pays en voie d'industrialisation industrializing country

pays[2], e /pei, peiz/ NM,F (*dial* = *compatriote*) ◆ **nous sommes ~** we come from the same village *ou* region *ou* part of the country ◆ **elle est ma ~e** she comes from the same village *ou* region *ou* part of the country as me

paysage /peizaʒ/ NM 1 (*gén*) landscape, scenery (*NonC*); (*Peinture*) landscape (painting) ◆ **on découvrait un ~ magnifique/un ~ de montagne** a magnificent/a mountainous landscape lay before us ◆ **nous avons traversé des ~s magnifiques** we drove through (some) magnificent scenery ◆ **les ~s orientaux** the landscape *ou* the scenery of the East ◆ **ce bâtiment nous gâche le ~** that building spoils our view ◆ **le ~ urbain** the urban landscape ◆ **ça fait bien dans le ~ !** (*iro*) it's all part of the image!, it fits the image! ◆ **il ne fait plus partie de mon ~** he's not part of my life anymore

2 (= *situation*) scene ◆ **le ~ politique/cinématographique** the political/film scene ◆ **dans le ~ audiovisuel français** on the French broadcasting scene

3 (*Ordin*) **mode ~** landscape mode

paysagé, e /peizaʒe/, **paysager, -ère** /peizaʒe, ɛʀ/ ADJ ◆ **parc paysager** landscaped garden ◆ **bureau ~** open-plan office

paysagiste /peizaʒist/ NMF (*Peinture*) landscape painter ◆ **architecte/jardinier ~** landscape architect/gardener

paysan, -anne /peizɑ̃, an/ ADJ 1 (= *agricole*) [*monde, problème*] farming (*épith*); [*agitation, revendications*] farmers', of the farmers; (= *rural*) [*vie, coutumes*] country (*épith*); (*péj*) [*air, manières*] peasant (*attrib*) 2 (*Culin*) **salade paysanne** *salad with onions and chopped bacon* ◆ **à la paysanne** *with onions and chopped bacon* NM (*gén*) (small) farmer; (*Hist*) peasant; (*péj*) peasant NF **paysanne** (*gén*) (small) farmer; (*Hist*) peasant (woman); (*péj*) peasant

paysannat /peizana/ NM (small) farmers

paysannerie /peizanʀi/ NF (*Hist ou péj*) peasantry

Pays-Bas /peiba/ NMPL ◆ **les ~** the Netherlands

PC /pese/ NM 1 (abrév de **parti communiste**) → **parti[1]** 2 (abrév de **poste de commandement**) → **poste[2]** 3 (*Ordin*) (abrév de **personal computer**) PC

PCB /pesebe/ NM (abrév de **polychlorobiphényle**) PCB

Pcc (abrév de **pour copie conforme**) → **copie**

PCF /peseɛf/ NM (abrév de **Parti communiste français**) *French political party*

pci /pesei/ NM (abrév de **Peripheral Component Interconnect**) (*Ordin*) PCI

PCV /peseve/ GRAMMAIRE ACTIVE 54.5, 54.6 NM (abrév de **percevoir**) (*Téléc*) ◆ **(appel en) ~** reverse-charge call (*Brit*), collect call (*US*) ◆ **appeler en ~** to make a reverse-charge call (*Brit*), to call collect (*US*)

pdf /pedeɛf/ NM (abrév de **Portable Document Format**) (*Ordin*) PDF

PDG /pedeʒe/ NM INV (abrév de **président-directeur général**) → **président**

PE /peə/ NM (abrév de **Parlement européen**) EP

PEA /peəa/ NM (abrév de **plan d'épargne en actions**) → **plan[1]**

péage /peaʒ/ NM (= *droit*) toll; (= *barrière*) tollgate ◆ **autoroute à ~** toll motorway (*Brit*), turnpike (*US*) ◆ **pont à ~** toll bridge ◆ **poste de ~** tollbooth ◆ **chaîne/télévision à ~** (*TV*) pay channel/TV

péagiste /peaʒist/ NMF tollbooth attendant

peau (pl **peaux**) /po/ NF 1 [*de personne*] skin ◆ **avoir une ~ de pêche** to have a peach-like complexion ◆ **soins de la/maladie de ~** skin care/disease ◆ **~x mortes** dead skin ◆ **n'avoir que la ~ et les os** to be all skin and bones ◆ **attraper qn par la ~ du cou *ou* du dos *ou* des fesses**⁑ (= *empoigner rudement*) to grab sb by the scruff of the neck; (= *s'en saisir à temps*) to grab hold of sb in the nick of time ◆ **faire ~ neuve** [*parti politique, administration*] to adopt *ou* find a new image; [*personne*] (*en changeant d'habit*) to change (one's clothes); (*en changeant de conduite*) to turn over a new leaf; → **coûter, fleur**

2 (* = *corps, vie*) **jouer *ou* risquer sa ~** to risk one's neck* *ou* hide* ◆ **il y a laissé sa ~** it cost him his life ◆ **sauver sa ~** to save one's skin *ou* hide* ◆ **tenir à sa ~** to value one's life ◆ **sa ~ ne vaut pas cher, je ne donnerai pas cher de sa ~** he's dead meat* ◆ **se faire crever *ou* trouer la ~**⁑ to get killed, to get a bullet in one's hide* ◆ **recevoir douze balles dans la ~** to be gunned down by a firing squad *ou* an execution squad ◆ **on lui fera la ~**⁑ we'll bump him off⁑ ◆ **je veux *ou* j'aurai sa ~ !** I'll have his hide for this!* ◆ **être bien/mal dans sa ~** (*physiquement*) to feel great*/awful ◆ **être bien dans sa ~** (*mentalement*) to be happy in o.s. ◆ **il est mal dans sa ~** he's not a happy person ◆ **avoir qn dans la ~*** to be crazy about sb* ◆ **avoir le jeu *etc* dans la ~** to have gambling *etc* in one's blood ◆ **se mettre dans la ~ de qn** to put o.s. in sb's place *ou* shoes ◆ **entrer dans la ~ du personnage** to get (right) into the part ◆ **je ne voudrais pas être dans sa ~** I wouldn't like to be in his shoes *ou* place ◆ **avoir la ~ dure** * (= *être solide*) to be hardy; (= *résister à la critique*) [*personne*] to be thick-skinned, to have a thick skin; [*idées, préjugés*] to be difficult to get rid of *ou* to overcome

3 [*d'animal*] (*gén*) skin; (= *cuir*) hide; (= *fourrure*) pelt; [*d'éléphant, buffle*] hide ◆ **gants/vêtements de ~** leather gloves/clothes ◆ **cuir pleine ~** full leather; → **vendre**

4 [*de fruit, lait, peinture*] skin; [*de fromage*] rind; (= *épluchure*) peel ◆ **enlever la ~ de** [+ *fruit*] to peel; [+ *fromage*] to take the rind off

5 ◆ **~ de balle!** ⁑ nothing doing!*, not a chance!*, no way!⁑

COMP **peau d'âne** † (= *diplôme*) diploma, sheepskin* (*US*)
peau de banane banana skin ◆ **glisser sur une ~ de banane** to slip on a banana skin ◆ **glisser *ou* placer des ~x de banane sous les pieds de qn** to try to trip sb up
peau de chagrin (*lit*) shagreen ◆ **diminuer *ou* rétrécir *ou* se réduire comme une ~ de chagrin** to shrink away
peau de chamois chamois leather, shammy
peau d'hareng* ◆ **quelle ~ d'hareng tu fais!** you naughty thing!*
peau lainée treated sheepskin
peau de mouton sheepskin ◆ **en ~ de mouton** sheepskin (*épith*)
peau d'orange (*Physiol*) orange peel effect
peau de porc pigskin
peau de serpent snakeskin
peau de tambour drumskin
peau de vache* (= *homme*) bastard*⁑; (= *femme*) bitch*⁑
peau de zénana *ou* de zébi ◆ **c'est en ~ de zénana *ou* de zébi** it's made of some sort of cheap stuff

peaucier /posje/ ADJ M, NM ◆ **(muscle) ~** platysma

peaufiner /pofine/ ▸ conjug 1 ◂ VT [+ *travail*] to polish up, to put the finishing touches to; [+ *style*] to polish

Peau-Rouge (pl **Peaux-Rouges**) /poʀuʒ/ NMF Red Indian, Redskin

peausserie /posʀi/ NF (= *articles*) leatherwear (*NonC*); (= *commerce*) skin trade; (= *boutique*) suede and leatherware shop

peaussier /posje/ ADJ M leather (*épith*) NM (= *ouvrier*) leatherworker; (= *commerçant*) leather dealer

pébroc*, **pébroque*** /pebʀɔk/ NM umbrella, brolly* (*Brit*)

pécan, pecan /pekɑ̃/ NM ◆ **(noix de) ~** pecan (nut)

pécari /pekaʀi/ NM peccary

peccadille /pekadij/ NF (= vétille) trifle; (= faute) peccadillo

pechblende /pɛʃblɛ̃d/ NF pitchblende

péché /peʃe/ NM sin ◆ **pour mes ~s** for my sins ◆ **à tout ~ miséricorde** every sin can be forgiven *ou* pardoned ◆ **vivre dans le ~** *(gén)* to lead a sinful life; *(sans être marié)* to live in sin ◆ **mourir en état de ~** to die a sinner ◆ **commettre un ~** to sin, to commit a sin
COMP **péché capital** deadly sin ◆ **les sept ~s capitaux** the seven deadly sins
péché de chair † sin of the flesh
péché de jeunesse youthful indiscretion
péché mignon ◆ **le whisky, c'est son ~ mignon** he's rather partial to whisky
péché mortel mortal sin
le péché d'orgueil the sin of pride
le péché originel original sin
péché véniel venial sin

pêche¹ /pɛʃ/ NF 1 (= fruit) peach ◆ **~-abricot, ~ jaune** *ou* **abricotée** yellow peach ◆ **~ blanche** white peach ◆ **~ de vigne** bush peach ◆ **avoir un teint de ~** to have a peaches and cream complexion; → **fendre, peau** 2 (* = vitalité) **avoir la ~** to be on form ◆ **avoir une ~ d'enfer** to be on top form, to be full of beans * *(Brit)* ◆ **ça donne la ~** it gets you going ◆ **il n'a pas la ~** he's feeling a bit low 3 (‡ = coup) punch, clout * *(Brit)* ◆ **donner une ~ à qn** to punch sb, to give sb a clout * *(Brit)* ADJ peach-coloured *(Brit)* ou -colored *(US)*

pêche² /pɛʃ/ NF 1 (= activité) fishing; (= saison) fishing season ◆ **la ~ à la ligne** *(en mer)* line fishing; *(en rivière)* angling ◆ **la ~ à la baleine** whaling ◆ **la ~ au gros** big-game fishing ◆ **grande ~ au large** deep-sea fishing ◆ **la ~ au harpon** harpoon fishing ◆ **la ~ à la crevette** shrimp fishing ◆ **la ~ à la truite** trout fishing ◆ **la ~ aux moules** mussel gathering ◆ **aller à la ~** *(lit)* to go fishing ◆ **aller à la ~ aux informations** to go fishing for information ◆ **aller à la ~ aux voix** to canvass, to go vote-catching * ◆ **filet/barque de ~** fishing net/boat; → **canne** 2 (= poissons) catch ◆ **faire une belle ~** to have *ou* make a good catch ◆ **la ~ miraculeuse** *(Bible)* the miraculous draught of fishes; *(fête foraine)* the bran tub *(Brit)*, the lucky dip *(Brit)*, the go-fish tub *(US)*

pécher /peʃe/ GRAMMAIRE ACTIVE 53.3 ► conjug 6 ◄ VI 1 *(Rel)* to sin ◆ **~ par orgueil** to commit the sin of pride 2 ◆ **~ contre la politesse/l'hospitalité** to break the rules of courtesy/of hospitality ◆ **~ par négligence/imprudence** to be too careless/reckless ◆ **~ par ignorance** to err through ignorance ◆ **~ par excès de prudence/d'optimisme** to be over-careful/over-optimistic, to err on the side of caution/of optimism ◆ **ça pèche par bien des points** *ou* **sur bien des côtés** it has a lot of weaknesses *ou* shortcomings

pêcher¹ /peʃe/ ► conjug 1 ◄ VT (= être pêcheur de) to fish for; (= attraper) to catch, to land ◆ **~ des coquillages** to gather shellfish ◆ **~ la baleine/la crevette** to go whaling/shrimping ◆ **~ la truite/la morue** to fish for trout/cod, to go trout-/cod-fishing ◆ **~ qch à la ligne/à l'asticot** to fish for sth with rod and line/with maggots ◆ **~ qch au chalut** to trawl for sth ◆ **où as-tu été ~ cette idée/cette boîte ?*** where did you dig that idea/that box up from? * ◆ **où a-t-il été ~ que ... ?*** wherever did he get the idea that ...? VI to fish, to go fishing; *(avec un chalut)* to trawl, to go trawling ◆ **~ à la ligne** to go angling ◆ **~ à l'asticot** to fish with maggots ◆ **~ à la mouche** to fly-fish ◆ **~ en eau trouble** *(fig)* to fish in troubled waters

pêcher² /peʃe/ NM (= arbre) peach tree

pêcherie /pɛʃʀi/ NF fishery, fishing ground

pécheur, pécheresse /peʃœʀ, peʃʀɛs/ ADJ sinful NM,F sinner

pêcheur /pɛʃœʀ/ NM fisherman; *(à la ligne)* angler ◆ **~ de crevettes** shrimper ◆ **~ de baleines** whaler ◆ **~ de palourdes** clamdigger ◆ **~ de perles** pearl diver ◆ **~ de corail** coral fisherman ADJ *[bateau]* fishing

pêcheuse /pɛʃøz/ NF fisherwoman; *(à la ligne)* (woman) angler

péchu, e* /peʃy/ ADJ ◆ **être ~** to be full of energy

pecnot /pɛkno/ NM ⇒ **péquenaud**

PECO /peko/ NMPL (abrév de **pays d'Europe centrale et orientale**) ◆ **les ~** the CEEC

pécore * /pekɔʀ/ NF *(péj = imbécile)* silly goose * NMF *(péj = paysan)* country bumpkin, yokel, hick * *(US)*

pectine /pɛktin/ NF pectin

pectique /pɛktik/ ADJ pectic

pectoral, e (mpl **-aux**) /pɛktɔʀal, o/ ADJ 1 *(= relatif à la poitrine)* pectoral 2 *[sirop, pastille]* throat *(épith)*, cough *(épith)*, expectorant *(SPÉC)* *(épith)* NM (= muscle) pectoral muscle ◆ **avoir de beaux pectoraux** to have big pecs * *ou* chest muscles

pécule /pekyl/ NM (= économies) savings, nest egg; *[de détenu, soldat]* earnings, wages *(paid on release or discharge)* ◆ **se faire** *ou* **se constituer un petit ~** to build up a little nest egg

pécuniaire /pekynjɛʀ/ ADJ *[embarras]* financial, pecuniary *(frm)*; *[aide, avantage, situation]* financial

pécuniairement /pekynjɛʀmɑ̃/ ADV financially

pédagogie /pedagɔʒi/ NF (= éducation) education; *(= art d'enseigner)* teaching skills; *(= méthodes d'enseignement)* educational methods ◆ **avoir beaucoup de ~** to have excellent teaching skills, to be a skilled teacher ◆ **il manque de ~** he's not a good teacher ◆ **faire œuvre de ~** to explain things clearly ◆ **il a dû faire œuvre de ~ auprès de ses collègues** he had to exercise great skills in persuading his colleagues

pédagogique /pedagɔʒik/ ADJ *[intérêt, contenu, théorie, moyens, méthode, projet]* educational, pedagogic(al) ◆ **outils ~s** teaching aids ◆ **stage (de formation) ~** teacher-training course ◆ **il a fait un exposé très ~** he gave a very clear lecture ◆ **ouvrage/musée à vocation ~** educational work/museum; → **conseiller²**

pédagogiquement /pedagɔʒikmɑ̃/ ADV *(= sur le plan de la pédagogie)* from an educational standpoint, pedagogically *(SPÉC)*; *(= avec pédagogie)* clearly

pédagogue /pedagɔg/ NMF (= professeur) teacher; *(= spécialiste)* teaching specialist, educationalist ◆ **c'est un bon ~, il est bon ~** he's a good teacher

pédale /pedal/ NF 1 *[de bicyclette, piano, voiture]* pedal; *[de machine à coudre ancienne, tour]* treadle 2 *(Mus)* **~ douce/forte** soft/sustaining pedal ◆ **(note de) ~** pedal (point) ◆ **~ wah-wah** wah-wah pedal ◆ **mettre la ~ douce** * *(fig)* to soft-pedal *, to go easy *; → **emmêler, perdre** 3 (‡ péj = homosexuel) queer‡, poof‡ *(Brit)*, fag‡ *(US)* ◆ **être de la ~** † to be (a) queer‡

pédaler /pedale/ ► conjug 1 ◄ VI to pedal; (* = se dépêcher) to hurry ◆ **~ dans la choucroute**‡ *ou* **la semoule**‡ *ou* **le yaourt**‡ *(= ne rien comprendre)* to be all at sea, to be at a complete loss; *(= ne pas progresser)* to get nowhere (fast) *

pédaleur, -euse /pedalœʀ, øz/ NM,F *(Cyclisme)* pedaller

pédalier /pedalje/ NM *[de bicyclette]* pedal and gear mechanism; *[d'orgue]* pedal-board, pedals

pédalo ® /pedalo/ NM pedalo, pedal boat ◆ **faire du ~** to go for a ride on a pedal boat

pédant, e /pedɑ̃, ɑ̃t/ ADJ pretentious NM,F pretentious person

pédanterie /pedɑ̃tʀi/ NF *(littér)* pretentiousness

pédantesque /pedɑ̃tɛsk/ ADJ abstruse

pédantisme /pedɑ̃tism/ NM ◆ **sans ~** without being pedantic

pédé‡ /pede/ NM (abrév de **pédéraste**) *(péj)* queer‡, poof‡ *(Brit)*, fag‡ *(US)* ◆ **être ~** to be (a) queer‡ *ou* a poof‡ *(Brit)* *ou* a fag‡ *(US)* ◆ **il est ~ comme un phoque**‡ he's as queer as a coot‡ *ou* as a three-dollar bill‡ *(US)*

pédéraste /pedeʀast/ NM pederast; *(par extension)* homosexual

pédérastie /pedeʀasti/ NF pederasty; *(par extension)* homosexuality

pédérastique /pedeʀastik/ ADJ pederast; *(par extension)* homosexual

pédestre /pedɛstʀ/ ADJ *(littér, hum)* ◆ **promenade** *ou* **circuit ~** walk, ramble, hike ◆ **sentier ~** pedestrian footpath

pédiatre /pedjatʀ/ NMF paediatrician *(Brit)*, pediatrician *(US)*

pédiatrie /pedjatʀi/ NF paediatrics *(sg)* *(Brit)*, pediatrics *(sg)* *(US)*

pédiatrique /pedjatʀik/ ADJ paediatric *(Brit)*, pediatric *(US)*

pedibus (cum jambis) /pedibys(kumʒɑ̃bis)/ ADV on foot, on Shanks' pony * *(Brit)* *ou* mare * *(US)*

pédicule /pedikyl/ NM *[d'organe]* pedicle; *[de plante]* peduncle

pédicure /pedikyʀ/ NMF chiropodist, podiatrist *(US)*

pédicurie /pedikyʀi/ NF (= soins médicaux) chiropody, podiatry *(US)*; (= soins de beauté) pedicure

pedigree /pedigʀe/ NM pedigree

pédologie /pedɔlɔʒi/ NF 1 *(Géol)* pedology 2 *(Méd)* paedology *(Brit)*, pedology *(US)*

pédologique /pedɔlɔʒik/ ADJ *(Géol)* pedological

pédologue /pedɔlɔg/ NMF *(Géol)* pedologist

pédoncule /pedɔ̃kyl/ NM peduncle ◆ **ôtez les ~s des poivrons** cut the stalks off the peppers

pédonculé, e /pedɔ̃kyle/ ADJ pedunculate(d) ◆ **chêne ~** pedunculate oak

pédophile /pedɔfil/ NM pedophile, paedophile *(Brit)* ADJ pedophile *(épith)*, paedophile *(épith)* *(Brit)*

pédophilie /pedɔfili/ NF pedophilia, paedophilia *(Brit)*

pédopsychiatre /pedopsikjatʀ/ NMF child psychiatrist

pedzouille‡ /pɛdzuj/ NM *(péj)* peasant, country bumpkin, hick * *(US)*

PEE /peəə/ NM (abrév de **plan d'épargne entreprise**) → **plan¹**

peeling /piliŋ/ NM (= gommage) facial scrub; *(Méd)* peel, dermabrasion ◆ **se faire un ~** to use a facial scrub; *(Méd)* to have dermabrasion

Pégase /pegaz/ NM Pegasus

PEGC /peəʒese/ NM (abrév de **professeur d'enseignement général des collèges**) → **professeur**

pègre /pɛgʀ/ NF ◆ **la ~** the underworld ◆ **membre de la ~** gangster, mobster

peignage /pɛɲaʒ/ NM *[de laine]* carding; *[de lin, chanvre]* carding, hackling

peigne /pɛɲ/ NM 1 *[de cheveux]* comb; *[de laine]* card; *[de lin, chanvre]* card, hackle; *[de métier]* reed ◆ **~ de poche** pocket comb ◆ **passer qch au ~ fin** *(fig)* to go through sth with a fine-tooth comb ◆ **se donner un coup de ~** to run a comb through one's hair ② *[de scorpion]* comb; *[d'oiseau]* pecten; (= *mollusque*) pecten

peigne-cul*‡ (pl **peigne-culs**) /pɛɲky/ **NM** *(péj)* (= *mesquin*) creep *; (= *inculte*) lout, yob * *(Brit)*

peignée * /peɲe/ **NF** (= *raclée*) thrashing, hiding * ◆ **donner/recevoir une** *ou* **la ~** to give/get a thrashing *ou* hiding *

peigner /peɲe/ ► conjug 1 ◄ **VT** *[+ cheveux]* to comb; *[+ laine]* to card; *[+ lin, chanvre]* to card, to hackle ◆ **~ qn** to comb sb's hair ◆ **être bien peigné** *[+ personne]* to have well-combed hair ◆ **des cheveux bien peignés** well-combed hair ◆ **mal peigné** dishevelled, tousled ◆ **faire ça ou ~ la girafe** *(hum)* it's either that or some other pointless task **VPR se peigner** to comb one's hair, to give one's hair a comb

peignoir /pɛɲwaʀ/ **NM** dressing gown ◆ **~ (de bain)** bathrobe

peinard, e * /penaʀ, aʀd/ **ADJ** ① (= *sans tracas*) *[travail, vie]* cushy *, easy ◆ **on est ~s dans ce service** we have a cushy * time of it in this department ◆ **il fait ses 35 heures,** ~ he does his 35 hours and that's it ◆ **rester** *ou* **se tenir ~** to keep out of trouble, to keep one's nose clean * ② (= *au calme*) *[coin]* quiet, peaceful ◆ **on va être ~s** *(pour se reposer)* we'll have a bit of peace, we can take it easy; *(pour agir)* we'll be left in peace ◆ **il vit ~ sur une île** he leads a nice quiet life on an island

peindre /pɛ̃dʀ/ ► conjug 52 ◄ **VT** *(gén)* to paint; *[+ mœurs]* to paint, to depict ◆ **~ qch en jaune** to paint sth yellow ◆ **~ à la chaux** to whitewash ◆ **tableau peint à l'huile** picture painted in oils ◆ **~ au pinceau/au rouleau** to paint with a brush/a roller ◆ **se faire ~ par qn** to have one's portrait painted by sb ◆ **romancier qui sait bien ~ ses personnages** novelist who portrays his characters well ◆ **il l'avait peint sous les traits d'un vieillard dans son livre** he had depicted *ou* portrayed him as an old man in his book ◆ **la cruauté était peinte sur son visage** his face was a mask of cruelty **VPR se peindre** (= *se décrire*) to portray o.s. ◆ **Montaigne s'est peint dans "Les Essais"** "Les Essais" are a self-portrayal of Montaigne ◆ **la consternation/le désespoir se peignait sur leur visage** dismay/despair was written on their faces

peine /pɛn/ **NF** ① (= *chagrin*) sorrow, sadness *(NonC)* ◆ **avoir de la ~** to be sad *ou* upset ◆ **être dans la ~** to be grief-stricken ◆ **faire de la ~ à qn** to upset sb, to make sb sad, to distress sb ◆ **elle m'a fait de la ~ et je lui ai donné de l'argent** I felt sorry for her and gave her some money ◆ **je ne voudrais pas te faire de (la) ~, mais ...** I don't want to disappoint you but ... ◆ **avoir des ~s de cœur** to have an unhappy love life ◆ **cela fait ~ à voir** it hurts to see it ◆ **il faisait ~ à voir** he looked a sorry *ou* pitiful sight; → **âme**

② (= *effort*) effort, trouble *(NonC)* ◆ **il faut se donner de la ~, cela demande de la ~** it requires an effort, you have to make an effort ◆ **se donner de la ~ pour faire qch** to go to a lot of trouble to do sth ◆ **si tu te mettais seulement en ~ d'essayer, si tu te donnais seulement la ~ d'essayer** if you would only bother to try *ou* take the trouble to try ◆ **il ne se donne aucune ~** he just doesn't try *ou* bother ◆ **donnez-vous** *ou* **prenez donc la ~ d'entrer/de vous asseoir** *(formule de politesse)* please *ou* do come in/sit down ◆ **ne vous donnez pas la ~ de venir me chercher** please don't bother to come and get me ◆ **c'est ~ perdue** it's a waste of time (and effort) ◆ **on lui a donné 50 € pour sa ~** he was given €50 for his trouble ◆ **en être pour sa ~** to get nothing for one's pains *ou* trouble ◆ **tu as été sage, pour la ~, tu auras un bonbon** here's a sweet for being good ◆ **ne vous mettez pas en ~ pour moi** don't go to *ou* put yourself to any trouble for me ◆ **toute ~ mérite salaire** the labourer is worthy of his hire *(Prov)* any effort should be rewarded ◆ **à chaque jour suffit sa ~** *(Prov)* sufficient unto the day is the evil thereof *(Prov)*

◆ **c'est/c'était + peine** ◆ **est-ce que c'est la ~ d'y aller ?** is it worth going? ◆ **ce n'est pas la ~ de me le répéter** there's no point in repeating that, you've no need to repeat that ◆ **ce n'est pas la ~** don't bother ◆ **c'était bien la ~ !** *(iro)* after all that trouble! ◆ **c'était bien la ~ de l'inviter ! ou qu'on l'invite !** *(iro)* it was a waste of time inviting him!

◆ **valoir la peine** ◆ **cela vaut la ~** it's worth it, it's worth the trouble ◆ **cela valait la ~ d'essayer** it was worth trying *ou* a try *ou* a go ◆ **ça vaut la ~ qu'il y aille** it's worth it for him to go, it's worth his while going ◆ **cela ne vaut pas la ~ d'en parler** (= *c'est trop mauvais*) it's not worth wasting one's breath over, it's not worth talking about; (= *c'est insignifiant*) it's hardly *ou* not worth mentioning

③ (= *difficulté*) difficulty ◆ **il a eu de la ~ à finir son repas/la course** he had difficulty finishing his meal/the race ◆ **il a eu de la ~ mais il y est arrivé** it wasn't easy (for him) but he managed it ◆ **avoir de la ~ à faire** to have difficulty in doing, to find it difficult *ou* hard to do ◆ **j'ai (de la) ~ à croire que ...** I find it hard to believe that ..., I can hardly believe that ... ◆ **avec ~** with difficulty ◆ **sans ~** without (any) difficulty, easily ◆ **il n'est pas en ~ pour trouver des secrétaires** he has no difficulty *ou* trouble finding secretaries ◆ **j'ai eu toutes les ~s du monde à le convaincre/à démarrer** I had a real job convincing him/getting the car started ◆ **je serais bien en ~ de vous le dire/d'en trouver** I'd be hard pushed * *ou* hard pressed to tell you/to find any

④ (= *punition*) punishment, penalty; *(Jur)* sentence ◆ **~ capitale** *ou* **de mort** capital punishment, death sentence *ou* penalty ◆ **~ de prison** prison sentence ◆ **~ alternative** *ou* **de substitution** alternative sentence ◆ **sous ~ de mort** on pain of death ◆ **"défense d'afficher sous peine d'amende"** "billposters will be fined" ◆ **"défense d'entrer sous peine de poursuites"** "trespassers will be prosecuted" ◆ **la ~ n'est pas toujours proportionnée au délit** the punishment does not always fit the crime ◆ **on ne peut rien lui dire, sous ~ d'être renvoyé** you daren't *ou* can't say anything to him for fear of being fired ◆ **pour la** *ou* **ta ~ tu mettras la table** for that you can set the table

◆ **à peine** hardly, scarcely, barely ◆ **il est à ~ 2 heures** it's only just 2 o'clock, it's only just turned 2 ◆ **il leur reste à ~ de quoi manger** they hardly have any food left ◆ **il gagne à ~ de quoi vivre** he hardly earns enough to keep body and soul together ◆ **il parle à ~** *[personne silencieuse]* he hardly says anything; *[enfant]* he can hardly *ou* barely talk ◆ **il était à ~ rentré qu'il a dû ressortir** he had only just got in when he had to go out again ◆ **à ~ dans la voiture, il s'est endormi** no sooner had he got in the car than he fell asleep ◆ **c'est à ~ si on l'entend** you can hardly hear him ◆ **il était à ~ aimable** he was barely civil ◆ **celui-ci est à ~ plus cher que les autres** this one is hardly any more expensive than the others

peiner /pene/ ► conjug 1 ◄ **VI** *[personne]* to work hard, to toil; *[moteur]* to labour *(Brit)*, to labor *(US)*; *[voiture, plante]* to struggle ◆ **~ sur un problème** to struggle with a problem ◆ **le coureur peinait dans les derniers mètres** the runner was struggling over the last few metres ◆ **le chien peine quand il fait chaud** the dog suffers when it's hot **VT** to grieve, to sadden ◆ **j'ai été peiné de l'apprendre** I was sad to hear it ◆ **... dit-il d'un ton peiné** *(gén)* ... he said in a sad voice; *(vexé)* ... he said in a hurt *ou* an aggrieved tone ◆ **il avait un air peiné** he looked upset

peintre /pɛ̃tʀ/ **NMF** *(lit)* painter ◆ **~ en bâtiment** house painter, painter and decorator ◆ **~-décorateur** painter and decorator ◆ **c'est un merveilleux ~ de notre société** *(écrivain)* he paints a marvellous picture of the society we live in

peinture /pɛ̃tyʀ/ **NF** ① (= *action, art*) painting ◆ **faire de la ~ (à l'huile/à l'eau)** to paint (in oils/in watercolours)

② (= *ouvrage*) painting, picture ◆ **vendre sa ~** to sell one's paintings; → **voir**

③ (= *surface peinte*) paintwork *(NonC)* ◆ **toutes les ~s sont à refaire** all the paintwork needs re-doing

④ (= *matière*) paint ◆ **"attention à la peinture", "peinture fraîche"** "wet paint" ◆ **donner un coup de ~ à un mur** to give a wall a coat of paint

⑤ *(fig)* (= *action*) portrayal; (= *résultat*) portrait ◆ **c'est une ~ des mœurs de l'époque** it portrays *ou* depicts the social customs of the period

COMP peinture abstraite *(NonC)* abstract art; (= *tableau*) abstract (painting)
peinture acrylique acrylic paint
peinture en bâtiment house painting, painting and decorating
peinture brillante gloss paint
peinture au doigt fingerpainting
peinture à l'eau (= *tableau, matière*) watercolour *(Brit)*, watercolor *(US)*; *(pour le bâtiment)* water(-based) paint
peinture à l'huile (= *tableau*) oil painting; (= *matière*) oil paint; *(pour le bâtiment)* oil-based paint
peinture laquée gloss paint
peinture mate matt emulsion (paint)
peinture métallisée metallic paint
peinture murale mural
peinture au pinceau painting with a brush
peinture au pistolet spray painting
peinture au rouleau roller painting
peinture satinée satin-finish paint
peinture sur soie silk painting

peinturer /pɛ̃tyʀe/ ► conjug 1 ◄ **VT** ① (* = *mal peindre*) to slap paint on ② *(Can)* to paint

peinturlurer * /pɛ̃tyʀlyʀe/ ► conjug 1 ◄ **VT** *(péj)* to daub (with paint) ◆ **~ qch de bleu** to daub sth with blue paint ◆ **visage peinturluré** painted face ◆ **lèvres peinturlurées en rouge** lips with a slash of red across them ◆ **se ~ le visage** to slap make-up on one's face

péjoratif, -ive /peʒɔʀatif, iv/ **ADJ** derogatory, pejorative **NM** *(Ling)* pejorative word

péjoration /peʒɔʀasjɔ̃/ **NF** pejoration

péjorativement /peʒɔʀativmɑ̃/ **ADV** in a derogatory fashion, pejoratively

Pékin /pekɛ̃/ **N** Beijing, Peking

pékin /pekɛ̃/ **NM** *(arg Mil)* civvy *(arg)* ◆ **s'habiller en ~** to dress in civvies *ou* mufti

pékinois, e /pekinwa, waz/ **ADJ** Pekinese **NM** ① (= *chien*) Pekinese, peke * ② (= *langue*) Mandarin (Chinese), Pekinese **NM,F Pékinois(e)** Pekinese

PEL /peœl/ **NM** (abrév de **plan d'épargne logement**) → **plan¹**

pelade /pəlad/ **NF** alopecia

pelage /pəlaʒ/ **NM** coat, fur

pélagique /pelaʒik/ **ADJ** pelagic

pélargonium /pelaʀgɔnjɔm/ **NM** pelargonium

pelé, e /pəle/ (ptp de **peler**) **ADJ** *[personne]* bald(-headed); *[animal]* hairless; *[vêtement]* threadbare; *[terrain, montagne]* bare **NM** (* = *personne*) bald-headed man, baldie*‡ ◆ **il n'y avait que trois** *ou* **quatre ~s et un tondu à la réunion** * there was hardly anyone at the meeting

pêle-mêle /pɛlmɛl/ ADV any old how ◆ **ils s'entassaient ~ dans l'autobus** they piled into the bus any old how ◆ **on y trouvait ~ des chapeaux, des rubans, des colliers** there were hats, ribbons and necklaces all mixed *ou* jumbled up together ◆ **un roman où l'on trouve ~ une rencontre avec Charlemagne, un voyage sur Mars ...** a novel containing a hotchpotch of meetings with Charlemagne, trips to Mars ... NM INV (= *cadre*) multiple photo frame

peler /pəle/ ▸ conjug 5 ◂ VTI (*gén*) to peel ◆ **ce fruit se pèle bien** this fruit peels easily *ou* is easy to peel ◆ **on pèle (de froid) ici !*** it's damn cold here!*, it's bloody freezing here!* (*Brit*)

pèlerin /pɛlʀɛ̃/ NM pilgrim ◆ **(faucon)** ~ peregrine falcon ◆ **(requin)** ~ basking shark ◆ **criquet** ~ migratory locust ◆ **qui c'est ce ~ ?*** (= *individu*) who's that guy?* *ou* bloke* (*Brit*)?

pèlerinage /pɛlʀinaʒ/ NM (= *voyage*) pilgrimage ◆ **(lieu de)** ~ place of pilgrimage, shrine ◆ **aller en** *ou* **faire un ~ à** to go on a pilgrimage to

pèlerine /pɛlʀin/ NF cape

pélican /pelikɑ̃/ NM pelican

pelisse /pəlis/ NF pelisse, dress-coat

pellagre /pelagʀ/ NF pellagra

pelle /pɛl/ NF 1 (*gén*) shovel; [*d'enfant*] spade ◆ **ramasser qch à la ~** to shovel sth up ◆ **on en ramasse** *ou* **il y en a à la ~** there are loads of them* ◆ **avoir de l'argent** *ou* **remuer l'argent à la ~** to have loads* *ou* pots* of money ◆ **(se) ramasser** *ou* **se prendre une ~*** (= *tomber, échouer*) to fall flat on one's face, to come a cropper* (*Brit*); (*après avoir demandé qch*) to be sent packing*; → **rond** 2 (* = *baiser*) **rouler une ~ à qn** to give sb a French kiss

COMP **pelle à charbon** coal shovel

pelle mécanique mechanical shovel *ou* digger

pelle à ordures dustpan

pelle à poisson fish slice

pelle à tarte cake *ou* pie server

pelletée /pɛlte/ NF shovelful, spadeful ◆ **des ~s de** masses of

pelleter /pɛlte/ ▸ conjug 4 ◂ VT to shovel (up)

pelleterie /pɛltʀi/ NF (= *commerce*) fur trade, furriery; (= *préparation*) fur dressing; (= *peau*) pelt

pelleteur /pɛltœʀ/ NM workman (*who does the digging*)

pelleteuse /pɛltøz/ NF mechanical shovel *ou* digger, excavator

pelletier, -ière /pɛltje, jɛʀ/ NM,F furrier

pellicule /pelikyl/ NF 1 (= *couche fine*) film, thin layer; (*Photo*) film ◆ **~ couleur/noir et blanc** colour/black and white film ◆ **ne gâche pas de la ~** don't waste film ◆ **(rouleau de)** ~ (roll of) film 2 (*Méd*) **~s** dandruff (*NonC*) ◆ **lotion contre les ~s** dandruff lotion

pelliculé, e /pelikyle/ ADJ [*pochette, couverture de livre*] plastic-coated

péloche* /pelɔʃ/ NF (= *film*) film; (= *rouleau*) roll of film

Péloponnèse /pelɔpɔnɛz/ NM ◆ **le ~** the Peloponnese ◆ **la guerre du ~** the Peloponnesian War

pelotage* /p(ə)lɔtaʒ/ NM petting* (*NonC*)

pelotari /p(ə)lɔtaʀi/ NM pelota player

pelote /p(ə)lɔt/ NF 1 [*de laine*] ball ◆ **mettre de la laine en ~** to wind wool into a ball ◆ **faire sa ~** † to feather one's nest, to make one's pile* ◆ **~ d'épingles** pin cushion ◆ **c'est une vraie ~ d'épingles** (*fig*) he (*ou* she) is really prickly; → **nerf** 2 (*Sport*) **~ (basque)** pelota 3 (*Zool*) **~ (plantaire)** pad

peloter* /p(ə)lɔte/ ▸ conjug 1 ◂ VT to feel up*, to touch up* ◆ **elle se faisait ~ par Paul** Paul was feeling* *ou* touching* her up ◆ **arrêtez de me ~ !** stop pawing me!*, keep your hands to yourself! ◆ **ils se pelotaient** they were petting*

peloteur, -euse* /p(ə)lɔtœʀ, øz/ ADJ ◆ **il a des gestes ~s** *ou* **des mains peloteuses** he can't keep his hands to himself NM,F groper* ◆ **c'est un ~** he can't keep his hands to himself

peloton /p(ə)lɔtɔ̃/ NM 1 [*de laine*] small ball 2 (= *groupe*) cluster, group; [*de pompiers, gendarmes*] squad; (*Mil*) platoon; (*Sport*) pack, bunch

COMP **peloton d'exécution** firing squad

peloton de tête (*Sport*) leaders, leading runners (*ou* riders *etc*) ◆ **être dans le ~ de tête** (*Sport*) to be up with the leaders; (*en classe*) to be among the top few [*pays, entreprise*] to be one of the front runners

pelotonner /p(ə)lɔtɔne/ ▸ conjug 1 ◂ VT [+ *laine*] to wind into a ball VPR **se pelotonner** to curl (o.s.) up ◆ **se ~ contre qn** to snuggle up to sb, to nestle close to sb ◆ **il s'est pelotonné entre mes bras** he snuggled up in my arms

pelouse /p(ə)luz/ NF lawn; (*Courses*) public enclosure; (*Ftbl, Rugby*) field, ground ◆ **"pelouse interdite"** "keep off the grass"

peluche /p(ə)lyʃ/ NF 1 (= *tissu*) plush; (= *poil*) fluff (*NonC*), bit of fluff ◆ **ce pull fait des ~s** this jumper pills 2 ◆ **(jouet en) ~** soft *ou* cuddly toy ◆ **chien/lapin en ~** stuffed *ou* fluffy (*Brit*) dog/rabbit; → **ours**

pelucher /p(ə)lyʃe/ ▸ conjug 1 ◂ VI (*par l'aspect*) to pill, to go fluffy; (= *perdre des poils*) to leave fluff

pelucheux, -euse /p(ə)lyʃø, øz/ ADJ fluffy

pelure /p(ə)lyʀ/ NF 1 (= *épluchure*) peel (*NonC*), peeling, piece of peel; (* *hum* = *manteau*) overcoat ◆ **~ d'oignon** (*Bot*) onion skin; (= *vin*) (pale) rosé wine; (= *couleur*) pinkish orange 2 ◆ **(papier) ~** flimsy (paper), copy *ou* bank paper; (= *feuille*) flimsy (copy)

pelvien, -ienne /pɛlvjɛ̃, jɛn/ ADJ pelvic; → **ceinture**

pelvis /pɛlvis/ NM pelvis

pénal, e (mpl **-aux**) /penal, o/ ADJ [*responsabilité, enquête, justice, loi*] criminal ◆ **le droit ~** criminal law ◆ **poursuivre qn au ~** to sue sb, to take legal action against sb; → **clause, code**

pénalement /penalmɑ̃/ ADV ◆ **être ~ responsable** to be criminally responsible ◆ **acte ~ répréhensible** act for which one is liable to prosecution

pénalisant, e /penalizɑ̃, ɑ̃t/ ADJ [*mesure, réforme*] disadvantageous ◆ **cette réglementation est très ~e pour notre industrie** this regulation puts our industry at a serious disadvantage *ou* severely penalizes our industry

pénalisation /penalizasjɔ̃/ NF 1 (*Sport*) (= *action*) penalization; (= *sanction*) penalty ◆ **points de ~** penalty points ◆ **cette mesure prévoit la ~ financière de certains produits polluants** this measure makes provision for imposing financial penalties *ou* sanctions against certain products that cause pollution 2 (*Jur*) [*d'usage, pratique*] criminalization

pénaliser /penalize/ ▸ conjug 1 ◂ VT [+ *contrevenant, faute, joueur*] to penalize; (= *défavoriser*) to penalize, to put at a disadvantage ◆ **ils ont été lourdement pénalisés par cette mesure** they were severely penalized by this measure

pénalité /penalite/ NF (*Fin, Sport* = *sanction*) penalty ◆ **~ de retard** (*Fin*) late payment penalty; (*pour retard de livraison*) late delivery penalty ◆ **coup de pied de ~** (*Ftbl, Rugby*) penalty (kick) ◆ **il a marqué sur un coup de ~** he scored from a penalty

penalty /penalti/ (pl **penalties** /penaltiz/) NM (*Ftbl*) (= *coup de pied*) penalty (kick); (= *sanction*) penalty ◆ **marquer sur ~** to score a penalty goal *ou* from a penalty ◆ **tirer un ~** to take a penalty (kick) ◆ **siffler le** *ou* **un ~** to award a penalty ◆ **point de ~** (= *endroit*) penalty spot

pénard, e* /penaʀ, aʀd/ ADJ ⇒ **peinard, e**

pénates /penat/ NMPL (*Myth*) Penates; (*fig hum*) home ◆ **regagner ses ~** to go back home ◆ **installer ses ~ quelque part** to settle down somewhere

penaud, e /pəno, od/ ADJ sheepish, contrite ◆ **d'un air ~** sheepishly, contritely ◆ **il en est resté tout ~** he became quite sheepish *ou* contrite

pence /pɛns/ NMPL pence

penchant /pɑ̃ʃɑ̃/ NM (= *tendance*) tendency, propensity (*à faire* to do); (= *faible*) liking, fondness (*pour qch* for sth); ◆ **avoir un ~ à faire qch** to be inclined *ou* have a tendency to do sth ◆ **avoir un ~ pour qch** to be fond of *ou* have a liking *ou* fondness for sth ◆ **avoir un ~ pour la boisson** to be partial to a drink ◆ **avoir du ~ pour qn** (*littér*) to be in love with sb ◆ **le ~ qu'ils ont l'un pour l'autre** the fondness they have for each other ◆ **mauvais ~s** baser instincts

penché, e /pɑ̃ʃe/ (ptp de **pencher**) ADJ [*tableau*] lop-sided; [*mur*] sloping; [*poteau, arbre, colonne*] leaning; [*écriture*] sloping, slanting; [*tête*] tilted (to one side) ◆ **le corps ~ en avant/en arrière** leaning forward/backward) ◆ **être ~ sur ses livres** [*personne*] to be bent over one's books; → **tour**[1]

pencher /pɑ̃ʃe/ ▸ conjug 1 ◂ VT [+ *meuble, bouteille*] to tip up, to tilt ◆ **~ son assiette** to tip one's plate up ◆ **~ la tête** (*en avant*) to bend one's head forward; (*sur le côté*) to tilt one's head

VI 1 (= *être incliné*) [*mur, arbre*] to lean; [*navire*] to list; [*objet en déséquilibre*] to tilt, to tip (to one side) ◆ **le tableau penche un peu de ce côté** the picture is leaning to this side, this side of the picture is lower than the other ◆ **faire ~ la balance** (*fig*) to tip the scales (*en faveur de* in favour of)

2 (= *être porté à*) **je penche pour la première hypothèse** I'm inclined to favour the first hypothesis ◆ **je penche à croire qu'il est sincère** I'm inclined to believe he's sincere

VPR **se pencher** 1 (= *s'incliner*) to lean over; (= *se baisser*) to bend down ◆ **se ~ en avant** to lean forward ◆ **se ~ par-dessus bord** to lean overboard ◆ **se ~ sur un livre** to bend over a book ◆ **"défense de se pencher au dehors** *ou* **par la fenêtre"** "do not lean out of the window"

2 (= *examiner*) **se ~ sur un problème/cas** to look into *ou* study a problem/case ◆ **se ~ sur les malheurs de qn** to turn one's attention to sb's misfortunes

pendable /pɑ̃dabl/ ADJ → **cas, tour**[2]

pendaison /pɑ̃dɛzɔ̃/ NF hanging ◆ **~ de crémaillère** house warming, house-warming party

pendant[1], **e** /pɑ̃dɑ̃, ɑ̃t/ ADJ 1 (= *qui pend*) [*bras, jambes*] hanging, dangling; [*langue*] hanging out (*attrib*); [*joue*] sagging; [*oreilles*] drooping; (*Jur*) [*fruits*] on the tree (*attrib*) ◆ **ne reste pas là les bras ~s** don't just stand there (doing nothing) ◆ **assis sur le mur les jambes ~es** sitting on the wall with his legs hanging down ◆ **le chien haletait la langue ~e** the dog was panting with its tongue hanging out ◆ **chien aux oreilles ~es** dog with drooping ears, lop-eared dog ◆ **les branches ~es du saule** the hanging *ou* drooping branches of the willow 2 (*Admin* = *en instance*) [*question*] outstanding, in abeyance (*attrib*); [*affaire*] pending (*attrib*); (*Jur*) [*procès*] pending (*attrib*)

pendant[2] /pɑ̃dɑ̃/ NM 1 (= *objet*) **~ (d'oreille)** drop earring, pendant earring ◆ **~ d'épée** frog 2 (= *contrepartie*) **le ~ de** [+ *œuvre d'art,* *meuble]* the matching piece to; *[+ personne, institution]* the counterpart of ◆ **faire ~ à** to match, to be the counterpart of ◆ **se faire** ~ to match ◆ **j'ai un chandelier et je cherche le** ~ I've got a candlestick and I'm looking for one to match it *ou* and I'm trying to make up a pair

pendant[3] /pɑ̃dɑ̃/ PRÉP (= *au cours de)* during; *(indiquant la durée)* for ◆ ~ **la journée/son séjour** during the day/his stay ◆ ~ **ce temps Paul attendait** during this time *ou* meanwhile Paul was waiting ◆ **qu'est-ce qu'il faisait ~ ce temps-là ?** what was he doing during that time? *ou* in the meantime? ◆ **à prendre ~ le repas** *[médicament]* to be taken at mealtimes *ou* with meals ◆ **on a marché ~ des kilomètres** we walked for miles ◆ **il a vécu en France ~ plusieurs années** he lived in France for several years ◆ ~ **quelques mois, il n'a pas pu travailler** for several months he was unable to work ◆ **on est resté sans nouvelles de lui ~ longtemps** we had no news from him for a long time ◆ ~ **un moment on a cru qu'il ne reviendrait pas** for a while we thought he would not return ◆ **avant la guerre et** ~ before and during the war

LOC CONJ **pendant que** while, whilst *(frm)* ◆ ~ **qu'elle se reposait, il écoutait la radio** while she was resting he would listen to the radio ◆ ~ **que vous serez à Paris, pourriez-vous aller le voir ?** while you're in Paris could you go and see him? ◆ ~ **que j'y pense, n'oubliez pas de fermer la porte à clé** while I think of it, don't forget to lock the door ◆ **arrosez le jardin et, ~ que vous y êtes, arrachez les mauvaises herbes** water the garden and do some weeding while you're at *ou* about it ◆ **finissez le plat ~ que vous y êtes !** *(iro)* why don't you eat it all (up) while you're at it! *(iro)* ◆ **dire que des gens doivent suivre un régime ~ que des enfants meurent de faim** to think that some people have to go on a diet while there are children dying of hunger

pendard, e †† /pɑ̃daʀ, aʀd/ NM,F *(hum)* scoundrel

pendeloque /pɑ̃d(ə)lɔk/ NF *[de boucles d'oreilles]* pendant; *[de lustre]* lustre, pendant

pendentif /pɑ̃dɑ̃tif/ NM (= *bijou)* pendant; *(Archit)* pendentive

penderie /pɑ̃dʀi/ NF (= *meuble)* wardrobe *(with hanging space only)*; (= *barre)* clothes rail ◆ **le placard du couloir nous sert de** ~ we hang our clothes in the hall cupboard *(Brit) ou* closet *(US)* ◆ **le côté ~ de l'armoire** the part of the wardrobe you hang things in

pendiller /pɑ̃dije/ ► conjug 1 ◄ VI *[clés, boucles d'oreilles, corde]* to dangle; *[linge]* to flap gently

Pendjab /pɛ̃dʒab/ NM ◆ **le** ~ the Punjab

pendouiller * /pɑ̃duje/ ► conjug 1 ◄ VI to dangle, to hang down

pendre /pɑ̃dʀ/ ► conjug 41 ◄ VT 1 *[+ rideau]* to hang, to put up (*à* at); *[+ tableau, manteau]* to hang (up) (*à* on); *[+ lustre]* to hang (up) (*à* from); ◆ ~ **le linge pour le faire sécher** *(dans la maison)* to hang up the washing to dry; *(dehors)* to hang out the washing to dry ◆ ~ **la crémaillère** to have a house-warming party *ou* a house warming

2 *[+ criminel]* to hang ◆ ~ **qn haut et court** *(Hist)* to hang sb ◆ **qu'il aille se faire ~ ailleurs !** * he can go hang! *, he can take a running jump! * ◆ **je veux être pendu si ...** I'll be damned * *ou* hanged if ... ◆ **dussé-je être pendu, je ne dirais jamais cela !** I wouldn't say that even if my life depended on it!; → **pis**[2]

VI 1 (= *être suspendu)* to hang (down) ◆ **des fruits pendaient aux branches** there was fruit hanging from the branches ◆ **cela lui pend au nez** * he's got it coming to him *

2 *[bras, jambes]* to dangle; *[joue]* to sag; *[langue]* to hang out; *[robe]* to dip, to hang down; *[cheveux]* to hang down ◆ **un lambeau de papier pendait** a strip of wallpaper was hanging off ◆ **laisser ~ ses jambes** to dangle one's legs

VPR **se pendre** 1 (= *se tuer)* to hang o.s.

2 (= *se suspendre)* **se ~ à une branche** to hang from a branch ◆ **se ~ au cou de qn** to throw one's arms round sb *ou* sb's neck

pendu, e /pɑ̃dy/ (ptp de **pendre**) ADJ 1 (= *accroché)* hung up, hanging up ◆ ~ **à** *(lit)* hanging from ◆ **être toujours ~ aux basques de qn** *(fig)* to keep pestering sb ◆ **il est toujours ~ aux jupes** *ou* **jupons de sa mère** he's always clinging to his mother's skirts, he's still tied to his mother's apron strings ◆ ~ **au bras de qn** holding on to sb's arm ◆ **elle est toujours ~e au téléphone** she spends all her time on the phone ◆ **ça fait deux heures qu'il est ~ au téléphone** he's been on the phone for two hours; → **langue** 2 (= *mort)* hanged NM,F hanged man *(ou* woman) ◆ **le (jeu du) ~** hangman ◆ **jouer au ~** to play hangman

pendulaire /pɑ̃dylɛʀ/ ADJ pendular ◆ **train ~** tilting train

pendule /pɑ̃dyl/ NF clock ◆ ~ **à coucou** cuckoo clock ◆ **remettre les ~s à l'heure** * *(fig)* to set the record straight ◆ **tu ne vas pas nous en chier** ** **une ~ (à treize coups) !** you're not going to make a fucking ** song and dance about it, are you? NM pendulum ◆ ~ **astronomique** pendulum clock ◆ **faire un ~** *[alpiniste]* to do a pendule *ou* a pendulum

pendulette /pɑ̃dylɛt/ NF small clock ◆ ~ **de voyage** travelling clock

pêne /pɛn/ NM *[de serrure]* bolt ◆ ~ **dormant** dead bolt ◆ ~ **demi-tour** latch *ou* spring bolt

Pénélope /penelɔp/ NF Penelope ◆ **c'est un travail de ~** it's a never-ending task

pénéplaine /peneplɛn/ NF peneplain, peneplane

pénétrabilité /penetʀabilite/ NF penetrability

pénétrable /penetʀabl/ ADJ *[endroit]* penetrable ◆ **difficilement ~** barely *ou* scarcely penetrable

pénétrant, e /penetʀɑ̃, ɑ̃t/ ADJ 1 *[pluie]* drenching; *[froid]* biting, bitter; *[odeur]* penetrating, pervasive; *[crème]* penetrating; *(Phys Nucl) [radiations, rayons]* penetrating 2 *[regard]* penetrating, searching, piercing; *[esprit]* penetrating, keen, shrewd; *[analyse, remarque]* penetrating, shrewd; *[charme]* irresistible NF **pénétrante** urban motorway *(Brit) ou* freeway *(US) (linking centre of town to inter-city routes)*

pénétration /penetʀasjɔ̃/ NF penetration ◆ **force de ~** *(Mil)* force of penetration ◆ **la ~ des idées nouvelles** the establishment *ou* penetration of new ideas ◆ **taux de ~** *[d'un marché]* penetration rate

pénétré, e /penetʀe/ (ptp de **pénétrer**) ADJ ◆ **être ~ de son importance** *ou* **de soi-même** to be full of self-importance, to be imbued *(frm)* with a sense of one's own importance ◆ ~ **de l'importance de son rôle** imbued *(frm)* with a sense of the importance of his role ◆ **orateur ~ de son sujet** speaker totally enthused by his subject ◆ **il est ~ de l'idée que ...** he is deeply convinced that ... ◆ ~ **de reconnaissance** full of gratitude ◆ **écouter qch d'un air ~** to listen to sth with solemn intensity

pénétrer /penetʀe/ ► conjug 6 ◄ VI 1 *[personne, véhicule]* ~ **dans** *[+ lieu]* to enter; *[+ groupe, milieu]* to get into ◆ **personne ne doit ~ ici** nobody must be allowed to enter ◆ ~ **chez qn par la force** to force an entry *ou* one's way into sb's home ◆ **les envahisseurs/les troupes ont pénétré dans le pays** the invaders/the troops have entered the country ◆ **il est difficile de ~ dans les milieux de la finance** it is hard to get into financial circles ◆ **faire ~ qn dans une pièce** to show sb into a room ◆ **des voleurs ont pénétré dans la maison en son absence** thieves broke into his house while he was away ◆ **l'habitude n'a pas encore pénétré dans les mœurs** the habit hasn't established itself yet ◆ **faire ~ une idée dans la tête de qn** to instil an idea in sb, to get an idea into sb's head

2 *[soleil]* to shine *ou* come in; *[vent]* to blow *ou* come in; *[air, liquide, insecte]* to come *ou* get in ◆ ~ **dans** to shine *ou* come *ou* blow into, to get into ◆ **la lumière pénétrait dans la cellule (par une lucarne)** light came into *ou* entered the cell (through a skylight) ◆ **le liquide pénètre à travers une membrane** the liquid comes *ou* penetrates through a membrane ◆ **la fumée/l'odeur pénètre par tous les interstices** the smoke/the smell comes *ou* gets in through all the gaps ◆ **faire ~ de l'air (dans)** to let fresh air in(to)

3 *(en s'enfonçant)* ~ **dans** *[crème, balle, verre]* to penetrate; *[aiguille]* to go in, to penetrate; *[habitude]* to make its way into; *[huile, encre]* to soak into ◆ **ce vernis pénètre dans le bois** this varnish soaks into the wood ◆ **faire ~ une crème (dans la peau)** to rub a cream in(to the skin)

VT 1 (= *percer) [froid, air]* to penetrate; *[odeur]* to spread through, to fill; *[liquide]* to penetrate, to soak through; *[regard]* to penetrate, to go through ◆ **le froid les pénétrait jusqu'aux os** the cold cut *ou* went right through them

2 (= *découvrir) [+ mystère, secret]* to fathom; *[+ intentions, idées, plans]* to fathom, to understand ◆ **il est difficile à ~** it is difficult to fathom him

3 (= *remplir)* **son sang-froid me pénètre d'admiration** his composure fills me with admiration ◆ **le remords pénétra sa conscience** he was filled with remorse, he was conscience-stricken ◆ **il se sentait pénétré de pitié/d'effroi** he was filled with pity/with fright

4 *[+ marché]* to penetrate, to break into

5 *(sexuellement)* to penetrate

VPR **se pénétrer** 1 ◆ **se ~ d'une idée** to get an idea firmly fixed *ou* set in one's mind ◆ **s'étant pénétré de l'importance de sa mission** firmly convinced of the importance of his mission ◆ **il faut bien vous ~ du fait que ...** you must be absolutely clear in your mind that *ou* have it firmly in your mind that ... ◆ **j'ai du mal à me ~ de l'utilité de tout cela** I find it difficult to convince myself of the usefulness of all this

2 (= *s'imbiber)* **se ~ d'eau/de gaz** to become permeated with water/with gas

> ⚠ Attention à ne pas traduire automatiquement **pénétrer** par **to penetrate** ; l'anglais préfère employer un verbe à particule.

pénibilité /penibilite/ NF difficulty

pénible /penibl/ ADJ 1 (= *fatigant, difficile) [travail, voyage, ascension]* hard; *[personne]* tiresome ◆ ~ **à lire** hard *ou* difficult to read ◆ **les derniers kilomètres ont été ~s (à parcourir)** the last few kilometres were heavy going *ou* hard going ◆ **l'hiver a été** ~ it's been a hard winter, the winter has been unpleasant ◆ **tout effort lui est ~** any effort is difficult for him, he finds it hard to make the slightest effort ◆ **il est vraiment ~** *[enfant]* he's a real nuisance; *[adulte]* he's a real pain in the neck * ◆ **sa façon de parler est vraiment ~ !** he's got a really irritating way of speaking!

2 (= *douloureux) [sujet, séparation, moment, maladie]* painful (*à* to); *[nouvelle, spectacle]* sad, painful; *[respiration]* laboured *(Brit)*, labored *(US)* ◆ **la lumière violente lui est ~** bright light hurts his eyes ◆ **ce bruit est ~ à supporter**

this noise is unpleasant *ou* painful to listen to ◆ **il m'est ~ de constater/d'avoir à vous dire que ...** I'm sorry to find/to have to tell you that ...

péniblement /penibləmɑ̃/ ADV (= *difficilement*) with difficulty; (= *tristement*) painfully; (= *tout juste*) only just ◆ **il a réussi ~ son examen** he scraped through the exam ◆ **leurs salaires atteignent ~ 500 euros par mois** they barely earn 500 euros a month

péniche /peniʃ/ NF (= *bateau*) barge ◆ **~ de débarquement** (*Mil*) landing craft ◆ **il a une vraie ~** * (= *grosse voiture*) he's got a great tank of a car ◆ **tu as vu ses ~s !** * (= *grands pieds*) did you see the size of his feet!

pénicilline /penisilin/ NF penicillin

pénil /penil/ NM mons veneris

péninsulaire /penɛ̃sylɛʀ/ ADJ peninsular

péninsule /penɛ̃syl/ NF peninsula ◆ **la ~ ibérique/italienne/coréenne** the Iberian/Italian/Korean peninsula ◆ **la ~ balkanique** the Balkan peninsula

pénis /penis/ NM penis

pénitence /penitɑ̃s/ NF [1] (*Rel*) (= *repentir*) penitence; (= *peine, sacrement*) penance ◆ **faire ~** to repent (*de* of); ◆ **pour votre ~** as a penance [2] (*gén, Scol* = *châtiment*) punishment ◆ **infliger une ~ à qn** to punish sb ◆ **mettre un enfant en ~** to make a child stand in the corner ◆ **pour ta ~** as a punishment (to you) [3] [*de jeux*] forfeit

pénitencier /penitɑ̃sje/ NM [1] (= *prison*) prison, penitentiary (*US*) [2] (*Rel*) penitentiary

pénitent, e /penitɑ̃, ɑ̃t/ ADJ, NM,F penitent

pénitentiaire /penitɑ̃sjɛʀ/ ADJ penitentiary, prison (*épith*) ◆ **établissement ~** penal establishment, prison; → **colonie**

penne /pɛn/ NF (= *plume*) large feather, penna (*SPÉC*); [*de flèche*] flight

Pennine /penin/ ADJ F ◆ **la chaîne ~** the Pennine Chain *ou* Range NFPL **Pennines** ◆ **les ~s** the Pennines

Pennsylvanie /pɛnsilvani/ NF Pennsylvania

penny (pl **pennies**) /peni/ NM penny

pénombre /penɔ̃bʀ/ NF (= *faible clarté*) half-light, shadowy light; (= *obscurité*) darkness; (*Astron*) penumbra ◆ **ses yeux s'étaient habitués à la ~** his eyes had got accustomed to the dark ◆ **demeurer dans la ~** (*fig*) to stay in the background

pensable /pɑ̃sabl/ ADJ thinkable ◆ **ce n'est pas ~** it's unthinkable

pensant, e /pɑ̃sɑ̃, ɑ̃t/ ADJ thinking

pense-bête (pl **pense-bêtes**) /pɑ̃sbɛt/ NM (*gén*) reminder; (= *objet*) note *ou* memo board

pensée[1] /pɑ̃se/ NF [1] (= *ce que l'on pense*) thought ◆ **sans déguiser sa ~** without hiding one's thoughts *ou* feelings ◆ **je l'ai fait dans la seule ~ de vous être utile** I only did it thinking it would help you, my only thought in doing it was to help you ◆ **recevez mes plus affectueuses ~s** with fondest love ◆ **saisir/deviner les ~s de qn** to grasp/guess sb's thoughts *ou* what sb is thinking (about) ◆ **plongé dans ses ~s** deep in thought ◆ **avoir une ~ pour qn** to think of sb ◆ **j'ai eu une ~ émue pour toi** (*hum*) I spared a thought for you (*hum*) ◆ **si vous voulez connaître le fond de ma ~** if you want to know what I really think (about it) *ou* how I really feel about it ◆ **aller jusqu'au bout de sa ~** (= *raisonner*) to carry one's line of thought through to its conclusion; (= *dire ce qu'on pense*) to say what's on one's mind ◆ **à la ~ de faire qch** at the thought of doing sth ◆ **à la ~ que ...** to think that ..., when one thinks that ...

[2] (= *faculté, fait de penser*) thought ◆ **la dignité de l'homme est dans la ~** human dignity lies in man's capacity for thought ◆ **arrêter sa ~ sur qch** (*littér*) to pause to think about sth

[3] (= *manière de penser*) thinking ◆ **~ claire/obscure** clear/muddled thinking

[4] (= *esprit*) thought, mind ◆ **venir à la ~ de qn** to occur to sb ◆ **se représenter qch par la ~** *ou* **en ~** to imagine sth in one's mind, to conjure up a mental picture of sth ◆ **transportons-nous par la ~ au XVIe siècle** let's imagine ourselves back in the 16th century ◆ **j'ai essayé de chasser ce souvenir de ma ~** I tried to banish this memory from my mind

[5] (= *doctrine*) thought, thinking ◆ **la ~ unique** (*péj gén*) doctrinaire approach; (*Pol*) *doctrinaire approach to government exclusively based on market forces and liberalism* ◆ **la ~ marxiste** Marxist thinking *ou* thought ◆ **la ~ de cet auteur est difficile à comprendre** it is difficult to understand what this author is trying to say

[6] (= *maxime*) thought ◆ **les ~s de Pascal** the thoughts of Pascal

pensée[2] /pɑ̃se/ NF (= *plante*) pansy ◆ **~ sauvage** wild pansy

penser /pɑ̃se/ GRAMMAIRE ACTIVE 28.1, 33.1, 35.1, 35.2, 53.2 ▸ conjug 1 ◂

VI [1] (= *réfléchir*) to think ◆ **façon de ~** way of thinking ◆ **une nouvelle qui donne** *ou* **laisse à ~** a piece of news which makes you (stop and) think *ou* which gives (you) food for thought ◆ **~ tout haut** to think aloud *ou* out loud

[2] ◆ **~ à** [+ *ami*] to think of *ou* about; [+ *problème, offre*] to think about *ou* over, to turn over in one's mind ◆ **pensez donc à ce que vous dites** just think about what you're saying ◆ **~ aux autres/aux malheureux** to think of others/of those who are unhappy ◆ **vous pensez à quelqu'un de précis pour ce travail ?** do you have anyone in particular in mind for this job? ◆ **tu vois à qui/à quoi je pense ?** you see who/what I'm thinking of? ◆ **faire ~ à** to make one think of, to remind one of ◆ **cette mélodie fait ~ à Debussy** this tune reminds you of Debussy *ou* is reminiscent of Debussy ◆ **il ne pense qu'à jouer** playing is all he ever thinks about ◆ **pensez-y avant d'accepter** think it over *ou* give it some thought before you accept ◆ **j'ai bien autre chose à ~** * I've got other things on my mind ◆ **il ne pense qu'à ça** * (*hum*) he's got a one-track mind * ◆ **il lui a donné un coup de pied où je pense** * he kicked him you know where * ◆ **faire/dire qch sans y ~** to do/say sth without thinking (about it) ◆ **n'y pensons plus !** let's forget it! ◆ **c'est simple mais il fallait y ~** it's simple when you know how ◆ **mais j'y pense, c'est aujourd'hui, l'anniversaire de Lisa !** I've just remembered, it's Lisa's birthday today! ◆ **ça me fait ~ qu'il ne m'a toujours pas répondu** that reminds me that he still hasn't replied

[3] ◆ **~ à** (= *prévoir*) to think of; (= *se souvenir de*) to remember ◆ **il pense à tout** he thinks of everything ◆ **~ à l'avenir/aux conséquences** to think of the future/of the consequences ◆ **a-t-il pensé à rapporter du pain ?** did he think of bringing *ou* did he remember to bring some bread? ◆ **pense à l'anniversaire de ta mère** remember *ou* don't forget your mother's birthday ◆ **fais m'y ~** remind me (about that), don't let me forget ◆ **il suffisait d'y ~** it was just a matter of thinking of it ◆ **voyons, pense un peu au danger !** just think of *ou* consider the danger!

[4] (*locutions excl*) **il vient ? – penses-tu ! ou pensez-vous !** is he coming? – is he heck! (*Brit*) * *ou* you must be joking! * ◆ **tu penses !** *ou* **vous pensez ! je le connais trop bien pour le croire** not likely! * I know him too well to believe him ◆ **il va accepter ? – je pense bien !** will he accept? – of course he will! *ou* I should think so! *ou* I should think he will! ◆ **mais vous n'y pensez pas, c'est bien trop dangereux !** don't even think about it, it's much too dangerous! ◆ **tu penses que je vais lui dire !** * you bet I'll tell him! *

VT [1] (= *avoir une opinion*) to think (*de* of, about); ◆ **~ du bien/du mal de qch/qn** to have a high/poor opinion of sth/sb ◆ **que pense-t-il du film ?** what does he think of the film? ◆ **que pensez-vous de ce projet ?** what do you think *ou* how do you feel about this plan? ◆ **il est difficile de savoir ce qu'il pense** it's difficult to know what he's thinking ◆ **je pense comme toi** I agree with you ◆ **je ne dis rien mais je n'en pense pas moins** I am not saying anything but that doesn't mean that I don't have an opinion ◆ **que penseriez-vous d'un voyage à Rome ?** what would you say to *ou* how would you fancy *ou* how about a trip to Rome?

[2] (= *supposer*) to think, to suppose, to believe; (= *imaginer*) to think, to expect, to imagine ◆ **il n'aurait jamais pensé qu'elle ferait cela** he would never have thought *ou* imagined *ou* dreamt she would do that, he would never have expected her to do that ◆ **quand on lui dit musique, il pense ennui** when you mention the word music to him, his only thought is that it's boring ◆ **je pense que non** I don't think so, I think not (*frm*) ◆ **je pense que oui** I think so ◆ **ce n'est pas si bête qu'on le pense** it's not such a silly idea as you might think *ou* suppose ◆ **pensez-vous qu'il vienne ?** *ou* **viendra ?** do you think he'll come?, are you expecting him to come? ◆ **je vous laisse à ~ s'il était content** you can imagine how pleased he was ◆ **pensez (qu')il est encore si jeune !** to think that he's still so young! ◆ **ils pensent avoir trouvé une maison** they think they've found a house ◆ **c'est bien ce que je pensais !** I thought as much!, just as *ou* what I thought! ◆ **vous pensez bien qu'elle a refusé** you can well imagine (that) she refused, as you may well expect, she refused ◆ **j'ai pensé mourir/m'évanouir** I thought I was going to die/faint ◆ **tout laisse à ~ qu'elle l'a quitté** there is every indication that she has left him

[3] ◆ **~ faire** (= *avoir l'intention de*) to be thinking of doing, to consider doing; (= *espérer*) to hope to do ◆ **il pense partir jeudi** he's thinking of going on Thursday ◆ **elle pense arriver demain** she's hoping *ou* expecting to arrive tomorrow

[4] (= *concevoir*) [+ *problème, projet, machine*] to think out ◆ **c'est bien/fortement pensé** it's well/very well thought out

NM (*littér*) thought

penseur /pɑ̃sœʀ/ NM thinker; → **libre** ADJ M † thoughtful

pensif, -ive /pɑ̃sif, iv/ ADJ thoughtful, pensive ◆ **il était tout ~** he was lost in thought ◆ **d'un air ~** pensively, thoughtfully

pension /pɑ̃sjɔ̃/ NF [1] (= *allocation*) pension ◆ **~ de guerre** war pension ◆ **~ d'invalidité** disablement pension ◆ **~ de retraite** old age pension, retirement pension ◆ **~ réversible** *ou* **de réversion** survivor's *ou* reversion pension, reversionary annuity ◆ **toucher sa ~** to draw one's pension

[2] (= *hôtel*) boarding house; [*de chats*] cattery; [*de chiens*] (boarding) kennels; [*de chevaux*] livery (stables) ◆ **mettre en ~** [+ *chien*] to put in kennels; [+ *cheval*] to put in livery (stables) ◆ **son poney est en ~** her pony's at livery

[3] (*Scol*) (boarding) school ◆ **mettre qn/être en ~** to send sb to/be at boarding school

[4] (= *hébergement*) [*de personne*] board and lodging, bed and board ◆ **la ~ coûte 60 € par jour** board and lodging is €60 a day ◆ **être en ~ chez qn** to board with sb *ou* at sb's ◆ **prendre ~ chez qn** (*lit*) to take board and lodging at sb's; (*hum*) to take up residence at sb's ◆ **prendre qn en ~** to take sb (in) as a lodger, to board sb ◆ **cham-**

bre sans ~ room *(with no meals provided)* ◆ **chambre avec** ~ **complète** full board ◆ **avoir en** ~ *(hum)* *[+ chat, chien]* to look after

5 *(Fin)* **taux de prise en** ~ repurchase rate

COMP **pension alimentaire** *[d'étudiant]* living allowance; *[de divorcée]* alimony, maintenance allowance

pension de famille ≃ boarding house

pensionnaire /pɑ̃sjɔnɛʀ/ NMF *(Scol)* boarder; *[de famille]* lodger; *[d'hôtel]* resident; *[de sanatorium]* patient; *[de Comédie-Française] salaried actor having no share in the profits*

pensionnat /pɑ̃sjɔna/ NM (boarding) school

pensionné, e /pɑ̃sjɔne/ (ptp de **pensionner**) ADJ who gets *ou* draws a pension NM,F pensioner

pensionner /pɑ̃sjɔne/ ▸ conjug 1 ◂ VT to give a pension to

pensivement /pɑ̃sivmɑ̃/ ADV pensively, thoughtfully

pensum † /pɛ̃sɔm/ NM *(Scol)* punishment, lines *(Brit)*; *(fig)* chore

pentaèdre /pɛ̃taɛdʀ/ ADJ pentahedral NM pentahedron

pentagonal, e (mpl **-aux**) /pɛ̃tagɔnal, o/ ADJ pentagonal

pentagone /pɛ̃tagɔn/ NM pentagon ◆ **le Pentagone** *(Mil)* the Pentagon

pentamètre /pɛ̃tamɛtʀ/ ADJ, NM pentameter

Pentateuque /pɛ̃tatøk/ NM Pentateuch

pentathlon /pɛ̃tatlɔ̃/ NM pentathlon

pentatonique /pɛ̃tatɔnik/ ADJ pentatonic

pente /pɑ̃t/ NF 1 *(gén)* slope ◆ **la** ~ **d'un toit** the pitch *ou* slope of a roof ◆ ~ **à 4%** *[de route]* gradient of 1 in 25, 4% gradient *ou* incline *(US)*

◆ **en pente** *[toit]* sloping; *[allée, pelouse]* on a slope *(attrib)* ◆ **de petites rues en** ~ **raide** steep little streets ◆ **garé dans une rue en** ~ parked on a slope ◆ **être en** ~ **douce/raide** to slope (down) gently/steeply

2 *(locutions)* **être sur une** *ou* **la mauvaise** ~ to be going downhill, to be on a downward path ◆ **remonter la** ~ *(fig)* to get back on one's feet again, to fight one's way back again ◆ **être sur une** ~ **glissante** *ou* **dangereuse** *ou* **savonneuse** *(fig)* to be on a slippery slope *(fig)* ◆ **suivre sa** ~ **naturelle** to follow one's natural bent *ou* inclination; → **dalle, rupture**

Pentecôte /pɑ̃tkot/ NF 1 *(Rel = dimanche)* Whit Sunday, Pentecost, Whitsun; *(= période)* Whit(suntide) ◆ **lundi de** ~ Whit Monday ◆ **de la** ~ Pentecostal, Whit *(épith)* 2 *(= fête juive)* Pentecost

pentecôtiste /pɑ̃tkotist/ ADJ *[personne]* Pentecostalist; *[église]* Pentecostal NMF Pentecostalist

penthotal ® /pɛ̃tɔtal/ NM Pentothal ®

pentu, e /pɑ̃ty/ ADJ sloping

penture /pɑ̃tyʀ/ NF *[de volet, porte]* strap hinge

pénultième /penyltjɛm/ ADJ penultimate NF penultimate (syllable)

pénurie /penyʀi/ NF shortage ◆ ~ **de** shortage *ou* lack of ◆ ~ **de main-d'œuvre/sucre** labour/sugar shortage ◆ **on ne peut guère qu'organiser la** ~ we must just make the best of a bad job* *ou* the best of what we've got

people /pipɔl/ ADJ INV ◆ **magazine/photo** ~ celebrity magazine/photo ◆ **émission** ~ programme with celebrity guests ◆ **rubrique** ~ gossip column

PEP /pɛp/ NM (abrév de **plan d'épargne populaire**) → **plan¹**

pep * /pɛp/ NM *(= dynamisme)* pep*, liveliness ◆ **elle a du** ~ she's full of pep* *ou* beans* *(Brit)* ◆ **ça m'a donné un coup de** ~ ! that pepped* me up! *ou* gave me a boost!

pépé * /pepe/ NM grandad*, grandpa*

pépée ‡ /pepe/ NF *(= fille)* girl, chick‡ *(US)*

pépère * /pepɛʀ/ NM 1 *(= pépé)* grandad*, grandpa* ◆ **un petit** ~ a little old man 2 ◆ **un gros** ~ *(enfant)* a bonny *(Brit)* *ou* cute *(US)* child; *(homme)* an old fatty* ADJ *[vie]* quiet, uneventful; *[travail]* cushy*, easy ◆ **un petit coin** ~ a nice quiet spot ◆ **avoir une conduite** ~ *(en voiture)* to potter *(Brit)* *ou* putter *(US)* along ◆ **c'est quelqu'un d'assez** ~ he's the stay-at-home type

pépettes, pépètes †* /pepɛt/ NFPL dough‡, lolly‡ *(Brit)* ◆ **avoir les** ~ *(= avoir peur)* to have the heebie-jeebies*

pépie /pepi/ NF *(= maladie aviaire)* pip ◆ **avoir la** ~ † to have a terrible thirst, to be parched*

pépiement /pepimɑ̃/ NM chirping *(NonC)*, chirruping *(NonC)*

pépier /pepje/ ▸ conjug 7 ◂ VI to chirp, to chirrup

Pépin /pepɛ̃/ NM ◆ ~ **le Bref** Pepin the Short

pépin /pepɛ̃/ NM 1 *(= graine)* pip ◆ **sans ~s** seedless 2 *(* = ennui)* snag, hitch ◆ **avoir un** ~ to hit a snag*, to have a spot of bother *(Brit)* ◆ **j'ai eu un** ~ **avec ma voiture** I had a problem with my car ◆ **gros/petit** ~ **de santé** major/slight health problem ◆ **c'est un gros** ~ **pour l'entreprise** it's a major setback for the company 3 *(* = parapluie)* umbrella, brolly* *(Brit)*

pépinière /pepinjɛʀ/ NF *(lit)* tree nursery; *(fig)* breeding-ground, nursery *(de* for); *(de formation en entreprise)* graduate training scheme ◆ ~ **d'entreprises** *(= parc)* enterprise zone

pépiniériste /pepinjeʀist/ NM nurseryman NF nurserywoman

pépite /pepit/ NF *[d'or]* nugget ◆ **~s de chocolat** chocolate chips

péplum /peplɔm/ NM *(Antiq)* peplos, peplum; *(= film)* epic *(set in antiquity)*

peps * /pɛps/ NM ⇒ **pep**

pepsine /pɛpsin/ NF pepsin

peptide /pɛptid/ NM peptide

peptique /pɛptik/ ADJ peptic

péquenaud, e ‡ /pekno, od/ ADJ peasant *(épith)* NM,F country bumpkin

péquenot /pekno/ ADJ, NM ⇒ **péquenaud**

péquin /pekɛ̃/ NM *(arg Mil)* ⇒ **pékin**

péquiste /pekist/ ADJ of the Parti québécois NMF member of the Parti québécois

PER /peəɛʀ/ NM (abrév de **plan d'épargne retraite**) → **plan¹**

perborate /pɛʀbɔʀat/ NM perborate

perçage /pɛʀsaʒ/ NM *[de trou]* boring, drilling; *[de matériau]* boring through

percale /pɛʀkal/ NF percale

percaline /pɛʀkalin/ NF percaline

perçant, e /pɛʀsɑ̃, ɑ̃t/ ADJ *[cri, voix]* piercing, shrill; *[froid]* biting, bitter; *[vue]* sharp, keen; *[regard]* piercing; *[esprit]* penetrating

per capita /pɛʀkapita/ LOC ADV per capita

perce /pɛʀs/ NF ◆ **mettre en** ~ *[+ tonneau]* to broach, to tap

percée /pɛʀse/ NF *(dans une forêt)* opening, clearing; *(dans un mur)* breach, gap; *(Mil, Sci, Écon)* breakthrough; *(Rugby)* break ◆ ~ **technologique** technological breakthrough ◆ **faire** *ou* **réaliser une** ~ **sur un marché/dans une élection** to achieve a breakthrough in a market/in an election

percement /pɛʀsəmɑ̃/ NM *[de trou]* piercing; *(avec perceuse)* drilling, boring; *[de rue]* building; *[de tunnel]* cutting, driving, boring; *[de fenêtre]* making

perce-neige (pl **perce-neige(s)**) /pɛʀsənɛʒ/ NM *ou* NF snowdrop

perce-oreille (pl **perce-oreilles**) /pɛʀsɔʀɛj/ NM earwig

percepteur, -trice /pɛʀsɛptœʀ, tʀis/ ADJ perceptive, of perception NM tax collector, tax man*

perceptibilité /pɛʀsɛptibilite/ NF perceptibility

perceptible /pɛʀsɛptibl/ ADJ 1 *[son, ironie]* perceptible *(à* to); ◆ **elle fit un mouvement à peine** ~ she moved almost imperceptibly ◆ **sa voix était à peine** ~ his voice was barely audible ◆ **une amélioration nettement** ~ a marked improvement 2 *[impôt]* collectable, payable

perceptif, -ive /pɛʀsɛptif, iv/ ADJ perceptive

perception /pɛʀsɛpsjɔ̃/ NF 1 *[d'objet, douleur, son]* perception ◆ ~ **visuelle** visual perception ◆ ~ **extra-sensorielle** extrasensory perception 2 *(= compréhension, appréhension)* perception ◆ **nous n'avons pas la même** ~ **de la situation** we don't perceive the situation in quite the same way ◆ **la** ~ **que nous avons de l'artiste/de la vie** our view of *ou* the way we perceive the artist/life 3 *[d'impôt, amende, péage]* collection; *[d'avantages financiers, allocation]* receipt; *(= bureau)* tax (collector's) office

percer /pɛʀse/ ▸ conjug 3 ◂ VT 1 *(gén = perforer)* to pierce, to make a hole in; *(avec perceuse)* to drill *ou* bore through, to drill *ou* bore a hole in; *[+ lobe d'oreille]* to pierce; *[+ chaussette, chaussure]* to wear a hole in; *[+ coffre-fort]* to break open, to crack*; *[+ tonneau]* to broach, to tap; *(Méd)* *[+ abcès]* to lance; *[+ tympan]* to burst ◆ **avoir une poche/une chaussure percée** to have a hole in one's pocket/shoe ◆ **percé de trous** full of holes, riddled with holes ◆ **la rouille avait percé le métal** rust had eaten into the metal ◆ **on a retrouvé son corps percé de coups de couteau** his body was found full of stab wounds ◆ **se faire** ~ **les oreilles** to have one's ears pierced; → **chaise, panier**

2 *[+ fenêtre, ouverture]* to pierce, to make; *[+ canal]* to build; *[+ tunnel]* to cut, to drive, to bore *(dans* through); ◆ ~ **un trou dans** to pierce *ou* make a hole in; *(avec perceuse)* to drill *ou* bore a hole through *ou* in ◆ **ils ont percé une nouvelle route à travers la forêt** they have built a new road through the forest ◆ ~ **une porte dans un mur** to make *ou* open a doorway in a wall ◆ **mur percé de petites fenêtres** wall with small windows set in it

3 *(= traverser)* ~ **l'air/le silence** to pierce the air/the silence ◆ ~ **les nuages/le front ennemi** to pierce *ou* break through the clouds/the enemy lines ◆ ~ **la foule** to force *ou* elbow one's way through the crowd ◆ **bruit qui perce les oreilles** ear-splitting noise ◆ ~ **qn du regard** to give sb a piercing look ◆ **ses yeux essayaient de** ~ **l'obscurité** he tried to peer through the darkness ◆ **cela m'a percé le cœur** † it cut me to the heart

4 *(= découvrir)* *[+ mystère]* to penetrate; *[+ complot]* to uncover ◆ ~ **qch à jour** to see (right) through sth

5 *[bébé]* ~ **des** *ou* **ses dents** to be teething, to cut one's teeth ◆ **il a percé deux dents** he has cut two teeth

VI 1 *[abcès]* to burst; *[plante]* to come up; *[soleil]* to come out, to break through; *(Mil)* to break through; *(Sport)* to make a break ◆ **il a une dent qui perce** he's cutting a tooth ◆ ~ **sur un nouveau marché** to break into a new market

2 *[sentiment, émotion]* to show; *[nouvelle]* to filter through *ou* out ◆ **rien n'a percé des négociations** no news of the negotiations has filtered through ◆ **il ne laisse jamais** ~ **ses sentiments** he never lets his feelings show ◆ **un ton où perçait l'ironie** a tone tinged with irony

3 *(= réussir, acquérir la notoriété)* to make a name for o.s.

perceur /pɛʀsœʀ/ **NM** 1 *(pour piercing)* (body) piercer 2 ~ **de coffre-fort*** safe-breaker, safe-cracker

perceuse /pɛʀsøz/ **NF** drill ◆ ~ **à percussion** hammer drill

percevable /pɛʀsəvabl/ **ADJ** *[impôt]* collectable, payable

percevoir /pɛʀsəvwaʀ/ GRAMMAIRE ACTIVE 33.1 ▸ conjug 28 ◂ **VT** 1 *(= ressentir) [+ objet, son, couleur]* to perceive; *[+ odeur, nuance, changement]* to detect; *[+ douleur, émotion]* to feel ◆ **j'ai cru ~ une légère hésitation dans sa voix** I thought I detected a slight note of hesitation in his voice 2 *(= comprendre) [+ situation]* to perceive ◆ **son action a été bien/mal perçue** what he did was well/badly received *ou* was perceived as something positive/negative ◆ **je le perçois comme quelqu'un de sensible** I see him as a sensitive person ◆ **il perçoit mal les problèmes** he hasn't got a clear grasp of the problems ◆ **c'est quelqu'un que je perçois mal** I can't make him out, I find it hard to get a sense of him ◆ **il perçoit bien les enfants** he understands children 3 *(= faire payer) [+ taxe, loyer]* to collect; *(= recevoir) [+ indemnité, revenu]* to receive, to be paid

perche[1] /pɛʀʃ/ **NF** *(= poisson)* perch ◆ ~ **de mer** sea perch

perche[2] /pɛʀʃ/ **NF** 1 *(gén)* pole; *[de tuteur]* stick; *[de téléski]* ski tow; *(Ciné, Radio, TV)* boom; → **saut, tendre[1]** 2 *(* = personne)* **(grande)** ~ beanpole* *(Brit)*, stringbean* *(US)*

perché, e /pɛʀʃe/ (ptp de **percher**) **ADJ** ◆ **voix haut ~e** high-pitched voice ◆ **~e sur des talons aiguille** perched on stilettos ◆ **village ~ sur la montagne** village set high up *ou* perched in the mountains

percher /pɛʀʃe/ ▸ conjug 1 ◂ **VI** *[oiseau]* to perch; *[volailles]* to roost; *[personne]* to live, to hang out*; *(pour la nuit)* to stay, to crash*; → **chat VT** to stick ◆ ~ **qch sur une armoire** to stick sth up on top of a cupboard ◆ **la valise est perchée sur l'armoire** the case is perched up on top of the wardrobe **VPR se percher** *[oiseau]* to perch; *(* = se jucher)* to perch

percheron, -onne /pɛʀʃəʀɔ̃, ɔn/ **ADJ** of *ou* from the Perche **NM,F Percheron(ne)** inhabitant *ou* native of the Perche **NM** *(= cheval)* Percheron

percheur, -euse /pɛʀʃœʀ, øz/ **ADJ** ◆ **oiseau ~** perching bird

perchiste /pɛʀʃist/ **NMF** *(Sport)* pole vaulter; *(Ciné, Radio, TV)* boom operator; *[de téléski]* ski lift *ou* ski tow attendant

perchoir /pɛʀʃwaʀ/ **NM** *(lit, fig)* perch; *[de volailles]* roost; *(Pol) seat of the president of the French National Assembly*

perclus, e /pɛʀkly, yz/ **ADJ** *(= paralysé)* crippled, paralyzed *(de* with); *(= ankylosé)* stiff; *(fig)* paralyzed

percolateur /pɛʀkɔlatœʀ/ **NM** coffee machine *(for making expresso, cappuccino etc)*

percussion /pɛʀkysjɔ̃/ **NF** *(Méd, Mus, Phys)* percussion ◆ **instrument à** *ou* **de ~** percussion instrument ◆ **les ~s** *[d'orchestre]* the percussion (section)

percussionniste /pɛʀkysjɔnist/ **NMF** percussionist

percutané, e /pɛʀkytane/ **ADJ** percutaneous

percutant, e /pɛʀkytɑ̃, ɑ̃t/ **ADJ** 1 *(Mil)* percussion *(épith)*; *(Phys)* percussive 2 *[slogan, titre]* snappy, punchy; *[réponse]* trenchant; *[analyse]* incisive; *[argument, discours, pensée]* forceful, powerful; *[images]* powerful ◆ **il n'a pas été très ~ pendant le débat** he didn't express himself very forcefully in the debate

percuter /pɛʀkyte/ ▸ conjug 1 ◂ **VT** *(Mil, Phys)* to strike; *(Méd)* to percuss; *[conducteur, véhicule]* to smash into *ou* crash into **VI** 1 ◆ ~ **contre** *[conducteur, véhicule]* to smash *ou* crash into; *[obus]* to strike 2 *(* = comprendre)* **il percute vite** he catches on* quickly, he's quick on the uptake ◆ **je n'ai pas percuté** I didn't twig* *ou* catch on*

percuteur /pɛʀkytœʀ/ **NM** firing pin, striker

perdant, e /pɛʀdɑ̃, ɑ̃t/ **ADJ** *[numéro, cheval]* losing *(épith)* ◆ **je suis ~** *(gén)* I lose out*; *(financièrement)* I'm out of pocket, I've lost out ◆ **tu es loin d'être ~** *(gén)* you're certainly not losing out; *(financièrement)* you're certainly not out of pocket *ou* not losing out **NM,F** loser ◆ **partir ~** to have lost before one starts ◆ **être bon/mauvais ~** to be a good/a bad loser

perdition /pɛʀdisjɔ̃/ **NF** *(Rel)* perdition ◆ **lieu de ~** den of iniquity ◆ **en ~** *[bateau]* in distress; *[jeunesse]* on the wrong path; *[entreprise]* on the road to ruin

perdre /pɛʀdʀ(ə)/ ▸ conjug 41 ◂ **VT** 1 *[+ match, guerre, procès, travail, avantage]* to lose; *[+ habitude]* to lose, to get out of; *(volontairement)* to break, to get out of ◆ **il a perdu son père à la guerre** he lost his father in the war ◆ **ce quartier est en train de ~ son cachet** this district is losing its distinctive charm ◆ **j'ai perdu le goût de manger** I've lost all interest in food ◆ **j'ai perdu le goût de rire** I don't feel like laughing any more ◆ **n'avoir rien à ~** *(fig)* to have nothing to lose ◆ ~ **un set/son service** *(Tennis)* to lose *ou* drop a set/one's serve ◆ **le Président perd 3 points dans le dernier sondage** the President is down 3 points in the latest poll ◆ **l'agriculture a perdu des milliers d'emplois** thousands of jobs have been lost in farming

2 *[+ objet] (= ne plus trouver)* to lose; *(= égarer)* to mislay ◆ ~ **(le souvenir de)** *[+ nom, date]* to forget ◆ ~ **sa page** *(en lisant)* to lose one's place ◆ ~ **son chemin** to lose one's way

3 *[+ membre, cheveux, dent]* to lose ◆ ~ **du poids** to lose weight ◆ ~ **l'appétit/la mémoire/la vie** to lose one's appetite/one's memory/one's life ◆ **il perd la vue** his sight is failing ◆ **il a perdu le souffle** he's out of breath ◆ ~ **la parole** to lose the power of speech ◆ **ce tableau a perdu beaucoup de valeur** this painting has lost a lot of its value ◆ ~ **l'équilibre** to lose one's balance ◆ ~ **espoir/patience** to lose hope/(one's) patience ◆ ~ **l'esprit** *ou* **la raison** to go out of one's mind, to take leave of one's senses ◆ ~ **courage** to lose heart, to be downhearted ◆ ~ **confiance** to lose one's confidence ◆ **elle a perdu les eaux** *[femme enceinte]* her waters have broken ◆ **la voiture perd de la vitesse** the car is losing speed; → **langue**

4 *[+ feuille, pétale, pelage, corne]* to lose, to shed ◆ **il perd son pantalon** his trousers are falling *ou* coming down ◆ **tu perds ton collier !** your necklace is coming off! ◆ **ce réservoir perd beaucoup d'eau** this tank leaks badly *ou* loses a lot of water

5 *(= gaspiller) [+ temps, peine, souffle, argent]* to waste *(à qch* on sth); *(= abîmer) [+ aliments]* to spoil ◆ **tu as du temps/de l'argent à ~ !** you've got time to waste/money to burn! ◆ **il a perdu une heure à la chercher** he wasted an hour looking for her ◆ **vous n'avez pas une minute à ~** you haven't (got) a minute to lose ◆ **sans ~ une minute** without wasting a minute

6 *(= manquer) [+ occasion]* to lose, to miss ◆ **tu ne l'as jamais vu ? tu n'y perds rien !** you've never seen him? you haven't missed anything! ◆ **il n'a pas perdu un mot/une miette de la conversation** he didn't miss a single word/a single syllable of the conversation ◆ **il ne perd rien pour attendre !** he's got it coming to him!* ◆ **rien n'est perdu !** nothing is lost!

7 *(= porter préjudice à)* to ruin, to be the ruin of ◆ ~ **qn dans l'esprit de qn** to lower sb's opinion of sb, to send sb down in sb's esteem ◆ **son ambition l'a perdu** ambition was his downfall *ou* the ruin of him, ambition proved his undoing ◆ **c'est le témoignage de son cousin qui l'a perdu** it was his cousin's evidence which was his undoing ◆ **ta bonté te perdra !** *(iro)* you're too kind! *(iro)*

8 *(locutions fig)* ~ **le nord*** to lose one's way ◆ **il ne perd pas le nord*** he keeps his wits about him ◆ **tu ne perds pas le nord, toi !*** you don't miss a trick! ◆ ~ **les pédales*** *(dans une explication)* to get all mixed up; *(= s'affoler)* to lose one's head *ou* one's grip; *[vieillard]* to lose one's marbles* ◆ ~ **ses moyens** to crack up* ◆ ~ **la tête** *(= s'affoler)* to lose one's head; *(= devenir fou)* to go mad *ou* crazy*; *[vieillard]* to lose one's marbles*; → **boule, face, illusion, pied etc**

VI 1 *(gén)* to lose ◆ ~ **sur un article** *(Comm)* to lose on an article, to sell an article at a loss ◆ **vous y perdez** *(dans une transaction)* you lose by it, you lose out on it; *(= vous ratez quelque chose)* it's your loss; → **change**

2 *[citerne, réservoir]* to leak

VPR se perdre 1 *(= s'égarer)* to get lost, to lose one's way

2 *(fig)* **se ~ dans les détails/dans ses explications** to get bogged down *ou* get lost in details/in one's explanations ◆ **se ~ en conjectures** to become lost in conjecture ◆ **se ~ dans ses pensées** to be lost in thought ◆ **il y a trop de chiffres, je m'y perds** there are too many figures, I'm all confused *ou* all at sea*

3 *(= disparaître)* to disappear, to vanish; *[coutume]* to be dying out; *(Naut)* to sink, to be wrecked ◆ **c'est un métier qui se perd** it's a dying trade ◆ **se ~ dans la foule** to disappear *ou* vanish into the crowd ◆ **son cri se perdit dans le vacarme** his shout was lost in the din *ou* was drowned (out) by the din ◆ **leurs silhouettes se perdirent dans la nuit** their figures vanished into the night *ou* were swallowed up by the darkness ◆ **ce sens s'est perdu** this meaning has died out *ou* has been lost ◆ **rien ne se perd, rien ne se crée(, tout se transforme)** matter can neither be created nor destroyed(, only transformed)

4 *(= devenir inutilisable)* to be wasted, to go to waste; *[denrées]* to go bad ◆ **il y a des gifles/des coups de pied qui se perdent*** *(fig)* he (*ou* she *etc*) deserves to be slapped *ou* a good slap/deserves a kick in the pants*

perdreau (pl **perdreaux**) /pɛʀdʀo/ **NM** (young) partridge

perdrix /pɛʀdʀi/ **NF** partridge ◆ ~ **blanche** *ou* **des neiges** ptarmigan ◆ ~ **de mer** pratincole

perdu, e /pɛʀdy/ (ptp de **perdre**) **ADJ** 1 *[bataille, cause, réputation, aventurier]* lost ◆ **il est ~** *[malade]* there's no hope for him ◆ **je suis ~ !** I'm done for!, it's all up with me!* *(Brit)* ◆ **quand il se vit ~** when he saw he was lost *ou* done for* ◆ **tout est ~** all is lost ◆ **rien n'est ~** nothing's lost, there's no harm done; → **corps**

2 *(= égaré) [personne, objet]* lost; *[balle, chien]* stray ◆ **ce n'est pas ~ pour tout le monde** somebody's made good use of it ◆ **un(e) de ~(e), dix de retrouvé(e)s** there are plenty more fish in the sea; → **salle**

3 *(= gaspillé) [occasion]* lost, wasted, missed; *[temps]* wasted ◆ **c'était une soirée de ~e** it was a wasted evening *ou* a waste of an evening ◆ **c'est de l'argent ~** it's money down the drain ◆ **il y a trop de place ~e** there's too much space wasted ◆ **à ses moments ~s, à temps ~** in his spare time; → **pain, peine**

4 *(= abîmé) [aliment]* spoilt, wasted; *[récolte]* ruined

5 *(= écarté) [pays, endroit]* out-of-the-way, isolated

6 *(= non consigné) [emballage, verre]* non-returnable, no-deposit *(épith)*

7 [personne] (= embrouillé) lost, all at sea* (attrib) ◆ ~ **dans ses pensées** (= absorbé) lost in thought

NM †† madman ◆ **crier/rire comme un** ~ to shout/laugh like a madman

perdurer /pɛʀdyʀe/ ▸ conjug 1 ◂ VI (littér) [tradition] to endure

père /pɛʀ/ NM 1 (gén) father ◆ **marié et ~ de trois enfants** married with three children ou and father of three children ◆ **il est ~ depuis hier** he became a father yesterday ◆ **Martin (le) ~** Martin senior ◆ **né de ~ inconnu** of an unknown father ◆ **c'est bien la fille de son ~ !** she really takes after her father! ◆ **à ~ avare, enfant ou fils prodigue** (Prov) a miser will father a spendthrift son ◆ **le coup du ~ François*** a stab in the back ◆ **il m'a fait le coup du ~ François** he stabbed me in the back; → **tel**

◆ **de père en fils** from father to son, from one generation to the next ◆ **ils sont bouchers de ~ en fils** they've been butchers for generations

2 (pl = ancêtres) **~s** forefathers, ancestors

3 (= inventeur) father ◆ **le ~ de la bombe H** the father of the H-bomb ◆ **~ fondateur** [de parti, association, idéologie] founding father

4 (Zool) [d'animal] sire

5 (Rel) father ◆ **le Père René** Father René ◆ **mon Père** Father; → **dieu**

6 (* = monsieur) **le ~ Benoît** old (man) Benoît* ◆ **un gros ~** (= homme) a big fat guy* ◆ **dis donc, petit ~** tell me old man ou buddy*

7 (* = enfant) **un brave petit ~** a fine little fellow* ◆ **un (bon) gros ~** a chubby chap*

COMP **père abbé** (Rel) abbot

les Pères blancs the White Fathers

les Pères de l'Église (Rel) the Church Fathers

le Père éternel (Rel) our Heavenly Father

père de famille (Jur) father ◆ **tu es ~ de famille, ne prends pas de risques** you have a wife and family to think about ou you're a family man, don't take risks ◆ **en bon ~ de famille, il ...** as a good father should, he ... ◆ **maintenant, c'est le vrai ~ de famille** (hum) now he's the serious family man

le père Fouettard the Bogeyman

le père Noël Father Christmas, Santa Claus

père peinard, père tranquille genial fellow

père spirituel [de groupe] spiritual leader; [de personne] spiritual father; → **croire, placement, valeur**

pérégrination /peʀegʀinasjɔ̃/ NF (surtout pl) peregrination

péremption /peʀɑ̃psjɔ̃/ NF (Jur) limitation period ◆ **il y a ~ au bout de trois ans** there is a three-year limitation period (after which claims are time-barred); → **date**

péremptoire /peʀɑ̃ptwaʀ/ ADJ [argument, ton] peremptory

péremptoirement /peʀɑ̃ptwaʀmɑ̃/ ADV peremptorily

pérennisation /peʀenizasjɔ̃/ NF perpetuation

pérenniser /peʀenize/ ▸ conjug 1 ◂ VT to perpetuate

pérennité /peʀenite/ NF [d'institution, goûts] durability; [de tradition] continuity, perpetuity; [de lignée] continuity

péréquation /peʀekwasjɔ̃/ NF [de prix, impôts] balancing out, evening out; [de notes] coordination, adjustment; [de salaires] adjustment, realignment

perestroïka /peʀɛstʀɔika/ NF perestroika

perfectibilité /pɛʀfɛktibilite/ NF perfectibility

perfectible /pɛʀfɛktibl/ ADJ perfectible

perfectif, -ive /pɛʀfɛktif, iv/ ADJ, NM perfective

perfection /pɛʀfɛksjɔ̃/ NF perfection ◆ **la ~ n'est pas de ce monde** there's no such thing as perfection, nothing's perfect ◆ **parvenir à ou atteindre la ~** to attain perfection

◆ **à la perfection** [jouer, fonctionner] to perfection; [connaître] perfectly ◆ **cela illustre à la ~ ce que je disais** that's a perfect illustration of ou that perfectly illustrates what I was saying

perfectionné, e /pɛʀfɛksjɔne/ (ptp de **perfectionner**) ADJ [dispositif, machine] sophisticated

perfectionnement /pɛʀfɛksjɔnmɑ̃/ NM 1 (NonC) (= amélioration) improving; (pour parfaire) perfecting ◆ **les ordinateurs ont atteint un tel degré de ~ que ...** computers have become so sophisticated that ... ◆ **des cours de ~ en danse/en anglais** advanced dance classes/English course 2 (= raffinement) improvement ◆ **ce logiciel nécessite encore quelques ~s** this software still needs a few improvements ◆ **les derniers ~s techniques** the latest technical developments ou improvements

perfectionner /pɛʀfɛksjɔne/ ▸ conjug 1 ◂ VT (= améliorer) to improve; (= parfaire) to perfect VPR **se perfectionner** [technique] to improve; [personne] to improve o.s. ◆ **se ~ en anglais** to improve one's English

perfectionnisme /pɛʀfɛksjɔnism/ NM perfectionism

perfectionniste /pɛʀfɛksjɔnist/ NMF perfectionist

perfide /pɛʀfid/ ADJ (littér) [personne, manœuvre, promesse] perfidious, treacherous, deceitful, false; [chose] treacherous NMF (littér) traitor; (en amour) perfidious ou falsehearted person

perfidement /pɛʀfidmɑ̃/ ADV (littér) perfidiously, treacherously

perfidie /pɛʀfidi/ NF (= caractère) perfidy, treachery; (= acte) act of perfidy ou treachery

perforage /pɛʀfɔʀaʒ/ NM (= poinçonnage) punching; (= forage) boring, drilling

perforant, e /pɛʀfɔʀɑ̃, ɑ̃t/ ADJ [instrument] perforating; [balle, obus] armour-piercing (Brit), armor-piercing (US)

perforateur, -trice /pɛʀfɔʀatœʀ, tʀis/ ADJ perforating NM,F (= ouvrier) punch-card operator NM (Méd) perforator NF **perforatrice** (= perceuse) drilling ou boring machine; (Ordin) card punch ◆ **perforatrice à clavier** key punch ◆ **perforatrice à air comprimé** compressed-air drill

perforation /pɛʀfɔʀasjɔ̃/ NF (gén, Méd) perforation; (Ordin) (= action) punching; (= trou) punched hole

perforer /pɛʀfɔʀe/ ▸ conjug 1 ◂ VT (= percer) to pierce; (Méd) to perforate; (= poinçonner) to punch ◆ **carte perforée** (Ordin) punch card ◆ **bande/feuille perforée** punched tape/sheet

perforeuse /pɛʀfɔʀøz/ NF card punch

performance /pɛʀfɔʀmɑ̃s/ NF 1 (= résultat) result, performance (NonC); (= exploit) feat, achievement ◆ **ses ~s en anglais** his results ou performance in English ◆ **s'il y parvient, ce sera une ~ remarquable** if he succeeds, it'll be an outstanding feat ou achievement ◆ **réussir une bonne ~** to achieve a good result 2 [de voiture, machine, économie, industrie] performance (NonC) 3 (Ling) **la ~** performance

performant, e /pɛʀfɔʀmɑ̃, ɑ̃t/ ADJ [machine, voiture] high-performance (épith); [résultat] outstanding, impressive; [entreprise, économie] successful; [investissement] high-return (épith); [administrateur, procédé] effective

performatif, -ive /pɛʀfɔʀmatif, iv/ ADJ, NM performative

perfuser /pɛʀfyze/ ▸ conjug 1 ◂ VT [+ patient] to put on a drip

perfusion /pɛʀfyzjɔ̃/ NF (Méd) drip (Brit), IV (US), perfusion ◆ **mettre qn/être sous ~** to put sb/be on a drip (Brit) ou an IV (US) ◆ **alimenter qn par ~** to drip-feed sb ◆ **le pays est encore sous ~ (financière)** this country is still heavily subsidized ou still dependent on subsidies

pergola /pɛʀgɔla/ NF pergola

péri /peʀi/ ADJ M, NM ◆ **(marin) ~ en mer** sailor lost at sea ◆ **au profit des ~s en mer** in aid of those lost at sea

périanthe /peʀjɑ̃t/ NM (Bot) perianth

péricarde /peʀikaʀd/ NM pericardium

péricarpe /peʀikaʀp/ NM (Bot) pericarp

péricliter /peʀiklite/ ▸ conjug 1 ◂ VI [affaire, économie] to be in a state of collapse, to collapse

péridot /peʀido/ NM peridot

péridural, e (mpl **-aux**) /peʀidyʀal, o/ ADJ epidural NF **péridurale** epidural ◆ **faire une ~e à qn** to give sb an epidural

périf* /peʀif/ NM (abrév de **(boulevard) périphérique**) → **périphérique**

périgée /peʀiʒe/ NM perigee

périglaciaire /peʀiglasjɛʀ/ ADJ periglacial

péri-informatique /peʀiɛ̃fɔʀmatik/ ADJ peripheral NF computer peripherals

péril /peʀil/ NM (littér) peril, danger ◆ **le ~ rouge/jaune** the red/yellow peril ◆ **au ~ de sa vie** at the risk of one's life ◆ **il n'y a pas ~ en la demeure** there's no need to hurry ◆ **il y a ~ à faire** it is perilous to do

◆ **en péril** [monument, institution] in peril ◆ **mettre en ~** to imperil, to endanger, to jeopardize

périlleusement /peʀijøzmɑ̃/ ADV (littér) perilously

périlleux, -euse /peʀijø, øz/ ADJ perilous; → **saut**

périmé, e /peʀime/ (ptp de **périmer**) ADJ [billet, bon] out-of-date (épith), no longer valid (attrib); [idée] dated, outdated; * [nourriture] past its use-by date ◆ **ce passeport est ~** this passport has expired

périmer /peʀime/ ▸ conjug 1 ◂ VI ◆ **laisser ~ un passeport/billet** to let a passport/ticket expire VPR **se périmer** (Jur) to lapse; [passeport, billet] to expire; [idée] to date, to become outdated

périmètre /peʀimɛtʀ/ NM (Math) perimeter; (= zone) area ◆ **dans un ~ de 3 km** within a 3 km radius ◆ **~ de sécurité** safety zone

périnatal, e (mpl **périnatals**) /peʀinatal/ ADJ perinatal

périnéal, e (mpl **-aux**) /peʀineal, o/ ADJ perineal

périnée /peʀine/ NM perineum

période /peʀjɔd/ NF 1 (gén) period ◆ **par ~s** from time to time ◆ **pendant la ~ des vacances** during the holiday period ◆ **en ~ scolaire** during termtime (Brit), while school is in session (US) ◆ **pendant la ~ électorale** at election time ◆ **~ (d'instruction)** (Mil) training (NonC) ◆ **~ d'essai** trial period ◆ **~ ensoleillée/de chaleur** sunny/warm spell ou period ◆ **c'est la bonne ~ pour les champignons** it's the right time for mushrooms ◆ **j'ai eu une ~ concert/théâtre*** I went through a period ou phase of going to concerts/the theatre a lot ◆ **elle a traversé une ~ difficile** she has been through a difficult period ou patch ◆ **la ~ bleue de Picasso** Picasso's blue period ◆ **~ bleue/blanche** (Transport) slack/relatively slack period during which discounts are available on tickets ◆ **~ rouge** peak period during which tickets are at their most expensive

2 (Math) [de fonction] period; [de fraction] repetend

3 (Phys) **~ radioactive** half-life

périodicité /perjɔdisite/ NF periodicity

périodique /perjɔdik/ ADJ (*gén, Chim, Phys*) periodic; (*Presse*) periodical; (*Méd*) [*fièvre*] recurring ◆ **fraction** ~ (*Math*) recurring decimal ◆ **fonction** ~ (*Math*) periodic function; → **garniture** NM (*Presse*) periodical

périodiquement /perjɔdikmɑ̃/ ADV periodically

périoste /perjɔst/ NM periosteum

péripatéticien, -ienne /peripatetisjɛ̃, jɛn/ ADJ, NM,F (*Philos*) peripatetic NF **péripatéticienne** (*hum = prostituée*) streetwalker

péripétie /peripesi/ NF 1 (= *épisode*) event, episode ◆ **les ~s d'une révolution/d'une exploration** the various episodes in a revolution/an exploration ◆ **après bien des ~s** after all sorts of incidents ◆ **voyage plein de ~s** eventful journey 2 (*Littérat*) peripeteia

périph * /perif/ NM (abrév de **(boulevard) périphérique**) → **périphérique**

périphérie /periferi/ NF (= *limite*) periphery; (= *banlieue*) outskirts ◆ **la proche** ~ the inner suburbs

périphérique /periferik/ ADJ (*Anat, Math*) peripheral; [*quartier*] outlying (*épith*); [*communes, régions, activités*] associated ◆ **poste** *ou* **radio** *ou* **station** ~ private radio station (*broadcasting from a neighbouring country*) NM 1 (*Ordin*) peripheral ◆ ~ **entrée-sortie** input-output device 2 ◆ **(boulevard)** ~ ring road (*Brit*), beltway (*US*) ◆ **(boulevard)** ~ **intérieur/extérieur** inner/outer ring road (*Brit*) *ou* beltway (*US*)

périphrase /perifraz/ NF circumlocution, periphrasis (*SPÉC*), periphrase (*SPÉC*)

périphrastique /perifrastik/ ADJ circumlocutory, periphrastic

périple /peripl/ NM (*par mer*) voyage; (*par terre*) tour, journey ◆ **au cours de son ~ américain** during his tour of the USA

périr /perir/ ► conjug 2 ◄ VI (*littér*) to perish (*littér*), to die; [*navire*] to go down, to sink; [*empire*] to perish, to fall ◆ ~ **noyé** to drown, to be drowned ◆ **faire** ~ [+ *personne, plante*] to kill ◆ **son souvenir ne périra jamais** his memory will never die *ou* perish (*littér*) ◆ ~ **d'ennui** (*fig*) to die of boredom

périscolaire /periskɔlɛr/ ADJ extracurricular

périscope /periskɔp/ NM periscope

périscopique /periskɔpik/ ADJ periscopic

périssable /perisabl/ ADJ perishable ◆ **denrées ~s** perishable goods, perishables

périssoire /periswar/ NF canoe

péristaltisme /peristaltism/ NM peristalsis

péristyle /peristil/ NM peristyle

péritel ® /peritɛl/ ADJ F, NF ◆ **(prise)** ~ SCART (socket)

péritoine /peritwan/ NM peritoneum

péritonite /peritɔnit/ NF peritonitis

périurbain, e /periyrbɛ̃, ɛn/ ADJ outlying ◆ **zone ~e** outlying suburbs, peri-urban area

perle /pɛrl/ NF 1 (= *bijou*) pearl; (= *boule*) bead ◆ **des dents de** ~ pearly teeth ◆ **c'est jeter** *ou* **donner des ~s aux pourceaux** it's like casting pearls before swine; → **enfiler** 2 (*littér* = *goutte*) [*d'eau, sang*] drop(let); [*de sueur*] bead 3 (= *personne, chose de valeur*) gem ◆ **la cuisinière est une** ~ the cook is an absolute gem *ou* a perfect treasure ◆ **c'est la ~ des maris** he's the best of husbands, you couldn't hope for a better husband ◆ **vous êtes une ~ rare** you're a (real) gem ◆ **la ~ d'une collection** the highlight of a collection 4 (= *erreur*) gem, howler
COMP **perle de culture** cultured pearl
perle fine, perle naturelle natural pearl
perle de rosée dewdrop

perlé, e /pɛrle/ (ptp de **perler**) ADJ [*orge*] pearl (*épith*); [*riz*] polished; [*coton, laine*] pearlized; [*tissu*] beaded; [*travail*] perfect, exquisite; [*rire*] rippling; → **grève**

perler /pɛrle/ ► conjug 1 ◄ VI [*sueur*] to form ◆ **la sueur perlait sur son front** beads of sweat stood out *ou* formed on his forehead VT † [+ *travail*] to take great pains over

perlier, -ière /pɛrlje, jɛr/ ADJ pearl (*épith*)

perlimpinpin /pɛrlɛ̃pɛ̃pɛ̃/ NM → **poudre**

perlouse*, **perlouze*** /pɛrluz/ NF (= *perle*) pearl; (= *pet*) smelly fart*

perm * /pɛrm/ NF 1 abrév de **permanence 3** 2 (*arg Mil*) abrév de **permission 2**

permafrost /pɛrmafrɔst/ NM permafrost

permanence /pɛrmanɑ̃s/ NF 1 (= *durée*) permanence, permanency

◆ **en permanence** [*siéger*] permanently; [*crier*] continuously ◆ **dans ce pays ce sont des émeutes/c'est la guerre en** ~ in that country there are constant *ou* continuous riots/there is a permanent state of war ◆ **elle ment en** ~ she's always lying

2 (= *service*) **être de** ~ to be on duty *ou* on call ◆ **une ~ est assurée le dimanche** there is someone on duty on Sundays, the office is manned on Sundays 3 (= *bureau*) (duty) office; (*Pol*) committee room; (*Scol*) study room *ou* hall (*US*) ◆ **heure de** ~ (*Scol*) private study period

permanent, e /pɛrmanɑ̃, ɑ̃t/ ADJ permanent; [*armée, comité*] standing (*épith*); [*spectacle, angoisse*] continuous; [*conflit, effort*] ongoing ◆ **« permanent de 14 heures à minuit »** (*Ciné*) "continuous showings from 2 o'clock to midnight" ◆ **cinéma** ~ cinema showing a continuous programme ◆ **ils sont en contact** ~ they are in constant contact ◆ **elle s'est installée en France de façon ~e** she has settled in France permanently ◆ **cela implique un travail ~ de recherche** this necessitates ongoing research work; → **formation** NM (*Pol*) (paid) official (*of union, political party*); (*dans une entreprise*) permanent employee ◆ **un ~ du parti** a party worker NF **permanente** (*Coiffure*) perm ◆ **se faire faire une ~e** to have one's hair permed, to get a perm

permanenter /pɛrmanɑ̃te/ ► conjug 1 ◄ VT to perm ◆ **se faire** ~ to have one's hair permed, to get a perm ◆ **cheveux permanentés** permed hair

permanganate /pɛrmɑ̃ganat/ NM permanganate

perméabilité /pɛrmeabilite/ NF [*de matière, frontière*] permeability (*à* to); ◆ ~ **à l'air** air permeability

perméable /pɛrmeabl/ ADJ 1 [*matière, frontière*] permeable (*à* to); ◆ ~ **à l'air** permeable to air 2 (= *réceptif*) ◆ ~ **à** [*personne*] receptive to, open to ◆ **trop ~ aux idées extrémistes** too easily influenced by extremist ideas

permettre /pɛrmɛtr/ GRAMMAIRE ACTIVE 28.1, 30, 36.1, 37.4 ► conjug 56 ◄

VT 1 (= *tolérer*) to allow, to permit ◆ ~ **à qn de faire qch,** ~ **que qn fasse qch** to allow *ou* permit sb to do sth, to let sb do sth ◆ **la loi le permet** it is allowed *ou* permitted by law, the law allows *ou* permits it ◆ **le docteur me permet l'alcool** the doctor allows me to drink *ou* lets me drink ◆ **il se croit tout permis** he thinks he can do what he likes *ou* as he pleases ◆ **est-il permis d'être aussi bête !** how can anyone be so stupid! ◆ **il est permis à tout le monde de se tromper !** anyone can make mistakes *ou* a mistake! ◆ **le professeur lui a permis de ne pas aller à l'école aujourd'hui** the teacher has given him permission to stay off school *ou* not to go to school today ◆ **il hurlait comme ce n'est pas permis** * he was yelling like mad *

2 (= *rendre possible*) to allow, to permit ◆ **ce diplôme va lui ~ de trouver du travail** this qualification will allow *ou* enable *ou* permit him to find a job ◆ **mes moyens ne me le permettent pas** I can't afford it ◆ **mes occupations ne me le permettent pas** I'm too busy to do that ◆ **sa santé ne le lui permet pas** his health doesn't allow him to do that ◆ **son attitude permet tous les soupçons** his way of behaving gives cause for suspicion ◆ **si le temps le permet** weather permitting ◆ **autant qu'il est permis d'en juger** as far as one can tell

3 (= *donner le droit*) to entitle ◆ **cette carte lui permet d'obtenir des réductions** this card entitles him to reductions ◆ **être majeur permet de voter** once you're 18 you're eligible to vote ◆ **qu'est-ce qui te permet de me juger ?** what gives you the right to judge me?

4 (*idée de sollicitation*) **vous permettez ?** may I? ◆ **permettez-moi de vous présenter ma sœur/de vous interrompre** may I introduce my sister/interrupt (you)? ◆ **s'il m'est permis de faire une objection** if I may *ou* might raise an objection ◆ **vous permettez que je fume ?** do you mind if I smoke? ◆ **vous permettez que je passe !** (*ton irrité*) if you don't mind I'd like to come past! ◆ **permettez ! je ne suis pas d'accord** I'm very sorry but I disagree! ◆ **permets-moi de te le dire** let me tell you

VPR **se permettre** 1 (= *s'offrir*) to allow o.s. ◆ **je me permets une petite fantaisie de temps en temps** I indulge myself from time to time ◆ **je ne peux pas me ~ d'acheter ce manteau** I can't afford this coat

2 (= *risquer*) [+ *grossièreté, plaisanterie*] to dare to make ◆ **ce sont des plaisanteries qu'on ne peut se ~ qu'entre amis** these jokes are only acceptable among friends ◆ **je me suis permis de sourire** *ou* **un sourire** I allowed myself *ou* ventured a smile ◆ **il s'est permis de partir sans permission** he took the liberty of going without permission ◆ **il se permet bien des choses** he takes a lot of liberties ◆ **je me permettrai de vous faire remarquer que …** I'd like to point out (to you) that … ◆ **puis-je me ~ de vous offrir un verre ?** will you let me buy you a drink? ◆ **je me permets de vous écrire au sujet de …** (*formule épistolaire*) I am writing to you in connection with …

> ⚠ Attention à ne pas traduire automatiquement **permettre** par **to permit**, qui est d'un usage moins courant que 'to get'.

permien, -ienne /pɛrmjɛ̃, jɛn/ ADJ permian NM ◆ **le** ~ the Permian era

permis, e /pɛrmi, iz/ GRAMMAIRE ACTIVE 36.1, 37.4 (ptp de **permettre**) ADJ [*limites*] permitted ◆ **il est ~ de s'interroger sur la nécessité de …** (*frm*) one might *ou* may well question the necessity of … NM permit, licence ◆ ~ **de chasse** hunting licence ◆ ~ **(de conduire)** (= *carte*) driving licence (*Brit*), driver's license (*US*); (= *épreuve*) driving test ◆ ~ **à points** *driving licence with a penalty point system* ◆ ~ **de construire** planning permission (*NonC*) ◆ ~ **d'inhumer** burial certificate ◆ ~ **bateau** boating licence ◆ ~ **moto** motorbike licence ◆ ~ **de pêche** fishing permit ◆ ~ **poids lourd** heavy-goods vehicle licence ◆ ~ **de port d'armes** gun licence ◆ ~ **de séjour** residence permit ◆ ~ **de travail** work permit

permissif, -ive /pɛrmisif, iv/ ADJ permissive

permission /pɛrmisjɔ̃/ NF 1 (= *autorisation*) permission ◆ **avec votre** ~ with your permission ◆ **accorder à qn la ~ de faire qch** to give sb permission to do sth ◆ **demander la** ~ to ask permission (*de* to); ◆ **je lui ai demandé la** ~ I asked his permission (*de* to); ◆ **demander à qn la** ~ to ask sb his permission (*de* to); ◆ **est-ce qu'il t'a donné la ~ (de le faire) ?** did he give you permission (to do it)? 2 (*Mil*) (= *congé*) leave, furlough; *(= certificat)* pass ◆ **en ~** on leave *ou* furlough ◆ **~ de minuit** late pass

permissionnaire /pɛʀmisjɔnɛʀ/ NM soldier on leave

permissivité /pɛʀmisivite/ NF permissiveness

permutabilité /pɛʀmytabilite/ NF permutability

permutable /pɛʀmytabl/ ADJ which can be changed *ou* swapped *ou* switched round; *(Math)* permutable

permutation /pɛʀmytasjɔ̃/ NF permutation

permuter /pɛʀmyte/ ► conjug 1 ◄ VT *(gén)* to change *ou* swap *ou* switch round, to permutate; *(Math)* to permutate, to permute VI to change, to swap, to switch (seats *ou* positions *ou* jobs *etc*)

pernicieusement /pɛʀnisjøzmɑ̃/ ADV *(littér)* perniciously

pernicieux, -ieuse /pɛʀnisjø, jøz/ ADJ *(gén, Méd)* pernicious ◆ **~ pour** injurious *ou* harmful to

péroné /peʀɔne/ NM fibula

péroniste /peʀɔnist/ ADJ Peronist NMF **Péroniste** Peronist

péronnelle /peʀɔnɛl/ NF *(péj)* silly goose * *(péj)*

péroraison /peʀɔʀɛzɔ̃/ NF *(Littérat = conclusion)* peroration, summing up; *(péj = discours)* windy discourse *(péj)*

pérorer /peʀɔʀe/ ► conjug 1 ◄ VI to hold forth *(péj)*, to declaim *(péj)*

Pérou /peʀu/ NM *(Géog)* Peru ◆ **ce qu'il gagne, ce n'est pas le ~ !*** he doesn't exactly earn a fortune ◆ **on a 60 € ? c'est le ~ !*** *(iro)* we've got €60? we're loaded! * *ou* we're rolling in it! *

Pérouse /peʀuz/ N Perugia

peroxyde /pɛʀɔksid/ NM peroxide ◆ **~ d'hydrogène** hydrogen peroxide

peroxydé, e /pɛʀɔkside/ ADJ ◆ **cheveux ~s** peroxide hair

perpendiculaire /pɛʀpɑ̃dikylɛʀ/ ADJ, NF perpendicular (*à* to)

perpendiculairement /pɛʀpɑ̃dikylɛʀmɑ̃/ ADV perpendicularly ◆ **~ à** at right angles to, perpendicular to

perpète * /pɛʀpɛt/ NF 1 *(= perpétuité)* **il a eu la ~** he got life * ◆ **jusqu'à ~** * *(= longtemps)* forever and a day * 2 *(= loin)* **à ~ (les oies)** miles away *

perpétration /pɛʀpetʀasjɔ̃/ NF perpetration

perpétrer /pɛʀpetʀe/ ► conjug 6 ◄ VT to perpetrate

perpette * /pɛʀpɛt/ NF ⇒ **perpète**

perpétuation /pɛʀpetɥasjɔ̃/ NF *(littér)* perpetuation

perpétuel, -elle /pɛʀpetɥɛl/ ADJ *(= pour toujours)* perpetual, everlasting; *(= incessant)* perpetual, never-ending; *[fonction, secrétaire]* permanent

perpétuellement /pɛʀpetɥɛlmɑ̃/ ADV *(= constamment)* constantly; *(littér = toujours)* perpetually

perpétuer /pɛʀpetɥe/ ► conjug 1 ◄ VT *(= immortaliser)* to perpetuate; *(= maintenir)* to perpetuate, to carry on VPR **se perpétuer** *[usage, abus]* to be perpetuated, to be carried on; *[espèce]* to survive ◆ **se ~ dans son œuvre/dans ses enfants** to live on in one's work/in one's children

perpétuité /pɛʀpetɥite/ NF perpetuity, perpetuation ◆ **à ~** *[condamnation]* for life; *[concession]* in perpetuity; → **réclusion**

perplexe /pɛʀplɛks/ ADJ perplexed, puzzled ◆ **rendre** *ou* **laisser ~** to perplex, to puzzle

perplexité /pɛʀplɛksite/ NF perplexity ◆ **je suis dans une grande ~** I just don't know what to think ◆ **être dans la plus complète ~** to be completely baffled *ou* utterly perplexed

perquisition /pɛʀkizisjɔ̃/ NF *(Police)* search ◆ **ils ont fait une ~** they carried out *ou* made a search, they searched the premises; → **mandat**

perquisitionner /pɛʀkizisjɔne/ ► conjug 1 ◄ VI to carry out a search, to make a search ◆ **~ au domicile de qn** to search sb's house, to carry out *ou* make a search of sb's house VT * to search

perron /peʀɔ̃/ NM steps *(leading to entrance)*, perron *(SPÉC)* ◆ **sur le ~ de l'Élysée** on the steps of the Élysée Palace

perroquet /peʀɔkɛ/ NM 1 *(= oiseau)* parrot ◆ **~ de mer** puffin ◆ **répéter qch comme un ~** to repeat sth parrot fashion 2 *(= voile)* topgallant (sail) 3 *(= boisson) apéritif made of pastis and mint syrup*

perruche /peʀyʃ/ NF 1 *(= oiseau)* budgerigar, budgie *; *(= femelle du perroquet)* female parrot 2 *(= voile)* mizzen topgallant (sail)

perruque /peʀyk/ NF 1 *(= coiffure)* wig; *(Hist)* wig, periwig, peruke 2 *(Pêche = enchevêtrement)* tangle 3 *(* = travail clandestin)* **faire des ~s** to work on the side *(during office hours)* ◆ **faire de la ~** *(= détournement de matériel)* to pilfer office equipment for personal use

perruquier, -ière /peʀykje, jɛʀ/ NM,F wigmaker

pers /pɛʀ/ ADJ M *[yeux]* greenish-blue, blue-green

persan, e /pɛʀsɑ̃, an/ ADJ Persian ◆ **(chat) ~** Persian (cat); → **tapis** NM *(= langue)* Persian NM,F **Persan(e)** Persian

perse /pɛʀs/ ADJ Persian NM *(= langue)* Persian NMF **Perse** Persian NF *(Géog)* ◆ **Perse** Persia

persécuté, e /pɛʀsekyte/ NM,F *(gén)* persecuted person; *(Psych)* person suffering from a persecution mania *ou* complex

persécuter /pɛʀsekyte/ ► conjug 1 ◄ VT *(= opprimer)* to persecute; *(= harceler)* to harass, to plague

persécuteur, -trice /pɛʀsekytœʀ, tʀis/ ADJ persecuting NM,F persecutor

persécution /pɛʀsekysjɔ̃/ NF persecution ◆ **délire de ~** persecution mania *ou* complex

Persée /pɛʀse/ NM Perseus

Perséphone /pɛʀsefɔn/ NF Persephone

persévérance /pɛʀseveʀɑ̃s/ NF perseverance

persévérant, e /pɛʀseveʀɑ̃, ɑ̃t/ ADJ persevering ◆ **être ~** to persevere, to be persevering

persévérer /pɛʀseveʀe/ ► conjug 6 ◄ VI to persevere ◆ **~ dans** *[+ effort, entreprise, recherches]* to persevere with *ou* in, to persist in; *[+ erreur, voie]* to persevere in ◆ **je persévère à le croire coupable** I continue to believe he's guilty

persienne /pɛʀsjɛn/ NF (louvred) shutter

persiflage /pɛʀsiflaʒ/ NM mockery *(NonC)*

persifler /pɛʀsifle/ ► conjug 1 ◄ VT to mock, to make fun of

persifleur, -euse /pɛʀsiflœʀ, øz/ ADJ mocking NM,F mocker

persil /pɛʀsi/ NM parsley ◆ **~ plat/frisé** flat-leaved/curly parsley ◆ **faux ~** fool's parsley

persillade /pɛʀsijad/ NF *(= sauce)* parsley vinaigrette; *(= viande) cold beef served with parsley vinaigrette*

persillé, e /pɛʀsije/ ADJ *[plat]* sprinkled with chopped parsley; *[viande]* marbled; *[fromage]* veined

persique /pɛʀsik/ ADJ Persian; → **golfe**

persistance /pɛʀsistɑ̃s/ NF *[de pluie, fièvre, douleur, odeur]* persistence; *[de personne]* persistence, persistency (*à faire* in doing); ◆ **cette ~ dans le mensonge** this persistent lying ◆ **avec ~** *(= tout le temps)* persistently; *(= avec obstination)* persistently, doggedly, stubbornly

persistant, e /pɛʀsistɑ̃, ɑ̃t/ ADJ *(gén)* persistent; *[feuilles]* evergreen, persistent *(SPÉC)* ◆ **arbre à feuillage ~** evergreen (tree)

persister /pɛʀsiste/ ► conjug 1 ◄ VI *[pluie]* to persist, to keep up; *[fièvre, douleur, odeur]* to persist, to linger; *[symptôme, personne]* to persist ◆ **la pluie/la douleur n'a pas persisté** the rain/the pain didn't last *ou* persist ◆ **~ dans qch/à faire qch** to persist in sth/in doing sth ◆ **il persiste dans son refus** he won't go back on his refusal ◆ **~ dans son opinion/ses projets** to stick to one's opinion/one's plans ◆ **il persiste dans son silence** he persists in keeping quiet ◆ **il persiste à faire cela** he persists in doing *ou* keeps (on) doing that ◆ **je persiste à croire que ...** I still believe that ... ◆ **c'est non, je persiste et signe !** *(fig)* the answer is no, and that's final! ◆ **il persistait une odeur de moisi** a musty smell lingered *ou* persisted ◆ **il persiste un doute** some doubt remains

perso * /pɛʀso/ ADJ (abrév de **personnel**) *(= privé)* personal; *(= égoïste)* selfish ◆ **jouer ~** *(gén)* to go one's own way, to go solo ◆ **il joue trop ~** *(Sport)* he tends to keep the ball to himself

persona /pɛʀsɔna/ NF ◆ **~ grata/non grata** persona grata/non grata

personnage /pɛʀsɔnaʒ/ NM 1 *(= individu)* character, individual ◆ **c'est un ~ !** he's (*ou* she's) quite a character!

2 *(= célébrité)* (very) important person ◆ **~ influent/haut placé** influential/highly placed person ◆ **~ connu** celebrity, well-known person ◆ **~ officiel** VIP ◆ **un grand ~** a great figure ◆ **grands ~s de l'État** State dignitaries ◆ **~s de l'Antiquité/historiques** great names of Antiquity/in history ◆ **il est devenu un ~** he's become a very important person *ou* a big name * ◆ **il se prend pour un grand ~** he really thinks he's someone important, he really thinks he's somebody *

3 *(Littérat)* character ◆ **liste des ~s** dramatis personae, list of characters ◆ **jouer un ~** *(lit, fig)* to play a part, to act a part *ou* role; → **peau**

4 *(Art) [de tableau]* figure

personnalisation /pɛʀsɔnalizasjɔ̃/ NF personalization

personnaliser /pɛʀsɔnalize/ ► conjug 1 ◄ VT *[+ produit] [fabricant]* to customize; *[propriétaire]* to personalize; *[+ appartement]* to give a personal touch to ◆ **crédit/service personnalisé** personalized loan/service

personnalité /pɛʀsɔnalite/ NF 1 *(Psych)* personality ◆ **avoir une forte ~/de la ~** to have a strong personality/lots of personality ◆ **sans ~** lacking in personality 2 *(= personne importante)* personality ◆ **il y aura de nombreuses ~s pour l'inauguration** there will be a number of key figures *ou* personalities at the opening 3 *(Jur)* **acquérir une ~ juridique** to acquire legal status

personne /pɛʀsɔn/ NF 1 *(= être humain)* person ◆ **deux ~s** two people ◆ **grande ~** adult, grown-up ◆ **le respect de la ~ humaine** respect for human dignity ◆ **les ~s qui ...** those who ..., the people who ... ◆ **c'est une ~ sympathique** he (*ou* she) is a very nice *ou* pleasant person ◆ **une ~ de connaissance m'a dit ...** someone *ou* a person I know told me ... ◆ **il n'y a pas ~ plus discrète que lui** there's no one more discreet than he is *ou* than him ◆ **c'est une drôle de petite/une jolie ~** † she's a funny little/a pretty little thing ◆ **trois gâteaux par ~** three cakes per person, three cakes each ◆ **15 € par ~** €15 each *ou* a head *ou* per person ◆ **par ~ interposée** through an intermediary, through a third party *ou* person ◆ **querelles/rivalités de ~s** personal quarrels/

rivalries ♦ **les droits de la** ~ *(Jur)* the rights of the individual; → **tiers**

2 *(= personnalité)* **toute sa** ~ **inspire confiance** everything about him inspires confidence ♦ **j'admire son œuvre mais je le méprise en tant que** ~ I admire his works but I have no time for him as a person ♦ **la** ~ **et l'œuvre de Balzac** Balzac, the man and his work

3 *(= corps)* **être bien (fait) de sa** ~ to be good-looking ♦ **exposer** *ou* **risquer sa** ~ to risk one's life *ou* one's neck ♦ **sur ma** ~ on my person ♦ **il semble toujours très content de sa petite** ~ he always seems very pleased with himself ♦ **il prend soin de sa petite** ~ he looks after himself

♦ **en personne** ♦ **je l'ai vu en** ~ I saw him in person ♦ **je m'en occupe en** ~ I'll see to it personally ♦ **c'est la paresse/la bonté en** ~ he's *ou* she's laziness/kindness itself *ou* personified

4 *(Gram)* person ♦ **à la première/troisième** ~ in the first/third person

PRON 1 *(= quelqu'un)* anyone, anybody ♦ **elle le sait mieux que** ~ **(au monde)** she knows that better than anyone *ou* anybody (else) ♦ **il est entré sans que** ~ **le voie** he came in without anyone *ou* anybody seeing him ♦ ~ **de blessé ?** is anyone *ou* anybody injured?, no one hurt? ♦ **elle sait faire le café comme** ~ she makes better coffee than anyone (else)

2 *(avec ne = aucun)* no one, nobody ♦ **presque** ~ hardly anyone *ou* anybody, practically no one *ou* nobody ♦ ~ **(d'autre) ne l'a vu** no one *ou* nobody (else) saw him ♦ **il n'a vu** ~ **(d'autre)** he didn't see anyone *ou* anybody (else), he saw no one *ou* nobody (else) ♦ ~ **d'autre que lui** no one *ou* nobody but him *ou* he ♦ **il n'y a** ~ there's no one *ou* nobody in, there isn't anyone *ou* anybody in ♦ **il n'y a eu** ~ **de blessé** no one *ou* nobody was injured, there wasn't anyone *ou* anybody injured ♦ **à qui as-tu demandé ? –** à ~ who did you ask? – no one *ou* nobody *ou* I didn't ask anyone *ou* anybody ♦ **ce n'est la faute de** ~ it's no one's *ou* nobody's fault ♦ **il n'y avait** ~ **d'intéressant à qui parler** there was no one *ou* nobody interesting to talk to ♦ **il n'y est pour** ~ he doesn't want to see anyone *ou* anybody ♦ **pour le travail, il n'y a plus** ~* *(iro)* as soon as there's a bit of work to be done, everyone disappears *ou* clears off* *ou* there's suddenly no one *ou* nobody around ♦ **n'y a-t-il** ~ **qui sache où il est ?** doesn't anyone *ou* anybody know where he is?

COMP **personne âgée** elderly person ♦ **mesure en faveur des ~s âgées** measure benefiting the elderly
personne à charge dependent
personne civile *(Jur)* legal entity
personnes déplacées *(Pol)* displaced persons
personne humaine potentielle potential human being
personne morale *(Jur)* ⇒ **personne civile**
personne physique *(Jur)* natural person

personnel, -elle /pɛʀsɔnɛl/ ADJ 1 *(= particulier, privé)* personal; *[appel téléphonique]* private ♦ **fortune personnelle** personal *ou* private fortune ♦ **strictement** ~ *[lettre]* highly confidential, private and personal; *[billet]* not transferable *(attrib)* ♦ **il a des idées/des opinions très personnelles sur la question** he has ideas/opinions of his own *ou* he has his own ideas/opinions on the subject ♦ **critiques personnelles** personal criticism

2 *(= égoïste)* selfish, self-centred; *(Sport) [joueur]* selfish

3 *(Gram) [pronom, nom, verbe]* personal; *[mode]* finite

NM *[d'école]* staff; *[de château, hôtel]* staff, employees; *[d'usine]* workforce, employees, personnel; *[de service public]* personnel, employees ♦ **manquer de** ~ to be shortstaffed *ou* understaffed ♦ **il y a trop de** ~ **dans ce service** this department is overstaffed ♦ **faire partie du** ~ to be on the staff ♦ **l'usine a 60 membres de** ~ *ou* **un** ~ **de 60** the factory has 60 people on the payroll, the factory has a workforce *ou* payroll of 60 ♦ ~ **de maison** domestic staff ♦ ~ **à terre/navigant** ground/flight personnel *ou* staff ♦ ~ **en civil/en tenue** plain-clothes/uniformed staff ♦ **bureau/chef du** ~ personnel office/officer

personnellement /pɛʀsɔnɛlmɑ̃/ GRAMMAIRE ACTIVE 33.2, 53.5 ADV personally ♦ **je lui dirai** ~ I'll tell him myself *ou* personally ♦ ~ **je veux bien** personally I don't mind, I for one don't mind

personnification /pɛʀsɔnifikasjɔ̃/ NF personification ♦ **c'est la** ~ **de la cruauté** he's the personification *ou* the embodiment of cruelty

personnifier /pɛʀsɔnifje/ ▸ conjug 7 ◂ VT to personify ♦ **cet homme personnifie le mal** this man is the embodiment of evil *ou* is evil itself *ou* is evil personified ♦ **être la bêtise personnifiée** to be stupidity itself *ou* personified ♦ **il personnifie son époque** he personifies *ou* typifies his age, he's the embodiment of his age

perspectif, -ive[1] /pɛʀspɛktif, iv/ ADJ perspective

perspective[2] /pɛʀspɛktiv/ NF 1 *(Art)* perspective ♦ **effet de** ~ 3-D *ou* 3 dimensional effect

2 *(= point de vue) (lit)* view; *(fig)* angle, viewpoint ♦ **dans une** ~ **historique** from a historical angle *ou* viewpoint, in a historical perspective ♦ **examiner une question sous des ~s différentes** to examine a question from different angles *ou* viewpoints

3 *(= événement en puissance)* prospect; *(= idée)* prospect, thought ♦ **des ~s d'avenir** future prospects ♦ **quelle** ~ **!** what a thought *ou* prospect!

4 *(locutions)*

♦ **à la perspective de** with the prospect of ♦ **l'optimisme est revenu à la** ~ **d'un accord** optimism has returned with the prospect of an agreement ♦ **à la** ~ **de le voir gagner les élections, ils ont formé une coalition** faced with the prospect of him winning the election, they formed a coalition

♦ **en perspective** *[dessin]* in perspective ♦ **il y a du travail en** ~ there's a lot of work ahead ♦ **mettre qch en** ~ to put sth in(to) perspective ♦ **il faut mettre les choses en** ~ you have to put things in(to) perspective ♦ **il propose une nouvelle mise en** ~ **de l'art moderne** he offers a new perspective on modern art ♦ **la mise en** ~ **historique de cette évolution s'impose** this development must be put into historical perspective

♦ **dans la perspective de** with the prospect of ♦ **dans la** ~ **de l'élection présidentielle, nous devrons …** with the presidential election coming up, we must …

perspicace /pɛʀspikas/ ADJ shrewd, perspicacious *(frm)*

perspicacité /pɛʀspikasite/ NF insight, perspicacity *(frm)*

persuader /pɛʀsɥade/ ▸ conjug 1 ◂ VT *(= convaincre)* to persuade, to convince *(qn de qch* sb of sth); ♦ ~ **qn (de faire qch)** to persuade sb (to do sth) ♦ **il les a persuadés que tout irait bien** he persuaded *ou* convinced them that all would be well ♦ **on l'a persuadé de partir** he was persuaded to leave ♦ **j'en suis persuadé** I'm quite sure *ou* convinced (of it) ♦ **il sait** ~ he's very persuasive, he knows how to convince people VI *(littér)* ♦ ~ **à qn (de faire)** to persuade sb (to do) ♦ **on lui a persuadé de rester** he was persuaded to stay VPR **se persuader** ♦ **se** ~ **de qch** to convince *ou* persuade o.s. of sth ♦ **se** ~ **que …** to convince *ou* persuade o.s. that …

persuasif, -ive /pɛʀsɥazif, iv/ ADJ *[ton, éloquence]* persuasive; *[argument, orateur]* persuasive, convincing

persuasion /pɛʀsɥazjɔ̃/ NF *(= action, art)* persuasion; *(= croyance)* conviction, belief

perte /pɛʀt/ GRAMMAIRE ACTIVE 51.4

NF 1 *(gén)* loss ♦ **vendre à** ~ to sell at a loss ♦ **la** ~ **d'une bataille/d'un procès** the loss of a battle/of a court case, losing a battle/a court case ♦ **essuyer une** ~ **importante** to suffer heavy losses ♦ **de lourdes ~s (en hommes)** *(Mil)* heavy losses (in men) ♦ **ce n'est pas une grosse** ~ it's not a serious loss ♦ **la** ~ **cruelle d'un être cher** the cruel *ou* grievous loss of a loved one; → **profit**

2 *(= ruine)* ruin ♦ **il a juré sa** ~ he has sworn to ruin him ♦ **il court à sa** ~ he is on the road to ruin

3 *(= déperdition)* loss; *(= gaspillage)* waste ♦ ~ **de chaleur/d'énergie** loss of heat/of energy, heat/energy loss ♦ ~ **de lumière** loss of light ♦ **c'est une** ~ **de temps/d'énergie** it's a waste of time/of energy

4 *(locutions)*

♦ **avec pertes et fracas** ♦ **mis à la porte avec ~s et fracas** thrown out ♦ **il a quitté le parti avec ~s et fracas** after a big scene he left the party

♦ **à perte de vue** *(= très loin)* as far as the eye can see; *(= longtemps)* interminably

COMP **pertes blanches** *(Méd)* vaginal discharge, leucorrhoea *(SPÉC)*
perte de charge pressure drop, drop in *ou* loss of pressure
perte de connaissance *ou* **de conscience** loss of consciousness ♦ **avoir une** ~ **de connaissance** *ou* **de conscience** to lose consciousness
perte de mémoire loss of memory, memory loss
perte de poids weight loss
pertes de sang *(Méd)* heavy bleeding
perte sèche *(Fin)* dead loss *(Fin)*, absolute loss
perte à la terre *(Élec)* earth *(Brit)* *ou* ground *(US)* leakage
perte de vitesse ♦ **être en** ~ **de vitesse** *[avion]* to lose lift *[mouvement]* to be losing momentum; *[entreprise, vedette]* to be going downhill

pertinemment /pɛʀtinamɑ̃/ ADV *[parler]* pertinently ♦ **il a répondu** ~ his reply was to the point ♦ **savoir** ~ **que …** to know full well that …, to know for a fact that …

pertinence /pɛʀtinɑ̃s/ NF 1 *(= à-propos) [de remarque, question, idée, analyse]* pertinence, relevance ♦ **il remarqua avec** ~ **que …** he aptly pointed out that … 2 *(Ling)* significance, distinctive nature

pertinent, e /pɛʀtinɑ̃, ɑ̃t/ ADJ 1 *[remarque, question, idée, analyse]* pertinent, relevant 2 *(Ling)* significant, distinctive

pertuis /pɛʀtɥi/ NM *(= détroit)* strait(s), channel; *[de fleuve]* narrows

pertuisane /pɛʀtɥizan/ NF partisan *(weapon)*

perturbant, e /pɛʀtyʀbɑ̃, ɑ̃t/ ADJ disturbing, perturbing ♦ **le divorce a été très** ~ **pour l'enfant** the divorce was a very disturbing *ou* unsettling experience for the child

perturbateur, -trice /pɛʀtyʀbatœʀ, tʀis/ ADJ disruptive NM,F *(gén)* troublemaker; *(dans un débat)* heckler

perturbation /pɛʀtyʀbasjɔ̃/ NF *[de services publics, travaux, cérémonie, réunion, transmission]* disruption; *(Astron)* perturbation ♦ **jeter** *ou* **semer la** ~ **dans** to disrupt ♦ **facteur de** ~ disruptive factor ♦ **~s dans l'acheminement du courrier** disruption(s) in the mail service ♦ **les ~s ont surtout affecté les lignes de banlieue** it was mainly the suburban lines that were disrupted ◆ ~ **(atmosphérique)** (atmospheric) disturbance

perturbé, e /pɛʀtyʀbe/ ADJ 1 *[personne]* upset 2 *[services publics, trafic]* disrupted ◆ **le trafic reste très** ~ traffic is still severely disrupted ◆ **j'ai un sommeil très** ~ I have trouble sleeping

perturber /pɛʀtyʀbe/ ▸ conjug 1 ◂ VT 1 *[+ services publics, travaux, cérémonie, réunion]* to disrupt; *(Radio, TV) [+ transmission]* to disrupt; *(Astron)* to perturb; *(Météo)* to disturb ◆ **le match/tournoi a été fortement perturbé par la pluie** the match/tournament was severely disrupted by rain 2 *(= déstabiliser) [+ personne]* to upset ◆ **son divorce l'a profondément perturbé** he was deeply upset by his divorce ◆ **qu'est-ce qui te perturbe ?** what's bothering you?

péruvien, -ienne /peʀyvjɛ̃, jɛn/ ADJ Peruvian NM,F **Péruvien(ne)** Peruvian

pervenche /pɛʀvɑ̃ʃ/ NF *(= plante)* periwinkle; *(* = contractuelle)* female traffic warden *(Brit)*, meter maid *(US)* ADJ INV periwinkle blue

pervers, e /pɛʀvɛʀ, ɛʀs/ ADJ *(littér) (= diabolique)* perverse; *(= vicieux)* perverted, depraved ◆ **les effets ~ de la publicité** the pernicious effects of advertising NM,F pervert ◆ ~ **sexuel** (sexual) pervert

perversion /pɛʀvɛʀsjɔ̃/ NF perversion, corruption; *(Méd, Psych)* perversion

perversité /pɛʀvɛʀsite/ NF perversity, depravity

pervertir /pɛʀvɛʀtiʀ/ ▸ conjug 2 ◂ VT *(= dépraver)* to corrupt, to pervert, to deprave; *(= altérer)* to pervert VPR **se pervertir** to become corrupt(ed) *ou* perverted *ou* depraved

pesage /pəzaʒ/ NM weighing; *[de jockey]* weigh-in; *(= salle)* weighing room; *(= enceinte)* enclosure

pesamment /pəzamɑ̃/ ADV *[chargé, tomber]* heavily; *[marcher]* with a heavy step *ou* tread, heavily

pesant, e /pəzɑ̃, ɑ̃t/ ADJ 1 *(= lourd) [paquet]* heavy, weighty; *[sommeil]* deep; *[démarche, pas, architecture]* heavy; *[esprit]* slow, sluggish; *[style, ton]* heavy, weighty, ponderous 2 *(= pénible) [charge, silence]* heavy; *[présence]* burdensome ◆ **il devient ~ avec ses questions** he's becoming a nuisance with all those questions NM ◆ **valoir son ~ d'or** *[personne]* to be worth one's weight in gold; *[diplôme]* to be worth its weight in gold ◆ **il faut le voir faire un discours, ça vaut son ~ d'or** *ou* **de cacahuètes*** *(hum)* you should hear him make a speech, it's priceless*

pesanteur /pəzɑ̃tœʀ/ NF 1 *(Phys)* gravity ◆ **défier les lois de la** ~ to defy (the laws of) gravity 2 *(= lourdeur) [de paquet]* heaviness, weightiness; *[de démarche]* heaviness; *[d'esprit]* slowness, sluggishness; *[d'architecture]* heaviness; *[de style]* heaviness, weightiness, ponderousness ◆ **avoir des ~s d'estomac** to have problems with one's digestion ◆ **les ~s administratives** cumbersome administrative procedures

pèse-acide (pl **pèse-acides**) /pɛzasid/ NM acidimeter

pèse-alcool (pl **pèse-alcools**) /pɛzalkɔl/ NM alcoholometer

pèse-bébé (pl **pèse-bébés**) /pɛzbebe/ NM (baby) scales

pesée /pəze/ NF 1 *(= action)* weighing ◆ **effectuer une** ~ to find out the weight 2 *(= pression, poussée)* push, thrust 3 *(Sport)* **aller à la** ~ to weigh in

pèse-lait (pl **pèse-laits**) /pɛzlɛ/ NM lactometer

pèse-lettre (pl **pèse-lettres**) /pɛzlɛtʀ/ NM letter scales

pèse-personne (pl **pèse-personnes**) /pɛzpɛʀsɔn/ NM scales; *(dans une salle de bains)* (bathroom) scales

peser /pəze/ GRAMMAIRE ACTIVE 53.4 ▸ conjug 5 ◂

VT 1 *[+ objet, personne]* to weigh ◆ ~ **qch dans sa main** to feel the weight of sth (in one's hand) ◆ **se** ~ to weigh o.s. ◆ **se faire** ~ *[sportif]* to get weighed in ◆ **il pèse 3 millions** he is worth 3 million

2 *(= évaluer)* to weigh (up) ◆ ~ **le pour et le contre** to weigh (up) the pros and cons ◆ ~ **ses mots/chances** to weigh one's words/chances ◆ **tout bien pesé** all things considered ◆ **ce qu'il dit est toujours pesé** what he says is always carefully thought out

VI 1 *(gén)* to weigh; *[sportif]* to weigh in ◆ **cela pèse beaucoup** it weighs a lot ◆ **cela pèse peu** it doesn't weigh much ◆ ~ **60 kg** to weigh 60 kg ◆ ~ **lourd** to be heavy ◆ **ce ministre ne pèse pas lourd*** this minister doesn't carry much weight *ou* doesn't count for much ◆ **il n'a pas pesé lourd (devant son adversaire)** he was no match for his opponent

2 *(= appuyer)* to press, to push ◆ ~ **sur/contre qch (de tout son poids)** to press *ou* push down on/against sth (with all one's weight) ◆ ~ **sur l'estomac** *[aliment, repas]* to lie (heavy) on the stomach ◆ **cela lui pèse sur le cœur** that makes him heavy-hearted ◆ **les remords lui pèsent sur la conscience** remorse lies heavy on his conscience, he is weighed down with remorse ◆ **le soupçon/l'accusation qui pèse sur lui** the suspicion/the accusation hanging *ou* which hangs over him ◆ **la menace/sentence qui pèse sur sa tête** the threat/sentence which hangs over his head ◆ **toute la responsabilité pèse sur lui** *ou* **sur ses épaules** all the responsibility is on him *ou* on his shoulders, he has to shoulder all the responsibility

3 *(= accabler)* ~ **à qn** to weigh sb down, to weigh heavy on sb ◆ **le silence/la solitude lui pèse** the silence/solitude is getting him down* *ou* weighs heavy on him ◆ **le temps lui pèse** time hangs heavy on his hands ◆ **ses responsabilités de maire lui pèsent** his responsibilities as mayor weigh heavy on him

4 *(= avoir de l'importance)* to carry weight ◆ **cela va ~ (dans la balance)** that will carry some weight ◆ **sa timidité a pesé dans leur décision** his shyness influenced their decision

peseta /pezeta/ NF peseta

peso /pezo, peso/ NM peso

pessaire /pesɛʀ/ NM pessary

pessimisme /pesimism/ NM pessimism

pessimiste /pesimist/ ADJ pessimistic *(sur* about) NMF pessimist

peste /pɛst/ NF *(Méd)* plague; *(péj = personne)* pest, nuisance ◆ **la ~ bubonique** the bubonic plague ◆ **la ~ noire** the black plague, the Black Death ◆ ~ **bovine** rinderpest, cattle plague ◆ **fuir qch/qn comme la** ~ to avoid sth/sb like the plague EXCL *(littér)* good gracious! ◆ ~ **soit de ...** a plague on ...

pester /pɛste/ ▸ conjug 1 ◂ VI to curse ◆ ~ **contre qn/qch** to curse sb/sth

pesticide /pɛstisid/ ADJ pesticidal NM pesticide

pestiféré, e /pɛstifeʀe/ ADJ plague-stricken NM,F plague victim ◆ **fuir qn comme un** ~ to avoid sb like the plague

pestilence /pɛstilɑ̃s/ NF stench

pestilentiel, -elle /pɛstilɑ̃sjɛl/ ADJ *(gén)* stinking, foul(-smelling); *(Méd)* pestilent

pet¹⁑ /pɛ/ NM 1 *(⁑ = gaz)* fart⁑ ◆ **faire** *ou* **lâcher un** ~ to break wind, to fart⁑ ◆ **il a toujours un ~ de travers** he's always got something wrong with him ◆ **partir comme un ~ (sur une toile cirée)** to scarper⁑ *(Brit)*, to split*; → **valoir** 2 († * = *guet*) **faire le** ~ to be on watch *ou* on look-out

pet²⁑ /pɛt/ NM *(= coup)* thump, bash; *(= marque)* dent ◆ **la table a pris un** ~ the table has taken a bash ◆ **il y a plein de ~s sur l'étagère** the shelf is all dented

pétainiste /petenist/ ADJ Pétain *(épith)* NMF **Pétainiste** Pétain supporter

pétale /petal/ NM petal

pétanque /petɑ̃k/ NF petanque *(type of bowls played in the South of France)*; → **BOULES**

pétant, e* /petɑ̃, ɑ̃t/ ADJ ◆ **à 2 heures ~(es)** at 2 on the dot*

pétaradant, e /petaʀadɑ̃, ɑ̃t/ ADJ *[moto]* noisy, spluttering, back-firing

pétarade /petaʀad/ NF *[de moteur, véhicule]* backfiring *(NonC)*; *[de feu d'artifice, fusillade]* crackling *(NonC)*

pétarader /petaʀade/ ▸ conjug 1 ◂ VI *[moteur, véhicule]* to backfire; *[feu d'artifice]* to go off ◆ **il les entendait ~ dans la cour** he could hear them revving up their engines in the backyard

pétard /petaʀ/ NM 1 *(= feu d'artifice)* firecracker, banger *(Brit)*; *(= accessoire de cotillon)* cracker; *(Rail)* detonator *(Brit)*, torpedo *(US)*; *(Mil)* petard, explosive charge ◆ **tirer** *ou* **faire partir un** ~ to let off a firecracker *ou* banger *(Brit)* ◆ **lancer un** ~ *(fig)* to drop a bombshell ◆ **c'était un ~ mouillé** *(fig)* it was a damp squib 2 *(⁑ = tapage)* din*, racket*, row* ◆ **il va y avoir du** ~ sparks will fly, there's going to be a hell of a row* ◆ **faire du** ~ *[nouvelle]* to cause a stir, to raise a stink*; *[personne]* to kick up a row* *ou* fuss* *ou* stink* ◆ **être en** ~ to be raging mad*, to be in a flaming temper *(contre* at) 3 *(⁑ = revolver)* gun 4 *(⁑ = derrière)* bottom*, bum* *(Brit)* 5 *(Drogue)* joint*, reefer*

pétasse⁑ /petas/ NF slut⁑

pétaudière /petodjɛʀ/ NF ◆ **c'est une** ~ it's bedlam ◆ **quelle ~ !** it's bedlam in here!

pet-de-nonne (pl **pets-de-nonne**) /pɛd(ə)nɔn/ NM fritter *(made with choux pastry)*

pété, e⁑ /pete/ (ptp de **péter**) ADJ 1 *(= ivre)* plastered⁑, pissed⁑ *(Brit)*; *(= drogué)* stoned⁑; *(= fou)* crazy, bonkers⁑ 2 ◆ ~ **de thunes*** rolling in it*

pet-en-l'air † /petɑ̃lɛʀ/ NM INV bumfreezer*

péter /pete/ ▸ conjug 6 ◂ VI 1 ⁑ *[personne]* to break wind, to fart⁑ ◆ **il veut ~ plus haut que son derrière** *ou* **son cul**⁑ he thinks he's it* ◆ **il m'a envoyé ~** he told me to go to hell⁑ ◆ ~ **dans la soie** to live in the lap of luxury

2 * *[détonation]* to go off; *[tuyau]* to burst; *[ballon]* to pop, to burst; *[ficelle]* to snap ◆ **la bombe lui a pété à la figure** the bomb went off *ou* blew up in his face ◆ **l'affaire lui a pété dans la main** the deal fell through ◆ **la crise est si grave qu'un jour ça va** ~ the crisis is so serious that one day all hell's going to break loose*

VT * 1 *[+ ficelle]* to snap; *[+ transistor, vase]* to bust* ◆ **je me suis pété une cheville** I did my ankle in* ◆ ~ **la gueule à qn**⁑ to smash sb's face in* ◆ **se ~ la gueule**⁑ *(= tomber)* to fall flat on one's face; *(= s'enivrer)* to get plastered⁑ *ou* pissed⁑ *(Brit)* ◆ **c'est un coup à se ~ la gueule**⁑ you'll *(ou* he'll *etc)* break your *(ou* his *etc)* neck doing that ◆ **il s'est pété la gueule en vélo**⁑ he smashed himself up when he came off his bike⁑

2 *(locutions)* ~ **le feu** *ou* **les flammes** *[personne]* to be full of go* *ou* beans* *(Brit)* ◆ ~ **la** *ou* **de santé** to be bursting with health ◆ **il pète la forme** he's on top form ◆ **ça va ~ des flammes** there's going to be a heck of a row* ◆ ~ **les plombs** *ou* **un plomb** *ou* **une durite*** to flip one's lid⁑ ◆ **il se la pète*** he thinks he's God's gift*

pète-sec * /pɛtsɛk/ **NMF INV, ADJ INV** ◆ **c'est un ~, il est très ~** he has a very curt *ou* abrupt manner

péteux, -euse * /petø, øz/ **ADJ** (= *peureux*) cowardly, yellow, yellow-bellied *; (= *honteux*) ashamed *(attrib)* **NM,F** (= *peureux*) coward, yellowbelly *; (= *prétentieux*) pretentious twit *

pétillant, e /petijɑ̃, ɑ̃t/ **ADJ** *[eau, vin]* sparkling; *[yeux]* sparkling, twinkling ◆ **discours ~ d'esprit** speech sparkling with wit

pétillement /petijmɑ̃/ **NM** *[de feu]* crackling *(NonC)*; *[de champagne, vin, eau]* bubbling *(NonC)*; *[de yeux]* sparkling *(NonC)*, twinkling *(NonC)* ◆ **entendre des ~s** to hear crackling *ou* crackles ◆ **ce ~ de malice dans son regard** the mischievous twinkle in his eye

pétiller /petije/ ▸ conjug 1 ◂ **VI** *[feu]* to crackle; *[champagne, vin, eau]* to bubble; *[joie]* to sparkle (*dans* in); *[yeux]* to sparkle, to twinkle (*de* with); ◆ **ses yeux pétillaient de malice** his eyes were sparkling *ou* twinkling mischievously ◆ **il pétillait de bonne humeur** he was bubbling (over) with good humour ◆ **~ d'intelligence** to sparkle with intelligence

pétiole /pesjɔl/ **NM** leafstalk, petiole *(SPÉC)*

petiot, e * /pətjo, jɔt/ **ADJ** teenyweeny *, tiny (little) **NM** little boy *ou* lad * *(Brit)* **NF** **petiote** little girl *ou* lass * *(US)*

petit, e /p(ə)ti, it/

1 ADJECTIF	4 NOM FÉMININ
2 LOC ADV	5 COMPOSÉS
3 NOM MASCULIN	

1 - ADJECTIF

Lorsque **petit** s'emploie dans des expressions telles que **les petites gens, entrer par la petite porte, ce n'est pas une petite affaire** etc., cherchez au nom.

1 gén, en dimension *[main, personne, objet, colline]* small, little *(épith)*; *[pointure]* small ◆ **~ et mince** short and thin ◆ **~ et carré** squat ◆ **et rond** dumpy ◆ **il est tout ~** he's very small *ou* a very small man; *(nuance affective)* he's a little *ou* a tiny (little) man ◆ **se faire tout ~** *(fig)* to keep a low profile, to make o.s. as inconspicuous as possible ◆ **depuis, il se fait tout ~ devant moi** ever since then, he's been acting like he's afraid of me ◆ **un ~ vieux** a little old man ◆ **ces chaussures sont un peu ~es/trop ~es pour moi** these shoes are a bit small *ou* rather a small fit/too small for me ◆ **~ poisson deviendra grand** *(Prov)* ◆ **les ~s ruisseaux font les grandes rivières** *(Prov)* great *ou* mighty oaks from little acorns grow *(Prov)*

◆ **en petit** ◆ **c'est écrit en ~** it's written in small letters ◆ **une cour d'école, c'est le monde en ~** a school playground is the world in miniature ◆ **le dessin est répété en ~ sur les fauteuils** there's a smaller version of the pattern on the armchairs, the pattern is the same on the armchairs but smaller

2 = mince *[tranche]* thin ◆ **avoir de ~s os** to be small-boned *ou* slight-boned ◆ **avoir de ~s bras** to have slender *ou* thin arms ◆ **une ~e pluie (fine) tombait** a (fine) drizzle was falling

3 = miniature, jouet toy *(épith)* ◆ **~e voiture** toy *ou* miniature car ◆ **~ train** (= *jouet*) toy train; (= *dans un parc*) miniature train ◆ **faire le ~ train** (= *jeu*) to play trains

4 = maladif **avoir une ~e santé** to be in poor health, to be frail ◆ **avoir une ~e figure** *ou* **mine** to look pale *ou* wan ◆ **tu as de ~s yeux ce matin** you're a bit bleary-eyed this morning

5 = jeune small, young; *(avec nuance affective)* little ◆ **quand il était ~** when he was small *ou* little ◆ **un ~ Anglais** an English boy ◆ **les ~s Anglais** English children ◆ **tu es encore trop ~ pour comprendre** you're still too young to understand ◆ **~ chat/chien** (little) kitten/puppy ◆ **~ lion/tigre/ours** lion/tiger/bear cub ◆ **dans sa ~e enfance** when he was very small, in his early childhood ◆ **~ garçon** little boy ◆ **je ne suis plus un ~ garçon !** I'm not a child anymore! ◆ **il fait très ~ garçon** he's very boyish ◆ **à côté de lui, Marc est un ~ garçon** *(fig)* compared to him, Marc is a babe in arms

6 = cadet **son ~ frère** his younger *ou* little brother; *(très petit)* his baby *ou* little brother ◆ **tu vas bientôt avoir une ~e sœur** you'll soon have a baby *ou* little sister

7 = court *[promenade, voyage]* short, little ◆ **sur une ~e distance** over a short distance ◆ **par ~es étapes** in short *ou* easy stages ◆ **c'est une ~e semaine/un ~ mois** *(écourtés par congé)* it's a short week/a short month ◆ **il est resté deux (pauvres) ~es heures** he stayed for a mere two hours ◆ **il en a pour une ~e heure** it will take him an hour at the most, it won't take him more than an hour ◆ **c'est à un ~ kilomètre d'ici** it's no more than *ou* just under a kilometre from here

8 = faible *[bruit]* faint, slight; *[cri]* little, faint; *[coup, tape]* light, gentle; *[pente]* gentle, slight; *[somme d'argent, budget]* small; *[loyer]* low ◆ **on entendit deux ~s coups à la porte** we heard two light *ou* gentle knocks on the door ◆ **il a un ~ appétit** he has a small appetite, he hasn't much of an appetite ◆ **une toute ~e voix** a tiny voice ◆ **film à ~ budget** low-budget film ◆ **c'est un ~ mardi** (= *la recette est faible*) it's a poor showing for a Tuesday ◆ **ils ont gagné par un ~ 1 à 0** *(Sport)* they won by a very slim 1-0; → **salaire**

9 = peu important *[commerçant, pays, entreprise, groupe]* small; *[opération, détail]* small, minor; *[amélioration, changement, inconvénient]* slight, minor; *[espoir, chance]* faint, slight; *[odeur, rhume]* slight; *[fonctionnaire, employé, romancier]* minor; *[cadeau, bibelot, soirée, réception]* little ◆ **le ~ commerce** small businesses ◆ **les ~es et moyennes entreprises/industries** small and medium-sized businesses/industries ◆ **chez le ~ épicier du coin** at the little grocer's down the street ◆ **avec un ~ effort** with a bit of an *ou* with a little effort ◆ **ce fait n'est connu que d'un ~ nombre** only a small number of people *ou* a few people are aware of this fact

10 péj = mesquin *[attitude, action]* mean, petty, low; *[personne]* petty ◆ **c'est ~ ce qu'il a fait là** that was a mean thing to do, that was mean of him

11 avec nuance affective ou euph little ◆ **vous prendrez bien un ~ dessert/verre ?** you'll have a little dessert/drink, won't you? ◆ **faire une ~e partie de cartes** to play a little game of cards ◆ **juste une ~e signature** can I just have your signature ◆ **un ~ coup de rouge** * a (little) glass of red wine ◆ **une ~e robe d'été** a light summer dress ◆ **ma ~e maman** my mummy ◆ **mon ~ papa** my daddy ◆ **mon ~ chou** *ou* **rat** *etc* (my little) darling ◆ **un ~ coin tranquille** a nice quiet spot ◆ **on va se faire un bon ~ souper** we'll make ourselves a nice little (bit of) supper ◆ **cela coûte une ~e fortune** it costs a small fortune ◆ **ce n'est pas grand-chose, mais c'est tout de même une ~e victoire** it's not much but it's a small victory nonetheless ◆ **il y a un ~ vent** *(agréable)* there's a bit of a breeze; *(désagréable)* it's a bit windy

12 pour déprécier **espèce de ~ impertinent** you cheeky little so-and-so * ◆ **je vous préviens, mon ~ ami** *ou* **monsieur** I warn you my good man *ou* dear fellow ◆ **~ con !** ** stupid jerk! **

13 locutions **c'est de la ~e bière** it's small beer *(Brit)*, it's small potatoes *(US)* ◆ **ce n'est pas de la ~e bière** it's no small matter, it's not without importance ◆ **être aux ~s soins pour qn** to wait on sb hand and foot; → **semaine, soulier** *etc*

2 - LOCUTION ADVERBIALE

petit à petit little by little, gradually ◆ **~ à ~, l'oiseau fait son nid** *(Prov)* with time and perseverance one accomplishes one's goals

3 - NOM MASCULIN

1 = enfant (little) boy ◆ **les ~s** the children ◆ **viens ici, ~** come here, son ◆ **pauvre ~** poor little thing ◆ **le ~ Durand** the Durands' son, the Durand boy ◆ **les ~s Durand** the Durand children ◆ **jeu pour ~s et grands** game for old and young (alike); → **tout-petit**

2 Scol junior (boy)

3 = jeune animal **les ~s** the young ◆ **la chatte et ses ~s** the cat and her kittens ◆ **la lionne et ses ~s** the lioness and her young *ou* cubs ◆ **faire des ~s** to have kittens *(ou* puppies *ou* lambs *etc)* ◆ **son argent a fait des ~s** *(fig)* his money has made more money

4 = personne de petite taille small man; (= *personne sans pouvoir*) little man ◆ **les ~s** small people ◆ **c'est toujours le ~ qui a tort** it's always the little man who's in the wrong

4 - NOM FÉMININ

petite (= *enfant*) (little) girl; (= *femme*) small woman ◆ **la ~e Durand** the Durands' daughter, the Durand girl ◆ **pauvre ~e** poor little thing ◆ **viens ici, ~e** come here, little one

5 - COMPOSÉS

petit ami boyfriend
petite amie girlfriend
petit banc low bench
les petits blancs poor white settlers
petit bleu † wire *(telegram)*
petits chevaux ◆ **jouer aux ~s chevaux** ≈ to play ludo *(Brit)*
le petit coin *(euph)* the smallest room *(euph)*, the bathroom *(euph)*, the toilet
petit cousin, petite cousine (= *enfant, jeune*) little *ou* young cousin; (= *enfant du cousin germain*) second cousin; (= *parent éloigné*) distant cousin
le petit endroit *(euph)* ⇒ **le petit coin**
petit four petit four
petit gâteau (sec) biscuit
le Petit Livre rouge the Little Red Book
petite main *(Couture)* apprentice seamstress; (= *subalterne*) minion
petit nom * (= *prénom*) Christian name, first name; (= *surnom*) nickname; *(entre amoureux)* pet name
petit pain ≈ bread roll ◆ **ça part** *ou* **se vend comme des ~s pains** * they're selling like hot cakes *
petit point *(Couture)* petit point
la petite reine (= *bicyclette*) the bicycle
petit salé *(Culin)* salt pork
la petite vérole smallpox
petite voiture (d'infirme) *(gén)* wheelchair; *(à moteur)* invalid carriage

petit-beurre (pl **petits-beurre**) /p(ə)tibœʀ/ **NM** petit beurre biscuit *(Brit)*, butter cookie *(US)*

petit-bourgeois, petite-bourgeoise (pl **petits-bourgeois**) /p(ə)tibuʀʒwa, p(ə)titbuʀʒwaz/ **ADJ** *(gén)* lower middle-class; *(péj)* petit-bourgeois, middle-class **NM,F** *(gén)* lower middle-class person; *(péj)* petit-bourgeois

petit(-)déjeuner (pl **petits(-)déjeuners**) /p(ə)tideʒœne/ **NM** breakfast ◆ **~ anglais/continental** English/continental breakfast **VI** **petit-déjeuner** * ▸ conjug 1 ◂ to have breakfast

petite-fille (pl **petites-filles**) /p(ə)titfij/ **NF** granddaughter

petite-maîtresse †† (pl **petites-maîtresses**) / p(ə)titmɛtʀɛs / **NF** lady of fashion

petitement / pətitmɑ̃ / **ADV** (= *chichement*) poorly; (= *mesquinement*) meanly, pettily ◆ **nous sommes ~ logés** our accommodation is cramped

petit-enfant (pl **petits-enfants**) / pətitɑ̃fɑ̃, pətizɑ̃fɑ̃ / **NM** grandchild

petite-nièce (pl **petites-nièces**) / p(ə)titnjɛs / **NF** great-niece, grand-niece

petitesse / p(ə)titɛs / **NF** *[de taille, endroit]* smallness, small size; *[de somme]* smallness, modesty; *[d'esprit, acte]* meanness *(NonC)*, pettiness *(NonC)*

petit-fils (pl **petits-fils**) / p(ə)tifis / **NM** grandson

petit-gris (pl **petits-gris**) / p(ə)tigʀi / **NM** 1 (= *escargot*) garden snail 2 (= *écureuil*) Siberian squirrel; (= *fourrure*) grey squirrel fur

pétition / petisjɔ̃ / **NF** 1 (= *demande, requête*) petition ◆ **faire une ~ auprès de qn** to petition sb ◆ **faire signer une ~** to set up a petition 2 *(Philos)* **~ de principe** petitio principii *(SPÉC)*, begging the question *(NonC)* ◆ **c'est une ~ de principe** it's begging the question

pétitionnaire / petisjɔnɛʀ / **NMF** petitioner

petit-lait (pl **petits-laits**) / p(ə)tilɛ / **NM** whey; → **lait**

petit-maître †† (mpl **petits-maîtres**) / p(ə)timɛtʀ / **NM** coxcomb ††, fop †

petit-nègre / pətinɛgʀ / **NM** *(péj)* pidgin French; (= *galimatias*) gibberish, gobbledygook *

petit-neveu (pl **petits-neveux**) / p(ə)tin(ə)vø / **NM** great-nephew, grand-nephew

petit-pois (pl **petits-pois**) / pətipwa / **NM** (garden) pea ◆ **il a un ~ dans la tête** *ou* **à la place de la cervelle** * he's a bit feather-brained

petit-suisse (pl **petits-suisses**) / p(ə)tisɥis / **NM** petit-suisse *(kind of cream cheese eaten as a dessert)*

pétochard, e * / petɔʃaʀ, aʀd / **ADJ** cowardly, yellow-bellied * **NM,F** coward, yellowbelly *

pétoche * / petɔʃ / **NF** ◆ **avoir la ~** to be scared silly * *ou* stiff * ◆ **flanquer la ~ à qn** to scare the living daylights out of sb *, to put the wind up sb * *(Brit)*

pétoire / petwaʀ / **NF** (= *sarbacane*) peashooter; (= *vieux fusil*) old gun; (= *cyclomoteur*) (motor) scooter

peton * / pətɔ̃ / **NM** (= *pied*) foot, tootsy *

pétoncle / petɔ̃kl / **NM** queen scallop

Pétrarque / petʀaʀk / **NM** Petrarch

pétrarquisme / petʀaʀkism / **NM** Petrarchism

pétrel / petʀɛl / **NM** (stormy) petrel

pétri, e / petʀi / (ptp de **pétrir**) **ADJ** ◆ **~ d'orgueil** filled with pride ◆ **il est ~ de qualités** he's got lots of good points ◆ **~ de contradictions** full of contradictions ◆ **~ de culture orientale/littérature slave** steeped in Eastern culture/Slavic literature

pétrifiant, e / petʀifjɑ̃, jɑ̃t / **ADJ** *[spectacle]* petrifying; *[nouvelle]* horrifying

pétrification / petʀifikasjɔ̃ / **NF** 1 *(Géol)* petrifaction, petrification 2 *[d'idées]* fossilization

pétrifier / petʀifje / ► conjug 7 ◄ **VT** 1 *(Géol)* to petrify 2 *[+ personne]* to paralyze, to transfix; *[+ idées]* to fossilize, to ossify ◆ **être pétrifié de terreur** to be petrified **VPR** **se pétrifier** 1 *(Géol)* to petrify, to become petrified 2 *[sourire]* to freeze; *[personne]* to be petrified; *[idées]* to become fossilized *ou* ossified

pétrin / petʀɛ̃ / **NM** 1 (* = *ennui*) mess *, jam *, fix * ◆ **tirer qn du ~** to get sb out of a mess * *ou* fix * *ou* tight spot * ◆ **être dans le ~** to be in a mess * *ou* jam * *ou* fix * ◆ **laisser qn dans le ~** to leave sb in *ou* jam * *ou* fix * ◆ **être/se mettre dans un beau ~** to be in/get (o.s.) into a fine mess * *ou* a jam * 2 *(Boulangerie)* kneading trough; *(mécanique)* kneading machine

pétrir / petʀiʀ / ► conjug 2 ◄ **VT** *[+ pâte, argile, muscle, main]* to knead; *[+ personne, esprit]* to mould, to shape

pétrissage / petʀisaʒ / **NM** *[de pâte]* kneading

pétrochimie / petʀoʃimi / **NF** petrochemistry

pétrochimique / petʀoʃimik / **ADJ** petrochemical

pétrochimiste / petʀoʃimist / **NMF** petrochemist

pétrodollar / petʀodɔlaʀ / **NM** petrodollar

pétrographie / petʀɔgʀafi / **NF** petrography

pétrographique / petʀɔgʀafik / **ADJ** petrographic(al)

pétrole / petʀɔl / **NM** *(brut)* oil, petroleum ◆ **~ (lampant)** paraffin (oil) *(Brit)*, kerosene *(US)* ◆ **~ brut** crude (oil), petroleum ◆ **lampe/réchaud à ~** paraffin *(Brit)* *ou* kerosene *(US)* *ou* oil lamp/heater ◆ **le ~ vert** agricultural produce *ou* resources

> ⚠ Attention à ne pas traduire automatiquement **pétrole** par le mot anglais **petrol**, qui a le sens de 'essence'.

pétrolette † / petʀɔlɛt / **NF** moped

pétroleuse / petʀɔløz / **NF** *(Hist)* pétroleuse *(female fire-raiser during the Commune)*; *(fig)* agitator

pétrolier, -ière / petʀɔlje, jɛʀ / **ADJ** *[industrie, produits]* petroleum *(épith)*, oil *(épith)*; *[port, société]* oil *(épith)*; *[pays]* oil-producing *(épith)* **NM** (= *navire*) (oil) tanker; (= *personne, financier*) oil magnate, oilman; (= *technicien*) petroleum engineer

pétrolifère / petʀɔlifɛʀ / **ADJ** *[roches, couches]* oil-bearing ◆ **gisement ~** oilfield

pétromonarchie / petʀomɔnaʀʃi / **NF** oil kingdom, oil-rich nation ◆ **les ~s du Golfe** the oil-kingdoms of the Gulf

P. et T. / peete / **NFPL** (abrév de **Postes et Télécommunications**) → **poste²**

pétulance / petylɑ̃s / **NF** exuberance, vivacity

pétulant, e / petylɑ̃, ɑ̃t / **ADJ** exuberant, vivacious

> ⚠ **pétulant** ne se traduit pas par le mot anglais **petulant**, qui a le sens de 'irritable' ou 'irrité'.

pétunia / petynja / **NM** petunia

peu / pø /

1 ADVERBE	3 NOM MASCULIN
2 PRONOM INDÉFINI	

1 - ADVERBE

> Lorsque **peu** suit un autre mot dans une locution figée telle que **avant peu, sous peu, quelque peu, si peu que**, cherchez sous l'autre mot.

1 = pas beaucoup little, not much ◆ **il gagne/mange/lit ~** he doesn't earn/eat/read much ◆ **il s'intéresse ~ à la peinture** he isn't very *ou* greatly interested in painting, he takes little interest in painting ◆ **il se contente de ~** it doesn't take much to satisfy him ◆ **il a donné 10 €, c'est ~** he gave €10, which isn't (very) much; → **dire**

◆ *adverbe* + **peu** ◆ **il gagne/mange/lit assez ~** he doesn't earn/eat/read very much ◆ **il gagne/mange/lit très ~** he earns/eats/reads very little ◆ **il y a bien ~ à faire/à voir ici** there's very little *ou* precious little * to do/see here, there's not much at all to do/see here ◆ **il boit trop ~** he doesn't drink enough ◆ **je le connais bien trop ~ pour le juger** I don't know him (nearly) well enough to judge him

◆ **à peu près** about ◆ **il pèse à ~ près 50 kilos** he weighs about 50 kilos ◆ **il sait à ~ près tout ce qui se passe** he knows just about everything that goes on ◆ **à ~ près terminé/cuit** almost finished/cooked, more or less finished/cooked; → **à-peu-près**

◆ **de peu** ◆ **il est le plus âgé de ~** he's slightly *ou* a little older ◆ **il l'a battu de ~** he just beat him ◆ **il a manqué le train de ~** he just missed the train; → **falloir**

◆ **peu de** *(quantité)* little, not much ◆ **nous avons eu (très) ~ de soleil** we had (very) little sunshine, we didn't have (very) much sunshine ◆ **du pain, il m'en reste très ~, il me reste très ~ de pain** I haven't very much bread left ◆ **il est ici depuis ~ de temps** he hasn't been here long, he's been here (only) for a short while *ou* time ◆ **il est ici pour ~ de temps** he isn't here for long, he's here for (only) a short time *ou* while ◆ **cela a ~ d'importance** that's not important, that's of little importance ◆ **il suffit de ~ de chose pour le choquer** it doesn't take much to shock him ◆ **ne me remerciez pas, c'est ~ de chose** there's no need to thank me, it's nothing
(nombre) few, not (very) many ◆ **nous avons eu ~ d'orages** we had few storms, we didn't have many storms ◆ **on attendait beaucoup de touristes, mais il en est venu (très) ~** we were expecting a lot of tourists but not (very) many came *ou* but (very) few came ◆ **~ de monde** *ou* **de gens** few people, not many people ◆ **en ~ de mots** briefly, in a few words ◆ **~ de choses ont changé** not much has changed

◆ **peu ou prou** *(littér)* to a greater or lesser degree, more or less ◆ **ils pensent tous ~ ou prou la même chose** they are all more or less of one mind

◆ **pour peu que** + *subjonctif* if ◆ **pour ~ qu'il soit sorti sans sa clé ...** if he should have come out without his key ... ◆ **je saurai le convaincre, pour ~ qu'il veuille bien m'écouter** I'll be able to persuade him if *ou* as long as he's willing to listen to me

2 = pas très

◆ **peu** + *adjectif* (a) little, not very ◆ **il est ~ sociable** he's not very sociable, he's unsociable ◆ **c'est ~ probable** it's unlikely *ou* not very likely

◆ *adverbe* + **peu** + *adjectif* ◆ **il est très ~ sociable** he is not very sociable at all, he is very unsociable ◆ **ils sont (bien) trop ~ nombreux** there are (far) too few of them ◆ **fort ~ intéressant** decidedly uninteresting, of very little interest ◆ **un auteur assez ~ connu** a relatively little-known *ou* relatively unknown author ◆ **il n'est pas ~ fier d'avoir réussi** he's as pleased as Punch about his success ◆ **elle n'est pas ~ soulagée d'être reçue** she's more than a little relieved at passing her exam

3 = pas longtemps **il était tombé malade ~ avant** he had been taken ill shortly before(hand) ◆ **je l'ai rencontré ~ avant Noël/midi** I met him shortly *ou* just before Christmas/midday ◆ **elle est arrivée ~ après** she arrived shortly *ou* soon after(wards) ◆ **~ après 11 heures/son arrivée** shortly after 11 o'clock/his arrival

4 = rarement **ils se voient ~** they don't see much of each other, they don't see each other very often ◆ **elle sort ~** she doesn't go out much

5 locutions

◆ **peu à peu** gradually, little by little ◆ **~ à ~, l'idée a gagné du terrain** little by little *ou* gradually *ou* bit by bit the idea has gained ground

2 - PRONOM INDÉFINI

= personnes ou choses en petit nombre ♦ **ils sont ~ à croire que ...** few believe that ..., there are few people *ou* there aren't many people who believe that ... ♦ **bien ~/trop ~ le savent** very few/too few people know ♦ **~ d'entre eux sont restés** few (of them) stayed, not many (of them) stayed

3 - NOM MASCULIN

1 = petite quantité little ♦ **j'ai oublié le ~ (de français) que j'avais appris** I've forgotten the little (French) I'd learnt ♦ **elle se contente du ~ (d'argent) qu'elle a** she is satisfied with what little (money) *ou* the little (money) she has ♦ **son ~ de compréhension/patience lui a nui** his lack of understanding/patience hasn't helped him ♦ **elle s'est aliéné le ~ d'amis qu'elle avait** she alienated the few friends she had ♦ **le ~ de cheveux qu'il lui reste** what little hair he has left

♦ **un peu de** a little, a bit of ♦ **un ~ d'eau** a little water, a drop of water ♦ **un ~ de patience** a little patience, a bit of patience ♦ **un ~ de silence/de calme, s'il vous plaît !** can we have some quiet *ou* a bit of quiet/some peace *ou* a bit of peace please! ♦ **il a un ~ de sinusite/bronchite** he has a touch of sinusitis/bronchitis ♦ **tu refuses parce que tu as peur ? – il y a un ~ de ça*** you're refusing because you're afraid? – that's partly it

♦ *verbe* + **un peu** a little, slightly, a bit ♦ **essaie de manger un ~** try to eat a little *ou* a bit ♦ **il boite un ~** he limps slightly *ou* a little *ou* a bit, he is slightly *ou* a bit lame ♦ **il te ressemble un ~** he looks rather *ou* a bit like you ♦ **restez encore un ~** stay a little longer ♦ **tu en veux encore ? – un (petit) ~** would you like some more? – a little bit *ou* just a little ♦ **un ~, beaucoup, passionnément, à la folie, pas du tout** *(en effeuillant la marguerite)* he loves me, he loves me not ♦ **il t'agace ? – un ~ beaucoup, oui !*** is he annoying you? – you could say that!

♦ **un peu** + *adverbe* ♦ **elle va un tout petit ~ mieux** she's slightly *ou* a little better ♦ **il y a un ~ moins de bruit** it is slightly *ou* a little less noisy, there's slightly *ou* a little less noise ♦ **nous avons un ~ moins de clients aujourd'hui** we don't have quite so many customers today ♦ **on trouve ce produit un ~ partout** you can get this product just about anywhere ♦ **j'aimerais avoir un ~ plus d'argent/d'amis** I'd like to have a bit *ou* a little more money/a few more friends ♦ **il y a un ~ plus d'un an** a little more than *ou* just over a year ago ♦ **un ~ plus et il écrasait le chien/oubliait son rendez-vous** he very nearly ran over the dog/forgot his appointment ♦ **un ~ plus et j'étais parti** I'd very nearly left ♦ **il travaille un ~ trop/un ~ trop lentement** he works a bit too much/a little *ou* a bit too slowly

♦ **un peu** + *adjectif* ♦ **c'est un ~ grand/petit** it's a little *ou* a bit (too) big/small ♦ **elle était un ~ perturbée** she was a bit *ou* rather upset ♦ **il est un ~ artiste** he's a bit of an artist, he's something of an artist

♦ **pour un peu** ♦ **pour un ~, il m'aurait accusé d'avoir volé** he all but *ou* just about* accused me of stealing ♦ **pour un ~, je l'aurais giflé !** I could have slapped him!

2 intensif **montre-moi donc un ~ comment tu fais** just (you) show me how you do it then ♦ **je me demande un ~ où sont les enfants** I just wonder where the children are *ou* can be ♦ **c'est un ~ fort !** that's a bit much!* ♦ **un ~ !*** and how!* ♦ **tu as vraiment vu l'accident ? – un ~ (mon neveu) !*** did you really see the accident? – you bet!* *ou* and how!* *ou* I sure did!* *(US)* ♦ **un ~, qu'il nous a menti !*** I'll say he lied to us!* ♦ **il nous a menti, et pas qu'un ~ !*** he lied to us bigtime!* ♦ **comme menteur/comique il est un ~ là !*** as liars/comedians go, he must be hard to beat!*; → **poser**

peuchère /pøʃɛʀ/ **EXCL** *(dial Midi)* well! well!

peuh /pø/ **EXCL** pooh!, bah!, phooey* *(US)*

peu(h)l, e /pøl/ **ADJ** Fulani **NM** *(= langue)* Fula(h), Fulani **NM,F** **Peu(h)l(e)** Fula(h), Fulani

peuplade /pœplad/ **NF** (small) tribe, people

peuple /pœpl/ **NM** 1 *(Pol = communauté)* people, nation ♦ **les ~s d'Europe** the peoples *ou* nations of Europe ♦ **le ~ élu** *(Rel)* the chosen people 2 *(= prolétariat)* **le ~** the people ♦ **les gens du ~** the common people, ordinary people ♦ **homme du ~** man of the people ♦ **le bas** *ou* **petit ~** †† *(péj)* the lower classes *(péj)* ♦ **faire ~** *(péj)* *(= ne pas être distingué)* to be common *(péj)*; *(= vouloir paraître simple)* to try to appear working-class ♦ **que demande le ~ !** *(hum)* what more could anyone want! ♦ **trois heures pour faire ça, il se moque** *ou* **se fiche du ~** 3 hours to do that, he must be joking! 3 *(= foule)* crowd (of people) ♦ **un ~ de badauds/d'admirateurs** *(littér)* a crowd of onlookers/of admirers ♦ **il y a du ~ !*** there's a big crowd!

peuplé, e /pœple/ (ptp de **peupler**) **ADJ** *[ville, région]* populated, inhabited ♦ **très/peu ~** densely/sparsely populated

peuplement /pœpləmɑ̃/ **NM** 1 *(= action)* *[de colonie]* populating; *[d'étang]* stocking; *[de forêt]* planting *(with trees)* 2 *(= population)* population

peupler /pœple/ ► conjug 1 ◄ **VT** 1 *(= pourvoir d'une population)* *[+ colonie]* to populate; *[+ étang]* to stock; *[+ forêt]* to plant out, to plant with trees; *(littér)* to fill (*de* with); ♦ **les rêves/souvenirs qui peuplent mon esprit** the dreams/memories that fill my mind ♦ **les cauchemars/monstres qui peuplent ses nuits** the nightmares/monsters which haunt his nights 2 *(= habiter)* *[+ terre]* to inhabit, to populate; *[+ maison]* to live in, to inhabit ♦ **maison peuplée de souvenirs** house filled with *ou* full of memories **VPR** **se peupler** *[ville, région]* to become populated; *(= s'animer)* to fill (up), to be filled (*de* with); ♦ **la rue se peuplait de cris** the street filled with cries

peupleraie /pøplʀɛ/ **NF** poplar grove

peuplier /pøplije/ **NM** poplar (tree)

peur /pœʀ/ **NF** fear ♦ **inspirer de la ~** to cause *ou* inspire fear ♦ **prendre ~** to take fright ♦ **la ~ lui donnait des ailes** fear lent him wings ♦ **être vert** *ou* **mort de ~** to be frightened *ou* scared out of one's wits, to be petrified (with fear) ♦ **la ~ de la punition/de mourir/du qu'en-dira-t-on** (the) fear of punishment/of death *ou* dying/of what people might say ♦ **la ~ de gagner** the fear of winning ♦ **la ~ du gendarme*** the fear of being caught ♦ **il y a eu plus de ~ que de mal** it was more frightening than anything else ♦ **être sans ~** to be fearless (*de* of); ♦ **faire qch sans ~** to do sth fearlessly

♦ **avoir** + **peur** ♦ **avoir ~** to be frightened *ou* afraid *ou* scared (*de* of); ♦ **avoir ~ pour qn** to be afraid for sb *ou* on sb's behalf, to fear for sb ♦ **avoir grand ~ que ...** to be very much afraid that ... ♦ **n'ayez pas ~** *(craindre)* don't be afraid *ou* frightened *ou* scared; *(s'inquiéter)* don't worry ♦ **il sera puni, n'aie pas ~ !** he will be punished – don't worry! ♦ **il veut faire ce voyage en deux jours, il n'a pas ~, lui au moins !*** he wants to do the trip in two days – well, he's a braver man than I! ♦ **il prétend qu'il a téléphoné, il n'a pas ~, lui au moins !*** he says he phoned – he's got a nerve! ♦ **n'ayez pas ~ de dire la vérité** don't be afraid *ou* scared to tell *ou* of telling the truth ♦ **il n'a ~ de rien** he's afraid of nothing, he's not afraid of anything ♦ **avoir ~ d'un rien** to frighten easily ♦ **avoir ~ de son ombre** to be frightened *ou* scared of one's own shadow ♦ **je n'ai pas ~ des mots** I'm not afraid of using plain language ♦ **j'ai bien ~/très ~ qu'il ne pleuve** I'm afraid/very much afraid it's going to rain *ou* it might rain ♦ **il va échouer ? – j'en ai (bien) ~** is he going to fail? – I'm (very much) afraid so *ou* I'm afraid he is ♦ **j'ai ~ qu'il ne vous ait menti/que cela ne vous gêne** I'm afraid *ou* worried *ou* I fear that he might have lied to you/that it might inconvenience you ♦ **je n'ai pas ~ qu'il dise la vérité** I'm not afraid *ou* frightened he'll tell the truth ♦ **il a eu plus de ~ que de mal** he was more frightened than hurt, he wasn't hurt so much as frightened ♦ **je n'ai qu'une ~, c'est qu'il ne revienne pas** my only fear is that he won't come back, I have only one fear, that he won't come back ♦ **il a eu une ~ bleue** he had a bad fright *ou* scare ♦ **il a une ~ bleue de sa femme** he's scared stiff* of his wife

♦ **faire** + **peur** ♦ **faire ~ à qn** *(= intimider)* to frighten *ou* scare sb; *(= causer une frayeur à)* to give sb a fright, to frighten *ou* scare sb ♦ **pour faire ~ aux oiseaux** to frighten *ou* scare the birds away *ou* off ♦ **l'idée de l'examen lui fait ~** the idea of sitting the exam frightens *ou* scares him, he's frightened *ou* scared at the idea of sitting the exam ♦ **cette pensée fait ~** it's a frightening *ou* scary* thought ♦ **il m'a fait une de ces ~s !** he gave me a horrible fright! *ou* scare!, he didn't half* give me a fright! *ou* scare! *(Brit)* ♦ **tout lui fait ~** he's afraid *ou* frightened *ou* scared of everything ♦ **le travail ne lui fait pas ~** he's not afraid of hard work ♦ **laid** *ou* **hideux à faire ~** frighteningly ugly ♦ **il est compétent, ça fait ~ !*** *(iro)* he's so efficient it's frightening! ♦ **il joue à se faire ~** he gets a kick out of being scared*

♦ **de peur de/que** for fear of ♦ **il a couru de ~ de manquer le train** he ran because he was afraid he might miss the train *ou* so as not to miss the train ♦ **il a accepté de ~ de les vexer** he accepted for fear of annoying them *ou* lest he (should) annoy them ♦ **il renonça, de ~ du ridicule** he gave up for fear of ridicule ♦ **j'ai fermé la porte, de ~ qu'elle ne prenne froid** I closed the door so that she didn't catch cold *ou* lest she (should) catch cold

peureusement /pøʀøzmɑ̃/ **ADV** fearfully, timorously *(frm)*

peureux, -euse /pøʀø, øz/ **ADJ** fearful, timorous *(frm)* **NM,F** fearful *ou* timorous *(frm)* person

peut-être /pøtɛtʀ/ **GRAMMAIRE ACTIVE 28.1, 42.3, 53.6** **ADV** perhaps, maybe ♦ **il est ~ intelligent, ~ est-il intelligent** perhaps *ou* maybe he's clever, he may *ou* might (well) be clever ♦ **il n'est ~ pas beau mais il est intelligent** he may *ou* might not be handsome but he is clever, maybe *ou* perhaps he's not handsome but he is clever ♦ **~ bien** perhaps (so), it could well be ♦ **~ pas** perhaps *ou* maybe not ♦ **~ bien mais ...** that's as may be but ..., perhaps so but ... ♦ **~ que ...** perhaps ... ♦ **~ bien qu'il pleuvra** it may well rain ♦ **~ que oui** perhaps so, perhaps he will (*ou* they are *etc*) ♦ **tu vas y aller ? – ~ bien que oui, ~ bien que non** will you go? – maybe, maybe not *ou* maybe I will, maybe I won't ♦ **je ne sais pas conduire ~ ?** who's (doing the) driving? *(iro)*, I do know how to drive, you know! ♦ **tu le sais mieux que moi ~ ?** so (you think) you know more about it than I do, do you?, I do know more about it than you, you know!

p.ex. (abrév de **par exemple**) e.g.

pèze* /pɛz/ **NM** *(= argent)* dough*, bread*

pff(t) /pf(t)/, **pfut** /pfyt/ **EXCL** pooh!, bah!

pH /peaʃ/ **NM** (abrév de **potentiel d'hydrogène**) pH

phacochère /fakɔʃɛʀ/ **NM** wart hog

Phaéton /faetɔ̃/ **NM** *(Myth)* Phaëthon

phaéton /faetɔ̃/ NM (= *calèche*) phaeton; (= *oiseau*) tropicbird

phagocyte /fagɔsit/ NM phagocyte

phagocyter /fagɔsite/ ▸ conjug 1 ◂ VT (*Bio*) to phagocytose; (*fig*) to absorb, to engulf

phagocytose /fagɔsitoz/ NF phagocytosis

phalange /falɑ̃ʒ/ NF (*Anat*) phalanx; (*Antiq, littér* = *armée*) phalanx ◆ **la ~** (*Pol : espagnole*) the Falange

phalangien, -ienne /falɑ̃ʒjɛ̃, jɛn/ ADJ (*Anat*) phalangeal

phalangiste /falɑ̃ʒist/ ADJ, NMF Falangist

phalanstère /falɑ̃stɛʀ/ NM phalanstery

phalène /falɛn/ NF *ou* m emerald, geometrid (*SPÉC*)

phallique /falik/ ADJ phallic

phallocrate /falɔkʀat/ ADJ chauvinist NM (male) chauvinist

phallocratie /falɔkʀasi/ NF male chauvinism

phallocratique /falɔkʀatik/ ADJ (male) chauvinist

phalloïde /falɔid/ ADJ phalloid; → **amanite**

phallus /falys/ NM (= *verge*) phallus; (= *champignon*) stinkhorn

phantasme /fɑ̃tasm/ NM ⇒ **fantasme**

pharamineux, -euse /faʀaminø, øz/ ADJ ⇒ **faramineux**

pharaon /faʀaɔ̃/ NM Pharaoh

pharaonien, -ienne /faʀaɔnjɛ̃, jɛn/, **pharaonique** /faʀaɔnik/ ADJ Pharaonic

phare /faʀ/ NM 1 (= *tour*) lighthouse; (*pour avions*) beacon ◆ **~ à feu fixe/tournant** fixed/revolving light *ou* beacon 2 [*de voiture*] headlight, headlamp ◆ **~ antibrouillard** fog lamp ◆ **~s longue portée** high intensity headlamps ◆ **~ à iode** quartz halogen lamp ◆ **rouler pleins ~s** *ou* **en ~s** to drive with one's headlights full on *ou* on full beam (*Brit*) *ou* with high beams on (*US*); → **appel, code** ADJ INV [*entreprise, produit, secteur, pays, titre boursier*] leading ◆ **l'émission ~ de notre chaîne** our channel's flagship programme ◆ **c'est un film ~** it's a seminal *ou* highly influential film ◆ **personnalité ~** leading light ◆ **c'est l'épreuve ~ de cette compétition** it's the main event *ou* it's the highlight of the competition

pharisaïque /faʀizaik/ ADJ (*Hist*) Pharisaic; (*fig*) pharisaic(al)

pharisaïsme /faʀizaism/ NM (*Hist*) Pharisaism, Phariseeism; (*fig*) pharisaism, phariseeism

pharisien, -ienne /faʀizjɛ̃, jɛn/ NM,F (*Hist*) Pharisee; (*fig*) pharisee

pharmaceutique /faʀmasøtik/ ADJ pharmaceutical, pharmaceutic

pharmacie /faʀmasi/ NF 1 (= *magasin*) pharmacy, chemist's (shop) (*Brit*), drugstore (*Can, US*); (= *officine*) dispensary; [*d'hôpital*] dispensary, pharmacy ◆ **ce produit est vendu en ~** this product is available in pharmacies *ou* from chemists (*Brit*) 2 (= *science*) pharmacy ◆ **laboratoire de ~** pharmaceutical laboratory 3 (= *produits*) medicines ◆ **(armoire à) ~** medicine chest *ou* cabinet *ou* cupboard

pharmacien, -ienne /faʀmasjɛ̃, jɛn/ NM,F (= *qui tient une pharmacie*) pharmacist, (dispensing) chemist (*Brit*), druggist (*US*); (= *préparateur*) pharmacist, chemist (*Brit*)

pharmacodépendance /faʀmakodepɑ̃dɑ̃s/ NF drug dependency

pharmacologie /faʀmakɔlɔʒi/ NF pharmacology

pharmacologique /faʀmakɔlɔʒik/ ADJ pharmacological

pharmacopée /faʀmakɔpe/ NF pharmacopoeia

pharyngal, e (mpl **-aux**) /faʀɛ̃gal, o/ ADJ pharyngeal NF **pharyngale** (*Ling*) pharyngeal

pharyngé, e /faʀɛ̃ʒe/, **pharyngien, -ienne** /faʀɛ̃ʒjɛ̃, jɛn/ ADJ pharyngeal, pharyngal

pharyngite /faʀɛ̃ʒit/ NF pharyngitis (*NonC*) ◆ **il a fait trois ~s** he had three bouts of pharyngitis

pharynx /faʀɛ̃ks/ NM pharynx

phase /fɑz/ NF (*gén, Méd*) phase, stage; (*Astron, Chim, Phys*) phase ◆ **la ~** (*Élec*) the live wire ◆ **~ de jeu** (*Sport*) passage of play ◆ **~ terminale** (*Méd*) terminal stage *ou* phase ◆ **l'économie a connu une longue ~ de croissance** the economy went through a long period of growth ◆ **être en ~** (*Phys*) to be in phase; [*personnes*] to be on the same wavelength; [*projets*] to be in line (*avec* with)

Phébus /febys/ NM Phoebus

Phèdre /fɛdʀ/ NF Phaedra

Phénicie /fenisi/ NF Phoenicia

phénicien, -ienne /fenisjɛ̃, jɛn/ ADJ Phoenician NM (= *langue*) Phoenician NM,F **Phénicien(ne)** Phoenician

phénix /feniks/ NM 1 (*Myth*) phoenix 2 († : *littér*) **ce n'est pas un ~*** he (*ou* she) is no genius 3 (= *plante*) ⇒ **phœnix**

phénobarbital (pl **phénobarbitals**) /fenɔbaʀbital/ NM phenobarbitone

phénol /fenɔl/ NM carbolic acid, phenol

phénoménal, e (mpl **-aux**) /fenɔmenal, o/ ADJ phenomenal

phénoménalement /fenɔmenalmɑ̃/ ADV phenomenally

phénomène /fenɔmɛn/ NM 1 (*gén, Philos*) phenomenon ◆ **~s** phenomena ◆ **~ de société/de mode** social/fashion phenomenon ◆ **les ~s de violence dans les écoles** incidents of violence *ou* violent incidents in schools 2 (= *monstre de foire*) freak (of nature); (* = *personne*) (*génial*) phenomenon; (*excentrique*) character*; (*anormal*) freak* ◆ **son petit dernier est un sacré ~ !** his youngest is a real devil!*

phénoménologie /fenɔmenɔlɔʒi/ NF phenomenology

phénoménologique /fenɔmenɔlɔʒik/ ADJ phenomenological

phénoménologue /fenɔmenɔlɔg/ NMF phenomenologist

phénotype /fenɔtip/ NM phenotype

phéromone /feʀɔmɔn/ NF pheromone

phi /fi/ NM phi

Philadelphie /filadɛlfi/ N Philadelphia

philanthrope /filɑ̃tʀɔp/ NMF philanthropist

philanthropie /filɑ̃tʀɔpi/ NF philanthropy

philanthropique /filɑ̃tʀɔpik/ ADJ philanthropic(al)

philatélie /filateli/ NF philately, stamp collecting

philatélique /filatelik/ ADJ philatelic

philatéliste /filatelist/ NMF philatelist, stamp collector

philharmonie /filaʀmɔni/ NF philharmonic society

philharmonique /filaʀmɔnik/ ADJ philharmonic

philhellène /filelɛn/ ADJ philhellenic NMF philhellene, philhellenist

philhellénique /filelenik/ ADJ philhellenic

philhellénisme /filelenism/ NM philhellenism

philippin, e /filipɛ̃, in/ ADJ Philippine NM,F **Philippin(e)** Filipino

Philippines /filipin/ NFPL ◆ **les ~** the Philippines

philippique /filipik/ NF (*littér*) diatribe, philippic (*littér*)

philistin /filistɛ̃/ ADJ M, NM (*Hist*) Philistine; (*fig*) philistine

philistinisme /filistinism/ NM philistinism

philo* /filo/ NF abrév de **philosophie**

philodendron /filɔdɛ̃dʀɔ̃/ NM philodendron

philologie /filɔlɔʒi/ NF philology

philologique /filɔlɔʒik/ ADJ philological

philologiquement /filɔlɔʒikmɑ̃/ ADV philologically

philologue /filɔlɔg/ NMF philologist

philosophale /filɔzɔfal/ ADJ F → **pierre**

philosophe /filɔzɔf/ NMF philosopher ADJ philosophical

philosopher /filɔzɔfe/ ▸ conjug 1 ◂ VI to philosophize (*sur* about)

philosophie /filɔzɔfi/ NF philosophy ◆ **il l'a accepté avec ~** he was philosophical about it ◆ **c'est ma ~ (de la vie)** it's my philosophy (of life)

philosophique /filɔzɔfik/ ADJ philosophical

philosophiquement /filɔzɔfikmɑ̃/ ADV philosophically

philtre /filtʀ/ NM philtre ◆ **~ d'amour** love potion

phishing /fiʃiŋ/ NM phishing

phlébite /flebit/ NF phlebitis

phlébologie /flebɔlɔʒi/ NF phlebology

phlébologue /flebɔlɔg/ NMF vein specialist

phlébotomie /flebɔtɔmi/ NF phlebotomy

phlegmon /flɛgmɔ̃/ NM abscess, phlegmon (*SPÉC*)

phlox /flɔks/ NM INV phlox

Phnom Penh /pnɔmpɛn/ N Phnom Penh

phobie /fɔbi/ NF phobia ◆ **avoir la ~ de** to have a phobia about

phobique /fɔbik/ ADJ, NMF phobic

phocéen, -enne /fɔseɛ̃, ɛn/ ADJ Phocaean ◆ **la cité phocéenne** Marseilles NM,F **Phocéen(ne)** Phocaean

phœnix /feniks/ NM (= *plante*) phoenix

phonateur, -trice /fɔnatœʀ, tʀis/ ADJ phonatory

phonation /fɔnasjɔ̃/ NF phonation

phonatoire /fɔnatwaʀ/ ADJ ⇒ **phonateur**

phone /fɔn/ NM phon

phonématique /fɔnematik/ NF phonology, phonemics (*sg*)

phonème /fɔnɛm/ NM phoneme

phonémique /fɔnemik/ ADJ phonemic NF ⇒ **phonématique**

phonéticien, -ienne /fɔnetisjɛ̃, jɛn/ NM,F phonetician

phonétique /fɔnetik/ NF phonetics (*sg*) ◆ **~ articulatoire/acoustique/auditoire** articulatory/acoustic/auditory phonetics ADJ phonetic ◆ **loi/système ~** phonetic law/system

phonétiquement /fɔnetikmɑ̃/ ADV phonetically

phoniatre /fɔnjatʀ/ NMF speech therapist

phoniatrie /fɔnjatʀi/ NF speech therapy

phonie /fɔni/ NF (*Téléc*) radiotelegraphy, wireless telegraphy (*Brit*)

phonique /fɔnik/ ADJ phonic

phono /fono/ NM abrév de **phonographe**

phonogramme /fɔnɔgʀam/ NM (= *signe*) phonogram

phonographe /fɔnɔgʀaf/ NM (*à rouleau*) phonograph; (*à disque*) (wind-up) gramophone, phonograph (US); (= *électrophone*) record player, phonograph (US)

phonographique /fɔnɔgʀafik/ ADJ phonographic

phonologie /fɔnɔlɔʒi/ NF phonology

phonologique /fɔnɔlɔʒik/ ADJ phonological

phonologue /fɔnɔlɔg/ NMF phonologist

phonothèque /fɔnɔtɛk/ NF sound archives

phoque /fɔk/ NM (= *animal*) seal; (= *fourrure*) sealskin; → **souffler**

phosphatage /fɔsfataʒ/ NM treating with phosphates

phosphate /fɔsfat/ NM phosphate

phosphaté, e /fɔsfate/ (ptp de **phosphater**) ADJ phosphatic, phosphated ◆ **engrais ~s** phosphate-enriched fertilizers

phosphater /fɔsfate/ ► conjug 1 ◄ VT to phosphatize, to phosphate, to treat with phosphates

phosphène /fɔsfɛn/ NM phosphene

phosphine /fɔsfin/ NF phosphine

phosphore /fɔsfɔʀ/ NM phosphorus

phosphoré, e /fɔsfɔʀe/ ADJ phosphorous

phosphorer * /fɔsfɔʀe/ ► conjug 1 ◄ VI to think hard

phosphorescence /fɔsfɔʀesɑ̃s/ NF luminosity, phosphorescence (*SPÉC*)

phosphorescent, e /fɔsfɔʀesɑ̃, ɑ̃t/ ADJ luminous, phosphorescent (*SPÉC*)

phosphoreux, -euse /fɔsfɔʀø, øz/ ADJ [*acide*] phosphorous; [*bronze*] phosphor (*épith*)

phosphorique /fɔsfɔʀik/ ADJ phosphoric

phosphure /fɔsfyʀ/ NM phosphide

phot /fɔt/ NM (*Phys*) phot

photo /fɔto/ NF (abrév de **photographie**) 1 (= *image*) photo, picture; (*instantané, d'amateur*) snap(shot); [*de film*] still ◆ **faire une ~ de, prendre en ~** to take a photo *ou* picture of ◆ **ça rend bien en ~** it looks good in a photo ◆ **j'ai mon fils en ~** I've got a photo *ou* picture of my son ◆ **elle est bien en ~** she takes a good photo, she's photogenic ◆ **qui est sur cette ~ ?** who is in this photo? *ou* picture? ◆ **~ de famille** (*gén*) family photo; (= *portrait*) family portrait; [*de collègues etc*] group photo ◆ **~ d'identité** passport photo ◆ **~ de mode** fashion photo *ou* shot ◆ **~s de vacances** holiday (*Brit*) *ou* vacation (*US*) photos *ou* snaps ◆ **tu veux ma ~ ?** * what are you staring at? ◆ **il n'y a pas ~** * there's no question about it ◆ **entre les deux candidats il n'y a pas ~** there's no competition between the two candidates; → **appareil**
2 (= *art*) photography ◆ **faire de la ~** (*en amateur*) to be an amateur photographer; (*en professionnel*) to be a (professional) photographer ◆ **je fais de la ~ à mes heures perdues** I take photo(graph)s in my spare time, I do photography in my spare time

photochimie /fɔtoʃimi/ NF photochemistry

photochimique /fɔtoʃimik/ ADJ photochemical

photocomposer /fɔtokɔ̃poze/ ► conjug 1 ◄ VT to photocompose, to filmset

photocomposeur /fɔtokɔ̃pozœʀ/ NM ⇒ **photocompositeur**

photocomposeuse /fɔtokɔ̃pozøz/ NF (= *machine*) photocomposer, filmsetter

photocompositeur /fɔtokɔ̃pozitœʀ/ NM (photo)typesetter

photocomposition /fɔtokɔ̃pozisjɔ̃/ NF filmsetting (*Brit*), photocomposition (*US*)

photoconducteur, -trice /fɔtokɔ̃dyktœʀ, tʀis/ ADJ photoconductive

photocopie /fɔtɔkɔpi/ NF (= *action*) photocopying; (= *copie*) photocopy

photocopier /fɔtɔkɔpje/ ► conjug 7 ◄ VT to photocopy ◆ **~ qch en trois exemplaires** to make three photocopies of sth

photocopieur /fɔtɔkɔpjœʀ/ NM, **photocopieuse** /fɔtɔkɔpjøz/ NF photocopier

photocopillage /fɔtɔkɔpijaʒ/ NM *illegal photocopying of copyright material*

photodissociation /fɔtodisɔsjasjɔ̃/ NF photodisintegration

photoélasticimétrie /fɔtoelastisimetʀi/ NF photoelasticity

photoélectricité /fɔtoelɛktʀisite/ NF photoelectricity

photoélectrique /fɔtoelɛktʀik/ ADJ photoelectric ◆ **cellule ~** photoelectric cell, photocell

photo-finish (pl **photos-finish**) /fɔtofiniʃ/ NM ◆ **l'arrivée de la deuxième course a dû être contrôlée au ~** the second race was a photo finish

photogénique /fɔtɔʒenik/ ADJ photogenic

photographe /fɔtɔgʀaf/ NMF (= *artiste*) photographer; (= *commerçant*) camera dealer ◆ **~ de mode/de presse** fashion/press photographer ◆ **vous trouverez cet article chez un ~** you will find this item at a camera shop *ou* store (*US*)

photographie /fɔtɔgʀafi/ NF 1 (= *art*) photography ◆ **faire de la ~** (*comme passe-temps*) to be an amateur photographer, to take photographs; (*en professionnel*) to be a (professional) photographer 2 (= *image*) photograph, picture ◆ **ce sondage est une ~ de l'opinion publique** this survey is a snapshot of public opinion; *pour autres loc voir* **photo**

photographier /fɔtɔgʀafje/ ► conjug 7 ◄ VT to photograph, to take a photo(graph) of, to take a picture of ◆ **se faire ~** to have one's photo(graph) *ou* picture taken ◆ **il avait photographié l'endroit** (= *mémoriser*) he had got the place firmly fixed in his mind *ou* in his mind's eye

photographique /fɔtɔgʀafik/ ADJ photographic; → **appareil**

photograveur /fɔtogʀavœʀ/ NM photoengraver

photogravure /fɔtɔgʀavyʀ/ NF photoengraving

photojournalisme /fɔtoʒuʀnalism/ NM photojournalism

photojournaliste /fɔtoʒuʀnalist/ NMF photojournalist

photolithographie /fɔtolitɔgʀafi/ NF photolithography

photoluminescence /fɔtolyminesɑ̃s/ NF photoluminescence

photolyse /fɔtɔliz/ NF photolysis

Photomaton ® /fɔtɔmatɔ̃/ NM automatic photo booth NF (photo booth) photo ◆ **se faire faire des ~s** to get one's pictures taken (in a photo booth)

photomètre /fɔtɔmɛtʀ/ NM photometer

photométrie /fɔtɔmetʀi/ NF photometry

photométrique /fɔtɔmetʀik/ ADJ photometric(al)

photomontage /fɔtɔmɔ̃taʒ/ NM photomontage

photomultiplicateur /fɔtomyltiplikatœʀ/ NM photomultiplier

photon /fɔtɔ̃/ NM photon

photopériode /fɔtopeʀjɔd/ NF photoperiod

photopériodisme /fɔtopeʀjɔdism/ NM photoperiodism

photophobie /fɔtɔfɔbi/ NF photophobia

photophore /fɔtɔfɔʀ/ NM [*de mineur*] (miner's) cap lamp; (*Anat*) photophore; (= *objet décoratif*) tealight holder

photopile /fɔtopil/ NF solar cell

photoréalisme /fɔtoʀealizm/ NM photorealism

photoreportage /fɔtoʀəpɔʀtaʒ/ NM photo story

photoroman /fɔtoʀɔmɑ̃/ NM photo story

photosensibilisant, e /fɔtosɑ̃sibilizɑ̃, ɑt/ ADJ [*médicament*] photosensitive

photosensible /fɔtosɑ̃sibl/ ADJ photosensitive ◆ **dispositif ~** photosensor

photosphère /fɔtɔsfɛʀ/ NF (*Astron*) photosphere

photostat /fɔtɔsta/ NM photostat

photostoppeur, -euse /fɔtɔstɔpœʀ, øz/ NM,F street photographer

photostyle /fɔtɔstil/ NM light pen

photosynthèse /fɔtosɛ̃tɛz/ NF photosynthesis

photothèque /fɔtɔtɛk/ NF photographic library, picture library

phrase /fʀɑz/ NF 1 (*Ling*) sentence; (= *propos*) words ◆ **faire des ~s** [*enfant*] to make sentences; (*péj*) to talk in flowery language ◆ **assez de grandes ~s !** enough of the rhetoric *ou* fine words! ◆ **il termina son discours sur cette ~** he closed his speech with these words ◆ **~ toute faite** stock phrase ◆ **citer une ~ célèbre** to quote a famous phrase *ou* saying ◆ **petite ~** (*Pol*) soundbite; → **membre** 2 (*Mus*) phrase

phrasé /fʀɑze/ NM (*Mus*) phrasing

phraséologie /fʀazeɔlɔʒi/ NF (*gén*) phraseology ◆ **la ~ marxiste/capitaliste** (*péj*) Marxist/capitalist jargon

phraser /fʀɑze/ ► conjug 1 ◄ VT (*Mus*) to phrase VI (*péj*) to use fine words (*péj*) *ou* high-flown language (*péj*)

phraseur, -euse /fʀɑzœʀ, øz/ NM,F man (*ou* woman) of fine words (*péj*)

phrastique /fʀastik/ ADJ phrasal

phréatique /fʀeatik/ ADJ → **nappe**

phrénique /fʀenik/ ADJ phrenic

phrénologie /fʀenɔlɔʒi/ NF phrenology

phrénologue /fʀenɔlɔg/, **phrénologiste** /fʀenɔlɔʒist/ NMF phrenologist

Phrygie /fʀiʒi/ NF Phrygia

phrygien, -ienne /fʀiʒjɛ̃, jɛn/ ADJ Phrygian; → **bonnet** NM,F **Phrygien(ne)** Phrygian

phtaléine /ftalein/ NF phthalein

phtisie /ftizi/ NF consumption, phthisis (*SPÉC*) ◆ **~ galopante** galloping consumption

phtisiologie /ftizjɔlɔʒi/ NF phthisiology

phtisiologue /ftizjɔlɔg/ NMF phthisiologist

phtisique /ftizik/ ADJ consumptive, phthisical (*SPÉC*)

phycologie /fikɔlɔʒi/ NF phycology

phylactère /filaktɛʀ/ NM phylactery

phylloxéra /filɔkseʀa/ NM phylloxera

phylogenèse /filoʒənɛz/ NF phylogenesis

phylogénétique /filɔʒenetik/ ADJ phylogenetic, phyletic

physicien, -ienne /fizisjɛ̃, jɛn/ NM,F physicist ◆ ~ **atomiste** *ou* **nucléaire** atomic *ou* nuclear physicist

> ⚠ **physicien** ne se traduit pas par le mot anglais **physician**, qui a le sens de 'médecin'.

physicochimie /fizikoʃimi/ NF physical chemistry

physicochimique /fizikoʃimik/ ADJ physicochemical

physicomathématique /fizikomatematik/ ADJ of mathematical physics

physiocrate /fizjɔkʀat/ NMF physiocrat ADJ physiocratic

physiocratie /fizjɔkʀasi/ NF physiocracy

physiologie /fizjɔlɔʒi/ NF physiology

physiologique /fizjɔlɔʒik/ ADJ physiological

physiologiquement /fizjɔlɔʒikmɑ̃/ ADV physiologically

physiologiste /fizjɔlɔʒist/ NMF physiologist ADJ physiological

physionomie /fizjɔnɔmi/ NF (= *traits du visage*) facial appearance (*NonC*), physiognomy (*frm*); (= *expression*) countenance (*frm*), face; (= *aspect*) appearance ◆ **en fonction de la ~ du marché** (*Bourse*) depending on how the market looks ◆ **la ~ de l'Europe a changé** the face of Europe has changed

physionomiste /fizjɔnɔmist/ ADJ ◆ **il est (très)** ~ he has a (very) good memory for faces

physiopathologie /fizjopatɔlɔʒi/ NF physiopathology

physiothérapeute /fizjoteʀapøt/ NMF *person practising natural medicine*

physiothérapie /fizjoteʀapi/ NF natural medicine

physique /fizik/ ADJ 1 (*gén*) physical ◆ **je ne peux pas le supporter, c'est** ~ I can't stand him, the very sight of him makes me sick; → **amour, culture, personne** *etc* 2 (= *athlétique*) [*joueur, match, jeu*] physical NM (= *aspect*) physical appearance; (= *stature, corps*) physique ◆ **elle sait se servir de son** ~ she knows how to use her looks ◆ **avoir un ~ agréable** to be good-looking ◆ **avoir le ~ de l'emploi** to look the part ◆ **au** ~ physically ◆ **il a un ~ de jeune premier** he looks really cute, he has the looks of a film star NF physics (*sg*) ◆ ~ **nucléaire/des particules** nuclear/particle physics

physiquement /fizikmɑ̃/ ADV physically ◆ **il est plutôt bien** ~ physically he's quite attractive

phytobiologie /fitobjɔlɔʒi/ NF phytology

phytogéographie /fitoʒeɔgʀafi/ NF phytogeography

phytopathologie /fitopatɔlɔʒi/ NF phytopathology

phytoplancton /fitoplɑ̃ktɔ̃/ NM phytoplankton

phytosanitaire /fitosanitɛʀ/ ADJ ◆ **produit** ~ (*de soins*) plant-care product; (= *pesticide*) pesticide; (= *herbicide*) weedkiller ◆ **contrôles ~s** phytosanitary regulations

phytothérapeute /fitoteʀapøt/ NMF (medical) herbalist, phytotherapist (*SPÉC*)

phytothérapie /fitoteʀapi/ NF herbal medicine

pi /pi/ NM (= *lettre, Math*) pi

p.i. (abrév de **par intérim**) acting, actg

piaf * /pjaf/ NM sparrow

piaffement /pjafmɑ̃/ NM [*de cheval*] stamping, pawing

piaffer /pjafe/ ▸ conjug 1 ◂ VI [*cheval*] to stamp, to paw the ground ◆ ~ **d'impatience** [*personne*] to be champing at the bit

piaillement * /pjɑjmɑ̃/ NM [*d'oiseau*] cheeping (*NonC*), peeping (*NonC*) ◆ **~s** (*péj*) [*d'enfant*] whining (*NonC*)

piailler * /pjɑje/ ▸ conjug 1 ◂ VI [*oiseau*] to cheep, to peep; [*enfant*] to whine

piaillerie * /pjɑjʀi/ NF ⇒ **piaillement**

piailleur, -euse * /pjɑjœʀ, øz/ ADJ [*oiseau*] cheeping, peeping; [*enfant*] whining NM,F whiner

piane-piane * /pjanpjan/ ADV gently ◆ **allez-y** ~ go gently *ou* easy*, easy *ou* gently does it* ◆ **le projet avance** ~ the project is coming along slowly but surely

pianissimo /pjanisimo/ ADV (*Mus*) pianissimo; (* *fig*) very gently NM (*Mus*) pianissimo

pianiste /pjanist/ NMF pianist, piano player

pianistique /pjanistik/ ADJ pianistic

piano[1] /pjano/ NM piano ◆ ~ **acoustique/électronique** acoustic/electric piano ◆ ~ **de concert/crapaud** concert grand/boudoir grand (piano) ◆ ~ **droit/à queue** upright/grand piano ◆ ~ **demi-queue/quart de queue** baby grand/miniature grand (piano) ◆ ~ **mécanique** player piano, piano organ, Pianola ® ◆ ~ **préparé** prepared piano ◆ ~ **à bretelles** (*hum*) accordion ◆ **faire** *ou* **jouer du** ~ to play the piano ◆ **se mettre au** ~ (= *apprendre*) to take up *ou* start the piano; (= *s'asseoir*) to sit down at the piano ◆ **accompagné au ~ par ...** accompanied on the piano by ...

piano[2] /pjano/ ADV (*Mus*) piano; (* *fig*) gently ◆ **allez-y** ~ easy *ou* gently does it*, go easy* *ou* gently

piano-bar (pl **pianos-bars**) /pjanobaʀ/ NM piano bar

piano(-)forte /pjanofɔʀte/ NM pianoforte

pianotage /pjanɔtaʒ/ NM (*sur un piano*) tinkling; (*sur un clavier*) tapping; (*sur une table*) drumming

pianoter /pjanɔte/ ▸ conjug 1 ◂ VI 1 (= *jouer du piano*) to tinkle away (at the piano) 2 (= *tapoter*) to drum one's fingers; (*sur un clavier*) to tap away ◆ **il pianotait sur son ordinateur** he was tapping away at his computer VT [+ *signal, code*] to tap out ◆ ~ **un air** to tinkle out a tune on the piano

piastre /pjastʀ/ NF piastre (*Brit*), piaster (*US*); (*Can* = *dollar*) (Canadian) dollar

piaule * /pjol/ NF (= *chambre louée*) room ◆ **ma** ~ my (bed)room

piaulement /pjolmɑ̃/ NM [*d'oiseau*] cheeping (*NonC*), peeping (*NonC*); (* : *péj*) [*d'enfant*] whining (*NonC*), whimpering (*NonC*)

piauler /pjole/ ▸ conjug 1 ◂ VI [*oiseau*] to cheep, to peep; (* : *péj*) [*enfant*] to whine, to whimper

PIB /peibe/ NM (abrév de **produit intérieur brut**) GDP

pic /pik/ NM 1 [*de montagne, courbe*] peak ◆ **à chaque ~ de pollution** whenever pollution levels peak *ou* reach a peak ◆ **atteindre un** ~ to reach *ou* hit a peak, to peak
◆ **à pic** [*rochers*] sheer, precipitous (*frm*); [*mont, chemin*] steep, precipitous (*frm*) ◆ **le chemin s'élève** *ou* **monte à** ~ the path rises steeply ◆ **la falaise plonge à ~ dans la mer** the cliff falls *ou* drops sheer (in)to the sea ◆ **arriver** *ou* **tomber à** ~ * to come just at the right time *ou* moment ◆ **vous arrivez à** ~ * you couldn't have come at a better time *ou* moment, you've come just at the right time *ou* moment
2 (= *pioche*) pick(axe) ◆ ~ **à glace** ice pick 3 (= *oiseau*) ~**(-vert)** (green) woodpecker ◆ ~ **épeiche** great-spotted woodpecker, pied woodpecker

pica /pika/ NM (*Typo*) pica

picaillons * /pikajɔ̃/ NMPL cash* (*NonC*)

picaresque /pikaʀɛsk/ ADJ picaresque

piccolo /pikɔlo/ NM piccolo

pichenette * /piʃnɛt/ NF flick ◆ **faire tomber qch d'une** ~ to flick sth off *ou* away

pichet /piʃɛ/ NM pitcher, jug ◆ **un ~ de vin** (*dans un restaurant*) ≃ a carafe of wine

pickpocket /pikpɔkɛt/ NM pickpocket

pick-up /pikœp/ NM INV 1 (= *véhicule*) pickup 2 († = *bras*) pickup; (= *électrophone*) record player

pico- /piko/ PRÉF pico- ◆ **~seconde** picosecond

picoler ⁑ /pikɔle/ ▸ conjug 1 ◂ VI to booze* ◆ **qu'est-ce qu'il peut ~ !** he sure can knock it back!* ◆ ~ **dur** (*habituellement*) to be a real boozer*; (*à l'occasion*) to hit the bottle* *ou* sauce* (*US*)

picoleur, -euse ⁑ /pikɔlœʀ, øz/ NM,F tippler*, boozer*

picorer /pikɔʀe/ ▸ conjug 1 ◂ VI to peck (about); (= *manger très peu*) to nibble VT to peck, to peck (away) at

picot /piko/ NM [*de dentelle*] picot; [*de planche*] burr; (= *petite pointe*) spike ◆ **dispositif d'entraînement à ~s** (*Ordin*) tractor drive

picotement /pikɔtmɑ̃/ NM [*de peau, membres*] tingling (*NonC*) ◆ **j'ai des ~s dans les yeux** my eyes are smarting *ou* stinging ◆ **j'ai des ~s dans la gorge** I've got a tickle in my throat ◆ **la décharge électrique provoque de légers ~s** the electrical discharge creates a slight tingling sensation

picoter /pikɔte/ ▸ conjug 1 ◂ VT 1 (= *provoquer des picotements*) ~ **la gorge** to tickle the throat ◆ ~ **la peau** to make the skin tingle ◆ ~ **les yeux** to make the eyes smart, to sting the eyes ◆ **j'ai les yeux qui me picotent** my eyes are stinging *ou* smarting 2 (*avec une épingle*) to prick 3 (= *picorer*) to peck, to peck (away) at VI [*gorge*] to tickle; [*peau*] to tingle; [*yeux*] to smart, to sting

picotin /pikɔtɛ̃/ NM (= *ration d'avoine*) oats, ration of oats; (= *mesure*) peck

picouse * /pikuz/ NF → **piquouse**

picrate /pikʀat/ NM (*Chim*) picrate; (* : *péj*) cheap wine, plonk* (*Brit*)

picrique /pikʀik/ ADJ ◆ **acide** ~ picric acid

picrocholin, e /pikʀɔkɔlɛ̃, in/ ADJ (*frm*) ◆ **guerre** *ou* **dispute ~e** petty wrangling (*NonC*)

Pictes /pikt/ NMPL Picts

pictogramme /piktɔgʀam/ NM pictogram

pictographie /piktɔgʀafi/ NF pictography

pictographique /piktɔgʀafik/ ADJ pictographic

pictural, e (mpl **-aux**) /piktyʀal, o/ ADJ pictorial

pidgin /pidʒin/ NM pidgin ◆ **~-english** pidgin English

Pie /pi/ NM Pius

pie[1] /pi/ NF (= *oiseau*) magpie; (* *péj* = *personne*) chatterbox*; → **bavard, voleur** ADJ INV [*cheval*] piebald; [*vache*] black and white; → **voiture**

pie[2] /pi/ ADJ F → **œuvre**

pièce /pjɛs/ NF 1 (= *fragment*) piece ◆ **en ~s** in pieces ◆ **mettre en ~s** (*lit*) (= *casser*) to smash to pieces; (= *déchirer*) to pull *ou* tear to pieces; (*fig*) to tear *ou* pull to pieces ◆ **c'est inventé** *ou* **forgé de toutes ~s** it's made up from start to finish, it's a complete fabrication ◆ **fait d'une seule** ~ made in one piece ◆ **fait de ~s et de morceaux** (*lit*) made with *ou* of bits and pieces; (*fig péj*) cobbled together ◆ **il est tout d'une** ~ he's very cut and dried about things; → **tailler**

2 *(gén = unité, objet)* piece; *[de jeu d'échecs, de dames]* piece; *[de tissu, drap]* length, piece; *(Mil)* gun; *(Chasse, Pêche = prise)* specimen ◆ **se vendre à la** ~ to be sold separately *ou* individually ◆ **2 F (la)** ~ 2 francs each *ou* apiece ◆ **travail à la** ~ *ou* **aux ~s** piecework ◆ **payé à la** ~ *ou* **aux ~s** on piece(work) rate, on piecework ◆ **on n'est pas aux ~s !*** there's no rush! ◆ **un deux-~s** *(Habillement) (= costume, tailleur)* a two-piece suit; *(= maillot de bain)* a two-piece (swimsuit) → **chef¹**

3 *[de machine, voiture]* part, component ◆ **~s (de rechange)** spares, (spare) parts ◆ ~ **d'origine** guaranteed genuine spare part

4 *(= document)* paper, document ◆ **avez-vous toutes les ~s nécessaires ?** have you got all the necessary papers? *ou* documents? ◆ **juger/décider sur ~s** to judge/decide on actual evidence ◆ **avec ~s à l'appui** with supporting documents ◆ **les plaintes doivent être accompagnées de ~s justificatives** *(Admin, Jur)* complaints must be documented *ou* accompanied by written proof *ou* evidence

5 *(pour vêtement abîmé, en chirurgie)* patch ◆ **mettre une ~ à qch** to put a patch on sth

6 *[de maison]* room ◆ **appartement de cinq ~s** five-room(ed) apartment *ou* flat *(Brit)* ◆ **un deux ~s (cuisine)** a two-room(ed) apartment *ou* flat *(Brit)* (with kitchen)

7 *(Théât)* play; *(Littérat, Mus)* piece ◆ **jouer** *ou* **monter une ~ de Racine** to put on a play by Racine ◆ **une ~ pour hautbois** a piece for oboe

8 ◆ ~ **(de monnaie)** coin ◆ ~ **d'argent/d'or** silver/gold coin ◆ **une ~ de 5 euros/de 50 centimes** a 5-euro/50-centime coin ◆ **~s jaunes** centime coins, ≃ coppers* *(Brit)* ◆ **donner la ~ à qn*** to give sb a tip, to tip sb; → **rendre**

9 *(littér)* **faire ~ à qn/à un projet** to thwart sb *ou* sb's plans/a project

COMP **pièce d'artifice** firework
pièce d'artillerie piece of ordnance, gun
pièce de bétail head of cattle ◆ **50 ~s de bétail** 50 head of cattle
pièce de blé wheat field, cornfield *(Brit)*
pièce de bois piece of wood *ou* timber *(for joinery etc)*
pièce du boucher *(Culin)* (large) steak
pièce de charpente member
pièce de collection collector's item *ou* piece
pièce comptable accounting record
pièce à conviction *(Jur)* exhibit
pièce détachée spare, (spare) part ◆ **livré en ~s détachées** (delivered) in kit form
pièce d'eau ornamental lake; *(plus petit)* ornamental pond
pièce d'identité identity paper ◆ **avez-vous une ~ d'identité ?** have you (got) any identification?
pièce maîtresse *[de collection, musée] (gén)* showpiece; *(en exposition)* showpiece, prize *ou* main exhibit; *[de politique, stratégie]* cornerstone
pièce montée *(Culin) pyramid-shaped cake made out of choux puffs, eaten on special occasions; (à un mariage)* ≃ wedding cake
pièce de musée museum piece
pièce rapportée *(Couture)* patch; *[de marqueterie, mosaïque]* insert, piece; *(* hum = belle-sœur, beau-frère etc)* in-law*; *(dans un groupe)* late addition
pièce de résistance main dish, pièce de résistance
pièce de terre piece *ou* patch of land
pièce de théâtre play
pièce de vers piece of poetry, short poem
pièce de viande side of meat
pièce de vin cask of wine

piécette /pjesɛt/ **NF** small coin

pied /pje/

1 NOM MASCULIN 2 COMPOSÉS

1 - NOM MASCULIN

1 Anat *[de personne, animal]* foot; *(= sabot) [de cheval, bœuf]* hoof; *[de mollusque]* foot ◆ **avoir les ~s plats** to have flat feet, to be flat-footed ◆ **sauter d'un ~ sur l'autre** to hop from one foot to the other ◆ **avoir** ~ *[nageur]* to be able to touch the bottom ◆ **je n'ai plus** ~ I'm out of my depth ◆ **avoir bon ~ bon œil** to be as fit as a fiddle, to be fighting fit, to be hale and hearty ◆ **avoir le ~ léger** to be light of step ◆ **avoir le ~ marin** to be a good sailor ◆ **avoir les (deux) ~s sur terre** to have one's feet firmly (planted) on the ground ◆ **avoir un ~ dans la tombe** to have one foot in the grave ◆ **avoir/garder un ~ dans l'entreprise** to have a foot/keep one's foot in the door, to have/maintain a foothold *ou* a toehold in the firm ◆ **conduire** *ou* **foncer (le) ~ au plancher** to drive with one's foot to the floor ◆ **faire du ~ à qn** *(= prévenir qn)* to give sb a warning kick; *(galamment)* to play footsie with sb* ◆ **faire le ~ de grue*** to stand about (waiting), to kick one's heels *(Brit)* ◆ **faire des ~s et des mains pour obtenir qch*** to move heaven and earth to get sth ◆ **cela lui fera les ~s*** that'll teach him (a thing or two)* ◆ **le ~ lui a manqué** he lost his footing, his foot slipped ◆ **mettre ~ à terre** to dismount ◆ **mettre les ~s chez qn** to set foot in sb's house ◆ **je n'y remettrai jamais les ~s** I'll never set foot (in) there again ◆ **je n'ai pas mis les ~s dehors aujourd'hui** I haven't been outside all day ◆ **mettre les ~s dans le plat*** *(= gaffer)* to boob‡, to put one's foot in it; *(= se fâcher)* to put one's foot down ◆ **il est incapable de mettre un ~ devant l'autre** he can't walk straight ◆ **partir du bon ~** to get off to a good start ◆ **partir** *ou* **sortir les ~s devant*** *(= mourir)* to go out feet first ◆ **perdre ~** *(lit, fig)* to be *ou* get out of one's depth; *(en montagne)* to lose one's footing ◆ **prendre ~ sur un marché** to gain *ou* get a foothold in a market ◆ **leur parti a pris ~ dans la région** their party has gained a foothold in the region ◆ **se prendre les ~s dans le tapis*** *(fig)* to slip up ◆ **il va prendre mon ~ au derrière !*** I'll give him a kick up the backside!* ◆ **repartir du bon ~** to make a clean *ou* fresh start ◆ **sans remuer** *ou* **bouger ni ~ ni patte*** without moving a muscle ◆ **avec lui, on ne sait jamais sur quel ~ danser** you never know where you stand with him ◆ **je ne sais pas sur quel ~ danser** I don't know what to do ◆ **il ne tient pas sur ses ~s** *(ivre)* he can hardly stand up; *(faible)* he's dead on his feet ◆ **"les pieds dans l'eau"** *(sur une annonce)* "on the waterfront" ◆ **"au pied !"** *(à un chien)* "heel!"; → **casser, deux, lâcher, retomber**

◆ **à pied** *(en marchant)* on foot ◆ **aller à ~** to go on foot, to walk ◆ **nous avons fait tout le chemin à ~** we walked all the way, we came all the way on foot ◆ **faire de la marche/course à ~** to go walking/running ◆ **ce type, on l'emmerde‡ à ~, à cheval et en voiture !** *(fig)* he can go to hell!‡ ◆ **mettre qn à ~** to suspend sb ◆ **mise à ~** suspension

◆ **à pied sec** without getting one's feet wet

◆ **à pieds joints** with one's feet together; → **sauter**

◆ **au pied levé** ◆ **remplacer qn au ~ levé** to stand in for sb at a moment's notice

◆ **aux pieds de** ◆ **le chien est couché aux ~s de son maître** the dog is lying at its master's feet ◆ **tomber aux ~s de qn** to fall at sb's feet

◆ **de pied en cap** from head to foot, from top to toe

◆ **de pied ferme** resolutely ◆ **s'il veut me créer des ennuis, je l'attends de ~ ferme** if he wants to create trouble for me, I'm ready and waiting for him

◆ **des pieds à la tête** from head to foot

◆ **en pied** *[portrait]* full-length; *[statue]* full-scale, full-size

◆ **le pied à l'étrier** ◆ **avoir le ~ à l'étrier** to be well on the way ◆ **mettre le ~ à l'étrier à qn** to give sb a boost *ou* a leg up *(Brit)*

◆ **pieds et poings liés** *(fig)* tied *ou* bound hand and foot

◆ **pied à pied** *[se défendre, lutter]* every inch of the way

◆ **sur pied** *(= levé, guéri)* ◆ **être sur ~** *[personne, malade]* to be up and about ◆ **remettre qn sur ~** to set sb back on his feet again
(= constitué) ◆ **maintenant que l'équipe est sur ~** ... now that the team has been set up ... ◆ **l'organisation sera sur ~ en mai** the organization will be operational in May ◆ **mettre qch sur ~** to set sth up ◆ **la mise sur ~ de qch** the setting up of sth
(= vivant, non coupé) ◆ **bétail sur ~** beef (*ou* mutton *etc*) on the hoof ◆ **blé sur ~** standing *ou* uncut corn *(Brit) ou* wheat *(US)*

◆ **coup de pied** *(gén, Sport)* kick ◆ **coup de ~ arrêté** free kick ◆ **un coup de ~ au derrière*** *ou* **aux fesses*** a kick in the pants* *ou* up the backside* ◆ **coup de ~ au cul‡** kick up the arse*‡ *(Brit) ou* in the ass*‡ *(US)* ◆ **donner un coup de ~ à** *ou* **dans** to kick ◆ **donner un coup de ~ dans la fourmilière** *(fig)* to stir things up ◆ **il a reçu un coup de ~** he was kicked ◆ **le coup de ~ de l'âne** *(fig)* delayed revenge; → **pénalité, touche**

2 = partie inférieure, base, support *[d'arbre, colline, échelle, lit, mur]* foot, bottom; *[de table]* leg; *[de champignon]* stalk; *[d'appareil-photo]* stand, tripod; *[de lampe]* base; *[de lampadaire]* stand; *[de verre]* stem; *[de colonne]* base, foot; *(Math) [de perpendiculaire]* foot; *[de chaussette]* foot ◆ **le ~ droit me va, mais le gauche est un peu grand** *(= chaussure)* the right shoe fits me, but the left one is a bit too big

◆ **au pied du mur** *(fig)* ◆ **être au ~ du mur** to have one's back to the wall ◆ **mettre qn au ~ du mur** to call sb's bluff

◆ **à pied d'œuvre** ready to get down to the job

3 Agr *[de salade, tomate]* plant ◆ ~ **de laitue** lettuce (plant) ◆ ~ **de céleri** head of celery ◆ ~ **de vigne** vine

4 Culin *[de porc, mouton, veau]* trotter ◆ **~s paquets** *dish made of mutton tripe and sheep's trotters*

5 = mesure foot ◆ **un poteau de six ~s** a six-foot pole ◆ **j'aurais voulu être à 100 ~s sous terre** I wished the ground would open up (and swallow me), I could have died*

6 Poésie foot

7 ‡ = idiot twit*, idiot ◆ **quel ~, celui-là !** what an idiot!, what a (useless) twit!*

◆ **comme un pied** ◆ **jouer comme un ~** to be a useless* *ou* lousy‡ player ◆ **il s'y prend comme un ~** he hasn't a clue how to go about it* ◆ **il conduit/chante comme un ~** he's a hopeless *ou* lousy‡ driver/singer

8 ‡ = plaisir **c'est le ~ !, quel ~ !** it's brilliant!* *ou* great!* ◆ **ce n'est pas le ~** it's no picnic* *ou* fun ◆ **c'est une solution, mais c'est pas le ~** it's a solution but it's not brilliant* *ou* great* ◆ **prendre son ~** *(= s'amuser)* to get one's kicks‡ *(avec* with*)*; *(sexuellement)* to have it away *ou* off‡ *(avec* with*)*

9 locutions

◆ **au petit pied** *(littér)* ◆ **un Balzac/un Versailles au petit ~** a poor man's Balzac/Versailles ◆ **un don Juan** *ou* **un séducteur au petit ~** a small-time Casanova

◆ **au pied de la lettre** literally ◆ **ne prends pas tout au ~ de la lettre !** don't take everything so literally! ◆ **il a suivi vos conseils au ~ de la lettre** he followed your advice to the letter

♦ **sur le pied de guerre** (all) ready to go, ready for action
♦ **sur un grand pied** ♦ **vivre sur un grand ~** to live in (great *ou* grand) style
♦ **sur un pied d'égalité, sur le même pied** *[être, mettre]* on an equal footing; *[traiter]* as equals

2 - COMPOSÉS

pied d'athlète *(Méd)* athlete's foot
pied autoréglable ⇒ **pied de nivellement**
pied de col NM *(Couture)* collarstand
pied à coulisse calliper rule
pied de fer (cobbler's) last
pied de lit footboard
pied de nez NM **faire un ~ de nez à qn** to thumb one's nose at sb, to cock a snook at sb *(Brit)*
les Pieds Nickelés *early 20th century French cartoon characters* ♦ **la bande de ~s nickelés qui traîne dans ce café*** the gang of good-for-nothings *ou* layabouts* who hang out* in this café
pied de nivellement *(sur un meuble)* self-levelling foot
pied de page footer

pied-à-terre /pjetatɛʀ/ NM INV pied-à-terre

pied-bot (pl **pieds-bots**) /pjebo/ NM person with a club-foot

pied-d'alouette (pl **pieds-d'alouette**) /pjedalwɛt/ NM larkspur

pied-de-biche (pl **pieds-de-biche**) /pjed(ə)biʃ/ NM *[de machine à coudre]* presser foot; *[de meuble]* cabriole leg; (= *levier*) wrecking bar; (= *arrache-clous*) nail puller *ou* extractor

pied-de-cheval (pl **pieds-de-cheval**) /pjed(ə)ʃəval/ NM *large specially cultivated oyster*

pied-de-loup (pl **pieds-de-loup**) /pjed(ə)lu/ NM club moss

pied-de-poule (pl **pieds-de-poule**) /pjed(ə)pul/ ADJ INV hound's-tooth, dog's-tooth NM hound's-tooth check *(NonC)*, dog's-tooth check *(NonC)*

pied-de-roi (pl **pieds-de-roi**) /pjed(ə)ʀwa/ NM *(Can)* folding foot-rule

pied-de-veau (pl **pieds-de-veau**) /pjed(ə)vo/ NM *(Bot)* lords and ladies, cuckoopint

pied-d'oiseau (pl **pieds-d'oiseau**) /pjedwazo/ NM (= *plante*) bird's-foot

piédestal (pl **-aux**) /pjedestal, o/ NM *(lit, fig)* pedestal ♦ **mettre** *ou* **placer qn sur un ~** to put sb on a pedestal ♦ **descendre/tomber de son ~** to come down from/fall off one's pedestal

pied-noir (pl **pieds-noirs**) /pjenwaʀ/ NMF pied-noir *(French colonial born in Algeria)*

pied-plat †† (pl **pieds-plats**) /pjepla/ NM lout

piégé, e /pjeʒe/ (ptp de **piéger**) ADJ ♦ **engin ~** booby trap ♦ **lettre ~e** letter bomb ♦ **colis** *ou* **paquet ~** parcel *ou* mail bomb ♦ **voiture ~e** car bomb

piège /pjɛʒ/ NM *(lit, fig)* trap; (= *fosse*) pit; (= *collet*) snare ♦ **~ à rats/à moineaux** rat-/sparrow-trap ♦ **~ à loups** mantrap ♦ **~ à touristes** tourist trap ♦ **c'est un ~ à cons**⁑ it's a con* *ou* a gyp⁑ *(US)* ♦ **prendre au ~** to (catch in a) trap ♦ **être pris à son propre ~** to be caught in *ou* fall into one's own trap ♦ **tendre un ~ (à qn)** to set a trap (for sb) ♦ **traduction/dictée pleine de ~s** translation/dictation full of pitfalls ♦ **donner** *ou* **tomber dans le ~** to fall into the trap, to be trapped ♦ **c'était un ~ et tu es tombé dedans !** *[question]* it was a trick question and you got caught out!

piégeage /pjeʒaʒ/ NM 1 *[d'animal]* trapping 2 *[de bois, arbre]* setting of traps (*de* in); *(avec des explosifs) [de colis, voiture]* setting of booby traps (*de* in)

piéger /pjeʒe/ ► conjug 3 et 6 ◄ VT 1 *[+ animal, substance]* to trap; *[+ personne] (gén)* to trap; *(par une question)* to trick ♦ **se faire ~ par un radar** to get caught in a radar trap ♦ **il s'est laissé ~ par un journaliste** he got caught out by a journalist ♦ **je me suis laissé ~ par son charme** I was completely taken in by his charm ♦ **l'eau se retrouve piégée dans la roche** the water gets trapped in the rock ♦ **la question était piégée** it was a trick question 2 *[+ bois, arbre]* to set a trap *ou* traps in; *(avec des explosifs) [+ engin, colis, voiture]* to booby-trap

pie-grièche (pl **pies-grièches**) /pigʀijɛʃ/ NF shrike, butcherbird

pie-mère (pl **pies-mères**) /pimɛʀ/ NF pia mater

Piémont /pjemɔ̃/ NM Piedmont

piémontais, e /pjemɔ̃tɛ, ɛz/ ADJ Piedmontese NM (= *dialecte*) Piedmontese NM,F **Piémontais(e)** Piedmontese

piercing /piʀsiŋ/ NM body piercing

piéride /pjeʀid/ NF pierid, pieridine butterfly ♦ **~ du chou** cabbage white (butterfly)

pierraille /pjeʀɑj/ NF *[de route, sentier]* loose stones, chippings; *[de pente, montagne]* scree *(NonC)*, loose stones

Pierre /pjɛʀ/ NM Peter ♦ **~ le Grand** *(Hist)* Peter the Great

pierre /pjɛʀ/ NF 1 *(gén, Méd)* stone ♦ **maison de** *ou* **en ~** stone(-built) house, house built of stone ♦ **mur en ~s sèches** dry-stone wall ♦ **attaquer qn à coups de ~s** to throw stones at sb ♦ **il resta** *ou* **son visage resta de ~** he remained stony-faced ♦ **jeter la première ~** to cast the first stone ♦ **je ne veux pas lui jeter la ~** I don't want to be too hard on him; → **âge, casseur**

2 (= *immobilier*) **la ~** bricks and mortar ♦ **investir dans la ~** to invest in bricks and mortar

3 *(locutions)* **faire d'une ~ deux coups** to kill two birds with one stone ♦ **il s'est mis une ~ au cou** he's taken on a heavy burden ♦ **~ qui roule n'amasse pas mousse** *(Prov)* a rolling stone gathers no moss *(Prov)* ♦ **c'est une ~ dans son jardin** it is a black mark against him ♦ **jour à marquer d'une ~ blanche** red-letter day ♦ **jour à marquer d'une ~ noire** black day ♦ **bâtir qch ~ à ~** to build sth up piece by piece *ou* stone by stone ♦ **ils n'ont pas laissé ~ sur ~** they didn't leave a stone standing ♦ **apporter sa ~ à qch** to add one's contribution to sth ♦ **aimer les vieilles ~s** to like old buildings

COMP **pierre à aiguiser** whetstone
pierre angulaire *(lit, fig)* cornerstone
pierre à bâtir building stone
pierre à briquet flint
pierre à chaux limestone
pierre à feu flint
pierre fine semiprecious stone
pierre funéraire tombstone, gravestone
pierre à fusil gunflint
pierre de lard French chalk, tailor's chalk
pierre levée standing stone
pierre de lune moonstone
pierre ollaire soapstone, steatite *(SPÉC)*
pierre philosophale philosopher's stone
pierre ponce pumice stone, pumice *(NonC)*
pierre précieuse precious stone, gem
la pierre de Rosette the Rosetta stone
pierre de taille freestone
pierre tombale tombstone, gravestone
pierre de touche *(lit, fig)* touchstone

pierreries /pjɛʀʀi/ NFPL gems, precious stones

pierreux, -euse /pjeʀø, øz/ ADJ *[terrain]* stony; *[fruit]* gritty; *(Méd)* calculous *(SPÉC)*

Pierrot /pjɛʀo/ NM *(Théât)* Pierrot

pierrot /pjɛʀo/ NM (= *oiseau*) sparrow

pietà /pjeta/ NF pietà

piétaille /pjetɑj/ NF *(péj) (Mil)* rank and file; (= *subalternes*) rank and file, menials; (= *piétons*) foot-sloggers*, pedestrians

piété /pjete/ NF *(Rel)* piety; (= *attachement*) devotion, reverence ♦ **~ filiale** filial devotion *ou* respect ♦ **articles/livre de ~** devotional articles/book ♦ **images de ~** pious images

piètement /pjɛtmɑ̃/ NM *[de meuble]* base

piétinement /pjetinmɑ̃/ NM 1 (= *stagnation*) **le ~ de la discussion** the fact that the discussion is not (*ou* was not) making (any) progress ♦ **vu le ~ de l'enquête** given that the investigation is (*ou* was) at a virtual standstill 2 (= *marche sur place*) standing about ♦ **ce fut moins un défilé qu'un gigantesque ~** it was more of a slow shuffle than a march 3 (= *bruit*) stamping

piétiner /pjetine/ ► conjug 1 ◄ VI 1 (= *trépigner*) to stamp (one's foot *ou* feet) ♦ **~ de colère/d'impatience** to stamp (one's feet) angrily/impatiently 2 (= *ne pas avancer*) *[personne]* to stand about; *[cortège]* to mark time; *[discussion]* to make no progress; *[affaire, enquête]* to be at a virtual standstill, to be making no headway; *[économie, science]* to stagnate, to be at a standstill ♦ **~ dans la boue** to trudge through the mud VT *[+ sol]* to trample on; *[+ victime] (fig) [+ adversaire]* to trample underfoot; *[+ parterres, fleurs]* to trample on, to trample underfoot, to tread on ♦ **plusieurs personnes furent piétinées** several people were trampled on *ou* trampled underfoot ♦ **~ les principes de qn** to trample sb's principles underfoot, to ride roughshod over sb's principles; → **plat**[1]

piétisme /pjetism/ NM pietism

piétiste /pjetist/ ADJ pietistic NMF pietist

piéton[1] /pjetɔ̃/ NM pedestrian

piéton[2], **-onne** /pjetɔ̃, ɔn/, **piétonnier, -ière** /pjetɔnje, jɛʀ/ ADJ pedestrian *(épith)* ♦ **rue piétonne** *ou* **piétonnière** *(gén)* pedestrianized street; *(commerciale)* pedestrian shopping street ♦ **zone piétonne** *ou* **piétonnière** *(gén)* pedestrian precinct; *(commerciale)* shopping precinct

piètre /pjɛtʀ/ ADJ *(frm) [adversaire, écrivain, roman]* very poor, mediocre; *[excuse]* paltry, lame ♦ **c'est une ~ consolation** it's small *ou* little comfort ♦ **dans un ~ état** in a very poor state ♦ **faire ~ figure** to cut a sorry figure ♦ **avoir ~ allure** to be a sorry *ou* wretched sight

piètrement /pjɛtʀəmɑ̃/ ADV very poorly

pieu (pl **pieux**) /pjø/ NM 1 (= *poteau*) post; *(pointu)* stake, pale; *(Constr)* pile 2 (⁑ = *lit*) bed ♦ **se mettre au ~** to hit the hay* *ou* sack*, to turn in*

pieusement /pjøzmɑ̃/ ADV *(Rel)* piously; (= *respectueusement*) reverently ♦ **un vieux tricot qu'il avait ~ conservé** *(hum)* an old sweater which he had lovingly kept

pieuter⁑ /pjøte/ ► conjug 1 ◄ VI ♦ **(aller) ~ chez qn** to crash *ou* kip *(Brit)* at sb's place⁑ VPR **se pieuter** to hit the hay* *ou* sack*, to turn in*

pieuvre /pjœvʀ/ NF 1 (= *animal*) octopus ♦ **cette entreprise est une ~** this is a very tentacular company ♦ **cette ville est une ~** this is a huge, sprawling city ♦ **la Pieuvre** (= *Mafia*) the Mob 2 (= *sandow*) spider

pieux, pieuse /pjø, pjøz/ ADJ *[personne]* (= *religieux*) pious, devout; (= *dévoué*) devoted, dutiful; *[pensée, souvenir, lecture, image]* pious; *[silence]* reverent, respectful ♦ **~ mensonge** white lie *(told out of pity etc)*

piézoélectricité /pjezoelɛktʀisite/ NF piezoelectricity

piézoélectrique /pjezoelɛktʀik/ ADJ piezoelectric

piézomètre /pjezɔmɛtʀ/ NM piezometer

pif[1]⁑ /pif/ NM (= *nez*) nose, conk⁑ *(Brit)*, schnozzle⁑ *(US)* ♦ **j'ai failli y aller, j'ai eu du ~**

I nearly went but I had a funny feeling about it ◆ **je l'ai dans le** ~ I can't stand *ou* stick* *(Brit)* him

◆ **au pif** *(= approximativement)* at a rough guess; *(= au hasard) [répondre, choisir]* at random ◆ **faire qch au** ~ *[+ plan, exercice, recette]* to do sth by guesswork

pif² /pif/ EXCL ◆ ~! **paf!** *(explosion)* bang! bang!; *(gifle)* smack! smack!, slap! slap!

pif(f)er ⁑ /pife/ ▸ conjug 1 ◂ VT ◆ **je ne peux pas le pif(f)er** I can't stand *ou* stick* *(Brit)* him

pifomètre ⁑ /pifɔmɛtʀ/ NM intuition, instinct ◆ **au pifomètre** at a rough guess ◆ **faire qch au** ~ to do sth by guesswork ◆ **j'y suis allé au** ~ I followed my nose*

pifrer ⁑ /pifʀe/ ▸ conjug 1 ◂ VT ⇒ **pif(f)er**

pige /piʒ/ NF ① *(⁑ = année)* **il a 50 ~s** he's 50 ◆ **à 60 ~s** at 60 ② *(Presse, Typo)* **être payé à la** ~ *[typographe]* to be paid at piecework rates; *[journaliste]* to be paid by the line; *[artiste]* to be paid per commission ◆ **faire des ~s pour un journal** to do freelance work for a newspaper ③ *(⁑ = surpasser)* **faire la ~ à qn** to leave sb standing*, to put sb in the shade

pigeon /piʒɔ̃/ NM ① *(= oiseau)* pigeon ② *(* = dupe)* mug⁑, sucker⁑
COMP **pigeon d'argile** clay pigeon
pigeon ramier woodpigeon, ring dove
pigeon vole *(= jeu)* game of forfeits, ≃ Simon says
pigeon voyageur carrier *ou* homing pigeon ◆ **par ~ voyageur** by pigeon post

pigeonnant, e /piʒɔnɑ̃, ɑt/ ADJ ◆ **soutien-gorge** ~ uplift bra ◆ **avoir une poitrine ~e** to have a lot of cleavage

pigeonne /piʒɔn/ NF hen-pigeon

pigeonneau (pl **pigeonneaux**) /piʒɔno/ NM young pigeon, squab

pigeonner /piʒɔne/ ▸ conjug 1 ◂ VT *(* = duper)* ◆ ~ **qn** to do sb⁑, to take sb for a ride⁑ ◆ **se laisser** *ou* **se faire** ~ to be done⁑, to be taken for a ride⁑, to be had* VI ◆ **ce soutien-gorge fait ~ les seins** this bra pushes the breasts up

pigeonnier /piʒɔnje/ NM pigeon house *ou* loft; *(* = logement)* garret, attic room

piger ⁑ /piʒe/ ▸ conjug 3 ◂ VT *(= comprendre)* to get it* ◆ **il a pigé** he's got it*, he's twigged* *(Brit)*, the penny has dropped* *(Brit)* ◆ **tu piges ?** (do you) get it?* ◆ **je ne pige rien à la chimie** chemistry's all Greek* *ou* double Dutch* *(Brit)* to me ◆ **je n'y pige rien** I just don't get it (at all)*, I can't make head (n)or tail of it ◆ **tu y piges quelque chose, toi ?** can you make anything of it?

pigiste /piʒist/ NMF *(= typographe)* (piecework) typesetter; *(= journaliste)* freelance journalist *(paid by the line)*; *(= artiste)* freelance artist

pigment /pigmɑ̃/ NM pigment

pigmentaire /pigmɑ̃tɛʀ/ ADJ pigmentary, pigmental

pigmentation /pigmɑ̃tasjɔ̃/ NF pigmentation

pigmenter /pigmɑ̃te/ ▸ conjug 1 ◂ VT to pigment

pigne /piɲ/ NF *(= pomme de pin)* pine cone; *(= graine)* pine kernel *ou* nut

pignocher /piɲɔʃe/ ▸ conjug 1 ◂ VI to pick *ou* nibble at one's food

pignon /piɲɔ̃/ NM ① *(Archit)* gable ◆ **à** ~ gabled ◆ **avoir ~ sur rue** *(fig)* to be well-established ② *(= roue dentée)* cog(wheel), gearwheel; *(= petite roue)* pinion ③ *(= fruit)* ~ **(de pin)** pine kernel *ou* nut

pignouf ⁑ /piɲuf/ NM peasant*, boor

pilaf /pilaf/ NM pilaf(f), pilau ◆ **riz** ~ pilau rice

pilage /pilaʒ/ NM crushing, pounding

pilastre /pilastʀ/ NM pilaster

Pilate /pilat/ NM Pilate

pilchard /pilʃaʀ/ NM pilchard

pile /pil/ NF ① *(= tas)* pile, stack; *(Ordin)* stack
② *[de pont]* support, pile, pier
③ *(Élec)* battery ◆ **à ~(s)** battery *(épith)*, battery-operated ◆ ~ **sèche** dry cell *ou* battery ◆ ~ **bâton** pencil battery ◆ ~ **rechargeable** rechargeable battery ◆ ~ **plate/ronde** flat/round battery ◆ ~ **bouton** watch battery ◆ ~ **atomique** nuclear reactor, (atomic) pile ◆ ~ **solaire** solar cell ◆ **appareil à ~s** *ou* **fonctionnant sur ~s** battery-operated *ou* battery-driven appliance
④ ⁑ *(= coups)* belting, thrashing; *(= défaite)* hammering*, thrashing* ◆ **donner une ~ à qn** *(rosser)* to give sb a belting *ou* thrashing, to lay into sb⁑; *(vaincre)* to lick sb*, to beat sb hollow* *(Brit)* ◆ **prendre** *ou* **recevoir une** ~ *(coups)* to get a belting; *(défaite)* to be licked*, to be beaten hollow* *(Brit)*
⑤ *[de pièce]* **c'est tombé sur (le côté)** ~ it came down tails ◆ ~ **ou face ?** heads or tails? ◆ ~ **c'est moi, face c'est toi** tails it's me, heads it's you ◆ **sur le côté ~ il y a ...** on the reverse side there's ... ◆ **on va jouer** *ou* **tirer ça à ~ ou face** we'll toss (up) for it ◆ **tirer à ~ ou face pour savoir si ...** to toss up to find out if ...
⑥ *(Hér)* pile
ADV *(* = net)* ◆ **s'arrêter** ~ to stop dead* ◆ **ça l'a arrêté** ~ it stopped him dead* *ou* in his tracks, it brought him up short* ◆ **vous êtes tombé ~ en m'offrant ce cadeau** *[personne]* you've chosen exactly the right present for me ◆ **j'ai ouvert l'annuaire et je suis tombé ~ sur le numéro** I opened the directory and came up with the number right *ou* straight *(Brit)* away ◆ **il lâcha sa gomme qui tomba ~ dans la corbeille à papier** he let go of his eraser and it fell right *ou* straight into the wastepaper basket ◆ **ça tombe ~ !** that's just *ou* exactly what I (*ou* we *etc*) need(ed)! ◆ **on est six et il y en a douze – ça tombe** ~ there are six of us and twelve of them – that works out exactly *ou* evenly ◆ **son mariage tombe ~ le jour de son anniversaire** her wedding is on the same day as her birthday ◆ **tomber** *ou* **arriver** ~ *(survenir) [personne]* to turn up* just at the right moment *ou* time; *[chose]* to come just at the right moment *ou* time ◆ **à 2 heures** ~ (at) dead on 2*, at 2 on the dot* ◆ **il est 11 heures** ~ it's dead on 11*, it's 11 o'clock exactly ◆ **c'est ~ poil ce que je voulais*** it's just what I wanted ◆ **ça rentre ~ poil*** it just fits in

piler /pile/ ▸ conjug 1 ◂ VT ① *(lit)* to crush, to pound ② ~ **qn** * *(= rosser)* to lay into sb⁑, to give sb a hammering⁑ *ou* belting⁑; *(= vaincre)* to lick sb*, to beat sb hollow* *(Brit)* VI *(* = freiner)* to jam on the brakes

pileux, -euse /pilø, øz/ ADJ *[follicule]* hair *(épith)*; → **système**

pilier /pilje/ NM ① *(Anat, Constr)* pillar; *[de dispositif, institution, politique]* mainstay, linchpin; *(= personne) [d'organisation, parti]* mainstay ◆ **la famille, ~ de la société** the family, the bedrock of society ◆ **c'est un ~ de bar** *ou* **de bistro** he spends his life propping up the bar, he's a barfly* *(US)* ② *(Rugby)* prop (forward)

pillage /pijaʒ/ NM ① *[de ville]* pillage, plundering; *[de magasin, maison]* looting; *[d'église, tombe]* looting, plundering; *[de ruche]* robbing ◆ **mettre au ~** to pillage, to plunder, to loot ◆ **le ~ des caisses de l'État** plundering the state coffers ② *(= plagiat) [d'ouvrage, auteur]* plagiarism

pillard, e /pijaʀ, aʀd/ ADJ *[soldats, bande]* pillaging *(épith)*, looting *(épith)*; *[oiseau]* thieving *(épith)* NM,F pillager, plunderer, looter

piller /pije/ ▸ conjug 1 ◂ VT ① *[+ ville]* to pillage, to plunder; *[+ magasin, maison]* to loot; *[+ église, tombe]* to loot, to plunder; *[+ verger]* to raid ◆ ~ **les caisses de l'État/les richesses minières d'un pays** to plunder the state coffers/the mineral resources of a country ② *(= plagier) [+ ouvrage, auteur]* to plagiarize, to borrow wholesale from

pilleur, -euse /pijœʀ, øz/ NM,F pillager, plunderer, looter; († *= plagiaire)* literary pirate, plagiarist ◆ ~ **d'épaves** looter *(of wrecked ships)* ◆ ~ **de tombes** tomb robber

pilon /pilɔ̃/ NM *(= instrument)* pestle; *(= jambe)* wooden leg; *[de poulet]* drumstick ◆ **mettre un livre au ~** to pulp a book

pilonnage /pilɔnaʒ/ NM ① *(Mil)* shelling, bombardment ◆ **il y a eu des ~s intensifs** there has been intense *ou* heavy shelling ② *[de livres]* pulping ③ *(Culin, Pharm)* pounding, crushing

pilonner /pilɔne/ ▸ conjug 1 ◂ VT ① *(Mil)* to shell, to bombard ◆ **l'artillerie a pilonné la capitale** artillery pounded the capital ② *[+ livre]* to pulp ③ *(Culin, Pharm)* to pound, to crush

pilori /pilɔʀi/ NM pillory, stocks ◆ **mettre** *ou* **clouer au ~** *(lit)* to put in the stocks; *(fig)* to pillory ◆ **être condamné au ~** to be put in the stocks

pilosité /pilozite/ NF pilosity ◆ **avoir une ~ très développée** to be very hairy

pilotage /pilɔtaʒ/ NM ① *[d'avion]* piloting, flying; *[de bateau]* piloting ◆ **école de ~** *[d'avions]* flying school; *[de voitures]* driving school *(specializing in advanced driving skills)* ◆ ~ **automatique** automatic piloting ◆ **l'accident a été attribué à une erreur de ~** the accident was put down to pilot error; → **poste²** ② *[d'entreprise, économie, projet]* running, management; → **comité**

pilote /pilɔt/ NM ① *[d'avion, bateau]* pilot; *[de voiture]* driver; *(= guide)* guide ◆ **servir de ~ à qn** to show sb round, to be sb's guide ② *(Ordin)* driver ③ *(= poisson)* pilotfish ④ *(en apposition = expérimental) [école, ferme]* experimental; *[projet, entreprise, usine]* pilot *(épith)*; *[produit]* low-priced
COMP **pilote automatique** automatic pilot, autopilot ◆ **être/passer en ~ automatique** to be on/switch to automatic pilot *ou* autopilot
pilote automobile racing driver
pilote de chasse fighter pilot
pilote de course ⇒ **pilote automobile**
pilote d'essai test pilot
pilote de guerre fighter pilot
pilote de ligne airline pilot

piloter /pilɔte/ ▸ conjug 1 ◂ VT ① *[+ avion]* to pilot, to fly; *[+ navire]* to pilot; *[+ voiture]* to drive ② *[+ entreprise, projet]* to run, to manage ◆ ~ **qn** *(fig)* to show sb round

pilotis /pilɔti/ NM pile, pilotis *(SPÉC)* ◆ **sur ~** on piles

pilou /pilu/ NM flannelette

pilule /pilyl/ NF ① *(Pharm)* pill ◆ **prendre la ~, être sous ~** * *(contraceptive)* to be on *ou* be taking the pill ◆ ~ **abortive/du lendemain** abortion/morning-after pill ◆ **il a eu du mal à avaler la ~, il a trouvé la ~ un peu amère** *ou* **un peu dure à avaler** *(fig)* he found it a bitter pill to swallow, he found it hard to take ◆ **faire qch pour faire passer la ~** to do sth to sweeten *ou* sugar the pill; → **dorer** ② *(* = défaite)* thrashing*, hammering* ◆ **on a pris la ~** we were thrashed* *ou* hammered*

pimbêche /pɛ̃bɛʃ/ ADJ F stuck-up*, full of herself *(attrib)* NF stuck-up thing* ◆ **c'est une horrible ~** she's so full of herself, she's horribly stuck-up*

pimbina /pɛ̃bina/ NM *(Can)* pembina *(Can)* *(type of cranberry)*

piment /pimɑ̃/ NM ① *(= plante)* pepper, capsicum ◆ ~ **rouge** *(= épice)* chilli ◆ ~ **doux** *(= fruit)* pepper, capsicum; *(= poudre)* paprika ◆ ~ **vert** green chilli ② *(fig)* spice, piquancy ◆ **avoir du ~** to be spicy *ou* piquant ◆ **donner du ~ à une**

situation to add *ou* give spice to a situation ◆ **ça donne du ~ à la vie** it adds a bit of spice to life, it makes life more exciting ◆ **trouver du ~ à qch** to find sth spicy *ou* piquant

pimenté, e /pimɑ̃te/ (ptp de **pimenter**) ADJ *[plat]* hot, spicy; *[récit]* spicy

pimenter /pimɑ̃te/ ▸ conjug 1 ◂ VT *(Culin)* to put chilli in; *(fig)* to add *ou* give spice to

pimpant, e /pɛ̃pɑ̃, ɑt/ ADJ *[robe, personne]* spruce

pimprenelle /pɛ̃pʀənɛl/ NF *(à fleurs verdâtres)* (salad) burnet; *(à fleurs rouges)* great burnet

pin /pɛ̃/ NM *(= arbre)* pine (tree); *(= bois)* pine(wood); → **aiguille, pomme**

COMP **pin laricio** *ou* **noir** Corsican pine
pin maritime maritime pine
pin d'Oregon Oregon pine
pin parasol *ou* **pignon** umbrella pine
pin sylvestre Scots *ou* Scotch fir, Scots *ou* Scotch pine

pinacle /pinakl/ NM *(Archit)* pinnacle ◆ **être au ~** *(fig)* to be at the top ◆ **porter** *ou* **mettre qn au ~** *(fig)* to praise sb to the skies

pinacothèque /pinakɔtɛk/ NF art gallery

pinaillage* /pinɑjaʒ/ NM hair-splitting, quibbling

pinailler* /pinɑje/ ▸ conjug 1 ◂ VI to quibble, to split hairs ◆ **il pinaille sur tout** he's forever splitting hairs

pinailleur, -euse* /pinɑjœʀ, øz/ ADJ pernickety, nitpicking* *(épith)*, hair-splitting *(épith)* NM,F nitpicker*, quibbler

pinard⁑ /pinaʀ/ NM *(gén)* wine; *(péj)* cheap wine, plonk* *(Brit)*

pinardier* /pinaʀdje/ NM wine tanker

pince /pɛ̃s/ NF 1 *(= outil)* **~(s)** *(gén)* pair of pliers, pliers; *(à charbon)* pair of tongs, tongs
2 *(= levier)* crowbar
3 *[de crabe, homard]* pincer, claw
4 *(Couture)* dart ◆ **faire des ~s à** to put darts in ◆ **~ de poitrine** bust darts ◆ **pantalon à ~s** front-pleated trousers
5 (⁑ *= main)* hand, mitt⁑, paw* ◆ **je lui ai serré la ~** I shook hands with him
6 (⁑ *= jambe)* leg ◆ **aller à ~s** to foot* *ou* hoof⁑ it ◆ **j'ai fait 15 km à ~s** I footed it for 15 km*

COMP **pince à billets** note *(Brit) ou* bill *(US)* clip
pince à cheveux hair clip
pince coupante wire cutters
pince crocodile crocodile clip
pince de cycliste bicycle clip
pince à dénuder wire strippers, wire stripping pliers
pince à épiler (eyebrow) tweezers
pince à escargots *special tongs used for eating snails*
pince à glace ice tongs
pince à linge clothes peg *(Brit)*, clothespin *(US, Écos)*
pince multiprise ⇒ **pince crocodile**
pince à ongles nail clippers
pince plate flat-nose pliers
pince à sucre sugar tongs
pince universelle (universal) pliers
pince à vélo bicycle clip

pincé, e¹ /pɛ̃se/ (ptp de **pincer**) ADJ *[personne, air]* stiff, starchy; *[sourire]* stiff, tight-lipped; *[ton]* stiff ◆ **d'un air ~** stiffly ◆ **les lèvres ~es** with pursed lips ◆ **aux lèvres ~es** thin-lipped ◆ **instrument à cordes ~es** *(Mus)* plucked stringed instrument

pinceau (pl **pinceaux**) /pɛ̃so/ NM *(gén)* brush; *(Peinture)* (paint)brush; *(= manière de peindre)* brushwork; (⁑ *= pied)* foot ◆ **~ à colle** paste brush ◆ **~ lumineux** pencil of light ◆ **coup de ~** brushstroke, stroke of the brush ◆ **donner un coup de ~ à un mur** to give a wall a lick of paint ◆ **avoir un bon coup de ~** to paint well, to be a good painter

pincée² /pɛ̃se/ NF *[de sel, poivre]* pinch

pince-fesses †⁑ /pɛ̃sfɛs/ NM INV dance, hop*

pincement /pɛ̃smɑ̃/ NM *(Mus)* plucking; *(Agr)* pinching out ◆ **~ des roues** *(en voiture)* toe-in ◆ **elle a eu un ~ de cœur** she felt a twinge of sorrow

pince-monseigneur (pl **pinces-monseigneur**) /pɛ̃smɔ̃sɛɲœʀ/ NF jemmy *(Brit)*, crowbar

pince-nez /pɛ̃sne/ NM INV pince-nez

pince-oreille (pl **pince-oreilles**) /pɛ̃sɔʀɛj/ NM earwig

pincer /pɛ̃se/ ▸ conjug 3 ◂ VT 1 *(accidentellement, pour faire mal)* to pinch; *[froid]* to nip ◆ **je me suis pincé dans la porte/avec l'ouvre-boîte** I caught myself in the door/with the can opener ◆ **se (faire) ~ le doigt** to catch one's finger ◆ **se (faire) ~ le doigt dans une porte** to trap *ou* catch one's finger in a door ◆ **il s'est fait ~ par un crabe** he was nipped by a crab ◆ **pince-moi, je rêve !** pinch me, I'm dreaming!
2 *(= tenir, serrer)* to grip ◆ **~ les lèvres** to purse (up) one's lips ◆ **se ~ le nez** to hold one's nose ◆ **une robe qui pince la taille** a dress which is tight at the waist
3 *(Mus)* to pluck
4 *(Couture) [+ veste]* to put darts in
5 (* *= arrêter, prendre)* to catch, to cop⁑; *[police]* to cop⁑, to catch, to nick⁑ *(Brit)* ◆ **se faire ~** to get caught
6 *(Agr)* to pinch out, to nip out
7 ◆ **en ~ pour qn** * to be stuck on sb*, to be mad about sb* ◆ **il est pincé*** he's hooked*
VI ◆ **ça pince (dur)** ⁑ it's freezing (cold), it's bitterly cold

pince-sans-rire /pɛ̃ssɑ̃ʀiʀ/ ADJ INV deadpan NMF INV ◆ **c'est un ~** he's got a deadpan sense of humour

pincette /pɛ̃sɛt/ NF *(gén pl, pour le feu)* pair of (fire) tongs, (fire) tongs; *[d'horloger]* pair of tweezers, tweezers; *(Helv = pince à linge)* peg ◆ **il n'est pas à toucher** *ou* **prendre avec des ~s** *(sale)* he's filthy dirty; *(mécontent)* he's like a bear with a sore head

pinçon /pɛ̃sɔ̃/ NM pinch-mark

Pindare /pɛ̃daʀ/ NM Pindar

pindarique /pɛ̃daʀik/ ADJ Pindaric

pine**/pin/ NF cock**, prick**

pinéal, e (mpl **-aux**) /pineal, o/ ADJ pineal ◆ **glande ~e** pineal gland *ou* body

pinède /pinɛd/, **pineraie** /pinʀɛ/ NF pinewood, pine forest

pingouin /pɛ̃gwɛ̃/ NM auk; *(= manchot)* penguin ◆ **(petit) ~** razorbill ◆ **habillé en ~*** *(hum)* in tails ◆ **qui c'est ce ~ ?*** *(= individu)* who's that guy?* *ou* bloke* *(Brit)* ?

ping-pong /piŋpɔ̃g/ NM INV table tennis, Ping-Pong ®

pingre /pɛ̃gʀ/ *(péj)* ADJ stingy NMF skinflint

pingrerie /pɛ̃gʀəʀi/ NF *(péj)* stinginess

Pinocchio /pinɔkjo/ NM Pinocchio

pin-pon /pɛ̃pɔ̃/ EXCL nee naw!

pin's /pins/ NM INV lapel badge, pin

pinson /pɛ̃sɔ̃/ NM chaffinch ◆ **~ du nord** brambling; → **gai**

pintade /pɛ̃tad/ NF guinea-fowl

pintadeau (pl **pintadeaux**) /pɛ̃tado/ NM young guinea-fowl, guinea-poult *(SPÉC)*

pinte /pɛ̃t/ NF 1 *(= ancienne mesure)* ≈ quart *(0.93 litre)*; *(= mesure anglo-saxonne)* pint; *(Can)* quart *(1.136 litre)*; → **payer** 2 *(Helv = débit de boissons)* bar

pinté, e⁑ /pɛ̃te/ (ptp de **pinter**) ADJ smashed⁑, plastered⁑

pinter⁑ /pɛ̃te/ VI **se pinter** ⁑ VPR ▸ conjug 1 ◂ to booze*, to liquor up⁑ *(US)* ◆ **on s'est pintés au whisky** we got smashed⁑ *ou* plastered⁑ on whisky

pin up /pinœp/ NF INV *(= personne)* sexy (-looking) girl; *(= photo)* pinup

pioche /pjɔʃ/ NF 1 *(à deux pointes)* pick, pickaxe, pickax *(US)*; *(à pointe et à houe)* mattock, pickaxe, pickax *(US)*; → **tête** 2 *(= tas de dominos, cartes)* stock, pile ◆ **bonne/mauvaise ~ !** good/bad choice!

piocher /pjɔʃe/ ▸ conjug 1 ◂ VT *[+ terre]* to pickaxe, to pickax *(US)*; (* *= étudier) [+ sujet]* to swot up* *(Brit)*, to slave *ou* slog *(Brit)* away at*; *[+ examen]* to cram *ou* swot* *(Brit)* for; *(Jeux) [+ carte, domino]* to take (from the stock *ou* pile); *[+ numéro]* to take VI *(= creuser)* to dig (with a pick); (* *: Jeux)* to pick up *ou* take a card *(ou* domino) (from the stock *ou* pile) ◆ **~ dans le tas** *(nourriture)* to dig in; *(objets)* to dig into the pile ◆ **~ dans ses économies** to dip into one's savings

piocheur, -euse* /pjɔʃœʀ, øz/ ADJ hard-working NM,F swot* *(Brit)*, grind* *(US)*

piolet /pjɔlɛ/ NM ice axe

pion¹ /pjɔ̃/ NM *(Échecs)* pawn; *(Dames)* piece, draught *(Brit)*, checker *(US)* ◆ **n'être qu'un ~ (sur l'échiquier)** to be just a pawn *ou* be nothing but a pawn (in the game) ◆ **avancer** *ou* **pousser ses ~s** *(fig)* to position o.s.; → **damer**

pion², pionne /pjɔ̃, pjɔn/ NM,F *(arg Scol = surveillant)* supervisor *(student paid to supervise schoolchildren)*

pioncer⁑ /pjɔ̃se/ ▸ conjug 3 ◂ VI to sleep, to get some shut-eye* ◆ **j'ai pas pioncé de la nuit** I didn't get a wink of sleep (all night) ◆ **il a pioncé deux heures** he got two hours' sleep *ou* kip⁑ *(Brit)*

pionnier, -ière /pjɔnje, jɛʀ/ NM,F *(lit, fig)* pioneer

pioupiou* † /pjupju/ NM young soldier, tommy* † *(Brit)*

pipe /pip/ NF 1 *(à fumer) (= contenant)* pipe; *(= contenu)* pipeful, pipe ◆ **fumer la ~** *(gén)* to smoke a pipe; *(habituellement)* to be a pipe-smoker ◆ **~ de bruyère/de terre** briar/clay pipe; → **casser, fendre, tête** 2 (* *= cigarette)* cig*, fag⁑ *(Brit)* 3 *(= futaille)* pipe 4 (** *= acte sexuel)* blow job** ◆ **tailler une ~ à qn** to give sb a blow job**

pipeau (pl **pipeaux**) /pipo/ NM *(Mus)* (reed-) pipe; *[d'oiseleur]* bird call ◆ **~x** *(gluaux)* limed twigs ◆ **c'est du ~*** that's a load of rubbish*

pipelette* /piplɛt/ NF *(péj)* chatterbox

pipeline /piplin/ NM pipeline ◆ **traitement en ~** *(Ordin)* pipelining

piper /pipe/ ▸ conjug 1 ◂ VT *[+ cartes]* to mark; *[+ dés]* to load ◆ **les dés sont pipés** *(fig)* the dice are loaded ◆ **il n'a pas pipé (mot)*** he didn't breathe a word, he kept mum*

piperade /pipeʀad/ NF piperade *(kind of omelette with tomatoes and peppers)*

pipette /pipɛt/ NF pipette

pipi* /pipi/ NM pee*, wee*, wee-wee *(langage enfantin)* ◆ **faire ~** to have a pee* *ou* a wee*, to have a wee-wee *(langage enfantin)* ◆ **faire ~ au lit** to wet the bed ◆ **le chien a fait ~ sur le tapis** the dog has made a puddle* on *ou* has done a wee* on the carpet ◆ **c'est du ~ de chat** *[boisson]* it's dishwater*, it's like cat's piss**; *[livre, film, théorie]* it's pathetic*, it's a waste of time; → **dame**

pipi-room * (pl **pipi-rooms**) /pipiʀum/ **NM** loo * *(Brit)*, bathroom *(US)* ◆ **aller au** ~ to go and spend a penny * *(Brit)*, to go to the bathroom *(US)*

pipit /pipit/ **NM** pipit ◆ ~ **des arbres** tree pipit

piquage /pikaʒ/ **NM** *(Couture)* sewing up, stitching, machining

piquant, e /pikɑ̃, ɑ̃t/ **ADJ** 1 *[barbe]* prickly; *[tige]* thorny, prickly 2 *[goût, radis, sauce, moutarde]* hot; *[odeur]* pungent; *[fromage]* sharp; *[vin]* sour, tart ◆ **eau** ~**e** * fizzy water ◆ **sauce** ~**e** *(Culin)* sauce piquante, piquant sauce 3 *[air, froid]* biting 4 *[détail] (= paradoxal)* surprising; *(= grivois)* spicy; *[description, style]* racy, piquant; *[conversation, charme, beauté]* piquant 5 *(= mordant) [mot, réplique]* biting, cutting **NM** 1 *[de hérisson, oursin]* spine; *[de porc-épic]* quill; *[de rosier]* thorn, prickle; *[de chardon]* prickle; *[de barbelé]* barb 2 *[de style, description]* raciness; *[de conversation]* piquancy; *[d'aventure]* spice ◆ **le** ~ **de l'histoire, c'est que ..., et, détail qui ne manque pas de** ~, **...** the most entertaining thing (about it) is that ...

pique /pik/ **NF** *(= arme)* pike; *[de picador]* lance; *(= parole blessante)* dig, cutting remark ◆ **il n'a pas arrêté de me lancer des** ~**s** he kept making cutting remarks **NM** *(= carte)* spade; *(= couleur)* spades ◆ **le trois de** ~ the three of spades

piqué, e /pike/ (ptp de **piquer**) **ADJ** 1 *(Couture = cousu)* (machine-)stitched; *[couvre-lit]* quilted
2 *(= marqué) [linge]* mildewed, mildewy; *[miroir]* speckled; *[livre]* foxed; *[meuble]* worm-eaten; *(= aigre) [vin]* sour ◆ **visage** ~ **de taches de rousseur** freckled face ◆ ~ **de rouille** *[métal]* pitted with rust; *[linge]* covered in rust spots ◆ ~ **par l'acide** pitted with acid marks ◆ **pas** ~ **des hannetons** * *ou* **des vers** * *(= excellent)* brilliant *, great *; *(= excentrique)* wild * ◆ **son article n'est pas** ~ **des hannetons** * *ou* **des vers** * his article is spot on * ◆ **ce problème n'était pas** ~ **des hannetons !** * *ou* **des vers !** * it was a tough problem! *
3 *(* = fou)* nuts *, barmy * *(Brit)* ◆ **il est** ~**, c'est un** ~ he's nuts * *ou* barmy * *(Brit)*, he's a nutter * *(Brit)*
4 *(Mus) [note]* staccato
5 *(Phot) [d'objectif, image]* sharpness
NM 1 *(en avion)* dive ◆ **attaque en** ~ *(= bombardement)* dive bombing run; *(à la mitrailleuse)* strafing run ◆ **bombardement en** ~ dive bombing run ◆ **faire un** ~ to (go into a) dive
2 *(= tissu)* piqué

pique-assiette * (pl **pique-assiettes**) /pikasjɛt/ **NMF** scrounger *, sponger * *(for a free meal)*

pique-feu (pl **pique-feu(x)**) /pikfø/ **NM** poker

pique-fleurs /pikflœʀ/ **NM INV** flower-holder

pique-nique (pl **pique-niques**) /piknik/ **NM** picnic ◆ **faire un** ~ to picnic, to have a picnic ◆ **demain nous allons faire un** ~ tomorrow we're going for *ou* on a picnic

pique-niquer /piknike/ ▸ conjug 1 ◂ **VI** to have a picnic, to picnic

pique-niqueur, -euse (mpl **pique-niqueurs**) /piknikœʀ, øz/ **NM,F** picnicker

piquer /pike/ ▸ conjug 1 ◂ **VT** 1 *[guêpe]* to sting; *[moustique, serpent]* to bite; *(avec une épingle, une pointe)* to prick; *(Méd)* to give an injection to, to give a shot * *ou* jab * *(Brit)* to ◆ **se faire** ~ **contre la variole** to have a smallpox injection *ou* shot * *ou* jab * *(Brit)* ◆ **faire** ~ **qn contre qch** to have sb vaccinated *ou* inoculated against sth ◆ **faire** ~ **un chat/chien** *(euph)* to have a cat/dog put down *ou* put to sleep ◆ **se** ~ **le doigt** to prick one's finger ◆ **les ronces, ça pique** brambles are prickly; → **mouche**
2 *[+ aiguille, fourche, fléchette]* to stick, to stab, to jab *(dans* into); ◆ **rôti piqué d'ail** joint stuck with cloves of garlic ◆ **piqué de lardons** larded ◆ ~ **la viande avec une fourchette** to prick the meat with a fork ◆ ~ **des petits pois avec une fourchette** to stab peas with a fork ◆ ~ **qch au mur** to put *ou* stick sth up on the wall ◆ ~ **une fleur sur un corsage** to pin a flower on(to) a blouse ◆ ~ **une fleur dans ses cheveux** to stick a flower in one's hair ◆ **des papillons piqués sur une planche** butterflies pinned on a board ◆ ~ **(une frite/un haricot) dans le plat** * to help o.s. (to a chip/a bean or two) ◆ ~ **au hasard** * *ou* **dans le tas** * to choose *ou* pick at random
3 *(Couture)* ~ **qch (à la machine)** to machine sth, to (machine) stitch sth, to sew sth up ◆ **ta mère sait-elle** ~ **?** can your mother use a sewing machine?
4 *[barbe]* to prick, to prickle; *[ortie]* to sting ◆ **tissu qui pique (la peau)** prickly material, material that prickles the skin ◆ **liqueur qui pique la gorge** liqueur which burns the throat ◆ **la fumée me pique les yeux** the smoke is stinging my eyes *ou* making my eyes sting *ou* smart ◆ **le froid/le vent nous piquait le** *ou* **au visage** the cold/the wind stung our faces ◆ **ça (me) pique** *[démangeaison]* it's itching *ou* itchy, it's making me itch ◆ **les yeux me piquent, j'ai les yeux qui piquent** my eyes are smarting *ou* stinging ◆ **ma gorge me pique** my throat's burning ◆ **tu piques avec ta barbe** your beard's scratchy ◆ **attention, ça pique** OK now, this is going to sting; → **frotter**
5 *(= exciter) [+ bœufs]* to goad; *[+ curiosité]* to arouse, to excite; *[+ intérêt]* to arouse, to provoke; *(† = vexer) [+ personne]* to pique, to nettle; *[+ amour-propre]* to pique, to hurt ◆ ~ **qn au vif** to cut sb to the quick
6 *(* = faire brusquement)* ~ **un cent mètres** *ou* **un sprint** to (put on a) sprint, to put on a burst of speed ◆ ~ **un roupillon** * *ou* **un somme** to have forty winks * *ou* a nap, to get a bit of shut-eye ✱ ◆ ~ **un galop** to break into a gallop ◆ ~ **une** *ou* **sa crise** to throw a fit ◆ ~ **une crise de larmes** to have a crying fit ◆ ~ **une colère** to fly into a rage, to have a fit * ◆ ~ **un fard** to go (bright) red ◆ ~ **une suée** to break out in a sweat ◆ ~ **un plongeon** to dive ◆ ~ **une tête dans une piscine** to dive (headfirst) into a pool
7 *(* = attraper) [+ manie, maladie]* to pick up, to catch, to get
8 *(* = voler) [+ portefeuille]* to pinch *, to swipe *, to nick ✱ *(Brit)*; *[+ idée]* to pinch *, to steal *(à qn* from sb)
9 *(✱ = arrêter) [+ voleur]* to cop ✱, to nab *, to nick ✱ *(Brit)*
10 *(Mus)* ~ **les notes** to play staccato
VI 1 *[avion]* to go into a dive; *[oiseau]* to swoop down ◆ **le cavalier piqua droit sur nous** the horseman came straight at us ◆ **il faudrait** ~ **vers le village** we'll have to head towards the village ◆ ~ **du nez** *[avion]* to go into a nose-dive; *[bateau]* to dip its head; *[fleurs]* to droop; *[personne]* to fall headfirst ◆ ~ **du nez dans son assiette** * *(de sommeil)* to nod off * *ou* doze off * (during a meal); *(de honte)* to hang one's head in shame ◆ ~ **des deux** to go full tilt
2 *[moutarde, radis]* to be hot; *[vin]* to be sour, to have a sour taste; *[fromage]* to be sharp ◆ **eau qui pique** * fizzy water
VPR **se piquer** 1 *(= se blesser) (avec une aiguille)* to prick o.s.; *(dans les orties)* to get stung, to sting o.s.
2 *[morphinomane]* to shoot up; *[diabétique]* to give o.s. an injection, to inject o.s. ◆ **il se pique à l'héroïne** he uses heroin
3 *[bois, linge]* to go mildewed *ou* mildewy; *[livre]* to become foxed; *[miroir]* to become speckled; *[métal]* to be pitted; *[vin, cidre]* to go *ou* turn sour
4 *(= prétendre connaître ou pouvoir)* **se** ~ **de littérature/psychologie** to like to think one knows a lot about literature/psychology, to pride o.s. on one's knowledge of literature/psychology ◆ **se** ~ **de faire qch** to pride o.s. on one's ability to do sth
5 *(= se vexer)* to take offence
6 ◆ **il s'est piqué au jeu** he became quite taken with it

piquet /pikɛ/ **NM** 1 *(= pieu)* post, stake, picket; *[de tente]* peg; *(Ski)* (marker) pole; → **raide** 2 ~ **(de grève)** (strike-)picket, picket line ◆ **organiser un** ~ **de grève** to organize a picket line ◆ **il y a un** ~ **de grève à l'usine** there's a picket line at the factory ◆ ~ **d'incendie** *(Mil)* fire-fighting squad 3 *(Scol)* **mettre qn au** ~ to make sb stand *ou* put sb in the corner 4 *(Cartes)* piquet

piquetage /pik(ə)taʒ/ **NM** staking (out)

piqueter /pik(ə)te/ ▸ conjug 4 ◂ **VT** 1 *[+ allée]* to stake out, to put stakes along 2 *(= moucheter)* to dot *(de* with); ◆ **ciel piqueté d'étoiles** star-studded *ou* star-spangled sky, sky studded with stars

piquette /pikɛt/ **NF** 1 *(= cru local)* local wine; *(= mauvais vin)* cheap wine, plonk * *(Brit)* 2 *(✱ = défaite)* hammering *, thrashing * ◆ **prendre une** ~ to be hammered * *ou* thrashed *

piqueur, -euse /pikœʀ, øz/ **ADJ** *[insecte]* stinging *(épith)* **NM** 1 *[d'écurie]* groom; *(Chasse)* whip 2 *(= mineur)* hewer 3 *(= surveillant)* foreman 4 *(* = voleur)* thief **NM,F** *(Couture)* machinist

piquier /pikje/ **NM** pikeman

piquouse * /pikuz/ **NF** shot *, jab * ◆ **il m'a fait une** ~ he gave me a jab * *ou* an injection

piqûre /pikyʀ/ **NF** 1 *[d'insecte, moustique]* bite; *[de guêpe, ortie]* sting ◆ ~ **d'épingle** pinprick ◆ **la** ~ **faite par l'aiguille** *(= plaie)* the hole made by the needle 2 *(Méd)* injection, shot *, jab * *(Brit)* ◆ **faire une** ~ **à qn** to give sb an injection *ou* a shot * *ou* a jab * *(Brit)* ◆ **se faire faire une** ~ to have an injection *ou* a shot * *ou* a jab * *(Brit)* ◆ ~ **de rappel** booster injection *ou* shot *, booster *(Brit)* 3 *(= petit trou)* hole; *[de moisi, rouille]* speck, spot ◆ ~ **de ver** wormhole 4 *(Couture) (= point)* stitch; *(= rang)* stitching *(NonC)* ◆ **rang de** ~**s** row *ou* line of stitches *ou* stitching ◆ **jupe à** ~**s apparentes** skirt with overstitched seams

piranha /piʀana/ **NM** piranha

piratage /piʀataʒ/ **NM** *[de cassette, vidéo]* pirating; *[de ligne téléphonique]* hacking *(de* into); ◆ ~ **(informatique)** (computer) hacking

pirate /piʀat/ **NM** pirate; *(† = escroc)* swindler, shark * ◆ ~ **de l'air** hijacker, skyjacker * ◆ ~ **(informatique)** (computer) hacker ◆ **c'est un vrai** ~**, cet enfant !** that child's a little rascal! ◆ ~ **de la route** carjacker **ADJ** *[bateau, émission, radio, télévision]* pirate *(épith)*

pirater /piʀate/ ▸ conjug 1 ◂ **VT** *[+ cassette, film, logiciel]* to pirate; *[+ ligne téléphonique]* to hack into ◆ ~ **un ordinateur** to hack into a computer

piraterie /piʀatʀi/ **NF** *(NonC)* piracy; *(= acte)* act of piracy; *(fig)* swindle, swindling *(NonC)* ◆ ~ **commerciale** illegal copying, forgery *(of famous brand name goods)* ◆ **acte de** ~ act of piracy ◆ ~ **aérienne** hijacking, skyjacking * ◆ **c'est de la** ~ **!** it's daylight robbery!

piraya /piʀaja/ **NM** ⇒ **piranha**

pire /piʀ/ **ADJ** 1 *(compar)* worse ◆ **c'est bien** ~ it's much worse ◆ **c'est** ~ **que jamais** it's worse than ever ◆ **c'est** ~ **que tout** it's the worst thing you can imagine ◆ **c'est de** ~ **en** ~ it's getting worse and worse ◆ **il y a** ~ **comme chef** you could do worse for a boss ◆ **j'ai déjà entendu** ~ **!** I've heard worse! ◆ **il n'est** ~ **eau que l'eau qui dort** *(Prov)* still waters run deep *(Prov)* ◆ **il n'est** ~ **sourd que celui qui ne veut pas entendre** *(Prov)* there are none so deaf as those who will not hear *(Prov)*

2 (superl) **le ~, la ~** the worst ◆ **les ~s rumeurs/difficultés** the most terrible rumours/severe difficulties
NM ◆ **le ~** the worst ◆ **le ~ de tout c'est** the worst thing of all is ◆ **le ~ c'est que ...** the worst of it (all) is that ... ◆ **(en mettant les choses) au ~** at the (very) worst, if the worst comes to the worst ◆ **je m'attends au ~** I expect the worst ◆ **le ~ est à venir** the worst is yet to come; → **politique**

Pirée /piʀe/ **NM** ◆ **le ~** Piraeus

pirogue /piʀɔg/ **NF** dugout, canoe, pirogue ◆ **~ à balancier** outrigger

piroguier /piʀɔgje/ **NM** boatman *(in a pirogue)*

pirouette /piʀwɛt/ **NF** 1 *[de danseuse, cheval]* pirouette 2 *(= faux-fuyant)* evasive reply ◆ **répondre par une ~** to cleverly side-step *ou* evade the question ◆ **il s'est sorti de la situation par une ~** he managed to wriggle out of the situation

pirouetter /piʀwete/ ► conjug 1 ◄ **VI** to pirouette

pis¹ /pi/ **NM** *[de vache]* udder

pis² /pi/ *(littér)* **ADJ** worse ◆ **qui ~ est** what is worse **ADV** worse ◆ **aller de ~ en ~** to get worse and worse ◆ **dire ~ que pendre de qn** to badmouth* sb; → **mal¹, tant** **NM** ◆ **le ~** the worst (thing) ◆ **au ~** at the (very) worst ◆ **au ~ aller** if the worst comes to the worst

pis-aller /pizale/ **NM INV** stopgap ◆ **cette solution n'est qu'un ~** it's only a stopgap solution ◆ **nous verrons ce film en vidéo, c'est un ~** we'll have to make do with second best and watch the film on video ◆ **au ~** if the worst comes to the worst

piscicole /pisikɔl/ **ADJ** *[réserve, vie, élevage]* fish, piscicultural *(SPÉC)* ◆ **ferme ~** fish farm ◆ **la faune ~** fish life

pisciculteur, -trice /pisikyltœʀ, tʀis/ **NM,F** fish breeder *ou* farmer, pisciculturist *(SPÉC)*

pisciculture /pisikyltYʀ/ **NF** fish breeding *ou* farming, pisciculture *(SPÉC)*

pisciforme /pisifɔʀm/ **ADJ** pisciform

piscine /pisin/ **NF** 1 *(= bassin)* swimming pool; *[de réacteur nucléaire]* cooling pond ◆ **~ municipale** public (swimming) pool, public baths *(Brit)* ◆ **~ olympique** Olympic-size(d) (swimming) pool ◆ **faire de la gymnastique en ~** to do water gymnastics 2 *(arg Police)* **la ~** *the French secret service*

piscivore /pisivɔʀ/ **ADJ** fish-eating *(épith)*, piscivorous *(SPÉC)* **NM** fish eater

Pise /piz/ **N** Pisa; → **tour¹**

pisé /pize/ **NM** adobe, pisé

pissaladière /pisaladjɛʀ/ **NF** *(Culin) Provençal pizza with onions, anchovy fillets and olives*

pisse⁑ /pis/ **NF** pee*, piss⁑

pisse-copie /piskɔpi/ **NM INV** *(péj)* hack*

pisse-froid⁑ /pisfʀwa/ **NM INV** wet blanket*

pissement /pismɑ̃/ **NM** ◆ **~ de sang** passing of blood (with the urine)

pissenlit /pisɑ̃li/ **NM** dandelion ◆ **manger les ~s par la racine*** to be pushing up the daisies*, to be dead and buried

pisser⁑ /pise/ ► conjug 1 ◄ **VI** 1 *(= uriner) [personne]* to (have a) pee* *ou* piss⁑; *[animal]* to pee*, to piss⁑ ◆ **je vais ~ un coup** I'm going for a pee* *ou* a piss⁑ ◆ **il a pissé dans sa culotte** he wet his trousers, he peed in his pants* ◆ **~ au lit** to wet the *ou* one's bed, to pee in the bed* ◆ **il ne se sent plus ~** *(péj)* he thinks the sun shines out of his arse⁑*(Brit) ou* ass⁑ *(US)*, he thinks his shit doesn't stink⁑*(US)* ◆ **ça l'a pris comme une envie de ~** he suddenly got an urge to do it* ◆ **les principes, je leur pisse dessus !** I couldn't give a shit⁑ about principles! ◆ **c'est comme si on pissait dans un violon** it's like pissing in the wind⁑ ◆ **laisse ~ (le mérinos) !** forget it!*, let him *(ou them etc)* get on with it! ◆ **ça ne pisse pas loin** it's nothing to shout about *ou* to write home about*
2 *(= couler)* to gush; *(= fuir)* to gush out ◆ **ça pisse** *(= il pleut)* it's coming down in buckets*, it's pissing down⁑*(Brit)*
VT ◆ **~ du sang** to pass blood (with the urine) ◆ **son nez pissait le sang** blood was gushing *ou* pouring from his nose ◆ **il pissait le sang** the blood was gushing out of him ◆ **le réservoir pissait l'eau** water was gushing *ou* pouring out of the tank ◆ **~ de la copie*** *(péj)* to churn out garbage *ou* rubbish *(Brit)*

pissette* /pisɛt/ **NF** *(= filet de liquide)* trickle

pisseur, -euse¹ /pisœʀ, øz/ **NM,F** ⁑ weak-bladdered individual, person who is always going for a pee* *ou* a piss⁑ **NF** **pisseuse** ⁑ female *(péj)* **COMP** **pisseur de copie*** *writer (or journalist etc) who churns out rubbish*

pisseux, -euse²* /pisø, øz/ **ADJ** *[couleur]* wishy-washy*, insipid; *[aspect]* tatty*, scruffy ◆ **odeur pisseuse** smell of pee* *ou* piss⁑

pisse-vinaigre⁑ /pisvinɛgʀ/ **NM INV** *(= rabat-joie)* wet blanket*; *(= avare)* skinflint

pissoir /piswaʀ/ **NM** *(dial)* urinal

pissotière⁑ /pisɔtjɛʀ/ **NF** (street) urinal

pistache /pistaʃ/ **NF** pistachio (nut) **ADJ INV** pistachio (green)

pistachier /pistaʃje/ **NM** pistachio (tree)

pistage /pistaʒ/ **NM** *[de gibier]* tracking, trailing; *[de personne]* tailing

pistard /pistaʀ/ **NM** track cyclist, track racer *ou* specialist

piste /pist/ **NF** 1 *(= traces) [d'animal, suspect]* track, tracks, trail ◆ **suivre/perdre la ~** to follow/lose the trail ◆ **être/mettre qn sur la (bonne) ~** to be/put sb on the right track ◆ **être sur/perdre la ~ d'un meurtrier** to be on/lose a murderer's trail ◆ **se lancer sur la ~ de qn** to follow sb's trail, to set out to track sb down; → **brouiller, faux², jeu**
2 *(Police = indice)* lead
3 *(fig)* **c'est une ~ à explorer** it's an avenue worth exploring ◆ **il a proposé de nouvelles ~s de recherche** he suggested some new avenues of research ◆ **tu as trouvé un emploi ? – pas encore, mais j'ai quelques ~s** have you found a job? – not yet, but I've got some possibilities to follow up
4 *[d'hippodrome]* course; *[de vélodrome, autodrome, stade]* track; *[de patinage]* rink; *[de danse]* (dance) floor; *[de cirque]* ring
◆ **en piste** ◆ **en ~ !** *(cirque)* into the ring!; *(fig)* off you go! ◆ **être en ~** *(lit)* to be in the ring; *(dans un concours, une élection etc)* to be in the running ◆ **entrer en ~** *(lit)* to enter the ring; *(fig)* to enter the arena, to come on(to) the scene ◆ **dès leur entrée en ~** *(lit)* as soon as they entered the ring; *(fig)* as soon as they entered the arena *ou* came on(to) the scene
5 *(Ski)* (ski) run, piste; *[de ski de fond]* trail ◆ **il y a 30 km de ~ dans cette station** there are 30 km of pistes *ou* ski runs at this resort ◆ **~ artificielle** dry *ou* artificial ski slope ◆ **~ pour débutants** nursery slope ◆ **~ rouge/noire** red/black piste *ou* ski run ◆ **ski hors ~** off-piste skiing ◆ **faire du hors ~** to go off-piste skiing
6 *[d'aéroport]* runway; *[de petit aéroport]* airstrip ◆ **~ d'atterrissage/d'envol** landing/takeoff runway
7 *(= sentier)* track; *[de désert]* trail
8 *[de magnétophone]* track ◆ **à 2/4 ~s** 2/4 track ◆ **~ sonore** *(Ciné)* sound track ◆ **~ magnétique** *[de carte]* magnetic strip
COMP **piste cavalière** bridle path
piste cyclable *(sur route)* (bi)cycle lane; *(= voie séparée)* (bi)cycle path *ou* track

pister /piste/ ► conjug 1 ◄ **VT** *[+ gibier]* to track, to trail; *[police] [+ personne]* to tail

pisteur /pistœʀ/ **NM** (member of the) ski patrol ◆ **les ~s** the ski patrol

pistil /pistil/ **NM** pistil

pistole /pistɔl/ **NF** pistole

pistolet /pistɔlɛ/ **NM** *(= arme)* pistol, gun; *(= jouet)* (toy) pistol, (toy) gun; *[de peintre]* spray gun; *(* = urinal)* bed-bottle ◆ **peindre au ~** to spray-paint ◆ **un drôle de ~*** † an odd customer*, a weird duck* *(US)*
COMP **pistolet agrafeur** staple gun
pistolet à air comprimé airgun
pistolet d'alarme alarm gun
pistolet d'arçon horse pistol
pistolet à bouchon popgun
pistolet à capsules cap gun
pistolet à eau water pistol

pistolet-mitrailleur (pl **pistolets-mitrailleurs**) /pistɔlɛmitʀajœʀ/ **NM** submachine gun, tommy gun, Sten gun ® *(Brit)*

piston /pistɔ̃/ **NM** 1 *[de moteur]* piston 2 * string-pulling*, wire-pulling *(US)* ◆ **avoir du ~** to have friends in the right places* ◆ **il a eu le poste par ~** he got the job thanks to a bit of string-pulling* 3 *(Mus) (= valve)* valve; *(= instrument)* cornet

pistonner* /pistɔne/ ► conjug 1 ◄ **VT** to pull strings *ou* wires *(US)* for* *(auprès de* with); ◆ **il s'est fait ~** he got somebody to pull some strings *ou* wires *(US)* for him*

pistou /pistu/ **NM** ◆ **soupe au ~** *vegetable soup with basil and garlic*

pita /pita/ **NM** pitta (bread)

pitance † /pitɑ̃s/ **NF** *(péj)* (means of) sustenance † *(frm)*

pit-bull (pl **pit-bulls**) /pitbyl/ **NM** pit bull (terrier)

pitchpin /pitʃpɛ̃/ **NM** pitch pine

piteusement /pitøzmɑ̃/ **ADV** pathetically ◆ **échouer ~** to fail miserably

piteux, -euse /pitø, øz/ **ADJ** *(= minable) [apparence]* sorry *(épith)*, pitiful, pathetic; *[résultats]* pitiful, pathetic; *(= honteux) [personne, air]* ashamed, shamefaced ◆ **en ~ état** in a sorry *ou* pitiful state ◆ **faire piteuse figure** to cut a sorry figure, to be a sorry *ou* pitiful sight ◆ **avoir piteuse mine** to be shabby-looking

pithécanthrope /pitekɑ̃tʀɔp/ **NM** pithecanthrope

pithiviers /pitivje/ **NM** *pastry with an almond paste filling*

pitié /pitje/ **NF** 1 *(= compassion)* pity ◆ **avoir ~ de qn** to pity sb, to feel pity for sb ◆ **prendre qn en ~** to take pity on sb ◆ **il me fait ~** I feel sorry for him, I pity him ◆ **cela me faisait ~ de le voir si malheureux** it was pitiful to see him so unhappy ◆ **son sort me fit ~** I took pity on him ◆ **il est si maigre que c'est à faire ~** he is pitifully *ou* painfully thin ◆ **il ne fait pas ~ !** *(= il est gros, riche)* it's hard to feel sorry for him! ◆ **quelle ~ !, c'est une ~ !** what a pity!, it's such a pity! ◆ **c'est (une vraie) ~** *ou* **quelle ~ de voir ça** it's pitiful to see (that)
2 *(= miséricorde)* pity, mercy ◆ **avoir ~ d'un ennemi** to take pity on an enemy, to have pity *ou* mercy on an enemy ◆ **~ !** *(= grâce)* (have) mercy!; *(= assez)* for goodness' *ou* pity's *ou* Pete's sake!* ◆ **par ~ !** for pity's sake! ◆ **sans ~** *[agir]* pitilessly, mercilessly; *[regarder]* pitilessly ◆ **il est sans ~** he's pitiless *ou* merciless *ou* ruthless ◆ **un monde sans ~** a cruel world

piton /pitɔ̃/ **NM** 1 *(à anneau)* eye; *(à crochet)* hook; *(Alpinisme)* piton, peg 2 *(Géog)* peak

pitonner /pitɔne/ ► conjug 1 ◄ **VI** 1 *(Alpinisme)* to drive pitons *ou* pegs into the rock 2 *(Can) (= zapper)* to channel-hop, to zap from channel to channel; *(= saisir sur ordinateur)* to keyboard

VT *(Can)* *[+ numéro de téléphone]* to dial; *[+ code]* to enter **VT INDIR** **pitonner sur** *(Can)* *[+ clavier]* to tap away on

pitonneuse /pitɔnøz/ **NF** *(Can = télécommande)* channel-hopper, zapper

pitoyable /pitwajabl/ **ADJ** *(gén)* pitiful ◆ **il était dans un état** ~ he was in a pitiful *ou* a sorry state

pitoyablement /pitwajabləmɑ̃/ **ADV** pitifully ◆ **échouer** ~ to fail miserably

pitre /pitʀ/ **NM** *(lit, fig)* clown ◆ **faire le** ~ to clown *ou* fool about *ou* around, to act the fool

pitrerie /pitʀəʀi/ **NF** tomfoolery *(NonC)* ◆ **il n'arrête pas de faire des ~s** he's always *ou* he never stops clowning around *ou* acting the fool ◆ **arrête de faire des ~s !** stop fooling around!

pittoresque /pitɔʀɛsk/ **ADJ** *[site]* picturesque; *[personnage]* picturesque, colourful *(Brit)*, colorful *(US)*; *[récit, style, détail]* colourful *(Brit)*, colorful *(US)*, picturesque, vivid **NM** ◆ **le** ~ the picturesque ◆ **le** ~ **de qch** the picturesque quality of sth, the colourfulness *ou* vividness of sth ◆ **le** ~ **dans tout cela c'est que ...** *(fig)* the amusing *ou* ironic thing about it all is that ...

pivert /pivɛʀ/ **NM** green woodpecker

pivoine /pivwan/ **NF** peony; → **rouge**

pivot /pivo/ **NM** *(gén, Sport, Mil)* pivot; *(= chose essentielle)* mainspring, linchpin; *(= personne essentielle)* linchpin; *[de dent]* post; *(Bot) (= racine)* taproot ◆ **cours** ~ *(Écon)* central rate ◆ **il a eu un rôle** ~ he played a pivotal role

pivotant, e /pivɔtɑ̃, ɑ̃t/ **ADJ** *[bras, panneau]* pivoting *(épith)*, revolving *(épith)*; *[fauteuil]* swivel *(épith)*; → **racine**

pivoter /pivɔte/ ► conjug 1 ◄ **VI** *[porte]* to revolve, to pivot; *(Mil)* to wheel round ◆ ~ **(sur ses talons)** *[personne]* to turn *ou* swivel round, to turn on one's heels ◆ **faire** ~ **qch** to pivot *ou* swivel sth round

pixel /piksɛl/ **NM** pixel

pizza /pidza/ **NF** pizza

pizzeria /pidzɛʀja/ **NF** pizzeria

pizzicato /pidzikato/ (pl **pizzicatos** *ou* **pizzicati** /pidzikati/) **NM** pizzicato

PJ[1] (abrév de **pièce(s) jointe(s)**) enc, encl

PJ[2] /peʒi/ **NF** (abrév de **police judiciaire**) ≈ CID *(Brit)*, FBI *(US)*

PL (abrév de **poids lourd**) HGV *(Brit)*, heavy truck *(US)*

Pl (abrév de **place**) Pl

placage /plakaʒ/ **NM** 1 *(en bois)* veneering *(NonC)*, veneer; *(en marbre, pierre)* facing ◆ ~ **en acajou** mahogany veneer 2 *(Rugby)* ⇒ **plaquage**

placard /plakaʀ/ **NM** 1 *(= armoire)* cupboard ◆ ~ **à balai/de cuisine** broom/kitchen cupboard 2 *(= affiche)* poster, notice ◆ ~ **publicitaire** *[de journal]* display advertisement 3 *(Typo)* galley (proof) 4 *(* = couche)* thick layer, thick coating *(NonC)* 5 *(arg Police = casier judiciaire)* (police) record 6 *(locutions)* **mettre qn au** ~* *(en prison)* to put sb away*, to send sb down*; *(renvoyer)* to fire sb, to give sb the push*; *(mettre à l'écart)* to push sb to one side ◆ **mettre qch au** ~ to shelve sth

placarder /plakaʀde/ ► conjug 1 ◄ **VT** *[+ affiche]* to stick up, to put up; *[+ mur]* to stick posters on ◆ **mur placardé d'affiches** wall covered with posters

placardiser /plakaʀdize/ ► conjug 1 ◄ **VT** *[+ personne]* to sideline

place /plas/

GRAMMAIRE ACTIVE 28, 29

NOM FÉMININ

1 = esplanade square ◆ **la** ~ **Rouge** Red Square ◆ **la** ~ **du marché** the market square, the marketplace ◆ **ils ont porté le débat sur la** ~ **publique** they've brought the discussion into the public arena ◆ **étaler ses divergences sur la** ~ **publique** to air one's differences in public ◆ **clamer qch sur la** ~ **publique** to proclaim sth from the rooftops

2 d'objet place ◆ **changer la** ~ **de qch** to change the place of sth ◆ **changer qch de** ~ to move *ou* shift sth, to put sth in a different place ◆ **la** ~ **des mots dans la phrase** word order in sentences ◆ **une** ~ **pour chaque chose et chaque chose à sa** ~ *(Prov)* a place for everything and everything in its place *(Prov)*

3 de personne place; *(assise)* seat ◆ ~ **d'honneur** place *ou* seat of honour ◆ **à vos** ~**s !** to your places! ◆ **~s assises 20, ~s debout 40** seating capacity 20, standing passengers 40 ◆ **il n'y a que des ~s debout** it's standing room only ◆ **une (voiture de) 4 ~s** a 4-seater (car) ◆ **la** ~ **du mort** *(dans une voiture)* the (front) passenger seat ◆ **tente à 4 ~s** tent that sleeps 4, 4-man tent ◆ **j'ai trois ~s dans ma voiture** I've room for three in my car ◆ **avoir sa** ~ **dans le cœur de qn/l'histoire** to have a place in sb's heart/in history ◆ **il ne donnerait pas sa** ~ **pour un empire** he wouldn't change places with anyone for all the tea in China* *ou* for the world ◆ **sa** ~ **n'est pas ici** he doesn't belong here ◆ **se faire une** ~ **dans la société/dans la littérature** to carve out a place *ou* niche for o.s. in society/in literature ◆ **se faire une** ~ **au soleil** to find o.s. a place in the sun *(fig)* ◆ **laisser sa** ~ **à qn** *(lit)* to give (up) one's seat to sb; *(fig)* to hand over to sb ◆ **prenez** ~ take a seat ◆ **prendre la** ~ **de qn** to take sb's place; *(= remplacer qn)* to take over from sb, to take sb's place ◆ **la religion tient une** ~ **importante dans cette société** religion holds *ou* has an important place in this society ◆ **elle tient une grande** ~ **dans ma vie** she means a great deal *ou* a lot to me ◆ **tenir sa** ~ *(= faire bonne figure)* to put up a good show, to hold one's own ◆ **trouver** *ou* **prendre** ~ **parmi/dans** to find a place (for o.s.) among/in; → **chasse**[1]

4 = espace libre room, space ◆ **tenir** *ou* **prendre de la** ~ to take up a lot of room *ou* space ◆ **faire/gagner de la** ~ to make/save room *ou* space ◆ **j'ai trouvé une** ~ *ou* **de la** ~ **pour me garer** *ou* *(Helv)* **une** ~ **de parc** I've found a parking space *ou* place ◆ **pouvez-vous me faire une petite** ~ **?** can you make a bit of room for me? ◆ **il y a juste la** ~ **de mettre un lave-vaisselle** there's just enough room *ou* space for a dishwasher ◆ **on n'a pas la** ~ **de se retourner** there's no room to move *ou* not enough room to swing a cat* *(Brit)* ◆ **ne mange pas trop, garde une** ~ **pour le gâteau** don't eat too much, leave some room for the cake ◆ **ce journal accorde** *ou* **consacre une** ~ **importante au sport** this newspaper gives a lot of coverage to sport ◆ **dans notre société, il y a** ~ **pour de nouvelles initiatives** our company provides scope for new initiatives ◆ **faire** ~ **à qch** *(fig)* to give way to sth ◆ **faire** ~ **à qn** *(lit)* to let sb pass; *(fig)* to give way to sb ◆ ~ **aux jeunes !** make way for the young! ◆ **faire** ~ **nette** to make a clean sweep

5 = billet seat; *(= prix, trajet)* fare; *(= emplacement réservé)* space ◆ **louer** *ou* **réserver sa** ~ to book one's seat ◆ **il n'a pas payé sa** ~ he hasn't paid for his seat, he hasn't paid his fare ◆ **payer** ~ **entière** *(au cinéma etc)* to pay full price; *(dans le bus etc)* to pay full fare ◆ ~ **de parking** parking space ◆ **parking de 500 ~s** parking (space) for 500 cars ◆ **cinéma de 400 ~s** cinema seating 400 (people) *ou* with a seating capacity of 400

6 = rang *(Scol)* place (in class); *(Sport)* place, placing ◆ **il a eu une bonne** ~ he got a good place *ou* a good placing ◆ **être reçu dans les premières ~s** to get one of the top places, to be amongst the top ◆ **il a eu une première** ~ *ou* **une** ~ **de premier en histoire** he was *ou* came *(Brit)* first in history ◆ **ce champion a reconquis la première** ~ **mondiale** the champion has won back the number one world ranking *ou* title ◆ **l'entreprise occupe la seconde** ~ **sur le marché des ordinateurs** the company ranks second in the computer market ◆ **figurer en bonne** ~ *[personne]* to be prominent ◆ **son nom figure en bonne** ~ **dans la liste** his name is high on the list ◆ **la question figure en bonne** ~ **dans l'ordre du jour** the matter is *ou* features high on the agenda ◆ **ses livres trônent en bonne** ~ **dans la vitrine** his books have pride of place in the shop window

7 = emploi job; *[de domestique]* position, situation ◆ **une** ~ **de serveuse/coursier** a job as a waitress/courier ◆ **dans les médias, les ~s sont chères** there's a lot of competition for jobs in the media, jobs in the media are hard to come by

8 Mil ~ **(forte** *ou* **de guerre)** fortified town ◆ **le commandant de la** ~ the fortress commander ◆ **s'introduire/avoir des contacts dans la** ~ to get/have contacts on the inside ◆ **maintenant il est dans la** ~ *(fig)* now he's on the inside ◆ ~ **d'armes** parade ground

9 Comm, Fin market ◆ **vous ne trouverez pas moins cher sur la** ~ **de Paris** you won't find cheaper on the Paris market ◆ **dans toutes les ~s financières du monde** in all the money markets of the world ◆ ~ **bancaire/commerciale** banking/trade centre ◆ ~ **boursière** stock market

10 locutions

◆ **à la place** *(= en échange)* instead ◆ **si tu n'en veux pas, prends autre chose à la** ~ if you don't want any, take something else instead ◆ **ils ont démoli la maison et construit un immeuble à la** ~ they've demolished the house and built an apartment building in its place

◆ **à la place de** *(= au lieu de)* instead of ◆ **elle a emporté ma veste à la** ~ **de la sienne** she went off with my jacket instead of her own ◆ **ils ont construit un parking à la** ~ **de la maison** they've built a car park where the house used to be ◆ **faire une démarche à la** ~ **de qn** *(= en le remplaçant)* to take steps on sb's behalf ◆ **répondre à la** ~ **de qn** to reply in sb's place *ou* on sb's behalf ◆ **se mettre à la** ~ **de qn** to put o.s. in sb's place *ou* in sb's shoes

◆ **à sa (***ou* **ma** *etc***) place** *(= à l'endroit habituel ou convenable)* ◆ **cette lampe n'est pas à sa** ~ this lamp isn't in the right place *ou* in its proper place *ou* is in the wrong place ◆ **il n'est pas à sa** ~ **dans ce milieu** he feels out of place in this setting ◆ **remettre qch à sa** ~ to put sth back where it belongs *ou* in its proper place ◆ **remettre les choses à leur** ~ *(en perspective)* to put things in perspective; *(au clair)* to put the record straight ◆ **remettre qn à sa** ~ to put sb in his place, to take sb down a peg or two* ◆ **savoir rester à sa** ~ to know one's place ◆ **à votre/sa** ~ *(= si j'étais vous)* if I were you/him, in your/his place ◆ **je n'aimerais pas être à sa** ~ I wouldn't like to be in his shoes ◆ **à ma** ~**, tu aurais accepté ?** in my place *ou* position would you have agreed?, would you have accepted if you were in my shoes?

◆ **de place en place, par places** here and there, in places

◆ **en place** ◆ **les gens en** ~ *(= influents)* influential people; *(= décisionnaires)* decisionmakers ◆ **le pouvoir/régime en** ~ *(maintenant)* the current government/regime; *(à l'époque)* the government/regime at the time ◆ **l'arrivée d'un cadre de haut niveau peut inquiéter les gens en** ~ if a senior manager joins them, it can be worrying for the existing team ◆ **être en ~** *[plan]* to be ready; *[forces de l'ordre]* to be in position; † *[domestique]* to be in service (*chez* with); ◆ **maintenant qu'il est en ~** *(dans un emploi)* now that he has got the position ◆ **tout le monde est en ~** everyone is in place *ou* is seated ◆ **le gouvernement est en ~ depuis trois mois** the government has been in power *ou* office for three months ◆ **tout est en ~ pour le drame** the scene is set for the tragedy ◆ **en ~ pour la photo !** everybody take up your positions for the photograph! ◆ **mettre en ~** *[+ plan]* to set up, to organize; *[+ marchandises]* to put on the shelves; *[+ service d'ordre]* to deploy; *[+ mécanisme, dispositif]* to install ◆ **le dispositif d'évacuation s'est mis en ~** evacuation procedures have been set up ◆ **mise en ~** *[de plan]* setting up; *[de service d'ordre]* deployment ◆ **il a terminé la mise en ~ au rayon confiserie** *[de marchandises]* he finished stocking the shelves in the confectionery department ◆ **remettre qch en ~** to put sth back where it belongs *ou* in its proper place ◆ **il ne tient pas en ~** he can't keep *ou* stay still, he's always fidgeting

◆ **sur place** on the spot ◆ **être/rester/se rendre sur ~** to be/stay/go there ◆ **les sauveteurs sont déjà sur ~** rescuers are already on the spot *ou* at the scene ◆ **on annonce l'envoi sur ~ d'observateurs internationaux** it has been announced that international observers are being sent out there ◆ **la situation sur ~ est catastrophique** the situation on the ground is disastrous ◆ **on peut faire la réparation sur ~** we can repair it right here *ou* on the spot ◆ **sa présence sur ~ est indispensable** his presence on the spot *ou* on site is essential ◆ **vous trouverez des vélos/des brochures sur ~** bicycles/leaflets are available on site ◆ **(à consommer) sur ~ ou à emporter ?** *(Comm)* eat in or take away? ◆ **les produits fabriqués sur ~** *(dans la région)* locally-manufactured products; *(dans le magasin)* goods made on the premises ◆ **il s'est enfui, abandonnant sur ~ la moto volée** he abandoned the stolen motorbike and fled; → **clouer, sur-place**

---

placé, e /plase/ (ptp de **placer**) **ADJ** 1 *(gén)* **la fenêtre/leur maison est ~e à gauche** the window/their house is (situated) on the left ◆ **je suis ou je me trouve ~ dans une position délicate** I am (placed) in *ou* I find myself (placed) in a tricky position ◆ **être bien/mal ~** *[terrain]* to be well/badly situated, to be favourably/unfavourably situated; *[objet]* to be well/badly placed; *[de spectateur]* to have a good/a poor seat; *[concurrent]* to be in a good/bad position, to be well/badly placed ◆ **leur confiance a été bien/mal ~e** their trust was justified/misplaced ◆ **sa fierté est mal ~e** his pride is misplaced *ou* out of place ◆ **il est bien ~ pour gagner** he is in a good position *ou* well placed to win ◆ **il est bien ~ pour le savoir** he should know ◆ **je suis bien/mal ~ pour vous répondre** I'm in a/in no position to answer ◆ **tu es mal ~ pour te plaindre !*** you've got nothing to complain about!; → **haut**

2 *(Courses)* **arriver ~** to be placed ◆ **jouer (un cheval) ~** to back a horse each way *(Brit)*, to put an each-way *(Brit)* bet on (a horse), to back a horse across the board *(US)*

placebo /plasebo/ **NM** placebo ◆ **effet ~** placebo effect

placement /plasmɑ̃/ **NM** 1 *(Fin)* investment ◆ **faire un ~ d'argent** to invest (some) money ◆ **~ de père de famille** gilt-edged investment, safe investment 2 *[d'employés]* placing ◆ **l'école assure le ~ des élèves** the school ensures that the pupils find employment; → **bureau** 3 *(Psych)* **~ d'office** compulsory admission ◆ **~ volontaire** voluntary admission

placenta /plasɛ̃ta/ **NM** *(Anat)* placenta; *(= arrière-faix)* afterbirth, placenta

placentaire /plasɛ̃tɛʀ/ **ADJ** placental

placer /plase/ ▸ conjug 3 ◂ **VT** 1 *(= assigner une place à) [+ objet, personne]* to place, to put; *[+ invité]* to seat, to put; *[+ spectateur]* to seat, to give a seat to, to put; *[+ sentinelle]* to post, to station; *(Ftbl) [+ ballon]* to place; *(Boxe) [+ coup]* to land, to place; *(Tech = installer)* to put in, to fit ◆ **vous me placez dans une situation délicate** you're placing *ou* putting me in a tricky position ◆ **~ sa voix** to pitch one's voice ◆ **~ ses affaires bien en ordre** to tidy up one's things

2 *(= situer)* to place, to set, to put ◆ **il a placé l'action de son roman en Provence** he has set *ou* situated the action of his novel in Provence ◆ **où placez-vous Lyon ?** whereabouts do you think Lyons is?, where would you put Lyons? ◆ **~ l'honnêteté avant l'intelligence** to set *ou* put *ou* place honesty above intelligence ◆ **~ le bonheur dans la vie familiale** to consider that happiness is found in family life ◆ **~ un nom sur un visage** to put a name to a face ◆ **je ne peux pas ~ de nom sur son visage** I can't place him, I can't put a name to his face ◆ **~ ses espérances en qn/qch** to set *ou* pin one's hopes on sb/sth

3 *(= introduire) [+ remarque, anecdote, plaisanterie]* to put in, to get in ◆ **il n'a pas pu ~ un mot** he couldn't get a word in (edgeways)

4 *[+ ouvrier, malade, écolier]* to place (*dans* in); ◆ **~ qn comme vendeur** to get *ou* find sb a job as a salesman ◆ **~ qn comme apprenti (chez qn)** to apprentice sb (to sb) ◆ **~ qn à la comptabilité** to give sb a job *ou* place sb in the accounts department ◆ **~ qn à la tête d'une entreprise** to put sb at the head of a business, to put sb in charge of a business ◆ **ils n'ont pas encore pu ~ leur fille** *(hum)* they've still not been able to marry off their daughter *ou* to get their daughter off their hands ◆ **~ qn/qch sous l'autorité/les ordres de** to place *ou* put sb/sth under the authority/orders of

5 *(= vendre) [+ marchandise]* to place, to sell ◆ **elle a réussi à ~ sa vieille machine à laver** *(hum)* she managed to find a home *(hum)* *ou* a buyer for her old washing machine

6 *[+ argent] (à la Bourse)* to invest; *(à la caisse d'épargne, sur un compte)* to deposit ◆ **~ une somme sur son compte** to put *ou* pay a sum into one's account

VPR se placer 1 *[personne]* to take up a position; *(debout)* to stand; *(assis)* to sit (down); *[événement, action]* to take place ◆ **se ~ de face/contre le mur/en cercle** to stand face on/against the wall/in a circle ◆ **se ~ sur le chemin de qn** to stand in sb's path ◆ **cette démarche se place dans le cadre de nos revendications** these steps should be seen in the context of our claims ◆ **si nous nous plaçons à ce point de vue ou dans cette perspective** *(fig)* if we look at things from this point of view, if we view the situation in this way ◆ **plaçons-nous dans le cas où cela arriverait** let us suppose that this happens, let us put ourselves in the situation where this actually happens

2 *[cheval]* to be placed ◆ **se ~ 2e** *(Scol, Sport)* to be *ou* come 2nd, to be in 2nd place ◆ **il s'est bien placé dans la course** he was well placed in the race ◆ **se ~ parmi les premiers** to be in the first few

3 *(= prendre une place)* to get *ou* find a job *(comme* as); ◆ **retraité qui voudrait bien se ~ (dans une institution)** pensioner who would like to find a place in a home

placet /plasɛ/ **NM** *(Hist, Jur)* petition

placeur /plasœʀ/ **NM** *[de spectateurs, invités]* usher

placeuse /plasøz/ **NF** *[de spectateurs]* usherette

placide /plasid/ **ADJ** placid, calm

placidement /plasidmɑ̃/ **ADV** placidly, calmly

placidité /plasidite/ **NF** placidity, placidness, calmness

placier /plasje/ **NM** travelling salesman, traveller ◆ **~ en assurances** insurance broker

Placoplâtre ® /plakoplɑtʀ/ **NM** plasterboard

plafond /plafɔ̃/ **NM** 1 *[de salle]* ceiling; *[de voiture, caverne]* roof; *(Art)* ceiling painting ◆ **~ à caissons** coffered ceiling ◆ **pièce haute/basse de ~** high-ceilinged/low-ceilinged room, room with a high/low ceiling ◆ **il est bas de ~*** he hasn't got much up top*; → **araignée** 2 *(= limite) [de prix, loyer]* ceiling; *(= nuages)* ceiling, cloud cover; *(= altitude maximale d'un avion)* ceiling, maximum height; *(= vitesse maximale d'une voiture)* top *ou* maximum speed ◆ **niveau/prix-~** ceiling, ceiling *ou* maximum limit/price ◆ **âge(-)~** maximum age ◆ **~ de crédit** lending *ou* credit limit ◆ **~ de la Sécurité sociale** *upper limit on salary deductions for social security contributions* ◆ **le ~ est bas** *(Météo)* the cloud cover is low

plafonnement /plafɔnmɑ̃/ **NM** ◆ **il y a un ~ des salaires/cotisations** there is an upper limit on salaries/contributions

plafonner /plafɔne/ ▸ conjug 1 ◂ **VI** *[prix, écolier, salaire]* to reach a ceiling *ou* maximum; *(en avion)* to reach one's ceiling; *(en voiture)* to reach one's top speed *ou* maximum speed ◆ **les ventes plafonnent** sales have reached their *ou* a ceiling (limit) ◆ **la voiture plafonne à 100 km/h** the car can't do more than 100 km/h **VT** 1 *(Constr)* to put a ceiling in ◆ **grenier plafonné** loft which has had a ceiling put in 2 *[+ salaires]* to put an upper limit on ◆ **cotisations plafonnées à 250 €** contributions which have had their ceiling *ou* upper limit fixed at €250

plafonnier /plafɔnje/ **NM** *[de voiture]* courtesy *ou* interior light; *[de chambre]* ceiling light *ou* lamp

plage /plaʒ/ **NF** 1 *[de mer, rivière, lac]* beach ◆ **~ de sable/de galets** sandy/pebble beach ◆ **sac/serviette/robe de ~** beach bag/towel/robe 2 *(= ville)* (seaside) resort 3 *(= zone) (dans un barème, une progression)* range, bracket; *(dans un horaire etc)* (time) slot ◆ **~ d'ombre** band of shadow, shadowy area ◆ **temps d'écoute divisé en ~s (horaires)** listening time divided into slots ◆ **~ horaire** *(Scol)* slot (in timetable) ◆ **~ musicale** intermission ◆ **~ publicitaire** commercial break, commercials ◆ **~ de prix** price range *ou* bracket 4 *[de disque]* track

COMP plage arrière *[de bateau]* quarter-deck; *(de voiture)* parcel shelf, back shelf

plage avant *(de bateau)* forecastle (head *ou* deck), fo'c'sle

plagiaire /plaʒjɛʀ/ **NMF** plagiarist, plagiarizer

plagiat /plaʒja/ **NM** plagiarism, plagiary ◆ **c'est un véritable ~** it's absolute plagiarism ◆ **faire du ~** to plagiarize

plagier /plaʒje/ ▸ conjug 7 ◂ **VT** to plagiarize

plagiste /plaʒist/ **NM** beach manager *ou* attendant

plaid /plɛd/ **NM** *(= couverture)* car rug, lap robe *(US)*

plaidant, e /plɛdɑ̃, ɑt/ **ADJ** *[partie]* litigant; *[avocat]* pleading

plaider /plede/ ▸ conjug 1 ◂ **VT** to plead ◆ **~ coupable/non coupable/la légitime défense** to plead guilty/not guilty/self-defence ◆ **~ la cause de qn** *(fig)* to plead sb's cause, to argue *ou* speak in favour of sb; *(Jur)* to plead for sb, to plead sb's case, to defend sb ◆ **~ sa propre cause** to speak in one's own defence ◆ **l'affaire s'est plaidée à Paris/à huis clos** the case was heard in Paris/in closed court *ou* in camera **VI** 1 *[avocat]* to plead (*pour* for, on behalf of; *contre* against); ◆ **~ pour ou en faveur de qn/qch** *(fig)* to speak in favour of sb/sth ② *(= intenter un procès)* to go to court, to litigate ◆ ~ **contre qn** to take sb to court, to take proceedings against sb ◆ **ils ont plaidé pendant des années** their case has dragged on for years

plaideur, -euse /plɛdœʀ, øz/ **NM,F** litigant

plaidoirie /plɛdwaʀi/ **NF** *(Jur)* speech for the defence, defence speech; *(fig)* plea, appeal *(en faveur de* on behalf of)

plaidoyer /plɛdwaje/ **NM** *(Jur)* speech for the defence; *(fig)* defence, plea ◆ ~ **en faveur de/contre qch** *(fig)* plea for/against sth

plaie /plɛ/ **NF** *(physique, morale)* wound; *(= coupure)* cut; *(= fléau)* scourge ◆ **rouvrir une** ~ *(fig)* to open an old wound ◆ ~ **ouverte/béante/profonde/vive** open/gaping/deep/raw wound ◆ **quelle** ~ **!** * *(personne)* he's such a nuisance! *ou* pest*!; *(chose)* what a nuisance! *ou* bind* *(Brit)*! ◆ **remuer** *ou* **tourner le couteau** *ou* **le fer dans la** ~ to twist *ou* turn the knife in the wound, to rub salt in the wound ◆ ~ **d'argent n'est pas mortelle** *(Prov)* money isn't everything ◆ **les ~s d'Égypte** *(Bible)* the plagues of Egypt; → **rêver**

plaignant, e /plɛɲɑ̃, ɑ̃t/ **ADJ** ◆ **la partie ~e** the plaintiff, the complainant **NM,F** plaintiff, complainant

plain /plɛ̃/ **NM** *(= marée)* ◆ **le** ~ high tide

plain-chant (pl **plains-chants**) /plɛ̃ʃɑ̃/ **NM** plainchant *(NonC)*, plainsong *(NonC)*

plaindre /plɛ̃dʀ/ ▸ conjug 52 ◂ **VT** ① *[+ personne]* to pity, to feel sorry for ◆ **aimer se faire** ~ to like to be pitied ◆ **il est bien à** ~ he is to be pitied ◆ **elle n'est pas à** ~ *(= c'est bien fait)* she doesn't deserve (any) sympathy, she doesn't deserve to be pitied; *(= elle a de la chance)* she's got nothing to complain about ◆ **je vous plains de vivre avec lui** I pity you *ou* I sympathize with you (for) having to live with him

② *(* = donner chichement)* to begrudge, to grudge ◆ **donne-moi plus de papier, on dirait que tu le plains** give me some more paper – anybody would think you begrudged it (me) ◆ **il ne plaint pas son temps/sa peine** he doesn't grudge his time/his efforts

VPR se plaindre *(= gémir)* to moan; *(= protester)* to complain, to grumble, to moan* *(de* about); *(frm, Jur = réclamer)* to make a complaint *(de* about; *auprès de* to); ◆ **se** ~ **de** *(souffrir) [+ maux de tête etc]* to complain of ◆ **se** ~ **de qn/qch à qn** to complain to sb about sb/sth ◆ **de quoi te plains-tu ?** *(lit)* what are you complaining *ou* grumbling *ou* moaning* about?; *(iro)* what have you got to complain *ou* grumble *ou* moan* about? ◆ **il se plaint que les prix montent** he's complaining about rising prices *ou* that prices are going up ◆ **ne viens pas te** ~ **si tu es puni** don't come and complain *ou* moan* (to me) if you're punished ◆ **je vais me** ~ **à qui de droit** I'm going to make a formal complaint

plaine /plɛn/ **NF** plain ◆ **c'est de la** ~ it is flat open country ◆ **en** ~ in the plains ◆ **haute** ~ high plain ◆ **les Grandes Plaines** the Great Plains

plain-pied /plɛ̃pje/ **de plain-pied LOC ADV** *[pièce]* on the same level *(avec* as); *[maison]* (built) at street-level ◆ **entrer de** ~ **dans le sujet** to come straight to the point

plainte /plɛ̃t/ **NF** ① *(= gémissement)* moan, groan; *(littér) [de vent]* moaning ② *(= doléance)* complaint, moaning* *(NonC)* *(péj)* ③ *(Jur)* complaint ◆ **porter** ~ *ou* **déposer une** ~ **contre qn** to lodge *ou* register a complaint against sb ◆ **je vais porter** ~ **!** I'm going to make a formal complaint! ◆ **désirez-vous porter** ~ **?** do you wish to press charges? ◆ ~ **contre X** complaint against person or persons unknown

plaintif, -ive /plɛ̃tif, iv/ **ADJ** plaintive, doleful

plaintivement /plɛ̃tivmɑ̃/ **ADV** plaintively, dolefully

plaire /plɛʀ/ GRAMMAIRE ACTIVE 39.2, 41 ▸ conjug 54 ◂

VI ① *(= être apprécié)* **ce garçon me plaît** I like that boy ◆ **ce garçon ne me plaît pas** I don't like that boy, I don't care for that boy ◆ **ce spectacle/dîner/livre m'a plu** I liked *ou* enjoyed that show/dinner/book ◆ **ce genre de musique ne me plaît pas beaucoup** I don't really care for *ou* I'm not very keen on* *(Brit)* that kind of music, that kind of music doesn't appeal to me very much ◆ **ton nouveau travail te plaît ?** (how) do you like your new job?, how are you enjoying your new job? ◆ **les brunes me plaisent** I like *ou* go for* dark-haired girls, dark-haired girls appeal to me ◆ **tu ne me plais pas avec cette coiffure** I don't like you with your hair like that ◆ **c'est une chose qui me plairait beaucoup à faire** it's something I'd very much like to do *ou* I'd love to do ◆ **on ne peut pas** ~ **à tout le monde** you can't be liked by everyone ◆ **c'est le genre d'homme qui plaît aux femmes** he's the sort of man that women like *ou* who appeals to women ◆ **le désir de** ~ the desire to please ◆ **c'est le genre de personne qui plaît en société** he's the type of person that people like to have around ◆ **tu commences à me** ~ **(avec tes questions) !** * *(iro)* you're starting to get on my nerves (with your questions)!

② *(= convenir à)* **ce plan me plaît** this plan suits me ◆ **ça te plairait d'aller au théâtre ?** would you like to go to the theatre?, do you feel like *ou* do you fancy *(Brit)* going to the theatre? ◆ **j'irai si ça me plaît** I'll go if I feel like it *ou* if I want (to) ◆ **je travaille quand ça me plaît** I work when I feel like it *ou* when it suits me ◆ **je fais ce qui me plaît** I do what I like *ou* as I please ◆ **si ça ne te plaît pas c'est le même prix !** * if you don't like it (that's just) too bad! * *ou* that's tough! *

③ *(= avoir du succès)* **achète des fleurs, cela plaît toujours** buy some flowers, they're always appreciated *ou* welcome ◆ **la pièce/cette réponse a plu** the play/this reply went down well

VB IMPERS ◆ **ici, je fais ce qu'il me plaît** I do as I please *ou* like here ◆ **et s'il me plaît d'y aller ?** and what if I want to go? ◆ **vous plairait-il de venir dîner ce soir ?** would you care *ou* like to come for dinner this evening? ◆ **il lui plaît de croire que ...** *(littér)* he likes to think that ... ◆ **comme il vous plaira** just as you like *ou* please *ou* choose *ou* wish ◆ **plaise** *ou* **plût à Dieu** *ou* **au ciel qu'il réussisse !** *(littér)* please God that he succeed! *(littér)* ◆ **plaît-il ?** *(frm)* I beg your pardon?

♦ **s'il te/vous plaît** please ◆ **deux croissants, s'il vous plaît** two croissants, please ◆ **et elle a un manteau de vison, s'il vous plaît !** * and she's got a mink coat if you please! *ou* no less!

VPR se plaire ① *(= se sentir bien, à l'aise)* **il se plaît à Londres** he likes *ou* enjoys being in London, he likes it in London ◆ **j'espère qu'il s'y plaira** I hope he'll like it there ◆ **se** ~ **avec qn** to enjoy being with sb, to enjoy sb's company ◆ **te plais-tu avec tes nouveaux amis ?** do you like being with your new friends? ◆ **les fougères se plaisent à l'ombre** ferns like shade

② *(= s'apprécier)* **je ne me plais pas en robe** I don't like myself in a dress ◆ **tu te plais avec ce chapeau ?** do you like yourself in that hat? ◆ **ces deux-là se plaisent** those two get on *ou* along *(Brit)* well together, those two have really hit it off*

③ *(littér = prendre plaisir à)* **se** ~ **à lire** to take pleasure in reading, to like *ou* be fond of reading ◆ **se** ~ **à tout critiquer** to delight in criticizing everything ◆ **je me plais à penser que ...** I like to think that ...

plaisamment /plɛzamɑ̃/ **ADV** ① *(= agréablement)* pleasantly, agreeably ② *(= de façon amusante)* amusingly

plaisance /plɛzɑ̃s/ **NF** ◆ **la (navigation de)** ~ boating; *(à voile)* sailing, yachting; → **bateau, port**[1]

plaisancier /plɛzɑ̃sje/ **NM** (amateur) sailor *ou* yachtsman

plaisant, e /plɛzɑ̃, ɑ̃t/ **ADJ** ① *(= agréable) [personne, séjour, souvenir]* pleasant, agreeable; *[maison]* pleasant, nice ◆ ~ **à l'œil** pleasing to the eye, nice *ou* attractive to look at ◆ **ce n'est guère** ~ it's not exactly pleasant, it's not very nice ◆ **c'est une ville très ~e à vivre** it's a very pleasant *ou* nice town to live in ◆ **il n'est pas très** ~ **à vivre** he's not that easy to get along with; → **mauvais** ② *(= amusant) [histoire, aventure]* amusing, funny ◆ **le** ~ **de la chose** the funny side *ou* part of it, the funny thing about it ③ *(= ridicule)* laughable, ridiculous ④ († = *bizarre)* bizarre, singular ◆ **voilà qui est** ~ **!** it's quite bizarre!

plaisanter /plɛzɑ̃te/ ▸ conjug 1 ◂ **VI** to joke, to have a joke *(sur* about); ◆ **je ne suis pas d'humeur à** ~ I'm in no mood for jokes *ou* joking, I'm not in a joking mood ◆ **et je ne plaisante pas !** and I mean it!, and I'm not joking! ◆ **c'est quelqu'un qui ne plaisante pas** he's not the sort you can have a joke with ◆ **non, je plaisante !** * just kidding! * ◆ **vous plaisantez** you must be joking *ou* kidding*, you're joking *ou* kidding* ◆ **c'était juste pour** ~ it was just a joke ◆ **dit-il pour** ~ he said jokingly *ou* in jest ◆ **on ne plaisante pas avec cela** this is no joking *ou* laughing matter ◆ **il ne faut pas** ~ **avec les médicaments** you shouldn't mess around* with medicines ◆ **il ne plaisante pas sur la discipline/cette question** there's no joking with him over matters of discipline/this subject ◆ **on ne plaisante pas avec la police** the police are not to be trifled with

VT to make fun of, to tease ◆ ~ **qn sur qch** to tease sb about sth

plaisanterie /plɛzɑ̃tʀi/ **NF** ① *(= blague)* joke *(sur* about); ◆ **aimer la** ~ to be fond of a joke ◆ ~ **de corps de garde** barrack-room joke ◆ **par** ~ for fun *ou* a joke *ou* a laugh* ◆ **faire une** ~ to tell *ou* crack a joke ◆ **tourner qch en** ~ to make a joke of sth, to laugh sth off ◆ **les ~s les plus courtes sont (toujours) les meilleures** brevity is the soul of wit

② *(= raillerie)* joke ◆ **il est en butte aux ~s de ses amis** his friends are always making fun of him *ou* poking fun at him ◆ **faire des ~s sur** to joke *ou* make jokes about *ou* at the expense of ◆ **il comprend** *ou* **prend bien la** ~ he knows how to *ou* he can take a joke ◆ **il ne faudrait pas pousser la** ~ **trop loin** we mustn't take the joke too far

③ *(= farce)* (practical) joke, prank; → **mauvais**

④ *(locutions)* **résoudre ce problème/gagner la course est une** ~ **pour lui** he could solve this problem/win the race with his eyes shut *ou* standing on his head* ◆ **la** ~ **a assez duré !** this has gone far enough!, this has gone beyond a joke! ◆ **lui, se lever tôt ? c'est une** ~ **!** him, get up early? what a joke! *ou* you must be joking! *ou* you must be kidding! *

plaisantin /plɛzɑ̃tɛ̃/ **NM** ① *(= blagueur)* joker ◆ **c'est un petit** ~ he's quite a joker ② *(= fumiste)* phoney*

plaisir /plɛziʀ/ GRAMMAIRE ACTIVE 30, 36.2, 46.5, 51.1, 51.2 **NM** ① *(= joie)* pleasure ◆ **avoir du** ~ *ou* **prendre** ~ **à faire qch** to find *ou* take pleasure in doing sth, to delight in doing sth ◆ **prendre (un malin)** ~ **à faire qch** to take (a mischievous) delight in doing sth ◆ **j'ai le** ~ **de vous annoncer que ...** I am pleased to inform you that ..., I have great pleasure to inform you that ... ◆ **M. et Mme Lebrun ont le** ~ **de vous faire part de ...** Mr and Mrs Lebrun are pleased to announce ... ◆ **c'est un ~ de le voir** it's a pleasure to see him ◆ **c'est un ~ chaque fois renouvelé de te voir** it's always a pleasure to see you ◆ **par ~, pour le ~** *(gén)* for pleasure; *[bricoler, peindre]* as a hobby ◆ **ranger pour le ~ de ranger** to tidy up just for the sake of it ◆ **je vous souhaite bien du ~ !** *(iro)* good luck to you! *(iro)*, I wish you (the best of) luck! *(iro)* ◆ **ça nous promet du ~ (en perspective)** *(iro)* I can hardly wait! *(iro)* ◆ **avec (le plus grand) ~** with (the greatest of) pleasure ◆ **au ~ de vous revoir, au ~*** (I'll) see you again sometime, (I'll) be seeing you* ◆ **les ~s de la table** good food; → **durer, gêne**

2 *(sexuel)* pleasure ◆ **avoir du ~** to experience pleasure ◆ **le ~ solitaire** self-abuse ◆ **les ~s de la chair** the pleasures of the flesh

3 *(= distraction)* pleasure ◆ **les ~s de la vie** life's (little) pleasures ◆ **courir après les ~s** to be a pleasure-seeker ◆ **le golf est un ~ coûteux** golf is an expensive hobby *ou* pleasure ◆ **lieu de ~** house of pleasure

4 *(littér = volonté)* pleasure *(littér)*, wish ◆ **si c'est votre (bon) ~** if such is your will *ou* wish, if you so desire ◆ **les faits ont été grossis à ~** the facts have been wildly exaggerated ◆ **il s'inquiète/ment à ~** he worries/lies for the sake of it

5 *(locutions)* **faire ~ à qn** to please sb ◆ **ce cadeau m'a fait ~** I was very pleased with this gift, this gift gave me great pleasure ◆ **ça me fait ~ de vous entendre dire cela** I'm pleased *ou* delighted to hear you say that ◆ **cela fait ~ à voir** it is a pleasure to see *ou* to behold ◆ **ça t'a agacé ? – au contraire, ça m'a fait ~** did it annoy you? – no, I was pleased ◆ **pour me faire ~** (just) to please me ◆ **fais-moi ~ : mange ta soupe/arrête la radio** do me a favour, eat your soup/turn off the radio, be a dear and eat your soup/turn off the radio ◆ **voulez-vous me faire le ~ de venir dîner ?** *(frm)* I should be most pleased if you would come to dinner, would you do me the pleasure of dining with me (*ou* us)? *(frm)* ◆ **fais-moi le ~ de te taire !** would you mind being quiet!, do me a favour and shut up!* ◆ **il se fera un ~ de vous reconduire** he'll be (only too) pleased *ou* glad to drive you back, it will be a pleasure for him to drive you back ◆ **bon, c'est bien pour vous faire ~** *ou* **si cela peut vous faire ~** all right, if it will make you happy ◆ **j'irai, mais c'est bien pour vous faire ~** I'll go (just) to keep you happy ◆ **se faire ~** *(= s'amuser)* to enjoy o.s., to have fun ◆ **faites-vous ~, allez dîner au "Gourmet"** treat *ou* spoil yourself, go and have dinner at the "Gourmet"

plan[1] /plɑ̃/ NM 1 *[de maison]* plan, blueprint; *[de machine]* plan, scale drawing; *[de ville, métro]* map, plan; *[de région]* map ◆ **acheter une maison sur ~** to buy a house while it's still only a plan on paper ◆ **faire** *ou* **tracer** *ou* **tirer un ~** to draw a plan ◆ **tirer des ~s sur la comète*** to build castles in the air

2 *(Math, Phys = surface)* plane

3 *(Ciné, Photo)* shot ◆ **premier ~** *(Peinture, Photo)* foreground ◆ **dernier ~** background ◆ **au second ~** in the background ◆ **au deuxième ~** *(Peinture)* in the middle distance ◆ **~ américain** *(Ciné)* medium close shot; → **gros**

4 *(fig)* **mettre qch au deuxième ~** to consider sth of secondary importance ◆ **ce problème est au premier ~ de nos préoccupations** this problem is uppermost in our minds *ou* is one of our foremost preoccupations ◆ **parmi toutes ces questions, l'inflation vient au premier ~** *ou* **nous mettons l'inflation au premier ~** of all these questions, inflation is the key *ou* priority issue *ou* we consider inflation to be the most important ◆ **personnalité de premier ~** key figure ◆ **personnalité de second ~** minor figure ◆ **un savant de tout premier ~** a scientist of the first rank, one of our foremost scientists ◆ **au premier ~ de l'actualité** at the forefront of the news, very much in the news

5 *(= niveau)* level ◆ **mettre sur le même ~** to put on the same plane *ou* level ◆ **au ~ national/international** at the national/international level ◆ **sur le ~ du confort** as far as comfort is concerned, as regards comfort ◆ **sur le ~ moral/intellectuel** morally/intellectually speaking, on the moral/intellectual plane ◆ **sur tous les ~s** in every way, on all fronts

6 *(= projet)* plan, project; *(Écon)* plan, programme ◆ **avoir/exécuter un ~** to have/carry out a plan ◆ **~ de carrière** career path ◆ **~ de cinq ans** five-year plan ◆ **~ de relance** *ou* **de redressement de l'économie** economic recovery plan ◆ **~ d'action/d'attaque** plan of action/of attack ◆ **~ de paix** peace plan ◆ **~ de modernisation/de restructuration** modernization/restructuring plan ◆ **~ de développement économique et social** economic and social development plan ◆ **~ social** *ou* **de licenciements** redundancy scheme *ou* plan ◆ **~ média** media campaign

7 *(* = idée)* idea ◆ **tu as un ~ pour les vacances ?** have you any ideas for the holidays? *ou* about where to go on holiday? ◆ **c'est un super ~ !** *ou* **un ~ d'enfer !** it's a great idea! ◆ **il a toujours des ~s foireux**** he's full of madcap* ideas *ou* schemes ◆ **on s'est fait un ~ restau/ciné hier soir** we ate out/we went to the cinema last night

8 *[de livre, dissertation, devoir]* plan, outline ◆ **faire un ~ de qch** to make a plan for sth, to plan sth out

9 *(* : locutions)* **rester en ~** *[personne]* to be left stranded, to be left high and dry; *[voiture]* to be abandoned *ou* ditched*; *[projets]* to be abandoned in midstream, to be left (hanging) in mid air ◆ **laisser en ~** *[+ personne]* to leave in the lurch *ou* high and dry *ou* stranded; *[+ voiture]* to abandon, to ditch*; *[+ affaires]* to abandon; *[+ projet, travail]* to drop, to abandon ◆ **il a tout laissé en ~ pour venir me voir** he dropped everything to come and see me

COMP **plan d'affaires** business plan
plan d'aménagement rural rural development plan
plan d'amortissement *(pour un bien, un investissement)* depreciation schedule; *(pour un emprunt)* redemption plan
plan comptable *French accounting standards*
plan de cuisson hob *(Brit)*, stovetop *(US)*
plan directeur *(Mil) map of the combat area; (Écon)* blueprint, master plan
plan d'eau *(lac)* lake; *(sur un cours d'eau)* stretch of smooth water
plan d'épargne en actions stock portfolio *(with tax advantages)*
plan d'épargne entreprise company savings plan
plan d'épargne-logement *savings plan for property purchase*
plan d'épargne populaire individual savings plan
plan d'épargne-retraite personal pension plan *ou* scheme
plan d'équipement industrial development programme
plan d'études study plan *ou* programme
plan de faille fault plane
plan de financement financing plan
plan fixe *(Ciné)* static shot
plan incliné inclined plane ◆ **en ~ incliné** sloping
plan de niveau floor plan
plan d'occupation des sols land use plan *(Brit)*, zoning regulations *ou* ordinances *(US)*
plan ORSEC *scheme set up to deal with major civil emergencies*
plan rapproché *ou* **serré** *(Ciné)* close-up (shot)
plan séquence *(Ciné)* sequence shot
plan de travail *(dans une cuisine)* work-top, work(ing) surface *(Brit)*, counter (top) *(US)*; *(planning)* work plan *ou* programme *ou* schedule
plan de vol flight plan; → **plan-concave, plan-convexe**

plan[2], e /plɑ̃, plan/ ADJ 1 *[miroir]* flat; *[surface]* flat, level 2 *(Math)* plane

planant, e* /planɑ̃, ɑ̃t/ ADJ *[musique]* mind-blowing*

planche /plɑ̃ʃ/ NF 1 *(en bois)* plank; *(plus large)* board; *(= rayon)* shelf; *(Naut = passerelle)* gangplank; *(= plongeoir)* diving board; *(* = ski)* ski ◆ **cabine/sol en ~s** wooden hut/floor ◆ **dormir sur une ~** to sleep on a wooden board ◆ **quand il sera entre quatre ~s*** when he's six foot under*; → **pain**

2 *(= illustration)* plate

3 *(= plantation)* bed

4 *(Natation)* **faire la ~** to float on one's back

NFPL **planches** *(Théât)* **les ~s** the boards, the stage *(NonC)* ◆ **monter sur les ~s** *(= faire du théâtre)* to go on the stage, to tread the boards; → **brûler**

COMP **planche anatomique** anatomical chart
planche à billets banknote plate ◆ **faire marcher la ~ à billets*** to print money
planche à découper *[de cuisinière]* chopping board; *[de boucher]* chopping block
planche à dessin *ou* **à dessiner** drawing board
planche à laver washboard
planche à pain *(lit)* breadboard ◆ **c'est une ~ à pain** *(péj)* she's as flat as a board* *ou* pancake*
planche à pâtisserie pastry board
planche à repasser ironing board
planche à roulettes *(= objet)* skateboard; *(= sport)* skateboarding ◆ **faire de la ~ à roulettes** to skateboard, to go skateboarding
planche de salut *(= appui)* mainstay; *(= dernier espoir)* last hope
planche de surf surfboard
planche à voile *(= objet)* windsurfing board, sailboard; *(= sport)* windsurfing ◆ **faire de la ~ à voile** to windsurf, to go windsurfing

planche-contact (pl **planches-contacts**) /plɑ̃ʃkɔ̃takt/ NF *(Photo)* contact sheet

plancher[1] /plɑ̃ʃe/ NM 1 *(= sol)* floor ◆ **faux ~** false floor ◆ **le ~ des vaches*** dry land; → **débarrasser, pied** 2 *(= limite)* lower limit ◆ **~ des cotisations** lower limit on contributions ◆ **prix ~** minimum *ou* floor *ou* bottom price 3 *(Anat)* floor ◆ **~ pelvien** pelvic floor

plancher[2]* /plɑ̃ʃe/ ▸ conjug 1 ◂ VI *(= parler)* to talk ◆ **sur quoi as-tu planché ?** what did they get you to talk on? ◆ **~ sur un rapport** *(= travailler)* to work on a report

planchette /plɑ̃ʃɛt/ NF *(gén)* (small) board; *(= rayon)* (small) shelf

planchiste /plɑ̃ʃist/ NMF windsurfer

plan-concave (pl **plan-concaves**) /plɑ̃kɔ̃kav/ ADJ plano-concave

plan-convexe (pl **plan-convexes**) /plɑ̃kɔ̃vɛks/ ADJ plano-convex

plancton /plɑ̃ktɔ̃/ NM plankton

planéité /planeite/ NF 1 *[de miroir]* flatness; *[de surface]* flatness, levelness 2 *(Math)* planeness

planer /plane/ ▸ conjug 1 ◂ VI 1 *[oiseau, avion]* to glide; *[brume, fumée]* to hang ◆ **l'oiseau planait au-dessus de sa tête** the bird was hovering above his head *ou* overhead ◆ **il laissa son regard ~ sur la foule** his gaze swept over the crowd; → **vol[1]** 2 *[danger, soupçons]* **~ sur** to hang over ◆ **laisser ~ le doute/une incertitude (sur)** to allow some doubt/some uncertainty to remain (about) ◆ **il faisait ~ la menace d'un licenciement** he was using the threat of redundancy ◆ **il a laissé ~ le mystère sur ses intentions** he remained mysterious about his intentions 3 (* = *se détacher*) *[personne]* to have one's head in the clouds 4 *[drogué]* to be high* *ou* spaced out* ◆ **ça fait ~** *[musique, spectacle]* it's really trippy*

planétaire /planetɛʀ/ ADJ 1 *(Astron Tech)* planetary 2 (= *mondial*) *[réchauffement]* global; *[succès, réseau]* global, worldwide; *[dimension, événement, stratégie]* global, international ◆ **à l'échelle ~** on a global *ou* worldwide scale

planétarium /planetaʀjɔm/ NM planetarium

planète /planɛt/ NF planet ◆ **la ~ bleue/rouge** the blue/red planet ◆ **sur toute la ~** all over the world ◆ **l'épidémie s'est étendue à la ~ entière** the epidemic has spread throughout the world

planétologie /planetɔlɔʒi/ NF planetology

planeur /planœʀ/ NM glider ◆ **faire du ~** to go gliding

planificateur, -trice /planifikatœʀ, tʀis/ *(Écon)* ADJ planning *(épith)* NM,F planner

planification /planifikasjɔ̃/ NF ◆ **~ (économique)** (economic) planning ◆ **~ familiale** family planning

planifier /planifje/ ▸ conjug 7 ◂ VT to plan ◆ **économie planifiée** planned *ou* controlled economy

planimétrie /planimetʀi/ NF planimetry

planimétrique /planimetʀik/ ADJ planimetric(al)

planisphère /planisfɛʀ/ NM planisphere

planning /planiŋ/ NM schedule ◆ **je vais regarder mon ~** I'll just take a look at my schedule ◆ **avoir un ~ très serré** to have a very tight schedule ◆ **~ familial** family planning

plan-plan * /plɑ̃plɑ̃/ ADJ INV *[allure]* laid-back* ◆ **ils mènent une vie ~** they lead a humdrum life ◆ **c'était ~** it was easy going

planque * /plɑ̃k/ NF (= *cachette*) hideaway, hideout, hidey-hole*; *(Police)* hideout; (= *travail tranquille*) cushy job *ou* number* ◆ **c'est la ~ !** it's a real cushy number!*

planqué, e * /plɑ̃ke/ *(péj)* NM,F *(au travail)* ◆ **c'est un ~** he's got a cushy job* NM *(Mil)* (= *non mobilisé*) draft dodger; (*qui évite l'action*) soldier with a desk job

planquer *̣* /plɑ̃ke/ ▸ conjug 1 ◂ VT to hide (away), to stash away* VI **se planquer** VPR to hide

plan-relief (pl **plans-reliefs**) /plɑ̃ʀəljɛf/ NM (= *maquette*) architectural model, scale model *(of a building)*

plant /plɑ̃/ NM (= *plante*) *[de légume]* seedling, young plant; *[de fleur]* bedding plant; (= *plantation*) *[de légumes]* bed, (vegetable) patch; *[de fleurs]* (flower) bed; *[d'arbres]* plantation ◆ **un ~ de salade** a lettuce seedling, a young lettuce (plant) ◆ **un ~ de vigne/de bégonia** a young vine/begonia

plantage * /plɑ̃taʒ/ NM *(Ordin)* crash ◆ **il y a eu un ~ dans la comptabilité** someone made a mistake in the accounts

Plantagenêt /plɑ̃taʒnɛ/ NMF Plantagenet

plantain /plɑ̃tɛ̃/ NM (= *herbacée*) plantain ◆ **(banane) ~** plantain

plantaire /plɑ̃tɛʀ/ ADJ plantar ◆ **verrue ~** verruca *(Brit)*, plantar wart *(US)*; → **voûte**

plantation /plɑ̃tasjɔ̃/ NF 1 (= *action*) planting; (= *culture*) plant; (= *terrain*) *[de légumes]* bed, (vegetable) patch; *[de fleurs]* (flower) bed; *[d'arbres, café, coton]* plantation ◆ **faire des ~s de fleurs** to plant flowers (out) ◆ **comment vont tes ~s ?** how's your garden doing? 2 (= *exploitation agricole*) plantation

plante[1] /plɑ̃t/ NF *(Bot)* plant ◆ **~ annuelle** annual (plant) ◆ **~ d'appartement** *ou* **d'agrément** house *ou* pot plant ◆ **~ à fleurs** flowering plant ◆ **~ fourragère** fodder plant ◆ **~ grasse** succulent (plant) ◆ **~ grimpante** creeper ◆ **~s médicinales** medicinal plants ◆ **~ de serre** *(lit)* greenhouse *ou* hothouse plant; *(fig)* hothouse plant, delicate flower ◆ **~ textile** fibre *(Brit)* *ou* fiber *(US)* plant ◆ **~ verte** house plant, green (foliage) plant ◆ **c'est une belle ~** *(fig)* she's a lovely *ou* fine specimen

plante[2] /plɑ̃t/ NF *(Anat)* ◆ **~ (des pieds)** sole (of the foot)

planté, e /plɑ̃te/ (ptp de **planter**) ADJ ◆ **avoir les dents bien/mal ~es** to have straight/uneven teeth ◆ **ses cheveux sont ~s très bas** he has a very low hairline ◆ **être bien ~ (sur ses jambes)** to be sturdily built ◆ **il est resté ~ au milieu de la rue** he stood stock-still in the middle of the road ◆ **ne restez pas ~ (debout *ou* comme un piquet) à ne rien faire !** don't just stand there doing nothing! ◆ **rester ~ devant une vitrine** to stand looking in a shop window

planter /plɑ̃te/ ▸ conjug 1 ◂ VT 1 *[+ plante, graine]* to plant, to put in; *[+ jardin]* to put plants in; (= *repiquer*) to plant out ◆ **on a planté la région en vignes** the region was planted with vines ◆ **~ un terrain en gazon** to grass over a piece of ground ◆ **avenue plantée d'arbres** tree-lined avenue ◆ **aller ~ ses choux** *(fig)* to retire to the country

2 (= *enfoncer*) *[+ clou]* to hammer in, to knock in; *[+ pieu]* to drive in ◆ **~ un poignard dans le dos de qn** to stick a knife into sb's back, to knife *ou* stab sb in the back ◆ **l'ours planta ses griffes dans son bras** the bear stuck its claws into his arm ◆ **se ~ une épine dans le doigt** to get a thorn stuck in one's finger ◆ **la flèche se planta dans la cible** the arrow hit the target

3 (= *mettre*) to stick, to put ◆ **il planta son chapeau sur sa tête** he stuck his hat on his head ◆ **il a planté sa voiture au milieu de la rue et il est parti** he stuck his car in the middle of the road and went off ◆ **il nous a plantés sur le trottoir pour aller chercher un journal** he left us hanging about* *ou* standing on the pavement while he went to get a paper ◆ **~ un baiser sur la joue de qn** to plant a kiss on sb's cheek ◆ **~ son regard *ou* ses yeux sur qn** to fix one's eyes on sb ◆ **il se planta devant moi** he planted *ou* plonked* himself in front of me ◆ **~ là** (= *laisser sur place*) *[+ personne]* to dump*, to leave behind; *[+ voiture]* to dump*, to ditch*; *[+ travail, outils]* to dump*, to drop; (= *délaisser*) *[+ épouse]* to walk out on*, to ditch*; *[+ travail]* to pack in

4 (= *installer*) *[+ échelle, drapeau]* to put up; *[+ tente]* to put up, to pitch ◆ **~ une échelle contre un mur** to put a ladder (up) *ou* stand a ladder (up) against a wall ◆ **~ le décor** *(Théât)* to put up *ou* set up the scenery; *[auteur]* to set the scene ◆ **cet auteur sait ~ ses personnages** this author is good at characterization

5 (*̣ = *poignarder*) to stab

VPR **se planter** * 1 (= *se tromper*) to mess up* ◆ **il s'est planté dans ses calculs** he got his calculations wrong ◆ **se ~ à un examen** to fail *ou* flunk* an exam, to blow it* in an exam *(US)* ◆ **je me suis planté en histoire** I flunked* history, I really blew it* in history ◆ **l'ordinateur s'est planté** the computer crashed

2 (= *avoir un accident*) to crash ◆ **il s'est planté en moto** he had a motorbike crash, he crashed his motorbike

VI (= *tomber en panne*) ◆ **l'ordinateur a planté, on a planté** the computer crashed

planteur /plɑ̃tœʀ/ NM 1 (= *colon*) planter 2 (= *cocktail*) planter's punch

planteuse /plɑ̃tøz/ NF *(Agr)* (potato) planter

plantigrade /plɑ̃tigʀad/ ADJ, NM plantigrade

plantoir /plɑ̃twaʀ/ NM dibble, dibber

planton /plɑ̃tɔ̃/ NM *(Mil)* orderly ◆ **être de ~** to be on orderly duty ◆ **faire le ~*** to hang about*, to stand around *ou* about (waiting)

plantureux, -euse /plɑ̃tyʀø, øz/ ADJ 1 *[repas]* copious, lavish; *[femme]* buxom; *[poitrine]* ample 2 *[région, terre]* fertile ◆ **année plantureuse** bumper year

plaquage /plakaʒ/ NM 1 *(de bois)* veneering; *(de métal)* plating 2 *(Rugby)* tackling *(NonC)*, tackle ◆ **~ à retardement** late tackle 3 (*̣ = *abandon*) *[de fiancé]* jilting*, ditching*, chucking*̣; *[d'épouse]* ditching*; *[d'emploi]* chucking (in *ou* up)*, packing in* *(Brit)*

plaque /plak/ NF 1 *[de métal, verre]* sheet, plate; *[de marbre]* slab; *[de chocolat]* block; *[de beurre]* pack; (= *revêtement*) plate, cover(ing) ◆ **légumes surgelés vendus en ~s** frozen vegetables sold in blocks

2 *[de verglas]* sheet, patch

3 (= *tache sur la peau*) patch, blotch, plaque *(SPÉC)*; *[d'eczéma]* patch; → **sclérose**

4 *(portant une inscription)* plaque; (= *insigne*) badge; *(au casino)* chip ◆ **poser *ou* visser sa ~** *[de médecin, avocat]* to set up in practice

5 *(Élec, Photo)* plate

6 *(Géol)* plate ◆ **~ continentale/océanique** continental/oceanic plate

7 (*̣ = 10 000 F) ten thousand francs

8 *(locutions)* **il est à côté de la ~*** he hasn't got a clue* ◆ **j'ai mis à côté de la ~*** I got it completely wrong, I was way off the mark

COMP **plaque de blindage** armour-plate *(NonC)*, armour-plating *(NonC)*

plaque chauffante *[de cuisinière]* hotplate

plaque de cheminée fireback

plaque commémorative commemorative plaque *ou* plate

plaque de cuisson *[de four]* baking tray; (= *table de cuisson*) hob, cooktop

plaque dentaire dental plaque

plaque d'égout manhole cover

plaque de four baking tray

plaque à gâteau *(Helv)* baking tin

plaque d'identité *[de soldat]* identity disc; *[de chien]* name tag, identity disc; *[de bracelet]* nameplate

plaque d'immatriculation *ou* **minéralogique** *ou* **de police** number plate, registration plate *(Brit)*, license plate *(US)*

plaque de propreté fingerplate

plaque sensible *(Photo)* sensitive plate

plaque tournante *(Rail)* turntable; *(fig)* (= *lien*) hub; (= *personne*) linchpin

plaqué, e /plake/ (ptp de **plaquer**) ADJ *[bracelet]* plated; *[poches]* patch *(épith)*; *[accord]* non-arpeggiated ◆ **~ or/argent** gold-/silver-plated ◆ **~ chêne** oak-veneered NM 1 *(Orfèvrerie)* plate ◆ **en ~** plated ◆ **c'est du ~** it's plated 2 *(Menuiserie)* veneer

plaquer /plake/ ▸ conjug 1 ◂ VT 1 *(Tech)* *[+ bois]* to veneer; *[+ bijoux]* to plate ◆ **~ du métal sur du bois** to plate wood with metal ◆ **~ des bijoux d'or/d'argent** to plate jewellery with gold/silver, to gold-plate/silver-plate jewellery

2 (= *surajouter*) to tack on ◆ **ce passage semble plaqué sur le reste du texte** this passage looks like it has just been stuck onto *ou* tacked onto the rest of the text

3 (*̣ = *abandonner*) *[+ fiancé]* to jilt*, to ditch*; *[+ époux]* to ditch*, to walk out on; *[+ emploi]* to chuck (in *ou* up)*̣, to pack in* *(Brit)* ◆ **elle a tout plaqué pour le suivre** she chucked up*̣ *ou* packed in* *(Brit)* everything to follow him

4 (= *aplatir*) *[+ cheveux]* to plaster down ◆ **la sueur plaquait sa chemise contre son corps** the sweat made his shirt cling *ou* stick to his body ◆ **le vent plaquait la neige contre le mur** the wind was flattening *ou* plastering the

snow up against the wall ◆ ~ **une personne contre un mur/au sol** to pin a person to a wall/to the ground ◆ **se ~ les cheveux** to plaster one's hair down (*sur* on, over); ◆ **se ~ au sol/contre un mur** to flatten o.s. on the ground/against a wall

5 *(= appliquer)* **elle lui plaqua un baiser sur la joue** she planted a kiss on his cheek ◆ ~ **sa main sur la bouche de qn** to slap one's hand over sb's mouth

6 *(Rugby)* to tackle, to bring down

7 *(Mus) [+ accord]* to strike, to play

plaquette /plakɛt/ NF 1 *(= petite plaque) [de métal]* plaque; *[de marbre]* tablet 2 *[de chocolat]* block, bar; *[de pilules]* blister *ou* bubble pack *ou* package; *[de beurre]* small pack *(Brit)*, ≃ stick *(US)* ◆ ~ **de frein** brake pad 3 *(= livre)* small volume ◆ ~ **(publicitaire** *ou* **promotionnelle)** (promotional) leaflet ◆ ~ **de présentation** presentation brochure ◆ ~ **d'information** information leaflet 4 *[de sang]* platelet

plasma /plasma/ NM *(Anat, Phys)* plasma ◆ ~ **sanguin** blood plasma

plastic /plastik/ NM plastic explosive

plasticage /plastikaʒ/ NM bombing (*de* of) bomb attack (*de* on)

plasticien, -ienne /plastisjɛ̃, jɛn/ NM,F 1 *(Art)* visual artist 2 *(= chirurgien)* plastic surgeon 3 *(Tech)* plastics specialist

plasticité /plastisite/ NF *(lit)* plasticity; *(fig)* malleability, plasticity

plastie /plasti/ NF plastic surgery ◆ **elle a subi une ~ des doigts** she had plastic surgery on her fingers

plastifiant, e /plastifjɑ̃, jɑ̃t/ ADJ plasticizing NM plasticizer

plastification /plastifikasjɔ̃/ NF ◆ ~ **de documents** lamination of documents

plastifier /plastifje/ ▸ conjug 7 ◂ VT to coat with plastic; *[+ document]* to laminate ◆ **plastifié** plastic-coated; *[document]* laminated

plastiquage /plastikaʒ/ NM ⇒ **plasticage**

plastique /plastik/ ADJ 1 *(Art)* plastic ◆ **chirurgie ~** plastic surgery 2 *(= malléable)* malleable, plastic ◆ **en matière ~** plastic NM plastic ◆ **en ~** plastic NF *[de sculpteur]* modelling, plastic art; *[de statue]* modelling; *(= arts)* plastic arts; *[de personne]* physique

plastiquement /plastikmɑ̃/ ADV from the point of view of form, plastically *(SPÉC)*

plastiquer /plastike/ ▸ conjug 1 ◂ VT to blow up, to carry out a bomb attack on

plastiqueur /plastikœʀ/ NM terrorist *(planting a plastic bomb)*

plastoc* /plastɔk/ NM plastic ◆ **en ~** plastic *(épith)*

plastron /plastʀɔ̃/ NM *(Habillement) [de corsage]* front; *[de chemise]* shirt front; *(amovible)* false shirt front, dicky*; *[d'escrimeur]* plastron; *[d'armure]* plastron, breastplate

plastronner /plastʀɔne/ ▸ conjug 1 ◂ VI to swagger VT to put a plastron on

plat¹, plate /pla, plat/ ADJ 1 *[surface, pays, couture, pli]* flat; *[mer]* smooth, still; *[eau]* plain, still; *(Géom) [angle]* straight; *[encéphalogramme, ventre, poitrine]* flat; *[cheveux]* straight ◆ **bateau à fond ~** flat-bottomed boat ◆ **chaussure ~e** *ou* **à talon ~** flat(-heeled) *ou* low(-heeled) shoe ◆ **elle est ~e de poitrine, elle a la poitrine ~e** she is flat-chested ◆ **elle est ~e comme une galette*** *ou* **une limande*** *ou* **une planche à pain*** she's as flat as a board*; → **assiette, battre**

2 *(= fade) [style]* flat, dull, unimaginative; *[dissertation, livre]* dull, unremarkable, unimaginative; *[adaptation]* unimaginative, unremarkable; *[voix]* flat, dull; *[vin]* insipid; *[personne, vie]* dull, uninteresting ◆ **ce qu'il écrit est très ~** what he writes is very dull *ou* flat

3 *(= obséquieux) [personne]* obsequious, ingratiating *(épith)* ◆ **il nous a fait ses plus ~es excuses** he made the humblest of apologies to us

NM *(= partie plate)* flat (part); *[de main]* flat ◆ **il y a 15 km de ~ avant la montagne** there is a 15 km flat stretch before the mountain ◆ **course de ~** flat race ◆ **faire un ~** *(Natation)* to (do a) belly flop ◆ **faire du ~ à*** *[+ supérieur]* to crawl *ou* grovel *ou* toady to; *[+ femme]* to try to pick up, to chat up* *(Brit)*

◆ **à plat** ◆ **mettre** *ou* **poser qch à ~** to lay sth (down) flat ◆ **posez le ruban bien à ~** lay the ribbon down nice and flat ◆ **mettre qch à ~** *(fig)* to have a close look at things ◆ **remettre qch à ~** *(fig)* to reexamine sth from every angle ◆ **remise à ~** *[de dossier, problème, situation]* complete *ou* thorough review ◆ **poser la main à ~ sur qch** to lay one's hand flat on sth ◆ **être à ~** *[pneu, batterie]* to be flat; * *[personne]* to be washed out* *ou* run down ◆ **la grippe l'a mis à ~*** he was laid low by (the) flu ◆ **être/rouler à ~** *[automobiliste]* to have/drive on a flat (tyre) ◆ **tomber à ~** *[remarque, plaisanterie]* to fall flat ◆ **tomber à ~ ventre** to fall flat on one's face, to fall full-length ◆ **se mettre à ~ ventre** to lie face down ◆ **se mettre à ~ ventre devant qn** *(fig)* to crawl *ou* grovel *ou* toady to sb

NF **plate** *(= bateau)* punt, flat-bottomed boat

COMP **plat de côtes, plates côtes** middle *ou* best *ou* short *(US)* rib

plat² /pla/ NM *(= récipient, mets)* dish; *(= partie du repas)* course; *(= contenu)* dish, plate(ful) ◆ ~ **à gratin** gratin dish ◆ **on en était au ~ de viande** we had reached the meat course ◆ **deux ~s de viande au choix** a choice of two meat dishes *ou* courses ◆ **il en a fait tout un ~*** he made a song and dance* *ou* a great fuss* about it ◆ **il voudrait qu'on lui apporte tout sur un ~ (d'argent)** he wants everything handed to him on a plate *(Brit)* *ou* a silver platter *(US)* ◆ **mettre les petits ~s dans les grands** to lay on a first-rate meal ◆ **il lui prépare de bons petits ~s** he makes tasty little dishes for her ◆ **pour un ~ de lentilles** *(Bible, fig)* for a mess of potage ◆ **quel ~ de nouilles !*** *(péj)* he's (*ou* she's) such an idiot!; → **œuf, pied**

COMP **plat à barbe** shaving mug
plat cuisiné *(chez un traiteur)* ready-made meal
plat à four oven dish
plat garni main course (served with vegetables)
plat du jour dish of the day, plat du jour ◆ **quel est le ~ du jour ?** what's today's special?
plat de résistance main course; *(fig)* pièce de résistance
plat de service serving dish

platane /platan/ NM plane tree ◆ **faux ~** sycamore ◆ **rentrer dans un ~*** to crash into a tree

plat-bord (pl **plats-bords**) /plabɔʀ/ NM gunwale

plateau (pl **plateaux**) /plato/ NM 1 *(gén)* tray ◆ ~ **à fromages** cheeseboard ◆ ~ **de fromages** cheeseboard, choice of cheeses *(on a menu)* ◆ ~ **d'huîtres** plate of oysters ◆ ~ **de fruits de mer** seafood platter ◆ **il faut tout lui apporter sur un ~ (d'argent)** *(fig)* he wants everything to be handed to him on a plate *(Brit)* *ou* a silver platter *(US)* ◆ **la victoire leur a été offerte sur un ~ (d'argent)** victory was handed to them on a plate

2 *[de balance]* pan; *[d'électrophone]* turntable, deck; *[de table]* top; *[de graphique]* plateau ◆ **la courbe fait un ~ avant de redescendre** the curve levels off *ou* reaches a plateau before falling again ◆ **arriver à un ~** *(dans une activité, une progression)* to reach a plateau ◆ **mettre qch dans** *ou* **sur les ~x de la balance** *(fig)* to weigh sth up *(fig)*

3 *(Géog)* plateau ◆ **haut ~** high plateau

4 *(Théât)* stage; *(Ciné, TV)* set ◆ **nous avons un ~ exceptionnel ce soir** *(= invités)* we have an exceptional line-up this evening ◆ **sur le ~ de l'émission** on the set

5 *(Rail) (= wagon)* flat wagon *(Brit)* *ou* car *(US)*; *(= plate-forme roulante)* trailer

6 *[de pédalier]* chain wheel

7 *(de ball-trap)* clay pigeon

COMP **plateau continental** continental shelf
plateau d'embrayage *[de voiture]* pressure plate
plateau sous-marin submarine plateau
plateau technique *[d'hôpital etc]* technical wherewithal *ou* capacity
plateau télé TV dinner
plateau de tournage *(Ciné)* film set

plateau-repas (pl **plateaux-repas**) /platoʀəpa/ NM *(en avion, en train)* tray meal; *(devant la télévision)* TV dinner

plate-bande (pl **plates-bandes**), **platebande** /platbɑ̃d/ NF *(de fleurs)* flower bed; *(Archit)* platband ◆ **marcher sur** *ou* **piétiner les plates-bandes de qn*** to encroach on sb's preserve, to poach on sb's territory

platée /plate/ NF dish(ful), plate(ful)

plate-forme (pl **plates-formes**), **plateforme** /platfɔʀm/ NF 1 *(gén = terrasse, estrade)* platform; *[d'autobus]* platform; *(Rail = wagon)* flat wagon *(Brit)* *ou* car *(US)* ◆ ~ **continentale** *(Géog)* continental shelf ◆ ~ **(de forage en mer)** (off-shore) oil rig ◆ ~ **flottante** floating rig 2 *(Ordin)* platform ◆ ~ **logiciel/matériel** software/hardware platform 3 *(Pol)* platform ◆ ~ **électorale** election platform

platement /platmɑ̃/ ADV *[écrire, s'exprimer]* dully, unimaginatively; *[s'excuser]* humbly

platine¹ /platin/ NM platinum ◆ ~ **iridié** platinum-iridium alloy ADJ INV *(= couleur)* platinum *(épith)* ◆ **blond ~** platinum blond

platine² /platin/ NF *[d'électrophone]* deck, turntable; *[de microscope]* stage; *[de presse]* platen; *[de montre, serrure]* plate; *[de machine à coudre]* throat plate ◆ ~ **laser** laser disk player ◆ ~ **cassette** cassette deck

platiné, e /platine/ ADJ *[cheveux]* platinum *(épith)* ◆ **une blonde ~e** a platinum blonde; → **vis**

platitude /platityd/ NF 1 *[de style]* flatness, dullness; *[de livre, film, discours, remarque]* dullness, lack of imagination (*de* in, of); *[de vie, personnage]* dullness 2 *(= propos)* platitude ◆ **dire des ~s** to make trite remarks, to utter platitudes 3 † *(= servilité) [de personne]* obsequiousness; *[d'excuse]* humility; *(= acte)* obsequiousness *(NonC)*

Platon /platɔ̃/ NM Plato

platonicien, -ienne /platɔnisjɛ̃, jɛn/ ADJ Platonic NM,F Platonist

platonique /platɔnik/ ADJ *[amour]* platonic ◆ **avoir un intérêt ~ pour qch** *(hum = de pure forme)* to have a casual *ou* passing interest in sth ◆ **les déclarations de l'ONU paraissent plutôt ~s** the statements issued by the UN seem to be nothing more than talk *ou* a matter of pure form

platoniquement /platɔnikmɑ̃/ ADV platonically

platonisme /platɔnism/ NM Platonism

plâtrage /plɑtʀaʒ/ NM 1 *[de mur]* plastering 2 *(Méd) [de membre]* setting *ou* putting in plaster; *[d'estomac]* lining 3 *(Agr) [de prairie]* liming

plâtras /plɑtʀɑ/ NM *(= débris)* rubble; *(= morceau de plâtre)* chunk *ou* lump of plaster

plâtre /plɑtʀ/ NM 1 (= *matière*) (*gén*) plaster; (*Agr*) lime ◆ **mettre une jambe dans le ~** to put *ou* set a leg in plaster ◆ **j'avais une jambe dans le ~** I had my leg in plaster ◆ **c'est du ~ !** [*fromage*] it's like chalk!; → **battre** 2 (*Art, Chirurgie = objet*) plaster cast ◆ **les ~s** (*Constr*) the plasterwork (*NonC*) ◆ **porter un ~ au bras** to have one's arm in plaster ◆ **~ de marche** walking plaster (*Brit*) *ou* cast (*US*); → **essuyer**

plâtrer /plɑtʀe/ ▸ conjug 1 ◂ VT 1 [+ *mur*] to plaster 2 (*Méd*) [+ *membre*] to set *ou* put in plaster; [+ *estomac*] to line ◆ **il a la jambe plâtrée** his leg is in plaster ◆ **elle est plâtrée du genou à la cheville** her leg is in plaster from her knee down to her ankle 3 (*Agr*) [+ *prairie*] to lime

plâtrerie /plɑtʀəʀi/ NF (= *usine*) plaster works

plâtreux, -euse /plɑtʀø, øz/ ADJ [*sol*] limey, chalky; [*surface*] plastered, coated with plaster; [*fromage*] chalky

plâtrier /plɑtʀije/ NM plasterer

plâtrière /plɑtʀijɛʀ/ NF (= *carrière*) gypsum *ou* lime quarry; (= *four*) gypsum kiln

plausibilité /plozibilite/ NF plausibility, plausibleness

plausible /plozibl/ ADJ plausible

plausiblement /plozibləmɑ̃/ ADV plausibly

Plaute /plot/ NM Plautus

play-back /plɛbak/ NM INV lip-synching ◆ **c'est du ~** they're (*ou* he is *etc*) just miming to a prerecorded tape *ou* lip-synching ◆ **chanter en ~** to mime to a prerecorded tape, to lip-synch

play-boy (pl **play-boys**) /plɛbɔj/ NM playboy

plèbe /plɛb/ NF ◆ **la ~** (*péj*) the plebs, the proles; (*Hist*) the plebeians

plébéien, -ienne /plebejɛ̃, jɛn/ ADJ (*Hist*) plebeian; [*goûts*] plebeian, common NM,F plebeian

plébiscitaire /plebisitɛʀ/ ADJ of a plebiscite

plébiscite /plebisit/ NM plebiscite ◆ **faire** *ou* **organiser un ~** to hold a referendum

plébisciter /plebisite/ ▸ conjug 1 ◂ VT (*Pol*) (*lit*) to elect by plebiscite; (= *élire à la majorité*) to elect by an overwhelming majority ◆ **se faire ~** [*candidat*] to be elected by an overwhelming majority ◆ **le public a plébiscité ce nouveau magazine** this new magazine has proved a tremendous success with the public

plectre /plɛktʀ/ NM plectrum

pléiade /plejad/ NF (= *groupe*) group ◆ **la Pléiade** (*Littérat*) the Pléiade ◆ **une ~ d'artistes** a whole host of stars NFPL **Pléiades** (*Astron*) **les Pléiades** the Pleiades

plein, pleine /plɛ̃, plɛn/

1 ADJECTIF
2 ADVERBE
3 NOM MASCULIN

Lorsque **plein** s'emploie dans des locutions telles que **de plein droit, à plein régime, en plein air, en mettre plein la vue** etc, cherchez au nom.

1 - ADJECTIF

1 = rempli [*boîte*] full; [*bus, salle*] full (up); [*crustacé, coquillage*] full; [*vie, journée*] full, busy ◆ **~ à craquer** [*valise*] full to bursting, crammed full; [*salle, bus, train*] packed (out), crammed full, full to bursting ◆ **un ~ verre de vin** a full glass of wine ◆ **un ~ panier de pommes** a whole basketful of apples, a full basket of apples ◆ **j'ai les mains ~es** my hands are full, I've got my hands full ◆ **~ comme un œuf** * [*tiroir*] chock-a-block * (*Brit*), chock-full *; [*nez*] stuffed up ◆ **être ~ aux as**‡ to be rolling in money * *ou* in it *, to be filthy rich‡ ◆ **un gros ~ de soupe** * (*péj*) a big fat slob‡ (*péj*)

◆ **plein de**

Lorsque **plein de** signifie 'couvert de', il ne se traduit pas par **full of**.

[*bonne volonté, admiration, fautes, vie*] full of; (= *couvert de*) [*taches, graisse*] covered in *ou* with ◆ **salle ~e de monde** room full of people, crowded room ◆ **j'ai la tête ~e de projets** I'm full of ideas ◆ **son film est ~ de sensualité** his film is very sensual ◆ **leur maison est ~e d'enfants/de fleurs** their house is full of children/of flowers ◆ **voilà une remarque ~e de finesse** that's a very shrewd remark ◆ **il est ~ de santé/d'idées** he's bursting with health/with ideas ◆ **il est ~ de son sujet/de sa nouvelle voiture** he's full of his subject/of his new car ◆ **mets ~ de saveur** dish full of flavour, tasty dish ◆ **être ~ de soi-même** to be full of o.s. *ou* of one's own importance

2 = complet [*succès*] complete; [*confiance*] complete, total; [*satisfaction*] full, complete, total ◆ **vous avez mon ~ accord** you have my wholehearted consent *ou* approval ◆ **au ~ sens du terme** in the full *ou* fullest sense of the word ◆ **absent un jour ~** absent for a whole day ◆ **il a ~ pouvoir pour agir** he has full power *ou* authority to act ◆ **avoir les ~s pouvoirs** to have full powers; → **arc, temps**[1]

3 = à son maximum **~e lune** (*Astron*) full moon ◆ **la mer est ~e, c'est la ~e mer** (*Naut*) the tide is in, it's high tide

4 = entier **deux volumes, reliure ~ cuir** two volumes fully bound in leather ◆ **manteau de fourrure ~e peau** fur coat made of solid *ou* full skins

5 = non creux [*paroi, porte, pneu, roue*] solid; [*trait*] unbroken, continuous; [*son*] solid; [*voix*] rich, sonorous; (= *rond*) [*visage*] full; [*joues*] chubby

6 ‡ = ivre plastered‡, stoned‡ (*US*) ◆ **~ comme une barrique** as drunk as a lord *

7 = gravide pregnant, in calf (*ou* foal *ou* lamb *etc*)

8 indiquant l'intensité **la ~e lumière le fatiguait** he found the bright light tiring ◆ **avoir ~e conscience de qch** to be fully aware of sth ◆ **heurter qch de ~ fouet** to crash headlong into sth ◆ **rincer le sol à ~s seaux** to rinse the floor with bucketfuls of water ◆ **ramasser qch à ~s bras/à ~es mains** to pick up armfuls/handfuls of sth ◆ **prendre qch à ~es mains** to lay a firm hold on sth, to grasp sth firmly

9 locutions

◆ **en plein** + *nom* (= *au milieu de, au plus fort de*) ◆ **en ~e poitrine** full *ou* right in the chest ◆ **en ~e tête** right in the head ◆ **arriver en ~ (milieu du) cours/en ~e répétition** to arrive (right) in the middle of the class/rehearsal ◆ **en ~ cœur de la ville** right in the centre of the town ◆ **c'est arrivé en ~ Paris/en ~e rue** it happened in the middle of Paris/in the middle of the street ◆ **restaurant en ~ ciel** restaurant up in the sky ◆ **en ~ jour** in broad daylight ◆ **en ~e nuit** in the middle of the night, at dead of night ◆ **en ~ hiver** in the depths *ou* middle of winter ◆ **son visage était en ~e lumière** the light was shining straight into his face *ou* at him ◆ **en ~e obscurité** in complete *ou* utter darkness ◆ **oiseau en ~ vol** bird in full flight ◆ **je suis en ~ travail** I'm in the middle of (my) work, I'm hard at work ◆ **arriver en ~ drame** to arrive in the middle of a crisis ◆ **enfant en ~e croissance** child who is growing fast *ou* shooting up ◆ **affaire en ~ essor** rapidly expanding *ou* growing business

2 - ADVERBE

1 = en grande quantité dans, partout sur **il a des bonbons ~ les poches** his pockets are full of *ou* stuffed with sweets ◆ **j'ai de l'encre ~ les mains** I've got ink all over my hands, my hands are covered in ink ◆ **il a des jouets ~ son placard** he's got a cupboardful *ou* a cupboard full of toys ◆ **en avoir ~ le dos** * *ou* **le cul** *‡ **de qch** to be fed up with sth *, to be sick and tired of sth *, to be pissed off *‡ with sth ◆ **en avoir ~ les jambes** * *ou* **les bottes** * *ou* **les pattes** * to be all-in *

2 * = beaucoup

◆ **plein de** lots of, loads of * ◆ **il y a ~ de bouteilles dans la cave/de gens dans la rue** the cellar/street is full of bottles/people, there are lots *ou* loads of bottles in the cellar/people in the street ◆ **un gâteau avec ~ de crème** a cake with lots of *ou* plenty of cream ◆ **il a mis ~ de chocolat sur sa veste** he's got chocolate all over his jacket ◆ **tu as des romans ? – j'en ai ~** have you any novels? – I've got loads; → **tout**

3 = exactement vers **se diriger/donner ~ ouest** to head/face due west

4 locutions

◆ **à plein** [*fonctionner, tourner*] at full capacity; [*exploiter*] to the full *ou* maximum ◆ **utiliser à ~ son potentiel/une machine/ses connaissances** to use one's potential/a machine/one's knowledge to the full, to make full use of one's potential/a machine/one's knowledge ◆ **il faut profiter à ~ de ces jours de congé** you should make the very most of your time off ◆ **le partenariat joue à ~ dans notre entreprise** partnership plays a full role in our company

◆ **en plein** ◆ **la lumière frappait son visage en ~** the light was shining straight *ou* right into his face

◆ **en plein dans/sur/dedans** ◆ **en ~ dans l'eau/l'œil** right *ou* straight in the water/the eye ◆ **la branche est tombée en ~ sur la voiture** the branch fell right on top of the car ◆ **j'ai marché en ~ dedans** I stepped right in it

3 - NOM MASCULIN

1 de carburant full tank, tankful ◆ **faire le ~ (d'essence)** to fill up ◆ **(faites) le ~, s'il vous plaît** fill it *ou* her * up please ◆ **on a fait deux ~s pour descendre jusqu'à Nice** we had to fill up twice to get down to Nice ◆ **faire le ~ d'eau/d'huile** to top up the water/the oil ◆ **le théâtre fait le ~ tous les soirs** the theatre has a full house every night ◆ **faire le ~ de soleil** to get a good dose of the sun ◆ **mangez des fruits, faites le ~ de vitamines** eat fruit and get a full dose of vitamins ◆ **la gauche a fait le ~ des voix aux élections** the left got their maximum possible vote in the elections ◆ **la coalition n'a pas fait le ~ de ses voix** the coalition didn't pick up its full quota of votes ◆ **j'ai fait le ~ de sensations fortes au cours de ce voyage** I had lots of exciting experiences during the trip ◆ **j'ai fait le ~ de souvenirs** I came back with lots of memories ◆ **tu as acheté beaucoup de conserves/livres – oui, j'ai fait le ~** * you bought lots of tins/books – yes I stocked up; → **battre**

2 Archit solid

3 Calligraphie downstroke

pleinement /plɛnmɑ̃/ ADV [*approuver*] wholeheartedly, fully ◆ **utiliser qch ~** to make full use of sth, to use sth to the full *ou* fully ◆ **jouir ~ de qch** to enjoy full use of sth ◆ **vivre ~** to live life to the full ◆ **~ responsable/satisfait de** wholly *ou* entirely *ou* fully responsible for/satisfied with ◆ **~ rassuré** completely *ou* totally reassured

plein-emploi, plein emploi /plɛnɑ̃plwa/ NM full employment

plein-temps (pl **pleins-temps**) /plɛ̃tɑ̃/ NM (= *emploi*) full-time job ◆ **je fais un ~** I work full time

pléistocène /pleistɔsɛn/ ADJ Pleistocene NM ◆ **le ~** the Pleistocene (period)

plénier, -ière /plenje, jɛʀ/ ADJ plenary

plénipotentiaire /plenipɔtɑ̃sjɛʀ/ ADJ, NM plenipotentiary; → **ministre**

plénitude /plenityd/ NF *[de forme]* plenitude *(littér)*, fullness; *[de son]* fullness, richness; *[de droit]* completeness ◆ **réaliser ses désirs dans leur** ~ to realize one's desires in their entirety ◆ **vivre la vie avec** ~ to live one's life to the full ◆ **dans la** ~ **de sa jeunesse/beauté** in the fullness of his youth/beauty *(littér)*

plenum /plenɔm/ NM plenary session *ou* meeting

pléonasme /pleɔnasm/ NM pleonasm

pléonastique /pleɔnastik/ ADJ pleonastic

plésiosaure /plezjɔzɔʀ/ NM plesiosaurus

pléthore /pletɔʀ/ NF overabundance, plethora

pléthorique /pletɔʀik/ ADJ 1 *[production, nombre]* excessive; *[offre]* excess; *[administration, bureaucratie]* bloated, excessive; *[majorité]* massive ◆ **avoir un personnel** ~ *ou* **des effectifs ~s** *[entreprise]* to be overmanned, to have excess staff ◆ **des classes aux effectifs ~s** overcrowded classes 2 *(Méd)* obese

pleur /plœʀ/ NM 1 *(littér)* (= *larme*) tear; (= *sanglot*) sob ◆ **verser un** ~ *(hum)* to shed a tear 2 *(locutions)* **en ~s** in tears ◆ **il y aura des ~s et des grincements de dents quand ...** there'll be much wailing and gnashing of teeth when ... ◆ **essuyer** *ou* **sécher les ~s de qn** to wipe away *ou* dry sb's tears 3 *(Bot)* bleeding

pleurage /plœʀaʒ/ NM *(Élec)* wow

pleural, e (mpl **-aux**) /plœʀal, o/ ADJ pleural

pleurant /plœʀɑ̃/ NM *(Art)* weeping figure

pleurard, e /plœʀaʀ, aʀd/ *(péj)* ADJ *[enfant]* whining *(épith)*, who never stops crying; *[ton]* whimpering *(épith)*, whining *(épith)* NM,F crybaby*, whiner

pleurer /plœʀe/ ► conjug 1 ◄ VI 1 (= *larmoyer*) *[personne]* to cry, to weep; *[yeux]* to water, to run ◆ **s'endormir en pleurant** to cry oneself to sleep ◆ ~ **de rire** to shed tears of laughter, to laugh until one cries ◆ ~ **de rage** to weep *ou* cry with rage, to shed tears of rage ◆ ~ **de joie** to cry *ou* weep for joy, to shed tears of joy ◆ ~ **d'avoir fait qch** to cry *ou* weep at *ou* over having done sth ◆ **j'ai perdu mon sac, j'en aurais pleuré** I lost my bag – I could have cried *ou* wept ◆ **il vaut mieux en rire que d'en** ~ it's better to laugh (about it) than cry about *ou* over it ◆ **faire** ~ **qn** to make sb cry, to bring tears to sb's eyes ◆ **les oignons me font** ~ onions make my eyes water *ou* make me cry ◆ ~ **comme un veau** *(péj) ou* **une Madeleine** *ou* **à chaudes larmes** to cry one's eyes *ou* one's heart out ◆ **être sur le point de** ~ to be almost in tears, to be on the point *ou* verge of tears ◆ **aller** ~ **dans le gilet de qn*** to run crying to sb ◆ **triste à (faire)** ~ dreadfully *ou* terribly sad ◆ **bête à (faire)** ~ pitifully stupid ◆ **c'est bête à (faire)** ~ it's enough to make you weep

2 ◆ ~ **sur** to lament (over) ◆ ~ **sur son propre sort** to bemoan one's lot

3 *(péj = réclamer)* **elle est tout le temps à** ~ she's always whining *ou* begging for something ◆ ~ **après qch** to shout for sth ◆ **il a été** ~ **à la direction pour obtenir une augmentation** he's been whingeing to the management about getting a rise

4 *(littér) [sirène, violon]* to wail

VT 1 *[+ personne]* to mourn (for); *[+ chose]* to bemoan; *[+ faute]* to bewail, to bemoan, to lament ◆ **mourir sans être pleuré** to die unlamented *ou* unmourned ◆ ~ **des larmes de joie** to weep *ou* shed tears of joy, to weep for joy ◆ ~ **des larmes de sang** to shed tears of blood ◆ ~ **tout son soûl** *ou* **toutes les larmes de son corps** to cry one's eyes out ◆ ~ **misère** to cry poverty ◆ ~ **sa jeunesse** to mourn for one's lost youth

2 *(péj)* (= *quémander*) *[+ augmentation, objet]* to beg for; (= *lésiner sur*) *[+ nourriture, fournitures]* to begrudge, to stint ◆ **il ne pleure pas sa peine*** he spares no effort ◆ **il ne pleure pas son argent*** he's very free with his money

pleurésie /plœʀezi/ NF pleurisy ◆ **avoir une** ~ to have pleurisy

pleurétique /plœʀetik/ ADJ pleuritic

pleureur, -euse /plœʀœʀ, øz/ ADJ 1 *[enfant]* whining *(épith)*, always crying *(attrib)*; *[ton]* tearful, whimpering *(épith)* ◆ **c'est un ~/une pleureuse** *(pleurard)* he/she is always crying; *(péj : quémandeur)* he/she is always begging for something 2 *(Bot) [frêne, mûrier etc]* weeping; → **saule** NF **pleureuse** (hired) mourner

pleurnichard, e /plœʀniʃaʀ, aʀd/ ADJ, NM,F ⇒ **pleurnicheur**

pleurnichement /plœʀniʃmɑ̃/ NM ⇒ **pleurnicherie**

pleurnicher /plœʀniʃe/ ► conjug 1 ◄ VI to snivel*, to whine

pleurnicherie /plœʀniʃʀi/ NF snivelling* *(NonC)*, whining *(NonC)*, grizzling* *(Brit) (NonC)*

pleurnicheur, -euse /plœʀniʃœʀ, øz/ ADJ *[enfant]* snivelling* *(épith)*, whining *(épith)*, grizzling* *(Brit) (épith)*; *[ton]* whining *(épith)* NM,F crybaby*

pleuropneumonie /plœʀopnømɔni/ NF pleuropneumonia

pleurote /plœʀɔt/ NF oyster mushroom, pleurotus *(SPÉC)*

pleurotomie /plœʀɔtɔmi/ NF pleurotomy

pleutre /pløtʀ/ *(littér)* ADJ cowardly NM coward

pleutrerie /pløtʀəʀi/ NF *(littér)* (= *caractère*) cowardice; (= *acte*) act of cowardice

pleuvasser /pløvase/, **pleuviner** /pløvine/, **pleuvioter** /pløvjɔte/ VB IMPERS ► conjug 1 ◄ (= *crachiner*) to drizzle, to spit (with rain); *(par averses)* to be showery

pleuvoir /pløvwaʀ/ ► conjug 23 ◄ VB IMPERS to rain ◆ **il pleut** it's raining ◆ **les jours où il pleut** on rainy days ◆ **on dirait qu'il va** ~ it looks like rain ◆ **il pleut à grosses gouttes** it's raining heavily ◆ **il pleut à flots** *ou* **à torrents** *ou* **à seaux** *ou* **à verse, il pleut des cordes** *ou* **des hallebardes** it's pouring (with rain) ◆ **il pleut comme vache qui pisse**** it's pouring down, it's pissing it down** *(Brit)* ◆ **qu'il pleuve ou qu'il vente** (come) rain or shine ◆ **il a reçu des cadeaux comme s'il en pleuvait** he was showered with presents ◆ **il ramasse de l'argent comme s'il en pleuvait*** he's raking it in*, he's raking in the money* ◆ **tu vas faire** ~ **!** *(hum) (à une personne qui chante mal)* you'll shatter the (glass in the) windows! *(hum)*

VI *[coups, projectiles]* to rain down; *[critiques, invitations]* to shower down ◆ **faire** ~ **des coups sur qn** to rain blows on sb ◆ **faire** ~ **des injures sur qn** to shower insults on sb, to subject sb to a torrent of insults *ou* abuse ◆ **les invitations pleuvaient sur lui** he was showered with invitations, invitations were showered on him

pleuvoter /pløvɔte/ ► conjug 1 ◄ VB IMPERS ⇒ **pleuvasser**

plèvre /plɛvʀ/ NF pleura

Plexiglas ® /plɛksiglas/ NM Perspex ®, Plexiglass ® *(US)*

plexus /plɛksys/ NM plexus ◆ ~ **solaire** solar plexus

pli /pli/ NM 1 *[de tissu, rideau, ourlet, accordéon]* fold; *(Couture)* pleat ◆ **(faux)** ~ crease ◆ **faire un** ~ **à un pantalon** *(au fer)* to put a crease in a pair of trousers; *(par négligence)* to crease a pair of trousers ◆ **jupe/robe à ~s** pleated skirt/dress ◆ **son manteau est plein de ~s** his coat is all creased ◆ **ton manteau fait un** ~ **dans le dos** your coat has a crease at the back, your coat creases (up) at the back ◆ **son corsage est trop étroit, il fait des ~s** her blouse is too tight – it's all puckered (up) ◆ **les ~s et les replis de sa cape** the many folds of her cloak ◆ **il va refuser, cela ne fait pas un** ~* he'll refuse, no doubt about it ◆ **j'avais dit qu'elle oublierait, ça n'a pas fait de** ~ **!** I'd said she'd forget and sure enough she did!

2 (= *jointure*) *[de genou, bras]* bend; (= *bourrelet*) *[de menton, ventre]* (skin-)fold; (= *ligne*) *[de bouche, yeux]* crease; (= *ride*) *[de front]* crease, furrow, line ◆ **sa peau faisait des ~s au coin des yeux/sur son ventre** his skin was creased round his eyes/made folds on his stomach ◆ **le** ~ **de l'aine** the (fold of the) groin ◆ **les ~s et les replis de son menton** the many folds under his chin, his quadruple chin *(hum)*

3 (= *forme*) *[de vêtement]* shape ◆ **garder un beau** *ou* **bon** ~ to keep its shape ◆ **prendre un mauvais** ~ *[vêtement]* to get crushed; *[cheveux]* to curl the wrong way; → **mise²**

4 (= *habitude*) habit ◆ **prendre le** ~ **de faire qch** to get into the habit of doing sth ◆ **il a pris un mauvais** ~ he's got into a bad habit ◆ **c'est un** ~ **à prendre !** you get used to it!

5 (= *enveloppe*) envelope; *(Admin = lettre)* letter ◆ **sous ce** ~ enclosed, herewith ◆ **sous** ~ **cacheté** in a sealed envelope

6 *(Cartes)* trick ◆ **faire un** ~ to win *ou* take a trick

7 *(Géol)* fold

COMP **pli d'aisance** *(Couture)* inverted pleat
pli creux *(Couture)* box pleat
pli de pantalon trouser crease
pli plat *(Couture)* flat pleat
pli de terrain fold in the ground, undulation

pliable /plijabl/ ADJ *[chaise, trottinette]* folding

pliage /plijaʒ/ NM (= *action*) folding; (= *feuille*) folded piece of paper ◆ **l'art du** ~ origami

pliant, e /plijɑ̃, ɑt/ ADJ *[lit, table, vélo]* collapsible, folding *(épith)*; *[mètre]* folding *(épith)*; *[canot]* collapsible NM folding *ou* collapsible (canvas) stool, campstool

plie /pli/ NF plaice

plier /plije/ ► conjug 7 ◄ VT 1 *[+ papier, tissu] (gén)* to fold; (= *ranger*) to fold up ◆ ~ **le coin d'une page** to fold over *ou* fold down *ou* turn down the corner of a page

2 (= *rabattre*) *[+ lit, table, tente]* to fold up; *[+ éventail]* to fold; *[+ livre, cahier]* to close (up); *[+ volets]* to fold back ◆ ~ **bagage** *(fig)* to pack up (and go)

3 (= *ployer*) *[+ branche]* to bend; *[+ genou, bras]* to bend, to flex ◆ ~ **le genou devant qn** *(lit)* to go down on one knee before sb; *(fig)* to bow before sb ◆ **être plié par l'âge** to be bent (double) with age ◆ **être plié (en deux), être plié de rire** to be doubled up with laughter ◆ **être plié de douleur** to be doubled up with pain

4 *[+ personne]* ~ **qn à une discipline** to force a discipline upon sb ◆ ~ **qn à sa volonté** to bend sb to one's will ◆ ~ **qn à sa loi** to lay down the law to sb

5 (* = *endommager*) *[+ voiture]* to wreck ◆ **sa voiture est complètement pliée** his car is a wreck *ou* a write-off* *(Brit)*

VI 1 *[arbre, branche]* to bend (over); *[plancher, paroi]* to sag, to bend over ◆ **les branches pliant sous le poids des pêches** the branches bending *ou* sagging under the weight of the peaches ◆ **faire** ~ **le plancher sous son poids** to make the floor sag beneath one's weight ◆ ~ **sous le poids des soucis/des ans** to be weighed down by worry/the years

2 (= *céder*) *[personne]* to yield, to give in, to knuckle under; *[armée]* to give way, to lose ground; *[résistance]* to give way ◆ ~ **devant l'autorité** to give in *ou* yield *ou* bow to authority ◆ **faire** ~ **qn** to make sb give in *ou* knuckle

under ♦ **notre défense plie mais ne rompt pas** *(Sport)* our defence is weakening but isn't breaking down completely

VPR se plier 1 *[meuble, objet]* to fold (up)

2 ♦ **se ~ à** *[+ règle]* to submit to, to abide by; *[+ discipline]* to submit o.s. to; *[+ circonstances]* to bow to, to submit to, to yield to; *[+ désirs, caprices de qn]* to give in to, to submit to

Pline /plin/ **NM** Pliny

plinthe /plɛ̃t/ **NF** *(gén)* skirting board; *(Archit)* plinth

pliocène /plijɔsɛn/ **ADJ** Pliocene **NM** ♦ **le ~** the Pliocene

plissage /plisaʒ/ **NM** pleating

plissé, e /plise/ (ptp de **plisser**) **ADJ** *[jupe]* pleated; *[terrain]* folded; *[peau]* creased, wrinkled **NM** pleats ♦ **~ soleil** sunray pleats

plissement /plismɑ̃/ **NM** 1 *[de lèvres]* puckering (up); *[de yeux]* screwing up; *[de front]* creasing; *[de nez]* wrinkling 2 *[de papier]* folding 3 *(Géol)* folding ♦ **le ~ alpin** the folding of the Alps ♦ **~ de terrain** fold

plisser /plise/ ► conjug 1 ◄ **VT** 1 *[+ jupe]* to pleat, to put pleats in; *[+ papier]* to fold (over) 2 *[+ lèvres, bouche]* to pucker (up); *[+ yeux]* to screw up; *[+ nez]* to wrinkle ♦ **un sourire plissa son visage** his face creased into a smile ♦ **il plissa le front** he knitted his brow ♦ **une ride lui plissa le front** a wrinkle furrowed his brow 3 *(= froisser) [+ vêtement]* to crease 4 *(Géol)* to fold **VI** *[vêtement]* to be creased ♦ **elle a les bas qui plissent** her stockings are wrinkled **VPR se plisser** 1 *[front]* to crease, to furrow; *[lèvres, bouche]* to pucker (up); *[nez]* to wrinkle 2 *(= se froisser)* to become creased ♦ **le lin se plisse très facilement** linen creases easily *ou* is easily creased

plissure /plisyʀ/ **NF** pleats

pliure /plijyʀ/ **NF** fold; *[de bras, genou]* bend; *(Typo)* folding

ploc /plɔk/ **EXCL** plop!

ploiement /plwamɑ̃/ **NM** bending

plomb /plɔ̃/ **NM** 1 *(= métal)* lead ♦ **de ~** *[tuyau]* lead; *[soldat]* tin; *[ciel]* leaden; *[soleil]* blazing; *[sommeil]* deep, heavy ♦ **j'ai des jambes de ~** my legs are *ou* feel like lead ♦ **sans ~** *[essence]* unleaded, lead-free ♦ **il n'a pas de ~ dans la tête** *ou* **la cervelle** he's feather brained ♦ **ça lui mettra du ~ dans la tête** *ou* **la cervelle** that will knock some sense into him

2 *(Chasse)* (lead) shot *(NonC)* ♦ **j'ai trouvé trois ~s dans le lièvre en le mangeant** I found three pieces of (lead) shot in the hare when I was eating it ♦ **du gros ~** buckshot ♦ **du petit ~** small shot ♦ **avoir du ~ dans l'aile** *(fig)* to be in a bad way

3 *(Pêche)* sinker; *(Typo)* type; *[de vitrail]* lead; *(= sceau)* (lead) seal; *(Élec = fusible)* fuse; *(Couture)* lead weight ♦ **~ (de sonde)** *(Naut)* sounding lead ♦ **les ~s ont sauté** the fuses have blown *ou* gone; → **péter vt 2**

4 *(locutions)* **mettre un mur à ~** to plumb a wall ♦ **le soleil tombe à ~** the sun is blazing straight down

plombage /plɔ̃baʒ/ **NM** 1 *[de dent]* filling ♦ **j'ai perdu mon ~** my filling has come out 2 *[de canne, ligne, rideaux]* weighting (with lead) 3 *[de colis, wagon]* sealing (with lead)

plombe* /plɔ̃b/ **NF** hour ♦ **ça fait deux ~s que j'attends** I've been waiting two hours now ♦ **à trois ~s du matin** at three o'clock in the morning

plombé, e /plɔ̃be/ (ptp de **plomber**) **ADJ** 1 *[teint, couleur, ciel]* leaden 2 *[essence]* leaded; *[dent]* filled ♦ **canne ~e** *ou* **à bout ~** walking stick with a lead(en) tip **NF plombée** *(= arme)* bludgeon; *(Pêche)* sinkers, weights

plomber /plɔ̃be/ ► conjug 1 ◄ **VT** 1 *[+ dent]* to fill, to put a filling in 2 *(= garnir de plomb) [+ canne, ligne, rideaux]* to weight (with lead) 3 *(= sceller) [+ colis, wagon]* to seal (with lead), to put a lead seal on 4 *(Constr) [+ mur]* to plumb 5 *(Agr)* to tamp (down) 6 *(= colorer en gris)* to turn leaden 7 *(= handicaper) [+ marché]* to drag down, to cripple; *[+ projet]* to hamper ♦ **un système bancaire plombé par d'énormes créances** a banking system crippled by heavy debts ♦ **les nouveaux investissements ont plombé les comptes de l'entreprise** the new investments have been a drain on the company accounts 8 (* = *contaminer*) to infect **VPR se plomber** *[ciel]* to turn leaden; *[visage]* to become livid

plomberie /plɔ̃bʀi/ **NF** *(= métier, installations)* plumbing; *(= atelier)* plumber's (work)shop; *(= industrie)* lead industry ♦ **faire de la ~** to do some plumbing

plombier /plɔ̃bje/ **NM** 1 *(= ouvrier)* plumber 2 *(* = agent secret)* mole*, spy *(who plants bugs)*

plombières /plɔ̃bjɛʀ/ **NF INV** tutti-frutti (ice cream)

plombifère /plɔ̃bifɛʀ/ **ADJ** plumbiferous

plonge* /plɔ̃ʒ/ **NF** dishwashing, washing-up *(in restaurant)* ♦ **faire la ~** to do the washing-up

plongé, e[1] /plɔ̃ʒe/ (ptp de **plonger**) **ADJ** ♦ **~ dans** *[+ obscurité, désespoir, misère]* plunged in; *[+ vice]* steeped in; *[+ méditation, pensées]* immersed in, deep in ♦ **~ dans la lecture d'un livre** buried *ou* immersed in a book ♦ **~ dans le sommeil** sound asleep, in a deep sleep

plongeant, e /plɔ̃ʒɑ̃, ɑ̃t/ **ADJ** *[décolleté, tir]* plunging ♦ **vue ~e** view from above

plongée[2] /plɔ̃ʒe/ **NF** 1 *[de nageur, sous-marin, gardien de but]* dive ♦ **faire de la ~** to go diving ♦ **effectuer plusieurs ~s** to make several dives ♦ **en ~, le sous-marin ...** when diving, the submarine ... ♦ **~ libre** free(-)diving ♦ **~ sous-marine** *(gén)* diving; *(avec scaphandre autonome)* skin *ou* scuba diving ♦ **~ avec tuba** snorkelling ♦ **~ avec bouteille(s)** diving with breathing apparatus ♦ **l'avion a fait une ~ sur la ville** the plane swooped down over the town ♦ **cette ~ dans la préhistoire/le passé** this journey deep into prehistory/the past 2 *[de cours, monnaie]* (nose-)dive 3 *(Ciné = prise de vue)* high angle shot ♦ **faire une ~ sur qch** to take a high angle shot of sth ♦ **en ~ verticale** from above

plongeoir /plɔ̃ʒwaʀ/ **NM** diving board

plongeon[1] /plɔ̃ʒɔ̃/ **NM** *(Ftbl, Natation)* dive ♦ **faire un ~** *[nageur]* to dive; *[gardien de but]* to make a dive, to dive; *(= tomber)* to go head over heels ♦ **faire le ~** *[société]* to go under suddenly; *[prix, valeurs]* to nose-dive, to take a nose dive

plongeon[2] /plɔ̃ʒɔ̃/ **NM** *(= oiseau)* diver *(Brit)*, loon *(US)*

plonger /plɔ̃ʒe/ ► conjug 3 ◄ **VI** 1 *[personne, sous-marin]* to dive (*dans* into; *sur* on, onto); *[avion, oiseau]* to dive, to swoop; *[gardien de but]* to dive, to make a dive ♦ **l'avion a plongé sur son objectif** the plane dived (down) *ou* swooped down towards its target ♦ **l'oiseau plongea sur sa proie** the bird swooped (down) onto its prey

2 *[route, terrain]* to plunge (down), to dip (sharply *ou* steeply); *[racines]* to go down ♦ **~ dans le sommeil** to fall (straight) into a deep sleep ♦ **mon regard plongeait sur la vallée** I gazed down on the valley ♦ **il a plongé dans l'alcool/la drogue** he turned to drink/to drugs ♦ **il a plongé dans la dépression** he sank into a deep depression

3 *[société]* to go under; *[prix, valeurs]* to nose-dive, to take a nose-dive, to plummet; *[notes scolaires]* to plummet

4 *(arg Crime) [truand]* to get busted* *ou* done* *(Brit)* (*pour* for)

VT ♦ **~ qch dans** *[+ sac]* to plunge *ou* thrust sth into; *[+ eau]* to plunge sth into ♦ **~ qn dans** *[+ obscurité, misère, sommeil, méditation, vice]* to plunge sb into; *[+ désespoir]* to throw *ou* plunge sb into ♦ **il plongea sa main dans sa poche pour prendre son mouchoir** he plunged his hand into his pocket to get his handkerchief out ♦ **~ qn dans la surprise** to surprise sb greatly ♦ **vous me plongez dans l'embarras** you've put me in a difficult position ♦ **il lui plongea un poignard dans le cœur** he plunged a dagger into his heart ♦ **plante qui plonge ses racines dans le sol** plant that thrusts its roots deep into the ground ♦ **~ son regard sur/vers** to cast one's eyes at/towards ♦ **il plongea son regard dans mes yeux** he looked deeply into my eyes

VPR se plonger ♦ **se ~ dans** *[+ études, lecture]* to bury *ou* immerse o.s. in, to throw o.s. into; *[+ dossier, eau, bain]* to plunge into, to immerse o.s. in ♦ **se ~ dans le vice** to throw o.s. into a life of vice

plongeur, -euse /plɔ̃ʒœʀ, øz/ **ADJ** diving **NM,F** 1 *(Sport)* diver ♦ **~ sous-marin** *(gén)* diver; *(sans scaphandre)* skin diver; → **cloche** 2 *[de restaurant]* dishwasher, washer-up *(Brit)* **NM** *(= oiseau)* diver *(Brit)*, loon *(US)*

plosive /ploziv/ **NF** plosive

plot /plo/ **NM** *(Élec)* contact; *[de billard électrique]* pin ♦ **~ (de départ)** *[de piscine]* (starting) block

plouc* /pluk/ **NM** *(péj)* *(= paysan)* country bumpkin; *(= crétin)* ninny* **ADJ** ♦ **il est ~** he's a ninny* ♦ **sa robe fait ~** her dress looks dowdy

plouf /pluf/ **EXCL** splash! ♦ **il est tombé dans l'eau avec un gros ~** he fell into the water with a splash ♦ **la pierre a fait ~ en tombant dans l'eau** the stone made a splash as it fell into the water

ploutocrate /plutɔkʀat/ **NM** plutocrat

ploutocratie /plutɔkʀasi/ **NF** plutocracy

ploutocratique /plutɔkʀatik/ **ADJ** plutocratic

ployer /plwaje/ ► conjug 8 ◄ *(littér)* **VI** *[branche, dos]* to bend; *[poutre, plancher]* to sag; *[genoux, jambes]* to give way, to bend; *[armée]* to yield, to give in; *[résistance]* to give way ♦ **faire ~ le plancher sous son poids** to make the floor sag beneath one's weight ♦ **~ sous l'impôt** to be weighed down by taxes ♦ **notre défense ploie mais ne rompt pas** *(Sport)* our defence is weakening but not breaking down completely ♦ **~ sous le joug** *(fig)* to bend beneath the yoke **VT** to bend ♦ **~ un pays sous son autorité** to make a country bow down *ou* submit to one's authority

pluches /plyʃ/ **NFPL** 1 *(arg Mil)* **être de (corvée de) ~** to be on potato-peeling *ou* spud-bashing* *(Brit)* duty 2 *(Culin)* **~ de cerfeuil** chervil sprigs

pluie /plɥi/ **NF** 1 *(gén)* rain; *(= averse)* shower (of rain) ♦ **les ~s** the rains ♦ **la saison des ~s** the rainy season ♦ **le temps est à la ~** we're in for some rain, it looks like rain ♦ **jour/temps de ~** wet *ou* rainy day/weather ♦ **sous la ~** in the rain ♦ **~ battante** driving *ou* lashing rain ♦ **~ diluvienne** pouring rain *(NonC)*, downpour ♦ **~ fine** drizzle ♦ **une ~ fine tombait** it was drizzling ♦ **~ jaune/acide** yellow/acid rain

2 *[de cadeaux, cendres]* shower; *[de balles, pierres, coups]* hail, shower ♦ **en ~** in a shower ♦ **tomber en ~** to shower down ♦ **versez le riz en ~** *(Culin)* add the rice gradually

3 *(locutions)* **après la ~ (vient) le beau temps** *(lit)* the sun is shining again after the rain; *(fig)* everything's fine again ♦ **faire la ~ et le beau temps** *(fig)* to call the shots* ♦ **il n'est pas né** *ou* **tombé de la dernière ~** *(fig)* he wasn't born yesterday ♦ **petite ~ abat grand vent** *(Prov)* a small effort can go a long way; → **ennuyeux, parler**

plumage /plymaʒ/ **NM** plumage *(NonC)*, feathers

plumard* /plymaʀ/ **NM** bed ♦ **aller au ~** to turn in*, to hit the hay* *ou* the sack*

plume /plym/ **NF** 1 *[d'oiseau]* feather ♦ **chapeau à ~s** feathered hat, hat with feathers ♦ **oreiller/lit de ~s** feather pillow/bed ♦ **être aussi léger qu'une ~, ne pas peser plus lourd qu'une ~** to be as light as a feather ♦ **soulever qch comme une ~** to lift sth up as if it weighed practically nothing ♦ **se mettre dans les ~s*** to hit the sack* *ou* the hay*, to turn in* ♦ **il y a laissé des ~s*** *(gén)* he came off badly; *(financièrement)* he got his fingers burnt ♦ **il perd ses ~s*** *(hum)* his hair is falling out, he's going bald; → **gibier, poids, voler**[1]

2 *(pour écrire, d'oiseau)* quill (pen); *(en acier)* (pen) nib ♦ **écrire à la ~** *(= stylo)* to write with a fountain pen ♦ **~ d'oie** goose quill ♦ **dessin à la ~** pen-and-ink drawing ♦ **écrire au fil** *ou* **courant de la ~** to write just as the ideas come to one *ou* come into one's head ♦ **il a la ~ facile** writing comes easy to him ♦ **vivre de sa ~** to live by writing *ou* by one's pen ♦ **prendre la ~ pour ...** to take up one's pen to ..., to put pen to paper to ... ♦ **il a pris sa plus belle ~ pour écrire au percepteur** *(hum)* he wrote the tax inspector a very elaborate letter ♦ **je lui passe la ~** *(dans une lettre)* I'll hand over to him, I'll let him carry on ♦ **tremper sa ~ dans le poison** *(fig)* to steep one's pen in venom; → **homme**

3 *(Pêche)* quill

4 *[de coquille]* pen

NM ⇒ **plumard**

COMP **plume à vaccin** vaccine point

plumeau (pl **plumeaux**) /plymo/ **NM** feather duster

plumer /plyme/ ► conjug 1 ◄ **VT** 1 *[+ volaille]* to pluck 2 * *[+ personne]* to fleece* ♦ **se faire ~** to be *ou* get fleeced*

plumet /plymɛ/ **NM** plume

plumetis /plym(ə)ti/ **NM** *(= tissu)* Swiss muslin; *(= broderie)* raised satin stitch

plumeux, -euse /plymø, øz/ **ADJ** feathery

plumier /plymje/ **NM** pencil box

plumitif /plymitif/ **NM** *(péj)* *(= employé)* penpusher *(péj)*; *(= écrivain)* scribbler *(péj)*

plupart /plypaʀ/ GRAMMAIRE ACTIVE 53.1 **NF** ♦ **la ~ des gens** most people, the majority of people ♦ **la ~ des gens qui se trouvaient là** most of the people there ♦ **la ~ (d'entre eux) pensent que ...** most (of them) *ou* the majority (of them) think that ... ♦ **dans la ~ des cas** in most cases, in the majority of cases ♦ **pour la ~** mostly, for the most part ♦ **ces gens qui, pour la ~, avaient tout perdu** these people who, for the most part, had lost everything, these people, most of whom had lost everything ♦ **la ~ du temps** most of the time ♦ **la ~ de mon temps** most of my time, the greater part of my time

plural, e (mpl **-aux**) /plyʀal, o/ **ADJ** *[vote]* plural

pluralisme /plyʀalism/ **NM** pluralism

pluraliste /plyʀalist/ **ADJ** pluralistic **NMF** pluralist

pluralité /plyʀalite/ **NF** multiplicity, plurality

pluriannuel, -elle /plyʀianɥɛl/ **ADJ** *[contrat]* long-term; *[plante]* perennial

pluriculturel, -elle /plyʀikyltyʀɛl/ **ADJ** multicultural

pluridisciplinaire /plyʀidisiplinɛʀ/ **ADJ** *(Scol)* pluridisciplinary, multidisciplinary

pluridisciplinarité /plyʀidisiplinaʀite/ **NF** pluridisciplinarity, multidisciplinary nature

pluriel, -elle /plyʀjɛl/ **ADJ** 1 *(Ling)* plural 2 *(= composite)* *[musique]* that draws on several sources; *[sanctions]* various ♦ **la gauche ~le** *(Pol)* the left coalition ♦ **liste ~le** *single voting list with candidates from different parties* ♦ **c'est une œuvre plurielle** *[livre, pièce de théâtre]* it is a work which can be read *(ou* understood *etc)* on many different levels **NM** plural ♦ **au ~** in the plural ♦ **la première personne du ~** the first person plural ♦ **le ~ de majesté** the royal "we" ♦ **le ~ de "cheval" est "chevaux"** the plural of "cheval" is "chevaux"

pluriethnique /plyʀiɛtnik/ **ADJ** multiethnic

plurifonctionnalité /plyʀifɔ̃ksjɔnalite/ **NF** *[d'appareil, salle]* versatility

plurilatéral, e (mpl **-aux**) /plyʀilateʀal, o/ **ADJ** multilateral

plurilingue /plyʀilɛ̃g/ **ADJ** multilingual

plurilinguisme /plyʀilɛ̃gɥism/ **NM** multilingualism

pluripartisme /plyʀipaʀtism/ **NM** *(Pol)* multiparty system

plurivalent, e /plyʀivalɑ̃, ɑ̃t/ **ADJ** multivalent, polyvalent

plus /ply, plys/

1 ADVERBE DE NÉGATION
2 ADVERBE (EMPLOI COMPARATIF)
3 ADVERBE (EMPLOI SUPERLATIF)
4 CONJONCTION
5 NOM MASCULIN

Lorsque **plus** s'emploie dans des locutions telles que **d'autant plus, raison de plus, tant et plus, à plus forte raison, non ... plus** etc, cherchez à l'autre mot.

1 - ADVERBE DE NÉGATION

plus adverbe de négation se prononce [ply] devant une consonne et en fin de phrase, [plyz] devant une voyelle.

♦ **(ne +)** *verbe* + **plus** *(temps)* not any longer *ou* any more, no longer; *(quantité)* no more, not any more ♦ **il ne la voit ~** he no longer sees her, he doesn't see her any more ♦ **il n'a ~ besoin de son parapluie** he doesn't need his umbrella any longer *ou* any more ♦ **il n'a ~ à s'inquiéter/travailler maintenant** he doesn't need to worry/work any more now ♦ **je ne reviendrai ~/~ jamais** I won't/I'll never come back again ♦ **il n'a ~ dit un mot** he didn't say another word (after that) ♦ **il n'est ~ là, il est ~ là*** he isn't here anymore ♦ **son père n'est ~** *(euph)* his father has passed away *(euph)* ♦ **elle n'est ~ très jeune** she's not as young as she used to be ♦ **~ besoin de rester !** there's no need to stay now ♦ **t'as ~ faim ?*** aren't you hungry any more?

♦ **plus de** + *nom* ♦ **elle n'a ~ de pain/d'argent** she's got no more *ou* she hasn't got any more bread/money, she's got no (more) bread/money left ♦ **elle ne veut ~ de pain** she doesn't want any more bread ♦ **il n'y a ~ guère** *ou* **beaucoup de pain** there's hardly any bread left ♦ **il n'y a ~ d'enfants/de jeunesse !** *(hum)* children/young people aren't what they used to be! ♦ **~ de doute !** there's no longer any doubt about it ♦ **~ de vin, merci** no more wine, thank you ♦ **des fruits ? y en a ~*** fruit? there's none left *ou* there's no more left *ou* there isn't any (more) left

♦ **plus que** *(= seulement)* ♦ **il n'y a ~ que des miettes** there are only crumbs left, there's nothing left but crumbs ♦ **ça ne tient ~ qu'à elle** it's up to her now ♦ **il n'y a (guère) ~ que huit jours avant les vacances** there's only (about) a week to go before the holidays ♦ **il ne nous reste ~ qu'à attendre** all we've got to do now is wait ♦ **il ne me reste ~ qu'à vous dire au revoir** it only remains for me to say goodbye ♦ **~ que 5 km à faire** only another 5 km to go

♦ **plus rien/personne/aucun** ♦ **il n'y a ~ rien** there's nothing left ♦ **il n'y a ~ rien d'autre à faire** there's nothing else to do ♦ **on n'y voit presque ~ rien** you can hardly see anything now ♦ **(il n'y a) ~ personne à la maison** there's no one left in the house ♦ **il n'y a ~ aucun espoir** there's no hope left

2 - ADVERBE (EMPLOI COMPARATIF)

plus comparatif se prononce [ply] devant une consonne, [plyz] devant une voyelle, [plys] en fin de phrase, [ply(s)] devant **que**.

1

♦ *verbe* + **plus (que)** ♦ **il devrait sortir/lire ~** he should go out/read more ♦ **vous travaillez ~ (que nous)** you work more (than us) ♦ **il ne gagne pas ~ (que vous)** he doesn't earn any more (than you) ♦ **j'aime la poésie ~ que tout au monde** I like poetry more than anything (else) in the world ♦ **~ fait douceur que violence** *(Prov)* kindness succeeds where force will fail

2

♦ **plus** + *adjectif ou adverbe court* (+ **que**)

Lorsque l'adjectif ou l'adverbe est court, c'est-à-dire qu'il n'a qu'une ou deux syllabes, son comparatif se forme généralement avec **-er**.

♦ **il est ~ foncé/large (que l'autre)** it's darker/wider (than the other one) ♦ **elle n'est pas ~ grande (que sa sœur)** she isn't any taller *ou* she is no taller (than her sister) ♦ **il est ~ vieux qu'elle de 10 ans** he's 10 years older than her *ou* than she is *ou* than she *(frm)* ♦ **il court ~ vite (qu'elle)** he runs faster (than her *ou* than she does) ♦ **une heure ~ tôt/tard** an hour earlier/later ♦ **ne venez pas ~ tard que 6 heures** don't come any later than 6 o'clock

Lorsque l'adjectif se termine par **y**, son comparatif est formé avec **-ier**.

♦ **elle est ~ jolie/bête** she's prettier/sillier ♦ **c'était ~ drôle** it was funnier

Lorsque l'adjectif n'a qu'une syllabe avec une voyelle brève et se termine par une consonne, il y a doublement de cette consonne finale.

♦ **il est ~ gros/mince** he's bigger/slimmer

Certains mots de deux syllabes admettent les deux types de comparatifs mais l'usage privilégie une forme plutôt que l'autre.

♦ **c'est ~ simple** it's simpler, it's more simple ♦ **cette méthode est ~ courante que l'autre** this method is more common *ou* is commoner than the other one ♦ **~ souvent que tu ne le penses** more often than you think, oftener than you think

Certaines terminaisons telles que **-ing, -ed, -s, -ly** interdisent l'ajout du suffixe de comparaison sur des mots de deux syllabes.

♦ **il est ~ malin** he's more cunning ♦ **c'est encore ~ pompeux** it's even more pompous ♦ **pour y arriver ~ rapidement** to get there more quickly ♦ **prends-le ~ doucement** take hold of it more gently

Attention aux comparatifs irréguliers.

♦ **c'est ~ loin** it's further, it's farther

Notez les autres traductions possibles lorsque la comparaison porte sur une même personne ou un même objet.

♦ **il est ~ bête que méchant** he's stupid rather than malicious, he's more stupid than malicious ♦ **c'est ~ agaçant que douloureux** it's not so much painful as annoying, it's more annoying than painful

3
◆ **plus** *+ adjectif ou adverbe long*

Lorsque l'adjectif ou l'adverbe anglais est long (au moins trois syllabes), son comparatif se forme généralement avec **more**.

◆ **il est ~ compétent (que vous/moi)** he is more competent (than you (are)/than me *ou* than I am *ou* than I *(frm)*) ◆ **beaucoup ~ facilement** much more *ou* a lot more easily MAIS **il est ~ malheureux que jamais** he's unhappier than ever

Notez l'emploi possible de **as** pour traduire les expressions avec **fois**.

◆ **deux fois ~ souvent que ...** twice as often as ... ◆ **deux ou trois fois ~ cher que ...** two or three times more expensive than ..., two or three times as expensive as ... ◆ **il est deux fois ~ âgé qu'elle** he's twice as old as her, he's twice her age

◆ **à plus tard!, à plus!** * see you later!

4 constructions

◆ **plus que** *+ adjectif ou adverbe* ◆ **il est ~ qu'intelligent** he's clever to say the least ◆ **un résultat ~ qu'honorable** a more than honourable result, an honourable result to say the least ◆ **~ que jamais** more than ever ◆ **je lui ai parlé ~ que gentiment** I spoke to him most kindly ◆ **j'en ai ~ qu'assez !** I've had more than enough of this!

◆ **de plus** *(comparaison)* ◆ **elle a 10 ans de ~ (que lui)** she's 10 years older (than him) ◆ **il y a dix personnes de ~ (qu'hier)** there are ten more people (than yesterday) ◆ **ça leur a pris dix minutes de ~ (que la veille)** it took them ten minutes longer (than the day before)
(= en outre) furthermore, what is more, moreover
(= encore) ◆ **une fois de ~** once more, once again ◆ **il me faut une heure de ~** I need one more *ou* another hour

◆ **de plus en plus** more and more ◆ **il fait de ~ en ~ beau** the weather's getting better and better ◆ **aller de ~ en ~ vite** to go faster and faster ◆ **de ~ en ~ drôle** funnier and funnier, more and more funny

◆ **en plus** *(= en supplément)* ◆ **les frais d'envoi sont en ~** postal charges are extra *ou* are not included ◆ **on nous a donné deux verres en ~** we were given two more *ou* extra glasses; *(= de trop)* we were given two glasses too many; *(= en prime)* we were given two glasses free ◆ **vous n'avez pas une chaise en ~ ?** you wouldn't have a spare chair? ◆ **elle a choisi le même chapeau avec les fleurs en ~** she chose the same hat but with flowers on it ◆ **il est doué, rapide, et en ~ il travaille !** he's talented, quick and on top of that *ou* and what's more he's a good worker!

◆ **en plus** *+ adjectif* ◆ **il ressemble à sa mère, mais en ~ blond** he's like his mother only fairer ◆ **je cherche le même genre de maison en ~ grand** I'm looking for the same kind of house only bigger

◆ **en plus de** ◆ **en ~ de son travail, il prend des cours du soir** on top of his work, he's taking evening classes ◆ **en ~ de cela** on top of (all) that, in addition to that

◆ **... et plus** ◆ **les enfants de six ans et ~** children aged six and over ◆ **les familles de trois enfants et ~** families with three or more children ◆ **10 000 € et ~** €10,000 and more *ou* and over

◆ **ni plus ni moins** ◆ **il est compétent, mais ni ~ ni moins que sa sœur** he's competent, but neither more (so) nor less so than his sister ◆ **elle est secrétaire, ni ~ ni moins** she's just a secretary, no more no less ◆ **c'est du vol, ni ~ ni moins** it's sheer *ou* daylight robbery ◆ **il envisage, ni ~ ni moins, de licencier la moitié du personnel** *(iro)* he's considering sacking half of the staff, no less

◆ **plus de** *(= davantage de)* ◆ **(un peu) ~ de pain** (a little *ou* a bit) more bread ◆ **j'ai ~ de pain que vous** I've got more bread than you (have) ◆ **il y aura (beaucoup) ~ de monde demain** there will be (a lot *ou* many) more people tomorrow ◆ **il n'y aura pas ~ de monde demain** there won't be any more people tomorrow
(= au-delà de) ◆ **il y aura ~ de 100 personnes** there will be more than *ou* over 100 people ◆ **à ~ de 100 mètres d'ici** more than *ou* over 100 metres from here ◆ **il roulait à ~ de 100 km/h** he was driving at over 100 km per hour ◆ **les enfants de ~ de 4 ans** children over 4 ◆ **les ~ de 30/40 ans** the over 30s/40s ◆ **il n'y avait pas ~ de 10 personnes** there were no more than 10 people ◆ **il est ~ de 9 heures** it's after *ou* past *ou* gone * 9 o'clock ◆ **~ d'un** more than one ◆ **~ d'un aurait refusé** many would have refused

◆ **plus ..., moins ...** the more ..., the less ... ◆ **~ on le connaît, moins on l'apprécie** the more you get to know him, the less you like him

◆ **plus ..., plus ...** the more ..., the more ... ◆ **~ il en a, ~ il en veut** the more he has, the more he wants ◆ **~ on boit, ~ on a soif** the more you drink, the thirstier you get ◆ **~ on est de fous, ~ on rit** *ou* **s'amuse** *(Prov)* the more the merrier

◆ **plus ou moins** *(= à peu près, presque)* more or less ◆ **ils sont ~ ou moins fiancés** they're more or less engaged ◆ **des pratiques ~ ou moins douteuses** more or less shady practices ◆ **à ~ ou moins long terme** sooner or later ◆ **je l'ai trouvé ~ ou moins sympathique** *(= pas très)* I didn't find him very friendly ◆ **est-elle efficace ? – ~ ou moins** is she efficient? – not particularly ◆ **les gens sont ~ ou moins réceptifs à la publicité** *(variant avec les individus)* some people are more receptive to advertising than others; *(selon leur humeur etc)* people can be more or less receptive to advertising ◆ **il supporte ~ ou moins bien cette situation** he just about puts up with the situation ◆ **je le connais ~ ou moins** I know him vaguely ◆ **ils utilisent cette méthode avec ~ ou moins de succès/d'enthousiasme** they use this method with varying degrees of success/of enthusiasm

◆ **qui plus est** furthermore, what's more, moreover

3 - ADVERBE (EMPLOI SUPERLATIF)

plus superlatif se prononce [ply(s)] devant une consonne, [plyz] devant une voyelle, [plys] en fin de phrase.

◆ *verbe +* **le plus** ◆ **ce qui m'a frappé le ~** what struck me most ◆ **ce qui les a le ~ étonnés** what surprised them (the) most ◆ **ce que j'aime le ~** what I most like, what I like (the) most *ou* (the) best

◆ **le plus** *+ adjectif ou adverbe court*

Lorsque l'adjectif ou l'adverbe est court, c'est-à-dire qu'il n'a qu'une ou deux syllabes, son superlatif se forme avec **-est**.

◆ **c'est le ~ grand peintre qui ait jamais vécu** he is the greatest painter that ever lived ◆ **il a couru le ~ vite** he ran the fastest

Lorsque l'adjectif se termine par **y** son superlatif se forme avec **-iest**.

◆ **c'est la ~ jolie/bête** she's the prettiest/silliest ◆ **c'était le moment le ~ drôle du film** that was the funniest part of the film

Lorsque l'adjectif n'a qu'une syllabe avec une voyelle brève et se termine par une consonne, il y a doublement de cette consonne finale.

◆ **c'est le ~ gros/mince** he's the biggest/slimmest

Certains mots de deux syllabes admettent les deux types de superlatifs mais l'usage privilégie une forme plutôt que l'autre.

◆ **c'est le ~ simple** it's the simplest, it's the most simple ◆ **c'est la méthode la ~ courante** it's the commonest *ou* the most common method

Certaines terminaisons telles que **-ing, -ed, -s, -ly** interdisent l'ajout du suffixe sur des mots de deux syllabes.

◆ **l'enfant le ~ doué que je connaisse/de la classe** the most gifted child I've (ever) met/in the class ◆ **c'est la partie la ~ ennuyeuse** it's the most boring part ◆ **c'est ce que j'ai de ~ précieux** it's the most precious thing I possess ◆ **c'est le livre que je lis le ~ souvent** it's the book I read most often

Attention aux superlatifs irréguliers.

◆ **c'est le ~ loin** it's the furthest, it's the farthest

Lorsque la comparaison se fait entre deux personnes ou deux choses, on utilise la forme du comparatif.

◆ **le ~ petit (des deux)** the smaller (of the two) MAIS **le ~ petit (de tous)** the smallest (of all)

◆ **le plus** *+ adjectif ou adverbe long*

Lorsque l'adjectif ou l'adverbe est long, c'est-à-dire qu'il a au moins trois syllabes, son superlatif se forme généralement avec **the most**.

◆ **c'est le ~ intéressant** it's the most interesting ◆ **le ~ beau de tous mes livres** the most beautiful of all my books MAIS **c'est la personne la ~ désordonnée que je connaisse** she's the untidiest person I know

Attention : lorsque la comparaison se fait entre deux personnes ou deux choses, on utilise la forme du comparatif.

◆ **le ~ beau (des deux)** the more beautiful (of the two)

◆ **le plus de** *+ nom* ◆ **c'est nous qui avons cueilli le ~ de fleurs** we've picked the most flowers ◆ **c'est le samedi qu'il y a le ~ de monde** it's on Saturdays that there are the most people ◆ **les films qui rapportent le ~ d'argent** the films that make the most money ◆ **ce qui m'a donné le ~ de mal** the thing I found (the) most difficult ◆ **celui qui a le ~ de chances de gagner** the one who has the most chances of winning

◆ **le plus (...) possible** ◆ **pour y arriver le ~ rapidement possible** to get there as quickly as possible ◆ **il a couru le ~ vite possible** he ran as fast as possible *ou* as fast as he could ◆ **prends-en le ~ possible** take as much (*ou* as many) as possible *ou* as you can ◆ **prends le ~ possible de livres/de beurre** take as many books/as much butter as possible

◆ **au plus** at the most ◆ **il y a au ~ un quart d'heure qu'il est parti** he left a quarter of an hour ago at the most ◆ **ça vaut 15 € au ~** its worth €15 maximum *ou* at (the) most ◆ **ils étaient une vingtaine au ~** there were twenty of them at (the) most *ou* at the outside

◆ **au plus** *+ adverbe* ◆ **rappelle-moi au ~ vite** call me back as soon as you can *ou* as soon as possible; → **tard, tôt**

◆ **des plus** *+ adjectif* ◆ **une situation des ~ embarrassantes** a most embarrassing situation ◆ **l'entreprise est des ~ rentables** the company is highly profitable ◆ **ses craintes sont des ~ justifiées** he has every reason to be afraid

◆ **tout au plus** at the very most ◆ **il a trente ans, tout au ~** he's thirty at (the) most *ou* at the outside ◆ **tout au ~ peut-on** *ou* **on peut**

tout au ~ affirmer que ... all we can say is that ..., the best we can say is that ...

4 - CONJONCTION

plus conjonction se prononce /plys/

/plys/ plus, and ♦ **deux ~ deux font quatre** two and two are four, two plus two make four ♦ **tous les voisins, ~ leurs enfants** all the neighbours, plus their children *ou* and their children (as well) ♦ **il paie sa chambre, ~ le téléphone et l'électricité** he pays for his room, plus the telephone and electricity bills ♦ **il fait ~ deux aujourd'hui** it's plus two (degrees) today, it's two above freezing today

5 - NOM MASCULIN

plus nom se prononce /plys/

1 Math **(signe)** ~ plus (sign)

2 = avantage plus ♦ **ici, parler breton est un ~ indéniable** being able to speak Breton is definitely a plus *ou* is quite an asset here ♦ **les ~ de ce nouveau modèle : ABS, airbag etc** the new model's plus points: ABS, airbag etc ♦ **quels sont les ~ de ce produit par rapport aux autres ?** what does this product have that the others don't?

plusieurs /plyzjœʀ/ ADJ INDÉF PL several ♦ **on ne peut pas être en ~ endroits à la fois** you can't be in more than one place at once ♦ **ils sont ~** there are several (of them), there are a number of them ♦ **ils sont ~ à vouloir venir** several of them want to come ♦ **un ou ~** one or more ♦ **~ fois, à ~ reprises** several times, on several occasions ♦ **payer en ~ fois** to pay in instalments PRON INDÉF PL several (people) ♦ **~ (d'entre eux)** several (of them) ♦ **ils se sont mis à ~ pour ...** several people got together to ... ♦ **nous nous sommes mis à ~ pour ...** several of us got together to ...

plus-que-parfait /plyskəpaʀfɛ/ NM *(Gram)* pluperfect (tense), past perfect

plus-value (pl **plus-values**) /plyvaly/ NF 1 *(= accroissement de valeur)* appreciation *(NonC)*, increase in value; *(= bénéfice réalisé)* capital gain; *(= excédent)* surplus, profit ♦ **réaliser** *ou* **faire** *ou* **dégager une ~** *[personne]* to make a profit ♦ **ces actions ont enregistré une ~ importante** the shares have yielded a substantial capital gain; → **impôt** 2 *(dans la pensée marxiste)* surplus value

Plutarque /plytaʀk/ NM Plutarch

Pluton /plytɔ̃/ NM *(Astron, Myth)* Pluto

plutonium /plytɔnjɔm/ NM plutonium

plutôt /plyto/ ADV 1 *(= de préférence)* rather; *(= à la place)* instead ♦ **ne lis pas ce livre, prends ~ celui-ci** don't read that book, take this one instead ♦ **prends ce livre ~ que celui-là** take this book rather than *ou* instead of that one ♦ **cette maladie affecte ~ les enfants** this illness affects children for the most part *ou* tends to affect children ♦ **je préfère ~ celui-ci** *(= je voudrais celui-ci de préférence)* I'd rather *ou* sooner have this one; *(= j'aime mieux celui-ci)* I prefer this one, I like this one better ♦ **~ mourir que souffrir** it is better to die than to suffer ♦ **~ que de me regarder, viens m'aider** instead of (just) watching me, come and help ♦ **n'importe quoi ~ que cela !** anything but that!, anything rather than that! ♦ **~ mourir (que de ...) !** I'd sooner die (than ...)!

2 *(= plus exactement)* rather ♦ **il n'est pas paresseux mais ~ apathique** he's not so much lazy as apathetic ♦ **il est ignorant ~ que sot** he's more ignorant than stupid, he's not so much stupid as ignorant ♦ **ou ~, c'est ce qu'il pense** or rather that's what he thinks ♦ **c'est un journaliste ~ qu'un romancier** he's more of a journalist than a novelist, he's a journalist more *ou* rather than a novelist ♦ **il s'y habitue ~ qu'il n'oublie** he's getting used to it rather than *ou* more than forgetting about it

3 *(= assez) [chaud, bon]* rather, quite, fairly ♦ **il remange, c'est ~ bon signe** he's eating again – that's quite a good sign ♦ **nos vacances sont ~ compromises avec cet événement** our holidays are somewhat in the balance because of this incident ♦ **un homme brun, ~ petit** a dark-haired man, rather *ou* somewhat on the short side *ou* rather short ♦ **il est ~ pénible, celui-là !** he's a bit of a pain in the neck!* ♦ **il faisait beau ? – non, il faisait ~ frais** was the weather good? – no, if anything it was cool ♦ **qu'est-ce qu'il est pénible, celui-là ! – ah oui, ~ !*** what a pain in the neck he is!* – you said it!* *ou* you're telling me!*

pluvial, e (mpl **-iaux**) /plyvjal, jo/ ADJ *[régime, écoulement]* pluvial ♦ **eau ~e** rainwater

pluvier /plyvje/ NM plover ♦ **~ guignard** dotterel

pluvieux, -ieuse /plyvjø, jøz/ ADJ *[journée, temps]* rainy, wet; *[été, climat]* wet

pluviner /plyvine/ ► conjug 1 ◄ VB IMPERS ⇒ **pleuvasser**

pluviomètre /plyvjɔmɛtʀ/ NM pluviometer *(SPÉC)*, rain gauge

pluviométrie /plyvjɔmetʀi/ NF pluviometry

pluviométrique /plyvjɔmetʀik/ ADJ pluviometric(al) ♦ **carte ~** isopluvial map ♦ **courbe ~** rainfall graph

pluviôse /plyvjoz/ NM Pluviôse *(fifth month in the French Republican calendar)*

pluviosité /plyvjozite/ NF *[de temps, saison]* raininess, wetness; *(= pluie tombée)* (average) rainfall

PLV /peɛlve/ NF (abrév de **publicité sur le lieu de vente**) → **publicité**

PM /peɛm/ NF 1 (abrév de **préparation militaire**) → **préparation** 2 (abrév de **police militaire**) MP NM 1 abrév de **pistolet-mitrailleur** 2 (abrév de **poids moléculaire**) → **poids**

PMA /peɛma/ NF (abrév de **procréation médicale(ment) assistée**) → **procréation** NMPL (abrév de **pays les moins avancés**) LDCs

PME /peɛmə/ NF INV (abrév de **petite et moyenne entreprise**) small (*ou* medium-sized) business, SME ♦ **les ~** small (and medium-sized) businesses, SMEs ♦ **les ~-PMI** small and medium-sized businesses and industries, SMEs/SMIs

PMI /peɛmi/ NF 1 (abrév de **petite et moyenne industrie**) small (*ou* medium-sized) industry, SMI ♦ **les ~** small and medium-sized industries, SMIs 2 (abrév de **protection maternelle et infantile**) → **protection**

PMU /peɛmy/ NM (abrév de **Pari mutuel urbain**) pari-mutuel, ≃ tote* *(Brit)* ♦ **jouer au ~** to bet on the horses, ≃ to bet on the tote* *(Brit)* ♦ **le bureau du ~** the betting office; → **PMU**

PNB /peɛnbe/ NM (abrév de **Produit national brut**) GNP

pneu /pnø/ NM (abrév de **pneumatique**) 1 *[de véhicule]* tyre *(Brit)*, tire *(US)* ♦ **~ clouté** studded tyre ♦ **~ sans chambre** *ou* **tubeless** tubeless tyre ♦ **~-neige** snow tyre ♦ **~ plein** solid tyre ♦ **~ radial** *ou* **à carcasse radiale** radial(ply) tyre 2 *(= message)* letter sent by pneumatic dispatch *ou* tube ♦ **par ~** by pneumatic dispatch *ou* tube

pneumatique /pnømatik/ ADJ *(Sci)* pneumatic; *(= gonflable)* inflatable; → **canot, marteau, matelas** NF pneumatics *(sg)* NM ⇒ **pneu**

pneumectomie /pnømɛktomi/ NF pneumectomy

pneumoconiose /pnømokɔnjoz/ NF pneumoconiosis

pneumocoque /pnømɔkɔk/ NM pneumococcus

pneumocystose /pnømosistoz/ NF pneumocystis carinii pneumonia, PCP

pneumogastrique /pnømogastʀik/ ADJ pneumogastric NM vagus nerve

pneumologie /pnømɔlɔʒi/ NF pneumology

pneumologue /pnømɔlɔg/ NMF lung specialist

pneumonectomie /pnømɔnɛktɔmi/ NF pneumonectomy

pneumonie /pnømɔni/ NF pneumonia *(NonC)* ♦ **faire** *ou* **avoir une ~** to have pneumonia

pneumonique /pnømɔnik/ ADJ pneumonic NMF pneumonia patient

pneumothorax /pnømotɔʀaks/ NM pneumothorax

Pnom-Penh /pnɔmpɛn/ N Phnom Penh

PO (abrév de **petites ondes**) MW

Pô /po/ NM ♦ **le ~** the Po

pochade /pɔʃad/ NF *(= dessin)* quick sketch *(in colour)*; *(= histoire)* humorous piece

pochard, e* /pɔʃaʀ, aʀd/ NM,F drunk, lush*

poche[1] /pɔʃ/ NF 1 *[de vêtement, sac]* pocket ♦ **~ revolver/intérieure** hip/inside pocket ♦ **~ de pantalon** trouser pocket ♦ **~ appliquée** *ou* **plaquée** patch pocket ♦ **~ coupée** inset pocket ♦ **fausse ~** false pocket

2 *(locutions)* **connaître un endroit comme sa ~** to know a place like the back of one's hand *ou* inside out ♦ **faire les ~s à qn*** to go through sb's pockets ♦ **s'en mettre plein les ~s*, se remplir les ~s*** to line one's pockets ♦ **en être de sa ~*** to be out of pocket, to lose out* (financially) ♦ **il a payé de sa ~** it came *ou* he paid for it out of his (own) pocket ♦ **de ~** *[collection, livre]* paperback *(épith)*; *[sous-marin, couteau, mouchoir]* pocket *(épith)*; *[jeu, ordinateur]* pocket-size *(épith)*

♦ **dans + poche** ♦ **il a mis le maire dans sa ~** he's got the mayor in his pocket ♦ **c'est dans la ~ !*** it's in the bag!* ♦ **ce n'est pas dans la ~ !*** it's not in the bag yet!* ♦ **mets ça dans ta ~ (et ton mouchoir par-dessus)** *[+ somme d'argent]* put that in your pocket (and forget about it); *[+ renseignement]* keep it under your hat*

♦ **en poche** ♦ **j'avais 5 euros/je n'avais pas un sou en ~** I had 5 euros/I didn't have a penny on me ♦ **(son) diplôme en ~, il a cherché du travail** armed with his diploma *ou* with his diploma under his belt, he started looking for a job ♦ **il a sa nomination en ~** his appointment is in the bag* ♦ **sans diplôme en ~, on ne peut rien faire** you can't do anything without qualifications

3 *(= déformation)* **faire des ~s** *[veste]* to lose its shape; *[pantalon]* to go baggy ♦ **avoir des ~s sous les yeux** to have bags under one's eyes

4 *(Helv = sac)* (carrier) bag

5 *[de kangourou]* pouch

6 *(= cavité)* pocket ♦ **~ d'air** air pocket ♦ **~ d'eau** pocket of water ♦ **~ de pus** pus sac ♦ **~ de sang** haematoma *(Brit)*, hematoma *(US)* ♦ **~ des eaux** amniotic sac

7 *(Culin)* **~ à douille** piping bag

8 *(= secteur)* **~ de résistance** pocket of resistance ♦ **~ de chômage/pauvreté** pocket of unemployment/poverty

9 *(Méd)* colostomy bag

poche[2] /pɔʃ/ NM *(= livre)* paperback ♦ **ce roman est paru en ~** this novel has come out in paperback

pocher /pɔʃe/ ► conjug 1 ◄ VT *(Culin)* to poach; *(Art)* to sketch ♦ **~ un œil à qn** to give sb a black eye VI *[pantalon]* ♦ **~ aux genoux** to go baggy at the knees ♦ **~ derrière** to go baggy in the bottom *ou* seat *(Brit)*

pochetron, -onne‡ /pɔʃtʀɔ̃, ɔn/ NM,F ⇒ **pochard, e**

pochette /pɔʃɛt/ NF (= *mouchoir*) pocket handkerchief; (= *petite poche*) breast pocket; (= *sac*) clutch *ou* envelope bag; [*de timbres, photos*] wallet, envelope; [*de serviette, aiguilles*] case; [*de disque*] sleeve, jacket (*US*) ◆ ~ **d'allumettes** book of matches

pochette-surprise (pl **pochettes-surprises**) /pɔʃɛtsyʀpʀiz/ NF lucky bag, Cracker Jack ® (*US*) ◆ **il a eu son permis dans une ~ !** (*hum*) God knows where he got his driving licence from! ◆ **elle a eu son diplôme dans une ~** (*hum*) she's got a Mickey Mouse * degree

pocheuse /pɔʃøz/ NF (egg)poacher

pochoir /pɔʃwaʀ/ NM (= *cache*) stencil; (= *tampon*) transfer ◆ **dessin au ~** stencil drawing ◆ **faire** *ou* **peindre qch au ~** to stencil sth

podagre /pɔdagʀ/ NF †† gout ADJ † suffering from gout

podcasting /pɔdkastiŋ/ NM podcasting

podium /pɔdjɔm/ NM (= *estrade*) podium; [*de défilé de mode*] catwalk ◆ **il peut espérer une place sur le ~ (du 400 m haies)** [*sportif*] he can hope to come away with a medal (in the 400 metre hurdles) ◆ **pour assurer notre présence sur les ~s olympiques** to ensure that we are among the Olympic medal winners ◆ **monter sur le ~** to mount the podium ◆ **monter sur la plus haute marche du ~** [*sportif, équipe*] (*gén*) to be the winner; (*aux Jeux olympiques*) to get the gold medal

podologie /pɔdɔlɔʒi/ NF chiropody, podiatry (*US*)

podologue /pɔdɔlɔg/ NMF chiropodist, podiatrist (*US*)

podomètre /pɔdɔmɛtʀ/ NM pedometer

poêle[1] /pwal/ NF ◆ ~ **(à frire)** frying pan; (* = *détecteur de métaux*) metal detector ◆ **passer qch à la ~** to fry sth ◆ ~ **à crêpes** pancake (*Brit*) *ou* crêpe pan ◆ ~ **à marrons** chestnut-roasting pan

poêle[2] /pwal/ NM stove ◆ ~ **à mazout/à pétrole** oil/paraffin (*Brit*) *ou* kerosene (*US*) stove ◆ ~ **à bois** wood(-burning) stove

poêle[3] /pwal/ NM [*de cercueil*] pall

poêlée /pwale/ NF ◆ **une ~ de** a frying pan full of ◆ ~ **de champignons/de légumes** (= *plat*) mixed fried mushrooms/vegetables

poêler /pwale/ ▸ conjug 1 ◂ VT to fry

poêlon /pwalɔ̃/ NM casserole

poème /pɔɛm/ NM poem ◆ ~ **en prose/symphonique** prose/symphonic poem ◆ **c'est tout un ~** * (= *c'est compliqué*) it's a whole lot of hassle *, it's a real palaver * (*Brit*)

poésie /pɔezi/ NF (= *art, qualité*) poetry; (= *poème*) poem, piece of poetry ◆ **faire de la ~** to write poetry ◆ **roman/film plein de ~** poetic novel/film

poète /pɔɛt/ NM poet; (= *rêveur*) poet, dreamer; → **œillet** ADJ [*tempérament*] poetic ◆ **être ~** to be a poet ◆ **femme ~** poetess

poétesse /pɔetɛs/ NF poetess

poétique /pɔetik/ ADJ poetic, poetical (*frm*) NF poetics (*sg*)

poétiquement /pɔetikmɑ̃/ ADV poetically

poétisation /pɔetizasjɔ̃/ NF (= *action*) poetizing; (= *résultat*) poetic depiction

poétiser /pɔetize/ ▸ conjug 1 ◂ VT to poetize

pogne‡ /pɔɲ/ NF mitt‡, paw * ◆ **être à la ~ de qn** to be under sb's thumb ◆ **avoir qn à sa ~** to have sb under one's thumb

pognon‡ /pɔɲɔ̃/ NM cash, dough‡ ◆ **ils sont pleins de ~**‡ they're loaded *

pogrom(e) /pɔgʀɔm/ NM pogrom

poids /pwɑ/ NM 1 (*gén*) weight ◆ **prendre du ~** [*adulte*] to put on *ou* gain weight; [*bébé*] to gain weight ◆ **perdre du ~** to lose weight ◆ **ce genre d'alimentation favorise la prise de ~** this kind of food makes you put on weight ◆ **quel ~ fait-il ?** how much does he weigh?, what's his weight? ◆ **vendu au ~** sold by weight ◆ **ces bijoux d'argent seront vendus au ~ du métal** this silver jewellery will be sold by the weight of the metal ◆ **la branche pliait sous le ~ des fruits** the branch was weighed down with (the) fruit *ou* was bending beneath the weight of the fruit ◆ **elle s'appuyait contre lui de tout son ~** she leaned against him with all her weight ◆ **elle a ajouté une pomme pour faire le ~** she put in an extra apple to make up the weight ◆ **faire bon ~** to give good weight ◆ **notre entreprise ne fait vraiment pas le ~** our firm really doesn't measure up ◆ **il ne fait pas le ~ face à son adversaire** he's no match for his opponent ◆ **faire deux ~, deux mesures** to have double standards

2 (= *objet*) [*de balance, horloge*] weight; (*Sport*) shot ◆ **lancer le ~** (*Sport*) to put(t) the shot; → **deux**

3 (= *charge*) weight ◆ **tout le ~ de l'entreprise repose sur lui** he carries the weight of the whole business on his shoulders ◆ **syndicat qui a beaucoup de ~** union which carries a lot of weight ◆ **plier sous le ~ des soucis/des impôts** to be weighed down by worries/taxes ◆ **être courbé sous le ~ des ans** to be bent by (the weight of) years ◆ **c'est le ~ des ans** (*hum*) old age never comes alone (*hum*) ◆ **enlever un ~ (de la conscience) à qn** to take a weight *ou* a load off sb's mind ◆ **c'est un ~ sur sa conscience** it lies *ou* weighs heavy on his conscience, it's a weight on his conscience ◆ **avoir** *ou* **se sentir un ~ sur l'estomac** to have something lying heavy on one's stomach ◆ **j'ai un ~ sur la poitrine** my chest feels tight

4 (= *force, influence*) weight ◆ **argument de ~** weighty *ou* forceful argument, argument of great weight ◆ **homme de ~** man who carries weight *ou* influence ◆ **cela donne du ~ à son hypothèse** that gives *ou* lends weight to his hypothesis ◆ **ses arguments ont eu beaucoup de ~ dans les négociations** his arguments carried a lot of weight in the negotiations

5 (*Boxe*) ~ **coq** bantamweight ◆ ~ **léger** lightweight ◆ ~ **mi-lourd** light heavyweight ◆ ~ **mi-mouche** light flyweight ◆ ~ **mi-moyen** *ou* **welter** welterweight ◆ ~ **mouche** flyweight ◆ ~ **moyen** middleweight ◆ ~ **plume** featherweight ◆ **c'est un ~ plume** * [*personne légère*] he's (*ou* she's) as light as a feather; [*objet*] it's as light as a feather; [*personne peu importante*] he's (*ou* she's) a lightweight ◆ **c'est un tissu ~ plume** it's an ultra-light fabric ◆ ~ **super-léger** light welterweight ◆ ~ **superwelter** *ou* **super-mi-moyen** light middleweight; → aussi **comp**

COMP **poids atomique** † atomic weight

poids brut gross weight

poids et haltères (*Sport*) NMPL weightlifting ◆ **faire des ~ et haltères** (*spécialité*) to be a weightlifter; (*pour s'entraîner*) to do weight training *ou* weightlifting

poids lourd (= *boxeur*) heavyweight; (= *camion*) heavy goods vehicle, heavy truck (*US*); (= *entreprise*) big name *; (= *personne*) heavyweight, big name * ◆ **c'est un ~ lourd de la finance/de l'industrie** he's a financial/industrial heavyweight, he's a big name in finance/in industry ◆ **le championnat du monde (des) ~ lourds** (*Boxe*) the world heavyweight championship

poids et mesures NMPL weights and measures

poids moléculaire molecular weight

poids mort (*Tech, péj*) dead weight

poids net net weight

poids net égoutté drained weight

poids spécifique specific gravity

poids total autorisé en charge gross weight

poids utile net weight

poids à vide [*de véhicule*] tare

poignant, e /pwaɲɑ̃, ɑ̃t/ ADJ [*témoignage*] heartbreaking; [*texte, roman, histoire, voix, simplicité*] deeply moving; [*tristesse*] extreme ◆ **c'était ~** it was heartrending

poignard /pwaɲaʀ/ NM dagger ◆ **coup de ~** (*lit*) stab ◆ **frappé d'un coup de ~ en plein cœur** stabbed in *ou* through the heart ◆ **on l'a tué à coups de ~** he was stabbed to death ◆ **cette décision est un coup de ~ au processus de paix** this decision is a serious blow for the peace process ◆ **c'est un coup de ~ dans le dos** it's a stab in the back

poignarder /pwaɲaʀde/ ▸ conjug 1 ◂ VT to stab, to knife ◆ **mortellement poignardé** stabbed to death ◆ ~ **qn dans le dos** (*lit, fig*) to stab sb in the back

poigne /pwaɲ/ NF (= *étreinte*) grip; (= *main*) hand; (= *autorité*) firm-handedness ◆ **avoir de la ~** (*lit*) to have a strong grip; (*fig*) to rule with a firm hand ◆ **à ~** [*personne, gouvernement*] firm-handed

poignée /pwaɲe/ NF 1 (*lit* = *quantité*) handful; [*de billets de banque*] fistful; (= *petit nombre*) handful ◆ **ajoutez une ~ de sel** add a handful of salt ◆ **à** *ou* **par ~s** in handfuls ◆ **je perds mes cheveux par ~s** my hair is coming out in handfuls 2 [*de porte, tiroir, valise*] handle; [*d'épée*] handle, hilt ◆ ~ **de frein** brake handle ◆ ~**s d'amour** (*hum*) love handles COMP **poignée de main** handshake ◆ **donner une ~ de main à qn** to shake hands with sb, to shake sb's hand *ou* sb by the hand

poignet /pwaɲɛ/ NM (*Anat*) wrist; [*de vêtement*] cuff ◆ ~ **de force** wrist band; → **force**

poil /pwal/ NM 1 [*d'humain*] hair ◆ **avoir du ~** *ou* **des ~s sur la poitrine** to have a hairy chest ◆ **avoir du ~ aux pattes**‡ to have hairy legs ◆ **les ~s de sa barbe** (*entretenue*) the bristles *ou* hairs of his beard; (*mal rasée*) the stubble on his face ◆ **sans ~s** [*poitrine, bras*] hairless ◆ **il n'a pas un ~ sur le caillou** * he's as bald as a coot * *ou* an egg * ◆ **il n'a pas un ~ de sec** * (*pluie*) he's drenched, he's soaked to the skin; (*sueur*) he's drenched with sweat

2 [*d'animal*] hair; (= *pelage*) coat ◆ **animal à ~ ras/court/long** smooth-/short-/long-haired animal ◆ **animal au ~ soyeux/roux** animal with a silky/ginger coat ◆ **en ~ de chèvre** goathair (*épith*) ◆ **en ~ de chameau** camelhair (*épith*) ◆ **caresser dans le sens du ~** [+ *chat*] to stroke the right way; [+ *personne*] to butter up; → **gibier**

3 [*de brosse à dents, pinceau*] bristle; [*de tapis, étoffe*] strand; (*Bot*) [*de plante*] down (*NonC*); [*d'artichaut*] choke (*NonC*) ◆ **les ~s d'un tapis** the pile of a carpet ◆ **les ~s d'un tissu** the pile *ou* nap of a fabric

4 (* = *un petit peu*) **s'il avait un ~ de bon sens** if he had an iota *ou* an ounce of good sense ◆ **à un ~ près, l'armoire ne passait pas dans la porte** a fraction more and the cupboard wouldn't have gone through the doorway ◆ **ça mesure environ un mètre, à un ~ près** it measures one metre as near as makes no difference ◆ **il n'y a pas un ~ de différence entre les deux** there isn't the slightest difference between the two ◆ **pousser qch d'un ~** to shift sth a fraction ◆ **il s'en est fallu d'un ~** it was a near *ou* close thing *ou* a close shave *; → **quart**

5 (*locutions*) **avoir un ~ dans la main** * to be bone-idle * ◆ **ce n'est plus un ~ qu'il a dans la main, c'est une canne !** *ou* **un bambou !** * he's as lazy as they come ◆ **un jeune blanc-bec qui n'a même pas de ~ au menton** * (*péj*) a young guy who's still wet behind the ears * (*péj*), a

babe in arms *(péj)* ◆ **tu parleras quand tu auras du ~ au menton** you can have your say when you're out of short pants* ◆ **être de bon/de mauvais ~*** to be in a good/bad mood ◆ **avoir qn sur le ~*** to have sb breathing down one's neck ◆ **tomber sur le ~ à qn*** *(agresser)* to go for* *ou* lay into* sb; *[police]* to pounce on sb*; *[fisc]* to come down on sb ◆ **reprendre du ~ de la bête*** *[malade]* to pick up (again), to regain strength; *[plante]* to pick up (again); *[rebelles, mouvement]* to regain strength; *[parti]* to be on the way up again ◆ **réglé au quart de ~*** strictly regulated

◆ **à poil‡** (= *nu*) stark naked, starkers‡ *(Brit)* ◆ **des mecs*/des filles à ~** naked guys*/girls ◆ **à ~ !** (= *déshabillez-vous*) get your clothes off!, get 'em off!‡ *(Brit)*; *(à chanteur, orateur)* get off!* ◆ **se mettre à ~** to strip off ◆ **se baigner à ~** to go skinny-dipping*

◆ **au poil*** (= *magnifique*) great*, fantastic*; (= *précisément*) *[réglé, convenir]* perfectly ◆ **tu arrives au ~, j'allais partir** you've come just at the right moment - I was just about to leave ◆ **ça me va au ~*** it suits me fine* *ou* to a T*

◆ **de tout poil, de tous poils** of all sorts *ou* kinds ◆ **des artistes de tout ~** all sorts *ou* kinds of artists

COMP **poil de carotte** *[personne]* red-haired, red-headed; *[cheveux]* red, carroty
poils follets down *(NonC)*
poil à gratter itching powder; *(fig)* provocateur

poilant, e‡ /pwalɑ̃, ɑ̃t/ ADJ hilarious

poiler (se)‡ /pwale/ ▸ conjug 1 ◂ VPR to kill o.s. (laughing)‡

poilu, e /pwaly/ ADJ hairy NM poilu *(French soldier in First World War)*

poinçon /pwɛ̃sɔ̃/ NM 1 (= *outil*) *[de cordonnier]* awl; *[de menuisier]* awl, bradawl; *[de brodeuse]* bodkin; *[de graveur]* style; *[de bijou, or]* die, stamp 2 (= *estampille*) hallmark 3 (= *matrice*) pattern

poinçonnage /pwɛ̃sɔnaʒ/, **poinçonnement** /pwɛ̃sɔnmɑ̃/ NM 1 *[de marchandise]* stamping; *[de pièce d'orfèvrerie]* hallmarking 2 *[de billet]* punching, clipping 3 *[de tôle]* punching

poinçonner /pwɛ̃sɔne/ ▸ conjug 1 ◂ VT 1 (= *estampiller*) *[+ marchandise]* to stamp; *[+ pièce d'orfèvrerie]* to hallmark 2 (= *perforer*) *[+ billet]* to punch (a hole in), to clip 3 (= *découper*) *[+ tôle]* to punch

poinçonneur, -euse /pwɛ̃sɔnœʀ, øz/ NM,F *(Hist = personne)* ticket-puncher NF **poinçonneuse** (= *machine*) punching machine, punch press

poindre /pwɛ̃dʀ/ ▸ conjug 49 ◂ VI *(littér)* *[jour]* to break, to dawn; *[aube]* to break; *[plante]* to come up, to peep through ◆ **un sentiment de jalousie/haine commençait à ~** he (*ou* she) began to feel the first stirrings of jealousy/hatred VT *(littér)* *[tristesse]* to afflict; *[douleur, amour]* to sting *(littér)*

poing /pwɛ̃/ NM 1 *(gén)* fist ◆ **les ~s sur les hanches** with (one's) hands on (one's) hips, with (one's) arms akimbo ◆ **lever le ~** *(gén)* to raise one's fist; *(salut)* to give the clenched fist salute ◆ **ils défilaient le ~ levé** they marched with clenched fists raised ◆ **montrer le ~** to shake one's fist ◆ **menacer qn du ~** to shake one's fist at sb ◆ **taper** *ou* **frapper du ~ sur la table** *(lit)* to thump the table (with one's fist), to bang *ou* thump one's fist on the table; *(fig)* to put one's foot down ◆ **revolver au ~** revolver in hand ◆ **je vais t'envoyer** *ou* **te coller* mon ~ dans la figure** you'll get my fist in your face* ◆ **tu veux mon ~ dans** *ou* **sur la gueule ?‡** do you want my fist in your face?, do you want a knuckle sandwich?‡; → **dormir, pied, serrer** *etc*

2 ◆ **coup de ~** punch ◆ **donner un coup de ~** *ou* **des coups de ~ à qn** to punch sb ◆ **donner des coups de ~ dans une porte** to bang on a door ◆ **il a reçu** *ou* **pris un coup de ~ dans la figure** he was punched in the face ◆ **faire le coup de ~ avec qn/contre qn** to fight alongside sb/against sb ◆ **opération coup de ~** (= *raid*) lightning raid; (= *action d'envergure*) blitz ◆ **opération coup de ~ contre le chômage/les fraudeurs** assault on unemployment/blitz *ou* crackdown on tax dodgers ◆ **"opération coup de poing sur les prix"** "prices slashed"

COMP **poing américain** (= *arme*) knuckle-duster

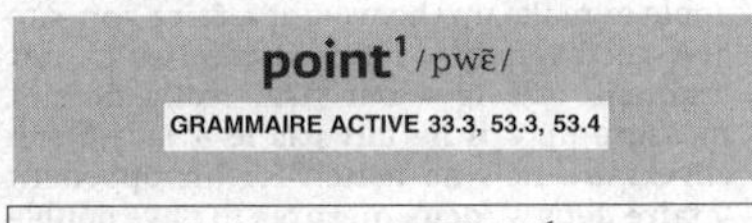

point[1] /pwɛ̃/

GRAMMAIRE ACTIVE 33.3, 53.3, 53.4

1 NOM MASCULIN 2 COMPOSÉS

1 - NOM MASCULIN

1 = endroit point, place; *(Astron, Géom)* point ◆ **pour aller d'un ~ à un autre** to go from one point *ou* place to another ◆ **fixer un ~ précis dans l'espace** to stare at a fixed point in space ◆ **le fleuve déborde en plusieurs ~s** the river overflows at several points *ou* in several places ◆ **ils étaient venus de tous les ~s de l'horizon** they had come from the four corners of the earth ◆ **je reprends mon discours au ~ où je l'ai laissé** I take up my speech where I left off

2 = situation point, stage ◆ **avoir atteint le ~ où ..., en être arrivé au ~ où ...** to have reached the point *ou* stage where ... ◆ **nous en sommes toujours au même ~** we haven't got any further, we're no further forward ◆ **c'est bête d'en être (arrivé) à ce ~-là et de ne pas finir** it's silly to have got so far *ou* to have reached this point *ou* stage and not to finish ◆ **au ~ où en sont les choses** as matters *ou* things stand ◆ **au ~ où nous en sommes, cela ne changera pas grand-chose** considering the situation we're in, it won't make much difference ◆ **on continue ? - au ~ où on en est** shall we go on? - we've got this far so we might as well

3 locutions

◆ **au point** *[image, photo]* in focus; *[affaire]* completely finalized *ou* settled; *[procédé, technique, machine]* perfected; *[discours, ouvrage]* finalized, up to scratch *(attrib)* ◆ **ce n'est pas encore au ~** *[machine, spectacle, organisation]* it isn't quite up to scratch yet; *[discours, devoir]* it's not quite finalized yet, it still needs some working on ◆ **ce n'est pas au ~** *[appareil photo, caméra]* it's out of focus

◆ **mettre + au point** *[+ photo, caméra]* to (bring into) focus; *[+ stratégie, technique]* to perfect; *[+ médicament, invention, système]* to develop; *[+ moteur]* to tune; *[+ mécanisme]* to tune, to adjust; *[+ projet]* to finalize ◆ **mettre une affaire au ~ avec qn** to finalize *ou* settle all the details of a matter with sb

◆ **mise au point** *[d'appareil photo, caméra]* focusing; *[de stratégie, technique]* perfecting; *[de médicament, invention, système]* development; *[de moteur]* tuning; *[de mécanisme]* tuning, adjustment; *(Ordin)* debugging; *[d'affaire, projet]* finalizing; *(fig = explication, correction)* clarification ◆ **publier une mise au ~** to issue a statement *(setting the record straight or clarifying a point)*

4 = degré, niveau *(gén)* point, stage; *(Sci)* point ◆ **~ d'ébullition/de congélation** boiling/freezing point ◆ **est-il possible d'être bête à ce ~(-là) !** how stupid can you get?* ◆ **il n'est pas inquiet à ce ~-là** he's not that worried ◆ **il s'est montré grossier au dernier ~** *(littér)* he was extremely rude ◆ **vous voyez à quel ~ il est généreux** you see how (very) generous he is *ou* the extent of his generosity ◆ **sa colère avait atteint un ~ tel** *ou* **un tel ~ que ...** he was so (very) angry that ..., his anger was such that ... ◆ **il en était arrivé à un tel ~ d'avarice que ...** he had become so miserly that ..., his miserliness had reached such proportions that ...

◆ **à ce** *ou* **tel point que ...** ◆ **c'était à ce ~ absurde que ...** it was so (very) absurd that ... ◆ **elles se ressemblent à ce** *ou* **tel ~ qu'on pourrait les confondre** they look so alike that you could easily mistake one for the other ◆ **son invention a eu du succès, à tel ~ qu'il est devenu célèbre** his invention was a success, so much so that *ou* to such an extent *ou* degree that he became famous

◆ **à point** *(Culin)* (= *bon à consommer*) *[fruit]* just ripe *(attrib)*, nicely ripe; *[fromage]* just right for eating *(attrib)*; *[viande]* medium ◆ **quelle cuisson ? - à ~** how would you like it cooked? - medium rare ◆ **le rôti est cuit à ~** the roast is cooked *ou* done to a turn

◆ **au plus haut point** *[détester, admirer]* intensely ◆ **se méfier au plus haut ~ de qch** to be extremely mistrustful of *ou* highly sceptical about sth ◆ **être au plus haut ~ de la gloire** to be at the peak *ou* summit of glory

◆ **au point de** + *infinitif* so much that ◆ **il ne pleut pas au ~ de mettre des bottes** it isn't raining enough for you to put boots on, it isn't raining so much that you need boots ◆ **tirer sur une corde au ~ de la casser** to pull on a rope so hard that it breaks, to pull a rope to the point where it breaks

◆ **au point que** ⇒ **à ce** *ou* **tel point que**

5 = aspect, détail, subdivision point ◆ **exposé en trois ~s** three-point presentation ◆ **~ de théologie/de philosophie** point of theology/of philosophy ◆ **passons au ~ suivant de l'ordre du jour** let us move on to the next item on the agenda ◆ **~ d'accord/de désaccord** point of agreement/of disagreement ◆ **~ mineur** *ou* **de détail** minor point, point of detail ◆ **nous abordons maintenant un ~ capital** we now come to a crucial point *ou* issue ◆ **voilà déjà un ~ acquis** *ou* **réglé** that's one thing *ou* point settled ◆ **avoir des ~s communs** to have things in common ◆ **je n'ai aucun ~ commun avec elle** I have nothing in common with her ◆ **ils sont d'accord sur ce ~/sur tous les ~s** they agree on this point *ou* score/on all points *ou* scores *ou* counts ◆ **exécutez ces instructions de ~ en ~** *(frm)* carry these instructions out point by point *ou* in every detail

◆ **en tout point, en tous points** in every respect ◆ **ils se ressemblent en tout ~** they resemble each other in every respect ◆ **ce fut en tous ~s réussi** it was an all-round *ou* unqualified success

◆ **jusqu'à un certain point** up to a point, to a certain extent

◆ **point par point** point by point ◆ **nous avons repris la question ~ par ~** we went over the question point by point ◆ **il répondit ~ par ~ aux accusations** he answered the charges point by point *ou* taking each point in turn

6 temps

◆ **à point (nommé)** *[arriver, venir]* just at the right moment, just when needed ◆ **cela tombe à ~ (nommé)** that comes just at the right moment, that's just *ou* exactly what I (*ou* we *etc*) need

◆ **sur le point de** + *infinitif* ◆ **être sur le ~ de faire qch** to be (just) about to do sth, to be just going to do sth, to be on the point of doing sth ◆ **j'étais sur le ~ de faire du café** I was just going to *ou* (just) about to make some coffee ◆ **une bombe sur le ~ d'exploser** a bomb about to go off ◆ **elle est sur le ~ de quitter son mari** she is about to leave *ou* is on the verge of leaving her husband

7 [= position] *[d'avion, bateau]* position • **recevoir le ~ par radio** to be given one's position by radio • **faire le ~** *(en mer)* to take a bearing, to plot one's position • **faire le ~ cartographique** *ou* **géographique** *(Mil)* to take a bearing • **faire le ~ horaire** to give regular bulletins, to have regular updates • **faire le ~ de la situation** *(= examiner)* to take stock of the situation, to review the situation; *(= faire un compte rendu)* to sum up the situation • **nous allons faire le ~ sur les derniers événements** let's have an update on the latest events • **et maintenant, le ~ sur la grève des transports** *(Journalisme)* and now, the latest (update) on the transport strike • **~ fixe** *(en avion)* (engine) run-up

8 [= marque] *(gén, Mus, en morse, sur i)* dot; *(= ponctuation)* full stop *(Brit)*, period *(US)*; *(= petite tache)* spot, speck; *[de dé]* pip • **le bateau n'était plus qu'un ~ à l'horizon** the ship was now nothing but a dot *ou* speck *ou* spot on the horizon • **mettre les ~s sur les i** *(fig)* to spell it out • **il a toujours besoin qu'on lui mette les ~s sur les i** you always have to spell things out to him • **~, à la ligne** *(lit)* new paragraph; *(fig)* full stop *(Brit)*, period *(US)* • **tu n'iras pas, un ~ c'est tout** you're not going and that's all there is to it *ou* and that's that, you're not going – full stop *(Brit) ou* period *(US)*

9 [d'un score] *(Cartes, Sport)* point; *(Scol, Univ)* mark, point • **~s d'honneurs/de distribution** *(Cartes)* points for honours/for distribution • **je n'ai pas les ~s d'annonce** *(Cartes)* I haven't got enough points to open the bidding • **gagner aux ~s** *(Boxe)* to win on points • **il a échoué d'un ~** he failed by one mark *ou* point • **la partie se joue en 15 ~s** the winner is the first person to get to *ou* to score 15 (points) • **on joue le ~** *(Tennis)* let's play on • **faire** *ou* **marquer le ~** *(Tennis)* to win the point • **rendre des ~s à qn** *(fig)* to give sb points, to give sb a (head) start • **enlever un ~ par faute** *(Scol)* to take a mark *ou* point off for every mistake • **bon/mauvais ~** good/bad mark *(for conduct etc)*; *(fig)* plus/minus (mark) • **la maîtresse m'a donné deux bons ~s** † ≈ the teacher gave me two stars • **un bon ~ pour vous !** *(fig)* that's a point in your favour!; → **compter, marquer**

10 [= pour cent] point • **sa cote de popularité a baissé de 3 ~s** his popularity rating has fallen (by) 3 points *ou* is down 3 points • **~ de base** basis point

11 [Méd] **avoir un ~ dans le dos** to have a twinge (of pain) in one's back • **vous avez un ~ de congestion là** you have a spot of congestion there

12 [TV, Typo] point • **caractère de 8/10 ~s** 8-/10-point type

2 - COMPOSÉS

point d'appui *(Mil)* base of operations; *[de levier]* fulcrum; *[de personne] (lit, fig)* support • **chercher un ~ d'appui** to look for something to lean on • **l'échelle a glissé de son ~ d'appui** the ladder slipped from where it was leaning

point barre * *(= c'est tout)* **je fais mon travail, ~ barre** I do my job, full stop *(Brit) ou* period *(US)* • **c'est non, ~ barre** the answer is no, and that's all there is to it

points cardinaux points of the compass, cardinal points

point chaud *(Mil)* trouble spot, hot spot; *(fig) (= endroit)* trouble spot • **c'est un des ~s chauds de l'actualité** *(= fait)* it's one of the burning *ou* most topical issues of the moment

point de chute *(lit)* landing place • **vous avez un ~ de chute à Rome ?** do you have somewhere to stay in Rome? • **l'ex-ministre est à la recherche d'un ~ de chute dans l'industrie** *(emploi)* the former minister is looking for a job in industry to retire into

point com *(Internet)* dotcom, dot.com

points de conduite *(Typo)* dot leaders

point de contrôle checkpoint

point de côté stitch, pain in the side

point critique *(Phys, fig)* critical point

point culminant *[de gloire, réussite, panique, épidémie]* height; *[d'affaire, scandale]* climax, culmination; *[de montagne]* peak, summit; *[de carrière]* height, zenith

point de départ *[de train, autobus]* point of departure; *[de science, réussite, aventure]* starting point; *[d'enquête]* point of departure, starting point; *(Sport)* start • **revenir à son ~ de départ** to come back to where it *(ou* one) started • **nous voilà revenus au ~ de départ** *(fig)* (so) we're back to square one *, we're back where we started

point de distribution *[d'eau]* supply point; *(Comm)* distribution outlet

point de droit point of law

point d'eau *(= source)* watering place; *[de camping]* water (supply) point

point d'équilibre *(Phys)* equilibrium point; *(Fin)* break-even point • **le gouvernement doit trouver le ~ d'équilibre** *(fig)* the government needs to find the right balance *ou* the happy medium

point d'exclamation exclamation mark *(Brit) ou* point *(US)*

point faible weak point

point final *(lit)* full stop *(Brit)*, period *(US)* • **je refuse, ~ final** *(fig)* I refuse, full stop *(Brit) ou* period *(US)*, I refuse and that's final • **mettre un ~ final à qch** *(fig)* to put an end to sth, to bring sth to an end

point fort strong point

point géométrique (geometrical) point

point d'honneur point of honour • **mettre un ~ d'honneur à** *ou* **se faire un ~ d'honneur de faire qch** to make it a point of honour to do sth

point d'impact point of impact

point d'incidence point of incidence

point d'information point of information

point d'interrogation question mark • **qui sera élu, c'est là le ~ d'interrogation** who will be elected – that's the big question (mark) *ou* that's the 64,000-dollar question *

point d'intersection point of intersection

point du jour daybreak, break of day

point lumineux dot *ou* spot of light

point mort *(Tech)* dead centre; *(en voiture)* neutral; *(Fin)* break-even point • **au ~ mort** *(en voiture)* in neutral; *[de négociations, affaires]* at a standstill

point névralgique *(Méd)* nerve centre; *(fig)* sensitive spot

point noir *(= comédon)* blackhead; *(= problème)* problem, difficulty; *(= lieu d'accidents)* blackspot

point de non-retour point of no return

point d'ordre point of order

point d'orgue *(Mus)* pause; *[de festival]* grand finale

point de passage *(lit)* crossing point • **ce café est le ~ de passage obligé du tout-Paris médiatique** this café is the place to be seen in Parisian media circles

point de presse press briefing

point de ralliement rallying point

point de rassemblement *(à l'aéroport etc)* meeting point; *(dans un bateau)* muster station

point de ravitaillement *(en nourriture)* refreshment point, staging point; *(en essence)* refuelling point

points de reprise *(Mus)* repeat marks

points de retraite *points calculated on the basis of social security contributions that count towards retirement pensions*

point de rouille spot *ou* speck of rust

point de saturation *(Sci, fig)* saturation point

point sensible *(sur la peau)* tender spot; *(Mil)* trouble spot; *(fig)* sensitive area, sore point

point de soudure spot *ou* blob of solder

point stratégique key point

points de suspension *(gén)* suspension points; *(en dictant)* dot, dot, dot

point de tangence tangential point

point de vente point of sale, sales outlet • **"points de vente dans toute la France"** "on sale throughout France" • **liste des ~s de vente** list of stockists *ou* retailers

point de vue *(lit)* view(point); *(fig)* point of view, standpoint • **du** *ou* **au ~ de vue moral** from a moral point of view, from a moral standpoint • **au ~ de vue argent** as regards money, moneywise * • **nous aimerions connaître votre ~ de vue sur ce sujet** we should like to know your point of view *ou* standpoint *ou* where you stand in this matter

---

point² / pwɛ̃ / NM *(Couture, Tricot)* stitch • **bâtir à grands ~s** to tack • **coudre à grands ~s** to sew using a long stitch • **faire un (petit) ~ à qch** to put a stitch in sth

COMP **point d'Alençon** Alençon lace

point d'arrêt finishing-off stitch

point arrière backstitch

point de chaînette chain stitch

point de chausson *(Couture)* blind hem stitch; *(Broderie)* closed herringbone stitch

point de couture stitch

point de croix cross-stitch

point devant running stitch

point d'épine feather stitch

point de feston blanket stitch

point de jersey stocking stitch

point mousse garter stitch

point d'ourlet hem-stitch

point de riz moss stitch

point de suture *(Méd)* stitch • **faire des ~s de suture à qch** to put stitches in sth, to stitch sth up

point de tapisserie canvas stitch

point de tige stem stitch

point de torsade cable stitch

point de tricot *(gén)* knitting stitch; *(maille à l'endroit)* knit stitch

point de Venise rose point

point³ / pwɛ̃ / ADV *(littér, hum)* ⇒ **pas²**

pointage / pwɛ̃taʒ / NM 1 *(= fait de cocher)* ticking *ou* checking *ou* marking off; *[de personnel] (à l'arrivée)* clocking in *ou* on; *(au départ)* clocking out • **procéder au ~ des voix** to count the votes 2 *[de fusil]* pointing, aiming, levelling *(vers, sur* at); *[de jumelles, lunette, télescope]* training *(vers, sur* on); *[de lampe]* directing *(vers, sur* towards) 3 *(Mus) [de note]* dotting 4 *[de trou de vis]* starting off 5 *(= contrôle)* check

pointe / pwɛ̃t / NF 1 *(= extrémité) [d'aiguille, épée]* point; *[de flèche, lance]* head, point; *[de couteau, crayon, clocher, clou]* point, tip; *[de canne]* (pointed) end, tip, point; *[de montagne]* peak, top; *[de menton, nez, langue, sein, ski]* tip; *[de moustache, col]* point; *[de chaussure]* toe, tip • **à la ~ de l'île** at the tip of the island • **chasser l'ennemi à la ~ de l'épée/de la baïonnette** to chase away the enemy with swords drawn/at bayonet point

2 *(= partie saillante) [de grillage]* spike; *[de côte]* headland • **la côte forme une ~** *ou* **s'avance en ~ à cet endroit** the coast juts out (into the sea) *ou* forms a headland at that point • **objet qui forme une ~** object that tapers (in)to a point

3 *(= clou)* tack; *[de chaussure de football, d'alpiniste]* spike; *(= outil pointu)* point • **tu cours avec des tennis ou avec des ~s ?** do you run in trainers or spikes?

4 *(Danse)* **(chaussons à) ~s** points, point shoes • **faire des ~s** to dance on points

5 *(= foulard)* triangular (neck)scarf; *(† = couche de bébé)* (triangular-shaped) nappy *(Brit) ou* diaper *(US)*

6 *(= allusion ironique)* pointed remark; *(= trait d'esprit)* witticism

7 *(= petite quantité)* **une ~ d'ail/d'ironie/de jalousie** a touch *ou* hint of garlic/of irony/of jealousy ◆ **il a une ~ d'accent** he has the merest hint of an accent *ou* a very slight accent

8 *(= maximum)* peak ◆ **faire** *ou* **pousser une ~ jusqu'à Paris** *(en voiture)* to push *ou* press on as far as Paris ◆ **faire** *ou* **pousser une ~ de vitesse** *[athlète, cycliste, automobiliste]* to put on a burst of speed, to put on a spurt ◆ **j'ai fait une ~ (de vitesse) de 180 (km/h)** I hit 180 km/h ◆ **faire du 200 km/h en ~** to have a top *ou* maximum speed of 200 km/h

9 *[de compas]* point

10 *(locutions)* **à la ~ du combat** in the forefront of (the) battle ◆ **à la ~ de l'actualité** in the forefront of current affairs *ou* of the news ◆ **à la ~ du progrès** in the forefront *ou* the front line *ou* at the leading edge of progress

◆ **de pointe** *[industrie]* leading, high-tech; *[technique]* latest, ultramodern, advanced; *[vitesse]* top, maximum ◆ **heure** *ou* **période de ~** *(gaz, électricité, téléphone)* peak period; *(circulation)* rush *ou* peak hour; *(magasin)* peak shopping period, busy period

◆ **en pointe** *[barbe, col]* pointed ◆ **décolleté en ~** V-neckline ◆ **tailler en ~** *[+ arbre, barbe]* to cut *ou* trim into a point; *[+ crayon]* to sharpen (in)to a point ◆ **canne qui se termine en ~** pointed stick

COMP **pointe d'asperge** asparagus tip *ou* spear

pointe Bic ® Biro ® *(Brit)*, Bic (pen) ® *(US)*

pointe fibre *(stylo)* fibre-tip (pen) *(Brit)*, fiber-tip (pen) *(US)*

pointe du jour *(littér)* **à la ~ du jour** at daybreak, at the crack of dawn

la pointe des pieds the toes ◆ **(se mettre) sur la ~ des pieds** (to stand) on tiptoe *ou* on one's toes ◆ **marcher/entrer sur la ~ des pieds** to walk/come in on tiptoe *ou* on one's toes, to tiptoe in/out ◆ **il faut y aller sur la ~ des pieds (avec lui)** *(fig)* you have to tread very carefully (when dealing with him)

pointe sèche *(Art)* dry-point ◆ **gravure à la ~ sèche** dry-point engraving

pointe du sein nipple

pointe de terre spit *ou* tongue of land, headland

pointeau (pl **pointeaux**) /pwɛ̃to/ NM 1 *[de carburateur, graveur]* needle 2 *(Ind = surveillant)* timekeeper

pointer[1] /pwɛ̃te/ ► conjug 1 ◄ VT 1 *(= cocher)* to tick off, to check off, to mark off ◆ **~ (sa position sur) la carte** *(en mer)* to prick off *ou* plot one's position; → **zéro**

2 *[personnel] (à l'arrivée)* to clock in *ou* on; *(au départ)* to clock out

3 *(= braquer) [+ fusil]* to point, to aim, to level *(vers, sur* at); *[+ jumelles]* to train *(vers, sur* on); *[+ lampe]* to direct *(vers, sur* towards); *[+ boule de pétanque]* to roll *(as opposed to throw)* ◆ **il pointa vers elle un index accusateur** he pointed an accusing finger at her

4 *(Mus) [+ note]* to dot ◆ **notes pointées** dotted rhythm

5 *[+ trou de vis]* to start off

VI *[employé] (à l'arrivée)* to clock in *ou* on; *(au départ)* to clock out ◆ **~ à l'ANPE** to sign on *(at the national employment agency)* ◆ **il pointe au chômage depuis trois mois** he's been on the dole * *(Brit) ou* on welfare *(US)* for three months

VPR **se pointer** * *(= arriver)* to turn up *, to show up *

COMP **pointer-cliquer** *(Ordin)* point-and-click

pointer[2] /pwɛ̃te/ ► conjug 1 ◄ VT 1 *(= piquer)* to stick *(dans* into); ◆ **il lui pointa sa lance dans le dos** he stuck his lance into his back 2 *(= dresser)* **église qui pointe ses tours vers le ciel** church whose towers soar (up) into the sky ◆ **le chien pointa les oreilles** the dog pricked up its ears VI *(littér)* 1 *(= s'élever) [tour]* to soar up 2 *(= apparaître) [plante]* to peep out; *[ironie]* to pierce through ◆ **ses seins pointaient sous la robe** her nipples showed beneath her dress ◆ **le jour pointait** day was breaking *ou* dawning

pointer[3] /pwɛ̃tœʀ/ NM *(= chien)* pointer

pointeur /pwɛ̃tœʀ/ NM *(dans une usine, pour athlètes)* timekeeper; *(Ordin)* pointer; *[de boules] player who aims at the jack; [de canon]* gun-layer

pointeuse /pwɛ̃tøz/ NF *(= personne)* timekeeper; *(= machine-outil)* jig borer ◆ **(horloge) ~** time clock

pointillage /pwɛ̃tijaʒ/ NM stipple, stippling

pointillé, e /pwɛ̃tije/ (ptp de **pointiller**) ADJ dotted NM 1 *(Art) (= procédé)* stipple, stippling; *(= gravure)* stipple 2 *(= trait)* dotted line; *(= perforations)* perforation(s) ◆ **"détacher** *ou* **découper suivant le pointillé"** "tear *ou* cut along the dotted line"

◆ **en pointillé** *(lit)* dotted; *[sous-entendu]* hinted at; *(= discontinu) [carrière, vie]* marked by stops and starts ◆ **un nouvel accord se dessine en ~** the first signs of a new agreement are emerging

pointillement /pwɛ̃tijmɑ̃/ NM ⇒ **pointillage**

pointiller /pwɛ̃tije/ ► conjug 1 ◄ *(Art)* VI to draw *(ou* engrave) in stipple VT to stipple

pointilleux, -euse /pwɛ̃tijø, øz/ ADJ particular, pernickety *(péj)*, fussy *(péj) (sur* about)

pointillisme /pwɛ̃tijism/ NM pointillism

pointilliste /pwɛ̃tijist/ ADJ, NMF pointillist

pointu, e /pwɛ̃ty/ ADJ 1 *(= en forme de pointe)* pointed; *(= aiguisé)* sharp 2 *(péj) [air]* peeved; *[caractère]* touchy, peevish; *[voix, ton]* shrill ◆ **accent ~** northern French accent 3 *(= précis) [domaine, connaissances, compétence]* specialized; *[question]* well-informed; *[analyse]* in-depth; *[diagnostic]* precise ◆ **des normes d'hygiène de plus en plus ~es** increasingly stringent *ou* rigorous standards of hygiene ADV ◆ **parler ~** to speak with *ou* have a northern French accent

pointure /pwɛ̃tyʀ/ NF *[de gant, chaussure]* size ◆ **quelle est votre ~ ?, quelle ~ faites-vous ?** what size do you take? *ou* are you? ◆ **c'est une (grande** *ou* **grosse) ~ dans la chanson/ce domaine** * he's a big name * in songwriting/this field

point-virgule (pl **points-virgules**) /pwɛ̃viʀgyl/ NM semi-colon

poire /pwaʀ/ NF 1 *(= fruit)* pear ◆ **il m'a dit cela entre la ~ et le fromage** he told me that quite casually over lunch *(ou* dinner); → **couper, garder**

2 *(* = tête)* mug *, face ◆ **il a une bonne ~** he's got a nice enough face ◆ **se ficher de** *ou* **se payer la ~ de qn** *(ridiculiser)* to have a good laugh at sb's expense, to take the mickey out of sb * *(Brit)*; *(tromper)* to take sb for a ride * ◆ **en pleine ~** right in the face

3 *(* = dupe)* sucker *, mug * *(Brit)* ◆ **c'est une bonne ~** he's a real sucker * *ou* mug * *(Brit)* ◆ **et moi, bonne ~, j'ai dit oui** and like a sucker * *ou* mug * *(Brit)* I said yes

4 *[de vaporisateur]* squeezer

ADJ ◆ **être ~** * to be a sucker * *ou* mug * *(Brit)*

COMP **poire Belle-Hélène** *stewed pear with chocolate sauce and cream*

poire électrique (pear-shaped) switch

poire à injections douche, syringe

poire à lavement enema syringe

poire à poudre powder horn

poiré /pwaʀe/ NM perry

poireau (pl **poireaux**) /pwaʀo/ NM leek ◆ **faire le ~** * to hang about *

poireauter * /pwaʀote/ ► conjug 1 ◄ VI to hang about * ◆ **faire ~ qn** to leave sb hanging about *

poirée /pwaʀe/ NF *(= bette)* Swiss chard

poirier /pwaʀje/ NM *(= arbre)* pear tree ◆ **faire le ~** *(= acrobatie)* to do a headstand

poiroter * /pwaʀote/ ► conjug 1 ◄ VI ⇒ **poireauter**

pois /pwɑ/ NM 1 *(= légume)* pea ◆ **petits ~** (garden) peas 2 *(Habillement)* (polka) dot, spot ◆ **robe à ~** spotted *ou* polka dot dress; → **purée**

COMP **pois cassés** split peas

pois chiche chickpea, garbanzo (bean) ◆ **il a un ~ chiche dans la tête** * he's a pea-brain *, he's short on grey matter *

pois gourmands mangetout peas

pois de senteur sweet pea; → **mange-tout**

poiscaille * /pwaskaj/ NF *ou* m *(souvent péj)* fish

poison /pwazɔ̃/ NM *(lit, fig)* poison NMF * *(= personne)* nuisance; *(= enfant)* little horror *; *(= chose)* drag *, bind * *(Brit)*

poissard, e /pwasaʀ, aʀd/ ADJ *[accent, langage]* vulgar, coarse NF **poissarde** ◆ **parler comme une ~e** to talk like a fishwife

poisse ⁑ /pwas/ NF rotten luck *, bad luck ◆ **avoir la ~** to have rotten * *ou* bad luck ◆ **quelle ~ !, c'est la ~ !** just my *(ou* our) (rotten) luck! * ◆ **ne le fais pas, ça porte la ~** don't do that – it's bad luck *ou* it's unlucky ◆ **ça leur a porté la ~** it brought them bad luck

poisser /pwase/ ► conjug 1 ◄ VT 1 *(⁑ = attraper)* to nab *, to cop ⁑ 2 *(= salir)* to make sticky; *(= engluer) [+ cordage]* to pitch ◆ **ça poisse** it's all sticky

poisseux, -euse /pwasø, øz/ ADJ *[mains, surface]* sticky

poisson /pwasɔ̃/ NM 1 *(gén)* fish ◆ **pêcher du ~** to fish ◆ **deux ~s** two fish *ou* fishes ◆ **fourchette/couteau à ~** fish fork/knife ◆ **être (heureux) comme un ~ dans l'eau** to be in one's element ◆ **être comme un ~ hors de l'eau** to be like a fish out of water ◆ **engueuler qn comme du ~ pourri** ⁑ to call sb all the names under the sun, to bawl sb out ◆ **un gros ~** * a big fish *; → **petit, queue**

2 *(Astron)* **les Poissons** Pisces, the Fishes ◆ **c'est un Poissons, il est (du signe du) Poissons** he's a Pisces

COMP **poisson d'argent** silverfish

poisson d'avril! April fool! ◆ **c'est un ~ d'avril** it's an April fool's trick

poisson d'eau douce freshwater fish

poisson lune sunfish

poisson de mer saltwater fish

poisson pilote pilotfish

poisson plat flatfish

poisson rouge goldfish

poisson volant flying fish

POISSON D'AVRIL

In France, as in Britain, 1 April is a day for playing practical jokes. The expression **poisson d'avril** comes from the tradition of pinning or sticking a paper fish on the back of an unsuspecting person, though by extension it can also refer to any form of practical joke played on 1 April.

poisson-chat (pl **poissons-chats**) /pwasɔ̃ʃa/ NM catfish

poisson-épée (pl **poissons-épées**) /pwasɔ̃epe/ NM swordfish

poissonnerie /pwasɔnʀi/ NF *(= boutique)* fish shop, fishmonger's (shop) *(surtout Brit)*; *(= métier)* fish trade

poissonneux, -euse /pwasɔnø, øz/ **ADJ** full of fish *(attrib)*, well-stocked with fish

poissonnier /pwasɔnje/ **NM** fishmonger *(surtout Brit)*, fish merchant *(US)*

poissonnière /pwasɔnjɛʀ/ **NF** 1 *(= personne)* (woman) fishmonger *(surtout Brit)*, fish merchant *(US)* 2 *(= ustensile)* fish kettle

poisson-perroquet (pl **poissons-perroquets**) /pwasɔ̃peʀɔkɛ/ **NM** parrotfish

poisson-scie (pl **poissons-scies**) /pwasɔ̃si/ **NM** sawfish

poitrail /pwatʀaj/ **NM** *[d'animal]* breast; *(hum = poitrine)* chest; *(Constr)* lintel

poitrinaire † /pwatʀinɛʀ/ **ADJ** ◆ **être** ~ to have TB, to be tuberculous *(SPÉC)* **NMF** tuberculosis sufferer

poitrine /pwatʀin/ **NF** *(gén)* chest, breast *(littér)*; *(= seins)* bust, bosom; *(Culin) [de veau, mouton]* breast; *[de porc]* belly ◆ ~ **salée** (ou **fumée**) ≈ streaky bacon ◆ ~ **de bœuf** brisket (of beef) ◆ **maladie de** ~ † chest complaint ◆ **elle a beaucoup de** ~ she's got a big bust ou bosom, she's big-busted ◆ **elle n'a pas de** ~ she's flat-chested ◆ **un cri jaillit de sa** ~ he uttered a cry; → **fluxion, tour², voix**

poivrade /pwavʀad/ **NF** 1 *(= sauce)* vinaigrette (sauce) with pepper ◆ **(à la)** ~ with salt and pepper 2 ◆ **(artichaut)** ~ *baby artichoke*

poivre /pwavʀ/ **NM** pepper; → **moulin, steak**

COMP **poivre blanc** white pepper

poivre de Cayenne Cayenne pepper

poivre en grains whole pepper, peppercorns

poivre gris black pepper

poivre moulu ground pepper

poivre noir black pepper

poivre en poudre ⇒ **poivre moulu**

poivre rouge red pepper

poivre et sel **ADJ INV** *[cheveux]* pepper-and-salt

poivre vert green pepper *(spice)*

poivré, e /pwavʀe/ (ptp de **poivrer**) **ADJ** 1 *[plat, goût, odeur]* peppery; *[histoire]* spicy, juicy *, saucy * 2 (* = *soûl)* pickled *, plastered *

poivrer /pwavʀe/ ▸ conjug 1 ◂ **VT** to pepper, to put pepper in ou on **VPR** **se poivrer** * (= *se soûler)* to get pickled * ou plastered *

poivrier /pwavʀije/ **NM** 1 *(= plante)* pepper plant 2 *(= récipient)* pepperpot, pepper shaker *(US)*

poivrière /pwavʀijɛʀ/ **NF** 1 *(Culin)* pepperpot, pepper shaker *(US)* 2 *(= plantation)* pepper plantation 3 *(Archit)* pepper-box

poivron /pwavʀɔ̃/ **NM** ◆ ~ **(doux)** (sweet) pepper, capsicum ◆ ~ **(vert)** green pepper ◆ ~ **rouge** red pepper

poivrot, e * /pwavʀo, ɔt/ **NM,F** drunkard, wino *

poix /pwa/ **NF** pitch *(tar)*

poker /pɔkɛʀ/ **NM** *(Cartes) (= jeu)* poker; *(= partie)* game of poker ◆ **faire un** ~ to have a game of poker ◆ ~ **d'as/de dames** four aces/queens ◆ ~ **d'as** *(= jeu)* poker dice ◆ ~ **menteur** *type of poker* ◆ **c'est une partie de** ~ **menteur, ils jouent au** ~ **menteur** *(fig)* they're calling his (ou their *etc)* bluff ◆ **coup de** ~ gamble ◆ **tenter un coup de** ~ to take a gamble ◆ **tout s'est joué sur un coup de** ~ it was all a big gamble ◆ **on ne joue pas sa carrière sur un coup de** ~ you don't gamble ou risk your entire career on a throw of the dice

polaire /pɔlɛʀ/ **ADJ** *(Chim, Géog, Math)* polar ◆ **froid** ~ arctic cold ◆ **laine** ~ *(= tissu)* fleece ◆ **(sweat en) laine** ~ fleece (sweatshirt); → **cercle, étoile** **NF** 1 *(Math)* polar 2 *(= vêtement)* fleece jacket (ou sweatshirt *etc)*

polaque ** /pɔlak/ **NM** *(injurieux)* Polack ** *(injurieux)*

polar¹ * /pɔlaʀ/ **NM** *(= roman)* detective novel

polar² /pɔlaʀ/ **NM** *(arg Scol)* swot * *(Brit)*, grind * *(US)*

polarisant, e /pɔlaʀizɑ̃, ɑ̃t/ **ADJ** *(Élec, Phys)* polarizing

polarisation /pɔlaʀizasjɔ̃/ **NF** *(Élec, Phys)* polarization; *(fig)* focusing

polariser /pɔlaʀize/ ▸ conjug 1 ◂ **VT** 1 *(Élec, Phys)* to polarize ◆ **lumière polarisée** polarized light 2 *(= faire converger sur soi) [+ attention, regards]* to attract ◆ **ce problème polarise tout le mécontentement** this problem is the focus of all the discontent 3 *(= concentrer)* ◆ **son attention/ses efforts sur qch** to focus ou centre one's attention/one's efforts on sth ◆ ~ **son énergie sur qch** to bring all one's energies to bear on sth **VPR** **se polariser** *(Phys)* to polarize ◆ **se** ~ ou **être polarisé sur qch** *[débat, mécontentement, critiques]* to be centred around ou upon sth, to be focused upon sth; *[personne]* to focus ou centre one's attention on sth ◆ **elle est trop polarisée sur sa réussite professionnelle** she's too bound up ou wrapped up in her career

polariseur /pɔlaʀizœʀ/ **ADJ, NM** ◆ **(prisme)** ~ polarizer

polarité /pɔlaʀite/ **NF** *(Bio, Ling, Math, Phys)* polarity

Polaroïd ® /pɔlaʀɔid/ **N** Polaroid ® ◆ **(appareil-photo)** ~ Polaroid ® (camera)

polder /pɔldɛʀ/ **NM** polder

poldérisation /pɔldeʀizasjɔ̃/ **NF** converting into a polder

pôle /pol/ **NM** 1 *(Sci)* pole ◆ **le** ~ **Nord/Sud** the North/South Pole ◆ ~ **magnétique** magnetic pole 2 *(= centre)* ~ **d'activité** *[d'entreprise]* area of activity ◆ ~ **de conversion** relocation area ◆ ~ **de développement** pole of development ◆ ~ **universitaire** university centre ◆ **la ville est devenue un** ~ **d'attraction pour les artistes/les investisseurs** the town has become a magnet for artists/investors, the town is drawing artists/investors like a magnet ◆ **Montpellier est le** ~ **économique de la région** Montpellier is the economic hub of the region

polémique /pɔlemik/ **ADJ** *[sujet]* controversial, contentious; *[écrit, article]* polemical ◆ **j'ai pris part à la discussion sans aucun esprit** ~ I took part in the discussion without wanting to be contentious **NF** *(= controverse)* controversy, argument (*sur* about, over); ◆ **chercher à faire de la** ~ to try to stir up controversy ◆ **engager une** ~ **avec qn** to enter into an argument with sb ◆ **une violente** ~ **s'est engagée sur** ... a fierce controversy has flared up about ... ◆ **relancer une** ~ to rekindle a controversy

polémiquer /pɔlemike/ ▸ conjug 1 ◂ **VI** to argue (*sur* about, over); ◆ **sans vouloir** ~, **j'ai toujours pensé que** ... I don't want to be controversial, but I've always thought that ... ◆ **je ne veux pas** ~ **sur ce point** I don't want to be drawn into an argument on this issue

polémiste /pɔlemist/ **NMF** polemicist

polémologie /pɔlemɔlɔʒi/ **NF** study of war

polenta /pɔlɛnta/ **NF** polenta

pole position /polpozisjɔ̃/ **NF** pole position ◆ **être en** ~ to be in pole position

poli¹, e /pɔli/ **ADJ** polite ◆ **ce n'est pas** ~ **de parler la bouche pleine** it's bad manners ou it's rude ou it's not nice to talk with your mouth full ◆ **ce n'est pas très** ~ **de dire ça** that's a rather rude thing to say, it's rather rude to say that ◆ **soyez** ~ ! don't be rude! ◆ **elle a été tout juste** ~**e avec moi** she was barely civil to me

poli², e /pɔli/ (ptp de **polir**) **ADJ** *[bois, ivoire]* polished; *[métal]* burnished, polished; *[caillou]* smooth **NM** shine ◆ **donner du** ~ **à** to put a shine on, to polish (up)

police¹ /pɔlis/ **NF** 1

L'anglais **police** se construit généralement avec un verbe au pluriel.

(= corps) police (NonC), police force ◆ **voiture de** ~ police car ◆ **être dans** ou **de la** ~ to be in the police (force) ◆ **la** ~ **est à ses trousses** the police are after him ou are on his tail ◆ **la guerre des** ~**s** the rivalry between different branches of the police ◆ **toutes les** ~**s de France** the police throughout France ◆ **après avoir passé la douane et les formalités de** ~ once you've gone through customs and immigration; → **plaque, salle**

2 *(= maintien de l'ordre)* policing, enforcement of (law and) order ◆ **les pouvoirs de** ~ **dans la société** powers to enforce ou maintain law and order in society ◆ **exercer** ou **faire la** ~ to keep (law and) order ◆ **faire la** ~ **dans une classe** to keep order in a class, to keep a class in order ◆ **faire sa propre** ~ to do one's own policing, to keep (law and) order for o.s.

COMP **police de l'air et des frontières** border police

police à cheval *(Can)* mounted police, Mounties *

police de la circulation traffic police

police judiciaire ≈ Criminal Investigation Department

police des mœurs, **police mondaine** ≈ vice squad

police montée *(Can)* mounted police, Mounties *

police municipale ≈ local police

police nationale national police force

police parallèle ≈ secret police

la police des polices Complaints and Discipline Branch *(Brit)*, Internal Affairs *(US)*

police privée private police force

police de la route traffic police *(Brit)*, state highway patrol *(US)*

police secours ≈ emergency services ◆ **appeler** ~ **secours** ≈ to dial 999 *(Brit)* ou 911 *(US)*, to call the emergency services

police secrète secret police

police² /pɔlis/ **NF** 1 *(Assurances)* (insurance) policy ◆ ~ **d'assurance vie** life insurance ou assurance policy ◆ ~ **d'assurance contre l'incendie** fire insurance policy 2 *(Typo, Ordin)* ~ **(de caractères)** font

policé, e /pɔlise/ (ptp de **policer**) **ADJ** *(frm) [musique, société]* refined; *[langue, manières]* refined, polished

policer /pɔlise/ ▸ conjug 3 ◂ **VT** *(littér* ou ††) to civilize

polichinelle /pɔliʃinɛl/ **NM** 1 *(Théât)* **Polichinelle** Punchinello; → **secret** 2 *(= marionnette)* Punch ◆ **avoir un** ~ **dans le tiroir** * to have a bun in the oven * 3 *(péj = personne)* buffoon ◆ **faire le** ~ to act the buffoon

policier, -ière /pɔlisje, jɛʀ/ **ADJ** *[chien, enquête, régime]* police *(épith)*; *[film, roman]* detective *(épith)* **NM** 1 *(= agent)* policeman, police officer ◆ **femme** ~ policewoman, woman police officer 2 *(= roman)* detective novel; *(= film)* detective film **NF** **policière** policewoman, woman police officer

policlinique /pɔliklinik/ **NF** out-patients' clinic

poliment /pɔlimɑ̃/ **ADV** politely

polio /pɔljo/ **NF** (abrév de **poliomyélite**) polio **NMF** (* abrév de **poliomyélitique**) polio victim

poliomyélite /pɔljɔmjelit/ **NF** poliomyelitis, polio

poliomyélitique /pɔljɔmjelitik/ **ADJ** suffering from polio **NMF** polio victim

polir /pɔliʀ/ ▸ conjug 2 ◂ **VT** 1 *[+ meuble, chaussures, pierre, verre]* to polish; *[+ métal]* to polish, to burnish, to buff ◆ **se ~ les ongles** to buff one's nails 2 *(= parfaire) [+ discours, style, phrase]* to polish; *[+ manières]* to polish, to refine

polissage /pɔlisaʒ/ NM *[de meuble, chaussures, pierre, verre]* polishing; *[de métal]* polishing, burnishing, buffing; *[d'ongles]* buffing

polisseur, -euse /pɔlisœʀ, øz/ NM,F polisher NF **polisseuse** *(= machine)* polisher, polishing machine

polissoir /pɔliswaʀ/ NM polisher, polishing machine ◆ **~ à ongles** nail buffer

polisson, -onne /pɔlisɔ̃, ɔn/ ADJ 1 *(= espiègle) [enfant, air]* naughty, mischievous 2 *(= grivois) [chanson]* naughty, saucy; *[regard]* saucy, randy* NM,F *(= enfant)* (little) rascal, (little) devil*, mischief*; *(= personne égrillarde)* saucy devil*; *(†† = petit vagabond)* street urchin

polissonner † /pɔlisɔne/ ▸ conjug 1 ◂ VI to be naughty

polissonnerie /pɔlisɔnʀi/ NF 1 *(= espièglerie)* naughty trick 2 *(= grivoiserie, parole)* naughty *ou* saucy remark; *(= action)* naughty thing

politesse /pɔlitɛs/ NF 1 *(= savoir-vivre)* politeness, courtesy ◆ **par ~** out of politeness, to be polite ◆ **je vais t'apprendre la ~ !** I'll teach you some manners! ◆ **tu aurais pu avoir la ~ de lui répondre** you could at least have had the courtesy to reply to him ◆ **il a eu la ~ de ne rien dire** he was polite enough to say nothing, he politely said nothing; → **brûler, formule, visite** 2 *(= parole)* polite remark; *(= action)* polite gesture ◆ **rendre une ~** to return a favour ◆ **se faire des ~s** *(paroles)* to exchange polite remarks; *(actions)* to make polite gestures to one another ◆ **ce serait la moindre des ~s** it's the least you *(ou he etc)* can do, it would only be polite

politicaillerie* /pɔlitikajʀi/ NF *(péj)* politicking *(péj)*

politicard, e /pɔlitikaʀ, aʀd/ *(péj)* ADJ *[ambitions]* petty political NM,F politician, political schemer *(péj)*

politicien, -ienne /pɔlitisjɛ̃, jɛn/ ADJ *(péj) [manœuvre, querelle]* (petty) political ◆ **la politique politicienne** politicking NM,F politician, political schemer *(péj)*

politico- /pɔlitiko/ PRÉF politico- ◆ **des questions politico-religieuses** politico-religious issues

politique /pɔlitik/ ADJ 1 *[institutions, économie, parti, prisonnier, pouvoir, réfugié]* political; *[carrière]* political, in politics ◆ **compte rendu de la semaine ~** report on the week in politics; → **homme, science**

2 *(littér = habile) [personne]* diplomatic; *[acte, invitation]* diplomatic, politic

NF 1 *(= science, carrière)* politics *(sg)* ◆ **parler ~** to talk politics ◆ **faire de la ~** *(militantisme)* to be a political activist; *(métier)* to be in politics

2 *(Pol) (= ligne de conduite)* policy; *(= manière de gouverner)* policies ◆ **~ intérieure/industrielle/sociale** domestic/industrial/social policy ◆ **il critique la ~ du gouvernement** he criticizes the government's policies ◆ **avoir une ~ de gauche/droite** to follow left-/right-wing policies ◆ **discours** *ou* **déclaration de ~ générale** policy speech ◆ **~ agricole commune** *(Europe)* common agricultural policy

3 *(= manière d'agir)* policy ◆ **il est de bonne ~ de ...** it is good policy to ... ◆ **la ~ du moindre effort** the principle of least effort ◆ **la ~ du pire** *making things worse in order to further one's own ends* ◆ **faire** *ou* **pratiquer la ~ de la chaise vide** to make a show of non-attendance ◆ **pratiquer la ~ de l'autruche** to bury one's head in the sand ◆ **c'est la ~ de l'autruche** it's like burying one's head in the sand

NM *(= politicien)* politician ◆ **le ~** *(= aspects politiques)* politics *(sg)*

politique-fiction /pɔlitikfiksjɔ̃/ NF political fantasy *ou* fiction ◆ **film de ~** political thriller ◆ **ce n'est pas de la ~, ces lois existent** this does not belong to the realms of political fantasy, these laws exist

politiquement /pɔlitikmɑ̃/ ADV *(lit)* politically; *(littér)* diplomatically ◆ **~ correct** politically correct, PC ◆ **~ incorrect** politically incorrect, non-PC

politiquer * † /pɔlitike/ ▸ conjug 1 ◂ VI to talk (about) politics

politisation /pɔlitizasjɔ̃/ NF politicization

politiser /pɔlitize/ ▸ conjug 1 ◂ VT *[+ débat]* to politicize, to bring politics into; *[+ événement]* to make a political issue of; *[+ personne, mouvement, action]* to politicize ◆ **être très politisé** *[personne]* to be highly politicized, to be politically aware VPR **se politiser** *[action, mouvement, débat]* to become politicized; *[personne]* to become politicized *ou* politically aware

politiste /pɔlitist/ NMF political scientist

politologie /pɔlitɔlɔʒi/ NF political science

politologue /pɔlitɔlɔg/ NMF political pundit *ou* analyst *ou* expert

polka /pɔlka/ NF polka

pollen /pɔlɛn/ NM pollen

pollinisateur, -trice /pɔlinizatœʀ, tʀis/ ADJ ◆ **insecte ~** insect pollinator, pollinating insect

pollinisation /pɔlinizasjɔ̃/ NF pollination

polluant, e /pɔlɥɑ̃, ɑ̃t/ ADJ polluting ◆ **produit ~** pollutant, polluting agent ◆ **non ~** non-polluting, environment-friendly ◆ **c'est très/peu ~** it produces a lot of/little pollution ◆ **industrie très ~e** highly polluting industry

polluer /pɔlɥe/ ▸ conjug 1 ◂ VT to pollute ◆ **ça me pollue la vie*** it really makes life hell for me*

pollueur, -euse /pɔlɥœʀ, øz/ ADJ polluting NM,F *(= substance)* pollutant, polluting agent; *(= industrie, personne)* polluter ◆ **le principe ~-payeur** the polluter-pays principle

pollution /pɔlysjɔ̃/ NF pollution ◆ **~ atmosphérique/radioactive** atmospheric/radioactive pollution ◆ **~ sonore** noise pollution ◆ **~ de l'air/des eaux/de l'environnement** air/water/environmental pollution ◆ **~ génétique** genetic pollution ◆ **~ par les nitrates** nitrate pollution ◆ **~s nocturnes** *(Méd)* nocturnal emissions *(SPÉC)*, wet dreams

polo /pɔlo/ NM 1 *(Sport)* polo 2 *(= chemise)* polo shirt

polochon* /pɔlɔʃɔ̃/ NM bolster ◆ **sac ~** duffel bag

Pologne /pɔlɔɲ/ NF Poland

polonais, e /pɔlonɛ, ɛz/ ADJ Polish NM 1 *(= langue)* Polish 2 ◆ **Polonais** Pole; → **soûl** NF **polonaise** 1 ◆ **Polonaise** Pole 2 *(= danse, Mus)* polonaise 3 *(= gâteau)* polonaise *(meringue-covered sponge cake containing preserved fruit and Kirsch)*

polonium /pɔlɔnjɔm/ NM polonium

poltron, -onne /pɔltʀɔ̃, ɔn/ ADJ cowardly, craven *(littér)* NM,F coward

poltronnerie /pɔltʀɔnʀi/ NF cowardice

polyacide /pɔliasid/ ADJ, NM polyacid

polyamide /pɔliamid/ NM polyamide

polyandre /pɔljɑ̃dʀ/ ADJ polyandrous

polyandrie /pɔliɑ̃dʀi/ NF polyandry

polyarchie /pɔljaʀʃi/ NF polyarchy

polyarthrite /pɔliaʀtʀit/ NF polyarthritis

polycarburant /pɔlikaʀbyʀɑ̃/ ADJ M *[moteur]* multifuel *(épith)*

polychlorure /pɔliklɔʀyʀ/ NM ◆ **~ de vinyle** polyvinyl chloride

polychrome /pɔlikʀom/ ADJ polychrome, polychromatic

polyclinique /pɔliklinik/ NF private general hospital

polycopie /pɔlikɔpi/ NF duplication, stencilling ◆ **tiré à la ~** duplicated, stencilled

polycopié /pɔlikɔpje/ NM *(Univ)* duplicated lecture notes

polycopier /pɔlikɔpje/ ▸ conjug 7 ◂ VT to duplicate, to stencil ◆ **cours polycopiés** duplicated lecture notes ◆ **machine à ~** duplicator

polyculture /pɔlikyltyʀ/ NF mixed farming

polyèdre /pɔljɛdʀ/ ADJ *[angle, solide]* polyhedral NM polyhedron

polyédrique /pɔljedʀik/ ADJ polyhedral

polyester /pɔliɛstɛʀ/ NM polyester

polyéthylène /pɔlietilɛn/ NM polyethylene

polygame /pɔligam/ ADJ polygamous NM polygamist

polygamie /pɔligami/ NF polygamy

polyglotte /pɔliglɔt/ ADJ, NMF polyglot

polygonal, e (mpl **-aux**) /pɔligɔnal, o/ ADJ polygonal, many-sided

polygone /pɔligɔn/ NM *(Math)* polygon ◆ **~ de tir** *(Mil)* rifle range

polygraphe /pɔligʀaf/ NMF polygraph

polyhandicapé, e /pɔliɑ̃dikape/ ADJ with multiple disabilities NM,F person with multiple disabilities

poly-insaturé, e /pɔliɛ̃satyʀe/ ADJ polyunsaturated

polymère /pɔlimɛʀ/ ADJ polymeric NM polymer

polymérisation /pɔlimeʀizasjɔ̃/ NF polymerization

polymériser VT, **se polymériser** VPR /pɔlimeʀize/ ▸ conjug 1 ◂ to polymerize

polymorphe /pɔlimɔʀf/ ADJ polymorphous, polymorphic

polymorphie /pɔlimɔʀfi/ NF, **polymorphisme** /pɔlimɔʀfism/ NM polymorphism

Polynésie /pɔlinezi/ NF Polynesia ◆ **~ française** French Polynesia

polynésien, -ienne /pɔlinezjɛ̃, jɛn/ ADJ Polynesian NM *(= langue)* Polynesian NM,F **Polynésien(ne)** Polynesian

polynévrite /pɔlinevʀit/ NF polyneuritis

polynôme /pɔlinom/ NM polynomial *(Math)*

polynucléaire /pɔlinykleɛʀ/ ADJ polynuclear, multinuclear NM polymorphonuclear leucocyte

polype /pɔlip/ NM *(= animal)* polyp; *(= tumeur)* polyp, polypus *(SPÉC)*

polyphasé, e /pɔlifaze/ ADJ polyphase

polyphonie /pɔlifɔni/ NF polyphony *(Mus)*

polyphonique /pɔlifɔnik/ ADJ polyphonic *(Mus)*

polyphosphate /pɔlifɔsfat/ NM polyphosphate

polypier /pɔlipje/ NM polypary

polypore /pɔlipɔʀ/ NM polyporus

polypropylène /pɔlipʀɔpilɛn/ NM *(Chim)* polypropylene

polysémie /pɔlisemi/ NF polysemy

polysémique /pɔlisemik/ ADJ polysemous, polysemic

polystyrène /pɔlistiʀɛn/ NM polystyrene ◆ **~ expansé** expanded polystyrene

polysyllabe /pɔlisi(l)lab/ ADJ polysyllabic NM polysyllable

polysyllabique /pɔlisi(l)labik/ ADJ polysyllabic ◆ **mot** ~ polysyllable

polytechnicien, -ienne /pɔlitɛknisjɛ̃, jɛn/ NM,F *student or ex-student of the École polytechnique*

polytechnique /pɔlitɛknik/ ADJ, NF ◆ **l'École** ~, **Polytechnique** the École polytechnique

> **POLYTECHNIQUE**
>
> The term **Polytechnique** is not to be confused with the English word « polytechnic » which used to refer to a particular kind of higher education establishment in Britain. In France, **Polytechnique** is the name of one of the most prestigious engineering schools, also known as l'« X ». → GRANDES ÉCOLES

polythéisme /pɔliteism/ NM polytheism

polythéiste /pɔliteist/ ADJ polytheistic NMF polytheist

polythérapie /pɔliteʀapi/ NF combination therapy

polytoxicomanie /pɔlitɔksikɔmani/ NF multiple (drug) addiction

polytransfusé, e /pɔlitʀɑ̃sfyze/ NM,F *person who has been given multiple blood transfusions*

polyuréthan(n)e /pɔliyʀetan/ NM polyurethan(e) ◆ **mousse de polyuréthan(n)e** polyurethan(e) foam

polyvalence /pɔlivalɑ̃s/ NF *(Chim, Méd)* polyvalency; *[de personne, mot]* versatility

polyvalent, e /pɔlivalɑ̃, ɑ̃t/ ADJ 1 *[salle]* multipurpose *(épith)*; *[personne]* versatile ◆ **formation ~e** comprehensive training ◆ **professeur ~** *teacher who teaches a variety of subjects* ◆ **nous recherchons une personne ~e** we're looking for a good all-rounder *(Brit)* ou for someone who's good all-around *(US)* 2 *[sérum, vaccin]* polyvalent 3 *(Chim)* polyvalent NM tax inspector *(sent to examine company's books)* NF **polyvalente** *(Can) secondary school teaching academic and vocational subjects*

> ⚠ **polyvalent** se traduit par le mot anglais **polyvalent** uniquement dans les domaines médical et chimique.

polyvinylique /pɔlivinilik/ ADJ polyvinyl *(épith)*

pomélo /pɔmelo/ NM grapefruit, pomelo *(US)*

Poméranie /pɔmeʀani/ NF Pomerania; → **loulou**[1]

pommade /pɔmad/ NF *(pour la peau)* ointment; *(pour les cheveux)* cream, pomade ◆ ~ **pour les lèvres** lip salve ou balm ◆ **beurre en ~** *(Culin)* softened butter ◆ **passer de la ~ à qn*** to butter sb up*, to soft-soap sb* *(Brit)*

pommader /pɔmade/ ▸ conjug 1 ◂ VT *[+ cheveux]* to pomade

pomme /pɔm/ NF 1 *(= fruit)* apple; *(= pomme de terre)* potato ◆ **tomber dans les ~s*** to faint, to pass out ◆ **elle est restée longtemps dans les ~s*** she was out (cold)* for some time ◆ **c'est aux ~s !*** it's ace!*; → **haut**

2 *[de chou, laitue]* heart; *[de canne, lit]* knob; *[d'arrosoir]* rose; *[de mât]* truck ◆ ~ **de douche** showerhead

3 *(* = tête)* head, nut*; *(= visage)* face, mug* ◆ **c'est pour ma ~** *(gén)* it's for me ou for yours truly*; *(qch de désagréable)* it's for yours truly* ou for muggins here‡ *(Brit)* ◆ **je m'occupe d'abord de ma ~** I'm looking after number one* ◆ **c'est pour ta ~** it's for you

4 *(* = naïf, indulgent)* sucker*, mug* *(Brit)* ◆ **et moi, bonne ~, j'ai dit oui** and like a sucker* ou mug* *(Brit)* I said yes

COMP **pomme d'Adam** Adam's apple

pommes allumettes matchstick potatoes

pomme d'amour *(= sucrerie)* toffee apple; *(= tomate)* love apple

pomme d'api *type of small apple*

pommes boulangère *(Culin)* fried potatoes with onions

pomme cannelle custard apple, sweetsop *(Brit)*

pomme à cidre cider apple

pomme à couteau eating apple

pomme à cuire cooking apple, cooker*

pommes dauphine pommes dauphine, ≃ potato croquettes *(without breadcrumbs)*

pomme de discorde *(fig)* bone of contention

pomme fruit apple

pommes mousseline mashed potatoes

pommes noisettes ≃ mini potato croquettes *(without breadcrumbs)*

pommes paille straw potatoes, ≃ shoestring potatoes *(US)*

pomme de pin pine ou fir cone

pomme sauvage crab apple

pomme de terre potato

pommes vapeur boiled potatoes; → **frite**[2]

pommé, e /pɔme/ (ptp de **pommer**) ADJ *[chou]* firm and round; *[laitue]* with a good heart

pommeau (pl **pommeaux**) /pɔmo/ NM *[d'épée, selle]* pommel; *[de canne]* knob

pommelé, e /pɔm(ə)le/ (ptp de **pommeler**) ADJ *[cheval]* dappled; *[ciel]* full of fluffy ou fleecy clouds ◆ **gris ~** dapple-grey

pommeler (se) /pɔm(ə)le/ ▸ conjug 4 ◂ VPR *[ciel]* to become full of fluffy ou fleecy clouds; *[chou, laitue]* to form a head ou heart

pommelle /pɔmɛl/ NF filter *(over a pipe)*

pommer /pɔme/ ▸ conjug 1 ◂ VI *[chou, laitue]* to form a head ou heart

pommeraie /pɔm(ə)ʀɛ/ NF apple orchard

pommette /pɔmɛt/ NF cheekbone ◆ **le rouge lui monta aux ~s** his cheeks reddened ◆ **~s saillantes** high cheekbones

pommier /pɔmje/ NM apple tree ◆ ~ **sauvage** crab-apple tree ◆ ~ **du Japon** Japan (flowering) quince (tree)

pompage /pɔ̃paʒ/ NM pumping ◆ ~ **optique** optical pumping

pompe[1] /pɔ̃p/ NF 1 *(= machine)* pump ◆ ~ **à air/à vide/de bicyclette** air/vacuum/bicycle pump

2 *(* = chaussure)* shoe ◆ **être à l'aise ou bien dans ses ~s** *(fig)* to feel good ◆ **je suis à côté de mes ~s en ce moment** I'm not quite with it* at the moment ◆ **ce type est vraiment à côté de ses ~s** that guy's really out of it*

3 *(* : locutions)* **(soldat de) deuxième ~** private ◆ **faire des ~s** *(Sport)* to do press-ups *(Brit)* ou push-ups *(US)* ◆ **c'est juste un petit coup de ~** I'm (ou we're) just feeling a bit drained ◆ **j'ai eu un** ou **le coup de ~** I felt drained, I was shattered*

◆ **à toute pompe** at top speed, flat out*

COMP **pompe aspirante** suction ou lift pump ◆ ~ **aspirante et foulante** suction and force pump

pompe à chaleur heat pump

pompe à essence *(= distributeur)* petrol *(Brit)* ou gas(oline) *(US)* pump; *(= station)* petrol *(Brit)* ou gas *(US)* station

pompe foulante force pump

pompe à incendie fire engine *(apparatus)*

pompe[2] /pɔ̃p/ NF 1 *(littér = solennité)* pomp ◆ **en grande ~** with great pomp 2 *(Rel = vanités)* **~s** pomps and vanities ◆ **renoncer au monde et à ses ~s** to renounce the world and all its pomps and vanities COMP **pompes funèbres** undertaker's, funeral director's *(Brit)*, mortician's *(US)* ◆ **entreprise de ~s funèbres** funeral home, funeral director's *(Brit)*, funeral parlor *(US)* ◆ **employé des ~s funèbres** undertaker's ou mortician's *(US)* assistant

pompé, e‡ /pɔ̃pe/ (ptp de **pomper**) ADJ *(= fatigué)* dead-beat*, knackered‡ *(Brit)*, pooped* *(US)*

Pompée /pɔ̃pe/ NM Pompey

Pompéi /pɔ̃pei/ N Pompeii

pompéien, -ienne /pɔ̃pejɛ̃, jɛn/ ADJ Pompeiian NM,F **Pompéien(ne)** Pompeiian

pomper /pɔ̃pe/ ▸ conjug 1 ◂ VT 1 *[+ air, liquide]* to pump; *[moustique]* to suck; *(= évacuer)* to pump out; *(= faire monter)* to pump up ◆ ~ **de l'eau** to get water from the pump, to pump water out ◆ **tu me pompes (l'air)**‡ you're getting on my nerves, I'm fed up with you‡ ◆ **il m'a pompé pas mal d'argent**‡ he sponged* quite a lot of money off me ◆ **les impôts nous pompent tout notre argent*** all our money gets eaten up in tax

2 *[éponge, buvard]* to soak up

3 *(arg Scol = copier)* to crib* *(sur* from*)*; ◆ **il m'a pompé toutes mes idées** he copied ou lifted* all my ideas ◆ **elle a pompé mon style** she has copied ou imitated my style

4 *(* = boire)* to knock back* ◆ **qu'est-ce qu'il pompe !** he can't half *(Brit)* ou he sure can *(US)* knock it back!*

5 *(* = épuiser)* to wear out, to tire out ◆ **tout ce travail m'a pompé** I'm worn out* ou knackered‡ *(Brit)* ou pooped* *(US)* after all that work

pompette* /pɔ̃pɛt/ ADJ tipsy*, tiddly* *(Brit)* ◆ **être/se sentir ~** to be/feel a bit tipsy* ou tiddly* *(Brit)*

pompeusement /pɔ̃pøzmɑ̃/ ADV pompously, pretentiously

pompeux, -euse /pɔ̃pø, øz/ ADJ *(= ampoulé)* pompous, pretentious; *(= imposant)* solemn

pompier, -ière /pɔ̃pje, jɛʀ/ ADJ *(péj)* *[style, écrivain]* pompous, pretentious; *[morceau de musique]* slushy* ◆ **art ~** official art NM 1 *(= personne)* fireman, firefighter ◆ **appeler les ~s** to call the fire brigade *(Brit)* ou department *(US)*; → **fumer** 2 *(*‡ = acte sexuel)* blow job*‡ ◆ **faire un ~ à qn** to give sb a blow job*‡

pompiste /pɔ̃pist/ NMF petrol pump *(Brit)* ou gas station *(US)* attendant

pompon /pɔ̃pɔ̃/ NM *[de chapeau, coussin]* pompom; *[de frange, instrument]* bobble ◆ **c'est le ~ !*** it's the last straw!, that beats everything!*, that's the limit!* ◆ **décrocher le ~** *(fig, aussi iro)* to hit the jackpot ◆ **décerner le ~ à qn** to give first prize to sb; → **rose**

pomponner /pɔ̃pɔne/ ▸ conjug 1 ◂ VT to titivate, to doll up*; *[+ bébé]* to dress up ◆ **bien pomponné** all dolled up* ou dressed up VPR **se pomponner** to doll o.s. up*, to get dolled up* ou dressed up

ponant /pɔnɑ̃/ NM *(littér)* west

ponçage /pɔ̃saʒ/ NM 1 *(avec du papier de verre)* sanding (down), sandpapering; *(avec une ponceuse)* sanding (down) 2 *(avec une pierre ponce)* pumicing

ponce /pɔ̃s/ NF 1 ◆ **(pierre) ~** pumice (stone) 2 *(Art)* pounce box

ponceau (pl **ponceaux**) /pɔ̃so/ NM *(= fleur)* corn ou Flanders ou field poppy, coquelicot; *(= colorant)* ponceau ADJ ponceau, dark red

Ponce Pilate /pɔ̃spilat/ NM Pontius Pilate

poncer /pɔ̃se/ ▸ conjug 3 ◂ VT 1 *(= décaper) (avec du papier de verre)* to sand (down), to sandpaper; *(avec une ponceuse)* to sand (down) ◆ **il faut commencer par ~** it needs sanding down first 2 *(avec une pierre ponce = polir)* to pumice 3 *(Art)* *[+ dessin]* to pounce

ponceuse /pɔ̃søz/ NF sander

poncho /pɔ̃(t)ʃo/ NM *(= cape)* poncho

poncif /pɔ̃sif/ NM 1 *(= cliché)* commonplace, cliché 2 *(Art)* stencil *(for pouncing)*

ponction /pɔ̃ksjɔ̃/ NF 1 *(Méd)* *(lombaire)* puncture; *(pulmonaire)* tapping ◆ **faire une ~ lombaire à qn** to perform a lumbar puncture on sb ◆ **faire une ~ pulmonaire à qn** to drain fluid from sb's lungs 2 *[d'argent]* draining ◆ **~ fiscale** (tax) levy *(sur* on); ◆ **les ~s opérées sur nos bénéfices** the levies on our profits ◆ **les ~s massives opérées sur notre pouvoir d'achat** the huge drain on our spending power ◆ **par de fréquentes ~s il a épuisé son capital** he has dipped into *ou* drawn on his capital so often he has used it all up ◆ **faire une sérieuse ~ dans ses économies** *[impôt]* to make a large hole in *ou* make serious inroads into one's savings; *[personne]* to draw heavily on one's savings

ponctionner /pɔ̃ksjɔne/ ► conjug 1 ◄ VT *[+ région lombaire]* to puncture; *[+ poumon]* to tap; *[+ réserves]* to tap; *[+ contribuable, entreprise]* to tax

ponctualité /pɔ̃ktɥalite/ NF *(= exactitude)* punctuality; *(= assiduité)* punctiliousness *(frm)*, meticulousness

ponctuation /pɔ̃ktɥasjɔ̃/ NF punctuation

ponctuel, -elle /pɔ̃ktɥɛl/ ADJ 1 *(= à l'heure)* punctual; *(= scrupuleux)* punctilious *(frm)*, meticulous 2 *(= limité, ciblé)* *[mesure, mission, projet]* specific; *[opération, coopération, accord, partenariat]* one-off; *[étude]* limited; *[événement]* particular ◆ **ces terroristes se livrent à des actions ponctuelles** the terrorists make sporadic attacks ◆ **je n'ai fait que quelques modifications ponctuelles** I've only changed a few details 3 *(Ling)* *[aspect]* punctual 4 *(Phys)* punctual

> ⚠ Au sens de 'limité', 'ciblé', **ponctuel** ne se traduit pas par le mot anglais **punctual**.

ponctuellement /pɔ̃ktɥɛlmɑ̃/ ADV 1 *(= avec exactitude)* *[arriver]* punctually 2 *(= de temps en temps)* from time to time; *(= ici et là)* here and there

ponctuer /pɔ̃ktɥe/ ► conjug 1 ◄ VT *(lit, fig)* to punctuate *(de* with); *(Mus)* to phrase

pondéral, e (mpl **-aux**) /pɔ̃deʀal, o/ ADJ weight *(épith)*; → **surcharge**

pondérateur, -trice /pɔ̃deʀatœʀ, tʀis/ ADJ *[influence]* stabilizing, steadying

pondération /pɔ̃deʀasjɔ̃/ NF 1 *[de personne]* level-headedness 2 *(= équilibrage)* balancing; *(Écon, Math)* weighting ◆ **~ des pouvoirs** balance of powers ◆ **le coefficient de ~ est 3** it's weighted by a factor of 3

pondéré, e /pɔ̃deʀe/ (ptp de **pondérer**) ADJ 1 *[personne, attitude]* level-headed 2 *(Écon)* **indice ~** weighted index

pondérer /pɔ̃deʀe/ ► conjug 6 ◄ VT *(= équilibrer)* to balance; *(= compenser)* to counterbalance *(par* by); *(Écon)* *[+ indice]* to weight

pondéreux, -euse /pɔ̃deʀø, øz/ ADJ *[marchandises, produits]* heavy NMPL heavy goods

pondeur /pɔ̃dœʀ/ NM *(péj)* ◆ **~ de romans** writer who churns out books

pondeuse /pɔ̃døz/ NF ◆ **(poule) ~** good layer; *(* : péj ou hum)* prolific child-bearer *(hum)*

pondre /pɔ̃dʀ/ ► conjug 41 ◄ VT *[+ œuf]* to lay; * *[+ enfant]* to produce; *[+ devoir, texte]* to produce, to turn out* ◆ **œuf frais pondu** new-laid egg VI *[poule]* to lay; *[poisson, insecte]* to lay its eggs

poney /pɔnɛ/ NM pony

pongé(e) /pɔ̃ʒe/ NM *(Tex)* pongee

pongiste /pɔ̃ʒist/ NMF table tennis player

pont /pɔ̃/ NM 1 *(= construction)* bridge; *(= lien)* bridge, link *(entre* between); ◆ **passer un ~** to go over *ou* cross a bridge ◆ **vivre** *ou* **coucher sous les ~s** to sleep rough, to live on the streets ◆ **solide comme le Pont-Neuf** (as) strong as an ox ◆ **se porter comme le Pont-Neuf*** to be hale and hearty ◆ **faire un ~ d'or à qn** *(pour l'employer)* to offer sb a fortune *(to take on a job)* ◆ **couper les ~s avec qn** to sever all links with sb ◆ **jeter un ~ sur une rivière** to bridge a river, to throw a bridge over a river ◆ **jeter un ~ entre les générations/deux cultures** to build bridges between generations/two cultures; → **eau**

2 *(= acrobatie)* crab ◆ **faire le ~** to do a crab

3 *[de bateau]* deck ◆ **~ avant/arrière** fore/rear deck ◆ **~ principal/supérieur** main/upper *ou* top deck ◆ **navire à deux/trois ~s** two/three decker ◆ **tout le monde sur le ~ !** all hands on deck!

4 *(= essieu)* axle ◆ **~ avant/arrière** front/rear axle

5 *(Mécanique)* **~ (élévateur)** (hydraulic) ramp ◆ **mettre une voiture sur le ~** to put a car on the ramp

6 *(= vacances)* extra day(s) off *(taken between two public holidays or a public holiday and a weekend)* ◆ **on a un ~ de trois jours pour Noël** we have three extra days (off) for *ou* at Christmas ◆ **faire le ~** to take the extra day (off), to make a long weekend of it; → **FÊTES LÉGALES**

7 *(Antiq)* **(royaume du) Pont** Pontus

8 *(Ftbl)* **petit ~** nutmeg *(Brit)*, between-the-leg pass *(US)* ◆ **faire un grand ~ à qn** to send the ball round sb's legs ◆ **faire un petit ~ à qn** to send the ball between sb's legs, to nutmeg sb *(Brit)*

9 *(Élec)* bridge (circuit) ◆ **~ de Wheatstone** Wheatstone bridge

COMP **pont aérien** airlift

pont aux ânes pons asinorum ◆ **c'est le ~ aux ânes** *(fig)* any fool knows that

pont basculant bascule bridge

les Ponts et Chaussées *(= service)* the highways department, the department of civil engineering; *(= école)* school of civil engineering ◆ **ingénieur des ~s et chaussées** civil engineer

pont d'envol *[de porte-avions]* flight deck

pont flottant pontoon bridge

pont garage car deck, vehicle deck

pont de glace *(Can)* ice bridge *ou* road

pont de graissage ramp *(in a garage)*

pont mobile movable bridge

pont à péage tollbridge

pont promenade *[de bateau]* promenade deck

pont roulant *(Rail)* travelling crane

pont suspendu suspension bridge

pont tournant swing bridge

pont transbordeur transporter bridge; → **hauban**

pontage /pɔ̃taʒ/ NM 1 *[de bateau]* decking 2 ◆ **~ (cardiaque)** *(Méd)* (heart) bypass operation *ou* surgery *(NonC)* ◆ **~ coronarien** coronary bypass operation *ou* surgery *(NonC)* ◆ **faire un ~ à qn** to carry out a (heart) bypass operation on sb ◆ **on lui a fait un triple ~** he had triple bypass surgery *ou* a triple bypass operation

pont-canal (pl **ponts-canaux**) /pɔ̃kanal, o/ NM canal bridge

ponte[1] /pɔ̃t/ NF *(= action)* laying (of eggs); *(= œufs)* eggs, clutch; *(= saison)* (egg-)laying season ◆ **~ ovulaire** ovulation

ponte[2] /pɔ̃t/ NM 1 *(* = pontife)* bigwig* ◆ **les grands ~s de l'université/du parti** the academic/party bigwigs ◆ **un ~ de la médecine** a leading light in the medical world ◆ **un ~ de la banque** a bigshot* in the banking world 2 *(Jeux)* punter

ponter[1] /pɔ̃te/ ► conjug 1 ◄ VT *[+ bateau]* to deck, to lay the deck of

ponter[2] /pɔ̃te/ ► conjug 1 ◄ *(Jeux)* VI to punt VT to bet

Pont-Euxin /pɔ̃tøksɛ̃/ NM ◆ **le ~** the Euxine Sea

pontife /pɔ̃tif/ NM 1 *(Rel)* pontiff; → **souverain** 2 *(* = personne importante)* big shot*, pundit*

pontifiant, e* /pɔ̃tifjɑ̃, jɑ̃t/ ADJ *[personne, ton]* pontificating

pontifical, e (mpl **-aux**) /pɔ̃tifikal, o/ ADJ *(Antiq)* pontifical; *(Rel)* *[messe]* pontifical; *[siège, gardes, États]* papal

pontificat /pɔ̃tifika/ NM pontificate

pontifier /pɔ̃tifje/ ► conjug 7 ◄ VI to pontificate

pont-levis (pl **ponts-levis**) /pɔ̃l(ə)vi/ NM drawbridge

ponton /pɔ̃tɔ̃/ NM *(= plate-forme)* pontoon, (floating) landing stage; *(= chaland)* lighter; *(= navire)* hulk

ponton-grue (pl **pontons-grues**) /pɔ̃tɔ̃gʀy/ NM floating crane

pontonnier /pɔ̃tɔnje/ NM *(Mil)* pontoneer

pool /pul/ NM *[de producteurs, dactylos]* pool ◆ **~ bancaire** banking pool

pop /pɔp/ ADJ INV *[musique, art]* pop NM INV ◆ **le ~** *(= musique)* pop (music); *(= art)* pop art

pop art, pop'art /pɔpaʀt/ NM pop art

pop-corn /pɔpkɔʀn/ NM INV popcorn

pope /pɔp/ NM (Orthodox) priest

popeline /pɔplin/ NF poplin

popote /pɔpɔt/ NF 1 *(* = cuisine)* cooking ◆ **faire la ~** to cook 2 *(Mil)* mess, canteen ◆ **j'ai fait le tour des ~s*** *(pour collecter des informations)* I asked around ADJ INV * stay-at-home *(épith)*, home-loving ◆ **il est très ~** he likes his home comforts

popotin */pɔpɔtɛ̃/ NM bottom*; → **se magner**

populace /pɔpylas/ NF *(péj)* rabble, mob

populaire /pɔpylɛʀ/ ADJ 1 *(= du peuple)* *[gouvernement, front, croyance, tradition]* popular; *[démocratie]* popular, people's; *[république]* people's; *[mouvement, manifestation]* mass ◆ **la République ~ de ...** the People's Republic of ... 2 *(= pour la masse)* *[roman, art, chanson]* popular; *[édition]* cheap; → **bal, soupe** 3 *(= plébéien)* *[goût]* common; *(= ouvrier)* *[milieu, quartier, origines]* working-class ◆ **les classes ~s** the working classes 4 *(= qui plaît)* popular, well-liked ◆ **très ~ auprès des jeunes** very popular with young people 5 *(Ling)* *[mot, expression]* vernacular; *[étymologie]* popular; *[latin]* popular

populairement /pɔpylɛʀmɑ̃/ ADV *(gén)* popularly; *[parler]* in the vernacular

popularisation /pɔpylaʀizasjɔ̃/ NF *(= vulgarisation)* popularization ◆ **avec la ~ des concepts freudiens** *(= propagation)* with Freudian theories becoming more widely known ◆ **la télévision a joué un rôle important dans la ~ de l'art lyrique** television played an important role in making opera accessible to *ou* in bringing opera to the general public

populariser /pɔpylaʀize/ ► conjug 1 ◄ VT to popularize VPR **se populariser** to become more (and more) popular

popularité /pɔpylaʀite/ NF popularity

population /pɔpylasjɔ̃/ NF population ◆ **région à ~ musulmane/mixte** area with a large Muslim population/with a mixed population ◆ **~ active/agricole** working/farming population ◆ **~ carcérale/civile/scolaire** prison/civilian/school population ◆ **mouvement de ~** population movement ◆ **l'attentat a fait quatre victimes parmi la ~** the bomb attack claimed four civilian casualties

populeux, -euse /pɔpylø, øz/ ADJ *[pays, ville]* densely populated, populous; *[rue]* crowded

populisme /pɔpylism/ NM 1 *(Pol)* populism 2 *(Littérat)* populisme *(a literary movement of the 1920s and 1930s which sets out to describe the lives of ordinary people)*

populiste /pɔpylist/ ADJ, NMF populist

populo* /pɔpylo/ NM *(péj = peuple)* ordinary people *ou* folks*; *(= foule)* crowd (of people)

porc /pɔʀ/ NM 1 *(= animal)* pig, hog *(US)*; *(= viande)* pork; *(= peau)* pigskin 2 *(* péj)* pig, swine*

porcelaine /pɔʀsəlɛn/ NF 1 *(= matière)* porcelain, china; *(= objet)* piece of porcelain ◆ ~ **dure/tendre** soft-paste/hard-paste porcelain ◆ ~ **tendre naturelle** bone china ◆ ~ **vitreuse** vitreous china ◆ ~ **de Saxe/de Sèvres** Dresden/Sèvres china ◆ ~ **de Chine** China ◆ **de Limoges** Limoges porcelain ◆ **de** *ou* **en** ~ china, porcelain 2 *(= coquillage)* cowrie

porcelainier, -ière /pɔʀsəlenje, jɛʀ/ ADJ china *(épith)*, porcelain *(épith)* NM *(= fabricant)* porcelain *ou* china manufacturer

porcelet /pɔʀsəlɛ/ NM piglet; *(Culin)* sucking pig

porc-épic (pl **porcs-épics**) /pɔʀkepik/ NM porcupine; *(= personne irritable)* prickly customer* ◆ **tu es un vrai** ~ ! *(= homme mal rasé)* you're all bristly!

porche /pɔʀʃ/ NM porch ◆ **sous le** ~ **de l'immeuble** in the entrance to the building

porcher, -ère /pɔʀʃe, ɛʀ/ NM,F pig-keeper, swineherd †

porcherie /pɔʀʃəʀi/ NF *(lit, fig)* pigsty, pigpen *(US)*

porcin, e /pɔʀsɛ̃, in/ ADJ *(lit)* porcine; *(fig)* piglike NM pig ◆ **les** ~**s** pigs

pore /pɔʀ/ NM pore ◆ **il sue l'arrogance par tous les** ~**s** he exudes arrogance from every pore

poreux, -euse /pɔʀø, øz/ ADJ porous

porno * /pɔʀno/ ADJ (abrév de **pornographique**) porn*, porno* ◆ **film/revue/cinéma** ~ porn(o)* film/magazine/cinema NM (abrév de **pornographie**) porn*

pornographe /pɔʀnɔgʀaf/ NMF pornographer ADJ of pornography *(attrib)*, pornographic

pornographie /pɔʀnɔgʀafi/ NF pornography

pornographique /pɔʀnɔgʀafik/ ADJ pornographic

porosité /pɔʀozite/ NF porosity

porphyre /pɔʀfiʀ/ NM porphyry

porphyrique /pɔʀfiʀik/ ADJ porphyritic

port[1] /pɔʀ/ NM 1 *(= bassin)* harbour *(Brit)*, harbor *(US)*; *(commercial)* port; *(= ville)* port; *(littér = abri)* port, haven ◆ **se promener sur le** ~ to walk around the harbour *ou* along the quayside ◆ **sortir du** ~ to leave port *ou* harbour ◆ **arriver au** ~ *(Naut)* to dock; *(fig)* to reach one's destination ◆ **arriver à bon** ~ to arrive intact, to arrive safe and sound ◆ **un** ~ **dans la tempête** *(fig)* a port in a storm

2 *(dans les Pyrénées)* pass

3 *(Ordin)* port ◆ ~ **parallèle/série** parallel/serial port

COMP **port artificiel** artificial harbour *(Brit) ou* harbor *(US)*

port d'attache *(Naut)* port of registry; *(fig)* home base

port autonome *(= gestion)* port authority; *(= lieu)* port *(publicly managed)*

port de commerce commercial port

port fluvial river port

port franc free port

port de guerre naval base

port maritime, port de mer sea port

port militaire military port

port de pêche fishing port

port de plaisance *(= bassin)* marina; *(= ville)* sailing *ou* yachting resort

port[2] /pɔʀ/ NM 1 *(= fait de porter) [d'objet]* carrying; *[d'habit, barbe, décoration]* wearing ◆ **le** ~ **du casque est obligatoire sur le chantier** hard hats must be worn on the building site ◆ ~ **d'armes prohibé** illegal carrying of firearms ◆ **se mettre au** ~ **d'armes** *(Mil)* to shoulder arms 2 *(= prix) (poste)* postage; *(= transport)* carriage ◆ **franco** *ou* **franc de** ~ carriage paid ◆ **(en)** ~ **dû/payé** postage due/paid 3 *(= comportement)* bearing, carriage ◆ **elle a un** ~ **majestueux** *ou* **de reine** she has a noble *ou* majestic *ou* queenly bearing ◆ **elle a un joli** ~ **de tête** she holds her head very nicely 4 *(Mus)* ~ **de voix** portamento

portabilité /pɔʀtabilite/ NF *(gén, Ordin)* portability

portable /pɔʀtabl/ ADJ 1 *(= portatif) (gén)* portable; *[téléphone]* mobile ◆ **logiciels** ~**s** portable software 2 *[vêtement]* wearable NM *(Ordin, gén)* portable; *(= qui tient sur les genoux)* laptop; *(= téléphone)* mobile phone, mobile*

portage /pɔʀtaʒ/ NM *[de marchandise]* porterage; *(Naut, Can)* portage ◆ ~ **à domicile** *(Presse)* home delivery ◆ **randonnée avec/sans** ~ hike with/without pack transfers

portager /pɔʀtaʒe/ ▸ conjug 3 ◂ VI *(Can)* to portage

portail /pɔʀtaj/ NM *(= porte)* gate; *(Internet)* portal

portance /pɔʀtɑ̃s/ NF *[d'une aile]* lift; *[d'un sol]* load-bearing capacity

portant, e /pɔʀtɑ̃, ɑ̃t/ ADJ 1 *[mur]* structural, supporting; *[roue]* running ◆ **surface** ~**e** *(Aviat)* aerofoil *(Brit)*, airfoil *(US)* ◆ **vent** ~ *(Naut)* fair wind 2 ◆ **être bien/mal** ~ to be healthy *ou* in good health/in poor health; → **bout** NM *(= anse)* handle; *(Théât)* upright; *(= présentoir)* rack

portatif, -ive /pɔʀtatif, iv/ ADJ portable

Port-au-Prince /pɔʀopʀɛ̃s/ N Port-au-Prince

porte /pɔʀt/ NF 1 *[de maison, voiture, meuble]* door; *[de forteresse, jardin, stade, ville]* gate; *(= seuil)* doorstep; *(= embrasure)* doorway ◆ ~ **pliante/coulissante** folding/sliding door ◆ **franchir** *ou* **passer la** ~ to go through *ou* come through the door(way) ◆ **sonner à la** ~ to ring the (door)bell ◆ **c'est à ma** ~ it's close by, it's on the doorstep ◆ **le bus me descend** *ou* **met à ma** ~ the bus takes me right to my door ◆ **j'ai trouvé ce colis à ma** ~ I found this parcel on my doorstep ◆ **ils se réfugièrent sous la** ~ they took shelter in the doorway ◆ **une (voiture) 3/5** ~**s** a 3-door/5-door (car) ◆ **il y a 100 km/j'ai mis deux heures (de)** ~ **à** ~ it's 100 km/it took me two hours (from) door to door ◆ **de** ~ **en** ~ from house to house ◆ **faire du** ~ **à** ~ *(= vendre)* to sell from door to door, to be a door-to-door salesman, to do doorstep selling *(Brit)*; *(= chercher du travail)* to go around knocking on doors ◆ **l'ennemi est à nos** ~**s** the enemy is at our gate(s) ◆ **Dijon,** ~ **de la Bourgogne** Dijon, the gateway to Burgundy; → **casser, clé** *etc*

2 *[d'aéroport]* gate

3 *[d'écluse]* (lock) gate; *(Ski)* gate

4 *(locutions)* **c'est/ce n'est pas la** ~ **à côté*** it's practically/it's not exactly on our *(ou my etc)* doorstep ◆ **la** ~ **!*** (shut the) door! ◆ **(à) la** ~ **!** (get) out! ◆ **être à la** ~ to be locked out ◆ **mettre** *ou* **flanquer qn à la** ~* *(licencier)* to fire sb*, to sack sb* *(Brit)*, to give sb the sack* *(Brit)*; *(Scol)* to expel sb; *(Univ)* to send sb down *(Brit)*, to flunk sb out* *(US)*; *(éjecter)* to throw *ou* boot* sb out ◆ **montrer la** ~ **à qn** to show sb the door ◆ **claquer/fermer la** ~ **au nez de qn** to slam/shut the door in sb's face ◆ **entrer** *ou* **passer par la petite/la grande** ~ *(fig)* to start at the bottom (rung of the ladder)/at the top ◆ **le ministre est sorti** *ou* **s'est en allé par la petite** ~ the minister left quietly *ou* made a discreet exit ◆ **ça lui a permis de sortir par la grande** ~ this allowed him to leave with dignity *ou* without losing face ◆ **fermer** *ou* **refuser sa** ~ **à qn** to close the door to sb, to bar sb from one's house ◆ **fermer la** ~ **à qch** *(fig)* to close the door on sth ◆ **j'ai trouvé** ~ **close** *ou* **de bois** *(Belg) (maison)* no one answered the door; *(magasin, bâtiment public)* it was closed ◆ **vous avez frappé** *ou* **sonné à la bonne/mauvaise** ~ *(fig)* you've come to the right/wrong person *ou* place ◆ **c'est la** ~ **ouverte** *ou* **c'est ouvrir la** ~ **à tous les abus** *(fig)* it means leaving the door wide open *ou* the way open to all sorts of abuses ◆ **toutes les** ~**s lui sont ouvertes** every door is open to him ◆ **laisser la** ~ **ouverte à un compromis** to leave the way open for compromise ◆ **journée** ~**(s) ouverte(s)** open day *(Brit)*, open house *(US)* ◆ **opération** ~**(s) ouverte(s)** open day event ◆ **il faut qu'une** ~ **soit ouverte ou fermée** you can't have it both ways ◆ **aux** ~**s de la mort** at death's door ◆ **parler à qn entre deux** ~**s** to have a quick word with sb, to speak to sb very briefly *ou* in passing ◆ **recevoir qn entre deux** ~**s** to meet sb very briefly ◆ **prendre la** ~ to go away, to leave ◆ **aimable** *ou* **souriant comme une** ~ **de prison** like a bear with a sore head

ADJ ◆ **veine** ~ portal vein

COMP **porte accordéon** folding door

les portes du Ciel the gates of Heaven

porte cochère carriage entrance, porte-cochère

porte à deux battants double door *ou* gate

porte d'embarquement *(dans aéroport)* departure gate

les portes de l'Enfer the gates of Hell

porte d'entrée front door

les Portes de Fer *(Géog)* the Iron Gate(s)

porte palière front door *(of an apartment)*

porte de secours emergency exit *ou* door

porte de service rear *ou* tradesman's *(surtout Brit)* entrance

porte de sortie *(lit)* exit, way out *(surtout Brit)*; *(fig)* way out, let-out* *(Brit)* ◆ **se ménager une** ~ **de sortie** to leave o.s. a way out *ou* loophole

porté, e[1] /pɔʀte/ (ptp de **porter**) ADJ ◆ **être** ~ **à faire qch** to be apt *ou* inclined to do sth, to tend to do sth ◆ **nous sommes** ~**s à croire que …** we are inclined to believe that … ◆ **être** ~ **à la colère/à l'exagération** to be prone to anger/to exaggeration ◆ **être** ~ **sur qch** to be fond of *ou* keen on *(Brit)* sth, to be partial to sth ◆ **être** ~ **sur la chose*** to have a one-track mind* NM *(Danse)* lift

porte-aéronefs /pɔʀtaeʀɔnɛf/ NM INV aircraft carrier

porte-à-faux /pɔʀtafo/ NM INV *[de mur]* slant; *[de rocher]* precarious balance, overhang; *(Archit)* cantilever ◆ **en** ~ *[mur, construction]* slanting, out of plumb; *[rocher]* precariously balanced; *(fig) [personne] (= dans une situation délicate)* in an awkward position; *(= en décalage, isolé)* out on a limb ◆ **être** *ou* **se trouver en** ~ **par rapport à** *ou* **avec qch** to be at odds *ou* out of step with sth ◆ **mettre qn en** ~ to put sb in an awkward position

porte-aiguilles /pɔʀtegɥij/ NM INV *(= boîte)* needle case; *(en tissu)* needle book

porte-avions /pɔʀtavjɔ̃/ NM INV aircraft carrier

porte-bagages /pɔʀt(ə)bagaʒ/ NM INV *[de vélo]* rack; *[de train]* (luggage) rack

porte-bébé (pl **porte-bébés**) /pɔʀt(ə)bebe/ NM *(= nacelle)* carrycot *(Brit)*; *(à bretelles)* baby sling, baby carrier

porte-billets /pɔʀt(ə)bijɛ/ NM INV wallet, notecase, billfold *(US)*

porte-bonheur /pɔʀt(ə)bɔnœʀ/ NM INV lucky charm ◆ **acheter du muguet** ~ to buy lily of the valley for good luck

porte-bouquet (pl **porte-bouquets**) /pɔʀt(ə)bukɛ/ NM flower holder

porte-bouteille(s) (pl **porte-bouteilles**) /pɔʀt(ə)butɛj/ NM (*à anse*) bottle-carrier; (*à casiers*) wine rack; (*= hérisson*) bottle-drainer

porte-cartes /pɔʀt(ə)kaʀt/ NM INV [*de papiers d'identité*] card wallet *ou* holder; [*de cartes géographiques*] map wallet

porte-chéquier (pl **porte-chéquier**) /pɔʀt(ə)ʃekje/ NM chequebook (*Brit*) *ou* checkbook (*US*) holder

porte-cigares /pɔʀt(ə)sigaʀ/ NM INV cigar case

porte-cigarettes /pɔʀt(ə)sigaʀɛt/ NM INV cigarette case

porte-clés /pɔʀt(ə)kle/ NM INV 1 (*= anneau*) key ring; (*= étui*) key case 2 (†† *= geôlier*) turnkey (††)

porte-conteneurs /pɔʀt(ə)kɔ̃t(ə)nœʀ/ NM INV container ship

porte-copie (pl **porte-copies**) /pɔʀt(ə)kɔpi/ NM copy holder

porte-couteau (pl **porte-couteaux**) /pɔʀt(ə)kuto/ NM knife rest

porte-crayon (pl **porte-crayons**) /pɔʀt(ə)kʀɛjɔ̃/ NM pencil holder

porte-croix /pɔʀt(ə)kʀwa/ NM INV cross bearer

porte-documents /pɔʀt(ə)dɔkymɑ̃/ NM INV briefcase, attaché case, document case

porte-drapeau (pl **porte-drapeaux**) /pɔʀt(ə)dʀapo/ NM (*lit, fig*) standard bearer

portée² /pɔʀte/ NF 1 (*= distance*) range, reach; [*de fusil, radar*] range; [*de cri, voix*] carrying-distance, reach ◆ **canon à faible/longue ~** short-/long-range gun ◆ **missile de moyenne ~** intermediate-range weapon ◆ **à ~ de la main** within (arm's) reach, at *ou* on hand ◆ **restez à ~ de voix** stay within earshot ◆ **restez à ~ de vue** don't go out of sight ◆ **cet hôtel est/n'est pas à la ~ de toutes les bourses** this hotel is/is not within everyone's means, this hotel suits/does not suit everyone's purse ◆ **ne laissez pas les médicaments à ~ de main** *ou* **à la ~ des enfants** keep medicines out of the reach of children ◆ **hors de ~** (*lit*) out of reach *ou* range; (*fig*) beyond reach ◆ **hors de ~ de fusil/de voix** out of rifle range/earshot

2 (*= capacité*) [*d'intelligence*] reach, scope, capacity; (*= niveau*) level ◆ **ce concept dépasse la ~ de l'intelligence ordinaire** this concept is beyond the reach *ou* scope *ou* capacity of the average mind ◆ **être à la ~ de qn** to be understandable to sb ◆ **il faut savoir se mettre à la ~ des enfants** you have to be able to come down to a child's level ◆ **mettre la science à la ~ de tous** to bring science within everyone's reach

3 (*= effet*) [*de parole, écrit*] impact, import; [*d'acte*] significance, consequences ◆ **il ne mesure pas la ~ de ses paroles/ses actes** he doesn't think about the import of what he's saying/the consequences of his actions ◆ **la ~ de cet événement est incalculable** it is impossible to foresee the consequences of this event ◆ **sans ~ pratique** of no practical consequence *ou* importance *ou* significance

4 (*Archit*) (*= poussée*) loading; (*= distance*) span

5 (*Mus*) stave, staff

6 (*= bébés animaux*) litter

porte-étendard (pl **porte-étendards**) /pɔʀtetɑ̃daʀ/ NM (*lit, fig*) standard bearer

porte-étrivière (pl **porte-étrivières**) /pɔʀtetʀivjɛʀ/ NM stirrup leather holder

portefaix †† /pɔʀtəfɛ/ NM INV porter

porte-fenêtre (pl **portes-fenêtres**) /pɔʀt(ə)fənɛtʀ/ NF French window (*Brit*) *ou* door (*US*)

portefeuille /pɔʀtəfœj/ NM [*d'argent*] wallet, billfold (*US*); (*Assurances, Bourse, Pol*) portfolio ◆ **société de ~** holding *ou* investment company ◆ **avoir un ~ bien garni** to be well-off ◆ **ils ont dû mettre la main au ~** they had to fork out * *ou* pay; → **lit, ministre**

porte-flingue* /pɔʀtəflɛ̃g/ NM INV henchman

porte-fusibles /pɔʀtəfyzibl/ NM INV fuse box

porte-greffe (pl **porte-greffes**) /pɔʀtəgʀɛf/ NM (*Agr*) stock (*for graft*)

porte-hélicoptères /pɔʀtelikɔptɛʀ/ NM INV helicopter carrier

porte-jarretelles /pɔʀt(ə)ʒaʀtɛl/ NM INV suspender belt (*Brit*), garter belt (*US*)

porte-jupe (pl **porte-jupes**) /pɔʀtəʒyp/ NM skirt hanger

porte-malheur /pɔʀt(ə)malœʀ/ NM INV (*= chose*) jinx; (*= personne*) jinx, Jonah

portemanteau (pl **portemanteaux**) /pɔʀt(ə)mɑ̃to/ NM 1 (*= cintre*) coat hanger; (*accroché au mur*) coat rack; (*sur pied*) hat stand ◆ **accrocher une veste au ~** to hang up a jacket 2 (†† *= malle*) portmanteau

porte-menu (pl **porte-menus**) /pɔʀt(ə)məny/ NM menu holder

portemine /pɔʀtəmin/ NM propelling pencil

porte-monnaie /pɔʀt(ə)mɔnɛ/ NM INV (*gén*) purse (*Brit*), coin purse (*US*); (*pour homme*) wallet ◆ **~ électronique** electronic purse ◆ **on fait souvent appel au ~ du contribuable** the taxpayer is often asked to dip into his pocket ◆ **avoir le ~ bien garni** to be well-off

porte-musique /pɔʀt(ə)myzik/ NM INV music case

porte-objet (pl **porte-objets**) /pɔʀt(ə)ɔbʒɛ/ NM (*= lamelle*) slide; (*= platine*) stage

porte-outil (pl **porte-outils**) /pɔʀtuti/ NM (*Tech*) chuck

porte-parapluies /pɔʀt(ə)paʀaplɥi/ NM INV umbrella stand

porte-parole /pɔʀt(ə)paʀɔl/ NMF INV spokesperson; (*= homme*) spokesman; (*= femme*) spokeswoman ◆ **le ~ du gouvernement** the government spokesperson, ≈ the press secretary (*US*) ◆ **se faire le ~ de qn** to act as spokesman for sb, to speak on sb's behalf ◆ **leur journal est le ~ du parti** their newspaper is the mouthpiece *ou* organ of the party

porte-plume (pl **porte-plumes**) /pɔʀtəplym/ NM penholder ◆ **prise ~** (*Ping-Pong*) penholder grip

porter /pɔʀte/ ▸ conjug 1 ◂ VT 1 [*+ parapluie, paquet, valise*] to carry; [*+ responsabilité*] to bear, to carry ◆ **~ un enfant dans ses bras/sur son dos** to carry a child in one's arms/on one's back ◆ **pouvez-vous me ~ ma valise ?** can you carry my case for me? ◆ **laisse-toi ~ par la vague** let yourself be carried by the waves ◆ **ses jambes ne le portent plus** his legs can no longer carry him ◆ **ce pont n'est pas fait pour ~ des camions** this bridge isn't meant to carry lorries *ou* meant for lorries *ou* can't take the weight of a lorry ◆ **portez ... arme !** (*Mil*) present ... arms! ◆ **la tige qui porte la fleur** the stem which bears the flower, the stem with the flower on ◆ **cette poutre porte tout le poids du plafond** this beam bears *ou* carries *ou* takes the whole weight of the ceiling ◆ **~ sa croix** to carry *ou* bear one's cross ◆ **~ le poids de ses fautes** to bear the weight of one's mistakes

2 (*= apporter*) to take ◆ **~ qch à qn** to take sth to sb ◆ **porte-lui ce livre** take this book to him, take him this book ◆ **le facteur porte les lettres et les colis** the postman delivers letters and parcels ◆ **je vais ~ la lettre à la boîte** I'm going to take the letter to the postbox, I'm going to put this letter in the postbox ◆ **~ les plats sur la table** to take the dishes (out *ou* over) to the table ◆ **porte-la sur le lit** put *ou* lay her on the bed ◆ **~ la main à son front** to put one's hand to one's brow ◆ **~ la main à son chapeau** to lift one's hand to one's hat ◆ **~ la main sur qn** to raise one's hand to sb ◆ **~ qch à sa bouche** to lift *ou* put sth to one's lips ◆ **~ de l'argent à la banque** to take some money to the bank ◆ **se faire ~ à manger** to have food brought (to one) ◆ **~ l'affaire sur la place publique/devant les tribunaux** to take *ou* carry the matter into the public arena/before the courts ◆ **~ la nouvelle à qn** to take *ou* bring the news to sb ◆ **~ une œuvre à l'écran/à la scène** to transfer a work to the screen/to the stage ◆ **~ chance** *ou* **bonheur/malheur (à qn)** to be lucky/unlucky (for sb), to bring (sb) (good) luck/bad luck ◆ **ça porte bonheur !** it brings good luck!, it's lucky! ◆ **~ de l'eau à la rivière** (*Prov*) to carry coals to Newcastle ◆ **portant partout la terreur et la mort** (*littér*) carrying fear and death everywhere

3 [*+ vêtement, bague, laine, lunettes*] to wear; [*+ armes héraldiques*] to bear; [*+ barbe*] to have, to wear; [*+ nom*] to have, to bear ◆ **~ les cheveux longs** to wear one's hair long, to have long hair ◆ **~ le nom d'une fleur** to be called after a flower ◆ **~ le nom de Jérôme** to be called Jerome ◆ **il porte bien son nom** his name suits him ◆ **elle porte bien son âge** she looks good for her age ◆ **elle porte bien le pantalon** trousers suit her ◆ **c'est elle qui porte le pantalon** *ou* **la culotte** (*fig*) she's the one that wears trousers (*Brit*) *ou* pants (*US*) ◆ **je ne veux pas ~ le chapeau** * (*fig*) I don't want to carry the can * *ou* take the rap * (*pour* for); ◆ **on lui a fait ~ le chapeau** * he carried the can * *ou* took the rap *

4 (*= tenir*) to hold, to keep ◆ **~ la tête haute** (*lit*) to hold *ou* keep one's head up; (*fig*) to hold one's head high ◆ **~ le corps en avant** to lean *ou* stoop forward

5 (*= montrer*) [*+ signe, trace*] to show, to bear; [*+ blessure, cicatrice*] to have, to bear; [*+ inscription, date*] to bear ◆ **il porte la bonté sur son visage** he has a very kind(-looking) face, his face is a picture of kindness ◆ **ce livre porte un beau titre** this book has a good title ◆ **la lettre porte la date du 12 mai** the letter is dated *ou* bears the date of 12 May ◆ **~ la marque de** (*Ling*) to be marked for

6 (*= inscrire*) [*+ nom*] to write down, to put down (*sur* on, in); (*Comm*) [*+ somme*] to enter (*sur* in); ◆ **~ de l'argent au crédit d'un compte** to credit an account with some money ◆ **nous portons cette somme à votre débit** we are debiting this sum from your account ◆ **se faire ~ absent** to go absent ◆ **se faire ~ malade** to report *ou* go sick ◆ **~ qn absent** (*Mil*) to report sb absent; (*Scol*) to mark sb absent ◆ **porté disparu/au nombre des morts** reported missing/dead ◆ **porté manquant** unaccounted for

7 (*= diriger*) [*+ regard*] to direct, to turn (*sur, vers* towards); [*+ attention*] to turn, to give (*sur* to) to focus (*sur* on); [*+ effort*] to direct (*sur* towards); [*+ pas*] to turn (*vers* towards); [*+ coup*] to deal (*à* to); [*+ accusation*] to make (*contre* against); [*+ attaque*] to make (*contre* on); ◆ **il fit ~ son attention sur ce détail** he turned his attention to *ou* focused his attention on this detail ◆ **il fit ~ son choix sur ce livre** he chose this book, his choice fell on this book

8 (*= ressentir*) [*+ amour, haine*] to feel (*à* for); [*+ reconnaissance*] to feel (*à* to, towards); ◆ **~ de l'amitié à qn** to feel friendship towards sb

9 (*= être enceinte de*) to carry

10 (*Fin*) [*+ intérêts*] to yield; (*Bot*) [*+ graines, fruit*] to bear; [*+ récolte, moisson*] to yield ◆ **cette ardeur/haine qu'il portait en lui** the passion/hatred which he carried with him ◆ **idée qui porte en soi les germes de sa propre destruction** idea which carries (within itself) *ou* bears

the seeds of its own destruction ◆ ~ **ses fruits** *(fig)* to bear fruit

11 *(= conduire, amener)* to carry; *(= entraîner) [foi]* to carry along; *[vent]* to carry away ◆ **se laisser ~ par la foule** to (let o.s.) be carried away by the crowd ◆ ~ **qn au pouvoir** to bring *ou* carry sb to power ◆ ~ **qch à sa perfection/à son paroxysme/à l'apogée** to bring sth to perfection/to a peak/to a climax ◆ ~ **la température à 800°/le salaire à 2 000 €/la vitesse à 30 nœuds** to bring the temperature up to 800°/the salary up to €2,000/the speed up to 30 knots ◆ **cela porte le nombre de blessés à 20** that brings the number of casualties (up) to 20

12 *(= inciter)* ~ **qn à faire qch** to prompt *ou* induce *ou* lead sb to do sth ◆ **ça le portera à l'indulgence** that will prompt him to be indulgent, that will make him indulgent ◆ **tout (nous) porte à croire que ...** everything leads us to believe that ...; → **porté**

13 *(Ordin) [+ logiciel]* to port *(sous* to*)*

VI 1 *[bruit, voix, canon]* to carry ◆ **le son/le coup a porté à 500 mètres** the sound/the shot carried 500 metres ◆ **le fusil porte à 300 mètres** the rifle has a range of 300 metres

2 *[reproche, coup]* ~ **(juste)** to hit *ou* strike home ◆ **tous les coups portaient** every blow told ◆ **un coup qui porte** a telling blow ◆ **ses conseils ont porté** his advice had some effect *ou* was of some use

3 *(Méd) [femme]* to carry her child *ou* baby; *[animal]* to carry its young

4 *(= frapper)* **sa tête a porté sur le bord du trottoir** his head struck the edge of the pavement ◆ **c'est la tête qui a porté** his head took the blow

5 *(= reposer) [édifice, pilier]* to be supported by *ou* on ◆ **tout le poids du plafond porte sur cette poutre** the whole weight of the ceiling is supported by this beam, this beam bears the whole weight of the ceiling ◆ ~ **à faux** *[mur]* to be out of plumb *ou* true; *[rocher]* to be precariously balanced; *(fig) [remarque]* to be out of place

6 ◆ ~ **sur** *(= concerner) [débat, cours]* to turn on, to revolve around, to be about; *[revendications, objection]* to concern; *[étude, effort, action]* to be concerned with, to focus on; *[accent]* to fall on ◆ **la question portait sur des auteurs au programme** the question was on some of the authors on the syllabus ◆ **il a fait ~ son exposé sur la situation économique** in his talk he concentrated *ou* focused on the economic situation

VPR se porter 1 *[personne]* **se ~ bien/mal** to be well/unwell *ou* in poor health ◆ **comment vous portez-vous ? – je me porte bien** how are you? – I'm fine *ou* I'm very well ◆ **se ~ comme un charme** to be fighting fit, to be as fit as a fiddle* ◆ **buvez moins, vous ne vous en porterez que mieux** drink less and you'll feel (all the) better for it ◆ **et je ne m'en suis pas plus mal porté** and I didn't come off any worse for it, and I was no worse off for it; → **pont**

2 *(= se présenter comme)* **se ~ candidat** to put o.s. up *ou* stand *(Brit) ou* run as a candidate ◆ **se ~ acquéreur (de)** to put in a bid (for) ◆ **se ~ fort pour qn** to answer for sb; → **caution** *etc*

3 *(= aller)* to go ◆ **se ~ à la rencontre** *ou* **au-devant de qn** to go to meet sb ◆ **se ~ à** *(= se laisser aller à) [+ voies de fait, violences]* to commit ◆ **se ~ à des extrémités** to go to extremes ◆ **se ~ sur** *(= se diriger vers) [soupçon, choix]* to fall on ◆ **son regard se porta sur moi** his eyes *ou* gaze fell on me, he looked towards me ◆ **son attention se porta sur ce point** he focused *ou* concentrated his attention on this point

4 *(= être porté) [vêtement]* **les jupes se portent très courtes** the fashion's for very short skirts, skirts are being worn very short ◆ **ça ne se porte plus** that's out of fashion, nobody wears that any more

porte-revues /pɔʀt(ə)ʀəvy/ **NM INV** magazine rack

porte-savon (pl **porte-savons**) /pɔʀt(ə)savɔ̃/ **NM** soapdish

porte-serviette /pɔʀt(ə)sɛʀvjɛt/ **NM INV** *(= pochette)* napkin-holder; *(péj Pol)* sidekick*, flunkey

porte-serviettes /pɔʀt(ə)sɛʀvjɛt/ **NM INV** towel rail ◆ ~ **chauffant** heated towel rail

porte-skis /pɔʀtəski/ **NM INV** ski rack

porteur, -euse /pɔʀtœʀ, øz/ **ADJ** *[fusée]* booster *(épith)*; *[courant]* carrier *(épith)*; *[mur]* load-bearing ◆ **thème ~** key theme ◆ **marché/créneau ~** *(Écon)* growth market/area ◆ **onde porteuse** *(Phys)* carrier (wave); → **mère**

NM,F 1 *[de valise, colis]* porter; *[de message]* messenger; *[de chèque]* bearer; *[de titre, actions]* holder ◆ ~ **d'eau** water carrier ◆ ~ **de journaux** newsboy, paper boy ◆ **le ~ du message** the bearer of the message ◆ **il arriva ~ d'une lettre/d'une nouvelle alarmante** he came bearing *ou* with a letter/an alarming piece of news ◆ **il était ~ de faux papiers** he was carrying forged papers ◆ **être ~ d'espoir** to bring hope ◆ **le ~ du ballon** the person with the ball *ou* who has (possession of) the ball ◆ **payable au ~** payable to bearer ◆ **les petits/gros ~s** *(Fin)* small/big shareholders

2 *(Méd)* carrier ◆ ~ **de germes** germ carrier ◆ ~ **sain** carrier ◆ **il est ~ du virus** he is carrying the virus

porte-vélos /pɔʀtəvelo/ **NM INV** bicycle rack

porte-voix /pɔʀtəvwa/ **NM INV** megaphone; *(électrique)* loudhailer ◆ **mettre ses mains en ~** to cup one's hands round one's mouth ◆ **il était le ~ des SDF** he spoke out on behalf of the homeless

portfolio /pɔʀtfɔljo/ **NM** *[de gravures, photographies]* portfolio

portier /pɔʀtje/ **NM** 1 *(= garde)* porter, commissionaire *(Brit, Can)* ◆ **(frère)** ~ *(Rel)* porter ◆ ~ **de nuit** night porter ◆ ~ **électronique** entrance intercom, entry phone 2 *(Ftbl)* goalkeeper

portière /pɔʀtjɛʀ/ **NF** 1 *(= porte)* door 2 *(= rideau)* portiere 3 *(Rel)* **(sœur)** ~ portress

portillon /pɔʀtijɔ̃/ **NM** gate; *[de métro]* gate, barrier ◆ ~ **automatique** (automatic) ticket barrier; → **bousculer**

portion /pɔʀsjɔ̃/ **NF** *[d'héritage]* portion, share; *[de nourriture]* portion, helping; *(= partie)* portion, section, part ◆ **fromage en ~s** cheese portions ◆ **être réduit à la ~ congrue** *(fig)* to get the smallest *ou* meanest share ◆ **bonne/mauvaise ~ de route** good/bad stretch of road

portique /pɔʀtik/ **NM** *(Archit)* portico; *(Sport)* crossbar and stands *(for holding gymnastic apparatus)*; *(= appareil de levage)* gantry ◆ ~ **électronique** *ou* **de sécurité** *ou* **de détection** *(à l'aéroport)* metal detector, diver's gate *(SPÉC)* ◆ ~ **à signaux** *(Rail)* signal gantry

Port-Louis /pɔʀlui/ **N** Port-Louis

Port Moresby /pɔʀmɔʀɛsbi/ **N** Port Moresby

Porto /pɔʀto/ **N** Oporto, Porto

porto /pɔʀto/ **NM** port (wine) ◆ **verre à ~** sherry *ou* Madeira *ou* port glass

Port of Spain /pɔʀɔfspɛjn/ **N** Port of Spain

Porto-Novo /pɔʀtonovo/ **N** Porto Novo

portoricain, e /pɔʀtɔʀikɛ̃, ɛn/ **ADJ** Puerto Rican **NM,F Portoricain(e)** Puerto Rican

Porto Rico /pɔʀtɔʀiko/ **NF** Puerto Rico

portrait /pɔʀtʀɛ/ **NM** 1 *(= peinture)* portrait; *(= photo)* photograph ◆ ~ **fidèle** good likeness ◆ ~ **de famille** family portrait ◆ ~ **de groupe** group portrait ◆ ~ **en pied/en buste** full-length/head-and-shoulders portrait ◆ **c'est tout le ~ de son père** he's the spitting image of his father ◆ **faire le ~ de qn** *(lit)* to paint sb's portrait ◆ **se faire tirer le ~*** to have one's photograph taken ◆ **se faire abîmer** *ou* **esquinter le ~*** to get one's face *ou* head bashed in* *ou* smashed in* ◆ **il t'a bien abîmé le ~ !*** he made a real mess of your face!

2 *(= description) [de personne]* portrait, description; *[de situation]* picture ◆ **faire** *ou* **brosser** *ou* **dresser le ~ de qn** to draw *ou* paint a portrait of sb, to paint a picture of sb ◆ **elle en a fait un ~ flatteur** she painted a flattering picture *ou* portrait of him ◆ **~-charge** caricature ◆ **jouer au ~** to play twenty questions ◆ ~ **chinois** *series of questions following the set pattern "if you were (an animal, a plant, a book etc), what would you be?"*

3 *(= genre)* **le ~** portraiture

portraitiste /pɔʀtʀɛtist/ **NMF** portrait painter, portraitist

portrait-robot (pl **portraits-robots**) /pɔʀtʀɛʀɔbo/ **NM** Identikit ® picture, Photofit ® (picture) ◆ **la police a diffusé** *ou* **donné le ~ du suspect** the police issued a Photofit *ou* Identikit (picture) of the suspect ◆ **faire le ~ de** *[+ criminel]* to make up a Photofit *ou* Identikit (picture) of ◆ **faire le ~ du Français moyen** to draw the profile of the average Frenchman

portraiturer /pɔʀtʀɛtyʀe/ ► conjug 1 ◄ **VT** *(lit, fig)* to portray

portuaire /pɔʀtɥɛʀ/ **ADJ** port *(épith)*, harbour *(épith) (Brit)*, harbor *(épith) (US)*

portugais, e /pɔʀtygɛ, ɛz/ **ADJ** Portuguese **NM** 1 *(= langue)* Portuguese 2 ◆ **Portugais** Portuguese **NF portugaise** 1 ◆ **Portugaise** Portuguese 2 *(= huître)* Portuguese oyster ◆ **il a les ~es ensablées*** *(= oreille)* he's as deaf as a post

Portugal /pɔʀtygal/ **NM** Portugal

Port-Vila /pɔʀvila/ **N** Port Vila

POS /peoɛs/ **NM** (abrév de **plan d'occupation des sols**) → **plan¹**

pose /poz/ **NF** 1 *(= installation) [de tableau, rideaux]* hanging, putting up; *[de tapis]* laying, putting down; *[de moquette]* fitting, laying; *[de vitre]* putting in, fixing; *[de serrure]* fitting; *[de chauffage]* installation, putting in; *[de gaz, électricité]* laying on, installation; *[de canalisations]* laying, putting in; *[de fondations, mines, voie ferrée]* laying

2 *(= attitude)* pose, posture; *(Art)* pose ◆ **garder la ~** to hold the pose ◆ **prendre une ~** to strike a pose ◆ **prendre des ~s (devant le miroir)** to pose (in front of the mirror) ◆ **faire prendre une ~ à qn** to pose sb

3 *(Photo = vue)* exposure ◆ **un film (de) 36 ~s** a 36-exposure film ◆ **déterminer le temps de ~** to decide on the exposure (time) ◆ **indice de ~** exposure index ◆ **mettre le bouton sur ~** to set the button to time exposure ◆ **prendre une photo en ~** *ou* **à la ~** to take a photo in time exposure

4 *(= affectation)* posing, pretension

posé, e /poze/ (ptp de **poser**) **ADJ** 1 *(= pondéré) [personne]* level-headed ◆ **d'un ton ~ mais ferme** calmly but firmly 2 *(Mus)* **bien/mal ~** *[voix]* steady/unsteady

Poséidon /poseidɔ̃/ **NM** Poseidon

posément /pozemɑ̃/ **ADV** *[parler]* calmly, deliberately; *[agir]* calmly, unhurriedly

posemètre /pozmɛtʀ/ **NM** exposure meter

poser /poze/ ► conjug 1 ◄ **VT** 1 *(= placer) [+ objet]* to put down, to lay down, to set down; *(debout)* to stand (up), to put (up) ◆ ~ **son manteau/chapeau** *(= ôter)* to take off one's coat/hat ◆ ~ **qch sur une table/par terre** to put sth (down) on the table/on the floor ◆ ~ **sa main/tête sur l'épaule de qn** to put *ou* lay one's hand/head on sb's shoulder ◆ ~ **sa tête sur l'oreiller** to lay one's head on the pillow ◆ ~ **une échelle contre un mur** to lean *ou* stand *ou* put (up) a ladder against a wall ◆ **où ai-je posé mes lunettes ?** where have I put my glasses? ◆ **pose ton journal et viens à table** put your paper down and come and have your dinner ◆ **il a posé son regard** *ou* **les yeux sur elle** he looked at her, his gaze came to rest on her ◆ **le pilote posa son avion en douceur** the pilot brought his plane down *ou* landed his plane gently ◆ ~ **la voix de qn** *(Mus)* to train sb's voice

2 *(= installer) [+ tableau, rideaux]* to hang, to put up; *[+ antenne]* to put up; *[+ tapis, carrelage]* to lay, to put down; *[+ moquette]* to fit, to lay; *[+ vitre]* to put in; *[+ serrure]* to fit; *[+ chauffage]* to put in, to install *(Brit)*, to instal *(US)*; *[+ gaz, électricité]* to lay on, to install *(Brit)*, to instal *(US)*; *[+ canalisations]* to lay, to put in; *[+ fondations, mines, voie ferrée]* to lay; *[+ bombe]* to plant ◆ ~ **la première pierre** *(lit, fig)* to lay the foundation stone ◆ ~ **des étagères au mur** to put up some shelves; → **jalon**

3 *[+ opération, chiffres]* to write, to set down ◆ **je pose 4 et je retiens 3** (I) put down 4 and carry 3, 4 and 3 to carry

4 *(= énoncer) [+ principe, condition]* to lay *ou* set down, to set out; *[+ question]* to ask; *(à un examen)* to set; *[+ devinette]* to set, to ask ◆ ~ **sa candidature à un poste** to apply for a post, to put in *ou* submit an application for a post ◆ ~ **sa candidature** *(Pol)* to put o.s. up *ou* run *(US)* for election ◆ **dire cela, c'est** ~ **que ...** in saying that, one is supposing that *ou* taking it for granted that ... ◆ **ceci posé** supposing that this is (*ou* was *etc*) the case, assuming this to be the case ◆ **posons que ...** let us suppose *ou* assume *ou* take it that ...; → **problème, question**

5 *(= demander)* ~ **des jours de congé** to put in a request for leave

6 ◆ ~ **qn** *(= lui donner de l'importance)* to give standing to sb; *(professionnellement)* to establish sb's reputation ◆ **voilà ce qui pose un homme** that's what sets a man up ◆ **avoir un frère ministre, ça vous pose !*** having a brother who's a cabinet minister really makes people look up to you! *ou* gives you real status! ◆ **une maison comme ça, ça (vous) pose*** with a house like that people really think you're somebody

VI 1 *(Art, Photo)* to pose, to sit *(pour* for); *(= chercher à se faire remarquer)* to swank *(Brit)*, to show off, to put on airs ◆ ~ **pour la postérité** *(hum)* to pose for posterity ◆ ~ **pour la galerie** *(fig)* to play to the gallery ◆ **faire** ~ **qn*** *(= faire attendre)* to keep sb hanging about* *ou* around*

2 ◆ ~ **à** *(= jouer à)* ~ **au grand patron/à l'artiste** to play *ou* act *ou* come* the big businessman/the artist, to pretend to be a big businessman/an artist ◆ ~ **au martyr** to play the martyr

3 *(Constr)* ~ **sur** *[poutre]* to bear *ou* rest on, to be supported by

VPR se poser 1 *[insecte, oiseau]* to land, to settle *(sur* on); *[avion]* to land; *[regard]* to (come to) rest, to settle, to fix *(sur* on); ◆ **se** ~ **en catastrophe/sur le ventre** *[avion]* to make an emergency landing/a belly-landing ◆ **son regard se posa sur la pendule** he turned his eyes to the clock, his glance fell on the clock ◆ **une main se posa soudain sur son épaule** he suddenly felt a hand on his shoulder ◆ **pose-toi là*** sit down here

2 *[question, problème]* to come up, to crop up, to arise; → aussi **problème, question**

3 *(= se présenter)* **se** ~ **en chef/en expert** to pass o.s. off as *ou* pose as a leader/an expert ◆ **se** ~ **comme victime** to pretend *ou* claim to be a victim ◆ **se** ~ **en défenseur des droits de l'homme** to claim to be a defender of human rights

4 *(* : locutions)* **comme menteur, vous vous posez (un peu) là !** you're a terrible *ou* an awful liar! ◆ **comme erreur, ça se posait (un peu) là !** that was some mistake! *ou* some blunder!* ◆ **tu as vu leur chien/père ? – il se pose là !** have you seen their dog/father? – it's/he's enormous! *ou* huge! *ou* massive!

poseur, -euse /pozœʀ, øz/ **ADJ** affected **NM,F** 1 *(péj)* show-off, poseur 2 *(= ouvrier)* ~ **de carrelage/de tuyaux** tile/pipe layer ◆ ~ **d'affiches** billposter, billsticker *(Brit)* ◆ ~ **de bombes** terrorist *(who plants bombs)*

posidonie /pozidɔni/ **NF** Posidonia (oceanica)

positif, -ive /pozitif, iv/ **ADJ** *(gén, Ling, Sci)* positive; *[cuti]* positive; *[fait, preuve]* positive, definite; *[personne, esprit]* pragmatic, down-to-earth; *[action, idée]* positive, constructive; *[avantage]* positive, real ◆ **Rhésus** ~ *(sang)* Rhesus positive **NM** 1 *(= réel)* positive, concrete ◆ **je veux du** ~ ! I want something positive! 2 *(Mus) (= clavier d'un orgue)* choir organ *(division of organ)*; *(= instrument)* positive organ 3 *(Photo)* positive 4 *(Ling)* positive (degree) ◆ **au** ~ in the positive (form)

position /pozisjɔ̃/ **NF** 1 *(gén = emplacement)* position; *[de navire]* bearings, position ◆ ~ **de défense/fortifiée** defensive/fortified position ◆ **rester sur ses ~s** *(lit)* to stand one's ground ◆ **rester** *ou* **camper sur ses ~s** *(fig)* to stand one's ground, to stick to one's guns *ou* line ◆ **abandonner ses ~s** to retreat, to abandon one's position, to withdraw ◆ **avoir une** ~ **de repli** *(Mil, fig)* to have a fallback position ◆ **la ville jouit d'une** ~ **idéale** the town is ideally situated ◆ **les joueurs ont changé de** ~ the players have changed position(s) ◆ **être en première/seconde** ~ *(dans une course)* to be in the lead/in second place; *(sur une liste)* to be at the top of/second on the list ◆ **être en dernière** ~ *(dans une course)* to be last, to bring up the rear; *(sur une liste)* to be at the bottom *ou* end of the list ◆ **arriver en première/deuxième/dernière** ~ to come first/second/last ◆ **en première** ~, **Banjo** *(dans une course)* (and it's) Banjo leading *ou* in the lead ◆ **syllabe en** ~ **forte/faible** *(Ling)* stressed/unstressed syllable, syllable in (a) stressed/(an) unstressed position ◆ **voyelle en** ~ **forte/faible** *(Ling)* stressed *ou* strong/unstressed *ou* weak vowel; → **feu¹, guerre**

2 *(= posture)* position ◆ **dormir dans une mauvaise** ~ to sleep in the wrong position *ou* in an awkward position ◆ **être assis/couché dans une mauvaise** ~ to be sitting/lying in an awkward position ◆ **se mettre en** ~ *(Mil, gén)* to take up (one's) position(s), to get into position ◆ **en** ~ ! (get to your) positions! ◆ **en** ~ **de combat** in a fighting position ◆ **en** ~ **allongée/assise/verticale** in a reclining/sitting/vertical *ou* upright position ◆ **la** ~ **du missionnaire** the missionary position

3 *(= situation)* position, situation; *(dans la société)* position ◆ **être dans une** ~ **délicate/fausse** to be in a difficult *ou* an awkward/in a false position ◆ **être en** ~ **de force pour négocier** to be bargaining from a position of strength ◆ **être en** ~ **de faire qch** to be in a position to do sth ◆ **dans sa** ~ **il ne peut se permettre une incartade** a man in his position dare not commit an indiscretion ◆ **il occupe une** ~ **importante** he holds an important position

4 *(= attitude)* position, stance ◆ **le gouvernement doit définir sa** ~ **sur cette question** the government must make its position *ou* stance on this question clear ◆ **prendre** ~ to take a stand, to declare o.s. ◆ **prendre (fermement)** ~ **en faveur de qch** to come down (strongly) in favour of sth ◆ **prise de** ~ stand ◆ **sa politique est en contradiction avec ses prises de** ~ his policy is at odds with the stands that he takes ◆ **revoir sa** ~ to review one's position

5 *[de compte bancaire]* position, balance ◆ **demander sa** ~ to ask for the balance of one's account

6 *(Bourse)* position ◆ ~ **acheteur/vendeur** bull *ou* long/bear *ou* short position

positionnement /pozisjɔnmɑ̃/ **NM** *[d'objet, produit, entreprise]* positioning ◆ ~ **avant/arrière** *(en avion)* nose out/in positioning

positionner /pozisjɔne/ ▸ conjug 1 ◂ **VT** 1 *(= placer)* to position 2 *(= repérer) [+ navire, troupes]* to locate 3 *[+ compte bancaire]* to establish the position *ou* balance of **VPR se positionner** *(gén)* to position o.s.; *[troupe]* to take up (one's) position, to get into position; *(dans un débat)* to take a stand ◆ **comment se positionne ce produit sur le marché ?** what slot does this product fill in the market? ◆ **comment vous positionnez-vous dans ce débat ?** what's your position *ou* stand in this debate?

positivement /pozitivmɑ̃/ **ADV** *(gén, Sci)* positively ◆ **je ne le sais pas** ~ I'm not positive about it

positiver /pozitive/ ▸ conjug 1 ◂ **VT** ◆ ~ **son angoisse/son stress** to channel one's anxiety/one's stress ◆ **essayez de** ~ **votre choix** try to concentrate on the positive aspects *ou* the plus side of your decision ◆ **ils essaient de** ~ **l'opinion des employés envers les cadres** they're trying to get the workers to have a more positive attitude towards *ou* to be more favourably disposed towards management **VI** to think positive, to look on the bright side (of things)

positivisme /pozitivism/ **NM** positivism

positiviste /pozitivist/ **ADJ, NMF** positivist

positivité /pozitivite/ **NF** positivity

positon /pozitɔ̃/, **positron** /pozitʀɔ̃/ **NM** positron

posologie /pozɔlɔʒi/ **NF** *(= étude)* posology; *(= indications)* directions for use, dosage

possédant, e /pɔsedɑ̃, ɑ̃t/ **ADJ** propertied, wealthy **NM** ◆ **les ~s** the wealthy, the rich

possédé, e /pɔsede/ (ptp de **posséder**) **ADJ** possessed *(de* by); ◆ ~ **du démon** possessed by the devil **NM,F** person possessed ◆ **crier comme un** ~ to cry like one possessed

posséder /pɔsede/ ▸ conjug 6 ◂ **VT** 1 *[+ bien, maison, fortune]* to possess, to own, to have ◆ **c'est tout ce que je possède** it's all I possess *ou* all I've got ◆ ~ **une femme** † to possess a woman ◆ **pour** ~ **le cœur d'une femme** to capture a woman's heart

2 *[+ caractéristique, qualité, territoire]* to have, to possess; *[+ expérience]* to have (had); *[+ diplôme, titre]* to have, to hold ◆ **cette maison possède une vue magnifique/deux entrées** this house has a magnificent view/two entrances ◆ **il croit** ~ **la vérité** he believes that he possesses the truth

3 *(= bien connaître) [+ métier]* to have a thorough knowledge of, to know inside out; *[+ technique]* to have mastered; *[+ langue]* to have a good command of ◆ **elle possède parfaitement l'anglais** she has a perfect command of English ◆ ~ **la clé de l'énigme** to possess *ou* have the key to the mystery ◆ **bien** ~ **son rôle** to be really on top of *ou* into* one's role *ou* part

4 *(= égarer) [démon]* to possess ◆ **la fureur/jalousie le possède** he is beside himself with *ou* he is overcome *ou* consumed with rage/jealousy ◆ **quel démon** *ou* **quelle rage te possède ?** what's got into you?*, what's come over you?; → **possédé**

5 *(* = duper)* ~ **qn** to take sb in* ◆ **se faire** ~ to be taken in*, to be had*

VPR **se posséder** ◆ **elle ne se possédait plus de joie** she was beside herself *ou* was overcome with joy ◆ **lorsqu'il est en colère, il ne se possède pas** when he's angry he loses all self-control *ou* all control of himself

possesseur /pɔsesœʀ/ **NM** *[de bien]* possessor, owner; *[de diplôme, titre, secret]* holder, possessor; *[de billet de loterie]* holder ◆ **être ~ de** *[+ objet]* to have; *[+ diplôme]* to hold; *[+ secret]* to possess, to have

possessif, -ive /pɔsesif, iv/ **ADJ** *(gén, Ling)* possessive **NM** *(Ling)* possessive

possession /pɔsesjɔ̃/ **NF** 1 *(= fait de posséder) [de bien]* possession, ownership; *[de diplôme, titre]* holding, possession; *[de billet de loterie]* holding ◆ **la ~ d'une arme/de cet avantage le rendait confiant** having a weapon/this advantage made him feel confident ◆ **~ vaut titre** possession amounts to title ◆ **prendre ~ de, entrer en ~ de** *[+ fonction]* to take up; *[+ bien, héritage]* to take possession of, to enter into possession of; *[+ appartement]* to take possession of; *[+ voiture]* to take delivery of ◆ **à la prise de ~ des terres** when he *(ou* they *etc)* took possession of the land

◆ **en + possession** ◆ **avoir qch en sa ~** to have sth in one's possession ◆ **être en ~ de qch** to be in possession of sth ◆ **tomber en la ~ de qn** to come into sb's possession ◆ **être en ~ de toutes ses facultés** to be in possession of all one's faculties ◆ **il était en pleine ~ de ses moyens** he was in full possession of his faculties ◆ **entrer en ~ de** to take possession of; *[+ voiture]* to take delivery of

2 *(= chose possédée)* possession ◆ **nos ~s à l'étranger** our overseas possessions

3 *(= maîtrise)* **~ de soi** self-control ◆ **reprendre ~ de soi-même** to regain one's self-control *ou* one's composure

4 *(= connaissance) [de langue]* command, mastery

5 *(Rel = envoûtement)* possession

possessivité /pɔsesivite/ **NF** possessiveness

possibilité /pɔsibilite/ GRAMMAIRE ACTIVE 43.3 **NF** *(gén)* possibility ◆ **~ non nulle** *(Stat)* non-zero probability ◆ **il y a plusieurs ~s** there are several possibilities ◆ **je ne vois pas d'autre ~ (que de ...)** I don't see any other possibility (than to ...) ◆ **ai-je la ~ de faire du feu/de parler librement ?** is it possible for me to light a fire/to speak freely? ◆ **~s** *(= moyens)* means; *(= potentiel)* possibilities, potential ◆ **quelles sont vos ~s financières ?** how much money can you put up?, what is your financial situation? ◆ **quelles sont vos ~s de logement ?** how many people can you accommodate? *ou* put up? ◆ **les ~s d'une découverte/d'un pays neuf** the possibilities *ou* potential of a discovery/of a new country ◆ **~ (de réalisation)** *[d'entreprise, projet]* feasibility

possible /pɔsibl/ GRAMMAIRE ACTIVE 31, 36.1, 42.3, 43.3

ADJ 1 *(= faisable) [solution]* possible; *[projet, entreprise]* feasible ◆ **il est ~/il n'est pas ~ de ...** it is possible/impossible to ... ◆ **nous avons fait tout ce qu'il était humainement ~ de faire** we've done everything that was humanly possible ◆ **lui serait-il ~ d'arriver plus tôt ?** could he possibly *ou* would it be possible for him to come earlier? ◆ **arrivez tôt si (c'est) ~** arrive early if possible *ou* if you can ◆ **c'est parfaitement ~** it's perfectly possible *ou* feasible ◆ **ce n'est pas ~ autrement** there's no other way, otherwise it's impossible ◆ **il n'est pas ~ qu'il soit aussi bête qu'il en a l'air** he can't possibly be as stupid as he looks ◆ **c'est dans les choses ~s** it's a possibility ◆ **la paix a rendu ~ leur rencontre** peace has made a meeting between them possible *ou* has made it possible for them to meet

2 *(= éventuel) (gén)* possible; *[danger]* possible, potential ◆ **une erreur est toujours ~** a mistake is always possible ◆ **il est ~ qu'il vienne/qu'il ne vienne pas** he may *ou* might come/not come, it's possible (that) he'll come/he won't come ◆ **il est bien ~ qu'il se soit perdu en route** he may very well have *ou* it could well be *ou* it's quite possible that he has lost his way ◆ **c'est (bien) ~/très ~** possibly/very possibly ◆ **son ~ retour sur la scène politique** his possible return to the political stage

3 *(= indiquant une limite)* possible ◆ **dans le meilleur des mondes ~s** in the best of all possible worlds ◆ **il a essayé tous les moyens ~s** he tried every possible means *ou* every means possible ◆ **il a eu toutes les difficultés ~s et imaginables à obtenir un visa** he had all kinds of problems getting a visa, he had every possible *ou* conceivable difficulty getting a visa ◆ **venez aussi vite/aussitôt que ~** come as quickly as possible *ou* as you (possibly) can/as soon as possible *ou* as you (possibly) can ◆ **venez le plus longtemps ~** come for as long as you (possibly) can ◆ **venez le plus vite/tôt ~** come as quickly/as soon as you (possibly) can ◆ **il sort le plus (souvent)/le moins (souvent) ~** he goes out as often/as little as possible *ou* as he can ◆ **il a acheté la valise la plus légère ~** he bought the lightest possible suitcase *ou* the lightest suitcase possible ◆ **le plus grand nombre ~ de personnes** as many people as possible, the greatest possible number of people; → **autant**

4 *(* : nég = acceptable)* **cette situation n'est plus ~** the situation has become impossible ◆ **il n'est pas ~ de travailler dans ce bruit** it just isn't possible *ou* it's (quite) impossible to work in this noise ◆ **un bruit/une puanteur pas ~*** an incredible racket*/stink* ◆ **il est d'une méchanceté pas ~*** he's incredibly *ou* unbelievably nasty

5 *(locutions)* **est-ce ~ !** I don't believe it! ◆ **c'est pas ~ !*** *(faux)* that can't be true! *ou* right!; *(étonnant)* well I never! *; *(irréalisable)* it's out of the question!, it's impossible! ◆ **ce n'est pas ~ d'être aussi bête !** how can anyone be so stupid!, how stupid can you get! * ◆ **elle voudrait vous parler – c'est (bien) ~, mais il faut que je parte** she'd like a word with you – that's as may be, but I've got to go ◆ **il devrait se reposer ! – c'est (bien) ~, mais il n'a pas le temps** he ought to take a rest! – maybe (he should), but he's too busy

NM ◆ **faire reculer les limites du ~** to push back the frontiers of what is possible *ou* of the possible ◆ **essayons, dans les limites du ~, de ...** let's try, as far as possible, to ... ◆ **c'est dans le domaine** *ou* **dans les limites du ~** it's within the realms of possibility ◆ **faire (tout) son ~** to do one's utmost *ou* one's best, to do all one can *(pour* to; *pour que* to make sure that); ◆ **il a été grossier/aimable au ~** he couldn't have been ruder/nicer (if he'd tried), he was as rude/nice as it's possible to be ◆ **c'est énervant au ~** it's extremely annoying; → **mesure**

possiblement /pɔsibləmɑ̃/ **ADV** possibly

post- /pɔst/ **PRÉF** post- ◆ **~électoral/-surréaliste** post-election *(épith)*/-surrealist ◆ **grossesse ~ménopausique** post-menopausal pregnancy ◆ **~baccalauréat** *[formation, classe, enseignement]* post-baccalauréat

postal, e (mpl **-aux**) /pɔstal, o/ **ADJ** *[service, taxe, voiture]* postal, mail; *[train, avion]* mail; *[colis]* sent by post *ou* mail ◆ **sac ~** postbag, mailbag; → **car¹, carte, chèque, code, franchise**

postcolonial, e (pl **-iaux**) /pɔstkɔlɔnjal, jo/ **ADJ** postcolonial

postcommunisme /pɔstkɔmynism/ **NM** post-communism

postcommuniste /pɔstkɔmynist/ **ADJ** *[ère]* postcommunist

postcure /pɔstkyʀ/ **NF** aftercare

postdater /pɔstdate/ ► conjug 1 ◄ **VT** to postdate

postdoctoral, e (mpl **-aux**) /pɔstdɔktɔʀal, o/ **ADJ** postdoctoral

poste¹ /pɔst/ **NF** 1 *(= administration, bureau)* post office ◆ **employé/ingénieur des ~s** post office worker/engineer ◆ **les Postes et Télécommunications, les Postes, Télécommunications et Télédiffusion** † *French post office and telecommunications service* ◆ **la grande ~, la ~ principale, le bureau de ~ principal** the main *ou* head post office 2 *(= service postal)* mail, post *(surtout Brit)*, postal *ou* mail service ◆ **envoyer qch par la ~** to send sth by post *ou* mail ◆ **mettre une lettre à la ~** to post *ou* mail a letter; → **cachet** 3 *(Hist)* post ◆ **maître de ~** postmaster ◆ **cheval de ~** post horse ◆ **courir la ~** to go posthaste; → **chaise, voiture**

COMP **poste aérienne** airmail
poste auxiliaire sub post office
poste restante poste restante *(Brit)*, general delivery *(US)*

poste² /pɔst/ GRAMMAIRE ACTIVE 54.2, 54.4, 54.7, 46

NM 1 *(= emplacement)* post ◆ **~ de douane** customs post ◆ **être/rester à son ~** to be/stay at one's post ◆ **mourir à son ~** to die at one's post ◆ **à vos ~s !** to your stations! *ou* posts! ◆ **à vos ~s de combat !** action stations! ◆ **toujours fidèle au ~ ?** *(hum)* still manning the fort?

2 *(Police)* **~ (de police)** (police) station ◆ **conduire** *ou* **emmener qn au ~** to take sb to the police station ◆ **il a passé la nuit au ~** he spent the night in the cells

3 *(= emploi) (gén)* job; *[de fonctionnaire]* post, appointment *(frm)*; *(dans une hiérarchie)* position; *(= nomination)* appointment ◆ **être en ~ à l'étranger** to hold an appointment *ou* a post abroad ◆ **il a trouvé un ~ de bibliothécaire** he has found a post *ou* job as a librarian ◆ **il a un ~ de professeur/en fac** he is a teacher/a university lecturer ◆ **la liste des ~s vacants** the list of positions available *ou* of unfilled appointments ◆ **~ d'enseignant** teaching position *ou* post *ou* job

4 *(Radio, TV)* set ◆ **~ émetteur/récepteur** transmitting/receiving set, transmitter/receiver ◆ **~ de radio/de télévision** radio/television (set) ◆ **ils l'ont dit au ~*** *(à la radio)* they said so on the radio; *(à la télévision)* they said so on the TV *ou* the box* *(Brit)*

5 *(Téléc = ligne)* extension

6 *(Fin = opération)* item, entry; *[de budget]* item, element

7 *(= période de travail)* shift ◆ **~ de huit heures** eight-hour shift

COMP **poste d'aiguillage** *(Rail)* signal box
poste avancé *(Mil)* advanced post
poste budgétaire budget item
poste de commande position of responsibility ◆ **ceux qui sont aux ~s de commande du pays** those at the helm of the country, the country's leaders
poste de commandement headquarters
poste de contrôle checkpoint
poste d'équipage *[de bateau]* crew's quarters
poste d'essence filling station, petrol *(Brit)* *ou* gas *(US)* station
poste frontière border *ou* frontier post
poste de garde *(Mil)* guardroom
poste d'incendie fire point
poste de lavage *(= lave-auto)* car wash
poste d'observation observation post
poste de pilotage cockpit
poste de police *(Police)* police station; *(Mil)* guard-room, guardhouse
poste de secours first-aid post
poste téléphonique telephone
poste de travail *(Ordin)* work station; *(= emplacement)* post; *(= emploi)* job, post

posté, e /pɔste/ (ptp de **poster**) ADJ ◆ **travail/travailleur ~** shift work/worker

poster¹ /pɔste/ ▸ conjug 1 ◂ VT 1 *[+ lettre]* to post *(surtout Brit)*, to mail *(surtout US)* 2 *[+ sentinelle]* to post, to station VPR **se poster** to take up (a) position, to position o.s., to station o.s.

poster² /pɔstɛʀ/ NM poster

postérieur, e /pɔsteʀjœʀ/ ADJ *(dans le temps) [date, document]* later; *[événement]* subsequent, later; *(dans l'espace) [partie]* back, posterior *(frm)*; *[membre]* hind, rear, back; *[voyelle]* back ◆ **ce document est légèrement/très ~ à cette date** this document dates from slightly later/much later ◆ **l'événement est ~ à 1850** the event took place later than *ou* after 1850 ◆ **~ à 1800** after 1800 NM * behind *, rear, posterior *(hum)*

postérieurement /pɔsteʀjœʀmɑ̃/ ADV later, subsequently ◆ **~ à** after

posteriori /pɔsteʀjɔʀi/ → **a posteriori**

postériorité /pɔsteʀjɔʀite/ NF posteriority

postérité /pɔsteʀite/ NF *(= descendants)* descendants; *(= avenir)* posterity ◆ **mourir sans ~** *(frm)* to die without issue ◆ **être jugé par la ~** to be judged by posterity ◆ **entrer dans la ~, passer à la ~** to go down in history

postface /pɔstfas/ NF postscript, postface

postglaciaire /pɔstglasjɛʀ/ ADJ postglacial

posthume /pɔstym/ ADJ posthumous ◆ **à titre ~** posthumously

postiche /pɔstiʃ/ ADJ *[cheveux, moustache]* false; *[ornement, fioriture]* postiche, superadded; *[sentiment]* fake; *(Ling) [élément, symbole]* dummy NM *(pour homme)* toupee; *(pour femme)* hairpiece, postiche

postier, -ière /pɔstje, jɛʀ/ NM,F post office worker ◆ **grève des ~s** postal strike

postillon /pɔstijɔ̃/ NM 1 *(* = salive)* sputter ◆ **envoyer des ~s** to sputter, to splutter 2 *(Hist = cocher)* postilion

postillonner * /pɔstijɔne/ ▸ conjug 1 ◂ VI to sputter, to splutter

postimpressionnisme /pɔstɛ̃pʀesjɔnism/ NM postimpressionism

postimpressionniste /pɔstɛ̃pʀesjɔnist/ ADJ, NMF postimpressionist

post(-)industriel, -elle /pɔstɛ̃dystʀijɛl/ ADJ post-industrial

Post-it ® /pɔstit/ NM INV Post-it ®

postmoderne /pɔstmɔdɛʀn/ ADJ postmodern

postmodernisme /pɔstmɔdɛʀnism/ NM postmodernism

post mortem /pɔstmɔʀtɛm/ LOC ADJ *[prélèvement, examen]* post-mortem

postnatal, e (mpl **postnatals**) /pɔstnatal/ ADJ postnatal

postopératoire /pɔstɔpeʀatwaʀ/ ADJ postoperative

postposer /pɔstpoze/ ▸ conjug 1 ◂ VT to place after the verb (*ou* noun etc) ◆ **sujet postposé** postpositive subject, subject placed after the verb

postposition /pɔstpozisjɔ̃/ NF postposition ◆ **verbe à ~** phrasal verb

postprandial, e (mpl **-iaux**) /pɔstpʀɑ̃djal, jo/ ADJ postprandial

post-production, postproduction /pɔstpʀɔdyksjɔ̃/ NF *(Ciné)* postproduction

postscolaire /pɔstskɔlɛʀ/ ADJ *[enseignement]* further *(épith)*, continuing *(épith)*

post-scriptum /pɔstskʀiptɔm/ NM INV postscript

postsonorisation /pɔstsɔnɔʀizasjɔ̃/ NF dubbing

postsonoriser /pɔstsɔnɔʀize/ ▸ conjug 1 ◂ VT to dub

postsynchronisation /pɔstsɛ̃kʀɔnizasjɔ̃/ NF *(Ciné)* dubbing

postsynchroniser /pɔstsɛ̃kʀɔnize/ ▸ conjug 1 ◂ VT *(Ciné)* to dub

postulant, e /pɔstylɑ̃, ɑ̃t/ NM,F applicant; *(Rel)* postulant

postulat /pɔstyla/ NM premise; *(Philos)* postulate ◆ **~ de base** *ou* **de départ** basic premise ◆ **partant du ~ que ...** starting from the premise that ...

postuler /pɔstyle/ ▸ conjug 1 ◂ VT 1 *[+ emploi]* to apply for, to put in for 2 *[+ principe]* to postulate VI 1 ◆ **~ à** *ou* **pour un emploi** to apply for a job 2 *(Jur)* **~ pour** to represent

posture /pɔstyʀ/ NF posture, position ◆ **être en bonne ~** to be in a good position ◆ **être en très mauvaise ~** to be in a really bad position *ou* a tight corner ◆ **en ~ de faire qch** † *(littér)* in a position to do sth

pot /po/ NM 1 *(= récipient) (en verre)* jar; *(en terre)* pot; *(en métal)* can, tin *(Brit)*, pot; *(en carton)* carton ◆ **petit ~ (pour bébé)** jar of baby food ◆ **il ne mange encore que des petits ~s** all he eats at the moment is baby food ◆ **~ à confiture** jamjar, jampot *(Brit)* ◆ **~ de confiture** jar *ou* pot *(Brit)* of jam ◆ **mettre en ~** *[+ fleur]* to pot; *[+ confiture]* to put in jars, to pot *(Brit)* ◆ **plantes en ~** pot plants ◆ **mettre un enfant sur le ~** to put a child on the potty ◆ **tourner autour du ~** *(fig)* to beat about *ou* around the bush; → **cuiller, découvrir, fortune** *etc*

2 * *(= boisson)* drink; *(= réunion)* drinks party ◆ **~ d'adieu** farewell party ◆ **~ de départ** *(à la retraite etc)* leaving party *ou* do * *(Brit)* ◆ **tu viens prendre** *ou* **boire un ~ ?** * are you coming for a drink?

3 *(* = chance)* luck ◆ **avoir du ~** to be lucky ◆ **tu as du ~ !** some people have all the luck!, you're a lucky beggar! * ◆ **t'as du ~, il est encore là** you're lucky *ou* in luck, he's still here ◆ **je n'ai jamais eu de ~ dans la vie/avec les hommes** I've always been unlucky *ou* I've never had any luck in life/with men ◆ **manquer de ~** to be unlucky *ou* out of luck ◆ **pas de** *ou* **manque de ~ !** just his (*ou* your *etc*) luck! ◆ **c'est un vrai coup de ~ !** what a stroke of luck!

4 *(Cartes) (= enjeu)* kitty; *(= restant)* pile

5 ◆ **plein ~** * **rouler plein ~** to drive flat out * ◆ **payer plein ~** to pay the full whack *

COMP **pot à bière** *(en verre)* beer mug; *(en terre ou en métal)* tankard

pot catalytique catalytic converter

pot de chambre chamber pot

pot de colle *(lit)* pot of glue; *(péj = crampon)* leech ◆ **il est du genre ~ de colle !** you just can't shake him off!, he sticks like a leech!

pot commun kitty

pot à eau *(pour se laver)* water jug, pitcher; *(pour boire)* water jug

pot d'échappement exhaust pipe; *(silencieux)* silencer *(Brit)*, muffler *(US)*

pot de fleurs *(= récipient)* plant pot, flowerpot; *(= fleurs)* pot plant ◆ **elle fait un peu ~ de fleurs** *(péj ou hum)* she just sits there and looks pretty

pot à lait *(pour transporter)* milk can; *(sur la table)* milk jug

pot(-)au(-)noir *(Naut)* doldrums

pot de peinture can *ou* pot *ou* tin *(Brit)* of paint ◆ **c'est un vrai ~ de peinture** * *(péj)* she wears far too much make-up, she plasters herself with make-up *

pot à tabac *(lit)* tobacco jar; *(† fig)* dumpy little person

pot de terre earthenware pot ◆ **un particulier qui se bat contre l'administration, c'est le ~ de terre contre le ~ de fer** one individual struggling against the authorities can't hope to win

pot de yaourt *(en verre)* pot of yoghurt; *(en carton)* carton *ou* pot of yoghurt

potabilité /pɔtabilite/ NF *[d'eau]* drinkability, potability *(SPÉC)*

potable /pɔtabl/ ADJ *(lit)* drinkable, potable *(frm)*; *(* = acceptable)* passable, decent ◆ **eau ~** drinking water ◆ **eau non ~** water which is not for drinking, non-drinking water ◆ **il ne peut pas faire un travail ~** he can't do a decent piece of work ◆ **le film est ~** the film isn't bad ◆ **ce travail est tout juste ~** this piece of work is barely passable *ou* acceptable

potache * /pɔtaʃ/ NM schoolboy, schoolkid * ◆ **plaisanteries (de) ~** schoolboy pranks

potage /pɔtaʒ/ NM soup ◆ **être dans le ~** * *(mal réveillé)* to be in a daze; *(désorienté)* to be in a muddle; *(en mauvaise posture)* to be in the soup *

potager, -ère /pɔtaʒe, ɛʀ/ ADJ *[plante]* edible ◆ **jardin ~** kitchen *ou* vegetable garden NM 1 *(= jardin)* kitchen *ou* vegetable garden 2 *(Helv = cuisinière)* cooker

potasse /pɔtas/ NF *(= hydroxide)* potassium hydroxide, caustic potash; *(= carbonate)* potash *(impure potassium carbonate)*

potasser * /pɔtase/ ▸ conjug 1 ◂ VT *[+ livre, discours, examen]* to cram *ou* bone up * *ou* swot up * *(Brit)* for; *[+ sujet]* to bone up (on) *, to swot up (on) * *(Brit)* VI to cram, to swot * *(Brit)*

potassique /pɔtasik/ ADJ potassic

potassium /pɔtasjɔm/ NM potassium

pot-au-feu /pɔtofø/ NM INV *(= plat)* boiled beef with vegetables; *(= viande)* stewing beef ◆ **~ de la mer** assorted boiled fish

pot-de-vin (pl **pots-de-vin**) /pod(ə)vɛ̃/ NM bribe, backhander * *(Brit)*, payola *(US)* ◆ **donner un ~ à qn** to bribe sb, to grease sb's palm, to give sb a backhander * *(Brit)*

pote * /pɔt/ NM pal *, mate * *(Brit)*, buddy * *(US)* ◆ **salut, mon ~ !** hi there! *

poteau (pl **poteaux**) /pɔto/ NM 1 *(= pilier)* post ◆ **rester au ~** *(Courses)* to be left at the (starting) post ◆ **elle a les jambes comme des ~x** * she's got legs like tree trunks * 2 ◆ **~ (d'exécution)** execution post, stake *(for execution by shooting)* ◆ **envoyer au ~** to sentence to execution by firing squad ◆ **au ~ !** lynch him!, string him up! * ◆ **le directeur au ~ !** down with the boss! 3 *(† * = ami)* pal *, buddy * *(US)*

COMP **poteau d'arrivée** winning *ou* finishing post

poteau de but goal-post

poteau de départ starting post

poteau électrique electricity pole

poteau indicateur signpost

poteau télégraphique telegraph post *ou* pole

poteau de torture torture post

potée /pɔte/ NF 1 *(Culin)* ≈ hotpot *(of pork and cabbage)* 2 *(Tech)* ~ **d'étain** tin putty, putty powder

potelé, e /pɔt(ə)le/ ADJ *[enfant]* chubby; *[bras]* plump

potence /pɔtɑ̃s/ NF 1 *(= gibet)* gallows *(sg)*; → **gibier** 2 *(= support)* bracket ◆ **en ~** *(= en équerre)* L-shaped; *(= en T)* T-shaped

potentat /pɔtɑ̃ta/ NM *(lit)* potentate; *(péj)* despot

potentialiser /pɔtɑ̃sjalize/ ▸ conjug 1 ◂ VT *(Pharm)* to potentiate; *[+ mécanisme]* to maximize the potential of, to potentiate

potentialité /pɔtɑ̃sjalite/ NF potentiality

potentiel, -ielle /pɔtɑ̃sjɛl/ ADJ *[marché, risque, client]* potential NM 1 *(Sci)* potential ◆ **~ électrique** electric potential 2 *(= capacité)* potential ◆ **~ industriel/militaire/nucléaire** industrial/military/nuclear potential ◆ **ce**

candidat a un bon ~ this applicant has good potential ◆ **ce pays a un énorme ~ économique/de croissance** this country has huge economic/growth potential

potentiellement /pɔtɑ̃sjɛlmɑ̃/ ADV potentially

potentille /pɔtɑ̃tij/ NF potentilla

potentiomètre /pɔtɑ̃sjɔmɛtʀ/ NM potentiometer

poterie /pɔtʀi/ NF (= *atelier, art*) pottery; (= *objet*) piece of pottery ◆ **~s** earthenware, pieces of pottery

poterne /pɔtɛʀn/ NF postern

potiche /pɔtiʃ/ NF (large) oriental vase; (*péj* = *prête-nom*) figurehead ◆ **il ne veut pas être un juge/président** ~ he doesn't want to be a mere figurehead judge/president ◆ **elle ne veut pas jouer les ~s** she doesn't want to just sit there and look pretty

potier, -ière /pɔtje, jɛʀ/ NM,F potter

potimarron /pɔtimaʀɔ̃/ NM *variety of small pumpkin*

potin * /pɔtɛ̃/ NM 1 (= *vacarme*) din*, racket* ◆ **faire du** ~ (*lit*) to make a noise; (*fig*) to kick up a fuss* ◆ **ça va faire du** ~ (*lit*) there'll be a lot of noise, it'll be noisy; (*fig*) this is going to stir things up*, there'll be quite a rumpus (over this) 2 (= *commérage*) **~s** gossip, tittle-tattle

potiner /pɔtine/ ▸ conjug 1 ◂ VI to gossip

potion /posjɔ̃/ NF (*lit*) potion ◆ **~ magique** (*lit, fig*) magic potion; (*fig*) ◆ **~ amère** bitter pill ◆ **la ~ sera amère** it will be a bitter pill to swallow

potiron /pɔtiʀɔ̃/ NM pumpkin

pot-pourri (pl **pots-pourris**) /popuʀi/ NM (= *fleurs*) pot-pourri; (*Mus*) potpourri, medley; (*fig*) mixture, medley

potron-minet * /pɔtʀɔ̃minɛ/ **dès potron-minet** LOC ADV at the crack of dawn, at daybreak

pou (pl **poux**) /pu/ NM louse ◆ **~ du pubis** pubic louse, crab (louse)⁑ ◆ **couvert de ~x** covered in lice, lice-ridden; → **chercher, laid**

pouah /pwa/ EXCL ugh!, yuk!

poubelle /pubɛl/ NF 1 [*d'ordures*] (dust-)bin (*Brit*), trash *ou* garbage can (*US*) ◆ **descendre/sortir la** ~ to take down/put out the bin (*Brit*) *ou* the garbage (*US*) *ou* trash (*US*) ◆ **les ~s sont passées ?*** have the binmen (*Brit*) *ou* the garbage men (*US*) been? ◆ **allez, hop ! à la ~ !** right! (let's) throw it out! ◆ **jeter/mettre qch à la** ~ to throw/put sth in the (dust)bin (*Brit*) *ou* trash can (*US*) *ou* garbage can (*US*) ◆ **c'est bon à mettre à la** ~ it's only fit for the (dust)bin (*Brit*), you can put it right into the trash *ou* garbage can (*US*) ◆ **faire les ~s** to rummage through bins (*Brit*) *ou* garbage cans (*US*) ◆ **il roule dans une ~*** his car is a real tip* (*Brit*), his car is a garbage can on wheels (*US*) ◆ **ça appartient aux ~s de l'histoire** that has been consigned to the scrap heap of history

2 (*Ordin*) trash

3 (*en apposition*) **camion(-)~** bin lorry (*Brit*), garbage truck (*US*) ◆ **classe(-)~** class of rejects ◆ **chaîne(-)~** trashy* television channel ◆ **navire(-)~** coffin ship (*often transporting dangerous nuclear waste etc*) ◆ **la presse(-)~** the gutter press

COMP **poubelle de table** *container placed on a table for bones, wrappers etc*

pouce /pus/ NM 1 (*Anat*) [*de main*] thumb; [*de pied*] big toe ◆ **se tourner** *ou* **se rouler les ~s** to twiddle one's thumbs ◆ **mettre les ~s*** to give in *ou* up ◆ **~ !** (*au jeu*) truce!, pax! (*Brit*) ◆ **on a déjeuné** *ou* **on a pris un morceau sur le ~*** we had a quick snack *ou* a bite to eat* ◆ **faire du ~***, **voyager sur le** ~ (* *Can*) to thumb* a lift, to hitch*, to hitch-hike ◆ **coup de** ~ (*pour aider qn*) nudge in the right direction ◆ **donner un coup de ~ aux ventes** to give sales a bit of a boost ◆ **donner un coup de ~ à un projet** to help a project along

2 (= *mesure*) inch ◆ **ils n'ont pas cédé un ~ de terrain** (*fig*) [*armée*] they haven't yielded an inch of land ◆ **son travail n'a pas avancé d'un** ~ he hasn't made the least *ou* the slightest bit of progress in his work ◆ **il n'a pas bougé d'un** ~ (*dans sa prise de position*) he refused to budge, he wouldn't budge an inch ◆ **la situation/ville n'a pas changé d'un** ~ the situation/town hasn't changed in the slightest *ou* hasn't changed the least little bit ◆ **il n'a pas varié** *ou* **dévié d'un ~ dans sa politique** he hasn't altered his policy in the slightest ◆ **et le ~ !*** and the rest!

Poucet /pusɛ/ NM ◆ **le Petit Poucet** "Tom Thumb"

Pouchkine /puʃkin/ NM Pushkin

pouding /pudiŋ/ NM ⇒ **pudding**

poudingue /pudɛ̃g/ NM (*Géol*) pudding stone

poudre /pudʀ/ NF (*gén*) powder; (= *poussière*) dust; (= *fard*) (face) powder; (= *explosif*) (gun) powder; (*Méd*) powder; (*arg Drogue* = *héroïne*) smack⁑ ◆ **~ d'or/de diamant** gold/diamond dust ◆ **réduire qch en** ~ to reduce *ou* grind sth to powder, to powder sth ◆ **en** ~ [*lait, œufs*] dried, powdered ◆ **chocolat en** ~ cocoa powder ◆ **se mettre de la** ~ to powder one's face *ou* nose ◆ **se mettre de la ~ sur** to powder ◆ **~ libre/compacte** loose/pressed powder ◆ **prendre la ~ d'escampette*** to take to one's heels, to skedaddle* ◆ **de la ~ de perlimpinpin** magical cure ◆ **jeter de la ~ aux yeux de qn** to impress sb ◆ **c'est de la ~ aux yeux** it's all just for show; → **feu¹, inventer**

COMP **poudre à canon** gunpowder
poudre dentifrice tooth powder
poudre à éternuer sneezing powder
poudre à laver washing powder (*Brit*), soap powder (*Brit*), (powdered) laundry detergent (*US*)
poudre à lever (*surtout Helv*) baking powder
poudre à récurer scouring powder
poudre de riz face powder

poudrer /pudʀe/ ▸ conjug 1 ◂ VT to powder VI (*Can*) [*neige*] to drift VPR **se poudrer** to powder one's face *ou* nose

poudrerie¹ /pudʀəʀi/ NF (= *fabrique*) gunpowder *ou* explosives factory

poudrerie² /pudʀəʀi/ NF (*Can*) drifting snow

poudreux, -euse /pudʀø, øz/ ADJ (= *poussiéreux*) dusty ◆ **neige poudreuse** powder snow NF **poudreuse** 1 (= *neige*) powder snow 2 (= *meuble*) dressing table 3 (*Agr*) duster

poudrier /pudʀije/ NM (powder) compact

poudrière /pudʀijɛʀ/ NF powder magazine; (*fig*) powder keg (*fig*)

poudroiement /pudʀwamɑ̃/ NM dust haze

poudroyer /pudʀwaje/ ▸ conjug 8 ◂ VI [*poussière*] to rise in clouds; [*neige*] to rise in a flurry ◆ **la route poudroyait** clouds of dust rose up from the road

pouet (pouet) * /puɛt(puɛt)/ EXCL (*klaxon*) beep! beep! ◆ **t'en sais rien, alors ~ ~ !** you don't know anything about it, so just shut up!*

pouf¹ /puf/ NM pouffe EXCL thud! ◆ **faire** ~ to tumble (over) ◆ **~ par terre !** whoops-a-daisy!

pouf², pouffe ⁑ /puf/ NF (*péj*) (= *femme*) tart⁑

pouffer /pufe/ ▸ conjug 1 ◂ VI ◆ **~ (de rire)** to burst out laughing

pouf(f)iasse ⁑ /pufjas/ NF (*péj*) tart⁑, slag⁑ (*Brit*); (= *prostituée*) whore, tart⁑

pouh /pu/ EXCL pooh!

pouillerie /pujʀi/ NF squalor

pouilleux, -euse /pujø, øz/ ADJ 1 (*lit*) lousy, flea-ridden, verminous 2 (= *sordide*) [*quartier, endroit*] squalid, seedy; [*personne*] dirty, filthy NM,F (= *pauvre*) down-and-out; (= *couvert de poux*) flea-ridden *ou* lice-ridden *ou* verminous person

pouillot /pujo/ NM warbler ◆ **~ fitis** willow warbler ◆ **~ véloce** chiffchaff

poujadisme /puʒadism/ NM Poujadism

poujadiste /puʒadist/ ADJ, NMF Poujadist

poulailler /pulɑje/ NM henhouse ◆ **le ~*** (*Théât*) the gallery, the gods* (*Brit*)

poulain /pulɛ̃/ NM 1 (= *cheval*) foal, colt; (*fig*) promising youngster; (= *protégé*) protégé 2 (*Tech*) **~ (de chargement)** skid

poulaine /pulɛn/ NF (*Hist* = *soulier*) poulaine, long pointed shoe

poularde /pulaʀd/ NF fattened chicken

poulbot /pulbo/ NM street urchin (*in Montmartre*)

poule¹ /pul/ NF 1 (= *oiseau*) hen; (*Culin*) (boiling) fowl ◆ **se lever avec les ~s** (*fig*) to be an early riser, to get up with the lark (*Brit*) *ou* birds (*US*) ◆ **se coucher avec les ~s** to go to bed early ◆ **quand les ~s auront des dents** never in a month of Sundays ◆ **être comme une ~ qui a trouvé un couteau** to be at a complete loss; → **chair, lait**

2 ⁑ (= *maîtresse*) mistress; (= *fille*) bird* (*Brit*), broad⁑ (*US*), chick* (*US*); (*prostituée*) whore, tart⁑, hooker⁑ (*US*) ◆ **~ de luxe** high-class prostitute

3 (= *terme affectueux*) **ma** ~ (my) pet ◆ **ça roule ma ~ !*** okey-doke!*

COMP **poule d'eau** moorhen
poule faisane hen pheasant
poule mouillée (= *lâche*) softy*, coward
la poule aux œufs d'or the goose that lays the golden eggs ◆ **tuer la ~ aux œufs d'or** to kill the goose that lays the golden eggs
poule pondeuse laying hen, layer
poule au pot boiled chicken ◆ **la ~ au pot tous les dimanches** (*Hist*) a chicken in the pot every Sunday
poule au riz chicken and rice

poule² /pul/ NF 1 (= *enjeu*) pool, kitty 2 (= *tournoi*) (*gén*) tournament; (*Escrime*) pool; (*Rugby*) group 3 (*Courses*) **~ d'essai** maiden race

poulet /pulɛ/ NM 1 (= *volaille*) chicken ◆ **~ de grain/fermier** corn-fed/free-range (*Brit*) chicken ◆ **mon (petit) ~ !*** (my) love! *ou* pet! (*Brit*) 2 (⁑ = *policier*) cop⁑ 3 († † = *billet doux*) love letter

poulette /pulɛt/ NF 1 (= *volaille*) pullet ◆ **ma ~ !*** (my) love *ou* pet (*Brit*)! 2 (* = *fille*) girl, lass*, bird* (*Brit*), chick* (*US*) 3 (*Culin*) **sauce** ~ sauce poulette (*made with eggs and lemon juice*)

pouliche /puliʃ/ NF filly

poulie /puli/ NF pulley; (*avec sa caisse*) block ◆ **~ simple/double/fixe** single/double/fixed block ◆ **~ folle** loose pulley

pouliner /puline/ ▸ conjug 1 ◂ VI to foal

poulinière /pulinjɛʀ/ ADJ F, NF ◆ **(jument)** ~ brood mare

poulot, -otte †* /pulo, ɔt/ NM,F ◆ **mon ~!, ma poulotte!** poppet!*, (my) pet! (*Brit*) *ou* love!

poulpe /pulp/ NM octopus

pouls /pu/ NM pulse ◆ **prendre** *ou* **tâter le ~ de qn** (*lit*) to feel *ou* take sb's pulse; (*fig*) to sound sb out ◆ **prendre** *ou* **tâter le ~ de** (*fig*) [+ *opinion publique*] to test, to sound out; [+ *économie*] to feel the pulse of

poumon /pumɔ̃/ NM (*Anat*) lung ◆ **respirer à pleins ~s** to breathe deeply ◆ **chanter/crier à pleins ~s** to sing/shout at the top of one's voice ◆ **~ artificiel/d'acier** artificial/iron lung ◆ **cette région est le ~ économique du pays** this region is the hub of the country's economy ◆ **la forêt amazonienne, ~ de la terre** the Amazon rainforest, the lungs of the earth ◆ **Hyde Park, le ~ de Londres** Hyde Park, London's green lung

poupard /pupaʀ/ **ADJ** † chubby(-cheeked) **NM** bouncing *ou* bonny *(Brit)* baby

poupe /pup/ **NF** *(Naut)* stern; → **vent**

poupée /pupe/ **NF** 1 *(= jouet)* doll ◆ **~(s) gigogne(s)** *ou* **russe(s)** nest of dolls, Russian dolls ◆ **~ gonflable** inflatable *ou* blow-up doll ◆ **~ de son** rag doll *(stuffed with bran)* ◆ **elle joue à la ~** she's playing with her doll(s); → **maison** 2 (* *= jolie femme)* doll * ◆ **bonjour, ~ !** hullo, doll! 3 *(= pansement)* finger bandage ◆ **faire une ~ à qn** to bandage sb's finger 4 *(Tech)* **~ fixe** headstock ◆ **~ mobile** tailstock

poupin, e /pupɛ̃, in/ **ADJ** chubby

poupon /pupɔ̃/ **NM** little baby, babe-in-arms

pouponner /pupɔne/ ► conjug 1 ◄ **VI** *[femme]* to play mother; *[homme]* to play father ◆ **tu vas bientôt (pouvoir) ~** soon you'll be fussing around like a fond mother *(ou* father *etc)*

pouponnière /pupɔnjɛʀ/ **NF** day nursery, crèche

pour /puʀ/

GRAMMAIRE ACTIVE 53.4

1 PRÉPOSITION 2 NOM MASCULIN

1 - PRÉPOSITION

1 direction for, to ◆ **partir ~ l'Espagne** to leave for Spain ◆ **il part ~ l'Espagne demain** he leaves for Spain *ou* he is off to Spain tomorrow ◆ **partir ~ l'étranger** to go abroad ◆ **un billet ~ Caen** a ticket to *ou* for Caen ◆ **le train ~ Londres** the London train, the train for London

2 temps for ◆ **tu restes à Paris ~ Noël ?** are you staying in Paris for Christmas? ◆ **il est absent ~ deux jours** he's away for two days ◆ **promettre qch ~ le mois prochain/~ dans huit jours/~ après les vacances** to promise sth for next month/for next week/for after the holidays ◆ **ce sera ~ l'an prochain** we'll have to wait for *ou* until next year ◆ **il lui faut sa voiture ~ demain** he must have his car for *ou* by tomorrow ◆ **~ le moment** *ou* **l'instant** for the moment ◆ **~ toujours** for ever

◆ **en avoir pour** *[+ durée]* ◆ **tu en as ~ combien de temps ?** how long are you going to be?, how long will it take you? ◆ **ne m'attendez pas, j'en ai encore ~ une heure** don't wait for me, I'll be another hour (yet) ◆ **elle en a bien ~ trois semaines** it'll take her at least three weeks ◆ **quand il se met à pleuvoir, on en a ~ trois jours** once it starts raining, it goes on *ou* sets in for three days ◆ **on en a encore ~ 20 km de cette mauvaise route** *(distance)* there's another 20 km of this awful road

3 intention, destination for ◆ **faire qch ~ qn** to do sth for sb ◆ **il ferait tout ~ elle/sa mère** he would do anything for her *ou* for her sake/his mother *ou* his mother's sake ◆ **faire qch ~ le plaisir** to do sth for pleasure ◆ **il n'est pas fait ~ le travail de bureau** he's not made for office work ◆ **c'est fait** *ou* **étudié ~ !** * that's what it's meant *ou* made for! ◆ **il travaille ~ un cabinet d'architectes** he works for a firm of architects ◆ **ce n'est pas un livre ~ (les) enfants** it's not a book for children, it's not a children's book ◆ **c'est mauvais/bon ~ vous/~ la santé** it's bad/good for you/for the health ◆ **c'est trop compliqué ~ elle** it's too complicated for her ◆ **son amour ~ elle/les bêtes** his love for her/of animals ◆ **il a été très gentil ~ ma mère** he was very kind to my mother ◆ **~ la plus grande joie des spectateurs** to the delight of the onlookers ◆ **coiffeur ~ dames** ladies' hairdresser ◆ **sirop ~ la toux** cough mixture *(Brit) ou* syrup *(US)* ◆ **pastilles ~ la gorge** throat tablets

◆ **pour** + *infinitif (= afin de)* to ◆ **trouvez un argument ~ le convaincre** find an argument to convince him *ou* that will convince him ◆ **il sera d'accord ~ nous aider** he'll agree to help us ◆ **~ mûrir, les tomates ont besoin de soleil** tomatoes need sunshine to ripen ◆ **je ne l'ai pas dit ~ le vexer** I didn't say that to annoy him ◆ **je n'ai rien dit ~ ne pas le blesser** I didn't say anything so as not to hurt him ◆ **elle se pencha ~ ramasser son gant** she bent down to pick up her glove ◆ **il tendit le bras ~ prendre la boîte** he reached for the box ◆ **creuser ~ trouver de l'eau/du pétrole** to dig for water/oil ◆ **il y a des gens assez innocents ~ le croire** some people are naive enough to believe him ◆ **il finissait le soir tard ~ reprendre le travail tôt le lendemain** he used to finish work late at night only to start again early the next morning ◆ **il est parti ~ ne plus revenir** he left never to return, he left and never came back again

◆ **pour que** + *subjonctif (= afin que)* so that, in order that *(frm)* ◆ **écris vite ta lettre ~ qu'elle parte ce soir** write your letter quickly so (that) it will go *ou* it goes this evening ◆ **il a mis une barrière ~ que les enfants ne sortent pas** he has put up a fence so that the children won't get out ◆ **c'est ça, laisse ton sac là ~ qu'on te le vole !** *(iro)* that's right, leave your bag there for someone to steal it! *ou* so that someone steals it! ◆ **il est trop tard ~ qu'on le prévienne** it's too late to warn him *ou* for him to be warned ◆ **elle est assez grande ~ qu'on puisse la laisser seule** *(iro)* she's old enough to be left on her own

4 cause ~ **quelle raison ?** for what reason?, why? ◆ **être condamné ~ vol** to be convicted for theft ◆ **"fermé pour réparations"** "closed for repairs" ◆ **il n'en est pas plus heureux ~ ça !** he's none the happier for all that!, he's no happier for all that! ◆ **on l'a félicité ~ son audace/~ son élection** he was congratulated on his daring/on his election ◆ **il est connu ~ sa générosité** he is known for his generosity ◆ **quelle histoire ~ si peu** what a fuss *ou* to-do * over *ou* about such a little thing ◆ **pourquoi se faire du souci ~ ça ?** why worry about that? ◆ **il est ~ quelque chose/~ beaucoup dans le succès de la pièce** he is partly/largely responsible for the success of the play, he had something/a lot to do with the play's success

◆ **pour** + *infinitif (introduisant une cause)* ◆ **elle a été punie ~ avoir menti** she was punished for lying *ou* having lied ◆ **on l'a félicité ~ avoir sauvé l'enfant** he was congratulated for having saved the child

(= susceptible de) ◆ **le travail n'est pas ~ l'effrayer** *ou* **~ lui faire peur** he's not afraid of hard work ◆ **ce n'est pas ~ arranger les choses** this isn't going to help matters, this will only make things worse

5 approbation for, in favour *(Brit) ou* favor *(US)* of ◆ **manifester ~ la paix** to demonstrate *ou* march for peace ◆ **je suis ~ les réformes/~ réduire** *ou* **qu'on réduise les dépenses** I'm in favour of the reforms/of reducing expenditure ◆ **je suis ~ !** * I'm all for it! *, I'm all in favour (of it)!

6 = du point de vue de qn ~ **lui, le projet n'est pas réalisable** as he sees it *ou* in his opinion *ou* in his view the plan isn't feasible ◆ **~ moi, elle était déjà au courant** if you ask me, she already knew ◆ **~ moi, je suis d'accord** personally *ou* for my part I agree ◆ **sa fille est tout ~ lui** his daughter is everything to him

7 = en ce qui concerne ~ **(ce qui est de) notre voyage, il faut y renoncer** as for our trip *ou* as far as our trip goes, we'll have to forget it ◆ **et ~ les billets, c'est toi qui t'en charges ?** so, are you going to take care of the tickets? ◆ **ça ne change rien ~ nous** that makes no difference as far as we're concerned ◆ **le plombier est venu/a téléphoné ~ la chaudière** the plumber came/phoned about the boiler

8 = à la place de, en échange de **payer ~ qn** to pay for sb ◆ **signez ~ moi** sign in my place *ou* for me ◆ **~ le directeur** *(Comm)* p.p. Manager ◆ **il a parlé ~ nous tous** he spoke on behalf of all of us *ou* on our behalf, he spoke for all of us ◆ **donnez-moi ~ 50 € d'essence** give me 50 euros' worth of petrol ◆ **il l'a eu ~ 2 €** he got it for €2

◆ **en avoir pour** *[+ prix]* ◆ **j'en ai eu ~ 10 € de photocopies** it cost me €10 to do the photocopies

9 rapport, comparaison for ◆ **il est petit ~ son âge** he is small for his age ◆ **il fait chaud ~ la saison** it's warm for the time of year ◆ **c'est bien trop cher ~ ce que c'est !** it's far too expensive for what it is! ◆ **~ un Anglais, il parle bien le français** he speaks French well for an Englishman ◆ **~ cent/mille** per cent/thousand ◆ **~ 500 g de farine, il te faut six œufs** for 500 grams of flour you need six eggs ◆ **~ un qui s'intéresse, il y en a dix qui bâillent** for every one that takes an interest there are ten who just sit there yawning ◆ **mourir ~ mourir, je préfère que ce soit ici** if I have to die I should prefer it to be here

10 = comme for, as ◆ **prendre qn ~ femme** to take sb as one's wife ◆ **il a ~ adjoint son cousin** he has his cousin as his deputy ◆ **il a ~ principe/méthode de faire ...** it is his principle/method to do ..., his principle /method is to do ... ◆ **ça a eu ~ effet de changer son comportement** this had the effect of changing his behaviour

11 emphatique ~ **un sale coup, c'est un sale coup !** * of all the unfortunate things (to happen)! ◆ **~ une vedette, c'en est une !** that's what I call a star! ◆ **~ être furieux, je suis furieux !** I am so angry!

12 indiquant une restriction ~ **avoir réussi, il n'en est pas plus heureux** he's no happier *ou* none the happier for having succeeded *ou* for his success ◆ **~ être petite, elle n'en est pas moins solide** she may be small but that doesn't mean she's not strong ◆ **~ riche qu'il soit, il n'est pas généreux** (as) rich as he is *ou* rich though he is, he's not generous

13 locutions

◆ **pour peu que** + *subjonctif* ◆ **~ peu qu'il soit sorti sans sa clé ...** if he's left without his key ... ◆ **il la convaincra, ~ peu qu'il sache s'y prendre** he'll convince her if he goes about it (in) the right way

◆ **être pour** + *infinitif* * ◆ **j'étais ~ partir** *(= être sur le point de)* I was just going, I was just about to go, I was on the point of leaving

2 - NOM MASCULIN

1 = arguments **le ~ et le contre** the arguments for and against, the pros and cons ◆ **il y a du ~ et du contre** there are arguments on both sides *ou* arguments for and against; → **peser**

2 = personne **les ~ ont la majorité** those in favour are in the majority ◆ **devant ses tableaux, il y a les ~ et les contre** people either like or dislike his paintings

pourboire /puʀbwaʀ/ **NM** tip ◆ **~ interdit** no gratuities, our staff do not accept gratuities ◆ **donner un ~ de 2 € à qn, donner 2 € de ~ à qn** to tip sb 2 euros, to give sb a 2 euro tip

pourceau (pl **pourceaux**) /puʀso/ **NM** *(littér, péj)* pig, swine *(inv)*; → **perle**

pour-cent /puʀsɑ̃/ **NM INV** *(= commission)* percentage, cut *

pourcentage /puʀsɑ̃taʒ/ **NM** percentage ◆ **résultat exprimé en ~** result expressed in percentages ◆ **fort ~ d'abstentions** high abstention rate ◆ **travailler** *ou* **être au ~** to work on commission ◆ **toucher un ~ sur les bénéfices** to get a share *ou* a cut* of the profits ◆ **côte à fort** ~ hill with a steep gradient, steep slope

pourchasser /puʀʃase/ ▸ conjug 1 ◂ VT *[police, chasseur, ennemi]* to pursue, to hunt down; *[créancier, importun]* to hound ◆ **~ la misère/le crime** to hunt out *ou* seek out poverty/crime ◆ **~ les fautes d'orthographe** to hunt out spelling mistakes

pourfendeur /puʀfɑ̃dœʀ/ NM *(hum)* destroyer

pourfendre /puʀfɑ̃dʀ/ ▸ conjug 41 ◂ VT *(littér)* *[+ adversaire]* to set about, to assail; *[+ abus]* to fight against, to combat

pourlécher (se) /puʀleʃe/ ▸ conjug 6 ◂ VPR *(lit, fig)* to lick one's lips ◆ **je m'en pourlèche déjà** *(lit)* my mouth is watering already; *(fig)* I can hardly wait ◆ **se ~ les babines** * *(lit)* to lick one's chops*; *(fig)* to lick *ou* smack one's lips

pourliche* /puʀliʃ/ NM tip

pourparlers /puʀpaʀle/ NMPL talks, negotiations, discussions ◆ **entrer en ~ avec qn** to start negotiations *ou* discussions with sb, to enter into talks with sb ◆ **être en ~ avec qn** to be negotiating with sb, to be having talks *ou* discussions with sb

pourpier /puʀpje/ NM portulaca; *(comestible)* purslane

pourpoint /puʀpwɛ̃/ NM doublet, pourpoint

pourpre /puʀpʀ/ ADJ *(gén)* crimson; *(Hér)* purpure ◆ **il devint ~** *(furieux)* he went purple (in the face); *(gêné)* he turned crimson *ou* scarlet NM ① *(= couleur)* crimson ◆ **~ rétinien** visual purple ② *(= coquillage)* murex NF *(= matière colorante, étoffe, symbole)* purple; *(= couleur)* scarlet ◆ **~ royale** royal purple ◆ **accéder à la ~ cardinalice** *ou* **romaine** to be given the red hat ◆ **né dans la ~** born to the purple

pourpré, e /puʀpʀe/ ADJ *(littér)* crimson

pourquoi /puʀkwa/ GRAMMAIRE ACTIVE 28.1

CONJ why ◆ **~ est-il venu ?** why did he come?, what did he come for? ◆ **~ les avoir oubliés ?** why did he *(ou* they *etc)* forget them? ◆ **c'est** *ou* **voilà ~ il n'est pas venu** that's (the reason) why he didn't come

ADV why ◆ **tu me le prêtes ? – ~ (donc) ?** can you lend me it? – why? *ou* what for? ◆ **tu viens ? – ~ pas ?** are you coming? – why not? ◆ **il a réussi, ~ pas vous ?** *(dans le futur)* he succeeded so why shouldn't you?; *(dans le passé)* he succeeded so why didn't you? *ou* so how come you didn't?* ◆ **je vais vous dire ~** I'll tell you why ◆ **il faut que ça marche, ou que ça dise ~** * it had better work or else*, it had better work, or I'll want to know why (not) ◆ **allez savoir** *ou* **comprendre ~ !*, je vous demande bien ~** I just can't imagine why!

NM INV *(= raison)* reason (*de* for); *(= question)* question ◆ **le ~ de son attitude** the reason for his attitude ◆ **il veut toujours savoir le ~ et le comment** he always wants to know the whys and wherefores ◆ **il est difficile de répondre à tous les ~ des enfants** it isn't easy to find an answer for everything children ask you

pourri, e /puʀi/ (ptp de **pourrir**) ADJ ① *[fruit]* rotten, bad; *[bois]* rotten; *[feuille]* decayed, rotting; *[viande]* bad; *[œuf]* rotten, bad, addled; *[enfant]* spoilt rotten *(attrib)*; *[cadavre]* decomposed, putrefied ◆ **être ~** *[pomme]* to have gone rotten *ou* bad; *[œuf]* to have gone bad; → **poisson** ② *[roche]* crumbling, rotten; *[neige]* melting, half-melted ③ *(= mauvais) [temps, été]* rotten; *[personne, société]* rotten, corrupt ◆ **flic ~**‡ bent copper* *(Brit)*, dirty *ou* bad cop* *(US)* ◆ **~ de fric**‡ stinking* *ou* filthy* rich ◆ **~ de défauts** full of *ou* riddled with faults ◆ **~ de talent** * oozing with talent NM ① *(= partie gâtée)* rotten *ou* bad part ◆ **sentir le ~** to smell rotten *ou* bad ② (‡ *= crapule)* swine‡ ◆ **bande de ~s !** (you) bastards!*‡ ③ (‡ *= policier corrompu)* bent copper* *(Brit)*, dirty *ou* bad cop* *(US)*

pourrir /puʀiʀ/ ▸ conjug 2 ◂ VI *[fruit]* to go rotten *ou* bad, to spoil; *[bois]* to rot (away); *[œuf]* to go bad; *[cadavre]* to rot (away); *[corps, membre]* to be eaten away; *[relations]* to deteriorate ◆ **récolte qui pourrit sur pied** harvest rotting on the stalk ◆ **~ dans la misère** to languish in poverty ◆ **~ en prison** to rot (away) in prison ◆ **laisser ~ la situation** to let the situation deteriorate *ou* get worse ◆ **laisser ~ une grève** to let a strike peter out VT ① *[+ fruit]* to rot, to spoil; *[+ bois]* to rot; *(= infecter) [+ corps]* to eat away (at) ② *(= gâter) [+ enfant]* to spoil rotten; *(= corrompre) [+ personne]* to corrupt, to spoil ◆ **ça me pourrit la vie** it's ruining my life VPR **se pourrir** *[fruit]* to go rotten *ou* bad, to spoil; *[bois]* to rot (away); *[relations, situation]* to deteriorate, to get worse

pourrissement /puʀismɑ̃/ NM *[de situation]* deterioration, worsening (*de* in, of)

pourriture /puʀityʀ/ NF ① *(lit, Agr)* rot; *[de société]* rottenness ◆ **odeur de ~** putrid smell ◆ **~ noble** noble rot, botrytis *(SPÉC)* ② (‡ *péj*) *(= homme)* louse‡, swine‡; *(= femme)* bitch*‡

pour-soi /puʀswa/ NM *(Philos)* pour-soi

poursuite /puʀsɥit/ NF ① *[de voleur, animal]* chase (*de* after) pursuit (*de* of); *[de bonheur, gloire]* pursuit (*de* of); ◆ **se mettre** *ou* **se lancer à la ~ de qn** to chase *ou* run after sb, to go in pursuit of sb ② *(Jur)* **~s (judiciaires)** legal proceedings ◆ **engager des ~s contre qn** to start legal proceedings against sb, to take legal action against sb ◆ **s'exposer à des ~s** to lay o.s. open to *ou* run the risk of prosecution ③ *(= continuation)* continuation ◆ **ils ont voté/décidé la ~ de la grève** they voted/decided to continue the strike ④ ◆ **(course) ~** *(Sport)* track race; *(Police)* chase, pursuit ◆ **~ individuelle** individual pursuit ◆ **~ en voiture** car chase

poursuiteur, -euse /puʀsɥitœʀ, øz/ NM,F track rider *ou* cyclist

poursuivant, e /puʀsɥivɑ̃, ɑt/ ADJ *(Jur)* ◆ **partie ~e** plaintiff NM,F *(= ennemi)* pursuer; *(Jur)* plaintiff

poursuivre /puʀsɥivʀ/ ▸ conjug 40 ◂ VT ① *(= courir après) [+ fugitif, ennemi]* to pursue; *[+ animal]* to chase (after), to hunt down, to pursue; *[+ malfaiteur]* to chase (after), to pursue ◆ **un enfant poursuivi par un chien** a child (being) chased *ou* pursued by a dog ◆ **les motards poursuivaient la voiture** the police motorcyclists were chasing the car *ou* were in pursuit of the car

② *(= harceler) [importun, souvenir]* to hound ◆ **être poursuivi par ses créanciers** to be hounded by one's creditors ◆ **~ qn de sa colère/de sa haine** to be bitterly angry with sb/hate sb bitterly ◆ **~ une femme de ses assiduités** to force one's attentions on a woman ◆ **cette idée le poursuit** he can't get the idea out of his mind, he's haunted by the idea ◆ **les photographes ont poursuivi l'actrice jusque chez elle** the photographers followed the actress all the way home

③ *(= chercher à atteindre) [+ fortune, gloire]* to seek (after); *[+ vérité]* to pursue, to seek (after); *[+ rêve]* to pursue, to follow; *[+ but, idéal]* to strive towards, to pursue

④ *(= continuer) (gén)* to continue, to go *ou* carry on with; *[+ avantage]* to follow up, to pursue ◆ **~ sa marche** to carry on walking

⑤ *(Jur)* **~ qn (en justice)** *(au criminel)* to prosecute sb, to bring proceedings against sb; *(au civil)* to sue sb, to bring proceedings against sb ◆ **être poursuivi pour vol** to be prosecuted for theft

VI ① *(= continuer)* to carry on, to go on, to continue ◆ **poursuivez, cela m'intéresse** go on *ou* tell me more, I'm interested ◆ **puis il poursuivit : voici pourquoi ...** then he went on *ou* continued: that's why ...

② *(= persévérer)* to keep at it, to keep it up

VPR **se poursuivre** *[négociations, débats]* to go on, to continue; *[enquête, recherches, travail]* to be going on ◆ **les débats se sont poursuivis jusqu'au matin** discussions went on *ou* continued until morning

pourtant /puʀtɑ̃/ ADV *(= néanmoins, en dépit de cela)* yet, nevertheless, all the same, even so; *(= cependant)* (and) yet ◆ **et ~** and yet, but nevertheless ◆ **frêle mais ~ résistant** frail but (nevertheless) resilient, frail (and) yet resilient ◆ **il faut ~ le faire** it's got to be done nevertheless *ou* all the same *ou* even so ◆ **il n'est ~ pas très intelligent** (and) yet he's not very clever, he's not very clever though ◆ **c'est ~ facile !** *(intensif)* but it's easy!, but it's not difficult! ◆ **on lui a ~ dit de faire attention** and yet we told him *ou* did tell him to be careful

pourtour /puʀtuʀ/ NM *[de cercle]* circumference; *[de rectangle]* perimeter; *(= bord)* surround ◆ **le ~ méditerranéen** the Mediterranean region ◆ **sur le ~ de** around

pourvoi /puʀvwa/ NM *(Jur)* appeal ◆ **~ en grâce** appeal for clemency ◆ **former un ~ en cassation** to (lodge an) appeal

pourvoir /puʀvwaʀ/ ▸ conjug 25 ◂ VT ① ◆ **~ qn de qch** to provide *ou* equip *ou* supply sb with sth ◆ **~ un enfant de vêtements chauds** to provide a child with warm clothes ◆ **la nature l'a pourvu d'une grande intelligence** nature has endowed him with great intelligence ◆ **la nature l'a pourvue d'une grande beauté** she is graced with great natural beauty ◆ **~ sa maison de tout le confort moderne** to fit one's house out *ou* equip one's house with all modern conveniences ◆ **~ sa cave de vin** to stock one's cellar with wine; → **pourvu¹**

② *[+ poste]* to fill ◆ **il y a deux postes à ~** there are two posts to fill

VT INDIR **pourvoir à** *[+ éventualité]* to provide for, to cater for; *[+ emploi]* to fill ◆ **~ aux besoins de qn** to provide for *ou* cater for *ou* supply sb's needs ◆ **~ à l'entretien du ménage** to provide for the upkeep of the household ◆ **j'y pourvoirai** I'll see to it *ou* deal with it

VPR **se pourvoir** ① ◆ **se ~ de** *[+ argent, vêtements]* to provide o.s. with; *[+ provisions, munitions]* to provide o.s. with, to equip o.s. with, to supply o.s. with

② *(Jur)* to appeal, to lodge an appeal ◆ **se ~ en appel** to take one's case to the Court of Appeal ◆ **se ~ en cassation** to (lodge an) appeal

pourvoyeur, -euse /puʀvwajœʀ, øz/ NM,F supplier, purveyor; *[de drogue]* supplier, pusher* NM *(Mil = servant de pièce)* artilleryman

pourvu¹, e /puʀvy/ (ptp de **pourvoir**) ADJ ① *[personne]* **être ~ de** *[+ intelligence, imagination]* to be gifted with, to be endowed with; *[+ grâce]* to be endowed with ◆ **avec ces provisions nous voilà ~s pour l'hiver** with these provisions we're stocked up for the winter ◆ **nous sommes très bien/très mal ~s en commerçants** we're very well-off/very badly off for shops ◆ **après l'héritage qu'il a fait c'est quelqu'un de bien ~** with the inheritance he's received, he's very well-off *ou* very well provided for ② *[chose]* **être ~ de** to be equipped *ou* fitted with ◆ **feuille de papier ~e d'une marge** sheet of paper with a margin ◆ **animal (qui est) ~ d'écailles** animal which has scales *ou* which is equipped with scales

pourvu² /puʀvy/ **pourvu que** LOC CONJ *(souhait)* let's hope; *(condition)* provided (that), so long as ◆ **~ que ça dure !** let's hope it lasts!

poussa(h) /pusa/ NM *(= jouet)* wobbly toy, Weeble ®; *(péj = homme)* potbellied man

pousse /pus/ NF ① *(= bourgeon)* shoot ◆ **~s de bambou** bamboo shoots ◆ **~s de soja** beansprouts ◆ **la plante fait des ~s** the plant is putting out shoots ◆ **jeune** ~ *(= entreprise)* start-up; *(= jeune talent)* new talent [2] *(= action) [de feuilles]* sprouting; *[de dents, cheveux]* growth

poussé, e¹ /puse/ (ptp de **pousser**) ADJ *[études]* advanced; *[enquête]* extensive, exhaustive; *[interrogatoire]* intensive; *[moteur]* souped-up* ◆ **très** ~ *[organisation, technique, dessin]* elaborate, sophisticated; *[précision]* high-level *(épith)*, extreme ◆ **il n'a pas eu une formation/éducation très** ~**e** he hasn't had much training/education ◆ **une plaisanterie un peu** ~**e** a joke which goes a bit too far NM *(Mus)* up-bow

pousse-au-crime * /pusokʀim/ NM INV *(= boisson)* firewater* ◆ **c'est du** ~ **!** *(fig) [décolleté, tenue]* it's an open invitation! ◆ **c'est une société** ~ it's a society that drives people to crime

pousse-café * /puskafe/ NM INV liqueur

poussée² /puse/ NF [1] *(= pression) [de foule]* pressure, pushing; *[d'arc, voûte, moteur]* thrust *(NonC)* ◆ **sous la** ~ under the pressure ◆ **la** ~ **d'Archimède** Archimedes' principle; *(Bot)* ◆ ~ **radiculaire** root pressure [2] *(= coup)* push, shove; *[d'ennemi]* thrust ◆ **écarter qn d'une** ~ to thrust *ou* push *ou* shove sb aside ◆ **enfoncer une porte d'une** ~ **violente** to break a door down with a violent heave *ou* shove [3] *(= éruption) [d'acné]* attack, eruption; *[de prix]* rise, upsurge, increase ◆ ~ **de fièvre** (sudden) high temperature ◆ **la** ~ **de la gauche/droite aux élections** the upsurge of the left/right in the elections ◆ **la** ~ **révolutionnaire de 1789** the revolutionary upsurge of 1789

pousse-pousse /puspus/ NM INV rickshaw; *(Helv = poussette)* pushchair *(Brit)*, stroller *(US)*

pousser /puse/ ► conjug 1 ◄ VT [1] *(gén) [+ voiture, meuble, personne]* to push; *[+ brouette, landau]* to push, to wheel; *[+ verrou] (= ouvrir)* to slide, to push back; *(= fermer)* to slide, to push to *ou* home; *[+ objet gênant]* to move, to shift, to push aside; *[+ pion]* to move ◆ ~ **une chaise contre le mur/près de la fenêtre/dehors** to push a chair (up) against the wall/over to the window/outside ◆ ~ **les gens vers la porte** to push the people towards *ou* to the door ◆ **il me poussa du genou/du coude** he nudged me with his knee/(with his elbow) ◆ ~ **un animal devant soi** to drive an animal in front of one ◆ ~ **la porte/la fenêtre** *(fermer)* to push the door/window to *ou* shut; *(ouvrir)* to push the door/window open ◆ ~ **un caillou du pied** to kick a stone (along) ◆ **le vent nous poussait vers la côte** the wind was blowing *ou* pushing *ou* driving us towards the shore ◆ **le courant poussait le bateau vers les rochers** the current was carrying the boat towards the rocks ◆ **peux-tu me** ~ **?** *(balançoire, voiture en panne)* can you give me a push? ◆ **peux-tu** ~ **ta voiture ?** can you move your car (out of the way)? ◆ **pousse tes fesses !**** shift your backside!**, shove over!** ◆ **(ne) poussez pas, il y a des enfants !** don't push *ou* stop pushing, there are children here! ◆ **il m'a poussé** he pushed me ◆ **il y a une voiture qui me pousse au derrière** * *ou* **au cul****the car behind me is right up my backside** *(Brit)*, there's a car riding my ass**(US) ◆ **faut pas** ~ **(grand-mère dans les orties) !** ** that's going a bit far!, you *(ou* he) must be kidding!* ◆ ~ **un peu loin le bouchon** to push it*, to go a bit far ◆ **ne pousse pas le bouchon trop loin** don't push it*, don't push your luck; → **pointe**

[2] *(= stimuler) [+ élève, ouvrier]* to urge on, to egg on, to push; *[+ cheval]* to ride hard, to push; *[+ moteur] (techniquement)* to soup up, to hot up, to hop up *(US)*; *(en accélérant)* to flog* *(surtout Brit)*, to drive hard; *[+ voiture]* to drive hard *ou* fast; *[+ machine]* to work hard; *[+ feu]* to stoke up; *[+ chauffage]* to turn up; *(= mettre en valeur) [+ candidat, protégé]* to push; *[+ dossier]* to help along ◆ **c'est l'ambition qui le pousse** he is driven by ambition, it's ambition which drives him on ◆ **dans ce lycée on pousse trop les élèves** the pupils are worked *ou* driven *ou* pushed too hard in this school ◆ **ce prof l'a beaucoup poussé en maths** this teacher has really pushed him *ou* made him get on in maths ◆ **pousse le son, on n'entend rien !** turn it up a bit, we can't hear a thing!

[3] ◆ ~ **qn à faire qch** *[faim, curiosité]* to drive sb to do sth; *[personne] (= inciter)* to urge *ou* press sb to do sth; *(= persuader)* to persuade sb to do sth, to talk sb into doing sth ◆ **ses parents le poussent à entrer à l'université/vers une carrière médicale** his parents are urging *ou* encouraging *ou* pushing him to go to university/to take up a career in medicine ◆ **c'est elle qui l'a poussé à acheter cette maison** she talked him into *ou* pushed him into buying this house ◆ **son échec nous pousse à croire que ...** his failure leads us to think that ..., because of his failure we're tempted to think that ... ◆ ~ **qn au crime/au désespoir** to drive sb to crime/to despair ◆ ~ **qn à la consommation** to encourage sb to buy *(ou* eat *ou* drink *etc)* ◆ ~ **qn à la dépense** to encourage sb to spend money ◆ **le sentiment qui le poussait vers sa bien-aimée** the feeling which drove him to his beloved ◆ ~ **qn sur un sujet** to get sb onto a subject

[4] *(= poursuivre) [+ études, discussion]* to continue, to carry on (with), to go on with; *[+ avantage]* to press (home), to follow up; *[+ affaire]* to follow up, to pursue; *[+ marche, progression]* to continue, to carry on with ◆ ~ **l'enquête/les recherches plus loin** to carry on *ou* press on with the inquiry/the research ◆ ~ **la curiosité/la plaisanterie un peu (trop) loin** to take curiosity/the joke a bit (too) far ◆ ~ **qch à la perfection** to carry *ou* bring sth to perfection ◆ **il pousse les choses au noir** he always looks on the black side (of things) *ou* takes a black view of things ◆ **il a poussé le dévouement/la gentillesse/la malhonnêteté jusqu'à faire ...** he was devoted/kind/dishonest enough to do ..., his devotion/kindness/dishonesty was such that he did ... ◆ ~ **l'indulgence jusqu'à la faiblesse** to carry indulgence to the point of weakness ◆ ~ **qn à bout** to push sb to breaking point, to drive sb to his wits' end *ou* the limit

[5] *[+ cri, hurlement]* to let out, to utter, to give; *[+ soupir]* to heave, to give ◆ ~ **des cris** to shout, to scream ◆ ~ **des rugissements** to roar ◆ **les enfants poussaient des cris perçants** the children were shrieking ◆ **le chien poussait de petits jappements plaintifs** the dog was yelping pitifully ◆ ~ **la chansonnette** *ou* **la romance, en** ~ **une*** *(hum)* to sing a (little) song

VI [1] *[plante] (= sortir de terre)* to sprout; *(= se développer)* to grow; *[barbe, enfant]* to grow; *[dent]* to come through; *[ville]* to grow, to expand ◆ **alors, les enfants, ça pousse ?*** and how are the kids doing?* ◆ **son bébé pousse bien*** her baby's growing well ◆ **mes choux poussent bien** my cabbages are coming on *ou* doing nicely *ou* well ◆ **tout pousse bien dans cette région** everything grows well in this region ◆ **ils font** ~ **des tomates par ici** they grow tomatoes in these parts, this is a tomato-growing area ◆ **la pluie fait** ~ **les mauvaises herbes** the rain makes the weeds grow ◆ **ça pousse comme du chiendent** they grow like weeds ◆ **il se fait** *ou* **se laisse** ~ **la barbe** he's growing a beard ◆ **il se fait** *ou* **se laisse** ~ **les cheveux** he's growing his hair, he's letting his hair grow ◆ **il a une dent qui pousse** he's cutting a tooth, he's got a tooth coming through ◆ ~ **comme un champignon** to be shooting up ◆ **de nouvelles villes poussaient comme des champignons** new towns were springing up *ou* sprouting like mushrooms, new towns were mushrooming

[2] *(= faire un effort) (pour accoucher, aller à la selle)* to push ◆ ~ **à la roue** *(fig)* to do a bit of pushing, to push a bit ◆ ~ **(à la roue) pour que qn fasse qch** to keep nudging *ou* pushing sb to get him to do sth ◆ ~ **à la hausse** *(Fin)* to push prices up ◆ ~ **à la baisse** *(Fin)* to force prices down

[3] *(= aller)* **nous allons** ~ **un peu plus avant** we're going to go on *ou* push on a bit further ◆ ~ **jusqu'à Lyon** to go on *ou* push on as far as *ou* carry on to Lyons

[4] *(* = exagérer)* to go too far, to overdo it ◆ **tu pousses !** that's going a bit far! ◆ **faut pas** ~ **!** that's going a bit far!, that's overdoing it a bit!

[5] *[vin]* to referment in spring

VPR **se pousser** [1] *(= se déplacer)* to move, to shift; *(= faire de la place)* to move *ou* shift over *(ou* up *ou* along *ou* down); *(en voiture)* to move ◆ **pousse-toi de là que je m'y mette*** move over and make room for me

[2] *(= essayer de s'élever)* **se** ~ **(dans la société)** to make one's way *ou* push o.s. up in society *ou* in the world

poussette /pusɛt/ NF *(pour enfant)* pushchair *(Brit)*, stroller *(US)*; *(Helv)* pram *(Brit)*, baby carriage *(US)*; *(à provisions)* shopping trolley *(Brit)*, shopping cart *(US)*; *(arg Cyclisme)* push *(given to a cyclist to spur him on in a race)*

poussette-canne (pl **poussettes-cannes**) /pusɛtkan/ NF baby buggy, (folding) stroller *(US)*

poussier /pusje/ NM coaldust, screenings *(SPÉC)*

poussière /pusjɛʀ/ NF [1] *(= particules)* dust ◆ **faire** *ou* **soulever de la** ~ to raise a lot of dust ◆ **prendre la** ~ to collect *ou* gather dust ◆ **faire la** ~* to do the dusting ◆ **couvert de** ~ dusty, covered in dust ◆ **avoir une** ~ **dans l'œil** to have a speck of dust in one's eye ◆ **leur** ~ **repose dans ces tombes** *(frm)* their ashes *ou* mortal remains lie in these tombs ◆ **une** ~ **de** *(fig)* a myriad of ◆ **réduire/tomber en** ~ to reduce to/crumble into dust

[2] *(locutions)* **5 € et des** ~**s*** just over €5 ◆ **il a 50 ans et des** ~**s** he's just over 50 ◆ **il était 22 heures et des** ~**s** it was just gone *ou* a little after 10 o'clock

COMP **poussière d'ange** *(= drogue)* angel dust
poussière de charbon coaldust
poussière cosmique cosmic dust
poussière d'étoiles stardust
poussière d'or gold dust
poussière radioactive radioactive particles *ou* dust *(NonC)*
poussière volcanique volcanic ash *ou* dust

poussiéreux, -euse /pusjeʀø, øz/ ADJ *(lit)* dusty, covered in dust; *(fig)* fusty

poussif, -ive /pusif, iv/ ADJ *[personne]* wheezy, short-winded; *[cheval]* broken-winded; *[moteur]* puffing, wheezing; *[style]* laboured *(Brit)*, labored *(US)*

poussin /pusɛ̃/ NM [1] *(= oiseau)* chick ◆ **mon** ~ **!*** *(terme affectueux)* pet!, poppet!* [2] *(Sport)* under eleven, junior [3] *(arg Mil) first-year cadet in the air force*

poussivement /pusivmɑ̃/ ADV ◆ **il monta** ~ **la côte/l'escalier** he wheezed up *ou* puffed up the hill/the stairs

poussoir /puswaʀ/ NM *[de sonnette]* button ◆ ~ **(de soupape)** *(dans moteur)* tappet

poutre /putʀ/ NF *(en bois)* beam; *(en métal)* girder; *(Gym)* beam ◆ ~**s apparentes** exposed beams; → **maître, paille**

poutrelle /putʀɛl/ NF *(en bois)* beam; *(en métal)* girder

poutse*, **poutze** * /puts/ NF *(Helv = nettoyage)* cleaning

poutser *, **poutzer** * /putse/ ► conjug 1 ◄ VT (*Helv*) to clean

pouvoir[1] /puvwaʀ/
► conjug 33 ◄
GRAMMAIRE ACTIVE 28.1, 30, 31, 36, 42, 43

1 VERBE AUXILIAIRE
2 VERBE IMPERSONNEL
3 VERBE TRANSITIF
4 VERBE PRONOMINAL

1 - VERBE AUXILIAIRE

1 permission

Lorsque **pouvoir** exprime la permission donnée par le locuteur à quelqu'un, il peut se traduire par **can** ou **may** ; **can** est le plus courant et couvre la majorité des cas ; **may** appartient à une langue plus soutenue et indique nettement un ton de supériorité.

◆ **tu peux le garder si tu veux** you can keep it if you want ◆ **maintenant, tu peux aller jouer** now you can *ou* may go and play ◆ **vous pouvez desservir** you can *ou* may (*frm*) clear the table

On emploie **can** ou **be allowed to** lorsque la permission dépend d'une tierce personne ou d'une autorité.

◆ **vous ne pouvez pas avoir accès à ces documents** you are not allowed access to these documents ◆ **crois-tu qu'il pourra venir ?** do you think he'll be allowed to come? ◆ **sa mère a dit qu'il ne pouvait pas rester** his mother said he couldn't stay *ou* wasn't (allowed) to stay ◆ **on ne peut pas marcher sur les pelouses** you can't walk *ou* you aren't allowed to walk on the grass ◆ **elle ne pourra lui rendre visite qu'une fois par semaine** she'll only be allowed to visit him once a week ◆ **arrêtez de la taquiner ! – si on ne peut plus s'amuser maintenant !** stop teasing her! – we can have a bit of fun, can't we?

Notez l'usage de **have to, be obliged to** lorsque la proposition infinitive est une négative.

◆ **il peut ne pas venir** he doesn't have to come, he's not obliged to come ◆ **tu peux très bien ne pas accepter** you don't have to accept

2 demande

Lorsque l'on demande à quelqu'un la permission de faire quelque chose, on utilise **can** ou la forme plus polie **could** ; **may** appartient à un registre plus soutenu et **might** appartient à une langue très recherchée.

◆ **est-ce que je peux fermer la fenêtre ?, puis-je** (*frm*) **fermer la fenêtre ?** can I *ou* may I (*frm*) shut the window? ◆ **puis-je emprunter votre stylo ?** can *ou* could *ou* may I borrow your pen? ◆ **pourrais-je vous parler ?, puis-je** (*frm*) **vous parler ?** can *ou* could *ou* may *ou* might (*frm*) I have a word with you? ◆ **puis-je vous être utile ?** can I be of any help (to you)?, can *ou* may I be of assistance?

Lorsque l'on demande un service à quelqu'un ou qu'on lui donne un ordre poli, on utilise **can** ou la forme plus courtoise **could**.

◆ **tu peux m'ouvrir la porte, s'il te plaît ?** can you *ou* could you open the door for me, please? ◆ **pourriez-vous nous apporter du thé ?** could you bring us some tea?

3 = avoir de bonnes raisons pour should ◆ **je suis désolé – tu peux (l'être) !** I'm sorry – so you should be! ◆ **ils se sont excusés – ils peuvent !** they said they were sorry – I should think they did! ◆ **elle s'est plainte/a demandé une indemnité – elle peut !** she complained/demanded compensation – I should think she did!

4 possibilité

Lorsque **pouvoir** exprime une possibilité ou une capacité physique, intellectuelle ou psychologique, il se traduit généralement par **can** ou par **be able to** ; **can** étant un verbe défectif, **be able to** le remplace aux temps où il ne peut être conjugué.

◆ **peut-il venir ?** can he come? ◆ **ne peut-il pas venir ?** can't he come?, isn't he able to come? ◆ **il ne peut pas ne pas venir** he can't not come ◆ **il ne peut pas venir** he can't come, he isn't able to *ou* is unable to come ◆ **peut-il marcher sans canne ?** can he walk *ou* is he able to walk without a stick? ◆ **il ne pourra plus jamais marcher** he will never be able to walk again ◆ **je ne peux que vous féliciter** I can only congratulate you ◆ **je voudrais ~ vous aider** I would like to be able to help you, I wish I could help you ◆ **il pourrait venir demain si vous aviez besoin de lui** he could come tomorrow if you needed him ◆ **il aurait pu venir s'il avait été prévenu plus tôt** he could have come *ou* he would have been able to come if he had been told earlier ◆ **il n'a (pas) pu** *ou* **ne put** (*littér*) **venir** he couldn't come, he wasn't able to *ou* was unable to come ◆ **comment as-tu pu (faire ça) !** how could you (do such a thing)! ◆ **la salle peut contenir 100 personnes** the auditorium can seat 100 people ◆ **la nouvelle moto pourra faire du 300 km/h** the new motorcycle will be able to do 300 km/h ◆ **c'est fait de telle manière qu'on ne puisse pas l'ouvrir** it's made so that it's impossible to open *ou* so that you can't open it ◆ **j'ai essayé de le joindre, mais je n'ai pas pu** I tried to get in touch with him but I couldn't *ou* but I wasn't able to ◆ **à l'époque, je pouvais soulever 100 kg** in those days, I could lift *ou* I was able to lift 100 kilos ◆ **on peut dire ce qu'on veut, les diplômes c'est utile** whatever anyone says *ou* you can say what you like, a degree is useful

Lorsque **pouvoir** implique la notion de réussite, on peut également employer **to manage** ; dans ces exemples, **can, could** ne peuvent pas être utilisés.

◆ **il a pu réparer la machine à laver** he was able to *ou* he managed to fix the washing machine ◆ **tu as pu lui téléphoner ?** did you manage to phone him?

5 probabilité, hypothèse

Lorsque **pouvoir** exprime une probabilité, une éventualité, une hypothèse ou un risque, il se traduit par **may** ou **could** ; **might** implique une plus grande incertitude.

◆ **il peut être italien** he may *ou* could *ou* might be Italian ◆ **peut-il être italien ?** could *ou* might he be Italian? ◆ **il peut ne pas être italien** he may *ou* might not be Italian ◆ **il pourrait être italien** he might *ou* could be Italian ◆ **ça peut laisser une cicatrice** it might leave a scar ◆ **ça aurait pu être un voleur !** it might *ou* could have been a burglar! ◆ **vous pourrez en avoir besoin** you may *ou* might need it ◆ **les cambrioleurs ont pu entrer par la fenêtre** the burglars could *ou* may *ou* might have got in through the window ◆ **il pouvait être 2 heures du matin** it could *ou* may *ou* might have been 2 o'clock in the morning ◆ **cela pourrait arriver** that might *ou* could happen MAIS **il ne peut pas être italien** he can't be Italian ◆ **une lettre peut toujours se perdre** letters can *ou* do get lost

◆ **bien + pouvoir** ◆ **il pourrait bien avoir raison** he could *ou* may *ou* might well be right ◆ **où ai-je bien pu mettre mon stylo ?** where on earth can I have put my pen? ◆ **qu'est-ce qu'elle a bien pu lui raconter ?** what on earth can she have told him? ◆ **qu'est-ce qu'il peut bien faire ?** what on earth is he doing?, what CAN he be doing? ◆ **tu pourrais bien le regretter** you may *ou* might well regret it ◆ **il a très bien pu entrer sans qu'on le voie** he could very well have come in without anyone seeing him ◆ **qu'est-ce que cela peut bien lui faire ?** * what's it to him? *

6 suggestion could, can ◆ **je pourrais venir te chercher** I could come and pick you up ◆ **tu peux bien lui prêter ton livre !** you can lend him your book, can't you?, surely you can lend him your book ◆ **il peut bien faire cela** that's the least he can do

might peut être utilisé pour exprimer l'agacement.

◆ **elle pourrait arriver à l'heure !** she might *ou* could at least be on time! ◆ **tu aurais pu me dire ça plus tôt !** you might *ou* could have told me sooner!

7 souhaits

Dans une langue soutenue, **pouvoir** s'utilise au subjonctif pour exprimer les souhaits ; il se traduit alors différemment selon les contextes.

◆ **puisse Dieu/le ciel les aider !** (may) God/ Heaven help them! ◆ **puisse-t-il guérir rapidement !** let's hope he makes a speedy recovery! ◆ **puissiez-vous dire vrai !** let's pray *ou* hope you're right! ◆ **puissé-je le revoir un jour !** I only hope I see him again one day!

2 - VERBE IMPERSONNEL

La probabilité, l'éventualité, l'hypothèse ou le risque sont rendus par **may** ou **could** ; **might** implique une plus grande incertitude.

◆ **il peut** *ou* **pourrait pleuvoir** it may *ou* could *ou* might rain ◆ **il pourrait y avoir du monde** there may *ou* could *ou* might be a lot of people there ◆ **il aurait pu y avoir un accident !** there could have been an accident! ◆ **il pourrait s'agir d'un assassinat** it could be murder ◆ **il pourrait se faire qu'elle ne soit pas chez elle** she may *ou* might well not be at home

3 - VERBE TRANSITIF

= être capable ou avoir la possibilité de faire

est-ce qu'on peut quelque chose pour lui ? is there anything we can do for him? ◆ **il partira dès qu'il (le) pourra** he will leave as soon as he can ◆ **il fait ce qu'il peut** he does what he can ◆ **il a fait tout ce qu'il a pu** he did all he could *ou* everything in his power ◆ **il peut beaucoup** he can do a lot ◆ **que puis-je** (*frm*) **pour vous ?** what can I do for you?, can I do anything to help you? ◆ **qui peut le plus peut le moins** (*Prov*) he who can do more can do less

◆ **ne/n'y pouvoir rien** ◆ **on n'y peut rien** it can't be helped, nothing can be done about it ◆ **désolé, mais je n'y peux rien** I'm sorry, but I can't do anything *ou* there's nothing I can do about it ◆ **la justice ne peut rien contre eux** the law is powerless *ou* can do nothing against them ◆ **je ne peux rien faire pour vous** I can't do anything for you

◆ **on ne peut plus/mieux** ◆ **il a été on ne peut plus aimable/prudent** he couldn't have been kinder/more careful ◆ **il a été on ne peut plus clair** he couldn't have made it clearer ◆ **c'est on ne peut mieux** it couldn't be better ◆ **elle le connaît on ne peut mieux** no one knows him better than she does ◆ **ils sont on ne peut plus mal avec leurs voisins** they couldn't be on worse terms with their neighbours, they're on the worst possible terms with their neighbours

◆ **n'en pouvoir plus** ◆ **je n'en peux plus** (*fatigue*) I'm worn out *ou* exhausted, I've had it*; (*énervement*) I've had it (up to here)*; (*désespoir*) I can't go on, I can't take it any longer, I can't take any more; *(impatience)* I can't stand it any longer ◆ **je n'en pouvais plus dans la montée** I tired myself out on the way up ◆ **ma voiture n'en peut plus** *(usée)* my car's had it* ◆ **regarde-le sur sa moto, il n'en peut plus !*** *(de fierté)* look at him on that motorbike, he's as proud as punch!

♦ **n'en pouvoir plus de** + *nom* ◆ **elle n'en pouvait plus de joie** she was beside herself with joy ◆ **je n'en pouvais plus de honte** I was absolutely mortified ◆ **ils n'en peuvent plus des humiliations** they can't take any more humiliation, they've had enough of being humiliated ◆ **elle n'en peut plus de leur machisme** she's had enough of their macho attitude

♦ **n'en pouvoir plus de** + *infinitif* ◆ **il n'en peut plus d'attendre** he's fed up with waiting*, he can't bear to wait any longer ◆ **je n'en pouvais plus de rire** I laughed so much it hurt

♦ **n'en pouvoir mais** *(littér)* ◆ **il n'en pouvait mais** he could do nothing about it

4 - VERBE PRONOMINAL

se pouvoir

L'éventualité, l'hypothèse ou le risque sont rendus par **may**, **might**, **could**, **be possible** ou un adverbe.

◆ **ça se peut*** possibly, perhaps, maybe, it's possible ◆ **tu crois qu'il va pleuvoir ? – ça se pourrait bien** do you think it's going to rain? – it might ◆ **ça ne se peut pas*** that's impossible, that's not possible ◆ **essayez, s'il se peut, de la convaincre** *(frm)* try to convince her, if at all possible

♦ **il se peut/se pourrait que** + *subjonctif* ◆ **il se peut/se pourrait qu'elle vienne** she may/might come ◆ **il se pourrait bien qu'il pleuve** it might *ou* could well rain ◆ **se peut-il que … ?** is it possible that …?, could *ou* might it be that …? ◆ **comment se peut-il que le dossier soit perdu ?** how can the file possibly be lost? ◆ **il se peut, éventuellement, que …** it may possibly be that …

pouvoir² /puvwaʀ/ NM 1 *(= faculté)* power; *(= capacité)* ability, capacity; *(Phys)* power ◆ **avoir le ~ de faire qch** to have the power *ou* ability to do sth ◆ **il a le ~ de se faire des amis partout** he has the ability *ou* he is able to make friends everywhere ◆ **il a un extraordinaire ~ d'éloquence/de conviction** he has remarkable *ou* exceptional powers of oratory/of persuasion ◆ **ce n'est pas en mon ~** it's not within *ou* in my power, it's beyond my power ◆ **il n'est pas en son ~ de vous aider** it's beyond *ou* it doesn't lie within his power to help you ◆ **il fera tout ce qui est en son ~** he will do everything (that is) in his power *ou* all that he possibly can ◆ **~ absorbant** absorption power, absorption factor *(SPÉC)* ◆ **~ d'attraction** *[de ville, idée]* appeal, attractiveness ◆ **~ couvrant/éclairant** covering/lighting power

2 *(= autorité)* power; *(= influence)* influence ◆ **avoir beaucoup de ~** to have a lot of power *ou* influence, to be very powerful *ou* influential ◆ **avoir du ~ sur qn** to have influence *ou* power over sb ◆ **n'avoir aucun ~ sur qn** to have no influence *ou* authority over sb ◆ **le père a ~ sur ses enfants** a father has power over his children ◆ **tenir qn en son ~** to hold sb in one's power ◆ **le pays entier est en son ~** the whole country is in his power, he has the whole country in his power ◆ **avoir du ~ sur soi-même** to have self-control ◆ **le troisième ~** *(= magistrature)* the magistracy ◆ **le quatrième ~** *(= presse)* the press, the fourth estate

3 *(= droit, attribution)* power ◆ **dépasser ses ~s** to exceed one's powers ◆ **en vertu des ~s qui me sont conférés** by virtue of the power which has been vested in me ◆ **séparation des ~s** separation *ou* division of powers ◆ **avoir ~ de faire qch** *(autorisation)* to have authority to do sth; *(droit)* to have the right to do sth ◆ **je n'ai pas ~ pour vous répondre** I have no authority to reply to you; → **plein**

4 *(Pol)* **le ~** *(= direction des pays)* power; *(= dirigeants)* the government ◆ **~ absolu** absolute power ◆ **~ central** central government ◆ **le parti (politique) au ~** the (political) party in power *ou* in office, the ruling party ◆ **avoir le ~** to have *ou* hold power ◆ **exercer le ~** to exercise power, to rule, to govern ◆ **prendre le ~, arriver au ~** *(légalement)* to come to power *ou* into office; *(illégalement)* to seize power ◆ **prise de ou du ~** *(légal)* coming to power; *(illégal, par la force)* seizure of power ◆ **des milieux proches du ~** sources close to the government ◆ **le ~ actuel dans ce pays** the present régime in this country ◆ **l'opinion et le ~** public opinion and the authorities, us and them *

5 *(Jur = procuration)* proxy ◆ **~ par-devant notaire** power of attorney ◆ **donner ~ à qn de faire qch** to give sb proxy to do sth *(Jur)*, to empower sb to do, to give sb authority to do; → **fondé**

COMP **pouvoir d'achat** purchasing *ou* buying power
pouvoir de concentration powers of concentration
les pouvoirs constitués the powers that be
pouvoir de décision decision-making power(s)
pouvoir disciplinaire disciplinary power(s)
pouvoirs exceptionnels emergency powers
le pouvoir exécutif executive power
le pouvoir judiciaire judicial power
le pouvoir législatif legislative power
pouvoirs publics authorities
pouvoir spirituel spiritual power
pouvoir temporel temporal power

pp (abrév de **pages**) pp

p.p. (abrév de **per procurationem**) p.p.

ppcm /pepeseɛm/ NM (abrév de **plus petit commun multiple**) LCM

PQ /peky/ NM abrév de **Parti québécois** *et de* **Province de Québec** NM *(* = papier hygiénique)* bog paper* *(Brit)*, loo paper * *(Brit)*, TP * *(US)*

PR /peɛʀ/ NM (abrév de **parti républicain**) *French political party* NF (abrév de **poste restante**) → **poste¹**

Pr (abrév de **professeur**) Prof

practice /pʀaktis/ NM *[de golf]* driving range

præsidium /pʀezidjɔm/ NM praesidium ◆ **le ~ suprême** the praesidium of the Supreme Soviet

pragmatique /pʀagmatik/ ADJ pragmatic NF ◆ **la ~** pragmatics *(sg)*

pragmatisme /pʀagmatism/ NM pragmatism

pragmatiste /pʀagmatist/ ADJ pragmatic, pragmatist NMF pragmatist

Prague /pʀag/ N Prague

praire /pʀɛʀ/ NF clam

prairial /pʀɛʀjal/ NM Prairial *(ninth month of French Republican calendar)*

prairie /pʀeʀi/ NF meadow ◆ **la ~** *(aux USA)* the prairie ◆ **des hectares de ~** acres of grassland

pralin /pʀalɛ̃/ NM *(Culin)* praline *(filling for chocolates)*

praline /pʀalin/ NF 1 *(Culin)* *(à l'amande)* praline, sugared almond; *(à la cacahuète)* caramelized peanut; *(Belg = chocolat)* chocolate 2 * *(= balle)* bullet ◆ **il lui a envoyé une ~** *(Ftbl etc)* he blasted the ball to him

praliné, e /pʀaline/ ADJ *[amande]* sugared; *[glace, crème]* praline-flavoured NM praline-flavoured ice cream

prame /pʀam/ NF *(Naut)* pram, praam

praséodyme /pʀazeɔdim/ NM praseodymium

praticable /pʀatikabl/ ADJ 1 *[projet, moyen, opération]* practicable, feasible; *[chemin]* passable, negotiable, practicable ◆ **route difficilement ~ en hiver** road which is almost impassable in winter 2 *(Théât)* *[porte, décor]* working NM *(Théât = décor)* piece of working scenery; *(Ciné = plate-forme)* gantry; *(Sport)* floor mat

praticien, -ienne /pʀatisjɛ̃, jɛn/ NM,F *(gén, Méd)* practitioner ◆ **~ hospitalier** hospital doctor

pratiquant, e /pʀatikɑ̃, ɑt/ ADJ practising *(épith)*, practicing *(épith) (US)* ◆ **catholique/juif/musulman ~** practising Catholic/Jew/Muslim ◆ **il est très/peu ~** *(allant à l'église)* he's/he isn't a regular churchgoer, he goes to *ou* attends/he doesn't go to church regularly ◆ **c'est un catholique non ~** he's a non-practising Catholic ◆ **elle n'est pas ~e** she isn't a practising Christian *(ou* Catholic *etc)* NM,F practising Christian *(ou Catholic etc)*; *(qui va à l'église)* (regular) churchgoer; *(= adepte)* follower ◆ **cette religion compte 30 millions de ~s** the religion has 30 million followers *ou* 30 million faithful

pratique /pʀatik/ ADJ 1 *(= non théorique)* *[jugement, connaissance]* practical; *(Scol)* *[exercice, cours]* practical ◆ **considération d'ordre ~** practical consideration; → **travail¹**

2 *(= réaliste)* *[personne]* practical(-minded) ◆ **il faut être ~ dans la vie** you have to be practical in life ◆ **avoir le sens** *ou* **l'esprit ~** to be practical-minded

3 *(= commode)* *[livre, moyen, vêtement, solution]* practical; *[instrument]* practical, handy; *[emploi du temps]* convenient ◆ **c'est très ~, j'habite à côté du bureau** it's very convenient *ou* handy, I live next door to the office

NF 1 *(= application)* practice ◆ **dans la ~** in practice ◆ **dans la ~ de tous les jours** in the ordinary run of things, in the normal course of events ◆ **en ~** in practice ◆ **mettre qch en ~** to put sth into practice ◆ **la mise en ~ ne sera pas aisée** putting it into practice won't be easy, it won't be easy to put it into practice *ou* to carry it out in practice

2 *(= expérience)* practical experience ◆ **il a une longue ~ des élèves** he has a lot of practical teaching experience ◆ **il a perdu la ~** he is out of practice, he's lost the knack ◆ **avoir la ~ du monde** †† to be well-versed in *ou* be familiar with the ways of society

3 *(= coutume, procédé)* practice ◆ **c'est une ~ générale** it is widespread practice ◆ **des ~s malhonnêtes** dishonest practices, sharp practice ◆ **~s religieuses/sexuelles** religious/sexual practices

4 *(= exercice, observance)* *[de règle]* observance; *[de médecine]* practising, exercise; *[de sport]* practising; *[de vertu]* exercise, practice ◆ **la ~ de l'escrime/du cheval/du golf développe les réflexes** fencing/horse-riding/golfing *ou* (playing) golf develops the reflexes ◆ **la ~ du yoga** the practice of yoga, doing yoga ◆ **~ (religieuse)** religious practice *ou* observance ◆ **condamné pour ~ illégale de la médecine** convicted of practising medicine illegally

5 (†† *= clientèle)* *[de commerçant]* custom (NonC), clientele (NonC); *[d'avocat]* practice, clientele (NonC) ◆ **donner sa ~ à un commerçant** to give a tradesman one's custom

6 (†† *= client)* *[de commerçant]* customer; *[d'avocat]* client

7 (†† *= fréquentation)* *[de personne, société]* frequenting, frequentation; *[d'auteur]* close study

pratiquement /pʀatikmɑ̃/ ADV *(= en pratique, en réalité)* in practice; *(= presque)* practically, virtually ◆ **c'est ~ la même chose, ça revient ~ au même** it's practically *ou* basically the same (thing) ◆ **il n'y en a ~ plus** there are virtually *ou* practically none left, there are hardly any left ◆ **je ne l'ai ~ jamais utilisé** I've hardly ever used it ◆ **je ne les ai ~ pas vus** I hardly saw them ◆ **~, la méthode consiste à ...** in practical terms, the method involves ...

pratiquer /pʀatike/ GRAMMAIRE ACTIVE 46.2
► conjug 1 ◄
VT 1 *(= mettre en pratique) [+ philosophie, politique]* to put into practice, to practise *(Brit)*, to practice *(US)*; *[+ règle]* to observe; *[+ religion, vertu, charité]* to practise *(Brit)*, to practice *(US)*
2 *(= exercer) [+ profession, art]* to practise *(Brit)*, to practice *(US)*; *[+ football, golf]* to play ◆ **~ l'escrime/le cheval/la pêche** to go fencing/horse-riding/fishing ◆ **~ la photo** to do photography ◆ **il est recommandé de ~ un sport** it is considered advisable to play *ou* do a sport ◆ **ils pratiquent l'exploitation systématique du touriste** they systematically exploit tourists
3 *(= faire) [+ ouverture, trou]* to make; *[+ route]* to make, to build; *(Méd) [+ intervention]* to carry out *(sur* on*)*
4 *(= utiliser) [+ méthode]* to practise *(Brit)*, to practice *(US)*, to use; *[+ système]* to use ◆ **~ le chantage** to use blackmail ◆ **~ le bluff** to bluff
5 *[+ rabais]* to give ◆ **ils pratiquent des prix élevés** they keep their prices high
6 *(†† = fréquenter) [+ auteur]* to study closely; *[+ personne, haute société]* to frequent
VI 1 *(Rel)* to practise *(Brit) ou* practice *(US)* one's religion *ou* faith, to be a practising *(Brit) ou* practicing *(US)* Christian *(ou* Muslim *etc)*; *(= aller à l'église)* to go to church, to be a churchgoer
2 *(Méd)* to be in practice, to have a practice
VPR **se pratiquer** *[méthode]* to be used; *[religion]* to be practised *(Brit) ou* practiced *(US)*; *[sport]* to be played ◆ **cela se pratique encore dans les villages** people still do it in the villages ◆ **comme cela se pratique en général** as is the usual practice ◆ **les prix qui se pratiquent à Paris** Paris prices ◆ **le vaudou se pratique encore dans cette région** voodoo is still practised in this region

praxis /pʀaksis/ NF praxis

pré /pʀe/ NM meadow ◆ **aller sur le ~** *(Hist)* to fight a duel ◆ **mettre un cheval au ~** to put a horse out to pasture COMP **pré carré** private preserve *ou* domain *ou* territory

préachat, pré-achat (pl **pré-achats**) /pʀeaʃa/ NM *[de billet]* buying in advance, advance purchasing; *[de film, droits de diffusion]* buying up

pré-acheter /pʀeaʃ(ə)te/ ► conjug 5 ◄ VT *[+ billet]* to buy *ou* purchase in advance; *[+ film, scénario]* to buy up

préadolescent, e /pʀeadɔlesɑ̃, ɑ̃t/ ADJ preadolescent, pre-teenage *(épith)* NM,F preadolescent, pre-teenager

préalable /pʀealabl/ ADJ *[entretien, condition, étude]* preliminary; *[accord, avis]* prior, previous ◆ **faites un essai ~ sur une petite zone** test first on a small area ◆ **~ à** preceding ◆ **lors des entretiens ~s aux négociations** during the discussions (which took place) prior to the negotiations ◆ **vous ne pouvez pas partir sans l'accord ~ du directeur** you cannot leave without first obtaining the director's permission *ou* without the prior agreement of the director ◆ **sans avis** *ou* **avertissement ~** without prior *ou* previous notice NM *(= condition)* precondition, prerequisite; *(† = préparation)* preliminary ◆ **poser qch comme ~ à** to lay sth down as a preliminary condition for
◆ **au préalable** first, beforehand

préalablement /pʀealabləmɑ̃/ ADV first, beforehand ◆ **~ à** prior to ◆ **~ à toute négociation** before any negotiation can take place, prior to any negotiation

Préalpes /pʀealp/ NFPL ◆ **les ~** the Pre-Alps

préalpin, e /pʀealpɛ̃, in/ ADJ of the Pre-Alps

préambule /pʀeɑ̃byl/ NM *[de discours, loi]* preamble *(de* to*)*; *[de contrat]* recitals; *(= prélude)* prelude *(à* to*)*; ◆ **sans ~** without any preliminaries, straight off

préau (pl **préaux**) /pʀeo/ NM *[d'école]* covered playground; *[de prison]* (exercise) yard; *[de couvent]* inner courtyard ◆ **sous le ~ de l'école** in the covered part of the school playground

préavis /pʀeavi/ NM (advance) notice ◆ **un ~ d'un mois** a month's notice *ou* warning ◆ **~ de licenciement** notice (of termination) ◆ **~ de grève** strike notice ◆ **déposer un ~ de grève** to give notice *ou* warning of strike action ◆ **sans ~** *[faire grève, partir]* without (previous) notice, without advance warning; *[retirer de l'argent]* on demand, without advance *ou* previous notice

prébende /pʀebɑ̃d/ NF *(Rel)* prebend; *(péj)* emoluments, payment *(NonC)*

prébendé, e /pʀebɑ̃de/ ADJ prebendal

prébendier /pʀebɑ̃dje/ NM prebendary

prébiotique /pʀebjɔtik/ ADJ *[chimie, molécule]* prebiotic

précaire /pʀekɛʀ/ ADJ *[position, situation, bonheur, équilibre, paix]* precarious; *[emploi]* insecure; *[santé]* shaky, precarious; *[abri]* makeshift ◆ **possesseur/possession (à titre) ~** *(Jur)* precarious holder/tenure

précairement /pʀekɛʀmɑ̃/ ADV precariously

précambrien, -ienne /pʀekɑ̃bʀijɛ̃, ijɛn/ ADJ, NM Precambrian

précancéreux, -euse /pʀekɑ̃seʀø, øz/ ADJ *[état, lésion]* precancerous

précarisation /pʀekaʀizasjɔ̃/ NF *[de situation]* jeopardizing; *[d'emploi]* casualization

précariser /pʀekaʀize/ ► conjug 1 ◄ VT *[+ situation, statut]* to jeopardize; *[+ emploi]* to make insecure ◆ **un tel taux de chômage précarise la société** such a high unemployment rate is a threat to *ou* undermines social stability

précarité /pʀekaʀite/ NF *(gén, Jur)* precariousness ◆ **~ de l'emploi** lack of job security ◆ **prime/indemnité de ~** *bonus/allowance paid to an employee to compensate for lack of job security* ◆ **la ~ des installations nucléaires** the hazards of *ou* the potential dangers of nuclear plants

précaution /pʀekosjɔ̃/ NF 1 *(= disposition)* precaution ◆ **prendre la ~ de faire qch** to take the precaution of doing sth ◆ **prendre des** *ou* **ses ~s** to take precautions ◆ **s'entourer de ~s** to take a lot of precautions ◆ **prendre** *ou* **s'entourer de ~s oratoires** to choose one's words with great care ◆ **il ne s'est pas embarrassé de ~s oratoires** he didn't beat about the bush ◆ **faire qch avec les plus grandes ~s** to do sth with the utmost care *ou* the greatest precaution ◆ **~s d'emploi** *(pour appareil)* safety instructions; *(pour médicament)* precautions before use; → **deux**
2 *(= prudence)* caution, care ◆ **avec ~** cautiously ◆ **"à manipuler avec précaution"** "handle with care" ◆ **par ~** as a precaution *(contre* against*)*; ◆ **par mesure de ~** as a precautionary measure ◆ **pour plus de ~** to be on the safe side ◆ **le principe de ~** the safety-first principle ◆ **sans ~** carelessly

précautionner (se) /pʀekosjɔne/ ► conjug 1 ◄ VPR to take precautions *(contre* against*)*

précautionneusement /pʀekosjɔnøzmɑ̃/ ADV *(= par précaution)* cautiously; *(= avec soin)* carefully

précautionneux, -euse /pʀekosjɔnø, øz/ ADJ *(= prudent)* cautious; *(= soigneux)* careful

précédemment /pʀesedamɑ̃/ ADV before, previously

précédent, e /pʀesedɑ̃, ɑ̃t/ ADJ previous ◆ **un discours/article ~** a previous *ou* an earlier speech/article ◆ **le discours/film ~** the preceding *ou* previous speech/film ◆ **le jour/mois ~** the previous day/month, the day/month before NM *(= fait, décision)* precedent ◆ **sans ~** unprecedented, without precedent ◆ **créer un ~** to create *ou* set a precedent

> ⚠ L'adjectif **précédent** se traduit rarement par le mot anglais **precedent**.

précéder /pʀesede/ ► conjug 6 ◄ VT 1 *(= venir avant) (dans le temps, dans une hiérarchie)* to precede, to come before; *(dans l'espace)* to precede, to be in front of, to come before; *(dans une file de véhicules)* to be in front *ou* ahead of, to precede ◆ **les jours qui ont précédé le coup d'État** the days preceding *ou* leading up to the coup d'état ◆ **être précédé de** to be preceded by ◆ **faire ~ son discours d'un préambule** to precede one's speech by *ou* preface one's speech with an introduction, to give a short introduction to one's speech
2 *(= devancer) (dans le temps, l'espace)* to precede, to go in front *ou* ahead of; *(dans une carrière etc)* to precede, to get ahead of ◆ **quand j'y suis arrivé, j'ai vu que quelqu'un m'avait précédé** when I got there I saw that someone had got there before me *ou* ahead of me *ou* had preceded me ◆ **il le précéda dans la chambre** he went into the room in front of him, he entered the room ahead of *ou* in front of him ◆ **il m'a précédé de cinq minutes** he got there five minutes before me *ou* ahead of me ◆ **sa mauvaise réputation l'avait précédé** his bad reputation had gone before *ou* preceded him
VI to precede, to go before ◆ **les jours qui ont précédé** the preceding days ◆ **dans tout ce qui a précédé** in all that has been said *(ou* written *etc)* before *ou* so far ◆ **dans le chapitre/la semaine qui précède** in the preceding chapter/week

précepte /pʀesɛpt/ NM precept

précepteur /pʀesɛptœʀ/ NM private tutor

préceptorat /pʀesɛptɔʀa/ NM tutorship, tutorage *(frm)*

préceptrice /pʀesɛptʀis/ NF governess

préchauffage /pʀeʃofaʒ/ NM preheating

préchauffer /pʀeʃofe/ ► conjug 1 ◄ VT to preheat

prêche /pʀɛʃ/ NM *(lit, fig)* sermon

prêcher /pʀeʃe/ ► conjug 1 ◄ VT 1 *(Rel, fig)* to preach; *[+ personne]* to preach to ◆ **~ un converti** to preach to the converted; → **parole** 2 *(= recommander) [+ modération, non-violence, tolérance]* to advocate ◆ **~ le faux pour savoir le vrai** to make false statements in order to discover the truth VI *(Rel)* to preach; *(fig)* to preach, to preachify, to sermonize ◆ **~ dans le désert** *(fig)* to preach in the wilderness ◆ **~ d'exemple** *ou* **par l'exemple** to practise what one preaches, to preach by example ◆ **~ pour son saint** *ou* **sa paroisse** to look after one's own interests, to look after *ou* take care of number one*

prêcheur, -euse /pʀɛʃœʀ, øz/ ADJ *[personne, ton]* moralizing ◆ **frères ~s** *(Rel)* preaching friars NM,F *(Rel)* preacher; *(fig)* moralizer

prêchi-prêcha /pʀeʃipʀeʃa/ NM INV *(péj)* preachifying *(NonC)*, continuous moralizing *(NonC) ou* sermonizing *(NonC)*

précieusement /pʀesjøzmɑ̃/ ADV 1 *(= soigneusement) [conserver]* carefully ◆ **garde ces lettres ~** take great care of these letters 2 *(= de manière affectée) [parler]* in an affected manner

précieux, -ieuse /pʀesjø, jøz/ ADJ 1 *(= de valeur) [pierre, métal, bois, bijou]* precious 2 *(= très utile) [collaborateur, aide, conseil]* invaluable *(à* to*)*; ◆ **votre aide m'est précieuse** your help is invaluable to me [3] *(= cher) [ami]* valued, precious [4] *(= affecté)* precious, affected [5] *(Littérat) [écrivain, salon]* précieux, precious **NF précieuse** précieuse

préciosité /pʀesjozite/ **NF** [1] ◆ **la ~** *(Littérat)* preciosity; *(= affectation)* preciosity, affectation [2] *(= formule, trait)* stylistic affectation, euphuism *(frm)*

précipice /pʀesipis/ **NM** [1] *(= gouffre)* chasm; *(= paroi abrupte)* precipice ◆ **un ~ de plusieurs centaines de mètres** a drop of several hundred metres ◆ **la voiture s'immobilisa au bord du ~/tomba dans le ~** the car stopped at the very edge *ou* brink of the precipice/went over the precipice ◆ **ne t'aventure pas près du ~** you mustn't go too near the edge [2] *(fig)* abyss ◆ **être au bord du ~** to be at the edge of the abyss

précipitamment /pʀesipitamɑ̃/ **ADV** hurriedly, hastily, precipitately *(frm)* ◆ **sortir ~** to rush *ou* dash out

précipitation /pʀesipitasjɔ̃/ **NF** [1] *(= hâte)* haste; *(= hâte excessive)* great haste, violent hurry ◆ **dans ma ~, je l'ai oublié chez moi** in my haste, I left it at home ◆ **avec ~** in great haste, in a great rush *ou* hurry [2] *(Chim)* precipitation **NFPL précipitations** *(Météo)* rainfall, precipitation ◆ **de fortes ~s** heavy rainfall ◆ **de nouvelles ~s sont prévues** more rain is forecast

précipité, e /pʀesipite/ (ptp de **précipiter**) **ADJ** *[départ, décision]* hurried, hasty, precipitate *(frm)*; *[fuite]* headlong; *[pas]* hurried; *[pouls, respiration, rythme]* fast, rapid ◆ **tout cela est trop ~** it's all happening too fast **NM** *(Chim)* precipitate

précipiter /pʀesipite/ ▸ conjug 1 ◂ **VT** [1] *(= jeter) [+ personne]* to throw, to push; *[+ objet]* to throw, to hurl *(contre* against, at; *vers* towards, at); ◆ **~ qn du haut d'une falaise** to push sb off a cliff ◆ **~ qn dans un escalier** to push sb downstairs ◆ **le choc l'a précipité contre le pare-brise** the shock threw *ou* hurled him against the windscreen ◆ **~ qn dans le malheur** to plunge sb into misfortune

[2] *(= hâter) [+ pas]* to quicken, to speed up; *[+ événement]* to hasten, to precipitate; *[+ départ]* to hasten ◆ **il ne faut rien ~** we mustn't be too hasty, we mustn't rush things

[3] *(Chim)* to precipitate

VI *(Chim)* to precipitate

VPR se précipiter [1] *(= se jeter) [personne]* **se ~ dans le vide** to hurl o.s. into space ◆ **se ~ du haut d'une falaise** to jump off *ou* throw o.s. off a cliff

[2] *(= se ruer)* **se ~ vers** to rush *ou* race towards ◆ **se ~ sur** to rush at ◆ **se ~ contre** *[personne]* to rush at, to throw o.s. against; *[voiture]* to smash into ◆ **se ~ au devant de qn/aux pieds de qn** to throw o.s. in front of sb/at sb's feet ◆ **se ~ sur l'ennemi** to rush at *ou* hurl o.s. on *ou* at the enemy ◆ **elle se précipita dans ses bras** she rushed into *ou* threw herself into *ou* flew into his arms ◆ **il se précipita à la porte pour ouvrir** he rushed to open the door ◆ **il se précipita sur le balcon** he raced *ou* dashed *ou* rushed out onto the balcony

[3] *(= s'accélérer) [rythme]* to speed up; *[pouls]* to quicken, to speed up ◆ **les choses** *ou* **événements se précipitaient** everything was happening at once

[4] *(= se dépêcher)* to hurry, to rush ◆ **ne nous précipitons pas** let's not rush things

précis, e /pʀesi, iz/ **ADJ** [1] *(= exact) [style, vocabulaire, terme, indication, témoignage]* precise; *[sens]* precise, exact; *[description]* accurate, precise; *[chiffre, calcul]* accurate, precise; *[instrument, tir, montre]* accurate ◆ **sois plus ~ dans le choix de tes mots** be more precise in your choice of words, choose your words more carefully

[2] *(= bien défini, particulier) [idée, donnée, règle]* precise, definite; *[heure, date]* precise, exact; *[ordre, demande]* precise; *[fait, raison]* precise, particular, specific; *[souvenir]* clear ◆ **sans raison ~e** for no particular *ou* precise reason ◆ **sans but ~** with no clear aim, with no particular aim in mind ◆ **je ne pense à rien de ~** I'm not thinking of anything in particular ◆ **à cet instant ~** at that precise *ou* very moment ◆ **au moment ~ où ...** at the precise *ou* exact *ou* very moment when ... ◆ **à 4 heures ~es** at 4 o'clock sharp *ou* on the dot*, at 4 o'clock precisely ◆ **à l'endroit ~ où ...** at the exact place where ... ◆ **sans que l'on puisse dire de façon ~e ...** although we can't say precisely *ou* with any precision ... ◆ **se référer à un texte de façon ~e** to make precise reference to a text

[3] *(= net) [point]* precise, exact; *[contours]* precise, distinct; *[geste, esprit]* precise; *[trait]* distinct

NM *(= résumé)* précis, summary; *(= manuel)* handbook

précisément /pʀesizemɑ̃/ **GRAMMAIRE ACTIVE 40.2, 53.1 ADV** [1] *(= avec précision) [décrire, chiffrer]* accurately, precisely; *[définir, déterminer, expliquer]* clearly ◆ **ou plus ~** or more precisely *ou* exactly, or to be more precise

[2] *(= justement)* **je venais ~ de sortir** I had in fact just gone out, as it happened I'd just gone out ◆ **c'est lui ~ qui m'avait conseillé de le faire** as a matter of fact it was he *ou* it so happens that it was he who advised me to do it ◆ **c'est ~ la raison pour laquelle** *ou* **c'est ~ pour cela que je viens vous voir** that's precisely *ou* just why I've come to see you, it's for that very *ou* precise reason that I've come to see you ◆ **mais je ne l'ai pas vu ! – ~ !** but I didn't see him! – precisely! *ou* exactly! *ou* that's just it! *ou* that's just the point!

[3] *(= exactement)* exactly, precisely ◆ **c'est ~ ce que je cherchais** that's exactly *ou* precisely *ou* just what I was looking for ◆ **il est arrivé ~ à ce moment-là** he arrived right *ou* just at that moment *ou* at that exact *ou* precise *ou* very moment ◆ **ce n'est pas ~ un chef-d'œuvre** it's not exactly what I'd call a masterpiece

préciser /pʀesize/ ▸ conjug 1 ◂ **VT** *[+ idée, intention]* to specify, to make clear, to clarify; *[+ fait, point]* to be more specific about, to clarify; *[+ destination]* to name, to specify ◆ **je vous préciserai la date de la réunion plus tard** I'll let you know the exact date of the meeting *ou* precisely when the meeting is later ◆ **il a précisé que ...** he explained that ..., he made it clear that ... ◆ **je dois ~ que ...** I must point out *ou* add that ... ◆ **pourriez-vous ~ quand cela est arrivé ?** could you say exactly when it happened? ◆ **pourriez-vous ~ ?** could you be more precise? *ou* specific? **VPR se préciser** *[idée]* to take shape; *[danger, intention]* to become clear *ou* clearer ◆ **la situation commence à se ~** we are beginning to see the situation more clearly ◆ **ça se précise !*** we're getting there!

précision /pʀesizjɔ̃/ **NF** [1] *(gén)* precision; *[de description, instrument]* precision, accuracy; *[de contours]* precision, distinctness; *[de trait]* distinctness ◆ **avec ~** precisely, with precision ◆ **de ~** precision *(épith)* ◆ **de haute ~** high-precision *(épith)*

[2] *(= détail)* point, piece of information ◆ **j'aimerais vous demander une ~/des ~s** I'd like to ask you to explain one thing/for further information ◆ **il a apporté des ~s intéressantes** he revealed some interesting points *ou* facts *ou* information ◆ **il n'a donné aucune ~ sur ce point** he didn't go into any detail on this point ◆ **encore une ~** one more point *ou* thing ◆ **sans autre ~** without any further information *ou* details ◆ **il m'a dit cela sans autre ~** he told me no more than that

précité, e /pʀesite/ **ADJ** aforesaid, aforementioned; *(par écrit)* aforesaid, above(-mentioned)

précoce /pʀekɔs/ **ADJ** *[fruit, saison, gelée]* early; *[plante]* early-flowering, early-fruiting, precocious *(SPÉC)*; *[calvitie, sénilité]* premature; *[mariage]* young *(épith)*, early *(épith)*; *[diagnostic]* early; *[enfant] (intellectuellement)* precocious, advanced for his *(ou* her) age *(attrib)*; *(sexuellement)* sexually precocious

précocement /pʀekɔsmɑ̃/ **ADV** precociously

précocité /pʀekɔsite/ **NF** *[de fruit, saison]* earliness; *[d'enfant] (intellectuelle)* precocity, precociousness; *(sexuelle)* sexual precocity *ou* precociousness

précolombien, -ienne /pʀekɔlɔ̃bjɛ̃, jɛn/ **ADJ** pre-Columbian

précombustion /pʀekɔ̃bystjɔ̃/ **NF** precombustion

précompte /pʀekɔ̃t/ **NM** *(= évaluation)* estimate ◆ **~ (fiscal)** *(= déduction)* tax withholding

précompter /pʀekɔ̃te/ ▸ conjug 1 ◂ **VT** *(= évaluer)* to estimate; *(= déduire)* to deduct *(sur* from)

préconception /pʀekɔ̃sɛpsjɔ̃/ **NF** preconception

préconçu, e /pʀekɔ̃sy/ **ADJ** preconceived ◆ **idée ~e** preconceived idea

préconisation /pʀekɔnizasjɔ̃/ **NF** recommendation

préconiser /pʀekɔnize/ ▸ conjug 1 ◂ **VT** *[+ remède]* to recommend; *[+ méthode, mode de vie, plan, solution]* to advocate

précontraint, e /pʀekɔ̃tʀɛ̃, ɛt/ **ADJ, NM** ◆ **(béton) ~** prestressed concrete **NF précontrainte** *(Tech)* prestressing

précuit, e /pʀekɥi, it/ **ADJ** precooked

précurseur /pʀekyʀsœʀ/ **ADJ M** precursory ◆ **~ de** preceding; → **signe NM** *(= personne)* forerunner, precursor; *(Bio)* precursor ◆ **il fait figure de ~ dans ce domaine** he's something of a trail-blazer in this field

prédateur, -trice /pʀedatœʀ, tʀis/ **ADJ** predatory **NM** *(gén)* predator; *(Écon)* raider

prédation /pʀedasjɔ̃/ **NF** predation

prédécesseur /pʀedesesœʀ/ **NM** predecessor

prédécoupé, e /pʀedekupe/ **ADJ** precut

prédéfinir /pʀedefiniʀ/ ▸ conjug 2 ◂ **VT** to predefine

prédestination /pʀedɛstinasjɔ̃/ **NF** predestination

prédestiné, e /pʀedɛstine/ (ptp de **prédestiner**) **ADJ** predestined *(à qch* for sth; *à faire* to do) fated *(à faire* to do); ◆ **elle portait un nom ~** she bore a prophetic name

prédestiner /pʀedɛstine/ ▸ conjug 1 ◂ **VT** to predestine *(à qch* for sth; *à faire* to do); ◆ **rien ne le prédestinait à devenir président** nothing about him suggested that he might one day become president

prédétermination /pʀedetɛʀminasjɔ̃/ **NF** predetermination

prédéterminer /pʀedetɛʀmine/ ▸ conjug 1 ◂ **VT** to predetermine

prédicant /pʀedikɑ̃/ **NM** preacher

prédicat /pʀedika/ **NM** predicate

prédicateur /pʀedikatœʀ/ **NM** preacher

prédicatif, -ive /pʀedikatif, iv/ **ADJ** predicative

prédication¹ /pʀedikasjɔ̃/ **NF** *(= activité)* preaching; *(= sermon)* sermon

prédication² /pʀedikasjɔ̃/ **NF** *(Ling)* predication

prédiction /pʀediksjɔ̃/ **NF** prediction

prédigéré, e /pʀediʒeʀe/ ADJ predigested

prédilection /pʀedilɛksjɔ̃/ NF (*pour qn, qch*) predilection, partiality (*pour* for); ◆ **avoir une ~ pour qch** to be partial to sth ◆ **de ~** favourite

prédire /pʀediʀ/ ▸ conjug 37 ◂ VT [*prophète*] to foretell; (*gén*) to predict ◆ **~ l'avenir** to tell *ou* predict the future ◆ **~ qch à qn** to predict sth for sb ◆ **il m'a prédit que je ...** he predicted (that) I ..., he told me (that) I ...

prédisposer /pʀedispoze/ ▸ conjug 1 ◂ VT to predispose (*à qch* to sth; *à faire qch* to do sth); ◆ **être prédisposé à une maladie** to be predisposed *ou* prone to an illness ◆ **être prédisposé en faveur de qn** to be predisposed in sb's favour ◆ **cela peut entraîner une prise de poids chez les sujets prédisposés** this may cause people to put on weight if they are prone to it

prédisposition /pʀedispozisjɔ̃/ NF predisposition (*à qch* to sth; *à faire qch* to do sth); ◆ **~ génétique** genetic (pre)disposition ◆ **avoir une ~ à l'obésité/à l'hypertension** to have a tendency to put on weight/to high blood pressure ◆ **elle avait des ~s pour la peinture** she showed a talent for painting

prédominance /pʀedɔminɑ̃s/ NF (*gén*) predominance, predominancy (*sur* over); [*de couleur*] predominance, prominence ◆ **population à ~ protestante** predominantly Protestant population ◆ **œuvres à ~ littéraire** mainly literary works

prédominant, e /pʀedɔminɑ̃, ɑ̃t/ ADJ (*gén*) predominant; [*avis, impression*] prevailing; [*couleur*] predominant, most prominent ◆ **ce pays occupe une place ~e sur le marché européen** this country occupies a dominant position in the European market

prédominer /pʀedɔmine/ ▸ conjug 1 ◂ VI (*gén*) to predominate; [*avis, impression*] to prevail; [*couleur*] to predominate, to be most prominent ◆ **le souci qui prédomine dans mon esprit** the worry which is uppermost in my mind

pré-électoral, e (mpl **-aux**) /pʀeelɛktɔʀal, o/ ADJ pre-election (*épith*)

préemballé, e /pʀeɑ̃bale/ ADJ prepacked, prepackaged

préembauche /pʀeɑ̃boʃ/ NF INV pre-recruitment

prééminence /pʀeeminɑ̃s/ NF pre-eminence ◆ **donner la ~ à qch** to give pre-eminence to sth

prééminent, e /pʀeeminɑ̃, ɑ̃t/ ADJ pre-eminent

préempter /pʀeɑ̃pte/ ▸ conjug 1 ◂ VT (*Jur*) to pre-empt

préemption /pʀeɑ̃psjɔ̃/ NF pre-emption ◆ **droit de ~** pre-emptive right

préencollé, e /pʀeɑ̃kɔle/ ADJ ◆ **papier peint ~** pre-pasted *ou* ready-pasted wallpaper ◆ **enveloppe ~e** gummed envelope

préenregistré, e /pʀeɑ̃ʀ(ə)ʒistʀe/ ADJ [*émission*] prerecorded ◆ **rires ~s** canned laughter

préenregistrement /pʀeɑ̃ʀ(ə)ʒistʀəmɑ̃/ NM [*de son, d'image*] pre-recording. [*de bagages*] check-in

préenregistrer /pʀeɑ̃ʀ(ə)ʒistʀe/ VT [*+ son, image*] to pre-record ◆ **vous pouvez ~ vos bagages** you can check in your luggage in advance

préétabli, e /pʀeetabli/ (ptp de **préétablir**) ADJ [*schéma, plan*] preestablished ◆ **harmonie ~e** (*Philos*) preestablished harmony

préétablir /pʀeetabliʀ/ ▸ conjug 2 ◂ VT to pre-establish

préexistant, e /pʀeɛgzistɑ̃, ɑ̃t/ ADJ pre-existent, pre-existing

préexistence /pʀeɛgzistɑ̃s/ NF pre-existence

préexister /pʀeɛgziste/ ▸ conjug 1 ◂ VI to pre-exist ◆ **~ à** to exist before

préfabrication /pʀefabʀikasjɔ̃/ NF prefabrication

préfabriqué, e /pʀefabʀike/ ADJ prefabricated NM (*= maison*) prefabricated house, prefab*; (*= matériau*) prefabricated material ◆ **en ~** prefabricated

préface /pʀefas/ NF preface; (*fig = prélude*) preface, prelude (*à* to)

préfacer /pʀefase/ ▸ conjug 3 ◂ VT [*+ livre*] to write a preface for, to preface

préfacier /pʀefasje/ NM preface writer

préfectoral, e (mpl **-aux**) /pʀefɛktɔʀal, o/ ADJ (*Admin française, Antiq*) prefectorial, prefectural; → **arrêté**

préfecture /pʀefɛktyʀ/ NF prefecture ◆ **~ de police** police headquarters ◆ **~ maritime** *police port authority*

> **PRÉFECTURE, PRÉFET**
>
> In France, a **préfet** is a high-ranking civil servant who represents the State at the level of the « département » or the « région ». Besides a range of important administrative duties, the role of the **préfet** is to ensure that government decisions are carried out properly at local level. The term **préfecture** refers to the area over which the **préfet** has authority, to the town where the administrative offices of the **préfet** are situated, and to these offices themselves. Official documents such as driving licences are issued by the **préfecture**. → DÉPARTEMENT, RÉGION

préférable /pʀefeʀabl/ ADJ preferable (*à qch* to sth); ◆ **il est ~ que je parte** it is preferable *ou* better that I should leave *ou* for me to leave ◆ **il serait ~ d'y aller *ou* que vous y alliez** it would be better if you went *ou* for you to go ◆ **il est ~ de ...** it is preferable *ou* better to ...

préférablement /pʀefeʀabləmɑ̃/ ADV preferably ◆ **~ à** in preference to

préféré, e /pʀefeʀe/ GRAMMAIRE ACTIVE 34.1 ADJ, NM,F favourite (*Brit*), favorite (*US*)

préférence /pʀefeʀɑ̃s/ GRAMMAIRE ACTIVE 34.5 NF preference ◆ **donner la ~ à** to give preference to ◆ **avoir une ~ marquée pour ...** to have a marked preference for ... ◆ **avoir la ~ sur** to have preference over ◆ **je n'ai pas de ~** I have no preference, I don't mind ◆ **par ordre de ~** in order of preference ◆ **la ~ communautaire** (*Europe*) Community preference ◆ **la ~ nationale** (*Pol*) *discrimination in favour of a country's own nationals*

◆ **de préférence** (*= plutôt*) preferably ◆ **de ~ à** in preference to, rather than

préférentiel, -ielle /pʀefeʀɑ̃sjɛl/ ADJ preferential ◆ **tarif ~** (*gén*) preferential *ou* special rate; (*Douane*) preferential tariff ◆ **action préférentielle** (*Bourse*) preferred *ou* preference share

préférentiellement /pʀefeʀɑ̃sjɛlmɑ̃/ ADV preferentially

préférer /pʀefeʀe/ GRAMMAIRE ACTIVE 31, 34.1, 34.4, 35.5 ▸ conjug 6 ◂ VT to prefer (*à* to); ◆ **je préfère ce manteau à l'autre** I prefer this coat to the other one, I like this coat better than the other one ◆ **je te préfère avec les cheveux courts** I like you better *ou* prefer you with short hair ◆ **je préfère aller au cinéma** I prefer to go *ou* I would rather go to the cinema ◆ **il préfère que ce soit vous qui le fassiez** he would rather you did it ◆ **nous avons préféré attendre avant de vous le dire** we thought it better to wait before telling you ◆ **nous avons préféré attendre que d'y aller tout de suite** we preferred to wait *ou* thought it better to wait rather than go straight away ◆ **que préférez-vous, du thé ou du café ?** what would you rather have *ou* what would you prefer – tea or coffee? ◆ **si tu préfères** if you prefer, if you like, if you'd rather ◆ **comme vous préférez** as you prefer *ou* like *ou* wish *ou* please ◆ **j'aurais préféré ne jamais l'avoir rencontré** I wish I'd never met him

préfet /pʀefɛ/ NM (*Admin française, Antiq*) prefect; (*Belg = directeur*) headmaster, principal (*of a college*), head (*Brit*) ◆ **~ de police** prefect of police, chief of police

préfète /pʀefɛt/ NF 1 (*= femme préfet*) (female *ou* woman) prefect; (*= femme du préfet*) prefect's wife 2 (*Belg = directrice*) headmistress, principal (*of a college*), head (*Brit*)

préfiguration /pʀefigyʀasjɔ̃/ NF prefiguration, foreshadowing

préfigurer /pʀefigyʀe/ ▸ conjug 1 ◂ VT to prefigure, to foreshadow

préfixal, e (mpl **-aux**) /pʀefiksal, o/ ADJ prefixal

préfixation /pʀefiksasjɔ̃/ NF prefixation

préfixe /pʀefiks/ NM prefix

préfixer /pʀefikse/ ▸ conjug 1 ◂ VT to prefix

préglaciaire /pʀeglasjɛʀ/ ADJ preglacial

prégnance /pʀegnɑ̃s/ NF (*littér*) [*de souvenir*] vividness; [*de tradition*] resonance; (*Psych*) pregnance (*SPÉC*), Prägnanz (*SPÉC*)

prégnant, e /pʀegnɑ̃, ɑ̃t/ ADJ (*littér*) [*souvenir*] vivid; [*débat*] meaningful ◆ **cette tradition est encore très ~e** this tradition still has great resonance

préhenseur /pʀeɑ̃sœʀ/ ADJ M prehensile

préhensile /pʀeɑ̃sil/ ADJ prehensile

préhension /pʀeɑ̃sjɔ̃/ NF prehension

préhispanique /pʀeispanik/ ADJ [*civilisation, culture*] pre-Hispanic

préhistoire /pʀeistwaʀ/ NF prehistory ◆ **les hommes de la ~** prehistoric men ◆ **depuis la ~** since prehistoric times

préhistorien, -ienne /pʀeistɔʀjɛ̃, jɛn/ NM,F prehistorian

préhistorique /pʀeistɔʀik/ ADJ prehistoric; (*= suranné*) antediluvian, ancient

préimplantatoire /pʀeɛ̃plɑ̃tatwaʀ/ ADJ ◆ **diagnostic ~** pre-implantation screening

préindustriel, -ielle /pʀeɛ̃dystʀijɛl/ ADJ preindustrial ◆ **la Grande-Bretagne préindustrielle** preindustrial Britain, Great Britain before the industrial revolution

préinscription /pʀeɛ̃skʀipsjɔ̃/ NF (*à l'université*) preregistration (*à* at); (*à un concours*) preregistration (*à* for)

préjudice /pʀeʒydis/ NM (*matériel, financier*) loss; (*moral*) harm (*NonC*), damage (*NonC*), wrong ◆ **~ commercial/financier** commercial/financial loss ◆ **~ matériel** material loss *ou* damage ◆ **~ moral** moral wrong ◆ **subir un ~** (*matériel*) to sustain a loss; (*moral*) to be wronged ◆ **le ~ subi par la victime** (*financier, matériel*) the loss sustained by the victim; (*moral*) the moral wrong *ou* damage suffered by the victim ◆ **causer un ~ *ou* porter ~ à qn** (*gén*) to do sb harm, to harm sb; [*décision*] to be detrimental to sb *ou* to sb's interests ◆ **ce supermarché a porté ~ aux petits commerçants** this supermarket was detrimental to (the interests of) small tradesmen ◆ **je ne voudrais pas vous porter ~ en leur racontant cela** I wouldn't like to harm you *ou* your case *ou* make difficulties for you by telling them about this

◆ **au préjudice de** ◆ **au ~ de sa santé/de M. Dufeu** to the detriment of health/of M. Dufeu ◆ **au ~ de la vérité** at the expense of truth

♦ **sans préjudice de** without prejudice to

> ⚠ Attention à ne pas traduire automatiquement **préjudice** par le mot anglais **prejudice**, qui a le sens de 'préjugé'.

préjudiciable /pʀeʒydisjabl/ **ADJ** prejudicial, detrimental, harmful (*à* to)

préjugé /pʀeʒyʒe/ **NM** prejudice ♦ **avoir un ~ contre** to be prejudiced *ou* biased against ♦ **sans ~** unprejudiced, unbiased ♦ **bénéficier d'un ~ favorable** to be favourably considered ♦ **~s de classe** class bias ♦ **~ de race** racial prejudice

préjuger /pʀeʒyʒe/ ▸ conjug 3 ◂ **préjuger de** **VT INDIR** to prejudge ♦ **~ d'une réaction** to foresee a reaction, to judge what a reaction might be ♦ **autant qu'on peut le ~, à ce qu'on en peut ~** as far as it is possible to judge in advance

prélasser (se) /pʀelɑse/ ▸ conjug 1 ◂ **VPR** *(dans un fauteuil)* to sprawl, to lounge; *(au soleil)* to bask

prélat /pʀela/ **NM** prelate

prélature /pʀelatyʀ/ **NF** prelacy

prélavage /pʀelavaʒ/ **NM** prewash

prélaver /pʀelave/ ▸ conjug 1 ◂ **VT** to prewash

prélèvement /pʀelɛvmɑ̃/ **NM** [1] *(Méd, Sci)* *[d'échantillon]* taking (NonC); *[d'organe]* removal ♦ **faire un ~ de sang** *ou* **sanguin** to take a blood sample [2] *(Fin)* *[de montant, pourcentage]* deduction; *(sur un compte, par le titulaire)* withdrawal, drawing out (NonC); *(par un créancier)* debit ♦ **~ automatique** *[de somme fixe]* standing order; *[de somme variable]* direct debit ♦ **~ bancaire** standing *ou* banker's order *(Brit)*, automatic deduction *(US)* [3] *[d'impôt]* levying (NonC), levy, imposition ♦ **~ fiscal/compensatoire/sur le capital/à l'importation** tax/compensatory/capital/import levy ♦ **~s obligatoires** tax and social security deductions

prélever /pʀel(ə)ve/ ▸ conjug 5 ◂ **VT** [1] *(Méd, Sci)* *[+ échantillon]* to take *(sur* from*)*; *[+ sang]* to take (a sample of); *[+ organe]* to remove [2] *(Fin)* *[+ montant, pourcentage]* to deduct *(sur* from*)*; *[+ somme] (sur un compte) [titulaire]* to withdraw *(sur* from*)*; *[créancier]* to debit *(sur* from*)*; ♦ **ses factures d'électricité sont automatiquement prélevées sur son compte** his electricity bills are debited *ou* automatically deducted from his account [3] *[+ impôt]* to levy, to impose *(sur* on*)*

préliminaire /pʀeliminɛʀ/ **ADJ** *(gén)* preliminary; *[discours]* introductory **NMPL** **préliminaires** preliminaries; *[de négociations]* preliminary talks

prélude /pʀelyd/ **NM** *(Mus = morceau)* prelude; *(pour se préparer)* warm-up; *(fig)* prelude *(à* to*)*

préluder /pʀelyde/ ▸ conjug 1 ◂ **VI** *(Mus)* to warm up ♦ **~ par qch** to begin with sth **VT INDIR** **préluder à** to be a prelude to, to lead up to

prématuré, e /pʀematyʀe/ **ADJ** *[bébé, nouvelle]* premature; *[mort]* untimely, premature ♦ **il est ~ de ...** it is premature to ..., it's too early to ... ♦ **de 3 semaines** 3 weeks premature *ou* early **NM,F** premature baby

prématurément /pʀematyʀemɑ̃/ **ADV** prematurely ♦ **une cruelle maladie l'a enlevé ~ à notre affection** a grievous illness brought his untimely departure from our midst

prémédication /pʀemedikasjɔ̃/ **NF** premedication, premed*

préméditation /pʀemeditasjɔ̃/ **NF** premeditation ♦ **avec ~** *[crime]* premeditated; *[tuer]* with intent, with malice aforethought ♦ **meurtre sans ~** unpremeditated murder

préméditer /pʀemedite/ ▸ conjug 1 ◂ **VT** to premeditate ♦ **~ de faire qch** to plan to do sth ♦ **meurtre prémédité** premeditated *ou* wilful murder

prémenstruel, -elle /pʀemɑ̃stʀyɛl/ **ADJ** premenstrual ♦ **syndrome ~** premenstrual tension *ou* syndrome

prémices /pʀemis/ **NFPL** *(littér)* beginnings; *[de récolte]* first fruits; *[d'animaux]* first-born (animals); *[de guerre, crise]* first *ou* warning signs; *[d'évolution]* beginnings

premier, -ière[1] /pʀəmje, jɛʀ/ GRAMMAIRE ACTIVE 53.2, 53.5

ADJ [1] *(dans le temps)* first; *[impression]* first, initial ♦ **les premières heures du jour** the early hours (of the morning), the small hours ♦ **dès les ~s jours** from the very first days ♦ **ses ~s poèmes** his first *ou* early poems ♦ **les ~s habitants de la Terre** the earliest *ou* first inhabitants of the Earth ♦ **les premières années de sa vie** the first few *ou* the early years of his life ♦ **c'est la première et la dernière fois que je suis tes conseils** it's the first and last time I follow your advice ♦ **au ~ signe de résistance** at the first *ou* slightest sign of resistance ♦ **à mon ~ signal** at the first signal from me, as soon as you see my signal; → **art, lit, main** *etc*; → aussi **sixième**

[2] *(dans un ordre)* first; *(à un examen)* first, top; *(en importance)* leading, foremost, top ♦ **~ commis/clerc** chief shop *(Brit)* *ou* store *(US)* assistant/clerk ♦ **le ~ constructeur automobile européen** the leading European car manufacturer ♦ **le ~ personnage de l'État** the country's leading *ou* most senior statesman ♦ **arriver/être ~** to arrive/be first ♦ **il est toujours ~ en classe** he's always top of the class *ou* first in the class ♦ **être reçu ~** to come first

[3] *(dans l'espace)* *[branche]* lower, bottom; *[rangée]* front ♦ **la première marche de l'escalier** *(en bas)* the bottom step; *(en haut)* the top step ♦ **le ~ barreau de l'échelle** the bottom *ou* first *ou* lowest rung of the ladder ♦ **le ~ mouchoir de la pile** the first handkerchief in the pile, the top handkerchief in the pile ♦ **les 100 premières pages** the first 100 pages ♦ **en première page** *(Presse)* on the front page ♦ **lire un livre de la première à la dernière ligne** to read a book from beginning to end *ou* from cover to cover

[4] *(= de base)* *[échelon, grade]* bottom; *[ébauche, projet]* first, rough ♦ **quel est votre ~ prix pour ce type de voyage ?** what do your prices start at for this kind of trip? ♦ **apprendre les ~s rudiments d'une science** to learn the first *ou* basic rudiments of a science

[5] *(après n = originel, fondamental)* *[cause, donnée]* basic; *[principe]* first, basic; *[objectif]* basic, primary, prime; *[état]* initial, original ♦ **c'est la qualité première d'un chef d'État** it's the prime *ou* essential quality for a head of state ♦ **retrouver sa vivacité première/son éclat ~** to regain one's former *ou* initial liveliness/sparkle

NM,F [1] *(dans le temps, l'espace)* first (one) ♦ **parler/passer/sortir le ~** to speak/go/go out first ♦ **arriver les ~s** to arrive (the) first ♦ **arriver dans les ~s** to be one of *ou* be among the first to arrive ♦ **les ~s arrivés seront les ~s servis** first come, first served ♦ **elle sera servie la première** she will be served first ♦ **au ~ de ces messieurs** next gentleman please ♦ **il a été le ~ à reconnaître ses torts** he was the first to admit that he was in the wrong ♦ **elle fut l'une des premières à ...** she was one of the first to ...; → **né**

[2] *(dans une hiérarchie, un ordre)* **il a été reçu dans** *ou* **parmi les ~s** *(Scol, Univ)* he was in the top *ou* first few ♦ **il est le ~ de sa classe** he is top of his class ♦ **il a une tête de ~ de la classe** *(péj)* he looks like a real egghead* *ou* swot* *(Brit)* ♦ **il s'est classé dans les dix ~s** *(Sport)* he was ranked in *ou* among the top *ou* first ten ♦ **les ~s seront les derniers (, et les derniers seront les ~s)** *(Bible)* the last shall be first (, and the first last); → **jeune**

[3] *(dans une série, une comparaison)* **Pierre et Paul sont cousins, le ~ est médecin** Peter and Paul are cousins, the former is a doctor ♦ **le ~ semble mieux** *(entre deux)* the first one seems better; *(dans une série)* the first one seems best

NM *(gén)* first; *(= étage)* first floor *(Brit)*, second floor *(US)* ♦ **c'est leur ~** *(= enfant)* it's their first child ♦ **mon ~ est ...** *(charade)* my first is in ...

♦ **en premier** *[arriver, parler]* first ♦ **je l'ai servi en ~** I served him first ♦ **en ~ je dirai que ...** firstly *ou* first *ou* to start with I'd like to say that ... ♦ **cela vient en ~ dans ma liste de priorités** that's first on *ou* top of my list of priorities ♦ **pour lui, la famille vient toujours en ~** his family always comes first

COMP **le premier de l'an** New Year's Day
le premier avril the first of April, April Fool's Day, All Fools' Day
le Premier Mai the first of May, May Day

première[2] /pʀəmjɛʀ/ **NF** [1] *(gén)* first; *(Aut)* first (gear); *(Hippisme)* first (race) ♦ **être en/passer la ~** *(= vitesse)* to be in/go into first (gear)

[2] *(Théât)* first night; *(Ciné)* première; *(= exploit) (gén)* first; *(Alpinisme)* first ascent ♦ **le soir de la ~, il ...** *(Ciné)* on the opening night, he ... ♦ **le public des grandes ~s** firstnighters ♦ **c'est une ~ mondiale** *(gén)* it's a world first; *(Ciné)* it's a world première ♦ **c'est une grande ~ pour notre équipe** it's a big first for our team

[3] *(= première classe)* first class ♦ **voyager en ~** to travel first-class ♦ **billet de ~** first-class ticket

[4] *(Scol)* **(classe de) ~** ≈ lower sixth (form) *(Brit)*, eleventh grade *(US)* ♦ **élève de ~** ≈ lower sixth former *(Brit)*, eleventh grader *(US)*, junior (in high school) *(US)*

[5] *(Couture)* head seamstress

[6] *(= semelle)* insole

LOC ADJ **de première** * ♦ **c'est de ~!** it's first-class! ♦ **il a fait un boulot de ~** he's done a first-class *ou* a first-rate job ♦ **c'est un salaud** **[*] **de ~ !** he's an out-and-out *ou* a right *(Brit)* bastard!*[*] ♦ **il est de ~ pour trouver les bons restaurants/pour les gaffes !** he's got a real knack* for *ou* he's great* at finding good restaurants/making blunders!

premièrement /pʀəmjɛʀmɑ̃/ GRAMMAIRE ACTIVE 53.5 **ADV** *(= d'abord)* first(ly); *(= en premier lieu)* in the first place; *(introduisant une objection)* for a start ♦ **~ il ne m'a rien dit, et en plus ...** for a start, he didn't say anything to me, and what's more ...

premier-maître (pl **premiers-maîtres**) /pʀəmjemɛtʀ/ **NM** chief petty officer

premier-né /pʀəmjene/, **première-née** /pʀəmjɛʀne/ (mpl **premiers-nés**) **ADJ, NM,F** first-born

prémisse /pʀemis/ **NF** premise, premiss

prémix /pʀemiks/ **NM** alcopop

prémolaire /pʀemɔlɛʀ/ **NF** premolar (tooth)

prémonition /pʀemɔnisjɔ̃/ **NF** premonition

prémonitoire /pʀemɔnitwaʀ/ **ADJ** premonitory

prémunir /pʀemyniʀ/ ▸ conjug 2 ◂ **VT** *(littér)* *(= mettre en garde)* to warn; *(= protéger)* to protect *(contre* against*)* **VPR** **se prémunir** to protect o.s. *(contre* from*)* to guard *(contre* against*)*

prenant, e /pʀənɑ̃, ɑt/ **ADJ** [1] *(= captivant)* *[film, livre]* absorbing, engrossing, compelling; *[voix]* fascinating, captivating [2] *(= qui prend du temps)* *[activité]* time-consuming ♦ **ce travail est trop ~** this job is too time-consuming *ou* takes up too much of my *(ou* our *etc)* time [3] *(Zool)* *[queue]* prehensile

prénatal, e (mpl **prénatals**) /pʀenatal/ **ADJ** *[diagnostic, dépistage, examen, visite]* antenatal, prenatal; *[allocation]* maternity *(épith)* ♦ **clinique ~e** antenatal clinic

prendre /pʀɑ̃dʀ/

► conjug 58 ◄

1 VERBE TRANSITIF
2 VERBE INTRANSITIF
3 VERBE PRONOMINAL

Lorsque **prendre** s'emploie dans des locutions telles que **prendre une photo/du poids/son temps, prendre en charge** etc, cherchez aussi au nom.

1 - VERBE TRANSITIF

1 = saisir *[+ objet]* to take ♦ **prends-le dans le placard/sur l'étagère** take it out of the cupboard/off *ou* (down) from the shelf ♦ **il l'a pris dans le tiroir** he took *ou* got it out of the drawer ♦ **il prit un journal/son crayon sur la table** he picked up *ou* took a newspaper/his pencil from the table ♦ **il la prit par le cou/par la taille** he put his arms round her neck/round her waist ♦ **~ qn par le bras/la taille** to take sb by the arm/the waist ♦ **~ qch des mains de qn** *(= débarrasser)* to take sth out of sb's hands; *(= enlever)* to take sth off sb *ou* away from sb ♦ **c'est toujours ça *ou* autant de pris** that's something at least ♦ **c'est à ~ ou à laisser** *[offre]* (you can) take it or leave it ♦ **je vous le fais à 80 €, c'est à ~ ou à laisser** I'll let you have it for €80, that's my final offer ♦ **avec lui, il faut en ~ et en laisser** you can only believe half of what he says, you must take what he tells you with a pinch of salt ♦ **je prends** *(dans un jeu de questions-réponses)* I'll answer; *(appel téléphonique)* I'll take it

2 = choisir to take ♦ **il y a plusieurs livres, lequel prends-tu ?** there are several books – which one are you going to take? *ou* which one do you want? ♦ **il a pris le bleu** he took the blue one

3 = se munir de *[+ instrument]* **tiens, prends ce marteau** here, use this hammer ♦ **il faut ~ un tournevis pour faire ça** you need a screwdriver for that ♦ **si tu sors, prends ton parapluie** if you go out, take your umbrella (with you) ♦ **prends ta chaise et viens t'asseoir ici** bring your chair and come and sit over here ♦ **as-tu pris les valises ?** have you brought the suitcases? ♦ **prends tes lunettes pour lire** put your glasses on to read

4 = aller chercher *[+ chose]* to pick up, to get, to fetch *(Brit)*; *[+ personne]* to pick up; *(= emmener)* to take ♦ **passer ~ qn à son bureau** to pick sb up *ou* call for sb at his office ♦ **je passerai les ~ chez toi** I'll come and collect *ou* get them *ou* I'll call in for them at your place ♦ **pouvez-vous me ~ (dans votre voiture) ?** can you give me a lift? ♦ **je ne veux plus de ce manteau, tu peux le ~** I don't want this coat any more – you can take *ou* have it ♦ **prends du beurre dans le réfrigérateur** get some butter out of the fridge

5 = s'emparer de force *[+ poisson, voleur]* to catch; *[+ argent, place, otage]* to take; *(Mil) [+ ville]* to take, to capture; *(Cartes, Échecs)* to take ♦ **un voleur lui a pris son portefeuille** a thief has taken *ou* stolen his wallet *ou* has robbed him of his wallet ♦ **il m'a pris mon idée** he has taken *ou* used *ou* pinched* *(Brit)* my idea ♦ **il prend tout ce qui lui tombe sous la main** he takes *ou* grabs everything he can lay his hands on ♦ **~ le service de qn** *(Tennis)* to break sb's service ♦ **se faire ~** *[voleur]* to be *ou* get caught ♦ **le voleur s'est fait ~** the robber was *ou* got caught; → **tel**

6 *: sexuellement *[+ personne]* to take ♦ **il l'a prise par devant/derrière** he took her from the front/from behind

7 = assaillir *[colère]* to come over; *[fièvre, douleur]* to strike ♦ **la colère le prit soudain** he was suddenly overcome with anger, anger suddenly overcame him ♦ **il fut pris d'un doute** he suddenly had a doubt, he felt doubtful all of a sudden ♦ **la douleur m'a pris au genou** I suddenly got a pain in my knee ♦ **les douleurs la prirent** her labour pains started ♦ **ça me prend dans le bas du dos et ça remonte*** it starts in my lower back and works its way up ♦ **qu'est-ce qui te prend ?*** what's the matter *ou* what's up* with you?, what's come over you?* ♦ **ça te prend souvent ?*** are you often like that? *(iro)* ♦ **quand ça me prend*, je peux rêvasser pendant des heures** I can daydream for hours when I feel like it *ou* when the mood takes me; → **tête**

8 = surprendre to catch ♦ **~ qn à faire qch** to catch sb doing sth ♦ **je vous y prends !** caught you! ♦ **si je t'y prends (encore), que je t'y prenne** *(menace)* just *ou* don't let me catch you doing that (again) *ou* at it (again) ♦ **~ qn sur le fait** to catch sb in the act *ou* red-handed ♦ **il s'est fait ~ en train de copier sur son voisin** he got caught copying from his neighbour

9 = duper to take in ♦ **on ne m'y prendra plus** I won't be taken in again, I won't be had a second time* ♦ **se laisser ~ à des paroles aimables** to let o.s. be sweet-talked *ou* taken in by sweet talk

10 = manger, boire *[+ aliment, boisson]* to have; *[+ médicament]* to take ♦ **prenez-vous du sucre ?** do you take sugar? ♦ **est-ce que vous prendrez du café ?** will you have *ou* would you like some coffee? ♦ **à ~ avant les repas** to be taken before meals ♦ **fais-lui ~ son médicament** give him his medicine ♦ **ce médicament se prend dans de l'eau** this medicine must be taken in water ♦ **as-tu pris de ce bon gâteau ?** have you had some of this nice cake? ♦ **il n'a rien pris depuis hier** he hasn't eaten anything since yesterday ♦ **le docteur m'interdit de ~ de l'alcool** the doctor won't allow me *ou* has forbidden me (to drink) alcohol

11 = voyager par *[+ métro, taxi]* to take, to travel *ou* go *ou* come by; *[+ voiture]* to take; *(= s'engager dans) [+ direction, rue]* to take ♦ **il prit le train puis l'avion de Paris à Londres** he took the train *ou* went by train then flew from Paris to London ♦ **j'ai pris l'avion/le train de 4 heures** I caught the 4 o'clock plane/train ♦ **je préfère ~ ma voiture** I'd rather take the car *ou* go in the car ♦ **ils ont pris la rue Blanche** they went down (*ou* up) the rue Blanche

12 = acheter *[+ billet, essence]* to get; *[+ voiture]* to buy; *(= réserver) [+ couchette, place]* to book ♦ **il prend toujours son pain à côté** he always gets *ou* buys his bread from the shop next door ♦ **peux-tu me ~ du pain ?** can you get me some bread? ♦ **nous avons pris une maison** *(loué)* we've taken *ou* rented a house; *(acheté)* we've bought a house ♦ **je prends du 38 (en chaussures/en robe)** I take a size 38 (shoe/dress)

13 = accepter *[+ client]* to take; *[+ passager]* to pick up; *[+ locataire]* to take (in); *[+ personnel]* to take on; *[+ domestique]* to engage, to take on ♦ **l'école ne prend plus de pensionnaires** the school no longer takes boarders ♦ **ce train ne prend pas de voyageurs** this train doesn't pick up passengers ♦ **il l'a prise comme interprète** he took her on as an interpreter

14 = noter *[+ renseignement, adresse, nom, rendez-vous]* to write down, to take down; *[+ mesures, température, empreintes]* to take; *(sous la dictée) [+ lettre]* to take (down) ♦ **~ des notes** to take notes

15 = adopter *[+ air, ton]* to put on, to assume; *[+ décision]* to take, to make, to come to; *[+ risque, mesure]* to take; *[+ attitude]* to strike, to take up ♦ **il prit un ton menaçant** a threatening note crept into his voice, his voice took on a threatening tone

16 = acquérir **~ de l'autorité** to gain authority ♦ **cela prend un sens particulier** it takes on a particular meaning

17 = s'accorder *[+ congé]* to take; *[+ vacances]* to take, to have, to go on; *[+ repos]* to have, to take ♦ **je prends quelques jours à Noël** I'm having a few days off at Christmas; → **temps¹**

18 = coûter *[+ temps, place, argent]* to take ♦ **cela me prend tout mon temps** it takes up all my time ♦ **la réparation a pris des heures** the repair took hours *ou* ages ♦ **attendez ici, ça ne prendra pas longtemps** wait here, it won't take long

19 = faire payer to charge ♦ **ils (m')ont pris 20 € pour une petite réparation** they charged (me) €20 for a minor repair ♦ **ce spécialiste prend très cher** this specialist charges very high fees, this specialist's charges *ou* fees are very high ♦ **ce plombier prend cher de l'heure** this plumber's hourly rate is high

20 = prélever *[+ pourcentage]* to take ♦ **ils prennent un pourcentage sur la vente** they charge a commission on the sale, they take a percentage on the sale ♦ **il prend sa commission sur la vente** he takes his commission on the sale ♦ **~ de l'argent à la banque/sur son compte** to draw (out) *ou* withdraw money from the bank/from one's account ♦ **la cotisation à la retraite est prise sur le salaire** the pension contribution is taken off one's salary *ou* deducted from one's salary ♦ **il a dû ~ sur ses économies pour payer les dégâts** he had to dip into *ou* go into his savings to pay for the damage ♦ **il a pris sur son temps pour venir m'aider** he gave up some of his time to help me

21 * = recevoir, subir *[+ coup, choc]* to get, to receive ♦ **il a pris la porte en pleine figure** the door hit *ou* got* him right in the face ♦ **qu'est-ce qu'on a pris !*, on en a pris plein la gueule‡ ou la tronche !‡, on s'en est pris plein la gueule‡ ou la tronche !‡** *(reproches)* we really got it in the neck!*, we really got what for!‡; *(défaite)* we got hammered!*; *(averse)* we got drenched! ♦ **il a pris pour les autres** *(emploi absolu)* he took the rap* ♦ **c'est toujours moi qui prends pour ma sœur !** I always get the blame for what my sister does! ♦ **le seau d'eau s'est renversé et c'est moi qui ai tout pris** the bucket of water tipped over and I got it all over me

22 = réagir à *[+ nouvelle]* to take ♦ **si vous le prenez ainsi ...** if that's how you want it ... ♦ **il a bien/mal pris la chose, il l'a bien/mal pris** he took it well/badly ♦ **il a bien pris ce que je lui ai dit** he took what I said in good part *ou* quite well ♦ **il a mal pris ce que je lui ai dit** he took exception *ou* didn't take kindly to what I said to him ♦ **~ qch avec bonne humeur** to take sth good-humouredly *ou* in good part ♦ **~ les choses comme elles sont/la vie comme elle vient** to take things as they come/life as it comes

23 = manier *[+ personne]* to handle; *[+ problème]* to handle, to tackle, to deal with, to cope with ♦ **elle sait le ~** she knows how to handle *ou* approach *ou* get round him ♦ **c'est quelqu'un de gentil mais il faut savoir le ~** he's nice but you have to keep on the right side of him ♦ **il y a plusieurs façons de ~ le problème** there are several ways of going about *ou* tackling the problem; → **bout**

24 locutions

♦ **prendre qn/qch pour** *(= considérer comme)* to take sb/sth for *(= utiliser comme)* to take sb/sth as ♦ **pour qui me prenez-vous ?** what *ou* who do you take me for?, what *ou* who do you think I am? ♦ **~ qn pour un autre** to take sb for *ou* think sb is somebody else, to mistake sb for somebody else ♦ **je n'aime pas qu'on me prenne pour un imbécile** I don't like being taken for a fool ♦ **~ qch pour prétexte/cible** to take sth as a pretext/target

♦ **prendre sur soi** (*= se maîtriser*) to grin and bear it ♦ **savoir ~ sur soi** to keep a grip on o.s. (*= assumer*) ♦ **j'ai dû ~ tout cela sur moi** I had to cope on my own ♦ **~ sur soi de faire qch** to take it upon o.s. to do sth

♦ **à tout prendre** on the whole, all in all

2 – VERBE INTRANSITIF

1 = durcir, épaissir [*ciment, pâte, crème*] to set; [*mayonnaise*] to thicken

2 = réussir [*plante*] to take (root); [*vaccin*] to take; [*mouvement, mode*] to catch on; [*livre, spectacle*] to be a success ♦ **le lilas a bien pris** the lilac's doing really well ♦ **la teinture prend mal avec ce tissu** this material is difficult to dye ♦ **la plaisanterie a pris** the joke was a great success ♦ **avec moi, ça ne prend pas*** it doesn't work with me*, it won't wash with me* (*Brit*)

3 = commencer à brûler [*feu*] (*gén*) to go; (*accidentellement*) to start; [*allumette*] to light; [*bois*] to catch fire ♦ **le feu ne veut pas ~** the fire won't go ♦ **le feu a pris sur le toit** the fire took hold in the roof

4 = se diriger to go ♦ **~ à gauche** to go *ou* turn *ou* bear left ♦ **~ par les petites rues** to take to *ou* go along *ou* keep to the side streets

3 – VERBE PRONOMINAL

se prendre

1 = se considérer **il se prend pour un intellectuel** he thinks *ou* likes to think he's an intellectual ♦ **pour qui se prend-il ?** (just) who does he think he is? ♦ **se ~ au sérieux** to take o.s. seriously

2 = accrocher, coincer to catch, to trap ♦ **le chat s'est pris la patte dans un piège** the cat got its paw trapped, the cat caught its paw in a trap ♦ **le rideau se prend dans la fenêtre** the curtain gets caught (up) *ou* stuck in the window ♦ **mon manteau s'est pris dans la porte** I caught *ou* trapped my coat in the door, my coat got trapped *ou* caught in the door ♦ **se ~ les pieds dans le tapis** (*lit*) to catch one's foot in the rug, to trip on the rug; (*fig*) to trip oneself up

3 locutions

♦ **se prendre à** + *infinitif* (*littér*) ♦ **se ~ à faire qch** (*= commencer*) to begin to do *ou* begin doing sth, to start to do *ou* start doing sth

♦ **s'en prendre à** [*+ personne*] (*= agresser*) to lay into*, to set about; (*= passer sa colère sur*) to take it out on; (*= blâmer*) to lay *ou* put the blame on, to attack ♦ **tu ne peux t'en ~ qu'à toi-même** you've only got yourself to blame

[*+ chose*] (*= remettre en question*) [*+ tradition, préjugé*] to challenge; (*= critiquer*) [*+ autorité, organisation*] to attack, to take on ♦ **il s'en est pris à son ordinateur** he took it out on his computer

♦ **s'y prendre** to set about (doing) it ♦ **il ne sait pas s'y ~** he doesn't know how to go *ou* set about it ♦ **je ne sais pas comment tu t'y prends** I don't know how you manage it ♦ **il ne s'y serait pas pris autrement s'il avait voulu tout faire échouer** he couldn't have done better if he had actually set out to ruin the whole thing ♦ **il fallait s'y ~ à temps** you should have done something about it *ou* started before it was too late ♦ **il faut s'y ~ à l'avance** you have to do it in advance ♦ **il s'y est bien/mal pris (pour le faire)** he went about it the right/wrong way ♦ **il s'y est pris drôlement pour le faire** he chose the oddest way of doing it, he went about it in the strangest way ♦ **s'y ~ à deux fois/plusieurs fois pour faire qch** to try twice/several times to do sth, to make two/several attempts to do sth ♦ **il faut s'y ~ à deux** it needs two of us (to do it) ♦ **s'y ~ bien** *ou* **savoir s'y ~ avec qn** to handle sb the right way ♦ **il sait s'y ~ avec les enfants** he really knows how to deal with children

preneur, -euse /pʀənœʀ, øz/ NM,F (*= acheteur*) buyer; (*= locataire*) lessee (*Jur*), tenant ♦ **~ de son** (*Ciné*) sound engineer ♦ **~ d'otages** hostage taker ♦ **trouver ~** to find a buyer ♦ **ces restes de gâteau vont vite trouver ~** there'll be no problem finding a taker for the rest of this cake ♦ **cet objet n'avait pas trouvé ~** there were no takers for this object ♦ **je suis ~ à 30 €** I'll buy *ou* take it for €30 ♦ **je ne suis pas ~** I'm not interested

prénom /pʀenɔ̃/ NM (*gén*) Christian name, first name; (*Admin*) forename, given name (*US*) ♦ **~ usuel** name by which one is known ♦ **il a dû se faire un ~** he had to make a name for himself in his own right

prénommé, e /pʀenɔme/ (ptp de **prénommer**) ADJ ♦ **le ~ Paul** the said Paul NM,F (*Jur*) above-named

prénommer /pʀenɔme/ ▸ conjug 1 ◂ VT to call, to name, to give a name to ♦ **on l'a prénommé comme son oncle** he was called *ou* named after his uncle, he was given the same name as his uncle VPR **se prénommer** to be called *ou* named

prénuptial, e (mpl **-aux**) /pʀenypsjal, o/ ADJ premarital

préoccupant, e /pʀeɔkypɑ̃, ɑ̃t/ ADJ worrying

préoccupation /pʀeɔkypasjɔ̃/ NF 1 (*= souci*) worry, anxiety ♦ **sa mauvaise santé était une ~ supplémentaire pour ses parents** his ill health was a further worry to *ou* cause for concern to his parents 2 (*= priorité*) preoccupation, concern ♦ **sa seule ~ était de ...** his one concern *ou* preoccupation was to ...

préoccupé, e /pʀeɔkype/ (ptp de **préoccuper**) ADJ (*= absorbé*) preoccupied (*de qch* with sth; *de faire qch* with doing sth); (*= soucieux*) concerned (*de qch* about sth; *de faire qch* to do sth) worried (*de qch* about sth; *de faire qch* about doing sth); ♦ **tu as l'air ~** you look worried

préoccuper /pʀeɔkype/ GRAMMAIRE ACTIVE 53.1, 53.2 ▸ conjug 1 ◂

VT 1 (*= inquiéter*) to worry ♦ **il y a quelque chose qui le préoccupe** something is worrying *ou* bothering him, he's got *ou* there's something on his mind ♦ **l'avenir de son fils le préoccupe** he's concerned *ou* anxious about his son's future

2 (*= absorber*) to preoccupy ♦ **cette idée lui préoccupe l'esprit** *ou* **le préoccupe** he is preoccupied with the idea ♦ **il est uniquement préoccupé de sa petite personne** all he ever thinks about is himself, he's totally wrapped up in himself

VPR **se préoccuper** to concern o.s. (*de* with) to be concerned (*de* with) to worry (*de* about); ♦ **se ~ de la santé de qn** to show (great) concern about sb's health ♦ **il ne se préoccupe pas beaucoup de notre sort** he isn't very worried *ou* he doesn't care very much about what happens to us ♦ **il ne s'en préoccupe guère** he hardly gives it a thought

préopératoire /pʀeɔpeʀatwaʀ/ ADJ preoperative

prépa /pʀepa/ NF (*arg Scol*) (abrév de **classe préparatoire**) → **préparatoire**

préparateur, -trice /pʀepaʀatœʀ, tʀis/ NM,F (*gén*) assistant; (*Univ*) demonstrator ♦ **~ en pharmacie** pharmaceutical *ou* chemist's (*Brit*) assistant

préparatifs /pʀepaʀatif/ NMPL preparations (*de* for); ♦ **nous en sommes aux ~ de départ** we're getting ready *ou* we're preparing to leave

préparation /pʀepaʀasjɔ̃/ NF 1 (*= confection*) (*gén*) preparation; [*de repas*] preparation, making; [*de médicament*] preparation, making up; [*de complot*] laying, hatching; [*de plan*] preparation, working out, drawing up ♦ **la ~ de ce plat demande des soins minutieux** this dish requires very careful preparation

2 (*= apprêt*) (*gén*) preparation; [*de table*] laying, getting ready; [*de peaux, poisson, volaille*] dressing; [*d'attaque, départ, voyage*] preparation (*de* for); ♦ **la ~ de l'avenir** preparing *ou* preparation for the future ♦ **attaque après ~ d'artillerie** attack following initial assault by the artillery ♦ **elle a plusieurs livres en ~** she has several books in the pipeline

3 (*= étude*) [*d'examen*] preparation, getting ready (*de* for)

4 (*= entraînement*) [*de personne*] (*à un examen*) preparation (*à* for); (*à une épreuve sportive*) preparation, training (*à* for); ♦ **annoncer quelque chose sans ~** to announce something abruptly *ou* without preparation

5 (*Chim, Pharm*) preparation

6 (*Scol*) **faire une ~ à Polytechnique** (*= classe préparatoire*) to prepare for entrance to the École polytechnique (*in one of the classes préparatoires*) ♦ **une ~ française** (*= devoir*) a French exercise, a piece of French homework ♦ **faire sa ~ militaire** (*Mil*) to do a training course in preparation for one's military service

préparatoire /pʀepaʀatwaʀ/ ADJ [*travail, démarche, conversation*] preparatory, preliminary ♦ **classe ~ (aux Grandes Écoles)** *class which prepares students for the entry exams to the Grandes Écoles*; → **cours**

CLASSES PRÉPARATOIRES

Classes préparatoires is the term given to the two years of intensive study required to sit the competitive entrance examinations to the « grandes écoles ». They are extremely demanding post-baccalauréat courses, usually taken in a « lycée ». Schools which provide such classes are more highly regarded than those which do not. → **BACCALAURÉAT, CONCOURS, GRANDES ÉCOLES, LYCÉE**

préparer /pʀepaʀe/ ▸ conjug 1 ◂ VT 1 (*= confectionner*) (*gén*) to prepare; [*+ repas*] to prepare, to make; [*+ médicament*] to prepare, to make up; [*+ piège, complot*] to lay, to hatch; [*+ plan*] to draw up, to work out, to prepare; [*+ cours, discours*] to prepare; [*+ thèse*] to be doing, to be working on, to prepare ♦ **elle nous prépare une tasse de thé** she's making a cup of tea for us, she's getting us a cup of tea ♦ **il lui prépare de bons petits plats** he makes *ou* cooks *ou* prepares tasty dishes for her ♦ **plat préparé** ready(-made) meal

2 (*= apprêter*) (*gén*) to prepare; [*+ table*] to lay, to get ready; [*+ affaires, bagages, chambre*] to prepare, to get ready; [*+ peaux, poisson, volaille*] to dress; (*Agr*) [*+ terre*] to prepare; [*+ attaque, rentrée, voyage*] to prepare (for), to get ready for; [*+ transition*] to prepare for ♦ **~ le départ** to get ready *ou* prepare to leave, to make ready for one's departure (*frm*) ♦ **~ l'avenir** to prepare for the future ♦ **~ ses effets** to time one's effects carefully, to prepare one's effects ♦ **il a préparé la rencontre des deux ministres** he made the preparations for *ou* he organized *ou* he set up the meeting between the two ministers ♦ **l'attaque avait été soigneusement préparée** the attack had been carefully prepared *ou* organized ♦ **le coup avait été préparé de longue main** they (*ou* he *etc*) had been preparing for it for a long time ♦ **~ le terrain** (*Mil, fig*) to prepare the ground

3 (*Scol*) [*+ examen*] to prepare for, to study for ♦ **~ Normale Sup** to study for entrance to the École normale supérieure

4 (*= habituer, entraîner*) **~ qn à qch/à faire qch** to prepare sb for sth/to do sth ♦ **~ les esprits** to prepare people('s minds) (*à qch* for sth); ♦ **~ qn à un examen** to prepare *ou* coach sb for an exam ♦ **il a essayé de la ~ à la triste nouvelle**

he tried to prepare her for the sad news ◆ **je n'y étais pas préparé** I wasn't prepared for it, I wasn't expecting it

5 *(= réserver)* ~ **qch à qn** to have sth in store for sb ◆ **je me demande ce qu'elle nous prépare** I wonder what she's got in store for us *ou* she's cooking up for us* ◆ **on ne sait pas ce que l'avenir nous prépare** we don't know what the future holds (in store) for us *ou* has in store for us ◆ **il nous prépare une surprise** he has a surprise in store for us, he's got a surprise up his sleeve ◆ **ce temps nous prépare de joyeuses vacances !** *(iro)* if this weather continues the holidays will be just great! * *(iro)* ◆ **il nous prépare un bon rhume** he's getting a cold

VPR **se préparer** 1 *(= s'apprêter)* to prepare (o.s.), to get ready *(à qch* for sth; *à faire* to do); ◆ **attendez, elle se prépare** wait a minute, she's getting ready ◆ **se ~ à une mauvaise nouvelle** to prepare o.s. for some bad news ◆ **se ~ au combat** *ou* **à combattre** to prepare to fight *ou* to do battle ◆ **se ~ pour les Jeux olympiques** to prepare *ou* train for the Olympics ◆ **préparez-vous au pire** prepare for the worst ◆ **je ne m'y étais pas préparé** I hadn't prepared myself for it, I wasn't expecting it ◆ **se ~ pour un bal/pour sortir dîner en ville** to get ready *ou* dressed for a dance/to go out to dinner ◆ **préparez-vous à être appelé d'urgence** be prepared to be called out urgently ◆ **vous vous préparez des ennuis** you're making trouble *ou* storing up trouble for yourself

2 *(= approcher) [orage]* to be brewing ◆ **il se prépare une bagarre** there's going to be a fight ◆ **il se prépare quelque chose de louche** there's something fishy going on*

prépayé, e /pʀepeje/ ADJ *[billet]* prepaid, paid in advance

prépondérance /pʀepɔ̃deʀɑ̃s/ NF *[de nation, groupe]* ascendancy, preponderance, supremacy *(sur* over); *[d'idée, croyance, théorie]* supremacy *(sur* over); *[de trait de caractère]* domination *(sur* over)

prépondérant, e /pʀepɔ̃deʀɑ̃, ɑ̃t/ ADJ *[rôle]* dominating, preponderant ◆ **voix ~e** *(Pol)* casting vote

préposé /pʀepoze/ NM *(gén)* employee; *(= facteur)* postman *(Brit)*, mailman *(US)*; *[de douane]* official, officer; *[de vestiaire]* attendant

préposée /pʀepoze/ NF *(gén)* employee; *(= factrice)* postwoman *(Brit)*, mailwoman *(US)*; *[de vestiaire]* attendant

préposer /pʀepoze/ ► conjug 1 ◄ VT to appoint *(à* to); ◆ **préposé à** in charge of

prépositif, -ive /pʀepozitif, iv/ ADJ prepositional

préposition /pʀepozisjɔ̃/ NF preposition

prépositionnel, -elle /pʀepozisjɔnɛl/ ADJ prepositional

prépositivement /pʀepozitivmɑ̃/ ADV prepositionally, as a preposition

pré(-)presse /pʀepʀɛs/ NF prepress

préprogrammé, e /pʀepʀɔgʀame/ ADJ *(Ordin)* preprogrammed

prépuce /pʀepys/ NM foreskin, prepuce *(SPÉC)*

préraphaélisme /pʀeʀafaelism/ NM Pre-Raphaelitism

préraphaélite /pʀeʀafaelit/ ADJ, NM Pre-Raphaelite

prérégler /pʀeʀegle/ ► conjug 6 ◄ VT to preset

prérentrée /pʀeʀɑ̃tʀe/ NF *(Scol) preparatory day for teachers before school term starts*

préretraite /pʀeʀ(ə)tʀɛt/ NF *(= état)* early retirement; *(= pension)* early retirement pension ◆ **partir en ~** to take early retirement ◆ **être mis en ~** to be given early retirement, to be retired early

préretraité, e /pʀeʀətʀete/ NM,F *person who has taken early retirement*

prérogative /pʀeʀɔgativ/ NF prerogative

préroman, e /pʀeʀɔmɑ̃, an/ ADJ *[art]* pre-Romanesque

préromantique /pʀeʀɔmɑ̃tik/ ADJ pre-Romantic ◆ **les ~s** the pre-Romantics, the pre-Romantic poets *(ou* musicians *etc)*

préromantisme /pʀeʀɔmɑ̃tism/ NM pre-Romanticism

près /pʀɛ/ ADV 1 *(dans l'espace)* near(by), close (by); *(dans le temps)* near, close ◆ **la gare est tout ~** we're very close to the station, the station is very nearby ◆ **il habite assez/tout ~** he lives quite/very near(by) *ou* close (by) ◆ **ne te mets pas trop ~** don't get too close *ou* near ◆ **c'est plus/moins ~ que je ne croyais** *(espace)* it's nearer *ou* closer than/further than I thought; *(temps)* it's nearer *ou* sooner *ou* closer than/not as near *ou* soon as I thought *ou* further off than I thought ◆ **Noël est très ~ maintenant** Christmas is (getting) very near *ou* close now, it'll very soon be Christmas now

2 *(locutions)* **c'est terminé à peu de chose ~** it's more or less *ou* pretty well* finished ◆ **ce n'est pas aussi bon, à beaucoup ~** it's nothing like *ou* nowhere near as good ◆ **ils sont identiques, à la couleur ~** they are identical apart from *ou* except for the colour ◆ **à cela ~ que ...** if it weren't for *ou* apart from the fact that ... ◆ **je vais vous donner le chiffre à un franc/à un centimètre ~** I'll give you the figure to within about a franc/a centimetre ◆ **cela fait 15 € à quelque chose** *ou* **à peu de chose(s) ~** that comes to €15, or as near as makes no difference ◆ **il a raté le bus à une minute ~** he missed the bus by a minute or so ◆ **il n'est pas à 10 minutes/à un kilo de sucre/à 15 € ~** he can spare 10 minutes/a kilo of sugar/€15 ◆ **il n'est pas à un crime ~** he won't let a crime stop him ◆ **il n'est plus à 10 minutes ~** he can wait another 10 minutes; → aussi **peu**

PRÉP *(littér ou Admin) (lieu)* near ◆ **ambassadeur ~ le roi de ...** ambassador to the king of ...

LOC PRÉP **près de** 1 *(dans l'espace)* close to, near (to) ◆ **leur maison est ~ de l'église** their house is close to *ou* near the church ◆ **le plus/moins ~ possible de la porte/de Noël** as close *ou* near to/as far away as possible from the door/Christmas ◆ **une robe ~ du corps** a close-fitting dress ◆ **ils étaient très ~ l'un de l'autre** they were very close to each other ◆ **elle est ~ de sa mère** she's with her mother ◆ **être très ~ du but** to be very close *ou* near to one's goal ◆ **être ~ de son argent** *ou* **de ses sous** * *(fig)* to be close- *ou* tight-fisted

2 *(dans le temps)* close to ◆ **il est ~ de minuit** it's close to midnight, it's nearly midnight ◆ **il est ~ de la retraite** he's close to *ou* nearing retirement ◆ **arriver ~ de la fin d'un voyage** to be nearing the end *ou* coming near *ou* close to the end of a journey ◆ **il est ~ de la cinquantaine** he's nearly *ou* almost fifty, he's going on fifty, he's coming up to fifty *(Brit)*

3 *(approximativement)* nearly, almost ◆ **il a dépensé ~ de la moitié de son salaire** he has spent nearly *ou* almost half his salary ◆ **il y a ~ de 5 ans qu'ils sont partis** they left nearly *ou* close on 5 years ago, it's nearly 5 years since they left

4 *(avec verbe à l'infinitif = sur le point de)* **être très ~ d'avoir trouvé la solution** to have almost *ou* nearly found the solution ◆ **elle a été très ~ de refuser** she was on the point of refusing, she was about to refuse, she came close to refusing ◆ **je suis très ~ de croire que ...** I'm (almost) beginning to think that ... ◆ **je ne suis pas ~ de partir/de réussir** at this rate, I'm not likely to be going (yet)/to succeed ◆ **je ne suis pas ~ d'y retourner/de recommencer** I won't go back there/do that again in a hurry, you won't catch me going back there/doing that again in a hurry

LOC ADV **de près** ◆ **le coup a été tiré de ~** the shot was fired at close range ◆ **il voit mal/bien de ~** he can't see very well/he can see all right close to ◆ **surveiller qn de ~** to keep a close watch on sb, to watch sb closely ◆ **il a vu la mort de ~** he has stared *ou* looked death in the face ◆ **il faudra examiner cette affaire de plus ~** we must have *ou* take a closer look at *ou* look more closely into this business ◆ **on a frôlé de très ~ la catastrophe** we came within an inch of disaster, we had a close shave *ou* a narrow escape ◆ **de ~ ou de loin** *[ressembler]* more or less ◆ **tout ce qui touche de ~ ou de loin au cinéma** everything remotely connected with cinema; → **rasé, regarder**

présage /pʀezaʒ/ NM omen, presage *(littér)* ◆ **bon/mauvais/heureux ~** good/ill/happy omen ◆ **ces bons résultats sont le ~ de jours meilleurs** these good results are the sign of better days to come

présager /pʀezaʒe/ ► conjug 3 ◄ VT *(= annoncer)* to be a sign *ou* an omen of, to presage *(littér)*; *(= prévoir)* to predict, to foresee ◆ **cela ne présage rien de bon** nothing good will come of it, that's an ominous sign ◆ **cela nous laisse ~ que ...** it leads us to predict *ou* expect that ... ◆ **rien ne laissait ~ la catastrophe** there was nothing to suggest that such a disaster might happen ◆ **rien ne laissait ~ que ...** there was nothing to suggest that ...

pré-salé (pl **prés-salés**) /pʀesale/ NM ◆ **(agneau/mouton de) ~** salt meadow lamb/sheep; *(= viande)* salt meadow lamb/mutton

presbyte /pʀɛsbit/ ADJ long-sighted, far-sighted *(US)*, presbyopic *(SPÉC)*

presbytère /pʀɛsbitɛʀ/ NM presbytery

presbytérianisme /pʀɛsbiteʀjanism/ NM Presbyterianism

presbytérien, -ienne /pʀɛsbiteʀjɛ̃, jɛn/ ADJ, NM,F Presbyterian

presbytie /pʀɛsbisi/ NF long-sightedness, far-sightedness *(US)*, presbyopia *(SPÉC)*

prescience /pʀesjɑ̃s/ NF prescience, foresight

prescient, e /pʀesjɑ̃, jɑ̃t/ ADJ prescient, far-sighted

préscolaire /pʀeskɔlɛʀ/ ADJ preschool *(épith)* ◆ **enfant d'âge ~** preschool child, child of preschool age

prescripteur, -trice /pʀɛskʀiptœʀ, tʀis/ NM,F *(Comm)* prescriber; *(Scol)* teacher *(who recommends schoolbooks)* ◆ **(médecin) ~** consultant

prescriptible /pʀɛskʀiptibl/ ADJ prescriptible

prescription /pʀɛskʀipsjɔ̃/ NF 1 *(Méd)* prescription, directions ◆ **"se conformer aux prescriptions du médecin"** "to be taken in accordance with the doctor's instructions" ◆ **obtenu sur ~ médicale** obtained on prescription 2 *(= ordre) (gén)* order, instruction; *[de morale, règlement]* dictate; *(= recommandation) [d'ouvrage, méthode]* recommendation ◆ **~s techniques** technical requirements 3 *(Jur) (droit civil)* prescription; *(droit pénal)* statute of limitations ◆ **au bout de sept ans il y a ~** the statute of limitations is seven years ◆ **il y a ~ maintenant, on peut en parler** *(hum)* it's ancient history now so it's all right to talk about it

prescrire /pʀɛskʀiʀ/ ► conjug 39 ◄ VT *(Méd, Jur)* to prescribe; *[+ objet, méthode, livre]* to recommend; *[morale, honneur, loi]* to stipulate, to lay down; *(= ordonner)* to order, to command ◆ **à la date prescrite** on the prescribed date, on the date stipulated ◆ **"ne pas dépasser la dose prescrite"** *(Méd)* "do not exceed the prescribed dose" ◆ **être prescrit, se** ~ *[peine, dette]* to lapse

préséance /pʀeseɑ̃s/ NF precedence *(NonC)* ◆ **par ordre de** ~ in order of precedence

présélecteur /pʀeselɛktœʀ/ NM preselector

présélection /pʀeselɛksjɔ̃/ NF *(gén)* pre-selection; *[de candidats]* pre-selection, shortlisting *(Brit)*; *(Helv : sur route)* lane ◆ **bouton** *ou* **touche de** ~ *(Radio)* preset button ◆ **programme de** ~ preset programme ◆ **effectuer une** ~ **des candidats** to shortlist *ou* pre-select applicants ◆ **boîte de vitesses à** ~ pre-selector gearbox

présélectionner /pʀeselɛksjɔne/ ► conjug 1 ◄ VT *[+ chaîne de radio]* to preset, to pre-select; *[+ candidats]* to pre-select, to short-list *(Brit)*; *[+ sportifs]* to pre-select

présence /pʀezɑ̃s/ NF 1 *[de personne, chose, pays]* presence; *(au bureau, à l'école)* attendance; *(Rel)* presence ◆ **la** ~ **aux cours est obligatoire** attendance at classes is compulsory ◆ **fuir la** ~ **de qn** to avoid sb, to keep well away from sb ◆ **Monsieur le maire nous a honoré de sa** ~ *(frm)* the Mayor honoured us with his presence ◆ **j'ai juste à faire de la** ~ I just have to be there *ou* present ◆ ~ **assidue au bureau** regular attendance at the office ◆ ~ **policière** police presence

◆ **en présence** ◆ **les forces en** ~ the opposing armies ◆ **mettre deux personnes en** ~ to bring two people together *ou* face to face ◆ **les parties en** ~ *(Jur)* the litigants, the opposing parties

◆ **en présence de** in the presence of ◆ **en** ~ **de tels incidents** faced with *ou* in the face of such incidents ◆ **mettre qn en** ~ **de qn/qch** to bring sb face to face with sb/sth ◆ **cela s'est produit en ma** ~ it happened while I was there *ou* in my presence

2 *(= personnalité)* presence ◆ **avoir de la** ~ to have (a) great presence ◆ **elle a beaucoup de** ~ **à l'écran/sur scène** she has great screen/stage presence

3 *(= être)* **j'ai senti une** ~ I felt a presence, I suddenly felt that I was not alone

COMP **présence d'esprit** presence of mind

présent¹, e /pʀezɑ̃, ɑ̃t/ ADJ 1 *[personne]* present; *(Rel)* present ◆ **les personnes ici ~es** *(frm)* those present, the persons here present *(frm)* ◆ **les personnes (qui étaient) ~es au moment de l'incident** the people who were present *ou* there when the incident occurred ◆ **être** ~ **à une cérémonie** to be present at *ou* attend a ceremony ◆ **être** ~ **à l'appel** to be present at roll call ◆ ~ **!** present! ◆ **répondre** ~ *(lit)* to answer "present" ◆ **il a toujours répondu** ~ **quand j'ai eu besoin de lui** *(fig)* he always came through *ou* he was always there when I needed him ◆ **cette année au festival, beaucoup de jeunes musiciens ont répondu ~(s)** many young musicians attended this year's festival ◆ **pour un bon repas, il est toujours** ~ **!** *(hum)* you can always count on him to be there when there's good food around! ◆ **je suis** ~ **en pensée** my thoughts are with you *(ou him etc)*, I'm thinking of you *(ou him etc)*

2 *[chose]* present ◆ **métal** ~ **dans un minerai** metal present *ou* found in an ore ◆ **son pessimisme est partout** ~ **dans son dernier roman** his pessimism runs right through *ou* is evident throughout his latest novel ◆ **sa gentillesse est ~e dans chacun de ses actes** his kindness is evident in everything he does ◆ **avoir qch** ~ **à l'esprit** to have sth fresh in one's mind ◆ **je n'ai pas les chiffres ~s à l'esprit** I can't bring the figures to mind, I can't remember the figures off-hand ◆ **j'aurai toujours ce souvenir** ~ **à l'esprit** this memory will be ever-present in my mind *ou* will always be fresh in my mind ◆ **gardez ceci** ~ **à l'esprit** keep *ou* bear this in mind

3 *(= actuel) [circonstances, état, heure, époque]* present ◆ **le 15 du mois** ~ on the 15th of this month

4 *(Gram) [temps, participe]* present

5 *(= dont il est question)* present ◆ **le** ~ **récit** the present account, this account ◆ **nous vous signalons par la ~e lettre que ...** *(Admin)* we hereby inform you that ...

6 *(= actif)* **ils sont très ~s dans le secteur informatique** they have a strong foothold in the computer sector ◆ **il est très** ~ **sur le terrain** *(Sport)* he covers the field really well ◆ **elle est très ~e au filet** *(Tennis)* she covers the net really well

NM 1 *(= époque)* **le** ~ the present

◆ **à présent** *(= en ce moment)* at present, presently *(US)*; *(= maintenant)* now; *(= de nos jours)* now, nowadays ◆ **la jeunesse/les gens d'à** ~ young people/people of today, young people/people nowadays

◆ **à présent que** ◆ **à** ~ **que nous savons** now that we know

2 *(Gram)* present (tense) ◆ **au** ~ in the present (tense) ◆ ~ **de l'indicatif** present indicative ◆ ~ **historique** *ou* **de narration** historic(al) *ou* narrative present

3 *(= personne)* **les ~s et les absents** those present and those absent ◆ **il n'y avait que cinq ~s** there were only five people present *ou* there

NF **présente** *(Admin)* **veuillez recevoir par la ~e ...** *(= lettre)* please find enclosed ... ◆ **nous vous signalons par la ~e que ...** we hereby inform you that ... ◆ **le contrat annexé à la ~e** the contract enclosed herewith

présent² /pʀezɑ̃/ NM *(littér)* gift, present ◆ **faire** ~ **de qch à qn** to present sb with sth

présentable /pʀezɑ̃tabl/ ADJ presentable ◆ **avec cet œil au beurre noir, je ne suis pas** ~ with this black eye, I'm not fit to be seen

présentateur, -trice /pʀezɑ̃tatœʀ, tʀis/ NM,F *(Radio, TV) [de jeu, causerie, variétés]* host, compere *(Brit)*, emcee *(US)*; *[de débat]* presenter; *[de nouvelles]* newscaster, newsreader

présentation /pʀezɑ̃tasjɔ̃/ NF 1 *(gén)* presentation ◆ **sur** ~ **d'une pièce d'identité** on presentation of proof of identity

2 *[de nouveau venu, conférencier]* introduction; *(frm : à la cour)* presentation ◆ **faire les ~s** to make the introductions, to introduce people to one another

3 *(au public) [de tableaux, pièce]* presentation; *[de marchandises]* presentation, display; *[de film]* presentation, showing; *(Radio, TV) [d'émission]* presentation, introduction ◆ ~ **de mode** fashion show

4 *(= manière de présenter) [d'idée, produit, travail]* presentation ◆ **avoir une bonne/mauvaise** ~ *[personne]* to have a good *ou* pleasant/an unattractive *ou* off-putting appearance

5 *(Rel)* **la Présentation** the Presentation

6 *(Méd) [de fœtus]* presentation ◆ ~ **par la tête/le siège** head/breech presentation

7 *(Fin)* presentation ◆ **payable sur** ~ payable on presentation *ou* at call *ou* at sight *ou* over the counter

présentement /pʀezɑ̃tmɑ̃/ ADV *(= en ce moment)* at present, presently *(US)*; *(= maintenant)* now

présenter /pʀezɑ̃te/ ► conjug 1 ◄ VT 1 *[+ personne] (à qn d'autre, à un groupe)* to introduce *(à* to; *dans* into); *(au roi, à la cour)* to present *(à* to) ◆ **je vous présente ma femme** this is my wife, have you met my wife?, may I introduce my wife (to you)?

2 *(= montrer) [+ billet, passeport]* to present, to show, to produce ◆ **il présentait une apparence de calme** he appeared calm ◆ **la ville présente un aspect inhabituel** the town looks different from usual *ou* doesn't look the same as it usually does

3 *(= proposer au public) [+ marchandises]* to present, to display *(à* to) to set out *(à* before); *(Théât) [+ acteur, pièce]* to present; *(Radio, TV) [+ émission]* to present, to introduce; *[+ jeux]* to present, to compère *(Brit)*; *[+ mode, tableaux]* to present ◆ **c'est lui qui présente les nouvelles** *(TV)* he presents *ou* reports the news

4 *(= offrir) [+ plat]* to present, to hold out; *[+ rafraîchissements]* to offer, to hand round; *[+ bouquet]* to present ◆ ~ **son bras à qn** to offer one's arm to sb

5 *(= exposer) [+ problème]* to set out, to explain; *[+ idées]* to present, to set *ou* lay out; *[+ théorie]* to expound, to set out ◆ **un travail bien/mal présenté** a well-/badly presented *ou* laid-out piece of work ◆ **les plats sont bien/mal présentés** the food is/isn't nicely *ou* attractively presented ◆ **présentez-lui cela avec tact** explain it to him *ou* put it to him tactfully ◆ **il nous a présenté son ami comme un héros** he spoke of his friend as a hero; → **jour**

6 *(= exprimer) [+ excuses]* to present, to offer, to make; *[+ condoléances, félicitations]* to present, to offer; *[+ respects]* to present, to pay; *[+ objection]* to raise

7 *(= comporter) [+ avantage, intérêt]* to present, to afford; *[+ différences]* to reveal, to present; *[+ risque, difficulté, obstacle]* to present ◆ **ce malade présente des symptômes de tuberculose** this patient presents *ou* shows symptoms of tuberculosis ◆ **ce tissu présente de nombreux défauts** this material has a number of flaws ◆ **le budget présente un déficit important** there is a big deficit in the budget ◆ **la situation présente un caractère d'urgence** the situation is *ou* appears urgent

8 *(= soumettre) [+ note, facture, devis, bilan]* to present, to submit; *[+ thèse]* to submit; *[+ motion]* to move; *[+ projet de loi]* to present, to introduce; *[+ rapport, requête]* to present, to put in, to submit ◆ ~ **sa candidature à un poste** to apply for *ou* put in for a job ◆ **il a présenté sa démission** he has handed in his resignation ◆ ~ **un candidat à un concours** to put a candidate in *ou* enter a candidate for a competitive examination ◆ **à l'examen, il a présenté un texte de Camus** *(Scol)* he chose *ou* did a text by Camus for the exam

9 *(= tourner dans la direction de)* to turn ◆ ~ **le flanc à l'ennemi** to turn one's flank towards the enemy ◆ **bateau qui présente le travers au vent** ship turning *ou* sailing broadside on to the wind

10 *(Mil) [+ armes]* to present; *[+ troupes]* to present *(for inspection)*; → **arme**

11 *(Tech = placer)* to position, to line up

VI *[personne]* ◆ ~ **bien/mal** to have a good *ou* pleasant/an unattractive *ou* off-putting *(Brit)* appearance

VPR **se présenter** 1 *(= se rendre)* to go, to come, to appear ◆ **se** ~ **chez qn** to go to sb's house ◆ **il ose encore se** ~ **chez toi !** does he still dare to show himself *ou* to appear at your house! ◆ **il ne s'est présenté personne** no one turned up *ou* came *ou* appeared ◆ **je ne peux pas me** ~ **dans cette tenue** I can't appear dressed like this ◆ **"ne pas écrire, se présenter"** *(dans une annonce)* "(interested) applicants should apply in person" ◆ **se** ~ **à l'audience** *(Jur)* to appear in court, to make a court appearance

2 *(= être candidat)* to come forward ◆ **se** ~ **pour un emploi** to put in *ou* apply for a job ◆ **se** ~ **à** *[+ examen]* to sit *(Brit)*, to take; *[+ concours]* to go in for, to enter ◆ **se** ~ **aux élections** to stand *(Brit) ou* run *(surtout US)* for election, to stand *(Brit) ou* run *(surtout US)* in the elections ◆ **se** ~ **aux élections présidentielles** to stand for president *ou* in the presidential elections *(Brit)*, to run for president *(surtout US)* ◆ **se** ~

comme candidat *(aux élections)* to be a candidate, to stand *(Brit) ou* run *(surtout US)* as a candidate *(à in)*; *(à un poste)* to apply *(à for)*

3 *(= se faire connaître : gén)* to introduce o.s. *(à to)*

4 *(= surgir) [d'occasion]* to arise, to present itself; *[de difficulté]* to crop *ou* come up, to arise, to present itself; *[de solution]* to come to mind, to present itself ◆ **un problème se présente à nous** we are faced *ou* confronted with a problem ◆ **il lit tout ce qui se présente** he reads everything he can get his hands on, he reads anything that's going* ◆ **il faut attendre que quelque chose se présente** we must wait until something turns up ◆ **deux noms se présentent à l'esprit** two names come *ou* spring to mind ◆ **un spectacle magnifique se présenta à ses yeux** a magnificent sight met his eyes

5 *(= apparaître)* **cela se présente sous forme de cachets** it's presented *ou* it comes in tablet form ◆ **l'affaire se présente bien/mal** things are looking good/aren't looking too good ◆ **les choses se présentent sous un nouveau jour** things appear in a new light ◆ **comment se présente le problème ?** what exactly is the problem?, what is the nature of the problem? ◆ **comment l'enfant se présente-t-il ?** *(Méd)* how is the baby presenting?

présentoir /prezɑ̃twaʀ/ **NM** *(= étagère)* display

présérie /preseri/ **NF** pilot production

préservateur, -trice /prezɛʀvatœʀ, tʀis/ **ADJ** preventive, protective **NM** *(Chim)* preservative

préservatif, -ive /prezɛʀvatif, iv/ **ADJ** preventive, protective **NM** ◆ **~ (masculin)** condom ◆ **~ féminin** female condom ◆ **refuser le ~** to refuse to wear a condom

> ⚠ Le nom **préservatif** ne se traduit pas par le mot anglais **preservative** qui a le sens de 'agent de conservation'.

préservation /prezɛʀvasjɔ̃/ **NF** *[d'environnement, espèce, patrimoine]* preservation, protection; *[d'identité culturelle]* preservation; *[d'emploi]* protection ◆ **les gens sont obnubilés par la ~ de leur emploi** people are obsessed with holding on to their jobs

préserver /prezɛʀve/ ▸ conjug 1 ◂ **VT** *[+ emploi, droits]* to safeguard, to preserve; *[+ identité culturelle, paix, liberté, valeurs, équilibre, indépendance]* to preserve; *[+ environnement, patrimoine, intérêts]* to preserve, to protect *(de* from, against); *[+ vie] (= protéger)* to protect; *(= sauver)* to save ◆ **se ~ du soleil** to protect o.s. from the sun ◆ **le ciel** *ou* **Dieu m'en préserve !** Heaven preserve me!, Heaven forbid!

pré-sida /presida/ **ADJ** *[traitement, époque]* pre-AIDS

présidence /prezidɑ̃s/ **NF** 1 *[d'État, tribunal]* presidency; *[de comité, réunion]* chairmanship; *[de firme]* chairmanship, directorship; *[d'université]* vice-chancellorship *(Brit)*, presidency *(US)* ◆ **candidat à la ~** *(Pol)* presidential candidate 2 *(= résidence)* presidential residence *ou* palace

président /prezidɑ̃/ **NM** 1 *(Pol)* president ◆ **Monsieur/Madame le ~** Mr/Madam President ◆ **~ de la République française/des États-Unis** President of the French Republic/of the United States

2 *[de comité, réunion, conseil d'administration, commission]* chairman; *[de club, société savante]* president; *[de firme]* chairman, president, chief operating officer; *[de jury d'examen]* chairman, chief examiner; *[d'université]* vice-chancellor *(Brit)*, president *(US)*, chancellor *(US)*

3 *(Jur) [de tribunal]* presiding judge *ou* magistrate; *[de jury]* foreman ◆ **Monsieur** *(ou* **Madame) le ~** Your Honour

COMP président de l'Assemblée nationale President of the National Assembly

président du Conseil *(Hist)* Prime Minister

président-directeur général chairman and managing director *(Brit)*, chief executive officer *(US)*

le président Mao Chairman Mao

président du Parlement européen President of the European Parliament

président du Sénat President of the Senate

président à vie life president

présidente /prezidɑ̃t/ **NF** 1 *(en titre : Pol)* president; *[de comité, réunion, conseil d'administration, commission]* chairwoman; *[de club, société savante]* president; *[de firme]* chairwoman, president; *[de jury d'examen]* chairwoman; *[d'université]* vice-chancellor *(Brit)*, president *(US)*, chancellor *(US)*; *(Jur) [de tribunal]* presiding judge *ou* magistrate; *[de jury]* forewoman 2 († *= épouse) (gén)* president's *ou* chairman's wife; *(Pol)* president's wife, first lady

présidentiable /prezidɑ̃sjabl/ **ADJ** ◆ **être ~** to be a possible *ou* potential presidential candidate

présidentialisation /prezidɑ̃sjalizasjɔ̃/ **NF** ◆ **il prône la ~ du régime** he wants the president to play a more important role in the government

présidentialiser /prezidɑ̃sjalize/ ▸ conjug 1 ◂ **VT** ◆ **~ un régime** to give the president a more important role in the government

présidentialisme /prezidɑ̃sjalism/ **NM** presidentialism

présidentiel, -ielle /prezidɑ̃sjɛl/ **ADJ** presidential ◆ **les (élections) présidentielles** the presidential elections; → **ÉLECTIONS**

présider /prezide/ ▸ conjug 1 ◂ **VT** *[+ tribunal, conseil, assemblée]* to preside over; *[+ comité, débat, séance]* to chair ◆ **~ un dîner** to be the guest of honour at a dinner ◆ **c'est M. Leblanc qui préside** *[+ séance]* Mr Leblanc is in *ou* taking the chair; *[+ club]* Mr Leblanc is president

VT INDIR présider à *[+ préparatifs, décisions, exécution]* to direct, to be in charge *ou* command of; *[+ destinées]* to rule over; *[+ cérémonie]* to preside over ◆ **règles qui président à qch** rules which govern sth ◆ **la volonté de conciliation a présidé aux discussions** a conciliatory spirit prevailed throughout the talks

présidium /prezidjɔm/ **NM** presidium

présocratique /presɔkʀatik/ **ADJ, NM** pre-Socratic

présomptif, -ive /prezɔ̃ptif, iv/ **ADJ** ◆ **héritier ~** heir apparent

présomption /prezɔ̃psjɔ̃/ **NF** 1 *(= supposition)* presumption, assumption; *(Jur)* presumption ◆ **de lourdes ~s pèsent sur lui** he is under grave suspicion ◆ **il a été condamné sur de simples ~s** he was convicted on suspicion alone ◆ **~ de paternité** presumption of paternity ◆ **~ d'innocence** presumption of innocence ◆ **faire respecter la ~ d'innocence** to respect the principle that the defendant is innocent until proven guilty 2 *(= prétention)* presumptuousness, presumption

présomptueusement /prezɔ̃ptɥøzmɑ̃/ **ADV** presumptuously

présomptueux, -euse /prezɔ̃ptɥø, øz/ **ADJ** presumptuous, self-assured ◆ **d'un ton** *ou* **d'un air ~** presumptuously

presque /pʀɛsk/ **ADV** 1 *(contexte positif)* almost, nearly, virtually ◆ **j'ai ~ terminé** I've almost *ou* nearly *ou* as good as finished ◆ **~ à chaque pas** at almost every step ◆ **une espèce d'inquiétude, ~ d'angoisse** a kind of anxiety – almost anguish ◆ **c'est ~ de la folie** it's little short of madness ◆ **c'est ~ impossible** it's almost *ou* virtually *ou* well-nigh impossible ◆ **c'est sûr ou ~** it's almost *ou* practically *ou* virtually certain

2 *(contexte négatif)* hardly, scarcely, almost, virtually ◆ **personne/rien ou ~, ~ personne/rien** hardly *ou* scarcely anyone/anything, almost nobody/nothing, next to nobody/nothing ◆ **as-tu trouvé des fautes ? – ~ pas** did you find any mistakes? – hardly any ◆ **a-t-il dormi ? – ~ pas** did he sleep? – hardly at all *ou* no, not really ◆ **je ne l'ai ~ pas entendu** I hardly *ou* scarcely heard him ◆ **il n'y a ~ plus de vin** there's hardly any wine left, the wine has nearly all gone ◆ **ça n'arrive ~ jamais** it hardly *ou* scarcely ever happens, it almost *ou* practically never happens

3 *(avant n)* **dans la ~ obscurité** in the near darkness ◆ **la ~ totalité des lecteurs** almost *ou* nearly all the readers ◆ **j'en ai la ~ certitude** I'm almost *ou* virtually certain

presqu' île /pʀɛskil/ **NF** peninsula

pressage /pʀesaʒ/ **NM** *[de disque, raisin]* pressing

pressant, e /pʀesɑ̃, ɑ̃t/ **ADJ** *[besoin, danger, invitation]* urgent, pressing *(épith)*; *[situation, travail, désir, demande]* urgent; *[personne]* insistent ◆ **demander qch de façon ~e** to ask for sth urgently ◆ **le créancier a été/s'est fait ~** the creditor was insistent/started to insist *ou* started to press him *(ou* me *etc)* ◆ **avoir un besoin ~** *ou* **une envie ~e** *(euph)* to need to answer an urgent call of nature

press-book (pl **press-books**) /pʀɛsbuk/ **NM** *[de mannequin]* portfolio

presse /pʀɛs/ **NF** 1 *(= institution)* press; *(= journaux)* (news)papers ◆ **la grande ~, la ~ à grand tirage** the popular press ◆ **la ~ écrite** the press ◆ **c'est dans toute la ~** it's in all the papers ◆ **la ~ périodique** periodicals, journals ◆ **~ régionale/mensuelle** regional/monthly press *ou* papers ◆ **~ féminine/automobile** women's/car magazines ◆ **~ d'opinion** papers specializing in analysis and commentary ◆ **~ d'information** newspapers ◆ **~ à scandale** *ou* **à sensation** gutter press ◆ **~ du cœur** romance magazines ◆ **avoir bonne/mauvaise ~** *(lit)* to get *ou* have a good/bad press; *(fig)* to be well/badly thought of ◆ **agence/attaché/conférence de ~** press agency/attaché/conference; → **délit, liberté, service**

2 *(= appareil) (gén)* press; *(Typo)* (printing) press ◆ **~ à cylindres/à bras** cylinder/hand press ◆ **~ de musculation** weight training machine ◆ **mettre sous ~** *[+ livre]* to send to press; *[+ journal]* to put to bed ◆ **le livre a été mis sous ~** the book has gone to press ◆ **le journal a été mis sous ~** the (news)paper has gone to bed ◆ **livre sous ~** book in press ◆ **correct au moment de la mise sous ~** correct at the time of going to press

3 *(littér = foule)* throng *(littér)*, press *(littér)*

4 *(= urgence)* **pendant les moments de ~** when things get busy ◆ **il n'y a pas de ~*** there's no rush *ou* hurry

pressé, e /pʀese/ (ptp de **presser**) **ADJ** 1 *[pas]* hurried ◆ **avoir un air ~** to look as though one is in a hurry ◆ **marcher d'un pas ~** to hurry along ◆ **je suis (très) ~** I'm in a (great) hurry *ou* (very) pressed for time ◆ **je ne suis pas ~** I'm in no hurry *ou* not in any hurry ◆ **être ~ de partir** to be in a hurry to leave 2 *(= urgent) [travail, lettre]* urgent ◆ **c'est ~ ?** is it urgent? ◆ **il n'a eu rien de plus ~ que de faire ...** he wasted no time doing ..., he just couldn't wait to do ... ◆ **si tu n'as rien de plus ~ à faire que de ...** if you have nothing more urgent to do than ... ◆ **il faut parer au plus ~** we must do the most urgent thing(s) first, first things first

presse-agrumes /pʀɛsagʀym/ **NM INV** *(électrique)* (electric) juice extractor *(Brit)*, (electric) juicer *(US)*; *(manuel)* orange *(ou* lemon *etc)* squeezer

presse-ail /pʀɛsaj/ NM INV garlic press *ou* crusher

presse-bouton /pʀɛsbutɔ̃/ ADJ INV push-button

presse-citron (pl **presse-citrons**) /pʀɛssitʀɔ̃/ NM lemon squeezer

pressentiment /pʀesɑ̃timɑ̃/ NM (= *intuition*) foreboding, presentiment, premonition; (= *idée*) feeling ◆ **j'ai comme un ~ qu'il ne viendra pas** I've got a feeling he won't come ◆ **avoir le ~ de qch/que ...** to have a premonition of sth/that ...

pressentir /pʀesɑ̃tiʀ/ ► conjug 16 ◄ VT ① [*+ danger*] to sense, to have a foreboding *ou* a premonition of ◆ **~ que ...** to have a feeling *ou* a premonition that ... ◆ **j'avais pressenti quelque chose** I had sensed something ◆ **il n'a rien laissé ~ de ses projets** he gave no hint of his plans ◆ **rien ne laissait ~ cette catastrophe** there was nothing to suggest that such a disaster might happen ② [*+ personne*] to sound out, to approach ◆ **il a été pressenti pour le poste** he has been sounded out *ou* approached about taking the job ◆ **ministre pressenti** prospective minister

presse-papiers /pʀɛspapje/ NM INV paperweight; (*Ordin*) clipboard

presse-purée /pʀɛspyʀe/ NM INV potato-masher

presser /pʀese/ ► conjug 1 ◄ VT ① [*+ éponge, fruit*] to squeeze; [*+ raisin*] to press ◆ **un citron pressé** a glass of freshly-squeezed lemon juice ◆ **~ qn comme un citron** to squeeze sb dry ◆ **on presse l'orange ou le citron et on jette l'écorce** (*fig*) you use people as long as they can be of service to you and then you cast them aside ◆ **si on lui pressait le nez, il en sortirait du lait** (*hum*) he's barely out of nappies (*Brit*) *ou* diapers (*US*)

② (= *serrer*) [*+ objet*] to squeeze ◆ **les gens étaient pressés les uns contre les autres** people were squashed up *ou* crushed up against one another ◆ **~ qn dans ses bras** to hug sb ◆ **~ qn contre sa poitrine** to clasp sb to one's chest ◆ **~ la main de ou à qn** to squeeze sb's hand, to give sb's hand a squeeze

③ (= *appuyer sur*) [*+ bouton, sonnette*] to press, to push ◆ **~ une matrice dans la cire** to press a mould into the wax

④ (= *façonner*) [*+ disque, pli de pantalon*] to press

⑤ (= *inciter à*) **~ qn de faire qch** to urge *ou* press sb to do sth

⑥ (= *hâter*) [*+ affaire*] to speed up; [*+ départ*] to hasten, to speed up ◆ **(faire) ~ qn** to hurry sb (up) ◆ **(faire) ~ les choses** to speed things up ◆ **~ le pas ou l'allure** to speed up, to hurry on ◆ **il fit ~ l'allure** he speeded up *ou* quickened the pace ◆ **~ le mouvement** to hurry up, to pick up the pace ◆ **qu'est-ce qui vous presse ?** what's the hurry? ◆ **rien ne vous presse** there's no hurry

⑦ (= *harceler*) [*+ débiteur*] to press, to put pressure on; (*littér, Mil*) [*+ ennemi*] to press ◆ **être pressé par le besoin** to be driven *ou* pressed by need ◆ **le désir qui le presse** (*littér*) the desire which drives him ◆ **~ qn de questions** to ply sb with questions

VI (= *être urgent*) to be urgent ◆ **l'affaire presse** it's urgent ◆ **le temps presse** time is short ◆ **cela ne presse pas, rien ne presse** there's no hurry *ou* rush *ou* urgency, there's no need to rush *ou* hurry

VPR **se presser** ① (= *se serrer*) **se ~ contre qn** to squeeze up against sb ◆ **les gens se pressaient pour entrer** people were pushing to get in, there was a crush to get in ◆ **les gens se pressaient autour de la vedette** people were pressing *ou* crowding round the star

② (= *se hâter*) to hurry (up) ◆ **ils allaient/travaillaient sans se ~** they went/were working at a leisurely pace ◆ **pressez-vous, il est tard** hurry up *ou* get a move on*, it's getting late ◆ **il faut se ~** we must hurry up *ou* get cracking* *ou* get a move on* ◆ **presse-toi de partir** hurry up and go ◆ **allons, pressons(-nous) !** come on, come on!, come on, we must hurry!

presse-raquette (pl **presse-raquettes**) /pʀɛsʀakɛt/ NM racket press

pressing /pʀesiŋ/ NM ① (= *établissement*) dry-cleaner's ② (*Sport*) pressure ◆ **faire le ~ sur qn** to put the pressure on sb

pression /pʀesjɔ̃/ NF ① (= *action*) pressure ◆ **je sentais la ~ de sa main sur la mienne** I could feel the pressure of his hand on mine *ou* his hand pressing on mine ◆ **une simple ~ du doigt suffit pour l'ouvrir** to open it, just press ◆ **faire ~ sur le couvercle d'une boîte** (*pour fermer*) to press (down) on the lid of a box; (*pour ouvrir*) to push up the lid of a box

② (*Méd, Phys*) pressure ◆ **~ artérielle/atmosphérique** blood/atmospheric pressure ◆ **à haute/basse ~** high/low pressure (*épith*) ◆ **être sous ~** [*machine*] to be under pressure; [*cabine*] to be pressurized; [*personne*] to be keyed up, to be tense ◆ **mettre sous ~, je suis sous ~ en ce moment** (*excès de travail*) I am under pressure just now ◆ **faire monter/baisser la ~** (*fig*) to increase/reduce the pressure

③ (= *contrainte*) pressure ◆ **~ sociale/fiscale** social/tax pressure ◆ **sous la ~ des événements** under the pressure of events ◆ **faire ~ ou exercer une ~ sur qn (pour qu'il fasse qch)** to put pressure on sb (to do sth), to bring pressure to bear on sb (to do sth), to pressurize sb (into doing sth) ◆ **être soumis à des ~s** to be under pressure; → **groupe**

◊ **mettre la pression** ◆ **en deuxième mi-temps, les Bordelais ont mis la ~** the Bordeaux team put the pressure on in then second half ◆ **mettre la ~ sur** to pressurize, to put pressure on ◆ **je ne voulais pas le faire, on m'a mis la ~*** I didn't want to do it, I was pressurized (into it)

④ ◆ **bière à la ~** draught (*Brit*) *ou* draft (*US*) beer, beer on draught (*Brit*) *ou* draft (*US*) ◆ **deux ~(s)*, s'il vous plaît** two (draught) beers, please

⑤ (= *bouton*) press stud (*Brit*), snap (fastener) (*US*), popper* (*Brit*)

pressoir /pʀeswaʀ/ NM ① (= *appareil*) [*de vin*] wine press; [*de cidre*] cider press; [*d'huile*] oil press ② (= *local*) press-house

pressothérapie /pʀesoteʀapi/ NF pressotherapy

pressurage /pʀesyʀaʒ/ NM [*de fruit*] pressing

pressurer /pʀesyʀe/ ► conjug 1 ◄ VT [*+ fruit*] to press; [*+ personne*] to pressurize, to put under pressure ◆ **se ~ le cerveau*** to rack one's brains

pressurisation /pʀesyʀizasjɔ̃/ NF pressurization

pressuriser /pʀesyʀize/ ► conjug 1 ◄ VT to pressurize ◆ **cabine pressurisée** pressurized cabin

prestance /pʀɛstɑ̃s/ NF presence ◆ **avoir de la ~** to have great presence

prestataire /pʀɛstatɛʀ/ NM ① (= *fournisseur*) **~ de service** service provider ◆ **nous avons des ~s extérieurs** we outsource some of our work ② (= *bénéficiaire*) person receiving benefits *ou* allowances

prestation /pʀɛstasjɔ̃/ NF ① (= *allocation*) [*d'assurance*] benefit ② (*gén pl* = *service*) service ◆ **"prestations luxueuses"** [*de maison*] "luxuriously appointed" ③ (= *performance*) [*d'artiste, sportif*] performance ◆ **faire une bonne ~** to put up a good performance, to perform well

COMP **prestations familiales** State benefits paid to the family (*maternity benefit, family income supplement, rent rebate etc*)

prestation d'invalidité disablement benefit *ou* allowance

prestation en nature payment in kind

prestation de serment taking the oath ◆ **la ~ de serment du président a eu lieu hier** the president was sworn in yesterday

prestation de service provision of a service

prestations sociales social security benefits, welfare payments

prestation de vieillesse old age pension

preste /pʀɛst/ ADJ (*littér*) nimble

prestement /pʀɛstəmɑ̃/ ADV (*littér*) nimbly

prestesse /pʀɛstɛs/ NF (*littér*) nimbleness

prestidigitateur, -trice /pʀɛstidiʒitatœʀ, tʀis/ NM,F conjurer, magician

prestidigitation /pʀɛstidiʒitasjɔ̃/ NF conjuring ◆ **faire de la ~** to do conjuring tricks ◆ **tour de ~** conjuring trick ◆ **ça relève de la ~ !** (*hum*) it's pure wizardry!

prestige /pʀɛstiʒ/ NM (*gén*) prestige ◆ **le ~ de l'uniforme** the glamour of uniforms ◆ **de ~** [*politique, opération, voiture*] prestige (*épith*) ◆ **faire qch pour le ~** to do sth for the glory of it *ou* for (the) prestige

prestigieux, -ieuse /pʀɛstiʒjø, jøz/ ADJ prestigious ◆ **une marque prestigieuse de voiture** a famous *ou* prestigious make of car

presto /pʀɛsto/ ADV (*Mus*) presto; (* *fig*) double-quick*

présumable /pʀezymabl/ ADJ presumable ◆ **il est ~ que ...** it may be presumed that ...

présumer /pʀezyme/ ► conjug 1 ◄ VT to presume, to assume ◆ **présumé innocent** presumed innocent ◆ **l'auteur présumé du livre** the presumed author of the book ◆ **le meurtrier présumé** the alleged killer ◆ **affaire de corruption présumée** alleged corruption affair ◆ **le père présumé** (*Jur*) the putative father VT INDIR **présumer de** ◆ **trop ~ de qch/qn** to overestimate *ou* overrate sth/sb ◆ **(trop) ~ de ses forces** to overestimate one's strength

présupposé /pʀesypoze/ NM presupposition

présupposer /pʀesypoze/ ► conjug 1 ◄ VT to presuppose

présupposition /pʀesypozisjɔ̃/ NF presupposition

présure /pʀezyʀ/ NF rennet

prêt¹, prête /pʀɛ, pʀɛt/ ADJ ① (= *préparé*) ready ◆ **~ à ou pour qch/à ou pour faire qch** ready for sth/to do sth ◆ **~ à fonctionner ou à l'emploi** ready for use ◆ **poulet ~ à cuire ou rôtir** oven-ready chicken ◆ **~ au départ ou à partir** ready to go *ou* leave, ready for the off* (*Brit*) ◆ **être fin ~ (au départ)** to be all set, to be raring* to go ◆ **tout est (fin) ~** everything is (quite) ready ◆ **se tenir ~ à qch/à faire qch** to hold o.s. *ou* be ready for sth/to do sth ◆ **tiens ta monnaie ~e pour payer** have your money ready to pay ◆ **il est ~ à tout** (*criminel*) he'll do anything, he'll stop at nothing ◆ **on m'a averti : je suis ~ à tout** they've warned me and I'm ready for anything ◆ **toujours ~ !** (*devise scoute*) be prepared!; → **marque**

② (= *disposé*) **~ à** ready *ou* prepared *ou* willing to ◆ **être tout ~ à faire qch** to be quite ready *ou* prepared *ou* willing to do sth

prêt² /pʀɛ/ NM ① (= *action*) loaning, lending; (= *somme*) loan ◆ **le service de ~ d'une bibliothèque** the lending department of a library ◆ **~ inter-bibliothèques** inter-library loan ◆ **~ sur gages** (= *service*) pawnbroking; (= *somme*) loan against security; → **bibliothèque** ② (*Mil*) pay ③ (= *avance*) advance

COMP **prêt aidé d'accession à la propriété** *loan for first-time home buyers*

prêt bancaire bank loan ◆ **~ (à taux) bonifié** subsidized *ou* guaranteed loan

prêt à la construction building loan
prêt conventionné regulated mortgage loan
prêt d'honneur *(government) loan made with no guarantee of repayment*
prêt immobilier ≃ mortgage (loan), real-estate loan *(US)*
prêt locatif aidé (d'insertion) *low-cost subsidized housing loan*
prêt personnel personal loan
prêt privilégié guaranteed loan
prêt relais bridging loan

prêt-à-coudre (pl **prêts-à-coudre**) /pʀetakudʀ/ NM ready-to-sew garment

prêt-à-manger (pl **prêts-à-manger**) /pʀetamɑ̃ʒe/ NM ready-made meals

prêt-à-monter (pl **prêts-à-monter**) /pʀetamɔ̃te/ NM kit

prêt-à-porter (pl **prêts-à-porter**) /pʀetapɔʀte/ NM ready-to-wear (clothes) • **acheter qch en ~** to buy sth ready to wear *ou* off the peg *(Brit) ou* off the rack *(US)* • **je n'achète que du ~** I only buy ready-to-wear *ou* off-the-peg *(Brit) ou* off-the-rack *(US)* clothes

prêt-bail (pl **prêts-bails**) /pʀɛbaj/ NM leasing

prêté /pʀete/ NM • **c'est un ~ pour un rendu** it's tit for tat

prétendant, e /pʀetɑ̃dɑ̃, ɑt/ NM *(= prince)* pretender; *(littér = galant)* suitor NM,F *(= candidat)* candidate *(à* for)

prétendre /pʀetɑ̃dʀ/ ▸ conjug 41 ◂ VT 1 *(= affirmer)* to claim, to maintain • **il prétend être** *ou* **qu'il est le premier à avoir trouvé la réponse** he claims he was the first to find the answer • **il se prétend insulté/médecin** he claims he's been insulted/he's a doctor • **je ne prétends pas qu'il l'ait fait** I don't say *ou* I'm not saying he did it • **on le prétend très riche** he is said to be very rich • **en prétendant qu'il venait chercher un livre** on the pretence of coming to get a book • **à ce qu'il prétend** according to him *ou* to what he says, if what he says is true • **à ce qu'on prétend** allegedly
2 *(= avoir la prétention de)* to pretend • **je ne prétends pas être expert** I don't pretend to be an expert • **tu ne prétends pas le faire tout seul ?** you don't expect to do it on your own? • **je ne prétends pas me défendre** I'm not trying to justify myself
3 *(littér) (= vouloir)* to want; *(= avoir l'intention de)* to mean, to intend • **que prétendez-vous de moi ?** what do you want of me? *(littér)* • **que prétend-il faire ?** what does he mean *ou* intend to do? • **je prétends être obéi** *ou* **qu'on m'obéisse** I mean to be obeyed
VT INDIR **prétendre à** *[+ honneurs, emploi]* to lay claim to, to aspire to; *[+ femme]* to aspire to • **~ à faire qch** to aspire to do sth

prétendu, e /pʀetɑ̃dy/ (ptp de **prétendre**) ADJ *[ami, expert]* so-called, supposed; *[alibi, preuves, déclaration]* alleged NM,F († *= fiancé*) intended †

prétendument /pʀetɑ̃dymɑ̃/ ADV supposedly, allegedly

prête-nom (pl **prête-noms**) /pʀɛtnɔ̃/ NM frontman

prétentaine † /pʀetɑ̃tɛn/ NF • **courir la ~** to go gallivanting

prétentieusement /pʀetɑ̃sjøzmɑ̃/ ADV pretentiously

prétentieux, -ieuse /pʀetɑ̃sjø, jøz/ ADJ *[personne, manières, ton]* pretentious, conceited; *[appellation]* pretentious, fancy; *[maison]* pretentious, showy NM,F conceited person • **c'est un petit ~ !** he's so conceited!

prétention /pʀetɑ̃sjɔ̃/ NF 1 *(= exigence)* claim • **avoir des ~s à** *ou* **sur** to lay claim to • **quelles sont vos ~s ?** *(= salaire)* what sort of salary do you expect? *ou* are you looking for?* • **écrire avec CV et ~s** write enclosing CV and stating expected salary
2 *(= ambition)* pretension, claim *(à* to); • **avoir la ~ de faire qch** to claim to be able to do sth, to like to think one can do sth • **je n'ai pas la ~ de rivaliser avec lui** I don't claim *ou* expect *ou* pretend (to be able) to compete with him • **il n'a pas la ~ de tout savoir** he makes no pretence of knowing everything, he doesn't pretend *ou* claim to know everything • **sa ~ à l'élégance** her claims *ou* pretensions to elegance • **sans ~** *[maison, repas]* unpretentious; *[robe]* simple
3 *(= vanité)* pretentiousness, pretension, conceitedness • **avec ~** pretentiously, conceitedly

prêter /pʀete/ ▸ conjug 1 ◂ VT 1 *[+ objet, argent]* to lend • **~ qch à qn** to lend sth to sb, to lend sb sth • **peux-tu me ~ ton stylo ?** can you lend me your pen, can I borrow your pen? • **ils prêtent à 10%** they lend (money) at 10%, they give loans at 10% • **ils m'ont prêté 20 €** they lent me €20 • **~ sur gages** to lend against security • **on ne prête qu'aux riches** *(Prov)* unto those that have shall more be given *(Prov)*
2 *(= attribuer) [+ sentiment, facultés]* to attribute, to ascribe • **on lui prête l'intention de démissionner** he is alleged *ou* said to be intending to resign • **on me prête des paroles que je n'ai pas dites** people are claiming I said things that I didn't • **nous prêtons une grande importance à ces problèmes** we consider these problems of great importance, we accord a great deal of importance to these problems
3 *(= apporter, offrir) [+ aide, appui]* to give, to lend • **~ assistance/secours à qn** to go to sb's assistance/aid • **~ main forte à qn** to lend sb a hand, to come to sb's assistance, to come to help sb • **~ son concours à** to give one's assistance to • **~ sa voix à une cause** to speak on behalf of *ou* in support of a cause • **~ sa voix pour un gala** to sing at a gala performance • **dans cette émission il prêtait sa voix à Napoléon** in this broadcast he played *ou* spoke the part of Napoleon • **~ son nom à** to lend one's name to • **~ la main à une entreprise/un complot** to be *ou* get involved in *ou* take part in an undertaking/a plot • **~ attention à** to pay attention to, to take notice of • **il faut ~ la plus grande attention à mes paroles** you must listen very closely *ou* you must pay very close attention to what I have to say • **~ le flanc à la critique** to lay o.s. open to criticism, to invite criticism • **~ l'oreille** to listen, to lend an ear *(à* to); • **~ serment** to take an *ou* the oath • **faire ~ serment à qn** to administer the oath to sb • **si Dieu me prête vie** *(hum)* if God grants me life, if I am spared *(hum)*
VT INDIR **prêter à** • **son attitude prête à équivoque/à la critique/aux commentaires** his attitude is ambiguous/is open to criticism/is likely to make people talk • **cette décision prête à (la) discussion** the decision is open to debate • **sa conduite prête à rire** his behaviour makes you want to laugh *ou* is laughable
VI *[tissu, cuir]* to give, to stretch
VPR **se prêter** 1 *(= consentir)* **se ~ à** *[+ expérience]* to participate in; *[+ projet, jeu]* to fall in with, to go along with • **il n'a pas voulu se ~ à leurs manœuvres** he didn't want any part in *ou* refused to have anything to do with their schemes
2 *(= s'adapter)* **se ~ (bien) à qch** to lend itself (well) to sth • **la salle se prête mal à une réunion intime** the room doesn't lend itself to informal meetings
3 *[chaussures, cuir]* to give, to stretch

prétérit /pʀeteʀit/ NM preterite (tense) • **au ~** in the preterite (tense)

prétérition /pʀeteʀisjɔ̃/ NF paralipsis, paraleipsis

préteur /pʀetœʀ/ NM *(Antiq)* praetor

prêteur, -euse /pʀɛtœʀ, øz/ ADJ unselfish • **il n'est pas ~** *[enfant]* he's possessive about his toys *ou* belongings, he doesn't like lending his things; *[adulte]* he isn't willing to lend things, he doesn't believe in lending (things) NM,F (money) lender • **~ sur gages** pawnbroker

prétexte /pʀetɛkst/ GRAMMAIRE ACTIVE 44.1 NM pretext, excuse • **mauvais ~** poor *ou* lame excuse • **sous ~ d'aider son frère** on the pretext *ou* pretence *ou* under (the) pretext of helping his brother • **sous (le) ~ que ...** on *ou* under the pretext that ..., on the pretence that ... • **sous ~ qu'elle est jeune on lui passe tout** just because she's young she gets away with everything • **sous aucun ~** on no account • **il a pris ~ du froid** *ou* **il a donné le froid comme ~ pour rester chez lui** he used the cold weather as a pretext *ou* an excuse for staying at home • **tous les ~s sont bons pour ne pas aller chez le dentiste** any excuse will do not to go to the dentist • **servir de ~ à qch/à faire qch** to be a pretext *ou* an excuse for sth/to do sth • **ça lui a servi de ~** *ou* **ça lui a donné un ~ pour refuser** it provided him with an excuse to refuse *ou* with a pretext for refusing • **il saisit le premier ~ venu pour partir** he made the first excuse he could think of for leaving • **ce n'est qu'un ~** it's just an excuse • **pour elle tout est ~ à se plaindre** she'll complain about anything and everything

prétexter /pʀetɛkste/ ▸ conjug 1 ◂ VT to give as a pretext *ou* an excuse • **il a prétexté qu'il était trop fatigué** he said he was too tired • **en prétextant que ...** on the pretext that ... • **~ une angine pour refuser une invitation** to say one has a sore throat to get out of an invitation

prétimbré, e /pʀetɛ̃bʀe/ ADJ *[enveloppe]* stamped

prétoire /pʀetwaʀ/ NM *(Antiq)* praetorium; *(Jur : frm)* court

Pretoria /pʀetɔʀja/ N Pretoria

prétorien, -ienne /pʀetɔʀjɛ̃, jɛn/ ADJ, NM *(Antiq)* praetorian

prêtraille /pʀɛtʀɑj/ NF *(péj)* • **la ~** priests, the clergy

prêtre /pʀɛtʀ/ NM priest • **se faire ~** to become a priest • **grand ~** high priest • **les grands ~s du monétarisme** the high priests of monetarism

prêt-relais (pl **prêts-relais**) /pʀɛʀəlɛ/ NM bridging loan

prêtre-ouvrier (pl **prêtres-ouvriers**) /pʀɛtʀuvʀije/ NM worker priest

prêtresse /pʀɛtʀɛs/ NF priestess

prêtrise /pʀɛtʀiz/ NF priesthood • **recevoir la ~** to be ordained

preuve /pʀœv/ NF 1 *(= démonstration)* proof, evidence • **faire la ~ de qch/que** to prove sth/that • **avoir la ~ de/que** to have proof *ou* evidence of/that • **pouvez-vous apporter la ~ de ce que vous dites ?** can you prove *ou* can you produce proof *ou* evidence of what you're saying? • **(c'est la) ~ que ...** that proves that ... • **j'avais prévu cela, la ~, j'ai déjà mon billet*** I'd thought of that, and to prove it I've already got my ticket • **jusqu'à ~ (du) contraire** until we find proof *ou* evidence to the contrary, until there's proof *ou* evidence that it's not the case • **n'importe qui peut conduire, à ~ mon fils*** anyone can drive, just look at *ou* take my son (for instance) • **il a réussi, à ~ qu'il ne faut jamais désespérer*** he succeeded, which just goes to show *ou* prove you should never give up hope
2 *(= indice)* proof *(NonC)*, evidence *(NonC)*, piece of evidence • **je n'ai pas de ~s** I have no proof *ou* evidence • **c'est une ~ supplémen-**

taire de sa culpabilité it's further proof *ou* it's further evidence of his guilt ◆ **il y a trois ~s irréfutables qu'il ment** there are three definite pieces of evidence which prove quite clearly that he's lying ◆ **affirmer qch ~s en mains** to back sth up with concrete proof *ou* evidence

3 (= *marque*) proof (*NonC*) ◆ **c'est une ~ de bonne volonté/d'amour** it's proof of his good intentions/of his love

4 (*Math*) [*d'opération*] proof ◆ **faire la ~ par neuf** to cast out the nines

5 (*locutions*) **faire ~ de** to show ◆ **faire ses ~s** [*personne*] to prove o.s., to show one's ability; [*voiture*] to prove itself ◆ **cette nouvelle technique n'a pas encore fait ses ~s** this new technique hasn't yet proved its worth

COMP **preuve par l'absurde** reductio ad absurdum

preuve concluante conclusive *ou* positive proof

preuve a contrario a contrario proof

preuve matérielle material evidence (*NonC*)

preux †† / prø / ADJ valiant †, gallant † NM valiant knight †

prévaloir / prevalwar / ▸ conjug 29 ◂ VI (*littér*) to prevail (*sur* over; *contre* against); ◆ **faire ~ ses droits** to insist upon one's rights ◆ **faire ~ son opinion** to win agreement *ou* acceptance for one's opinion ◆ **son opinion a prévalu sur celle de ses collègues** his opinion prevailed over *ou* overrode that of his colleagues ◆ **rien ne peut ~ contre ses préjugés** nothing can overcome his prejudices VPR **se prévaloir** 1 (= *se flatter*) **se ~ de** to pride o.s. on 2 (= *profiter*) **se ~ de** to take advantage of

prévaricateur, -trice / prevarikatœr, tris / ADJ corrupt NM,F corrupt official

prévarication / prevarikasjɔ̃ / NF corrupt practices

> ⚠ **prévarication** ne se traduit pas par le mot anglais **prevarication**, qui a le sens de 'faux-fuyants'.

prévariquer / prevarike / ▸ conjug 1 ◂ VI to be guilty of corrupt practices

prévenance / prev(ə)nɑ̃s / NF thoughtfulness (*NonC*), consideration (*NonC*), kindness (*NonC*) ◆ **toutes les ~s que vous avez eues pour moi** all the consideration *ou* kindness you've shown me ◆ **entourer qn de ~s** to be very considerate to *ou* towards sb ◆ **il n'a aucune ~ pour les autres** he shows *ou* has no consideration for others, he's very thoughtless

prévenant, e / prev(ə)nɑ̃, ɑ̃t / ADJ [*personne*] considerate, kind (*envers* to) thoughtful (*envers* of); [*manières*] kind, attentive

prévendre / prevɑ̃dʀ / ▸ conjug 41 ◂ VT [+ *billets, marchandises*] to pre-sell

prévenir / prev(ə)niʀ / GRAMMAIRE ACTIVE 29.3 ▸ conjug 22 ◂ VT 1 (= *avertir*) to warn (*de qch* about *ou* against *ou* of sth); (= *aviser*) to inform, to tell (*de qch* about sth); ◆ **qui faut-il ~ en cas d'accident ?** who should be informed *ou* told if there's an accident? ◆ **~ le médecin/la police** to call the doctor/the police ◆ **tu es prévenu !** you've been warned! ◆ **partir sans ~** to leave without warning, to leave without telling anyone ◆ **il aurait pu ~** he could have let us know

2 (= *empêcher*) [+ *accident, catastrophe*] to prevent, to avert, to avoid; [+ *maladie*] to prevent, to guard against; [+ *danger*] to avert, to avoid; [+ *malheur*] to ward off, to avoid, to provide against; → **mieux**

3 (= *devancer*) [+ *besoin, désir*] to anticipate; [+ *question, objection*] to forestall ◆ **il voulait arriver le premier mais son frère l'avait prévenu** (*littér*) he wanted to be the first to arrive but his brother had anticipated him *ou* had got there before him

4 (*frm* = *influencer*) **~ qn contre qn** to prejudice *ou* bias sb against sb ◆ **~ qn en faveur de qn** to prejudice *ou* predispose sb in sb's favour

prévente / prevɑ̃t / NF pre-selling

préventif, -ive / prevɑ̃tif, iv / ADJ [*mesure, médecine*] preventive ◆ **à titre ~** as a precaution *ou* preventive measure ◆ **la lutte préventive contre le sida** AIDS prevention NF (*Jur*) ◆ **être en préventive** to be on remand, to be remanded in custody ◆ **mettre qn en préventive** to remand sb in custody, to hold sb on remand ◆ **il a fait 6 mois de (prison) préventive** he was remanded in custody for 6 months

prévention / prevɑ̃sjɔ̃ / NF 1 [*d'accident, crime, corruption, maladie, délinquance*] prevention ◆ **~ routière** road safety ◆ **faire de la ~** to take preventive action ◆ **campagne/politique de ~** prevention campaign/policy ◆ **mesures de ~** preventive measures 2 (*Jur*) custody, detention ◆ **mettre en ~** to detain, to remand in *ou* take into custody 3 (= *préjugé*) prejudice (*contre* against); (= *réserve*) reservation ◆ **considérer qch sans ~** to take an unprejudiced *ou* unbiased view of sth

préventivement / prevɑ̃tivmɑ̃ / ADV [*agir*] preventively, as a precaution *ou* preventive measure ◆ **être incarcéré ~** (*Jur*) to be remanded *ou* held in custody *ou* detention (awaiting trial)

prévenu, e / prev(ə)ny / (ptp de **prévenir**) ADJ (*Jur*) charged ◆ **être ~ d'un délit** to be charged with *ou* accused of a crime NM,F (*Jur*) defendant, accused (person)

préverbe / prevɛʀb / NM verbal prefix, preverb

prévisibilité / previzibilite / NF foreseeable nature

prévisible / previzibl / ADJ [*réaction, résultat, personne*] predictable; [*événement, évolution*] foreseeable, predictable ◆ **difficilement ~** difficult to foresee ◆ **dans un avenir ~** in the foreseeable future ◆ **une amélioration est ~ dans les prochains mois** an improvement can be expected *ou* is foreseeable within the next few months ◆ **il était ~ que ...** it was to be expected that ..., it was predictable that ...

prévision / previzjɔ̃ / NF 1 (*gén pl* = *prédiction*) prediction, expectation; (*Fin*) forecast, estimate, prediction ◆ **~s budgétaires** budget estimates ◆ **~s météorologiques** weather forecast ◆ **~ à court/long terme** short-term/long-term forecast ◆ **~ en temps réel** nowcast ◆ **il a réussi au-delà de toute ~** he has succeeded beyond all expectations 2 (= *action*) **la ~ du temps** weather forecasting ◆ **la ~ de ses réactions est impossible** it's impossible to predict his reactions *ou* to foresee what his reactions will be ◆ **en ~ de son arrivée/d'une augmentation du trafic** in anticipation *ou* expectation of his arrival/of an increase in the traffic

prévisionnel, -elle / previzjɔnɛl / ADJ [*mesure, plan*] forward-looking; [*budget*] projected

prévisionniste / previzjɔnist / NMF (economic) forecaster

prévoir / prevwaʀ / ▸ conjug 24 ◂ VT 1 (= *anticiper*) [+ *événement, conséquence*] to foresee, to anticipate; [+ *temps*] to forecast; [+ *réaction, contretemps*] to expect, to reckon on, to anticipate ◆ **~ le pire** to expect the worst ◆ **il faut ~ les erreurs éventuelles** we must allow for *ou* make provision for possible errors ◆ **nous n'avions pas prévu qu'il refuserait** we hadn't reckoned on his refusing, we hadn't anticipated *ou* foreseen that he'd refuse ◆ **cela fait** *ou* **laisse ~ un malheur** it bodes ill ◆ **rien ne laisse ~ une amélioration rapide** there's no prospect *ou* suggestion of a quick improvement ◆ **tout laisse ~ une issue rapide/qu'il refusera** everything points *ou* all the signs point to a rapid solution/to his refusing ◆ **rien ne faisait** *ou* **ne laissait ~ que ...** there was nothing to suggest *ou* to make us think that ... ◆ **on ne peut pas tout ~** you can't think of everything ◆ **plus tôt que prévu** earlier than expected *ou* anticipated; → **programme**

2 (= *projeter*) [+ *voyage, construction*] to plan ◆ **~ de faire qch** to plan to do *ou* on doing sth ◆ **pour quand prévoyez-vous votre arrivée ?** when do you plan to arrive? ◆ **au moment prévu** at the appointed *ou* scheduled *ou* prescribed time ◆ **comme prévu** as planned, according to plan ◆ **"ouverture prévue pour la fin de l'année"** [*autoroute*] "scheduled to open at the end of the year"

3 (= *préparer, envisager*) to allow ◆ **il faudra ~ des trous pour l'écoulement des eaux** you must leave *ou* provide some holes for drainage ◆ **prévoyez de l'argent en plus pour les faux frais** allow some extra money for incidental expenses ◆ **il vaut mieux ~ quelques couvertures en plus** you'd better allow a few extra blankets *ou* bring (along) a few extra blankets ◆ **il faudrait ~ un repas** you ought to make plans for *ou* to organize a meal ◆ **tout est prévu pour l'arrivée de nos hôtes** everything is in hand *ou* organized for the arrival of our guests ◆ **cette voiture est prévue pour quatre personnes** this car is designed for four people ◆ **vous avez prévu grand** you've planned things on a grand scale ◆ **déposez vos lettres dans la boîte prévue à cet effet** put your letters in the box provided ◆ **on a prévu des douches** (*à installer*) they have made provision for showers to be built; (*déjà installées*) they have laid on *ou* provided showers

4 (*Jur*) [*loi, règlement*] to provide for, to make provision for ◆ **c'est prévu à l'article 8** article 8 makes provision for that, it's provided for in article 8 ◆ **le code pénal prévoit que ...** the penal code holds that ... ◆ **la loi prévoit une peine de prison** the law makes provision for a prison sentence ◆ **ce n'est pas prévu dans le contrat** it is not provided for in the contract, the contract makes no provision for it

prévôt / prevo / NM (*Hist, Rel*) provost; (*Mil*) provost marshal

prévôtal, e (mpl **-aux**) / prevotal, o / ADJ of a provost

prévôté / prevote / NF (*Hist*) provostship; (*Mil*) military police

prévoyance / prevwajɑ̃s / NF foresight, forethought ◆ **caisse de ~** contingency fund ◆ **société de ~** provident society

prévoyant, e / prevwajɑ̃, ɑ̃t / ADJ provident

Priam / pʀijam / NM Priam

priapisme / pʀijapism / NM priapism

prie-Dieu / pʀidjø / NM INV prie-dieu

prier / pʀije / GRAMMAIRE ACTIVE 31 ▸ conjug 7 ◂

VT 1 [+ *Dieu, saint*] to pray to ◆ **~ Dieu de faire un miracle** to pray for a miracle ◆ **je prie Dieu que cela soit vrai** pray God that it is true

2 (= *implorer*) to beg, to beseech (*littér*) ◆ **elle le pria de rester** she begged *ou* urged *ou* pressed him to stay ◆ **je vous prie de me pardonner** please forgive me ◆ **dites oui, je vous en prie !** please say yes! ◆ **Pierre, je t'en prie, calme-toi !** Pierre, for heaven's sake, calm down! ◆ **je t'en prie, ça suffit !** please, that's quite enough!

3 (= *inviter*) to invite, to ask; (*frm*) to request (*frm*) ◆ **il m'a prié à déjeuner** *ou* **de venir déjeuner** he has invited *ou* asked me to lunch ◆ **vous êtes prié de vous présenter à 9 heures** you are requested to present yourself at 9 o'clock ◆ **on l'a prié d'assister à la cérémonie** he was invited to attend the ceremony ◆ **nous vous prions d'honorer de votre présence la cérémonie** we request the honour *ou* pleasure of your company at the ceremony

4 (= *ordonner*) **je vous prie de sortir** will you please leave the room ◆ **vous êtes prié de répondre quand on vous parle/de rester assis** please reply when spoken to/remain seated ◆ **taisez-vous, je vous prie** would you please be quiet

5 (*formules de politesse*) **je vous en prie** (= *faites donc*) please do, of course; (= *après vous*) after you; (*idée d'irritation*) do you mind! ◆ **excusez-moi – je vous en prie** I'm sorry – not at all ◆ **merci beaucoup – je vous en prie** thank you – don't mention it *ou* you're welcome ◆ **voulez-vous ouvrir la fenêtre je vous prie ?** would you mind opening the window please?, would you be so kind as to open the window please?; → **agréer**

6 (*locutions*) **il s'est fait** ~ he needed coaxing *ou* persuading ◆ **il ne s'est pas fait** ~ he didn't need persuading, he didn't wait to be asked twice, he was only too willing (to do it) ◆ **il a accepté l'offre sans se faire** ~ he accepted the offer without hesitation ◆ **allez, viens, ne te fais pas** ~ **!** come on! don't be such a bore!

VI to pray (*pour* for); ◆ **prions, mes frères** brothers, let us pray

prière /pʀijɛʀ/ **NF** 1 (*Rel* = *oraison, office*) prayer ◆ **être en** ~ to be praying *ou* at prayer ◆ **dire** *ou* **faire ses ~s** to say one's prayers ◆ **se rendre à la** ~ to go to prayer ◆ **ne m'oubliez pas dans vos ~s** (*hum*) remember me in your prayers, pray for me; → **livre¹, moulin**

2 (= *demande*) plea, entreaty ◆ **céder aux ~s de qn** to give in to sb's requests ◆ **à la** ~ **de qn** at sb's request *ou* behest (*littér*) ◆ **j'ai une** ~ **à vous adresser** I have a request to make to you ◆ **il est resté sourd à mes ~s** he turned a deaf ear to my pleas *ou* entreaties

◆ **prière de ...** please ... ◆ ~ **de répondre par retour du courrier** please reply by return of post ◆ ~ **de vous présenter à 9 heures** you are requested to present yourself *ou* please present yourself at 9 o'clock ◆ **"prière de ne pas fumer"** "no smoking (please)" ◆ **"prière de ne pas se pencher à la fenêtre"** "(please) do not lean out of the window" ◆ ~ **d'insérer** (*Édition*) please insert

prieur /pʀijœʀ/ **NM** ◆ **(père)** ~ prior

prieure /pʀijœʀ/ **NF** ◆ **(mère)** ~ prioress

prieuré /pʀijœʀe/ **NM** (= *couvent*) priory; (= *église*) priory (church)

prima donna /pʀimadɔna/ (pl inv *ou* **prime donne** /pʀimedɔne/) **NF** prima donna

primaire /pʀimɛʀ/ **ADJ** 1 primary ◆ **délinquant** ~ first offender ◆ **école** ~ primary *ou* elementary school, grade school (*US*) ◆ **ère** ~ primary *ou* palaeozoic era 2 (*péj* = *simpliste*) [*personne*] simple-minded, limited*; [*raisonnement*] simplistic; [*plaisanterie*] obvious **NM** (*Scol*) primary school *ou* education; (*Élec*) primary; (*Géol*) Primary, Palaeozoic ◆ **être en** ~ (*Scol*) to be in primary school **NF** (*Pol*) primary (election)

primal, e (mpl **-aux**) /pʀimal, o/ **ADJ** ◆ **cri** ~ primal scream ◆ **thérapie** ~**e** primal (scream) therapy, scream therapy

primarité /pʀimaʀite/ **NF** primarity

primat /pʀima/ **NM** 1 (*Rel*) primate 2 (*littér* = *primauté*) primacy

primate /pʀimat/ **NM** 1 (= *animal*) primate 2 (* *péj* = *personne*) ape*

primatologie /pʀimatɔlɔʒi/ **NF** primatology

primatologue /pʀimatɔlɔg/ **NMF** primatologist

primauté /pʀimote/ **NF** (*Rel*) primacy; (*fig*) primacy, pre-eminence (*sur* over); ◆ **donner la** ~ **à qch** to prioritize sth

prime¹ /pʀim/ **NF** 1 (= *cadeau*) free gift ◆ **donné en** ~ **avec qch** given away *ou* given as a free gift with sth ◆ **cette année il a eu la rougeole, la varicelle et les oreillons en** ~ **!** (*iro*) this year he had the measles, chickenpox and the mumps to boot! *ou* on top of that!

2 (= *bonus*) bonus; (= *subvention*) premium, subsidy; (= *indemnité*) allowance ◆ ~ **d'allaitement** nursing mother's allowance ◆ ~ **d'ancienneté** seniority bonus *ou* pay ◆ ~ **de déménagement** relocation allowance ◆ ~ **de départ** *bonus paid to an employee when leaving a job;* (*importante*) golden handshake ◆ ~ **à l'emploi** *financial incentive to promote employment* ◆ ~ **à l'exportation** export premium *ou* subsidy ◆ ~ **de fin d'année/de rendement** Christmas/ productivity bonus ◆ ~ **d'intéressement** performance(-related) bonus ◆ ~ **de licenciement** severance pay, redundancy payment ◆ ~ **de risque** danger money (*NonC*) ◆ ~ **de transport** transport allowance ◆ **c'est donner une** ~ **à la paresse !** it's just paying people to sit around doing nothing!; → **précarité**

3 (*Assurances, Bourse*) premium ◆ ~ **d'assurances** insurance premium ◆ ~ **d'émission** issuing share *ou* premium ◆ ~ **de remboursement** redemption premium ◆ **faire** ~ to be at a premium

prime² /pʀim/ **ADJ** 1 ◆ **de** ~ **abord** at first glance ◆ **dès sa** ~ **jeunesse** from his earliest youth ◆ **il n'est plus de** ~ **jeunesse** he's no longer in the prime of youth *ou* the first flush of youth 2 (*Math*) prime ◆ **n** ~ n prime

primé, e /pʀime/ (ptp de **primer**) **ADJ** [*film, reportage, auteur, cinéaste*] award-winning (*épith*); [*animal*] prize(-winning); [*invention, produit*] prize-winning ◆ **ce film a été plusieurs fois** ~ this film has won several awards

primer /pʀime/ ▸ conjug 1 ◂ **VT** 1 (= *surpasser*) to prevail over, to take precedence over ◆ **chez elle, l'intelligence prime la générosité** in her case, intelligence is more in evidence *ou* to the fore than generosity 2 (= *récompenser*) to award a prize to; (= *subventionner*) to subsidize **VI** (= *dominer*) to be the prime *ou* dominant feature, to dominate; (= *compter, valoir*) to be of prime importance, to take first place ◆ **c'est le bleu qui prime dans ce tableau** blue is the dominant colour in this picture ◆ **pour moi ce sont les qualités de cœur qui priment** the qualities of the heart are what count the most for me

primerose /pʀimʀoz/ **NF** hollyhock

primesautier, -ière /pʀimsotje, jɛʀ/ **ADJ** impulsive ◆ **être d'humeur primesautière** to have an impulsive temperament *ou* nature

prime time /pʀajmtajm/ **NM INV** (*TV*) prime time ◆ **diffusé en** ~ broadcast on prime-time television *ou* in prime time

primeur /pʀimœʀ/ **NFPL** ◆ **~s** (= *fruits et légumes*) early fruit and vegetables ◆ **marchand de ~s** greengrocer (*Brit*), grocer (*US*) (*specializing in early produce*) **NF** 1 (*Presse* = *nouvelle*) scoop ◆ **avoir la** ~ **d'une nouvelle** to be the first to hear a piece of news ◆ **je vous réserve la** ~ **de mon manuscrit** I'll let you be the first to read my manuscript 2 ◆ **vin (de)** ~ nouveau wine, wine of the latest vintage

primevère /pʀimvɛʀ/ **NF** (*sauvage*) primrose; (*cultivée*) primula; (*jaune*) primrose

primigeste /pʀimiʒɛst/ **NF** primigravida

primipare /pʀimipaʀ/ **ADJ** primiparous **NF** primipara

primitif, -ive /pʀimitif, iv/ **ADJ** 1 (= *originel*) [*forme, état*] original, primitive; [*projet, question, préoccupation*] original, first; [*église*] primitive, early; [*peintre*] primitive; (*Logique*) [*proposition, concept*] basic; (*Art*) [*couleurs*] primary; (*Géol*) [*terrain*] primitive, primeval ◆ **ville construite sur le site** ~ **d'une cité romaine** town built on the original site of a Roman city ◆ **je préfère revenir à mon projet ~/à mon idée primitive** I'd rather revert to my original *ou* initial *ou* first plan/idea 2 (*Sociol*) [*peuple, art, mœurs*] primitive 3 (= *sommaire*) [*installation*] primitive, crude 4 (*Ling*) [*temps, langue*] basic; [*mot*] primitive; [*sens*] original 5 (*Math*) **fonction primitive** primitive **NM,F** (*Art, Sociol*) primitive **NF primitive** (*Math*) primitive

primitivement /pʀimitivmɑ̃/ **ADV** originally

primitivisme /pʀimitivism/ **NM** (*Art*) primitivism

primo /pʀimo/ **ADV** first (of all), firstly

primo-accédant, e (pl **primo-accédants**) /pʀimoaksedɑ̃, ɑt/ **NM,F** ◆ ~ **(à la propriété)** first-time (home-)buyer

primogéniture /pʀimoʒenityʀ/ **NF** primogeniture

primo-infection (pl **primo-infections**) /pʀimoɛ̃fɛksjɔ̃/ **NF** primary infection

primordial, e (mpl **-iaux**) /pʀimɔʀdjal, jo/ **ADJ** 1 (= *vital*) [*élément, question*] essential, vital; [*objectif, préoccupation*] chief, main; [*rôle*] crucial, key (*épith*) ◆ **d'une importance** ~**e** of the utmost *ou* of paramount *ou* primordial importance 2 (*littér* = *originel*) primordial

primordialement /pʀimɔʀdjalmɑ̃/ **ADV** essentially

prince /pʀɛ̃s/ **NM** 1 (*lit*) prince ◆ **le** ~ **des chanteurs** *etc* (*fig*) the prince *ou* king of singers *etc* ◆ **Robin des bois, le** ~ **des voleurs** Robin Hood, Prince of Thieves; → **fait¹**

2 (*locutions*) **être** *ou* **se montrer bon** ~ to be magnanimous *ou* generous, to behave generously ◆ **être habillé/vivre comme un** ~ to be dressed/live like a prince

COMP prince des apôtres Prince of the apostles

le Prince charmant Prince Charming ◆ **elle attend le** *ou* **son** ~ **charmant** she's waiting for her Prince Charming *ou* for Mr. Right* to come along, she's waiting for her knight in shining armour

prince consort Prince Consort

prince de l'Église prince of the Church

prince de Galles Prince of Wales; (= *tissu*) Prince of Wales check

prince héritier crown prince

prince du sang prince of royal blood

le Prince des ténèbres *ou* **des démons** the prince of darkness

princeps /pʀɛ̃sɛps/ **ADJ** [*édition*] first

princesse /pʀɛ̃sɛs/ **NF** princess ◆ **faire la** *ou* **sa** ~**, prendre des airs de** ~ to put on airs ◆ **robe** ~ princess dress; → **frais²**

princier, -ière /pʀɛ̃sje, jɛʀ/ **ADJ** (*lit, fig*) princely

princièrement /pʀɛ̃sjɛʀmɑ̃/ **ADV** in (a) princely fashion

principal, e (mpl **-aux**) /pʀɛ̃sipal, o/ **GRAMMAIRE ACTIVE 53.2 ADJ** 1 [*entrée, bâtiment, résidence*] main; [*clerc, employé*] chief, head; [*question, raison, but*] principal, main; [*personnage, rôle*] leading, main, principal ◆ **elle a eu l'un des rôles principaux dans l'affaire** she played a major role *ou* she was one of the leading *ou* main figures in the business 2 (*Gram*) [*proposition*] main **NM** 1 (*Fin*) principal 2 (*Scol*) headmaster, principal, head (*Brit*); (*Admin*) chief clerk 3 (= *chose importante*) **le** ~ the most important thing, the main point ◆ **c'est le** ~ that's the main thing 4 (*Mus*) principal **NF principale** 1 (*Gram*) main clause 2 (*Scol*) headmistress, principal, head (*Brit*)

principalement /pʀɛ̃sipalmɑ̃/ **ADV** principally, mainly, chiefly

principat /pʀɛ̃sipa/ **NM** princedom

principauté /pʀɛ̃sipote/ **NF** principality ◆ **la Principauté (de Monaco)** Monaco

principe /pʀɛ̃sip/ **NM** 1 (= *règle*) [*de science, géométrie*] principle ◆ **il nous a expliqué le** ~ **de la machine** he explained the principle on which the machine worked ◆ **le ~ d'Archimède** Archimedes' principle; → **pétition**

2 *(= hypothèse)* principle, assumption ◆ **partir du ~ que ..., poser comme ~ que ...** to work on the principle *ou* assumption that ...; → **accord**

3 *(= règle morale)* principle ◆ **il a des ~s** he's a man of principle, he's got principles ◆ **il n'a pas de ~s** he's unprincipled, he has no principles ◆ **avoir pour ~ de faire qch** to make it a principle to do sth, to make a point of doing sth ◆ **je ne mens pas, c'est un ~ chez moi** I make a point of not telling lies, it's a rule with me that I don't tell lies ◆ **il n'est pas dans mes ~s de ...** I make it a principle not to ... ◆ **il a manqué à ses ~s** he has failed to stick to his principles

4 *(= origine)* principle ◆ **remonter jusqu'au ~ des choses** to go back to first principles

5 *(= élément)* principle, element, constituent ◆ **~ nécessaire à la nutrition** necessary principle of nutrition

6 *(= rudiment)* **~s** rudiments, principles

7 *(locutions)* **faire qch pour le ~** to do sth on principle *ou* for the sake of it

◆ **de principe** *[hostilité, objection, opposition, soutien]* systematic, automatic ◆ **décision de ~** decision in principle ◆ **c'est une question de ~** it's a matter of principle

◆ **en principe** *(= d'habitude, en général)* as a rule; *(= théoriquement)* in principle, theoretically

◆ **par principe** on principle

printanier, -ière /pʀɛ̃tanje, jɛʀ/ **ADJ** *[soleil, couleur, temps, vêtement]* spring *(épith)*; *[atmosphère]* spring-like ◆ **navarin (d'agneau) ~** *(Culin)* navarin of lamb with spring vegetables

printemps /pʀɛ̃tɑ̃/ **NM** spring ◆ **au ~** in (the) spring(time) ◆ **au ~ de la vie** *(littér)* in the springtime of life ◆ **mes 40 ~** *(hum)* my 40 summers *(hum)*

prion /pʀijɔ̃/ **NM** prion

priorat /pʀijɔʀa/ **NM** priorate

priori /pʀijɔʀi/ → **a priori**

prioritaire /pʀijɔʀitɛʀ/ **ADJ** 1 *[projet, opération]* priority *(épith)* ◆ **être ~** *[personne, projet]* to take *ou* have priority 2 **être ~** *[véhicule, automobiliste]* to have priority *ou* right of way ◆ **il était sur une route ~** he had right of way, he was on the main road **NMF** *(= automobiliste)* person who has right of way *ou* priority

prioritairement /pʀijɔʀitɛʀmɑ̃/ **ADV** *(gén)* first and foremost; *[traiter]* as a (matter of) priority ◆ **ces places sont ~ réservées aux handicapés** the disabled have priority for these seats, these seats are reserved first and foremost for the disabled

priorité /pʀijɔʀite/ **NF** 1 *(gén)* priority ◆ **donner la ~ absolue à qch** to give top priority to sth ◆ **il faut établir une ~ dans les questions à régler** we must prioritize the questions to be dealt with ◆ **l'une des ~s essentielles** one of the first *ou* top priorities

◆ **en + priorité** ◆ **discuter qch en ~** to discuss sth as a (matter of) priority ◆ **venir en ~** to come first ◆ **l'une des choses à faire en grande ~, il nous faudrait en ~ des vivres** first and foremost we need supplies, we need supplies as a matter of urgency

2 *(sur la route)* priority, right of way ◆ **avoir la ~** to have right of way *(sur* over); ◆ **~ à droite** *(principe) system of giving way to traffic coming from the right; (panneau)* give way to the vehicles on your right ◆ **laisser** *ou* **céder la ~ à qn** to give way to sb *(Brit)*, to yield to sb *(US)*; → **refus**

pris, prise¹ /pʀi, pʀiz/ (ptp de **prendre**) **ADJ** 1 *[place]* taken ◆ **avoir les mains ~es** to have one's hands full ◆ **tous les billets sont ~** the tickets are sold out, all the tickets have been sold ◆ **toutes les places sont ~es** all the seats are taken *ou* have gone ◆ **toute ma journée est ~e** I'm busy all day ◆ **ça me fera 50 €, c'est toujours ça de ~*** I'll get €50, that's better than nothing

2 *[personne]* busy ◆ **le directeur est très ~ cette semaine** the manager is very busy this week ◆ **si vous n'êtes pas ~ ce soir ...** if you're free *ou* if you've got nothing on *ou* if you're not doing anything this evening ... ◆ **désolé, je suis ~** sorry, I'm busy

3 *(Méd) [nez]* stuffy, stuffed-up; *[gorge]* hoarse ◆ **j'ai le nez ~** my nose is stuffed up ◆ **j'ai la gorge ~e** my throat is hoarse ◆ **les poumons sont ~** the lungs are (now) affected

4 *(Culin) [crème, gelée]* set ◆ **mer ~e par les glaces** frozen sea

5 † **avoir la taille bien ~e** to have a neat waist ◆ **la taille ~e dans un manteau de bonne coupe** wearing a well-cut coat to show off a neat waist

6 *(= envahi par)* **~ de peur/remords** stricken with *ou* by fear/remorse ◆ **~ d'une inquiétude soudaine** seized by a sudden anxiety ◆ **j'ai été ~ d'une envie soudaine de chocolat** I had a sudden urge to eat some chocolate ◆ **~ de boisson** *(frm)* under the influence*, the worse for drink

prise² /pʀiz/ **NF** 1 *(= moyen d'empoigner, de prendre)* hold (NonC), grip (NonC); *(pour soulever, faire levier)* purchase (NonC); *(Catch, Judo)* hold; *(Alpinisme)* hold; *(Sport : sur raquette, club, batte)* grip ◆ **faire une ~ de judo à qn** to get sb in a judo hold ◆ **on n'a pas de ~ pour soulever la caisse** there's no purchase to lift the chest, you can't get a hold on the chest to lift it ◆ **cette construction offre trop de ~ au vent** this building catches the wind very badly ◆ **avoir ~ sur** to have a hold on *ou* over ◆ **on n'a aucune ~ sur lui** no one has any hold *ou* influence over him ◆ **ces théories n'ont que trop de ~ sur elle** these theories have all too great a hold on *ou* over her ◆ **donner ~ à** to give rise to ◆ **son attitude donne ~ aux soupçons** his attitude gives rise to *ou* lays him open to suspicion; → **lâcher**

2 *(Chasse, Pêche = butin)* catch; *(= saisie) [de contrebande, drogue]* capture, seizure; *(Mil) [de ville, navire]* capture; *(Échecs, Dames)* capture

3 *(Élec)* **~ (de courant)** *(mâle)* plug; *(femelle)* socket, point, power point (SPÉC); *(au mur)* socket ◆ **~ multiple** adaptor; *(avec rallonge)* trailing socket ◆ **triple ~** three-way adaptor ◆ **~ pour rasoir électrique** razor point; → aussi **comp**

4 *[de tabac]* pinch of snuff; *[de cocaïne]* snort‡

5 *(Méd)* **à administrer en plusieurs ~s par jour** to be given *ou* administered at intervals throughout the day ◆ **arrêter la ~ de la pilule** to stop taking the pill ◆ **la ~ de ce médicament est déconseillée pendant la grossesse** it is not recommended that this medicine be taken during pregnancy

6 *(= durcissement) [de ciment, enduit]* setting ◆ **à ~ rapide** quick-setting

7 *(locutions)*

◆ **aux prises (avec)** ◆ **être** *ou* **se trouver aux ~s avec des difficultés** to be battling *ou* grappling *ou* wrestling with difficulties ◆ **être aux ~s avec un créancier** to be battling against *ou* doing battle with a creditor ◆ **cette campagne met aux ~s deux hommes bien différents** this campaign pits two extremely different men against each other ◆ **je l'ai trouvé aux ~s avec son ordinateur** *(hum)* I found him battling with *ou* trying to get to grips with his computer

◆ **en prise** ◆ **être/mettre en ~** *(en voiture)* to be in/put the car into gear ◆ **en ~ (directe)** in direct drive ◆ **en ~ (directe) avec** *ou* **sur** *(fig)* tuned into ◆ **un gouvernement en ~ avec les réalités du pays** a government in tune with *ou* that is tuned into the realities of the country ◆ **littérature en ~ directe avec les mutations de la société** writing that has its finger on the pulse of a changing society

COMP **prise d'air** air inlet *ou* intake

prise d'armes military review *ou* parade

la prise de la Bastille the storming of the Bastille

prise de bec* row*, set-to* ◆ **avoir une ~ de bec avec qn** to have a row* *ou* a set-to* with sb, to fall out with sb

prise de corps *(Jur)* arrest

prise d'eau water (supply) point; *(= robinet)* tap *(Brit)*, faucet *(US)*

prise de guerre spoils of war

prise péritel → **péritel**

prise de sang blood test ◆ **faire une ~ de sang à qn** to take a blood sample from sb

prise de son *(Ciné, Radio, TV)* sound recording ◆ **~ de son : J. Dupont** sound (engineer): J. Dupont

prise de téléphone phone socket

prise de terre *(Élec, Radio)* earth *(Brit)*, ground *(US)* ◆ **la machine à laver n'a pas de ~ de terre** the washing machine isn't earthed *(Brit) ou* grounded *(US)*

prise de tête quelle **~ de tête ces maths/son copain !** maths/her boyfriend drives me crazy! ou does my head in‡

prise de vue(s) *(Ciné, TV)* filming, shooting ◆ **~ de vue** *(= photographie)* shot ◆ **~ de vue(s) : J. Dupont** camera(work): J. Dupont; → **charge, conscience, contact, main** *etc*

priser¹ /pʀize/ ▸ conjug 1 ◂ **VT** *(littér)* to prize, to value ◆ **très prisé** highly prized ◆ **je prise fort peu ce genre de plaisanterie** I don't appreciate this sort of joke at all

priser² /pʀize/ ▸ conjug 1 ◂ **VT** *[+ tabac]* to take; *[+ drogue]* to take, to snort‡; → **tabac** **VI** to take snuff

priseur, -euse /pʀizœʀ, øz/ **NM,F** snuff taker

prismatique /pʀismatik/ **ADJ** prismatic

prisme /pʀism/ **NM** prism

prison /pʀizɔ̃/ **NF** 1 *(= lieu)* prison, jail, penitentiary *(US)*; *(= demeure sombre)* prison ◆ **~ pour dettes** *(Hist)* debtors' prison ◆ **mettre qn en ~** to send sb to prison *ou* jail, to imprison sb ◆ **~ ouverte** open prison ◆ **elle vit dans une ~ dorée** she's like a bird in a gilded cage; → **porte** 2 *(= emprisonnement)* prison, jail ◆ **peine de ~** prison sentence ◆ **faire de la ~** to go to *ou* be in prison ◆ **faire 6 mois de ~** to spend 6 months in jail *ou* prison ◆ **condamné à 3 mois de ~ ferme/à la ~ à vie** sentenced to 3 months' imprisonment/to life imprisonment

prisonnier, -ière /pʀizɔnje, jɛʀ/ **ADJ** *[soldat]* captive ◆ **être ~** *(enfermé)* to be trapped, to be a prisoner; *(en prison)* to be imprisoned, to be a prisoner ◆ **être ~ de ses vêtements** to be hampered by one's clothes ◆ **être ~ de ses préjugés/de l'ennemi** to be a prisoner of one's prejudices/of the enemy **NM,F** prisoner ◆ **~ d'opinion** prisoner of conscience ◆ **~ politique** political prisoner ◆ **faire/retenir qn ~** to take/hold sb prisoner ◆ **~ de guerre** prisoner of war; → **camp, constituer**

Prisunic ® /pʀizynik/ **NM** department store *(for inexpensive goods)*, ≃ Woolworth's ®, five and dime *(US)* ◆ **de ~** *(péj)* cheap

privatif, -ive /pʀivatif, iv/ **ADJ** 1 *(Gram)* privative 2 *(Jur = qui prive)* which deprives of rights *(ou* liberties *etc)* 3 *(Jur = privé)* private ◆ **avec jardin ~** with private garden ◆ **"jardin privatif"** *(sur annonce)* "own garden"; → **carte** **NM** *(Gram)* privative (prefix *ou* element)

privation /pʀivasjɔ̃/ **NF** 1 *(= suppression)* deprivation ◆ **la ~ des droits civiques** *(Jur)* the forfeiture *ou* deprivation of civil rights ◆ **la ~ de liberté** the loss of liberty ◆ **la ~ de la vue/d'un membre** the loss of one's sight/of a limb ◆ **la ~ de nourriture/sommeil** food/sleep deprivation 2 *(gén pl = sacrifice)* privation, hardship ◆ **les ~s que je me suis imposées** the things I went ou did ou managed without, the hardships I bore ◆ **souffrir de ~s** to endure hardship

privatisation /pʀivatizasjɔ̃/ **NF** privatization ◆ **~ partielle/totale** partial/wholesale privatization ◆ **entreprise en cours de ~** company undergoing privatization

privatiser /pʀivatize/ ► conjug 1 ◄ **VT** *[+ entreprise]* to privatize ◆ **entreprise privatisée** privatized company

privautés /pʀivote/ **NFPL** liberties ◆ **prendre des ~ avec** to take liberties with ◆ **~ de langage** familiar ou coarse language

privé, e /pʀive/ **ADJ** *(gén)* private; *(Presse) [source]* unofficial; *(Jur) [droit]* civil; *[télévision, radio]* independent ◆ **personne ~e** private person ◆ **en séjour (à titre) ~** on a private visit **NM** [1] ◆ **le ~** *(= vie)* private life; *(= secteur)* the private sector ◆ **dans le ~** *(= vie privée)* in one's private life; *(= secteur privé)* in the private sector

◆ **en privé** *[conversation, réunion]* private, in private *(attrib)*; *[parler]* privately, in private

[2] *(* = détective)* private eye *, private detective

privément /pʀivemɑ̃/ **ADV** *(littér)* privately

priver /pʀive/ ► conjug 1 ◄ **VT** [1] *(délibérément, pour punir)* **~ qn de qch** to deprive sb of sth ◆ **il a été privé de dessert** he was deprived of dessert, he had to go without his dessert ◆ **il a été privé de récréation** he was kept in at playtime ◆ **on l'a privé de sa liberté/ses droits** he was deprived of his freedom/his rights

[2] *(= faire perdre)* **~ qn de ses moyens** to deprive sb of ou strip sb of his means ◆ **cette perte m'a privé de ma seule joie** this loss has deprived me of my only joy ou has taken my only joy from me ◆ **l'accident l'a privé d'un bras** he lost an arm in the accident ◆ **privé de connaissance** unconscious ◆ **privé de voix** speechless, unable to speak ◆ **un discours privé de l'essentiel** a speech from which the main content had been removed ou which was stripped of its essential content

[3] *(= démunir)* **nous avons été privés d'électricité pendant 3 jours** we were without ou we had no ou we were deprived of electricity for 3 days ◆ **il a été privé de sommeil** he didn't get any sleep ◆ **on m'interdit le sel, ça me prive beaucoup** I'm not allowed salt and I must say I miss it ou and I don't like having to go ou do without it ◆ **cela ne me prive pas du tout** *(de vous le donner)* I can spare it (quite easily); *(de ne plus en manger)* I don't miss it at all; *(de ne pas y aller)* I don't mind at all

VPR **se priver** [1] *(par économie)* to go without, to do without ◆ **se ~ de qch** to go ou do ou manage without sth ◆ **ils ont dû se ~ pour leurs enfants** they had to go ou do without for the sake of their children ◆ **je n'ai pas l'intention de me ~** I've no intention of going ou doing without, I don't intend to go short *(Brit)*

[2] *(= se passer de)* **se ~ de** to manage without, to do without, to deny o.s., to forego ◆ **il se prive de dessert par crainte de grossir** he does without dessert for fear of putting on weight ◆ **se ~ de cigarettes** to deny o.s. cigarettes ◆ **ils ont dû se ~ d'une partie de leur personnel** they had to manage without ou do without some of their staff ◆ **tu te prives d'un beau spectacle en refusant d'y aller** you'll miss out on * ou you'll deprive yourself of a fine show by not going

[3] *(gén nég = se retenir)* **il ne s'est pas privé de le dire/le critiquer** he made no bones about ou he had no hesitation in saying it/criticizing him ◆ **j'aime bien manger et quand j'en ai l'occasion je ne m'en prive pas** I love eating and whenever I get the chance I don't hold back ◆ **si tu veux y aller, ne t'en prive pas pour moi** if you want to go don't stop yourself because of me

privilège /pʀivilɛʒ/ **NM** *(gén)* privilege ◆ **j'ai eu le ~ d'assister à la cérémonie** I had the privilege of attending ou I was privileged to attend the ceremony ◆ **avoir le triste ~ de faire qch** to have the unhappy privilege of doing sth ◆ **ce pays a le triste ~ d'être le pays le plus pollué** this country has the dubious distinction ou privilege of being the most polluted country

privilégié, e /pʀivileʒje/ (ptp de **privilégier**) **ADJ** [1] *(= exceptionnel) [lieu, moyen, traitement, tarif, site, climat]* special; *[accès]* privileged, special ◆ **la France est le partenaire ~ de l'Allemagne dans la construction européenne** France and Germany have a special relationship in the building of Europe ◆ **entretenir des relations ~es avec qn** to have a special ou privileged relationship with sb ◆ **ils ont un accès ~ au marché** they have privileged ou special access to the market ◆ **j'ai été le témoin ~ de ces mutations** I was privileged to witness these changes

[2] *(= riche)* privileged ◆ **les classes ~es** the privileged classes

[3] *(= qui a de la chance)* fortunate

[4] *(Fin) [action]* preference *(épith)* *(Brit)*, preferred *(US)*; *[créancier]* preferential

NM,F privileged person ◆ **c'est un ~** he is fortunate ou lucky ◆ **quelques ~s** a privileged ou lucky few

privilégier /pʀivileʒje/ ► conjug 7 ◄ **VT** to favour *(Brit)*, to favor *(US)* ◆ **privilégié par le sort** fortunate, lucky ◆ **la police semble ~ la thèse de l'attentat** the police appear to favour the theory that it was a terrorist attack ◆ **il a été privilégié par la nature** nature has been kind to him

prix /pʀi/ **NM** [1] *(= coût) [d'objet, produit]* price; *[de location, transport]* cost ◆ **le ~ d'un billet Paris-Lyon** the fare between Paris and Lyons, the price of a ticket between Paris and Lyons ◆ **à quel ~ vend-il/sont ses tapis ?** what price is he asking for/are his carpets?, how much is he charging ou asking for/are his carpets? ◆ **quel ~ veut-elle de sa maison ?** what (price) is she asking ou how much does she want for her house? ◆ **quels sont vos ~ ?** *(pour service)* what are your rates?; *(pour objet)* what sort of prices do you charge? ◆ **je l'ai payé 80 € ! – c'est le ~** I paid 80 euros for it! – that's the going rate ◆ **1 000 €, ~ à débattre** €1,000 or nearest offer, €1,000 o.n.o. *(Brit)* ◆ **au ~ que ça coûte, il ne faut pas le gaspiller** at that price we'd better not waste any ◆ **au ~ où sont les choses ou où est le beurre !** * with prices what they are! ◆ **votre ~ sera le mien** name ou state your price ◆ **c'était le premier ~** it was the cheapest ◆ **quel est votre dernier ~ ?** *(pour vendre)* what's the lowest you'll go?; *(pour acheter)* what's your final offer? ◆ **acheter qch à ~ d'or** to pay a (small) fortune for sth ◆ **payer le ~ fort** *(lit)* to pay the full price; *(fig)* to pay a heavy price ◆ **faire payer le ~ fort** to charge the full price ◆ **au ~ fort** at the highest possible price ◆ **à bas ~** *[produit, terrain]* cheap; *[acheter, vendre]* cheaply ◆ **je l'ai eu à bas ~** I got it cheap ◆ **ça n'a pas de ~** it's priceless ◆ **je vous fais un ~ (d'ami)** I'll let you have it cheap ou at a reduced price, I'll knock a bit off for you * ◆ **j'y ai mis le ~ (qu'il fallait)** I had to pay a lot ou quite a price for it, it cost me a lot ◆ **il faut y mettre le ~** you have to be prepared to pay for it ◆ **il n'a pas voulu y mettre le ~** he didn't want to pay that much ◆ **je cherche une robe – dans quels ~ ?** I'm looking for a dress – in what price range? ◆ **c'est dans mes ~** that's affordable ou within my price range ◆ **c'est hors de ~** it's outrageously expensive ◆ **cette table est hors de ~** the price of this table is exorbitant ou outrageous ◆ **ce magasin est hors de ~** the prices in this shop are exorbitant ou outrageous ◆ **c'est un objet qui n'a pas de ~** it's a priceless object ◆ **mettre qch à ~** *(enchères)* to set a reserve price *(Brit)* ou an upset price *(US)* on sth ◆ **mettre à ~ la tête de qn** to put a price on sb's head, to offer a reward for sb's capture ◆ **mise à ~ : 200 €** *(enchères)* reserve *(Brit)* ou upset *(US)* price: €200 ◆ **objet de ~** expensive item; → **bas**[1]

[2] *(fig)* price ◆ **le ~ du succès/de la gloire** the price of success/of glory ◆ **j'apprécie votre geste à son juste ~** I appreciate the true worth of what you did ◆ **son amitié n'a pas de ~ pour moi** I cannot put a price on his friendship ◆ **donner du ~ à** *[+ exploit, aide]* to make (even) more worthwhile ◆ **leur pauvreté donne encore plus de ~ à leur cadeau** their poverty makes their present even more precious ou impressive, their poverty increases the value ou worth of their gift even more

[3] *(= récompense, Scol)* prize ◆ **(livre de) ~** *(Scol)* prize(-book) ◆ **le ~ Nobel de la paix** the Nobel Peace Prize

[4] *(= vainqueur, personne)* prizewinner; *(= livre)* prizewinning book ◆ **premier ~ du Conservatoire** first prizewinner at the Conservatoire ◆ **as-tu lu le dernier ~ Goncourt ?** have you read the book that won the last ou latest Prix Goncourt?

[5] *(Courses)* race ◆ **Grand Prix (automobile)** Grand Prix

[6] *(locutions)* **à tout ~** at all costs, at any price ◆ **à aucun ~** on no account, not at any price ◆ **au ~ de grands efforts/sacrifices** after much effort/many sacrifices

COMP **prix d'achat** purchase price
prix actuel going price *(de* for)
prix agricoles *(Europe)* agricultural prices
prix d'appel introductory price
prix conseillé manufacturer's recommended price, recommended retail price
prix coûtant cost price
prix de départ asking price
prix de détail retail price
prix d'encouragement special prize *(for promising entrant)*
prix d'excellence *(Scol)* prize for coming first in the class ou for being top of the form
prix de fabrique factory price
prix fixe *(gén)* set price; *(menu)* set (price) menu ◆ **(repas à) ~ fixe** set (price) meal
prix forfaitaire contract price
prix de gros wholesale price
prix imposé *(Comm)* regulation price
prix d'interprétation féminine/masculine *(Ciné, Théât)* prize for best actress/actor
prix d'intervention intervention price
prix de lancement introductory price
prix littéraire literary prize
prix marqué marked price
prix à la production ou au producteur farm gate price
prix public retail ou list ou base price
prix de revient cost price
prix sortie d'usine factory price
prix de vente selling price, sale price
prix de vertu paragon of virtue

PRIX LITTÉRAIRES

The prix Goncourt, France's best-known annual literary prize, is awarded for the year's finest prose work (usually a novel). The winner is chosen by a jury made up of members of the Académie Goncourt, who make their final decision over lunch at Drouant, a famous Paris restaurant.

There are over 100 other important literary prizes in France, the most coveted of which include the Prix Femina, the Prix Interallié, the Prix Renaudot and the Prix Médicis.

pro * /pʀo/ **NMF** (abrév de **professionnel**) pro * ◆ **c'est un travail de ~** it's a professional job

◆ **il est très ~** he's very professional, he's a real pro*

pro- /pʀo/ **PRÉF** pro- ◆ **~américain/chinois** pro-American/-Chinese ◆ **~Maastricht** pro-Maastricht

proactif, -ive /pʀoaktif, iv/ **ADJ** proactive

probabilisme /pʀɔbabilism/ **NM** probabilism

probabiliste /pʀɔbabilist/ **ADJ** *(Stat)* probability *(épith)*

probabilité /pʀɔbabilite/ **GRAMMAIRE ACTIVE 42.2** **NF** 1 *(= vraisemblance) [d'événement, hypothèse]* probability, likelihood ◆ **selon toute ~** in all probability *ou* likelihood 2 *(Math, Stat)* probability ◆ **calcul/théorie des ~s** probability calculus/theory

probable /pʀɔbabl/ **GRAMMAIRE ACTIVE 42.2, 43.2** **ADJ** 1 *(= vraisemblable) [événement, hypothèse, évolution]* probable, likely ◆ **il est ~ qu'il gagnera** it's likely that he will win, he's likely to win, he'll probably win, the chances are (that) he'll win ◆ **il est peu ~ qu'il vienne** he's unlikely to come, there's little chance of his coming, the chances are (that) he won't come ◆ **il est fort ~ qu'il ait raison** in all likelihood he's right, it's highly likely that he's right ◆ **c'est (très) ~** it's (very *ou* highly) probable, (most *ou* very) probably, it's (highly) likely ◆ **c'est son successeur ~** he's likely to succeed him 2 *(Math, Stat)* probable **ADV** * ◆ **j'ai dû l'oublier dans le bus – ~** *(= sûrement)* I must have left it on the bus – most likely

probablement /pʀɔbabləmɑ̃/ **GRAMMAIRE ACTIVE 42.2, 43.2, 53.6** **ADV** probably ◆ **il viendra ~** he's likely to come, he'll probably come ◆ **~ pas** probably not

probant, e /pʀɔbɑ̃, ɑ̃t/ **ADJ** *[argument, expérience]* convincing; *(Jur)* probative

probation /pʀɔbasjɔ̃/ **NF** *(Jur, Rel)* probation ◆ **stage de ~** trial *ou* probationary period

probatoire /pʀɔbatwaʀ/ **ADJ** *[examen, test]* grading, preliminary ◆ **stage ~** trial *ou* probationary period

probe /pʀɔb/ **ADJ** *(littér)* upright, honest

probité /pʀɔbite/ **NF** probity, integrity

problématique /pʀɔblematik/ **ADJ** problematic(al) **NF** *(= problème)* problem, issue; *(= science)* problematics *(sg)*

problème /pʀɔblɛm/ **GRAMMAIRE ACTIVE 53.1, 53.2, 53.3** **NM** 1 *(= difficulté)* problem; *(= question débattue)* problem, issue ◆ **le ~ du logement** the housing problem, the problem of housing ◆ **~ de santé** health problem ◆ **j'ai eu quelques ~s de santé dernièrement** I've had some problems with my health *ou* health problems recently, my health hasn't been too good recently ◆ **c'est tout un ~** it's a real problem ◆ **elle risque d'avoir de sérieux ~s avec la police** she could run into serious trouble with the police ◆ **soulever un ~** to raise a problem ◆ **faire ~** to pose problems ◆ **(il n'y a) pas de ~ !*** no problem!, no sweat!* ◆ **ça lui pose un ~ de conscience** this is troubling his conscience ◆ **il a bien su poser le ~** he put *ou* formulated the problem well ◆ **ce retard pose un ~** this delay poses a problem *ou* confronts us with a problem ◆ **son admission au club pose des ~s** his joining the club is problematic *ou* is not straightforward ◆ **son cas nous pose un sérieux ~** his case poses a difficult problem for us, his case presents us with a difficult problem ◆ **le ~ qui se pose** the problem we are faced with *ou* we must face ◆ **si tu viens en voiture, le ~ ne se pose pas** if you come by car the problem doesn't arise ◆ **le ~ ne se pose pas dans ces termes** that isn't the problem, the problem shouldn't be stated in these terms

◆ **à problèmes** *[peau, cheveux, enfant]* problem *(épith)* ◆ **famille à ~s** problem *ou* dysfunctional family ◆ **quartier/banlieue à ~s** problem area/suburb *(in which there is a lot of crime)*

2 *(Math)* problem ◆ **~s de robinets** *(Scol)* sums about the volume of water in containers ◆ **le prof nous a posé un ~ difficile** the teacher set us a difficult problem

pro bono /pʀobono/ **ADJ, ADV** pro bono

procédé /pʀɔsede/ **NM** 1 *(= méthode)* process ◆ **~ de fabrication** manufacturing process 2 *(= conduite)* behaviour *(Brit) (NonC)*, behavior *(US) (NonC)*, conduct *(NonC)* ◆ **avoir recours à un ~ malhonnête** to do something in a dishonest way, to resort to dishonest behaviour ◆ **ce sont là des ~s peu recommandables** that's pretty disreputable behaviour; → **échange** 3 *(Billard)* tip

procéder /pʀɔsede/ ▸ conjug 6 ◂ **VI** *(= agir)* to proceed; *(moralement)* to behave ◆ **~ par ordre** to take things one by one, to do one thing at a time ◆ **~ avec prudence** to proceed with caution ◆ **~ par élimination** to use a process of elimination ◆ **je n'aime pas sa façon de ~ (envers les gens)** I don't like the way he behaves (towards people)

VT INDIR **procéder à** *(= opérer) [+ enquête, expérience]* to conduct, to carry out; *[+ dépouillement]* to start ◆ **ils ont procédé à l'ouverture du coffre** they proceeded to open the chest, they set about opening the chest ◆ **nous avons fait ~ à une étude sur ...** we have initiated *ou* set up a study on ... ◆ **~ au vote** to take a vote *(sur* on) ◆ **~ à une élection** to hold an election ◆ **~ à l'élection du nouveau président** to hold an election for the new president, to elect the new president

VT INDIR **procéder de** *(frm = provenir de)* to come from, to proceed from, to originate in; *(Rel)* to proceed from ◆ **cette philosophie procède de celle de Platon** this philosophy originates in *ou* is a development from that of Plato ◆ **cela procède d'une mauvaise organisation** it comes from *ou* is due to bad organization

procédural, e (mpl **-aux**) /pʀɔsedyʀal, o/ **ADJ** procedural

procédure /pʀɔsedyʀ/ **NF** 1 *(= marche à suivre)* procedure ◆ **quelle ~ doit-on suivre pour obtenir ... ?** what procedure must one follow to obtain ...?, what's the (usual) procedure for obtaining ...? 2 *(Jur) (= règles)* procedure; *(= procès)* proceedings ◆ **~ accélérée** expeditious procedure ◆ **~ de conciliation** conciliation procedure ◆ **~ civile** civil (law) procedure ◆ **~ pénale** criminal (law) procedure ◆ **problème de ~** procedural problem

procédurier, -ière /pʀɔsedyʀje, jɛʀ/ **ADJ** *(péj) [tempérament, attitude]* quibbling *(épith)*, pettifogging *(épith)* ◆ **il est très ~** he's a real stickler for the regulations

procès /pʀɔsɛ/ **NM** 1 *(Jur = poursuite)* (legal) proceedings, (court) action, lawsuit; *[de cour d'assises]* trial ◆ **faire/intenter un ~ à qn** to take/start *ou* institute *(frm)* (legal) proceedings against sb ◆ **engager un ~ contre qn** to take (court) action against sb, to bring an action against sb, to take sb to court, to sue sb ◆ **intenter un ~ en divorce** to institute divorce proceedings ◆ **être en ~ avec qn** to be involved in a lawsuit with sb ◆ **gagner/perdre son ~** to win/lose one's case ◆ **réviser un ~** to review a case *ou* judgment

2 *(fig)* **faire le ~ de qn/la société capitaliste** to put sb/capitalism on trial *ou* in the dock ◆ **faire le ~ de qch** to pick holes in sth, to criticize sth ◆ **là tu me fais un ~ d'intention** you're putting words into my mouth ◆ **vous me faites un mauvais ~** you're making unfounded *ou* groundless accusations against me; → **forme**

3 *(Anat, Ling)* process

COMP **procès civil** civil proceedings *ou* action
procès criminel criminal proceedings *ou* trial

processeur /pʀɔsesœʀ/ **NM** processor

procession /pʀɔsesjɔ̃/ **NF** procession ◆ **marcher en ~** to walk in procession

processionnaire /pʀɔsesjɔnɛʀ/ **ADJ** processionary **NF** processionary caterpillar

processionnel, -elle /pʀɔsesjɔnɛl/ **ADJ** processional

processionnellement /pʀɔsesjɔnɛlmɑ̃/ **ADV** in procession

processus /pʀɔsesys/ **NM** 1 *(= procédure)* process ◆ **~ de paix** peace process ◆ **le ~ d'intégration européenne** the European integration process 2 *[de maladie]* progress ◆ **l'apparition d'un ~ cancéreux** the appearance of a cancerous growth 3 *(Anat)* process

procès-verbal (pl **procès-verbaux**) /pʀɔsɛvɛʀbal, o/ **NM** *(= compte rendu)* minutes; *(Jur = constat)* report, statement; *(de contravention)* statement ◆ **dresser (un) ~ à un automobiliste** to give a ticket to *ou* book *(Brit)* a motorist

prochain, e /pʀɔʃɛ̃, ɛn/ **ADJ** 1 *(= suivant) [réunion, numéro, semaine]* next ◆ **lundi/le mois ~** next Monday/month ◆ **le 8 septembre ~** on 8 September (of this year) ◆ **la ~e rencontre aura lieu à Paris** the next meeting will take place in Paris ◆ **la ~e fois que tu viendras** (the) next time you come ◆ **la ~e fois** *ou* **la fois ~e, je le saurai** I'll know next time ◆ **je ne peux pas rester dîner aujourd'hui, ce sera pour une ~e fois** I can't stay for dinner today – it'll have to be *ou* I'll have to come some other time ◆ **au revoir, à une ~e fois !** goodbye, see you again!* ◆ **je descends à la ~e*** I'm getting off at the next stop *(ou* station *etc)* ◆ **à la ~e occasion** at the next *ou* first opportunity

◆ **à la prochaine!*** *(= salut)* see you!*, be seeing you!*

2 *(= proche) [arrivée, départ]* impending, imminent; *[mort]* imminent; *[avenir]* near, immediate ◆ **un jour ~** soon, in the near future ◆ **un de ces ~s jours** one of these days, before long

3 *[village] (= suivant)* next; *(= voisin)* neighbouring *(Brit)*, neighboring *(US)*, nearby; *(= plus près)* nearest

4 *(littér) [cause]* immediate

NM fellow man; *(Rel)* neighbour *(Brit)*, neighbor *(US)*

prochainement /pʀɔʃɛnmɑ̃/ **ADV** soon, shortly ◆ **~ (sur vos écrans) ...** *(Ciné)* coming soon *ou* shortly ...

proche /pʀɔʃ/ **ADJ** 1 *(dans l'espace) [village]* neighbouring *(Brit) (épith)*, neighboring *(US) (épith)*, nearby *(épith)*; *[rue]* nearby *(épith)* ◆ **être (tout) ~** to be (very) near *ou* close, to be (quite) close by ◆ **le magasin le plus ~** the nearest shop

2 *(= imminent) [mort]* close *(attrib)*, at hand *(attrib)*; *[départ]* imminent, at hand *(attrib)* ◆ **dans un ~ avenir** in the near *ou* immediate future ◆ **être ~** *[de fin, but]* to be drawing near, to be near at hand ◆ **la nuit est ~** it's nearly nightfall ◆ **l'heure est ~ où ...** the time is at hand when ...; → **futur**

3 *(= récent) [événement]* close *(attrib)*, recent

4 *[parent]* close, near ◆ **mes plus ~s parents** my nearest *ou* closest relatives, my next of kin *(Admin)*

5 *[ami]* close ◆ **je me sens très ~ d'elle** I feel very close to her ◆ **les ~s conseillers/collaborateurs du président** the president's closest *ou* immediate advisers/associates

6 *(= semblable)* similar ◆ **nos positions sont très ~s** our positions are very similar, we take a very similar position *ou* line

7 *(locutions)*

♦ **proche de** *(= avoisinant)* close to, near; *(= parent de)* closely related to ♦ ~ **de la ville** near the town, close to the town ♦ **être ~ de** *[+ fin, victoire]* to be nearing, to be close to; *[+ dénouement]* to be nearing, to be drawing close to ♦ **être ~ de la mort** to be near death *ou* close to death ♦ **les maisons sont très ~s les unes des autres** the houses are very close together ♦ **l'italien est ~ du latin** Italian is closely related to Latin ♦ **une désinvolture ~ de l'insolence** off-handedness verging on insolence ♦ **selon des sources ~s de l'ONU** according to sources close to the UN

ADV

♦ **de proche en proche** step by step, gradually ♦ **la nouvelle se répandit de ~ en ~** the news gradually spread

NM *(surtout pl)* close relation ♦ **les ~s** close relations, next of kin *(Admin)*

Proche-Orient /pʀɔʃɔʀjɑ̃/ **NM** ♦ **le ~** the Near East ♦ **du ~** Near Eastern, in *ou* from the Near East

proche-oriental, e (mpl **proche-orientaux**) /pʀɔʃɔʀjɑ̃tal, o/ **ADJ** Near Eastern

proclamateur, -trice /pʀɔklamatœʀ, tʀis/ **NM,F** proclaimer

proclamation /pʀɔklamasjɔ̃/ **NF** 1 *(= reconnaissance officielle) [de république, état d'urgence]* proclamation, declaration; *[de verdict, résultats d'élection, résultats d'examen]* announcement ♦ ~ **de l'indépendance** declaration of independence 2 *(= texte)* proclamation

proclamer /pʀɔklame/ ► conjug 1 ◄ **VT** 1 *(= affirmer) [+ conviction, vérité]* to proclaim ♦ ~ **son innocence** to proclaim *ou* declare one's innocence ♦ ~ **que ...** to proclaim *ou* declare *ou* assert that ... ♦ **il se proclamait le sauveur du pays** he proclaimed *ou* declared himself (to be) the saviour of the country ♦ **chez eux, tout proclamait la pauvreté** *(littér)* everything in their house proclaimed their poverty 2 *(= reconnaître officiellement) [+ république, état d'urgence, état de siège, indépendance]* to proclaim, to declare; *[+ décret]* to publish; *[+ verdict, résultats]* to announce ♦ ~ **qn roi** to proclaim sb king

proclitique /pʀɔklitik/ **ADJ, NM** proclitic

proconsul /pʀɔkɔ̃syl/ **NM** proconsul

procrastination /pʀɔkʀastinasjɔ̃/ **NF** *(littér)* procrastination

procréateur, -trice /pʀɔkʀeatœʀ, tʀis/ *(littér)* **ADJ** procreative **NM,F** procreator

procréation /pʀɔkʀeasjɔ̃/ **NF** *(littér)* procreation *(littér)*, reproduction ♦ ~ **artificielle** *ou* **médicale(ment) assistée** artificial *ou* assisted reproduction

procréer /pʀɔkʀee/ ► conjug 1 ◄ **VT** *(littér)* to procreate

procuration /pʀɔkyʀasjɔ̃/ **NF** *(Jur)* *(pour voter, représenter qn)* proxy; *(pour toucher de l'argent)* power of attorney ♦ **avoir (une) ~** to have power of attorney *ou* an authorization ♦ **avoir ~ sur un compte en banque** to have power of attorney over a bank account ♦ **donner (une) ~ à qn** to give sb power of attorney, to authorize sb ♦ **par ~** *(lit)* by proxy; *(fig) [vivre, voyager]* vicariously

procurer /pʀɔkyʀe/ ► conjug 1 ◄ **VT** 1 *(= faire obtenir)* ~ **qch à qn** to get *ou* obtain sth for sb, to find sth for sb, to provide sb with sth 2 *(= apporter) [+ joie, ennuis]* to bring; *[+ avantage]* to bring, to give, to procure ♦ **le plaisir que procure le jardinage** the pleasure that gardening brings *ou* that one gets from gardening **VPR** **se procurer** *(= obtenir)* to get, to procure, to obtain (for o.s.); *(= trouver)* to find, to come by; *(= acheter)* to get, to buy (o.s.)

procureur /pʀɔkyʀœʀ/ **NM** 1 *(Jur)* ~ **(de la République)** public *ou* state prosecutor ♦ ~ **général** public prosecutor *(in appeal courts)* ♦ ~ **de la Couronne** *(Can)* Crown prosecutor *(Can)* 2 *(Rel)* procurator

prodigalité /pʀɔdigalite/ **NF** 1 *(= caractère)* prodigality, extravagance 2 *(= dépenses)* ~**s** extravagance 3 *(littér = profusion) [de détails]* abundance, profusion, wealth

prodige /pʀɔdiʒ/ **NM** *(= événement)* marvel, wonder; *(= personne)* prodigy ♦ **un ~ de la nature/science** a wonder of nature/science ♦ **tenir du ~** to be astounding *ou* extraordinary ♦ **faire des ~s** to work wonders ♦ **grâce à des ~s de courage/patience** thanks to his (*ou* her *etc*) prodigious *ou* extraordinary courage/patience **ADJ** ♦ **enfant ~** child prodigy

prodigieusement /pʀɔdiʒjøzmɑ̃/ **ADV** *[ennuyeux, long, compliqué, cher]* incredibly ♦ ~ **doué** prodigiously talented ♦ **cela nous a agacé ~** we found it intensely irritating

prodigieux, -ieuse /pʀɔdiʒjø, jøz/ **ADJ** *[foule, force, bêtise]* prodigious, incredible, phenomenal; *[personne, génie]* prodigious, phenomenal; *[effort]* prodigious, tremendous, fantastic

prodigue /pʀɔdig/ **ADJ** *(= dépensier)* extravagant, wasteful, prodigal; *(= généreux)* generous ♦ **être ~ de ses compliments** to be lavish with one's praise ♦ **être ~ de conseils** to be full of advice *ou* free with one's advice ♦ **lui, en général si peu ~ de compliments/conseils** he who is usually so sparing of compliments/advice ♦ **être ~ de son temps** to be unsparing *ou* unstinting of one's time ♦ **être ~ de son bien** to be lavish with one's money ♦ **l'enfant** *ou* **le fils ~** *(Rel)* the prodigal son **NMF** spendthrift

prodiguer /pʀɔdige/ ► conjug 1 ◄ **VT** *[+ compliments, conseils]* to be full of, to pour out; *[+ argent]* to be lavish with ♦ ~ **des compliments/conseils à qn** to lavish compliments/advice on sb, to pour out compliments/advice to sb ♦ **elle me prodigua ses soins** she lavished care on me ♦ **malgré les soins que le médecin lui a prodigués** in spite of the care *ou* treatment the doctor gave him ♦ **se ~ sans compter** to spare no effort, to give unsparingly *ou* unstintingly of o.s.

pro domo /pʀodomo/ **LOC ADJ** ♦ **faire un plaidoyer ~** *(Jur)* to defend o.s., to plead one's own case; *(fig)* to justify o.s. ♦ **le discours du ministre était un véritable plaidoyer ~** the minister's speech was a real exercise in self-justification

prodrome /pʀodʀom/ **NM** *(littér)* forerunner; *(Méd)* prodrome

producteur, -trice /pʀɔdyktœʀ, tʀis/ **ADJ** ♦ **pays ~ de pétrole** oil-producing country, oil producer ♦ **pays ~ de blé** wheat-growing country, wheat producer ♦ **société productrice** *(Ciné)* film company **NM,F** 1 *(Comm)* producer; *[de blé, tomates]* grower, producer ♦ **du ~ au consommateur** from the producer to the consumer 2 *(Ciné, TV)* producer ♦ ~**-réalisateur** *(TV)* producer and director

productible /pʀɔdyktibl/ **ADJ** producible

productif, -ive /pʀɔdyktif, iv/ **ADJ** productive ♦ ~ **d'intérêts** *(Fin)* that bears interest, interest-bearing

production /pʀɔdyksjɔ̃/ **NF** 1 *(NonC)* *(gén)* production; *(Agr)* production, growing

2 *(= ensemble de produits, rendement) [d'usine]* production, output; *[d'exploitation agricole]* production, yield ♦ ~ **annuelle de blé** annual wheat production *ou* yield ♦ **notre ~ est inférieure à nos besoins** our output is lower than our needs ♦ ~ **brute** gross output ♦ **capacité/coûts de ~** production capacity/costs ♦ **directeur de la ~** production manager; → **moyen²**

3 *(= produit)* product ♦ ~**s** *(agricoles)* produce; *(industriels, commerciaux)* products, goods

4 *(= œuvre)* work; *(= ensemble de l'œuvre)* works ♦ **la ~ cinématographique/dramatique du XXᵉ siècle** 20th-century cinema/plays ♦ **les ~s de l'esprit** creations of the mind

5 *(Jur) [de document]* presentation

6 *(Ciné, Radio, TV)* production ♦ **assistant/directeur de ~** production assistant/manager; → **société**

productique /pʀɔdyktik/ **NF** factory *ou* industrial automation

productivisme /pʀɔdyktivism/ **NM** emphasis on high productivity, productivism *(SPÉC)*

productiviste /pʀɔdyktivist/ **ADJ** *[société]* that puts strong emphasis on high productivity, productivist *(SPÉC)* ♦ **pour rompre avec la logique ~** to break away from the over-emphasis on high productivity **NMF** advocate of high productivity, productivist *(SPÉC)*

productivité /pʀɔdyktivite/ **NF** productivity

produire /pʀɔdɥiʀ/ ► conjug 38 ◄ **VT** 1 *(en fabriquant)* to produce; *(en cultivant)* to produce, to grow ♦ **pays qui produit du pétrole** country which produces oil, oil-producing country ♦ **cette école a produit plusieurs savants** this school has produced several scientists

2 *(= créer) [+ roman]* to produce, to write; *[+ tableau]* to produce, to paint ♦ **un poète qui ne produit pas beaucoup** a poet who doesn't write much

3 *(Fin) [+ intérêt]* to yield, to return ♦ **arbre/terre qui produit de bons fruits** tree/soil which yields *ou* produces good fruit ♦ **certains sols produisent plus que d'autres** some soils are more productive *ou* give a better yield than others

4 *(= causer) [+ rouille, humidité, son]* to produce, to make; *[+ effet]* to produce, to have; *[+ changement]* to produce, to bring about; *[+ résultat]* to produce, to give; *[+ sensation]* to cause, to create ♦ ~ **une bonne/mauvaise impression sur qn** to make a good/bad impression on sb ♦ **il a produit une forte impression sur les examinateurs** he made a great impression on the examiners, the examiners were highly impressed by him

5 *(Jur) [+ document]* to present, to produce; *[+ témoin]* to produce

6 *(Ciné, Radio, TV) [+ film, émission]* to produce

VPR **se produire** 1 *(= survenir)* to happen, to occur, to take place ♦ **cela peut se ~** it can happen ♦ **ce cas ne s'était jamais produit** this kind of case had never come up before ♦ **il s'est produit un revirement dans l'opinion** there has been a complete change in public opinion ♦ **le changement qui s'est produit en lui** the change that has come over him *ou* taken place in him

2 *[acteur, chanteur]* to perform, to give a performance, to appear ♦ **se ~ sur scène** to appear live *ou* on stage ♦ **se ~ en public** to appear in public, to give a public performance

produit /pʀɔdɥi/ **NM** 1 *(= denrée, article)* product ♦ ~**s** *(agricoles)* produce; *(industriels, commerciaux)* goods, products ♦ **il faudrait acheter un ~ pour nettoyer les carreaux** we'll have to buy something to clean the windows (with) ♦ **il y avait plein de ~s dans le placard** there was all sorts of stuff in the cupboard ♦ **chef** *ou* **responsable (de) ~** product manager, brand manager ♦ **un ~ typique de notre université** *(fig)* a typical product of our university ♦ **c'est le (pur) ~ de ton imagination** it's a (pure) figment of your imagination

2 *(= rapport)* product, yield; *(= bénéfice)* profit; *(= revenu)* income ♦ **le ~ de la collecte sera donné à une bonne œuvre** the proceeds from the collection will be given to charity ♦ **vivre du ~ de sa terre** to live off the land

3 *(Math)* product

4 *(Chim)* product, chemical

5 *(= petit d'animal)* offspring *(inv)*

COMP **produits agricoles** agricultural *ou* farm produce
produits alimentaires foodstuffs
produit d'appel loss leader
produit bancaire banking product
produits de beauté cosmetics, beauty products
produits blancs white goods
produits bruns brown goods
produit brut *(= bénéfice)* gross profit; *(= objet)* unfinished product
produit chimique chemical
produit de consommation consumable ◆ ~ **de consommation courante** basic consumable ◆ **~s de grande consommation** consumer goods
produits dérivés *(Comm, Fin)* derivatives
produit d'entretien clean(s)ing product
produit d'épargne savings product
produit financier financial product
produit de l'impôt tax yield
produits industriels industrial goods *ou* products
produit intérieur brut gross domestic product
produits manufacturés manufactured goods
produit national brut gross national product
produit net net profit
produit pétrolier oil product
produit pharmaceutique pharmaceutical (product)
produits de première nécessité vital commodities
produits de toilette toiletries
produit pour la vaisselle washing-up liquid *(Brit)*, dish soap *(US)*
produit des ventes income *ou* proceeds from sales; → **substitution**

proéminence /pʀɔeminɑ̃s/ NF prominence, protuberance

proéminent, e /pʀɔeminɑ̃, ɑ̃t/ ADJ prominent, protuberant

prof* /pʀɔf/ NMF (abrév de **professeur**) *(Scol)* teacher; *(Univ)* ≈ lecturer *(Brit)*, instructor *(US)*, prof* *(US)*; *(avec chaire)* prof*

profanateur, -trice /pʀɔfanatœʀ, tʀis/ ADJ profaning *(épith)*, profane NM,F profaner

profanation /pʀɔfanasjɔ̃/ NF 1 *[d'église, autel, hostie, sépulture]* desecration 2 *[de sentiment, souvenir, nom]* defilement; *[d'institution]* debasement; *[de talent]* prostitution, debasement

profane /pʀɔfan/ ADJ 1 *(= non spécialiste)* **je suis ~ en la matière** I'm a layman in the field, I don't know (very) much about the subject 2 *(= non religieux)* *[fête]* secular; *[auteur, littérature, musique]* secular, profane *(littér)* NMF 1 *(gén)* layman, lay person ◆ **aux yeux du** ~ to the layman *ou* the uninitiated ◆ **un ~ en art** a person who knows nothing about art 2 *(Rel)* non-believer NM *(Rel)* ◆ **le ~** the secular, the profane *(littér)* ◆ **le ~ et le sacré** the sacred and the profane

> ⚠ **profane** se traduit par le mot anglais **profane** uniquement au sens de 'non religieux'.

profaner /pʀɔfane/ ▸ conjug 1 ◂ VT 1 *[+ église, autel, hostie, sépulture]* to desecrate 2 *[+ sentiments, souvenir, nom]* to defile; *[+ institution]* to debase; *[+ talent]* to prostitute, to debase

proférer /pʀɔfeʀe/ ▸ conjug 6 ◂ VT *[+ parole]* to utter; *[+ injures]* to utter, to pour out

professer /pʀɔfese/ ▸ conjug 1 ◂ VT 1 *[+ idées, opinions]* to put forward; *[+ doctrine, admiration, mépris]* to proclaim; *[+ foi]* to profess; *(fig)* to proclaim ◆ ~ **que ...** to proclaim that ... 2 *(Scol)* to teach

professeur /pʀɔfesœʀ/ NM *(gén)* teacher; *[de lycée, collège]* (school) teacher; *(Univ)* ≈ lecturer *(Brit)*, instructor *(US)*; *(avec chaire)* professor ◆ **elle est ~** she's a (school) teacher ◆ **(Monsieur) le ~ Durand** *(Univ)* Professor Durand ◆ ~ **de piano/de chant** piano/singing teacher *ou* master *(Brit) ou* mistress *(Brit)* ◆ ~ **de droit** lecturer in law, professor of law ◆ **l'ensemble des ~s** the teaching staff

COMP **professeur agrégé** *(gén)* qualified schoolteacher *(who has passed the agrégation)*; *(en médecine)* professor of medicine *(holder of the agrégation)*; *(Can Univ)* associate professor
professeur certifié qualified schoolteacher *(who has passed the CAPES)*
professeur des écoles primary school teacher
professeur d'enseignement général des collèges basic-grade schoolteacher *(in a collège)*
professeur principal ≈ class teacher *(Brit)*, form tutor *(Brit)*, homeroom teacher *(US)*; → **associé**

professeure /pʀɔfesœʀ/ NF *(surtout Can)* → **professeur**

profession /pʀɔfesjɔ̃/ NF 1 *(gén)* occupation; *(manuelle)* trade; *(libérale)* profession ◆ **exercer la ~ de médecin** to be a doctor by profession, to practise as a doctor *(Brit)*, to practice medicine *(US)* ◆ **menuisier de ~** carpenter by trade ◆ **menteur de ~** *(hum)* professional liar ◆ **"sans profession"** *(Admin)* "unemployed"
2 *(= personnes)* **(les gens de) la ~** *(gén)* the people in the profession; *(= artisans)* the people in the trade
3 *(locutions)* **faire ~ de non-conformisme** to profess nonconformism ◆ **ceux qui font ~ de démocratiser l'information** those who proclaim that they want to make information available to all

COMP **profession de foi** *(Rel, fig)* profession of faith
profession libérale (liberal) profession ◆ **les membres des ~s libérales** professional people, the members of the (liberal) professions

professionnalisation /pʀɔfesjɔnalizasjɔ̃/ NF *[d'armée, recherche]* professionalization ◆ **la ~ des études est renforcée par les stages en entreprise** work experience schemes in companies help to give a vocational focus to studies

professionnaliser /pʀɔfesjɔnalize/ ▸ conjug 1 ◂ VT *[+ armée, métier]* to professionalize; *[+ sportif]* to make professional ◆ **filière/formation professionnalisée** vocational course/training VPR **se professionnaliser** *[sport, activité]* to become professionalized, to professionalize; *[sportif]* to turn professional

professionnalisme /pʀɔfesjɔnalism/ NM professionalism

professionnel, -elle /pʀɔfesjɔnɛl/ ADJ 1 *[activité, maladie]* occupational *(épith)*; *[école]* technical *(épith)* ◆ **faute professionnelle** (professional) negligence *(NonC)*; *(Méd)* malpractice ◆ **formation/orientation professionnelle** vocational training/guidance ◆ **cours ~** vocational training course ◆ **frais ~s** business expenses ◆ **(être tenu par) le secret ~** (to be bound by) professional secrecy; → **certificat, conscience, déformation**
2 *[écrivain, sportif]* professional; *(hum)* *[menteur]* professional, adept ◆ **il est très ~ (dans ce qu'il fait)** he's very professional, he has a very professional attitude
NM,F 1 *(gén, Sport)* professional ◆ **c'est un travail de ~** *(pour un professionnel)* it's a job for a professional; *(bien fait)* it's a professional job ◆ **passer ~** to turn professional ◆ **les ~s du tourisme** people working in the tourist industry
2 *(catégorie d'ouvrier)* skilled worker

professionnellement /pʀɔfesjɔnɛlmɑ̃/ ADV professionally

professoral, e (mpl **-aux**) /pʀɔfesɔʀal, o/ ADJ *[ton, attitude]* professorial ◆ **le corps ~** *(gén)* (the) teachers, the teaching profession; *[d'école]* the teaching staff

professorat /pʀɔfesɔʀa/ NM ◆ **le ~** the teaching profession ◆ **le ~ de français** French teaching, the teaching of French

profil /pʀɔfil/ NM 1 *(= silhouette)* *[de personne]* profile; *[d'édifice]* outline, profile; *[de voiture]* line ◆ **de ~** *[dessiner]* in profile; *[regarder]* sideways on, in profile ◆ **un ~ de médaille** a finely chiselled profile ◆ **garder (le) ~ bas, prendre** *ou* **adopter un ~ bas** to keep a low profile 2 *(= coupe)* *[de bâtiment, route]* profile; *(Géol)* *[de sol]* section 3 *(Psych)* profile ◆ ~ **de carrière** career profile ◆ **le ~ d'un étudiant** the profile of a student's performance ◆ **il a le bon ~ pour le métier** his previous experience *ou* his career to date *ou* his career profile seems right for the job

profilé, e /pʀɔfile/ (ptp de **profiler**) ADJ *(gén)* shaped; *(= aérodynamique)* streamlined NM *(Tech)* ◆ ~ **(métallique)** metal section

profiler /pʀɔfile/ ▸ conjug 1 ◂ VT 1 *(Tech)* *(= dessiner)* to profile, to represent in profile; *(= fabriquer)* to shape; *(= rendre aérodynamique)* to streamline 2 *(= faire ressortir)* **la cathédrale profile ses tours contre le ciel** the cathedral towers stand out *ou* stand outlined *ou* are silhouetted against the sky VPR **se profiler** *[objet]* to stand out (in profile), to be outlined *(sur, contre* against); *[ennuis, solution]* to emerge ◆ **se ~ à l'horizon** *[obstacles, menace]* to loom on the horizon; *[élections]* to loom ◆ **une solution politique se profile à l'horizon** we can see the beginnings of a political solution

profileur, -euse /pʀɔfilœʀ, øz/ NM,F profiler

profit /pʀɔfi/ NM 1 *(Comm, Fin = gain)* profit ◆ **(faire) passer qch par** *ou* **aux ~s et pertes** *(lit, fig)* to write sth off (as a loss) ◆ **il n'y a pas de petit(s) ~(s)** great oaks from little acorns grow *(Prov)* look after the pennies and the pounds will look after themselves *(Brit)*; → **compte**
2 *(= avantage)* benefit, advantage ◆ **être d'un grand ~ à qn** to be of great benefit *ou* most useful to sb ◆ **faire du ~** *(gén)* to be economical, to be good value (for money); * *[de vêtement]* to wear well; *[de rôti]* to go a long way ◆ **ce rôti n'a pas fait de ~** that roast didn't go very far ◆ **ses vacances lui ont fait beaucoup de ~** *ou* **lui ont été d'un grand ~** his holiday did him a lot of good, he greatly benefited from his holiday ◆ **il fait (son) ~ de tout** he turns everything to (his) advantage ◆ **vous avez ~ à faire cela** it's in your interest *ou* to your advantage to do that ◆ **s'il le fait, c'est qu'il y trouve son ~** if he does it, it's because it's to his advantage *ou* in his interest *ou* because he's getting something out of it* ◆ **il a suivi les cours sans (en tirer) aucun ~** he attended the classes without deriving any benefit from them ◆ **il a suivi les cours avec ~** he attended the classes and got a lot out of them *ou* and gained a lot from them ◆ **tirer ~ de** *[+ leçon, affaire]* to profit *ou* benefit from ◆ **tirer ~ du malheur des autres** to profit from *ou* take advantage of other people's misfortune
3 *(locutions)*
♦ **à profit** ◆ **mettre à ~** *[+ idée, invention]* to turn to (good) account; *[+ jeunesse, temps libre, sa beauté]* to make the most of, to take advantage of ◆ **tourner qch à ~** to turn sth to good account ◆ **il a mis à ~ le mauvais temps pour ranger le grenier** he made the most of *ou* took advantage of the bad weather to tidy the attic, he turned the bad weather to (good) account by tidying up the attic

♦ **au profit de** *(gén)* for; *(= pour aider)* in aid of ◆ **il est soupçonné d'espionnage au ~ d'un pays étranger** he's suspected of spying for a foreign country ◆ **collecte au ~ des aveugles** collection in aid of the blind ◆ **ils ont perdu du terrain/la ville au ~ des socialistes** they've lost ground/the town to the socialists ◆ **il sacrifie sa vie de famille au ~ de son travail** he sacrifices his family life to his work ◆ **le dessin a disparu au ~ de la photo** drawing has been replaced *ou* supplanted by photography ◆ **le fioul a été abandonné au ~ du gaz** oil has been dropped in favour of gas

profitabilité /pʀɔfitabilite/ NF profitability

profitable /pʀɔfitabl/ ADJ *(= utile)* beneficial, of benefit *(attrib)*; *(= lucratif)* profitable *(à* to); ◆ **le stage lui a été très ~** he got a lot out of the training course, the training course was of great benefit to him

profiter /pʀɔfite/ ► conjug 1 ◄ VT INDIR **profiter de** *(= tirer avantage de)* [+ *situation, privilège, occasion, crédulité*] to take advantage of; *(= jouir de)* [+ *jeunesse, vacances*] to make the most of, to take advantage of ◆ **ils ont profité de ce que le professeur était sorti pour se battre** they took advantage of the fact that the teacher had gone out to have a fight ◆ **elle en a profité pour se sauver** she took advantage of the opportunity to slip away ◆ **profitez de la vie !** make the most of life! ◆ **je n'ai pas assez profité de mes enfants (quand ils étaient petits)** I wasn't able to enjoy being with my children as much as I would have liked (when they were small)

VT INDIR **profiter à** *(= rapporter à)* ~ **à qn** *(financièrement)* to be profitable to sb; [*situation*] to be to sb's advantage; [*repos*] to benefit sb, to be beneficial to sb; [*conseil*] to benefit sb ◆ **à qui cela profite-t-il ?** who stands to gain by it?, who will that help? ◆ **à qui profite le crime ?** who would benefit from the crime?; → **bien**

VI * *(= se développer)* [*enfant*] to thrive, to grow; *(= être économique)* [*plat*] to go a long way, to be economical; [*vêtement*] to wear well

profiterole /pʀɔfitʀɔl/ NF profiterole

profiteur, -euse /pʀɔfitœʀ, øz/ NM,F profiteer ◆ ~ **de guerre** war profiteer

profond, e /pʀɔfɔ̃, ɔ̃d/ ADJ 1 *(lit)* deep ◆ **décolleté** ~ plunging neckline ◆ **peu** ~ [*eau, vallée, puits*] shallow; [*coupure*] superficial ◆ ~ **de 3 mètres** 3 metres deep ◆ **forage** ~ deep-sea drilling; → **eau**

2 *(= grand, extrême)* [*soupir, silence*] deep, heavy; [*sommeil*] deep, sound; [*coma, respect*] deep; [*mystère, malaise*] deep, profound; *(littér)* [*nuit*] deep *(littér)*, dark; [*changement, joie, foi, différence, influence*] profound; [*erreur*] serious; [*ignorance*] profound, extreme; [*intérêt, sentiment*] profound, keen; [*ennui*] profound, acute; [*révérence*] low, deep ◆ **les couches ~es** [*de peau*] the deeper *ou* lower layers; [*de sol*] the (earth's) substrata

3 *(= caché, secret)* [*cause, signification*] underlying, deeper; *(Ling)* [*structure*] deep; [*tendance*] deep-seated, underlying ◆ **son comportement traduit sa nature ~e** his true nature is reflected in his behaviour ◆ **la France ~e** *(gén)* the broad mass of French people; *(des campagnes)* rural France ◆ **l'Amérique ~e** middle America

4 *(= pénétrant)* [*penseur, réflexion*] profound, deep; [*esprit, remarque*] profound

5 [*couleur, regard, voix*] deep

ADV [*creuser*] deep; [*planter*] deep (down)

LOC PRÉP **au plus profond de** [+ *désespoir, forêt*] in the depths of ◆ **au plus ~ de la mer** at the (very) bottom of the sea, in the depths of the sea ◆ **au plus ~ de la nuit** at dead of night ◆ **au plus ~ de mon être** in the depths of my being, in my deepest being

profondément /pʀɔfɔ̃demɑ̃/ ADV [*choqué, ému*] deeply, profoundly; [*préoccupé*] deeply, intensely; [*attristé, bouleversé*] deeply; [*convaincu*] deeply, utterly; [*différent*] profoundly, vastly; [*influencer, se tromper*] profoundly; [*réfléchir*] deeply, profoundly; [*aimer, ressentir, regretter*] deeply; [*respirer*] deep(ly); [*creuser, pénétrer*] deep; [*s'incliner*] low ◆ **il dort** ~ *(en général)* he sleeps soundly, he's a sound sleeper; *(en ce moment)* he's sound *ou* fast asleep ◆ **s'ennuyer** ~ to be utterly *ou* acutely *ou* profoundly bored ◆ **idée ~ ancrée dans les esprits** idea deeply rooted in people's minds ◆ **une tradition ~ enracinée** a deeply-rooted tradition ◆ **ça m'est ~ égal** I really couldn't care less

profondeur /pʀɔfɔ̃dœʀ/ NF 1 [*de boîte, mer, trou*] depth; [*de plaie*] deepness, depth ◆ **à cause du peu de ~ de la rivière** because of the shallowness of the river ◆ **cela manque de ~** it's not deep enough ◆ **creuser en ~** to dig deep ◆ **creuser jusqu'à 3 mètres de ~** to dig down to a depth of 3 metres ◆ **avoir 10 mètres de ~** to be 10 metres deep *ou* in depth ◆ **à 10 mètres de ~** 10 metres down, at a depth of 10 metres ◆ ~ **de champ** *(Photo)* depth of field

2 *(= fond)* ~**s** [*de métro, mine, poche*] depths ◆ **les ~s de l'être** the depths of the human psyche ◆ **se retrouver dans les ~s du classement** *(Sport)* to be at the bottom of the table(s)

3 [*de personne*] profoundness, profundity, depth; [*d'esprit, remarque*] profoundness, profundity; [*de sentiment*] depth, keenness; [*de sommeil*] soundness, depth; [*de regard*] depth; [*de couleur, voix*] deepness

LOC ADV, LOC ADJ **en profondeur** [*agir, exprimer*] in depth; [*réformer*] radically, completely; [*nettoyage*] thorough; [*réforme*] radical, thorough-(going) ◆ **cette pommade agit en ~** this cream works deep into the skin

pro forma /pʀofɔʀma/ ADJ INV ◆ **facture ~** pro forma invoice

profus, e /pʀɔfy, yz/ ADJ *(littér)* profuse

profusément /pʀɔfyzemɑ̃/ ADV *(littér)* profusely, abundantly

profusion /pʀɔfyzjɔ̃/ NF [*de fleurs, lumière*] profusion; [*d'idées, conseils*] wealth, abundance, profusion ◆ **il nous a décrit la scène avec une incroyable ~ de détails** he described the scene to us in the most elaborate detail ◆ **nous ne nous attendions pas à une telle ~ de candidatures** we didn't expect such a flood of applicants *ou* such a large number of applications

♦ **à profusion** ◆ **il y a des fruits à ~ sur le marché** there is plenty of fruit on the market ◆ **nous en avons à ~** we've got plenty *ou* masses *

progéniture /pʀɔʒenityʀ/ NF [*d'homme, animal*] offspring, progeny *(littér)*; *(hum = famille)* offspring *(hum)*

progéria /pʀɔʒeʀja/ NM progeria

progestatif /pʀɔʒɛstatif/ NM progestogen, progestin

progestérone /pʀɔʒɛsteʀɔn/ NF progesterone

progiciel /pʀɔʒisjɛl/ NM software package

programmable /pʀɔgʀamabl/ ADJ programmable ◆ **touche ~** user-definable key ◆ **l'enchaînement des titres est ~ (à l'avance)** *(Hi-fi)* the sequence of tracks can be preset

programmateur, -trice /pʀɔgʀamatœʀ, tʀis/ NM,F *(Radio, TV)* programme *(Brit) ou* program *(US)* planner NM *(= appareil) (gén)* time switch; [*de four*] autotimer

programmation /pʀɔgʀamasjɔ̃/ NF *(Radio, TV)* programming, programme *(Brit) ou* program *(US)* planning; *(Ordin)* programming

programmatique /pʀɔgʀamatik/ ADJ *(Pol)* programmatic ◆ **document ~** policy document

programme /pʀɔgʀam/ NM 1 *(= éléments prévus)* [*de cinéma, concert, radio, télévision*] programme *(Brit)*, program *(US)* ◆ **au ~** on the programme ◆ **voici le ~ de la matinée** *(Radio, TV)* here is a rundown of the morning's programmes ◆ **fin de nos ~s à minuit** *(Radio, TV)* our programmes will end at midnight, closedown will be at midnight *(Brit)*, we will be closing down at midnight *(Brit)* ◆ **changement de ~** change in (the) *ou* of programme

2 *(= brochure)* [*de cinéma, théâtre, concert*] programme *(Brit)*, program *(US)*; [*de radio, télévision*] *(gén)* guide, listings magazine; *(= section de journal)* listings

3 *(Scol)* [*de matière*] syllabus; [*de classe, école*] curriculum ◆ **le ~ de français** the French syllabus ◆ **quel est le ~ cette année ?** what's (on) the curriculum this year? ◆ **les œuvres du** *ou* **au ~** the set *(Brit) ou* assigned *(US)* books *ou* works, the books on the syllabus

4 *(= projet, Pol)* programme *(Brit)*, program *(US)* ◆ ~ **d'action/de travail** programme of action/of work ◆ ~ **commun** joint programme ◆ ~ **économique/nucléaire/de recherches** economic/nuclear/research programme ◆ ~ **électoral** election programme *ou* platform ◆ **le ~ européen Socrates** the European Socrates programme ◆ **c'est tout un ~ !*, vaste ~ !*** that'll take some doing!

5 *(= calendrier)* programme *(Brit)*, program *(US)* ◆ **quel est le ~ de la journée ?** *ou* **des réjouissances ?*** what's the programme for the day?, what's on the agenda? * ◆ **j'ai un ~ très chargé** I have a very busy timetable ◆ **il y a un changement de ~** there's been a change of plan ◆ **ce n'était pas prévu au ~** it wasn't expected, that wasn't on the agenda ◆ **son frère n'était pas prévu au ~** his brother wasn't supposed to come along

6 [*de machine à laver*] programme *(Brit)*, program *(US)*; *(Ordin)* (computer) program ◆ ~ **source/objet** source/object program

7 *(Sport)* programme *(Brit)*, program *(US)* ◆ ~ **libre** [*de patinage artistique*] free skating

programmer /pʀɔgʀame/ ► conjug 1 ◄ VT 1 [+ *émission*] to schedule; [+ *machine*] to programme *(Brit)*, to program *(US)*; [+ *magnétoscope*] to set, to programme *(Brit)*, to program *(US)*; [+ *ordinateur*] to program ◆ **composition programmée** *(Typo)* computer(ized) *ou* electronic typesetting ◆ ~ **à l'avance** [+ *magnétoscope*] to preset 2 *(= prévoir, organiser)* [+ *opération, naissance, vacances*] to plan ◆ **son dernier concert est programmé à Paris** his last concert is scheduled to take place in Paris ◆ **ce bébé n'était pas vraiment programmé*** this baby wasn't really planned VI *(Ordin)* to (write a) program

programmeur, -euse /pʀɔgʀamœʀ, øz/ NM,F (computer) programmer

progrès /pʀɔgʀɛ/ NM 1 *(= amélioration)* progress *(NonC)* ◆ **faire des ~/de petits ~** to make progress/a little progress ◆ **il y a du ~ !** *(gén)* there is some progress *ou* improvement; *(iro)* you're *(ou* he's *etc)* improving! *ou* getting better! *(iro)* ◆ **c'est un grand ~** it's a great advance, it's a great step forward ◆ **il a fait de grands ~** he has made great progress *ou* shown (a) great improvement ◆ **nos ventes ont enregistré un léger/net ~** our sales have increased slightly/sharply ◆ **les ~ de la médecine** advances in medicine ◆ **les grands ~ technologiques de ces dix dernières années** the great strides forward *ou* the great advances made in technology in the last ten years

2 ◆ **le ~** *(= évolution)* progress *(NonC)* ◆ **le ~ économique** economic progress *ou* development ◆ **le ~ social** social progress ◆ **c'est le ~ !** that's progress! ◆ **on n'arrête pas le ~ !** you can't stop progress!; *(iro)* that's progress for you! ◆ **les forces de ~** *(Pol)* the forces of

progress ◆ **les hommes et les femmes de ~** progressives, progressive people

3 *(= progression) [d'incendie, inondation]* spread, progress; *[de maladie]* progression, progress; *[d'armée]* progress, advance; *[de criminalité, délinquance]* rise (*de* in); ◆ **suivre les ~ de** *[+ incendie, maladie]* to monitor the progress of

LOC ADV **en progrès** ◆ **être en ~** *[élève]* to be making progress; *[résultats d'un élève]* to be improving; *[résultats économiques]* to be improving, to show an increase; *[productivité, rentabilité]* to be increasing *ou* improving; *[monnaie]* to gain ground ◆ **le franc est en léger ~** the franc is up slightly ◆ **hier, le dollar était en net ~** yesterday the dollar rose sharply ◆ **avec le PIB en ~ de 2%** with GDP up by 2% ◆ **leur parti est en ~ par rapport aux dernières élections** their party has gained ground since the last elections ◆ **il est en net ~ dans les sondages** he's gaining a lot of ground in the polls

progresser /pʀɔgʀese/ ► conjug 1 ◄ VI 1 *(= s'améliorer) [élève]* to progress, to make progress ◆ **il a beaucoup progressé cette année** he has made a lot of progress *ou* has come on well this year

2 *(= augmenter) [prix, ventes, production, chômage]* to rise, to increase, to go up; *[monnaie]* to rise; *[criminalité, délinquance]* to be on the increase ◆ **le mark a progressé de 3% face au franc** the mark rose 3% against the franc ◆ **la criminalité a encore progressé** crime is on the rise again ◆ **il a progressé dans les sondages** he has gained ground in the polls ◆ **elle a progressé de 3 points dans les sondages** she has gained 3 points in the polls

3 *(= avancer) [ennemi, explorateurs, sauveteurs]* to advance, to make headway *ou* progress; *[maladie]* to progress; *[recherches, science]* to advance, to progress; *[projet]* to progress; *[idée, théorie]* to gain ground, to make headway ◆ **afin que notre monde/la science progresse** so that our world/science goes forward *ou* progresses *ou* makes progress

progressif, -ive /pʀɔgʀesif, iv/ ADJ 1 *(= graduel) [détérioration, réduction, développement]* progressive, gradual; *[impôt, taux]* progressive ◆ **de manière progressive** gradually, progressively 2 *[lunettes]* varifocal; *[verres]* progressive 3 *(Ling)* progressive

progression /pʀɔgʀesjɔ̃/ NF 1 *[d'élève, explorateurs]* progress; *[d'ennemi]* advance; *[de maladie]* progression, spread; *[de science]* progress, advance; *[d'idées]* spread, advance ◆ **il faut stopper la ~ du racisme** we must stop the spread of racism, we must stop racism from spreading

◆ **en progression** ◆ **être en ~** *[chiffre d'affaires, ventes]* to be increasing, to be up; *[monnaie]* to be gaining ground ◆ **ventes en ~** rising *ou* increasing sales ◆ **le PIB est en ~ de 3%** GDP is up *ou* has risen by 3% ◆ **le chômage est en ~ constante/de 5%** unemployment is steadily increasing/has increased by 5% ◆ **le chiffre d'affaires est en ~ par rapport à l'année dernière** turnover is up on last year

2 *(Math, Mus)* progression ◆ **~ arithmétique/géométrique** arithmetic/geometric progression ◆ **~ économique** economic advance

progressisme /pʀɔgʀesism/ NM progressivism

progressiste /pʀɔgʀesist/ ADJ, NMF progressive

progressivement /pʀɔgʀesivmɑ̃/ ADV gradually, progressively

progressivité /pʀɔgʀesivite/ NF progressiveness

prohibé, e /pʀɔibe/ (ptp de **prohiber**) ADJ *[marchandise, action]* prohibited, forbidden; *[arme]* illegal

prohiber /pʀɔibe/ ► conjug 1 ◄ VT to prohibit, to ban, to forbid

prohibitif, -ive /pʀɔibitif, iv/ ADJ *[prix]* prohibitive; *[mesure]* prohibitory, prohibitive

prohibition /pʀɔibisjɔ̃/ NF *(gén)* prohibition (*de* of, on); ◆ **la Prohibition** *(Hist US)* Prohibition ◆ **~ du port d'armes** ban on the carrying of weapons ◆ **ils veulent imposer la ~ de l'alcool** they want a ban on alcohol to be introduced

prohibitionnisme /pʀɔibisjɔnism/ NM prohibitionism

prohibitionniste /pʀɔibisjɔnist/ ADJ, NMF prohibitionist

proie /pʀwɑ/ NF *(lit, fig)* prey *(NonC)* ◆ **c'est une ~ facile pour des escrocs** he's easy prey *ou* game* for swindlers ◆ **être la ~ de** to fall prey *ou* victim to ◆ **le pays fut la ~ des envahisseurs** the country fell prey to invaders ◆ **la maison était la ~ des flammes** the house was engulfed in flames ◆ **lâcher** *ou* **laisser la ~ pour l'ombre** *(fig)* to give up what one has (already) for some uncertain *ou* fanciful alternative; → **oiseau**

◆ **en proie à** ◆ **être en ~ à** *[+ guerre, crise, violence, récession]* to be plagued by, to be in the grip of; *[+ difficultés financières]* to be plagued *ou* beset by; *[+ doute, émotion]* to be prey to; *[+ colère]* to be seething with; *[+ douleur]* to be racked *ou* tortured by ◆ **il était en ~ au remords** he was stricken with *ou* racked by remorse ◆ **en ~ au désespoir** racked by despair ◆ **en ~ à la panique** panic-stricken

projecteur /pʀɔʒɛktœʀ/ NM 1 *[de diapositives, film]* projector ◆ **~ sonore** sound projector 2 *(= lumière) [de théâtre]* spotlight; *[de prison, bateau]* searchlight; *[de monument public, stade]* floodlight; *[de voiture]* headlamp unit *ou* assembly, headlight ◆ **être (placé) sous les ~s (de l'actualité)** *(fig)* to be in the spotlight *ou* limelight ◆ **braquer les ~s de l'actualité sur qch** to turn the spotlight on sth ◆ **jeter un coup de ~ sur qch** *(fig)* to put sth under the spotlight

projectif, -ive /pʀɔʒɛktif, iv/ ADJ projective

projectile /pʀɔʒɛktil/ NM *(gén)* missile; *(Mil, Tech)* projectile

projection /pʀɔʒɛksjɔ̃/ NF 1 *(= action) [de film]* projection, screening, showing; *(= séance)* screening, showing ◆ **~ privée/publique** private/public screening *ou* showing ◆ **~ vidéo** video screening ◆ **appareil de ~** projector ◆ **conférence avec des ~s (de diapositives)** lecture (illustrated) with slides, slide lecture; → **cabine, salle**

2 *(= prévision)* forecast ◆ **selon les ~s officielles, le déficit public devrait augmenter** according to official forecasts *ou* predictions, the public deficit is going to rise ◆ **faire des ~s** to make forecasts ◆ **si nous faisons des ~s sur sept ans** if we forecast seven years ahead *ou* make forecasts for the next seven years

3 *(Math, Psych)* projection (*sur* onto); ◆ **~ de Mercator** Mercator's projection

4 *[d'ombre]* casting

5 *(= lancement) [de liquide, vapeur]* discharge, ejection ◆ **~s volcaniques** volcanic ejections *ou* ejecta ◆ **~ de cendres** emission of ash ◆ **des ~s de graisse/d'acide** splashes of fat/acid

projectionniste /pʀɔʒɛksjɔnist/ NMF projectionist

projet /pʀɔʒɛ/ NM 1 *(= dessein, intention)* plan ◆ **~s criminels/de vacances** criminal/holiday plans ◆ **faire des ~s d'avenir** to make plans for the future, to make future plans ◆ **faire** *ou* **former le ~ de faire qch** to plan to do sth ◆ **ce ~ de livre/d'agrandissement** this plan for a book/for an extension ◆ **quels sont vos ~s pour le mois prochain ?** what are your plans *ou* what plans have you got for next month? ◆ **ce n'est encore qu'un ~, c'est encore à l'état de ~** *ou* **en ~** it's still only at the planning stage ◆ **c'est resté à l'état de ~** *(gén)* it never came to anything; *[réforme, mesure]* it never got off the drawing-board

2 *(= ébauche) [de roman]* (preliminary) draft; *[de maison, ville]* plan ◆ **~ de budget** budget proposal ◆ **~ de loi** bill ◆ **~ de réforme** reform bill ◆ **~ de réforme constitutionnelle** constitutional amendment bill ◆ **~ de résolution de l'ONU** UN draft resolution ◆ **établir un ~ d'accord/de contrat** to draft an agreement/a contract, to produce a draft agreement/contract ◆ **~ de société** vision of society ◆ **~ de vie** life plan

3 *(= travail en cours)* project ◆ **~ de construction de logements** house-building scheme *ou* project

⚠ Au sens de 'intention', **projet** se traduit rarement par **project**.

projeter /pʀɔʒ(ə)te/ GRAMMAIRE ACTIVE 35.2 ► conjug 4 ◄

VT 1 *(= envisager)* to plan (*de faire* to do); ◆ **as-tu projeté quelque chose pour les vacances ?** have you made any plans *ou* have you planned anything for your holidays?

2 *(= jeter) [+ gravillons]* to throw up; *[+ étincelles]* to throw off; *[+ fumée]* to send out, to discharge; *[+ lave]* to eject, to throw out ◆ **attention ! la poêle projette de la graisse** careful! the frying pan is spitting (out) fat ◆ **être projeté hors de** to be thrown *ou* hurled *ou* flung out of ◆ **on lui a projeté de l'eau dans les yeux** someone threw water into his eyes

3 *(= envoyer) [+ ombre, reflet]* to cast, to project, to throw; *[+ film, diapositive]* to project; *(= montrer)* to show ◆ **on peut ~ ce film sur un petit écran** this film may be projected onto *ou* shown on a small screen ◆ **on nous a projeté des diapositives** we were shown some slides

4 *(Math, Psych)* to project (*sur* onto)

VPR **se projeter** *[ombre]* to be cast, to fall (*sur* on)

projeteur, -euse /pʀɔʒ(ə)tœʀ, øz/ NM,F project designer

projo* /pʀɔʒo/ NM abrév de **projecteur**

prolapsus /pʀolapsys/ NM prolapse

prolégomènes /pʀɔlegɔmɛn/ NMPL prolegomena

prolepse /pʀɔlɛps/ NF *(Littérat)* prolepsis

prolétaire /pʀɔletɛʀ/ ADJ proletarian NMF proletarian ◆ **les enfants de ~s** children of working-class people ◆ **~s de tous les pays, unissez-vous !** workers of the world, unite!

prolétariat /pʀɔletaʀja/ NM proletariat

prolétarien, -ienne /pʀɔletaʀjɛ̃, jɛn/ ADJ proletarian

prolétarisation /pʀɔletaʀizasjɔ̃/ NF proletarianization

prolétariser /pʀɔletaʀize/ ► conjug 1 ◄ VT to proletarianize

prolifération /pʀɔlifeʀasjɔ̃/ NF proliferation ◆ **la ~ nucléaire** nuclear proliferation

proliférer /pʀɔlifeʀe/ ► conjug 6 ◄ VI to proliferate ◆ **les guerres civiles prolifèrent** civil wars are breaking out all over the world

prolifique /pʀɔlifik/ ADJ prolific

prolixe /pʀɔliks/ ADJ *[orateur, discours]* verbose, prolix *(frm)* ◆ **il n'a pas été très ~** he wasn't very forthcoming

prolixité /pʀɔliksite/ NF verbosity, prolixity *(frm)*

prolo* /pʀolo/ (abrév de **prolétaire**) NMF working-class person ADJ *[quartier, personne]* working-class ◆ **ça fait ~** it's common

prologue /pʀɔlɔg/ NM prologue (*à* to)

prolongateur /pʀɔlɔ̃gatœʀ/ NM extension cable *ou* lead

prolongation /pʀɔlɔ̃gasjɔ̃/ **NF** 1 *(dans le temps) [de séjour, trêve, séance, visa, délai, contrat]* extension; *[de vie, maladie]* prolongation; *(Mus) [de note]* prolongation ◆ **~s** *(Ftbl)* extra time *(NonC) (Brit)*, overtime *(NonC) (US)* ◆ **obtenir une ~** to get an extension ◆ **ils ont joué les ~s** *(Ftbl)* they played extra time *(Brit) ou* overtime *(US)*, the game ou they went into extra time *(Brit) ou* overtime *(US)*; *(hum : en vacances, pour un travail)* they stayed on 2 *(dans l'espace) [de rue]* extension; *(Math) [de ligne]* prolongation

prolonge /pʀɔlɔ̃ʒ/ **NF** ammunition wagon ◆ **~ d'artillerie** gun carriage

prolongé, e /pʀɔlɔ̃ʒe/ (ptp de **prolonger**) **ADJ** *[débat, séjour, absence]* prolonged, lengthy; *[rire, cri, sécheresse]* prolonged; *[effort]* prolonged, sustained ◆ **exposition ~e au soleil** prolonged exposure to the sun ◆ **jeune fille ~e** *(hum ou †)* old maid ◆ **c'est un adolescent ~** he's an overgrown teenager ◆ **rue de la Paix ~e** continuation of Rue de la Paix ◆ **en cas d'arrêt ~** in case of prolonged stoppage ◆ **week-end ~** long weekend ◆ **la station assise/debout ~e peut provoquer des douleurs** sitting/standing in the same position for an extended period of time can cause aches and pains ◆ **ce déodorant a une action ~e** this deodorant has a long-lasting effect ◆ **"pas d'utilisation prolongée sans avis médical"** "not to be taken for long periods without medical advice"

prolongement /pʀɔlɔ̃ʒmɑ̃/ **NM** 1 *[de bâtiment, voie ferrée, ligne de métro, route, délai, période]* extension ◆ **l'outil doit être un ~ du bras** the tool should be like an extension of one's arm ◆ **décider le ~ d'une route** to decide to extend *ou* continue a road ◆ **cette rue se trouve dans le ~ de l'autre** this street runs on from the other *ou* is the continuation of the other

2 *(= suite) [d'affaire, politique, rapport]* repercussion, consequence ◆ **c'est le ~ logique de la politique entreprise** it's the logical extension *ou* consequence of the policy that has been undertaken ◆ **ce rapport est dans le ~ du précédent** this report follows on from the previous one ◆ **dans le ~ de ce que je disais ce matin** following on from *ou* to continue with what I was saying this morning ◆ **dans le ~ de la réflexion amorcée en 1998, il a déclaré que ...** expanding on *ou* developing the line of thought first outlined in 1998, he declared that ...

prolonger /pʀɔlɔ̃ʒe/ ▸ conjug 3 ◂ **VT** 1 *(dans le temps) [+ séjour, trêve, séance, délai, contrat]* to extend, to prolong; *[+ visa]* to extend; *[+ vie, maladie]* to prolong; *(Mus) [+ note]* to prolong ◆ **nous ne pouvons ~ notre séjour** we can't stay any longer, we can't prolong our stay

2 *(dans l'espace) [+ rue]* to extend, to continue; *(Math) [+ ligne]* to prolong, to produce ◆ **on a prolongé le mur jusqu'au garage** we extended *ou* continued the wall as far as *ou* up to the garage ◆ **ce bâtiment prolonge l'aile principale** this building is an extension *ou* a continuation of the main wing

VPR se prolonger 1 *(= continuer) [attente]* to go on; *[situation]* to go on, to last, to persist; *[effet]* to last, to persist; *[débat]* to last, to go on, to carry on; *[maladie]* to continue, to persist ◆ **il voudrait se ~ dans ses enfants** *(= se perpétuer)* he would like to live on in his children

2 *(= s'étendre) [rue, chemin]* to go on, to carry on *(Brit)*, to continue

promenade /pʀɔm(ə)nad/ **NF** 1 *(à pied)* walk, stroll; *(en voiture)* drive, ride; *(en bateau)* sail; *(en vélo, à cheval)* ride ◆ **partir en ~, faire une ~** to go for a walk *ou* stroll *(ou drive etc)* ◆ **être en ~** to be out walking *ou* out for a walk ◆ **faire faire une ~ à qn** to take sb (out) for a walk ◆ **cette course a été une vraie ~ pour lui** the race was a walkover for him ◆ **ça n'a pas été une ~ de santé** it was no picnic* 2 *(= avenue)* walk, esplanade; *(= front de mer)* promenade

promener /pʀɔm(ə)ne/ ▸ conjug 5 ◂ **VT** 1 ◆ **(emmener) ~ qn** to take sb (out) for a walk *ou* stroll ◆ **~ le chien** to walk the dog, to take the dog out (for a walk) ◆ **~ des amis à travers une ville** to show *ou* take friends round a town ◆ **cela te promènera** it will get you out for a while ◆ **il promène son nounours partout*** he trails his teddy bear around everywhere with him ◆ **est-ce qu'il va nous ~ encore longtemps à travers ces bureaux ?*** is he going to trail us round these offices much longer?; → **envoyer**

2 *(fig)* ◆ **~ son regard sur qch** to run *ou* cast one's eyes over sth ◆ **~ ses doigts sur qch** to run *ou* pass one's fingers over sth ◆ **il promène sa tristesse/son ennui** he goes around looking sad/bored all the time ◆ **il promenait sa caméra/son micro dans les rues de New York** he roved the streets of New York with his camera/his microphone

VPR se promener 1 *(= aller en promenade)* to go for a walk *ou* stroll *(ou drive etc)* ◆ **aller se ~** to go (out) for a walk *ou* stroll *(ou drive etc)* ◆ **viens te ~ avec maman** come for a walk with mummy ◆ **se ~ dans sa chambre** to walk *ou* pace up and down in one's room ◆ **allez vous ~ !*** go and take a running jump!*, get lost!* ◆ **je ne vais pas laisser tes chiens se ~ dans mon jardin** I'm not going to let your dogs wander round my garden ◆ **il s'est vraiment promené dans cette course** *(Sport)* the race was a walkover for him

2 *[pensées, regard, doigts]* to wander ◆ **son crayon se promenait sur le papier** he let his pencil wander over the paper, his pencil wandered over the paper ◆ **ses affaires se promènent toujours partout*** he always leaves his things lying around

promeneur, -euse /pʀɔm(ə)nœʀ, øz/ **NM,F** walker, stroller ◆ **les ~s du dimanche** people out for a Sunday walk *ou* stroll

promenoir /pʀɔm(ə)nwaʀ/ **NM** *(†: Théât)* promenade (gallery), standing gallery; *[d'école, prison]* (covered) walk

promesse /pʀɔmɛs/ **NF** *(= assurance)* promise; *(= parole)* promise, word; *(Comm)* commitment, undertaking ◆ **~ de mariage** promise of marriage ◆ **~ en l'air** *ou* **d'ivrogne** *ou* **de Gascon** empty *ou* vain promise ◆ **~ d'achat/de vente** agreement to buy/to sell, purchase/sales agreement ◆ **fausses ~s** empty *ou* false promises ◆ **méfiez-vous des belles ~s des politiques** beware of politicians and their big promises ◆ **faire une ~** to make a promise, to give one's word ◆ **il m'en a fait la ~** he gave me his word ◆ **manquer à/tenir sa ~** to break/keep one's promise *ou* word ◆ **honorer/respecter ses ~s** to honour/keep one's promises ◆ **j'ai sa ~** I have his word for it, he has promised me ◆ **auteur plein de ~s** writer showing much promise *ou* full of promise, very promising writer ◆ **sourire plein de ~s** smile that promised *(ou* promises) much ◆ **des ~s, toujours des ~s !** promises, promises!

Prométhée /pʀɔmete/ **NM** Prometheus

prométhéen, -enne /pʀɔmeteɛ̃, ɛn/ **ADJ** Promethean ◆ **le rêve ~** *man's dream of becoming master of his own destiny*

prométhium /pʀɔmetjɔm/ **NM** promethium

prometteur, -euse /pʀɔmetœʀ, øz/ **ADJ** *[début, signe]* promising; *[acteur, politicien]* up-and-coming, promising

promettre /pʀɔmɛtʀ/ ▸ conjug 56 ◂ **VT** 1 *[+ chose, aide]* to promise ◆ **je lui ai promis un cadeau** I promised him a present ◆ **je te le promets** I promise (you) ◆ **il n'a rien osé ~** he couldn't promise anything, he didn't dare commit himself ◆ **il a promis de venir** he promised to come ◆ **il m'a promis de venir** *ou* **qu'il viendrait** he promised me (that) he would *ou* he'd come ◆ **~ la lune, ~ monts et merveilles** to promise the moon *ou* the earth ◆ **tu as promis, il faut y aller** you've promised *ou* you've given your word so you have to go ◆ **il ne faut pas ~ quand on ne peut pas tenir** one mustn't make promises that one cannot keep ◆ **~ le secret** to promise to keep a secret ◆ **~ son cœur/sa main/son amour** to pledge one's heart/one's hand/one's love

2 *(= prédire)* to promise ◆ **je vous promets qu'il ne recommencera pas** I (can) promise you he won't do that again ◆ **il sera furieux, je te le promets** he'll be furious, I can promise you that ◆ **on nous promet du beau temps/un été pluvieux** we are promised *ou* we are in for* some fine weather/a rainy summer ◆ **ces nuages nous promettent de la pluie** these clouds mean *ou* promise rain ◆ **cela ne nous promet rien de bon** this doesn't look at all hopeful *ou* good (for us)

3 *(= faire espérer)* to promise ◆ **le spectacle/dîner promet d'être réussi** the show/dinner promises to be a success ◆ **cet enfant promet** this child shows promise *ou* is promising, he's *(ou* she's) a promising child ◆ **ça promet !** *(iro)* that's a good start! *(iro)*, that's promising! *(iro)* ◆ **ça promet pour l'avenir/pour l'hiver !** *(iro)* that bodes well for the future/(the) winter! *(iro)*

VPR se promettre ◆ **se ~ du bon temps** *ou* **du plaisir** to promise o.s. a good time ◆ **je me suis promis un petit voyage** I've promised myself a little trip ◆ **se ~ de faire qch** to mean *ou* resolve to do sth ◆ **je me suis bien promis de ne jamais plus l'inviter** I vowed never to invite him again ◆ **elles se sont promis de garder le secret** they promised each other they'd keep it a secret

promis, e /pʀɔmi, iz/ (ptp de **promettre**) **ADJ** 1 *(= assuré)* promised ◆ **comme ~, il est venu** as promised, he came ◆ **voilà la photo ~e** here's the photograph I promised you ◆ **tu le feras ? – ~(, juré) !** *ou* **c'est ~ !** you'll do it? – yes, cross my heart! *ou* I promise! 2 *(= destiné)* **être ~ à un bel avenir** *[personne]* to be destined for great things, to have a bright future ahead of one; *[invention]* to have a bright future ◆ **quartier ~ à la démolition** area earmarked *ou* scheduled for demolition; → **chose, terre** **NM,F** *(††, dial)* betrothed †

promiscuité /pʀɔmiskɥite/ **NF** 1 *[de lieu public]* crowding *(NonC) (de* in); *[de chambre]* lack of privacy *(NonC) (de* in); ◆ **vivre dans la ~** to live in very close quarters, to live on top of one another 2 ◆ **~ sexuelle** (sexual) promiscuity

promo* /pʀɔmo/ **NF** abrév de **promotion**

promontoire /pʀɔmɔ̃twaʀ/ **NM** *(Géog)* headland, promontory

promoteur, -trice /pʀɔmɔtœʀ, tʀis/ **NM,F** *(= instigateur)* promoter ◆ **~ (immobilier)** property developer ◆ **~ de ventes** sales promoter **NM** *(Chim)* promoter

promotion /pʀɔmosjɔ̃/ **NF** 1 *(= avancement)* promotion *(à un poste* to a job); ◆ **~ sociale** social advancement 2 *(Scol)* year, class *(US)* ◆ **être le premier de sa ~** to be first in one's year *ou* class *(US)* 3 *(Comm = réclame)* special offer ◆ **notre ~ de la semaine** this week's special offer ◆ **article en ~** item on special offer ◆ **il y a une ~ sur les chemises** shirts are on special offer, there's a special on shirts *(US)* ◆ **~ des ventes** sales promotion 4 *(= encouragement)* promotion ◆ **faire la ~ de** *[+ politique, idée, technique]* to promote **NFPL promotions** *(Helv Scol)* end of term party

promotionnel, -elle /pʀɔmosjɔnɛl/ **ADJ** *[article]* on (special) offer; *[vente, campagne]* promotional ◆ **tarif ~** special offer ◆ **offre promotionnelle** special offer, special *(US)* ◆ **matériel ~** publicity material

promouvoir /pʀɔmuvwaʀ/ ▸ conjug 27 ◂ VT to promote ◆ **il a été promu directeur** he was promoted *ou* upgraded to (the rank of) manager

prompt, prompte /pʀɔ̃(pt), pʀɔ̃(p)t/ ADJ *[réaction, départ]* prompt, swift; *[changement]* quick, swift ◆ **je vous souhaite un ~ rétablissement** get well soon, I wish you a speedy recovery ◆ **~ à l'injure/aux excuses/à réagir/à critiquer** quick to insult/to apologize/to react/to criticize ◆ **avoir le geste ~** to be quick to act ◆ **il a l'esprit ~** he has a quick *ou* ready wit ◆ **~ comme l'éclair** *ou* **la foudre** as quick as lightning ◆ **dans l'espoir d'une ~e réponse** hoping for an early reply

promptement /pʀɔ̃ptəmɑ̃/ ADV *[agir, réagir]* quickly, swiftly; *[finir]* quickly; *[répondre, riposter]* promptly

prompteur /pʀɔ̃ptœʀ/ NM Autocue® *(Brit)*, teleprompter® *(US)*

promptitude /pʀɔ̃(p)tityd/ NF *[de répartie, riposte]* quickness; *[de réaction]* promptness, swiftness; *[de départ, changement]* suddenness; *[de guérison]* speed ◆ **il a réagi avec ~** he was quick to react

promulgation /pʀɔmylgasjɔ̃/ NF promulgation

promulguer /pʀɔmylge/ ▸ conjug 1 ◂ VT to promulgate

pronateur /pʀɔnatœʀ/ ADJ M, NM ◆ **(muscle) ~** pronator

pronation /pʀɔnasjɔ̃/ NF pronation

prône /pʀon/ NM sermon

prôner /pʀone/ ▸ conjug 1 ◂ VT 1 *(= préconiser)* to advocate, to recommend 2 *(= vanter)* to laud, to extol

pronom /pʀɔnɔ̃/ NM pronoun

pronominal, e (mpl **-aux**) /pʀɔnɔminal, o/ ADJ pronominal ◆ **(verbe) ~** pronominal *ou* reflexive (verb) ◆ **mettre un verbe à la forme ~e** to put a verb in its pronominal *ou* reflexive form

pronominalement /pʀɔnɔminalmɑ̃/ ADV pronominally, reflexively

prononçable /pʀɔnɔ̃sabl/ ADJ pronounceable ◆ **son nom est difficilement ~** his name is hard to pronounce ◆ **ce mot n'est pas ~** that word is unpronounceable

prononcé, e /pʀɔnɔ̃se/ (ptp de **prononcer**) ADJ *[accent, goût, trait]* pronounced, strong NM *(Jur)* pronouncement

prononcer /pʀɔnɔ̃se/ GRAMMAIRE ACTIVE 33.3 ▸ conjug 3 ◂

VT 1 *(= articuler) [+ mot, son]* to pronounce ◆ **son nom est impossible à ~** his name is impossible to pronounce *ou* is unpronounceable ◆ **comment est-ce que ça se prononce ?** how is it pronounced?, how do you pronounce it? ◆ **cette lettre ne se prononce pas** that letter is silent *ou* is not pronounced ◆ **tu prononces mal** your pronunciation is poor ◆ **mal ~ un mot** to mispronounce a word, to pronounce a word badly ◆ **~ distinctement** to speak clearly, to pronounce one's words clearly

2 *(= dire) [+ parole, nom]* to utter; *[+ souhait]* to utter, to make; *[+ discours]* to make, to deliver ◆ **sortir sans ~ un mot** to go out without uttering a word ◆ **ne prononcez plus jamais ce nom !** don't you ever mention *ou* utter that name again! ◆ **~ ses vœux** *(Rel)* to take one's vows

3 *[+ sentence]* to pronounce, to pass; *[+ dissolution, excommunication]* to pronounce ◆ **~ le huis clos** to order that a case (should) be heard in camera

VI *(Jur)* to deliver *ou* give a verdict ◆ **~ en faveur de/contre** *(littér)* to come down *ou* pronounce in favour of/against

VPR **se prononcer** *(= se décider) (gén)* to reach *ou* come to a decision *(sur* on, about); *(Jur)* to reach a verdict *(sur* on); *(= s'exprimer) (avis)* to give *ou* express an opinion *(sur* on); *(décision)* to give a decision *(sur* on); *(Jur)* to give a verdict *(sur* on); ◆ **le médecin ne s'est toujours pas prononcé** the doctor still hasn't given a verdict *ou* a firm opinion ◆ **se ~ en faveur de qn/pour qch** to come down *ou* pronounce o.s. in favour of sb/in favour of sth ◆ **se ~ contre une décision** to declare one's opposition to *ou* pronounce o.s. against a decision ◆ **"ne se prononcent pas"** *(sondage)* "don't know"

prononciation /pʀɔnɔ̃sjasjɔ̃/ NF 1 *(gén)* pronunciation ◆ **la ~ de ce mot est difficile** this word is hard to pronounce ◆ **il a une bonne/mauvaise ~** he speaks/doesn't speak clearly, he pronounces/doesn't pronounce his words clearly; *(dans une langue étrangère)* his pronunciation is good/poor ◆ **faute** *ou* **erreur de ~** pronunciation error, error of pronunciation ◆ **faire une faute de ~** to mispronounce a word ◆ **défaut** *ou* **vice de ~** speech impediment *ou* defect 2 *(Jur)* pronouncement

pronostic /pʀɔnɔstik/ NM *(gén)* forecast, prognostication *(frm)*; *(Méd)* prognosis; *(Courses)* tip; *(Sport)* forecast ◆ **quels sont vos ~s ?** what's your forecast? ◆ **au ~ infaillible** unerring in his *(ou* her *etc)* forecasts ◆ **elle a fait le bon ~** *(gén)* her prediction proved correct; *(Méd)* she made the right prognosis ◆ **se tromper dans ses ~s** *(gén)* to get one's forecasts wrong ◆ **mes ~s donnaient le 11 gagnant** *(Courses)* I tipped number 11 to win ◆ **faire des ~s sur les matchs de football** to forecast the football results

pronostiquer /pʀɔnɔstike/ ▸ conjug 1 ◂ VT *(= prédire)* to forecast, to prognosticate *(frm)*; *(= être le signe de)* to foretell, to be a sign of; *(Courses)* to tip

pronostiqueur, -euse /pʀɔnɔstikœʀ, øz/ NM,F *(gén)* forecaster, prognosticator *(frm)*; *(Courses)* tipster

pronunciamiento /pʀɔnunsjamjento/ NM pronunciamento

pro-occidental, e (mpl **pro-occidentaux**) /pʀɔɔksidɑ̃tal, o/ ADJ pro-Western

propagande /pʀɔpagɑ̃d/ NF propaganda ◆ **~ électorale/de guerre** electioneering/war propaganda ◆ **faire de la ~ pour qch/qn** to push *ou* plug* sth/sb ◆ **je ne ferai pas de ~ pour ce commerçant/ce produit** I certainly won't be doing any advertising for *ou* plugging* this trader/this product ◆ **journal de ~** propaganda sheet *ou* newspaper ◆ **film/discours de ~** propaganda film/speech ◆ **discours de ~ électorale** electioneering speech

propagandiste /pʀɔpagɑ̃dist/ NMF propagandist

propagateur, -trice /pʀɔpagatœʀ, tʀis/ NM,F *[de méthode, religion, théorie]* propagator; *[de nouvelle]* spreader

propagation /pʀɔpagasjɔ̃/ NF 1 *[de foi, idée]* propagation; *[de nouvelle]* spreading; *[de maladie, épidémie]* spread; *[de rumeur]* spreading, putting about *(Brit)* ◆ **pour arrêter la ~ de l'incendie** to stop the fire spreading 2 *(Phys) [de son, onde, lumière, chaleur]* propagation ◆ **vitesse de ~** velocity of propagation 3 *(Bio)* propagation

propager /pʀɔpaʒe/ ▸ conjug 3 ◂ VT 1 *(= diffuser) [+ foi, idée]* to propagate; *[+ nouvelle, maladie]* to spread; *[+ rumeur]* to spread, to put about *(Brit)* 2 *(Phys) [+ son, lumière, onde]* to propagate 3 *(Bio) [+ espèce]* to propagate VPR **se propager** 1 *(= se répandre) [incendie, idée, nouvelle, maladie]* to spread 2 *(Phys) [onde]* to be propagated 3 *(Bio) [espèce]* to propagate

propane /pʀɔpan/ NM propane

propédeutique † /pʀɔpedøtik/ NF *(Univ) foundation course for first-year university students*

propène /pʀɔpɛn/ NM propene

propension /pʀɔpɑ̃sjɔ̃/ NF proclivity *(frm) (à qch* to *ou* towards sth; *à faire* to do) propensity *(à qch* for sth; *à faire* to do); ◆ **~ à consommer/économiser** *(Écon)* propensity to spend/save

propergol /pʀɔpɛʀgɔl/ NM *[de fusée]* propellant, propellent

prophète /pʀɔfɛt/ NM *(gén)* prophet, seer; *(Rel)* prophet ◆ **faux ~** false prophet ◆ **~ de malheur** prophet of doom, doomsayer ◆ **les (livres des) Prophètes** *(Bible)* the Books of (the) Prophets; → **nul**

prophétesse /pʀɔfetɛs/ NF *(gén)* prophetess, seer; *(Rel)* prophetess

prophétie /pʀɔfesi/ NF prophecy

prophétique /pʀɔfetik/ ADJ prophetic

prophétiquement /pʀɔfetikmɑ̃/ ADV prophetically

prophétiser /pʀɔfetize/ ▸ conjug 1 ◂ VT to prophesy ◆ **il est facile de ~** it's easy to make predictions *ou* prophesies

prophylactique /pʀɔfilaktik/ ADJ prophylactic

prophylaxie /pʀɔfilaksi/ NF disease prevention, prophylaxis *(SPÉC)*

propice /pʀɔpis/ ADJ *[circonstance, occasion]* favourable *(Brit)*, favorable *(US)*, auspicious, propitious; *[milieu, terrain]* favourable *(Brit)*, favorable *(US)* ◆ **attendre le moment ~** to wait for the right moment *ou* an opportune *(frm)* moment ◆ **cherchons un endroit plus ~ pour discuter** let's look for a more suitable place to talk ◆ **être ~ à qch** to favour sth, to be favourable to sth ◆ **un climat ~ à la négociation** an atmosphere favourable *ou* conducive to negotiation ◆ **que les dieux vous soient ~s !** *(littér, hum)* may the gods look kindly *ou* smile upon you! *(littér, hum)*

propitiation /pʀɔpisjasjɔ̃/ NF propitiation ◆ **victime de ~** propitiatory victim

propitiatoire /pʀɔpisjatwaʀ/ ADJ propitiatory

propolis /pʀɔpɔlis/ NF propolis

proportion /pʀɔpɔʀsjɔ̃/ NF proportion ◆ **la ~ hommes/femmes** the proportion *ou* ratio of men to women ◆ **hors de (toute) ~** out of (all) proportion *(avec* with); ◆ **sans ~ avec** out of proportion to ◆ **toute(s) ~(s) gardée(s)** relatively speaking, making due allowance(s)

◆ **à proportion de** in proportion to, proportionally to

◆ **en proportion** proportionately, in proportion ◆ **si le chiffre d'affaires augmente, les salaires seront augmentés en ~** if turnover increases, salaries will be raised proportionately *ou* commensurately ◆ **il a un poste élevé et un salaire en ~** he has a top position and a correspondingly high salary ◆ **pour maintenir un tel train de vie, il faut avoir des revenus en ~** to maintain such a lavish lifestyle, you must have an income to match

◆ **en proportion de** *(= relatif à)* proportional *ou* proportionate to, in proportion to, relative to; *(= relativement à)* proportionally to ◆ **l'entreprise investira en ~ de son chiffre d'affaires** the amount of money the company invests will be relative *ou* proportional to its turnover ◆ **c'est bien peu, en ~ du service qu'il m'a rendu** it's nothing, compared to all the favours he has done me

NFPL **proportions** *(= taille, importance)* proportions ◆ **édifice de belles ~s** well-proportioned building ◆ **cela a pris des ~s considérables** it reached considerable proportions ◆ **il faut ramener l'affaire à de justes ~s** this matter must be put into perspective ◆ **augmenter/réduire qch dans des ~s considérables** to increase/reduce sth considerably

proportionnalité /pʀɔpɔʀsjɔnalite/ **NF** proportionality; *(Pol)* proportional representation ◆ **~ de l'impôt** proportional taxation (system)

proportionné, e /pʀɔpɔʀsjɔne/ (ptp de **proportionner**) **ADJ** ◆ **~ à** proportional *ou* proportionate to ◆ **bien** ~ well-proportioned ◆ **admirablement** ~ admirably well-proportioned

proportionnel, -elle /pʀɔpɔʀsjɔnɛl/ **ADJ** *(gén, Math, Pol)* proportional ◆ **~ à** proportional *ou* proportionate to, in proportion to *ou* with ◆ **directement/inversement ~ à** directly/inversely proportional to, in direct/inverse proportion to **NF proportionnelle** *(Math)* proportional ◆ **la proportionnelle (intégrale)** *(Pol)* (pure) proportional representation ◆ **élu à la proportionnelle** elected by proportional representation

proportionnellement /pʀɔpɔʀsjɔnɛlmɑ̃/ **ADV** proportionally, proportionately ◆ **~ plus grand** proportionally *ou* proportionately bigger ◆ **~ à** in proportion to, proportionally to

proportionner /pʀɔpɔʀsjɔne/ ► conjug 1 ◄ **VT** to proportion, to make proportional, to adjust *(à* to)

propos /pʀɔpo/ **NM** [1] *(gén pl)* words ◆ **ses ~ ont irrité tout le monde** what he said annoyed everyone ◆ **ce sont des ~ en l'air** it's just empty *ou* idle talk *ou* hot air* ◆ **tenir des ~ blessants** to say hurtful things, to make hurtful remarks ◆ **tenir des ~ désobligeants à l'égard de qn** to make offensive remarks about sb, to say offensive things about sb ◆ **des ~ de personne soûle** *(péj)* drunken ramblings

[2] *(frm = intention)* intention, aim ◆ **mon ~ est de vous expliquer ...** my intention *ou* aim is to explain to you ... ◆ **il n'entre pas dans mon ~ de ...** it is not my intention to ... ◆ **tel n'était pas mon ~** that was not my intention ◆ **avoir le ferme ~ de faire qch** to have the firm intention of doing sth ◆ **faire qch de ~ délibéré** to do sth deliberately *ou* on purpose

[3] *(= sujet)* **à quel ~ voulait-il me voir ?** what did he want to see me about? ◆ **à quel ~ est-il venu ?** what was his reason for coming?, what brought him?* ◆ **c'est à quel ~ ?** what is it about?, what is it in connection with? ◆ **à ~ de ta voiture** about your car, on the subject of your car ◆ **je vous écris à ~ de l'annonce** I am writing regarding *ou* concerning the advertisement *ou* in connection with the advertisement ◆ **à tout ~** (= *sans arrêt*) every other minute ◆ **il se plaint à tout ~** he complains at the slightest (little) thing ◆ **il se met en colère à ~ de tout et de rien** *ou* **à tout ~** he loses his temper at the slightest (little) thing *ou* for no reason at all ◆ **à ce ~** in this connection, (while) on this subject ◆ **hors de ~** irrelevant

[4] ◆ **à ~** *[décision]* well-timed, opportune, timely; *[remarque]* apt, pertinent, apposite; *[arriver]* at the right moment *ou* time ◆ **tomber** *ou* **arriver mal à ~** to happen (just) at the wrong moment *ou* time ◆ **voilà qui tombe à ~/mal à ~ !** it couldn't have come at a better/worse time! *ou* moment! ◆ **il a jugé à ~ de nous prévenir** he thought it right to let us know, he saw fit to let us know ◆ **à ~, dis-moi ...** incidentally *ou* by the way, tell me ...

proposer /pʀɔpoze/ GRAMMAIRE ACTIVE 28.1 ► conjug 1 ◄

VT [1] *(= suggérer)* *[+ arrangement, interprétation, projet, appellation]* to suggest, to propose; *[+ solution, interprétation]* to suggest, to put forward, to propose; *[+ candidat]* to propose, to nominate, to put forward; *(Scol, Univ)* *[+ sujet, texte]* to set *(Brit)*, to assign *(US)*; *(Pol)* *[+ loi]* to move, to propose ◆ **on a proposé mon nom pour ce poste** my name has been put forward for this post ◆ **~ qch à qn** to suggest *ou* put sth to sb ◆ **~ de faire qch** to suggest *ou* propose doing sth ◆ **le film que nous vous proposons (de voir) ce soir** *(TV)* the film we are showing this evening, our film this evening ◆ **l'homme propose, Dieu dispose** *(Prov)* man proposes, God disposes *(Prov)* ◆ **je vous propose de passer me voir** I suggest that you come round and see me ◆ **qu'est-ce que tu proposes ?** what do you suggest? ◆ **~ qu'une motion soit mise aux voix** to move that a motion be put to the vote

[2] *(= offrir)* *[+ aide, prix, situation]* to offer ◆ **~ qch à qn** to offer sth to sb, to offer sb sth ◆ **~ de faire qch** to offer to do sth ◆ **on me propose une nouvelle voiture** I am being offered *ou* I have the offer of a new car ◆ **je lui ai proposé de la raccompagner** I offered to see her home

VPR se proposer [1] *(= offrir ses services)* to offer one's services ◆ **elle s'est proposée pour garder les enfants** she offered to look after the children

[2] *(= envisager)* *[+ but, tâche]* to set o.s. ◆ **se ~ de faire qch** to intend *ou* mean *ou* propose to do sth ◆ **il se proposait de prouver que ...** he set out to prove that ...

> ⚠ Au sens de 'offrir', **proposer** ne se traduit pas par **to propose**.

proposition /pʀɔpozisjɔ̃/ **NF** [1] *(= suggestion)* proposal, suggestion; *(Comm)* proposition; *(Pol = recommandation)* proposal ◆ **~s de paix** peace proposals ◆ **~ de réforme** reform proposal ◆ **~ de résolution** *(Jur)* proposal *ou* motion for a resolution ◆ **~ de loi** *(Pol)* private bill, private member's bill *(Brit)* ◆ **sur (la) ~ de** at the suggestion of, on the proposal of ◆ **sur sa ~, il a été décidé d'attendre** at his suggestion it was decided to wait ◆ **la ~ de qn à un grade supérieur** the nomination of sb to a higher position ◆ **faire une ~ (à qn)** to make (sb) a proposition ◆ **faire des ~s (malhonnêtes) à une femme** to proposition a woman ◆ **il a eu plusieurs ~s de films** he's been approached by several film directors

[2] *(Math, Philos)* *(= postulat)* proposition; *(= déclaration)* proposition, assertion

[3] *(Gram)* clause ◆ **~ principale/subordonnée/indépendante** main/subordinate/independent clause ◆ **~ consécutive** *ou* **de conséquence** consecutive *ou* result clause

propositionnel, -elle /pʀɔpozisjɔnɛl/ **ADJ** propositional

propre¹ /pʀɔpʀ/ **ADJ** [1] *(= pas sali, nettoyé)* *[linge, mains, maison, personne]* clean ◆ **des draps bien ~s** nice clean sheets ◆ **~ comme un sou neuf** as clean as a new pin ◆ **leurs enfants sont toujours (tenus) très ~s** their children are always very neat and tidy *ou* very neatly turned out ◆ **ce n'est pas ~ de manger avec les doigts** it's dirty to eat with your fingers ◆ **nous voilà ~s !*** now we're in a fine *ou* proper mess!* ◆ **c'est quelqu'un de très ~ sur lui*** he's very clean-cut ◆ **~ en ordre** *(Helv hum)* excessively clean and tidy

[2] *(= soigné)* *[travail, exécution]* neat, neatly done; *[cahier, copie]* neat; *[personne]* tidy, neat

[3] *(= qui ne salit pas)* *[chien, chat]* house-trained; *[enfant]* toilet-trained, potty-trained*; *(= non polluant)* *[moteur, voiture, produit]* clean ◆ **il n'est pas encore ~** he isn't toilet-trained *ou* potty-trained* yet

[4] *(= honnête)* *[personne]* honest, decent; *[affaire, argent]* honest; *[mœurs]* decent ◆ **il n'a jamais rien fait de ~** he's never done a decent *ou* an honest thing in his life ◆ **une affaire pas très ~** a slightly suspect *ou* shady piece of business ◆ **ce garçon-là, ce n'est pas grand-chose de ~*** that young man hasn't got much to recommend him *ou* isn't up to much*

NM ◆ **sentir le ~*** to smell clean ◆ **mettre** *ou* **recopier qch au ~** to make a fair copy of sth, to copy sth out neatly ◆ **c'est du ~ !*** *(gâchis)* what a mess!, what a shambles!*; *(comportement)* what a way to behave!, it's an absolute disgrace!

propre² /pʀɔpʀ/ **ADJ** [1] *(intensif possessif)* own ◆ **il a sa ~ voiture** he's got his own car *ou* a car of his own ◆ **ce sont ses ~s mots** those are his own *ou* his very *ou* his actual words ◆ **de mes ~s yeux** with my own eyes ◆ **ils ont leurs caractères/qualités ~s** they have their own (specific) *ou* their particular characters/qualities; → **chef², initiative, main, moyen²**

[2] *(= particulier, spécifique)* **c'est un trait qui lui est ~** it's a trait which is peculiar to him, it's a distinctive *ou* specific characteristic of his ◆ **les coutumes ~s à certaines régions** the customs peculiar to *ou* characteristic of *ou* proper to *(frm)* certain regions ◆ **biens ~s** *(Jur)* personal property; → **fonds, nom, sens**

[3] *(= qui convient)* suitable, appropriate *(à* for); ◆ **le mot ~** the right *ou* proper word ◆ **ce n'est pas un lieu ~ à la conversation** it isn't a suitable *ou* an appropriate place for talking ◆ **sol ~ à la culture du blé** soil suitable for *ou* suited to wheat-growing ◆ **on l'a jugé ~ à s'occuper de l'affaire** he was considered the right man for *ou* suitable for the job

[4] *(= de nature à)* **un poste ~ à lui apporter des satisfactions** a job likely to bring him satisfaction ◆ **exercice ~ à développer les muscles des épaules** exercise that will develop the shoulder muscles ◆ **un lieu/une musique ~ au recueillement** a place/a type of music favourable *ou* conducive to meditation ◆ **c'est bien ~ à vous dégoûter de la politique** it's (exactly) the sort of thing that turns you *ou* to turn you right off politics, it's guaranteed to put you off politics

NM [1] *(= qualité distinctive)* peculiarity, (exclusive *ou* distinctive) feature ◆ **la raison est le ~ de l'homme** reason is a (distinctive) feature of man, reason is peculiar to man ◆ **la parole est le ~ de l'homme** speech is man's special gift *ou* attribute ◆ **c'est le ~ de ce système d'éducation de fabriquer des paresseux** it's a peculiarity *ou* feature of this educational system that it turns out idlers ◆ **avoir un domaine en ~** to be the sole owner of an estate, to have exclusive possession of an estate ◆ **cette caractéristique que la France possède en ~** this feature which is peculiar *ou* exclusive to France

[2] *(Ling)* **au ~** in the literal sense *ou* meaning, literally

> ⚠ **propre** se traduit par **proper** uniquement au sens de 'qui convient'.

propre-à-rien (pl **propres-à-rien**) /pʀɔpʀaʀjɛ̃/ **NMF** good-for-nothing, ne'er-do-well, waster

proprement /pʀɔpʀəmɑ̃/ **ADV** [1] *(= avec propreté)* cleanly; *(= avec netteté)* neatly, tidily; *(= comme il faut)* properly; *(= décemment)* decently ◆ **tenir une maison très ~** to keep a house very clean ◆ **mange ~ !** don't make such a mess (when you're eating)!, eat properly! ◆ **se conduire ~** to behave properly *ou* correctly

[2] *(= exactement)* exactly, literally; *(= exclusivement)* specifically, strictly; *(= vraiment)* absolutely ◆ **à ~ parler** strictly speaking ◆ **le village ~ dit** the actual village, the village itself ◆ **la linguistique ~ dite** linguistics proper ◆ **c'est un problème ~ français** it's a specifically French problem ◆ **c'est ~ scandaleux** it's absolutely disgraceful ◆ **il m'a ~ fermé la porte au nez** he simply shut the door in my face ◆ **on l'a ~ rossé** he was well and truly beaten up

propret, -ette /pʀɔpʀɛ, ɛt/ **ADJ** *[personne]* neat (and tidy); *[chose]* neat (and tidy), spick-and-span *(attrib)*

propreté /pʀɔpʀəte/ **NF** [1] *[de linge, mains, maison, personne]* cleanliness, cleanness ◆ **ils n'ont aucune notion de** ~ they have no notion of hygiene ◆ **l'apprentissage de la ~ chez l'enfant** toilet-training in the child ◆ **apprendre la ~ à un chiot** to house-train a puppy ◆ **d'une ~ méticuleuse** scrupulously clean ◆ **d'une ~ douteuse** not very clean ◆ **des meubles luisants de** ~ sparkling clean furniture; → **plaque** [2] *[de travail, exécution d'un morceau de musique]* neatness; *(Scol) [de cahier, copie]* neatness

propriétaire /pʀɔpʀijetɛʀ/ **NM** [1] *[de voiture, chien, maison]* owner; *[d'hôtel, entreprise]* proprietor, owner ◆ **il est ~ (de sa maison)** he owns his (own) house ◆ **quand on est ~, il faut ...** when one is a home-owner *ou* house-owner one has to ...; → **tour²**

[2] *[de location]* landlord, owner ◆ **mis à la porte par son** ~ thrown out by his landlord

[3] *[de terres, immeubles]* owner ◆ **~ éleveur** breeder ◆ **~ récoltant** grower ◆ **achat direct au** ~ direct purchase from the grower ◆ **~ terrien** landowner ◆ **~ foncier** property owner ◆ **les petits ~s** smallholders

NF *(gén)* owner; *[d'hôtel, entreprise]* proprietress, owner; *[de location]* landlady, owner

ADJ *(Ordin) [logiciel, système]* proprietary

> ⚠ **propriétaire** se traduit par **proprietor** uniquement quand on parle d'un hôtel, d'un restaurant ou d'une entreprise.

propriété /pʀɔpʀijete/ **NF** [1] *(= droit)* ownership, property *(frm) (Jur)*; *(= possession)* property ◆ **~ de l'État/collective** state/collective ownership ◆ **la petite ~** *(gén)* small estates; *(Agr)* smallholdings ◆ **la grande ~** large estates; *(Agr)* large farms ◆ **posséder qch en toute ~** to be the sole owner of sth, to have sole ownership of sth ◆ **recevoir qch en pleine ~** to acquire the freehold of sth; → **accession, titre**

[2] *(= immeuble, maison)* property; *(= terres)* property *(NonC)*, land *(NonC)*, estate ◆ **revenu d'une ~** revenue from a property *ou* a piece of land

[3] *(= qualité)* property ◆ **~s chimiques/physiques/thérapeutiques** chemical/physical/therapeutic properties

[4] *(= correction) [de mot]* appropriateness, suitability, correctness

COMP **propriété artistique** artistic copyright
propriété bâtie developed property
propriété commerciale security of tenure *(of industrial or commercial tenant)*
propriété foncière property ownership
propriétés immobilières real estate *(NonC)*, realty *(NonC) (Jur)*
propriété industrielle patent rights
propriété intellectuelle intellectual property
propriété littéraire author's copyright
propriété non bâtie undeveloped property
propriété privée private property
propriété publique public property

> ⚠ **propriété** ne se traduit pas par le mot anglais **propriety**, qui a le sens de 'bienséance'.

proprio* /pʀɔpʀijo/ **NMF** (abrév de **propriétaire**) *(= homme)* landlord; *(= femme)* landlady

propulser /pʀɔpylse/ ▸ conjug 1 ◂ **VT** [1] *[+ voiture]* to propel, to drive (along *ou* forward); *[+ missile]* to propel, to power

[2] *(= projeter)* to hurl, to fling ◆ **il a été propulsé contre le mur** he was hurled *ou* flung against the wall

[3] *(= promouvoir)* **on l'a propulsé à la direction du service** he suddenly found himself at the head of the department ◆ **avant de se retrouver propulsé au sommet de la hiérarchie** before suddenly finding himself at the top of *ou* thrust to the top of the hierarchy ◆ **le voilà propulsé au rang de star/à la tête de l'entreprise** and now he's suddenly become a star/the head of the company ◆ **on se retrouve propulsés dans un monde féerique** we suddenly find ourselves transported to a magical world

VPR **se propulser** *(= avancer)* to propel o.s. ◆ **l'entreprise s'est propulsée à la première place du marché** the company has shot into the lead

propulseur /pʀɔpylsœʀ/ **ADJ M** propulsive, driving *(épith)* **NM** [1] *[de fusée]* thruster ◆ **~ d'appoint** booster [2] *[de lance, harpon]* throwing stick

propulsif, -ive /pʀɔpylsif, iv/ **ADJ** propelling, propellent

propulsion /pʀɔpylsjɔ̃/ **NF** propulsion ◆ **moteur à ~** propulsion engine ◆ **système de ~** propulsion system ◆ **à ~ atomique/nucléaire** atomic-/nuclear-powered ◆ **sous-marin à ~ classique** conventionally-powered submarine

propylène /pʀɔpilɛn/ **NM** propylene

prorata /pʀɔʀata/ **NM INV** proportional share, proportion ◆ **au ~ de** in proportion to, proportionally to, on the basis of ◆ **paiement au ~** payment on a pro rata basis

prorogation /pʀɔʀɔgasjɔ̃/ **NF** [1] *[de délai, durée]* extension; *[d'échéance]* putting back, deferment [2] *[de séance]* adjournment; *(Parl)* prorogation

proroger /pʀɔʀɔʒe/ ▸ conjug 3 ◂ **VT** [1] *(= prolonger) [+ délai, durée]* to extend; *(= reporter) [+ échéance]* to put back, to defer [2] *(= ajourner) [+ séance]* to adjourn; *(Parl)* to prorogue ◆ **le parlement s'est prorogé jusqu'en octobre** the parliament has adjourned *ou* prorogued until October

prosaïque /pʀozaik/ **ADJ** *[esprit, personne, vie, style, remarque, détail]* mundane, prosaic; *[goûts]* mundane, commonplace

prosaïquement /pʀozaikmɑ̃/ **ADV** prosaically ◆ **vivre ~** to lead a mundane life *ou* a prosaic existence ◆ **plus ~, je dirais ...** more prosaically, I would say ...

prosaïsme /pʀozaism/ **NM** mundanity, mundaneness

prosateur /pʀozatœʀ/ **NM** prose-writer, writer of prose

proscription /pʀɔskʀipsjɔ̃/ **NF** [1] *[d'idéologie, activité, drogue, mot]* banning, prohibition, proscription [2] *[de personne] (= mise hors la loi)* outlawing *(NonC)*; *(= exil)* banishment, exiling *(NonC)*

proscrire /pʀɔskʀiʀ/ ▸ conjug 39 ◂ **VT** [1] *[+ idéologie, activité]* to ban, to proscribe; *[+ drogue, mot]* to ban, to prohibit the use of, to proscribe ◆ **~ une expression de son vocabulaire** to banish an expression from one's vocabulary ◆ **c'est à ~ absolument !** it is to be avoided at all costs! [2] *[+ personne] (= mettre hors la loi)* to outlaw; *(= exiler)* to banish, to exile

proscrit, e /pʀɔskʀi, it/ (ptp de **proscrire**) **NM,F** *(= hors-la-loi)* outlaw; *(= exilé)* exile

prose /pʀoz/ **NF** *(gén)* prose; *(= style)* prose (style) ◆ **poème/tragédie en ~** prose poem/tragedy ◆ **écrire en ~** to write in prose ◆ **faire de la ~** to write prose ◆ **la ~ administrative** *(péj)* officialese ◆ **je viens de lire sa ~** *(péj) (lettre)* I've just read his epistle *(hum)*; *(devoir, roman)* I've just read his great work *(iro, hum)*

prosélyte /pʀozelit/ **NMF** proselyte *(frm)*, convert ◆ **les ~s des médecines douces** converts to alternative medicine

prosélytisme /pʀozelitism/ **NM** proselytism ◆ **faire du ~** to proselytize, to preach

prosodie /pʀɔzɔdi/ **NF** prosody

prosodique /pʀɔzɔdik/ **ADJ** prosodic ◆ **trait ~** prosodic feature

prosopopée /pʀɔzɔpɔpe/ **NF** prosopopoeia, prosopopeia

prospect /pʀɔspɛ(kt)/ **NM** *(Écon)* prospect, prospective customer

prospecter /pʀɔspɛkte/ ▸ conjug 1 ◂ **VT** [1] *(Min)* to prospect [2] *(Comm) [+ marché]* to explore; *[+ région, clientèle]* to canvass ◆ **j'ai prospecté le quartier pour trouver une maison** I scoured *ou* searched the area to find a house

prospecteur, -trice /pʀɔspɛktœʀ, tʀis/ **NM,F** prospector

prospecteur-placier (pl **prospecteurs-placiers**) /pʀɔspɛktœʀplasje/ **NM** employment officer, job placement officer *(Brit)*

prospectif, -ive /pʀɔspɛktif, iv/ **ADJ** *(Écon)* ◆ **analyse prospective** forecast ◆ **cellule prospective** group of economic forecasters ◆ **ils ont fait des études prospectives** they made some forecasts ◆ **nous manquons d'une vision prospective sur ces marchés** we can't predict what will happen in these markets **NF** **prospective** *(gén)* futurology; *(Écon)* economic forecasting

> ⚠ L'adjectif **prospectif** se traduit rarement par **prospective**, qui a le sens de 'futur'.

prospection /pʀɔspɛksjɔ̃/ **NF** [1] *(Min)* prospecting ◆ **ils font de la ~ pétrolière** they are prospecting for oil [2] *(Comm) [de marché]* exploring; *[de région, clientèle]* canvassing ◆ **faire de la ~** to canvass for business

prospectiviste /pʀɔspɛktivist/ **NMF** *(gén)* futurologist; *(Écon)* (economic) forecaster

prospectus /pʀɔspɛktys/ **NM** leaflet ◆ **~ publicitaire** publicity *ou* advertising leaflet ◆ **ma boîte aux lettres était pleine de ~** my letter box was full of junk mail

prospère /pʀɔspɛʀ/ **ADJ** [1] *[commerce, pays, collectivité]* prosperous, thriving, flourishing; *[période]* prosperous [2] *[personne]* blooming with health *(attrib)* ◆ **avoir une mine ~** to look healthy ◆ **être d'une santé ~** to be blooming with health

prospérer /pʀɔspeʀe/ ▸ conjug 6 ◂ **VI** *[commerce]* to prosper, to thrive, to flourish; *[personne]* to prosper, to do well; *[animal, activité, plante]* to thrive, to flourish

prospérité /pʀɔspeʀite/ **NF** [1] *(matérielle)* prosperity; *(économique)* prosperity, affluence [2] *(= santé)* (flourishing) health

prostaglandine /pʀɔstaglɑ̃din/ **NF** prostaglandin

prostate /pʀɔstat/ **NF** prostate (gland)

prostatectomie /pʀɔstatɛktɔmi/ **NF** prostatectomy

prostatique /pʀɔstatik/ **ADJ** prostatic **NM** prostate sufferer

prosternation /pʀɔstɛʀnasjɔ̃/ **NF** prostration

prosterné, e /pʀɔstɛʀne/ (ptp de **prosterner**) **ADJ** prostrate

prosternement /pʀɔstɛʀnəmɑ̃/ **NM** *(= action)* prostration; *(= attitude)* prostrate attitude; *(fig)* grovelling

prosterner /pʀɔstɛʀne/ ▸ conjug 1 ◂ **VT** *(littér)* to bow low ◆ **il prosterna le corps** he prostrated himself **VPR** **se prosterner** *(= s'incliner)* to bow low, to bow down, to prostrate o.s. *(devant* before); *(= s'humilier)* to grovel *(devant* before) to kowtow *(devant* to)

prostitué /pʀɔstitɥe/ **NM** male prostitute, rent boy* *(Brit)*

prostituée /pʀɔstitɥe/ NF prostitute

prostituer /pʀɔstitɥe/ ▸ conjug 1 ◂ VT (lit) ◆ ~ qn to make a prostitute of sb VPR **se prostituer** (lit, fig) to prostitute o.s.

prostitution /pʀɔstitysjɔ̃/ NF (lit, fig) prostitution

prostration /pʀɔstʀasjɔ̃/ NF (Méd, Rel) prostration

prostré, e /pʀɔstʀe/ ADJ (fig) prostrate, prostrated; (Méd) prostrate

protactinium /pʀɔtaktinjɔm/ NM protactinium

protagoniste /pʀɔtagɔnist/ NMF protagonist ◆ **les principaux ~s de l'affaire/du conflit** the main players ou protagonists in the affair/the conflict

protecteur, -trice /pʀɔtɛktœʀ, tʀis/ ADJ 1 (gén, Chim, Écon) protective (de of); (Cosmétique) [film] protective ◆ **crème protectrice** protective ou barrier cream; → **société** 2 [ton, air] patronizing NM,F (= défenseur) protector, guardian; [d'arts] patron ◆ ~ **de la nature/l'environnement** protector of nature/the environment NM (= souteneur) pimp (péj); († = galant) fancy man †

protection /pʀɔtɛksjɔ̃/ NF 1 (= défense) protection (contre against, from); ◆ ~ **contre les rayonnements** radiation protection ◆ **assurer la ~ de** to protect ◆ **chargé d'assurer la ~ rapprochée du chef de l'État** in charge of the close protection ou personal safety of the head of state ◆ **zone sous ~ policière/militaire** area under police/military protection ◆ **région sous ~ de l'ONU** UN protection zone, area under UN protection ◆ **sous la ~ de** under the protection of ◆ **elle a été placée sous la ~ de la police** she was given police protection ◆ **prendre qn sous sa ~** to give sb one's protection, to take sb under one's wing ◆ **l'ambassade est sous haute ~ policière** the embassy is under heavy police guard ◆ **crème solaire/indice haute ~** high-protection sun cream/factor ◆ **rapports sexuels sans ~** unprotected sex

2 ◆ **de ~** [équipement, grille, lunettes, mesures] protective ◆ **zone de ~** [de population] safe haven ◆ **système de ~** security system

3 (= patronage) (gén) protection; [de personne puissante, mécène] patronage ◆ **placer un enfant sous la ~ de qn** to place a child in sb's care ◆ **prendre qn sous sa ~** to give sb one's patronage, to take sb under one's wing ◆ **obtenir une place par ~** to get a post by pulling strings

4 (= dispositif) (pour une partie du corps) item of protective clothing (ou gear); (= blindage) [de navire] armour(-plating) (Brit), armor (-plating) (US)

5 (Ordin) protection ◆ ~ **contre l'écriture** write protection

COMP **protection aérienne** air ou aerial protection

protection civile (lors de catastrophes) disaster and emergency services; (en temps de guerre) civil defence

protection du consommateur consumer protection

protection des données data protection

protection de l'emploi job protection

protection de l'enfance child welfare

protection de l'environnement environmental protection

protection maternelle et infantile mother and child care

protection de la nature nature conservation

protection périodique sanitary towel (Brit) ou napkin (US)

protection des sites preservation ou protection of beauty spots

protection sociale social welfare ◆ **personnes sans ~ sociale** people not covered by social security ou with no social welfare cover

protection solaire (= produit) sun cream (ou lotion)

protectionnisme /pʀɔtɛksjɔnism/ NM protectionism

protectionniste /pʀɔtɛksjɔnist/ ADJ, NMF protectionist

protectorat /pʀɔtɛktɔʀa/ NM protectorate

protégé, e /pʀɔteʒe/ ADJ 1 [espèce, site, zone] protected; (Écon) [secteur, marché] protected; (Ordin) [disquette] write-protected; [logiciel] copy-protected ◆ ~ **en écriture** write-protected ◆ **la reproduction d'œuvres ~es** the reproduction of works under copyright protection ou of copyright works ◆ **rapports sexuels ~s/non ~s** safe/unprotected sex; → **passage** 2 (pour handicapé) **atelier** ~ sheltered workshop ◆ **emploi** ~ job in a sheltered workshop NM protégé; (* = chouchou) favourite, pet * NF **protégée** protégée; (* = favorite) favourite, pet *

protège-bas /pʀɔtɛʒba/ NM INV sockette

protège-cahier (pl **protège-cahiers**) /pʀɔtɛʒkaje/ NM exercise-book cover

protège-dents /pʀɔtɛʒdɑ̃/ NM INV gum-shield

protège-poignet /pʀɔtɛʒpwaɲɛ/ (pl **protège-poignets**) NM wrist guard

protéger /pʀɔteʒe/ ▸ conjug 6 et 3 ◂ VT 1 (gén) to protect (de, contre from); ◆ ~ **les intérêts de qn** to protect sb's interests ◆ **crème qui protège contre le soleil** cream that gives (good) protection against the sun

2 (= patronner) [+ personne] to be a patron of; [+ carrière] to further; [+ arts, sports, artisanat] to patronize

VPR **se protéger** to protect o.s. (de from; contre against); ◆ **se ~ contre le** ou **du sida/contre le** ou **du soleil** to protect o.s. against AIDS/against the sun ◆ **se ~ du froid/contre les piqûres d'insectes** to protect o.s. from the cold/against insect bites

protège-slip (pl **protège-slips**) /pʀɔtɛʒslip/ NM panty liner

protège-tibia (pl **protège-tibias**) /pʀɔtɛʒtibja/ NM shin guard

protéiforme /pʀɔteifɔʀm/ ADJ protean

protéine /pʀɔtein/ NF protein

protéiné, e /pʀɔteine/ ADJ ◆ **diète ~e** high-protein diet

protéique /pʀɔteik/ ADJ protein (épith), proteinic

protestable /pʀɔtɛstabl/ ADJ protestable, which may be protested

protestant, e /pʀɔtɛstɑ̃, ɑt/ ADJ, NM,F Protestant

protestantisme /pʀɔtɛstɑ̃tism/ NM Protestantism

protestataire /pʀɔtɛstatɛʀ/ ADJ [personne] protesting (épith); [marche, mesure] protest (épith) NMF protester

protestation /pʀɔtɛstasjɔ̃/ NF 1 (= plainte) protest (contre against); (Jur) protesting, protestation ◆ **en signe de ~** as a (sign of) protest ◆ **lettre/marche/mouvement de ~** protest letter/march/movement 2 (souvent pl = déclaration) protestation, profession ◆ **faire des ~s d'amitié à qn** to profess one's friendship to sb

protester /pʀɔtɛste/ GRAMMAIRE ACTIVE 41 ▸ conjug 1 ◂ VI to protest (contre against, about); ◆ ~ **de son innocence/de sa loyauté** to protest one's innocence/one's loyalty ◆ **"mais non", protesta-t-il** "no", he protested VT (Jur) to protest; (frm = déclarer) to declare, to affirm, to profess ◆ **il protesta la plus vive admiration pour elle** (frm) he declared that he had the keenest admiration for her

protêt /pʀɔtɛ/ NM (Comm, Jur) protest

prothèse /pʀɔtɛz/ NF 1 (= appareil) prosthesis (SPÉC); (= membre artificiel) artificial limb (ou hand ou arm etc), prosthesis (SPÉC) ◆ ~ **dentaire** dentures, false teeth, dental prosthesis (SPÉC) ◆ ~ **auditive** hearing aid ◆ ~ **mammaire** breast prosthesis ◆ **pose d'une ~ de hanche** hip replacement (operation) 2 (= science, technique) prosthetics (sg) ◆ **la ~ dentaire** prosthodontics (sg)

prothésiste /pʀɔtezist/ NMF prosthetist, prosthetic technician ◆ ~ **(dentaire)** dental technician, prosthodontist

protide /pʀɔtid/ NM protein

proto... /pʀɔto/ PRÉF proto...

protocolaire /pʀɔtɔkɔlɛʀ/ ADJ [invitation, cérémonie] formal ◆ **question ~** question of protocol ◆ **ce n'est pas très ~ !** it doesn't show much regard for protocol!

protocole /pʀɔtɔkɔl/ NM 1 (= étiquette) etiquette; (Pol) protocol ◆ **il est très attaché au ~** he's a stickler for form ◆ **chef du ~** chief ou head of protocol 2 (= procès-verbal) protocol; (= résolutions) agreement ◆ ~ **d'accord/de coopération/financier** draft/cooperation/financial agreement 3 (Ordin, Sci) protocol ◆ ~ **de transfert de fichiers** file transfer protocol; (rédaction d'ouvrage) style guide ◆ ~ **thérapeutique** medical protocol

proton /pʀɔtɔ̃/ NM proton

protoplasma /pʀɔtɔplasma/, **protoplasme** /pʀɔtɔplasm/ NM protoplasm

protoplasmique /pʀɔtɔplasmik/ ADJ protoplasmic

prototype /pʀɔtɔtip/ NM prototype ◆ ~ **d'avion** prototype aircraft

protoxyde /pʀɔtɔksid/ NM protoxide

protozoaire /pʀɔtɔzɔɛʀ/ NM protozoon ◆ ~**s** protozoa

protubérance /pʀɔtybeʀɑ̃s/ NF bulge, protuberance ◆ ~ **solaire** (Astron) (solar) prominence

protubérant, e /pʀɔtybeʀɑ̃, ɑt/ ADJ [ventre, yeux] bulging, protuberant, protruding; [nez, menton] protuberant, protruding

prou /pʀu/ ADV → **peu**

proue /pʀu/ NF bow, bows, prow; → **figure**

prouesse /pʀuɛs/ NF (frm) feat ◆ **faire des ~s** to work miracles, to perform amazing feats ◆ **il a fallu faire des ~s pour le convaincre** it was quite a feat to convince him ◆ **il nous racontait ses ~s (sexuelles)** he regaled us with tales of his sexual exploits ◆ **cela n'a pu être réalisé qu'au prix de ~s techniques** this could not have been achieved without technical wizardry ◆ **ses ~s d'haltérophile** his prowess as a weight lifter

proustien, -ienne /pʀustjɛ̃, jɛn/ ADJ Proustian

prout * /pʀut/ NM ◆ **faire (un) ~** to fart‡ ◆ **elle est très ~ ~ ma chère** she's terribly la-di-da *

prouvable /pʀuvabl/ ADJ provable ◆ **allégations difficilement ~s** allegations which are difficult to prove

prouver /pʀuve/ GRAMMAIRE ACTIVE 53.4 ▸ conjug 1 ◂ VT to prove ◆ **les faits ont prouvé qu'il avait raison/qu'il était innocent** the facts proved him (to be) right/innocent ou proved that he was right/innocent ◆ **il est prouvé que ...** it has been proved that ... ◆ **cela prouve que ...** it proves ou shows that ... ◆ **il n'est pas prouvé qu'il soit coupable** there is no proof that he is guilty ou of his guilt ◆ **cela n'est pas prouvé** there's no proof of it, that hasn't been proved, that remains to be proved ◆ **sa culpabilité reste à ~** it has yet to be proved that he is guilty ◆ **cette réponse prouve de l'esprit** that answer gives proof of his (*ou* her *etc*) wit *ou* shows wit ◆ **comment vous ~ ma reconnaissance ?** how can I show *ou* demonstrate my gratitude to you? ◆ **il a voulu se ~ (à lui-même) qu'il en était capable** he wanted to prove to himself that he was capable of it ◆ **son efficacité n'est plus à ~** its effectiveness is no longer in doubt *ou* in question ◆ **j'ai 25 ans d'expérience, je n'ai plus rien à ~** I have 25 years' experience, I have nothing to prove; → **A¹, absurde**

provenance /pʀɔv(ə)nɑ̃s/ NF origin, provenance (*frm*) ◆ **j'ignore la ~ de cette lettre** I don't know where this letter comes *ou* came *ou* was sent from ◆ **pays de ~** country of origin ◆ **des objets de toutes ~s** articles of every possible origin ◆ **de ~ étrangère** of foreign origin ◆ **le train en ~ de Cherbourg** the train from Cherbourg

provençal, e (mpl **-aux**) /pʀɔvɑ̃sal, o/ ADJ Provençal ◆ **(à la) ~e** (*Culin*) (à la) Provençale NM (= *langue*) Provençal NM,F **Provençal(e)** Provençal

Provence /pʀɔvɑ̃s/ NF Provence

provenir /pʀɔv(ə)niʀ/ ▸ conjug 22 ◂ **provenir de** VT INDIR (= *venir de*) [+ *pays*] to come from, to be from; (= *résulter de*) [+ *cause*] to be due to, to be the result of ◆ **son genre de vie provient de son éducation** his life style is the result of his upbringing ◆ **mot qui provient d'une racine grecque** word which comes *ou* derives from a Greek root ◆ **cette fortune provient d'une lointaine cousine** this fortune comes from a distant cousin ◆ **vase provenant de Chine** vase (that comes) from China ◆ **je me demande d'où provient sa fortune** I wonder where he got his money from, I wonder how he came by so much money

proverbe /pʀɔvɛʀb/ NM proverb ◆ **comme dit le ~** as the saying goes ◆ **passer en ~** to become proverbial ◆ **le livre des Proverbes** (*Bible*) the (Book of) Proverbs

proverbial, e (mpl **-iaux**) /pʀɔvɛʀbjal, jo/ ADJ proverbial

proverbialement /pʀɔvɛʀbjalmɑ̃/ ADV proverbially

providence /pʀɔvidɑ̃s/ NF (*Rel*) providence; (= *sauveur*) guardian angel ◆ **cette bouteille d'eau a été notre ~** that bottle of water was our salvation *ou* was a lifesaver ◆ **vous êtes ma ~ !** you're my salvation!; → **état**

providentiel, -ielle /pʀɔvidɑ̃sjɛl/ ADJ providential ◆ **voici l'homme ~** here's the man we need

providentiellement /pʀɔvidɑ̃sjɛlmɑ̃/ ADV providentially

province /pʀɔvɛ̃s/ NF 1 (= *région*) province ◆ **Paris et la ~** Paris and the provinces ◆ **vivre en ~** to live in the provinces ◆ **ville de ~** provincial town ◆ **il arrive de sa ~** (*péj*) where has he been? ◆ **elle fait très ~** (*péj*) she's very provincial ◆ **les Provinces Unies** (*Hist*) the United Provinces 2 (*au Canada*) province ◆ **les Provinces maritimes** the Maritime Provinces, the Maritimes (*Can*) ◆ **habitant des Provinces maritimes** Maritimer ◆ **les Provinces des prairies** the Prairie Provinces (*Can*) ◆ **la Belle Province** Quebec

provincial, e (mpl **-iaux**) /pʀɔvɛ̃sjal, jo/ ADJ 1 (*gén, Rel*) provincial 2 (*au Canada*) **gouvernement ~** Provincial government NM,F provincial ◆ **les provinciaux** people who live in the provinces, provincials NM 1 (*Rel*) Provincial 2 (*au Canada*) **le ~** the Provincial Government

provincialiser (se) /pʀɔvɛ̃sjalize/ ▸ conjug 1 ◂ VPR [*ville*] to become more provincial

provincialisme /pʀɔvɛ̃sjalism/ NM provincialism

proviseur /pʀɔvizœʀ/ NM [*de lycée*] headmaster, principal, head (*Brit*) ◆ **~-adjoint** ≈ deputy *ou* assistant head (*Brit*), assistant *ou* vice-principal (*US*)

provision /pʀɔvizjɔ̃/ NF 1 (= *réserve*) [*de vivres, cartouches*] stock, supply; [*d'eau*] supply ◆ **faire (une) ~ de** [+ *nourriture, papier*] to stock up with, to lay *ou* get in a stock of; [+ *énergie, courage*] to build up a stock of ◆ **j'ai acheté toute une ~ de bonbons** I've bought a good supply *ou* stock of sweets ◆ **j'ai une bonne ~ de conserves** I have a good stock of canned food ◆ **avoir une bonne ~ de courage** to have considerable reserves of courage

2 (= *vivres*) **~s** provisions, food (*NonC*) ◆ **faire ses ~s, aller aux ~s*** to go shopping (for groceries *ou* food) ◆ **elle posa ses ~s sur la table** she put her groceries on the table ◆ **faire des ~s pour l'hiver** (*lit*) to stock up (with food *ou* provisions) for the winter; (*hum : financièrement*) to put something away for a rainy day ◆ **tu fais des ~s pour l'hiver ?** (*hum : à qn qui mange trop*) are you fattening yourself up for the winter? ◆ **~s de guerre** war supplies ◆ **~s de bouche** provisions ◆ **filet/panier à ~s** shopping bag/basket ◆ **armoire** *ou* **placard à ~s** food cupboard

3 (= *arrhes*) (*chez un avocat*) retainer, retaining fee; (*pour un achat*) deposit ◆ **y a-t-il ~ au compte ?** (*Banque*) are there sufficient funds in the account? ◆ **~s sur charges** (*immeuble d'habitation*) interim payment for maintenance *ou* service charges ◆ **~s pour créances douteuses** provision for bad debts ◆ **~s pour risques** contingency reserve; → **chèque**

> ⚠ **provision** se traduit par le mot anglais **provision** uniquement au pluriel, au sens de 'vivres'.

provisionnel, -elle /pʀɔvizjɔnɛl/ ADJ (*Jur*) provisional ◆ **acompte** *ou* **tiers ~** provisional payment (*towards one's income tax*); → **IMPÔTS**

provisionner /pʀɔvizjɔne/ ▸ conjug 1 ◂ VT (*Banque*) [+ *compte*] to pay money *ou* funds into ◆ **la banque a provisionné à 20% ses risques sur l'immobilier** the bank has set aside 20% of its capital in provision against *ou* to cover real estate losses

provisoire /pʀɔvizwaʀ/ ADJ [*mesure, solution*] temporary, provisional; [*bonheur, liaison, installation*] temporary; [*arrêt, jugement*] provisional; [*adjoint*] temporary, acting (*épith*); [*gouvernement*] provisional, interim (*épith*) ◆ **à titre ~** temporarily, provisionally; → **liberté** NM ◆ **c'est du ~** it's a temporary *ou* provisional arrangement

provisoirement /pʀɔvizwaʀmɑ̃/ ADV (= *momentanément*) temporarily; (= *pour l'instant*) for the time being

provitamine /pʀovitamin/ NF provitamin

provoc* /pʀɔvɔk/ NF abrév de **provocation**

provocant, e /pʀɔvɔkɑ̃, ɑ̃t/ ADJ provocative

provocateur, -trice /pʀɔvɔkatœʀ, tʀis/ ADJ provocative; → **agent** NM agitator

provocation /pʀɔvɔkasjɔ̃/ NF 1 (= *défi*) provocation ◆ **ils ont accusé les manifestants de faire de la ~** they accused the demonstrators of being provocative *ou* of trying to provoke trouble ◆ **il l'a fait par pure ~** he did it just to be provocative *ou* to get a reaction ◆ **leur façon de s'habiller, c'est de la ~** (*gén*) they're out to shock people by the way they dress; (*pour exciter*) they dress to be provocative ◆ **il a multiplié les ~s à l'égard des autorités** he has increasingly tried to provoke the authorities ◆ **~ en duel** challenge to a duel 2 (= *incitation*) **~ à (faire) qch** incitement to (do) sth ◆ **~ à la haine raciale/au crime** incitement to racial hatred/to commit a crime ◆ **~ au suicide** ≈ assisted suicide

provoquer /pʀɔvɔke/ GRAMMAIRE ACTIVE 44.2 ▸ conjug 1 ◂ VT 1 (= *défier*) to provoke ◆ **elle aime ~ les hommes** she likes to provoke men ◆ **~ qn du regard** to give sb a defiant look; (*pour exciter*) to give sb a provocative look ◆ **les deux adversaires s'étaient provoqués** the two opponents had provoked each other ◆ **~ qn en duel** to challenge sb to a duel

2 (= *causer*) [+ *accident, incendie, explosion, dégâts*] to cause; [+ *réaction, changement d'attitude*] to provoke, to prompt, to produce; [+ *courant d'air*] to create, to cause; [+ *crise, révolte*] to cause, to bring about, to provoke; [+ *commentaires*] to give rise to, to provoke, to prompt; [+ *colère*] to arouse, to spark off; [+ *curiosité*] to arouse, to excite; [+ *gaieté*] to cause, to provoke; [+ *aveux, explications*] to prompt; [+ *accouchement*] to induce ◆ **l'accident a provoqué la mort de six personnes** six people were killed in the accident ◆ **médicament qui provoque le sommeil** sleep-inducing drug ◆ **le malade est sous sommeil provoqué** the patient is in an induced sleep ◆ **l'élévation de température a provoqué cette réaction** (*Chim*) the rise in temperature brought about *ou* triggered off *ou* started up this reaction ◆ **les émeutes ont provoqué la chute du régime** rioting brought about *ou* led to the fall of the regime ◆ **~ des élections anticipées** to force an early election

3 (= *inciter*) **~ qn à** to incite sb to

proxénète /pʀɔksenɛt/ NMF procurer

proxénétisme /pʀɔksenetism/ NM procuring ◆ **il a été condamné pour ~** he was convicted of living off immoral earnings

proximité /pʀɔksimite/ NF 1 (*dans l'espace*) proximity, nearness, closeness ◆ **à cause de la ~ de l'aéroport** because the airport is so close, because of the proximity of the airport

◆ **à proximité** nearby, close by

◆ **à proximité de** near (to), close to, in the vicinity of

◆ **de proximité** ◆ **commerce de ~** local shop (*Brit*) *ou* store (*US*), neighborhood store (*US*) ◆ **emploi de ~** *job created at local community level, typically involving childminding, domestic work, caring for old people etc* ◆ **la police de ~** community policing ◆ **il faut développer les services de ~** we need to develop local community-based services

2 (*dans le temps*) closeness ◆ **c'est lié à la ~ de l'élection** it's connected to the fact that the elections are so close

pruche /pʀyʃ/ NF (*Can*) hemlock spruce

prude /pʀyd/ ADJ prudish NF prude ◆ **faire la ~, jouer les ~s** to behave prudishly

prudemment /pʀydamɑ̃/ ADV [*conduire*] carefully; [*avancer, répondre*] cautiously ◆ **garder ~ le silence** to keep a cautious silence

prudence /pʀydɑ̃s/ NF 1 (= *circonspection*) care, caution, prudence; (= *réserve*) caution ◆ **~ ! ça glisse** careful! it's slippery ◆ **faire preuve de ~** to be cautious *ou* careful ◆ **il a manqué de ~** he wasn't cautious *ou* careful enough ◆ **par (mesure de) ~** as a precaution ◆ **avec la plus grande ~** with the greatest caution, extremely carefully *ou* cautiously ◆ **il faudra lui annoncer la nouvelle avec beaucoup de ~** the news must be broken to him very carefully ◆ **~ est mère de sûreté** (*Prov*) discretion is the better part of valour (*Prov*) 2 (= *sagesse*) wisdom ◆ **il a eu la ~ de partir** he had the good sense to leave

prudent, e /pʀydɑ̃, ɑ̃t/ GRAMMAIRE ACTIVE 29.2 ADJ 1 (= *circonspect*) careful, cautious, prudent; (= *réservé*) cautious ◆ **soyez ~ !** (*gén*) be careful!, take care!; (*sur la route*) drive carefully! ◆ **il s'est montré très ~ au sujet du résultat** he was very cautious *ou* cagey about the result ◆ **c'est un ~** he's a careful *ou* cautious man ◆ **avancer à pas ~s** to move forward cautiously *ou* with cautious steps ◆ **soyez plus ~ à l'avenir** be more careful in future ◆ **il n'est pas très ~ en voiture** he's not a careful driver

2 (= sage) wise, sensible ◆ **il est ~ de faire** it is wise *ou* advisable to do ◆ **il serait ~ de vous munir d'un parapluie** it would be wise *ou* sensible to take an umbrella, you would be well-advised to take an umbrella ◆ **ce n'est pas ~** it's not advisable, it's not a good idea ◆ **ce n'est pas ~ de boire avant de conduire** it's not sensible *ou* wise *ou* advisable to drink before driving ◆ **c'est plus ~** it's wiser *ou* safer *ou* more sensible ◆ **il jugea plus ~ de se taire** he thought it wiser *ou* more sensible to keep quiet

pruderie /pʀydʀi/ NF (*littér*) prudishness (*NonC*), prudery

prud'homal, e (mpl **-aux**) /pʀydɔmal, o/ ADJ of an industrial tribunal (*Brit*) *ou* labor relations board (*US*)

prud'homie /pʀydɔmi/ NF jurisdiction of an industrial tribunal (*Brit*) *ou* labor relations board (*US*); → **prud'homme**

prud'homme /pʀydɔm/ NM ≈ member of an industrial tribunal (*Brit*) *ou* labor relations board (*US*) ◆ **conseil des ~s, les ~s** ≈ industrial tribunal (*Brit*), labor relations board (*US*) (*with wide administrative and advisory powers*) ◆ **aller aux** *ou* **devant les ~s** ≈ to go before an industrial tribunal (*Brit*) *ou* the labor relations board (*US*)

prudhommerie /pʀydɔmʀi/ NF sententiousness, pomposity

prudhommesque /pʀydɔmɛsk/ ADJ sententious, pompous

prune /pʀyn/ NF 1 (= *fruit*) plum; (= *alcool*) plum brandy ◆ **pour des ~s** * for nothing ◆ **des ~s !** * not likely! *, not on your life! *, no way! * 2 (* = *contravention*) ticket (*for speeding, illegal parking etc*) ◆ **il m'a filé une ~** he gave me a ticket, he booked me (*Brit*) 3 († * = *coup*) clout * ◆ **filer une ~ à qn** * to give sb a clout *, to clout * sb ADJ INV plum-coloured (*Brit*) *ou* -colored (*US*)

> ⚠ **prune** ne se traduit pas par le mot anglais **prune**, qui a le sens de 'pruneau'.

pruneau (pl **pruneaux**) /pʀyno/ NM 1 (= *fruit sec*) prune; (*Helv* = *quetsche*) kind of dark-red plum 2 (* = *balle*) slug *

prunelle /pʀynɛl/ NF 1 (= *fruit*) sloe; (= *eau-de-vie*) sloe gin 2 (= *pupille*) pupil; (= *œil*) eye ◆ **il y tient comme à la ~ de ses yeux** (*objet*) he treasures *ou* cherishes it; (*personne*) she (*ou* he) is the apple of his eye, she (*ou* he) is very precious to him ◆ **il/elle jouait de la ~** * he/she was giving her/him the eye *

prunellier /pʀynəlje/ NM sloe, blackthorn

prunier /pʀynje/ NM plum tree; → **secouer**

prunus /pʀynys/ NM prunus, Japanese flowering cherry

prurigineux, -euse /pʀyʀiʒinø, øz/ ADJ pruriginous

prurigo /pʀyʀigo/ NM prurigo

prurit /pʀyʀit/ NM (*Méd*) pruritus ◆ **leur ~ réformateur/égalitaire** (*hum*) their zeal for reform/egalitarianism ◆ **le ~ de l'écriture le démange** he's got the writing bug

Prusse /pʀys/ NF Prussia; → **bleu**

prussien, -ienne /pʀysjɛ̃, jɛn/ ADJ Prussian NM,F **Prussien(ne)** Prussian

prytanée /pʀitane/ NM (*Antiq*) prytaneum ◆ **~ militaire** military academy

PS /peɛs/ NM (abrév de **parti socialiste**) *French political party*

P.-S., PS /peɛs/ NM (abrév de **post-scriptum**) ps

psallette /psalɛt/ NF choir

psalmiste /psalmist/ NM psalmist

psalmodie /psalmɔdi/ NF (*Rel*) psalmody, chant; (*littér*) drone (*NonC*)

psalmodier /psalmɔdje/ ► conjug 7 ◄ VT (*Rel*) to chant; (*littér*) to drone out VI to chant; (*littér*) to drone (on *ou* away)

psaume /psom/ NM psalm ◆ **le livre des Psaumes** (*Bible*) the Book of Psalms

psautier /psotje/ NM psalter

pschitt /pʃit/ EXCL hiss NM (* = *atomiseur*) spray ◆ **vaporisez deux coups de ~ sur un chiffon** spray twice onto a cloth

pseudo * /psødo/ NM abrév de **pseudonyme**

pseudo- /psødo/ PRÉF (*gén*) pseudo- ◆ **~historien** pseudo-historian ◆ **~science/-réalité** pseudo-science/-reality ◆ **les ~révélations parues dans leur journal** the pseudo-revelations *ou* so-called revelations published in their newspaper

pseudonyme /psødɔnim/ NM (*gén*) assumed *ou* fictitious name; [*d'écrivain*] pen name, pseudonym; [*de comédien*] stage name; (*Jur, hum*) alias; (*Internet*) handle, nick

psitt /psit/ EXCL ps(s)t!

psittacisme /psitasism/ NM (= *répétition mécanique*) parrotry; (*Psych*) psittacism

psittacose /psitakoz/ NF psittacosis

psoriasis /psɔʀjazis/ NM psoriasis

psy * /psi/ ADJ INV abrév de **psychologique, psychique, psychosomatique** NMF (abrév de **psychiatre, psychologue, psychothérapeute, psychanalyste**) ◆ **il va chez son ~ toutes les semaines** he goes to see his analyst *ou* shrink * every week NF abrév de **psychiatrie, psychologie**

psychanalyse /psikanaliz/ NF [*de personne*] psychoanalysis, analysis; [*de texte*] psychoanalytical study ◆ **entreprendre/faire/suivre une ~** to start/do/undergo analysis

psychanalyser /psikanalize/ ► conjug 1 ◄ VT [+ *personne*] to psychoanalyze; [+ *texte*] to study from a psychoanalytical viewpoint ◆ **se faire ~** to have o.s. psychoanalyzed

psychanalyste /psikanalist/ NMF psychoanalyst, analyst

psychanalytique /psikanalitik/ ADJ psychoanalytic(al)

psyché /psiʃe/ NF 1 (*Psych*) psyche 2 (= *miroir*) cheval glass, swing mirror 3 (*Myth*) **Psyché** Psyche

psychédélique /psikedelik/ ADJ psychedelic

psychédélisme /psikedelism/ NM psychedelic state

psychiatre /psikjatʀ/ NMF psychiatrist

psychiatrie /psikjatʀi/ NF psychiatry

psychiatrique /psikjatʀik/ ADJ [*troubles*] psychiatric; [*hôpital*] psychiatric, mental (*épith*)

psychique /psiʃik/ ADJ psychological, psychic(al)

psychiquement /psiʃikmɑ̃/ ADV psychologically

psychisme /psiʃism/ NM psyche, mind

psycho * /psiko/ NF abrév de **psychologie**

psychodrame /psikodʀam/ NM (*Psych*) psychodrama; (= *drame*) drama

psychogène /psikɔʒɛn/ ADJ psychogenic

psychokinésie /psikokinezi/ NF psychokinesis

psycholinguistique /psikolɛ̃gɥistik/ ADJ psycholinguistic NF psycholinguistics (*sg*)

psychologie /psikɔlɔʒi/ NF psychology ◆ **la ~ de l'enfant/des foules/du comportement** child/crowd/behavioural psychology ◆ **il faut faire preuve de ~** you have to be perceptive about people, you have to have good insight into people ◆ **il manque complètement de ~** he's completely unperceptive about people, he's got absolutely no insight into people

psychologique /psikɔlɔʒik/ ADJ psychological ◆ **tu sais, mon vieux, c'est ~ !** it's psychological *ou* it's all in the mind, my friend!; → **moment**

psychologiquement /psikɔlɔʒikmɑ̃/ ADV psychologically

psychologue /psikɔlɔg/ ADJ (= *intuitif*) ◆ **il est/il n'est pas très ~** he's very/he's not very perceptive about people NMF psychologist ◆ **~ d'entreprise** industrial psychologist ◆ **~ scolaire** educational psychologist

psychométrie /psikɔmetʀi/ NF psychometry, psychometrics (*sg*)

psychométrique /psikɔmetʀik/ ADJ psychometric

psychomoteur, -trice /psikomɔtœʀ, tʀis/ ADJ psychomotor

psychopathe /psikɔpat/ NMF psychopath ◆ **tueur ~** psychopathic killer

psychopathie /psikɔpati/ NF psychopathy

psychopathologie /psikopatɔlɔʒi/ NF psychopathology

psychopédagogie /psikopedagɔʒi/ NF educational psychology

psychopédagogique /psikopedagɔʒik/ ADJ [*études, formation*] in educational psychology

psychophysiologie /psikofizjɔlɔʒi/ NF psychophysiology

psychophysiologique /psikofizjɔlɔʒik/ ADJ psychophysiological

psychose /psikoz/ NF (*Psych*) psychosis; (= *obsession*) obsessive fear ◆ **~ maniacodépressive** manic depressive psychosis ◆ **~ collective** mass hysteria, collective hysteria ◆ **~ de guerre** war psychosis *ou* hysteria

psychosensoriel, -ielle /psikosɑ̃sɔʀjɛl/ ADJ psychosensory

psychosocial, e (mpl **-iaux**) /psikososjal, jo/ ADJ psychosocial

psychosociologie /psikososjɔlɔʒi/ NF psychosociology

psychosomatique /psikosɔmatik/ ADJ psychosomatic NF psychosomatics (*sg*)

psychotechnicien, -ienne /psikoteknisjɛ̃, jɛn/ NM,F psychotechnician, psychotechnologist

psychotechnique /psikoteknik/ ADJ psychotechnical, psychotechnological NF psychotechnics (*sg*), psychotechnology

psychothérapeute /psikoteʀapøt/ NMF psychotherapist

psychothérapie /psikoteʀapi/ NF psychotherapy ◆ **~ de soutien** supportive therapy ◆ **entreprendre/faire/suivre une ~** to start/do/undergo (a course of) psychotherapy

psychothérapique /psikoteʀapik/ ADJ psychotherapeutic

psychotique /psikɔtik/ ADJ, NMF psychotic

Pte abrév de **porte**

ptérodactyle /pteʀɔdaktil/ NM pterodactyl

Ptolémée /ptɔleme/ NM Ptolemy

ptose /ptoz/ NF ptosis

P.T.T. /petete/ NFPL (abrév de **Postes, Télécommunications et Télédiffusion**) → **poste**[1]

ptyaline /ptjalin/ NF ptyalin

puant, e /pɥɑ̃, pɥɑ̃t/ ADJ 1 (*lit*) stinking, foul-smelling 2 (* : *péj*) [*personne, attitude*] arrogant ◆ **il est ~, c'est un type ~** he's an arrogant creep * ◆ **~ d'orgueil** bloated with pride

puanteur /pɥɑ̃tœʀ/ NF stink, stench

pub[1] /pœb/ NM (= *bar*) pub

pub[2] * /pyb/ NF (= *annonce*) ad *, advert * *(Brit)*; *(Ciné, TV)* commercial, ad *, advert * *(Brit)* ◆ **la ~** *(métier)* advertising ◆ **faire de la ~ pour qch** *(Comm)* to advertise sth; (= *inciter à acheter qch*) to plug sth *, to give sth a plug * ◆ **ça lui a fait de la ~** it was a plug * for him ◆ **coup de ~** publicity stunt ◆ **ses disques ne se vendent qu'à coups de ~** his records are selling only as a result of heavy advertising

pubère /pybɛʀ/ ADJ pubescent

puberté /pybɛʀte/ NF puberty

pubien, -ienne /pybjɛ̃, jɛn/ ADJ pubic ◆ **région pubienne** pubic region, pubes

pubis /pybis/ NM (= *os*) pubis; (= *bas-ventre*) pubes ◆ **os ~** pubic bone

publiable /pyblijabl/ ADJ publishable ◆ **ce n'est pas ~** it's not fit for publication

public, -ique /pyblik/ ADJ [1] (= *non privé*) *[intérêt, lieu, opinion, vie]* public; *[vente, réunion]* public, open to the public *(attrib)* ◆ **danger/ennemi/homme ~** public danger/enemy/figure ◆ **la nouvelle est maintenant publique** the news is now common *ou* public knowledge ◆ **la nouvelle a été rendue publique hier** the news was made public *ou* was released yesterday; → **domaine, droit**[3]**, notoriété**

[2] (= *de l'État*) *[services, secteur, finances]* public; *[école, instruction]* State *(épith)*, public *(US)*; → **charge, chose, dette** *etc*

NM [1] (= *population*) **le ~** the (general) public ◆ **"interdit au public"** "no admittance to the public"

[2] (= *audience, assistance*) audience ◆ **œuvre conçue pour un jeune ~** work written for a young audience ◆ **le ~ parisien est très exigeant** Paris audiences are very demanding ◆ **des huées s'élevèrent du ~** the audience started booing ◆ **cet écrivain s'adresse à un vaste ~** this author writes for a wide readership ◆ **cet acteur a son ~** this actor has his fans *ou* followers ◆ **cet ouvrage plaira à tous les ~s** this work will be appreciated by all kinds of readers ◆ **un ~ clairsemé assistait au match** the match was attended by very few spectators ◆ **le ~ est informé que ...** the public is advised that ... ◆ **en ~** in public ◆ **le grand ~** the general public ◆ **roman destiné au grand ~** novel written for the general reader *ou* public ◆ **appareils électroniques grand ~** consumer electronics ◆ **film grand ~** film with mass appeal ◆ **il lui faut toujours un ~** *(fig)* he always needs an audience ◆ **être bon/mauvais ~** to be easy/hard to please

[3] (= *secteur*) **le ~** the public sector

publicain /pyblikɛ̃/ NM *(Hist romaine)* publican, tax-gatherer

publication /pyblikasjɔ̃/ NF (= *action*) publication, publishing; (= *écrit publié*) publication ◆ **après sa ~ aux États-Unis** after being published *ou* after its publication in the United States ◆ **ce livre a été interdit de ~** this book has been banned ◆ **~ des bans (de mariage)** publication *ou* reading of the banns ◆ **~ assistée par ordinateur** desktop publishing

publiciste /pyblisist/ NMF [1] (* = *publicitaire*) advertising executive [2] *(Jur)* public law specialist

publicitaire /pyblisitɛʀ/ ADJ *[budget, affiche, agence, campagne]* advertising *(épith)*; *[film]* promotional ◆ **annonce ~** advertisement ◆ **échantillon ~** give-away, free sample ◆ **grande vente ~** big promotional sale ◆ **matériel ~** publicity material ◆ **rédacteur ~** copywriter NMF advertising executive

publicité /pyblisite/ NF [1] *(Comm = méthode, profession)* advertising ◆ **il travaille dans la ~** he's in advertising, he's an adman * ◆ **faire de la ~ pour qch** *(Comm)* to advertise sth; (= *inciter à acheter qch*) to plug sth * ◆ **il sait bien faire sa propre ~** he's good at selling himself ◆ **cette marque fait beaucoup de ~** this make does a lot of advertising ◆ **son livre a été lancé à grand renfort de ~** his book was launched amid a blaze of publicity *ou* amid much media hype * ◆ **coup de ~** publicity stunt ◆ **~ par affichage** poster advertising ◆ **~ collective/comparative** collective/comparative advertising ◆ **~ directe** direct advertising ◆ **~ de rappel** reminder advertising ◆ **~ mensongère** misleading advertising ◆ **~ sur les lieux de vente** point-of-sale advertising ◆ **matériel de ~** *(Comm)* publicity material ◆ **dépenses de ~** advertising costs ◆ **campagne de ~** publicity *ou* advertising campaign; → **agence** *etc*

[2] (= *annonce*) advertisement, ad *, advert * *(Brit)*; *(Ciné, TV)* commercial, advertisement ◆ **~ rédactionnelle** special advertising feature, advertorial *(US)*

[3] (= *révélations*) publicity ◆ **on a fait trop de ~ autour de cette affaire** this affair has had *ou* has been given too much publicity

[4] *(Jur)* **la ~ des débats** the public nature of the proceedings

publier /pyblije/ ► conjug 7 ◄ VT [1] *[+ livre] [auteur]* to publish; *[éditeur]* to publish, to bring out [2] *[+ bans, décret]* to publish; *(littér)* *[+ nouvelle]* to publish (abroad) *(littér)*, to make public ◆ **ça vient d'être publié** it's just out, it has just come out *ou* been published ◆ **~ un communiqué** to release a statement *(au sujet de* about)

publiphone ® /pyblifɔn/ NM public telephone, payphone ◆ **~ à carte** card phone

publipostage /pyblipɔstaʒ/ NM mailshot, mass mailing

publiquement /pyblikmɑ̃/ ADV publicly ◆ **le ministre a exprimé ~ son désaccord** the minister went on the record to express his disagreement, the minister publicly expressed his disagreement ◆ **le président a dû intervenir ~** the president had to issue a public statement

publireportage /pybliʀ(ə)pɔʀtaʒ/ NM special advertising feature, advertorial *(US)*

puce /pys/ NF [1] (= *insecte*) flea ◆ **~ de mer** *ou* **de sable** sand flea ◆ **~ d'eau** water flea ◆ **ça m'a mis la ~ à l'oreille** that started *ou* got me thinking ◆ **le marché aux ~s, les ~s** the flea market ◆ **oui, ma ~** * yes, pet * ◆ **c'est une petite ~** *(fig)* she's a tiny little thing ◆ **être agité** *ou* **excité comme une ~** to be all excited; → **sac**[1]**, secouer** [2] ◆ **jeu de ~s** tiddlywinks ◆ **jouer aux ~s** to play tiddlywinks [3] *(Ordin)* (silicon) chip ◆ **~ électronique** microchip ◆ **~ mémoire** memory chip ADJ INV (= *couleur*) puce

puceau * (pl **puceaux**) /pyso/ ADJ M ◆ **être ~** to be a virgin NM virgin

pucelage * /pys(ə)laʒ/ NM virginity

pucelle †† * /pysɛl/ *(hum)* ADJ F ◆ **être ~** to be a virgin ◆ **elle n'est plus ~** she has lost her virginity, she's not a virgin NF virgin, maid(en) *(littér)* ◆ **la Pucelle d'Orléans** *(Hist)* the Maid of Orleans *(Joan of Arc)*

puceron /pys(ə)ʀɔ̃/ NM aphid, greenfly ◆ **~ cendré** blackfly

pucier ‡ /pysje/ NM bed

pudding /pudiŋ/ NM *close-textured fruit sponge*

puddlage /pydlaʒ/ NM puddling

pudeur /pydœʀ/ NF [1] *(concernant le corps)* modesty ◆ **elle a beaucoup de ~** she has a keen sense of modesty ◆ **elle est sans ~, elle n'a aucune ~** she has no modesty, she's quite shameless ◆ **expliquer qch sans fausse ~** to explain sth without undue prudery *ou* quite openly ◆ **il parle de sa maladie sans fausse ~** he talks about his illness quite openly; → **attentat, outrage** [2] (= *délicatesse*) sense of propriety *ou* decency ◆ **agir sans ~** to act with no regard to propriety ◆ **il aurait pu avoir la ~ de ne pas en parler** he could have had the decency not to talk about it

pudibond, e /pydibɔ̃, ɔ̃d/ ADJ (excessively) prudish, prim and proper

pudibonderie /pydibɔ̃dʀi/ NF (excessive) prudishness, (excessive) primness

pudicité /pydisite/ NF *(littér)* (= *chasteté*) modesty; (= *discrétion*) discretion

pudique /pydik/ ADJ [1] (= *chaste*) *[personne, geste]* modest [2] (= *discret*) *[allusion]* discreet ◆ **un terme ~ pour désigner ...** a nice way of saying ..., a euphemism for ...

pudiquement /pydikmɑ̃/ ADV [1] (= *chastement*) modestly [2] (= *avec tact*) discreetly ◆ **ils détournaient les yeux ~** they looked away discreetly *ou* out of a sense of decency [3] (= *par euphémisme*) discreetly ◆ **cela désigne ~ ...** it's a nice way of saying ..., it's a euphemism for ...

puer /pɥe/ ► conjug 1 ◄ VI to stink ◆ **il pue des pieds** his feet stink, he has smelly feet ◆ **il pue de la gueule** his breath stinks ◆ **ça pue !** it stinks! VT to stink *ou* reek of ◆ **ça pue l'argent** it reeks *ou* stinks of money

puériculteur, -trice /pɥeʀikyltœʀ, tʀis/ NM,F *(dans un hôpital)* paediatric *(Brit)* *ou* pediatric *(US)* nurse; *(dans une crèche)* nursery nurse

puériculture /pɥeʀikyltyʀ/ NF *(gén)* infant care; *(dans une crèche)* nursery nursing; *(en pédiatrie)* paediatric *(Brit)* *ou* pediatric *(US)* nursing ◆ **donner des cours de ~ aux mamans** to give courses on infant care to mothers

puéril, e /pɥeʀil/ ADJ puerile, childish

puérilement /pɥeʀilmɑ̃/ ADV childishly

puérilité /pɥeʀilite/ NF (= *caractère*) puerility, childishness; (= *acte*) childish behaviour *(Brit)* *ou* behavior *(US)* *(NonC)*

puerpéral, e (mpl **-aux**) /pɥɛʀpeʀal, o/ ADJ puerperal

pugilat /pyʒila/ NM (fist) fight

pugiliste /pyʒilist/ NM *(littér)* pugilist *(littér)*

pugilistique /pyʒilistik/ ADJ *(littér)* pugilistic *(littér, frm)*

pugnace /pygnas/ ADJ pugnacious

pugnacité /pygnasite/ NF *(littér)* pugnacity

puîné, e † /pɥine/ ADJ (= *de deux*) younger; (= *de plusieurs*) youngest NM,F (*de deux*) younger brother (*ou* sister); (*de plusieurs*) youngest brother (*ou* sister)

puis /pɥi/ ADV (= *ensuite*) then; (*dans une énumération*) then, next ◆ **et ~** (= *en outre*) and besides ◆ **et ~ ensuite** *ou* **après** and then, and after that ◆ **et ~ c'est tout** and that's all *ou* that's it *ou* that's all there is to it ◆ **il est parti, et ~ voilà !** off he went, and that was that! ◆ **et ~ après tout** and after all ◆ **et ~ après ?** (= *ensuite*) and what next?, and then (what)?; (= *et alors ?*) so what? *, what of it? ◆ **et ~ quoi ?** (= *quoi d'autre*) well, what?, and then what?; (= *et alors ?*) so what? *, what of it? ◆ **et ~ quoi encore ?** (= *tu exagères*) whatever next?

puisage /pɥizaʒ/ NM drawing (of water)

puisard /pɥizaʀ/ NM *(gén)* cesspool, sink; *(dans un bateau)* well

puisatier /pɥizatje/ NM well-digger

puiser /pɥize/ ► conjug 1 ◄ VT *[+ eau]* to draw *(dans* from); *[+ exemple, renseignement, inspiration]* to draw, to take *(dans* from); ◆ **les deux auteurs ont puisé aux mêmes sources** the two authors drew on the same sources ◆ **~ dans son sac/ses économies** to dip into one's bag/one's savings ◆ **j'ai dû ~ dans mes réserves pour finir la course** I had to draw on my reserves to finish the race

puisque /pɥisk(ə)/ GRAMMAIRE ACTIVE 44.1 CONJ [1] (= *du moment que*) since, seeing that ◆ **ces ani-**

maux sont donc des mammifères, puisqu'ils allaitent leurs petits these animals are therefore mammals, seeing that *ou* since they suckle their young ◆ **ça doit être vrai, puisqu'il le dit** it must be true since he says so
2 *(= comme)* as, since, seeing that ◆ ~ **vous êtes là, venez m'aider** as *ou* since *ou* seeing that you're here come and help me ◆ **ces escrocs, puisqu'il faut les appeler ainsi ...** these crooks – as *ou* since one must call them that ... ◆ **son échec, ~ échec il y a ...** his failure, given that he has indeed failed ..., his failure, seeing as that is what it amounts to ... ◆ ~ **c'est comme ça, je ne viendrai plus !** if that's how it is, I won't come anymore!
3 *(valeur intensive)* ◆ **je te le dis !** I'm telling you (so)! ◆ ~ **je te dis que c'est vrai !** I'm telling you it's true!

puissamment /pɥisamɑ̃/ **ADV** *(= fortement)* powerfully; *(= beaucoup)* greatly ◆ ~ **raisonné !** *(iro)* what brilliant reasoning! *(iro)*

puissance /pɥisɑ̃s/ **NF** 1 *(= force) [d'armée, muscle, impulsion]* power, strength; *[de vent]* strength, force
2 *(Élec, Phys)* power; *[de microscope]* (magnifying) power; *[de moteur, voiture, haut-parleur]* power ◆ ~ **en watts** wattage ◆ ~ **de sortie** *[de chaîne hi-fi]* output ◆ ~ **de calcul/de traitement** *(Ordin)* computing/processing power *ou* capacity ◆ **modifier la ~ de l'éclairage** to adjust the lighting ◆ ~ **effective d'un moteur** engine power output ◆ **bombe de forte ~** powerful *ou* high-powered bomb ◆ **bombe de faible ~** low-power bomb ◆ **la ~ de destruction de ce missile** this missile's destructive potential
3 *(= capacité)* power ◆ **la ~ d'évocation de la musique** the evocative power of music ◆ **une grande ~ de séduction/suggestion** great seductive/suggestive power(s), great powers of seduction/suggestion ◆ **la ~ d'attraction de la capitale** the pull of the capital ◆ **grâce à la ~ de sa volonté** thanks to his willpower *ou* his strength of will ◆ **avoir une grande ~ de travail** to have a great capacity for work ◆ **avoir une grande ~ d'imagination** to have a very powerful imagination *ou* great powers of imagination
4 *(= pouvoir) [de classe sociale, pays, argent]* power ◆ **l'or/le pétrole est une ~** gold/oil confers power ◆ **les ~s qui agissent sur le monde** the powers that influence the world
◆ **en puissance** *[délinquant, dictateur]* potential ◆ **l'homme est en ~ dans l'enfant** the man is latent in the child ◆ **exister en ~** to have a potential existence ◆ **c'est là en ~** it is potentially present ◆ **monter en ~** *[idée, théorie]* to gain ground ◆ **montée en ~** *[de pays, mouvement, personne]* increase in power; *[de secteur]* increase in importance
5 *(Pol)* power ◆ **grande ~** major *ou* great power, superpower ◆ **la première ~ économique/nucléaire mondiale** the world's leading economic/nuclear power
6 *(Math)* power ◆ **élever un nombre à la ~ 10** to raise a number to the power of 10 ◆ **10 ~ 4** 10 to the power of 4, 10 to the 4th
COMP **puissance administrative** *[de moteur]* engine rating
les puissances d'argent the forces of money
puissance de feu *(Mil)* fire power
puissance fiscale ⇒ **puissance administrative**
puissance au frein *[de véhicule]* brake horsepower; *[de moteur]* power output
puissance maritale *(Jur)* marital rights
les puissances occultes unseen *ou* hidden powers
puissance paternelle *(Jur)* parental rights *ou* authority ◆ **exercer/être déchu de sa ~ paternelle** to exercise/have lost one's parental rights
la puissance publique the public authorities
les puissances des ténèbres the powers of darkness

puissant, e /pɥisɑ̃, ɑ̃t/ **ADJ** powerful; *[drogue, remède]* potent, powerful ◆ **c'est ~ !*** *(= formidable)* it's great!* **NM** ◆ **les ~s** the mighty *ou* powerful

puits /pɥi/ **NM** *[d'eau, pétrole]* well; *(Min)* shaft; *(Constr)* well, shaft ◆ **c'est un ~ sans fond** *(fig)* it's a bottomless pit
COMP **puits d'aérage** *ou* **d'aération** ventilation shaft
puits d'amour ≃ cream puff
puits artésien artesian well
puits à ciel ouvert *(Min)* opencast mine
puits d'érudition ⇒ **puits de science**
puits d'extraction winding shaft
puits de jour *ou* **de lumière** *(Constr)* light shaft
puits de mine mine shaft
puits perdu cesspool, sink
puits de pétrole oil well
puits de science fount of knowledge

pull /pyl/ **NM** pullover, sweater, jumper *(Brit)* ◆ ~ **chaussette** skinnyrib sweater

pullman /pulman/ **NM** Pullman (car)

pull-over (pl **pull-overs**) /pylɔvɛʀ/ **NM** pullover, sweater, jumper *(Brit)*

pullulation /pylylasjɔ̃/ **NF**, **pullulement** /pylylmɑ̃/ **NM** *(= action)* proliferation; *(= profusion) [d'insectes]* multitude; *[d'insectes volants]* swarm, multitude

pulluler /pylyle/ ▸ conjug 1 ◂ **VI** *(= se reproduire)* to proliferate, to multiply, to pullulate *(frm)*; *(= grouiller)* to swarm, to pullulate *(frm)*; *[erreurs, contrefaçons]* to abound, to pullulate *(frm)* ◆ **la ville pullule de touristes** the town is swarming with tourists ◆ **la rivière pullule de truites** the river is teeming with trout

pulmonaire /pylmɔnɛʀ/ **ADJ** *[maladie]* pulmonary, lung *(épith)*; *[artère]* pulmonary ◆ **congestion ~** congestion of the lungs

pulpe /pylp/ **NF** *[de fruit, dent, bois]* pulp; *[de doigt]* pad ◆ **boisson/yaourt à la ~ de fruits** real fruit drink/yoghurt

pulpeux, -euse /pylpø, øz/ **ADJ** *[fruit]* pulpy; *[lèvres]* full, fleshy; *[femme]* curvaceous

pulsar /pylsaʀ/ **NM** pulsar

pulsation /pylsasjɔ̃/ **NF** *(Méd) [de cœur, pouls]* beating *(NonC)*, beat, pulsation *(SPÉC)*; *(Phys)* pulsation; *(Élec)* pulsatance ◆ **~s (du cœur)** *(= rythme cardiaque)* heartbeat; *(= battements)* heartbeats

pulsé /pylse/ **ADJ M** ◆ **chauffage à air ~** forced air heating

pulsion /pylsjɔ̃/ **NF** *(Psych)* drive, urge ◆ **la ~ sexuelle** the sex drive ◆ **~s sexuelles** sexual urges ◆ ~ **de mort** death wish ◆ ~ **meurtrière/suicidaire** murderous/suicidal impulse ◆ ~ **de vie** life instinct

pulsionnel, -elle /pylsjɔnɛl/ **ADJ** *[comportement]* instinctual ◆ **réaction pulsionnelle** impulsive reaction

pulvérisable /pylveʀizabl/ **ADJ** *[+ liquide, médicament]* in spray form

pulvérisateur /pylveʀizatœʀ/ **NM** *(à parfum)* spray, atomizer; *(à peinture)* spray; *(pour médicament)* spray, vaporizer ◆ ~ **d'insecticide** *(Agr)* (crop) duster

pulvérisation /pylveʀizasjɔ̃/ **NF** 1 *(= broyage)* pulverizing, pulverization 2 *(= vaporisation)* spraying ◆ **"trois pulvérisations dans chaque narine"** *(Méd)* "spray three times into each nostril" ◆ **le médecin a ordonné des ~s (nasales)** the doctor prescribed a nasal spray 3 *(= anéantissement) [d'adversaire]* pulverizing, demolishing; * *[de record]* smashing*, shattering*; *[d'argument]* demolition, demolishing

pulvériser /pylveʀize/ ▸ conjug 1 ◂ **VT** 1 *(= broyer)* to pulverize, to reduce to powder 2 *[+ liquide, insecticide]* to spray ◆ ~ **des insecticides sur un champ** to spray a field with insecticides 3 *(= anéantir) [+ adversaire]* to pulverize, to demolish; * *[+ record]* to smash*, to shatter*; *[+ argument]* to demolish, to pull to pieces ◆ **bâtiment pulvérisé par l'explosion** building reduced to rubble by the explosion

pulvériseur /pylveʀizœʀ/ **NM** disc harrow

pulvérulence /pylveʀylɑ̃s/ **NF** pulverulence

pulvérulent, e /pylveʀylɑ̃, ɑ̃t/ **ADJ** pulverulent

puma /pyma/ **NM** puma, cougar, mountain lion

punaise /pynɛz/ **NF** 1 *(= insecte)* bug ◆ ~ **d'eau** water stick insect ◆ **c'est une vraie ~** *(péj)* he's a real mischief-maker ◆ ~ **!*** well!, blimey!* *(Brit)*, gee!* *(US)* ◆ ~ **de sacristie*** *(péj)* churchy woman 2 *(= clou)* drawing pin *(Brit)*, thumbtack *(US)*

punaiser /pyneze/ ▸ conjug 1 ◂ **VT** to pin up *(ou* down *ou* on etc) ◆ ~ **une affiche au mur** to pin up a poster, to pin a poster up on the wall

punch[1] /pɔ̃ʃ/ **NM** *(= boisson)* punch

punch[2] /pœnʃ/ **NM** 1 *(= énergie)* punch ◆ **avoir du ~** *[personne]* to have lots of drive, to have a lot of get up and go; *[slogan]* to be catchy* *ou* punchy*; *[cheveux]* to have lots of bounce ◆ **pour donner du ~ à vos cheveux** to give new life to your hair ◆ **manquer de ~** *[personne]* to lack dynamism *ou* drive; *[entreprise, économie]* to lack dynamism ◆ **cette mise en scène manque de ~** the production isn't punchy* enough 2 *(Boxe)* punching ability ◆ **avoir du ~** to pack *ou* have a good punch

puncheur /pœnʃœʀ/ **NM** good puncher, hard hitter

punching-ball (pl **punching-balls**) /pœnʃiŋbol/ **NM** punching bag, punchbag *(Brit)*, punchball ◆ **je lui sers de ~** he uses me as a punching bag

punique /pynik/ **ADJ** Punic

punir /pyniʀ/ ▸ conjug 2 ◂ **VT** 1 *[+ criminel, enfant]* to punish *(pour* for); ◆ **être puni de prison/de mort** to be sentenced to prison/to death
2 *(= faire souffrir)* to punish ◆ **il a été puni de son imprudence** he was punished for his recklessness, he suffered for his recklessness ◆ **tu as été malade, ça te punira de ta gourmandise** you've been ill – that'll teach you not to be greedy ◆ **il est orgueilleux, et l'en voilà bien puni** he's paying the penalty for *ou* being made to suffer for his pride ◆ **il est puni par où il a péché** he has got his (just) deserts, he's paying for his sins
3 *(= sanctionner) [+ faute, infraction, crime]* to punish ◆ **tout abus sera puni (de prison)** all abuses are punishable *ou* will be punished (by prison) ◆ **ce crime est puni par la loi/puni de mort** this crime is punishable by law/punishable by death

punissable /pynisabl/ **ADJ** punishable *(de* by)

punitif, -ive /pynitif, iv/ **ADJ** ◆ **action punitive** punitive action *(NonC)* ◆ **expédition punitive** *[d'armée, rebelles]* punitive expedition *ou* raid; *[de criminels, gang]* revenge killing

punition /pynisjɔ̃/ **NF** punishment *(de qch* for sth); ◆ **avoir une ~** *(Scol)* to be given a punishment ◆ ~ **corporelle** corporal punishment *(NonC)* ◆ **en ~ de ses fautes** as a punishment for his mistakes ◆ **pour ta ~** as a punishment

punk /pœk/ **ADJ INV, NMF** punk

pupille[1] /pypij/ **NF** *(Anat)* pupil

pupille² /pypij/ NMF (= *enfant*) ward ◆ ~ **de l'État** child in (local authority) care ◆ ~ **de la Nation** war orphan

pupitre /pypitʀ/ NM (*Scol*) desk; (*Rel*) lectern; [*de musicien*] music stand; [*de piano*] music rest; [*de chef d'orchestre*] rostrum; (*Ordin*) console ◆ **au ~, Henri Dupont** (*Mus*) at the rostrum – Henri Dupont, conducting – Henri Dupont ◆ **chef de** ~ (*Mus*) head of section

pupitreur, -euse /pypitʀœʀ, øz/ NM,F (*Ordin*) system operator

pur, e /pyʀ/ ADJ [1] (= *sans mélange*) [*alcool, eau, race, métal*] pure; [*vin*] undiluted; [*whisky, gin*] neat, straight; [*ciel*] clear; [*voyelle*] pure; [*diamant*] flawless ◆ ~ **fruit** [*confiture*] real fruit (*épith*) ◆ ~ **beurre** [*sablé*] all butter ◆ ~ **porc** [*saucisson*] pure pork ◆ **~e laine** pure wool ◆ **c'est un communiste/capitaliste ~ jus** *ou* **sucre** he's a dyed-in-the-wool communist/capitalist ◆ **c'est un Parisien ~ jus** *ou* **sucre** he's a Parisian through and through *ou* to the core ◆ **c'est du Woody Allen ~ jus** it's stock Woody Allen ◆ **un ~ produit de la bourgeoisie** a pure product of the middle class ◆ **un Australien de ~e souche** an Australian born and bred ◆ **boire son vin** ~ to drink one's wine without water *ou* undiluted ◆ **à l'état** ~ (*Chim*) in the pure state ◆ **l'air ~ de la campagne** the pure *ou* fresh country air; → **esprit, pur-sang**

[2] (= *théorique*) [*science, mathématiques*] pure

[3] (= *innocent*) [*âme, cœur, intentions, pensées*] pure; [*personne*] pure, pure-hearted; [*conscience*] clear; [*regard*] frank

[4] (= *parfait*) [*style*] pure; (= *limpide*) [*voix*] pure, clear ◆ **un visage d'un ovale très** ~ a perfectly oval face ◆ **elle parle un français très** ~ she speaks very pure French

[5] (= *exact, strict*) pure, sheer ◆ **c'est de la folie ~e** it's pure *ou* sheer *ou* utter madness ◆ **c'est de la poésie/de l'imagination toute ~e** it's pure *ou* sheer poetry/imagination ◆ **c'est de l'insubordination ~e et simple** it's insubordination pure and simple ◆ **c'était du racisme ~ et simple** *ou* **à l'état** ~ it was straight *ou* plain racism ◆ **ils réclament la suppression ~e et simple de la loi** they're quite simply asking for the law to be withdrawn ◆ **il ne s'agit pas d'une ~e et simple déclaration publique** it's not just *ou* it's not purely and simply a public statement ◆ **cela relève de la ~e fiction** it's pure fiction ◆ **il a dit cela par ~e méchanceté** he said that out of pure spite ◆ **œuvre de ~e imagination** work of pure imagination ◆ **c'est une question de ~e forme** it's merely *ou* purely a question of form ◆ **c'est par ~ hasard que je l'ai vu** I saw it by sheer chance *ou* purely by chance ◆ **c'est la ~e vérité** it's the plain *ou* simple (unadulterated) truth ◆ **en ~e perte** for absolutely nothing, fruitlessly ◆ **il a travaillé en ~e perte** absolutely nothing came of his work, his work was fruitless ◆ **par ~e ignorance** out of sheer ignorance ◆ ~ **et dur** (*Pol*) hard-line

NM,F (*Pol*) ◆ ~ **(et dur)** hard-liner

purée /pyʀe/ NF ◆ ~ **(de pommes de terre)** mashed potato(es) ◆ ~ **de marrons/de tomates** chestnut/tomato purée ◆ **c'est de la ~ de pois** (= *brouillard*) it's murky fog *ou* a peasouper* ◆ **être dans la** ~* to be in a real mess* ◆ ~**, je l'ai oublié !*** darn (it)* *ou* sugar*, I forgot!

purement /pyʀmɑ̃/ ADV purely ◆ ~ **et simplement** purely and simply

pureté /pyʀte/ NF [1] (*Chim*) [*de métal, substance*] purity [2] (= *perfection*) [*de traits*] perfection; [*de style*] purity; [*d'air, eau, son*] purity, pureness; [*de voix*] purity, clarity; [*de diamant*] flawlessness [3] (= *innocence*) [*d'âme, cœur, personne, intentions, pensées*] purity; [*de conscience*] clearness; [*de regard*] frankness

purgatif, -ive /pyʀgatif, iv/ ADJ purgative NM purgative, purge

purgation /pyʀgasjɔ̃/ NF (*Méd*) (= *action*) purgation; (= *remède*) purgative, purge

purgatoire /pyʀgatwaʀ/ NM (*Rel, fig*) purgatory ◆ **elle a déjà fait son** ~ she's already done her penance

purge /pyʀʒ/ NF (*Méd*) purge, purgative; (*Pol*) purge; (*Tech*) [*de conduite*] flushing out, draining; [*de freins, radiateur*] bleeding

purger /pyʀʒe/ ► conjug 3 ◄ VT [1] (*Jur*) [+ *peine*] to serve [2] (= *vidanger*) [+ *conduite, radiateur*] to bleed, to flush (out), to drain; [+ *circuit hydraulique, freins*] to bleed [3] (*Méd*) to purge, to give a purgative to [4] (= *débarrasser*) to purge, to cleanse, to rid (*de* of) VPR **se purger** to take a purgative *ou* purge

purgeur /pyʀʒœʀ/ NM [*de tuyauterie*] drain-cock, tap (*Brit*); [*de radiateur*] bleed-tap

purifiant, e /pyʀifjɑ̃, jɑ̃t/ ADJ purifying, cleansing

purificateur, -trice /pyʀifikatœʀ, tʀis/ ADJ purifying, cleansing, purificatory NM (= *appareil*) (air) purifier

purification /pyʀifikasjɔ̃/ NF [*d'air, liquide, langue*] purification, purifying; [*de métal*] refinement; [*d'âme*] cleansing, purging ◆ ~ **ethnique** ethnic cleansing ◆ **la Purification** (*Rel*) the Purification

purificatoire /pyʀifikatwaʀ/ ADJ (*littér*) purificatory, purifying, cleansing

purifier /pyʀifje/ ► conjug 7 ◄ VT (*gén*) to purify, to cleanse; [+ *air, langue, liquide*] to purify; [+ *métal*] to refine; (*littér*) [+ *âme*] to cleanse, to purge ◆ ~ **l'atmosphère** (*lit*) to purify the atmosphere *ou* air; (*fig*) to clear the air VPR **se purifier** to cleanse o.s.

purin /pyʀɛ̃/ NM slurry

purisme /pyʀism/ NM purism

puriste /pyʀist/ ADJ, NMF purist

puritain, e /pyʀitɛ̃, ɛn/ ADJ puritan(ical); (*Hist*) Puritan NM,F puritan; (*Hist*) Puritan

puritanisme /pyʀitanism/ NM puritanism; (*Hist*) Puritanism

purpurin, e /pyʀpyʀɛ̃, in/ ADJ (*littér*) crimson

pur-sang /pyʀsɑ̃/ NM INV thoroughbred, purebred

purulence /pyʀylɑ̃s/ NF purulence, purulency

purulent, e /pyʀylɑ̃, ɑ̃t/ ADJ purulent

pus /py/ NM pus

pusillanime /pyzi(l)lanim/ ADJ (*littér*) pusillanimous (*littér*), fainthearted

pusillanimité /pyzi(l)lanimite/ NF (*littér*) pusillanimity (*littér*), faintheartedness

pustule /pystyl/ NF pustule

pustuleux, -euse /pystylø, øz/ ADJ pustular

putain* /pytɛ̃/ NF [1] (= *prostituée*) whore, hooker*, hustler* (*US*); (= *fille facile*) slut*, slag* (*Brit*) ◆ **faire la** ~* (*lit*) to be a whore *ou* hooker* *ou* hustler* (*US*), to turn tricks* (*US*); (*fig*) to sell one's soul, to sell out* [2] (*en exclamation*) ~ **!** bloody hell!* (*Brit*), goddammit!* (*US*) ◆ **cette ~ de guerre** (*intensif*) this bloody* (*Brit*) awful *ou* goddamn* (*US*) war ◆ **ce ~ de réveil !** that bloody* (*Brit*) *ou* goddamn* (*US*) alarm clock! ◆ **quel ~ de vent !** this fucking** wind!, this bloody* (*Brit*) awful wind!

putassier, -ière* /pytasje, jɛʀ/ ADJ [1] [*personne, mœurs*] sluttish; [*maquillage, tenue*] sluttish, tarty* ◆ **avoir un langage** ~ to swear like a trooper, to be foul-mouthed [2] (= *servile*) **comportement** ~ bootlicking, arse-licking** (*Brit*), ass-licking** (*US*)

putatif, -ive /pytatif, iv/ ADJ putative, presumed ◆ **père** ~ putative father

pute** /pyt/ NF whore, hooker*, hustler* (*US*) ◆ **aller aux** *ou* **chez les ~s** to go and see a whore

putois /pytwa/ NM (= *animal*) polecat; (= *fourrure*) fitch ◆ **crier comme un** ~ to shout *ou* scream one's head off (in protest), to scream *ou* yell blue murder* (*Brit*)

putréfaction /pytʀefaksjɔ̃/ NF putrefaction ◆ **cadavre en** ~ body in a state of putrefaction, putrefying *ou* rotting body

putréfiable /pytʀefjabl/ ADJ putrefiable

putréfier /pytʀefje/ ► conjug 7 ◄ VT to putrefy, to rot VPR **se putréfier** to putrefy, to rot, to go rotten

putrescence /pytʀesɑ̃s/ NF putrescence

putrescent, e /pytʀesɑ̃, ɑ̃t/ ADJ putrescent

putrescible /pytʀesibl/ ADJ putrescible

putride /pytʀid/ ADJ putrid

putridité /pytʀidite/ NF putridity, putridness

putsch /putʃ/ NM putsch

putschiste /putʃist/ NM putschist

puvathérapie /pyvateʀapi/ NF PUVA treatment *ou* therapy

puzzle /pœzl/ NM (*lit*) jigsaw (puzzle); (*fig*) jigsaw ◆ **faire un** ~ to do a jigsaw ◆ **reconstituer le ~, rassembler toutes les pièces du** ~ (*fig*) to fit *ou* put the pieces of the jigsaw together again

p.-v., PV* /peve/ NM (abrév de **procès-verbal**) (*gén*) fine; (*pour stationnement interdit*) (parking) ticket; (*pour excès de vitesse*) speeding ticket ◆ **je me suis pris un** ~ I got a ticket, I got booked (*Brit*)

PVC /pevese/ NM INV (abrév de **polyvinyl chloride**) PVC ◆ **en (plastique)** ~ PVC (*épith*)

pygargue /pigaʀg/ NM white-tailed eagle

Pygmalion /pigmaljɔ̃/ NM Pygmalion ◆ **il a voulu jouer les ~s avec elle** he wanted to be her Pygmalion

pygmée /pigme/ ADJ, NMF pygmy, pigmy ◆ **c'est un vrai** ~ (*péj*) he's a dwarf

pyjama /piʒama/ NM pyjamas, pajamas (*US*) ◆ **il était en ~(s)** he was in his pyjamas ◆ **acheter un** ~ to buy a pair of pyjamas, to buy some pyjamas ◆ **deux ~s** two pairs of pyjamas; → **veste**

pylône /pilon/ NM pylon ◆ ~ **électrique** electricity pylon

pylore /pilɔʀ/ NM pylorus

pylorique /pilɔʀik/ ADJ pyloric

Pyongyang /pjɔŋjaŋ/ N Pyongyang

pyorrhée /pjɔʀe/ NF pyorrhoea, pyorrhea

pyralène ® /piʀalɛn/ NM Pyralene ®

pyramidal, e (mpl **-aux**) /piʀamidal, o/ ADJ pyramid-shaped, pyramid-like, pyramidal (*SPÉC*)

pyramide /piʀamid/ NF pyramid ◆ ~ **inversée** inverted pyramid ◆ ~ **humaine** human pyramid ◆ ~ **des âges** population pyramid ◆ **~s rénales** *ou* **de Malpighi** (*Anat*) Malpighian pyramids ◆ **structure/organisation en** ~ pyramidal structure/organization

pyrénéen, -enne /piʀeneɛ̃, ɛn/ ADJ Pyrenean NM,F **Pyrénéen(ne)** inhabitant *ou* native of the Pyrenees, Pyrenean

Pyrénées /piʀene/ NFPL ◆ **les** ~ the Pyrenees

pyrex ® /piʀɛks/ NM Pyrex ® ◆ **assiette en** ~ Pyrex dish

pyrite /piʀit/ NF pyrites

pyrograver /piʀogʀave/ ► conjug 1 ◄ VT to do pyrography *ou* poker-work

pyrograveur, -euse /piʀɔgʀavœʀ, øz/ **NM,F** pyrographer

pyrogravure /piʀɔgʀavyʀ/ **NF** (*Art*) pyrography, poker-work; (*= objet*) pyrograph

pyrolyse /piʀɔliz/ **NF** pyrolysis ◆ **four à ~** pyrolytic oven

pyromane /piʀɔman/ **NMF** (*Méd*) pyromaniac; (*gén, Jur*) arsonist, fire raiser

pyromanie /piʀɔmani/ **NF** pyromania

pyromètre /piʀɔmɛtʀ/ **NM** pyrometer

pyrométrie /piʀɔmetʀi/ **NF** pyrometry

pyrométrique /piʀɔmetʀik/ **ADJ** pyrometric

pyrotechnie /piʀɔtɛkni/ **NF** pyrotechnics (*sg*), pyrotechny

pyrotechnique /piʀɔtɛknik/ **ADJ** pyrotechnic ◆ **spectacle ~** firework display

Pyrrhus /piʀys/ **NM** Pyrrhus; → **victoire**

Pythagore /pitagɔʀ/ **NM** Pythagoras

pythagoricien, -ienne /pitagɔʀisjɛ̃, jɛn/ **ADJ, NM,F** Pythagorean

pythagorique /pitagɔʀik/ **ADJ** Pythagorean

Pythie /piti/ **NF** 1 (*Antiq*) **la ~ (de Delphes)** the Pythia 2 ◆ **pythie** (*= devineresse*) prophetess ◆ **jouer la pythie** to be a seer *ou* soothsayer

python /pitɔ̃/ **NM** python

pythonisse /pitɔnis/ **NF** prophetess

Qq

Q, q /ky/ NM (= *lettre*) Q, q ◆ **fièvre Q** Q fever

qat /kat/ NM k(h)at

Qatar /katar/ NM Qatar

qatari, e /katari/ ADJ Qatari NM,F **Qatari(e)** Qatari ◆ **les Qatari** Qataris

qch (abrév de **quelque chose**) sth

QCM /kyseem/ NM (abrév de **questionnaire à choix multiple**) → **questionnaire**

QF /kyef/ NM (abrév de **quotient familial**) → **quotient**

QG /kyʒe/ NM (abrév de **quartier général**) HQ

QHS † /kyaʃes/ NM (abrév de **quartier de haute sécurité**) → **quartier**

QI /kyi/ NM (abrév de **quotient intellectuel**) IQ

qn (abrév de **quelqu'un**) sb

qq abrév de **quelque**

qu' /k/ → **que**

quadra * /k(w)adra/ NMF (abrév de **quadragénaire**) person in his (*ou* her) forties ◆ **les ~s** forty somethings * ◆ **les ~s du gouvernement** the forty-year-olds in the government

quadragénaire /k(w)adraʒener/ ADJ (= *de quarante ans*) forty-year-old (*épith*) ◆ **il est ~** (= *de quarante à cinquante ans*) he's in his forties ◆ **maintenant que tu es ~** now that you're forty (years old), now that you've reached forty NMF forty-year-old man (*ou* woman)

Quadragésime /kwadraʒezim/ NF Quadragesima

quadrangle /k(w)adrɑ̃gl/ NM (*Géom*) quadrangle

quadrangulaire /k(w)adrɑ̃gyler/ ADJ quadrangular

quadrant /kadrɑ̃/ NM quadrant

quadrature /k(w)adratyr/ NF (*gén*) quadrature ◆ **~ du cercle** (*Math*) quadrature *ou* squaring of the circle ◆ **c'est la ~ du cercle** (*fig*) it's like trying to square the circle, it's attempting the impossible

quadriceps /k(w)adriseps/ NM quadriceps

quadrichromie /k(w)adrikrɔmi/ NF four-colour (printing) process

quadriennal, e (mpl **-aux**) /k(w)adrijenal, o/ ADJ four-year (*épith*), quadrennial ◆ **assolement ~** four-year rotation

quadrige /k(w)adriʒ/ NM quadriga

quadrijumeaux /k(w)adriʒymo/ ADJ MPL → **tubercule**

quadrilatéral, e (mpl **-aux**) /k(w)adrilateral, o/ ADJ quadrilateral

quadrilatère /k(w)adrilater/ NM (*Géom, Mil*) quadrilateral

quadrilingue /k(w)adrilɛ̃g/ ADJ quadrilingual

quadrillage /kadrijaʒ/ NM 1 (= *dessin*) [*de papier*] square pattern; [*de tissu*] check pattern; [*de rues*] criss-cross *ou* grid pattern *ou* layout 2 [*de ville, pays*] (*gén*) covering; (*Mil, Police*) covering, control(ling) ◆ **la police a établi un ~ serré du quartier** the area is under close *ou* tight police control

quadrille /kadrij/ NM (= *danse, danseurs*) quadrille ◆ **~ des lanciers** lancers

quadrillé, e /kadrije/ (ptp de **quadriller**) ADJ [*papier, feuille*] squared

quadriller /kadrije/ ▸ conjug 1 ◂ VT [+ *papier*] to mark out in squares; [+ *ville, pays*] (*gén*) to cover; (*Mil, Police*) to cover, to control ◆ **la ville est étroitement quadrillée par la police** the town is under close *ou* tight police control ◆ **la ville est quadrillée par un réseau de rues** the town is criss-crossed by a network of streets

quadrillion /k(w)adriljɔ̃/ NM quadrillion (*Brit*), septillion (*US*)

quadrimoteur /kadrimɔtœr/ ADJ M four-engined NM four-engined plane

quadriparti, e /k(w)adriparti/, **quadripartite** /k(w)adripartit/ ADJ (*Bot*) quadripartite ◆ **conférence quadripartite** (*Pol*) (*entre pays*) four-power conference; (*entre partis*) four-party conference

quadriphonie /k(w)adrifɔni/ NF quadraphony

quadriphonique /k(w)adrifɔnik/ ADJ quadraphonic

quadriréacteur /k(w)adrireaktœr/ ADJ M four-engined NM four-engined jet *ou* plane

quadrumane /k(w)adryman/ ADJ quadrumanous NM quadrumane

quadrupède /k(w)adrypɛd/ ADJ fourfooted, quadruped NM quadruped

quadruple /k(w)adrypl/ ADJ [*nombre, quantité, rangée*] quadruple ◆ **une quantité ~ de l'autre** a quantity four times (as great as) the other ◆ **en ~ exemplaire** in four copies ◆ **la ~ championne d'Europe** the European champion four times over; → **croche** NM (*Math, gén*) quadruple ◆ **je l'ai payé le ~/le ~ de l'autre** I paid four times as much for it/four times as much as the other for it ◆ **augmenter qch au ~** to increase sth fourfold

quadrupler /k(w)adryple/ ▸ conjug 1 ◂ VTI to quadruple, to increase fourfold

quadruplés, -ées /k(w)adryple/ NM,F PL quadruplets, quads *

quadruplex /k(w)adryplɛks/ NM (*Téléc*) quadruplex system

quai /ke/ NM [*de port*] (*gén*) quay; (*pour marchandises*) wharf, quay; [*de gare*] platform; [*de rivière*] bank, embankment; (= *route*) riverside road ◆ **droits de ~** dockage, wharfage ◆ **être à ~** [*bateau*] to be alongside (the quay); [*de train*] to be in (the station) ◆ **venir à ~** [*bateau*] to berth ◆ **rester à ~** [*bateau*] to remain in dock; [*train*] to remain in the station ◆ **sur les ~s de la Seine** on the banks of the Seine; → **accès, billet**

COMP **le Quai des Orfèvres** police headquarters (*in Paris*), ≃ (New) Scotland Yard (*Brit*), the FBI (*US*)

le Quai (d'Orsay) *the French Foreign Office*

> **QUAI**
>
> In French towns, the word **quai** refers to a street running along the river, and appears in the street name itself. In Paris, some of these street names are used by extension to refer to the famous institutions situated there: the **Quai Conti** refers to the Académie française, the **Quai des Orfèvres** to the headquarters of the police force, and the **Quai d'Orsay** to the Foreign Office.

quaker, quakeresse /kwɛkœr, kwekrɛs/ NM,F Quaker

quakerisme /kwɛkœrism/ NM Quakerism

qualifiable /kalifjabl/ ADJ 1 (= *qui peut se qualifier*) (*Sport*) [*équipe, joueur*] able to qualify 2 (= *qui peut être nommé*) (*Jur*) **cet acte n'est pas juridiquement ~** this act cannot be legally defined ◆ **un délit ~ de haute trahison** a treasonable offence ◆ **une telle conduite n'est pas ~** such behaviour is beyond description *ou* defies description

qualifiant, e /kalifjɑ̃, jɑ̃t/ ADJ [*formation*] leading to a qualification

qualificateur /kalifikatœr/ NM (*Ling*) qualifier

qualificatif, -ive /kalifikatif, iv/ ADJ [*adjectif*] qualifying ◆ **épreuves qualificatives** (*Sport*) qualifying heats *ou* rounds NM (*Ling*) qualifier; (= *mot*) term ◆ **ce produit mérite le ~ de révolutionnaire** this product deserves to be described as revolutionary

qualification /kalifikasjɔ̃/ GRAMMAIRE ACTIVE 42.4 NF 1 (*Sport*) **obtenir sa ~** to qualify (*en, pour* for); ◆ **la ~ de notre équipe demeure incertaine** it's still not certain whether our team will qualify ◆ **épreuves de ~** qualifying heats *ou* rounds, qualifiers ◆ **c'est le but de la ~** this goal secures the team's qualification 2 (= *ap-*

titude) skill; *(= diplôme)* qualification ◆ ~ **professionnelle** professional qualification ◆ **sans** ~ *[personne]* *(= sans compétence)* unskilled; *(= sans diplômes)* unqualified ◆ **ce travail demande un haut niveau de** ~ this is highly skilled work 3 *(Jur)* **la** ~ **d'homicide involontaire a été retenue contre lui** he was charged with manslaughter 4 *(Ling)* qualification 5 *(= nom)* label, description

qualifié, e /kalifje/ (ptp de **qualifier**) ADJ 1 *(= compétent) (gén)* qualified; *(Ind) [emploi, main-d'œuvre, ouvrier]* skilled ◆ **non** ~ *[emploi, main-d'œuvre, ouvrier]* unskilled ◆ **emploi/ouvrier très** ~ highly skilled job/worker ◆ **il n'est pas** ~ **pour ce poste/gérer le service** he isn't qualified for this post/to manage the department ◆ **je ne suis pas** ~ **pour en parler** I'm not qualified to talk about it ◆ **majorité** ~**e** *(Pol)* qualified majority 2 *(Sport)* **les joueurs** ~**s pour la finale** the players who have qualified for the final, the qualifiers for the final 3 *(Jur) [vol, délit]* aggravated ◆ **c'est du vol** ~ *(fig)* it's daylight robbery ◆ **c'est de l'hypocrisie** ~**e** it's blatant hypocrisy

qualifier /kalifje/ ▸ conjug 7 ◂ VT 1 *[+ conduite, projet]* to describe *(de* as); ◆ **cet accord a été qualifié d'historique** this agreement has been described as historic ◆ **sa maison qu'il qualifiait pompeusement (de) manoir** his house which he described pompously as a manor ◆ ~ **qn de menteur** to call sb a liar 2 *(Sport)* ~ **une équipe** to ensure a team qualifies 3 *(Ling)* to qualify VPR **se qualifier** *(Sport)* to qualify *(pour* for); ◆ **il se qualifie d'artiste** *(hum)* he describes himself as an artist, he calls himself an artist

qualitatif, -ive /kalitatif, iv/ ADJ qualitative

qualitativement /kalitativmɑ̃/ ADV qualitatively ◆ **c'est une œuvre** ~ **discutable** the quality of the work is debatable

qualité /kalite/ NF 1 *[de marchandise]* quality ◆ **la** ~ **de (la) vie** the quality of life ◆ **de** ~ *[article, ouvrage, spectacle]* quality *(épith)* ◆ **de bonne/mauvaise** ~ of good *ou* high/bad *ou* poor quality ◆ **produits de haute** ~ high-quality products ◆ **article de première** ~ top-quality article, article of the highest quality ◆ **fruits de** ~ **supérieure** fruit of superior quality, superior-quality fruit ◆ ~ **courrier** *(Ordin)* near letter quality ◆ **service** ~ quality (control) department ◆ **responsable** ~ quality controller

2 *[de personne]* *(= vertu)* quality; *(= don)* skill ◆ ~**s humaines/personnelles** human/personal qualities ◆ **ses** ~**s de cœur** his noble-heartedness ◆ ~**s professionnelles** professional skills ◆ ~**s de gestionnaire** management *ou* managerial skills ◆ **cette œuvre a de grandes** ~**s littéraires** this work has great literary qualities

3 *(= fonction)* position ◆ **sa** ~ **de directeur** his position as manager ◆ **en sa** ~ **de maire** in his capacity as mayor ◆ **en (ma)** ~ **d'auteur/de femme mariée** as an author/a married woman ◆ **sa** ~ **d'étranger** his alien status ◆ **la** ~ **de Français** status as a French citizen ◆ **vos nom, prénom et** ~ *(Admin)* surname, forename *(Brit) ou* given name *(US)* and occupation ◆ **avoir** ~ **pour** *(Jur)* to have authority to

4 († *= noblesse)* quality ◆ **les gens/un homme de** ~ people/a man of quality

qualiticien, -ienne /kalitisjɛ̃, jɛn/ NM,F quality controller *(Brit) ou* controler *(US)*

quand /kɑ̃/ CONJ when ◆ ~ **ce sera fini, nous irons prendre un café** when it's finished we'll go and have a coffee ◆ **sais-tu de** ~ **était sa dernière lettre ?** do you know when his last letter was written? *ou* what was the date of his last letter? ◆ ~ **je te le disais !** I told you so! ◆ ~ **je pense que ... !** when I think that ...!, to think that ...! ◆ **on y va ?** – ~ **tu veux** shall we go? – ready when you are ◆ **c'est** ~ **tu veux !*** *(ton irrité)* take your time! ◆ **pour la bière, c'est** ~ **il veut !*** *(iro)* he's taking his time with that beer! ◆ **pourquoi ne pas acheter une voiture** ~ **nous pouvons nous le permettre ?** why not buy a car when we can afford it? ◆ **pourquoi vivre ici** ~ **tu pourrais avoir une belle maison ?** why live here when you could have a beautiful house?

◆ **quand bien même** even though *ou* if ◆ ~ **bien même tu aurais raison, je n'irais pas** even though *ou* even if you were right, I wouldn't go; → **même**

ADV when ◆ ~ **pars-tu ?,** ~ **est-ce que tu pars ?, tu pars** ~ **?*** when are you leaving? ◆ **dis-moi** ~ **tu pars** tell me when you're leaving *ou* when you'll be leaving ◆ **à** ~ **le voyage ?** when are you going? ◆ **c'est pour** ~ **?** *(devoir)* when is it due? *ou* for?; *(rendez-vous)* when is it?; *(naissance)* when is it to be? ◆ **ça date de** ~ **?** *(événement)* when did it happen?; *(lettre)* what's the date on it?, when was it written?; → **depuis, importer², jusque**

quant /kɑ̃/ ADV ◆ ~ **à** *(= pour ce qui est de)* as for, as to; *(= au sujet de)* as regards, regarding ◆ ~ **à moi, je pense qu'il est fou** as far as I'm concerned, he's mad ◆ ~ **à moi, je pars** as for me, I'm leaving ◆ ~ **à affirmer cela ...** as for stating that ... ◆ **je n'ai rien su** ~ **à ce qui s'est passé** I knew nothing about *ou* of what happened ◆ ~ **à cela, tu peux en être sûr** you can be quite sure about that ◆ ~ **à cela, je n'en sais rien** as to that *ou* as regards that *ou* as far as that goes, I know nothing about it

quanta /k(w)ɑ̃ta/ (pl de **quantum**)

quant-à-soi /kɑ̃taswa/ NM INV reserve ◆ **il est resté sur** *ou* **a gardé son** ~ he kept his own counsel

quantième /kɑ̃tjɛm/ NM *(Admin)* day *(of the month)*

quantifiable /kɑ̃tifjabl/ ADJ quantifiable ◆ **facteurs non** ~**s** factors which cannot be quantified, unquantifiable factors

quantificateur /kɑ̃tifikatœʀ/ NM quantifier

quantification /kɑ̃tifikasjɔ̃/ NF *(gén, Philos)* quantification; *(Phys)* quantization

quantifier /kɑ̃tifje/ ▸ conjug 7 ◂ VT *(gén, Philos)* to quantify; *(Phys)* to quantize

quantifieur /kɑ̃tifjœʀ/ NM ⇒ **quantificateur**

quantique /k(w)ɑ̃tik/ ADJ quantum *(épith)* NF quantum physics

quantitatif, -ive /kɑ̃titatif, iv/ ADJ quantitative

quantitativement /kɑ̃titativmɑ̃/ ADV quantitatively

quantité /kɑ̃tite/ NF 1 *(= nombre, somme)* quantity, amount ◆ **la** ~ **d'eau nécessaire à l'organisme** the amount *ou* quantity of water necessary for the body ◆ **la** ~ **de gens qui ne paient pas leurs impôts** the number of people who don't pay their taxes ◆ **quelle** ~ **de pétrole s'est déversée dans la mer ?** how much oil was spilled into the sea? ◆ **en** ~**s industrielles** in vast quantities *ou* amounts ◆ **en grande/petite** ~ in large/small quantities *ou* amounts ◆ **en** ~ **suffisante** in sufficient quantities

2 *(= grand nombre)* **(une)** ~ **de** *[+ raisons, personnes]* a great many, a lot of ◆ **des** ~**s** *ou* **(une)** ~ **de gens croient que ...** a great many people *ou* a lot of people believe that ... ◆ ~ **d'indices révèlent que ...** many signs *ou* a (great) number of signs indicate that ... ◆ **il y a des fruits en (grande) !** ~ fruit is in plentiful supply ◆ **il y a eu des accidents en** ~ there have been a great number of *ou* a lot of *ou* a great many accidents ◆ **du travail en** ~ a great deal of work

3 *(Ling, Sci)* quantity ◆ ~ **négligeable** negligible quantity *ou* amount ◆ **considérer qn comme** ~ **négligeable** to consider sb of minimal importance

quantum /k(w)ɑ̃tɔm/ (pl **quanta** /k(w)ɑ̃ta/) NM *(Jur, Phys)* quantum ◆ **la théorie des quanta** quantum theory

quarantaine /kaʀɑ̃tɛn/ NF 1 *(= âge, nombre)* about forty; *pour loc voir* **soixantaine** 2 *(Méd, Naut)* quarantine ◆ **mettre en** ~ *(lit) [+ animal, malade, navire]* to quarantine, to put in quarantine; *(= ostraciser) [+ personne]* to blacklist, to send to Coventry *(Brit)*; *[+ pays]* to blacklist; → **pavillon**

quarante /kaʀɑ̃t/ ADJ INV, NM INV forty ◆ **les Quarante** *the members of the French Academy* ◆ **un** ~**-cinq tours** *(= disque)* a single, a forty-five; *pour autres loc voir* **soixante, an;** → **ACADÉMIE**

quarantenaire /kaʀɑ̃tnɛʀ/ ADJ 1 *[période]* forty-year *(épith)* 2 *(Méd, Naut)* quarantine *(épith)* NM *(= anniversaire)* fortieth anniversary

quarantième /kaʀɑ̃tjɛm/ ADJ, NMF fortieth ◆ **les** ~**s rugissants** *(Naut)* the Roaring Forties

quark /kwaʀk/ NM quark

quart /kaʀ/ NM 1 *(= fraction)* quarter; *(= 250 g)* ≃ half a pound; *(= 250 ml)* quarter litre ◆ **un** ~ **de poulet** a quarter chicken ◆ **un** ~ **de beurre** 250 g of butter ◆ **un** ~ **de vin** a quarter-litre carafe of wine ◆ **un kilo/une livre un** ~ *ou* **et** ~ a kilo/a pound and a quarter ◆ **on n'a pas fait le** ~ **du travail** we haven't done a quarter of the work ◆ **c'est réglé au** ~ **de poil*** it's finely *ou* perfectly tuned; → **tiers, trois**

2 *(Mil = gobelet)* beaker *(of 1/4 litre capacity)*

3 *(dans le temps)* ~ **d'heure** quarter of an hour, quarter-hour *(surtout US)* ◆ **3 heures moins le** ~ (a) quarter to *ou* of *(US)* 3 ◆ **3 heures et** ~, **3 heures un** ~ (a) quarter past *ou* after *(US)* 3 ◆ **il est le** ~**/moins le** ~ it's (a) quarter past/(a) quarter to ◆ **de** ~ **d'heure en** ~ **d'heure** every quarter of an hour ◆ **passer un mauvais** *ou* **sale** ~ **d'heure** to have a bad *ou* hard time of it ◆ **il lui a fait passer un mauvais** ~ **d'heure** he gave him a bad *ou* hard time ◆ ~ **d'heure américain** lady's choice ◆ **un** ~ **de seconde** *(lit)* a quarter of a second; *(fig)* a split second ◆ **en un** ~ **de seconde** *(lit)* in a quarter of a second; *(fig)* in no time at all ◆ **un** ~ **de siècle** a quarter of a century

4 *(Naut)* watch ◆ **être de** ~ to keep the watch ◆ **prendre le** ~ to take the watch ◆ **de** ~ *[homme, matelot]* on watch ◆ **officier de** ~ officer of the watch ◆ **petit** ~ dogwatch ◆ **grand** ~ six-hour watch

COMP **quart de cercle** quarter-circle

quarts de finale quarter finals ◆ **être en** ~**s de finale** to be in the quarter finals

quart de soupir semiquaver rest *(Brit)*, sixteenth rest *(US)*

quart de ton quarter tone

quart de tour quarter turn ◆ **donner un** ~ **de tour à un bouton de porte** to turn a knob round a quarter of the way, to give a knob a quarter turn ◆ **démarrer** *ou* **partir au** ~ **de tour** *[engin]* to start (up) first time; * *[personne]* to have a short fuse ◆ **comprendre au** ~ **de tour*** to understand straight off*, to be quick on the uptake

quart-de-rond (pl **quarts-de-rond**) /kaʀdəʀɔ̃/ NM ovolo, quarter round

quarte /k(w)aʀt/ NF *(Escrime)* quarte; *(Cartes)* quart; *(Mus)* fourth; *(Hist = deux pintes)* quart ADJ F → **fièvre**

quarté /k(w)aʀte/ NM *French system of forecast betting on four horses in a race*

quarteron, -onne /kaʀtəʀɔ̃, ɔn/ NM,F *(= métis)* quadroon NM *(péj = groupe)* small *ou* insignificant band, minor group

quartette /k(w)aʀtɛt/ NM *(Mus)* jazz quartet(te)

quartier /kaʀtje/ NM **1** *[de ville] (Admin = division)* district, area; *(gén = partie)* neighbourhood *(Brit)*, neighborhood *(US)*, area ◆ **le ~ chinois** Chinatown, the Chinese quarter *ou* area ◆ **le ~ juif** the Jewish quarter *ou* area ◆ **les vieux ~s de la ville** the old part of the town ◆ **les gens du ~** the local people, the people in the neighbourhood ◆ **vous êtes du ~ ?** do you live around here? ◆ **le ~ est/ouest de la ville** the east/west end *ou* side of (the) town ◆ **~ commerçant** shopping area *ou* district ◆ **le ~ des affaires** the business district *ou* area ◆ **le Quartier latin** the Latin Quarter ◆ **de ~** *[cinéma, épicier]* local *(épith)* ◆ **association/maison de ~** community association/centre ◆ **la vie de ~** community life; → **bas¹, beau**

2 *(= portion) [de bœuf]* quarter; *[de viande]* large piece, chunk; *[de fruit]* piece, segment ◆ **mettre en ~s** *(lit, fig)* to tear to pieces

3 *(Astron, Hér)* quarter

4 *(† = grâce, pitié)* quarter † ◆ **demander/faire ~** to ask for/give quarter ◆ **ne pas faire de ~** to give no quarter ◆ **pas de ~ !** show no mercy!

5 *(Mil)* **~(s)** quarters ◆ **rentrer au(x) ~(s)** to return to quarters ◆ **avoir ~(s) libre(s)** *(Mil)* to have leave from barracks; *[élèves, touristes]* to be free (for a few hours) ◆ **prendre ses ~s d'hiver** *(lit, fig)* to go into winter quarters ◆ **c'est là que nous tenons nos ~s** *(fig)* this is where we have our headquarters

COMP **quartier général** *(Mil, fig)* headquarters ◆ **grand ~ général** *(Mil)* general headquarters

quartier de haute sécurité, quartier de sécurité renforcée *[de prison]* high *ou* maximum *ou* top security wing

quartier de noblesse *(lit)* degree of noble lineage *(representing one generation)* ◆ **avoir ses ~s de noblesse** *(fig)* to be well established and respected, to have earned one's colours

quartier réservé red-light district

quartier-maître (pl **quartiers-maîtres**) / kaʀtjemɛtʀ / NM *(Naut)* ≈ leading seaman ◆ **~ de 1re classe** leading rating *(Brit)*, petty officer third class *(US)*

quartile /kwaʀtil/ NM quartile

quart-monde (pl **quarts-mondes**) /kaʀmɔ̃d/ NM ◆ **le ~** *(= démunis)* the underclass; *(= pays)* the Fourth World

quarto /kwaʀto/ ADV fourthly

quartz /kwaʀts/ NM quartz

quartzite /kwaʀtsit/ NM quartzite

quasar /kazaʀ/ NM quasar

quasi¹ /kazi/ NM *(Culin) cut of meat from upper part of leg of veal*

quasi² /kazi/ ADV almost, nearly PRÉF near, quasi- *(surtout US)* ◆ **~-certitude/-obscurité** near certainty/darkness ◆ **~-monnaie** near money ◆ **~-contrat** quasi-contract ◆ **~-collision** *(avions)* near miss ◆ **la ~-totalité des dépenses** almost all (of) the expenditure

quasi-délit (pl **quasi-délits**) /kazideli/ NM *(Jur)* technical offence *(Brit) ou* offense *(US)*

quasiment /kazimɑ̃/ ADV *(dans une affirmation)* practically ◆ **c'est ~ fait** it's as good as done ◆ **~ jamais** hardly ever ◆ **il n'a ~ pas parlé/dormi** he hardly said a word/slept ◆ **je n'y vais ~ plus** I hardly ever *ou* almost never go there anymore

Quasimodo /kazimɔdo/ NF ◆ **la ~, le dimanche de ~** Low Sunday

quaternaire /kwatɛʀnɛʀ/ ADJ *(gén, Chim)* quaternary; *(Géol)* Quaternary NM *(Géol)* ◆ **le ~** the Quaternary (period)

quatorze /katɔʀz/ ADJ INV, NM INV fourteen ◆ **avant/après (la guerre de) ~** before/after the First World War ◆ **le ~ juillet** the Fourteenth of July, Bastille Day *(French national holiday)*; → **chercher, repartir²**; *pour autres loc voir* **six**; → LE QUATORZE JUILLET

quatorzième /katɔʀzjɛm/ ADJ INV, NMF fourteenth; *pour loc voir* **sixième**

quatrain /katʀɛ̃/ NM quatrain

quatre /katʀ/ ADJ INV, NM INV four ◆ **aux ~ coins de** *(lit, fig)* in the four corners of ◆ **à ~ mains** *(Mus) [morceau]* for four hands, four-handed *[jouer]* four-handed ◆ **marcher à ~ pattes** to walk on all fours ◆ **nos amis à ~ pattes** our four-legged friends ◆ **les ~ grands** *(Pol)* the Big Four ◆ **monter/descendre (l'escalier) ~ à ~** to rush up/down the stairs four at a time ◆ **manger comme ~** to eat like a horse ◆ **une robe de ~ sous** a cheap dress ◆ **il avait ~ sous d'économies** he had a modest amount of savings ◆ **s'il avait ~ sous de bon sens** if he had a scrap *ou* modicum of common sense ◆ **être tiré à ~ épingles** to be dressed up to the nines ◆ **un de ces ~ (matins)** * one of these (fine) days ◆ **je ne vais pas recommencer tous les ~ matins !** * I'm not going to keep doing it! ◆ **faire les ~ cents coups** to lead a wild life ◆ **tomber les ~ fers en l'air** to fall flat on one's back ◆ **faire ses ~ volontés** to do exactly as one pleases ◆ **faire les ~ volontés de qn** to satisfy sb's every whim ◆ **dire à qn ses ~ vérités** to tell sb a few plain *ou* home truths ◆ **se mettre** *ou* **se couper en ~ pour (aider) qn** to bend over backwards to help sb * ◆ **elle se tenait à ~ pour ne pas rire/pour ne pas le gifler** she was doing all she could to keep from laughing/to keep from smacking him ◆ **je n'irai pas par ~ chemins** I'm not going to beat about the bush ◆ **entre ~ murs** within *ou* between four walls ◆ **je n'ai pas ~ bras !** * I've only got one pair of hands! ◆ **quand il sera entre ~ planches** * when he's six foot under * ◆ **entre ~ z'yeux** *, **entre quat-z-yeux** * *(= directement)* face to face; *(= en privé)* in private; → **trèfle, vent,** *etc*; *pour autres loc voir* **six**

NM *(en aviron)* ◆ **~ barré** coxed four ◆ **~ sans barreur** coxless four

quatre-cent-vingt-et-un /kat(ʀə)sɑ̃vɛ̃teœ̃/ NM INV *dice game*

quatre-épices /katʀepis/ NM INV allspice

quatre-heures * /katʀœʀ/ NM INV *(langage enfantin)* afternoon tea *(Brit) ou* snack

quatre-huit /kat(ʀə)ɥit/ NM INV *(Mus)* common time

quatre-mâts /kat(ʀə)mɑ/ NM INV four-master

quatre-quarts /kat(ʀə)kaʀ/ NM INV *(Culin)* pound cake

quatre-quatre /kat(ʀə)katʀ/ ADJ INV, NM INV four-wheel drive

quatre-vingt-dix /katʀəvɛ̃dis/ ADJ INV, NM INV ninety

quatre-vingt-dixième /katʀəvɛ̃dizjɛm/ ADJ INV, NMF ninetieth

quatre-vingt-et-un /katvɛ̃teœ̃/ NM INV ⇒ **quatre-cent-vingt-et-un**

quatre-vingtième /katʀəvɛ̃tjɛm/ ADJ INV, NMF eightieth

quatre-vingt-onze /katʀəvɛ̃ɔ̃z/ ADJ INV, NM INV ninety-one

quatre-vingt-onzième /katʀəvɛ̃ɔ̃zjɛm/ ADJ INV, NMF ninety-first

quatre-vingts /katʀəvɛ̃/ ADJ INV, NM INV eighty

quatre-vingt-un /katʀəvɛ̃œ̃/ ADJ INV, NM INV eighty-one

quatre-vingt-unième /katʀəvɛ̃ynjɛm/ ADJ INV, NMF eighty-first

quatrième /katʀijɛm/ ADJ fourth ◆ **le ~ pouvoir** the fourth estate ◆ **le ~ âge** *(= personnes)* the over 75s; *(= état)* the fourth age *(75 onwards)* ◆ **faire qch en ~ vitesse** to do sth at top speed; *pour autres loc voir* **sixième** NMF *(= joueur de cartes)* fourth player NF *(= vitesse)* fourth gear; *(Cartes = quarte)* quart; *(Scol = classe)* ≈ third form *ou* year *(Brit)*, third year (in junior high school) *(US)* ◆ **~ de couverture** *[de livre]* back cover

quatrièmement /katʀijɛmmɑ̃/ ADV fourthly, in the fourth place

quatrillion /k(w)atʀiljɔ̃/ NM quadrillion *(Brit)*, septillion *(US)*

quattrocento /kwatʀotʃento/ NM ◆ **le ~** the quattrocento

quatuor /kwatɥɔʀ/ NM *(= œuvre, musiciens)* quartet(te); *(fig)* quartet(te), foursome ◆ **~ à cordes** string quartet(te)

que /kə/

Devant voyelle ou **h** muet = **qu'**.

1 CONJONCTION	3 PRONOM RELATIF
2 ADVERBE	4 PRONOM INTERROGATIF

1 - CONJONCTION

Lorsque **que** sert à former des locutions conjonctives (**afin que, à mesure que, dès que, tant que, tel que, plus/moins ... que etc**), reportez-vous à l'autre mot.

1 *(complétive)*

Lorsque **que** introduit une subordonnée complétive, il se traduit généralement par **that** mais est souvent omis.

◆ **elle sait ~ tu es prêt** she knows (that) you're ready ◆ **tu crois qu'il réussira ?** do you think he'll succeed? ◆ **c'est agréable qu'il fasse beau** it's nice that the weather's fine ◆ **c'est dommage qu'il pleuve** it's a pity (that) it's raining ◆ **l'idée qu'il pourrait échouer** the idea of him *ou* his failing, the idea that he might fail

Avec un verbe de volonté, l'anglais emploie une proposition infinitive.

◆ **je veux/j'aimerais qu'il vienne** I want him/would like him to come ◆ **je ne veux pas qu'il vienne** I don't want him to come MAIS **j'aimerais qu'il ne vienne pas** I'd rather he didn't come

Avec les verbes d'opinion tels que **penser, croire** suivis de **oui, si, non, que** n'est pas traduit.

◆ **je pense ~ oui/non** I think/don't think so ◆ **mais il n'a pas de voiture ! – il dit ~ si** but he has no car! – he says he has; → **craindre, douter, peur,** *etc*

2 *(remplaçant « si », « quand », « comme », etc.)*

Lorsque **que** est précédé d'une proposition introduite par **si, quand, comme, que, etc** il ne se traduit pas.

◆ **si vous êtes sages et qu'il fait beau, nous sortirons** if you are good and the weather is fine, we'll go out ◆ **il vous recevra quand il rentrera et qu'il aura déjeuné** he'll see you when he comes home and he's had a meal ◆ **comme la maison est petite et qu'il n'y a pas de jardin ...** as the house is small and there's no garden ... ◆ **bien qu'il soit en retard et ~ nous soyons pressés** although he's late and we're in a hurry

3 hypothèse = si whether ◆ **il ira, qu'il le veuille ou non** he'll go whether he wants to or not *ou* whether he likes it or not ◆ **qu'il parte ou qu'il reste, ça m'est égal** whether he leaves or stays, it's all the same to me, he can leave or he can stay, it's all the same to me

4 but **tenez-le, qu'il ne tombe pas** hold him in case he falls *ou* so that he won't fall ◆ **venez**

~ **nous causions** come along and we'll have *ou* so that we can have a chat

5 temps **elle venait à peine de sortir qu'il se mit à pleuvoir** she had no sooner gone out than it started raining, she had hardly *ou* just gone out when it started raining ◆ **ils ne se connaissaient pas depuis 10 minutes qu'ils étaient déjà amis** they had only known each other for 10 minutes and already they were friends; → **faire, ne, si²**

6 ordre, souhait, résignation

Lorsque **que** suivi d'une 3ᵉ personne exprime l'ordre, le souhait, la résignation ou la menace, il se traduit par un verbe, un adverbe ou une conjonction.

◆ **qu'il se taise !** I wish he would be quiet! ◆ ~ **la lumière soit** let there be light ◆ ~ **la guerre finisse !** if only the war would end! ◆ **qu'ils me laissent en paix !** I wish they'd leave me in peace! ◆ **eh bien, qu'il vienne !** all right, he can come! *ou* let him come! ◆ ~ **le Seigneur ait pitié de lui !** (may) the Lord have mercy upon him! ◆ **qu'elle vienne me reprocher quelque chose(, je saurai la recevoir) !** she'd better not start criticizing! ◆ **qu'il essaie seulement !** just let him try!

7 *(renforçant affirmation)*

Notez l'emploi d'adverbes ou de l'auxiliaire en anglais lorsque **que** renforce une affirmation ou une négation.

◆ ~ **oui !** yes indeed! ◆ **il était fâché ?** – ~ **oui !** was he angry? – was he ever! ◆ ~ **non !** certainly not!, not at all! ◆ **tu viens ?** – ~ **non/oui !** are you coming? – no I am not!/you bet I am! * ◆ **mais il n'en veut pas !** – ~ **si/non** but he doesn't want any! – yes he does/no he doesn't

8 pour reprendre ce qui vient d'être dit ~ **tu crois !** * that's what YOU think! ◆ ~ **je l'aide ? tu plaisantes !** me, help him? you must be joking! ◆ ~ **tu y ailles seul ? c'est trop dangereux !** go on your own? that's far too dangerous!

9 après un discours rapporté **"viens ici !", qu'il me crie** * "come here", he shouted ◆ **"et pourquoi ?" ~ je lui fais** * "why's that?", I go to him *

10 locutions

◆ **que ... ne ...** *(littér)* ◆ **il ne se passe pas une minute ~ je ne pense à lui** *(= sans que)* not a minute goes by when I don't think about him *ou* without me thinking about him ◆ **ils pourraient me supplier ~ je n'accepterais pas** even if they begged me I wouldn't accept ◆ **j'avais déjà fini de déjeuner qu'elle n'avait pas commencé** I'd already finished my lunch and she hadn't even started

2 - ADVERBE

1 valeur intensive

◆ **que, qu'est-ce que** *(devant adjectif, adverbe)* how; *(devant nom singulier)* what a; *(devant nom pluriel)* what a lot of ◆ **(qu'est-ce) ~ tu es lent !** you're so slow!, how slow you are! ◆ **qu'est-ce qu'il est bête !** he's such an idiot! ◆ ~ **de monde !, qu'est-ce qu'il y a comme monde !** what a crowd (there is)!, what a lot of people! ◆ ~ **de voitures !, qu'est-ce qu'il y a comme circulation !** there's so much traffic! ◆ ~ **de mal vous vous donnez !** what a lot of trouble you're taking! ◆ **(qu'est-ce) qu'il joue bien !** doesn't he play well!, what a good player he is!

2 dans des interrogatives = pourquoi why ◆ **qu'avais-tu besoin de lui en parler ?** why did you have to go and talk to him about it? ◆ ~ **n'es-tu venu me voir ?** *(littér)* why didn't you come to see me?

3 - PRONOM RELATIF

1 antécédent personne

que se traduit par **who** ou par **that**, ce dernier étant souvent omis ; dans une langue plus soutenue, on peut employer **whom**.

◆ **la fille qu'il a rencontrée là-bas et qu'il a épousée par la suite** the girl (that) he met there and later married ◆ **les enfants ~ tu vois jouer dans la rue** the children (that) you see playing in the street ◆ **la femme qu'il aime toujours** the woman (whom *(frm)*) he still loves

Quand l'antécédent est un nom propre, on traduit obligatoirement par **who** ou **whom**.

◆ **il y avait David Legrand, ~ je n'avais pas vu depuis des années** David Legrand, who *ou* whom *(frm)* I hadn't seen for years, was there

2 antécédent animal ou chose

que se traduit par **which** ou **that**, ce dernier étant souvent omis.

◆ **le chaton qu'il a trouvé dans la cave** the kitten (that) he found in the cellar ◆ **j'ai déjà les livres qu'il m'a offerts** I've already got the books he gave me ◆ **la raison qu'il a donnée** the reason (that *ou* which) he gave

3 en incise

Notez que lorsque la relative est en incise, on n'emploie jamais **that**.

◆ **un certain M. Leduc, ~ je ne connais même pas, m'a appelé** a certain Mr Leduc, who *ou* whom *(frm)* I don't even know, called me ◆ **l'étiquette, ~ j'avais pourtant bien collée, est tombée** the label, which I'd stuck on properly, fell off all the same

4 temps when ◆ **un jour/un été ~ ...** * one day/one summer when ... ◆ **tu te souviens de l'hiver qu'il a fait si froid ?** * do you remember the winter (when) it was so cold?; → **temps¹**

5 dans des formes attributives **quel homme charmant ~ votre voisin !** what a charming man your neighbour is! ◆ **tout distrait qu'il est, il s'en est aperçu** absent-minded though he is, he still noticed it ◆ **et moi, aveugle ~ j'étais, je ne m'en suis pas aperçu** and blind as I was, I didn't see it ◆ **pour ignorante qu'elle soit** ignorant though she may be, however ignorant she is *ou* may be ◆ **c'est un inconvénient ~ de ne pas avoir de voiture** it's inconvenient not having a car ◆ **de brune qu'elle était, elle est devenue blonde** once a brunette, she has now turned blonde ◆ **en bon fils qu'il est** being the good son (that) he is ◆ **plein d'attentions qu'il était** *, **ce jeune homme !** he was so considerate that young man was! *

4 - PRONOM INTERROGATIF

what ◆ ~ **fais-tu ?, qu'est-ce ~ tu fais ?** what are you doing? ◆ **qu'est-ce qu'il voulait ?** what did he want? ◆ **qu'en sais-tu ?** what do you know about it?

Notez que dans les cas où il y a discrimination ou choix, on emploie **which**.

◆ **qu'est-ce ~ tu préfères, le rouge ou le noir ?** which (one) do you prefer, the red or the black?

◆ **qu'est-ce qui** what ◆ **qu'est-ce qui l'a mis en colère ?** what made him so angry? ◆ **qu'est-ce qui t'empêchait de le faire ?** what stopped you from doing it?

Québec /kebɛk/ N *(= ville)* Quebec (City) NM *(= province)* ◆ **le ~** Quebec

Québec

Quebec's history as a French-speaking province of Canada has meant that the French spoken there has developed many distinctive characteristics. Since the 1970s, the government of Quebec has been actively promoting the use of French terms instead of anglicisms in everyday life in order to preserve the Francophone identity of the province, over 80% of whose inhabitants have French as their mother tongue. → **Office de la langue française, Révolution tranquille**

québécisme /kebesism/ NM *expression (ou word etc) used in Quebec*

québécois, e /kebekwa, waz/ ADJ Quebec *(épith)* ◆ **le Parti ~** the Parti Québécois NM *(= variété du français)* Quebec French NM,F **Québécois(e)** Quebecker, Quebecer, Québécois *(Can)*

quechua /ketʃwa/ ADJ, NM Quechua, Kechua

Queensland /kwinzlɑ̃d/ NM Queensland

quel, quelle /kɛl/ ADJ 1 *(interrog : dir, indir, être animé : attrib)* who; *(être animé : épith)* what; *(chose)* what ◆ ~ **est cet auteur ?** who is that author? ◆ **sur ~ auteur va-t-il parler ?** what author is he going to talk about? ◆ **quelles ont été les raisons de son départ ?** what were the reasons for his leaving? *ou* departure? ◆ **dans ~s pays êtes-vous allé ?** what countries have you been to? ◆ **lui avez-vous dit à quelle adresse (il faut) envoyer la lettre ?** have you told him the *ou* what address to send the letter to? ◆ **j'ignore ~ est l'auteur de ces poèmes** I don't know who wrote these poems *ou* who the author of these poems is

2 *(interrog discriminatif)* which ◆ ~ **acteur préférez-vous ?** which actor do you prefer? ◆ ~ **est le vin le moins cher des trois ?** which wine is the cheapest of the three?

3 *(excl)* what ◆ **quelle surprise/coïncidence !** what a surprise/coincidence! ◆ ~ **courage !** what courage! ◆ ~**s charmants enfants !** what charming children! ◆ ~ **imbécile je suis !** what a fool I am! ◆ ~ **(sale) temps !** what rotten weather! ◆ **il a vu ~s amis fidèles il avait** he saw what faithful friends he had ◆ **j'ai remarqué avec quelle attention ils écoutaient** I noticed how attentively they were listening

4 *(relatif, être animé)* whoever; *(chose)* whatever; *(discriminatif)* whichever, whatever ◆ **quelle que soit** *ou* **quelle que puisse être votre décision, écrivez-nous** write to us whatever your decision may be *ou* whatever you decide ◆ ~ **que soit le train que vous preniez, vous arriverez trop tard** whichever *ou* whatever train you take, you will be too late ◆ **quelles que soient les conséquences** whatever the consequences (may be) ◆ **quelle que soit la personne qui vous répondra** whoever answers you ◆ ~ **qu'il soit, le prix sera toujours trop élevé** whatever the price (is), it will still be too high ◆ **les hommes, ~s qu'ils soient** all men, irrespective of who they are

PRON INTERROG which ◆ **de tous ces enfants, ~ est le plus intelligent ?** of all these children, which (one) is the most intelligent? ◆ **des deux solutions quelle est celle que vous préférez ?** of the two solutions, which (one) do you prefer?

quelconque /kɛlkɔ̃k/ ADJ 1 *(= n'importe quel)* some (or other), any ◆ **une lettre envoyée par un ami ~** *ou* **par un ~ de ses amis** a letter sent by some friend of his *ou* by some friend or other (of his) ◆ **choisis un stylo ~ parmi ceux-là** choose any one of those pens ◆ **sous un prétexte ~** on some pretext or other ◆ **pour une raison ~** for some reason (or other) ◆ **à**

partir d'un point ~ du cercle from any point on the circle; → **triangle**

2 (= *moindre*) **un** *ou* **une** ~ any, the least *ou* slightest ◆ **il n'a pas manifesté un désir ~ d'y aller** he didn't show the slightest *ou* least desire *ou* any desire to go ◆ **avez-vous une ~ idée de l'endroit où ça se trouve ?** have you any idea where it might be?

3 (= *médiocre*) [*repas*] poor, indifferent; [*élève, devoir*] poor; [*acteur*] poor, second-rate ◆ **c'est un repas/devoir** ~ this is a poor meal/essay, this meal/essay isn't up to much* (*Brit*) ◆ **c'est quelqu'un de très** ~ (*laid*) he's not very good-looking at all; (*ordinaire*) he's pretty nondescript

quelque /kɛlk(ə)/

1 ADJECTIF INDÉFINI 2 ADVERBE

1 - ADJECTIF INDÉFINI

1 au singulier some ◆ **il habite à ~ distance d'ici** he lives some distance *ou* way from here ◆ **dans ~ temps** before long, in a (little) while ◆ **attendre ~ temps** to wait a while ◆ **je ne le vois plus depuis ~ temps** I haven't seen him for some time *ou* for a while, it's some time *ou* a while since I've seen him ◆ **il faut trouver ~ autre solution** we'll have to find some other solution ◆ **j'ai ~ peine à croire cela** I find that rather *ou* somewhat difficult to believe, I have some difficulty in believing that ◆ **avec ~ impatience/inquiétude** with some impatience/anxiety ◆ **désirez-vous ~ autre chose ?** would you like something *ou* anything else?

◆ **en quelque sorte** (= *pour ainsi dire*) as it were, so to speak; (= *bref*) in a word; (= *d'une certaine manière*) in a way ◆ **le liquide s'était en ~ sorte solidifié** the liquid had solidified as it were *ou* so to speak ◆ **en ~ sorte, tu refuses** in a word, you refuse ◆ **on pourrait dire en ~ sorte que ...** you could say in a way that ...

◆ **quelque chose** something; (*avec interrogation*) anything, something ◆ **~ chose d'extraordinaire** something extraordinary ◆ **~ chose d'autre** something else ◆ **puis-je faire ~ chose pour vous ?** is there anything *ou* something I can do for you? ◆ **il a ~ chose (qui ne va pas)** (*maladie*) there's something wrong *ou* the matter with him; (*ennuis*) there's something the matter (with him) ◆ **vous prendrez bien ~ chose (à boire)** do have something to drink ◆ **il/ça y est pour ~ chose** he/it has got something to do with it ◆ **il y a ~ chose comme une semaine** something like a week ago, a week or so ago ◆ **je t'ai apporté un petit ~ chose** I've brought you a little something; → **déjà, dire, malheur**

◆ **faire ~ chose à qn** to have an effect on sb ◆ **ça m'a fait ~ chose d'apprendre sa mort** I was upset when I heard he had died ◆ **quand il me prend dans ses bras, ça me fait ~ chose** it does something to me when he takes me in his arms

(* : *intensif*) ◆ **il a plu ~ chose (de bien) !** it rained like anything!*, it didn't half rain!* (*Brit*) ◆ **je tiens ~ chose comme rhume !** I've got a terrible *ou* a dreadful cold! ◆ **il se prend pour ~ chose** he thinks he's quite something ◆ **ce film/être pilote, c'est ~ chose !** that film/being a pilot is quite something! ◆ **ça alors, c'est ~ chose !** (*ton irrité*) that's (a bit) too much!, that's a bit stiff!* (*Brit*)

◆ **quelque part** somewhere ◆ **posez votre paquet ~ part dans un coin** put your parcel down in a corner somewhere ◆ **je vais ~ part** (*euph = toilettes*) I'm going to wash my hands (*euph*) ◆ **tu veux mon pied ~ part ?*** (*euph*) do you want a kick up the backside?*

2 au pluriel ~s a few, some ◆ **M. Dupont va vous dire ~s mots** Mr Dupont is going to say a few words (to you) ◆ **~s milliers (de)** a few thousand ◆ **il ne peut rester que ~s instants** he can only stay (for) a few moments ◆ **~s autres** some *ou* a few others ◆ **avez-vous ~s feuilles de papier à me passer ?** could you let me have a few sheets of paper?

◆ **et quelques** ◆ **20 kg et ~s*** a bit over 20 kg* ◆ **il doit être trois heures et ~s*** it must be a bit* *ou* a little after three

◆ **les** *ou* **ces** *ou* **ses** *etc* **quelques ...** ◆ **les ~s enfants qui étaient venus** the few children who had come ◆ **ces ~s poèmes** these few poems ◆ **les ~s centaines/milliers de personnes qui ...** the few hundred/thousand people who ...

3 locutions

◆ **quelque ... que** whatever; (*discriminatif*) whichever, whatever ◆ **de ~ façon que l'on envisage le problème** whatever *ou* whichever way you look at the problem ◆ **par ~ temps qu'il fasse** whatever the weather (may be *ou* is like) ◆ **il veut l'acheter, à ~ prix que ce soit, par ~ moyen que ce soit** he wants to buy it no matter what the cost and no matter how

2 - ADVERBE

1 = environ, à peu près some, about ◆ **il y a ~ 20 ans qu'il enseigne ici** he has been teaching here for some *ou* about 20 years *ou* for 20 years or so ◆ **ça a augmenté de ~ 10 €** it's gone up by about €10 *ou* by €10 or so *ou* by some €10

2 locutions

◆ **quelque peu** rather, somewhat ◆ **~ peu déçu** rather *ou* somewhat disappointed ◆ **~ peu grivois** a touch *ou* somewhat risqué ◆ **il est ~ peu menteur** he is something of *ou* a bit of a liar

◆ **quelque ... que** (*littér*) however ◆ **~ pénible que soit la tâche** however laborious the task may be

---

quelquefois /kɛlkəfwa/ **ADV** sometimes, occasionally, at times

quelques-uns, -unes /kɛlkəzœ̃, yn/ **PRON INDÉF PL** some, a few ◆ **~ de nos lecteurs/ses amis** some *ou* a few of our readers/his friends ◆ **privilège réservé à ~** privilege reserved for a very few

quelqu'un /kɛlkœ̃/ **PRON INDÉF** 1 (*gén*) somebody, someone; (*avec interrog*) anybody, anyone ◆ **~ d'autre** somebody *ou* someone else ◆ **c'est ~ de sûr/d'important** he's a reliable/an important person, he's someone reliable/important ◆ **Claire, c'est ~ de bien** Claire is a nice person ◆ **il faudrait ~ de plus** we need one more person ◆ **~ pourrait-il répondre ?** could somebody answer? ◆ **il y a ~ ?** is there anybody there?

2 (*intensif*) **c'est vraiment ~ cette fille** that girl's really something else* ◆ **c'est ~ (d'important) dans le monde du cinéma** she's really somebody in cinema ◆ **dans ce métier, c'est difficile de devenir ~*** it's not easy to make a name for yourself in this profession ◆ **ça alors, c'est ~ ! †*** that's (a bit) too much!, that's a bit stiff!* (*Brit*)

quémander /kemɑ̃de/ ► conjug 1 ◄ **VT** [+ *argent, faveur*] to beg for; [+ *louanges*] to beg *ou* fish *ou* angle for

quémandeur, -euse /kemɑ̃dœʀ, øz/ **NM,F** (*littér*) beggar

qu'en-dira-t-on /kɑ̃diʀatɔ̃/ **NM INV** (= *commérage*) ◆ **le ~** gossip ◆ **il se moque du ~** he doesn't care what people say, he doesn't care about gossip

quenelle /kənɛl/ **NF** (*Culin*) quenelle

quenotte /kənɔt/ **NF** (*langage enfantin*) tooth, toothy-peg (*Brit*) (*langage enfantin*)

quenouille /kənuj/ **NF** distaff ◆ **tomber en ~** (*Hist*) to pass into female hands; (= *échouer*) to fall through; (= *être abandonné*) [*pouvoir, privilège*] to be forsaken

quéquette* /kekɛt/ **NF** (*langage enfantin*) willy* (*Brit*), peter* (*US*)

querelle /kəʀɛl/ **NF** 1 (= *dispute*) quarrel ◆ **~ d'amoureux** lovers' tiff ◆ **~ d'ivrognes** drunken row ◆ **~ d'Allemand, mauvaise ~** quarrel over nothing ◆ **chercher une ~ d'Allemand** *ou* **une mauvaise ~ à qn** to pick a quarrel with sb for nothing *ou* for no reason at all ◆ **~ de famille** *ou* **familiale** family quarrel *ou* squabble; (*grave*) family feud ◆ **~ de chapelle** *ou* **de clocher** petty squabbling (*NonC*) *ou* in-fighting (*NonC*) 2 (= *polémique*) dispute (*sur* over, about); ◆ **la ~ sur l'enseignement privé** the dispute over private education 3 (††, *littér* = *cause, parti*) cause, quarrel † ◆ **épouser** *ou* **embrasser la ~ de qn** to take up *ou* fight sb's cause; → **chercher, vider**

quereller /kəʀele/ ► conjug 1 ◄ **VT** († = *gronder*) to scold **VPR** **se quereller** to quarrel (with one another) ◆ **se ~ au sujet** *ou* **à propos de qch** to quarrel *ou* squabble over *ou* about sth

querelleur, -euse /kəʀelœʀ, øz/ **ADJ** quarrelsome

quérir /keʀiʀ/ ► conjug 21 ◄ **VT** (*littér* = *chercher*) ◆ **envoyer** *ou* **faire ~ qn** to summon sb, to bid sb (to) come † ◆ **aller ~ qn** to go seek sb †, to go in quest of sb †

questeur /kɛstœʀ/ **NM** (*Antiq*) quaestor (*Brit*), questor (*US*); (*Pol française*) questeur (*administrative and financial officer elected to the French Parliament*)

question /kɛstjɔ̃/ GRAMMAIRE ACTIVE 39.3, 43.3, 53.1, 53.2, 53.6 **NF** 1 (= *demande*) (*gén*) question; (*pour lever un doute*) query, question ◆ **~ piège** (*d'apparence facile*) trick question; (*pour nuire à qn*) loaded question ◆ **~ subsidiaire** tiebreaker ◆ **évidemment ! cette ~ ! ou quelle ~ !** obviously! what a question! ◆ **c'est la grande ~** (*problème*) it's the main *ou* major issue *ou* question ◆ **c'est la grande ~, c'est la ~ à mille francs*** (*interrogation*) it's the big question *ou* the sixty-four thousand dollar question*

2 (*Pol*) **~ écrite/orale** written/oral question ◆ **séance de ~s au gouvernement** question and answer session (*at the French National Assembly*), ≃ question time (*Brit*)

3 (= *problème*) question, matter, issue ◆ **~s économiques/sociales** economic/social questions *ou* matters *ou* issues ◆ **pour des ~s de sécurité/d'hygiène** for reasons of security/of hygiene ◆ **~ d'actualité** (*Presse*) topical question ◆ **la ~ est délicate** it's a delicate question *ou* matter ◆ **la ~ est de savoir si ...** the question is whether ... ◆ **la ~ sociale** the social question *ou* issue ◆ **sortir de la ~** to stray *ou* wander from the point ◆ **la ~ n'est pas là, là n'est pas la ~** that's not the point ◆ **c'est toute la ~, c'est la grosse** *ou* **grande ~** that's the big question, that's the crux of the matter, that's the whole point ◆ **il n'y a pas de ~, c'est lui le meilleur** he is indisputably *ou* unquestionably the best, there's no question about it – he's the best ◆ **cela ne fait pas ~** there's no question about it ◆ **c'est une ~ de temps** it's a question *ou* matter of time ◆ **c'est une ~ d'heures/de vie ou de mort/d'habitude** it's a matter *ou* question of time/of life or death/of habit ◆ **je ne céderai pas, c'est une ~ de principe** I won't give in, it's a matter of principle ◆ **"autres questions"** (*ordre du jour*) "any other business"; → **autre**

4 (* = *en ce qui concerne*) **~ argent** as far as money goes, money-wise* ◆ **~ bêtise, il se**

pose là ! he's a prize idiot! ◆ ~ **cuisine, elle est nulle** when it comes to cooking, she's useless*

5 *(avec poser, se poser)* **poser une ~ à qn** to ask sb a question, to put a question to sb ◆ **l'ambiguïté de son attitude pose la ~ de son honnêteté** his ambivalent attitude makes you wonder how honest he is *ou* makes you question his honesty ◆ **sans poser de ~s** without asking any questions, without raising any queries ◆ **la ~ me semble mal posée** I think the question is badly put ◆ **poser la ~ de confiance** *(Pol)* to ask for a vote of confidence ◆ **la ~ qui se pose** the question which must be asked *ou* considered ◆ **il y a une ~ que je me pose** there's one thing I'd like to know, I wonder about one thing ◆ **je me pose la ~** that's the question, that's what I'm wondering ◆ **il commence à se poser des ~s** he's beginning to wonder *ou* to have doubts ◆ **il l'a fait sans se poser de ~s** he did it without a second thought

6 *(locutions)* **de quoi est-il ~ ?** what is it about? ◆ **il fut d'abord ~ du budget** first they spoke about *ou* discussed the budget ◆ **il est ~ de lui comme ministre** *ou* **qu'il soit ministre** there's some question *ou* talk of his being a minister ◆ **il n'est plus ~ de ce fait dans la suite** no further mention of this fact is made subsequently, there is no further reference to this fact thereafter ◆ **il n'est pas ~ que nous y renoncions/d'y renoncer** there's no question of our *ou* us giving it up/of giving it up ◆ **il n'en est pas ~ !** that's out of the question! ◆ **moi y aller ? pas ~ !*** me go? nothing doing!* *ou* no way!* ◆ **c'est hors de ~** it is out of the question

7 *(locutions)* **en ~** *(= dont on parle)* in question ◆ **c'est votre vie qui est en ~** *(= en jeu)* it's your life which is at stake voir**Graal**osa**mettre** *ou* **remettre en ~** *[+ autorité, théorie]* to question, to challenge; *[+ compétence, honnêteté, pratique]* to question, to call *ou* bring into question ◆ **la remise en ~ de nos accords** the fact that our agreements are being called into question ◆ **cela remet sa compétence en ~** this puts a question mark over his competence ◆ **le projet est sans cesse remis en ~** the project is continually being called into question ◆ **il faut se remettre en ~ de temps en temps** it's important to do some soul-searching *ou* to take a good look at oneself from time to time ◆ **elle ne se remet jamais en ~** she never questions herself

8 *(Hist = torture)* question ◆ **soumettre qn à la ~, infliger la ~ à qn** to put sb to the question

questionnaire /kɛstjɔnɛʀ/ **NM** questionnaire ◆ ~ **à choix multiple** multiple choice question paper

questionnement /kɛstjɔnmɑ̃/ **NM** 1 *(= remise en cause)* questioning ◆ **le ~ des valeurs de notre temps** the questioning *ou* the calling into question of contemporary values 2 *[de personne]* questioning *(sur* about); ◆ **le ~ des philosophes** *(= questions)* the questions philosophers are asking themselves

questionner /kɛstjɔne/ ▸ **conjug 1** ◂ **VT** *(= interroger)* to question *(sur* about); ◆ **arrête de ~ toujours comme ça** stop pestering me with questions all the time, stop questioning me all the time

questionneur, -euse /kɛstjɔnœʀ, øz/ **NM,F** questioner

questure /kɛstyʀ/ **NF** *(Antic)* quaestorship *(Brit)*, questorship *(US)*; *(Pol française) administrative and financial commission at the French Parliament*

quétaine * /ketɛn/ **ADJ** (Can) tacky *

quête /kɛt/ **NF** 1 *(= collecte)* collection ◆ **faire la ~** *(à l'église)* to take (the) collection; *[artiste de rue]* to go round with the hat; *[association caritative]* to collect for charity 2 *(= recherche)* search, quest ◆ **sa ~ spirituelle** his spiritual quest; → **Graal**

◆ **en + quête de** in search of ◆ **se mettre en ~ de** *[+ pain]* to go to get; *[+ champignons]* to go in search of ◆ **se mettre en ~ d'un appartement** to start looking for an apartment *ou* flat *(Brit)*, to start flat-hunting *(Brit)* ◆ **être en ~ de travail** to be looking for *ou* seeking work ◆ **des jeunes en ~ d'absolu/d'identité** young people in search of the absolute/of an identity ◆ **des publicitaires en ~ permanente d'idées** advertising people always on the lookout for ideas

quêter /kete/ ▸ **conjug 1** ◂ **VI** *(à l'église)* to take (the) collection; *(dans la rue)* to collect money ◆ ~ **pour les aveugles** to collect for the blind **VT** *[+ louanges]* to seek (after), to fish *ou* angle for; *[+ suffrages]* to seek; *[+ sourire, regard]* to seek, to try to win

quêteur, -euse /kɛtœʀ, øz/ **NM,F** *(dans la rue, à l'église)* collector

quetsche /kwɛtʃ/ **NF** *kind of dark-red plum*

quetzal /kɛtzal/ **NM** *(= oiseau, monnaie)* que(t)zal

queue /kø/ **NF** 1 *[d'animal, avion, comète, lettre, note]* tail; *[d'orage]* tail end; *[de classement]* bottom; *[de casserole, poêle]* handle; *[de feuille, fruit]* stalk; *[de fleur]* stem, stalk; *[de colonne, train]* rear ◆ **en ~ de phrase** at the end of the sentence ◆ **en ~ de liste/classe** at the bottom of the list/class ◆ **être en ~ de peloton** *(lit)* to be at the back of the pack; *(fig)* to be lagging behind ◆ **en ~ (de train)** at the rear of the train ◆ **compartiments de ~** rear compartments; → **diable**

2 *(= file de personnes)* queue *(Brit)*, line *(US)* ◆ **faire la ~** to queue (up) *(Brit)*, to stand in line *(US)* ◆ **il y a trois heures de ~** there's a three-hour queue *(Brit) ou* line *(US)* ◆ **mettez-vous à la ~** join the queue *(Brit) ou* line *(US)*

3 *(**= pénis)* cock**, prick**

4 *(locutions)* **la ~ basse*** *ou* **entre les jambes*** with one's tail between one's legs ◆ **à la ~ leu leu** *[arriver, marcher]* in single file; *[venir se plaindre]* one after the other ◆ **il n'y en avait pas la ~ d'un*** there wasn't a single one ◆ **faire une ~ de poisson à qn** *(en conduisant)* to cut in front of sb ◆ **finir en ~ de poisson** to come to an abrupt end ◆ **histoire sans ~ ni tête*** cock-and-bull story ◆ **mettre des ~s aux zéros** *[marchand]* to overcharge ◆ **faire une fausse ~** *(Billard)* to miscue

COMP queue d'aronde dovetail ◆ **assemblage en ~ d'aronde** dovetail joint
queue de billard (billiard) cue
queue de cheval ponytail ◆ **se faire une ~ de cheval** to put one's hair in a ponytail
queue de vache ADJ INV *[couleur, cheveux]* reddish-brown

queue-de-morue (pl **queues-de-morue**) /kød(ə)mɔʀy/ **NF** 1 *(= pinceau)* (medium) paintbrush 2 †† *(= basques)* tails; *(= habit)* tail coat

queue-de-pie (pl **queues-de-pie**) /kød(ə)pi/ **NF** *(habit)* tails, tail coat

queue-de-rat (pl **queues-de-rat**) /kød(ə)ʀa/ **NF** *(= lime)* round file

queue-de-renard (pl **queues-de-renard**) /kød(ə)ʀənaʀ/ **NF** *(= plante)* ◆ **à épi vert clair** green amaranth ◆ ~ **des jardins** love-lies-bleeding

queux /kø/ **NM** → **maître**

qui /ki/

1 PRONOM INTERROGATIF 2 PRONOM RELATIF

Pour les proverbes commençant par **qui**, cherchez sous le verbe, le nom ou l'adjectif.

1 - PRONOM INTERROGATIF

1 sujet

Lorsque **qui** ou **qui est-ce qui** sont sujets, ils se traduisent par **who**.

◆ ~ **l'a vu ?, ~ est-ce ~ l'a vu ?** who saw him? ◆ **vous devinez ~ me l'a dit !** you can guess who told me! ◆ **on m'a raconté … – ~ ça ?** somebody told me … – who was that? ◆ ~ **va là ?** who goes there? ◆ **je me demande ~ est là** I wonder who's there

Notez l'emploi de **which** lorsqu'il y a discrimination entre plusieurs personnes.

◆ ~ **d'entre eux** *ou* **parmi eux saurait ?** which of them would know? ◆ **~, parmi les candidats, pourrait répondre ?** which (one) of the candidates could reply?

2 objet

Lorsque **qui** est objet, il se traduit par **who** dans la langue courante et par **whom** dans une langue plus soutenue.

◆ ~ **a-t-elle vu ?** who *ou* whom *(frm)* did she see? ◆ **elle a vu ~ ?*, ~ est-ce qu'elle a vu ?** who did she see? ◆ **elle a vu ~ ?** *(surprise)* she saw who?, who did she see? ◆ **je me demande ~ il a invité** I wonder who *ou* whom *(frm)* he has invited

3 avec préposition

Notez la place de la préposition en anglais : avec **who** et **whose**, elle est rejetée en fin de proposition, alors qu'elle précède toujours **whom**.

◆ **à** *ou* **avec ~ voulez-vous parler ?** who would you like to speak to? ◆ **à ~ donc parlais-tu ?** who were you talking to?, who was it you were talking to? ◆ **elle ne sait pas à ~ parler** she doesn't know who to talk to ◆ **à ~ est ce sac ?** *(sens possessif)* whose bag is this?, who does this bag belong to?, whose is this bag? ◆ **chez ~ allez-vous ?** whose house are you going to? ◆ **de ~ parles-tu ?** who are you talking about? ◆ **de ~ est la pièce ?** who is the play by? ◆ **pour ~ ont-ils voté ?** who did they vote for?, for whom *(frm)* did they vote?

2 - PRONOM RELATIF

1 sujet

Lorsque **qui** est sujet, il se traduit par **who** ou **that** quand l'antécédent est une personne ; si c'est un nom propre, on traduit obligatoirement par **who**.

◆ **je connais des gens ~ se plaindraient** I know some people who *ou* that would complain ◆ **j'ai rencontré Luc ~ m'a raconté que …** I met Luc, who told me that …

qui sujet se traduit par **that** ou **which** quand l'antécédent est un animal ou une chose.

◆ **il a un perroquet ~ parle** he's got a parrot that *ou* which talks

Notez que lorsque la relative est en incise, on n'emploie jamais **that**.

◆ **Tom, ~ travaille à la poste, m'a dit …** Tom, who works at the post office, told me … ◆ **la table, ~ était en acajou, était très lourde** the table, which was made of mahogany, was very heavy

Lorsque la proposition définit ou qualifie l'antécédent, le pronom peut être omis.

◆ **les amis ~ viennent ce soir sont américains** the friends (who *ou* that are) coming tonight are American ◆ **prends le plat ~ est sur la table** take the dish which *ou* that is on the table ◆ **Paul, ~ traversait la rue, trébucha** Paul tripped (as he was) crossing the street ◆ **je la vis ~ nageait vers le pont** I saw her swimming towards the bridge ◆ **moi ~ espérais rentrer tôt !** and there I was thinking I was going to get home early tonight!; → **ce², moi, toi**

2 avec préposition

Le pronom relatif est parfois omis en anglais ; notez la place de la préposition (voir aussi **pron interrog 3**).

◆ **la personne à ~ j'ai parlé** the person (who *ou* that) I spoke to ◆ **l' élève de ~ il attendait de meilleurs résultats** the pupil (who *ou* that) he was expecting better results from, the pupil from whom *(frm)* he was expecting better results ◆ **le patron pour ~ il travaille** the employer (that *ou* who) he works for, the employer for whom *(frm)* he works ◆ **la femme sans ~ il ne pouvait vivre** the woman (who *ou* that) he couldn't live without

3 sans antécédent

Lorsque **qui** n'a pas d'antécédent, il représente toujours un être animé ou plusieurs, et se traduit par **whoever**, **anyone who**, **anyone that**.

◆ **ira ~ voudra** whoever wants *ou* anyone who wants to go can go ◆ **il a dit à ~ voulait l'entendre que ...** he told anyone who *ou* that would listen that ..., he told whoever would listen that ... ◆ **amenez ~ vous voulez** bring along whoever you like *ou* anyone (that) you like ◆ **~ les verrait ensemble ne devinerait jamais ça** anyone seeing them together would never guess, anyone who *ou* that saw them together would never guess ◆ **pour ~ s'intéresse à la physique, ce livre est indispensable** for anyone (who *ou* that is) interested in physics this book is indispensable ◆ **ils ont pris tout ce qu'ils ont pu : ~ une chaise, ~ une table, ~ un livre** they took whatever they could: one took a chair, one a table, another a book ◆ **c'est à ~ des deux mangera le plus vite** each tries to eat faster than the other ◆ **c'est à ~ criera le plus fort** each tries to shout louder than the other

◆ **à qui mieux mieux** *(gén)* each one more so than the other; *(crier)* each one louder than the other; *(frapper)* each one harder than the other

◆ **qui de droit** *(Admin)* ◆ **"à qui de droit"** "to whom it may concern" ◆ **je le dirai à ~ de droit** I will tell whoever is concerned *ou* is the proper authority ◆ **le tableau a été restitué à ~ de droit** the painting was returned to its rightful owner ◆ **je remercierai ~ de droit** I'll thank whoever I have to thank

◆ **qui que ce soit** anybody, anyone ◆ **j'interdis à ~ que ce soit d'entrer ici** I forbid anybody *ou* anyone to come in here

◆ **qui tu sais, qui vous savez** ◆ **cela m'a été dit par ~ vous savez** I was told that by you-know-who*

---

quia /kɥija/ ADV ◆ **mettre à ~** to confound sb †, to nonplus sb ◆ **être à ~** to be at a loss for an answer

quiche /kiʃ/ NF ◆ **~ (lorraine)** quiche (Lorraine) ◆ **~ au crabe** crab quiche

quick /kwik/ NM ◆ **court** *ou* **terrain (de tennis) en ~** all-weather court, hard court

quiconque /kikɔ̃k/ PRON REL *(= celui qui)* whoever, anyone who, whosoever † ◆ **~ a tué sera jugé** whoever has killed will be judged ◆ **la loi punit ~ est coupable** the law punishes anyone who is guilty PRON INDÉF *(= n'importe qui, personne)* anyone, anybody ◆ **je le sais mieux que ~** I know better than anyone (else) ◆ **il ne veut recevoir d'ordres de ~** he won't take orders from anyone *ou* anybody

quid /kwid/ PRON INTERROG ◆ **~ de la démocratie ?** *(= et au sujet de la démocratie ?)* and what about democracy?; *(= que va-t-il advenir de la démocratie ?)* whither democracy?

quidam † /k(ɥ)idam/ NM *(hum = individu)* fellow, chap *(Brit)*, cove † *(Brit)*

quiet, quiète †† /kjɛ, kjɛt/ ADJ *(littér)* calm, tranquil

quiétisme /kjetism/ NM quietism

quiétiste /kjetist/ ADJ, NMF quietist

quiétude /kjetyd/ NF *(littér) [de lieu]* quiet, tranquility; *[de personne]* peace (of mind) ◆ **en toute ~** *(= sans soucis)* with complete peace of mind; *(= sans obstacle)* in (complete) peace ◆ **les voleurs ont pu opérer en toute ~** the thieves were able to go about their business undisturbed

quignon /kiɲɔ̃/ NM ◆ **~ (de pain)** *(= croûton)* crust (of bread), heel of the loaf; *(= morceau)* hunk *ou* chunk of bread

quille /kij/ NF 1 *(Jeux)* skittle ◆ **(jeu de) ~s** ninepins, skittles; → **chien** 2 *(* = jambe)* pin* 3 *(arg Mil)* **la ~** demob *(arg Mil Brit)* 4 *(Naut)* keel ◆ **la ~ en l'air** bottom up(wards), keel up

quincaillerie /kɛ̃kajʀi/ NF *(= métier, ustensiles)* hardware, ironmongery *(Brit)*; *(= magasin)* hardware shop *ou* store, ironmonger's (shop) *(Brit)*; *(péj = bijoux)* cheap(-looking) jewellery *(Brit)* *ou* jewelry *(US)* ◆ **elle a sorti toute sa ~** she's put on all her trinkets

quincaillier, -ière /kɛ̃kaje, jɛʀ/ NM,F hardware dealer, ironmonger *(Brit)*

quinconce /kɛ̃kɔ̃s/ **en quinconce** LOC ADV in staggered rows

quinine /kinin/ NF quinine

quinqua * /kɛ̃ka/ NMF (abrév de **quinquagénaire**) person in his (*ou* her) fifties ◆ **les ~s** fifty somethings*

quinquagénaire /kɛ̃kaʒenɛʀ/ ADJ *(= de cinquante ans)* fifty-year-old *(épith)* ◆ **il est ~** *(= de cinquante à soixante ans)* he is in his fifties ◆ **maintenant que tu es ~** *(hum)* now that you're fifty (years old), now that you've reached fifty NMF fifty-year-old man (*ou* woman)

Quinquagésime /kɥɛ̃kwaʒezim/ NF Quinquagesima

quinquennal, e (mpl **-aux**) /kɛ̃kenal, o/ ADJ five-year *(épith)*, quinquennial ◆ **assolement ~** five-year rotation

quinquennat /kɛ̃kena/ NM *(Pol)* five year term (of office)

quinquet /kɛ̃kɛ/ NM *(Hist)* oil lamp ◆ **~s*** *(† = yeux)* peepers* *(hum)*

quinquina /kɛ̃kina/ NM *(Bot, Pharm)* cinchona ◆ **(apéritif au) ~** *quinine tonic wine*

quint /kɛ̃/ ADJ → **Charles**

quintal (pl **-aux**) /kɛ̃tal, o/ NM quintal *(100 kg)*; *(Can)* hundredweight

quinte /kɛ̃t/ NF 1 *(Méd)* **~ (de toux)** coughing fit 2 *(Mus)* fifth; *(Escrime)* quinte; *(Cartes)* quint

quinté /kɛ̃te/ NM *French forecast system involving betting on five horses*

quintessence /kɛ̃tesɑ̃s/ NF *(Chim, Philos, fig)* quintessence ◆ **abstracteur de ~** *(hum)* hair-splitter

quintet /k(ɥ)ɛ̃tɛ/ NM *(Jazz)* jazz quintet

quintette /k(ɥ)ɛ̃tɛt/ NM *(= morceau, musiciens)* quintet(te) ◆ **~ à cordes/à vent** string/wind quintet

quinteux, -euse †† /kɛ̃tø, øz/ ADJ *(littér) [vieillard]* crotchety, crabbed †

quintillion /kɛ̃tiljɔ̃/ NM quintillion *(Brit)*, nonillion *(US)*

quintuple /kɛ̃typl/ ADJ *[quantité, rangée, nombre]* quintuple ◆ **une quantité ~ de l'autre** a quantity five times (as great as) the other ◆ **en ~ exemplaire/partie** in five copies/parts ◆ **le ~ champion du monde** the world champion five times over NM *(Math, gén)* quintuple *(de* of); ◆ **je l'ai payé le ~/le ~ de l'autre** I paid five times as much for it/five times as much as the other for it ◆ **je vous le rendrai au ~** I'll repay you five times over ◆ **augmenter au ~** to increase fivefold

quintupler /kɛ̃typle/ ▸ conjug 1 ◂ VTI to quintuple, to increase fivefold *ou* five times

quintuplés, -ées /kɛ̃typle/ NM,F PL quintuplets, quins* *(Brit)*, quints* *(US)*

quinzaine /kɛ̃zɛn/ NF *(= nombre)* about fifteen, fifteen or so; *(= salaire)* two weeks' *ou* fortnightly *(Brit)* *ou* fortnight's *(Brit)* pay ◆ **une ~ (de jours)** *(= deux semaines)* two weeks, a fortnight *(Brit)* ◆ **~ publicitaire** *ou* **commerciale** (two-week) sale ◆ **~ du blanc** (two-week) linen sale ◆ **"quinzaine des soldes"** "two-week sale", "sales fortnight" *(Brit)*

quinze /kɛ̃z/ NM INV fifteen ◆ **le ~ de France** *(Rugby)* the French fifteen; *pour autres loc voir* **six** ADJ INV fifteen ◆ **le ~ août** 15 August, Assumption ◆ **demain en ~** a fortnight tomorrow *(Brit)*, two weeks from tomorrow *(US)* ◆ **lundi en ~** a fortnight on Monday *(Brit)*, two weeks from Monday *(US)* ◆ **dans ~ jours** in two weeks, in a fortnight *(Brit)*, in a fortnight's time *(Brit)*, in two weeks' time *(Brit)* ◆ **tous les ~ jours** every two weeks, every fortnight *(Brit)*; → **FÊTES LÉGALES**

quinzième /kɛ̃zjɛm/ ADJ, NMF fifteenth; *pour loc voir* **sixième**

quinzièmement /kɛ̃zjɛmmɑ̃/ ADV in the fifteenth place, fifteenthly

quiproquo /kipʀɔko/ NM 1 *(= méprise sur une personne)* mistake; *(= malentendu sur un sujet)* misunderstanding ◆ **le ~ durait depuis un quart d'heure, sans qu'ils s'en rendent compte** they had been talking at cross-purposes for a quarter of an hour without realizing it 2 *(Théât)* (case of) mistaken identity

Quito /kito/ N Quito

quittance /kitɑ̃s/ NF *(= reçu)* receipt; *(= facture)* bill ◆ **~ d'électricité** receipt *(to show one has paid one's electricity bill)* ◆ **~ de loyer** rent receipt ◆ **donner ~ à qn de qch** *(frm)* to acquit sb of sth *(frm)*

quitte /kit/ ADJ 1 ◆ **être ~ envers qn** to be quits* *ou* all square with sb, to be no longer in sb's debt ◆ **être ~ envers sa patrie** to have served one's country ◆ **être ~ envers la société** to have paid one's debt to society ◆ **nous sommes ~s** *(dette)* we're quits* *ou* all square; *(méchanceté)* we're even *ou* quits* *ou* all square ◆ **tu es ~ pour cette fois** I'll let you off this time, I'll let you get away with it this time ◆ **je ne vous tiens pas ~** you still owe me

2 ◆ **être/tenir qn ~ d'une dette/obligation** to be/consider sb rid *ou* clear of a debt/an obligation ◆ **je suis ~ de mes dettes envers vous** all my debts to you are clear *ou* are paid off ◆ **nous en sommes ~s pour la peur** we got off with a fright

3 ◆ **~ à** *(idée de risque)* even if it means ◆ **~ à s'ennuyer, ils préfèrent rester chez eux** they prefer to stay at home even if it means getting bored ◆ **~ à aller au restaurant, autant en**

choisir un bon *(idée de nécessité)* if we're going to a restaurant, we might as well go to a good one

4 ◆ ~ **ou double** *(= jeu)* double or quits ◆ **c'est (du) ~ ou double, c'est jouer à ~ ou double** *(fig)* it's a big gamble, it's risking a lot

quitter /kite/ GRAMMAIRE ACTIVE 54.3, 54.4, 54.5 ▸ conjug 1 ◂

VT 1 *[+ école, pays, personne]* to leave; *[+ métier]* to leave, to quit, to give up ◆ **il n'a pas quitté la maison depuis trois jours** he hasn't been outside *ou* he hasn't set foot outside the house for three days, he hasn't left the house for three days ◆ **je suis pressé, il faut que je vous quitte** I'm in a hurry so I must leave you *ou* I must be off* ◆ **il a quitté sa femme** he's left his wife ◆ **ne pas ~ la chambre** to be confined to one's room ◆ **"les clients sont priés de quitter la chambre avant 11 heures"** "guests are requested to vacate their rooms before 11 o'clock" ◆ ~ **l'autoroute à Lyon** to turn off *ou* leave the motorway at Lyon ◆ **le camion a quitté la route** the lorry ran off *ou* left the road ◆ **le train a quitté la voie** *ou* **les rails** the train derailed *ou* jumped the rails ◆ **il a quitté ce monde** *(euph)* he has departed this world ◆ ~ **la place** *(fig)* to withdraw, to retire ◆ **si je le quitte des yeux une seconde** if I take my eyes off him for a second, if I let him out of my sight for a second ◆ **ne quittez pas** *(Téléc)* hold the line, hold on a moment; → **lieu¹, semelle**

2 *(= renoncer à) [+ espoir, illusion]* to give up, to forsake; *(= abandonner) [crainte, énergie]* to leave, to desert ◆ **tout son courage l'a quitté** all his courage left *ou* deserted him

3 *(† = enlever) [+ vêtement]* to take off ◆ ~ **le deuil** to come out of mourning ◆ ~ **l'habit** *ou* **la robe** *(fig)* to leave the priesthood ◆ ~ **l'uniforme** *(Mil)* to leave the army *(ou navy etc)*

4 *(Ordin)* to quit, to exit

VPR se quitter *[couple]* to split up, to part ◆ **nous nous sommes quittés bons amis** we parted good friends ◆ **ils ne se quittent pas** they are always together, you never see them apart ◆ **nous nous sommes quittés à 11 heures** we left each other at 11

quitus /kitys/ **NM** *(Comm)* full discharge, quietus

qui-vive /kiviv/ **NM INV** ◆ **être sur le ~** to be on the alert

quiz(z) /kwiz/ **NM INV** quiz ◆ **~z télévisé** TV quiz show

quoi /kwa/ **PRON INTERROG** 1 what ◆ **on joue ~ au cinéma ?*** what's on at the cinema? ◆ ~ **faire/lui dire ?** what are we (going) to do/to say to him? ◆ ~ **encore ?** *(gén)* what else?; *(exaspération)* what is it now? ◆ ~ **de plus beau que … ?** what can be more beautiful than …? ◆ ~ **de neuf ?** *ou* **de nouveau ?** what's new? ◆ **je ne sais ~ lui donner** I don't know what to give him ◆ **je ne vois pas avec ~/sur ~ vous allez écrire** I don't see what you are going to write with/on ◆ **vers ~ allons-nous ?** what are we heading for? ◆ **en ~ est cette statue ?** what is this statue made of? ◆ **en ~ puis-je vous aider ?** how can I help you? ◆ **il voudrait savoir en ~ cela le concerne** he would like to know what that's got to do with him; → **comme, sans**

2 *(en exclamatif)* ~ **! tu oses l'accuser ?** what! you dare to accuse him! ◆ ~ **? qu'est-ce qu'il a dit ?** *(pour faire répéter)* what was it *ou* what was that he said? ◆ **et puis ~ encore !** *(iro)* what next! ◆ **puisque je te le dis, ~ !*** I'm telling you it's true!*

3 *(locutions)*

◆ **à quoi** ◆ **à ~ reconnaissez-vous le cristal ?** how can you tell that something is crystal? ◆ **à ~ bon (faire) ?** what's the use (of doing)? ◆ **à ~ ça sert ?*** what's that for? ◆ **dites-nous à ~ cela sert** tell us what that's for ◆ **je sais à ~ tu fais allusion** I know what (it is) you're referring to

◆ **de quoi** ◆ **de ~ parles-tu ?, tu parles de ~ ?*** what are you talking about?, what are you on about?* *(Brit)* ◆ **il voudrait savoir de ~ il est question** he would like to know what it's about

PRONOM RELATIF ◆ **as-tu de ~ écrire ?** have you got a pen? ◆ **ils n'ont même pas de ~ vivre** they haven't even got enough to live on ◆ **il n'y a pas de ~ rire** it's no laughing matter, there's nothing to laugh about ◆ **il n'y a pas de ~ pleurer** it's not worth crying over *ou* about, there's nothing to cry about ◆ **il n'y a pas de ~ s'étonner** there's nothing surprising about *ou* in that ◆ **ils ont de ~ occuper leurs vacances** they've got enough *ou* plenty to occupy them on their holiday ◆ **avoir/emporter de ~ manger** to have/take something to eat ◆ **avoir de ~** to have means ◆ **des gens qui ont de ~** people of means ◆ **merci beaucoup ! – il n'y a pas de ~** many thanks! – don't mention it *ou* (it's) a pleasure *ou* not at all *ou* you're welcome ◆ **ils n'ont pas de ~ s'acheter une voiture** they can't afford to buy a car ◆ **de ~ (de ~) !*** what's all this nonsense! ◆ **c'est en ~ tu te trompes** that's where you're wrong

◆ **quoi que** *+ subj* ◆ ~ **qu'il arrive** whatever happens ◆ ~ **qu'il en soit** be that as it may, however that may be ◆ ~ **qu'on en dise/qu'elle fasse** whatever *ou* no matter what people say/she does ◆ **si vous avez besoin de ~ que ce soit** if there's anything (at all) you need

quoique /kwak(ə)/ **CONJ** *(= bien que)* although, though ◆ **quoiqu'il soit malade et qu'il n'ait pas d'argent** although *ou* though he is ill and has no money ◆ **je ne pense pas qu'il faisait semblant, ~ …** I don't think he was pretending, but then *ou* there again …

quolibet † /kɔlibɛ/ **NM** *(= raillerie)* gibe, jeer ◆ **couvrir qn de ~s** to gibe *ou* jeer at sb

quorum /kɔʀɔm/ **NM** quorum ◆ **le ~ a/n'a pas été atteint** there was/was not a quorum, we *(ou they etc)* had/did not have a quorum

quota /k(w)ɔta/ **NM** *(Admin)* quota ◆ **~s d'importation** import quotas ◆ **1 000 personnes sélectionnées selon la méthode des ~s** a quota sample of 1,000 people

quote-part (pl **quotes-parts**) /kɔtpaʀ/ **NF** *(lit, fig)* share

quotidien, -ienne /kɔtidjɛ̃, jɛn/ **ADJ** *(= journalier) [nourriture, trajet, travail]* daily *(épith)*; *(= banal) [incident]* everyday *(épith)*, daily *(épith)*; *[existence]* everyday *(épith)*, humdrum ◆ **dans la vie quotidienne** in everyday *ou* daily life; → **pain** **NM** 1 *(= journal)* daily (paper), (news) paper ◆ **les grands ~s** the big national dailies 2 *(= routine)* **le ~** everyday life ◆ **la pratique médicale/l'enseignement au ~** day-to-day medical practice/teaching

quotidiennement /kɔtidjɛnmɑ̃/ **ADV** daily, every day

quotidienneté /kɔtidjɛnte/ **NF** everyday nature

quotient /kɔsjɑ̃/ **NM** *(Math)* quotient ◆ ~ **intellectuel** intelligence quotient, IQ ◆ ~ **familial** *(Impôts)* dependents' allowance set against tax

quotité /kɔtite/ **NF** *(Fin)* quota ◆ ~ **disponible** *(Jur) portion of estate of which testator may dispose at his discretion*

QWERTY /kwɛʀti/ **ADV** ◆ **clavier ~** QWERTY keyboard

R, r /ɛʀ/ **NM** *(= lettre)* R, r; → **mois**

rab* /ʀab/ **NM** 1 *[de nourriture]* extra ◆ **est-ce qu'il y a du ~ ?** is there any extra (left)?, is there any extra food (left)? ◆ **qui veut du ~ ?** anyone for seconds? ◆ **il reste un ~ de viande, il reste de la viande en ~** there is some meat left 2 *[de temps] (gén, Mil)* extra time ◆ **un ~ de 5 minutes** *ou* **5 minutes de ~ pour finir le devoir** 5 minutes' extra time *ou* 5 minutes extra to finish off the exercise ◆ **faire du ~** *(travail)* to do *ou* work extra time; *(Mil)* to do *ou* serve extra time

rabâchage /ʀabɑʃaʒ/ **NM** *(= répétition)* boring repetition; *(= révision)* going over and over ◆ **ses conférences, c'est du ~** his lectures are just a rehash of old stuff ◆ **un ~ de généralités inconsistantes** a rehash of empty generalities

rabâcher /ʀabɑʃe/ ▸ conjug 1 ◂ **VT** *(= ressasser) [+ histoire]* to harp on about*, to keep (on) repeating; *(= réviser) [+ leçon]* to go over and over, to keep going back over *(à qn* for sb); ◆ **il rabâche toujours la même chose** he keeps rambling *ou* harping on about the same (old) thing **VI** *(= radoter)* to keep repeating o.s.

rabâcheur, -euse /ʀabɑʃœʀ, øz/ **NM,F** repetitive *ou* repetitious bore ◆ **il est du genre ~** he's the type who never stops repeating himself *ou* harping on*

rabais /ʀabɛ/ **NM** reduction, discount ◆ **5 € de ~, ~ de 5 €** reduction *ou* discount of €5, €5 off ◆ **faire un ~ de 5 € sur qch** to give a reduction *ou* discount of €5 on sth, to knock €5 off (the price of) sth

◆ **au rabais** *[acheter, vendre]* at a reduced price, (on the) cheap; *(péj) [acteur, journaliste]* third-rate; *(péj) [enseignement, médecine]* cheap-rate, on the cheap *(attrib)* ◆ **je ne veux pas travailler au ~** *(péj)* I won't work for a pittance

rabaissant, e /ʀabɛsɑ̃, ɑ̃t/ **ADJ** *[remarque]* disparaging, derogatory; *[métier]* degrading

rabaisser /ʀabese/ ▸ conjug 1 ◂ **VT** 1 *(= dénigrer) [+ personne]* to disparage; *[+ efforts, talent, travail]* to belittle, to disparage 2 *(= réduire) [+ pouvoirs]* to reduce, to decrease; *[+ orgueil]* to humble; *[+ exigences]* to moderate, to reduce; *[+ qualité]* to impair ◆ **il voulait 10 000 € par mois, mais il a dû ~ ses prétentions** he wanted €10,000 a month but he had to lower his sights; → **caquet** 3 *(= diminuer) [+ prix]* to reduce, to knock down, to bring down 4 *(= baisser) [+ robe, store]* to pull (back) down **VPR** **se rabaisser** to belittle o.s. ◆ **elle se rabaisse toujours** she never gives herself enough credit, she's always belittling herself *ou* running herself down ◆ **se ~ devant qn** to humble o.s. *ou* bow before sb

rabane /ʀaban/ **NF** raffia fabric

Rabat /ʀaba/ **N** Rabat

rabat /ʀaba/ **NM** 1 *[de table]* flap, leaf; *[de poche, enveloppe, livre]* flap; *[de drap]* fold *(over the covers)*; *[d'avocat, prêtre]* bands ◆ **poche à ~** flapped pocket 2 ⇒ **rabattage**

rabat-joie /ʀabaʒwa/ **NM INV** killjoy, spoilsport, wet blanket* ◆ **faire le ~** to spoil the fun, to act like *ou* be a spoilsport, to be a wet blanket* ◆ **il est drôlement ~** he's an awful killjoy *ou* spoilsport *ou* wet blanket*

rabattable /ʀabatabl/ **ADJ** *[siège]* folding *(épith)*

rabattage /ʀabataʒ/ **NM** *(Chasse)* beating

rabatteur, -euse /ʀabatœʀ, øz/ **NM,F** *(Chasse)* beater; *(fig : péj)* tout; *[de prostituée]* procurer, pimp ◆ **le ~ de l'hôtel** the hotel tout **NM** *[de moissonneuse]* reel

rabattre /ʀabatʀ/ ▸ conjug 41 ◂ **VT** 1 *[+ capot, clapet]* to close, to shut; *[+ couvercle]* to close; *[+ drap]* to fold over *ou* back; *[+ col]* to turn down; *[+ bord de chapeau]* to turn *ou* pull down; *[+ strapontin] (= ouvrir)* to pull down; *(= fermer)* to put up; *[+ jupe]* to pull down ◆ **le vent rabat la fumée** the wind blows the smoke back down ◆ **il rabattit ses cheveux sur son front** he brushed his hair down over his forehead ◆ **le chapeau rabattu sur les yeux** his hat pulled down over his eyes ◆ **~ les couvertures** *(pour couvrir)* to pull the blankets up; *(pour découvrir)* to push *ou* throw back the blankets

2 *(= diminuer)* to reduce; *(= déduire)* to deduct, to take off ◆ **il n'a pas voulu ~ un centime (du prix)** he wouldn't take *ou* knock a halfpenny (Brit) *ou* cent (US) off (the price), he wouldn't come down (by) one centime (on the price) ◆ **~ l'orgueil de qn** to humble sb's pride

◆ **en rabattre** *(de ses prétentions)* to climb down; *(de ses ambitions)* to lower one's sights; *(de ses illusions)* to lose one's illusions

3 *(Chasse) [+ gibier]* to drive; *[+ terrain]* to beat ◆ **~ des clients*** *[prostituée]* to tout for customers

4 *(Tricot)* **~ des mailles** to cast off ◆ **~ une couture** *(Couture)* to stitch down a seam

5 *(Arboriculture) [+ arbre]* to cut back

VPR **se rabattre** 1 *[voiture]* to cut in; *[coureur]* to cut in, to cut across ◆ **se ~ devant qn** *[voiture]* to cut in front of sb; *[coureur]* to cut *ou* swing in front of *ou* across sb ◆ **le coureur s'est rabattu à la corde** the runner cut *ou* swung across to the inside lane

2 *(= prendre faute de mieux)* **se ~ sur** *[+ marchandise, personne]* to fall back on, to make do with

3 *(= se refermer) [porte]* to fall *ou* slam shut; *[couvercle]* to close; *[dossier]* to fold down, to fold away ◆ **la porte se rabattit sur lui** the door closed *ou* shut on *ou* behind him

rabattu, e /ʀabaty/ (ptp de **rabattre**) **ADJ** *[col, bords]* turned down; *[poche]* flapped

rabbin /ʀabɛ̃/ **NM** rabbi ◆ **grand ~** chief rabbi

rabbinat /ʀabina/ **NM** rabbinate

rabbinique /ʀabinik/ **ADJ** rabbinic(al)

rabbinisme /ʀabinism/ **NM** rabbinism

rabelaisien, -ienne /ʀablɛzjɛ̃, jɛn/ **ADJ** Rabelaisian

rabibochage* /ʀabibɔʃaʒ/ **NM** *(= réconciliation)* reconciliation

rabibocher* /ʀabibɔʃe/ ▸ conjug 1 ◂ **VT** *(= réconcilier) [+ amis, époux]* to patch things up between **VPR** **se rabibocher** to make it up, to patch things up *(avec* with) ◆ **ils se sont rabibochés** they've patched things up

rabiot* /ʀabjo/ **NM** ⇒ **rab**

rabioter* /ʀabjɔte/ ▸ conjug 1 ◂ **VT** 1 *(= obtenir)* to wangle* ◆ **j'ai rabioté cinq minutes de sommeil** I managed to snatch another five minutes' sleep 2 *(= voler) [+ temps, argent]* to fiddle* *(Brit) (qch à qn* sth from sb); ◆ **le plombier m'a rabioté 10 €/un quart d'heure** the plumber swindled *ou* did* me out of €10/a quarter of an hour ◆ **un commerçant qui rabiote** a shopkeeper who makes a bit on the side ◆ **~ sur la quantité** to give short measure

rabioteur, -euse* /ʀabjɔtœʀ, øz/ **NM,F** *(= qui vole)* ◆ **c'est un vrai ~** he's always trying to make a bit on the side, he's always on the fiddle* *(Brit)*

rabique /ʀabik/ **ADJ** rabies *(épith)*

râble /ʀɑbl/ **NM** *[d'un animal]* back; *(* = dos)* small of the back ◆ **tomber** *ou* **sauter sur le ~ de qn*** to set on sb*, to go for sb* ◆ **le pauvre, il ne sait pas ce qui va lui tomber sur le ~ !*** the poor guy doesn't know what he's in for! ◆ **~ de lièvre** *(Culin)* saddle of hare

râblé, e /ʀɑble/ **ADJ** *[homme]* stocky, well-set *(Brit)*, heavy-set *(US)*; *[cheval]* broad-backed

rabot /ʀabo/ **NM** plane ◆ **passer qch au ~** to plane sth (down)

rabotage /ʀabɔtaʒ/ **NM** planing (down)

raboter /ʀabɔte/ ▸ conjug 1 ◂ **VT** 1 *(Menuiserie)* to plane (down) 2 *(* = racler) [+ objet]* to scrape; *[+ partie du corps]* to graze, to scrape ◆ **mon pare-chocs a raboté le mur** my bumper scraped the wall ◆ **baisse-toi si tu ne veux pas te ~ la tête contre le plafond** bend down if you don't want to scrape your head on the ceiling 3 (*fig* = *diminuer*) to reduce ◆ **crédits/salaires rabotés** reduced credits/wages

raboteur /ʀabɔtœʀ/ NM (= *ouvrier*) planer

raboteuse¹ /ʀabɔtøz/ NF (= *machine*) planing machine

raboteux, -euse² /ʀabɔtø, øz/ ADJ (= *rugueux*) [*surface, arête*] uneven, rough; [*chemin*] rugged, uneven, bumpy; (*littér*) [*style*] rough, rugged; [*voix*] rough

rabougri, e /ʀabugʀi/ (ptp de **rabougrir**) ADJ (= *chétif*) [*plante*] stunted, scraggy; [*personne*] stunted, puny; (= *desséché*) [*plante*] shrivelled; [*vieillard*] wizened, shrivelled

rabougrir /ʀabugʀiʀ/ ▸ conjug 2 ◂ VT [+ *personne*] to (cause to) shrivel up; [+ *plante*] (= *dessécher*) to shrivel (up); (= *étioler*) to stunt VPR **se rabougrir** [*personne*] to become shrivelled (with age), to become wizened; [*plante*] to shrivel (up), to become stunted

rabougrissement /ʀabugʀismɑ̃/ NM (= *action*) [*de plante*] stunting, shrivelling (up); [*de personne*] shrivelling up; (= *résultat*) [*de plante*] scragginess; [*de personne*] stunted appearance; [*de vieillard*] wizened appearance

rabouter /ʀabute/ ▸ conjug 1 ◂ VT [+ *tubes, planches*] to join (together) (end to end); [+ *étoffes*] to seam *ou* sew together

rabrouer /ʀabʀue/ ▸ conjug 1 ◂ VT to snub, to rebuff ◆ **elle me rabroue tout le temps** she rebuffs me all the time ◆ **se faire ~** to be rebuffed

racaille /ʀakɑj/ NF 1 (= *populace*) rabble, riffraff 2 * (= *individu*) chav * (*Brit*), punk * (*US*)

raccommodable /ʀakɔmɔdabl/ ADJ [*vêtement*] repairable, mendable

raccommodage /ʀakɔmɔdaʒ/ NM 1 (= *action*) [*de vêtement, accroc, filet*] mending, repairing; [*de chaussettes*] darning, mending ◆ **faire du ~** *ou* **des ~s** (*pour soi*) to do some mending; (*comme métier*) to take in mending 2 (= *endroit réparé*) (*gén*) mend, repair; [*de chaussette*] darn

raccommodement* /ʀakɔmɔdmɑ̃/ NM (= *réconciliation*) reconciliation

raccommoder /ʀakɔmɔde/ ▸ conjug 1 ◂ VT 1 [+ *vêtements, accroc*] to mend, to repair; [+ *chaussette*] to darn, to mend 2 * [+ *ennemis*] to bring together again, to patch things up between VPR **se raccommoder** * to make it up, to be reconciled

raccommodeur, -euse /ʀakɔmɔdœʀ, øz/ NM,F [*de linge, filets*] mender ◆ **~ de porcelaines** †† china restorer

raccompagner /ʀakɔ̃paɲe/ ▸ conjug 1 ◂ VT to take back (*à* to) ◆ **~ qn (chez lui)** to take sb home ◆ **~ qn au bureau en voiture** to drive sb back to the office ◆ **~ qn au bureau à pied** to walk sb back to the office ◆ **~ qn à la gare** to take sb to the station ◆ **~ qn (jusqu')à la porte** to see sb to the door ◆ **il l'a raccompagnée jusqu'à sa voiture** he saw her to her car ◆ **je vous raccompagne** (*chez vous*) I'll take you home; (*à la sortie*) I'll see you out

raccord /ʀakɔʀ/ NM 1 [*de papier peint*] join ◆ **~ (de maçonnerie)** pointing (*NonC*) ◆ **faire un ~** (*de papier peint*) to line up the pattern ◆ **faire un ~ de peinture/de maquillage** to touch up the paintwork/one's makeup ◆ **on ne voit pas les ~s (de peinture)** you can't see where the paint has been touched up ◆ **les ~s sont mal faits** (*papier peint*) the pattern isn't matched properly ◆ **papier peint sans ~s** random match wallpaper 2 [*de texte, discours*] link, join; (*Ciné*) [*de séquence*] continuity; [*de scène*] link shot; (= *collage*) [*de film, bande magnétique*] splice ◆ **à cause des coupures, nous avons dû faire des ~s** (*Ciné*) because of the cuts, we had to do some link shots ◆ **ce plan n'est pas ~** this shot doesn't follow on from the preceding one 3 (= *pièce, joint*) link; [*de pompe à vélo*] nozzle

raccordement /ʀakɔʀdəmɑ̃/ NM 1 (*NonC*) [*de routes, bâtiments, voies ferrées*] linking, joining, connecting; [*de fils électriques*] joining; [*de tuyaux*] joining, connecting; (*Ciné*) linking ◆ **~ (au réseau)** (*Téléc*) connection (to the phone network); (*à l'électricité*) connection (to the mains) ◆ **ils sont venus faire le ~** (*Téléc*) they've come to connect the phone; (*à l'électricité*) they've come to connect the electricity; → **bretelle, taxe, voie** 2 (= *soudure, épissure*) join; (= *tunnel, passage*) connecting passage; (= *carrefour, voie ferrée*) junction

raccorder /ʀakɔʀde/ ▸ conjug 1 ◂ VT 1 [+ *routes, bâtiments, voies ferrées*] to link up, to join (up), to connect (*à* with, to); [+ *fils électriques*] to join; [+ *tuyaux*] to join, to connect (*à* to); ◆ **les motifs du papier peint sont parfaitement raccordés** the wallpaper is perfectly lined up 2 (*Ciné*) [+ *plans, scènes*] to link up 3 ◆ **~ qn au réseau** (*Téléc*) to connect sb's phone; (*à l'électricité*) to connect sb to the mains ◆ **quand les deux tuyaux seront raccordés** when the two pipes are joined together *ou* connected 4 (= *établir une relation entre*) to connect VPR **se raccorder** [*routes*] to link *ou* join up (*à* with); ◆ **se ~ à** [*faits*] to tie up *ou* in with

raccourci /ʀakuʀsi/ NM 1 (= *chemin*) short cut ◆ **prendre un ~ par la forêt** to take a short cut through the forest ◆ **~ clavier** (*Ordin*) hot key 2 (= *formule frappante*) pithy turn of phrase; (= *résumé*) summary ◆ **en ~** (= *en miniature*) in miniature; (= *dans les grandes lignes*) in (broad) outline; (= *en bref*) in a nutshell, in brief ◆ **cet article donne un ~ saisissant de leurs pratiques** this article provides a graphic resumé of their methods ◆ **dans** *ou* **un ~ saisissant, il écrit que ...** in a graphic phrase, he writes that ... 3 (*Art*) foreshortening ◆ **figure en ~** foreshortened figure

raccourcir /ʀakuʀsiʀ/ ▸ conjug 2 ◂ VT 1 [+ *distance, temps*] to shorten; [+ *vêtement*] to shorten, to take up; [+ *vacances*] to shorten, to cut short; [+ *texte*] to cut ◆ **j'ai raccourci le chapitre de trois pages** I cut *ou* shortened the chapter by three pages ◆ **ça raccourcit le trajet de 5 km** it cuts *ou* knocks 5 km off the journey ◆ **passons par là, ça (nous) raccourcit** let's go this way, it's shorter *ou* quicker ◆ **les vêtements amples raccourcissent la silhouette** baggy clothes make people look shorter 2 (* *hum*) **~ qn** (= *décapiter*) to chop sb's head off VI [*jours*] to grow shorter, to draw in; [*vêtement*] (*au lavage*) to shrink ◆ **les jupes ont raccourci cette année** (*Mode*) skirts are shorter this year, hemlines have gone up this year

raccourcissement /ʀakuʀsismɑ̃/ NM [*de distance, temps, jour, vacances, texte*] shortening; [*de vêtement*] (*en cousant*) shortening; (*au lavage*) shrinking

raccoutumer /ʀakutyme/ ▸ conjug 1 ◂ VT ⇒ **réaccoutumer**

raccroc /ʀakʀo/ NM (*frm*) ◆ **par ~** (= *par hasard*) by chance; (= *par un heureux hasard*) by a stroke of good fortune

raccrocher /ʀakʀɔʃe/ GRAMMAIRE ACTIVE 54.3, 54.5 ▸ conjug 1 ◂

VI 1 (*Téléc*) to hang up, to ring off (*surtout Brit*) ◆ **ne raccroche pas** hold on, don't hang up *ou* ring off (*surtout Brit*) ◆ **~ au nez de qn** * to put the phone down on sb, to hang up on sb

2 (*arg Sport*) to retire

VT 1 [+ *vêtement, tableau*] to hang back up; (*Téléc*) [+ *combiné*] to put down ◆ **j'avais mal raccroché** I hadn't put the receiver down properly ◆ **~ les gants/chaussures** (*Sport*) to hang up one's gloves/boots

2 (= *racoler*) [*vendeur, portier*] to tout for ◆ **~ le client** [*prostituée*] to solicit, to accost customers

3 (= *attraper*) [+ *personne, bonne affaire*] to grab *ou* get hold of ◆ **il m'a raccroché dans la rue** he stopped *ou* waylaid *ou* button-holed me in the street

4 (= *relier*) [+ *wagons, faits*] to link, to connect (*à* to, with)

5 (* = *rattraper*) [+ *affaire, contrat*] to save, to rescue

VPR **se raccrocher** ◆ **se ~ à** [+ *branche, rampe*] to catch *ou* grab (hold of); [+ *espoir, personne*] to cling to, to hang on to ◆ **cette idée se raccroche à la précédente** this idea ties in with the previous one; → **branche**

race /ʀas/ NF 1 [*de personnes*] race ◆ **la ~ humaine** the human race ◆ **être de ~ indienne** to be of Indian stock *ou* blood ◆ **un individu de ~ blanche/noire** a white/black person ◆ **c'est de la sale ~ !** ** (*péj*) they're just scum! ** 2 [*d'animaux*] breed ◆ **la ~ chevaline** horses ◆ **la ~ bovine normande** Normandy cattle ◆ **de ~** (*gén*) pedigree (*épith*), purebred (*épith*); [*cheval*] thoroughbred ◆ **avoir de la ~** to be of good stock; → **chien** 3 (= *ancêtres*) stock, race ◆ **être de ~ noble** to be of noble stock *ou* blood *ou* race ◆ **avoir de la ~** to have breeding 4 (= *catégorie*) breed ◆ **lui et les gens de sa ~** him and others like him ◆ **les cordonniers, c'est une ~ qui disparaît** cobblers are a dying breed *ou* race ◆ **il est de la ~ des héros** he's the stuff heroes are made of

racé, e /ʀase/ ADJ [*animal*] purebred (*épith*), pedigree (*épith*); [*cheval*] thoroughbred; [*personne*] distinguished; [*voiture, voilier, ligne*] sleek

rachat /ʀaʃa/ NM 1 [*d'objet que l'on possédait avant*] buying back, repurchase; [*d'objet d'occasion*] buying, purchase; [*d'usine en faillite*] buying up *ou* out *ou* over; [*de dette, rente*] redemption ◆ **~ d'entreprise par l'encadrement/par les salariés** management/employee buyout ◆ **option** *ou* **possibilité de ~** buy-back option ◆ **après le ~ du journal par le groupe** after the group bought the paper back 2 [*d'esclave, otage*] ransom, ransoming 3 (= *réparation*) redemption, atonement; (*Rel*) redemption

rachetable /ʀaʃ(ə)tabl/ ADJ [*dette, rente*] redeemable; [*péché*] expiable; [*pécheur*] redeemable ◆ **cette faute n'est pas ~** you can't make up for this mistake

racheter /ʀaʃ(ə)te/ ▸ conjug 5 ◂ VT 1 [+ *objet que l'on possédait avant*] to buy back, to repurchase; [+ *nouvel objet*] to buy *ou* purchase another; [+ *pain, lait*] to buy some more; [+ *objet d'occasion*] to buy, to purchase; [+ *entreprise*] to buy out, to take over; [+ *usine en faillite*] to buy up *ou* out *ou* over ◆ **je lui ai racheté son vieux vélo** I bought his old bike from *ou* off him ◆ **il a racheté toutes les parts de son associé** he bought his partner out, he bought up all his partner's shares ◆ **j'ai dû ~ du tissu/des verres** I had to buy some more material/some more glasses

2 [+ *dette, rente*] to redeem

3 [+ *esclave, otage*] to ransom, to pay a ransom for

4 (= *réparer*) [+ *péché, crime*] to atone for, to expiate; [+ *mauvaise conduite, faute*] to make amends for, to make up for; [+ *imperfection*] to make up *ou* compensate for; [+ *pécheur*] to redeem ◆ **il n'y en a pas un pour ~ l'autre** * they're both (just) as bad as each other

5 (*Scol*) [+ *candidat*] to mark up

6 (*Archit*) to modify

VPR **se racheter** [*pécheur*] to redeem o.s.; [*criminel*] to make amends ◆ **se ~ aux yeux de qn** to redeem o.s. in sb's eyes ◆ **essaie de te ~ en t'excusant** try and make up for it *ou* try to make amends by apologizing

rachidien, -ienne /ʀaʃidjɛ̃, jɛn/ ADJ of the spinal column, rachidian (*SPÉC*)

rachis /ʀaʃis/ NM *(Anat)* vertebral *ou* spinal column

rachitique /ʀaʃitik/ ADJ *[personne] (Méd)* suffering from rickets, rachitic *(SPÉC)*; *(= maigre)* puny; *[arbre, poulet]* scraggy, scrawny ◆ **c'est un ~, il est ~** he suffers from rickets

rachitisme /ʀaʃitism/ NM rickets *(sg)*, rachitis *(SPÉC)* ◆ **faire du ~** to have rickets

racial, e (mpl **-iaux**) /ʀasjal, jo/ ADJ racial; *[discrimination, lois]* racial, race *(épith)*; *[émeutes, relations]* race *(épith)* ◆ **son appartenance ~e** his race

racine /ʀasin/ NF 1 *(gén)* root ◆ **la carotte est une ~** the carrot is a root (vegetable), carrots are a root crop ◆ **prendre ~** *(lit)* to take *ou* strike root(s), to put out roots; *(fig = s'établir)* to put down (one's) roots; *(* : chez qn, à attendre)* to take root* ◆ **prendre le mal à la ~, s'attaquer aux ~s du mal** to get to the root of the problem; → **rougir** 2 *(Math)* root ◆ **~ carrée/cubique/dixième** square/cube/tenth root 3 *[de mot]* root NFPL **racines** *(= attaches, origines)* roots ◆ **il est sans ~s** he's rootless, he belongs nowhere ◆ **cette idée a des ~s profondes dans notre société** this idea is deeply rooted in our society

COMP **racine adventive** adventitious root
racine aérienne aerial root
racine fasciculée fascicled root
racine pivotante taproot

racinien, -ienne /ʀasinjɛ̃, jɛn/ ADJ Racinian

racisme /ʀasism/ NM racism ◆ **~ anti-arabe** racism against Arabs ◆ **~ anticorse** prejudice against Corsicans ◆ **~ antijeunes** discrimination against young people

raciste /ʀasist/ ADJ, NMF racist

racket /ʀakɛt/ NM *(= activité)* racketeering *(NonC)*; *(= vol)* (extortion) racket ◆ **~ scolaire** *bullying other children for money etc* ◆ **faire du ~, se livrer au ~** *(contre protection)* to run a protection racket ◆ **c'est du ~ !** it's daylight robbery!

racketter /ʀakete/ ► conjug 1 ◄ VT ◆ **~ qn** to extort money from sb ◆ **il se fait ~ à l'école** children bully him into giving them money (*ou* his personal belongings *etc*) at school

racketteur /ʀaketœʀ/ NM racketeer

raclage /ʀɑklaʒ/ NM *(Tech)* scraping

raclée* /ʀɑkle/ NF *(= coups)* hiding, thrashing; *(= défaite)* thrashing* ◆ **flanquer une bonne ~ à qn** to give sb a good hiding ◆ **il a pris une bonne ~ aux élections** he got thrashed* *ou* hammered* in the elections

raclement /ʀɑkləmɑ̃/ NM *(= bruit)* scraping (noise) ◆ **on entendit un ~ de gorge** someone could be heard clearing their throat

racler /ʀɑkle/ ► conjug 1 ◄ VT 1 *(gén, Méd, Tech)* to scrape; *[+ fond de casserole]* to scrape out; *[+ parquet]* to scrape (down) ◆ **ce vin racle le gosier** this wine is really rough ◆ **se ~ la gorge** to clear one's throat; → **fond** 2 *(= ratisser) [+ allée, gravier, sable]* to rake 3 *(= enlever) [+ tache, croûte]* to scrape away *ou* off; *[+ peinture, écailles]* to scrape off ◆ **~ la boue de ses semelles** to scrape the mud off one's shoes 4 *(péj) [+ violon]* to scrape *ou* saw (a tune) on; *[+ guitare]* to strum (a tune) on

raclette /ʀɑklɛt/ NF 1 *(= outil)* scraper 2 *(Culin)* raclette *(melted cheese served with boiled potatoes and cold meats)*

racloir /ʀɑklwaʀ/ NM scraper

raclure /ʀɑklyʀ/ NF 1 *(gén pl = déchet)* scraping 2 *(*✻ *péj)* louse*

racolage /ʀakɔlaʒ/ NM 1 *(par une prostituée)* soliciting 2 *(péj : par un agent électoral, un portier, un vendeur)* soliciting, touting ◆ **faire du ~** to solicit, to tout ◆ **cette émission fait du ~ émotionnel** this programme deliberately plays on people's emotions

racoler /ʀakɔle/ ► conjug 1 ◄ VT 1 *[prostituée]* **~ des clients** to solicit for clients ◆ **~ en voiture** to solicit in a car 2 *(péj) [agent électoral, portier, vendeur]* to solicit, to tout for 3 *(Hist) [+ soldats]* to pressgang

racoleur, -euse /ʀakɔlœʀ, øz/ NM *(pour spectacle)* tout; *(† Mil)* crimp; *(péj Pol)* canvasser NF **racoleuse** *(= prostituée)* streetwalker, whore ADJ 1 *[slogan, publicité] (gén)* eye-catching, enticing; *(Pol)* vote-catching 2 *(péj) [reportage, article]* sensationalistic; *[film, titre]* too sensational ◆ **c'est trop ~** it plays too much on people's emotions

racontable /ʀakɔ̃tabl/ ADJ repeatable ◆ **cette histoire n'est pas ~ devant des enfants** this story is not fit to be told in front of children

racontar /ʀakɔ̃taʀ/ NM story, bit of gossip ◆ **ce ne sont que des ~s !** it's just gossip!

raconter /ʀakɔ̃te/ ► conjug 1 ◄ VT 1 *(= relater) [+ histoire, légende]* to tell ◆ **~ qch à qn** to tell sb sth ◆ **~ sa vie** to tell one's life story ◆ **il nous a raconté ses malheurs** he told us about his misfortunes ◆ **il raconte qu'il a vu la reine** he says that he's seen the queen ◆ **elle m'a raconté qu'elle t'avait rencontré** she told me that she had met you ◆ **on raconte que ...** people say that ... ◆ **à ce qu'on raconte** from what people say ◆ **il est un peu radin à ce qu'on raconte** he's a bit mean by all accounts *ou* from what people say ◆ **le témoin a raconté ce qui s'était passé** the witness described *ou* recounted what had happened ◆ **il raconte bien** he tells a good story, he's a good storyteller ◆ **alors, raconte !** come on, tell me! (*ou* us!) ◆ **alors, qu'est-ce que tu racontes ?*** so, what's new?*, so, how are things with you?* ◆ **je te raconte pas !*** you can imagine!
2 *(= dire de mauvaise foi)* **qu'est-ce que tu racontes ?** what on earth are you talking about?, what are you (going) on about?* ◆ **il raconte n'importe quoi** he's talking nonsense *ou* rubbish* *(Brit)* ◆ **~ des histoires, en ~** to tell stories, to spin yarns ◆ **il a été ~ qu'on allait divorcer** he's been (going around) telling people we're getting divorced
VPR **se raconter** *[écrivain]* to talk about o.s. ◆ **se ~ des histoires** *(= se leurrer)* to lie to o.s. ◆ **il se la raconte*** he thinks he's God's gift*

raconteur, -euse /ʀakɔ̃tœʀ, øz/ NM,F storyteller ◆ **~ de** narrator of

racornir /ʀakɔʀniʀ/ ► conjug 2 ◄ VT 1 *(= durcir) [+ peau, cuir]* to toughen, to harden; *[+ cœur, personne]* to harden ◆ **cuir racorni** hardened *ou* dried-up leather ◆ **dans son cœur racorni** in his hard heart 2 *(= ratatiner) [+ personne, plante]* to shrivel (up) ◆ **un vieillard racorni** a shrivelled(-up) *ou* wizened old man VPR **se racornir** 1 *(= se durcir) [peau, cuir, cœur, personne]* to become tough *ou* hard 2 *(= se ratatiner) [personne, plante]* to shrivel (up), to become shrivelled (up)

racornissement /ʀakɔʀnismɑ̃/ NM *[de peau, cuir]* toughening, hardening; *[de plante]* shrivelling (up)

rad /ʀad/ NM rad

radar /ʀadaʀ/ NM radar ◆ **système/écran ~** radar system/screen ◆ **contrôle ~** *(sur route)* speed check ◆ **il s'est fait prendre au ~*** he was caught by a speed trap* ◆ **marcher** *ou* **fonctionner au ~*** *(fig)* to be on automatic pilot*

radariste /ʀadaʀist/ NMF radar operator

radasse✻ /ʀadas/ NF *(péj)* tart✻

rade /ʀad/ NF *(= port)* (natural) harbour *(Brit) ou* harbor *(US)*, roads *(SPÉC)*, roadstead *(SPÉC)*
♦ **en rade** *[bateau]* in harbour, in the roads *(SPÉC)* ◆ **en ~ de Brest** in Brest harbour ◆ **laisser en ~*** *[+ personne]* to leave in the lurch, to leave high and dry; *[+ projet]* to forget about, to drop, to shelve; *[+ voiture]* to leave behind ◆ **elle/sa voiture est restée en ~*** she/her car was left stranded ◆ **tomber en ~*** *(panne d'essence)* to run out of petrol *(Brit) ou* gas *(US)*; *(ennuis mécaniques)* to break down

radeau (pl **radeaux**) /ʀado/ NM raft; *(= train de bois)* timber float *ou* raft ◆ **~ de sauvetage/pneumatique** rescue/inflatable raft

radial, e (mpl **-iaux**) /ʀadjal, jo/ ADJ *(gén)* radial NF **radiale** *(= route)* urban motorway *(Brit) ou* highway *(US)*

radian /ʀadjɑ̃/ NM radian

radiant, e /ʀadjɑ̃, jɑ̃t/ ADJ *[énergie]* radiant ◆ **(point) ~** *(Astron)* radiant

radiateur /ʀadjatœʀ/ NM *(à eau, à huile)* radiator; *(à gaz, à barres chauffantes)* heater; *[de voiture]* radiator ◆ **~ à accumulation** storage radiator *ou* heater ◆ **~ électrique** electric heater ◆ **~ extraplat** slimline radiator ◆ **~ soufflant** fan heater ◆ **~ parabolique** electric fire

radiation /ʀadjasjɔ̃/ NF 1 *(Phys)* radiation 2 *[de nom, mention]* crossing *ou* striking off ◆ **on a demandé sa ~ du club** there have been calls for him to be expelled from the club *ou* for his club membership to be cancelled

radical, e (mpl **-aux**) /ʀadikal, o/ ADJ *[changement, mesure, solution]* radical, drastic; *(Bot, Math, Hist, Pol)* radical ◆ **une rupture ~e avec les pratiques passées** a complete break with past practices ◆ **essayez ce remède, c'est ~*** try this remedy, it works like a charm *ou* it really does the trick* ◆ **un mois de ce régime et tu maigris, c'est ~ !*** one month on this diet and you lose weight, it never fails! NM *[de mot]* stem, radical, root; *(Chim, Pol)* radical; *(Math)* radical sign ◆ **radicaux libres** *(Chim)* (free) radicals

radicalement /ʀadikalmɑ̃/ ADV *[changer, différer]* radically; *[faux, nouveau]* completely ◆ **~ opposé à/différent** radically opposed to/different ◆ **rompre ~ avec** to make a complete break with

radicalisation /ʀadikalizasjɔ̃/ NF *[de position, revendications]* toughening; *[de conflit]* intensification; *[de régime, parti]* radicalization ◆ **certains élus préconisent une ~ du texte** some representatives would like the text to be made even more radical

radicaliser /ʀadikalize/ ► conjug 1 ◄ VT *[+ position]* to toughen, to harden; *[+ politique]* to toughen VPR **se radicaliser** *[personne, parti, position, politique]* to become more radical; *[conflit]* to intensify

radicalisme /ʀadikalism/ NM *(Pol)* radicalism

radical-socialisme /ʀadikalsɔsjalism/ NM radical socialism

radical-socialiste, radicale-socialiste /ʀadikalsɔsjalist/ (mpl **radicaux-socialistes** /ʀadikosɔsjalist/) ADJ, NMF radical socialist

radicelle /ʀadisɛl/ NF rootlet, radicle *(SPÉC)*

radiculaire /ʀadikylɛʀ/ ADJ radicular

radicule /ʀadikyl/ NF radicle

radié, e /ʀadje/ (ptp de **radier**) ADJ *(= rayonné)* rayed, radiate

radier /ʀadje/ ► conjug 7 ◄ VT *[+ mention, nom]* to cross off, to strike off ◆ **il a été radié de l'Ordre des médecins** he has been struck off the medical register

radiesthésie /ʀadjɛstezi/ NF (power of) divination, dowsing *(based on the detection of radiation)*

radiesthésiste /ʀadjɛstezist/ NMF diviner, dowser

radieusement /ʀadjøzmɑ̃/ ADV radiantly ◆ **~ beau** *[personne]* radiantly *ou* dazzlingly beautiful

radieux, -ieuse /ʀadjø, jøz/ ADJ *[personne, sourire, beauté]* radiant; *[journée, temps]* beautiful

radin, e * /ʀadɛ̃, in/ ADJ stingy, mean (Brit) NM,F skinflint ◆ **quel** ~ ! how mean can you get!, mean, or what? *

radiner * VI, **se radiner** * VPR /ʀadine/ ▸ conjug 1 ◂ (= arriver) to turn up, to show up *, to roll up *; (= accourir) to rush over, to dash over ◆ **allez, radine(-toi) !** come on, step on it! * ou get your skates on! * (Brit)

radinerie * /ʀadinʀi/ NF stinginess (NonC), meanness (Brit)

radio /ʀadjo/ NF 1 (= poste) radio ◆ **mets la** ~ turn on ou put on the radio; → **poste²**

2 (= radiodiffusion) **la** ~ (the) radio ◆ **avoir la** ~ to have a radio ◆ **parler à la** ~ to speak on the radio ◆ **passer à la** ~ to be on the radio ◆ **travailler à la** ~ to work in broadcasting ou on the radio ◆ **antenne/fréquence** ~ radio aerial/frequency

3 (= station) radio station ◆ ~ **pirate** pirate radio station ◆ **la** ~ **du Caire** Cairo radio ◆ ~ **libre** ou **locale privée** independent local radio station

4 (= radiotéléphonie) radio ◆ **message** ~ radio message ◆ **la** ~ **de bord du navire** the ship's radio

5 (= radiographie) X-ray (photograph) ◆ **passer une** ~ to have an X-ray (taken) ◆ **on lui a fait passer une** ~ he was X-rayed

NM (= opérateur) radio operator; († = message) radiogram, radiotelegram

> ⚠ Au sens de 'radiographie', **radio** ne se traduit pas par le mot anglais **radio**.

radioactif, -ive /ʀadjoaktif, iv/ ADJ radioactive ◆ **déchets faiblement/hautement** ~**s** low-level/highly ou high-level radioactive waste

radioactivité /ʀadjoaktivite/ NF radioactivity ◆ ~ **naturelle** natural ou naturally-occurring radioactivity

radioalignement /ʀadjoaliɲ(ə)mɑ̃/ NM radio navigation system

radioamateur /ʀadjoamatœʀ/ NM radio ham *

radioastronome /ʀadjoastʀɔnɔm/ NMF radio astronomer

radioastronomie /ʀadjoastʀɔnɔmi/ NF radio astronomy

radiobalisage /ʀadjobalizaʒ/ NM radio beacon signalling

radiobalise /ʀadjobaliz/ NF radio beacon

radiobaliser /ʀadjobalize/ ▸ conjug 1 ◂ VT to equip with a radio beacon system

radiobiologie /ʀadjobjɔlɔʒi/ NF radiobiology

radiocarbone /ʀadjokaʀbɔn/ NM radiocarbon, radioactive carbon

radiocassette /ʀadjokasɛt/ NM cassette radio, radio cassette player

radiocobalt /ʀadjokɔbalt/ NM radio cobalt, radioactive cobalt

radiocommande /ʀadjokɔmɑ̃d/ NF radio control

radiocommunication /ʀadjokɔmynikasjɔ̃/ NF radio communication

radiocompas /ʀadjokɔ̃pɑ/ NM radio compass

radioconducteur /ʀadjokɔ̃dyktœʀ/ NM detector

radiodiagnostic /ʀadjodjagnɔstik/ NM radiodiagnosis

radiodiffuser /ʀadjodifyze/ ▸ conjug 1 ◂ VT to broadcast (by radio) ◆ **interview radiodiffusée** broadcast ou radio interview

radiodiffuseur /ʀadjodifyzœʀ/ NM (radio) broadcaster

radiodiffusion /ʀadjodifyzjɔ̃/ NF broadcasting (by radio)

radioélectricien, -ienne /ʀadjoelɛktʀisjɛ̃, jɛn/ NM,F radio-engineer

radioélectricité /ʀadjoelɛktʀisite/ NF radio-engineering

radioélectrique /ʀadjoelɛktʀik/ ADJ radio (épith)

radioélément /ʀadjoelemɑ̃/ NM radio-element

radiofréquence /ʀadjofʀekɑ̃s/ NF radio frequency

radiogénique /ʀadjoʒenik/ ADJ radiogenic

radiogoniomètre /ʀadjogɔnjɔmɛtʀ/ NM direction finder, radiogoniometer

radiogoniométrie /ʀadjogɔnjɔmetʀi/ NF radio direction finding, radiogoniometry

radiogramme /ʀadjɔgʀam/ NM (= télégramme) radiogram, radiotelegram; (= film) radiograph, radiogram

radiographie /ʀadjɔgʀafi/ NF 1 (= technique) radiography, X-ray photography ◆ **passer une** ~ to have an X-ray (taken), to be X-rayed 2 (= photographie) X-ray (photograph), radiograph

radiographier /ʀadjɔgʀafje/ ▸ conjug 7 ◂ VT to X-ray

radiographique /ʀadjɔgʀafik/ ADJ X-ray (épith)

radioguidage /ʀadjogidaʒ/ NM (en avion) radio control, radiodirection ◆ **le** ~ **des automobilistes** (Radio) broadcasting traffic reports to motorists

radioguidé, e /ʀadjogide/ ADJ radio-controlled

radioguider /ʀadjogide/ ▸ conjug 1 ◂ VT to radio-control

radio-isotope (pl **radio-isotopes**) /ʀadjoizɔtɔp/ NM radio-isotope

radiologie /ʀadjɔlɔʒi/ NF radiology

radiologique /ʀadjɔlɔʒik/ ADJ radiological

radiologiste /ʀadjɔlɔʒist/, **radiologue** /ʀadjɔlɔg/ NMF radiologist

radiomessagerie /ʀadjomesaʒʀi/ NF radiopaging

radiomètre /ʀadjɔmɛtʀ/ NM radiometer

radio-moquette * /ʀadjomɔkɛt/ NF rumours (Brit), rumors (US)

radionavigant /ʀadjonavigɑ̃/ NM radio officer

radionavigation /ʀadjonavigasjɔ̃/ NF radio navigation

radiophare /ʀadjofaʀ/ NM radio beacon

radiophonie /ʀadjɔfɔni/ NF radiotelephony

radiophonique /ʀadjɔfɔnik/ ADJ radio (épith)

radioprotection /ʀadjopʀɔtɛksjɔ̃/ NF radiation protection

radioreportage /ʀadjoʀ(ə)pɔʀtaʒ/ NM radio report

radioreporter /ʀadjoʀ(ə)pɔʀtɛʀ/ NM radio reporter

radio-réveil (pl **radio-réveils**) /ʀadjoʀevɛj/ NM radio-alarm, clock-radio

radioscopie /ʀadjɔskɔpi/ NF radioscopy

radioscopique /ʀadjɔskɔpik/ ADJ radioscopic

radiosondage /ʀadjosɔ̃daʒ/ NM (Météo) radiosonde exploration; (Géol) seismic prospecting

radiosonde /ʀadjosɔ̃d/ NF radiosonde

radiosource /ʀadjosuʀs/ NF radio source, star source

radio-taxi (pl **radio-taxis**) /ʀadjotaksi/ NM radio taxi, radio cab

radiotechnique /ʀadjotɛknik/ NF radio technology ADJ radiotechnological

radiotélégraphie /ʀadjotelegʀafi/ NF radiotelegraphy, wireless telegraphy

radiotélégraphique /ʀadjotelegʀafik/ ADJ radiotelegraphic

radiotélégraphiste /ʀadjotelegʀafist/ NMF radiotelegrapher

radiotéléphone /ʀadjotelefɔn/ NM radiotelephone

radiotéléphonie /ʀadjotelefɔni/ NF radiotelephony, wireless telephony

radiotélescope /ʀadjotelɛskɔp/ NM radio telescope

radiotélévisé, e /ʀadjotelevize/ ADJ broadcast on both radio and television, broadcast and televised

radiotélévision /ʀadjotelevizjɔ̃/ NF radio and television

radiothérapeute /ʀadjoteʀapøt/ NMF radiotherapist

radiothérapie /ʀadjoteʀapi/ NF radiotherapy

radis /ʀadi/ NM 1 (= légume) radish ◆ ~ **noir** black winter radish 2 (* = sou) penny, cent (US) ◆ **je n'ai pas un** ~ I haven't got a penny (to my name) (Brit) ou a cent * ou a bean (US) * ◆ **ça ne vaut pas un** ~ it's not worth a penny ou a bean (Brit) *

radium /ʀadjɔm/ NM radium

radius /ʀadjys/ NM (Anat) radius

radjah /ʀadʒa/ NM rajah

radome /ʀadom/ NM radome

radon /ʀadɔ̃/ NM radon

radotage /ʀadɔtaʒ/ NM (péj) drivel (NonC), rambling

radoter /ʀadɔte/ ▸ conjug 1 ◂ VI (péj) to ramble on ou drivel (on) ◆ **tu radotes** * you're talking a load of drivel * VT (péj) ◆ **il radote toujours les mêmes histoires** * he's always going on ou wittering on * about the same old things

radoteur, -euse /ʀadɔtœʀ, øz/ NM,F (péj) driveling (old) fool, (old) driveller

radoub /ʀadu/ NM (Naut) refitting ◆ **navire au** ~ ship under repair ou undergoing a refit; → **bassin**

radouber /ʀadube/ ▸ conjug 1 ◂ VT [+ navire] to repair, to refit; [+ filet de pêche] to repair, to mend

radoucir /ʀadusiʀ/ ▸ conjug 2 ◂ VT [+ ton, attitude] to soften; [+ temps] to make milder VPR **se radoucir** [personne] (après une colère) to calm down, to be mollified; (avec l'âge) to mellow; [voix] to soften, to become milder; [temps] to become milder

radoucissement /ʀadusismɑ̃/ NM 1 (Météo) ~ **(de la température)** rise in (the) temperature ◆ **on prévoit un léger/net** ~ the forecast is for slightly/much milder weather 2 [de ton, attitude] softening; [de personne] calming down

rafale /ʀafal/ NF [de vent] gust; [de pluie] sudden shower; [de neige] flurry ◆ **une soudaine** ~ **(de vent)** a sudden gust of wind ◆ ~ **de mitrailleuse** burst of machine gun fire ◆ **en** ou **par** ~**s** [souffler] in gusts; [tirer] in bursts ◆ **tir en** ~**s** firing ou shooting in bursts ◆ **une** ~ ou **des** ~**s de balles** a hail of bullets ◆ **le gouvernement publiait des communiqués en** ~**s** the government issued statements in rapid-fire succession

raffermir /ʀafɛʀmiʀ/ ▸ conjug 2 ◂ VT 1 [+ muscle] to harden, to tone up; [+ chair] to firm up, to make firm(er); [+ peau] to tone up; [+ voix] to steady 2 [+ gouvernement, popularité] to strengthen, to reinforce; [+ prix, marché, cours] to steady; [+ courage, résolution] to strengthen VPR **se raffermir** 1 [muscle] to harden; [chair] to firm up, to become firm(er) 2 [autorité] to strengthen, to become strengthened ou reinforced; *[prix, marché, cours, voix]* to become steadier ◆ **son visage se raffermit** his face became more composed ◆ **ma résolution se raffermit** I grew stronger in my resolve ◆ **se ~ dans ses intentions** to strengthen one's resolve ◆ **le cours du dollar s'est légèrement raffermi** the dollar is slightly steadier

raffermissant, e /ʀafɛʀmisɑ̃, ɑ̃t/ ADJ *(Cosmétique)* toning

raffermissement /ʀafɛʀmismɑ̃/ NM ① *[de muscle]* strengthening; *[de chair]* firming; *[de peau]* firming up; *[de voix]* steadying ② *[de gouvernement, popularité]* reinforcement; *[de cours, monnaie]* steadying; *[de courage, résolution]* strengthening ◆ **la nouvelle a provoqué un ~ du dollar** the news steadied the dollar

raffinage /ʀafinaʒ/ NM refining

raffiné, e /ʀafine/ (ptp de **raffiner**) ADJ ① *[pétrole, sucre]* refined ② *[personne, mœurs, style]* refined, polished, sophisticated; *[esprit, gourmet, goûts]* discriminating, refined; *[confort, décor]* elegant; *[cuisine, élégance]* refined ◆ **peu ~** unrefined, unsophisticated ◆ **supplice ~** slow torture

raffinement /ʀafinmɑ̃/ NM ① *(= caractère) [de personne, civilisation]* refinement, sophistication ② *(gén pl = détail raffiné)* nicety, refinement ③ *(= excès)* **c'est du ~** that's being oversubtle ◆ **avec un ~ de luxe/de cruauté** with refinements of luxury/of cruelty

raffiner /ʀafine/ ▸ conjug 1 ◂ VT ① *[+ pétrole, sucre, papier]* to refine ② *[+ langage, manières]* to refine, to polish VI *(dans le raisonnement)* to be oversubtle; *(sur les détails)* to be (over)meticulous

raffinerie /ʀafinʀi/ NF refinery ◆ **~ de pétrole/de sucre** oil/sugar refinery

raffineur, -euse /ʀafinœʀ, øz/ NM,F refiner

raffoler /ʀafɔle/ ▸ conjug 1 ◂ **raffoler de** VT INDIR to be mad *ou* crazy* *ou* wild* about ◆ **le chocolat, j'en raffole !** I'm mad* about chocolate!

raffut * /ʀafy/ NM *(= vacarme)* row, racket ◆ **faire du ~** *(= être bruyant)* to make a row *ou* racket; *(= protester)* to kick up a fuss *ou* stink* ◆ **ils ont fait un ~ de tous les diables** they made a hell* of a racket ◆ **sa démission va faire du ~** his resignation will cause a row *ou* a stink*

rafiot /ʀafjo/ NM *(péj = bateau)* (old) tub *(péj)*

rafistolage * /ʀafistɔlaʒ/ NM *(= action : lit, fig)* patching up ◆ **ce n'est qu'un** *ou* **que du ~** *(lit)* it's only a patched-up *ou* makeshift repair; *(fig)* it's just a stopgap (solution)

rafistoler * /ʀafistɔle/ ▸ conjug 1 ◂ VT *(= réparer)* to patch up

rafle /ʀɑfl/ NF (police) roundup *ou* raid, swoop ◆ **la police a fait une ~** the police rounded up some suspects ◆ **être pris dans une ~** to be caught in a roundup *ou* a raid ◆ **la ~ du Vél' d'Hiv** *(Hist) the roundup of Jews in the Paris Vélodrome d'Hiver during the Second World War*

rafler * /ʀɑfle/ ▸ conjug 1 ◂ VT *(= prendre) [+ récompenses]* to run off with; *[+ place]* to bag*, to grab; *(= voler) [+ bijoux]* to swipe** ◆ **les clients avaient tout raflé** the customers had swept up *ou* snaffled* everything ◆ **elle a raflé tous les prix** she ran away *ou* off with all the prizes, she made a clean sweep of the prizes ◆ **le film a raflé sept Oscars** the film scooped seven Oscars

rafraîchir /ʀafʀeʃiʀ/ ▸ conjug 2 ◂ VT ① *(= refroidir) [+ air]* to cool (down), to freshen; *[+ vin]* to chill; *[+ boisson]* to cool, to make cooler; *[+ haleine]* to freshen; → **fruit¹**
② *(= redonner du tonus à) [+ visage, corps]* to freshen (up)
③ *(= désaltérer) [boisson]* to refresh
④ *(= rénover) [+ vêtement]* to smarten up, to brighten up; *[+ tableau, couleur]* to brighten up, to freshen up; *[+ appartement]* to do up, to brighten up; *[+ connaissances]* to brush up ◆ **"à rafraîchir"** *[+ appartement]* "needs some work" ◆ **se faire ~ les cheveux** to have a trim, to have one's hair trimmed ◆ **~ la mémoire** *ou* **les idées de qn** to jog *ou* refresh sb's memory
⑤ *(Ordin) [+ écran]* to refresh
VI *[vin etc]* to cool (down) ◆ **mettre à ~** *[+ vin, dessert]* to chill
VPR **se rafraîchir** ① *(Météo)* **le temps/ça se rafraîchit** the weather/it's getting cooler *ou* colder
② *(en se lavant)* to freshen (o.s.) up; *(en buvant)* to refresh o.s. ◆ **on se rafraîchirait volontiers** a cool drink would be very welcome

rafraîchissant, e /ʀafʀeʃisɑ̃, ɑ̃t/ ADJ *[vent]* refreshing, cooling; *[boisson]* refreshing; *(fig) [idée, œuvre]* refreshing

rafraîchissement /ʀafʀeʃismɑ̃/ NM ① *[de température]* cooling ◆ **dû au ~ de la température** due to the cooler weather *ou* the cooling of the weather ◆ **on s'attend à un ~ rapide de la température** we expect temperatures to drop sharply, we expect the weather to get rapidly cooler ② *(= boisson)* cool *ou* cold drink ◆ **~s** *(= glaces, fruits)* refreshments ③ *(Ordin)* refresh ◆ **fréquence de ~** refresh rate

raft /ʀaft/ NM raft

rafting /ʀaftiŋ/ NM rafting ◆ **faire du ~** to raft, to go rafting

ragaillardir /ʀagajaʀdiʀ/ ▸ conjug 2 ◂ VT to perk up, to buck up* ◆ **tout ragaillardi par cette nouvelle** bucked up by this news*

rage /ʀaʒ/ NF ① *(= colère)* rage, fury ◆ **la ~ au cœur** seething with rage *ou* anger ◆ **mettre qn en ~** to infuriate *ou* enrage sb, to make sb's blood boil ◆ **être dans une ~ folle, être ivre** *ou* **fou de ~** to be mad with rage, to be in a raging temper ◆ **être en ~, avoir la ~**** to be in a rage ◆ **suffoquer** *ou* **étouffer de ~** to choke with anger *ou* rage ◆ **dans sa ~ de ne pouvoir l'obtenir, il …** in his rage *ou* fury at not being able to get it, he … ◆ **être pris d'une ~ aveugle** *ou* **destructrice** to go into a blind rage; → **amour**
② *(= envie violente)* **avoir la ~ de (faire) qch** to have a passion for (doing) sth ◆ **sa ~ de vaincre** his dogged determination to win ◆ **sa ~ de vivre** his lust for life
③ ◆ **faire ~** *[guerre, incendie, tempête, polémique]* to rage; *[concurrence]* to be fierce
④ *(Méd)* **la ~** rabies *(sg)*; → **noyer²**
⑤ ◆ **~ de dents** raging toothache

rageant, e * /ʀaʒɑ̃, ɑ̃t/ ADJ infuriating, maddening ◆ **ce qui est ~ avec lui, c'est que …** the infuriating *ou* maddening thing about him is that …

rager /ʀaʒe/ ▸ conjug 3 ◂ VI to fume ◆ **ça (me) fait ~ !** it makes me fume! *ou* furious! *ou* mad! ◆ **rageant de voir que les autres n'étaient pas punis** furious that the others weren't punished

rageur, -euse /ʀaʒœʀ, øz/ ADJ *[enfant]* hot-tempered, quick-tempered; *[voix, geste]* bad-tempered, angry ◆ **il était ~** he was furious *ou* livid

rageusement /ʀaʒøzmɑ̃/ ADV angrily

ragga /ʀaga/ NM *(Mus)* ragga (music)

raglan /ʀaglɑ̃/ NM, ADJ INV raglan

ragondin /ʀagɔ̃dɛ̃/ NM *(= animal)* coypu; *(= fourrure)* nutria

ragot * /ʀago/ NM piece of (malicious) gossip *ou* tittle-tattle ◆ **~s** gossip, tittle-tattle

ragougnasse * /ʀaguɲas/ NF *(péj = nourriture)* pigswill *(NonC)*

ragoût /ʀagu/ NM stew, ragout ◆ **~ de mouton** lamb stew ◆ **en ~** stewed

ragoûtant, e /ʀagutɑ̃, ɑ̃t/ ADJ ◆ **peu ~** *[mets]* unappetizing; *[individu]* unsavoury; *[travail]* unwholesome, unpalatable ◆ **ce n'est guère ~** that's not very inviting *ou* tempting

ragtime /ʀagtajm/ NM ragtime

rahat-loukoum (pl **rahat-loukoums**) /ʀaatlukum/ NM ⇒ **loukoum**

rai /ʀɛ/ NM ① *(littér = rayon)* ray ② *[de roue]* spoke *(of wooden wheel)*

raï /ʀaj/ ADJ INV rai *(épith)* NM INV rai

raid /ʀɛd/ NM ① *(Mil)* raid, hit-and-run attack ◆ **~ aérien** air raid ◆ **~ boursier** raid ◆ **faire un ~ sur** *(Fin, Mil)* to raid ② *(Sport)* **~ automobile/à skis** long-distance car/ski trek

raide /ʀɛd/ ADJ ① *[corps, membre, geste, étoffe]* stiff; *[cheveux]* straight; *[câble]* taut, tight ◆ **être** *ou* **se tenir ~ comme un échalas** *ou* **un piquet** *ou* **un manche à balai** *ou* **la justice** to be (as) stiff as a poker ◆ **assis ~ sur sa chaise** sitting bolt upright on his chair ◆ **avoir une jambe ~** to have a stiff leg ◆ **ses cheveux sont ~s comme des baguettes de tambour** her hair is dead straight; → **corde**
② *[pente, escalier]* steep, abrupt
③ *(= inflexible) [attitude, morale, personne]* rigid, inflexible; *[manières]* stiff, starchy; *[démarche]* stiff
④ *(= fort, âpre) [alcool]* rough
⑤ *(* = difficile à croire)* **c'est un peu ~** that's a bit hard to swallow *ou* a bit far-fetched ◆ **elle est ~ celle-là !** that's a bit much!* ◆ **il en a vu de ~s** he's seen a thing or two*
⑥ *(* = osé)* **assez** *ou* **un peu ~** *[propos, passage, scène]* daring ◆ **il s'en passe de ~s, chez eux** all sorts of things go on at their place ◆ **il en raconte de ~s** he tells some pretty daring stories
⑦ *(** = sans argent)* broke* ◆ **être ~ comme un passe-lacet** to be flat *ou* stony *(Brit)* broke*
⑧ ** *(= ivre)* drunk, sloshed*; *(= drogué)* stoned**, high* ◆ **être complètement ~** *(sous l'effet d'une drogue)* to be completely stoned**, to be as high as a kite*; *(sous l'effet de l'alcool)* to be blind drunk*
ADV ① *(= en pente)* **ça montait/descendait ~** *(ascension, descente)* it was a steep climb/climb down; *(pente)* it climbed/fell steeply
② *(= net)* **tomber ~** to drop to the ground *ou* floor ◆ **quand elle m'a dit ça, j'en suis tombé ~*** I was thunderstruck when she told me ◆ **tomber ~ mort** to drop *ou* fall down dead ◆ **tuer qn ~*** to kill sb outright *ou* stone dead *(Brit)* ◆ **il l'a étendu ~ (mort)*** he laid him out cold* ◆ **être ~ fou** *ou* **dingue*** to be completely crazy *ou* nuts*

raider /ʀɛdœʀ/ NM *(Bourse)* raider

raideur /ʀɛdœʀ/ NF ① *[de corps, membre, geste, étoffe]* stiffness; *[de cheveux]* straightness; *[de câble]* tautness, tightness ◆ **j'ai une ~ dans la nuque** I've got a stiff neck ② *[de pente, escalier]* steepness, abruptness ③ *[d'attitude, morale, personne]* rigidity, inflexibility; *[de manières]* stiffness, starchiness; *[de démarche]* stiffness ◆ **avec ~** *[répondre, saluer, marcher]* stiffly ④ *(= âpreté) [d'alcool]* roughness

raidillon /ʀɛdijɔ̃/ NM steep path

raidir /ʀɛdiʀ/ ▸ conjug 2 ◂ VT *[+ drap, tissu]* to stiffen; *[+ corde, fil de fer]* to pull taut *ou* tight, to tighten ◆ **~ ses muscles** to tense *ou* stiffen one's muscles ◆ **des corps raidis par la mort** stiff corpses ◆ **~ sa position** *(fig)* to harden *ou* toughen one's position, to take a hard(er) *ou* tough(er) line VPR **se raidir** ① *[toile, tissu]* to stiffen, to become stiff(er); *[corde]* to grow taut; *(fig) [position]* to harden ② *[personne] (= perdre sa souplesse)* to become stiff(er); *(= bander ses muscles)* to stiffen; *(= se préparer moralement)* to brace *ou* steel o.s.; *(= s'entêter)* to take a hard(er) *ou* tough(er) line

raidissement /ʀedismɑ̃/ **NM** *(= perte de souplesse)* stiffening ◆ **ce ~ soudain du parti adverse** *(= intransigeance)* this sudden tough(er) line taken by the opposing party

raidisseur /ʀedisœʀ/ **NM** *(= tendeur)* tightener

raie[1] /ʀɛ/ **NF** 1 *(= trait)* line; *(Agr = sillon)* furrow; *(= éraflure)* mark, scratch ◆ **faire une ~** to draw a line ◆ **attention, tu vas faire des ~s** careful, you'll scratch it ◆ **la ~ des fesses** the cleft between the buttocks 2 *(= bande)* stripe ◆ **chemise avec des ~s** striped *ou* stripy *(Brit)* shirt ◆ **les ~s de son pelage** the stripes on its fur ◆ **~ d'absorption/d'émission** *(Phys)* absorption/emission line 3 *(Coiffure)* parting *(Brit)*, part *(US)* ◆ **avoir la ~ au milieu/sur le côté** to have a centre/side parting *(Brit) ou* part *(US)*, to have one's hair parted in the middle/to the side

raie[2] /ʀɛ/ **NF** *(= poisson)* skate, ray; *(Culin)* skate ◆ **~ bouclée** thornback ray ◆ **~ manta** manta ray ◆ **~ électrique** electric ray; → **gueule**

raifort /ʀɛfɔʀ/ **NM** *(= aromate)* horseradish; *(= radis noir)* black winter radish

rail /ʀɑj/ **NM** 1 *(= barre)* rail ◆ **les ~s** *(= voie)* the rails, the track ◆ **~ conducteur** live rail ◆ **~ de sécurité** guardrail, crash barrier *(Brit)* ◆ **le ~ est plus pratique que la route** it's more practical to travel by train than by road ◆ **être sur les ~s** *(fig)* to be under way ◆ **remettre sur les ~s** *(lit, fig)* to put back on the rails ◆ **quitter les ~s, sortir des ~s** to jump the rails, to go off the rails ◆ **transport ~-route** road-rail transport ◆ **~ de travelling** *(Ciné)* dolly 2 *(Naut)* lane

railler /ʀɑje/ ▸ conjug 1 ◂ **VT** *(frm = se moquer de)* [+ *personne, chose*] to scoff at, to jeer at, to mock at **VI** († † = *plaisanter*) to jest ◆ **vous raillez ?** you jest? ◆ **..., dit-il en raillant ...,** he quipped **VPR se railler** † † to scoff, to jeer, to mock *(de* at)

raillerie /ʀɑjʀi/ **NF** *(frm)* *(= ironie)* mockery, scoffing; *(= remarque)* gibe ◆ **il sortit de scène sous les ~s du public** he left the stage to the booing *ou* catcalls of the audience

railleur, -euse /ʀɑjœʀ, øz/ **ADJ** mocking, derisive, scoffing **NM** scoffer, mocker

railleusement /ʀɑjøzmɑ̃/ **ADV** mockingly, derisively, scoffingly

rainer /ʀene/ ▸ conjug 1 ◂ **VT** to groove

rainette /ʀenɛt/ **NF** 1 *(= grenouille)* tree frog 2 ⇒ **reinette**

rainurage /ʀenyʀaʒ/ **NM** grooved surface

rainure /ʀenyʀ/ **NF** *(longue, formant glissière)* groove; *(courte, pour emboîtage)* slot ◆ **les ~s du parquet** the gaps between the floorboards

rainurer /ʀenyʀe/ ▸ conjug 1 ◂ **VT** to groove

rais /ʀɛ/ **NM** ⇒ **rai**

raïs /ʀais/ **NM** head of state *(of an Arab country)*

raisin /ʀɛzɛ̃/ **NM** 1 *(= espèce)* grape ◆ **du ~, des ~s** *(= fruit)* grapes ◆ **~ noir/blanc** black/white grape ◆ **c'est un ~ qui donne du bon vin** it's a grape that yields a good wine; → **grain, grappe, jus** 2 *(= papier)* ≈ royal 3 *(= œufs)* **~s de mer** *[de seiche]* cuttlefish eggs; *[de poulpe]* octopus eggs

COMP raisins de Corinthe currants
raisins secs raisins
raisins de Smyrne sultanas
raisin de table dessert *ou* eating grapes

raisiné /ʀezine/ **NM** *(= jus)* grape jelly; *(= confiture) pear or quince jam made with grape jelly;* († * = *sang)* blood

raisinet /ʀezine/ **NM** *(Helv = groseille rouge)* red currant

raison /ʀɛzɔ̃/ GRAMMAIRE ACTIVE 38.1, 40.3, 44.1, 53.2, 53.3

NF 1 *(gén, Philos = faculté de discernement)* reason ◆ **seul l'homme est doué de ~** man alone is endowed with reason ◆ **conforme/contraire à la ~** reasonable/unreasonable ◆ **il n'a plus sa ~, il a perdu la ~** he has lost his reason, he has taken leave of his senses, he is not in his right mind ◆ **si tu avais toute ta ~ tu verrais que ...** if you were in your right mind, you would see that ... ◆ **manger/boire plus que de ~** to eat/drink more than is sensible *ou* more than one should; → **âge, mariage, rime**

2 *(= motif)* reason ◆ **la ~ pour laquelle je suis venu** the reason (why *ou* that) I came ◆ **pour quelles ~s l'avez-vous renvoyé ?** why *ou* on what grounds did you fire him?, what were your reasons for firing him? ◆ **la ~ de cette réaction** the reason for this reaction ◆ **il n'y a pas de ~ de s'arrêter** there's no reason to stop ◆ **j'ai mes ~s** I have my reasons ◆ **pour (des) ~s politiques/familiales** for political/family reasons ◆ **pour ~s de santé** for health reasons, on grounds of (ill) health ◆ **~s cachées** hidden motives *ou* reasons ◆ **il a refusé pour la simple ~ que ...** he refused simply on the grounds that ..., he refused simply because ... ◆ **pour la simple et bonne ~ que je ne veux pas** for the simple reason that I don't want to ◆ **j'ai de bonnes ~s de penser que ...** I have good *ou* every reason to think that ... ◆ **la ~ en est que ...** the reason is that ...

3 *(= argument, explication, excuse)* reason ◆ **sans ~** without reason ◆ **sans ~ valable** for no valid reason ◆ **il a toujours de bonnes ~s !** *(iro)* he's always got a good excuse! *ou* reason! ◆ **la ~ du plus fort est toujours la meilleure** *(Prov)* might is right *(Prov)* ◆ **ce n'est pas une ~ !** that's no excuse! *ou* reason!; → **comparaison, rendre**

4 *(Math)* ratio ◆ **~ directe/inverse** direct/inverse ratio *ou* proportion

5 *(locutions)* **pour une ~ ou pour une autre** for some reason or other, for one reason or another ◆ **rire sans ~** to laugh for no reason ◆ **non sans ~** not without reason ◆ **se faire une ~** to accept it ◆ **entendre ~, se rendre à la ~** to listen to *ou* see reason ◆ **faire entendre ~ à qn, ramener qn à la ~** to make sb see sense *ou* reason ◆ **mettre qn à la ~** † to bring sb to their senses, to make sb see sense *ou* reason, to talk (some) sense into sb ◆ **demander ~ à qn de** *(littér)* [+ *offense*] to demand satisfaction from sb for *(frm)*

◆ **avoir raison** to be right *(de faire* in doing, to do); ◆ **tu as bien ~ !** you're absolutely *ou* dead* right! ◆ **avoir ~ de qn/qch** to get the better of sb/sth

◆ **donner raison à qn** *[événement]* to prove sb right ◆ **tu donnes toujours ~ à ta fille** you're always siding with your daughter, you're always on your daughter's side ◆ **la justice a fini par lui donner ~** the court eventually decided in his favour

◆ **raison de plus** all the more reason *(pour faire* for doing, to do)

◆ **à raison de** ◆ **à ~ de 25 € par caisse** at the rate of €25 per crate ◆ **payé à ~ de 40 lignes par page** paid on the basis of 40 lines a page ◆ **à ~ de 3 fois par semaine** 3 times a week

◆ **avec (juste) raison, à juste raison** rightly, justifiably, with good reason

◆ **à plus forte raison** ◆ **à plus forte ~, je n'irai pas** all the more reason for me not to go ◆ **à plus forte ~ si/quand ...** all the more so if/when ...

◆ **comme de raison** as one might expect

◆ **en raison de** ◆ **en ~ du froid** because of *ou* owing to the cold weather ◆ **en ~ de son jeune âge** because of *ou* on the grounds of his youth ◆ **on est payé en ~ du travail fourni** we are paid according to *ou* in proportion to the work produced

COMP raison d'État reasons of state
raison d'être raison d'être ◆ **cet enfant est toute sa ~ d'être** this child is her whole life *ou* her entire reason for living *ou* her entire raison d'être ◆ **cette association n'a aucune ~ d'être** this association has no reason to exist *ou* no raison d'être
raison sociale *[d'entreprise]* corporate name
raison de vivre reason for living

raisonnable /ʀɛzɔnabl/ **ADJ** 1 *(= sensé)* [*personne, solution, conduite*] sensible, reasonable; [*conseil, opinion, propos*] sensible ◆ **soyez ~** be reasonable ◆ **elle devrait être plus ~ à son âge** she should know better *ou* she should have more sense at her age ◆ **réaction bien peu ~** very unreasonable reaction ◆ **boire trop avant un match, ce n'est pas ~** it isn't sensible *ou* it's silly to drink too much before a match ◆ **250 € pour cette vieillerie, ce n'est pas ~ !** €250 for this old thing, that's crazy! *ou* ridiculous! ◆ **est-ce bien ~ ?** *(hum)* is it wise?

2 *(= décent)* [*prix, demande, salaire, quantité*] reasonable, fair; [*heure, limite, délai*] reasonable ◆ **le déficit budgétaire reste ~** the budget deficit is still at a reasonable level

3 *(littér = doué de raison)* rational, reasoning

raisonnablement /ʀɛzɔnabləmɑ̃/ **ADV** [*conseiller*] sensibly, soundly; [*agir*] sensibly, reasonably; [*boire*] in moderation; [*dépenser*] moderately; [*travailler, rétribuer*] reasonably *ou* fairly well ◆ **on peut ~ espérer que ...** one can reasonably hope that ...

raisonné, e /ʀɛzɔne/ (ptp de **raisonner**) **ADJ** 1 *(= mûri, réfléchi)* [*attitude, projet*] well thought-out, reasoned; *(= mesuré)* [*confiance, optimisme*] cautious ◆ **il a pris une décision ~e** he made a reasoned decision ◆ **c'est bien ~** it's well reasoned *ou* argued 2 *(= systématique)* **grammaire/méthode ~e de français** reasoned grammar/primer of French ◆ **catalogue ~** catalogue raisonné

raisonnement /ʀɛzɔnmɑ̃/ **NM** 1 *(= activité de la raison)* reasoning (NonC); *(= faculté de penser)* power of reasoning; *(= façon de réfléchir)* way of thinking; *(= cheminement de la pensée)* thought process ◆ **~ analogique/par déduction/par induction** analogical/deductive/inductive reasoning ◆ **~ économique/politique** economic/political thinking ◆ **prouver qch par le ~** to prove sth by one's reasoning *ou* by the use of reason; → **absurde**

2 *(= argumentation)* argument ◆ **il tient le ~ suivant** his argument *ou* reasoning is as follows ◆ **il m'a tenu ce ~** he gave me this explanation ◆ **si l'on tient le même ~ que lui** if you take the same line as he does ◆ **si tu tiens ce ~** if this is the view you hold *ou* take, if this is how you think ◆ **j'ai du mal à suivre son ~** I'm having trouble following his argument *ou* his line of thought ◆ **un ~ logique** a logical argument, a logical line *ou* chain of reasoning ◆ **ses ~s m'étonnent** his reasoning surprises me ◆ **ce n'est pas un ~ !*** that's not a valid argument!

3 *(péj = ergotages)* **~s** arguing, argument ◆ **tous les ~s ne changeront pas ma décision** no amount of arguing *ou* argument will alter my decision

raisonner /ʀɛzɔne/ ▸ conjug 1 ◂ **VI** 1 *(= penser, réfléchir)* to reason *(sur* about); ◆ **~ par induction/déduction** to reason by induction/deduction ◆ **il raisonne juste/mal** his reasoning is/isn't very sound ◆ **il raisonne comme une pantoufle*** he can't follow his own argument 2 *(= discourir, argumenter)* to argue *(sur* about); ◆ **on ne peut pas ~ avec lui** you (just) can't argue *ou* reason with him 3 *(péj = ergoter)* to argue, to quibble *(avec* with) **VT** 1 *(= sermonner)* to reason with ◆ **inutile d'essayer de le ~** it's useless to try and reason with him 2 *(= justifier par la raison)* [+ *croyance, conduite, démarche*] to reason out **VPR se raisonner** to reason with o.s., to make o.s. see reason ◆ **raisonne-toi** try to be reasonable *ou* to make yourself see reason ◆ **l'amour ne se raisonne pas** love cannot be reasoned *ou* knows no reason

raisonneur, -euse /ʀɛzɔnœʀ, øz/ ADJ 1 *(péj)* quibbling *(épith)*, argumentative 2 *(= réfléchi)* reasoning *(épith)* NM,F 1 *(péj = ergoteur)* arguer, quibbler ◆ **ne fais pas le ~** stop arguing *ou* quibbling 2 *(= penseur)* reasoner

rajah /ʀa(d)ʒa/ NM rajah

rajeunir /ʀaʒœniʀ/ ▸ conjug 2 ◂ VT 1 ◆ **~ qn** *[cure]* to rejuvenate sb; *[repos, expérience]* to make sb feel younger; *[soins de beauté, vêtement]* to make sb look younger ◆ **l'amour/ce chapeau la rajeunit de 10 ans** being in love/that hat takes 10 years off her* *ou* makes her look 10 years younger ◆ **tu le rajeunis (de 5 ans), il est né en 1950** you're making him out to be (5 years) younger than he is – he was born in 1950 ◆ **ça ne nous rajeunit pas !** *(hum)* that makes you realize we're not getting any younger!

2 *[+ institution]* to modernize; *[+ installation, mobilier]* to modernize, to give a new look to; *[+ manuel, image de marque]* to update, to bring up to date; *[+ vieux habits]* to give a new look to, to brighten up; *[+ personnel, entreprise]* to bring new *ou* young blood into, to recruit younger people into; *[+ thème, théorie]* to inject new life into ◆ **ils cherchent à ~ leur clientèle/public** they're trying to attract younger customers/a younger audience

VI *[personne]* *(= se sentir plus jeune)* to feel younger; *(= paraître plus jeune)* to look younger; *[institution, quartier]* *(= se moderniser)* to be modernized; *(= avoir un personnel, des habitants plus jeunes)* to have a younger feel ◆ **notre public rajeunit** our audience is getting younger ◆ **avec les enfants, la vieille demeure rajeunissait** with the children around, the old house had a younger feel to it

VPR **se rajeunir** *(= se prétendre moins âgé)* to make o.s. younger than one is; *(= se faire paraître moins âgé)* to make o.s. look younger

rajeunissant, e /ʀaʒœnisɑ̃, ɑ̃t/ ADJ *[traitement, crème]* rejuvenating

rajeunissement /ʀaʒœnismɑ̃/ NM *[de personne]* rejuvenation; *[de manuel]* updating; *[d'installation, mobilier]* modernization; *[de vieux habits]* brightening up ◆ **~ du personnel** injection of new *ou* young blood into the staff ◆ **nous assistons à un ~ de la population/clientèle** the population is/the customers are getting younger ◆ **la cathédrale a subi une cure de ~** the cathedral has been given a face-lift

rajout /ʀaʒu/ NM addition *(sur to)*

rajouter /ʀaʒute/ ▸ conjug 1 ◂ VT *[+ du sucre]* to put on *ou* put in *ou* add (some) more; *[+ un sucre]* to add another ◆ **après avoir donné 20 €, il en rajouta 5** having already given 20 euros he added another 5 ◆ **il rajouta que ...** he added that ... ◆ **en ~*** *(fig)* to lay it on (thick)*, to exaggerate ◆ **il ne faut pas croire tout ce qu'il dit, il en rajoute* toujours** you mustn't believe everything he says, he always exaggerates

rajustement /ʀaʒystəmɑ̃/ NM ⇒ **réajustement**

rajuster /ʀaʒyste/ ▸ conjug 1 ◂ VT ⇒ **réajuster**

raki /ʀaki/ NM raki

râlant, e* /ʀɑlɑ̃, ɑ̃t/ ADJ infuriating ◆ **attendre pour rien, c'est ~ !** it's infuriating, all this waiting around for nothing!

râle[1] /ʀɑl/ NM 1 *[de blessé]* groan ◆ **~ (d'agonie *ou* de la mort)** *[de mourant]* death rattle 2 *(Méd)* rale

râle[2] /ʀɑl/ NM *(= oiseau)* rail ◆ **~ des genêts** corncrake ◆ **~ d'eau, ~ noir** water rail

ralenti, e /ʀalɑ̃ti/ (ptp de **ralentir**) ADJ *[vie]* slow-moving, slow; *[mouvement]* slow NM 1 *(Ciné)* slow motion ◆ **en *ou* au ~** *[filmer, projeter]* in slow motion 2 *[de moteur]* **régler le ~** to adjust the idle *ou* the tick-over *(Brit)* ◆ **le moteur est un peu faible au ~** the engine doesn't idle too well *ou* doesn't tick over *(Brit)* ◆ **tourner au ~** to idle, to tick over *(Brit)* ◆ **vivre au ~** to live at a slower pace ◆ **cette existence paisible, au ~** this peaceful, slow existence ◆ **usine qui tourne au ~** factory which is just idling *ou* ticking over *(Brit)* ◆ **ça tourne au ~ chez lui !** *(péj)* he's a bit slow!*

ralentir /ʀalɑ̃tiʀ/ ▸ conjug 2 ◂ VT *[+ processus, véhicule]* to slow down; *[+ mouvement, expansion]* to slow down *ou* up; *(Mil)* *[+ avance]* to check, to hold up; *[+ effort, zèle]* to slacken ◆ **~ l'allure** to slow down *ou* up, to reduce speed ◆ **~ le pas** to slacken one's *ou* the pace, to slow down VI *[marcheur]* to slow down, to slacken one's pace; *[véhicule, automobiliste]* to slow down, to reduce speed ◆ **"ralentir"** *(panneau)* "slow", "reduce speed now" VPR **se ralentir** *[production]* to slow down *ou* up, to slacken (off); *(Mil)* *[offensive]* to let up, to ease off; *[ardeur, zèle]* to flag; *(Physiol)* *[fonctions]* to slow down; *[rythme]* to slow (down) ◆ **sa respiration s'est ralentie** he is breathing more slowly ◆ **l'inflation s'est ralentie** inflation has slowed down

ralentissement /ʀalɑ̃tismɑ̃/ NM 1 *[de processus, véhicule, automobiliste, marcheur]* slowing down; *[de mouvement, expansion]* slowing down *ou* up; *(Mil)* *[d'avance]* checking, holding up; *[d'effort, zèle]* slackening ◆ **un ~ de l'activité économique** a slowdown in economic activity ◆ **un ~ sur 3 km** a 3 km tailback *(Brit)* *ou* hold-up *(US)* 2 *[de production]* falloff; *(Mil)* *[d'offensive]* letting up, easing; *[d'ardeur, zèle]* flagging; *(Physiol)* *[de fonctions]* slowing down ◆ **provoquer le ~ de qch** to slow sth down

ralentisseur /ʀalɑ̃tisœʀ/ NM 1 *[de camion]* speed reducer 2 *(sur route)* speed bump, sleeping policeman *(Brit)* 3 *(Phys)* moderator

râler /ʀɑle/ ▸ conjug 1 ◂ VI 1 *[blessé]* to groan, to moan; *[mourant]* to give the death rattle 2 *(* = protester)* to moan* ◆ **il est allé ~ chez le prof** he went to moan* to the teacher ◆ **il râlait contre *ou* après moi** he was moaning* about me ◆ **faire ~ qn** to infuriate sb ◆ **ça (vous) fait ~** it's infuriating ◆ **arrête de ~ !** stop moaning!

râleur, -euse* /ʀɑlœʀ, øz/ ADJ ◆ **des gens ~s** moaners* ◆ **il est ~** he never stops moaning NM,F moaner* ◆ **quel ~, celui-là !** he never stops moaning!

ralingue /ʀalɛ̃g/ NF boltrope

ralliement /ʀalimɑ̃/ NM 1 *(Chasse, Mil, Naut)* rallying; *(= union)* *[de groupe, parti]* rallying, uniting ◆ **le ~ des troupes** the rallying of troops 2 *(= adhésion)* *[de personne, groupe]* winning over, rallying ◆ **~ à** joining, going over to ◆ **je suis étonné de son ~ (à notre cause)** I am surprised by the fact that he joined (our cause) ◆ **signe/cri de ~** rallying sign/cry ◆ **point de ~** *(en cas d'incendie)* assembly point; *(fig)* rallying point

rallier /ʀalje/ ▸ conjug 7 ◂ VT 1 *(Chasse, Mil, Naut = regrouper)* to rally 2 *(= gagner)* *[+ personne, groupe]* to win over, to rally *(à to)*; *[+ suffrages]* to bring in, to win ◆ **~ qn à son avis/sa cause** to bring sb round *(Brit)* *ou* win sb over to one's way of thinking/one's cause 3 *(= unir)* *[+ groupe, parti]* to rally, to unite ◆ **groupe rallié autour d'un idéal** group united by an ideal 4 *(= rejoindre)* *(Mil, Naut)* to rejoin ◆ **~ la majorité** *(Pol)* to rejoin the majority ◆ **~ le bord** *(Naut)* to rejoin ship ◆ **~ la côte *ou* la terre** to make landfall VPR **se rallier** 1 *(= suivre)* **se ~ à** *[+ parti]* to join; *[+ ennemi]* to go over to; *[+ chef]* to rally round *ou* to; *[+ avis]* to come over *ou* round to; *[+ doctrine, cause]* to be won over to 2 *(Mil, Naut = se regrouper)* to rally

rallonge /ʀalɔ̃ʒ/ NF 1 *[de table]* (extra) leaf; *[de fil électrique]* extension lead *ou* cord *ou* cable *(Brit)*; *[de vêtement]* piece *(used to lengthen an item of clothing)*; *[de compas]* extension arm; *[de perche]* extension piece ◆ **table à ~(s)** extendable table 2 *(* = supplément)* **une ~ d'argent** a bit of extra *ou* some extra money ◆ **une ~ de vacances** a few extra days holiday ◆ **obtenir une ~ de crédit** to get an extension of credit ◆ **une ~ de deux jours** an extra two days, a two-day extension 3 *(péj)* **histoire à ~** never-ending story ◆ **nom à ~** *(gén)* long, complicated surname; *(en deux mots)* double-barrelled name

rallongement /ʀalɔ̃ʒmɑ̃/ NM *[de vêtement]* *(en ajoutant du tissu)* lengthening; *(en défaisant l'ourlet)* letting down; *[de vacances, fil, table, bâtiment]* extension

rallonger /ʀalɔ̃ʒe/ ▸ conjug 3 ◂ VT *[+ vêtement]* *(en ajoutant)* to lengthen, to make longer; *(en défaisant l'ourlet)* to let down; *[+ texte, service militaire, piste]* to lengthen, to extend, to make longer; *[+ vacances, fil, table, bâtiment]* to extend ◆ **~ une robe de 2 cm** to let down a dress by 2 cm ◆ **j'ai rallongé le texte de trois pages** I added three pages to the text ◆ **par ce chemin/en bus, ça me rallonge de 10 minutes*** this way/by bus, it takes me 10 minutes longer VI * ◆ **les jours rallongent** the days are getting longer ◆ **les jupes rallongent** hemlines are going down VPR **se rallonger** *[personne]* to lie down again; *(= devenir plus long)* to get longer

rallumer /ʀalyme/ ▸ conjug 1 ◂ VT 1 *(lit)* *[+ feu]* to light again, to relight; *[+ cigarette]* to relight, to light up again; *[+ lampe]* to switch *ou* turn *ou* put on again ◆ **~ (l'électricité *ou* la lumière)** to switch *ou* turn *ou* put the light(s) on again ◆ **~ (dans) le bureau** to switch *ou* turn *ou* put the light(s) on again in the office 2 *(fig)* *[+ courage, haine, querelle]* to revive, to rekindle; *[+ conflit, guerre]* to stir up again, to revive, to rekindle VPR **se rallumer** 1 *[incendie]* to flare up again; *[lampe]* to come on again ◆ **le bureau se ralluma** the light(s) in the office went *ou* came on again 2 *[guerre, querelle]* to flare up again; *[haine, courage]* to revive, to be revived

rallye /ʀali/ NM 1 *(automobile)* (car) rally 2 *(mondain)* series of society parties *(organized to enable young people to meet suitable friends)*

RAM /ʀam/ NF (abrév de **Random Access Memory**) *(Ordin)* RAM

Ramadan, ramadan /ʀamadɑ̃/ NM Ramadan ◆ **faire *ou* observer le ~** to observe Ramadan

ramage /ʀamaʒ/ NM 1 *(littér = chant)* song, warbling *(NonC)* 2 *(= branchages, dessin)* **~(s)** foliage ◆ **tissu à ~s** fabric with a leafy design *ou* pattern

ramassage /ʀamasaʒ/ NM 1 *(gén)* collection; *[de cahiers, copies]* taking in, collection ◆ **~ scolaire** *(= service)* school bus service; *(= action)* picking up of pupils ◆ **point de ~** pick-up point ◆ **quels sont les horaires de ~ des poubelles ?** what time is the waste collected? 2 *(= cueillette)* *[de bois mort, coquillages, foin]* gathering; *[d'épis, fruits tombés]* gathering (up); *[de champignons]* picking, gathering; *[de pommes de terre]* digging up, lifting; *[de balles de tennis]* picking up ◆ **faire l'objet d'un ~** *[de valeur boursière]* to be snapped up

ramasse‡ /ʀamas/ NF ◆ **il est à la ~** *(= fatigué)* he's shattered*; *(= nul)* he's hopeless*; *(= fou)* he's crazy*

ramassé, e /ʀamɑse/ (ptp de **ramasser**) ADJ *(pour se protéger)* huddled (up); *(pour bondir)* crouched; *(= trapu)* squat, stocky; *(= concis)* compact, condensed ◆ **le petit village ~ dans le fond de la vallée** the little village nestling in the heart of the valley

ramasse-miettes /ʀamɑsmjɛt/ NM INV table tidy *(Brit)*, silent butler *(US)*

ramasse-monnaie /ʀamasmɔnɛ/ NM INV (change-)tray

ramasser /ʀamɑse/ ► conjug 1 ◄ VT 1 *(lit, fig = prendre) [+ objet, personne]* to pick up ◆ **il était à ~ à la petite cuiller*** *(blessé)* they had to scrape him off the ground; *(fatigué)* he was completely shattered* ◆ **~ une bûche*** ou **un gadin*** ou **une gamelle*** ou **une pelle*** to fall flat on one's face, to come a cropper* *(Brit)*
2 *(= collecter) [+ objets épars]* to pick up, to gather up; *[+ cartes, idées, informations]* to pick up; *[+ élèves]* to pick up, to collect; *[+ copies, cahiers]* to collect, to take in; *[+ cotisations, ordures]* to collect; * *[+ argent]* to pick up, to pocket*
3 *(= récolter) [+ bois, feuilles, coquillages]* to gather, to collect; *[+ fruits tombés]* to gather (up); *[+ foin]* to gather; *[+ pommes de terre]* to lift, to dig up; *[+ champignons]* to pick, to gather; *(Bourse) [+ titres]* to snap up ◆ **~ qch à la pelle** *(lit)* to shovel sth up; *(fig : en abondance)* to get loads* ou stacks* of sth
4 *(= resserrer) [+ jupons, draps, cheveux]* to gather (up); *[+ style]* to condense
5 *(* = attraper) [+ rhume, maladie]* to catch, to get; *[+ réprimande, coups]* to collect, to get; *[+ amende]* to pick up, to collect, to get; *[+ mauvaise note]* to get ◆ **il a ramassé 50 € (d'amende)** he picked up ou collected a 50-euro fine, he was done for 50 euros* *(Brit)* ◆ **où as-tu ramassé ce mec ?**‡ where the hell did you find that guy?‡
6 *(* = échouer)* **se faire ~** *[candidat]* to fail; *[dragueur]* to get the cold shoulder* ◆ **il va se faire ~ par sa mère** *(= se faire réprimander)* he'll get told off ou ticked off *(Brit)* by his mother* ◆ **il s'est fait ~ en anglais** he failed his English ◆ **se faire ~ dans une manif*** to get picked up at a demo*
VPR **se ramasser** 1 *(= se pelotonner)* to curl up; *(pour bondir)* to crouch
2 *(= se relever)* to pick o.s. up
3 *(* = tomber)* to fall over ou down, to come a cropper* *(Brit)*; *(* = échouer) [candidat]* to come a cropper* *(Brit)*, to take a flat beating *(US)*

ramasseur, -euse /ʀamɑsœʀ, øz/ NM,F *(= personne)* collector ◆ **~ de lait** milk collector ◆ **~/ramasseuse de balles** *(Tennis)* ballboy/ballgirl ◆ **~ de pommes de terre/champignons** potato/mushroom picker NM *(= outil, machine)* pickup NF **ramasseuse** *(= machine)* **ramasseuse-presse** baler

ramassis /ʀamɑsi/ NM *(péj)* ◆ **~ de** *[+ voyous]* pack ou bunch of; *[+ doctrines, objets]* jumble of *[+ mensonges]* pack of ◆ **un ~ de conneries**‡ a load of rubbish* *(Brit)*, a bunch of garbage* *(US)*

ramassoire /ʀamaswaʀ/ NF *(Helv = pelle à ordures)* dustpan

rambarde /ʀɑ̃baʀd/ NF guardrail

ramdam‡ /ʀamdam/ NM *(= tapage)* racket, row *(surtout Brit)*; *(= protestation)* row ◆ **faire du ~** *(bruit)* to kick up* ou make a racket ou row; *(protestation)* to kick up* a fuss ou a row*; *(scandale)* to cause a stir

rame /ʀam/ NF 1 *(= aviron)* oar ◆ **aller à la ~** to row ◆ **faire force de ~s** *(littér)* to ply the oars *(littér)*, to row hard ◆ **il n'en fiche pas une ~**‡ he doesn't do a damned‡ thing, he doesn't do a stroke (of work) 2 *(Rail)* train ◆ **~ (de métro)** (underground *(Brit)* ou subway *(US)*) train 3 *[de papier]* ream; 4 *[pour sécher les tissus]* tenter 5 *(= tuteur)* stake, stick; → **haricot**

rameau (pl **rameaux**) /ʀamo/ NM *(lit)* (small) branch; *(fig)* branch; *(Anat)* ramification ◆ **~ d'olivier** *(lit, fig)* olive branch ◆ **(dimanche des) Rameaux** *(Rel)* Palm Sunday

ramée /ʀame/ NF *(littér = feuillage)* leafy boughs *(littér)*; *(coupé)* leafy ou green branches ◆ **il n'en fiche pas une ~**‡ he doesn't do a damned* thing, he doesn't do a stroke (of work)

ramener /ʀam(ə)ne/ ► conjug 5 ◄ VT 1 *[+ personne, objet]* to bring back, to take back; *[+ paix, ordre]* to bring back, to restore ◆ **je vais te ~ en voiture** I'll drive you back (home), I'll take you back (home) in the car ◆ **ramène du pain/les enfants** bring ou fetch *(Brit)* some bread/the children back *(de* from); ◆ **ça l'a ramené en prison** it put ou landed* him back in prison ◆ **l'été a ramené les accidents/la mode des chapeaux** summer has seen a resurgence of accidents/has brought hats back into fashion
2 *(= tirer) [+ voile]* to draw; *[+ couverture]* to pull, to draw ◆ **il a ramené la couverture sur lui** he pulled the blanket up ◆ **~ ses cheveux sur son front/en arrière** to brush one's hair forward/back ◆ **~ les épaules en arrière** to pull one's shoulders back
3 *(= faire revenir à)* **~ à** to bring back to ◆ **~ à la vie** *[+ personne]* to revive, to bring back to life; *[+ région]* to revitalize, to bring back to life ◆ **~ le compteur à zéro** to put the meter back to zero, to reset the meter at zero ◆ **~ les prix à un juste niveau** to bring prices back (down) ou restore prices to a reasonable level ◆ **il ramène toujours tout à lui** he always brings everything back to himself ◆ **~ un incident à de plus justes proportions** to get ou bring an incident into proportion ◆ **ils ont ramené ces bagarres au rang de simple incident** they played down the fighting, passing it off as a mere incident ◆ **~ la conversation sur un sujet** to bring ou steer ou lead the conversation back (on)to a subject ◆ **cela nous ramène 20 ans en arrière** it takes us back 20 years; → **raison**
4 *(= réduire à)* **~ à** to reduce to ◆ **~ l'inflation à moins de 3%** to reduce inflation to less than 3%, to bring inflation back down to below 3%
5 *(locutions)* **la ~**‡, **~ sa fraise**‡ ou **sa gueule**‡ *(= protester)* to kick up a fuss* ou a row *(surtout Brit)*; *(= intervenir)* to interfere, to put ou shove one's oar in* *(Brit)*
VPR **se ramener** 1 *(= se réduire à)* **se ~ à** *[problèmes]* to come down to, to boil down to; *(Math) [fraction]* to reduce to, to be reduced to
2 *(‡ = arriver)* to roll up*, to turn up*

ramequin /ʀamkɛ̃/ NM ramekin, ramequin

ramer[1] /ʀame/ ► conjug 1 ◄ VI 1 *(Sport)* to row ◆ **~ en couple** to scull 2 *(* = travailler dur)* to work hard, to slog one's guts out‡ *(Brit)* ◆ **elle a ramé six mois avant de trouver du travail** *(= avoir des difficultés)* she struggled for six long hard months before she found a job ◆ **je rame complètement** *(= être perdu)* I haven't got a clue what I'm doing

ramer[2] /ʀame/ ► conjug 1 ◄ VT *(Agr)* to stake

ramette /ʀamɛt/ NF *[de papier à lettres]* ream

rameur /ʀamœʀ/ NM *(= sportif)* oarsman, rower; *(= galérien)* rower ◆ **~ en couple** sculler

rameuse /ʀamøz/ NF *(= sportive)* oarswoman, rower

rameuter /ʀamøte/ ► conjug 1 ◄ VT *[+ foule, partisans]* to gather together, to round up; *[+ chiens]* to round up, to form into a pack again ◆ **les gens s'étaient rameutés** people had formed a crowd

rami /ʀami/ NM rummy ◆ **faire ~** to get rummy

ramier /ʀamje/ NM ◆ **(pigeon) ~** woodpigeon, ringdove

ramification /ʀamifikasjɔ̃/ NF *(Bot, Anat)* ramification, branching; *[de réseau routier]* branch; *[de voie ferrée]* branch line; *[d'organisation, maffia]* branch ◆ **les ~s du complot/scandale** the ramifications of the plot/scandal

ramifié, e /ʀamifje/ (ptp de **se ramifier**) ADJ *(lit, fig)* ramified

ramifier (se) /ʀamifje/ ► conjug 7 ◄ VPR *[veines]* to ramify; *[routes, branches, famille]* to branch out *(en* into); ◆ **cette science s'est ramifiée en plusieurs disciplines** this science has branched out into several different disciplines

ramille /ʀamij/ NF *(= brindille)* twig

ramolli, e /ʀamɔli/ (ptp de **ramollir**) ADJ *[biscuit, beurre]* soft; *[personne] (= avachi)* soft; *(= stupide)* soft (in the head), soft-headed ◆ **il a le cerveau ~** *(péj)* he is ou has gone soft in the head*

ramollir /ʀamɔliʀ/ ► conjug 2 ◄ VT *[+ matière]* to soften; *[+ courage, résolution]* to weaken ◆ **~ qn** *[plaisir]* to soften sb; *[climat]* to enervate sb VI **se ramollir** VPR *[beurre, argile]* to soften (up), to go soft; *[personne]* to go to seed ◆ **depuis que j'ai arrêté le tennis, je me suis ramolli** I've been out of condition since I've stopped playing tennis ◆ **son cerveau se ramollit** *(hum)* he's going soft in the head*

ramollissement /ʀamɔlismɑ̃/ NM softening ◆ **~ cérébral** softening of the brain

ramollo* /ʀamɔlo/ ADJ *(= avachi)* droopy; *(= gâteux)* soft (in the head)

ramonage /ʀamɔnaʒ/ NM chimney-sweeping; *(Alpinisme)* chimney-climbing

ramoner /ʀamɔne/ ► conjug 1 ◄ VT *[+ cheminée]* to sweep; *[+ pipe]* to clean out VI *(Alpinisme)* to climb a chimney

ramoneur /ʀamɔnœʀ/ NM (chimney) sweep

rampant, e /ʀɑ̃pɑ̃, ɑ̃t/ ADJ 1 *[animal]* crawling, creeping; *[plante, inflation]* creeping; *[caractère, employé]* grovelling, cringing ◆ **personnel ~** *(= personnel au sol)* ground crew ou staff 2 *(Héraldique)* rampant ◆ **lion ~** lion rampant NM 1 *(= membre du personnel au sol)* member of the ground crew ou staff ◆ **les ~s** the ground crew ou staff 2 *(Archit)* pitch

rampe /ʀɑ̃p/ NF 1 *(= voie d'accès)* ramp, slope; *(= côte)* slope, incline, gradient 2 *[d'escalier]* banister(s); *[de chemin]* handrail 3 *(Théât = projecteurs)* **la ~** the footlights, the floats *(Brit)* ◆ **passer la ~** to get across to the audience 4 *(locutions)* **tenez bon la ~*** hold on to your hat* ◆ **elle tient bon la ~*** she's still going strong ◆ **lâcher la ~*** *(= mourir)* to kick the bucket‡
COMP **rampe d'accès** approach ramp
rampe de balisage runway lights
rampe de débarquement disembarkation ramp
rampe de graissage oil gallery
rampe de lancement launching pad; *(fig)* springboard

ramper /ʀɑ̃pe/ ► conjug 1 ◄ VI 1 *[serpent]* to crawl, to slither; *[quadrupède, homme]* to crawl; *[plante, ombre, feu]* to creep; *[sentiment, brouillard, mal, maladie]* to lurk ◆ **entrer/sortir en rampant** to crawl in/out ◆ **le lierre rampe contre le mur** the ivy creeps up the wall 2 *(fig péj = s'abaisser)* to grovel *(devant* before) to crawl, to cringe *(devant* to)

rampon /ʀɑ̃pɔ̃/ NM *(Helv = mâche)* lamb's lettuce

ramponneau‡ (pl **ramponneaux**) /ʀɑ̃pɔno/ NM bump, knock ◆ **donner un ~ à qn** to bump ou knock sb

Ramsès /ʀamsɛs/ NM Rameses, Ramses

ramure /ʀamyʀ/ NF *[de cerf]* antlers; *[d'arbre]* boughs, foliage

rancard‡ /ʀɑ̃kaʀ/ NM 1 *(= renseignement)* tip 2 *(= rendez-vous) (gén)* meeting, date; *[d'amoureux]* date ◆ **donner (un) ~ à qn** to arrange to meet sb, to make a date with sb ◆ **avoir (un) ~ avec qn** to have a meeting with sb, to have a date with sb ◆ **j'ai ~ avec lui dans une heure** I'm meeting him in an hour

rancarder‡ /ʀɑ̃kaʀde/ ► conjug 1 ◄ VT *(= renseigner)* to tip off ◆ **il m'a rancardé sur le voyage** he told me about ou genned me up on* *(Brit)* the trip VPR **se rancarder** *(= s'informer)* **se**

~ **sur qch** to get information on sth, to find out about sth

rancart /ʀɑ̃kaʀ/ **au rancart** ⁑ LOC ADV ◆ **mettre au** ~ *[+ objet, idée, projet]* to chuck out⁑, to scrap; *[+ personne]* to throw on the scrap heap* ◆ **bon à mettre au** ~ fit for the scrap heap

rance /ʀɑ̃s/ ADJ *[beurre]* rancid; *[odeur]* rank, rancid; *(fig)* stale ◆ **sentir le** ~ to smell rancid *ou* rank ◆ **odeur de** ~ rank *ou* rancid smell

ranch (pl **ranchs** *ou* **ranches**) /ʀɑ̃tʃ/ NM ranch

ranci, e /ʀɑ̃si/ (ptp de **rancir**) ADJ *[beurre]* rancid; *(péj) [personne]* stale NM ◆ **sentir le** ~ to smell rank *ou* rancid

rancir /ʀɑ̃siʀ/ ► conjug 2 ◄ VI *[lard, beurre]* to go rancid *ou* off* *(Brit)*; *(fig)* to grow stale

rancœur /ʀɑ̃kœʀ/ NF *(frm)* resentment *(NonC)*, rancour *(Brit) (NonC)*, rancor *(US) (NonC)* ◆ **avoir de la** ~ **contre qn** to feel resentment against *ou* towards sb ◆ **les ~s s'étaient accumulées depuis des années** the resentment had been building up for years

rançon /ʀɑ̃sɔ̃/ NF *(lit)* ransom ◆ **c'est la** ~ **de la gloire/du progrès** *(fig)* that's the price of fame/of progress ◆ **mettre à** ~ *(littér)* to hold to ransom

rançonner /ʀɑ̃sɔne/ ► conjug 1 ◄ VT *(= voler) [+ convoi, voyageurs]* to demand a ransom from; *[+ contribuables, clients]* to fleece

rançonneur, -euse /ʀɑ̃sɔnœʀ, øz/ NM,F *(lit)* person demanding a ransom, ransomer; *(fig)* extortioner, extortionist

rancune /ʀɑ̃kyn/ NF grudge, rancour *(Brit) (NonC) (frm)*, rancor *(US) (NonC)* ◆ **avoir de la** ~ **à l'égard de** *ou* **contre qn, garder** ~ **à qn** to hold *ou* harbour a grudge against sb, to bear sb a grudge *(de qch* for sth); ◆ **oubliez vos vieilles ~s** put aside your old grudges ◆ **sans** ~ **!** no hard *ou* ill feelings!

rancunier, -ière /ʀɑ̃kynje, jɛʀ/ ADJ ◆ **être** ~ to bear grudges ◆ **qu'est-ce que tu peux être** ~ **!** you're certainly one to bear a grudge!, you don't know how to forgive and forget, do you?

rand /ʀɑ̃d/ NM rand

rando* /ʀɑ̃do/ NF (abrév de **randonnée**) hike

randomiser /ʀɑ̃dɔmize/ ► conjug 1 ◄ VT to randomize

randonnée /ʀɑ̃dɔne/ NF 1 *(= promenade) (à pied)* walk ◆ ~ **(à bicyclette)** (bike) ride ◆ ~ **pédestre** *ou* **à pied** *(courte, à la campagne)* walk; *(longue, en montagne)* hike ◆ **faire une** ~ **à ski** to go cross-country skiing ◆ ~ **équestre** *ou* **à cheval** pony trek ◆ **partir en** ~ *(courte)* to go for a walk; *(longue)* to go hiking 2 *(= activité)* **la** ~ rambling; *(promenades plus longues)* hiking ◆ **la** ~ **équestre** pony trekking ◆ **chaussures de** ~ hiking boots ◆ **ski de** ~ cross-country skiing ◆ **sentier de grande** ~ (registered) hiking trail

randonner /ʀɑ̃dɔne/ ► conjug 1 ◄ VI *(gén)* to go walking *ou* rambling; *(promenades plus longues)* to go hiking ◆ **ils ont découvert les Pyrénées en randonnant** they got to know the Pyrenees by going hiking there

randonneur, -euse /ʀɑ̃dɔnœʀ, øz/ NM,F hiker

rang /ʀɑ̃/ NM 1 *(= rangée) [de maisons, personnes, objets, tricot]* row; *(= file)* line; *(Mil)* rank ◆ **collier à trois ~s (de perles)** necklace with three rows of pearls ◆ **porter un** ~ **de perles** to wear a string *ou* rope *ou* row of pearls ◆ **assis au troisième** ~ sitting in the third row ◆ **deux jours de** ~ *(= d'affilée)* two days running *ou* in succession ◆ **en ~s serrés** in close order, in serried ranks ◆ **en** ~ **d'oignons** in a row *ou* line ◆ **en** ~ **par deux/quatre** two/four abreast ◆ **sur deux/quatre ~s** two/four deep ◆ **se mettre sur un** ~ to get into *ou* form a line ◆ **se mettre en ~s par quatre** *(Scol)* to line up in fours; *(Mil)* to form fours ◆ **plusieurs personnes sont sur** *ou* **se sont mises sur les ~s pour l'acheter** several people are in the running *ou* have got themselves lined up to buy it, several people have indicated an interest in buying it ◆ **servir dans les ~s de** *(Mil)* to serve in the ranks of ◆ **grossir les ~s de** *(fig)* to swell the ranks of ◆ **nous l'avons admis dans nos ~s** *(fig)* we allowed him to enter our ranks ◆ **à vos ~s, fixe !** *(Mil)* fall in! ◆ **officier sorti du** ~ officer who has risen through *ou* from the ranks; → **rentrer, rompre, serrer**

2 *(Can)* country road *(bordered by farms at right angles)*, concession road *(in Quebec)* ◆ **les ~s** the country

3 *(= condition)* station ◆ **de haut** ~ *(= noble)* noble; *[officier]* high-ranking *(épith)* ◆ **du plus haut** ~ of the highest standing ◆ **tenir** *ou* **garder son** ~ to maintain one's rank

4 *(hiérarchique = grade, place)* rank ◆ **avoir** ~ **de** to hold the rank of ◆ **avoir** ~ **parmi** to rank among ◆ **par** ~ **d'âge/de taille** in order of age/of size *ou* height ◆ **être reçu dans un bon** ~ to be in the top few ◆ **13e, c'est un bon** ~ 13th place isn't bad ◆ **être placé au deuxième** ~ to be ranked *ou* placed second ◆ **ce pays se situe au troisième** ~ **mondial des exportateurs de pétrole** this country is the third largest oil exporter in the world ◆ **mettre un écrivain au** ~ **des plus grands** to rank a writer among the greatest ◆ **c'est au premier/dernier** ~ **de mes préoccupations** that's the first/last thing on my mind ◆ **il est au premier** ~ **des artistes contemporains** he is one of the highest ranking of *ou* he ranks among the best of contemporary artists ◆ **écrivain/journaliste de second** ~ second-rate writer/journalist

LES RANGS

In Quebec, rural areas are divided into districts known as **rangs**. The word **rang** refers to a series of rectangular fields (each known as a « lot »), usually laid out between a river and a road (the road itself also being called a **rang**). The **rangs** are numbered or given names so that they can be easily identified and used in addresses (e.g. « le deuxième rang », « le rang Saint-Claude »). In Quebec, the expression « dans les rangs » means « in the countryside ».

rangé, e[1] /ʀɑ̃ʒe/ (ptp de **ranger**) ADJ *(= ordonné)* orderly; *(= sans excès)* settled, steady ◆ **il est** ~ **(des voitures⁑) maintenant** *[escroc]* he's going straight now; *[séducteur]* he's settled down now ◆ **petite vie bien ~e** well-ordered existence ◆ **jeune fille ~e** well-behaved young lady; → **bataille**

range-CD /ʀɑ̃ʒ(ə)sede/ NM INV CD rack

rangée[2] /ʀɑ̃ʒe/ NF *[de maisons, arbres]* row, line; *[d'objets, spectateurs, perles]* row

rangement /ʀɑ̃ʒmɑ̃/ NM 1 *(= action) [d'objets, linge]* putting away; *[de pièce, meuble]* tidying (up) ◆ **faire du** ~ to do some tidying up ◆ **capacité de** ~ **d'une bibliothèque** shelf space of a bookcase ◆ **la maison manque d'espaces de** ~ the house lacks storage *ou* cupboard space 2 *(= espace) [d'appartement]* cupboard space; *[de remise]* storage space ◆ **il faut que j'achète un** ~ **pour mes CD** I must buy something to keep my CDs in, I must buy a rack for my CDs; → **meuble** 3 *(= arrangement)* arrangement

ranger[1] /ʀɑ̃ʒe/ ► conjug 3 ◄ VT 1 *(= mettre en ordre) [+ tiroir, maison]* to tidy (up); *[+ dossiers, papiers]* to tidy (up), to arrange; *[+ mots, chiffres]* to arrange, to order ◆ **tout est toujours bien rangé chez elle** it's always (nice and) tidy at her place ◆ **rangé par ordre alphabétique** listed *ou* arranged alphabetically *ou* in alphabetical order

2 *(= mettre à sa place) [+ papiers, vêtements]* to put away; *[+ bateau]* to moor, to berth; *[+ voiture, vélo] (au garage)* to put away; *(dans la rue)* to park ◆ **où se rangent les tasses ?** where do the cups go? *ou* belong? ◆ **je le range parmi les meilleurs** I rank *ou* put it among the best ◆ **ce roman est à** ~ **parmi les meilleurs** this novel ranks *ou* is to be ranked among the best

3 *(= disposer) [+ écoliers]* to line up, to put *ou* form into rows; *[+ soldats]* to draw up; *[+ invités]* to place ◆ ~ **qn sous son autorité** *(fig)* to bring sb under one's authority

4 *(Naut)* ~ **la côte** to sail along the coast

VPR **se ranger** 1 *[automobiliste] (= stationner)* to park; *(= venir s'arrêter)* to pull in *ou* up, to draw up ◆ **la voiture se rangea contre le trottoir** the car pulled in *ou* up *ou* drew up at the kerb ◆ **le navire se rangea contre le quai** the ship moored *ou* berthed *ou* came alongside the quay

2 *(= s'écarter) [piéton]* to step *ou* stand aside, to make way; *[véhicule]* to pull over ◆ **il se rangea pour la laisser passer** he stepped *ou* stood aside to let her go by, he made way for her

3 *(= se mettre en rang)* to line up, to get into line *ou* rows ◆ **se** ~ **par deux/quatre** to line up in twos/fours, to get into rows of two/four

4 *(= se rallier à)* **se** ~ **à** *[+ décision]* to go along with, to abide by; *[+ avis]* to come round *ou* over to, to fall in with ◆ **se** ~ **du côté de qn** to side with sb

5 *(* = cesser son activité)* **se** ~ **(des voitures)** *[escroc]* to go straight; *[séducteur]* to settle down

ranger[2] /ʀɑ̃dʒɛʀ/ NM *(= soldat)* ranger; *(= scout)* rover; *(= chaussure)* canvas walking boot

Rangoon /ʀɑ̃gun/ N Rangoon

rani /ʀani/ NF rani, ranee

ranimer /ʀanime/ ► conjug 1 ◄ VT *[+ blessé]* to revive, to bring to, to bring round *(Brit)*; *[+ feu, braises]* to rekindle; *[+ région, souvenir, conversation]* to revive, to bring back to life; *[+ rancune, querelle]* to rake up, to revive; *[+ forces, ardeur]* to renew, to restore; *[+ amour, haine, espoir]* to rekindle, to renew; *[+ douleur]* to revive, to renew; *[+ couleurs]* to brighten up, to revive VPR **se ranimer** *[personne]* to revive, to come to, to come round *(Brit)*; *[feu, braises]* to rekindle, to be rekindled; *[haine, passion]* to be rekindled; *[conversation, débat]* to pick up (again); *[souvenirs, espoirs]* to be revived

raout † /ʀaut/ NM *(= réception)* Society ball

rap /ʀap/ NM *(= musique)* rap (music); *(= technique)* rapping

rapace /ʀapas/ NM *(= oiseau)* bird of prey, raptor *(SPÉC)*; *(fig)* vulture ADJ predatory, raptorial *(SPÉC)*; *(fig)* rapacious, grasping

rapacité /ʀapasite/ NF *(lit, fig)* rapaciousness, rapacity

râpage /ʀɑpaʒ/ NM *[de carottes, fromage]* grating; *[de bois]* rasping; *[de tabac]* grinding

rapatrié, e /ʀapatʀije/ (ptp de **rapatrier**) ADJ repatriated NM,F repatriate ◆ **les ~s d'Algérie** *French settlers repatriated after Algerian independence*

rapatriement /ʀapatʀimɑ̃/ NM repatriation ◆ ~ **sanitaire** repatriation on medical grounds ◆ ~ **volontaire** voluntary repatriation

rapatrier /ʀapatʀije/ ► conjug 7 ◄ VT *[+ personne, capitaux]* to repatriate; *[+ objet]* to send *ou* bring back (home) ◆ **il a fait** ~ **le corps de son fils** he had his son's body sent back home

râpe /ʀɑp/ NF *(= ustensile de cuisine)* grater; *(pour le bois)* rasp; *(pour le tabac)* grinder ◆ ~ **à fromage** cheese grater

râpé, e /ʀɑpe/ (ptp de **râper**) ADJ *(= usé) [veste]* threadbare; *[coude]* through, worn *(attrib)*; *[carottes, fromage]* grated ◆ **c'est** ~ **pour ce soir** *(* = raté)* we've had it for tonight* NM *(= fromage)* grated cheese

râper /ʀɑpe/ ► conjug 1 ◄ VT *[+ carottes, fromage]* to grate; *[+ bois]* to rasp; *[+ tabac]* to grind ◆ **vin**

qui râpe la gorge *ou* **le gosier** rough wine ◆ **tissu qui râpe la peau** scratchy material

rapetassage* /ʀap(ə)tasaʒ/ NM patching up

rapetasser* /ʀap(ə)tase/ ▸ conjug 1 ◂ VT to patch up

rapetissement /ʀap(ə)tismɑ̃/ NM [1] *[de manteau]* taking up, shortening; *[de taille, encolure]* taking in; *[d'objet]* shortening, shrinking [2] *(= rabaissement)* belittling [3] *(= action de faire paraître plus petit)* dwarfing ◆ **le ~ des objets dû à la distance** the fact that objects look smaller when seen from a distance

rapetisser /ʀap(ə)tise/ ▸ conjug 1 ◂ VT [1] *(= raccourcir) [+ manteau]* to take up, to shorten; *[+ taille, encolure]* to take in; *[+ objet]* to shorten ◆ **l'âge l'avait rapetissé** he had shrunk with age [2] *(= rabaisser)* to belittle [3] *(= faire paraître plus petit)* ~ **qch** to make sth seem *ou* look small(er) ◆ **le château rapetissait toutes les maisons alentour** the castle dwarfed all the surrounding houses, the castle made all the surrounding houses look *ou* seem small VI * *[jours]* to get shorter ◆ **les objets rapetissent à distance** objects look smaller from a distance VPR **se rapetisser** [1] *[vieillard]* to shrink, to grow shorter *ou* smaller [2] *(= se rabaisser)* **se ~ aux yeux de qn** to belittle o.s. in sb's eyes

râpeux, -euse /ʀɑpø, øz/ ADJ rough

Raphaël /ʀafaɛl/ NM Raphael

raphaélique /ʀafaelik/ ADJ Raphaelesque

raphia /ʀafja/ NM raffia

rapiat, e /ʀapja, jat/ *(péj)* ADJ niggardly, stingy, tight-fisted NM,F niggard, skinflint

rapide /ʀapid/ ADJ [1] *(en déplacement) [coureur, marche, pas]* fast, quick; *[véhicule, route]* fast; *[animal]* fast(-moving); *[fleuve]* fast(-flowing), swift-flowing ◆ ~ **comme une flèche** *ou* **l'éclair** incredibly fast ◆ **il est ~ à la course** he's a fast runner ◆ **elle marchait d'un pas ~** she was walking quickly; → **voie**

[2] *(dans le temps) [travail, guérison, progrès, remède, réponse]* quick, fast; *[intervention, visite, fortune, recette]* quick; *[poison]* quick-acting, fast-acting; *[accord]* speedy, swift ◆ **examen (trop) ~ de qch** cursory examination of sth ◆ **décision trop ~** hasty decision ◆ **faire un calcul ~** to do a quick calculation ◆ **c'est ~ à faire** *(plat)* it's very quick to make

[3] *[pente, descente]* steep

[4] *[mouvement, coup d'œil]* rapid, quick; *[esprit, intelligence]* quick; *[travailleur]* quick, fast ◆ **d'une main ~** *(= vite)* quickly, rapidly; *(= adroitement)* deftly ◆ **avoir des réflexes ~s** to have quick reflexes ◆ **tu n'es pas très ~ ce matin** you're a bit slow *ou* you re not on the ball* this morning ◆ **c'est une ~** *(qui agit vite)* she's a fast worker; *(qui comprend vite)* she's quick on the uptake ◆ **ce n'est pas un ~** he's a bit slow

[5] *(en fréquence) [pouls, rythme, respiration]* fast, rapid

[6] *[style, récit]* lively

[7] *[pellicule]* fast; *[ciment]* quick-setting

NM [1] *(= train)* express (train), fast train ◆ **le ~ Paris-Nice** the Paris-Nice express

[2] *[de cours d'eau]* rapids ◆ **descendre des ~s en kayak** to canoe down some rapids, to shoot rapids in a canoe

> ⚠ Attention à ne pas traduire automatiquement l'adjectif **rapide** par le mot anglais **rapid**.

rapidement /ʀapidmɑ̃/ ADV quickly ◆ **la situation se dégrade ~** the situation is fast deteriorating, the situation is getting worse every minute ◆ **les pompiers sont intervenus ~** the fire brigade arrived very quickly ◆ **il faut mettre ~ un terme à ce conflit** we must put a swift end to the conflict ◆ **j'ai parcouru ~ le journal** I quickly skimmed through the paper

rapidité /ʀapidite/ NF *(gén)* speed; *[de changements, développement]* rapidity; *[de réponse, geste]* swiftness, quickness; *[de style]* briskness, liveliness; *[de pouls]* quickness ◆ **~ d'esprit** quickness of mind ◆ **~ de décision** quick *ou* speedy decision-making ◆ **la ~ de sa réaction m'a étonné** I was surprised by the speed of his reaction ◆ **la ~ d'adaptation est essentielle dans ce métier** the ability to adapt quickly is essential in this profession ◆ **avec ~** quickly ◆ **avec la ~ de l'éclair** *ou* **de la foudre** *ou* **d'une flèche** with lightning speed

> ⚠ Attention à ne pas traduire automatiquement **rapidité** par **rapidity**.

rapido* /ʀapido/, **rapidos*** /ʀapidos/ ADV pronto*

rapiéçage /ʀapjesaʒ/, **rapiècement** /ʀapjesmɑ̃/ NM [1] *[de vêtement, pneu]* patching (up); *[de chaussure]* mending, repairing [2] *(= pièce)* patch

rapiécer /ʀapjese/ ▸ conjug 3 et 6 ◂ VT *[+ vêtement, pneu]* to patch (up), to put a patch in; *[+ chaussure]* to mend, to repair ◆ **il portait une veste toute rapiécée** he was wearing a patched-up old jacket

rapière /ʀapjɛʀ/ NF rapier

rapin /ʀapɛ̃/ NM *(† ou péj = artiste peintre)* painter, dauber

rapine /ʀapin/ NF *(littér)* plundering, plunder ◆ **vivre de ~(s)** to live by plunder

rapiner /ʀapine/ ▸ conjug 1 ◂ VTI *(littér)* to plunder

raplapla* /ʀaplapla/ ADJ INV *(= fatigué)* done in*; *(= plat)* flat

raplatir /ʀaplatiʀ/ ▸ conjug 2 ◂ VT to flatten out

rappareiller /ʀapaʀeje/ ▸ conjug 1 ◂ VT to match up

rapparier /ʀapaʀje/ ▸ conjug 7 ◂ VT to pair up, to match up

rappel /ʀapɛl/ NM [1] *[d'ambassadeur]* recall, recalling; *(Mil) [de réservistes]* recall; *[de marchandises défectueuses]* callback ◆ **il y a eu trois ~s** *(Théât)* there were three curtain calls; *(à un concert)* they *(ou he etc)* came back on stage for three encores; → **battre**

[2] *[d'événement]* reminder; *(Comm) [de référence]* quote; *(Admin = deuxième avis)* reminder; *(Admin = somme due)* back pay *(NonC)*; *(= vaccination)* booster ◆ **au ~ de cette bévue, il rougit** he blushed at being reminded of this blunder ◆ **toucher un ~ (de salaire)** to get some back pay ◆ **~ de limitation de vitesse** *(= panneau)* speed limit sign, reminder of the speed limit ◆ **~ des titres de l'actualité** *(Radio, TV)* summary of the day's headlines ◆ **~ à l'ordre** call to order ◆ **~ de couleur** colour repeat

[3] *(Tech) [de pièce, levier]* return ◆ **~ (de corde)** *(Alpinisme) (= technique)* abseiling, roping down; *(= opération)* abseil ◆ **faire un ~, descendre en ~** to abseil, to rope down ◆ **faire du ~** *(Naut)* to sit out ◆ **ressort de ~** *(Tech)* return spring; → **descente**

rappelé /ʀap(ə)le/ NM recalled soldier

rappeler /ʀap(ə)le/ GRAMMAIRE ACTIVE 54.2, 54.3, 54.5, 28.1 ▸ conjug 4 ◂

VT [1] *(= faire revenir) [+ personne, acteur, chien]* to call back; *(Mil) [+ réservistes, classe]* to recall, to call up (again); *[+ diplomate]* to recall ◆ **~ qn au chevet d'un malade** *ou* **auprès d'un malade** to call *ou* summon sb back to a sick person's bedside ◆ **ses affaires l'ont rappelé à Paris** he was called back to Paris on business ◆ **Dieu l'a rappelé à lui** *(frm)* he (has) departed this world *ou* life ◆ **~ des réservistes au front** to recall reservists to the front ◆ **~ un fichier (à l'écran)** to call up a file (onto the screen)

[2] ◆ **~ qch à qn** *(= évoquer, remettre en mémoire)* to remind sb of sth ◆ **il rappela les qualités du défunt** he evoked *ou* mentioned the qualities of the deceased, he reminded the audience of the qualities of the deceased ◆ **faut-il ~ que ... ?** must I remind you that ...?, must it be repeated that ...? ◆ **ces dessins rappellent l'art arabe** those drawings are reminiscent of *ou* remind one of Arabian art ◆ **le motif des poches rappelle celui du bas de la robe** the design on the pockets is repeated round the hem of the dress ◆ **cela ne te rappelle rien ?** doesn't that remind you of anything? ◆ **tu me rappelles ma tante** you remind me of my aunt ◆ **rappelle-moi mon rendez-vous** remind me about my appointment ◆ **rappelez-moi votre nom** sorry - could you tell me your name again? ◆ **attends, ça me rappelle quelque chose** wait, it rings a bell ◆ **rappelez-moi à son bon souvenir** *(frm)* please remember me to him, please give him my kind regards

[3] ◆ **~ qn à la vie** *ou* **à lui** to bring sb back to life, to revive sb ◆ **~ qn à l'ordre** to call sb to order ◆ **~ qn à son devoir** to remind sb of their duty ◆ **~ qn à de meilleurs sentiments** to put sb in a better frame of mind

[4] *(= retéléphoner à)* to call *ou* phone *ou* ring back *(Brit)* ◆ **il vient de ~** he's just called *ou* phoned back *ou* rung *(Brit)*

[5] *(Comm) [+ référence]* to quote

[6] *(= tirer) (Tech) [+ pièce, levier]* to return; *(Alpinisme) [+ corde]* to pull to *ou* through

VPR **se rappeler** to remember ◆ **se ~ que ...** to remember that ... ◆ **autant que je me rappelle** as far as I can remember ◆ **mais si, rappelle-toi, il était là !** come on, you remember, he was there!, he was there, surely you remember! ◆ **je me permets de me ~ à votre bon souvenir** *(frm)* I send you my kindest regards ◆ **rappelle-toi que ton honneur est en jeu** remember (that) your honour is at stake ◆ **il ne se rappelle plus (rien)** he doesn't *ou* can't remember a thing

rapper /ʀape/ ▸ conjug 1 ◂ VI to rap, to play rap music

rappeur, -euse /ʀapœʀ, øz/ NM,F *(Mus)* rapper

rappliquer* /ʀaplike/ ▸ conjug 1 ◂ VI *(= revenir)* to come back; *(= arriver)* to turn up, to show up* ◆ **rapplique tout de suite à la maison !** come home right away!, get yourself back here right away!*

rapport /ʀapɔʀ/ GRAMMAIRE ACTIVE 32.1 NM [1] *(= lien, corrélation)* connection, relationship, link ◆ **établir un ~/des ~s entre deux incidents** to establish a link *ou* connection/links *ou* connections between two incidents ◆ **avoir un certain ~/beaucoup de ~ avec qch** to have something/a lot to do with sth, to have some/a definite connection with sth ◆ **avoir ~ à qch** to bear some relation to sth, to have something to do *ou* some connection with sth ◆ **n'avoir aucun ~ avec** *ou* **être sans ~ avec qch** to bear no relation to sth, to have nothing to do *ou* no connection with sth ◆ **les deux incidents n'ont aucun ~** the two incidents have nothing to do with each other *ou* are unconnected ◆ **je ne vois pas le ~** I don't see the connection

◆ **être en ~ avec qch** to be in keeping with sth ◆ **une situation en ~ avec ses goûts** a job in keeping *ou* in harmony *ou* in line with his tastes ◆ **son train de vie n'est pas en ~ avec son salaire** his lifestyle doesn't match *ou* isn't in keeping with his salary

[2] *(= relation personnelle)* relationship *(à, avec)*; ◆ **~s** relations ◆ **~s sociaux/humains** social/human relations ◆ **les ~s d'amitié entre les deux peuples** the friendly relations *ou* the ties of friendship between the two nations

♦ **les ~s entre (les) professeurs et (les) étudiants** relations between teachers and students, student-teacher *ou* student-staff relations ♦ **son ~ à l'argent est bizarre** he has a strange relationship with money ♦ **ses ~s avec les autres sont difficiles** he has problems dealing with *ou* getting along *ou* on *(Brit)* with people ♦ **avoir** *ou* **entretenir de bons/mauvais ~s avec qn** to be on good/bad terms with sb

♦ **être en ~ avec qn** to be in touch *ou* contact with sb ♦ **nous n'avons jamais été en ~ avec cette société** we have never had any dealings *ou* anything to do with that company ♦ **se mettre en ~ avec qn** to get in touch *ou* contact with sb ♦ **mettre qn en ~ avec qn d'autre** to put sb in touch *ou* contact with sb else

3 ♦ **~ (sexuel)** sexual intercourse *(NonC)* ♦ **avoir des ~s (sexuels)** to have (sexual) intercourse *ou* sexual relations *ou* sex ♦ **~s protégés** safe sex ♦ **~s non protégés** unprotected sex

4 *(= exposé, compte rendu)* report; *(Mil = réunion)* (post-exercise) conference ♦ **au ~ !** *(Mil)* read!; *(hum)* let's hear what you've got to say! ♦ **~ (annuel) d'activité** *(Écon)* annual report ♦ **~ d'inspection** *(Scol)* evaluation (report) ♦ **~ de police** police report

5 *(= revenu, profit)* yield, return, revenue ♦ **~s** *[de tiercé]* winnings ♦ **être d'un bon ~** to give a good profit, to have a good yield, to give a good return ♦ **ces champs sont en plein ~** these fields are bringing in a full yield; → **immeuble, maison**

6 *(Math, Tech)* ratio ♦ **~ de transmission** *[de moteur]* gear ratio ♦ **dans le ~ de 1 à 100/de 100 contre 1** in a ratio of 1 to 100/of 100 to 1 ♦ **le ~ qualité-prix** the quality-price ratio ♦ **il y a un bon ~ qualité-prix** it's really good value for money ♦ **ce n'est pas d'un bon ~ qualité-prix** it's not good value for money

7 *(locutions)* **le ~ de** *ou* **des forces entre les deux blocs** the balance of power between the two blocs ♦ **envisager des relations sous l'angle d'un ~ de forces** to see relationships in terms of a power struggle ♦ **il n'y a aucune inquiétude à avoir sous le ~ de l'honnêteté** from the point of view of honesty *ou* as far as honesty is concerned there's nothing to worry about

♦ **rapport à*** about, in connection with, concerning ♦ **je viens vous voir ~ à votre annonce*** I've come (to see you) about your advertisement

♦ **par rapport à** *(= comparé à)* in comparison with, in relation to; *(= en fonction de)* in relation to; *(= envers)* with respect *ou* regard to, towards ♦ **le cours de la livre par ~ au dollar** the price of the pound against the dollar

♦ **sous tous (les) rapports** in every respect ♦ **jeune homme bien sous tous ~s** *(hum)* clean-living young man

rapportage /ʀapɔʀtaʒ/ **NM** *(arg Scol = mouchardage)* tale-telling *(NonC)*, tattling *(NonC) (US)*

rapporté, e /ʀapɔʀte/ (ptp de **rapporter**) **ADJ** *(gén)* added; *(Couture)* sewn-on; *[terre]* piled-up ♦ **poche ~e** patch pocket; → **pièce**

rapporter /ʀapɔʀte/ ► conjug 1 ◄ **VT** 1 *(= apporter)* *[+ objet, souvenir, réponse]* to bring back; *[chien] [+ gibier]* to retrieve ♦ **Toby, rapporte !** *(à un chien)* fetch, Toby! ♦ **~ qch à qn** to bring *ou* take sth back to sb ♦ **n'oublie pas de lui ~ son parapluie** don't forget to return his umbrella to him ♦ **il rapportera du pain en rentrant** he'll bring some bread when he gets back ♦ **~ une bonne impression de qch** to come back *ou* come away with a good impression of sth ♦ **quand doit-il ~ la réponse ?** when does he have to come *ou* be back with the answer?

2 *(= produire un gain)* *[actions, terre]* to yield (a return of), to bring in (a yield *ou* revenue of); *[métier]* to bring in; *[vente]* to bring in (a profit *ou* revenue of) ♦ **placement qui rapporte du 5%** investment that yields (a return of) 5% ♦ **ça rapporte beaucoup d'argent** it's extremely profitable, it brings in a lot of money, it gives a high return ♦ **ça ne lui rapportera rien** *[mauvaise action]* it won't do him any good ♦ **ça leur a rapporté 25 € net** they netted €25, it brought them in €25 net

3 *(= faire un compte rendu de)* *[+ fait]* to report; *(= mentionner)* to mention; *(= citer) [+ mot célèbre]* to quote; *(= répéter pour dénoncer)* to report ♦ **on nous a rapporté que son projet n'avait pas été bien accueilli** we were told that his project hadn't been well received ♦ **~ à qn les actions de qn** to report sb's actions to sb ♦ **il a rapporté à la maîtresse ce qu'avaient dit ses camarades** he told the teacher what his classmates had said, he reported what his classmates had said to the teacher

4 *(= ajouter)* *(gén)* to add; *[+ bande de tissu, poche]* to sew on ♦ **~ une aile à une maison** to build an extra wing onto a house ♦ **~ un peu de terre pour surélever le sol** to pile up some earth to raise the level of the ground ♦ **c'est un élément rapporté** it's been added on

5 *(= rattacher à)* **~ à** to relate to ♦ **il faut tout ~ à la même échelle de valeurs** everything has to be related *ou* referred to the same scale of values ♦ **il rapporte tout à lui** he brings everything back to himself

6 *(= annuler)* *[+ décret, décision, mesure]* to revoke

7 *(Math)* **~ un angle** to plot an angle

VI 1 *(Chasse) [chien]* to retrieve

2 *[investissement]* to give a good return *ou* yield ♦ **ça rapporte bien** *ou* **gros** *[domaine d'activité]* it's very profitable, it brings in a lot of money; *[travail]* it pays very well

3 *(arg Scol)* **~ (sur ses camarades)** *(= moucharder)* to tell tales *ou* sneak* (on one's friends), to tell on *(Brit)** *ou* tattle on* *(US)* one's friends

VPR **se rapporter** 1 ♦ **se ~ à qch** to relate to sth ♦ **se ~ à** *(Gram) (= antécédent)* to relate *ou* refer to ♦ **ce paragraphe ne se rapporte pas du tout au sujet** this paragraph bears no relation at all to the subject, this paragraph is totally irrelevant to *ou* unconnected with the subject ♦ **ça se rapporte à ce que je disais tout à l'heure** that ties *ou* links up with *ou* relates to what I was saying just now

2 ♦ **s'en ~ à qn** to rely on sb ♦ **s'en ~ au jugement/témoignage de qn** to rely on sb's judgment/account

rapporteur, -euse /ʀapɔʀtœʀ, øz/ **NM,F** *(= mouchard)* telltale, sneak*, tattler* *(US)* ♦ **elle est rapporteuse** she's a telltale *ou* sneak* *ou* tattler *(US)* **NM** 1 *(Jur) [de tribunal]* (court) reporter; *[de commission]* rapporteur, reporter *(member acting as spokesman)* 2 *(Géom)* protractor

rapprendre /ʀapʀɑ̃dʀ/ ► conjug 58 ◄ **VT** ⇒ **réapprendre**

rapproché, e /ʀapʀɔʃe/ (ptp de **rapprocher**) **ADJ** 1 *(= proche)* *[échéance, objet, bruit]* close ♦ **l'objet le plus ~ de toi** the object closest *ou* nearest to you ♦ **à une date ~e, dans un avenir ~** in the near *ou* not too distant future ♦ **elle a des yeux très ~s** she's got close-set eyes, her eyes are very close together ♦ **surveillance ~e** close surveillance; → **combat, garde¹, protection**

2 *(= répété)* *[incidents]* frequent ♦ **des crises de plus en plus ~es** increasingly frequent crises, crises which have become more and more frequent ♦ **trois explosions très ~es** three explosions in quick succession *ou* very close together ♦ **à intervalles ~s** in quick succession, at short *ou* close intervals ♦ **des grossesses ~es** (a series of) pregnancies at short *ou* close intervals

rapprochement /ʀapʀɔʃmɑ̃/ **NM** 1 *(= action de rapprocher)* *[d'objet, meuble]* bringing closer *ou* nearer; *[d'objets, meubles]* bringing closer *ou* nearer to each other; *[d'ennemis]* bringing together, reconciliation; *[de partis, factions]* bringing together; *[de points de vue, textes]* comparison, bringing together, comparing ♦ **le ~ des lèvres d'une plaie** *(Méd)* joining the edges of a wound, closing (the lips of) a wound

2 *(= action de se rapprocher)* *[de bruit]* coming closer; *[d'ennemis, famille]* coming together, reconciliation; *[de partis, factions]* coming together, rapprochement ♦ **ce ~ avec la droite nous inquiète** *(Pol)* their moving closer to the right worries us ♦ **le ~ des bruits de pas** the noise of footsteps drawing *ou* coming closer

3 *(= lien, rapport)* parallel ♦ **je n'avais pas fait le ~ (entre ces deux incidents)** I hadn't made *ou* established the connection *ou* link (between the two incidents) ♦ **il y a de nombreux ~s intéressants/troublants** there are many interesting/disturbing parallels *ou* comparisons to be made

rapprocher /ʀapʀɔʃe/ ► conjug 1 ◄ **VT** 1 *(= approcher)* to bring closer *ou* nearer *(de* to); ♦ **~ sa chaise (de la table)** to pull *ou* draw one's chair up (to the table) ♦ **~ deux objets l'un de l'autre** to move two objects (closer) together ♦ **~ les lèvres d'une plaie** to join the edges of a wound, to close (the lips of) a wound ♦ **il a changé d'emploi : ça le rapproche de chez lui** he has changed jobs – that brings him closer *ou* nearer to home

2 *(= réconcilier, réunir)* *[+ ennemis]* to bring together ♦ **nous nous sentions rapprochés par un malheur commun** we felt drawn together by a common misfortune, we felt that a common misfortune had brought *ou* drawn us together ♦ **leur amour de la chasse les rapproche** their love of hunting brings them together *ou* draws them to *ou* towards each other ♦ **cette expérience m'a rapproché d'elle** the experience brought me closer to her

3 *(= mettre en parallèle, confronter)* *[+ indices, textes]* to put together *ou* side by side, to compare, to bring together; *(= établir un lien entre, assimiler)* *[+ indices, textes]* to establish a connection *ou* link *ou* parallel between ♦ **essayons de ~ ces indices de ceux-là** let's try and put *ou* bring these two sets of clues together, let's try and compare these two sets of clues ♦ **on peut ~ cela du poème de Villon** we can relate *ou* connect that to Villon's poem, we can establish a connection *ou* link *ou* parallel between that and Villon's poem ♦ **c'est à ~ de ce qu'on disait tout à l'heure** that ties up *ou* connects with *ou* relates to what we were saying earlier

VPR **se rapprocher** 1 *(= approcher)* *[échéance, personne, véhicule, orage]* to get closer *ou* nearer, to approach ♦ **rapproche-toi (de moi)** come closer *ou* nearer (to me) ♦ **il se rapprocha d'elle sur la banquette** he edged his way towards her *ou* drew closer to her on the bench ♦ **pour se ~ de chez lui, il a changé d'emploi** to get closer *ou* nearer to home he changed jobs ♦ **plus on se rapprochait de l'examen …** the closer *ou* nearer we came *ou* got to the exam … ♦ **se ~ de la vérité** to come close *ou* get near *ou* close to the truth ♦ **les bruits se rapprochèrent** the noises got closer *ou* nearer

2 *(dans le temps)* *[crises, bruits]* to become more frequent

3 *(= se réconcilier)* *[ennemis]* to come together, to be reconciled; *(= trouver un terrain d'entente)* *[points de vue]* to draw closer together; *[société]* to form links ♦ **il s'est rapproché de ses parents** he became *ou* drew closer to his parents ♦ **il a essayé de se ~ de la droite** *(Pol)* he tried to move *ou* draw closer to the right ♦ **leur position s'est rapprochée de la nôtre** their position has drawn closer to ours ♦ **se ~ des autres actionnaires** to join forces with the other shareholders

4 *(= s'apparenter à)* to be close to ♦ **ça se rapproche de ce qu'on disait tout à l'heure** that's

close to *ou* ties up *ou* connects with what we were saying earlier ♦ **ses opinions se rapprochent beaucoup des miennes** his opinions are very close *ou* similar to mine

rapsode /Rapsɔd/ NM ⇒ **rhapsode**

rapsodie /Rapsɔdi/ NF ⇒ **rhapsodie**

rapt /Rapt/ NM (= *enlèvement*) abduction

raquer* /Rake/ ▸ conjug 1 ◂ VTI (= *payer*) to fork out* ♦ **d'accord, mais il va falloir ~ !** OK, but it'll cost you! *

raquette /Rakɛt/ NF 1 *(Tennis, Squash)* racket; *(Ping-Pong)* bat ♦ **c'est une bonne ~** (= *joueur*) he's a good tennis (*ou* squash) player 2 *(à neige)* snowshoe 3 *(Basket)* free-throw area 4 (= *plante*) nopal, prickly pear

raquetteur, -euse /Raketœr, øz/ NM,F *(Can)* snowshoer

rare /RɑR/ ADJ 1 (= *peu commun*) *[objet, mot, édition]* rare ♦ **ça n'a rien de ~** there's nothing uncommon *ou* unusual about this ♦ **il est ~ qu'on puisse reprocher à un roman d'être trop court** it's not often that you can criticize a novel for being too short ♦ **il n'est pas ~ qu'en plein été, il fasse un temps d'hiver** quite often, in the middle of summer, it's like winter ♦ **c'est ~ de le voir fatigué** you rarely *ou* don't often see him looking tired; → **oiseau, perle**

2 (= *peu nombreux*) *[cas, exemples]* rare, few; *[visites]* rare; *[passants, voitures]* few ♦ **les ~s voitures qui passaient** the few cars that went by ♦ **les ~s amis qui lui restent** the few friends he still has ♦ **à de ~s intervalles** at rare intervals ♦ **les ~s fois où ...** on the rare occasions (when) ... ♦ **il est l'un des ~s qui ...** he's one of the few (people) who ... ♦ **à cette heure les clients sont ~s** at this time of day there are very few customers, at this time of day customers are few and far between ♦ **à de ~s exceptions près** with very few exceptions

3 (= *peu abondant*) *[main d'œuvre]* scarce; *[barbe, cheveux]* thin, sparse; *[végétation]* sparse ♦ **il a le cheveu ~** he's rather thin on top ♦ **se faire ~** *[argent]* to be tight, to be in short supply; *[nourriture]* to become scarce, to be in short supply ♦ **vous vous faites ~** *(hum)* you've been keeping a low profile

4 (= *exceptionnel*) *[talent, qualité, sentiment, beauté]* rare; *[homme, énergie]* exceptional, singular; *[saveur, moment]* exquisite; *(hum) [imbécile, imprudence]* utter ♦ **avec un ~ courage** with rare *ou* singular *ou* exceptional courage ♦ **une attaque d'une ~ violence** an exceptionally *ou* extremely violent attack ♦ **d'une ~ beauté** exceptionally *ou* extremely beautiful ♦ **il est d'une ~ stupidité** he's utterly stupid

5 *(Chim) [gaz]* rare

raréfaction /Rarefaksjɔ̃/ NF *[d'oxygène]* rarefaction; *[de nourriture]* (= *action*) increased scarcity; (= *résultat*) scarcity, short supply

raréfiable /Rarefjabl/ ADJ rarefiable

raréfier /Rarefje/ ▸ conjug 7 ◂ VT *[+ air]* to rarefy ♦ **gaz raréfié** rarefied gas VPR **se raréfier** *[oxygène]* to rarefy; *[argent, nourriture]* to grow *ou* become scarce, to be in short supply

rarement /RɑRmɑ̃/ ADV rarely, seldom ♦ **le règlement est ~ respecté** the rule is rarely *ou* seldom observed ♦ **il ne rate que ~ sa cible** he only rarely misses his target ♦ **cela arrive plus ~** it happens less often *ou* frequently

rareté /RɑRte/ NF 1 *[d'édition, objet]* rarity; *[de mot, cas]* rareness, rarity; *[de vivres, argent]* scarcity ♦ **la ~ des touristes/visiteurs** the small numbers of tourists/visitors ♦ **se plaindre de la ~ des lettres/visites de qn** to complain of the infrequency of sb's letters/visits 2 (= *objet précieux*) rarity, rare object ♦ **une telle erreur de sa part, c'est une ~** it's a rare *ou* an unusual occurrence for him to make a mistake like that

rarissime /Rarisim/ ADJ extremely rare ♦ **fait ~, la pièce est restée six mois à l'affiche** the play ran for six months, which is very rare

ras[1] /Rɑs/ NM (= *titre éthiopien*) ras

ras[2]**, e** /Rɑ, Rɑz/ ADJ 1 *[poil, herbe]* short; *[cheveux]* close-cropped; *[étoffe]* with a short pile; *[mesure, tasse]* full ♦ **il avait la tête ~e** he had close-cropped hair ♦ **à poil ~** *[chien]* short-haired; *[étoffe]* with a short pile ♦ **ongles/cheveux coupés ~** *ou* **à ~** nails/hair cut short

2 *(locutions)* **pull ~ du cou** crew-neck *ou* round-neck sweater ♦ **j'en ai ~ le bol*** *ou* **le pompon*** *ou* **la casquette*** **(de tout ça)** I'm sick to death of it*, I'm fed up to the back teeth (with it all) *(Brit)**

♦ **à** *ou* **au ras de** (= *au niveau de*) ♦ **au ~ de la terre** *ou* **du sol/de l'eau** level with the ground/the water ♦ **arbre coupé à ~ de terre** tree cut down to the ground ♦ **ses cheveux lui arrivent au ~ des fesses** she can almost sit on her hair ♦ **ça lui arrive au ~ des chevilles** it comes down to her ankles ♦ **voler au ~ du sol/au ~ de l'eau** (= *tout près de*) to fly close to *ou* just above the ground/the water, to skim the ground/the water ♦ **le projectile lui est passé au ~ de la tête/du visage** the projectile skimmed his head/his face ♦ **la discussion est au ~ des pâquerettes*** the discussion is pretty lowbrow ♦ **soyons pragmatiques, restons au ~ des pâquerettes*** let's be pragmatic and keep our feet on the ground

♦ **à ras bord(s)** to the brim ♦ **remplir un verre à ~ bord** to fill a glass to the brim *ou* top ♦ **plein à ~ bord** *[verre]* full to the brim, brimful; *[baignoire]* full to overflowing *ou* to the brim

♦ **en rase campagne** in open country

R.A.S. /ɛRaɛs/ (abrév de **rien à signaler**) → **rien**

rasade /Rɑzad/ NF glassful

rasage /Rɑzaʒ/ NM 1 *[de barbe]* shaving; → **lotion** 2 *[de velours]* shearing

rasant, e /Rɑzɑ̃, ɑ̃t/ ADJ 1 (* = *ennuyeux*) boring ♦ **qu'il est ~ !** he's a (real) bore! *ou* drag!* 2 *[lumière]* low-angled; *[fortification]* low-built ♦ **tir ~** grazing fire

rascasse /Raskas/ NF scorpion fish

rasé, e /Rɑze/ (ptp de **raser**) ADJ *[menton]* (clean-) shaven; *[tête]* shaven ♦ **être bien/mal ~** to be shaven/unshaven ♦ **~ de près** close-shaven ♦ **~ de frais** freshly shaven ♦ **avoir les cheveux ~s** to have a shaven head ♦ **les crânes ~s** (= *personnes*) skinheads

rase-mottes /Rɑzmɔt/ NM INV hedgehopping ♦ **faire du ~, voler en ~** to hedgehop ♦ **vol en ~** hedgehopping flight

raser /Rɑze/ ▸ conjug 1 ◂ VT 1 (= *tondre*) *[+ barbe, cheveux]* to shave off; *[+ menton, tête]* to shave; *[+ malade]* to shave ♦ **~ un prêtre/condamné** to shave a priest's/convict's head ♦ **se faire ~ la tête** to have one's head shaved ♦ **à ~** *[crème, gel, mousse]* shaving *(épith)* 2 (= *effleurer*) *[projectile, véhicule]* to graze, to scrape; *[oiseau, balle de tennis]* to skim (over) ♦ **~ les murs** to hug the walls 3 (= *abattre*) *[+ maison]* to raze (to the ground) ♦ **~ un navire** to bring a ship's masts down 4 (* = *ennuyer*) to bore ♦ **ça me rase !** it bores me stiff! * *ou* to tears! * 5 *(Tech) [+ mesure à grains]* to strike; *[+ velours]* to shear VPR **se raser** 1 *(toilette)* to shave, to have a shave ♦ **se ~ la tête/les jambes** to shave one's head/one's legs 2 (* = *s'ennuyer*) to be bored stiff* *ou* to tears*

raseur, -euse* /RɑzœR, øz/ ADJ boring ♦ **qu'il est ~ !** he's a (real) bore! *ou* drag!* NM,F bore

rasibus* /Rɑzibys/ ADV *[couper]* very close *ou* fine ♦ **passer ~** *[projectile]* to whizz past very close

ras-le-bol* /Rɑl(ə)bɔl/ EXCL enough is enough! NM INV (= *mécontentement*) discontent ♦ **provoquer le ~ général** to cause widespread discontent ♦ **le ~ étudiant** student unrest; → **table**

rasoir /RɑzwaR/ NM razor ♦ **~ électrique** (electric) shaver, electric razor ♦ **~ mécanique** *ou* **de sûreté** safety razor ♦ **~ à main** *ou* **de coiffeur** cut-throat *ou* straight razor ♦ **~ jetable** disposable *ou* throwaway razor ♦ **se donner un coup de ~** to have a quick shave; → **feu**[1]**, fil** etc ADJ (* = *ennuyeux*) *[film, livre]* dead boring* ♦ **qu'il est ~ !** what a bore *ou* drag* he is!

Raspoutine /Rasputin/ NM Rasputin

rassasier /Rasazje/ ▸ conjug 7 ◂ *(frm)* VT 1 (= *assouvir*) *[+ faim, curiosité, désirs]* to satisfy

2 (= *nourrir*) **~ qn** *[aliment]* to satisfy sb *ou* sb's appetite ♦ **~ qn de qch** (= *lui en donner suffisamment*) to satisfy sb with sth *ou* sb's appetite *ou* hunger with sth; (= *lui en donner trop*) to give sb too much of sth ♦ **être rassasié** (= *n'avoir plus faim*) to be satisfied, to have eaten one's fill; (= *en être dégoûté*) to be satiated *ou* sated, to have had more than enough ♦ **on ne peut pas le ~ de chocolats** you can't give him too many chocolates ♦ **~ ses yeux de qch** to feast one's eyes on sth ♦ **je suis rassasié de toutes ces histoires !** I've had quite enough of all this!

VPR **se rassasier** (= *se nourrir*) to satisfy one's hunger, to eat one's fill ♦ **se ~ d'un spectacle** to feast one's eyes on a sight ♦ **je ne me rassasierai jamais de ...** I'll never tire *ou* have enough of ...

rassemblement /Rasɑ̃bləmɑ̃/ NM 1 (= *action de regrouper*) *[de troupeau]* rounding up; *[d'objets, documents]* gathering, collecting 2 *[de pièces, mécanisme]* reassembly 3 *(Équitation) [de cheval]* collecting 4 (= *réunion, attroupement*) *(gén)* assembly, gathering; *[de manifestants]* rally ♦ **~ !** *(Mil)* fall in! ♦ **~ à 9 heures sur le quai** we'll meet at 9 o'clock on the platform ♦ **~ pour la paix** *(Pol)* peace rally; → **point**[1] 5 **le Rassemblement pour la République** *centre-right political party*

rassembler /Rasɑ̃ble/ ▸ conjug 1 ◂ VT 1 (= *regrouper*) *[+ personnes]* to gather, to assemble; *[+ troupes]* to muster; *[+ troupeau]* to round up; *[+ objets épars]* to gather together, to collect ♦ **il rassembla les élèves dans la cour** he gathered *ou* assembled the pupils in the playground ♦ **le festival rassemble les meilleurs musiciens** the festival brings together the best musicians

2 (= *rallier*) to rally; *[+ sympathisants]* to round up, to rally ♦ **cette cause a rassemblé des gens de tous horizons** people from all walks of life have rallied to this cause

3 *[+ documents, manuscrits, notes]* to gather together, to collect, to assemble

4 *[+ idées, souvenirs]* to collect; *[+ courage, forces]* to summon up, to muster ♦ **~ ses esprits** to collect one's thoughts

5 (= *remonter*) *[+ pièces, mécanisme]* to put back together, to reassemble

6 *(Équitation) [+ cheval]* to collect

VPR **se rassembler** 1 *[se regrouper]* to gather; *[soldats, participants]* to assemble, to gather ♦ **nous nous rassemblons deux fois par semaine** we get together twice a week ♦ **en cas d'urgence, rassemblez-vous sur le pont** *(Naut)* in an emergency, assemble on deck ♦ **rassemblés autour du feu** gathered round the fire ♦ **toute la famille était rassemblée** the whole family was gathered together

2 (= *s'unir*) **nous devons nous ~ autour du président/pour lutter contre ...** we must unite behind the president/to fight against ...

3 *(Sport)* to bend *(to gather one's strength)*

rassembleur, -euse /Rasɑ̃blœR, øz/ ADJ *[discours]* rallying; *[thème, projet]* unifying NM,F unifier ♦ **il fut le ~ d'une nation divisée** he was the unifier of *ou* he unified a divided nation

rasseoir /raswar/ ▸ conjug 26 ◂ VT [+ bébé] to sit back up (straight); [+ objet] to put back up straight VPR **se rasseoir** to sit down again ◆ **faire (se)** ~ **qn** to make sb sit down again ◆ **rassieds-toi !** sit down!

rasséréné, e /raseʀene/ (ptp de **rasséréner**) ADJ [ciel, personne, visage] serene

rasséréner /raseʀene/ ▸ conjug 6 ◂ VT to make serene again VPR **se rasséréner** [personne, visage, ciel] to become serene again, to recover one's (ou its) serenity

rassir VI, **se rassir** VPR /rasiʀ/ ▸ conjug 2 ◂ to go stale

rassis, e /rasi, iz/ (ptp de **rassir, rasseoir**) ADJ 1 [pain] stale; [viande] hung 2 [personne] (= pondéré) composed, calm; (péj) stale

rassortiment /rasɔʀtimɑ̃/ NM ⇒ **réassortiment**

rassortir /rasɔʀtiʀ/ ▸ conjug 2 ◂ VT ⇒ **réassortir**

rassurant, e /rasyʀɑ̃, ɑ̃t/ ADJ [nouvelle, voix] reassuring, comforting; [discours, présence, visage] reassuring; [indice] encouraging ◆ **"ne vous inquiétez pas", dit-il d'un ton** ~ "don't worry", he said reassuringly ◆ **il a tenu des propos peu ~s** he said some rather worrying things ◆ **c'est ~ !** (iro) that's very reassuring! (iro), that's a great comfort!* (iro) ◆ **le gouvernement se veut** ~ the government is seeking to reassure the public ◆ **son discours se voulait** ~ what he said was intended to reassure people

rassurer /rasyʀe/ ▸ conjug 1 ◂ VT ◆ ~ **qn** to put sb's mind at ease ou rest, to reassure sb ◆ **le médecin m'a rassuré sur son état de santé** the doctor reassured me about the state of his health ◆ **me voilà rassuré maintenant** I've got nothing to worry about now, that's put my mind at rest VPR **se rassurer** ◆ **à cette nouvelle, il se rassura** the news put his mind at ease ou rest, he was relieved ou reassured when he heard the news ◆ **il essayait de se** ~ **en se disant que c'était impossible** he tried to reassure himself by saying it was impossible ◆ **rassure-toi** don't worry

rasta[1] /rasta/ ADJ, NMF (abrév de **rastafari**) Rasta

rasta[2] * /rasta/ ADJ, NM abrév de **rastaquouère**

rastafari /rastafaʀi/ ADJ, NM Rastafarian

rastaquouère /rastakwɛʀ/ NM (péj) flashy foreigner (péj)

rat /ʀa/ NM (= animal) rat; (péj = avare) miser ◆ **c'est un vrai ~, ce type** that guy's really stingy* ou a real skinflint* ◆ **les ~s quittent le navire** (fig) the rats are leaving the sinking ship ◆ **s'ennuyer** ou **s'emmerder**‡ **comme un ~ mort** to be bored stiff* ou to death* ◆ **mon (petit)** ~ (terme d'affection) (my) pet, darling ◆ **petit ~ de l'Opéra** pupil of the Opéra de Paris ballet class (working as an extra); → **chat, fait**[2]

COMP **rat d'Amérique** muskrat, musquash (Brit)
rat de bibliothèque bookworm (who spends all his time in libraries)
rat de cave spiral candlestick used in a cellar or on a staircase
rat des champs fieldmouse
rat d'eau water vole
rat d'égout sewer rat
rat d'hôtel hotel thief
rat musqué muskrat, musquash (Brit)
rat palmiste ground squirrel

rata † /ʀata/ NM (arg Mil) (= nourriture) grub*; (= ragoût) stew

ratafia /ʀatafja/ NM (= liqueur) ratafia

ratage * /ʀataʒ/ NM 1 (= échec) failure ◆ **des ~s successifs** successive failures ◆ **son film est un ~ complet** his film is a complete failure ou flop 2 (= action) [de travail, affaire] messing up, spoiling; [de mayonnaise, sauce] spoiling; [d'examen] failing, flunking*

rataplan /ʀataplɑ̃/ EXCL, NM rat-a-tat-tat

ratatiné, e /ʀatatine/ (ptp de **ratatiner**) ADJ 1 [pomme] dried-up, shrivelled; [visage, personne] wrinkled, wizened 2 ‡ [voiture] smashed-up*, banjaxed* (US); [personne] exhausted, knackered‡ (Brit)

ratatiner /ʀatatine/ ▸ conjug 1 ◂ VT 1 [+ pomme] to dry up, to shrivel ◆ **ratatiné par l'âge** [visage, personne] wrinkled ou wizened with age 2 (‡ = détruire) [+ maison] to wreck; [+ machine, voiture] to smash to bits ou pieces ◆ **se faire** ~ (battre) to get thrashed ou a thrashing; (tuer) to get done in‡ ou bumped off‡ ◆ **sa voiture a été complètement ratatinée** his car was a complete write-off (Brit), his car was totaled* (US) VPR **se ratatiner** [pomme] to shrivel ou dry up; [visage] to become wrinkled ou wizened; [personne] (par l'âge) to become wrinkled ou wizened; (pour tenir moins de place) to curl up

ratatouille /ʀatatuj/ NF (Culin) ◆ ~ **(niçoise)** ratatouille; (péj) (= ragoût) bad stew; (= cuisine) lousy* food

rate[1] /ʀat/ NF (= organe) spleen; → **dilater, fouler**

rate[2] /ʀat/ NF (= animal) female rat

raté, e /ʀate/ ADJ [tentative, mariage, artiste] failed; [vie] wasted; [départ] bad, poor ◆ **un film** ~ a flop ◆ **ma mayonnaise/la dernière scène est complètement ~e** my mayonnaise/the last scene is a complete disaster ◆ **encore une occasion ~e !** another missed opportunity! NM,F (* = personne) failure NM 1 (en voiture : gén pl) misfiring (NonC) ◆ **avoir des ~s** to misfire ◆ **il y a eu des ~s dans les négociations** there were some hiccups in the negotiations 2 [d'arme à feu] misfire

râteau (pl **râteaux**) /ʀɑto/ NM (Agr, Roulette) rake; [de métier à tisser] comb ◆ **se prendre un ~** * (avec une fille, un garçon) to get blown out*

râtelier /ʀɑtəlje/ NM [de bétail, armes, outils] rack; (* = dentier) (set of) false teeth ◆ ~ **à pipes** pipe rack; → **manger**

rater /ʀate/ ▸ conjug 1 ◂ VI 1 [projet, affaire] to fail, to fall through ◆ **ce contretemps/cette erreur risque de tout faire** ~ this hitch/this mistake could well ruin everything ◆ **je t'avais dit qu'elle y allait : ça n'a pas raté*** I told you she'd go and I was dead right* (Brit) ou and (so) she did ◆ **ça ne rate jamais !** it never fails!
2 [arme] to fail to go off, to misfire
VT 1 (= manquer) [+ balle, cible, occasion, train, rendez-vous, spectacle, personne] to miss ◆ **c'est une occasion à ne pas** ~ it's an opportunity not to be missed ◆ **raté !** missed! ◆ **ils se sont ratés de peu** they just missed each other ◆ **si tu croyais m'impressionner, c'est raté** if you were trying to impress me, it hasn't worked! ◆ **il n'en rate pas une !** (iro) he's always putting his foot in it!* ◆ **je ne te raterai pas !** I'll get you!*, I'll show you! ◆ **il voulait faire le malin mais je ne l'ai pas raté** he tried to be smart but I soon sorted him out I didn't let him get away with it ◆ **il ne t'a pas raté !** he really got you there!*
2 (= ne pas réussir) [+ travail, affaire] to mess up, to spoil; [+ mayonnaise, sauce, plat] to make a mess of; [+ examen] to fail, to flunk* ◆ **ces photos sont complètement ratées** these photos are a complete disaster ◆ **un écrivain raté** a failed writer ◆ ~ **son entrée** to miss one's entrance ◆ **j'ai raté mon effet** I didn't achieve the effect I was hoping for ◆ ~ **sa vie** to make a mess of one's life ◆ **il a raté son coup** he didn't pull it off ◆ **il a raté son suicide, il s'est raté** he bungled his suicide attempt ◆ **le coiffeur m'a raté** the hairdresser made a mess of my hair

ratiboiser‡ /ʀatibwaze/ ▸ conjug 1 ◂ VT 1 (= rafler) ~ **qch à qn** (au jeu) to clean sb out of sth*; (en le volant) to pinch* ou nick‡ (Brit) sth from sb ◆ **on lui a ratiboisé son portefeuille, il s'est fait ~ son portefeuille** he got his wallet pinched* ou nicked‡ (Brit) 2 (= dépouiller) ~ **qn** to skin sb (alive)*, to clean sb out* 3 (= abattre) [+ maison] to wreck ◆ **il a été ratiboisé en moins de deux** [personne] in next to no time he was dead 4 (= couper les cheveux à) [+ personne] to scalp* (fig) ◆ **se faire** ~ to be scalped*

raticide /ʀatisid/ NM rat poison

ratier /ʀatje/ NM ◆ **(chien)** ~ ratter

ratière /ʀatjɛʀ/ NF rattrap

ratification /ʀatifikasjɔ̃/ NF (Admin, Jur) ratification ◆ ~ **de vente** sales confirmation

ratifier /ʀatifje/ ▸ conjug 7 ◂ VT (Admin, Jur) to ratify; (littér = confirmer) to confirm, to ratify

ratine /ʀatin/ NF ratine

rating /ʀatiŋ, ʀetiŋ/ NM (Écon, Naut) rating

ratio /ʀasjo/ NM ratio

ratiocination /ʀasjɔsinasjɔ̃/ NF (littér péj) (= action) hair-splitting, quibbling; (= raisonnement) hair-splitting argument, quibbling (NonC)

ratiociner /ʀasjɔsine/ ▸ conjug 1 ◂ VI (littér péj) to split hairs, to quibble (sur over)

ratiocineur, -euse /ʀasjɔsinœʀ, øz/ NM,F (littér péj) hair-splitter, quibbler

ration /ʀasjɔ̃/ NF (= portion limitée) ration; [de soldat] rations; [d'animal] (feed) intake; [d'organisme] (food) intake ◆ ~ **de viande/fourrage** meat/fodder ration ◆ ~ **alimentaire** food intake ◆ ~ **d'entretien** minimum daily requirement ◆ ~ **de survie** survival rations ◆ **il a eu sa ~ d'épreuves/de soucis** he had his share of trials/of worries

rationalisation /ʀasjɔnalizasjɔ̃/ NF rationalization

rationaliser /ʀasjɔnalize/ ▸ conjug 1 ◂ VT to rationalize

rationalisme /ʀasjɔnalism/ NM rationalism

rationaliste /ʀasjɔnalist/ ADJ, NMF rationalist

rationalité /ʀasjɔnalite/ NF rationality

rationnel, -elle /ʀasjɔnɛl/ ADJ rational

rationnellement /ʀasjɔnɛlmɑ̃/ ADV rationally

rationnement /ʀasjɔnmɑ̃/ NM rationing; → **carte**

rationner /ʀasjɔne/ ▸ conjug 1 ◂ VT [+ pain, eau] to ration; [+ personne] (lit) to put on rations; (fig hum = ne pas donner assez à) to give short rations to VPR **se rationner** to ration o.s.

ratissage /ʀatisaʒ/ NM (Agr) raking; (Mil, Police) combing

ratisser /ʀatise/ ▸ conjug 1 ◂ VT [+ gravier] to rake; [+ feuilles] to rake up; (Mil, Police) to comb; (Rugby) [+ ballon] to heel; (* = dépouiller au jeu) to clean out* ◆ ~ **large** to cast the net wide ◆ **il s'est fait ~ (au jeu)*** he was cleaned out* ou he lost everything at the gambling table

raton /ʀatɔ̃/ NM 1 (= rat) young rat ◆ ~ **laveur** racoon 2 (*‡, raciste) racist term applied to North Africans in France 3 (= terme d'affection) **mon ~ !** (my) pet!

raton(n)ade /ʀatɔnad/ NF racist attack (mainly on North African Arabs)

RATP /ɛʀatepe/ NF (abrév de **Régie autonome des transports parisiens**) → **régie**

rattachement /ʀataʃmɑ̃/ NM (Admin, Pol) uniting (à with) joining (à to); ◆ **le ~ de la Savoie à la France** the incorporation of Savoy into France ◆ **demander son ~ à** to ask to be united with ou joined to ◆ **quel est votre service de ~ ?** which service are you attached to?

rattacher /ʀataʃe/ ▸ conjug 1 ◂ VT 1 (= attacher de nouveau) [+ animal, prisonnier, colis] to tie up again; [+ ceinture, lacets, jupe] to do up ou fasten again 2 (= annexer, incorporer) [+ territoire] to incorporate (*à* into); *[+ commune, service]* to join (*à* to) to unite (*à* with); *[+ employé, fonctionnaire]* to attach (*à* to) 3 *(= comparer, rapprocher) [+ problème, question]* to link, to connect, to tie up (*à* with); *[+ fait]* to relate (*à* to); ◆ **cela peut se ~ au premier problème** that can be related to *ou* tied up with the first problem ◆ **on peut ~ cette langue au groupe slave** this language can be related to *ou* linked with the Slavonic group 4 *(= relier) [+ personne]* to bind, to tie (*à* to); ◆ **rien ne le rattache plus à sa famille** he has no more ties with his family, nothing binds *ou* ties him to his family any more

rattrapable /RatRapabl/ **ADJ** *[erreur, gaffe]* which can be put right; *[heure, journée]* which can be made up

rattrapage /RatRapaʒ/ **NM** *[de maille]* picking up; *[d'erreur]* making good; *[de candidat d'examen]* passing ◆ **le ~ d'une bêtise/d'un oubli** making up for something silly/for an omission ◆ **le ~ du retard** *[d'élève]* catching up, making up for lost time; *[de conducteur]* making up for lost time ◆ **~ scolaire** remedial teaching *ou* classes ◆ **cours de ~** remedial class *ou* course ◆ **suivre des cours de ~** to go to remedial classes ◆ **épreuve de ~** *(Scol) additional exam for borderline cases* ◆ **session de ~** *(Scol)* retakes, resits *(Brit)* ◆ **pour permettre le ~ économique de certains pays européens** to allow certain European economies to catch up ◆ **le ~ des salaires sur les prix** an increase in salaries to keep up with *ou* keep pace with prices

rattraper /RatRape/ ▸ conjug 1 ◂ **VT** 1 *(= reprendre) [+ animal échappé, prisonnier]* to recapture

2 *(= retenir) [+ objet, personne qui tombe]* to catch (hold of)

3 *(= réparer) [+ maille]* to pick up; *[+ mayonnaise]* to salvage; *[+ erreur]* to make good, to make up for; *[+ bêtise, parole malheureuse, oubli]* to make up for ◆ **je vais essayer de ~ le coup*** I'll try and sort this out

4 *(= regagner) [+ argent perdu]* to recover, to get back, to recoup; *[+ sommeil]* to catch up on; *[+ temps perdu]* to make up for ◆ **le conducteur a rattrapé son retard** the driver made up for lost time ◆ **cet élève ne pourra jamais ~ son retard** this pupil will never be able to catch up ◆ **ce qu'il perd d'un côté, il le rattrape de l'autre** what he loses in one way he gains in another, what he loses on the swings he gains on the roundabouts *(Brit)*

5 *(= rejoindre)* **~ qn** *(lit, fig)* to catch sb up, to catch up with sb ◆ **le coût de la vie a rattrapé l'augmentation de salaire** the cost of living has caught up with the increase in salaries

6 *(Scol)* **~ qn** *(= repêcher)* to give sb a pass, to let sb get through

VPR se rattraper 1 *(= reprendre son équilibre)* to stop o.s. falling, to catch o.s. (just) in time ◆ **se ~ à la rampe/à qn** to catch hold of the banister/of sb to stop o.s. falling ◆ **j'ai failli gaffer, mais je me suis rattrapé in extremis** I nearly put my foot in it but stopped myself just in time; → **branche**

2 *(= compenser)* to make up for it ◆ **j'ai passé trois nuits sans dormir, mais hier je me suis rattrapé** I had three sleepless nights, but I made up for it yesterday ◆ **les plats ne sont pas chers mais ils se rattrapent sur les vins** the food isn't expensive but they make up for it on the wine ◆ **les fabricants comptent sur les marchés extérieurs pour se ~** manufacturers are looking to foreign markets to make up their losses ◆ **le joueur avait perdu les deux premiers sets, mais il s'est rattrapé au troisième** the player had lost the first two sets but he pulled back in the third

rature /RatyR/ **NF** deletion, erasure, crossing out ◆ **faire une ~** to make a deletion *ou* an erasure ◆ **sans ~s ni surcharges** *(Admin)* without deletions or alterations

raturer /RatyRe/ ▸ conjug 1 ◂ **VT** *(= corriger) [+ mot, phrase, texte]* to make an alteration *ou* alterations to; *(= barrer) [+ lettre, mot]* to cross out, to erase, to delete

RAU † /ɛRay/ **NF** (abrév de **République arabe unie**) UAR †

rauque /Rok/ **ADJ** *[voix] (gén)* hoarse; *(chanteuse de blues)* husky, throaty; *[cri]* raucous

ravage /Ravaʒ/ **NM** 1 *(littér = action) [de pays, ville]* pillaging 2 *(gén pl = dégâts)* ravages ◆ **les ~s de la guerre/du sida** the devastation caused by war/AIDS, the ravages of war/AIDS ◆ **les ~s du chômage** the devastating effects *ou* the ravages of unemployment ◆ **les ~s du temps** the ravages of time ◆ **les ~s de la maladie** the devastating effects of the disease

◆ **faire des ravages** *[tempête, grêle]* to wreak havoc; *[séducteur]* to be a real heartbreaker; *[doctrine]* to gain a lot of ground ◆ **l'épidémie a fait de terribles ~s parmi les jeunes** the epidemic has wrought terrible devastation among young people

ravagé, e /Ravaʒe/ (ptp de **ravager**) **ADJ** 1 *(= tourmenté) [visage]* harrowed, haggard ◆ **avoir les traits ~s** to have harrowed *ou* ravaged *ou* haggard features ◆ **visage ~ par la maladie** face ravaged by illness 2 *(* = fou)* **il est complètement ~** he's completely nuts* *ou* bonkers* *(Brit)*, he's off his head*

ravager /Ravaʒe/ ▸ conjug 3 ◂ **VT** *[+ pays]* to lay waste, to ravage, to devastate; *[+ maison, ville]* to ravage, to devastate; *[+ visage] [maladie]* to ravage; *[chagrin, soucis]* to harrow; *[+ personne, vie]* to wreak havoc upon

ravageur, -euse /RavaʒœR, øz/ **ADJ** *[passion, sourire]* devastating; *[humour]* scathing ◆ **insectes ~s** pests ◆ **les effets ~s de la drogue** the devastating effects of drugs **NM** *(= animal nuisible)* pest

ravalement /Ravalmɑ̃/ **NM** 1 *(Constr) (= nettoyage)* cleaning; *(= remise en état) [de façade, mur]* restoration; *[d'immeuble]* renovation, facelift* ◆ **faire le ~ de** to clean, to restore, to give a facelift to* ◆ **faire un ~*** *(= retoucher son maquillage)* to fix one's warpaint* 2 *(littér = avilissement) [de dignité, personne, mérite]* lowering

ravaler /Ravale/ ▸ conjug 1 ◂ **VT** 1 *(Constr) (= nettoyer)* to clean; *(= remettre en état) [+ façade, mur]* to do up, to restore; *[+ immeuble]* to renovate, to give a facelift to* ◆ **se faire ~ la façade*** to have a facelift 2 *(= avaler) [+ salive, dégoût]* to swallow; *[+ sanglots]* to swallow, to choke back; *[+ colère]* to stifle; *[+ larmes]* to hold *ou* choke back; *[+ sourire]* to suppress ◆ **faire ~ ses paroles à qn** to make sb take back *ou* swallow their words 3 *(littér) [+ dignité, personne, mérite]* to lower ◆ **ce genre d'acte ravale l'homme au rang de la bête** this kind of behaviour brings man down *ou* reduces man to the level of animals **VPR se ravaler** 1 *(= s'abaisser)* to lower o.s. ◆ **se ~ au rang de ...** to reduce o.s. to the level of ... 2 * **se ~ la façade** to slap on* some make-up

ravaleur /RavalœR/ **NM** *(= maçon)* stone restorer

ravaudage /Ravodaʒ/ **NM** *[de vêtement]* mending, repairing; *[de chaussette]* darning; *[d'objet]* makeshift repair ◆ **faire du ~** to mend, to darn

ravauder /Ravode/ ▸ conjug 1 ◂ **VT** *(littér = repriser) [+ vêtement]* to repair, to mend; *[+ chaussette]* to darn

rave /Rav/ **NF** *(= navet)* turnip; *(= radis)* radish; → **céleri**

ravenelle /Ravnɛl/ **NF** *(= giroflée)* wallflower; *(= radis)* wild radish

Ravenne /Ravɛn/ **N** Ravenna

ravi, e /Ravi/ (ptp de **ravir**) **ADJ** *(= enchanté)* delighted ◆ **je n'étais pas franchement ~ de sa décision** I wasn't exactly overjoyed about his decision ◆ **~ de vous connaître** delighted *ou* pleased to meet you

ravier /Ravje/ **NM** hors d'oeuvres dish

ravigotant, e * /Ravigɔtɑ̃, ɑ̃t/ **ADJ** *[air]* bracing ◆ **ce vin est ~** this wine bucks you up* *ou* puts new life into you

ravigote /Ravigɔt/ **NF** *(= vinaigrette)* (oil and vinegar) dressing *(with hard-boiled eggs, shallot and herbs)*

ravigoter * /Ravigɔte/ ▸ conjug 1 ◂ **VT** *[alcool]* to buck up*, to pick up; *[repas, douche, nouvelle, chaleur]* to buck up*, to put new life into ◆ **(tout) ravigoté par une bonne nuit** feeling refreshed after a good night's sleep

ravin /Ravɛ̃/ **NM** *(gén)* gully; *(encaissé)* ravine

ravine /Ravin/ **NF** (small) ravine, gully

ravinement /Ravinmɑ̃/ **NM** *(= action)* gullying *(Géog)* ◆ **~s** *(= rigoles, ravins)* gullies ◆ **le ~ de ces pentes** *(= aspect)* the (numerous) gullies furrowing these slopes ◆ **le ~ affecte particulièrement ces sols** gully erosion *ou* gullying affects these kinds of soil in particular

raviner /Ravine/ ▸ conjug 1 ◂ **VT** *[+ visage, chemin]* to furrow; *[+ versant]* to gully *(Géog)* ◆ **visage raviné par les larmes** tear-streaked face, face streaked with tears ◆ **les bords ravinés de la rivière** the gullied *(Géog) ou* furrowed banks of the river

ravioli /Ravjɔli/ **NM** ◆ **~s** ravioli *(NonC)*

ravir /RaviR/ ▸ conjug 2 ◂ **VT** *(littér)* 1 *(= charmer)* to delight ◆ **cela lui va à ~** that suits her beautifully, she looks delightful in it ◆ **il danse à ~** he's a beautiful dancer ◆ **elle est jolie à ~** she's as pretty as a picture 2 *(= enlever)* **~ à qn** *[+ trésor, être aimé, honneur]* to rob sb of, to take (away) from sb ◆ **elle lui a ravi son titre de championne d'Europe** she took the European championship title off her; → **vedette** 3 *(† = kidnapper)* to ravish †, to abduct

raviser (se) /Ravize/ ▸ conjug 1 ◂ **VPR** to change one's mind, to decide otherwise ◆ **après avoir dit oui, il s'est ravisé** after saying yes he changed his mind *ou* decided otherwise *ou* decided against it ◆ **il s'est ravisé** he decided against it, he thought better of it

ravissant, e /Ravisɑ̃, ɑ̃t/ **ADJ** *[beauté]* ravishing; *[femme, robe]* ravishing, beautiful; *[maison, tableau]* delightful, beautiful

ravissement /Ravismɑ̃/ **NM** 1 *(gén, Rel)* rapture ◆ **plonger qn dans le ~** to send sb into raptures ◆ **plongé dans le ~** in raptures ◆ **regarder qn avec ~** to look at sb rapturously 2 *(† ou littér = enlèvement)* ravishing †, abduction

ravisseur, -euse /RavisœR, øz/ **NM,F** kidnapper, abductor

ravitaillement /Ravitajmɑ̃/ **NM** 1 *(NonC, en vivres, munitions) [d'armée, ville, navire]* resupplying; *[de coureurs, skieurs]* getting fresh supplies to; *(en carburant) [de véhicule, avion, embarcation]* refuelling ◆ **~ en vol** in-flight refuelling ◆ **le ~ des troupes (en vivres/munitions)** supplying the troops (with food/ammunition), the provision *ou* providing of the troops with fresh supplies (of food/ammunition) ◆ **aller au ~*** to go for fresh supplies ◆ **les voies de ~ sont bloquées** supply routes are blocked ◆ **convoi de ~** supply convoy 2 *(= provisions)* supplies

ravitailler /Ravitaje/ ▸ conjug 1 ◂ **VT** *(en vivres, munitions) [+ armée, ville, navire]* to provide with fresh supplies, to resupply; *[+ coureurs, skieurs]* to give fresh supplies to; *(en carburant) [+ véhicule, avion, embarcation]* to refuel ◆ **~ une ville en combustible** to provide a town with fresh supplies of fuel ◆ **~ un avion en vol** to refuel an aircraft in flight **VPR se ravitailler** *[ville, armée, coureurs, skieurs]* to get fresh supplies; *[véhicule, avion]* to refuel; *(= faire des courses)* to stock up

ravitailleur /ʀavitajœʀ/ NM (Mil) (= navire) supply ship; (= avion) supply plane; (= véhicule) supply vehicle ◆ ~ **en vol** aerial tanker ADJ [navire, avion, véhicule] supply (épith)

raviver /ʀavive/ ▸ conjug 1 ◂ VT [+ feu, sentiment, douleur] to revive, to rekindle; [+ couleur] to brighten up; [+ souvenir] to revive, to bring back to life; (Tech) [+ métal] to clean; (Méd) [+ plaie] to reopen ◆ **sa douleur/sa jalousie s'est ravivée** his grief/his jealousy was revived ou rekindled

ravoir /ʀavwaʀ/ ▸ conjug 34 ◂ VT 1 (= recouvrer) to have ou get back 2 (* = nettoyer : gén nég) [+ tissu, métal] to get clean ◆ **cette casserole est difficile à** ~ this saucepan is hard to clean, it's hard to get this saucepan clean

rayage /ʀɛjaʒ/ NM 1 [de nom] crossing ou scoring out 2 [de canon] rifling

rayé, e /ʀeje/ (ptp de **rayer**) ADJ 1 [tissu, pelage] striped; [papier à lettres] ruled, lined 2 [surface] scratched; [disque] scratched, scratchy 3 (Tech) [canon] rifled

rayer /ʀeje/ ▸ conjug 8 ◂ VT 1 (= marquer de raies) [+ papier à lettres] to rule, to line ◆ **des cicatrices lui rayaient le visage** scars lined his face 2 (= érafler) to scratch 3 (= biffer) to cross ou score out 4 (= exclure) ~ **qn de** to cross sb ou sb's name off ◆ **il a été rayé de la liste** he ou his name has been crossed ou struck off the list ◆ **"rayer la mention inutile"** "cross out where not applicable", "delete where inapplicable" ◆ ~ **qch de sa mémoire** to blot out ou erase sth from one's memory ◆ ~ **un pays/une ville de la carte** to wipe a country/a town off the map ◆ **je l'ai rayé de mes tablettes** I want nothing to do with him ever again 5 (Tech) [+ canon] to rifle

ray-grass /ʀɛgʀɑs/ NM INV rye-grass, English meadow grass

rayon /ʀɛjɔ̃/ NM 1 (gén = trait, faisceau, Opt, Phys) ray; [d'astre] ray; [de lumière, jour] ray, beam; [de phare] beam

2 (= radiations) ~**s** rays ◆ ~**s infrarouges/ultraviolets** infrared/ultraviolet rays ◆ ~**s alpha/bêta** alpha/beta rays ◆ ~**s X** X-rays ◆ **traitement par les** ~**s** radiation treatment ◆ **on lui fait des** ~**s** he's having radiation treatment

3 (fig = lueur) ray ◆ ~ **d'espoir** ray ou gleam of hope

4 (Math) radius

5 [de roue] spoke

6 (= planche) shelf; [de bibliothèque] (book)shelf ◆ **le livre n'est pas en** ~ the book is not on display ou on the shelves

7 (dans un magasin) department; (petit) counter ◆ **le** ~ **(de l')alimentation/(de la) parfumerie** (= comptoir) the food/perfume counter; (= section) the food/perfume department ◆ **le** ~ **frais** the fresh food department ◆ **le** ~ **enfants** the children's department ◆ **c'est/ce n'est pas son** ~ (spécialité) that's/that isn't his line; (responsabilité) that's/that's not his concern ou responsibility ou department* ◆ **il en connaît un** ~* he knows masses about it*, he's really clued up about it* (Brit)

8 [de ruche] (honey)comb

9 (= périmètre) radius ◆ **dans un** ~ **de 10 km** within a radius of 10 km ou a 10-km radius

10 (Agr = sillon) drill

COMP **rayon d'action** (lit) range; (fig) field of action, scope, range ◆ **engin à grand** ~ **d'action** long-range missile
rayon de braquage [de voiture] turning circle, (steering) lock (Brit)
rayon cathodique cathode ray
rayons cosmiques cosmic rays
rayon de courbure radius of curvature
rayons gamma gamma rays ou radiation
rayon ionisant ionizing radiation
rayon laser laser beam
rayon de lune moonbeam
le rayon de la mort the death ray
rayon de soleil (lit) ray of sunlight ou sunshine, sunbeam; (fig) ray of sunshine ◆ **aux premiers** ~**s de soleil** at sunrise
rayon vert green flash
rayon visuel (Opt) line of vision ou sight

rayonnage /ʀɛjɔnaʒ/ NM 1 (= planches) set of shelves, shelving (NonC) ◆ ~**s** (sets of) shelves, shelving 2 (Agr) drilling

rayonnant, e /ʀɛjɔnɑ̃, ɑt/ ADJ 1 (= radieux) [beauté, air, personne] radiant; [sourire] radiant, beaming (épith); [visage] wreathed in smiles, beaming ◆ **visage** ~ **de joie/santé** face radiant with joy/glowing ou radiant with health 2 (= en étoile) [motif, fleur] radiating ◆ **le style (gothique)** ~ High Gothic ◆ **chapelles** ~**es** radiating chapels 3 (Phys) [énergie, chaleur] radiant; (Méd) [douleur] spreading

rayonne /ʀɛjɔn/ NF rayon ◆ **en** ~ rayon (épith)

rayonnement /ʀɛjɔnmɑ̃/ NM 1 (= influence) influence; (= magnétisme) charisma ◆ **le** ~ **international de la France** the influence exerted internationally by France ◆ **le** ~ **de la culture française, le** ~ **culturel de la France** France's cultural influence ◆ **une université au** ~ **international** a university with an international reputation 2 (= éclat) [de jeunesse, beauté] radiance ◆ **dans tout le** ~ **de sa jeunesse** in the full radiance of his youth ◆ **le** ~ **de son bonheur** his radiant happiness 3 (= lumière) [d'astre, soleil] radiance 4 (= radiations) [de chaleur, lumière, astre] radiation ◆ ~ **ionisant** ionizing radiation ◆ **chauffage par** ~ radiant heating ◆ ~ **fossile** background radiation

rayonner /ʀɛjɔne/ ▸ conjug 1 ◂ VI 1 (= étinceler) [influence, culture, personnalité] to shine forth ◆ ~ **sur/dans** (= se répandre) [influence, prestige] to extend over/in, to make itself felt over/in; [culture] to extend over/in, to be influential over/in, to exert its influence over/in; [personnalité] to be influential over/in

2 (= être éclatant) [joie, bonheur] to shine ou beam forth; [beauté] to shine forth, to be radiant; [visage, personne] (de joie, de beauté) to be radiant (de with); ◆ **le bonheur faisait** ~ **son visage** his face glowed with happiness ◆ **l'amour rayonne dans ses yeux** love shines ou sparkles in his eyes ◆ ~ **de bonheur** to be radiant ou glowing ou beaming with happiness ◆ ~ **de beauté** to be radiantly ou dazzlingly beautiful

3 (littér = briller) [lumière, astre] to shine (forth), to be radiant

4 (Phys = émettre un rayonnement) [chaleur, énergie, lumière] to radiate

5 (= faire un circuit) ~ **autour d'une ville** [touristes] to use a town as a base for touring (around a region); [cars] to service the area around a town ◆ ~ **dans une région** [touristes] to tour around a region (from a base); [cars] to service a region

6 (= aller en rayons) [avenues, lignes] to radiate (autour de from, out from)

VT (= garnir de rayonnages) to shelve

rayure /ʀejyʀ/ NF (= dessin) stripe; (= éraflure) scratch; [de fusil] groove ◆ **papier/tissu à** ~**s** striped paper/material ◆ **à** ~**s noires** with black stripes, black-striped ◆ **costume à** ~**s fines** pinstriped suit

raz-de-marée, raz de marée /ʀɑdmaʀe/ NM INV (lit, fig) tidal wave ◆ ~ **électoral** (victoire) landslide (election) victory; (changement) big swing (to a party in an election)

razzia /ʀa(d)zja/ NF raid, foray, razzia ◆ **faire une** ~ **dans une maison/le frigo*** (fig) to raid a house/the fridge

razzier /ʀa(d)zje/ ▸ conjug 7 ◂ VT (lit, fig = piller) to raid, to plunder

RCS /ɛʀseɛs/ (abrév de **registre du commerce et des sociétés**) CRO

RDA † /ɛʀdea/ NF (abrév de **République démocratique allemande**) GDR †

rdc abrév de **rez-de-chaussée**

RDS /ɛʀdeɛs/ NM (abrév de **remboursement de la dette sociale**) → **remboursement**

ré /ʀe/ NM (Mus) D; (en chantant la gamme) re, ray ◆ **en** ~ **mineur** in D minor

réabonnement /ʀeabɔnmɑ̃/ NM renewal of subscription ◆ **le** ~ **doit se faire dans les huit jours** renewal of subscription must be made within a week, subscriptions must be renewed within a week

réabonner /ʀeabɔne/ ▸ conjug 1 ◂ VT ◆ ~ **qn** to renew sb's subscription (à to) VPR **se réabonner** to renew one's subscription, to take out a new subscription (à to)

réabsorber /ʀeapsɔʀbe/ ▸ conjug 1 ◂ VT to reabsorb

réabsorption /ʀeapsɔʀpsjɔ̃/ NF reabsorption

réac* /ʀeak/ ADJ, NMF abrév de **réactionnaire**

réaccoutumer /ʀeakutyme/ ▸ conjug 1 ◂ VT to reaccustom VPR **se réaccoutumer** to reaccustom o.s., to become reaccustomed (à to)

réacheminer /ʀeaʃəmine/ ▸ conjug 1 ◂ VT [+ courrier, vivres] to redirect

réacteur /ʀeaktœʀ/ NM [d'avion] jet engine; (Chim, Phys) reactor ◆ ~ **nucléaire** nuclear reactor ◆ ~ **thermique** thermal reactor ◆ ~ **à neutrons rapides** fast-breeder reactor ◆ ~ **à eau pressurisée** pressurised water reactor

réactif, -ive /ʀeaktif, iv/ ADJ reactive ◆ **papier** ~ reagent ou test paper ◆ **peau réactive** sensitive skin NM (Chim) reagent

réaction /ʀeaksjɔ̃/ GRAMMAIRE ACTIVE 33.1 NF 1 (gén, Sci) reaction ◆ **être** ou **rester sans** ~ to show no reaction ◆ ~ **de défense/en chaîne** defence/chain reaction ◆ **une** ~ **de rejet à l'égard de ce parti** a rejection of this party ◆ **cette décision a provoqué** ou **suscité de violentes** ~**s dans l'opinion publique** there was strong public reaction to this decision ◆ **la** ~ **des marchés boursiers a été immédiate** the stock markets reacted immediately ◆ **sa** ~ **a été excessive** he overreacted ◆ **cette voiture a de bonnes** ~**s** this car responds well

◆ **en réaction** ◆ **être en** ~ **contre** to be in reaction against ◆ **en** ~ **contre les abus, ils ...** as a reaction against the abuses, they ...

◆ **en réaction à** [propos, décision] in reaction ou response to

2 **moteur à** ~ jet engine ◆ **propulsion par** ~ jet propulsion; → **avion**

réactionnaire /ʀeaksjɔnɛʀ/ ADJ, NMF reactionary

réactionnel, -elle /ʀeaksjɔnɛl/ ADJ (Chim, Physiol) reactional; (Psych) reactive ◆ **psychose réactionnelle** reactive psychosis

réactivation /ʀeaktivasjɔ̃/ NF reactivation

réactiver /ʀeaktive/ ▸ conjug 1 ◂ VT [+ négociations, processus de paix, programme] to revive, to restart; [+ croissance, économie, mesures, projet] to revive; [+ machine, système] to reactivate

réactivité /ʀeaktivite/ NF 1 (Phys, Méd) reactivity 2 [d'employé] adaptability, resourcefulness

réactualisation /ʀeaktɥalizasjɔ̃/ NF updating, bringing up to date; (Ordin) refresh

réactualiser /ʀeaktɥalize/ ▸ conjug 1 ◂ VT to update, to bring up to date; (Ordin) to refresh

réadaptation /ʀeadaptasjɔ̃/ NF [de personne] readjustment; (Méd) rehabilitation; [de muscle] re-education ◆ **centre de** ~ **à la vie sauvage** animal sanctuary (where animals are prepared for *release into the wild)* ◆ ~ **fonctionnelle** *(Méd)* rehabilitation

réadapter /Readapte/ ▸ conjug 1 ◂ VT *[+ personne]* to readjust *(à* to) VPR **se réadapter** to readjust, to become readjusted *(à* to)

réadmettre /ReadmɛtR/ ▸ conjug 56 ◂ VT to readmit

réadmission /Readmisjɔ̃/ NF readmission, readmittance

ready-made /Redimɛd/ NM INV *(Art)* ready-made

réaffectation /Reafɛktasjɔ̃/ NF *[de crédits, terrain, personne]* reallocation

réaffecter /Reafɛkte/ ▸ conjug 1 ◂ VT *(surtout passif) [+ crédits, terrain, personne]* to reallocate *(à* to)

réaffirmation /ReafiRmasjɔ̃/ NF reaffirmation

réaffirmer /ReafiRme/ ▸ conjug 1 ◂ VT to reaffirm, to reassert

réagir /ReaʒiR/ ▸ conjug 2 ◂ VI 1 *(gén, Chim)* to react *(à* to; *contre* against); *(= répondre)* to respond *(à* to); ◆ **il a réagi positivement à ma proposition** he reacted positively to my proposal ◆ **tu réagis trop violemment** you're overreacting ◆ **ils ont assisté à la scène sans** ~ they saw what happened, but did nothing ◆ **il faut** ~ **!** you have to do something! ◆ **souhaitez-vous** ~ **à cette déclaration ?** would you like to respond to that statement? ◆ **il réagit bien au traitement** he's responding well to treatment ◆ **sa voiture réagit mal au freinage** his brakes aren't very responsive ◆ **les organes des sens réagissent aux excitations** sense organs respond to stimuli 2 ◆ ~ **sur** to have an effect on, to affect ◆ **cet événement a réagi sur les sondages** this event affected the polls

réajustement /Reaʒystəmɑ̃/ NM *[de prix, loyer, salaires, taux]* adjustment

réajuster /Reaʒyste/ ▸ conjug 1 ◂ VT 1 *(= remettre en place) [+ mécanisme]* to readjust; *[+ vêtement]* to straighten (out), to tidy; *[+ cravate, lunettes]* to straighten, to adjust; *[+ coiffure]* to rearrange, to tidy ◆ **elle réajusta sa toilette** she straightened her clothes 2 *(= recentrer) [+ tir]* to (re)adjust; *[+ loyers, prix, salaires, taux]* to adjust VPR **se réajuster** *[personne]* to tidy *ou* straighten o.s. up

réalignement /Realiɲ(ə)mɑ̃/ NM *(Écon) [de monnaie, taux]* realignment

réalisable /Realizabl/ ADJ *[rêve]* attainable; *(Fin) [capital]* realizable; *[projet]* workable, feasible ◆ **difficilement** ~ hard to achieve

réalisateur, -trice /RealizatœR, tRis/ NM,F *(Ciné)* (film) director, film-maker; *(Radio, TV)* director

réalisation /Realizasjɔ̃/ NF 1 *[de rêve, ambition]* fulfilment ◆ **aura-t-il les moyens nécessaires à la** ~ **de son ambition ?** will he have what's needed to achieve *ou* fulfil his ambition? ◆ **plusieurs projets sont en cours de** ~ several projects are in the pipeline *ou* are under way ◆ **pour accélérer la** ~ **du projet d'autoroute** to hasten the completion of the motorway ◆ **le constructeur automobile a joué un rôle actif dans la** ~ **de cet exploit** the car manufacturer played an active role in achieving this feat
2 *[de meuble, bijou]* making; *[d'étude, sondage]* carrying out ◆ **une sauce dont la** ~ **est très délicate** a sauce that is very tricky to make ◆ **de** ~ **facile** easy to make ◆ **j'étais chargé de la** ~ **de cette étude** I was asked to carry out this piece of research
3 *(Fin) [de capital, valeurs, patrimoine]* realization
4 *(Comm)* realization; *[de vente, contrat]* conclusion
5 *(= création)* achievement, creation ◆ **c'est la plus belle** ~ **de l'architecte** it is the architect's finest achievement
6 *(Ciné)* direction; *(Radio, TV)* production ◆ **"réalisation (de) John Huston"** "directed by John Huston" ◆ **la** ~ **du film a duré six mois** the film took six months to make ◆ **assistant à la** ~ production assistant
7 *(Mus)* realization

réaliser /Realize/ ▸ conjug 1 ◂ VT 1 *[+ ambition]* to achieve; *[+ désir]* to fulfil; *[+ effort]* to make; *[+ exploit]* to achieve, to carry off; *[+ projet]* to carry out, to carry through ◆ ~ **un rêve** to fulfil *ou* achieve a dream ◆ **il a réalisé le meilleur temps aux essais** he got the best time in the trials ◆ **le sentiment d'avoir réalisé un exploit** the feeling that one has achieved something
2 *(= effectuer) [+ meuble, bijou]* to make; *[+ étude, sondage]* to carry out, to do ◆ **c'est lui qui a réalisé tous les maquillages** he did all the makeup
3 (* *= saisir)* to realize ◆ ~ **l'importance de qch** to realize the importance of sth ◆ **je n'ai pas encore réalisé** it hasn't sunk in yet
4 *(Ciné)* to direct; *(Radio, TV)* to produce ◆ **il vient de** ~ **son premier film** he's just made his first film ◆ **émission conçue et réalisée par ...** programme devised and produced by ...
5 *(Comm)* to realize; *[+ achat, vente, bénéfice, économie]* to make; *[+ contrat]* to conclude ◆ **l'entreprise réalise un chiffre d'affaires de 15 000 € par semaine** the firm has a turnover of *ou* turns over €15,000 a week
6 *(Fin) [+ capital, biens]* to realize ◆ **la banque a réalisé une partie de son portefeuille** part of the bank's portfolio was liquidated
7 *(Mus)* to realize
VPR **se réaliser** 1 *[rêve, vœu]* to come true; *[prédiction]* to be fulfilled; *[projet]* to be carried out, to be achieved
2 *[caractère, personnalité]* to be fulfilled ◆ **il s'est complètement réalisé dans son métier** he's completely fulfilled in his job

⚠ Attention à ne pas traduire automatiquement **réaliser** par **to realize**.

réalisme /Realism/ NM realism ◆ **le** ~ **socialiste** socialist realism

réaliste /Realist/ ADJ *[description, négociateur]* realistic; *(Art, Littérat)* realist NMF realist

réalité /Realite/ GRAMMAIRE ACTIVE 53.3, 53.4, 53.6 NF 1 *(= existence effective)* reality *(NonC)* ◆ **différentes** ~**s** different types of reality ◆ ~ **virtuelle** virtual reality
◆ **en réalité** in (actual) fact, in reality 2 *(= chose réelle)* reality ◆ **c'est une** ~ **incontournable** it's an inescapable fact ◆ **parfois la** ~ **dépasse la fiction** (sometimes) truth can be stranger than fiction ◆ **oublieux des** ~**s de la vie en communauté** neglecting the realities *ou* facts of communal life ◆ **détaché des** ~**s de ce monde** divorced from the realities of this world ◆ **ce sont les dures** ~**s de la vie** those are the harsh realities of life ◆ **son rêve est devenu (une)** ~ his dream became (a) reality *ou* came true; → **désir, sens**

reality show, reality-show (pl **reality(-)shows**) /Realitiʃo/ NM *(TV)* reality TV show; *(= feuilleton)* real-life soap

realpolitik /Realpɔlitik/ NF realpolitik

réaménagement /Reamenaʒmɑ̃/ NM *[de site, espace]* redevelopment; *[de pièce]* refitting; *[de calendrier, horaires, structure, service]* reorganization ◆ ~ **monétaire** currency readjustment

réaménager /Reamenaʒe/ ▸ conjug 3 ◂ VT *[+ site]* to redevelop; *[+ appartement, bâtiment]* to refit, to refurbish; *[+ horaires, structure, service]* to reorganize; *[+ taux d'intérêt]* to adjust

réamorcer /ReamɔRse/ ▸ conjug 3 ◂ VT 1 *[+ ordinateur]* to reboot; *[+ pompe]* to prime again ◆ ~ **la pompe** *(fig)* to get things going again, to set things in motion again ◆ **ces investissements permettront de** ~ **la pompe de l'économie** these investments will give the economy a kickstart 2 *[+ dialogue, négociations, processus]* to start again, to reinitiate

réanimateur, -trice /ReanimatœR, tRis/ NM,F *(= personne)* resuscitator NM *(= respirateur)* ventilator, respirator

réanimation /Reanimasjɔ̃/ NF resuscitation; *(fig)* revival ◆ **être en (service de)** ~ to be in the intensive care unit, to be in intensive care

réanimer /Reanime/ ▸ conjug 1 ◂ VT 1 *[+ personne]* to resuscitate, to revive 2 *(= faire revivre) [+ quartier, région]* to revive

réapparaître /ReapaRɛtR/ ▸ conjug 57 ◂ VI *[soleil]* to come out again, to reappear; *[maladie, symptôme]* to recur; *[personne]* to reappear, to come back

réapparition /ReapaRisjɔ̃/ NF *[de soleil]* reappearance; *[de maladie, symptôme]* recurrence; *[d'artiste]* comeback ◆ **faire sa** ~ to reappear ◆ **la mode des chapeaux a fait sa** ~ hats are back in fashion

réapprendre /ReapRɑ̃dR/ ▸ conjug 58 ◂ VT *(gén)* to relearn, to learn again; *(littér) [+ solitude, liberté]* to get to know again, to relearn *(littér)*, to learn again *(littér)* ◆ ~ **qch à qn** to teach sth to sb again, to teach sb sth again ◆ ~ **à faire qch** to learn to do sth again

réapprentissage /ReapRɑ̃tisaʒ/ NM ◆ **le** ~ **de qch** relearning sth, learning sth again ◆ **cela va demander un long** ~ that will take a long time to relearn *ou* to learn again

réapprovisionnement /ReapRɔvizjɔnmɑ̃/ NM 1 *(Fin)* **le** ~ **d'un compte en banque** putting (more) money into a bank account 2 *(= ravitaillement)* resupplying 3 *[de magasin]* restocking, stocking up again

réapprovisionner /ReapRɔvizjɔne/ ▸ conjug 1 ◂ VT 1 *[+ compte en banque]* to put (more) money into 2 *(= ravitailler)* to resupply 3 *[+ magasin]* to restock *(en* with) VPR **se réapprovisionner** to stock up again *(en* with)

réargenter /RearʒɑRte/ ▸ conjug 1 ◂ VT to resilver VPR **se réargenter** * *(= se renflouer)* to get back on a sound financial footing

réarmement /RearRməmɑ̃/ NM 1 *[de fusil]* reloading; *[d'appareil-photo]* winding on 2 *(Naut) [de navire]* refitting 3 *[de pays]* rearmament ◆ **politique de** ~ policy of rearmament

réarmer /RearRme/ ▸ conjug 1 ◂ VT 1 *[+ fusil]* to reload; *[+ appareil-photo]* to wind on 2 *(Naut) [+ bateau]* to refit 3 *[+ pays]* to rearm VI **se réarmer** VPR *[pays]* to rearm

réarrangement /RearRɑ̃ʒmɑ̃/ NM rearrangement ◆ ~ **moléculaire** *(Phys)* molecular rearrangement

réarranger /RearRɑ̃ʒe/ ▸ conjug 3 ◂ VT *[+ coiffure, fleurs, chambre]* to rearrange; *[+ cravate, jupe]* to straighten (up) again; *[+ entrevue]* to rearrange

réassignation /Reasiɲasjɔ̃/ NF *(Jur)* resummons *(sg)*; *(Fin)* reallocation

réassigner /Reasiɲe/ ▸ conjug 1 ◂ VT *(gén)* to reassign; *(Jur)* to resummon; *(Fin)* to reallocate

réassort /ReasɔR/ NM *(= action)* restocking; *(= marchandises)* fresh stock *ou* supply

réassortiment /ReasɔRtimɑ̃/ NM *(= action) [de stock]* replenishment; *[de verres]* replacement, matching (up); *[de service de table, tissu]* matching (up); *(= marchandises)* new *ou* fresh stock

réassortir /ReasɔRtiR/ ▸ conjug 2 ◂ VT *[+ magasin]* to restock *(en* with); *[+ stock]* to replenish; *[+ service de table]* to match (up); *[+ verres]* to replace, to match (up) VPR **se réassortir** *(Comm)* to stock up again (*de* with) to replenish one's stock(s) (*de* of)

réassurance /ReasyRɑ̃s/ NF reinsurance

réassurer VT, **se réassurer** VPR /ReasyRe/ ► conjug 1 ◄ to reinsure

réassureur /ReasyRœR/ NM reinsurer, reinsurance underwriter

rebaisser /R(ə)bese/ ► conjug 1 ◄ VI *[prix]* to go down again; *[température, niveau d'eau]* to fall again VT *[+ prix]* to bring back down, to bring down again, to lower again; *[+ radio, son, chauffage]* to turn down again; *[+ store, levier]* to pull down again, to lower again

rebaptiser /R(ə)batize/ ► conjug 1 ◄ VT *[+ enfant]* to rebaptize; *[+ rue]* to rename; *[+ navire]* to rechristen

rébarbatif, -ive /RebaRbatif, iv/ ADJ (= *rebutant*) *[mine]* forbidding, unprepossessing; *[sujet, tâche]* daunting, forbidding; *[style]* off-putting

rebâtir /R(ə)bɑtiR/ ► conjug 2 ◄ VT to rebuild

rebattre /R(ə)batR/ ► conjug 41 ◄ VT [1] *(Cartes)* to reshuffle [2] ◆ **il m'a rebattu les oreilles de son succès** he kept harping on about his success ◆ **il en parlait toute la journée, j'en avais les oreilles rebattues** he talked of it all day long until I was sick and tired of hearing about it*

rebattu, e /R(ə)baty/ (ptp de **rebattre**) ADJ *[sujet, citation]* hackneyed

rebec /Rəbɛk/ NM rebec(k)

rebelle /Rəbɛl/ ADJ *[troupes, soldat]* rebel *(épith)*; *[enfant, esprit, cœur]* rebellious; *[cheval]* restive; *[fièvre, maladie]* stubborn; *[mèche, cheveux]* unruly

◆ **rebelle à** ◆ **des mouvements de guérilla ~s à l'autorité de Delhi** guerilla movements resisting the Delhi government ◆ **des adolescents ~s aux activités intellectuelles** teenagers who resist *ou* rebel against intellectual activities ◆ **cette maladie est ~ aux médicaments** this disease does not respond to drugs ◆ **cheveux ~s à la brosse** unruly hair NMF rebel

rebeller (se) /R(ə)bele/ ► conjug 1 ◄ VPR to rebel *(contre* against)

rébellion /Rebeljɔ̃/ NF (= *révolte*) rebellion ◆ **la ~** (= *rebelles*) the rebels

rebelote /Rəbəlɔt/ EXCL *(Cartes)* rebelote! *(said when the king of trumps is played after the queen or the queen of trumps is played after the king)*; (* *fig*) here we go again!

rebeu‡ /Rəbø/ NM *second-generation North African living in France*

rebiffer (se)* /R(ə)bife/ ► conjug 1 ◄ VPR (= *résister*) *[personne]* to hit *ou* strike back *(contre* at); *(fig) [corps, conscience]* to rebel *(contre* against)

rebiquer* /R(ə)bike/ ► conjug 1 ◄ VI (= *se redresser*) *[mèche de cheveux]* to stick up; *[col]* to curl up at the ends ◆ **ta veste rebique derrière** your jacket sticks out at the back

reblanchir /R(ə)blɑ̃ʃiR/ ► conjug 2 ◄ VT *(gén)* to rewhiten; *[+ mur]* to rewhitewash

reblochon /Rəblɔʃɔ̃/ NM *kind of cheese from Savoie*

reboisement /R(ə)bwazmɑ̃/ NM reforestation, reafforestation

reboiser /R(ə)bwaze/ ► conjug 1 ◄ VT to reforest, to reafforest

rebond /R(ə)bɔ̃/ NM [1] *[de balle]* *(sur le sol)* bounce; *(contre un mur)* rebound ◆ **rattraper une balle au ~** to catch a ball on the bounce [2] *[d'histoire]* development [3] (= *amélioration*) *[d'activité économique, marché]* recovery ◆ **on note un léger ~ de la consommation** consumption has picked up slightly

rebondi, e /R(ə)bɔ̃di/ (ptp de **rebondir**) ADJ *[objet, bouteille, forme]* potbellied; *[croupe]* rounded; *[poitrine]* well-developed; *[ventre]* fat; *[joues, visage]* chubby; *[femme]* curvaceous, amply proportioned; *[homme]* portly, corpulent; *[porte-monnaie]* well-lined ◆ **elle avait des formes ~es** she was amply proportioned ◆ **il a un ventre ~** he has a paunch, he has a fat stomach

rebondir /R(ə)bɔ̃diR/ ► conjug 2 ◄ VI [1] *[balle]* *(sur le sol)* to bounce; *(contre un mur)* to rebound ◆ **faire ~ une balle par terre/contre un mur** to bounce a ball on the ground/against a wall [2] *[conversation]* to get going *ou* moving again; *[scandale, affaire, procès]* to be revived; *(Théât) [action, intrigue]* to get moving again, to take off again ◆ **l'affaire n'en finit pas de ~** there are new developments in the affair all the time ◆ **faire ~** *[+ conversation]* to give new impetus to, to set *ou* get going again; *[+ action d'une pièce]* to get *ou* set moving again; *[+ scandale, procès]* to revive [3] *[économie, marché, actions]* to pick up again ◆ **ça l'a aidé à ~ après son licenciement/son divorce** it helped him get back on his feet again after his dismissal/his divorce

rebondissement /R(ə)bɔ̃dismɑ̃/ NM (= *développement*) (sudden new) development (*de* in); (= *réapparition*) sudden revival (NonC) (*de* of); ◆ **feuilleton/récit à ~s** action-packed serial/story ◆ **l'affaire vient de connaître un nouveau ~** there has been a new development in the affair ◆ **le ~ de la controverse sur la peine de mort** the sudden revival of the controversy about the death penalty

rebord /R(ə)bɔR/ NM [1] *[d'assiette, tuyau, plat, pot]* rim; *[de puits, falaise]* edge; *[de corniche, table, buffet]* (projecting) edge ◆ **le ~ de la cheminée** the mantelpiece *ou* mantelshelf ◆ **le ~ de la fenêtre** the windowsill, the window ledge [2] *[de vêtement]* hem

reborder /R(ə)bɔRde/ ► conjug 1 ◄ VT *[+ vêtement]* to put a new edging on; *[+ enfant]* to tuck in again

reboucher /R(ə)buʃe/ ► conjug 1 ◄ VT *[+ trou]* to fill in again; *[+ bouteille]* to recork; *[+ carafe]* to put the stopper back in; *[+ tube]* to put the cap back on VPR **se reboucher** *[tuyau]* to get blocked again

rebours /R(ə)buR/ **à rebours** LOC ADV [1] (= *à rebrousse-poil*) **caresser un chat à ~** to stroke a cat the wrong way ◆ **lisser un tissu à ~** to smooth out a fabric against the nap *ou* pile ◆ **prendre qn à ~** to rub sb up the wrong way [2] (= *à l'envers*) **faire un trajet à ~** to make a trip the other way round ◆ **prendre une rue en sens unique à ~** to go the wrong way up a one-way street ◆ **feuilleter un magazine à ~** to flip through a magazine from back to front ◆ **compter à ~** to count backwards ◆ **prendre l'ennemi à ~** *(Mil)* to surprise the enemy from behind; → **compte** [3] (= *de travers*) **comprendre à ~** to misunderstand, to get the wrong idea, to get the wrong end of the stick* ◆ **faire tout à ~** to do everything the wrong way round *ou* back to front *(Brit)* [4] (= *à l'opposé de*) **à ~ de** against ◆ **aller à ~ de la tendance générale** to go against *ou* run counter to the general trend ◆ **c'est à ~ du bon sens !** it goes against *ou* flies in the face of common sense!

rebouteur, -euse /R(ə)butœR, øz/, **rebouteux, -euse** /R(ə)butø, øz/ NM,F bonesetter

reboutonner /R(ə)butɔne/ ► conjug 1 ◄ VT to button up again, to rebutton VPR **se reboutonner** to do o.s. up again, to do up one's buttons again

rebrousse-poil /Rəbruspwal/ **à rebrousse-poil** LOC ADV *[caresser]* the wrong way ◆ **lisser un tissu à ~** to smooth out a fabric against the pile *ou* nap ◆ **prendre qn à ~** *(fig)* to rub sb up the wrong way ◆ **cette évolution prend toutes les habitudes à ~** this development goes right against the grain of established habits

rebrousser /R(ə)bRuse/ ► conjug 1 ◄ VT [1] ◆ **~ chemin** to turn back, to turn round and go back [2] *[+ poil]* to brush up; *[+ cheveux]* to brush back; *(Tech) [+ cuir]* to strike ◆ **~ le poil de qn** *(fig)* to rub sb up the wrong way

rebuffade /R(ə)byfad/ NF rebuff ◆ **essuyer une ~** to be rebuffed, to suffer a rebuff

rébus /Rebys/ NM (= *jeu*) rebus; *(fig* = *énigme)* puzzle

rebut /Rəby/ NM [1] (= *déchets*) scrap ◆ **c'est du ~** *(objets)* it's scrap; *(vêtements)* they're just cast-offs ◆ **c'est le ~ de la cave** it's all the unwanted stuff from the cellar ◆ **mettre** *ou* **jeter au ~** to scrap, to throw out, to discard; *[+ vêtements]* to discard, to throw out ◆ **ces vieux journaux vont aller au ~** these old papers are going to be thrown out *ou* discarded ◆ **marchandises de ~** trash goods ◆ **bois de ~** old wood [2] *(péj* = *racaille)* **le ~ de la société** the scum *ou* dregs of society [3] *(Poste)* **~s** dead letters

rebutant, e /R(ə)bytɑ̃, ɑ̃t/ ADJ (= *dégoûtant*) repellent; (= *décourageant*) disheartening, off-putting

rebuter /R(ə)byte/ ► conjug 1 ◄ VT (= *décourager*) to dishearten, to discourage, to put off; (= *répugner*) to repel; *(littér* = *repousser durement)* to repulse ◆ **il ne faut pas te ~ tout de suite** don't be deterred *ou* put off straight away

recacheter /R(ə)kaʃ(ə)te/ ► conjug 4 ◄ VT to reseal

recadrage /R(ə)kɑdRaʒ/ NM [1] *(Ciné, Photo)* cropping, reframing [2] *[de politique]* refocusing ◆ **le projet a subi de nombreux ~s** the project has been altered and redefined on numerous occasions

recadrer /R(ə)kɑdRe/ ► conjug 1 ◄ VT [1] *(Ciné, Photo)* to crop, to reframe [2] *[+ politique]* to refocus; *[+ action, projet]* to redefine the terms of ◆ **il faut ~ nos priorités** we need to redefine our priorities ◆ **le gouvernement a recadré sa réflexion sur l'éducation** the government has redefined *ou* rethought its position on education

récalcitrant, e /Rekalsitrɑ̃, ɑ̃t/ ADJ (= *indocile*) *[animal]* refractory, stubborn; *[personne]* recalcitrant, refractory; *[appareil, pièce]* unmanageable NM,F recalcitrant

recalculer /R(ə)kalkyle/ ► conjug 1 ◄ VT *[+ budget]* to recalculate

recalé, e /R(ə)kale/ (ptp de **recaler**) ADJ *(Scol, Univ) [étudiant]* failed, who has been failed ◆ **les (candidats) ~s à la session de juin** the exam candidates who were failed in June

recaler /R(ə)kale/ ► conjug 1 ◄ VT *(Scol* = *refuser)* to fail ◆ **se faire ~** *ou* **être recalé en histoire** to fail (in) *ou* flunk* history ◆ **il a été recalé trois fois au permis de conduire** he failed his driving test three times

recapitalisation /R(ə)kapitalizasjɔ̃/ NF *(Écon)* recapitalization

recapitaliser /R(ə)kapitalize/ ► conjug 1 ◄ VT *(Écon)* to recapitalize

récapitulatif, -ive /Rekapitylatif, iv/ ADJ *[chapitre]* recapitulative, recapitulatory; *[état, tableau]* summary *(épith)* ◆ **dresser un état ~ d'un compte** to draw up a summary statement of an account NM summary, recapitulation

récapitulation /Rekapitylasjɔ̃/ NF recapitulation ◆ **faire la ~ de** to recapitulate

récapituler /Rekapityle/ ► conjug 1 ◄ VT to recapitulate, to recap

recarreler /R(ə)kaRle/ ► conjug 4 ◄ VT to retile

recaser* /R(ə)kɑze/ ► conjug 1 ◄ VT *[+ chômeur]* to find a new job for; *[+ réfugié]* to rehouse ◆ **il a**

pu se ~ *[veuf, divorcé]* he managed to get hitched* again *ou* to find himself someone new; *[chômeur]* he managed to find a new job

recauser* /R(ə)koze/ ▸ conjug 1 ◂ VI ◆ ~ **de qch** to talk about sth again ◆ **je vous en recauserai** we'll talk about it again

recéder /R(ə)sede/ ▸ conjug 6 ◂ VT (= *rétrocéder*) to give *ou* sell back; (= *vendre*) to resell

recel /Rəsɛl/ NM ◆ ~ **(d'objets volés)** (= *action*) receiving (stolen goods); (= *résultat*) possession of *ou* possessing stolen goods ◆ ~ **de malfaiteur** harbouring a criminal ◆ **condamné pour** ~ sentenced for possession of stolen goods *ou* for receiving (stolen goods)

receler /R(ə)səle/ ▸ conjug 5 ◂ VT 1 *(Jur)* *[+ objet volé]* to receive, to fence*; *[+ malfaiteur]* to harbour 2 (= *contenir*) *[+ secret, erreur, trésor]* to conceal

receleur, -euse /R(ə)səlœR, øz/ NM,F *(Jur)* receiver of stolen goods, fence*

récemment /Resamɑ̃/ ADV 1 (= *depuis peu*) recently ◆ **la pluie ~ tombée rendait la route glissante** the rain which had fallen recently *ou* had just fallen made the road slippery ◆ ~ **publié** recently published 2 (= *dernièrement*) recently, lately *(gén dans phrases nég ou interrog)* ◆ **l'as-tu vu ~ ?** have you seen him lately *ou* recently? ◆ **encore (tout) ~ il était très en forme** just recently *ou* even quite recently he was still in tiptop form

recensement /R(ə)sɑ̃smɑ̃/ NM *[de population]* census; *[d'objets]* inventory; *(Mil)* registration *(of young men eligible for military service)* ◆ **faire le ~ de la population** to take a *ou* the census of the population, to make *ou* take a population census ◆ **faire le ~ des besoins en matériel** to take *ou* make an inventory of equipment requirements

recenser /R(ə)sɑ̃se/ ▸ conjug 1 ◂ VT *[+ population]* to take a *ou* the census of, to make a census of; *[+ objets]* to make *ou* take an inventory of; *[+ futurs conscrits]* to compile a register of; *[+ malades, victimes]* to make a list of ◆ **le pays compte trois millions de chômeurs recensés** the country has three million people registered as unemployed *ou* officially unemployed

recenseur, -euse /R(ə)sɑ̃sœR, øz/ ADJ M, NM,F ◆ **(agent)** ~ census taker

recension /R(ə)sɑ̃sjɔ̃/ NF *(littér)* (= *collationnement*) recension, critical revision *(of a text)*; (= *inventaire*) *[de documents, faits]* inventory; (= *analyse*) *[d'œuvre littéraire]* review

récent, e /Resɑ̃, ɑ̃t/ ADJ (= *survenu récemment*) recent; (= *nouveau, de fraîche date*) new ◆ **les chiffres les plus ~s montrent que ...** the latest *ou* most recent figures show that ... ◆ **jusqu'à une période ~e** until recently ◆ **ce phénomène est relativement** ~ this phenomenon is relatively recent *ou* new ◆ **ce bâtiment est tout** ~ this building is quite new

recentrage /R(ə)sɑ̃tRaʒ/ NM *[de parti]* movement towards the centre; *[de politique]* redefinition, reorientation; *(Écon)* *[d'activités]* refocusing

recentralisation /R(ə)sɑ̃tRalizasjɔ̃/ NF recentralization

recentraliser /R(ə)sɑ̃tRalize/ ▸ conjug 1 ◂ VT to recentralize

recentrer /R(ə)sɑ̃tRe/ ▸ conjug 1 ◂ VT *(Ftbl)* to centre again; *[+ politique]* to redefine, to reorient; *[+ débat]* to bring back to the main point; *(Écon)* *[+ activités]* to refocus VPR **se recentrer** ◆ **se ~ sur une activité** to refocus on an activity

récépissé /Resepise/ NM (= *reçu*) receipt

réceptacle /Reseptakl/ NM (= *déversoir*) *(gén, Bot)* receptacle; *(Géog)* catchment basin

récepteur, -trice /ReseptœR, tRis/ ADJ receiving ◆ **poste** ~ receiver NM *(gén, Télec)* receiver; *(TV)* (receiving) set; *(Bio, Physiol)* receptor ◆ ~ **(de télévision)** television set ◆ ~ **téléphonique** (telephone) receiver

> ⚠ **récepteur** se traduit par le mot anglais **receptor** uniquement en biochimie et physiologie.

réceptif, -ive /Reseptif, iv/ ADJ receptive (*à* to); *(Méd)* susceptible (*à* to)

réception /Resepsjɔ̃/ GRAMMAIRE ACTIVE 47.2, 52.1 NF 1 (= *accueil*) welcome, reception ◆ **discours de** ~ welcoming speech ◆ **heures de ~ de 14 à 16 heures** consultations between 2 and 4 pm ◆ **quelles sont vos heures de ~ ?** *(Scol)* when are you available to see parents?; *(Univ)* when are you available to see students?

2 (= *bureau*) reception, reception desk; (= *entrée, salon*) *[d'hôtel]* entrance hall; *[d'appartement, villa]* reception room ◆ **adressez-vous à la** ~ ask at reception *ou* at the reception desk ◆ **salle de** ~ function room ◆ **salons de** ~ reception rooms

3 (= *réunion, fête*) reception; → **jour**

4 (= *action de recevoir*) *[de paquet, lettre]* receipt; *(Bio, Radio, TV)* reception ◆ **à la ~ de sa lettre** on receipt of *ou* on receiving his letter ◆ **c'est lui qui s'occupe de la ~ des marchandises** he is the one who takes delivery of the goods ◆ **la ~ est mauvaise aujourd'hui** *(Radio)* reception is bad *ou* poor today; → **accusé, accuser**

5 *(Sport)* (= *prise, blocage*) *(Ftbl, Rugby)* stopping, trapping; *(Volley)* catching; (= *atterrissage*) *[de sauteur, parachutiste]* landing ◆ **le footballeur a manqué sa** ~ the player missed the ball *ou* failed to take the pass ◆ **il a manqué sa** ~ *[sauteur]* he made a bad landing *ou* landed badly

6 *(Constr)* ~ **des travaux** acceptance of work done *(after verification)*

réceptionnaire /Resepsjɔnɛr/ NMF *[d'hôtel]* head of reception; *(Comm)* *[de marchandises]* receiving clerk; *(Jur)* receiving agent

réceptionner /Resepsjɔne/ ▸ conjug 1 ◂ VT *[+ marchandises]* to receive, to take delivery of, to check and sign for; *[+ client]* to receive, to welcome; *(Sport)* *[+ balle]* to receive VPR **se réceptionner** *(Sport)* to land

réceptionniste /Resepsjɔnist/ NMF receptionist ◆ **~-standardiste** receptionist and telephonist

réceptivité /Reseptivite/ NF *(gén)* receptivity, receptiveness; *(Méd)* susceptibility (*à* to)

récessif, -ive /Resesif, iv/ ADJ *(Bio)* recessive

récession /Resesjɔ̃/ NF recession ◆ **de** ~ recessionary ◆ ~ **avec inflation** slumpflation

récessionniste /Resesjɔnist/ ADJ recessionary ◆ **tendance** ~ recessionary trend

récessivité /Resesivite/ NF recessiveness

recette /R(ə)sɛt/ NF 1 *(Culin)* recipe; *(Chim)* *[de teinture, produit]* formula; *(fig = truc, secret)* formula, recipe (*de* for) 2 (= *encaisse*) takings ◆ **aujourd'hui, j'ai fait une bonne** ~ I've made a good day's takings, the takings were good today ◆ **faire** ~ (= *avoir du succès*) to be a big success, to be a winner 3 (= *rentrées d'argent*) **~s** receipts ◆ **l'excédent des ~s sur les dépenses** the excess of receipts *ou* revenue over expenses *ou* outlay ◆ **~s fiscales** tax revenue(s), revenue from taxation 4 *(Impôts)* (= *recouvrement*) collection; (= *bureau*) tax (collector's) office, revenue office ◆ ~ **municipale** local tax office ◆ **~(-perception)** tax office ◆ ~ **principale** main tax office; → **garçon**

recevabilité /R(ə)səvabilite/ NF *(Jur)* *[de pourvoi, témoignage]* admissibility

recevable /R(ə)səvabl/ ADJ *(Jur)* *[demande, appel, pourvoi]* admissible, allowable; *[personne]* competent ◆ **témoignage non** ~ inadmissible evidence

receveur /R(ə)səvœR/ NM 1 *(Méd)* recipient ◆ ~ **universel** universal recipient 2 ◆ ~ **(d'autobus)** conductor ◆ ~ **(des contributions)** tax collector *ou* officer ◆ ~ **(des postes)** postmaster ◆ ~ **municipal** local tax officer

receveuse /R(ə)səvøz/ NF 1 *(Méd)* recipient ◆ ~ **universelle** universal recipient 2 ◆ ~ **(d'autobus)** conductress ◆ ~ **(des contributions)** tax collector *ou* officer ◆ ~ **(des postes)** postmistress

recevoir /R(ə)səvwaR/ ▸ conjug 28 ◂ VT 1 *(gén)* to get, to receive; *[+ approbation, refus]* to get, to meet with; *[+ modifications]* to undergo; *[+ confession]* to hear; *(Rel)* *[+ vœux, sacrement]* to receive ◆ ~ **les ordres** *(Rel)* to take holy orders ◆ **nous avons bien reçu votre lettre du 15 juillet** we acknowledge *ou* confirm receipt of your letter of 15 July ◆ **je vous reçois cinq sur cinq** *(Radio, fig)* I'm receiving you loud and clear ◆ **un procédé qui a reçu le nom de son inventeur** a process which took its name from the inventor ◆ **l'affaire recevra toute notre attention** the matter will receive our full attention ◆ **nous avons reçu la pluie** we got *ou* had rain ◆ **j'ai reçu le caillou sur la tête** the stone hit me on the head, I got hit on the head by the stone ◆ **il a reçu un coup de pied/un coup de poing dans la figure** he got kicked/punched in the face, he got a kick/a punch in the face ◆ **c'est lui qui a tout reçu** *(blâme, coups)* he bore the brunt of it; *(sauce, éclaboussures)* most of it went on him ◆ **recevez, cher Monsieur (ou chère Madame), l'expression de mes sentiments distingués** *(formule épistolaire)* yours faithfully *(Brit)* *ou* truly *(US)*; → **leçon, ordre²**

2 *[+ invité]* (= *accueillir*) to welcome, to greet, to receive *(frm)*; (= *traiter*) to entertain; (= *loger*) to put up, to have to stay; *[+ jeux olympiques, championnat]* to host; *(Admin)* *[+ employé, demandeur]* to see; *[+ demande, déposition, plainte]* to admit ◆ ~ **qn à dîner** to have sb to dinner ◆ **ils ont reçu le roi** they entertained the king ◆ **être bien/mal reçu** *[proposition, nouvelles]* to be well/badly received; *[personne]* to receive a warm welcome/frosty reception ◆ **on est toujours bien/mal reçu chez eux** they always/never make you feel welcome ◆ ~ **qn à bras ouverts** to welcome sb with open arms ◆ **il est reçu partout dans la haute société** all doors are open to him in society ◆ **les Dupont reçoivent beaucoup** the Duponts entertain a lot ◆ **la baronne reçoit le jeudi** the baroness is at home (to visitors) on Thursdays ◆ **le directeur reçoit le jeudi** the principal receives visitors on Thursdays ◆ **le docteur reçoit de 10 h à 12 h** the doctor's surgery is from 10 am till noon *(Brit)*, the doctor is in his office from 10 till noon *(US)* ◆ ~ **la visite de qn/d'un cambrioleur** to get a visit from sb/from a burglar ◆ **se faire ~*** to get shouted at; → **chien**

3 *(Scol, Univ)* *[+ candidat]* to pass ◆ **être reçu à un examen** to pass an exam ◆ **il a été reçu dans les premiers/dans les derniers** he was near the top/bottom in the exam ◆ **il a été reçu premier/deuxième/dernier** he came first/second/last *ou* bottom in the exam; → **reçu**

4 (= *contenir*) *[hôtel, lycée]* to take, to accommodate; (= *récolter*) *[gouttière]* to collect ◆ **par manque de locaux on n'a pas pu ~ plus d'élèves cette année** we didn't have room to take more pupils this year ◆ ~ **un affluent** *[rivière]* to be joined by a tributary ◆ **leur chambre ne reçoit jamais le soleil** their room never gets any sun

5 *(Tech)* *[+ pièce mobile]* to take ◆ **cette encoche reçoit le crochet qui assure la fermeture de la porte** this notch takes the hook which keeps the door shut, the hook that keeps the door shut fits into this ring

VPR **se recevoir** ① *(= tomber)* to land ◆ **se ~ sur une jambe/sur les mains** to land on one leg/on one's hands ◆ **il s'est mal reçu** he landed awkwardly

② *(† = se fréquenter)* **elles se connaissent mais ne se reçoivent pas** they know each other but they are not on visiting terms

rechange /ʀ(ə)ʃɑ̃ʒ/ NM ① ◆ **~ (de vêtements)** change of clothes ◆ **as-tu ton ~ ?** have you got a change of clothes? ② ◆ **de ~** *(= de remplacement) [solution, politique]* alternative; *(= de secours) [outil]* spare ◆ **avoir du linge de ~** to have a change of clothes ◆ **j'ai apporté des chaussures de ~** I brought a spare *ou* an extra pair of shoes; → **pièce**

rechanger /ʀ(ə)ʃɑ̃ʒe/ ▸ conjug 3 ◂ VT to change again

rechanter /ʀ(ə)ʃɑ̃te/ ▸ conjug 1 ◂ VT to sing again

rechapage /ʀ(ə)ʃapaʒ/ NM *(= opération)* retreading, remoulding *(Brit)* ◆ **le ~ n'a pas duré** *(= résultat)* the retread *ou* remould *(Brit)* didn't last long

rechaper /ʀ(ə)ʃape/ ▸ conjug 1 ◂ VT *[+ pneu]* to retread, to remould *(Brit)* ◆ **pneus rechapés** retreads, remoulds *(Brit)*

réchappé, e /ʀeʃape/ (ptp de **réchapper**) NM,F survivor *(de* of*)*; ◆ **les ~s du naufrage** the survivors of the shipwreck

réchapper /ʀeʃape/ ▸ conjug 1 ◂ VI ◆ **~ de** *ou* **à** *[+ accident, maladie]* to come through ◆ **tu as eu de la chance d'en ~** you were lucky to escape with your life ◆ **si jamais j'en réchappe** if ever I come through this

recharge /ʀ(ə)ʃaʀʒ/ NF ① *(= action) (Élec)* recharging; *(Mil)* reloading ② *(= cartouche) [d'arme]* reload; *[de stylo, agenda]* refill

rechargeable /ʀ(ə)ʃaʀʒabl/ ADJ *[batterie, pile, appareil électrique, carte à puce]* rechargeable; *[stylo, vaporisateur, aérosol]* refillable; *[briquet]* refillable, rechargeable

rechargement /ʀ(ə)ʃaʀʒəmɑ̃/ NM ① *[de stylo]* refilling; *[de briquet]* refilling, recharging; *[de batterie, pile]* recharging ◆ **~ en combustible d'un réacteur nucléaire** refuelling a nuclear reactor ② *(Tech) [de route]* remetalling; *[de voie, rails]* relaying

recharger /ʀ(ə)ʃaʀʒe/ ▸ conjug 3 ◂ VT ① *[+ arme, appareil-photo]* to reload; *[+ briquet]* to refill, to recharge; *[+ batterie, pile]* to recharge ◆ **~ ses batteries** *ou* **ses accus** * *(fig)* to recharge one's batteries ② *[+ véhicule]* reload, to load up again ③ *(Tech) [+ route]* to remetal; *[+ voie, rails]* to relay VPR **se recharger** *(= être rechargeable) [stylo]* to be refillable; *[briquet, batterie, pile]* to be rechargeable; *(= se charger à nouveau) [batterie, pile]* to recharge

réchaud /ʀeʃo/ NM ① *(= appareil de cuisson)* (portable) stove ◆ **~ à gaz** gas stove *ou* ring *(Brit)* ◆ **~ à alcool** spirit stove ② *(= chauffe-plat)* platewarmer ③ *(= cassolette)* burner *(for incense etc)*

réchauffage /ʀeʃofaʒ/ NM *[d'aliment]* reheating

réchauffé, e /ʀeʃofe/ (ptp de **réchauffer**) ADJ *[nourriture]* reheated, warmed-up; *(péj) [plaisanterie]* stale, old hat *(attrib)*; *[théories]* rehashed, old hat *(attrib)* ◆ **des manches courtes en décembre ? eh bien ! tu es ~ !** * you're wearing short sleeves in December? you don't feel the cold, do you! NM ◆ **c'est du ~** *(ragoût)* it's reheated *ou* warmed-up; *(vieille affaire)* it's old hat

réchauffement /ʀeʃofmɑ̃/ NM *[d'eau, membres, personne]* warming (up) ◆ **le ~ de la planète** global warming ◆ **on constate un ~ de la température** the temperature is rising ◆ **on espère un ~ de la température** we're hoping for warmer weather ◆ **ceci a favorisé le ~ des relations entre les deux pays** this has made for warmer relations between the two countries

réchauffer /ʀeʃofe/ ▸ conjug 1 ◂ VT ① *[+ aliment]* to reheat, to heat *ou* warm up again ◆ **réchauffe** *ou* **fais ~ la soupe, mets la soupe à ~** reheat the soup, heat *ou* warm the soup up again

② *[+ personne]* to warm up ◆ **une bonne soupe, ça réchauffe** a nice bowl of soup warms you up ◆ **~ un serpent dans son sein** *(littér, hum)* to nurse a viper in one's bosom

③ *(= réconforter) [+ cœur]* to warm; *(= ranimer) [+ courage]* to stir up, to rekindle ◆ **cela m'a réchauffé le cœur de les voir** it did my heart good *ou* it was heartwarming to see them

④ *[soleil]* to heat up, to warm up ◆ **le soleil réchauffe la terre** the sun warms the earth ◆ **ce rayon de soleil va ~ l'atmosphère** this ray of sunshine will warm up the air ◆ **les tons bruns réchauffent la pièce** the browns make the room seem warmer

VPR **se réchauffer** ① *[temps, température]* to get warmer, to warm up ◆ **on dirait que ça se réchauffe** it feels as if it's getting warmer *ou* warming up

② *[personne]* to warm o.s. (up) ◆ **alors tu te réchauffes un peu ?** are you warming up now? *ou* feeling a bit warmer now? ◆ **se ~ les doigts, ~ ses doigts** to warm one's fingers (up)

réchauffeur /ʀeʃofœʀ/ NM heater

rechausser /ʀ(ə)ʃose/ ▸ conjug 1 ◂ VT ① *(Agr) [+ arbre]* to earth up; *(Constr) [+ mur]* to consolidate ② ◆ **~ un enfant** *(chaussures enlevées)* to put a child's shoes back on; *(chaussures neuves)* to buy a child new shoes ◆ **~ une voiture** to put new tyres *(Brit) ou* tires *(US)* on a car ③ ◆ **~ ses skis** to put one's skis back on VPR **se rechausser** to put one's shoes back on; *(= acheter de nouvelles chaussures)* to buy (o.s.) new shoes

rêche /ʀɛʃ/ ADJ *(au toucher) [tissu, peau]* rough, harsh; *(au goût) [vin]* rough; *[fruit vert]* harsh; *(péj) [personne]* abrasive

recherche /ʀ(ə)ʃɛʀʃ/ NF ① *(= action de rechercher)* search *(de* for*)*; ◆ **la ~ de ce document m'a pris plusieurs heures** it took me several hours to search for the document ◆ **la ~ de l'albumine dans le sang est faite en laboratoire** tests to detect albumin in the blood are performed in a laboratory

◆ **à la recherche de** in search of ◆ **être/se mettre à la ~ de qch/qn** to be/go in search of sth/sb, to search for sth/sb ◆ **je suis à la ~ de mes lunettes** I'm searching *ou* looking for my glasses ◆ **ils sont à la ~ d'un appartement** they're looking for a flat *(Brit) ou* an apartment *(US)* ◆ **nous avons fait toute la ville à la ~ d'un livre sur la Norvège** we looked all over town for a book about Norway ◆ **il a dû se mettre à la ~ d'une nouvelle situation** he had to start looking for a new job ◆ **il est toujours à la ~ d'une bonne excuse** he's always looking for *ou* on the look-out for a good excuse

② *(= enquête)* **~s** investigations ◆ **faire des ~s** to make *ou* pursue investigations ◆ **malgré toutes leurs ~s, ils n'ont pas trouvé le document** despite all their searching they couldn't find the document ◆ **toutes nos ~s pour retrouver l'enfant sont demeurées sans résultat** all our attempts to find the child remained fruitless ◆ **jusqu'ici il a échappé aux ~s de la police** until now he has eluded the police

③ *(Scol, Univ)* **la ~** *(= activité intellectuelle, métier, spécialité)* research ◆ **~s** *(= études, enquêtes)* research ◆ **faire des ~s sur un sujet** to do *ou* carry out research into a subject ◆ **que fait-il comme ~s ?** what is he doing research on?, what is his field of research? ◆ **être dans la ~** to be a researcher ◆ **faire de la ~** to do research ◆ **il fait de la ~ en chimie** he's doing research in chemistry ◆ **bourse/étudiant de ~** research grant/student ◆ **travail de ~** research work ◆ **~ appliquée/fondamentale** applied/basic research ◆ **~ clinique** clinical research ◆ **~ et développement** research and development, R & D ◆ **~ opérationnelle** operational research

④ *(fig = poursuite)* pursuit *(de* of*)* search *(de* for*)*; ◆ **la ~ de la gloire** the pursuit of fame ◆ **la ~ de la perfection** the search *ou* quest for perfection ◆ **la ~ des plaisirs** the pursuit of pleasure

⑤ *(= raffinement) [de tenue, ameublement]* studied elegance; *(péj = affectation)* affectation ◆ **être habillé avec ~/sans ~** to be dressed with studied elegance/carelessly

⑥ *(Ordin)* search

> ⚠ **recherche** se traduit par **research** uniquement quand il désigne une activité intellectuelle.

recherché, e /ʀ(ə)ʃɛʀʃe/ (ptp de **rechercher**) ADJ ① *[tableau, livre]* much sought-after; *[produits, acteur, conférencier]* in great demand *(attrib)*, much sought-after; *(= apprécié des connaisseurs) [morceau délicat, plaisir]* choice *(épith)*, exquisite ② *(= étudié, soigné) [style]* mannered; *[expression]* studied; *[vocabulaire]* recherché, carefully chosen; *[tenue]* meticulous; *(péj)* affected

recherche-développement /ʀ(ə)ʃɛʀʃ dev(ə)lɔpmɑ̃/ NF research and development, R and D

rechercher /ʀ(ə)ʃɛʀʃe/ ▸ conjug 1 ◂ VT ① *(= chercher à trouver) [+ objet, enfant]* to search for; *[+ coupable, témoin]* to try to find, to look for; *[+ cause]* to try to discover ◆ **~ l'albumine dans le sang** to check for albumin in the blood ◆ **~ comment/pourquoi** to try to find out how/why ◆ **~ qch dans sa mémoire** to search one's memory for sth ◆ **il faudra ~ ce document dans tous les vieux dossiers** we'll have to search through all the old files to find this document ◆ **~ un mot dans un fichier** *(Ordin)* to search a file for a word ◆ **"on recherche femme de ménage"** *(annonce)* "cleaner required" ◆ **recherché pour meurtre** wanted for murder ◆ **les policiers le recherchent depuis deux ans** the police have been looking for him for two years ◆ **la police recherche ...** the police want to interview ...

② *(= viser à) [+ honneurs]* to seek; *[+ succès, plaisir]* to pursue; *[+ danger]* to court; *[+ compliments]* to fish for ◆ **~ la perfection** to strive for *ou* seek perfection ◆ **~ l'amitié/la compagnie de qn** to seek sb's friendship/company ◆ **un photographe qui recherche l'insolite** a photographer who strives to capture the unusual

③ *(= chercher à nouveau)* to search for *ou* look for again ◆ **il faudra que je recherche dans mon sac** I must have another look (for it) in my bag, I must look in my bag again ◆ **recherche donc cette lettre** have another look for that letter

④ *(= reprendre) [+ personne]* to collect, to fetch

> ⚠ **rechercher** se traduit rarement par **to research**, qui a le sens de 'faire des recherches sur'.

rechigner /ʀ(ə)ʃiɲe/ ▸ conjug 1 ◂ VI *(= renâcler)* to balk, to jib *(à, devant qch* at sth; *à faire* at doing*)*; ◆ **quand je lui ai dit de m'aider, il a rechigné** when I told him to help me he balked *ou* he made a sour face ◆ **faire qch en rechignant** to do sth with bad grace *ou* reluctantly ◆ **il m'a obéi sans trop ~** he obeyed me without making too much fuss

rechute /ʀ(ə)ʃyt/ NF *(Méd)* relapse; *(fig : dans l'erreur, le vice)* lapse *(dans* into*)*; ◆ **faire** *ou* **avoir une ~** *(Méd)* to have a relapse

rechuter /ʀ(ə)ʃyte/ ▸ conjug 1 ◂ VI *(Méd)* to relapse, to have a relapse

récidivant, e /ʀesidivɑ̃, ɑ̃t/ ADJ *(Méd)* recurring

récidive /ʀesidiv/ NF 1 *(Jur)* second *ou* subsequent offence *(Brit) ou* offense *(US)* ◆ **en cas de ~** in the event of a second *ou* subsequent offence, in the event of a repetition of the offence ◆ **escroquerie avec ~** second offence of fraud ◆ **être en ~** to reoffend, to be a recidivist *(SPÉC)* ◆ **les cas de ~ se multiplient chez les jeunes délinquants** reoffending *ou* recidivism *(SPÉC)* is on the increase among juvenile delinquents ◆ **à la première ~, je le fiche à la porte** if he does that once again, I'll throw him out 2 *(Méd)* recurrence; *(fig = nouvelle incartade)* repetition *(of one's bad ways)*

récidiver /ʀesidive/ ► conjug 1 ◄ VI *(Jur)* to reoffend; *[enfant, élève]* to do it again; *(Méd)* to recur ◆ **il a récidivé 15 minutes plus tard avec un second but** he did it again* 15 minutes later with a second goal

récidivisme /ʀesidivism/ NM reoffending, recidivism *(SPÉC)*

récidiviste /ʀesidivist/ NMF second offender, recidivist *(SPÉC)*; *(plusieurs répétitions)* habitual offender, recidivist *(SPÉC)* ◆ **condamné ~** recidivist

récidivité /ʀesidivite/ NF *(Méd)* recurring nature

récif /ʀesif/ NM reef ◆ **~ corallien** *ou* **de corail** coral reef ◆ **~ frangeant** fringing reef ◆ **~-barrière** barrier reef

récipiendaire /ʀesipjɑ̃dɛʀ/ NM *(Univ)* recipient *(of a diploma)*; *[de société]* newly elected member, member elect

récipient /ʀesipjɑ̃/ NM container

> ⚠ **récipient** ne se traduit pas par le mot anglais **recipient**.

réciprocité /ʀesipʀɔsite/ NF reciprocity

réciproque /ʀesipʀɔk/ ADJ *[sentiments, confiance, tolérance, concessions]* reciprocal, mutual; *(Math) [figure, transformation]* reciprocal; *[adjectif, verbe, pronom]* reciprocal ◆ **propositions ~s** *(Logique)* converse propositions ◆ **je lui fais confiance et c'est ~** I trust him and he trusts me ◆ **il la détestait et c'était ~** he hated her and the feeling was mutual NF ◆ **la ~** *(= l'inverse) (gén)* the opposite, the reverse; *(Logique)* the converse; *(= la pareille)* the same (treatment) ◆ **il me déteste mais la ~ n'est pas vraie** he hates me but the opposite *ou* reverse isn't true ◆ **s'attendre à la ~** to expect the same (treatment) *ou* to be paid back

réciproquement /ʀesipʀɔkmɑ̃/ ADV 1 *(= l'un l'autre)* each other, one another ◆ **ils se félicitaient ~** they congratulated each other *ou* one another 2 *(= vice versa)* vice versa ◆ **il me déteste et ~** he hates me and I hate him *ou* and the feeling is mutual ◆ **un employé doit avoir de l'estime pour son chef et ~** an employee should respect his boss and vice versa

réciproquer /ʀesipʀɔke/ ► conjug 1 ◄ VT *(Belg) [+ vœux, aide]* to reciprocate

récit /ʀesi/ NM 1 *(= action de raconter)* account, story; *(= histoire)* story; *(= genre)* narrative ◆ **~ autobiographique** autobiographical account ◆ **~ de voyage** travel story ◆ **faire le ~ de** to give an account of, to tell the story of ◆ **au ~ de ces exploits** on hearing the story of these exploits 2 *(Théât = monologue)* (narrative) monologue

récital (pl **récitals**) /ʀesital/ NM recital ◆ **donner un ~ de piano** to give a piano recital

récitant, e /ʀesitɑ̃, ɑ̃t/ ADJ *(Mus)* solo NM,F *(Mus, Radio, Théât, TV)* narrator

récitatif /ʀesitatif/ NM recitative

récitation /ʀesitasjɔ̃/ NF 1 *(= matière, classe)* recitation ◆ **composition de ~** recitation test ◆ **leçon de ~** verse to be recited by heart 2 *(= texte, poème)* recitation, piece (to be recited) 3 *(= action)* recital, reciting

réciter /ʀesite/ ► conjug 1 ◄ VT 1 *[+ leçon, chapelet, prière]* to recite 2 *(péj) [+ profession de foi, témoignage]* to trot out, to recite

réclamation /ʀeklamasjɔ̃/ NF 1 *(= plainte)* complaint; *(Sport)* objection ◆ **faire/déposer une ~** to make/lodge a complaint ◆ **adressez vos ~s à ..., pour toute ~ s'adresser à ...** all complaints should be referred to ... ◆ **"(bureau** *ou* **service des) réclamations"** "complaints department *ou* office" ◆ **téléphonez aux ~s** *(Téléc)* ring the engineers 2 *(= récrimination)* protest, complaint

> ⚠ **réclamation** ne se traduit pas par le mot anglais **reclamation**, qui a le sens de 'récupération'.

réclame /ʀeklam/ NF *(= annonce publicitaire)* advertisement, ad*, advert *(Brit)* ◆ **la ~** *(= publicité)* advertising, publicity ◆ **faire de la ~ pour un produit** to advertise *ou* publicize a product ◆ **ça ne leur fait pas de ~** that's not very good publicity for them ◆ **je ne vais pas lui faire de la ~** *(fig)* I'm not going to give him free publicity ◆ **en ~** on (special) offer ◆ **article ~** special offer

réclamer /ʀeklame/ ► conjug 1 ◄ VT 1 *(= demander) [+ silence, paix, aide]* to ask *ou* call for; *[+ argent, augmentation]* to ask for; *[+ pain]* to ask *ou* beg for ◆ **je lui ai réclamé mon stylo** I asked him for my pen back ◆ **~ qch avec insistance** *ou* **haut et fort** to clamour for sth ◆ **~ l'indulgence de qn** to beg *ou* crave sb's indulgence ◆ **je réclame la parole !** I want to say something! ◆ **il m'a réclamé à boire/un jouet** he asked me for a drink/a toy ◆ **je n'aime pas les enfants qui réclament** I don't like children who are always asking for things ◆ **l'enfant malade réclame sa mère** the sick child is calling *ou* asking for his mother, the sick child wants his mother

2 *(= exiger) [+ droit, dû]* to claim; *(plus énergique) [+ rançon]* to demand; *[+ part]* to claim, to lay claim to ◆ **~ justice** to demand justice ◆ **les policiers lui ont réclamé ses papiers d'identité** the police officers demanded (to see) his identity papers ◆ **certains réclament que cette question soit inscrite à l'ordre du jour** some people are insisting that this issue be put on the agenda ◆ **~ la démission du ministre** to call for the minister to resign *ou* for the minister's resignation

3 *(= nécessiter) [+ patience, soin]* to call for, to demand, to require

VI *(= protester)* to complain ◆ **si vous n'êtes pas content, allez ~ ailleurs** if you're not happy, go and complain *ou* make your complaints elsewhere ◆ **~ contre qch** to cry out against sth

VPR **se réclamer** ◆ **se ~ de** *[+ parti, organisation]* to claim to represent; *[+ théorie, principe]* to claim to adhere to; *[+ personne]* to claim to be a follower of ◆ **doctrine politique qui se réclame de la Révolution française** political doctrine that claims to go back to the spirit of *ou* that claims to have its roots in the French Revolution ◆ **il se réclame de l'école romantique** he claims to draw *ou* take his inspiration from the romantic school ◆ **il s'est réclamé du ministre pour obtenir ce poste** he used the minister's name (as a reference) to obtain this position

> ⚠ **réclamer** ne se traduit pas par **to reclaim**, qui a le sens de 'reconquérir', 'récupérer'.

reclassement /ʀ(ə)klasmɑ̃/ NM 1 *[de salarié]* redeployment; *[de chômeur]* placement; *[d'ex-prisonnier]* rehabilitation ◆ **~ externe** outplacement 2 *[d'objet, dossier]* reclassifying 3 *[de salaires, fonctionnaire]* regrading ◆ **~ de la fonction publique** establishing a new wage scale for the public sector

reclasser /ʀ(ə)klase/ ► conjug 1 ◄ VT 1 *(= réinsérer) [+ salarié]* to redeploy; *[+ chômeur]* to place; *[+ ex-prisonnier]* to rehabilitate 2 *[+ objet, dossier]* to reclassify 3 *(= ajuster le salaire de)* to regrade VPR **se reclasser** *(= se réinsérer)* to find a placement ◆ **elle s'est reclassée dans la restauration** she changed direction and went into catering

reclouer /ʀ(ə)klue/ ► conjug 1 ◄ VT to nail back on, to nail back together

reclus, e /ʀəkly, yz/ ADJ cloistered ◆ **il vit ~, il a** *ou* **mène une vie ~e** he leads the life of a recluse, he leads a cloistered life ◆ **une vieille dame ~e dans sa chambre** an old lady shut up in her room NM,F recluse

réclusion /ʀeklyzjɔ̃/ NF 1 *(= emprisonnement)* **~ (criminelle)** imprisonment ◆ **~ criminelle à perpétuité** life imprisonment ◆ **condamné à dix ans de ~ (criminelle)** sentenced to ten years' imprisonment 2 *(littér) (= retraite)* reclusion *(littér)*

réclusionnaire /ʀeklyzjɔnɛʀ/ NMF *(Jur)* convict

recoiffer /ʀ(ə)kwafe/ ► conjug 1 ◄ VT ◆ **~ ses cheveux** to do one's hair ◆ **~ qn** to do sb's hair VPR **se recoiffer** *(= se peigner)* to do one's hair; *(= remettre son chapeau)* to put one's hat back on

recoin /ʀəkwɛ̃/ NM *(lit)* nook; *(fig)* hidden *ou* innermost recess ◆ **les ~s du grenier** the nooks and crannies of the attic ◆ **dans les ~s de sa mémoire** in the recesses of his mind ◆ **il connaît les moindres ~s des Pyrénées** he knows the Pyrenees like the back of his hand, he knows every nook and cranny of the Pyrenees; → **coin**

recollage /ʀ(ə)kɔlaʒ/ NM *[d'étiquette]* resticking; *[de morceaux, vase]* sticking back together again; *[d'enveloppe]* resticking

recoller /ʀ(ə)kɔle/ ► conjug 1 ◄ VT 1 *[+ étiquette]* to stick back on *ou* down, to restick; *[+ morceaux, vase]* to stick back together; *[+ enveloppe]* to stick back down, to restick ◆ **~ les morceaux** *(= réconcilier)* to patch things up

2 *(= remettre)* **~ son oreille à la porte** to stick one's ear against the door again ◆ **~ qn en prison*** to stick sb back in prison* ◆ **ne recolle pas tes affaires dans ce coin !*** don't just stick your things back down in that corner!*

3 *(* = redonner)* **~ une amende à qn** to fine sb again ◆ **on nous a recollé le même moniteur que l'année dernière** we got stuck with the same group leader as last year ◆ **arrête ou je t'en recolle une*** stop it or you'll get another slap

VT INDIR **recoller à** *(Sport)* **le coureur a recollé au peloton** the runner caught up with *ou* closed the gap with the rest of the pack

VPR **se recoller** 1 *[os]* to mend, to knit (together)

2 *(* = subir)* **il a fallu se ~ la vaisselle** we got stuck with the washing-up again

3 *(* = se remettre)* **on va se ~ au boulot** let's get back down to work ◆ **allez, on s'y recolle !** come on, let's get back to it!

4 *(* = se remettre en ménage)* to get back together

récoltant, e /ʀekɔltɑ̃, ɑ̃t/ ADJ, NM,F ◆ **(propriétaire) ~** farmer *(who harvests his own crop)*, grower

récolte /ʀekɔlt/ NF 1 *(= activité) (gén)* harvesting; *[de perles]* gathering ◆ **il y a deux ~s par an** there are two harvests a year ◆ **faire la ~ des pommes de terre** to harvest potatoes 2 *[de souvenirs, documents, signatures]* collecting, gathering; *[d'argent]* collecting 3 *(= produit) [de blé, maïs, etc]* harvest, crop; *[de pommes de terre,* *fraises, raisin, miel]* crop ◆ **cette année, on a fait une excellente ~ (de fruits)** this year we had an excellent crop (of fruit) ◆ **~ sur pied** standing crop ◆ **la saison des ~s** harvest time 4 *[de documents, souvenirs]* collection; *(= argent récolté)* takings ◆ **la ~ est maigre** *(= documents)* I didn't get much information

récolter /ʀekɔlte/ ► conjug 1 ◄ **VT** 1 *(gén)* to harvest; *[+ perles]* to gather ◆ **~ ce qu'on a semé** *(fig)* to reap what one has sown; → **semer** 2 *(= recueillir) [+ souvenirs, documents, signatures]* to collect, to gather; *[+ argent]* to collect; *[+ renseignements]* to gather; * *[+ contravention, coups, mauvaise note]* to get; *(Pol) [+ suffrages, points, voix]* to gain ◆ **je n'ai récolté que des ennuis** all I got was a lot of trouble

recombinant, e /ʀ(ə)kɔ̃binɑ̃, ɑt/ **ADJ** *(Méd) [produit, virus]* recombinant

recommandable /ʀ(ə)kɔmɑ̃dabl/ **ADJ** *(= estimable)* commendable ◆ **peu ~** *[personne]* disreputable; *[comportement, moyen]* not very commendable

recommandation /ʀ(ə)kɔmɑ̃dasjɔ̃/ **NF** 1 *(= conseil) (gén, Pol)* recommendation ◆ **faire des ~s à qn** to make recommendations to sb ◆ **~s de l'ONU** UN recommendations ◆ **c'est la ~ officielle pour "jet-stream"** *(Ling)* it's the recommended official French word for "jet-stream" 2 *(= avis favorable) [d'hôtel, livre, etc]* recommendation ◆ **je l'ai acheté sur sa ~** I bought it on his recommendation 3 *(= appui)* recommendation ◆ **sur la ~ de qn** on sb's recommendation ◆ **donner une ~ à qn pour un employeur** to give sb a reference (for an employer); → **lettre** 4 *(Poste) [de lettre, paquet]* recording; *(avec valeur assurée)* registration 5 *(Rel)* commandation

recommandé, e /ʀ(ə)kɔmɑ̃de/ (ptp de **recommander**) **ADJ** 1 *(Poste) [lettre, paquet]* recorded delivery; *(avec valeur assurée)* registered ◆ **"envoi (en) recommandé"** "recorded delivery" *(Brit)*, "certified mail" *(US)*; *(avec valeur assurée)* "registered mail", "registered post" *(Brit)* ◆ **envoyer qch en ~** to send sth recorded delivery *(Brit)* ou by certified mail *(US)*; *(avec valeur assurée)* to send sth by registered mail ou post *(Brit)*; → **lettre** 2 *(= conseillé) [produit, hôtel]* recommended; *[mesure, initiative]* advisable, recommended ◆ **est-ce bien ~ ?** is it advisable? *(de faire qch* to do sth); ◆ **il est ~ de ...** it's advisable ou recommended to ... ◆ **ce n'est pas très ~** * it's not very ou really advisable, it's not really recommended

recommander /ʀ(ə)kɔmɑ̃de/ GRAMMAIRE ACTIVE 28.1, 46.4 ► conjug 1 ◄

VT 1 *(= appuyer) [+ candidat]* to recommend *(à* to); ◆ **est-il recommandé ?** has he been recommended? ◆ **sa probité intellectuelle le recommande autant que ses découvertes** his intellectual honesty commends him as much as his discoveries

2 *(= conseiller) [+ hôtel, livre, film, produit]* to recommend *(à* to); ◆ **~ à qn de faire qch** to recommend ou advise sb to do sth ◆ **le médecin lui a recommandé le repos** the doctor advised him to rest ◆ **je te recommande la modération/la discrétion** I advise you to be moderate/discreet, I recommend that you be moderate/discreet ◆ **je te recommande (de lire) ce livre** I recommend (that you read) this book ◆ **je te recommande de partir** *(ton menaçant)* I strongly advise you to leave ◆ **je ne saurais trop vous ~ de faire cette démarche** I strongly urge you to do this ◆ **est-ce bien à ~ ?** is it advisable?

3 *(Rel)* **~ son âme à Dieu** to commend one's soul to God

4 *(Poste)* to record; *(avec valeur assurée)* to register

VPR se recommander 1 *(= se réclamer de)* **se ~ de qn** to give sb's name as a reference

2 *(= s'en remettre à)* **se ~ à qn/Dieu** to commend o.s. to sb/God

3 *(= montrer sa valeur)* **il se recommande par son talent/son expérience** his talent/his experience commends him

recommencement /ʀ(ə)kɔmɑ̃smɑ̃/ **NM** ◆ **l'histoire/la vie est un éternel ~** history/life is a process of constant renewal ◆ **les ~s sont toujours difficiles** beginning again ou making a fresh start is always difficult

recommencer /ʀ(ə)kɔmɑ̃se/ ► conjug 3 ◄ **VT** 1 *(= continuer) [+ récit, lecture]* to go on with; *[+ lutte, combat]* to resume ◆ **ça fait la troisième fois que je recommence** this is the third time I've had to do it ◆ **~ à** ou **de** *(littér)* **faire qch** to begin ou start to do sth again, to begin ou start doing sth again ◆ **il a recommencé à neiger** it started to snow again ◆ **il recommence à neiger** it's snowing again

2 *(= refaire) [+ travail, expérience]* to start again *(Brit)*, to start over *(US)*; *(= répéter) [+ erreur]* to make again ◆ **laisser bouillir 5 minutes, ~ l'opération trois fois** leave to boil for 5 minutes, repeat three times ◆ **~ sa vie** to make a fresh start (in life) ◆ **si c'était à ~** if I could start ou have it over again ◆ **tout est à ~** we *(ou* I *etc)* will have to start all over again ◆ **on prend les mêmes et on recommence !** * it's always the same old people!; → **zéro**

VI *[pluie, orage]* to begin ou start again; *[combat]* to start up again, to start afresh, to resume ◆ **la pluie recommence** it's beginning ou starting to rain again, the rain is beginning ou starting again ◆ **en septembre, l'école recommence** school begins ou starts again ou resumes in September ◆ **je leur ai dit de se taire, et voilà que ça recommence !** I told them to be quiet and now they're at it again! ◆ **ça y est, ça recommence !** * here we go again! ◆ **on lui dit de ne pas le faire, mais deux minutes plus tard, il recommence** he is told not to do it but two minutes later he does it again ou he's at it again ◆ **il m'a promis qu'il ne recommencerait plus** he promised he wouldn't do it again

recomparaître /ʀ(ə)kɔ̃paʀɛtʀ/ ► conjug 57 ◄ **VI** *(Jur)* to appear (in court) again

récompense /ʀekɔ̃pɑ̃s/ **NF** *(= action, chose)* reward; *(= prix)* award ◆ **en ~ de** in return for, as a reward for ◆ **en ~ de vos services** in return for your services ◆ **je me sacrifie et voilà ma ~** I make sacrifices and that's all the reward I get ◆ **sa réussite est la ~ de son travail** his success is just reward for his work ◆ **"forte récompense"** *(dans une annonce)* "generous reward" ◆ **obtenir la plus haute ~ pour qch** to receive the highest honour for sth

> ⚠ Attention à ne pas traduire automatiquement **récompense** par le mot anglais **recompense**, qui est d'un registre plus soutenu et a le sens de 'dédommagement'.

récompenser /ʀekɔ̃pɑ̃se/ ► conjug 1 ◄ **VT** to reward ◆ **être récompensé d'avoir fait qch** to be rewarded for having done sth ◆ **j'ai été largement récompensé de mes efforts** I have been amply rewarded for my efforts ◆ **le biologiste a été récompensé pour sa découverte** the biologist got ou was given an award for his discovery ◆ **ce prix récompense le premier roman d'un auteur** this prize is awarded for an author's first novel

recomposé, e /ʀ(ə)kɔ̃poze/ (ptp de **recomposer**) **ADJ** *[passé]* reconstructed ◆ **une famille ~e** a reconstituted family, a blended family *(that includes step-parents and stepchildren)*

recomposer /ʀ(ə)kɔ̃poze/ ► conjug 1 ◄ **VT** 1 *(Téléc) [+ numéro]* to dial again, to redial 2 *[+ scène, image, passé]* to reconstruct; *[+ puzzle] (fig)* to piece together ◆ **~ une famille** to build another family 3 *(Chim)* to recompose 4 *(Typo) [+ ligne, texte]* to reset

recomposition /ʀ(ə)kɔ̃pozisjɔ̃/ **NF** 1 *(de mémoire)* reconstitution 2 *(Chim)* recomposition 3 *(Téléc) [de numéro]* redialling 4 *(Typo)* resetting

recompter /ʀ(ə)kɔ̃te/ ► conjug 1 ◄ **VT** to count again, to recount

réconciliateur, -trice /ʀekɔ̃siljatœʀ, tʀis/ **NM,F** reconciler

réconciliation /ʀekɔ̃siljasjɔ̃/ **NF** reconciliation

réconcilier /ʀekɔ̃silje/ GRAMMAIRE ACTIVE 53.4 ► conjug 7 ◄ **VT** *(Rel)* to reconcile; *[+ personnes, théories]* to reconcile *(avec* with); ◆ **~ qn avec une idée** to reconcile sb to an idea ◆ **cette émission m'a réconcilié avec la télévision** this programme restored my faith in television **VPR se réconcilier** to be ou become reconciled *(avec* with); ◆ **ils se sont réconciliés** they have made their peace with one another, they've patched things up ◆ **se ~ avec soi-même** to feel ou be at peace with o.s.

reconductible /ʀ(ə)kɔ̃dyktibl/ **ADJ** renewable

reconduction /ʀ(ə)kɔ̃dyksjɔ̃/ **NF** renewal ◆ **tacite ~** renewal by tacit agreement

reconduire /ʀ(ə)kɔ̃dɥiʀ/ ► conjug 38 ◄ **VT** 1 *(= continuer) [+ politique, budget, bail]* to renew ◆ **commande tacitement reconduite** order renewed by tacit agreement 2 *(= raccompagner)* **~ qn chez lui/à la gare** to see ou take sb (back) home/to the station ◆ **il a été reconduit à la frontière par les policiers** he was escorted (back) to the frontier by the police ◆ **~ qn à pied/en voiture chez lui** to walk/drive sb (back) home ◆ **il m'a reconduit à la porte** he showed me to the door

reconduite /ʀ(ə)kɔ̃dɥit/ **NF** *[de personne en situation irrégulière]* ◆ **~ (à la frontière)** escorting (back) to the border ◆ **le nombre de ~s exécutées** the number of people who were escorted back to the border

reconfiguration /ʀ(ə)kɔ̃figyʀasjɔ̃/ **NF** 1 *(Ordin)* reconfiguration 2 *(Écon) [d'entreprise]* re-engineering

reconfigurer /ʀ(ə)kɔ̃figyʀe/ ► conjug 1 ◄ **VT** 1 *(Ordin)* to reconfigure 2 *(Écon) [+ entreprise]* to re-engineer

réconfort /ʀekɔ̃fɔʀ/ **NM** comfort ◆ **avoir besoin de ~** to need comforting ◆ **sa présence m'a apporté un grand ~** his presence was a great comfort to me ◆ **~ moral** solace ◆ **elle a trouvé un ~ dans la lecture** she found some consolation in reading

réconfortant, e /ʀekɔ̃fɔʀtɑ̃, ɑt/ **ADJ** *(= rassurant) [parole, idée]* comforting; *(= stimulant) [remède]* tonic *(épith)*, fortifying; *[aliment]* fortifying

réconforter /ʀekɔ̃fɔʀte/ ► conjug 1 ◄ **VT** *[paroles, présence]* to comfort; *[alcool, aliment, remède]* to fortify **VPR se réconforter** *(moralement)* to comfort o.s., to cheer o.s. up, to make o.s. feel better; *(physiquement)* to fortify o.s.

reconnaissable /ʀ(ə)kɔnɛsabl/ **ADJ** recognizable *(à* by, from); ◆ **il n'était pas ~** he was unrecognizable, you wouldn't have recognized him ◆ **son style est ~ entre mille** his style is unmistakable ◆ **difficilement ~** hard to recognize

reconnaissance /ʀ(ə)kɔnɛsɑ̃s/ GRAMMAIRE ACTIVE 49

NF 1 *(= gratitude)* gratitude *(à qn* to ou towards sb); ◆ **avoir/éprouver de la ~ pour qn** to be/feel grateful to sb ◆ **en ~ de ses services/de son aide** in recognition of ou acknowledgement of ou gratitude for his services/his help ◆ **être pénétré de ~ pour la générosité de qn** to be filled with gratitude to sb for his generosity ◆ **je lui voue une ~ éternelle** I am eternally grateful to him ◆ **il n'a même pas la ~ du ventre** *(hum)* he's not even grateful for what he's been given

2 *(Pol)* *[d'État, indépendance]* recognition; *(Jur)* *[de droit]* recognition, acknowledgement; *[de diplôme, rôle, statut]* recognition ◆ **il a soif de ~ sociale** he craves social recognition

3 *(= exploration)* reconnaissance, survey; *(Mil)* reconnaissance, recce* ◆ **envoyer en ~** *(lit, fig)* to send (out) on reconnaissance *ou* on a recce* ◆ **partir en ~** *(lit, fig)* to go and reconnoitre (the ground) ◆ **faire** *ou* **pousser une ~** *(Mil)* to make a reconnaissance, to go on reconnaissance ◆ **mission/patrouille de ~** reconnaissance mission/patrol

4 *(= identification)* recognition ◆ **il lui fit un petit signe de ~** he gave her a little sign of recognition ◆ **il tenait un journal en signe de ~** he was carrying a newspaper so that he could be recognized *ou* identified

5 *(littér = aveu)* acknowledgement, admission

6 *(Ordin)* recognition ◆ **~ vocale** *ou* **de la parole** speech recognition ◆ **~ de formes** pattern recognition ◆ **~ optique de caractères** optical character recognition, OCR

COMP **reconnaissance de dette** acknowledgement of a debt, IOU
reconnaissance d'enfant legal recognition of a child
reconnaissance du mont-de-piété pawn ticket
reconnaissance d'utilité publique official approval

reconnaissant, e /ʀ(ə)kɔnɛsɑ̃, ɑt/ GRAMMAIRE ACTIVE 29.1, 31, 46.1, 46.3, 46.4, 47.1, 48.1, 49 ADJ grateful *(à qn de qch* to sb for sth); ◆ **se montrer ~ envers qn** to show one's gratitude to sb ◆ **je vous serais ~ de me répondre rapidement** I would be grateful if you would reply quickly *ou* for a speedy reply

reconnaître /ʀ(ə)kɔnɛtʀ/ GRAMMAIRE ACTIVE 38.1, 40.2, 45.2, 53.6 ▸ conjug 57 ◂

VT 1 *(gén = identifier)* to recognize ◆ **je l'ai reconnu à sa voix** I recognized him *ou* I knew it was him *ou* I could tell it was him from *ou* by (the sound of) his voice ◆ **je le reconnaîtrais entre mille** I'd recognize him anywhere ◆ **elle reconnut l'enfant à son foulard rouge** she recognized the child by his red scarf ◆ **~ la voix/le pas de qn** to recognize sb's voice/walk ◆ **~ le corps** *(d'un mort)* to identify the body ◆ **ces jumeaux sont impossibles à ~** these twins are impossible to tell apart, it's impossible to tell which of these twins is which ◆ **on reconnaît un gros fumeur à ses doigts jaunis** you can tell *ou* recognize a heavy smoker by his stained fingers ◆ **on reconnaît bien là sa paresse** that's just typical of his laziness ◆ **je le reconnais bien là !** that's just like him!, that's him all over! ◆ **méfiez-vous, il sait ~ un mensonge** be careful – he knows *ou* recognizes *ou* he can spot a lie when he hears one ◆ **on ne le reconnaît plus** you wouldn't know *ou* recognize him now

2 *(= convenir de)* *[+ innocence, supériorité, valeur]* to recognize, to acknowledge; *(= avouer)* *[+ torts]* to recognize, to acknowledge, to admit ◆ **il reconnut peu à peu la difficulté de la tâche** he gradually came to recognize the difficulty of the task ◆ **il faut ~ les faits** we must face *ou* recognize the facts ◆ **on lui reconnaît une qualité, il est honnête** he is recognized as having one quality – he is honest ◆ **il faut ~ qu'il faisait très froid** admittedly it was very cold ◆ **il a reconnu s'être trompé/qu'il s'était trompé** he admitted to *ou* acknowledged making a mistake/that he had made a mistake ◆ **je reconnais que j'avais tout à fait oublié ce rendez-vous** I must confess *ou* admit (that) I had completely forgotten this appointment

3 *(= admettre)* *[+ maître, chef]* to recognize; *(Pol)* *[+ État, gouvernement]* to recognize; *(Jur)* *[+ enfant]* to recognize legally, to acknowledge; *[+ dette]* to acknowledge; *[+ diplôme]* to recognize ◆ **~ qn pour** *ou* **comme chef** to acknowledge *ou* recognize sb as (one's) leader ◆ **~ la compétence d'un tribunal** to acknowledge *ou* recognize the competence of a court ◆ **~ qn coupable** to find sb guilty ◆ **~ sa signature** to acknowledge one's signature ◆ **il ne reconnaît à personne le droit d'intervenir** he doesn't acknowledge that anyone has the right to intervene

4 *(Mil)* *[+ côte, île, terrain]* to reconnoitre ◆ **on va aller ~ les lieux** *ou* **le terrain** we're going to see how the land lies, we're going to reconnoitre (the ground) ◆ **les gangsters étaient certainement venus ~ les lieux auparavant** the gangsters had probably been to look over the place beforehand

5 *(littér = montrer de la gratitude pour)* to recognize, to acknowledge

VPR **se reconnaître** 1 *(dans la glace)* to recognize o.s.; *(entre personnes)* to recognize each other ◆ **elle ne se reconnaît pas du tout dans ses filles** she (just) can't see any likeness between herself and her daughters

2 *(lit, fig = se retrouver)* to find one's way about *ou* around ◆ **je ne m'y reconnais plus** I'm completely lost ◆ **je commence à me ~** I'm beginning to find my bearings

3 *(= être reconnaissable)* to be recognizable *(à* by); ◆ **le pêcher se reconnaît à ses fleurs roses** the peach tree is recognizable by its pink flowers, you can tell a peach tree by its pink flowers

4 *(= s'avouer)* **se ~ vaincu** to admit *ou* acknowledge defeat ◆ **se ~ coupable** to admit *ou* acknowledge one's guilt

reconnecter VT, **se reconnecter** VPR /ʀ(ə)kɔnɛkte/ ▸ conjug 1 ◂ *(gén)* to reconnect *(à* to); *(Ordin)* to log on again

reconnu, e /ʀ(ə)kɔny/ (ptp de **reconnaître**) ADJ *[fait]* recognized, accepted; *[auteur, chef, diplôme]* recognized ◆ **c'est un fait ~ que ...** it's a recognized *ou* an accepted fact that ... ◆ **il est ~ que ...** it is recognized *ou* accepted *ou* acknowledged that ...

reconquérir /ʀ(ə)kɔ̃keʀiʀ/ ▸ conjug 21 ◂ VT *(Mil)* to reconquer, to recapture, to capture back; *[+ personne, titre, siège de député]* to win back; *[+ dignité, liberté]* to recover, to win back

reconquête /ʀ(ə)kɔ̃kɛt/ NF *(Mil)* reconquest, recapture; *[de droit, liberté]* recovery

reconsidérer /ʀ(ə)kɔ̃sideʀe/ ▸ conjug 6 ◂ VT to reconsider

reconstituant, e /ʀ(ə)kɔ̃stitɥɑ̃, ɑt/ ADJ *[aliment, régime]* energy-giving NM energy-giving food, energizer

reconstituer /ʀ(ə)kɔ̃stitɥe/ ▸ conjug 1 ◂ VT 1 *[+ parti, armée, association]* to re-form; *[+ fortune, capital, réserves]* to build up again ◆ **bifteck haché reconstitué** mincemeat *(Brit)* *ou* hamburger *(US)* patty 2 *[+ crime, faits, histoire]* to reconstruct, to piece together; *[+ décor]* to recreate; *[+ puzzle]* to piece together; *[+ fichier]* to rebuild; *[+ texte]* to restore, to reconstitute; *[+ édifice, vieux quartier]* to reconstruct 3 *[+ objet brisé]* to put *ou* piece together 4 *(Bio)* *[+ organisme]* to regenerate VPR **se reconstituer** *[équipe, parti]* to re-form; *[+ réserves]* to be built up again

reconstitution /ʀ(ə)kɔ̃stitysjɔ̃/ NF 1 *[de parti, armée, association]* re-forming; *[de fortune, capital, réserves]* rebuilding 2 *[de crime, faits, puzzle, histoire]* reconstruction, piecing together; *[de fichier]* rebuilding; *[de texte]* restoration, reconstitution ◆ **la ~ du crime** the reconstruction of the crime *(in the presence of the examining magistrate and the accused)* 3 *[d'objet brisé]* repairing 4 *(Bio)* *[d'organisme]* regeneration

reconstructeur, -trice /ʀ(ə)kɔ̃stʀyktœʀ, tʀis/ ADJ *[chirurgie]* reconstructive

reconstruction /ʀ(ə)kɔ̃stʀyksjɔ̃/ NF *[de maison, ville, pays]* rebuilding, reconstruction; *[de fortune]* rebuilding

reconstructive /ʀəkɔ̃stʀyktiv/ ADJ F **chirurgie reconstructive** reconstructive surgery

reconstruire /ʀ(ə)kɔ̃stʀɥiʀ/ ▸ conjug 38 ◂ VT *[+ maison, ville, pays]* to rebuild, to reconstruct; *[+ fortune]* to build up again, to rebuild ◆ **il a dû ~ sa vie** he had to rebuild his life

recontacter /ʀ(ə)kɔ̃takte/ ▸ conjug 1 ◂ VT ◆ **~ qn** to get in touch with sb again ◆ **je vous recontacterai quand j'aurai pris une décision** I'll get in touch with you again when I've made a decision

reconversion /ʀ(ə)kɔ̃vɛʀsjɔ̃/ NF *[d'usine]* reconversion; *[de personnel]* redeployment, retraining; *[de région]* redevelopment; *[d'économie]* restructuring ◆ **stage/plan de ~** retraining course/scheme

reconvertir /ʀ(ə)kɔ̃vɛʀtiʀ/ ▸ conjug 2 ◂ VT *[+ personnel]* to retrain; *[+ région]* to redevelop; *[+ économie, entreprise]* to restructure ◆ **l'ancienne fabrique a été reconvertie en école** the old factory has been converted into a school VPR **se reconvertir** *[personne]* to move into *ou* turn to a new type of employment; *[entreprise]* to change activity ◆ **il s'est reconverti dans la publicité** he has changed direction and gone into advertising ◆ **nous nous sommes reconvertis dans le textile** we have moved over *ou* gone over into textiles

recopier /ʀ(ə)kɔpje/ ▸ conjug 7 ◂ VT *(= transcrire)* to copy out, to write out; *(= recommencer)* to copy out *ou* write out again ◆ **~ ses notes au propre** to write up one's notes, to make a clean *ou* fair *(Brit)* copy of one's notes

record /ʀ(ə)kɔʀ/ NM *(Sport)* record ◆ **~ masculin/féminin** men's/women's record ◆ **~ de vitesse/d'altitude** speed/altitude record ◆ **~ du monde/d'Europe** world/European record ◆ **le yen a battu son ~ historique** the yen has hit *ou* reached a record high *ou* an all-time high ◆ **le ministre bat tous les ~s d'impopularité** the minister breaks *ou* beats all the records for unpopularity ◆ **ça bat (tous) les ~s !*** that beats everything! ◆ **ce film a connu des ~s d'affluence** the film broke box-office records ◆ **un ~ d'abstentions** a record number of abstentions ◆ **j'ai lu deux livres en une semaine, c'est mon ~** I read two books within a week, it's a personal record

ADJ INV *[chiffre, niveau, production, taux]* record *(épith)* ◆ **les bénéfices ont atteint un montant ~ de 5 milliards** profits reached a record total of 5 billion ◆ **en un temps ~** in record time

recorder /ʀ(ə)kɔʀde/ ▸ conjug 1 ◂ VT *[+ raquette]* to restring

recordman /ʀ(ə)kɔʀdman/ (pl **recordmen** /ʀ(ə)kɔʀdmɛn/) NM (men's) record holder

> ⚠ **recordman** ne se traduit pas par **record man**, qui n'existe pas en anglais.

recordwoman /ʀ(ə)kɔʀdwuman/ (pl **recordwomen** /ʀ(ə)kɔʀdwumɛn/) NF (women's) record holder

> ⚠ **recordwoman** ne se traduit pas par **record woman**, qui n'existe pas en anglais.

recorriger /ʀəkɔʀiʒe/ ▸ conjug 3 ◂ VT to recorrect, to correct again; *(Scol)* to mark *ou* grade again

recoucher /ʀ(ə)kuʃe/ ▸ conjug 1 ◂ VT *[+ enfant]* to put back to bed; *[+ objet]* to lay *ou* put down again VPR **se recoucher** to go back to bed

recoudre /ʀ(ə)kudʀ/ ▸ conjug 48 ◂ VT *[+ ourlet]* to sew up again; *[+ bouton]* to sew back on, to sew on again; *[+ plaie]* to stitch up (again), to put stitches (back) in; *[+ opéré]* to stitch (back) up

recoupement /R(ə)kupmɑ̃/ NM cross-check, cross-checking *(NonC)* ◆ **par** ~ by cross-checking ◆ **faire des ~s** to cross-check

recouper /R(ə)kupe/ ▸ conjug 1 ◂ VT 1 *(gén)* to cut again; *[+ vêtement]* to recut; *[+ route]* to intersect ◆ ~ **du pain** to cut (some) more bread ◆ **elle m'a recoupé une tranche de viande** she cut me another slice of meat 2 *[+ vin]* to blend 3 *[témoignage]* to tie up *ou* match up with, to confirm, to support VI *(Cartes)* to cut again VPR **se recouper** *[faits]* to tie *ou* match up, to confirm *ou* support one another; *[droites, cercles]* to intersect; *[chiffres, résultats]* to add up

recourbé, e /R(ə)kuRbe/ (ptp de **recourber**) ADJ *(gén)* curved; *(accidentellement)* bent; *[bec]* curved, hooked ◆ **nez** ~ hooknose

recourber /R(ə)kuRbe/ ▸ conjug 1 ◂ VT *[+ bois]* to bend (over); *[+ métal]* to bend, to curve VPR **se recourber** to curve (up), to bend (up)

recourir /R(ə)kuRiR/ ▸ conjug 11 ◂ VT *(Sport)* to run again VT INDIR **recourir à** *[+ opération, emprunt]* to resort to, to have recourse to; *[+ force]* to resort to; *[+ personne]* to turn to, to appeal to ◆ **j'ai recouru à son aide** I turned *ou* appealed to him for help VI 1 *(Sport)* to race again, to run again ◆ **j'ai recouru le chercher** I ran back *ou* raced back *ou* nipped back* *(Brit)* to get it 2 *(Jur)* ~ **contre qn** to (lodge an) appeal against sb

recours /R(ə)kuR/ NM resort, recourse; *(Jur)* appeal ◆ **le ~ à la violence ne sert à rien** resorting to violence doesn't do any good ◆ **nous n'avons plus qu'un** ~ there's only one course (of action) left open to us ◆ **il n'y a aucun ~ contre cette décision** there is no way of changing this decision, there is no appeal possible ◆ **il n'y a aucun ~ contre cette maladie** there is no cure *ou* remedy for this disease ◆ **la situation est sans** ~ there's nothing we can do about the situation, there's no way out of the situation

◆ **avoir recours à** *[+ mesure, solution]* to resort to, to have recourse to; *[+ force]* to resort to; *[+ personne]* to turn to, to appeal to

◆ **en dernier recours** as a last resort ◆ **la banque n'effectuera des licenciements qu'en dernier** ~ the bank will not make people redundant except as a last resort ◆ **en dernier ~, un tirage au sort aura lieu** if all else fails there will be a draw

COMP **recours en cassation** appeal to the supreme court

recours contentieux *submission for a legal settlement*

recours en grâce *(= remise de peine)* plea for pardon; *(= commutation de peine)* plea for clemency

recours gracieux *submission for an out-of-court settlement*

recours hiérarchique disciplinary complaint

recouvrable /R(ə)kuvRabl/ ADJ 1 *[impôt]* collectable, which can be collected; *[créance]* recoverable, reclaimable, retrievable 2 *[peinture]* recoatable

recouvrement /R(ə)kuvRəmɑ̃/ NM 1 *(= action)* covering (up); *(= résultat)* cover ◆ **assemblage à** ~ *(Constr)* lap joint 2 *(Fin) [de cotisations]* collection, payment; *[d'impôt]* collection, levying; *(littér) [de créance]* recovery 3 *(littér) [de forces, santé]* recovery

recouvrer /R(ə)kuvRe/ ▸ conjug 1 ◂ VT 1 *[+ santé, vue]* to recover, to regain; *[+ liberté]* to regain; *[+ amitié]* to win back ◆ ~ **la raison** to recover one's senses, to come back to one's senses 2 *(Fin) [+ cotisation]* to collect; *[+ impôt]* to collect, to levy; *(littér) [+ créance]* to recover

recouvrir /R(ə)kuvRiR/ ▸ conjug 18 ◂ VT 1 *(entièrement)* to cover ◆ **la neige recouvre le sol** snow covers the ground ◆ **recouvert d'écailles/d'eau** covered in *ou* with scales/water ◆ ~ **un mur de papier peint/de carreaux** to paper/tile a wall ◆ **le sol était recouvert d'un tapis** the floor was carpeted, there was a carpet on the floor ◆ **le visage recouvert d'un voile** her face covered by a veil ◆ **elle avait la tête recouverte d'un fichu** she had a shawl around her head ◆ **recouvre la casserole/les haricots** put the lid on the saucepan/the beans

2 *(à nouveau) [+ fauteuil, livre]* to re-cover, to put a new cover on; *[+ casserole]* to put the lid back on ◆ ~ **un enfant qui dort** to cover (up) a sleeping child again

3 *(= cacher) [+ intentions]* to conceal, to hide, to mask; *(= englober) [+ aspects, questions]* to cover

VPR **se recouvrir** 1 *(= se garnir)* **se ~ d'eau/de terre** to become covered in *ou* with water/earth ◆ **le ciel se recouvre** the sky is getting cloudy *ou* becoming overcast again

2 *(= se chevaucher)* to overlap ◆ **les deux feuilles se recouvrent partiellement** the two sheets overlap slightly

recracher /R(ə)kRaʃe/ ▸ conjug 1 ◂ VT to spit out (again) ◆ **l'usine recrachait ses eaux usées dans la rivière** the factory spewed out its waste water into the river VI to spit again

récré* /RekRe/ NF (abrév de **récréation**) break, recess *(US)* ◆ **à la** ~ at break time, at recess time *(US)*

récréatif, -ive /RekReatif, iv/ ADJ *[lecture]* light *(épith)* ◆ **soirée récréative** evening's recreation *ou* entertainment

récréation /RekReasjɔ̃/ NF 1 *(Scol)* break, recess *(US)* ◆ **aller en** ~ to go out for (the) break ◆ **les enfants sont en** ~ the children are having their break, the children are on recess *(US)*; → **cour** 2 *(gén = détente)* recreation, relaxation

> ⚠ Au sens scolaire, **récréation** ne se traduit généralement pas par le mot anglais **recreation**.

recréer /R(ə)kRee/ ▸ conjug 1 ◂ VT to re-create

récréer /RekRee/ ▸ conjug 1 ◂ *(littér)* VT to entertain, to amuse VPR **se récréer** to amuse o.s.

recrépir /R(ə)kRepiR/ ▸ conjug 2 ◂ VT to resurface (with roughcast *ou* pebble dash) ◆ **faire ~ sa maison** to have the roughcast *ou* pebble dash redone on one's house

recreuser /R(ə)kRøze/ ▸ conjug 1 ◂ VT *[+ trou] (de nouveau)* to dig again; *(davantage)* to dig deeper; *[+ question]* to go further *ou* deeper into, to dig deeper into

récrier (se) /RekRije/ ▸ conjug 7 ◂ VPR *(littér)* to exclaim ◆ **se ~ d'admiration/d'indignation/de surprise** to exclaim *ou* cry out in admiration/in indignation/in surprise ◆ **se ~ contre qch** to cry out against sth

récriminateur, -trice /RekRiminatœR, tRis/ ADJ remonstrative, complaining

récrimination /RekRiminasjɔ̃/ NF recrimination, remonstration, complaint

récriminatoire /RekRiminatwaR/ ADJ *[discours, propos]* remonstrative

récriminer /RekRimine/ ▸ conjug 1 ◂ VI to recriminate, to remonstrate *(contre* against) to complain bitterly *(contre* about)

récrire /RekRiR/ ▸ conjug 39 ◂ VT ⇒ **réécrire**

recroquevillé, e /R(ə)kRɔk(ə)vije/ (ptp de **recroqueviller**) ADJ *[feuille, fleur]* shrivelled (up), curled (up); *[personne]* hunched *ou* huddled up ◆ **il était tout ~ dans un coin** he was all hunched up *ou* huddled up in a corner

recroqueviller (se) /R(ə)kRɔk(ə)vije/ ▸ conjug 1 ◂ VPR *[feuille, fleur]* to shrivel up, to curl up; *[personne]* to huddle *ou* curl o.s. up

recru, e¹ /RəkRy/ ADJ *(littér)* ◆ ~ **(de fatigue)** exhausted, tired out

recrudescence /R(ə)kRydesɑ̃s/ NF *[de criminalité, combats]* (fresh *ou* new) upsurge *ou* outbreak; *[d'épidémie]* (fresh *ou* new) outbreak ◆ **devant la ~ des vols** in view of the increasing number of thefts ◆ **il y a eu une ~ de froid** there was another spell of even colder weather

recrudescent, e /R(ə)kRydesɑ̃, ɑ̃t/ ADJ *(littér)* recrudescent ◆ **épidémie ~e** epidemic which is on the increase *ou* upsurge again

recrue² /RəkRy/ NF *(Mil)* recruit; *(fig)* recruit, new member ◆ **faire une (nouvelle)** ~ *(fig)* to gain a (new) recruit, to recruit a new member

recrutement /R(ə)kRytmɑ̃/ NM *(= action)* recruitment, recruiting; *(= recrues)* recruits ◆ ~ **externe/interne** external/internal recruitment

recruter /R(ə)kRyte/ ▸ conjug 1 ◂ VT *(Mil, fig)* to recruit ◆ **se ~ dans** *ou* **parmi** to be recruited from, to come from ◆ ~ **des cadres pour une entreprise** to headhunt for a company

recruteur, -euse /R(ə)kRytœR, øz/ NM,F *(Mil)* recruiting officer; *(pour cadres)* headhunter ADJ recruiting ◆ **agent** ~ recruiting agent

recta †* /Rɛkta/ ADV *[payer]* promptly, on the nail*; *[arriver]* on the dot* ◆ **quand j'ai les pieds mouillés, c'est ~, j'attrape un rhume** whenever I get my feet wet that's it*, I catch a cold

rectal, e (mpl **-aux**) /Rɛktal, o/ ADJ rectal

rectangle /Rɛktɑ̃gl/ NM *(gén)* rectangle, oblong; *(Math)* rectangle ◆ ~ **blanc** † *(TV)* "suitable for adults only" sign ADJ right-angled

rectangulaire /Rɛktɑ̃gylɛR/ ADJ rectangular, oblong

recteur /Rɛktœr/ NM 1 ◆ ~ **(d'académie)** ~ **chancelier des universités** ≃ chief education officer *(Brit)*, director of education *(Brit)*, commissioner of education *(US)*; → **ACADÉMIE** 2 *(Rel) (= prêtre)* priest; *(= directeur)* rector

rectifiable /Rɛktifjabl/ ADJ *[erreur]* rectifiable, which can be put right *ou* corrected; *[alcool]* rectifiable

rectificateur /Rɛktifikatœr/ NM *(Chim)* rectifier

rectificatif, -ive /Rɛktifikatif, iv/ ADJ *[compte]* rectified, corrected ◆ **acte ~, note rectificative** correction NM correction ◆ **apporter un** ~ to make a correction

rectification /Rɛktifikasjɔ̃/ NF 1 *[d'erreur]* rectification, correction; *[de paroles, texte]* correction ◆ **permettez-moi une petite** ~ if I might make a small rectification ◆ **apporter des ~s** to make some corrections 2 *[de route, tracé, virage]* straightening; *[de mauvaise position]* correction 3 *(Tech) [de pièce]* truing up, making true 4 *(Chim, Math)* rectification

rectifier /Rɛktifje/ ▸ conjug 7 ◂ VT 1 *(= corriger) [+ calcul, erreur]* to correct, to rectify; *[+ paroles, texte]* to correct; *[+ facture, contrat]* to amend ◆ **"non, ils étaient deux" rectifia-t-il** "no, actually there were two of them" he said ◆ **je voudrais ~ une ou deux choses qui ont été dites** I'd like to set the record straight

2 *(= ajuster, modifier) (gén)* to adjust; *[+ route, tracé]* to straighten; *[+ virage]* to straighten (out); *[+ mauvaise position]* to correct; *[+ assaisonnement]* to correct ◆ ~ **sa position/l'alignement** *(Mil)* to correct one's stance/the alignment ◆ ~ **le tir** *(lit)* to adjust one's aim; *(fig)* to change one's tack ◆ **il rectifia la position du rétroviseur** he adjusted his driving mirror

3 *(Tech) [+ pièce]* to true (up), to adjust

4 *(Chim, Math)* to rectify

5 (* = tuer) **il a été rectifié, il s'est fait** ~ they did away with him *, he got himself killed *ou* bumped off * *(Brit)*

rectifieur, -ieuse /ʀɛktifjœʀ, jøz/ NM,F (= ouvrier) grinding machine operator NF **rectifieuse** (= machine) grinding machine

rectiligne /ʀɛktiliɲ/ ADJ *(gén)* straight; *[mouvement]* rectilinear; *(Géom)* rectilinear NM *(Géom)* rectilinear angle

rectitude /ʀɛktityd/ NF *[de caractère]* rectitude, uprightness; *[de jugement]* soundness, rectitude; *(littér) [de ligne]* straightness

recto /ʀɛkto/ NM front (of a page), first side, recto *(frm)* ♦ ~ **verso** on both sides (of the page) ♦ **voir au** ~ see other side

rectoral, e (pl **-aux**) /ʀɛktɔʀal, o/ ADJ of the education office *ou* authority

rectorat /ʀɛktɔʀa/ NM (= bureaux) education offices; (= administration) education authority

rectrice /ʀɛktʀis/ ADJ F, NF ♦ **(plume)** ~ rectrix

rectum /ʀɛktɔm/ NM rectum

reçu, e /ʀ(ə)sy/ (ptp de **recevoir**) ADJ 1 *[usages, coutumes]* accepted; → **idée** 2 *[candidat]* successful NM 1 (= quittance) receipt 2 (= candidat) successful candidate ♦ **il y a eu 50 ~s** there were 50 passes *ou* successful candidates

recueil /ʀəkœj/ NM *(gén)* book, collection; *[de documents]* compendium ♦ ~ **de poèmes** anthology *ou* collection of poems ♦ ~ **de morceaux choisis** anthology ♦ ~ **de faits** *(fig)* collection of facts

recueillement /ʀ(ə)kœjmɑ̃/ NM meditation, contemplation ♦ **écouter avec un grand ~** to listen reverently ♦ **écouter avec un ~ quasi religieux** to listen with almost religious respect *ou* reverence

recueilli, e /ʀ(ə)kœji/ (ptp de **recueillir**) ADJ meditative, contemplative

recueillir /ʀ(ə)kœjiʀ/ ▸ conjug 12 ◂ VT 1 (= récolter) *[+ graines]* to gather, to collect; *[+ argent, documents]* to collect; *[+ liquide]* to collect, to catch; *[+ suffrages]* to win; *[+ héritage]* to inherit ♦ ~ **le fruit de ses efforts** to reap the rewards of one's efforts ♦ ~ **de vifs applaudissements** *[orateur, discours]* to be enthusiastically *ou* warmly applauded ♦ **il a recueilli 100 voix** he got *ou* polled 100 votes 2 (= accueillir) *[+ réfugié]* to take in ♦ ~ **qn sous son toit** to receive sb in one's home, to welcome sb into one's home 3 (= enregistrer) *[+ déposition, chansons anciennes]* to take down, to take note of; *[+ opinion]* to record VPR **se recueillir** *(Rel, gén)* to collect *ou* gather one's thoughts, to commune with o.s. ♦ **aller se ~ sur la tombe de qn** to go and meditate at sb's grave

recuire /ʀ(ə)kɥiʀ/ ▸ conjug 38 ◂ VT *[+ viande]* to recook, to cook again; *[+ pain, gâteaux]* to rebake, to bake again; *[+ poterie]* to bake *ou* fire again; *(Tech) [+ métal]* to anneal VI *[viande]* to cook for a further length of time ♦ **faire ~** *[+ viande]* to cook a little longer; *[+ gâteau]* to bake a little longer

recuit, e /ʀəkɥi, it/ ADJ *[visage, peau]* sunburnt; *(littér) [haine]* deep-rooted

recul /ʀ(ə)kyl/ NM 1 (= éloignement dans le temps, l'espace) distance ♦ **avec le ~ (du temps), on juge mieux les événements** when some time has elapsed one can judge events better ♦ **prendre du ~** *(lit)* to step back, to stand back; *(fig)* to stand back *(par rapport à* from); ♦ **après cette dispute, j'ai besoin de prendre un peu de ~** after that quarrel I need to take stock ♦ **avec du** *ou* **le ~** with (the benefit of) hindsight ♦ **il manque de ~** *(pour faire demi-tour)* he hasn't got enough room; *(pour prendre une photo)* he's too close; *(pour juger objectivement)* he's too involved ♦ **nous manquons de ~** *ou* **nous n'avons pas assez de ~ pour mesurer les effets à long terme** not enough time has passed *ou* it is still too soon for us to assess the long-term effects ♦ **cette salle n'a pas assez de ~** you can't get back far enough in this room

2 (= retraite) *[d'armée]* retreat; *[de patron, négociateur]* climb-down * *(par rapport à* from); ♦ **j'ai été étonné de son ~ devant la menace de grève** I was amazed at how he caved in once there was a threat of a strike ♦ **avoir un mouvement de ~** to recoil, to shrink back *(devant, par rapport à* from)

3 (= déclin) *[de civilisation, langue, épidémie]* decline *(de* of); *[d'investissements, ventes, prix, taux]* decline, fall, drop *(de* in); ♦ **être en ~** *[épidémie]* to be on the decline, to be subsiding; *[chômage]* to be on the decline, to be going down; *[monnaie]* to be falling, to lose value; *[parti]* to be losing ground ♦ **un ~ de la majorité aux élections** a setback for the ruling party in the election ♦ **le ~ du dollar par rapport à l'euro** the fall of the dollar against the euro ♦ **le ~ de la livre sur les marchés internationaux** the loss of value of the pound on the international markets ♦ **le dollar est en net ~ par rapport à hier** the dollar has dropped sharply since yesterday ♦ **le ~ de l'influence française en Afrique** the decline of French influence in Africa

4 *[d'arme à feu]* recoil, kick

5 (= report) *[d'échéance]* postponement

6 (= déplacement) *[de véhicule]* backward movement; → **phare**

reculade /ʀ(ə)kylad/ NF *(Mil)* retreat, withdrawal; *(fig péj)* retreat, climb-down * ♦ **c'est la ~ générale** they're all backing down

reculé, e /ʀ(ə)kyle/ (ptp de **reculer**) ADJ *[époque]* remote, distant; *[région, village]* remote, out-of-the-way *(épith)*, out of the way *(attrib)* ♦ **en ces temps ~s** in those far-off times

reculer /ʀ(ə)kyle/ ▸ conjug 1 ◂ VI 1 *[personne]* to move *ou* step back; *(par peur)* to draw back, to back away; *[automobiliste, automobile]* to reverse, to back (up), to move back; *[cheval]* to back; *[mer]* to recede; *(Mil)* to retreat ♦ ~ **de deux pas** to go back *ou* move back two paces, to take two paces back ♦ ~ **devant l'ennemi** to retreat from *ou* draw back from the enemy ♦ ~ **d'horreur** to draw back *ou* shrink back in horror, to recoil (in horror) ♦ **c'est ~ pour mieux sauter** it's just putting off the evil day ♦ **faire ~** *[+ foule]* to move back, to force back; *[+ cheval]* to move back; *[+ ennemi]* to push *ou* force back; *[+ désert]* to drive back ♦ **ce spectacle le fit ~** he recoiled at the sight

2 (= hésiter) to shrink back; (= changer d'avis) to back down, to back out ♦ **tu ne peux plus ~ maintenant** you can't back out *ou* back down now ♦ ~ **devant la dépense/difficulté** to shrink from the expense/difficulty ♦ **je ne reculerai devant rien, rien ne me fera ~** I'll stop *ou* stick *(Brit)* at nothing, nothing will stop me ♦ **il ne faut pas ~ devant ses obligations** you mustn't shrink from your obligations ♦ **il ne recule pas devant la dénonciation** he doesn't flinch at *ou* shrink from informing on people ♦ **cette condition ferait ~ de plus braves** this condition would make braver men (than I *ou* you *etc*) draw back *ou* hesitate

3 (= diminuer) *(gén)* to be on the decline; *[patois]* to be on the decline, to lose ground; *[chômage]* to decline, to subside, to go down; *[eaux]* to subside, to recede, to go down; *[incendie]* to subside, to lose ground; *[civilisation, science]* to be on the decline ♦ **il a reculé en français** *[élève]* he's gone down in French ♦ **faire ~ l'épidémie** to get the epidemic under control ♦ **faire ~ le chômage** to reduce the number of unemployed ♦ **faire ~ l'inflation** to curb inflation ♦ **les mines d'or ont reculé d'un point** *(Bourse)* gold shares fell back a point

4 *[arme à feu]* to recoil

VT *[+ chaise, meuble]* to move back, to push back; *[+ véhicule]* to reverse, to back (up); *[+ frontières]* to extend, to push *ou* move back; *[+ livraison, date]* to put back, to postpone; *[+ décision]* to put off, to defer, to postpone; *[+ échéance]* to defer, to postpone

VPR **se reculer** to stand *ou* step *ou* move back, to take a step back

reculons /ʀ(ə)kylɔ̃/ **à reculons** LOC ADV *[aller, marcher]* backwards; *[accepter]* reluctantly, unwillingly ♦ **sortir à ~ d'une pièce/d'un garage** to back out of a room/a garage ♦ **ce pays entre à ~ dans l'Europe** this country is reluctant about going into Europe ♦ **ils y vont à ~** *(fig)* they're dragging their feet

récup * /ʀekyp/ NF (abrév de **récupération**) *[de déchets, ferraille, chiffons, emballages]* recycling; *[de chaleur, énergie]* recovery; *[de délinquant]* rehabilitation ♦ **matériaux de ~** salvaged materials ♦ **son appartement est meublé avec de la ~** his flat is furnished with stuff salvaged from skips ♦ **l'art de la ~** making things out of junk

récupérable /ʀekypeʀabl/ ADJ *[créance]* recoverable; *[heures]* which can be made up; *[ferraille]* which can be salvaged; *[vieux habits]* usable ♦ **un délinquant qui n'est plus ~** an offender with no potential for rehabilitation ♦ **il n'est plus ~** there is no hope of reforming him

récupérateur, -trice /ʀekypeʀatœʀ, tʀis/ ADJ *(péj) [discours, procédé]* designed to win over dissenting opinion (*ou* groups *etc*) NM,F (= personne) *[de carton, plastique, papier]* salvage dealer; *[de métal]* scrap metal dealer, scrap merchant NM *(Tech) [de chaleur]* recuperator, regenerator; *[d'arme]* recuperator

récupération /ʀekypeʀasjɔ̃/ NF 1 *[d'argent, biens, forces]* recovery; *(Ordin) [+ de données, fichier]* retrieval, recovery ♦ **la capacité de ~ de l'organisme** the body's powers of recuperation *ou* recovery 2 *[de déchets, ferraille, chiffons, emballages]* recycling; *[de chaleur, énergie]* recovery; *[de délinquant]* rehabilitation ♦ **matériaux de ~** salvaged materials 3 *[de journées de travail]* making up ♦ **deux jours de ~** two days to make up 4 *(Pol : péj) [de mouvement, personnes]* takeover, hijacking

récupérer /ʀekypeʀe/ ▸ conjug 6 ◂ VT 1 *[+ argent, biens, territoire]* to get back, to recover; *[+ objet prêté]* to get back; *[+ forces]* to recover, to get back, to regain; *(Ordin)* to retrieve, to recover; (= aller chercher) *[+ enfant, bagages]* to pick up, to collect; *[+ sièges, voix]* (= reprendre à un autre) to take; (= s'approprier) to win, to take ♦ **il a récupéré son siège** *(Pol)* he won back his seat ♦ **ils sont allés ~ les pilotes abattus en territoire ennemi** they went to rescue the pilots that had been shot down in enemy territory

2 (= réhabiliter) *[+ délinquant]* to rehabilitate, to reform

3 *[+ ferraille, chiffons, emballages]* to salvage, to reclaim; *[+ chaleur, énergie]* to recover; *[+ déchets]* to recycle; *[+ délinquant]* to rehabilitate ♦ **toutes les pêches étaient pourries, je n'ai rien pu ~** all the peaches were rotten, I couldn't use any of them ♦ **regarde si tu peux ~ quelque chose dans ces vieux habits** see if you can find anything usable among these old clothes ♦ **où es-tu allé ~ ce chat ?** * wherever did you find that cat?

4 *[+ journées de travail]* to make up ♦ **on récupérera samedi** we'll make it up *ou* we'll make the time up on Saturday

5 *(Pol : péj) [+ personne, mouvement]* to take over, to hijack ♦ **se faire ~ par la gauche/la droite** to be taken over by the left/the right ♦ ~ **une situation/un événement à son profit** to cash in on a situation/an event

VI (*après des efforts, une maladie*) to recover, to recuperate

récurage /ʀekyʀaʒ/ NM scouring

récurer /ʀekyʀe/ ► conjug 1 ◄ VT to scour; → **poudre**

récurrence /ʀekyʀɑ̃s/ NF (*Math, Méd, littér = répétition*) recurrence

récurrent, e /ʀekyʀɑ̃, ɑ̃t/ ADJ [*cauchemar, phénomène, problème, thème*] recurring, recurrent; (*Anat, Ling, Méd*) recurrent ◆ **série ~e** (*Math*) recursion series ◆ **ces rumeurs apparaissent de façon ~e** these rumours are always going round

récursif, -ive /ʀekyʀsif, iv/ ADJ recursive

récursivité /ʀekyʀsivite/ NF recursiveness

récusable /ʀekyzabl/ ADJ [*témoin*] challengeable; [*témoignage*] impugnable

récusation /ʀekyzasjɔ̃/ NF [*de témoin, juge, juré*] challenging (*NonC*), objection; [*de témoignage*] impugnment, challenging (*NonC*), challenge ◆ **droit de ~** right to challenge

récuser /ʀekyze/ ► conjug 1 ◄ VT [*+ témoin, juge, juré*] to challenge, to object to; [*+ témoignage*] to impugn, to challenge; [*+ accusation*] to deny, to refute ◆ **~ un argument** (*Jur*) to make objection to an argument ◆ **~ la compétence d'un tribunal** to challenge the competence of a court VPR **se récuser** to decline to give an opinion *ou* accept responsibility; (*Jur*) [*juge*] to decline to act

recyclable /ʀ(ə)siklabl/ ADJ recyclable

recyclage /ʀ(ə)siklaʒ/ NM 1 [*d'élève*] reorientation; [*d'employé*] retraining ◆ **stage de ~** retraining *ou* refresher course 2 [*d'eaux usées, déchets*] recycling 3 (*Fin*) reinvestment ◆ **le ~ d'argent sale** money-laundering

recycler /ʀ(ə)sikle/ ► conjug 1 ◄ VT 1 [*+ employé*] (*dans son domaine*) to send on a refresher course; (*pour un nouveau métier*) to retrain; [*+ élève*] to reorientate 2 (*Tech*) [*+ déchets, eaux usées*] to recycle ◆ **papier recyclé** recycled paper 3 (*Fin*) (*= réinvestir*) to reinvest; (*= blanchir*) to launder VPR **se recycler** [*personne*] (*dans son domaine*) to go on a refresher course; (*pour un nouveau métier*) to retrain ◆ **elle s'est recyclée dans la restauration** she changed direction and went into catering ◆ **je ne peux pas me ~ à mon âge** I can't learn a new job *ou* trade at my age ◆ **se ~ en permanence** to be constantly updating one's skills ◆ **il a besoin de se ~ !*** he needs to get with it!*

recycleur /ʀəsiklœʀ/ NM (*= industriel*) recycler

rédacteur, -trice /ʀedaktœʀ, tʀis/ NM,F (*Presse*) sub-editor; [*d'article*] writer; [*de loi*] drafter; [*d'encyclopédie, dictionnaire*] compiler, editor ◆ **~ politique/économique** political/economics editor ◆ **~ sportif** sports editor, sportswriter

COMP **rédacteur en chef** editor
rédacteur publicitaire copywriter
rédacteur technique technical writer

rédaction /ʀedaksjɔ̃/ NF 1 [*de contrat, projet*] drafting, drawing up; [*de thèse, article*] writing; [*d'encyclopédie, dictionnaire*] compiling, compilation; (*Admin, Jur*) wording ◆ **ce n'est que la première ~** it's only the first draft ◆ **~ technique** technical writing 2 (*Presse*) (*= personnel*) editorial staff; (*= bureaux*) editorial offices; → **salle, secrétaire** 3 (*Scol*) essay, composition

rédactionnel, -elle /ʀedaksjɔnɛl/ ADJ editorial

reddition /ʀedisjɔ̃/ NF (*Mil*) surrender; [*de comptes*] rendering ◆ **~ sans conditions** unconditional surrender

redécoupage /ʀədekupaʒ/ NM ◆ **effectuer un ~ électoral** to make boundary changes

redécouverte /ʀ(ə)dekuvɛʀt/ NF rediscovery

redécouvrir /ʀ(ə)dekuvʀiʀ/ ► conjug 18 ◄ VT to rediscover

redéfaire /ʀ(ə)defɛʀ/ ► conjug 60 ◄ VT [*+ paquet, lacet*] to undo again; [*+ manteau*] to take off again; [*+ couture*] to unpick again ◆ **le nœud s'est redéfait** the knot has come undone *ou* come untied again

redéfinir /ʀ(ə)definiʀ/ ► conjug 2 ◄ VT to redefine

redéfinition /ʀ(ə)definisjɔ̃/ NF redefinition

redemander /ʀəd(ə)mɑ̃de, ʀ(ə)dəmɑ̃de/ ► conjug 1 ◄ VT [*+ adresse*] to ask again for; [*+ aliment*] to ask for more; [*+ bouteille*] to ask for another ◆ **redemande-le-lui** (*une nouvelle fois*) ask him for it again; (*récupère-le*) ask him to give it back to you, ask him for it back ◆ **~ du poulet** to ask for more chicken *ou* another helping of chicken ◆ **en ~*** (*iro*) to ask for more*

redémarrage /ʀ(ə)demaʀaʒ/ NM 1 [*de moteur, réacteur, usine*] starting up again ◆ **pendant le ~** (*Ordin*) while the computer restarts 2 (*= reprise*) [*d'économie, activité, ventes*] resurgence, upturn; [*d'inflation*] resurgence; [*de croissance*] pickup (*de* in)

redémarrer /ʀ(ə)demaʀe/ ► conjug 1 ◄ VI 1 [*moteur*] to start up again; [*véhicule*] to move off again; [*réacteur*] to be started up again ◆ **le chauffeur a redémarré au feu vert** the driver moved *ou* drove off again when the light turned green 2 [*processus*] to start again; [*économie*] to get going again, to take off again; [*croissance*] to pick up again; [*inflation*] to rise again ◆ **il tente de faire ~ son entreprise** he's trying to get his company started again 3 (*Ordin*) to restart

rédempteur, -trice /ʀedɑ̃ptœʀ, tʀis/ ADJ redemptive, redeeming NM,F redeemer

rédemption /ʀedɑ̃psjɔ̃/ NF 1 (*Rel*) redemption 2 (*Jur*) [*de rente*] redemption; [*de droit*] recovery

redéploiement /ʀ(ə)deplwamɑ̃/ NM [*d'armée, effectifs*] redeployment; [*de groupe industriel, activités, crédits*] restructuring

redéployer /ʀ(ə)deplwaje/ ► conjug 8 ◄ VT [*+ efforts, ressources, troupes*] to redeploy; [*+ crédits, effectifs*] to redeploy, to reassign ◆ **l'entreprise a redéployé ses activités autour de trois pôles** the company has reorganized its operations around three core areas ◆ **un nouveau musée a été construit pour ~ l'ensemble des collections** a new museum has been built so that the collection can be displayed in a new way VPR **se redéployer** [*armée, effectifs*] to redeploy; [*entreprise*] to reorganize its operations

redescendre /ʀ(ə)desɑ̃dʀ/ ► conjug 41 ◄ VT (*avec aux avoir*) 1 [*+ escalier*] to go *ou* come (back) down again ◆ **la balle a redescendu la pente** the ball rolled down the slope again *ou* rolled back down the slope

2 [*+ objet*] (*à la cave*) to take downstairs again; (*du grenier*) to bring downstairs again; (*d'un rayon*) to get *ou* lift (back) down again; (*d'un crochet*) to take (back) down again ◆ **~ qch d'un cran** to put sth one notch lower down

VI (*avec aux être*) 1 (*dans l'escalier*) to go *ou* come (back) downstairs again; (*d'une colline*) to go *ou* come (back) down again ◆ **l'alpiniste redescend** (*à pied*) the mountaineer climbs down again; (*avec une corde*) the mountaineer ropes down again ◆ **~ de voiture** to get *ou* climb out of the car again

2 [*ascenseur, avion*] to go down again; [*marée*] to go out again, to go back out; [*chemin*] to go *ou* slope down again; [*baromètre, fièvre*] to fall again

redessiner /ʀ(ə)desine/ ► conjug 1 ◄ VT [*+ paysage, jardin*] to redesign; [*+ frontière*] to redraw

redevable /ʀ(ə)dəvabl/ ADJ 1 (*Fin*) **être ~ de 20 € à qn** to owe sb €20 ◆ **~ de l'impôt** liable for tax 2 (*fig*) **être ~ à qn de** [*+ aide, service*] to be indebted to sb for ◆ **je vous suis ~ de la vie** I owe you my life

redevance /ʀ(ə)dəvɑ̃s/ NF 1 (*= impôt*) tax; (*Radio, TV*) *annual fee paid to the government to cover the costs of public television*, licence fee (*Brit*); (*Téléc*) rental charge 2 (*= bail, rente*) dues, fees; (*touchée par l'inventeur*) royalties

redevenir /ʀ(ə)dəv(ə)niʀ/ ► conjug 22 ◄ VI to become again ◆ **le temps est redevenu glacial** the weather has become *ou* gone very cold again ◆ **il est redevenu lui-même** he is his old self again

redevoir /ʀ(ə)dəvwaʀ/ ► conjug 28 ◄ VT ◆ **il me redoit 1 500 €** he still owes me €1,500

rédhibitoire /ʀedibitwaʀ/ ADJ [*défaut*] crippling, damning; [*conditions*] totally unacceptable ◆ **un échec n'est pas forcément ~** one failure does not necessarily spell the end of everything ◆ **sa mauvaise foi est vraiment ~** his insincerity puts him quite beyond the pale ◆ **il est un peu menteur, mais ce n'est pas ~** he's a bit of a liar but that doesn't rule him out altogether ◆ **vice ~** (*Jur*) latent defect

rediffuser /ʀ(ə)difyze/ ► conjug 1 ◄ VT [*+ émission*] to repeat, to rerun

rediffusion /ʀ(ə)difyzjɔ̃/ NF [*d'émission*] repeat, rerun

rédiger /ʀediʒe/ ► conjug 3 ◄ VT [*+ article, lettre*] to write, to compose; (*à partir de notes*) to write up; [*+ encyclopédie, dictionnaire*] to compile, to write; [*+ contrat*] to draw up, to draft ◆ **bien rédigé** well-written

redimensionnement /ʀədimɑ̃sjɔnmɑ̃/ NM resizing

redimensionner /ʀ(ə)dimɑ̃sjɔne/ ► conjug 1 ◄ VT [*+ entreprise, comité, image*] to resize

redingote /ʀ(ə)dɛ̃gɔt/ NF (*Hist*) frock coat ◆ **manteau ~** [*de femme*] fitted coat

redire /ʀ(ə)diʀ/ ► conjug 37 ◄ VT 1 [*+ affirmation*] to say again, to repeat; [*+ histoire*] to tell again, to repeat; [*+ médisance*] to (go and) tell, to repeat ◆ **~ qch à qn** to say sth to sb again, to tell sb sth again, to repeat sth to sb ◆ **il redit toujours la même chose** he's always saying *ou* he keeps saying the same thing ◆ **je te l'ai dit et redit** I've told you that over and over again *ou* time and time again ◆ **je lui ai redit cent fois que …** I've told him countless times that … ◆ **redis-le après moi** repeat after me ◆ **ne le lui redites pas** don't go and tell him *ou* don't go and repeat (to him) what I've said ◆ **il ne se le fait pas ~ deux fois** he doesn't need telling *ou* to be told twice

2 ◆ **avoir** *ou* **trouver à ~ à qch** to find fault with sth ◆ **il trouve à ~ à tout** he finds fault with everything, he's always ready to criticize ◆ **on ne peut rien trouver à ~ là-dessus** there's nothing to say *ou* you can say to that ◆ **je ne vois rien à ~ (à cela)** I don't have any complaint(s) about that, I can't see anything wrong with that

rediriger /ʀ(ə)diʀiʒe/ ► conjug 3 ◄ VT [*+ appel, personne*] to redirect

rediscuter /ʀ(ə)diskyte/ ► conjug 1 ◄ VT to discuss again, to have further discussion on

redistribuer /ʀ(ə)distʀibɥe/ ► conjug 1 ◄ VT [*+ biens*] to redistribute; [*+ emplois, rôles, tâches*] to reallocate; [*+ cartes*] to deal again ◆ **cet événement va ~ les cartes dans la bataille électorale** this event will change the face of the electoral battle

redistributif, -ive /ʀ(ə)distʀibytif, iv/ ADJ (*Écon*) [*effet, fiscalité*] redistributive

redistribution /ʀ(ə)distʀibysjɔ̃/ NF [*de richesses, revenus, pouvoirs*] redistribution; [*de rôles, terres*] reallocation; [*de cartes*] redeal ◆ **la ~ des cartes dans le secteur des télécommunications** the reorganization of the telecommunications sector

redite /ʀ(ə)dit/ NF (needless) repetition

redondance /ʀ(ə)dɔ̃dɑ̃s/ NF 1 *[de style]* redundancy *(NonC)*, diffuseness *(NonC)*; *(Ling, Ordin)* redundancy *(NonC)* 2 *(= expression)* unnecessary *ou* superfluous expression ◆ **votre devoir est plein de ~s** your homework is full of repetitions

redondant, e /ʀ(ə)dɔ̃dɑ̃, ɑ̃t/ ADJ *[mot]* superfluous, redundant; *[style]* redundant, diffuse; *(Ling, Ordin)* redundant

redonner /ʀ(ə)dɔne/ ▸ conjug 1 ◂ VT 1 *(= rendre) [+ objet, bien]* to give back, to return; *[+ forme, idéal]* to give back, to give again; *[+ espoir, énergie]* to restore, to give back ◆ **l'air frais te redonnera des couleurs** the fresh air will put some colour back in your cheeks *ou* bring some colour back to your cheeks ◆ **cela te redonnera des forces** that will build your strength back up *ou* put new strength into you *ou* restore your strength ◆ **cette crème redonnera du tonus à votre peau** this cream will revitalize your skin ◆ **~ de la confiance/du courage à qn** to give sb new *ou* fresh confidence/courage, to restore sb's confidence/courage ◆ **ce voyage m'a redonné goût à la vie** this trip restored my appetite for life ◆ **~ la parole à qn** to let sb speak again ◆ **~ vie à un quartier/un village** to give an area/a village a new lease of life ◆ **ça a redonné le même résultat** it produced the same result as before

2 *(= donner de nouveau) [+ adresse]* to give again; *[+ pain, eau]* to give some more ◆ **~ une couche de peinture** to give another coat of paint ◆ **redonne-toi un coup de peigne** give your hair another quick comb ◆ **tu peux me ~ de la viande/ des carottes ?** can you give me some more meat/some more carrots? *ou* another helping of meat/of carrots? ◆ **redonne-lui une bière/à boire** give him another beer/another drink

3 *(Théât)* to put on again

redorer /ʀ(ə)dɔʀe/ ▸ conjug 1 ◂ VT to regild ◆ **~ son blason** *[famille]* to boost the family fortunes by marrying into money; *[entreprise, émission]* to regain prestige

redormir /ʀ(ə)dɔʀmiʀ/ ▸ conjug 16 ◂ VI to sleep some more ◆ **j'ai redormi trois heures** I slept for three more hours

redoublant, e /ʀ(ə)dublɑ̃, ɑ̃t/ NM,F *(Scol)* pupil who is repeating *(ou* has repeated) a year at school, repeater *(US)*

redoublement /ʀ(ə)dubləmɑ̃/ NM 1 *(= accroissement)* increase *(de* in), intensification *(de* of) ◆ **je vous demande un ~ d'attention** I need you to pay even closer attention, I need your increased attention ◆ **avec un ~ de larmes** with a fresh flood of tears 2 *(Scol)* **le ~ permet aux élèves faibles de rattraper** repeating a year *ou* a grade *(US) ou* being kept down *(Brit)* helps the weaker pupils to catch up 3 *(Ling)* reduplication

redoubler /ʀ(ə)duble/ ▸ conjug 1 ◂ VT 1 *(= accroître) [+ joie, douleur, craintes]* to increase, to intensify; *[+ efforts]* to step up, to redouble ◆ **frapper à coups redoublés** to bang twice as hard, to bang even harder ◆ **hurler à cris redoublés** to yell twice as loud

2 *(Ling) [+ syllabe]* to reduplicate; *(Couture) [+ vêtement]* to reline ◆ **~ (une classe)** *(Scol)* to repeat a year *ou* a grade *(US)*, to be held back *ou* kept down *(Brit)* a year

VT INDIR **redoubler de** ◆ **~ d'efforts** to step up *ou* redouble one's efforts, to try extra hard ◆ **~ de prudence/de vigilance** to be extra careful/vigilant, to be doubly careful/vigilant ◆ **le vent redouble de violence** the wind is getting even stronger *ou* is blowing even more strongly

VI *(gén)* to increase, to intensify; *[froid, douleur]* to become twice as bad, to get even worse; *[vent]* to become twice as strong; *[joie]* to become even more intense; *[larmes]* to flow *ou* fall even faster; *[cris]* to get even louder *ou* twice as loud

redoutable /ʀ(ə)dutabl/ ADJ *[arme, adversaire, concurrence]* formidable, fearsome; *[maladie]* dreadful; *[problème]* formidable, dreadful; *[question]* tough, difficult ◆ **son charme ~** his devastating charm ◆ **elle est d'une efficacité ~** she's frighteningly efficient

redoutablement /ʀ(ə)dutabləmɑ̃/ ADV *[agile, efficace]* formidably; *[dangereux]* extremely ◆ **un couteau ~ effilé** a dangerously sharp knife

redoute /ʀədut/ NF *(Mil)* redoubt

redouter /ʀ(ə)dute/ ▸ conjug 1 ◂ VT *[+ ennemi, avenir, conséquence]* to dread, to fear ◆ **je redoute de l'apprendre** I dread finding out about it ◆ **je redoute qu'il ne l'apprenne** I dread his finding out about it

redoux /ʀədu/ NM *(= temps plus chaud)* spell of milder weather; *(= dégel)* thaw

redresse /ʀ(ə)dʀɛs/ **à la redresse** ✲† LOC ADJ *[personne]* tough

redressement /ʀ(ə)dʀɛsmɑ̃/ NM 1 *[de poteau]* setting upright, righting; *[de tige]* straightening (up); *[de tôle]* straightening out, knocking out; *[de courant]* rectification; *[de buste, corps]* straightening up 2 *[de bateau]* righting; *[de roue, voiture, avion]* straightening up 3 *[de situation] (= action)* putting right; *(= résultat)* recovery 4 *[d'économie]* recovery, upturn; *[d'entreprise]* recovery, turnaround ◆ **plan de ~** recovery package ◆ **~ économique/financier** economic/financial recovery ◆ **être mis** *ou* **placé en ~ judiciaire** *(Jur)* to be put into receivership *ou* administration 5 *[d'erreur]* righting, putting right; *[d'abus, torts]* righting, redress; *[de jugement]* correcting ◆ **~ fiscal** *(Fin)* tax adjustment; → **maison**

redresser /ʀ(ə)dʀese/ ▸ conjug 1 ◂ VT 1 *(= relever)* to straighten up; *[+ tôle cabossée]* to knock out; *[+ courant]* to rectify; *(Opt) [+ image]* to straighten ◆ **~ un malade sur son oreiller** to sit *ou* prop a patient up against his pillow ◆ **~ les épaules** to straighten one's shoulders, to throw one's shoulders back ◆ **~ le corps (en arrière)** to stand up straight, to straighten up ◆ **~ la tête** *(lit)* to hold up *ou* lift (up) one's head; *(fig = être fier)* to hold one's head up high; *(fig = se révolter)* to show signs of rebellion ◆ **se faire ~ les dents** to have one's teeth straightened

2 *(= rediriger) [+ roue, voiture]* to straighten up; *[+ bateau]* to right; *[+ avion]* to lift the nose of, to straighten up ◆ **redresse !** straighten up!; → **barre**

3 *(= rétablir) [+ économie]* to put *ou* set right; *[+ entreprise déficitaire]* to turn round; *[+ situation]* to put right, to straighten out ◆ **~ le pays** to get *ou* put the country on its feet again

4 *(littér = corriger) [+ erreur]* to rectify, to put right; *[+ torts, abus]* to remedy ◆ **~ le jugement défavorable de qn** to change sb's unfavourable opinion

VPR **se redresser** 1 *(= se mettre assis)* to sit up; *(= se mettre debout)* to stand up; *(= se mettre droit)* to stand up straight; *(après s'être courbé)* to straighten up; *(fig = être fier)* to hold one's head up high ◆ **redresse-toi !** sit *ou* stand up straight!

2 *[bateau]* to right itself; *[avion]* to flatten out, to straighten up; *[voiture]* to straighten up; *[pays, économie]* to recover; *[situation]* to correct itself

3 *[coin replié, cheveux]* to stick up ◆ **les blés, couchés par le vent, se redressèrent** the wheat, which had been flattened by the wind, stood up straight again

redresseur /ʀ(ə)dʀesœʀ/ NM 1 *(Hist, iro)* **~ de torts** righter of wrongs ◆ **~ d'entreprises** corporate rescuer 2 *(Élec)* rectifier ADJ M *[muscle]* erector; *[prisme]* erecting

réduc * /ʀedyk/ NF abrév de **réduction 2**

réducteur, -trice /ʀedyktœʀ, tʀis/ ADJ 1 *(Chim)* reducing; *[engrenage]* reduction 2 *(péj = simplificateur) [analyse, concept]* simplistic NM *(Chim)* reducing agent; *(Photo)* reducer ◆ **~ (de vitesse)** speed reducer ◆ **~ de tête** head shrinker

réductibilité /ʀedyktibilite/ NF reducibility

réductible /ʀedyktibl/ ADJ *(Chim, Math)* reducible *(en, à* to); *(Méd) [fracture]* which can be reduced *(SPÉC) ou* set; *[quantité]* which can be reduced

réduction /ʀedyksjɔ̃/ NF 1 *(= diminution) [de dépenses, personnel, production, déficit]* reduction, cut *(de* in); ◆ **~ de salaire/d'impôts** wage/tax cut, cut in wages/in taxes ◆ **~ du temps de travail** cut *ou* reduction in working time *ou* hours ◆ **obtenir une ~ de peine** to get a reduced sentence

2 *(= rabais)* discount, reduction ◆ **faire/obtenir une ~** to give/get a reduction ◆ **une ~ de 10% a 10%** discount ◆ **~ (pour les) étudiants/chômeurs** concessions for students/the unemployed ◆ **carte de ~** discount card ◆ **bénéficier d'une carte de ~ dans les transports** *(trains)* to have a railcard; *(bus)* to have a bus pass

3 *(= reproduction) [de plan, photo]* reduction ◆ **en ~** *(fig)* in miniature

4 *(Méd) [de fracture]* reduction *(SPÉC)*, setting; *(Bio, Chim, Math)* reduction

5 *(Culin)* reduction (by boiling)

6 *(Mil) [de ville]* capture; *[de rebelles]* quelling

réductionnisme /ʀedyksjɔnism/ NM reductionism

réductionniste /ʀedyksjɔnist/ ADJ, NMF reductionist

réduire /ʀedɥiʀ/ ▸ conjug 38 ◂ VT 1 *(= diminuer) [+ hauteur, vitesse, temps de travail, inégalités]* to reduce; *[+ peine, impôt, consommation]* to reduce, to cut; *[+ prix]* to reduce, to cut, to bring down; *[+ pression]* to reduce, to lessen; *[+ texte]* to shorten, to cut; *[+ production]* to reduce, to cut (back), to lower; *[+ dépenses]* to reduce, to cut, to cut down *ou* back (on); *[+ risques]* to reduce, to lower; *[+ voilure]* to shorten; *[+ tête coupée]* to shrink ◆ **il va falloir ~ notre train de vie** we'll have to cut down on *ou* curb our spending ◆ **~ petit à petit l'autorité de qn/la portée d'une loi** to chip away at sb's authority/a law

2 *(= reproduire) [+ dessin, plan]* to reduce, to scale down; *[+ photographie]* to reduce, to make smaller; *[+ figure géométrique]* to scale down

3 *(= contraindre)* **~ à** *[+ soumission, désespoir]* to reduce to ◆ **~ qn à l'obéissance/en esclavage** to reduce sb to obedience/to slavery ◆ **après son accident, il a été réduit à l'inaction** since his accident he's been unable to get about ◆ **il en est réduit à mendier** he has been reduced to begging

4 ◆ **~ à** *(= ramener à)* to reduce to, to bring down to; *(= limiter à)* to limit to, to confine to ◆ **~ des fractions à un dénominateur commun** to reduce *ou* bring down fractions to a common denominator ◆ **~ des éléments différents à un type commun** to reduce different elements to one general type ◆ **je réduirai mon étude à quelques aspects** I shall limit *ou* confine my study to a few aspects ◆ **~ à sa plus simple expression** *(Math) [+ polynôme]* to reduce to its simplest expression; *(fig) [+ mobilier, repas]* to reduce to the absolute *ou* bare minimum ◆ **~ qch à néant** *ou* **à rien** *ou* **à zéro** to reduce sth to nothing

5 *(= transformer)* ~ **en** to reduce to ◆ **réduisez les grammes en milligrammes** convert the grammes to milligrammes ◆ ~ **qch en miettes/en morceaux** to smash sth to tiny pieces/to pieces ◆ ~ **qch en bouillie** to crush *ou* reduce sth to a pulp ◆ ~ **qch en poudre** to grind *ou* reduce sth to a powder ◆ **sa maison était réduite en cendres** his house was reduced to ashes *ou* burnt to the ground ◆ **les cadavres étaient réduits en charpie** the bodies were torn to shreds

6 *(Méd) [+ fracture]* to set, to reduce *(SPÉC)*; *(Chim) [+ minerai, oxyde]* to reduce; *(Culin) [+ sauce]* to reduce (by boiling)

7 *(Mil) [+ place forte]* to capture; *[+ rebelles]* to quell ◆ ~ **l'opposition** to silence the opposition

VI *(Culin) [sauce]* to reduce ◆ **faire** *ou* **laisser** ~ **la sauce** simmer the sauce to reduce it ◆ **les épinards réduisent à la cuisson** spinach shrinks when you cook it

VPR se réduire 1 ◆ **se** ~ **à** *[affaire, incident]* to boil down to, to amount to; *[somme, quantité]* to amount to ◆ **mon profit se réduit à bien peu de chose** the profit I've made amounts to very little ◆ **notre action ne se réduit pas à quelques discours** the action we are taking involves more than *ou* isn't just a matter of a few speeches ◆ **je me réduirai à quelques exemples** I'll limit *ou* confine myself to a few examples, I'll just select *ou* quote a few examples

2 ◆ **se** ~ **en** to be reduced to ◆ **se** ~ **en cendres** to be burnt *ou* reduced to ashes ◆ **se** ~ **en poussière** to be reduced *ou* crumble away *ou* turn to dust ◆ **se** ~ **en bouillie** to be crushed to a pulp

3 *(= dépenser moins)* to cut down on one's spending *ou* expenditure

réduit, e /ʀedɥi, it/ (ptp de **réduire**) **ADJ** 1 *(= petit)* small ◆ **de taille** *ou* **dimension** ~**e** small ◆ **reproduction à échelle** ~**e** small-scale reproduction ◆ **un nombre** ~ **de ...** a small number of ... ◆ **métal à teneur en plomb** ~**e** metal with a low lead content; → **modèle**

2 *(= diminué) [tarif, prix, taux]* reduced; *[délai]* shorter; *[moyens, débouchés]* limited ◆ **livres à prix** ~**s** cut-price books, books at a reduced price *ou* at reduced prices ◆ **avancer à vitesse** ~**e** to move forward at low speed *ou* at a reduced speed ◆ **maintenant ils produisent ces voitures en nombre** ~ they're now producing a smaller number of these cars *ou* fewer of these cars ◆ **travail à temps** ~ short-time work ◆ **chômeur ayant exercé une activité** ~**e** unemployed person who has worked a limited number of hours ◆ **"service réduit le dimanche"** "reduced service on Sundays" ◆ **tête** ~**e** shrunken head

NM *(= pièce)* tiny room; *(péj)* cubbyhole, poky little hole; *(= recoin)* recess; *(Mil)* enclave; *[de maquisards]* hideout

redynamiser /ʀ(ə)dinamize/ ▸ conjug 1 ◂ **VT** *[+ économie, secteur, tourisme]* to give a new boost to

rééchelonnement /ʀeeʃ(ə)lɔnmɑ̃/ **NM** *[de dettes]* rescheduling

rééchelonner /ʀeeʃ(ə)lɔne/ ▸ conjug 1 ◂ **VT** *[+ dettes]* to reschedule

réécrire /ʀeekʀiʀ/ ▸ conjug 39 ◂ **VT** *[+ roman, inscription]* to rewrite; *[+ lettre]* to write again ◆ ~ **l'histoire** *(fig)* to rewrite history ◆ **il m'a réécrit** he has written to me again, he has written me another letter

réécriture /ʀeekʀityʀ/ **NF** rewriting ◆ **règle de** ~ *(Ling)* rewrite *ou* rewriting rule

réédification /ʀeedifikasjɔ̃/ **NF** rebuilding, reconstruction

réédifier /ʀeedifje/ ▸ conjug 7 ◂ **VT** to rebuild, to reconstruct; *(fig)* to rebuild

rééditer /ʀeedite/ ▸ conjug 1 ◂ **VT** to republish; *(fig)* to repeat

réédition /ʀeedisjɔ̃/ **NF** new edition; *(fig)* repetition, repeat

rééducateur, -trice /ʀeedykatœʀ, tʀis/ **NM,F** *(= kinésithérapeute)* physiotherapist; *(= psychologue)* counsellor

rééducation /ʀeedykasjɔ̃/ **NF** 1 *(Méd) [de malade]* rehabilitation; *[de membre]* re-education; *(= spécialité médicale)* physiotherapy, physical therapy *(US)* ◆ **faire de la** ~ to undergo *ou* have physiotherapy, to have physical therapy *(US)* ◆ **exercice de** ~ physiotherapy exercise ◆ ~ **de la parole** speech therapy ◆ **centre de** ~ rehabilitation centre 2 *(gén, lit, Pol)* re-education; *[de délinquant]* rehabilitation

rééduquer /ʀeedyke/ ▸ conjug 1 ◂ **VT** 1 *(Méd) [+ malade]* to rehabilitate; *[+ membre]* to re-educate 2 *(gén, Pol, lit)* to re-educate; *[+ délinquant]* to rehabilitate

réel, -elle /ʀeɛl/ **ADJ** 1 *[fait, chef, existence, avantage]* real; *[besoin, cause]* real, true; *[danger, plaisir, amélioration, douleur]* real, genuine ◆ **faire de réelles économies** to make significant *ou* real savings ◆ **son héros est très** ~ his hero is very lifelike *ou* realistic 2 *(Math, Opt, Philos, Phys)* real; *(Fin) [valeur, salaire]* real, actual ◆ **taux d'intérêt** ~ effective interest rate **NM** ◆ **le** ~ reality, the real

réélection /ʀeelɛksjɔ̃/ **NF** re-election

rééligibilité /ʀeeliʒibilite/ **NF** re-eligibility

rééligible /ʀeeliʒibl/ **ADJ** re-eligible

réélire /ʀeeliʀ/ ▸ conjug 43 ◂ **VT** to re-elect ◆ **ne pas** ~ **qn** to vote sb out

réellement /ʀeɛlmɑ̃/ **ADV** really, truly ◆ **je suis** ~ **désolé** I'm really *ou* truly sorry ◆ **ça m'a** ~ **consterné/aidé** that really worried/helped me, that was a genuine worry/help to me ◆ ~, **tu exagères !** really *ou* honestly, you're going too far!

réembarquer /ʀeɑ̃baʀke/ ▸ conjug 1 ◂ **VTI** ⇒ **rembarquer**

réembaucher /ʀeɑ̃boʃe/ ▸ conjug 1 ◂ **VT** to take on again, to re-employ ◆ **l'entreprise réembauchera à l'automne prochain** the company will start hiring again next autumn

réembobiner /ʀeɑ̃bɔbine/ ▸ conjug 1 ◂ **VT** ⇒ **rembobiner**

réémergence /ʀeemɛʀʒɑ̃s/ **NF** re-emergence

réemploi /ʀeɑ̃plwa/ **NM** 1 *[de méthode, produit]* re-use 2 *(= réinvestissement)* reinvestment 3 *(= nouvelle embauche)* re-employment

réemployer /ʀeɑ̃plwaje/ ▸ conjug 8 ◂ **VT** 1 *[+ méthode, produit]* to re-use 2 *(= réinvestir)* to reinvest 3 *(= réembaucher)* to re-employ, to take back on

réemprunter /ʀeɑ̃pʀœ̃te/ ▸ conjug 1 ◂ **VT** 1 *[+ argent, objet] (une nouvelle fois)* to borrow again; *(davantage)* to borrow more 2 ◆ ~ **le même chemin** to take the same road again, to go the same way again

réengagement /ʀeɑ̃gaʒmɑ̃/ **NM** ⇒ **rengagement**

réengager /ʀeɑ̃gaʒe/ ▸ conjug 3 ◂ **VT** ⇒ **rengager**

réenregistrable /ʀeɑ̃ʀ(ə)ʒistʀabl/ **ADJ** *[CD]* recordable

réenregistrement /ʀeɑ̃ʀ(ə)ʒistʀəmɑ̃/ **NM** *[de disque]* re-recording

réenregistrer /ʀeɑ̃ʀ(ə)ʒistʀe/ ▸ conjug 1 ◂ **VT** *[+ musique, titre]* to re-record ◆ **j'ai réenregistré un documentaire par-dessus le film** I recorded a documentary over the film

réentendre /ʀeɑ̃tɑ̃dʀ/ ▸ conjug 41 ◂ **VT** to hear again

rééquilibrage /ʀeekilibʀaʒ/ **NM** *[de chargement]* readjustment; *[de budget, finances, comptes]* rebalancing; *[de pouvoirs]* restoring the balance ◆ **le** ~ **des roues** *(d'une voiture)* balancing the wheels ◆ **le** ~ **des forces au sein du gouvernement** the redistribution of power within the government

rééquilibrer /ʀeekilibʀe/ ▸ conjug 1 ◂ **VT** *[+ chargement]* to readjust; *[+ roues de voiture]* to balance; *[+ économie]* to restabilize, to find a new equilibrium for; *[+ budget, comptes, finances]* to rebalance ◆ ~ **les pouvoirs/la balance commerciale** to restore the balance of power/the balance of trade

réescompte /ʀeɛskɔ̃t/ **NM** rediscount

réescompter /ʀeɛskɔ̃te/ ▸ conjug 1 ◂ **VT** to rediscount

réessayer /ʀeeseje/ ▸ conjug 8 ◂ **VT** *[+ robe]* to try on again; *[+ recette]* to try again ◆ **je réessaierai plus tard** I'll try again later

réétudier /ʀeetydje/ ▸ conjug 7 ◂ **VT** *[+ dossier, question]* to reexamine

réévaluation /ʀeevalɥasjɔ̃/ **NF** 1 *[de monnaie]* revaluation; *[de salaire] (à la hausse)* upgrading; *(à la baisse)* downgrading 2 *[de situation, place, méthode]* reappraisal, reassessment

réévaluer /ʀeevalɥe/ ▸ conjug 1 ◂ **VT** 1 *[+ monnaie]* to revalue *(par rapport à* against); *[+ salaire] (à la hausse)* to upgrade; *(à la baisse)* to downgrade 2 *[+ situation, place, méthode]* to reappraise, to reassess

réexamen /ʀeɛgzamɛ̃/ **NM** *[de malade]* re-examination; *[de problème, situation, dossier, candidature, décision]* reconsideration ◆ **demander un** ~ **de la situation** to ask for the situation to be reconsidered

réexaminer /ʀeɛgzamine/ ▸ conjug 1 ◂ **VT** *[+ malade]* to re-examine; *[+ problème, situation, candidature, décision]* to examine again, to reconsider

réexpédier /ʀeɛkspedje/ ▸ conjug 7 ◂ **VT** 1 *(= retourner, renvoyer)* to return, to send back ◆ **on l'a réexpédié dans son pays** he was sent back to his country 2 *(= faire suivre)* to send on, to forward

réexpédition /ʀeɛkspedisjɔ̃/ **NF** 1 *(= retour)* returning 2 *(= fait de faire suivre)* forwarding ◆ **enveloppe/frais de** ~ forwarding envelope/charges

réexportation /ʀeɛkspɔʀtasjɔ̃/ **NF** re-export

réexporter /ʀeɛkspɔʀte/ ▸ conjug 1 ◂ **VT** to re-export

réf. (abrév de **référence**) ref.

refaçonner /ʀ(ə)fasɔne/ ▸ conjug 1 ◂ **VT** *[+ sculpture]* to remodel; *[+ émission]* to redesign; *[+ phrase, texte]* to rework

réfaction /ʀefaksjɔ̃/ **NF** *(Comm)* allowance, rebate

refacturer /ʀ(ə)faktyʀe/ ▸ conjug 1 ◂ **VT** ◆ ~ **qch à qn** to pass on the cost of sth to sb ◆ **les coûts sont en partie refacturés au client** some of the costs are passed on to the customer

refaire /ʀ(ə)fɛʀ/ ▸ conjug 60 ◂ **VT** 1 *(= recommencer) (gén) [+ travail, dessin]* to redo, to do again; *[+ maquillage]* to redo; *[+ voyage]* to make again; *[+ article, devoir]* to rewrite; *[+ nœud]* to retie; *[+ paquet]* to do up again ◆ **il a refait mon pansement** he put on a new bandage for me ◆ **elle a refait sa vie avec lui** she started a new relationship with him ◆ **il m'a refait une visite** he paid me another call, he called on me again ◆ **il refait (du) soleil** the sun has come out again ◆ **tu refais toujours la même faute** you always make the same mistake ◆ **il a refait de la fièvre/de l'asthme** he has had another bout of fever/of asthma ◆ **il refait du vélo** he has taken up cycling again ◆ **il va falloir tout** ~ **depuis le début** it will have to be done all over again, we'll have to start again from scratch ◆ **si vous refaites du bruit** if you start making a noise again, if there's any further noise from you ◆ **il va falloir ~ de la soupe** we'll have to make some more soup ◆ **je vais me ~ une tasse de café** I'm going to make myself another cup of coffee ◆ **~ le monde** *(en parlant)* to try to solve the world's problems ◆ **si c'était à ~ !** if I had my time over again! ◆ **à ~** *(Cartes)* re-deal

2 *(= retaper)* *[+ toit]* to redo, to renew; *[+ route]* to repair; *[+ mur]* to rebuild, to repair; *[+ meuble]* to do up, to renovate, to restore; *[+ chambre]* to decorate ◆ **on refera les peintures/les papiers au printemps** we'll repaint/repaper in the spring, we'll redo the paintwork/the wallpaper in the spring ◆ **nous allons faire ~ le carrelage du salon** we're going to have the sitting room floor re-tiled ◆ **se faire ~ le nez** to have one's nose remodelled *(Brit)* *ou* remodeled *(US)*, to have a nose job* ◆ **~ qch à neuf** to do sth up like new ◆ **~ ses forces/sa santé** to recover one's strength/one's health ◆ **à son âge, tu ne la referas pas** at her age, you won't change her

3 *(* = duper)* to take in ◆ **il a été refait, il s'est fait ~** he has been taken in *ou* had* ◆ **il m'a refait de 10 €** he did* *ou* diddled* *(Brit)* me out of €10

VPR **se refaire** *(= retrouver une santé)* to recuperate, to recover; *(= regagner son argent)* to make up one's losses ◆ **se ~ une santé dans le Midi** to (go and) recuperate in the south of France, to recover *ou* regain one's health in the south of France ◆ **se ~ une beauté** to freshen up ◆ **que voulez-vous, on ne se refait pas !** what can you expect – you can't change how you're made! * *ou* you can't change your own character!; → **virginité**

réfection /ʀefɛksjɔ̃/ NF *[de route]* repairing; *[de mur, maison]* rebuilding, repairing ◆ **la ~ de la route va durer trois semaines** the road repairs *ou* the repairs to the road will take three weeks

réfectoire /ʀefɛktwaʀ/ NM *(Scol)* dining hall, canteen; *(Rel)* refectory; *[d'usine]* canteen

refend /ʀəfɑ̃/ NM ◆ **mur de ~** supporting (partition) wall ◆ **bois de ~** wood in planks

référé /ʀefeʀe/ NM *(Jur)* ◆ **(procédure en) ~** summary proceedings ◆ **(arrêt *ou* jugement en) ~** interim ruling ◆ **assigner qn en ~** to apply for summary judgment against sb ◆ **juge des ~s** judge in chambers

référence /ʀefeʀɑ̃s/ NF 1 *(= renvoi)* reference; *(en bas de page)* reference, footnote ◆ **par ~ à** in reference to ◆ **en ~ à votre courrier du 2 juin** with reference to your letter of 2 June ◆ **l'auteur cité en ~** *(plus haut)* the abovementioned author ◆ **ouvrage/numéro de ~** reference book/number ◆ **période/prix de ~** base *ou* reference period/price ◆ **taux de ~** *(Fin)* benchmark *ou* reference rate ◆ **prendre qch comme point de ~** to use sth as a point of reference ◆ **faire ~ à** to refer to, to make (a) reference to ◆ **servir de ~** *[chiffres, indice, taux]* to be used as a benchmark; *[personne]* to be a role model ◆ **c'est un livre qui fait ~** it is a standard reference work; → **année**

2 *(= recommandation)* *(gén)* reference ◆ **cet employé a-t-il des ~s ?** *(d'un employeur)* has this employee got a reference? *ou* a testimonial? *(Brit)*; *(de plusieurs employeurs)* has this employee got references? *ou* testimonials? *(Brit)* ◆ **lettre de ~** letter of reference, testimonial *(Brit)* ◆ **il a un doctorat, c'est quand même une ~** he has a doctorate which is not a bad recommendation *ou* which is something to go by ◆ **ce n'est pas une ~** *(iro)* that's no recommendation

3 *(Ling)* reference

référencement /ʀefeʀɑ̃smɑ̃/ NM *[de produit]* referencing

référencer /ʀefeʀɑ̃se/ ▸ conjug 3 ◂ VT to reference

référendaire /ʀefeʀɑ̃dɛʀ/ ADJ *(pour un référendum)* referendum *(épith)* NM ◆ **(conseiller) ~** public auditor

référendum /ʀefeʀɛ̃dɔm/ NM referendum ◆ **faire *ou* organiser un ~** to hold a referendum

référent /ʀefeʀɑ̃/ NM referent

référentiel, -elle /ʀefeʀɑ̃sjɛl/ ADJ referential NM system of reference

référer /ʀefeʀe/ GRAMMAIRE ACTIVE 46.1 ▸ conjug 6 ◂ VT INDIR **en référer à** ◆ **en ~ à qn** to refer *ou* submit a matter *ou* question to sb VPR **se référer** ◆ **se ~ à** *(= consulter)* to consult; *(= faire référence à)* to refer to; *(= s'en remettre à)* to refer to ◆ **si l'on s'en réfère à son dernier article** if we refer to his most recent article

refermer /ʀ(ə)fɛʀme/ ▸ conjug 1 ◂ VT to close *ou* shut again ◆ **peux-tu ~ la porte ?** can you close *ou* shut the door? ◆ **~ un dossier** *(fig)* to close a file VPR **se refermer** *[plaie]* to close up, to heal up; *[fleur]* to close up (again); *[fenêtre, porte]* to close *ou* shut (again) ◆ **le piège se referma sur lui** the trap closed *ou* shut on him

refiler* /ʀ(ə)file/ ▸ conjug 1 ◂ VT to give *(à qn* to sb); ◆ **refile-moi ton livre** let me have your book, give me your book ◆ **il m'a refilé la rougeole** I've caught measles off him, he has passed his measles on to me ◆ **il s'est fait ~ une fausse pièce** someone has palmed *ou* fobbed a forged coin off on him*; → **bébé**

refinancement /ʀ(ə)finɑ̃smɑ̃/ NM refinancing ◆ **plan de ~** refinancing plan

refinancer /ʀ(ə)finɑ̃se/ ▸ conjug 1 ◂ VT to refinance

réfléchi, e /ʀefleʃi/ (ptp de **réfléchir**) ADJ 1 *(= pondéré)* *[action]* well-thought-out *(épith)*, well thought out *(attrib)*, well-considered; *[personne, air]* thoughtful ◆ **tout bien ~** after careful consideration *ou* thought, having weighed up all the pros and cons ◆ **c'est tout ~** my mind is made up, I've made my mind up 2 *(Gram)* reflexive 3 *(Opt)* reflected NM *(Gram)* reflexive

réfléchir /ʀefleʃiʀ/ GRAMMAIRE ACTIVE 29.3 ▸ conjug 2 ◂

VI to think, to reflect ◆ **prends le temps de ~** take time to reflect *ou* to think about it *ou* to consider it ◆ **cela donne à ~** it's food for thought, it makes you think ◆ **cet accident, ça fait ~** an accident like that makes you think ◆ **il faut ~ avant d'agir** you must think before you act ◆ **je demande à ~** I'd like time to consider it *ou* to think things over ◆ **elle a accepté sans ~** she accepted without thinking ◆ **la prochaine fois, tâche de ~** next time just try and think a bit *ou* try and use your brains a bit ◆ **j'ai longuement réfléchi et je suis arrivé à cette conclusion** I have given it a lot of thought and have come to this conclusion

VT INDIR **réfléchir à *ou* sur qch** to think about sth, to turn sth over in one's mind ◆ **réfléchissez-y** think about it, think it over ◆ **réfléchis à ce que tu vas faire** think about what you're going to do ◆ **à bien y ~..., en y réfléchissant (bien)...** when you really think about it ...

VT 1 ◆ **~ que** to realize that ◆ **il n'avait pas réfléchi qu'il ne pourrait pas venir** he hadn't thought *ou* realized that *ou* it hadn't occurred to him that he wouldn't be able to come

2 *[+ lumière, son]* to reflect ◆ **les arbres se réfléchissent dans le lac** the trees are reflected in the lake, you can see the reflection of the trees in the lake

réfléchissant, e /ʀefleʃisɑ̃, ɑ̃t/ ADJ reflective

réflecteur, -trice /ʀeflɛktœʀ, tʀis/ ADJ reflecting NM *(gén)* reflector

reflet /ʀ(ə)flɛ/ NM 1 *(= éclat)* *(gén)* reflection; *[de cheveux]* *(naturel)* glint, light; *(artificiel)* highlight ◆ **les ~s moirés de la soie** the shimmering play of light on silk ◆ **les ~s du soleil sur la mer** the reflection *ou* glint *ou* flash of the sun on the sea ◆ **la lame projetait des ~s sur le mur** the reflection of the blade shone on the wall, the blade threw a reflection onto the wall ◆ **se faire faire des ~s (dans les cheveux)** to have one's hair highlighted

2 *(lit = image)* reflection ◆ **le ~ de son visage dans le lac** the reflection of his face in the lake

3 *(fig = représentation)* reflection ◆ **les habits sont le ~ d'une époque/d'une personnalité** clothes reflect *ou* are the reflection of an era/of one's personality ◆ **c'est le pâle ~ de son prédécesseur** he's a pale reflection of his predecessor ◆ **c'est le ~ de son père** he's the image of his father

refléter /ʀ(ə)flete/ ▸ conjug 6 ◂ VT *(lit, fig)* to reflect, to mirror ◆ **son visage reflète la bonté** his kindness shows in his face VPR **se refléter** to be reflected, to be mirrored *(dans* in; *sur* on); ◆ **son trouble se reflétait sur son visage** his agitation showed on his face

refleurir /ʀ(ə)flœʀiʀ/ ▸ conjug 2 ◂ VI *(= fleurir à nouveau)* to flower *ou* blossom again; *(= renaître)* to flourish *ou* blossom again VT *[+ tombe]* to put fresh flowers on

reflex /ʀeflɛks/ ADJ reflex NM reflex camera ◆ **~ à un objectif/deux objectifs** single-lens/twin-lens reflex (camera)

réflexe /ʀeflɛks/ ADJ reflex

NM *(Physiol)* reflex; *(= réaction)* reaction ◆ **~ rotulien** knee jerk ◆ **~ conditionné *ou* conditionnel** conditioned reflex *ou* response ◆ **~ de défense** *(Physiol)* defence reflex; *(gén)* defensive reaction ◆ **~ de survie** instinct for survival ◆ **~ de solidarité** instinctive feeling of solidarity ◆ **avoir de bons/mauvais ~s** to have quick *ou* good/slow *ou* poor reflexes ◆ **il eut le ~ de couper l'électricité** his immediate *ou* instant reaction was to switch off the electricity, he instinctively switched off the electricity ◆ **manquer de ~** to be slow to react ◆ **son premier ~ a été d'appeler la police** his first reaction was to call the police ◆ **par ~, j'ai regardé derrière moi** I instinctively looked behind me ◆ **il a freiné par ~** he braked instinctively

réflexibilité /ʀeflɛksibilite/ NF reflexibility

réflexible /ʀeflɛksibl/ ADJ reflexible

réflexif, -ive /ʀeflɛksif, iv/ ADJ *(Math)* reflexive; *(Psych)* introspective

réflexion /ʀeflɛksjɔ̃/ NF 1 *(= méditation)* thought, reflection *(NonC)* ◆ **plongé *ou* absorbé dans ses ~s** deep *ou* lost in thought ◆ **ceci donne matière à ~** this is food for thought, this gives you something to think about ◆ **ceci mérite ~** *[offre]* this is worth thinking about *ou* considering; *[problème]* this needs thinking about *ou* over ◆ **ceci nécessite une ~ plus approfondie sur les problèmes** further thought needs to be given to the problems ◆ **avec ~** thoughtfully ◆ **elle a fait son choix au terme d'une longue ~ personnelle** she made her choice after much heart-searching ◆ **~ faite *ou* à la ~, je reste** on reflection *ou* on second thoughts, I'll stay ◆ **à la ~, on s'aperçoit que c'est faux** when you think about it you can see that it's wrong ◆ **groupe *ou* cellule *ou* cercle de ~** *(Pol)* think-tank ◆ **laissez-moi un délai *ou* un temps de ~** give me time to think ◆ **après un temps de ~, il ajouta ...** after a moment's thought, he added ... ◆ **nous organiserons une journée de ~ sur ce thème** we will organise a one-day conference on this topic; → **mûr**

2 *(= remarque)* remark; *(= idée)* thought ◆ **consigner ses ~s dans un cahier** to write down one's thoughts in a notebook ◆ **je m'en**

suis moi-même fait la ~ I noticed that myself ◆ **je ne me suis pas fait cette** ~ I didn't think of that ◆ **garde tes ~s pour toi** keep your remarks *ou* comments to yourself ◆ **les clients commencent à faire des ~s** the customers are beginning to make comments ◆ **on m'a fait des ~s sur son travail** people have complained to me *ou* made complaints to me about his work

③ *(Phys)* reflection

> ⚠ Attention à ne pas traduire automatiquement **réflexion** au sens de 'pensée' par le mot anglais **reflection**.

réflexivité /ʀeflɛksivite/ NF reflexiveness; *(Math)* reflexivity

réflexologie /ʀeflɛksɔlɔʒi/ NF reflexology

refluer /ʀ(ə)flye/ ► conjug 1 ◄ VI *[liquide]* to flow back; *[marée]* to go back, to ebb; *[foule]* to pour *ou* surge back; *[sang]* to rush back; *[fumée]* to blow back down; *[souvenirs]* to rush *ou* flood back ◆ **faire ~ la foule** to push *ou* force the crowd back

reflux /ʀəfly/ NM *[de foule]* backward surge; *[de marée]* ebb; *(Méd)* reflux; → **flux**

refondateur, -trice /ʀ(ə)fɔ̃datœʀ, tʀis/ ADJ *[courant]* radically reformist NM,F radical reformer

refondation /ʀ(ə)fɔ̃dasjɔ̃/ NF *[de parti politique]* radical reform

refonder /ʀ(ə)fɔ̃de/ ► conjug 1 ◄ VT *[+ alliance]* to reforge; *[+ parti politique]* to radically reform; *[+ système, modèle]* to build on new foundations ◆ **elle voudrait ~ son foyer sur des bases plus saines** she'd like to start her family life over again on a sounder basis

refondre /ʀ(ə)fɔ̃dʀ/ ► conjug 41 ◄ VT ① *[+ métal]* to remelt, to melt down again; *[+ cloche]* to recast ② *(= réviser) [+ texte, dictionnaire]* to revise; *[+ système, programme]* to overhaul ◆ **édition entièrement refondue et mise à jour** completely revised and updated edition VI to melt again

refonte /ʀ(ə)fɔ̃t/ NF ① *[de métal]* remelting; *[de cloche]* recasting ② *[de texte, dictionnaire]* revision; *[de système, programme]* overhaul ◆ **l'opposition exige une ~ radicale de la politique économique** the opposition is demanding a radical rethink of economic policy

reforestation /ʀ(ə)fɔʀɛstasjɔ̃/ NF re(af)forestation

réformable /ʀefɔʀmabl/ ADJ *(gén)* reformable; *[jugement]* which may be reversed; *[loi]* which may be amended *ou* reformed

reformatage /ʀ(ə)fɔʀmataʒ/ NM *(Ordin, TV)* reformatting

reformater /ʀ(ə)fɔʀmate/ ► conjug 1 ◄ VT *[+ disquette, grille de programmes]* to reformat

réformateur, -trice /ʀefɔʀmatœʀ, tʀis/ ADJ reforming NM,F reformer

réformation /ʀefɔʀmasjɔ̃/ NF reformation, reform ◆ **la Réformation** *(Rel)* the Reformation

réforme /ʀefɔʀm/ NF ① *(= changement)* reform ◆ **~ agraire/de l'orthographe** land/spelling reform ② *(Mil) [d'appelé]* declaration of unfitness for service; *[de soldat]* discharge ◆ **mettre à la ~** *[+ objets]* to scrap; *[+ cheval]* to put out to grass ◆ **mise à la ~** *[de soldat]* discharge; *[d'objets]* scrapping ③ *(Rel)* reformation

réformé, e /ʀefɔʀme/ (ptp de **réformer**) ADJ ① *(Rel)* Reformed ◆ **la religion ~e** the Protestant Reformed religion ② *(Mil) [appelé]* declared unfit for service; *[soldat]* discharged, invalided out *(Brit)* NM,F *(Rel)* Protestant

reformer /ʀ(ə)fɔʀme/ ► conjug 1 ◄ VT to re-form ◆ **~ les rangs** *(Mil)* to fall in again, to fall into line again VPR **se reformer** *[armée, nuage]* to re-form; *[parti]* to re-form, to be re-formed; *[groupe, rangs]* to form up again

réformer /ʀefɔʀme/ ► conjug 1 ◄ VT ① *(= améliorer) [+ loi, mœurs, religion]* to reform; *[+ abus]* to correct, to (put) right, to reform; *[+ méthode]* to improve, to reform; *[+ administration]* to reform, to overhaul ② *(Jur) [+ jugement]* to reverse, to quash *(Brit)* ③ *(Mil) [+ appelé]* to declare unfit for service; *[+ soldat]* to discharge, to invalid out *(Brit)*; *[+ matériel]* to scrap ◆ **il s'est fait ~** he got himself declared unfit for service, he got himself discharged on health grounds *ou* invalided out *(Brit)* VPR **se réformer** to change one's ways, to turn over a new leaf

réformette * /ʀefɔʀmɛt/ NF so-called reform

réformisme /ʀefɔʀmism/ NM reformism

réformiste /ʀefɔʀmist/ ADJ, NMF reformist

reformuler /ʀ(ə)fɔʀmyle/ ► conjug 1 ◄ VT *[+ proposition, théorie]* to reformulate; *[+ demande, plainte]* to change the wording of; *[+ question]* to rephrase; *(Chim)* to reformulate

refoulé, e /ʀ(ə)fule/ (ptp de **refouler**) ADJ *[personne]* repressed, inhibited; *[conflits, sentiments, sexualité]* repressed NM,F *(= personne)* repressed *ou* inhibited person NM *(Psych)* ◆ **le ~** the repressed

refoulement /ʀ(ə)fulmɑ̃/ NM ① *[d'envahisseur, attaque]* driving back, repulsing; *[de manifestants]* driving back; *[d'immigré, étranger]* turning back ② *[de désir, instinct, souvenir]* repression, suppression; *[de colère]* repression; *(Psych)* repression ③ *[de liquide]* **le ~ de l'eau** the reversal of the flow of the water ④ *(Rail)* backing, reversing

refouler /ʀ(ə)fule/ ► conjug 1 ◄ VT ① *[+ envahisseur, attaque]* to drive back, to repulse; *[+ manifestant]* to drive back; *[+ immigré, étranger]* to turn back ◆ **les clandestins ont été refoulés à la frontière** the illegal immigrants were turned back at the border ② *[+ larmes]* to force *ou* hold back, to repress; *[+ désir, instinct, souvenir]* to repress, to suppress; *[+ colère]* to repress, to hold in check; *[+ sanglots]* to choke back, to force back; *(Psych)* to repress ③ *(= faire refluer) [+ liquide]* to force back, to reverse *ou* invert the flow of ④ *(Rail)* to back, to reverse ⑤ *(Naut) [+ courant, marée]* to stem VI *[siphon, tuyauterie]* to flow back; *[cheminée]* to smoke

refourguer * /ʀ(ə)fuʀge/ ► conjug 1 ◄ VT *(= vendre)* to flog * *(à* to) to unload * *(à* onto); ◆ **~ à qn** *(= donner, se débarrasser de) [+ problème]* to unload onto sb, to palm off onto sb *; *[+ responsabilités]* to unload onto sb ◆ **elle m'a refourgué un dossier gênant** she offloaded a difficult case onto me ◆ **il m'a refourgué un faux billet** he palmed a forged banknote off onto me

refoutre ✱ /ʀ(ə)futʀ/ VT ◆ **refous-le là** shove * it back in there ◆ **refous un peu de colle dessus** stick some more glue on it ◆ **ne refous plus jamais les pieds ici !** don't you dare show your face in here again!

réfractaire /ʀefʀaktɛʀ/ ADJ ① ◆ **~ à** *[+ autorité, virus, influence]* resistant to ◆ **maladie ~** stubborn illness ◆ **je suis ~ à la poésie** poetry is a closed book to me, poetry does nothing for me ◆ **être ~ à la discipline** to resist discipline ◆ **prêtre ~** *(Hist)* non-juring priest ② *[métal]* refractory; *[brique, argile]* fire *(épith)*; *[plat]* ovenproof, heat-resistant NM *(Hist, Mil)* draft dodger, draft evader ◆ **les ~s au STO** *French civilians who refused to work in Germany during the Second World War*

réfracter /ʀefʀakte/ ► conjug 1 ◄ VT to refract VPR **se réfracter** to be refracted

réfracteur, -trice /ʀefʀaktœʀ, tʀis/ ADJ refractive, refracting *(épith)*

réfraction /ʀefʀaksjɔ̃/ NF refraction ◆ **indice de ~** refractive index

réfractomètre /ʀefʀaktɔmɛtʀ/ NM refractometer

refrain /ʀ(ə)fʀɛ̃/ NM *(Mus : en fin de couplet)* refrain, chorus; *(= chanson)* tune ◆ **c'est toujours le même ~** * it's always the same old story ◆ **change de ~ !** change the record! *, give it a rest! *

refréner /ʀ(ə)fʀene/ ► conjug 6 ◄ VT *[+ désir, impatience]* to curb, to hold in check, to check

réfrigérant, e /ʀefʀiʒeʀɑ̃, ɑ̃t/ ADJ *[fluide]* refrigerant, refrigerating; *[accueil, personne]* icy, frosty; → **mélange** NM *(Tech)* cooler

réfrigérateur /ʀefʀiʒeʀatœʀ/ NM refrigerator, fridge ◆ **mettre un projet au ~** to put a plan on ice

réfrigération /ʀefʀiʒeʀasjɔ̃/ NF refrigeration; *(Tech)* cooling

réfrigérer /ʀefʀiʒeʀe/ ► conjug 6 ◄ VT ① *(gén)* to refrigerate; *(Tech)* to cool; *[+ local]* to cool ◆ **véhicule réfrigéré** refrigerated vehicle ◆ **vitrine réfrigérée** refrigerated display ◆ **je suis réfrigéré** * I'm frozen stiff * ② *(fig) [+ enthousiasme]* to put a damper on, to cool; *[+ personne]* to have a cooling *ou* dampening effect on

réfringence /ʀefʀɛ̃ʒɑ̃s/ NF refringence

réfringent, e /ʀefʀɛ̃ʒɑ̃, ɑ̃t/ ADJ refringent

refroidir /ʀ(ə)fʀwadiʀ/ ► conjug 2 ◄ VT ① *[+ nourriture]* to cool (down) ② *(fig) [+ personne]* to put off, to have a cooling effect on; *[+ zèle]* to cool, to put a damper on, to dampen ◆ **ça m'a un peu refroidi** it put me off a bit ③ (✱ = *tuer*) to do in ✱, to bump off ✱ VI *(= cesser d'être trop chaud)* to cool (down); *(= devenir trop froid)* to get cold ◆ **laisser** *ou* **faire ~** *[+ mets trop chaud]* to leave to cool, to let cool (down); *(involontairement)* to let get cold; *[+ moteur]* to let cool; *(péj) [+ projet]* to let slide *ou* slip ◆ **mettre qch à ~** to put sth to cool (down) ◆ **tu refroidis !** *(jeu)* you're getting cold! VPR **se refroidir** *[ardeur]* to cool (off); *[mets]* to get cold; *[temps]* to get cooler *ou* colder; *[personne] (= avoir froid)* to get cold; *(= attraper un rhume)* to catch a chill

refroidissement /ʀ(ə)fʀwadismɑ̃/ NM ① *[d'air, liquide]* cooling ◆ **~ par air/eau** air-/water-cooling ◆ **~ de la température** drop in temperature ◆ **on observe un ~ du temps** the weather is getting cooler *ou* colder ◆ **tour de ~** cooling tower ② *(Méd)* chill ◆ **prendre un ~** to catch a chill ③ *(fig) [de passion]* cooling (off) ◆ **on note un ~ des relations entre les deux pays** relations between the two countries are cooling

refroidisseur, -euse /ʀ(ə)fʀwadisœʀ, øz/ ADJ cooling NM cooler; *(en industrie)* cooling tower

refuge /ʀ(ə)fyʒ/ NM *(gén)* refuge; *(pour piétons)* refuge, (traffic) island; *(en montagne)* refuge, (mountain) hut ◆ **lieu de ~** place of refuge *ou* safety ◆ **valeur ~** *(Bourse)* safe investment ◆ **chercher/trouver ~** to seek/find refuge *(dans* in; *auprès de* with); ◆ **il a cherché ~ dans une église** he sought refuge *ou* sanctuary in a church ◆ **la forêt lui a servi de ~** he found refuge in the forest

réfugié, e /ʀefyʒje/ (ptp de **se réfugier**) ADJ, NM,F refugee ◆ **~ politique** political refugee

réfugier (se) /ʀefyʒje/ ► conjug 7 ◄ VPR *(lit, fig)* to take refuge

refus /ʀ(ə)fy/ NM *(gén, Équitation)* refusal ◆ **~ de comparaître** *(Jur)* refusal to appear (in court) ◆ **~ de priorité** *(en conduisant)* refusal to give way *(Brit) ou* to yield *(US)* ◆ **~ d'obéissance** *(gén)* refusal to obey; *(Mil)* insubordination ◆ **ce n'est pas de ~** * I wouldn't say no ◆ **en cas de ~ de paiement** *ou* **de payer, il peut être poursuivi** if he refuses to pay, he may be taken to court ◆ **ils persistent dans leur ~ de négocier/de signer** they are still refusing to negotiate/to sign

refuser /ʀ(ə)fyze/ GRAMMAIRE ACTIVE 35.5, 39.3, 46.5, 52.5 ► conjug 1 ◄

VT 1 *(= ne pas accepter)* *[+ cadeau]* to refuse; *[+ offre, invitation]* to refuse, to decline, to turn down; *[+ manuscrit]* to reject, to turn down, to refuse; *[+ marchandise, racisme, inégalité]* to reject, to refuse to accept; *[+ politique, méthodes]* to refuse, to reject ◆ ~ **la lutte** *ou* **le combat** to refuse to fight ◆ **le cheval a refusé (l'obstacle)** the horse refused (the fence) ◆ ~ **le risque** to refuse to take risks ◆ **il a toujours refusé la vie routinière** he has always refused to accept a routine life

2 *(= ne pas accorder)* *[+ permission, entrée, consentement]* to refuse; *[+ demande]* to refuse, to turn down; *[+ compétence, qualité]* to deny ◆ ~ **l'entrée à qn** to refuse admittance *ou* entry to sb, to turn sb away ◆ ~ **sa porte à qn** to bar one's door to sb ◆ **je me suis vu ~ un verre d'eau** I was refused a glass of water ◆ **on lui a refusé l'accès aux archives** he was refused *ou* denied access to the records ◆ **il m'a refusé la priorité** *[automobiliste]* he didn't give me right of way *(Brit)*, he didn't yield to me *(US)* ◆ **elle est si gentille, on ne peut rien lui** ~ she's so nice, you just can't say no to her ◆ **je lui refuse toute générosité** I refuse to accept *ou* admit that he has any generosity

3 *[+ client]* to turn away; *[+ candidat]* *(à un examen)* to fail; *(à un poste)* to turn down, to reject ◆ **il s'est fait ~ au permis de conduire** he failed his driving test ◆ **on a dû ~ du monde** they had to turn people away

4 ◆ ~ **de faire qch** to refuse to do sth ◆ **il a refusé net (de le faire)** he refused point-blank (to do it) ◆ **la voiture refuse de démarrer** the car won't start

VI *[pieu]* to resist; *[vent]* to haul

VPR **se refuser** 1 *(= se priver de)* to refuse o.s., to deny o.s. ◆ **tu ne te refuses rien !** *(iro)* you certainly spoil yourself!

2 ◆ **ça ne se refuse pas** *[offre]* it is not to be turned down *ou* refused ◆ **un apéritif, ça ne se refuse pas** I wouldn't say no to an apéritif

3 ◆ **se ~ à** *[+ méthode, solution]* to refuse (to accept), to reject ◆ **se ~ à tout commentaire** to refuse to (make any) comment ◆ **elle s'est refusée à lui** *(frm)* she refused to give herself to him ◆ **se ~ à faire qch** to refuse to do sth

réfutable /ʀefytabl/ ADJ refutable, which can be disproved *ou* refuted ◆ **facilement** ~ easily refuted *ou* disproved

réfutation /ʀefytasjɔ̃/ NF refutation ◆ **fait qui apporte la ~ d'une allégation** fact which refutes *ou* disproves an allegation

réfuter /ʀefyte/ ► conjug 1 ◄ VT to refute, to disprove

regagner /ʀ(ə)gaɲe/ ► conjug 1 ◄ VT 1 *(= récupérer)* *[+ amitié, faveur]* to regain, to win back; *[+ argent perdu au jeu]* to win back; *[+ confiance]* to regain, to recover, to get back; *[+ parts de marché]* to get back, to regain ◆ ~ **du terrain** *(Mil, fig)* to regain ground ◆ ~ **le terrain perdu** to win back lost ground ◆ **il a regagné sa place en tête du classement** he regained his place *ou* position at the top of the league 2 *[+ lieu]* to get *ou* go back to; *[+ pays]* to arrive back in, to get back to ◆ **les sinistrés ont pu ~ leur domicile** the disaster victims were able to return to their homes ◆ **il regagna enfin sa maison** he finally arrived back home *ou* got back home ◆ ~ **sa place** to return to one's place *ou* seat ◆ **les spationautes ont regagné la Terre** the astronauts returned to earth

regain /ʀəgɛ̃/ NM 1 ◆ ~ **de** *[+ jeunesse]* renewal of; *[+ popularité]* revival of; *[+ activité, influence]* renewal *ou* revival of ◆ **un ~ d'intérêt/d'optimisme/d'énergie** renewed interest/optimism/energy ◆ ~ **de violence** new *ou* fresh outbreak of violence, renewed (outbreak of) violence ◆ ~ **de tension** *(Pol)* rise in tension 2 *(Agr)* second crop of hay, aftermath †

régal (pl **régals**) /ʀegal/ NM delight, treat ◆ **ce gâteau est un ~ !, ce gâteau, quel ~ !** this cake is absolutely delicious! ◆ **c'est un ~ pour les yeux** it is a sight for sore eyes, it is a delight *ou* treat to look at ◆ **quel ~ de manger des cerises** what a treat to have cherries

régalade /ʀegalad/ **à la régalade** LOC ADV *[boire]* without letting one's lips touch the bottle (*ou* glass *etc*)

régaler /ʀegale/ ► conjug 1 ◄ VT ◆ ~ **qn** to treat sb to a delicious meal ◆ **c'est moi qui régale** I'm treating everyone, it's my treat ◆ **c'est le patron qui régale** it's on the house ◆ **chaque soir, il nous régalait de ses histoires** in the evenings he would regale us with his stories

VPR **se régaler** *(= bien manger)* to have a delicious meal; *(= éprouver du plaisir)* to have a wonderful time* ◆ **se ~ de gâteaux** to have a feast of cakes ◆ **on s'est (bien) régalé** *(au repas)* it was delicious; *(au cinéma, théâtre)* we had a great time*, we really enjoyed ourselves ◆ **je me régale !** this is delicious! ◆ **il y en a qui se sont régalés dans cette vente** *(péj)* some people did really well out of that sale ◆ **les cafetiers se régalent avec cette vague de chaleur** the café owners are making a mint* *ou* doing really well in this heatwave ◆ **se ~ de romans** *(habituellement)* to be a keen reader of *ou* very keen on *(Brit)* novels; *(en vacances etc)* to gorge o.s. on novels, to have a feast of novel-reading

régalien, -ienne /ʀegaljɛ̃, jɛn/ ADJ *[droits]* kingly

regard /ʀ(ə)gaʀ/ NM 1 *(= yeux)* eyes ◆ **son ~ bleu/noir** his blue/black eyes ◆ **son ~ se posa sur moi** his gaze *ou* eyes came to rest on me ◆ **soustraire qch aux ~s** to hide sth from sight *ou* from view, to put sth out of sight ◆ **cela attire tous les ~s** it catches everyone's eye *ou* attention ◆ **tous les ~s étaient fixés sur elle** all eyes were on her *ou* were turned towards her ◆ **il restait assis, le ~ perdu (dans le vide)** he was sitting there, staring into space ◆ **son ~ était dur/tendre** he had a hard/tender look in his eye ◆ **il avançait, le ~ fixe** he was walking along with a fixed stare ◆ **dévorer/menacer qn du ~** to look hungrily/threateningly at sb, to fix sb with a hungry/threatening look *ou* stare ◆ **sous le ~ attentif de sa mère** under his mother's watchful eye ◆ **sous le ~ des caméras** in front of the cameras; → **chercher, croiser, détourner**

2 *(= coup d'œil)* look, glance ◆ **échanger des ~s avec qn** to exchange looks *ou* glances with sb ◆ **échanger des ~s d'intelligence** to exchange knowing looks ◆ **lancer un ~ de colère à qn** to glare at sb, to cast an angry look *ou* glare at sb ◆ **au premier ~** at first glance *ou* sight ◆ ~ **en coin** *ou* **en coulisse** sideways *ou* sidelong glance ◆ **il lui lança un ~ noir** he shot him a black *ou* dark look ◆ **il jeta un dernier ~ en arrière** he took one last look behind him, he looked back one last time

3 *(= point de vue, opinion)* **porter** *ou* **jeter un ~ critique sur qch** to take a critical look at sth, to look critically at sth ◆ **porter un ~ extérieur sur qch** to look at sth from the outside ◆ **il mène sa vie sans se soucier du ~ des autres** he lives his own life and isn't concerned about what other people think

4 *[d'égout]* manhole; *[de baignoire]* inspection hole

5 *(locutions)*

◆ **au regard de** ◆ **au ~ de la loi** in the eyes of the law, from the legal viewpoint

◆ **en regard** ◆ **texte avec photos en ~** text with photos on the opposite *ou* facing page

◆ **en regard de** ◆ **en ~ de ce qu'il gagne** compared with *ou* in comparison with what he earns

regardant, e /ʀ(ə)gaʀdɑ̃, ɑ̃t/ ADJ careful with money ◆ **il n'est pas ~** he's quite free with his money ◆ **ils sont/ne sont pas ~s sur l'argent de poche** they are not very/they are quite generous with pocket money ◆ **il n'est pas très ~ sur la propreté/les manières** he's not very particular about cleanliness/manners

regarder /ʀ(ə)gaʀde/ ► conjug 1 ◄ VT 1 *(= diriger son regard vers)* *[+ paysage, scène]* to look at; *[+ action en déroulement, film, match]* to watch ◆ **elle regardait les voitures sur le parking** she was looking at the cars in the car park ◆ **elle regardait les voitures défiler** *ou* **qui défilaient** she was watching the cars driving past *ou* the cars as they drove past ◆ ~ **tomber la pluie** *ou* **la pluie tomber** to watch the rain falling ◆ **il regarda sa montre** he looked at *ou* had a look at his watch ◆ **regarde, il pleut** look, it's raining ◆ **regarde bien, il va sauter** watch *ou* look, he's going to jump ◆ ~ **la télévision/une émission à la télévision** to watch television/a programme on television ◆ ~ **le journal** to look at *ou* have a look at the paper ◆ ~ **sur le livre de qn** *(= partager)* to share sb's book; *(= tricher)* to look at sb's book ◆ ~ **par la fenêtre** *(du dedans)* to look out of the window; *(du dehors)* to look in through the window ◆ **regarde les oiseaux par la fenêtre** look through *ou* out of the window at the birds, watch the birds through *ou* out of the window ◆ **regarde devant toi/derrière toi** look in front of you/behind you ◆ **regarde où tu marches** watch *ou* look where you're going *ou* putting your feet ◆ **regarde voir* dans l'armoire** take *ou* have a look in the wardrobe ◆ **regarde voir* s'il arrive** look *ou* have a look and see if he's coming ◆ **attends, je vais ~** hang on, I'll go and look *ou* I'll take a look ◆ **regardez-moi ça/son écriture*** just (take a) look at that/at his writing ◆ **tu ne m'as pas regardé !*** what do you take me for!*, who do you think I am!* ◆ **j'ai regardé partout, je n'ai rien trouvé** I looked everywhere but I couldn't find anything ◆ **regarde à la pendule quelle heure il est** look at the clock to see what time it is, look and see what time it is by the clock ◆ **regardez-le faire** *(gén)* watch him *ou* look at him do it; *(pour apprendre)* watch *ou* look how he does it ◆ **elles sont allées ~ les vitrines/les magasins** they've gone to do some window-shopping/to have a look around the shops ◆ **sans ~** *[traverser]* without looking; *[payer]* regardless of cost *ou* the expense; → **chien**

2 *(rapidement)* to glance at, to have a glance *ou* a (quick) look at; *(furtivement)* to steal a glance at, to glance sidelong at; *(longuement)* to gaze at; *(fixement)* to stare at ◆ ~ **un texte rapidement** to glance at *ou* through a text, to have a quick look *ou* glance at *ou* through a text ◆ ~ **(qch) par le trou de la serrure** to peep *ou* look (at sth) through the keyhole ◆ ~ **qch de près/de plus près** to have a close/closer look at sth, to look closely/more closely at sth ◆ ~ **sans voir** to look with unseeing eyes ◆ ~ **qn avec colère** to glare angrily at sb ◆ ~ **qn avec méfiance** to look at *ou* eye sb suspiciously ◆ ~ **qn de haut** to give sb a scornful look, to look scornfully at sb ◆ ~ **qn droit dans les yeux/bien en face** *(lit, fig)* to look sb straight in the eye/straight in the face ◆ ~ **qn dans le blanc des yeux** to look sb straight in the face *ou* eye

3 *(= vérifier)* *[+ appareil, malade]* to look at; *[+ huile, essence]* to look at, to check ◆ **peux-tu ~ la lampe ? elle ne marche pas** can you have *ou* take a look at the lamp? it doesn't work ◆ **regarde dans l'annuaire** look in the phone book ◆ ~ **un mot dans le dictionnaire** to look up *ou* check a word in the dictionary

4 *(= considérer)* *[+ situation, problème]* to view ◆ ~ **l'avenir avec appréhension** to view the future

with trepidation ◆ **il ne regarde que son propre intérêt** he is only concerned with *ou* he only thinks about his own interests ◆ **nous le regardons comme un ami** we look upon him *ou* we regard him as a friend

[5] *(= concerner)* to concern ◆ **cette affaire me regarde quand même un peu** this business does concern me a little ◆ **en quoi cela te regarde-t-il ?** *(= de quoi te mêles-tu ?)* what business is it of yours?, what has it to do with you?; *(= en quoi es-tu touché ?)* how does it affect *ou* concern you? ◆ **fais ce que je te dis, la suite me regarde** do what I tell you, what happens next is my concern *ou* business ◆ **que vas-tu faire ? – ça me regarde** what will you do? – that's my business *ou* my concern ◆ **non mais, ça vous regarde !*** what business is it of yours? ◆ **cela ne le regarde pas** *ou* **en rien** that's none of his business, that's no concern of his ◆ **mêlez-vous de ce qui vous regarde** mind your own business

[6] *(= être orienté vers)* ~ **(vers)** *[maison]* to face

VT INDIR **regarder à** to think of *ou* about ◆ **y ~ à deux fois avant de faire qch** to think twice before doing sth ◆ **il n'y regarde pas de si près** he's not that fussy *ou* particular ◆ **à y bien ~** on thinking it over ◆ **c'est quelqu'un qui va ~ à deux francs** he's the sort of person who will niggle over *ou* worry about two francs ◆ **il regarde à s'acheter un costume neuf** he always thinks twice before laying out money for a new suit ◆ **quand il fait un cadeau, il ne regarde pas à la dépense** when he gives somebody a present he doesn't worry how much he spends ◆ **acheter qch sans ~ à la dépense** to buy sth without bothering about the expense

VPR **se regarder** [1] *(soi-même)* ◆ **se ~ dans une glace** to look at o.s. in a mirror ◆ **elle ne peut plus se ~ dans une glace** *(fig)* she's ashamed of herself ◆ **il ne s'est pas regardé !** *(iro)* he should take a look at himself!

[2] *(mutuellement) [personnes]* to look at each other *ou* one another; *[maisons]* to face each other *ou* one another

regarnir /ʀ(ə)gaʀniʀ/ ► conjug 2 ◄ VT *[+ magasin, rayon]* to stock up again, to restock; *[+ trousse]* to refill, to replenish; *[+ réfrigérateur]* to fill (up) again; *[+ coussin]* to refill

régate /ʀegat/ NF ◆ **~(s)** regatta

régater /ʀegate/ ► conjug 1 ◄ VI to sail in a regatta

régatier, -ière /ʀegatje, jɛʀ/ NM,F regatta competitor

regeler /ʀəʒ(ə)le, ʀ(ə)ʒəle/ ► conjug 5 ◄ VT, VB IMPERS to freeze again

régence /ʀeʒɑ̃s/ NF *(Pol)* regency ◆ **la Régence** *(Hist)* the Regency ADJ INV *[meuble] (en France)* (French) Regency; *(en Grande-Bretagne)* Regency; *(fig) [personne, mœurs]* overrefined

régénérant, e /ʀeʒeneʀɑ̃, ʀɑ̃t/ ADJ *[lait, crème]* regenerating

régénérateur, -trice /ʀeʒeneʀatœʀ, tʀis/ ADJ regenerative NM regenerator

régénération /ʀeʒeneʀasjɔ̃/ NF regeneration

régénérer /ʀeʒeneʀe/ ► conjug 6 ◄ VT *(Bio, Rel)* to regenerate; *[+ personne, forces]* to revive, to restore

régent, e /ʀeʒɑ̃, ɑ̃t/ ADJ regent ◆ **prince ~** prince regent NM,F *(Pol)* regent; *(Admin = directeur)* manager

régenter /ʀeʒɑ̃te/ ► conjug 1 ◄ VT *(gén)* to rule over; *[+ personne]* to dictate to ◆ **il veut tout ~** he wants to run the whole show*

reggae /ʀege/ NM reggae

régicide /ʀeʒisid/ ADJ regicidal NMF *(= personne)* regicide NM *(= crime)* regicide

régie /ʀeʒi/ NF [1] *(= gestion) [d'État]* state control; *[de commune]* local government control (*de* over); ◆ **en ~** under state (*ou* local government) control ◆ **~ directe** *ou* **simple** direct state control ◆ **~ intéressée** public service concession ◆ **travaux en ~** public work contracting *(by the government)* [2] *(= société)* ~ **(d'État)** state-owned company, government corporation ◆ **la Régie française des tabacs** *the French national tobacco company* ◆ **la Régie autonome des transports parisiens** *the Paris city transport authority* ◆ **~ publicitaire** advertising sales division [3] *(Ciné, Théât, TV)* production department; *(Radio, TV = salle de contrôle)* control room

regimber /ʀ(ə)ʒɛ̃be/ ► conjug 1 ◄ VI *[personne]* to rebel (*contre* against); *[cheval]* to jib ◆ **fais-le sans ~** do it without grumbling ◆ **quand je lui ai demandé de le faire, il a regimbé** when I asked him to do it he jibbed at the idea

régime[1] /ʀeʒim/ NM [1] *(Pol) (= mode)* system (of government); *(= gouvernement)* government; *(péj)* régime ◆ **~ monarchique/républicain** monarchical/republican system (of government); → **ancien**

[2] *(Admin) (= système)* scheme, system; *(= règlements)* regulations ◆ **~ douanier/des hôpitaux** *(= système)* customs/hospital system; *(= règle)* customs/hospital regulations ◆ **~ de la Sécurité sociale** Social Security system ◆ **~ maladie** health insurance scheme *(Brit) ou* plan *(US)* ◆ **~ vieillesse** pension scheme

[3] *(Jur)* ~ **(matrimonial)** marriage settlement ◆ **se marier sous le ~ de la communauté/de la séparation de biens** to opt for a marriage settlement based on joint ownership of property/on separate ownership of property

[4] *(Méd)* diet ◆ **être/mettre qn au ~** to be/put sb on a diet ◆ **suivre un ~ (alimentaire)** *(gén)* to be on a diet; *(scrupuleusement)* to follow *ou* keep to a diet ◆ **~ sec/sans sel/lacté/basses calories/amaigrissant** alcohol-free/salt-free/milk/low-calorie/slimming *(Brit) ou* reducing *(US)* diet ◆ **chocolat/produit de ~** diet chocolate/product ◆ **être/se mettre au ~ jockey*** *(hum)* to be/go on a starvation *ou* crash diet

[5] *[de moteur]* (engine *ou* running) speed ◆ **ce moteur est bruyant à haut ~** this engine is noisy when it's revving hard ◆ **~ de croisière** cruising speed ◆ **à ce ~, nous n'aurons bientôt plus d'argent** (if we go on) at this rate *ou* at the rate we're going we'll soon have no money left ◆ **fonctionner** *ou* **marcher** *ou* **tourner à plein ~** *[moteur]* to run at top speed, to be on *ou* at full throttle; *[usine]* to run at full capacity ◆ **baisse de ~** *(= ralentissement)* slowdown ◆ **il a disputé trois sets sans la moindre baisse de ~** he played three sets without once slackening his *ou* the pace ◆ **montée en ~** *[de moteur]* revving (up); *[de secteur, économie]* gearing up ◆ **la montée en ~ de l'entreprise** the increased activity in the company

[6] *(Météo) [de pluies, fleuve]* régime

[7] *(Gram)* object ◆ **~ direct/indirect** direct/indirect object ◆ **cas ~** objective case

[8] *(Phys) [d'écoulement]* rate of flow

régime[2] /ʀeʒim/ NM *[de dattes]* cluster, bunch; *[de bananes]* bunch

régiment /ʀeʒimɑ̃/ NM [1] *(Mil) (= corps)* regiment; *(* = service militaire)* military *ou* national service ◆ **être au ~*** to be doing (one's) national *ou* military service ◆ **aller au ~*** to go into the army, to be called up [2] *(* = masse) [de personnes]* regiment, army; *[de choses]* mass(es), loads ◆ **il y en a pour tout un ~** there's enough for a whole army

régimentaire /ʀeʒimɑ̃tɛʀ/ ADJ regimental

région /ʀeʒjɔ̃/ NF *(Admin, Géog) (étendue)* region; *(limitée)* area; *(Anat)* region, area; *(= conseil régional)* regional council; *(fig = domaine)* region ◆ **~s polaires/équatoriales** polar/equatorial regions ◆ **la ~ parisienne/londonienne** the Paris/London area ◆ **Toulouse et sa ~** Toulouse and the surrounding area ◆ **ça se trouve dans la ~ de Lyon** it's in the Lyons area *ou* around Lyons ◆ **si vous passez dans la ~, allez les voir** if you are in the area *ou* if you go that way, go and see them ◆ **les habitants de la ~** the local inhabitants ◆ **je ne suis pas de la ~** I'm not from around here ◆ **dans nos ~s** *(= où nous sommes)* in these parts, in our part of the world; *(= d'où nous venons)* where we come from ◆ **en ~** in the provinces

RÉGION

The 22 **régions** are the largest administrative divisions in France, each being made up of several « départements ». Each **région** is administered by a « conseil régional », whose members (« les conseillers régionaux ») are elected for a six-year term in the « élections régionales ». The expression « la **région** » is also used by extension to refer to the regional council itself. → DÉPARTEMENT, ÉLECTIONS

régional, e (mpl **-aux**) /ʀeʒjɔnal, o/ ADJ *[presse, élections]* regional NM *(Cyclisme)* ◆ **le ~ de l'étape** *cyclist from the particular region through which the Tour de France is passing* NFPL **régionales** *(= élections)* regional elections; *(= nouvelles)* regional news *(NonC)*

régionalisation /ʀeʒjɔnalizasjɔ̃/ NF regionalization

régionaliser /ʀeʒjɔnalize/ ► conjug 1 ◄ VT to regionalize

régionalisme /ʀeʒjɔnalism/ NM [1] *(Pol)* regionalism [2] *(Ling)* regionalism, regional expression

régionaliste /ʀeʒjɔnalist/ ADJ regionalist(ic) NMF regionalist

régir /ʀeʒiʀ/ ► conjug 2 ◄ VT *(gén, Ling)* to govern

régisseur, -euse /ʀeʒisœʀ, øz/ NM,F *[de propriété]* steward; *(Théât)* stage manager; *(Ciné, TV)* assistant director ◆ **~ de plateau** studio director

registre /ʀəʒistʀ/ NM [1] *(= livre)* register ◆ **~ maritime/d'hôtel/du commerce** shipping/hotel/trade register ◆ **~ de notes** *(Scol)* mark book *(Brit)*, grade book *ou* register *(US)* ◆ **~ d'absences** *(Scol)* attendance register [2] *(Mus) [d'orgue]* stop; *[de voix] (= étage)* register; *(= étendue)* register, range [3] *(Ling) (= niveau)* register, level (of language); *(= style)* register, style [4] *(Tech) [de fourneau]* damper, register; *(Ordin, Typo)* register [5] *(fig = genre, ton)* mood, vein ◆ **il a complètement changé de ~** *[écrivain]* he's completely changed his style ◆ **cet auteur joue sur tous les ~s** this author has a very varied style

COMP **Registre du commerce et des sociétés** *(= service)* Companies Registration Office; *(= fichier)* trade *ou* company *ou* corporate *(US)* register

registre de comptabilité ledger

registre de l'état civil register of births, marriages and deaths

registre mortuaire register of deaths

registre de vapeur throttle valve

réglable /ʀeglabl/ ADJ [1] *[mécanisme, débit]* adjustable ◆ **siège à dossier ~** reclining seat [2] *(= payable)* payable

réglage /ʀeglaʒ/ NM [1] *[de mécanisme, débit]* regulation, adjustment; *[de moteur]* tuning; *[d'allumage, thermostat]* setting, adjustment; *[de dossier de chaise, tir]* adjustment [2] *[de papier]* ruling

réglé, e /ʀegle/ (ptp de **régler**) ADJ [1] *(= régulier) [vie]* (well-)ordered, regular; *[personne]* steady, stable ◆ **c'est ~ comme du papier à musique*, il arrive tous les jours à 8 heures** he arrives at 8 o'clock every day, as regular as clockwork ◆ **être ~ comme une horloge** to be as regular as clockwork [2] *[adolescente]* **elle n'est pas encore ~e** she hasn't started having periods yet ◆ **elle est bien ~e** her periods are regular [3] *[papier]* ruled, lined

règle /ʀɛgl/ **NF** [1] *(= loi, principe)* rule ◆ **~ de conduite** rule of conduct ◆ **~ de 3** rule of 3 ◆ **les ~s de la bienséance/de l'honneur** the rules of propriety/of honour ◆ **~ d'or** golden rule ◆ **~s de sécurité** safety regulations ◆ **respecter les ~s élémentaires d'hygiène** to observe the basic hygiene rules, to observe basic hygiene ◆ **me lever à 7 heures, j'en ai fait une ~ de vie** I've made it a rule to get up at 7 in the morning ◆ **ils ont pour ~ de se réunir chaque jour** they make it a rule to meet every day ◆ **c'est la ~ du jeu** *(lit, fig)* those are the rules of the game ◆ **se plier aux ~s du jeu** *(lit, fig)* to play the game according to the rules ◆ **c'est la ~ (de la maison)** that's the rule (of the house) ◆ **cela n'échappe pas à la ~** that's no exception to the rule ◆ **laisser jouer la ~ de l'avantage** *(Sport)* to play the advantage rule

◆ **dans les règles** ◆ **il faut faire la demande dans les ~s** you must apply through the proper channels *ou* according to the rules ◆ **dans les ~s de l'art** *(lit)* carried out professionally; *(hum)* according to the rule book

◆ **de règle** ◆ **il est de ~ qu'on fasse** *ou* **de faire un cadeau** it's usual *ou* it's standard practice *ou* the done thing to give a present ◆ **dans ce métier, la prudence est de ~** in this profession, caution is the rule

◆ **en règle** *[comptabilité, papiers]* in order; *[avertissement]* given according to the rules; *[réclamation]* made according to the rules; *[attaque, critique]* all-out *(épith)* ◆ **il lui a fait une cour en ~** he did all the right things to win her hand ◆ **être en ~ avec les autorités** to be straight with *ou* in order with the authorities ◆ **se mettre en ~ avec les autorités** to sort out *ou* straighten out one's position with the authorities ◆ **je ne suis pas en ~** my papers are not in order ◆ **se mettre en ~ avec Dieu** to make things right with God

◆ **en règle générale** as a (general) rule

[2] *(= instrument)* ruler ◆ **trait tiré à la ~** line drawn with a ruler ◆ **~ à calcul** *ou* **à calculer** slide rule

[3] *(= menstruation)* **~s** period(s) ◆ **avoir ses ~s** to have one's period(s) ◆ **pendant la période des ~s** during menstruation ◆ **avoir des ~s douloureuses** to suffer from *ou* get period pains, to have painful periods

[4] *(Rel)* rule

règlement /ʀɛgləmɑ̃/ GRAMMAIRE ACTIVE 47.5 **NM** [1] *(Admin, Police, Univ) (= règle)* regulation; *(= réglementation)* rules, regulations ◆ **c'est contraire au ~** it's against the rules *ou* against regulations ◆ **~ de service** administrative rule *ou* regulation ◆ **~ intérieur** *(Scol)* school rules; *[d'entreprise]* policies and procedures (manual) ◆ **d'après le ~ communautaire** *ou* **européen du 2 mars** *(Europe)* under the community *ou* European regulation of 2 March

[2] *[d'affaire, conflit]* settlement, settling; *[de facture, dette]* settlement, payment ◆ **~ en espèces** cash settlement *ou* payment ◆ **faire un ~ par chèque** to pay *ou* make a payment by cheque ◆ **la date de ~ est inscrite sur la facture** the due date *ou* the date when payment is due appears on the bill ◆ **marché à ~ mensuel** *(Bourse)* forward market ◆ **~ judiciaire** *(Jur)* (compulsory) liquidation ◆ **être mis en ~ judiciaire** to be put into receivership, to be put into the hands of the receiver ◆ **~ (à l')amiable** *(Jur)* amicable settlement, out-of-court settlement ◆ **~ de compte(s)** *(fig)* settling of scores; *(de gangsters)* gangland killing ◆ **le ~ de votre dossier interviendra sous un mois** your request will be dealt with within a month

réglementaire /ʀɛgləmɑ̃tɛʀ/ **ADJ** *[uniforme, taille]* regulation *(épith)*; *[procédure]* statutory, laid down in the regulations ◆ **ça n'est pas très ~** that isn't really allowed, that's really against the rules ◆ **dans le temps ~** in the prescribed time ◆ **ce certificat n'est pas ~** this certificate doesn't conform to the regulations ◆ **dispositions ~s** regulations ◆ **pouvoir ~** power to make regulations

réglementairement /ʀɛgləmɑ̃tɛʀmɑ̃/ **ADV** in accordance with *ou* according to the regulations, statutorily

réglementation /ʀɛgləmɑ̃tasjɔ̃/ **NF** *(= règles)* regulations; *(= contrôle) [de prix, loyers]* control, regulation ◆ **~ des changes** exchange control regulations

réglementer /ʀɛgləmɑ̃te/ ► conjug 1 ◄ **VT** to regulate, to control ◆ **la vente des médicaments est très réglementée** the sale of medicines is strictly controlled; → **stationnement**

régler /ʀegle/ GRAMMAIRE ACTIVE 47.5 ► conjug 6 ◄ **VT** [1] *(= conclure) [+ affaire, conflit]* to settle; *[+ problème]* to settle, to sort out; *[+ dossier]* to deal with ◆ **~ qch à l'amiable** *(gén)* to settle sth amicably; *(Jur)* to settle sth out of court ◆ **alors, c'est une affaire réglée** *ou* **c'est réglé ?** right, is that settled then? ◆ **on va ~ ça tout de suite** we'll get that settled *ou* sorted out straightaway

[2] *(= payer) [+ note, dette]* to settle (up), to pay (up); *[+ compte]* to settle; *[+ commerçant, créancier]* to settle up with, to pay; *[+ travaux]* to settle up for, to pay for ◆ **est-ce que je peux ~ ?** can I settle up (with you)? *ou* settle *ou* pay the bill? ◆ **je viens ~ mes dettes** I've come to settle my debts *ou* to square up with you* ◆ **~ qch en espèces** to pay for sth in cash ◆ **est-ce que je peux (vous) ~ par chèque ?** can I give you a cheque?, can I pay (you) by cheque? ◆ **~ son compte à un employé*** *(lit)* to settle up with an employee*; *(fig = renvoyer)* to give an employee his cards *(Brit) ou* books* *(Brit) ou* pink slip* *(US)* ◆ **j'ai un compte à ~ avec lui** I've got a score to settle with him, I've got a bone to pick with him ◆ **on lui a réglé son compte !*** *(vengeance)* they've settled his hash*; *(assassinat)* they've taken care of him *(euph)* ◆ **les deux bandes veulent ~ leurs comptes** the two gangs want to settle the score*

[3] *[+ mécanisme, débit, machine]* to regulate, to adjust; *[+ dossier de chaise, tir]* to adjust; *[+ moteur]* to tune; *[+ allumage, ralenti]* to set, to adjust; *[+ réveil]* to set ◆ **~ le thermostat à 18°** to set the thermostat to *ou* at 18° ◆ **~ une montre** *(mettre à l'heure)* to put a watch right *(sur* by); *(réparer)* to regulate a watch ◆ **le carburateur est mal réglé** the carburettor is badly tuned

[4] *(= fixer) [+ modalités, date, programme]* to settle (on), to fix (up), to decide on; *[+ conduite, réactions]* to determine ◆ **~ l'ordre d'une cérémonie** to settle *ou* fix (up) the order of (a) ceremony ◆ **il ne sait pas ~ l'emploi de ses journées** he is incapable of planning out *ou* organizing his daily routine ◆ **~ le sort de qn** to decide *ou* determine sb's fate

[5] *(= prendre comme modèle)* **~ qch sur** to model sth on, to adjust sth to ◆ **~ sa vie sur (celle de) son père** to model one's life on that of one's father ◆ **~ sa conduite sur les circonstances** to adjust one's conduct *ou* behaviour to the circumstances ◆ **se ~ sur qn d'autre** to model o.s. on sb else ◆ **il essaya de ~ son pas sur celui de son père** he tried to walk in step with his father ◆ **~ sa vitesse sur celle de l'autre voiture** to adjust *ou* match one's speed to that of the other car

[6] *[+ papier]* to rule (lines on)

réglette /ʀeglɛt/ **NF** *(Typo)* setting stick; *(= petite règle)* small ruler

régleur, -euse /ʀeglœʀ, øz/ **NM,F** *(= ouvrier)* setter, adjuster **NF** **régleuse** ruling machine

réglisse /ʀeglis/ **NF** *ou* **nm** liquorice ◆ **bâton/rouleau de ~** liquorice stick/roll

réglo* /ʀeglo/ **ADJ INV** *[personne]* straight*, honest, dependable ◆ **c'est ~** it's OK*, it's in order ◆ **ce n'est pas très ~** it's not really right, it's not really on* *(Brit)*

régnant, e /ʀeɲɑ̃, ɑ̃t/ **ADJ** *[famille, prince]* reigning *(épith)*; *[théorie, idée]* reigning *(épith)*, prevailing *(épith)*

règne /ʀɛɲ/ **NM** [1] *[de roi, tyran] (= période)* reign; *(= domination)* rule ◆ **sous le ~ de Louis XIV** *(période)* during the reign of Louis XIV; *(domination)* under the rule of Louis XIV [2] *(fig)* **le ~ de (la) terreur** the rule of terror ◆ **le ~ de la loi** the rule of law ◆ **ces temps de ~ de l'image** these times when image is all *ou* all-important ◆ **le ~ du chacun-pour-soi** an ethos of every man for himself [3] ◆ **~ animal/végétal/minéral** animal/vegetable *ou* plant/mineral kingdom

régner /ʀeɲe/ ► conjug 6 ◄ **VI** [1] *(= être sur le trône)* to reign; *(= exercer sa domination)* to rule *(sur* over) ◆ **il règne (en maître) sur le village** *(fig)* he reigns *ou* rules (supreme) over the village ◆ **elle règne dans la cuisine** she reigns over *ou* rules in the kitchen ◆ **~ sur nos passions** *(littér)* to rule over *ou* govern our passions; → **diviser**

[2] *(= prédominer) [paix, silence]* to reign *(sur* over) ◆ **le silence régnait au déjeuner** they ate in silence ◆ **la confiance qui règne entre les deux partenaires** the trust (that exists) between the two partners ◆ **la confiance ne règne pas vraiment ici** there's no real (feeling of) confidence here ◆ **la confiance règne !** *(iro)* you see how much they *(ou* you *etc)* trust us! ◆ **la peur continue de ~ dans les rues de la ville** fear still pervades the streets of the town ◆ **la peur du chômage règne partout** everywhere there is the fear of unemployment ◆ **la plus grande confusion continue de ~** there is still tremendous confusion ◆ **une maison où l'ordre règne** a house in which everything is tidy ◆ **il a fait ~ la terreur** he imposed a reign of terror ◆ **faire ~ l'ordre/la loi** to impose order/the rule of law

regonflage /ʀ(ə)gɔ̃flaʒ/, **regonflement** /ʀ(ə)gɔ̃fləmɑ̃/ **NM** blowing up (again), reinflating; *(avec une pompe à main)* pumping up (again)

regonfler /ʀ(ə)gɔ̃fle/ ► conjug 1 ◄ **VT** [1] *(= gonfler à nouveau)* to blow up again, to reinflate; *(avec une pompe à main)* to pump up again [2] *(= gonfler davantage)* to blow up harder, to pump up further [3] * *[+ personne]* to cheer up; *[+ ventes, bénéfices]* to boost ◆ **il est regonflé (à bloc)** he's back on top of things* ◆ **~ le moral de qn** to bolster sb up **VI** *[rivière]* to swell *ou* rise again; *(Méd)* to swell up again

regorgement /ʀ(ə)gɔʀʒəmɑ̃/ **NM** overflow

regorger /ʀ(ə)gɔʀʒe/ ► conjug 3 ◄ **VI** [1] ◆ **~ de** *[région, pays]* to abound in; *[maison, magasin]* to be packed *ou* crammed with ◆ **la région regorge d'ananas** pineapples are plentiful in the region, the region abounds in pineapples ◆ **cette année le marché regorge de fruits** this year there is a glut *ou* an abundance of fruit on the market ◆ **le pays regorge d'argent** the country has enormous financial assets ◆ **il regorge d'argent** he is rolling in money*, he has got plenty of money ◆ **sa maison regorgeait de livres/d'invités** his house was packed with *ou* crammed with *ou* cram-full of books/guests ◆ **la rue regorge de petits étals** the street is packed with little market stalls ◆ **la ville regorge de festivaliers** the town is swarming with festival-goers ◆ **son livre regorge de bonnes idées/de fautes** his book is (jam-)packed *ou* crammed with good ideas/is riddled with mistakes

[2] *[liquide]* to overflow

régresser /ʀegʀese/ ▸ conjug 1 ◂ VI [*science, enfant*] to regress; [*douleur, épidémie*] to recede, to diminish; [*chiffre d'affaires, ventes*] to drop, to fall ◆ **le taux de chômage a nettement régressé** the rate of unemployment has dropped sharply

régressif, -ive /ʀegʀesif, iv/ ADJ [*évolution, raisonnement*] regressive; [*marche*] backward (*épith*); (*Phon*) anticipatory ◆ **érosion régressive** (*Géol*) headward erosion ◆ **forme régressive** regressive *ou* recessive form ◆ **dérivation régressive** (*Ling*) back formation ◆ **impôt ~** (*Fin*) regressive tax

régression /ʀegʀesjɔ̃/ NF (*gén*) regression, decline; (*Bio, Math, Psych*) regression ◆ **être en (voie de) ~** to be on the decline *ou* decrease, to be declining *ou* decreasing ◆ **~ marine** (*Géol*) marine regression

regret /ʀ(ə)gʀɛ/ GRAMMAIRE ACTIVE 36.3, 45.3, 46.5, 52.5 NM 1 [*de décision, faute*] regret (*de* for); [*de passé*] regret (*de* about); ◆ **le ~ d'une occasion manquée la faisait pleurer** she wept with regret at the lost opportunity, she wept in regret at losing the opportunity ◆ **les ~s causés par une occasion manquée** the regrets felt at *ou* for a missed opportunity ◆ **le ~ du pays natal** homesickness ◆ **le ~ d'avoir échoué** the regret that he had failed *ou* at having failed ◆ **vivre dans le ~ d'une faute** to spend one's life regretting a mistake ◆ **c'est avec ~ que je vous le dis** I am sorry *ou* I regret to have to tell you this ◆ **sans ~** with no regrets ◆ **je te le donne – sans ~s ?** take this – are you (really) sure? ◆ **~s éternels** (*sur une tombe*) sorely missed

2 (*locutions*) **je suis au ~ de ne pouvoir ...** I'm sorry *ou* I regret that I am unable to ... ◆ **j'ai le ~ de vous informer que ...** I regret to inform you that ..., I must regretfully inform you that ... (*frm*) ◆ **à mon grand ~** to my great regret

◆ **à regret** [*partir*] with regret, regretfully; [*accepter, donner*] with regret, reluctantly

regrettable /ʀ(ə)gʀetabl/ GRAMMAIRE ACTIVE 45.3 ADJ [*incident, conséquence*] regrettable, unfortunate ◆ **il est ~ que ...** it's unfortunate *ou* regrettable that ...

regrettablement /ʀ(ə)gʀetabləmɑ̃/ ADV (*littér*) regrettably

regretter /ʀ(ə)gʀete/ GRAMMAIRE ACTIVE 45.3, 47.2 ▸ conjug 1 ◂ VT 1 [*+ ce que l'on n'a plus*] to miss; [*+ occasion manquée*] to regret ◆ **il regrette sa jeunesse** he thinks back (nostalgically) to his youth ◆ **il regrette le temps où tout était simple** he looks back nostalgically *ou* wistfully to the time when everything was simple ◆ **ne regrettez-vous pas le temps perdu ?** aren't you sorry this time has gone? ◆ **il regrette son argent** he wishes he hadn't spent the money ◆ **c'était cher, mais je ne regrette pas mon argent** it was expensive but I don't regret buying it *ou* spending the money ◆ **notre regretté président** our late lamented president ◆ **on le regrette beaucoup dans le village** he is greatly *ou* sadly missed in the village

2 (= *se repentir de*) [*+ décision, imprudence*] to regret ◆ **tu le regretteras** you'll regret it, you'll be sorry for it ◆ **tu ne le regretteras pas** you won't regret it ◆ **je ne regrette rien** I have no regrets ◆ **je regrette mon geste** I wish I hadn't done that ◆ **elles regrettent d'avoir parlé** they're sorry they spoke, they wish they hadn't spoken

3 (= *désapprouver*) to deplore, to regret ◆ **les médecins regrettent que le grand public ne soit pas mieux informé des symptômes de l'infarctus** doctors deplore the fact that the public is not better informed about the symptoms of heart attack ◆ **on regrettera que la traduction ait été bâclée** it is regrettable that the translation is so slapdash

4 (= *être désolé*) to be sorry, to regret ◆ **je regrette, mais il est trop tard** I'm sorry, but it's too late, I'm afraid it's too late ◆ **ah non ! je regrette, il était avec moi** no, sorry, he was with me ◆ **nous avons beaucoup regretté votre absence** we were very sorry that you weren't able to join us ◆ **nous regrettons qu'il soit malade** we are sorry that he is ill

◆ **regretter de** ◆ **je regrette de ne pas lui avoir écrit** I'm sorry *ou* I regret that I didn't write to him ◆ **je regrette de vous avoir fait attendre** I'm sorry to have kept you waiting ◆ **je ne regrette pas d'être venu** I'm not sorry *ou* I'm glad I came ◆ **sa femme regrette de ne pas être présente** his wife is sorry that she cannot be present ◆ **je regrette de ne pouvoir donner une suite favorable à votre demande** I am sorry that I cannot meet your request

> ⚠ Attention à ne pas traduire automatiquement **regretter** par **to regret** ; l'anglais préfère une tournure contenant le mot 'sorry'.

regrimper /ʀ(ə)gʀɛ̃pe/ ▸ conjug 1 ◂ VT [*+ pente, escalier*] to climb (up) again VI [*route*] to climb (up) again; [*fièvre*] to go up *ou* rise again; [*prix*] to go up *ou* climb again ◆ **~ dans le train** to climb back into the train ◆ **ça va faire ~ les prix/la fièvre** it'll put up prices/his temperature again

regrossir /ʀ(ə)gʀosiʀ/ ▸ conjug 2 ◂ VI to put on weight again

regroupement /ʀ(ə)gʀupmɑ̃/ NM 1 [*d'objets, pièces de collection*] bringing together; [*d'industries, partis, parcelles*] grouping together ◆ **~s de sociétés** (*Fin, Jur*) groupings of companies 2 (= *fait de réunir de nouveau*) [*d'armée, personnes*] reassembling; [*de bétail*] rounding up again ◆ **~ familial** (*Jur*) family reunification 3 (*Sport*) [*de coureurs*] bunching together; [*de rugbymen*] loose scrum

regrouper /ʀ(ə)gʀupe/ ▸ conjug 1 ◂ VT 1 (= *réunir*) [*+ objets*] to put *ou* group together; [*+ pièces de collection*] to bring together; [*+ industries, partis, parcelles*] to group together; [*+ territoires*] to consolidate; (= *fusionner*) [*+ services, classes*] to merge 2 (= *réunir de nouveau*) [*+ armée, personnes*] to reassemble; [*+ parti*] to regroup; [*+ bétail*] to round up, to herd together VPR **se regrouper** 1 (= *se réunir*) [*personnes*] to gather (together), to assemble; [*entreprises*] to group together ◆ **se ~ autour d'une cause** to unite behind a cause 2 (*Sport*) [*coureurs*] to bunch together again; [*rugbymen*] to form a loose scrum

régularisable /ʀegylaʀizabl/ ADJ [*personne*] whose status can be made legal ◆ **les personnes non ~s** people whose status cannot be regularized

régularisation /ʀegylaʀizasjɔ̃/ NF 1 [*de situation*] regularization; [*de passeport, papiers*] sorting out 2 [*de mécanisme, débit*] regulation 3 (*Fin*) equalization ◆ **~ des cours** price stabilization

régulariser /ʀegylaʀize/ ▸ conjug 1 ◂ VT 1 [*+ passeport, papiers*] to sort out ◆ **~ sa situation** (*gén*) to get one's situation sorted out; [*immigré*] to get one's papers in order, to have one's (immigration) status regularized ◆ **ils ont fini par ~** * (= *ils se sont mariés*) they ended up making it official ◆ **faire ~ ses papiers** to have one's papers put in order *ou* sorted out 2 (= *régler*) [*+ mécanisme, débit*] to regulate ◆ **~ le cours d'un fleuve** to regulate the flow of a river 3 (*Méd*) [*+ pouls, respiration, rythme cardiaque, circulation*] to regulate 4 (*Fin*) [*+ monnaie*] to equalize VPR **se régulariser** [*pouls, respiration, rythme cardiaque, circulation*] to return to normal

régularité /ʀegylaʀite/ NF 1 [*de pouls, travail, effort, respiration, rythme*] regularity, steadiness; [*de qualité, résultats*] consistency, evenness; [*de vitesse, vent*] steadiness; [*d'habitudes, progrès, paiement, visites, service de transport*] regularity ◆ **avec ~** [*se produire*] regularly; [*progresser*] steadily 2 (= *uniformité*) [*de répartition, couche, ligne*] evenness; (= *symétrie*) symmetry; (= *harmonie*) [*de traits, paysage*] regularity, evenness; [*d'écriture*] regularity; (= *égalité*) [*d'humeur*] steadiness, evenness; (*Math*) [*de polygone*] regularity 3 (= *légalité*) [*d'élection, procédure*] legality, lawfulness

régulateur, -trice /ʀegylatœʀ, tʀis/ ADJ regulating NM (*Tech, fig*) regulator ◆ **~ de vitesse/de température** speed/temperature control *ou* regulator

régulation /ʀegylasjɔ̃/ NF [*d'économie, trafic*] regulation; [*de mécanisme*] regulation, adjustment ◆ **~ des naissances** birth control ◆ **~ thermique** (*Physiol*) regulation of body temperature, thermotaxis (*SPÉC*) ◆ **~ de la circulation** traffic control, regulation of traffic flow

réguler /ʀegyle/ ▸ conjug 1 ◂ VT [*+ flux, marché, taux*] to regulate ◆ **~ la circulation routière** to regulate the flow of traffic, to control traffic

régulier, -ière /ʀegylje, jɛʀ/ ADJ 1 (*en fréquence, en force*) [*pouls, rythme, respiration*] regular, steady; [*effort*] sustained; [*qualité, résultats*] consistent; [*progrès, vitesse, vent*] steady; [*habitudes, paiement, revenus, visites*] regular; (*Transports*) [*ligne, vol*] scheduled; [*service de train, bus*] regular ◆ **incapable d'un travail ~, il voulait devenir comédien** unable to do a regular job, he wanted to become an actor ◆ **à intervalles ~s** at regular intervals ◆ **prendre ses repas à (des) heures régulières** to eat regular meals ◆ **exercer une pression régulière sur qch** to exert steady pressure on sth ◆ **être en correspondance régulière avec qn** to correspond regularly with sb, to write regularly to sb

2 (= *uniforme*) [*répartition, couche, ligne*] even; [*façade*] regular; [*traits*] regular, even; [*écriture*] regular, neat; (*Math*) [*polygone*] regular; [*humeur*] steady, even; [*vie*] ordered ◆ **avoir un visage ~** to have regular features ◆ **il faut que la pression soit bien régulière partout** the pressure must be evenly distributed

3 (= *légal*) [*gouvernement*] legitimate; [*procédure*] in order (*attrib*); [*jugement*] regular, in order (*attrib*); [*tribunal*] legal, official ◆ **être en situation régulière** to have one's papers in order

4 (= *honnête*) [*opération, coup*] aboveboard (*attrib*); [*homme d'affaires*] on the level (*attrib*) ◆ **vous me faites faire quelque chose qui n'est pas très ~** (= *correct*) what you're asking me to do is a bit dodgy * (*Brit*), if I do what you ask, I'll be sailing a bit close to the wind ◆ **être ~ en affaires** to be straight *ou* honest in business ◆ **coup ~** (*Boxe*) fair blow; (*Échecs*) correct move

5 (*Mil*) [*troupes*] regular; [*armée*] regular, standing; (*Rel*) [*clergé, ordre*] regular

6 [*vers, verbe, pluriel*] regular

7 (*Can* = *normal*) normal, regular (*US*)

NM (= *client, Mil, Rel*) regular

NF **régulière** (*, †) (= *femme*) missus *, old woman *; (= *maîtresse*) lady-love (*hum*)

LOC ADV **à la régulière** * [*battre*] fair and square

régulièrement /ʀegyljɛʀmɑ̃/ ADV 1 (= *souvent*) regularly ◆ **il est ~ en retard** he's habitually late 2 (= *uniformément*) [*répartir, disposer*] evenly; [*progresser*] steadily 3 (= *selon les règles*) properly ◆ **élu ~** properly elected, elected in accordance with the rules 4 * (= *en principe*) normally; (= *d'habitude*) normally, usually

régurgitation /ʀegyʀʒitasjɔ̃/ NF regurgitation

régurgiter /ʀegyʀʒite/ ▸ conjug 1 ◂ VT to regurgitate

réhabilitation /ʀeabilitasjɔ̃/ NF 1 (*Jur*) [*de condamné*] clearing (the name of), rehabilitation; [*de failli*] discharge ◆ **obtenir la ~ de qn** to get sb's name cleared, to get sb rehabilitated 2 *(= revalorisation) [de profession, art, idéologie]* restoring to favour 3 *(= rénovation) [de quartier, immeuble]* restoration, rehabilitation ◆ **~ des sites** *(École)* site remediation

réhabiliter /ʀeabilite/ ► conjug 1 ◄ VT 1 *(= blanchir) [+ condamné]* to clear (the name of); *[+ failli]* to discharge ◆ **~ la mémoire de qn** to restore sb's good name 2 *(= revaloriser) [+ profession, art, idéologie]* to bring back into favour, to restore to favour 3 *(= rénover) [+ quartier, immeuble]* to restore, to rehabilitate; *(École) [+ sites]* to remediate, to rehabilitate 4 *(= rétablir)* **~ qn dans ses fonctions** to reinstate sb (in their job) ◆ **~ qn dans ses droits** to restore sb's rights (to them) VPR **se réhabiliter** to rehabilitate o.s.

réhabituer /ʀeabitɥe/ ► conjug 1 ◄ VT ◆ **~ qn à (faire) qch** to get sb used to (doing) sth again, to reaccustom sb to (doing) sth VPR **se réhabituer** ◆ **se ~ à (faire) qch** to get used to (doing) sth again, to reaccustom o.s. to (doing) sth ◆ **ça va être dur de se ~** it will be difficult to get used to it again

rehaussement /ʀəosmɑ̃/ NM 1 *[de mur, clôture]* heightening; *[de plafond, chaise]* raising, heightening 2 *(Fin) [de plafond]* raising

rehausser /ʀəose/ ► conjug 1 ◄ VT 1 *[+ mur, clôture]* to heighten, to make higher; *[+ plafond, chaise]* to raise, to heighten ◆ **on va le ~ avec un coussin** *[+ enfant]* we'll put a cushion under him so he's sitting up a bit higher 2 *(= augmenter, souligner) [+ beauté, couleur, image de marque]* to enhance; *[+ goût]* to bring out; *[+ mérite, prestige]* to enhance, to increase; *[+ popularité]* to increase; *[+ détail]* to bring out, to accentuate, to underline ◆ **les épices rehaussent la saveur d'un plat** spices bring out the flavour of a dish 3 *(= orner) [+ tableau, robe]* to brighten up, to liven up ◆ **rehaussé de** embellished with

rehausseur /ʀəosœʀ/ ADJ M, NM *[de siège d'enfant]* ◆ **~ de siège, siège ~** booster seat

réhumaniser /ʀeymanize/ ► conjug 1 ◄ VT *[+ ville, justice]* to make more human

réhydratation /ʀeidʀatasjɔ̃/ NF *(gén)* rehydration; *[de peau]* moisturizing

réhydrater /ʀeidʀate/ ► conjug 1 ◄ VT *(gén)* to rehydrate; *[+ peau]* to moisturize

réification /ʀeifikasjɔ̃/ NF reification

réifier /ʀeifje/ ► conjug 7 ◄ VT to reify

reiki /ʀeki/ NM reiki

réimperméabilisation /ʀeɛ̃pɛʀmeabilizasjɔ̃/ NF reproofing

réimperméabiliser /ʀeɛ̃pɛʀmeabilize/ ► conjug 1 ◄ VT to reproof

réimplantation /ʀeɛ̃plɑ̃tasjɔ̃/ NF *[d'embryon, organe]* reimplantation

réimplanter /ʀeɛ̃plɑ̃te/ ► conjug 1 ◄ VT *[+ entreprise existante]* to relocate; *[+ nouvelle entreprise]* to set up; *[+ embryon, organe]* to reimplant VPR **se réimplanter** *[entreprise]* to relocate; *[personne]* to reestablish oneself

réimportation /ʀeɛ̃pɔʀtasjɔ̃/ NF reimportation

réimporter /ʀeɛ̃pɔʀte/ ► conjug 1 ◄ VT to reimport

réimposer /ʀeɛ̃poze/ ► conjug 1 ◄ VT 1 *(Fin)* to impose a new *ou* further tax on 2 *(Typo)* to reimpose

réimposition /ʀeɛ̃pozisjɔ̃/ NF 1 *(Fin)* further taxation 2 *(Typo)* reimposition

réimpression /ʀeɛ̃pʀesjɔ̃/ NF *(= action)* reprinting; *(= livre)* reprint ◆ **l'ouvrage est en cours de ~** the book is being reprinted

réimprimer /ʀeɛ̃pʀime/ ► conjug 1 ◄ VT to reprint

Reims /ʀɛ̃s/ N Rheims

rein /ʀɛ̃/ NM *(= organe)* kidney ◆ **être sous ~ artificiel** to be on a kidney machine ◆ **~ flottant** renal ptosis NMPL **reins** *(= région)* small of the back; *(= taille)* waist ◆ **avoir mal aux ~s** to have backache *(in the lower back)*, to have an ache in the small of one's back ◆ **ses cheveux tombent sur ses ~s** her hair comes down to her waist ◆ **il donna un coup de ~s pour se relever** he heaved himself up ◆ **donner un coup de ~s pour soulever qch** to heave sth up ◆ **avoir les ~s solides** *(lit)* to have a strong *ou* sturdy back ◆ **ils ont/n'ont pas les ~s assez solides** *(fig)* they are/aren't in a strong enough financial position ◆ **casser** *ou* **briser les ~s à qn** *(fig)* to ruin *ou* break sb ◆ **il m'a mis l'épée dans les ~s** *(fig)* he really turned on the pressure; → **creux**

réincarcération /ʀeɛ̃kaʀseʀasjɔ̃/ NF reimprisonment, reincarceration

réincarcérer /ʀeɛ̃kaʀseʀe/ ► conjug 6 ◄ VT to reimprison, to reincarcerate

réincarnation /ʀeɛ̃kaʀnasjɔ̃/ NF reincarnation

réincarner (se) /ʀeɛ̃kaʀne/ ► conjug 1 ◄ VPR to be reincarnated *(en* as)

réincorporer /ʀeɛ̃kɔʀpɔʀe/ ► conjug 1 ◄ VT *[+ soldat]* to re-enlist ◆ **~ son régiment** to re-enlist in one's regiment

reine /ʀɛn/ NF queen ◆ **la ~ de Saba** the Queen of Sheba ◆ **la ~ d'Angleterre** the Queen of England ◆ **la ~ Élisabeth** Queen Elizabeth ◆ **la ~ mère** *(lit)* the Queen mother; *(* fig)* her ladyship* ◆ **la ~ du bal** the queen *ou* the belle of the ball ◆ **~ de beauté** beauty queen ◆ **la ~ des abeilles/des fourmis** the queen bee/ant ◆ **comme une ~** *[vivre]* in the lap of luxury; *[traiter]* like a queen ◆ **être vêtue comme une ~** to look like a queen ◆ **la ~ de cœur/pique** *(Cartes)* the queen of hearts/spades ◆ **c'est la ~ des idiotes*** she's a prize idiot*; → **bouchée², petit, port²** COMP **reine des reinettes** rennet

reine-claude (pl **reines-claudes**) /ʀɛnklod/ NF greengage

reine-des-prés (pl **reines-des-prés**) /ʀɛndepʀe/ NF meadowsweet

reine-marguerite (pl **reines-marguerites**) /ʀɛnmaʀgəʀit/ NF (China) aster

reinette /ʀɛnɛt/ NF ≈ (Cox's orange) pippin ◆ **~ grise** russet

réinfecter /ʀeɛ̃fɛkte/ ► conjug 1 ◄ VT to reinfect ◆ **la plaie s'est réinfectée** the wound has become infected again

réinfection /ʀeɛ̃fɛksjɔ̃/ NF reinfection

réingénierie /ʀeɛ̃ʒeniʀi/ NF re-engineering

réinitialiser /ʀeinisjalize/ ► conjug 1 ◄ VT *(Ordin)* to reboot

réinjecter /ʀeɛ̃ʒɛkte/ ► conjug 1 ◄ VT *(Méd)* to re-inject ◆ **~ des fonds dans une entreprise** to pump more money into a company ◆ **ils ont réinjecté une partie des bénéfices dans la recherche** they put some of the profits back into research

réinscriptible /ʀeɛ̃skʀiptibl/ ADJ *(Ordin) [disque]* rewriteable

réinscription /ʀeɛ̃skʀipsjɔ̃/ NF reregistration, re-enrolment (Brit), re-enrollment (US)

réinscrire /ʀeɛ̃skʀiʀ/ ► conjug 39 ◄ VT *[+ épitaphe]* to reinscribe; *[+ date, nom]* to put down again; *[+ élève]* to re-enrol, to reregister ◆ **je n'ai pas réinscrit mon fils à la cantine cette année** I haven't put my son's name down for school meals this year VPR **se réinscrire** to re-enrol, to reregister *(à* for)

réinsérer /ʀeɛ̃seʀe/ ► conjug 6 ◄ VT 1 *[+ délinquant, handicapé]* to rehabilitate ◆ **se ~ dans la société** to reintegrate into society 2 *[+ publicité, feuillet]* to reinsert

réinsertion /ʀeɛ̃sɛʀsjɔ̃/ NF 1 *[de délinquant, handicapé]* rehabilitation ◆ **la ~ sociale des anciens détenus** the rehabilitation of ex-prisoners 2 *[de publicité, feuillet]* reinsertion

> ⚠ Au sens de 'réintégration', **réinsertion** ne se traduit pas par le mot anglais **reinsertion**.

réinstallation /ʀeɛ̃stalasjɔ̃/ NF 1 *(= remise en place) [de cuisinière]* putting back, reinstallation; *[d'étagère]* putting up again; *[de téléphone]* reinstallation 2 *(= réaménagement)* **notre ~ à Paris/dans l'appartement va poser des problèmes** moving back to Paris/into the flat is going to create problems

réinstaller /ʀeɛ̃stale/ ► conjug 1 ◄ VT 1 *(= remettre en place) [+ cuisinière]* to put back; *[+ étagère]* to put back up, to put up again; *[+ téléphone]* to reconnect 2 *(= réaménager) [+ pièce, appartement]* to refurnish ◆ **les bureaux ont été réinstallés à Paris** the offices were moved back to Paris 3 *(= rétablir)* **~ qn chez lui** to move sb back into their own home ◆ **~ qn dans ses fonctions** to reinstate sb in their job, to give sb their job back VPR **se réinstaller** *(dans un fauteuil)* to settle down again *(dans* in); *(dans une maison)* to move back *(dans* into) ◆ **il s'est réinstallé à Paris** *(gén)* he's moved back to Paris; *[commerçant]* he's set up in business again in Paris ◆ **se ~ au pouvoir** to come back to power

réinstaurer /ʀeɛ̃stɔʀe/ VT to re-establish

réintégration /ʀeɛ̃tegʀasjɔ̃/ NF 1 *[d'employé]* reinstatement *(dans* in) 2 *(= retour)* return *(de* to); ◆ **~ du domicile conjugal** returning to the marital home

réintégrer /ʀeɛ̃tegʀe/ ► conjug 6 ◄ VT 1 *(= rétablir)* **~ qn (dans ses fonctions)** to reinstate sb (in their job), to restore sb to their (former) position ◆ **~ qn dans ses droits** to restore sb's rights 2 *(= regagner)* to return to, to go back to ◆ **~ le domicile conjugal** to return to the marital home

réinterpréter /ʀeɛ̃tɛʀpʀete/ ► conjug 6 ◄ VT to reinterpret

réintroduction /ʀeɛ̃tʀɔdyksjɔ̃/ NF *[de personne, mode, projet de loi]* reintroduction ◆ **la ~ d'espèces en voie de disparition** reintroducing endangered species

réintroduire /ʀeɛ̃tʀɔdɥiʀ/ ► conjug 38 ◄ VT 1 *(= réinsérer) [+ objet]* to reinsert ◆ **~ une clé dans une serrure** to put a key back into a lock ◆ **~ des erreurs dans un texte** to reintroduce errors *ou* put errors back into a text 2 *(= présenter de nouveau) [+ personne]* to introduce again; *[+ projet de loi]* to reintroduce 3 *(= relancer) [+ mode]* to reintroduce, to introduce again VPR **se réintroduire** ◆ **se ~ dans** *[+ lieu, milieu]* to get back into

réinventer /ʀeɛ̃vɑ̃te/ ► conjug 1 ◄ VT to reinvent ◆ **inutile de ~ la roue** there's no point reinventing the wheel

réinvention /ʀeɛ̃vɑ̃sjɔ̃/ NF reinvention

réinvestir /ʀeɛ̃vɛstiʀ/ ► conjug 2 ◄ VT *(Fin) [+ capital]* to reinvest *(dans* in); ◆ **une partie des bénéfices a été réinvestie dans l'entreprise** some of the profits have been reinvested in *ou* have gone straight back into the company

réinviter /ʀeɛ̃vite/ ► conjug 1 ◄ VT to invite back, to ask back again, to reinvite

réislamisation /ʀeislamizasjɔ̃/ NF revival of Islam ◆ **cela a conduit à une ~ du pays/des mœurs** this has led to a revival of Islam in the country/in people's lives

réitératif, -ive /ʀeiteʀatif, iv/ ADJ reiterative

réitération /ʀeiteʀasjɔ̃/ **NF** reiteration, repetition

réitérer /ʀeiteʀe/ ► conjug 6 ◄ **VT** *[+ promesse, ordre, question]* to reiterate, to repeat; *[+ demande, exploit]* to repeat ◆ **attaques réitérées** repeated attacks ◆ **le criminel a réitéré** the criminal has repeated his crime *ou* has done it again

reître /ʀɛtʀ/ **NM** *(littér)* ruffianly *ou* roughneck soldier

rejaillir /ʀ(ə)ʒajiʀ/ ► conjug 2 ◄ **VI** 1 *(= éclabousser) [liquide]* to splash back *ou* up *(sur* onto, at); *(avec force)* to spurt back *ou* up *(sur* onto, at); *[boue]* to splash up *(sur* onto, at); ◆ **l'huile m'a rejailli à la figure** the oil splashed up in my face 2 *(= retomber)* ~ **sur qn** *[scandale, honte]* to rebound on sb; *[gloire]* to be reflected on sb ◆ **les bienfaits de cette invention rejailliront sur tous** everyone stands to benefit from this invention ◆ **sa renommée a rejailli sur ses collègues** his fame brought his colleagues some reflected glory

rejaillissement /ʀ(ə)ʒajismɑ̃/ **NM** 1 *[de liquide, boue]* splashing up; *(avec force)* spurting up 2 *[de scandale, honte]* rebounding; *[de gloire]* reflection

rejet /ʀəʒɛ/ **NM** 1 *[d'épave, corps]* casting up, washing up 2 *[de fumée, gaz, déchets]* discharge; *[de lave]* throwing out, spewing out 3 *(= refus) [de candidat, candidature, manuscrit, projet de loi, offre] [demande, conseil]* rejection; *[de recours en grâce, hypothèse]* rejection, dismissal 4 *(Littérat)* enjamb(e) ment, rejet 5 *(Ling)* **le ~ de la préposition à la fin de la phrase** putting the preposition at the end of the sentence 6 *(Bot)* shoot 7 *(Géol)* throw 8 *(Méd) [de greffe]* rejection ◆ **phénomène de ~** *(lit, fig)* rejection ◆ **faire un ~** *(Méd)* to reject a transplant ◆ **la musique baroque, moi je fais un ~*** I can't bear baroque music 9 *(Ordin)* reject

rejeter /ʀəʒ(ə)te, ʀ(ə)ʒəte/ GRAMMAIRE ACTIVE 39.1 ► conjug 4 ◄

VT 1 *(= refuser) [+ domination, amant, candidat, candidature, manuscrit]* to reject; *[+ projet de loi]* to reject, to throw out; *[+ accusation]* to refute, to deny; *[+ offre, demande, conseil]* to reject, to turn down; *[+ recours en grâce, hypothèse]* to reject, to dismiss; *[+ indésirable]* to cast out, to expel; *[+ envahisseur]* to push back, to drive back ◆ **la machine rejette les mauvaises pièces de monnaie** the machine rejects *ou* refuses invalid coins ◆ **la proposition de paix a été rejetée** the peace proposal has been rejected ◆ **le village l'a rejeté après ce dernier scandale** the village has cast him out after this latest scandal ◆ **~ qn d'un parti** to expel sb from *ou* throw sb out of a party

2 *(= relancer) [+ objet]* to throw back *(à* to); ◆ **~ un poisson à l'eau** to throw a fish back (into the water)

3 *[+ fumée, gaz, déchets]* to discharge ◆ **il** *ou* **son estomac rejette toute nourriture** his stomach rejects everything, he can't keep anything down ◆ **le volcan rejette de la lave** the volcano is spewing *ou* throwing out lava ◆ **le cadavre a été rejeté par la mer** the corpse was washed up on the shore

4 *(= faire porter)* **~ une faute sur qn/qch** to put the blame on sb/sth, to blame sb/sth ◆ **il rejette la responsabilité sur moi** he blames me, he lays the responsibility at my door

5 *(= placer)* **la préposition est rejetée à la fin** the preposition is put at the end ◆ **~ la tête en arrière** to throw *ou* toss one's head back ◆ **~ ses cheveux en arrière** *(avec la main)* to push one's hair back; *(en se coiffant)* to comb *ou* brush one's hair back; *(d'un mouvement de la tête)* to toss one's hair back ◆ **~ les épaules en arrière** to pull one's shoulders back ◆ **~ la terre hors d'une tranchée** to throw the earth out of a trench

6 *(Méd) [+ greffon]* to reject

7 *(Ordin)* to reject

VPR se rejeter 1 *(= se reculer)* **se ~ en arrière** to jump *ou* leap back(wards)

2 *(= se jeter de nouveau)* **il s'est rejeté dans l'eau** he jumped back *ou* threw himself back into the water

3 *(= se renvoyer)* **ils se rejettent (mutuellement) la responsabilité de la rupture** they lay the responsibility for the break-up at each other's door, each wants the other to take responsibility for the break-up

rejeton /ʀəʒ(ə)tɔ̃, ʀ(ə)ʒətɔ̃/ **NM** 1 *(* = enfant)* kid* ◆ **ils sont venus avec leurs ~s** they brought their kids* *ou* offspring *(hum)* with them 2 *(Bot)* shoot; *(fig)* offshoot

rejoindre /ʀ(ə)ʒwɛ̃dʀ/ ► conjug 49 ◄ **VT** 1 *(= regagner, retrouver) [+ lieu]* to get (back) to; *[+ route]* to (re)join, to get (back) (on)to; *[+ personne]* to (re-)join, to meet (again); *[+ poste, régiment]* to rejoin, to return to ◆ **la route rejoint la voie ferrée à …** the road meets (up with) *ou* (re)joins the railway line at …

2 *(= rattraper)* to catch up (with) ◆ **je n'arrive pas à le ~** I can't catch up with him *ou* catch him up *(Brit)*

3 *(= se rallier à) [+ parti]* to join; *[+ point de vue]* to agree with ◆ **je vous rejoins sur ce point** I agree with you on that point ◆ **mon idée rejoint la vôtre** my idea is closely akin to yours *ou* is very much like yours ◆ **c'est ici que la prudence rejoint la lâcheté** this is where prudence comes close to *ou* is closely akin to cowardice

4 *(= réunir) [+ personnes]* to reunite, to bring back together; *[+ choses]* to bring together (again); *[+ lèvres d'une plaie]* to close

VPR se rejoindre *[routes]* to join, to meet; *[idées]* to be very similar; *[personnes] (pour rendez-vous)* to meet (up) (again); *(sur point de vue)* to agree

rejointoyer /ʀ(ə)ʒwɛ̃twaje/ ► conjug 8 ◄ **VT** to repoint, to regrout

rejouer /ʀ(ə)ʒwe/ ► conjug 1 ◄ **VT** *(gén)* to play again; *[+ match]* to replay ◆ **~ cœur** *(Cartes)* to lead hearts again ◆ **on rejoue une partie ?** shall we have *ou* play another game? ◆ **~ une pièce** *[acteurs]* to perform a play again, to give another performance of a play; *[théâtre]* to put on a play again ◆ **nous rejouons demain à Marseille** *[acteurs]* we're performing again tomorrow in Marseilles; *[joueurs]* we're playing again tomorrow in Marseilles **VI** *[enfants, joueurs]* to play again; *[musicien]* to play *ou* perform again ◆ **acteur qui ne pourra plus jamais ~** actor who will never be able to act *ou* perform again

réjoui, e /ʀeʒwi/ (ptp de **réjouir**) **ADJ** ◆ **avoir l'air ~, avoir une mine ~e** to look delighted

réjouir /ʀeʒwiʀ/ GRAMMAIRE ACTIVE 38.2 ► conjug 2 ◄

VT *[+ personne, regard]* to delight; *[+ cœur]* to gladden ◆ **cette perspective le réjouit** this prospect delights *ou* thrills him, he is delighted *ou* thrilled at this prospect ◆ **cette idée ne me réjouit pas beaucoup** I don't find the thought of it particularly appealing

VPR se réjouir to be delighted *ou* thrilled *(de faire* to do); ◆ **se ~ de** *[+ nouvelle, événement]* to be delighted *ou* thrilled about *ou* at; *[+ malheur]* to take delight in, to rejoice over; *(surtout Helv : à l'avance)* to look forward to ◆ **vous avez gagné et je m'en réjouis pour vous** you've won and I'm delighted for you ◆ **se ~ (à la pensée) que …** to be delighted *ou* thrilled (at the thought) that … ◆ **je me réjouis à l'avance de les voir** I am greatly looking forward to seeing them ◆ **réjouissez-vous !** rejoice! ◆ **je me réjouis que tu aies réussi** I'm delighted *ou* thrilled that you've succeeded

réjouissance /ʀeʒwisɑ̃s/ **NF** rejoicing ◆ **~s** festivities, merrymaking *(NonC)* ◆ **quel est le programme des ~s pour la journée ?** *(hum)* what delights are in store (for us) today? *(hum)*, what's on the agenda for today?*

réjouissant, e /ʀeʒwisɑ̃, ɑ̃t/ **ADJ** *[histoire]* amusing, entertaining; *[nouvelle]* cheering ◆ **quelle perspective ~e !** *(iro)* what a delightful prospect! *(iro)* ◆ **les prévisions ne sont guère ~es** the forecasts aren't very encouraging *ou* heartening ◆ **ce n'est pas ~ !** it's no joke!

rejuger /ʀ(ə)ʒyʒe/ ► conjug 3 ◄ **VT** *(Jur) [+ affaire, accusé]* to retry

relâche /ʀəlɑʃ/ **NM** *ou* **NF** 1 *(littér = répit)* respite, rest ◆ **prendre un peu de ~** to take a short rest *ou* break ◆ **se donner ~** to give o.s. a rest *ou* a break ◆ **sans ~** relentlessly 2 *(Théât)* closure ◆ **faire ~** to be closed, to close ◆ **"relâche"** "no performance(s) (today *ou* this week *etc*)" ◆ **le lundi est le jour de ~ du cinéma local** the local cinema is closed on Monday(s) **NF** *(Naut)* port of call ◆ **faire ~ dans un port** to put in at *ou* call at a port

relâché, e /ʀ(ə)lɑʃe/ (ptp de **relâcher**) **ADJ** *[style]* loose, limp; *[conduite, mœurs]* lax; *[discipline, autorité]* lax, slack; *[prononciation]* lax

relâchement /ʀ(ə)lɑʃmɑ̃/ **NM** 1 *[d'étreinte]* relaxation, loosening; *[de lien]* loosening, slackening; *[de muscle]* relaxation; *[de ressort]* release 2 *[de discipline, effort, zèle]* relaxation, slackening; *[de surveillance]* relaxation; *[de courage, attention]* flagging ◆ **il y a du ~ dans la discipline** discipline is getting lax *ou* slack ◆ **~ des mœurs** loosening *ou* slackening of moral standards

relâcher /ʀ(ə)lɑʃe/ ► conjug 1 ◄ **VT** 1 *[+ étreinte]* to relax, to loosen; *[+ lien]* to loosen, to slacken (off); *[+ muscle]* to relax; *[+ ressort]* to release ◆ **il a relâché le poisson dans l'eau** he threw the fish back (into the water) ◆ **~ les intestins** to loosen the bowels

2 *[+ discipline, surveillance]* to relax; *[+ effort]* to relax, to let up ◆ **ils relâchent leur attention** their attention is wandering

3 *[+ prisonnier, otage, gibier]* to release, to let go, to set free

4 *(= refaire tomber) [+ objet]* to drop (again), to let go of (again) ◆ **ne relâche pas la corde** don't let go of the rope (again)

VI *(Naut)* ◆ **~ (dans un port)** to put into port

VPR se relâcher 1 *[courroie]* to loosen, to go *ou* get loose *ou* slack; *[muscle]* to relax

2 *[surveillance, discipline]* to become *ou* get lax *ou* slack; *[mœurs]* to become *ou* get lax; *[style]* to become sloppy; *[courage, attention]* to flag; *[zèle]* to slacken, to flag; *[effort]* to let up ◆ **il se relâche** he's letting up ◆ **ne te relâche pas maintenant !** don't let up *ou* slack(en) off now! ◆ **il se relâche dans son travail** he's growing slack in his work, his work is getting slack

relais /ʀ(ə)lɛ/ **NM** 1 *(Sport)* relay (race); *(Alpinisme)* stance ◆ **~ 4 fois 100 mètres** 4 by 100 metres (relay) ◆ **passer le ~ à son coéquipier** to hand over to one's team-mate ◆ **à cause du mauvais passage de ~** because one of the runners fumbled the baton *ou* pass

2 *(au travail)* **ouvriers/équipe de ~** shift workers/team ◆ **travail par ~** shift work ◆ **passer le ~ à qn** to hand over to sb ◆ **le passage de ~ entre l'ancien et le nouveau directeur** the handover from the old manager to the new one ◆ **prendre le ~ (de qn)** to take over (from sb) ◆ **servir de ~** *(dans une transaction)* to act as an intermediary *ou* a go-between ◆ **la pluie ayant cessé, c'est la neige qui a pris le ~** once the rain had stopped the snow took over *ou* set in; → **crédit-relais, prêt²**

3 *(= chevaux, chiens)* relay ◆ **~ (de poste)** *(Hist = auberge)* post house, coaching inn; *(Mil)* stag-

ing post ◆ ~ **routier** transport café (*Brit*), truck stop (*US*) ◆ **ville** ~ stopover; → **cheval**

4 (*Élec, Radio, Téléc*) (= *action*) relaying; (= *dispositif*) relay ◆ ~ **de télévision** television relay station ◆ ~ **hertzien** radio relay ◆ **avion/satellite de** ~ relay plane/satellite

relance / Rəlɑ̃s / NF 1 (= *reprise*) [*d'économie, industrie, emploi*] boosting, stimulation; [*d'idée, projet*] revival, relaunching; [*de négociations*] reopening; (*Écon*) reflation ◆ **pour permettre la ~ du processus de paix** in order to restart the peace process ◆ **la ~ de l'économie n'a pas duré** the boost (given) to the economy did not last ◆ **la ~ du terrorisme est due à ...** the fresh outburst of *ou* upsurge in terrorism is due to ... ◆ **provoquer la ~ de** [+ *économie*] to give a boost to, to boost, to stimulate; [+ *projet*] to revive, to relaunch ◆ **mesures/politique de ~** reflationary measures/policy 2 (*Poker*) **faire une ~** to raise the stakes, to make a higher bid ◆ **limiter la ~** to limit the stakes 3 [*de débiteur*] chasing up; [*de client*] following up ◆ **lettre de ~** reminder

relancer / R(ə)lɑ̃se / ► conjug 3 ◄ VT 1 (= *renvoyer*) [+ *objet, ballon*] to throw back (again) 2 (= *faire repartir*) [+ *gibier*] to start (again); [+ *moteur*] to restart; [+ *idée, projet*] to revive, to relaunch; [+ *polémique, dialogue, négociations*] to reopen; [+ *économie, industrie, emploi, inflation*] to boost, to give a boost to, to stimulate ◆ ~ **la machine économique** to kick-start the economy 3 (= *harceler*) [+ *débiteur*] to chase up; (*sexuellement*) [+ *personne*] to harass, to pester, to chase after ◆ ~ **un client par téléphone** to make a follow-up call to a customer 4 (*Cartes*) [+ *enjeu*] to raise 5 (*Ordin*) to restart

relaps, e / Rəlaps / ADJ relapsed NM,F relapsed heretic

relater / R(ə)late / ► conjug 1 ◄ VT (*littér*) [+ *événement, aventure*] to relate, to recount; (*Jur*) [+ *pièce, fait*] to record ◆ **le journaliste relate que ...** the journalist says that ... *ou* tells us that ... ◆ **pourriez-vous ~ les faits tels que vous les avez observés ?** could you state the facts exactly as you observed them?

relatif, -ive / R(ə)latif, iv / ADJ (*gén, Gram, Mus*) relative; [*silence, luxe*] relative, comparative ◆ **tout est ~** everything is relative ◆ **discussions relatives à un sujet** discussions relating to *ou* connected with a subject ◆ **faire preuve d'un enthousiasme tout ~** to be less than enthusiastic ◆ **faire preuve d'un optimisme ~** to be guardedly optimistic ◆ **(ton) majeur/mineur ~** (*Mus*) relative major/minor (key) NM 1 (*Gram*) relative pronoun 2 ◆ **avoir le sens du ~** to have a sense of proportion NF **relative** (*Gram*) relative clause

relation / R(ə)lasjɔ̃ / NF 1 (*gén, Math, Philos*) relation(ship) ◆ ~ **de cause à effet** relation(ship) of cause and effect ◆ **la ~ entre l'homme et l'environnement** the relation(ship) between man and the environment ◆ **il y a une ~ évidente entre ...** there is an obvious connection *ou* relation(ship) between ... ◆ **c'est sans ~** *ou* **cela n'a aucune ~ avec ...** it has no connection with ..., it bears no relation to ... ◆ **faire la ~ entre deux événements** to make the connection between two events

2 (= *personne*) acquaintance ◆ **une de mes ~s** an acquaintance of mine, someone I know ◆ **trouver un poste par ~s** to find a job through one's connections, to find a job by knowing somebody *ou* by knowing the right people ◆ **avoir des ~s** to have (influential) connections, to know the right people

3 (= *récit*) account, report ◆ ~ **orale/écrite** oral/written account *ou* report ◆ **d'après la ~ d'un témoin** according to a witness's account ◆ **faire la ~ des événements/de son voyage** to give an account of *ou* relate the events/one's journey

NFPL **relations** relations; (= *rapports*) (*gén*) relations; (*sur le plan personnel*) relationship, relations ◆ **~s diplomatiques/culturelles/publiques/internationales** diplomatic/cultural/public/international relations ◆ **opération de ~s publiques** PR exercise ◆ **~s patrons-ouvriers/patronat-syndicats** labour-management/union-management relations ◆ **~s humaines** human relationships ◆ **les ~s sont tendues/cordiales entre nous** relations between us are strained/cordial, the relationship between us *ou* our relationship is strained/cordial ◆ **avoir des ~s (sexuelles) avec qn** to have sexual relations *ou* (sexual) intercourse with sb ◆ **avoir des ~s amoureuses avec qn** to have an affair *ou* a love affair with sb ◆ **avoir de bonnes ~s/des ~s amicales avec qn** to be on good/friendly terms with sb, to have a good/friendly relationship with sb ◆ **être en ~s d'affaires avec qn** to have business relations *ou* business dealings *ou* a business relationship with sb ◆ **être/rester en ~(s) avec qn** to be/keep in touch *ou* contact with sb ◆ **entrer** *ou* **se mettre en ~(s) avec qn** to get in touch *ou* make contact with sb ◆ **nous sommes en ~s suivies** we are in constant *ou* close contact

relationnel, -elle / R(ə)lasjɔnɛl / ADJ 1 [*problèmes*] relationship (*épith*) ◆ **réseau ~** network of contacts ◆ **sur le plan ~, il a toujours eu des problèmes** he's always had problems relating to other people ◆ **le ~ est de plus en plus important en entreprise** human relations are more and more important in the workplace 2 [*grammaire*] relational ◆ **base de données relationnelle** relational data base

relativement / R(ə)lativmɑ̃ / ADV 1 [*facile, honnête, rare*] relatively, comparatively 2 ◆ ~ **à** (= *par comparaison à*) in relation to, compared to; (= *concernant*) with regard to, concerning

relativisation / Rəlativizasjɔ̃ / NF relativization

relativiser / R(ə)lativize / ► conjug 1 ◄ VT to relativize ◆ **il faut ~** you have to put things into perspective

relativisme / R(ə)lativism / NM relativism

relativiste / R(ə)lativist / ADJ relativistic NMF relativist

relativité / R(ə)lativite / NF relativity ◆ **découvrir la ~ des choses/des valeurs** to realize that things/values are relative ◆ **(théorie de la) ~ générale/restreinte** general/special (theory of) relativity

relaver / R(ə)lave / ► conjug 1 ◄ VT to wash again, to rewash

relax* / Rəlaks / ADJ ⇒ **relaxe²**

relaxant, e / R(ə)laksɑ̃, ɑt / ADJ relaxing

relaxation / R(ə)laksasjɔ̃ / NF relaxation ◆ **j'ai besoin de ~** I need to relax, I need a bit of relaxation ◆ **faire de la ~** to do relaxation exercises

relaxe¹ / Rəlaks / NF (= *acquittement*) acquittal, discharge; (= *libération*) release

relaxe²* / Rəlaks / ADJ [*ambiance*] relaxed, informal, laid back*; [*tenue*] informal, casual; [*personne*] relaxed, easy-going, laid-back*; [*vacances*] relaxing ◆ **siège** *ou* **fauteuil ~** reclining chair, recliner

relaxer¹ / R(ə)lakse / ► conjug 1 ◄ VT (= *acquitter*) to acquit, to discharge; (= *libérer*) to release

relaxer² / R(ə)lakse / ► conjug 1 ◄ VT [+ *muscles*] to relax VPR **se relaxer** to relax

relayer / R(ə)leje / ► conjug 8 ◄ VT 1 [+ *personne*] to relieve, to take over from; [+ *appareil*] to replace; [+ *initiative*] to take over ◆ **se faire ~** to get somebody to take over, to hand over to somebody else 2 (*Radio, TV*) to relay ◆ ~ **l'information** to pass the message on, to relay the message VPR **se relayer** to take turns (*pour faire* to do, at doing), to take it in turns (*pour faire* to do); (*dans un relais*) to take over from one another

> ⚠ **relayer qn** ne se traduit pas par **to relay sb.**

relayeur, -euse / R(ə)lɛjœR, øz / NM,F relay runner

relecture / R(ə)lɛktyR / NF rereading ◆ ~ **d'épreuves** proofreading ◆ **cet auteur nous propose une ~ de l'histoire contemporaine** this author offers us a rereading of contemporary history

relégation / R(ə)legasjɔ̃ / NF 1 [*de personne, problème, objet*] relegation 2 (*Sport*) relegation (*en* to) 3 (*Jur* = *exil*) relegation, banishment

reléguer / R(ə)lege / ► conjug 6 ◄ VT 1 (= *confiner*) [+ *personne, problème*] to relegate (*à* to); [+ *objet*] to consign, to relegate (*à, dans* to); ◆ ~ **qch/qn au second plan** to relegate sth/sb to a position of secondary importance 2 (*Sport*) to relegate (*en* to); ◆ **ils se trouvent relégués à la dixième place/en deuxième division** they have been relegated to tenth place/to the second division 3 (*Jur* = *exiler*) to relegate, to banish

relent / Rəlɑ̃ / NM foul smell, stench (*NonC*) ◆ **un ~** *ou* **des ~s de poisson pourri** a stench *ou* foul smell of rotten fish, the reek of rotten fish ◆ **des ~s de vengeance** a whiff of revenge ◆ **ça a des ~s de racisme** it smacks of racism

relevable / Rəl(ə)vabl, R(ə)ləvabl / ADJ [*siège*] tip-up (*épith*), fold-away (*épith*)

relevage / Rəl(ə)vaʒ / NM ◆ **station de ~** sewage treatment plant, sewage pumping station

relevé, e / Rəl(ə)ve / (ptp de **relever**) ADJ 1 [*col*] turned-up; [*virage*] banked; [*manches*] rolled-up; [*tête*] (*lit*) held up; (*fig*) held high ◆ **chapeau à bords ~s** hat with a turned-up brim ◆ **porter les cheveux ~s** to wear one's hair up ◆ **pas ~** (*Équitation*) high-step

2 (= *noble*) [*style, langue, sentiments*] elevated, lofty; [*conversation*] refined, sophisticated ◆ **cette expression n'est pas très ~e** it's not a very choice *ou* refined expression ◆ **plaisanterie peu ~e** rather crude joke

3 (*Culin*) [*sauce, mets*] highly-seasoned, spicy, hot

NM 1 [*de dépenses*] summary, statement; [*de cote*] plotting; [*de citations, adresses*] list; (= *facture*) bill; [*de construction, plan*] layout ◆ **faire un ~ de** [+ *citations, erreurs*] to list, to note down; [+ *notes*] to take down; [+ *compteur*] to read ◆ **prochain ~ du compteur dans deux mois** next meter reading in two months ◆ ~ **de gaz/de téléphone** gas/telephone bill ◆ ~ **bancaire**, ~ **de compte** bank statement ◆ ~ **de condamnations** police record ◆ ~ **d'identité bancaire** particulars of one's bank account ◆ ~ **d'identité postal** particulars of one's post-office bank account ◆ ~ **de notes** marks sheet (*Brit*), grade sheet (*US*)

2 (*Danse*) relevé

relève / R(ə)lɛv / NF 1 (= *personne*) relief; (= *travailleurs*) relief (team); (= *troupe*) relief (troops); (= *sentinelles*) relief (guard) 2 (= *action*) relief ◆ **la ~ de la garde** the changing of the guard ◆ **assurer** *ou* **prendre la ~ de qn** (*lit*) to relieve sb, to take over from sb; (*fig*) to take over (from sb)

relèvement / R(ə)lɛvmɑ̃ / NM 1 (= *redressement*) recovery ◆ **on assiste à un ~ spectaculaire du pays/de l'économie** the country/the economy is making a spectacular recovery 2 (= *rehaussement*) [*de niveau*] raising; [*de cours, salaires, impôts, taux*] raising ◆ **le ~ du plancher** raising the level of the floor ◆ **un ~ de 5%** a 5% rise ◆ **le ~ du salaire minimum** (*action*) the raising of the minimum wage; (*résultat*) the rise in the minimum wage 3 (*Naut*) **faire un ~ de sa position** to plot one's position

relever /ʀəl(ə)ve, ʀ(ə)ləve/ ▸ conjug 5 ◂ VT 1 *(= redresser) [+ statue, meuble]* to stand up (again); *[+ chaise]* to stand up (again), to pick up; *[+ véhicule, bateau]* to right; *[+ personne]* to help (back) up, to help (back) to his feet; *[+ blessé]* to pick up ◆ **~ une vieille dame tombée dans la rue** to help up an old lady who has fallen in the street ◆ **l'arbitre a fait ~ les joueurs** the referee made the players get up ◆ **~ la tête** *(lit)* to lift *ou* hold up one's head; *(fig) (= se rebeller)* to raise one's head, to show signs of rebelling; *(fig) (= être fier)* to hold one's head up *ou* high

2 *(= remonter) [+ col]* to turn up; *[+ chaussettes]* to pull up; *[+ jupe]* to raise, to lift; *[+ manche, pantalon]* to roll up; *[+ voile]* to lift, to raise; *[+ cheveux]* to put up; *[+ vitre] (en poussant)* to push up; *(avec bouton ou manivelle)* to wind up; *[+ store]* to roll up, to raise; *[+ siège]* to tip up; *[+ manette]* to push up; *[+ couvercle]* to lift (up) ◆ **lorsqu'il releva les yeux** when he lifted (up) *ou* raised his eyes, when he looked up ◆ **elle avait les cheveux relevés** she had *ou* was wearing her hair up

3 *(= mettre plus haut) [+ mur, étagère, plafond]* to raise, to heighten; *[+ niveau]* to raise, to bring up

4 *(= remettre en état) [+ ruines]* to rebuild; *[+ économie]* to rebuild, to restore; *[+ pays, entreprise]* to put back on its feet

5 *(= augmenter, faire monter) [+ salaire, impôts]* to raise, to increase, to put up; *[+ niveau de vie]* to raise; *[+ chiffre d'affaires]* to increase ◆ **j'ai dû ~ toutes les notes de deux points** I had to raise *ou* increase all the marks by two points ◆ **cela ne l'a pas relevé dans mon estime** that didn't raise him in my esteem, that didn't improve my opinion of him ◆ **il n'y en a pas un pour ~ l'autre** * *(péj)* they're both (just) as bad as one another ◆ **pour ~ le moral des troupes** to boost the morale of the troops

6 *[+ sauce, plat]* to season ◆ **~ le goût d'un mets avec des épices** to bring out the flavour of a dish with spices ◆ **ce plat aurait pu être un peu plus relevé** this dish could have done with a bit more seasoning ◆ **mettre des touches de couleurs claires pour ~ un tableau un peu terne** *(fig)* to add dabs of light colour to brighten *ou* liven up a rather dull picture ◆ **bijoux qui relèvent la beauté d'une femme** jewellery that enhances a woman's beauty

7 *(= relayer) [+ sentinelle]* to relieve, to take over from ◆ **à quelle heure viendra-t-on me ~ ?** when will I be relieved?, when is someone coming to take over from me? ◆ **~ la garde** to change the guard

8 *(= remarquer) [+ faute, fait]* to pick out, to find; *[+ contradiction]* to find; *[+ traces, empreintes]* to find, to discover ◆ **les charges relevées contre l'accusé** *(Jur)* the charges laid *ou* brought against the accused

9 *(= enregistrer) [+ adresse, renseignement]* to take down, to note (down); *[+ notes]* to take down; *[+ plan]* to copy out, to sketch; *(Naut) [+ point]* to plot; *[+ compteur, électricité, gaz]* to read ◆ **j'ai fait ~ le nom des témoins** I had the name of the witnesses noted (down) *ou* taken down ◆ **~ une cote** to plot an altitude ◆ **les températures relevées sous abri** temperatures recorded in the shade ◆ **~ des empreintes digitales** to take fingerprints ◆ **~ les compteurs** ⁂ *[proxénète]* to collect the takings

10 *(= réagir à) [+ injure, calomnie]* to react to, to reply to; *[+ défi]* to accept, to take up, to answer ◆ **je n'ai pas relevé cette insinuation** I ignored this insinuation, I did not react *ou* reply to this insinuation ◆ **il a dit un gros mot mais je n'ai pas relevé** he said a rude word but I didn't react *ou* I ignored it

11 *(= ramasser) [+ copies, cahiers]* to collect (in), to take in ◆ **relevez 40 mailles autour de l'encolure** *(Tricot)* pick up 40 stitches around the neck; → **gant**

12 ◆ **~ qn de qch** to release sb from sth ◆ **je te relève de ta promesse** I release you from your promise ◆ **~ un fonctionnaire de ses fonctions** to relieve an official of his duties

VT INDIR **relever de** 1 *(= se rétablir)* **~ de maladie** to recover from *ou* get over an illness, to get back on one's feet (after an illness) ◆ **elle relève de couches** she's just had a baby

2 *(= être du ressort de)* to be a matter for, to be the concern of; *(= être sous la tutelle de)* to come under ◆ **cela relève de la Sécurité sociale** that is a matter for the Social Security ◆ **cela relève de la théologie** that comes *ou* falls within the province of theology ◆ **son cas relève de la psychanalyse** he needs to see a psychoanalyst ◆ **ce service relève du ministère de l'Intérieur** this department comes under the authority of the Home Office ◆ **cette affaire ne relève pas de ma compétence** this matter does not come within my remit ◆ **ça relève de l'imagination la plus fantaisiste** that is a product of pure fancy; → **miracle**

VI *(= remonter) [vêtement]* to pull up, to go up ◆ **cette jupe relève par devant** this skirt rides up at the front

VPR **se relever** 1 *(= se remettre debout)* to stand *ou* get up (again), to get back (on)to one's feet (again) ◆ **le boxeur se releva** the boxer got up again *ou* got back to his feet *ou* picked himself up ◆ **il l'a aidée à se ~** he helped her up

2 *(= sortir du lit)* to get up; *(= ressortir du lit)* to get up again ◆ **se ~ la nuit** to get up in the night ◆ **il m'a fait (me) ~ pour que je lui apporte à boire** he made me get up to fetch him a drink

3 *(= remonter) [strapontin]* to tip up; *[couvercle, tête de lit]* to lift up ◆ **ses lèvres se relevaient dans un sourire** his mouth curled into a smile ◆ **est-ce que cette fenêtre se relève ?** does this window go up? ◆ **à l'heure où tous les stores de magasins se relèvent** when the shopkeepers roll up their shutters

4 *(= se remettre)* **se ~ de** *[+ deuil, chagrin, honte]* to recover from, to get over ◆ **se ~ de ses ruines/cendres** to rise from its ruins/ashes ◆ **il ne s'en est jamais relevé** he never got over it

releveur, -euse /ʀəl(ə)vœʀ, øz/ ADJ ◆ **muscle ~** levator (muscle) NM *(Anat)* levator NM,F *[de compteur]* meter reader ◆ **~ du gaz/de l'électricité** gasman/electricity man

relief /ʀəljɛf/ NM 1 *(Géog)* relief *(SPÉC)*, landscape ◆ **avoir un ~ accidenté** to be mountainous ◆ **région de peu de ~** rather flat region ◆ **le ~ sous-marin** the relief of the sea bed ◆ **le ~ tourmenté de la Planète rouge** the rugged landscape *ou* surface of the red planet

2 *(= saillies) [de visage]* contours; *[de médaille]* embossed *ou* raised design; *(Art)* relief ◆ **la pierre ne présentait aucun ~** the stone was quite smooth ◆ **l'artiste a utilisé le ~ naturel de la paroi** the artist made use of the natural contours of the rock wall

3 *(= profondeur, contraste) [de dessin]* depth; *[de style]* relief ◆ **portrait/photographie qui a beaucoup de ~** portrait/photograph which has plenty of depth ◆ **~ acoustique *ou* sonore** depth of sound ◆ **personnage qui manque de ~** rather flat *ou* uninteresting character ◆ **votre dissertation manque de ~** your essay is rather flat

4 ◆ **en ~** *[motif]* in relief, raised; *[caractères]* raised, embossed; *[carte de visite]* embossed; *[photographie, cinéma]* three-dimensional, 3-D, stereoscopic ◆ **l'impression est en ~** the printing is embossed ◆ **carte en ~** relief map ◆ **mettre en ~** *[+ intelligence]* to bring out; *[+ beauté, qualités]* to set *ou* show off; *[+ idée]* to bring out ◆ **l'éclairage mettait en ~ les imperfections de son visage** the lighting showed up the imperfections of her face ◆ **je tiens à mettre ce point en ~** I wish to underline *ou* stress *ou* emphasize this point ◆ **il essayait de se mettre en ~ en monopolisant la conversation** he was trying to get himself noticed by monopolizing the conversation

NMPL **reliefs** *(littér : d'un repas)* remains, leftovers ◆ **les ~s de sa gloire** *(littér)* the remnants of his glory

> ⚠ Attention à ne pas traduire automatiquement **relief** au sens géographique par le mot anglais **relief**, qui est un terme technique.

relier /ʀəlje/ ▸ conjug 7 ◂ VT 1 *[+ points, mots]* to join *ou* link up *ou* together; *(Élec)* to connect (up); *[+ villes]* to link (up); *[+ idées]* to link (up *ou* together); *[+ faits]* to connect (together), to link (up *ou* together) ◆ **~ deux choses entre elles** to link *ou* join up two things, to link *ou* join two things together ◆ **des vols fréquents relient Paris à New York** frequent flights link *ou* connect Paris and *ou* with New York ◆ **nous sommes reliés au studio par voiture-radio** we have a radio-car link to the studio ◆ **ce verbe est relié à son complément par une préposition** this verb is linked to its complement by a preposition ◆ **~ le passé au présent** to link the past to the present, to link the past and the present (together)

2 *[+ livre]* to bind; *[+ tonneau]* to hoop ◆ **livre relié** bound volume, hardback (book) ◆ **livre relié (en) cuir** leather-bound book, book bound in leather

relieur, -ieuse /ʀəljœʀ, jøz/ NM,F (book)binder

religieusement /ʀ(ə)liʒjøzmɑ̃/ ADV *(Rel, fig)* religiously; *[écouter]* religiously, reverently; *[tenir sa parole]* scrupulously, religiously ◆ **conserver *ou* garder ~** *[+ objet]* to keep lovingly; *[+ secret]* to keep scrupulously ◆ **se marier ~** to have a church wedding, to get married in church ◆ **il a été élevé ~** he had a religious upbringing

religieux, -ieuse /ʀ(ə)liʒjø, jøz/ ADJ 1 *(Rel) [édifice, secte, cérémonie, opinion]* religious; *[art]* sacred, religious; *[école, mariage, musique]* church *(épith)*; *[vie, ordres, personne]* religious ◆ **l'habit ~** the monk's *(ou* nun's) habit 2 *(fig) [respect, soin]* religious; *[silence]* reverent; → **mante** NM *(gén)* person belonging to a religious order; *(= moine)* monk, friar NF **religieuse** 1 *(= nonne)* nun 2 *(Culin)* iced *ou* frosted *(US)* cream puff *(made with choux pastry)*

religion /ʀ(ə)liʒjɔ̃/ NF 1 *(= culte)* religion, (religious) faith ◆ **la ~** *(= ensemble de croyances)* religion ◆ **la ~ chrétienne/musulmane** the Christian/Muslim religion *ou* faith ◆ **avoir de la ~** to be religious ◆ **les gens sans ~** people who have no religion *ou* without religion ◆ **c'est contraire à ma ~, ma ~ me l'interdit** *(hum)* it's against my religion *(hum)*

2 *(= vie monastique)* monastic life ◆ **entrer en ~** to take one's vows ◆ **Anne Dupuis, en ~ sœur Claire** Anne Dupuis, whose religious name is Sister Claire

3 *(fig)* **se faire une ~ de qch** to make a religion of sth ◆ **il a la ~ de la nature** he's a nature lover ◆ **sur ce point, sa ~ était faite** *(= conviction)* he was absolutely convinced of this ◆ **je n'ai pas encore fait ma ~ là-dessus** I haven't made up my mind yet

religiosité /ʀ(ə)liʒjozite/ NF religiosity

reliquaire /ʀəlikɛʀ/ NM reliquary

reliquat /ʀəlika/ NM *[de dette]* remainder, outstanding amount *ou* balance; *[de compte]* balance; *[de somme]* remainder ◆ **il subsiste un ~ très important/un petit ~** there's a very large/a small amount left (over) *ou* remaining ◆ **arrangez-vous pour qu'il n'y ait pas de ~** work it so that there is nothing left over

relique /ʀəlik/ NF *(Rel, fig)* relic; *(Bio)* relict ◆ **garder *ou* conserver qch comme une ~** to treasure sth

relire /ʀ(ə)liʀ/ ▸ conjug 43 ◂ VT *[+ roman]* to read again, to reread; *[+ manuscrit]* to read through again, to read over (again), to reread ◆ **je n'arrive pas à me ~** I can't read what I've written

reliure /ʀəljyʀ/ **NF** *(= couverture)* binding; *(= art, action)* (book)binding ◆ **~ pleine** full binding ◆ **donner un livre à la ~** to send a book for binding *ou* to the binder('s)

relocalisation /ʀ(ə)lɔkalizasjɔ̃/ **NF** *[d'entreprise, production]* relocation, transfer

relogement /ʀ(ə)lɔʒmɑ̃/ **NM** rehousing

reloger /ʀ(ə)lɔʒe/ ▸ conjug 3 ◂ **VT** to rehouse

relookage /ʀ(ə)lukaʒ/ **NM** *[de produit]* rebranding

relooker* /ʀ(ə)luke/ ▸ conjug 1 ◂ **VT** *[+ produit]* to give a new look to; *[+ personne] (physiquement)* to give a new look to; *(changer son image de marque)* to revamp the image of ◆ **relooké pour l'occasion, il ...** specially groomed for the occasion, he ...

> ⚠ Le verbe **to relook** n'existe pas en anglais.

relou* /ʀəlu/ **ADJ** *(= bête)* stupid ◆ **qu'est-ce qu'il est ~ !** what a jerk!* ◆ **c'est un peu ~ ce film !** what a stupid film! ◆ **t'es ~ avec tes questions !** *(= énervant)* you're a real pain* with all your questions !

relouer /ʀəlwe/ ▸ conjug 1 ◂ **VT** *[locataire]* to rent again; *[propriétaire]* to rent out again, to relet *(Brit)* ◆ **cette année je reloue dans le Midi** I'm renting a place in the South of France again this year

reluire /ʀ(ə)lɥiʀ/ ▸ conjug 38 ◂ **VI** *[meuble, chaussures]* to shine, to gleam; *[métal, carrosserie] (au soleil)* to gleam, to shine; *(sous la pluie)* to glisten ◆ **faire ~ qch** to polish *ou* shine sth up, to make sth shine; → **brosse**

reluisant, e /ʀ(ə)lɥizɑ̃, ɑ̃t/ **ADJ** 1 *[meubles, parquet, cuivres]* shining, shiny, gleaming ◆ **~ de graisse** shiny with grease ◆ **~ de pluie** glistening in the rain ◆ **~ de propreté** spotless 2 *(fig iro)* **peu** *ou* **pas très ~** *[avenir, résultat, situation]* far from brilliant *(attrib)*; *[personne]* despicable

reluquer* /ʀ(ə)lyke/ ▸ conjug 1 ◂ **VT** *[+ personne]* to eye (up)*, to ogle*; *[+ passant]* to eye, to squint at*; *[+ objet, poste]* to have one's eye on

rem /ʀɛm/ **NM** rem

remâcher /ʀ(ə)mɑʃe/ ▸ conjug 1 ◂ **VT** *[ruminant]* to ruminate; *[personne] [+ passé, soucis, échec]* to ruminate over *ou* on, to chew over, to brood on *ou* over; *[+ colère]* to nurse

remailler /ʀ(ə)mɑje/ ▸ conjug 1 ◂ **VT** ⇒ **remmailler**

remake /ʀimɛk/ **NM** *(Ciné)* remake; *[de livre, spectacle]* new version

rémanence /ʀemanɑ̃s/ **NF** *(Phys)* remanence ◆ **~ des images visuelles** persistence of vision

rémanent, e /ʀemanɑ̃, ɑ̃t/ **ADJ** *[magnétisme]* residual; *[pesticide]* persistent ◆ **image ~e** after-image

remanger /ʀ(ə)mɑ̃ʒe/ ▸ conjug 3 ◂ **VT** *(= manger de nouveau)* to have again; *(= reprendre)* to have *ou* eat some more ◆ **on a remangé du poulet aujourd'hui** we had chicken again today ◆ **j'en remangerais bien** I'd like to have that again, I could eat that again **VI** to eat again, to have something to eat again

remaniement /ʀ(ə)manimɑ̃/ **NM** 1 *[de roman, discours]* reworking; *[de programme]* modification, reorganization; *[de plan, constitution]* revision, amendment ◆ **apporter un ~ à qch** to revise *ou* reshape *ou* modify *etc* sth 2 *[d'équipe]* reorganization; *(Pol) [de cabinet, ministère]* reshuffle ◆ **~ ministériel** cabinet reshuffle

remanier /ʀ(ə)manje/ ▸ conjug 7 ◂ **VT** 1 *[+ roman, discours]* to rework; *[+ encyclopédie]* to revise; *[+ programme]* to modify, to reorganize; *[+ plan, constitution]* to revise, to amend 2 *[+ équipe]* to reorganize; *(Pol) [+ cabinet, ministère]* to reshuffle

remaquiller /ʀ(ə)makije/ ▸ conjug 1 ◂ **VT** ◆ **~ qn** to make sb up again **VPR** **se remaquiller** *(complètement)* to make o.s. up again, to redo one's face; *(rapidement)* to touch up one's make-up

remarcher /ʀ(ə)maʀʃe/ ▸ conjug 1 ◂ **VI** *[personne]* to walk again; *[appareil]* to work again

remariage /ʀ(ə)maʀjaʒ/ **NM** second marriage, remarriage

remarier /ʀ(ə)maʀje/ ▸ conjug 7 ◂ **VT** ◆ **il aimerait ~ son fils** he'd like to see his son remarried *ou* married again **VPR** **se remarier** to remarry, to marry again

remarquable /ʀ(ə)maʀkabl/ **ADJ** *[personne, exploit, réussite]* remarkable, outstanding; *[événement, fait]* noteworthy, remarkable ◆ **il est ~ par sa taille** he is notable for *ou* he stands out because of his height ◆ **elle est ~ par son intelligence** she is outstandingly intelligent

remarquablement /ʀ(ə)maʀkabləmɑ̃/ **ADV** *[beau, doué]* remarkably, outstandingly; *[réussir, jouer]* remarkably *ou* outstandingly well

remarque /ʀ(ə)maʀk/ **NF** *(= observation)* remark, comment; *(= critique)* critical remark; *(= annotation)* note ◆ **faire une ~ désobligeante/pertinente** to make an unpleasant/a pertinent comment ◆ **il m'en a fait la ~** he remarked *ou* commented on it to me ◆ **je m'en suis moi-même fait la ~** that occurred to me as well, I thought that myself ◆ **faire une ~ à qn** to criticize sb ◆ **il m'a fait des ~s sur ma tenue** he passed comment on the way I was dressed ◆ **elle a écrit des ~s sur mon devoir** she wrote some comments on my essay

remarqué, e /ʀ(ə)maʀke/ (ptp de **remarquer**) **ADJ** *[entrée, absence]* conspicuous ◆ **il a fait une intervention très ~e** his speech attracted a lot of attention

remarquer /ʀ(ə)maʀke/ GRAMMAIRE ACTIVE 53.5 ▸ conjug 1 ◂

VT 1 *(= apercevoir)* to notice ◆ **je l'ai remarqué dans la foule** I caught sight of *ou* noticed him in the crowd ◆ **avec ce chapeau, comment ne pas la ~ !** how can you fail to notice her when she's wearing that hat? ◆ **il entra sans qu'on le remarque** *ou* **sans se faire ~** he came in unnoticed *ou* without being noticed ◆ **il aime se faire ~** he likes to be noticed *ou* to draw attention to himself ◆ **je remarque que vous avez une cravate** I notice *ou* see that you are wearing a tie ◆ **je remarque que vous ne vous êtes pas excusé** I note that you did not apologize

2 *(= faire une remarque)* to remark, to observe ◆ **tu es sot, remarqua son frère** you're stupid, his brother remarked *ou* observed ◆ **il remarqua qu'il faisait froid** he remarked *ou* commented that it was cold ◆ **remarquez (bien) que je n'en sais rien** I don't really know though, mind you I don't know *(Brit)* ◆ **ça m'est tout à fait égal, remarque !** I couldn't care less, by the way!, I couldn't care less, if you want the truth!

3 ◆ **faire ~** *[+ détail, erreur]* to point out, to draw attention to ◆ **il me fit ~ qu'il faisait nuit/qu'il était tard** he reminded me that it was dark/late ◆ **je te ferai seulement ~ que tu n'as pas de preuves** I'd just like to point out that you have no proof

4 *(= marquer de nouveau)* to re-mark, to mark again

VPR **se remarquer** *[défaut, gêne, jalousie]* to be obvious, to be noticeable ◆ **cette tache se remarque beaucoup/à peine** this stain is quite/hardly noticeable, this stain really/hardly shows ◆ **ça ne se remarquera pas** no one will notice it ◆ **ça finirait par se ~** people would start to notice *ou* start noticing

> ⚠ Au sens de 'apercevoir', **to remark** est d'un registre plus soutenu que **remarquer**.

remballer /ʀɑ̃bale/ ▸ conjug 1 ◂ **VT** 1 *(= ranger)* to pack (up) again; *(dans du papier)* to rewrap ◆ **remballe ta marchandise !*** you can clear off and take that stuff with you!* ◆ **tu peux ~ tes commentaires !*** you know what you can do with your remarks!* 2 *(* = rabrouer)* **on s'est fait ~** we were sent packing*, they told us to get lost*

rembarquement /ʀɑ̃baʀkəmɑ̃/ **NM** *[de passagers]* re-embarkation; *[de marchandises]* reloading

rembarquer /ʀɑ̃baʀke/ ▸ conjug 1 ◂ **VT** *[+ passagers]* to re-embark; *[+ marchandises]* to reload **VI** to re-embark, to go back on board (ship) ◆ **faire ~ les passagers** to re-embark the passengers **VPR** **se rembarquer** 1 *(sur un bateau)* to re-embark, to go back on board (ship) 2 *(= s'engager)* **elle s'est rembarquée dans une drôle d'affaire** she's got herself involved in something really weird again

rembarrer* /ʀɑ̃baʀe/ ▸ conjug 1 ◂ **VT** ◆ **~ qn** *(= recevoir avec froideur)* to brush sb aside, to rebuff sb; *(= remettre à sa place)* to put sb in their place, to take sb down a peg or two ◆ **on s'est fait ~** we were sent packing*, they told us to get lost*

remblai /ʀɑ̃blɛ/ **NM** *(Rail, pour route)* embankment; *(Constr)* cut ◆ **(terre de) ~** *(Rail)* ballast, remblai; *(pour route)* hard core; *(Constr)* backfill ◆ **travaux de ~** *(Rail, pour route)* embankment work; *(Constr)* cutting work ◆ **~s récents** *(sur route)* soft verges

remblayage /ʀɑ̃blɛjaʒ/ **NM** *[de route, voie ferrée]* banking up; *[de fossé]* filling in *ou* up

remblayer /ʀɑ̃bleje/ ▸ conjug 8 ◂ **VT** *[+ route, voie ferrée]* to bank up; *[+ fossé]* to fill in *ou* up

rembobiner /ʀɑ̃bɔbine/ ▸ conjug 1 ◂ **VT** *[+ film, bande magnétique]* to rewind, to wind back; *[+ fil]* to rewind, to wind up again

remboîtage /ʀɑ̃bwataʒ/, **remboîtement** /ʀɑ̃bwatmɑ̃/ **NM** 1 *[de tuyaux]* fitting together, reassembly; *(Méd) [d'os]* putting back (into place) 2 *(Tech) [de livre]* recasing

remboîter /ʀɑ̃bwate/ ▸ conjug 1 ◂ **VT** 1 *[+ tuyaux]* to fit together again, to reassemble; *(Méd) [+ os]* to put back (into place) 2 *(Tech) [+ livre]* to recase

rembourrage /ʀɑ̃buʀaʒ/ **NM** *[de fauteuil, matelas]* stuffing; *[de vêtement]* padding

rembourrer /ʀɑ̃buʀe/ ▸ conjug 1 ◂ **VT** *[+ fauteuil, matelas]* to stuff; *[+ vêtement]* to pad ◆ **veste rembourrée de plume d'oie** goosedown jacket ◆ **bien rembourré** *[+ coussin]* well-filled, well-padded; * *[+ personne]* well-padded ◆ **rembourré avec des noyaux de pêches*** *(hum)* rock hard

remboursable /ʀɑ̃buʀsabl/ **ADJ** *[billet, médicament]* refundable; *[emprunt]* repayable

remboursement /ʀɑ̃buʀsəmɑ̃/ **NM** *[de dette]* repayment, settlement; *[d'emprunt]* repayment; *[de somme]* reimbursement, repayment; *[de créancier]* repayment, reimbursement; *[de frais médicaux]* reimbursement ◆ **obtenir le ~ de son repas** to get one's money back for one's meal, to get a refund on one's meal ◆ **envoi contre ~** cash with order ◆ **(contribution au) ~ de la dette sociale** *tax introduced in 1996 in order to help pay off the deficit in the French social security budget*

rembourser /ʀɑ̃buʀse/ ▸ conjug 1 ◂ **VT** 1 *[+ dette]* to pay off, to repay, to settle; *[+ emprunt, créancier]* to pay back *ou* off, to repay; *[+ somme]* to repay, to pay back ◆ **~ qn de qch** to reimburse sth to sb, to reimburse sb for sth, to repay sb sth ◆ **je te rembourserai demain** I'll pay you back *ou* repay you tomorrow

2 *[+ dépenses professionnelles]* to refund, to reimburse; *[+ article acheté]* to refund the price of; *[+ billet]* to reimburse ◆ **~ la différence** to refund the difference ◆ **je me suis fait ~ mon repas/voyage** I claimed for my meal/travel ◆ **est-ce remboursé par la Sécurité sociale ?** ≈ can you get it on the NHS *(Brit) ou* can you get it paid for by Medicaid *(US)* ? ◆ **c'est remboursé à 75%** *[médicament, lunettes, etc]* you get 75% of the cost paid ◆ **"satisfait ou remboursé"** "satisfaction or your money back" ◆ **remboursez !** *(Théât)* we want our money back! *ou* a refund!

> ⚠ **rembourser** se traduit par **to reimburse** uniquement quand il s'agit de frais ou de dommages-intérêts.

rembrunir (se) /ʀɑ̃bʀyniʀ/ ► conjug 2 ◄ **VPR** *[visage, traits]* to darken, to cloud (over); *[personne]* to bristle, to stiffen; *[ciel]* to become overcast, to darken, to cloud over ◆ **le temps se rembrunit** it's clouding over, it's getting cloudy

rembrunissement /ʀɑ̃bʀynismɑ̃/ **NM** *(littér) [de visage, front]* darkening

remède /ʀ(ə)mɛd/ **NM** 1 *(Méd) (= traitement)* remedy, cure; *(= médicament)* medicine ◆ **prescrire/prendre un ~ pour un lumbago** to give/take something *ou* some medicine for lumbago ◆ **~ de bonne femme** folk cure *ou* remedy ◆ **~ souverain/de cheval** * sovereign/drastic remedy ◆ **~ universel** cure-all, universal cure *ou* remedy 2 *(fig)* remedy, cure ◆ **porter ~ à qch** to remedy sth ◆ **la situation est sans ~** there's nothing that can be done about the situation, the situation is hopeless ◆ **le ~ est pire que le mal** the cure is worse than the disease ◆ **il n'y a pas de ~ miracle** there is no miracle cure ◆ **c'est un ~ à** *ou* **contre l'amour !** * it's (*ou* he's *ou* she's *etc*) a real turn-off! *; → **mal²**

remédiable /ʀ(ə)medjabl/ **ADJ** *[mal]* that can be remedied *ou* cured, remediable

remédier /ʀ(ə)medje/ ► conjug 7 ◄ **remédier à VT INDIR** *(lit) [+ maladie]* to cure; *(fig) [+ mal, situation]* to remedy, to put right; *[+ abus]* to remedy, to right; *[+ perte]* to remedy, to make good; *[+ besoin]* to remedy; *[+ inconvénient]* to remedy, to find a remedy for; *[+ difficulté]* to find a solution for, to solve

remembrement /ʀ(ə)mɑ̃bʀəmɑ̃/ **NM** land consolidation

remembrer /ʀ(ə)mɑ̃bʀe/ ► conjug 1 ◄ **VT** *[+ terres, exploitation]* to consolidate

remémoration /ʀ(ə)memɔʀasjɔ̃/ **NF** recall, recollection

remémorer (se) /ʀ(ə)memɔʀe/ ► conjug 1 ◄ **VPR** to recall, to recollect

remerciement /ʀ(ə)mɛʀsimɑ̃/ GRAMMAIRE ACTIVE 49

NM *(= action)* thanks *(pl)*, thanking ◆ **~s** *(dans un livre, film)* acknowledgements ◆ **exprimer ses profonds/sincères ~s à qn** to express one's deep/sincere gratitude to sb ◆ **il lui bredouilla un ~** he mumbled his thanks to her ◆ **lettre de ~** thank-you letter, letter of thanks ◆ **elle adressa quelques mots de ~ à ses électeurs** she made a brief thank-you speech to the people who voted for her ◆ **il a reçu une récompense en ~ de ses services** he received an award in recognition of his services ◆ **en ~, il m'a envoyé des fleurs** he sent me some flowers by way of thanks *ou* to thank me

NMPL remerciements ◆ **avec tous mes ~s** with many thanks ◆ **adresser ses ~s à qn** to express one's thanks to sb

remercier /ʀ(ə)mɛʀsje/ GRAMMAIRE ACTIVE 47.1, 47.2, 49 ► conjug 7 ◄ **VT** 1 *(= dire merci)* to thank *(qn de ou pour qch* sb for sth; *qn d'avoir fait qch* sb for doing sth); ◆ **~ le ciel** *ou* **Dieu** to thank God ◆ **~ qn par un cadeau/d'un pourboire** to thank sb with a present/with a tip, to give sb a present/a tip by way of thanks ◆ **je ne sais comment vous ~** I can't thank you enough, I don't know how to thank you ◆ **il me remercia d'un sourire** he thanked me with a smile, he smiled his thanks ◆ **je vous remercie** thank you ◆ **tu peux me ~ !** you've got me to thank for that! ◆ **je te remercie de tes conseils** *(iro)* thanks for the advice *(iro)*, I can do without your advice (thank you)

2 *(= refuser poliment)* **vous voulez boire ? – je vous remercie** would you like a drink? – no thank you ◆ **sortir avec lui ? je te remercie !** *(iro)* go out with him? no thanks!

3 *(euph = renvoyer) [+ employé]* to dismiss *(from his job)*

réméré /ʀemeʀe/ **NM** *(Fin)* ◆ **faculté de ~** option of repurchase, repurchase agreement ◆ **vente à ~** sale with option of purchase ◆ **clause de ~** repurchase clause

remettant /ʀ(ə)metɑ̃/ **NM** *(Fin)* remitter

remettre /ʀ(ə)mɛtʀ/ ► conjug 56 ◄ **VT** 1 *(= replacer) [+ objet]* to put back, to replace *(dans* in(to); *sur* on); *[+ os luxé]* to put back in place ◆ **~ un enfant au lit** to put a child back (in)to bed ◆ **~ un enfant à l'école** to send a child back to school ◆ **~ qch à cuire** to put sth on to cook again ◆ **~ debout** *[+ enfant]* to stand back on his feet; *[+ objet]* to stand up again ◆ **~ qch droit** to put *ou* set sth straight again ◆ **~ un bouton à une veste** to sew *ou* put a button back on a jacket ◆ **il a remis l'étagère/la porte qu'il avait enlevée** he put the shelf back up/rehung the door that he had taken down ◆ **je ne veux plus ~ les pieds ici !** I never want to set foot in here again! ◆ **~ qn sur la bonne voie** *ou* **sur les rails** to put sb back on the right track ◆ **~ le couvert** * *(gén)* to go at it * again; *(sexuellement)* to be at it again *

2 *(= porter de nouveau) [+ vêtement, chapeau]* to put back on, to put on again ◆ **j'ai remis mon manteau d'hiver** I'm wearing my winter coat again

3 *(= replacer dans une situation)* **~ un appareil en marche** to restart a machine, to start a machine (up) again, to set a machine going again ◆ **~ un moteur en marche** to start up an engine again ◆ **~ une coutume en usage** to revive a custom ◆ **~ en question** *[+ institution, autorité]* to (call into) question, to challenge; *[+ projet, accord]* to cast doubt over ◆ **tout est remis en question** *ou* **en cause à cause du mauvais temps** everything's in the balance again because of the bad weather, the bad weather throws the whole thing back into question ◆ **~ une pendule à l'heure** to set *ou* put *(Brit)* a clock right ◆ **~ les pendules à l'heure** * *(fig)* to set the record straight ◆ **~ les idées en place à qn** * to teach sb a lesson * ◆ **~ qch à neuf** to make sth as good as new again ◆ **~ qch en état** to repair *ou* mend sth ◆ **le repos l'a remise (sur pied)** the rest has set her back on her feet ◆ **~ qn en confiance** to restore sb's confidence ◆ **~ de l'ordre dans qch** *(= ranger)* to tidy sth up; *(= classer)* to sort sth out; → **cause, jour, place** *etc*

4 *(= donner) [+ lettre, paquet]* to hand over, to deliver; *[+ clés]* to hand in *ou* over, to give in, to return; *[+ récompense]* to present; *[+ devoir]* to hand in, to give in; *[+ rançon]* to hand over; *[+ démission]* to hand in, to give in, to tender *(à* to); ◆ **il s'est fait ~ les clés par la concierge** he got the keys from the concierge ◆ **~ un enfant à ses parents** to return a child to his parents ◆ **~ un criminel à la justice** to hand a criminal over to the law ◆ **~ à qn un porte-monnaie volé** to hand *ou* give back *ou* return a stolen purse to sb

5 *(= ajourner) [+ réunion]* to put off, to postpone *(à* until) to put back *(Brit) (à* to); *(Jur)* to adjourn *(à* until); *[+ décision]* to put off, to postpone, to defer *(à* until); *[+ date]* to postpone, to put back *(Brit) (à* to); ◆ **une visite qui ne peut se ~ (à plus tard)** a visit that can't be postponed *ou* put off ◆ **~ un rendez-vous à jeudi/au 8** to put off *ou* postpone an appointment till Thursday/the 8th ◆ **il ne faut jamais ~ à demain** *ou* **au lendemain ce qu'on peut faire le jour même** *(Prov)* never put off till tomorrow what you can do today *(Prov)*

6 *(= se rappeler)* to remember ◆ **je vous remets très bien** I remember you very well ◆ **je ne le remets pas** I can't place him, I don't remember him ◆ **~ qch en esprit** *ou* **en mémoire à qn** *(= rappeler)* to remind sb of sth, to recall sth to sb ◆ **ce livre m'a remis ces événements en mémoire** this book reminded me of these events *ou* brought these events to mind

7 *(= rajouter) [+ vinaigre, sel]* to add more, to put in (some) more; *[+ verre, coussin]* to add; *[+ maquillage]* to put on (some) more ◆ **j'ai froid, je vais ~ un tricot** I'm cold – I'll go and put another jersey on ◆ **~ de l'huile dans un moteur** to top up an engine with oil ◆ **en remettant un peu d'argent, vous pourriez avoir le grand modèle** if you paid a bit more you could have the large size ◆ **il faut ~ de l'argent sur le compte, nous sommes débiteurs** we'll have to put some money into the account as we're overdrawn ◆ **en ~** * to overdo it, to lay it on a bit thick *

8 *(= rallumer, rétablir) [+ radio, chauffage]* to put *ou* turn *ou* switch on again ◆ **il y a eu une coupure mais le courant a été remis à midi** there was a power cut but the electricity came back on again *ou* was put back on again at midday ◆ **~ le contact** to turn the ignition on again

9 *(= faire grâce de) [+ dette, peine]* to remit; *[+ péché]* to forgive, to pardon, to remit ◆ **~ une dette à qn** to remit sb's debt, to let sb off a debt ◆ **~ une peine à un condamné** to remit a prisoner's sentence

10 *(= confier)* **~ son sort/sa vie entre les mains de qn** to put one's fate/one's life into sb's hands ◆ **~ son âme à Dieu** to commit one's soul to God *ou* into God's keeping

11 ◆ **~ ça** * *(= recommencer)* **dire qu'il va falloir ~ ça !** to think that we'll have to go through all that again! ◆ **quand est-ce qu'on remet ça ?** when can we do it again? ◆ **on remet ça ?** *[+ partie de cartes]* shall we have another game?; *(au café)* shall we have another drink? *ou* round?; *[+ travail]* let's get back to it *, let's get down to it again, let's get going again * ◆ **garçon, remettez-nous ça !** (the) same again please! * ◆ **les voilà qui remettent ça !** *[+ bruit, commentaires]* here *ou* there they go again! *, they're at it again! * ◆ **tu ne vas pas ~ ça avec tes critiques** you're not criticizing again, are you? ◆ **le gouvernement va ~ ça avec les économies d'énergie** the government is going to start trying to save energy again

VPR se remettre 1 *(= recouvrer la santé)* to recover, to get better; *(psychologiquement)* to cheer up ◆ **se ~ d'une maladie/d'un accident** to recover from *ou* get over an illness/an accident ◆ **remettez-vous !** pull yourself together! ◆ **elle ne s'en remettra pas** she won't get over it

2 *(= recommencer)* **se ~ à (faire) qch** to start (doing) sth again ◆ **se ~ à fumer** to take up *ou* start smoking again ◆ **il s'est remis au tennis/au latin** he has taken up tennis/Latin again ◆ **après son départ il se remit à travailler** *ou* **au travail** after she had gone he started working again *ou* went back *ou* got back to work ◆ **il se remet à faire froid** the weather *ou* it is getting *ou* turning cold again ◆ **le temps s'est remis au beau** the weather has turned fine again, the weather has picked up again ◆ **se ~ en selle** to remount, to get back on one's horse ◆ **se ~ debout** to get back

to one's feet, to get (back) up again, to stand up again

[3] *(= se confier)* **se ~ entre les mains de qn** to put o.s. in sb's hands ◆ **je m'en remets à vous** I'll leave it (up) to you, I'll leave the matter in your hands ◆ **s'en ~ à la décision de qn** to leave it to sb to decide ◆ **s'en ~ à la discrétion de qn** to leave it to sb's discretion

[4] *(= se réconcilier)* **se ~ avec qn** to make it up with sb, to make *ou* patch up one's differences with sb ◆ **ils se sont remis ensemble** they're back together again

remeubler /ʀ(ə)mœble/ ▸ conjug 1 ◂ VT to refurnish VPR **se remeubler** to refurnish one's house, to get new furniture

rémige /ʀemiʒ/ NF remex

remilitarisation /ʀ(ə)militaʀizasjɔ̃/ NF remilitarization

remilitariser /ʀ(ə)militaʀize/ ▸ conjug 1 ◂ VT to remilitarize

reminéralisant, e /ʀ(ə)mineʀalizɑ̃, ɑ̃t/ ADJ *[produit, substance]* remineralizing

reminéralisation /ʀ(ə)mineʀalizasjɔ̃/ NF remineralization

reminéraliser /ʀ(ə)mineʀalize/ ▸ conjug 1 ◂ VT to remineralize

réminiscence /ʀeminisɑ̃s/ NF *(= faculté mentale) (Philos, Psych)* reminiscence; *(= souvenir)* reminiscence, vague recollection ◆ **sa conversation était truffée de ~s littéraires** literary influences were constantly in evidence in his conversation ◆ **mon latin est bien rouillé, mais j'ai encore quelques ~s** my Latin is very rusty but I can still remember some ◆ **on trouve des ~s de Rabelais dans l'œuvre de cet auteur** there are echoes of Rabelais in this author's work, parts of this author's work are reminiscent of Rabelais

remisage /ʀ(ə)mizaʒ/ NM *[d'outil, voiture]* putting away

remise /ʀ(ə)miz/ NF [1] *(= livraison) [de lettre, paquet]* delivery; *[de clés]* handing over; *[de récompense]* presentation; *[de devoir, rapport]* handing in; *[de rançon]* handing over, handover; *[d'armes]* surrender, handover ◆ **~ de parts** *(Jur)* transfer *ou* conveyance of legacy ◆ **la ~ des prix/médailles/diplômes** the prize-giving/medal/graduation ceremony; → **cause, touche**

[2] *(= réduction) [de peine]* remission, reduction *(de of, in)*; ◆ **le condamné a bénéficié d'une importante ~ de peine** the prisoner was granted a large reduction in his sentence

[3] *(= rabais)* discount, reduction ◆ **ils font une ~ de 5% sur les livres scolaires** they're giving *ou* allowing (a) 5% discount *ou* reduction on school books ◆ **~ de dette** *(Fin)* condonation, remission of a debt

[4] *(pour outils, véhicules = local)* shed

[5] *(= ajournement) [de réunion]* postponement, deferment, putting off *ou* back *(Brit)*; *[de décision]* putting off ◆ **~ à huitaine d'un débat** postponement of a debate for a week

remiser /ʀ(ə)mize/ ▸ conjug 1 ◂ VT *[+ voiture, outil, valise]* to put away VI *(Jeux)* to make another bet, to bet again VPR **se remiser** *[gibier]* to take cover

remisier /ʀ(ə)mizje/ NM *(Bourse)* intermediate broker

rémissible /ʀemisibl/ ADJ remissible

rémission /ʀemisjɔ̃/ NF [1] *[de péchés]* remission, forgiveness; *(Jur)* remission [2] *(Méd) [de maladie]* remission; *[de douleur, fièvre]* subsidence, abatement; *(fig littér : dans la tempête, le travail)* lull [3] ◆ **sans ~** *[travailler, torturer, poursuivre]* unremittingly, relentlessly; *[payer]* without fail; *[mal, maladie]* irremediable ◆ **si tu recommences, tu seras puni sans ~** if you do it again you'll be punished without fail

remix /ʀəmiks/ NM *(Mus)* remix

remixage /ʀ(ə)miksaʒ/ NM *[de chanson]* remix

remixer /ʀ(ə)mikse/ ▸ conjug 1 ◂ VT *[+ chanson]* to remix ◆ **version remixée** remix version

remixeur /ʀ(ə)miksœʀ/ NM *(= personne)* remixer

remmailler /ʀɑ̃maje/ ▸ conjug 1 ◂ VT *[+ tricot, bas]* to darn; *[+ filet]* to mend

remmailleuse /ʀɑ̃majøz/ NF darner

remmailloter /ʀɑ̃majɔte/ ▸ conjug 1 ◂ VT *[+ bébé]* to change

remmancher /ʀɑ̃mɑ̃ʃe/ ▸ conjug 1 ◂ VT *[+ couteau, balai] (= remettre le manche)* to put the handle back on; *(= remplacer le manche)* to put a new handle on

remmener /ʀɑ̃m(ə)ne/ ▸ conjug 5 ◂ VT to take back, to bring back ◆ **~ qn chez lui** to take sb back home ◆ **~ qn à pied** to walk sb back ◆ **~ qn en voiture** to give sb a lift back, to drive sb back

remodelage /ʀ(ə)mɔd(ə)laʒ/ NM [1] *[de visage, silhouette]* remodelling; *[de nez, joues]* reshaping; *[de ville]* remodelling, replanning [2] *[de profession, organisation]* reorganization, restructuring

remodeler /ʀ(ə)mɔd(ə)le/ ▸ conjug 5 ◂ VT [1] *[+ visage, silhouette]* to remodel; *[+ nez, joues]* to reshape; *[+ ville]* to remodel, to replan [2] *[+ profession, organisation]* to reorganize, to restructure

remontage /ʀ(ə)mɔ̃taʒ/ NM *[de montre]* rewinding, winding up; *[de machine, meuble]* reassembly, putting back together; *[de tuyau]* putting back

remontant, e /ʀ(ə)mɔ̃tɑ̃, ɑ̃t/ ADJ [1] *[boisson]* invigorating, fortifying [2] *[rosier]* reflowering, remontant *(SPÉC)*; *[fraisier, framboisier]* double-cropping, double-fruiting NM tonic, pick-me-up*

remonte /ʀ(ə)mɔ̃t/ NF [1] *[de bateau]* sailing upstream, ascent; *[de poissons]* run [2] *(Équitation) (= fourniture de chevaux)* remount; *(= service)* remount department

remonté, e[1]* /ʀ(ə)mɔ̃te/ (ptp de **remonter**) ADJ [1] *(= en colère)* furious *(contre qn* with sb) mad* *(contre qn* at sb); ◆ **être ~ contre qch** to be wound up* about sth ◆ **être ~ contre qn** to be livid* *ou* mad* *ou* furious with sb ◆ **il est ~ aujourd'hui** he's in a foul mood *ou* temper today [2] *(= dynamique)* **il est ~** he's full of energy ◆ **je suis ~ à bloc** *(gén)* I'm on top form; *(avant un examen, un entretien)* I'm all keyed up *ou* psyched up*

remontée[2] /ʀ(ə)mɔ̃te/ NF *[de côte]* ascent, climbing; *[de rivière]* ascent; *[d'eaux]* rising; *[de prix, taux d'intérêt]* rise ◆ **la ~ des mineurs par l'ascenseur** bringing miners up by lift ◆ **il ne faut pas que la ~ du plongeur soit trop rapide** the diver must not come back up too quickly ◆ **la ~ de l'or à la Bourse** the rise in the price *ou* value of gold on the stock exchange ◆ **faire une (belle) ~** to make a (good) recovery ◆ **faire une ~ spectaculaire (de la 30e à la 2e place)** to make a spectacular recovery (from 30th to 2nd place) ◆ **le président effectue une ~ spectaculaire dans les sondages** the president is rising swiftly in the opinion polls ◆ **~s mécaniques** *(Sport)* ski-lifts

remonte-pente (pl **remonte-pentes**) /ʀ(ə)mɔ̃tpɑ̃t/ NM ski tow

remonter /ʀ(ə)mɔ̃te/ GRAMMAIRE ACTIVE 44.2 ▸ conjug 1 ◂

VI *(surtout avec aux être)* [1] *(= monter à nouveau)* to go *ou* come back up ◆ **il remonta à pied** he walked back up ◆ **remonte me voir** come back up and see me ◆ **je remonte demain à Paris (en voiture)** I'm driving back up to Paris tomorrow ◆ **il remonta sur la table** he climbed back (up) onto the table ◆ **~ sur le trône** to come back *ou* return to the throne ◆ **~ sur les planches** *(Théât)* to go back on the stage

[2] *(dans un moyen de transport)* **~ en voiture** to get back into one's car, to get into one's car again ◆ **~ à cheval** *(= se remettre en selle)* to remount (one's horse), to get back on(to) one's horse; *(= se remettre à faire du cheval)* to take up riding again ◆ **~ à bord** *(Naut)* to go back on board (ship)

[3] *(= s'élever de nouveau) [marée]* to come in again; *[prix, température, baromètre]* to rise again, to go up again; *[colline, route]* to go up again, to rise again ◆ **la mer remonte** the tide is coming in again ◆ **la fièvre remonte** his temperature is rising *ou* going up again, the fever is getting worse again ◆ **les bénéfices ont remonté au dernier trimestre** profits were up again in the last quarter ◆ **les prix ont remonté en flèche** prices shot up *ou* rocketed again ◆ **ses actions remontent** *(fig)* things are looking up for him (again), his fortunes are picking up (again) ◆ **il remonte dans mon estime** my opinion of him is improving again ◆ **il est remonté de la 7e à la 3e place** he has come up from 7th to 3rd place

[4] *[vêtement]* to go up, to pull up ◆ **sa robe remonte sur le côté** her dress goes *ou* pulls up at the side *ou* is higher on one side ◆ **sa jupe remonte quand elle s'assied** her skirt rides up *ou* pulls up *ou* goes up when she sits down

[5] *(= réapparaître)* to come back ◆ **les souvenirs qui remontent à ma mémoire** memories which come back to me *ou* to my mind ◆ **~ à la surface** to come back up to the surface, to resurface ◆ **sous-marin qui remonte en surface** submarine which is coming back up to the surface *ou* which is resurfacing ◆ **une mauvaise odeur remontait de l'égout** a bad smell was coming *ou* wafting up out of the drain

[6] *(= retourner)* to return, to go back ◆ **~ à la source/cause** to go back *ou* return to the source/cause ◆ **~ de l'effet à la cause** to go back from the effect to the cause ◆ **~ au vent** *ou* **dans le vent** *(Naut)* to tack close to the wind ◆ **il faut ~ plus haut** *ou* **plus loin pour comprendre l'affaire** you must go *ou* look further back to understand this business ◆ **~ jusqu'au coupable** to trace the guilty person ◆ **aussi loin que remontent ses souvenirs** as far back as he can remember ◆ **~ dans le temps** to go back in time

[7] ◆ **~ à** *(= dater de)* **cette histoire remonte à une époque reculée/à plusieurs années** all this dates back *ou* goes back a very long time/several years ◆ **tout cela remonte au déluge !** *(hum) (= c'est très ancien)* all that's as old as the hills!; *(= c'est passé depuis longtemps)* all that was ages ago! ◆ **on ne va pas ~ au déluge !** we're not going back over ancient history again! ◆ **la famille remonte aux croisades** the family goes *ou* dates back to the time of the Crusades

VT *(avec aux avoir)* [1] *[+ étage, côte, marche]* to go *ou* climb back up; *[+ rue]* to go *ou* come back up ◆ **~ l'escalier en courant** to rush *ou* run back upstairs ◆ **~ la rue à pas lents** to walk slowly (back) up the street ◆ **~ le courant/une rivière** *(à la nage)* to swim (back) upstream/up a river; *(en barque)* to sail *ou* row (back) upstream/up a river ◆ **~ le courant** *ou* **la pente** *(fig)* to begin to get back on one's feet again ◆ **~ le cours du temps** to go back in time ◆ **machine à ~ le temps** time machine

[2] *(= rattraper) [+ adversaire]* to catch up with ◆ **~ le cortège** to move up towards *ou* work one's way towards the front of the pageant ◆ **se faire ~ par un adversaire** to let o.s. be caught up by an opponent ◆ **il a 15 points/places à ~ pour être 2e** he has 15 marks/places to catch up in order to be 2nd

[3] *(= relever) [+ mur]* to raise, to heighten; *[+ tableau, étagère]* to raise, to put higher up; *[+ vitre]*

(en poussant) to push up; *(avec bouton ou manivelle)* to wind up; *[+ store]* to roll up, to raise; *[+ pantalon, manche]* to pull up; *(en roulant)* to roll up; *(d'une saccade)* to hitch up; *[+ chaussettes]* to pull up; *[+ col]* to turn up; *[+ jupe]* to pick up, to raise; *(fig) [+ mauvaise note]* to put up, to raise ◆ **~ les bretelles à qn** * *(fig)* to give sb a piece of one's mind * ◆ **il s'est fait ~ les bretelles par le patron** * the boss gave him a real tongue-lashing * *ou* dressing-down

[4] *(= remporter)* to take *ou* bring back up ◆ **~ une malle au grenier** to take *ou* carry a trunk back up to the attic

[5] *[+ montre, mécanisme]* to wind up

[6] *(= réinstaller) [+ machine, moteur, meuble]* to put together again, to put back together (again), to reassemble; *[+ robinet, tuyau]* to put back ◆ **ils ont remonté une usine à Lyon** they have set up *ou* built another factory in Lyon ◆ **il a eu du mal à ~ les roues de sa bicyclette** he had a job putting *ou* getting the wheels back on his bicycle

[7] *(= réassortir) [+ garde-robe]* to renew, to replenish; *[+ magasin]* to restock ◆ **mon père nous a remontés en vaisselle** my father has given us a whole new set of crockery ◆ **~ son ménage** *(en meubles)* to buy new furniture; *(en linge)* to buy new linen

[8] *(= remettre en état) [+ personne] (physiquement)* to set *ou* buck * up (again); *(moralement)* to cheer *ou* buck * up (again); *[+ entreprise]* to put *ou* set back on its feet; *[+ mur en ruines]* to rebuild ◆ **le nouveau directeur a bien remonté cette entreprise** the new manager has really got this firm back on its feet ◆ **ce contrat remonterait bien mes affaires** this contract would really give business a boost for me; → **moral**

[9] *(Théât) [+ pièce]* to restage, to put on again

VPR se remonter [1] *(= refaire des provisions)* ◆ **se ~ en boîtes de conserves** to get in (further) stocks of canned food, to replenish one's stocks of canned food ◆ **se ~ en chaussures** to get some new shoes

[2] *(= récupérer) (physiquement)* to buck * *ou* set o.s. up (again) ◆ **se ~ (le moral)** *(moralement)* to raise (one's spirits), to cheer *ou* buck * o.s. up

remontoir /ʀ(ə)mɔ̃twaʀ/ **NM** *[de montre]* winder; *[de jouet, horloge]* winding mechanism

remontrance /ʀ(ə)mɔ̃tʀɑ̃s/ **NF** [1] *(= reproche)* remonstrance, reproof, reprimand, admonition *(frm)* ◆ **faire des ~s à qn (au sujet de qch)** to remonstrate with sb (about sth), to reprove *ou* reprimand *ou* admonish *(frm)* sb (for sth) [2] *(Hist)* remonstrance

remontrer /ʀ(ə)mɔ̃tʀe/ ► conjug 1 ◄ **VT** [1] *(= montrer de nouveau)* to show again ◆ **remontrez-moi la bleue** show me the blue one again, let me have another look at the blue one ◆ **ne te remontre plus ici** don't show your face *ou* yourself here again [2] *(= donner des leçons)* **en ~ à qn** to teach sb a thing or two ◆ **dans ce domaine, il pourrait t'en ~** he could teach you a thing or two about this ◆ **n'essaie pas de m'en ~** *(= montrer sa supériorité)* don't bother trying to teach me anything [3] *(†, littér)* **~ à qn que** to point out to sb that

remords /ʀ(ə)mɔʀ/ **NM** remorse *(NonC)* ◆ **j'éprouve quelques ~ à l'avoir laissé seul** I feel some remorse at having left him alone ◆ **j'ai eu un ~ de conscience, je suis allé vérifier** I had second thoughts *ou* I thought better of it and went to check ◆ **~ cuisants** agonies of remorse ◆ **avoir des ~** to feel remorse ◆ **être pris de ~** to be stricken *ou* smitten with remorse ◆ **n'avoir aucun ~** to have no (feeling of) remorse, to feel no remorse ◆ **je le tuerais sans (le moindre) ~** I'd kill him without (the slightest) compunction *ou* remorse ◆ **je te le donne – (c'est) sans ~ ?** here you are – are you sure?

remorquage /ʀ(ə)mɔʀkaʒ/ **NM** *[de voiture, caravane]* towing; *[de train]* pulling, hauling; *[de bateau]* towing, tugging

remorque /ʀ(ə)mɔʀk/ **NF** [1] *(= véhicule)* trailer; *(= câble)* towrope, towline; → **camion** [2] *(locutions)* **prendre une voiture en ~** to tow a car ◆ **"en remorque"** "on tow" ◆ **quand ils vont se promener ils ont toujours la belle-sœur en ~** whenever they go for a walk they always have the sister-in-law in tow *ou* they always drag along their sister-in-law ◆ **être à la ~** *(péj)* to trail behind ◆ **être à la ~ de** *(péj)* to tag along behind ◆ **être à la ~ d'une grande puissance** *[pays]* to tag along *ou* to trail behind a great power

remorquer /ʀ(ə)mɔʀke/ ► conjug 1 ◄ **VT** [1] *[+ voiture, caravane]* to tow; *[+ train]* to pull, to haul; *[+ bateau]* to tow, to tug ◆ **je suis tombé en panne et j'ai dû me faire ~ jusqu'au village** I had a breakdown and had to get a tow *ou* get myself towed as far as the village [2] *[+ personne]* to drag along ◆ **~ toute la famille derrière soi** to have the whole family in tow, to drag the whole family along

remorqueur /ʀ(ə)mɔʀkœʀ/ **NM** *(= bateau)* tug(boat)

remotivation /ʀ(ə)mɔtivasjɔ̃/ **NF** remotivation

remotiver /ʀ(ə)mɔtive/ ► conjug 1 ◄ **VT** *[+ personne, personnel]* to remotivate

remouiller /ʀ(ə)muje/ ► conjug 1 ◄ **VT** [1] *(= mouiller de nouveau)* to wet again ◆ **~ du linge à repasser** to dampen washing ready for ironing ◆ **se faire ~ (par la pluie)** to get wet (in the rain) again ◆ **je viens de m'essuyer les mains, je ne veux pas me les ~** I've just dried my hands and I don't want to get them wet again [2] *(Naut)* **~ (l'ancre)** to drop anchor again

rémoulade /ʀemulad/ **NF** remoulade, rémoulade *(dressing containing mustard and herbs)*; → **céleri**

remoulage /ʀ(ə)mulaʒ/ **NM** [1] *(Art)* recasting [2] *[de café, pièce métallique]* regrinding; *[de farine] (= action)* remilling; *(= résultat)* middlings

remouler /ʀ(ə)mule/ ► conjug 1 ◄ **VT** *[+ statue]* to recast

rémouleur /ʀemulœʀ/ **NM** (knife- *ou* scissor-) grinder

remous /ʀəmu/ **NM** [1] *[de bateau]* (back-)wash *(NonC)*; *[d'eau]* swirl, eddy; *[d'air]* eddy ◆ **emporté par les ~ de la foule** swept along by the bustling *ou* milling crowd; → **bain** [2] *(= agitation)* stir *(NonC)* ◆ **~ d'idées** whirl *ou* swirl of ideas ◆ **l'affaire a provoqué de vifs ~ politiques** the affair caused a stir in political circles ◆ **cette décision n'a suscité aucun ~** this decision didn't raise any eyebrows

rempaillage /ʀɑ̃pɑjaʒ/ **NM** *[de chaise]* reseating, rebottoming *(with straw)*

rempailler /ʀɑ̃pɑje/ ► conjug 1 ◄ **VT** *[+ chaise]* to reseat, to rebottom *(with straw)*

rempailleur, -euse /ʀɑ̃pɑjœʀ, øz/ **NM,F** *[de chaise]* chair-bottomer

rempaqueter /ʀɑ̃pak(ə)te/ ► conjug 4 ◄ **VT** to wrap up again, to rewrap

rempart /ʀɑ̃paʀ/ **NM** [1] *(Mil)* rampart ◆ **~s** *[de ville]* city walls, ramparts; *[de château fort]* battlements, ramparts [2] *(fig)* bastion, rampart *(littér)* ◆ **le dernier ~ contre** the last bastion against ◆ **il lui fit un ~ de son corps** he shielded him with his body

rempiler /ʀɑ̃pile/ ► conjug 1 ◄ **VT** *[+ objets]* to pile *ou* stack up again **VI** *(arg Mil)* to join up again, to re-enlist

remplaçable /ʀɑ̃plasabl/ **ADJ** replaceable ◆ **difficilement ~** hard to replace

remplaçant, e /ʀɑ̃plasɑ̃, ɑ̃t/ **NM,F** *(gén)* replacement, substitute; *[de médecin]* replacement, locum *(Brit)*; *(Sport)* reserve; *(pendant un match)* substitute; *(Théât)* understudy; *(Scol)* supply *(Brit) ou* substitute *(US)* teacher ◆ **être le ~ de qn** to stand in for sb ◆ **trouver un ~ à un professeur malade** to get sb to stand in *ou* substitute for a sick teacher ◆ **il faut lui trouver un ~** we must find a replacement *ou* a substitute for him

remplacement /ʀɑ̃plasmɑ̃/ **NM** [1] *(= intérim) [d'acteur malade, médecin en vacances]* standing in (*de* for); *[de joueur, professeur malade]* standing in (*de* for) substitution (*de* for) deputizing (*de* for); ◆ **assurer le ~ d'un collègue pendant sa maladie** to stand in for a colleague during his illness ◆ **faire des ~s** *[secrétaire]* to temp *, to do temporary work; *[professeur]* to do supply teaching *(Brit)*, to work as a supply *(Brit) ou* substitute *(US)* teacher ◆ **j'ai fait trois ~s cette semaine** I've had three temporary replacement jobs this week

[2] *(= substitution)* replacement (*de* of) taking over (*de* from); *[d'employé, objet usagé]* replacement ◆ **effectuer le ~ d'une pièce défectueuse** to replace a faulty part ◆ **film présenté en ~ d'une émission annulée** film shown in place of a cancelled programme ◆ **je n'ai plus de stylos, en ~ je vous donne un crayon** I have no more pens so I'll give you a pencil instead ◆ **le ~ du nom par le pronom** the replacement of the noun by the pronoun ◆ **il va falloir trouver une solution de ~** we'll have to find an alternative (solution) ◆ **produit/matériel de ~** substitute (product/material)

remplacer /ʀɑ̃plase/ ► conjug 3 ◄ **VT** [1] *(= assurer l'intérim de) [+ acteur]* to stand in for; *[+ joueur, professeur]* to stand in for, to substitute for; *[+ médecin]* to stand in for, to do a locum for *(Brit)* ◆ **je me suis fait ~** I got someone to stand in for me *ou* to cover for me

[2] *(= succéder à)* to replace, to take over from, to take the place of ◆ **le train a remplacé la diligence** the train replaced *ou* took the place of the stagecoach ◆ **son fils l'a remplacé comme directeur** his son has taken over from him *ou* has replaced him as director ◆ **~ une sentinelle** to take over from *ou* relieve a sentry

[3] *(= tenir lieu de)* to take the place of, to replace ◆ **le miel peut ~ le sucre** honey can be used in place of *ou* used as a substitute for sugar ◆ **le pronom remplace le nom dans la phrase** the pronoun takes the place of *ou* replaces the noun in the sentence ◆ **on peut ~ le beurre par de l'huile d'olive** you can use olive oil instead of butter ◆ **rien ne remplace le vrai beurre** there's nothing like *ou* you can't beat real butter ◆ **une autre femme l'a vite remplacée (dans son cœur)** she was soon replaced (in his affections) by another woman

[4] *(= changer) [+ employé]* to replace; *[+ objet usagé]* to replace, to change ◆ **~ un vieux lit par un neuf** to replace an old bed with a new one, to change an old bed for a new one ◆ **les pièces défectueuses seront remplacées gratuitement** faulty parts will be replaced free of charge ◆ **~ un carreau cassé** to replace a broken windowpane ◆ **remplacez les pointillés par des pronoms** put pronouns in place of the dotted lines ◆ **un homme comme lui ne se remplace pas aisément** a man like that isn't easy to replace

rempli[1], e /ʀɑ̃pli/ (ptp de **remplir**) **ADJ** *[récipient, théâtre]* full (*de* of) filled (*de* with); *[joue, visage]* full, plump; *[journée, vie]* full, busy ◆ **il avait les yeux ~s de larmes** his eyes were brimming with *ou* full of tears ◆ **avoir l'estomac bien ~** to have a full stomach, to have eaten one's fill ◆ **texte ~ de fautes** text riddled *ou* packed with mistakes ◆ **sa tête était ~e de souvenirs** his mind was filled with *ou* full of memories ◆ **no-**

tre carnet de commandes est bien ~ our order book is full ◆ **il est** ~ **de son importance/de lui-même** he's full of his own importance/of himself

rempli² /Rɑ̃pli/ NM *(Couture)* tuck

remplir /Rɑ̃pliR/ ▸ conjug 2 ◂ VT 1 *(= emplir) (gén)* to fill (*de* with); *[+ récipient]* to fill (up); *(à nouveau)* to refill; *[+ questionnaire]* to fill in *ou* out ◆ ~ **qch à moitié** to half fill sth, to fill sth half full ◆ **il en a rempli 15 pages** he filled 15 pages with it, he wrote 15 pages on it ◆ **ce chanteur ne remplira pas la salle** this singer won't fill the hall *ou* won't get a full house ◆ **ces tâches routinières ont rempli sa vie** these routine tasks have filled his life, his life has been filled with these routine tasks ◆ **ça remplit la première page des journaux** it fills *ou* covers the front page of the newspapers ◆ **ce résultat me remplit d'admiration** this result fills me with admiration, I am filled with admiration at this result ◆ ~ **son temps** to fill one's time ◆ **il remplit bien ses journées** he gets a lot done in (the course of) a day, he packs a lot into his days
2 *(= s'acquitter de) [+ contrat, mission, obligation]* to fulfil, to carry out; *[+ devoir]* to carry out, to do; *[+ rôle]* to fill, to play; *[+ besoin]* to fulfil, to answer, to meet ◆ ~ **ses engagements** to meet one's commitments ◆ ~ **ses fonctions** to do *ou* carry out one's job, to carry out *ou* perform one's functions ◆ **objet qui remplit une fonction précise** object that fulfils a precise purpose ◆ **vous ne remplissez pas les conditions** you do not fulfil *ou* satisfy *ou* meet the conditions
VPR **se remplir** *[récipient, salle]* to fill (up) (*de* with); ◆ **se** ~ **les poches** * to line one's pockets ◆ **on s'est bien rempli la panse** * we stuffed ourselves *, we pigged out *

remplissage /Rɑ̃plisaʒ/ NM *[de tonneau, bassin]* filling (up); *(péj : dans un livre)* padding ◆ **faire du** ~ to pad out one's work (*ou* speech *etc*) ◆ **taux de** ~ **des avions/hôtels** air passenger/hotel occupancy rate

remploi /Rɑ̃plwa/ NM ⇒ **réemploi**

remployer /Rɑ̃plwaje/ ▸ conjug 8 ◂ VT ⇒ **réemployer**

remplumer (se) * /Rɑ̃plyme/ ▸ conjug 1 ◂ VPR *(physiquement)* to fill out again, to get a bit of flesh on one's bones again; *(financièrement)* to get back on one's feet, to have some money in one's pocket again

rempocher /Rɑ̃pɔʃe/ ▸ conjug 1 ◂ VT to put back in one's pocket ◆ **le ministre a dû** ~ **son projet de réforme** the minister had to shelve his reform plan

rempoissonnement /Rɑ̃pwasɔnmɑ̃/ NM restocking (with fish)

rempoissonner /Rɑ̃pwasɔne/ ▸ conjug 1 ◂ VT to restock (with fish)

remporter /Rɑ̃pɔRte/ ▸ conjug 1 ◂ VT 1 *(= reprendre)* to take away (again), to take back 2 *[+ championnat, élections, contrat]* to win; *[+ prix]* to win, to carry off ◆ ~ **la victoire** to win ◆ ~ **un (vif) succès** to achieve (a great) success

rempotage /Rɑ̃pɔtaʒ/ NM repotting

rempoter /Rɑ̃pɔte/ ▸ conjug 1 ◂ VT to repot

remuant, e /Rəmɥɑ̃, ɑ̃t/ ADJ *[enfant]* *(= agité)* fidgety; *(= turbulent)* boisterous; *[public]* rowdy; *[opposition]* active

remue-ménage /R(ə)mymenaʒ/ NM INV *(= bruit)* commotion *(NonC)*; *(= activité)* hurly-burly *(NonC)*, hustle and bustle *(NonC)* ◆ **il y a du** ~ **chez les voisins** the neighbours are making a great commotion ◆ **faire du** ~ to make a commotion ◆ **le** ~ **électoral** the electoral hurly-burly

remue-méninges /R(ə)mymenɛ̃ʒ/ NM INV brainstorming

remuement /R(ə)mymɑ̃/ NM *(littér)* moving, movement

remuer /Rəmɥe/ ▸ conjug 1 ◂ VT 1 *(= bouger) [+ tête, bras, lèvres]* to move; *[+ oreille]* to twitch ◆ ~ **la queue** *[vache, écureuil]* to flick its tail; *[chien]* to wag its tail ◆ ~ **les bras** *ou* **les mains en parlant** to wave one's arms about *ou* gesticulate as one speaks ◆ ~ **les épaules/les hanches en marchant** to swing *ou* sway one's shoulders/one's hips as one walks; → **doigt**
2 *[+ objet]* *(= déplacer)* to move, to shift; *(= secouer)* to shake ◆ **il essaya de** ~ **la pierre** he tried to move *ou* shift the stone ◆ **sa valise est si lourde que je ne peux même pas la** ~ his suitcase is so heavy that I can't even shift *ou* move *ou* budge it ◆ **arrête de** ~ **ta chaise** stop moving your chair about ◆ **ne remue pas** *ou* **ne fais pas** ~ **la table, je suis en train d'écrire** don't shake *ou* move *ou* wobble the table – I'm trying to write
3 *(= brasser) [+ café]* to stir; *[+ sable]* to stir up; *[+ salade]* to toss; *[+ terre]* to dig *ou* turn over ◆ **il a remué la sauce/les braises** he gave the sauce a stir/the fire a poke, he stirred the sauce/poked the fire ◆ **il a tout remué dans le tiroir** he turned the whole drawer *ou* everything in the drawer upside down ◆ **la brise remuait les feuilles** the breeze stirred the leaves ◆ **une odeur de terre remuée** a smell of fresh earth *ou* of freshly turned *ou* dug earth ◆ ~ **de l'argent (à la pelle)** to deal with *ou* handle vast amounts of money ◆ ~ **ciel et terre pour** *(fig)* to move heaven and earth (in order) to ◆ ~ **des souvenirs** *[personne nostalgique]* to turn *ou* go over old memories in one's mind; *[évocation]* to stir up *ou* arouse old memories
4 *[+ personne]* *(= émouvoir)* to move; *(= bouleverser)* to upset ◆ **ça vous remue les tripes** * it really tugs at your heartstrings ◆ **elle était toute remuée par cette nouvelle** she was very upset when she heard the news
VI 1 *(= bouger) [personne]* to move; *[dent, tuile]* to be loose ◆ **cesse de** ~ **!** keep still!, stop fidgeting! ◆ **le vent faisait** ~ **les branchages** the wind was stirring the branches, the branches were stirring *ou* swaying in the wind ◆ **ça a remué pendant la traversée** * the crossing was pretty rough * ◆ **il a remué toute la nuit** he tossed and turned all night ◆ **j'ai entendu** ~ **dans la cuisine** I heard someone moving about in the kitchen; → **nez**
2 *(fig = se rebeller)* to show signs of unrest
VPR **se remuer** 1 *(= bouger)* to move; *(= se déplacer)* to move about
2 * *(= se mettre en route)* to get going; *(= s'activer)* to get a move on *, to shift *ou* stir o.s. * ◆ **remue-toi un peu !** get a move on! * ◆ **il s'est beaucoup remué pour leur trouver une maison** he's gone to a lot of trouble to find them a house ◆ **il ne s'est pas beaucoup remué** he didn't exactly strain himself *ou* put himself out

remugle /Rəmygl/ NM *(littér)* mustiness, fustiness

rémunérateur, -trice /RemyneRatœR, tRis/ ADJ *[emploi]* remunerative, lucrative

rémunération /RemyneRasjɔ̃/ NF *[de personne]* payment, remuneration (*de* of); *[d'investissement, capital]* return (*de* on) ◆ **la** ~ **moyenne des cadres** average executive pay ◆ **en** ~ **de vos services** in payment for your services ◆ **mode de** ~ *[de salarié]* method of payment; *[d'investissement]* type of return ◆ **emploi à faible/forte** ~ low-paid/highly-paid job ◆ **toucher une** ~ **de 1 500 €** to be paid €1,500 ◆ **placement à faible/forte** ~ low-return *ou* low-yield/high-return *ou* high-yield investment

rémunérer /RemyneRe/ ▸ conjug 6 ◂ VT *[+ personne]* to pay, to remunerate ◆ ~ **le travail de qn** to pay sb for their work ◆ **travail bien/mal rémunéré** well-paid/badly-paid job ◆ **avoir une activité rémunérée** to be in salaried employment ◆ **emploi rémunéré à 1 500 €** job that pays €1,500 ◆ **placement rémunéré à 4,5%** investment yielding 4.5%; → **compte**

> ⚠ **rémunérer** se traduit rarement par **to remunerate**, qui est d'un registre plus soutenu.

renâcler /R(ə)nɑkle/ ▸ conjug 1 ◂ VI *[animal]* to snort; *(fig) [personne]* to grumble, to complain, to show (one's) reluctance ◆ ~ **à la besogne** *ou* **à la tâche** to grumble, to complain *(about having to do a job)* ◆ ~ **à faire qch** to do sth reluctantly *ou* grudgingly ◆ **sans** ~ uncomplainingly, without grumbling ◆ **faire qch en renâclant** to do sth grudgingly *ou* reluctantly *ou* with (a) bad grace

renaissance /R(ə)nɛsɑ̃s/ NF *(Rel, fig)* rebirth ◆ **la Renaissance** *(Hist)* the Renaissance ADJ INV *[mobilier, style]* Renaissance

renaissant, e /R(ə)nɛsɑ̃, ɑ̃t/ ADJ 1 *[forces]* returning; *[économie]* reviving, recovering; *[espoir, intérêt]* renewed ◆ **toujours** *ou* **sans cesse** ~ *[difficultés]* constantly recurring, that keep cropping up; *[obstacles]* that keep cropping up; *[doutes, hésitations, intérêt]* constantly renewed 2 *(Hist)* Renaissance *(épith)*

renaître /R(ə)nɛtR/ ▸ conjug 59 ◂ VI 1 *[joie]* to spring up again, to be revived (*dans* in); *[espoir, doute]* to be revived (*dans* in) to be reborn *(littér)*; *[conflit]* to spring up again, to break out again; *[difficulté]* to recur, to crop up again; *[économie]* to revive, to recover; *[sourire]* to return (*sur* to) to reappear (*sur* on); *[plante]* to come *ou* spring up again; *[jour]* to dawn, to break ◆ **le printemps renaît** spring is reawakening ◆ **la nature renaît au printemps** nature comes back to life in spring ◆ **faire** ~ *[+ sentiment, passé]* to bring back, to revive; *[+ problème, sourire]* to bring back; *[+ espoir, conflit]* to revive
2 *(= revivre) (gén)* to come to life again; *(Rel)* to be born again (*en* in); ◆ ~ **de ses cendres** *(Myth, fig)* to rise from one's ashes ◆ **je me sens** ~ I feel as if I've been given a new lease of life
3 *(littér)* ~ **au bonheur** to find happiness again ◆ ~ **à l'espérance** to find fresh hope ◆ ~ **à la vie** to take on a new lease of life

rénal, e (mpl **-aux**) /Renal, o/ ADJ renal *(SPÉC)*, kidney *(épith)*

renard /R(ə)naR/ NM *(= animal)* fox; *(= fourrure)* fox(-fur) ◆ ~ **argenté/bleu** silver/blue fox ◆ ~ **des sables** fennec ◆ **c'est un vieux** ~ *(fig)* he's a sly old fox *ou* dog

renarde /R(ə)naRd/ NF vixen

renardeau (pl **renardeaux**) /R(ə)naRdo/ NM fox cub

renardière /R(ə)naRdjɛR/ NF *(= terrier)* fox's den; *(Can)* fox farm

renationalisation /R(ə)nasjɔnalizasjɔ̃/ NF *[d'entreprise]* renationalization

renationaliser /R(ə)nasjɔnalize/ ▸ conjug 1 ◂ VT *[+ entreprise]* to renationalize

renauder * † /Rənode/ ▸ conjug 1 ◂ VI to grouse *, to grouch *

rencaisser /Rɑ̃kese/ ▸ conjug 1 ◂ VT 1 *[+ argent]* to put back in the till 2 *[+ plantes]* to rebox

rencard ✻ /Rɑ̃kaR/ NM ⇒ **rancard**

rencarder ✻ /Rɑ̃kaRde/ ▸ conjug 1 ◂ VT ⇒ **rancarder**

renchérir /Rɑ̃ʃeRiR/ ▸ conjug 2 ◂ VI 1 *(en paroles, en actes)* to go further, to go one better *(péj)* ◆ ~ **sur ce que qn dit** to add something to what sb says, to go further *ou* one better *(péj)* than sb ◆ ~ **sur ce que qn fait** to go further than sb ◆ **"et je n'en ai nul besoin" renchérit-il** "and I don't need it in the least", he added ◆ **il faut**

toujours qu'il renchérisse (sur ce qu'on dit) he always has to go one better [2] *[prix]* to get dearer *ou* more expensive ◆ **la vie renchérit** the cost of living is going up *ou* rising [3] *(dans une vente : sur l'offre de qn)* to make a higher bid, to bid higher *(sur* than); *(sur son offre)* to raise one's bid **VT** *[+ coût]* to put up, to increase; *[+ produit]* to make more expensive, to put up the price of

renchérissement /ʀɑ̃ʃeʀismɑ̃/ **NM** *[de marchandises]* rise *ou* increase in (the) price *(de* of); *[de loyers]* rise, increase *(de* in); ◆ **le ~ de la vie** the rise *ou* increase in the cost of living

rencogner (se)* /ʀɑ̃kɔɲe/ ► conjug 1 ◄ **VPR** to huddle up, to curl up (in a corner)

rencontre /ʀɑ̃kɔ̃tʀ/ **NF** [1] *(imprévue)* encounter, meeting ◆ **le hasard d'une ~ a changé ma vie** a chance encounter *ou* meeting changed my life ◆ **~ du premier/deuxième/troisième type** close encounter of the first/second/third kind

◆ **faire + rencontre(s)** ◆ **faire la ~ de qn** to meet sb; *(imprévue)* to meet sb, to run into sb ◆ **faire une mauvaise ~** to have an unpleasant encounter ◆ **faire une ~ inattendue** to have an unexpected encounter ◆ **j'ai peur qu'il ne fasse de mauvaises ~s** I'm afraid that he might get involved with the wrong sort of people ◆ **j'ai fait des ~s intéressantes** I met some interesting people

◆ **à la rencontre de** ◆ **aller à la ~ de qn** to go and meet sb, to go to meet sb ◆ **(partir) à la ~ des Incas** (to go) in search of the Incas

◆ **de rencontre** ◆ **lieu/point de ~** meeting place/point ◆ **amours/amis de ~** casual love affairs/friends ◆ **compagnons de ~** chance companions; → **club**

[2] *(organisée) (Pol)* meeting ◆ **~ au sommet** summit meeting ◆ **le festival propose des ateliers et des ~s avec les artistes** the festival offers workshops and interviews with the artists ◆ **~s musicales/théâtrales** *(= événement culturel)* music/theatre festival

[3] *(= compétition)* match; *(Athlétisme)* meeting; *(Ftbl etc)* game ◆ **la ~ (des deux équipes) aura lieu le 15** the game will be on the 15th ◆ **~ de boxe** boxing match

[4] *(Mil)* skirmish, encounter, engagement; *(= duel)* encounter, meeting

[5] *[d'éléments]* conjunction; *[de rivières]* confluence; *[de routes]* junction; *[de voitures]* collision; *[de voyelles]* juxtaposition ◆ **la ~ des deux routes/rivières se fait ici** the roads/rivers merge here

rencontrer /ʀɑ̃kɔ̃tʀe/ ► conjug 1 ◄ **VT** [1] *(gén)* to meet; *(par hasard)* to meet, to run *ou* bump into* ◆ **j'ai rencontré Paul en ville** I met *ou* ran into* *ou* bumped into* Paul in town ◆ **le Premier ministre a rencontré son homologue allemand** the Prime Minister has had a meeting with *ou* has met his German counterpart ◆ **mon regard rencontra le sien** our eyes met, my eyes met his

[2] *(= trouver) [+ expression]* to find, to come across; *[+ occasion]* to meet with ◆ **des gens/sites comme on n'en rencontre plus** the sort of people/places you don't find any more ◆ **arrête-toi au premier garage que nous rencontrerons** stop at the first garage you come across *ou* find ◆ **avec lui, j'ai rencontré le bonheur** I have found happiness with him

[3] *(= heurter)* to strike; *(= toucher)* to meet (with) ◆ **la lame rencontra un os** the blade struck a bone ◆ **sa main ne rencontra que le vide** his hand met with nothing but empty space

[4] *[+ obstacle, difficulté, opposition]* to meet with, to encounter, to come up against; *[+ résistance]* to meet with, to come up against

[5] *(Sport) [+ équipe]* to meet, to play (against); *[+ boxeur]* to meet, to fight (against)

VPR **se rencontrer** [1] *[personnes, regards]* to meet; *[rivières, routes]* to meet, to join; *[équipes]* to meet, to play (each other); *[boxeurs]* to meet, to fight (each other); *[véhicules]* to collide (with each other) ◆ **faire se ~ deux personnes** to arrange for two people to meet, to arrange a meeting between two people ◆ **je me suis déjà rencontré avec lui** *(frm)* I have already met him ◆ **nous nous sommes déjà rencontrés** we have already met

[2] *(= avoir les mêmes idées)* **se ~ (avec qn)** to be of the same opinion *ou* mind (as sb); → **esprit**

[3] *(= exister) [coïncidence, curiosité]* to be found ◆ **cela ne se rencontre plus de nos jours** that isn't found *ou* one doesn't come across that any more nowadays ◆ **il se rencontre des gens qui ...** you do find people who ..., there are people who ...

rendement /ʀɑ̃dmɑ̃/ **NM** *[de champ]* yield; *[de machine]* output; *[d'entreprise] (= productivité)* productivity; *(= production)* output; *[de personne]* output; *(Phys)* efficiency; *(Fin) [d'investissement]* return *(de* on) yield *(de* of); ◆ **taux de ~** *[d'investissement]* (rate of) return, yield ◆ **l'entreprise marche à plein ~** the business is working at full capacity ◆ **placement d'un ~ médiocre** low-yielding investment ◆ **il travaille beaucoup, mais il n'a pas de ~*** he works hard but he isn't very productive

rendez-vous /ʀɑ̃devu/ **NM INV** [1] *(gén)* appointment; *(d'amoureux)* date ◆ **donner** *ou* **fixer un ~ à qn, prendre ~ avec qn** *(pour affaires, consultation)* to make an appointment with sb; *(entre amis)* to arrange to see *ou* meet sb ◆ **j'ai (un) ~ à 10 heures** I have an appointment *ou* I have to meet someone at 10 o'clock ◆ **nous nous étions donné ~ à l'aéroport** we had arranged to meet at the airport ◆ **ma parole, vous vous êtes donné ~ !** my goodness, you must have planned this! ◆ **le soleil était au ~ pour le mariage** it was a sunny day for the wedding ◆ **la croissance espérée n'est pas au ~** the expected growth has not materialized ◆ **avoir ~ avec la mort** *(littér)* to have an appointment with death ◆ **~ d'affaires** business appointment ◆ **~ spatial** docking (in space) ◆ **prendre (un) ~ chez le dentiste/coiffeur** to make a dental/hair appointment ◆ **j'ai ~ chez le médecin** I've got a doctor's appointment *ou* an appointment at the doctor's ◆ **le médecin ne reçoit que sur ~** the doctor only sees patients by appointment ◆ **ce match sera le grand ~ sportif de l'année** this match will be the big sporting event of the year ◆ **le festival est le ~ annuel des cinéphiles** the festival brings cinema lovers together once a year ◆ **~ manqué** *(fig)* missed *ou* wasted opportunity; → **galant**

[2] *(= lieu)* meeting place ◆ **~ de chasse** meet; → **maison**

[3] *(* = personne)* **votre ~ est arrivé** the person you're waiting for has arrived

COMP **rendez-vous citoyen** *training course replacing military service in France*

rendormir /ʀɑ̃dɔʀmiʀ/ ► conjug 16 ◄ **VT** to put to sleep again, to put back to sleep **VPR** **se rendormir** to go back to sleep, to fall asleep again

rendosser /ʀɑ̃dose/ ► conjug 1 ◄ **VT** to put on again

rendre /ʀɑ̃dʀ/ ► conjug 41 ◄ **VT** [1] *(= restituer) (gén)* to give back, to return, to take *ou* bring back; *[+ marchandises défectueuses, bouteille vide]* to return, to take back; *[+ argent]* to pay *ou* give back, to return; *[+ objet volé]* to give back, to return; *[+ otage]* to return; *[+ cadeau, bague]* to return, to give back; *(Scol) [+ copie]* to hand in ◆ **quand pourriez-vous me ~ votre réponse ?** when will you be able to give me *ou* let me have your reply? ◆ **~ son devoir en retard** to hand *ou* give in one's essay late ◆ **~ sa parole à qn** to release sb from a promise, to let sb off (his promise) ◆ **~ la liberté à qn** to set sb free, to give sb his freedom ◆ **~ la santé à qn** to restore sb to health ◆ **~ la vue à qn** to restore sb's sight, to give sb back his sight ◆ **cela lui a rendu toutes ses forces/son courage** that gave him back *ou* restored all his strength/his courage ◆ **~ la vie à qn** to save sb's life *(fig)* ◆ **rendu à la vie civile** back in civilian life ◆ **cette lessive rend à votre linge l'éclat du neuf** this powder makes your washing as good as new

[2] *(Jur) [+ jugement, arrêt]* to pronounce, to render; *[+ verdict]* to return

[3] *(= donner en retour) [+ hospitalité, invitation]* to return, to repay; *[+ salut, coup, baiser]* to return ◆ **je lui ai rendu sa visite** I returned *ou* repaid his visit ◆ **~ coup pour coup** to return blow for blow ◆ **il m'a joué un sale tour, mais je le lui rendrai** he played a dirty trick on me, but I'll get even with him *ou* I'll get my own back on him* ◆ **je lui ai rendu injure pour injure** I gave him as good as I got ◆ **Dieu vous le rendra au centuple** God will return it to you a hundredfold ◆ **~ la politesse à qn** to return sb's kindness ◆ **il la déteste, et elle le lui rend bien** he hates her and she feels exactly the same (way) about him ◆ **~ la monnaie à qn** to give sb his change ◆ **il m'a donné 10 € et je lui en ai rendu 5** he gave me 10 euros and I gave him 5 euros back *ou* 5 euros change ◆ **~ la pareille à qn** to pay sb back in his own coin; → aussi **monnaie**

[4] *(avec adj)* to make ◆ **~ qn heureux** to make sb happy ◆ **~ qch public** to make sth public ◆ **~ qn responsable de qch** to make sb responsible for sth ◆ **son discours l'a rendu célèbre** his speech has made him famous ◆ **c'est à vous ~ fou !** it's enough to drive you mad!

[5] *(= exprimer par un autre moyen) [+ mot, expression, atmosphère]* to render ◆ **cela ne rend pas bien sa pensée** that doesn't render *ou* convey his thoughts very well ◆ **le portrait ne rend pas son expression** this portrait has not caught *ou* captured his expression

[6] *(= produire) [+ liquide]* to give out; *[+ son]* to produce, to make ◆ **le concombre rend beaucoup d'eau** cucumbers give out a lot of water ◆ **l'enquête n'a rien rendu** the inquiry drew a blank *ou* didn't come to anything *ou* produced nothing ◆ **ça ne rend pas grand-chose** *[photo, décor, musique]* it's a bit disappointing

[7] *(= vomir) [+ bile]* to vomit, to bring up; *[+ déjeuner]* to vomit, to bring back *ou* up ◆ **~ tripes et boyaux*** to be as sick as a dog* ◆ **~ du sang (par la bouche)** to cough up *ou* vomit blood

[8] *(Sport)* **~ du poids** *[cheval]* to have a weight handicap ◆ **~ 3 kg** to give *ou* carry 3 kg ◆ **~ de la distance** *[coureur]* to have a handicap ◆ **~ 100 mètres** to have a 100-metre handicap ◆ **~ des points à qn** *(fig)* to give sb points *ou* a head start

[9] *(Mil) [+ place forte]* to surrender ◆ **~ les armes** to lay down one's arms

[10] *(locutions)* **~ l'âme** *ou* **le dernier soupir** *[personne]* to breathe one's last, to give up the ghost ◆ **ma voiture/mon frigo a rendu l'âme*** my car/my fridge has given up the ghost* ◆ **~ gloire à** *[+ Dieu]* to glorify; *[+ hommes]* to pay homage to ◆ **~ grâce(s) à qn** to give *ou* render *(frm)* thanks to sb; → **compte, service, visite** *etc*

VI [1] *[arbres, terre]* to yield, to be productive ◆ **les pommiers ont bien rendu** the apple trees have given a good yield *ou* crop ◆ **la pêche a bien rendu** we have got a good catch (of fish) ◆ **ma petite expérience n'a pas rendu** *(fig)* my little experiment didn't pay off *ou* didn't come to anything

[2] *(= vomir)* to be sick, to vomit ◆ **avoir envie de ~** to feel sick

[3] *(= produire un effet)* **la pendule rendrait mieux dans l'entrée** the clock would look better in the hall ◆ **ça rend mal en photo** a

photograph doesn't do it justice ◆ **ça rend bien** it looks good

VPR **se rendre** 1 (= *céder*) *[soldat, criminel]* to give o.s. up, to surrender; *[troupe]* to surrender ◆ **se ~ à l'avis de qn** to bow to sb's opinion ◆ **se ~ à l'évidence** (= *regarder les choses en face*) to face facts; (= *admettre son tort*) to bow before the evidence ◆ **se ~ aux prières de qn** to give way *ou* give in *ou* yield to sb's pleas ◆ **se ~ aux raisons de qn** to bow to *ou* accept sb's reasons

2 (= *aller*) **se ~ à** to go to ◆ **il se rend à son travail à pied/en voiture** he walks/drives to work, he goes to work on foot/by car ◆ **alors qu'il se rendait à ...** as he was on his way to ... *ou* going to ... ◆ **la police s'est rendue sur les lieux** the police went to *ou* arrived on the scene ◆ **se ~ à l'appel de qn** to respond to sb's appeal; → **lieu¹**

3 (*avec adj*) **se ~ utile/indispensable** to make o.s. useful/indispensable ◆ **il se rend ridicule** he's making a fool of himself, he's making himself look foolish ◆ **vous allez vous ~ malade** you're going to make yourself ill

rendu, e /ʀɑ̃dy/ (ptp de **rendre**) ADJ 1 (= *arrivé*) **être ~** to have arrived ◆ **nous voilà ~s !** here we are then! ◆ **on est plus vite ~ par le train** you get there quicker by train 2 (= *remis*) **~ à domicile** delivered to the house 3 (= *fatigué*) exhausted, tired out, worn out NM 1 (*Comm*) return; → **prêté** 2 (*Art*) rendering

rêne /ʀɛn/ NF rein ◆ **prendre les ~s d'une affaire** (*fig*) to take over a business, to assume control *ou* take control of a business ◆ **lâcher les ~s** (*lit*) to loosen *ou* slacken the reins; (*fig*) to let go ◆ **c'est lui qui tient les ~s du gouvernement** (*fig*) it's he who holds the reins of government *ou* who is in the saddle

renégat, e /ʀənega, at/ NM,F (*Rel*) renegade; (*gén, Pol*) renegade, turncoat

renégociation /ʀ(ə)negɔsjasjɔ̃/ NF renegotiation

renégocier /ʀ(ə)negɔsje/ ► conjug 7 ◄ VT, VI to renegotiate

reneiger /ʀ(ə)neʒe/ ► conjug 3 ◄ VB IMPERS to snow again

renfermé, e /ʀɑ̃fɛʀme/ (ptp de **renfermer**) ADJ *[personne]* withdrawn, uncommunicative NM ◆ **ça sent le ~** it smells musty *ou* stuffy (in here); → **odeur**

renfermer /ʀɑ̃fɛʀme/ ► conjug 1 ◄ VT 1 (= *contenir*) *[+ trésors]* to contain, to hold; *[+ erreurs, vérités]* to contain ◆ **phrase qui renferme plusieurs idées** sentence that encompasses *ou* contains several ideas 2 (†: *à clé*) to lock again, to lock back up VPR **se renfermer** ◆ **se ~ (en soi-même)** to withdraw into o.s. ◆ **se ~ dans sa coquille** to withdraw into one's shell

renfiler /ʀɑ̃file/ ► conjug 1 ◄ VT *[+ perles]* to restring; *[+ aiguille]* to thread again, to rethread; *[+ bas, manteau]* to slip back into

renflé, e /ʀɑ̃fle/ (ptp de **renfler**) ADJ bulging (*épith*), bulbous

renflement /ʀɑ̃fləmɑ̃/ NM bulge

renfler /ʀɑ̃fle/ ► conjug 1 ◄ VT to make a bulge in; *[+ joues]* to blow out VPR **se renfler** to bulge (out)

renflouage /ʀɑ̃fluaʒ/, **renflouement** /ʀɑ̃flumɑ̃/ NM 1 *[de navire]* refloating 2 *[d'entreprise]* refloating, bailing out; *[de personne]* bailing out

renflouer /ʀɑ̃flue/ ► conjug 1 ◄ VT 1 *[+ navire]* to refloat 2 *[+ entreprise]* to refloat, to bail out; *[+ personne]* to set back on their feet again, to bail out VPR **se renflouer** *[personne]* to get back on one's feet again (*financially*)

renfoncement /ʀɑ̃fɔ̃smɑ̃/ NM recess ◆ **caché dans le ~ d'une porte** hidden in a doorway

renfoncer /ʀɑ̃fɔ̃se/ ► conjug 3 ◄ VT 1 *[+ clou]* to knock further in; *[+ bouchon]* to push further in ◆ **il renfonça son chapeau (sur sa tête)** he pulled his hat down (further) 2 (*Typo*) to indent

renforçateur /ʀɑ̃fɔʀsatœʀ/ NM (*Photo*) intensifier; (*Psych*) reinforcer ◆ **~ de goût** flavour enhancer

renforcement /ʀɑ̃fɔʀsəmɑ̃/ NM 1 *[de vêtement, mur]* reinforcement; *[de poutre]* reinforcement, trussing; *[de régime, position, monnaie, amitié]* strengthening; *[de paix, pouvoir]* consolidating 2 *[d'équipe, armée]* reinforcement ◆ **~ des effectifs de la police** increasing the number of police officers 3 *[de crainte, soupçon]* reinforcement, increase; *[d'argument]* reinforcement, strengthening 4 *[de pression, effort, surveillance, contrôle]* intensification, stepping up; *[de couleur, ton, expression]* intensification ◆ **un ~ des sanctions économiques** toughening *ou* stepping up economic sanctions ◆ **un ~ du dialogue Nord-Sud** stepping up dialogue between North and South

renforcer /ʀɑ̃fɔʀse/ ► conjug 3 ◄ VT 1 *[+ vêtement, mur]* to reinforce; *[+ poutre]* to reinforce; *[+ régime, position, monnaie, amitié]* to strengthen; *[+ paix, pouvoir]* to consolidate ◆ **bas à talon renforcé** stocking with reinforced heel

2 *[+ équipe, armée, effectifs]* to reinforce ◆ **des réservistes sont venus ~ nos effectifs** reservists arrived as reinforcements *ou* to swell our numbers

3 *[+ crainte, soupçon]* to reinforce, to increase; *[+ argument]* to reinforce, to strengthen ◆ **~ qn dans une opinion** to confirm sb's opinion, to confirm sb in an opinion ◆ **ça renforce ce que je dis** that backs up what I'm saying

4 *[+ pression, effort, surveillance, contrôle]* to intensify, to step up; *[+ couleur, son, expression]* to intensify ◆ **(cours d')anglais renforcé** (*Scol*) remedial English (class)

VPR **se renforcer** *[craintes]* to increase; *[amitié]* to strengthen; *[pression]* to intensify ◆ **notre équipe s'est renforcée de deux nouveaux joueurs** our team has been strengthened by two new players

renfort /ʀɑ̃fɔʀ/ NM 1 (*gén*) help, helpers ◆ **~s** (*Mil*) (*en hommes*) reinforcements; (*en matériel*) (further) supplies ◆ **recevoir un ~ de troupes/d'artillerie** to receive more troops/guns, to receive reinforcements/a further supply of guns

2 (*Tech*) reinforcement, strengthening piece

3 (*Couture*) patch ◆ **collants avec ~s aux talons** tights with reinforced heels

4 (*locutions*) **de ~** *[barre, toile]* strengthening; *[troupe]* back-up, supporting; *[personnel]* extra, additional ◆ **envoyer qn en ~** to send sb as an extra *ou* sb to augment the numbers ◆ **les 500 soldats appelés en ~** the 500 soldiers called in as reinforcements ◆ **embaucher du personnel en ~** to employ extra *ou* additional staff

◆ **à grand renfort de** ◆ **parfum lancé à grand ~ de publicité** perfume launched amid much publicity *ou* a blaze of publicity ◆ **à grand ~ de gestes/d'explications** with a great many gestures/explanations ◆ **à grand ~ de citations/d'arguments** with the help *ou* support of a great many quotations/arguments

renfrogné, e /ʀɑ̃fʀɔɲe/ (ptp de **se renfrogner**) ADJ *[visage]* sullen, scowling (*épith*), sulky; *[air, personne]* sullen, sulky

renfrognement /ʀɑ̃fʀɔɲmɑ̃/ NM scowling, sullenness

renfrogner (se) /ʀɑ̃fʀɔɲe/ ► conjug 1 ◄ VPR *[personne]* to scowl, to pull a sour face

rengagé /ʀɑ̃gaʒe/ ADJ M *[soldat]* re-enlisted NM re-enlisted soldier

rengagement /ʀɑ̃gaʒmɑ̃/ NM 1 *[de discussion]* starting up again; *[de combat]* re-engagement 2 (= *réinvestissement*) reinvestment 3 (= *nouveau recrutement*) *[de soldat]* re-enlistment; *[d'ouvrier]* taking back

rengager /ʀɑ̃gaʒe/ ► conjug 3 ◄ VT 1 *[+ discussion]* to start up again; *[+ combat]* to re-engage 2 (= *réinvestir*) to reinvest 3 (= *recruter de nouveau*) *[+ soldat]* to re-enlist; *[+ ouvrier]* to take back 4 (= *réintroduire*) **~ une clé dans une serrure** to put a key back into a lock ◆ **~ sa voiture dans une rue** to drive (back) into a street again VI (*Mil*) to join up again, to re-enlist VPR **se rengager** 1 (*Mil*) to join up again, to re-enlist 2 *[discussion]* to start up again 3 (= *entrer à nouveau*) **se ~ dans une rue** to enter a street again

rengaine /ʀɑ̃gɛn/ NF (= *formule*) hackneyed expression; (= *chanson*) old (repetitive) song *ou* melody ◆ **c'est toujours la même ~*** it's always the same old refrain (*Brit*) *ou* song* (*US*)

rengainer /ʀɑ̃gene/ ► conjug 1 ◄ VT 1 * *[+ compliment]* to save, to withhold; *[+ sentiments]* to contain, to hold back ◆ **rengaine tes beaux discours !** (you can) save *ou* keep your fine speeches! 2 *[+ épée]* to sheathe, to put up; *[+ revolver]* to put back in its holster

rengorger (se) /ʀɑ̃gɔʀʒe/ ► conjug 3 ◄ VPR *[oiseau]* to puff out its throat; *[personne]* to puff o.s. up ◆ **se ~ d'avoir fait qch** to be full of o.s. for having done sth

reniement /ʀənimɑ̃/ NM *[de foi, opinion]* renunciation; *[de frère, patrie, signature, passé, cause, parti]* disowning, repudiation; *[de promesse, engagement]* breaking; (*Rel*) denial ◆ **le ~ de Jésus par saint Pierre** St Peter's denial of Christ

renier /ʀənje/ ► conjug 7 ◄ VT *[+ foi, opinion]* to renounce; *[+ personne, patrie, signature, passé, cause, parti]* to disown; *[+ promesse, engagement]* to go back on, to break ◆ **il renia Jésus-Christ** (*Rel*) he denied Christ ◆ **~ Dieu** to renounce God VPR **se renier** to go back on what one has said *ou* done

reniflement /ʀ(ə)nifləmɑ̃/ NM 1 (= *action*) *[de fleur, objet]* sniffing (*NonC*); *[de cheval]* snorting (*NonC*); (*à cause d'un rhume, en pleurant*) sniffing (*NonC*), snuffling (*NonC*), sniffling (*NonC*) 2 (= *bruit*) sniff, sniffle, snuffle; (*plus fort*) snort

renifler /ʀ(ə)nifle/ ► conjug 1 ◄ VT 1 *[+ cocaïne]* to snort, to take a snort of; *[+ colle]* to sniff 2 *[+ fleur, objet, odeur]* to sniff 3 (* = *pressentir*) *[+ bonne affaire, arnaque]* to sniff out* ◆ **~ quelque chose de louche** to smell a rat VI *[personne]* to sniff; (*en pleurant*) to sniff, to snuffle, to sniffle; *[cheval]* to snort ◆ **arrête de ~, mouche-toi !** stop sniffing and blow your nose!

renifleur, -euse /ʀ(ə)niflœʀ, øz/ ADJ sniffing, snuffling NM,F * sniffer, snuffer; → **avion**

renne /ʀɛn/ NM reindeer

renom /ʀənɔ̃/ NM 1 (= *notoriété*) renown, repute, fame ◆ **vin de grand ~** famous wine ◆ **restaurant en ~** celebrated *ou* renowned *ou* famous restaurant ◆ **acquérir du ~** to win renown, to become famous ◆ **avoir du ~** to be famous *ou* renowned 2 (*frm* = *réputation*) reputation ◆ **son ~ de sévérité** his reputation for severity ◆ **bon/mauvais ~** good/bad reputation *ou* name

renommé, e¹ /ʀ(ə)nɔme/ (ptp de **renommer**) ADJ celebrated, renowned, famous ◆ **~ pour** renowned *ou* famed for

renommée² /ʀ(ə)nɔme/ NF 1 (= *célébrité*) fame, renown ◆ **marque/savant de ~ mondiale** world-famous make/scholar ◆ **de grande ~** of great renown 2 (*littér* = *opinion publique*) public report 3 (*littér* = *réputation*) reputation ◆ **bonne/mauvaise ~** good/bad reputation *ou* name

renommer /ʀ(ə)nɔme/ ► conjug 1 ◄ VT 1 *[+ personne]* to reappoint 2 *(Ordin)* *[+ fichier, répertoire]* to rename

renonce /ʀ(ə)nɔ̃s/ NF *(Cartes)* ◆ **faire une ~** to revoke, to renegue, to fail to follow suit

renoncement /ʀ(ə)nɔ̃smɑ̃/ NM *(= action)* renouncement *(à of)*; *(= sacrifice)* renunciation ◆ **~ à soi-même** self-abnegation, self-renunciation ◆ **mener une vie de ~** to live a life of renunciation *ou* abnegation

renoncer /ʀ(ə)nɔ̃se/ ► conjug 3 ◄ VT INDIR **renoncer à** *[+ projet, lutte]* to give up, to renounce; *[+ fonction, héritage, titre, pouvoir, trône]* to renounce, to relinquish; *[+ habitude]* to give up; *[+ métier]* to abandon, to give up ◆ **~ à un voyage/au mariage** to give up *ou* abandon the idea of a journey/of marriage ◆ **~ à qn** to give sb up ◆ **~ au tabac** to give up smoking ◆ **~ à comprendre** to give up trying to understand ◆ **~ à lutter** to give up the struggle ◆ **~ à se marier** to give up *ou* abandon the idea of getting married ◆ **~ aux plaisirs/au monde** to renounce pleasures/the world ◆ **je *ou* j'y renonce** I give up ◆ **~ à cœur** *(Cartes)* to fail to follow (in) hearts ◆ **~ à toute prétention** *(Jur)* to abandon any claim

VT *(littér)* *[+ ami]* to give up

⚠ Attention à ne pas traduire automatiquement **renoncer à** par **to renounce**, qui ne s'utilise que dans certains contextes.

renonciation /ʀənɔ̃sjasjɔ̃/ NF *[de fonction, héritage, titre, pouvoir, trône]* renunciation, relinquishment *(à of)*; *[d'opinion, croyance, idée, projet, lutte]* giving up

renoncule /ʀənɔ̃kyl/ NF *(sauvage)* buttercup; *(cultivée)* globeflower, ranunculus *(SPÉC)*

renouer /ʀənwe/ ► conjug 1 ◄ VT *[+ lacet, nœud]* to tie (up) again, to re-tie; *[+ cravate]* to reknot, to knot again; *[+ conversation, liaison]* to renew, to resume VI ◆ **~ avec qn** to take up with sb again, to become friends with sb again ◆ **~ avec une habitude** to take up a habit again ◆ **~ avec une tradition** to revive a tradition ◆ **ils ont renoué avec la victoire** they came back on top

renouveau (pl **renouveaux**) /ʀ(ə)nuvo/ NM 1 *(= transformation)* revival ◆ **le ~ des sciences et des arts à la Renaissance** the revival of the sciences and the arts *ou* the renewed interest in *ou* the renewal of interest in the sciences and arts during the Renaissance 2 *(= regain)* **~ de succès/faveur** renewed success/favour ◆ **connaître un ~ de faveur** to enjoy renewed favour, to come back into favour 3 *(littér = printemps)* **le ~** springtide *(littér)*

renouvelable /ʀ(ə)nuv(ə)labl/ ADJ *[bail, contrat, énergie, passeport]* renewable; *[expérience]* which can be tried again *ou* repeated; *[congé]* which can be re-granted; *[assemblée]* that must be re-elected ◆ **le mandat présidentiel est ~ tous les 5 ans** the president must run *ou* stand *(Brit)* for re-election every 5 years ◆ **ressources naturelles non ~s** non-renewable natural resources ◆ **crédit ~** revolving credit

renouveler /ʀ(ə)nuv(ə)le/ ► conjug 4 ◄ VT 1 *[+ matériel, personnel, équipe]* to renew, to replace; *[+ stock]* to renew, to replenish; *[+ pansement]* to renew, to change; *[+ conseil d'administration]* to re-elect ◆ **~ l'air d'une pièce** to air a room ◆ **~ l'eau d'une piscine** to renew the water in a swimming pool ◆ **~ sa garde-robe** to renew one's wardrobe, to buy some new clothes ◆ **la chambre doit être renouvelée tous les cinq ans** *(Pol)* the house must be re-elected every five years

2 *[+ mode, théorie]* to renew, to revive ◆ **cette découverte a complètement renouvelé notre vision des choses** this discovery has given us a whole new insight into things *ou* has cast a whole new light on things for us ◆ **les poètes de la Pléiade renouvelèrent la langue française** the poets of the Pléiade gave new *ou* renewed life to the French language

3 *[+ passeport, contrat, abonnement, bail, prêt, mandat]* to renew ◆ **à ~** *(Méd)* to be renewed

4 *[+ douleur]* to revive

5 *[+ candidature]* to renew; *[+ demande, offre, promesse, erreur]* to renew, to repeat; *[+ expérience, exploit]* to repeat, to do again; *(Rel)* *[+ vœux]* to renew ◆ **l'énergie sans cesse renouvelée que requiert ce métier** the constantly renewed energy which this job requires ◆ **avec mes remerciements renouvelés** *(dans une lettre)* with renewed thanks, thanking you once more *ou* once again ◆ **la chambre a renouvelé sa confiance au gouvernement** the house reaffirmed *ou* reasserted its confidence in the government

6 *(littér = emprunter)* **épisode renouvelé de l'Antiquité** episode taken *ou* borrowed from Antiquity

VPR **se renouveler** 1 *(= se répéter)* *[incident]* to recur, to be repeated ◆ **cette petite scène se renouvelle tous les jours** this little scene recurs *ou* is repeated every day ◆ **et que ça ne se renouvelle plus !** and don't let it happen again!

2 *(= être remplacé)* to be renewed *ou* replaced ◆ **les cellules de notre corps se renouvellent constamment** the cells of our body are constantly being renewed *ou* replaced ◆ **les hommes au pouvoir ne se renouvellent pas assez** men in power aren't replaced often enough

3 *(= innover)* *[auteur, peintre]* to change one's style, to try something new ◆ **il ne se renouvelle pas** *[comique]* he always tells the same old jokes *ou* stories

renouvellement /ʀ(ə)nuvɛlmɑ̃/ NM 1 *[de matériel, personnel, équipe]* renewal, replacement; *[de stock]* renewal, replenishment; *[de pansement]* renewal, changing; *[de garde-robe]* changing; *[de cellules]* renewal 2 *[de mode, théorie, art, langue]* renewal, revival; *[de genre littéraire]* revival ◆ **elle éprouve un besoin de ~** she feels she needs to start afresh 3 *[de passeport, contrat, abonnement, bail, prêt]* renewal ◆ **solliciter le ~ de son mandat** *(Pol)* to run *ou* stand *(Brit)* for re-election 4 *[de candidature]* renewal; *[de demande, offre, promesse, erreur]* renewal, repetition; *[d'expérience, exploit]* repetition; *[d'incident]* recurrence; *[de douleur]* revival; *(Rel)* *[de vœux]* renewal ◆ **faire son ~** to renew one's first communion promises

rénovateur, -trice /ʀenɔvatœʀ, tʀis/ ADJ *[doctrine]* which seeks a renewal, reformist; *[influence]* renewing *(épith)*, reforming *(épith)* NM,F *(de la morale, Pol)* reformer ◆ **il est considéré comme le ~ de cette science/de cet art** he's considered as having been the one who injected new life into this science/into this art form NM *(= produit d'entretien)* restorer

rénovation /ʀenɔvasjɔ̃/ NF 1 *[de maison]* renovation; *(= nouvelle décoration)* refurbishment; *[de quartier]* renovation, refurbishment; *[de meuble]* restoration ◆ **en (cours de) ~** under renovation ◆ **le musée est en ~** the museum is being renovated *ou* restored ◆ **travaux de ~** renovations, renovation work 2 *[d'enseignement, institution]* reform; *[de science]* renewal, bringing up to date; *[de méthode]* reform

rénover /ʀenɔve/ ► conjug 1 ◄ VT 1 *[+ maison]* to renovate; *(nouvelle décoration)* to refurbish; *[+ quartier]* to renovate; *[+ meuble]* to restore 2 *[+ enseignement, institution]* to reform; *[+ méthode, parti]* to reform

renseignement /ʀɑ̃sɛɲmɑ̃/ GRAMMAIRE ACTIVE 54.1, 54.5, 47.1 NM 1 *(gén)* information *(NonC)*, piece of information ◆ **un ~ intéressant** an interesting piece of information, some interesting information ◆ **demander un ~ *ou* des ~s à qn** to ask sb for information ◆ **il est allé aux ~s** he has gone to find out ◆ **prendre ses ~s *ou* demander des ~s sur qn** to make inquiries *ou* ask for information about sb ◆ **~s pris, aucun élève n'était absent ce jour-là** (when asked) the school said no pupils were absent that day ◆ **avoir de bons ~s sur le compte de qn** to have good *ou* favourable reports about *ou* on sb ◆ **pourriez-vous me donner un ~ ?** I'd like some information, could you give me some information? ◆ **veuillez m'envoyer de plus amples ~s sur ...** please send me further details of ... *ou* further information about ... ◆ **je peux te demander un ~ ?** can I ask you something?, could you tell me something? ◆ **merci pour le ~** thanks for the information, thanks for telling me *ou* letting me know ◆ **guichet/bureau des ~s** information *ou* inquiry *(Brit)* desk/office ◆ **"renseignements"** *(panneau)* "information", "inquiries" *(Brit)* ◆ **(service des) ~s** *(Téléc)* directory inquiries *(Brit)*, information *(US)*

2 *(Mil)* intelligence *(NonC)*, piece of intelligence ◆ **agent/service de ~s** intelligence agent/service ◆ **travailler dans le ~** to work in intelligence ◆ **les ~s généraux** *the security branch of the police force*

renseigner /ʀɑ̃seɲe/ ► conjug 1 ◄ VT 1 ◆ **~ un client/un touriste** to give some information to a customer/a tourist ◆ **~ la police/l'ennemi** to give information to the police/the enemy *(sur about)*; ◆ **~ un passant/un automobiliste** *(sur le chemin à prendre)* to give directions to a passer-by/a driver, to tell a passer-by/a driver the way ◆ **qui pourrait me ~ sur le prix de la voiture/sur lui ?** who could tell me the price of the car/something about him?, who could give me some information *ou* particulars about the price of the car/about him? ◆ **puis-je vous ~ ?** can I help you? ◆ **il pourra peut-être te ~** perhaps he'll be able to give you some information (about it), perhaps he'll be able to tell you *ou* to help you ◆ **document qui renseigne utilement** document which gives useful information ◆ **ça ne nous renseigne pas beaucoup !** that doesn't get us very far!, that doesn't tell us very much! *ou* give us much to go on! ◆ **il a l'air bien renseigné** he seems to be well informed *ou* to know a lot about it ◆ **il est mal renseigné** he doesn't know much about it, he isn't very well informed ◆ **j'ai été mal renseigné** I was misinformed *ou* given the wrong information

2 *(= remplir)* *[+ case, champ de données]* to fill in

VPR **se renseigner** *(= demander des renseignements)* to make enquiries, to ask for information *(sur about)*; *(= obtenir des renseignements)* to find out *(sur about)*; ◆ **je vais me ~ auprès de lui** I'll ask him for information *ou* for particulars, I'll ask him about it ◆ **renseignez-vous auprès de l'office du tourisme/à l'accueil** enquire at *ou* ask at the tourist office/at reception (for details) ◆ **j'essaierai de me ~** I'll try to find out, I'll try and get some information ◆ **je vais me ~ sur son compte** I'll make enquiries about him, I'll find out about him ◆ **je voudrais me ~ sur les caméscopes** I'd like some information *ou* particulars about camcorders

rentabilisation /ʀɑ̃tabilizasjɔ̃/ NF *[de produit, entreprise]* making profitable; *[d'invention]* marketing, commercializing ◆ **la ~ des investissements** securing a return on investments, making investments pay

rentabiliser /ʀɑ̃tabilize/ ► conjug 1 ◄ VT *[+ entreprise, activité]* to make profitable, to make pay; *[+ investissements]* to secure a return on, to make pay; *[+ équipements]* to make cost-effective, to make pay ◆ **notre investissement a été très vite rentabilisé** we got a quick return on our investment ◆ **~ son temps** to make the best use of one's time

rentabilité /ʀɑ̃tabilite/ NF profitability ◆ **~ des investissements** return on investments ◆ **ce placement a une faible/forte ~** this is a low-return *ou* low-yield/high-return *ou* high-yield investment

rentable /ʀɑ̃tabl/ ADJ *[entreprise, activité]* profitable ◆ **c'est une affaire très ~** this is a very profitable business, this business really pays ◆ **au prix où est l'essence, les transports privés ne sont pas ~s** with fuel the price it is, private transport isn't a paying *ou* viable proposition *ou* private transport doesn't pay ◆ **il travaille beaucoup mais il n'est pas ~** he works a lot but he isn't very productive ◆ **ce n'est plus du tout ~** *(lit)* it's no longer financially viable; *(fig)* it just isn't worth it any more ◆ **cette prise de position s'est avérée politiquement ~** taking this stand paid off *ou* was a good move politically

rentamer /ʀɑ̃tame/ ▸ conjug 1 ◂ VT *[+ discours]* to begin *ou* start again

rente /ʀɑ̃t/ NF ① *(= pension)* annuity, pension; *(fournie par la famille)* allowance ◆ **~ de situation** secure *ou* guaranteed income ◆ **~ viagère** life annuity ◆ **faire une ~ à qn** to give an allowance to sb ② *(= emprunt d'État)* government stock *ou* loan *ou* bond ◆ **~s perpétuelles** perpetual loans, irredeemable securities ③ *(locutions)* **avoir des ~s** to have a private *ou* an unearned income, to have private *ou* independent means ◆ **vivre de ses ~s** to live on *ou* off one's private income

> ⚠ **rente** ne se traduit pas par le mot anglais **rent**, qui a le sens de 'loyer'.

rentier, -ière /ʀɑ̃tje, jɛʀ/ NM,F person of independent *ou* private means ◆ **c'est un petit ~** he has a small private income ◆ **mener une vie de ~** to live a life of ease *ou* leisure

rentrant, e /ʀɑ̃tʀɑ̃, ɑ̃t/ ADJ *[train d'atterrissage]* retractable; *(Math) [angle]* reflex

rentré, e[1] /ʀɑ̃tʀe/ (ptp de **rentrer**) ADJ *[colère]* suppressed; *[yeux]* sunken; *[joues]* sunken, hollow NM *(Couture)* hem

rentre-dedans‡ /ʀɑ̃t(ʀə)dədɑ̃/ NM INV ◆ **il m'a fait du ~** *[dragueur]* he came on really strong to me*; *[vendeur]* he was really pushy*

rentrée[2] /ʀɑ̃tʀe/ NF ① ◆ **~ (scolaire** *ou* **des classes)** start of the new school year, time when the schools go back ◆ **~ universitaire** start of the new academic year; *(du trimestre)* start of the new (school *ou* university) term ◆ **acheter des cahiers pour la ~ (des classes)** to buy exercise books for the new school year ◆ **la ~ aura lieu lundi** the new term begins on Monday, school starts again on Monday ◆ **la ~ s'est bien passée** the term began well ◆ **"les affaires de la rentrée"** *(dans un magasin)* "back-to-school bargains" ◆ **à la ~ de Noël** at the start of (the) term after the Christmas holidays ◆ **cette langue sera enseignée à partir de la ~ 2004** this language will be part of the syllabus as from autumn 2004 *ou* as from the start of the 2004-5 school year

② *[de tribunaux]* reopening; *[de parlement]* reopening, reassembly ◆ **la ~ parlementaire aura lieu cette semaine** parliament reassembles *ou* reopens this week, the new session of parliament starts this week ◆ **les députés font leur ~ aujourd'hui** the deputies are returning *ou* reassembling today (for the start of the new session) ◆ **faire sa ~ politique** *(après les vacances d'été)* to start the new political season, to begin one's autumn campaign; *(après avoir fait autre chose)* to make a *ou* one's political comeback ◆ **c'est la ~ des théâtres parisiens** it's the start of the theatrical season in Paris ◆ **la ~ littéraire** the start of the literary season *ou* calendar ◆ **on craint une ~ sociale agitée** it is feared that there will be some social unrest this autumn ◆ **la réforme entrera en vigueur à la ~ prochaine** the reform will come into effect next autumn ◆ **leur album sortira à la ~ de septembre** their album will come out in September ◆ **la mode de la ~** the autumn fashions ◆ **on verra ça à la ~** we'll see about that after the holidays *ou* when we come back from holiday

③ *[d'acteur, sportif]* comeback

④ *(= retour)* return ◆ **pour faciliter la ~ dans la capitale** to make getting back into *ou* the return into the capital easier ◆ **la ~ des ouvriers à l'usine le lundi matin** the workers' return to work on a Monday morning ◆ **à l'heure des ~s dans Paris** when everyone is coming back into Paris ◆ **il m'a reproché mes ~s tardives** he told me off for coming in late ◆ **~ dans l'atmosphère** *(Espace)* re-entry into the atmosphere ◆ **effectuer sa ~ dans l'atmosphère** to re-enter the atmosphere ◆ **~ en touche** *(Sport)* throw-in

⑤ *[de récolte]* bringing in ◆ **faire la ~ du blé** to bring in the wheat

⑥ *(Cartes)* cards picked up

⑦ *(Comm, Fin)* **~s** income ◆ **~ d'argent** sum of money (coming in) ◆ **je compte sur une ~ d'argent très prochaine** I'm expecting a sum of money *ou* some money very soon ◆ **les ~s de l'impôt** tax revenue

> **RENTRÉE**
>
> **La rentrée (des classes)** in September each year is not only the time when French children and teachers go back to school; it is also the time when political and social life begins again after the long summer break. The expression « à la rentrée » is thus not restricted to an educational context, but can refer in general to the renewed activity that takes place throughout the country in the autumn.

rentrer /ʀɑ̃tʀe/ ▸ conjug 1 ◂ VI *(avec aux être)* ① *(= entrer à nouveau) (vu de l'extérieur)* to go back in; *(vu de l'intérieur)* to come back in ◆ **il pleut trop, rentrez un instant** it's raining too hard so come back in for a while ◆ **il est rentré dans la maison/la pièce** he went back (*ou* came back) into the house/the room ◆ **la navette est rentrée dans l'atmosphère** the shuttle re-entered the atmosphere ◆ **il était sorti sans ses clés, il a dû ~ par la fenêtre** he'd gone out without his keys and he had to get back in through the window ◆ **l'acteur est rentré en scène** the actor came on again

② *(= revenir chez soi)* to come back, to come (back) home, to return (home); *(= s'en aller chez soi)* to go (back) home, to return home; *(= arriver chez soi)* to get (back) home, to return home ◆ **~ déjeuner/dîner** to go (back) home for lunch/dinner ◆ **est-ce qu'il est rentré ?** is he back? ◆ **elle est rentrée très tard hier soir** she came *ou* got in *ou* back very late last night ◆ **je l'ai rencontré en rentrant** I met him on my way home ◆ **~ de l'école/du bureau** to come back from school/from the office, to come (*ou* go) home from school/from the office ◆ **il a dû ~ de voyage d'urgence** he had to come back *ou* come home from his trip urgently, he had to return home urgently ◆ **~ à Paris/de Paris** to go back *ou* come back *ou* return to Paris/from Paris ◆ **je rentre en voiture** I'm driving back, I'm going back by car ◆ **dépêche-toi de ~, ta mère a besoin de toi** hurry home *ou* back, your mother needs you ◆ **~ à sa base** *[avion]* to return *ou* go back to base ◆ **le navire rentre au port** the ship is coming back in

③ *(= reprendre ses activités) [élèves]* to go back to school, to start school again; *[université]* to start again; *[tribunaux]* to reopen; *[parlement]* to reassemble; *[députés]* to return, to reassemble ◆ **les enfants rentrent en classe** *ou* **à l'école lundi** the children go back to school *ou* start school again on Monday ◆ **le trimestre prochain, on rentrera un lundi** next term starts *ou* next term we start on a Monday ◆ **elle rentre au lycée l'année prochaine** she's starting secondary school next year

④ *(= entrer) [personne]* to go in, to come in; *[chose]* to go in ◆ **il pleuvait, nous sommes rentrés dans un café** it was raining so we went into a cafe ◆ **les voleurs sont rentrés par la fenêtre** the thieves got in by the window ◆ **cette clé ne rentre pas (dans la serrure)** this key doesn't fit (into the lock), I can't get this key in (the lock) ◆ **j'ai grossi, je ne rentre plus dans cette jupe** I've put on weight, I can't get into this skirt any more ◆ **faire ~ qch dans la tête de qn** to get sth into sb's head ◆ **il a le cou qui lui rentre dans les épaules** he has a very short neck ◆ **il était exténué, les jambes lui rentraient dans le corps** he was so exhausted his legs were giving way under him ◆ **tout cela ne rentrera pas dans ta valise** that won't all go *ou* fit into your suitcase, you won't get all that into your suitcase ◆ **cubes qui rentrent les uns dans les autres** cubes that fit into one another; → aussi **entrer**

⑤ *(= devenir membre de)* **~ dans** *[+ police, entreprise, fonction publique]* to join, to go into; *[+ industrie, banque]* to go into ◆ **c'est son père qui l'a fait ~ dans l'usine** his father helped him (to) get a job in the factory *ou* (to) get into the factory

⑥ *(= se heurter à)* **~ dans** to crash into, to collide with ◆ **sa voiture a dérapé, il est rentré dans un arbre** his car skidded and he crashed into a tree ◆ **furieux, il voulait lui ~ dedans*** *ou* **dans le chou*** *(= agresser)* he was so furious he felt like smashing his head in* ◆ **rentrez-leur dedans !**‡ get them!* ◆ **il lui est rentré dans le lard**‡ *ou* **le mou**‡ *ou* **le buffet**‡ he beat him up*

⑦ *(= être compris dans)* **~ dans** to be included in, to be part of ◆ **cela ne rentre pas dans ses attributions** that is not included in *ou* part of his duties ◆ **les frais de déplacement ne devraient pas ~ dans la note** travelling expenses should not be included in the bill *ou* should not be put on the bill ◆ **~ dans une catégorie** to fall *ou* come into a category

⑧ *[argent]* to come in ◆ **l'argent ne rentre pas en ce moment** the money isn't coming in at the moment ◆ **l'argent rentre difficilement/bien en ce moment** there isn't much money/there's plenty of money coming in at the moment ◆ **faire ~ les impôts/les fonds** to collect the taxes/the funds ◆ **faire ~ l'argent** to get the money in

⑨ * **la grammaire/les maths, ça ne rentre pas** *[connaissances]* he can't take grammar/maths in, he can't get the hang of grammar/maths* ◆ **l'anglais, ça commence à ~** English is beginning to sink in

⑩ *(locutions)* **~ dans ses droits** to recover one's rights ◆ **~ dans son argent/dans ses frais** to recover *ou* get back one's money/one's expenses ◆ **~ dans ses fonds** to recoup one's costs ◆ **tout est rentré dans l'ordre** *(dans son état normal)* everything is back to normal again; *(dans le calme)* order has returned, order has been restored; *(= tout a été clarifié)* everything is sorted out now ◆ **~ dans le rang** to come *ou* fall back into line; → **coquille, grâce, terre** *etc*

VT *(avec aux avoir)* ① *[+ foins, moisson]* to bring in, to get in; *[+ marchandises, animaux] (en venant)* to bring in; *(en allant)* to take in ◆ **~ sa voiture (au garage)** to put the car away (in the garage) ◆ **ne laisse pas ton vélo sous la pluie, rentre-le** don't leave your bicycle out in the rain, put it away *ou* bring it in ◆ **~ les bêtes à l'étable** to bring the cattle into the cowshed

2 [+ train d'atterrissage] to raise; (lit, fig) [+ griffes] to draw in • ~ **sa chemise (dans son pantalon)** to tuck one's shirt in (one's trousers) • ~ **le cou dans les épaules** to hunch up one's shoulders • **ne me rentre pas ton coude dans le ventre** don't jab *ou* stick your elbow in(to) my stomach • ~ **le** *ou* **son ventre** to pull one's stomach in • ~ **ses larmes** to hold back *ou* choke back the tears • ~ **sa rage** to hold back *ou* suppress one's anger • ~ **un but** (*Sport*) to score a goal

3 (*Ordin*) [+ données] to enter

VPR **se rentrer** 1 (= pouvoir être rentré) **ce lit se rentre sous l'autre** this bed fits under the other one

2 (*mutuellement*) **ils se sont rentrés dedans** (= heurtés) they crashed into each other; * (= battus) they laid into each other

renversant, e * /ʀɑ̃vɛʀsɑ̃, ɑ̃t/ ADJ [nouvelle] staggering*, astounding; [personne] amazing, incredible

renverse /ʀɑ̃vɛʀs/ NF 1 (*Naut*) [de vent] change; [de courant] turn 2 • **tomber à la** ~ to fall backwards, to fall flat on one's back • **il y a de quoi tomber à la** ~ ! (*fig*) it's astounding! *ou* staggering!*

renversé, e /ʀɑ̃vɛʀse/ (ptp de **renverser**) ADJ 1 (= à l'envers) [objet] upside down (*attrib*); [fraction] inverted; [image] inverted, reversed; → **crème** 2 (= stupéfait) **être** ~ to be bowled over, to be staggered* 3 (= penché) [écriture] backhand (*épith*)

renversement /ʀɑ̃vɛʀsəmɑ̃/ NM 1 [d'image, fraction] inversion; [d'ordre des mots] inversion, reversal; [de vapeur] reversing; [de situation] reversal; (*Mus*) [d'intervalles, accord] inversion 2 [d'alliances, valeurs, rôles] reversal; [de ministre] removal from office; [de gouvernement] (par un coup d'État) overthrow; (par un vote) defeat, voting *ou* turning out of office • **un ~ de tendance de l'opinion publique** a shift *ou* swing in public opinion 3 [de buste, tête] tilting *ou* tipping back 4 [de courant] changing of direction; [de marée, vent] turning, changing of direction

renverser /ʀɑ̃vɛʀse/ ▸ conjug 1 ◂ VT 1 (= faire tomber) [+ personne] to knock over; [+ chaise] to knock over, to overturn; [+ vase, bouteille] to knock over, to upset; [+ piéton] to knock down, to run over • **elle l'a renversé d'un coup de poing** she knocked him to the ground • **un camion a renversé son chargement sur la route** a lorry has shed its load

2 (= répandre) [+ liquide] to spill, to upset • ~ **du vin sur la nappe** to spill *ou* upset some wine on the tablecloth

3 (= mettre à l'envers) to turn upside down • ~ **un seau (pour monter dessus)** to turn a bucket upside down (so as to stand on it)

4 (= abattre) [+ obstacles] (lit) to knock down; (fig) to overcome; [+ ordre établi, tradition, royauté] to overthrow; [+ ministre] to put *ou* throw out of office, to remove from office • ~ **le gouvernement** (par un coup d'État) to overthrow *ou* overturn *ou* topple the government; (par un vote) to defeat the government, to vote *ou* throw the government out of office

5 (= pencher) ~ **la tête en arrière** to tip *ou* tilt one's head back • ~ **le corps en arrière** to lean back • **elle lui renversa la tête en arrière** she tipped *ou* put his head back

6 (= inverser) [+ ordre des mots, courant] to reverse; [+ fraction] to invert; (*Opt*) [+ image] to invert, to reverse • ~ **la situation** to reverse the situation, to turn things (a)round • **il ne faudrait pas ~ les rôles** don't try to turn the situation round • ~ **la vapeur** (lit) [bateau] to go astern; (fig) to change tack

7 (* = étonner) to bowl over, to stagger • **la nouvelle l'a renversé** the news bowled him over *ou* staggered him

VI (*Naut*) [marée] to turn

VPR **se renverser** 1 • **se ~ en arrière** to lean back • **se ~ sur le dos** to lie down (on one's back) • **se ~ sur sa chaise** to lean back on one's chair, to tip one's chair back

2 [voiture, camion] to overturn; [bateau] to overturn, to capsize; [verre, vase] to fall over, to be overturned

renvoi /ʀɑ̃vwa/ NM 1 [d'employé] dismissal, sacking (*Brit*); [d'élève, étudiant] (définitif) expulsion; (temporaire) suspension • **menacer de ~** [+ employé] to threaten with dismissal; (*Scol*) to threaten to expel *ou* with expulsion • **j'ai demandé son ~ du club** I asked for him to be expelled from the club

2 [d'accusé, troupes] discharge

3 [de lettre, colis, cadeau] sending back, return

4 (*Sport*) [de balle] sending back; (au pied) kicking back; (à la main) throwing back; (*Tennis*) return • ~ **aux 22 mètres** (*Rugby*) drop-out • **à la suite d'un mauvais ~ du gardien, la balle a été interceptée** as a result of a poor return *ou* throw by the goalkeeper the ball was intercepted

5 (*Téléc*) [d'appel] transfer • ~ **temporaire de ligne** call diversion

6 [de lecteur] referral (à to)

7 [de rendez-vous] postponement • ~ **à date ultérieure** postponement to a later date • ~ **à huitaine** (*Jur*) adjournment for a week

8 (= envoi, *Jur*) **le ~ d'un projet de loi en commission** referral of a bill to a committee • **demande de ~ devant une autre juridiction** application for transfer of proceedings

9 (= référence) cross-reference; (en bas de page) footnote • **faire un ~ aux notes de l'appendice** to cross-refer to the notes in the appendix

10 (= rot) belch, burp • **avoir un ~** (*gén*) to belch, to burp; [bébé] to burp • **avoir des ~s** to have wind (*Brit*) *ou* gas (*US*) • **ça me donne des ~s** it makes me belch, it gives me wind (*Brit*)

11 (*Tech*) **levier de ~** reversing lever • **poulie de ~** return pulley

12 (*Mus*) repeat mark *ou* sign

renvoyer /ʀɑ̃vwaje/ ▸ conjug 8 ◂ VT 1 [+ employé] to dismiss, to fire*, to sack (*Brit*); [+ membre d'un club] to expel; [+ élève, étudiant] (définitivement) to expel; (temporairement) to suspend • **il s'est fait ~ de son travail** he was dismissed *ou* fired* *ou* sacked (*Brit*) from his job

2 (= faire retourner) to send back; (= faire repartir) to send away; (= libérer) [+ accusé, troupes] to discharge; [+ importun, créancier] to send away • **je l'ai renvoyé chez lui** I sent him back home • ~ **dans leurs foyers** [+ soldats] to discharge, to send (back) home; [+ femmes, enfants] to send (back) home • **les électeurs ont renvoyé les démocrates dans leurs foyers** the voters sent the democrats packing* • ~ **un projet de loi en commission** to refer a bill back *ou* send a bill for further discussion

3 (= réexpédier) [+ lettre, colis] to send back, to return; [+ cadeau non voulu, bague de fiançailles] to return, to give back • **je te renvoie le compliment !** and the same to you!

4 (= relancer) [+ balle] to send back; (au pied) to kick back; (à la main) to throw back; (*Tennis*) to return (à to); • **il m'a renvoyé la balle** (*fig* : argument) he threw the *ou* my argument back at me, he came back at me with the same argument; (responsabilité) he handed the responsibility over to me, he left it up to me • **ils se renvoient la balle** (argument) they come back at each other with the same argument; (responsabilité) they each refuse to take responsibility, they're both trying to pass the buck* • ~ **l'ascenseur** (*fig*) to return the favour

5 (= référer) [+ lecteur] to refer (à to); • ~ **aux notes de l'appendice** to (cross-)refer to notes in the appendix • ~ **un procès en Haute Cour** to refer a case to the high court • ~ **le prévenu en cour d'assises** to send the accused for trial by the Crown Court • ~ **qn de service en service** to send sb from one department to another • **cela (nous) renvoie à l'Antiquité/à la notion d'éthique** this takes us back to ancient times/to the notion of ethics

6 (*Téléc*) [+ appel] to transfer

7 (= différer) [+ rendez-vous] to postpone, to put off • **l'affaire a été renvoyée à huitaine** (*Jur*) the case was postponed *ou* put off for a week • ~ **qch aux calendes grecques** to postpone sth *ou* put sth off indefinitely

8 (= réfléchir) [+ lumière, chaleur, image] to reflect; [+ son] to echo

9 (*Cartes*) ~ **carreau/pique** to play diamonds/spades again, to lead diamonds/spades again

réoccupation /ʀeɔkypasjɔ̃/ NF (*Mil*) reoccupation • **depuis la ~ du village sinistré par les habitants** since the inhabitants of the stricken village moved back in *ou* came back

réoccuper /ʀeɔkype/ ▸ conjug 1 ◂ VT [+ territoire] to reoccupy; [+ fonction] to take up again • **les grévistes ont réoccupé les locaux** the strikers have staged another sit-in • ~ **une maison** to move back into a house

réopérer /ʀeɔpeʀe/ ▸ conjug 6 ◂ VT to operate again • **elle s'est fait ~** she had another operation, she was operated on again

réorchestration /ʀeɔʀkɛstʀasjɔ̃/ NF reorchestration

réorchestrer /ʀeɔʀkɛstʀe/ ▸ conjug 1 ◂ VT to reorchestrate

réorganisateur, -trice /ʀeɔʀganizatœʀ, tʀis/ NM,F reorganizer

réorganisation /ʀeɔʀganizasjɔ̃/ NF reorganization

réorganiser /ʀeɔʀganize/ ▸ conjug 1 ◂ VT to reorganize VPR **se réorganiser** [pays, parti] to get reorganized, to reorganize itself

réorientation /ʀeɔʀjɑ̃tasjɔ̃/ NF [de politique] redirecting, reorientation • ~ **scolaire** streaming

réorienter /ʀeɔʀjɑ̃te/ ▸ conjug 1 ◂ VT [+ politique] to redirect, to reorient(ate); [+ élève] to put into a new stream • ~ **sa carrière** to take one's career in a new direction

réouverture /ʀeuvɛʀtyʀ/ NF [de magasin, théâtre] reopening; [de débat] resumption, reopening

repaire /ʀ(ə)pɛʀ/ NM [d'animal] den, lair; (*fig*) den, hideout • **cette taverne est un ~ de brigands** this inn is a thieves' den *ou* a haunt of robbers

repaître /ʀəpɛtʀ/ ▸ conjug 57 ◂ VT (*littér*) • ~ **ses yeux de qch** to feast one's eyes on sth • ~ **son esprit de lectures** to feed one's mind on books

VPR **se repaître** 1 • **se ~ de** [+ crimes] to wallow in; [+ lectures, films] to revel in; [+ illusions] to revel in, to feed on 2 (= manger) [animal] to eat its fill; [personne] to eat one's fill • **se ~ de qch** to gorge o.s. on sth

répandre /ʀepɑ̃dʀ/ ▸ conjug 41 ◂ VT 1 (= renverser) [+ soupe, vin] to spill; [+ grains] to scatter; (volontairement) [+ sciure, produit] to spread • **le camion a répandu son chargement sur la chaussée** the truck shed its load • ~ **du sable sur le sol** to spread *ou* sprinkle sand on the ground • **la rivière répand ses eaux dans la vallée** the waters of the river spread over *ou* out across the valley

2 (*littér*) [+ larmes] to shed • ~ **son sang** to shed one's blood • ~ **le sang** to spill *ou* shed blood • **beaucoup de sang a été répandu** a lot of blood was shed *ou* spilled, there was a lot of bloodshed

3 (= être source de) [+ lumière] to shed, to give out; [+ odeur] to give off; [+ chaleur] to give out *ou* off • ~ **de la fumée** [cheminée] to give out smoke; [feu] to give off *ou* out smoke

4 *(= propager) [+ nouvelle, mode, joie, terreur]* to spread; *[+ dons]* to lavish, to pour out

VPR **se répandre** 1 *(= couler) [liquide]* to spill, to be spilled; *[grains]* to scatter, to be scattered *(sur* over); ◆ **le verre a débordé, et le vin s'est répandu par terre** the glass overflowed and the wine spilled onto the floor ◆ **le sang se répand dans les tissus** blood spreads through the tissues ◆ **la foule se répand dans les rues** the crowd spills out *ou* pours out into the streets

2 *(= se dégager) [chaleur, odeur, lumière]* to spread *(dans* through); *[son]* to carry *(dans* through); ◆ **il se répandit une forte odeur de caoutchouc brûlé** a strong smell of burning rubber was given off

3 *(= se propager) [doctrine, mode, nouvelle]* to spread *(dans, à travers* through); *[méthode, opinion]* to become widespread *(dans, parmi* among); *[coutume, pratique]* to take hold, to become widespread ◆ **la peur se répandit sur son visage** a look of fear spread over his face; → **traînée**

4 ◆ **se ~ en calomnies/excuses/menaces** to pour out *ou* pour forth slanderous remarks/excuses/threats ◆ **se ~ en invectives** to let out a torrent of abuse, to pour out a stream of abuse

répandu, e /repɑ̃dy/ (ptp de **répandre**) ADJ *[opinion, préjugé]* widespread; *[méthode]* widespread, widely used ◆ **idée très ~e** widely *ou* commonly held idea ◆ **une pratique largement ~e dans le monde** a practice that is very common throughout the world ◆ **profession peu ~e** rather unusual profession ◆ **les ordinateurs individuels étaient encore peu ~s** personal computers were still not very widespread *ou* common

réparable /reparabl/ ADJ *[objet]* repairable, which can be repaired *ou* mended; *[erreur]* which can be put right *ou* corrected; *[perte, faute]* which can be made up for ◆ **ce n'est pas ~** *[objet]* it is beyond repair; *[faute]* there's no way of making up for it; *[erreur]* it can't be put right ◆ **les dégâts sont facilement ~s** the damage can easily be repaired ◆ **cette maladresse sera difficilement ~** it will be hard to put such a blunder right *ou* to make up for such a blunder

reparaître /ʀ(ə)paʀɛtʀ/ ▸ conjug 57 ◂ VI *[personne, trait héréditaire]* to reappear; *[lune]* to reappear, to come out again; *[roman, texte]* to be republished; *[journal, magazine]* to be back in print

réparateur, -trice /reparatœr, tris/ ADJ *[sommeil]* refreshing ◆ **crème réparatrice** *(Cosmétique)* conditioning cream; → **chirurgie**

NM,F repairer ◆ **~ d'objets d'art** restorer of works of art ◆ **~ de porcelaine** porcelain restorer ◆ **le ~ de télévision** the television *ou* TV repairman *ou* engineer

réparation /reparasjɔ̃/ NF 1 *[de machine, montre, chaussures, voiture]* mending, repairing, repair; *[d'accroc, fuite]* mending, repair; *[de maison]* repairing; *[d'objet d'art]* restoration, repair ◆ **la voiture est en ~** the car is being repaired ◆ **on va faire des ~s dans la maison** we're going to have some repairs done in the house ◆ **pendant les ~s** during the repairs, while the repairs are (*ou* were) being carried out ◆ **atelier de ~** repair shop

2 *[d'erreur]* correction; *[d'oubli, négligence]* rectification

3 *[de faute, offense]* atonement *(de* for); *[de tort]* redress *(de* for); *[de perte]* compensation *(de* for); ◆ **en ~ du dommage causé** as reparation for the damage caused ◆ **obtenir ~ (d'un affront)** to obtain redress (for an insult) ◆ **demander ~ par les armes** to demand a duel

4 *(Ftbl)* **coup de pied/points/surface de ~** penalty kick/points/area

5 *(= recouvrement) [de forces]* recovery ◆ **la ~ des tissus sera longue** the tissues will take a long time to heal ◆ **~ cellulaire** cell repair

6 *(= dommages-intérêts)* damages, compensation ◆ **~s** *(Hist)* reparations

réparer /repare/ ▸ conjug 1 ◂ VT 1 *(= raccommoder) [+ chaussures, montre, machine, voiture]* to mend, to repair, to fix; *[+ accroc, fuite, route]* to mend, to repair; *[+ objet d'art]* to restore, to repair ◆ **donner qch à ~** to take sth to be mended *ou* repaired ◆ **faire ~ qch** to get *ou* have sth mended *ou* repaired ◆ **~ sommairement qch** to patch sth up ◆ **j'ai emmené la voiture à ~** * I took the car in (to be repaired)

2 *(= corriger) [+ erreur]* to correct, to put right; *[+ oubli, négligence]* to put right, to rectify

3 *(= compenser) [+ faute]* to make up for, to make amends for; *[+ tort]* to put right, to redress; *[+ offense]* to atone for, to make up for; *[+ perte]* to make good, to make up for, to compensate for ◆ **tu ne pourras jamais ~ le mal que tu m'as fait** you'll never put right *ou* never undo the harm you've done me ◆ **comment pourrais-je ~ ?** what could I do to make up for it? *ou* to make amends? ◆ **comment pourrais-je ~ ma bêtise ?** how could I make amends for *ou* make up for my stupidity? ◆ **cela ne pourra jamais ~ le dommage que j'ai subi** that'll never make up for *ou* compensate for the harm I've suffered ◆ **vous devez ~ en l'épousant** † you'll have to make amends by marrying her, you'll have to make an honest woman of her

4 *(= recouvrer) [+ forces, santé]* to restore

5 *(locutions)* **il va falloir ~ les dégâts** *(lit)* we'll have to repair the damage; (* *fig)* we'll have to repair the damage *ou* pick up the pieces ◆ **~ le désordre de sa toilette** *(littér)* to straighten *ou* tidy one's clothes

reparler /ʀ(ə)paʀle/ ▸ conjug 1 ◂ VI ◆ **~ de qch** to talk about sth again ◆ **~ à qn** to speak to sb again ◆ **nous en reparlerons** *(lit)* we'll talk about it again *ou* discuss it again later; *(dit avec scepticisme)* we'll see about that ◆ **c'est un romancier dont on reparlera** he's a very promising novelist, we'll be hearing more of this novelist ◆ **il commence à ~** *[accidenté, malade]* he's starting to speak again VPR **se reparler** to speak to each other again, to be on speaking terms again, to be back on speaking terms

repartie, répartie /reparti/ NF retort, rejoinder *(frm)* ◆ **avoir de la ~, avoir la ~ facile** to be good *ou* quick at repartee ◆ **avoir l'esprit de ~** to have a talent *ou* gift for repartee

repartir[1] /repartir, ʀ(ə)partir/, **répartir**[1] /repartir/ ▸ conjug 16 ◂ VT *(littér = répliquer)* to retort, to reply

repartir[2] /ʀ(ə)partir/ ▸ conjug 16 ◂ VI *[voyageur]* to set *ou* start off again; *[machine]* to start (up) again, to restart; *[affaire, discussion]* to get going again ◆ **~ chez soi** to go back *ou* return home ◆ **il est reparti hier** he left again yesterday ◆ **il est reparti comme il était venu** he left as he came ◆ **~ en campagne** *(Pol)* to go back on the campaign trail, to start campaigning again ◆ **~ à l'assaut** to launch another attack *(de* on); ◆ **~ sur des bases nouvelles** to make a fresh start ◆ **les achats de véhicules neufs sont repartis à la hausse** sales of new cars have taken off *ou* picked up again ◆ **la croissance repart** growth is picking up again ◆ **heureusement, c'est bien reparti** fortunately, things have got off to a good start this time ◆ **ça y est, les voilà repartis sur la politique !** *(dans une discussion)* that's it, they're off again *ou* there they go again, talking politics! ◆ **c'est reparti pour un tour !** * *ou* **comme en 14 !** * *ou* **comme en 40 !** * here we go again! ◆ **faire ~** *[+ entreprise, économie]* to get going again; *[+ moteur]* to start up again; → **zéro**

répartir[2] /repartir/ ▸ conjug 2 ◂ VT 1 *(= diviser) [+ ressources, travail]* to share out, to distribute *(entre* among); *[+ impôts, charges]* to share out *(en* into; *entre* among) to apportion; *[+ butin, récompenses]* to share out, to divide up *(entre* among); *[+ rôles]* to distribute *(entre* among); *[+ poids, volume, chaleur]* to distribute ◆ **on avait réparti les joueurs en deux groupes** the players had been divided *ou* split (up) into two groups ◆ **répartissez le mélange dans des coupelles** *(Culin)* divide the mixture equally into small bowls

2 *(= étaler) [+ paiement, cours, horaire]* to spread *(sur* over); ◆ **on a mal réparti les bagages dans le coffre** the luggage hasn't been evenly distributed in the boot ◆ **les troupes sont réparties le long de la frontière** troops are spread out along the border ◆ **le programme est réparti sur deux ans** the programme is spread (out) over a two-year period

VPR **se répartir** 1 *(= se décomposer)* **les charges se répartissent comme suit** the expenses are divided up as follows ◆ **ils se répartissent en deux ensembles** they can be divided into two sets ◆ **ils se sont répartis en deux groupes** they divided themselves *ou* they split into two groups

2 *(= se partager)* **ils se sont réparti le travail** they shared the work out *ou* divided the work up among themselves

répartiteur, -trice /repartitœr, tris/ NM,F *(gén, littér)* distributor, apportioner; *[d'impôt]* assessor ◆ **~ d'avaries** averager, average adjuster NM *(Tech) [d'électricité]* divider; *[de fluides]* regulator

répartition /repartisjɔ̃/ NF 1 *[de ressources, travail]* sharing out (NonC), distribution; *[d'impôts, charges]* sharing out (NonC); *[de butin, récompenses]* sharing out (NonC), dividing up (NonC); *[de poids, volume, chaleur]* dividing up (NonC), distribution; *[de population, faune, flore, richesses, rôles]* distribution; *(= agencement) [de pièces, salles]* layout, distribution ◆ **~ par âge/sexe** distribution by age/sex ◆ **~ géographique** geographical distribution ◆ **la ~ des pouvoirs entre le Président et le Premier ministre** the distribution of power between the President and the Prime Minister 2 *[de paiement, cours, horaires]* spreading (NonC); *(Comm)* dispatching

reparution /ʀ(ə)paʀysjɔ̃/ NF *[de journal]* reappearance ◆ **depuis la ~ du magazine en 1989** since the magazine resumed publication in 1989, since the magazine's reappearance in 1989 ◆ **la ~ de l'album en disque compact** the release of the CD version of the album

repas /ʀ(ə)pɑ/ NM meal ◆ **~ d'affaires** *(= déjeuner)* business lunch; *(= dîner)* business dinner ◆ **~ à la carte** à la carte meal ◆ **~ léger** light meal ◆ **~ de midi** midday *ou* noon (US) meal, lunch ◆ **~ de noces** reception ◆ **~ de Noël** Christmas dinner ◆ **~ scolaire** school lunch ◆ **~ du soir** evening meal, dinner ◆ **il prend tous ses ~ au restaurant** he always eats out ◆ **faire 3 ~ par jour** to have 3 meals a day ◆ **~ complet** three-course meal ◆ **médicament à prendre avant/à chaque ~** medicine to be taken before/with meals ◆ **assister au ~ des fauves** to watch the big cats being fed ◆ **à l'heure du ~, aux heures des ~** at mealtimes ◆ **manger en dehors des ~** *ou* **entre les ~** to eat between meals

repassage /ʀ(ə)pɑsaʒ/ NM *[de linge]* ironing; *[de couteau]* sharpening ◆ **faire le ~** to do the ironing ◆ **"repassage superflu"** "wash-and-wear", "non-iron"

repasser /ʀ(ə)pɑse/ ▸ conjug 1 ◂ VT 1 *(au fer à repasser)* to iron; *(à la pattemouille)* to press ◆ **le nylon ne se repasse pas** nylon doesn't need ironing; → **fer, planche, table**

2 *[+ examen]* to take again, to resit *(Brit)*; *[+ permis de conduire]* to take again ◆ ~ **une visite médicale** to have another medical
3 *[+ souvenir, leçon, rôle]* to go (back) over, to go over again ◆ ~ **qch dans son esprit** to go over sth again *ou* go back over sth in one's mind
4 *[+ plat]* to hand round again; *[+ film]* to show again; *[+ émission]* to repeat; *[+ disque, chanson]* to play again ◆ ~ **un plat au four** to put a dish in the oven again *ou* back in the oven
5 *(* = transmettre) [+ affaire, travail]* to hand over *ou* on; *[+ maladie]* to pass on *(à qn* to sb); ◆ **il m'a repassé le tuyau** he passed the tip on to me ◆ **je te repasse ta mère** *(au téléphone)* I'll hand you back to your mother ◆ **je vous repasse le standard** I'll put you back through to the operator
6 *[+ rivière, montagne, frontière]* to cross again, to go *ou* come back across
7 *[+ couteau, lame]* to sharpen (up)
VI 1 *(= retourner)* to come back, to go back ◆ **je repasserai** I'll come back, I'll call (in) again ◆ **si vous repassez par Paris** *(au retour)* if you come back through Paris; *(une autre fois)* if you're passing through Paris again ◆ **ils sont repassés en Belgique** they crossed back *ou* went back over into Belgium ◆ **il va falloir que je repasse sur le billard*** I've got to have another operation ◆ **tu peux toujours ~ !*** you don't have a prayer!, you've got a hope!* *(Brit)*
2 *(devant un même lieu)* to go *ou* come past again; *(sur un même trait)* to go over again, to go back over ◆ **je passai et repassai devant la vitrine** I kept walking backwards and forwards in front of the shop window ◆ **souvenirs qui repassent dans la mémoire** memories that are running through one's mind ◆ **quand il fait un travail, il faut toujours ~ derrière lui** when he does some work you always have to go over it again

repasseur /ʀ(ə)pɑsœʀ/ NM *(= rémouleur)* knife-grinder *ou* -sharpener

repasseuse /ʀ(ə)pɑsøz/ NF *(= femme)* ironer; *(= machine)* ironer, ironing machine

repavage /ʀ(ə)pavaʒ/ NM repaving

repaver /ʀ(ə)pave/ ▸ conjug 1 ◂ VT to repave

repayer /ʀ(ə)peje/ ▸ conjug 8 ◂ VT to pay again

repêchage /ʀ(ə)peʃaʒ/ NM 1 *[d'objet, noyé]* recovery 2 *(Scol) [de candidat]* letting through, passing ◆ **épreuve/question de** ~ exam/question to give candidates a second chance

repêcher /ʀ(ə)peʃe/ ▸ conjug 1 ◂ VT 1 *[+ objet, noyé]* to recover, to fish out ◆ **je suis allé ~ la lettre dans la poubelle** I went and fished the letter out of the bin 2 *(Scol) [+ candidat]* to let through, to pass *(with less than the official pass mark)*; *[+ athlète]* to give a second chance to ◆ **il a été repêché à l'oral** he scraped through *ou* just got a pass thanks to the oral

repeindre /ʀ(ə)pɛ̃dʀ/ ▸ conjug 52 ◂ VT to repaint

rependre /ʀ(ə)pɑ̃dʀ/ ▸ conjug 41 ◂ VT to re-hang, to hang again

repenser /ʀ(ə)pɑ̃se/ ▸ conjug 1 ◂ VT INDIR **repenser à** ◆ ~ **à qch** to think about sth again ◆ **plus j'y repense** the more I think of it ◆ **je n'y ai plus repensé** *(plus avant)* I haven't thought about it again (since), I haven't given it any further thought (since); *(= j'ai oublié)* it completely slipped my mind ◆ **j'y repenserai** I'll think about it again, I'll have another think about it VT *[+ concept]* to rethink ◆ **il faut ~ tout l'enseignement** the whole issue of education will have to be rethought ◆ ~ **la question** to rethink the question

repentant, e /ʀ(ə)pɑ̃tɑ̃, ɑ̃t/ ADJ repentant, penitent

repenti, e /ʀ(ə)pɑ̃ti/ (ptp de **se repentir**) ADJ repentant, penitent ◆ **buveur/joueur** ~ reformed drinker/gambler NM,F *(gén)* reformed man *(ou* woman); *(= ancien malfaiteur)* criminal turned informer ◆ **un ~ de la Mafia** a Mafia turncoat

repentir (se)[1] /ʀ(ə)pɑ̃tiʀ/ ▸ conjug 16 ◂ VPR 1 *(Rel)* to repent ◆ **se ~ d'une faute/d'avoir commis une faute** to repent of a fault/of having committed a fault 2 *(= regretter)* **se ~ de qch/d'avoir fait qch** to regret sth/having done sth, to be sorry for sth/for having done sth ◆ **tu t'en repentiras !** you'll be sorry!

repentir[2] /ʀ(ə)pɑ̃tiʀ/ NM *(Rel)* repentance *(NonC)*; *(= regret)* regret

repérable /ʀ(ə)peʀabl/ ADJ which can be spotted ◆ ~ **de loin** easily spotted from a distance ◆ **difficilement** ~ *(gén)* difficult to spot; *(Mil)* difficult to locate

repérage /ʀ(ə)peʀaʒ/ NM location ◆ **le ~ d'un point sur la carte** locating a point on the map, pinpointing a spot on the map ◆ **faire des ~s** *(Ciné)* to research locations ◆ **partir en** ~ *(Ciné)* to go looking for locations

répercussion /ʀepɛʀkysjɔ̃/ NF *(gén)* repercussion *(sur, dans* on); ◆ **la hausse des taux d'intérêt a eu des ~s sur l'économie** the rise in interest rates has had a knock-on effect on the economy ◆ **la ~ d'une taxe sur le client** *(Fin)* passing a tax on *ou* along *(US)* to the customer

répercuter /ʀepɛʀkyte/ ▸ conjug 1 ◂ VT 1 *[+ son]* to echo; *[+ écho]* to send back, to throw back; *[+ lumière]* to reflect 2 *(= transmettre)* ~ **une augmentation sur le client** to pass an increase in cost on to the customer ◆ ~ **un impôt sur le consommateur** to pass on *ou* along *(US)* a tax to the consumer VPR **se répercuter** 1 *[son]* to reverberate, to echo; *[lumière]* to be reflected, to reflect 2 ◆ **se ~ sur** to have repercussions on, to affect

reperdre /ʀ(ə)pɛʀdʀ/ ▸ conjug 41 ◂ VT to lose again

repère /ʀ(ə)pɛʀ/ NM 1 *(= marque, trait)* mark; *(= jalon, balise)* marker; *(= monument, accident de terrain)* landmark; *(= événement)* landmark; *(= date)* reference point ◆ ~ **de niveau** bench mark ◆ **j'ai laissé des branches comme ~s pour retrouver notre chemin** I've left branches as markers so that we can find the way back again

◆ **point de repère** *(dans l'espace)* landmark; *(dans le temps, fig)* point of reference
2 *(fig)* **perdre ses ~s** *[personne]* to lose one's bearings, to become disorientated; *[société]* to lose its points of reference ◆ **dans un monde sans ~s** in a world that has lost its way ◆ **la disparition des ~s traditionnels** the loss of traditional points of reference ◆ **les adolescents ont besoin de ~s** adolescents need points of reference ◆ **les toxicomanes sont souvent des jeunes qui ont perdu leurs ~s** drug addicts are often youths who've lost their way ◆ **j'essaie de donner des ~s à mon fils** I'm trying to give my son guidance

repérer /ʀ(ə)peʀe/ ▸ conjug 6 ◂ VT 1 *(* = localiser) [+ erreur, personne]* to spot; *[+ endroit, chemin]* to locate, to find ◆ **se faire** ~ *(lit)* to be spotted; *(fig)* to be found out, to get caught ◆ **il avait repéré un petit restaurant** he had discovered a little restaurant ◆ **tu vas nous faire** ~ we'll be spotted because of you, you'll get us caught 2 *(Mil)* to locate, to pinpoint 3 *(Tech = jalonner) [+ niveau, alignement]* to mark out *ou* off, to stake out VPR **se repérer** *(gén = se diriger)* to find one's way about *ou* around; *(= établir sa position)* to find *ou* get one's bearings ◆ **j'ai du mal à me ~ dans cette intrigue** I have difficulty getting my bearings in this plot

répertoire /ʀepɛʀtwaʀ/ NM 1 *(= carnet)* notebook *(with alphabetical thumb index)*; *(= liste)* (alphabetical) list; *(= catalogue)* catalogue ◆ **noter un mot dans un** ~ to write a word down in an alphabetical index, to index a word
2 *[d'un théâtre]* repertoire; *[de chanteur, musicien]* repertoire, repertory ◆ **les plus grandes œuvres du ~ classique/contemporain** the greatest works in the classic/modern repertory ◆ **les plus grandes œuvres du ~ lyrique/symphonique** the greatest operas/symphonies ◆ **les grandes œuvres du** ~ the great works of the repertoire, the classics ◆ **elle n'a que deux chansons à son** ~ she's only got two songs in her repertoire ◆ **elle a tout un ~ de jurons/d'histoires drôles** *(fig)* she has quite a repertoire of swearwords/of jokes
3 *(Ordin)* directory, folder
COMP **répertoire d'adresses** address book
répertoire alphabétique alphabetical index *ou* list
répertoire des rues *(sur un plan)* street index

répertorier /ʀepɛʀtɔʀje/ ▸ conjug 7 ◂ VT *[+ information]* to list; *[+ cas, maladie]* to record; *[+ œuvre]* to index ◆ **non répertorié** unlisted ◆ **les restaurants sont répertoriés par quartiers** the restaurants are listed by area ◆ **90 espèces de coccinelles ont été répertoriées** 90 species of ladybird have been listed *ou* recorded

repeser /ʀ(ə)pəze/ ▸ conjug 5 ◂ VT to reweigh, to weigh again

répète * /ʀepɛt/ NF abrév de **répétition**

répéter /ʀepete/ GRAMMAIRE ACTIVE 54.4 ▸ conjug 6 ◂
VT 1 *(= redire) [+ explication, question]* to repeat; *[+ mot]* to repeat, to say again; *[+ histoire]* to repeat, to tell again ◆ ~ **à qn que** ... to tell sb again that ... ◆ **pourriez-vous me ~ cette phrase ?** could you repeat that sentence?, could you say that sentence (to me) again? ◆ **répète-moi le numéro du code** tell me *ou* give me the code number again, tell me what the code number is again ◆ **je l'ai répété/je te l'ai répété dix fois** I've said that/I've told you that a dozen times ◆ **il répète toujours la même chose** he keeps saying *ou* repeating the same thing ◆ **répète !** *(ton de menace)* say that again! ◆ **il ne se l'est pas fait ~** he didn't have to be told *ou* asked twice, he didn't need asking *ou* telling twice ◆ **on ne répétera jamais assez que** ... it cannot be said often enough that ...
2 *(= rapporter) [+ calomnie]* to repeat, to spread about; *[+ histoire]* to repeat ◆ **elle est allée tout ~ à son père** she went and repeated everything to her father, she went and told her father everything ◆ **je vais vous ~ exactement ce qu'il m'a dit** I'll repeat exactly what he said ◆ **c'est un secret, ne le répétez pas !** it's a secret, don't repeat it! *ou* don't tell anyone! ◆ **il m'a répété tous les détails de l'événement** he went over all the details of the event for me, he related all the details of the event to me
3 *(= refaire) [+ expérience, exploit]* to repeat, to do again; *[+ proposition]* to repeat, to renew; *[+ essai]* to repeat ◆ **nous répéterons une nouvelle fois la tentative** we'll repeat the attempt one more time, we'll have another try ◆ **tentatives répétées de suicide/d'évasion** repeated suicide/escape attempts
4 *[+ pièce, symphonie, émission]* to rehearse; *[+ rôle, leçon]* to learn, to go over; *[+ morceau de piano]* to practise ◆ **nous répétons à 4 heures** we rehearse at 4 o'clock, the rehearsal is at 4 o'clock ◆ **ma mère m'a fait ~ ma leçon/mon rôle** I went over my homework/my part with my mother
5 *(= reproduire) [+ motif]* to repeat; *(Mus) [+ thème]* to repeat, to restate ◆ **les miroirs répétaient son image** his image was reflected again and again in the mirrors
VPR **se répéter** 1 *(= redire, radoter)* to repeat o.s. ◆ **se ~ qch à soi-même** to repeat sth to o.s. ◆ **la nouvelle que toute la ville se répète** the

news which is being repeated all round the town ◆ **je ne voudrais pas me ~, mais ...** I don't want to repeat myself *ou* say the same thing twice, but ...

2 *(= se reproduire)* to be repeated, to reoccur, to recur ◆ **ces incidents se répétèrent fréquemment** these incidents were frequently repeated, these incidents kept recurring *ou* occurred repeatedly ◆ **que cela ne se répète pas !** (just) don't let that happen again! ◆ **l'histoire ne se répète jamais** history never repeats itself

répétiteur, -trice /ʀepetitœʀ, tʀis/ **NM,F** *(Scol)* tutor, coach **NM** *(Tech)* ◆ **~ de signaux** repeater

répétitif, -ive /ʀepetitif, iv/ **ADJ** repetitive

répétition /ʀepetisjɔ̃/ **NF** 1 *(= redite)* repetition ◆ **il y a beaucoup de ~s** there is a lot of repetition, there are numerous repetitions

2 *(= révision)* repetition; *[de pièce, symphonie]* rehearsal; *[de rôle]* learning; *[de morceau de piano]* practising ◆ **~ générale** (final) dress rehearsal ◆ **pour éviter la ~ d'une telle mésaventure** to prevent such a mishap happening again ◆ **la ~ d'un tel exploit est difficile** repeating a feat like that *ou* doing a feat like that again is difficult ◆ **la chorale est en ~** the choir is rehearsing *ou* practising

3 *(= nouvelle occurrence)* ◆ **pour éviter la ~ d'une telle mésaventure** to prevent such a mishap happening again

◆ **à répétition** ◆ **faire des rhumes/des angines à ~** to have one cold/one sore throat after another ◆ **scandales/grèves à ~** one scandal/strike after another, endless scandals/strikes ◆ **fusil/montre à ~** repeater rifle/watch

répétitivité /ʀepetitivite/ **NF** repetitiveness

repeuplement /ʀ(ə)pœpləmɑ̃/ **NM** *[de région]* repopulation; *[d'étang, chasse]* restocking; *[de forêt]* replanting

repeupler /ʀ(ə)pœple/ ► conjug 1 ◄ **VT** *[+ région]* to repopulate; *[+ étang, chasse]* to restock *(de* with); *[+ forêt]* to replant *(de* with) **VPR** **se repeupler** *[région]* to be *ou* become repopulated ◆ **le village commence à se ~** people have started moving back into the village

repincer /ʀ(ə)pɛ̃se/ ► conjug 3 ◄ **VT** *(lit)* to pinch *ou* nip again; *(* fig)* to catch again, to nab* again ◆ **se faire ~** to get caught *ou* nabbed* again

repiquage /ʀ(ə)pikaʒ/ **NM** 1 *[de plantes]* pricking out; *[de riz]* transplanting 2 *(bactériologique)* subculturing 3 *[de photo]* touching up, retouching 4 *(= réenregistrement)* rerecording; *(= copie)* recording, tape

repiquer /ʀ(ə)pike/ ► conjug 1 ◄ **VT** 1 *[+ plantes]* to prick out; *[+ riz]* to transplant ◆ **plantes à ~** bedding plants 2 *(Bio)* to subculture 3 *[+ photo]* to touch up, to retouch 4 *(= réenregistrer)* to rerecord; *(= faire une copie de) [+ disque]* to record, to tape; *[+ logiciel]* to make a copy of 5 *(* = reprendre)* to catch again ◆ **il s'est fait ~ à la frontière** the police caught up with him again at the border 6 *[moustique]* to bite again; *[épine]* to prick again ◆ **~ un vêtement à la machine** *(Couture)* to restitch a garment **VT INDIR** **repiquer à** * ◆ **~ au plat** to take a second helping ◆ **~ au truc** to go back to one's old ways, to be at it again* ◆ **elle a repiqué aux somnifères** she's back on sleeping tablets again

répit /ʀepi/ **NM** *(= rémission)* respite *(frm)*; *(= repos)* respite *(frm)*, rest ◆ **la douleur ne lui laisse pas de ~** the pain never gives him any respite ◆ **s'accorder un peu de ~** to have a bit of a rest ◆ **donnez-moi un petit ~ pour vous payer** give me a bit more time to pay you ◆ **accordez-nous 5 minutes de ~** give us 5 minutes' rest *ou* respite

◆ **sans répit** ◆ **travailler sans ~** to work continuously *ou* without respite ◆ **harceler qn sans ~** to harass sb relentlessly

replacement /ʀ(ə)plasmɑ̃/ **NM** *[d'objet]* replacing, putting back; *[d'employé]* redeployment

replacer /ʀ(ə)plase/ ► conjug 3 ◄ **VT** 1 *(= remettre) [+ objet]* to replace, to put back (in its place) ◆ **~ une vertèbre** to put *ou* ease a vertebra back into place 2 *(= resituer)* **il faut ~ les choses dans leur contexte** we must put things back in their context 3 *[+ employé]* to find a new job for, to redeploy 4 * **il faudra que je la replace, celle-là !** *[+ plaisanterie, expression]* I must remember to use that one again! **VPR** **se replacer** 1 *[employé]* to find a new job 2 *(= s'imaginer)* **se ~ dans les mêmes conditions** to put o.s. in the same situation ◆ **replaçons-nous au 16e siècle** let's go *ou* look back to the 16th century

replantation /ʀ(ə)plɑ̃tasjɔ̃/ **NF** *[de forêt]* replanting

replanter /ʀ(ə)plɑ̃te/ ► conjug 1 ◄ **VT** *[+ plante]* to replant, to plant out; *[+ forêt, arbre]* to replant ◆ **~ un bois en conifères** to replant a wood with conifers

replat /ʀəpla/ **NM** projecting ledge *ou* shelf

replâtrage /ʀ(ə)plɑtʀaʒ/ **NM** 1 *[de mur]* replastering 2 * *[d'amitié, gouvernement]* patching up ◆ **~ ministériel** *(Pol)* patching together *ou* patch-up of the cabinet

replâtrer /ʀ(ə)plɑtʀe/ ► conjug 1 ◄ **VT** 1 *[+ mur]* to replaster; *[+ membre]* to put another cast on 2 * *[+ amitié, gouvernement]* to patch up

replet, -ète /ʀəplɛ, ɛt/ **ADJ** *[personne]* podgy, fat; *[visage]* chubby

repleuvoir /ʀ(ə)plœvwaʀ/ ► conjug 23 ◄ **VB IMPERS** to rain again, to start raining again ◆ **il repleut** it is raining again, it has started raining again

repli /ʀəpli/ **NM** 1 *[de terrain, papier]* fold; *[d'intestin, serpent]* coil; *[de rivière]* bend, twist; *[de peau] (dû à l'âge)* wrinkle; *(d'embonpoint)* fold *(de* in) 2 *(Couture) [d'ourlet, étoffe]* fold, turn *(de* in) 3 *(Mil)* withdrawal, falling back ◆ **position de ~** *(Mil, fig)* fallback position ◆ **~ stratégique** *(Mil, fig)* strategic withdrawal 4 *(Bourse)* fall, drop ◆ **le cours de l'étain a accentué son ~** the price of tin has weakened further ◆ **le dollar est en ~ à 1 €** the dollar has fallen back to €1 ◆ **mouvement de ~ des taux d'intérêt** downward trend in interest rates 5 *(= réserve)* withdrawal ◆ **~ sur soi-même** withdrawal (into oneself), turning in on oneself ◆ **le ~ identitaire** clinging to identity 6 *(= recoin) [de cœur, conscience]* hidden *ou* innermost recess, innermost reaches

repliable /ʀ(ə)plijabl/ **ADJ** folding *(épith)*

réplication /ʀeplikasjɔ̃/ **NF** replication

repliement /ʀ(ə)plimɑ̃/ **NM** ◆ **~ (sur soi-même)** withdrawal (into oneself), turning in on oneself

replier /ʀ(ə)plije/ ► conjug 7 ◄ **VT** 1 *[+ carte, journal, robe]* to fold up (again), to fold back up; *[+ manche, bas de pantalon]* to roll up, to fold up; *[+ coin de feuille]* to fold over; *[+ ailes]* to fold (back); *[+ jambes]* to tuck up; *[+ couteau]* to close ◆ **les jambes repliées sous lui** sitting back with his legs tucked under him ◆ **~ le drap sur la couverture** to fold the sheet back over *ou* down over the blanket 2 *(Mil) [+ troupes]* to withdraw; *[+ civils]* to move back *ou* away **VPR** **se replier** *[serpent]* to curl up, to coil up; *[chat]* to curl up; *[lame de couteau]* to fold back; *(Mil)* to fall back, to withdraw *(sur* to); *(Bourse) [valeurs]* to fall (back), to drop ◆ **se ~ (sur soi-même)** to withdraw into oneself, to turn in on oneself ◆ **communauté repliée sur elle-même** inward-looking community

réplique /ʀeplik/ **NF** 1 *(= réponse)* retort ◆ **il a la ~ facile** he's always ready with an answer, he's never at a loss for an answer *ou* a reply ◆ **et pas de ~ !** and don't answer back! ◆ **"non", dit-il d'un ton sans ~** "no", he said in a tone that brooked no reply ◆ **argument sans ~** irrefutable argument

2 *(= contre-attaque)* counter-attack ◆ **la ~ ne se fit pas attendre** they weren't slow to retaliate

3 *(Théât)* line ◆ **dialogue aux ~s spirituelles** dialogue with some witty lines ◆ **oublier sa ~** to forget one's lines *ou* words ◆ **l'acteur a manqué sa ~** the actor missed his cue ◆ **c'est Belon qui vous donnera la ~** *(pour répéter)* Belon will give you your cue; *(dans une scène)* Belon will play opposite you ◆ **je saurai lui donner la ~** *(fig)* I can match him (in an argument), I can give as good as I get

4 *(Art)* replica ◆ **il est la ~ de son jumeau** *(fig)* he's the (spitting) image of his twin brother

5 *[de tremblement de terre]* after-shock

répliquer /ʀeplike/ ► conjug 1 ◄ **VT** to reply ◆ **il (lui) répliqua que ...** he replied *ou* retorted that ... ◆ **il n'y a rien à ~ à cela** there's no answer to that ◆ **il trouve toujours quelque chose à ~** he's always got an answer for everything **VI** 1 *(= répondre)* to reply ◆ **~ à la critique** to reply to criticism ◆ **et ne réplique pas !** *(insolence)* and don't answer back!; *(protestation)* and no protests! 2 *(= contre-attaquer)* to retaliate ◆ **il répliqua par des coups de poing/des injures** he retaliated with his fists/with foul language

replonger /ʀ(ə)plɔ̃ʒe/ ► conjug 3 ◄ **VT** *[+ rame, cuiller]* to dip back *(dans* into); ◆ **replongé dans la pauvreté/la guerre/l'obscurité** plunged into poverty/war/darkness again, plunged back into poverty/war/darkness ◆ **replongeant sa main dans l'eau** dipping his hand into the water again ◆ **ce film nous replonge dans l'univers des années 30** this film takes us right back to the 1930s ◆ **elle replongea son nez dans ses dossiers** she buried herself in her files again

VI 1 *(dans une piscine)* to dive back, to dive again *(dans* into)

2 * *[drogué]* to become hooked* again; *[délinquant]* to go back to one's old ways; *[alcoolique]* to go back to drinking

VPR **se replonger** to dive back *ou* again *(dans* into); ◆ **il se replongea dans sa lecture** he immersed himself in his book again, he went back to his reading ◆ **se ~ dans les études** to throw oneself into one's studies again

repolir /ʀ(ə)pɔliʀ/ ► conjug 2 ◄ **VT** *[+ objet]* to repolish; *(fig) [+ discours]* to polish up again, to touch up again

répondant, e /ʀepɔ̃dɑ̃, ɑt/ **NM,F** guarantor, surety ◆ **servir de ~ à qn** *(Fin)* to stand surety for sb, to be sb's guarantor; *(fig)* to vouch for sb **NM** 1 *(Fin)* **il a du ~** *(compte approvisionné)* he has money behind him; *(* : beaucoup d'argent)* he has something to fall back on; *(* : le sens de la répartie)* he has a talent for repartee 2 *(Rel)* server

répondeur, -euse /ʀepɔ̃dœʀ, øz/ **ADJ** * impertinent, cheeky* *(Brit)*, sassy* *(US)* ◆ **je n'aime pas les enfants ~s** I don't like children who answer back **NM** ◆ **~ (téléphonique)** (telephone) answering machine *(simply giving a recorded message)* ◆ **~ (enregistreur)** (telephone) answering machine, answerphone *(on which you can leave a message)* ◆ **je suis tombé sur un ~** I got a recorded message; → **interrogeable**

répondre /ʀepɔ̃dʀ/ **GRAMMAIRE ACTIVE 54.4, 54.5, 54.7** ► conjug 41 ◄

VT 1 *(gén)* to answer, to reply ◆ **il a répondu une grossièreté** he replied with a rude remark, he made a rude remark in reply ◆ **il m'a répondu oui/non** he said *ou* answered yes/no ◆ **il m'a répondu (par) une lettre** he sent me a written reply ◆ **il a répondu qu'il le savait** he answered *ou* replied that he knew ◆ **il m'a répondu qu'il viendrait** he told me (in reply) that he would come ◆ **je lui ai répondu de se taire** *ou* **qu'il se taise** I told him to be quiet

◆ **vous me demandez si j'accepte, je (vous) réponds que non** you're asking me if I accept and I'm telling you I don't *ou* and my answer is no ◆ **je me suis vu ~ que …, il me fut répondu que …** I was told that … ◆ **~ présent à l'appel** *(lit)* to answer present at roll call; *(fig)* to come forward, to make oneself known ◆ **réponds quelque chose, même si c'est faux** give an answer, even if it's wrong ◆ **(c'est) bien répondu !** well said! ◆ **qu'avez-vous à ~ ?** what have you got to say in reply? ◆ **il n'y a rien à ~** there's no answer to that ◆ **qu'est-ce que vous voulez ~ à cela ?** what can you say to that?

2 *(Rel)* **~ la messe** to serve (at) mass

VI 1 *(gén)* to answer, to reply ◆ **réponds donc !** well answer (then)! ◆ **~ en claquant la porte** to slam the door by way of reply *ou* by way of an answer ◆ **~ à qn/à une question/à une convocation** to reply to *ou* answer sb/a question/a summons ◆ **seul l'écho lui répondit** only the echo answered him ◆ **je ne lui ai pas encore répondu** I haven't yet replied to his letter *ou* answered his letter *ou* written back to him ◆ **je lui répondrai par écrit** I'll reply *ou* answer in writing, I'll let him have a written reply *ou* answer ◆ **avez-vous répondu à son invitation ?** did you reply to his invitation? ◆ **il répond au nom de Louis** he answers to the name of Louis ◆ **~ par oui ou par non** to reply *ou* answer *ou* say yes or no ◆ **~ par monosyllabes** to reply in words of one syllable ◆ **instruments de musique qui se répondent** musical instruments that answer each other ◆ **~ par un sourire/en hochant la tête** to smile/nod in reply ◆ **elle répondit à son salut par un sourire** she replied to *ou* answered his greeting with a smile ◆ **il a répondu par des injures** he replied with a string of insults, he replied by insulting us *(ou* them *etc)*

2 *(= aller ouvrir ou décrocher)* ◆ **~ (à la porte *ou* à la sonnette)** to answer the door ◆ **~ (au téléphone)** to answer the telephone ◆ **son poste ne répond pas** there's no reply from his extension ◆ **personne ne répond, ça ne répond pas** there's no answer *ou* reply, no one's answering ◆ **on a sonné, va ~** there's the doorbell - go and see who it is ◆ **personne n'a répondu à mon coup de sonnette** no one answered the door *ou* the bell when I rang, I got no answer when I rang the bell

3 *(= être impertinent)* to answer back ◆ **il a répondu à la maîtresse** he answered the teacher back

4 *(= réagir) [voiture, commandes, membres]* to respond *(à* to); ◆ **son cerveau ne répond plus aux excitations** his brain no longer responds to stimuli ◆ **les freins ne répondaient plus** the brakes were no longer responding

VT INDIR répondre à 1 *(= correspondre à) [+ besoin]* to answer, to meet; *[+ signalement]* to answer, to fit; *[+ norme, condition]* to meet ◆ **ça répond tout à fait à l'idée que je m'en faisais** that corresponds exactly to what I imagined it to be like ◆ **cela répond/ne répond pas à ce que nous cherchons** this meets/doesn't meet *ou* falls short of our requirements ◆ **ça répond/ne répond pas à mon attente *ou* à mes espérances** it comes up to/falls short of my expectations ◆ **cela répond à une certaine logique** it's quite logical

2 *(= payer de retour) [+ attaque, avances]* to respond to; *[+ amour, affection, salut]* to return; *[+ politesse, gentillesse, invitation]* to repay, to pay back ◆ **peu de gens ont répondu à cet appel** few people responded to this appeal, there was little response to this appeal ◆ **~ à la force par la force** to answer *ou* meet force with force ◆ **s'ils lancent une attaque, nous saurons y ~** if they launch an attack we'll fight back *ou* retaliate

3 *(= être identique à) [+ dessin, façade]* to match ◆ **les deux ailes du bâtiment se répondent** the two wings of the building match (each other)

VT INDIR répondre de 1 *(= être garant de) [+ personne]* to answer for ◆ **~ de l'innocence/l'honnêteté de qn** to answer *ou* vouch for sb's innocence/honesty ◆ **~ des dettes de qn** to answer for sb's debts, to be answerable for sb's debts ◆ **si vous agissez ainsi, je ne réponds plus de rien** if you behave like that, I'll accept no further responsibility ◆ **il viendra, je vous en réponds !** he'll come all right, you can take my word for it! ◆ **ça ne se passera pas comme ça, je t'en réponds !** you can take it from me that it won't happen like that!, it won't happen like that, you take it from me!

2 *(= rendre compte de) [+ actes, décision]* to be accountable for ◆ **~ de ses crimes** *(Jur)* to answer for one's crimes

répons /ʀepɔ̃/ **NM** *(Rel)* response

réponse /ʀepɔ̃s/ GRAMMAIRE ACTIVE 46.4 **NF** 1 *(à demande, lettre, objection)* reply, response; *(à coup de sonnette, prière, question,)* answer, reply; *(à énigme, examen, problème)* answer *(à* to); *(Mus)* recapitulation ◆ **en ~ à votre question** in answer *ou* reply *ou* response to your question ◆ **en ~ aux accusations portées contre lui** in response *ou* reply to the accusations brought against him ◆ **pour toute ~, il grogna** he just grunted in reply ◆ **pour toute ~, il me raccrocha au nez** he just hung up on me ◆ **ma ~ est non** my answer is no ◆ **télégramme avec ~ payée** reply-paid telegram ◆ **ma lettre est restée sans ~** my letter remained unanswered ◆ **sa demande est restée sans ~** there has been no reply *ou* response to his request ◆ **apporter une ~ au problème** to find an answer to the problem ◆ **la ~ ne s'est pas fait attendre** *(Mil, fig)* they were *(ou* he was *etc)* quick to retaliate

2 *(Physiol, Tech = réaction)* response; *(à un appel, un sentiment = écho)* response ◆ **~ immunitaire** immune response

3 *(locutions)* **avoir ~ à tout** to have an answer for everything ◆ **c'est la ~ du berger à la bergère** it's tit for tat ◆ **il me fit une ~ de Normand** he wouldn't say yes or no, he wouldn't give me a straight answer ◆ **il fait les demandes et les ~s** he doesn't let anyone get a word in edgeways* *(Brit) ou* edgewise *(US)*

> ⚠ Attention à ne pas traduire automatiquement **réponse** par **response**, qui, sauf au sens de 'réaction', est d'un registre plus soutenu.

repopulation /ʀ(ə)pɔpylasjɔ̃/ **NF** *[de ville]* repopulation; *[d'étang]* restocking

report /ʀəpɔʀ/ **NM** 1 *[de match]* postponement, putting off; *[de procès]* postponement; *[de décision]* putting off, deferment; *[de date]* putting off, putting back, deferment ◆ **~ d'échéance** *(Fin)* extension of due date ◆ **"report"** *(en bas de page)* "carried forward"; *(en haut de page)* "brought forward" 2 *[de chiffres, indications]* transfer, writing out, copying out; *(Comm) [d'écritures]* posting; *[de somme]* carrying forward *ou* over; *(Photo)* transfer ◆ **faire le ~ de** *[+ somme]* to carry forward *ou* over; *[+ écritures]* to post ◆ **les ~s de voix entre les deux partis se sont bien effectués au deuxième tour** *(Pol)* the votes were satisfactorily transferred to the party with more votes after the first round of the election

reportage /ʀ(ə)pɔʀtaʒ/ **NM** 1 *(Presse, Radio, TV)* report *(sur* on); *(sur le vif) [de match, événement]* commentary ◆ **~ photographique/télévisé** illustrated/television report ◆ **~ en direct** live commentary ◆ **faire un ~ sur** *(Presse)* to write a report on; *(Radio, TV)* to report on ◆ **faire *ou* assurer le ~ d'une cérémonie** to cover a ceremony, to do the coverage of a ceremony ◆ **être en ~** *(Presse)* to be out on a story, to be covering a story; *(Radio, TV)* to be (out) reporting ◆ **c'était un ~ de Julie Durand** that report was from Julie Durand, that was Julie Durand reporting

2 *(= métier)* (news) reporting ◆ **il fait du ~** he's a (news) reporter ◆ **le grand ~** the coverage of major international events ◆ **il a fait plusieurs grands ~s pour …** he has covered several big stories for …

3 *(NonC) (= photographie documentaire)* reportage

reporter¹ /ʀ(ə)pɔʀte/ GRAMMAIRE ACTIVE 48.3 ▸ conjug 1 ◂

VT 1 *(= ramener) [+ objet]* to take back; *(par la pensée)* to take back *(à* to); ◆ **cette chanson nous reporte aux années trente** this song takes us back to the thirties

2 *(= différer) [+ match]* to postpone, to put off; *[+ décision]* to put off, to defer; *[+ date]* to put off *ou* back *(Brit)*, to defer ◆ **la réunion est reportée à demain/d'une semaine** the meeting has been postponed until tomorrow/for a week ◆ **le jugement est reporté à huitaine** *(Jur)* (the) sentence has been deferred for a week

3 *[+ chiffres, indications]* to transfer *(sur* to) to write out, to copy out *(sur* on); *(Comm) [+ écritures]* to post; *(Photo)* to transfer *(sur* to); ◆ **~ une somme sur la page suivante** to carry an amount forward *ou* over to the next page

4 *(= transférer)* **~ son affection/son vote sur** to transfer one's affection/one's vote to ◆ **~ son gain sur un autre cheval/numéro** to put *ou* place one's winnings on *ou* transfer one's bet to another horse/number

VT INDIR reporter à *(= en référer à) (hiérarchiquement)* to report to

VPR se reporter 1 *(= se référer à)* **se ~ à** to refer to ◆ **reportez-vous à la page 5** turn to *ou* refer to *ou* see page 5

2 *(par la pensée)* **se ~ à** to think back to, to cast one's mind back to ◆ **reportez-vous (par l'esprit) aux années 50** cast your mind back to the fifties ◆ **si l'on se reporte à l'Angleterre de cette époque** if one thinks back to the England of that period

3 *(= se transférer)* **son affection s'est reportée sur ses chats** he transferred his affection to his cats

reporter² /ʀ(ə)pɔʀtɛʀ/ **NM** reporter ◆ **grand ~** special correspondent ◆ **~(-)photographe** reporter and photographer ◆ **~-cameraman** news reporter and cameraman; → **radioreporter**

reporteur /ʀ(ə)pɔʀtœʀ/ **NM** 1 *(Bourse)* taker (of stock) 2 *(Typo)* transfer 3 *(TV)* reporter ◆ **~ d'images** reporter-cameraman

reporting /ʀipɔʀtiŋ/ **NM** notification ◆ **ses méthodes de ~ étaient déficientes** his notification procedures were unsatisfactory

repos /ʀ(ə)po/ **NM** 1 *(= détente)* rest ◆ **prendre du ~/un peu de ~** to take *ou* have a rest/a bit of a rest ◆ **il ne peut pas rester *ou* demeurer en ~ 5 minutes** he can't rest *ou* relax for (even) 5 minutes ◆ **le médecin lui a ordonné le ~ complet** the doctor has ordered him to rest *ou* ordered complete rest ◆ **après une matinée/journée de ~, il allait mieux** after a morning's/day's rest he felt better ◆ **respecter le ~ dominical** to observe Sunday as a day of rest ◆ **le ~ du guerrier** *(hum)* a well-earned rest; → **lit, maison**

2 *(= congé)* **avoir droit à deux jours de ~ hebdomadaire** to be entitled to two days off a week ◆ **le médecin lui a donné du ~/huit jours de ~** the doctor has given him some time off/a week off

3 *(= tranquillité)* peace and quiet; *(= quiétude morale)* peace of mind; *(littér = sommeil, mort)* rest, sleep ◆ **il n'y aura pas de ~ pour lui tant que …** he'll have no peace of mind until …, he

won't get any rest until ... ♦ **le ~ de la tombe** the sleep of the dead ♦ **le ~ éternel** eternal rest
4 *(= pause)* *[de discours]* pause; *[de vers]* rest; *(Mus)* cadence
5 *(= petit palier)* half landing
6 *(locutions)* ~ ! *(Mil)* (stand) at ease! ♦ **muscle à l'état de ~** relaxed muscle
♦ **au repos** *[soldat]* standing at ease; *[masse, machine, animal]* at rest; *[muscle]* relaxed
♦ **de + repos** ♦ **être de ~** to be off ♦ **de tout ~** *[situation, entreprise]* secure, safe; *[placement]* gilt-edged, safe; *[travail]* easy ♦ **ce n'est pas de tout ~ !** it's not exactly restful!, it's no picnic! *
♦ **en repos** ♦ **être en ~** to be resting ♦ **avoir la conscience en ~** to have an easy *ou* a clear conscience ♦ **pour avoir l'esprit en ~** to put my *(ou your etc)* mind at rest ♦ **laisser qn en ~** *(frm)* to leave sb in peace *ou* alone
♦ **sans repos** *[travailler]* without stopping, relentlessly; *[marcher]* without a break *ou* a rest, without stopping; *[quête]* uninterrupted, relentless

reposant, e /ʀ(ə)pozɑ̃, ɑ̃t/ **ADJ** *[sommeil]* refreshing; *[couleur, lieu]* restful; *[musique, vacances]* restful, relaxing ♦ **c'est ~ pour la vue** it's (very) restful on *ou* to the eyes

repose /ʀ(ə)poz/ **NF** *[d'appareil]* refitting, reinstallation; *[de tapis]* relaying, putting (back) down again

reposé, e¹ /ʀ(ə)poze/ (ptp de **reposer**) **ADJ** *[air, teint, cheval]* fresh, rested *(attrib)* ♦ **elle avait le visage ~** she looked rested ♦ **j'ai l'esprit ~** my mind is fresh ♦ **maintenant que vous êtes bien ~ ...** now (that) you've had a good rest ...; → **tête**

repose-bras /ʀ(ə)pozbʀɑ/ **NM INV** armrest

repose-pied (pl **repose-pieds**) /ʀ(ə)pozpje/ **NM** footrest

reposer /ʀ(ə)poze/ ▸ conjug 1 ◂ **VT** 1 *(= poser à nouveau)* *[+ verre, livre]* to put back down, to put down again; *[+ tapis]* to relay, to put back down; *[+ objet démonté]* to put back together ♦ **~ ses yeux sur qch** to look at sth again ♦ **va ~ ce livre où tu l'as trouvé** go and put that book back where you found it ♦ **reposez armes !** *(Mil)* order arms!
2 *(= soulager, délasser)* *[+ yeux, corps, membres]* to rest; *[+ esprit]* to rest, to relax ♦ **se ~ l'esprit** to rest one's mind, to give one's mind *ou* brain a rest ♦ **les lunettes de soleil reposent les yeux *ou* la vue** sunglasses rest the eyes, sunglasses are restful to the eyes ♦ **~ sa tête/jambe sur un coussin** to rest one's head/leg on a cushion ♦ **cela repose de ne voir personne (pendant une journée)** it makes a restful change not to see anyone (for a whole day); → **tête**
3 *(= répéter)* *[+ question]* to repeat, to ask again; *[+ problème]* to bring up again, to raise again ♦ **cela va ~ le problème** that will raise the (whole) problem again *ou* bring the (whole) problem up again ♦ **cet incident va (nous) ~ un problème** this incident is going to pose us a new problem *ou* bring up a new problem for us
VT INDIR **reposer sur** *[bâtiment]* to be built on; *[route]* to rest on, to be supported by; *[supposition]* to rest on, to be based on; *[résultat]* to depend on ♦ **sa jambe reposait sur un coussin** his leg was resting on a cushion ♦ **sa théorie ne repose sur rien de précis** his theory doesn't rest on *ou* isn't based on anything specific ♦ **tout repose sur son témoignage** everything hinges on *ou* rests on his evidence
VI 1 *(littér)* *(= être étendu)* to rest, to lie (down); *(= dormir)* to sleep, to rest; *(= être enterré)* to rest ♦ **faire ~ son cheval** to rest one's horse ♦ **tout reposait dans la campagne** everything was sleeping *ou* resting in the countryside ♦ **ici repose ...** here lies ... ♦ **qu'il repose en paix** may he rest in peace ♦ **l'épave repose par 20 mètres de fond** the wreck is lying 20 metres down
2 ♦ **laisser ~** *[+ liquide]* to leave to settle, to let settle *ou* stand; *[+ pâte à pain]* to leave to rise, to let rise; *[+ pâte feuilletée]* to (allow to) rest; *[+ pâte à crêpes]* to leave (to stand) ♦ **laisser ~ la terre** to let the earth lie fallow
VPR **se reposer** 1 *(= se délasser)* to rest ♦ **se ~ sur ses lauriers** to rest on one's laurels
2 ♦ **se ~ sur qn** to rely on sb ♦ **je me repose sur vous pour régler cette affaire** I'll leave it to you *ou* I'm relying on you to sort this business out ♦ **elle se repose sur lui pour tout** she relies on him for everything
3 *(= se poser à nouveau)* *[oiseau, poussière]* to settle again; *[problème]* to crop up again

repose-tête (pl **repose-têtes**) /ʀ(ə)poztɛt/ **NM** headrest

repositionner /ʀ(ə)pozisjɔne/ ▸ conjug 1 ◂ **VT** to reposition ♦ **ils désirent ~ la chaîne sur le marché** they are looking to reposition the chain in the market **VPR** **se repositionner** to reposition o.s. ♦ **nous cherchons à nous ~ dans le haut de gamme** we are seeking to reposition ourselves at the higher end of the market

reposoir /ʀ(ə)pozwaʀ/ **NM** *[d'église, procession]* altar of repose; *[de maison privée]* household altar

repoussage /ʀ(ə)pusaʒ/ **NM** *[de cuir, métal]* repoussé work, embossing

repoussant, e /ʀ(ə)pusɑ̃, ɑ̃t/ **ADJ** *[odeur, saleté, visage]* repulsive, repugnant ♦ **d'une laideur ~e** repulsive

repousse /ʀ(ə)pus/ **NF** *[de cheveux, gazon]* regrowth ♦ **pour accélérer la ~ des cheveux** to help the hair grow again *ou* grow back in

repousse-peaux /ʀəpuspo/ **NM INV** orange stick

repousser /ʀ(ə)puse/ ▸ conjug 1 ◂ **VT** 1 *(= écarter, refouler)* *[+ objet encombrant]* to push out of the way, to push away; *[+ ennemi, attaque]* to repel, to repulse, to drive back; *[+ coups]* to ward off; *[+ soupirant, quémandeur, malheureux]* to turn away ♦ **~ qch du pied** to kick sth out of the way, to kick sth away ♦ **il me repoussa avec brusquerie** he pushed me away *ou* out of the way roughly ♦ **elle parvint à ~ son agresseur** she managed to drive off *ou* beat off her attacker ♦ **les électrons se repoussent** electrons repel each other
2 *(= refuser)* *[+ demande, conseil, aide]* to turn down, to reject; *[+ hypothèse]* to dismiss, to rule out; *[+ tentation]* to reject, to resist, to repel; *[+ projet de loi]* to reject; *[+ objections, arguments]* to brush aside, to dismiss ♦ **la police ne repousse pas l'hypothèse du suicide** the police do not rule out the possibility of suicide
3 *(= remettre en place)* *[+ meuble]* to push back; *[+ tiroir]* to push back in; *[+ porte]* to push to ♦ **repousse la table contre le mur** push the table back *ou* up against the wall
4 *(= différer)* *[+ date, réunion]* to put off *ou* back *(Brit)*, to postpone, to defer ♦ **la date de l'examen a été repoussée (à huitaine/à lundi)** the exam has been put off *ou* postponed (for a week/till Monday), the date of the exam has been put back *(Brit)* (a week/till Monday)
5 *(= dégoûter)* to repel, to repulse ♦ **tout en lui me repousse** everything about him repels *ou* repulses me
6 *(Tech)* *[+ cuir, métal]* to emboss (by hand), to work in repoussé ♦ **en cuir/métal repoussé** in repoussé leather/metal
VI *[feuilles, cheveux]* to grow again ♦ **laisser ~ sa barbe** to let one's beard grow again

repoussoir /ʀ(ə)puswaʀ/ **NM** 1 *(à cuir, métal)* snarling iron; *(à ongles)* orange stick 2 *(Art)* repoussoir, high-toned foreground; *(fig = faire-valoir)* foil ♦ **servir de ~ à qn** to act as a foil to sb 3 *(péj, * = personne laide)* ugly so-and-so * ♦ **c'est un ~ !** he's *(ou she's)* ugly as sin! *

répréhensible /ʀepʀeɑ̃sibl/ **ADJ** *[acte, personne]* reprehensible ♦ **je ne vois pas ce qu'il y a de ~ à ça !** I don't see what's wrong with that!

reprendre /ʀ(ə)pʀɑ̃dʀ/ ▸ conjug 58 ◂ **VT** 1 *(= récupérer)* *[+ ville]* to recapture; *[+ prisonnier]* to recapture, to catch again; *[+ employé]* to take back; *[+ objet prêté]* to take back, to get back ♦ **~ sa place** *(sur un siège)* to go back to one's seat, to resume one's seat; *(dans un emploi)* to go back to work ♦ **la photo avait repris sa place sur la cheminée** the photo was back in its (usual) place on the mantelpiece ♦ **passer ~ qn** to go back *ou* come back for sb ♦ **il a repris sa parole** he went back on his word ♦ **j'irai ~ mon manteau chez le teinturier** I'll go and get my coat (back) from the cleaner's ♦ **~ son nom de jeune fille** to take one's maiden name again, to go back to *ou* revert to one's maiden name
2 *(= se resservir de)* *[+ plat]* to have *ou* take (some) more ♦ **voulez-vous ~ des légumes ?** would you like a second helping of *ou* some more vegetables?
3 *(= retrouver)* *[+ espoir, droits, forces]* to regain, to recover ♦ **~ des couleurs** to get some colour back in one's cheeks ♦ **~ confiance/courage** to regain *ou* recover one's confidence/courage ♦ **~ ses droits** to reassert itself ♦ **~ ses habitudes** to get back into one's old habits, to take up one's old habits again ♦ **~ contact avec qn** to get in touch with sb again ♦ **~ ses esprits *ou* ses sens** to come to, to regain consciousness, to come round *(Brit)* ♦ **~ sa liberté** to regain one's freedom ♦ **~ haleine *ou* son souffle** to get one's breath back; → **connaissance, conscience, dessus** *etc*
4 *(Comm)* *[+ marchandises]* to take back; *(contre un nouvel achat)* to take in part exchange; *[+ fonds de commerce, usine]* to take over ♦ **les articles en solde ne sont ni repris ni échangés** sale goods cannot be returned or exchanged ♦ **ils m'ont repris ma vieille télé** they bought my old TV set off me (in part exchange) ♦ **j'ai acheté une voiture neuve et ils ont repris la vieille** I bought a new car and traded in the old one *ou* and they took the old one in part exchange ♦ **il a repris l'affaire de son père** he has taken on *ou* over his father's business
5 *(= recommencer, poursuivre)* *[+ travaux]* to resume; *[+ études, fonctions, lutte]* to take up again, to resume; *[+ livre]* to pick up again, to go back to; *[+ lecture]* to go back to, to resume; *[+ conversation, récit]* to resume, to carry on (with); *[+ promenade]* to resume, to continue; *[+ hostilités]* to reopen, to start again; *[+ pièce de théâtre]* to put on again ♦ **~ la route *ou* son chemin** *[voyageur]* to set off again ♦ **~ la route** *[routier]* to go back on the road again ♦ **~ la mer** *[marin]* to go back to sea ♦ **après déjeuner ils reprirent la route** after lunch they continued their journey *ou* they set off again ♦ **~ la plume** to take up the pen again ♦ **reprenez votre histoire au début** start your story from the beginning again, go back to the beginning of your story again ♦ **reprenons les faits un par un** let's go over the facts again one by one ♦ **il reprendra la parole après vous** he will speak again after you ♦ **~ le travail** *(après maladie, grève)* to go back to work, to start work again; *(après le repas)* to get back to work, to start work again ♦ **la vie reprend son cours** life is back to normal again ♦ **il a repris le rôle de Hamlet** *(Théât)* he has taken on the role of Hamlet; → **collier**
6 *(= saisir à nouveau)* **son mal de gorge l'a repris** his sore throat is troubling *ou* bothering him again ♦ **ses douleurs l'ont repris** he is in pain again ♦ **voilà que ça le reprend !** *(iro)* there he goes again!, he's off again! * ♦ **ses doutes le reprirent** he started feeling doubtful again

7 *(= attraper à nouveau)* to catch again ◆ **on ne m'y reprendra plus** *(fig)* I won't let myself be caught (out) again ◆ **que je ne t'y reprenne pas !** *(menace)* don't let me catch you doing that again!
8 *(Sport = rattraper) [+ balle]* to catch ◆ **revers bien repris par Legrand** *(Tennis)* backhand well returned by Legrand
9 *(= retoucher, corriger) [+ tableau]* to touch up; *[+ article, chapitre]* to go over again; *[+ manteau] (gén)* to alter; *(trop grand)* to take in; *(trop petit)* to let out; *(trop long)* to take up; *(trop court)* to let down ◆ **il n'y a rien à ~** there's not a single correction *ou* alteration to be made ◆ **il y a beaucoup de choses à ~ dans ce travail** there are lots of improvements to be made to this work, there are a lot of things that need improving in this work ◆ **il faut ~ un centimètre à droite** *(Couture)* we'll have to take it in half an inch on the right
10 *(= réprimander) [+ personne]* to reprimand, to tell off *; *(pour faute de langue)* to pull up ◆ **~ un élève qui se trompe** to correct a pupil
11 *(= répéter) [+ refrain]* to take up; *[+ critique]* to repeat ◆ **il reprend toujours les mêmes arguments** he always repeats the same arguments, he always comes out with the same old arguments ◆ **reprenez les 5 dernières mesures** *(Mus)* let's have *ou* take the last 5 bars again ◆ **ils reprirent la chanson en chœur** they all joined in *ou* took up the song
12 *(= réutiliser) [+ idée, suggestion]* to take up (again), to use (again) ◆ **l'incident a été repris par les journaux** the incident was taken up by the newspapers
VI 1 *(= retrouver de la vigueur) [plante]* to recover; *[affaires]* to pick up ◆ **la vie reprenait peu à peu** life gradually returned to normal ◆ **il a bien repris depuis son opération** he has made a good recovery since his operation ◆ **pour faire ~ le feu** to get the fire going (again); → **affaire**
2 *(= recommencer) [bruit, pluie, incendie, grève]* to start again; *[fièvre, douleur]* to come back again; *(Scol, Univ)* to start again, to go back ◆ **le froid a repris depuis hier** it has turned cold again since yesterday
3 *(= dire)* **"ce n'est pas moi", reprit-il** "it's not me", he went on
VPR se reprendre 1 *(= se corriger)* to correct o.s.; *(= s'interrompre)* to stop o.s. ◆ **il allait plaisanter, il s'est repris à temps** he was going to make a joke but he stopped himself *ou* pulled himself up in time
2 *(= recommencer)* **se ~ à plusieurs fois pour faire qch** to make several attempts to do sth *ou* at doing sth ◆ **il a dû s'y ~ à deux fois pour ouvrir la porte** he had to make two attempts before he could open the door ◆ **il se reprit à penser à elle** he went back to thinking about her, his thoughts went back to her ◆ **il se reprit à craindre que ...** once more he began to be afraid that ... ◆ **chacun se reprit à espérer** everyone began to hope again, everyone's hopes began to revive again
3 *(= se ressaisir)* **après une période de découragement, il s'est repris** after feeling quite despondent for a while he's got a grip on himself *ou* pulled himself together (again) ◆ **le coureur s'est bien repris sur la fin** the runner made a good recovery *ou* caught up well towards the end

repreneur /R(ə)pRənœR/ **NM** *[d'entreprise]* (corporate) rescuer; *(péj)* raider ◆ **trouver ~** to find a buyer

représailles /R(ə)pRezɑj/ **NFPL** *(Pol, fig)* reprisals, retaliation *(NonC)* ◆ **user de ~, exercer des ~** to take reprisals, to retaliate *(envers, contre, sur* against); ◆ **par ~** in retaliation, as a reprisal ◆ **en ~ de** as a reprisal for, in retaliation for ◆ **menacer un pays de ~ commerciales** to threaten a country with trade reprisals ◆ **mesures de ~** retaliatory measures ◆ **attends-toi à des ~ !** you can expect reprisals!

représentable /R(ə)pRezɑ̃tabl/ **ADJ** *[phénomène]* representable, that can be represented ◆ **c'est difficilement ~** it is difficult to represent it

représentant, e /R(ə)pRezɑ̃tɑ̃, ɑ̃t/ **NM,F** *(gén)* representative ◆ **~ du personnel** staff representative ◆ **~ syndical** union representative, shop steward *(Brit)* ◆ **~ de commerce** sales representative, rep * ◆ **~ des forces de l'ordre** police officer ◆ **~ en justice** legal representative ◆ **il est ~ en cosmétiques** he's a representative *ou* a rep * for a cosmetics firm ◆ **~ multicarte** sales representative acting for several firms

représentatif, -ive /R(ə)pRezɑ̃tatif, iv/ **ADJ** *(gén)* representative ◆ **~ de** *(= typique de)* representative of ◆ **signes ~s d'une fonction** signs representing *ou* which represent a function ◆ **échantillon ~ de la population** representative sample of the population

représentation /R(ə)pRezɑ̃tasjɔ̃/ **NF** 1 *(= notation, transcription) [d'objet, phénomène, son]* representation; *[de paysage, société]* portrayal; *[de faits]* representation, description ◆ **~ graphique** graphic(al) representation ◆ **c'est une ~ erronée de la réalité** it's a misrepresentation of reality ◆ **~ en arbre** *(Ling)* tree diagram
2 *(= évocation, perception)* representation ◆ **~s visuelles/auditives** visual/auditory representations
3 *(Théât = action, séance)* performance ◆ **troupe en ~** company on tour ◆ **on a toujours l'impression qu'il est en ~** *(fig)* he always seems to be playing a role
4 *[de pays, citoyens, mandant]* representation; *(= mandataires, délégation)* representatives ◆ **il assure la ~ de son gouvernement auprès de notre pays** he represents his government in our country ◆ **~ diplomatique/proportionnelle/en justice** diplomatic/proportional/legal representation
5 *(Comm)* sales representation ◆ **faire de la ~** to be a (sales) representative *ou* a rep * ◆ **la ~ entre pour beaucoup dans les frais** *(= les représentants)* the sales force is a major factor in costs
6 *(= réception)* entertainment
7 *(frm = reproches)* **faire des ~s à** to make representations to

représentativité /R(ə)pRezɑ̃tativite/ **NF** representativeness ◆ **reconnaître la ~ d'une organisation** to recognize an organization as a representative body

représenter /R(ə)pRezɑ̃te/ ► conjug 1 ◄ **VT** 1 *(= décrire) [peintre, romancier]* to depict, to portray, to show; *[photographie]* to show ◆ **ce dessin représente un cheval** this is a drawing of a horse ◆ **la scène représente une rue** *(Théât)* the scene is a street ◆ **~ fidèlement les faits** to describe *ou* set out the facts faithfully ◆ **on le représente comme un escroc** he's portrayed as a crook ◆ **il a voulu ~ la société du 19e siècle** he wanted to depict *ou* portray 19th-century society
2 *(= symboliser)* to represent; *(= signifier)* to represent, to mean ◆ **les parents représentent l'autorité** parents represent authority ◆ **ce poste représente beaucoup pour moi** this job means a lot to me ◆ **ce trait représente un arbre** this line represents a tree ◆ **ça va ~ beaucoup de travail** this is going to mean *ou* involve a lot of work ◆ **ça représente une part importante des dépenses** this is *ou* represents a large part of the costs ◆ **ils représentent 12% de la population** they make up *ou* represent *ou* are 12% of the population
3 *(Théât) (= jouer)* to perform, to play; *(= mettre à l'affiche)* to perform, to put on, to stage ◆ **on va ~ quatre pièces cette année** we *(ou* they *etc)* will perform *ou* put on four plays this year ◆ **"Hamlet" fut représenté pour la première fois en 1603** "Hamlet" was first performed in 1603
4 *(= agir au nom de) [+ ministre, pays]* to represent ◆ **il s'est fait ~ par son notaire** he was represented by his lawyer ◆ **les personnes qui ne peuvent pas assister à la réunion doivent se faire ~ (par un tiers)** people who cannot attend the meeting should send a proxy
5 ◆ **~ une maison de commerce** to represent a firm, to be a representative for a firm
6 *(littér)* **~ qch à qn** to point sth out to sb, to (try to) impress sth on sb ◆ **il lui représenta les inconvénients de la situation** he pointed out the drawbacks to him
VI † ◆ **il représente bien/ne représente pas bien** *(= en imposer)* he cuts a fine/a poor *ou* sorry figure
VPR se représenter 1 *(= s'imaginer)* to imagine ◆ **je ne pouvais plus me ~ son visage** I could no longer bring his face to mind *ou* visualize his face ◆ **on se le représente bien en Hamlet** you can well imagine him as Hamlet ◆ **tu te représentes la scène quand il a annoncé sa démission !** you can just imagine the scene when he announced his resignation!
2 *(= survenir à nouveau)* **l'idée se représenta à lui** the idea occurred to him again ◆ **si l'occasion se représente** if the occasion presents itself again ◆ **le même problème va se ~** the same problem will crop up again
3 *(= se présenter à nouveau) (Scol, Univ)* to retake, to resit *(Brit)*; *(Pol)* to run again, to stand again *(Brit)* ◆ **se ~ à un examen** to retake *ou* resit *(Brit)* an exam ◆ **se ~ à une élection** to run *ou* stand *(Brit)* for re-election

répressif, -ive /RepResif, iv/ **ADJ** repressive

répression /RepResjɔ̃/ **NF** 1 *[de crime, abus]* curbing; *[de révolte]* suppression, quelling, repression ◆ **la ~** *(Pol)* repression ◆ **la ~ qui a suivi le coup d'État** the repression *ou* crackdown which followed the coup ◆ **prendre des mesures de ~ contre le crime** to crack down on crime ◆ **le service de la ~ des fraudes** the Fraud Squad 2 *(Bio, Psych)* repression

réprimande /RepRimɑ̃d/ **NF** reprimand, rebuke ◆ **adresser une sévère ~ à un enfant** to scold *ou* rebuke a child severely ◆ **son attitude mérite une ~** he deserves a reprimand for his attitude ◆ **faire des ~s à qn** to reprimand *ou* rebuke sb

réprimander /RepRimɑ̃de/ ► conjug 1 ◄ **VT** to reprimand, to rebuke ◆ **se faire ~ par** to be reprimanded *ou* rebuked by

réprimer /RepRime/ ► conjug 1 ◄ **VT** *[+ insurrection]* to quell, to repress, to put down; *[+ crimes, abus]* to curb, to crack down on; *[+ sentiment, désir]* to repress, to suppress; *[+ rire, bâillement]* to suppress, to stifle; *[+ larmes, colère]* to hold back, to swallow

repris /R(ə)pRi/ **NM INV** ◆ **il s'agit d'un ~ de justice** the man has previous convictions, the man is an ex-prisoner *ou* an ex-convict ◆ **un dangereux ~ de justice** a dangerous known criminal

reprisage /R(ə)pRizaʒ/ **NM** *[de chaussette, lainage]* darning; *[de collant, drap, accroc]* mending

reprise /R(ə)pRiz/ **NF** 1 *(= recommencement) [d'activité, cours, travaux]* resumption; *[d'hostilités]* resumption, re-opening, renewal; *[de froid]* return; *(Théât)* revival; *(Ciné)* rerun, reshowing *(NonC)*; *(Mus = passage répété)* repeat; *(Radio, TV = rediffusion)* repeat ◆ **la ~ des violons** *(Mus)* the re-entry of the violins ◆ **la ~ des combats est imminente** fighting will begin again *ou* will be resumed again very soon ◆ **pour éviter la ~ de l'inflation** to stop inflation taking off again ◆ **avec la ~ du mauvais temps** with the return of the bad weather

◆ **les ouvriers ont décidé la ~ du travail** the men have decided to go back to *ou* to return to work ◆ **on espère une ~ des affaires** we're hoping that business will pick up again ◆ **la ~ (économique) est assez forte dans certains secteurs** the (economic) revival *ou* recovery is quite marked in certain sectors

2 (*= accélération*) **avoir de bonnes ~s** *ou* **de la ~** to have good acceleration, to accelerate well ◆ **sa voiture n'a pas de ~s** his car has no acceleration

3 (*Boxe*) round; (*Escrime*) reprise; (*Équitation*) (*pour le cavalier*) riding lesson; (*pour le cheval*) dressage lesson ◆ **à la ~** (*Ftbl*) at the start of the second half ◆ **~ de volée** (*Tennis*) volleyed return ◆ **~ !** (*après arrêt*) time!

4 (*Comm*) [*de marchandise*] taking back; (*pour nouvel achat*) trade-in, part exchange (*Brit*); (*pour occuper des locaux*) key money ◆ **valeur de ~ d'une voiture** trade-in value *ou* part-exchange value (*Brit*) of a car ◆ **nous vous offrons une ~ de 1 000 € pour l'achat d'un nouveau modèle** we'll give you €1,000 when you trade your old one in ◆ **~ des bouteilles vides** return of empties ◆ **la maison ne fait pas de ~** goods cannot be returned *ou* exchanged ◆ **payer une ~ de 1 000 € à l'ancien locataire** to pay the outgoing tenant €1,000 for improvements made to the property

5 (*= réutilisation*) [*d'idée, suggestion*] re-using, taking up again

6 [*de chaussette*] darn; [*de drap, chemise*] mend ◆ **faire une ~ perdue** to darn (*ou* mend) invisibly ◆ **faire une ~** *ou* **des ~s à un drap** to mend a sheet

7 (*Constr*) **~ en sous-œuvre** underpinning

8 (*locutions*) **à deux ou trois ~s** on two or three occasions, two or three times ◆ **à maintes/plusieurs ~s** on many/several occasions, many/several times

repriser /ʀ(ə)pʀize/ ► conjug 1 ◄ **VT** [*+ chaussette, lainage*] to darn; [*+ collant, drap*] to mend; [*+ accroc*] to mend, to stitch up; → **aiguille, coton, œuf**

réprobateur, -trice /ʀepʀɔbatœʀ, tʀis/ **ADJ** reproachful, reproving ◆ **elle me lança un regard ~** she gave me a reproachful *ou* reproving look, she looked at me reproachfully ◆ **d'un ton ~** reproachfully

réprobation /ʀepʀɔbasjɔ̃/ **NF** 1 (*= blâme*) disapproval, reprobation (*frm*) ◆ **air/ton de ~** reproachful *ou* reproving look/tone 2 (*Rel*) reprobation

reproche /ʀ(ə)pʀɔʃ/ **NM** criticism ◆ **faire** *ou* **adresser des ~s à qn** to criticize sb ◆ **conduite qui mérite des ~s** blameworthy *ou* reprehensible behaviour ◆ **faire ~ à qn d'avoir menti** (*frm*) to reproach sb for lying ◆ **je me fais de grands ~s** I hold myself very much to blame ◆ **avec ~** reproachfully ◆ **ton/regard de ~** reproachful tone/look ◆ **il est sans ~** he's beyond *ou* above reproach ◆ **sans ~, permettez-moi de vous dire que …, je ne vous fais pas de ~ mais permettez-moi de vous dire que …** I'm not blaming you but let me say that … ◆ **ce n'est pas un ~ !** this isn't a criticism! ◆ **soit dit sans ~, tu devrais maigrir un peu** no offence meant but you should lose a bit of weight ◆ **le seul ~ que je ferais à cette cuisine …** the only criticism I have to make about the kitchen …

reprocher /ʀ(ə)pʀɔʃe/ ► conjug 1 ◄ **VT** 1 ◆ **~ qch à qn** to criticize sb for sth ◆ **~ à qn de faire qch** to criticize sb for doing sth ◆ **les faits qui lui sont reprochés** (*Jur*) the charges against him ◆ **on lui a reproché sa maladresse** they criticized him for being clumsy ◆ **on lui reproche de nombreuses malhonnêtetés** he is accused of several instances of dishonesty ◆ **il me reproche mon succès/ma fortune** he resents my success/my wealth, he holds my success/my wealth against me ◆ **je ne te reproche rien** I'm not blaming you for anything ◆ **je me reproche de ne pas l'avoir fait** I regret not doing it ◆ **je n'ai rien à me ~** I've nothing to reproach myself with, I've nothing to be ashamed of ◆ **qu'est-ce qu'elle lui reproche ?** what has she got against him? ◆ **qu'est-ce que tu me reproches ?** what have I done wrong? ◆ **il est très minutieux mais on ne peut pas le lui ~** he's very meticulous but there's nothing wrong with that *ou* but that's no bad thing

2 (*= critiquer*) **qu'as-tu à ~ à mon plan/ce tableau ?** what have you got against my plan/this picture?, what don't you like about my plan/this picture? ◆ **je reproche à ce tissu d'être trop salissant** my criticism of this material is that it shows the dirt ◆ **je ne vois rien à ~ à son travail** I can't find any faults *ou* I can't find anything to criticize in his work

reproducteur, -trice /ʀ(ə)pʀɔdyktœʀ, tʀis/ **ADJ** (*Bio*) reproductive ◆ **cheval ~** studhorse, stallion **NM** 1 (*= animal*) breeder ◆ **~s** breeding stock (*NonC*) 2 (*Tech = gabarit*) template

reproductible /ʀ(ə)pʀɔdyktibl/ **ADJ** which can be reproduced, reproducible

reproductif, -ive /ʀ(ə)pʀɔdyktif, iv/ **ADJ** reproductive

reproduction /ʀ(ə)pʀɔdyksjɔ̃/ **NF** 1 [*de son, mouvement*] reproduction; [*de modèle, tableau*] reproduction, copying; (*par reprographie*) reproduction, duplication; [*de texte*] reprinting; [*de clé*] copying ◆ **"reproduction interdite"** "all rights (of reproduction) reserved" 2 (*= copie*) reproduction ◆ **livre contenant de nombreuses ~s** book containing many reproductions ◆ **ce n'est qu'une ~** it's only a copy 3 [*de plantes, animaux*] reproduction, breeding ◆ **~ artificielle** artificial reproduction ◆ **organes de ~** reproductive organs ◆ **~ par mitose** *ou* **par division cellulaire** replication

reproduire /ʀ(ə)pʀɔdɥiʀ/ ► conjug 38 ◄ **VT** 1 (*= restituer*) [*+ son, mouvement*] to reproduce

2 (*= copier*) [*+ modèle, tableau*] to reproduce, to copy; (*par reprographie*) to reproduce, to duplicate; (*par moulage*) to reproduce; [*+ clé*] to make a copy of ◆ **la photo est reproduite en page 3** the picture is shown *ou* reproduced on page 3 ◆ **le texte de la conférence sera reproduit dans notre magazine** the text of the lecture will be printed in our magazine

3 (*= répéter*) [*+ erreur, expérience*] to repeat

4 (*= imiter*) to copy ◆ **essayant de ~ les gestes de son professeur** trying to copy his teacher's gestures

VPR se reproduire 1 [*plantes, animaux*] to reproduce, to breed ◆ **se ~ par mitose** *ou* **par division cellulaire** (*Bio*) to replicate

2 (*= se répéter*) [*phénomène*] to recur, to happen again; [*erreur*] to reappear, to recur ◆ **et que cela ne se reproduise plus !** and don't let it happen again! ◆ **ce genre d'incident se reproduit régulièrement** this kind of thing happens quite regularly

reprofilage /ʀ(ə)pʀɔfilaʒ/ **NM** rejigging

reprofiler /ʀ(ə)pʀɔfile/ ► conjug 1 ◄ **VT** [*+ organisation, cotisation*] to rejig; [*+ bâtiment*] to give a new look to

reprogrammer /ʀ(ə)pʀɔgʀame/ ► conjug 1 ◄ **VT** 1 [*+ ordinateur, magnétoscope*] to reprogram 2 (*Ciné, TV*) to reschedule

reprographie /ʀ(ə)pʀɔgʀafi/ **NF** (*= procédés*) reprographics (*SPÉC*) ◆ **la ~ sauvage** illegal copying ◆ **le service de ~** the photocopying department ◆ **'~'** (*en vitrine*) 'photocopying available'

reprographier /ʀ(ə)pʀɔgʀafje/ ► conjug 7 ◄ **VT** to (photo)copy, to duplicate

réprouvé, e /ʀepʀuve/ (ptp de **réprouver**) **NM,F** (*Rel*) reprobate; (*fig*) outcast, reprobate

réprouver /ʀepʀuve/ GRAMMAIRE ACTIVE 41 ► conjug 1 ◄ **VT** 1 [*+ personne*] to reprove; [*+ attitude, comportement*] to reprove, to condemn; [*+ projet*] to condemn, to disapprove of ◆ **des actes que la morale réprouve** immoral acts 2 (*Rel*) to damn, to reprobate

reps /ʀɛps/ **NM** rep(p)

reptation /ʀɛptasjɔ̃/ **NF** crawling

reptile /ʀɛptil/ **NM** (*= animal*) reptile; (*= serpent*) snake; (*péj = personne*) reptile

reptilien, -ienne /ʀɛptiljɛ̃, jɛn/ **ADJ** reptilian

repu, e /ʀəpy/ (ptp de **repaître**) **ADJ** [*animal*] sated; [*personne*] full up* (*attrib*) ◆ **je suis ~** I'm full, I've eaten my fill ◆ **il est ~ de cinéma** he has had his fill of the cinema

républicain, e /ʀepyblikɛ̃, ɛn/ **ADJ, NM,F** republican; (*Pol US*) Republican ◆ **le calendrier ~** the French Revolutionary calendar; → **garde²**

republier /ʀəpyblije/ ► conjug 7 ◄ **VT** to republish

république /ʀepyblik/ **NF** republic ◆ **on est en ~ !** it's a free country! ◆ **la ~ des Lettres** (*fig*) the republic of letters ◆ **la République française** the French Republic ◆ **la Cinquième République** the Fifth Republic ◆ **la République arabe unie** (*Hist*) the United Arab Republic ◆ **la République d'Irlande** the Irish Republic ◆ **la République démocratique allemande** (*Hist*) the German Democratic Republic ◆ **la République fédérale d'Allemagne** the Federal Republic of Germany ◆ **la République islamique d'Iran** the Islamic Republic of Iran ◆ **la République populaire de Chine** the Chinese People's Republic, the People's Republic of China ◆ **la République tchèque** the Czech Republic ◆ **sous la République de Weimar** in the Weimar Republic ◆ **~ bananière** banana republic

LA CINQUIÈME RÉPUBLIQUE

The term « the Fifth Republic » refers to the French Republic since the presidency of General de Gaulle (1959-1969), during which a new Constitution was established.

répudiation /ʀepydjasjɔ̃/ **NF** 1 [*d'épouse*] repudiation 2 [*d'opinion, foi, engagement*] renouncement 3 (*Jur*) [*de nationalité, succession*] renouncement, relinquishment

répudier /ʀepydje/ ► conjug 7 ◄ **VT** 1 [*+ épouse*] to repudiate 2 [*+ opinion, foi*] to renounce; [*+ engagement*] to renounce, to go back on 3 (*Jur*) [*+ nationalité, succession*] to renounce, to relinquish

répugnance /ʀepyɲɑ̃s/ **NF** 1 (*= répulsion*) (*pour personnes*) repugnance (*pour* for) disgust (*pour* for) loathing (*pour* of); (*pour nourriture, mensonge*) disgust (*pour* for) loathing (*pour* of); ◆ **avoir de la ~ pour** to loathe, to have a loathing of ◆ **j'éprouve de la ~ à la vue de ce spectacle** this sight fills me with disgust, I find this sight quite repugnant *ou* disgusting 2 (*= hésitation*) reluctance (*à faire qch* to do sth); ◆ **il éprouvait une certaine ~ à nous le dire** he was rather loath *ou* reluctant to tell us ◆ **faire qch avec ~** to do sth reluctantly *ou* unwillingly

répugnant, e /ʀepyɲɑ, ɑt/ **ADJ** [*individu*] repugnant; [*laideur*] revolting; [*action*] disgusting, loathsome; [*travail, odeur, nourriture*] disgusting, revolting

répugner /ʀepyɲe/ ► conjug 1 ◄ **VT INDIR répugner à** 1 (*= dégoûter*) to repel, to disgust, to be repugnant to ◆ **cet individu me répugne profondément** I find that man absolutely repellent ◆ **manger du poisson lui répugnait** the thought of eating fish made him feel sick ◆ **cette odeur lui répugnait** the smell made him feel sick, he was repelled by the smell

♦ **cette idée ne lui répugnait pas du tout** he didn't find this idea off-putting in the least

2 *(= hésiter)* ~ **à faire qch** to be loath *ou* reluctant to do sth ♦ **il répugnait à parler en public/à accepter cette aide** he was loath *ou* reluctant to speak in public/to accept this help ♦ **il ne répugnait pas à mentir quand cela lui semblait nécessaire** he had no qualms about lying if he thought it necessary

VB IMPERS *(frm)* ♦ **il me répugne de devoir vous le dire** it's very distasteful to me to have to tell you this

VT *(littér)* → **vt indir 1**

répulsif, -ive /ʀepylsif, iv/ ADJ *(gén, Phys)* repulsive NM repellent, repellant

répulsion /ʀepylsjɔ̃/ NF *(gén)* repulsion, disgust; *(Phys)* repulsion ♦ **éprouver** *ou* **avoir de la ~ pour qqch** to be repelled by sth, to find sth repellent

réputation /ʀepytasjɔ̃/ NF 1 *(= honneur)* reputation, good name ♦ **préserver sa ~** to keep up *ou* protect one's reputation *ou* good name

2 *(= renommée)* reputation ♦ **avoir bonne/mauvaise ~** to have a good/bad reputation ♦ **se faire une ~** to make a name *ou* a reputation for o.s. ♦ **sa ~ n'est plus à faire** his reputation is firmly established ♦ **ce film a fait sa ~** this film made his reputation *ou* name ♦ **produit de ~ mondiale** product which has a world-wide reputation ♦ **connaître qn/qch de ~ (seulement)** to know sb/sth (only) by repute ♦ **sa ~ de gynécologue** his reputation as a gynaecologist ♦ **il a une ~ d'avarice** he has a reputation for miserliness ♦ **il a la ~ d'être avare** he has a reputation for *ou* of being miserly, he is reputed to be miserly

réputé, e /ʀepyte/ ADJ 1 *(= célèbre)* *[vin, artiste]* reputable, renowned, of repute ♦ **l'un des médecins les plus ~s de la ville** one of the town's most reputable doctors, one of the best-known doctors in town ♦ **c'est un fromage/vin hautement ~** it's a cheese/wine of great repute *ou* renown ♦ **orateur ~ pour ses bons mots** speaker renowned for his witticisms ♦ **ville ~e pour sa cuisine/ses monuments** town which is renowned for *ou* which has a great reputation for its food/its monuments ♦ **il n'est pas ~ pour son honnêteté !** he's not exactly renowned *ou* famous for his honesty!

2 *(= considéré comme)* reputed ♦ **remède ~ infaillible** cure which is reputed *ou* supposed *ou* said to be infallible ♦ **professeur ~ pour être très sévère** teacher who has the reputation of being *ou* who is reputed to be *ou* said to be very strict

requalification /ʀ(ə)kalifikasjɔ̃/ NF 1 *(= recyclage)* retraining 2 *(Jur)* **la ~ des faits** amendment of the charges

requalifier /ʀ(ə)kalifje/ ► conjug 7 ◄ VT 1 *[+ personne]* to retrain 2 *(Jur)* *[+ faits, délit]* to amend

requérant, e /ʀəkeʀɑ̃, ɑ̃t/ NM,F *(Jur)* applicant

requérir /ʀəkeʀiʀ/ ► conjug 21 ◄ VT 1 *(= nécessiter)* *[+ soins, prudence]* to call for, to require ♦ **ceci requiert toute notre attention** this calls for *ou* requires *ou* demands our full attention 2 *(= solliciter)* *[+ aide, service]* to request; *(= exiger)* *[+ justification]* to require; *(= réquisitionner)* *[+ personne]* to call upon ♦ ~ **l'intervention de la police** to require *ou* necessitate police intervention ♦ **je vous requiers de me suivre** *(frm)* I call on you to follow me 3 *(Jur)* *[+ peine]* to call for, to demand ♦ **le procureur était en train de ~** the prosecutor was summing up

requête /ʀəkɛt/ NF 1 *(= demande)* request ♦ **à** *ou* **sur la ~ de qn** at sb's request, at the request of sb 2 *(Jur)* petition ♦ **adresser une ~ à un juge** to petition a judge ♦ ~ **en cassation** appeal ♦ ~ **civile** *appeal to a court against its judgment* 3 *(Ordin)* query

requiem /ʀekɥijɛm/ NM INV requiem

requin /ʀəkɛ̃/ NM *(lit, fig)* shark ♦ ~ **marteau** hammerhead (shark) ♦ ~ **blanc/bleu/pèlerin** white/blue/basking shark ♦ ~**-baleine/ -tigre** whale/tiger shark ♦ **les ~s de la finance** the sharks of the financial world

requinquer* /ʀ(ə)kɛ̃ke/ ► conjug 1 ◄ VT to pep up*, to buck up* ♦ **un whisky vous requinquera** a whisky will pep you up* *ou* buck you up* ♦ **avec un peu de repos, dans trois jours vous serez requinqué** with a bit of a rest in three days you'll be your old (perky) self again* *ou* you'll be back on form again *(Brit)*

VPR **se requinquer** to perk up*

requis, e /ʀəki, iz/ (ptp de **requérir**) ADJ 1 *(= nécessaire)* *[majorité, niveau]* required, necessary; *[qualités, compétence, diplômes]* necessary, required, requisite ♦ **avoir les qualifications ~es pour un poste** to have the necessary *ou* requisite qualifications for a job ♦ **dans les temps** *ou* **délais ~** in the required time ♦ **satisfaire aux conditions ~es** to meet the requirements *ou* the necessary conditions ♦ **avoir l'âge ~** to meet the age requirements ♦ **il a la voix ~e pour ce rôle** he's got the right (kind of) voice for this part 2 *(= réquisitionné)* conscripted

réquisition /ʀekizisjɔ̃/ NF 1 *[de biens]* requisitioning, commandeering; *[d'hommes]* conscription, requisitioning ♦ ~ **de la force armée** requisitioning of *ou* calling out of the army 2 *(Jur)* ~**s** *(= plaidoirie)* summing-up for the prosecution

réquisitionner /ʀekizisjɔne/ ► conjug 1 ◄ VT *[+ biens]* to requisition, to commandeer; *[+ hommes]* to conscript, to requisition ♦ **j'ai été réquisitionné pour faire la vaisselle** *(hum)* I have been drafted in *ou* requisitioned to do the dishes *(hum)*

réquisitoire /ʀekizitwaʀ/ NM 1 *(Jur)* *(= plaidoirie)* summing-up for the prosecution *(specifying appropriate sentence)*; *(= acte écrit)* instruction, brief *(to examining magistrate)* 2 *(fig)* indictment *(contre of)*; ♦ **son discours fut un ~ contre le capitalisme** his speech was an indictment of capitalism

RER /ɛʀøɛʀ/ NM (abrév de **réseau express régional**) → **réseau**

reroutage /ʀəʀutaʒ/ NM *(Téléc)* rerouting

rerouter /ʀəʀute/ ► conjug 1 ◄ VT *(Téléc)* *[+ message]* to reroute

rerouteur /ʀəʀutœʀ/ NM *(Téléc)* rerouter

RES /ʀɛs, ɛʀəɛs/ NM (abrév de **rachat d'entreprise par ses salariés**) → **rachat**

resaler /ʀ(ə)sale/ ► conjug 1 ◄ VT to add more salt to, to put more salt in

resalir /ʀ(ə)saliʀ/ ► conjug 2 ◄ VT *[+ tapis, mur, sol, vêtement]* to get dirty again ♦ **ne va pas te ~** don't go and get yourself dirty *ou* in a mess again ♦ **se ~ les mains** to get one's hands dirty again, to dirty one's hands again

rescapé, e /ʀɛskape/ ADJ *[personne]* surviving NM,F *(lit, fig)* survivor *(de of, from)*

rescolarisation /ʀ(ə)skɔlaʀizasjɔ̃/ NF *[d'enfant]* return to school

rescolariser /ʀ(ə)skɔlaʀize/ ► conjug 1 ◄ VT *[+ enfant]* to send back to school

rescousse /ʀɛskus/ NF ♦ **venir** *ou* **aller à la ~ de qn** to go to sb's rescue *ou* aid ♦ **appeler qn à la ~** to call to sb for help ♦ **ils arrivèrent à la ~** they came to the rescue

rescrit /ʀɛskʀi/ NM rescript

réseau (pl **réseaux**) /ʀezo/ NM 1 *(gén)* network ♦ ~ **routier/ferroviaire/téléphonique** road/rail/telephone network ♦ ~ **bancaire** banking network ♦ ~ **de communication/d'information/ de distribution** communications / information / distribution network ♦ ~ **commercial** *ou* **de vente** sales network ♦ ~ **électrique** electricity network *ou* grid *(Brit)* ♦ ~ **express régional** *rapid-transit train service between Paris and the suburbs* ♦ ~ **d'assainissement** sewer *ou* sewerage system ♦ ~ **fluvial** river system, network of rivers ♦ ~ **de transports en commun** public transport system *ou* network ♦ **les abonnés du ~ sont avisés que …** *(Téléc)* telephone subscribers are advised that … ♦ **sur l'ensemble du ~** over the whole network; → **câblé, hertzien**

2 *[d'amis, relations]* network; *[de prostitution, trafiquants, terroristes]* ring ♦ ~ **d'espionnage** spy network *ou* ring ♦ ~ **de résistants** resistance network ♦ ~ **d'intrigues** web of intrigue ♦ ~ **d'influence** network of influence

3 *(Ordin, Sci)* network ♦ **le ~ des ~x** *(= Internet)* the Internet ♦ ~ **étendu** wide-area network, WAN ♦ ~ **local** local area network, LAN ♦ ~ **neuronal** neural net(work) ♦ **sur le ~ Internet** on the Internet

♦ **en réseau** ♦ **être en ~** *[personnes, entreprises]* to be on the network ♦ **mettre des ordinateurs en ~** to network computers ♦ **entreprise en ~** networked company, company on the network ♦ **travailler en ~** to work on a network ♦ **la mise en ~ de l'information** information networking

4 *(= estomac de ruminant)* reticulum

5 *(Phys)* ~ **de diffraction** diffraction pattern ♦ ~ **cristallin** crystal lattice

réséda /ʀezeda/ NM reseda, mignonette

réservataire /ʀezɛʀvatɛʀ/ ADJ, NM ♦ **(héritier) ~** *rightful heir to the réserve légale*

réservation /ʀezɛʀvasjɔ̃/ GRAMMAIRE ACTIVE 48.3 NF *(à l'hôtel)* reservation; *(des places)* reservation, booking; *(Jur)* reservation ♦ ~ **de groupes** *(Tourisme)* group booking ♦ **bureau de ~** booking office ♦ **faire une ~ dans un hôtel/restaurant** to make a booking *ou* a reservation in a hotel/restaurant, to book *ou* reserve a room (in a hotel)/a table (in a restaurant) ♦ **"réservation obligatoire"** *(Rail)* "passengers with reservations only" ♦ **sur ~** by prior arrangement

réserve /ʀezɛʀv/ GRAMMAIRE ACTIVE 53.6 NF 1 *(= provision)* supply, reserve; *[de marchandises]* stock ♦ **les enfants ont une ~ énorme d'énergie** children have an enormous supply *ou* enormous reserves of energy ♦ **faire des ~s de sucre** to get in *ou* lay in a stock of sugar ♦ **heureusement, ils avaient une petite ~ (d'argent)** fortunately they had a little money put by *ou* a little money in reserve ♦ **monnaie de ~** *(Fin)* reserve currency ♦ **les ~s mondiales de pétrole** the world's oil reserves ♦ **les ~s (nutritives) de l'organisme** the organism's food reserves ♦ **il peut jeûner, il a des ~s !** *(hum)* it's no problem for him to go without food, he can live off his fat!

♦ **de** *ou* **en réserve** ♦ **avoir des provisions de** *ou* **en ~** to have provisions in reserve *ou* put by ♦ **mettre qch en ~** to put sth by, to put sth in reserve ♦ **avoir/garder qch en ~** *(gén)* to have/keep sth in reserve; *(Comm)* to have/keep sth in stock

2 *(= restriction)* reservation ♦ **faire** *ou* **émettre des ~s sur qch** to have reservations about sth

♦ **sans réserve** *[soutien]* unreserved; *[admiration]* unreserved, unqualified; *[consentement]* full; *[approuver, accepter]* unreservedly, without reservation, unhesitatingly

♦ **sous réserve de** subject to

♦ **sous réserve que** ♦ **le projet est accepté sous ~ que les délais soient respectés** the project has been approved on condition that the deadlines are met

♦ **sous toutes réserves** ♦ **je vous le dis sous toutes ~s** I can't vouch for *ou* guarantee the truth of what I'm telling you ♦ **tarif/horaire publié sous toutes ~s** prices/timetable correct at time of going to press

③ *(= prudence, discrétion)* reserve ◆ **être/demeurer** *ou* **se tenir sur la** ~ to be/remain very reserved ◆ **il m'a parlé sans** ~ he talked to me quite unreservedly *ou* openly ◆ **elle est d'une grande** ~ she's very reserved, she keeps herself to herself ◆ **devoir** *ou* **obligation de** ~ duty to preserve secrecy

④ *(Mil)* **la** ~ the reserve ◆ **les ~s** the reserves ◆ **officiers/armée de** ~ reserve officers/army

⑤ *(Sport)* **équipe/joueur de** ~ reserve *ou* second string *(US)* team/player

⑥ *(= territoire) [de nature, animaux]* reserve; *[d'Indiens]* reservation ◆ ~ **de pêche/chasse** fishing/hunting preserve ◆ ~ **naturelle** nature reserve ◆ ~ **ornithologique** *ou* **d'oiseaux** bird sanctuary

⑦ *[de musée]* reserve collection; *[de bibliothèque]* reserved section *(for valuable books)* ◆ **le livre est à la** ~ the book is in the reserved section

⑧ *(= entrepôt)* storehouse; *(= pièce)* storeroom; *(d'un magasin)* stockroom

⑨ *(Jur)* ~ **(héréditaire** *ou* **légale)** *part of the legacy which cannot be withheld from the rightful heirs*

réservé, e /ʀezɛʀve/ (ptp de **réserver**) **ADJ** ① *[place, salle]* reserved *(à qn/qch* for sb/sth); ◆ **chasse/pêche ~e** private hunting/fishing ◆ **cuvée ~e** vintage cuvée ◆ **j'ai une table ~e** I've got a table reserved *ou* booked ◆ **tous droits ~s** all rights reserved ◆ **voie ~e aux autobus** bus lane; → **quartier** ② *(= discret) [caractère, personne]* reserved ③ *(= dubitatif)* **il s'est montré très ~ sur la faisabilité du projet** he sounded very doubtful as to the feasibility of the project ◆ **je suis très ~ quant à sa réussite** I'm not too optimistic about his chances of success

réserver /ʀezɛʀve/ GRAMMAIRE ACTIVE 48.3 ▸ conjug 1 ◂

VT ① *(= louer) [+ place, chambre, table] [voyageur]* to book, to reserve; *[agence]* to reserve

② *(= mettre à part) [+ objets]* to keep, to save, to reserve *(à, pour* for); *[+ marchandises]* to keep, to put aside *ou* on one side *(à* for); ◆ **il nous a réservé deux places à côté de lui** he's kept *ou* saved us two seats beside him ◆ **on vous a réservé ce bureau** we've reserved this office for you ◆ ~ **le meilleur pour la fin** to keep *ou* save the best till last ◆ **ils réservent ces fauteuils pour les cérémonies** they keep these armchairs for (special) ceremonies ◆ **ces emplacements sont strictement réservés aux voitures du personnel** these parking places are strictly reserved for members of staff ◆ **nous réservons toujours un peu d'argent pour les dépenses imprévues** we always keep *ou* put a bit of money on one side for unexpected expenses

③ *(= destiner) [+ dangers, désagréments, joies]* to have in store *(à* for); *[+ accueil, châtiment]* to have in store, to reserve *(à* for); ◆ **cette expédition devait leur ~ bien des surprises** there were many surprises in store for them on that expedition ◆ **nous ne savons pas ce que l'avenir nous réserve** we don't know what the future has in store for us *ou* holds for us ◆ **le sort qui lui est réservé est peu enviable** he has an unenviable fate in store for him *ou* reserved for him ◆ **c'est à lui qu'il était réservé de marcher le premier sur la Lune** he was to be the first man to walk on the Moon ◆ **c'est à lui que fut réservé l'honneur de porter le drapeau** the honour of carrying the flag fell to him ◆ **tu me réserves ta soirée ?** are you free tonight? *ou* this evening?, could we do something this evening?

④ *(= remettre à plus tard) [+ réponse, opinion]* to reserve ◆ **le médecin préfère ~ son diagnostic** the doctor would rather not make a diagnosis yet

VPR **se réserver** ① *(= prélever)* to keep *ou* reserve for o.s. ◆ **il s'est réservé le meilleur morceau** he kept *ou* saved the best bit for himself

② *(= se ménager)* to save o.s. ◆ **se ~ pour une autre occasion** to save o.s. for another time ◆ **il ne mange pas maintenant, il se réserve pour le banquet** he isn't eating now - he's saving himself for the banquet ◆ **il faut savoir se ~** *(Sport)* one must learn to conserve *ou* save one's strength

③ ◆ **il se réserve d'intervenir plus tard** he's holding his fire ◆ **se ~ le droit de faire qch** to reserve the right to do sth

réserviste /ʀezɛʀvist/ **NM** reservist

réservoir /ʀezɛʀvwaʀ/ **NM** *(= cuve)* tank; *(= plan d'eau)* reservoir; *[de poissons]* fishpond; *[d'usine à gaz]* gasometer, gasholder; *(Bio) [d'infection]* reservoir ◆ **ce pays est un ~ de talents/de main-d'œuvre** *(fig)* this country has a wealth of talent/a huge pool of labour to draw on ◆ ~ **d'eau** *(gén, de voiture)* water tank; *(pour une maison)* water cistern; *(pour eau de pluie, en bois)* water butt; *(en ciment)* water tank ◆ ~ **d'essence** petrol *(Brit) ou* gas *(US)* tank

résidant, e /ʀezidɑ̃, ɑt/ **ADJ** resident

résidence /ʀezidɑ̃s/ **NF** *(gén)* residence; *(= immeuble)* (block of) residential flats *(Brit)*, residential apartment building *(US)* ◆ **établir sa ~ à** to take up residence in ◆ **changer de ~** to move (house) ◆ **en ~ à** *(Admin)* in residence at ◆ **en ~ surveillée** *ou* **forcée** under house arrest ◆ **la ~** *(Diplomatie)* the residency; → **assigner, certificat**

COMP **résidence hôtelière** residential *ou* apartment *(US)* hotel
résidence principale main home
résidence secondaire second home
résidence universitaire (university) hall(s) of residence, residence hall *(US)*, dormitory *(US)*

résident, e /ʀezidɑ̃, ɑt/ **NM,F** *(= étranger)* foreign national *ou* resident; *(= diplomate)* resident ◆ **ministre ~** resident minister ◆ **avoir le statut de ~ permanent en France** to have permanent resident status in France **ADJ** *(Ordin)* resident

résidentiel, -ielle /ʀezidɑ̃sjɛl/ **ADJ** *(= riche) [banlieue, quartier]* affluent, plush; *(= d'habitations)* residential

> ⚠ **résidentiel** au sens de 'riche' ne se traduit pas par **residential**.

résider /ʀezide/ ▸ conjug 1 ◂ **VI** *(lit, fig)* to reside; *[difficulté]* to lie *(en, dans* in); ◆ **il réside à cet hôtel/à Dijon** he resides *(frm)* at this hotel/in Dijon ◆ **après avoir résidé quelques temps en France** after living *ou* residing *(frm)* in France for some time, after having been resident in France for some time ◆ **le problème réside en ceci que ...** the problem lies in the fact that ...

résidu /ʀezidy/ **NM** ① *(= reste, Chim, fig)* residue *(NonC)*; *(Math)* remainder ② *(= déchets)* **~s** remnants, residue *(NonC)* ◆ **~s industriels** industrial waste

résiduel, -elle /ʀezidɥɛl/ **ADJ** residual

résignation /ʀeziɲasjɔ̃/ **NF** resignation *(à* to); ◆ **avec ~** with resignation, resignedly

résigné, e /ʀeziɲe/ (ptp de **résigner**) **ADJ** *[air, geste, ton]* resigned ◆ ~ **à son sort** resigned to his fate ◆ **il est ~** he is resigned to it ◆ **dire qch d'un air ~** to say sth resignedly

résigner /ʀeziɲe/ ▸ conjug 1 ◂ **VPR** **se résigner** to resign o.s. *(à* to); ◆ **il faudra s'y ~** we'll have to resign ourselves to it *ou* put up with it **VT** *(littér) [+ charge, fonction]* to relinquish, to resign

résiliable /ʀeziljabl/ **ADJ** *[contrat] (à terme)* which can be terminated, terminable; *(en cours)* which can be cancelled, cancellable, which can be rescinded

résiliation /ʀeziljasjɔ̃/ **NF** *[de contrat, bail, marché, abonnement] (à terme)* termination; *(en cours)* cancellation, rescinding; *[d'engagement]* cancellation

résilience /ʀeziljɑ̃s/ **NF** ① *[de métal]* ductility ② *(Psych)* resilience

résilient, e /ʀeziljɑ̃, jɑ̃t/ **ADJ** ① *[métal]* ductile ② *[personne]* resilient

résilier /ʀezilje/ ▸ conjug 7 ◂ **VT** *[+ contrat, bail, marché, abonnement] (à terme)* to terminate; *(en cours)* to cancel, to rescind; *[+ engagement]* to cancel

résille /ʀezij/ **NF** *(gén = filet)* net, netting *(NonC)*; *(pour les cheveux)* hairnet; *[de vitrail]* cames *(SPÉC)*, lead(s), leading *(NonC)*; → **bas²**

résine /ʀezin/ **NF** resin ◆ ~ **époxy** epoxy (resin) ◆ ~ **de synthèse** synthetic resin

résiné, e /ʀezine/ **ADJ, NM** ◆ **(vin) ~** retsina

résineux, -euse /ʀezinø, øz/ **ADJ** resinous **NM** coniferous tree ◆ **forêt de ~** coniferous forest

résistance /ʀezistɑ̃s/ **NF** ① *(= opposition)* resistance *(NonC) (à, contre* to); ◆ **la Résistance** *(Hist)* the (French) Resistance ◆ ~ **active/passive/armée** active/passive/armed resistance ◆ **l'armée dut se rendre après une ~ héroïque** the army was forced to surrender after putting up a heroic resistance *ou* a heroic fight ◆ **opposer une ~ farouche à un projet** to put up a fierce resistance to a project, to make a very determined stand against a project ◆ **malgré les ~s des syndicats** in spite of resistance from the trade unions ◆ **cela ne se fera pas sans ~** that won't be done without some opposition *ou* resistance ◆ **faire de la ~** *(fig)* to put up a fight; → **noyau**

② *(= endurance)* resistance, stamina ◆ ~ **à la fatigue** resistance to fatigue ◆ **il a une grande ~** *ou* **beaucoup de ~** he has great *ou* a lot of resistance *ou* stamina ◆ **coureur qui a de la ~/qui n'a pas de ~** runner who has lots of/who has no staying power ◆ **ce matériau offre une grande ~ au feu/aux chocs** this material is very heat-/shock-resistant ◆ **acier/béton à haute ~** high-tensile *ou* high-strength steel/concrete; → **pièce, plat²**

③ *(Élec) [de réchaud, radiateur]* element; *(= mesure)* resistance ◆ **unité de ~** unit of (electrical) resistance

④ *(Phys = force)* resistance ◆ ~ **d'un corps/de l'air** resistance of a body/of the air ◆ ~ **mécanique** mechanical resistance ◆ ~ **des matériaux** strength of materials ◆ **quand il voulut ouvrir la porte, il sentit une ~** when he tried to open the door he felt some resistance

résistant, e /ʀezistɑ̃, ɑt/ **ADJ** *[personne]* robust, tough; *[plante]* hardy; *[tissu, vêtements, métal]* strong, hard-wearing; *[couleur]* fast; *[bois]* hard ◆ **il est très ~** *(gén)* he has a lot of stamina; *(athlète)* he has lots of staying power ◆ ~ **à la chaleur** heatproof, heat-resistant ◆ ~ **aux chocs** shockproof, shock-resistant ◆ **bactéries ~es aux antibiotiques** bacteria that are resistant to antibiotics, antibiotic-resistant bacteria **NM,F** *(Hist)* (French) Resistance fighter ◆ **il a été ~** he was in the Resistance

résister /ʀeziste/ GRAMMAIRE ACTIVE 53.3 ▸ conjug 1 ◂ **résister à** **VT INDIR** ① *(= s'opposer à)* to resist ◆ **inutile de ~** it's pointless to resist, it's *ou* there's no point resisting ◆ ~ **au courant d'une rivière** to fight against the current of a river ◆ ~ **à la volonté de qn** to hold out against *ou* resist sb's will ◆ **il n'ose pas ~ à sa fille** he daren't stand up to his daughter ◆ **je n'aime pas que mes enfants me résistent** I don't like my children defying me ◆ **je n'ai pas résisté à cette robe** I couldn't resist (buying) this dress

② *(= surmonter) [+ émotion, adversité]* to overcome; *[+ fatigue]* to conquer; *[+ privations, cha-*

grin] to rise above; [+ douleur] to stand, to withstand ◆ **leur amour ne résista pas à cette infidélité** their relationship did not survive this infidelity

3 (= supporter) [+ sécheresse, gelée, vent] to withstand, to stand up to, to resist ◆ **ça a bien résisté à l'épreuve du temps** it has really stood the test of time ◆ **le plancher ne pourra pas ~ au poids** the floor won't support *ou* take the weight ◆ **la porte a résisté** the door held *ou* didn't give ◆ **couleur qui résiste au lavage** fast colour ◆ **tissu qui résiste au lavage en machine** machine-washable material, material which can be machine-washed ◆ **cette vaisselle résiste au feu** these dishes are heat-resistant *ou* heatproof ◆ **ce raisonnement ne résiste pas à l'analyse** this reasoning does not stand up to analysis

résistivité /Rezistivite/ NF (*Élec*) resistivity ◆ **la ~ du cuivre est très faible** copper has a very low resistance

resituer /R(ə)sitɥe/ ▸ conjug 1 ◂ VT [+ action, événement] to put back in its context ◆ **resituons cet événement dans son contexte économique** let's place this event in its economic context

résolu, e /Rezɔly/ GRAMMAIRE ACTIVE 35.2 (ptp de **résoudre**) ADJ [personne, ton, air] resolute ◆ **il est bien ~ à partir** he is firmly resolved *ou* he is determined to leave, he is set on leaving

résoluble /Rezɔlybl/ ADJ [problème] soluble; (*Chim*) resolvable; (*Jur*) [contrat] annullable, cancellable

résolument /Rezɔlymɑ̃/ ADV 1 (= totalement) resolutely ◆ **je suis ~ contre** I'm firmly against it, I'm resolutely opposed to it 2 (= courageusement) resolutely, steadfastly

résolutif, -ive /Rezɔlytif, iv/ ADJ, NM resolvent

résolution /Rezɔlysjɔ̃/ NF 1 (*gén, Pol* = *décision*) resolution ◆ **prendre la ~ de faire qch** to make a resolution to do sth, to resolve to do sth ◆ **ma ~ est prise** I've made my resolution ◆ **bonnes ~s** good resolutions ◆ **prendre de bonnes ~s pour le nouvel an** to make New Year's resolutions ◆ **adopter une ~** to adopt a resolution ◆ **la ~ 240 du Conseil de sécurité** Security Council resolution 240 ◆ **projet/proposition de ~** draft/proposed resolution

2 (= énergie) resolve, resolution ◆ **la ~ se lisait sur son visage** he had a determined *ou* resolute expression on his face

3 (= solution) solution ◆ **il attendait de moi la ~ de son problème** he expected me to give him a solution to his problem *ou* to solve his problem for him ◆ **la ~ du conflit** the resolution of the conflict ◆ **~ d'une équation** (*Math*) (re)solution of an equation ◆ **~ d'un triangle** resolution of a triangle

4 (*Jur* = *annulation*) [de contrat, vente] cancellation, annulment

5 (*Méd, Mus, Phys*) resolution ◆ **~ de l'eau en vapeur** resolution of water into steam

6 [d'image] resolution ◆ **image de haute ~** high-resolution image ◆ **écran (à) haute ~** high-resolution screen

résolutoire /RezɔlytwaR/ ADJ (*Jur*) resolutive

résonance /Rezɔnɑ̃s/ NF (*gén, Élec, Phon, Phys*) resonance (*NonC*); (*fig*) echo ◆ **être/entrer en ~** to be/start resonating ◆ **~ magnétique nucléaire** nuclear magnetic resonance ◆ **ce poème éveille en moi des ~s** (*littér*) this poem strikes a chord with me ◆ **le peintre a su rester en ~ avec son époque** the painter managed to stay in tune with his times; → **caisse**

résonateur /RezɔnatœR/ NM resonator ◆ **~ nucléaire** nuclear resonator

résonnant, e /Rezɔnɑ̃, ɑ̃t/ ADJ [voix] resonant

résonner /Rezɔne/ ▸ conjug 1 ◂ VI [son] to resonate, to reverberate, to resound; [pas] to resound; [salle] to be resonant ◆ **cloche qui résonne bien/faiblement** bell which resounds well/rings feebly ◆ **ne parle pas trop fort, ça résonne** don't speak too loudly because it echoes ◆ **~ de** to resound *ou* ring *ou* resonate with

résorber /RezɔRbe/ ▸ conjug 1 ◂ VT 1 (*Méd*) [+ tumeur, épanchement] to resorb ◆ **les cicatrices sont résorbées** the scar tissue has healed 2 (= éliminer) [+ chômage, inflation] to bring down, to reduce (gradually); [+ déficit, surplus] to absorb; [+ stocks] to reduce ◆ **trouver un moyen pour ~ la crise économique** to find some way of resolving the economic crisis VPR **se résorber** 1 (*Méd*) to be resorbed 2 [chômage] to be brought down *ou* reduced; [déficit] to be absorbed ◆ **l'embouteillage se résorbe peu à peu** the traffic jam is gradually breaking up

résorption /RezɔRpsjɔ̃/ NF 1 (*Méd*) [de tumeur, épanchement] resorption 2 [de chômage, inflation] bringing down, gradual reduction (*de* in); [de déficit, surplus] absorption

résoudre /RezudR/ ▸ conjug 51 ◂ VT 1 [+ mystère, équation, problème de maths] to solve; [+ dilemme, crise] to solve, to resolve; [+ difficultés] to solve, to resolve, to settle; [+ conflit] to settle, to resolve ◆ **j'ignore comment ce problème va se ~** *ou* **va être résolu** I can't see how this problem will be solved *ou* resolved

2 (= décider) [+ exécution, mort] to decide on, to determine on ◆ **~ de faire qch** to decide *ou* resolve to do sth, to make up one's mind to do sth ◆ **~ qn à faire qch** to prevail upon sb *ou* induce sb to do sth

3 (*Méd*) [+ tumeur] to resolve

4 (*Jur* = *annuler*) [+ contrat, vente] to cancel, to annul

5 (*Mus*) [+ dissonance] to resolve

6 (= transformer) **~ qch en cendres** to reduce sth to ashes ◆ **les nuages se résolvent en pluie/grêle** the clouds turn into rain/hail

VPR **se résoudre** ◆ **se ~ à faire qch** (= *se décider*) to resolve *ou* decide to do sth, to make up one's mind to do sth; (= *se résigner*) to resign *ou* reconcile o.s. to doing sth ◆ **il n'a pas pu se ~ à la quitter** he couldn't bring himself to leave her

respect /Rɛspɛ/ NM 1 (= considération) respect (*de, pour* for); ◆ **le ~ des principes démocratiques** respect for democratic principles ◆ **le ~ humain** † fear of the judgment of others ◆ **~ de soi** self-respect ◆ **avoir du ~ pour qn** to respect sb, to have respect for sb ◆ **il n'a aucun ~ pour le bien d'autrui** he has no respect *ou* consideration *ou* regard for other people's property ◆ **manquer de ~ à** *ou* **envers qn** to be disrespectful to(wards) sb ◆ **agir dans le ~ des règles/des droits de l'homme** to act in accordance with the rules/with human rights ◆ **par ~ pour sa mémoire** out of respect *ou* consideration for his memory ◆ **malgré** *ou* **sauf le ~ que je vous dois, sauf votre ~** († *ou hum*) with (all) respect, with all due respect

2 (= formule de politesse) **présenter ses ~s à qn** to pay one's respects to sb ◆ **présentez mes ~s à votre femme** give my regards *ou* pay my respects to your wife ◆ **mes ~s, mon colonel** good day to you, sir

3 (*locutions*) **tenir qn en ~** (*avec une arme*) to keep sb at a respectful distance *ou* at bay; (*fig*) to keep sb at bay

respectabilité /Rɛspɛktabilite/ NF respectability

respectable /Rɛspɛktabl/ ADJ (= honorable) respectable; (= important) respectable, sizeable ◆ **il avait un ventre ~** * (*hum*) he had quite a paunch

respecter /Rɛspɛkte/ GRAMMAIRE ACTIVE 38.3 ▸ conjug 1 ◂

VT 1 [+ personne] to respect, to have respect for ◆ **~ une femme** † to respect a woman's honour ◆ **faire ~ l'interdiction/l'embargo** to maintain the ban/embargo ◆ **se faire ~** to win respect ◆ **notre très respecté confrère** our highly esteemed colleague

2 [+ formes, loi, droits, environnement] to respect; [+ traditions] to respect, to have respect for; [+ calendrier, délais] to keep to; [+ cahier des charges, clause contractuelle] to abide by, to respect; [+ cessez-le-feu] to observe; [+ interdiction] to observe, to obey; [+ parole donnée, promesse] to keep ◆ **~ ses engagements** to honour one's commitments ◆ **les opinions de qn** to respect sb's opinions ◆ **respectez son sommeil** let him sleep, don't disturb him while he's asleep ◆ **respectez le matériel !** be careful with the equipment! ◆ **lessive qui respecte les couleurs** washing powder that is kind to colours ◆ **"respectez les pelouses"** "keep off the grass" ◆ **~ une minute de silence** to observe a minute's silence ◆ **ces voyous ne respectent rien** those louts show no respect for anything ◆ **classer des livres en respectant l'ordre alphabétique** to arrange books in alphabetical order ◆ **faire ~ la loi** to enforce the law ◆ **le programme a été scrupuleusement respecté** the programme was strictly adhered to

VPR **se respecter** to respect o.s. ◆ **tout professeur/juge/plombier qui se respecte** (*hum*) any self-respecting teacher/judge/plumber ◆ **il se respecte trop pour faire cela** he has too much self-respect to do that

respectif, -ive /Rɛspɛktif, iv/ ADJ respective

respectivement /Rɛspɛktivmɑ̃/ ADV respectively ◆ **ils ont ~ 9 et 12 ans** they are 9 and 12 years old respectively

respectueusement /Rɛspɛktɥøzmɑ̃/ ADV respectfully, with respect

respectueux, -euse /Rɛspɛktɥø, øz/ ADJ [langage, personne, silence] respectful (*envers, pour* to); ◆ **se montrer ~ du bien d'autrui** to show respect *ou* consideration for other people's property ◆ **~ des traditions** respectful of traditions ◆ **~ de la loi** respectful of the law, law-abiding ◆ **projet ~ de l'environnement** environment-friendly *ou* environmentally sound project ◆ **pays ~ des droits de l'homme** country that respects human rights ◆ **être peu ~ des autres** to show little respect for others ◆ **veuillez agréer, Monsieur (***ou* **Madame), mes salutations respectueuses** yours sincerely *ou* faithfully (*Brit*) ◆ **voulez-vous transmettre à votre mère mes hommages ~** please give my best regards *ou* my respects to your mother; → **distance**

NF **respectueuse** * (= prostituée) whore, prostitute, tart *

respirable /RɛspiRabl/ ADJ breathable ◆ **l'air n'y est pas ~** the air there is unbreathable ◆ **l'atmosphère n'est pas ~ dans cette famille** (*fig*) the atmosphere in this family is suffocating

respirateur /RɛspiRatœR/ NM ◆ **~ (artificiel)** (*gén*) respirator; (*pour malade dans le coma*) ventilator

respiration /RɛspiRasjɔ̃/ NF 1 (= fonction, action naturelle) breathing, respiration (*SPÉC*); (= souffle) breath ◆ **~ pulmonaire/cutanée/artificielle** *ou* **assistée** pulmonary/cutaneous/artificial respiration ◆ **~ entrecoupée** irregular breathing ◆ **~ courte** shortness of breath ◆ **avoir la ~ difficile** to have difficulty (in) *ou* trouble breathing ◆ **avoir la ~ bruyante** to breathe heavily *ou* noisily ◆ **faites trois ~s complètes** breathe in and out three times; → **couper, retenir** 2 (*Mus*) phrasing ◆ **respecter les ~s d'un poème** to respect the phrasing of a poem

respiratoire /ʀɛspiʀatwaʀ/ ADJ *[système, voies]* respiratory; *[troubles]* breathing *(épith)*, respiratory

respirer /ʀɛspiʀe/ ▸ conjug 1 ◂ VI 1 *(lit, Bio)* to breathe, to respire *(SPÉC)* ♦ **"respirez !"** *(chez le médecin)* "breathe in!", "take a deep breath!" ♦ **~ par la bouche/le nez** to breathe through one's mouth/one's nose ♦ **est-ce qu'il respire (encore) ?** is he (still) breathing? ♦ **~ avec difficulté** to have difficulty (in) *ou* trouble breathing, to breathe with difficulty ♦ **~ profondément** to breathe deeply, to take a deep breath ♦ **~ à pleins poumons** to breathe deeply; → **mentir**

2 *(fig)* (= *se détendre*) to get one's breath; (= *se rassurer*) to breathe again *ou* easy ♦ **ouf, on respire !** phew, we can breathe again!

VT 1 (= *inhaler*) to breathe (in), to inhale ♦ **~ un air vicié/le grand air** to breathe in foul air/ the fresh air ♦ **faire ~ des sels à qn** to make sb inhale smelling salts

2 (= *exprimer*) *[+ calme, bonheur, santé]* to radiate; *[+ honnêteté, franchise, orgueil, ennui]* to exude, to emanate ♦ **son attitude respirait la méfiance** his whole attitude was mistrustful, his attitude was clearly one of mistrust

resplendir /ʀɛsplɑ̃diʀ/ ▸ conjug 2 ◂ VI *[soleil, lune]* to shine; *[surface métallique]* to gleam, to shine ♦ **le lac/la neige resplendissait sous le soleil** the lake/the snow glistened *ou* glittered in the sun ♦ **le ciel resplendit au coucher du soleil** the sky is radiant *ou* ablaze at sunset ♦ **toute la cuisine resplendissait** the whole kitchen shone *ou* gleamed ♦ **il resplendissait de joie/de bonheur** he was aglow *ou* radiant with joy/with happiness

resplendissant, e /ʀɛsplɑ̃disɑ̃, ɑ̃t/ ADJ 1 *(lit* = *brillant) [soleil]* radiant, dazzling; *[lune]* shining, beaming; *[surface métallique]* gleaming, shining; *[lac, neige]* glistening, glittering; *[ciel]* radiant 2 *(fig* = *éclatant) [beauté, santé]* radiant; *[visage, yeux]* shining ♦ **avoir une mine ~e** to look radiant ♦ **être ~ de santé/de joie** to be glowing *ou* radiant with health/with joy

resplendissement /ʀɛsplɑ̃dismɑ̃/ NM *[de beauté, soleil]* brilliance

responsabilisation /ʀɛspɔ̃sabilizasjɔ̃/ NF ♦ **pour encourager la ~ des employés/des parents** to encourage employees/parents to assume more responsibility

responsabiliser /ʀɛspɔ̃sabilize/ ▸ conjug 1 ◂ VT ♦ **~ qn** (= *le rendre conscient de ses responsabilités*) to make sb aware of their responsibilities, to give sb a sense of responsibility; (= *lui donner des responsabilités*) to give sb responsibilities

responsabilité /ʀɛspɔ̃sabilite/ GRAMMAIRE ACTIVE 47.3

NF 1 (= *charge*) responsibility ♦ **de lourdes ~s** heavy responsibilities ♦ **assumer la ~ d'une affaire** to take on the responsibility for a matter ♦ **avoir la ~ de qn** to take *ou* have responsibility for sb ♦ **avoir la ~ de la gestion/de la sécurité** to be responsible for management/ for security ♦ **il fuit les ~s** he shuns (any) responsibility ♦ **il serait temps qu'il prenne ses ~s** it's (high) time he faced up to his responsibilities ♦ **ce poste comporte d'importantes ~s** this post involves *ou* carries considerable responsibilities ♦ **il a un poste de ~** he's in a position of responsibility ♦ **accéder à de hautes ~s** to reach a position of great responsibility

2 *(légale)* liability *(de* for); *(morale)* responsibility; *(ministérielle)* responsibility; *(financière)* (financial) accountability ♦ **emmener ces enfants en montagne, c'est une ~** it's a responsibility taking these children to the mountains ♦ **le Premier ministre a engagé la ~ de son gouvernement** ≈ the prime minister has sought a vote of confidence in his government ♦ **porter la ~ de qch** to take responsibility for sth ♦ **faire porter la ~ de qch à** *ou* **sur qn** to hold sb responsible for sth, to blame sb for sth ♦ **les bagages sont sous ta ~** you're responsible for *ou* in charge of the luggage, the luggage is your responsibility ♦ **ces élèves sont sous ma ~** I'm responsible for these pupils, these pupils are my responsibility *ou* are in my charge; → **assurance, société**

COMP **responsabilité atténuée** diminished responsibility
responsabilité civile civil liability
responsabilité collective collective responsibility
responsabilité contractuelle contractual liability
responsabilité pénale criminal responsibility
responsabilité pleine et entière full and entire responsibility

responsable /ʀɛspɔ̃sabl/ ADJ 1 (= *coupable*) responsible, to blame ♦ **Dupont, ~ de l'échec, a été renvoyé** Dupont, who was responsible *ou* to blame for the failure, has been dismissed ♦ **ils considèrent l'état défectueux des freins comme ~ (de l'accident)** they consider that defective brakes were to blame *ou* were responsible for the accident

2 *(légalement, de dégâts)* liable, responsible *(de* for); *(de délits)* responsible (de for); *(moralement)* responsible, accountable *(de* for; *devant qn* to sb); ♦ **reconnu ~ de ses actes** held responsible for his actions ♦ **il n'est pas ~ des délits/ dégâts commis par ses enfants** he is not responsible for the misdemeanours of/liable *ou* responsible for damage caused by his children ♦ **je le tiens pour ~ de l'accident** I hold him responsible *ou* I blame him for the accident ♦ **civilement/pénalement ~** liable in civil/criminal law ♦ **le ministre est ~ de ses décisions (devant le parlement)** the minister is responsible *ou* accountable (to Parliament) for his decisions

3 (= *chargé de*) **~ de** responsible for, in charge of

4 (= *sérieux*) *[attitude, employé, étudiant]* responsible ♦ **agir de manière ~** to behave responsibly

NMF 1 (= *coupable*) person responsible *ou* to blame ♦ **il faut trouver les ~s (de cette erreur)** we must find those responsible *ou* those who are to blame (for this error) ♦ **le seul ~ est l'alcool** alcohol alone is to blame *ou* is the culprit

2 (= *personne compétente*) person in charge ♦ **adressez-vous au ~** see the person in charge

3 (= *chef*) manager ♦ **~ des ventes** sales manager ♦ **~ marketing** marketing manager

4 (= *dirigeant*) official ♦ **les ~s du parti** the party officials ♦ **~ syndical** trade union official ♦ **~ politique** politician

> ⚠ Quand **responsable** est un nom, il ne se traduit pas par le mot anglais **responsible**.

resquillage* /ʀɛskijaʒ/ NM, **resquille*** /ʀɛskij/ NF *(dans l'autobus, le métro)* fare-dodging*, grabbing a free ride; *(au match, cinéma)* sneaking in, getting in on the sly

resquiller* /ʀɛskije/ ▸ conjug 1 ◂ VI (= *ne pas payer) (dans l'autobus, le métro)* to sneak a free ride, to dodge the fare; *(au match, cinéma)* to get in on the sly, to sneak in; (= *ne pas faire la queue*) to jump the queue *(Brit)*, to cut in (at the beginning of) the line *(US)* VT *[+ place]* to wangle*, to fiddle*

resquilleur, -euse* /ʀɛskijœʀ, øz/ NM,F (= *qui n'attend pas son tour) person who doesn't wait his or her turn*, queue-jumper *(Brit)*; (= *qui ne paie pas) (dans l'autobus)* fare-dodger* ♦ **expulser les ~s** *(au stade)* to throw out the people who have wangled their way in without paying

ressac /ʀəsak/ NM ♦ **le ~** (= *mouvement*) the backwash, the undertow; (= *vague*) the surf

ressaisir /ʀ(ə)seziʀ/ ▸ conjug 2 ◂ VT 1 *[+ branche, bouée]* to catch hold of again; *[+ pouvoir, occasion, prétexte]* to seize again; *(Jur) [+ biens]* to recover possession of 2 *[peur]* to grip (once) again; *[délire, désir]* to take hold of again 3 *(Jur)* **~ un tribunal d'une affaire** to lay a matter before a court again VPR **se ressaisir** 1 (= *reprendre son sang-froid*) to regain one's self-control; *(Sport : après avoir flanché)* to rally, to recover ♦ **ressaisissez-vous !** pull yourself together!, get a grip on yourself! ♦ **le coureur s'est bien ressaisi sur la fin** the runner rallied *ou* recovered well towards the end 2 ♦ **se ~ de** *[+ objet]* to recover; *[+ pouvoir]* to seize again

ressaisissement /ʀ(ə)sezismɑ̃/ NM recovery

ressassé, e /ʀ(ə)sase/ (ptp de **ressasser**) ADJ *[plaisanterie, thème]* worn out, hackneyed

ressasser /ʀ(ə)sase/ ▸ conjug 1 ◂ VT *[+ pensées, regrets]* to keep turning over; *[+ plaisanteries, conseil]* to keep trotting out

ressaut /ʀəso/ NM *(Géog)* (= *plan vertical*) rise; (= *plan horizontal*) shelf; *(Archit)* projection

ressauter /ʀ(ə)sote/ ▸ conjug 1 ◂ VI to jump again VT *[+ obstacle]* to jump (over) again

ressayer /ʀeseje/ ▸ conjug 8 ◂ VT, VI *(gén)* to try again; *(Couture)* ⇒ **réessayer**

ressemblance /ʀ(ə)sɑ̃blɑ̃s/ NF 1 (= *similitude visuelle*) resemblance, likeness; (= *analogie de composition*) similarity ♦ **~ presque parfaite entre deux substances** near perfect similarity of two substances ♦ **avoir** *ou* **offrir une ~ avec qch** to bear a resemblance *ou* likeness to sth ♦ **la ~ entre père et fils/ces montagnes est frappante** the resemblance between father and son/these mountains is striking ♦ **ce peintre s'inquiète peu de la ~** this painter cares very little about getting a good likeness ♦ **toute ~ avec des personnes existant ou ayant existé est purement fortuite** any resemblance to any person living or dead is purely accidental 2 (= *trait*) resemblance; (= *analogie*) similarity

ressemblant, e /ʀ(ə)sɑ̃blɑ̃, ɑ̃t/ ADJ *[photo, portrait]* lifelike, true to life ♦ **vous êtes très ~ sur cette photo** this is a very good photo of you ♦ **il a fait d'elle un portrait très ~** he painted a very good likeness of her ♦ **ce n'est pas très ~** it's not a very good likeness

ressembler /ʀ(ə)sɑ̃ble/ GRAMMAIRE ACTIVE 32.4, 32.5 ▸ conjug 1 ◂

VT INDIR **ressembler à** 1 (= *être semblable à*) to be like; *(physiquement)* to be *ou* look like, to resemble ♦ **il me ressemble beaucoup physiquement/moralement** he is very like me in looks/in character ♦ **juste quelques accrochages, rien qui ressemble à une offensive** just a few skirmishes - nothing that you could call a real offensive ♦ **il ne ressemble en rien à l'image que je me faisais de lui** he's nothing like how I imagined him ♦ **à quoi ressemble-t-il ?*** what does he look like?, what's he like? ♦ **ton fils s'est roulé dans la boue, regarde à quoi il ressemble !*** your son has been rolling in the mud - just look at the state of him! ♦ **ça ne ressemble à rien !*** *[attitude]* it makes no sense at all!; *[peinture, objet]* it's like nothing on earth! ♦ **à quoi ça ressemble de crier comme ça !*** what do you mean by shouting like that!

2 (= *être typique de*) **cela lui ressemble bien de dire ça** it's just like him *ou* it's typical of him to say that ♦ **cela ne te ressemble pas** that's (most) unlike you *ou* not like you

VPR **se ressembler** *(physiquement, visuellement)* to look *ou* be alike; *(moralement, par ses éléments)* to be alike ♦ **ils se ressemblent comme deux**

gouttes d'eau they're as like as two peas (in a pod) ◆ **tu ne te ressembles plus depuis ton accident** you're not yourself since your accident ◆ **aucune ville ne se ressemble** no two towns are alike ◆ **dans cette rue, il n'y a pas deux maisons qui se ressemblent** no two houses are the same in this street ◆ **toutes les grandes villes se ressemblent** all big towns are alike *ou* the same ◆ **qui se ressemble s'assemble** *(Prov)* birds of a feather flock together *(Prov)* → **jour**

> ⚠ Attention à ne pas traduire automatiquement **ressembler** par **to resemble**, qui est d'un registre plus soutenu.

ressemelage /ʀ(ə)səm(ə)laʒ/ **NM** soling, resoling

ressemeler /ʀ(ə)səm(ə)le/ ▸ conjug 4 ◂ **VT** to sole, to resole

ressemer /ʀəs(ə)me, ʀ(ə)səme/ ▸ conjug 5 ◂ **VT** to resow, to sow again **VPR** **se ressemer** ◆ **ça s'est ressemé tout seul** it (re)seeded itself

ressentiment /ʀ(ə)sɑ̃timɑ̃/ **NM** resentment *(contre* against; *de* at); ◆ **éprouver du ~** to feel resentful *(à l'égard de* towards); ◆ **il en a gardé du ~** it has remained a sore point with him ◆ **avec ~** resentfully, with resentment

ressentir /ʀ(ə)sɑ̃tiʀ/ ▸ conjug 16 ◂ **VT** *[+ douleur, sentiment, coup]* to feel; *[+ sensation]* to feel, to experience; *[+ perte, insulte, privation]* to feel, to be affected by ◆ **il ressentit les effets de cette nuit de beuverie** he felt the effects of that night's drinking ◆ **il ressent toute chose profondément** he feels everything deeply, he is deeply affected by everything **VPR** **se ressentir** 1 ◆ **se ~ de** *[travail, qualité]* to show the effects of; *[personne, communauté]* to feel the effects of ◆ **la qualité/son travail s'en ressent** the quality/his work is affected, it is telling on the quality/his work ◆ **l'athlète se ressentait du manque de préparation** the athlete's lack of preparation told on his performance 2 * **s'en ~ pour** to feel up to ◆ **il ne s'en ressent pas pour faire ça** he doesn't feel up to doing that

resserre /ʀəsɛʀ/ **NF** *(= cabane)* shed; *(= réduit)* store, storeroom

resserré, e /ʀ(ə)seʀe/ (ptp de **resserrer**) **ADJ** *[chemin, vallée]* narrow ◆ **maison ~e entre des immeubles** house squeezed between high buildings ◆ **veste ~e à la taille** jacket fitted at the waist

resserrement /ʀ(ə)sɛʀmɑ̃/ **NM** 1 *(= action) [de nœud, étreinte]* tightening; *[de pores]* closing; *[de liens, amitié]* strengthening; *[de vallée]* narrowing; *[de crédits]* tightening, squeezing 2 *(= goulet) [de route, vallée]* narrow part

resserrer /ʀ(ə)seʀe/ ▸ conjug 1 ◂ **VT** 1 *[+ vis]* to tighten (up); *[+ nœud, ceinture, étreinte]* to tighten ◆ **produit qui resserre les pores** product which helps (to) close the pores; → **boulon** 2 *[+ discipline]* to tighten up; *[+ cercle, filets]* to draw tighter, to tighten; *[+ liens, amitié]* to strengthen; *[+ récit]* to tighten up, to compress; *[+ crédits]* to tighten, to squeeze ◆ **l'armée resserre son étau autour de la capitale** the army is tightening its grip *ou* the noose around the capital **VPR** **se resserrer** 1 *[nœud, étreinte]* to tighten; *[pores, mâchoire]* to close; *[chemin, vallée]* to narrow ◆ **l'étau se resserre** *(fig)* the noose is tightening 2 *[liens affectifs]* to grow stronger; *[cercle, groupe]* to draw in ◆ **le filet/l'enquête se resserrait autour de lui** the net/the inquiry was closing in on him

resservir /ʀ(ə)sɛʀviʀ/ ▸ conjug 14 ◂ **VT** 1 *(= servir à nouveau) [+ plat]* to serve (up) again *(à* to) to dish up again * *(péj) (à* for)
2 *(= servir davantage) [+ dîneur]* to give another *ou* a second helping to ◆ **~ de la soupe/viande** to give another *ou* a second helping of soup/meat
3 *[+ thème, histoire]* to trot out again ◆ **les thèmes qu'ils nous resservent depuis des années** the themes that they have been feeding us with *ou* trotting out to us for years
VI 1 *[vêtement usagé, outil]* to serve again, to do again ◆ **ça peut toujours ~** it may come in handy *ou* be useful again ◆ **cet emballage peut ~** this packaging can be used again ◆ **ce manteau pourra te ~** you may find this coat useful again (some time)
2 *(Tennis)* to serve again
VPR **se resservir** 1 *[dîneur]* to help o.s. again, to take another helping ◆ **se ~ de fromage/viande** to help o.s. to some more cheese/meat, to take another helping of cheese/meat
2 *(= réutiliser)* **se ~ de** *[+ outil]* to use again; *[+ vêtement]* to wear again

ressort¹ /ʀ(ə)sɔʀ/ **NM** 1 *(= pièce de métal)* spring ◆ **faire ~** to spring back ◆ **à ~** *[mécanisme, pièce]* spring-loaded; → **matelas, mouvoir**
2 *(= énergie)* spirit ◆ **avoir du/manquer de ~** to have/lack spirit ◆ **un être sans ~** a spiritless individual
3 *(littér = motivation)* **les ~s psychologiques de qn** sb's psychological motives ◆ **les ~s qui le font agir** what motivates him, what makes him tick* ◆ **les ~s secrets de l'esprit humain/de l'organisation** the inner *ou* secret workings of the human mind/the organization ◆ **les ~s secrets de cette affaire** the hidden undercurrents of this affair
4 († = *élasticité)* resilience
COMP **ressort à boudin** spiral spring
ressort hélicoïdal helical *ou* coil spring
ressort à lames leafspring
ressort de montre hairspring
ressort de suspension suspension spring
ressort de traction drawspring

ressort² /ʀ(ə)sɔʀ/ **NM** 1 *(Admin, Jur = compétence)* **être du ~ de** to be *ou* fall within the competence of ◆ **c'est du ~ de la justice/du chef de service** that is for the law/the head of department to deal with, that is the law's/the head of department's responsibility ◆ **ce n'est pas de mon ~** *(fig)* this is not my responsibility, this is outside my remit 2 *(Jur = circonscription)* jurisdiction ◆ **dans le ~ du tribunal de Paris** in the jurisdiction of the courts of Paris 3 *(Jur)* **en dernier ~** without appeal; *(fig = en dernier recours)* as a last resort; *(= finalement)* in the last resort *ou* instance

ressortir¹ /ʀ(ə)sɔʀtiʀ/ ▸ conjug 16 ◂ **VI** *(avec aux être)* 1 *[personne]* to go *ou* come out; *[objet]* to come out; *(une nouvelle fois)* to go *(ou* come) out again ◆ **je suis ressorti faire des courses** I went out shopping again ◆ **il a jeté un coup d'œil aux journaux et il est ressorti** he glanced at the newspapers and went (back) out again ◆ **des désirs refoulés/des souvenirs qui ressortent** repressed desires/memories which resurface *ou* come back up to the surface ◆ **le rouge/7 est ressorti** the red/7 came out *ou* up again ◆ **ce film ressort sur nos écrans** this film is showing again *ou* has been re-released
2 *(= contraster) [détail, couleur, qualité]* to stand out ◆ **faire ~ qch** to make sth stand out, to bring out sth
VT INDIR **ressortir de** *(= résulter)* to emerge from, to be the result of ◆ **il ressort de tout cela que personne ne savait** what emerges from all that is that no one knew
VT *(avec aux avoir : à nouveau) [+ vêtements d'hiver, outil]* to take out again; *[+ film]* to re-release, to bring out again; *(Comm) [+ modèle]* to bring out again ◆ **le soleil revenant, ils ont ressorti les chaises sur la terrasse** when the sun came out again, they took *ou* brought the chairs back onto the terrace ◆ **j'ai encore besoin du registre, ressors-le** I still need the register so take *ou* get it (back) out again ◆ **il (nous) ressort toujours les mêmes blagues** he always trots out the same old jokes ◆ **~ un vieux projet d'un tiroir** to dust off an old project

ressortir² /ʀ(ə)sɔʀtiʀ/ ▸ conjug 2 ◂ **ressortir à VT INDIR** *[+ tribunal]* to come under the jurisdiction of; *(frm) [+ domaine]* to be the concern *ou* province of, to pertain to ◆ **ceci ressort à une autre juridiction** this comes under *ou* belongs to a separate jurisdiction

ressortissant, e /ʀ(ə)sɔʀtisɑ̃, ɑ̃t/ **NM,F** national ◆ **~ français** French national *ou* citizen

ressouder /ʀ(ə)sude/ ▸ conjug 1 ◂ **VT** *[+ objet brisé]* to solder together again; *(= souder à nouveau) [+ petite pièce]* to resolder; *[+ grosse pièce]* to reweld; *[+ amitié]* to patch up, to renew the bonds of; *[+ équipe, parti]* to reunite **VPR** **se ressouder** *[os, fracture]* to knit, to mend; *[amitié]* to mend ◆ **l'opposition s'est ressoudée autour de son chef** the opposition has reunited around its leader

ressource /ʀ(ə)suʀs/ **NF** 1 *(= moyens matériels, financiers)* **~s** *[de pays]* resources; *[de famille, personne]* resources, means ◆ **~s personnelles** personal resources ◆ **avoir de maigres ~s** to have limited *ou* slender resources *ou* means ◆ **une famille sans ~s** a family with no means of support *ou* no resources ◆ **~s naturelles/pétrolières** natural/petroleum resources ◆ **les ~s en hommes d'un pays** the manpower resources of a country ◆ **les ~s de l'État** *ou* **du Trésor** the financial resources of the state ◆ **directeur/responsable des ~s humaines** director/head of human resources
2 *(= possibilités)* **~s** *[d'artiste, aventurier, sportif]* resources; *[d'art, technique, système]* possibilities ◆ **les ~s de son talent/imagination** the resources of one's talent/imagination ◆ **ce système a des ~s variées** this system has a wide range of possible applications ◆ **les ~s de la langue française** the resources of the French language ◆ **les ~s de la photographie** the various possibilities of photography ◆ **être à bout de ~s** to have exhausted all the possibilities, to be at the end of one's resources ◆ **homme/femme de ~(s)** man/woman of resource, resourceful man/woman
3 *(= recours)* **n'ayant pas la ~ de lui parler** having no means *ou* possibility of speaking to him ◆ **je n'ai d'autre ~ que de lui téléphoner** the only course open to me is to phone him, I have no other option but to phone him ◆ **sa seule ~ était de ...** the only way *ou* course open to him was to ... ◆ **vous êtes ma dernière ~** you are my last resort ◆ **en dernière ~** as a last resort
4 *(Ordin)* resource
5 ◆ **avoir de la ~** *[cheval, sportif]* to have strength in reserve ◆ **il y a de la ~** * there's plenty more where that came from

ressourcer (se) /ʀ(ə)suʀse/ ▸ conjug 3 ◂ **VPR** *(= retrouver ses racines)* to go back to one's roots; *(= recouvrer ses forces)* to recharge one's batteries

ressouvenir (se) /ʀ(ə)suv(ə)niʀ/ ▸ conjug 22 ◂ **VPR** *(littér)* ◆ **se ~ de** to remember, to recall ◆ **faire (se) ~ qn de qch** to remind sb of sth ◆ **ce bruit le fit se ~** *ou (littér)* **lui fit ~ de son accident** when he heard the noise he was reminded of his accident

ressurgir /ʀ(ə)syʀʒiʀ/ ▸ conjug 2 ◂ **VI** ⇒ **resurgir**

ressusciter /ʀesysite/ ▸ conjug 1 ◂ **VI** 1 *(Rel)* to rise (from the dead) ◆ **Christ est ressuscité !** Christ is risen! ◆ **le Christ ressuscité** the risen Christ ◆ **ressuscité d'entre les morts** risen from the dead
2 *(fig = renaître) [malade]* to come back to life, to revive; *[sentiment, souvenir]* to revive, to reawaken

VT [1] *(lit)* *[+ mourant]* to resuscitate, to restore *ou* bring back to life; *(Rel)* to raise (from the dead) ◆ **buvez ça, ça ressusciterait un mort*** drink that - it'll put new life into you ◆ **bruit à ~ les morts** noise that could wake the dead
[2] *(= régénérer)* *[+ malade]* to revive; *[+ projet, entreprise]* to inject new life into, to revive
[3] *(= faire revivre)* *[+ sentiment]* to revive, to reawaken; *[+ héros, mode]* to bring back, to resurrect *(péj)*; *[+ passé, coutume, loi]* to revive, to resurrect *(péj)*

> ⚠ **ressusciter** se traduit par **to resuscitate** uniquement au sens de 'ranimer'.

restant, e /ʀɛstɑ̃, ɑ̃t/ ADJ remaining ◆ **le seul cousin ~** the sole *ou* one remaining cousin, the only *ou* one cousin left *ou* remaining; → **poste¹** NM [1] *(= l'autre partie)* **le ~** the rest, the remainder ◆ **tout le ~ des provisions était perdu** all the rest *ou* remainder of the supplies were lost ◆ **pour le ~ de mes jours** *ou* **de ma vie** for the rest of my life [2] *(= ce qui est en trop)* **accommoder un ~ de poulet** to make a dish with some left-over chicken ◆ **faire une écharpe dans un ~ de tissu** to make a scarf out of some left-over material

restau* /ʀɛsto/ NM (abrév de **restaurant**) ⇒ **resto**

restaurant /ʀɛstɔʀɑ̃/ NM restaurant ◆ **on va au ~ ?** shall we go to a restaurant?, shall we eat out?
COMP **restaurant d'entreprise** staff canteen, staff dining room
restaurant gastronomique gourmet restaurant
restaurant libre-service self-service restaurant, cafeteria
restaurant rapide fast-food restaurant
restaurant scolaire school canteen
restaurant self-service ⇒ **restaurant libre-service**
restaurant à thème themed restaurant
restaurant universitaire university refectory *ou* canteen *ou* cafeteria

restaurateur, -trice /ʀɛstɔʀatœʀ, tʀis/ NM,F [1] *[de tableau, dynastie]* restorer [2] *(= aubergiste)* restaurant owner, restaurateur

restauration /ʀɛstɔʀasjɔ̃/ NF [1] *(= rétablissement, réparation)* restoration ◆ **la Restauration** *(Hist)* the Restoration *(of the Bourbons in 1830)* ◆ **la ~ de la démocratie est en bonne voie dans ce pays** democracy is well on the way to being restored in this country [2] *(= hôtellerie)* catering ◆ **il travaille dans la ~** he works in catering ◆ **la ~ rapide** the fast-food industry *ou* trade ◆ **la ~ collective/scolaire** institutional/school catering [3] *(Ordin)* *[de fichier]* restore

> ⚠ Au sens culinaire, **restauration** ne se traduit pas par le mot anglais **restoration**.

restaurer /ʀɛstɔʀe/ ► conjug 1 ◄ VT [1] *[+ dynastie, paix, tableau]* to restore [2] *(= nourrir)* to feed [3] *(Ordin)* to restore VPR **se restaurer** to have something to eat

restauroute /ʀɛstɔʀut/ NM ⇒ **restoroute**

reste /ʀɛst/ NM [1] *(= l'autre partie)* **le ~** the rest ◆ **le ~ de sa vie/du temps/des hommes** the rest of his life/of the time/of humanity ◆ **j'ai lu trois chapitres, je lirai le ~ (du livre) demain** I've read three chapters and I'll read the rest (of the book) tomorrow ◆ **le ~ du lait** the rest of the milk, what is left of the milk ◆ **préparez les bagages, je m'occupe du ~** get the luggage ready and I'll see to the rest *ou* to everything else
[2] *(= ce qui est en trop)* **il y a un ~ de fromage/de tissu** there's some *ou* a piece of cheese/material left over ◆ **s'il y a un ~, je fais une omelette/une écharpe** if there's some *ou* any left *ou* left over I'll make an omelette/a scarf ◆ **ce ~ de poulet ne suffira pas** this left-over chicken won't be enough ◆ **s'il y a un ~ (de laine), j'aimerais faire une écharpe** if there's some spare (wool) *ou* some (wool) to spare, I'd like to make a scarf ◆ **un ~ de tendresse/de pitié la poussa à rester** a last trace *ou* a remnant of tenderness/of pity moved her to stay
[3] *(Math = différence)* remainder
[4] *(locutions)* **avoir de l'argent/du temps de ~** to have money/time left over *ou* in hand *ou* to spare ◆ **il ne voulait pas être** *ou* **demeurer en ~ avec eux** he didn't want to be outdone by them *ou* one down on them* *(Brit)* ◆ **sans demander son ~** *(= sans plus de cérémonie)* without further ado; *(= sans protester)* without a murmur ◆ **il a empoché l'argent sans demander son ~** he pocketed the money without asking any questions ◆ **il est menteur, paresseux et (tout) le ~** he's untruthful, lazy and everything else as well ◆ **avec la grève, la neige et (tout) le ~, ils ne peuvent pas venir** what with the strike, the snow and everything else *ou* all the rest, they can't come ◆ **pour le ~** *ou* **quant au ~ (nous verrons bien)** (as) for the rest (we'll have to see) ◆ **il a été opéré, le temps fera le ~** he's had an operation, time will do the rest
◆ **du reste, au reste** *(littér)* (and) besides, (and) what's more ◆ **nous la connaissons, du ~, très peu** besides *ou* moreover, we hardly know her at all
NMPL **restes** *(= nourriture)* the left-overs; *(frm = dépouille mortelle)* the (mortal) remains ◆ **les ~s de** *[+ repas]* the remains of, the leftovers from; *[+ fortune, bâtiment]* the remains of, what is (*ou* was) left of ◆ **donner les ~s au chien** to give the scraps *ou* leftovers to the dog ◆ **elle a de beaux ~s** *(hum)* she's still a fine(-looking) woman

rester /ʀɛste/ ► conjug 1 ◄ VI [1] *(dans un lieu)* to stay, to remain; *(* = habiter)* to live ◆ **~ au lit** *[paresseux]* to stay *ou* lie in bed; *[malade]* to stay in bed ◆ **~ à la maison** to stay *ou* remain in the house *ou* indoors ◆ **~ chez soi** to stay at home *ou* in ◆ **~ au** *ou* **dans le jardin/à la campagne/à l'étranger** to stay *ou* remain in the garden/in the country/abroad ◆ **~ (à) dîner/déjeuner** to stay for *ou* to dinner/lunch ◆ **je ne peux ~ que 10 minutes** I can only stay *ou* stop* 10 minutes ◆ **la voiture est restée dehors/au garage** the car stayed *ou* remained outside/in the garage ◆ **la lettre va certainement ~ dans sa poche** the letter is sure to stay in his pocket ◆ **un os lui est resté dans la gorge** a bone got stuck in his throat ◆ **ça m'est resté là*** *ou* **en travers de la gorge** *(lit, fig)* it stuck in my throat ◆ **restez où vous êtes** stay *ou* remain where you are ◆ **~ à regarder la télévision** to stay watching television ◆ **nous sommes restés deux heures à l'attendre** we stayed there waiting for him for two hours ◆ **naturellement, ça reste entre nous** of course we shall keep this to ourselves *ou* this is strictly between ourselves ◆ **il ne peut pas ~ en place** he can't keep still
[2] *(dans un état)* to stay, to remain ◆ **~ éveillé/immobile** to keep *ou* stay awake/still ◆ **~ sans bouger/sans rien dire** to stay *ou* remain motionless/silent ◆ **~ indifférent devant qch/insensible à qch** to remain indifferent to sth/impervious to sth ◆ **~ maître de soi** to maintain one's composure ◆ **~ célibataire** to stay single, to remain unmarried ◆ **~ handicapé à vie** to be handicapped for life ◆ **~ dans l'ignorance** to remain in ignorance ◆ **~ en fonction** to remain in office ◆ **~ debout** *(lit)* to stand, to remain standing; *(= ne pas se coucher)* to stay up ◆ **je suis resté assis/debout toute la journée** I've been sitting/standing (up) all day ◆ **ne reste pas là les bras croisés** don't just stand there with your arms folded ◆ **il est resté très timide** he has remained *ou* he is still very shy ◆ **il est et restera toujours maladroit** he is clumsy and he always will be ◆ **cette coutume est restée en honneur dans certains pays** this custom is still honoured in certain countries ◆ **le centre-ville est resté paralysé toute la journée** the city centre was choked with traffic *ou* gridlocked all day; → **lettre, panne¹, plan¹**
[3] *(= subsister)* to be left, to remain ◆ **rien ne reste de l'ancien château** nothing is left *ou* remains of the old castle ◆ **c'est le seul parent qui leur reste** he's their only remaining relative, he's the only relative they have left ◆ **c'est tout l'argent qui leur reste** that's all the money they have left ◆ **10 km restaient à faire** there were still 10 km to go
[4] *(= durer)* to last, to live on ◆ **c'est une œuvre qui restera** it's a work which will live on *ou* which will last ◆ **le désir passe, la tendresse reste** desire passes, tenderness lives on ◆ **le surnom lui est resté** the nickname stayed with him, the nickname stuck
[5] *(locutions)*
◆ **rester sur** ◆ **rester sur une impression** to retain an impression ◆ **je suis resté sur ma faim** *(après un repas)* I still felt hungry; *(à la fin d'une histoire)* I felt there was something missing ◆ **sa remarque m'est restée sur le cœur** his remark (still) rankles (in my mind) ◆ **mon déjeuner m'est resté sur l'estomac** my lunch is still sitting there ◆ **ça m'est resté sur l'estomac*** *(fig)* it still riles me*, I still feel sore about it* ◆ **ne restons pas sur un échec** let's not give up just because we failed
◆ **en ~ à** *(= ne pas dépasser)* to go no further than ◆ **ils en sont restés à quelques baisers/des discussions préliminaires** they got no further than a few kisses/preliminary discussions ◆ **les gens du village en sont restés à la bougie** the villagers are still using candles ◆ **les pourparlers en sont restés là** they only got that far *ou* that is as far as they got in their discussions ◆ **les choses en sont restées là jusqu'à ...** nothing more happened until ..., nothing more was done (about it) until ... ◆ **où en étions-nous restés dans notre lecture ?** where did we leave off in our reading? ◆ **restons-en là** let's leave off there, let's leave it at that
◆ **y rester*** *(= mourir)* to die ◆ **il a bien failli y ~** that was nearly the end of him
VB IMPERS ◆ **il reste encore un peu de jour/de pain** there's still a little daylight/bread left ◆ **il leur reste juste de quoi vivre** they have just enough left to live on ◆ **il me reste à faire ceci** I still have this to do, there's still this for me to do ◆ **il reste beaucoup à faire** much remains to be done, there's a lot left to do ◆ **il nous reste son souvenir** we still have our memories of him ◆ **il ne me reste que toi** you're all I have left ◆ **il n'est rien resté de leur maison/des provisions** nothing remained *ou* was left of their house/of the supplies ◆ **le peu de temps qu'il lui restait à vivre** the short time that he had left to live ◆ **il ne me reste qu'à vous remercier** it only remains for me to thank you ◆ **il restait à faire 50 km** there were 50 km still *ou* left to go ◆ **est-ce qu'il vous reste assez de force pour terminer ce travail ?** do you have enough strength left to finish this job? ◆ **quand on a été en prison, il en reste toujours quelque chose** when you've been in prison something of it always stays with you ◆ **(il) reste à savoir si/à prouver que ...** it remains to be seen if/to be proved that ... ◆ **il reste que ..., il n'en reste pas moins que ...** the fact remains (nonetheless) that ..., it is nevertheless a fact that ... ◆ **il reste entendu que ...** it remains *ou* is still quite understood that ...

restituer /ʀɛstitɥe/ ► conjug 1 ◄ VT [1] *(= redonner)* *[+ objet volé]* to return, to restore *(à qn* to sb); *[+ argent]* to return, to refund *(à qn* to sb)

2 *(= reconstituer)* *[+ fresque, texte, inscription]* to reconstruct, to restore; *[+ son]* to reproduce ◆ **un texte enfin restitué dans son intégralité** a text finally restored in its entirety
3 *(= recréer)* to recreate ◆ **le film restitue bien l'atmosphère de l'époque** the film successfully recreates the atmosphere of the period ◆ **appareil qui restitue fidèlement les sons** apparatus which gives faithful sound reproduction ◆ **il n'a pas su ~ la complexité des sentiments du héros** he wasn't able to render the complexity of the hero's feelings
4 *(= libérer)* *[+ énergie, chaleur]* to release ◆ **l'énergie emmagasinée est entièrement restituée sous forme de chaleur** the energy stored up is entirely released in the form of heat

restitution /ʀɛstitysjɔ̃/ **NF** 1 *[d'objet volé, argent]* return ◆ **pour obtenir la ~ des territoires** to secure the return of the territories 2 *[de fresque, texte, inscription]* reconstruction, restoration; *[de son]* reproduction 3 *[d'énergie, chaleur]* release

resto * /ʀɛsto/ **NM** (abrév de **restaurant**) restaurant ◆ **~ U** university refectory *ou* canteen *ou* cafeteria ◆ **les Restos du cœur** *charity set up to provide food for the homeless during the winter*

restoroute ® /ʀɛstoʀut/ **NM** *[de route]* roadside restaurant; *[d'autoroute]* motorway *(Brit)* *ou* highway *(US)* restaurant

restreindre /ʀɛstʀɛ̃dʀ/ ► conjug 52 ◄ **VT** *[+ quantité, production, dépenses]* to restrict, to limit, to cut down; *[+ ambition]* to restrict, to limit, to curb ◆ **nous restreindrons notre étude à quelques exemples** we will restrict our study to a few examples ◆ **~ le crédit** to restrict credit **VPR** **se restreindre** 1 *(dans ses dépenses, sur la nourriture)* to cut down (*sur* on) 2 *(= diminuer)* *[production, tirage]* to decrease, to go down; *[espace]* to decrease, to diminish; *[ambition, champ d'action]* to narrow; *[sens d'un mot]* to become more restricted ◆ **le champ de leur enquête se restreint** the scope of their inquiry is narrowing

restreint, e /ʀɛstʀɛ̃, ɛ̃t/ (ptp de **restreindre**) **ADJ** *[autorité, emploi, production, vocabulaire]* limited, restricted; *[espace, moyens, nombre, personnel]* limited; *[sens]* restricted ◆ **~ à** confined *ou* restricted *ou* limited to; → **comité, suffrage**

restrictif, -ive /ʀɛstʀiktif, iv/ **ADJ** restrictive

restriction /ʀɛstʀiksjɔ̃/ **NF** 1 *(= action)* restriction, limiting, limitation
2 *(= réduction)* restriction ◆ **~s** *[de personnel, consommation, crédit]* restrictions ◆ **~s budgétaires** budget(ary) constraints *ou* restrictions ◆ **prendre des mesures de ~** to adopt restrictive measures ◆ **~s à l'exportation/importation** export/import restraints
3 *(= condition)* qualification; *(= réticence)* reservation ◆ **~ mentale** mental reservation ◆ **faire** *ou* **émettre des ~s** to express some reservations ◆ **avec ~** *ou* **des ~s** with some qualification(s) *ou* reservation(s)
◆ **sans restriction** *[soutien, attachement]* unqualified, unconditional; *[accepter, soutenir]* unreservedly ◆ **approuver qch sans ~** to give one's unqualified approval to sth, to accept sth without reservation ◆ **ce régime alimentaire autorise sans ~ les fruits** this diet places no restriction on the consumption of fruit ◆ **ce pays accueille sans ~ les immigrants** this country allows unrestricted entry to *ou* has an open door policy towards immigrants

restructuration /ʀəstʀyktyʀasjɔ̃/ **NF** restructuring ◆ **notre groupe est en pleine ~** our company is going through a major restructuring (programme) ◆ **la ~ du quartier** the reorganization of the area

restructurer /ʀəstʀyktyʀe/ ► conjug 1 ◄ **VT** to restructure **VPR** **se restructurer** to restructure

resucée * /ʀ(ə)syse/ **NF** 1 *[de boisson]* **veux-tu une ~ de whisky ?** would you like another drop *ou* shot of whisky? 2 *(fig)* *[de film, musique, théorie]* rehash *

résultante /ʀezyltɑ̃t/ **NF** *(Sci)* resultant; *(fig = conséquence)* outcome, result, consequence

résultat /ʀezylta/ GRAMMAIRE ACTIVE 53.4 **NM** 1 *(= conséquence)* result, outcome ◆ **cette tentative a eu des ~s désastreux** this attempt had disastrous results *ou* a disastrous outcome ◆ **cette démarche eut pour ~ une amélioration de la situation** *ou* **d'améliorer la situation** this measure resulted in *ou* led to an improvement in the situation ◆ **on l'a laissé seul : ~, il a fait des bêtises** we left him alone, and what happens? – he goes and does something silly ◆ **il n'y a que le ~ qui compte** the only thing that matters is the result ◆ **on a voulu lui faire confiance, le ~ est là !** we trusted him and look what happened!
2 *(= chose obtenue, réalisation)* result ◆ **c'est un ~ remarquable** it is a remarkable result *ou* achievement ◆ **il a promis d'obtenir des ~s** he promised to get results ◆ **beau ~ !** *(iro)* well done! *(iro)* ◆ **il essaya, sans ~, de le convaincre** he tried to convince him but to no effect *ou* avail ◆ **le traitement fut sans ~** the treatment had no effect *ou* didn't work
3 *(= solution)* *[d'addition, problème]* result
4 *(= classement)* *[d'élection, examen]* results ◆ **et maintenant, les ~s sportifs** and now for the sports results ◆ **le ~ des courses** *(Sport)* the racing results; *(fig)* the upshot ◆ **voici quelques ~s partiels de l'élection** here are some of the election results so far
5 *(Fin gén)* result; *(= chiffres)* figures; *(= bénéfices)* profit; *(= revenu)* income; *(= gains)* earnings ◆ **~s** results ◆ **~ bénéficiaire** profit ◆ **~ net** net profit *ou* income *ou* earnings ◆ **~ brut d'exploitation** gross trading profit

résulter /ʀezylte/ ► conjug 1 ◄ **VI** ◆ **~ de** to result from, to be the result of ◆ **rien de bon ne peut en ~** no good can come of it ◆ **les avantages économiques qui en résultent** the resulting economic benefits ◆ **ce qui a résulté de la discussion est que ...** the result *ou* outcome of the discussion was that ..., what came out of the discussion was that ... **VB IMPERS** ◆ **il résulte de tout ceci que ...** the result of all this is that ... ◆ **il en résulte que c'est impossible** the result is that it's impossible ◆ **qu'en résultera-t-il ?** what will be the result? *ou* outcome?

résumé /ʀezyme/ GRAMMAIRE ACTIVE 53.4 **NM** *(= texte, ouvrage)* summary ◆ **faire un ~ de** to sum up, to give a brief summary of ◆ **un ~ des opérations menées depuis 1998** a review of the operations carried out since 1998 ◆ **"résumé des chapitres précédents"** "the story so far" ◆ **~ des informations** *(Radio, TV)* news roundup
◆ **en résumé** *(= en bref)* in short, in brief; *(= pour conclure)* to sum up; *(= en miniature)* in miniature

résumer /ʀezyme/ GRAMMAIRE ACTIVE 53.1, 53.4 ► conjug 1 ◄ **VT** *(= abréger)* to summarize; *(= récapituler, aussi Jur)* to sum up; *(= symboliser)* to epitomize, to typify **VPR** **se résumer** 1 *[personne]* to sum up (one's ideas) 2 *(= être contenu)* **les faits se résument en quelques mots** the facts can be summed up *ou* summarized in a few words 3 *(= se réduire à)* **se ~ à** to amount to, to come down to, to boil down to ◆ **l'affaire se résume à peu de chose** the affair amounts to *ou* comes down to nothing really

⚠ **résumer** ne se traduit pas par **to resume**, qui a le sens de 'recommencer'.

résurgence /ʀezyʀʒɑ̃s/ **NF** *(Géol)* reappearance *(of river)*, resurgence; *[d'idée, mythe]* resurgence

résurgent, e /ʀezyʀʒɑ̃, ɑ̃t/ **ADJ** *(Géol)* *[eaux]* re-emergent

resurgir /ʀ(ə)syʀʒiʀ/ ► conjug 2 ◄ **VI** *[cours d'eau]* to come up again, to resurface; *[personne, passé, souvenir]* to resurface; *[problème, idée, débat, menace]* to resurface, to re-emerge; *[conflit]* to blow up again

résurrection /ʀezyʀɛksjɔ̃/ **NF** *[de mort]* resurrection; *(fig = renouveau)* revival ◆ **la Résurrection** *(Rel)* the Resurrection ◆ **c'est une véritable ~ !** he has really come back to life!

retable /ʀətabl/ **NM** altarpiece, reredos

rétablir /ʀetabliʀ/ GRAMMAIRE ACTIVE 50.4 ► conjug 2 ◄
VT 1 *[+ courant, communications]* to restore
2 *[+ démocratie, monarchie]* to restore, to re-establish; *[+ droit, ordre, équilibre, confiance, forces, santé]* to restore; *[+ fait, vérité]* to re-establish; *[+ cessez-le-feu, paix]* to restore ◆ **~ les relations diplomatiques** to restore diplomatic relations ◆ **~ la situation** to rectify the situation, to get the situation back to normal ◆ **il était mené 5 jeux à rien mais il a réussi à ~ la situation** he was losing 5 games to love but managed to pull back
3 *(= réintégrer)* to reinstate ◆ **~ qn dans ses fonctions** to reinstate sb in *ou* restore sb to their post ◆ **~ qn dans ses droits** to restore sb's rights
4 *(= guérir)* **~ qn** to restore sb to health, to bring about sb's recovery
VPR **se rétablir** 1 *[personne, économie]* to recover ◆ **il s'est vite rétabli** he soon recovered
2 *(= revenir)* *[silence, calme]* to return, to be restored
3 *(Sport)* to pull o.s. up *(onto a ledge etc)*; *(après perte d'équilibre)* to regain one's balance

rétablissement /ʀetablismɑ̃/ GRAMMAIRE ACTIVE 50.4 **NM** 1 *[de courant, communications]* restoring; *[de démocratie, monarchie, droit, ordre, équilibre, forces, santé]* restoration; *[de fait, vérité]* re-establishment; *[de cessez-le-feu]* restoration ◆ **~ des relations diplomatiques** restoring diplomatic relations 2 *[de personne, économie]* recovery ◆ **en vous souhaitant un prompt ~** with my (*ou* our) good wishes for your swift recovery, hoping you will be better soon ◆ **tous nos vœux de prompt ~** our best wishes for a speedy recovery 3 *(Sport)* **faire** *ou* **opérer un ~** to do a pull-up *(into a standing position, onto a ledge etc)*

retailler /ʀ(ə)taje/ ► conjug 1 ◄ **VT** *[+ diamant, vêtement]* to re-cut; *[+ crayon]* to sharpen; *[+ arbre]* to (re-)prune

rétamage /ʀetamaʒ/ **NM** re-coating, re-tinning *(of pans)*

rétamé, e ‡ /ʀetame/ (ptp de **rétamer**) **ADJ** *(= fatigué)* worn out *, knackered ‡ *(Brit)*; *(= ivre)* plastered ‡, sloshed ‡; *(= détruit, démoli)* wiped out; *(= sans argent)* broke * ◆ **il a été ~ en un mois** *(= mort)* he was dead within a month, he was a goner within a month ‡

rétamer /ʀetame/ ► conjug 1 ◄ **VT** 1 *[+ casseroles]* to re-coat, to re-tin 2 ‡ *(= fatiguer)* to wear out *, to knacker ‡ *(Brit)*; *(= rendre ivre)* to knock out ‡; *(= démolir)* to wipe out; *(= dépouiller au jeu)* to clean out *; *(à un examen)* to flunk * ◆ **se faire ~ au poker** to be cleaned out * at poker **VPR** **se rétamer** ‡ *[candidat]* to flunk * ◆ **se ~ (par terre)** *(= tomber)* to take a dive *, to crash to the ground ◆ **la voiture s'est rétamée contre un arbre** the car crashed into a tree

rétameur /ʀetamœʀ/ **NM** tinker

retapage /R(ə)tapaʒ/ NM *[de maison, vêtement]* doing up; *[de voiture]* fixing up; *[de lit]* straightening

retape* /R(ə)tap/ NF ◆ **faire (de) la ~** *[prostituée]* to walk the streets*, to be on the game* *(Brit)*; *[agent publicitaire]* to tout (around) for business ◆ **faire de la ~ pour une compagnie de bateaux-mouches** to tout for a pleasure boat company

retaper /R(ə)tape/ ▸ conjug 1 ◂ VT 1 (* = *remettre en état) [+ maison, vêtement]* to do up; *[+ voiture]* to fix up; *[+ lit]* to straighten; *[+ malade, personne fatiguée]* to buck up* ◆ **la maison a été entièrement retapée** the house has been entirely redone *ou* redecorated ◆ **ça m'a retapé, ce whisky** that whisky has really bucked me up* 2 (= *dactylographier*) to retype, to type again VPR **se retaper*** 1 (= *guérir*) to get back on one's feet ◆ **il va se ~ en quelques semaines** he'll be back on his feet in a few weeks 2 (= *refaire*) **j'ai dû me ~ tout le trajet à pied** I had to walk all the way back home ◆ **j'ai dû me ~ la vaisselle** I got lumbered with the washing-up again

retapisser /R(ə)tapise/ ▸ conjug 1 ◂ VT *(de papier peint) [+ pièce]* to repaper; *(de tissu) [+ fauteuil]* to reupholster ◆ **j'ai retapissé la chambre de papier bleu** I repapered the bedroom in blue

retard /R(ə)taR/ NM 1 *[de personne attendue]* lateness *(NonC)* ◆ **ces ~s continuels seront punis** this constant lateness will be punished ◆ **plusieurs ~s dans la même semaine, c'est inadmissible** it won't do being late several times in one week ◆ **il a eu quatre ~s** *(Scol)* he was late four times ◆ **son ~ m'inquiète** I'm worried that he hasn't arrived yet ◆ **vous avez du ~** you're late ◆ **vous avez deux heures de ~** *ou* **un ~ de deux heures** you're two hours late ◆ **tu as un métro** *ou* **un train de ~ !*** *(hum)* (= *tu n'es pas au courant*) you must have been asleep!; (= *tu es lent à comprendre*) you're slow on the uptake!; (= *tu ne vis pas avec ton époque*) you're behind the times!; → **billet**
2 *[de train, concurrent]* delay ◆ **un ~ de trois heures est annoncé sur la ligne Paris-Brest** there will be a delay of three hours *ou* trains will run three hours late on the Paris-Brest line ◆ **le conducteur essayait de combler son ~** the driver was trying to make up the time he had lost ◆ **avoir 2 secondes de ~ sur le champion/le record** *(Sport)* to be 2 seconds slower than *ou* behind the champion/outside the record ◆ **elle a un ~ de règles** *(Méd)* her period's late, she's late with her period
3 *(Horlogerie)* **cette montre a du ~** this watch is slow ◆ **la pendule prend du ~** the clock is slow ◆ **la pendule prend un ~ de 3 minutes par jour** the clock loses 3 minutes a day
4 (= *non-observation des délais*) delay ◆ **des ~s successifs** a series of delays ◆ **s'il y a du ~ dans l'exécution d'une commande** if there is a delay in carrying out an order ◆ **sans ~** without delay ◆ **livrer qch avec ~** to deliver sth late, to be late (in) delivering sth
5 *(sur un programme)* delay ◆ **il avait un ~ scolaire considérable** he had fallen a long way behind at school ◆ **il doit combler son ~ en anglais** he has a lot of ground to make up in English ◆ **j'ai pris du ~ dans mes révisions** I have fallen behind in *ou* I am behind with my revision
6 (= *infériorité*) *[de pays, peuple]* backwardness ◆ **~ de croissance** *[d'enfant]* growth retardation; *(Écon)* slow growth ◆ **~ industriel** industrial backwardness ◆ **~ mental** backwardness ◆ **il vit avec un siècle de ~** he's a hundred years behind the times, he's living in the last century
7 *(Mus)* retardation
8 *(locutions)*
◆ **en retard** ◆ **tu es en ~** you're late ◆ **ils sont en ~ de deux heures** they're two hours late ◆ **ça/il m'a mis en ~** it/he made me late ◆ **je me suis mis en ~** I made myself late ◆ **paiement en ~** *(effectué)* late payment; *(non effectué)* overdue payment, payment overdue ◆ **vous êtes en ~ pour les inscriptions** you are late (in) registering ◆ **il est toujours en ~ pour payer sa cotisation** he is always behind with his subscription ◆ **payer qch en ~** to pay sth late, to be late (in) paying sth ◆ **j'ai du travail/courrier en ~** I'm behind with my work/mail, I have a backlog of work/mail ◆ **il est en ~ pour son âge** he's backward for his age ◆ **région en ~** under-developed *ou* economically backward region ◆ **ce pays est en ~ de cent ans du point de vue économique** this country's economy is one hundred years behind, this country is economically one hundred years behind ◆ **ils sont toujours en ~ d'une guerre** they're always fighting yesterday's battles ◆ **ils ne sont jamais en ~ d'une idée** they're never short of ideas
◆ **en retard sur** ◆ **nous sommes/les recherches sont en ~ sur le programme** we are/the research is behind schedule ◆ **le train est en ~ sur l'horaire** the train is running behind schedule ◆ **être en ~ (de 2 heures/2 km) sur le peloton** *(Sport)* to be (2 hours/2 km) behind the pack ◆ **être en ~ sur son temps** *ou* **siècle** to be behind the times
ADJ INV *(Pharm)* ◆ **insuline/effet ~** delayed insulin/effect
COMP **retard à l'allumage** *[de moteur]* retarded spark *ou* ignition ◆ **il a du ~ à l'allumage*** *(fig)* he's a bit slow on the uptake*

retardataire /R(ə)taRdatɛR/ ADJ *[arrivant]* late; *[théorie, méthode]* obsolete, outmoded NMF latecomer

retardateur, -trice /R(ə)taRdatœR, tRis/ ADJ *(Sci, Tech)* retarding NM *(Photo)* self-timer; *(Chim)* retarder

retardé, e /R(ə)taRde/ (ptp de **retarder**) ADJ *(scolairement)* backward, slow; *(intellectuellement)* retarded, backward; *(économiquement)* backward

retardement /R(ə)taRdəmɑ̃/ NM *[de processus, train]* delaying ◆ **manœuvres de ~** delaying tactics
◆ **à retardement** *[+ engin, torpille]* with a timing device; *[+ dispositif]* delayed-action *(épith)*; *(Photo) [+ mécanisme]* self-timing; * *[+ excuses, souhaits]* belated; *[comprendre, se fâcher, rire]* after the event, in retrospect ◆ **il comprend tout à ~** *(péj)* he's always a bit slow on the uptake* ◆ **il rit toujours à ~** *(péj)* it always takes him a while to see the joke

retarder /R(ə)taRde/ ▸ conjug 1 ◂ VT 1 (= *mettre en retard sur un horaire*) *[+ arrivant, arrivée]* to delay, to make late; *[+ personne ou véhicule en chemin]* to delay, to hold up ◆ **une visite inattendue m'a retardé** I was delayed by an unexpected visitor ◆ **je ne veux pas vous ~** I don't want to delay you *ou* make you late ◆ **ne te retarde pas (pour ça)** don't make yourself late for that ◆ **il a été retardé par les grèves** he has been delayed *ou* held up by the strikes
2 (= *mettre en retard sur un programme*) *[+ employé, élève]* to hinder, to set back; *[+ opération, vendange, chercheur]* to delay, to hold up ◆ **ça l'a retardé dans sa mission/ses études** this has set him back in *ou* hindered him in his mission/his studies
3 (= *remettre*) *[+ départ, moment, opération]* to delay; *[+ date]* to put back; *[+ allumage de moteur]* to retard ◆ **~ son départ d'une heure** to put back one's departure by an hour, to delay one's departure for an hour ◆ **porte à ouverture retardée** door with a time lock ◆ **parachute à ouverture retardée** parachute with fail-safe delayed opening
4 *[+ montre, réveil]* to put back ◆ **~ l'horloge d'une heure** to put the clock back an hour
VI 1 *[montre]* to be slow; *(régulièrement)* to lose time ◆ **je retarde (de 10 minutes)** my watch is (10 minutes) slow, I'm (10 minutes) slow
2 (= *être à un stade antérieur*) **~ sur son époque** *ou* **temps** *ou* **siècle** to be behind the times
3 (* = *être dépassé*) to be out of touch, to be behind the times* ◆ **ma voiture ? tu retardes, je l'ai vendue il y a deux ans** (= *n'être pas au courant*) my car? you're a bit behind the times* *ou* you're a bit out of touch – I sold it two years ago

retâter /R(ə)tɑte/ ▸ conjug 1 ◂ VT *[+ objet, pouls]* to feel again VI ◆ **~ de*** *[+ prison]* to get another taste of; *[+ métier]* to have another go at

reteindre /R(ə)tɛ̃dR/ ▸ conjug 52 ◂ VT to dye again, to redye

retéléphoner /R(ə)telefɔne/ ▸ conjug 1 ◂ VI to phone again, to call back ◆ **je lui retéléphonerai demain** I'll phone him again *ou* call him back tomorrow, I'll give him another call tomorrow

retendre /R(ə)tɑ̃dR/ ▸ conjug 41 ◂ VT 1 *[+ câble]* to stretch again, to pull taut again; *[+ peau, tissu]* to tauten; *[+ cordes de guitare, de raquette]* to (re)tighten 2 *[+ piège, filets]* to reset, to set again 3 ◆ **~ la main à qn** to stretch out one's hand again to sb

retenir /Rət(ə)niR, R(ə)təniR/ ▸ conjug 22 ◂ VT 1 *(lit, fig = maintenir) [+ personne, objet qui glisse]* to hold back; *[+ chien]* to hold back; *[+ cheval]* to rein in, to hold back ◆ **~ qn par le bras** to hold sb back by the arm ◆ **il allait tomber, une branche l'a retenu** he was about to fall but a branch held him back ◆ **le barrage retient l'eau** the dam holds back the water ◆ **~ la foule** to hold back the crowd ◆ **il se serait jeté par la fenêtre si on ne l'avait pas retenu** he would have thrown himself out of the window if he hadn't been held back *ou* stopped ◆ **retenez-moi ou je fais un malheur !*** hold me back *ou* stop me or I'll do something I'll regret! ◆ **une certaine timidité le retenait** a certain shyness held him back ◆ **~ qn de faire qch** to keep sb from doing sth, to stop sb doing sth ◆ **je ne sais pas ce qui me retient de lui dire ce que je pense** I don't know what keeps me from *ou* stops me telling him what I think
2 (= *garder*) *[+ personne]* to keep ◆ **~ qn à dîner** to have sb stay for dinner, to keep sb for dinner ◆ **j'ai été retenu** I was kept back *ou* detained *ou* held up ◆ **il m'a retenu une heure** he kept me for an hour ◆ **si tu veux partir, je ne te retiens pas** if you want to leave, I won't hold you back *ou* stop you ◆ **c'est la maladie de sa femme qui l'a retenu à Brest** it was his wife's illness that detained him in Brest ◆ **son travail le retenait ailleurs** his work detained *ou* kept him elsewhere ◆ **la grippe l'a retenu au lit/à la maison** flu kept him in bed/at home ◆ **~ qn prisonnier/en otage** to hold sb prisoner/hostage
3 (= *empêcher de se dissiper*) *[+ eau d'infiltration, odeur]* to retain; *[+ chaleur]* to retain, to keep in; *[+ lumière]* to reflect ◆ **cette terre retient l'eau** this soil retains water ◆ **le noir retient la chaleur** black retains the heat *ou* keeps in the heat
4 (= *fixer*) *[clou, nœud]* to hold ◆ **c'est un simple clou qui retient le tableau au mur** there's just a nail holding the picture on the wall ◆ **un ruban retenait ses cheveux** a ribbon kept *ou* held her hair in place, her hair was tied up with a ribbon
5 ◆ **~ l'attention de qn** to hold sb's attention ◆ **ce détail retient l'attention** this detail holds one's attention ◆ **votre demande a retenu toute notre attention** *(frm)* your request has been given full consideration
6 (= *louer, réserver*) *[+ chambre, place, table]* to book, to reserve; *[+ date]* to reserve, to set aside; *[+ domestique]* to engage

7 *(= se souvenir de)* *[+ donnée, leçon, nom]* to remember; *[+ impression]* to retain ◆ **je n'ai pas retenu son nom/la date** I can't remember his name/the date ◆ **je retiens de cette aventure qu'il est plus prudent de bien s'équiper** I've learnt from this adventure that it's wiser to be properly equipped ◆ **j'en retiens qu'il est pingre et borné, c'est tout** the only thing that stands out *ou* that sticks in my mind is that he's stingy and narrow-minded ◆ **un nom qu'on retient** a name that stays in your mind, a name you remember ◆ **retenez bien ce qu'on vous a dit** don't forget *ou* make sure you remember what you were told ◆ **celui-là, je le retiens !*** I'll remember him all right!, I won't forget him in a hurry! ◆ **ah ! toi, je te retiens*, avec tes idées lumineuses !** you and your bright ideas!

8 *(= contenir, réprimer)* *[+ cri, larmes]* to hold back *ou* in, to suppress; *[+ colère]* to hold back ◆ **~ son souffle** *ou* **sa respiration** to hold one's breath ◆ **il ne put ~ un sourire/un rire** he could not hold back *ou* suppress a smile/a laugh, he could not help smiling/laughing ◆ **il retint les mots qui lui venaient à la bouche** he held back *ou* bit back *(Brit)* the words that came to him

9 *(Math)* to carry ◆ **je pose 4 et je retiens 2** 4 down and 2 to carry, put down 4 and carry 2

10 *(= garder)* *[+ salaire]* to stop, to withhold; *[+ possessions, bagages d'un client]* to retain

11 *(= prélever, retrancher)* to deduct, to keep back ◆ **ils nous retiennent 200 € (sur notre salaire) pour les assurances** they deduct €200 (from our wages) for insurance ◆ **~ une certaine somme pour la retraite** to deduct a certain sum for a pension scheme ◆ **~ les impôts à la base** to deduct taxes at source

12 *(= accepter)* *[+ plan, proposition]* to accept; *[+ candidature, nom]* to retain, to accept ◆ **le jury a retenu la préméditation** *(Jur)* the jury accepted the charge of premeditation ◆ **c'est notre projet qui a été retenu** it's our project that has been accepted

VPR se retenir 1 *(= s'accrocher)* **se ~ à qch** to hold on to sth

2 *(= se contenir)* to restrain o.s.; *(= s'abstenir)* to stop o.s. *(de faire* doing); *(de faire ses besoins naturels)* to hold on, to hold o.s. in ◆ **se ~ de pleurer** *ou* **pour ne pas pleurer** to hold back one's tears ◆ **malgré sa colère, il essaya de se ~** despite his anger, he tried to restrain *ou* contain himself ◆ **il se retint de lui faire remarquer que ...** he refrained from pointing out to him that ...

retenter /ʀ(ə)tɑ̃te/ ▸ conjug 1 ◂ **VT** *(gén)* to try again, to make another attempt at, to have another go at; *[+ épreuve, saut]* to try again; *[+ action, opération]* to reattempt ◆ **~ sa chance** to try one's luck again ◆ **~ de faire qch** to try to do sth again

rétention /ʀetɑ̃sjɔ̃/ **NF** 1 *(Méd)* retention ◆ **~ d'eau/d'urine** retention of water/of urine 2 ◆ **~ d'informations** withholding information ◆ **~ administrative** *(Jur)* detention *(of asylum seekers)* ◆ **centre de ~** detention centre

retentir /ʀ(ə)tɑ̃tiʀ/ ▸ conjug 2 ◂ **VI** 1 *[sonnerie]* to ring; *[bruit métallique, cris, détonation, explosion]* to ring out; *[écho, tonnerre]* to reverberate ◆ **à minuit, des explosions retentirent** explosions were heard at midnight ◆ **des tirs sporadiques ont à nouveau retenti dans la ville** sporadic gunfire rang out again in the city ◆ **ces mots retentissent encore à mes oreilles** those words are still ringing *ou* echoing in my ears 2 *(= résonner de)* **~ de** to ring with, to be full of the sound of 3 *(= affecter)* **~ sur** to have an effect upon, to affect

retentissant, e /ʀ(ə)tɑ̃tisɑ̃, ɑ̃t/ **ADJ** 1 *(= fort, sonore)* *[son, voix]* ringing *(épith)*; *[bruit, choc, claque]* resounding *(épith)* 2 *(= éclatant, frappant)* *[échec, succès]* resounding *(épith)*; *[scandale]* tremendous; *[faillite, procès]* spectacular; *[déclaration, discours]* sensational ◆ **son film a fait un bide ~*** his film was a resounding flop*

retentissement /ʀ(ə)tɑ̃tismɑ̃/ **NM** 1 *(= répercussion)* repercussion, (after-)effect ◆ **les ~s de l'affaire** the repercussions of the affair 2 *(= éclat)* stir, effect ◆ **cette nouvelle eut un grand ~ dans l'opinion** this piece of news created a considerable stir in public opinion ◆ **son œuvre fut sans grand ~** his work went virtually unnoticed ◆ **l'affaire a eu un énorme ~ médiatique** the affair created a media sensation 3 *(littér)* *[de son, cloche]* ringing; *[de voix]* echoing sound

retenu, e[1] /ʀət(ə)ny/ (ptp de **retenir**) **ADJ** *(littér = discret)* *[charme, grâce]* reserved, restrained

retenue[2] /ʀət(ə)ny/ **NF** 1 *(= prélèvement)* deduction ◆ **opérer une ~ de 10% sur un salaire** to deduct 10% from a salary ◆ **~ pour la retraite** deductions for a pension scheme ◆ **système de ~ à la source** *system of deducting income tax at source*, ≃ PAYE *ou* pay-as-you-earn system *(Brit)*

2 *(= modération)* self-control, (self-)restraint; *(= réserve)* reserve ◆ **avoir de la ~** to be reserved ◆ **faire preuve de ~** to show restraint ◆ **parler/s'exprimer sans ~** to talk/express o.s. quite openly ◆ **rire sans ~** to laugh without restraint *ou* unrestrainedly ◆ **il n'a aucune ~ dans ses propos** he shows no restraint in what he says ◆ **il s'est confié à moi sans aucune ~** he confided in me quite freely *ou* unreservedly ◆ **un peu de ~ !** show some restraint!, control yourself! ◆ **dans sa colère, elle perdit toute ~** she was so enraged that she lost all self-control

3 *(Math)* **n'oublie pas la ~** don't forget what to carry (over)

4 *(Scol)* detention ◆ **être en ~** to be in detention, to be kept in ◆ **il les a mis en ~** he kept them in, he gave them detention ◆ **il a eu deux heures de ~** he got two hours' detention, he was kept in for two hours (after school)

5 *(Tech)* **la ~ du barrage** the volume of water behind the dam ◆ **barrage à faible ~** low-volume dam ◆ **bassin de ~** balancing *ou* compensating reservoir

6 *(= embouteillage)* tailback *(Brit)*, (traffic) backup *(US)*

7 *(Naut)* guest rope

8 *(Constr)* (under)pinning

rétiaire /ʀetjɛʀ/ **NM** *(Antiq)* retiarius

réticence /ʀetisɑ̃s/ **NF** 1 *(= hésitation)* hesitation, reluctance *(NonC)* ◆ **avec ~** reluctantly, with some hesitation ◆ **sans ~** without (any) hesitation ◆ **cette proposition suscite quelques ~s chez les éditeurs** publishers are a bit hesitant about *ou* are reluctant to go along with this proposal ◆ **compte tenu des ~s manifestées par les syndicats** *(= réserve)* given the misgivings *ou* reservations expressed by the unions 2 *(† = omission)* reticence *(NonC)* ◆ **parler sans ~** to speak openly, to conceal nothing

réticent, e /ʀetisɑ̃, ɑ̃t/ **ADJ** 1 *(= hésitant)* hesitant ◆ **se montrer ~** to be hesitant ◆ **le gouvernement reste très ~ à l'égard de toute baisse des taux d'intérêt** the government remains very doubtful about any cut in interest rates 2 *(= réservé)* reticent

> ⚠ **réticent** se traduit par le mot anglais **reticent** uniquement au sens de 'réservé'.

réticulaire /ʀetikylɛʀ/ **ADJ** reticular

réticule /ʀetikyl/ **NM** *(Opt)* reticle; *(= sac)* reticule

réticulé, e /ʀetikyle/ **ADJ** *(Anat, Géol)* reticulate; *(Archit)* reticulated

rétif, -ive /ʀetif, iv/ **ADJ** *[animal]* stubborn; *[personne]* rebellious, restive

rétine /ʀetin/ **NF** retina

rétinien, -ienne /ʀetinjɛ̃, jɛn/ **ADJ** retinal

rétinite /ʀetinit/ **NF** retinitis

retirage /ʀ(ə)tiʀaʒ/ **NM** reprint

retiré, e /ʀ(ə)tiʀe/ (ptp de **retirer**) **ADJ** 1 *(= solitaire)* *[lieu]* remote, out-of-the-way; *[maison]* isolated; *[vie]* secluded ◆ **vivre ~, mener une vie ~e** to live in isolation *ou* seclusion, to lead a secluded life ◆ **il vivait ~ du reste du monde** he lived withdrawn *ou* cut off from the rest of the world ◆ **~ quelque part dans le Béarn** living quietly somewhere in the Béarn 2 *(= en retraite)* retired ◆ **~ des affaires** retired from business

retirer /ʀ(ə)tiʀe/ ▸ conjug 1 ◂ **VT** 1 *(lit, fig = enlever)* *[+ gants, lunettes, manteau]* to take off, to remove; *[+ privilèges]* to withdraw ◆ **~ son collier au chien** to take the dog's collar off, to remove the dog's collar ◆ **retire-lui ses chaussures** take his shoes off (for him) ◆ **retire-lui ce couteau des mains** take that knife (away) from him ◆ **~ à qn son emploi** to take sb's job away (from them), to deprive sb of their job ◆ **~ son permis (de conduire) à qn** to take away *ou* revoke sb's (driving) licence, to disqualify sb from driving ◆ **~ une pièce de l'affiche** to take off *ou* close a play ◆ **on lui a retiré la garde des enfants** he was deprived of custody of the children ◆ **je lui ai retiré ma confiance** I don't trust him any more ◆ **~ la parole à qn** to make sb stand down *(Brit)*, to take the floor from sb *(US)*

2 *(= sortir)* to take out, to remove *(de* from); ◆ **~ un bouchon** to pull out *ou* take out *ou* remove a cork ◆ **~ un corps de l'eau/qn de dessous les décombres** to pull a body out of the water/sb out of *ou* out from under the rubble ◆ **~ un plat du four/les bagages du coffre** to take a dish out of the oven/the luggage out of the boot ◆ **ils ont retiré leur fils du lycée** they have taken their son away from *ou* removed their son from the school ◆ **se faire ~ une dent** to have a tooth out ◆ **je ne peux pas ~ la clé de la serrure** I can't get the key out of the lock ◆ **retire les mains de tes poches** take your hands out of your pockets ◆ **on lui retirera difficilement de l'idée** *ou* **de la tête qu'il est menacé*** we'll have difficulty *ou* a job convincing him that he's not being threatened

3 *(= reprendre possession de)* *[+ bagages, billets réservés]* to collect, to pick up; *[+ argent en dépôt]* to withdraw, to take out; *[+ gage]* to redeem ◆ **~ de l'argent (de la banque)** to withdraw money (from the bank), to take money out (of the bank) ◆ **votre commande est prête à être retirée** your order is now awaiting collection *ou* ready for collection

4 *(= ramener en arrière)* to take away, to remove, to withdraw ◆ **~ sa tête/sa main (pour éviter un coup)** to remove *ou* withdraw one's head/one's hand (to avoid being hit) ◆ **il retira prestement sa main** he whisked *ou* snatched his hand away

5 *(= annuler)* *[+ candidature]* to withdraw; *[+ accusation, plainte]* to withdraw, to take back ◆ **je retire ce que j'ai dit** I take back what I said ◆ **~ sa candidature** *(Pol)* to withdraw one's candidature, to stand down *(Brit)* ◆ **~ un produit du commerce** *ou* **du marché** to take a product off the market

6 *(= obtenir)* *[+ avantages]* to get, to gain *ou* derive *(de* from); ◆ **les bénéfices qu'on en retire** the profits to be had *ou* gained from it ◆ **il en a retiré un grand profit** he profited *ou* gained greatly by it ◆ **il n'en a retiré que des ennuis** it caused him nothing but trouble ◆ **tout ce qu'il en a retiré, c'est ...** the only thing he has got out of it is ..., all he has gained is ...

7 (= extraire) [+ extrait, huile, minerai] to obtain ◆ **une substance dont on retire une huile précieuse** a substance from which a valuable oil is obtained

8 (Photo) to reprint ◆ **faire ~ des photos** to have reprints of one's photographs done

VPR **se retirer** 1 (= partir) to retire, to withdraw; (= aller se coucher) to retire (to bed); (= prendre sa retraite) to retire; (= retirer sa candidature) to withdraw, to stand down (Brit) (en faveur de in favour of); ◆ **se ~ discrètement** to withdraw discreetly ◆ **ils se sont retirés dans un coin pour discuter affaires** they withdrew ou retired to a corner to talk business ◆ **se ~ dans sa chambre** to go ou withdraw (frm) ou retire (frm) to one's room ◆ **se ~ dans sa tour d'ivoire** (fig) to take refuge ou lock o.s. up in an ivory tower ◆ **ils ont décidé de se ~ à la campagne** they've decided to retire to the country ◆ **elle s'est retirée dans un couvent** she retired ou withdrew to a convent

2 (= reculer) (pour laisser passer qn, éviter un coup) to move out of the way; [troupes] to withdraw; [marée, mer] to recede, to go back, to ebb; [eaux d'inondation] to recede, to go down; [glacier] to recede ◆ **retire-toi d'ici ou de là, tu me gênes** stand somewhere else – you're in my way

3 (= quitter) **se ~ de** to withdraw from ◆ **se ~ d'une compétition/d'un marché** to withdraw from a competition/from a market ◆ **se ~ des affaires** to retire from business ◆ **se ~ du monde** to withdraw from society ◆ **se ~ de la partie** to drop out

retombant, e /ʀ(ə)tɔ̃bɑ̃, ɑ̃t/ ADJ [moustache] drooping; [branches] hanging ◆ **plantes ~es ou à port ~** trailing plants

retombée /ʀ(ə)tɔ̃be/ NF 1 ◆ **~s (radioactives ou atomiques)** (radioactive) fallout (NonC) 2 (gén pl = répercussion) [de scandale] consequence, effect; [d'invention] spin-off ◆ **les ~s financières d'une opération** the financial spin-offs of a deal ◆ **l'accord a eu des ~s économiques immédiates** the agreement had an immediate knock-on effect on the economy ou immediate economic repercussions ◆ **le gouvernement redoute les ~s médiatiques de l'événement** the government is concerned about the effects media coverage of this event might have 3 (Archit) spring, springing

retomber /ʀ(ə)tɔ̃be/ ▸ conjug 1 ◂ VI 1 (= faire une nouvelle chute) to fall again ◆ **le lendemain, il est retombé dans la piscine** the next day he fell into the swimming pool again ◆ **~ dans la misère** to fall on hard times again ◆ **~ dans le découragement** to lose heart again ◆ **~ dans l'erreur/le péché** to fall back ou lapse into error/sin ◆ **son roman est retombé dans l'oubli** his novel has sunk back into oblivion ◆ **le pays retomba dans la guerre civile** the country lapsed into civil war again ◆ **je vais ~ dans l'ennui** I'll start being bored again ◆ **la conversation retomba sur le même sujet** the conversation turned once again ou came round again to the same subject

2 (= redevenir) **~ amoureux/enceinte/malade** to fall in love/get pregnant/fall ill again ◆ **ils sont retombés d'accord** they reached agreement again

3 [neige, pluie] to fall again, to come down again ◆ **la neige retombait de plus belle** the snow was falling again still more heavily

4 (= tomber après s'être élevé) [personne] to land; [chose lancée, liquide] to come down; [gâteau, soufflé] to collapse; [abattant, capot, herse] to fall back down; [fusée, missile] to land, to come back to earth; [conversation] to fall away, to die; [intérêt] to fall away, to fall off; (Pol) [tension] to subside; [vent] to subside, to die down; [silence] to fall ou descend again ◆ **~ comme un soufflé** to fade away to nothing ◆ **il est retombé lourdement (sur le dos)** he landed heavily (on his back) ◆ **elle saute bien mais elle ne sait pas ~** she can jump well but she doesn't know how to land ◆ **le chat retombe toujours sur ses pattes** cats always land on their feet ◆ **il retombera toujours sur ses pattes ou pieds** he'll always land ou fall on his feet ◆ **se laisser ~ sur son oreiller** to fall back ou sink back onto one's pillow ◆ **laissez ~ les bras** (Sport) let your arms drop ou fall (by your sides) ◆ **il laissa ~ le rideau** he let the curtain fall back ◆ **l'eau retombait en cascades** the water fell back in cascades ◆ **ça lui est retombé sur le nez*** it backfired on him ◆ **le brouillard est retombé en fin de matinée** the fog fell again ou came down again ou closed in again towards lunchtime ◆ **l'inflation est retombée à 4%** inflation has fallen to 4%

5 (= pendre) [cheveux, rideaux] to fall, to hang (down) ◆ **de petites boucles blondes retombaient sur son front** little blond curls tumbled ou fell onto her forehead

6 (= échoir à) **la responsabilité retombera sur toi** the responsibility will fall ou land* on you ◆ **les frais retombèrent sur nous** we were landed* ou saddled with the expense ◆ **faire ~ sur qn la responsabilité de qch/les frais de qch** to pass the responsibility for sth/the cost of sth on to sb, to land* sb with the responsibility for sth/the cost of sth ◆ **ça va me ~ dessus*** (gén) I'll get the blame ou take the flak* (for it); [travail] I'll get lumbered ou landed with it* ◆ **le péché du père retombera sur la tête des enfants** the sins of the fathers will be visited on the sons

7 ◆ **Noël retombe un samedi** Christmas falls on a Saturday again ◆ **~ en enfance** to lapse into second childhood ◆ **je suis retombé sur lui le lendemain, au même endroit** I came across him again the next day in the same place ◆ **ils nous sont retombés dessus le lendemain** they landed* on us again the next day

retordre /ʀ(ə)tɔʀdʀ/ ▸ conjug 41 ◂ VT [+ câbles] to twist again; [+ linge] to wring (out) again; → **fil**

rétorquer /ʀetɔʀke/ ▸ conjug 1 ◂ VT to retort

retors, e /ʀətɔʀ, ɔʀs/ ADJ 1 **fil ~** twisted yarn 2 (= rusé) sly, wily, underhand

rétorsion /ʀetɔʀsjɔ̃/ NF (frm, Jur, Pol) retortion, retaliation ◆ **user de ~ envers un État** to retaliate ou use retortion against a state; → **mesure**

retouche /ʀ(ə)tuʃ/ NF [de photo, peinture] touching up (NonC); [de texte, vêtement] alteration ◆ **faire une ~ à une photo** to touch up a photo ◆ **faire une ~** (à une photo, une peinture) to do some touching up; (à un vêtement) to make an alteration ◆ **~ d'images** retouching

retoucher /ʀ(ə)tuʃe/ ▸ conjug 1 ◂ VT 1 (= améliorer) [+ peinture, photo] to touch up, to retouch; [+ texte, vêtement] to alter, to make alterations to ◆ **il faudra ~ cette veste au col** this jacket will have to be altered at the neck ◆ **on voit tout de suite que cette photo est retouchée** you can see straight away that this photo has been touched up 2 (= toucher de nouveau) to touch again; (= blesser de nouveau) to hit again

VI ◆ **~ à qch** to touch sth again ◆ **s'il retouche à ma sœur, gare à lui !** if he lays hands on ou touches my sister again he'd better look out! ◆ **je n'ai plus jamais retouché à l'alcool** I never touched a drop of alcohol again

retoucheur, -euse /ʀ(ə)tuʃœʀ, øz/ NM,F ◆ **~ (en confection)** dressmaker in charge of alterations ◆ **~ photographe** retoucher

retour /ʀ(ə)tuʀ/ NM 1 (= fait d'être revenu) (gén) return; (à la maison) homecoming, return home; (= chemin, trajet) return (journey), way back, journey back; (= billet) return (ticket) ◆ **il fallait déjà penser au ~** it was already time to think about going back ◆ **être sur le (chemin du) ~** to be on one's way back ◆ **pendant le ~** on the way back, during the return journey (Brit) ◆ **elle n'a pas assez pour payer son ~** she hasn't enough for her ticket home ◆ **(être) de ~ (de)** (to be) back (from) ◆ **à votre ~, écrivez-nous** write to us when you get back ◆ **à leur ~, ils trouvèrent la maison vide** when they got back ou on their return, they found the house empty ◆ **de ~ à la maison** back home ◆ **au ~ de notre voyage** when we got back from our trip ◆ **à son ~ d'Afrique** on his return from Africa, when he got back from Africa; → **cheval**

2 (à un état antérieur) **~ à** return to ◆ **le ~ à une vie normale** the return to (a) normal life ◆ **ils considèrent le ~ à l'emploi comme une priorité** they regard getting people back to work as a priority ◆ **~ à la nature/la terre** return to nature/the land ◆ **c'est un ~ aux sources pour lui** he is going back to his beginnings ◆ **~ à la normale** return to normal ◆ **il y a un ~ progressif à la normale** things are getting back to normal ◆ **~ au calme** return to a state of calm ◆ **son ~ à la politique** his return to politics, his political comeback

3 (= réapparition) return; (= répétition régulière) [de cadence, motif, thème] recurrence ◆ **le ~ du printemps/de la paix** the return of spring/of peace ◆ **on prévoit un ~ du froid** the forecasters say the cold weather is coming back ◆ **un ~ offensif de la grippe** a renewed outbreak of flu

4 (Comm, Poste) [d'emballage, objets invendus, récipient] return ◆ **~ à l'envoyeur ou à l'expéditeur** return to sender ◆ **avec faculté de ~** on approval, on sale or return ◆ **clause de ~** (Fin) no protest clause

5 (Jur) **(droit de) ~** reversion

6 (littér = changement d'avis) change of heart ◆ **~s** (= revirements) reversals ◆ **les ~s de la fortune** the twists of fortune ◆ **un ~ soudain dans l'opinion publique** a sudden turnabout in public opinion

7 (Tech) [de chariot de machine, pièce mobile] return; (= partie de bureau) (desk) extension ◆ **touche ~** (Ordin) return key

8 (Élec) **~ à la terre ou à la masse** earth (Brit) ou ground (US) return

9 (Tennis) return ◆ **~ de service** return of service ou serve ◆ **match ~** (Sport) return match, second ou return leg

10 (Fin) return ◆ **~ sur investissements** return on investments

11 (locutions) **en ~** in return ◆ **choc ou effet en ~** backlash ◆ **bâtiment en ~ (d'équerre)** building constructed at right angles ◆ **être sur le ~*** (péj) to be over the hill*, to be a bit past it* (Brit) ◆ **faire ~ à** to revert to ◆ **par un juste ~ des choses, il a été cette fois récompensé** events went his way ou fate was fair to him this time and he got his just reward ◆ **par un juste ~ des choses, il a été puni** he was punished, which served him right ◆ **par ~ (du courrier)** by return (of post) ◆ **sans ~** [partir] for ever ◆ **voyage sans ~** journey from which there is no return ◆ **faire un ~ sur soi-même** to take stock of o.s., to do some soul-searching; → **payer**

COMP **retour d'âge** change of life

retour en arrière (Ciné, Littérat) flashback; (= souvenir) look back; (= mesure rétrograde) retreat ◆ **faire un ~ en arrière** to take a look back, to look back; (Ciné) to flash back

retour de bâton (= contrecoup) backlash ◆ **ils ont dépensé sans compter pendant des années, maintenant c'est le ~ de bâton** they spent money recklessly for years - but now the chickens are coming home to roost

retour de couches first period (after pregnancy), return of menstruation

retour éternel (Philos) eternal recurrence

retour de flamme (dans un moteur) backfire; (fig) rekindling of passion ◆ **il y a eu un ~ de flamme** (feu) the flames leapt out

retour en force ◆ **il y a eu un ~ en force du**

racisme racism is back with a vengeance ◆ **on assiste à un ~ en force de leur parti sur la scène politique** their party is making a big comeback
retour de manivelle (*lit*) kick ◆ **il y aura un ~ de manivelle** (*fig*) it'll backfire (on them)

retourne /ʀ(ə)tuʀn/ NF 1 (*Ftbl*) overhead kick 2 (*Cartes*) *card turned over to determine the trump*

retournement /ʀ(ə)tuʀnəmɑ̃/ NM [*de situation, opinion publique*] reversal (*de* of) turnaround (*de* in)

retourner /ʀ(ə)tuʀne/ ► conjug 1 ◄ VT (*avec aux avoir*) 1 (= *mettre dans l'autre sens*) [+ *caisse, seau*] to turn upside down; [+ *matelas*] to turn (over); [+ *carte*] to turn up *ou* over; [+ *omelette, poisson, viande*] to turn over; [+ *crêpe*] (*avec une spatule*) to turn over; (*en lançant*) to toss ◆ **~ un tableau contre le mur** to turn a picture to face the wall ◆ **elle l'a retourné (comme une crêpe *ou* un gant)*** (*fig*) she soon changed his mind for him ◆ **~ la situation** to reverse the situation
2 (*en remuant, secouant*) [+ *sol, terre*] to turn over; [+ *salade*] to toss; [+ *foin*] to toss, to turn (over)
3 (= *mettre l'intérieur à l'extérieur*) [+ *parapluie, sac, vêtement*] to turn inside out; (*Couture*) [+ *col, vêtement*] to turn ◆ **~ ses poches pour trouver qch** to turn one's pockets inside out *ou* turn out one's pockets to find sth ◆ **son col est retourné** (*par mégarde*) his collar is sticking up; → **veste**
4 (= *orienter dans le sens opposé*) [+ *mot, phrase*] to turn round ◆ **~ un argument contre qn** to turn an argument back on sb *ou* against sb ◆ **il retourna le pistolet contre lui-même** he turned the gun on himself ◆ **~ un compliment** to return a compliment ◆ **je pourrais vous ~ votre critique** I could criticize you in the same way
5 (= *renvoyer*) [+ *lettre, marchandise*] to return, to send back
6 (* *fig* = *bouleverser*) [+ *maison, pièce*] to turn upside down; [+ *personne*] to shake ◆ **il a tout retourné dans la maison pour retrouver ce livre** he turned the whole house upside down to find that book ◆ **la nouvelle l'a complètement retourné** the news has severely shaken him ◆ **ce spectacle m'a retourné** this sight moved me deeply
7 (= *tourner plusieurs fois*) **~ une pensée/une idée dans sa tête** to turn a thought/an idea over (and over) in one's mind ◆ **~ le couteau *ou* le poignard dans la plaie** (*fig*) to twist the knife in the wound; → **tourner**
VI (*avec aux être*) 1 (= *aller à nouveau*) to return, to go back ◆ **~ en Italie/à la mer** to go back *ou* return to Italy/to the seaside ◆ **je devrai ~ chez le médecin** I'll have to go back to the doctor's ◆ **~ en arrière *ou* sur ses pas** to turn back, to retrace one's steps ◆ **il retourne demain à son travail/à l'école** he's going back to work/to school tomorrow ◆ **elle est retournée chez elle chercher son parapluie** she went back home to get her umbrella
2 (*à un état antérieur*) **~ à** to return to, to go back to ◆ **~ à la vie sauvage** to revert *ou* go back to the wild state ◆ **~ à Dieu** to return to God ◆ **il est retourné à son ancien métier/à la physique** he has gone back to his old job/to physics
3 (= *être restitué*) **la maison retournera à son frère** the house will go back *ou* revert to his brother
VB IMPERS ◆ **nous voudrions bien savoir de quoi il retourne** we'd really like to know what it's all about
VPR **se retourner** 1 [*personne couchée*] to turn over; [*automobiliste, véhicule*] to turn over, to overturn; [*bateau*] to capsize, to keel over ◆ **se ~ sur le dos/le ventre** to turn (over) onto one's back/one's stomach ◆ **se ~ dans son lit toute la nuit** to toss and turn all night in bed ◆ **il doit se ~ dans sa tombe !** (*hum*) he must be turning in his grave! (*hum*) ◆ **la voiture s'est retournée** the car overturned ◆ **laissez-lui le temps de se ~** (*fig*) give him time to sort himself out ◆ **il sait se ~** (*fig*) he knows how to cope
2 (= *tourner la tête*) to turn round ◆ **partir sans se ~** to go off without looking back *ou* without a backward glance ◆ **tout le monde se retournait sur lui *ou* sur son passage** everyone turned round as he went by
3 (*fig*) [*situation*] to be reversed ◆ **se ~ contre qn** [*personne*] to turn against sb; [*acte, situation*] to backfire on sb, to rebound on sb; (*Jur* = *poursuivre*) to take (court) action *ou* proceedings against sb ◆ **il ne savait vers qui se ~** he didn't know who to turn to
4 (= *tordre*) [+ *pouce*] to wrench, to twist
5 (*littér* = *cheminer*) **s'en ~** to journey back; (= *partir*) to depart, to leave ◆ **il s'en retourna comme il était venu** he left as he had come ◆ **s'en ~ dans son pays (natal)** to return to one's native country

> ⚠ Attention à ne pas traduire automatiquement **retourner** par **to return** ; l'anglais préfère employer un verbe à particule.

retracer /ʀ(ə)tʀase/ ► conjug 3 ◄ VT 1 (= *raconter*) [+ *histoire, vie*] to relate, to recount ◆ **le film retrace la carrière de l'artiste** the film goes back over *ou* traces the artist's career 2 (= *tracer à nouveau*) [+ *trait effacé*] to redraw, to draw again

rétractable /ʀetʀaktabl/ ADJ (*Jur*) revocable ◆ **crayon à pointe ~** retractable pencil ◆ **volant ~ (en cas de choc)** collapsible steering wheel ◆ **clavier ~** (*Ordin*) pull-out keyboard ◆ **emballé sous film ~** shrink-wrapped

rétractation /ʀetʀaktasjɔ̃/ NF [*d'aveux, promesse, témoignage*] retraction, withdrawal

rétracter /ʀetʀakte/ ► conjug 1 ◄ VT 1 (= *contracter, rentrer*) [+ *griffe*] to draw in, to retract 2 (*littér* = *revenir sur*) [+ *parole, opinion*] to retract, to withdraw, to take back VPR **se rétracter** 1 (= *se retirer*) [*griffe, antenne*] to retract ◆ **au moindre reproche, elle se rétractait** (*littér*) she would shrink at the slightest reproach 2 (= *se dédire, Jur*) to retract, to withdraw one's statement ◆ **je ne veux pas avoir l'air de me ~** I don't want to appear to back down

rétractile /ʀetʀaktil/ ADJ retractile

rétraction /ʀetʀaksjɔ̃/ NF (*Méd*) retraction

retraduction /ʀ(ə)tʀadyksjɔ̃/ NF retranslation

retraduire /ʀ(ə)tʀadɥiʀ/ ► conjug 38 ◄ VT (= *traduire de nouveau*) to retranslate, to translate again; (= *traduire dans la langue de départ*) to translate back

retrait /ʀ(ə)tʀɛ/ NM 1 (= *départ*) [*de mer*] ebb; [*d'eaux, glacier*] retreat; [*de candidat, candidature, troupes*] withdrawal ◆ **on vient d'annoncer le ~ du marché de ce produit** it's just been announced that this product has been withdrawn from sale *ou* taken off the market
2 [*de somme d'argent*] withdrawal; [*de bagages*] collection; [*d'objet en gage*] redemption ◆ **le ~ des bagages peut se faire à toute heure** luggage may be collected at any time ◆ **faire un ~ de 50 €** to withdraw €50 ◆ **~ à vue** withdrawal on demand
3 (= *suppression*) [*de demande, projet*] withdrawal ◆ **~ du permis (de conduire)** disqualification from driving, driving ban, revocation of a driving licence ◆ **il a eu un ~ de deux points** his licence was endorsed with two points ◆ **~ d'emploi** (*Admin*) deprivation of office ◆ **~ de plainte** (*Jur*) nonsuit ◆ **les étudiants réclament le ~ du projet de loi** the students are demanding that the bill be withdrawn *ou* shelved
4 (= *rétrécissement*) [*de ciment*] shrinkage, contraction; [*de tissu*] shrinkage ◆ **il y a du ~** there's some shrinkage
5 (*locutions*)
◆ **en retrait** ◆ **situé en ~** set back ◆ **se tenant en ~** standing back ◆ **rester en ~** [*personne*] to stay in the background ◆ **faire une passe en ~** (*Ftbl*) to pass back ◆ **ces propositions sont en ~ sur les précédentes** these offers do not go as far as the previous ones ◆ **notre chiffre d'affaires est en léger ~ par rapport aux années précédentes** our turnover is slightly down *ou* has fallen slightly compared to previous years
◆ **en retrait de** set back from ◆ **une petite maison, un peu en ~ de la route** a little house, set back a bit from the road

retraite /ʀ(ə)tʀɛt/ NF 1 (*Mil* = *fuite*) retreat ◆ **battre/sonner la ~** to beat/sound the retreat ◆ **battre en ~** to beat a retreat
2 (= *cessation de travail*) retirement ◆ **être en *ou* à la ~** to be retired *ou* in retirement ◆ **travailleur en ~** retired worker, pensioner ◆ **mettre qn à la ~** to pension sb off, to superannuate sb ◆ **mise à la ~ (d'office)** (compulsory) retirement ◆ **mettre qn à la ~ d'office** to make sb take compulsory retirement ◆ **prendre sa ~** to retire, to go into retirement ◆ **prendre une ~ anticipée** to retire early, to take early retirement ◆ **pour lui, c'est la ~ forcée** he has had retirement forced on him, he has had to retire early
3 (= *pension*) pension ◆ **toucher *ou* percevoir une petite ~** to receive *ou* draw a small pension; → **caisse, maison**
4 (*littér* = *refuge*) [*de poète, amants*] retreat, refuge; [*d'ours, loup*] lair; [*de voleurs*] hideout, hiding place
5 (*Rel* = *récollection*) retreat ◆ **faire *ou* suivre une ~** to be in retreat, to go into retreat
6 (*Constr*) tapering
COMP **retraite des cadres** management pension
retraite par capitalisation self-funded retirement scheme (*Brit*) *ou* plan (*US*)
retraite complémentaire supplementary pension
retraite aux flambeaux torchlight procession
retraite par répartition contributory pension scheme (*Brit*) *ou* plan (*US*)
retraite des vieux †* (old age) pension
retraite des vieux travailleurs retirement pension

retraité, e /ʀ(ə)tʀete/ ADJ 1 [*personne*] retired 2 [*déchets*] reprocessed NM,F (old age) pensioner ◆ **les ~s** retired people, pensioners ◆ **~s actifs** active retired people

retraitement /ʀ(ə)tʀɛtmɑ̃/ NM reprocessing ◆ **usine de ~ des déchets nucléaires** nuclear reprocessing plant

retraiter /ʀ(ə)tʀete/ ► conjug 1 ◄ VT to reprocess

retranchement /ʀ(ə)tʀɑ̃ʃmɑ̃/ NM (*Mil*) entrenchment, retrenchment ◆ **pousser qn dans ses derniers ~s** to drive *ou* hound sb into a corner ◆ **poussé dans ses derniers ~s, il dut admettre les faits** he was driven into a corner and had to admit the facts

retrancher /ʀ(ə)tʀɑ̃ʃe/ ► conjug 1 ◄ VT 1 (= *enlever*) [+ *quantité*] to take away, to subtract (*de* from); [+ *somme d'argent*] to deduct, to dock, to take off; [+ *passage, mot*] to take out, to remove, to omit (*de* from); ◆ **~ 10 de 15** to take 10 (away) from 15, to subtract 10 from 15 ◆ **~ une somme d'un salaire** to deduct *ou* dock a sum from a salary ◆ **si l'on retranche ceux qui n'ont pas de licence** if you leave out *ou* omit the non-graduates ◆ **ils étaient décidés à me ~ du monde des vivants** (*hum*) they were set on removing me from the land of the living

2 (littér = couper) [+ chair gangrenée] to remove, to cut off; [+ organe malade] to remove, to cut out
3 (littér = séparer) to cut off ◆ **son argent le retranchait des autres** his money cut him off from other people
4 († Mil = fortifier) to entrench
VPR **se retrancher** 1 (Mil = se fortifier) **se ~ derrière/dans** to entrench o.s. behind/in ◆ **se ~ sur une position** to entrench o.s. in a position
2 (fig) **se ~ dans son mutisme** to take refuge in silence ◆ **se ~ dans sa douleur** to shut o.s. away with one's grief ◆ **se ~ derrière la loi/le secret professionnel** to take refuge behind ou hide behind the law/professional secrecy

retranscription /ʀ(ə)tʀɑ̃skʀipsjɔ̃/ NF (= action) retranscription; (= résultat) new transcript

retranscrire /ʀ(ə)tʀɑ̃skʀiʀ/ ▸ conjug 39 ◂ VT to retranscribe

retransmettre /ʀ(ə)tʀɑ̃smɛtʀ/ ▸ conjug 56 ◂ VT 1 [+ match, émission, concert] (Radio) to broadcast; (TV) to show, to broadcast ◆ **~ qch en différé** (Radio) to broadcast a recording of sth; (TV) to show ou broadcast a recording of sth ◆ **~ qch en direct** (Radio) to broadcast sth live; (TV) to show ou broadcast sth live ◆ **retransmis par satellite** relayed by satellite 2 [+ nouvelle, ordre] to pass on

retransmission /ʀ(ə)tʀɑ̃smisjɔ̃/ NF 1 [de match, émission, concert] (Radio) broadcast; (TV) broadcast, showing ◆ **~ en direct/différé** live/recorded broadcast ◆ **la ~ du match aura lieu à 23 heures** the match will be shown at 11 pm 2 [de nouvelle, ordre] passing on

retravailler /ʀ(ə)tʀavaje/ ▸ conjug 1 ◂ VI 1 (= recommencer le travail) to start work again ◆ **il retravaille depuis le mois dernier** he has been back at work since last month 2 (= se remettre à) **~ à qch** to start work on sth again, to work at sth again VT [+ question] to give (some) more thought to; [+ discours, ouvrage] to work on again; [+ pâte à pain] to knead again; [+ argile] to work again; [+ minerai] to reprocess

retraverser /ʀ(ə)tʀavɛʀse/ ▸ conjug 1 ◂ VT (de nouveau) to recross; (dans l'autre sens) to cross back over

rétréci, e /ʀetʀesi/ ADJ [tricot, vêtement] shrunk, shrunken; [pupille] contracted; (péj) [esprit] narrow; (Écon) [marché] shrinking ◆ **"chaussée rétrécie"** "road narrows"

rétrécir /ʀetʀesiʀ/ ▸ conjug 2 ◂ VT [+ vêtement] to take in; [+ tissu] to shrink; [+ pupille] to contract; [+ conduit, orifice, rue] to narrow, to make narrower; [+ bague] to tighten, to make smaller; (fig) [+ champ d'activité, esprit] to narrow VI [laine, tissu] to shrink; [pupille] to contract; [rue, vallée] to narrow, to become ou get narrower; [esprit] to grow narrow; [cercle d'amis] to grow smaller, to dwindle; (Écon) [marché] to shrink, to contract ◆ **~ au lavage** to shrink in the wash ◆ **faire ~** [+ tissu] to shrink VPR **se rétrécir** → vi

rétrécissement /ʀetʀesismɑ̃/ NM [de laine, tricot] shrinkage; [de pupille] contraction; [de conduit, rue, vallée] narrowing; (Écon) [de marché] shrinking, contracting; [de vêtement] taking in; (Méd) [d'aorte, rectum] stricture

retrempe /ʀətʀɑ̃p/ NF [d'acier] requenching

retremper /ʀ(ə)tʀɑ̃pe/ ▸ conjug 1 ◂ VT 1 [+ acier] to requench ◆ **~ son courage aux dangers du front** to try ou test one's courage again amid the dangers at the front 2 (= réimprégner) to resoak VPR **se retremper** [baigneur] to go back into the water ◆ **se ~ dans l'ambiance familiale** to reimmerse o.s. in the family atmosphere

rétribuer /ʀetʀibɥe/ ▸ conjug 1 ◂ VT [+ ouvrier] to pay ◆ **~ le travail/les services de qn** to pay sb for their work/their services

rétribution /ʀetʀibysjɔ̃/ NF (= paiement) payment, remuneration (NonC); (littér = récompense) reward, recompense (de for)

> ⚠ **rétribution** ne se traduit pas par le mot anglais **retribution**, qui a le sens de 'châtiment'.

retriever /ʀetʀivœʀ/ NM retriever

rétro[1] * /ʀetʀo/ NM 1 abrév de **rétroviseur** 2 (Billard) screw-back stroke

rétro[2] /ʀetʀo/ ADJ INV ◆ **la mode/le style ~** retro fashions/style ◆ **robe ~** retro-style dress NM ◆ **le ~** retro

rétroactes /ʀetʀoakt/ NMPL (Belg = antécédents) antecedents ◆ **elle ignorait les ~ de l'affaire** she knew nothing about the background to the affair

rétroactif, -ive /ʀetʀoaktif, iv/ ADJ retroactive, retrospective ◆ **mesure/augmentation de salaire avec effet ~** retroactive ou backdated measure/pay rise ◆ **loi à effet ~** ex post facto law ◆ **la loi est entrée en vigueur avec effet ~ à compter du 1er octobre** the law came into force, retroactive to 1 October

rétroaction /ʀetʀoaksjɔ̃/ NF retroactive ou retrospective effect

rétroactivement /ʀetʀoaktivmɑ̃/ ADV retroactively, retrospectively

rétroactivité /ʀetʀoaktivite/ NF retroactivity

rétrocéder /ʀetʀosede/ ▸ conjug 6 ◂ VT (Jur) to retrocede, to cede back

rétrocession /ʀetʀosesjɔ̃/ NF (Jur) retrocession, retrocedence ◆ **la ~ de Hong-Kong à la Chine** the handover of Hong Kong to China

rétroéclairé, e /ʀetʀoeklɛʀe/ ADJ [document] back-lit

rétroflexe /ʀetʀoflɛks/ ADJ retroflex

rétrofusée /ʀetʀofyze/ NF retrorocket

rétrogradation /ʀetʀɔgʀadasjɔ̃/ NF (littér = régression) regression, retrogression; (Admin) [d'officier] demotion; [de fonctionnaire] demotion, downgrading; (Astron) retrogradation

rétrograde /ʀetʀɔgʀad/ ADJ 1 (péj = arriéré) [esprit] reactionary; [idées, mesures, politique] retrograde, reactionary 2 (= de recul) [mouvement, sens] backward, retrograde; (Littérat) [rimes, vers] palindromic; (Astron) retrograde ◆ **effet ~** (Billard) screw-back ◆ **amnésie ~** retrograde amnesia

rétrograder /ʀetʀɔgʀade/ ▸ conjug 1 ◂ VI 1 (en conduisant) to change down ◆ **~ de troisième en seconde** to change down from third to second 2 (= régresser) (dans une hiérarchie) to regress, to move down; (contre le progrès) to go backward, to regress; (= perdre son avance) to fall back; (= reculer) to move back ◆ **il rétrograde de la 2e à la 6e place** he's moved ou dropped* back from second to sixth place 3 (Astron) to retrograde VT [+ officier] to demote; [+ fonctionnaire] to demote, to downgrade

rétropédalage /ʀetʀopedalaʒ/ NM back-pedalling (lit)

rétroplanning /ʀetʀoplaniŋ/ NM reverse schedule

rétroprojecteur /ʀetʀopʀɔʒɛktœʀ/ NM overhead projector

rétropropulsion /ʀetʀopʀɔpylsjɔ̃/ NF reverse thrust

rétrospectif, -ive /ʀetʀɔspɛktif, iv/ ADJ [étude, peur] retrospective NF **rétrospective** (Art = exposition) retrospective ◆ **rétrospective Buster Keaton** (Ciné = projections) Buster Keaton season

rétrospectivement /ʀetʀɔspɛktivmɑ̃/ ADV [apparaître] in retrospect, retrospectively; [avoir peur, être jaloux] in retrospect, looking back ◆ **ces faits me sont apparus ~ sous un jour inquiétant** looking back on it ou in retrospect I saw the worrying side of these facts

retroussé, e /ʀ(ə)tʀuse/ ADJ [jupe] hitched up; [manche, pantalon] rolled up; [nez] turned-up, snub; [moustaches, lèvres] curled up

retrousser /ʀ(ə)tʀuse/ ▸ conjug 1 ◂ VT [+ jupe] to hitch up; [+ manche, pantalon] to roll up; [+ lèvres] to curl up ◆ **~ ses manches** (lit, fig) to roll up one's sleeves ◆ **~ ses babines** [animal] to snarl

retroussis /ʀ(ə)tʀusi/ NM (= partie retroussée) lip

retrouvailles /ʀ(ə)tʀuvaj/ NFPL (après une séparation) reunion ◆ **ses ~ avec son pays natal** his homecoming, his return to his homeland ◆ **aspirer aux ~ avec la nature** to dream of getting back to nature ◆ **les ~ franco-vietnamiennes** (Pol) the renewal of ties between France and Vietnam

retrouver /ʀ(ə)tʀuve/ ▸ conjug 1 ◂ VT 1 (= récupérer) [+ objet personnel, enfant] to find (again); [+ fugitif, objet égaré par un tiers] to find ◆ **~ son chemin** to find one's way again ◆ **on retrouva son cadavre sur une plage** his body was found on a beach ◆ **on les a retrouvés vivants** they were found alive ◆ **après sa maladie, il a retrouvé son poste** he got his job back again after his illness ◆ **une chienne ou une chatte n'y retrouverait pas ses petits, une poule n'y retrouverait pas ses poussins** it's in absolute chaos, it's an absolute shambles ou an unholy mess*
2 (= se remémorer) to think of, to remember, to recall ◆ **je ne retrouve plus son nom** I can't think of ou remember ou recall his name
3 (= revoir) [+ personne] to meet (up with) again; [+ endroit] to be back in, to see again ◆ **je l'ai retrouvé par hasard en Italie** I met up with him again by chance in Italy, I happened to come across him again in Italy ◆ **je l'ai retrouvé grandi/vieilli** I found him taller/looking older ◆ **et que je ne te retrouve pas ici !** and don't let me catch ou find you here again! ◆ **je serai ravi de vous ~** I'll be delighted to see ou meet you again
4 (= rejoindre) to join, to meet (again), to see (again) ◆ **je vous retrouve à 5 heures au Café de la Poste** I'll join ou meet ou see you at 5 o'clock at the Café de la Poste ◆ **après le pont, vous retrouverez la route de Caen** after the bridge you'll be back on the road to Caen
5 (= recouvrer) [+ forces, santé, calme] to regain; [+ joie, foi] to find again ◆ **~ le sommeil** to go ou get back to sleep (again) ◆ **elle mit longtemps à ~ la santé/le calme** she took a long time to regain her health/composure, it was a long time before she regained her health/composure ◆ **très vite elle retrouva son sourire** she very soon found her smile again
6 (= redécouvrir) [+ secret] to rediscover; [+ recette] to rediscover, to uncover; [+ article en vente, situation, poste] to find again ◆ **je voudrais ~ des rideaux de la même couleur** I'd like to find curtains in the same colour again ◆ **~ du travail** to find work again ◆ **il a bien cherché, mais une situation pareille ne se retrouve pas facilement** he looked around but it's not easy to come by ou find another job like that ◆ **une telle occasion ne se retrouvera jamais** an opportunity like this will never occur again ou crop up again
7 (= reconnaître) to recognize ◆ **on retrouve chez Louis le sourire de son père** you can see ou recognize his father's smile in Louis, you can see Louis has his father's smile ◆ **je retrouve bien là mon fils !** that's my son all right!

8 *(= trouver, rencontrer)* to find, to encounter ◆ **on retrouve sans cesse les mêmes tournures dans ses romans** you find the same expressions all the time in his novels

VPR **se retrouver** 1 *(= se réunir)* to meet, to meet up; *(= se revoir après une absence)* to meet again ◆ **après le travail, ils se sont tous retrouvés au café** after work they all met in the café ◆ **ils se sont retrouvés par hasard à Paris** they met again by chance in Paris ◆ **un club où l'on se retrouve entre sportifs** a club where sportsmen get together ◆ **comme on se retrouve !** fancy *ou* imagine meeting *ou* seeing you here! ◆ **on se retrouvera !** *(menace)* I'll get even with you!, I'll get my own back! *(Brit)*

2 *(= être de nouveau)* to find o.s. back ◆ **il se retrouva place de la Concorde** he found himself back at the Place de la Concorde ◆ **se ~ dans la même situation** to find o.s. back in the same situation ◆ **se ~ seul** *(sans amis)* to be left on one's own *ou* with no one; *(loin des autres, de la foule)* to be alone *ou* on one's own

3 *(* = finir)* **il s'est retrouvé en prison/dans le fossé** he ended up in prison/in the ditch, he wound up* *ou* landed up* *(Brit)* in prison/in the ditch ◆ **se ~ sur le trottoir*** to be back on the streets* ◆ **se ~ à la rue** *(= sans logement)* to be out on the street(s)

4 *(= voir clair, mettre de l'ordre)* **il ne se** *ou* **s'y retrouve pas dans ses calculs/la numération binaire** he can't make sense of his calculations/binary notation ◆ **on a de la peine à s'y ~, dans ces digressions/raisonnements** it's hard to find one's way through *ou* to make sense of these digressions/arguments ◆ **allez donc vous (y) ~ dans un désordre pareil !** let's see you try and straighten out this awful mess! ◆ **je ne m'y retrouve plus** I'm completely lost

5 *(* = rentrer dans ses frais)* **s'y ~** to break even ◆ **les frais furent énormes mais il s'y est largement retrouvé** his costs were enormous but he did very well out of the deal ◆ **tout ce que j'espère, c'est qu'on s'y retrouve** all I hope is that we don't lose on it *ou* that we break even ◆ **s'il te prête cet argent c'est qu'il s'y retrouve** if he's lending you this money it's because there's something in it for him

6 *(= trouver son chemin)* **se ~, s'y ~** to find one's way ◆ **la ville a tellement changé que je ne m'y retrouve plus** the town has changed so much I can't find my way around any more

7 *(littér = faire un retour sur soi-même)* to find o.s. again

8 *(= être présent)* **ces caractéristiques se retrouvent aussi chez les cervidés** these characteristics are also found *ou* encountered in the deer family

rétroviral, e (mpl **-aux**) /ʀetʀoviʀal, o/ retroviral

rétrovirus /ʀetʀoviʀys/ NM retrovirus

rétroviseur /ʀetʀɔvizœʀ/ NM rear-view mirror, (driving) mirror ◆ **~ latéral** wing mirror *(Brit)*, side-view mirror *(US)*

rets /ʀɛ/ NMPL *(littér = piège)* snare ◆ **prendre** *ou* **attraper qn dans ses ~** to ensnare sb ◆ **se laisser prendre** *ou* **tomber dans les ~ de qn** to be ensnared by sb

reubeu* /ʀøbø/ NM Arab

réuni, e /ʀeyni/ (ptp de **réunir**) ADJ 1 *(= pris ensemble)* **~s** (put) together, combined ◆ **aussi fort que les Français et les Anglais ~s** as strong as the French and the English put together *ou* combined 2 *(Comm = associés)* **~s** associated ◆ **les Transporteurs Réunis** Associated Carriers

réunification /ʀeynifikasjɔ̃/ NF reunification

réunifier /ʀeynifje/ ► conjug 7 ◄ VT to reunify, to reunite ◆ **l'Allemagne réunifiée** reunited *ou* reunified Germany VPR **se réunifier** to reunify

Réunion /ʀeynjɔ̃/ NF *(Géog)* ◆ **(l'île de) la ~** Réunion (Island)

réunion /ʀeynjɔ̃/ NF 1 *(= séance)* meeting ◆ **notre prochaine ~ sera le 10** our next meeting will be on the 10th ◆ **dans une ~** at *ou* in a meeting ◆ **~ d'information** briefing (session) ◆ **~ syndicale** union meeting ◆ **~ de travail** work session ◆ **être en ~** to be at *ou* in a meeting

2 *(Sport)* **~ cycliste** cycle rally ◆ **~ d'athlétisme** athletics meeting ◆ **~ hippique** *(= concours)* horse show; *(= course)* race meeting ◆ **~ sportive** sports meeting

3 *[d'entreprises]* merging; *[d'États]* union; *[de fleuves]* confluence, merging; *[de rues]* junction, joining; *[d'idées]* meeting

4 *[de faits, objets]* collection, gathering; *[de fonds]* raising; *[d'amis, membres d'une famille, d'un club]* bringing together, reunion, reuniting; *[d'éléments, parties]* combination; *(Math) [d'ensembles]* union ◆ **la ~ d'une province à un État** the union of a province with a state ◆ **~ de famille** family gathering

réunionite* /ʀeynjɔnit/ NF mania for meetings

réunionnais, e /ʀeynjɔnɛ, ɛz/ ADJ of *ou* from Réunion NM,F **Réunionnais(e)** inhabitant *ou* native of Réunion

réunir /ʀeyniʀ/ ► conjug 2 ◄ VT 1 *(= rassembler)* *[+ objets]* to gather *ou* collect (together); *[+ faits, preuves]* to put together ◆ **~ tout son linge en un paquet** to collect all one's washing into a bundle ◆ **~ des papiers par une épingle** to pin papers together, to fix papers together with a pin

2 *(= recueillir)* *[+ fonds]* to raise, to get together; *[+ preuves]* to collect, to gather (together); *[+ pièces de collection, timbres]* to collect

3 *(= cumuler)* to combine ◆ **ce livre réunit diverses tendances stylistiques** this book combines various styles, this book is a combination of different styles ◆ **~ toutes les conditions exigées** to satisfy *ou* meet all the requirements

4 *(= assembler)* *[+ participants]* to gather, to collect; *(= convoquer)* *[+ membres d'un parti]* to call together, to call a meeting of; *(= inviter)* *[+ amis, famille]* to entertain, to have over *ou* round *(Brit)*; *(= rapprocher)* *[+ antagonistes, ennemis]* to bring together, to reunite; *[+ anciens amis]* to bring together again, to reunite ◆ **on avait réuni les participants dans la cour** they had gathered those taking part in the yard ◆ **ce congrès a réuni des écrivains de toutes tendances** this congress gathered *ou* brought together writers of all kinds ◆ **nous réunissons nos amis tous les mercredis** we entertain our friends every Wednesday, we have our friends over *ou* round *(Brit)* every Wednesday ◆ **après une brouille de plusieurs années, ce deuil les a réunis** after a quarrel which lasted several years, this bereavement brought them together again *ou* reunited them

5 *(= raccorder)* *[+ éléments, parties]* to join ◆ **le couloir réunit les deux ailes du bâtiment** the corridor joins *ou* links the two wings of the building

6 *(= relier)* to join (up *ou* together) ◆ **~ deux fils** to tie two threads together ◆ **~ les bords d'une plaie/d'un accroc** to bring together the edges of a wound/of a tear

7 *(= rattacher à)* **~ à** *[+ province]* to unite to

VPR **se réunir** 1 *(= se rencontrer)* to meet, to get together ◆ **se ~ entre amis** to get together with (some) friends, to have a friendly get-together ◆ **le petit groupe se réunissait dans un bar** the little group would meet *ou* get together in a bar

2 *(= s'associer)* *[entreprises]* to combine, to merge; *[États]* to unite

3 *(= se joindre)* *[États]* to unite; *[fleuves]* to flow into each other, to merge; *[rues]* to join, to converge; *[idées]* to unite, to be united

réussi, e /ʀeysi/ (ptp de **réussir**) ADJ *(= couronné de succès)* *[dîner, mariage, soirée]* successful; *(= bien exécuté)* *[mouvement]* good, well executed *(frm)*; *[photo, roman]* successful; *[mélange, tournure]* effective ◆ **c'était vraiment très ~** it really was a great success *ou* very successful ◆ **eh bien, c'est ~ !** *(iro)* well that's just great! * *(iro)*, very clever! *(iro)*

réussir /ʀeysiʀ/ GRAMMAIRE ACTIVE 50.5 ► conjug 2 ◄

VI 1 *[affaire, entreprise, projet]* to succeed, to be a success, to be successful; *[culture, plantation]* to thrive, to do well; *[manœuvre, ruse]* to pay off ◆ **pourquoi l'entreprise n'a-t-elle pas réussi ?** why wasn't the venture a success?, why didn't the venture come off *ou* succeed? ◆ **le culot réussit parfois où la prudence échoue** sometimes nerve succeeds *ou* works where caution fails ◆ **la vigne ne réussit pas partout** vines don't thrive everywhere *ou* do not do well everywhere ◆ **tout lui/rien ne lui réussit** everything/nothing goes right for him, everything/nothing works for him ◆ **cela lui a mal réussi, cela ne lui a pas réussi** that didn't do him any good

2 *[personne]* *(dans une entreprise)* to succeed, to be successful; *(à un examen)* to pass ◆ **~ dans la vie** to succeed *ou* get on in life ◆ **~ dans les affaires/dans ses études** to succeed *ou* do well in business/in one's studies ◆ **et leur expédition au Pôle, ont-ils réussi ? – ils n'ont pas réussi** what about their expedition to the Pole, did they succeed? *ou* did they pull it off* ? – they failed ◆ **il a réussi/il n'a pas réussi à l'examen** he passed/he failed the exam ◆ **il a réussi dans tout ce qu'il a entrepris** he has made a success of *ou* been successful *ou* succeeded in all his undertakings ◆ **tous leurs enfants ont bien réussi** all their children have done well ◆ **il réussit bien en anglais/à l'école** he's a success at *ou* he does well at English/at school

3 ◆ **~ à faire qch** to succeed in doing sth, to manage to do sth ◆ **il a réussi à les convaincre** he succeeded in convincing them, he managed to convince them ◆ **cette maladroite a réussi à se brûler*** *(iro)* this clumsy girl has managed to burn herself *ou* has gone and burnt herself*

4 *(= être bénéfique à)* **~ à** to agree with ◆ **l'air de la mer/la vie active lui réussit** sea air/an active life agrees with him ◆ **le curry ne me réussit pas** curry doesn't agree with me

VT 1 *(= bien exécuter)* *[+ entreprise, film]* to make a success of ◆ **~ sa carrière** to have a successful career ◆ **~ sa vie** to make a success of one's life ◆ **ce plat est facile/difficile à ~** this dish is easy/difficult to make ◆ **elle a bien réussi sa sauce** her sauce was a great success ◆ **le Premier ministre a réussi son examen de passage** the Prime Minister has passed the test ◆ **vont-ils ~ leur coup ?** will they manage to carry *ou* pull it off? ◆ **il a réussi son coup : 1 500 € de raflés* en 10 minutes !** he pulled the job off – €1,500 swiped in 10 minutes flat* ◆ **je l'ai bien réussi, mon fils** *(hum)* I did a good job on my son *(hum)* ◆ **~ l'impossible** to manage to do the impossible ◆ **il a réussi le tour de force** *ou* **la prouesse de les réconcilier** he miraculously managed to bring about a reconciliation between them ◆ **elle a réussi une prouesse** she pulled off a remarkable feat ◆ **elle a réussi son effet** she achieved the effect she wanted

2 *(= exécuter)* *[+ but, essai]* to bring off, to pull off; *[+ tâche]* to bring off, to manage successfully ◆ **il a réussi deux très jolies photos** he

managed two very nice photographs, he took two very successful photographs

réussite /Reysit/ NF 1 success ◆ **ce fut une ~ complète** it was a complete *ou* an unqualified success ◆ **sa ~ sociale a été fulgurante** his rise to success was dazzling ◆ **c'est un signe de ~ sociale** it's a sign of social success ◆ **je me suis fait teindre les cheveux mais ce n'est pas une ~ !** I had my hair dyed but it hasn't turned out very well! ◆ **~ scolaire** academic success ◆ **le taux de ~ au concours est de 10%** there is a 10% success rate in the exam ◆ **les chances de ~ de cet accord** the agreement's chances of success *ou* of succeeding ◆ **ce n'est pas une franche ~** it's not a great success 2 *(Cartes)* patience ◆ **faire une ~** to play patience

réutilisable /Reytilizabl/ ADJ reusable ◆ **emballage non-~** disposable *ou* non-reusable packaging

réutiliser /Reytilize/ ► conjug 1 ◄ VT to reuse

revaccination /R(ə)vaksinasjɔ̃/ NF revaccination

revacciner /R(ə)vaksine/ ► conjug 1 ◄ VT to revaccinate

revaloir /R(ə)valwaR/ ► conjug 29 ◄ VT to pay back ◆ **je te revaudrai ça, je te le revaudrai** *(hostile)* I'll pay you back for this, I'll get even with you for this, I'll get back at you for this; *(reconnaissant)* I'll repay you some day

revalorisation /R(ə)valɔRizasjɔ̃/ NF *[de monnaie]* revaluation ◆ **~ salariale** *ou* **des salaires** wage increase ◆ **ils prônent la ~ des carrières de l'enseignement** they want to improve the image *ou* to restore the prestige of the teaching profession

revaloriser /R(ə)valɔRize/ ► conjug 1 ◄ VT 1 *[+ monnaie]* to revalue; *[+ titre]* to increase the value of 2 *[+ salaire]* to raise; *[+ conditions de travail]* to improve 3 *(= promouvoir) [+ méthode]* to promote again; *[+ valeur morale, institution, tradition]* to reassert the value of ◆ **l'entreprise veut ~ son image** the company wants to boost its image

revanchard, e /R(ə)vɑ̃ʃaR, aRd/ *(péj)* ADJ *[politique]* of revenge *(especially against enemy country)*; *[politicien]* who is an advocate of *ou* who advocates revenge; *[pays]* bent on revenge *(attrib)*; *[attitude, propos]* vengeful NM,F advocate of revenge, revanchist *(frm)*

revanche /R(ə)vɑ̃ʃ/ NF *(après défaite, humiliation)* revenge; *(Sport)* revenge match; *(Jeux)* return game; *(Boxe)* return fight *ou* bout ◆ **prendre sa ~ (sur qn)** to take one's revenge (on sb), to get one's own back (on sb) * *(Brit)* ◆ **prendre une ~ éclatante (sur qn)** to take a spectacular revenge (on sb) ◆ **donner sa ~ à qn** *(Jeux, Sport)* to let sb have *ou* give sb their revenge ◆ **le mépris est la ~ des faibles** contempt is the revenge of the weak

◆ **en revanche** on the other hand

revanchisme /R(ə)vɑ̃ʃism/ NM *(Pol)* revanchism

rêvasser /Revase/ ► conjug 1 ◄ VI to daydream, to let one's mind wander, to muse *(littér)*

rêvasserie /RevasRi/ NF *(= rêve)* daydreaming *(NonC)*; *(= chimère)* (idle) dream, (idle) fancy, daydreaming *(NonC)*

rêve /Rev/ NM 1 *(pendant le sommeil)* dream; *(éveillé)* dream, daydream; *(fig = chimère)* dream ◆ **le ~ et la réalité** dream and reality ◆ **le ~, les ~s** *(Psych)* dreaming, dreams ◆ **le ~ éveillé** *(Psych)* daydreaming ◆ **j'ai fait un ~ affreux** I had a horrible dream ◆ **~ prémonitoire** premonitory dream ◆ **mauvais ~** bad dream, nightmare ◆ **faire des ~s** to dream, to have dreams ◆ **faites de beaux ~s !** sweet dreams! ◆ **il est perdu dans ses ~s** he's (day)dreaming, he's in a world of his own ◆ **sortir d'un ~** to come out of a dream

2 *(locutions)* **c'était un beau ~ !** it was a lovely dream! ◆ **le ~ américain** the American dream ◆ **c'est un de mes ~s de jeunesse** it's one of the things I've always dreamt of *ou* wanted ◆ **c'est le ~ de leur vie** it's their life-long dream ◆ **mon ~ s'est enfin réalisé** my dream has finally come true ◆ **disparaître** *ou* **s'évanouir comme un ~** to vanish *ou* fade like a dream ◆ **disparaître comme dans un ~** to be gone *ou* disappear in a trice ◆ **ça, c'est le ~ *** that would be ideal *ou* (just) perfect ◆ **une maison comme ça, ce n'est pas le ~ *** it's not exactly a dream house

◆ **de rêve** ◆ **voiture/maison de ~** dream car/ house ◆ **créature de ~** gorgeous *ou* lovely creature ◆ **il fait un temps de ~ pour une balade à la campagne** it's perfect weather for a walk in the country ◆ **il mène une vie de ~** he leads an idyllic life ◆ **il a un corps de ~** he's got a superb body

◆ **de mes/ses** *etc* **rêves** ◆ **la voiture/la femme de ses ~s** the car/the woman of his dreams, his dream car/woman

◆ **en rêve** ◆ **voir/entendre qch en ~** to see/ hear sth in a dream ◆ **créer qch en ~** to dream sth up ◆ **même pas en ~ !** * in your dreams! *

rêvé, e /Reve/ (ptp de **rêver**) ADJ ideal, perfect ◆ **c'est l'occasion ~e !** it's the ideal *ou* a golden opportunity!

revêche /Rəvɛʃ/ ADJ *[air, ton]* surly; *[personne]* sour-tempered

réveil /Revɛj/ NM 1 *[de dormeur]* waking (up) *(NonC)*, wakening *(littér)*; *[de personne évanouie]* coming to *(NonC)*; *(fig = retour à la réalité)* awakening ◆ **à mon ~, je vis qu'il était parti** when I woke up *ou* on waking I found he was gone ◆ **il a le ~ difficile** he finds it hard to wake up, he finds waking up difficult ◆ **il eut un ~ brutal** he was rudely woken up *ou* awakened ◆ **dès le ~, il chante** as soon as he's awake *ou* he wakes up he starts singing ◆ **il a passé une nuit entrecoupée de ~s en sursaut** he had a bad night, waking with a start every so often ◆ **~ téléphonique** alarm call ◆ **le ~ fut pénible** *(fig)* he (*ou* I *etc*) had a rude awakening

2 *(fig = renaissance) [de nature, sentiment, souvenir]* reawakening; *[de volcan]* fresh stirrings; *[de douleur]* return ◆ **le ~ des nationalismes** the resurgence of nationalism

3 *(Mil)* reveille ◆ **sonner le ~** to sound the reveille ◆ **battre le ~** *to wake soldiers up to the sound of drums* ◆ **~ en fanfare** reveille on the bugle ◆ **ce matin, j'ai eu droit à un ~ en fanfare !** *(fig)* I was treated to a rowdy awakening this morning!

4 *(= réveille-matin)* alarm (clock) ◆ **mets le ~ à 8 heures** set the alarm for 8 (o'clock) ◆ **~ de voyage** travel alarm (clock)

réveillé, e /Reveje/ ADJ *(= à l'état de veille)* awake; *(* = dégourdi)* bright ◆ **à moitié ~** half asleep ◆ **il était mal ~** he was still half asleep, he hadn't woken up properly

réveille-matin /Revɛjmatɛ̃/ NM INV alarm clock

réveiller /Reveje/ ► conjug 1 ◄ VT 1 *[+ dormeur]* to wake (up), to waken, to awaken *(littér)*; *(= ranimer) [+ personne évanouie]* to bring round, to revive; *(= ramener à la réalité) [+ rêveur]* to wake up, to waken ◆ **réveillez-moi à 5 heures** wake me (up) at 5 (o'clock) ◆ **voulez-vous qu'on vous réveille ?** *(dans un hôtel)* would you like a wake-up call? ◆ **se faire ~ tous les matins à la même heure** to be woken up every morning at the same time ◆ **être réveillé en sursaut** to be woken (up) with a start ◆ **faire un vacarme à ~ les morts** to make a racket that would waken the dead ◆ **ne réveillez pas le chat qui dort** *(Prov)* let sleeping dogs lie *(Prov)*

2 *(= raviver) [+ appétit, courage]* to rouse, to awaken; *[+ douleur] (physique)* to start up again; *(mentale)* to revive, to reawaken; *[+ jalousie, rancune]* to reawaken, to rouse; *[+ souvenir]* to awaken, to revive, to bring back

3 *(= ranimer) [+ membre ankylosé]* to bring some sensation *ou* feeling back into ◆ **~ les consciences** to awaken *ou* stir people's consciences

VPR **se réveiller** 1 *[dormeur]* to wake (up), to awake, to awaken *(littér)*; *[personne évanouie]* to come round *(Brit) ou* around *(US)*, to come to, to regain consciousness; *[paresseux, rêveur]* to wake up *(de* from); ◆ **réveille-toi !** wake up! ◆ **se réveillant de sa torpeur** rousing himself from his lethargy ◆ **se ~ en sursaut** to wake up with a start

2 *(= se raviver) [appétit, courage]* to be roused; *[douleur]* to return; *[jalousie, rancune]* to be reawakened *ou* roused; *[souvenir]* to return, to come back, to reawaken *(littér)*

3 *(= se ranimer) [nature]* to reawaken; *[volcan]* to stir again ◆ **mon pied se réveille** the feeling's coming back into my foot, I'm getting some feeling back in my foot

réveillon /Revɛjɔ̃/ NM ◆ **~ (de Noël/du Nouvel An)** *(= repas)* Christmas Eve/New Year's Eve dinner; *(= fête)* Christmas Eve/New Year's (Eve) party; *(= date)* Christmas/New Year's Eve ◆ **on ne va pas passer le ~ là-dessus !** * let's not make a meal of this!

réveillonner /Revɛjɔne/ ► conjug 1 ◄ VI to celebrate Christmas *ou* New Year's Eve *(with a dinner and a party)*

révélateur, -trice /RevelatœR, tRis/ GRAMMAIRE ACTIVE 53.6 ADJ *[détail]* telling, revealing; *[indice, symptôme]* revealing ◆ **film ~ d'une mode/d'une tendance** film revealing a fashion/a tendency ◆ **c'est ~ d'un malaise profond** it reveals a deep malaise; → **lapsus** NM 1 *(Photo)* developer 2 *(littér) (= personne)* enlightener; *(= événement, expérience)* revelation ◆ **ce conflit a été le ~ d'une crise plus profonde** this conflict revealed a much deeper crisis

révélation /Revelasjɔ̃/ NF 1 *[de fait, projet, secret]* revelation, disclosure 2 *[d'artiste]* revelation, discovery ◆ **ce livre est une ~** this book is a revelation ◆ **ce fut une véritable ~ !** it was quite a revelation! ◆ **ce jeune auteur a été la ~ de l'année** this young author was the discovery of the year 3 *[de sensations, talent, tendances]* revelation ◆ **avoir la ~ de qch** to discover sth 4 *(= confidence, aveu)* disclosure, revelation ◆ **faire des ~s importantes** to make important disclosures *ou* revelations 5 *(Rel)* revelation 6 *(Photo) [d'image]* developing

révélé, e /Revele/ (ptp de **révéler**) ADJ *(Rel) [dogme, religion]* revealed

révéler /Revele/ ► conjug 6 ◄ VT 1 *(= divulguer) [+ fait, projet]* to reveal, to make known, to disclose; *[+ secret]* to disclose, to give away, to reveal; *[+ opinion]* to make known ◆ **je ne peux encore rien ~** I can't disclose *ou* reveal anything yet, I can't give anything away yet ◆ **~ que** to reveal that ◆ **ça l'avait révélée à elle-même** this had given her a new awareness of herself

2 *(= témoigner de) [+ aptitude, caractère]* to reveal, to show; *[+ sentiments]* to show ◆ **œuvre qui révèle une grande sensibilité** work which reveals *ou* displays great sensitivity ◆ **sa physionomie révèle la bonté/une grande ambition** his features show kindness/great ambition ◆ **son décolleté révélait la délicatesse de sa peau** her low neckline showed *ou* revealed her delicate skin

3 *(= faire connaître) [+ artiste] [imprésario]* to discover; *[œuvre]* to bring to fame; *(Rel)* to reveal ◆ **le roman qui l'a révélé au public** the novel that introduced him to the public

4 *(Photo)* to develop

VPR **se révéler** 1 *[vérité, talent, tendance]* to be revealed, to reveal itself; *(Rel)* to reveal o.s. ◆ **des sensations nouvelles se révélaient à lui** he was becoming aware of new feelings

2 *[artiste]* to come into one's own ◆ **il ne s'est révélé que vers la quarantaine** he didn't really come into his own until he was nearly forty

3 (= *s'avérer*) **se ~ cruel/ambitieux** to show o.s. *ou* prove to be cruel/ambitious ◆ **se ~ difficile/aisé** to prove difficult/easy ◆ **son hypothèse se révéla fausse** his hypothesis proved (to be) *ou* was shown to be false

revenant, e /ʀ(ə)vənɑ̃, ɑ̃t/ **NM,F** ghost ◆ **tiens, un ~ !*** hello stranger! *; → **histoire**

revendeur, -euse /ʀ(ə)vɑ̃dœʀ, øz/ **NM,F** (= *détaillant*) retailer, dealer, stockist *(Brit)*; *(d'occasion)* secondhand dealer ◆ **chez votre ~ habituel** at your local dealer *ou* stockist *(Brit)* ◆ **~ (de drogue)** (drug-)pusher * *ou* dealer

revendicateur, -trice /ʀ(ə)vɑ̃dikatœʀ, tʀis/ **NM,F** protester **ADJ** ◆ **lettre revendicatrice** letter putting forward one's claims ◆ **déclaration revendicatrice** declaration of claims ◆ **avoir une attitude revendicatrice** to make a lot of demands

revendicatif, -ive /ʀ(ə)vɑ̃dikatif, iv/ **ADJ** *[mouvement]* protest *(épith)* ◆ **action revendicative** protest campaign ◆ **organiser une journée d'action revendicative** to organize a day of action *ou* protest (in support of one's claims) ◆ **les syndicats ont adopté une position plus revendicative** the unions have stepped up their demands

revendication /ʀ(ə)vɑ̃dikasjɔ̃/ **NF** 1 (= *action*) claiming ◆ **il n'y a pas eu de ~ de l'attentat** no one claimed responsibility for the attack 2 *(Pol, Syndicats = demande)* claim, demand ◆ **journée de ~** day of action *ou* of protest (in support of one's claims) ◆ **lettre de ~** letter putting forward one's claims ◆ **mouvement de ~** protest movement ◆ **~s salariales/territoriales** wage/territorial claims ◆ **~s sociales** workers' demands ◆ **~s d'autonomie** demands for autonomy; → **catégoriel**

revendiquer /ʀ(ə)vɑ̃dike/ ▸ **conjug 1** ◂ **VT** 1 (= *demander*) *[+ chose due, droits]* to claim, to demand ◆ **ils passent leur temps à ~** they're forever making demands ◆ **~ l'égalité des salaires** to demand equal pay 2 (= *assumer*) *[+ paternité, responsabilité]* to claim; *[+ attentat, explosion]* to claim responsibility for ◆ **l'attentat n'a pas été revendiqué** no one has claimed responsibility for the attack ◆ **il revendique son appartenance à la communauté juive** he asserts *ou* proclaims his Jewish identity **VPR se revendiquer** ◆ **il se revendique (comme) Basque** he asserts *ou* proclaims his Basque identity ◆ **elle se revendiquait du féminisme** she was a feminist and proud of it

revendre /ʀ(ə)vɑ̃dʀ/ ▸ **conjug 41** ◂ **VT** 1 (= *vendre d'occasion ou au détail*) to resell, to sell; *[+ actions, terres, filiale]* to sell off ◆ **acheté 5 €, cet article est revendu** *ou* **se revend 30 €** purchased for €5, this item is being resold at €30 ◆ **ça se revend facilement** that's easily resold *ou* sold again ◆ **il a revendu sa voiture pour payer ses dettes** he sold his car to pay off his debts

2 (= *vendre davantage*) **j'en ai vendu deux en janvier et j'en ai revendu quatre en février** I sold two in January and I sold another four in February ◆ **j'en ai vendu la semaine dernière mais je n'en ai pas revendu depuis** I sold some last week but I've sold no more since then

3 *(locutions)* **avoir de l'énergie/de l'intelligence à ~** to have energy/brains to spare ◆ **si tu veux un tableau, on en a à ~** if you want a picture, we've got lots of them ◆ **des chapeaux, elle en a à ~** she's got more hats than she knows what to do with

revenez-y /ʀəv(ə)nezi, ʀ(ə)vənezi/ **NM INV** → **goût**

revenir /ʀəv(ə)niʀ, ʀ(ə)vəniʀ/ ▸ conjug 22 ◂

1 VERBE INTRANSITIF 2 VERBE PRONOMINAL

1 – VERBE INTRANSITIF

1 [= repasser, venir de nouveau] to come back, to come again ◆ **il doit ~ nous voir demain** he's coming back to see us tomorrow, he's coming to see us again tomorrow ◆ **pouvez-vous ~ plus tard ?** can you come back later? ◆ **reviens ! je plaisantais** come back! I was joking ◆ **~ sur ses pas** to retrace one's steps

2 [= réapparaître] *[saison, mode]* to come back, to return; *[soleil, oiseaux]* to return, to reappear; *[fête, date]* to come (round) again; *[calme, ordre]* to return; *[thème, idée]* to recur, to reappear ◆ **~ à la mémoire** *[souvenir, idée]* to come back to mind ◆ **cette expression revient souvent dans ses livres** that expression often crops up in his books ◆ **Noël revient chaque année à la même date** Christmas comes (round) on the same date every year ◆ **sa lettre est revenue parce qu'il avait changé d'adresse** his letter was returned *ou* came back because he had changed his address

3 [= rentrer] to come back, to return ◆ **~ quelque part/de quelque part** to come back *ou* return (to) somewhere/from somewhere ◆ **~ chez soi** to come back *ou* return home ◆ **~ dans son pays** to come back *ou* return to one's country ◆ **~ en bateau/avion** to sail/fly back, to come back by boat/air ◆ **~ à la hâte** to hurry back ◆ **~ de voyage** to return from a trip ◆ **en revenant de l'école** on the way back *ou* home from school ◆ **je lui téléphonerai en revenant** I'll phone him when I get back ◆ **sa femme lui est revenue** his wife has come back to him ◆ **je reviens dans un instant** I'll be back in a minute, I'll be right back * ◆ **on va à la piscine ? – j'en reviens !** shall we go to the swimming pool? – I've just come back from there!

4 [= retourner] **~ en arrière** *(gén)* to go back ◆ **on ne peut pas ~ en arrière** *(dans le temps)* you can't turn *ou* put back the clock

5 [= coûter] **ça revient cher** it's expensive

6 [Culin] **faire ~** to brown ◆ **"faire revenir les oignons dans le beurre"** "brown *ou* fry the onions gently in the butter"

7 [locutions]

◆ **revenir à qch** (= *recommencer, reprendre*) *[+ études, sujet]* to go back to, to return to; *[+ méthode, procédé]* to go back to, to return to, to revert to ◆ **~ à ses premières amours** to go back *ou* return to one's first love ◆ **~ à de meilleurs sentiments** to return to a better frame of mind ◆ **~ à la religion** to come back to religion ◆ **~ à la vie** to come back to life ◆ **on y reviendra, à cette mode** this fashion will come back ◆ **nous y reviendrons dans un instant** we'll come back to that in a moment ◆ **n'y revenez plus !** (= *ne recommencez plus*) don't do that again!; (= *n'en redemandez plus*) that's all you're getting!, don't bother coming back! ◆ **j'en reviens toujours là, il faut ...** I still come back to this, we must ... ◆ **il n'y a pas à y ~** there's no going back on it ◆ **~ à la charge** to return to the attack

(= *équivaloir à*) to come down to, to amount to, to boil down to ◆ **cette hypothèse revient à une proposition très simple** this hypothesis comes down *ou* amounts to a very simple proposition ◆ **ça revient à une question d'argent** it all boils down to a question of money ◆ **cela revient à dire que ...** it amounts to saying that ... ◆ **ça revient au même** it amounts *ou* comes to the same thing

(= *coûter*) to amount to, to come to, to cost ◆ **ça revient à 20 €** it comes to *ou* amounts to €20 ◆ **à combien est-ce que cela va vous ~ ?** how much will that cost you?, how much will that set you back? * ◆ **~ à la marque** *ou* **au score** *(Sport)* to draw (even *ou* level)

◆ **revenir à qn** *[souvenir, idée]* to come back to sb ◆ **son nom me revient maintenant** his name has come back to me now ◆ **ça me revient !** I've got it now!, it's coming back to me now! *[courage, appétit, parole]* to come back to sb, to return (to sb) ◆ **le courage me revint** my courage came back to me *ou* returned ◆ **l'appétit m'est revenu** my appetite returned, I got my appetite back

[rumeur] ◆ **~ à qn** *ou* **aux oreilles de qn** to reach sb's ears, to get back to sb ◆ **il m'est revenu que ...** *(frm)* word has come back to me *ou* reached me that ...

(= *appartenir à*) *[droit, honneur, responsabilité]* to fall to sb; *[biens, somme d'argent]* (= *échoir à*) to come *ou* pass to sb; (= *être la part de*) to come *ou* go to sb ◆ **il lui revient de décider** (= *incomber à*) it is for him *ou* up to him to decide ◆ **ce titre lui revient de droit** this title is his by right ◆ **cet honneur lui revient** this honour is due to him *ou* is his by right ◆ **tout le mérite vous revient** all the credit goes to you, the credit is all yours ◆ **les biens de son père sont revenus à l'État** his father's property passed to the state ◆ **là-dessus, 15 € me reviennent** €15 of that comes to me

(* = *plaire à*) ◆ **il a une tête qui ne me revient pas** I don't like the look of him ◆ **elle ne me revient pas du tout cette fille** I don't like that girl at all

◆ **revenir à soi** *[personne]* to come to, to come round *(Brit)*

◆ **revenir de** (= *se remettre de*) *[+ maladie]* to recover from, to get over; *[+ syncope]* to come to after, to come round from *(Brit)*; *[+ égarement, surprise]* to get over; *[+ illusions]* to lose, to shake off; *[+ erreurs, théories]* to leave behind, to throw over, to put *ou* cast aside ◆ **il revient de loin** (= *il a frôlé la catastrophe*) he had a close shave; (= *il a eu des ennuis*) he had a tough time ◆ **crois-tu qu'il en reviendra ?** (= *qu'il en réchappera*) do you think he'll pull through? ◆ **je n'en reviens pas !** *(surprise)* I can't believe it! ◆ **ils sont déjà revenus de ces théories** they have already thrown over *ou* put aside these theories ◆ **elle est revenue de tout** she's seen it all before

◆ **revenir sur** (= *réexaminer*) *[+ affaire, problème]* to go back over (= *se dédire de*) *[+ promesse]* to go back on; *[+ décision]* to go back on, to reconsider *(Sport = rattraper)* to catch up with ◆ **ne revenons pas là-dessus** let's not go back over that ◆ **~ sur le passé** to go back over the past; → **tapis**

2 – VERBE PRONOMINAL

s'en revenir († *ou littér*) **comme il s'en revenait (du village), il aperçut un aigle** as he was coming back (from the village), he noticed an eagle ◆ **il s'en revint la queue basse** he came back with his tail between his legs ◆ **il s'en revint, le cœur plein d'allégresse** he came away with a joyful heart

revente /ʀ(ə)vɑ̃t/ **NF** resale ◆ **valeur à la ~** resale value ◆ **il a été inculpé de ~ de drogue** he was charged with drug dealing ◆ **la ~ de l'entreprise lui a rapporté beaucoup d'argent** he made a lot of money on the sale of the company

revenu /ʀəv(ə)ny/ **NM** *[de particulier]* income (NonC) (*de* from); *[d'État]* revenue (*de* from); *[de domaine, terre]* income (*de* from); *[de capital, investissement]* yield (*de* from, on); ◆ **~ annuel/brut/imposable/par habitant** annual/gross/assessed/per capita income ◆ **à ~ fixe** *(Fin)* *[valeurs]* fixed-yield ◆ **les pays à ~ élevé** high-income countries ◆ **famille/ménage à ~s modestes** low-income family/ household ◆ **avoir de gros ~s** to have a large income ◆ **personne sans ~s réguliers** person who has no regular income

COMP **revenus de l'État** public revenue
revenu fiscal tax revenue
revenu intérieur brut gross domestic income
revenu minimum d'insertion *minimum welfare payment given to those who are not entitled to unemployment benefit*, ≃ income support (Brit), welfare (US)
revenu national gross national product
revenu net d'impôts disposable income
revenu du travail earned income

rêver /ʀeve/ ▸ conjug 1 ◂ VI 1 *[dormeur]* to dream (*de*, *à* of, about); ◆ ~ **que** to dream that ◆ **j'ai rêvé de toi** I dreamt about *ou* of you ◆ **il en rêve la nuit** he dreams about it at night ◆ ~ **tout éveillé** to be lost in a daydream ◆ **je ne rêve pas, c'est bien vrai ?** I'm not imagining it *ou* dreaming, am I? – it's really true! ◆ **tu m'as appelé ? – moi ? tu rêves !** did you call me? – me? you must have been dreaming! *ou* you're imagining things! ◆ **une révolution, maintenant ? vous rêvez !** a revolution now? your imagination's running away with you! ◆ **on croit ~ !*** I can hardly believe it!, the mind boggles! * ◆ **(non,) mais je rêve !*** he (*ou* they *etc*) can't be serious! ◆ **(il ne) faut pas ~*** I wouldn't count on it * ◆ **on peut toujours ~** there's no harm in dreaming
2 (= *rêvasser*) to dream, to muse (*littér*), to daydream ◆ **travaille au lieu de ~ !** get on with your work instead of (day)dreaming! ◆ ~ **à des jours meilleurs** to dream of better days
3 (= *désirer*) to dream ◆ ~ **tout haut** to dream aloud ◆ ~ **de qch/de faire** to dream of sth/of doing ◆ **elle rêve d'une chaumière en pleine forêt** she dreams of a cottage in the heart of a forest ◆ ~ **de réussir** to long to succeed, to long for success ◆ ~ **de rencontrer la femme idéale** to dream of meeting *ou* long to meet the ideal woman ◆ **des images qui font ~** pictures that fire the imagination ◆ **ça fait ~ de l'entendre parler de ses voyages** hearing him talk about his travels really gets the imagination going
VT 1 *(en dormant)* to dream ◆ **j'ai rêvé la même chose qu'hier** I dreamt the same (thing) as last night
2 (*littér* = *imaginer*) to dream ◆ **il rêve sa vie au lieu de la vivre** he's dreaming his life away instead of living it ◆ **je n'ai jamais dit ça, c'est toi qui l'as rêvé !** (*péj*) I never said that – you must have dreamt it!
3 (= *désirer*) to dream of ◆ ~ **mariage/succès** (*littér*) to dream of marriage/success ◆ **il se rêve conquérant** (*littér*) he dreams of being a conqueror ◆ **il ne rêve que plaies et bosses** his mind is full of heroic dreams

réverbération /ʀevɛʀbeʀasjɔ̃/ NF *[de son]* reverberation; *[de chaleur, lumière]* reflection

réverbère /ʀevɛʀbɛʀ/ NM (*d'éclairage*) street lamp *ou* light; (*Tech*) reflector; → **allumeur**

réverbérer /ʀevɛʀbeʀe/ ▸ conjug 6 ◂ VT *[+ son]* to send back, to reverberate; *[+ chaleur, lumière]* to reflect

reverdir /ʀ(ə)vɛʀdiʀ/ ▸ conjug 2 ◂ VI *[plantes]* to grow green again VT (*Tech*) *[peaux]* to soak

révérence /ʀeveʀɑ̃s/ NF 1 (= *salut*) *[d'homme]* bow; *[de femme]* curtsey ◆ **faire une ~** *[homme]* to bow; *[femme]* to curtsey (*à qn* to sb); ◆ **tirer sa ~ (à qn)** (*lit*) to bow out, to make one's bow (and leave); (*fig*) to take one's leave (of sb) 2 (*littér* = *respect*) reverence (*envers, pour* for); ◆ ~ **parler** † with all due respect

révérencieux, -ieuse /ʀeveʀɑ̃sjø, jøz/ ADJ (*littér*) reverent ◆ **être peu ~ envers** to show scant respect for

révérend, e /ʀeveʀɑ̃, ɑ̃d/ ADJ, NM reverend ◆ **le Révérend Père Martin** Reverend Father Martin

révérendissime /ʀeveʀɑ̃disim/ ADJ most reverend

révérer /ʀeveʀe/ ▸ conjug 6 ◂ VT (*littér*) (*gén*) to revere; (*Rel*) to revere, to reverence

rêverie /ʀɛvʀi/ NF 1 (= *activité*) daydreaming, reverie (*littér*), musing (*littér*) 2 (= *rêve*) daydream, reverie (*littér*) 3 (*péj* = *chimère*) ~**s** daydreams, delusions, illusions

revérifier /ʀ(ə)veʀifje/ ▸ conjug 7 ◂ VT to double-check

revernir /ʀ(ə)vɛʀniʀ/ ▸ conjug 2 ◂ VT to revarnish

revers /ʀ(ə)vɛʀ/ GRAMMAIRE ACTIVE 53.3 NM 1 *[de feuille, papier]* back; *[d'étoffe]* wrong side ◆ **le ~ de la charité** (*littér*) the reverse of charity ◆ **prendre l'ennemi de** *ou* **à ~** to take the enemy from *ou* in the rear
2 *[de médaille, pièce d'argent]* reverse, reverse side, back ◆ **pièce frappée au ~ d'une effigie** coin struck with a portrait on the reverse ◆ **c'est le ~ de la médaille** (*fig*) that's the other side of the coin ◆ **toute médaille a son ~** (*fig*) every rose has its thorn (*Prov*)
3 *[de main]* back ◆ **d'un ~ de main** (*lit*) with the back of one's hand ◆ **il a balayé** *ou* **écarté nos arguments d'un ~ de (la) main** (*fig*) he brushed aside all our arguments, he dismissed all our arguments out of hand
4 (*Tennis*) backhand ◆ **faire un ~** to play a backhand shot ◆ **volée de ~** backhand volley ◆ ~ **à deux mains** double-handed *ou* two-handed backhand
5 (*Habillement*) *[de manteau, veste]* lapel, revers; *[de pantalon]* turn-up (*Brit*), cuff (*US*); *[de bottes]* top; *[de manche]* (turned-back) cuff ◆ **bottes à ~** turned-down boots ◆ **pantalons à ~** trousers with turn-ups (*Brit*) *ou* cuffs (*US*)
6 (= *coup du sort*) setback ◆ ~ **(de fortune)** reverse (of fortune) ◆ ~ **économiques/militaires** economic/military setbacks *ou* reverses

reversement /ʀ(ə)vɛʀsəmɑ̃/ NM (*Fin*) *[d'excédent, somme]* putting back, paying back (*dans, sur* into); *[de titre]* transfer

reverser /ʀ(ə)vɛʀse/ ▸ conjug 1 ◂ VT 1 *[+ liquide]* (= *verser davantage*) to pour out some more ◆ **reverse-moi du vin/un verre de vin** pour me (out) some more wine/another glass of wine ◆ **reversez le vin dans la bouteille** (= *remettre*) pour the wine back into the bottle 2 (*Fin*) *[+ excédent, somme]* to put back, to pay back (*dans, sur* into); *[+ titre]* to transfer

réversibilité /ʀevɛʀsibilite/ NF *[de pension]* reversibility; *[de mouvement]* (*Chim*) reversibility

réversible /ʀevɛʀsibl/ ADJ *[mouvement, vêtement, réaction chimique]* reversible; (*Jur*) revertible (*sur* to); ◆ **l'histoire n'est pas ~** history cannot be undone *ou* altered

réversion /ʀevɛʀsjɔ̃/ NF (*Bio, Jur*) reversion ◆ **pension de ~** reversion pension

revêtement /ʀ(ə)vɛtmɑ̃/ NM (= *enduit*) coating; (= *surface*) *[de route]* surface; (= *garniture, placage*) *[de mur extérieur]* facing, cladding; *[de mur intérieur]* covering ◆ ~ **(du sol)** flooring (*NonC*), floor-covering (*NonC*) ◆ ~ **mural** wall-covering (*NonC*) ◆ ~ **antiadhésif** *[de poêle]* nonstick coating

revêtir /ʀ(ə)vetiʀ/ ▸ conjug 20 ◂ VT 1 (*frm, hum* = *mettre*) *[+ uniforme, habit]* to don (*frm*), to put on
2 (= *prendre, avoir*) *[+ caractère, importance]* to take on, to assume; *[+ apparence, forme]* to assume, to take on ◆ **une rencontre qui revêt une importance particulière** a meeting which is especially important ◆ **cela ne revêt aucun caractère d'urgence** it is by no means urgent ◆ **le langage humain revêt les formes les plus variées** human language appears in *ou* takes on the most varied forms
3 (*frm, hum* = *habiller*) *[vêtement]* to adorn ◆ ~ **qn de** to dress sb in ◆ ~ **un prélat des vêtements sacerdotaux** to clothe a prelate in his priestly robes
4 (= *couvrir, déguiser*) ~ **qch de** to cloak sth in, to cover sth with
5 (*frm*) ~ **qn de** *[+ dignité, autorité]* (= *investir de*) to endow *ou* invest sb with
6 (*Admin, Jur*) ~ **un document de sa signature/d'un sceau** to append one's signature/a seal to a document
7 (= *enduire*) to coat (*de* with); (= *couvrir*) *[+ route]* to surface (*de* with); *[+ mur, sol]* to cover (*de* with); ◆ ~ **un mur de boiseries** to (wood-)panel a wall ◆ ~ **un mur de carreaux** to tile a wall, to cover a wall with tiles ◆ ~ **de plâtre** to plaster ◆ ~ **de crépi** to face with roughcast, to roughcast ◆ ~ **d'un enduit imperméable** to cover with a waterproof coating, to give a waterproof coating to ◆ **rue revêtue d'un pavage** street which has been paved over ◆ **sommets revêtus de neige** snow-clad *ou* snow-covered summits
VPR **se revêtir** (= *mettre*) **se ~ de** (*frm*) to array o.s. in (*frm*), to don (*frm*), to dress o.s. in ◆ **vers l'automne les sommets se revêtent de neige** (*littér*) as autumn draws near, the mountain tops don their snowy mantle (*littér*) *ou* are bedecked (*frm*) with snow

revêtu, e /ʀ(ə)vety/ (ptp de **revêtir**) ADJ 1 (= *habillé de*) ~ **de** dressed in, wearing 2 *[route]* surfaced ◆ **chemin non ~** unsurfaced road 3 ~ **de** (= *enduit de*) coated with

rêveur, -euse /ʀɛvœʀ, øz/ ADJ *[air, personne]* dreamy ◆ **il a l'esprit ~** he's inclined to be a dreamer ◆ **ça vous laisse ~*** it makes you wonder NM,F (*lit, péj*) dreamer

rêveusement /ʀɛvøzmɑ̃/ ADV (= *distraitement*) dreamily, as (if) in a dream; (= *avec perplexité*) distractedly

revient /ʀəvjɛ̃/ NM → **prix**

revigorant, e /ʀ(ə)vigɔʀɑ̃, ɑ̃t/ ADJ *[vent, air frais]* invigorating; *[repas, boisson]* reviving (*épith*); *[discours, promesse]* cheering, invigorating

revigorer /ʀ(ə)vigɔʀe/ ▸ conjug 1 ◂ VT *[vent, air frais]* to invigorate; *[repas, boisson]* to revive, to put new life into, to buck up*; *[discours, promesse]* to cheer, to invigorate, to buck up* ◆ **un petit vent frais qui revigore** a bracing *ou* an invigorating cool breeze ◆ **ces mesures vont ~ l'économie locale** these measures will give a boost to the local economy

revirement /ʀ(ə)viʀmɑ̃/ NM (= *changement d'avis*) change of mind, reversal (of opinion); (= *changement brusque*) *[de tendances]* reversal (*de* of); *[de goûts]* (abrupt) change (*de* in); ◆ ~ **d'opinion** change *ou* U-turn *ou* turnaround in public opinion ◆ **un ~ soudain de la situation** a sudden reversal of the situation

révisable /ʀevizabl/ ADJ 1 (= *qui peut être sujet à modification*) *[contrat, salaire]* revisable ◆ **prix ~ à la baisse/hausse** price that can be revised downwards/upwards ◆ **prêt à taux ~** (*gén*) loan with adjustable interest rate; (*immobilier*) ≃ adjustable-rate mortgage 2 (*Jur*) *[procès]* reviewable

réviser /ʀevize/ ▸ conjug 1 ◂ VT 1 *[+ procès, règlement]* to review; *[+ constitution, opinion]* to revise ◆ **j'ai révisé mon jugement sur lui** I've revised my opinion of him 2 *[+ comptes]* to audit; *[+ moteur, installation]* to overhaul, to service ◆ **faire ~ sa voiture** to have one's car serviced ◆ **j'ai fait ~ les freins** I've had the brakes looked at 3 (= *mettre à jour*) *[+ liste, estimation]* to revise ◆ ~ **à la hausse/à la baisse** to revise upwards/downwards 4 (= *corriger*) *[+ texte, manuscrit, épreuves]* to revise ◆ **nouvelle édition complètement révisée** new and completely revised edition 5 *(Scol)* *[+ sujet]* to revise ♦ ~ **son histoire** to revise history, to do one's history revision ♦ **commencer à** ~ to start revising *ou* (one's) revision

réviseur /ʀevizœʀ/ **NM** reviser ♦ ~**-comptable** independent auditor

révision /ʀevizjɔ̃/ **NF** 1 *(à l'école)* revision ♦ **faire ses ~s** to do one's revision, to revise 2 *[de voiture]* service; *[de moteur]* overhaul *(NonC)*; *(= examen)* servicing ♦ **prochaine ~ après 10 000 km** next major service due after 10,000 km 3 *[de procès, règlement]* review; *[de constitution]* revision 4 *(= correction)* *[de texte, manuscrit, épreuves]* revision 5 *(= mise à jour)* *[de liste]* revision *(NonC)* ♦ ~ **des listes électorales** revision of the electoral register; → **conseil** 6 *(= vérification)* *[de comptes]* audit; *[d'installation]* overhaul *(NonC)*

révisionnisme /ʀevizjɔnism/ **NM** revisionism

révisionniste /ʀevizjɔnist/ **ADJ, NMF** revisionist

revisiter /ʀ(ə)vizite/ ► conjug 1 ◄ **VT** *[+ musée, ville]* to revisit, to visit again; *[+ théorie]* to reexamine ♦ **la mode des années 30/la pièce de Molière revisitée par Anne Morand** thirties fashions/Molière's play reinterpreted by Anne Morand, a new take on thirties fashions/Molière's play by Anne Morand

revisser /ʀ(ə)vise/ ► conjug 1 ◄ **VT** to screw back again

revitalisant, e /ʀ(ə)vitalizɑ̃, ɑ̃t/ **ADJ** *[séjour, vacances]* revitalizing, restorative; *[crème de soin, lotion, shampoing]* revitalizing, regenerative

revitalisation /ʀ(ə)vitalizasjɔ̃/ **NF** revitalization

revitaliser /ʀ(ə)vitalize/ ► conjug 1 ◄ **VT** to revitalize

revivifier /ʀ(ə)vivifje/ ► conjug 7 ◄ **VT** *(littér)* *[+ personne, souvenir]* to revive

revivre /ʀ(ə)vivʀ/ ► conjug 46 ◄ **VI** 1 *(= être ressuscité)* to live again ♦ **on peut vraiment dire qu'il revit dans son fils** it's really true to say that he lives on in his son

2 *(= être revigoré)* to come alive again ♦ **je me sentais** ~ I felt alive again, I felt (like) a new man *(ou* woman) ♦ **ouf, je revis !** whew! what a relief! *ou* I can breathe again! *

3 *(= se renouveler)* *[coutumes, institution, mode]* to be revived

4 ♦ **faire** ~ *(= ressusciter)* to bring back to life, to restore to life; *(= revigorer)* to revive, to put new life in *ou* into; *(= remettre en honneur)* *[+ mode, époque, usage]* to revive; *(= remettre en mémoire)* to bring back ♦ **faire** ~ **un personnage/une époque dans un roman** to bring a character/an era back to life in a novel ♦ **le grand air m'a fait** ~ the fresh air put new life in me ♦ **cela faisait** ~ **tout un monde que j'avais cru oublié** it brought back a whole world I thought had been forgotten

VT *[+ passé, période]* *(lit)* to relive, to live (through) again; *(en imagination)* to relive, to live (over) again

révocabilité /ʀevɔkabilite/ **NF** *[de contrat]* revocability; *[de fonctionnaire]* removability

révocable /ʀevɔkabl/ **ADJ** *[legs, contrat]* revocable; *[fonctionnaire]* removable, dismissible

révocation /ʀevɔkasjɔ̃/ **NF** 1 *(= destitution)* *[de magistrat, fonctionnaire]* removal (from office), dismissal 2 *(= annulation)* *[de legs, contrat, édit]* revocation ♦ **la ~ de l'Édit de Nantes** *(Hist)* the Revocation of the Edict of Nantes

revoici * /ʀ(ə)vwasi/, **revoilà** * /ʀ(ə)vwala/ **PRÉP** ♦ ~ **Paul!** Paul's back (again)!, here's Paul again! ♦ **me ~ !** it's me again!, here I am again! ♦ **nous ~ à la maison/en France** here we are, back home/in France (again) ♦ ~ **la mer** here's the sea again ♦ **le revoilà qui se plaint !** there he goes complaining again! ♦ **les revoilà !** there they are again!

revoir /ʀ(ə)vwaʀ/ ► conjug 30 ◄ **VT** 1 *(= retrouver)* *[+ personne]* to see *ou* meet again; *[+ patrie, village]* to see again ♦ **je l'ai revu deux ou trois fois depuis** I've seen him *ou* we've met two or three times since ♦ **quand le revois-tu ?** when are you seeing *ou* meeting him again?

♦ **au revoir!** goodbye! ♦ **au ~ Monsieur/Madame** goodbye (Mr X/Mrs X) ♦ **dire au ~ à qn** to say goodbye to sb ♦ **faire au ~ de la main** to wave goodbye ♦ **ce n'était heureusement qu'un au** ~ fortunately it was farewell and not adieu

2 *(= apercevoir de nouveau)* to see again ♦ **filez, et qu'on ne vous revoie plus ici !** clear off, and don't show your face here again!

3 *(= regarder de nouveau)* to see again ♦ **je suis allé ~ ce film** I went to (see) that film again

4 *(= être à nouveau témoin de)* *[+ atrocités, scène]* to witness *ou* see again; *[+ conditions]* to see again ♦ **craignant de ~ augmenter le chômage** afraid of seeing unemployment increase again

5 *(= imaginer de nouveau)* to see again ♦ **je le revois encore, dans sa cuisine** I can still see him there in his kitchen

6 *(= réviser)* *[+ édition, texte]* to revise; *(Scol)* *[+ leçons]* to revise, to go over again; *(= examiner de nouveau)* *[+ position, stratégie]* to review, to reconsider ♦ **édition revue et corrigée/augmentée** revised and updated/expanded edition ♦ **l'histoire de France revue et corrigée par A. Leblanc** the history of France revised and updated *ou* given a new treatment by A. Leblanc ♦ **nos tarifs/objectifs ont été revus à la baisse/hausse** our prices/targets have been revised downwards/upwards ♦ ~ **sa copie** *(fig)* to review one's plans, to go back to the drawing board

VPR **se revoir** 1 *(réciproque)* to see each other again ♦ **on se revoit quand ?** when shall we see each other again? ♦ **nous nous revoyons de temps en temps** we still see each other from time to time

2 *(réfléchi)* **je me revoyais écolier** I saw myself as a schoolboy again

revoler /ʀ(ə)vɔle/ ► conjug 1 ◄ **VI** *[oiseau, pilote]* to fly again

révoltant, e /ʀevɔltɑ̃, ɑ̃t/ **ADJ** revolting, appalling

révolte /ʀevɔlt/ **NF** revolt, rebellion ♦ **les paysans sont en ~ contre ...** the peasants are in revolt against ... *ou* up in arms against ... ♦ **adolescent en** ~ rebellious adolescent ♦ **devant ce refus, elle a eu un mouvement de** ~ she bridled at this refusal ♦ **à 17 ans, Alex était en pleine** ~ at 17 Alex was going through a rebellious phase

révolté, e /ʀevɔlte/ (ptp de **révolter**) **ADJ** 1 *[paysans, adolescent]* rebellious 2 *(= outré)* outraged, incensed **NM,F** rebel

révolter /ʀevɔlte/ ► conjug 1 ◄ **VT** *(= indigner)* to revolt, to outrage, to appal ♦ **ceci nous révolte** we are revolted *ou* outraged by this **VPR** **se révolter** 1 *[personne]* *(= s'insurger)* to revolt, to rebel, to rise up *(contre* against); *(= se cabrer)* to rebel *(contre* against) 2 *(= s'indigner)* to be revolted *ou* repelled *ou* appalled *(contre* by) ♦ **l'esprit se révolte contre une telle propagande** one can only be revolted by such propaganda

révolu, e /ʀevɔly/ **ADJ** 1 *(littér = de jadis)* *[époque]* past, bygone *(épith)*, gone by ♦ **des jours ~s** past *ou* bygone days, days gone by ♦ **l'époque ~e des diligences** the bygone days of stagecoaches 2 *(= fini)* *[époque, jours]* past, in the past *(attrib)* ♦ **cette époque est ~e, nous devons penser à l'avenir** that era is in the past – we have to think of the future 3 *(Admin = complété)* **âgé de 20 ans ~s** over 20 years of age ♦ **avoir 20 ans ~s** to be over 20 years of age ♦ **après deux ans ~s** when two full years had *(ou* have) passed

révolution /ʀevɔlysjɔ̃/ **NF** 1 *(= rotation)* revolution ♦ **escalier à double** ~ double staircase

2 *(culturelle, industrielle = changement)* revolution ♦ ~ **pacifique/permanente/violente** peaceful/permanent/violent revolution ♦ **la Révolution (française)** the French Revolution ♦ **la ~ d'Octobre/de velours** the October/Velvet Revolution ♦ ~ **de palais** palace revolution *ou* coup ♦ **la ~ silencieuse/verte/sexuelle** the silent/green/sexual revolution ♦ **la ~ technologique** the technological revolution, the revolution in technology ♦ **ce nouveau produit constitue une véritable** ~ this new product is truly revolutionary ♦ **notre profession a subi une véritable** ~ our profession has been revolutionized *ou* has undergone a radical transformation

3 *(= parti, forces de la révolution)* **la** ~ the forces of revolution

4 *(locutions)* **être en** ~ *[rue, quartier]* to be in turmoil ♦ **créer une petite** ~ *[idée, invention, procédé]* to cause a stir

> **LA RÉVOLUTION TRANQUILLE**
>
> The term **la Révolution tranquille** refers to the important social, political and cultural transition that took place in Quebec from the early 1960s. As well as rapid economic expansion and a reorganization of political institutions, there was a growing sense of pride among Québécois in their specific identity as French-speaking citizens. The **Révolution tranquille** is thus seen as a strong affirmation of Quebec's identity as a French-speaking province. → **OFFICE DE LA LANGUE FRANÇAISE, QUÉBEC**

révolutionnaire /ʀevɔlysjɔnɛʀ/ **ADJ** *(gén)* revolutionary; *(Hist)* Revolutionary, of the French Revolution **NMF** *(gén)* revolutionary; *(Hist)* Revolutionary *(in the French Revolution)*

révolutionner /ʀevɔlysjɔne/ ► conjug 1 ◄ **VT** 1 *(= transformer radicalement)* to revolutionize 2 *(* = bouleverser)* *[+ personnes]* to stir up ♦ **son arrivée a révolutionné le quartier** his arrival stirred up the whole neighbourhood *ou* caused a great stir in the neighbourhood

revolver /ʀevɔlvɛʀ/ **NM** *(= pistolet)* *(gén)* pistol, (hand)gun; *(à barillet)* revolver ♦ **coup de** ~ pistol shot, gunshot ♦ **tué de plusieurs coups de** ~ gunned down ♦ **microscope à** ~ microscope with a revolving nosepiece ♦ **tour** ~ capstan lathe, turret lathe; → **poche**[1]

revolving /ʀevɔlviŋ/ **ADJ INV** ♦ **crédit** ~ revolving credit

révoquer /ʀevɔke/ ► conjug 1 ◄ **VT** 1 *(= destituer)* *[+ magistrat, fonctionnaire]* to remove from office, to dismiss 2 *(= annuler)* *[+ legs, contrat, édit]* to revoke 3 *(littér = contester)* ~ **qch en doute** to call sth into question, to question sth

revoter /ʀ(ə)vɔte/ ► conjug 1 ◄ **VI** to vote again **VT** ♦ ~ **un texte de loi** to vote on a bill again

revouloir * /ʀ(ə)vulwaʀ/ ► conjug 31 ◄ **VT** *[+ pain]* to want more; *[+ orange]* to want another ♦ **qui en reveut ?** *(gén)* who wants (some) more?; *(nourriture)* anyone for seconds? * ♦ **tu reveux du café/un morceau de gâteau ?** would you like some more coffee/another slice of cake? ♦ **il reveut le livre** *(qui est à lui)* he wants his book back; *(qu'on lui a déjà prêté)* he wants the book again

revoyure * /ʀ(ə)vwajyʀ/ **à la revoyure EXCL** see you! *, (I'll) be seeing you! *

revue /ʀ(ə)vy/ **NF** 1 *(= examen)* review ♦ **faire la ~ de** to review, to go through ♦ **une ~ de la**

presse hebdomadaire a review of the weekly press

2 *(Mil)* *(= inspection)* inspection, review; *(= parade)* march-past, review

3 *(= magazine)* *(à fort tirage, illustrée)* magazine; *(érudite)* review, journal ◆ ~ **automobile/de mode** car/fashion magazine ◆ ~ **littéraire/scientifique** literary/scientific journal *ou* review

4 *(= spectacle)* *(satirique)* revue; *(de variétés)* variety show *ou* performance ◆ ~ **à grand spectacle** extravaganza

5 *(locutions)* **passer en** ~ *(Mil)* to pass in review, to review, to inspect; *(fig = énumérer mentalement)* to go over in one's mind, to pass in review, to go through; *(= faire la liste de)* to list ◆ **être de la** ~ * to lose out

COMP **revue d'armement** *(Mil)* arms inspection
revue de détail *(Mil)* kit inspection
revue de presse review of the press *ou* papers

révulsé, e /ʀevylse/ (ptp de **se révulser**) ADJ *[yeux]* rolled upwards *(attrib)*; *[visage]* contorted

révulser /ʀevylse/ ▸ conjug 1 ◂ VT *(= dégoûter)* to disgust ◆ **ça me révulse** I find it repulsive *ou* disgusting VPR **se révulser** *[visage]* to contort; *[yeux]* to roll upwards

révulsif, -ive /ʀevylsif, iv/ *(Méd)* ADJ revulsant NM revulsant, revulsive

révulsion /ʀevylsjɔ̃/ NF *(Méd, fig)* revulsion

rewriter[1] /ʀiʀajte/ ▸ conjug 1 ◂ VT to edit, to rewrite *(US)*

rewriter[2] /ʀiʀajtœʀ/ NM editor, rewriter *(US)*

rewriting /ʀiʀajtiŋ/ NM editing, rewriting *(US)*

Reykjavik /ʀekjavik/ N Reykjavik

rez-de-chaussée /ʀed(ə)ʃose/ NM INV ground floor *(surtout Brit)*, first floor *(US)* ◆ **au** ~ on the ground floor ◆ **habiter un** ~ to live in a ground-floor flat *(Brit) ou* in a first-floor apartment *(US)*

rez-de-jardin /ʀed(ə)ʒaʀdɛ̃/ NM INV garden level ◆ **appartement en** ~ garden flat *(Brit) ou* apartment *(US)*

RF (abrév de **République française**) → **république**

RFA /ɛʀɛfa/ NF (abrév de **République fédérale d'Allemagne**) → **république**

RG /ɛʀʒe/ NMPL (abrév de **renseignements généraux**) → **renseignement**

Rh (abrév de **rhésus**) Rh

rhabiller /ʀabije/ ▸ conjug 1 ◂ VT 1 ◆ ~ **qn** *(lit)* to dress sb again, to put sb's clothes back on; *(= lui racheter des habits)* to fit sb out again, to reclothe sb 2 *[+ édifice]* to renovate ◆ **immeuble rhabillé façon moderne** renovated and modernized building 3 *(Tech)* *[+ montre, pendule]* to repair VPR **se rhabiller** to put one's clothes back on, to dress (o.s.) again ◆ **tu peux aller te** ~ **!** * you can forget it! *

rhapsode /ʀapsɔd/ NM rhapsode

rhapsodie /ʀapsɔdi/ NF rhapsody

rhème /ʀɛm/ NM rheme

rhénan, e /ʀenɑ̃, an/ ADJ *(Géog)* Rhine *(épith)*, of the Rhine; *(Art)* Rhenish

Rhénanie /ʀenani/ NF Rhineland ◆ **la ~-Palatinat** the Rhineland-Palatinate

rhénium /ʀenjɔm/ NM rhenium

rhéostat /ʀeɔsta/ NM rheostat

rhésus /ʀezys/ NM 1 *(Méd)* rhesus ◆ ~ **positif/négatif** rhesus *ou* Rh positive/negative; → **facteur** 2 *(= singe)* rhesus monkey

rhéteur /ʀetœʀ/ NM *(Hist)* rhetor

rhétique /ʀetik/ ADJ rhetic

rhétoricien, -ienne /ʀetɔʀisjɛ̃, jɛn/ NM,F *(lit, péj)* rhetorician

rhétorique /ʀetɔʀik/ NF rhetoric; → **figure, fleur** ADJ rhetorical

Rhin /ʀɛ̃/ NM ◆ **le** ~ the Rhine

rhinite /ʀinit/ NF rhinitis *(NonC)* *(SPÉC)*

rhinocéros /ʀinɔseʀɔs/ NM rhinoceros, rhino ◆ ~ **d'Asie** Indian rhinoceros ◆ ~ **d'Afrique** (African) white rhinoceros

rhinolaryngite /ʀinolaʀɛ̃ʒit/ NF sore throat, throat infection

rhinologie /ʀinɔlɔʒi/ NF rhinology

rhinopharyngé, e /ʀinofaʀɛ̃ʒe/, **rhinopharyngien, -ienne** /ʀinofaʀɛ̃ʒjɛ̃, jɛn/ ADJ nose and throat *(épith)*

rhinopharyngite /ʀinofaʀɛ̃ʒit/ NF sore throat, throat infection, rhinopharyngitis *(NonC)* *(SPÉC)*

rhinopharynx /ʀinofaʀɛ̃ks/ NM nose and throat, rhinopharynx *(SPÉC)*

rhinoplastie /ʀinoplasti/ NF rhinoplasty

rhizome /ʀizom/ NM rhizome

rho /ʀo/ NM *(= lettre grecque)* rho

rhodanien, -ienne /ʀɔdanjɛ̃, jɛn/ ADJ Rhone *(épith)*, of the Rhone; → **sillon**

Rhode Island /ʀɔdajlɑ̃d/ NM Rhode Island

Rhodes /ʀɔd/ N Rhodes ◆ **l'île de** ~ the island of Rhodes; → **colosse**

Rhodésie /ʀɔdezi/ NF Rhodesia

rhodésien, -ienne /ʀɔdezjɛ̃, jɛn/ ADJ Rhodesian NM,F **Rhodésien(ne)** Rhodesian

rhodium /ʀɔdjɔm/ NM rhodium

rhododendron /ʀɔdɔdɛ̃dʀɔ̃/ NM rhododendron

rhombe /ʀɔ̃b/ NM († = *losange*) rhomb, rhombus; *(= instrument)* bullroarer

rhombique /ʀɔ̃bik/ ADJ rhombic

rhomboïdal, e (mpl **-aux**) /ʀɔ̃bɔidal, o/ ADJ rhomboid

rhomboïde /ʀɔ̃bɔid/ NM rhomboid

Rhône /ʀon/ NM *(= fleuve)* ◆ **le** ~ the (river) Rhone

rhône-alpin, e /ʀonalpɛ̃, in/ ADJ in the Rhone-Alpes region NM,F **Rhône-Alpin(e)** person living in the Rhone-Alpes region

rhovyl ® /ʀɔvil/ NM Rhovyl ®

rhubarbe /ʀybaʀb/ NF rhubarb

rhum /ʀɔm/ NM rum ◆ ~ **blanc** *ou* **agricole/brun** white/dark rum ◆ **sorbet au** ~ rum-flavoured sorbet ◆ **glace ~-raisin** rum and raisin ice cream

rhumatisant, e /ʀymatizɑ̃, ɑ̃t/ ADJ, NM,F rheumatic

rhumatismal, e (mpl **-aux**) /ʀymatismal, o/ ADJ rheumatic

rhumatisme /ʀymatism/ NM rheumatism *(NonC)* ◆ **avoir un** ~ *ou* **des ~s dans le bras** to have rheumatism in one's arm ◆ ~ **articulaire** rheumatoid arthritis *(NonC)* ◆ ~ **déformant** polyarthritis *(NonC)*

rhumato * /ʀymato/ NF abrév de **rhumatologie** NMF abrév de **rhumatologue**

rhumatoïde /ʀymatoid/ ADJ → **polyarthrite**

rhumatologie /ʀymatɔlɔʒi/ NF rheumatology

rhumatologue /ʀymatɔlɔg/ NMF rheumatologist

rhume /ʀym/ NM cold ◆ **attraper un (gros)** ~ to catch a (bad *ou* heavy) cold ◆ ~ **de cerveau** head cold ◆ ~ **des foins** hay fever

rhumerie /ʀɔmʀi/ NF *(= distillerie)* rum distillery

rhyolit(h)e /ʀjɔlit/ NF rhyolite

rhythm and blues /ʀitmɛndbluz/, **rhythm'n'blues** /ʀitmənbluz/ NM rhythm and blues, rhythm'n'blues

ria /ʀija/ NF ria

riant, e /ʀ(i)jɑ̃, ɑ̃t/ ADJ *[paysage]* pleasant; *[atmosphère, perspective]* cheerful, happy; *[visage]* cheerful, smiling, happy

RIB /ʀib/ NM (abrév de **relevé d'identité bancaire**) → **relevé**

ribambelle /ʀibɑ̃bɛl/ NF ◆ **une** ~ **de** *[+ enfants]* a swarm *ou* herd *ou* flock of; *[+ animaux]* a herd of; *[+ noms]* a string of; *[+ objets]* a row of; *[+ choses à faire]* stacks of

ribaud /ʀibo/ NM (†† *ou hum*) bawdy *ou* ribald fellow

ribaude †† /ʀibod/ NF trollop †*, bawdy wench †

riboflavine /ʀiboflavin/ NF riboflavin

ribonucléique /ʀibonykleik/ ADJ ◆ **acide** ~ ribonucleic acid

ribosome /ʀibozom/ NM ribosome

ribote † * /ʀibɔt/ NF merrymaking *(NonC)*, revel, carousing † *(NonC)* ◆ **être en ~, faire** ~ to make merry, to carouse †

ribouldingue * † /ʀibuldɛ̃g/ NF spree, binge * ◆ **deux jours de** ~ a two-day spree * *ou* binge * ◆ **faire la** ~ to go on a spree *ou* a binge *

ricain, e * /ʀikɛ̃, ɛn/ *(hum, péj)* ADJ Yank(ee) * *(péj)* NM,F **Ricain(e)** Yank(ee) *

ricanant, e /ʀikanɑ̃, ɑ̃t/ ADJ *[personne, voix]* sniggering

ricanement /ʀikanmɑ̃/ NM *(méchant)* snigger, sniggering *(NonC)*; *(sot)* giggle, giggling *(NonC)*; *(gêné)* nervous laughter *(NonC)* ◆ **j'ai entendu des ~s** I heard someone sniggering

ricaner /ʀikane/ ▸ conjug 1 ◂ VI *(méchamment)* to snigger; *(sottement)* to giggle; *(avec gêne)* to laugh nervously, to give a nervous laugh

ricaneur, -euse /ʀikanœʀ, øz/ ADJ *(méchant)* sniggering; *(bête)* giggling NM,F *(= personne méchante)* sniggerer; *(= personne bête)* giggler

RICE /ʀis/ NM (abrév de **relevé d'identité de Caisse d'épargne**) → **relevé**

Richard /ʀiʃaʀ/ NM Richard ◆ ~ **Cœur de Lion** Richard (the) Lionheart

richard, e * /ʀiʃaʀ, aʀd/ NM,F *(péj)* rich person ◆ **un hôtel pour ~s** a posh * hotel

riche /ʀiʃ/ ADJ 1 *(= nanti)* *[personne]* rich, wealthy, well-off *(attrib)*; *[pays]* rich ◆ ~ **à millions** enormously wealthy ◆ ~ **comme Crésus** as rich as Croesus, fabulously rich *ou* wealthy ◆ **faire un** ~ **mariage** to marry into a wealthy family, to marry (into) money ◆ ~ **héritière** wealthy heiress ◆ **nous ne sommes pas ~s** we're by no means rich, we're not very well-off

2 *(= luxueux)* *[bijoux, étoffes]* rich, costly; *[coloris]* rich; *[mobilier]* sumptuous, costly ◆ **je vous donne ce stylo, mais ce n'est pas un** ~ **cadeau** I'll give you this pen but it's not much of a gift ◆ **ça fait** ~ * it looks expensive *ou* posh *

3 *(= consistant, fertile)* *[aliment, mélange, sujet, terre]* rich ◆ **le français est une langue** ~ French is a rich language ◆ **c'est une** ~ **nature** he (*ou* she) is a person of immense resources *ou* qualities ◆ **c'est une** ~ **idée** * that's a great * *ou* grand idea

4 *(= abondant)* *[moisson]* rich; *[végétation]* rich, lush; *[collection]* large, rich; *[vocabulaire]* rich, wide ◆ **il y a une documentation très** ~ **sur ce sujet** there is a wealth of *ou* a vast amount of information on this subject

5 *(locutions)*

♦ **riche de** *[+ espérances, possibilités]* full of ♦ **c'est une expérience ~ d'enseignements** you learn a great deal from this experience, it's a tremendous learning experience ♦ **il est revenu, ~ de souvenirs** he returned with a wealth of memories ♦ **acteur/marché ~ de promesses** highly promising actor/market ♦ **bibliothèque ~ de plusieurs millions d'ouvrages** library boasting several million books ♦ **~ de cette expérience, il ...** thanks to this experience, he ...

♦ **riche en** *[calories, gibier, monuments]* rich in ♦ **alimentation ~ en protéines/cellulose végétale** high-protein/high-fibre diet ♦ **région ~ en eau/pétrole** region rich in water/oil resources ♦ **je ne suis pas ~ en sucre** *(hum)* I'm not very well-off for sugar ♦ **année ~ en événements spectaculaires** year full of dramatic incidents, action-packed year

NMF rich *ou* wealthy person ♦ **les ~s** the rich, the wealthy ♦ **de ~(s)** *[vêtements, nourriture]* fancy ♦ **voiture de ~(s)** *(péj)* fancy *ou* flashy car; → **gosse, prêter**

richelieu /Riʃəljø/ NM *(= chaussure)* Oxford (shoe)

richement /Riʃmɑ̃/ ADV *[récompenser, vêtir]* richly; *[décoré, meublé]* richly, sumptuously ♦ **~ illustré** richly *ou* lavishly illustrated, with lavish *ou* copious illustrations; → **doter**

richesse /Riʃɛs/ NF 1 *[de pays, personne]* wealth ♦ **la ~ ne l'a pas changé** wealth *ou* being rich hasn't altered him ♦ **ce n'est pas la ~, mais c'est mieux que rien*** it's not exactly the lap of luxury but it's better than nothing ♦ **être d'une ~ insolente** to be obscenely rich ♦ **le tourisme est notre principale (source de) ~** tourism is our greatest asset ♦ **la ~ nationale** the country's national wealth

2 *[d'ameublement, décor]* sumptuousness, richness; *[de coloris, étoffe]* richness

3 *[d'aliment, collection, sol, texte]* richness; *[de végétation]* richness, lushness ♦ **la ~ de son vocabulaire** the richness of his vocabulary, his wide *ou* rich vocabulary ♦ **la ~ de cette documentation** the abundance of the information ♦ **la ~ en calcium de cet aliment** the high calcium content of this food ♦ **la ~ en matières premières/en gibier de cette région** the abundance of raw materials/of game in this region ♦ **la ~ en pétrole/en minéraux du pays** the country's abundant *ou* vast oil/mineral resources ♦ **une culture d'une ~ inouïe** an extraordinarily rich culture

4 *(= bien)* **notre ferme, c'est notre seule ~** this farm is all we have ♦ **la santé est une ~** good health is a great blessing *ou* is a boon, it's a blessing to be healthy

NFPL **richesses** *(= argent)* riches, wealth; *(= ressources)* wealth; *(fig = trésors)* treasures ♦ **entasser des ~s** to pile up riches ♦ **la répartition des ~s d'un pays** the distribution of a country's wealth ♦ **l'exploitation des ~s naturelles** the exploitation of natural resources ♦ **les ~s de l'art tibétain** the treasures of Tibetan art ♦ **montrez-nous toutes vos ~s** show us your treasures

richissime /Riʃisim/ ADJ fabulously rich *ou* wealthy

ricin /Risɛ̃/ NM castor oil plant; → **huile**

ricocher /Rikɔʃe/ ▸ conjug 1 ◂ VI *[balle de fusil]* to ricochet *(sur* off); *[pierre]* to rebound *(sur* off); *(sur l'eau)* to bounce *(sur* on); ♦ **faire ~ un galet sur l'eau** to skim a pebble across the water, to make a pebble bounce on the water

ricochet /Rikɔʃɛ/ NM *(gén)* rebound; *[de balle de fusil]* ricochet; *[de caillou sur l'eau]* bounce ♦ **faire ~** *(lit, fig)* to rebound ♦ **il a été blessé par ~** he was wounded by a ricocheting bullet ♦ **par ~, il a perdu son emploi** *(fig)* as an indirect result he lost his job ♦ **(s'amuser à) faire des ~s** to skim pebbles ♦ **il a fait quatre ~s** he made the pebble bounce four times

ric-rac* /RikRak/ ADV 1 *(= très exactement) [payer]* on the nail* 2 *(= de justesse) [réussir, échapper]* by the skin of one's teeth ♦ **côté finances, ce mois-ci, c'est ~** money is going to be tight this month, we'll just about make it through the month moneywise ♦ **ça va se jouer ~** it's going to be touch and go ♦ **j'ai eu mon train ~** I caught the train, but only just

rictus /Riktys/ NM *(grimaçant)* grin; *(effrayant)* snarl ♦ **~ moqueur/cruel** mocking *ou* sardonic/cruel grin

ride /Rid/ NF *[de peau, pomme]* wrinkle *(de* in); *[d'eau, sable]* ripple *(de* on, in) ridge *(de* in); ♦ **les ~s de son front** the wrinkles *ou* lines on his forehead ♦ **visage creusé de ~s** deeply lined face, wrinkled face ♦ **elle/ce roman n'a pas pris une ~** *(lit, fig)* she/this novel hasn't aged a bit

ridé, e /Ride/ (ptp de **rider**) ADJ *[peau, fruit]* wrinkled; *[front]* furrowed; *[eau, mer]* rippled ♦ **~e comme une vieille pomme** as wrinkled as a prune

rideau (pl **rideaux**) /Rido/ NM 1 *(= draperie)* curtain ♦ **tirer les ~x** *(fermer)* to draw *ou* close the curtains *ou* drapes (US), to draw the curtains to; *(ouvrir)* to draw the curtains, to pull *ou* draw the curtains back ♦ **tirer le ~ sur** *(fig) [+ défaut, passé]* to draw a veil over ♦ **tomber en ~*** to break down ♦ **je me suis retrouvé en ~ en pleine campagne*** there I was, broken down in the middle of nowhere

2 *(Théât)* curtain ♦ **~ à 20 heures** the curtain rises at 8 o'clock, the curtain's at 8 o'clock ♦ **~ !** *(= cri des spectateurs)* curtain!; *(* fig = assez)* that's enough!, I've had enough! ♦ **le ~ est tombé sur l'affaire** *(fig)* the curtain came down on the affair

3 *[de boutique]* shutter; *[de cheminée]* register, blower; *[de classeur, secrétaire]* roll shutter; *[d'appareil-photo]* shutter

4 *(= écran)* **~ de** *[+ arbres, verdure]* curtain *ou* screen of; *[+ policiers, troupes]* curtain of; *[+ pluie]* curtain *ou* sheet of ♦ **~ de fumée** smoke screen ♦ **~ de feu** sheet of flame *ou* fire

COMP **rideaux bonne femme** looped curtains *ou* drapes (US)

rideau de douche shower curtain

rideau de fer *ou* **métallique** *[de boutique]* metal shutter(s); *[de théâtre]* (metal) safety curtain, fire curtain ♦ **le ~ de fer** *(Hist)* the Iron Curtain ♦ **les pays au-delà du ~ de fer** the Iron Curtain countries, the countries behind the Iron Curtain

rideaux de lit bed hangings *ou* curtains

rideau de perles bead curtain

ridelle /Ridɛl/ NF *[de camion, charrette]* slatted side

rider /Ride/ ▸ conjug 1 ◂ VT *[+ fruit, peau]* to wrinkle; *[+ front] [colère, soucis]* to wrinkle; *[âge]* to line with wrinkles; *[+ eau]* to ripple, to ruffle the surface of; *[+ neige, sable]* to ruffle *ou* wrinkle the surface of; *(Naut)* to tighten VPR **se rider** *[peau, fruit, visage]* to become wrinkled, to become lined with wrinkles; *[eau, surface]* to ripple, to become rippled ♦ **à ces mots, son front se rida** his forehead wrinkled *ou* he wrinkled his forehead at these words

ridicule /Ridikyl/ ADJ 1 *(= grotesque) [conduite, personne, vêtement]* ridiculous, ludicrous, absurd; *[prétentions]* ridiculous, laughable; *[superstition]* ridiculous, silly ♦ **se rendre ~ aux yeux de tous** to make o.s. (look) ridiculous *ou* make a fool of o.s. *ou* make o.s. look a fool in everyone's eyes ♦ **ça le rend ~** it makes him look ridiculous *ou* (like) a fool ♦ **ne sois pas ~** don't be ridiculous *ou* silly *ou* absurd

2 *(= infime) [prix]* ridiculous, ridiculously low; *[quantité]* ridiculous, ridiculously small

NM 1 *(= absurdité)* ridiculousness, absurdity ♦ **le ~ de la conversation ne lui échappait pas** he was well aware of the absurdity of the conversation ♦ **je ne sais pas si vous saisissez tout le ~ de la situation** I don't know if you realize just how absurd *ou* ridiculous the situation is *ou* if you realize the full absurdity of the situation ♦ **il y a quelque ~ à faire ...** it is rather ridiculous to do ... ♦ **c'est d'un ~ achevé** it's perfectly *ou* utterly ridiculous ♦ **se donner le ~ de ...** to be ridiculous enough to ...; → **tourner**

2 ♦ **le ~** ridicule ♦ **tomber dans le ~** *[personne]* to make o.s. ridiculous, to become ridiculous; *[film]* to become ridiculous ♦ **s'exposer au ~** to expose o.s. *ou* lay o.s. open to ridicule ♦ **avoir le sens du ~** to have a sense of the ridiculous ♦ **la peur du ~** (the) fear of ridicule *ou* of appearing ridiculous ♦ **le ~ ne tue pas** ridicule has never been the unmaking of anyone, ridicule never killed anyone ♦ **tourner qn/qch en ~** to ridicule sb/sth, to make sb/sth an object of ridicule ♦ **couvrir qn de ~** to heap ridicule on sb, to make sb look ridiculous, to make a laughing stock of sb ♦ **il y en a qui n'ont pas peur du ~ !** some people aren't afraid of looking ridiculous!

NMPL **ridicules** *(= travers)* silliness *(NonC)*, ridiculous *ou* silly ways, absurdities ♦ **les ~s humains** the absurdities of human nature ♦ **les ~s d'une classe sociale** the ridiculous ways *ou* the (little) absurdities of a social class

ridiculement /Ridikylmɑ̃/ ADV *[bas, vêtu]* ridiculously; *[chanter, marcher]* in a ridiculous way

ridiculiser /Ridikylize/ ▸ conjug 1 ◂ VT *[+ défaut, doctrine, personne]* to ridicule, to hold up to ridicule VPR **se ridiculiser** to make o.s. (look) ridiculous, to make a fool of o.s.

ridule /Ridyl/ NF fine line *ou* wrinkle ♦ **rides et ~s** lines and wrinkles

rien /Rjɛ̃/

1 PRONOM INDÉFINI	3 LOC ADV
2 NOM MASCULIN	4 ADVERBE

1 – PRONOM INDÉFINI

1

♦ **rien + ne** *(= nulle chose)* nothing ♦ **~ ne le fera reculer** nothing will make him turn back ♦ **il n'y a ~ qui puisse m'empêcher de faire cela** there's nothing that could prevent me from doing that ♦ **il n'y a ~ que je ne fasse pour elle** there's nothing I wouldn't do for her ♦ **il n'y a plus ~** there's nothing left ♦ **on ne pouvait plus ~ pour elle** there was nothing more *ou* else to be done for her, nothing more could be done for her ♦ **je n'ai ~ entendu/compris** I didn't hear/understand anything *ou* a thing, I heard/understood nothing ♦ **je ne crois plus à ~** I don't believe in anything any more ♦ **elle ne mange presque ~** she hardly eats a thing, she eats hardly anything ♦ **il n'en sait ~** he has no idea ♦ **je n'en sais trop ~** I haven't a clue ♦ **(dans la vie) on n'a ~ sans ~** you only get out of life what you put into it ♦ **~ ne sert de courir, il faut partir à point** *ou* **temps** *(Prov)* slow and steady wins the race *(Prov)* → **risquer, valoir**

♦ **rien + avoir** ♦ **ils n'ont ~** *(possessions)* they have nothing; *(maladie, blessure)* there's nothing wrong with them ♦ **ça va, tu n'as ~ ?** are you OK? ♦ **n'avoir ~ contre qn** to have nothing against sb ♦ **il n'a ~ d'un politicien/d'un dictateur** he's got nothing of the politician/dictator in *ou* about him ♦ **il n'a ~ de son père** he is nothing *ou* not a bit like his father ♦ **j'en ai ~ à faire*** *ou* **à foutre*** I don't give a damn* *ou* toss*

♦ **rien + être** ♦ **n'être ~** *[personne]* to be a nobody; *[chose]* to be nothing ♦ **pour lui, 50 km à vélo, ce n'est ~** he thinks nothing of cycling 50 kilometres ♦ **n'être ~ en comparaison de ...** to be nothing compared to ... ♦ **il n'est ~ dans l'entreprise** he's a nobody *ou* he's nothing in the firm ♦ **il ne nous est ~** he's not connected with us, he's nothing to do with us ♦ **il n'est plus ~ pour moi** he means nothing to me anymore ♦ **il n'en est ~** it's nothing of the sort, that's not it at all ♦ **on le croyait blessé, mais il n'en est ~** we thought he was injured but he's not at all *ou* he's nothing of the sort ♦ **élever quatre enfants, ça n'est pas ~** bringing up four children is not exactly a picnic* *ou* is no mean feat ♦ **tu t'es fait mal ? – non, ce n'est** *ou* **c'est* ~** did you hurt yourself? – no, it's nothing ♦ **pardon ! – c'est* ~** sorry! – it doesn't matter *ou* it's alright ♦ **c'est ~ de le dire*** (and) that's putting it mildly*, (and) that's an understatement

♦ **rien + faire** ♦ **il ne fait (plus) ~** he doesn't work (any more) ♦ **huit jours sans ~ faire** a week doing nothing ♦ **il ne nous a ~ fait** he hasn't done anything to us ♦ **cela ne lui fait ~** he doesn't mind *ou* care ♦ **ça ne fait ~** it doesn't matter, never mind ♦ **ça ne fait ~ si j'amène un ami ?** is it all right if I bring a friend along? ♦ **il n'y a ~ à faire** *(gén)* there's nothing we can do, there's nothing to be done; *(= c'est inutile)* it's useless *ou* hopeless ♦ **~ à faire !** it's no good! ♦ **~ n'y fait !** nothing's any good!

♦ **en rien** *(= absolument pas)* ♦ **cela ne nous gêne en ~** it doesn't bother us in any way *ou* in the least *ou* at all ♦ **il n'est en ~ responsable de la situation** he's not in any way *ou* at all responsible for the situation, he's not the slightest bit responsible for the situation ♦ **ce tableau ne ressemble en ~ au reste de son œuvre** this picture is nothing like his other works

♦ **rien de** *+ adjectif ou adverbe* nothing ♦ **~ d'autre** nothing else ♦ **~ de plus** nothing more *ou* else *ou* further ♦ **~ de moins** nothing less ♦ **~ de neuf** nothing new ♦ **~ de plus facile** nothing easier ♦ **il n'y a ~ eu de volé** nothing was stolen, there was nothing stolen ♦ **nous n'avons ~ d'autre** *ou* **de plus à ajouter** we have nothing else *ou* more *ou* further to add ♦ **ça n'a ~ d'impossible** it's perfectly possible ♦ **(il n'y a) ~ de tel qu'une bonne douche chaude !** there's nothing like *ou* nothing to beat a nice hot shower!, you can't beat a nice hot shower! ♦ **je t'achèterai le journal ; ~ d'autre ?** *(sans ne)* I'll get you a newspaper – do you want anything else? ♦ **~ de grave, j'espère ?** *(après un accident, un incident)* nothing serious, I hope? ♦ **elle a fait ce qu'il fallait, ~ de plus, ~ de moins** she did all she had to, nothing more nor less *ou* nothing more, nothing less

2 *(= quelque chose)* anything ♦ **avez-vous jamais ~ fait pour l'aider ?** have you ever done anything to help him? ♦ **as-tu jamais ~ lu de plus drôle ?** did you ever read anything quite so funny? ♦ **as-tu jamais ~ vu de pareil ?** have you ever seen such a thing? *ou* anything like it? *ou* the like? ♦ **sans ~ qui le prouve** without anything to prove it ♦ **sans que/avant que tu en saches ~** without your knowing/before you know anything about it

3 *(Sport)* nil; *(Tennis)* love ♦ **~ partout** *(Sport)* nil all; *(Tennis)* love all ♦ **15 à ~** *(Tennis)* 15 love ♦ **il mène par deux sets à ~** he's leading by two sets to love

4 *(Jeux)* **~ ne va plus !** rien ne va plus!

5 *(expressions figées)*

♦ **deux** *ou* **trois fois rien** next to nothing

♦ **rien à rien** ♦ **il ne comprend ~ à ~** he hasn't got a clue

♦ **rien au monde** nothing on earth *ou* in the world ♦ **je ne connais ~ au monde de plus bête** I can't think of anything more stupid ♦ **il ne quitterait son pays pour ~ au monde** he wouldn't leave his country for anything *ou* for all the tea in China

♦ **rien de rien*** nothing, absolutely nothing ♦ **il ne fait ~, mais ~ de ~*** he does nothing, and I mean nothing *ou* but nothing (at all)

♦ **rien du tout** nothing at all ♦ **une petite blessure de ~ du tout** a trifling *ou* trivial little injury, a mere scratch ♦ **qu'est-ce que c'est que cette pomme/ce cadeau de ~ du tout ?** what on earth can I (*ou* you *etc*) do with this stupid little apple/present?

♦ **rien qui vaille** ♦ **ne faire/n'écrire ~ qui vaille** to do/write nothing useful *ou* worthwhile *ou* of any use ♦ **ça ne me dit ~ qui vaille** *(= je me méfie)* I don't like the look of that, that looks suspicious to me; *(= ça ne me tente pas)* it doesn't appeal to me in the least *ou* slightest

♦ **pour rien** *(= inutilement)* for nothing *(= pour peu d'argent)* for a song, for next to nothing ♦ **ce n'est pas pour ~ que ...** *(= sans cause)* it is not without cause *ou* good reason that ..., it's not for nothing that ...

♦ **on n'a ~ pour ~** everything has its price; → **compter, coup, être**

♦ **rien que** *(= seulement)* ♦ **la vérité, ~ que la vérité** the truth and nothing but the truth ♦ **~ que la chambre coûte déjà très cher** the room alone already costs a great deal ♦ **~ que dans cet immeuble, il y a eu six cambriolages** in this apartment building alone there have been six burglaries ♦ **~ qu'à le voir, j'ai deviné** I guessed by just looking at him ♦ **je voudrais vous voir, ~ qu'une minute** could I see you just for a minute? ♦ **je voudrais une pièce ~ que pour moi** I would like a room of my own ♦ **il le fait ~ que pour l'embêter*** he does it just to annoy him ♦ **~ que d'y penser*, ça me rend furieux** the very idea of it makes me furious ♦ **c'est à moi, ~ qu'à moi** it's mine and mine alone, it's mine and mine only ♦ **il voulait 100 €, ~ que ça !** *(iro)* he wanted a mere €100 *(iro)*, he just *ou* only wanted €100 *(iro)* ♦ **elle veut être actrice, ~ que ça !** *(iro)* she wants to be an actress, no less!

♦ **rien moins que** ♦ **~ moins que sûr** anything but sure, not at all sure

♦ **un monument ~ moins que colossal** an absolutely huge monument ♦ **il s'agit là de ~ moins qu'un crime** it's nothing less than a crime ♦ **il n'est question de ~ moins que d'abattre deux forêts** it will mean nothing less than chopping down two forests

6 *(autres locutions)* **~ à signaler/déclarer** nothing to report/declare ♦ **je vous remercie – de ~*** thank you – you're welcome *ou* don't mention it *ou* not at all ♦ **excusez-moi ! – de ~*** sorry! – no bother* *ou* no trouble (at all) ♦ **une fille de ~** † *(péj)* a worthless girl ♦ **c'est mieux que ~** it's better than nothing ♦ **c'est ça ou ~** it's that or nothing, take it or leave it ♦ **ce que tu fais ou ~ !** you may as well not bother!; → **comme, dire** *etc*

2 – NOM MASCULIN

1 *(= néant)* nothingness

2 *(= petite chose sans importance)* **un ~** a mere nothing ♦ **des ~s** trivia ♦ **un ~ l'effraie, il a peur d'un ~** every little thing *ou* the slightest thing frightens him ♦ **un ~ la fait rire** she laughs at every little thing *ou* at anything at all ♦ **un ~ l'habille** she looks good in anything ♦ **j'ai failli rater le train, il s'en est fallu d'un ~** I came within a hair's breadth of missing the train ♦ **il suffirait d'un ~ pour qu'ils se réconcilient** it would take nothing at all for them to make up

♦ **comme un rien** ♦ **il pourrait te casser le bras comme un ~*** he could break your arm, no trouble ♦ **ces vieilles savates, ça tue l'amour comme un ~ !** those old slippers are a real passion killer!

♦ **pour un rien** ♦ **il pleure pour un ~** he cries at the drop of a hat *ou* at the slightest little thing ♦ **il s'inquiète pour un ~** he worries about the slightest little thing

3 *(= petite quantité)*

♦ **un rien de** a touch *ou* hint of ♦ **mettez-y un ~ de muscade** add a touch *ou* a tiny pinch of nutmeg ♦ **un ~ de vin** a taste of wine ♦ **un ~ de fantaisie** a touch of fantasy ♦ **avec un ~ d'ironie** with a hint *ou* touch of irony ♦ **en un ~ de temps** in no time (at all), in next to no time

4 *(péj: désignant une personne)* **c'est un/une ~ du tout** *(socialement)* he/she is a nobody; *(moralement)* he/she is no good

3 – LOC ADV

un rien *(= un peu)* a (tiny) bit, a shade ♦ **c'est un ~ bruyant ici** it's a bit *ou* a shade noisy in here ♦ **un ~ plus grand/petit** a fraction bigger/smaller ♦ **moi pas, dit-elle un ~ insolente** I'm not, she said rather insolently

4 – ADVERBE

(†, ‡ = très) really, not half* *(Brit)* ♦ **il fait ~ froid ici** it's damned cold‡ *ou* it isn't half cold* *(Brit)* here ♦ **ils sont ~ snobs** they're really stuck-up*, they aren't half snobs* *(Brit)*

rieur, rieuse /ʀ(i)jœʀ, ʀ(i)jøz/ ADJ *[personne]* cheerful, merry; *[expression, yeux]* cheerful, laughing; → **mouette** NM,F ♦ **les ~s se turent** people stopped laughing ♦ **il avait les ~s de son côté** he had people laughing with him rather than at him

rififi /ʀififi/ NM *(arg Crime)* trouble

riflard /ʀiflaʀ/ NM *(= rabot)* jack plane; *(= lime à métaux)* rough file

rifle /ʀifl/ NM rifle; → **vingt-deux**

Riga /ʀiga/ N Riga

rigaudon /ʀigodɔ̃, ʀigodɔ̃/ NM rigadoon

rigide /ʀiʒid/ ADJ 1 *[armature, tige]* rigid, stiff; *[muscle, col, carton]* stiff ♦ **livre à couverture ~** hardback (book) 2 *[règle, morale, politique, discipline]* strict, rigid; *[caractère]* rigid, inflexible; *[classification, éducation]* strict; *[personne]* rigid

rigidement /ʀiʒidmɑ̃/ ADV *[élever un enfant]* strictly; *[appliquer un règlement]* strictly, rigidly

rigidifier /ʀiʒidifje/ ► conjug 7 ◄ VT *(lit)* to make rigid *ou* stiff; *(fig)* to rigidify

rigidité /ʀiʒidite/ NF 1 *[d'armature, tige]* rigidity, rigidness, stiffness; *[de muscle, carton, col]* stiffness ♦ **~ cadavérique** rigor mortis 2 *[de caractère, personne]* rigidity, inflexibility; *[de règle, morale, politique]* strictness, rigidity; *[de classification, éducation]* strictness

rigodon /ʀigɔdɔ̃/ NM ⇒ **rigaudon**

rigolade* /ʀigɔlad/ NF 1 *(= rire, amusement)* **il aime la ~** he likes a bit of fun *ou* a laugh* ♦ **on a eu une bonne partie** *ou* **séance de ~** it was *ou* we had a good laugh* *ou* a lot of fun ♦ **quelle ~, quand il est entré !** what a laugh* when he came in! ♦ **le dîner s'est terminé dans la plus franche ~** the dinner ended in uproarious laughter ♦ **il n'y a pas que la ~ dans la vie** having fun isn't the only thing in life ♦ **il prend tout à la ~** he thinks everything's a big joke *ou* laugh*, he makes a joke of everything

2 *(= plaisanterie)* **ce procès est une (vaste) ~** this trial is a (big) joke *ou* farce ♦ **démonter ça, c'est une** *ou* **de la ~** taking that to pieces is child's play *ou* is a cinch* ♦ **ce qu'il dit là, c'est de la ~** what he says is a lot of *ou* a load of hooey‡ ♦ **ce régime, c'est de la ~** this diet is a complete con*

rigolard, e* /ʀigɔlaʀ, aʀd/ ADJ *[air, personne]* jovial ♦ **c'est un ~** he's always ready for a laugh*, he likes a good laugh*

rigole /ʀigɔl/ NF (= *canal*) channel; (= *filet d'eau*) rivulet; (*Agr* = *sillon*) furrow ◆ **la pluie avait creusé des ~s dans le sol** the rain had cut channels *ou* furrows in the earth ◆ **~ d'irrigation** irrigation channel ◆ **~ d'écoulement** drain

rigoler* /ʀigɔle/ ▸ conjug 1 ◂ VI 1 (= *rire*) to laugh ◆ **quand il l'a su, il a bien rigolé** when he found out, he had a good laugh about it* ◆ **il nous a bien fait ~** he had us all laughing *ou* in stitches* ◆ **tu me fais ~** (*iro*) you make me laugh (*iro*) ◆ **ne me fais pas ~** (*iro*) don't make me laugh ◆ **il n'y a pas de quoi ~ !** that's nothing to laugh about!, what's so funny? ◆ **quand tu verras les dégâts, tu rigoleras moins** you'll be laughing on the other side of your face *ou* you won't be laughing when you see the damage

2 (= *s'amuser*) to have (a bit of) fun, to have a (bit of a) laugh* ◆ **il aime ~** he likes a bit of fun *ou* a good laugh* ◆ **on a bien rigolé** we had great fun *ou* a good laugh* ◆ **chez eux, on ne doit pas ~ tous les jours !** it can't be much fun in their house!

3 (= *plaisanter*) to joke ◆ **tu rigoles !** you're kidding!* *ou* joking! ◆ **je ne rigole pas** I'm not joking *ou* kidding* ◆ **le patron est quelqu'un qui ne rigole pas** the boss won't take any nonsense ◆ **il ne faut pas ~ avec ces médicaments** you shouldn't mess about* *ou* fool about* with medicines like these ◆ **il ne faut pas ~ avec ce genre de maladie** an illness like this has to be taken seriously *ou* can't be taken lightly ◆ **j'ai dit ça pour ~** it was only a joke, I only said it in fun *ou* for a laugh*

rigolo, -ote* /ʀigɔlo, ɔt/ ADJ [*histoire, film*] funny; [*personne*] funny, comical ◆ **il est ~** (*plaisantin*) he's funny, he's a laugh*; (*original*) he's comical *ou* funny ◆ **ce qui lui est arrivé n'est pas ~** what's happened to him is no joke *ou* is not funny ◆ **vous êtes ~, vous, mettez-vous à ma place !** (*iro*) you make me laugh – put yourself in my shoes! ◆ **c'est ~, je n'avais jamais remarqué cela** that's funny *ou* odd, I'd never noticed that ◆ **c'est ~ comme les gens sont égoïstes** (*iro*) it's funny how selfish people can be (*iro*) NM,F (= *comique*) comic, wag; (*péj* = *fumiste*) fraud, phoney ◆ **c'est un sacré ~** he likes a good laugh*, he's a real comic ◆ **c'est un (petit) ~** (*péj*) he's a (little) fraud NM († ⁑ = *revolver*) gun, rod (*US*)

rigorisme /ʀigɔʀism/ NM rigorism, austerity, rigid moral standards

rigoriste /ʀigɔʀist/ ADJ rigoristic, austere, rigid NMF rigorist, rigid moralist

rigoureusement /ʀiguʀøzmɑ̃/ ADV 1 [*punir, traiter*] harshly; [*démontrer, raisonner, sélectionner*] rigorously; [*appliquer, classifier*] rigorously, strictly ◆ **respecter ~ les consignes** to observe the regulations strictly 2 (= *absolument*) [*authentique, vrai*] absolutely, utterly, entirely; [*exact*] rigorously; [*interdit*] strictly; [*impossible*] utterly; [*identique*] absolutely ◆ **ça ne changera ~ rien** that'll change absolutely nothing

rigoureux, -euse /ʀiguʀø, øz/ ADJ 1 (= *sévère*) [*discipline, punition*] harsh, severe; [*mesures*] tough, drastic, harsh; [*maître, moraliste*] strict; [*sélection, gestion, suivi*] rigorous; [*climat*] harsh ◆ **hiver ~** hard *ou* harsh winter ◆ **avoir l'esprit ~** to have a rigorous mind ◆ **de façon rigoureuse** rigorously 2 (= *exact*) [*méthode, raisonnement, style, examen*] rigorous; [*classification, définition*] strict 3 (= *absolu*) [*interdiction, sens d'un mot*] strict ◆ **l'application rigoureuse de la loi** the strict enforcement of the law ◆ **ce n'est pas une règle rigoureuse** it's not a hard-and-fast rule

rigueur /ʀigœʀ/ NF 1 (= *sévérité*) [*de condamnation, discipline*] harshness, severity; [*de mesures*] harshness, severity; [*de climat, hiver*] harshness ◆ **punir qn avec toute la ~ de la loi** to punish sb with the maximum severity the law allows ◆ **faire preuve de ~ à l'égard de qn** to be strict with sb, to be hard on sb ◆ **traiter qn avec la plus grande ~** to treat sb with the utmost harshness *ou* severity ◆ **les ~s de l'hiver** (*littér*) the rigours of winter; → **arrêt, délai**

2 (= *austérité*) [*de morale*] rigidness, strictness; [*de personne*] sternness, strictness ◆ **la politique de ~ du gouvernement** the government's austerity measures ◆ **la ~ économique** economic austerity

3 (= *précision*) [*de pensée, raisonnement, style*] rigour; [*de calcul*] precision, exactness; [*de classification, définition*] strictness ◆ **manquer de ~** to lack rigour

4 (*locutions*) **tenir ~ à qn** to hold it against sb ◆ **il lui a tenu ~ de n'être pas venu** he held it against him that he didn't come ◆ **je ne vous en tiens pas ~** I don't hold it against you ◆ **en toute ~** strictly speaking

◆ **à la rigueur** ◆ **à la ~** at a pinch, if need be ◆ **on peut à l'extrême ~ remplacer le curry par du poivre** at a pinch *ou* if you really have to you can use pepper instead of curry powder ◆ **un délit, à la ~, mais un crime non : le mot est trop fort** a minor offence possibly *ou* perhaps, but not a crime - that's too strong a word ◆ **il pourrait à la ~ avoir gagné la côte, mais j'en doute** there is a faint possibility that he made it *ou* he may just possibly have made it back to the shore but I doubt it

◆ **de rigueur** ◆ **il est de ~ d'envoyer un petit mot de remerciement** it is the done thing to send a note of thanks ◆ **la tenue de ~ est ...** the dress to be worn is ..., the accepted dress *ou* attire (*frm*) is ... ◆ **"tenue de soirée de rigueur"** "evening dress", "dress: formal"

rikiki* /ʀikiki/ ADJ INV → **riquiqui**

rillettes /ʀijɛt/ NFPL rillettes (*type of potted meat or fish*) ◆ **~ pur porc** 100% pork rillettes

rillons /ʀijɔ̃/ NMPL *pork cooked in fat and served cold*

rimailler † /ʀimaje/ ▸ conjug 1 ◂ VI (*péj*) to write doggerel, to versify

rimailleur, -euse † /ʀimajœʀ, øz/ NM,F (*péj*) would-be poet, rhymester, poetaster †

rimaye /ʀimaj/ NF bergschrund

rime /ʀim/ NF rhyme ◆ **~ masculine/féminine** masculine/feminine rhyme ◆ **~ pauvre/riche** poor/rich rhyme ◆ **~s croisées** *ou* **alternées** alternate rhymes ◆ **~s plates** *ou* **suivies** rhyming couplets ◆ **~s embrassées** abba rhyme scheme ◆ **~s tiercées** terza rima ◆ **~ pour l'œil/l'oreille** rhyme for the eye/the ear ◆ **faire qch sans ~ ni raison** to do sth without either rhyme or reason ◆ **cela n'a ni ~ ni raison** there's neither rhyme nor reason to it

rimer /ʀime/ ▸ conjug 1 ◂ VI 1 [*mot*] to rhyme (*avec* with); ◆ **cela ne rime à rien** (*fig*) it doesn't make sense, there's no sense *ou* point in it ◆ **à quoi cela rime-t-il ?** what's the point of it? *ou* sense in it? ◆ **économie ne rime pas toujours avec profit** saving doesn't necessarily go together with profit, saving and profit don't necessarily go hand in hand 2 [*poète*] to write verse *ou* poetry VT to put into verse ◆ **poésie rimée** rhyming poetry *ou* verse

rimeur, -euse /ʀimœʀ, øz/ NM,F (*péj*) rhymester, would-be poet, poetaster †

rimmel ® /ʀimɛl/ NM mascara

rinçage /ʀɛ̃saʒ/ NM 1 (= *fait de passer à l'eau*) rinsing out *ou* through; (*pour enlever le savon*) rinsing; (= *opération*) rinse ◆ **cette machine à laver fait 3 ~s** this washing machine does 3 rinses ◆ **ajouter du vinaigre dans la dernière eau de ~** add some vinegar in the final rinse 2 (*pour cheveux*) (colour (*Brit*) *ou* color (*US*)) rinse ◆ **elle s'est fait faire un ~** she had a colour rinse

rinceau (pl **rinceaux**) /ʀɛ̃so/ NM (*Archit*) foliage (*NonC*), foliation (*NonC*)

rince-bouteille(s) (pl **rince-bouteilles**) /ʀɛ̃sbutɛj/ NM (= *machine*) bottle-washing machine; (= *brosse*) bottlebrush

rince-doigts /ʀɛ̃sdwa/ NM INV (= *bol*) finger-bowl; (*en papier*) finger wipe

rincée* /ʀɛ̃se/ NF (= *averse*) downpour; (= *défaite, volée*) thrashing*, licking*

rincer /ʀɛ̃se/ ▸ conjug 3 ◂ VT 1 [+ *bouteille, verre*] to rinse (out); (*pour enlever le savon*) to rinse ◆ **rince l'assiette** give the plate a rinse, rinse the plate 2 (⁑ = *offrir à boire*) **c'est lui qui rince** the drinks are on him 3 ◆ **se faire ~*** (*par la pluie*) to get drenched *ou* soaked; (*au jeu*) to get cleaned out* ◆ **il est rincé*** he's lost everything VPR **se rincer** (= *laver*) **se ~ la bouche** to rinse out one's mouth ◆ **se ~ les mains/les cheveux** to rinse one's hands/one's hair ◆ **se ~ l'œil**⁑ to get an eyeful* ◆ **se ~ le gosier** *ou* **la dalle**⁑ to wet one's whistle*

rincette* /ʀɛ̃sɛt/ NF nip of brandy *etc*, little drop of wine (*ou* brandy *etc*)

rinçure /ʀɛ̃syʀ/ NF (= *eau de lavage*) rinsing water; (*péj* = *mauvais vin*) plonk* (*Brit*), cheap wine

ring /ʀiŋ/ NM (boxing) ring ◆ **les champions du ~** boxing champions ◆ **monter sur le ~** (*pour un match*) to go into the ring; (= *faire carrière*) to take up boxing

ringard, e* /ʀɛ̃gaʀ, aʀd/ ADJ [*personne*] square*; [*vêtement*] dowdy, naff* (*Brit*); [*film, roman, chanson, décor*] tacky*, naff* (*Brit*) NM,F (= *dépassé*) square*; (= *médiocre*) loser*

ringardise* /ʀɛ̃gaʀdiz/ NF [*de vêtement*] dowdiness ◆ **ses films/chansons sont d'une ~ !** his films/songs are incredibly tacky!*

ringardiser* /ʀɛ̃gaʀdize/ ▸ conjug 1 ◂ VT ◆ **~ un parti/une idéologie** to make a party/an ideology look old hat ◆ **il ne veut pas se laisser ~** he doesn't want to appear out of step with the times

RIP /ʀip/ NM (abrév de **relevé d'identité postal**) → **relevé**

ripaille †* /ʀipaj/ NF (= *festin*) feast ◆ **faire ~** to have a feast, to have a good blow-out* (*Brit*)

ripailler †* /ʀipaje/ ▸ conjug 1 ◂ VI (= *festoyer*) to feast, to have a good blow-out* (*Brit*)

ripailleur, -euse †* /ʀipajœʀ, øz/ ADJ revelling NM,F reveller

ripaton⁑ /ʀipatɔ̃/ NM (= *pied*) foot

riper /ʀipe/ ▸ conjug 1 ◂ VI 1 (= *déraper*) to slip 2 (* = *s'en aller*) to take off VT 1 (*Tech* = *gratter*) to scrape 2 ◆ **(faire) ~** (= *déplacer*) [+ *meuble, pierre, véhicule*] to slide along

ripoliner /ʀipɔline/ ▸ conjug 1 ◂ VT to paint with gloss paint ◆ **murs ripolinés de vert** walls painted in green gloss

riposte /ʀipɔst/ NF (= *réponse*) retort, riposte; (= *contre-attaque*) counterattack, reprisal; (*Escrime*) riposte ◆ **en ~ à** in reply to ◆ **notre ~ sera impitoyable** we will retaliate mercilessly ◆ **il est prompt à la ~** he always has a ready answer *ou* a quick retort ◆ **la ~ ne s'est pas fait attendre** the reaction was not long in coming

riposter /ʀipɔste/ ▸ conjug 1 ◂ VI 1 (= *répondre*) to answer back, to riposte, to retaliate ◆ **~ à une insulte** to reply to an insult ◆ **il riposta (à cela) par une insulte** he answered back *ou* retorted with an insult, he flung back an insult ◆ **~ à une accusation par une insulte** to counter an accusation with an insult 2 (= *contre-attaquer*) to counterattack, to retaliate ◆ **~ à coups de grenades** to retaliate by throwing grenades ◆ **~ à une attaque** to counter an attack 3 (*Escrime*) to riposte VT ◆ **~ que** to retort *ou* riposte *ou* answer back that

ripou* (pl **ripous, ripoux**) /ʀipu/ ADJ crooked NM *(gén)* crook; *(= policier)* crooked cop*, bent copper* *(Brit)*

riquiqui* /ʀikiki/ ADJ INV tiny ◆ **ça fait un peu ~** *[portion]* it's a bit stingy*; *[manteau]* it's much too small

rire /ʀiʀ/ ▸ conjug 36 ◂ VI 1 *(gén)* to laugh ◆ **~ aux éclats** *ou* **à gorge déployée** to roar with laughter, to laugh one's head off ◆ **~ aux larmes** to laugh until one cries ◆ **~ franchement** *ou* **de bon cœur** to laugh heartily ◆ **~ bruyamment** to guffaw, to roar with laughter ◆ **~ comme un bossu** *ou* **comme une baleine** *(péj)* to be doubled up with laughter ◆ **c'est à mourir** *ou* **crever* de ~** it's hilarious, it's awfully funny ◆ **la plaisanterie fit ~** the joke raised a laugh *ou* made everyone laugh ◆ **ça ne me fait pas ~** I don't find it funny, it doesn't make me laugh ◆ **nous avons bien ri (de notre mésaventure)** we had a good laugh* (over our mishap) ◆ **ça m'a bien fait ~** it really made me laugh, it had me in fits* ◆ **on va ~ : il va essayer de sauter** we're in for a laugh* – he's going to try and jump ◆ **il vaut mieux en ~ qu'en pleurer** it's better to look on the bright side ◆ **il a pris les choses en riant** *(avec bonne humeur)* he saw the funny side of it; *(à la légère)* he laughed it off ◆ **il n'y a pas de quoi ~** there's nothing to laugh about, it's no laughing matter ◆ **rira bien qui rira le dernier** *(Prov)* he who laughs last laughs longest *(Brit)* *ou* best *(US)* *(Prov)*

2 *(littér)* *[yeux]* to sparkle *ou* shine with happiness *ou* laughter; *[visage]* to shine with happiness

3 *(= s'amuser)* to have fun, to have a laugh* ◆ **il ne pense qu'à ~** he only thinks of having fun ◆ **il passe son temps à ~ avec ses camarades** he spends his time fooling around *ou* playing about *ou* larking about *(Brit)* with his friends ◆ **~ aux dépens de qn** to laugh *ou* have a laugh at sb's expense ◆ **c'est un homme qui aime bien ~** he is a man who likes a bit of fun *ou* a good laugh* ◆ **c'est maintenant qu'on va ~ !** this is where the fun starts!; → **histoire**

4 *(= plaisanter)* to be joking ◆ **vous voulez ~ !** you're joking!, you must be joking! *ou* kidding!* ◆ **et je ne ris pas** and I'm not joking ◆ **il a dit cela pour ~** he was only joking, he said it in fun ◆ **il a fait cela pour ~** he did it for a joke *ou* laugh* ◆ **c'était une bagarre pour ~** it was only a pretend fight, it wasn't a real fight; → **mot**

5 *(locutions)* **~ dans sa barbe** *ou* **tout bas** to laugh to o.s., to chuckle (away) to o.s. ◆ **~ sous cape** to laugh up one's sleeve, to have a quiet laugh ◆ **~ au nez** *ou* **à la barbe de qn** to laugh in sb's face ◆ **~ du bout des dents** *ou* **des lèvres** to force o.s. to laugh, to laugh politely ◆ **il faisait semblant de trouver ça drôle, mais en fait il riait jaune** he pretended he found it funny but in fact he had to force himself to laugh ◆ **quand il apprendra la nouvelle, il rira jaune** when he hears the news he won't find it funny *ou* he'll be laughing on the other side of his face *(Brit)* ◆ **vous me faites ~ !, laissez-moi ~ !** *(iro)* don't make me laugh!, you make me laugh! *(iro)* ◆ **ça ne fait plus ~ personne** *(fig)* it's beyond a joke ◆ **sans ~, c'est vrai ?** joking apart *ou* aside, is it true?, seriously, is it true? ◆ **elle l'a quitté – oh ! sans ~ ?** she has left him – really? *ou* you're joking? *(iro)*

VT INDIR **rire de** *(= se moquer de)* *[+ personne, défaut, crainte]* to laugh at, to scoff at ◆ **il fait ~ de lui** people laugh at him *ou* make fun of him, he's a laughing stock

VPR **se rire** ◆ **se ~ de** *(= se jouer de)* *[+ difficultés, épreuve]* to make light of, to take in one's stride; *(= se moquer de)* *[+ menaces, recommandations]* to laugh at; *[+ personne]* to laugh at, to scoff at

NM *(= façon de rire)* laugh; *(= éclat de rire)* laughter *(NonC)*, laugh ◆ **~s** laughter ◆ **le ~** laughter ◆ **le ~ est le propre de l'homme** *(Prov)* laughter is unique to man ◆ **un gros ~** a loud laugh, a guffaw ◆ **un ~ homérique** a hearty *ou* booming laugh ◆ **un petit ~ bête** a stupid giggle *ou* titter ◆ **un ~ moqueur** a mocking *ou* scornful laugh ◆ **~s préenregistrés** *ou* **en boîte*** *(Radio, TV)* canned laughter ◆ **il y eut des ~s dans la salle quand ...** there was laughter in the audience when ... ◆ **elle a un ~ bête** she has a silly *ou* stupid laugh ◆ **elle eut un petit ~ méchant** she gave a wicked little laugh, she laughed wickedly ◆ **il eut un petit ~ de satisfaction** he gave a little chuckle of satisfaction, he chuckled with satisfaction ◆ **les ~s l'obligèrent à se taire** the laughter forced him to stop speaking, he was laughed down; → **éclater, fou**

ris¹ /ʀi/ NM 1 *(Culin)* **~ de veau** calf's sweetbread; *(sur un menu)* calves' sweetbreads 2 *(Naut)* reef

ris² /ʀi/ NM *(littér = rire)* laugh, laughter *(NonC)*

RISC /ɛʀiɛsse/ ADJ (abrév de **Reduced Instruction Set Computing**) *(Ordin)* RISC ◆ **technologie/système ~** RISC technology/system

risée /ʀize/ NF 1 *(= moquerie)* **s'exposer à la ~ générale** to lay o.s. open to ridicule ◆ **être un objet de ~** to be a laughing stock, to be an object of ridicule ◆ **être la ~ de toute l'Europe** to be the laughing stock of Europe 2 *(Naut)* **~(s)** light breeze

risette /ʀizɛt/ NF *(langage enfantin)* ◆ **faire (une) ~ à qn** to give sb a nice *ou* little smile ◆ **fais ~ (au monsieur)** smile nicely (at the gentleman) ◆ **être obligé de faire des ~s au patron** *(fig)* to have to smile politely to the boss

risible /ʀizibl/ ADJ *(= ridicule)* *[attitude]* laughable, ridiculous, silly; *(= comique)* *[aventure]* laughable, funny

risiblement /ʀiziblәmɑ̃/ ADV ridiculously, laughably

risque /ʀisk/ GRAMMAIRE ACTIVE 42.3 NM 1 *(gén, Assurances, Jur)* risk ◆ **~ calculé** calculated risk ◆ **entreprise pleine de ~s** high-risk business ◆ **c'est un ~ à courir** it's a risk one has to take *ou* run, one has to take *ou* run the risk ◆ **il y a du ~ à faire cela** there's a risk in doing that, it's risky doing that ◆ **le goût du ~** a taste for danger ◆ **ce qui paie, c'est le ~** it pays off to take risks, taking risks pays off ◆ **on n'a rien sans ~** you don't get anywhere without taking risks nothing ventured, nothing gained *(Prov)* ◆ **il y a (un) ~ d'émeute/d'épidémie** there's a risk of an uprising/an epidemic ◆ **à cause du ~ d'incendie** because of the fire risk *ou* the risk of fire ◆ **cela constitue un ~ pour la santé** that is a health hazard *ou* a health risk ◆ **~ de change** *(Fin)* exchange risk *ou* exposure ◆ **prendre des ~s** to take risks ◆ **ne prendre aucun ~** *(fig)* to play (it) safe, to take no risks ◆ **prise de ~(s)** risk-taking; → **assurance**

2 *(locutions)* **le ~ zéro n'existe pas** there's no such thing as zero risk ◆ **ce sont les ~s du métier** *(hum)* that's an occupational hazard *(hum)* ◆ **il n'y a pas de ~ qu'il refuse** there's no risk *ou* chance of his refusing ◆ **au ~ de le mécontenter/de se tuer/de sa vie** at the risk of displeasing him/of killing himself/of his life ◆ **c'est à tes ~s et périls** you do it at your own risk, on your own head be it!

◆ **à + risque** *(Méd)* *[groupe]* high-risk; *(Fin)* *[placement]* risky ◆ **à haut ~** high-risk *(épith)* ◆ **pratique à ~** (high-)risk behaviour *(NonC)* *(Brit)* *ou* behavior *(NonC)* *(US)*

risqué, e /ʀiske/ (ptp de **risquer**) ADJ *(= hasardeux)* risky, dicey* *(Brit)*; *(= licencieux)* risqué, daring, off-color *(US)*

risquer /ʀiske/ GRAMMAIRE ACTIVE 29.3 ▸ conjug 1 ◂

VT 1 *(= s'exposer à)* **il risque la mort** he risks being killed ◆ **parler politique, c'est ~ la prison** if you talk about politics you could end up in prison ◆ **il risque la prison à vie** he could get life imprisonment ◆ **il risque le renvoi** he could be sacked ◆ **qu'est-ce qu'on risque ?** *(= quels sont les risques ?)* what are the risks *ou* dangers?; *(= c'est sans danger)* what have we got to lose?, where's *ou* what's the risk? ◆ **bien emballé, ce vase ne risque rien** if it's properly packed the vase will be okay ◆ **ce vieux chapeau ne risque rien** it doesn't matter what happens to this old hat ◆ **ça ne risque pas !** not a chance!

2 *(= tenter)* to risk ◆ **~ le tout pour le tout** to risk everything ◆ **~ le paquet*** to go for broke* ◆ **risquons le coup** let's chance *ou* risk it ◆ **qui ne risque rien n'a rien** *(Prov)* nothing ventured, nothing gained *(Prov)* ◆ **tu risques gros** you're taking a big risk

3 *(= mettre en danger)* *[+ fortune, réputation, vie]* to risk

4 *(= hasarder)* **je ne risquerais pas un gros mot devant mon grand-père** I wouldn't dare use bad language in front of my grandfather ◆ **~ un œil au dehors** to take a peep *ou* a quick look outside ◆ **~ un orteil dans l'eau** *(hum)* to venture a toe in the water

5 *(locutions)*

◆ **risquer de** ◆ **tu risques de le perdre** *(éventualité)* you might *ou* could lose it; *(forte possibilité)* you could easily lose it; *(probabilité)* you'll probably lose it ◆ **il risque de pleuvoir** it could *ou* may rain, there's a chance of rain ◆ **le feu risque de s'éteindre** the fire might go out ◆ **avec ces embouteillages, il risque d'être en retard** with these traffic jams, he may *ou* could well be late ◆ **on risque fort d'être en retard** we're very likely to be late ◆ **pourquoi ~ de tout perdre ?** why risk losing everything? ◆ **ça ne risque pas d'arriver !** not a chance!, that's not likely to happen! ◆ **il ne risque pas de gagner** he hasn't got much chance of winning, he isn't likely to win

◆ **risquer que** ◆ **tu risques qu'on te le vole** there's a danger it'll be stolen, it might be stolen

VPR **se risquer** ◆ **se ~ dans une grotte/sur une corniche** to venture inside a cave/onto a ledge ◆ **se ~ à faire qch** to venture *ou* dare to do sth ◆ **à ta place, je ne m'y risquerais pas** if I were you, I wouldn't risk it ◆ **je vais me ~ à faire un soufflé** I'm going to try my hand *ou* have a go at making a soufflé

> ⚠ **risquer de** se traduit rarement par **to risk** ; les tournures avec des auxiliaires modaux sont plus courantes en anglais.

risque-tout /ʀiskәtu/ NMF INV daredevil ◆ **elle est ~, c'est une ~** she's a daredevil

rissole /ʀisɔl/ NF rissole

rissoler /ʀisɔle/ ▸ conjug 1 ◂ VT *(Culin)* ◆ **(faire) ~** to brown ◆ **pommes rissolées** fried potatoes VI *(Culin)* to brown

ristourne /ʀistuʀn/ NF *(sur achat)* discount; *(sur cotisation)* rebate; *(= commission)* commission ◆ **faire une ~ à qn** to give sb a discount ◆ **je lui ai demandé 10% de ~** I asked him for a 10% discount

ristourner /ʀistuʀne/ ▸ conjug 1 ◂ VT 1 *(= accorder une réduction de)* to give a discount of; *(= rembourser un trop-perçu de)* to refund the difference of; *(= donner une commission de)* to give a commission of ◆ **ils m'ont ristourné 80 €** they gave me 80 euros back ◆ **une partie de la taxe est ristournée au pays exportateur** part of the tax is refunded to the exporting country 2 *(Jur, Naut)* *[+ police d'assurance]* to cancel

ristrette /ʀistʀɛt/, **ristretto** /ʀistʀeto/ NM *(Helv)* espresso

rital*/ʀital/ NM (injurieux = Italien) wop*(injurieux), Eyetie*(injurieux)

rite /ʀit/ NM (gén, Rel) rite; (fig = habitude) ritual ◆ **~s sociaux** social rituals ◆ **~s d'initiation** ou **initiatiques** initiation rites ◆ ~ **de passage** rite of passage

ritournelle /ʀituʀnɛl/ NF (Mus) ritornello ◆ **c'est toujours la même** ~ (fig) it's always the same (old) story

ritualiser /ʀitɥalize/ ▸ conjug 1 ◂ VT to ritualize

ritualisme /ʀitɥalism/ NM ritualism

ritualiste /ʀitɥalist/ ADJ ritualistic NM,F ritualist

rituel, -elle /ʀitɥɛl/ ADJ ritual NM ritual ◆ **le ~ du départ était toujours le même** the ritual was always the same when we left

rituellement /ʀitɥɛlmɑ̃/ ADV (= religieusement) religiously, ritually; (hum = invariablement) invariably, unfailingly

rivage /ʀivaʒ/ NM shore

rival, e (mpl **-aux**) /ʀival, o/ ADJ, NM,F rival ◆ **sans ~** unrivalled

rivaliser /ʀivalize/ GRAMMAIRE ACTIVE 32.2, 32.3 ▸ conjug 1 ◂ VI ◆ ~ **avec** [personne] to rival, to compete with, to vie with; [chose] to hold its own against, to compare with ◆ ~ **de générosité/de bons mots avec qn** to vie with sb ou try to outdo sb in generosity/wit, to rival sb in generosity/wit ◆ **il essaie de ~ avec moi** he's trying to emulate me ou to vie with me ◆ **ses tableaux rivalisent avec les plus grands chefs-d'œuvre** his paintings rival the greatest masterpieces ou can hold their own against the greatest masterpieces

rivalité /ʀivalite/ NF rivalry ◆ **~s internes** (gén) internal rivalries; (Pol) internecine strife ou rivalries ◆ **~s de personnes** rivalry between people

rive /ʀiv/ NF 1 [de mer, lac] shore; [de rivière] bank ◆ **la ~ gauche/droite de la Tamise** the north/south bank of the Thames ◆ **la ~ gauche/droite (de la Seine)** the left/right bank (of the Seine) 2 (Tech) [de four] lip ◆ **planche de** ~ [de toit] eaves fascia

RIVE GAUCHE, RIVE DROITE

The terms **rive gauche** and **rive droite** are social and cultural notions as well as geographical ones. The Left Bank of the Seine (ie, the southern half of Paris) is traditionally associated with the arts (especially literature), with students and with a somewhat Bohemian lifestyle. The Right Bank is generally viewed as being more traditionalist, commercially-minded and conformist.

rivé, e /ʀive/ (ptp de **river**) ADJ ◆ ~ **à** [+ bureau, travail] tethered ou tied to; [+ chaise] glued ou riveted to ◆ **les yeux ~s sur moi/la tache de sang** (with) his eyes riveted on me/the bloodstain ◆ **rester ~ sur place** to be ou stand riveted ou rooted to the spot ◆ ~ **à la télé*** glued to the TV*

river /ʀive/ ▸ conjug 1 ◂ VT 1 (Tech) [+ clou] to clinch; [+ plaques] to rivet together ◆ ~ **son clou à qn*** (fig) to shut sb up* 2 (littér = fixer) ~ **qch au mur/sol** to nail sth to the wall/floor ◆ **il la rivait au sol** he pinned her to the ground ◆ **la haine/le sentiment qui les rivait ensemble** ou **l'un à l'autre** the hatred/the emotional bond which held them to each other

riverain, e /ʀiv(ə)ʀɛ̃, ɛn/ NM,F resident ◆ **les ~s se plaignent du bruit des voitures** the residents complain about traffic noise ◆ **"interdit sauf aux riverains"** "no entry except for access", "residents only" ADJ (d'un lac) lakeside; (d'une rivière) riverside, riparian (SPÉC) ◆ **les propriétés ~es** (d'une route) the houses along the road ◆ **les propriétés ~es de la Seine** the houses along the banks of the Seine

rivet /ʀivɛ/ NM rivet

rivetage /ʀiv(ə)taʒ/ NM riveting

riveter /ʀiv(ə)te/ ▸ conjug 4 ◂ VT to rivet (together)

riveteuse /ʀiv(ə)tøz/, **riveuse** /ʀivøz/ NF riveting machine

rivière /ʀivjɛʀ/ NF (lit, fig) river; (Équitation) water jump ◆ ~ **de diamants** diamond rivière; → **petit**

rixe /ʀiks/ NF brawl, fight, scuffle

Riyad /ʀijad/ N Riyadh

riyal /ʀijal/ NM riyal

riz /ʀi/ NM rice ◆ ~ **Caroline** ou **à grains longs** long-grain rice ◆ ~ **à grains ronds** round-grain rice ◆ ~ **basmati** basmati rice ◆ ~ **brun** ou **complet** brown rice ◆ ~ **cantonais** fried rice ◆ ~ **créole** creole rice ◆ ~ **gluant** sticky rice ◆ ~ **au lait** rice pudding ◆ ~ **pilaf** pilaf(f) ou pilau rice ◆ ~ **sauvage** wild rice; → **gâteau, paille**

rizerie /ʀizʀi/ NF rice-processing factory

riziculture /ʀizikyltyʀ/ NF rice-growing

rizière /ʀizjɛʀ/ NF paddy-field, ricefield

RM /ɛʀɛm/ NM (abrév de **règlement mensuel**) → **règlement**

RMI /ɛʀɛmi/ NM (abrév de **revenu minimum d'insertion**) → **revenu**

rmiste, Rmiste /ɛʀɛmist/ NMF person receiving welfare payment, ≃ person on income support (Brit), person on welfare (US)

RMN /ɛʀɛmɛn/ NF (abrév de **résonance magnétique nucléaire**) NMR

RN /ɛʀɛn/ NF (abrév de **route nationale**) → **route** NM (abrév de **revenu national**) → **revenu**

RNIS /ɛʀɛniɛs/ NM (abrév de **Réseau Numérique à Intégration de Service**) ISDN

robe /ʀɔb/ NF 1 [de femme, fillette] dress ◆ ~ **courte/décolletée/d'été** short/low-necked/summer dress

2 [de magistrat, prélat] robe; [de professeur] gown ◆ **la ~** (Hist Jur) the legal profession; → **gens**[1], **homme, noblesse**

3 (= pelage) [de cheval, fauve] coat

4 (= peau) [d'oignon] skin; [de fève] husk

5 [de cigare] wrapper, outer leaf

6 (= couleur) [de vin] colour (Brit), color (US)

COMP **robe bain de soleil** sundress

robe de bal ball gown ou dress

robe de baptême christening ou baptism robe

robe bustier off-the-shoulder dress

robe de chambre dressing gown ◆ **pommes de terre en ~ de chambre** ou **des champs** (Culin) baked ou jacket (Brit) potatoes, potatoes in their jackets

robe chasuble pinafore dress

robe chaussette ⇒ **robe tube**

robe chemisier shirtwaister (dress) (Brit), shirtwaist (dress) (US)

robe de cocktail cocktail dress

robe de communion ou **de communiant(e)** first communion dress

robe de grossesse maternity dress

robe d'hôtesse hostess gown

robe d'intérieur housecoat

robe kimono kimono (dress)

robe de mariée wedding dress ou gown

robe du soir evening dress ou gown

robe tube tube

robe tunique smock

robe-manteau (pl **robes-manteaux**) /ʀɔbmɑ̃to/ NF coat dress

roberts‡ /ʀɔbɛʀ/ NMPL (= seins) tits‡, boobs‡

robe-sac (pl **robes-sacs**) /ʀɔbsak/ NF sack dress

robe-tablier (pl **robes-tabliers**) /ʀɔbtablije/ NF overall

Robin /ʀɔbɛ̃/ NM Robin ◆ ~ **des Bois** Robin Hood ◆ **c'est le ~ des Bois de la politique française** (hum = justicier) he's the Robin Hood of French politics

robinet /ʀɔbinɛ/ NM 1 [d'évier, baignoire, tonneau] tap (Brit), faucet (US) ◆ ~ **d'eau chaude/froide** hot/cold (water) tap (Brit) ou faucet (US) ◆ ~ **mélangeur**, ~ **mitigeur** mixer tap (Brit) ou faucet (US) ◆ ~ **du gaz** gas tap ◆ ~ **d'arrêt** stopcock; → **problème** 2 (*, langage enfantin = pénis) willy* (Brit), peter* (US)

robinetterie /ʀɔbinɛtʀi/ NF (= installations) taps (Brit), faucets (US), plumbing (NonC); (= usine) tap (Brit) ou faucet (US) factory; (= commerce) tap (Brit) ou faucet (US) trade

robinier /ʀɔbinje/ NM locust tree, false acacia

Robinson Crusoé /ʀɔbɛ̃sɔ̃kʀyzɔe/ NM Robinson Crusoe

roboratif, -ive /ʀɔbɔʀatif, iv/ ADJ (littér) [climat] bracing; [activité] invigorating; [liqueur, vin] tonic, stimulating

robot /ʀɔbo/ NM (lit, fig) robot ◆ ~ **ménager** ou **de cuisine** food processor

roboticien, -ienne /ʀɔbɔtisjɛ̃, jɛn/ NM,F robotics specialist

robotique /ʀɔbɔtik/ NF robotics (sg)

robotisation /ʀɔbɔtizasjɔ̃/ NF [d'atelier, usine] automation ◆ **il redoute la ~ de l'humanité** he fears that human beings are being turned into robots

robotiser /ʀɔbɔtize/ ▸ conjug 1 ◂ VT [+ atelier, usine] to automate ◆ **des gens complètement robotisés** people who have been turned into robots

robre /ʀɔbʀ/ NM (Bridge) rubber

robusta /ʀɔbysta/ NM (= café) robusta

robuste /ʀɔbyst/ ADJ (= fort et résistant) strong; (= d'apparence) solidly-built ◆ **de ~ constitution** of strong ou robust constitution ◆ **d'une santé** ~ in excellent health

robustement /ʀɔbystəmɑ̃/ ADV robustly

robustesse /ʀɔbystɛs/ NF strength; [de voiture, bateau] sturdiness ◆ **ils sont confiants dans la ~ de la croissance** they are confident that growth is strong

roc[1] /ʀɔk/ NM (lit, fig) rock; → **bâtir, dur**

roc[2] /ʀɔk/ NM (Myth) ◆ **(oiseau) ~** roc

rocade /ʀɔkad/ NF (= route) bypass; (Mil) communications line

rocaille /ʀɔkaj/ NF 1 (= cailloux) loose stones; (= terrain) rocky ou stony ground 2 (= jardin) rockery, rock garden ◆ **plantes de ~** rock plants 3 (Constr) **grotte/fontaine en ~** grotto/fountain in rockwork ADJ [objet, style] rocaille

rocailleux, -euse /ʀɔkajø, øz/ ADJ [terrain] rocky, stony; [style] rugged; [son, voix] harsh, grating

rocambole /ʀɔkɑ̃bɔl/ NF rocambole

rocambolesque /ʀɔkɑ̃bɔlɛsk/ ADJ [aventures, péripéties] fantastic, incredible

rochassier, -ière /ʀɔʃasje, jɛʀ/ NM,F rock climber

roche /ʀɔʃ/ NF (gén) rock ◆ **~s sédimentaires/volcaniques** sedimentary/volcanic rock(s) ◆ ~ **lunaire** moon rock ◆ ~ **mère** parent rock ◆ **la ~ Tarpéienne** the Tarpeian Rock ◆ **fond de ~** (Naut) rock bottom; → **anguille, coq**[1], **cristal**

rocher /ʀɔʃe/ NM 1 (= bloc) rock; (gros, lisse) boulder; (= substance) rock ◆ **le ~ de Sisyphe** the rock of Sisyphus ◆ **le ~ de Gibraltar, le Rocher** the Rock (of Gibraltar) ◆ **faire du ~**

(Alpinisme) to go rock-climbing [2] *(Anat)* petrosal bone [3] *(en chocolat)* chocolate

rochet /ʀɔʃɛ/ NM [1] *(Rel)* ratchet [2] *(Tech)* **roue à ~** ratchet wheel

rocheux, -euse /ʀɔʃø, øz/ ADJ rocky ◆ **paroi rocheuse** rock face NFPL **Rocheuses** ◆ **les (montagnes) Rocheuses** the Rocky Mountains, the Rockies

rock[1] /ʀɔk/ NM *(Myth)* ⇒ **roc**[2]

rock[2] /ʀɔk/ *(Mus)* ADJ rock NM *(= musique)* rock; *(= danse)* jive, rock 'n' roll ◆ **le ~ punk/alternatif** punk/alternative rock ◆ **danser le ~** to rock, to jive ◆ **~ and roll, ~ 'n' roll** rock 'n' roll ◆ **~ acrobatique** acrobatic dancing

rocker /ʀɔkœʀ/ NM ⇒ **rockeur**

rockeur, -euse /ʀɔkœʀ, øz/ NM,F *(= chanteur)* rock singer; *(= musicien)* rock musician; *(= fan)* rock fan, rocker

rocking-chair (pl **rocking-chairs**) /ʀɔkiŋ(t)ʃɛʀ/ NM rocking chair

rococo /ʀɔkɔko/ NM *(Art)* rococo ADJ INV *(Art)* rococo; *(péj)* old-fashioned, outdated

rodage /ʀɔdaʒ/ NM [1] *[de véhicule, moteur]* running in *(Brit)*, breaking in *(US)* ◆ **"en rodage"** "running in" *(Brit)*, "breaking in" *(US)* ◆ **pendant le ~** during the running-in *(Brit)* *ou* breaking-in *(US)* period ◆ **la voiture était en ~** the car was being run in *(Brit)* *ou* broken in *(US)* [2] *[de soupape]* grinding [3] *(= mise au point)* **on a dû prévoir une période de ~** we had to allow some time to get up to speed ◆ **ce spectacle a demandé un certain ~** the show took a little while to get over its teething troubles *ou* get into its stride ◆ **le nouveau gouvernement est encore en ~** the new government is still cutting its teeth

rodéo /ʀɔdeo/ NM *(= sport)* rodeo; *(= poursuite)* high-speed car chase ◆ **~ (automobile** *ou* **motorisé), ~ de voitures volées** joy riding *(NonC)*

roder /ʀɔde/ ▸ conjug 1 ◂ VT [1] *[+ véhicule, moteur]* to run in *(Brit)*, to break in *(US)* [2] *[+ soupape]* to grind [3] *(= mettre au point)* **il faut ~ ce spectacle/ce nouveau service** we have to let this show/this new service get into its stride, we have to give this show/this new service time to get over its teething troubles ◆ **ce spectacle est maintenant bien rodé** the show is really running well *ou* smoothly now, all the initial problems in the show have been ironed out ◆ **il n'est pas encore rodé** *[personne]* he hasn't quite got the hang of it yet; *[organisme]* it hasn't yet got into its stride

rôder /ʀode/ ▸ conjug 1 ◂ VI *(au hasard)* to roam *ou* wander about; *(de façon suspecte)* to loiter *ou* lurk (about *ou* around); *(= être en maraude)* to prowl about, to be on the prowl ◆ **~ autour d'un magasin** to hang *ou* lurk around a shop ◆ **~ autour de qn** to hang around sb

rôdeur, -euse /ʀodœʀ, øz/ NM,F prowler

rodomontade /ʀɔdɔmɔ̃tad/ NF *(littér)* *(= vantardise)* bragging *(NonC)*, boasting *(NonC)*; *(= menace)* sabre rattling *(NonC)*

Rogations /ʀɔgasjɔ̃/ NFPL *(Rel)* Rogations

rogatoire /ʀɔgatwaʀ/ ADJ *(Jur)* rogatory; → **commission**

rogatons /ʀɔgatɔ̃/ NMPL *(péj)* *(= nourriture)* scraps (of food), left-overs; *(= objets)* pieces of junk; *(= vêtements)* old rags

rogne* /ʀɔɲ/ NF anger ◆ **être en ~** to be (really *ou* hopping* *(Brit)*) mad *ou* really ratty* *(Brit)* ◆ **se mettre en ~** to get (really *ou* hopping* *(Brit)*) mad *ou* really ratty* *(Brit)*, to blow one's top* *(contre* at); ◆ **mettre qn en ~** to make sb (really *ou* hopping* *(Brit)*) mad *ou* really ratty* *(Brit)*, to make sb lose their temper ◆ **il était dans une telle ~ que ...** he was in such a (foul) temper that ..., he was so mad* *ou* ratty* *(Brit)* that ... ◆ **ses ~s duraient des jours** his tempers lasted for days

rogner /ʀɔɲe/ ▸ conjug 1 ◂ VT [1] *(= couper)* *[+ ongle, page, plaque]* to trim; *[+ griffe]* to clip, to trim; *[+ aile, pièce d'or]* to clip ◆ **~ les ailes à qn** to clip sb's wings [2] *(= réduire)* *[+ prix]* to whittle down, to cut down; *[+ salaire]* to cut back *ou* down, to whittle down ◆ **~ sur** *[+ dépense, prix]* to cut down on, to cut back on; *[+ nourriture, sorties]* to cut down on

rognon /ʀɔɲɔ̃/ NM [1] *(Culin)* kidney ◆ **~s blancs** ram's testicles [2] *(Géol)* nodule

rognures /ʀɔɲyʀ/ NFPL *[de métal]* clippings, trimmings; *[de cuir, papier]* clippings; *[d'ongles]* clippings, parings; *[de viande]* scraps

rogomme /ʀɔgɔm/ NM ◆ **voix de ~** hoarse *ou* rasping voice

rogue /ʀɔg/ ADJ *(= arrogant)* haughty, arrogant

roi /ʀwa/ NM [1] *(= souverain, Cartes, Échecs)* king ◆ **le livre des Rois** *(Bible)* (the Book of) Kings ◆ **le jour des Rois** *(gén)* Twelfth Night; *(Rel)* Epiphany ◆ **tirer les ~s** to eat Twelfth Night cake ◆ **le ~ n'est pas son cousin !** he's very full of himself! ◆ **travailler pour le ~ de Prusse** to receive no reward for one's pains; → **bleu, camelot, heureux** *etc*

[2] *(fig)* king ◆ **le ~ des animaux/de la forêt** the king of the beasts/of the forest ◆ **~ du pétrole** oil king ◆ **les ~s de la finance** the kings of finance ◆ **un des ~s de la presse/du textile** one of the press/textile barons *ou* magnates *ou* tycoons ◆ **c'est le ~ des fromages** it's the prince of cheeses ◆ **c'est le ~ de la resquille !*** he's a master *ou* an ace* at getting something for nothing ◆ **tu es vraiment le ~ (des imbéciles) !*** you really are a prize idiot!*, you really take the cake (for sheer stupidity)!* ◆ **c'est le ~ des cons**** he's an utter cretin** *(Brit)* *ou* a total asshole** *(US)* ◆ **c'est le ~ des salauds**** he's the world's biggest bastard**

COMP **les rois fainéants** *(Hist)* *the last Merovingian kings*
le Roi des Juifs the King of the Jews
le Roi des Rois the King of Kings
le Roi Très Chrétien the King of France; → **mage**

LES ROIS

At Epiphany, it is traditional for French people to get together and share a « galette des rois », a round, flat pastry filled with almond paste. A small figurine (« la fève ») is baked inside the pastry, and the person who finds it in his or her portion is given a cardboard crown to wear. This tradition is known as « tirer les rois ». In some families, a child goes under the table while the pastry is being shared out and says who should receive each portion.

roide /ʀwad/ ADJ, **roideur** /ʀwadœʀ/ NF, **roidir** /ʀwadiʀ/ VT (†† *ou* littér) ⇒ **raide, raideur, raidir**

roiller* /ʀɔje/ VB IMPERS *(Helv = pleuvoir)* to rain

Roi-Soleil /ʀwasɔlɛj/ NM ◆ **le ~** the Sun King

roitelet /ʀwat(ə)lɛ/ NM [1] *(péj = roi)* kinglet, petty king [2] *(= oiseau)* wren ◆ **~ (huppé)** goldcrest

rôle /ʀol/ NM [1] *(Théât, fig)* role, part ◆ **jouer un ~** *[personne]* *(Théât)* to play a part (*dans* in); *(fig)* to put on an act; *[fait, circonstance]* to play a part, to have a role (*dans* in); ◆ **premier ~** lead, leading *ou* major role *ou* part ◆ **avoir le premier ~ dans qch** *(fig)* to play a leading part in sth ◆ **second/petit ~** supporting/minor role *ou* part ◆ **jouer les seconds ~s** *(Ciné)* to play minor parts *ou* supporting roles; *(fig : en politique)* to play second fiddle ◆ **~ muet** non-speaking part ◆ **~ de composition** character part *ou* role ◆ **savoir son ~** to know one's part *ou* lines ◆ **distribuer les ~s** to cast the parts ◆ **je lui ai donné le ~ de Lear** I gave him the role *ou* part of Lear, I cast him as Lear ◆ **il joue bien son ~ de jeune cadre** he's a success in the role of the young executive ◆ **inverser** *ou* **renverser les ~s** to reverse *ou* switch roles ◆ **avoir le beau ~** to show o.s. in a good light, to come off best; → **jeu**

[2] *(= fonction, statut)* *[de personne]* role; *[d'institution, système]* role, function; *(= contribution)* part; *(= devoir, travail)* job ◆ **il a un ~ important dans l'organisation** he has an important role in the organization ◆ **quel a été son ~ dans cette affaire ?** what was his role in all this? ◆ **ce n'est pas mon ~ de vous sermonner mais ...** it isn't my job *ou* place to lecture you but ... ◆ **en donnant cet avertissement, il est dans son ~** *(= il fait ce qu'il a à faire)* in issuing this warning, he's simply doing his job ◆ **le ~ de la métaphore chez Lawrence** the role *ou* function of metaphor in Lawrence ◆ **la télévision a pour ~ de ...** the role *ou* function of television is to ...

[3] *(= registre, Admin)* roll; *(Jur)* cause list ◆ **~ d'équipage** muster (roll) ◆ **~ des impôts** tax list *ou* roll; → **tour**[2]

rôle-titre (pl **rôles-titres**) /ʀoltitʀ/ NM title role

roller /ʀɔlœʀ/ NM roller skate ◆ **~ en ligne** rollerblade, in-line roller skate ◆ **faire du ~** to roller-skate ◆ **faire du ~ en ligne** to rollerblade

rollmops /ʀɔlmɔps/ NM rollmop

Rolls ® /ʀɔls/ NF *(lit)* Rolls, Rolls Royce ®; *(fig)* Rolls Royce

ROM /ʀɔm/ NF [1] (abrév de **Read Only Memory**) *(Ordin)* ROM [2] (abrév de **Région d'outre-mer**) *French overseas region* → **DOM**

romain, e /ʀɔmɛ̃, ɛn/ ADJ *(gén)* Roman NM *(Typo)* roman NM,F **Romain(e)** Roman; → **travail**[1] NF **romaine** ◆ **(laitue) ~e** cos (lettuce) *(Brit)*, romaine (lettuce) *(US)* ◆ **(balance) ~e** steelyard ◆ **être bon comme la ~e** *(trop bon)* to be too nice for one's own good; *(menacé)* to be in for it*

romaïque /ʀɔmaik/ ADJ, NM Romaic, demotic Greek

roman[1] /ʀɔmɑ̃/ NM [1] *(= livre)* novel; *(fig = récit)* story ◆ **le ~** *(= genre)* the novel ◆ **ils ne publient que des ~s** they only publish novels *ou* fiction ◆ **ça n'arrive que dans les ~s** it only happens in novels *ou* fiction *ou* stories ◆ **sa vie est un vrai ~** his life is like something out of a novel ◆ **c'est tout un ~ *** it's a long story, it's a real saga ◆ **Éric et sa mère, c'est un vrai ~** *ou* **tout un ~ !** you could write a book about Eric and his mother! ◆ **ça se lit comme un ~** it reads like a novel; → **eau, nouveau**

[2] *(Littérat = œuvre médiévale)* romance ◆ **~ courtois** courtly romance

COMP **roman d'amour** *(lit)* love story; *(fig)* love story, (storybook) romance
roman d'analyse psychological novel
roman d'anticipation futuristic novel, science-fiction novel
roman d'aventures adventure story
roman de cape et d'épée swashbuckler
roman de chevalerie tale of chivalry
roman à clés roman à clés
roman d'épouvante horror story
roman d'espionnage spy thriller *ou* story
roman familial *(Psych)* family romance
roman de gare airport novel
roman historique historical novel
roman de mœurs social novel
roman noir *(Hist)* Gothic novel; *(policier)* violent thriller
roman policier detective novel *ou* story, whodunit*
roman de science-fiction science-fiction novel
roman (de) série noire thriller

roman², e /ʀɔmɑ̃, an/ ADJ *(Ling)* Romance *(épith)*, Romanic; *(Archit)* Romanesque; *(en Grande-Bretagne)* Norman NM **le ~ (commun)** *(= langue)* late vulgar Latin ◆ **le ~** *(Archit)* the Romanesque

> ⚠ L'adjectif **roman** ne se traduit pas par le mot anglais **Roman**, qui a le sens de 'romain'.

romance /ʀɔmɑ̃s/ NF [1] *(= chanson)* sentimental ballad, lovesong ◆ **les ~s napolitaines** the Neapolitan lovesongs; → **pousser** [2] *(Littérat, Mus)* ballad, romance

romancer /ʀɔmɑ̃se/ ► conjug 3 ◄ VT *(= présenter sous forme de roman)* to make into a novel; *(= agrémenter)* to romanticize ◆ **histoire romancée** fictionalized history; → **biographie**

romanche /ʀɔmɑ̃ʃ/ ADJ, NM Romans(c)h

romancier /ʀɔmɑ̃sje/ NM novelist

romancière /ʀɔmɑ̃sjɛʀ/ NF (woman) novelist

romand, e /ʀɔmɑ̃, ɑ̃d/ ADJ of French-speaking Switzerland ◆ **les Romands** the French-speaking Swiss; → **suisse**

romanesque /ʀɔmanɛsk/ ADJ [1] *[amours]* storybook *(épith)*; *[aventures]* storybook *(épith)*; *[histoire, imagination, personne, tempérament]* romantic [2] *(Littérat) [traitement, récit]* novelistic ◆ **la technique ~** the technique(s) of the novel ◆ **œuvres ~s** novels, fiction *(NonC)* NM *[d'imagination, personne]* romantic side ◆ **elle se réfugiait dans le ~** she took refuge in a world of romance

> ⚠ L'adjectif **romanesque** ne se traduit pas par le mot anglais **Romanesque**, qui désigne le style 'roman'.

roman-feuilleton (pl **romans-feuilletons**) /ʀɔmɑ̃fœjtɔ̃/ NM serialized novel, serial ◆ **son histoire, c'est un vrai ~** his story is like something out of a soap opera

roman-fleuve (pl **romans-fleuves**) /ʀɔmɑ̃flœv/ NM roman fleuve, saga

romanichel, -elle ⁎⁎ /ʀɔmaniʃɛl/ NM,F *(souvent injurieux)* gipsy, gyppo ⁎⁎ *(injurieux)*

romanisant, e /ʀɔmanizɑ̃, ɑ̃t/ ADJ *(Rel)* romanist; *(Ling)* specializing in Romance languages NM,F *(= linguiste)* romanist, specialist in Romance languages

romaniser /ʀɔmanize/ ► conjug 1 ◄ VT *(gén)* to romanize

romaniste /ʀɔmanist/ NMF *(Jur, Rel)* romanist; *(Ling)* romanist, specialist in Romance languages

romanité /ʀɔmanite/ NF *(= civilisation)* Roman civilization; *(= pays)* Roman Empire

romano ⁎⁎ /ʀɔmano/ NMF *(injurieux)* gyppo ⁎⁎ *(injurieux)*

roman-photo (pl **romans-photos**) /ʀɔmɑ̃fɔto/ NM photo romance, photo love story ◆ **une héroïne de ~** *(hum)* a Mills and Boon *(Brit)* ou Harlequin Romance *(US)* type heroine

romantique /ʀɔmɑ̃tik/ ADJ romantic NMF romantic

romantisme /ʀɔmɑ̃tism/ NM romanticism ◆ **le ~** *(Art, Littérat)* the Romantic Movement

romarin /ʀɔmaʀɛ̃/ NM rosemary

rombière ⁎ /ʀɔ̃bjɛʀ/ NF *(péj)* ◆ **(vieille) ~** old biddy ⁎ *(péj)*

Rome /ʀɔm/ N Rome ◆ **la ~ antique** Ancient Rome; → **tout**

Roméo /ʀɔmeo/ NM Romeo

rompre /ʀɔ̃pʀ/ ► conjug 41 ◄ VT [1] *(= faire cesser) [+ fiançailles, pourparlers, relations diplomatiques]* to break off; *[+ enchantement, monotonie, silence]* to break; *[+ solitude, isolement]* to put an end to; *[+ liens, contrat, traité]* to break ◆ **~ l'équilibre** to upset the balance ◆ **l'équilibre écologique est rompu** the ecological balance has been upset ou disturbed ◆ **~ le Carême** to break Lent ou the Lenten fast ◆ **~ le charme** *(littér)* to break the spell

[2] *(= casser) [+ branche]* to break; *[+ pain]* to break (up) ◆ **~ ses chaînes** *(lit, fig)* to break one's chains ◆ **~ ses amarres** *[bateau]* to break (loose from) its moorings ◆ **il a rompu les amarres avec son pays natal** he has cut himself off completely from ou broken all links with his native country ◆ **~ le front de l'ennemi** to break through the enemy front ◆ **la mer a rompu les digues** the sea has broken (through) ou burst the dykes; → **applaudir, glace¹**

[3] *(littér = habituer)* **~ qn à un exercice** to break sb in to an exercise

[4] *(locutions)* **~ une lance** ou **des lances pour qn** to take up the cudgels for sb ◆ **~ une lance** ou **des lances contre qn** to cross swords with sb ◆ **~ les rangs** *(Mil)* to fall out, to dismiss ◆ **rompez (les rangs) !** *(Mil)* dismiss!, fall out!

VI [1] *(= se séparer de)* **~ avec qn** to break with sb, to break off one's relations with sb ◆ **il n'a pas le courage de ~** he hasn't got the courage to break it off ◆ **~ avec de vieilles habitudes/la tradition** to break with old habits/tradition

[2] *[corde]* to break, to snap; *[digue]* to burst, to break

[3] *(Boxe, Escrime)* to break ◆ **~ en visière avec** *(fig)* to quarrel openly with ◆ **~ le combat** *(Mil)* to withdraw from the engagement

VPR **se rompre** *(= se briser) [branche, câble, chaîne, corde]* to break, to snap; *[digue]* to burst, to break; *[vaisseau sanguin]* to burst, to rupture ◆ **il va se ~ les os** ou **le cou** he's going to break his neck

rompu, e /ʀɔ̃py/ (ptp de **rompre**) ADJ [1] *(= fourbu)* **~ (de fatigue)** exhausted, worn-out, tired out ◆ **~ de travail** exhausted by over work [2] *(= expérimenté)* **être ~ aux affaires** to have wide business experience ◆ **~ aux privations/à la discipline** accustomed ou inured to hardship/to discipline ◆ **il est ~ à toutes les ficelles du métier/au maniement des armes** he is experienced in ou familiar with all the tricks of the trade/the handling of firearms ◆ **~ aux techniques militaires/à l'art de la diplomatie** well-versed in military techniques/in the art of diplomacy; → **bâton**

romsteck /ʀɔmstɛk/ NM *(= viande)* rumpsteak *(NonC)*; *(= tranche)* piece of rumpsteak

ronce /ʀɔ̃s/ NF [1] *(= branche)* bramble branch ◆ **~s** *(= buissons)* brambles, thorns ◆ **~ (des haies)** blackberry bush, bramble (bush) ◆ **il a déchiré son pantalon dans les ~s** he tore his trousers on ou in the brambles [2] *(Menuiserie)* burr ◆ **~ de noyer** burr walnut ◆ **~ d'acajou** figured mahogany

ronceraie /ʀɔ̃sʀɛ/ NF bramble patch, briar patch

Roncevaux /ʀɔ̃s(ə)vo/ N Roncesvalles

ronchon, -onne /ʀɔ̃ʃɔ̃, ɔn/ ADJ grumpy, grouchy ⁎ NM,F grumbler

ronchonnement /ʀɔ̃ʃɔnmɑ̃/ NM grumbling

ronchonner /ʀɔ̃ʃɔne/ ► conjug 1 ◄ VI to grumble *(après at)*

ronchonneur, -euse /ʀɔ̃ʃɔnœʀ, øz/ ADJ grumpy, grouchy ⁎ NM,F grumbler

rond, e¹ /ʀɔ̃, ʀɔ̃d/ ADJ [1] *[forme, objet]* round; *[pièce, lit]* circular, round; → **dos, œil, table**

[2] *(= rebondi) [joues, visage]* round; *[épaules]* fleshy; *[fesses]* plump, well-rounded; *[hanches]* rounded, curvaceous; *[mollet]* well-rounded; *[poitrine]* full, (well-)rounded; *[ventre]* tubby, round; *[bébé]* chubby ◆ **une petite femme toute ~e** a plump little woman ◆ **un petit homme ~** a chubby ou tubby little man

[3] *(= net)* round ◆ **chiffre ~** round number ou figure ◆ **ça fait 10 € tout ~** it comes to exactly €10 ◆ **ça fait un compte ~** it makes a round number ou figure ◆ **être ~ en affaires** to be straightforward ou straight ⁎ ou on the level ⁎ in business matters

[4] *(⁎ = soûl)* drunk, tight ⁎ ◆ **être ~ comme une bille** ou **comme une queue de pelle** to be blind ou rolling drunk ⁎

NM [1] *(= cercle)* circle, ring ◆ **faire des ~s de fumée** to blow smoke rings ◆ **faire des ~s dans l'eau** to make rings ou circular ripples in the water; *(en bateau)* to potter about *(Brit)* ou putter around *(US)* in a boat ◆ **le verre a fait des ~s sur la table** the glass has made rings on the table

◆ **en rond** in a circle ou ring ◆ **s'asseoir/danser en ~** to sit/dance in a circle ou ring ◆ **tourner en ~** *(à pied)* to walk round and round; *(en voiture)* to drive round in circles; *[enquête, discussion]* to get nowhere, to go round in circles ◆ **nous tournons en ~ depuis trois mois** we've been marking time ou going round in circles for three months

[2] *(= objet) [de cuisinière]* ring ◆ **~ de serviette** napkin ou serviette *(Brit)* ring ◆ **il en est resté comme deux ~s de flan** ⁎ you could have knocked him down with a feather; → **baver**

[3] *(⁎ = sou)* **~s** lolly ⁎ *(NonC)*, cash ⁎ *(NonC)* ◆ **avoir des ~s** to be loaded ⁎, to be rolling in it ⁎, to have plenty of cash ⁎ ◆ **il n'a pas le** ou **un ~** he hasn't got a penny (to his name) ou a (red) cent *(US)*, he doesn't have two pennies ou cents *(US)* to rub together ◆ **il n'a plus un** ou **le ~** he's (flat ou stony *(Brit)* ou stone *(US)*) broke ⁎ ◆ **je l'ai eu pour pas un ~** it didn't cost me a penny ou a cent *(US)* ◆ **ça doit valoir des ~s !** that must be worth a mint! ⁎ ou a pretty penny! ⁎ ou a penny or two! *(Brit)*

ADV ◆ **avaler qch tout ~** to swallow sth whole ◆ **tourner ~** to run smoothly ◆ **ça ne tourne pas ~ chez elle** ⁎, **elle ne tourne pas ~** ⁎ she's got a screw loose ⁎ ◆ **qu'est-ce qui ne tourne pas ~ ?** ⁎ what's the matter?, what's wrong?, what's up? ⁎

COMP **rond de jambes** *(Danse)* rond de jambe ◆ **faire des ~s de jambes** *(péj)* to bow and scrape *(péj)*

rond de sorcière *(= champignons)* fairy ring

rond-de-cuir (pl **ronds-de-cuir**) /ʀɔ̃d(ə)kɥiʀ/ NM *(péj)* penpusher *(Brit)*, pencil pusher *(US)*

ronde² /ʀɔ̃d/ NF [1] *(= tour de surveillance) [de gardien, vigile, soldats]* rounds, patrol; *[de policier]* beat, patrol, rounds; *(= patrouille)* patrol ◆ **faire sa ~** to be on one's rounds ou on the beat ou on patrol ◆ **sa ~ dura plus longtemps** he took longer doing his rounds ◆ **il a fait trois ~s aujourd'hui** he has been on his rounds three times today, he has covered his beat three times today ◆ **~ de nuit** *(= action)* night rounds, night watch ou patrol; *(= soldats)* night patrol ◆ **ils virent passer la ~** they saw the soldiers pass on their rounds; → **chemin**

[2] *(= danse)* round (dance), dance in a ring; *(= danseurs)* circle, ring ◆ **~ villageoise/enfantine** villagers'/children's dance *(in a ring)* ◆ **faites la ~** dance round in a circle ou ring ◆ **la ~ des hélicoptères dans le ciel** the helicopters coming and going in the sky ◆ **la ~ des voitures sur la place** the constant flow of traffic round the square ◆ **la ~ des saisons** *(littér)* the cycle of the seasons ◆ **sa vie n'est qu'une ~ continue de fêtes et de sorties** his life is a non-stop social whirl

[3] *(Mus = note)* semibreve *(Brit)*, whole note *(US)*

[4] *(Écriture)* roundhand

LOC ADV **à la ronde à 10 km à la ~** within a 10-km radius ◆ **à des kilomètres à la ~** for miles around ◆ **passer qch à la ~** to pass sth round

rondeau (pl **rondeaux**) /ʀɔ̃do/ NM (*Littérat*) rondeau; (*Mus*) rondo

ronde-bosse (pl **rondes-bosses**) /ʀɔ̃dbɔs/ NF (*= technique*) sculpture in the round ◆ **personnages en** ~ figures in the round

rondelet, -ette /ʀɔ̃dlɛ, ɛt/ ADJ [*adulte*] plumpish; [*enfant*] chubby; [*salaire, somme*] tidy (*épith*)

rondelle /ʀɔ̃dɛl/ NF [1] [*de carotte, saucisson*] slice, round (*Brit*) ◆ ~ **de citron/d'orange** slice of lemon/of orange ◆ **couper en** ~**s** to slice, to cut into slices *ou* rounds (*Brit*); [*+ personne*] to dismember [2] (*= disque de carton, plastique*) disc; [*de boulon*] washer; [*de bâton de ski*] basket

rondement /ʀɔ̃dmɑ̃/ ADV [1] (*= efficacement*) efficiently ◆ **il a mené** ~ **cette enquête/réunion** he conducted the investigation/meeting quickly and efficiently ◆ **c'est quelqu'un qui mène** ~ **les affaires** he's someone who gets things done ◆ **le film est** ~ **mené** the film is well-paced [2] (*= franchement*) frankly, outspokenly

rondeur /ʀɔ̃dœʀ/ NF [1] [*de bras, joues, personne*] plumpness, chubbiness; [*de visage*] roundness, chubbiness; [*de poitrine*] fullness; [*de mollet*] roundness ◆ **les** ~**s d'une femme** (*hum*) a woman's curves [2] (*= forme sphérique*) roundness [3] (*= bonhomie*) friendly straightforwardness, easy-going directness ◆ **avec** ~ with (an) easy-going directness

rondin /ʀɔ̃dɛ̃/ NM log; → **cabane**

rondo /ʀɔ̃do/ NM rondo

rondouillard, e* /ʀɔ̃dujaʀ, aʀd/ ADJ tubby, podgy (*Brit*), pudgy (*US*) ◆ **c'est un petit** ~ he's a tubby *ou* podgy little guy* *ou* chap (*Brit*)

rond-point (pl **ronds-points**) /ʀɔ̃pwɛ̃/ NM (*= carrefour*) roundabout (*Brit*), traffic circle (*US*); (*dans un nom de lieu = place*) ≃ circus (*Brit*)

Ronéo ® /ʀɔneo/ NF mimeo, Roneo ®

ronéoter /ʀɔneɔte/, **ronéotyper** /ʀɔneɔtipe/ ▸ conjug 1 ◂ VT to duplicate, to roneo ®, to mimeo

ronflant, e /ʀɔ̃flɑ̃, ɑ̃t/ ADJ [*moteur*] purring; (*péj*) [*discours*] high-flown, grand(-sounding); [*titre*] grand(-sounding); [*style*] bombastic

ronflement /ʀɔ̃fləmɑ̃/ NM [1] [*de dormeur*] snore, snoring (*NonC*) ◆ **j'entendais des** ~**s** I could hear (somebody) snoring [2] [*de poêle, feu*] (*sourd*) hum(ming) (*NonC*); (*plus fort*) roar, roaring (*NonC*); [*de moteur*] purr(ing) (*NonC*), throbbing (*NonC*); (*= vrombissement*) roar, roaring (*NonC*)

ronfler /ʀɔ̃fle/ ▸ conjug 1 ◂ VI [1] [*dormeur*] to snore [2] [*poêle, feu*] to hum; (*plus fort*) to roar; [*moteur*] (*sourdement*) to purr, to throb ◆ **faire** ~ **son moteur** to rev up one's engine ◆ **il actionna le démarreur et le moteur ronfla** he pressed the starter and the engine throbbed *ou* roared into action [3] (** = dormir*) to snore away, to be out for the count* (*Brit*)

ronfleur, -euse /ʀɔ̃flœʀ, øz/ NM,F snorer NM [*de téléphone*] buzzer

ronger /ʀɔ̃ʒe/ ▸ conjug 3 ◂ VT [1] [*souris*] to gnaw *ou* eat away at, to gnaw *ou* eat into; [*acide, pourriture, rouille, vers*] to eat into; [*mer*] to wear away, to eat into; [*eczéma*] to pit ◆ ~ **un os** [*chien*] to gnaw (at) a bone; [*personne*] to pick a bone, to gnaw (at) a bone ◆ **les chenilles rongent les feuilles** caterpillars are eating away *ou* are nibbling (at) the leaves ◆ **rongé par les vers** worm-eaten ◆ **rongé par la rouille** eaten into by rust, pitted with rust ◆ **fresques rongées par l'humidité** mildewed frescoes ◆ ~ **son frein** (*lit, fig*) to champ at the bit; → **os**
[2] [*maladie*] to sap (the strength of); [*chagrin, pensée*] to gnaw *ou* eat away at ◆ **le mal qui le ronge** the evil which is gnawing *ou* eating away at him ◆ **rongé par la maladie** sapped by illness ◆ **rongé par la drogue** ravaged by drugs ◆ **le chômage, ce cancer qui ronge la société** the cancer of unemployment that is eating away at society ◆ **une démocratie rongée de l'intérieur** a democracy that is being undermined from within
VPR **se ronger** [1] ◆ **se** ~ **les ongles** to bite one's nails; → **sang**
[2] (*fig*) **elle se ronge** (*de chagrin*) she's eating her heart out, she's tormented with grief; (*d'inquiétude*) she's worrying herself sick, she's making herself sick with worry

rongeur, -euse /ʀɔ̃ʒœʀ, øz/ ADJ, NM rodent

ronron /ʀɔ̃ʀɔ̃/ NM [*de chat*] purr(ing) (*NonC*); * [*de moteur*] purr(ing) (*NonC*), hum(ming) (*NonC*); (*péj*) [*de discours*] drone (*NonC*), droning (on) (*NonC*) ◆ **le** ~ **de la vie quotidienne*** the humdrum routine of daily life

ronronnement /ʀɔ̃ʀɔnmɑ̃/ NM [*de chat*] purr(ing) (*NonC*); [*de moteur*] purr(ing) (*NonC*), hum(ming) (*NonC*) ◆ **un** ~ **conformiste** stultifying conformism

ronronner /ʀɔ̃ʀɔne/ ▸ conjug 1 ◂ VI [*chat*] to purr; [*moteur*] to purr, to hum ◆ **il ronronnait de satisfaction** (*fig*) he was purring with satisfaction ◆ **ça ronronne dans ce service** things are ticking over nicely in the department

roque /ʀɔk/ NM (*Échecs*) castling ◆ **grand/petit** ~ castling queen's/king's side

roquefort /ʀɔkfɔʀ/ NM Roquefort (cheese)

roquer /ʀɔke/ ▸ conjug 1 ◂ VI (*Échecs*) to castle; (*Croquet*) to roquet

roquet /ʀɔkɛ/ NM (*péj*) (*= chien*) (nasty little) dog; (*= personne*) ill-tempered little runt*

roquette[1] /ʀɔkɛt/ NF (*Mil*) rocket ◆ ~ **antichar** anti-tank rocket

roquette[2] /ʀɔkɛt/ NF (*Bot, Culin*) rocket, arugula (*US*)

rorqual (pl **rorquals**) /ʀɔʀk(w)al/ NM rorqual, finback

rosace /ʀozas/ NF [*de cathédrale*] rose window, rosace; [*de plafond*] (ceiling) rose; (*Broderie*) Teneriffe motif; (*= figure géométrique*) rosette

rosacé, e /ʀozase/ ADJ (*Bot*) rosaceous NF **rosacée** [1] (*Méd*) rosacea [2] (*= plante*) rosaceous plant ◆ ~**es** Rosaceae, rosaceous plants

rosaire /ʀozɛʀ/ NM rosary ◆ **réciter son** ~ to say *ou* recite the rosary, to tell one's beads †

rosat /ʀoza/ ADJ INV [*miel, pommade*] rose (*épith*) ◆ **huile** ~ attar of roses

rosâtre /ʀozɑtʀ/ ADJ pinkish

rosbif /ʀɔsbif/ NM [1] (*= rôti*) roast beef (*NonC*); (*à rôtir*) roasting beef (*NonC*) ◆ **un** ~ a joint of (roast) beef, a joint of (roasting) beef [2] († *, *péj = Anglais*) Brit*

rose /ʀoz/ NF (*= fleur*) rose; (*= vitrail*) rose window; (*= diamant*) rose diamond ◆ **il n'y a pas de** ~**s sans épines** (*Prov*) there's no rose without a thorn (*Prov*) → **bois, découvrir, envoyer**
NM (*= couleur*) pink; → **vieux**
ADJ [1] (*gén*) pink; [*joues, teint*] pink; (*= plein de santé*) rosy ◆ ~ **bonbon** candy pink ◆ ~ **saumoné** *ou* **saumon** salmon pink ◆ ~ **indien** hot pink ◆ **la ville** ~ Toulouse (*so called because of the pink stone of which it is largely built*); → **crevette, flamant**
[2] (*hum = socialiste*) left-wing, pink (*hum*)
[3] (*= érotique*) **messageries** ~**s** sex chatlines (*on Minitel*) ◆ **téléphone** ~ sex chatlines, phone sex; → **Minitel**
[4] (*locutions*) **voir la vie** *ou* **tout en** ~ to see life through rose-tinted *ou* rose-coloured glasses ◆ **ce roman montre la vie en** ~ this novel gives a rosy picture *ou* view of life ◆ **tout n'est pas** ~**, ce n'est pas tout** ~ it's not all roses *ou* all rosy, it's no bed of roses ◆ **sa vie n'était pas bien** ~ his life was no bed of roses
COMP **rose d'Inde** African marigold
rose de Jéricho resurrection plant, rose of Jericho
rose de Noël Christmas rose
rose pompon button rose
rose des sables gypsum flower
rose trémière hollyhock
rose des vents compass rose

rosé, e[1] /ʀoze/ ADJ [*couleur*] pinkish; [*vin*] rosé; [*viande cuite*] pink NM (*= vin*) rosé (wine) ◆ ~ **(des prés)** (*= champignon*) field mushroom

roseau (pl **roseaux**) /ʀozo/ NM reed

rose-croix /ʀozkʀwa/ NF INV ◆ **la Rose-Croix** (*= confrérie*) the Rosicrucians NM INV (*= membre*) Rosicrucian; (*= grade de franc-maçonnerie*) Rose-croix

rosée[2] /ʀoze/ NF dew ◆ **couvert** *ou* **humide de** ~ [*herbe, prés*] dewy, covered in *ou* with dew; [*sac de couchage, objet laissé dehors*] wet with dew ◆ **point de** ~ (*Phys*) dew point; → **goutte**

roséole /ʀozeɔl/ NF (*Méd = éruption*) roseola

roseraie /ʀozʀɛ/ NF (*= jardin*) rose garden; (*= plantation*) rose-nursery

rose(-)thé (pl **roses(-)thé**) /ʀozte/ NF tea rose ADJ tea-rose (*épith*)

rosette /ʀozɛt/ NF (*= nœud*) bow; (*= insigne*) rosette; (*Archit, Art, Bot*) rosette ◆ **avoir la** ~ to be an officer of the Légion d'honneur ◆ ~ **de Lyon** (*Culin*) *type of slicing sausage*; → LÉGION D'HONNEUR

rosicrucien, -ienne /ʀozikʀysjɛ̃, jɛn/ ADJ, NM,F Rosicrucian

rosier /ʀozje/ NM rosebush, rose tree ◆ ~ **nain/grimpant** dwarf/climbing rose

rosière /ʀozjɛʀ/ NF (*Hist*) *village maiden publicly rewarded for her chastity*; (*hum*) innocent maiden

rosiériste /ʀozjeʀist/ NMF rose grower

rosir /ʀoziʀ/ ▸ conjug 2 ◂ VI [*ciel, neige*] to grow *ou* turn pink; [*personne, visage*] (*de confusion*) to go pink, to blush slightly; (*de santé*) to get one's colour back VT [*+ ciel, neige*] to give a pink(ish) hue *ou* tinge to

rosse /ʀɔs/ NF [1] (†, *péj = cheval*) nag [2] (** = méchant*) (*homme*) swine*, beast*; (*femme*) cow*, beast* ◆ **ah les** ~**s !** the (rotten) swine!*, the (rotten) beasts!* ADJ (*péj*) [*critique, chansonnier, caricature*] nasty, vicious; [*coup, action*] lousy*, rotten*; [*homme*] horrid; [*femme*] bitchy*, horrid ◆ **tu as vraiment été** ~ **(avec lui)** you were really horrid (to him)

rossée †* /ʀɔse/ NF thrashing, (good) hiding, hammering*

rosser /ʀɔse/ ▸ conjug 1 ◂ VT [1] (*= frapper*) to thrash, to give a (good) hiding to ◆ **se faire** ~ to get a (good) hiding *ou* a thrashing *ou* a hammering* [2] (** = vaincre*) to thrash, to lick*, to hammer*

rosserie /ʀɔsʀi/ NF [1] (*= méchanceté*) (*gén*) horridness; [*de critique, chansonnier, caricature*] nastiness, viciousness; [*d'action*] lousiness*, rottenness* [2] (*= propos*) nasty *ou* bitchy* remark; (*= acte*) lousy* *ou* rotten* trick

rossignol /ʀɔsiɲɔl/ NM [1] (*= oiseau*) nightingale [2] (** = invendu*) unsaleable article, piece of junk* [3] (*= clé*) picklock

rossinante † /ʀɔsinɑ̃t/ NF (*hum*) (old) jade, old nag

rostre /ʀɔstʀ/ NM (*= éperon*) rostrum NMPL **rostres** (*= tribune*) rostrum

rot /ʀo/ NM (*= renvoi*) belch, burp*; [*de bébé*] burp ◆ **faire** *ou* **lâcher un** ~ to belch, to burp*, to let out a belch *ou* burp* ◆ **le bébé a fait son** ~ the baby has done his (little) burp ◆ **faire faire son** ~ **à un bébé** to burp *ou* wind (*Brit*) a baby

rôt †† /ʀo/ NM roast

rotatif, -ive /ʀɔtatif, iv/ ADJ rotary ◆ **mouvement** ~ rotating movement, rotary movement *ou* motion NF **rotative** rotary press

rotation /ʀɔtasjɔ̃/ NF [1] *(= mouvement)* rotation ◆ **mouvement de** ~ rotating movement, rotary movement *ou* motion ◆ **corps en** ~ rotating body, body in rotation ◆ **vitesse de** ~ speed of rotation ◆ **la Terre effectue une** ~ **sur elle-même en 24 heures** the Earth completes a full rotation in 24 hours

[2] *(= alternance) [de matériel, stock]* turnover; *[d'avions, bateaux]* frequency (of service) ◆ **la** ~ **du personnel** *(à des tâches successives)* the rotation of staff; *(= départs et embauches)* the turnover of staff ◆ **taux de** ~ **(du personnel)** (staff) turnover rate ◆ ~ **des cultures** rotation of crops, crop rotation ◆ **15 ~s quotidiennes Paris-Lyon** *(= vols)* 15 daily return flights between Paris and Lyon ◆ **les médecins sont de garde par** ~ **tous les mois** the doctors are on duty each month on a rota basis *ou* system

rotatoire /ʀɔtatwaʀ/ ADJ rotatory, rotary

roter * /ʀɔte/ ► conjug 1 ◄ VI to burp *, to belch

rôti /ʀoti/ NM *(Culin) (cru)* joint, roasting meat *(NonC)*; *(cuit)* joint, roast, roast meat *(NonC)* ◆ **un** ~ **de bœuf/porc** a joint of beef/pork ◆ **du** ~ **de bœuf/porc** *(cru)* roasting beef/pork; *(cuit)* roast beef/pork

rôtie /ʀoti/ NF *(Can ou archaïque)* piece *ou* slice of toast

rotin /ʀɔtɛ̃/ NM [1] *(= fibre)* rattan (cane) ◆ **chaise de** *ou* **en** ~ rattan chair [2] *(† * = sou)* penny, cent ◆ **il n'a pas un** ~ he hasn't got a penny *ou* cent to his name

rôtir /ʀotiʀ/ ► conjug 2 ◄ VT *(Culin)* ◆ **(faire)** ~ to roast ◆ **poulet/agneau rôti** roast chicken/lamb ◆ **il attend toujours que ça lui tombe tout rôti dans le bec** * he expects everything to be handed to him on a plate *ou* a silver platter *(US)* VI *(Culin)* to roast; * *[baigneur, estivants]* to roast ◆ **mettre un canard à** ~ to put a duck in the oven to roast VPR **se rôtir** ◆ **se** ~ **au soleil** * to bask in the sun

rôtisserie /ʀotisʀi/ NF *(dans nom de restaurant)* steakhouse, grill; *(= boutique) shop selling roast meat*

rôtisseur, -euse /ʀotisœʀ, øz/ NM,F *(= traiteur) seller of roast meat; (= restaurateur)* steakhouse proprietor

rôtissoire /ʀotiswaʀ/ NF rotisserie, (roasting) spit

rotogravure /ʀɔtɔgʀavyʀ/ NF rotogravure

rotonde /ʀɔtɔ̃d/ NF *(Archit)* rotunda; *(Rail)* engine shed *(Brit)*, roundhouse *(US)*; *(dans un bus) row of seats at rear of bus* ◆ **édifice en** ~ circular building

rotondité /ʀɔtɔ̃dite/ NF [1] *(= sphéricité)* roundness, rotundity *(frm)* [2] *(hum = embonpoint)* plumpness, rotundity *(hum)*

rotor /ʀɔtɔʀ/ NM rotor

rottweil(l)er /ʀɔtvajlœʀ/ NM Rottweiler

rotule /ʀɔtyl/ NF [1] *(Anat)* kneecap, patella *(SPÉC)* ◆ **être sur les ~s** * to be dead beat * *ou* all in * [2] *(Tech)* ball-and-socket joint

rotulien, -ienne /ʀɔtyljɛ̃, jɛn/ ADJ patellar; → **réflexe**

roture /ʀɔtyʀ/ NF *(= absence de noblesse)* common rank; *[de fief]* roture ◆ **la** ~ *(= roturiers)* the commoners, the common people

roturier, -ière /ʀɔtyʀje, jɛʀ/ ADJ *(Hist)* common, of common birth; *(fig = vulgaire)* common, plebeian NM,F commoner

rouage /ʀwaʒ/ NM *[d'engrenage]* cog(wheel), gearwheel; *[de montre]* part ◆ **les ~s d'une montre** the works *ou* parts of a watch ◆ **il n'est qu'un** ~ **dans cette organisation** he's merely a cog in this organization ◆ **les ~s de l'État** the machinery of state ◆ **les ~s administratifs** the administrative machinery ◆ **organisation aux ~s compliqués** organization with complex structures

roubignoles ** /ʀubiɲɔl/ NFPL *(= testicules)* balls **, nuts **

roublard, e * /ʀublaʀ, aʀd/ ADJ crafty, wily, artful NM,F crafty *ou* artful devil * ◆ **ce** ~ **de Paul** crafty old Paul *

roublardise * /ʀublaʀdiz/ NF *(= caractère)* craftiness, wiliness, artfulness; *(= acte, tour)* crafty *ou* artful trick

rouble /ʀubl/ NM rouble

roucoulade /ʀukulad/ NF, **roucoulement** /ʀukulmɑ̃/ NM *(gén pl) [d'oiseau]* cooing *(NonC)*; * *[d'amoureux]* (billing and) cooing *(NonC)*; *(péj) [de chanteur]* crooning *(NonC)*

roucouler /ʀukule/ ► conjug 1 ◄ VI *[oiseau]* to coo; * *[amoureux]* to bill and coo; *(péj) [chanteur]* to croon VT *(péj) [+ chanson]* to croon; * *[+ mots d'amour]* to coo ◆ **il lui roucoulait des mots tendres** he was whispering sweet nothings to her

roudoudou /ʀududu/ NM *children's sweet in the form of a small shell filled with hard confectionery*

roue /ʀu/ NF *[de véhicule, loterie, moulin]* wheel; *[d'engrenage]* cog(wheel), (gear)wheel ◆ **véhicule à deux/quatre ~s** two-/four-wheeled vehicle ◆ ~ **avant/arrière** front/back wheel ◆ **(supplice de) la** ~ *(Hist)* (torture of) the wheel ◆ **la** ~ **de la Fortune** the wheel of Fortune ◆ **la** ~ **tourne !** how things change! ◆ **faire la** ~ *[paon]* to spread *ou* fan its tail; *[personne] (= se pavaner)* to strut about, to swagger (about); *(Gym)* to do a cartwheel ◆ **la grande** ~ *(fête foraine)* the big wheel *(Brit)*, the Ferris Wheel *(US)* ◆ **il s'est jeté sous les ~s de la voiture** he threw himself under the car ◆ **son bureau est à quelques tours de** ~ **de la tour Eiffel** his office is a short car-ride away from the Eiffel Tower ◆ **le coureur est revenu dans la** ~ **de son adversaire** the cyclist closed in right behind his opponent ◆ **être** ~ **à** *ou* **dans** ~ to be neck and neck; → **bâton, chapeau, cinquième, pousser**

COMP **roue à aubes** *[de bateau]* paddle wheel
roue dentée cogwheel
roue à friction friction wheel
roue à godets bucket wheel
roue de gouvernail (steering) wheel, helm
roue hydraulique waterwheel
roue libre freewheel ◆ **descendre une côte en** ~ **libre** to freewheel *ou* coast down a hill ◆ **pédaler en** ~ **libre** to freewheel, to coast (along) ◆ **il s'est mis en** ~ **libre** * *(= il ne se surmène pas)* he's taking it easy
roue motrice driving wheel ◆ **véhicule à 4 ~s motrices** 4-wheel drive vehicle
roue de secours spare wheel *(Brit) ou* tire *(US)*
roue de transmission driving wheel

roué, e /ʀwe/ (ptp de **rouer**) ADJ *(= rusé)* cunning, wily, sly NM,F cunning *ou* sly individual ◆ **c'est une petite ~e** she's a cunning *ou* wily *ou* sly little minx NM *(Hist = débauché)* rake, roué NF **rouée** *(Hist = débauchée)* hussy

rouelle /ʀwɛl/ NF ◆ ~ slice

rouer /ʀwe/ ► conjug 1 ◄ VT [1] ◆ ~ **qn de coups** to give sb a beating *ou* thrashing, to beat sb black and blue [2] *(Hist) [+ condamné]* to put on the wheel

rouerie /ʀuʀi/ NF *(littér) (= caractère)* cunning, wiliness, slyness; *(= action)* cunning *ou* wily *ou* sly trick

rouet /ʀwɛ/ NM *(à filer)* spinning wheel

rouflaquettes * /ʀuflakɛt/ NFPL *(= favoris)* sideburns, sideboards *(Brit)*

rouge /ʀuʒ/ ADJ [1] *(gén, Pol)* red; → **armée**[2]

[2] *(= incandescent) [métal]* red-hot; *[tison]* glowing red *(attrib)*, red-hot

[3] *[visage, yeux]* red ◆ ~ **de colère/confusion/honte** red *ou* flushed with anger/embarrassment/shame ◆ ~ **d'émotion** flushed with emotion ◆ **devenir** ~ **comme une cerise** to blush, to go quite pink, to go red in the face ◆ **il est** ~ **comme un coq** *ou* **un coquelicot** *ou* **un homard** *ou* **une pivoine** *ou* **une écrevisse** *ou* **une tomate** he's as red as a beetroot *ou* a lobster ◆ **il était** ~ **d'avoir couru** he was red in the face *ou* his face was flushed from running

[4] *(= roux) [cheveux, pelage]* red

ADV ◆ **voir** ~ to see red ◆ **voter** ~ *(Pol)* to vote Communist; → **fâcher**

NM [1] *(= couleur)* red ◆ **le feu est au** ~ the lights are red ◆ **passer au** ~ *[feu]* to change to red; *(= redémarrer trop tôt)* to jump the lights; *(= ne pas s'arrêter)* to go through a red light, to run a red light *(US)* ◆ **tout miser sur le** ~ *(Jeux)* to put all one's chips on the red ◆ **être dans le** ~ * *(Fin)* to be in the red * ◆ **sortir du** ~ * to get out of the red *; → **bordeaux**

[2] *(= signe d'émotion)* **ça lui a fait monter le** ~ **aux joues** it made him blush ◆ **le** ~ **lui monta aux joues** his cheeks flushed, he went red (in the face) ◆ **le** ~ **(de la confusion/de la honte) lui monta au front** his face went red *ou* flushed *ou* he blushed (with embarrassment/with shame)

[3] *(= vin)* red wine ◆ **boire un coup de** ~ * to have a glass of red wine; → **gros**

[4] *(= fard) (à joues)* rouge †, blusher; *(à lèvres)* lipstick; → **bâton, tube**

[5] *(= incandescence)* **fer porté** *ou* **chauffé au** ~ red-hot iron

NMF *(péj = communiste)* Red * *(péj)*, Commie * *(péj)*

COMP **rouge brique** ADJ INV brick red
rouge cerise ADJ INV cherry-red
rouge à joues rouge †, blusher ◆ **se mettre du** ~ **à joues** to rouge one's cheeks †, to put blusher on
rouge à lèvres lipstick
rouge sang ADJ INV blood red

rougeâtre /ʀuʒɑtʀ/ ADJ reddish

rougeaud, e /ʀuʒo, od/ ADJ red-faced ◆ **ce gros** ~ **la dégoûtait** she found this fat red-faced man repellent

rouge-gorge (pl **rouges-gorges**) /ʀuʒgɔʀʒ/ NM robin

rougeoiement /ʀuʒwamɑ̃/ NM *[de couchant, incendie]* red *ou* reddish glow; *[de ciel]* reddening

rougeole /ʀuʒɔl/ NF ◆ **la** ~ (the) measles *(sg)* ◆ **il a eu une très forte** ~ he had a very bad bout of measles

rougeoyant, e /ʀuʒwajɑ̃, ɑ̃t/ ADJ *[ciel]* reddening; *[cendres]* glowing red *(attrib)*, glowing ◆ **des reflets ~s** a glimmering red glow

rougeoyer /ʀuʒwaje/ ► conjug 8 ◄ VI *[couchant, feu, incendie]* to glow red; *[ciel]* to turn red, to take on a reddish hue

rouge-queue (pl **rouges-queues**) /ʀuʒkø/ NM redstart

rouget /ʀuʒɛ/ NM mullet ◆ ~ **barbet** *ou* **de vase** red *ou* striped mullet, goatfish *(US)* ◆ ~ **grondin** gurnard ◆ ~ **de roche** surmullet

rougeur /ʀuʒœʀ/ NF [1] *(= teinte)* redness [2] *[de personne] (due à la course, un échauffement, une émotion)* red face, flushing *(NonC)*; *(due à la honte, gêne)* red face, blushing *(NonC)*, blushes; *[de visage, joues]* redness, flushing *(NonC)* ◆ **sa** ~ **a trahi son émotion/sa gêne** her red face *ou* her blushes betrayed her emotion/her embarrassment ◆ **la** ~ **de ses joues** his red face *ou* cheeks, his blushing ◆ **avoir des ~s de jeune fille** to blush like a young girl ◆ **elle était sujette à des ~s subites** she was inclined to blush suddenly [3] *(Méd = tache)* red blotch *ou* patch

rough /RœF/ **NM** *(Golf)* rough

rougir /RuʒiR/ ▸ conjug 2 ◂ **VI** [1] *(de honte, gêne)* to blush, to go red, to redden *(de* with*)*; *(de plaisir, d'émotion)* to flush, to go red, to redden *(de* with*)*; ◆ **il rougit de colère** he *ou* his face flushed *ou* reddened with anger ◆ **à ces mots, elle rougit** she blushed *ou* went red *ou* reddened at the words ◆ ~ **jusqu'au blanc des yeux** *ou* **jusqu'aux yeux,** ~ **jusqu'aux oreilles,** ~ **jusqu'à la racine des cheveux** to go bright red, to blush to the roots of one's hair ◆ **faire** ~ **qn** *(lit, fig)* to make sb blush ◆ **dire qch sans** ~ to say sth without blushing *ou* unblushingly
[2] *(fig = avoir honte)* ~ **de** to be ashamed of ◆ **je n'ai pas à** ~ **de cela** that is nothing for me to be ashamed of ◆ **il ne rougit de rien** he's quite shameless, he has no shame ◆ **j'en rougis pour lui** I blush for him, I'm ashamed for him
[3] *(après un coup de soleil)* to go red
[4] *[ciel, feuille, neige]* to go *ou* turn red, to redden; *[métal]* to become *ou* get red-hot; *[crustacés cuits, fraises, tomates]* to redden, to turn red
VT *[+ ciel]* to turn red, to give a red glow to, to redden; *[+ arbres, feuilles]* to turn red, to redden; *[+ métal]* to heat to red heat, to make red-hot ◆ ~ **son eau** to put a dash *ou* drop of red wine in one's water ◆ **boire de l'eau rougie** to drink water with a few drops of red wine in it ◆ ~ **la terre de son sang** *(lit)* to stain the ground with one's blood; *(fig)* to shed one's blood ◆ **les yeux rougis** *(par les larmes)* with red eyes, red-eyed; *(par l'alcool, la drogue)* with bloodshot eyes

rougissant, e /Ruʒisɑ̃, ɑ̃t/ **ADJ** *[personne, visage]* blushing; *[ciel, feuille]* reddening

rougissement /Ruʒismɑ̃/ **NM** *(de honte)* blush, blushing *(NonC)*; *(d'émotion)* flush, flushing *(NonC)*

rouille /Ruj/ **NF** [1] *(Bot, Chim)* rust [2] *(Culin)* spicy Provençal sauce eaten with fish **ADJ INV** rust(-coloured), rusty

rouillé, e /Ruje/ (ptp de **rouiller**) **ADJ** [1] *[métal]* rusty, rusted; *(littér) [écorce, roche]* rust-coloured [2] *[personne] (intellectuellement)* rusty; *(physiquement)* out of practice; *[mémoire]* rusty; *[muscles]* stiff [3] *[blé]* rusty

rouiller /Ruje/ ▸ conjug 1 ◂ **VI** to rust, to go *ou* get rusty ◆ **laisser** ~ **qch** to let sth go *ou* get rusty **VT** *[+ esprit, métal]* to make rusty **VPR se rouiller** *[métal]* to go *ou* get rusty, to rust; *[esprit, mémoire]* to become *ou* go rusty; *[corps, muscles]* to grow *ou* get stiff; *[sportif]* to get rusty, to get out of practice ◆ **mon italien se rouille** my Italian is getting a bit rusty

rouir /RwiR/ ▸ conjug 2 ◂ **VT, VI** ◆ **(faire)** ~ to ret

rouissage /Rwisaʒ/ **NM** retting

roulade /Rulad/ **NF** [1] *(Mus)* roulade, run; *[d'oiseau]* trill [2] *(Culin)* roulade ◆ ~ **de veau** veal roulade [3] *(Sport)* roll ◆ ~ **avant/arrière** forward/backward roll ◆ **faire des** ~**s** to do rolls

roulage /Rulaʒ/ **NM** († *Min = camionnage, transport)* haulage; *(Agr)* rolling

roulant, e /Rulɑ̃, ɑ̃t/ **ADJ** [1] *(= mobile) [meuble]* on wheels; → **cuisine, fauteuil, table** [2] *(Rail)* **matériel** ~ rolling stock ◆ **personnel** ~ train crews [3] *[trottoir, surface transporteuse]* moving; → **escalier, feu¹, pont** [4] *[route, piste]* fast **NMPL roulants** *(arg Rail)* **les** ~**s** train crews **NF roulante** *(arg Mil)* field kitchen

roulé, e /Rule/ (ptp de **rouler**) **ADJ** [1] *[bord de chapeau]* curved; *[bord de foulard, morceau de boucherie]* rolled; *[journal, tapis]* rolled up; → **col** [2] * **elle est bien** ~**e** she's got all the right curves in all the right places, she's well put together [3] *(Ling)* rolled ◆ **r** ~ trilled *ou* rolled r **NM** *(= gâteau)* Swiss roll; *(= viande)* rolled meat *(NonC)* ◆ ~ **de veau** rolled veal *(NonC)* ◆ ~ **au fromage** *puff-pastry roll with cheese filling*

rouleau (pl **rouleaux**) /Rulo/ **NM** [1] *(= bande enroulée)* roll ◆ ~ **de papier/tissu/pellicule** roll of paper/material/film ◆ **un** ~ **de cheveux blonds** *(= boucle)* a ringlet of blond hair; *(= cheveux roulés sur la nuque)* a coil of blond hair *(rolled at the nape of the neck)*; → **bout**
[2] *(= cylindre) [de pièces, tabac]* roll ◆ ~ **de réglisse** liquorice roll
[3] *(= outil, ustensile)* roller; *[de machine à écrire]* platen, roller ◆ **passer une pelouse au** ~ to roll a lawn ◆ **avoir des** ~**x dans les cheveux** to have one's hair in curlers *ou* rollers, to have curlers *ou* rollers in one's hair ◆ **peindre au** ~ to paint with a roller
[4] *(= vague)* roller
[5] *(Sport = saut)* roll
COMP rouleau compresseur *(lit)* steamroller, roadroller; *(fig)* steamroller, bulldozer
rouleau dorsal *(Sport)* Fosbury flop
rouleau encreur ⇒ **rouleau imprimeur**
rouleau essuie-mains roller towel
rouleau imprimeur ink roller
rouleau de papier hygiénique toilet roll, roll of toilet paper *ou* tissue
rouleau de papyrus papyrus scroll
rouleau de parchemin scroll *ou* roll of parchment
rouleau à pâtisserie, rouleau à pâte *(Helv)* rolling pin
rouleau de printemps *(Culin)* spring roll
rouleau ventral *(Sport)* western roll

roulé-boulé (pl **roulés-boulés**) /Rulebule/ **NM** roll ◆ **faire un** ~ to roll over, to curl up ◆ **tomber en** ~ to roll (down)

roulement /Rulmɑ̃/ **NM** [1] *(= rotation) [d'équipe, ouvriers]* rotation ◆ **travailler par** ~ to work on a rota basis *ou* system, to work in rotation ◆ **pour le ménage, on fait un** ~ we take it in turns to do the housework [2] *(= circulation) [de train, voiture]* movement ◆ **route usée/pneu usé par le** ~ road/tyre worn through use; → **bande¹** [3] *(= bruit) [de camion, train]* rumble, rumbling *(NonC)*; *[de charrette]* rattle, rattling *(NonC)* ◆ **entendre le** ~ **du tonnerre** to hear thunder ◆ **il y eut un** ~ **de tonnerre** there was a rumble *ou* peal *ou* roll of thunder ◆ ~ **de tambour** drum roll [4] *[de capitaux]* circulation; → **fonds** [5] *(= mouvement) [d'œil]* rolling; *[de hanche]* wiggling **COMP roulement (à billes)** ball bearings ◆ **monté sur** ~ **à billes** mounted on ball bearings

rouler /Rule/ ▸ conjug 1 ◂ **VT** [1] *(= pousser) [+ meuble]* to wheel (along), to roll (along); *[+ chariot, brouette]* to wheel (along), to trundle along; *[+ boule, tonneau]* to roll (along)
[2] *(= enrouler) [+ tapis, tissu, carte]* to roll up; *[+ cigarette]* to roll; *[+ ficelle, fil de fer]* to wind up, to roll up; *[+ viande, parapluie, mèche de cheveux]* to roll (up) ◆ ~ **qn dans une couverture** to wrap *ou* roll sb (up) in a blanket ◆ ~ **un pansement autour d'un bras** to wrap *ou* wind a bandage round an arm ◆ ~ **ses manches jusqu'au coude** to roll up one's sleeves to one's elbows
[3] *(= tourner et retourner)* to roll ◆ ~ **des boulettes dans de la farine** to roll meatballs in flour ◆ **la mer roulait les galets sur la plage** the sea rolled the pebbles along the beach ◆ **il roulait mille projets dans sa tête** *(fig)* he was turning thousands of plans over (and over) in his mind ◆ **le fleuve roulait des flots boueux** *(littér)* the river flowed muddily along
[4] *(= passer au rouleau) [+ court de tennis, pelouse]* to roll; *(Culin) [+ pâte]* to roll out
[5] *(* = duper)* to con‡; *(sur le prix, le poids)* to diddle* *(Brit)*, to do* *(sur* over*)*; ◆ **je l'ai bien roulé** I really conned him‡, I really took him for a ride* ◆ **elle m'a roulé de 5 €** she's diddled* *(Brit) ou* done* me out of €5 ◆ **se faire** ~ to be conned‡ *ou* had* *ou* done* *ou* diddled* *(Brit)* ◆ **il s'est fait** ~ **dans la farine*** he was had*
[6] *(= balancer, faire bouger)* ~ **les** *ou* **des épaules (en marchant)** to sway one's shoulders (as one walks along) ◆ ~ **les** *ou* **des mécaniques‡** *(en marchant)* to (walk with a) swagger; *(= montrer sa force, ses muscles)* to show off one's muscles; *(intellectuellement)* to show off ◆ ~ **les** *ou* **des hanches** to wiggle one's hips ◆ ~ **les yeux** to roll one's eyes ◆ **il a roulé sa bosse*** he's been around*; → **patin, pelle**
[7] *(Ling)* ~ **les "r"** to roll one's r's
VI [1] *[voiture, train]* to go, to run ◆ **le train roulait/roulait à vive allure à travers la campagne** the train was going along/was racing (along) through the countryside ◆ **cette voiture a très peu/beaucoup roulé** this car has a very low/high mileage ◆ **cette voiture a 10 ans et elle roule encore** this car is 10 years old but it's still going *ou* running ◆ **la voiture roule bien depuis la révision** the car is running *ou* going well since its service ◆ **les voitures ne roulent pas bien sur le sable** cars don't run well on sand ◆ **le véhicule roulait à gauche** the vehicle was driving (along) on the left ◆ ~ **au pas** *(par prudence)* to go at a walking pace, to go dead slow *(Brit)*; *(dans un embouteillage)* to crawl along ◆ **le train roulait à 150 à l'heure au moment de l'accident** the train was doing 150 *ou* going at 150 kilometres an hour at the time of the accident ◆ **sa voiture roule au super/au gazole** his car runs on four-star/diesel
[2] *[passager, conducteur]* to drive ◆ ~ **à 80 km à l'heure** to do 80 km per hour, to drive at 80 km per hour ◆ **on a bien roulé*** we made good time ◆ **ça roule/ça ne roule pas bien** the traffic is/is not flowing well ◆ **nous roulions sur la N7 quand soudain ...** we were driving along the N7 when suddenly ... ◆ **dans son métier, il roule beaucoup** he does a lot of driving in his job ◆ **il roule en 2CV** he drives a 2CV ◆ **il roule en Rolls** he drives (around in) a Rolls ◆ ~ **carrosse** (†, *hum)* to live in high style ◆ ~ **pour qn*** *(= être à la solde de qn)* to be for sb ◆ **il roule tout seul*** *(fig)* he's a loner
[3] *[boule, bille, dé]* to roll; *[presse]* to roll, to run ◆ **allez, roulez !** let's roll it!*, off we go! ◆ **une larme roula sur sa joue** a tear rolled down his cheek ◆ **une secousse le fit** ~ **à bas de sa couchette** there was a jolt and he rolled off his couchette ◆ **il a roulé en bas de l'escalier** he rolled right down the stairs ◆ **un coup de poing l'envoya** ~ **dans la poussière** a punch sent him rolling in the dust ◆ **il a roulé sous la table** *(ivre)* he was legless* *ou* under the table ◆ **faire** ~ *[+ boule]* to roll; *[+ cerceau]* to roll along; → **pierre**
[4] *[bateau]* to roll ◆ **ça roulait*** the boat was rolling quite a bit
[5] *(* = bourlinguer)* to knock about* ◆ **il a pas mal roulé** he has knocked about* quite a bit, he's been around*
[6] *[argent, capitaux]* to turn over, to circulate
[7] *(= faire un bruit sourd) [tambour]* to roll; *[tonnerre]* to roll, to rumble
[8] *[conversation]* ~ **sur** to turn on, to be centred on
[9] *(* = aller bien)* **ça roule ?** how's things?*, how's life? ◆ **c'est une affaire qui roule** it's going well
[10] ◆ ~ **sur l'or** to be rolling in money*, to have pots of money* ◆ **ils ne roulent pas sur l'or depuis qu'ils sont à la retraite** they're not exactly living in the lap of luxury *ou* they're not terribly well-off now they've retired
VPR se rouler [1] *(allongé sur le sol ou sur qch)* to roll (about) ◆ **se** ~ **par terre/dans l'herbe** to roll (about) on the ground/in the grass ◆ **se** ~ **par terre de rire** *(fig)* to roll on the ground

with laughter, to fall about* (laughing) *(Brit)* ◆ **c'est à se ~ (par terre)*** it's a scream*; → **pouce**
[2] *(= s'enrouler)* **se ~ dans une couverture** to roll *ou* wrap o.s. up in a blanket ◆ **se ~ en boule** to roll o.s. (up) into a ball

roulette /ʀulɛt/ NF [1] *[de meuble]* caster, castor ◆ **fauteuil à ~s** armchair on casters *ou* castors ◆ **ça a marché** *ou* **été comme sur des ~s*** *[plan]* it went like clockwork *ou* very smoothly; *[interview, soirée]* it went off very smoothly *ou* like a dream; → **patin** [2] *(= outil) [de pâtissier]* pastry (cutting) wheel; *[de relieur]* fillet; *[de couturière]* tracing wheel; *[de vitrier]* steel(-wheel) glass cutter ◆ **~ de dentiste** dentist's drill [3] *(= jeu)* roulette; *(= instrument)* roulette wheel ◆ **jouer à la ~** to play roulette ◆ **~ russe** Russian roulette

rouleur /ʀulœʀ/ NM *(Cyclisme)* flat racer ◆ **c'est un bon ~** he's good on the flat ◆ **quel ~ de mécaniques !*** he likes to strut his stuff!*

roulier /ʀulje/ NM *(Hist)* cart driver, wagoner; *(Naut)* roll-on roll-off ferry, ro-ro ferry

roulis /ʀuli/ NM *(Naut)* roll(ing) *(NonC)* ◆ **il y a beaucoup de ~** the ship is rolling a lot ◆ **coup de ~** roll

roulotte /ʀulɔt/ NF caravan *(Brit)*, trailer *(US)* ◆ **visitez l'Irlande en ~** tour around Ireland in a horse-drawn *ou* gypsy caravan

roulotté, e /ʀulɔte/ ADJ *(Couture)* rolled ◆ **foulard ~ (à la) main** hand-rolled scarf NM rolled hem

roulure* /ʀulyʀ/ NF *(péj)* slut *(péj)*, trollop † *(péj)*

roumain, e /ʀumɛ̃, ɛn/ ADJ Romanian, Rumanian NM *(= langue)* Romanian, Rumanian NM,F **Roumain(e)** Romanian, Rumanian

Roumanie /ʀumani/ NF Romania, Rumania

round /ʀaund/ NM *(Boxe)* round

roupettes* /ʀupɛt/ NFPL *(= testicules)* balls*, nuts*

roupie /ʀupi/ NF [1] *(= monnaie)* rupee [2] († *) **c'est de la ~ de sansonnet** it's a load of (old) rubbish *ou* junk*, it's absolute trash* ◆ **ce n'est pas de la ~ de sansonnet** it's none of your cheap rubbish *ou* junk*

roupiller* /ʀupije/ ▸ conjug 1 ◂ VI *(= dormir)* to sleep; *(= faire un petit somme)* to have a snooze* *ou* a nap *ou* a kip* *(Brit)* ◆ **j'ai besoin de ~** I must get some shut-eye* ◆ **je n'arrive pas à ~** I can't get any shut-eye* ◆ **je vais ~** I'll be turning in*, I'm off to hit the hay* ◆ **viens ~ chez nous** come and bed down *ou* kip down *(Brit)* at our place* ◆ **secouez-vous, vous roupillez !** pull yourself together – you're half asleep! *ou* you're dozing!

roupillon* /ʀupijɔ̃/ NM snooze*, nap, kip* *(Brit)* ◆ **piquer** *ou* **faire un ~** to have a snooze* *ou* a nap *ou* a kip* *(Brit)*

rouquin, e* /ʀukɛ̃, in/ ADJ *[personne]* red-haired; *[cheveux]* red, carroty* *(péj)* NM,F red-head

rouscailler* /ʀuskɑje/ ▸ conjug 1 ◂ VI to moan*, to bellyache*

rouspétance* /ʀuspetɑ̃s/ NF *(= ronchonnement)* moaning* *(NonC)*, grousing* *(NonC)*, grouching* *(NonC)*; *(= protestation)* moaning* *(NonC)*, grumbling *(NonC)* ◆ **pas de ~ !** no grumbling!

rouspéter* /ʀuspete/ ▸ conjug 6 ◂ VI *(= ronchonner)* to moan*, to grouse*, to grouch*; *(= protester)* to moan*, to grumble *(après, contre* at); ◆ **se faire ~ par qn** to get an earful from sb*

rouspéteur, -euse* /ʀuspetœʀ, øz/ ADJ grumpy NM,F moaner*

roussâtre /ʀusɑtʀ/ ADJ reddish, russet

rousse[1] †* /ʀus/ NF *(arg Crime)* ◆ **la ~** *(= police)* the fuzz *(arg Crime)*, the cops*

rousserolle /ʀus(ə)ʀɔl/ NF ◆ **~ verderolle** marsh warbler ◆ **~ effarvatte** reed warbler

roussette /ʀusɛt/ NF [1] *(= poisson)* dogfish; *(Culin)* rock salmon [2] *(= chauve-souris)* flying fox [3] *(= grenouille)* common frog

rousseur /ʀusœʀ/ NF [1] *[de cheveux, barbe]* redness; *(orangé)* gingery colour; *[de pelage, robe, feuille]* russet colour; → **tache** [2] *(sur le papier)* **~s** brownish marks *ou* stains; *(sur la peau)* liver spots

roussi /ʀusi/ NM ◆ **odeur de ~** smell of (something) burning *ou* scorching *ou* singeing ◆ **ça sent le ~ !** *(lit)* there's a smell of (something) burning *ou* scorching *ou* singeing; *(fig)* I can smell trouble

roussir /ʀusiʀ/ ▸ conjug 2 ◂ VT *[fer à repasser]* to scorch, to singe; *[flamme]* to singe ◆ **~ l'herbe** *[gelée]* to turn the grass brown *ou* yellow; *[chaleur]* to scorch the grass VI [1] *[feuilles, forêt]* to turn *ou* go brown *ou* russet [2] *(Culin)* **faire ~** to brown

rouste* /ʀust/ NF *(= coups)* hiding, thrashing; *(= défaite)* hammering* ◆ **prendre une ~** *(lit)* to get a hiding, to get thrashed; *(fig)* to get a hammering*, to get thrashed* ◆ **flanquer** *ou* **filer une ~ à qn** *(lit)* to give sb a hiding *ou* thrashing; *(fig)* to give sb a hammering*, to thrash sb

roustons* /ʀustɔ̃/ NMPL *(= testicules)* balls*, nuts*

routage /ʀutaʒ/ NM [1] *(= distribution)* sorting and mailing ◆ **entreprise de ~** mailing firm *ou* service [2] *(Naut)* plotting a course *(de* for)

routard, e /ʀutaʀ, aʀd/ NM,F backpacker

route /ʀut/ NF [1] *(= voie de communication)* road ◆ **~ nationale** main road, ≃ A road *(Brit)* trunk road *(Brit)* ◆ **~ départementale** minor road, ≃ B road *(Brit)* ◆ **~ secondaire** minor *ou* secondary road ◆ **~ de montagne** mountain road ◆ **prenez la ~ de Lyon** take the road to Lyon *ou* the Lyon road ◆ **"route barrée"** "road closed"; → **barrer, grand-route**
[2] *(= moyen de transport)* **la ~** road ◆ **la ~ est plus économique que le rail** road is cheaper than rail ◆ **la ~ est meurtrière** the road is a killer ◆ **arriver par la ~** to arrive by road ◆ **faire de la ~** to do a lot of mileage; → **accident, blessé, code**
[3] *(= chemin à suivre)* way; *(Naut = direction, cap)* course ◆ **je ne l'emmène pas, ce n'est pas (sur) ma ~** I'm not taking him – it's not on my way ◆ **indiquer/montrer la ~ à qn** to point out/show the way to sb ◆ **perdre/retrouver sa ~** to lose/find one's way
[4] *(= ligne de communication)* route ◆ **~ aérienne/maritime** air/sea route ◆ **la ~ du sel/de l'opium/des épices** the salt/opium/spice route *ou* trail ◆ **la ~ de la soie** the Silk Road *ou* Route ◆ **la ~ des vins** the wine trail ◆ **la ~ des Indes** the route to India
[5] *(= trajet)* trip, journey *(Brit)* ◆ **bonne ~ !** have a good trip! *ou* journey! *(Brit)* ◆ **carnet** *ou* **journal de ~** travel diary *ou* journal ◆ **la ~ sera longue** *(gén)* it'll be a long journey; *(en voiture)* it'll be a long drive *ou* ride ◆ **il y a trois heures de ~** *(en voiture)* it's a three-hour drive *ou* ride *ou* journey *(Brit)*; *(à bicyclette)* it's a three-hour (cycle-)ride ◆ **ils ont fait toute la ~ à pied/à bicyclette** they walked/cycled the whole way, they did the whole journey *(Brit)* on foot/by bicycle; → **compagnon**
[6] *(= ligne de conduite, voie)* path, road, way ◆ **la ~ à suivre** the path *ou* road to follow ◆ **la ~ du bonheur** the road *ou* path *ou* way to happiness ◆ **nos ~s se sont croisées** our paths crossed ◆ **votre ~ est toute tracée** your path is set out for you ◆ **être sur la bonne ~** *(dans la vie)* to be on the right road *ou* path; *(dans un problème)* to be on the right track ◆ **remettre qn sur la bonne ~** to put sb back on the right road *ou* path *ou* track ◆ **c'est lui qui a ouvert la ~** he's the one who opened (up) the road *ou* way; → **faux²**
[7] *(locutions)* **faire ~** *(Naut)* to be under way ◆ **faire ~ avec qn** to travel with sb ◆ **prendre la ~** to start out, to set off *ou* out, to get under way ◆ **reprendre la ~, se remettre en ~** to start out again, to set off *ou* out again, to resume one's journey *(Brit)* ◆ **en cours de ~** *(lit, fig)* along the way ◆ **tenir la ~** *[voiture]* to hold the road; * *[matériel]* to be well-made *ou* serviceable; * *[argument, raisonnement]* to hold water; *[solution, politique]* to be viable ◆ **tracer la ~*** to push ahead

◆ **en route** on the way *ou* journey *(Brit)*, en route ◆ **en ~ !** let's go!, let's be off! ◆ **en ~, mauvaise troupe !** *(hum)* off we go! ◆ **en ~ pour** bound for, heading for, on its way to ◆ **avoir plusieurs projets en ~** to have several projects on the go ◆ **mettre en ~** *[+ machine, moteur]* to start (up); *[+ processus, projet, réforme]* to set in motion, to get under way ◆ **mettre le repas en ~** to get the meal started ◆ **ils ont attendu longtemps avant de mettre un bébé en ~** they waited a long time before starting a family ◆ **remettre en ~ le moteur/le processus de paix** to restart the engine/the peace process, to get the engine/peace process going again ◆ **mise en ~** *[de machine]* starting up; *[de processus, projet]* setting in motion ◆ **la mise en ~ des réformes sera difficile** it will be difficult to implement the reforms *ou* to get the reforms under way ◆ **depuis la remise en ~ des machines** since the machines have been restarted *ou* started up again ◆ **ils envisagent la remise en ~ de l'usine** they're considering bringing the factory back into operation ◆ **se mettre en ~** to start out, to set off *ou* out, to get under way ◆ **se remettre en ~** to start out again, to set off *ou* out again, to resume one's journey *(Brit)*

router /ʀute/ ▸ conjug 1 ◂ VT [1] *[+ journaux]* to pack and mail; *(Ordin) [+ informations, fichiers, messages]* to route [2] *(Naut)* to plot a course for

routeur, -euse /ʀutœʀ, øz/ NM,F *(Naut)* route planner NM *(Ordin)* router

routier, -ière /ʀutje, jɛʀ/ ADJ *[carte, circulation, réseau, transport]* road *(épith)*; → **gare¹** NM *(= camionneur)* long-distance truck *ou* lorry *(Brit)* driver; *(= restaurant)* ≃ roadside café, transport café *(Brit)*, truckstop *(US)*; *(= cycliste)* road racer *ou* rider; *(Naut = carte)* route chart; († = *scout)* rover ◆ **un vieux ~ de la politique** a wily old politician, an old hand at politics NF **routière** *(= voiture)* touring car, tourer *(Brit)*; *(= moto)* road bike ◆ **grande routière** high-performance touring car *ou* tourer *(Brit)*

routine /ʀutin/ NF [1] *(= habitude)* routine ◆ **la ~ quotidienne** the daily routine *ou* grind ◆ **s'enfoncer/tomber dans la ~** to settle/fall into a routine ◆ **par ~** as a matter of routine ◆ **contrôle/opération de ~** routine check/operation [2] *(Ordin)* routine

routinier, -ière /ʀutinje, jɛʀ/ ADJ *[procédé, travail, vie]* humdrum, routine; *[personne]* routine-minded, addicted to routine *(attrib)* ◆ **il a l'esprit ~** he's completely tied to (his) routine ◆ **c'est un travail un peu ~** the work is a bit routine *ou* humdrum ◆ **c'est un ~** he's a creature of habit

rouvre /ʀuvʀ/ ADJ, NM ◆ **(chêne) ~** durmast *ou* sessile oak

rouvrir /ʀuvʀiʀ/ ▸ conjug 18 ◂ VT *(gén)* to reopen; *[+ porte, yeux]* to reopen, to open again ◆ **le stade rouvrira ses portes dimanche** the stadium will reopen its doors on Sunday VI *[magasin, musée, théâtre]* to reopen, to open again VPR **se rouvrir** *[porte]* to reopen, to open again; *[plaie, blessure]* to open up again, to reopen

roux, rousse² /ʀu, ʀus/ ADJ *[cheveux] (foncé)* red, auburn; *(clair)* ginger; *[barbe] (foncé)* red; *(clair)* ginger; *[pelage, robe, feuilles]* russet, red-dish-brown; → **blond, lune** NM,F redhead NM 1 *(= couleur) [de cheveux]* red, auburn; *[de barbe]* red; *(= orangé)* ginger; *[de pelage, robe feuille]* russet, reddish-brown ◆ **cheveux d'un ~ flamboyant** flaming red hair 2 *(Culin)* roux

royal, e (mpl **-aux**) /ʀwajal, o/ ADJ 1 *(gén)* royal ◆ **la famille ~e** the Royal Family ou royal family; → **gelée², voie** 2 *[magnificence, maintien]* kingly, regal; *[cadeau, demeure, repas]* fit for a king *(attrib)*; *[salaire]* princely; → **aigle, tigre** 3 *(intensif) [indifférence, mépris]* majestic, lofty, regal ◆ **il m'a fichu une paix ~e*** he left me in perfect peace NF 1 * **la Royale** *(Naut)* the French Navy 2 *(Culin)* **lièvre à la ~e** hare royale

royalement /ʀwajalmɑ̃/ ADV 1 *(= magnifiquement, généreusement)* **vous serez traité ~** you will be treated like a king ◆ **il l'a reçue ~** he gave her a wonderful reception ◆ **il a accueilli ~ la presse internationale** he gave a lavish welcome to the international press ◆ **ils sont payés ~ 1 000 € brut par mois** they are paid the princely sum of €1,000 a month 2 *(= complètement)* * **il se moque ~ de sa situation*** he couldn't care less* ou he doesn't care two hoots* about his position

⚠ Le mot **royally** existe, mais les traductions données ici sont plus courantes.

royalisme /ʀwajalism/ NM royalism

royaliste /ʀwajalist/ ADJ royalist ◆ **être plus ~ que le roi** *(fig)* to carry things to extremes, to be more Catholic than the Pope ◆ **puisqu'on ne te demande rien, pourquoi être plus ~ que le roi ?** since you haven't be been asked to do anything, why put yourself out? ou why be so zealous? NMF royalist

royalties /ʀwajalti/ NFPL royalties ◆ **toucher des ~** to receive royalties

royaume /ʀwajom/ NM *(lit)* kingdom, realm; *(fig = domaine)* domain ◆ **le vieux grenier était son ~** the old attic was his domain ◆ **le ~ céleste** ou **des cieux** ou **de Dieu** *(Rel)* the kingdom of heaven ou God ◆ **le ~ des morts** the kingdom of the dead ◆ **le ~ des ombres** the land of the shades, the valley of the shadows ◆ **au ~ des aveugles les borgnes sont rois** *(Prov)* in the kingdom of the blind the one-eyed man is king *(Prov)*

Royaume-Uni /ʀwajomyni/ NM ◆ **le ~ (de Grande-Bretagne et d'Irlande du Nord)** the United Kingdom (of Great Britain and Northern Ireland)

royauté /ʀwajote/ NF *(= régime)* monarchy; *(= fonction, dignité)* kingship

RP NM (abrév de **Révérend Père**) → **révérend** NF (abrév de **recette principale**) → **recette** NFPL (abrév de **relations publiques**) PR

RPR /ɛʀpeɛʀ/ NM (abrév de **Rassemblement pour la République**) *centre-right political party*

RSVP /ɛʀɛsvepe/ (abrév de **répondez s'il vous plaît**) RSVP

Rte abrév de **route**

RTT /ɛʀtete/ NF (abrév de **réduction du temps de travail**) reduction of working hours

RU /ʀy/ NM (abrév de **restaurant universitaire**) → **restaurant**

ru † /ʀy/ NM brook, rivulet *(littér)*

ruade /ʀɥad/ NF kick ◆ **tué par une ~** killed by a kick from a horse ◆ **le cheval lui a cassé la jambe d'une ~** the horse kicked ou lashed out at him and broke his leg ◆ **décocher** ou **lancer une ~** to lash ou kick out

ruban /ʀybɑ̃/ NM *(gén, fig)* ribbon; *[de machine à écrire]* ribbon; *[de couture, ourlet]* binding, tape ◆ **le ~ (rouge)** *(de la Légion d'honneur) the ribbon of the Légion d'Honneur* ◆ **le ~ argenté du Rhône** *(fig)* the silver ribbon of the Rhone ◆ **le double ~ de l'autoroute** the two ou twin lines of the motorway; → LÉGION D'HONNEUR

COMP **ruban d'acier** steel band ou strip
ruban adhésif adhesive tape, sticky tape
le ruban bleu *(Naut)* the Blue Riband ou Ribbon *(of the Atlantic)* ◆ **détenir le ~ bleu (de qch)** *(fig)* to be the world leader (in sth)
ruban de chapeau hat band
ruban d'eau *(= plante)* bur reed
ruban encreur typewriter ribbon
ruban isolant insulating tape
ruban perforé *(Ordin)* paper tape

rubato /ʀybato/ ADV, NM rubato

rubéole /ʀybeɔl/ NF German measles *(sg)*, rubella *(SPÉC)*

Rubicon /ʀybikɔ̃/ NM Rubicon; → **franchir**

rubicond, e /ʀybikɔ̃, ɔ̃d/ ADJ rubicund, ruddy

rubidium /ʀybidjɔm/ NM rubidium

rubis /ʀybi/ NM *(= pierre)* ruby; *(= couleur)* ruby (colour); *[d'horloge, montre]* jewel; → **payer** ADJ INV ruby(-coloured)

rubrique /ʀybʀik/ NF 1 *(= article, chronique)* column ◆ **~ sportive/littéraire/des spectacles** sports/literary/entertainments column ◆ **il tient la ~ scientifique du journal** he writes the newspaper's science column 2 *(= catégorie, titre)* heading, rubric ◆ **sous cette même ~** under the same heading ou rubric 3 *(Rel)* rubric

ruche /ʀyʃ/ NF 1 *(en bois)* (bee) hive; *(en paille)* (bee) hive, skep *(SPÉC)*; *(= essaim)* hive ◆ **nos bureaux sont une véritable ~** ou **une ~ bourdonnante** *(fig)* our offices are a real hive of activity 2 *(Couture)* ruche

ruché /ʀyʃe/ NM *(Couture)* ruching *(NonC)*, ruche

rucher /ʀyʃe/ NM apiary

rude /ʀyd/ ADJ 1 *(= rêche) [surface, barbe, peau]* rough; *(= rauque) [voix, sons]* harsh
2 *[métier, vie, combat]* hard, tough; *[montée]* stiff, tough, hard; *[adversaire]* tough; *[climat, hiver]* harsh, hard, severe ◆ **c'est un ~ coup pour elle/notre équipe** it's a hard ou harsh ou severe blow for her/our team ◆ **être mis à ~ épreuve** *[personne]* to be severely tested, to be put through the mill; *[tissu, métal]* to receive ou have rough treatment ◆ **mes nerfs ont été mis à ~ épreuve** it was a great strain on my nerves ◆ **il a été à ~ école dans sa jeunesse** he learned life the hard way when he was young, he went to the school of hard knocks ◆ **en faire voir de ~s à qn** to give sb a hard ou tough time ◆ **en voir de ~s** to have a hard ou tough time (of it)
3 *(= fruste) [manières]* unpolished, crude, unrefined; *[traits]* rugged; *[montagnards]* rugged, tough
4 *(= sévère, bourru) [personne, caractère]* harsh, hard, severe; *[manières]* rough ◆ **tu as été trop ~ avec elle** you were too hard on her
5 *(* : intensif)* **un ~ gaillard** a hearty fellow ◆ **avoir un ~ appétit/estomac** to have a hearty appetite/an iron stomach ◆ **il a une ~ veine** he's a lucky beggar* *(Brit)* ou son-of-a-gun* *(US)* ◆ **ça m'a fait une ~ peur** it gave me a dreadful ou real fright ◆ **recevoir un ~ coup de poing** to get a real ou proper* *(Brit)* thump

⚠ **rude** se traduit rarement par **rude**, qui a le sens de 'impoli'.

rudement /ʀydmɑ̃/ ADV 1 *[heurter, frapper, tomber]* hard; *[répondre]* harshly; *[traiter]* roughly, harshly 2 *(* = très) [bon, content]* terribly*, awfully*, jolly* *(Brit)*; *[cher, fatigant, mauvais]* dreadfully, terribly, awfully ◆ **il a fallu ~ travailler** we had to work really hard ◆ **elle danse ~ bien** she dances awfully ou jolly *(Brit)* well, she's quite a dancer ◆ **ça me change ~ de faire ça** it's a real change ou quite a change for me to do that ◆ **elle avait ~ changé** she had really changed, she hadn't half changed* *(Brit)* ◆ **il est ~ plus généreux que toi** he's a great deal ou darned sight* more generous than you ◆ **j'ai eu ~ peur** it gave me a dreadful ou real fright

rudesse /ʀydɛs/ NF 1 *[de surface, barbe, peau]* roughness; *[de voix, sons]* harshness 2 *[de métier, vie, combat, montée]* hardness, toughness; *[d'adversaire]* toughness; *[de climat, hiver]* harshness, hardness, severity 3 *[de manières]* crudeness; *[de traits]* ruggedness; *[de montagnards]* ruggedness, toughness 4 *[de personne, caractère]* harshness, hardness, severity; *[de manières]* roughness ◆ **traiter qn avec ~** to treat sb roughly ou harshly

rudiment /ʀydimɑ̃/ NM rudiment NMPL **rudiments** *[de discipline]* rudiments; *[de système, théorie]* principles ◆ **~s d'algèbre** principles ou rudiments of algebra ◆ **avoir quelques ~s de chimie** to have some basic knowledge of chemistry, to know some basic chemistry ◆ **avoir quelques ~s d'anglais** to have a smattering of English ou some basic knowledge of English ◆ **nous n'en sommes qu'aux ~s, on en est encore aux ~s** we're still at a rudimentary stage

rudimentaire /ʀydimɑ̃tɛʀ/ ADJ *(gén)* rudimentary; *[connaissances]* rudimentary, elementary ◆ **les installations de l'hôpital sont très ~s** the hospital facilities are rather rough-and-ready ou a bit basic ◆ **elle parle un anglais ~** she speaks basic English

rudoiement /ʀydwamɑ̃/ NM *(littér)* rough ou harsh treatment

rudologie /ʀydɔlɔʒi/ NF garbology

rudoyer /ʀydwaje/ ► conjug 8 ◄ VT to treat harshly

rue¹ /ʀy/ NF 1 *(= voie, habitants)* street ◆ **~ à sens unique** one-way street ◆ **scènes de la ~** street scenes ◆ **élevé dans la ~** brought up in the street(s) ◆ **être à la ~** to be on the streets ◆ **jeter qn à la ~** to put sb out ou throw sb out (into the street) ◆ **descendre dans la ~** *(= manifester)* to take to the streets; → **coin, combat, piéton², plein** *etc* 2 *(péj = populace)* **la ~** the mob

RUE

Many Paris street names are used, especially in the press, to refer to the famous institutions that have their homes there. The Ministry of Education is on the **rue de Grenelle**; the **rue de Solférino** refers to Socialist Party headquarters; the **rue d'Ulm** is where the « École normale supérieure » is situated, and the **rue de Valois** is the home of the Ministry of Culture. → QUAI

rue² /ʀy/ NF *(= plante)* rue

ruée /ʀɥe/ NF rush; *(péj)* stampede ◆ **à l'ouverture, ce fut la ~ vers l'entrée du magasin** when the shop opened, there was a (great) rush ou a stampede for the entrance, as soon as the doors opened there was a stampede ou a mad scramble to get into the shop ◆ **la ~ des touristes ne prend fin qu'à l'automne** the influx of tourists doesn't tail off until the autumn, the tourist invasion doesn't end until the autumn ◆ **dès que quelqu'un prend sa retraite ou démissionne, c'est la ~** *(fig)* the moment someone retires or resigns there's a scramble for their job ◆ **dans la ~, il fut renversé** he was knocked over in the rush ou stampede ◆ **cet événement a entraîné une ~ sur le dollar** this event caused a run on the dollar ◆ **la ~ vers l'or** the gold rush

ruelle /ʀɥɛl/ NF *(= rue)* alley(way), lane; †† *[de chambre]* ruelle †, space (between bed and wall); *(Hist, Littérat)* ruelle *(room used in 17th century to hold literary salons)*

ruer /ʀɥe/ ▸ conjug 1 ◂ VI *[cheval]* to kick (out) ◆ **~ dans les brancards** *(fig)* to rebel, to kick over the traces VPR **se ruer** ◆ **se ~ sur** *[+ article en vente, nourriture, personne]* to pounce on; *[+ emplois vacants]* to fling o.s. at, to pounce at ◆ **se ~ vers** *[+ porte, sortie]* to dash *ou* rush for *ou* towards ◆ **se ~ dans/hors de** *[+ maison, pièce]* to dash *ou* rush *ou* tear into/out of ◆ **se ~ dans l'escalier** *(monter)* to tear *ou* dash up the stairs; *(descendre)* to tear down the stairs, to hurl o.s. down the stairs ◆ **se ~ à l'assaut** to hurl *ou* fling o.s. into the attack

ruf(f)ian /ʀyfjɑ̃/ NM *(littér, = aventurier)* rogue

ruflette ® /ʀyflɛt/ NF curtain *ou* heading tape

rugby /ʀygbi/ NM rugby (football) ◆ **~ à quinze** Rugby Union ◆ **~ à treize** Rugby League ◆ **jouer au ~, faire du ~** to play rugby

rugbyman /ʀygbiman/ (pl **rugbymen** /ʀygbimɛn/) NM rugby player

> ⚠ **rugbyman** ne se traduit pas par **rugby man**, qui n'existe pas en anglais.

rugir /ʀyʒiʀ/ ▸ conjug 2 ◂ VI *[fauve, mer, moteur]* to roar; *[vent, tempête]* to howl, to roar ◆ **~ de douleur** to howl *ou* roar with pain ◆ **~ de colère** to bellow *ou* roar with anger ◆ **faire ~ son moteur** to rev (up) one's engine VT *[+ ordres, menaces]* to roar *ou* bellow out

rugissant, e /ʀyʒisɑ̃, ɑ̃t/ ADJ roaring, howling; → **quarantième**

rugissement /ʀyʒismɑ̃/ NM *[de fauve, mer, moteur]* roar, roaring (NonC); *[de vent, tempête]* howl, howling (NonC) ◆ **~ de douleur** howl *ou* roar of pain ◆ **~ de colère** roar of anger ◆ **j'entendais des ~s de lions** I could hear lions roaring *ou* the roar of lions ◆ **pousser un ~ de rage** to roar with anger

rugosité /ʀygozite/ NF 1 (NonC) *[d'écorce, surface, vin]* roughness; *[de peau, tissu]* roughness, coarseness; *[de sol]* ruggedness, roughness, bumpiness 2 *(= aspérité)* rough patch, bump ◆ **poncer les ~s** to sand down the rough areas

rugueux, -euse /ʀygø, øz/ ADJ *[écorce, surface, vin]* rough; *[peau, tissu]* rough, coarse; *[sol]* rugged, rough, bumpy

Ruhr /ʀuʀ/ NF ◆ **la ~** the Ruhr

ruine /ʀɥin/ NF 1 *(= décombres, destruction, perte de fortune)* ruin ◆ **~s romaines** Roman ruins ◆ **acheter une ~ à la campagne** to buy a ruin in the country ◆ **~ (humaine)** *(péj)* (human) wreck ◆ **causer la ~ de** *[+ monarchie]* to bring about the ruin *ou* downfall of; *[+ carrière, réputation, santé]* to ruin, to bring about the ruin of; *[+ banquier, entreprise]* to ruin, to bring ruin upon ◆ **c'est la ~ de tous mes espoirs** that means the ruin of *ou* that puts paid to *(Brit)* all my hopes ◆ **courir** *ou* **aller à sa ~** to be on the road to ruin, to be heading for ruin

◆ **en ruine(s)** in ruin(s), ruined *(épith)* ◆ **tomber en ~** to fall in ruins

2 *(= acquisition coûteuse)* ◆ **cette voiture est une vraie ~** that car will ruin me ◆ **20 €, c'est pas la ~ !** * 20 euros won't break the bank! *

ruiner /ʀɥine/ ▸ conjug 1 ◂ VT 1 *[+ pays, personne]* to ruin, to cause the ruin of ◆ **ça ne va pas te ~ !** * it won't break * *ou* ruin you! 2 *[+ réputation, santé]* to ruin; *[+ carrière]* to ruin, to wreck; *[+ espoirs]* to shatter, to dash, to ruin; *[+ efforts]* to destroy, to ruin VPR **se ruiner** *(= dépenser tout son argent)* to ruin *ou* bankrupt o.s.; *(fig = dépenser trop)* to spend a fortune ◆ **se ~ en fleurs** to spend a fortune on flowers ◆ **quelques conseils pour partir en vacances sans se ~** a few tips for going on holiday without spending a fortune *ou* breaking the bank * ◆ **se ~ au jeu** to lose all one's money gambling

ruineux, -euse /ʀɥinø, øz/ ADJ *[goût]* extravagant; *[acquisition, voiture]* *(prix élevé)* ruinously expensive; *(entretien coûteux)* expensive to run *(ou* keep) ◆ **ce n'est pas ~ !** it won't break the bank!

ruisseau (pl **ruisseaux**) /ʀɥiso/ NM 1 *(= cours d'eau)* stream, brook ◆ **des ~x de** *(fig)* *[+ larmes]* floods of; *[+ lave, sang]* streams of; → **petit** 2 *(= caniveau)* gutter ◆ **élevé dans le ~** *(fig)* brought up in the gutter ◆ **tirer qn du ~** *(fig)* to pull *ou* drag sb out of the gutter

ruisselant, e /ʀɥis(ə)lɑ̃, ɑ̃t/ ADJ *[visage]* streaming; *[personne]* dripping wet, streaming ◆ **le mur était ~** the wall had water running down it ◆ **son front ~ de sueur** his forehead bathed in *ou* dripping with sweat ◆ **le visage ~ de larmes** his face streaming with tears, with tears streaming down his face

ruisseler /ʀɥis(ə)le/ ▸ conjug 4 ◂ VI 1 *(= couler)* *[lumière]* to stream; *[cheveux]* to flow, to stream *(sur* over); *[liquide, pluie]* to stream, to flow *(sur* down) 2 *(= être couvert d'eau)* **~ (d'eau)** *[mur]* to have water running down it; *[visage]* to stream (with water) ◆ **~ de lumière/larmes** to stream with light/tears ◆ **~ de sueur** to drip *ou* stream with sweat

ruisselet /ʀɥis(ə)lɛ/ NM rivulet, brooklet

ruissellement /ʀɥisɛlmɑ̃/ NM ◆ **le ~ de la pluie/de l'eau sur le mur** the rain/water streaming *ou* running *ou* flowing down the wall ◆ **eaux de ~** runoff ◆ **le ~ de sa chevelure sur ses épaules** her hair flowing *ou* tumbling over her shoulders ◆ **un ~ de pierreries** a glistening *ou* glittering cascade of jewels ◆ **ébloui par ce ~ de lumière** dazzled by this stream of light COMP **ruissellement pluvial** *(Géol)* run-off

rumba /ʀumba/ NF rumba

rumeur /ʀymœʀ/ NF 1 *(= nouvelle imprécise)* rumour ◆ **selon certaines ~s, elle ...** rumour has it that she ..., it is rumoured that she ... ◆ **il dément les ~s selon lesquelles le boxeur était dopé** he denies the rumours that the boxer was doped ◆ **si l'on en croit la ~ publique, il ...** if you believe what is publicly rumoured, he ... ◆ **faire courir de fausses ~s** to spread rumours 2 *(= son)* *[de vagues, vent]* murmur(ing) (NonC); *[de circulation, rue, ville]* hum (NonC); *[d'émeute]* rumbling; *[de bureau, conversation]* buzz (NonC) 3 *(= protestation)* rumblings ◆ **~ de mécontentement** rumblings of discontent ◆ **une ~ s'éleva** *ou* **des ~s s'élevèrent de la foule** angry sounds rose up from the crowd

ruminant, e /ʀyminɑ̃/ ADJ, NM ruminant

rumination /ʀyminasjɔ̃/ NF rumination

ruminer /ʀymine/ ▸ conjug 1 ◂ VT *[animal]* to ruminate; *[+ projet]* to ruminate on *ou* over, to chew over; *[+ chagrin]* to brood over; *[+ vengeance]* to ponder, to meditate ◆ **toujours dans son coin à ~ (ses pensées)** always in his corner chewing the cud *ou* chewing things over *ou* pondering (things) VI *(Zool)* to ruminate, to chew the cud

rumsteck /ʀɔmstɛk/ NM ⇒ **romsteck**

rune /ʀyn/ NF rune

runique /ʀynik/ ADJ runic

rupestre /ʀypɛstʀ/ ADJ 1 *(Art)* rupestrian (SPÉC), rupestral (SPÉC), rock *(épith)* ◆ **peintures ~s** *(gén)* rock paintings; *(dans une grotte)* cave *ou* rock paintings 2 *(Bot)* rupestrine (SPÉC), rock *(épith)*

rupin, e * /ʀypɛ̃, in/ ADJ *[appartement, quartier]* ritzy *, plush *, swanky *; *[personne]* stinking *ou* filthy rich * NM,F rich person ◆ **c'est un ~** he's rolling in it * ◆ **les ~s** the rich

rupteur /ʀyptœʀ/ NM (contact) breaker

rupture /ʀyptyʀ/ NF 1 *(= annulation)* *[de relations diplomatiques]* breaking off, severing, rupture; *[de fiançailles, pourparlers]* breaking off ◆ **la ~ du traité/contrat par ce pays** the breach of the treaty/contract by this country ◆ **après la ~ des négociations** after negotiations broke down, after the breakdown of the negotiations ◆ **la ~ de leurs fiançailles m'a surpris** I was surprised when they broke off their engagement ◆ **la ~ du jeûne** the breaking of the fast ◆ **il est 19h05, l'heure de ~ du jeûne** it's five past seven, when fasting ends

◆ **en rupture** ◆ **des jeunes en ~ familiale** young people who have broken off relations with their families ◆ **il est en ~ avec son parti** he has broken with his party ◆ **être en ~ avec le monde/les idées de son temps** to be at odds with the world/the ideas of one's time ◆ **cette initiative est en ~ avec la tradition** this initiative marks a break with tradition

2 *(= séparation amoureuse)* break-up, split ◆ **sa ~ (d')avec Louise** his split *ou* break-up with Louise ◆ **~ passagère** temporary break-up

3 *(= cassure, déchirure)* *[de câble, branche, corde, poutre]* breaking; *[de digue]* bursting, breach(ing); *[de veine]* bursting, rupture; *[d'organe]* rupture; *[de tendon]* rupture, tearing ◆ **en cas de ~ du barrage** should the dam burst ◆ **point de ~** *(gén)* breaking point; *(Ordin)* breakpoint

4 *(= solution de continuité)* break ◆ **~ entre le passé et le présent** break between the past and the present ◆ **~ de rythme** (sudden) break in (the) rhythm ◆ **~ de ton** abrupt change in *ou* of tone ◆ **la ~ d'approvisionnement provoquée par les grèves** the disruption in supplies caused by the strikes ◆ **cela marque une ~ avec la tendance des années précédentes** this marks a break with the tendency of the preceding years

COMP **rupture d'anévrisme** aneurysmal rupture

rupture de ban *illegal return from banishment* ◆ **en ~ de ban** *(Jur)* *illegally returning from banishment;* *(fig)* in defiance of the accepted code of conduct ◆ **en ~ de ban avec la société** at odds with society

rupture de charge *(Transport)* transshipment

rupture de circuit *(Élec)* break in the circuit

rupture de contrat breach of contract

rupture de direction steering failure

rupture d'équilibre *(lit)* loss of balance ◆ **une ~ d'équilibre est à craindre entre ces nations** *(fig)* an upset in the balance of power is to be feared among these states

rupture d'essieu broken axle

rupture du jeûne breaking of a fast

rupture de pente change of incline *ou* gradient

rupture de séquence *(Ordin)* jump

rupture de stock stock shortage, stockout (US) ◆ **être en ~ de stock** to be out of stock

rural, e (mpl **-aux**) /ʀyʀal, o/ ADJ *(gén)* country *(épith)*, rural; *(Admin)* rural ◆ **le monde ~** *(gén)* rural society; *(= agriculteurs)* the farming community; → **exode** NM,F country person, rustic ◆ **les ruraux** country people, countryfolk

rurbain, e /ʀyʀbɛ̃, ɛn/ ADJ ◆ **l'espace ~** the outer suburbs NM,F person who lives in the outer suburbs

ruse /ʀyz/ NF 1 (NonC, *pour gagner, obtenir un avantage*) cunning, craftiness, slyness; *(pour tromper)* trickery, guile ◆ **obtenir qch par ~** to obtain sth by *ou* through trickery *ou* by guile 2 *(= subterfuge)* trick, ruse ◆ **~ de guerre** *(lit, hum)* stratagem, tactics ◆ **avec des ~s de Sioux** with crafty tactics

rusé, e /ʀyze/ (ptp de **ruser**) ADJ *[personne]* cunning, crafty, sly, wily; *[air]* sly, wily ◆ **~ comme un (vieux) renard** as sly *ou* cunning as a fox ◆ **c'est un ~** he's a crafty *ou* sly one

ruser /ʀyze/ ► conjug 1 ◄ **VI** (*= être habile*) (*pour gagner, obtenir un avantage*) to use cunning; (*pour tromper*) to use trickery ◆ **ne ruse pas avec moi !** don't try and be clever *ou* smart* with me! ◆ **il va falloir ~ si l'on veut entrer** we'll have to use a bit of cunning *ou* be a bit crafty if we want to get in

rush /ʀœʃ/ **NM** (*= afflux*) rush; (*Ciné*) rush

russe /ʀys/ **ADJ** Russian ◆ **boire à la ~** to drink (and cast one's glass aside) in the Russian style; → **montagne, roulette** **NM** (*= langue*) Russian **NMF** **Russe** Russian ◆ **Russe blanc(he)** White Russian

Russie /ʀysi/ **NF** Russia ◆ **la ~ blanche** White Russia ◆ **la ~ soviétique** Soviet Russia

russification /ʀysifikasjɔ̃/ **NF** russianization, russification

russifier /ʀysifje/ ► conjug 7 ◄ **VT** to russianize, to russify

russophile /ʀysɔfil/ **ADJ, NMF** Russophil(e)

russophone /ʀysɔfɔn/ **ADJ** [*population, communauté, minorité*] Russian-speaking **NMF** (*= personne*) Russian speaker

rustaud, e /ʀysto, od/ **ADJ** countrified, rustic **NM,F** (*péj*) country bumpkin, yokel, hillbilly (*US*)

rusticité /ʀystisite/ **NF** 1 [*de manières, personne*] rustic simplicity, rusticity (*littér*) 2 (*Agr*) hardiness

rustine ® /ʀystin/ **NF** rubber repair patch (*for bicycle tyre*) ◆ **il ne suffira pas de coller quelques ~s pour sauver l'entreprise** (*fig*) it'll take more than stopgap measures *ou* cosmetic improvements to save the company

rustique /ʀystik/ **ADJ** 1 [*mobilier*] rustic; [*maçonnerie*] rustic, rusticated ◆ **bois ~** rustic wood 2 (*littér*) [*maison*] rustic (*épith*); [*manières, vie*] rustic, country (*épith*) 3 [*plante*] hardy **NM** (*= style*) rustic style ◆ **meubler une maison en ~** to furnish a house in the rustic style *ou* with rustic furniture

rustre /ʀystʀ/ **NM** 1 (*péj = brute*) lout, boor 2 († = *paysan*) peasant **ADJ** brutish, boorish

rut /ʀyt/ **NM** (*= état*) [*de mâle*] rut; [*de femelle*] heat; (*= période*) [*de mâle*] rutting (period); [*de femelle*] heat period ◆ **être en ~** [*mâle*] to be rutting; [*femelle*] to be on (*Brit*) *ou* in (*US*) heat

rutabaga /ʀytabaga/ **NM** swede, rutabaga (*US*)

ruthénium /ʀytenjɔm/ **NM** ruthenium

rutilant, e /ʀytilɑ̃, ɑ̃t/ **ADJ** (*= brillant*) brightly shining, gleaming; (*= rouge ardent*) rutilant ◆ **vêtu d'un uniforme ~** very spick and span *ou* very spruce in his uniform

rutiler /ʀytile/ ► conjug 1 ◄ **VI** to gleam, to shine brightly

rv abrév de **rendez-vous**

Rwanda /ʀwɑ̃da/ **NM** Rwanda

rwandais, e /ʀwɑ̃dɛ, ɛz/ **ADJ** Rwandan **NM,F** **Rwandais(e)** Rwandan

rythme /ʀitm/ **NM** 1 (*Art, Littérat, Mus*) rhythm ◆ **marquer le ~** to beat time ◆ **au ~ de** (*Mus*) to the beat *ou* rhythm of ◆ **avoir le sens du ~** to have a sense of rhythm ◆ **une pièce qui manque de ~** (*Théât*) a slow-moving play
2 (*= cadence*) [*de cœur, respiration, saisons*] rhythm ◆ **interrompant le ~ de sa respiration** interrupting the rhythm of his breathing
3 (*= vitesse*) [*de respiration*] rate; [*de battements du cœur*] rate, speed; [*de travail, vie*]tempo, pace; [*de production*] rate ◆ **à un ~ infernal/régulier** at a phenomenal *ou* terrific/steady rate ◆ **le ~ soutenu de la croissance économique** the sustained rate of economic growth ◆ **~ cardiaque** (rate of) heartbeat ◆ **~ biologique** biological rhythm ◆ **les ~s scolaires** the way the school year is organized *ou* divided up ◆ **à ce ~-là, il ne va plus en rester** at that rate there won't be any left ◆ **il n'arrive pas à suivre le ~** he can't keep up (the pace) ◆ **produire des voitures au ~ de 1 000 par jour** to produce cars at the rate of 1,000 a *ou* per day ◆ **changer au ~ des saisons** to change with the seasons ◆ **vivez au ~des habitants** live like the locals ◆ **des vacances au ~ des Antilles** a typical Caribbean holiday

rythmé, e /ʀitme/ (ptp de **rythmer**) **ADJ** rhythmic(al) ◆ **bien ~** highly rhythmic(al)

rythmer /ʀitme/ ► conjug 1 ◄ **VT** (*= cadencer*) [*+ phrase, prose, travail*] to give rhythm to, to punctuate ◆ **les saisons rythmaient leur vie** their lives were governed by the rhythm of the seasons

rythmique /ʀitmik/ **ADJ** rhythmic(al); → **section** **NF** (*Littérat*) rhythmics (*sg*) ◆ **la (danse) ~** rhythmics (*sg*)

S s

S[1], **s**[1] /ɛs/ NM [1] *(= lettre)* S, s [2] *(= figure)* zigzag; *(= virages)* double bend, S bend ◆ **faire des s** to zigzag ◆ **en s** *[route]* zigzagging *(épith)*, winding; *[barre]* S-shaped

S[2] (abrév de **Sud**) S

s[2] (abrév de **seconde**) s

s' /s/ → **se, si**[1]

s/ abrév de **sur**

SA /ɛsa/ NF (abrév de **société anonyme**) *(gén)* limited company; *(ouverte au public)* public limited company ◆ **Raymond** ~ Raymond Ltd *(Brit)*, Raymond Inc. *(US)*; *(ouverte au public)* Raymond plc

sa /sa/ ADJ POSS → **son**[1]

Saba /saba/ NF Sheba ◆ **la reine de** ~ the Queen of Sheba

sabayon /sabajɔ̃/ NM *(= dessert)* zabaglione; *(= sauce)* sabayon

sabbat /saba/ NM [1] *(Rel)* Sabbath [2] *(* = bruit)* racket, row* [3] *[de sorcières]* (witches') sabbath

sabbatique /sabatik/ ADJ *(Rel, Univ)* *[année, congé]* sabbatical ◆ **prendre une année** ~ *(Univ)* to take a sabbatical year *ou* a year's sabbatical (leave); *[étudiant, employé]* to take a year off *ou* out ◆ **être en congé** ~ *(Univ)* to be on sabbatical (leave); *[employé]* to be taking a year off *ou* out

sabin, e[1] /sabɛ̃, in/ ADJ Sabine NM,F **Sabin(e)** Sabine; → **enlèvement**

sabir /sabiʀ/ NM *(= parlé dans le Levant)* sabir; *(Ling)* ≃ pidgin; *(péj = jargon)* jargon; *(incompréhensible)* mumbo jumbo* ◆ **un curieux ~ fait de français et d'arabe** a strange mixture of French and Arabic

sablage /sablaʒ/ NM *[d'allée, route]* sanding; *[de façade]* sandblasting

sable[1] /sabl/ NM sand ◆ **de** ~ *[dune]* sand *(épith)*; *[fond, plage]* sandy ◆ **vent de** ~ sandstorm ◆ **~s mouvants** quicksand(s) ◆ **ville ensevelie sous les ~s** city buried in the sands ◆ **être sur le** ~* *(sans argent)* to be (stony *(Brit) ou* stone *(US)*) broke*, to be skint* *(Brit)*; *(sans travail)* to be out of a job, to be jobless; → **bac**[2], **bâtir, grain, marchand** ADJ INV sandy, sand-coloured *(Brit) ou* -colored *(US)*

sable[2] /sabl/ NM *(Hér)* sable

sablé, e /sable/ (ptp de **sabler**) ADJ [1] **gâteau** ~ shortbread biscuit *(Brit) ou* cookie *(US)*; → **pâte** [2] *[route]* sandy, sanded NM *(= gâteau)* shortbread biscuit *(Brit) ou* cookie *(US)*

sabler /sable/ ► conjug 1 ◄ VT [1] *[+ route]* to sand; *[+ façade]* to sandblast [2] ◆ ~ **le champagne** *(lit)* to crack open a bottle of champagne; *(fig)* to celebrate with champagne

sableux, -euse /sablø, øz/ ADJ *[alluvions, sol]* sandy; *[coquillages]* gritty, sandy NF **sableuse** *(= machine)* sandblaster

sablier /sablije/ NM *(gén)* hourglass, sandglass; *(Culin)* egg timer

sablière /sablijɛʀ/ NF *(= carrière)* sand quarry; *(Constr)* string-piece; *(Rail)* sand-box

sablonneux, -euse /sablɔnø, øz/ ADJ sandy

sablonnière /sablɔnjɛʀ/ NF sand quarry

sabord /sabɔʀ/ NM *(Naut)* scuttle ◆ **mille ~s !*** *(hum)* blistering barnacles!* *(hum)*

sabordage /sabɔʀdaʒ/, **sabordement** /sabɔʀdəmɑ̃/ NM *[de bateau]* scuppering, scuttling; *[d'entreprise]* winding up

saborder /sabɔʀde/ ► conjug 1 ◄ VT *[+ bateau]* to scupper, to scuttle; *[+ entreprise]* to wind up; *[+ négociations, projet]* to put paid to, to scupper VPR **se saborder** *(Naut)* to scupper *ou* scuttle one's ship; *[candidat]* to write o.s. off, to scupper one's chances; *[parti]* to wind (itself) up; *[entreprise]* to wind (itself) up, to fold ◆ **il a décidé de se** ~ *(patron)* he decided to wind up the company

sabot /sabo/ NM [1] *(= chaussure)* clog; → **baignoire, venir** [2] *[d'animal]* hoof ◆ **animal à ~s** hoofed animal ◆ **le cheval lui donna un coup de** ~ the horse kicked out at him [3] *(*: péj)* **c'est un vrai** ~ † *(voiture, machine)* it's a piece of old junk* ◆ **il travaille comme un** ~ he's a shoddy worker ◆ **il joue comme un** ~ he's a hopeless *ou* pathetic* player [4] *(= toupie)* (whipping) top [5] *[de pied de table, poteau]* ferrule ◆ ~ **de frein** brake shoe ◆ ~ **(de Denver)** wheel clamp, Denver boot *(US)* ◆ **mettre un ~ à une voiture** to clamp a car

sabotage /sabɔtaʒ/ NM [1] *(Mil, Pol, fig)* *(= action)* sabotage; *(= acte)* act of sabotage ◆ ~ **industriel** industrial sabotage [2] *(= bâclage)* botching

sabot-de-Vénus (pl **sabots-de-Vénus**) /sabod(ə)venys/ NM *(= plante)* lady's slipper

saboter /sabɔte/ ► conjug 1 ◄ VT [1] *(Mil, Pol, fig)* to sabotage [2] *(= bâcler)* to make a (proper) mess of, to botch; *(= abîmer)* to mess up, to ruin

saboteur, -euse /sabɔtœʀ, øz/ NM,F *(Mil, Pol)* saboteur; *(= bâcleur)* shoddy worker

sabotier, -ière /sabɔtje, jɛʀ/ NM,F *(= fabricant)* clog-maker; *(= marchand)* clog-seller

sabra /sabʀa/ NMF sabra

sabre /sɑbʀ/ NM sabre *(Brit)*, saber *(US)* ◆ ~ **d'abordage** cutlass ◆ ~ **de cavalerie** riding sabre ◆ **mettre ~ au clair** to draw one's sword ◆ **charger ~ au clair** to charge with swords drawn ◆ **le ~ et le goupillon** the Army and the Church ◆ **bruits de** ~ *(Pol)* sabre-rattling

sabrer /sabʀe/ ► conjug 1 ◄ VT [1] *(Mil)* to sabre *(Brit)*, to saber *(US)*, to cut down ◆ ~ **le champagne** *to open a bottle of champagne using a sabre; (fig)* to celebrate with champagne [2] *(littér = marquer)* **la ride qui sabrait son front** the deep line across his brow ◆ **dessin sabré de coups de crayon rageurs** drawing scored with angry pencil strokes [3] *(* = biffer)* *[+ texte]* to slash (great) chunks out of*; *[+ passage, phrase]* to cut out, to scrub (out)*; *[+ projet]* to axe, to chop* [4] *(* = recaler)* *[+ étudiant]* to flunk*; *(= renvoyer)* *[+ employé]* to fire*, to sack* *(Brit)* ◆ **se faire** ~ *[étudiant]* to be flunked*; *[employé]* to get fired* *ou* sacked* *(Brit)*, to get the sack* *(Brit)* [5] *(* = critiquer)* *[+ devoir]* to tear to pieces *ou* to shreds; *[+ livre, pièce]* to slam*, to pan* [6] *(* = bâcler)* *[+ travail]* to knock off* (in a rush)

sabreur /sabʀœʀ/ NM *(péj = soldat)* fighting cock *(péj)*; *(= escrimeur)* swordsman

sac[1] /sak/ NM [1] *(gén)* bag; *(de grande taille, en toile)* sack; *(= cartable)* (school) bag; *(à bretelles)* satchel; *(pour achats)* shopping bag, carrier bag *(Brit)* ◆ ~ **(en) plastique** plastic bag ◆ ~ **(à poussières)** *(pour aspirateur)* dust bag, vacuum cleaner bag, Hoover ® bag *(Brit)* ◆ **mettre en ~(s)** to bag; → **course**

[2] *(= contenu)* *(gén)* bag(ful); *(de grande taille, en toile)* sack(ful)

[3] *(‡ = 10 francs)* **dix/trente ~s** one hundred/three hundred francs

[4] *(locutions)* **habillé comme un** ~ dressed like a tramp ◆ **ils sont tous à mettre dans le même** ~* *(péj)* they're all as bad as each other ◆ **l'affaire est** *ou* **c'est dans le** ~* it's in the bag* ◆ **des gens de ~ et de corde** †† gallows birds ◆ **le ~ et la cendre** *(Rel)* sackcloth and ashes; → **main, tour**[2]

[5] *(Anat)* sac ◆ ~ **embryonnaire/lacrymal** embryo/lacrimal sac

COMP **sac à bandoulière** shoulder bag
sac de couchage sleeping bag
sac à dos rucksack, backpack
sac d'embrouilles * muddle
sac à main handbag, purse *(US)*, pocketbook *(US)*
sac à malice bag of tricks
sac de marin kitbag
sac de nœuds * ⇒ **sac d'embrouilles**
sac d'os (*, *péj*) bag of bones
sac à ouvrage workbag
sac de plage beach bag
sac polochon sausage bag
sac à provisions shopping bag

sac à puces (*, péj = lit) fleabag*
sac reporter organizer bag
sac de sable (Constr, Mil) sandbag; (Boxe) punching bag, punchbag (Brit)
sac de sport sports bag
sac à viande (Camping) sleeping bag sheet
sac à vin * (old) soak*, wino*, drunkard
sac de voyage travelling bag; (pour l'avion) flight bag, carry-on bag

sac[2] /sak/ NM ◆ **(mise à)** ~ *[de ville]* sack, sacking *(NonC)*; *[de maison, pièce]* ransacking *(NonC)* ◆ **mettre à** ~ *[+ ville]* to sack; *[+ maison, pièce]* to ransack

saccade /sakad/ NF jerk ◆ **avancer par ~s** to jerk along, to move along in fits and starts *ou* jerkily ◆ **parler par ~s** to speak haltingly

saccadé, e /sakade/ ADJ *[démarche, gestes, style]* jerky; *[débit, respiration]* spasmodic, halting; *[bruit]* staccato; *[sommeil]* fitful

saccage /sakaʒ/ NM *(= destruction) [de pièce, bâtiment]* ransacking; *[de jardin]* wrecking; *[de forêt, littoral, planète]* destruction; *(= pillage) [de pays, ville]* sack, sacking *(NonC)*; *[de maison]* ransacking

saccager /sakaʒe/ ▸ conjug 3 ◂ VT [1] *(= dévaster) [+ pièce]* to turn upside down, to wreck; *[+ jardin, bâtiment]* to wreck; *[+ forêt, littoral, planète]* to destroy ◆ **ils ont tout saccagé dans la maison** they turned the whole house upside down ◆ **l'appartement était entièrement saccagé** the flat was completely wrecked ◆ **champ saccagé par la grêle** field laid waste *ou* devastated by the hail [2] *(= piller) [+ pays, ville]* to sack, to lay waste; *[+ maison]* to ransack

saccageur, -euse /sakaʒœʀ, øz/ NM,F *(= dévastateur)* vandal; *(= pillard)* pillager, plunderer

saccharification /sakaʀifikasjɔ̃/ NF saccharification

saccharifier /sakaʀifje/ ▸ conjug 7 ◂ VT to saccharify

saccharine /sakaʀin/ NF saccharin(e)

saccharose /sakaʀoz/ NM sucrose, saccharose

SACEM /sasɛm/ NF (abrév de **Société des auteurs, compositeurs et éditeurs de musique**) *French body responsible for collecting and distributing music royalties,* ≃ PRS *(Brit)*

sacerdoce /sasɛʀdɔs/ NM *(Rel)* priesthood; *(fig)* calling, vocation

sacerdotal, e (mpl **-aux**) /sasɛʀdɔtal, o/ ADJ priestly, sacerdotal

sachem /saʃɛm/ NM sachem

sachet /saʃɛ/ NM *[de bonbons, thé]* bag; *[de levure, sucre vanillé]* sachet; *[de drogue]* (small) bag; *[de soupe]* packet ◆ ~ **de lavande** lavender bag *ou* sachet ◆ ~ **d'aspirine** sachet of (powdered) aspirin ◆ **soupe en ~(s)** packet soup ◆ **thé en ~(s)** tea bags ◆ **café en ~s individuels** individual sachets of coffee

sacoche /sakɔʃ/ NF *(gén)* bag; *(pour outils)* toolbag; *[de cycliste] (de selle)* saddlebag; *(de porte-bagages)* pannier; *[d'écolier]* (school) bag; *(à bretelles)* satchel; *[d'encaisseur]* (money) bag; *[de facteur]* (post-)bag

sac-poubelle, sac poubelle (pl **sacs(-)poubelles**) /sakpubɛl/ NM bin liner *(Brit)*, garbage bag *(US)*

sacquer * /sake/ ▸ conjug 1 ◂ VT [1] *[+ employé]* ~ **qn** to fire sb, to kick sb out‡, to give sb the push‡ *ou* the boot‡ *ou* the sack* *(Brit)* ◆ **se faire** ~ to get the push‡ *ou* boot‡ *ou* sack* *(Brit)*, to get (o.s.) kicked out‡ [2] *[+ élève]* to mark *(Brit)* *ou* grade *(US)* strictly ◆ **je me suis fait ~ à l'examen** the examiner gave me lousy* marks *(Brit) ou* grades *(US)* [3] *(= détester)* **je ne peux pas le** ~ I can't stand him, I hate his guts‡

sacral, e (mpl **-aux**) /sakʀal, o/ ADJ sacred

sacralisation /sakʀalizasjɔ̃/ NF ◆ **la ~ des loisirs/de la famille** the sanctification of leisure time/the family

sacraliser /sakʀalize/ ▸ conjug 1 ◂ VT to regard as sacred, to make sacred ◆ ~ **la réussite sociale/la famille** to regard social success/the family as sacred

sacralité /sakʀalite/ NF *[de personne]* sacred status; *[d'institution]* sacredness

sacramentel, -elle /sakʀamɑ̃tɛl/ ADJ [1] *(fig = rituel)* ritual, ritualistic [2] *(Rel) [rite, formule]* sacramental

sacre /sakʀ/ NM [1] *[de roi]* coronation; *[d'évêque]* consecration ◆ **"le Sacre du Printemps"** *(Mus)* "the Rite of Spring" [2] *(= oiseau)* saker [3] *(Can = juron)* (blasphemous) swearword

sacré[1], **e** /sakʀe/ (ptp de **sacrer**) ADJ [1] *(après n : Rel) [lieu, objet, texte]* sacred, holy; *[art, musique]* sacred; *[horreur, terreur]* holy; *[droit]* hallowed, sacred ◆ **le Sacré Collège** the Sacred College (of Cardinals); → **feu**[1], **union**
[2] *(après n = inviolable) [droit, promesse]* sacred ◆ **son sommeil, c'est** ~ his sleep is sacred; → **monstre**
[3] (* : *avant n = maudit)* blasted*, confounded*, damned‡ ◆ ~ **nom de nom !**‡ hell and damnation!‡ ◆ **elle a un ~ caractère** she's got a lousy* temper
[4] (* : *avant n = considérable)* **c'est un ~ imbécile** he's a real idiot ◆ **c'est un ~ menteur** he's a terrible liar ◆ **il a un ~ toupet** he's got a *ou* one heck* *ou* hell‡ of a nerve, he's got a right cheek* *(Brit)* ◆ **elle a eu une ~e chance** she was damn(ed) lucky‡
[5] (* : *avant n : admiration, surprise)* ~ **farceur !** you old devil (you)!* ◆ **ce ~ Paul a encore gagné aux courses** Paul's gone and won on the horses again, the lucky devil*
NM ◆ **le** ~ the sacred

sacré[2], **e** /sakʀe/ ADJ *(Anat)* sacral

sacrebleu * /sakʀəblø/ EXCL (††, *hum*) confound it!*, strewth!* *(Brit)*

Sacré-Cœur /sakʀekœʀ/ NM [1] *(Rel)* **le** ~ the Sacred Heart ◆ **la fête du** ~ the Feast of the Sacred Heart [2] *(= église)* **le ~, la basilique du** ~ the Sacré-Cœur

sacrement /sakʀəmɑ̃/ NM sacrament ◆ **recevoir les derniers ~s** to receive the last rites *ou* sacraments ◆ **il est mort, muni des ~s de l'Église** he died fortified with the (last) rites *ou* sacraments of the Church

sacrément * /sakʀemɑ̃/ ADV *[froid, intéressant, laid]* damned‡, jolly* *(Brit)* ◆ **j'ai eu ~ peur** I was damned‡ *ou* jolly* *(Brit)* scared ◆ **ça m'a ~ plu** I really liked it, I liked it ever so much ◆ **il est ~ menteur** he's a downright *ou* an out-and-out liar

sacrer /sakʀe/ ▸ conjug 1 ◂ VT *[+ roi]* to crown; *[+ évêque]* to consecrate ◆ **il a été sacré champion du monde/meilleur joueur** he was crowned world champion/best player VI (††, * = *jurer*) to curse, to swear

sacrificateur, -trice /sakʀifikatœʀ, tʀis/ NM,F *(Hist)* sacrificer ◆ **grand** ~ high priest

sacrifice /sakʀifis/ NM *(Rel, fig)* sacrifice ◆ ~ **financier/humain** financial/human sacrifice ◆ **faire un ~/des ~s** to make a sacrifice/sacrifices ◆ **faire le ~ de sa vie/d'une journée de vacances** to sacrifice one's life/a day's holiday ◆ **offrir qch en** ~ to offer sth as a sacrifice *(à* to*)*; ◆ **être prêt à tous les ~s pour qn/qch** to be prepared to sacrifice everything for sb/sth ◆ ~ **de soi** self-sacrifice; → **saint**

sacrificiel, -ielle /sakʀifisjɛl/ ADJ sacrificial

sacrifié, e /sakʀifje/ (ptp de **sacrifier**) ADJ [1] *[peuple, troupe]* sacrificed ◆ **les ~s du plan de restructuration** the victims of *ou* those who have been sacrificed in the restructuring plan [2] *(Comm)* **articles ~s** give-aways*, items given away at knockdown prices ◆ **"prix sacrifiés"** "giveaway prices", "rock-bottom prices", "prices slashed"

sacrifier /sakʀifje/ ▸ conjug 7 ◂ VT [1] *(gén)* to sacrifice *(à* to; *pour* for*)*; *(= abandonner)* to give up ◆ ~ **sa vie pour sa patrie** to lay down *ou* sacrifice one's life for one's country ◆ **il a sacrifié sa carrière au profit de sa famille** he sacrificed his career for (the sake of) his family ◆ **il a dû ~ ses vacances** he had to give up his holidays [2] *(Comm) [+ marchandises]* to give away (at a knockdown price) VT INDIR **sacrifier à** *[+ mode, préjugés, tradition]* to conform to VPR **se sacrifier** to sacrifice o.s. *(à* to; *pour* for*)*; ◆ **il ne reste qu'un chocolat … je me sacrifie !** *(iro)* there's only one chocolate left … I'll just have to eat it myself!

sacrilège /sakʀilɛʒ/ ADJ *(Rel, fig)* sacrilegious ◆ **acte** ~ sacrilegious act, act of sacrilege NM *(Rel, fig)* sacrilege ◆ **ce serait un ~ de …** it would be (a) sacrilege to … ◆ **commettre un** ~ to commit sacrilege ◆ **il a coupé son vin avec de l'eau, quel ~ !** he put water in his wine, what sacrilege! NMF sacrilegious person

sacripant /sakʀipɑ̃/ NM (††, *hum*) rogue, scoundrel

sacristain /sakʀistɛ̃/ NM *[de sacristie]* sacristan; *[d'église]* sexton

sacristaine /sakʀistɛn/ NF sacristan

sacristie /sakʀisti/ NF *(catholique)* sacristy; *(protestante)* vestry; → **punaise**

sacristine /sakʀistin/ NF ⇒ **sacristaine**

sacro-iliaque /sakʀoiljak/ ADJ sacroiliac

sacro-saint, e /sakʀosɛ̃, sɛ̃t/ ADJ *(lit, iro)* sacrosanct

sacrum /sakʀɔm/ NM sacrum

sadique /sadik/ ADJ sadistic ◆ **stade ~ anal** *(Psych)* anal stage NMF sadist

sadiquement /sadikmɑ̃/ ADV sadistically

sadisme /sadism/ NM sadism

sado * /sado/ ADJ sadistic ◆ **il est ~-maso** he's into S&M NMF sadist

sadomasochisme /sadomazɔʃism/ NM sadomasochism

sadomasochiste /sadomazɔʃist/ ADJ sadomasochistic NMF sadomasochist

SAE /ɛsaø/ ADJ (abrév de **Society of Automotive Engineers**) SAE ◆ **classification/numéro** ~ SAE classification/number

safari /safaʀi/ NM safari ◆ **faire un** ~ to go on safari

safari-photo (pl **safaris-photos**) /safaʀifɔto/ NM photo(graphic) safari

safran /safʀɑ̃/ NM [1] *(= couleur, plante, épice)* saffron ◆ ~ **des prés** autumn crocus, meadow saffron, colchicum (SPÉC) ◆ **riz au** ~ saffron rice [2] *[de gouvernail]* rudder blade ADJ INV saffron(-coloured *(Brit) ou* -colored *(US)*) ◆ **jaune** ~ saffron yellow

safrané, e /safʀane/ ADJ *[plat, sauce]* with saffron; *[tissu]* saffron(-coloured *(Brit) ou* -colored *(US)*), saffron (yellow) ◆ **de couleur ~e** saffron-coloured

saga /saga/ NF saga

sagace /sagas/ ADJ *(littér)* sagacious, shrewd

sagacité /sagasite/ NF sagacity, shrewdness ◆ **avec** ~ shrewdly

sagaie /sagɛ/ NF assegai, assagai

sage /saʒ/ ADJ [1] *(= avisé) [conseil]* sound, sensible, wise; *[action, démarche, décision, précaution]* wise, sensible; *[personne]* wise ◆ **il serait plus ~ de …** it would be wiser *ou* more sensible to …, you *(ou* he *etc)* would be better advised to … [2] *(euph = chaste) [jeune fille]* good, well-behaved

♦ **elle n'est pas très ~** she's a bit wild 3 *(= docile) [animal, enfant]* good, well-behaved ♦ **sois ~** be good, behave yourself, be a good boy *(ou* girl) ♦ **~ comme une image** (as) good as gold ♦ **il a été très ~ chez son oncle** he was very well-behaved *ou* he behaved (himself) very well at his uncle's ♦ **est-ce que tu as été ~ ?** have you been a good boy *(ou* girl)? 4 *(= décent, modéré) [goûts]* sober, moderate; *[roman]* restrained, tame; *[prix]* moderate; *[vêtement]* sensible **NM** wise man; *(Antiq)* sage

sage-femme (pl **sages-femmes**) /saʒfam/ **NF** midwife

sagement /saʒmɑ̃/ **ADV** 1 *(= avec bon sens) [conseiller, agir]* wisely, sensibly; *[décider]* wisely 2 *(= chastement)* properly ♦ **se conduire ~** to be good, to behave o.s. (properly) 3 *(= docilement)* quietly ♦ **il est resté ~ assis sans rien dire** *[enfant]* he sat quietly *ou* he sat like a good boy and said nothing ♦ **va bien ~ te coucher** be a good boy *(ou* girl) and go to bed, off you go to bed like a good boy *(ou* girl) ♦ **des paires de chaussures ~ alignées** pairs of shoes neatly lined up 4 *(= modérément)* wisely, moderately ♦ **savoir user ~ de qch** to know how to use sth wisely *ou* in moderation *ou* moderately

sagesse /saʒɛs/ **NF** 1 *(= bon sens) [de personne]* wisdom, (good) sense; *[de conseil]* soundness; *[d'action, démarche, décision]* wisdom ♦ **faire preuve de ~** to be sensible ♦ **il a eu la ~ de ...** he had the wisdom *ou* (good) sense to ..., he was wise *ou* sensible enough to ... ♦ **dans son infinie ~, il m'a conseillé de ...** in his infinite wisdom, he advised me to ... ♦ **écouter la voix de la ~** to listen to the voice of reason ♦ **la ~ populaire/des nations** popular/traditional wisdom

2 *(euph = chasteté)* chastity

3 *(= docilité) [d'enfant]* good behaviour *(Brit) ou* behavior *(US)* ♦ **il est la ~ même** he's incredibly well-behaved ♦ **il a été d'une ~ exemplaire** he has been very good, he has behaved himself very well; → **dent**

4 *(= modération)* moderation ♦ **savoir utiliser qch avec ~** to know how to use sth wisely *ou* in moderation

Sagittaire /saʒitɛʀ/ **NM** ♦ **le ~** Sagittarius ♦ **il est ~, il est (du signe) du ~** he's (a) Sagittarius *ou* a Sagittarian

sagittal, e (mpl **-aux**) /saʒital, o/ **ADJ** sagittal

sagouin, e /sagwɛ̃, in/ **NM** 1 *(= singe)* marmoset 2 *(* = homme) (sale)* filthy pig*; filthy slob*; *(méchant)* swine*; *(incompétent)* bungling idiot* ♦ **il mange comme un ~** he eats like a pig ♦ **il travaille comme un ~** he's a very sloppy worker **NF sagouine** * *(sale)* filthy slob*; *(méchante)* bitch**, cow* *(Brit)*; *(incompétente)* bungling idiot*

Sahara /saaʀa/ **NM** ♦ **le ~** the Sahara (desert) ♦ **au ~** in the Sahara ♦ **le ~ occidental** the Western Sahara

saharien, -ienne /saaʀjɛ̃, jɛn/ **ADJ** *(= du Sahara)* Saharan; *[chaleur, climat]* desert *(épith)* ♦ **ensemble ~** *(= costume)* safari suit **NF saharienne** *(= veste)* safari jacket; *(= chemise)* safari shirt

Sahel /saɛl/ **NM** ♦ **le ~** the Sahel

sahélien, -ienne /saeljɛ̃, jɛn/ **ADJ** Sahelian **NM,F Sahélien(ne)** Sahelian

sahraoui, e /saʀawi/ **ADJ** Western Saharan **NM,F Sahraoui(e)** Western Saharan

saignant, e /sɛɲɑ̃, ɑ̃t/ **ADJ** 1 *[plaie]* bleeding; *[entrecôte]* rare ♦ **je n'aime pas la viande ~e** I don't like rare *ou* underdone meat 2 * *[commentaires, critiques]* scathing **NM** ♦ **je n'aime pas le ~** I don't like rare *ou* underdone meat

saignée /seɲe/ **NF** 1 *(Méd) (= épanchement)* bleeding *(NonC)*; *(= opération)* bloodletting *(NonC)*, bleeding *(NonC)* ♦ **faire une ~ à qn** to bleed sb, to let sb's blood 2 *[de budget]* savage cut *(à, dans* in); ♦ **les ~s que j'ai dû faire sur mon salaire/mes économies pour ...** the huge holes I had to make in my salary/my savings to ... ♦ **les ~s faites dans le pays par la guerre** the heavy losses incurred by the country in the war 3 *(Anat)* **la ~ du bras** the crook of the elbow 4 *(= sillon) [de sol]* trench, ditch; *[de mur]* groove ♦ **faire une ~ à un arbre** to make a tap-hole in a tree

saignement /sɛɲmɑ̃/ **NM** bleeding *(NonC)* ♦ **~ de nez** nosebleed

saigner /seɲe/ ► conjug 1 ◄ **VI** 1 *(lit)* to bleed ♦ **il saignait comme un bœuf*** the blood was pouring out of him ♦ **il saignait du nez** he had a nosebleed, his nose was bleeding ♦ **ça va ~ !** * *(fig)* the fur will fly!* 2 *(littér) [dignité, orgueil]* to sting ♦ **mon cœur saigne** *ou* **le cœur me saigne encore** my heart is still bleeding *(littér)* **VT** 1 *[+ animal]* to kill *(by bleeding)*; *[+ malade]* to bleed 2 *(= exploiter)* to bleed ♦ **~ qn à blanc** to bleed sb dry *ou* white ♦ **nation/ville saignée à blanc** nation/town that has been bled dry *ou* white 3 *[+ arbre]* to tap **VPR se saigner** ♦ **se ~ (aux quatre veines) pour qn** to bleed o.s. dry *ou* white for sb

Saïgon /sajgɔ̃/ **N** Saigon

saillant, e /sajɑ̃, ɑ̃t/ **ADJ** 1 *[menton, front, pommette, veine]* prominent; *[yeux, muscle]* bulging *(épith)*; *[corniche]* projecting *(épith)*; → **angle** 2 *(= frappant) [point]* salient *(frm)*, key; *[trait]* outstanding, key; *[événement]* striking ♦ **l'exemple le plus ~ est ...** the most striking example is ... 3 *(Hér)* salient **NM** *(= avancée)* salient

saillie /saji/ **NF** 1 *(= aspérité)* projection ♦ **faire ~** to project, to jut out ♦ **qui forme ~, en ~** projecting, overhanging ♦ **rocher qui s'avance en ~** rock which sticks *ou* juts out, overhang 2 *(littér = boutade)* sally, witticism 3 *(= accouplement d'animaux)* covering, servicing, serving

saillir[1] /sajiʀ/ ► conjug 13 ◄ **VI** *[balcon, corniche]* to jut out, to stick out, to project; *[menton, poitrine, pommette]* to be prominent; *[muscle, veine]* to protrude, to stand out; *[yeux]* to bulge

saillir[2] /sajiʀ/ ► conjug 2 ◄ **VI** *(littér = jaillir)* to gush forth **VT** *[+ animal]* to cover, to service, to serve

sain, saine /sɛ̃, sɛn/ **ADJ** 1 *(= en bonne santé) [personne, cellules]* healthy; *[constitution, dents]* healthy, sound ♦ **être/arriver ~ et sauf** to be/arrive safe and sound ♦ **il est sorti ~ et sauf de l'accident** he escaped unharmed *ou* unscathed from the accident ♦ **~ de corps et d'esprit** *(gén)* sound in body and mind; *(dans testament)* being of sound mind ♦ **être ~ d'esprit** to be of sound mind, to be sane; → **porteur**

2 *(= salubre, bon pour la santé) [climat, vie]* healthy; *[nourriture]* healthy, wholesome ♦ **il n'est pas ~ de si peu manger** it's not good *ou* it's not healthy to eat so little ♦ **il est ~ de rire de temps en temps** it does you good to laugh from time to time

3 *(= non abîmé) [fondations, mur]* sound; *[affaire, économie, gestion]* sound ♦ **établir qch sur des bases ~es** to establish sth on a sound basis

4 *(moralement) [personne]* sane; *[jugement, politique]* sound, sane; *[goûts, idées]* healthy; *[lectures]* wholesome ♦ **ce n'est pas ~ pour la démocratie/notre économie** it's not healthy for democracy/our economy

5 *(Naut) [côte]* safe

saindoux /sɛ̃du/ **NM** lard

sainement /sɛnmɑ̃/ **ADV** *[manger]* healthily; *[juger]* sanely; *[raisonner]* soundly ♦ **vivre ~** to lead a healthy life, to live healthily

sainfoin /sɛ̃fwɛ̃/ **NM** sainfoin

saint, sainte /sɛ̃, sɛ̃t/ **ADJ** 1 *(= sacré) [image, semaine]* holy ♦ **la ~e Bible** the Holy Bible ♦ **les Saintes Écritures** the Holy Scriptures, Holy Scripture ♦ **les ~es huiles** the holy oils ♦ **la ~e Croix/Sainte Famille** the Holy Cross/Family ♦ **les ~es femmes** the holy women ♦ **la semaine ~e** Holy Week ♦ **le mardi/ mercredi ~** Tuesday/Wednesday before Easter, the Tuesday/Wednesday of Holy Week ♦ **le jeudi ~** Maundy Thursday ♦ **le vendredi ~** Good Friday ♦ **le samedi ~** Holy *ou* Easter Saturday ♦ **s'approcher de la ~e table** to take communion; → **guerre, lieu**[1]**, semaine, terre**

2 *(devant prénom)* Saint ♦ **~ Pierre/Paul** *(apôtre)* Saint Peter/Paul ♦ **Saint-Pierre/-Paul** *(église)* Saint Peter's/Paul's ♦ **ils ont fêté la Saint-Pierre** *(fête)* they celebrated the feast of Saint Peter ♦ **le jour de la Saint-Pierre, à la Saint-Pierre** *(jour)* (on) Saint Peter's day ♦ **à la Saint-Michel/-Martin** at Michaelmas/ Martinmas; → aussi **saint-pierre**

3 *(= pieux) [pensée, personne]* saintly, godly; *[vie, action]* pious, saintly, holy ♦ **sa mère est une ~e femme** his mother is a real saint

4 *(* locutions)* **toute la ~e journée** the whole blessed day* ♦ **avoir une ~e horreur de qch** to have a holy horror of sth* ♦ **être saisi d'une ~e colère** to fly into an almighty *ou* a holy rage **NM,F** *(lit, fig)* saint ♦ **il veut se faire passer pour un (petit) ~** he wants to pass for a saint ♦ **ce n'est pas un ~** he's no saint ♦ **elle a la patience d'une ~e** she has the patience of a saint *ou* of Job ♦ **un ~ de bois/pierre** a wooden/ stone statue of a saint ♦ **la fête de tous les ~s** All Saints' Day ♦ **~ laïc** secular saint ♦ **comme on connaît ses ~s on les honore** *(Prov)* we treat people according to their merits; → **prêcher, savoir**

COMP le saint chrême the chrism, the holy oil
le Saint Empire romain germanique the Holy Roman Empire
les saints de glace the 11th, 12th and 13th of May
Saint-Jacques-de-Compostelle Santiago de Compostela
Saint Louis Saint Louis
sainte nitouche *(péj)* (pious *ou* saintly) hypocrite ♦ **c'est une ~e nitouche** she looks as if butter wouldn't melt in her mouth ♦ **de ~e nitouche** *[attitude, air]* hypocritically pious
saint patron patron saint
le saint sacrifice the Holy Sacrifice of the Mass
le Saint des Saints *(Rel)* the Holy of Holies; *(fig)* the holy of holies
le saint suaire the Holy Shroud ♦ **le ~ suaire de Turin** the Turin Shroud
la sainte Trinité the Holy Trinity
la Sainte Vierge the Blessed Virgin

Saint-Barthélemy /sɛ̃baʀtelemi/ **N** *(Géog)* Saint-Barthélemy, Saint Bartholomew, Saint Bart's **NF** ♦ **(le massacre de) la ~** the Saint Bartholomew's Day Massacre

saint-bernard (pl **saint(s)-bernard(s)**) /sɛ̃bɛʀnaʀ/ **NM** *(= chien)* St Bernard; *(hum = personne)* good Samaritan

Saint-Cyr /sɛ̃siʀ/ **N** *French military academy*

saint-cyrien (pl **saint-cyriens**) /sɛ̃siʀjɛ̃/ **NM** (military) cadet *(of the Saint-Cyr academy)*

Saint-Domingue /sɛ̃dɔmɛ̃g/ **N** Santo Domingo

Sainte-Alliance /sɛ̃taljɑ̃s/ **NF** ♦ **la ~** the Holy Alliance

Sainte-Hélène /sɛ̃telɛn/ **N** Saint Helena

Sainte-Lucie /sɛ̃tlysi/ **N** Saint Lucia

saintement /sɛ̃tmɑ̃/ **ADV** *[agir, mourir]* like a saint ♦ **vivre ~** to lead a saintly *ou* holy life, to live like a saint

Sainte-Sophie /sɛ̃tsɔfi/ **NF** Saint Sophia

Saint-Esprit /sɛ̃tɛspʀi/ NM 1 le ~ the Holy Spirit *ou* Ghost; → **opération** 2 **saint-esprit** *(= croix) type of cross bearing the emblem of the Holy Ghost, sometimes worn by French Protestant women*

sainteté /sɛ̃təte/ NF 1 *[de personne]* saintliness, godliness; *[d'Évangile, Vierge]* holiness; *[de lieu]* holiness, sanctity; *[de mariage]* sanctity; → **odeur** 2 ◆ **Sa Sainteté (le pape)** His Holiness (the Pope)

saint-frusquin † /sɛ̃fʀyskɛ̃/ NM ◆ **il est arrivé avec tout son ~** he arrived with all his gear* *ou* clobber *(Brit)** ◆ **et tout le ~** *(= et tout le reste)* and all the rest

saint-glinglin /sɛ̃glɛ̃glɛ̃/ **à la saint-glinglin** * LOC ADV ◆ **il te le rendra à la ~** he'll never give it back to you in a month of Sundays ◆ **attendre jusqu'à la ~** to wait forever ◆ **on ne va pas rester là jusqu'à la ~** we're not going to hang around here forever*

saint-honoré (pl **saint-honoré(s)**) /sɛ̃tɔnɔʀe/ NM *(Culin)* Saint Honoré (gâteau)

Saint-Jean /sɛ̃ʒɑ̃/ NF ◆ **la ~** Midsummer('s) Day ◆ **les feux de la ~** *bonfires lit to celebrate Midsummer Night*

Saint-Laurent /sɛ̃lɔʀɑ̃/ NM ◆ **le ~** the St Lawrence (river)

Saint-Marin /sɛ̃maʀɛ̃/ NM San Marino

Saint-Nicolas /sɛ̃nikɔla/ NF ◆ **la ~** St Nicholas's Day

Saint-Office /sɛ̃tɔfis/ NM ◆ **le ~** the Holy Office

Saint-Père /sɛ̃pɛʀ/ NM ◆ **le ~** the Holy Father

saint-pierre /sɛ̃pjɛʀ/ NM INV *(= poisson)* dory, John Dory

Saint-Pierre-et-Miquelon /sɛ̃pjɛʀemiklɔ̃/ N Saint Pierre and Miquelon

Saint-Sacrement /sɛ̃sakʀəmɑ̃/ NM ◆ **le ~** the Blessed Sacrament ◆ **porter qch comme le ~** † to carry sth with infinite care *ou* as if it were the Crown Jewels

Saint-Sépulcre /sɛ̃sepylkʀ/ NM ◆ **le ~** the Holy Sepulchre

Saint-Siège /sɛ̃sjɛʒ/ NM ◆ **le ~** the Holy See

saint-simonien, -ienne (mpl **saint-simoniens**) /sɛ̃simɔnjɛ̃, jɛn/ ADJ, NM,F Saint-Simonian

saint-simonisme /sɛ̃simɔnism/ NM Saint-Simonism

Saints-Innocents /sɛ̃zinɔsɑ̃/ NMPL ◆ **le jour des ~** Holy Innocents' Day

Saint-Sylvestre /sɛ̃silvɛstʀ/ NF ◆ **la ~** New Year's Eve

Saint-Synode /sɛ̃sinɔd/ NM ◆ **le ~** the Holy Synod

Saint-Valentin /sɛ̃valɑ̃tɛ̃/ NF ◆ **la ~** (Saint) Valentine's Day

Saint-Vincent-et-(les-)Grenadines /sɛ̃vɛ̃sɑ̃e(le)gʀənadin/ NPL Saint Vincent and the Grenadines

saisi, e /sezi/ (ptp de **saisir**) ADJ *(Jur)* ◆ **tiers ~** garnishee NM *(Jur)* distrainee

saisie /sezi/ NF 1 *[de biens]* seizure, distraint *(SPÉC)*, distress *(SPÉC)* ◆ **opérer une ~** to make a seizure 2 *[de documents, articles prohibés]* seizure, confiscation; *[de drogue]* seizure 3 *(= capture)* capture 4 *(Ordin)* ~ **de données** *(gén)* data capture; *(sur clavier)* keyboarding ◆ ~ **manuelle** (manual) data entry ◆ ~ **automatique** *(gén)* automatic data capture; *(au scanner)* optical reading *ou* scanning ◆ **faire de la ~ (de données)** *(gén)* to capture data; *(sur clavier)* to key(board) data

COMP **saisie conservatoire** seizure of goods *(to prevent sale etc)*
saisie immobilière seizure of property
saisie mobilière ⇒ **saisie-exécution**

saisie-arrêt (pl **saisies-arrêts**) /seziaʀɛ/ NF distraint, attachment

saisie-exécution (pl **saisies-exécutions**) /seziegzekysjɔ̃/ NF distraint *(for sale by court order)*

saisie-gagerie (pl **saisies-gageries**) /sezigaʒʀi/ NF seizure of goods *(by landlord in lieu of unpaid rent)*

saisine /sezin/ NF 1 *(Jur)* submission of a case to the court 2 *(Naut = cordage)* lashing

saisir /seziʀ/ ► conjug 2 ◄ VT 1 *(= prendre)* to take hold of, to catch hold of; *(= s'emparer de)* to seize, to grab ◆ ~ **qn à la gorge** to grab *ou* seize sb by the throat ◆ ~ **un ballon au vol** to catch a ball (in mid air) ◆ **il lui saisit le bras pour l'empêcher de sauter** he grabbed his arm to stop him jumping ◆ **ils le saisirent à bras-le-corps** they took hold of *ou* seized him bodily

2 *[+ occasion]* to seize; *[+ prétexte]* to seize (on) ◆ ~ **sa chance** to seize *ou* grab one's chance ◆ ~ **l'occasion/la chance au vol** to jump at the opportunity/the chance, to take the opportunity/the chance when it arises ◆ ~ **la balle au bond** to jump at the opportunity (while the going is good)

3 *(= entendre) [+ nom, mot]* to catch, to get; *(= comprendre) [+ explications]* to grasp, to understand, to get ◆ **il a saisi quelques noms au vol** he caught *ou* overheard a few names in passing ◆ **d'un coup d'œil, il saisit ce qui se passait** he saw what was going on at a glance ◆ **tu saisis ce que je veux dire ?** do you get it?*, do you get what I mean?

4 *[peur]* to take hold of, to seize, to grip; *[allégresse, colère]* to take hold of, to come over; *[malaise]* to come over ◆ **le froid l'a saisi** *ou* **il a été saisi par le froid en sortant** he was gripped by the cold as he went out ◆ **il a été saisi de mouvements convulsifs** he was seized with convulsions ◆ **saisi de joie** overcome with joy ◆ **saisi de peur** overcome by fear ◆ **saisi de panique/d'horreur** panic-/horror-stricken ◆ **je fus saisi de l'envie de ...** I suddenly had the urge to ...

5 *(= impressionner, surprendre)* to strike ◆ **la ressemblance entre les deux sœurs le saisit** he was struck by the resemblance between the two sisters ◆ **elle fut tellement saisie que ...** she was so surprised that ...

6 *(Jur) [+ biens]* to seize, to distrain *(SPÉC)*; *[+ documents, drogue]* to seize, to confiscate; *[+ personne]* to take into custody, to seize

7 *(Jur) [+ juridiction]* to submit *ou* refer a case to ◆ ~ **le Conseil de sécurité d'une affaire** to submit *ou* refer a matter to the Security Council ◆ ~ **la Cour de justice** to complain to the Court of Justice ◆ **la cour a été saisie de l'affaire** *ou* **du dossier** the case has been submitted *ou* referred to the court

8 *(Culin) [+ viande]* to seal, to sear

9 *(Ordin) [+ données] (gén)* to capture; *(sur clavier)* to key (in), to keyboard

VPR **se saisir** ◆ **se ~ de qch/qn** to seize sth/sb, to catch *ou* grab hold of sth/sb ◆ **le gouvernement/le Conseil de sécurité s'est saisi du dossier** the government/Security Council has taken up the issue

⚠ Attention à ne pas traduire automatiquement **saisir** par **to seize**, qui est d'un registre plus soutenu.

saisissable /sezisabl/ ADJ 1 *[nuance, sensation]* perceptible 2 *(Jur)* seizable, distrainable *(SPÉC)*

saisissant, e /sezisɑ̃, ɑt/ ADJ 1 *[spectacle]* gripping; *[contraste, ressemblance]* striking, startling; *[froid]* biting, piercing; → **raccourci** 2 *(Jur)* distraining NM *(Jur)* distrainer

saisissement /sezismɑ̃/ NM *(= émotion)* shock; *(† = frisson de froid)* sudden chill

saison /sɛzɔ̃/ NF 1 *(= division de l'année)* season ◆ **la belle/mauvaise ~** the summer/winter months ◆ **en cette ~** at this time of year ◆ **en toutes ~s** all (the) year round ◆ **il n'y a plus de ~s !** there are no seasons any more!

2 *(= époque)* season ◆ ~ **des amours/des fraises/théâtrale/touristique** mating/strawberry/theatre/tourist season ◆ **la ~ des pluies** the rainy *ou* wet season ◆ **la ~ sèche** the dry season ◆ **la ~ des moissons/des vendanges** harvest/grape-harvesting time ◆ **les nouvelles couleurs de la ~** the new season's colours ◆ **nous faisons la ~ sur la Côte d'Azur** we're working on the Côte d'Azur during the season ◆ **les hôteliers ont fait une bonne ~** hoteliers have had a good season ◆ **haute/basse ~** high *ou* peak/low *ou* off season ◆ **en (haute) ~ les prix sont plus chers** in the high season *ou* at the height of the season prices are higher ◆ **en pleine ~** at the height *ou* peak of the season; → **marchand, voiture**

3 *(= cure)* stay *(at a spa)*, cure

4 *(locutions)*

♦ **de saison** *[fruits, légumes]* seasonal ◆ **il fait un temps de ~** the weather is right *ou* what one would expect for the time of year, the weather is seasonable ◆ **faire preuve d'un optimisme de ~** to show fitting optimism ◆ **vos plaisanteries ne sont pas de ~** *(frm)* your jokes are totally out of place

♦ **hors saison** *[plante]* out of season *(attrib)*; *[prix]* off-season *(épith)*, low-season *(épith)* ◆ **prendre ses vacances hors ~** to go on holiday in the off season *ou* low season

♦ **hors de saison** *(lit)* out of season; *(frm)* *(= inopportun)* untimely, out of place

saisonnalité /sɛzɔnalite/ NF seasonality

saisonnier, -ière /sɛzɔnje, jɛʀ/ ADJ *[commerce, emploi, travailleur]* seasonal ◆ **variations saisonnières** seasonal variations *ou* fluctuations ◆ **dépression saisonnière** *(Psych)* seasonal affective disorder, SAD NM,F *(= ouvrier)* seasonal worker

saké /sake/ NM sake

salace /salas/ ADJ *(littér)* salacious

salacité /salasite/ NF *(littér)* salaciousness, salacity

salade /salad/ NF 1 *(= plante)* lettuce; *(= scarole)* escarole ◆ **la laitue est une ~** lettuce is a salad vegetable 2 *(= plat)* green salad ◆ ~ **de tomates/de fruits/russe** tomato/fruit/Russian salad ◆ ~ **niçoise** salade niçoise ◆ ~ **composée** mixed salad ◆ ~ **cuite** cooked salad greens ◆ **haricots en ~** bean salad; → **panier** 3 (* = *confusion*) tangle, muddle 4 (* = *mensonge*) **~s** stories* ◆ **raconter des ~s** to spin yarns, to tell stories* ◆ **vendre sa ~** *[représentant]* to make one's sales pitch*

saladier /saladje/ NM *(= récipient)* salad bowl; *(= contenu)* bowlful

salage /salaʒ/ NM salting

salaire /salɛʀ/ GRAMMAIRE ACTIVE 46.2 NM 1 *(mensuel, annuel)* salary; *(journalier, hebdomadaire)* wage(s), pay ◆ ~ **horaire** hourly wage ◆ **famille à ~ unique** single income family ◆ **toucher le ~ unique** *(allocation)* ≈ to get income support *(Brit)* ◆ ~ **de famine** *ou* **de misère** starvation wage ◆ ~ **minimum** minimum wage ◆ ~ **minimum agricole garanti** *guaranteed minimum agricultural wage* ◆ ~ **minimum interprofessionnel de croissance,** ~ **minimum interprofessionnel garanti** † (index-linked) guaranteed minimum wage ◆ ~ **d'embauche** starting salary ◆ ~ **de base** basic pay *ou* salary ◆ ~ **indirect** employer's contributions ◆ ~ **brut/net** gross/net *ou* take-home pay ◆ ~ **nominal/réel** nominal/real wage ◆ ~ **imposable** taxable income ◆ **les petits ~s** *(= personnes)* low-wage earners ◆ **les gros ~s** high earners; → **bulletin, échelle, peine** *etc*

2 *(= récompense)* reward *(de* for); *(= châtiment)* reward, retribution, recompense *(de* for) → **peine**

salaison /salɛzɔ̃/ NF 1 (= *procédé*) salting 2 (= *viande*) salt meat; (= *poisson*) salt fish

salaisonnerie /salɛzɔnʀi/ NF (= *secteur*) ham curing; (= *entreprise*) ham producer

salaisonnier /salɛzɔnje/ NM *person working in the cured meat industry*

salamalecs* /salamalɛk/ NMPL (*péj*) bowing and scraping ◆ **faire des** ~ to bow and scrape

salamandre /salamɑ̃dʀ/ NF 1 (= *animal*) salamander 2 (= *poêle*) slow-combustion stove

salami /salami/ NM salami

Salamine /salamin/ N Salamis

salant /salɑ̃/ ADJ M, NM ◆ **(marais)** ~ (*gén*) salt marsh; (*exploité*) saltern

salarial, e (mpl **-iaux**) /salaʀjal, jo/ ADJ 1 (= *des salaires*) [*accord, politique, exigences, revendications*] wage (*épith*), pay (*épith*) 2 (= *des salariés*) **cotisations ~es** employee contributions ◆ **charges ~es** payroll *ou* wage costs; → **masse**

salariat /salaʀja/ NM 1 (= *salariés*) wage-earners ◆ **le ~ et le patronat** employees and employers 2 (= *rémunération*) (*au mois*) payment by salary; (*au jour, à la semaine*) payment by wages 3 (= *état*) (being in) employment ◆ **être réduit au ~ après avoir été patron** to be reduced to the ranks of the employees *ou* of the salaried staff after having been in a senior position

salarié, e /salaʀje/ ADJ [*travailleur*] (*au mois*) salaried (*épith*); (*à la journée, à la semaine*) wage-earning; [*travail, emploi*] paid ◆ **elle est ~e** she gets a salary, she's on the payroll ◆ **travailleur non ~** non-salaried worker NM,F (*payé au mois*) salaried employee; (*payé au jour, à la semaine*) wage-earner ◆ **le statut de ~** employee status ◆ **notre entreprise compte 55 ~s** our company has 55 employees on the payroll *ou* has a payroll of 55 employees

salarier /salaʀje/ ▸ conjug 7 ◂ VT to put on a salary ◆ **il préférerait se faire ~** he would prefer to have a salaried job *ou* to be put on a salary ◆ **la direction a salarié cinq personnes** management have put five people on the company payroll

salaud‡ /salo/ NM bastard*‡, swine‡ ◆ **quel beau ~ !** what an absolute bastard!*‡ ◆ **alors mon ~, tu ne t'en fais pas !** well you old bugger*‡, you're not exactly overdoing it! ◆ **1 500 € ? ben, mon ~ !** €1,500? I'll be damned* ◆ **tous des ~s !** they're all bastards!*‡ ADJ ◆ **tu es ~** you're an absolute bastard*‡ *ou* swine‡ ◆ **il a été ~ avec elle** he was a real bastard to her*‡ ◆ **il n'a pas été ~ avec toi** he's been nice to you ◆ **c'est ~ d'avoir fait ça** that was a shitty‡ thing to do ◆ **sois pas ~ !** don't be so mean!

salazarisme /salazaʀism/ NM Salazarism

sale /sal/ ADJ 1 (= *crasseux*) dirty ◆ **~ comme un cochon** *ou* **un porc** *ou* **un peigne** filthy (dirty) ◆ **oh la ~ !** you dirty girl! ◆ **c'est pas ~ !*** it's not bad!* ◆ **l'argent ~** dirty money; → **laver**

2 (= *ordurier*) [*histoire*] dirty, filthy

3 (* : *avant n* = *mauvais*) [*affaire, maladie, habitude*] nasty; [*guerre*] dirty ◆ **~ coup** (= *mauvais tour*) dirty trick; (= *choc*) terrible *ou* dreadful blow ◆ **faire un ~ coup à qn** to play a (dirty) trick on sb ◆ **c'est un ~ coup pour l'entreprise** it's bad news for the company, it's dealt a heavy blow to the company ◆ **(c'est un) ~ coup pour la fanfare** it's a real blow ◆ **~ tour** dirty trick ◆ **~ temps** filthy* *ou* foul *ou* lousy* weather ◆ **~ temps pour les petites entreprises** bad days *ou* hard times for small businesses ◆ **~ démago**‡ bloody‡ (*Brit*) *ou* goddamn* (*US*) demagogue ◆ **avoir une ~ tête*** (= *sembler malade*) to look awful, to look like death warmed up* (*Brit*) *ou* over* (*US*); (= *faire peur*) to look evil ◆ **faire une ~ tête** (= *être mécontent*) to have a face like thunder ◆ **il a fait une ~ tête** (= *il était dépité*) his face fell ◆ **il m'est arrivé une ~ histoire** something awful happened to me ◆ **faire le ~ travail** *ou* **boulot*** to do the dirty work; → **besogne, délit**

NM ◆ **mettre qch au ~** to put sth in the wash ◆ **aller/être au ~** to go/be in the wash

salé, e /sale/ (ptp de **saler**) ADJ 1 (= *contenant du sel*) [*mer, saveur*] salty; (= *additionné de sel*) [*amande, plat*] salted; [*gâteau*] (= *non sucré*) savoury (*Brit*), savory (*US*); (= *au goût salé*) salty; (= *conservé au sel*) [*poisson, viande*] salt (*épith*); [*beurre*] salted ◆ **ce serait meilleur plus ~** it would be better if it had more salt in; → **eau** 2 (* = *grivois*) spicy, juicy, fruity* ◆ **plaisanterie ~e** dirty joke 3 (* = *sévère*) [*punition*] stiff; [*facture*] steep ◆ **la note s'annonce ~e** the bill is going to be a bit steep NM (= *nourriture*) ◆ **le ~** (*gén*) salty foods; (*par opposition à sucré*) savoury (*Brit*) *ou* savory (*US*) foods ◆ **petit ~** (= *porc*) salt pork ADV ◆ **manger ~** to like a lot of salt on one's food, to like one's food well salted ◆ **il ne peut pas manger trop ~** he can't have his food too salty

salement /salmɑ̃/ ADV 1 (= *malproprement, bassement*) dirtily 2 (‡ = *très, beaucoup*) [*dur, embêtant*] damned‡, bloody‡ (*Brit*) ◆ **j'ai ~ mal** it's damned *ou* bloody (*Brit*) painful‡, it hurts like mad* ◆ **j'ai eu ~ peur** I had a *ou* one hell of a fright‡, I was damned *ou* bloody (*Brit*) scared‡

saler /sale/ ▸ conjug 1 ◂ VT 1 [+ *plat, soupe*] to put salt in, to salt; (*pour conserver*) to salt; [+ *chaussée*] to salt ◆ **tu ne sales pas assez** you don't put enough salt in, you don't use enough salt 2 * [+ *client*] to do*, to fleece; [+ *facture*] to bump up*; [+ *inculpé*] to be tough on*

saleté /salte/ NF 1 (= *malpropreté*) [*de lieu, personne*] dirtiness ◆ **il est/c'est d'une ~ incroyable** he's/it's absolutely filthy

2 (= *crasse*) dirt, filth ◆ **murs couverts de ~** walls covered in dirt *ou* filth ◆ **vivre dans la ~** to live in filth *ou* squalor ◆ **le chauffage au charbon fait de la ~** coal heating makes a lot of mess *ou* dirt

3 (= *ordure, impureté*) dirt (NonC) ◆ **il y a une ~ par terre/sur ta robe** there's some dirt on the floor/on your dress ◆ **j'ai une ~ dans l'œil** I've got some dirt in my eye ◆ **tu as fait des ~s partout en perçant le mur** you've made a mess all over the place drilling the wall ◆ **enlève tes ~s de ma chambre** get your junk* *ou* rubbish (*Brit*) *ou* trash (*US*) out of my room ◆ **le chat a fait des ~s** *ou* **ses ~s dans le salon** the cat has made a mess in the lounge

4 (* = *chose sans valeur*) piece of junk* ◆ **ce réfrigérateur est une ~** *ou* **de la vraie ~** this fridge is a piece of junk* ◆ **c'est une ~ qu'ils ont achetée hier** it's some (old) junk* *ou* rubbish (*Brit*) *ou* trash* (*US*) they bought yesterday ◆ **chez eux, il n'y a que des ~s** their place is full of junk* *ou* trash (*US*) ◆ **il se bourre de ~s avant le repas** he stuffs himself* with junk food before meals

5 (* = *maladie*) **je me demande où j'ai bien pu attraper cette ~-là** I wonder where on earth I could have caught this blasted thing* ◆ **je récolte toutes les ~s qui traînent** I catch every blasted thing going*

6 (* = *obscénité*) dirty *ou* filthy thing (to say)* ◆ **dire des ~s** to say filthy things*, to talk dirty*

7 (* = *méchanceté*) dirty trick ◆ **faire une ~ à qn** to play a dirty trick on sb ◆ **on en a vu des ~s pendant la guerre** we saw plenty of disgusting things during the war

8 (* = *personne méprisable*) nasty piece of work*, nasty character

9 (* : *intensif*) ◆ **~ de virus !** this blasted virus! ◆ **~ de guerre !** what a damned‡ *ou* bloody‡ (*Brit*) awful war!

salicorne /salikɔʀn/ NF samphire

salicylate /salisilat/ NM salicylate

salicylique /salisilik/ ADJ ◆ **acide ~** salicylic acid

salière /saljɛʀ/ NF 1 (= *récipient*) saltcellar; (*à trous*) saltcellar (*Brit*), salt shaker (*US*) 2 [*de clavicule*] saltcellar

salification /salifikasjɔ̃/ NF salification

salifier /salifje/ ▸ conjug 7 ◂ VT to salify

saligaud‡ /saligo/ NM (= *malpropre*) dirty *ou* filthy pig‡; (= *salaud*) swine‡, bastard*‡

salin, e /salɛ̃, in/ ADJ saline NM salt marsh NF(PL) **saline(s)** (= *entreprise*) saltworks; (= *salin*) salt marsh

salinité /salinite/ NF salinity

salique /salik/ ADJ Salic, Salian ◆ **loi ~** Salic law

salir /saliʀ/ ▸ conjug 2 ◂ VT 1 [+ *lieu*] to make dirty, to mess up*, to make a mess in; [+ *objet*] to make dirty ◆ **le charbon salit** coal is messy *ou* dirty 2 [+ *imagination*] to corrupt, to defile; [+ *réputation*] to sully, to soil, to tarnish ◆ **~ qn** to tarnish *ou* sully sb's reputation ◆ **il a été sali par ces rumeurs** his reputation has been tarnished by these rumours VPR **se salir** 1 [*tissu*] to get dirty *ou* soiled; [*personne*] to get dirty ◆ **le blanc se salit facilement** white shows the dirt (easily), white soils easily ◆ **se ~ les mains** (*lit, fig*) to get one's hands dirty, to dirty one's hands 2 (= *se déshonorer*) to sully *ou* soil *ou* tarnish one's reputation

salissant, e /salisɑ̃, ɑ̃t/ ADJ [*étoffe*] which shows the dirt, which soils easily; [*travail*] dirty, messy ◆ **ce tissu est très ~** this material really shows the dirt

salissure /salisyʀ/ NF (= *saleté*) dirt, filth; (= *tache*) dirty mark

salivaire /salivɛʀ/ ADJ salivary

salivation /salivasjɔ̃/ NF salivation

salive /saliv/ NF saliva, spittle ◆ **avaler sa ~** to gulp ◆ **épargne** *ou* **ne gaspille pas ta ~** save your breath, don't waste your breath ◆ **dépenser** *ou* **user beaucoup de ~ pour convaincre qn** to have to do a lot of talking *ou* use a lot of breath to persuade sb

saliver /salive/ ▸ conjug 1 ◂ VI to salivate; [*animal*] (*péj*) to drool ◆ **ça le faisait ~** [*nourriture*] it made his mouth water; [*spectacle*] it made him drool

salle /sal/ NF 1 [*de café, musée*] room; [*de château*] hall; [*de restaurant*] (dining) room; [*d'hôpital*] ward ◆ **en ~** (*Sport*) [*record, athlétisme*] indoor; → **fille, garçon**

2 (*Ciné, Théât*) (= *auditorium*) auditorium, theatre (*Brit*), theater (*US*); (= *cinéma*) cinema (*Brit*), movie theater (*US*); (= *public*) audience ◆ **plusieurs ~s de quartier ont dû fermer** several local cinemas had to close down ◆ **faire ~ comble** *ou* **pleine** [*comédien*] to play to a packed *ou* full house, to have a full house; [*spectacle*] to play to a packed *ou* full house ◆ **cinéma à plusieurs ~s** cinema with several screens ◆ **film projeté dans la ~ 3** film showing on screen 3 ◆ **le film sort en ~** *ou* **dans les ~s mercredi prochain** the film will be in cinemas *ou* on general release next Wednesday ◆ **sortie en ~** [*de film*] cinema release

COMP **salle d'arcade** video *ou* amusement (*Brit*) arcade
salle d'armes arms room
salle d'attente waiting room
salle d'audience courtroom
salle de bain(s) bathroom
salle de bal ballroom
salle de banquets [*de château*] banqueting hall
salle basse lower hall
salle de billard billiard room
salle blanche clean room

salle du chapitre *(Rel)* chapter room
salle de cinéma cinema *(Brit)*, movie theater *(US)*
salle de classe classroom
salle des coffres strongroom, vault
salle commune *[de colonie de vacances]* commonroom; *[d'hôpital]* ward
salle de concert concert hall
salle de conférences lecture *ou* conference room; *(grande)* lecture hall *ou* theatre
salle de cours classroom
salle de douches shower-room, showers
salle d'eau shower-room
salle d'embarquement *[d'aéroport]* departure lounge
salle d'étude(s) prep room
salle d'exposition *(Comm)* showroom
salle des fêtes village hall
salle de garde staff waiting room *(in hospital)*
salle des gardes *[de château]* guardroom
salle de jeu *(pour enfants)* playroom, rumpus room *(US)*; *[de casino]* gaming room
salle de lecture reading room
salle des machines engine room
salle à manger *(= pièce)* dining room; *(= meubles)* dining-room suite
salle de montage cutting room
salle de musculation weights room
les salles obscures cinemas *(Brit)*, movie theaters *(US)*
salle d'opération operating theatre *(Brit) ou* room *(US)*
salle des pas perdus (waiting) hall
salle de permanence ⇒ **salle d'étude(s)**
salle de police guardhouse, guardroom
salle des professeurs common room, staff room
salle de projection film theatre
salle de réanimation recovery room
salle de rédaction (newspaper) office
salle de réunion meeting room
salle de réveil observation ward
salle de séjour living room
salle de soins treatment room
salle de spectacle *(= cinéma)* cinema, movie theater *(US)*; *(= théâtre)* theatre *(Brit)*, theater *(US)*
salle de sport gym
salle de travail *[d'hôpital]* labour room
salle du trône throne room
salle des ventes saleroom, auction room

salmigondis /salmigɔ̃di/ **NM** *(Culin, fig)* hotchpotch *(Brit)*, hodgepodge *(US)*

salmis /salmi/ **NM** salmi *(rich stew)*

salmonella /salmɔnela/, **salmonelle** /salmɔnɛl/ **NF** salmonella

salmonellose /salmɔneloz/ **NF** salmonellosis

salmoniculture /salmɔnikyltyʀ/ **NF** salmon farming

saloir /salwaʀ/ **NM** salting-tub

Salomé /salɔme/ **NF** Salome

Salomon /salɔmɔ̃/ **NM** Solomon ◆ **le jugement de** ~ the judgment of Solomon ◆ **les îles** ~ the Solomon Islands

salon /salɔ̃/ **NM** 1 *[de maison]* sitting *ou* living room, lounge *(Brit)*; *[de navire]* saloon, lounge ◆ **coin** ~ living area
2 *[d'hôtel] (pour les clients)* lounge; *(pour conférences, réceptions)* function room
3 *(= meubles)* living-room suite; *(= canapé et deux fauteuils)* three-piece suite ◆ ~ **de jardin** set of garden furniture
4 *(= exposition)* exhibition, show
5 *(= cercle littéraire)* salon ◆ **tenir** ~ *(Littérat)* to hold a salon ◆ **faire** *ou* **tenir** ~ *(hum)* to have a natter* ◆ **c'est le dernier** ~ **où l'on cause !** *(péj hum)* what a lot of chatterboxes (you are)!*
COMP **Salon des Arts ménagers** *home improvements exhibition*, ≃ Ideal Home Exhibition *(Brit)*
salon d'attente waiting room
le Salon de l'Auto the Motor *ou* Car Show
salon de beauté beauty salon *ou* parlour *(Brit) ou* parlor *(US)*
salon de coiffure hairdressing salon
salon d'essayage fitting room
salon funéraire *(Can)* funeral home, funeral parlour *(Brit) ou* parlor *(US)*
le Salon du Livre the Book Fair
salon particulier private room
salon professionnel trade fair *ou* show
salon de réception *[de maison]* reception room; *[d'hôtel]* function room
salon-salle à manger living-cum-dining room *(Brit)*, living room-dining room *(US)*
salon de thé tearoom

saloon /salun/ **NM** *(Far-West)* saloon

salop* /salo/ **NM** ⇒ **salaud**

salopard* /salɔpaʀ/ **NM** bastard**, swine*

salope** /salɔp/ **NF** *(= déloyale, méchante)* bitch**, cow* *(Brit)*; *(= dévergondée, sale)* slut*

saloper* /salɔpe/ ▸ conjug 1 ◂ **VT** *(= bâcler)* to botch, to bungle, to make a mess of; *(= salir)* to mess up*, to muck up*

saloperie* /salɔpʀi/ **NF** 1 *(= chose sans valeur)* piece of junk* ◆ **cette radio est une** ~ *ou* **de la vraie** ~ this radio is a piece of junk* *ou* is absolute crap** ◆ **ils n'achètent que des ~s** they only buy junk* *ou* crap** ◆ **le grenier est plein de ~s** the attic is full of junk *ou* rubbish* *(Brit)*
2 *(= mauvaise nourriture)* muck* *(NonC)*, rubbish* *(NonC) (Brit)* ◆ **ils nous ont fait manger de la** ~ *ou* **des ~s** they gave us some awful muck *ou* rubbish *(Brit)* to eat* ◆ **c'est bon, ces petites ~s** these little things are really good ◆ **il se bourre de ~s avant le repas** he stuffs himself* with junk food before meals
3 *(= maladie)* **il a dû attraper une** ~ he must have caught some blasted bug* ◆ **il récolte toutes les ~s** he gets every blasted thing going*
4 *(= ordure)* dirt *(NonC)*, mess *(NonC)*, muck* *(NonC)* ◆ **quand on ramone la cheminée, ça fait des ~s** *ou* **de la** ~ **partout** when the chimney's swept the dirt gets everywhere ◆ **va faire tes ~s ailleurs** go and make your mess somewhere else
5 *(= action)* dirty trick; *(= parole)* bitchy remark* ◆ **faire une** ~ **à qn** to play a dirty *ou* a lousy* trick on sb, to do the dirty on sb*
6 *(= obscénités)* **~s** dirty *ou* filthy remarks ◆ **dire des ~s** to talk dirty*
7 *(= crasse)* filth

salopette /salɔpɛt/ **NF** dungarees; *[d'ouvrier]* overall(s); *(Ski)* ski pants, salopettes *(Brit)*

salpêtre /salpɛtʀ/ **NM** saltpetre *(Brit)*, saltpeter *(US)*

salpêtrer /salpetʀe/ ▸ conjug 1 ◂ **VT** 1 *(Agr) [+ terre]* to add saltpetre *(Brit) ou* saltpeter *(US)* to 2 *[+ mur]* to cover with saltpetre *(Brit) ou* saltpeter *(US)* ◆ **cave salpêtrée** cellar covered with saltpetre

salpingite /salpɛ̃ʒit/ **NF** salpingitis

salsa /salsa/ **NF** salsa ◆ **danser la** ~ to dance *ou* do the salsa

salsifis /salsifi/ **NM** *(= plante)* salsify, oysterplant

SALT /salt/ (abrév de **Strategic Arms Limitation Talks**) SALT

saltimbanque /saltɛ̃bɑ̃k/ **NMF** *(= acrobate)* acrobat; *(= forain)* (travelling) performer; *(= professionnel du spectacle)* entertainer

salto /salto/ **NM** *(Sport)* somersault, flip ◆ ~ **avant/arrière** forward/backward somersault ◆ **double** ~ double somersault *ou* flip

salubre /salybʀ/ **ADJ** *[air, climat]* healthy, salubrious *(frm)*; *[logement]* salubrious *(frm)*

salubrité /salybʀite/ **NF** *[de lieu, climat]* healthiness, salubrity *(frm)*, salubriousness *(frm)* ◆ **par mesure de** ~ as a health measure ◆ ~ **publique** public health

saluer /salɥe/ ▸ conjug 1 ◂ **VT** 1 *(= dire bonjour à)* to greet ◆ **se découvrir/s'incliner pour** ~ **qn** to raise one's hat/bow to sb (in greeting) ◆ ~ **qn** to wave to sb (in greeting) ◆ ~ **qn d'un signe de tête** to nod (a greeting) to sb ◆ ~ **qn à son arrivée** to greet sb on their arrival ◆ **saluez-le de ma part** give him my regards
2 *(= dire au revoir à)* to say goodbye to, to take one's leave of ◆ **il nous salua et sortit** he said goodbye *ou* took his leave and went out ◆ **il salua (le public)** he bowed (to the audience)
3 *(Mil, Naut) [+ supérieur, drapeau, navire]* to salute
4 *(= témoigner son respect pour) [+ ennemi vaincu, courage, héroïsme]* to salute ◆ ~ **la mémoire/les efforts de qn** to pay tribute to sb's memory/efforts ◆ **nous saluons en vous l'homme qui a sauvé tant de vies** we salute you as the man who has saved so many lives
5 *(= accueillir) [+ initiative]* to welcome; *(= acclamer)* to hail ◆ **"je vous salue, Marie"** *(Rel)* "Hail, Mary" ◆ ~ **qch comme un succès/une victoire** to hail sth as a success/a victory ◆ **l'événement a été salué comme historique** it was hailed as an historic event ◆ **cette déclaration a été saluée par une ovation** this announcement was greeted with thunderous applause ◆ **elle/son arrivée fut saluée par des huées** *(hum)* she/her arrival was greeted with *ou* by booing

⚠ Au sens de 'dire bonjour *ou* au revoir à', **saluer** ne se traduit généralement pas par **to salute**.

salut /saly/ **NM** 1 *(de la main)* wave (of the hand); *(de la tête)* nod (of the head); *(du buste)* bow; *(Mil, Naut)* salute ◆ **faire un** ~ *(de la main)* to wave (one's hand); *(de la tête)* to nod (one's head); *(du buste)* to bow ◆ **faire le** ~ **militaire** to give the military salute ◆ ~ **au drapeau** salute to the colours
2 *(= sauvegarde) [de personne]* (personal) safety; *[de nation]* safety ◆ **trouver/chercher son** ~ **dans la fuite** to find/seek safety *ou* refuge in flight ◆ **elle n'a dû son** ~ **qu'à son courage** only her courage saved her ◆ **mesures de** ~ **public** state security measures, measures to protect national security ◆ **ancre** *ou* **planche de** ~ sheet anchor *(fig)*
3 *(Rel = rédemption)* salvation; → **armée², hors**
EXCL 1 * *(= bonjour)* hello!, hi!*; *(= au revoir)* see you!*, bye!*, cheerio!* *(Brit)* ◆ ~, **les gars !** hi guys!* ◆ ~ **!** *(= rien à faire)* no thanks!
2 *(littér)* (all) hail ◆ ~ **(à toi) puissant seigneur !** (all) hail (to thee) mighty lord! ◆ ~, **forêt de mon enfance !** hail (to thee), o forest of my childhood!

salutaire /salytɛʀ/ **ADJ** 1 *[conseil]* salutary *(épith)*, profitable *(épith)*; *[choc, épreuve]* salutary *(épith)*; *[influence]* healthy *(épith)*, salutary *(épith)*; *[dégoût]* healthy *(épith)* ◆ **cette déception lui a été** ~ that disappointment was good for him *ou* did him some good ◆ **l'autodérision est un exercice** ~ it is good to be able to laugh at oneself 2 *[air]* healthy, salubrious *(frm)*; *[remède]* beneficial ◆ **ce petit repos m'a été** ~ that little rest did me good *ou* was good for me

salutation /salytasjɔ̃/ **NF** greeting ◆ **après les ~s d'usage** after the usual greetings ◆ **meilleures ~s** *(pour clore une lettre)* kind regards

salutiste /salytist/ **ADJ, NMF** Salvationist

Salvador /salvadɔʀ/ **NM** ◆ **le** ~ El Salvador ◆ **au** ~ in El Salvador

salvadorien, -ienne /salvadɔʀjɛ̃, jɛn/ **ADJ** Salvadorian, Salvadorean, Salvadoran **NM,F** **Sal-**

vadorien(ne) Salvadorian, Salvadorean, Salvadoran

salvateur, -trice /salvatœʀ, tʀis/ ADJ *(littér)* *[eau]* life-saving; *[effet]* salutary ◆ **jouer un rôle** ~ to be a life-saver

salve /salv/ NF *[d'artillerie, roquettes]* salvo ◆ **une ~ de 21 coups de canon** a 21-gun salute ◆ **tirer une ~ d'honneur** to fire a salute ◆ **une ~ d'applaudissements** a burst *ou* round of applause ◆ **une ~ de critiques/d'injures** a volley of criticism/of abuse

Salzbourg /salzbuʀ/ N Salzburg

Samarie /samaʀi/ NF Samaria

samaritain, e /samaʀitɛ̃, ɛn/ ADJ Samaritan NM,F **Samaritain(e)** Samaritan ◆ **les Samaritains** the Samaritans ◆ **bon Samaritain** *(Bible)* good Samaritan ◆ **jouer les bons Samaritains** to play the good Samaritan

samba /sɑ̃(m)ba/ NF samba

samedi /samdi/ NM Saturday ◆ **nous irons** ~ we'll go on Saturday ◆ ~ **nous sommes allés ...** on Saturday *ou* last Saturday we went ... ◆ **pas ~ qui vient mais l'autre** not this (coming) Saturday but the next *ou* but the one after that ◆ **ce ~(-ci), ~ qui vient** this (coming) Saturday ◆ **un ~ sur deux** every other *ou* second Saturday ◆ **nous sommes ~ (aujourd'hui)** it's Saturday (today) ◆ **le ~ 18 décembre** Saturday the 18th of December; *(à l'écrit)* Saturday 18 December ◆ **la réunion aura lieu le ~ 23 janvier** the meeting will take place on Saturday 23 January ◆ ~ **matin/après-midi** (on) Saturday morning/afternoon ◆ ~ **soir** (on) Saturday evening *ou* night ◆ **la nuit de** ~ Saturday night ◆ **dans la nuit de ~ à dimanche** on Saturday night ◆ **l'édition de ~ ou du ~** the Saturday edition; → **huit**

samit /sami/ NM samite

Samoa /samɔa/ NM ◆ **les îles** ~ Samoa, the Samoa Islands ◆ **les ~-occidentales/-américaines** Western/American Samoa

samoan, e /samɔɑ̃, an/ ADJ Samoan NM,F **Samoan(e)** Samoan

samosa /samosa/ NM samosa

samouraï /samuʀaj/ NM samurai

samovar /samɔvaʀ/ NM samovar

sampan(g) /sɑ̃pɑ̃/ NM sampan

sampling /sɑ̃pliŋ/ NM *(Mus)* sampling

Samson /sɑ̃sɔ̃/ NM Samson ◆ ~ **et Dalila** Samson and Delilah

SAMU /samy/ NM (abrév de **Service d'assistance médicale d'urgence**) ◆ ~ **social** *mobile emergency medical service for homeless people;* → **service**

samuraï /samuʀaj/ NM ⇒ **samouraï**

sana * /sana/ NM abrév de **sanatorium**

Sanaa /sanaa/ N San'a, Sanaa

sanatorium /sanatɔʀjɔm/ NM sanatorium, sanitarium *(US)*

sancerre /sɑ̃sɛʀ/ NM Sancerre *(type of wine from the Loire valley)*

Sancho Pança /sɑ̃ʃopɑ̃sa/ NM Sancho Panza

sanctification /sɑ̃ktifikasjɔ̃/ NF sanctification

sanctifié, e /sɑ̃ktifje/ (ptp de **sanctifier**) ADJ blessed

sanctifier /sɑ̃ktifje/ ▸ conjug 7 ◂ VT to sanctify, to hallow, to bless ◆ ~ **le jour du Seigneur** to observe the Sabbath ◆ **"que ton nom soit sanctifié"** *(Rel)* "hallowed be Thy name"

sanction /sɑ̃ksjɔ̃/ NF 1 *(= condamnation)* *(Jur)* sanction, penalty; *(Écon, Pol)* sanction; *(Scol)* punishment; *(= conséquence)* penalty *(de* for); ◆ ~ **administrative/disciplinaire** administrative/disciplinary action *(NonC)* ◆ ~ **pénale** penalty ◆ **~s commerciales/économiques** trade/economic sanctions ◆ **prendre des ~s** *(Écon, Pol)* to impose sanctions *(contre, à l'encontre de* on); ◆ **prendre des ~s contre un joueur/club/ministre** to take disciplinary action against a player/club/minister ◆ **prendre des ~s contre un élève** to punish *ou* discipline a pupil ◆ **la ~ électorale a été sévère** the electorate's rejection was complete

2 *(= ratification)* sanction *(NonC)*, approval *(NonC)* ◆ **recevoir la ~ de qn** to obtain sb's sanction *ou* approval ◆ **c'est la ~ du progrès** *(= conséquence)* it's the price of progress ◆ **ce mot a reçu la ~ de l'usage** this word has been sanctioned by use

sanctionner /sɑ̃ksjɔne/ ▸ conjug 1 ◂ VT 1 *(= punir)* to penalize; *(mesures disciplinaires)* to take disciplinary action against; *(sanctions économiques)* to impose sanctions on ◆ **tout manquement à ce principe sera sévèrement sanctionné** any party found in breach of this principle will be heavily penalized ◆ **les électeurs ont sanctionné la politique du précédent gouvernement** the electorate rejected the policy of the previous government 2 *(= consacrer, ratifier)* to sanction, to approve; *[+ loi]* to sanction ◆ **ce diplôme sanctionne les études secondaires** this diploma marks the successful conclusion of secondary education

> ⚠ Attention à ne pas traduire automatiquement **sanctionner** par **to sanction**, qui a le sens de 'approuver'.

sanctuaire /sɑ̃ktɥɛʀ/ NM 1 *(Rel = lieu saint)* sanctuary, shrine; *[de temple, église]* sanctuary 2 *(littér)* sanctuary 3 *(Pol)* sanctuary

sanctus /sɑ̃ktys/ NM Sanctus

sandale /sɑ̃dal/ NF sandal

sandalette /sɑ̃dalɛt/ NF (light) sandal

sandiniste /sɑ̃dinist/ ADJ, NMF Sandinist(a)

sandow ® /sɑ̃do/ NM *(= attache)* luggage elastic; *(pour planeur)* catapult

sandre /sɑ̃dʀ/ NM pikeperch, zander

sandwich (pl **sandwiches** *ou* **sandwichs**) /sɑ̃dwi(t)ʃ/ NM sandwich ◆ ~ **au jambon** ham sandwich ◆ **(pris) en ~ (entre)** * sandwiched (between) ◆ **les deux voitures l'ont pris en ~** * he was sandwiched between the two cars

sandwicherie /sɑ̃dwi(t)ʃəʀi/ NF sandwich shop *ou* bar

San Francisco /sɑ̃ fʀɑ̃sisko/ N San Francisco

sang /sɑ̃/ NM 1 *(lit, fig)* blood ◆ ~ **artériel/veineux** arterial/venous blood ◆ ~ **contaminé** infected *ou* contaminated blood ◆ **animal à ~ froid/chaud** cold-/warmblooded animal ◆ **le ~ a coulé** blood has flowed ◆ **verser** *ou* **faire couler le** ~ to shed *ou* spill blood ◆ **cela finira dans le** ~ blood will be shed ◆ **il va y avoir du ~ !** * *(fig)* the fur will fly! * ◆ **avoir du ~ sur les mains** *(fig)* to have blood on one's hands ◆ **son ~ crie vengeance** his blood cries (for) vengeance ◆ **il était en** ~ he was covered in *ou* with blood ◆ **pincer qn (jusqu')au** ~ to pinch sb till he bleeds *ou* till the blood comes ◆ **mordre qn jusqu'au** ~ to bite sb and draw blood ◆ **payer son crime de son** ~ to pay for one's crime with one's life ◆ **donner son ~ pour un malade** to give *ou* donate one's blood for somebody who is ill ◆ **donner son ~ pour sa patrie** to shed one's blood for one's country; → **donneur, feu¹, noyer², pinte**

2 *(= race, famille)* blood ◆ **de ~ royal** of royal blood ◆ **avoir du ~ bleu** to have blue blood, to be blue-blooded ◆ **du même** ~ of the same flesh and blood ◆ **liens du** ~ blood ties, ties of blood; → **prince, voix**

3 *(locutions)* **avoir le ~ chaud** *(= s'emporter facilement)* to be hotheaded; *(= être sensuel)* to be hot-blooded ◆ **un apport de ~ neuf** an injection of new *ou* fresh blood *(dans* into); ◆ **se faire un ~ d'encre** to be worried sick *ou* stiff * ◆ **se faire du mauvais** ~ to worry, to get in a state ◆ **avoir du ~ dans les veines** to have courage *ou* guts * ◆ **il n'a pas de ~ dans les veines, il a du ~ de navet** *ou* **de poulet** *(manque de courage)* he's a spineless individual, he's got no guts *; *(manque d'énergie)* he's very lethargic ◆ **il a le jeu/le jazz dans le** ~ he's got gambling/jazz in his blood ◆ **le ~ lui monta au visage** the blood rushed to his face ◆ **bon ~ !** ‡ dammit! ‡ ◆ **coup de** ~ *(Méd)* stroke ◆ **attraper un coup de** ~ *(fig = colère)* to fly into a rage ◆ **mon ~ n'a fait qu'un tour** *(émotion, peur)* my heart missed *ou* skipped a beat; *(colère, indignation)* I saw red ◆ **se ronger** *ou* **se manger les ~s** to worry (o.s.), to fret ◆ **se ronger les ~s pour savoir comment faire qch** to agonize over how to do sth ◆ **tourner les ~s à qn** to shake sb up ◆ **histoire à glacer le** ~ bloodcurdling story ◆ **son ~ se glaça dans ses veines** his blood froze *ou* ran cold in his veins; → **suer**

sang-froid /sɑ̃fʀwa/ NM INV calm, cool *, sangfroid *(frm)* ◆ **garder/perdre son** ~ to keep/lose one's head *ou* one's cool * ◆ **faire qch de** ~ to do sth in cold blood *ou* cold-bloodedly ◆ **répondre avec** ~ to reply coolly *ou* calmly ◆ **crime commis de** ~ cold-blooded murder

sanglant, e /sɑ̃glɑ̃, ɑt/ ADJ 1 *[couteau, plaie]* bloody; *[bandage, habits]* blood-soaked, bloody; *[mains, visage]* covered in blood, bloody 2 *[répression, affrontement, attentat, dictature, guerre]* bloody 3 *(fig)* *[insulte, reproche, défaite]* cruel ◆ **ils se sont disputés, ça a été ~ !** they really laid into each other! 4 *(littér = couleur)* blood-red

sangle /sɑ̃gl/ NF *(gén)* strap; *[de selle]* girth ◆ **~s** *[de siège]* webbing ◆ ~ **d'ouverture automatique** *[de parachute]* ripcord ◆ ~ **abdominale** *(Anat)* abdominal muscles; → **lit**

sangler /sɑ̃gle/ ▸ conjug 1 ◂ VT *[+ cheval]* to girth; *[+ colis, corps]* to strap up ◆ **sanglé dans son uniforme** done up *ou* strapped up tight in one's uniform VPR **se sangler** to do one's belt up tight

sanglier /sɑ̃glije/ NM (wild) boar

sanglot /sɑ̃glo/ NM sob ◆ **avec des ~s dans la voix** in a voice choked with emotion ◆ **elle répondit dans un ~ que ...** she answered with a sob that ... ◆ **elle essayait de me parler entre deux ~s** she tried to speak to me between sobs; → **éclater**

sangloter /sɑ̃glɔte/ ▸ conjug 1 ◂ VI to sob

sang-mêlé /sɑ̃mele/ NMF INV *person of mixed blood*

sangria /sɑ̃gʀija/ NF sangria

sangsue /sɑ̃sy/ NF *(lit, fig)* leech

sanguin, e /sɑ̃gɛ̃, in/ ADJ 1 *[caractère, personne]* fiery; *[visage]* ruddy, sanguine *(frm)* 2 *(Anat)* blood *(épith)* ◆ **produits ~s** blood products NF **sanguine** 1 ◆ **(orange) ~e** blood orange 2 *(= dessin)* red chalk drawing; *(= crayon)* red chalk, sanguine *(SPÉC)*

sanguinaire /sɑ̃ginɛʀ/ ADJ *[personne]* bloodthirsty, sanguinary *(littér)*; *[combat, dictature]* bloody, sanguinary *(littér)* ◆ **monstre** ~ bloodthirsty monster NF *(= plante)* bloodroot, sanguinaria

sanguinolent, e /sɑ̃ginɔlɑ̃, ɑt/ ADJ *[crachat]* streaked with blood; *[plaie]* oozing blood *(attrib)*, bloody

Sanisette ® /sanizɛt/ NF *coin-operated public toilet*, Superloo ® *(Brit)*

sanitaire /sanitɛʀ/ ADJ 1 *(Méd)* *[services, mesures]* health *(épith)*; *[conditions]* sanitary ◆ **campagne** ~ campaign to improve sanitary conditions; → **cordon, train** 2 *(Plomberie)* **l'installation ~ est défectueuse** the bathroom plumbing is faulty ◆ **appareil** ~ bathroom *ou* sanitary appliance NM ◆ **le** ~ bathroom installations ◆ **les ~s** *(= lieu)* the bathroom; (= *appareils*) the bathroom (suite); (= *plomberie*) the bathroom plumbing

San José / sɑ̃ʒoze / N San José

San Juan / sɑ̃ʒyɑ / N San Juan

sans / sɑ̃ / PRÉP 1 *(privation, absence)* without ◆ **être ~ père/mère** to have no father/mother, to be fatherless/motherless ◆ **il est ~ secrétaire en ce moment** he is without a secretary at the moment, he has no secretary at the moment ◆ **ils sont ~ argent** they have no money, they are penniless ◆ **je suis sorti ~ chapeau ni manteau** I went out without a hat or coat *ou* with no hat or coat ◆ **repas à 10 € ~ le vin** meal at €10 exclusive of wine *ou* not including wine ◆ **on a retrouvé le sac, mais ~ l'argent** they found the bag minus the money *ou* but without the money ◆ **être ~ abri** to be homeless

2 *(manière, caractérisation)* without ◆ **manger ~ fourchette** to eat without a fork ◆ **boire ~ soif** to drink without being thirsty ◆ **il est parti ~ même** *ou* **~ seulement un mot de remerciement** he left without even a word of thanks ◆ **l'histoire n'est pas ~ intérêt** the story is not devoid of interest *ou* is not without interest ◆ **nous avons trouvé sa maison ~ mal** we found his house with no difficulty *ou* with no trouble *ou* without difficulty ◆ **marcher ~ chaussures** to walk barefoot ◆ **promenade ~ but** aimless walk ◆ **une Europe ~ frontières** a Europe without borders ◆ **je le connais, ~ plus** I know him but no more than that ◆ **tu as aimé ce film ? – ~ plus** did you like the film? – it was all right (I suppose); → **cesse, doute, effort** *etc*

3 *(cause ou condition négative)* but for ◆ **~ moi, il ne les aurait jamais retrouvés** but for me *ou* had it not been for me, he would never have found them ◆ **~ cette réunion, il aurait pu partir ce soir** if it had not been for *ou* were it not for *ou* but for this meeting he could have left tonight ◆ **~ sa présence d'esprit, il se tuait** had he not had such presence of mind *ou* without *ou* but for his presence of mind he would have been killed

4 *(avec infin)* without ◆ **il est entré ~ faire de bruit** he came in without making a noise *ou* noiselessly ◆ **je n'irai pas ~ être invité** I won't go without being invited *ou* unless I am invited ◆ **j'y crois ~ y croire** I believe it and I don't ◆ **je ne suis pas ~ avoir des doutes sur son honnêteté** I have my doubts *ou* I am not without some doubts as to his honesty ◆ **la situation n'est pas ~ nous inquiéter** the situation is somewhat disturbing; → **attendre, dire, jamais, savoir**

5 *(locutions)*

♦ **sans que** + *subj* ◆ **il est entré ~ (même** *ou* **seulement) que je l'entende** he came in without my (even) hearing him ◆ **~ (même) que nous le sachions, il avait écrit** he had written without our (even) knowing ◆ **il peut jouer de la musique ~ que cela m'empêche de travailler** he can play music without it making it impossible for me to work ◆ **il ne se passe pas de jour ~ qu'il lui écrive** not a day goes by without his writing to her

♦ **sans ça***, **sans quoi*** otherwise ◆ **si on m'offre un bon prix je vends ma voiture, ~ ça** *ou* **~ quoi je la garde** I'll sell my car if I'm offered a good price for it but otherwise *ou* if not, I'll keep it ◆ **sois sage, ~ ça ... !** be good or else ...!

♦ **non sans** ◆ **non ~ peine** *ou* **mal** *ou* **difficulté** not without difficulty ◆ **il l'a fait non ~ rechigner** he did it albeit reluctantly ◆ **l'incendie a été maîtrisé, non ~ que les pompiers aient dû intervenir** the fire was brought under control but not until the fire brigade were brought in

ADV * ◆ **votre parapluie ! vous alliez partir ~** your umbrella! you were going to go off without it ◆ **il a oublié ses lunettes et il ne peut pas conduire ~** he's forgotten his glasses, and he can't drive without them

COMP **sans domicile fixe** ADJ INV of no fixed abode NMF INV homeless person ◆ **les ~ domicile fixe** the homeless

sans faute [*téléphoner, prévenir*] without fail

sans-abri / sɑ̃zabʀi / NMF INV homeless person ◆ **les ~** the homeless

San Salvador / sɑ̃salvadɔʀ / N San Salvador

sans-cœur / sɑ̃kœʀ / ADJ INV heartless NMF INV heartless person

sanscrit, e / sɑ̃skʀi, it / ADJ, NM ⇒ **sanskrit**

sans-culotte (pl **sans-culottes**) / sɑ̃kylɔt / NM *(Hist)* sans culotte

sans-emploi / sɑ̃zɑ̃plwa / NMF INV unemployed person ◆ **les ~** the jobless, the unemployed ◆ **le nombre des ~** the number of unemployed *ou* of people out of work, the jobless figure

sans-façon / sɑ̃fasɔ̃ / NM INV casualness, offhandedness

sans-faute / sɑ̃fot / NM INV *(Équitation)* clear round; *(Sport)* faultless performance ◆ **faire un ~** *(Équitation)* to do a clear round; *(Sport)* to put up a faultless performance, not to put a foot wrong ◆ **son cursus scolaire est un ~** his academic record is impeccable ◆ **jusqu'à présent, il a réussi un ~** *(gén)* he hasn't put a foot wrong so far; *(dans un jeu avec questions)* he has got all the answers right so far

sans-fil / sɑ̃fil / NM (= *téléphone*) cordless telephone; († = *radio*) wireless telegraphy ◆ **le marché du ~** the cordless telephone market; → aussi **fil**

sans-filiste † (pl **sans-filistes**) / sɑ̃filist / NMF wireless enthusiast

sans-gêne / sɑ̃ʒɛn / ADJ INV inconsiderate ◆ **il est vraiment ~ !** he's got a nerve! * NM INV lack of consideration (for others), inconsiderateness ◆ **elle est d'un ~ incroyable !** she's got an incredible nerve! * NMF INV inconsiderate person

sans-grade / sɑ̃gʀad / NMF INV 1 *(Mil)* serviceman, enlisted man (US) 2 (= *subalterne*) underling, peon (US) ◆ **les ~** *(dans une hiérarchie)* the underlings, the small fry; *(dans la société, un milieu)* the nobodies, the nonentities

sanskrit, e / sɑ̃skʀi, it / ADJ, NM Sanskrit

sans-le-sou * / sɑ̃l(ə)su / NMF INV ◆ **c'est un ~** he's penniless ◆ **les ~** the have-nots

sans-logis / sɑ̃lɔʒi / NMF *(gén pl)* homeless person ◆ **les ~** the homeless

sansonnet / sɑ̃sɔnɛ / NM starling; → **roupie**

sans-papiers / sɑ̃papje / NMF INV undocumented immigrant

sans-parti / sɑ̃paʀti / NMF INV *(gén) person who is not a member of a political party;* (= *candidat*) independent (candidate)

sans-patrie / sɑ̃patʀi / NMF INV stateless person

sans-soin † / sɑ̃swɛ̃ / NMF INV careless person

sans-souci † / sɑ̃susi / NMF INV carefree *ou* happy-go-lucky person

sans-travail / sɑ̃tʀavaj / NMF INV ⇒ **sans-emploi**

sans-voix / sɑ̃vwa / NMPL ◆ **les ~** people with no voice

santal / sɑ̃tal / NM sandal, sandalwood ◆ **bois de ~** sandalwood ◆ **huile de ~** sandalwood oil

santé / sɑ̃te / NF 1 [*de personne, esprit, pays*] health ◆ **~ mentale** mental health ◆ **en bonne/mauvaise ~** in good/bad health ◆ **avoir des problèmes** *ou* **ennuis de ~** to have health problems ◆ **la bonne ~ du franc** the good health of the Franc ◆ **la mauvaise ~ financière d'une entreprise** a company's poor financial health ◆ **c'est bon/mauvais pour la ~** it's good/bad for the health *ou* for you ◆ **être en pleine ~** to be in perfect health ◆ **avoir la ~** to be healthy, to be in good health ◆ **il a la ~ !** * *(fig = énergie)* he must have lots of energy! ◆ **il n'a pas de ~, il a une petite ~** he's in poor health ◆ **avoir une ~ de fer** to have an iron constitution ◆ **comment va la ~ ?** * how are you doing? * *ou* keeping? * *(Brit)* ◆ **meilleure ~ !** get well soon!; → **maison, raison, respirer**

2 *(Admin)* **la ~ publique** public health ◆ **la ~** *(Naut)* the quarantine service ◆ **services de ~** *(Admin)* health services ◆ **les dépenses de ~** health spending ◆ **le système de ~** the health system ◆ **les professions de ~** health (care) professions; → **ministère, ministre**

3 *(en trinquant)* **à votre ~ !, ~ !** * cheers!, (your) good health! ◆ **à la ~ de Paul !** (here's) to Paul! ◆ **boire à la ~ de qn** to drink to sb's health

santiag / sɑ̃tjag / NM cowboy boot

Santiago / sɑ̃tjago / N Santiago

santoméen, -enne / sɑ̃tomeɛ̃, ɛn / ADJ of *ou* from São Tomé e Principe NM,F **Santoméen(ne)** inhabitant of São Tomé e Principe

santon / sɑ̃tɔ̃ / NM (ornamental) figure *(in a Christmas crib)*

São Tomé / saotɔme / N ◆ **~ et Principe** São Tomé e Principe

saoudien, -ienne / saudjɛ̃, jɛn / ADJ Saudi Arabian NM,F **Saoudien(ne)** Saudi Arabian

saoul, e / su, sul / ADJ ⇒ **soûl**

saoulard, e * / sulaʀ, aʀd / NM,F ⇒ **soûlard**

sapajou / sapaʒu / NM (= *singe*) capuchin monkey, sapajou

sape / sap / NF 1 *(lit, fig)* (= *action*) undermining, sapping; (= *tranchée*) approach *ou* sapping trench ◆ **travail de ~** *(Mil)* sap; *(fig)* chipping away 2 (= *habits*) **~s*** gear* *(NonC)*, clobber* *(NonC)* *(Brit)*

saper / sape / ▸ conjug 1 ◂ VT *(lit, fig)* to undermine, to sap ◆ **~ le moral à qn** * to knock the stuffing out of sb* VPR **se saper** * to get all dressed up* ◆ **il s'était sapé pour aller danser** he'd got all dressed up to go dancing* ◆ **bien sapé** well-dressed

saperlipopette † * / sapɛʀlipɔpɛt / EXCL *(hum)* gad! † *(hum)*, gadzooks! † *(hum)*

sapeur / sapœʀ / NM *(Mil)* sapper; → **fumer**

sapeur-pompier (pl **sapeurs-pompiers**) / sapœʀpɔ̃pje / NM firefighter, fireman *(Brit)*

saphène / safɛn / ADJ saphenous NF saphena

saphique / safik / ADJ, NM *(Littérat)* Sapphic

saphir / safiʀ / NM (= *pierre*) sapphire; (= *aiguille*) needle; [*de tourne-disque*] stylus ADJ INV sapphire

saphisme / safism / NM sapphism

sapide / sapid / ADJ sapid

sapidité / sapidite / NF sapidity; → **agent**

sapience † / sapjɑ̃s / NF sapience *(frm)*, wisdom

sapin / sapɛ̃ / NM (= *arbre*) fir (tree); (= *bois*) fir ◆ **~ de Noël** Christmas tree ◆ **toux qui sent le ~** * graveyard cough ◆ **costume en ~*** wooden overcoat* ◆ **ça sent le ~** *(hum, *)* he's *(ou you've etc)* got one foot in the grave

sapinière / sapinjɛʀ / NF fir plantation *ou* forest

saponacé, e / sapɔnase / ADJ saponaceous

saponaire / sapɔnɛʀ / NF saponin

saponification / sapɔnifikasjɔ̃ / NF saponification

saponifier / sapɔnifje / ▸ conjug 7 ◂ VT to saponify

sapristi * † / sapʀisti / EXCL *(colère)* for God's sake!*; *(surprise)* good grief!*, (good) heavens!

saprophage /sapʀɔfaʒ/ ADJ saprophagous NM saprophagous animal

saprophyte /sapʀɔfit/ ADJ, NM (*Bio, Méd*) saprophyte

saquer* /sake/ ▸ conjug 1 ◂ VT ⇒ **sacquer**

S.A.R. (abrév de **Son Altesse Royale**) HRH

sarabande /saʀabɑ̃d/ NF (= *danse*) saraband; (* = *tapage*) racket, hullabaloo*; (= *succession*) jumble ◆ **faire la ~*** to make a racket *ou* a hullabaloo* ◆ **les souvenirs/chiffres qui dansent la ~ dans ma tête** the memories/figures whirling around in my head

Saragosse /saʀagɔs/ N Saragossa

sarajévien, -ienne /saʀajevjɛ̃, ɛn/ ADJ Sarajevan NM,F **Sarajévien(ne)** Sarajevan

Sarajevo /saʀajevo/ N Sarajevo

sarbacane /saʀbakan/ NF (= *arme*) blowpipe, blowgun; (= *jouet*) peashooter

sarcasme /saʀkasm/ NM (= *ironie*) sarcasm; (= *remarque*) sarcastic remark

sarcastique /saʀkastik/ ADJ sarcastic

sarcastiquement /saʀkastikmɑ̃/ ADV sarcastically

sarcelle /saʀsɛl/ NF teal

sarclage /saʀklaʒ/ NM [*de jardin, culture*] weeding; [*de mauvaise herbe*] hoeing

sarcler /saʀkle/ ▸ conjug 1 ◂ VT [+ *jardin, culture*] to weed; [+ *mauvaises herbes*] to hoe

sarclette /saʀklɛt/ NF (small) hoe

sarcomateux, -euse /saʀkɔmatø, øz/ ADJ sarcomatoid, sarcomatous

sarcome /saʀkom/ NM sarcoma ◆ **~ de Kaposi** Kaposi's Sarcoma

sarcophage /saʀkɔfaʒ/ NM (*pour corps, installation nucléaire*) sarcophagus

Sardaigne /saʀdɛɲ/ NF Sardinia

sarde /saʀd/ ADJ Sardinian NM (= *langue*) Sardinian NMF **Sarde** Sardinian

sardine /saʀdin/ NF 1 (= *poisson*) sardine ◆ **une boîte de ~s à l'huile** a tin (*Brit*) *ou* can (*US*) of sardines in oil ◆ **serrés *ou* tassés comme des ~s (en boîte)** packed *ou* squashed together like sardines (in a tin (*Brit*) *ou* can (*US*)) 2 (* *Camping*) tent peg 3 (*arg Mil*) stripe

sardinerie /saʀdinʀi/ NF sardine cannery

sardinier, -ière /saʀdinje, jɛʀ/ ADJ sardine (*épith*) NM,F (= *ouvrier*) sardine canner NM (= *bateau*) sardine boat; (= *pêcheur*) sardine fisher

sardonique /saʀdɔnik/ ADJ sardonic

sargasse /saʀgas/ NF sargasso, gulfweed; → **mer**

sari /saʀi/ NM sari

sarigue /saʀig/ NF (o)possum

sarin /saʀɛ̃/ NM ◆ **(gaz) ~** sarin (gas)

SARL /ɛsaɛʀɛl/ NF (abrév de **société à responsabilité limitée**) limited liability company ◆ **Raymond ~** Raymond Ltd (*Brit*), Raymond Inc. (*US*); → **société**

sarment /saʀmɑ̃/ NM (= *tige*) twining *ou* climbing stem, bine (*SPÉC*) ◆ **~ (de vigne)** vine shoot

sarmenteux, -euse /saʀmɑ̃tø, øz/ ADJ [*plante*] climbing (*épith*); [*tige*] climbing (*épith*), twining (*épith*)

saroual /saʀwal/, **sarouel** /saʀwɛl/ NM baggy trousers (*worn in North Africa*)

sarrasin[1], **e** /saʀazɛ̃, in/ (*Hist*) ADJ Saracen NM,F **Sarrasin(e)** Saracen

sarrasin[2] /saʀazɛ̃/ NM (= *plante*) buckwheat ◆ **galette de ~** buckwheat pancake

sarrau /saʀo/ NM smock

sarriette /saʀjɛt/ NF savory

sas /sɑs/ NM 1 (*Espace, Naut*) airlock; [*d'écluse*] lock; [*de banque*] double-entrance security door ◆ **~ de décompression** decompression airlock 2 (= *tamis*) sieve, screen

S.A.S. /ɛsaɛs/ (abrév de **Son Altesse Sérénissime**) HSH

sashimi /saʃimi/ NM sashimi

sassafras /sasafʀa/ NM sassafras

sasser /sɑse/ ▸ conjug 1 ◂ VT [+ *farine*] to sift, to screen; [+ *péniche*] to take through a lock

Satan /satɑ̃/ NM Satan

satané, e* /satane/ ADJ blasted*, confounded* ◆ **c'est un ~ menteur !** he's a damned liar!* ◆ **~s embouteillages !** blasted traffic jams!*

satanique /satanik/ ADJ (= *de Satan*) satanic; (*fig*) [*plaisir, rire*] fiendish, satanic, wicked; [*ruse*] fiendish

sataniser /satanize/ ▸ conjug 1 ◂ VT [+ *personne*] to demonize

satanisme /satanism/ NM (= *culte*) Satanism; (*fig*) fiendishness, wickedness

sataniste /satanist/ ADJ satanic NMF Satanist

satellisation /satelizasjɔ̃/ NF 1 [*de fusée*] (launching and) putting into orbit ◆ **programme de ~** satellite launching programme 2 [*de pays*] satellization ◆ **la ~ de cet État est à craindre** it is feared that this state will become a satellite

satelliser /satelize/ ▸ conjug 1 ◂ VT [+ *fusée*] to put into orbit (round the earth); [+ *pays*] to make a satellite of, to make into a satellite ◆ **ils ont été satellisés dans les filiales** they have been sidelined into various subsidiaries

satellitaire /satelitɛʀ/ ADJ [*diffusion, système, téléphone*] satellite (*épith*); → **antenne**

satellite /satelit/ NM 1 (*Astron, Espace, Pol*) satellite ◆ **~ artificiel/naturel** artificial/natural satellite ◆ **~ de communication/télécommunications/radiodiffusion** communications/telecommunications/broadcast satellite ◆ **~ météorologique/d'observation** weather/observation satellite ◆ **~ antisatellite, ~ d'intervention** killer satellite ◆ **~-espion** spy satellite, spy-in-the-sky* ◆ **diffusion par ~** satellite broadcasting, broadcasting by satellite ◆ **j'ai le ~** (* = *télévision*) I have satellite TV 2 (*en apposition*) [*chaîne, image, photo, liaison, pays, ville*] satellite (*épith*) ◆ **ordinateur ~** satellite *ou* peripheral computer 3 [*d'aérogare*] satellite ◆ **~ numéro 5** satellite number 5 4 (*Tech*) **(pignon) ~** bevel pinion

satiété /sasjete/ NF satiation, satiety ◆ **(jusqu')à ~** [*répéter*] ad nauseam ◆ **boire/manger jusqu'à ~** to eat/drink until one can eat/drink no more ◆ **j'en ai à ~** I've got more than enough

satin /satɛ̃/ NM satin ◆ **~ de laine/de coton** wool/cotton satin ◆ **elle avait une peau de ~** her skin was (like) satin, she had satin (-smooth) skin

satiné, e /satine/ (ptp de **satiner**) ADJ [*aspect, tissu*] satiny, satin-like; [*peau*] satin (*épith*), satin-smooth; [*papier, peinture*] with a silk finish NM satin(-like) *ou* satiny quality

satiner /satine/ ▸ conjug 1 ◂ VT [+ *étoffe*] to put a satin finish on, to satinize; [+ *papier, photo*] to give a silk finish to ◆ **la lumière satinait sa peau** the light gave her skin a satin-like quality *ou* gloss

satinette /satinɛt/ NF (*en coton et soie*) satinet; (*en coton*) sateen

satire /satiʀ/ NF (*gén*) satire; (*écrite*) satire, lampoon ◆ **faire la ~ de qch** to satirize sth, to lampoon sth

satirique /satiʀik/ ADJ satirical, satiric

satiriquement /satiʀikmɑ̃/ ADV satirically

satiriste /satiʀist/ NMF satirist

satisfaction /satisfaksjɔ̃/ NF 1 (= *contentement*) satisfaction ◆ **éprouver une certaine ~ à faire qch** to feel a certain satisfaction in doing sth, to get a certain satisfaction out of doing sth *ou* from doing sth ◆ **cet employé/cette lessive me donne (toute *ou* entière) ~** I'm (completely) satisfied with this employee/this washing powder ◆ **je vois avec ~ que ...** I'm pleased *ou* gratified to see that ... ◆ **à la ~ générale *ou* de tous** to everybody's satisfaction ◆ **à leur grande ~** to their great satisfaction ◆ **la ~ du devoir accompli** the satisfaction of having done one's duty

2 (= *sujet de contentement*) satisfaction ◆ **mon travail/mon fils me procure de grandes ~s** my job/my son gives me great satisfaction, I get a lot of satisfaction out of *ou* from my job/my son ◆ **ma fille ne m'a donné que des ~s** my daughter has always been a (source of) great satisfaction to me ◆ **c'est une ~ qu'il pourrait m'accorder** he might grant me that satisfaction ◆ **~ d'amour-propre** gratification of one's self-esteem

3 (*en réponse à une attente, des exigences*) **donner ~ à qn** to satisfy sb ◆ **il ne faut pas donner ~ aux terroristes** we mustn't give in to the terrorists' demands ◆ **obtenir ~** to get *ou* obtain satisfaction, to get what one wants ◆ **ils ont obtenu ~ (sur tous les points)** they got what they wanted (on all counts)

4 (*frm* = *assouvissement*) [*de faim, passion*] satisfaction, appeasement; [*de soif*] satisfaction, quenching; [*d'envie*] satisfaction; [*de désir*] satisfaction, gratification

5 (*Rel*) satisfaction

satisfaire /satisfɛʀ/ ▸ conjug 60 ◂ VT [+ *curiosité, personne*] to satisfy; [+ *désir*] to satisfy, to fulfil (*Brit*), to fulfill (*US*); [+ *faim, passion*] to satisfy, to appease; [+ *soif*] to quench, to satisfy; [+ *besoin, demande, revendications, goûts*] to meet, to satisfy; [+ *clientèle*] to satisfy, to please ◆ **votre nouvel assistant vous satisfait-il ?** are you satisfied with your new assistant? ◆ **j'espère que cette solution vous satisfait** I hope you find this solution satisfactory, I hope you are satisfied *ou* happy with this solution ◆ **je suis désolé que vous n'en soyez pas satisfait** I am sorry it was not satisfactory *ou* you were not satisfied ◆ **on ne peut pas ~ tout le monde (et son père*)** you can't please all the people (all the time), you can't please everyone ◆ **~ l'attente de qn** to come up to sb's expectations ◆ **arriver à ~ la demande** to keep up with demand

VT INDIR **satisfaire à** [+ *désir*] to satisfy, to fulfil (*Brit*), to fulfill (*US*); [+ *engagement, promesse*] to fulfil (*Brit*), to fulfill (*US*); [+ *demande, revendication, critères*] to meet, to satisfy; [+ *condition, exigences*] to meet, to fulfil (*Brit*), to fulfill (*US*), to satisfy; [+ *test de qualité*] to pass ◆ **avez-vous satisfait à vos obligations militaires ?** have you completed your military service? ◆ **cette installation ne satisfait pas aux normes** this installation does not comply with *ou* satisfy standard requirements

VPR **se satisfaire** to be satisfied (*de* with); (*euph* = *uriner*) to relieve o.s. ◆ **se ~ de peu** to be easily satisfied ◆ **tu as vu son mari ?, elle se satisfait de peu !** (*hum*) have you seen her husband? she's not exactly choosy!* ◆ **il ne se satisfait pas de mots, il a besoin d'agir** words aren't enough for him, he needs to act

satisfaisant, e /satisfəzɑ̃, ɑ̃t/ ADJ (= *acceptable*) satisfactory; (= *qui fait plaisir*) satisfying ◆ **de façon ~e** satisfactorily ◆ **ces questions n'ont toujours pas reçu de réponses ~es** these questions have still not been answered satisfactorily ◆ **son état est jugé ~** [*de malade*] his condition is said to be satisfactory ◆ **peu ~** [*bilan, résultats, solution, travail*] unsatisfactory

satisfait, e /satisfɛ, ɛt/ (ptp de **satisfaire**) ADJ *[air, besoin, désir, personne]* satisfied ◆ **"satisfait ou remboursé"** "satisfaction or your money back" ◆ **être ~ de** *[+ personne]* to be satisfied with; *[+ décision, solution]* to be satisfied with, to be happy with *ou* about; *[+ soirée]* to be pleased with ◆ **être ~ de soi** to be satisfied *ou* pleased with o.s. ◆ **il est toujours très ~ de lui** he's so self-satisfied ◆ **il est ~ de son sort** he is satisfied *ou* happy with his lot ◆ **te voilà ~ !** *(iro)* are you satisfied?

satisfecit /satisfesit/ NM INV *(Scol)* ≈ star, merit point ◆ **je lui donne un ~ pour la façon dont il a mené l'affaire** I'll give him full marks *(Brit)* *ou* full points *(US)* for the way he conducted the business

satrape /satʀap/ NM *(Hist)* satrap; *(littér = despote)* satrap, despot; *(menant grand train)* nabob

saturant, e /satyʀɑ̃, ɑ̃t/ ADJ saturating ◆ **vapeur ~e** saturated vapour

saturateur /satyʀatœʀ/ NM *[de radiateur]* humidifier; *(Sci)* saturator

saturation /satyʀasjɔ̃/ NF *(gén, Sci)* saturation *(de* of); ◆ **arriver à ~** to reach saturation point ◆ **à cause de la ~ des lignes téléphoniques** because the telephone lines are all engaged *(Brit)* *ou* busy *(US)* ◆ **pour éviter la ~ du réseau routier** to prevent the road network from getting clogged up *ou* becoming saturated ◆ **j'en ai jusqu'à ~** I've had more than I can take

saturé, e /satyʀe/ (ptp de **saturer**) ADJ 1 *(Chim)* *[solution]* saturated 2 *(= imprégné)* *[sol, terre]* saturated *(de* with) 3 *(= encombré)* *[autoroute]* heavily congested; *[marché]* saturated, glutted; *(Téléc)* *[réseau]* overloaded, saturated; *[standard, lignes]* jammed; *(Ordin)* *[mémoire]* full 4 *[personne]* **je suis ~** *(par trop de travail)* I'm up to my eyes in work, I've got more work than I can cope with ◆ **les gens sont ~s de publicité** people have had their fill of *ou* are sick of advertising ◆ **j'ai mangé tant de fraises que j'en suis ~** I couldn't eat another strawberry, I've had so many 5 *(Peinture)* **couleur ~e** saturated colour *(Brit)* *ou* color *(US)*

saturer /satyʀe/ ► conjug 1 ◄ VT *(gén, Sci)* to saturate *(de* with); ◆ **~ les électeurs de promesses** to swamp the electors with promises VI 1 *[appareil hi-fi]* to distort 2 * **après six heures de ce travail, je sature** after six hours of this work, I've had enough

saturnales /satyʀnal/ NFPL *(lit)* Saturnalia; *(fig)* saturnalia

Saturne /satyʀn/ NM *(Myth)* Saturn NF *(Astron)* Saturn ◆ **extrait** *ou* **sel de saturne** *(Pharm)* lead acetate

saturnien, -ienne /satyʀnjɛ̃, jɛn/ ADJ *(littér)* saturnine

saturnin, e /satyʀnɛ̃, in/ ADJ saturnine

saturnisme /satyʀnism/ NM lead poisoning, saturnism *(SPÉC)*

satyre /satiʀ/ NM *(= divinité, papillon)* satyr; (* *= obsédé)* sex maniac

satyrique /satiʀik/ ADJ satyric

sauce /sos/ NF 1 *(Culin)* sauce; *[de salade]* dressing; *(= jus de viande)* gravy ◆ **viande en ~** meat cooked in a sauce ◆ **~ béarnaise/béchamel/blanche/moutarde/ piquante/ tomate** béarnaise/béchamel/white/mustard/piquant/tomato sauce ◆ **~ vinaigrette** vinaigrette, French dressing *(Brit)* ◆ **~ à l'orange/aux câpres** orange/caper sauce ◆ **~ chasseur/mousseline** sauce chasseur/mousseline ◆ **~ madère/suprême/hollandaise** Madeira/suprême/hollandaise sauce

2 *(* = remplissage)* padding* ◆ **reprendre un vieux discours en changeant la ~** *(= présentation)* to take an old speech and dress it up ◆ **c'est la même chose avec une autre ~** same meat, different gravy ◆ **il faudrait rallonger la ~ pour ce devoir** you'll have to pad out this essay

3 *(locutions)* **à quelle ~ allons-nous être mangés ?** I wonder what fate has in store for us ◆ **mettre qn à toutes les ~s** to make sb do any job going* ◆ **mettre un exemple à toutes les ~s** to turn *ou* adapt an example to fit any case ◆ **mettre la ~*** *(en voiture)* to step on the gas*; *(gén = se dépêcher)* to step on it* ◆ **mettre toute la ~*** to go flat out* ◆ **recevoir la ~*** to get soaked *ou* drenched ◆ **faire monter la ~** to build up the hype*

4 *(= crayon à estomper)* soft black crayon

saucée* /sose/ NF downpour ◆ **recevoir** *ou* **prendre une ~** to get soaked *ou* drenched

saucer /sose/ ► conjug 3 ◄ VT *[+ assiette]* to mop up the sauce from; *[+ pain]* to use to mop up the sauce ◆ **prends du pain pour ~** have some bread to mop up the sauce ◆ **se faire ~*, être saucé*** to get soaked *ou* drenched

saucier /sosje/ NM sauce chef *ou* cook

saucière /sosjɛʀ/ NF *(gén)* sauceboat; *[de jus de viande]* gravy boat

sauciflard‡ /sosiflaʀ/ NM sausage *(eaten cold in slices)*

saucisse /sosis/ NF 1 *(Culin)* sausage ◆ **~ de Morteau** *type of smoked sausage* ◆ **~ de Strasbourg** *type of beef sausage* ◆ **~ de Francfort** frankfurter; → **attacher, chair** 2 *(= idiot)* **(grande) ~**‡ nincompoop*, great ninny*

saucisson /sosisɔ̃/ NM 1 *(Culin)* sausage *(eaten cold in slices)* ◆ **~ à l'ail** garlic sausage ◆ **~ sec** (dry) pork and beef sausage ◆ **~ pur porc** 100% pork sausage; → **ficeler** 2 *(= pain)* (cylindrical) loaf 3 *[de poudre]* *canvas tube filled with gunpowder*, saucisson *(US)*

saucissonnage* /sosisɔnaʒ/ NM *[de livre, émission]* chopping up ◆ **les gens se plaignent du ~ des émissions par la publicité** people are complaining about television programmes being chopped up *ou* constantly interrupted by commercial breaks

saucissonné, e* /sosisɔne/ (ptp de **saucissonner**) ADJ *(= ligoté)* trussed up

saucissonner /sosisɔne/ ► conjug 1 ◄ VI († * *= pique-niquer)* to (have a) picnic VT 1 *(hum = ligoter)* *[+ personne]* to truss up 2 *(= découper)* *[+ livre, émission]* to chop up; *[+ entreprise, territoire]* to carve *ou* slice up *(en* into); ◆ **des films saucissonnés par la publicité** films chopped up by commercials

sauf[1], sauve /sof, sov/ ADJ *[personne]* unharmed, unhurt; *[honneur]* intact ◆ **il a eu la vie sauve** his life was spared ◆ **laisser la vie sauve à qn** to spare sb's life ◆ **il dut à sa franchise d'avoir la vie sauve** he owed his life to his frankness, it was thanks to his frankness that his life was spared; → **sain**

sauf[2] /sof/ PRÉP 1 *(= à part)* except, but, save *(frm)* ◆ **tout le monde ~ lui** everyone except *ou* but *ou* save *(frm)* him ◆ **~ accord** *ou* **convention contraire** *(Jur)* unless otherwise agreed ◆ **~ dispositions contraires** except as otherwise provided ◆ **~ cas exceptionnel** except in exceptional circumstances ◆ **le repas était excellent ~ le dessert** *ou* **~ pour ce qui est du dessert** the meal was excellent except for *ou* apart from *ou* aside from *(surtout US)* the dessert ◆ **tout ~ ça !** anything but that!

2 *(avec conj)* **~ si** unless ◆ **nous irons demain, ~ s'il pleut** we'll go tomorrow unless it rains ◆ **nous sortons tout le temps ~ quand il pleut** we always go out except when it's raining ◆ **~ que** except that

3 *(locutions : littér)* **il accepte de nous aider, ~ à nous critiquer si nous échouons** he agrees to help us even if he does (reserve the right to) criticize us if we fail ◆ **~ le respect que je vous dois, ~ votre respect** with all due respect

sauf-conduit (pl **sauf-conduits**) /sofkɔ̃dɥi/ NM safe-conduct

sauge /soʒ/ NF *(Culin)* sage; *(ornementale)* salvia

saugrenu, e /sogʀəny/ ADJ preposterous, ludicrous ◆ **voilà une question bien ~e !** what a ridiculous question! ◆ **quelle idée ~e !** what a ridiculous idea!

Saül /sayl/ NM Saul

saulaie /solɛ/ NF willow plantation

saule /sol/ NM willow (tree) ◆ **~ blanc/pleureur** white/weeping willow

saumâtre /somatʀ/ ADJ 1 *[eau]* brackish; *[goût]* briny 2 *[humeur, impression, plaisanterie]* nasty, unpleasant ◆ **il l'a trouvée ~*** he was not amused

saumon /somɔ̃/ NM 1 *(= poisson)* salmon ◆ **~ fumé** smoked salmon, lox *(US)* ◆ **~ cru mariné à l'aneth** gravadlax, gravlax, salmon marinated in dill 2 *(Tech)* *(= lingot)* pig ADJ INV salmon (pink)

saumoné, e /somɔne/ ADJ *[couleur]* salmon (pink); → **truite**

saumure /somyʀ/ NF brine

saumuré, e /somyʀe/ ADJ *[hareng]* pickled (in brine)

sauna /sona/ NM sauna

saunier /sonje/ NM *(= ouvrier)* worker in a saltworks; *(= exploitant)* salt merchant

saupiquet /sopikɛ/ NM *(= sauce, ragoût)* spicy sauce or stew

saupoudrage /sopudʀaʒ/ NM 1 *(gén)* sprinkling; *(Culin)* sprinkling, dusting 2 *[crédits, subventions]* spreading thinly ◆ **ils accusent le gouvernement de faire du ~ de subventions** they are accusing the government of spreading the subsidies too thinly

saupoudrer /sopudʀe/ ► conjug 1 ◄ VT 1 *(gén)* to sprinkle; *(Culin)* to sprinkle, to dust *(de* with); ◆ **se ~ les mains de talc** to sprinkle talc on one's hands 2 *[+ crédits]* to spread thinly, to give sparingly ◆ **il saupoudre sa conversation de mots anglais** he peppers *ou* sprinkles his conversation with English words

saupoudreuse /sopudʀøz/ NF (sugar *ou* flour *etc*) dredger

saur /sɔʀ/ ADJ M → **hareng**

saurer /sɔʀe/ ► conjug 1 ◄ VT to smoke, to cure

saurien /sɔʀjɛ̃/ NM saurian ◆ **~s** Sauria *(SPÉC)*, saurians

saurissage /sɔʀisaʒ/ NM smoking, curing

saut /so/ NM 1 *(lit, fig = bond)* jump, leap ◆ **~ avec/sans élan** *(Sport)* running/standing jump ◆ **faire un ~** to (make a) jump *ou* leap ◆ **faire un ~ dans l'inconnu/le vide** to (make a) leap into the unknown/the void ◆ **le véhicule fit un ~ de 100 mètres dans le ravin** the vehicle fell *ou* dropped 100 metres into the ravine ◆ **se lever d'un ~** to jump *ou* leap up, to jump *ou* leap to one's feet ◆ **quittons Louis XIV et faisons un ~ d'un siècle** let us leave Louis XIV and jump forward a century ◆ **progresser** *ou* **avancer par ~s** *(fig)* to go forward by *ou* in stages

2 *(Sport)* jumping ◆ **épreuves de ~** jumping events; → **triple**

3 *(Géog = cascade)* waterfall, falls

4 *(Math, Ordin)* jump

5 *(locutions)* **faire qch au ~ du lit** to do sth as soon as one gets up *ou* gets out of bed ◆ **prendre qn au ~ du lit** to find sb just out of bed (when one calls) ◆ **faire le ~** to take the plunge ◆ **faire le grand ~** *(= mourir)* to pass on ◆ **faire un ~ chez qn** to pop over *ou* round *(Brit)* to sb's place*, to drop in on sb ◆ **faire un ~ à la banque** to drop in at the bank ◆ **il a fait un ~**

jusqu'à Bordeaux he made a flying visit to Bordeaux

COMP **saut de l'ange** *(Natation)* swallow dive *(Brit)*, swan dive *(US)*
saut de carpe jack-knife dive, pike *(Brit)*
saut de chat pas de chat
saut en chute libre *(= sport)* free-fall parachuting; *(= bond)* free-fall jump
saut en ciseaux scissors (jump)
saut à la corde skipping *(Brit)*, jumping rope *(US)*
saut à l'élastique bungee jumping
saut groupé tuck
saut de haies hurdling
saut en hauteur *(= sport)* high jump; *(= bond)* (high) jump
saut de ligne *(Ordin)* line break
saut en longueur *(= sport)* long jump; *(= bond)* (long) jump
saut de la mort leap of death
saut de page page break
saut en parachute *(= sport)* parachuting, parachute jumping; *(= bond)* parachute jump
saut à la perche *(= sport)* pole vaulting; *(= bond)* (pole) vault
saut périlleux somersault
saut à pieds joints standing jump
saut de puce ◆ **l'avion fait des ~s de puce** the plane makes several stopovers
saut en rouleau western roll.
saut de séquence *(Ordin)* jump
saut à skis *(= sport)* skijumping; *(= bond)* jump

saut-de-lit (pl **sauts-de-lit**) /sod(ə)li/ NM negligée

saut-de-loup (pl **sauts-de-loup**) /sod(ə)lu/ NM (wide) ditch

saut-de-mouton (pl **sauts-de-mouton**) /sod(ə)mutɔ̃/ NM flyover *(Brit)*, overpass *(US)*

saute /sot/ NF sudden change ◆ **~ de vent** sudden change (in the direction) of the wind ◆ **~ d'humeur** sudden change of mood ◆ **~ de température** jump in temperature ◆ **pour empêcher les ~s d'images** *(TV)* to stop the picture jumping, to keep the picture steady

sauté, e /sote/ (ptp de **sauter**) ADJ, NM sautéed, sauté ◆ **~ de veau** sauté of veal

saute-mouton /sotmutɔ̃/ NM INV leapfrog ◆ **jouer à ~** *(lit)* to play leapfrog ◆ **le scénario joue à ~ par dessus les siècles** the film script leapfrogs from one century to the next

sauter /sote/ ▸ conjug 1 ◂ VI [1] *[personne]* to jump, to leap *(dans* into; *par-dessus* over); *(vers le bas)* to jump *ou* leap (down); *(vers le haut)* to jump *ou* leap (up); *[oiseau]* to hop; *[insecte]* to jump, to hop; *[kangourou]* to jump ◆ **~ à pieds joints** to make a standing jump ◆ **~ à pieds joints dans qch** *(fig)* to jump into sth with both feet, to rush headlong into sth ◆ **~ à cloche-pied** to hop ◆ **~ à la corde** to skip *(Brit)*, to jump rope *(US)* ◆ **~ à la perche** to pole-vault ◆ **~ en parachute** *(gén, Sport)* to parachute, to make a parachute jump; *[parachutistes]* to parachute, to be dropped *(sur* over); *(en cas d'accident)* to bale out *(Brit)*, to bail out *(US)*, to make an emergency (parachute) jump ◆ **~ en ciseaux** to do a scissors jump ◆ **~ en hauteur/en longueur** to do the high/the long jump ◆ **faire ~ un enfant sur ses genoux** to bounce *ou* dandle † a child on one's knee ◆ **les cahots faisaient ~ les passagers** the passengers jolted *ou* bounced along over the bumps ◆ **il sauta de la table** he jumped *ou* leapt (down) off *ou* from the table ◆ **~ en l'air** to jump *ou* leap *ou* spring into the air ◆ **~ en l'air** *ou* **au plafond** *(de colère)* to hit the roof *; *(de joie)* to jump for joy; *(de surprise, de peur)* to jump (out of one's skin) ◆ **~ de joie** *(lit, fig)* to jump for joy

[2] *(= se précipiter)* **~ (à bas) du lit** to jump *ou* leap *ou* spring out of bed ◆ **~ en selle** to jump *ou* leap *ou* spring into the saddle ◆ **~ à la gorge de qn** to fly *ou* leap at sb's throat ◆ **~ au cou de qn** to fly into sb's arms ◆ **~ dans un taxi/un autobus** to jump *ou* leap into a taxi/onto a bus ◆ **~ par la fenêtre** to jump *ou* leap out of the window ◆ **~ d'un train en marche** to jump *ou* leap from a moving train ◆ **~ sur une occasion/une proposition** to jump *ou* leap at an opportunity/an offer ◆ **il m'a sauté dessus** he pounced on me ◆ **saute-lui dessus * quand il sortira du bureau pour lui demander ...** *(fig)* grab him when he comes out of the office and ask him ... ◆ **va faire tes devoirs, et que ça saute !*** go and do your homework and be quick about it! ◆ **il est malade, cela saute aux yeux** he's ill – it sticks out a mile *ou* it's (quite) obvious ◆ **sa malhonnêteté saute aux yeux** his dishonesty sticks out a mile *ou* is (quite) obvious

[3] *(indiquant la discontinuité)* to jump, to leap ◆ **~ d'un sujet à l'autre** to jump *ou* skip from one subject to another

[4] *[bouchon]* to pop *ou* fly out; *[bouton]* to fly *ou* pop off; *[chaîne de vélo]* to come off; * *[classe, cours]* to be cancelled ◆ **faire ~ un cours** to cancel a class *ou* a lecture ◆ **faire ~ une crêpe** to toss a pancake ◆ **faire ~ une serrure** to burst *ou* break open a lock ◆ **faire ~ le(s) verrou(s)** *(fig)* to break down the barrier(s) ◆ **faire ~ une contravention** * to get a fine taken care of *ou* quashed *(Brit)*

[5] *(= exploser) [bâtiment, bombe, pont]* to blow up, to explode; *(Élec) [fil, circuit]* to fuse; *[fusible]* to blow ◆ **~ sur une mine** *[personne]* to step on a mine; *[véhicule]* to go over a mine ◆ **faire ~** *[+ train, édifice]* to blow up; *(Élec) [+ plombs]* to blow ◆ **faire ~ une mine** *(pour la détruire)* to blow up a mine; *(pour détruire un bâtiment)* to set off a mine ◆ **il s'est fait ~ avec les otages** he blew himself up with the hostages ◆ **se faire ~ la cervelle** * *ou* **le caisson** ‡ to blow one's brains out * ◆ **faire ~ la banque** *(Casino)* to break the bank

[6] *(* = être renvoyé) [directeur]* to get fired, to get the push ‡ *ou* the sack * *(Brit)*; *[gouvernement]* to get kicked out * ◆ **faire ~ qn** *(gén)* to fire sb, to give sb the push ‡ *ou* the sack * *(Brit)*; *[+ gouvernement]* to kick out *

[7] *(Culin)* **faire ~** to sauté, to (shallow) fry

[8] *(= clignoter) [paupière]* to twitch; *[image de télévision]* to flicker, to jump

VT [1] *(= franchir) [+ obstacle, mur]* to jump (over), to leap (over) ◆ **il saute 5 mètres** he can jump 5 metres ◆ **il sauta le fossé d'un bond** he jumped *ou* cleared the ditch with one bound ◆ **~ le pas** *(fig)* to take the plunge

[2] *(= omettre) [+ étape, page, repas]* to skip, to miss ◆ **~ une classe** *(Scol)* to skip a year ◆ **ces caractères héréditaires peuvent ~ une génération** these hereditary characteristics can skip a generation ◆ **on la saute ici !‡** we're starving to death here! *

[3] *(‡ = avoir des rapports sexuels avec)* to fuck *‡, to screw *‡ ◆ **elle s'est fait ~ par Pierre‡** she had it off with Pierre‡, she got laid by Pierre‡

sauterelle /sotʀɛl/ NF [1] *(gén)* grasshopper; *(= criquet)* locust ◆ **nuage** *ou* **nuée de ~s** *(lit, fig)* swarm of locusts ◆ **(grande) ~** * *(= personne maigre)* beanpole *(Brit)*, string bean *(US)* [2] *(= fausse équerre)* bevel; *(= appareil de manutention)* conveyor belt

sauterie † /sotʀi/ NF party ◆ **je donne une petite ~ demain** I'm giving *ou* throwing a little party tomorrow

saute-ruisseau (pl **saute-ruisseaux**) /sotʀɥiso/ NM († *ou littér*) errand boy, office boy *(in a lawyer's office)*

sauteur, -euse /sotœʀ, øz/ ADJ *[insecte]* jumping *(épith)*; *[oiseau]* hopping *(épith)*; → **scie** NM,F [1] *(= athlète, cheval)* jumper [2] *(* = fumiste)* unreliable person NF **sauteuse** [1] *(Culin)* high-sided frying pan [2] *(* = dévergondée)* floozy *

COMP **sauteur en hauteur** high jumper
sauteur en longueur long jumper
sauteur à la perche pole vaulter
sauteur à skis skijumper

sautillant, e /sotijɑ̃, ɑ̃t/ ADJ *[démarche]* hopping, skipping; *[oiseau]* hopping; *[enfant]* skipping; *(sur un pied)* hopping; *[musique]* bouncy; *[style]* jumpy, jerky ◆ **les images ~es des films d'époque** the flickering images of vintage films

sautillement /sotijmɑ̃/ NM *[d'oiseau]* hopping; *[d'enfant]* skipping; *(sur un pied)* hopping

sautiller /sotije/ ▸ conjug 1 ◂ VI *[oiseau]* to hop; *[enfant]* to skip; *(sur un pied)* to hop

sautoir /sotwaʀ/ NM [1] *(Bijouterie)* chain ◆ **~ de perles** string of pearls ◆ **porter qch en ~** to wear sth (on a chain) round one's neck [2] *(Sport)* jumping pit [3] *(Hér)* saltire ◆ **épées en ~** crossed swords

sauvage /sovaʒ/ ADJ [1] *[animal, plante, fleur, lieu]* wild; *[peuplade]* primitive, savage ◆ **côte ~** wild coast ◆ **enfant ~** wild child ◆ **vivre à l'état ~** to live wild ◆ **retourner à l'état ~** *[jardin]* to go wild; *[animal]* to revert to its wild state; → **soie**

[2] *(= farouche) [animal]* wild; *[personne]* unsociable

[3] *(= brutal) [cri]* wild; *[conduite]* savage, wild; *[combat]* savage

[4] *(= illégal) [vente]* unauthorized; *[concurrence]* unfair; *[crèche, école]* unofficial; *[urbanisation]* unplanned; *[immigration, importations]* illegal; *[capitalisme, libéralisme]* unrestrained, untrammelled ◆ **faire du camping ~** *(illégal)* to camp on unauthorized sites; *(dans la nature)* to camp in the wild, to go wilderness camping *(US)* ◆ **décharge ~** illicit rubbish *(Brit)* *ou* garbage *(US)* dump ◆ **il a été condamné pour affichage ~** he was prosecuted for flyposting; → **grève, parking**

NMF [1] *(= solitaire)* recluse ◆ **vivre en ~** to live a secluded life, to live as a recluse

[2] *(= brute)* brute, savage ◆ **mœurs de ~s** brutish *ou* savage ways

[3] *(= indigène)* savage ◆ **on n'est pas des ~s !*** we're not savages!

sauvagement /sovaʒmɑ̃/ ADV *[frapper, tuer]* savagely, brutally; *[assassiné]* brutally; *[torturé]* severely, brutally

sauvageon, -onne /sovaʒɔ̃, ɔn/ NM,F little savage NM wild stock *(for grafting)*

sauvagerie /sovaʒʀi/ NF *(= cruauté)* savagery, savageness, brutality; *(= insociabilité)* unsociability, unsociableness

sauvagin, e /sovaʒɛ̃, in/ ADJ *[odeur, goût]* of wildfowl NF **sauvagine** wildfowl ◆ **chasse à la ~e** wildfowling

sauve /sov/ ADJ F → **sauf**[1]

sauvegarde[1] /sovgaʀd/ NF [1] *(= action) [de droits, emploi, environnement]* protection, safeguarding; *[de dignité, réputation]* protecting, safeguarding; *[d'ordre public, paix]* upholding, maintenance; *(Ordin)* saving ◆ **sous la ~ de** under the protection of ◆ **clause de ~** safety clause ◆ **la ~ des droits de l'homme** the protection of human rights, safeguarding human rights ◆ **faire la ~ d'un fichier** *(Ordin)* to save a file ◆ **de ~** *(Ordin) [copie, disquette, fichier]* backup *(épith)* [2] *(= garantie)* safeguard ◆ **être la ~ de** to safeguard, to be the safeguard of *ou* for

sauvegarde[2] /sovgaʀd/ NF *(Naut)* protective rope

sauvegarder /sovgaʀde/ ▸ conjug 1 ◂ VT *[+ droits, emploi, environnement, dignité, réputation]* to protect, to safeguard; *[+ ordre public, paix]* to uphold, to maintain; *(Ordin)* to save

sauve-qui-peut /sovkipø/ NM INV *(= cri)* (cry of) run for your life; *(= panique)* stampede, mad rush

sauver /sove/ ▸ conjug 1 ◂ VT 1 *(= épargner la mort, la faillite à)* to save; *(= porter secours à)* to rescue ◆ **elle est sauvée !** *[malade]* she's come through!; *[accidentée, otage]* she's been rescued! ◆ **nous sommes sauvés !*** we're saved! ◆ ~ **qn/qch de** *[+ danger, désastre]* to save *ou* rescue sb/sth from ◆ **un mot de lui peut tout** ~ a word from him can save the day *ou* situation

2 *(= sauvegarder) [+ biens, cargaison, mobilier]* to salvage, to save, to rescue; *[+ honneur, emplois, planète, processus de paix]* to save

3 *(Rel) [+ âme, pécheurs]* to save

4 *(= racheter)* to save, to redeem ◆ **ce sont les illustrations qui sauvent le livre** it's the illustrations which save *ou* redeem the book, the illustrations are the redeeming feature *ou* the saving grace of the book

5 *(locutions)* ~ **la vie à** *ou* **de qn** to save sb's life ◆ ~ **sa peau*** *ou* **sa tête*** to save one's skin *ou* hide* ◆ ~ **les meubles** * *(fig)* to salvage *ou* save something from the wreckage ◆ ~ **la situation** to save *ou* retrieve the situation ◆ ~ **les apparences** to keep up appearances ◆ ~ **la face** to save face ◆ **il m'a sauvé la mise** he bailed me out, he got me out of a tight corner ◆ **être sauvé par le gong** *[boxeur, candidat]* to be saved by the bell

VPR **se sauver** 1 *(= s'enfuir)* to run away *(de* from); *(* = partir)* to be off*, to get going ◆ **il s'est sauvé à toutes jambes** he ran away as fast as his legs could carry him ◆ **sauve-toi*, il est déjà 8 heures** you'd better be off* *ou* get going, it's already 8 o'clock ◆ **bon, je me sauve*** right, I'm off* ◆ **vite, le lait se sauve*** quick, the milk's boiling over ◆ **sauve qui peut !** run for your life!; → aussi **sauve-qui-peut**

2 ◆ **se** ~ **de** *[+ danger, désastre]* to escape

sauvetage /sov(ə)taʒ/ NM 1 *[de personnes]* rescue; *(moral)* salvation; *[de biens]* salvaging ◆ ~ **en mer/montagne** sea/mountain rescue ◆ **le** ~ **des naufragés** rescuing the survivors of the shipwreck ◆ **opérer le** ~ **de** *[+ personnes]* to rescue; *[+ biens]* to salvage ◆ **de** ~ *[matériel, équipe]* rescue *(épith)* ◆ **opération de** ~ *[de personnes]* rescue operation; *[de biens]* salvage operation ◆ **plan de** ~ **d'une entreprise** *(Écon)* rescue plan for a firm; → **bateau, bouée, canot** *etc* 2 *(= technique)* **le** ~ life-saving ◆ **cours de** ~ life-saving lessons

sauveteur /sov(ə)tœʀ/ NM rescuer

sauvette* /sovɛt/ **à la sauvette** LOC ADV *(= vite)* hastily, hurriedly; *(= en cachette)* on the sly ◆ **ils se sont mariés à la** ~ they married in haste ◆ **la réforme a été votée à la** ~ the reform was rushed through parliament ◆ **images tournées à la** ~ pictures shot on the sly ◆ **vente à la** ~ (unauthorized) street hawking *ou* peddling ◆ **vendre qch à la** ~ to hawk *ou* peddle sth on the streets *(without authorization)* ◆ **vendeur** *ou* **marchand à la** ~ street hawker ◆ **acheter son billet à un revendeur à la** ~ to buy one's ticket from an unauthorized source *ou* from a ticket tout *(Brit)*

sauveur /sovœʀ/ ADJ M ◆ **le Dieu** ~ God the Saviour *(Brit)* *ou* Savior *(US)* NM saviour *(Brit)*, savior *(US)* ◆ **le Sauveur** *(Rel)* the Saviour ◆ **tu es mon** ~ **!** *(hum)* you're my saviour!

sauvignon /soviɲɔ̃/ NM Sauvignon *(type of wine from the Loire valley)*

SAV /esave/ NM (abrév de **service après-vente**) → **service**

savamment /savamɑ̃/ ADV *(= avec érudition)* learnedly; *(= adroitement)* cleverly, skilfully *(Brit)*, skillfully *(US)* ◆ **j'en parle** ~ *(= par expérience)* I know what I'm talking about ◆ ~ **dosé/entretenu/orchestré** skilfully controlled/maintained/orchestrated

savane /savan/ NF savannah; *(* Can)* swamp

savant, e /savɑ̃, ɑt/ ADJ 1 *(= érudit) [personne]* learned, scholarly; *[édition]* scholarly; *[mot, société]* learned ◆ **être** ~ **en qch** to be learned in sth ◆ **c'est trop** ~ **pour moi** *(hum) [discussion, livre]* it's too highbrow for me; *[problème]* it's too difficult *ou* complicated for me 2 *(= habile) [arrangement, dosage, stratagème]* clever, skilful *(Brit)*, skillful *(US)* ◆ **le** ~ **désordre de sa tenue** the studied carelessness of his dress ◆ **un** ~ **mélange de...** a clever mixture of... 3 *[chien, puce]* performing *(épith)* NM *(sciences)* scientist; *(lettres)* scholar

savarin /savaʀɛ̃/ NM *(Culin)* savarin

savate* /savat/ NF 1 *(= pantoufle)* worn-out old slipper; *(= chaussure)* worn-out old shoe ◆ **être en** ~**s** to be in one's slippers; → **traîner** 2 *(* = maladroit)* clumsy idiot *ou* oaf 3 *(Sport)* **la** ~ kickboxing

savetier †† /sav(ə)tje/ NM cobbler †

saveur /savœʀ/ NF *(lit = goût)* flavour *(Brit)*, flavor *(US)*; *(fig = piment)* spice ◆ **sans** ~ flavourless *(Brit)*, flavorless *(US)* ◆ **venez déguster les** ~**s de notre terroir** come and taste our local specialities ◆ **c'est ce lait qui fait toute la** ~ **du fromage** it's this milk that gives the cheese its flavour ◆ **ce sont les expressions dialectales qui donnent toute sa** ~ **au roman** it's the regional expressions that spice up the novel

Savoie /savwa/ NF *(= région)* ◆ **la** ~ Savoy; → **biscuit**

savoir /savwaʀ/ GRAMMAIRE ACTIVE 43.1, 43.4, 53.1 ▸ conjug 32 ◂

VT 1 *(gén)* to know ◆ ~ **le nom/l'adresse de qn** to know sb's name/address ◆ **c'est difficile à** ~ it's difficult to know *ou* ascertain ◆ **je ne savais quoi** *ou* **que dire/faire** I didn't know what to say/do ◆ **oui, je (le) sais** yes, I know ◆ **je savais qu'elle était malade, je la savais malade** I knew (that) she was ill ◆ **on ne lui savait pas de parents/de fortune** we didn't know whether *ou* if he had any relatives/money; *(en fait il en a)* we didn't know (that) he had any relatives/money ◆ **savez-vous quand/comment il vient ?** do you know when/how he's coming? ◆ **vous savez la nouvelle ?** have you heard *ou* do you know the news? ◆ **elle sait cela par** *ou* **de son boucher** she heard it from her butcher ◆ **tout le village sut bientôt la catastrophe** the whole village soon knew *ou* heard about the disaster ◆ **il ne savait pas s'il devait accepter** he didn't know whether to accept (or not) ◆ **je crois** ~ **que ...** I believe *ou* understand that ..., I am led to believe *ou* understand that ... ◆ **je n'en sais rien** I don't know, I have no idea ◆ **il ment – qu'en savez-vous ?** he is lying – how do you know? ◆ **leur politique ne marchera jamais – qu'en sais-tu ?** their policy will never work – what do you know about it? ◆ **je voudrais en** ~ **davantage** I'd like to know more about it ◆ **il nous a fait** ~ **que ...** he informed us *ou* let us know that ... ◆ **ça se saurait si c'était vrai** if it was true people would know about it ◆ **ça finira bien par se** ~ it'll get out in the end

2 *(= avoir des connaissances sur)* to know ◆ ~ **le grec/son rôle/sa leçon** to know Greek/one's part/one's lesson ◆ **dites-nous ce que vous savez de l'affaire** tell us what you know about *ou* of the matter ◆ **en** ~ **trop (long)** to know too much ◆ **il croit tout** ~ he thinks he knows everything *ou* knows it all ◆ **Monsieur (*ou* Madame *ou* Mademoiselle) je-sais-tout*** *(péj)* smart-alec(k)*, know-all ◆ **tu en sais, des choses*** you certainly know a thing or two, don't you! ◆ **il ne sait ni A ni B, il ne sait rien de rien** he hasn't a clue about anything

3 *(avec infin = être capable de)* to know how to ◆ **elle sait lire et écrire** she can read and write, she knows how to read and write ◆ **il ne sait pas nager** he can't swim, he doesn't know how to swim ◆ ~ **plaire** to know how to please ◆ **il sait parler aux enfants** he's good at talking to children, he knows how to talk to children, he can talk to children ◆ **elle saura bien se défendre** she'll be quite capable of looking after herself ◆ **ça, je sais (le) faire** that I can do ◆ **il a toujours su y faire** *ou* **s'y prendre** he's always known how to go about things (the right way) ◆ **il sait écouter** he's a good listener ◆ **il faut** ~ **attendre/se contenter de peu** you have to learn to be patient *ou* to wait/be content with little ◆ **on ne saurait penser à tout** *(littér hum)* you can't think of everything ◆ **je ne saurais vous exprimer toute ma gratitude** *(littér)* I shall never be able to express my gratitude ◆ **je ne saurais pas vous répondre/vous renseigner** I'm afraid I can't answer you/give you any information ◆ **ces explications ont su éclairer et rassurer** these explanations proved both enlightening and reassuring

4 *(= se rendre compte de)* to know ◆ **il ne sait plus ce qu'il dit** he doesn't know *ou* realize what he's saying, he isn't aware of what he's saying ◆ **je ne sais plus ce que je dis** I no longer know what I'm saying ◆ **il ne sait pas ce qu'il veut** he doesn't know what he wants, he doesn't know his own mind ◆ **il se savait très malade** he knew he was very ill ◆ **elle sait bien qu'il ment** she's well aware of the fact that he's lying, she knows very well *ou* full well that he's lying ◆ **sans le** ~ *(= sans s'en rendre compte)* without knowing *ou* realizing (it), unknowingly; *(= sans le faire exprès)* unwittingly, unknowingly ◆ **c'est un artiste sans le** ~ he's an artist but he doesn't know it

5 *(Belg) (= pouvoir)* to be able to ◆ **je ne saurai pas le porter, c'est trop lourd** I can't carry it, it's too heavy

6 *(locutions)* **qui sait ?** who knows? ◆ **et que sais-je encore** and I don't know what else ◆ **(à)** ~ **si ça va lui plaire !** there's no knowing whether he'll like it or not! ◆ **tu veux celui-ci ou celui-là, faudrait** ~ **!*** do you want this one or that one, make up your mind, will you? ◆ **ils vont renouveler nos contrats ou pas, faudrait** ~ **!*** so are they going to renew our contracts or not, it's about time we knew! ◆ **je sais ce que je sais** I know what I know ◆ **je sais bien, mais ...** I know, but ... ◆ **et puis, tu sais, nous serons très heureux de t'aider** and you know, we'll be very happy to help you ◆ **il nous a emmenés je ne sais où** he took us goodness knows where ◆ **je ne sais qui de ses amis m'a dit que ...** one of his friends, whose name I forget, told me that ... ◆ **il y a je ne sais combien de temps qu'il ne l'a vue** it's been I don't know how long since he last saw her, I don't how long it is *ou* it has been since he (last) saw her ◆ **cette pièce avait je ne sais quoi de sinistre** the room had something strangely sinister about it ◆ **elle ne sait pas quoi faire** *ou* **elle ne sait que faire pour l'aider/le consoler** she's at a loss to know how to help him/comfort him ◆ **il n'a rien voulu** ~ he didn't want to know ◆ **on ne sait jamais** you never know ◆ **(pour autant) que je sache** as far as I know, to the best of my knowledge ◆ **je ne l'y ai pas autorisé, que je sache** I didn't give him permission to do so, as far as I know ◆ **pas que je sache** not as far as I know, not to my knowledge ◆ **je ne sache pas que je vous ai invité !** I'm not aware that *ou* I didn't know that I invited you! ◆ **sachons-le bien, si ...** let's be quite clear, if ... ◆ **sachez (bien) que jamais je n'accepterai !** I'll have you know *ou* let me tell you I shall never accept! ◆ **oui, mais sachez qu'à l'origine, c'est elle-même qui ne le voulait pas** yes, but you should know that it was she who didn't want to in the first place ◆ **à** ~ that is, namely, i.e. ◆ **l'objet/la personne que vous savez sera là demain** *(hum)* you-know-what/you-know-who will be there tomorrow ◆ **vous n'êtes pas sans** ~ **que ...** *(frm)* you are not *ou* will not be

unaware (of the fact) that … *(frm)*, you will not be ignorant of the fact that … *(frm)* ◆ **il m'a su gré/il ne m'a su aucun gré de l'avoir averti** he was grateful to me/he wasn't in the least grateful to me for having warned him ◆ **il ne savait à quel saint se vouer** he didn't know which way to turn ◆ **si je savais, j'irais la chercher** if I knew (for sure) *ou* if I could be sure, I would go and look for her ◆ **si j'avais su** had I known, if I had known ◆ **elle ne savait où donner de la tête** she didn't know whether she was coming or going ◆ **il ne savait où se mettre** he didn't know where to put himself ◆ **tout ce que vous avez toujours voulu ~ sur …** everything you always wanted to know about … ◆ **toi-même tu le sais*** you know perfectly well; → **dieu, qui**

NM ◆ **le ~** learning, knowledge

savoir-être /savwaʀɛtʀ/ NM INV inter-personal skills

savoir-faire /savwaʀfɛʀ/ NM INV *(gén)* know-how*; *(dans un métier)* expertise ◆ **acquérir un ~** to acquire expertise ◆ **il a beaucoup/il manque de ~ avec les enfants** he's very good/isn't very good with children

savoir-vivre /savwaʀvivʀ/ NM INV manners ◆ **il n'a aucun ~** he has no manners ◆ **les règles du ~** the rules of (social) etiquette

savon /savɔ̃/ NM 1 *(= matière)* soap *(NonC)*; *(= morceau)* bar of soap ◆ **~ liquide/noir** liquid/soft soap ◆ **~ à barbe/de toilette/de Marseille** shaving/toilet/household soap ◆ **~ en paillettes/en poudre** soap flakes/powder; → **pain** 2

2 *(* = remontrance)* **il m'a passé/j'ai reçu un (bon) ~** he gave me/I got a (real) telling-off* *ou* dressing-down*, he really tore me off a strip* *(Brit)*

savonnage /savɔnaʒ/ NM soaping *(NonC)*

savonner /savɔne/ ► conjug 1 ◄ VT *[+ enfant, linge, corps]* to soap; *[+ barbe]* to lather, to soap ◆ **~ la tête de qn*** to give sb a dressing-down*, to haul sb over the coals ◆ **~ la planche à qn*** to make life difficult for sb* ◆ **se ~ les mains/le visage** to soap one's hands/one's face, to put soap on one's hands/one's face

savonnerie /savɔnʀi/ NF 1 *(= usine)* soap factory 2 *(= tapis)* Savonnerie carpet

savonnette /savɔnɛt/ NF bar of (toilet) soap

savonneux, -euse /savɔnø, øz/ ADJ soapy; → **pente**

savourer /savuʀe/ ► conjug 1 ◄ VT *[+ plat, boisson, plaisanterie, triomphe]* to savour *(Brit)*, to savor *(US)*

savoureux, -euse /savuʀø, øz/ ADJ *[plat]* delicious, very tasty; *[anecdote, moment, personne]* delightful

savoyard, e /savwajaʀ, aʀd/ ADJ Savoyard; → **fondue** NM,F **Savoyard(e)** Savoyard

sax* /saks/ NM (abrév de **saxophone**) sax*

Saxe /saks/ NF Saxony; → **porcelaine**

saxe /saks/ NM *(= matière)* Dresden china *(NonC)*; *(= objet)* piece of Dresden china

saxhorn /saksɔʀn/ NM saxhorn

saxifrage /saksifʀaʒ/ NF saxifrage

saxo* /sakso/ NM *(= instrument)* sax* NM,F *(= musicien)* sax player*

saxon, -onne /saksɔ̃, ɔn/ ADJ Saxon NM *(= langue)* Saxon NM,F **Saxon(ne)** Saxon

saxophone /saksɔfɔn/ NM saxophone

saxophoniste /saksɔfɔnist/ NMF saxophonist, saxophone player

saynète /sɛnɛt/ NF playlet

sbire /sbiʀ/ NM *(péj)* henchman

s/c (abrév de **sous couvert de**) ≈ c/o

scabieux, -ieuse /skabjø, jøz/ ADJ scabious NF **scabieuse** scabious

scabreux, -euse /skabʀø, øz/ ADJ *(= indécent)* improper, shocking; *(= dangereux)* risky

scalaire /skalɛʀ/ ADJ *(Math)* scalar NM *(= poisson)* angel fish, scalare

scalène /skalɛn/ ADJ *(Anat, Math)* scalene NM ◆ **(muscle) ~** scalenus

scalp /skalp/ NM *(= action)* scalping; *(= chevelure)* scalp

scalpel /skalpɛl/ NM scalpel

scalper /skalpe/ ► conjug 1 ◄ VT to scalp

scampi /skɑ̃pi/ NMPL scampi

scandale /skɑ̃dal/ NM 1 *(= fait choquant, affaire, Rel)* scandal ◆ **~ financier/public** financial/public scandal ◆ **c'est un ~ !** it's scandalous! *ou* outrageous!, it's a scandal! ◆ **sa tenue a fait ~** people were shocked by his outfit ◆ **son livre a fait ~** his book caused a scandal ◆ **au grand ~ de mon père, j'ai voulu épouser un étranger** I wanted to marry a foreigner, which scandalized my father ◆ **elle va crier au ~** she'll make a big fuss about it ◆ **les gens vont crier au ~** there'll be an outcry ◆ **celui/celle par qui le ~ arrive** the one who broke the scandal ◆ **à ~** *[couple, livre]* controversial, headline-hitting* *(épith)* ◆ **journal à ~** scandal sheet

2 *(= scène, tapage)* scene, fuss ◆ **faire un *ou* du ~** to make a scene, to kick up a fuss* ◆ **et pas de ~ !** and don't make a fuss! ◆ **condamné pour ~ sur la voie publique** fined for disturbing the peace *ou* for creating a public disturbance

scandaleusement /skɑ̃daløzmɑ̃/ ADV *[se comporter]* scandalously, outrageously, shockingly; *[cher]* scandalously, outrageously, prohibitively; *[laid, mauvais]* appallingly; *[exagéré, sous-estimé]* grossly

scandaleux, -euse /skɑ̃dalø, øz/ ADJ *[conduite, prix, propos]* scandalous, outrageous, shocking; *[chronique, littérature]* outrageous, shocking ◆ **vie scandaleuse** life of scandal, scandalous life ◆ **c'est ~ !** it's scandalous! ◆ **50 € pour ça, ce n'est pas ~** €50 for that is hardly exorbitant

scandaliser /skɑ̃dalize/ ► conjug 1 ◄ VT to scandalize, to shock deeply ◆ **se ~ de qch** to be deeply shocked at sth, to be scandalized by sth

scander /skɑ̃de/ ► conjug 1 ◄ VT *[+ vers]* to scan; *[+ discours]* to give emphasis to; *[+ mots]* to articulate separately; *[+ nom, slogan]* to chant

scandinave /skɑ̃dinav/ ADJ Scandinavian NMF **Scandinave** Scandinavian

Scandinavie /skɑ̃dinavi/ NF Scandinavia

scandium /skɑ̃djɔm/ NM scandium

scanner[1] /skanɛʀ/ NM *(Opt)* (optical) scanner ◆ **(examen au) ~** *(Méd)* scan ◆ **passer un ~** to have a scan ◆ **~ à plat** flatbed scanner

scanner[2] /skane/, **scannériser** /skaneʀize/ ► conjug 1 ◄ VT *(Ordin)* to scan

scanneur /skanœʀ/ NM ⇒ **scanner**[1]

scanographe /skanɔgʀaf/ NM *(Méd)* scanner

scanographie /skanɔgʀafi/ NF *(= science)* (body) scanning; *(= photo)* scan ◆ **~ du cerveau** brain scan

scansion /skɑ̃sjɔ̃/ NF scanning, scansion

scaphandre /skafɑ̃dʀ/ NM *[de plongeur]* diving suit; *[de cosmonaute]* spacesuit ◆ **~ autonome** aqualung, scuba

scaphandrier /skafɑ̃dʀije/ NM (deep-sea) diver

scapulaire /skapylɛʀ/ ADJ, NM *(Anat, Méd, Rel)* scapular

scarabée /skaʀabe/ NM *(= insecte)* beetle, scarab *(SPÉC)*; *(= bijou)* scarab

scarificateur /skaʀifikatœʀ/ NM *(Méd)* scarificator; *(Agr)* scarifier

scarification /skaʀifikasjɔ̃/ NF scarification

scarifier /skaʀifje/ ► conjug 7 ◄ VT *(Agr, Méd)* to scarify

scarlatine /skaʀlatin/ NF scarlet fever, scarlatina *(SPÉC)*

scarole /skaʀɔl/ NF escarole

scato* /skato/ ADJ abrév de **scatologique**

scatologie /skatɔlɔʒi/ NF scatology

scatologique /skatɔlɔʒik/ ADJ scatological

sceau (pl **sceaux**) /so/ NM *(= cachet, estampille)* seal; *(fig = marque)* stamp, mark ◆ **mettre son ~ sur** to put one's seal to *ou* on ◆ **apposer son ~ sur** to affix one's seal to ◆ **porter le ~ du génie** to bear the stamp *ou* mark of genius ◆ **sous le ~ du secret** under the seal of secrecy; → **garde**[2]

scélérat, e † /seleʀa, at/ ADJ *(littér)* *(= criminel)* villainous, blackguardly †; *(= méchant)* wicked NM,F *(littér = criminel)* villain, blackguard † ◆ **petit ~ !*** (you) little rascal!

scélératesse † /seleʀatɛs/ NF *(littér)* *(= caractère)* villainy, wickedness; *(= acte)* villainous *ou* wicked *ou* blackguardly † deed

scellement /sɛlmɑ̃/ NM 1 *[d'acte, document, sac]* sealing 2 *(Constr)* embedding *(NonC)* 3 *(Méd)* *[de couronne, prothèse]* lute, luting

sceller /sele/ ► conjug 1 ◄ VT 1 *(= cacheter)* *[+ acte, document, sac]* to seal 2 *(Constr)* to embed 3 *(Méd)* *[+ couronne, prothèse]* to lute 4 *(= sanctionner)* *[+ amitié, pacte, réconciliation]* to seal ◆ **son destin était scellé** his fate was sealed

scellés /sele/ NMPL seals ◆ **apposer *ou* mettre les ~ sur une porte** to put the seals on a door, to affix the seals to a door ◆ **lever les ~** to take the seals off ◆ **mettre *ou* placer qch sous ~** to put *ou* place sth under seal

scénario /senaʀjo/ NM 1 *(Ciné, Théât = plan)* scenario; *(Ciné = découpage et dialogues)* screenplay, (film) script 2 *(= évolution possible)* scenario ◆ **ça s'est déroulé selon le ~ habituel** it followed the usual pattern ◆ **c'est toujours le même ~*** it's always the same old ritual *ou* carry-on* *(Brit)*; → **catastrophe**

scénarisation /senaʀizasjɔ̃/ NF scripting

scénariser /senaʀize/ ► conjug 1 ◄ VT *(TV)* to script

scénariste /senaʀist/ NMF *(Ciné)* scriptwriter

scénaristique /senaʀistik/ ADJ ◆ **l'écriture ~** script writing ◆ **la structure *ou* construction ~** the plot structure ◆ **le meurtre n'est qu'un prétexte ~** the murder is just a plot device

scène /sɛn/ NF 1 *(= estrade)* stage ◆ **~ tournante** revolving stage ◆ **sortir de ~, quitter la ~** to go off stage, to exit ◆ **occuper le devant de la ~** *(lit)* to be in the foreground, to be at the front of the stage; *(fig)* to be in the forefront ◆ **en fond de ~** at the back of the stage, in the background ◆ **sur (la) ~** on stage ◆ **il se produira *ou* sera sur la ~ de l'Olympia en janvier** he'll be performing *ou* appearing at the Olympia in January

2 *(= le théâtre)* **la ~** the stage ◆ **une vedette de la ~ française** a star of the French stage ◆ **il a quitté la ~ à 75 ans** he gave up the stage at the age of 75 ◆ **à la ~ comme à la ville** (both) on stage and off, both on and off (the) stage ◆ **porter une œuvre à la ~** to bring a work to the stage, to stage a work ◆ **adapter un film pour la ~** to adapt a film for the stage

3 *(Ciné, Théât = division)* scene ◆ **dans la première ~** in the first *ou* opening scene, in scene one ◆ **~ d'action** *(Ciné)* action scene *ou* sequence ◆ **~ d'amour** love scene ◆ **elle m'a joué la grande ~ du deux*** she made an almighty fuss

4 *(= décor)* scene ◆ **changement de ~** scene change

5 *(Ciné, Théât = lieu de l'action)* scene ◆ **la ~ est *ou* se passe à Rome** the scene is set in Rome

6 *(= spectacle)* scene ◆ **il a assisté à toute la** ~ he witnessed the whole scene ◆ ~ **de panique/de violence** scene of panic/of violence ◆ **la** ~ **originaire** *ou* **primitive** *(Psych)* the primal scene

7 *(= confrontation, dispute)* scene ◆ ~ **de jalousie/de rupture** jealous/break-up scene ◆ **il m'a fait une** ~ **de jalousie** he exploded at me in a fit of jealousy ◆ ~ **de ménage** domestic fight *ou* quarrel ◆ **faire une** ~ to make a scene ◆ **il m'a fait une** ~ **parce que j'avais oublié la clé** he made a scene because I had forgotten the key ◆ **avoir une** ~ **(avec qn)** to have a scene (with sb)

8 *(= domaine)* scene ◆ **sur la** ~ **politique/internationale/littéraire** on the political/international/literary scene ◆ **la** ~ **publique** the public arena ◆ **il s'est retiré de la** ~ **publique** he has retired from public life

9 *(Art = tableau)* scene ◆ ~ **d'intérieur/mythologique** indoor/mythological scene ◆ ~ **de genre** genre painting

10 *(locutions)*

◆ **en scène** on stage ◆ **tout le monde en** ~ **!** everybody on stage! ◆ **être en** ~ to be on stage ◆ **entrer en** ~ *(Théât)* to come on stage; *[politicien, sportif]* to arrive on *ou* enter the scene ◆ **c'est là que l'informatique entre en** ~ this is where computing comes in ◆ **entrée en** ~ *(Théât)* entrance; *(fig)* arrival on the scene ◆ **par ordre d'entrée en** ~ in order of appearance → **metteur**

◆ **mettre en scène** *(Théât) [+ histoire, personnage]* to present; *[+ auteur]* to stage *ou* produce the play(s) of; *[+ pièce de théâtre]* to stage, to direct; *[+ film]* to direct

◆ **mise en scène** *(Ciné, Théât = production)* production ◆ **il a révolutionné la mise en** ~ *(= art)* he revolutionized directing *ou* stagecraft ◆ **mise en** ~ **de Vilar** directed by Vilar ◆ **c'est de la mise en** ~ *(fig, péj)* it's all put on ◆ **toute cette mise en** ~ **pour nous faire croire que ...** this whole performance was to make us believe that ...

scénique /senik/ ADJ theatrical; → **indication**

scéniquement /senikmɑ̃/ ADV *(Théât)* theatrically

scénographe /senɔgʀaf/ NMF *(Théât)* stage *ou* theatre *(Brit) ou* theater *(US)* designer

scénographie /senɔgʀafi/ NF 1 *(Art)* scenography 2 *(Théât)* stage design

scénographique /senɔgʀafik/ ADJ *(Théât) [conditions]* relating to stage *ou* theatre *(Brit) ou* theater *(US)* design ◆ **quelle que soit la solution** ~ **retenue** whatever way the director decides to handle the scene

scepticisme /septisism/ NM scepticism *(Brit)*, skepticism *(US)* ◆ **exprimer son** ~ **à l'égard de** *ou* **sur qch** to express scepticism about sth

sceptique /septik/ ADJ sceptical *(Brit)*, skeptical *(US)* ◆ **d'un air** ~ sceptically *(Brit)*, skeptically *(US)* ◆ **être** *ou* **se montrer** ~ to be sceptical *(à l'égard de, sur, quant à* about); ◆ **ses arguments me laissent** ~ his arguments don't convince me NMF sceptic *(Brit)*, skeptic *(US)*; *(Philos)* Sceptic *(Brit)*, Skeptic *(US)*

sceptre /septʀ/ NM *(lit, fig)* sceptre *(Brit)*, scepter *(US)*

Schéhérazade /ʃeeʀazad/ NF Sheherazade

schelling /ʃ(ə)lɛ̃/ NM ⇒ **schilling**

schéma /ʃema/ NM 1 *(= diagramme)* diagram, sketch ◆ ~ **de montage** assembly diagram *ou* instructions ◆ ~ **de principe** (wiring) diagram ◆ **je vais te faire un petit** ~ I'll draw you a little diagram 2 *(= plan)* plan (of action); *(= organisation)* set-up ◆ **les choses ne se déroulaient pas suivant le** ~ **classique** things didn't follow their usual pattern ◆ ~ **d'aménagement,** ~ **directeur** *(Admin)* urban development plan ◆ **cela n'entre pas dans mes** ~**s** *(= principes)* it goes against my principles 3 *(= résumé)* outline ◆ **faire le** ~ **de l'opération** to give an outline of the operation 4 *(Psych)* ~ **corporel** body image

schématique /ʃematik/ ADJ *[dessin]* diagrammatic(al), schematic; *(péj) [interprétation, conception]* oversimplified

schématiquement /ʃematikmɑ̃/ ADV *[représenter]* diagrammatically, schematically ◆ **il exposa l'affaire** ~ he gave an outline of the affair, he outlined the affair ◆ **très** ~**, voici de quoi il s'agit** briefly, this is what it's all about

schématisation /ʃematizasjɔ̃/ NF schematization; *(péj)* (over)simplification

schématiser /ʃematize/ ► conjug 1 ◄ VT to schematize; *(péj)* to (over)simplify

schématisme /ʃematism/ NM *(péj)* oversimplicity

schème /ʃɛm/ NM *(Philos)* schema; *(Art)* design, scheme

Schengen /ʃengɛn/ N ◆ **l'espace** ~ the Schengen zone ◆ **les accords de** ~ the Schengen agreement

scherzando /skɛʀtsando/ ADV scherzando

scherzo /skɛʀdzo/ NM scherzo ADV scherzando

schilling /ʃiliŋ/ NM schilling

schismatique /ʃismatik/ ADJ, NMF schismatic

schisme /ʃism/ NM *(Rel)* schism; *(Pol)* split

schiste /ʃist/ NM *(métamorphique)* schist, shale ◆ ~ **bitumineux** oil shale ◆ **huile de** ~ shale oil

schisteux, -euse /ʃistø, øz/ ADJ schistose

schizo * /skizo/ ADJ, NMF (abrév de **schizophrène**) schizo *

schizoïde /skizɔid/ ADJ, NMF schizoid

schizophrène /skizɔfʀɛn/ ADJ, NMF *(Méd, fig)* schizophrenic

schizophrénie /skizɔfʀeni/ NF *(Méd, fig)* schizophrenia

schizophrénique /skizɔfʀenik/ ADJ schizophrenic

schlague /ʃlag/ NF *(Mil Hist)* ◆ **la** ~ drubbing, flogging ◆ **ils n'obéissent qu'à la** ~ ** they only do as they're told if you really lay into them ** *ou* if you give them what-for **

schlass ** /ʃlas/ ADJ INV *(= ivre)* sozzled **, plastered ** NM *(= couteau)* knife

schlinguer ** /ʃlɛ̃ge/ ► conjug 1 ◄ VI to pong **, to stink to high heaven *

schlitte /ʃlit/ NF sledge *(for transporting wood)*

schlitter /ʃlite/ ► conjug 1 ◄ VT to sledge *(wood)*

schmilblik * /ʃmilblik/ NM ◆ **faire avancer le** ~ to help things along ◆ **ça ne fait pas avancer le** ~ that doesn't get anybody anywhere, that doesn't get us very far

schnaps /ʃnaps/ NM schnap(p)s

schnock ** /ʃnɔk/ NM ⇒ **chnoque**

schnouff † /ʃnuf/ NF *(arg Drogue)* dope **

Schtroumpf /ʃtʀumf/ NM Smurf

schuss /ʃus/ NM schuss ADV ◆ **descendre (tout)** ~ to schuss (down)

schwa /ʃva/ NM schwa(h)

Schweppes ® /ʃwɛps/ NM tonic (water)

SCI /ɛssei/ NF (abrév de **société civile immobilière**) → **société**

sciage /sjaʒ/ NM *[de bois, métal]* sawing

sciatique /sjatik/ NF sciatica ADJ sciatic

scie /si/ NF 1 *(= outil)* saw ◆ ~ **à bois** wood saw ◆ ~ **circulaire** circular saw ◆ ~ **à chantourner** *ou* **découper** fretsaw ◆ ~ **électrique** power saw ◆ ~ **à guichet** panel saw ◆ ~ **à métaux** hacksaw ◆ ~ **musicale** musical saw ◆ ~ **à ruban** bandsaw ◆ ~ **sauteuse** jigsaw; → **dent** 2 *(péj)* *(= chanson)* repetitive song; *(= personne)* bore

sciemment /sjamɑ̃/ ADV knowingly

science /sjɑ̃s/ NF 1 *(= domaine scientifique)* science ◆ **les** ~**s** *(gén)* the sciences; *(Scol)* science ◆ **la** ~ **du beau** the science of beauty ◆ ~**s appliquées/exactes/pures/ humaines/ occultes** applied/exact/pure/social/ occult sciences ◆ ~**s expérimentales** experimental sciences ◆ **les** ~**s dures/molles** the hard/soft sciences ◆ **institut des** ~**s sociales** *(Univ)* institute of social science ◆ ~**s naturelles** † *(Scol)* natural science † ◆ ~**s physiques** physical science ◆ ~**s marines** *ou* **de la mer** marine science ◆ **les** ~**s de la vie** the life sciences ◆ **sciences de la vie et de la terre** *(Scol)* ≈ biology ◆ ~**s d'observation** observational sciences ◆ ~**s économiques** economics *(sg)* ◆ ~**s politiques** political science ◆ **Sciences Po** *(Univ)* *French school of political science*; → **homme**

2 *(= art, habileté)* **la** ~ **de la guerre** the science *ou* art of war ◆ **faire qch avec une** ~ **consommée** to do sth with consummate skill ◆ **sa** ~ **des couleurs** his skilful use of colour

3 *(= érudition)* knowledge ◆ **je n'ai pas la** ~ **infuse** I have no way of knowing ◆ **la** ~ **du bien et du mal** *(Rel)* the knowledge of good and evil ◆ **savoir de** ~ **certaine que ...** to know for a fact *ou* for certain that ... ◆ **il faut toujours qu'il étale sa** ~ he's always showing off his knowledge; → **puits**

science-fiction /sjɑ̃sfiksjɔ̃/ NF science fiction, sci-fi * ◆ **film/roman de** ~ science fiction *ou* sci-fi * film/novel ◆ **c'est** *ou* **ça relève de la** ~ it's like something out of science fiction

scientificité /sjɑ̃tifisite/ NF scientific character *ou* nature

scientifique /sjɑ̃tifik/ ADJ scientific NMF scientist

scientifiquement /sjɑ̃tifikmɑ̃/ ADV scientifically

scientisme /sjɑ̃tism/ NM scientism

scientiste /sjɑ̃tist/ NMF 1 *(= adepte du scientisme)* believer in the authority of science 2 *(= chrétien)* Christian Scientist ADJ scientistic

scientologie /sjɑ̃tɔlɔʒi/ NF Scientology ®

scientologue /sjɑ̃tɔlɔg/ ADJ, NMF Scientologist

scier /sje/ ► conjug 7 ◄ VT 1 *[+ bois, métal]* to saw; *[+ bûche]* to saw (up); *[+ partie en trop]* to saw off ◆ ~ **une branche pour faire des bûches** to saw (up) a branch into logs ◆ ~ **la branche sur laquelle on est assis** *(fig)* to dig one's own grave 2 *(* = stupéfier)* **ça m'a scié !** it bowled me over! *, it staggered me! * ◆ **c'est vraiment sciant !** it's absolutely staggering! * 3 *(* = ennuyer)* ~ **qn** to bore sb rigid * *ou* stiff *

scierie /siʀi/ NF sawmill

scieur /sjœʀ/ NM sawyer ◆ ~ **de long** pit sawyer

scille /sil/ NF scilla

Scilly /sili/ N ◆ **les îles** ~ the Scilly Isles

scinder /sɛ̃de/ ► conjug 1 ◄ VT to split (up), to divide (up) *(en* in, into) VPR **se scinder** to split (up) *(en* in, into)

scintigraphie /sɛ̃tigʀafi/ NF scintigraphy

scintillant, e /sɛ̃tijɑ̃, ɑ̃t/ ADJ *[diamant, yeux, neige]* sparkling; *[étoile, lumières]* twinkling; *[robe]* shimmering; *[goutte d'eau]* glistening; *[esprit]* sparkling, scintillating

scintillation /sɛ̃tijasjɔ̃/ NF *(Astron, Phys)* scintillation ◆ **compteur à** ~**s** scintillation counter

scintillement /sɛ̃tijmɑ̃/ NM *[de diamant, yeux]* sparkling; *[d'étoile, lumières]* twinkling; *[de goutte d'eau]* glistening; *[d'esprit]* sparkling, scintillating ◆ **le** ~ **de son esprit** his scintillating mind ◆ **le** ~ **de ses yeux** his sparkling eyes

scintiller /sɛ̃tije/ ▸ conjug 1 ◂ VI *[diamant, yeux]* to sparkle; *[étoile, lumières]* to twinkle; *[goutte d'eau]* to glisten; *[esprit]* to sparkle, to scintillate

scion /sjɔ̃/ NM *(Bot)* *(gén)* twig; *(= greffe)* scion; *(Pêche)* top piece

Scipion /sipjɔ̃/ NM Scipio ◆ **~ l'Africain** Scipio Africanus

scission /sisjɔ̃/ NF 1 *(= schisme)* split, scission *(frm)* ◆ **faire ~** to split away, to secede 2 *(Écon)* demerger 3 *(Bot, Phys)* fission

scissioniste /sisjɔnist/ ADJ, NMF secessionist

scissipare /sisipaʀ/ ADJ fissiparous, schizogenetic

scissiparité /sisipaʀite/ NF fissiparousness, schizogenesis

scissure /sisyʀ/ NF fissure, sulcus ◆ **~ interhémisphérique** longitudinal fissure of the cerebrum ◆ **~ latérale** *ou* **de Sylvius** fissure of Sylvius, lateral fissure

sciure /sjyʀ/ NF ◆ **~ (de bois)** sawdust

scléreux, -euse /skleʀø, øz/ ADJ sclerotic, sclerous

sclérosant, e /skleʀozɑ̃, ɑ̃t/ ADJ *(fig)* ossifying

sclérose /skleʀoz/ NF 1 *(Méd)* sclerosis ◆ **~ artérielle** hardening of the arteries, arteriosclerosis *(SPÉC)* ◆ **~ en plaques** multiple sclerosis 2 *(fig)* ossification

sclérosé, e /skleʀoze/ (ptp de **se scléroser**) ADJ *(lit)* sclerosed, sclerotic; *(fig)* ossified

scléroser /skleʀoze/ ▸ conjug 1 ◂ VPR **se scléroser** *(Méd)* to become sclerotic *ou* sclerosed; *(fig)* to become ossified VT *[+ tissus]* to cause sclerosis of

sclérotique /skleʀɔtik/ NF sclera, sclerotic

scolaire /skɔlɛʀ/ ADJ 1 *(gén)* school *(épith)* ◆ **ses succès ~s** his success in *ou* at school ◆ **enfant d'âge ~** child of school age ◆ **en milieu ~** in schools ◆ **les ~s** schoolchildren; → **établissement, groupe, livret** *etc* 2 *(péj)* *[style]* unimaginative ◆ **son livre est un peu ~ par endroits** his book is a bit starchy in places

scolairement /skɔlɛʀmɑ̃/ ADV ◆ **il réussit très bien ~** he's doing very well at school ◆ **il faut intégrer ces enfants ~ et socialement** these children need to be helped to fit in, both at school and in society

scolarisable /skɔlaʀizabl/ ADJ *[handicapé]* educable, capable of attending school

scolarisation /skɔlaʀizasjɔ̃/ NF *[d'enfant]* schooling ◆ **la ~ d'une population/d'un pays** providing a population with schooling/a country with schools ◆ **taux de ~** percentage of children in full-time education

scolariser /skɔlaʀize/ ▸ conjug 1 ◂ VT *[+ enfant]* to provide with schooling, to send to school; *[+ pays]* to provide with schools *ou* schooling

scolarité /skɔlaʀite/ NF schooling ◆ **~ primaire/secondaire** primary/secondary schooling *ou* education ◆ **la ~ a été prolongée jusqu'à 16 ans** the school-leaving age has been raised to 16 ◆ **pendant mes années de ~** during my school years *ou* years at school ◆ **~ obligatoire** compulsory education *ou* schooling ◆ **service de la ~** *(Univ)* registrar's office ◆ **il a suivi une ~ normale** he had a normal education ◆ **il a eu une ~ difficile** he had difficulties at school; → **certificat, frais²**

scolastique /skɔlastik/ ADJ *(Philos, péj)* scholastic NF scholasticism NM *(Philos)* scholastic, schoolman; *(= séminariste)* seminarian, seminarist; *(péj)* scholastic

scoliose /skɔljoz/ NF curvature of the spine, scoliosis *(SPÉC)*

scolopendre /skɔlɔpɑ̃dʀ/ NF 1 *(= animal)* centipede, scolopendra *(SPÉC)* 2 *(= plante)* hart's-tongue, scolopendrium *(SPÉC)*

sconse /skɔ̃s/ NM skunk (fur)

scoop * /skup/ NM scoop

scooter /skutœʀ/ NM (motor) scooter ◆ **~ des mers** jet ski ◆ **~ des neiges** Skidoo ® ◆ **faire du ~** to ride a scooter

scopie ** /skɔpi/ NF abrév de **radioscopie**

scorbut /skɔʀbyt/ NM scurvy

scorbutique /skɔʀbytik/ ADJ *[symptômes]* of scurvy, scorbutic *(SPÉC)*; *[personne]* suffering from scurvy, scorbutic *(SPÉC)* NMF person with *ou* suffering from scurvy

score /skɔʀ/ NM *(gén, Sport)* score ◆ **faire un bon/mauvais ~** *(Pol, Scol, Sport)* to do well/badly ◆ **obtenir un ~ de 48% aux élections** to get 48% of the votes ◆ **mener au ~** to be in the lead

scorie /skɔʀi/ NF *(gén pl)* 1 *(= résidu)* slag *(NonC)*, scoria *(NonC)*, clinker *(NonC)* ◆ **~s (volcaniques)** (volcanic) scoria 2 *(fig)* dross *(NonC)* ◆ **il reste beaucoup de ~s dans le texte** there are still a lot of errors in the text

scorpion /skɔʀpjɔ̃/ NM 1 *(= animal)* scorpion ◆ **~ d'eau** water-scorpion ◆ **~ de mer** scorpion-fish 2 *(Astron)* **le Scorpion** Scorpio ◆ **il est Scorpion, il est (du signe) du Scorpion** he's (a) Scorpio

scotch /skɔtʃ/ NM 1 *(= boisson)* scotch (whisky *(Brit)* *ou* whiskey *(US, Ir)*) 2 *(= adhésif)* **Scotch** ® Sellotape ® *(Brit)*, Scotchtape ® *(US)*

scotcher /skɔtʃe/ ▸ conjug 1 ◂ VT to sellotape *(Brit)*, to stick with Scotchtape ® *(US)* ◆ **je suis resté scotché** * *(= stupéfait)* I was flabbergasted *ou* gobsmacked * *(Brit)* ◆ **elle était scotchée sur son siège** she was glued to her seat ◆ **il reste des heures scotché** * **devant sa télévision** he spends hours glued to the television

scotch-terrier (pl **scotch-terriers**) /skɔtʃtɛʀje/ NM Scottish *ou* Scotch terrier

scoubidou /skubidu/ NM *strip of plaited plastic threads*

scoumoune ** /skumun/ NF *(arg Crime)* tough *ou* rotten luck *

scout, e /skut/ ADJ *[camp, mouvement]* scout *(épith)* ◆ **avoir un côté ~** *(péj)* to be a bit of a boy scout NM (boy) scout ◆ **les ~s de France** French scouts NF **scoute** (girl) scout

scoutisme /skutism/ NM *(= mouvement)* scout movement; *(= activité)* scouting ◆ **faire du ~** to be a scout

SCP /ɛssepe/ NF (abrév de **société civile professionnelle**) → **société**

SCPI /ɛssepei/ NF (abrév de **société civile de placement immobilier**) → **société**

Scrabble ® /skʀabl/ NM Scrabble ® ◆ **faire un ~** to play Scrabble ®, to have a game of Scrabble ®

scratch /skʀatʃ/ NM 1 *(= bande Velcro ®)* Velcro strip 2 *(Mus)* scratch

scratcher /skʀatʃe/ ▸ conjug 1 ◂ VT *(Sport)* to scratch VPR **se scratcher** * to get smashed up *

scriban /skʀibɑ̃/ NM *(avec cabinet)* bureau bookcase; *(sans cabinet)* slant-front bureau

scribe /skʀib/ NM *(péj = bureaucrate)* penpusher *(Brit)*, pencil pusher *(US)*; *(Hist)* scribe

scribouillard, e /skʀibujaʀ, aʀd/ NM,F *(péj)* penpusher *(Brit)*, pencil pusher *(US)*

scribouilleur, -euse * /skʀibujœʀ, øz/ NM,F *(péj)* hack (writer), scribbler

script /skʀipt/ NM 1 ◆ **(écriture) ~** printing ◆ **apprendre le ~** to learn how to print (letters) ◆ **écrire en ~** to print 2 *(Ciné)* (shooting) script 3 *(Ordin)* script NF ⇒ **script-girl**

scripte /skʀipt/ NF *(Ciné)* continuity girl

scripteur /skʀiptœʀ/ NM *(Ling)* writer

script-girl † (pl **script-girls**) /skʀiptgœʀl/ NF continuity girl

scriptural, e (mpl **-aux**) /skʀiptyʀal, o/ ADJ → **monnaie**

scrofulaire /skʀɔfylɛʀ/ NF figwort

scrofule /skʀɔfyl/ NF *(Méd)* scrofula ◆ **~s** *(Hist Méd)* scrofula, king's evil

scrogneugneu † /skʀɔɲøɲø/ EXCL damnation!

scrotal, e (mpl **-aux**) /skʀɔtal, o/ ADJ scrotal

scrotum /skʀɔtɔm/ NM scrotum

scrupule /skʀypyl/ NM scruple ◆ **avoir des ~s to have scruples** ◆ **avoir des ~s à faire qch, se faire ~ de faire qch** to have scruples *ou* misgivings *ou* qualms about doing sth ◆ **faire taire ses ~s** to silence one's scruples ◆ **je n'aurais aucun ~ à refuser** I wouldn't have any scruples *ou* qualms *ou* misgivings about refusing ◆ **son honnêteté est poussée jusqu'au ~** he's scrupulously honest ◆ **il est dénué de ~s** he has no scruples, he is completely unscrupulous ◆ **sans ~s** *[personne]* unscrupulous, without scruples; *[agir]* unscrupulously ◆ **vos ~s vous honorent** your scrupulousness is a credit to you ◆ **je comprends votre ~** *ou* **vos ~s** I understand your scruples ◆ **dans** *ou* **par un ~ d'honnêteté/d'exactitude historique** *(= par souci de)* in scrupulous regard for honesty/for historical exactness

scrupuleusement /skʀypyløzmɑ̃/ ADV scrupulously

scrupuleux, -euse /skʀypylø, øz/ ADJ scrupulous ◆ **peu ~** unscrupulous ◆ **ils réclament le respect ~ des règles démocratiques** they demand that the rules of democracy be scrupulously respected ◆ **avec un soin ~** with scrupulous care

scrutateur, -trice /skʀytatœʀ, tʀis/ ADJ *(littér)* *[caractère, regard]* searching ◆ **sous l'œil ~ du maître** under the watchful eye of the master NM *(Pol)* teller, scrutineer *(Brit)*

scruter /skʀyte/ ▸ conjug 1 ◂ VT *[+ horizon]* to scan, to search, to scrutinize; *[+ objet, personne]* to scrutinize, to examine; *[+ pénombre]* to peer into, to search

scrutin /skʀytɛ̃/ NM 1 *(= vote)* ballot ◆ **par voie de ~** by ballot ◆ **voter au ~ secret** to vote by secret ballot ◆ **il a été élu au troisième tour de ~** he was elected on *ou* at the third ballot *ou* round ◆ **dépouiller le ~** to count the votes 2 *(= élection)* poll ◆ **le jour du ~** polling day ◆ **ouverture/clôture du ~** start/close of polling 3 *(= modalité)* ◆ **~ de liste** list system ◆ **~ d'arrondissement** district election system ◆ **~ majoritaire** election on a majority basis ◆ **~ proportionnel** proportional representation ◆ **~ de ballottage** second ballot, second round of voting ◆ **~ uninominal** uninominal system

sculpter /skylte/ ▸ conjug 1 ◂ VT *[+ marbre, statue]* to sculpt; *[+ meuble]* to carve, to sculpt; *[+ bâton, bois]* to carve ◆ **~ qch dans du bois** to carve sth out of wood

sculpteur /skyltœʀ/ NM *(= homme)* sculptor; *(= femme)* sculptor, sculptress ◆ **~ sur bois** woodcarver

sculptural, e (mpl **-aux**) /skyltyʀal, o/ ADJ *(Art)* sculptural; *(fig)* *[beauté, corps, formes]* statuesque

sculpture /skyltyʀ/ NF 1 *(= art, objet)* sculpture ◆ **faire de la ~** to sculpt ◆ **~ sur bois** woodcarving ◆ **une ~ sur marbre/neige/glace** a marble/snow/an ice sculpture 2 *[pneu]* tread (pattern) ◆ **~s** tread

Scylla /sila/ NF Scylla; → **Charybde**

scythe /sit/ ADJ Scythian NM (= langue) Scythian NM,F **Scythe** Scythian

Scythie /siti/ NF Scythia

SDF /ɛsdeɛf/ NMF INV (abrév de **sans domicile fixe**) homeless person ♦ **les ~** the homeless

SDN /ɛsdeɛn/ NF (abrév de **Société des Nations**) → **société**

se /sə/ PRON 1 *(réfléchi, sg, indéfini)* oneself; *(homme)* himself; *(femme)* herself; *(sujet non humain)* itself; *(pl)* themselves ♦ **~ regarder dans la glace** to look at o.s. in the mirror ♦ **~ raser/laver** to shave/wash ♦ **~ mouiller/salir** to get wet/dirty ♦ **~ brûler/couper** to burn/cut o.s.; → **écouter, faire**

2 *(réciproque)* each other, one another ♦ **deux personnes qui s'aiment** two people who love each other *ou* one another ♦ **des gens qui ~ haïssent** people who hate each other *ou* one another

3 *(possessif)* **~ casser la jambe** to break one's leg ♦ **il ~ lave les mains** he is washing his hands ♦ **elle s'est coupé les cheveux** she has cut her hair

4 *(passif)* **cela ne ~ fait pas** that's not done ♦ **cela ~ répare/recolle facilement** it can easily be repaired/glued together again ♦ **la vérité finira par ~ savoir** the truth will out in the end, the truth will finally be found out ♦ **l'anglais ~ parle dans le monde entier** English is spoken throughout the world ♦ **cela ~ vend bien** it sells well ♦ **les escargots ~ ~rvent dans la coquille** snails are served in their shells

5 *(impersonnel)* **il ~ peut que ...** it may be that ..., it is possible that ... ♦ **comment ~ fait-il que ... ?** how is it that ...?

S.E. (abrév de **Son Excellence**) HE

S.É. (abrév de **Son Éminence**) HE

séance /seɑ̃s/ NF 1 *(= réunion) [de conseil municipal]* meeting, session; *[de parlement, tribunal]* session, sitting; *[de comité]* session ♦ **être en ~** to be in session, to sit ♦ **la ~ est levée** the meeting is over ♦ **~ extraordinaire** extraordinary meeting ♦ **la proposition sera examinée en ~ publique** the proposal will be considered at *ou* in a public session *ou* meeting ♦ **ils l'ont fusillé ~ tenante** they shot him there and then *ou* on the spot ♦ **nous partirons ~ tenante** we shall leave forthwith *ou* without further ado; → **suspension**

2 *(= période)* session ♦ **~ de photographie/rééducation/gymnastique** photographic *ou* photography/physiotherapy/gymnastics session ♦ **~ de pose** sitting ♦ **~ de spiritisme** séance ♦ **~ de travail** working session ♦ **~ de torture** torture session

3 *(= représentation) (Théât)* performance ♦ **~ privée** private showing *ou* performance ♦ **~ (de cinéma)** film ♦ **première/dernière ~** *(Ciné)* first/last showing ♦ **la ~ est à 21h, et le film 15 minutes plus tard** the programme starts at 9 o'clock and the film 15 minutes later

4 *(Bourse)* day of trading, session ♦ **après plusieurs ~s de hausse** after several sessions *ou* days of bullish trading ♦ **en début/fin de ~** at the opening/close (of the day's trading) ♦ **l'indice a gagné 10 points en cours de ~** the index gained 10 points during (the day's) trading

séant[1] /seɑ̃/ NM *(hum = derrière)* posterior *(hum)* ♦ **se mettre sur son ~** *(frm)* to sit up *(from a lying position)*

séant[2], séante /seɑ̃, seɑ̃t/ ADJ *(littér = convenable)* seemly, fitting ♦ **il n'est pas ~ de dire cela** it is unseemly *ou* unfitting to say such things

seau (pl **seaux**) /so/ NM (= *récipient*) bucket, pail *(surtout US)*; *(= contenu)* bucket(ful), pail(ful) *(surtout US)* ♦ **il pleut à ~x, la pluie tombe à ~x** it's coming *ou* pouring down in buckets*, it's raining buckets* ♦ **~ à champagne/glace** champagne/ice bucket ♦ **~ à charbon** coal scuttle ♦ **~ hygiénique** slop pail

sébacé, e /sebase/ ADJ *[glande]* sebaceous

sébile /sebil/ NF begging bowl ♦ **tendre la ~** *(lit)* to beg; *(fig)* to bring out *ou* hold out the begging bowl

séborrhée /sebɔʀe/ NF seborrhoea *(Brit)*, seborrhea *(US)*

sébum /sebɔm/ NM sebum

sec, sèche[1] /sɛk, sɛʃ/ ADJ 1 *[air, bois, climat, linge, temps, saison, toux]* dry; *[fruit]* dried ♦ **elle le regarda partir, l'œil ~** she watched him go, dry-eyed ♦ **j'avais la gorge sèche** my throat was dry ♦ **il est au régime ~** he's not allowed to drink alcohol ♦ **lorsque la peinture est sèche au toucher** when the paint is dry to the touch; → **cale[1], cinq, cul**

2 *(= sans graisse) [cheveu, peau]* dry

3 *(= maigre) [bras, personne]* lean ♦ **il est ~ comme un coup de trique*** *ou* **comme un hareng*** he's as thin as a rake

4 *(= sans douceur) [rire, vin]* dry; *[style]* terse; *[cœur]* cold, hard; *[réponse]* curt ♦ **elle a été très sèche avec moi** she was very curt with me ♦ **il lui a écrit une lettre très sèche** he wrote him a very curt letter ♦ **se casser avec un bruit ~** to break with a (sharp) snap, to snap ♦ **"non", dit-il d'un ton ~** "no", he said curtly ♦ **placage ~** *(Sport)* hard tackle; → **coup**

5 *(= sans eau) [alcool]* neat ♦ **il prend son whisky ~** he takes *ou* drinks his whisky neat *ou* straight

6 *(Cartes)* **atout/valet ~** singleton trump/jack ♦ **son valet était ~** his jack was a singleton

7 *(Tennis)* **il a été battu en trois sets ~s** he was beaten in three straight sets

8 *(= sans prestations supplémentaires)* **le vol ~ coûte 250 €** the flight-only price is €250 ♦ **licenciement ~** compulsory lay-off *ou* redundancy *(Brit) (without any compensation)*

9 *(locutions)* **être** *ou* **rester ~*** to be stumped* ♦ **je suis resté ~ sur ce sujet** I drew a blank on the subject

ADV * *[frapper]* hard ♦ **il boit ~** he really knocks it back*, he's a hard *ou* heavy drinker ♦ **démarrer ~** *(en voiture) (sans douceur)* to start (up) with a jolt *ou* jerk; *(rapidement)* to tear off ♦ **ça démarre ~ ce soir** the evening's off to a good start ♦ **conduire ~** to drive like a racing driver ♦ **et lui, aussi ~, a répondu que ...** and he replied straight off that ... ♦ **il est arrivé et reparti aussi ~** he arrived and left again just as quickly ♦ **je l'ai eu ~*** I was really shocked

NM

♦ **au sec** ♦ **tenir** *ou* **conserver qch au ~** to keep sth in a dry place ♦ **rester au ~** to stay in the dry ♦ **pour garder les pieds au ~** to keep your feet dry

♦ **à sec** ♦ **être à ~** *[puits, torrent]* to be dry *ou* dried-up; *(* = être sans argent) [personne]* to be broke* *ou* skint* *(Brit)*; *[caisse]* to be empty ♦ **mettre à ~ un étang** *[personne]* to drain a pond; *[soleil]* to dry up a pond ♦ **il l'a mis à ~** *(au jeu) [+ joueur]* he cleaned him out*, he took him to the cleaner's*

sécable /sekabl/ ADJ *[comprimé]* divisible

SECAM /sekam/ ADJ, NM (abrév de **séquentiel couleur à mémoire**) SECAM

sécant, e /sekɑ̃, ɑ̃t/ ADJ secant NF **sécante** secant

sécateur /sekatœʀ/ NM (pair of) secateurs, (pair of) pruning shears

sécession /sesesjɔ̃/ NF secession ♦ **faire ~** to secede, to break away; → **guerre**

sécessionniste /sesesjɔnist/ ADJ, NMF secessionist ♦ **république ~** breakaway republic

séchage /seʃaʒ/ NM *[de cheveux, linge]* drying; *[de bois]* seasoning ♦ **le ~ (en) machine n'est pas recommandé pour ce tissu** it is not recommended that this fabric be dried in a clothes dryer ♦ **"séchage à plat"** "dry flat" ♦ **vernis/colle à ~ rapide** quick-drying varnish/glue

sèche[2]* /sɛʃ/ NF *(= cigarette)* cigarette, cig*, fag* *(Brit)*

sèche-cheveux /sɛʃʃəvø/ NM INV hairdryer

sèche-linge /sɛʃlɛ̃ʒ/ NM INV *(= armoire)* drying cabinet; *(= machine)* tumble-dryer

sèche-mains /sɛʃmɛ̃/ NM INV hand-dryer, blower

sèchement /sɛʃmɑ̃/ ADV *[répondre]* curtly

sécher /seʃe/ ▸ conjug 6 ◂ VT 1 *(gén)* to dry ♦ **sèche tes larmes** dry your tears *ou* eyes ♦ **~ les larmes** *ou* **les pleurs de qn** *(= le consoler)* to wipe away sb's tears ♦ **~ son verre*** to drain one's glass

2 *(arg Scol = manquer) [+ cours]* to skip* ♦ **il a séché l'école pendant trois jours** he skipped school* *ou* skived off school *(Brit)** for three days

3 *(* = faire tomber) [+ adversaire]* to bring down

VI 1 *[surface mouillée, peinture]* to dry (off); *[substance imbibée de liquide]* to dry (out); *[linge]* to dry ♦ **faire** *ou* **laisser ~ du linge, mettre du linge à ~** *(à l'intérieur)* to put *ou* hang washing up to dry; *(à l'extérieur)* to put *ou* hang washing out to dry ♦ **"faire sécher sans essorer"** "do not spin (dry)" ♦ **"faire sécher à plat"** "dry flat"

2 *(= se déshydrater) [bois]* to dry out; *[fleur]* to dry up *ou* out ♦ **le caoutchouc a séché** the rubber has dried up *ou* gone dry ♦ **~ sur pied** *[plante]* to wither on the stalk ♦ **faire ~** *[+ fleurs, fruits, viande]* to dry; *[+ bois]* to season ♦ **boue/fleur/viande séchée** dried mud/flower/meat

3 *(arg Scol = rester sec)* to be stumped* ♦ **j'ai séché en chimie** I drew a (complete) blank *ou* I dried up* completely in chemistry

VPR **se sécher** to dry o.s. (off) ♦ **se ~ les cheveux/mains** to dry one's hair/hands ♦ **se ~ au soleil/avec une serviette** to dry o.s. in the sun/with a towel ♦ **se ~ devant le feu** to dry o.s. *ou* dry (o.s.) off in front of the fire

sécheresse /sɛʃʀɛs/ NF 1 *[de climat, sol, style, ton]* dryness; *[de réponse]* curtness; *[de cœur]* coldness, hardness ♦ **~ vaginale** vaginal dryness ♦ **~ cutanée/oculaire** dry skin/eyes, dryness of the skin/eyes ♦ **dire qch avec ~** to say sth curtly 2 *(= absence de pluie)* drought ♦ **année/période de ~** year/period of drought

sécherie /sɛʃʀi/ NF *(= machine)* drier, dryer, drying machine; *(= installations)* drying plant

séchoir /seʃwaʀ/ NM *(= local) (pour nourriture)* drying shed; *(pour linge)* drying room; *(= appareil)* dryer ♦ **~ à linge** *(pliant)* clothes-horse; *(rotatif)* tumble dryer; *(à cordes)* clothes airer ♦ **~ à chanvre/à tabac** hemp/tobacco drying shed ♦ **~ à cheveux** hairdryer ♦ **~ à tambour** tumble-dryer

second, e[1] /s(ə)gɔ̃, ɔ̃d/ ADJ 1 *(chronologiquement)* second ♦ **la ~e fois** the second time ♦ **je vous le dis pour la ~e fois, vous n'aurez rien** I repeat, you'll get nothing ♦ **chapitre, chapitre ~** chapter two; → **main, noce**

2 *(hiérarchiquement)* second ♦ **intelligence/malhonnêteté à nulle autre ~e** unparalleled intelligence/dishonesty; → **couteau, marché, plan[1]**

3 *(= autre, nouveau)* second ♦ **une ~e jeunesse** a second youth ♦ **dans une ~e vie** in a second life ♦ **cet écrivain est un ~ Hugo** this writer is a second Hugo ♦ **chez lui, c'est une ~e nature** with him it's second nature; → **état, habitude, souffle, vue[2]**

4 *(= dérivé) [cause]* secondary

NM,F second ◆ **le ~ de ses fils** his second son ◆ **il a été reçu ~ (en physique)** he came *ou* was second (in physics) ◆ **sans ~** *(littér)* second to none, peerless *(littér)* ◆ **~ (de cordée)** *(Alpinisme)* second (on the rope)

NM 1 *(= adjoint)* second in command; *(Naut)* first mate; *(en duel)* second

◆ **en second** ◆ **officier** *ou* **capitaine en ~** first mate ◆ **passer en ~** to be second ◆ **sa famille passe en ~** his family comes second *ou* takes second place

2 *(= étage)* second floor *(Brit)*, third floor *(US)* ◆ **la dame du ~** the lady on the second floor *(Brit) ou* the third floor *(US)*

3 *(dans une charade)* second ◆ **mon ~ est ...** my second is ...

NF seconde 1 *(Transport)* second class; *(billet)* second-class ticket ◆ **les ~es sont à l'avant** *(dans un train)* the second-class seats *ou* carriages are at the front ◆ **voyager en ~e** to travel second-class

2 *(Scol)* **(classe de) ~e** ≃ fifth form *(Brit) (in secondary school)*, tenth grade *(US) (in high school)*, sophomore year *(US) (in high school)*; → LYCÉE

3 *(= vitesse)* second (gear) ◆ **être en/passer la** *ou* **en ~e** to be in/change into second (gear)

4 *(Mus)* second

5 *(Danse)* second (position)

6 *(Escrime)* seconde; → aussi **seconde²**

secondaire /s(ə)gɔ̃dɛʀ/ **ADJ** *(gén, Chim, Scol)* secondary; *(Géol)* mesozoic, secondary † ◆ **c'est ~** that's of secondary importance ◆ **caractères sexuels ~s** *(Psych)* secondary sexual characteristics ◆ **intrigue ~** *(Littérat)* subplot ◆ **effets ~s** side effects ◆ **ligne ~** *(Rail)* branch line; → **route, secteur NM** 1 *(Scol)* **le ~** secondary (school) *(Brit) ou* high-school *(US)* education ◆ **les professeurs du ~** secondary school *(Brit) ou* high-school *(US)* teachers 2 *(Écon)* **le ~** the secondary sector 3 *(Géol)* **le ~** the Mesozoic, the Secondary Era † 4 *(Élec = enroulement)* secondary (winding)

secondairement /s(ə)gɔ̃dɛʀmɑ̃/ **ADV** secondarily

secondariser /s(ə)gɔ̃daʀize/ ► conjug 1 ◄ **VT** *[+ études supérieures, université]* to lower standards in

seconde² /s(ə)gɔ̃d/ **NF** *(gén, Géom)* second ◆ **(attends) une ~ !** just a *ou* one second! *ou* sec! * ◆ **à la ~ où il la vit ...** the (very) moment he saw her ..., the second he saw her ... ◆ **avec elle, tout doit être fait à la ~** with her, things have to be done instantly; → **fraction, quart**

secondement /s(ə)gɔ̃dmɑ̃/ **ADV** second(ly)

seconder /s(ə)gɔ̃de/ ► conjug 1 ◄ **VT** *(lit, fig)* to assist, to aid, to help ◆ **bien secondé par ...** ably assisted by ...

secouer /s(ə)kwe/ ► conjug 1 ◄ **VT** 1 *[+ arbre, salade]* to shake; *[+ miettes, poussière, oppression, paresse]* to shake off; *[+ tapis]* to shake (out) ◆ **~ le joug de** *[+ dictature, tyrannie]* to throw off *ou* cast off the yoke of ◆ **arrête de me ~ comme un prunier !*** stop shaking me! ◆ **~ la tête** *(pour dire oui)* to nod (one's head); *(pour dire non)* to shake one's head ◆ **l'explosion secoua l'hôtel** the explosion shook *ou* rocked the hotel ◆ **on est drôlement secoué** *(dans un autocar)* you really get shaken about; *(dans un bateau)* you really get tossed about ◆ **le vent secouait le petit bateau** the wind tossed the little boat about ◆ **la ville a été fortement secouée par le tremblement de terre** the town was rocked by the earthquake ◆ **le malade était secoué de spasmes/sanglots** spasms/great sobs shook the patient's body, the patient was racked with *ou* by spasms/great sobs ◆ **j'en ai rien à ~**** I don't give a damn** *ou* toss**

2 *(= traumatiser)* to shake ◆ **ce deuil l'a beaucoup secoué** this bereavement has really shaken him ◆ **t'es complètement secoué !**** *(= fou)* you're completely mad!

3 *(= ébranler)* to shake, to rock ◆ **cela a durement secoué le franc** this has severely shaken the franc ◆ **un gouvernement secoué par des affaires de corruption** a government rocked *ou* shaken by corruption scandals

4 *(= bousculer)* to shake up ◆ **il ne travaille que lorsqu'on le secoue** he only works if you push him ◆ **il faut ~ la torpeur de notre pays** this country needs to be shaken from *ou* out of its torpor ◆ **~ les puces à qn*** *(= le réprimander)* to tell *ou* tick* *(Brit)* sb off, to give sb a telling-off *ou* a ticking-off* *(Brit)*; *(= le stimuler)* to give sb a good shake ◆ **secoue tes puces*** *ou* **ta graisse**** *(= cesse de te morfondre)* snap out of it*; *(= fais vite)* get a move on* ◆ **~ le cocotier*** to get rid of the deadwood*

VPR se secouer *(lit)* to shake o.s.; *(* = faire un effort)* to make an effort; *(* = se dépêcher)* to get a move on*

secourable /s(ə)kuʀabl/ **ADJ** *[personne]* helpful; → **main**

secourir /s(ə)kuʀiʀ/ ► conjug 11 ◄ **VT** *[+ blessé, pauvre]* to help, to assist; *[+ alpiniste, skieur]* to rescue

secourisme /s(ə)kuʀism/ **NM** first aid ◆ **brevet de ~** first-aid certificate ◆ **apprendre les gestes élémentaires de ~** to learn basic first-aid skills

secouriste /s(ə)kuʀist/ **NMF** first-aid worker

secours /s(ə)kuʀ/ **NM** 1 *(= aide)* help, aid, assistance ◆ **appeler qn à son ~** to call to sb for help ◆ **demander du ~** to ask for help *ou* assistance ◆ **crier au ~** to shout *ou* call (out) for help ◆ **au ~ !** help! ◆ **aller au ~ de qn** to go to sb's aid *ou* assistance ◆ **porter ~ à qn** to give sb help *ou* assistance ◆ **le Secours catholique** *Catholic charity organization giving assistance to the poor* ◆ **le Secours populaire** *charity organization giving assistance to the poor*

2 *(= vivres, argent)* aid (NonC) ◆ **distribuer/recevoir des ~** to distribute/receive aid ◆ **~ humanitaires** humanitarian aid *ou* assistance ◆ **société de ~ mutuel** *(Hist)* friendly *(Brit) ou* benefit *(US)* society

3 *(= sauvetage)* aid (NonC), assistance (NonC) ◆ **~ aux blessés** aid *ou* assistance for the wounded ◆ **~ d'urgence** emergency aid *ou* assistance ◆ **le ~ en montagne/en mer** mountain/sea rescue ◆ **équipe de ~** rescue party *ou* team ◆ **quand les ~ arrivèrent** when help *ou* the rescue party arrived ◆ **porter ~ à un alpiniste** to rescue a mountaineer ◆ **les premiers ~ sont arrivés très rapidement** the emergency services were soon at the scene ◆ **apporter les premiers ~ à qn** to give first aid to sb; → **poste²**

4 *(Mil)* relief (NonC) ◆ **la colonne de ~** the relief column ◆ **les ~ sont attendus** relief is expected

5 *(Rel)* **mourir avec/sans les ~ de la religion** to die with/without the last rites

6 *(locutions)* **cela m'a été/ne m'a pas été d'un grand ~** this has been a *ou* of great help/of little help to me ◆ **éclairage de ~** emergency lighting ◆ **batterie de ~** spare battery; → **escalier, issue², poste², roue**

secousse /s(ə)kus/ **NF** 1 *(= cahot) [de train, voiture]* jolt, bump; *[d'avion]* bump ◆ **sans (une) ~** *[s'arrêter]* without a jolt, smoothly; *[transporter]* smoothly ◆ **avancer par ~s** to jolt along 2 *(= choc)* jerk, jolt; *(= traction)* tug, pull ◆ **~ (électrique)** (electric) shock ◆ **il a donné des ~s à la corde** he tugged the rope ◆ **~ (tellurique** *ou* **sismique)** (earth) tremor ◆ **il n'en fiche pas une ~ †*** he never does a stroke of work 3 *(= bouleversement)* jolt, shock ◆ **~s politiques/monétaires** political/monetary upheavals

secret, -ète /səkʀɛ, ɛt/ **ADJ** 1 *(= confidentiel)* secret ◆ **garder** *ou* **tenir qch ~** to keep sth secret ◆ **dans un lieu tenu ~** in a secret location ◆ **des informations classées secrètes** classified information; → **agent, fonds, service**

2 *(= caché) [tiroir, porte, pressentiment, vie]* secret ◆ **nos plus secrètes pensées** our most secret *ou* our innermost thoughts ◆ **avoir un charme ~** to have a hidden charm

3 *(= renfermé) [personne]* secretive

NM 1 *(= cachotterie)* secret ◆ **c'est son ~** it's his secret ◆ **il a gardé le ~ de notre projet** he kept our plan secret ◆ **ne pas avoir de ~(s) pour qn** *[personne]* to have no secrets from sb, to keep nothing from sb; *[sujet]* to have *ou* hold no secrets for sb ◆ **l'informatique n'a plus de ~(s) pour elle** computing holds no secrets for her now ◆ **confier un ~ à qn** to confide a secret to sb ◆ **il n'en fait pas un ~** he makes no secret about *ou* of it ◆ **~s d'alcôve** intimate talk ◆ **un ~ d'État** a state *ou* official secret ◆ **faire un ~ d'État de qch** *(fig)* to make a big secret of sth, to act as if sth were a state secret ◆ **"secret(-)défense"** "official secret" ◆ **couvert par le ~(-)défense** ≃ covered by the Official Secrets Act ◆ **~ de Polichinelle** open secret ◆ **ce n'est un ~ pour personne que ...** it's no secret that ...

2 *(= mécanisme, moyen)* secret ◆ **~ industriel/de fabrication** industrial/trade secret ◆ **le ~ du bonheur/de la réussite** the secret of happiness/of success ◆ **une sauce/un tour de passe-passe dont il a le ~** a sauce/a conjuring trick of which he (alone) has the secret ◆ **il a le ~ de ces plaisanteries stupides** he's got a knack for telling stupid jokes ◆ **tiroir à ~** drawer with a secret lock ◆ **cadenas à ~** combination lock

3 *(= discrétion, silence)* secrecy ◆ **demander/exiger/promettre le ~ (absolu)** to ask for/demand/promise (absolute) secrecy ◆ **trahir le ~** to betray the oath of secrecy ◆ **le ~ professionnel/bancaire** professional/bank secrecy ◆ **le ~ médical** medical confidentiality ◆ **le ~ de la confession** the seal of the confessional ◆ **le gouvernement a gardé le ~ sur les négociations** the government has maintained silence *ou* remained silent about the negotiations; → **sceau**

4 *(= mystère)* secret ◆ **les ~s de la nature** the secrets of nature, nature's secrets ◆ **pénétrer dans le ~ des cœurs** to penetrate the secrets of the heart ◆ **ce dossier n'a pas encore livré tous ses ~s** this file has not given up all its secrets yet

5 *(locutions)* **faire ~ de tout** to be secretive about everything

◆ **dans + secret** ◆ **dans le ~** in secret *ou* secrecy, secretly ◆ **négociations menées dans le plus grand ~** negotiations carried out in the strictest *ou* utmost secrecy ◆ **mettre qn dans le ~** to let sb into *ou* in on the secret, to let sb in on it* ◆ **être dans le ~** to be in on the secret, to be in on it* ◆ **je ne suis pas dans le ~ des dieux** I don't share the secrets of the powers that be

◆ **en secret** *(= sans témoins)* in secret *ou* secrecy, secretly; *(= intérieurement)* secretly, inwardly

◆ **au secret** *(Prison)* in solitary confinement, in solitary*

secrétaire /s(ə)kʀetɛʀ/ **NMF** secretary ◆ **~ médicale/commerciale/particulière/juridique** medical/business *ou* commercial/private/legal secretary ◆ **premier ~** *(Pol)* first secretary

NM *(= meuble)* writing desk, secretaire *(Brit)*, secretary *(US)*

COMP secrétaire d'ambassade embassy secretary

secrétaire de direction executive secretary, personal assistant

secrétaire d'État ≃ junior minister *(à* for); *(US Pol = ministre des Affaires étrangères)* Secretary

of State ◆ **le ~ d'État américain au Trésor** the American Treasury Secretary
secrétaire général secretary-general, general secretary ◆ **le ~ général des Nations unies** the Secretary-General of the United Nations
secrétaire de mairie ≃ town clerk *(in charge of records and legal business)*
secrétaire perpétuel permanent secretary *(of one of the Académies françaises)*
secrétaire de production *(Ciné)* production secretary
secrétaire de rédaction sub-editor *(Brit)*, copy editor *(US)*

secrétariat /s(ə)kʀetaʀja/ **NM** [1] *(= fonction officielle)* secretaryship, post *ou* office of secretary; *(= durée de fonction)* secretaryship, term (of office) as secretary ◆ **~ d'État** *(= fonction)* post of junior minister; *(= bureau)* ≃ junior minister's office ◆ **~ général des Nations Unies** United Nations Secretariat [2] *(= profession, travail)* secretarial work; *(= bureaux) [d'école]* (secretary's) office; *[d'usine, administration]* secretarial offices; *[d'organisation internationale]* secretariat; *(= personnel)* secretarial staff ◆ **école de ~** secretarial college ◆ **~ de rédaction** editorial office

secrètement /səkʀɛtmɑ̃/ **ADV** *[négocier, se rencontrer]* secretly, in secret; *[espérer]* secretly

sécréter /sekʀete/ ▸ conjug 6 ◂ **VT** *[+ substance]* to secrete; *[+ ennui]* to exude

sécréteur, -euse *ou* **-trice** /sekʀetœʀ, øz, tʀis/ **ADJ** secretory

sécrétion /sekʀesjɔ̃/ **NF** secretion

sécrétoire /sekʀetwaʀ/ **ADJ** secretory

sectaire /sɛktɛʀ/ **ADJ, NMF** sectarian

sectarisme /sɛktaʀism/ **NM** sectarianism

secte /sɛkt/ **NF** sect

secteur /sɛktœʀ/ **NM** [1] *(gén, Mil)* sector; *(Admin)* district; *(= zone, domaine)* area; *(= partie)* part; *[d'agent de police]* beat ◆ **~ postal** *(Mil)* postal area, ≃ BFPO area *(Brit)* ◆ **dans le ~*** *(= ici)* round here; *(= là-bas)* round there ◆ **changer de ~*** to move elsewhere ◆ **~ sauvegardé** *(Admin)* conservation area ◆ **~ géographique** *(de recrutement scolaire)* catchment area *(Brit)*, school district *(US)*
[2] *(Élec) (= zone)* local supply area ◆ **le ~** *(= circuit)* the mains (supply) ◆ **panne de ~** local supply breakdown ◆ **fonctionne sur pile et ~** battery or mains operated
[3] *(Écon)* **~ (économique)** (economic) sector ◆ **~ agricole/bancaire/industriel/pétrolier** agricultural/banking/industrial/oil sector ◆ **~ public/semi-public/privé** public *ou* state/semi-public/private sector ◆ **le ~ nationalisé** nationalized industries ◆ **~ d'activité** branch of industry ◆ **~ primaire** primary sector ◆ **~ secondaire** manufacturing *ou* secondary sector ◆ **~ tertiaire** service industries, service *ou* tertiary sector
[4] *(Géom)* sector ◆ **~ angulaire** sector ◆ **~ circulaire** sector of circle ◆ **~ sphérique** spherical sector, sector of sphere
[5] *(Ordin)* sector

section /sɛksjɔ̃/ **NF** [1] *(= coupe) (gén)* section; *[de fil électrique]* gauge ◆ **fil de petite/grosse ~** thin-/heavy-gauge wire ◆ **prenons un tube de ~ double** let's use a tube which is twice the bore ◆ **dessiner la ~ d'un os/d'une tige** to draw the section of a bone/of a stem, to draw a bone/a stem in section ◆ **la ~ (de ce câble) est toute rouillée** the end (of this cable) is all rusted
[2] *(Scol)* ≃ course ◆ **il est en ~ littéraire/scientifique** he's doing a literature/science course
[3] *(Univ)* department
[4] *(Admin)* section, department; *(Pol)* branch ◆ **~ du Conseil d'État** department of the Council of State ◆ **~ (du) contentieux** legal section *ou* department ◆ **~ électorale** ward ◆ **~ syndicale** (trade) union group
[5] *(= partie) [d'ouvrage]* section; *[de route, rivière, voie ferrée]* section; *(en autobus)* fare stage; → **fin²**
[6] *(Mus)* section ◆ **~ mélodique/rythmique** melody/rhythm section
[7] *(Mil)* platoon
[8] *(Math)* section ◆ **~ conique/plane** conic/plane section
[9] *(Méd = ablation)* severing

sectionnement /sɛksjɔnmɑ̃/ **NM** [1] *[de tube, fil, artère]* severing [2] *[de circonscription, groupe]* division

sectionner /sɛksjɔne/ ▸ conjug 1 ◂ **VT** [1] *[+ tube, fil, artère, membre]* to sever [2] *[+ circonscription, groupe]* to divide (up), to split (up) *(en into)* **VPR**
se sectionner [1] *[tube, fil, artère, membre]* to be severed [2] *[circonscription, groupe]* to divide *ou* split (up)

sectoriel, -ielle /sɛktɔʀjɛl/ **ADJ** sectional

sectorisation /sɛktɔʀizasjɔ̃/ **NF** division into sectors

sectoriser /sɛktɔʀize/ ▸ conjug 1 ◂ **VT** to divide into sectors, to sector

Sécu* /seky/ **NF** (abrév de **Sécurité sociale**) → **sécurité**

séculaire /sekylɛʀ/ **ADJ** [1] *(= très vieux) [pratiques, traditions, conflit, histoire, croyance]* age-old; *[arbre]* ancient [2] *(= qui a lieu tous les cent ans) [fête, jeux]* centennial ◆ **année ~** last year of the century [3] *(= centenaire)* **ces forêts/maisons sont quatre fois ~s** these forests/houses are four centuries old

sécularisation /sekylaʀizasjɔ̃/ **NF** secularization

séculariser /sekylaʀize/ ▸ conjug 1 ◂ **VT** to secularize

séculier, -ière /sekylje, jɛʀ/ **ADJ** *[clergé, autorité]* secular; → **bras** **NM** secular

secundo /səgɔ̃do/ **ADV** second(ly), in the second place

sécurisant, e /sekyʀizɑ̃, ɑ̃t/ **ADJ** reassuring ◆ **telles quelles, les pistes cyclables sont peu ~es pour leurs utilisateurs** as they are at present, cycle paths do not make their users feel safe

sécurisation /sekyʀizasjɔ̃/ **NF** [1] *[de personne]* reassuring ◆ **des opérations de ~ de la population** measures to reassure the people *ou* to make the people feel more secure [2] *(Internet) [d'informations, paiement, transaction]* securing, making secure ◆ **outils de ~** security tools

sécuriser /sekyʀize/ ▸ conjug 1 ◂ **VT** [1] *(= rassurer)* **~ qn** to give (a feeling of) security to sb, to make sb feel secure ◆ **~ l'opinion** to reassure people ◆ **être/se sentir sécurisé par qn/qch** to be/feel reassured by sb/sth [2] *(= accroître la sécurité de) [+ informations, paiement, site, résidence, réseau]* to secure ◆ **~ les transports de fonds** to increase the security of transfers of funds ◆ **~ l'accès à qch** to make access to sth more secure ◆ **les Casques bleus ont sécurisé la zone** the Blue Berets improved security in the area

Securit ® /sekyʀit/ **NM** ◆ **verre ~** Triplex (glass) ®

sécuritaire /sekyʀitɛʀ/ **ADJ** *[politique]* law-and-order *(épith)*; *[idéologie]* that concentrates on law and order ◆ **mesures ~s** security measures ◆ **il rompt avec le discours ~ de son parti** he's distancing himself from his party's stance on law and order ◆ **il y a une dégradation de la situation ~ dans la région** law and order is breaking down in the region ◆ **le tout ~** overemphasis on law and order

sécurité /sekyʀite/ **NF** [1] *(= absence de danger)* safety; *(= conditions d'ordre, absence de troubles)* security ◆ **une fausse impression de ~** a false sense of security ◆ **cette retraite représentait pour lui une ~** this pension meant security for him ◆ **la ~ de l'emploi** security of employment, job security ◆ **la ~ matérielle** material security ◆ **assurer la ~ d'un personnage important/des ouvriers/des installations** to ensure the safety of an important person/of workers/of the equipment ◆ **l'État assure la ~ des citoyens** the state looks after the security *ou* safety of its citizens ◆ **la ~ nationale/internationale** national/international security ◆ **pacte/traité de ~ collective** collective security pact/treaty ◆ **mesures de ~** *(contre incendie)* safety measures *ou* precautions; *(contre attentat)* security measures ◆ **des mesures de ~ très strictes avaient été prises** very strict security precautions *ou* measures had been taken, security was very tight
◆ **en + sécurité** ◆ **être/se sentir en ~** to be/feel safe, to be/feel secure ◆ **mettre qch en ~** to put sth in a safe place ◆ **en toute ~** safely, in complete safety
[2] *(= mécanisme)* safety catch, safety *(US)* ◆ **mettre la ~** *[d'arme à feu]* to put on the safety catch *ou* the safety *(US)* ◆ **de ~** *[dispositif]* safety *(épith)* ◆ **(porte à) ~ enfants** *(dans une voiture)* childproof lock, child lock ◆ **~ informatique** computer security ◆ **assurer la ~ d'un système** to ensure that a system is secure, to ensure system security; → **cran**
[3] *(= service)* security ◆ **la ~ militaire** military security

COMP **la sécurité civile** *emergency services dealing with natural disasters, bomb disposal etc*
la sécurité publique law and order ◆ **agent de la ~ publique** officer of the law
la sécurité routière road safety
la Sécurité sociale *(pour la santé)* ≃ the National Health Service *(Brit)*, Medicaid *(US)*; *(pour vieillesse etc)* ≃ the Social Security, Medicare *(US)* ◆ **prestations de la Sécurité sociale** ≃ Social Security benefits

SÉCURITÉ SOCIALE

The French public welfare system is financed by compulsory contributions paid directly from salaries and by employers. It covers essential health care, pensions and other basic benefits. In many cases, costs not covered by the **Sécurité sociale** may be met by a **mutuelle**. → MUTUELLE

sédatif, -ive /sedatif, iv/ **ADJ** sedative **NM** sedative ◆ **sous ~s** under sedation

sédation /sedasjɔ̃/ **NF** sedation

sédentaire /sedɑ̃tɛʀ/ **ADJ** *[personne, travail, vie]* sedentary; *[population]* settled, sedentary; *(Mil)* permanently garrisoned ◆ **personnel ~** office staff

sédentarisation /sedɑ̃taʀizasjɔ̃/ **NF** settling process

sédentariser /sedɑ̃taʀize/ ▸ conjug 1 ◂ **VT** to settle ◆ **population sédentarisée** settled population

sédentarité /sedɑ̃taʀite/ **NF** *[de population]* settled way of life; *[de travail]* sedentary nature

sédiment /sedimɑ̃/ **NM** *(Géol)* deposit, sediment; *(Méd)* sediment ◆ **~s marins** marine sediments

sédimentaire /sedimɑ̃tɛʀ/ **ADJ** sedimentary

sédimentation /sedimɑ̃tasjɔ̃/ **NF** sedimentation; → **vitesse**

sédimenter /sedimɑ̃te/ ▸ conjug 1 ◂ **VI** to deposit sediment

séditieux, -ieuse /sedisjø, jøz/ ADJ (= *en sédition) [général, troupes]* insurrectionary *(épith)*, insurgent *(épith)*; (= *agitateur) [esprit, propos, réunion]* seditious NM,F insurrectionary, insurgent

sédition /sedisjɔ̃/ NF insurrection, sedition ◆ **esprit de ~** spirit of sedition *ou* insurrection *ou* revolt

séducteur, -trice /sedyktœʀ, tʀis/ ADJ seductive NM (= *débaucheur*) seducer; *(péj* = *Don Juan)* womanizer *(péj)* NF **séductrice** seductress

séduction /sedyksjɔ̃/ NF 1 (= *charme)* charm; (= *action)* seduction ◆ **scène de ~** seduction scene ◆ **il y a toujours un jeu de ~ entre un homme et une femme** there is always an element of flirtation between a man and a woman ◆ **il a un grand pouvoir de ~** he has great charm ◆ **le pouvoir de ~ de l'argent** the lure *ou* seductive power of money ◆ **leur opération de ~ en direction du public/des électeurs** the charm offensive they aimed at the public/the voters ◆ **leurs tentatives de ~ pour se concilier l'ONU** their attempts to win over the UN

2 (= *attrait) [style, projet, idéologie]* appeal ◆ **exercer une forte ~ sur qn** to have a great deal of appeal for sb ◆ **les ~s de la vie estudiantine** the attractions *ou* appeal of student life

3 *(Jur) [de femme]* seduction; *[de mineur]* corruption

> ⚠ Attention à ne pas traduire automatiquement **séduction** par le mot anglais **seduction**, qui désigne uniquement l'action de séduire.

séduire /sedɥiʀ/ ▸ conjug 38 ◂ VT 1 *(par son physique, son charme)* to charm ◆ **qu'est-ce qui t'a séduit chez** *ou* **en elle ?** what attracted you to her? ◆ **elle sait ~** she knows how to use her charms

2 (= *plaire) [style, qualité, projet]* to appeal to ◆ **une des qualités qui me séduisent le plus** one of the qualities which most appeal to me *ou* which I find most appealing ◆ **ils ont essayé de nous ~ avec ces propositions** they tried to win us over *ou* to tempt us with these proposals ◆ **cette idée va-t-elle les ~ ?** is this idea going to tempt them? *ou* appeal to them? ◆ **leur projet/style de vie me séduit mais ...** their plan/lifestyle does appeal to me *ou* does have some appeal for me but ... ◆ **essayez cette crème, vous serez séduite** try this cream, you'll love it ◆ **séduit par les apparences** (= *tromper)* taken in by appearances

3 *(† : sexuellement)* to seduce

séduisant, e /sedɥizɑ̃, ɑ̃t/ ADJ 1 *[personne, visage]* attractive; *[beauté]* seductive 2 *[genre de vie, projet, style, tenue, endroit]* appealing, attractive; *[solution, théorie, produit]* attractive

> ⚠ L'adjectif **séduisant** ne se traduit pas par **seducing**.

sedum /sedɔm/ NM sedum

séfarade /sefaʀad/ ADJ Sephardic NMF Sephardi

segment /sɛgmɑ̃/ NM *(gén)* segment ◆ **~ de frein** brake shoe ◆ **~ de piston** piston ring ◆ **~ de programme** *(Ordin)* segment ◆ **~ de marché** market segment, segment of the market

segmental, e (mpl **-aux**) /sɛgmɑ̃tal, o/ ADJ *(Ling)* segmental

segmentation /sɛgmɑ̃tasjɔ̃/ NF *(gén)* segmentation

segmenter /sɛgmɑ̃te/ ▸ conjug 1 ◂ VT to segment VPR **se segmenter** to segment, to form *ou* break into segments ◆ **dans un marché de plus en plus segmenté** on an increasingly fragmented market

ségrégatif, -ive /segʀegatif, iv/ ADJ segregative

ségrégation /segʀegasjɔ̃/ NF segregation ◆ **~ raciale** racial segregation

ségrégationnisme /segʀegasjɔnism/ NM racial segregation, segregationism

ségrégationniste /segʀegasjɔnist/ ADJ *[manifestant]* segregationist; *[problème]* of segregation; *[troubles]* due to segregation NMF segregationist

ségréger /segʀeʒe/ ▸ conjug 3 ou 6 ◂, **ségréguer** /segʀege/ ▸ conjug 6 ◂ VT to segregate ◆ **une nation de plus en plus ségréguée** a nation that has become increasingly segregated

seiche /sɛʃ/ NF cuttlefish; → **os**

séide /seid/ NM (fanatically devoted) henchman

seigle /sɛgl/ NM rye; → **pain**

seigneur /sɛɲœʀ/ NM 1 *(Hist* = *suzerain, noble)* lord; *(fig* = *maître)* overlord ◆ **mon ~ et maître** *(hum)* my lord and master ◆ **grand ~** great *ou* powerful lord ◆ **se montrer grand ~ avec qn** to behave in a lordly fashion towards sb ◆ **faire le grand ~** to play *ou* act the grand *ou* fine gentleman ◆ **faire le grand ~ avec qn** to lord it over sb ◆ **à tout ~ tout honneur** *(Prov)* honour to whom honour is due *(Prov)* 2 *(Rel)* **le Seigneur** the Lord ◆ **Notre-Seigneur Jésus-Christ** Our Lord Jesus Christ ◆ **Seigneur Dieu !** good Lord!; → **jour, vigne**

seigneurial, e (mpl **-iaux**) /sɛɲœʀjal, jo/ ADJ *[château, domaine]* seigniorial; *[allure, luxe]* lordly, stately

seigneurie /sɛɲœʀi/ NF 1 ◆ **Votre/Sa Seigneurie** your/his Lordship 2 (= *terre)* (lord's) domain, seigniory; (= *droits féodaux)* seigniory

sein /sɛ̃/ NM 1 (= *mamelle)* breast ◆ **donner le ~ à un bébé** (= *méthode)* to breast-feed a baby, to suckle *ou* nurse a baby; (= *être en train d'allaiter)* to feed a baby (at the breast), to suckle *ou* nurse a baby; (= *présenter le sein)* to give a baby the breast ◆ **prendre le ~** to take the breast ◆ **elle était ~s nus** she was topless ◆ **ça me ferait mal aux ~s*** (= *me déplairait)* that would really get (to) me*; → **faux², nourrir**

2 *(locutions)*

◆ **au sein de** (= *parmi, dans)* in, within ◆ **ils sont pour la libre concurrence au ~ de l'Union européenne** they are in favour of free competition within the European Union ◆ **il a fait toute sa carrière au ~ du parti/de l'armée** he has spent his entire career in the party/in the army ◆ **sa présence au ~ de l'équipe** his presence in *ou* on the team

3 *(littér)* (= *poitrine)* breast *(littér)*, bosom *(littér)*; (= *matrice)* womb; (= *giron, milieu)* bosom ◆ **serrer qn/qch contre son ~** to clasp sb/sth to one's bosom ◆ **porter un enfant dans son ~** to carry a child in one's womb ◆ **le ~ de Dieu** the bosom of the Father ◆ **dans le ~ de l'église** in the bosom of the church; → **réchauffer**

Seine /sɛn/ NF ◆ **la ~** the Seine

seine /sɛn/ NF (= *filet)* seine

seing /sɛ̃/ NM †† signature ◆ **acte sous ~ privé** *(Jur)* private agreement *(document not legally certified)*

séisme /seism/ NM 1 *(Géog)* earthquake, seism *(SPÉC)* 2 (= *bouleversement)* upheaval ◆ **cela a provoqué un véritable ~ dans le gouvernement** this caused a major upheaval in the government

séismique /seismik/ ADJ ⇒ **sismique**

séismographe /seismɔgʀaf/ NM ⇒ **sismographe**

séismologie /seismɔlɔʒi/ NF ⇒ **sismologie**

seize /sɛz/ ADJ INV, NM INV sixteen ◆ **film tourné en ~ millimètres** film shot in sixteen millimetres; *pour loc voir* **six**

seizième /sɛzjɛm/ ADJ, NMF sixteenth ◆ **~s de finale** *(Sport)* first round *(of 5-round knockout competition)* ◆ **le ~ (arrondissement)** the sixteenth arrondissement *(wealthy area in Paris)* ◆ **être très ~** to be typical of the sixteenth arrondissement; *pour loc voir* **sixième**

seizièmement /sɛzjɛmmɑ̃/ ADV in the sixteenth place, sixteenth

séjour /seʒuʀ/ NM 1 (= *visite)* stay ◆ **faire un ~ de trois semaines à Paris** to stay (for) three weeks in Paris, to have a three-week stay in Paris ◆ **faire un ~ à l'étranger** to spend time abroad ◆ **j'ai fait plusieurs ~s en Australie** I've been to Australia several times ◆ **c'est mon deuxième ~ aux États-Unis** it's my second stay in *ou* trip to the United States, it's the second time I've been to the United States ◆ **il a fait trois ~s en prison** he has been in prison three times before, he has had three spells in prison ◆ **elle a fait plusieurs ~s à l'hôpital** she has had several stays *ou* spells in hospital ◆ **~ officiel** *(Pol)* official visit ◆ **le ministre était en ~ privé en France** the minister was on a private holiday *(Brit) ou* on vacation *(US)* in France ◆ **il a fait un ~ linguistique en Irlande** he went to Ireland on a language course; → **interdit¹, permis, taxe**

2 (= *salon)* living room, lounge *(Brit)* ◆ **~ double** living-cum-dining room *(Brit)*, living room-dining room *(US)*; → **salle**

3 *(littér)* (= *endroit)* abode *(littér)*, dwelling place *(littér)*; (= *demeure temporaire)* sojourn *(littér)* ◆ **le ~ des dieux** the abode *ou* dwelling place of the gods

séjourner /seʒuʀne/ ▸ conjug 1 ◂ VI *[personne]* to stay; *[eau, neige]* to lie ◆ **~ chez qn** to stay with sb

sel /sɛl/ NM 1 *(gén, Chim)* salt ◆ **sans ~** *[biscottes, pain, régime]* salt-free *(épith)* ◆ **je mange sans ~** I don't put salt on my food; → **gros, poivre** 2 (= *humour)* wit; (= *piquant)* spice ◆ **la remarque ne manque pas de ~** it's quite a witty remark ◆ **c'est ce qui fait tout le ~ de l'aventure** that's what gives the adventure its spice ◆ **ils sont le ~ de la terre** *(littér)* they are the salt of the earth; → **grain** NMPL **sels** *(à respirer)* smelling salts

COMP **sel d'Angleterre** ⇒ **sel d'Epsom**
sel attique Attic salt *ou* wit
sels de bain bath salts
sels biliaires bile salts
sel de céleri celery salt
sel de cuisine cooking salt
sel d'Epsom Epsom salts
sel fin ⇒ **sel de table**
sel gemme rock salt
sel de Guérande sea salt from Guérande
sel marin *ou* **de mer** sea salt
sels minéraux mineral salts
sel de table table salt

sélacien, -ienne /selasjɛ̃, jɛn/ ADJ, NM selachian

select* /selɛkt/ ADJ INV, **sélect, e*** /selɛkt/ ADJ *[personne]* posh*, high-class; *[clientèle, club, endroit]* select, posh*

sélecteur /selɛktœʀ/ NM *[d'ordinateur, télévision, central téléphonique]* selector; *[de motocyclette]* gear lever ADJ M ◆ **comité ~** selection committee

sélectif, -ive /selɛktif, iv/ ADJ selective; → **tri**

sélection /selɛksjɔ̃/ NF 1 (= *action)* selection ◆ **~ naturelle** *(Bio)* natural selection ◆ **il y a une ~ (à l'entrée)** *(Scol, Univ)* admission is by selective entry ◆ **faire** *ou* **opérer** *ou* **effectuer une ~ parmi** to make a selection from among

2 (= *choix, gamme) [d'articles, produits, œuvres]* selection

3 (*Sport*) (*= choix*) selection; (*= équipe*) (*gén*) team; (*Ftbl, Rugby etc*) line-up ◆ **la ~ française au festival de Cannes** the French films selected to be shown at the Cannes film festival ◆ **comité de ~** selection committee ◆ **il a plus de 20 ~s à son actif en équipe nationale** he's been selected over 20 times for the national team, he's been capped more than 20 times (*Brit*), he has more than 20 caps to his credit (*Brit*) ◆ **match de ~** trial match ◆ **épreuves de ~** (selection) trials, heats

sélectionné, e /selɛksjɔne/ (ptp de **sélectionner**) ADJ (*= soigneusement choisi*) specially selected, choice (*épith*) NM,F (*Ftbl etc*) selected player; (*Athlétisme*) selected competitor ◆ **les ~s** (*Ftbl, Rugby*) the line-up ◆ **figurer parmi les ~s** to be in the line-up

sélectionner /selɛksjɔne/ ▸ conjug 1 ◂ VT to select (*parmi* from (among)); ◆ **un film sélectionné à Cannes** a film selected at the Cannes film festival ◆ **il a été sélectionné trois fois en équipe nationale** he has been selected three times for the national team

sélectionneur, -euse /selɛksjɔnœʀ, øz/ NM,F (*Sport*) selector

sélectivement /selɛktivmɑ̃/ ADV selectively ◆ **les lésions cérébrales altèrent ~ la mémoire** brain lesions affect only certain parts of the memory

sélectivité /selɛktivite/ NF (*Radio*) selectivity

sélénite /selenit/ ADJ moon (*épith*)

sélénium /selenjɔm/ NM selenium

self /sɛlf/ NM (* *= restaurant*) self-service restaurant, cafeteria NF (*Élec*) (*= propriété*) self-induction; (*= bobine*) self-induction coil

self-control /sɛlfkɔ̃tʀol/ NM self-control

self-inductance /sɛlfɛ̃dyktɑ̃s/ NF self-inductance

self-induction /sɛlfɛ̃dyksjɔ̃/ NF self-induction

self-made-man /sɛlfmɛdman/ (pl **self-made-men** /sɛlfmɛdmɛn/) NM self-made man

self-service (pl **self-services**) /sɛlfsɛʀvis/ NM self-service; (*= restaurant*) self-service restaurant, cafeteria; (*= station-service*) self-service petrol (*Brit*) *ou* gas (*US*) station

selle /sɛl/ NF 1 (*Cyclisme, Équitation*) saddle ◆ **monter sans ~** to ride bareback ◆ **se mettre en ~** to mount, to get into the saddle ◆ **mettre qn en ~** (*lit*) to put sb in the saddle; (*fig*) to give sb a boost *ou* a leg-up ◆ **se remettre en ~** (*lit*) to remount, to get back into the saddle; (*fig*) to get back in the saddle ◆ **être bien en ~** (*lit, fig*) to be firmly in the saddle; → **cheval** 2 (*Boucherie*) saddle 3 (*Art*) [*de sculpteur*] turntable 4 ◆ **êtes-vous allé à la ~ aujourd'hui?** have your bowels moved today? NFPL **selles** (*Méd*) stools, motions

seller /sele/ ▸ conjug 1 ◂ VT to saddle

sellerie /sɛlʀi/ NF (*= articles, métier, selles*) saddlery; (*= lieu de rangement*) tack room, harness room, saddle room

sellette /sɛlɛt/ NF 1 (*pour sculpteur*) turntable; (*pour statue, pot de fleur*) stand 2 (*Constr*) cradle 3 (*locutions*) ◆ **être/mettre qn sur la ~** to be/put sb in the hot seat

sellier /selje/ NM saddler

selon /s(ə)lɔ̃/ GRAMMAIRE ACTIVE 33.2, 53.3, 53.5 PRÉP 1 (*= conformément à*) in accordance with ◆ **agir ~ sa conscience** to follow the dictates of one's conscience, to act according to one's conscience ◆ **~ la volonté de qn** in accordance with sb's wishes ◆ **~ la formule** *ou* **l'expression consacrée** as the saying goes

2 (*= en proportion de, en fonction de*) according to ◆ **vivre ~ ses moyens** to live within one's means ◆ **donner ~ ses moyens** to give according to one's means ◆ **le nombre varie ~ la saison** the number varies (along) with *ou* according to the season ◆ **c'est ~ le cas/les circonstances** it all depends on the individual case/on the circumstances ◆ **c'est ~** * it (all) depends ◆ **il acceptera ou n'acceptera pas, ~ son humeur** he may or may not accept, depending on *ou* according to his mood *ou* how he feels

3 (*= suivant l'opinion de*) according to ◆ **~ lui** according to him ◆ **~ ses propres termes** in his own words ◆ **~ moi, c'est une mauvaise idée** in my opinion, it's a bad idea ◆ **qui l'a cassé ? – ~ toi ?** who broke it? – who do you think?

Seltz /sɛls/ NF → **eau**

semailles /s(ə)mɑj/ NFPL (*= action*) sowing (*NonC*); (*= période*) sowing period; (*= graine*) seed, seeds

semaine /s(ə)mɛn/ NF 1 (*gén*) week ◆ **la première ~ de mai** the first week in *ou* of May ◆ **en ~** during the week, on weekdays ◆ **louer à la ~** to let by the week ◆ **dans 2 ~s à partir d'aujourd'hui** 2 weeks *ou* a fortnight (*Brit*) (from) today ◆ **la ~ de 35 heures** the 35-hour (working) week ◆ **à la ~ prochaine !** I'll see you (*ou* talk to you) next week!; → **courant, fin**[2]

2 (*= salaire*) week's wages *ou* pay, weekly wage *ou* pay; (*= argent de poche*) week's *ou* weekly pocket money

3 (*Publicité*) week ◆ **~ publicitaire/commerciale** publicity/business week ◆ **la ~ du livre/du bricolage** book/do-it-yourself week ◆ **la ~ contre la faim** feed the hungry week ◆ **la ~ contre le SIDA** AIDS week ◆ **c'est sa ~ de bonté !** * (*hum*) it must be charity week! * (*hum*)

4 (*Bijouterie*) (*= bracelet*) (seven-band) bracelet; (*= bague*) (seven-band) ring

5 (*locutions*) **il te le rendra la ~ des quatre jeudis** he'll never give it back to you in a month of Sundays ◆ **faire la ~ anglaise** to work *ou* do a five-day week; (*Mil*) ◆ **être de ~** to be on duty (*for the week*) ◆ **officier de ~** officer on duty (*for the week*), officer of the week ◆ **gestion à la petite ~** short-sighted management ◆ **trafiquants à la petite ~** small-time dealers

semainier, -ière /s(ə)menje, jɛʀ/ NM,F (*= personne*) person on duty (*for the week*) NM (*= agenda*) desk diary; (*= meuble*) chest of (seven) drawers, semainier; (*= bracelet*) (seven-band) bracelet

sémanticien, -ienne /semɑ̃tisjɛ̃, jɛn/ NM,F semantician, semanticist

sémantique /semɑ̃tik/ ADJ semantic NF semantics (*sg*)

sémaphore /semafɔʀ/ NM (*Naut*) semaphore; (*Rail*) semaphore signal

semblable /sɑ̃blabl/ ADJ 1 (*= similaire*) similar ◆ **~ à** like, similar to ◆ **dans un cas ~** in a case like this, in such a case ◆ **je ne connais rien de ~** I've never come across anything like it ◆ **une maison ~ à tant d'autres** a house like so many others *ou* similar to so many others ◆ **il a prononcé un discours très ~ à celui de l'année dernière** he delivered a speech very much like *ou* very much in the same vein as last year's ◆ **en cette circonstance, il a été ~ à lui-même** on this occasion he behaved true to form *ou* as usual ◆ **elle était là, ~ à elle-même** she was there, the same as ever

2 (*avant n = tel*) such ◆ **de ~s calomnies sont inacceptables** such calumnies *ou* calumnies of this kind are unacceptable

3 (*= qui se ressemblent*) **~s** alike ◆ **les deux frères étaient ~s (en tout)** the two brothers were alike (in every way); → **triangle**

NMF fellow creature ◆ **aimer son ~** to love one's fellow creatures *ou* fellow men ◆ **toi et tes ~s** (*péj*) you and your kind (*péj*), you and people like you (*péj*) ◆ **il n'a pas son ~** there's no-one like him

semblablement /sɑ̃blabləmɑ̃/ ADV similarly, likewise

semblant /sɑ̃blɑ̃/ NM (*= apparence*) ◆ **un ~ de calme/bonheur/vie/vérité** a semblance of calm/happiness/life/truth ◆ **un ~ de réponse** some vague attempt at a reply ◆ **un ~ de soleil** a glimmer of sun ◆ **un ~ de sourire** the shadow *ou* ghost of a smile ◆ **nous avons un ~ de jardin** we've got a garden of sorts ◆ **pour redonner un ~ de cohérence à leur politique** to make their policy look more consistent

◆ **faire semblant** ◆ **il fait ~** he's pretending ◆ **faire ~ de dormir/lire** to pretend to be asleep/to be reading ◆ **il a fait ~ de ne pas me voir** he pretended not to see me, he acted as if he didn't see me ◆ **il fait ~ de rien** *, **mais il entend tout** he's pretending to take no notice but he can hear everything

sembler /sɑ̃ble/ GRAMMAIRE ACTIVE 33.2, 53.4, 53.5 ▸ conjug 1 ◂

VB IMPERS 1 (*= paraître*) **il semble bon/inutile de ...** it seems a good idea/useless to ... ◆ **il semblerait qu'il ne soit pas venu** it would seem *ou* appear that he didn't come, it looks as though *ou* as if he didn't come

2 (*= estimer*) **il peut te ~ démodé de ...** it may seem *ou* appear old-fashioned to you to ... ◆ **c'était lundi, il me semble** I think it was on Monday ◆ **il me semble que ...** it seems *ou* appears to me that ... ◆ **il me semble que oui/que non** I think so/I don't think so ◆ **il me semble que tu n'as pas le droit de ...** it seems *ou* appears to me that you don't have the right to ... ◆ **comme bon me/te semble** as I/you see fit, as I/you think best *ou* fit ◆ **ils se marieront quand bon leur semblera** they will get married when they see fit ◆ **prenez qui/ce que bon vous semble** take who/what you please *ou* wish

3 (*= croire*) **il me semble que** I think (that) ◆ **il me semblait bien que je l'avais posé là** I really thought *ou* did think I had put it down here ◆ **il me semble revoir mon grand-père** it's like seeing my grandfather again ◆ **il me semble vous l'avoir déjà dit** I have a feeling I've already told you

4 (*locutions*) **je vous connais, ce me semble** † methinks I know you †, it seems to me that I know you ◆ **je suis déjà venu ici, me semble-t-il** it seems to me (that) I've been here before, I seem to have been here before ◆ **il a, semble-t-il, essayé de me contacter** apparently he tried to contact me ◆ **à ce qu'il me semble, notre organisation est mauvaise** to my mind *ou* it seems to me (that) our organization is bad, our organization seems bad to me ◆ **que vous en semble ?** (*frm, hum*) what do you think (of it)?

VI to seem ◆ **la maison lui sembla magnifique** the house seemed magnificent to him ◆ **il semblait content/nerveux** he seemed (to be) *ou* appeared *ou* looked happy/nervous ◆ **elle me semble bien fatiguée** she seems *ou* looks very tired to me ◆ **vous me semblez bien pessimiste !** you do sound *ou* seem very pessimistic! ◆ **il ne semblait pas convaincu** he didn't seem (to be) convinced, he didn't look *ou* sound convinced ◆ **les frontières de la science semblent reculer** the frontiers of science seem *ou* appear to be retreating ◆ **tout semble indiquer que leur départ fut précipité** all the signs are that they left in a hurry ◆ **mes arguments ne semblent pas l'avoir convaincu** apparently he has not been convinced by my arguments

semé, e /s(ə)me/ (ptp de **semer**) ADJ ◆ **questions ~es de pièges** questions full of pitfalls ◆ **la**

route de la démocratie est ~e d'embûches/n'est pas ~e de roses the road to democracy is fraught with difficulties/is not easy ◆ **mer ~e d'écueils** sea scattered *ou* dotted with reefs ◆ **robe ~e de pierreries** dress studded with gems ◆ **récit ~ d'anecdotes** story interspersed *ou* sprinkled with anecdotes ◆ **tissu ~ de fleurs** flowery material ◆ **gazon ~ de fleurs** lawn dotted with flowers ◆ **campagne ~e d'arbres** countryside dotted with trees ◆ **la vie est ~e de joies et de peines** life is full of joys and sorrows

sème /sɛm/ NM seme

semelle /s(ə)mɛl/ NF [1] *[de chaussure]* sole ◆ **~s (intérieures)** insoles ◆ **~s compensées** platform soles ◆ **chaussures à ~s compensées** platform shoes ◆ **~s de plomb** lead boots ◆ **j'avais des ~s de plomb** *(fig)* my feet felt like lead weights ◆ **il va à l'école avec des ~s de plomb** he drags himself to school as if his feet were made of lead ◆ **c'est de la vraie ~*** *[viande]* it's as tough as old boots* *(Brit) ou* shoe leather *(US)*, it's like leather; → **battre, crêpe²**
[2] *(locutions)* **il n'a pas avancé/reculé d'une ~** he hasn't moved forward/moved back (so much as) a single inch *ou* an inch ◆ **il ne m'a pas quitté** *ou* **lâché d'une ~** he didn't leave me for a single second, he stuck to me like a leech ◆ **ne le lâche pas d'une ~ !** don't let him out of your sight!
[3] *(Tech)* *[de rail]* base plate pad; *[de machine]* bedplate; *[de fer à repasser]* sole plate; *[de ski]* running surface

semence /s(ə)mɑ̃s/ NF [1] *(Agr, fig)* seed ◆ **blé/pommes de terre de ~** seed corn/potatoes [2] *(= sperme)* semen, seed *(littér)* [3] *(= clou)* tack [4] *(Bijouterie)* **~ de diamants** diamond sparks ◆ **~ de perles** seed pearls

semer /s(ə)me/ ▸ conjug 5 ◂ VT [1] *(= répandre)* *[+ discorde, graines]* to sow; *[+ confusion, terreur]* to spread; *[+ clous, confettis]* to scatter; *[+ faux bruits]* to spread, to disseminate *(frm)* ◆ **~ la panique** to spread panic ◆ **ils ont semé la mort dans la région** they brought death and destruction to the region ◆ **~ le doute dans l'esprit de qn** to sow doubts in sb's mind ◆ **~ ses propos de citations** to intersperse *ou* sprinkle one's remarks with quotations ◆ **qui sème le vent récolte la tempête** *(Prov)* he who sows the wind shall reap the whirlwind *(Prov)* [2] *(* = perdre)* *[+ mouchoir]* to lose; *[+ poursuivant]* to lose, to shake off

semestre /s(ə)mɛstʀ/ NM [1] *(= période)* half-year, six-month period ◆ **tous les ~s** every six months, twice yearly *ou* a year ◆ **taxe payée par ~** tax paid half-yearly ◆ **pendant le premier/second ~ (de l'année)** during the first/second half of the year, during the first/second six-month period (of the year) [2] *(Univ)* semester [3] *(= loyer)* half-yearly *ou* six months' rent ◆ **je vous dois un ~** I owe you six months' *ou* half a year's rent [4] *[rente, pension]* half-yearly payment

semestriel, -ielle /s(ə)mɛstʀijɛl/ ADJ [1] *[assemblée]* six-monthly; *[revue, bulletin]* biannual; *[résultats]* half-yearly [2] *(Univ)* *[examen]* end-of-semester *(épith)*; *[cours]* one-semester *(épith)* [3] *[rente, pension]* half-yearly

semestriellement /s(ə)mɛstʀijɛlmɑ̃/ ADV *(gén)* half-yearly; *(Univ)* every *ou* each semester ◆ **les montants sont fixés ~** the amounts are set every six months

semeur, -euse /s(ə)mœʀ, øz/ NM,F sower ◆ **~ de trouble(s)** troublemaker ◆ **~ de discorde** sower of discord ◆ **ces ~s de mort** these merchants of death ◆ **la Semeuse** *figure of a woman sowing seeds that appears on some French coins*

semi- /səmi/ PRÉF semi- ◆ **~autonome/-professionnel** semi-autonomous/-professional

semi-aride /səmiaʀid/ ADJ semiarid

semi-automatique /səmiɔtɔmatik/ ADJ semi-automatic

semi-auxiliaire /səmioksiljɛʀ/ ADJ semiauxiliary NM semiauxiliary verb

semi-chenillé, e /səmiʃ(ə)nije/ ADJ half-tracked NM half-track

semi-circulaire /səmisiʀkylɛʀ/ ADJ semicircular

semi-conducteur, -trice /səmikɔ̃dyktœʀ, tʀis/ ADJ *[propriétés, cristaux]* semiconducting NM semiconductor

semi-conserve /səmikɔ̃sɛʀv/ NF semi-preserve

semi-consonne /səmikɔ̃sɔn/ NF semiconsonant

semi-fini, e /səmifini/ ADJ semi-finished ◆ **produits ~s** semi-finished goods *ou* products

semi-liberté /səmilibɛʀte/ NF *[de prisonnier]* ≈ partial release ◆ **les animaux vivent en ~** the animals live in relative liberty

sémillant, e /semijɑ̃, ɑt/ ADJ *(= alerte, vif)* *[personne]* vivacious, spirited; *[allure, esprit]* vivacious; *(= fringant)* dashing *(épith)*

séminaire /seminɛʀ/ NM *(Rel)* seminary; *(Univ)* seminar ◆ **grand ~** *(Rel)* (theological) seminary ◆ **petit ~** Catholic secondary school

séminal, e (mpl **-aux**) /seminal, o/ ADJ *(Bio)* seminal

séminariste /seminaʀist/ NM seminarian, seminarist

séminifère /seminifɛʀ/ ADJ seminiferous

semi-nomade /səminɔmad/ ADJ seminomadic NMF seminomad

semi-nomadisme /səminɔmadism/ NM seminomadism

semi-officiel, -elle /səmiɔfisjɛl/ ADJ semi-official

sémiologie /semjɔlɔʒi/ NF *(Ling, Méd)* semiology

sémiologique /semjɔlɔʒik/ ADJ semiological

sémiologue /semjɔlɔg/ NMF semiologist

sémioticien, -ienne /semjɔtisjɛ̃, jɛn/ NM,F semiotician

sémiotique /semjɔtik/ ADJ semiotic NF semiotics *(sg)*

semi-ouvré, e /səmiuvʀe/ ADJ semifinished

semi-perméable /səmipɛʀmeabl/ ADJ semipermeable

semi-précieux, -ieuse /səmipʀesjø, jøz/ ADJ *[pierre]* semiprecious

semi-produit /səmipʀɔdɥi/ NM semifinished product

semi-public, -ique /səmipyblik/ ADJ semi-public

sémique /semik/ ADJ semic ◆ **acte ~** semic *ou* meaningful act

Sémiramis /semiʀamis/ NF Semiramis

semi-remorque /səmiʀ(ə)mɔʀk/ NM *(= camion)* articulated lorry *(Brit)*, artic* *(Brit)*, trailer truck *(US)* NF *(= remorque)* trailer *(Brit)*, semitrailer *(US)*

semis /s(ə)mi/ NM *(= plante)* seedling; *(= opération)* sowing; *(= terrain)* seedbed, seed plot; *(= motif)* pattern, motif

sémite /semit/ ADJ Semitic NMF **Sémite** Semite

sémitique /semitik/ ADJ Semitic

sémitisme /semitism/ NM Semitism

semi-voyelle /səmivwajɛl/ NF semivowel

semoir /səmwaʀ/ NM [1] *(= machine)* sower, seeder ◆ **~ à engrais** muckspreader, manure spreader [2] *(= sac)* seed-bag, seed-lip

semonce /səmɔ̃s/ NF reprimand ◆ **coup de ~** *(Naut)* warning shot across the bows; *(fig)* warning ◆ **un coup de ~ pour le gouvernement** *(Pol)* a warning shot across the government's bows

semoule /s(ə)mul/ NF ◆ **~ (de blé dur)** *(gén)* semolina; *(pour couscous)* couscous ◆ **~ de maïs** corn meal; → **gâteau, sucre**

sempiternel, -elle /sɑ̃pitɛʀnɛl/ ADJ *[plaintes, reproches]* eternal *(épith)*, never-ending

sempiternellement /sɑ̃pitɛʀnɛlmɑ̃/ ADV eternally

sénat /sena/ NM *(gén, Hist)* senate ◆ **le Sénat** *(Pol)* the Senate ◆ **le Sénat américain** the American Senate; → **SÉNAT**

> **SÉNAT**
>
> The **Sénat**, the upper house of the French parliament, sits at the Palais du Luxembourg in Paris. One third of its members, known as « sénateurs », are elected for a nine-year term every three years by an electoral college consisting of « députés » and other electoral representatives. The **Sénat** has a wide range of powers but is overruled by the « Assemblée nationale » in cases of disagreement. → **ASSEMBLÉE NATIONALE, DÉPUTÉ, ÉLECTIONS**

sénateur, -trice /senatœʀ, tʀis/ NM,F senator; → **train**

sénatorial, e (mpl **-iaux**) /senatɔʀjal, jo/ ADJ *[commission]* senatorial; *[mission, rapport]* Senate *(épith)* ◆ **la majorité ~e** the majority in the Senate NFPL ◆ **les (élections) ~es** *(gén)* the senatorial elections; *(aux USA)* the Senate elections; → **ÉLECTIONS**

sénatus-consulte (pl **sénatus-consultes**) /senatyskɔ̃sylt/ NM *(Antiq, Hist)* senatus consultum

séné /sene/ NM senna

sénéchal (pl **-aux**) /seneʃal, o/ NM *(Hist)* seneschal

séneçon /sɛnsɔ̃/ NM groundsel

Sénégal /senegal/ NM Senegal

sénégalais, e /senegalɛ, ɛz/ ADJ Senegalese NM,F **Sénégalais(e)** Senegalese

Sénèque /senɛk/ NM Seneca

sénescence /senesɑ̃s/ NF senescence

sénescent, e /senesɑ̃, ɑt/ ADJ senescent

sénevé /sɛnve/ NM *(= plante)* wild mustard; *(= graine)* wild mustard seed

sénile /senil/ ADJ *(péj, Méd)* senile

sénilité /senilite/ NF senility

senior /senjɔʀ/ ADJ, NMF *(Sport)* senior ◆ **les ~s** *(= personnes de plus de 50 ans)* the over-fifties

senne /sɛn/ NF ⇒ **seine**

sens /sɑ̃s/ NM [1] *(= goût, vue etc)* sense ◆ **les ~** the senses ◆ **avoir le ~ de l'odorat/de l'ouïe très développé** to have a highly developed *ou* a very keen sense of smell/of hearing ◆ **reprendre ses ~** to regain consciousness ◆ **sixième ~** sixth sense; → **organe**
[2] *(= instinct)* sense ◆ **avoir le ~ du rythme/de l'humour/du ridicule** to have a sense of rhythm/of humour/of the ridiculous ◆ **il n'a aucun ~ moral/pratique** he has no moral/practical sense ◆ **avoir le ~ des réalités** to have a sense of reality ◆ **avoir le ~ de l'orientation** to have a (good) sense of direction ◆ **avoir le ~ des responsabilités/des valeurs** to have a sense of responsibility/of moral values ◆ **avoir le ~ des affaires** to have business acumen *ou* good business sense, to have a good head for business

[3] *(= avis, jugement)* sense ◆ **ce qu'il dit est plein de ~** what he is saying makes (good) sense *ou* is very sensible ◆ **cela n'a pas de ~** that doesn't make (any) sense ◆ **il a perdu le ~ (commun)** he's lost his hold on common sense ◆ **cela tombe sous le ~** it's (perfectly) obvious, it stands to reason ◆ **à mon ~** to my mind, in my opinion, the way I see it

♦ **bon sens** common sense ◆ **homme de bon ~** man of (good) sense ◆ **le bon ~ voudrait qu'il refuse** the sensible thing would be for him to refuse, the sensible thing for him to do would be to refuse ◆ **c'est une question de bon ~** it's a matter of common sense ◆ **interprétations qui défient le bon ~** interpretations that fly in the face of common sense ◆ **ça semble de bon ~** it seems to make sense ◆ **c'est le bon ~ même de ...** it's only common sense *ou* it only makes sense to ...

[4] *(= signification) [de parole, geste]* meaning ◆ **ce qui donne un ~ à la vie/à son action** what gives (a) meaning to life/to what he did ◆ **au ~ propre/figuré** in the literal *ou* true/figurative sense ◆ **au ~ large/strict du terme** in the general/strict sense of the word ◆ **dans tous les ~ du terme** in every sense of the word ◆ **dans le bon ~ du terme** in the best sense of the word ◆ **faire ~** to make sense ◆ **qui n'a pas de ~, dépourvu de ~, vide de ~** meaningless, which has no meaning ◆ **en un (certain) ~** in a (certain) sense ◆ **en ce ~ que ...** in the sense that ... ◆ **la culture, au ~ où il l'entend** culture, as he understands it; → **double, faux(-)sens**

[5] *(= direction)* direction ◆ **aller** *ou* **être dans le bon/mauvais ~** to go *ou* be in the right/wrong direction, to go the right/wrong way ◆ **mesurer/fendre qch dans le ~ de la longueur** to measure/split sth along its length *ou* lengthwise *ou* lengthways ◆ **ça fait dix mètres dans le ~ de la longueur** it's ten metres in length ◆ **dans le ~ de la largeur** across its width, in width, widthwise ◆ **dans le ~ du bois** with the grain (of the wood) ◆ **arriver/venir en ~ contraire** *ou* **inverse** to arrive/come from the opposite direction ◆ **aller en ~ contraire** to go in the opposite direction ◆ **dans le ~ des aiguilles d'une montre** clockwise ◆ **dans le ~ inverse des aiguilles d'une montre** anticlockwise *(Brit)*, counterclockwise *(US)* ◆ **dans le ~ de la marche** facing the front (of the train), facing the engine ◆ **il retourna la boîte dans tous les ~ avant de l'ouvrir** he turned the box this way and that before opening it ◆ **ça va** *ou* **part dans tous les ~** *(fig)* it's going all over the place ◆ **une voie de circulation a été mise en ~ inverse sur ...** there is a contraflow system in operation on ... ◆ **la circulation dans le ~ Paris-province/dans le ~ province-Paris** traffic out of Paris/into Paris

♦ **sens dessus dessous** ◆ **être/mettre ~ dessus dessous** *(lit, fig)* to be/turn upside down

♦ **sens devant derrière** back to front, the wrong way round

[6] *(= ligne directrice)* **il a répondu dans le même ~** he replied more or less in the same way *ou* along the same lines ◆ **il a agi dans le même ~** he acted along the same lines, he did more or less the same thing ◆ **j'ai donné des directives dans ce ~** I've given instructions to that effect *ou* end ◆ **dans quel ~ allez-vous orienter votre politique ?** along what lines are you going to direct your policy? ◆ **cette réforme va dans le bon ~** this reform is a step in the right direction ◆ **le ~ de l'histoire** the course of history

COMP **sens giratoire** *(Aut)* roundabout *(Brit)*, traffic circle *(US)* ◆ **la place est en ~ giratoire** the square forms a roundabout

sens interdit *(Aut)* one-way street ◆ **vous êtes en ~ interdit** you are in a one-way street, you are going the wrong way (up a one-way street)

sens unique *(Aut)* one-way street ◆ **à ~ unique** *[rue]* one-way; *[concession]* one-sided ◆ **c'est toujours à ~ unique avec lui** everything is so one-sided with him

sensass * /sɑ̃sas/ ADJ INV fantastic*, terrific*, sensational

sensation /sɑ̃sasjɔ̃/ NF [1] *(= perception)* sensation; *(= impression)* feeling, sensation ◆ **il eut une ~ d'étouffement** he felt he was suffocating ◆ **éprouver une ~ de bien-être** to have a feeling of well-being ◆ **éprouver une ~ de faim/froid** to feel cold/hungry ◆ **avoir une ~ de malaise** *(psychologiquement)* to feel ill at ease; *(physiquement)* to feel weak ◆ ◆ **~ de brûlure** burning sensation ◆ **ça laisse une ~ de fraîcheur** *[déodorant]* it leaves you feeling refreshed ◆ ◆ **~ de liberté/plénitude/puissance** feeling *ou* sense of freedom/bliss/power ◆ **j'ai la ~ de l'avoir déjà vu** I have a feeling I've seen him before ◆ **quelle ~ cela te procure-t-il ?** how does it make you feel?, what kind of sensation does it give you? ◆ **les amateurs de ~s fortes** thrill-seekers, people who like big thrills

[2] *(= effet)* **faire ~** to cause *ou* create a sensation

♦ **à sensation** *[littérature, roman, procès]* sensational; *[magazine]* sensationalist ◆ **journal à ~** tabloid, scandal sheet; → **presse**

sensationnalisme /sɑ̃sasjɔnalism/ NM sensationalism

sensationnaliste /sɑ̃sasjɔnalist/ ADJ sensationalist

sensationnel, -elle /sɑ̃sasjɔnɛl/ ADJ *(* = merveilleux)* fantastic*, terrific*, sensational; *(= qui fait sensation)* sensational NM ◆ **le ~** the sensational ◆ **des journalistes à l'affût du ~** journalists on the lookout for sensational stories

sensé, e /sɑ̃se/ ADJ *[question, personne, mesure]* sensible ◆ **tenir des propos ~s** to talk sense

sensément /sɑ̃semɑ̃/ ADV sensibly ◆ **je ne peux ~ pas lui proposer cela** it would be unreasonable of me to suggest that to him

sensibilisateur, -trice /sɑ̃sibilizatœʀ, tʀis/ ADJ sensitizing NM sensitizer

sensibilisation /sɑ̃sibilizasjɔ̃/ NF [1] *[de personnes]* **la ~ de l'opinion publique à ce problème est récente** public opinion has only recently become sensitive *ou* alive to this problem ◆ **campagne de ~** public awareness campaign, consciousness-raising campaign ◆ **mener des actions de ~ à l'écologie** to attempt to raise public awareness of ecological issues [2] *(Bio, Photo)* sensitization

sensibilisé, e /sɑ̃sibilize/ (ptp de **sensibiliser**) ADJ **sensibilisé à** *(gén)* sensitive *ou* alive to ◆ **~ aux problèmes sociaux** socially aware ◆ **~ aux problèmes de santé** aware of health issues

sensibiliser /sɑ̃sibilize/ ▸ conjug 1 ◂ VT [1] ◆ **~ qn** to make sb sensitive *(à* to); ◆ **~ l'opinion publique à un problème** to heighten public awareness of a problem, to make the public aware of a problem [2] *(Bio, Photo)* to sensitize

sensibilité /sɑ̃sibilite/ NF [1] *[de personne]* sensitivity; *[d'artiste]* sensibility, sensitivity ◆ **n'avoir aucune ~** to have no sensitivity ◆ **être d'une grande ~** to be extremely sensitive ◆ **faire preuve d'une ~ exacerbée** to be hypersensitive ◆ **exprimer sa ~** to express one's feelings ◆ **l'évolution de la ~ artistique** the development of artistic sensibility ◆ **cela heurte notre ~** it offends our sensibilities ◆ **certaines scènes peuvent heurter la ~ des plus jeunes** some scenes may be unsuitable for a younger audience

[2] *(Pol)* **~ politique** political sensitivity ◆ **il a une ~ de gauche/de droite** his sympathies lie with the left/the right ◆ **les maires, toutes ~s politiques confondues, sont d'accord** mayors of all political tendencies agree

[3] *[d'instrument, muscle, pellicule, marché, secteur]* sensitivity

sensible /sɑ̃sibl/ GRAMMAIRE ACTIVE 49 ADJ [1] *(= impressionnable) [personne]* sensitive *(à* to); ◆ **film déconseillé aux personnes ~s** film not recommended for people of a nervous disposition ◆ **elle a le cœur ~** she is tender-hearted ◆ **être ~ au charme de qn** to be susceptible to sb's charm ◆ **j'ai été très ~ à ses attentions** I was really touched by how considerate he was ◆ **les gens sont de plus en plus ~s à la qualité du cadre de vie** people are more and more aware of the importance of their surroundings ◆ **il est très ~ à la poésie** he has a great feeling for poetry ◆ **il est peu ~ à ce genre d'argument** he's unlikely to be convinced by that kind of argument ◆ **ils ne sont pas du tout ~s à notre humour** they don't appreciate our sense of humour at all ◆ **l'opinion publique est très ~ aux problèmes des réfugiés** public opinion is very much alive to the refugees' problems; → **âme, point¹**

[2] *(= notable) [hausse, changement, progrès]* appreciable, noticeable, palpable *(épith)* ◆ **la différence n'est pas ~** the difference is hardly noticeable *ou* appreciable ◆ **de façon ~** appreciably

[3] *(= tangible)* perceptible ◆ **le vent était à peine ~** the wind was scarcely *ou* hardly perceptible ◆ **~ à la vue/l'ouïe** perceptible to the eye/the ear

[4] *[blessure, organe, peau]* sensitive ◆ **avoir l'ouïe ~** to have sensitive *ou* keen hearing ◆ **~ au chaud/froid** sensitive to (the) heat/cold ◆ **être ~ de la bouche/gorge** to have a sensitive mouth/throat

[5] *(= qui varie)* **~ à** *[marché, secteur]* sensitive to ◆ **les valeurs (les plus) ~s à l'évolution des taux d'intérêt** shares that are (most) sensitive to fluctuating interest rates

[6] *(= difficile) [dossier, projet, secteur]* sensitive; *[établissement scolaire, quartier]* problem *(épith)* ◆ **zone ~** *(= quartier)* problem area; *(Mil)* sensitive area

[7] *[balance, baromètre, papier]* sensitive; → **corde**

[8] *(Mus)* **(note) ~** leading note

[9] *(Philos)* **intuition ~** sensory intuition ◆ **un être ~** a sentient being ◆ **le monde ~** the physical world, the world as perceived by the senses

> ⚠ Évitez de traduire **sensible** par le mot anglais **sensible**, qui a le sens de 'raisonnable'.

sensiblement /sɑ̃sibləmɑ̃/ ADV [1] *(= presque)* approximately, more or less ◆ **être ~ du même âge/de la même taille** to be approximately *ou* more or less the same age/the same height [2] *(= notablement) [meilleur]* appreciably, noticeably; *[différent]* noticeably, markedly; *[inférieur] [améliorer]* noticeably ◆ **le risque en sera très ~ réduit** the risk will be considerably reduced

> ⚠ Évitez de traduire **sensiblement** par **sensibly**, qui a le sens de 'avec bon sens'.

sensiblerie /sɑ̃siblǝʀi/ NF *(= sentimentalité)* sentimentality, mawkishness; *(= impressionnabilité)* squeamishness

sensitif, -ive /sɑ̃sitif, iv/ ADJ *(Anat) [nerf]* sensory; *(littér)* oversensitive NF **sensitive** *(= plante)* sensitive plant

sensoriel, -ielle /sɑ̃sɔʀjɛl/ ADJ sensory, sensorial ◆ **organe ~** sense organ, sensory organ

sensorimoteur, -trice /sɑ̃sɔʀimɔtœʀ, tʀis/ ADJ sensorimotor

sensualisme /sɑ̃sɥalism/ NM *(Philos)* sensualism

sensualiste /sɑ̃sɥalist/ *(Philos)* ADJ sensualist, sensualistic NMF sensualist

sensualité /sɑ̃sɥalite/ NF (*gén*) sensuality; [*de langage, style*] sensuousness

sensuel, -uelle /sɑ̃sɥɛl/ ADJ (*gén*) sensual; [*langage, style*] sensuous

sensuellement /sɑ̃sɥɛlmɑ̃/ ADV sensually

sent-bon /sɑ̃bɔ̃/ NM INV (*langage enfantin*) perfume

sente /sɑ̃t/ NF (*littér*) (foot)path

sentence /sɑ̃tɑ̃s/ NF (= *verdict*) sentence; (= *adage*) maxim

sentencieusement /sɑ̃tɑ̃sjøzmɑ̃/ ADV sententiously

sentencieux, -ieuse /sɑ̃tɑ̃sjø, jøz/ ADJ sententious

senteur /sɑ̃tœʀ/ NF (*littér*) scent, perfume; → **pois**

senti, e /sɑ̃ti/ (ptp de **sentir**) ADJ (= *sincère*) heartfelt, sincere ♦ **quelques vérités bien ~es** a few home truths ♦ **quelques mots bien ~s** (*bien choisis*) a few well-chosen *ou* well-expressed words; (*de blâme*) a few well-chosen words ♦ **un discours bien** ~ a well-delivered *ou* heartfelt speech

sentier /sɑ̃tje/ NM (*lit*) (foot)path; (*fig*) path ♦ **sortir des ~s battus** to go *ou* venture off the beaten track ♦ **hors** *ou* **loin des ~s battus** off the beaten track ♦ **les ~s de la gloire** (*littér*) the path to glory ♦ **être sur le ~ de la guerre** (*lit, fig*) to be on the warpath ♦ **le Sentier lumineux** (*Pol*) the Shining Path; → **randonnée**

sentiériste /sɑ̃tjerist/ NMF Shining Path guerrilla

sentiment /sɑ̃timɑ̃/ GRAMMAIRE ACTIVE 33.1 NM 1 (= *émotion*) feeling, sentiment (*frm*) ♦ ~ **de pitié/tendresse/haine** feeling of pity/tenderness/hatred ♦ ~ **de culpabilité** feeling of guilt, guilty feeling ♦ **avoir de bons/mauvais ~s à l'égard de qn** to be well-/ill-disposed towards sb ♦ **bons ~s** finer feelings ♦ **dans ce cas, il faut savoir oublier les ~s** in this case, we have to put sentiment to one side *ou* to disregard our own feelings ♦ **prendre qn par les ~s** to appeal to sb's feelings ♦ **ça n'empêche pas les ~s** * (*souvent iro*) that doesn't mean we (*ou* they *etc*) don't love each other

2 (= *sensibilité*) **le** ~ feeling, emotion ♦ **être capable de** ~ to be capable of emotion ♦ **être dépourvu de** ~ to be devoid of all feeling *ou* emotion ♦ **jouer/danser avec** ~ to play/dance with feeling ♦ **agir par** ~ to be guided by *ou* listen to one's feelings ♦ **faire du** ~ (*péj*) to sentimentalize, to be sentimental ♦ **tu ne m'auras pas au** ~ * you won't get round me like that, you can't sweet-talk me *

3 (= *conscience*) **avoir le ~ de** to be aware of ♦ **avoir le ~ que quelque chose va arriver** to have a feeling that something is going to happen ♦ **je n'ai jamais eu le ~ qu'il mentait/de renier mes principes** I never felt that he was lying/that I was going against my principles ♦ **elle avait le ~ très vif de sa valeur** she had a keen sense of her worth

4 (*formule de politesse*) **transmettez-lui nos meilleurs ~s** give him our best wishes; → **agréer**

5 (*frm* = *opinion*) feeling ♦ **quel est votre ~ ?** what are your feelings *ou* what is your feeling (about that)? ♦ **je n'ai aucun ~ particulier sur la question** I have no particular opinion about the matter

sentimental, e (mpl **-aux**) /sɑ̃timɑ̃tal, o/ ADJ 1 (= *tendre*) [*personne*] romantic 2 (= *affectif*) [*raisons, voyage*] sentimental ♦ **cette bague a pour moi une grande valeur ~e** this ring is of great sentimental value to me 3 (= *amoureux*) [*aventure, vie*] love (*épith*) ♦ **sur le plan** ~ (*dans horoscope*) on the romantic *ou* love front ♦ **sa vie était un échec sur le plan** ~ as far as relationships were concerned, his life was a failure ♦ **il a des problèmes sentimentaux** he has problems with his love life ♦ **déception ~e** disappointment in love ♦ **drame** ~ tragic love story 4 (*péj*) [*chanson, film, personne*] sentimental, soppy * ♦ **ne sois pas si** ~ don't be so soft *ou* soppy * *ou* sentimental NM,F sentimentalist ♦ **c'est un grand** ~ he's a great romantic

sentimentalement /sɑ̃timɑ̃talmɑ̃/ ADV sentimentally; (*péj*) soppily *

sentimentalisme /sɑ̃timɑ̃talism/ NM sentimentalism

sentimentalité /sɑ̃timɑ̃talite/ NF sentimentality; (*péj*) soppiness *

sentinelle /sɑ̃tinɛl/ NF sentry, sentinel (*littér*) ♦ **être en** ~ (*Mil*) to be on sentry duty, to stand sentry ♦ **mets-toi en ~ à la fenêtre** (*fig*) stand guard *ou* keep watch at the window

sentir /sɑ̃tiʀ/ ▸ conjug 16 ◂ VT 1 (= *percevoir*) (*par l'odorat*) to smell; (*au goût*) to taste; (*au toucher, contact*) to feel ♦ ~ **un courant d'air** to feel a draught ♦ ~ **son cœur battre/ses yeux se fermer** to feel one's heart beating/one's eyes closing ♦ **il ne sent pas la différence entre le beurre et la margarine** he can't taste *ou* tell the difference between butter and margarine ♦ **elle sentit une odeur de gaz/de brûlé** she smelled *ou* smelt (*Brit*) gas/burning ♦ **on sent qu'il y a de l'ail dans ce plat** you can taste the garlic in this dish, you can tell there's garlic in this dish ♦ **il ne sent jamais le froid/la fatigue** he never feels the cold/feels tired ♦ **elle sentit qu'on lui tapait sur l'épaule** she felt somebody tapping her on the shoulder ♦ **je suis enrhumé, je ne sens plus rien** I have a cold and can't smell anything *ou* and I've lost my sense of smell ♦ **je ne sens plus mes doigts** (*de froid*) I have lost all sensation in my fingers, I can't feel my fingers ♦ **je ne sens plus mes jambes** (*de fatigue*) my legs are dropping off * (*Brit*), my legs are folding under me (*US*) ♦ **je l'ai senti passer** * [*+ facture, opération*] I really felt it * ♦ ~ **l'écurie** * [*personne*] to get the smell *ou* scent of home in one's nostrils ♦ **je ne le sens pas, ce type** * I don't like the look of him ♦ **je le sens mal ce voyage** * I'm not (at all) happy about this trip

2 (= *dégager une certaine odeur*) to smell; (= *avoir un certain goût*) to taste ♦ ~ **bon/mauvais** to smell good *ou* nice/bad ♦ ~ **des pieds/de la bouche** to have smelly feet/bad breath ♦ **son manteau sent la fumée** his coat smells of smoke ♦ **ce poisson commence à** ~ this fish is beginning to smell ♦ **ce thé sent le jasmin** (*goût*) this tea tastes of jasmine; (*odeur*) this tea smells of jasmine ♦ **la pièce sent le renfermé/le moisi** the room smells stale/musty ♦ **ça ne sent pas la rose !** * that doesn't smell too good!

3 (= *dénoter*) to be indicative of, to reveal, to smack of ♦ **une certaine arrogance qui sent la petite bourgeoisie** a certain arrogance indicative of *ou* which reveals *ou* suggests a middle-class background

4 (= *annoncer*) **ça sent le fagot/l'autoritarisme** it smacks of heresy/of authoritarianism ♦ **ça sent le piège** there's a trap *ou* catch ♦ **ça sent la pluie/la neige** it looks *ou* feels like rain/snow ♦ **ça sent l'orage** there's a storm in the air ♦ **ça sent le printemps** spring is in the air ♦ **ça sent la punition** someone's in for a telling off *, someone's going to be punished ♦ **cela sent la poudre** things could flare up; → **roussi, sapin**

5 (= *avoir conscience de*) [*+ changement, fatigue*] to feel, to be aware *ou* conscious of; [*+ importance de qch*] to be aware *ou* conscious of; (= *apprécier*) [*+ beauté, élégance de qch*] to appreciate; (= *pressentir*) [*+ danger, difficulté*] to sense ♦ **il sentait la panique le gagner** he felt panic rising within him ♦ **sentant le but proche ...** sensing the goal was at hand ... ♦ **il ne sent pas sa force** he doesn't know *ou* realize his own strength ♦ **elle sent maintenant le vide causé par son départ** now she is feeling the emptiness left by his departure ♦ **sentez-vous la beauté de ce passage ?** do you feel *ou* appreciate the beauty of this passage? ♦ **le cheval sentait (venir) l'orage** the horse sensed the storm (coming) ♦ **c'est sa façon de ~ (les choses)** that's the way he feels (about things) ♦ ~ **que** to be aware *ou* conscious that; (= *pressentir*) to sense that ♦ **il sentit qu'il ne reviendrait jamais** he sensed *ou* felt that he would never come back (again) ♦ **faire ~ son autorité** to make one's authority felt ♦ **faire ~ la beauté d'une œuvre d'art** to bring out *ou* demonstrate the beauty of a work of art ♦ **il m'a fait ~ que j'étais de trop** he let me know I wasn't wanted ♦ **j'ai senti le coup** * I knew what was coming

6 (= *supporter*) **il ne peut pas le** ~ * he can't stand *ou* bear (the sight of) him

VPR **se sentir** 1 [*personne*] **se ~ mal** (*physiquement*) to feel ill *ou* unwell *ou* sick, not to feel very well; (*psychologiquement*) to be unhappy ♦ **se ~ bien** (*physiquement, psychologiquement*) to feel good ♦ **se ~ mieux/fatigué** to feel better/tired ♦ **se ~ revivre/rajeunir** to feel o.s. coming alive again/growing young again ♦ **il ne se sent pas la force/le courage de le lui dire** he doesn't feel strong/brave enough to tell him ♦ **ne pas se ~ de joie** to be beside o.s. with joy ♦ **il ne se sent plus !** * he really thinks he's arrived! ♦ **non, mais tu ne te sens pas bien !** * are you out of your mind! *

2 (= *être perceptible*) [*effet*] to be felt, to show ♦ **cette amélioration/augmentation se sent** this improvement/increase can be felt *ou* shows ♦ **les effets des grèves vont se faire ~ à la fin du mois** the effect of the strikes will be felt *ou* will show at the end of the month ♦ **nul besoin de réfléchir, cela se sent** there's no need to think about it - you can feel *ou* sense it ♦ **il est inquiet, ça se sent** you can tell he's worried ♦ **30 euros d'augmentation par mois, ça se sentirait à peine** a 30 euro monthly pay rise would be hardly noticeable

3 (= *se supporter*) **ils ne peuvent pas se** ~ * they can't stand *ou* bear each other

4 (* = *être d'accord*) **tu te sens pour aller faire un tour ?** do you feel like going for a walk?

seoir /swaʀ/ ▸ conjug 26 ◂ (*frm*) VI (= *convenir*) ♦ ~ **à qn** to become sb VB IMPERS ♦ **il sied de/que** it is proper *ou* fitting to/that ♦ **comme il sied** as is proper *ou* fitting ♦ **il lui sied/ne lui sied pas de faire cela** it befits *ou* becomes/ill befits *ou* ill becomes him to do that

Séoul /seul/ N Seoul

sep /sɛp/ NM ⇒ **cep**

sépale /sepal/ NM sepal

séparable /sepaʀabl/ ADJ separable (*de* from); ♦ **deux concepts difficilement ~s** two concepts which are difficult to separate

séparateur, -trice /sepaʀatœʀ, tʀis/ ADJ separating (*épith*), separative ♦ **pouvoir ~ de l'œil/d'un instrument d'optique** resolving power of the eye/of an optical instrument NM (*Élec, Tech*) separator; (*Ordin*) delimiter ♦ ~ **d'isotopes** isotope separator

séparation /sepaʀasjɔ̃/ NF 1 (= *dissociation*) [*éléments, gaz, liquides*] separation ♦ ~ **isotopique** *ou* **des isotopes** isotope separation

2 (= *division*) [*de territoire*] division, splitting

3 [*d'amis, parents*] separation ♦ **une longue ~ avait transformé leurs rapports** a long (period of) separation had changed their relationship ♦ **après cinq ans de** ~ after five years' separation ♦ **au moment de la** ~ [*de manifestants*] when they dispersed; [*de convives*] when they parted ♦ ~ **de corps** (*Jur*) legal separation ♦ ~ **de fait** de facto separation ♦ ~ **à l'amiable** voluntary separation

[4] *[de notions, services]* separation ◆ **la ~ des pouvoirs** *(Pol)* the separation of powers ◆ **la ~ de l'Église et de l'État** the separation of the Church and the State ◆ **mariés sous le régime de la ~ de biens** *(Jur)* married under separation of property
[5] *(= démarcation)* division, partition ◆ **mur de ~** separating *ou* dividing wall ◆ **un paravent sert de ~ entre les deux parties de la pièce** a screen separates the two parts of the room
[6] *(= distinction)* dividing line ◆ **il faut établir une ~ très nette entre ces problèmes** you must draw a very clear dividing line between these problems

séparatisme /sepaʀatism/ NM *(Pol, Rel)* separatism

séparatiste /sepaʀatist/ ADJ, NMF *(Pol)* separatist; *(Hist US = sudiste)* secessionist ◆ **mouvement/organisation ~** separatist movement/organization

séparé, e /sepaʀe/ (ptp de **séparer**) ADJ [1] *(= distinct) [analyses, entités, mondes, notions, paix]* separate ◆ **ces colis feront l'objet d'un envoi ~** these parcels will be sent separately ◆ **accord ~** separate agreement ◆ **ils dorment dans deux chambres ~es** they sleep in separate rooms ◆ **le développement ~** *(Pol)* (racial) separate development [2] *[personnes] (Jur = désuni)* separated; *(gén = éloigné)* parted *(attrib)*, apart *(attrib)* ◆ **vivre ~** to live apart, to be separated *(de* from)

séparément /sepaʀemɑ̃/ ADV separately

séparer /sepaʀe/ ▸ conjug 1 ◂ VT [1] *(= détacher) (gén)* to separate; *[+ écorce, peau, enveloppe]* to pull off, to pull away *(de* from); *(= extraire) [+ éléments, gaz, liquides]* to separate (out) *(de* from); ◆ **~ la tête du tronc** to separate *ou* sever the head from the trunk ◆ **~ la noix de sa coquille** to separate the nut from its shell ◆ **~ le grain du son** to separate the grain from the bran ◆ **~ un minerai de ses impuretés** to separate an ore from its impurities ◆ **séparez les blancs des jaunes** *(Culin)* separate the whites from the yolks ◆ **~ le bon grain de l'ivraie** *(Bible)* to separate the wheat from the chaff
[2] *(= diviser)* to part, to split, to divide ◆ **~ un territoire (en deux) par une frontière** to split *ou* divide a territory (in two) by a frontier
[3] *(= désunir) [+ amis, alliés]* to part, to drive apart; *[+ adversaires, combattants]* to separate, to pull apart, to part ◆ **ils se battaient, je les ai séparés** they were fighting and I separated them *ou* pulled them apart *ou* parted them ◆ **~ qn et** *ou* **de qn d'autre** to separate *ou* part sb from sb else ◆ **dans cet hôpital, les hommes et les femmes sont séparés** men and women are separated in this hospital ◆ **ils avaient séparé l'enfant de sa mère** they had separated the child from its mother ◆ **rien ne pourra jamais nous ~** nothing will ever come between us *ou* drive us apart ◆ **la vie les a séparés** they went their separate ways in life ◆ **la mort les a séparés** they were parted by death
[4] *(= se dresser entre) [+ territoires, classes sociales, générations]* to separate ◆ **une barrière sépare les spectateurs des** *ou* **et les joueurs** a barrier separates the spectators from the players ◆ **un simple grillage nous séparait des lions** a wire fence was all that separated us from the lions ◆ **une chaîne de montagnes sépare la France et** *ou* **de l'Espagne** a chain of mountains separates France from *ou* and Spain ◆ **un seul obstacle le séparait encore du but** only one obstacle stood *ou* remained between him and his goal ◆ **près de deux heures le séparaient de la ville** he was nearly two hours away from the city ◆ **3 kilomètres séparent le village de la mer** the village is 3 kilometres from the sea ◆ **les 200 mètres qui séparent la poste et la gare** the 200 metres between the post office and the station ◆ **les six ans qui séparent l'audience de la date du drame** the six years that have elapsed between the hearing and the date of the tragedy ◆ **tout les séparait** they were worlds apart, they had nothing in common
[5] *(= différencier) [+ questions, aspects]* to distinguish between ◆ **~ l'érudition de** *ou* **et l'intelligence** to distinguish *ou* differentiate between learning and intelligence

VPR **se séparer** [1] *(= se défaire de)* **se ~ de** *[+ employé, objet personnel]* to part with ◆ **en voyage, ne vous séparez jamais de votre passeport** keep your passport on you at all times when travelling
[2] *(= s'écarter)* to divide, to part *(de* from); *(= se détacher)* to split off, to separate off *(de* from); ◆ **l'écorce se sépare du tronc** the bark is coming away from the trunk ◆ **l'endroit où les branches se séparent du tronc** the place where the branches split *ou* separate off from the trunk ◆ **le premier étage de la fusée s'est séparé (de la base)** the first stage of the rocket has split off (from the base) *ou* separated (off) from the base ◆ **à cet endroit, le fleuve/la route se sépare en deux** at this point the river/the road forks ◆ **les routes/branches se séparent** the roads/branches divide *ou* part ◆ **c'est là que nos routes** *ou* **chemins se séparent** this is where we go our separate ways
[3] *(= se disperser) [adversaires]* to separate, to break apart; *[manifestants, participants]* to disperse; *[assemblée]* to break up
[4] *(= se quitter) [convives]* to leave each other, to part; *[époux]* to separate *(aussi Jur)*, to part, to split up ◆ **se ~ de son mari/sa femme** to part *ou* separate from one's husband/one's wife ◆ **ils se sont séparés à l'amiable** their separation was amicable

sépharade /sefaʀad/ ADJ, NMF ⇒ **séfarade**

sépia /sepja/ NF *(= encre de seiche)* cuttlefish ink, sepia; *(= couleur, dessin, substance)* sepia ◆ **(dessin à la) ~** sepia (drawing)

sept /sɛt/ ADJ INV, NM INV seven ◆ **~ jours sur ~** seven days a week ◆ **les ~ péchés capitaux** the seven deadly sins ◆ **les Sept Merveilles du monde** the seven wonders of the world ◆ **les ~ familles** *(Cartes)* Happy Families ◆ **les ~ pays les plus industrialisés** the Group of Seven (industrialized nations) ◆ **les Sept d'or** *television awards; pour loc voir* **six**

septain /sɛtɛ̃/ NM *seven-line stanza or poem*

septantaine /sɛptɑ̃tɛn/ NF *(Belg, Helv)* about seventy, seventy or so ◆ **il doit avoir la ~** he must be about seventy

septante /sɛptɑ̃t/ ADJ INV *(Belg, Helv)* seventy ◆ **la version des Septante** *(Bible)* the Septuagint

septantième /sɛptɑ̃tjɛm/ ADJ, NMF *(Belg, Helv)* seventieth

septembre /sɛptɑ̃bʀ/ NM September ◆ **le mois de ~** the month of September ◆ **le premier/dix ~ tombe un mercredi** the first/tenth of September falls on a Wednesday ◆ **nous avons rendez-vous le premier/dix ~** we have an appointment on the first/tenth of September ◆ **en ~** in September ◆ **au mois de ~** in (the month of) September ◆ **au début (du mois) de ~, début ~** at the beginning of September, in early September ◆ **au milieu (du mois) de ~, à la mi-~** in the middle of September, in mid-September ◆ **à la fin (du mois) de ~, fin ~** at the end of September ◆ **pendant le mois de ~** during September ◆ **vers la fin de ~** late in September, in late September, towards the end of September ◆ **~ a été très froid** September was very cold ◆ **~ prochain/dernier** next/last September

septennal, e (mpl **-aux**) /sɛptenal, o/ ADJ *(durée) [mandat, période]* seven-year *(épith)*; *(fréquence) [festival]* septennial

septennat /sɛptena/ NM *[de président]* seven-year term (of office) ◆ **au cours de son ~** during his time in office *ou* his presidency ◆ **briguer un second ~** to run for a second term in office, to seek a second term of office

septentrion /sɛptɑ̃tʀijɔ̃/ NM (†† *littér)* north

septentrional, e (mpl **-aux**) /sɛptɑ̃tʀijɔnal, o/ ADJ northern

septicémie /sɛptisemi/ NF blood poisoning, septicaemia *(SPÉC) (Brit)*, septicemia *(SPÉC) (US)*

septicémique /sɛptisemik/ ADJ septicaemic *(Brit)*, septicemic *(US)*

septicité /sɛptisite/ NF septicity

septième /sɛtjɛm/ ADJ, NM seventh ◆ **le ~ art** the cinema ◆ **être au ~ ciel** to be in seventh heaven, to be on cloud nine *; *pour autres loc voir* **sixième** NF [1] *(Scol) sixth year in primary school,* fifth grade *(US)* [2] *(Mus)* seventh

septièmement /sɛtjɛmmɑ̃/ ADV seventhly; *pour loc voir* **sixièmement**

septique /sɛptik/ ADJ *[bactérie, fièvre]* septic; → **fosse**

septuagénaire /sɛptɥaʒenɛʀ/ ADJ septuagenarian, seventy-year-old *(épith)* NMF septuagenarian, seventy-year-old man (*ou* woman)

septuagésime /sɛptɥaʒezim/ NF Septuagesima

septuor /sɛptɥɔʀ/ NM septet(te)

septuple /sɛptypl/ ADJ *[nombre, quantité, rangée]* septuple ◆ **une quantité ~ de l'autre** a quantity seven times (as great as) the other ◆ **en ~ exemplaire** in seven copies NM *(gén, Math)* ◆ **je l'ai payé le ~/le ~ de l'autre** I paid seven times as much for it/seven times as much as the other for it ◆ **augmenter au ~** to increase sevenfold *ou* seven times

septuplé, e /sɛptyple/ NM,F septuplet

septupler /sɛptyple/ ▸ conjug 1 ◂ VTI to increase sevenfold *ou* seven times

sépulcral, e (mpl **-aux**) /sepylkʀal, o/ ADJ *[atmosphère, voix]* sepulchral; *[salle]* tomb-like

sépulcre /sepylkʀ/ NM sepulchre *(Brit)*, sepulcher *(US)*

sépulture /sepyltyʀ/ NF [1] *(† littér = inhumation)* sepulture *(littér)*, burial ◆ **être privé de ~** to be refused burial [2] *(= lieu)* burial place; *(= tombe)* grave; *(= pierre tombale)* gravestone, tombstone; → **violation**

séquelle /sekɛl/ NF *(souvent pl) [de maladie, accident]* after-effect; *(= conséquence) [de guerre]* aftermath *(NonC)* ◆ **les ~s du colonialisme** the legacy of colonialism ◆ **elle n'a gardé aucune ~ psychologique de son agression** she was not psychologically scarred by the attack ◆ **ça a laissé des ~s** *[blessure, incident]* it had serious after-effects *ou* consequences ◆ **la lutte entre les différents courants du parti a laissé des ~s** the struggle between the different factions has left its mark on the party

séquençage /sekɑ̃saʒ/ NM *(Bio)* sequencing

séquence /sekɑ̃s/ NF *(Ciné, Mus, Rel)* sequence; *(Cartes)* run; *(Ling, Ordin)* sequence, string ◆ **~ d'ADN/d'ARN** DNA/RNA sequence ◆ **~ génétique** gene sequence; → **plan**[1]

séquencer /sekɑ̃se/ ▸ conjug 3 ◂ VT *[+ génome]* to sequence

séquenceur /sekɑ̃sœʀ/ NM sequencer

séquentiel, -ielle /sekɑ̃sjɛl/ ADJ sequential ◆ **accès ~** *(Ordin)* sequential *ou* serial access ◆ **accomplir des tâches de façon séquentielle** to perform tasks in sequence *ou* sequentially

séquestration /sekɛstʀasjɔ̃/ **NF** 1 *[d'otage]* holding ◆ **~ (arbitraire)** *(Jur)* false imprisonment 2 *[de biens]* sequestration, impoundment 3 *(Chim, Méd)* sequestration

séquestre /sekɛstʀ/ **NM** 1 *(Jur, Pol) (= action)* confiscation, impoundment, sequestration; *(= dépositaire)* depository ◆ **mettre** *ou* **placer des biens sous ~** to sequester goods ◆ **biens sous ~** sequestrated property ◆ **mise sous ~** sequestration 2 *(Méd)* sequestrum

séquestrer /sekɛstʀe/ ▸ conjug 1 ◂ **VT** 1 *(Jur)* *[+ personne]* to confine illegally; *[+ otage]* to hold ◆ **les ouvriers en grève ont séquestré le directeur dans son bureau** the strikers confined the manager to his office 2 *(= saisir)* *[+ biens]* to sequester, to impound *(pending decision over ownership)*

sequin /səkɛ̃/ **NM** *(Hist)* sequin *(gold coin)*

séquoia /sekɔja/ **NM** sequoia, redwood

sérac /seʀak/ **NM** serac

sérail /seʀaj/ **NM** *(lit)* seraglio, serail; *(fig)* inner circle ◆ **c'est un homme du ~** he's an establishment figure *ou* man ◆ **il est issu du ~ politique** he's from a political background

séraphin /seʀafɛ̃/ **NM** seraph

séraphique /seʀafik/ **ADJ** *(Rel, fig)* seraphic

serbe /sɛʀb/ **ADJ** Serbian **NM** *(= langue)* Serbian **NMF** **Serbe** Serb

Serbie /sɛʀbi/ **NF** Serbia ◆ **la République de ~** the Serbian Republic

serbo-croate (pl **serbo-croates**) /sɛʀbo kʀɔat/ **ADJ** Serbo-Croat(ian) **NM** *(= langue)* Serbo-Croat

Sercq /sɛʀk/ **NM** Sark

séré /seʀe/ **NM** *(Helv)* soft white cheese

serein, e /səʀɛ̃, ɛn/ **ADJ** 1 *(= confiant)* confident ◆ **je suis tout à fait ~, je suis sûr que son innocence sera prouvée** I'm quite confident, I'm sure he'll be proved innocent 2 *(= calme)* *[âme, foi, visage, personne]* serene, calm 3 *(= impartial)* *[jugement, critique]* calm, dispassionate 4 *(= clair)* *[ciel, nuit, jour]* clear

> ⚠ Au sens de 'confiant', **serein** ne se traduit pas par le mot anglais **serene**.

sereinement /səʀɛnmɑ̃/ **ADV** calmly; *[regarder]* serenely; *[juger]* impartially, dispassionately ◆ **ils envisagent l'avenir ~** they view the future with equanimity, they feel confident about the future

sérénade /seʀenad/ **NF** 1 *(Mus = concert, pièce)* serenade ◆ **donner une ~ à qn** to serenade sb 2 *(* hum = charivari)* racket, hullabaloo* ◆ **faire toute une ~ à propos de qch** to make a big fuss *ou* a song and dance about sth ◆ **c'est toujours la même ~ !** it's always the same scenario!

sérénissime /seʀenisim/ **ADJ** ◆ **Son Altesse ~** His (*ou* Her) Most Serene Highness ◆ **la république ~, la Sérénissime** *(Hist)* the Venetian Republic, the *ou* la Serenissima

sérénité /seʀenite/ **NF** 1 *[de ciel, nuit, jour]* clearness, clarity 2 *[d'âme, foi, visage]* serenity, calmness ◆ **elle affiche une ~ étonnante** she's incredibly serene *ou* calm ◆ **j'ai retrouvé la ~** I feel serene *ou* calm again ◆ **il envisage l'avenir avec une relative ~** he views the future with relative equanimity, he feels quite calm about the future 3 *[de jugement, critique]* impartiality, dispassionateness

séreux, -euse /seʀø, øz/ **ADJ** serous **NF** **séreuse** serous membrane

serf, serve /sɛʀ(f), sɛʀv/ **ADJ** *[personne]* in serfdom *(attrib)* ◆ **condition serve** (state of) serfdom ◆ **terre serve** land held in villein tenure **NM,F** serf

serfouette /sɛʀfwɛt/ **NF** hoe-fork, weeding hoe

serge /sɛʀʒ/ **NF** serge

sergent[1] /sɛʀʒɑ̃/ **NM** *(Mil)* sergeant ◆ **~-chef** staff sergeant ◆ **~ de ville** † policeman ◆ **~(-)fourrier** quartermaster sergeant ◆ **~ instructeur** drill sergeant ◆ **~-major** ≈ quartermaster sergeant *(in charge of accounts etc)*

sergent[2] /sɛʀʒɑ̃/ **NM** *(= serre-joint)* cramp, clamp

séricicole /seʀisikɔl/ **ADJ** silkworm-breeding *(épith)*, sericultural *(SPÉC)*

sériciculteur, -trice /seʀisikyltœʀ, tʀis/ **NM,F** silkworm breeder, sericulturist *(SPÉC)*

sériciculture /seʀisikyltyʀ/ **NF** silkworm breeding, sericulture *(SPÉC)*

série /seʀi/ **NF** 1 *(= suite)* *[de timbres]* set, series; *[de clés, casseroles, volumes]* set; *[de tests]* series, battery; *[d'accidents, ennuis, succès]* series, string; *[de mesures, réformes]* series ◆ **(toute) une ~ de ...** *(beaucoup)* a (whole) series *ou* string of ... ◆ **dans la ~ les ennuis continuent, la voiture est tombée en panne !** *(hum)* and now something else has gone wrong, the car has broken down! ◆ **(ouvrages de) ~ noire** *(Littérat)* crime thrillers, whodunnits* ◆ **c'est la ~ noire** *(fig)* it's one disaster after another, it's a chain of disasters; → **loi**

2 *(Radio, TV)* series ◆ **~ télévisée** television series

3 *(= catégorie, Naut)* class; *(Sport = épreuve de qualification)* qualifying heat *ou* round ◆ **joueur de deuxième ~** second-rank player ◆ **film de ~ B** B film *ou* movie ◆ **les différentes ~s du baccalauréat** the different baccalauréat options; → **tête;** → **BACCALAURÉAT**

4 *[d'objets fabriqués]* ◆ **limitée/spéciale** limited/special series ◆ **article/voiture de ~** standard article/car ◆ **modèle de ~** production model ◆ **hors ~** *[table, machine]* made-to-order, custom-built; *[talent, don]* incomparable, outstanding ◆ **numéro hors ~** *(Presse)* special issue; → **fin²;** → aussi **hors-série**

5 *(Chim, Math, Mus, Phon)* series; *(Billard)* break ◆ **monté en ~** *(Élec)* connected in series ◆ **imprimante/port ~** serial printer/port

6 *(locutions)*

◆ **de série** ◆ **numéro de ~** *[de véhicule]* serial number ◆ **prix de ~** standard price

◆ **en série** ◆ **fabrication** *ou* **production en ~** mass production ◆ **fabriqué** *ou* **produit en ~** mass-produced ◆ **la direction assistée est (livrée) en ~** power steering is standard ◆ **meurtres en ~** serial killings ◆ **tueur en ~** serial killer

sériel, -ielle /seʀjɛl/ **ADJ** *[ordre]* serial; *[musique]* serial, twelve-note *(épith)*, dodecaphonic; *[compositeur]* dodecaphonic

sérier /seʀje/ ▸ conjug 7 ◂ **VT** *[+ problèmes, questions]* to separate out

sérieusement /seʀjøzmɑ̃/ **ADV** 1 *(= consciencieusement)* *[travailler]* conscientiously 2 *(= sans rire)* *[parler, envisager]* seriously ◆ **elle envisage ~ de divorcer** she's seriously considering divorce ◆ **(tu parles) ~ ?** are you serious?, do you really mean it? ◆ **non, il l'a dit ~** no – he was quite serious, no – he really meant it 3 *(= vraiment)* really ◆ **ça commence ~ à m'agacer** it's really beginning to annoy me 4 *(= gravement)* *[blesser]* seriously ◆ **l'un des reins est ~ atteint** one of the kidneys is seriously damaged

sérieux, -ieuse /seʀjø, jøz/ **ADJ** 1 *(= grave)* *[personne, air]* serious ◆ **~ comme un pape*** deadly serious

2 *(= digne de confiance)* *[personne]* reliable, dependable; *(= fiable)* *[acquéreur, promesses, raison, proposition, annonce]* genuine, serious; *[renseignement, source]* genuine, reliable ◆ **un client ~** a good customer ◆ **"pas sérieux s'abstenir"** "no time wasters", "genuine inquiries only"

3 *(= réfléchi)* *[personne]* serious, serious-minded; *(= consciencieux)* *[employé, élève, apprenti]* conscientious; *[études]* serious; *[travail, artisan]* careful, painstaking ◆ **elle est très sérieuse dans son travail** she's a very conscientious worker ◆ **vous annulez le rendez-vous une heure avant, ce n'est pas ~ !** you cancel the appointment just one hour beforehand – it's just not good enough! ◆ **ça ne fait pas très ~** it doesn't look good ◆ **partir skier pendant les examens, ce n'est vraiment pas ~ !** it's not very responsible to go off skiing during the exams! ◆ **un nom comme ça, ça fait ~** a name like that makes a good impression *ou* is quite impressive ◆ **si tu veux faire ~, mets un costume** if you want to be taken seriously *ou* if you want to come across, well you should wear a suit

4 *(= convenable)* *[jeune homme, jeune fille]* responsible, trustworthy

5 *(= qui ne plaisante pas)* serious ◆ **ce n'est pas ~ !, vous n'êtes pas ~ !** you can't be serious!, you must be joking! ◆ **ce n'est pas ~, il ne le fera jamais** he doesn't really mean it – he'll never do it! ◆ **non, il était ~** no, he was serious *ou* he meant it ◆ **c'est ~, ce que vous dites ?** are you serious?, do you really mean that?

6 *(= important)* *[conversation, livre, projet]* serious ◆ **passons aux affaires** *ou* **choses sérieuses** let's move on to more serious matters, let's get down to business

7 *(= préoccupant)* *[situation, affaire, maladie, blessure]* serious

8 *(intensif)* *[coup]* serious; *[somme, différence]* considerable, sizeable ◆ **de sérieuses chances de ...** a strong *ou* good chance of ... ◆ **il a de sérieuses raisons de ...** he has very good reasons to ... ◆ **je n'avais aucune raison sérieuse de penser qu'il mettrait sa menace à exécution** I had no real reason to think he would carry out his threat ◆ **ils ont une sérieuse avance** they have a strong *ou* good *ou* sizeable lead ◆ **ils ont un ~ retard** they're seriously behind schedule ◆ **il pourrait avoir de ~ ennuis** he could have real *ou* serious problems ◆ **elle a un ~ besoin d'argent/de vacances** she's in real *ou* serious need of money/of a holiday ◆ **il devra faire de ~ efforts pour rattraper son retard** he'll have to make a real effort to catch up

NM 1 *(= gravité)* *[de personne, air]* seriousness, earnestness; *[de conversation, livre, projet]* seriousness ◆ **garder son ~** to keep a straight face ◆ **perdre son ~** to give way to laughter ◆ **prendre qch/qn au ~** to take sth/sb seriously ◆ **se prendre au ~** to take o.s. seriously ◆ **c'est du ~** it's to be taken seriously

2 *(= fiabilité)* *[de personne]* reliability, dependability; *[d'acquéreur, promesses, intentions]* genuineness, seriousness; *[de renseignement, sources]* genuineness, reliability; *[d'employé, élève, apprenti]* conscientiousness ◆ **travailler avec ~** to be a conscientious worker ◆ **il fait preuve de beaucoup de ~ dans son travail/ses études** he takes his work/his studies very seriously, he's a conscientious worker/student

3 *(= sagesse)* *[de jeune homme, jeune fille]* trustworthiness

4 *(= caractère préoccupant)* *[de situation, affaire, maladie]* seriousness

sérigraphie /seʀigʀafi/ **NF** *(= technique)* silk-screen printing, serigraphy *(SPÉC)*; *(= estampe)* screen print, serigraph *(SPÉC)*

serin /s(ə)ʀɛ̃/ **NM** *(= oiseau)* canary; († : *péj = niais*) ninny*

seriner /s(ə)ʀine/ ▸ conjug 1 ◂ **VT** 1 *(péj = rabâcher)* **~ qch à qn** to drum sth into sb ◆ **tais-toi, tu nous serines !*** oh, be quiet, we're tired of hearing the same thing over and over again! 2 ◆ ~ **(un air à) un oiseau** to teach a bird a tune *(using a bird organ)*

seringa(t) /s(ə)ʀɛ̃ga/ NM syringa, mock orange

seringue /s(ə)ʀɛ̃g/ NF syringe

serment /sɛʀmɑ̃/ NM 1 *(solennel)* oath ◆ **faire un ~** to take an oath ◆ ~ **sur l'honneur** solemn oath ◆ **sous ~** on *ou* under oath ◆ ~ **d'Hippocrate** Hippocratic oath ◆ **le ~ du Jeu de paume** *(Hist)* the Tennis Court Oath ◆ ~ **professionnel** oath of office; → **prestation, prêter** 2 *(= promesse)* pledge ◆ **échanger des ~s (d'amour)** to exchange vows *ou* pledges of love ◆ ~ **d'ivrogne** *(fig)* empty vow, vain resolution ◆ **je te fais le ~ de ne plus jouer** I (solemnly) swear to you *ou* I'll make you a solemn promise that I'll never gamble again; → **faux²**

sermon /sɛʀmɔ̃/ NM *(Rel)* sermon; *(péj)* lecture, sermon

sermonner /sɛʀmɔne/ ▸ conjug 1 ◂ VT ◆ ~ **qn** to lecture sb, to sermonize sb

sermonneur, -euse /sɛʀmɔnœʀ, øz/ NM,F *(péj)* sermonizer, preacher

SERNAM /sɛʀnam/ NF (abrév de **Service national des messageries**) *French national parcels service*

séroconversion /seʀokɔ̃vɛʀsjɔ̃/ NF seroconversion

sérodiagnostic /seʀodjagnɔstik/ NM serodiagnosis

sérologie /seʀɔlɔʒi/ NF serology

sérologique /seʀɔlɔʒik/ ADJ serologic(al)

sérologiste /seʀɔlɔʒist/ NMF serologist

séronégatif, -ive /seʀonegatif, iv/ ADJ *(gén)* seronegative; *(Sida)* HIV negative NM,F *(gén)* person who is seronegative; *(Sida)* person who is HIV negative

séronégativité /seʀonegativite/ NF *(gén)* seronegativity; *(Sida)* HIV-negative status

séropo * /seʀopo/ ADJ, NM,F abrév de **séropositif, ive**

séropositif, -ive /seʀopozitif, iv/ ADJ *(gén)* seropositive; *(Sida)* HIV positive NM,F *(gén)* person who is seropositive; *(Sida)* person who is HIV positive, person with HIV

séropositivité /seʀopozitivite/ NF *(gén)* seropositivity; *(Sida)* HIV infection, seropositivity *(SPÉC)* ◆ **quand il a appris sa ~** when he learned that he was HIV positive *ou* that he was infected with HIV

séroprévalence /seʀopʀevalɑ̃s/ NF HIV prevalence ◆ **taux de ~** HIV prevalence rate

sérosité /seʀozite/ NF serous fluid, serosity

sérothérapie /seʀoteʀapi/ NF serotherapy

sérovaccination /seʀovaksinasjɔ̃/ NF serovaccination

serpe /sɛʀp/ NF billhook, bill ◆ **visage taillé à la ~** *ou* **à coups de ~** craggy *ou* rugged face

serpent /sɛʀpɑ̃/ NM 1 *(= animal)* snake; *(péj = personne)* viper *(péj)* ◆ **le ~** *(Rel)* the serpent ◆ **c'est le ~ qui se mord la queue** *(fig)* it's a vicious circle; → **charmeur, réchauffer** 2 *(Mus)* bass horn 3 *(= ruban)* ribbon ◆ **un ~ de fumée** a ribbon of smoke ◆ **le ~ argenté du fleuve** the silvery ribbon of the river

COMP **serpent d'eau** water snake

serpent à lunettes Indian cobra

serpent de mer *(hum Presse)* trite news story *(that journalists fall back on in the absence of more important news)*

le serpent monétaire (européen) the (European) currency snake

serpent à plumes *(Myth)* plumed serpent

serpent à sonnettes rattlesnake

serpentaire /sɛʀpɑ̃tɛʀ/ NM *(= oiseau)* secretary bird, serpent-eater NF *(= plante)* snakeroot

serpenteau (pl **serpenteaux**) /sɛʀpɑ̃to/ NM *(= animal)* young snake; *(= feu d'artifice)* serpent

serpenter /sɛʀpɑ̃te/ ▸ conjug 1 ◂ VI *[chemin, rivière]* to snake, to meander, to wind; *[vallée]* to wind ◆ **la route descendait en serpentant vers la plaine** the road snaked *ou* wound (its way) down to the plain

serpentin, e /sɛʀpɑ̃tɛ̃, in/ ADJ *(gén)* serpentine NM *(= ruban)* streamer; *(Chim)* coil NF **serpentine** *(Minér)* serpentine

serpette /sɛʀpɛt/ NF pruning knife

serpillière /sɛʀpijɛʀ/ NF floorcloth ◆ **passer la ~** to mop the floor

serpolet /sɛʀpɔlɛ/ NM mother-of-thyme, wild thyme

serrage /seʀaʒ/ NM *[d'écrou, vis]* tightening; *[de joint]* clamping; *[de nœud]* tightening, pulling tight; → **bague, collier, vis**

serre¹ /sɛʀ/ NF *(pour cultures)* greenhouse, glasshouse; *(attenant à une maison)* conservatory ◆ **pousser en ~** to grow under glass ◆ ~ **chaude** hothouse ◆ ~ **froide** cold greenhouse; → **effet**

serre² /sɛʀ/ NF *(= griffe)* talon, claw

serré, e /seʀe/ (ptp de **serrer**) ADJ 1 *[chaussures, vêtement]* tight ◆ **robe ~e à la taille** dress fitted at the waist ◆ **elle porte des jeans ~s** she wears tight-fitting jeans

2 *[passagers, spectateurs]* (tightly) packed ◆ **être ~s comme des harengs** *ou* **sardines** to be packed like sardines ◆ **mettez-vous ailleurs, nous sommes trop ~s à cette table** sit somewhere else, it's too crowded at this table; → **rang**

3 *[tissu]* closely woven; *[réseau]* dense; *[écriture, mailles]* close; *[blés, herbe, forêt]* dense; *[virage]* sharp; *[style]* tight, concise; *[horaire]* tight ◆ **une petite pluie fine et ~e** a steady drizzle ◆ **un café (bien) ~** a (good) strong coffee ◆ **pousser en touffes ~es** to grow in thick clumps ◆ **nous avons un calendrier très ~** we have a very tight schedule ◆ **plan ~** *(Ciné)* tight shot, close-up

4 *(= bloqué) [bandage, nœud]* tight ◆ **trop ~** too tight ◆ **pas assez ~** not tight enough

5 *(= contracté)* **les mâchoires/dents ~es** with set jaws/clenched teeth ◆ **les lèvres ~es** with tight lips, tight-lipped ◆ **les poings ~s** with clenched fists ◆ **avoir le cœur ~** to feel a pang of anguish ◆ **je le regardai partir, le cœur ~** I felt sick at heart as I watched him go ◆ **avoir la gorge ~e** to have a lump in one's throat

6 *[discussion, négociations]* closely argued; *[jeu, lutte, match]* tight, close-fought; *[budget]* tight; *[prix]* keen; *[gestion]* strict ◆ **arrivée ~e** *(Sport)* close finish ◆ **les deux candidats sont en ballottage très ~** the two candidates are fighting it out in a very close second round, the two candidates are running neck and neck in the second round of voting ◆ **la partie est ~e, nous jouons une partie ~e** it's a tight game, we're in a tight game

ADV ◆ **écrire ~** to write one's letters close together, to write in a cramped hand ◆ **jouer ~** *(fig)* to play it tight, to play a tight game ◆ **vivre ~** to live on a tight budget

serre-file (pl **serre-files**) /sɛʀfil/ NM *(Mil)* file closer, serrefile; *(Naut)* tail-end Charlie

serre-joint (pl **serre-joints**) /sɛʀʒwɛ̃/ NM clamp, cramp

serre-livres /sɛʀlivʀ/ NM INV bookend

serrement /sɛʀmɑ̃/ NM 1 ◆ ~ **de main** handshake ◆ ~ **de cœur** pang of anguish ◆ ~ **de gorge** tightening in the throat 2 *(Min)* dam

serrer /seʀe/ ▸ conjug 1 ◂ VT 1 *(= maintenir, presser)* to grip, to hold tight ◆ ~ **qch dans sa main** to clutch sth ◆ ~ **une pipe/un os entre ses dents** to clench *ou* have a pipe/a bone between one's teeth ◆ ~ **qn dans ses bras/contre son cœur** to clasp sb in one's arms/to one's chest ◆ ~ **la main à** *ou* **de qn** *(= la donner)* to shake sb's hand, to shake hands with sb; *(= la presser)* to squeeze *ou* press sb's hand ◆ **se ~ la main** to shake hands ◆ ~ **qn à la gorge** to grab sb by the throat; → **kiki**

2 *(= contracter)* ~ **le poing/les mâchoires** to clench one's fist/one's jaws ◆ ~ **les lèvres** to set one's lips ◆ **avoir le cœur serré par l'émotion** to feel a pang of emotion ◆ **avoir la gorge serrée par l'émotion** to be choked by emotion ◆ **cela serre le cœur** *ou* **c'est à vous ~ le cœur de les voir si malheureux** it makes your heart bleed to see them so unhappy ◆ ~ **les dents** *(lit)* to clench one's teeth; *(fig)* to grit one's teeth ◆ ~ **les fesses** *(= se retenir)* to hold on; *(* = avoir peur)* to be scared stiff *ou* out of one's wits *

3 *(= comprimer)* to be too tight for; *(= mouler)* to fit tightly ◆ **mon pantalon me serre** my trousers are too tight (for me) ◆ **cette jupe me serre (à) la taille** this skirt is too tight round the waist ◆ **ces chaussures me serrent (le pied)** these shoes are too tight

4 *(= bloquer) [+ écrou, vis]* to tighten; *[+ pansement]* to wind tightly; *[+ joint]* to clamp; *[+ robinet]* to turn off tight; *[+ ceinture, lacet, nœud]* to tighten, to pull tight; *(= tendre) [+ câble]* to tauten, to make taut, to tighten; *(Naut) [+ voile]* to make fast, to belay *(SPÉC)* ◆ ~ **les prix** to keep prices down ◆ ~ **le frein à main** to put on the handbrake ◆ ~ **la vis à qn** * to crack down on sb *

5 *(= se tenir près de) (par derrière)* to keep close behind; *(latéralement) [+ automobile, concurrent]* to squeeze *(contre* up against); ◆ ~ **qn de près** to follow close behind sb ◆ ~ **une femme de près** * *(fig)* to come on strong * to a woman ◆ ~ **de près l'ennemi** to be snapping at the enemy's heels ◆ ~ **qn dans un coin** to wedge sb in a corner ◆ ~ **un cycliste contre le trottoir** to squeeze a cyclist against the pavement ◆ ~ **le trottoir** to hug the kerb ◆ ~ **sa droite** *(en voiture)* to keep to the right ◆ **ne serre pas cette voiture de trop près** don't get too close to *ou* behind that car ◆ ~ **une question de plus près** to study a question more closely ◆ ~ **le texte** to follow the text closely, to keep close to the text ◆ ~ **la côte** *(en mer)* to sail close to the shore, to hug the shore ◆ ~ **le vent** *(en mer)* to hug the wind

6 *(* = emprisonner)* to nab * ◆ **se faire ~ par la police** to get nabbed * by the police

7 *(= rapprocher) [+ objets alignés, lignes, mots]* to close up, to put close together ◆ ~ **les rangs** *(Mil)* to close ranks ◆ **serrez !** *(Mil)* close ranks! ◆ ~ **son style** to write concisely, to write in a condensed *ou* concise style ◆ **il faudra ~ les invités, la table est petite** we'll have to squeeze the guests up *ou* together as the table is so small

8 *(dial,* † *= ranger)* to put away

VI *(en voiture)* ◆ ~ **à droite/gauche** to move in to the right-/left-hand lane ◆ **"véhicules lents serrez à droite"** "slow-moving vehicles keep to the right"

VPR **se serrer** 1 *(= se rapprocher)* **se ~ contre qn** to huddle (up) against sb; *(tendrement)* to cuddle *ou* snuggle up to sb ◆ **se ~ autour de la table/du feu** to squeeze *ou* crowd round the table/the fire ◆ **se ~ pour faire de la place** to squeeze up to make room ◆ **serrez-vous un peu** squeeze up a bit; → **ceinture, coude**

2 *(= se contracter)* **à cette vue, son cœur se serra** at the sight of this he felt a pang of anguish ◆ **ses poings se serrèrent, presque malgré lui** his fists clenched *ou* he clenched his fists almost in spite of himself

serre-tête (pl **serre-tête(s)**) /sɛʀtɛt/ NM hairband

serrure /seʀyʀ/ NF *[de porte, coffre-fort, valise]* lock; *(Rail)* interlocking switch ◆ ~ **encastrée** mortise lock ◆ ~ **de sûreté** safety lock ◆ ~ **à**

pompe spring lock ◆ ~ **à combinaison** combination lock ◆ ~ **trois points** three-point security lock; → **trou**

serrurerie /seʀyʀʀi/ NF (= *métier*) locksmithing, locksmith's trade; (= *ferronnerie, objets*) ironwork ◆ ~ **d'art** ornamental ironwork, wrought-iron work ◆ **grosse** ~ heavy ironwork

serrurier /seʀyʀje/ NM (= *fabriquant de clés, serrures*) locksmith; (= *ferronnier*) ironsmith

sertir /sɛʀtiʀ/ ▸ conjug 2 ◂ VT 1 (= *monter*) [+ *pierre précieuse*] to set ◆ **bague sertie de diamants** ring set with diamonds 2 (*Tech*) [+ *pièces de tôle*] to crimp

sertissage /sɛʀtisaʒ/ NM 1 [*de pierre précieuse*] setting 2 (*Tech*) [*de pièces de tôle*] crimping

sertisseur, -euse /sɛʀtisœʀ, øz/ NM,F 1 [*de pierre précieuse*] setter 2 (*Tech*) [*de pièces de tôle*] crimper

sertissure /sɛʀtisyʀ/ NF [*de pierre précieuse*] (= *procédé*) setting; (= *objet*) bezel

sérum /seʀɔm/ NM 1 (*Physiol*) ~ **(sanguin)** (blood) serum ◆ ~ **artificiel** *ou* **physiologique** normal *ou* physiological salt solution 2 (*Méd*) serum ◆ ~ **antidiphtérique/antitétanique/antivenimeux** anti-diphtheric/antitetanus/snakebite serum ◆ ~ **de vérité** truth drug

servage /sɛʀvaʒ/ NM (*Hist*) serfdom; (*fig*) bondage, thraldom

serval (pl **-s**) /sɛʀval/ NM serval

servant, e /sɛʀvɑ̃, ɑ̃t/ ADJ ◆ **chevalier** *ou* **cavalier** ~ escort NM (*Rel*) server; (*Mil*) [*de pièce d'artillerie*] server ◆ ~ **d'autel** altar boy NF **servante** (= *domestique*) servant, maidservant

serveur /sɛʀvœʀ/ NM 1 [*de restaurant*] waiter; [*de bar*] barman 2 (= *ouvrier*) [*de machine*] feeder 3 (*Tennis*) server 4 (*Cartes*) dealer 5 (*Ordin*) server ◆ **centre** ~ service centre, retrieval centre ◆ ~ **Internet** Internet server ◆ ~ **de fichiers** file server ◆ ~ **vocal** answering service

serveuse /sɛʀvøz/ NF [*de restaurant*] waitress; [*de bar*] barmaid

serviabilité /sɛʀvjabilite/ NF helpfulness

serviable /sɛʀvjabl/ ADJ helpful

service /sɛʀvis/

1 NOM MASCULIN 2 COMPOSÉS

1 - NOM MASCULIN

1 [= travail] duty; [*de domestique*] (domestic) service ◆ ~ **de jour/nuit** day/night duty ◆ **on ne fume pas pendant le** ~ smoking is not allowed while on duty ◆ **un peu de vin ? – non merci, jamais pendant le** ~ a little wine? – no, thank you, not while I'm on duty ◆ **heures de** ~ hours of service *ou* duty ◆ **il est très ~(-)~** * he's a stickler for the regulations ◆ **avoir 25 ans de** ~ (*Admin, Mil*) to have completed 25 years' service ◆ **10 ans de ~ chez le même employeur** 10 years with the same employer ◆ **après 10 ans de bons et loyaux ~s** after 10 years' loyal service ◆ **qui est de ~ cette nuit ?** who's on duty tonight?, who's on night duty? ◆ **être en** ~ **commandé** to be acting under orders, to be on an official assignment ◆ **prendre/quitter son** ~ to come on/off duty ◆ **reprendre du** ~ [*personne*] to go back to work; [*objet*] to have a new lease of life ◆ **être en ~ chez qn** [*domestique*] to be in service with sb; → **escalier, note, règlement**

◆ **au service de** ◆ **être au ~ de** [+ *maître, Dieu*] to be in the service of; [+ *cause*] to serve ◆ **nos conseillers sont à votre** ~ our advisers are at your service ◆ **se mettre au ~ de** [+ *maître*] to enter the service of, to go into service with; [+ *cause*] to begin to serve; [+ *Dieu, État*] to place o.s. in the service of ◆ **prendre qn à son** ~ to take sb into one's service

2 [= prestation] service ◆ **s'assurer les ~s de qn** to enlist sb's services ◆ **offrir** *ou* **proposer ses ~s à qn** to offer sb one's services ◆ **nous serons obligés de nous passer de vos ~s** we will have to let you go ◆ ~ **de base d'un réseau câblé** (*Télec*) basic range of channels available to cable television subscribers

3 [Écon: au pl] **les biens et les ~s** goods and services ◆ **la part des ~s dans l'économie** (= *secteur*) the role of service industries in the economy; → **emploi, société**

4 [Mil] **le ~ (militaire** *ou* **national)** military *ou* national service ◆ ~ **civil** non-military national service ◆ **bon pour le** ~ fit for military service ◆ **faire son** ~ to do one's military *ou* national service ◆ ~ **armé** combatant service; → **état**

5 [Admin] (= *administration*) service; (= *département*) department ◆ **les ~s d'un ministère** the departments of a ministry ◆ **les ~s de santé/postaux** health (care)/postal services ◆ **les ~s de police** the police department (*US*) ◆ **les ~s financiers de la Ville de Paris** the treasury department of the City of Paris ◆ **les ~s sociaux** the social services ◆ **le ~ social de la ville** the local social services ◆ ~ **hospitalier** hospital service ◆ ~ **de réanimation** intensive care unit ◆ ~ **du contentieux/des achats/de la communication** legal/buying/PR department ◆ ~ **consommateurs** customer service department ◆ **les ~s généraux** (*dans une entreprise*) the maintenance department ◆ ~ **informatique** computer department ◆ ~ **de surveillance/contrôle** surveillance/monitoring service; → **chef¹**

6 [Rel = office, messe] service ◆ ~ **funèbre** funeral service

7 [= faveur, aide] service ◆ **rendre ~ à qn** (= *aider qn*) to do sb a service *ou* a good turn; (= *s'avérer utile*) to come in useful *ou* handy for sb, to be of use to sb ◆ **il aime rendre** ~ he likes to do good turns *ou* be helpful ◆ **rendre un petit ~ à qn** (*fig*) to do sb a favour, to do sb a small service ◆ **tous les ~s qu'il m'a rendus** all the favours *ou* services he has done me ◆ **décoré pour ~s rendus pendant la guerre** decorated for services rendered during the war ◆ **rendre un mauvais ~ à qn** to do sb a disservice ◆ **qu'y a-t-il pour votre ~ ?** (*frm*) how can I be of service to you? ◆ **merci ! – ~ !**(*Helv*) thank you! – you're welcome!

8 [à table, au restaurant] service; (= *pourboire*) service charge ◆ **Marc fera le** ~ Marc will serve ◆ **passe-moi les amuse-gueules, je vais faire le** ~ hand me the appetizers, I'll pass them round ◆ **la nourriture est bonne mais le ~ est trop lent** the food is good but the service is too slow ◆ **ils ont oublié de compter le** ~ they have forgotten to include the service (charge) on the bill ◆ ~ **compris/non compris** service included/not included, inclusive/exclusive of service ◆ **premier/deuxième** ~ (= *série de repas*) first/second sitting

9 [= assortiment] [*de couverts, linge de table*] set; [*de verres, vaisselle*] service, set ◆ ~ **de table** (= *linge*) set of table linen; (= *vaisselle*) set of tableware ◆ ~ **à café/thé** coffee/tea set *ou* service ◆ ~ **à liqueurs** set of liqueur glasses ◆ ~ **à poisson** (= *vaisselle*) set of fish plates; (= *couverts*) fish service ◆ ~ **à fondue** fondue set ◆ ~ **à gâteaux** (= *couverts*) set of cake knives and forks; (= *vaisselle*) set of cake plates ◆ ~ **trois pièces** ‡ (= *sexe masculin*) wedding tackle * (*hum*)

10 [Transport] service ◆ **un ~ d'autocars dessert ces localités** there is a coach service to these districts ◆ **assurer le ~ entre** to provide a service between ◆ ~ **d'hiver/d'été** winter/summer service ◆ ~ **partiel** [*d'autobus*] limited service ◆ **le ~ est interrompu sur la ligne 3** service is suspended on line 3

11 [Tennis] service ◆ **être au** ~ to have the service ◆ **prendre le ~ (de qn)** to win the service (from sb) ◆ **il a un excellent** ~ he has an excellent service *ou* serve ◆ ~ **Dupont !** Dupont to serve! ◆ ~ **canon** bullet-like serve *ou* service ◆ ~**-volée** serve and volley

12 [= fonctionnement] [*de machine, installation*] operation, working ◆ **faire le ~ d'une pièce d'artillerie** to operate *ou* work a piece of artillery

◆ **en service** [*installation, usine*] in service ◆ **entrer en** ~ to come into service ◆ **mettre en** ~ to put *ou* bring into service ◆ **la mise en ~ des nouveaux autobus est prévue pour juin** the new buses are due to be put into service in June ◆ **remise en** ~ [*d'aéroport, réacteur, voie ferrée*] reopening

◆ **hors service** [*appareil*] out of order (*attrib*); * [*personne*] shattered *, done in *

2 - COMPOSÉS

service après-vente after-sales service
Service d'assistance médicale d'urgence mobile emergency medical service
service en ligne (*Ordin*) on-line service
service minimum skeleton service
service d'ordre (= *policiers*) police contingent; (= *manifestants*) team of stewards (*responsible for crowd control etc*) ◆ **pour assurer le ~ d'ordre** to maintain (good) order
service de presse [*de ministère, entreprise*] press relations department; (= *distribution*) distribution of review copies; (= *ouvrage*) review copy ◆ **ce livre m'a été envoyé en ~ de presse** I got a review copy of the book
service public public service ◆ **les ~s publics** the (public) utilities ◆ **une télévision de ~ public** a public television company
service régional de police judiciaire regional crime squad
les services secrets the secret service
service de sécurité (*d'un pays*) security service ◆ **le ~ de sécurité de l'aéroport** airport security
les services spéciaux the secret service
Service du travail obligatoire (*Hist*) *forced labour instituted in France by the Nazis during World War II*

SERVICE MILITAIRE

Until 1997, all French men over eighteen years of age were required to do ten months' **service militaire** if passed fit. The call-up could be delayed if the conscript was a full-time student in higher education. Conscientious objectors were required to do two years' public service. The entire system has now been phased out.

serviette /sɛʀvjɛt/ NF 1 (*en tissu*) ~ **(de toilette)** (hand) towel ◆ ~ **(de table)** (table) napkin, serviette (*Brit*); → **mélanger, rond** 2 (= *cartable*) [*d'écolier, homme d'affaires*] briefcase

COMP **serviette de bain** bath towel
serviette(-)éponge terry towel
serviette hygiénique sanitary towel (*Brit*) *ou* napkin (*US*)
serviette en papier paper (table) napkin, paper serviette (*Brit*)
serviette périodique ⇒ **serviette hygiénique**
serviette de plage beach towel

servile /sɛʀvil/ ADJ 1 (= *obséquieux*) [*personne*] servile; [*obéissance*] slavish; [*flatterie*] fawning 2 (= *sans originalité*) [*traduction, imitation*] slavish 3 (*littér* = *de serf*) [*condition, travail*] servile

servilement /sɛʀvilmɑ̃/ ADV [*obéir, imiter, traduire, copier*] slavishly ◆ **flatter qn** ~ to fawn on sb

servilité /sɛʀvilite/ NF 1 (= obséquiosité) servility 2 [de traduction, imitation] slavishness 3 (littér) [de condition, travail] servility

servir /sɛʀviʀ/ ▸ conjug 14 ◂ VT 1 (= être au service de) [+ pays, cause] to serve; (emploi absolu = être soldat) to serve (dans in); ◆ ~ **la messe** (Rel) to serve mass

2 [domestique] [+ patron] to serve, to wait on ◆ **il sert comme chauffeur** he works as a chauffeur ◆ **il servait dans la même famille depuis 20 ans** he had been in service with the same family for 20 years ◆ **elle aime se faire** ~ she likes to be waited on ◆ **on n'est jamais si bien servi que par soi-même** (Prov) if you want something doing, do it yourself

3 (= aider) [+ personne] to be of service to, to aid ◆ ~ **les ambitions/intérêts de qn** to serve ou aid sb's ambitions/interests ◆ **ceci nous sert** this serves our interests ◆ **sa prudence l'a servi auprès des autorités** his caution served him well ou stood him in good stead in his dealings with the authorities ◆ **il a été servi par les circonstances** he was aided by circumstances ◆ **il a été servi par une bonne mémoire** his memory served him well

4 (dans un magasin) [+ client] to serve, to attend to; [+ consommateur] to serve; [+ dîneur] to wait on; (chez soi, à table) to serve ◆ **ce boucher nous sert depuis des années** this butcher has supplied us for years, we've been going to this butcher for years ◆ **le boucher m'a bien servi** (en qualité) the butcher has given me good meat; (en quantité) the butcher has given me a good amount for my money ◆ **on vous sert, Madame ?** are you being served? ◆ **on n'arrive pas à se faire** ~ **ici** it's difficult to get served here ◆ **prenez, n'attendez pas qu'on vous serve** help yourself – don't wait to be served ◆ **"Madame est servie"** "dinner is served" ◆ **pour vous** ~ † at your service ◆ **des garçons en livrée servaient** waiters in livery waited ou served at table ◆ **les paysans voulaient la pluie, ils ont été servis !** the farmers wanted rain - well, they've certainly got what they wanted! ◆ **en fait d'ennuis, elle a été servie** she's had more than her fair share of problems

5 (Mil) [+ pièce d'artillerie] to serve

6 (= donner) [+ rafraîchissement, plat] to serve ◆ ~ **qch à qn** to serve sb with sth, to help sb to sth ◆ ~ **le déjeuner/dîner** to serve (up) lunch/dinner ◆ **"servir frais"** "serve chilled" ◆ ~ **à déjeuner/dîner** to serve lunch/dinner (à qn to sb); ◆ ~ **à boire** to serve drinks ◆ ~ **à boire à qn** to serve a drink to sb ◆ ~ **le café** to serve ou pour the coffee ◆ **on nous a servi le petit déjeuner au lit** we were served (our) breakfast in bed ◆ **il a faim, servez-le bien** he's hungry so give him a good helping ◆ **à table, c'est servi !** come and sit down now, it's ready! ◆ **il nous sert toujours les mêmes plaisanteries** he always trots out the same old jokes ◆ **toutes ces émissions stupides qu'ils nous servent** all these stupid programmes they expect us to watch; → **soupe**

7 (= verser) to pay ◆ ~ **une rente/une pension/des intérêts à qn** to pay sb an income/a pension/interest

8 (Cartes) to deal

9 (Tennis, Ping-pong, Volley) to serve ◆ **à vous de** ~ your service, it's your turn to serve

VT INDIR **servir à** (= être utile à) [+ personne] to be of use ou help to; [+ usage, opération] to be of use in, to be useful for ◆ ~ **à faire qch** to be used for doing sth ◆ **ça m'a servi à réparer ce fauteuil** I used it to mend this armchair ◆ **ça ne sert à rien** [objet] it's no use, it's useless; [démarche] there's no point ◆ **cela ne sert à rien de pleurer/réclamer** it's no use ou there's no point crying/complaining, crying/complaining won't help ◆ **à quoi sert cet objet ?** what's this thing used for? ◆ **à quoi servirait de réclamer ?** what use would it be to complain?, what would be the point of complaining? ◆ **cela ne servirait pas à grand-chose de dire ...** there's little point in saying ..., it wouldn't be much use saying ... ◆ **est-ce que cela pourrait vous** ~ **?** could this be (of) any use to you?, could you make use of this? ◆ **vos conseils lui ont bien servi** your advice has been very useful ou helpful to him ◆ **ces projecteurs servent à guider les avions** these floodlights are used to guide ou for guiding the planes ◆ **cet instrument sert à beaucoup de choses** this instrument has many uses ou is used for many things ◆ **cela a servi à nous faire comprendre les difficultés** this served to help us understand the difficulties ◆ **cet héritage n'a servi qu'à les brouiller** the inheritance only served to drive a wedge between them ◆ **ne jette pas cette boîte, ça peut toujours** ~ don't throw that box away – it may still come in handy ou still be of some use ◆ **ce mot a beaucoup servi dans les années 60** the word was much used in the sixties ◆ **cette valise n'a jamais servi** this suitcase has never been used; → **rien**

VT INDIR **servir de** (= être utilisé comme) [personne] to act as; [ustensile, objet] to serve as ◆ **elle lui a servi d'interprète/de témoin** she acted as his interpreter/as a witness (for him) ◆ **cette pièce sert de chambre d'amis** this room serves as ou is used as a guest room ◆ **cela pourrait te** ~ **de table** you could use that as a table, that would serve ou do as a table for you; → **exemple, leçon**

VPR **se servir** 1 (à table, dans une distribution) to help o.s. ◆ **se** ~ **chez Leblanc** (chez un fournisseur) to buy ou shop at Leblanc's ◆ **se** ~ **en viande chez Leblanc** to buy one's meat at Leblanc's, to go to Leblanc's for one's meat ◆ **servez-vous donc de viande** do help yourself to some meat ◆ **tu t'es mal servi** you haven't given yourself a very big portion ◆ **ne te gêne pas, sers-toi !** (iro) go ahead, help yourself! (iro)

2 ◆ **se** ~ **de** (= utiliser) [+ outil, mot, main-d'œuvre] to use; [+ personne] to use, to make use of ◆ **il sait bien se** ~ **de cet outil** he knows how to use this tool ◆ **t'es-tu servi de ce vêtement ?** have you ever worn this? ◆ **il se sert de sa voiture pour aller au bureau** he uses his car to go to the office ◆ **se** ~ **de ses relations** to make use of ou use one's acquaintances ◆ **il s'est servi de moi** he used me

3 (sens passif) **ce vin se sert très frais** this wine should be served chilled

serviteur /sɛʀvitœʀ/ NM 1 (= domestique) servant ◆ **en ce qui concerne votre** ~ **...** (hum) as far as yours truly is concerned ... (hum) 2 (pour cheminée) fire irons

servitude /sɛʀvityd/ NF 1 (= esclavage) servitude, bondage 2 (gén pl = contrainte) constraint 3 (Jur) easement ◆ ~ **de passage** right of way

servocommande /sɛʀvokɔmɑ̃d/ NF servo-mechanism

servodirection /sɛʀvodiʀɛksjɔ̃/ NF servo(-assisted) steering

servofrein /sɛʀvofʀɛ̃/ NM servo(-assisted) brake

servomécanisme /sɛʀvomekanism/ NM servo system

servomoteur /sɛʀvomɔtœʀ/ NM servo-motor

servovalve /sɛʀvovalv/ NF servo valve

ses /se/ ADJ POSS → **son¹**

sésame /sezam/ NM sesame ◆ **graines de** ~ sesame seeds ◆ **pain au** ~ sesame seed loaf ◆ **"Sésame ouvre-toi"** "open Sesame" ◆ **ce diplôme est un** ~ **pour l'emploi** this degree opens doors in the job market ◆ **le système informatisé de la bibliothèque est le véritable** ~ **de ses trésors** the library's computer system opens up all its treasures

sessile /sesil/ ADJ (Bot) sessile; → **chêne**

session /sesjɔ̃/ NF 1 (Jur, Parl) session, sitting ◆ ~ **extraordinaire** (Parl) special session 2 (Scol, Univ) session ◆ **la** ~ **de printemps/d'automne** the spring/autumn session ◆ ~ **d'examen** exam session ◆ **la** ~ **de juin** the June exams ◆ **la** ~ **de septembre** the (September) retakes ou resits (Brit) ◆ ~ **de rattrapage** special session of the baccalauréat for students who are unable to take the exam the first time around 3 (= cours, stage) course ◆ ~ **de formation** training course

sesterce /sɛstɛʀs/ NM (Hist) (= monnaie) sesterce, sestertius; (= mille unités) sestertium

set /sɛt/ NM 1 (Tennis) set; → **balle¹** 2 ◆ ~ **(de table)** (= ensemble) set of tablemats ou place mats; (= napperon) tablemat, place mat

setter /setɛʀ/ NM setter ◆ ~ **irlandais** Irish setter

seuil /sœj/ NM 1 [de porte] (= marche) doorstep; (= entrée) doorway, threshold †; (fig) threshold ◆ **se tenir sur le** ~ **de sa maison** to stand in the doorway of one's house ◆ **il m'a reçu sur le** ~ he kept me on the doorstep ou at the door ◆ **avoir la campagne au** ~ **de sa maison** to have the country on ou at one's doorstep ◆ **le** ~ **de** (fig = début) [+ période] the threshold of ◆ **au** ~ **de la mort** at death's door ◆ **le** ~ **du désert** the edge of the desert

2 (Géog, Tech) sill

3 (= limite) threshold; (Psych) threshold, limen (SPÉC) ◆ ~ **auditif** auditory threshold ◆ ~ **de la douleur** pain threshold ◆ ~ **de rentabilité** break-even point ◆ ~ **de tolérance** threshold of tolerance ◆ ~ **de pauvreté** poverty line ou level ◆ **vivre en dessous du** ~ **de pauvreté** to live below ou beneath the poverty line ◆ ~ **de résistance** (Bourse) resistance level ◆ **le dollar est passé sous le** ~ **d'un euro** the dollar fell below the 1 euro level ◆ ~ **d'imposition** tax threshold ◆ **relever les** ~**s sociaux** (Jur) to raise the minimum number of employees required to establish works councils, delegates' committees etc

seul, e /sœl/ ADJ 1 (après n ou attrib) [personne] (= sans compagnie, non accompagné) alone (attrib), on one's own (attrib), by oneself (attrib); (= isolé) lonely; [objet, mot] alone (attrib), on its own (attrib), by itself (attrib) ◆ **être/rester** ~ to be/remain alone ou on one's own ou by oneself ◆ **laissez-moi** ~ **quelques instants** leave me alone ou on my own ou by myself for a moment ◆ ~ **avec qn/ses pensées/son chagrin** alone with sb/one's thoughts/one's grief ◆ **ils se retrouvèrent enfin** ~**s** they were alone (together) ou on their own ou by themselves at last ◆ **un homme** ~**/une femme** ~**e peut très bien se débrouiller** a man on his own/a woman on her own ou a single man/woman can manage perfectly well ◆ **au bal, il y avait beaucoup d'hommes** ~**s** at the dance there were many men on their own ◆ **se sentir (très)** ~ to feel (very) lonely ou lonesome ◆ ~ **au monde** alone in the world ◆ **les amoureux sont** ~**s au monde** lovers behave as if they are the only ones in the world ◆ **être** ~ **contre tous** to be alone against the world ◆ **il s'est battu,** ~ **contre tous** he fought single-handedly ◆ **mot employé** ~ word used alone ou on its own ou by itself ◆ **la lampe** ~**e ne suffit pas** the lamp alone ou on its own is not enough, the lamp is not enough on its own ou by itself ◆ **il est tout** ~ he's all alone ◆ **il était tout** ~ **dans un coin** he was all by himself ou all alone in a corner ◆ **il l'a fait tout** ~ he did it all by himself ou (all) on his own ◆ **cette tasse ne s'est pas cassée toute** ~**e !** this cup didn't break all by itself!; → **cavalier**

2 (avant n = unique) **un** ~ **homme/livre** (et non plusieurs) one man/book, a single man/book;

(*à l'exception de tout autre*) only one man/book ◆ **le ~ homme/livre** the one man/book, the only man/book, the sole man/book ◆ **les ~es personnes/conditions** the only people/conditions ◆ **un ~ livre suffit** one book *ou* a single book will do ◆ **un ~ homme peut vous aider : Paul** only one man can help you and that's Paul ◆ **pour cette ~e raison** for this reason alone *ou* only, for this one reason ◆ **son ~ souci est de ...** his only *ou* sole *ou* one concern is to ... ◆ **un ~ moment d'inattention** one *ou* a single moment's lapse of concentration ◆ **il n'y a qu'un ~ Dieu** there is only one God, there is one God only *ou* alone ◆ **une ~e fois** only once, once only ◆ **la ~e chose, c'est que ça ferme à 6 heures** the only thing is (that) it shuts at 6

3 (*en apposition*) only ◆ **~ le résultat compte** the result alone counts, only the result counts ◆ **~s les parents sont admis** only parents are admitted ◆ **~e Gabrielle peut le faire** only Gabrielle *ou* Gabrielle alone can do it ◆ **~e l'imprudence peut être la cause de cet accident** only carelessness can have caused this accident ◆ **lui ~ est venu en voiture** he alone *ou* only he came by car ◆ **à eux ~s, ils ont bu dix bouteilles** they drank ten bottles between them ◆ **je l'ai fait à moi (tout)** ~ I did it (all) on my own *ou* (all) by myself, I did it single-handed

4 (*locutions*) **~ et unique** one and only ◆ **c'est la ~e et même personne** they're one and the same (person) ◆ **~ de son espèce** the only one of its kind ◆ **d'un ~ coup** (= *subitement*) suddenly; (= *en une seule fois*) in one go ◆ **vous êtes ~ juge** you alone can judge ◆ **à ~e fin de ...** with the sole purpose of ... ◆ **dans la ~e intention de ...** with the one *ou* sole intention of ... ◆ **du ~ fait que ...** by the very fact that ... ◆ **à la ~e pensée de ...** at the mere thought of ... ◆ **la ~e pensée d'y retourner la remplissait de frayeur** the mere *ou* very thought of going back there filled her with fear ◆ **parler à qn ~ à ~** to speak to sb in private *ou* privately *ou* alone ◆ **se retrouver ~ à ~ avec qn** to find o.s. alone with sb ◆ **comme un ~ homme** (*fig*) as one man ◆ **d'une ~e voix** with one voice

ADV 1 (= *sans compagnie*) **parler/rire ~** to talk/laugh to oneself ◆ **vivre/travailler ~** to live/work alone *ou* by oneself *ou* on one's own

2 (= *sans aide*) by oneself, on one's own, unaided ◆ **faire qch (tout) ~** to do sth (all) by oneself *ou* (all) on one's own, to do sth unaided *ou* single-handed ◆ **ça va tout ~** it's all going smoothly

NM,F ◆ **un ~ peut le faire** (*et non plusieurs*) one man can do it, a single man can do it; (*à l'exception de tout autre*) only one man can do it ◆ **un ~ contre tous** one (man) against all ◆ **le ~ que j'aime** the only one I love ◆ **vous n'êtes pas la ~e à vous plaindre** you aren't the only one to complain, you aren't alone in complaining ◆ **une ~e de ses peintures n'a pas été détruite dans l'incendie** only one of his paintings was not destroyed in the fire ◆ **il n'en reste pas un ~** there isn't a single *ou* solitary one left

seulement /sœlmɑ̃/ ADV 1 (*quantité = pas davantage*) only ◆ **cinq personnes ~ sont venues** only five people came ◆ **nous serons ~ quatre** there will only be four of us ◆ **je pars pour deux jours ~** I'm only going away for two days

2 (= *exclusivement*) only, alone, solely ◆ **on ne vit pas ~ de pain** you can't live on bread alone ◆ **ce n'est pas ~ sa maladie qui le déprime** it's not only *ou* just his illness that depresses him ◆ **250 €, c'est ~ le prix de la chambre** €250 is the price for just the room *ou* is the price for the room only ◆ **on leur permet de lire ~ le soir** they are only allowed to read at night ◆ **il fait cela ~ pour nous ennuyer** he only does that to annoy us

3 (*temps = pas avant*) only ◆ **il vient ~ d'entrer** he's only just (now) come in ◆ **ce fut ~ vers 10 heures qu'il arriva** he only got there at about 10 o'clock ◆ **il est parti ~ ce matin** he left only this morning, he only left this morning

4 (*en tête de proposition = mais, toutefois*) only, but ◆ **je connais un bon chirurgien, ~ il est cher** I know a good surgeon, only *ou* but he is expensive ◆ **j'avais tout organisé, ~ voilà, ils ne sont même pas venus** I'd organized everything, the only thing was they didn't turn up

5 (*locutions*) **non ~ il ne travaille pas mais (encore) il empêche les autres de travailler** not only does he not work but he stops the others working too ◆ **non ~ le directeur mais aussi** *ou* **encore les employés** not only *ou* just the manager but the employees too *ou* as well ◆ **non ~ il a plu, mais (encore) il a fait froid** it didn't only rain but it was cold too, it not only rained but it was also cold ◆ **on ne nous a pas ~ donné un verre d'eau** (*même pas*) we were not even given a glass of water, we were not given so much as a glass of water ◆ **il n'a pas ~ de quoi se payer un costume** he hasn't even got enough to buy himself a suit ◆ **il est parti sans ~ nous prévenir** he left without so much as *ou* without even telling us ◆ **si ~** if only; → **si**

seulet, -ette †* /sœlɛ, ɛt/ ADJ (*hum*) lonesome, lonely, all alone ◆ **se sentir bien ~** to feel all alone *ou* very lonesome

sève /sɛv/ NF [*d'arbre*] sap; (*fig*) sap, life, vigour (*Brit*), vigor (*US*) ◆ **~ ascendante/brute/descendante élaborée** rising/crude/falling elaborated sap ◆ **les arbres sont en pleine ~** the sap has risen in the trees ◆ **la jeunesse est débordante de ~** young people are brimming with strength and vigour

sévère /sevɛʀ/ ADJ 1 (= *dur, strict*) [*maître, juge, climat, mesures, règlement, sanctions*] severe, harsh; [*parent, éducation, ton*] strict, severe; [*jugement*] severe, harsh; [*regard, visage*] severe, stern; [*verdict*] harsh ◆ **elle suit un régime ~** she's on a strict diet ◆ **après une sélection ~** after a rigorous selection process ◆ **une morale ~** a strict *ou* stern moral code ◆ **ne soyez pas trop ~ avec elle** don't be too harsh on her *ou* strict with her ◆ **la critique a été très ~ avec son film** the critics were very hard on his film ◆ **son rapport est très ~ sur l'état de nos prisons** his report is highly critical of the state of our prisons

2 (= *austère*) [*style, architecture*] severe; [*traits du visage, tenue*] severe, stern ◆ **une beauté ~** a severe beauty

3 (= *important*) [*pertes, échec*] severe, heavy; [*concurrence*] tough; [*défaite*] heavy ◆ **ils ont dû faire des coupes ~s dans le budget militaire** they had to make heavy *ou* severe cuts in the military budget

ADV (* : *intensif*) ◆ **il s'est fait engueuler, (mais alors) ~ !** he got a real bollocking‡ ◆ **elle s'est fait amocher, ~ !** she got badly beaten up

sévèrement /sevɛʀmɑ̃/ ADV 1 (= *durement*) [*punir*] severely; [*juger, critiquer*] harshly, severely; [*contrôler, réglementer*] strictly ◆ **les visites sont ~ contrôlées** visits are under strict control 2 (= *gravement*) [*éprouver, affecter*] severely ◆ **cette ville est ~ affectée par la crise** the town has been severely hit by the crisis ◆ **un malade ~ atteint** a severely affected patient

sévérité /seveʀite/ NF 1 (= *dureté, rigueur*) [*de maître, juge, jugement, climat, mesures, règlement*] severity, harshness; [*de parent, éducation, ton*] strictness, severity; [*de regard*] severity, sternness; [*de verdict*] harshness ◆ **elle a élevé ses enfants avec une grande ~** she was very strict with her children ◆ **il se juge avec trop de ~** he's too hard on himself ◆ **tu manques de ~ avec lui** you're not strict enough with him, you're too soft on him 2 (= *austérité*) [*de style, architecture*] severity; [*de tenue, mœurs, traits du visage*] severity, sternness 3 (= *gravité*) [*de pertes, échec, récession*] severity

sévices /sevis/ NMPL physical cruelty (*NonC*), ill treatment (*NonC*) ◆ **~ corporels/sexuels** physical/sexual abuse (*NonC*) ◆ **faire subir des ~ à la population** to treat the population brutally *ou* cruelly ◆ **exercer des ~ sur un enfant** (*gén*) to ill-treat a child; (*sexuels*) to abuse a child ◆ **être victime de ~** to be ill-treated *ou* abused

Séville /sevil/ N Seville

sévir /seviʀ/ ► conjug 2 ◄ VI 1 (= *punir*) to act ruthlessly ◆ **~ contre** [+ *personne, abus, pratique*] to deal ruthlessly with ◆ **si vous continuez, je vais devoir ~** if you carry on, I shall have to deal severely with you *ou* use harsh measures 2 (= *exercer ses ravages*) [*virus*] to be rife; [*doctrine*] to hold sway ◆ **ce fléau sévit encore en Asie** the illness is still rife in Asia ◆ **la pauvreté sévissait** poverty was rampant *ou* rife ◆ **il sévit à la télé/dans notre service depuis 20 ans** (*hum*) he's been plaguing our screens/our department for 20 years now (*hum*) ◆ **est-ce qu'il sévit encore à l'université ?** (*hum*) do they still let him loose on the students? (*hum*)

sevrage /səvʀaʒ/ NM 1 [*de nourrisson, jeune animal*] weaning 2 (*Hort*) [*de marcotte*] separation 3 (*Méd*) **une méthode de ~ des toxicomanes** a method of weaning addicts off drugs ◆ **les cures de ~ des toxicomanes** drug withdrawal programmes ◆ **pour faciliter le ~ tabagique** to make it easier for people to give up *ou* to stop smoking ◆ **il lui faudra un ~ pharmacologique** he'll need some kind of prop *ou* substitute product to help him give up

sevrer /səvʀe/ ► conjug 5 ◄ VT 1 [+ *nourrisson, jeune animal*] to wean ◆ **~ un toxicomane** to wean an addict off drugs ◆ **pour ~ les fumeurs** to help smokers give up 2 (*Hort*) [+ *marcotte*] to separate 3 (*littér = priver*) **~ qn de qch** to deprive sb of sth ◆ **nous avons été sevrés de théâtre** we have been deprived of theatre outings

sèvres /sɛvʀ/ NM (= *porcelaine*) Sèvres porcelain; (= *objet*) piece of Sèvres porcelain

sexagénaire /sɛksaʒenɛʀ/ ADJ sixty-year-old (*épith*), sexagenarian NMF sixty-year-old, sexagenarian

sexagésimal, e (mpl **-aux**) /sɛgzaʒezimal, o/ ADJ sexagesimal

sexagésime /sɛgzaʒezim/ NF (*Rel*) Sexagesima (Sunday)

sex-appeal /sɛksapil/ NM sex appeal

sexe /sɛks/ NM 1 (= *catégorie*) sex ◆ **enfant de** *ou* **du ~ masculin/féminin** male/female child ◆ **nous recherchons une personne de ~ féminin/masculin** we are looking for a woman/man ◆ **le ~ faible/fort** the weaker/stronger sex ◆ **le (beau) ~** (*littér*) the fair sex ◆ **discuter du ~ des anges*** to discuss futilities 2 (= *sexualité*) sex ◆ **ce journal ne parle que de ~** this paper is full of nothing but sex 3 (= *organes génitaux*) genitals, sex organs; (= *verge*) penis

sexisme /sɛksism/ NM sexism ◆ **être accusé de ~** to be accused of sexism *ou* of being sexist

sexiste /sɛksist/ ADJ, NMF sexist

sexologie /sɛksɔlɔʒi/ NF sexology

sexologue /sɛksɔlɔg/ NMF sexologist, sex specialist

sexothérapeute /sɛksoteʀapøt/ NMF sex therapist

sex-shop (pl **sex-shops**) /sɛksʃɔp/ NM sex-shop

sex-symbol (pl **sex-symbols**) /sɛkssɛ̃bɔl/ NM sex symbol

sextant /sɛkstɑ̃/ NM (= *instrument*) sextant; (*Math = arc*) sextant arc

sextuor /sɛkstɥɔʀ/ NM (*Mus*) sextet(te)

sextuple /sɛkstypl/ ADJ *[nombre, quantité, rangée]* sextuple ◆ **une quantité ~ de l'autre** a quantity six times (as great as) the other ◆ **en ~ exemplaire** in six copies NM *(gén, Math)* ◆ **je l'ai payé le ~/le ~ de l'autre** I paid six times as much for it/six times as much as the other for it ◆ **augmenter au ~** to increase sixfold *ou* six times

sextupler /sɛkstyple/ ▸ conjug 1 ◂ VTI to increase six times *ou* sixfold

sextuplés, -ées /sɛkstyple/ NM,F PL sextuplets

sexualiser /sɛksɥalize/ ▸ conjug 1 ◂ VT to sexualize

sexualité /sɛksɥalite/ NF sexuality ◆ **troubles de la ~** sexual problems ◆ **avoir une ~ épanouie** to have a full sex life

sexué, e /sɛksɥe/ ADJ *[mammifères, plantes]* sexed, sexual; *[reproduction]* sexual

sexuel, -elle /sɛksɥɛl/ ADJ *[caractère, instinct, plaisir]* sexual; *[éducation, hormone, organe, partenaire]* sexual, sex *(épith)*; *[abus, comportement, sévices]* sexual ◆ **avoir une activité sexuelle importante** to have a very active sex life; → **rapport**

sexuellement /sɛksɥɛlmɑ̃/ ADV sexually; → **maladie**

sexy * /sɛksi/ ADJ INV sexy *

seyant, e /sɛjɑ̃, ɑt/ ADJ *[vêtement]* becoming ◆ **elle portait une jupe très ~e** she was wearing a skirt that really suited her

Seychelles /sɛʃɛl/ NFPL ◆ **les ~** the Seychelles

seychellois, e /sɛʃɛlwa, az/ ADJ of *ou* from the Seychelles NM,F **Seychellois(e)** inhabitant *ou* native of the Seychelles

SF * /ɛsɛf/ NF (abrév de **science-fiction**) sci-fi * ◆ **film/roman de ~** sci-fi * film/novel

SG /ɛsʒe/ NM (abrév de **secrétaire général**) → **secrétaire**

SGBD /ɛsʒebede/ NM (abrév de **système de gestion de bases de données**) → **système**

SGML /ɛsʒeɛmɛl/ NM (abrév de **Standard Generalized Mark-Up Language**) *(Ordin)* SGML

shabbat /ʃabat/ NM ⇒ **sabbat**

shah /ʃa/ NM shah

shaker /ʃɛkœʀ/ NM cocktail shaker

shakespearien, -ienne /ʃɛkspiʀjɛ̃, jɛn/ ADJ Shakespearian

shako /ʃako/ NM shako

shampoing, shampooing /ʃɑ̃pwɛ̃/ NM (= *lavage, produit)* shampoo ◆ **faire un ~ à qn** to give sb a shampoo, to shampoo *ou* wash sb's hair ◆ **se faire un ~** to shampoo one's hair ◆ **à appliquer après chaque ~** apply every time after shampooing ◆ **~ colorant** shampoo-in hair colourant *(Brit) ou* colorant *(US)* ◆ **~ crème** cream shampoo ◆ **~ à moquette** carpet shampoo

shampouiner, shampooiner /ʃɑ̃pwine/ ▸ conjug 1 ◂ VT to shampoo ◆ **se ~ la tête** to shampoo one's hair

shampouineur, -euse, shampooineur, -euse /ʃɑ̃pwinœʀ, øz/ NM,F trainee hairdresser *(who washes hair)*, junior NF **shampouineuse, shampooineuse** (= *machine)* carpet shampooer

shant(o)ung /ʃɑtuŋ/ NM shantung (silk)

Shape, SHAPE /ʃap/ (abrév de **Supreme Headquarters Allied Powers Europe**) NM SHAPE

shareware /ʃɛʀwɛʀ/ NM shareware

shekel /ʃekɛl/ NM shekel

shérif /ʃeʀif/ NM *[de western]* sheriff, marshal

sherpa /ʃɛʀpa/ NM (= *guide)* Sherpa; *(Pol)* aide *(helping with preparations for summit talks)*

sherry /ʃeʀi/ NM sherry

shetland /ʃɛtlɑ̃d/ NM (= *laine)* Shetland wool; (= *tricot)* Shetland pullover NFPL **Shetland** ◆ **les (îles) Shetland** the Shetlands, the Shetland Islands ◆ **les (îles) Shetland-du-Sud** the South Shetlands

shetlandais, e /ʃɛtlɑ̃dɛ, ɛz/ ADJ Shetland *(épith)* NM,F **Shetlandais(e)** Shetlander

shilling /ʃiliŋ/ NM shilling

shimmy /ʃimi/ NM (= *danse, flottement de roues)* shimmy

shinto /ʃinto/, **shintoïsme** /ʃintɔism/ NM Shinto, Shintoism

shintoïste /ʃintɔist/ ADJ, NMF Shintoist

shit /ʃit/ NM *(arg Drogue)* dope *, hash *

Shiva /ʃiva/ NM ⇒ **Siva**

Shoah /ʃɔa/ NF Shoah

shog(o)un /ʃɔgun/ NM shogun

shoot /ʃut/ NM 1 *(Ftbl)* shot 2 *(arg Drogue)* fix * ◆ **se faire un ~ d'héroïne** to shoot up * with heroin

shooter /ʃute/ ▸ conjug 1 ◂ VI *(Ftbl)* to shoot, to make a shot VT ◆ **~ un penalty** to take a penalty (kick *ou* shot) VPR **se shooter** *(arg Drogue)* to shoot up * ◆ **se ~ à l'héroïne** to mainline * heroin, to shoot up * with heroin ◆ **il s'est shooté pendant dix ans** he mainlined * drugs for ten years ◆ **je me shoote au café** * I need to have my daily fix * of coffee ◆ **on l'a complètement shooté aux médicaments** * he's been drugged *ou* doped up to the eyeballs *

shopping /ʃɔpiŋ/ NM shopping ◆ **faire du ~** to go shopping ◆ **faire son ~** to do one's shopping

short /ʃɔʀt/ NM ◆ **~(s)** pair of shorts, shorts ◆ **être en ~(s)** to be in shorts *ou* wearing shorts; → **tailler** ADJ (* = *juste)* ◆ **3 bouteilles de vin pour 9, c'est un peu ~** 3 bottles of wine for 9 people, that's not really enough ◆ **5 minutes pour aller à la gare, c'est un peu ~** 5 minutes to get to the station, that's cutting it a bit fine ◆ **je suis un peu ~ en pain** I'm a bit low on bread

show /ʃo/ NM show ◆ **faire son ~** to put on a show

showbiz * /ʃobiz/ NM INV (abrév de **show-business**) show biz *

show-business /ʃobiznɛs/ NM INV show business

show-room (pl **show-rooms**) /ʃoʀum/ NM showroom

shrapnel(l) /ʃʀapnɛl/ NM shrapnel

shunt /ʃœt/ NM *(Élec)* shunt

shunter /ʃœte/ ▸ conjug 1 ◂ VT *(Élec)* to shunt; * *[+ personne, service]* to bypass

SI 1 (abrév de **syndicat d'initiative**) → **syndicat** 2 (abrév de **Système international (d'unités)**) SI

si[1] /si/ GRAMMAIRE ACTIVE 30

CONJ 1 *(éventualité, condition)* if ◆ **s'il fait beau demain (et ~ j'en ai** *ou* **et que j'en aie le temps), je sortirai** if it's fine tomorrow (and (if) I have time), I'll go out

2 *(hypothèse)* if ◆ **~ et seulement ~** *(Math)* if and only if ◆ **~ j'avais de l'argent, j'achèterais une voiture** if I had any money *ou* had I any money, I would buy a car ◆ **même s'il s'excusait, je ne lui pardonnerais pas** even if he were to apologize I wouldn't forgive him ◆ **~ nous n'avions pas été prévenus, nous serions arrivés** *ou* **nous arrivions trop tard** if we hadn't been warned, we would have arrived too late ◆ **il a déclaré que ~ on ne l'augmentait pas, il partirait** *ou* **il partait** he said that if he didn't get a rise he would leave *ou* he was leaving ◆ **viendras-tu ? ~ oui, préviens-moi à l'avance** are you coming? if so *ou* if you are, tell me in advance; → **comme**

3 *(répétition = toutes les fois que)* if, when ◆ **s'il faisait beau, il allait se promener** if *ou* when it was nice he used to go for a walk ◆ **~ je sors sans parapluie, il pleut** if *ou* whenever I go out without an umbrella it always rains

4 *(opposition)* while, whilst *(surtout Brit)* ◆ **~ lui est aimable, sa femme (par contre) est arrogante** while *ou* whereas he is very pleasant his wife (on the other hand) is arrogant

5 *(exposant un fait)* **s'il ne joue plus, c'est qu'il s'est cassé la jambe** if he doesn't play any more it's because he has broken his leg, the reason he no longer plays is that he has broken his leg ◆ **c'est un miracle ~ la voiture n'a pas pris feu** it's a miracle (that) the car didn't catch fire ◆ **excusez-nous** *ou* **pardonnez-nous ~ nous n'avons pas pu venir** please excuse *ou* forgive us for not being able to come

6 *(dans une interrogation indirecte)* if, whether ◆ **il ignore/se demande ~ elle viendra (ou non)** he doesn't know/is wondering whether *ou* if she'll come (or not) ◆ **il faut s'assurer ~ la télé marche** we must make sure that the TV is working ◆ **vous imaginez s'ils étaient fiers !** you can imagine how proud they were! ◆ **~ je veux y aller ! quelle question !** do I want to go! what a question!

7 *(en corrélation avec proposition implicite)* if ◆ **~ j'avais su !** if I had only known!, had I (only) known! ◆ **~ je le tenais !** if I could (only) lay my hands on him! ◆ **et s'il refusait ?** and what if he refused?, and what if he should refuse?, and supposing he refused? ◆ **~ tu lui téléphonais ?** how *ou* what about phoning him?, supposing *ou* suppose you phoned him? ◆ **~ nous allions nous promener ?** what *ou* how about going for a walk?, what would you say to a walk?

8 *(locutions)* **~ j'ai bien compris/entendu** if I understood correctly/heard properly ◆ **~ seulement il venait/était venu** if only he was coming/had come ◆ **brave homme s'il en fut** a fine man if ever there was one ◆ **~ c'est ça** *, **je m'en vais** if that's how it is, I'm off *

◆ **si + dire** ◆ **~ j'ose dire** *(frm, hum)* if I may say so ◆ **~ je puis dire** *(frm)* if I may put it like that ◆ **~ l'on peut dire** *(frm)* in a way, as it were, so to speak, in a manner of speaking

◆ **si ce n'est** ◆ **qui peut le savoir, ~ ce n'est lui ?** if he doesn't know, who will? ◆ **~ ce n'est elle, qui aurait osé ?** who but she would have dared? ◆ **~ ce n'était la crainte de les décourager** if it were not *ou* were it not for the fear of putting them off ◆ **il n'avait rien emporté, ~ ce n'est quelques biscuits et une pomme** he had taken nothing with him apart from *ou* other than a few biscuits and an apple ◆ **une des plus belles, ~ ce n'est la plus belle** one of the most beautiful, if not the most beautiful ◆ **elle se porte bien, ~ ce n'est qu'elle est très fatiguée** she's quite well apart from the fact that she is very tired *ou* apart from feeling very tired

◆ **si tant est que** so long as, provided *ou* providing that ◆ **invite-les tous, ~ tant est que nous ayons assez de verres** invite them all, so long as we have enough glasses *ou* if we have enough glasses that is ◆ **ils sont sous-payés, ~ tant est qu'on les paie** they are underpaid, if they are paid at all

NM INV if ◆ **avec des ~ (et des mais), on mettrait Paris en bouteille** if ifs and ands were pots and pans there'd be no need for tinkers

si[2] /si/ ADV 1 *(affirmatif)* **vous ne venez pas ? – ~/mais ~/que ~** aren't you coming? – yes I am/of course I am/indeed I am *ou* I certainly am ◆ **vous n'avez rien mangé ? – ~, une pomme** haven't you had anything to eat? – yes (I have), an apple ◆ **~, ~, il faut venir** oh but you must come! ◆ **il n'a pas voulu, moi** ~ he didn't want to, but I did ◆ **il n'a pas écrit ? – il semble bien** *ou* **il paraît que** ~ hasn't he written? – yes, it seems that he has ◆ **je pensais qu'il ne viendrait pas, mais quand je lui en ai parlé il m'a répondu que** ~ I thought he wouldn't come but when I mentioned it to him he told me he would ◆ **je croyais qu'elle ne voulait pas venir, mais il m'a dit que** ~ I thought she didn't want to come but he said she did ◆ ~ **fait** † indeed yes

2 *(intensif = tellement) (modifiant attrib, adv)* so ◆ **un ami** ~ **gentil** *(modifiant épith)* such a kind friend, so kind a friend *(frm)* ◆ **des amis** ~ **gentils, de** ~ **gentils amis** such kind friends ◆ **il parle** ~ **bas qu'on ne l'entend pas** he speaks so low *ou* in such a low voice that you can't hear him ◆ **j'ai** ~ **faim** I'm so hungry ◆ **elle n'est pas** ~ **stupide qu'elle ne puisse comprendre ceci** she's not so stupid that she can't understand this ◆ **il est stupide, non ? –** ~ **peu !** *(iro)* he's stupid, isn't he? – and how! * *ou* too right! *

◆ **si bien que** so that, with the result that

3 *(concessif = aussi)* however ◆ ~ **bête soit-il** *ou* **qu'il soit, il comprendra** however stupid he is he will understand ◆ ~ **rapidement qu'il progresse** however rapidly he progresses ◆ ~ **adroitement qu'il ait parlé, il n'a convaincu personne** for all that he spoke very cleverly *ou* however cleverly he may have spoken he didn't convince anyone ◆ ~ **beau qu'il fasse, il ne peut encore sortir** however good the weather is, he can't go out yet ◆ ~ **peu que ce soit** however little it may be, little as *ou* though it may be

4 *(égalité = aussi)* as, so ◆ **elle n'est pas** ~ **timide que vous croyez** she's not so *ou* as shy as you think ◆ **il ne travaille pas** ~ **lentement qu'il en a l'air** he doesn't work as slowly as he seems to ◆ **ce n'est pas** ~ **facile** *ou* **simple** it's not as simple as that

si³ /si/ NM INV *(Mus)* B; *(en chantant la gamme)* ti, te

Siam /sjam/ NM Siam

siamois, e /sjamwa, waz/ ADJ *(† Géog)* Siamese; *[chat]* Siamese ◆ **frères** ~, **sœurs ~es** Siamese twins NM,F 1 † **Siamois(e)** *(Géog)* Siamese 2 *(pl = jumeaux)* Siamese twins NM *(= chat)* Siamese

Sibérie /siberi/ NF Siberia

sibérien, -ienne /siberjɛ̃, jɛn/ ADJ *(Géog, fig)* Siberian NM,F **Sibérien(ne)** Siberian

sibylle /sibil/ NF sibyl

sibyllin, e /sibilɛ̃, in/ ADJ *(Myth)* sibylline; *[phrase, personne]* cryptic, sibylline *(frm)* ◆ **tenir des propos ~s** to talk in riddles ◆ **de façon** *ou* **de manière ~e** cryptically

sic /sik/ ADV sic

SICAV, sicav /sikav/ NF INV (abrév de **société d'investissement à capital variable**) *(= fonds)* unit trust *(Brit)*, open-end investment trust *(US)*, mutual fund *(US)*; *(= part)* share in a unit trust *(Brit) ou* an open-end investment trust *(US) ou* a mutual fund *(US)* ◆ **sicav monétaire** money market fund ◆ **sicav obligataire** bond fund ◆ **sicav de trésorerie** cash management unit trust *ou* mutual fund

siccatif, -ive /sikatif, iv/ ADJ, NM siccative

Sicile /sisil/ NF Sicily

sicilien, -ienne /sisiljɛ̃, jɛn/ ADJ Sicilian NM 1 *(= dialecte)* Sicilian 2 ◆ **Sicilien** Sicilian NF **sicilienne** 1 ◆ **Sicilienne** Sicilian 2 *(= danse)* Siciliano, Sicilienne

SIDA, sida /sida/ NM (abrév de **syndrome d'immunodéficience acquise**) AIDS, Aids ◆ **avoir le/être atteint du sida** to have/be suffering from AIDS ◆ **le virus du sida** the AIDS virus ◆ **la lutte contre le sida** the battle against AIDS

side-car (pl **side-cars**) /sidkar/ NM *(= habitacle)* sidecar; *(= véhicule entier)* motorcycle and sidecar

sidéen, -enne /sideɛ̃, ɛn/ ADJ *[personne]* (infected) with AIDS *ou* Aids NM,F AIDS *ou* Aids sufferer, person with AIDS, PWA

sidéral, e (mpl **-aux**) /sideral, o/ ADJ sidereal ◆ **l'espace** ~ outer space

sidérant, e* /siderɑ̃, ɑt/ ADJ staggering *

sidération /siderasjɔ̃/ NF *(Méd)* sideration

sidérer /sidere/ ► conjug 6 ◄ VT 1 *(* = abasourdir)* to stagger * ◆ **cette nouvelle m'a sidéré** I was staggered * *ou* dumbfounded by the news ◆ **je suis sidéré par son intelligence/son insolence** I'm dumbfounded *ou* amazed by his intelligence/his insolence ◆ **la foule regardait, sidérée** the crowd watched, dumbfounded 2 *(Méd)* to siderate

sidérurgie /sideryrʒi/ NF *(= fabrication)* (iron and) steel metallurgy; *(= industrie)* (iron and) steel industry

sidérurgique /sideryrʒik/ ADJ *[procédé]* (iron and) steel-manufacturing *(épith)*; *[industrie]* iron and steel *(épith)*

sidérurgiste /sideryrʒist/ NMF *(= industriel)* steel manufacturer; *(= ouvrier)* steel worker

sidi † /sidi/ NM *(injurieux) North African immigrant (resident in France)*

Sidon /sidɔ̃/ N Sidon

siècle /sjɛkl/ NM 1 *(gén)* century ◆ **au 3e** ~ **avant Jésus-Christ/après Jésus-Christ** *ou* **de notre ère** in the 3rd century B.C./A.D. ◆ **au** ~ **dernier** in the last century ◆ **le Grand Siècle** the 17th century *(in France)*, the grand siècle ◆ **le hold-up/match du** ~ * the hold-up/match of the century ◆ **cet arbre a/ces ruines ont des ~s** this tree is/these ruins are centuries old ◆ **après des ~s de colonisation, le pays ...** after centuries of colonial rule, the country ... ◆ **il est né avec le** ~, **il a l'âge du** ~ he's as old as the century; → **consommation, fin², mal²**

2 *(= époque)* age ◆ **être de son ~/d'un autre** ~ to belong to one's age/to another age ◆ **de** ~ **en** ~ from age to age, through the ages ◆ **le** ~ **de Périclès/d'Auguste** the age of Pericles/of Augustus ◆ **le Siècle des lumières** (the Age of) the Enlightenment ◆ **il y a un** ~ *ou* **des ~s que nous ne nous sommes vus** * it has been *ou* it is years *ou* ages since we last saw each other

3 *(Rel = monde)* **le** ~ the world ◆ **les plaisirs du** ~ worldly pleasures, the pleasures of the world

siège¹ /sjɛʒ/ NM 1 *(= meuble)* seat ◆ ~ **de jardin/de bureau** garden/office chair ◆ **le** ~ **des toilettes** the toilet seat ◆ **donner/offrir un** ~ **à qn** to give/offer sb a seat ◆ **prenez un** ~ take a seat ◆ **Dupont, le spécialiste du** ~ **de bureau** Dupont, the specialist in office seating ◆ ~ **avant/arrière** front/back seat

2 *(frm, Méd = postérieur)* seat ◆ **l'enfant se présente par le** ~ the baby's in the breech position; → **bain**

3 *(Pol = fonction)* seat ◆ ~ **vacant** vacant seat ◆ **retrouver son** ~ **de député** to win back one's parliamentary seat

4 *(Jur) [de magistrat]* bench; → **magistrature**

5 *(= résidence principale) [de firme]* head office; *[de parti, organisation internationale]* headquarters; *[d'assemblée, tribunal]* seat ◆ ~ **social** registered office ◆ ~ **épiscopal/pontifical** episcopal/pontifical see ◆ **cette organisation, dont le** ~ **est à Genève** this Geneva-based organization, this organization which is based in Geneva *ou* which has its headquarters in Geneva

6 *(= centre) [de maladie, passions, rébellion]* seat; *(Physiol) [de faculté, sensation]* centre *(Brit)*, center *(US)*

COMP **siège-auto** *(pour bébé)* baby (car) seat
siège baquet bucket seat
siège pour bébé(s) baby (car) seat
siège éjectable ejector seat ◆ **il est sur un** ~ **éjectable** *(fig)* he could be fired any time

siège² /sjɛʒ/ NM *[de place forte]* siege ◆ **mettre le** ~ **devant une ville** to besiege a town ◆ **faire le** ~ **de** *(lit, fig)* to lay siege to; → **état, lever¹**

siéger /sjeʒe/ ► conjug 3 et 6 ◄ VI 1 *(= être en session) [assemblée, tribunal]* to be in session 2 *(= être membre de)* ~ **à** *[+ conseil, comité]* to sit *ou* be on 3 *(= être situé à)* ~ **à** *[tribunal, organisme]* to have its headquarters in, to be headquartered in *(US)* 4 *(= résider)* **voilà où siège le mal** that's where the trouble lies

sien, sienne /sjɛ̃, sjɛn/ PRON POSS ◆ **le** ~, **la sienne, les** ~**s, les siennes** *[d'homme]* his (own); *[de femme]* hers, her own; *[de chose, animal]* its own; *[de nation]* its own, hers, her own; *(indéf)* one's own ◆ **ce sac/cette robe est le ~/la sienne** this bag/this dress is hers, this is her bag/dress ◆ **il est parti avec une veste qui n'est pas la sienne** he left with a jacket which isn't his *ou* with somebody else's jacket ◆ **mes enfants sont sortis avec deux des ~s/les deux ~s** my children have gone out with two of hers/her two ◆ **cet oiseau préfère les nids des autres au** ~ this bird prefers other birds' nests to its own ◆ **je préfère mes ciseaux, les ~s ne coupent pas** I prefer my scissors because hers don't cut ◆ **la sienne de voiture est plus rapide** * *(emphatique)* his car is faster, his is a faster car ◆ **de tous les pays, on préfère toujours le** ~ of all countries one always prefers one's own

NM 1 ◆ **les choses s'arrangent depuis qu'elle y a mis du** ~ things are beginning to sort themselves out since she began to pull her weight ◆ **chacun doit être prêt à y mettre du** ~ everyone must be prepared to pull his weight *ou* to make some effort

2 ◆ **les ~s** *(= famille)* one's family, one's folks *; *(= partisans)* one's (own) people ◆ **Dieu reconnaît les ~s** God knows his own *ou* his people

NFPL **siennes** ◆ **il/elle a encore fait des siennes** * he/she has (gone and) done it again * ◆ **le mal de mer commençait à faire des siennes parmi les passagers** seasickness was beginning to claim some victims among the passengers

ADJ POSS *(† ou littér)* ◆ **un** ~ **cousin** a cousin of his *(ou* hers) ◆ **il fait siennes toutes les opinions de son père** he adopts all his father's opinions

Sienne /sjɛn/ N Siena; → **terre**

sierra /sjera/ NF sierra ◆ **la** ~ **Madre/Nevada** the Sierra Madre/Nevada

Sierra Leone /sjeraleɔn(e)/ NF Sierra Leone

sierra-léonien, -ienne /sjeraleɔnjɛ̃, jɛn/ ADJ Sierra Leonean NM,F **Sierra-Léonien(ne)** Sierra Leonean

sieste /sjɛst/ NF *(gén)* nap, snooze *; *(en Espagne etc)* siesta ◆ **faire la** ~ *(gén)* to have *ou* take a nap; *(en Espagne etc)* to have a siesta ◆ **je vais faire une petite** ~ I'm going to take a little nap ◆ **c'est l'heure de la** ~ **!** it's time for a snooze! * *ou* an afternoon nap! ◆ **on a fait une** ~ **crapuleuse** * we spent the afternoon in bed having sex

sieur /sjœr/ NM ◆ **le** ~ **Leblanc** *(††, Jur)* Mr Leblanc; *(péj, hum)* Master Leblanc

sifflant, e /siflɑ̃, ɑt/ ADJ *[sonorité]* whistling; *[toux]* wheezing; *[prononciation]* hissing, whistling NF **sifflante** ◆ **(consonne) ~e** sibilant

sifflement /sifləmɑ̃/ NM 1 *[de personne, oiseau, train, bouilloire, vent]* whistling (NonC); *[de serpent, vapeur, gaz, machine à vapeur]* hissing (NonC); *[de voix, respiration]* wheezing (NonC); *[de projectile]* whistling (NonC), hissing (NonC) ◆ **un** ~ a whistle, a hiss ◆ **un** ~ **d'admiration**

ou **admiratif** a whistle of admiration ◆ **un ~ mélodieux** a tuneful whistle ◆ **des ~s se firent entendre** there was the sound of whistling ◆ **j'entendis le ~ aigu/les ~s de la locomotive** I heard the shrill whistle/the whistling of the locomotive ◆ **des ~s** whistling noises, hissing noises ◆ **~ d'oreilles** ringing in the ears

2 *(gén pl = huées)* booing *(NonC)*, hissing *(NonC)* ◆ **il quitta la scène sous les ~s du public** he was booed off the stage

siffler /sifle/ ▸ conjug 1 ◂ VI *[personne]* to whistle; *(avec un sifflet)* to blow one's *ou* a whistle; *[oiseau, train, bouilloire, vent]* to whistle; *[serpent, vapeur, gaz, machine à vapeur]* to hiss; *[voix, respiration]* to wheeze; *[projectile]* to whistle, to hiss ◆ **~ comme un merle** to whistle like a bird ◆ **la balle/l'obus siffla à ses oreilles** the bullet/the shell whistled past his ears ◆ **il siffle en respirant** he wheezes ◆ **j'ai les oreilles qui sifflent** my ears are ringing

VT 1 *(= appeler) [+ chien, personne]* to whistle for; *[+ fille]* to whistle at; *[+ automobiliste ou joueur en faute]* to blow one's whistle at; *(= signaler) [+ départ, faute]* to blow one's whistle for ◆ **~ la fin du match/la mi-temps** *(Ftbl)* to blow the final whistle/the half-time whistle, to blow for time/for half time ◆ **elle s'est fait ~ dans la rue** someone wolf-whistled at her in the street

2 *(= huer) [+ orateur, acteur, pièce]* to hiss, to boo ◆ **se faire ~** to get booed

3 *(= moduler) [+ air, chanson]* to whistle

4 (* = *avaler)* to guzzle *, to knock back *

sifflet /siflɛ/ NM 1 *(= instrument, son)* whistle ◆ **~ à roulette** whistle ◆ **~ à vapeur** steam whistle ◆ **~ d'alarme** alarm whistle ◆ **coup de ~** whistle; → **couper** 2 *(= huées)* **~s** whistles of disapproval, hissing, booing, catcalls ◆ **il est sorti sous les ~s du public** he was booed off the stage

siffleur, -euse /siflœʀ, øz/ ADJ *[merle]* whistling; *[serpent]* hissing ◆ **(canard) ~** widgeon NM,F *(= qui sifflote)* whistler; *(= qui hue)* hisser, booer

siffleux * /siflø/ NM *(Can)* groundhog, woodchuck, whistler *(US, Can)*

sifflotement /siflɔtmɑ̃/ NM whistling *(NonC)*

siffloter /siflɔte/ ▸ conjug 1 ◂ VI to whistle (a tune) ◆ **~ entre ses dents** to whistle under one's breath VT *[+ air]* to whistle

sigillé, e /siʒile/ ADJ sigillated

sigisbée † /siʒizbe/ NM *(hum = amant)* beau †

sigle /sigl/ NM *(prononcé lettre par lettre)* (set of) initials, abbreviation; *(= acronyme)* acronym

siglé, e /sigle/ ADJ *[objet]* bearing the initials of a designer ◆ **sac ~** designer bag ◆ **boutons ~s ARA** buttons with ARA engraved on them

sigma /sigma/ NM sigma

signal (pl **-aux**) /siɲal, o/ NM 1 *(= signe convenu) (Psych = stimulus)* signal; *(= indice)* sign ◆ **~ de détresse** distress signal ◆ **c'était le ~ de la fin du repas** it was the signal that the meal was over ◆ **cette émeute fut le ~ d'une véritable révolution** the riot signalled the outbreak of a virtual revolution ◆ **à mon ~ tous se levèrent** when I gave the signal everyone got up ◆ **donner un ~ à** *(lit)* to give a signal to; *(fig)* to send a signal to ◆ **le gouvernement voulait donner un ~ fort/clair aux employeurs** the government wanted to send a strong/clear signal to employers ◆ **ça été le ~ du déclenchement de la crise** it was the trigger for the crisis ◆ **donner le ~ de** *(lit)* to give the signal for; *(= déclencher)* to be the signal for, to signal ◆ **donner le ~ du départ** to give the starting signal

2 *(Naut, Rail = écriteau, avertisseur)* signal; *(Aut = écriteau)* (road) sign ◆ **signaux (lumineux)** *(= feux)* traffic signals *ou* lights ◆ **~ automatique** *(Rail)* automatic signal ◆ **~ sonore** *ou* **acoustique** sound *ou* acoustic signal ◆ **~ optique/lumineux** visual/light signal

3 *(Ling, Ordin, Téléc)* signal ◆ **~ horaire** time signal ◆ **"signal d'appel"** *(Téléc : option)* "call waiting"

COMP **signal d'alarme** alarm ◆ **ça a déclenché le ~ d'alarme** it set the alarm off ◆ **tirer le ~ d'alarme** *(lit)* to pull the alarm, to pull the communication cord *(Brit)*; *(fig)* to sound the alarm ◆ **les climatologues avaient tiré un premier ~ d'alarme dans les années 80** climatologists had first sounded the alarm in the 1980s

signal d'alerte warning signal

signalé, e /siɲale/ (ptp de **signaler**) ADJ *(littér = remarquable) [récompense, service]* signal *(littér)* *(épith)*

signalement /siɲalmɑ̃/ NM *[de personne, véhicule]* description, particulars ◆ **donner le ~ de qn** to describe sb

signaler /siɲale/ GRAMMAIRE ACTIVE 47.4 ▸ conjug 1 ◂

VT 1 *(= être l'indice de)* to indicate, to be a sign of ◆ **des empreintes qui signalent la présence de qn** footprints indicating sb's presence

2 *[écriteau, sonnerie]* to signal; *[personne] (= faire un signe)* to signal; *(en mettant un écriteau ou une indication)* to indicate ◆ **on signale l'arrivée d'un train au moyen d'une sonnerie** the arrival of a train is signalled by a bell ringing, a bell warns of *ou* signals the arrival of a train ◆ **sur ma carte, on signale l'existence d'une source près du village** my map indicates that there's a spring near the village ◆ **signalez que vous allez tourner en tendant le bras** indicate *ou* signal that you are turning by putting out your arm

3 *[+ détail, erreur]* to indicate, to point out; *[+ fait nouveau, perte, vol]* to report ◆ **rien à ~** nothing to report ◆ **son père a signalé sa disparition à la police** his father had reported him missing to the police ◆ **~ qn à l'attention de qn** to bring sb to sb's attention ◆ **on signale l'arrivée du bateau** it has just been announced that the boat is coming in ◆ **on a signalé leur présence à Paris** they are reported to be in Paris ◆ **nous vous signalons en outre que ...** we would further point out to you that ... ◆ **nous vous signalons qu'il ...** for your information, he ... ◆ **signalons la parution du livre en format poche** we should mention that the book is now available in pocket format ◆ **il a klaxonné pour ~ sa présence** he hooted to show that he was there ◆ **un rapport avait déjà signalé la présence d'hormones dans la viande** a report had already pointed to the presence of hormones in the meat ◆ **personne ne nous avait signalé l'existence de ce manuscrit** nobody had told us that this manuscript existed ◆ **je te signale que je t'attends depuis une heure !** I'd like you to know that I've been waiting for you for an hour! ◆ **il est déjà 11 heures, je te signale !** * it's already 11 o'clock, I'll have you know!

VPR **se signaler** 1 *(= s'illustrer)* to distinguish o.s., to stand out ◆ **il s'est signalé à plusieurs reprises par son courage** he showed exceptional bravery on several occasions ◆ **enfin, un film qui se signale par la beauté des dialogues** at last a film that is distinguished by the beauty of its scripts

2 *(= attirer l'attention)* to draw attention to o.s. ◆ **se ~ à l'attention de qn** to attract sb's attention, to bring o.s. to sb's attention

signalétique /siɲaletik/ ADJ *[détail]* identifying, descriptive ◆ **fiche ~** identification sheet NF means of signalling

signalisation /siɲalizasjɔ̃/ NF 1 *(= balisage) [de route, réseau]* erection of (road)signs (and signals) (de on); *[de piste]* laying out of runway markings and lights (de on); *[de voie]* putting signals (de on); ◆ **"absence de signalisation"** "no road markings" ◆ **~ automatique** *(sur voie ferrée)* automatic signalling ◆ **erreur de ~** *(sur route)* signposting error; *(sur voie ferrée)* signalling error ◆ **moyens de ~** means of signalling; → **feu¹**, **panneau** 2 *(= panneaux sur route)* signs; *(= signaux sur voie ferrée)* signals ◆ **~ routière** roadsigns and markings ◆ **~ horizontale** *(sur route)* road markings ◆ **~ verticale** roadsigns

signaliser /siɲalize/ ▸ conjug 1 ◂ VT *[+ route, réseau]* to put up (road)signs on; *[+ piste]* to put runway markings and lights on; *[+ voie de chemin de fer]* to put signals on ◆ **bien signalisé** *[+ route]* well signposted; *[+ piste]* clearly marked; *[+ voie de chemin de fer]* with clear signals ◆ **la frontière n'est pas toujours signalisée** the border isn't always marked

signataire /siɲatɛʀ/ ADJ signatory ◆ **pays ~s** signatory countries NMF *[de traité, paix]* signatory ◆ **les ~s** those signing, the signatories

signature /siɲatyʀ/ NF 1 *(= action)* signing; *(= marque, nom)* signature ◆ **avant la ~ du contrat** before the contract is signed ◆ **les fondés de pouvoir ont la ~** the senior executives may sign for the company ◆ **ouvrage publié sous la ~ d'un journaliste** work published under the name of a journalist ◆ **donner un document à la ~** to give a document to be signed ◆ **le traité sera soumis à la ~ de tous les États** the treaty will be presented to all the states for signature ◆ **les négociations ont abouti à la ~ d'un accord** the talks ended with the signing of an agreement ◆ **~ électronique** *(Internet)* electronic signature

2 *(= signe distinctif)* mark ◆ **l'attentat porte leur ~** the attack bears their mark *ou* has their name written all over it *

3 *(Typo = cahier)* signature

signe /siɲ/ NM 1 *(= geste) (de la main)* sign, gesture; *(de l'expression)* sign ◆ **s'exprimer par ~s** to use signs to communicate ◆ **langage** *ou* **langue des ~s** sign language ◆ **faire un ~ à qn** to make a sign to sb, to sign to sb ◆ **un ~ de tête affirmatif/négatif** a nod/a shake of the head ◆ **ils se faisaient des ~s** they were making signs to each other ◆ **un ~ d'adieu/de refus** a sign of farewell/of refusal ◆ **elle m'a fait un ~ d'adieu** she waved goodbye to me

2 *(= indice)* sign ◆ **~ précurseur** *ou* **avant-coureur** portent, omen, forewarning ◆ **elle t'a invité ? c'est un ~ !** she invited you? that's a good sign! ◆ **il recommence à manger, c'est bon ~** he's beginning to eat again, that's a good sign ◆ **c'est (un) ~ de pluie** it's a sign of rain ◆ **c'est ~ qu'il va pleuvoir/qu'il est de retour** it shows *ou* it's a sign that it's going to rain/that he's back ◆ **c'est mauvais ~** it's a bad sign ◆ **y a-t-il des ~s de vie sur Mars ?** are there signs of life on Mars? ◆ **il n'a plus jamais donné ~ de vie** we've never heard from him since ◆ **c'est un ~ des temps** it's a sign of the times ◆ **c'est un ~ révélateur** it's very revealing ◆ **c'est un ~ qui ne trompe pas** the signs are unmistakable ◆ **montrer** *ou* **donner des ~s de faiblesse** *ou* **de fatigue** *[personne]* to show signs of tiredness; *[appareil, montre]* to be on its last legs; *[coalition]* to be showing signs of strain; *[monnaie]* to be weakening ◆ **~ clinique** *(Méd)* clinical sign

3 *(= trait)* mark ◆ **"signes particuliers : néant"** "distinguishing marks: none" ◆ **~ distinctif** distinguishing feature ◆ **leur argot est un ~ de reconnaissance** using slang is a way for them to recognize each other

4 *(= symbole) (gén, Ling, Math, Mus)* sign; *(Typo) [de correcteurs]* mark ◆ **le ~ moins/plus/égal** the minus/plus/equal(s) sign ◆ **~ (typogra-**

phique) character ◆ **~s d'expression** *(Mus)* expression marks ◆ ~ **accidentel** *(Mus)* accidental

5 *(Astrol)* ~ **du zodiaque** sign of the zodiac ◆ **sous quel ~ es-tu né ?** what sign were you born under?, what's your sign?

◆ **sous le signe de** ◆ **une rencontre placée sous le ~ de l'amitié franco-britannique** a meeting where the dominant theme was Franco-British friendship ◆ **cette semaine a été placée sous le ~ de l'optimisme** this week was marked by optimism ◆ **l'action gouvernementale sera placée sous le double ~ de la lutte contre le chômage et contre la pauvreté** government action will focus on fighting both unemployment and poverty

6 *(locutions)* **faire ~ à qn** *(lit)* to make a sign to sb; *(= contacter)* to get in touch with sb, to contact sb ◆ **faire ~ à qn d'entrer** to motion sb in, to make a sign for sb to come in ◆ **de la tête, il m'a fait ~ de ne pas bouger** he shook his head to tell me not to move ◆ **il a fait ~ à la voiture de franchir les grilles** he waved the car through the gates ◆ **faire ~ du doigt à qn** to beckon (to) sb ◆ **faire ~ que oui** to nod (in agreement) ◆ **faire ~ que non** *(de la tête)* to shake one's head (in disagreement *ou* disapproval); *(de la main)* to make a gesture of refusal (*ou* disagreement *ou* disapproval)

◆ **en signe de** ◆ **en ~ de protestation** as a sign *ou* mark of protest ◆ **en ~ de reconnaissance** as a token of gratitude ◆ **en ~ de respect** as a sign *ou* mark *ou* token of respect ◆ **en ~ de solidarité/de deuil** as a sign of solidarity/of mourning

COMP **signe cabalistique** cabalistic sign
signe de la croix sign of the cross ◆ **faire le ~ de la croix** *ou* **un ~ de croix** to make the sign of the cross, to cross o.s.
signes extérieurs de richesse outward signs of wealth
signes héraldiques coat of arms
signe de ponctuation punctuation mark
signe de ralliement rallying symbol

signer /siɲe/ ► conjug 1 ◄ VT 1 *[+ document, traité, œuvre d'art]* to sign ◆ ~ **la paix** to sign a peace treaty ◆ **signez au bas de la page/en marge** sign at the bottom of the page/in the margin ◆ ~ **un chèque en blanc** *(lit, fig)* to sign a blank cheque ◆ ~ **son nom** to sign one's name ◆ **elle signe "Malou"** she signs herself "Malou" ◆ **il a signé avec le club italien** *(Sport)* he's signed for the Italian club ◆ ~ **d'une croix/de son vrai nom** to sign with a cross/with one's real name ◆ ~ **de son sang** to sign in blood ◆ **tableau non signé** unsigned painting ◆ **œuvre signée de la main de l'artiste** work signed by the artist ◆ **cela a signé la fin de leur collaboration** that signalled the end of their collaboration; → **arrêt**

2 *(= être l'auteur de)* to make ◆ **elle vient de ~ son deuxième film** she's just made her second film ◆ **il signe le troisième but de la partie** *(Sport)* he's scored the third goal of the match ◆ **cravate/carrosserie signée Paul** tie/coachwork by Paul ◆ **il signe le meilleur temps aux essais** he got the best times in the trials ◆ **c'est signé Louis !*** it has Louis written all over it!* ◆ **c'est signé !*** it's obvious who did it!

3 *(= engager) [+ sportif, artiste, auteur]* to sign

4 *(Tech) (au poinçon)* to hallmark

VPR **se signer** *(Rel)* to cross o.s.

signet /siɲɛ/ NM *(livre, Internet)* bookmark

signifiant, e /siɲifjɑ̃, jɑ̃t/ ADJ *(littér)* significative, meaningful NM *(Ling)* signifier, significant

significatif, -ive /siɲifikatif, iv/ ADJ 1 *(= révélateur) [exemple, mot]* significant, revealing; *[geste, sourire]* meaningful ◆ **ces oublis sont ~s de son état d'esprit** his forgetfulness reflects his state of mind 2 *(= visible) [amélioration, baisse, changement, progrès]* significant, considerable ◆ **de manière significative** significantly 3 *(= expressif) [symbole]* meaningful, significant

signification /siɲifikasjɔ̃/ NF 1 *[de fait, chiffres]* significance (NonC) ◆ **une omission lourde de ~** a highly significant omission ◆ **cette mesure n'a pas grande ~** this measure is not very significant 2 *[de mot, symbole]* meaning ◆ **la ~** *(Ling)* signification ◆ **quelle est la ~ de ce dessin ?** what does this drawing mean? 3 *(Jur) [de décision judiciaire]* notification ◆ ~ **d'actes** service of documents

significativement /siɲifikativmɑ̃/ ADV *[améliorer, augmenter, réduire]* significantly, to a significant extent; *[meilleur, supérieur]* significantly ◆ **les commentaires ont été assez ~ unanimes** significantly, most people made the same kind of comments

signifié /siɲifje/ NM *(Ling)* signified, signifié

signifier /siɲifje/ ► conjug 7 ◄ VT 1 *(= avoir pour sens)* to mean, to signify ◆ **que signifie ce mot/son silence ?** what is the meaning of this word/his silence?, what does this word/his silence mean *ou* signify? ◆ **les symboles signifient** *(Ling)* symbols convey meaning ◆ **que signifie cette cérémonie ?** what is the significance of this ceremony?, what does this ceremony signify? ◆ **ses colères ne signifient rien** his tempers don't mean anything ◆ **bonté ne signifie pas forcément faiblesse** kindness does not necessarily mean *ou* signify *ou* imply weakness *ou* is not necessarily synonymous with weakness ◆ **cela signifie que l'automne est proche** it means *ou* shows that autumn is near, it marks *ou* signifies the approach of autumn ◆ **qu'est-ce que cela signifie ?** what's the meaning of this?; *(après remarque hostile)* what's that supposed to mean?; *(à un enfant qui fait une scène)* what's all this in aid of?

2 *(frm = faire connaître)* to make known ◆ ~ **ses intentions/sa volonté à qn** to make one's intentions/one's wishes known to sb, to inform sb of one's intentions/one's wishes ◆ ~ **son congé à qn** *(= renvoyer qn)* to give sb notice of dismissal, to give sb their notice ◆ **son regard me signifiait tout son mépris** his look conveyed to me his utter scorn ◆ **signifiez-lui qu'il doit se rendre à cette convocation** inform him that he is to answer this summons

3 *(Jur) [+ exploit, décision judiciaire]* to serve notice of (*à* on) to notify (*à* to)

signofile /siɲofil/ NM *(Helv = clignotant)* indicator

sikh /sik/ ADJ Sikh NMF **Sikh** Sikh

silence /silɑ̃s/ NM 1 *(= absence de bruits, de conversation)* silence ◆ **garder le ~** to keep silent, to say nothing ◆ **faire ~** to be silent ◆ **réclamer le ~** to ask for silence ◆ **il n'arrive pas à faire le ~ dans sa classe** he can't get his pupils to be quiet ◆ **sortez vos livres et en ~ !** get out your books and no talking! ◆ **(faites) ~ !** silence!; *(en classe)* silence!, no talking! ◆ ~ **! on tourne** *(Ciné)* quiet everybody, action! ◆ **il prononça son discours dans un ~ absolu** there was dead silence while he made his speech ◆ **un ~ de mort** a deathly hush *ou* silence; → **minute, parole**

◆ **en silence** in silence; *[pleurer]* quietly ◆ **souffrir en ~** to suffer in silence ◆ **vous pouvez jouer, mais en ~** you can play, but don't make any noise ◆ **il l'a aimée en ~ pendant plus de 20 ans** he loved her secretly for more than 20 years

2 *(= pause) (dans la conversation, un récit)* pause; *(Mus)* rest ◆ **récit entrecoupé de longs ~s** account broken by lengthy pauses ◆ **il y eut un ~ gêné** there was an embarrassed silence ◆ **à son entrée il y eut un ~** there was a hush when he came in

3 *(= impossibilité ou refus de s'exprimer)* silence ◆ **les journaux gardèrent le ~ sur cette grève** the newspapers kept silent *ou* were silent on this strike ◆ **promets-moi un ~ absolu** promise me you won't breathe a word ◆ **garder un ~ absolu sur qch** to say absolutely nothing about sth, to keep completely quiet about sth ◆ **contraindre l'opposition au ~** to force the opposition to keep silent ◆ **réduire qn au ~** to silence sb, to reduce sb to silence ◆ **acheter le ~ de qn** to buy sb's silence ◆ **briser** *ou* **rompre le ~** to break one's silence ◆ **passer qch sous ~** to pass sth over in silence ◆ **le sujet est passé sous ~** the subject was not mentioned ◆ **surprise préparée dans le plus grand ~** surprise prepared in the greatest secrecy ◆ ~ **radio** *(lit)* radio silence, blackout; *(fig)* total silence ◆ **le célèbre compositeur vient de sortir de 12 années de ~** the famous composer has just broken 12 years of silence ◆ **le ~ de la loi sur ce sujet** the lack *ou* absence of legislation on this matter; → **loi**

4 *(= paix)* silence, still(ness) ◆ **dans le grand ~ de la plaine** in the great silence *ou* stillness of the plain ◆ **vivre dans la solitude et le ~** to live in solitary silence

silencieusement /silɑ̃sjøzmɑ̃/ ADV *[avancer, défiler, regarder]* in silence; *[pleurer]* quietly ◆ **la cérémonie s'est déroulée ~** the ceremony took place in silence

silencieux, -ieuse /silɑ̃sjø, jøz/ ADJ 1 *(= peu bruyant) [mouvement, pas, personne]* silent, quiet; *[moteur, machine]* quiet, noiseless; *[lieu, cloître]* silent, still ◆ **le voyage du retour fut ~** the return journey took place in silence 2 *(= peu communicatif)* quiet; *(= qui ne veut ou ne peut s'exprimer)* silent ◆ **rester ~** to remain silent (*sur, à propos de* about) → **majorité** NM *[d'arme à feu]* silencer; *[de pot d'échappement]* silencer (Brit), muffler (US)

Silésie /silezi/ NF Silesia

silex /silɛks/ NM flint ◆ **des (armes en) ~** *(Archéol)* flints

silhouette /silwɛt/ NF 1 *(= contours)* outline, silhouette; *[de voiture]* shape ◆ **la ~ du château se détache sur le couchant** the château is silhouetted against the sunset ◆ **on le voyait en ~, à contre-jour** he could be seen silhouetted against the light 2 *(= personne)* figure ◆ **je distinguais une ~ dans le brouillard** I could make out a figure in the fog ◆ **~s de tir** *(Mil)* figure targets ◆ **faire des ~s** *[figurant]* to have walk-on parts 3 *(= allure)* figure ◆ **une ~ massive/élégante** a heavy/an elegant figure

silhouetter /silwete/ ► conjug 1 ◄ VT 1 *(Art)* to outline ◆ **l'artiste silhouetta un corps de femme** the artist outlined *ou* drew an outline of a woman's body 2 *(Photo)* to block out VPR **se silhouetter** to be silhouetted ◆ **le clocher se silhouette sur le ciel** the bell tower is silhouetted *ou* outlined against the sky

silicate /silikat/ NM silicate

silice /silis/ NF silica ◆ ~ **fondue** *ou* **vitreuse** silica glass

siliceux, -euse /silisø, øz/ ADJ siliceous, silicious

silicium /silisjɔm/ NM silicon

silicone /silikon/ NF silicone ◆ **gel de ~** silicone gel

siliconer /silikone/ ► conjug 1 ◄ VT to cover with silicone ◆ **pare-brise siliconé** silicone-coated windscreen ◆ **sa poitrine siliconée** *(péj ou hum)* her silicone breasts

silicose /silikoz/ NF silicosis

sillage /sijaʒ/ NM 1 *[d'embarcation]* wake; *[d'avion à réaction] (= déplacement d'air)* slipstream; *(= trace)* (vapour (Brit) *ou* vapor (US)) trail; *[de personne, animal, parfum]* trail ◆ **dans le ~ de qn** *(lit, fig)* (following) in sb's wake ◆ **mar-**

cher dans le ~ de qn to follow in sb's footsteps [2] *(Phys)* wake

sillon /sijɔ̃/ NM [1] *[de champ]* furrow ◆ **les ~s** *(littér)* the (ploughed *(Brit)* *ou* plowed *(US)*) fields [2] *(= ride, rayure)* furrow [3] *(Anat)* fissure [4] *[de disque]* groove [5] ◆ **le ~ rhodanien** the Rhone valley

sillonner /sijɔne/ ▸ conjug 1 ◂ VT [1] *(= traverser)* *[avion, bateau, routes]* to cut across, to cross ◆ **les canaux qui sillonnent la Hollande** the canals which cut across *ou* which criss-cross Holland ◆ **région sillonnée de canaux/routes** region criss-crossed by canals/roads ◆ **des avions ont sillonné le ciel toute la journée** planes have been droning backwards and forwards *ou* to and fro across the sky all day ◆ **des éclairs sillonnaient le ciel** flashes of lightning criss-crossed the sky ◆ **~ les routes** to travel the country ◆ **les touristes sillonnent la France en été** tourists travel to every corner *ou* throughout the length and breadth of France in the summer

[2] *(= creuser)* *[rides, ravins, crevasses]* to furrow ◆ **visage sillonné de rides** face furrowed with wrinkles ◆ **front sillonné d'une ride profonde** deeply furrowed brow

silo /silo/ NM *(Aviat, Mil)* silo ◆ **~ à céréales** *ou* **à grains/fourrage** grain/fodder silo ◆ **mettre en ~** to put in a silo, to silo

silure /silyʀ/ NM silurid *(giant catfish)*

silurien, -ienne /silyʀjɛ̃, jɛn/ ADJ Silurian NM ◆ **le ~** the Silurian

simagrées /simagʀe/ NFPL fuss *(NonC)*, playacting *(NonC)* ◆ **faire des ~** to playact ◆ **arrête tes ~!** stop your playacting! ◆ **elle a fait beaucoup de ~ avant d'accepter son cadeau** she made a great fuss (about it) *ou* she put on a great show of reluctance before she accepted his present

simien, -ienne /simjɛ̃, jɛn/ ADJ, NM simian

simiesque /simjɛsk/ ADJ monkey-like, ape-like

similaire /similɛʀ/ ADJ similar *(à* to*)*; ◆ **le rouge à lèvres, le fond de teint et produits ~s** lipstick, foundation and similar products *ou* products of a similar nature

similarité /similaʀite/ NF similarity *(entre* between; *avec* with*)*

simili /simili/ PRÉF imitation *(épith)*, artificial ◆ **en ~ fourrure** fun fur *(épith)* ◆ **des ~-prophètes** *(péj)* pseudo prophets NM imitation ◆ **bijoux en ~** imitation *ou* costume jewellery NF * abrév de **similigravure**

similicuir /similikɥiʀ/ NM imitation leather, Leatherette ®

similigravure /similigʀavyʀ/ NF half-tone engraving

similitude /similityd/ NF [1] *(= ressemblance)* similarity ◆ **il y a certaines ~s entre ces méthodes** there are certain similarities between these methods [2] *(Géom)* similarity

simonie /simɔni/ NF simony

simoun /simun/ NM simoom, simoon

simple /sɛ̃pl/ ADJ [1] *(= non composé, non multiple)* *[fleur]* simple; *[nœud, cornet de glace]* single; *(Chim)* *[corps]* simple; *(Math)* *[racine]* simple ◆ **en ~ épaisseur** in a single layer *ou* thickness; → **passé**

[2] *(= peu complexe)* simple ◆ **réduit à sa plus ~ expression** reduced to a minimum ◆ **sa situation est loin d'être ~** his situation is far from being simple *ou* straightforward ◆ **~ comme bonjour** * (as) easy as falling off a log* *ou* as pie* ◆ **dans ce cas, c'est bien ~ : je m'en vais** * in that case it's quite simple *ou* straightforward – I'm leaving ◆ **pourquoi faire ~ quand on peut faire compliqué ?** * *(hum)* why not make things really complicated! *(hum)* ◆ **ce serait trop ~ !** that would be too easy! *ou* too simple! ◆ **ce n'est pas si ~** it's not as simple as that ◆ **il y a un moyen ~ pour ...** there is an easy way of ...

[3] *(= modeste)* *[personne]* unaffected ◆ **il a su rester ~** he hasn't let it go to his head

[4] *(= peu sophistiqué)* *[vie, goûts]* simple; *[robe, repas, style]* simple, plain ◆ **être ~ dans sa mise** to dress simply *ou* plainly ◆ **dans le plus ~ appareil** *(hum)* in one's birthday suit, in the altogether *

[5] *(= de condition modeste)* modest ◆ **ce sont des gens ~s** they are simple folk

[6] *(= naïf)* simple ◆ **il est un peu ~** he's a bit simple ◆ **il est ~ d'esprit, c'est un ~ d'esprit** he's simple-minded

[7] *(= ordinaire)* *[particulier, salarié]* ordinary ◆ **un ~ soldat** a private

[8] *(valeur restrictive)* **une ~ formalité** a mere formality ◆ **un ~ regard/une ~ remarque la déconcertait** just a *ou* a mere look/comment would upset her ◆ **d'un ~ geste de la main** with a simple movement *ou* with just a movement of his hand ◆ **par ~ curiosité** out of pure curiosity ◆ **sur ~ présentation de votre carte d'étudiant** simply *ou* just show your student card ◆ **vous obtiendrez des informations sur ~ appel (téléphonique)** simply pick up the phone and you will get all the information you need; → **pur**

NM [1] ◆ **passer du ~ au double** to double ◆ **les prix peuvent varier du ~ au double** prices can vary by as much as 100%

[2] *(Bot)* medicinal plant, simple †

[3] *(Tennis)* singles ◆ **~ messieurs/dames** men's/women's *ou* ladies' singles

simplement /sɛ̃pləmɑ̃/ ADV [1] *(= sans sophistication)* simply ◆ **elle s'habille très ~** she dresses very simply ◆ **ils vivent très ~** they lead a very simple life [2] *(= seulement)* simply, merely, just ◆ **je vous demande ~ de me prévenir** I simply *ou* just want you to warn me, all I ask is that you warn me ◆ **je veux ~ dire que ...** I simply *ou* merely *ou* just want to say that ... [3] *(= tout à fait)* **tout ~** *[remarquable, insupportable, incroyable]* quite simply, just ◆ **c'est tout ~ inadmissible** it's quite simply intolerable; → **purement** [4] *(= facilement)* easily ◆ **cela s'explique très ~** that's easily explained

simplet, -ette /sɛ̃plɛ, ɛt/ ADJ [1] *[personne]* simple(-minded), ingenuous [2] *[question, raisonnement]* simplistic, naïve; *[intrigue, roman]* simple, unsophisticated

simplex /sɛ̃plɛks/ NM *(Ordin)* simplex

simplicité /sɛ̃plisite/ NF [1] *(= facilité)* simplicity ◆ **un appareil d'une grande ~ d'emploi** an easy-to-use appliance, an appliance that is very easy to use ◆ **cet exercice est d'une ~ biblique** *ou* **enfantine** this exercise is child's play *ou* is simplicity itself

[2] *(= manque de sophistication)* *[de vie, goûts]* simplicity; *[de robe, repas, style]* simplicity, plainness ◆ **habillé avec ~** dressed simply ◆ **décor d'une grande ~** very simple decor ◆ **"c'est une vocation", dit-elle en toute ~** "it's a vocation", she said modestly ◆ **venez dîner demain, ce sera en toute ~** come for dinner tomorrow – it won't be anything fancy ◆ **il dit en toute ~ être un sculpteur de génie** *(iro)* he very modestly says that he's a brilliant sculptor *(iro)*

[3] *(= naïveté)* simpleness ◆ **j'avais la ~ de croire que cela durerait toujours** I was naïve enough to think that it would last forever

[4] *(= modestie, naturel)* unaffectedness ◆ **il manque de ~** he's rather affected

simplifiable /sɛ̃plifjabl/ ADJ *(gén)* *[méthode]* that can be simplified; *(Math)* *[fraction]* reducible

simplificateur, -trice /sɛ̃plifikatœʀ, tʀis/ ADJ simplifying *(épith)*

simplification /sɛ̃plifikasjɔ̃/ NF simplification

simplifier /sɛ̃plifje/ ▸ conjug 7 ◂ VT *(gén, Math)* to simplify ◆ **disons, pour ~ les choses, que ...** to simplify matters, let's say that ... ◆ **~ à l'extrême** *ou* **à l'excès, trop ~** to oversimplify ◆ **des procédures très simplifiées** streamlined procedures

simplisme /sɛ̃plism/ NM *(péj)* simplism

simplissime /sɛ̃plisim/ ADJ ◆ **c'est ~** it couldn't be simpler

simpliste /sɛ̃plist/ ADJ *(péj)* simplistic

simulacre /simylakʀ/ NM [1] *(= action simulée)* enactment ◆ **les acteurs firent un ~ de sacrifice humain** the actors enacted a human sacrifice [2] *(péj = fausse apparence)* **un ~ de justice** a pretence of justice ◆ **un ~ de gouvernement/de procès** a sham government/trial, a mockery of a government/of a trial

simulateur, -trice /simylatœʀ, tʀis/ NM,F *(gén)* pretender; *(= qui feint la maladie)* malingerer NM simulator ◆ **~ de conduite** (driving) simulator ◆ **~ de vol** flight simulator

simulation /simylasjɔ̃/ NF simulation ◆ **il n'est pas malade, c'est de la ~** he isn't ill – it's all put on *ou* he's just malingering ◆ **logiciel de ~** simulation software

simulé, e /simyle/ (ptp de **simuler**) ADJ *[attaque, retraite]* simulated; *[amabilité, gravité]* feigned; *[accident, suicide]* fake *(épith)*; *[conditions, situation, essais nucléaires]* simulated ◆ **~ sur ordinateur** computer-simulated

simuler /simyle/ ▸ conjug 1 ◂ VT [1] *(= feindre)* *[+ sentiment, attaque]* to feign, to simulate *(frm)* ◆ **~ une maladie** to feign illness, to pretend to be ill, to malinger [2] *(= avoir l'apparence de)* to simulate ◆ **ce papier peint simule une boiserie** this wallpaper is made to look like *ou* simulates wood panelling [3] *(Ordin, Tech = reproduire)* to simulate [4] *(Jur)* *[+ contrat, vente]* to effect fictitiously

simultané, e /simyltane/ ADJ simultaneous ◆ **la présence ~e de deux personnes dans un même lieu** the presence of two people in the same place at the same time ◆ **de manière ~e** at the same time, simultaneously ◆ **diffusion en ~** simultaneous broadcast ◆ **c'était en ~** it was shown *ou* broadcast simultaneously; → **traduction** NF **simultanée** *(Échecs)* simultaneous, simul

simultanéisme /simyltaneism/ NM *(Littérat = procédé narratif)* (use of) simultaneous action

simultanéité /simyltaneite/ NF simultaneousness, simultaneity

simultanément /simyltanemɑ̃/ ADV simultaneously

Sinaï /sinai/ NM Sinai; → **mont**

sinapisé /sinapize/ ADJ ◆ **bain/cataplasme ~** mustard bath/poultice

sinapisme /sinapism/ NM mustard poultice *ou* plaster

sincère /sɛ̃sɛʀ/ GRAMMAIRE ACTIVE 49 ADJ [1] *(= franc, loyal)* *[personne, aveu, paroles]* sincere; *[réponse, explication]* sincere, honest ◆ **est-il ~ dans son amitié ?** is he sincere in his friendship?, is his friendship sincere? *ou* genuine? ◆ **sois ~ avec toi-même** be honest with yourself [2] *(= réel)* *[repentir, amour, partisan, admiration]* sincere, genuine, true ◆ **son chagrin est ~** he's genuinely upset, his sorrow is genuine ◆ **un ami ~ des arts** a true *ou* genuine friend of the arts ◆ **mes ~s condoléances** *(formules épistolaires)* my sincere *ou* heartfelt condolences ◆ **mes regrets les plus ~s** my sincerest regrets ◆ **mes ~s salutations** yours sincerely ◆ **nos vœux les plus ~s** with our best wishes

sincèrement /sɛ̃sɛʀmɑ̃/ ADV [1] *(= réellement)* *[espérer, croire, penser, regretter, remercier]* sincerely; *[aimer]* truly ◆ **je vous souhaite ~ de réussir** I sincerely hope you will succeed ◆ **je**

suis ~ **désolé que** ... I am sincerely *ou* truly *ou* genuinely sorry that ... ◆ **il a paru ~ étonné** he seemed genuinely surprised 2 *(= franchement)* honestly, really ◆ **~, vous feriez mieux de refuser** to be honest you'd be better off saying no

sincérité /sɛ̃seʀite/ NF 1 *(= franchise, loyauté) [de personne, aveu, paroles]* sincerity; *[de réponse, explications]* sincerity, honesty ◆ **en toute** ~ in all sincerity ◆ **répondez-moi en toute** ~ give me an honest answer 2 *[de repentir, amour, admiration]* sincerity, genuineness

sinécure /sinekyʀ/ NF sinecure ◆ **ce n'est pas une** ~ * it's no picnic *

sine die /sinedje/ LOC ADV sine die

sine qua non /sinekwanɔn/ GRAMMAIRE ACTIVE 37.1 LOC ADJ ◆ **une condition** ~ an indispensable condition, a prerequisite, a sine qua non ◆ **c'est la condition ~ de la réussite/pour enrayer la récession** it's a sine qua non of success/for curbing the recession

Singapour /sɛ̃gapuʀ/ N Singapore

singapourien, -ienne /sɛ̃gapuʀjɛ̃, jɛn/ ADJ Singaporean NM,F **Singapourien(ne)** Singaporean

singe /sɛ̃ʒ/ NM 1 *(= animal) (à longue queue)* monkey; *(à queue courte ou sans queue)* ape ◆ **les grands ~s** the big apes 2 *(péj) (= personne laide)* horror; *(= enfant espiègle)* monkey ◆ **c'est un vrai** ~ *(très agile)* he's very agile 3 *(arg Mil = corned beef)* bully beef * 4 *(* = patron)* boss * 5 *(locutions)* **faire le** ~ to monkey about ◆ **être laid comme un** ~ to be as ugly as sin; → **apprendre, malin, monnaie**

COMP **singe-araignée** spider monkey
singe-écureuil squirrel monkey
singe hurleur howler monkey

singer /sɛ̃ʒe/ ► conjug 3 ◄ VT *[+ démarche, personne]* to ape, to mimic, to take off; *[+ sentiments]* to feign

singerie /sɛ̃ʒʀi/ NF 1 *(gén pl = grimaces et pitreries)* antics, clowning *(NonC)* ◆ **faire des ~s** to clown about, to play the fool 2 *(= simagrées)* **~s** antics 3 *(= cage)* monkey house

single /siŋgœl/ NM *(= chambre)* single room; *(= disque)* single

singleton /sɛ̃glətɔ̃/ NM singleton

singulariser /sɛ̃gylaʀize/ ► conjug 1 ◄ VT to mark out, to make conspicuous VPR **se singulariser** *(= se faire remarquer)* to call attention to o.s., to make o.s. conspicuous ◆ **se ~ par qch** to distinguish o.s. by sth ◆ **cette église se singularise par son étrange clocher** this church is remarkable for its strange steeple

singularité /sɛ̃gylaʀite/ NF 1 *(= particularité)* singularity ◆ **cet orchestre a pour ~** *ou* **présente la ~ de jouer sans chef** this orchestra is unusual in that it doesn't have a conductor ◆ **il cultive sa ~** he likes to stand out from the crowd *ou* to be different 2 *(= bizarrerie)* peculiarity ◆ **le manuscrit présente plusieurs ~s** the manuscript is odd in several respects

singulier, -ière /sɛ̃gylje, jɛʀ/ ADJ 1 *(= étonnant, peu commun)* remarkable, singular *(frm)* ◆ **un visage d'une beauté singulière** a face of remarkable *ou* singular *(frm)* beauty ◆ **c'est un personnage** ~ he's an unusual character 2 *(= étrange)* odd, strange ◆ **je trouve ~ qu'il n'ait pas jugé bon de ...** I find it odd *ou* strange that he didn't see fit to ... ◆ **singulière façon de se comporter !** what a strange way to behave! 3 *(Ling)* singular NM *(Ling)* singular ◆ **au ~** in the singular ◆ **à la deuxième personne du ~** in the second person singular

singulièrement /sɛ̃gyljɛʀmɑ̃/ ADV 1 *(= étrangement)* in a peculiar way, oddly, strangely 2 *(= beaucoup, très) [intéressant, fort]* remarkably, extremely ◆ **cela leur complique ~ la tâche** that makes things particularly difficult for them ◆ **il manque ~ d'imagination** he is singularly lacking in imagination ◆ **sa marge de manœuvre est ~ réduite** his room for manoeuvre has been greatly *ou* severely reduced ◆ **trancher** *ou* **contraster ~ avec qch** to be in singular contrast with sth 3 *(= en particulier)* particularly, especially

sinisation /sinizasjɔ̃/ NF sinicization

siniser /sinize/ ► conjug 1 ◄ VT *[+ culture, région]* to sinicize ◆ **une population fortement sinisée** a people strongly influenced by Chinese culture VPR **se siniser** to become sinicized

sinistre /sinistʀ/ ADJ 1 *(= lugubre) [voix, air]* gloomy; *[personne]* grim-looking; *[soirée, réunion]* grim, deadly (boring)*; *[image, tableau]* grim ◆ **c'est vraiment ~ ici** *(= glauque)* it's really miserable in here; *(= effrayant)* it's really creepy in here ◆ **tu es ~ ce soir !** you're cheerful tonight! *(iro)* ◆ **le patron est ~** the boss gives me the creeps *
2 *(avant n) [personnage]* appalling, evil ◆ **un pénitencier de ~ réputation** a prison of evil repute ◆ **ce pays détient le ~ record du nombre de tués sur la route** this country holds the gruesome record for road fatalities ◆ **une ~ liste d'assassinats** a grim list of killings ◆ **un ~ avertissement** a grim warning ◆ **une ~ réalité** a grim reality; → **mémoire¹**
3 *(intensif)* **un ~ voyou/imbécile** an absolute lout/idiot
4 *(= de mauvais augure) [bruit, projet]* sinister
NM *(= catastrophe)* disaster; *(= incendie)* blaze; *(Assurances = cas)* accident ◆ **l'assuré doit déclarer le ~ dans les 24 heures** any (accident) claim must be notified within 24 hours ◆ **évaluer l'importance d'un ~** *(Assurances)* to appraise the extent of the damage *(ou loss etc)*

> ⚠ L'adjectif **sinistre** se traduit par le mot anglais **sinister** uniquement au sens de 'de mauvais augure'.

sinistré, e /sinistʀe/ ADJ *[région, pays]* (disaster-) stricken *(épith)*; *[secteur économique]* devastated ◆ **zone ~e** disaster area ◆ **ville ~e sur le plan de l'emploi** town devastated *ou* blighted by unemployment ◆ **les personnes ~es** the disaster victims NM,F disaster victim

sinistrement /sinistʀəmɑ̃/ ADV in a sinister way ◆ **nom ~ célèbre** infamous name

sinistrose /sinistʀoz/ NF pessimism

Sinn Fein /sinfejn/ NM *(Pol)* Sinn Féin

sino- /sinɔ/ PRÉF Sino- ◆ **~américain/tibétain** Sino-American/Tibetan

sinologie /sinɔlɔʒi/ NF sinology

sinologue /sinɔlɔg/ NMF sinologist, specialist in Chinese affairs

sinon /sinɔ̃/ CONJ 1 *(= autrement)* otherwise, or else ◆ **fais-le, ~ nous aurons des ennuis** do it, otherwise *ou* or else we will be in trouble ◆ **fais-tes-le, vous vous exposerez ~ à des ennuis** do it - you're likely to get into trouble otherwise ◆ **elle doit être malade, ~ elle serait déjà venue** she must be ill, otherwise *ou* or else she would have already come ◆ **fais-le, ~ ...** *(pour indiquer la menace)* do it, or else ...
2 *(concession = si ce n'est)* if not ◆ **il faut le faire, ~ pour le plaisir, du moins par devoir** it must be done, if not for pleasure, (then) at least out of a sense of duty ◆ **il avait leur approbation, ~ leur enthousiasme** he had their approval, if not their enthusiasm ◆ **cette histoire est savoureuse, ~ très morale** *(frm)* this story is spicy, if not very moral ◆ **ils y étaient opposés, ~ hostiles** *(frm)* they were opposed, if not (actively) hostile, to it
3 *(frm = sauf)* except, other than, save *(frm)* ◆ **on ne possède jamais rien, ~ soi-même** there is nothing one ever possesses, except (for) *ou* other than oneself ◆ **à quoi peut bien servir cette manœuvre ~ à nous intimider ?** what can be the purpose of this manoeuvre other than *ou* if not to intimidate us?
◆ **sinon que** only that, other than that ◆ **je ne sais pas grand-chose, ~ qu'il a démissionné** I don't know much about it, only that *ou* other than that he has resigned

sinophile /sinɔfil/ ADJ, NMF sinophile

sinoque †* /sinɔk/ ADJ crazy *, batty *, nutty * NMF loony *, nutcase *

sinuer /sinɥe/ ► conjug 1 ◄ VI *(littér) [rivière, route]* to meander, to wind

sinueux, -euse /sinɥø, øz/ ADJ 1 *[rivière]* winding *(épith)*, meandering *(épith)*; *[route, chemin]* winding *(épith)*; *[ligne]* sinuous 2 *[pensée, raisonnement]* tortuous ◆ **il a eu un parcours ~** his career followed a tortuous path *ou* route

sinuosité /sinɥozite/ NF *(NonC) [de route]* winding; *[de rivière]* winding, meandering; *[de pensée, raisonnement]* tortuousness ◆ **les ~s du chemin/de la rivière** the twists and turns of the path/of the river ◆ **les ~s de sa pensée** his tortuous train of thought, his convoluted thought processes ◆ **les ~s de la politique** the tortuous course of politics

sinus¹ /sinys/ NM *(Anat)* sinus ◆ **~ frontal/maxillaire** frontal/maxillary sinus

sinus² /sinys/ NM *(Math)* sine

sinusite /sinyzit/ NF sinusitis *(NonC)*

sinusoïdal, e (mpl **-aux**) /sinyzɔidal, o/ ADJ sinusoidal

sinusoïde /sinyzɔid/ NF sinusoid, sine curve

Sion /sjɔ̃/ N Zion

sionisme /sjɔnism/ NM Zionism

sioniste /sjɔnist/ ADJ, NMF Zionist

sioux /sju/ ADJ INV Sioux NM *(= langue)* Sioux NMF **Sioux** Sioux; → **ruse**

siphon /sifɔ̃/ NM 1 *(= tube, bouteille)* siphon; *[d'évier, W-C]* U-bend 2 *(Spéléologie)* sump 3 *[d'animal marin]* siphon

siphonné, e * /sifɔne/ ADJ *(= fou)* crazy *

siphonner /sifɔne/ ► conjug 1 ◄ VT to siphon

sire /siʀ/ NM 1 *(au roi)* **Sire** Sire 2 *(Hist = seigneur)* lord 3 ◆ **un triste ~** an unsavoury *(Brit)* *ou* unsavory *(US)* individual ◆ **un pauvre ~** † a poor *ou* penniless fellow

sirène /siʀɛn/ NF 1 *(Myth)* siren; *(à queue de poisson)* mermaid ◆ **écouter le chant des ~s** to listen to the sirens' song ◆ **céder à l'appel des ~s nationalistes** to give in to the lure of nationalist ideas 2 *(= appareil) [d'ambulance, bateau]* siren; *[d'usine]* hooter *(Brit)*, siren *(US)*; *[de pompiers]* fire siren ◆ **~ d'alarme** *(en temps de guerre)* air-raid siren; *(en temps de paix)* fire alarm ◆ **la police est arrivée toutes ~s hurlantes** the police cars arrived with their sirens wailing

Sirius /siʀjys/ NM Sirius

sirocco /siʀɔko/ NM sirocco

sirop /siʀo/ NM 1 *(= médicament)* syrup, mixture; *(= boisson)* fruit drink *ou* cordial *(Brit)* ◆ **~ d'orgeat** barley water ◆ **~ de groseille/d'ananas/de menthe** redcurrant/pineapple/mint cordial *(Brit)* *ou* beverage *(US)* ◆ **~ d'érable** maple syrup ◆ **~ de maïs** corn syrup ◆ **~ contre la toux** cough mixture *ou* syrup *ou* linctus *(Brit)* 2 *(* : péj)* schmaltz * ◆ **cette musique, c'est du ~** this music is schmaltz * *ou* very syrupy

siroter * /siʀɔte/ ► conjug 1 ◄ VT to sip

sirupeux, -euse /siʀypø, øz/ ADJ *[liquide]* syrupy; *(péj) [musique]* schmaltzy *, syrupy

sis, sise /si, siz/ ADJ *(Admin, Jur)* located

sisal /sizal/ NM sisal

sismal, e (mpl **-aux**) /sismal, o/ ADJ ♦ **ligne ~e** path of an earthquake

sismicité /sismisite/ NF seismicity

sismique /sismik/ ADJ seismic; → **secousse**

sismogramme /sismɔgʀam/ NM seismogram

sismographe /sismɔgʀaf/ NM seismograph

sismographie /sismɔgʀafi/ NF seismography

sismologie /sismɔlɔʒi/ NF seismology

sismologue /sismɔlɔg/ NMF seismologist

sismothérapie /sismoteʀapi/ NF shock therapy

sistre /sistʀ/ NM sistrum

Sisyphe /sizif/ NM Sisyphus; → **rocher**

sitar /sitaʀ/ NM sitar

sitcom /sitkɔm/ NM ou NF (abrév de **situation comedy**) sitcom

site /sit/ NM [1] *(= environnement)* setting; *(= endroit remarquable)* beauty spot ♦ **dans un ~ merveilleux/très sauvage** in a marvellous/very wild setting ♦ **~ naturel/historique** natural/historic site ♦ **les ~s pittoresques de la région** the beauty spots of the area ♦ **~ touristique** tourist spot *ou* attraction ♦ **la protection des ~s** the conservation of places of interest ♦ **~ protégé** *ou* **classé** conservation area ♦ **"Beaumanoir, ses plages, ses hôtels, ses sites"** "Beaumanoir for beaches, hotels and places to visit"

[2] *(= emplacement) (industriel, militaire)* site ♦ **~ archéologique/olympique/de production** archeological/Olympic/production site ♦ **pistes cyclables en ~ propre** separate bicycle lanes ♦ **ligne de bus en ~ propre** bus lane system *(with a physical barrier between the bus lane and the street)*

[3] *(Mil)* **(angle de)** ~ (angle of) sight ♦ **ligne de ~** line of sight

[4] *(Ordin)* site ♦ **~ Web** website ♦ **~ miroir** mirror site

[5] *(locutions)*

♦ **sur site** on site ♦ **dépannage sur ~** on-site repairs

sit-in /sitin/ NM INV sit-in ♦ **faire un ~** to stage a sit-in

sitôt /sito/ ADV [1] *(= dès que)* **~ couchée, elle s'endormit** as soon as she was in bed she fell asleep, she was no sooner in bed *ou* no sooner was she in bed than she fell asleep ♦ **~ dit, ~ fait** no sooner said than done ♦ **~ après la guerre** immediately *ou* straight *(Brit) ou* right after the war, immediately the war was over *(Brit)*

[2] *(avec nég)* **il ne reviendra pas de ~** he won't be back for quite a while *ou* for (quite) some time, he won't be back in a hurry ♦ **il a été si bien puni qu'il ne recommencera pas de ~ !** he was so severely punished that he won't be doing that again for a while! *ou* in a hurry!

PRÉP *(littér)* ♦ **~ ton retour, il faudra que ...** as soon as you're back, we must ... ♦ **~ les vacances, elle partait** she would go away as soon as the holidays started, the holidays had no sooner begun than she would go away

LOC CONJ **sitôt (après) que** as soon as, no sooner than ♦ **~ (après) que le docteur fut parti, elle se sentit mieux** as soon as the doctor had left she felt better, the doctor had no sooner left than she felt better ♦ **~ qu'il sera guéri, il reprendra le travail** as soon as he is better he'll go back to work

sittelle /sitel/ NF nuthatch

situation /sitɥasjɔ̃/ GRAMMAIRE ACTIVE 46.2 NF [1] *(= emplacement)* situation, location ♦ **la ~ de cette villa est excellente** this villa is very well situated *ou* is in an excellent location

[2] *(= conjoncture, circonstances)* situation ♦ **tu vois la ~ où je me trouve** you see the situation *ou* position I'm in ♦ **être dans une ~ délicate** *ou* **difficile** to be in a difficult position *ou* situation ♦ **être en ~ de faire qch** to be in a position to do sth ♦ **~ de fait** de facto situation ♦ **~ de famille** marital status ♦ **~ financière/politique** financial/political situation ♦ **étranger en ~ irrégulière** foreigner whose papers are not in order ♦ **dans une ~ désespérée** in a desperate plight ♦ **l'entreprise est en ~ de monopole** the company has a monopoly on the market ♦ **faire face à une ~ d'urgence** to cope with an emergency situation ♦ **c'est l'homme de la ~** he's the right man for the job; → **comique, renverser**

[3] *(= emploi)* post, job, position ♦ **chercher une/perdre sa ~** to look for a/lose one's post *ou* job ♦ **il a une belle ~** he has an excellent job ♦ **il s'est fait une belle ~ dans l'édition** he's worked up to a good position in publishing

[4] *(Fin = état)* statement of finances ♦ **~ de trésorerie** cash flow statement

[5] *(locutions)* **en ~** in a real-life situation

situationnisme /sitɥasjɔnism/ NM situationism

situationniste /sitɥasjɔnist/ NMF situationist

situé, e /sitɥe/ (ptp de **situer**) ADJ situated ♦ **bien/mal ~** well/poorly situated

situer /sitɥe/ ► conjug 1 ◄ VT [1] *(lit = placer, construire)* to site, to situate, to locate

[2] *(par la pensée) (= localiser)* to set, to place; (* *= catégoriser) [+ personne]* to place ♦ **on ne le situe pas bien** * you just can't figure him out *

VPR **se situer** [1] *(emploi réfléchi)* to place o.s. ♦ **essayer de se ~ par rapport à qn/qch** to try to place o.s. in relation to sb/sth ♦ **il se situe à gauche** *(Pol)* he's on the left, he leans towards the left

[2] *(= se trouver) (dans l'espace)* to be situated; *(dans le temps)* to take place; *(par rapport à des notions)* to stand ♦ **l'action/cette scène se situe à Paris** the action/this scene is set *ou* takes place in Paris ♦ **la hausse des prix se situera entre 5% et 10%** prices will rise by between 5% and 10%, there will be price rises of between 5% and 10% ♦ **la France se situe dans le peloton de tête** France is among the leading countries

Siva /ʃiva/ NM Siva, Shiva

six /sis, *devant n commençant par consonne* si, *devant n commençant par voyelle ou h muet* siz/ ADJ CARDINAL INV six ♦ **il y avait ~ mille personnes** there were six thousand people ♦ **ils sont ~ enfants** there are six children ♦ **je suis resté ~ heures/jours** I stayed six hours/days ♦ **les ~ huitièmes de cette somme** six eighths of this sum ♦ **il a ~ ans** he is six (years old) ♦ **un enfant de ~ ans** a six-year-old (child), a child of six ♦ **un objet de 6 €** an item costing €6 ♦ **polygone à ~ faces** six-sided polygon ♦ **couper qch en ~ morceaux** to cut sth into six pieces ♦ **j'en ai pris trois, il en reste ~** I've taken three (of them) and there are six (of them) left ♦ **il est ~ heures** it's six o'clock ♦ **il est ~ heures du soir** it's 6 pm, it's six in the evening ♦ **il est ~ heures du matin** it's 6 am, it's six in the morning ♦ **il est trois heures moins ~** it is six minutes to three ♦ **il est trois heures ~** it is six minutes past *ou* after *(US)* three ♦ **par vingt voix contre ~** by twenty votes to six ♦ **cinq jours/fois sur ~** five days/times out of six ♦ **ils sont venus tous les ~** all six of them came ♦ **ils ont porté la table à eux ~** the six of them carried the table ♦ **ils ont mangé le jambon à eux ~** the six of them ate the ham, they ate the ham between the six of them ♦ **partagez cela entre vous ~** share that among the six of you ♦ **ils viennent à ~ pour déjeuner** there are six coming to lunch ♦ **on peut s'asseoir à ~ autour de cette table** this table can seat six (people) ♦ **ils vivent à ~ dans une seule pièce** there are six of them living in one room ♦ **se battre à ~ contre un/à un contre ~** to fight six against one/one against six ♦ **entrer ~ par ~** to come in by sixes *ou* six at a time *ou* six by six ♦ **se mettre en rangs par ~** to form rows of six

ADJ ORDINAL INV ♦ **arriver le ~ septembre** to arrive on the sixth of September *ou* (on) September the sixth *ou* (on) September sixth ♦ **Louis ~** Louis the Sixth ♦ **chapitre/page/article ~** chapter/page/article six ♦ **le numéro ~ gagne un lot** number six wins a prize ♦ **il habite au numéro ~ de la rue Arthur** he lives at number six Rue Arthur

NM INV [1] *(= nombre)* six ♦ **trente-/quarante-~** thirty-/forty-six ♦ **quatre et deux font ~** four and two are *ou* make six ♦ **il fait mal ses ~** he writes his sixes badly ♦ **c'est le ~ qui a gagné** number six has won ♦ **il habite au ~ (de la rue)** he lives at number six ♦ **il habite ~ rue de Paris** he lives at six, Rue de Paris ♦ **nous sommes le ~ aujourd'hui** it's the sixth today ♦ **il est venu le ~** he came on the sixth ♦ **il est payé le ~** *ou* **tous les ~ de chaque mois** he is paid on the sixth of each month ♦ **le ~ de cœur** *(Cartes)* the six of hearts ♦ **le ~ et deux** *(Dominos)* the six-two ♦ **la facture est datée du ~** the bill is dated the 6th

[2] *(Pol)* **les Six, l'Europe des Six** *(jusqu'en 1973)* the Six, the Europe of the Six

sixain /sizɛ̃/ NM ⇒ **sizain**

six-huit /sisɥit/ NM INV *(Mus)* six-eight (time) ♦ **mesure à ~** bar in six-eight (time)

sixième /sizjɛm/ ADJ sixth ♦ **vingt-/trente-~** twenty-/thirty-sixth ♦ **recevoir la ~ partie d'un héritage** to receive a sixth of a bequest ♦ **demeurer dans le ~ (arrondissement)** to live in the sixth arrondissement *(in Paris)* ♦ **habiter au ~ (étage)** to live on the sixth floor *(Brit) ou* the seventh floor *(US)*

NMF *(gén)* sixth (person) ♦ **se classer ~** to come sixth ♦ **nous avons besoin d'un ~ pour compléter l'équipe** we need a sixth (person) to complete the team ♦ **elle est arrivée (la) ~ dans la course** she came (in) sixth in the race

NM *(= portion)* sixth ♦ **calculer le ~ d'un nombre** to work out the sixth of a number ♦ **recevoir le ~** *ou* **un ~ d'une somme** to receive a sixth of a sum ♦ **(les) deux ~s du budget seront consacrés à ...** two sixths of the budget will be given over to ...

NF *(Scol)* ≈ first form *(Brit)*, sixth grade *(US)* ♦ **entrer en (classe de) ~** ≈ to go into the first form *(Brit) ou* sixth grade *(US)* ♦ **élève de ~** ≈ first form *(Brit) ou* sixth-grade *(US)* pupil

sixièmement /sizjɛmmɑ̃/ ADV in the sixth place, sixthly

six-mâts /sima/ NM INV *(Naut)* six-master

six-quatre-deux * /siskatdø/ **à la six-quatre-deux** LOC ADV *[faire]* in a slapdash way, any old way, any old how * *(Brit)*

sixte /sikst/ NF *(Mus)* sixth; *(Escrime)* sixte

Sixtine /sixtin/ ADJ, NF ♦ **la (chapelle) ~** the Sistine Chapel

sizain /sizɛ̃/ NM *(Littérat)* six-line stanza; *(Cartes) packet of six packs of cards*

ska /ska/ NM ska

skaï ® /skaj/ NM Leatherette ® ♦ **en ~** Leatherette *(épith)*

skate(-board), skateboard /skɛt(bɔʀd)/ NM skateboard ♦ **le ~(-board)** *(= activité)* skateboarding ♦ **faire du ~(-board)** to skateboard

skateur, -euse /skɛtœʀ, øz/ NM,F skateboarder

sketch (pl **sketches**) /skɛtʃ/ NM (variety) sketch; → **film**

ski /ski/ NM *(= objet)* ski; *(= sport)* skiing ♦ **s'acheter des ~s** to buy o.s. a pair of skis *ou* some skis ♦ **~ amont/aval** uphill/downhill ski ♦ **aller quelque part à** *ou* **en ~s** to go somewhere on skis, to ski somewhere ◆ **faire du** ~ to ski, to go skiing ◆ **aller au** ~ * to go skiing ◆ **vacances/équipement de** ~ ski(ing) holiday/equipment ◆ **chaussures/moniteur/épreuve/station de** ~ ski boots/instructor/race/resort; → **lunette, piste**

COMP **ski acrobatique** hot-dogging, free-styling
ski alpin *(= discipline)* Alpine skiing; *(opposé à ski de fond)* downhill skiing
ski artistique ski ballet
ski sur bosses mogul skiing
ski court short ski
ski de descente downhill skiing
ski d'été glacier skiing
ski évolutif short ski method, ski évolutif
ski de fond *(= sport)* cross-country skiing, ski touring *(US)*, langlauf; *(= objet)* cross-country ski
ski sur glacier glacier skiing
ski de haute montagne ski-mountaineering
ski nautique water-skiing
ski nordique Nordic skiing
ski parabolique parabolic ski
ski de piste downhill skiing
ski de randonnée ⇒ **ski de fond**

skiable /skjabl/ ADJ *[neige, piste]* skiable ◆ **ils ont un grand domaine** ~ they have a lot of ski slopes *ou* pistes

ski-bob (pl **ski-bobs**) /skibɔb/ NM skibob ◆ **faire du** ~ to go skibobbing

skidoo /skidu/ NM skidoo, snow scooter ◆ **faire du** ~ to skidoo ◆ **il y est allé en** ~ he went there on a skidoo *ou* on a snow scooter

skier /skje/ ► conjug 7 ◄ VI to ski

skieur, skieuse /skjœʀ, skjøz/ NM,F skier; *(Ski nautique)* water-skier ◆ ~ **de fond** cross-country *ou* langlauf skier ◆ ~ **hors piste** off-piste skier ◆ **deux ~s hors piste ont été tués** two people skiing off-piste were killed

skif(f) /skif/ NM skiff

skin * /skin/ NM skin *

skinhead /skinɛd/ NM skinhead

skipper /skipœʀ/ NM *(Voile)* skipper

Skopje /skɔpje/ N Skopje

slalom /slalɔm/ NM *(= épreuve, piste)* slalom; *(= mouvement)* slalom *ou* weaving movement; *(entre divers obstacles)* zigzag ◆ **faire du** ~ to slalom *(entre, parmi* between); ◆ ~ **géant/spécial** giant/special slalom ◆ **le** ~ **nautique** slalom canoeing; → **descente**

slalomer /slalɔme/ ► conjug 1 ◄ VI *(Sport)* to slalom ◆ **il slalomait entre les voitures** he was weaving in and out of the traffic *ou* zigzagging through the traffic ◆ **le serveur slalomait entre les tables** the waiter was weaving between the tables

slalomeur, -euse /slalɔmœʀ, øz/ NM,F slalom skier *ou* specialist *ou* racer

slave /slav/ ADJ Slav(onic), Slavic; *[langue]* Slavic, Slavonic ◆ **le charme** ~ Slavonic charm
NMF **Slave** Slav

slavisant, e /slavizɑ̃, ɑt/ NM,F Slavist

Slavonie /slavɔni/ NF Slavonia

slavophile /slavɔfil/ ADJ, NMF Slavophile

sleeping † /slipiŋ/ NM sleeping car

slice /slajs/ NM *(Tennis etc)* slice

slicer /slajse/ ► conjug 3 ◄ VT *(Tennis etc)* to slice ◆ **revers slicé** sliced backhand

slip /slip/ NM 1 *[d'homme]* briefs, underpants; *[de femme]* pants *(Brit)*, panties *(US)*, briefs ◆ ~ **de bain** *[d'homme]* (bathing *ou* swimming) trunks; *(bikini)* bikini bottom(s) ◆ ~ **brésilien** tanga ◆ ~ **kangourou** Y-fronts ◆ **j'ai acheté deux ~s** I bought two pairs of briefs *ou* pants ◆ **se retrouver en** ~ * *(fig)* to lose one's shirt 2 *(Naut)* slipway

> ⚠ Au sens français, **slip** ne se traduit pas par le mot anglais **slip**.

slipé, e /slipe/ ADJ *[collant]* with integral pants *(Brit) ou* panty *(US)*

slogan /slɔgɑ̃/ NM slogan

sloop /slup/ NM sloop

slovaque /slɔvak/ ADJ Slovak NMF **Slovaque** Slovak

Slovaquie /slɔvaki/ NF Slovakia

slovène /slɔvɛn/ ADJ Slovene NM *(= langue)* Slovene NMF **Slovène** Slovene

Slovénie /slɔveni/ NF Slovenia

slow /slo/ NM *(= danse)* slow dance; *(= musique)* slow number; *(= fox-trot)* slow fox trot ◆ **danser un** ~ to do *ou* dance a slow dance

SMAG /smag/ NM (abrév de **salaire minimum agricole garanti**) → **salaire**

smala * /smala/ NF *(péj = troupe)* tribe * ◆ **ils ont débarqué avec toute la** ~ they turned up with all their family in tow

smash /sma(t)ʃ/ NM *(Tennis)* smash ◆ **faire un** ~ to do a smash, to smash (the ball)

smasher /sma(t)ʃe/ ► conjug 1 ◄ *(Tennis)* VT to smash VI to do a smash, to smash (the ball)

SME /ɛsɛmə/ NM (abrév de **système monétaire européen**) EMS

SMIC /smik/ NM (abrév de **salaire minimum interprofessionnel de croissance**) → **salaire**

smicard, e * /smikaʀ, aʀd/ NM,F minimum wage earner

SMIG † /smig/ NM (abrév de **salaire minimum interprofessionnel garanti**) → **salaire**

smocks /smɔk/ NMPL *(= fronces)* smocking *(NonC)* ◆ **robe à** ~ smocked dress

smog /smɔg/ NM smog

smok * /smɔk/ NM (abrév de **smoking**) DJ * *(Brit)*, tux * *(US)*

smoking /smɔkiŋ/ NM *(= costume)* dinner suit, evening suit, dress suit; *(= veston)* dinner jacket, DJ * *(Brit)*, tuxedo *(US)*, tux * *(US)*

> ⚠ **smoking** ne se traduit pas par le mot anglais **smoking**, qui a le sens de 'tabagisme'.

SMS /ɛsɛmɛs/ NM (abrév de **Short Message Service**) SMS

SMUR /smyʀ/ NM (abrév de **Service médical d'urgence et de réanimation**) *mobile emergency unit*

smurf /smœʀf/ NM *(Danse)* break dancing ◆ **danser le** ~ to break-dance

snack /snak/, **snack-bar** (pl **snack-bars** /snakbaʀ/) NM snack bar

SNCF /ɛsɛnseɛf/ NF (abrév de **Société nationale des chemins de fer français**) → **société**

snif(f) /snif/ EXCL boo hoo!

sniffer * /snife/ ► conjug 1 ◄ VT to sniff ◆ ~ **de la cocaïne/de la colle** to sniff cocaine/glue

sniper /snajpœʀ/ NM sniper

snob /snɔb/ NMF snob ADJ *[personne, attitude]* snobbish; *[quartier]* posh *

snober /snɔbe/ ► conjug 1 ◄ VT *[+ personne]* to snub, to give the cold shoulder to; *[+ endroit, réception]* to turn one's nose up at

snobinard, e * /snɔbinaʀ, aʀd/ *(péj)* ADJ snooty *, stuck-up *, snobbish NM,F stuck-up thing *, snob

snobisme /snɔbism/ NM snobbery, snobbishness ◆ ~ **à l'envers** *ou* **à rebours** inverted snobbery

snowboard /snobɔʀd/ NM snowboard ◆ **le** ~ *(= activité)* snowboarding ◆ **faire du** ~ to snowboard

snowboardeur, -euse /snobɔʀdœʀ, øz/ NM,F snowboarder

soap-opéra (pl **soap-opéras**) /sopɔpeʀa/ NM soap opera

sobre /sɔbʀ/ ADJ 1 *[personne] (= qui mange et boit peu)* abstemious; *(= qui ne boit pas d'alcool)* teetotal; *(= qui n'est pas ivre)* sober ◆ ~ **comme un chameau** * as sober as a judge 2 *(= mesuré, simple) [décor, style, éloquence]* sober, understated; *[tenue]* simple, plain; *[commentaire, vie]* simple ◆ ~ **de gestes/en paroles** sparing of gestures/of words ◆ **des vêtements de coupe** ~ clothes cut simply

sobrement /sɔbʀəmɑ̃/ ADV 1 *[vivre]* abstemiously 2 *(= simplement) [s'habiller]* simply, plainly; *[commenter, expliquer]* simply

sobriété /sɔbʀijete/ NF 1 *[de personne] (= fait de boire et manger peu)* temperance; *(= fait de ne pas boire d'alcool)* abstinence 2 *(= simplicité) [de style, éloquence]* sobriety; *[de mise en scène, décor]* simplicity ◆ ~ **de gestes/paroles** restraint in one's gestures/words

sobriquet /sɔbʀikɛ/ NM nickname

soc /sɔk/ NM ploughshare *(Brit)*, plowshare *(US)*

sociabilité /sɔsjabilite/ NF 1 *(Sociol)* sociability, social nature 2 *(= civilité) [de personne, caractère]* sociability

sociable /sɔsjabl/ ADJ 1 *(Sociol)* social 2 *(= ouvert, civil) [personne, caractère]* sociable; *[milieu]* hospitable ◆ **je ne suis pas d'humeur** ~ **aujourd'hui** I'm not in a sociable mood today, I don't feel like socializing today

social, e (mpl **-iaux**) /sɔsjal, jo/ ADJ 1 *[animal, créature, rapports, conventions]* social; → **science** 2 *[classe, questions, loi, politique, système]* social ◆ **œuvres ~es** charity activities; → **assistant, sécurité, siège**[1] 3 *(= du travail)* **revendications ~es** workers' demands ◆ **conflit** ~ industrial *ou* trade dispute ◆ **plan** ~ restructuring programme NM ◆ **le** ~ *(= questions)* social issues ◆ **faire du** ~ to tackle social issues

social-démocrate, sociale-démocrate (mpl **sociaux-démocrates**) /sɔsjaldemɔkʀat, sɔsjodemɔkʀat/ ADJ, NM,F Social Democrat

social-démocratie (pl **social-démocraties**) /sɔsjaldemɔkʀasi/ NF social democracy

socialement /sɔsjalmɑ̃/ ADV socially

socialisant, e /sɔsjalizɑ̃, ɑt/ ADJ *[idéologie]* with socialist leanings *ou* tendencies

socialisation /sɔsjalizasjɔ̃/ NF 1 *(Écon) [de moyens de production]* collectivization 2 *(Sociol) [de personne]* socialization

socialiser /sɔsjalize/ ► conjug 1 ◄ VT 1 *(Écon)* to socialize ◆ **le financement socialisé des dépenses médicales** socialized healthcare ◆ **ils ont décidé de** ~ **les pertes** they've decided that the state should pay for the losses 2 *(Sociol) [+ personne]* to socialize ◆ **les individus les plus socialisés** those who are most fully socialized VPR **se socialiser** *(Sociol) [personne]* to become socialized

socialisme /sɔsjalism/ NM socialism ◆ ~ **utopique/scientifique/révolutionnaire** utopian/scientific/revolutionary socialism ◆ ~ **d'État** state socialism

socialiste /sɔsjalist/ ADJ, NMF socialist

socialo /sɔsjalo/ PRÉF socialo ◆ **~-communiste** socialo-communist NMF (*, *souvent péj*) Socialist

sociétaire /sɔsjetɛʀ/ NMF member *(of a society)* ◆ ~ **de la Comédie-Française** (shareholding) member of the Comédie-Française

sociétal, e (mpl **-aux**) /sɔsjetal, o/ ADJ *[changement, structure]* societal ◆ **engagement** ~ community involvement

société /sɔsjete/ NF 1 *(= groupe, communauté)* society ◆ **la** ~ society ◆ **la vie en** ~ life in society ◆ ~ **sans classe** classless society ◆ **la** ~ **de consommation** the consumer society ◆ **la** ~ **de loisirs** the leisure society

2 *(= club) (littéraire)* society; *(sportif)* club ◆ ~ **de pêche/tir** angling/shooting club ◆ ~ **secrète/savante** secret/learned society ◆ **la Société protectrice des animaux** ≃ the Royal Society for the Prevention of Cruelty to Animals *(Brit)*, the American Society for the Prevention of Cruelty to Animals *(US)*

3 *(= entreprise)* company, firm ◆ ~ **financière** finance company ◆ ~ **immobilière** *(= compagnie)* property *(Brit)* ou real estate *(US)* company; *[de copropriétaires]* housing association

4 *(= classes supérieures)* **la** ~ society ◆ **dans la bonne** ~ in polite society ◆ **la haute** ~ high society

5 *(= assemblée)* company, gathering ◆ **il y venait une** ~ **assez mêlée/une** ~ **d'artistes et d'écrivains** a fairly mixed company ou gathering/a company ou gathering of artists and writers used to come ◆ **toute la** ~ **se leva pour l'acclamer** the whole company rose to acclaim him

6 *(= compagnie)* company, society *(frm) (littér)* ◆ **rechercher/priser la** ~ **de qn** to seek/value sb's company ou society *(littér)* ou companionship ◆ **dans la** ~ **de qn** in the company ou society *(frm, littér)* of sb; → **jeu, talent¹**

COMP **société par actions** joint-stock company
société anonyme *(gén)* ≃ limited (liability) company; *(ouverte au public)* ≃ public limited company
Société des auteurs, compositeurs et éditeurs de musique *French body responsible for collecting and distributing music royalties*, ≃ Publishing Rights Society *(Brit)*
société de Bourse brokerage ou broking firm
société à capital variable company with variable capital
société de capitaux joint-stock company
société civile *(Comm)* non-trading company; *(Philos)* civil society ◆ **personne de la** ~ **civile** *(Pol)* lay person
société civile immobilière non-trading property *(Brit)* ou real estate *(US)* company
société civile de placement immobilier non-trading property *(Brit)* ou real estate *(US)* investment trust
société civile professionnelle professional partnership
société en commandite limited partnership
société commerciale trading company
société commune joint-venture company
société de crédit credit ou finance company
société d'économie mixte semi-public company
société écran bogus ou dummy company
société d'exploitation development company
société d'investissement investment trust ◆ ~ **d'investissement à capital variable** unit trust *(Brit)*, open-end investment trust *(US)*, mutual fund *(US)*
la société de Jésus the Society of Jesus
Société nationale des chemins de fer français *French national railway company*
la Société des Nations *(Hist Pol)* the League of Nations
société en nom collectif general partnership
société en participation joint-venture company
société de personnes partnership
société de portefeuille holding company
société de production *(Audiov)* production company
société à responsabilité limitée limited liability company
société de services service company ◆ ~ **de services informatiques** software house
société de tempérance temperance society

> ⚠ Au sens de 'entreprise', **société** ne se traduit pas par **society**.

socio * /sɔsjo/ NF abrév de **sociologie**

sociobiologie /sɔsjobjɔlɔʒi/ NF sociobiology

socioculturel, -elle /sɔsjokyltyʀɛl/ ADJ sociocultural

sociodrame /sɔsjodʀam/ NM sociodrama

socio-économique (pl **socio-économiques**) /sɔsjoekɔnɔmik/ ADJ socioeconomic

socio-éducatif, -ive (mpl **socio-éducatifs**) /sɔsjoedykatif, iv/ ADJ socioeducational

sociogéographique /sɔsjoʒeɔgʀafik/ ADJ sociogeographic

sociogramme /sɔsjogʀam/ NM sociogram

sociolinguistique /sɔsjolɛ̃gɥistik/ ADJ sociolinguistic NF sociolinguistics *(sg)*

sociologie /sɔsjɔlɔʒi/ NF sociology

sociologique /sɔsjɔlɔʒik/ ADJ sociological

sociologiquement /sɔsjɔlɔʒikmɑ̃/ ADV sociologically

sociologue /sɔsjɔlɔg/ NMF sociologist

sociométrie /sɔsjɔmetʀi/ NF sociometry

sociopathe /sɔsjopat/ NMF sociopath

sociopolitique /sɔsjopɔlitik/ ADJ sociopolitical

socio(-)professionnel, -elle /sɔsjopʀɔfesjɔnɛl/ ADJ socio-professional

soclage /sɔklaʒ/ NM *[d'œuvre d'art]* mounting *(on a base)*

socle /sɔkl/ NM 1 *[de statue, colonne]* plinth, pedestal, socle *(SPÉC)*; *[de lampe, vase]* base 2 *(fig)* **le** ~ **de connaissances et de compétences commun à tous les élèves** the core knowledge and skills shared by all the pupils ◆ **ils cherchent à consolider leur** ~ **électoral** they are trying to strengthen their electoral base ◆ **le** ~ **sur lequel fut fondée notre république** the foundation stone of our republic 3 *(Géog)* basement ◆ ~ **continental** continental shelf ◆ ~ **rocheux** bedrock

socler /sɔkle/ ► conjug 1 ◄ VT *[+ œuvre d'art]* to mount *(on a base)*

socque /sɔk/ NM *(= sabot)* clog

socquette /sɔkɛt/ NF ankle sock *(Brit)*, anklet *(US)*

Socrate /sɔkʀat/ NM Socrates

socratique /sɔkʀatik/ ADJ Socratic

soda /sɔda/ NM fizzy drink *(Brit)*, soda *(US)*, pop* ◆ ~ **à l'orange** orangeade ◆ **whisky** ~ whisky and soda

sodé, e /sɔde/ ADJ sodium *(épith)*

sodium /sɔdjɔm/ NM sodium

Sodome /sɔdɔm/ N Sodom ◆ ~ **et Gomorrhe** Sodom and Gomorrah

sodomie /sɔdɔmi/ NF sodomy, buggery

sodomiser /sɔdɔmize/ ► conjug 1 ◄ VT to bugger, to have anal intercourse with

sodomite /sɔdɔmit/ NM sodomite

sœur /sœʀ/ NF 1 *(lit, fig)* sister ◆ **avec un dévouement de** ~ with a sister's ou with sisterly devotion ◆ **la poésie,** ~ **de la musique** poetry, sister of ou to music ◆ **peuplades/organisations ~s** sister peoples/organizations ◆ ~ **d'infortune** *(littér)* fellow sufferer ◆ **j'ai trouvé la** ~ **de cette commode chez un antiquaire** *(hum)* I found the partner to this chest of drawers in an antique shop ◆ **et ta** ~ **!*** get lost!*; → **âme, lait**

2 *(Rel)* nun, sister; *(comme titre)* Sister ◆ ~ **Jeanne** Sister Jeanne ◆ **elle a été élevée chez les ~s** she was convent-educated ◆ **elle était en pension chez les ~s** she went to a convent (boarding) school ◆ **les Petites ~s des pauvres** the Little Sisters of the Poor ◆ **les ~s de la Charité** the Sisters of Charity; → **bon¹**

sœurette * /sœʀɛt/ NF little sister, kid* sister ◆ **salut** ~ **!** hi sis!*

sofa /sɔfa/ NM sofa

Sofia /sɔfja/ N Sofia

SOFRES /sɔfʀɛs/ NF (abrév de **Société française d'enquêtes par sondage**) *French public opinion poll institute*, ≃ Gallup, MORI *(Brit)*

soft /sɔft/ ADJ INV *[film]* soft-porn*, soft-core* ◆ **érotisme** ~ soft(-core) porn* ◆ **l'ambiance** ~ **d'un salon de thé** the cosy atmosphere of a tearoom ◆ **c'est la version** ~ **de son premier livre** it's the watered-down version of his first book ◆ **la campagne électorale est plus** ~ **que la précédente** the electoral campaign is less aggressive than the previous one NM ◆ **le** ~ *(Ordin)* software; *(Ciné)* soft(-core) porn films*

software /sɔftwɛʀ/ NM software

soi /swa/ PRON PERS 1 *(gén)* one(self); *(fonction d'attribut)* oneself ◆ **n'aimer que** ~ to love only oneself ◆ **regarder devant/derrière** ~ to look in front of/behind one ◆ **malgré** ~ in spite of oneself ◆ **avoir confiance en** ~ to be self-confident ◆ **rester chez** ~ to stay at home

2 † *(= lui)* himself; *(= elle)* herself; *(= chose)* itself ◆ **il n'agissait que pour** ~ *(frm)* he was only acting for himself ou in his own interests ◆ **elle comprenait qu'il fût mécontent de** ~ *(évite une ambiguïté)* she understood his not being pleased with himself ◆ **il allait droit devant** ~ *(frm)* he was going straight ahead

3 *(locutions)* **aller de** ~ to be self-evident, to be obvious ◆ **cela va de** ~ it goes without saying, it's obvious, it stands to reason ◆ **il va de** ~ **que ...** it goes without saying ou it stands to reason that ... ◆ **en** ~ *(= intrinsèquement)* in itself ◆ **n'exister que pour** ~ to exist only for oneself ◆ **dans un groupe, on peut se rendre service entre** ~ in a group, people can help each other ou one another (out) ◆ **être/rester** ~ to be/remain oneself; → **chacun, hors, maître**

4 ◆ **~-même** oneself ◆ **on le fait ~-même** you do it yourself, one does it oneself *(frm)* ◆ **le respect de ~-même** self-respect ◆ **Monsieur Leblanc ? – ~-même !** *(hum)* Mr Leblanc? – in person! ou none other!; *pour autres loc voir* **même**

NM *(Philos, littér = personnalité, conscience)* self; *(Psych = inconscient)* id ◆ **la conscience de** ~ self-awareness, awareness of self; → **en-soi, pour-soi**

soi-disant /swadizɑ̃/ ADJ INV so-called ◆ **un** ~ **poète/professeur** a so-called ou would-be poet/teacher ADV supposedly ◆ **il était** ~ **parti à Rome** he had supposedly left for Rome, he was supposed to have left for Rome ◆ **il était venu** ~ **pour discuter** he had come to talk – or so he said, he had come ostensibly for a talk ◆ ~ **que*** ... it would appear that ..., apparently ...

soie /swa/ NF 1 *(= tissu, fil)* silk ◆ ~ **sauvage/végétale** wild/vegetal silk ◆ ~ **grège/lavée** raw/washed silk; → **papier, ver** 2 *(= poil) [de sanglier]* bristle ◆ **brosse en ~s de sanglier** (boar) bristle brush ◆ **brosse à dents en ~s de nylon** nylon (bristle) tooth brush, tooth brush with nylon bristles 3 *(Tech) [de lime, couteau]* tang

soierie /swaʀi/ NF *(= tissu)* silk; *(= industrie, commerce)* silk trade; *(= filature)* silk mill

soif /swaf/ NF [1] *(lit)* thirst ◆ **avoir** ~ *[personne]* to be thirsty; *[plante, terre]* to be dry *ou* thirsty ◆ **avoir grand** ~ † to be very thirsty ◆ **ça donne** ~ it makes you thirsty ◆ **il fait** ~* I'm parched* ◆ **jusqu'à plus** ~ *(lit)* till one's thirst is quenched; *(fig)* till one can't take any more ◆ **rester sur sa** ~ *(lit)* to remain thirsty; *(fig)* to be left unsatisfied; → **boire, étancher, garder, mourir** [2] *(= désir)* ~ **de** *[+ richesse, connaissances, vengeance, pouvoir]* thirst *ou* craving for ◆ ~ **de faire qch** craving to do sth

soiffard, e* † /swafaʀ, aʀd/ *(péj)* ADJ boozy* NM,F boozer*

soignant, e /swaɲɑ̃, ɑ̃t/ ADJ *[personnel]* nursing *(épith)* ◆ **équipe ~e** (team of) doctors and nurses

soigné, e /swaɲe/ (ptp de **soigner**) ADJ [1] *(= propre) [personne, chevelure]* well-groomed, neat, tidy; *[ongles]* manicured, well-kept; *[mains]* well-cared-for *(épith)*, well cared for *(attrib)* ◆ **peu** ~ *[personne]* untidy; *[cheveux]* unkempt, untidy; *[ongles, mains]* neglected (-looking) ◆ **il est très ~ de sa personne** he is very well turned-out *ou* well-groomed

[2] *(= consciencieux) [travail, style, présentation]* careful, meticulous; *[vitrine]* neat, carefully laid out; *[jardin]* well-kept; *[repas]* carefully prepared ◆ **peu** ~ *[travail]* careless, sloppy ◆ **ils font une cuisine très ~e** their food is beautifully prepared ◆ **c'est un film très** ~ it's a very polished *ou* well-crafted film

[3] *(*: intensif) [note]* massive*, whopping* *(épith)*; *[punition]* stiff* ◆ **avoir un rhume (quelque chose de)** ~ to have a real beauty* *ou* a whopper* of a cold ◆ **la note était ~e** it was some bill*, it was a massive* *ou* whopping* bill

soigner /swaɲe/ ▸ conjug 1 ◂ VT [1] *(= traiter) [+ patient, maladie] [médecin]* to treat; *[infirmière, mère]* to look after, to nurse ◆ ~ **les blessés** to tend *ou* nurse the wounded ◆ **tu devrais te faire** ~ you should see a doctor ◆ **il faut te faire ~ !*** you need your head examined *ou* examining! ◆ **rentrez chez vous pour ~ votre rhume** go back home and look after *ou* nurse that cold (of yours) ◆ **je soigne mes rhumatismes avec des pilules** I'm taking pills for my rheumatism ◆ **j'ai été très bien soigné dans cette clinique** I had very good treatment *ou* I was very well looked after in that clinic ◆ **un rhume mal soigné peut avoir de graves conséquences** if not treated properly a cold can lead to something more serious

[2] *(= entretenir) [+ chien, plantes, invité]* to look after; *[+ ongles, chevelure, outils, livres]* to look after, to take (good) care of; *[+ cheval]* to groom; *[+ tenue, travail, repas, style, présentation]* to take care over ◆ ~ **sa clientèle** to look after one's customers ◆ ~ **son image (de marque)** to be careful about one's image ◆ **le pays essaie de ~ son image à l'étranger** the country is trying to cultivate its image abroad

[3] *(* = maltraiter)* ~ **qn** to let sb have it* ◆ **5 € le café – ils nous ont soignés !** €5 for a coffee – what a rip-off!* *ou* we've been had!* *ou* done!* *(Brit)* ◆ **ils lui sont tombés dessus à quatre : j'aime autant te dire qu'ils l'ont soigné** four of them laid into him – I can tell you they really let him have it*; → **oignon**

VPR **se soigner** [1] *[personne] (= prendre des médicaments)* to take medicine ◆ **se ~ par les plantes** to take herbal medicine ◆ **soigne-toi bien** take good care of yourself, look after yourself ◆ **ils se soignent : champagne, saumon ... !** *(hum)* they take good care of *ou* they look after themselves (all right) – champagne, salmon, the lot!

[2] *[maladie]* **de nos jours, la tuberculose se soigne** these days tuberculosis can be treated ◆ **ça se soigne, tu sais !*** *(hum)* there's a cure for that, you know!

soigneur /swaɲœʀ/ NM *(Boxe)* second; *(Cyclisme, Ftbl)* trainer

soigneusement /swaɲøzmɑ̃/ ADV *[ranger, nettoyer, entretenir, éviter, choisir]* carefully; *[écrire, plier]* carefully, neatly ◆ ~ **préparé** carefully prepared, prepared with care ◆ **il pèse ~ ses mots** he weighs his words carefully

soigneux, -euse /swaɲø, øz/ ADJ [1] *(= propre, ordonné)* tidy, neat ◆ **ce garçon n'est pas assez** ~ that boy isn't tidy enough [2] *(= appliqué, minutieux) [travailleur]* careful, painstaking; *[travail]* careful, meticulous; *[recherche, examen]* careful ◆ **être ~ dans son travail** to take care over one's work [3] *(= soucieux)* **être ~ de sa santé** to be careful about one's health ◆ **être ~ de ses affaires** to be careful with one's belongings ◆ **être ~ de sa personne** to be careful about *ou* take care over one's appearance ◆ **être ~ de ses vêtements** to take care of *ou* look after one's clothes

soi-même /swamɛm/ PRON → **même, soi**

soin /swɛ̃/ NM [1] *(= application)* care; *(= ordre et propreté)* tidiness, neatness ◆ **être sans ~, n'avoir aucun** ~ to be careless *ou* untidy *ou* sloppy ◆ **faire qch sans** ~ to do sth carelessly ◆ **faire qch avec (grand)** ~ to do sth with (great) care *ou* (very) carefully ◆ **il nous évite avec un certain ~, il met un certain ~ à nous éviter** he takes great care *ou* he goes to some lengths to avoid us

[2] *(= charge, responsabilité)* care ◆ **confier à qn le ~ de ses affaires** to entrust sb with the care of one's affairs ◆ **confier à qn le ~ de faire qch** to entrust sb with the job *ou* task of doing sth ◆ **je vous laisse ce** ~ I leave this to you, I leave you to take care of this ◆ **son premier ~ fut de ...** his first concern was to ... ◆ **le ~ de son salut/avenir l'occupait tout entier** *(littér)* his thoughts were filled with the care of his salvation/future *(littér)*

[3] *(= traitement)* **le ~ du cheveu** hair care

[4] *(locutions)* **avoir** *ou* **prendre ~ de faire qch** to take care to do sth, to make a point of doing sth ◆ **avoir** *ou* **prendre ~ de qn/qch** to take care of *ou* look after sb/sth ◆ **il prend bien ~/grand ~ de sa petite personne** he takes good care/great care of his little self *ou* of number one* ◆ **ayez** *ou* **prenez ~ d'éteindre** take care *ou* be sure to turn out the lights, make sure you turn out the lights ◆ **avoir ~ que ...** to make sure that ...

NMPL **soins** [1] *(= entretien, hygiène)* care *(NonC)*; *(= traitement)* treatment *(NonC)* ◆ **~s esthétiques** *ou* **de beauté** beauty care ◆ **~s des cheveux/des ongles** hair/nail care ◆ **~s du visage** (facial) skin care ◆ **son état demande des ~s** his condition requires treatment *ou* (medical) attention ◆ **le blessé a reçu les premiers ~s** the injured man has been given first aid

[2] *(= attention)* care (and attention) *(NonC)* ◆ **l'enfant a besoin des ~s d'une mère** the child needs a mother's care (and attention) ◆ **confier qn/qch aux (bons) ~s de qn** to leave sb/sth in the hands *ou* care of sb ◆ **aux bons ~s de** *(sur lettre : frm)* care of, c/o ◆ **être aux petits ~s pour qn** to attend to sb's every need, to wait on sb hand and foot

[3] *(Rel)* **donner ses ~s à qn** to minister to sb

COMP **soins dentaires** dental treatment *ou* care

soins hospitaliers hospital care *ou* treatment

soins intensifs intensive care ◆ **unité de ~s intensifs** intensive care unit

soins médicaux medical *ou* health care

soir /swaʀ/ NM [1] evening ◆ **les ~s d'automne/d'hiver** autumn/winter evenings ◆ **le ~ descend** *ou* **tombe** night is falling, evening is closing in ◆ **le ~ où j'y suis allé** the evening I went ◆ **au ~ de la/de sa vie** *(littér)* in the evening of life/of his life *(littér)* ◆ **le grand** ~ the big night; *(Pol)* the revolution; → **matin**

◆ **du soir** ◆ **repas/journal du** ~ evening meal/paper ◆ **5 heures du** ~ 5 (o'clock) in the afternoon *ou* evening, 5 pm ◆ **8 heures du** ~ 8 (o'clock) in the evening, 8 o'clock at night, 8 pm ◆ **11 heures du** ~ 11 (o'clock) at night, 11 pm ◆ **être du** ~ to be a night owl*; → **cours, robe**

[2] *(locutions)* **le ~, je vais souvent les voir** I often go to see them in the evening ◆ **le ~, je suis allé les voir/il a plu** I went to see them/it rained in the evening ◆ **il pleut assez souvent le** ~ it quite often rains in the evening(s) ◆ **sortir le** ~ to go out in the evening ◆ **j'y vais ce** ~ I'm going this evening *ou* tonight ◆ **à ce ~ !** (I'll) see you (*ou* I'll talk to you) this evening! *ou* tonight! ◆ **vivement ce ~ qu'on se couche*** I can't wait until bedtime, roll on bedtime* *(Brit)* ◆ **tous les ~s, chaque** ~ every evening *ou* night ◆ **hier** ~ last night, yesterday evening ◆ **demain** ~ tomorrow evening *ou* night ◆ **dimanche** ~ Sunday evening *ou* night ◆ **hier au** ~ yesterday evening ◆ **le 17 au** ~ on the evening of the 17th ◆ **la veille au** ~ the previous evening ◆ **il est arrivé un (beau)** ~ he turned up one (fine) evening ◆ **viens nous voir un de ces ~s** come and see us one evening *ou* night

soirée /swaʀe/ GRAMMAIRE ACTIVE 52.2 NF [1] *(= soir)* evening ◆ **bonne ~ !** have a nice evening! ◆ **les longues ~s d'hiver** the long winter evenings [2] *(= réception)* party ◆ ~ **dansante** dance ◆ ~ **mondaine** society party; → **tenue²** [3] *(Ciné, Théât = séance)* evening performance ◆ **donner un spectacle/une pièce en** ~ to give an evening performance of a show/play ◆ ~ **thématique** (TV) *evening of programmes devoted to a theme* ◆ ~ **électorale** election night

soit /swa/ ADV *(frm = oui)* very well, so be it *(frm)* ◆ **eh bien, ~, qu'il y aille !** very well then, let him go!; → **tant**

CONJ [1] *(= ou)* ~ **l'un ~ l'autre** (either) one or the other ◆ ~ **avant ~ après** (either) before or after ◆ ~ **timidité, ~ mépris** *ou* ~ **timidité ou mépris, elle ne lui adressait jamais la parole** be it (out of) *ou* whether out of shyness or contempt, she never spoke to him ◆ ~ **qu'il soit fatigué, ~ qu'il en ait assez** whether he is tired or whether he has had enough ◆ ~ **qu'il n'entende pas, ou ne veuille pas entendre** whether he cannot hear or (whether) he does not wish to hear

[2] *(= à savoir)* that is to say ◆ **des détails importants, ~ l'approvisionnement, le transport, etc** important details, that is to say *ou* for instance provisions, transport, etc

[3] *(Math = posons)* ~ **un rectangle ABCD** let ABCD be a rectangle ◆ **soient deux triangles isocèles** given two isosceles triangles

soixantaine /swasɑ̃tɛn/ NF [1] *(= environ soixante)* sixty or so, (round) about sixty, sixty-odd* ◆ **il y avait une ~ de personnes/de livres** there were sixty or so *ou* about sixty people/books, there were sixty-odd* people/books ◆ **la ~ de spectateurs qui étaient là** the sixty or so *ou* the sixty-odd* people there ◆ **ils étaient une bonne** ~ there were a good sixty of them ◆ **il y a une ~/une bonne ~ d'années** sixty or so *ou* sixty-odd*/a good sixty years ago ◆ **ça doit coûter une ~ de mille (francs)** that must cost sixty thousand or so francs *ou* (round) about sixty thousand francs *ou* some sixty thousand francs

[2] *(= soixante unités)* sixty ◆ **sa collection n'atteint pas encore/a dépassé la** ~ his collection has not yet reached/has passed the sixty mark, there are not yet sixty/are now over sixty in his collection

[3] *(= âge)* sixty ◆ **approcher de la/atteindre la** ~ to near/reach sixty ◆ **un homme dans la** ~ a man in his sixties ◆ **d'une ~ d'années** *[per-*

sonne] of about sixty; *[arbre]* sixty or so years old ◆ **elle a la ~** she's sixtyish, she's about sixty

soixante /swasɑ̃t/ **ADJ INV, NM INV** sixty ◆ **à la page ~** on page sixty ◆ **habiter au ~** to live at number sixty ◆ **les années ~** the sixties, the 60s ◆ **~ et un** sixty-one ◆ **~ et unième** sixty-first ◆ **~-dix** seventy ◆ **~-dixième** seventieth ◆ **~ mille** sixty thousand ◆ **le (numéro) ~** *(jeu, rue)* number sixty ◆ **un ~-neuf**‡ *(= position sexuelle)* a soixante-neuf‡, a sixty-nine‡

soixante-huitard, e (mpl **soixante-huitards**) /swasɑ̃tɥitaʀ, aʀd/ **ADJ** *[personne]* who took part in the events of May 1968; *[idéologie, slogan]* inspired by the events of May 1968 **NM,F** *(en mai 68)* participant in the events of May 1968; *(après 1968)* proponent of the ideals of May 1968; → **MAI 68**

soixantième /swasɑ̃tjɛm/ **ADJ, NM** sixtieth

soja /sɔʒa/ **NM** *(= plante)* soya; *(= graines)* soya beans

sol[1] /sɔl/ **NM** *(gén)* ground; *(= plancher)* floor; *(= revêtement)* floor, flooring *(NonC)*; *(= territoire, terrain, Agr, Géol)* soil ◆ **étendu sur le ~** spread out on the ground ◆ **posé au ~** *ou* **à même le ~** (placed) on the ground *(ou* floor*)* ◆ **~ carrelé/cimenté** tiled/concrete floor ◆ **la surface au ~** the floor surface ◆ **la pose des ~s** *(Constr)* the laying of floors *ou* of flooring ◆ **~ natal** native soil ◆ **sur le ~ français** on French soil ◆ **personnel au ~** *[dans aéroport]* ground staff *ou* personnel ◆ **essais/vitesse au ~** *[d'avion]* ground tests/speed ◆ **exercices au ~** *(Sport)* floor exercises

sol[2] /sɔl/ **NM INV** *(Mus)* G; *(en chantant la gamme)* so(h); → **clé**

sol[3] /sɔl/ **NM** *(Chim)* sol

sol[4] /sɔl/ **NM** *(= monnaie)* sol

sol-air /sɔlɛʀ/ **ADJ INV** ground-to-air

solaire /sɔlɛʀ/ **ADJ** *(Astrol, Astron) [énergie, panneaux]* solar; *[crème, filtre]* sun *(attrib)*; *[calculatrice]* solar(-powered); → **cadran, plexus, spectre** **NM** *(= énergie)* ◆ **le ~** solar energy

solarisation /sɔlaʀizasjɔ̃/ **NF** *(= chauffage)* solar heating; *(Photo)* solarization

solarium /sɔlaʀjɔm/ **NM** solarium

soldanelle /sɔldanɛl/ **NF** *(= primulacée)* soldanella; *(= liseron)* sea bindweed

soldat /sɔlda/ **NM** *(gén)* soldier ◆ **(simple) ~, ~ de 2e classe** *(armée de terre)* private; *(armée de l'air)* aircraftman *(Brit)*, basic airman *(US)* ◆ **~ de 1re classe** *(armée de terre)* ≈ private *(Brit)*, private first class *(US)*; *(armée de l'air)* leading aircraftman *(Brit)*, airman first class *(US)* ◆ **se faire ~** to join the army, to enlist ◆ **~ de la liberté/du Christ** *(littér)* soldier of liberty/of Christ ◆ **jouer aux (petits) ~s** to play (at) soldiers ◆ **jouer au petit ~** *(fig)* to throw one's weight around; → **fille**

COMP **soldat du feu** firefighter
le Soldat inconnu the Unknown Soldier *ou* Warrior
soldat d'infanterie infantryman
soldats de la paix peacekeepers
soldat de plomb tin *ou* toy soldier

soldate /sɔldat/ **NF** woman soldier

soldatesque /sɔldatɛsk/ *(péj)* **NF** army rabble **ADJ** † barrack-room *(épith)*

solde[1] /sɔld/ **NF** [1] *[de soldat, matelot]* pay [2] *(péj)* **être à la ~ de qn** to be in the pay of sb ◆ **avoir qn à sa ~** to have sb in one's pay

solde[2] /sɔld/ **NM** [1] *(Fin = reliquat) (gén)* balance; *(= reste à payer)* balance outstanding ◆ **il y a un ~ de 25 € en votre faveur** there is a balance of €25 in your favour ◆ **~ débiteur/créditeur** debit/credit balance ◆ **~ de trésorerie** cash balance ◆ **pour ~ de (tout) compte** in settlement [2] *(Comm)* **~ (de marchandises)** remaining goods ◆ **vente de ~s** sale, sale of reduced items ◆ **mettre des marchandises en ~** to put goods in a sale ◆ **vendre/acheter qch en ~** to sell (off)/buy sth at sale price ◆ **article (vendu) en ~** sale(s) item *ou* article **NMPL** **soldes** *(parfois nfpl)* **"soldes"** *(pancarte)* "sale" ◆ **les ~s** the sales ◆ **je l'ai acheté dans les ~s** I bought it in the sales ◆ **faire les ~s** to go to the sales ◆ **la saison des ~s** the sales season

solder /sɔlde/ ▸ conjug 1 ◂ **VT** [1] *[+ compte] (= arrêter)* to wind up, to close; *(= acquitter)* to pay (off) the balance of, to settle
[2] *[+ marchandises]* to sell (off) at sale price ◆ **ils soldent ces pantalons à 20 €** they are selling off these trousers at *ou* for €20, they are selling these trousers in the sale at *ou* for €20 ◆ **je vous le solde à 5 €** I'll let you have it for €5, I'll knock it down * *ou* reduce it to €5 for you
VPR **se solder** ◆ **se ~ par** *(Comm) [exercice, budget]* to show; *(fig) [entreprise, opération]* to end in ◆ **les comptes se soldent par un bénéfice** the accounts show a profit ◆ **l'exercice se solde par un déficit/bénéfice de 50 millions** the end-of-year figures show a loss/profit of 50 million ◆ **l'entreprise/la conférence s'est soldée par un échec** the undertaking/the conference ended in failure *ou* came to nothing

solderie /sɔldəʀi/ **NF** discount store

soldeur, -euse /sɔldœʀ, øz/ **NM,F** *(= propriétaire)* discount store owner; *(= entreprise)* discount store

sole[1] /sɔl/ **NF** *(= poisson)* sole ◆ **~ meunière** *(Culin)* sole meunière

sole[2] /sɔl/ **NF** *[de four]* hearth; *[de sabot, bateau]* sole

solécisme /sɔlesism/ **NM** solecism *(in language)*

soleil /sɔlɛj/ **NM** [1] *(= astre, gén)* sun ◆ **le Soleil** *(Astron, Myth)* the Sun ◆ **orienté au ~ levant/couchant** facing the rising/setting sun ◆ **le ~ de minuit** the midnight sun ◆ **les ~s pâles/brumeux de l'hiver** *(littér)* the pale/misty winter sun ◆ **tu es mon (rayon de) ~** you are my sunshine; → **coucher, lever**[2]**, rayon**
[2] *(= chaleur)* sun, sunshine; *(= lumière)* sun, sunshine, sunlight ◆ **au ~** in the sun ◆ **être assis/se mettre au ~** to be sitting in/go into the sun(shine) ◆ **vivre au ~** to live in the sun ◆ **il y a du ~, il fait du ~, il fait ~** * the sun's shining, it's sunny ◆ **il fait un beau ~** it's nice and sunny ◆ **il fait un ~ de plomb** the sun is blazing down, there's a blazing sun ◆ **être en plein ~** to be right in the sun ◆ **rester en plein ~** to stay (out) in the sun ◆ **c'est une plante de plein ~** this plant thrives in full sun ◆ **des jours sans ~** sunless days ◆ **se chercher un coin au ~** to look for a spot in the sun(shine) *ou* a sunny spot ◆ **la couleur a passé au ~** the colour has faded in the sun
◆ **coup de soleil** sunburn *(NonC)* ◆ **attraper** *ou* **prendre un coup de ~** to get sunburned ◆ **j'ai (pris) un coup de ~ dans le dos** I burned my back, my back is sunburned
[3] *(= motif, ornement)* sun
[4] *(= feu d'artifice)* Catherine wheel
[5] *(= acrobatie)* grand circle ◆ **faire un ~** *(= culbute)* to turn *ou* do a somersault, to somersault
[6] *(= fleur)* sunflower
[7] *(locutions)* **se lever avec le ~** to rise with the sun, to be up with the sun *ou* the lark *(Brit)* ◆ **le ~ brille pour tout le monde** *(Prov)* nature belongs to everyone ◆ **rien de nouveau** *ou* **neuf sous le ~** there's nothing new under the sun ◆ **avoir du bien** *ou* **des biens au ~** to be the owner of property, to have property ◆ **se faire/avoir une place au ~** *(fig)* to find oneself/have a place in the sun

solennel, -elle /sɔlanɛl/ **ADJ** *(gén)* solemn; *[promesse, ton, occasion]* solemn, formal; *[séance]* ceremonious; → **communion**

solennellement /sɔlanɛlmɑ̃/ **ADV** *(gén)* solemnly; *[offrir, ouvrir]* ceremoniously

solenniser /sɔlanize/ ▸ conjug 1 ◂ **VT** to solemnize

solennité /sɔlanite/ **NF** [1] *(= caractère)* solemnity [2] *(= fête)* grand *ou* formal occasion [3] *(gén pl = formalité)* formality, solemnity

solénoïde /sɔlenɔid/ **NM** solenoid

soleret /sɔlʀɛ/ **NM** *(Hist)* solleret

Solex ® /sɔlɛks/ **NM** ≈ moped

solfège /sɔlfɛʒ/ **NM** *(= théorie)* music theory, musical notation; *(= livre)* (music) theory book; *(† = gamme)* (tonic) sol-fa ◆ **apprendre le ~** to learn music theory *ou* musical notation

solfier /sɔlfje/ ▸ conjug 7 ◂ **VTI** to sing naming the notes

solidaire /sɔlidɛʀ/ **ADJ** [1] *[personnes]* **être ~s** to show solidarity, to stand *ou* stick together ◆ **pendant les grèves les ouvriers sont ~s** during strikes workers stand *ou* stick together *ou* show solidarity ◆ **être ~ de** to stand by, to be behind ◆ **nous sommes ~s du gouvernement** we stand by *ou* are behind *ou* are backing the government ◆ **nous sommes ~s de leur combat** we support their struggle ◆ **être ~ des victimes d'un régime** to show solidarity with *ou* stand by *ou* support the victims of a régime ◆ **ils ne sont pas très ~s l'un de l'autre** they're not very supportive of each other ◆ **ces pays se sentent ~s** these countries feel they have each others' support *ou* feel a sense of solidarity ◆ **se montrer ~ de qn** to show solidarity with sb ◆ **il rêve d'une société plus ~** he dreams of a more united society
[2] *[mécanismes, pièces, systèmes]* interdependent ◆ **cette pièce est ~ de l'autre** the two parts are interdependent ◆ **ces trois objectifs sont étroitement ~s** these three objectives are closely interlinked
[3] *(Jur) [contrat, engagement]* binding all parties; *[débiteurs]* jointly liable; → **caution**

solidairement /sɔlidɛʀmɑ̃/ **ADV** jointly, jointly and severally (SPÉC)

solidariser /sɔlidaʀize/ ▸ conjug 1 ◂ **VT** *[+ personnes]* to unify; *[+ objets]* to interlock **VPR** **se solidariser** ◆ **se ~ avec** to show solidarity with

solidarité /sɔlidaʀite/ **NF** [1] *[de personnes]* solidarity ◆ **~ de classe/professionnelle** class/professional solidarity ◆ **~ ministérielle** ministerial solidarity *(whereby all ministers assume responsibility for a government's decisions)* ◆ **cesser le travail par ~ avec des grévistes** to come out *ou* stop work in sympathy with the strikers; → **grève** [2] *[de mécanismes, systèmes]* interdependence [3] *(Jur)* joint and several liability

solide /sɔlid/ **ADJ** [1] *(= non liquide) [nourriture, état, corps]* solid; *(Géom, Phys)* solid ◆ **ne lui donnez pas encore d'aliments ~s** don't give him any solid food *ou* any solids yet
[2] *(= robuste) [construction, meuble]* solid, sturdy; *[matériaux]* sturdy, hard-wearing; *[outil]* sturdy; *[monnaie, économie]* strong ◆ **c'est du ~** * *[meuble]* it's solid stuff ◆ **être ~ sur ses jambes** to be steady on one's legs ◆ **avoir une position ~** to have a secure position ◆ **ce n'est pas très ~** *[pont, chaise]* it's not very solid
[3] *(= durable, sérieux) [institutions, qualités, vertus]* solid, sound; *[bases]* solid, firm, sound; *[preuve, alibi, liens, expérience, amitié]* solid, firm; *[argument, formation, culture, connaissances, raisons]* sound ◆ **être doué d'un ~ bon sens** to have sound common sense ◆ **ces opinions/raisonnements ne reposent sur rien de ~** these opinions/arguments have no solid *ou* sound foundation ◆ **leur couple, c'est du ~** * they have a solid *ou* strong relationship
[4] *(= vigoureux) [personne]* sturdy, robust; *[poigne, jambes, bras]* sturdy, solid; *[santé, poumons,*

cœur, esprit, psychisme] sound ◆ **avoir la tête ~** *(lit)* to have a hard head; *(fig)* to have a good head on one's shoulders ◆ **il n'a plus la tête bien ~** his mind's not what it was ◆ **il n'a pas l'estomac très ~** he has a rather weak *ou* delicate stomach ◆ **il faut avoir les nerfs ~s** you need strong nerves *ou* nerves of steel; → **rein**
5 *(intensif) [coup de poing]* hefty*; *[revenus]* substantial; *[engueulade]* good, proper* *(Brit)* ◆ **il a un ~ appétit** *ou* **coup de fourchette*** he has a hearty appetite, he's a hearty eater ◆ **un ~ repas le remit d'aplomb** a (good) solid meal put him back on his feet
6 *(locutions)* **être ~ au poste** *(Mil)* to be loyal to one's post; *(fig)* to be completely dependable *ou* reliable ◆ **~ comme un roc** as solid as a rock
NM *(Géom, Phys)* solid

solidement /sɔlidmɑ̃/ ADV 1 *[installé, implanté, établi]* firmly; *[arrimé]* securely, firmly ◆ **rester ~ attaché aux traditions locales** to remain firmly attached to local traditions ◆ **être ~ attaché à qn/qch** to be deeply attached to sb/sth ◆ **une certitude ~ ancrée dans les esprits** a conviction firmly entrenched in people's minds ◆ **tradition ~ établie** long *ou* solidly established tradition 2 *[fixer, tenir]* firmly; *[fabriquer, construire]* solidly ◆ **résister ~** to put up a solid *ou* firm resistance

solidification /sɔlidifikasjɔ̃/ NF solidification

solidifier VT, **se solidifier** VPR /sɔlidifje/ ► conjug 7 ◄ to solidify

solidité /sɔlidite/ NF 1 (= robustesse) *[de matériaux, construction, meuble]* solidity, sturdiness; *[d'outil]* solidity ◆ **d'une ~ à toute épreuve** *[de construction, meuble]* strong enough to resist anything 2 (= stabilité) *[d'institutions]* solidity, soundness; *[de bases]* solidity, firmness, soundness; *[d'amitié, liens]* solidity, firmness; *[de monnaie, économie]* strength; *[de raisonnement]* soundness 3 (= vigueur) *[de personne]* sturdiness, robustness; *[de poigne, jambes, bras]* sturdiness, solidity

soliflore /sɔliflɔʀ/ NM bud vase

soliloque /sɔlilɔk/ NM soliloquy

soliloquer /sɔlilɔke/ ► conjug 1 ◄ VI to soliloquize

Soliman /sɔlimɑ̃/ NM ◆ **~ le Magnifique** Suleiman the Magnificent

solipède /sɔliped/ ADJ, NM solidungulate

solipsisme /sɔlipsism/ NM solipsism

soliste /sɔlist/ NMF soloist

solitaire /sɔlitɛʀ/ ADJ 1 (= isolé) *[passant]* solitary *(épith)*, lone *(épith)*; *[arbre, maison, rocher]* solitary *(épith)*, lonely *(épith)*, isolated ◆ **là vivaient quelques chasseurs/bûcherons ~s** a few solitary *ou* lone hunters/woodcutters lived there
2 (= désert) *[chemin, demeure, parc]* lonely *(épith)*, deserted
3 (= sans compagnie) *[adolescent, vieillard, vie]* solitary, lonely, lonesome *(US)*; *[caractère, passe-temps]* solitary; → **plaisir**
4 *(Bot) [fleur]* solitary; → **ver**
NMF loner
◆ **en solitaire** ◆ **il préfère travailler en ~** he prefers to work on his own ◆ **ascension/traversée en ~** solo climb/crossing ◆ **course en ~** single-handed *ou* solo race ◆ **partir/voyager en ~** to leave/travel alone *ou* on one's own ◆ **elle a fait le tour du monde en ~** *[navigatrice]* she sailed single-handed *ou* solo around the world
NM 1 (= sanglier) old boar
2 (= diamant) solitaire
3 (= jeu) solitaire

solitairement /sɔlitɛʀmɑ̃/ ADV *[souffrir]* alone ◆ **vivre ~** to lead a solitary life

solitude /sɔlityd/ NF 1 *[de personne]* (= tranquillité) solitude; (= manque de compagnie) loneliness, lonesomeness *(US)*; *[d'endroit]* loneliness ◆ **~ morale** moral isolation ◆ **la ~ à deux** shared solitude ◆ **éprouver un sentiment de ~** to feel lonely ◆ **dans les moments de grande ~** at times of great loneliness ◆ **aimer la ~** to like being on one's own, to like one's own company 2 (= désert) solitude ◆ **les ~s glacées du Grand Nord** *(littér)* the icy solitudes *ou* wastes of the far North *(littér)*

solive /sɔliv/ NF joist

sollicitation /sɔlisitasjɔ̃/ NF 1 (= démarche) entreaty, appeal ◆ **céder/répondre aux ~s de qn** to yield/respond to sb's entreaties 2 *(littér : gén pl = tentation)* solicitation *(littér)*, enticement 3 *(Tech = impulsion)* prompting ◆ **l'engin répondait aux moindres ~s de son pilote** the craft responded to the slightest touch (from the pilot)

solliciter /sɔlisite/ ► conjug 1 ◄ VT 1 *(frm = demander) [+ poste, explication]* to seek; *[+ faveur, audience]* to seek, to solicit *(frm)* (de qn from sb) 2 *(frm = faire appel à) [+ personne]* to appeal to ◆ **~ qn de faire qch** to appeal to sb *ou* request sb to do sth ◆ **je l'ai déjà sollicité à plusieurs reprises à ce sujet** I have already appealed to him *ou* approached him on several occasions over this matter ◆ **il est très sollicité** he's very much in demand 3 (= agir sur) *[+ curiosité, sens de qn]* to appeal to; *[+ attention]* to attract, to solicit ◆ **les attractions qui sollicitent le touriste** the attractions that are there to tempt *ou* entice the tourist ◆ **le moteur répondait immédiatement lorsque le pilote le sollicitait** the engine responded immediately to the pilot's touch ◆ **~ un cheval** to urge a horse on

solliciteur, -euse /sɔlisitœʀ, øz/ NM,F supplicant NM *(Can)* ◆ **~ général** Solicitor General

sollicitude /sɔlisityd/ NF concern (NonC), solicitude *(frm)* ◆ **demander/dire qch avec ~** to ask/say sth solicitously *ou* with concern ◆ **être** *ou* **se montrer plein de ~ envers qn** to be very attentive *ou* solicitous *(frm)* to(wards) sb ◆ **toutes leurs ~s finissaient par nous agacer** we found their constant concern (for our welfare) *ou* their solicitude *(frm)* annoying in the end

solo /solo/ (pl **solos** *ou* **soli** /soli/) ADJ INV, NM solo ◆ **~ de violon** violin solo ◆ **violon/flûte ~** solo violin/flute ◆ **(spectacle) ~** one-man (*ou* one-woman) show ◆ **carrière ~** solo career
◆ **en solo** ◆ **jouer/chanter en ~** to play/sing solo ◆ **l'escalade en ~** solo climbing ◆ **travailler en ~** to work on one's own ◆ **il a décidé d'agir en ~** he decided to go it alone*

sol-sol /sɔlsɔl/ ADJ INV ground-to-ground

solstice /sɔlstis/ NM solstice ◆ **~ d'hiver/d'été** winter/summer solstice

solubiliser /sɔlybilize/ ► conjug 1 ◄ VT to make soluble

solubilité /sɔlybilite/ NF solubility

soluble /sɔlybl/ ADJ 1 *[substance]* soluble ◆ **ce n'est pas ~ dans l'eau** it isn't soluble in water, it isn't water soluble ◆ **leur électorat n'est pas ~ dans la droite modérée** their voters cannot be absorbed into the moderate right; → **café** 2 *[problème]* soluble, solvable ◆ **c'est aisément/difficilement ~** it's easy/hard to solve

soluté /sɔlyte/ NM *(Chim, Pharm)* solution

solution /sɔlysjɔ̃/ NF 1 *[de problème, énigme, équation]* (= action) solution, solving (de of); (= résultat) solution, answer (de to) 2 *[de difficulté, situation]* (= issue) solution, answer (de to); (= moyens employés) solution (de to); ◆ **c'est une ~ de facilité** it's the easy way out ◆ **ce n'est pas une ~ à la crise qu'ils traversent** that's no way to resolve the crisis they're in ◆ **ce n'est pas une ~ !** that won't solve anything! ◆ **hâter la ~ d'une crise** to hasten the resolution *ou* settling of a crisis 3 *(Chim = action, mélange)* solution ◆ **en ~** in solution
COMP **solution de continuité** *(frm)* solution of continuity *(frm)*
la solution finale *(Hist Pol)* the Final Solution

solutionner /sɔlysjɔne/ ► conjug 1 ◄ VT to solve

solvabilisation /sɔlvabilizasjɔ̃/ NF *(Écon)* ◆ **pour faciliter la ~ de la demande** to stimulate demand

solvabiliser /sɔlvabilize/ ► conjug 1 ◄ VT 1 *[+ foyers, personne]* to give disposable income to 2 *[+ demande]* to stimulate

solvabilité /sɔlvabilite/ NF solvency, creditworthiness

solvable /sɔlvabl/ ADJ solvent, creditworthy

> ⚠ **solvable** ne se traduit pas par le mot anglais **solvable**, qui a le sens de 'soluble'.

solvant /sɔlvɑ̃/ NM *(Chim)* solvent ◆ **prise de ~s** (= toxicomanie) solvent abuse

soma /sɔma/ NM soma

somali /sɔmali/ NM (= langue) Somali NMPL **Somalis** Somalis

Somalie /sɔmali/ NF (= région) Somaliland; (= État) Somalia

somalien, -ienne /sɔmaljɛ̃, jɛn/ ADJ Somalian NM,F **Somalien(ne)** Somalian

somatique /sɔmatik/ ADJ *(Bio, Psych)* somatic

somatisation /sɔmatizasjɔ̃/ NF somatization

somatiser /sɔmatize/ ► conjug 1 ◄ VT to somatize ◆ **il a tendance à ~** he tends to have psychosomatic problems

sombre /sɔ̃bʀ/ ADJ 1 (= obscur, foncé) *[ciel, nuit, pièce]* dark ◆ **il fait déjà ~** it's already dark ◆ **bleu/vert ~** dark blue/green ◆ **de ~s abîmes** *(littér)* dark abysses ◆ **le ~ empire, les ~s rivages** *(Myth)* the underworld, the nether world; → **coupe²**
2 (= mélancolique) sombre *(Brit)*, somber *(US)*, gloomy, dismal; (= sinistre, funeste) *[période]* dark ◆ **d'un air ~** sombrely *(Brit)*, somberly *(US)*, gloomily ◆ **il avait le visage ~** he looked gloomy *ou* sombre ◆ **de ~s pensées** sombre *ou* gloomy *ou* dark thoughts ◆ **un ~ avenir** a dark *ou* gloomy *ou* dismal future ◆ **les moments** *ou* **heures ~s de notre histoire** the dark moments in our history
3 (*: valeur intensive) ◆ **~ idiot/brute** absolute idiot/brute ◆ **une ~ histoire de meurtre** a dark tale of murder ◆ **ils se sont disputés pour une ~ histoire d'argent** they argued over a sordid financial matter
4 *(Phon) [voyelle]* dark

sombrement /sɔ̃bʀ(ə)mɑ̃/ ADV *[dire]* sombrely *(Brit)*, somberly *(US)*, gloomily

sombrer /sɔ̃bʀe/ ► conjug 1 ◄ VI *[bateau]* to sink, to go down, to founder; *[empire]* to founder; *[fortune]* to be swallowed up; *[entreprise]* to collapse ◆ **sa raison a sombré** he has lost his reason, his mind has gone ◆ **~ dans** *[+ désespoir, sommeil, oubli]* to sink into; *[+ crise, anarchie, misère]* to slide into, to sink into; *[+ coma]* to sink into, to slip into ◆ **elle a sombré dans l'alcool** she sank into alcoholism ◆ **ils ont lentement sombré dans la délinquance** they drifted into crime ◆ **~ dans le ridicule** to become ridiculous

sombrero /sɔ̃bʀeʀo/ NM sombrero

sommaire /sɔmɛʀ/ ADJ 1 (= court) *[exposé, explication]* basic, summary *(épith)*, brief; *[réponse]* brief, summary *(épith)*; (= expéditif) *[justice, procédure, exécution]* summary *(épith)* 2 (= rudimentaire, superficiel) *[connaissances, éducation]* basic; *[examen]* brief, cursory, perfunctory; *[ana-*

lyse, description] brief, cursory; *[instruction, réparation, repas]* basic; *[décoration]* minimal NM (= *exposé*) summary; (= *résumé de chapitre*) summary, argument; *[de revue]* (table of) contents ◆ **au ~ du numéro spécial** appearing in *ou* featured in the special issue ◆ **au ~ de notre émission ce soir ...** in our programme tonight ...

sommairement /sɔmɛʀmɑ̃/ ADV 1 *[exposer, juger, exécuter]* summarily ◆ **il me l'a expliqué assez ~** he gave me a fairly basic explanation of it 2 (= *rudimentairement*) *[réparer]* superficially; *[meubler]* basically

sommation[1] /sɔmasjɔ̃/ NF *(Jur)* summons *(sg)*; *(frm = injonction)* demand; *(avant de faire feu)* warning ◆ **recevoir ~ de payer une dette** *(Jur)* to be served notice to pay a debt ◆ **faire les ~s d'usage** *(Mil, Police)* to give the standard *ou* customary warnings ◆ **tirer sans ~** to shoot without warning

sommation[2] /sɔmasjɔ̃/ NF *(Math, Physiol)* summation

somme[1] /sɔm/ NF → **bête**

somme[2] /sɔm/ NM (= *sieste*) nap, snooze ◆ **faire un petit ~** to have a (short) nap *ou* a (little) snooze *ou* forty winks *

somme[3] /sɔm/ GRAMMAIRE ACTIVE 47.5 NF 1 *(Math)* sum; (= *quantité*) amount ◆ **~ algébrique** algebraic sum ◆ **la ~ totale** the grand total, the sum total ◆ **faire la ~ de** to add up ◆ **la ~ des dégâts est considérable** the (total) amount of damage *ou* the total damage is considerable ◆ **une ~ de travail énorme** an enormous amount of work

2 ◆ **~ (d'argent)** sum *ou* amount (of money) ◆ **dépenser des ~s folles** * to spend vast amounts *ou* sums of money ◆ **c'est une ~ !** *(intensif)* it's quite a sum! ◆ **payer/toucher/atteindre une ~ de 150 €** to pay/get/fetch €150 ◆ **pour la coquette ~ de 2 millions d'euros** for the tidy sum of 2 million euros

3 (= *ouvrage de synthèse*) comprehensive survey ◆ **une ~ littéraire/scientifique** a comprehensive survey of literature/of science

4 *(locutions)*

◆ **en somme** (= *tout bien considéré*) all in all; (= *bref*) in short ◆ **en ~, il ne s'agit que d'un incident sans importance** in fact, it's only an incident of minor importance ◆ **en ~, vous n'en voulez plus ?** in short, you don't want any more?

◆ **somme toute** when all is said and done

sommeil /sɔmɛj/ NM 1 (= *fait de dormir*) sleep ◆ **huit heures de ~** eight hours' sleep ◆ **avoir le ~ léger/profond** to be a light/heavy sleeper, to sleep lightly/deeply ◆ **avoir un bon ~** to be a sound sleeper ◆ **dormir d'un ~ agité** to sleep fitfully ◆ **un ~ profond** *ou* **de plomb** a heavy *ou* deep sleep ◆ **le ~ paradoxal** REM sleep ◆ **premier ~** first hours of sleep ◆ **nuit sans ~** sleepless night ◆ **être en plein ~** to be fast asleep ◆ **la sonnerie du téléphone l'a tirée de son ~** she was woken (up) by the phone ringing ◆ **il en a perdu le ~** he lost sleep over it ◆ **le ~ éternel, le dernier ~** *(littér)* eternal rest ◆ **le ~ des morts** *(littér)* the sleep of the dead ◆ **avoir ~** to be *ou* feel sleepy ◆ **tomber de ~** to be asleep on one's feet, to be ready *ou* fit to drop * ◆ **chercher le ~** to try to sleep ◆ **il ne pouvait pas trouver le ~** he couldn't get to sleep ◆ **un ~ agréable l'envahissait** he was beginning to feel pleasantly sleepy; → **cure**[1], **dormir, maladie**

2 (= *inactivité*) **le ~ de la nature** nature's sleep *(littér)*, the dormant state of nature ◆ **laisser une affaire en ~** to leave a matter (lying) dormant, to leave a matter in abeyance ◆ **le ~ de la petite ville pendant l'hiver** the sleepiness of the little town during winter

sommeiller /sɔmeje/ ► conjug 1 ◄ VI *[personne]* to doze; *[qualité, défaut, nature, argent]* to lie dormant ◆ **l'artiste qui sommeillait en lui** the dormant artist within him; → **cochon**

sommelier /sɔməlje/ NM wine waiter

sommelière /sɔməljɛʀ/ NF (= *caviste*) wine waitress; *(Helv = serveuse)* waitress

sommer[1] /sɔme/ ► conjug 1 ◄ VT *(frm = enjoindre)* ◆ **~ qn de faire qch** to command *ou* enjoin sb to do sth *(frm)* ◆ **~ qn de** *ou* **à comparaître** *(Jur)* to summon sb to appear

sommer[2] /sɔme/ ► conjug 1 ◄ VT (= *additionner*) to add

sommet /sɔmɛ/ NM 1 (= *point culminant*) *[de montagne]* summit, top; *[de tour, arbre, toit, pente, hiérarchie]* top; *[de vague]* crest; *[de crâne]* crown, vertex *(SPÉC)*; *[d'angle]* vertex; *[de solide, figure, parabole]* vertex, apex ◆ **présentation du ~** *(Méd)* vertex presentation ◆ **au ~ de l'échelle sociale** at the top of the social ladder ◆ **les ~s de la gloire/des honneurs** the summits *ou* heights of fame/of honour ◆ **redescendons de ces ~s** *(littér, hum)* let us climb down from these lofty heights *(littér) (hum)* 2 (= *cime, montagne*) summit, mountain top ◆ **l'air pur des ~s** the pure air of the summits *ou* the mountain tops 3 *(Pol)* summit ◆ **au ~** *[réunion, discussions]* summit *(épith)*; → **conférence**

sommier /sɔmje/ NM 1 *[de lit]* **~ (à ressorts), ~ tapissier** *(s'encastrant dans le lit, fixé au lit)* springing *(NonC) (Brit)*, springs *(of bedstead)*; *(avec pieds)* bed base, box springs *(US)* ◆ **~ (métallique)** mesh-springing *(Brit)*, mesh-sprung bed base, mesh springs *(US)* ◆ **~ à lattes** slatted bed base ◆ **~ extra-plat** metal-framed bed base 2 *(Tech) [de voûte]* impost, springer; *[de clocher]* stock; *[de porte, fenêtre]* transom; *[de grille]* lower crossbar; *[d'orgue]* windchest 3 (= *registre*) ledger

sommité /sɔ(m)mite/ NF 1 (= *personne*) prominent person, leading light *(de* in); ◆ **les ~s du monde médical** leading medical experts 2 *(Bot)* head

somnambule /sɔmnɑ̃byl/ NMF sleepwalker, somnambulist *(SPÉC)* ◆ **marcher/agir comme un ~** to walk/act like a sleepwalker *ou* as if in a trance ADJ ◆ **être ~** to be a sleepwalker, to sleepwalk

somnambulisme /sɔmnɑ̃bylism/ NM sleepwalking, somnambulism *(SPÉC)*

somnifère /sɔmnifɛʀ/ NM sleeping drug, soporific; (= *pilule*) sleeping pill, sleeping tablet ADJ somniferous *(frm)*, sleepinducing, soporific

somnolence /sɔmnɔlɑ̃s/ NF *[de personne]* sleepiness *(NonC)*, drowsiness *(NonC)*, somnolence *(NonC) (frm)*; *[de marché, économie]* sluggishness ◆ **être dans un état de ~** to be in a drowsy state ◆ **"risques de somnolence attachés à ce médicament"** "this medicine can cause drowsiness"

somnolent, e /sɔmnɔlɑ̃, ɑ̃t/ ADJ *[personne]* sleepy, drowsy, somnolent *(frm)*; *[vie, province]* sleepy; *[faculté]* dormant, inert

somnoler /sɔmnɔle/ ► conjug 1 ◄ VI *[personne]* to doze; *[ville]* to be sleepy; *[économie, marché]* to be sluggish

somptuaire /sɔ̃ptɥɛʀ/ ADJ 1 *[loi, réforme]* sumptuary 2 *[projet, dépenses]* extravagant

somptueusement /sɔ̃ptɥøzmɑ̃/ ADV *[décorer, meubler, illustrer]* lavishly ◆ **il nous a reçus ~** he received us royally

somptueux, -euse /sɔ̃ptɥø, øz/ ADJ *[résidence, palais, décor, spectacle, fête]* magnificent, grand; *[habit, couleurs, paysage]* magnificent; *[train de vie, illustration, cadeau]* lavish; *[repas, festin]* lavish, sumptuous ◆ **tu es somptueuse ce soir** you look magnificent tonight

> ⚠ **somptueux** se traduit rarement par le mot anglais **sumptuous**, qui est d'un registre plus soutenu.

somptuosité /sɔ̃ptɥozite/ NF *[d'habit, résidence]* sumptuousness, magnificence; *[de train de vie]* lavishness; *[de cadeau]* handsomeness, sumptuousness; *[de repas, festin]* sumptuousness, lavishness ◆ **impressionné par la ~ des images** impressed by the sumptuous images

son[1] /sɔ̃/, **sa** /sa/ (pl **ses** /se/) ADJ POSS 1 *(homme)* his; *(emphatique)* his own; *(femme)* her; *(emphatique)* her own; *(nation)* its, her; *(emphatique)* its own, her own ◆ **Son Altesse Royale** *(prince)* His Royal Highness; *(princesse)* Her Royal Highness ◆ **Sa Majesté** *(roi)* His Majesty; *(reine)* Her Majesty ◆ **Sa Sainteté le pape** His Holiness the Pope ◆ **ce n'est pas ~ genre** he *(ou* she) is not that sort, it's not like him *(ou* her) ◆ **quand s'est passé ~ accident ?** when did he have his accident? ◆ **~ père et sa mère, ses père et mère** his *(ou* her) father and (his *ou* her) mother ◆ **~ jardin à lui/à elle est une vraie jungle** *(emphatique)* his *ou* his own/her *ou* her own garden is a real jungle ◆ **ses date et lieu de naissance** his *(ou* her) date and place of birth ◆ **à sa vue, elle poussa un cri** she screamed at the sight of him *(ou* her) ◆ **un de ses amis** one of his *(ou* her) friends, a friend of his *(ou* hers) ◆ **~ idiote de sœur** * that stupid sister of his *(ou* hers)

2 *[d'objet, abstraction]* its ◆ **l'hôtel est réputé pour sa cuisine** the hotel is famous for its food ◆ **pour comprendre ce crime il faut chercher ~ mobile** to understand this crime we must try to find the motive ◆ **ça a ~ importance** it has its *ou* a certain importance

3 *(à valeur d'indéfini)* one's; *(après chacun, personne)* his, her ◆ **faire ses études** to study ◆ **on ne connaît pas ~ bonheur** one never knows how fortunate one is, you never know how fortunate you are ◆ **être satisfait de sa situation** to be satisfied with one's situation ◆ **chacun selon ses possibilités** each according to his (own) capabilities ◆ **personne ne sait comment finira sa vie** no-one knows how his *ou* their life will end ◆ **quelqu'un a-t-il oublié sa veste ?** has someone left their jacket?

4 *(* : valeur affective, ironique, intensive)* **il doit (bien) gagner ~ million par an** he must be (easily) earning a million a year ◆ **avoir ~ samedi/dimanche** to have (one's) Saturday(s)/Sunday(s) off ◆ **il a passé tout ~ dimanche à travailler** he spent the whole of *ou* all Sunday working ◆ **~ M. Dupont ne me plaît pas du tout** I don't care for his *(ou* her) Mr Dupont at all ◆ **avoir ses petites manies** to have one's funny little ways ◆ **elle a ses jours !** she has her (good and bad) days! ◆ **il a sa crise de foie** he is having one of his bilious attacks ◆ **cet enfant ne ferme jamais ses portes** that child never shuts the door behind him ◆ **alors, on est content de revoir ses camarades ?** so, are you happy to see your friends again?; → **sentir**

son[2] /sɔ̃/ NM 1 (= *bruit*) sound ◆ **~ articulé/inarticulé** articulate/inarticulate sound ◆ **le timbre et la hauteur du ~ d'une cloche/d'un tambour/d'un avertisseur** the tone and pitch of (the sound of) a bell/of a drum/of an alarm ◆ **réveillé par le ~ des cloches/tambours/klaxons** woken by the sound of bells/drums/horns, woken by the ringing of bells/the beat of drums/the blare of horns ◆ **défiler au ~ d'une fanfare** to march past to the sound of a band ◆ **elle dansait au ~ de l'accordéon** she was dancing to the accordion ◆ **elle tressaillit au ~ de sa voix** she started at the sound of his voice ◆ **proclamer qch à ~ de trompe** to proclaim sth from the rooftops *ou* the housetops ◆ **n'entendre qu'un/entendre un autre ~ de cloche** *(fig)* to hear only one/another side of the story ◆ **j'aimerais bien entendre un autre ~ de cloche** I'd like to have a second opinion ◆ **même ~ de cloche chez les patrons/à l'ambassade** the bosses are/the embassy is telling the same story ◆ **c'est un autre**

~ **de cloche** that's quite another story ◆ **qui n'entend qu'une cloche n'entend qu'un** ~ *(Prov)* you should always get both sides of the story
[2] *(Ciné, Radio, TV)* sound ◆ **baisser le** ~ to turn down the sound *ou* volume ◆ **équipe/ingénieur du** ~ sound team/engineer ◆ **synchroniser le** ~ **et l'image** to synchronize the sound and the picture ◆ **(spectacle)** ~ **et lumière** son et lumière (show); → **numérique, stéréo**

son³ /sɔ̃/ **NM** *(= substance)* bran ◆ **farine de** ~ bran flour; → **pain, poupée, tache**

sonar /sɔnaʀ/ **NM** sonar

sonate /sɔnat/ **NF** sonata ◆ ~**s pour piano** sonatas for piano, piano sonatas

sonatine /sɔnatin/ **NF** sonatina

sondage /sɔ̃daʒ/ **NM** [1] *(= enquête) (succincte)* poll; *(approfondie)* survey ◆ ~ **d'opinion** opinion poll ◆ ~ **par téléphone** telephone poll ◆ **il remonte/baisse dans les** ~**s** he is going up again/down in the polls ◆ **faire un** ~ to take a poll, to conduct a survey *(auprès de* among); ◆ **procéder par** ~ to do a spot check; → **institut** [2] *(Tech = forage)* boring, drilling; *(Météo, Naut)* sounding; *(Méd)* probing *(NonC)*, probe; *(pour évacuer)* catheterization ◆ **puits de** ~ borehole

sonde /sɔ̃d/ **NF** [1] *(Naut) (= instrument)* lead line, sounding line; *(gén pl = relevé)* soundings ◆ **naviguer à la** ~ to navigate by soundings ◆ **jeter une** ~ to cast the lead; → **île** [2] *(Tech : de forage)* borer, drill [3] *(Méd)* probe; *(à canal central)* catheter; *(d'alimentation)* feeding tube ◆ **mettre une** ~ **à qn** to put a catheter in sb ◆ **alimenter un malade avec une** ~ to feed a patient through a tube [4] *(= aérostat)* sonde ◆ ~ **aérienne** sounding balloon ◆ ~ **atmosphérique** sonde ◆ ~ **moléculaire/spatiale** molecular/space probe [5] *(Douane : pour fouiller)* probe; *(Comm : pour prélever)* taster; *(à avalanche)* pole *(for locating victims)* ◆ ~ **à fromage** cheese taster

sondé, e /sɔ̃de/ **NM,F** *person taking part in an opinion poll* ◆ **la majorité des** ~**s était pour** the majority of those polled were in favour of the idea

sonder /sɔ̃de/ ▸ conjug 1 ◂ **VT** [1] *(Naut)* to sound; *(Tech)* [+ terrain] to bore, to drill; [+ bagages] to probe, to search (with a probe); [+ avalanche] to probe; *(Méd)* [+ plaie] to probe; [+ organe, malade] to catheterize ◆ ~ **l'atmosphère** to make soundings in the atmosphere ◆ **il sonda l'abîme du regard** *(littér)* his eyes probed the depths of the abyss [2] [+ personne] *(gén)* to sound out; *(par sondage d'opinion)* to poll; [+ conscience, avenir] to sound out, to probe ◆ **je l'ai sondé sur ses intentions** I sounded him out, I asked him what his intentions were ◆ ~ **les esprits** to sound out opinion ◆ ~ **l'opinion** to make a survey of (public) opinion; → **terrain**

sondeur, -euse /sɔ̃dœʀ, øz/ **NM** *(Tech)* sounder **NM,F** *[de sondage d'opinion]* pollster

songe /sɔ̃ʒ/ **NM** *(littér)* dream ◆ **en** ~ in a dream ◆ **faire un** ~ to have a dream ◆ ~, **mensonge** *(Prov)* dreams are just illusions

songe-creux † /sɔ̃ʒkʀø/ **NM INV** *(littér)* visionary

songer /sɔ̃ʒe/ GRAMMAIRE ACTIVE 28.1, 35.2 ▸ conjug 3 ◂
VI *(littér = rêver)* to dream
VT ◆ ~ **que ...** to reflect *ou* consider that ... ◆ **ils pourraient refuser, songeait-il** they could refuse, he reflected *ou* mused ◆ **songez que cela peut présenter de grands dangers** remember *ou* you must be aware that it can be very dangerous ◆ **il n'avait jamais songé qu'ils puissent réussir** he had never imagined they might be successful ◆ **cela me fait** ~ **que je voulais lui téléphoner** that reminds me – I wanted to phone him ◆ **songez donc !** just imagine! *ou* think!
VT INDIR songer à *(= considérer)* to consider, to think about ◆ ~ **à se marier** *ou* **au mariage** to contemplate marriage, to think of getting married ◆ **j'y ai sérieusement songé** I gave it some serious thought ◆ **elle songe sérieusement à s'expatrier** she's seriously thinking about *ou* considering going to live abroad ◆ **songez-y** think it over, give it some thought ◆ **il ne songe qu'à son avancement** all he thinks about is his own advancement ◆ **quand on songe à tout ce gaspillage** when you think of all this waste ◆ **il ne faut pas y** ~, **inutile d'y** ~ it's no use (even) thinking about it ◆ **vous n'y songez pas !** you must be joking!, you're not serious! ◆ **vous me faites** ~ **à mon frère** you remind me of my brother; → **mal² 5**

songerie /sɔ̃ʒʀi/ **NF** *(littér)* reverie

songeur, -euse /sɔ̃ʒœʀ, øz/ **ADJ** pensive ◆ **tu as l'air bien songeuse** you look very pensive ◆ **cela me laisse** ~ I just don't know what to think **NM,F** dreamer

sonique /sɔnik/ **ADJ** *[vitesse]* sonic ◆ **barrière** ~ sound barrier

sonnaille /sɔnɑj/ **NF** *(= cloche)* bell; *(= bruit)* ringing *(NonC)*

sonnant, e /sɔnɑ̃, ɑ̃t/ **ADJ** [1] *(= précis)* **à 4 heures** ~**es** on the stroke of 4, at 4 (o'clock) sharp [2] *[horloge]* chiming, striking [3] *[voix]* resonant; → **espèce**

sonné, e /sɔne/ (ptp de **sonner**) **ADJ** [1] *(= annoncé)* **il est midi** ~ it's past *ou* gone *(Brit)* twelve ◆ **avoir trente ans bien** ~**s*** *(= révolu)* to be on the wrong side of thirty* [2] *(* = fou)* cracked*, off one's rocker* *(attrib)* [3] *(* = assommé)* groggy

sonner /sɔne/ GRAMMAIRE ACTIVE 54.5 ▸ conjug 1 ◂
VT [1] [+ cloche] to ring; [+ tocsin, glas] to sound, to toll; [+ clairon] to sound ◆ ~ **trois coups à la porte** to ring three times at the door ◆ **se faire** ~ **les cloches*** to get a good telling-off* *ou* ticking-off* *(Brit)* ◆ ~ **les cloches à qn*** to give sb a roasting* *ou* a telling-off*
[2] *(= annoncer)* [+ messe, matines] to ring the bell for; [+ réveil, rassemblement, retraite] to sound ◆ ~ **l'alarme** to sound the alarm ◆ ~ **la charge** *(Mil)* to sound the charge; *(fig)* to declare war *(contre* on); ◆ ~ **l'heure** to strike the hour ◆ **la pendule sonnait 3 heures** the clock was striking 3 (o'clock)
[3] *(= appeler)* [+ portier, infirmière] to ring for ◆ **on ne t'a pas sonné !*** nobody asked you!
[4] *(* = étourdir) [chute, grippe]* to knock out; [+ nouvelle] to stagger*, to take aback ◆ **la nouvelle l'a un peu sonné** he was rather taken aback by the news
VI [1] *[cloches, téléphone]* to ring; *[réveil]* to go off; *[clairon]* to sound; *[tocsin, glas]* to sound, to toll ◆ **elle a mis le réveil à** ~ **pour** *ou* **à 7 heures** she set the alarm for 7 o'clock ◆ **la cloche a sonné** *(Scol)* the bell has gone *ou* rung ◆ ~ **à toute volée** to peal (out) ◆ **les oreilles lui sonnent** his ears are ringing
[2] *(son métallique) [marteau]* to ring; *[clés, monnaie]* to jangle, to jingle ◆ ~ **clair** to give a clear ring ◆ ~ **creux** *(lit)* to sound hollow; *[discours]* to have a hollow ring, to ring hollow ◆ ~ **faux** *(lit)* to sound out of tune; *[rire, paroles]* to ring *ou* sound false ◆ ~ **juste** *(lit)* to sound in tune; *[déclaration]* to ring true ◆ ~ **bien/mal** *(fig)* to sound good/bad ◆ **ce prénom sonne bien à l'oreille** that name has a nice ring to it, it's a nice-sounding name ◆ **l'argent sonna sur le comptoir** the money clattered onto the counter
[3] *(= être annoncé) [midi, minuit]* to strike ◆ **3 heures venaient de** ~ it had just struck 3 o'clock, 3 o'clock had just struck ◆ **la récréation a sonné** the bell has gone for break ◆ **la messe sonne** the bells are ringing *ou* going for mass; → **heure**
[4] *(= actionner une sonnette)* to ring ◆ **on a sonné** the bell has just gone, I just heard the bell, somebody just rang (the bell) ◆ ~ **chez qn** to ring at sb's door, to ring sb's doorbell ◆ **"sonner avant d'entrer"** "please ring before you enter"
[5] ◆ **faire** ~ *[+ nom, mot]* to say in a resonant voice
VT INDIR sonner de *[+ clairon, cor]* to sound

sonnerie /sɔnʀi/ **NF** [1] *(= son) [de sonnette, cloches]* ringing; *[de téléphone mobile]* ringtone ◆ **la** ~ **du clairon** the bugle call, the sound of the bugle ◆ **j'ai entendu la** ~ **du téléphone** I heard the telephone ringing ◆ **la** ~ **du téléphone l'a réveillé** he was woken by the telephone (ringing) ◆ **elle sursautait à chaque** ~ **du téléphone** she jumped every time the phone rang ◆ ~ **d'alarme** alarm bell ◆ ~ **polyphonique** polyphonic ringtone [2] *(Mil = air)* call ◆ **la** ~ **du réveil** (the sounding of) reveille ◆ **la** ~ **aux morts** the last post [3] *(= mécanisme) [de réveil]* alarm (mechanism), bell; *[de pendule]* chimes, chiming *ou* striking mechanism; *(= sonnette)* bell ◆ ~ **électrique/téléphonique** electric/telephone bell

sonnet /sɔnɛ/ **NM** sonnet

sonnette /sɔnɛt/ **NF** [1] *(électrique, de porte)* bell; *(= clochette)* (hand) bell ◆ **coup de** ~ ring ◆ **je n'ai pas entendu le coup de** ~ I didn't hear the bell (ring) ◆ ~ **de nuit** night bell ◆ ~ **d'alarme** alarm bell ◆ **tirer la** ~ **d'alarme** *(fig)* to set off *ou* sound the alarm (bell) ◆ **tirer les** ~**s** *(jeu d'enfants)* to ring doorbells (and run away); *(fig = démarcher)* to go knocking on doors; → **serpent** [2] *(Tech) (= engin)* pile driver

sonneur /sɔnœʀ/ **NM** [1] *[de cloches]* bell ringer [2] *(Tech) (= ouvrier)* pile driver operator

sono* /sɔno/ **NF** (abrév de **sonorisation**) *[de salle de conférences]* PA (system); *[de discothèque]* sound system ◆ **la** ~ **est trop forte** the sound's too loud

sonore /sɔnɔʀ/ **ADJ** [1] *[objet, surface en métal]* resonant; *[voix]* ringing *(épith)*, sonorous, resonant; *[rire]* ringing *(épith)*, resounding *(épith)*; *[baiser, gifle]* resounding *(épith)* [2] *[salle]* resonant; *[voûte]* echoing [3] *(péj) [paroles, mots]* high-sounding, sonorous [4] *(Acoustique) [niveau, onde, vibrations]* sound *(épith)* ◆ **fond** ~ *(= bruits)* background noise; *(= musique)* background music [5] *(Ciné) [film, effets]* sound *(épith)*; → **bande¹** [6] *(Ling)* voiced **NF** *(Ling)* voiced consonant

sonorisation /sɔnɔʀizasjɔ̃/ **NF** [1] *(Ciné)* adding the soundtrack *(de* to) dubbing *(de* of) [2] *(= action) [de salle de conférences]* fitting with a public address system; *[de discothèque]* fitting with a sound system; *(= équipement) [de salle de conférences]* public address system, PA (system); *[de discothèque]* sound system [3] *(Phon)* voicing

sonoriser /sɔnɔʀize/ ▸ conjug 1 ◂ **VT** [1] *[+ film]* to add the soundtrack to, to dub; *[+ salle de conférences]* to fit with a public address system *ou* a PA (system) [2] *(Phon)* to voice

sonorité /sɔnɔʀite/ **NF** [1] *(= timbre, son) [de radio, instrument de musique]* tone; *[de voix]* sonority, tone ◆ ~**s** *[de voix, instrument]* tones [2] *(Ling)* voicing [3] *(= résonance) [d'air]* sonority, resonance; *[de salle]* acoustics *(sg)*; *[de cirque rocheux, grotte]* resonance

sonothèque /sɔnɔtɛk/ **NF** sound (effects) library

sonotone ® /sɔnɔtɔn/ **NM** hearing aid

sophisme /sɔfism/ **NM** sophism

sophiste /sɔfist/ **NMF** sophist

sophistication /sɔfistikasjɔ̃/ **NF** sophistication; († *= altération)* adulteration

sophistique /sɔfistik/ ADJ sophistic NF sophistry

sophistiqué, e /sɔfistike/ (ptp de **sophistiquer**) ADJ *(gén)* sophisticated; († = *altéré*) adulterated

sophistiquer /sɔfistike/ ▸ conjug 1 ◂ VT († = *raffiner*) to make (more) sophisticated; († = *altérer*) to adulterate VPR **se sophistiquer** to become (more) sophisticated

Sophocle /sɔfɔkl/ NM Sophocles

sophrologie /sɔfʀɔlɔʒi/ NF relaxation therapy

sophrologue /sɔfʀɔlɔg/ NMF relaxation therapist

soporifique /sɔpɔʀifik/ ADJ *(lit)* soporific, sleep-inducing; *(péj)* soporific NM sleeping drug, soporific

soprane /sɔpʀan/ NMF ⇒ **soprano nmf**

sopraniste /sɔpʀanist/ NM (male) soprano

soprano /sɔpʀano/ (pl **sopranos** *ou* **soprani** /sɔpʀani/) ADJ ◆ **saxophone** ~ soprano (saxophone) NM (= *voix*) soprano (voice); (= *voix d'enfant*) soprano, treble NMF (= *personne*) soprano ◆ ~ **dramatique/lyrique** dramatic/lyric soprano

sorbe /sɔʀb/ NF sorb (apple)

sorbet /sɔʀbɛ/ NM sorbet, water ice *(Brit)*, sherbet *(US)* ◆ ~ **au citron/à l'orange** lemon/orange sorbet

sorbetière /sɔʀbətjɛʀ/ NF ice cream maker

sorbier /sɔʀbje/ NM service tree, sorb ◆ ~ **des oiseleurs** European mountain ash, rowan tree

sorbitol /sɔʀbitɔl/ NM sorbitol

sorbonnard, e /sɔʀbɔnaʀ, aʀd/ *(péj)* ADJ pedantic NM,F *student or teacher at the Sorbonne*

sorcellerie /sɔʀsɛlʀi/ NF witchcraft, sorcery ◆ **c'est de la** ~ **!** it's magic! ◆ **procès en** ~ *(fig)* witch hunt

sorcier /sɔʀsje/ NM *(lit)* sorcerer ◆ **il ne faut pas être** ~ **pour ...** *(fig)* you don't have to be a wizard to ...; → **apprenti** ADJ ◆ **ce n'est pas** ~ **!*** it's dead easy! *

sorcière /sɔʀsjɛʀ/ NF witch, sorceress ◆ **vieille** ~ **!** *(péj)* old witch! *ou* hag!; → **chasse¹**

sordide /sɔʀdid/ ADJ 1 *[bar, hôtel, quartier, banlieue]* seedy, squalid ◆ **des conditions de vie** ~**s** squalid living conditions 2 *[réalité, histoire, crime, querelle, affaire, détails]* sordid; *[action, mentalité, avarice, égoïsme]* base NM ◆ **le** ~ **de la situation** the sordidness of the situation

sordidement /sɔʀdidmɑ̃/ ADV *[vivre]* in squalor; *[agir]* basely ◆ **il a fini** ~ he came to a squalid *ou* sordid end

sorgho /sɔʀgo/ NM sorghum

Sorlingues /sɔʀlɛ̃g/ NFPL ◆ **les (îles)** ~ the Scilly Isles, the Isles of Scilly, the Scillies

sornettes † /sɔʀnɛt/ NFPL twaddle, balderdash ◆ ~ **!** fiddlesticks!

sort /sɔʀ/ NM 1 (= *condition*) lot ◆ **être content** *ou* **satisfait de son** ~ to be happy with one's lot (in life) ◆ **améliorer le** ~ **des pauvres/handicapés** to improve the lot of the poor/the handicapped ◆ **envier le** ~ **de qn** to envy sb's lot

2 (= *destinée*) fate ◆ **le** ~ **qui l'attend** the fate that awaits him ◆ **abandonner qn à son triste** ~ *(hum)* to abandon sb to his sad fate ◆ **sa proposition a eu** *ou* **subi le même** ~ **que les précédentes** his proposal met with the same fate as the previous ones ◆ **le** ~ **décidera** fate will decide ◆ **pour essayer de conjurer le (mauvais)** ~ to try to ward off fate ◆ **c'est un coup du** ~ it's a stroke of fate ◆ **faire un** ~ **à** (= *mettre en valeur*) to stress, to emphasize; (* = *se débarrasser de*) to get rid of, to get shot of* *(Brit)*; *[+ plat, bouteille]* to polish off*; → **caprice, ironie**

3 (= *hasard*) fate ◆ **le** ~ **est tombé sur lui** he was chosen by fate, it fell to him ◆ **le** ~ **en est jeté** the die is cast ◆ **tirer au** ~ to draw lots ◆ **tirer qch au** ~ to draw lots for sth; → **tirage**

4 *(Sorcellerie)* spell; (= *malédiction*) curse ◆ **il y a un** ~ **sur qn** there is a curse on sb ◆ **jeter un** ~ **à** *ou* **sur qn** to put *ou* cast a spell on, to put a curse *ou* jinx* on sb

sortable * /sɔʀtabl/ ADJ *(gén nég) [personne]* presentable ◆ **tu n'es pas** ~ **!** we (*ou* I) can't take you anywhere!

sortant, e /sɔʀtɑ̃, ɑ̃t/ ADJ *[député, maire]* outgoing *(épith)* ◆ **les numéros** ~**s** the numbers which come up NM (= *personne : gén pl*) ◆ **les** ~**s** the outgoing crowd; *(Pol)* the outgoing deputies

sorte /sɔʀt/ NF 1 (= *espèce*) sort, kind ◆ **toutes** ~**s de gens/choses** all kinds *ou* sorts *ou* manner of people/things ◆ **des vêtements de toutes (les)** ~**s** all kinds *ou* sorts *ou* manner of clothes ◆ **nous avons trois** ~**s de fleurs** we have three kinds *ou* types *ou* sorts of flower(s) ◆ **des roches de même** ~ rocks of the same sort *ou* kind *ou* type

2 ◆ **une** ~ **de** a sort *ou* kind of ◆ **une** ~ **de médecin/voiture** *(péj)* a doctor/car of sorts ◆ **robe taillée dans une** ~ **de satin** dress cut out of some sort *ou* kind of satin

3 *(locutions)*

◆ **de la sorte** (= *de cette façon*) in that way ◆ **accoutré de la** ~ dressed in that way ◆ **il n'a rien fait de la** ~ he did nothing of the kind *ou* no such thing

◆ **de sorte à** so as to, in order to

◆ **de (telle) sorte que, en sorte que** *(littér)* (= *de façon à ce que*) so that, in such a way that; (= *si bien que*) so much so that ◆ **faire en** ~ **que** to see to it that ◆ **faites en** ~ **que vous ayez fini** *ou* **d'avoir fini demain** see to it *ou* arrange it *ou* arrange things so that you finish tomorrow

◆ **en quelque sorte** in a way, sort of* ◆ **vous avouez l'avoir dit, en quelque** ~ you are in a way *ou* sort of* admitting to having said it ◆ **c'est un ami en quelque** ~ I suppose you could say he's a friend, he's sort of a friend *

sortie /sɔʀti/ NF 1 (= *action, moment*) *[de personne]* exit; *[de véhicule, bateau, armée occupante]* departure; *(Mil* = *mission)* sortie; *(Théât)* exit ◆ **elle attend la** ~ **des artistes** she's waiting for the performers to come out ◆ **à sa** ~**, tous se sont tus** when he went out *ou* left everybody fell silent ◆ **à sa** ~ **du salon** when he went out of *ou* left the lounge ◆ **il a fait une** ~ **remarquée** he made a dramatic exit ◆ **il a fait une** ~ **discrète** he made a discreet exit, he left discreetly ◆ **faire une** ~ *[avions, troupes]* to make a sortie ◆ **faire une** ~ **dans l'espace** to take *ou* make a space walk ◆ **tenter une** ~ *(Mil)* to attempt a sortie ◆ **les sauveteurs ont fait 30** ~**s en mer cette semaine** the lifeboatmen were called out 30 times this week ◆ **la** ~ **des classes est fixée au 29 juin** the schools will close for the summer on 29 June ◆ **à la** ~ **des ouvriers/bureaux/théâtres** when the workers/offices/theatres come out ◆ **sa mère l'attend tous les jours à la** ~ **de l'école** his mother waits for him every day after school *ou* when school comes out *ou* finishes ◆ **retrouvons-nous à la** ~ **(du concert)** let's meet at the end (of the concert) ◆ **à sa** ~ **de prison** when he comes (*ou* came) out of prison ◆ **c'est sa première** ~ **depuis sa maladie** it's the first time he's been out since his illness ◆ **elle a manqué sa** ~ **à l'acte 2** *(Théât)* she missed *ou* fluffed *(Brit)* her exit in act 2 ◆ **pousser qn vers la** ~ *(fig)* to push sb out; → **faux²**

2 (= *fin*) end ◆ **à la** ~ **de l'enfance** at the end of childhood ◆ **à la** ~ **de l'hiver** at the end of winter

3 (= *congé*) day off; (= *promenade*) outing; *(le soir : au théâtre, au cinéma etc)* evening *ou* night out ◆ **c'est le jour de** ~ **de la bonne** it's the maid's day off ◆ **c'est le jour de** ~ **des pensionnaires** it's the boarders' day out ◆ **il est de** ~ *[soldat, domestique]* it's his day off ◆ **nous sommes de** ~ **ce soir** we're going out tonight, we're having an evening out tonight ◆ **ils viennent déjeuner le dimanche, cela leur fait une petite** ~ they come to lunch on Sundays - it gives them a little outing *ou* it's a day out for them ◆ **elle s'est acheté une robe du soir pour leurs** ~**s** she's bought herself an evening dress for when they go out *ou* have a night out ◆ **faire une** ~ **en mer** to go on a boat trip *(at sea)* ◆ ~ **éducative** *ou* **scolaire** *(Scol)* field-trip, school outing *(Brit)*, school visit *(Brit)* ◆ **il dépense tout son argent pour ses** ~**s** he spends all his money on going out

4 (= *lieu*) exit, way out ◆ ~ **d'autoroute** motorway exit *(Brit)*, highway exit *(US)* ◆ ~ **de métro** metro exit, underground *(Brit) ou* subway *(US)* exit ◆ ~ **de secours** emergency exit ◆ ~ **des artistes** stage door ◆ **"attention, sortie d'usine"** "caution, factory entrance *ou* exit" ◆ **"sortie de camions"** "vehicle exit" ◆ **garé devant la** ~ **de l'école** parked in front of the school gates *ou* entrance ◆ **sa maison se trouve à la** ~ **du village** his house is at the edge of the village *ou* just as you come out of the village ◆ **les** ~**s de Paris sont encombrées** the roads out of Paris are congested ◆ **par ici la** ~ **!** this way out! ◆ **trouver une (porte de)** ~ *(fig)* to find a way out ◆ **il faut se ménager une (porte de)** ~ you must try to leave yourself a way out

5 (= *écoulement*) *[d'eau, gaz]* outflow ◆ **cela empêche la** ~ **des gaz** it prevents the gases from coming out *ou* escaping

6 (= *emportement*) outburst; (= *remarque drôle*) sally; (= *remarque incongrue*) peculiar *ou* odd remark ◆ **elle est sujette à ce genre de** ~ she's given to that kind of outburst ◆ **faire une** ~ **à qn** to let fly at sb ◆ **faire une** ~ **contre qch/qn** to lash out against sth/sb

7 *(Comm* = *mise en vente) [de voiture, modèle]* launching; *[de livre]* appearance, publication; *[de disque, film]* release ◆ **à la** ~ **du livre** when the book comes (*ou* came) out

8 *[de marchandises, devises]* export ◆ ~ **(de capitaux)** outflow (of capital) ◆ **la** ~ **de l'or/des devises/de certains produits est contingentée** there are controls on gold/currency/certain products leaving the country *ou* on the export of gold/currency/certain products ◆ **il y a eu d'importantes** ~**s de devises** large amounts of currency have been flowing out of *ou* leaving the country

9 (= *somme dépensée*) item of expenditure ◆ **il y a eu plus de** ~**s que de rentrées** there have been more outgoings than receipts ◆ ~**s de caisse** cash payments

10 *(Ordin)* output, readout ◆ ~ **(sur) imprimante** print-out

11 *(Sport)* ~ **en touche** going into touch ◆ **il y a** ~ **en touche si le ballon touche la ligne** the ball is in touch *ou* has gone into touch if it touches the line ◆ **ils ont marqué l'essai sur une** ~ **de mêlée** *(Rugby)* they scored a try straight out of the scrum ◆ **le ballon est allé en** ~ **de but** *(Ftbl)* the ball has gone into touch behind the back line ◆ **faire une** ~ *[gardien de but]* to leave the goalmouth, to come out of goal ◆ **lors de la dernière** ~ **de l'équipe de France contre l'Angleterre** when France last played (against) England ◆ **faire une** ~ **de route** *[voiture]* to go off the track

COMP **sortie de bain** bathrobe

sortilège /sɔʀtilɛʒ/ NM (magic) spell

sortir[1] /sɔʀtiʀ/

► conjug 16 ◄

1 VERBE INTRANSITIF
2 VERBE TRANSITIF
3 VERBE PRONOMINAL

1 - VERBE INTRANSITIF

avec auxiliaire être

1 *[personne] (= aller)* to go out, to leave; *(= venir)* to come out, to leave; *(à pied)* to walk out; *(en voiture)* to drive out, to go *ou* come out; *[véhicule]* to drive out, to go *ou* come out; *(Ordin)* to exit, to log out; *(Théât)* to exit, to leave (the stage) ◆ ~ **en voiture/à bicyclette** to go out for a drive/a cycle ride, to go out in one's car/on one's bike ◆ ~ **en courant** to run out ◆ ~ **en boitant** to limp out ◆ ~ **par la porte/par la fenêtre** to go *ou* get out *ou* leave by the door/by the window ◆ **ça me sort par les yeux** *ou* **les oreilles*** I've had more than I can take (of it) ◆ ~ **en mer** to put out to sea ◆ **depuis trois jours, les bateaux ne sont pas sortis** the boats haven't been out for three days ◆ **faites ~ ces gens** make these people go *ou* leave, get these people out ◆ **Madame, est-ce que je peux ~ ?** *(Scol)* Miss, can I be excused please? ◆ ~ **de** *[+ pièce]* to go *ou* come out of, to leave; *[+ région, pays]* to leave ◆ ~ **de chez qn** to go *ou* come out of sb's house, to leave sb's house ◆ **mais d'où sort-il (donc) ?*** *(= il est tout sale)* where has he been!; *(= il ne sait pas la nouvelle)* where has he been (all this time)?; *(= il est mal élevé)* where was he brought up? *(iro)*; *(= il est bête)* where did they find him? *(iro)* ◆ **il sortit discrètement (de la pièce)** he went out (of the room) *ou* left (the room) discreetly, he slipped out (of the room) ◆ **sors (d'ici) !** get out (of here)! ◆ **le train sort du tunnel** the train is coming out of the tunnel ◆ **les voiliers sortaient du port** the sailing boats were leaving the harbour ◆ **"la servante sort"** *(Théât)* "exit the maid" ◆ **"les 3 gardes sortent"** *(Théât)* "exeunt 3 guards" ◆ **laisser ~ qn** to let sb out, to let sb leave ◆ **ne laissez ~ personne** don't let anybody out *ou* leave ◆ **laisser ~ qn de** *[+ pièce, pays]* to let sb out of, to let sb leave; → **gond**

2 = partir de chez soi to go out ◆ ~ **faire des courses/prendre l'air** to go out shopping/for some fresh air ◆ ~ **acheter du pain** to go out to buy *ou* for some bread ◆ ~ **dîner/déjeuner** to go out for *ou* to dinner/lunch ◆ **mon père est sorti, puis-je prendre un message ?** *(au téléphone)* my father's gone out, can I take a message? ◆ **ils sortent beaucoup/ne sortent pas beaucoup** they go out a lot/don't go out much ◆ **tu ne les connais pas ? il faut ~ un peu** *ou* **le dimanche*** you don't know them? where have you been?* ◆ **mes parents ne me laissent pas ~** my parents don't let me (go) out ◆ **le médecin lui a permis de ~** the doctor has allowed him (to go) out ◆ **c'est le soir que les moustiques sortent** the mosquitoes come out in the evening ◆ **il n'est jamais sorti de son village** he has never been out of *ou* gone outside his village

3 Comm *[marchandises, devises]* to leave ◆ **tout ce qui sort (du pays) doit être déclaré** everything going out (of the country) *ou* leaving (the country) must be declared

4 = quitter to leave, to come out; *[élèves]* to get out; *[objet, pièce]* to come out ◆ **le joint est sorti de son logement** the joint has come out of its socket ◆ ~ **du théâtre** to go *ou* come out of *ou* leave the theatre ◆ ~ **de l'hôpital/de prison** to come out of hospital/of prison ◆ **quand sortil ?** *(de prison)* when does he come *ou* get out?; *(de l'hôpital)* when is he coming out? *ou* leaving? ◆ **je sors à 6 heures** *(du bureau, du lycée)* I finish at 6 ◆ ~ **de table** to leave the table ◆ ~ **de l'eau** to come out of the water ◆ ~ **du lit** to get out of bed, to get up ◆ ~ **de son lit** *[fleuve]* to overflow its banks ◆ ~ **de terre** *[plante]* to sprout ◆ ~ **des rails** *(Rail)* to go off the rails ◆ **la voiture est sortie de la route** the car left *ou* came off the road ◆ ~ **de convalescence/d'un profond sommeil** to come out of *ou* emerge from convalescence/a deep sleep ◆ ~ **de son calme** to lose one's calm ◆ ~ **de son indifférence** to overcome one's indifference ◆ ~ **indemne d'un accident** to come out of an accident unscathed ◆ **ce secret ne doit pas ~ de la famille** this secret must not go beyond *ou* outside family ◆ **c'est confidentiel, ça ne doit pas ~ d'ici** it's confidential, it must not leave this room ◆ ~ **de la récession** to get out of the recession ◆ **il a trop de copies à corriger, il n'en sort pas** he has too many papers to correct – there's no end to them ◆ **on n'est pas sortis de l'auberge*** we're not out of the woods yet ◆ **cela lui est sorti de la mémoire** *ou* **de l'esprit** it slipped his mind ◆ **ça m'est sorti de la tête** it went right out of my head; → **impasse, mauvais**

5 = fréquenter ~ **avec qn** to go out with sb ◆ **ils sortent ensemble depuis 2 ans** they've been going out together for 2 years

6 marquant le passé immédiat **il sortait tout juste de l'enfance quand ...** he was in his early teens when ... ◆ **on sortait de l'hiver** it was the end of winter ◆ **il sort d'ici** he's just left ◆ **il sort du lit** he's just got up, he's just out of bed ◆ **on ne dirait pas qu'elle sort de chez le coiffeur !** you'd never believe she'd just had her hair done! ◆ **il sort d'une bronchite** he's just had bronchitis, he's just recovering from a bout of bronchitis ◆ **il sort d'une période de cafard** he's just gone through *ou* had a spell of depression ◆ **il en est sorti grandi** *(d'une épreuve)* he came out of it a stronger person, he was better for it ◆ **je sors de lui parler*** I've just been talking to him ◆ **je sors d'en prendre*** I've had quite enough thank you *(iro)*

7 = s'écarter de ~ **du sujet/de la question** to go *ou* get off the subject/the point ◆ ~ **de la légalité** to overstep *ou* go outside *ou* go beyond the law ◆ ~ **des limites de** to go beyond the bounds of, to overstep the limits of ◆ ~ **(du jeu)** *(Sport) [balle, ballon]* to go out (of play) ◆ ~ **en touche** *[ballon]* to go into touch ◆ **la balle est sortie** *(Tennis)* the ball is out ◆ **cela sort de mes compétences** that's outside my field ◆ **vous sortez de votre rôle** that is not your responsibility *ou* part of your brief; → **ordinaire**

8 = être issu de ~ **d'une bonne famille/du peuple** to come from a good family/from the working class ◆ **il sort du lycée Victor Duruy** he was (educated) at the lycée Victor Duruy ◆ **il sort de l'université de Perpignan** he was *ou* he studied at the University of Perpignan ◆ **pas besoin de** *ou* **il ne faut pas ~ de Polytechnique pour comprendre ça*** you don't need a PhD to understand that ◆ **un ingénieur tout droit sorti de l'école** an engineer fresh out of college

9 = dépasser to stick out; *(= commencer à pousser) [blé, plante]* to come up; *[dent]* to come through; *[bouton]* to appear

10 = être fabriqué, publié to come out; *[disque, film]* to be released ◆ **le film sort sur les écrans le 2 mai** the film is on general release from 2 May ◆ **cette encyclopédie sort par fascicules** this encyclopaedia comes out *ou* is published in instalments ◆ **sa robe sort de chez un grand couturier** her dress is by one of the top fashion designers

11 Jeux, Loterie *[numéro, couleur]* to come up; *(Scol) [sujet d'examen]* to come up

12 = provenir de ~ **de** to come from ◆ **sait-on ce qui sortira de ces entrevues !** *(fig) (= résulter)* who knows what will come (out) of these talks! *ou* what these talks will lead to! ◆ **il n'est rien sorti de nos recherches** nothing came (out) of our research ◆ **que va-t-il ~ de tout cela ?** what will come of all this? ◆ **des mots qui sortent du cœur** words which come from the heart, heartfelt words ◆ **une odeur de brûlé sortait de la cuisine** a smell of burning came from the kitchen ◆ **une épaisse fumée sortait par les fenêtres** thick smoke was pouring out of the windows

13 = être dit **c'est sorti tout seul*** *[propos, remarque]* it just came out* ◆ **il fallait que ça sorte*** I *(ou he etc)* just had to say it

2 - VERBE TRANSITIF

avec auxiliaire avoir

1 = mener dehors *[+ personne, chien]* to take out; *(* = accompagner lors d'une sortie)* to take out; *(= expulser) [+ personne]* to throw out ◆ **sortez-le !** throw him out!, get him out of here! ◆ **va au cinéma, cela te sortira** go and see a film, that'll get you out a bit *ou* give you a change of scene

2 = extraire to take out; *[+ train d'atterrissage]* to lower ◆ ~ **des vêtements d'une armoire/une voiture du garage** to get *ou* take clothes out of a wardrobe/the car out of the garage ◆ **ils ont réussi à ~ les enfants de la grotte/le car du ravin** they managed to get the children out of the cave/the coach out of the ravine ◆ **il sortit de sa poche un mouchoir** he took *ou* brought *ou* pulled a handkerchief out of his pocket ◆ ~ **les mains de ses poches** to take one's hands out of one's pockets ◆ **il a sorti son passeport** he took out *ou* produced his passport ◆ **les douaniers ont tout sorti de sa valise** the customs men took everything out of his suitcase ◆ **sortons les fauteuils dans le jardin** let's take the armchairs out into the garden ◆ **il nous a sorti son vieux bordeaux** he got his old claret out for us ◆ **il faut le ~ de là** *(lit, fig) (d'un lieu)* we must get him out of there; *(d'une situation difficile)* we must get him out of it; → **affaire**

3 Comm **(faire)** ~ *[+ marchandises] (par la douane)* to take out; *(en fraude)* to smuggle out

4 = mettre en vente *[+ voiture, modèle]* to bring out; *[+ livre]* to bring out, to publish; *[+ disque, film] [artiste]* to bring out; *[compagnie]* to release ◆ **ils viennent de ~ un nouveau logiciel** they've just brought out a new software package

5 * = dire to come out with* ◆ **il vous sort de ces réflexions !** the things he comes out with!* ◆ **elle en a sorti une bien bonne** she came out with a good one* ◆ **qu'est-ce qu'il va encore nous ~ ?** what will he come out with next?* ◆ **c'est ce journal qui a sorti l'affaire** *(Journalisme = révéler)* this was the newspaper that first broke the story

6 * = éliminer d'un concours *[+ concurrent, adversaire]* to knock out *(fig)* ◆ **il s'est fait ~ dès le premier match** he was knocked out in the first match

3 - VERBE PRONOMINAL

se sortir ◆ **se ~ d'une situation difficile** to manage to get out of a difficult situation *ou* to extricate o.s. from a difficult situation ◆ **la voiture est en miettes, mais il s'en est sorti sans une égratignure** the car's a write-off but he came out of it without a scratch ◆ **tu crois qu'il va s'en ~ ?** *(il est malade)* do you think he'll pull through?; *(il est surchargé de travail)* do you think he'll ever get to *ou* see the end of it?; *(il est sur la sellette)* do you think he'll come through all right? ◆ **avec son salaire, il ne peut pas s'en ~** he can't get by on what he earns ◆ **va l'aider, il ne s'en sort pas** go and help him, he can't cope *ou* manage ◆ **j'ai trop de travail, je ne m'en sors pas** I've got too much work, I can't see the end of it ◆ **bravo, tu**

t'en es très bien sorti ! you've done really well!

sortir² /sɔʀtiʀ/ **NM** *(littér)* ◆ **au ~ de l'hiver/de l'enfance** as winter/childhood draws *(ou* drew) to a close ◆ **au ~ de la réunion** at the end of the meeting, when the meeting broke up

SOS /ɛsoɛs/ **NM** SOS ◆ **lancer un ~** to put out an SOS ◆ **envoyer un ~ à qn** to send an SOS to sb ◆ **~ médecins/dépannage** *etc* emergency medical/repair *etc* service

sosie /sɔzi/ **NM** (= *personne*) double ◆ **c'est le ~ de son frère** he's the (spitting) image of his brother

sot, sotte /so, sɔt/ **ADJ** silly, foolish, stupid ◆ **il n'y a pas de ~ métier(, il n'y a que de ~tes gens)** *(Prov)* every trade has its value ◆ **il est facteur – il n'y a pas de ~ métier !** he's a postman – well, there's nothing wrong with that! **NM,F** (†, *frm*) (= *niais*) fool; (= *enfant*) (little) idiot; *(Hist, Littérat* = *bouffon)* fool

sotie /sɔti/ **NF** *(Hist Littérat) satirical farce of 15th and 16th centuries*

sot-l'y-laisse /solilɛs/ **NM INV** *[de volaille]* oyster *(in chicken)*

sottement /sɔtmɑ̃/ **ADV** foolishly, stupidly

sottie /sɔti/ **NF** ⇒ **sotie**

sottise /sɔtiz/ **NF** 1 (= *caractère*) stupidity, foolishness ◆ **avoir la ~ de faire** to be foolish *ou* stupid enough to do sth, to have the stupidity to do sth 2 (= *parole*) silly *ou* foolish remark; (= *action*) silly *ou* foolish thing to do, folly † *(frm)* ◆ **dire des ~s** to say silly *ou* stupid *ou* foolish things, to make silly *ou* foolish remarks ◆ **faire une ~** *[adulte]* to do a silly *ou* foolish thing, to do something stupid ◆ **faire des ~s** *[enfant]* to misbehave, to be naughty

sottisier /sɔtizje/ **NM** (= *livre*) collection of howlers*; *(Radio, TV)* collection of out-takes

sou /su/ **NM** 1 (= *monnaie*) *(Hist)* sou, ≈ shilling *(Brit)*; (†, *Helv* = *cinq centimes*) 5 centimes; (* *Can*) cent ◆ **un trente ~s**‡ *(Can)* a quarter *(US, Can)*

2 *(locutions)* **un ~ est un ~** every penny counts ◆ **c'est une affaire** *ou* **une histoire de gros ~s** *(péj)* there's big money involved ◆ **donner/compter/économiser ~ à** *ou* **par ~** to give/count/save penny by penny ◆ **il n'a pas le (premier) ~, il n'a pas un ~ vaillant** he hasn't got a penny *ou* a cent *(US)* (to his name) ◆ **il est sans le** *ou* **un ~** he's penniless ◆ **il est toujours en train de compter ses ~s** he's always counting the pennies ◆ **ils en sont à leurs derniers ~s** they're down to their last few pennies ◆ **dépenser jusqu'à son dernier ~** to spend every last penny ◆ **y laisser jusqu'à son dernier ~** to lose everything, to lose one's last buck* *(US)* ◆ **il n'a pas pour un ~ de méchanceté/bon sens** he hasn't got an ounce of unkindness/good sense (in him) ◆ **il n'est pas hypocrite/raciste pour un ~** *ou* **deux ~s** he isn't at all *ou* (in) the least bit hypocritical/racist ◆ **propre/reluisant** *ou* **brillant comme un ~ neuf** (as) clean/bright as a new pin, spick and span; → **appareil, cent¹, machine, près, quatre**

soubassement /subasmɑ̃/ **NM** *[de maison]* base; *[de murs, fenêtre]* dado; *[de colonne]* crepidoma; *(Géol)* bedrock; *[de thèse]* basis ◆ **leur parti n'a aucun ~ idéologique** their party has no ideological base ◆ **un pays sans aucun ~ économique** a country with no economic base

soubresaut /subʀəso/ **NM** 1 (= *cahot*) jolt ◆ **le véhicule fit un ~** the vehicle gave a jolt 2 (= *tressaillement*) *(de peur)* start; *(d'agonie)* convulsive movement ◆ **avoir** *ou* **faire un ~** to give a start, to start

soubrette /subʀɛt/ **NF** (†, *hum* = *femme de chambre)* maid; *(Théât)* soubrette

souche /suʃ/ **NF** 1 *[d'arbre]* stump; *[de vigne]* stock ◆ **rester planté comme une ~** to stand stock-still; → **dormir** 2 *[de famille, race]* founder ◆ **faire ~** to found a line ◆ **de vieille ~** of old stock ◆ **elle est française de ~** she's of French origin *ou* extraction 3 *(Ling)* root ◆ **mot de ~ latine** word with a Latin root ◆ **mot ~** root word 4 *(Bio) [de bactéries, virus]* clone, strain ◆ **cellule ~** original cell 5 (= *talon)* counterfoil, stub ◆ **carnet à ~s** counterfoil book 6 *[de cheminée]* (chimney) stack

souci¹ /susi/ **NM** (= *fleur*) ◆ **~ (des jardins)** marigold ◆ **~ d'eau** *ou* **des marais** marsh marigold

souci² /susi/ **NM** 1 (= *inquiétude*) worry ◆ **se faire du ~** to worry *(pour* about); ◆ **avec un fils comme ça, ils ont du ~ à se faire !** with a son like that they've got reason to worry! ◆ **ils n'ont pas de ~ à se faire** they've got nothing to worry about ◆ **être sans ~** to be free of worries *ou* care(s) ◆ **cela t'éviterait bien du ~** it would save *ou* spare you a lot of worry ◆ **cela lui donne (bien) du ~** it worries him (a lot), he worries (a great deal) over it ◆ **~s d'argent** money worries, worries about money ◆ **pas de ~ !** no problem!

2 (= *préoccupation*) concern *(de* for); ◆ **avoir ~ du bien-être de son prochain** to be concerned about other people's well-being ◆ **sa carrière est son unique ~** his career is his sole concern *ou* is all he worries about ◆ **cet enfant est un ~ perpétuel pour ses parents** that child is a constant source of worry for his parents ◆ **avoir le ~ de bien faire** to be concerned about doing things well ◆ **dans le ~ de lui plaire** in his concern to please her ◆ **nous avons fait ce choix dans un ~ de cohérence** we made this choice with a view to being consistent *ou* for the sake of consistency ◆ **par ~ d'honnêteté** for honesty's sake ◆ **ils produisent sans ~ de qualité** they churn out products regardless of quality ◆ **c'est le moindre** *ou* **le cadet** *ou* **le dernier de mes ~s** that's the least of my worries

soucier /susje/ ▸ **conjug 7** ◂ **VPR** **se soucier** ◆ **se ~ de** to care about ◆ **se ~ des autres** to care about *ou* for others, to show concern for others ◆ **je ne m'en soucie guère** I am quite indifferent to it ◆ **il s'en soucie comme de sa première chemise** *ou* **comme de l'an quarante*** he doesn't give *ou* care a hoot* (about it)*, he couldn't care less (about it)* ◆ **il se soucie peu de plaire** *(littér)* he cares little *ou* he doesn't bother whether he is liked or not ◆ **il se soucie fort de ce qu'ils pensent** *(littér)* he cares very much what they think ◆ **sans se ~ de leur réaction** without worrying about their reaction ◆ **sans se ~ de fermer la porte à clé** without bothering to lock the door ◆ **elle a accepté sans se ~ des conséquences** she accepted without giving any thought to the consequences ◆ **se ~ que** *(littér)* (+ *subj*) to care that

VT to worry, to trouble

soucieux, -ieuse /susjø, jøz/ **ADJ** 1 (= *inquiet*) *[personne, air, ton]* concerned, worried 2 ◆ **être ~ de qch** to be concerned with *ou* about sth, to be preoccupied with sth ◆ **~ de son seul intérêt** concerned *ou* preoccupied solely with his own interests ◆ **être ~ de faire** to be anxious to do ◆ **~ que** *(frm)* concerned *ou* anxious that ◆ **peu ~ qu'on le voie** caring little *ou* unconcerned whether he be *ou* is seen or not

soucoupe /sukup/ **NF** saucer ◆ **~ volante** flying saucer; → **œil**

soudage /sudaʒ/ **NM** *(avec brasure, fil à souder)* soldering; *(autogène)* welding

soudain, e /sudɛ̃, ɛn/ **ADJ** *(gén)* sudden; *[mort]* sudden, unexpected **ADV** (= *tout à coup*) suddenly, all of a sudden ◆ **~, il se mit à pleurer** all of a sudden he started to cry, he suddenly started to cry

soudainement /sudɛnmɑ̃/ **ADV** suddenly, all of a sudden

soudaineté /sudɛnte/ **NF** suddenness

Soudan /sudɑ̃/ **NM** ◆ **le ~** (the) Sudan

soudanais, e /sudanɛ, ɛz/ **ADJ** Sudanese, of *ou* from (the) Sudan **NM,F** **Soudanais(e)** Sudanese, inhabitant *ou* native of (the) Sudan

soudard /sudaʀ/ **NM** *(péj)* ruffianly *ou* roughneck soldier

soude /sud/ **NF** 1 *(industrielle)* soda ◆ **~ caustique** caustic soda; → **bicarbonate, cristal** 2 (= *plante*) saltwort ◆ **(cendre de) ~** † *(Chim)* soda ash

soudé, e /sude/ (ptp de **souder**) **ADJ** *[organes, pétales]* joined (together); *[couple]* close, united; *[équipe]* closely-knit ◆ **notre équipe n'est pas assez ~e** our team isn't united enough ◆ **l'opposition est ~e derrière lui** the opposition is united behind him

souder /sude/ ▸ **conjug 1** ◂ **VT** 1 *[+ métal] (avec brasure, fil à souder)* to solder; *(soudure autogène)* to weld; *[+ plastique]* to weld, to seal ◆ **~ à chaud/froid** to hot-/cold-weld; → **fer, fil, lampe** 2 *(Méd) [+ os]* to knit 3 (= *unir*) *[+ choses, organismes]* to fuse (together); *(littér) [+ cœurs, êtres]* to bind *ou* knit together *(littér)*, to unite 4 *(Culin) [+ bords]* to seal **VPR** **se souder** 1 *[os]* to knit together; *[vertèbres]* to fuse 2 *[équipe, parti]* to pull together, to unite; (= *s'unir*) to be knit together *(littér)*

soudeur, -euse /sudœʀ, øz/ **NM,F** *[de métal] (avec brasure, fil à souder)* solderer; *(soudure autogène)* welder **NF** **soudeuse** (= *machine*) welder

soudoyer /sudwaje/ ▸ **conjug 8** ◂ **VT** to bribe

soudure /sudyʀ/ **NF** 1 (= *opération*) *[de métal] (avec brasure, fil à souder)* soldering; *(autogène)* welding; *[de plastique]* welding, sealing; (= *endroit*) soldered joint, weld; (= *substance*) solder ◆ **~ à l'arc** arc welding ◆ **~ autogène** welding ◆ **~ au chalumeau** torch welding ◆ **il faut faire une ~** it needs soldering *ou* welding ◆ **faire la ~ (entre)** *(fig)* to bridge the gap (between) ◆ **je dois faire la ~** (= *remplacer qn*) I've got to fill in 2 *[d'os]* knitting; *[d'organes, pétales]* join; *(littér) [de partis, cœurs]* binding *ou* knitting *(littér)* together, uniting

soufflage /suflaʒ/ **NM** 1 *(Métal)* blowing ◆ **~ du verre** glass-blowing 2 *(Naut)* sheathing

soufflant, e /suflɑ̃, ɑt/ **ADJ** 1 ◆ **(machine) ~e** blower ◆ **(radiateur) ~** fan heater 2 († * = *étonnant*) staggering, stunning **NM** *(arg Crime* = *pistolet)* pistol, rod‡ *(US)*

souffle /sufl/ **NM** 1 (= *expiration*) *(en soufflant)* blow, puff; *(en respirant)* breath ◆ **éteindre une bougie d'un ~** to blow a candle out ◆ **il murmura mon nom dans un ~** he breathed my name ◆ **le dernier ~ d'un agonisant** the last breath of a dying man ◆ **pour jouer d'un instrument à vent, il faut du ~** you need a lot of breath *ou* puff* *(Brit)* to play a wind instrument

2 (= *respiration*) breathing ◆ **on entendait un ~ dans l'obscurité** we heard (someone) breathing in the darkness ◆ **manquer de ~** *(lit)* to be short of breath; *(fig) [prose]* to be lacklustre *(Brit) ou* lackluster *(US)*; *[campagne électorale]* to be lacklustre *(Brit) ou* lackluster *(US)*, to be lacking (in) oomph* ◆ **son roman manque de ~** his novel flags in parts ◆ **il ne manque pas de ~ !*** (= *il a du toupet*) he's got a nerve!* ◆ **avoir le ~ court** to be short of breath, to be short-winded ◆ **retenir son ~** to hold one's breath ◆ **reprendre son ~** to get one's breath back ◆ **ne plus avoir de ~, être à bout de ~** to be out of breath ◆ **couper le ~ à qn** *(lit)* to wind sb; *(fig)* to take sb's breath away ◆ **j'en ai eu le ~ coupé** *(fig)* it (quite) took my breath away ◆ **c'est à vous couper le ~** it's breathtaking, it's enough to take your breath away ◆ **donner**

un ~ nouveau *ou* **redonner du ~ à** to give a new lease of life to, to breathe new life into ◆ **la dévaluation va redonner du ~ aux exportations** devaluation will give a fillip to exports ◆ **trouver son second ~** *(Sport, fig)* to get one's second wind; → **bout, second**

3 *(= déplacement d'air) [d'incendie, ventilateur, explosion]* blast

4 *(= vent)* puff *ou* breath of air, puff of wind ◆ **le ~ du vent dans les feuilles** the wind blowing through the leaves ◆ **un ~ d'air faisait bruire le feuillage** a slight breeze was rustling the leaves ◆ **il n'y avait pas un ~ (d'air** *ou* **de vent)** there was not a breath of air

5 *(= force créatrice)* inspiration ◆ **le ~ du génie** the inspiration born of genius ◆ **le ~ créateur** *(Rel)* the breath of God

6 *(Méd)* **~ cardiaque** *ou* **au cœur** cardiac *ou* heart murmur; → **bruit**

7 *(Téléc)* background noise

soufflé, e /sufle/ (ptp de **souffler**) ADJ 1 *(Culin)* soufflé *(épith)* 2 *(* = surpris)* flabbergasted*, staggered* NM *(Culin)* soufflé ◆ **~ au fromage** cheese soufflé; → **retomber**

souffler /sufle/ ▸ conjug 1 ◂ VI 1 *[vent, personne]* to blow ◆ **~ dans un instrument à vent** to blow (into) a wind instrument ◆ **~ sur une bougie (pour l'éteindre)** to blow out a candle ◆ **~ sur sa soupe (pour la faire refroidir)** to blow on one's soup (to cool it down) ◆ **~ sur ses doigts (pour les réchauffer)** to blow on one's fingers (to warm them up) ◆ **voir de quel côté souffle le vent** *(lit, fig)* to see which way the wind is blowing ◆ **le vent a soufflé si fort qu'il a abattu deux arbres** the wind was so strong *ou* blew so hard that it brought two trees down ◆ **le vent soufflait en rafales** the wind was blowing in gusts ◆ **le vent soufflait en tempête** it was blowing a gale ◆ **j'ai dû ~ dans le ballon*** *(alcootest)* I was breathalyzed, they gave me a breath test ◆ **~ sur le feu** *(lit)* to blow on the fire; *(fig)* to add fuel to the fire ◆ **il croit qu'il va y arriver en soufflant dessus** *(fig)* he thinks it's going to be a cinch*

2 *(= respirer avec peine)* to puff (and blow) ◆ **il ne peut monter les escaliers sans ~** he can't go up the stairs without puffing (and blowing) ◆ **~ comme un bœuf** *ou* **une locomotive** *ou* **un phoque*** to puff and blow like an old steam engine

3 *(= se reposer)* to get one's breath back ◆ **laisser ~ qn/un cheval** to let sb/a horse get his breath back ◆ **il ne prend jamais le temps de ~** he never lets up, he never stops to catch his breath ◆ **donnez-lui un peu de temps pour ~** *(pour se reposer)* give him time to get his breath back, give him a breather*; *(avant de payer)* give him a breather*

VT 1 *[+ bougie, feu]* to blow out

2 *(= envoyer)* **~ de la fumée au nez de qn** to blow smoke in(to) sb's face ◆ **~ des odeurs d'ail au visage de qn** to breathe garlic over sb *ou* into sb's face ◆ **le ventilateur soufflait des odeurs de graillon** the fan was blowing out greasy smells ◆ **le vent leur soufflait le sable dans les yeux** the wind was blowing the sand into their eyes ◆ **~ le chaud et le froid** *(fig)* to blow hot and cold

3 *(* = prendre)* to pinch*, to swipe*, to nick* *(Brit) (à qn* from sb); ◆ **il lui a soufflé sa petite amie/son poste** he's pinched* his girlfriend/his job ◆ **~ un pion** *(Dames)* to huff a draught ◆ **~ n'est pas jouer** *(Dames)* huffing isn't a real move

4 *[bombe, explosion]* to destroy ◆ **leur maison a été soufflée par une bombe** their house was destroyed by the blast from a bomb

5 *(= dire) [+ conseil, réponse, réplique]* to whisper *(à qn* to sb); ◆ **on lui a soufflé sa leçon** *(fig)* he was told what to say ◆ **~ son rôle à qn** *(Théât)* to prompt sb, to give sb a prompt ◆ **~ qch à l'oreille de qn** to whisper sth in sb's ear ◆ **on ne souffle pas !** *(en classe, dans un jeu)* no whispering! ◆ **il n'a pas soufflé mot** he didn't breathe a word ◆ **c'est lui qui m'en avait soufflé l'idée** he's the one who gave me the idea

6 *(* = étonner)* to flabbergast*, to stagger* ◆ **elle a été soufflée d'apprendre leur échec** she was flabbergasted* *ou* staggered* to hear they had failed ◆ **leur toupet m'a soufflé** I was flabbergasted* *ou* staggered* at their nerve

7 **~ le verre** to blow glass

soufflerie /sufləʀi/ NF *[d'orgue, forge]* bellows; *(Tech : d'aération)* ventilating fan; *(dans une usine)* blower ◆ **~ (aérodynamique)** wind tunnel

soufflet[1] /suflɛ/ NM 1 *[de forge]* bellows 2 *(Rail)* vestibule; *(Couture)* gusset; *[de sac, classeur]* extendible gusset; *[d'appareil photographique, instrument de musique]* bellows ◆ **classeur à ~s** accordion file

soufflet[2] /suflɛ/ NM *(littér = gifle)* slap in the face

souffleter /sufləte/ ▸ conjug 4 ◂ VT *(littér)* ◆ **~ qn** to give sb a slap in the face

souffleur, -euse /suflœʀ, øz/ NM 1 *(Géol)* fumarole 2 *(= baleine)* blower; *(= dauphin)* bottle-nose(d) dolphin 3 **~ de verre** glass-blower NM,F *(Théât)* prompter; → **trou** NF **souffleuse** *(Can)* snowblower

souffrance /sufʀɑ̃s/ NF 1 *(= douleur)* suffering ◆ **~ physique/morale** physical/mental suffering ◆ **les ~s infligées à la population** the suffering inflicted on the population ◆ **elle est morte dans d'atroces ~s** she died in agony *ou* great pain 2 ◆ **être en ~** *[marchandises, colis]* to be awaiting delivery, to be held up; *[affaire, dossier]* to be pending, to be waiting to be dealt with

souffrant, e /sufʀɑ̃, ɑ̃t/ ADJ 1 *(= malade) [personne]* unwell, poorly ◆ **avoir l'air ~** to look unwell *ou* poorly 2 *(littér)* **l'humanité ~e** suffering humanity ◆ **l'Église ~e** the Church suffering

souffre-douleur /sufʀədulœʀ/ NMF INV whipping boy, punch bag *(Brit)*, punching bag *(US)*

souffreteux, -euse /sufʀətø, øz/ ADJ *[personne, plante]* sickly, puny

souffrir /sufʀiʀ/ ▸ conjug 18 ◂ VI 1 *(physiquement)* to suffer ◆ **elle souffre beaucoup** she is in great pain *ou* is suffering a great deal ◆ **~ comme un damné** to suffer torture *ou* torment(s) ◆ **il faut ~ pour être belle** *(hum)* you have to suffer to be beautiful, no pain no gain ◆ **faire ~ qn** *[personne, blessure]* to hurt sb ◆ **mon bras me fait ~** my arm hurts *ou* is painful ◆ **~ de l'estomac/des reins** to have stomach/kidney trouble ◆ **il souffre d'une grave maladie/de rhumatismes** he is suffering from a serious illness/from rheumatism ◆ **~ du froid/de la chaleur** to suffer from the cold/from the heat

2 *(moralement)* to suffer *(de* from); ◆ **faire ~ qn** *[personne]* to make sb suffer; *[attitude, événement]* to cause sb pain ◆ **il a beaucoup souffert d'avoir été chassé de son pays** he has suffered a great deal from being forced to leave his country ◆ **je souffre de le voir si affaibli** it pains *ou* grieves me to see him so weak ◆ **j'en souffrais pour lui** I felt bad for him

3 *(= pâtir)* to suffer ◆ **les fraises souffrent de la chaleur** strawberries suffer in the heat ◆ **les fraises ont souffert du gel** the strawberries have suffered from *ou* have been hard hit by the frost ◆ **sa réputation en a souffert** his reputation suffered by it ◆ **le pays a souffert de la guerre** the country has suffered from the war

4 *(* = éprouver de la difficulté)* to have a hard time of it ◆ **on a fini par gagner, mais ils nous ont fait ~** *ou* **mais on a souffert** we won in the end but we had a hard time of it *ou* they gave us a rough time ◆ **je l'ai réparé mais j'ai souffert** I fixed it, but it wasn't easy

VT 1 *(= éprouver)* **~ le martyre** to go through agonies, to go through hell ◆ **sa jambe lui fait ~ le martyre** he goes through hell with that leg of his ◆ **~ mille morts** to die a thousand deaths

2 *(littér = supporter)* to bear ◆ **il ne peut pas ~ cette fille/le mensonge/les épinards** he can't stand *ou* bear that girl/lies/spinach ◆ **je ne peux ~ de te voir malheureux** I can't bear to see you unhappy ◆ **il ne peut pas ~ que ...** he cannot bear that ... ◆ **je ne souffrirai pas qu'il me donne des ordres** I won't take him giving me orders ◆ **souffrez que je vous contredise** allow *ou* permit me to contradict you

3 *(frm = admettre)* to admit of, to allow of ◆ **la règle souffre quelques exceptions** the rule admits of *ou* allows of a few exceptions ◆ **la règle ne peut ~ aucune exception** the rule admits of no exception ◆ **cette affaire ne peut ~ aucun retard** this matter simply cannot be delayed

VPR **se souffrir** *(= se supporter)* **ils ne peuvent pas se ~** they can't stand *ou* bear each other

soufi, e /sufi/ ADJ Sufi, Sufic NM,F Sufi

soufisme /sufism/ NM Sufism

soufrage /sufʀaʒ/ NM *[de vigne, laine]* sulphuration *(Brit)*, sulfuration *(US)*; *[d'allumettes]* sulphuring *(Brit)*, sulfuring *(US)*

soufre /sufʀ/ NM sulphur *(Brit)*, sulfur *(US)* ◆ **jaune ~** sulphur *(Brit)* *ou* sulfur *(US)* yellow ◆ **sentir le ~** *(fig)* to smack of heresy

soufré, e /sufʀe/ ADJ 1 *(= enduit de soufre)* coated with sulphur *(Brit)* *ou* sulfur *(US)* 2 *(= jaune)* sulphur *(Brit)* *ou* sulfur *(US)* yellow

soufrer /sufʀe/ ▸ conjug 1 ◂ VT *[+ vigne]* to (treat with) sulphur *(Brit)* *ou* sulfur *(US)*; *[+ allumettes]* to sulphur *(Brit)* *ou* sulfur *(US)*; *[+ laine]* to sulphurate *(Brit)* *ou* sulfurate *(US)*

soufrière /sufʀijɛʀ/ NF sulphur *(Brit)* *ou* sulfur *(US)* mine ◆ **la Soufrière** *(Géog)* the Soufrière

souhait /swɛ/ NM wish ◆ **formuler des ~s pour qch** to express one's best wishes for sth ◆ **les ~s de bonne année** New Year greetings, good wishes for the New Year ◆ **tous nos ~s de réussite** our best wishes for your success ◆ **à vos ~s !** bless you!, gesundheit! *(US)* ◆ **la viande était rôtie à ~** the meat was done to perfection *ou* done to a turn ◆ **le vin était fruité à ~** the wine was delightfully fruity ◆ **tout marchait à ~** everything went perfectly *ou* went like a dream ◆ **une chanson niaise à ~** *(hum)* an incredibly silly song

souhaitable /swetabl/ ADJ desirable ◆ **ce n'est guère ~** it is not really to be desired ◆ **sa présence n'a pas été jugée ~** his presence was deemed undesirable

souhaiter /swete/ GRAMMAIRE ACTIVE 28.1, 31, 50.1, 50.3 ▸ conjug 1 ◂ VT 1 *(= espérer) [+ réussite, changements]* to wish for ◆ **~ que** to hope that ◆ **il est à ~ que ...** it is to be hoped that ... ◆ **ce n'est pas à ~** it's not really to be desired ◆ **je souhaite qu'il réussisse** I hope he succeeds ◆ **je souhaite réussir** I hope to succeed ◆ **~ pouvoir étudier/partir à l'étranger** to hope to be able to study/go abroad ◆ **je le souhaitais différent/plus affectueux** I wished he were different/more affectionate ◆ **je souhaiterais parler à Jean** I'd like to speak to Jean, please ◆ **à quelle heure souhaitez-vous partir ?** what time would you like to leave? ◆ **"anglais souhaité"** *(dans une offre d'emploi)* "knowledge of English desirable"

2 *(= exprimer ses vœux)* **~ à qn le bonheur/la réussite** to wish sb happiness/success ◆ **je vous souhaite bien des choses** all the best ◆ **~ à qn de réussir** to wish sb success ◆ **je vous**

souhaite bien du plaisir !, je vous en souhaite !* *(iro)* (and the) best of luck to you! * *(iro)* ◆ ~ **la bonne année/bonne chance à qn** to wish sb a happy New Year/(the best of) luck ◆ **je vous la souhaite bonne et heureuse !*** here's hoping you have a really good New Year! ◆ **je ne souhaite à personne de connaître une telle horreur** I wouldn't wish such an awful thing on anybody ◆ **tout ce que je souhaite, c'est que tu sois heureux** all I want is for you to be happy

souiller /suje/ ▸ conjug 1 ◂ VT *(littér)* *[+ drap, vêtement]* to soil, to dirty; *[+ atmosphère]* to pollute; *[+ réputation, pureté, âme]* to sully, to tarnish ◆ **souillé de boue** spattered with mud ◆ ~ **ses mains du sang des innocents** to stain one's hands with the blood of innocents

souillon /sujɔ̃/ NF slattern, slut

souillure /sujyʀ/ NF *(littér, lit)* stain; *(fig)* blemish, stain ◆ **la ~ du péché** the stain of sin

souk /suk/ NM 1 *(= marché)* souk 2 * **c'est le ~ ici !** *(= désordre)* this place is absolute chaos! ◆ **c'est fini, ce ~ ?** *(= tintamarre)* will you stop that racket?

soul /sul/ *(Mus)* ADJ INV soul *(épith)* NF ou NM soul

soûl, soûle /su, sul/ ADJ *(= ivre)* drunk, drunken *(épith)* ◆ ~ **comme une bourrique*** ou **un Polonais*** ou **une grive** blind drunk*, (as) drunk as a lord *(surtout Brit)* NM *(= à satiété)* ◆ **manger tout son ~** to eat one's fill ◆ **chanter tout son ~** to sing one's heart out ◆ **elle a ri/pleuré tout son ~** she laughed/cried till she could laugh/cry no more

soulagement /sulaʒmɑ̃/ NM relief ◆ **j'ai éprouvé un immense ~** I felt an immense sense of relief, I felt immensely relieved ◆ **un murmure de ~ parcourut la foule** the crowd murmured in relief ◆ **ça a été un ~ d'apprendre que ...** it was a relief ou I was (ou we were etc) relieved to learn that ... ◆ **cette annonce a été accueillie avec ~** the announcement came as a relief ◆ **à mon grand ~** to my great relief

soulager /sulaʒe/ ▸ conjug 3 ◂ VT 1 *[+ personne] (physiquement)* to relieve; *(moralement)* to relieve, to soothe; *[+ douleur]* to relieve, to soothe; *[+ maux]* to relieve; *[+ conscience]* to ease ◆ **ça le soulage de s'étendre** it relieves the pain when he stretches out ◆ **ça le soulage de prendre ces pilules** these pills bring him relief ◆ **buvez, ça vous soulagera** drink this – it'll make you feel better ◆ **être soulagé d'avoir fait qch** to be relieved that one has done ou to have done sth ◆ **cet aveu l'a soulagé** this confession made him feel better ou eased his conscience ◆ **cela me soulage d'un grand poids** it's a great weight off my mind ◆ ~ **les pauvres/les déshérités** to bring relief to ou relieve the poor/the underprivileged ◆ **si ça peut te ~, sache que tu n'es pas le seul dans ce cas** if it's any consolation you should know that you're not the only one in this situation ◆ **mets de la crème, ça soulage** put some cream on, it's soothing ◆ **pleure un bon coup, ça soulage !** have a good cry, it'll make you feel better!

2 *(= décharger) [+ personne]* to relieve *(de* of); *(Archit) [+ mur, poutre]* to relieve the strain on ◆ ~ **qn de son portefeuille** *(hum)* to relieve sb of their wallet *(hum)*

VPR **se soulager** 1 *(= se décharger d'un souci)* to find relief, to ease one's feelings, to make o.s. feel better; *(= apaiser sa conscience)* to ease one's conscience ◆ **elle se soulageait en lui prodiguant des insultes** she found relief in ou eased her feelings by throwing insults at him ◆ **leur conscience se soulage à bon marché** their consciences can be eased at little expense

2 *(euph = uriner)* to relieve o.s.

soûlant, e* /sulɑ̃, ɑt/ ADJ wearing ◆ **tu es ~ avec tes questions** you're wearing me out ou tiring me out with your questions

soûlard, e‡ /sulaʀ, aʀd/, **soûlaud, e**‡ /sulo, od/ NM,F drunkard, old soak‡

soûler /sule/ ▸ conjug 1 ◂ VT 1 *(* = rendre ivre)* ~ **qn** *[personne]* to get sb drunk; *[boisson]* to make sb drunk

2 *(* = fatiguer)* ~ **qn** to make sb's head spin ou reel ◆ **tu nous soûles avec tes questions** you're driving us mad with all your questions ◆ ~ **qn de** *[+ théories]* to make sb's head spin ou reel with; *[+ questions, conseils]* to wear ou tire sb out with; *[+ luxe, sensations]* to intoxicate sb with ◆ **chaque fois qu'il vient, il nous soûle de paroles** every time he comes, he wears us out with all his talking

3 *(= griser qn) [parfum]* to go to sb's head, to intoxicate sb; *[vent, vitesse, théories]* to intoxicate sb, to make sb's head spin ou reel

VPR **se soûler** *(* = s'enivrer)* to get drunk ◆ **se ~ à la bière/au whisky** to get drunk on beer/on whisky ◆ **se ~ la gueule**‡ to get blind drunk*, to get pissed*‡ *(Brit)* ◆ **se ~ de** *[+ bruit, vitesse, vent, parfums]* to get drunk on; *[+ sensations]* to make o.s. drunk with ou on

soûlerie /sulʀi/ NF *(péj)* drunken binge

soulèvement /sulɛvmɑ̃/ NM 1 *(= révolte)* uprising 2 *(Géol)* upthrust, upheaval

soulever /sul(ə)ve/ GRAMMAIRE ACTIVE 53.2, 53.6 ▸ conjug 5 ◂

VT 1 *(= lever) [+ fardeau, malade, couvercle, rideau]* to lift (up) ◆ ~ **qn de terre** to lift sb (up) off the ground ◆ **cela me soulève le cœur** *[odeur]* it makes me feel sick ou want to heave*, it turns my stomach; *[attitude]* it makes me sick, it turns my stomach ◆ **odeur/spectacle qui soulève le cœur** nauseating ou sickening smell/sight ◆ **cette déclaration a permis de ~ un coin du voile** *(fig)* this declaration has thrown a little light on the matter

2 *(= remuer) [+ poussière]* to raise ◆ **le véhicule soulevait des nuages de poussière** the vehicle sent up ou raised clouds of dust ◆ **le bateau soulevait de grosses vagues** the boat was making great waves ◆ **le vent soulevait les vagues/le sable** the wind whipped up the waves/blew ou whipped up the sand

3 *(= indigner)* to stir up; *(= pousser à la révolte)* to stir up ou rouse (to revolt); *(= exalter)* to stir ◆ ~ **l'opinion publique (contre qn)** to stir up ou rouse public opinion (against sb)

4 *(= provoquer) [+ enthousiasme, colère]* to arouse; *[+ protestations, applaudissements]* to raise; *[+ difficultés, questions]* to raise, to bring up

5 *(= évoquer) [+ question, problème]* to raise, to bring up

6 *(‡ = voler)* ~ **qch (à qn)** to pinch* ou swipe‡ sth (from sb) ◆ **il lui a soulevé sa femme** he stole his wife

VPR **se soulever** 1 *(= se lever) [personne]* to lift o.s. up; *[poitrine]* to heave ◆ **soulève-toi pour que je redresse ton oreiller** lift yourself up ou sit up a bit so that I can plump up your pillow ◆ **il s'est soulevé sur un bras** he raised himself on one elbow

2 *[véhicule, couvercle, rideau]* to lift; *[vagues, mer]* to swell (up) ◆ **à cette vue, son cœur se souleva** his stomach turned at the sight

3 *(= s'insurger)* to rise up *(contre* against)

soulier /sulje/ NM shoe ◆ **~s bas/plats** low-heeled/flat shoes ◆ **~s montants** ankle boots ◆ **~s de marche** walking shoes ◆ **être dans ses petits ~s** *(fig)* to feel awkward ou ill at ease

soulignage /suliɲaʒ/, **soulignement** /suliɲmɑ̃/ NM underlining

souligner /suliɲe/ GRAMMAIRE ACTIVE 53.6 ▸ conjug 1 ◂ VT 1 *(lit)* to underline; *(fig = accentuer)* to accentuate, to emphasize ◆ ~ **qch d'un trait double** to underline sth twice, to double underline sth ◆ ~ **qch en rouge** to underline sth in red ◆ ~ **ses yeux de noir** to put on black eye-liner ◆ **ce tissu à rayures soulignait son embonpoint** that striped material emphasized ou accentuated his stoutness 2 *(= faire remarquer)* to underline, to stress, to emphasize ◆ **il souligna l'importance de cette rencontre** he underlined ou stressed ou emphasized the importance of this meeting

soûlographie * /sulɔgʀafi/ NF *(hum)* drunkenness, boozing‡ *(Brit)*

soumettre /sumɛtʀ/ ▸ conjug 56 ◂ VT 1 *(= dompter) [+ pays, peuple]* to subject, to subjugate; *[+ personne]* to subject; *[+ rebelles]* to put down, to subdue, to subjugate

2 *(= asservir)* ~ **qn à** *[+ maître, loi]* to subject sb to

3 *(= astreindre)* ~ **qn à** *[+ traitement, formalité, régime, impôt]* to subject sb to ◆ ~ **qch à** *[+ traitement, essai, taxe]* to subject sth to ◆ **être soumis à des règles strictes** to be subject to strict rules ◆ **soumis aux droits de douane** dutiable, subject to (customs) duty ◆ **soumis à l'impôt** subject to tax(ation), taxable

4 *(= présenter) [+ idée, cas, manuscrit]* to submit *(à* to); ◆ ~ **une idée/un projet/une question à qn** to submit an idea/a plan/a matter to sb, to put an idea/a plan/a matter before sb ◆ ~ **un document à la signature** to submit a document for signature ◆ ~ **un projet de loi à référendum** to submit ou put a bill to referendum

VPR **se soumettre** 1 *(= obéir)* to submit *(à* to)

2 ◆ **se ~ à** *[+ traitement, formalité]* to submit to; *[+ entraînement, régime]* to submit to, to subject o.s. to

soumis, e /sumi, iz/ (ptp de **soumettre**) ADJ *(= docile) [personne, air]* submissive ◆ **fille ~e** † ≃ registered prostitute

soumission /sumisjɔ̃/ NF 1 *(= obéissance)* submission *(à* to); ◆ **il est toujours d'une parfaite ~ à leur égard** he is always totally submissive to their wishes ◆ **il exigeait de moi une totale ~** he demanded that I submit completely to him, he demanded my complete submission 2 *(= reddition)* submission ◆ **ils ont fait leur ~** they have submitted *(à* to) 3 *(Comm)* tender ◆ **faire une ~ pour un contrat** to tender for a contract ◆ ~ **cachetée** sealed bid

soumissionnaire /sumisjɔnɛʀ/ NMF *(Comm)* bidder, tenderer

soumissionner /sumisjɔne/ ▸ conjug 1 ◂ VT *(Comm)* to bid for, to tender for

soupape /supap/ NF valve ◆ **moteur 16 ~s** 16-valve engine ◆ ~ **d'admission/d'échappement** inlet/exhaust valve ◆ **~s en tête/latérales** overhead/side valves ◆ ~ **de sûreté** ou **de sécurité** *(lit, fig)* safety valve

soupçon /supsɔ̃/ NM 1 *(= suspicion)* suspicion ◆ **conduite exempte de tout ~** conduct above suspicion ◆ **personne à l'abri de** ou **au-dessus de tout ~** person free from ou person above all ou any suspicion ◆ **de graves ~s pèsent sur lui** he's under serious suspicion ◆ **avoir des ~s (sur)** to have one's suspicions (about), to be suspicious (about) ◆ **j'en avais le ~ !** I suspected as much! ◆ **sa femme eut bientôt des ~s** his wife soon became suspicious ◆ **des difficultés dont il n'avait pas ~** difficulties of which he had no inkling ou no suspicion 2 *(= petite quantité) [d'assaisonnement, maquillage, vulgarité]* hint, touch; *[de vin, lait]* drop

soupçonnable /supsɔnabl/ ADJ *(gén nég)* that arouses suspicion(s) ◆ **il est peu ~ de sympathies racistes** he can hardly be accused of being a racist

soupçonner /supsɔne/ ▸ conjug 1 ◂ VT to suspect ◆ **il est soupçonné de vol** he is suspected of theft ◆ **on le soupçonne d'y avoir participé, on soupçonne qu'il y a participé** he is suspected of having taken part in it ◆ **il soupçonnait un piège** he suspected a trap ◆ **vous ne soupçonnez pas ce que ça demande comme travail** you've no idea how much work it involves

soupçonneux, -euse /supsɔnø, øz/ ADJ suspicious ◆ **il me lança un regard ~** he gave me a suspicious glance, he glanced at me suspiciously

soupe /sup/ NF 1 *(Culin)* soup ◆ **~ à l'oignon/aux légumes/de poisson** onion/vegetable/fish soup; → **cheveu, marchand, plein**

2 *(hum = nourriture)* grub‡, nosh‡ ◆ **à la ~ !** grub's up!‡, come and get it! ◆ **on en a assez de la ~ qu'ils nous servent à la télévision** we've had enough of the rubbish they put on television ◆ **ce n'est pas de la musique, c'est de la ~ !** that's not music, it's garbage!

3 *(* : Ski)* porridge*

4 *(locutions)* **par ici la bonne ~ !*** roll up! roll up! ◆ **il est allé à la ~** * *(fig)* he has taken a backhander* ◆ **servir la ~ à qn** * *(fig)* to crawl to sb*

COMP **soupe au lait** ◆ **il est (très) ~ au lait** ◆ **c'est une ~ au lait** he flies off the handle easily, he's very quick-tempered

soupe populaire *(= lieu)* soup kitchen; *(= nourriture)* free meals ◆ **se retrouver à la ~ populaire** *(fig)* to end up penniless

soupe primitive *(Bio)* primeval soup

soupente /supɑ̃t/ NF cupboard *(Brit)* ou closet *(US)* (under the stairs)

souper /supe/ NM supper; *(Belg, Can, Helv = dîner)* dinner, supper VI ► conjug 1 ◄ 1 *(lit)* to have supper; *(Belg, Can, Helv)* to have dinner ou supper ◆ **après le spectacle, nous sommes allés ~** after the show we went for supper 2 * **j'en ai soupé de ces histoires !** I'm sick and tired* ou I've had a bellyful‡ of all this fuss!

soupeser /supəze/ ► conjug 5 ◄ VT *(lit)* to weigh in one's hand(s), to feel the weight of; *(fig)* to weigh up

soupière /supjɛʀ/ NF (soup) tureen

soupir /supiʀ/ NM 1 *(gén)* sigh ◆ **~ de satisfaction** sigh of satisfaction, satisfied sigh ◆ **pousser un ~ de soulagement** to give ou heave a sigh of relief ◆ **pousser un gros ~** to let out ou give a heavy sigh, to sigh heavily ◆ **"oui", dit-il dans un ~** "yes", he said with a sigh ou he sighed ◆ **rendre le dernier ~** *(littér)* to breathe one's last *(littér)* ◆ **l'objet de ses ~s** *(littér)* the object of his desire 2 *(Mus)* crotchet rest *(Brit)*, quarter(-note) rest *(US)*; → **quart**

soupirail (pl **-aux**) /supiʀaj, o/ NM (small) basement window *(gen with bars)*

soupirant /supiʀɑ̃/ NM († ou hum) suitor † *(aussi hum)*, wooer † *(aussi hum)*

soupirer /supiʀe/ ► conjug 1 ◄ VI to sigh ◆ **~ d'aise** to sigh with contentment, to heave a contented sigh ◆ **~ après ou pour qch/qn** *(littér)* to sigh for sth/sb *(littér)*, to yearn for sth/sb ◆ **"j'ai tout perdu", soupira-t-il** "I've lost everything," he sighed ◆ **... dit-il en soupirant** ... he said with a sigh ou he sighed

souple /supl/ ADJ 1 *(= flexible) [corps, membres, poignet, cuir]* supple; *[branche, tige, lame]* flexible; *[plastique, brosse à dents, lentilles, col]* soft; *[peau, cheveux]* smooth, soft; *[trait]* gentle ◆ **des chaussures en cuir ~** soft leather shoes ◆ **couverture de livre ~** flexi-cover ◆ **il est ~ comme un verre de lampe** he's as stiff as a board ◆ **avoir une conduite ~** *[automobiliste]* to be a smooth driver; → **disque, échine**

2 *(= accommodant) [personne, caractère]* flexible, adaptable; *[attitude, discipline, règlement]* flexible ◆ **horaires ~s** flexible hours ◆ **c'est un mode de paiement plus ~** it's a more flexible mode of payment

3 *(= gracieux, fluide) [corps, silhouette]* lithe, lissom *(littér)*; *[démarche, taille]* lithe, supple; *[style]* fluid, flowing *(épith)* ◆ **~ comme un chat ou une chatte** as agile as a cat

> ⚠ Attention à ne pas traduire automatiquement **souple** par **supple** ; les deux mots ne se correspondent que dans certains contextes.

souplement /supləmɑ̃/ ADV *[utiliser]* flexibly ◆ **les mesures sont appliquées plus ~ dans ce pays** the measures are applied with greater flexibility in this country

souplesse /suplɛs/ NF 1 *(physique) [de corps, membres, cuir]* suppleness; *[de branche, tige, lame]* flexibility; *[de plastique]* softness ◆ **pour entretenir la ~ de la peau/des cheveux** to keep the skin/the hair soft ◆ **d'une grande ~ d'utilisation** very easy to use ◆ **je manque de ~** I'm not very supple 2 *(= adaptabilité) [de personne, caractère, esprit]* flexibility, adaptability; *[de discipline, forme d'expression, règlement]* flexibility ◆ **il manque de ~** he's quite inflexible ◆ **il faut introduire plus de ~ dans les horaires** we must bring in more flexible working hours 3 *(= grâce, fluidité) [de corps, silhouette]* litheness, lissomness *(littér)*; *[de démarche, taille]* litheness; *[de style]* fluidity ◆ **faire qch en ~** to do sth smoothly ◆ **un démarrage en ~** a smooth start

souquenille /suknij/ NF *(Hist)* smock

souquer /suke/ ► conjug 1 ◄ VT *(= serrer)* to tighten VI *(= ramer)* ◆ **~ ferme ou dur** to pull hard (at the oars)

sourate /suʀat/ NF sura

source /suʀs/ NF 1 *(= point d'eau)* spring ◆ **~ thermale/d'eau minérale** hot ou thermal/mineral spring; → **couler, eau**

2 *(= foyer)* source ◆ **~ de chaleur/d'énergie** source of heat/of energy ◆ **~ lumineuse ou de lumière** source of light, light source ◆ **~ sonore** source of sound

3 *[de cours d'eau]* source ◆ **cette rivière prend sa ~ dans le Massif central** this river has its source in the Massif Central

4 *(= origine)* source ◆ **~ de ridicule/d'inspiration** source of ridicule/of inspiration ◆ **~ de revenus** source of income ◆ **l'argent est la ~ de tous les maux** money is the root of all evil ◆ **cette voiture est une ~ de tracas** this car causes me a lot of trouble ◆ **de ~ sûre, de bonne ~** from a reliable source, on good authority ◆ **tenir qch de ~ sûre** to have sth on good authority, to get sth from a reliable source ◆ **de ~ généralement bien informée** from a usually well-informed ou accurate source ◆ **de ~ officielle ou autorisée** from an official source ◆ **citer ses ~s** to quote one's sources ◆ **langage/programme/fichier ~** *(Ordin)* source language/program/file ◆ **langue ~** *(Ling)* departure ou source language; → **retenue², retour**

sourcier, -ière /suʀsje, jɛʀ/ NM,F water diviner; → **baguette**

sourcil /suʀsi/ NM (eye)brow ◆ **aux ~s épais** heavy-browed, beetle-browed; → **froncer**

sourcilier, -ière /suʀsilje, jɛʀ/ ADJ superciliary; → **arcade**

sourciller /suʀsije/ ► conjug 1 ◄ VI ◆ **il n'a pas sourcillé** he didn't turn a hair ou bat an eyelid ◆ **écoutant sans ~ mes reproches** listening to my reproaches without turning a hair ou batting an eyelid

sourcilleux, -euse /suʀsijø, øz/ ADJ *(= pointilleux)* finicky; *(littér = hautain)* haughty

sourd, e /suʀ, suʀd/ ADJ 1 *[personne]* deaf ◆ **~ d'une oreille** deaf in one ear ◆ **être ~ comme un pot*** to be as deaf as a post ◆ **faire la ~e oreille** to turn a deaf ear *(à* to) → **naissance**

2 ◆ **~ à** *[+ conseils, prières]* deaf to; *[+ vacarme, environnement]* oblivious of ou to ◆ **rester ~ aux appels de qn** to remain deaf to sb's appeals

3 *[son, voix]* muffled, muted; *[couleur]* muted, subdued; *(Phon) [consonne]* voiceless, unvoiced ◆ **chambre ~e** anechoic room; → **lanterne**

4 *(= vague) [douleur]* dull; *[désir, angoisse, inquiétude]* muted, gnawing; *[colère]* subdued, muted

5 *(= caché) [lutte]* silent, hidden ◆ **se livrer à de ~es manigances** to be engaged in hidden manoeuvring

NM,F deaf person ◆ **les ~s** the deaf ◆ **taper ou frapper ou cogner comme un ~** * to bang with all one's might ◆ **crier ou hurler comme un ~** * to yell at the top of one's voice ou for all one is worth; → **dialogue, pire**

NF **sourde** *(Phon)* voiceless ou unvoiced consonant

sourdement /suʀdəmɑ̃/ ADV *(= avec un bruit assourdi)* dully; *(littér = secrètement)* silently ◆ **le tonnerre grondait ~ au loin** there was a muffled rumble of thunder ou thunder rumbled dully in the distance

sourdine /suʀdin/ NF *[de trompette, violon]* mute ◆ **mettre une ~ à** *[+ prétentions]* to tone down; *[+ enthousiasme]* to dampen, to mute

◆ **en sourdine** *[jouer]* softly, quietly; *[faire, suggérer]* quietly ◆ **on entendait une musique en ~** there was music playing softly in the background ◆ **mettre en ~** *[+ débat]* to relegate to the background; *[+ idée, querelle]* to pass over; *[+ critiques]* to tone down; *[+ revendications]* to set aside ◆ **mets-la en ~ !**‡ put a sock in it!‡, shut your mouth!‡

sourdingue‡ /suʀdɛ̃g/ ADJ deaf, cloth-eared‡

sourd-muet, sourde-muette (mpl **sourds-muets**) /suʀmɥɛ, suʀd(ə)mɥɛt/ ADJ deaf-and-dumb NM,F deaf-mute, deaf-and-dumb person

sourdre /suʀdʀ/ VI *(littér) [source]* to rise; *[eau]* to spring up, to rise; *[émotions]* to well up, to rise

souriant, e /suʀjɑ̃, jɑ̃t/ ADJ *[visage]* smiling; *[personne]* cheerful; *[pensée, philosophie]* benign, agreeable ◆ **la standardiste est très ~e** the receptionist is always smiling ou is very cheerful

souriceau (pl **souriceaux**) /suʀiso/ NM young mouse

souricière /suʀisjɛʀ/ NF *(lit)* mousetrap; *(fig)* trap ◆ **établir une ~** *(Police)* to set a trap

sourire /suʀiʀ/ NM smile ◆ **le ~ aux lèvres** with a smile on his lips ◆ **avec le ~** *[accueillir qn]* with a smile; *[travailler]* cheerfully ◆ **gardez le ~ !** keep smiling! ◆ **avoir le ~** *(lit, fig)* to have a smile on one's face ◆ **il avait un ~ jusqu'aux oreilles** he was grinning from ear to ear ◆ **faire ou adresser un ~ à qn** to give sb a smile ◆ **faire des ~s à qn** to keep smiling at sb ◆ **être tout ~** to be all smiles ◆ **un large ~** *(chaleureux)* a broad smile; *(amusé)* a (broad) grin, a broad smile; → **coin**

VI ► conjug 36 ◄ 1 *(gén)* to smile *(à qn* at sb) ◆ **~ à la vie** to enjoy being alive ◆ **~ aux anges** *[personne]* to have a great beam ou vacant grin on one's face; *[bébé]* to smile happily in one's sleep ◆ **cette remarque les fit ~** *(lit)* this remark made them smile ou brought a smile to their faces ◆ **ce projet fait ~** *(fig)* this project is laughable ◆ **il est difficile d'en ~** it's nothing to smile about ◆ **je souris de le voir si vaniteux** it makes me smile to see how vain he is ◆ **il sourit de nos efforts** he laughs at our efforts, our efforts make him smile ◆ **il ne faut pas ~ de ces menaces** these threats can't just be laughed ou shrugged off

2 ◆ **~ à** *(= plaire à)* to appeal to; *(= être favorable à)* to smile on, to favour *(Brit)*, to favor *(US)* ◆ **cette idée ne me sourit guère** that idea doesn't appeal to me, I don't fancy that idea*

(Brit) ◆ **l'idée de faire cela ne me sourit pas** I don't relish the thought of doing that, the idea of doing that doesn't appeal to me ◆ **la chance lui souriait** luck smiled on him ◆ **tout lui sourit** everything goes his way

souris[1] /suʀi/ NF 1 *(= animal)* mouse ◆ **~ blanche** white mouse ◆ **~ grise** house mouse ◆ **je voudrais bien être une petite ~** *(pour espionner)* I'd love to be a fly on the wall ◆ **la petite ~ viendra chercher ta dent** the tooth fairy will come; → **gris, jouer, trotter** 2 *(* = femme)* chick* ◆ **~ d'hôtel** sneak thief *(operating in hotels)* 3 *[de gigot]* knuckle-joint ◆ **~ d'agneau** lamb shank 4 *(Ordin)* mouse

souris[2] †† /suʀi/ NM *(= sourire)* smile

sournois, e /suʀnwa, waz/ ADJ *[personne, regard, air]* sly, shifty; *[méthode, attaque, manœuvres]* underhand; *[douleur, virus, maladie]* insidious NM,F sly person ◆ **c'est un petit ~** he's a sly little devil*

sournoisement /suʀnwazmɑ̃/ ADV *[agir, regarder]* slyly ◆ **il s'approcha ~ de lui** he stole *ou* crept stealthily up to him

sournoiserie /suʀnwazʀi/ NF *(littér) [de personne, regard, air]* slyness, shiftiness; *[de méthode, attaque]* underhand nature

sous /su/ GRAMMAIRE ACTIVE 53.6

PRÉP 1 *(position)* under, underneath, beneath; *(atmosphère)* in ◆ **~ terre** under the ground, underground ◆ **~ le canon** *ou* **le feu de l'ennemi** under enemy fire ◆ **nager ~ l'eau** to swim under water ◆ **s'abriter ~ un arbre/un parapluie** to shelter under *ou* underneath *ou* beneath a tree/an umbrella ◆ **porter son sac ~ le bras** to carry one's bag under one's arm ◆ **dormir ~ la tente** to sleep under canvas *ou* in a tent ◆ **une mèche dépassait de ~ son chapeau** a lock of hair hung down from under her hat ◆ **vous trouverez le renseignement ~ tel numéro/telle rubrique** you will find the information under such-and-such a number/such-and-such a heading ◆ **~ des dehors frustes/une apparence paisible, il ...** beneath *ou* under *ou* behind his rough/peaceful exterior, he ... ◆ **se promener ~ la pluie/~ le soleil** to take a walk in the rain/in the sunshine ◆ **le village est plus joli ~ la lune/la clarté des étoiles** the village is prettier in the *ou* by moonlight/by starlight ◆ **le pays était ~ la neige** the country was covered with *ou* in snow; → **clé, coup, manteau** *etc*

2 *(temps) (= à l'époque de)* under; *(= dans un délai de)* within ◆ **~ le règne/le pontificat de ...** under *ou* during the reign/the pontificate of ... ◆ **~ Charles X** under Charles X ◆ **~ la Révolution/la Ve République** at the time of *ou* during the Revolution/the Vth Republic ◆ **~ peu** shortly, before long ◆ **~ huitaine/quinzaine** within a week/two weeks *ou* a fortnight *(Brit)*

3 *(cause)* under ◆ **~ l'influence de qn/qch** under the influence of sb/sth ◆ **le rocher s'est effrité ~ l'action du soleil/du gel** the rock has crumbled away due to the action of the sun/of the frost ◆ **plier ~ le poids de qch** to bend beneath *ou* under the weight of sth

4 *(manière)* **examiner une question ~ tous ses angles** *ou* **toutes ses faces** to examine every angle *ou* facet of a question, to look at a question from every angle ◆ **~ un faux nom/une identité d'emprunt** under a false name/an assumed identity ◆ **~ certaines conditions, j'accepte** I accept on certain conditions ◆ **~ ce rapport** on that score, in this *ou* that respect ◆ **il a été peint ~ les traits d'un berger** he was painted as a shepherd *ou* in the guise of a shepherd

5 *(dépendance)* under ◆ **être ~ les ordres de qn** to be under sb's orders ◆ **~ un régime capitaliste/socialiste** under a capitalist/socialist régime ◆ **la valise est ~ sa garde** the suitcase is in his care ◆ **se mettre ~ la protection/la garde de qn** to commit o.s. to sb's protection/care ◆ **l'affaire est ~ sa direction** he is running *ou* managing the affair, the affair is under his management ◆ **l'affaire est ~ sa responsabilité** the affair is his responsibility *ou* comes within his sphere of responsibility

6 *(Méd)* **il est ~ calmants/antibiotiques** he's on tranquilizers/antibiotics

7 *(Tech)* **câble ~ gaine** sheathed *ou* encased cable ◆ **(emballé) ~ plastique** plastic-wrapped ◆ **~ tube** in (a) tube ◆ **(emballé) ~ vide** vacuum-packed

8 *(Ordin)* **travailler ~ DOS ®/UNIX ®** to work in DOS ®/UNIX ®

PRÉF *(pour les composés les plus fréquents, voir à l'ordre alphabétique)* 1 *(infériorité)* **c'est de la ~-littérature/du ~-Giono** it's substandard literature/Giono

2 *(subordination)* sub- ◆ **~-catégorie** subcategory ◆ **~-agence** *(Écon)* sub-branch

3 *(insuffisance)* **~-industrialisé** underindustrialized ◆ **~-peuplement** underpopulation ◆ **les dangers de la ~-productivité** the dangers of underproductivity ◆ **~-rémunéré** underpaid ◆ **la région est ~-urbanisée** the region is insufficiently urbanized

sous-alimentation /suzalimɑ̃tasjɔ̃/ NF undernourishment, malnutrition

sous-alimenté, e /suzalimɑ̃te/ ADJ undernourished, underfed

sous-amendement /suzamɑ̃dmɑ̃/ NM *amendment to an amendment*

sous-bibliothécaire /subiblijɔtekɛʀ/ NMF assistant librarian, sub-librarian

sous-bois /subwɑ/ NM INV undergrowth ◆ **se promener dans les** *ou* **en ~** to walk through the trees

sous-brigadier /subʀigadje/ NM deputy sergeant

sous-chef /suʃɛf/ NMF *(gén)* second-in-command ◆ **~ de bureau** *(Admin)* deputy chief clerk ◆ **~ de gare** deputy *ou* sub-stationmaster

sous-classe /suklɑs/ NF sub-class

sous-comité /sukɔmite/ NM subcommittee

sous-commission /sukɔmisjɔ̃/ NF subcommittee

sous-consommation /sukɔ̃sɔmasjɔ̃/ NF underconsumption

sous-continent /sukɔ̃tinɑ̃/ NM subcontinent

sous-couche /sukuʃ/ NF *[peinture]* undercoat; *[parquet, moquette]* underlay ◆ **la ~ de glace** the underlying layer of ice

souscripteur, -trice /suskʀiptœʀ, tʀis/ NM,F *[d'emprunt, publication]* subscriber *(de* to)

souscription /suskʀipsjɔ̃/ NF *(Fin) [d'actions]* subscription, application *(de* for); *[de police d'assurance]* taking out; *(= somme)* subscription, contribution ◆ **ouvrir une ~ en faveur de qch** to start a fund in aid of sth ◆ **livre en ~** book sold on a subscription basis ◆ **ce livre est offert en ~ jusqu'au 15 novembre au prix de 100** € this book is available to subscribers until 15 November at the prepublication price of €100

souscrire /suskʀiʀ/ ▸ conjug 39 ◂ VT INDIR **souscrire à** 1 *[+ emprunt, publication]* to subscribe to; *[+ émission d'actions]* to subscribe for, to apply for ◆ **il a souscrit pour 200 € à l'emprunt** he subscribed *ou* applied for 200 euros' worth of shares in the scheme 2 *[+ idée, opinion, projet]* to subscribe to ◆ **c'est une excellente idée et j'y souscris** it's an excellent idea and I subscribe to it *ou* and I'm all in favour of it VT *[+ abonnement, assurance]* to take out; *[+ actions]* to subscribe for, to apply for; *[+ emprunt]* to subscribe to; *[+ billet de commerce]* to sign ◆ **le capital a été entièrement souscrit** the capital was fully subscribed

souscrit, e /suskʀi, it/ (ptp de **souscrire**) ADJ ◆ **capital ~** subscribed capital

sous-cutané, e /sukytane/ ADJ subcutaneous ◆ **piqûre en ~** subcutaneous injection

sous-développé, e /sudev(ə)lɔpe/ ADJ underdeveloped ◆ **les pays ~s** the underdeveloped countries

sous-développement /sudev(ə)lɔpmɑ̃/ NM underdevelopment

sous-diacre /sudjakʀ/ NM subdeacon

sous-directeur, -trice /sudiʀɛktœʀ, tʀis/ NM,F assistant manager, sub-manager

sous-dominante /sudɔminɑ̃t/ NF subdominant

sous-doué, e /sudwe/ *(péj ou hum)* ADJ dim NM,F dimwit*

sous-effectif /suzefɛktif/ NM understaffing ◆ **en ~** *(Mil)* undermanned; *[entreprise, service]* understaffed; *[usine, police]* undermanned ◆ **nous travaillons en ~** we are understaffed

sous-embranchement /suzɑ̃bʀɑ̃ʃmɑ̃/ NM sub-branch

sous-emploi /suzɑ̃plwa/ NM underemployment

sous-employer /suzɑ̃plwaje/ ▸ conjug 8 ◂ VT to underuse

sous-ensemble /suzɑ̃sɑ̃bl/ NM subset

sous-entendre /suzɑ̃tɑ̃dʀ/ ▸ conjug 41 ◂ VT to imply, to infer ◆ **qu'est-ce qu'il sous-entend par là ?** what's he trying to imply *ou* what does he mean by that?

sous-entendu, e /suzɑ̃tɑ̃dy/ ADJ implied, understood ◆ **il me faut une personne jeune, ~ : plus jeune que vous** I need a young person, meaning: younger than you NM insinuation; *(surtout sexuel)* innuendo ◆ **d'une voix pleine** *ou* **chargée** *ou* **lourde de ~s** *(gén)* in a voice full of hidden meaning; *(avec connotations sexuelles)* in a voice full of *ou* charged with innuendo

sous-équipé, e /suzekipe/ ADJ underequipped

sous-équipement /suzekipmɑ̃/ NM lack of equipment

sous-espèce /suzɛspɛs/ NF subspecies

sous-estimation /suzɛstimasjɔ̃/ NF underestimate

sous-estimer /suzɛstime/ ▸ conjug 1 ◂ VT to underestimate

sous-évaluation /suzevalɥasjɔ̃/ NF *[de bijou, meuble, monnaie]* undervaluation; *[de compétence, adversaire]* underestimation

sous-évaluer /suzevalɥe/ ▸ conjug 1 ◂ VT *[+ objet, entreprise, monnaie]* to undervalue; *[+ sentiment, risque, conséquence]* to underestimate

sous-exploitation /suzɛksplwatasjɔ̃/ NF underexploitation, underuse

sous-exploiter /suzɛksplwate/ ▸ conjug 1 ◂ VT to underexploit, to underuse

sous-exposer /suzɛkspoze/ ▸ conjug 1 ◂ VT to underexpose

sous-exposition /suzɛkspozisjɔ̃/ NF underexposure

sous-fifre* /sufifʀ/ NM underling

sous-filiale /sufiljal/ NF sub-branch

sous-gouverneur /suguvɛʀnœʀ/ NM deputy governor

sous-groupe /sugʀup/ NM subgroup

sous-homme /suzɔm/ NM subhuman

sous-informé, e /suzɛ̃fɔʀme/ ADJ poorly informed

sous-jacent, e /suʒasɑ̃, ɑ̃t/ ADJ *[terrain, couche]* subjacent, underlying; *[raison, problème]* underlying

sous-lieutenant /suljøt(ə)nɑ̃/ NM *(armée de terre)* second lieutenant; *(marine)* sublieutenant; *(aviation)* pilot officer *(Brit)*, second lieutenant *(US)*

sous-locataire /sulɔkatɛʀ/ NMF subtenant

sous-location /sulɔkasjɔ̃/ NF *(= action)* subletting; *(= logement)* house *ou* apartment that is sublet

sous-louer /sulwe/ ► conjug 1 ◄ VT to sublet

sous-main /sumɛ̃/ NM INV desk blotter ◆ **en ~** *(fig) [agir, négocier]* secretly, behind the scenes

sous-maîtresse /sumɛtʀɛs/ NF brothel-keeper, madam

sous-marin, e /sumaʀɛ̃, in/ ADJ *[pêche, chasse]* underwater *(épith)*; *[végétation, faune]* submarine *(épith)*, underwater *(épith)*; *[câble]* undersea *(épith)*; → **plongée²**, **plongeur** NM 1 *(lit)* submarine ◆ **~ nucléaire d'attaque** nuclear hunter-killer (submarine), nuclear attack submarine ◆ **~ de poche** pocket *ou* midget submarine 2 *(= espion)* mole

sous-marinier /sumaʀinje/ NM submariner

sous-marque /sumaʀk/ NF sub-brand

sous-médicalisé, e /sumedikalize/ ADJ *[population, région]* underprovided with medical care; *[hôpital]* with inadequate medical facilities

sous-menu /suməny/ NM *(Ordin)* sub-menu

sous-ministre /suministʀ/ NM *(Can)* deputy minister

sous-multiple /sumyltipl/ NM submultiple

sous-nappe /sunap/ NF undercloth

sous-nutrition /sunytʀisjɔ̃/ NF malnutrition

sous-off* /suzɔf/ NM (abrév de **sous-officier**) non-com*

sous-officier /suzɔfisje/ NM non-commissioned officer, NCO

sous-ordre /suzɔʀdʀ/ GRAMMAIRE ACTIVE 26.6 NM 1 *[d'animaux]* suborder 2 *(= subalterne)* subordinate, underling

sous-payer /supeje/ ► conjug 8 ◄ VT to underpay

sous-peuplé, e /supœple/ ADJ underpopulated

sous-peuplement /supœpləmɑ̃/ NM underpopulation

sous-pied /supje/ NM (under)strap

sous-plat (pl **sous-plats**) /supla/ NM *(Belg = dessous-de-plat)* table mat *(for hot serving dishes)*

sous-préfecture /supʀefɛktyʀ/ NF sub-prefecture

sous-préfet /supʀefɛ/ NM sub-prefect

sous-préfète /supʀefɛt/ NF *(= fonctionnaire)* sub-prefect; *(= épouse)* sub-prefect's wife

sous-production /supʀɔdyksjɔ̃/ NF underproduction

sous-produit /supʀɔdɥi/ NM by-product; *(péj)* inferior product

sous-programme /supʀɔgʀam/ NM subroutine, subprogram

sous-prolétaire /supʀɔletɛʀ/ NMF member of the urban underclass

sous-prolétariat /supʀɔletaʀja/ NM underclass

sous-pull /supyl/ NM thin poloneck jersey

sous-qualifié, e /sukalifje/ ADJ *[emploi, main-d'œuvre]* underqualified

sous-secrétaire /sus(ə)kʀetɛʀ/ NM ◆ **~ d'État** Under-Secretary

sous-secrétariat /sus(ə)kʀetaʀja/ NM *(= fonction)* post of Under-Secretary; *(= bureau)* Under-Secretary's office

sous-seing /susɛ̃/ NM INV *(Jur)* private document *(not officially recorded)*, signed writing

soussigné, e /susiɲe/ ADJ, NM,F undersigned ◆ **je ~, Dupont Charles-Henri, déclare que …** I the undersigned, Charles-Henri Dupont, certify that … ◆ **les (témoins) ~s** we the undersigned

sous-sol /susɔl/ NM *(Géol)* subsoil, substratum; *[de maison]* basement; *[de magasin]* basement, lower ground floor ◆ **les richesses de notre ~** our mineral resources ◆ **parking en ~** underground car park ◆ **~ total** full basement

sous-tasse /sutɑs/ NF *(Belg, Helv)* saucer

sous-tendre /sutɑ̃dʀ/ ► conjug 41 ◄ VT *(Géom)* to subtend; *(fig)* to underlie, to underpin ◆ **l'idéologie qui sous-tend toutes ces publicités** the underlying ideology behind all these advertisements

sous-titrage /sutitʀaʒ/ NM subtitling *(NonC)*

sous-titre /sutitʀ/ NM *[de journal, livre]* subheading, subhead; *[de film]* subtitle

sous-titrer /sutitʀe/ ► conjug 1 ◄ VT to subtitle ◆ **en version originale sous-titrée** in the original (version) with subtitles

soustractif, -ive /sustʀaktif, iv/ ADJ subtractive

soustraction /sustʀaksjɔ̃/ NF 1 *(Math)* subtraction ◆ **faire la ~ de** *[+ somme]* to take away, to subtract ◆ **il faut encore déduire les frais de réparation : faites la ~ vous-même** then you still have to deduct repair costs - you can work it out for yourself 2 *(Jur)* removal ◆ **~ d'enfant** abduction of a child *(by non-custodial parent)*

soustraire /sustʀɛʀ/ ► conjug 50 ◄ VT 1 *(gén, Math = défalquer)* to subtract, to take away *(de* from) 2 *(frm) (= dérober)* to remove, to abstract; *(= cacher)* to conceal, to shield *(à* from); ◆ **~ qn à la justice/à la colère de qn** to shield sb from justice/from sb's anger ◆ **~ à la compétence de** *(Jur)* to exclude from the jurisdiction of VPR **se soustraire** *(frm)* **se ~ à** *[+ devoir]* to shirk; *[+ obligation, corvée]* to escape, to shirk; *[+ autorité]* to elude, to escape from; *[+ curiosité]* to conceal o.s. from, to escape from; *[+ regards, vue]* to conceal o.s. from ◆ **se ~ à la justice** to elude justice; *(en s'enfuyant)* to abscond ◆ **quelle corvée ! comment m'y ~ ?** what a chore! how can I get out of it?

sous-traitance /sutʀɛtɑ̃s/ NF subcontracting

sous-traitant /sutʀɛtɑ̃/ NM subcontractor

sous-traiter /sutʀete/ ► conjug 1 ◄ VI *[maître d'œuvre]* to subcontract work *ou* jobs, to contract out work; *[exécutant]* to be subcontracted ◆ **son entreprise sous-traite pour une grosse société** his company does contract work for a big firm VT *[+ affaire, tâche]* to subcontract, to contract out ◆ **cette marque sous-traite la fabrication des vêtements** this company contracts out *ou* subcontracts clothes manufacturing

sous-utiliser /suzytilize/ ► conjug 1 ◄ VT *[+ capacités, réseau]* to underuse

sous-ventrière /suvɑ̃tʀijɛʀ/ NF *[de cheval]* girth, bellyband ◆ **manger à s'en faire péter* la ~** to stuff o.s.

sous-verre /suvɛʀ/ NM *(= encadrement)* clip frame; *(= image encadrée)* clip-framed picture

sous-vêtement /suvɛtmɑ̃/ NM item of underwear, undergarment ◆ **~s** underwear

soutache /sutaʃ/ NF *(Couture)* frog, braid

soutane /sutan/ NF cassock, soutane ◆ **prendre la ~** *(fig)* to enter the Church ◆ **la ~** *(péj = le clergé)* priests, the cloth

soute /sut/ NF *[de navire]* hold ◆ **~ (à bagages)** *[de bateau, avion]* baggage hold ◆ **~ à charbon** coal bunker ◆ **~ à munitions** ammunition store ◆ **~ à mazout** oil tank ◆ **~ à bombes** bomb bay

soutenable /sut(ə)nabl/ ADJ 1 *(= défendable) [opinion]* tenable 2 *(= durable) [croissance, rythme, développement]* sustainable 3 *(= supportable)* **ce film est d'une violence difficilement ~** this film is almost unbearably violent

soutenance /sut(ə)nɑ̃s/ NF *(Univ)* ◆ **~ de thèse** ≃ viva (voce) *(Brit)*, defense *(US)*

soutènement /sutɛnmɑ̃/ NM ◆ **travaux de ~** support(ing) works ◆ **ouvrage de ~** support(ing) structure ◆ **mur de ~** retaining *ou* breast wall

souteneur /sut(ə)nœʀ/ NM *(= proxénète)* pimp, procurer

soutenir /sut(ə)niʀ/ GRAMMAIRE ACTIVE 40.2, 53.2, 53.5 ► conjug 22 ◄

VT 1 *(= servir d'appui à) [+ personne, toit, mur]* to support, to hold up; *[médicament, traitement]* to sustain ◆ **on lui a fait une piqûre pour ~ le cœur** they gave him an injection to sustain his heart *ou* to keep his heart going ◆ **ses jambes peuvent à peine le ~** his legs can hardly support him, he can hardly stand ◆ **prenez un peu d'alcool, cela soutient** have a little drink – it'll give you a lift* *ou* keep you going

2 *(= aider) [+ gouvernement, parti, candidat]* to support, to back; *[+ famille]* to support ◆ **~ le franc/l'économie** to support *ou* bolster the franc/the economy ◆ **elle soutient les enfants contre leur père** she takes the children's part *ou* she stands up for the children against their father ◆ **son amitié/il les a beaucoup soutenus dans leur épreuve** his friendship/he was a real support *ou* prop to them in their time of trouble ◆ **~ le moral des troupes** to keep the troops' morale up *ou* high

3 *(= faire durer) [+ attention, conversation, effort]* to keep up, to sustain; *[+ réputation]* to keep up, to maintain

4 *(= résister à) [+ assaut, combat]* to stand up to, to withstand; *[+ siège]* to withstand; *[+ regard]* to bear, to support ◆ **~ la comparaison avec** to bear *ou* stand comparison with, to compare (favourably) with

5 *(= affirmer) [+ opinion, doctrine]* to uphold, to support; *(= défendre) [+ droits]* to uphold, to defend ◆ **~ sa thèse** *(Univ)* to attend *ou* have one's viva *(Brit)*, to defend one's dissertation *(US)* ◆ **c'est une doctrine que je ne pourrai jamais ~** it is a doctrine which I shall never be able to support *ou* uphold ◆ **elle soutient toujours le contraire de ce qu'il dit** she always maintains the opposite of what he says ◆ **il a soutenu jusqu'au bout qu'il était innocent** he maintained to the end that he was innocent ◆ **il m'a soutenu (mordicus) qu'il avait écrit*** he swore (blind) that he'd written

VPR **se soutenir** 1 *(= se maintenir) (sur ses jambes)* to hold o.s. up, to support o.s.; *(dans l'eau)* to keep (o.s.) afloat *ou* up ◆ **il n'arrivait plus à se ~ sur ses jambes** his legs could no longer support him, he could no longer stand

2 *(= s'entraider)* to stand by each other ◆ **dans la famille, ils se soutiennent tous** the family all stand by each other *ou* stick together

3 *(= être défendu)* **ça peut se ~** it's a tenable point of view ◆ **un tel point de vue ne peut se ~** a point of view like that is indefensible *ou* untenable

soutenu, e /sut(ə)ny/ (ptp de **soutenir**) ADJ 1 *(= constant, assidu) [attention, effort, travail, croissance]* sustained; *[rythme]* steady ◆ **après plusieurs années de croissance très ~e** after several years of strong growth 2 *(= châtié) [style, langue]* formal, elevated 3 *(= intense) [couleur]* strong; *[marché]* buoyant

souterrain, e /sutɛʀɛ̃, ɛn/ ADJ 1 *[parking, laboratoire, autoroute, explosion, abri, nappe]* underground; *[cours d'eau, galerie]* subterranean, underground; → **passage** [2] *[action, influence]* subterranean; *[travail]* behind-the-scenes ◆ **économie ~e** underground economy NM *(= passage) (gén)* underground *ou* subterranean passage; *(pour piétons)* underpass, subway *(Brit)*; *(= cave)* underground *ou* subterranean room; *(Archéol)* souterrain

soutien /sutjɛ̃/ GRAMMAIRE ACTIVE 38.1, 38.2, 40.2 NM [1] *(= aide)* support ◆ **~ financier** financial backing ◆ **~ logistique/moral** logistical/moral support ◆ **cours de ~** *(Scol)* remedial course ◆ **~ en français** extra teaching in French ◆ **apporter son ~ à qn/qch** to give sb/sth one's support ◆ **psychothérapie de ~** supportive psychotherapy ◆ **~ psychologique** counselling *(Brit)*, counseling *(US)* ◆ **unité de ~** *(Mil)* support *ou* reserve unit [2] *(= personne)* support, prop; *[de parti]* supporter ◆ **tu es mon seul ~** you're my only support ◆ **l'un des ~s du régime** one of the mainstays of the regime ◆ **être ~ de famille** *(Admin)* to be the main wage-earner in the family [3] *(= action) [de voûte]* supporting ◆ **~ des prix** price support

soutien-gorge (pl **soutiens-gorge**) /sutjɛ̃gɔʀʒ/ NM bra ◆ **~ d'allaitement** nursing bra

soutier /sutje/ NM *(Naut)* coal-trimmer

soutif * /sutif/ NM (abrév de **soutien-gorge**) bra

soutirage /sutiʀaʒ/ NM *[de vin]* decanting

soutirer /sutiʀe/ ▸ conjug 1 ◂ VT [1] *(= prendre)* **~ qch à qn** *[+ argent]* to squeeze *ou* get sth out of sb; *[+ promesse]* to extract sth from sb, to worm sth out of sb [2] *[+ vin]* to decant, to rack

souvenance /suv(ə)nɑ̃s/ NF *(littér)* recollection ◆ **avoir ~ de** to recollect, to have a recollection of ◆ **à ma ~** *(frm)* as I recall

souvenir /suv(ə)niʀ/ GRAMMAIRE ACTIVE 48.2 NM [1] *(= réminiscence)* memory ◆ **~s** *(= mémoires écrits)* memoirs ◆ **elle a gardé de lui un bon/mauvais ~** she has good/bad memories of him ◆ **j'ai gardé un ~ ému de cette soirée** I have fond memories of that evening ◆ **ce n'est plus qu'un mauvais ~** it's just a bad memory now ◆ **je n'ai qu'un vague ~ de l'incident/de l'avoir rencontré** I have only a vague *ou* dim recollection of the incident/of having met him *ou* of meeting him ◆ **raconter des ~s d'enfance/de guerre** to recount memories of one's childhood/of the war ◆ **si mes ~s sont exacts** if my memory serves me right *ou* correctly, if memory serves ◆ **~-écran** *(Psych)* screen memory

[2] *(littér = fait de se souvenir)* recollection, remembrance *(littér)* ◆ **avoir le ~ de qch** to remember sth ◆ **garder** *ou* **conserver le ~ de qch** to remember sth, to retain the memory of sth ◆ **perdre le ~ de qch** to lose all recollection of sth ◆ **évoquer le ~ de qn** to recall *ou* evoke the memory of sb ◆ **je n'ai pas ~ d'avoir ...** *(frm)* I have no recollection *ou* memory of having ...

◆ **en souvenir de** *[+ personne disparue]* in memory *ou* remembrance of; *[+ occasion]* in memory of ◆ **en ~ du passé** for old times' sake

[3] *(= objet à valeur sentimentale)* keepsake, memento; *(pour touristes, marque d'un événement)* souvenir ◆ **photo ~** souvenir photo ◆ **garder qch comme ~ (de qn)** to keep sth as a memento (of sb) ◆ **cette cicatrice est un ~ de la guerre** this scar is a souvenir from the war ◆ **cette montre est un ~ de famille** this watch is a family heirloom ◆ **boutique** *ou* **magasin de ~s** souvenir shop

[4] *(= formule de politesse)* **amical** *ou* **affectueux ~** yours (ever) ◆ **meilleur** *ou* **amical ~ de Rome** *(sur une carte)* greetings from Rome ◆ **mon bon ~ à Jean, transmettez mon meilleur ~ à Jean** remember me to Jean, (give my) regards to Jean ◆ **rappelez-moi au bon ~ de votre mère** remember me to your mother, give my (kind) regards to your mother ◆ **croyez à mon fidèle ~** yours ever, yours sincerely

VPR **se souvenir** ▸ conjug 22 ◂ to remember ◆ **se ~ de qn** to remember sb ◆ **se ~ de qch/d'avoir fait qch/que ...** to remember *ou* recall *ou* recollect sth/doing sth/that ... ◆ **il a plu tout l'été, tu t'en souviens ?** *ou* **tu te souviens ?** * it rained all summer, do you remember?, it rained all summer, remember? * ◆ **elle lui a donné une leçon dont il se souviendra** she taught him a lesson he won't forget (in a hurry) ◆ **souvenez-vous qu'il est très puissant** bear in mind *ou* remember that he is very powerful ◆ **souviens-toi de ta promesse !** remember your promise! ◆ **autant que je m'en souvienne ...** as *ou* so far as I (can) remember ... ◆ **tu m'as fait me ~ que ..., tu m'as fait ~ que ...** *(littér)* you have reminded me that ... ◆ **je m'en souviendrai !** *(menace)* I won't forget!

VB IMPERS *(littér)* ◆ **il me souvient d'avoir entendu raconter cette histoire** I recollect *ou* recall *ou* remember having heard *ou* hearing that story

> ⚠ Le mot **souvenir** se traduit par l'anglais **souvenir** uniquement quand il désigne un objet.

souvent /suvɑ̃/ ADV often ◆ **le plus ~, ça marche bien** more often than not it works well ◆ **il ne vient pas ~ nous voir** he doesn't come to see us often, he doesn't often come and see us ◆ **on se voit ~ ces derniers temps** we have seen a lot of each other recently ◆ **il se trompe plus ~ qu'à son tour** he's very often mistaken ◆ **bien ~** very often ◆ **peu ~** seldom

souverain, e /suv(ə)ʀɛ̃, ɛn/ ADJ [1] *[État, puissance]* sovereign; *[assemblée, cour, juge]* supreme ◆ **le ~ pontife** the Supreme Pontiff, the Pope [2] *(= suprême)* sovereign ◆ **le ~ bien** the sovereign good ◆ **remède ~ contre qch** sovereign remedy against sth [3] *(intensif) [mépris]* supreme NM,F [1] *(= monarque)* sovereign, monarch ◆ **~ absolu/constitutionnel** absolute/constitutional monarch ◆ **la ~e britannique** the British sovereign, the Queen [2] *(fig)* sovereign ◆ **s'imposer en ~** to reign supreme ◆ **la philosophie est la ~e des disciplines de l'esprit** philosophy is the most noble *ou* the highest of the mental disciplines NM [1] *(Jur, Pol)* **le ~** the sovereign power [2] *(Hist Brit = monnaie)* sovereign

souverainement /suv(ə)ʀɛnmɑ̃/ ADV [1] *(= intensément)* supremely ◆ **ça me déplaît ~** I dislike it intensely [2] *(= en tant que souverain)* with sovereign power

souveraineté /suv(ə)ʀɛnte/ NF sovereignty

souverainiste /suv(ə)ʀɛnist/ ADJ, NMF *(au Canada)* Quebec separatist

soviet † /sɔvjɛt/ NM soviet † ◆ **le Soviet suprême** the Supreme Soviet † ◆ **les Soviets** * *(péj)* the Soviets †

soviétique /sɔvjetik/ ADJ Soviet NMF **Soviétique** Soviet citizen

soviétisation /sɔvjetizasjɔ̃/ NF sovietization

soviétiser /sɔvjetize/ ▸ conjug 1 ◂ VT to sovietize

soviétologue /sɔvjetɔlɔg/ NMF Kremlinologist

sovkhoze /sɔvkoz/ NM sovkhoz

soya /sɔja/ NM ⇒ **soja**

soyeux, -euse /swajø, øz/ ADJ silky NM silk manufacturer *(of Lyons)*, silk merchant *(of Lyons)*

SPA /ɛspea/ NF (abrév de **Société protectrice des animaux**) ≈ RSPCA *(Brit)*, ASPCA *(US)*

spacieusement /spasjøzmɑ̃/ ADV spaciously ◆ **~ aménagé** spaciously laid out ◆ **nous sommes ~ logés** we have ample room where we are staying

spacieux, -ieuse /spasjø, jøz/ ADJ spacious, roomy ◆ **nous avons déménagé dans des locaux plus ~** we have moved to bigger premises

spadassin /spadasɛ̃/ NM *(littér, † = mercenaire)* hired killer *ou* assassin; *(† = bretteur)* swordsman

spaghetti /spageti/ NM ◆ **des ~s** spaghetti ◆ **~s bolognaise** spaghetti Bolognaise ◆ **un ~** a strand of spaghetti; → **western**

spahi /spai/ NM *(Hist, Mil)* Spahi *(soldier of native cavalry corps of French army in North Africa)*

spam /spam/ NM *(Internet)* spam

spamming /spamiŋ/ NM *(Internet)* spamming

spanglish /spɑ̃gliʃ/ NM spanglish

sparadrap /spaʀadʀa/ NM Band-Aid ®, plaster *(Brit)*

Spartacus /spaʀtakys/ NM Spartacus

spartakiste /spaʀtakist/ NMF Spartacist

Sparte /spaʀt/ N Sparta

spartiate /spaʀsjat/ ADJ *(Hist, fig)* Spartan NMF *(Hist)* ◆ **Spartiate** Spartan NFPL **spartiates** *(= chaussures)* Roman sandals

spasme /spasm/ NM spasm

spasmodique /spasmɔdik/ ADJ spasmodic

spasmophile /spasmɔfil/ ADJ spasmophilic NMF person suffering from spasmophilia

spasmophilie /spasmɔfili/ NF spasmophilia

spath /spat/ NM *(Minér)* spar ◆ **~ fluor** fluorspar, fluorite *(US)*

spatial, e (mpl **-iaux**) /spasjal, jo/ ADJ *(opposé à temporel)* spatial; *(Espace)* space *(épith)*; → **combinaison, engin, station**

spatialisation /spasjalizasjɔ̃/ NF spatialization

spatialiser /spasjalize/ ▸ conjug 1 ◂ VT to spatialize

spatialité /spasjalite/ NF spatiality

spationaute /spasjonot/ NM astronaut, spaceman NF astronaut, spacewoman

spationef /spasjɔnɛf/ NM spaceship, spacecraft

spatiotemporel, -elle /spasjotɑ̃pɔʀɛl/ ADJ spatiotemporal

spatule /spatyl/ NF [1] *(= ustensile) [de peintre, cuisinier]* spatula ◆ **doigts en ~** spatula-shaped fingers [2] *(= bout) [de ski, manche de cuiller]* tip [3] *(= oiseau)* spoon-bill

speaker /spikœʀ/ NM *(Radio, TV) (= annonceur)* announcer; *(= journaliste)* newscaster, newsreader ◆ **le ~** *(Pol Brit et US)* the Speaker

speakerine † /spikʀin/ NF *(Radio, TV) (= annonceuse)* announcer; *(= journaliste)* newsreader, newscaster

spécial, e (mpl **-iaux**) /spesjal, jo/ ADJ [1] *(= spécifique)* special ◆ **une (émission) ~e élections** an election special ◆ **le prix ~ du jury** *(Ciné)* the special jury prize ◆ **épreuve ~e** *(Rallye)* special stage ◆ **crème ~ visage** face cream; → **édition, envoyé, service** [2] *(= bizarre)* peculiar ◆ **il a des mœurs un peu ~es** *(euph)* he's that way inclined * *(euph)* ◆ **il est très ~** he's very peculiar *ou* odd ◆ **la cuisine japonaise, c'est ~** Japanese food is not to everybody's taste NF **spéciale** [1] *(= huître)* top-quality oyster [2] *(Rallye) (= épreuve)* special stage [3] *(= émission)* special

spécialement /spesjalmɑ̃/ ADV *(= plus particulièrement)* especially, particularly; *(= tout exprès)* specially ◆ **pas ~ intéressant** not particularly *ou* especially interesting ◆ **tu es pressé ? – pas ~** * are you in a hurry? – not really *ou* especially ◆ **c'est très intéressant, ~ vers la fin** it is very interesting, especially *ou* particularly towards the end ◆ **on l'a choisi ~ pour ce travail** he was specially chosen for this job ◆ ~

construit pour cet usage specially built for this purpose

spécialisation /spesjalizasjɔ̃/ NF specialization ◆ **faire une ~ en qch** *(Univ)* to specialize in sth

spécialisé, e /spesjalize/ (ptp de **spécialiser**) ADJ *[travail, personne, ouvrage, revue]* specialized ◆ **être ~ dans** *[personne]* to be a specialist in; *[entreprise]* to specialize in; → **ouvrier**

spécialiser /spesjalize/ ▸ conjug 1 ◂ VPR **se spécialiser** to specialize *(dans* in) VT to specialize

spécialiste /spesjalist/ NMF *(gén, Méd)* specialist ◆ **c'est un ~ de la gaffe*** he's always putting his foot in it* ◆ **lecteur/public non ~** non-specialist reader/audience

spécialité /spesjalite/ NF *(gén, Culin)* speciality *(Brit)*, specialty *(US)*; *(Univ = branche)* special field, specialism *(Brit)* ◆ **~ pharmaceutique** patent medicine ◆ **~ médicale** area of medical specialization ◆ **sa ~, c'est la chirurgie** he specializes in surgery ◆ **~s régionales** *(Culin)* regional specialties ◆ **"la spécialité du chef"** "the chef's special *ou* speciality" ◆ **il est le meilleur dans sa ~** he's the best in his field ◆ **les gaffes, c'est sa ~** he's always putting his foot in it ◆ **il a la ~ de faire ...*** he has a special *ou* particular knack of doing ..., he specializes in doing ... ◆ **se faire une ~ de (faire) qch** to specialize in (doing) sth

spécieusement /spesjøzmɑ̃/ ADV speciously

spécieux, -ieuse /spesjø, jøz/ ADJ specious

spécification /spesifikasjɔ̃/ NF specification

spécificité /spesifisite/ NF specificity

spécifier /spesifje/ ▸ conjug 7 ◂ VT *(= préciser)* to specify, to state; *(= indiquer, mentionner)* to state ◆ **veuillez ~ le modèle que vous désirez** please specify the model that you require ◆ **en passant votre commande, n'oubliez pas de ~ votre adresse** when placing your order, don't forget to state your address ◆ **a-t-il spécifié l'heure ?** did he specify *ou* state the time? ◆ **j'avais bien spécifié qu'il devait venir le matin** I had stated specifically that he should come in the morning

spécifique /spesifik/ GRAMMAIRE ACTIVE 53.1 ADJ specific

spécifiquement /spesifikmɑ̃/ ADV *(= tout exprès)* specifically; *(= typiquement)* typically

spécimen /spesimɛn/ NM *(= échantillon, exemple)* specimen; *(= exemplaire publicitaire)* specimen *ou* sample copy ◆ **~ de signature** specimen signature ◆ **c'est un drôle de ~*** *(iro)* he's an odd character *ou* a queer fish* *(Brit)*

spectacle /spɛktakl/ NM 1 *(= vue, tableau)* sight; *(grandiose, magnifique)* sight, spectacle ◆ **au ~ de** at the sight of ◆ **j'étais ému par ce ~** I was moved by what I saw ◆ **se donner *ou* s'offrir en ~ (à qn)** *(péj)* to make a spectacle *ou* an exhibition of o.s. (in front of sb) ◆ **une vieille dame qui assistait au ~ de la foule/de la rue** an old lady who was watching the crowd/the bustle of the street

2 *(Ciné, Théât = représentation)* show ◆ **le ~** *(= branche)* show business, show biz* ◆ **les arts du ~, le ~ vivant** the performing arts ◆ **"spectacles"** *(= rubrique)* "entertainment" ◆ **le ~ va commencer** the show is about to begin ◆ **un ~ lyrique** an opera ◆ **un ~ dramatique** a play ◆ **~ de variétés** variety show ◆ **aller au ~** to go to a show ◆ **donner un ~** to put on a show ◆ **donner un ~ de danse/marionnettes** to put on a dance/puppet show ◆ **l'industrie du ~** the entertainment(s) industry ◆ **film à grand ~** epic (film), blockbuster; → **salle**

3 *(en apposition)* **l'information-~** news as entertainment ◆ **procès-~** show trial ◆ **politique-~** showbiz politics ◆ **c'est de la justice-~** it isn't justice, it's a circus

spectaculaire /spɛktakylɛʀ/ ADJ spectacular

spectaculairement /spɛktakylɛʀmɑ̃/ ADV 1 *(= d'une manière théâtrale)* **manifester ~ son soutien à une cause** to give a dramatic demonstration of one's support for a cause ◆ **il a ~ démissionné** he resigned in a blaze of publicity ◆ **affirmer qch ~** to state sth emphatically 2 *(= considérablement) [augmenter, améliorer, renforcer]* greatly; *[progresser]* enormously

spectateur, -trice /spɛktatœʀ, tʀis/ NM,F *[d'événement, accident]* onlooker, witness; *[d'œuvre d'art]* viewer; *(Sport)* spectator; *(Ciné, Théât)* member of the audience ◆ **les ~s** *(Ciné, Théât)* the audience ◆ **traverser la vie en ~** to go through life as an onlooker *ou* a spectator ◆ **allons-nous assister en ~s impuissants à cette horreur ?** are we just going to stand by helplessly and watch this horrific spectacle?

spectral, e (mpl **-aux**) /spɛktʀal, o/ ADJ 1 *(= fantomatique)* ghostly, spectral 2 *(Phys)* spectral; → **analyse**

spectre /spɛktʀ/ NM 1 *(= fantôme)* ghost; *(fig)* spectre *(Brit)*, specter *(US)* ◆ **comme s'il avait vu un ~** as if he'd seen a ghost ◆ **le ~ de l'inflation** the spectre of inflation ◆ **agiter *ou* brandir le ~ de la guerre civile** to raise the spectre of civil war 2 *(Phys)* spectrum ◆ **~ d'absorption/de masse/de résonance** absorption/mass/resonance spectrum ◆ **~ solaire** solar spectrum 3 *(= éventail) [de thèmes, partis politiques]* spectrum ◆ **aux deux extrémités du ~ politique** at both ends of the political spectrum ◆ **ils attirent un large ~ de lecteurs** they appeal to a wide and varied readership 4 *(Pharm)* spectrum ◆ **antibiotique à large ~** broad-spectrum antibiotic

spectrogramme /spɛktʀɔgʀam/ NM spectrogram

spectrographe /spɛktʀɔgʀaf/ NM spectrograph

spectrographie /spɛktʀɔgʀafi/ NF spectrography

spectromètre /spɛktʀɔmɛtʀ/ NM spectrometer

spectroscope /spɛktʀɔskɔp/ NM spectroscope

spectroscopie /spɛktʀɔskɔpi/ NF spectroscopy

spectroscopique /spɛktʀɔskɔpik/ ADJ spectroscopic

spéculaire /spekylɛʀ/ ADJ *(gén)* specular ◆ **écriture/image ~** mirror writing/image NF *(= plante)* Venus's looking-glass

spéculateur, -trice /spekylatœʀ, tʀis/ NM,F speculator ◆ **~ à la baisse** bear ◆ **~ à la hausse** bull

spéculatif, -ive /spekylatif, iv/ ADJ *(Fin, Philos)* speculative

spéculation /spekylasjɔ̃/ NF *(gén)* speculation ◆ **~ à la baisse/à la hausse** bear/bull operation ◆ **~ boursière/immobilière** stock-market/property *(Brit) ou* real-estate *(US)* speculation ◆ **ce ne sont que des ~s (hasardeuses)** it's pure speculation *ou* conjecture ◆ **cela a relancé les ~s sur l'éventualité d'un accord** this prompted new speculation about the possibility of an agreement

spéculer /spekyle/ ▸ conjug 1 ◂ VI 1 *(Bourse)* to speculate *(sur* in); ◆ **~ à la hausse/à la baisse** to bull/bear 2 *(Philos)* to speculate *(sur* on, about); ◆ **~ sur** *(fig = tabler sur)* to bank on, to rely on

spéculum /spekylɔm/ NM speculum

speech* /spitʃ/ NM *(= laïus)* speech ◆ **faire un ~** to make a speech ◆ **elle nous a fait son ~ sur le machisme** she gave us her speech *ou* spiel* on male chauvinism

speed* /spid/ ADJ *(= agité)* hyper* ◆ **elle est très ~** she's really hyper* NM *(arg Drogue)* speed

speedé, e* /spide/ ADJ *(= agité)* hyper*, hyped up*

speeder* /spide/ ▸ conjug 1 ◂ VI 1 ◆ **elle speede tout le temps** *(= va vite)* she just never stops; *(= est hyperactive)* she's really hyper* 2 *(= se droguer)* to take speed

spéléo* /speleo/ NF abrév de **spéléologie** NMF abrév de **spéléologue**

spéléologie /speleɔlɔʒi/ NF *(= étude)* speleology; *(= exploration)* caving, potholing *(Brit)*, spelunking *(US)*

spéléologique /speleɔlɔʒik/ ADJ *[recherche]* speleological; *[expédition]* caving *(épith)*, potholing *(Brit) (épith)*, spelunking *(US) (épith)*

spéléologue /speleɔlɔg/ NMF *(= spécialiste)* speleologist; *(= explorateur)* caver, potholer *(Brit)*, spelunker *(US)*

spencer /spɛnsœʀ/ NM short jacket, spencer; *(Mil)* mess jacket

spermaceti /spɛʀmaseti/ NM spermaceti

spermatique /spɛʀmatik/ ADJ spermatic ◆ **cordon ~** spermatic cord

spermatogénèse /spɛʀmatɔʒenɛz/ NF spermatogenesis

spermatozoïde /spɛʀmatɔzɔid/ NM sperm, spermatozoon

sperme /spɛʀm/ NM semen, sperm

spermicide /spɛʀmisid/ ADJ spermicide *(épith)*, spermicidal NM spermicide

spermogramme /spɛʀmɔgʀam/ NM semen analysis

sphaigne /sfɛɲ/ NF peat *ou* bog moss

sphénoïde /sfenɔid/ NM sphenoid bone

sphère /sfɛʀ/ NF *(Astron, fig)* sphere ◆ **~ céleste/terrestre** celestial/terrestrial sphere ◆ **~ d'influence/d'activité** sphere of influence/of activity ◆ **dans toutes les ~s de la vie privée/publique** in all spheres of private/public life ◆ **les hautes ~s de l'État** the higher *ou* highest echelons *ou* levels of government ◆ **il évolue dans les hautes ~s** he moves in influential circles

sphéricité /sfeʀisite/ NF sphericity

sphérique /sfeʀik/ ADJ spherical; → **calotte**

sphéroïde /sfeʀɔid/ NM spheroid

sphincter /sfɛ̃ktɛʀ/ NM sphincter

sphinx /sfɛ̃ks/ NM 1 *(Art, Myth, fig)* sphinx ◆ **le Sphinx** *(Myth)* the Sphinx ◆ **sourire de ~** sphinx-like smile 2 *(= papillon)* hawkmoth *(Brit)*, sphinx moth *(US)*

spi /spi/ NM ⇒ **spinnaker**

spina-bifida /spinabifida/ NM INV spina bifida

spinal, e (mpl **-aux**) /spinal, o/ ADJ spinal

spinnaker /spinakɛʀ/ NM spinnaker

spiral, e (mpl **-aux**) /spiʀal, o/ ADJ spiral NM ◆ **(ressort) ~** hairspring NF **spirale** spiral ◆ **s'élever/tomber en ~e** to spiral up(wards)/down(wards) ◆ **la ~e de l'inflation *ou* inflationniste** the inflationary spiral ◆ **pris dans une ~e de violence** caught up in a spiral of violence; → **cahier**

spiralé, e /spiʀale/ ADJ spiral *(épith)*

spirante /spiʀɑ̃t/ ADJ F, NF ◆ **(consonne) ~** spirant, fricative

spire /spiʀ/ NF *[d'hélice, spirale]* (single) turn; *[de coquille]* whorl; *[de ressort]* spiral

spirite /spiʀit/ ADJ, NMF spiritualist

spiritisme /spiʀitism/ NM spiritualism

spiritualiser /spiʀitɥalize/ ▸ conjug 1 ◂ VT to spiritualize

spiritualisme /spiʀitɥalism/ NM spiritualism

spiritualiste /spiʀitɥalist/ ADJ spiritualist(ic) NMF spiritualist

spiritualité /spiʀitɥalite/ NF spirituality

spirituel, -elle /spiʀitɥɛl/ ADJ 1 (= vif, fin) *[personne, remarque]* witty 2 *(Philos, Rel)* *[chef, maître, père, fils, pouvoir]* spiritual ◆ **musique spirituelle** sacred music ◆ **concert ~** concert of sacred music ◆ **le ~ et le temporel** the spiritual and the temporal

spirituellement /spiʀitɥɛlmɑ̃/ ADV 1 *[remarquer]* wittily 2 *(Philos, Rel)* spiritually

spiritueux, -euse /spiʀitɥø, øz/ ADJ spirituous NM spirit ◆ **les ~** spirits

spiroïdal, e (mpl **-aux**) /spiʀɔidal, o/ ADJ spiroid

spleen /splin/ NM *(littér)* melancholy, spleen (††) ◆ **avoir le ~** to feel melancholy

splendeur /splɑ̃dœʀ/ NF 1 *[de paysage, réception, résidence]* magnificence, splendour *(Brit)*, splendor *(US)* ◆ **ce tapis est une ~** this carpet is quite magnificent ◆ **les ~s de l'art africain** the splendours of African art ◆ **quelle ~ !** it's magnificent! 2 (= gloire) glory, splendour *(Brit)*, splendor *(US)* ◆ **du temps de sa ~** in the days of its *(ou his etc)* glory *ou* splendour ◆ **dans toute sa/leur ~** *(iro)* in all its/their splendour *ou* glory 3 *(littér = éclat, lumière)* brilliance, splendour *(Brit)*, splendor *(US)*

splendide /splɑ̃did/ ADJ *[temps, journée]* splendid, gorgeous, glorious; *[soleil]* glorious; *[réception, résidence, spectacle]* splendid, magnificent; *[femme]* magnificent, gorgeous; *[voix, œuvre, film, image, interprétation]* magnificent, wonderful ◆ **~ isolement** splendid isolation ◆ **tu as un teint** *ou* **une mine ~** you look wonderful

splendidement /splɑ̃didmɑ̃/ ADV splendidly, magnificently ◆ **un rôle ~ interprété par un jeune acteur** a wonderful *ou* magnificent performance by a young actor

spoiler /spɔjlɛʀ/ NM *[de voiture]* spoiler

spoliateur, -trice /spɔljatœʀ, tʀis/ ADJ *[loi]* spoliatory NM,F despoiler

spoliation /spɔljasjɔ̃/ NF despoilment *(de of)*

spolier /spɔlje/ ► conjug 7 ◄ VT to despoil *(de of)*

spondaïque /spɔ̃daik/ ADJ spondaic

spondée /spɔ̃de/ NM spondee

spongieux, -ieuse /spɔ̃ʒjø, jøz/ ADJ *(gén, Anat)* spongy

spongiforme /spɔ̃ʒifɔʀm/ ADJ spongiform; → **encéphalopathie**

sponsor /spɔ̃sɔʀ/ NM sponsor

sponsorisation /spɔ̃sɔʀizasjɔ̃/ NF sponsoring

sponsoriser /spɔ̃sɔʀize/ ► conjug 1 ◄ VT to sponsor ◆ **se faire ~ par une société** to get sponsorship from a company

spontané, e /spɔ̃tane/ ADJ *(gén)* spontaneous; *[candidature, témoignage]* unsolicited; *[aveux]* voluntary ◆ **c'est quelqu'un de très ~** he's very spontaneous ◆ **une grève ~e** a lightning strike; → **génération**

spontanéité /spɔ̃taneite/ NF spontaneity

spontanément /spɔ̃tanemɑ̃/ ADV spontaneously

Sporades /spɔʀad/ NFPL ◆ **les ~** the Sporades

sporadicité /spɔʀadisite/ NF sporadic nature *ou* occurrence

sporadique /spɔʀadik/ ADJ sporadic

sporadiquement /spɔʀadikmɑ̃/ ADV sporadically

sporange /spɔʀɑ̃ʒ/ NM spore case, sporangium *(SPÉC)*

spore /spɔʀ/ NF spore

sport /spɔʀ/ NM 1 (= activité) sport ◆ **faire du ~** to do sport ◆ **~ individuel/d'équipe** *ou* **collectif** individual/team sport ◆ **~ amateur/professionnel** amateur/professional sport ◆ **~ en salle/de plein air** indoor/outdoor sport ◆ **~ de compétition/de combat** competitive/combat sport ◆ **~ de loisir** recreational sport ◆ **les ~s d'hiver** winter sports ◆ **aller aux ~s d'hiver** to go on a winter sports holiday ◆ **~s nautiques/mécaniques** water/motor sports ◆ **~ cérébral** mental exercise ◆ **la corruption/la fraude fiscale est devenue un véritable ~ national** corruption/tax fraud has become a national pastime ◆ **(section) ~-études** *(Scol)* special course in secondary school for athletically-gifted pupils ◆ **de ~** *[vêtements, terrain, voiture]* sports *(épith)*
2 (* = action) **il va y avoir du ~ !** we're going to see some fun!* *ou* action!* ◆ **faire ça, c'est vraiment du ~** it's no picnic* ◆ **faire qch pour le ~** to do sth for the hell of it*
ADJ INV 1 (= décontracté) *[vêtement]* casual
2 († = chic, fair-play) sporting, fair

sportif, -ive /spɔʀtif, iv/ ADJ 1 *[épreuve, journal, résultats]* sports *(épith)*; *[pêche, marche]* competitive *(épith)* ◆ **pratiquer une activité sportive** to play *ou* practise a sport 2 *[personne, jeunesse]* athletic, fond of sports *(attrib)*; *[allure, démarche]* athletic ◆ **conduite sportive** sport driving ◆ **elle a une conduite sportive** she drives like a rally driver 3 *[attitude, mentalité, comportement]* sporting, sportsmanlike ◆ **faire preuve d'esprit ~** to be sportsmanlike NM sportsman NF **sportive** sportswoman

sportivement /spɔʀtivmɑ̃/ ADV sportingly

sportivité /spɔʀtivite/ NF sportsmanship

spot /spɔt/ NM 1 *(Phys)* light spot; *(Élec)* scanning spot; *[de radar]* blip 2 (= lampe, Ciné, Théât) spotlight, spot 3 (= publicité) ~ **(publicitaire)** commercial, advert* *(Brit)*, ad* ADJ INV *[crédit, marché, prix]* spot *(épith)*

spoutnik /sputnik/ NM sputnik

sprat /spʀat/ NM sprat

spray /spʀɛ/ NM (= aérosol) spray, aerosol ◆ **déodorant en ~** spray(-on) deodorant

sprint /spʀint/ NM *(de fin de course)* (final) sprint, final spurt; (= épreuve) sprint → **piquer**

sprinter[1] /spʀinte/ ► conjug 1 ◄ VI to sprint; *(en fin de course)* to put on a final spurt

sprinter[2] /spʀintœʀ/ NM, **sprinteur, -euse** /spʀintœʀ, øz/ NM,F sprinter; *(en fin de course)* fast finisher

squale /skwal/ NM shark

squame /skwam/ NF *(Méd)* scale, squama *(SPÉC)*

squameux, -euse /skwamø, øz/ ADJ *(Méd)* squamous, squamose; *(littér)* scaly

square /skwaʀ/ NM public garden(s)

squash /skwaʃ/ NM squash ◆ **faire du ~** to play squash

squat * /skwat/ NM (= logement) squat

squatter[1] /skwatœʀ/ NM squatter

squatter[2] /skwate/, **squattériser** /skwateʀize/ ► conjug 1 ◄ VT 1 *[+ logement]* to squat (in) 2 (* = utiliser) *[+ ordinateur]* to borrow ◆ **je peux ~ ton bureau quelques minutes ?** can I use your office for a few minutes?

squatteur /skwatœʀ/ NM ⇒ **squatter**[1]

squaw /skwo/ NF squaw

squeezer /skwize/ ► conjug 1 ◄ VT 1 *(au bridge)* to squeeze 2 (* = évincer) to bypass

squelette /skəlɛt/ NM *(lit, fig)* skeleton ◆ **après sa maladie, c'était un vrai ~** after his illness he was just a bag of bones *ou* he was like a skeleton ◆ **c'est un ~ ambulant*** he's a walking skeleton ◆ **un ~ dans le placard*** (= scandale) a skeleton in the cupboard *(Brit)* *ou* closet *(US)*

squelettique /skəletik/ ADJ *[personne, arbre]* scrawny; *[exposé]* sketchy, skimpy; *(Anat)* skeletal ◆ **d'une maigreur ~** skin and bone ◆ **il est ~** he's skin and bone, he's like a skeleton ◆ **des effectifs ~s** a skeleton staff

SRAS /sʀas/ NM (abrév de **syndrome respiratoire aigu sévère**) SARS

Sri Lanka /sʀilɑ̃ka/ NM Sri Lanka

sri-lankais, e /sʀilɑ̃kɛ, ɛz/ ADJ Sri-Lankan NM,F **Sri-Lankais(e)** Sri-Lankan

SRPJ /ɛsɛʀpeʒi/ NM (abrév de **service régional de la police judiciaire**) ≈ regional crime squad, CID *(Brit)*

S.S. /ɛsɛs/ NF 1 (abrév de **Sécurité sociale**) → **sécurité** 2 (abrév de **Sa Sainteté**) HH NM (= soldat) SS man

SSII /ɛsɛsii/ NF (abrév de **société de service et d'ingénierie en informatique**) computer engineering and maintenance company

St (abrév de **Saint**) St

stabilisant /stabilizɑ̃/ NM *(Chim)* stabilizer

stabilisateur, -trice /stabilizatœʀ, tʀis/ ADJ stabilizing ◆ **l'effet ~ de l'euro** the stabilizing effect of the euro NM *(Tech)* *[de véhicule]* anti-roll device; *[de navire, vélo]* stabilizer; *[d'avion]* *(horizontal)* tailplane; *(vertical)* fixed fin; *(Chim : pour aliments)* stabilizer

stabilisation /stabilizasjɔ̃/ NF stabilization

stabiliser /stabilize/ ► conjug 1 ◄ VT *[+ situation, prix]* to stabilize; *[+ terrain]* to consolidate ◆ **à 90 km/h en vitesse stabilisée** *(Aut)* at a constant 90 km/h; → **accotement** VPR **se stabiliser** *[situation, prix, cours]* to stabilize, to become stabilized; *[courbe de graphe]* to plateau; *[personne]* *(physiquement)* to find one's balance; *(dans la vie)* to settle down

stabilité /stabilite/ NF stability ◆ **~ des prix** price stability ◆ **~ monétaire/économique/politique** monetary/economic/political stability

stable /stabl/ ADJ *[monnaie, gouvernement, personne]* *(Chim, Phys)* stable; *[position, échelle]* stable, steady ◆ **~ sur ses jambes** steady on one's legs

stabulation /stabylasjɔ̃/ NF *[de bétail]* stalling; *[de chevaux]* stabling; *[de poissons]* storing in tanks

staccato /stakato/ ADV staccato NM staccato passage

stade /stad/ NM 1 *(sportif)* stadium 2 (= période, étape) stage ◆ **à ce ~** at this stage ◆ **à ce ~ de la maladie** at this stage in the development of the disease ◆ **il en est resté au ~ de l'adolescence** he never got beyond adolescence *ou* the adolescent phase ◆ **passer à un ~ supérieur** to go one step higher ◆ **~ oral/anal/génital** *(Psych)* oral/anal/genital stage

stadier /stadje/ NM steward *(working in a stadium)*

staff[1] /staf/ NM 1 (= personnel) staff 2 *(Méd = réunion de travail)* staff meeting

staff[2] /staf/ NM (= plâtre) staff

staffeur /stafœʀ/ NM plasterer *(working in staff)*

stage /staʒ/ GRAMMAIRE ACTIVE 46.1 NM 1 (= immersion dans une entreprise) (work) placement, internship *(US)* ◆ **faire un ~ (en entreprise)** to do a (work) placement *ou* an internship *(US)* ◆ **je vais faire un ~ de trois mois chez IBM** I'm going to do a three-month placement *ou* internship *(US)* with IBM 2 (= enseignement, cours) (training) course ◆ **faire** *ou* **suivre un ~** to go on a (training) course ◆ **faire un ~ de peinture/de roller/de plongée** to have painting/rollerblading/diving lessons, to go on a painting/rollerblading/diving course ◆ **faire**

un ~ d'informatique *(gén)* to go on a computing course; *(en entreprise)* to have in-service *ou* in-house training in computing 3 *[d'avocat]* articles ◆ **il a fait son ~ chez maître Legrand** he did his articles in Mr Legrand's practice

COMP **stage d'initiation** introductory course
stage d'insertion (professionnelle) *training scheme for the young unemployed to help them find work*
stage-parking* useless training course
stage pédagogique teaching practice, school placement
stage de perfectionnement (professionnel) vocational training course
stage de réinsertion retraining course

> ⚠ **stage** ne se traduit pas par le mot anglais **stage**, qui a le sens de 'étape' ou 'scène'.

stagflation /stagflasjɔ̃/ NF stagflation

stagiaire /staʒjɛʀ/ NMF trainee, intern *(US)* ADJ trainee *(épith)* ◆ **professeur ~** student *ou* trainee teacher

stagnant, e /stagnɑ̃, ɑ̃t/ ADJ *(lit, fig)* stagnant

stagnation /stagnasjɔ̃/ NF *(lit, fig)* stagnation ◆ **marché en ~** stagnating market

stagner /stagne/ ▸ conjug 1 ◂ VI *(lit, fig)* to stagnate

stakhanovisme /stakanɔvism/ NM Stakhanovism

stakhanoviste /stakanɔvist/ ADJ Stakhanovist NMF Stakhanovite

stalactite /stalaktit/ NF stalactite

stalag /stalag/ NM stalag

stalagmite /stalagmit/ NF stalagmite

Staline /stalin/ NM Stalin

stalinien, -ienne /stalinjɛ̃, jɛn/ ADJ, NM,F Stalinist

stalinisme /stalinism/ NM Stalinism

stalle /stal/ NF *[de cheval]* stall, box; *(Rel)* stall

stance /stɑ̃s/ NF († = *strophe)* stanza ◆ **~s** *(= poème) type of verse form (of lyrical poem)*

stand /stɑ̃d/ NM *[d'exposition]* stand; *[de foire]* stall ◆ **~ (de tir)** *[de foire]* *(Sport)* shooting range; *(Mil)* firing range ◆ **~ de ravitaillement** *(Sport)* pit

standard[1] /stɑ̃daʀ/ NM *(Téléc)* switchboard

standard[2] /stɑ̃daʀ/ NM 1 *(= norme)* standard ◆ **~ de vie** standard of living 2 *(Mus)* (jazz) standard ADJ INV standard *(épith)*; → **échange**

standardisation /stɑ̃daʀdizasjɔ̃/ NF standardization

standardiser /stɑ̃daʀdize/ ▸ conjug 1 ◂ VT to standardize

standardiste /stɑ̃daʀdist/ NMF switchboard operator ◆ **demandez à la ~** ask the operator

stand-by /stɑ̃dbaj/ ADJ INV stand-by *(épith)* ◆ **en ~** on stand-by NM INV stand-by passenger

standing /stɑ̃diŋ/ NM standing ◆ **immeuble de grand ~** block of luxury flats *(Brit) ou* apartments *(US)*

staphylocoque /stafilɔkɔk/ NM staphylococcus ◆ **~ doré** staphylococcus aureus

star /staʀ/ NF *(Ciné)* star ◆ **c'est une ~ du journalisme/de la politique** he's (*ou* she's) a big name in journalism/in politics ◆ **~ du tennis** top name in tennis, star tennis player

starisation /staʀizajɔ̃/ NF ◆ **il refuse la ~** he refuses to be made into a star *ou* turned into a celebrity

stariser* /staʀize/ ▸ conjug 1 ◂ VT *[+ personne]* to make into a star

starking /staʀkiŋ/ NF starking (apple)

starlette /staʀlɛt/ NF starlet

star-system (pl **star-systems**) /staʀsistɛm/ NM star system

START /staʀt/ (abrév de **Strategic Arms Reduction Talks**) START

starter /staʀtɛʀ/ NM 1 *[de moteur]* choke ◆ **mettre le ~** to pull the choke out ◆ **marcher au ~** to run with the choke out ◆ **~ automatique** automatic choke 2 *(Sport)* starter

> ⚠ **starter** se traduit par le mot anglais **starter** uniquement au sens sportif.

starting-block (pl **starting-blocks**) /staʀtiŋblɔk/ NM starting block ◆ **être dans les ~s** to be on the starting blocks

starting-gate (pl **starting-gates**) /staʀtiŋgɛt/ NM starting gate

start-up /staʀtœp/ NF INV *(= entreprise)* start-up

stase /stɑz/ NF stasis

stat* /stat/ NF (abrév de **statistique**) stat* ◆ **faire des ~s** to do stats*

station /stasjɔ̃/ NF 1 *(= lieu d'arrêt)* **~ (de métro)** (underground *(Brit) ou* subway *(US)*) station ◆ **~ (d'autobus)** (bus) stop ◆ **~ (de chemin de fer)** halt ◆ **~ de taxis** taxi rank
2 *(= poste, établissement)* station ◆ **~ d'observation/de recherches** observation/research station ◆ **~ agronomique/météorologique** agricultural research/meteorological station ◆ **~ d'épuration** water-treatment plant ◆ **~ de pompage** pumping station ◆ **~ géodésique** geodesic *ou* geodetic station ◆ **~ d'émission** *ou* **émettrice** transmitting station ◆ **~ (de) radar** radar tracking station ◆ **~ de radio** radio station ◆ **~ spatiale/orbitale** space/orbiting station ◆ **~ d'essence** service *ou* filling station, petrol *(Brit) ou* gas *(US)* station ◆ **~ de lavage** carwash
3 *(= site)* site; *[d'animaux, plantes]* station ◆ **~ préhistorique** prehistoric site ◆ **une ~ de gentianes** a gentian station
4 *(de vacances)* resort ◆ **~ balnéaire/climatique** sea *ou* seaside/health resort ◆ **~ de ski** *ou* **de sports d'hiver** winter sports *ou* (winter) ski resort ◆ **~ de montagne** *ou* **d'altitude** mountain resort ◆ **~ thermale** thermal spa
5 *(= posture)* posture, stance ◆ **~ verticale** upright position ◆ **la ~ debout lui est pénible** he finds standing upright painful
6 *(= halte)* stop ◆ **faire des ~s prolongées devant les vitrines** to linger in front of the shop windows
7 *(Rel)* station ◆ **les ~s de la Croix** the Stations of the Cross
8 *(Marine)* station
9 *(Astron)* stationary point
10 *(Ordin)* **~ d'accueil** docking station ◆ **~ de travail** workstation

stationnaire /stasjɔnɛʀ/ ADJ stationary ◆ **son état est ~** *(Méd)* his condition is stable ◆ **ondes ~s** *(Phys)* standing waves ◆ **l'hélicoptère était en vol ~** the helicopter was hovering overhead NM *(Naut)* station ship

stationnement /stasjɔnmɑ̃/ NM 1 *[de véhicule]* parking ◆ **~ alterné** parking on alternate sides ◆ **~ bilatéral/unilatéral** parking on both sides/on one side only ◆ **"stationnement gênant"** "limited parking" ◆ **"stationnement réglementé"** "restricted parking" ◆ **"stationnement interdit"** "no parking", "no waiting"; *(sur autoroute)* "no stopping" ◆ **"stationnement payant"** *(avec parcmètres)* "meter zone"; *(avec tickets)* "parking with ticket only" ◆ **en ~** *[véhicule]* parked; *(Mil)* stationed; → **disque, feu**[1] 2 *(Can = parking)* car park *(Brit)*, parking lot *(US)*

stationner /stasjɔne/ ▸ conjug 1 ◂ VI 1 *(= être garé)* to be parked; *(= se garer)* to park 2 *(= rester sur place) [personne]* to stay, to remain 3 *(Mil)* **armes nucléaires/troupes stationnées en Europe** nuclear weapons/troops stationed in Europe

station-service (pl **stations-service(s)**) /stasjɔ̃sɛʀvis/ NF service *ou* filling station, petrol *(Brit) ou* gas *(US)* station

statique /statik/ ADJ static NF statics *(sg)*

statiquement /statikmɑ̃/ ADV statically

statisme /statism/ NM stasis

statisticien, -ienne /statistisjɛ̃, jɛn/ NM,F statistician

statistique /statistik/ NF *(= science)* ◆ **la ~** statistics *(sg)* ◆ **des ~s** *(= données)* statistics ◆ **une ~** a statistic ADJ statistical ◆ **données ~s** statistical data

statistiquement /statistikmɑ̃/ ADV statistically

stator /statɔʀ/ NM stator

statuaire /statɥɛʀ/ NF statuary ADJ statuary NM *(littér)* sculptor

statue /staty/ NF statue ◆ **rester immobile comme une ~** to stand as still as a statue, to stand stock-still ◆ **elle était la ~ du désespoir** she was the picture of despair ◆ **changé en ~ de sel** *(Bible)* turned into a pillar of salt; *(fig)* transfixed, rooted to the spot

statuer /statɥe/ ▸ conjug 1 ◂ VI to give a verdict ◆ **~ sur** to rule on, to give a ruling on ◆ **~ sur le cas de qn** to decide sb's case

statuette /statɥɛt/ NF statuette

statufier /statyfje/ ▸ conjug 7 ◂ VT *(= immortaliser)* to erect a statue to; *(= pétrifier)* to transfix, to root to the spot

statu quo /statykwo/ NM INV status quo

stature /statyʀ/ NF *(= taille)* stature; *(fig = calibre)* calibre *(Brit)*, caliber *(US)* ◆ **de haute ~** of (great) stature ◆ **cet écrivain est d'une tout autre ~** this writer is in a different league altogether

statut /staty/ NM *(= position)* status ◆ **~ social/fiscal/juridique** social/tax/legal status ◆ **avoir/obtenir le ~ de salarié** to be on/be put on the payroll ◆ **il a obtenu le ~ de réfugié politique** he has been given *ou* granted political refugee status NMPL **statuts** *(= règlement)* statutes

statutaire /statytɛʀ/ ADJ statutory ◆ **horaire ~** regulation *ou* statutory number of working hours

statutairement /statytɛʀmɑ̃/ ADV in accordance with the statutes *ou* regulations, statutorily

Ste (abrév de **Sainte**) St

Sté (abrév de **société**) ◆ **et ~** and Co.

steak /stɛk/ NM steak ◆ **~ au poivre** steak au poivre, peppered steak ◆ **~ tartare** steak tartar(e) ◆ **~ frites** steak and chips *(Brit) ou* French fries *(US)* ◆ **~ haché** minced beef *(Brit)*, ground beef *(US)*; *(moulé)* hamburger ◆ **~ de thon** tuna steak

stéarine /steaʀin/ NF stearin

stéatite /steatit/ NF steatite

steeple /stipœl/ NM ◆ **~(-chase)** *(Athlétisme, Équitation)* steeplechase ◆ **le 3 000 mètres ~** the 3,000 metres steeplechase

stèle /stɛl/ NF stele

stellaire /stelɛʀ/ ADJ stellar NF stitchwort

stem(m) /stɛm/ NM *(Ski)* stem ◆ **faire du ~(m)** to stem

stencil /stɛnsil/ NM *(pour polycopie)* stencil

sténo /steno/ NMF (abrév de **sténographe**) shorthand typist, steno* *(US)* NF (abrév de **sténographie**) shorthand ◆ **prendre une lettre en ~** to take a letter (down) in shorthand

sténodactylo[1] /stenodaktilo/, **sténodactylographe** † /stenodaktilɔgʀaf/ NMF shorthand typist

sténodactylo[2] /stenodaktilo/, **sténodactylographie** † /stenodaktilɔgʀafi/ NF shorthand typing

sténographe † /stenɔgʀaf/ NMF shorthand typist, stenographer *(US)*

sténographie /stenɔgʀafi/ NF shorthand, stenography

sténographier /stenɔgʀafje/ ▸ conjug 7 ◂ VT to take down in shorthand

sténographique /stenɔgʀafik/ ADJ shorthand *(épith)*, stenographic

sténopé /stenɔpe/ NM *(Photo)* pinhole

sténotype /stenɔtip/ NF stenotype

sténotypie /stenɔtipi/ NF stenotypy

sténotypiste /stenɔtipist/ NMF stenotypist

stentor /stɑ̃tɔʀ/ NM [1] *(= homme)* stentor ◆ **une voix de** ~ a stentorian voice [2] *(= protozoaire)* stentor

steppe /stɛp/ NF steppe

stepper /stɛpœʀ/ NM *(= machine)* stepper

stercoraire /stɛʀkɔʀɛʀ/ NM skua

stère /stɛʀ/ NM stere

stéréo /steʀeo/ NF (abrév de **stéréophonie**) stereo ◆ **émission (en)** ~ programme in stereo ◆ **enregistrement (en)** ~ stereo recording ◆ **c'est en** ~ it's in stereo ADJ INV (abrév de **stéréophonique**) stereo ◆ **son** ~ stereo sound

stéréophonie /steʀeɔfɔni/ NF stereophony

stéréophonique /steʀeɔfɔnik/ ADJ stereophonic

stéréoscope /steʀeɔskɔp/ NM stereoscope

stéréoscopie /steʀeɔskɔpi/ NF stereoscopy

stéréoscopique /steʀeɔskɔpik/ ADJ stereoscopic

stéréotype /steʀeɔtip/ NM *(lit, fig)* stereotype

stéréotypé, e /steʀeɔtipe/ ADJ stereotyped

stérile /steʀil/ ADJ [1] *[personne, couple]* sterile, infertile; *[animal, plante, union]* sterile; *[terre, sol]* barren [2] *(= aseptique) [milieu, compresse, flacon, seringue]* sterile [3] *[sujet, réflexions, pensées]* sterile; *[discussion, effort, débat]* futile; *[écrivain, artiste]* unproductive; *[concurrence]* pointless ◆ **il faut éviter de se livrer au jeu ~ de la comparaison** you should avoid making pointless comparisons

stérilet /steʀilɛ/ NM coil, IUD, intra-uterine device

stérilisant, e /steʀilizɑ̃, ɑ̃t/ ADJ *(lit)* sterilizing; *(fig)* unproductive, fruitless

stérilisateur /steʀilizatœʀ/ NM sterilizer

stérilisation /steʀilizasjɔ̃/ NF sterilization

stériliser /steʀilize/ ▸ conjug 1 ◂ VT to sterilize ◆ **lait stérilisé** sterilized milk

stérilité /steʀilite/ NF [1] *[de personne]* infertility, sterility; *[d'animal, plante, union]* sterility; *[de terre, sol]* barrenness [2] *[de milieu, compresse, flacon]* sterility [3] *[de sujet, réflexion, pensées]* sterility; *[de discussion, débat, effort]* fruitlessness, futility; *[d'écrivain, artiste]* lack of creativity

sterling /stɛʀliŋ/ ADJ INV, NM INV sterling; → **livre**[2]

sterne /stɛʀn/ NF tern ◆ ~ **arctique** Arctic tern

sternum /stɛʀnɔm/ NM breastbone, sternum *(SPÉC)*

stéroïde /steʀɔid/ NM steroid ADJ steroidal

stéthoscope /stetɔskɔp/ NM stethoscope

Stetson ® /stɛtsɔn/ NM Stetson ®

steward /stiwaʀt/ NM steward, flight attendant

stick /stik/ NM *[de colle]* stick; *(Hockey)* stick; *(= groupe de parachutistes)* stick ◆ **déodorant en** ~ stick deodorant

stigmate /stigmat/ NM [1] *(= marque, Méd)* mark, scar ◆ **~s** *(Rel)* stigmata ◆ **~s du vice/de la bêtise** marks of vice/of stupidity ◆ **son corps porte encore les ~s de cette expédition** his body still bears scars from that expedition ◆ **les collines qui portent les ~s de la guerre** the battle-scarred hills ◆ **la colonisation y a laissé des ~s** colonisation has left its mark there [2] *(= orifice) [d'animal]* stigma, spiracle; *[de plante]* stigma

stigmatisation /stigmatizasjɔ̃/ NF *(Rel)* stigmatization; *(= blâme)* condemnation, denunciation

stigmatiser /stigmatize/ ▸ conjug 1 ◂ VT [1] *(= blâmer)* to denounce, to condemn ◆ **ces quartiers stigmatisés comme des zones de non-droit** these districts that are branded as no-go areas [2] *(Méd)* to mark, to scar

stimulant, e /stimylɑ̃, ɑ̃t/ ADJ stimulating ◆ **c'est intellectuellement très** ~ intellectually it's very stimulating NM *(physique)* stimulant; *(intellectuel)* stimulus, spur, incentive; *(= drogue)* upper*

stimulateur /stimylatœʀ/ NM ◆ ~ **cardiaque** pacemaker

stimulation /stimylasjɔ̃/ NF stimulation ◆ **mesures de ~ de la demande** *(Écon)* measures to stimulate *ou* boost demand

stimuler /stimyle/ ▸ conjug 1 ◂ VT *[+ personne]* to stimulate, to spur on; *[+ économie, croissance, demande]* to stimulate, to boost; *[+ appétit]* to stimulate ◆ **cet élève a besoin d'être stimulé sans arrêt** this pupil needs constant stimulation

stimulus /stimylys/ (pl **stimuli** /stimyli/) NM *(Physiol, Psych)* stimulus

stipendié, e /stipɑ̃dje/ (ptp de **stipendier**) ADJ *(littér, péj)* hired

stipendier /stipɑ̃dje/ ▸ conjug 7 ◂ VT *(littér, péj)* to hire, to take into one's pay

stipulation /stipylasjɔ̃/ NF stipulation

stipuler /stipyle/ ▸ conjug 1 ◂ VT *[clause, loi, condition]* to state, to stipulate; *(= faire savoir expressément)* to stipulate, to specify

STO /ɛsteo/ NM (abrév de **Service du travail obligatoire**) → **service**

stock /stɔk/ NM [1] *(Comm)* stock; *(fig)* stock, supply ◆ ~ **d'or** gold reserves ◆ **faire des ~s** to stock up *(de* on); ◆ **avoir qch en** ~ to have *ou* keep sth in stock ◆ **prends un crayon, j'en ai tout un** ~ take a pencil, I've got a whole stock of them ◆ **dans la limite des ~s disponibles** while stocks last ◆ **~s stratégiques/régulateurs** strategic/regulatory stocks; → **rupture** [2] *(Bio)* stock

stockage /stɔkaʒ/ NM [1] *(= accumulation)* stocking; *(= entreposage)* storage ◆ **le ~ de l'énergie** energy storage ◆ **le ~ des déchets radioactifs** the storage of nuclear waste [2] *(Ordin)* storage

stock-car (pl **stock-cars**) /stɔkkaʀ/ NM *(= sport)* stock-car racing; *(= voiture)* stock car ◆ **une course de** ~ a stock-car race

stocker /stɔke/ ▸ conjug 1 ◂ VT *(= accumuler)* to stock; *(= entreposer)* to store; *(péj : pour spéculer, amasser)* to stockpile ◆ ~ **(sur mémoire)** *(Ordin)* to store (in the memory)

Stockholm /stɔkɔlm/ N Stockholm

stockiste /stɔkist/ NMF *(Comm)* stockist *(Brit)*, dealer *(US)*; *[de voiture]* agent

stock-option /stɔkɔpsjɔ̃/ NF stock option

stoïcien, -ienne /stɔisjɛ̃, jɛn/ ADJ, NM,F stoic

stoïcisme /stɔisism/ NM *(Philos)* Stoicism; *(fig)* stoicism

stoïque /stɔik/ ADJ stoical, stoic NMF *(gén)* stoic; *(Philos)* Stoic

stoïquement /stɔikmɑ̃/ ADV stoically

stomacal, e (mpl **-aux**) /stɔmakal, o/ ADJ stomach *(épith)*, gastric

stomatologie /stɔmatɔlɔʒi/ NF stomatology

stomatologiste /stɔmatɔlɔʒist/, **stomatologue** /stɔmatɔlɔg/ NMF stomatologist

stop /stɔp/ EXCL [1] ◆ ~! stop! ◆ **tu me diras** ~ - ~ ! *(en servant qn)* say when - when! ◆ **il faut savoir dire** ~ you have to know when to say no ◆ **après deux ans sans vacances, j'ai dit ~ !** after two years without a holiday, I said enough is enough! [2] *(Téléc)* stop NM [1] *(= panneau)* stop *ou* halt sign; *(= feu arrière)* brakelight [2] (* abrév de **auto-stop**) **faire du** ~ to hitch(hike), to thumb * a lift *ou* a ride ◆ **faire le tour de l'Europe en** ~ to hitch round Europe ◆ **il a fait du ~ pour rentrer chez lui, il est rentré chez lui en** ~ he hitched (a lift) home ◆ **j'ai pris deux personnes en** ~ I picked up two hitchhikers ◆ **je l'ai pris en** ~ I gave him a lift *ou* ride

stop and go /stɔpɛndgo/ NM INV *(Écon)* stop and go ◆ **politique de** ~ stop-go policy

stoppage /stɔpaʒ/ NM invisible mending

stopper /stɔpe/ ▸ conjug 1 ◂ VI to halt, to stop VT [1] *(= arrêter)* to stop, to halt [2] *(Couture) [+ bas]* to mend ◆ **faire ~ un vêtement** to get a garment (invisibly) mended

stoppeur, -euse /stɔpœʀ, øz/ NM,F [1] *(Couture)* invisible mender [2] (* = *auto-stoppeur)* hitchhiker [3] *(Ftbl)* fullback

store /stɔʀ/ NM [1] *(en plastique, bois, tissu)* blind; *[de magasin] (en toile)* awning, shade; *(en métal)* shutters ◆ ~ **vénitien** *ou* **à lamelles orientables** Venetian blind ◆ ~ **à enrouleur** roller blind [2] *(= voilage)* net curtain

STP (abrév de **s'il te plaît**) pls, please

strabisme /stʀabism/ NM squinting *(Brit)*, strabismus *(SPÉC)* ◆ ~ **divergent** divergent squint ◆ ~ **convergent** convergent strabismus *(SPÉC)* ◆ **il souffre d'un léger** ~ he is slightly cross-eyed, he suffers from a slight strabismus *(SPÉC)*, he has a slight squint *(Brit)*

stradivarius /stʀadivaʀjys/ NM Stradivarius

strangulation /stʀɑ̃gylasjɔ̃/ NF strangulation

strapontin /stʀapɔ̃tɛ̃/ NM *(Aut, Théât)* jump seat, foldaway seat; *(fig = position subalterne)* minor role ◆ **il n'occupe qu'un ~ dans la commission** he has a very minor role in the commission

Strasbourg /stʀazbuʀ/ N Strasbourg

strasbourgeois, e /stʀazbuʀʒwa, waz/ ADJ of *ou* from Strasbourg NM,F **Strasbourgeois(e)** inhabitant *ou* native of Strasbourg

strass /stʀas/ NM *(lit)* paste; *(péj)* show, gloss ◆ **broche/collier en** ~ paste brooch/necklace

stratagème /stʀataʒɛm/ NM stratagem

strate /stʀat/ NF *(Géol, fig)* stratum ◆ **les différentes ~s de la société** the different strata of society

stratège /stʀatɛʒ/ NM *(Mil, fig)* strategist ◆ **c'est un grand** *ou* **fin** ~ he's a master strategist

stratégie /stʀateʒi/ NF strategy ◆ ~ **de communication/de vente** communication/selling strategy ◆ ~ **d'entreprise** corporate strategy

stratégique /stʀateʒik/ ADJ strategic

stratégiquement /stʀateʒikmɑ̃/ ADV strategically

stratification /stʀatifikasjɔ̃/ NF stratification

stratifié, e /stʀatifje/ (ptp de **stratifier**) ADJ stratified; *(Tech)* laminated NM laminate ◆ **en ~** laminated

stratifier /stʀatifje/ ► conjug 7 ◄ VT to stratify

stratigraphie /stʀatigʀafi/ NF *(Géol)* stratigraphy

stratocumulus /stʀatokymylys/ NM INV stratocumulus

stratosphère /stʀatɔsfɛʀ/ NF stratosphere

stratosphérique /stʀatɔsfeʀik/ ADJ stratospheric

stratus /stʀatys/ NM INV stratus

streptocoque /stʀɛptɔkɔk/ NM streptococcus

streptomycine /stʀɛptɔmisin/ NF streptomycin

stress /stʀɛs/ NM *(gén, Méd)* stress ◆ **être dans un état de ~ permanent** to be under constant stress

stressant, e /stʀesɑ̃, ɑ̃t/ ADJ *[situation, vie, métier]* stressful ◆ **qu'est-ce qu'il est ~ !** he really stresses me out! *

stresser /stʀese/ ► conjug 1 ◄ VT to put under stress, to stress out* ◆ **cette réunion m'a complètement stressé** the meeting really stressed me out*, I felt completely stressed after the meeting ◆ **être stressé** to be under stress ◆ **se sentir stressé** to feel stressed ◆ **les cadres stressés d'aujourd'hui** today's stressed(-out) executives VPR **se stresser** to get stressed

stretch /stʀɛtʃ/ ADJ INV stretch *(épith)*, stretchy NM ◆ **Stretch**® stretch fabric ◆ **jupe en Stretch** stretch skirt

stretching /stʀɛtʃiŋ/ NM *(Sport)* stretches ◆ **faire du ~** to do stretches ◆ **cours de ~** stretch class

striation /stʀijasjɔ̃/ NF striation

strict, e /stʀikt/ ADJ 1 *(= astreignant, étroit) [obligation, sens]* strict; *[interprétation]* literal; *(Math)* strict ◆ **au sens ~ du terme** in the strict sense of the word ◆ **la ~e observation du règlement** the strict observance of the rules

2 *(= sévère) [discipline, maître, morale, principes]* strict ◆ **il est très ~ sur la ponctualité** he is a stickler for punctuality, he's very strict about punctuality ◆ **il était très ~ avec nous** *ou* **à notre égard** he was very strict with us

3 *(= absolu)* **c'est son droit le plus ~** it is his most basic right ◆ **le ~ nécessaire/minimum** the bare essentials/minimum ◆ **c'est la ~e vérité** it is the plain *ou* simple truth ◆ **dans la plus ~e intimité** in the strictest privacy

4 *(= sobre) [tenue]* severe, plain; *[coiffure]* austere, severe ◆ **un uniforme/costume très ~** a very austere *ou* plain uniform/suit

strictement /stʀiktəmɑ̃/ ADV 1 *(= rigoureusement) [confidentiel, personnel]* strictly ◆ **les sanctions seront ~ appliquées** the sanctions will be strictly enforced ◆ **~ inférieur/supérieur** *(Math)* strictly lesser/greater 2 *(= sévèrement)* strictly ◆ **il a été élevé très ~** he had a very strict upbringing 3 *(= sobrement)* plainly

stricto sensu /stʀiktosɛ̃sy/ LOC ADV strictly speaking

strident, e /stʀidɑ̃, ɑ̃t/ ADJ shrill, strident; *(Phon)* strident

stridulation /stʀidylasjɔ̃/ NF stridulation, chirring *(NonC)*

striduler /stʀidyle/ ► conjug 1 ◄ VI to stridulate, to chirr

strie /stʀi/ NF *(de couleur)* streak; *(en relief)* ridge; *(en creux)* groove; *(Anat, Géol)* stria

strié, e /stʀije/ ADJ 1 *[coquille, roche, tige]* striated 2 *(Anat) [muscle]* striated ◆ **corps ~** (corpus) striatum

strier /stʀije/ ► conjug 7 ◄ VT *(de couleurs)* to streak; *(en relief)* to ridge; *(en creux)* to groove; *(Anat, Géol)* to striate ◆ **cheveux striés de blanc** hair streaked with grey ◆ **l'orage striait le ciel d'éclairs** lightning ripped through the sky; → **muscle**

string /stʀiŋ/ NM *(= sous-vêtement)* G-string; *(= maillot de bain)* tanga

striptease, strip-tease (pl **strip-teases**) /stʀiptiz/ NM *(= spectacle)* striptease ◆ **faire un ~** to do a striptease ◆ **faire du ~** to be a striptease artist, to be a stripper

strip-teaseur, -euse (mpl **strip-teaseurs**) /stʀiptizœʀ, øz/ NM,F stripper, striptease artist

striure /stʀijyʀ/ NF *[de couleurs]* streaking *(NonC)* ◆ **la ~** *ou* **les ~s de la pierre** the ridges *ou* grooves in the stone

stroboscope /stʀɔbɔskɔp/ NM stroboscope

stroboscopique /stʀɔbɔskɔpik/ ADJ stroboscopic, strobe *(épith)* ◆ **lumière ~** strobe lighting

strontium /stʀɔ̃sjɔm/ NM strontium

strophe /stʀɔf/ NF *(Littérat)* verse, stanza; *(Théât grec)* strophe

structural, e (mpl **-aux**) /stʀyktyʀal, o/ ADJ structural

structuralisme /stʀyktyʀalism/ NM structuralism

structuraliste /stʀyktyʀalist/ ADJ, NMF structuralist

structurant, e /stʀyktyʀɑ̃, ɑ̃t/ ADJ *[principe]* founding; *[expérience]* formative; → **gel**

structuration /stʀyktyʀasjɔ̃/ NF structuring

structure /stʀyktyʀ/ NF 1 *(gén)* structure ◆ **la ~ familiale** the family structure ◆ **~s d'accueil** *(gén)* facilities; *[d'hôpital]* reception facilities ◆ **la ~ des dépenses s'est modifiée** spending patterns have changed ◆ **~ profonde/superficielle** *ou* **de surface** *(Ling)* deep/surface structure ◆ **~ mentale** mindset ◆ **réformes de ~** structural reforms 2 *(= organisme)* organization

structuré, e /stʀyktyʀe/ (ptp de **structurer**) ADJ structured

structurel, -elle /stʀyktyʀɛl/ ADJ structural

structurellement /stʀyktyʀɛlmɑ̃/ ADV structurally ◆ **être ~ déficitaire** to have a structural deficit

structurer /stʀyktyʀe/ ► conjug 1 ◄ VT to structure, to give structure to VPR **se structurer** *[parti]* to develop a structure; *[enfant]* to form

strychnine /stʀiknin/ NF strychnine

stuc /styk/ NM stucco ◆ **en ~** stucco *(épith)*

studette /stydɛt/ NF small studio flat *(Brit)* *ou* apartment *(surtout US)*

studieusement /stydjøzmɑ̃/ ADV studiously

studieux, -ieuse /stydjø, jøz/ ADJ *[personne, ambiance]* studious ◆ **j'ai eu** *ou* **passé des vacances studieuses** I spent the holidays studying

studio /stydjo/ NM 1 *(d'habitation)* studio flat *(Brit)* *ou* apartment *(surtout US)*; *(d'artiste)* studio 2 *(Ciné, TV : de prise de vues)* studio; *(= salle de cinéma)* film theatre *(Brit)* *ou* theater *(US)* ◆ **tourner en ~** to film *ou* shoot in the studio ◆ **~ d'enregistrement** recording studio ◆ **à vous les ~s !** *(TV)* and now back to the studio!

stupéfaction /stypefaksjɔ̃/ NF *(= étonnement)* amazement, astonishment, stupefaction ◆ **à la ~ générale** to everyone's astonishment *ou* amazement

stupéfaire /stypefɛʀ/ ► conjug 60 ◄ VT to stun, to astound, to dumbfound

stupéfait, e /stypefɛ, ɛt/ (ptp de **stupéfaire**) ADJ stunned, dumbfounded, astounded *(de qch* at sth); ◆ **~ de voir que ...** astounded *ou* stunned to see that ...

stupéfiant, e /stypefjɑ̃, jɑ̃t/ ADJ 1 *(= étonnant)* astounding, staggering 2 *(Méd)* stupefying, stupefacient *(SPÉC)* NM drug, narcotic, stupefacient *(SPÉC)*; → **brigade**

stupéfié, e /stypefje/ (ptp de **stupéfier**) ADJ staggered, dumbfounded

stupéfier /stypefje/ ► conjug 7 ◄ VT *(= étonner)* to stagger, to astound; *(Méd, littér)* to stupefy

stupeur /stypœʀ/ NF *(= étonnement)* astonishment, amazement; *(Méd)* stupor ◆ **être frappé de ~** to be dumbfounded *ou* stunned ◆ **c'est avec ~ que j'appris la nouvelle** I was stunned when I heard the news ◆ **à la ~ générale** to everyone's astonishment *ou* amazement

stupide /stypid/ ADJ *(= inepte)* stupid; *(= hébété)* stunned, bemused; *(= imprévisible) [accident]* stupid, silly ◆ **c'est ~, j'ai oublié !** how stupid of me, I forgot!

stupidement /stypidmɑ̃/ ADV stupidly

stupidité /stypidite/ NF *(= caractère)* stupidity; *(= parole)* stupid thing to say; *(= acte)* stupid thing to do ◆ **c'est une vraie ~** *ou* **de la ~** that's really stupid

stupre † /stypʀ/ NM *(littér)* debauchery, depravity

stups * /styp/ NMPL (abrév de **stupéfiants**) → **brigade**

style /stil/ NM 1 *(gén, Art, Littérat, Sport)* style ◆ **meubles/reliure de ~** period furniture/binding ◆ **meubles de ~ Directoire/Louis XVI** Directoire/Louis XVI furniture ◆ **je reconnais bien là son ~** that is just his style ◆ **ce n'est pas son ~** *(vêtements)* it's not his style; *(comportement étonnant)* it's not like him ◆ **ou quelque chose de ce ~** *(fig)* or something along those lines ◆ **cet athlète a du ~** this athlete has style ◆ **offensive/opération de grand ~** full-scale *ou* large-scale offensive/operation ◆ **il a fait ~*** **celui qui ne m'entendait pas** he made as if* he didn't hear me; → **exercice**

2 *(= pointe, Bot)* style; *[de cylindre enregistreur]* stylus; *[de cadran solaire]* style, gnomon; *(Hist = poinçon)* style, stylus

COMP **style direct** *(Ling)* direct speech

style indirect *(Ling)* indirect *ou* reported speech ◆ **~ indirect libre** indirect free speech

style journalistique journalistic style, journalese *(péj)*

style télégraphique telegraphic style

style de vie lifestyle

stylé, e /stile/ ADJ *[domestique, personnel]* perfectly trained

stylet /stilɛ/ NM 1 *(= poignard)* stiletto, stylet 2 *(Méd)* stylet 3 *[d'animal]* proboscis, stylet

stylisation /stilizasjɔ̃/ NF stylization

styliser /stilize/ ► conjug 1 ◄ VT to stylize ◆ **colombe/fleur stylisée** stylized dove/flower

stylisme /stilism/ NM *(= métier)* dress designing; *(= snobisme)* concern for style

styliste /stilist/ NMF *(= dessinateur industriel)* designer; *(= écrivain)* stylist ◆ **~ de mode** clothes *ou* dress designer

stylisticien, -ienne /stilistisjɛ̃, jɛn/ NM,F stylistician, specialist in stylistics

stylistique /stilistik/ NF stylistics *(sg)* ADJ *[analyse, emploi]* stylistic

stylo /stilo/ NM pen ◆ **~-bille, ~ à bille** ballpoint (pen), Biro® *(Brit)*, Bic® *(US)* ◆ **~ à encre** *ou* **(à) plume** *ou* **à réservoir** fountain pen ◆ **~-feutre** felt-tip pen ◆ **~ à cartouche** cartridge pen ◆ **~ numérique** digital pen

stylographe † /stilɔgʀaf/ NM fountain pen

Styx /stiks/ NM ◆ **le** ~ the Styx

su, e /sy/ (ptp de **savoir**) ADJ known NM ◆ **au** ~ **de** → **vu¹**

suaire /sɥɛʀ/ NM *(littér = linceul)* shroud, winding sheet; *(fig)* shroud; → **saint**

suant, suante /sɥɑ̃, sɥɑ̃t/ ADJ 1 *(= en sueur)* sweaty 2 *(* = ennuyeux) [livre, cours]* deadly (dull)* ◆ **ce film est** ~* this film is a real drag* *ou* is deadly* ◆ **ce qu'il est** ~ **!*** what a drag* *ou* a pain (in the neck)* he is!

suave /sɥav/ ADJ *[personne, manières]* suave, smooth; *[voix]* smooth; *[musique, parfum]* sweet; *[couleurs]* mellow; *[formes]* smooth

suavement /sɥavmɑ̃/ ADV *[s'exprimer]* suavely

suavité /sɥavite/ NF *[de personne, manières, voix, regard]* suavity, smoothness; *[de musique, parfum]* sweetness; *[de couleurs]* mellowness; *[de formes]* smoothness

subaigu, -uë /sybegy/ ADJ subacute

subalterne /sybaltɛʀn/ ADJ *[rôle]* subordinate, subsidiary; *[employé, poste]* junior *(ép th)* ◆ **officier** ~ subaltern NMF subordinate, inferior

subantarctique /sybɑ̃taʀktik/ ADJ subantarctic

subaquatique /sybakwatik/ ADJ subaquatic, underwater *(épith)*

subarctique /sybaʀktik/ ADJ subarctic

subconscient, e /sypkɔ̃sjɑ̃, jɑ̃t/ ADJ, NM subconscious

subdiviser /sybdivize/ ► conjug 1 ◄ VT to subdivide *(en* into) VPR **se subdiviser** to be subdivided, to be further divided *(en* into)

subdivision /sybdivizjɔ̃/ NF *(gén)* subdivision; *[de classeur]* section

subéquatorial, e (mpl **-iaux**) /sybekwatɔʀjal, jo/ ADJ subequatorial

subir /sybiʀ/ ► conjug 2 ◄ VT 1 *(= être victime de)* *[+ affront]* to be subjected to, to suffer; *[+ violences, attaque, critique]* to undergo, to suffer, to be subjected to; *[+ perte, défaite, dégâts]* to suffer, to sustain; *[+ choc]* to suffer ◆ **faire** ~ **un affront/des tortures à qn** to subject sb to an insult/to torture ◆ **faire** ~ **des pertes/une défaite à l'ennemi** to inflict losses/defeat on the enemy

2 *(= être soumis à) [+ charme]* to be subject to, to be under the influence of; *[+ influence]* to be under; *[+ peine de prison]* to serve; *[+ examen]* to undergo, to go through; *[+ opération, interrogatoire]* to undergo ◆ ~ **les effets de qch** to be affected by sth ◆ ~ **la loi du plus fort** to be subjected to the law of the strongest ◆ ~ **les rigueurs de l'hiver** to undergo *ou* be subjected to the rigours of winter ◆ **faire** ~ **son influence à qn** to exert an influence over sb ◆ **faire** ~ **un examen à qn** to put sb through *ou* subject sb to an examination, to make sb undergo an examination

3 *(= endurer)* to suffer, to put up with, to endure ◆ **il faut** ~ **et se taire** you must suffer in silence ◆ **il va falloir le** ~ **pendant toute la journée*** we're going to have to put up with him all day ◆ **on subit sa famille, on choisit ses amis** you can pick your friends but not your family

4 *(= recevoir) [+ modification, transformation]* to undergo, to go through ◆ **les prix ont subi une hausse importante** there has been a considerable increase in prices, prices have undergone a considerable increase

subit, e /sybi, it/ ADJ sudden

subitement /sybitmɑ̃/ ADV suddenly, all of a sudden

subito (presto)* /sybito(pʀesto)/ LOC ADV *(= brusquement)* all of a sudden; *(= immédiatement)* at once

subjectif, -ive /sybʒɛktif, iv/ ADJ subjective ◆ **un danger** ~ a danger which one creates for oneself

subjectivement /sybʒɛktivmɑ̃/ ADV subjectively

subjectivisme /sybʒɛktivism/ NM subjectivism

subjectiviste /sybʒɛktivist/ ADJ subjectivistic NMF subjectivist

subjectivité /sybʒɛktivite/ NF subjectivity

subjonctif, -ive /sybʒɔ̃ktif, iv/ ADJ, NM subjunctive ◆ **au** ~ in the subjunctive

subjuguer /sybʒyge/ ► conjug 1 ◄ VT 1 *[+ auditoire, personne malléable]* to captivate, to enthrall ◆ **complètement subjugué par les thèses fascistes** in thrall to fascist ideas 2 *(littér)* *[+ peuple vaincu]* to subjugate ◆ **être subjugué par le charme/la personnalité de qn** to be captivated by sb's charm/personality

sublimation /syblimasjɔ̃/ NF *(Chim, Psych)* sublimation

sublime /syblim/ ADJ *(gén)* sublime; *[personne]* magnificent, wonderful ◆ ~ **de dévouement** sublimely dedicated ◆ **la Sublime Porte** *(Hist)* the Sublime Porte NM ◆ **le** ~ the sublime

sublimé, e /syblime/ (ptp de **sublimer**) ADJ sublimate(d) NM sublimate

sublimement /syblimmɑ̃/ ADV sublimely

sublimer /syblime/ ► conjug 1 ◄ VT *(Psych)* to sublimate; *(Chim)* to sublimate, to sublime

subliminaire /sybliminɛʀ/, **subliminal, e** (mpl **-aux**) /subliminal, o/ ADJ subliminal

sublimité /syblimite/ NF *(littér)* sublimeness *(NonC)*, sublimity

sublingual, e (mpl **-aux**) /syblɛ̃gwal, o/ ADJ sublingual ◆ **comprimé** ~ tablet to be dissolved under the tongue

submergé, e /sybmɛʀʒe/ (ptp de **submerger**) ADJ 1 *[terres, plaine]* flooded, submerged; *[récifs]* submerged 2 *(= débordé, dépassé)* swamped, snowed under ◆ ~ **de** *[+ appels téléphoniques, commandes]* snowed under *ou* swamped *ou* inundated with; *[+ douleur, plaisir, inquiétude]* overwhelmed *ou* overcome with ◆ **le standard est** ~ **d'appels** the switchboard is inundated *ou* flooded *ou* swamped with calls ◆ **les hôpitaux sont** ~**s de blessés** the hospitals are overflowing with wounded people ◆ ~ **de travail** snowed under *ou* swamped with work, up to one's eyes *(Brit) ou* ears *(US)* in work* ◆ **nous étions complètement** ~**s** we were completely snowed under, we were up to our eyes *(Brit) ou* ears *(US)* in it*

submerger /sybmɛʀʒe/ ► conjug 3 ◄ VT *(= inonder)* *[+ terres, plaine]* to flood, to submerge; *[+ barque]* to submerge ◆ ~ **qn** *[foule]* to engulf sb; *[ennemi]* to overwhelm sb; *[émotion]* to overcome sb, to overwhelm sb ◆ **ils nous submergeaient de travail** they swamped *ou* inundated us with work ◆ **les policiers ont été submergés par les manifestants** the police were overwhelmed by the demonstrators

submersible /sybmɛʀsibl/ ADJ *(Bot) [plante]* submerged NM *(Naut)* submersible

submersion /sybmɛʀsjɔ̃/ NF *[de terres]* flooding, submersion ◆ **mort par** ~ *(Méd)* death by drowning

subodorer /sybɔdɔʀe/ ► conjug 1 ◄ VT *(= soupçonner)* to suspect ◆ **aucun professeur n'avait subodoré son génie** none of the teachers realized how brilliant he was ◆ **elle subodorait un drame épouvantable** she sensed that a terrible tragedy was taking place

subordination /sybɔʀdinasjɔ̃/ NF subordination ◆ **je m'élève contre la** ~ **de cette décision à leurs plans** I object to this decision being subject to their plans ◆ **relation** *ou* **rapport de** ~ *(Ling)* relation of subordination; → **conjonction**

subordonné, e /sybɔʀdɔne/ (ptp de **subordonner**) ADJ *(gén, Ling)* subordinate *(à* to); ◆ **proposition** ~**e** *(Ling)* dependent *ou* subordinate clause NM,F subordinate NF **subordonnée** *(Ling)* dependent *ou* subordinate clause

subordonner /sybɔʀdɔne/ ► conjug 1 ◄ VT 1 *(dans une hiérarchie)* ~ **qn à** to subordinate sb to ◆ **accepter de se** ~ **à qn** to agree to subordinate o.s. to sb, to accept a subordinate position under sb 2 *(Ling)* to subordinate ◆ ~ **qch à** *(= placer au second rang)* to subordinate sth to ◆ **nous subordonnons notre décision à ses plans** *(= faire dépendre de)* our decision will be subject to his plans ◆ **leur départ est subordonné au résultat des examens** their departure is subject to *ou* depends on the exam results

subornation /sybɔʀnasjɔ̃/ NF *(Jur) [de témoins]* bribing, subornation *(SPÉC)*

suborner /sybɔʀne/ ► conjug 1 ◄ VT *(Jur) [+ témoins]* to bribe, to suborn *(SPÉC)*; *(littér) [+ jeune fille]* to lead astray, to seduce

suborneur † /sybɔʀnœʀ/ NM seducer

subreptice /sybʀɛptis/ ADJ *[moyen]* stealthy, surreptitious ◆ **acte** ~ *(Jur)* subreption

subrepticement /sybʀɛptismɑ̃/ ADV stealthily, surreptitiously

subrogation /sybʀɔgasjɔ̃/ NF *(Jur)* subrogation

subrogé, e /sybʀɔʒe/ (ptp de **subroger**) ADJ *(Jur)* ◆ ~**(-)tuteur** surrogate guardian ◆ **langage** ~ *(Ling)* subrogate language NM,F *(Jur)* surrogate

subroger /sybʀɔʒe/ ► conjug 3 ◄ VT *(Jur)* to subrogate, to substitute

subsaharien, -ienne /sybsaaʀjɛ̃, jɛn/ ADJ *[désert, pays]* sub-Saharan; → **Afrique**

subséquemment /sypsekamɑ̃/ ADV († , *Jur*) subsequently

subséquent, e /sypsekɑ̃, ɑ̃t/ ADJ († , *Jur, Géog*) subsequent

subside /sybzid/ NM grant ◆ **les modestes** ~**s qu'il recevait de son père** the small allowance he received from his father

subsidiaire /sybzidjɛʀ/ ADJ *[raison, motif]* subsidiary; → **question**

subsidiairement /sybzidjɛʀmɑ̃/ ADV subsidiarily

subsidiarité /sybzidjaʀite/ NF *(Pol)* subsidiarity ◆ **le principe de** ~ *(Europe)* the principle of subsidiarity

subsistance /sybzistɑ̃s/ NF *(= moyens d'existence)* subsistence ◆ **assurer la** ~ **de sa famille/de qn** to support *ou* maintain *ou* keep one's family/sb ◆ **assurer sa (propre)** ~ to keep *ou* support o.s. ◆ **ma** ~ **était assurée** I had enough to live on ◆ **ils tirent leur** ~ **de certaines racines** they live on certain root crops ◆ **moyens de** ~ means of subsistence ◆ **économie/agriculture de** ~ subsistence economy/agriculture

subsistant, e /sybzistɑ̃, ɑ̃t/ ADJ remaining *(épith)* NM *(Mil)* seconded serviceman

subsister /sybziste/ ► conjug 1 ◄ VI *[personne]* *(= ne pas périr)* to live on, to survive; *(= se nourrir, gagner sa vie)* to live, to stay alive, to subsist; *(= rester) [erreur, vestiges]* to remain ◆ **ils ont tout juste de quoi** ~ they have just enough to live on *ou* to keep body and soul together ◆ **le doute subsiste** *ou* **il subsiste un doute quant à** *ou* **sur** there is still some doubt as to, there remains some doubt as to ◆ **du château primitif, il ne subsiste que l'aile gauche** only the left wing of the original castle remains intact ◆ **il ne subsiste que quelques spécimens de**

cette plante there are only a few specimens of this plant left

subsonique /sypsɔnik/ ADJ subsonic

substance /sypstɑ̃s/ NF (gén, Philos) substance ♦ **la ~ de notre discussion** the substance *ou* gist of our discussion ♦ **c'était un discours sans ~, ce discours manquait de ~** the speech had no substance to it ♦ **~ blanche/grise** (Anat) white/grey matter ♦ **~ étrangère** foreign substance *ou* matter (NonC) ♦ **le lait est une ~ alimentaire** milk is a food ♦ **en ~** in substance ♦ **voilà, en ~, ce qu'ils ont dit** here is, in substance, what they said, here is the gist of what they said

substantialité /sypstɑ̃sjalite/ NF substantiality

substantiel, -ielle /sypstɑ̃sjɛl/ ADJ (gén, Philos) substantial

substantiellement /sypstɑ̃sjɛlmɑ̃/ ADV substantially

substantif, -ive /sypstɑ̃tif, iv/ NM noun, substantive ADJ [proposition] noun (épith); [emploi] nominal, substantival; [style] nominal

substantifique /sypstɑ̃tifik/ ADJ (hum) ♦ **la ~ moelle** the very substance

substantivation /sypstɑ̃tivasjɔ̃/ NF nominalization, substantivization

substantivement /sypstɑ̃tivmɑ̃/ ADV nominally, as a noun, substantively

substantiver /sypstɑ̃tive/ ► conjug 1 ◄ VT to nominalize, to substantivize

substituer /sypstitɥe/ ► conjug 1 ◄ VT 1 (= remplacer) **~ qch/qn à** to substitute sth/sb for 2 (Jur) [+ legs] to entail VPR **se substituer** ♦ **se ~ à qn** (en l'évinçant) to substitute o.s. for sb; (en le représentant) to substitute for sb, to act as a substitute for sb ♦ **l'adjoint s'est substitué au chef** the deputy is substituting for the boss

substitut /sypstity/ NM (= magistrat) deputy public prosecutor (Brit), assistant district attorney (US); (= succédané) substitute (de for); (Ling) pro-form substitute ♦ **~ maternel** (Psych) substitute mother ♦ **~ de repas** meal replacement

substitutif, -ive /sypstitytif, iv/ ADJ (Méd) ♦ **traitement ~** replacement therapy ♦ **traitement hormonal ~** hormone replacement therapy

substitution /sypstitysjɔ̃/ NF (gén, Chim) (intentionnelle) substitution (à for); (accidentelle) [de vêtements, bébés] mix-up (de of, in); ♦ **il y a eu ~ d'enfants** the babies were switched ♦ **produit de ~** substitute (product) ♦ **produit *ou* drogue de ~ à l'héroïne** heroin substitute ♦ **traitement de ~** *treatment of drug addicts with substitute drugs* ♦ **hormones de ~** replacement hormones ♦ **énergies de ~** alternative (sources of) energy ♦ **carburant de ~** substitute fuel ♦ **effet de ~** (dans l'emploi) substitution effect; → **mère, peine**

substrat /sypstʀa/ NM (Géol, Ling, Philos) substratum

subsumer /sypsyme/ ► conjug 1 ◄ VT to subsume

subterfuge /syptɛʀfyʒ/ NM subterfuge ♦ **user de ~s** to use subterfuge

subtil, e /syptil/ ADJ 1 (= sagace) [personne, esprit, intelligence, réponse, calcul] subtle ♦ **c'est un négociateur ~** he's a skilful negotiator 2 (= raffiné) [nuance, distinction] subtle, fine; [parfum, goût, raisonnement] subtle ♦ **un ~ mélange d'autorité et de tendresse** a subtle blend of authority and tenderness ♦ **c'est trop ~ pour moi** it's too subtle for me

subtilement /syptilmɑ̃/ ADV subtly, in a subtle way

subtilisation /syptilizasjɔ̃/ NF spiriting away

subtiliser /syptilize/ ► conjug 1 ◄ VT (= dérober) to steal ♦ **il s'est fait ~ sa valise** his suitcase was stolen VI (littér = raffiner) to subtilize

subtilité /syptilite/ NF subtlety ♦ **les ~s de la langue française** the subtleties of the French language

subtropical, e (mpl **-aux**) /sybtʀɔpikal, o/ ADJ subtropical ♦ **régions ~es** subtropical regions, subtropics

suburbain, e /sybyʀbɛ̃, ɛn/ ADJ suburban

subvenir /sybvəniʀ/ ► conjug 22 ◄ **subvenir à** VT INDIR [+ besoins] to provide for, to meet; [+ frais] to meet, to cover ♦ **~ aux besoins de sa famille** to provide for *ou* support one's family ♦ **~ à ses propres besoins** to support o.s.

subvention /sybvɑ̃sjɔ̃/ NF subsidy ♦ **ils reçoivent des ~s publiques** they receive public subsidies

subventionner /sybvɑ̃sjɔne/ ► conjug 1 ◄ VT to subsidize ♦ **théâtre subventionné** subsidized theatre ♦ **école subventionnée** grant-maintained school

subversif, -ive /sybvɛʀsif, iv/ ADJ subversive

subversion /sybvɛʀsjɔ̃/ NF subversion

subversivement /sybvɛʀsivmɑ̃/ ADV subversively

subvertir /sybvɛʀtiʀ/ ► conjug 2 ◄ VT [+ structure, valeurs] to undermine

suc /syk/ NM [de plante] sap; [de viande, fleur, fruit] juice; (littér) [d'œuvre] pith, meat ♦ **~s digestifs *ou* gastriques** gastric juices

succédané /syksedane/ NM (= substitut) substitute (de for); (= médicament) substitute, succedaneum (SPÉC) ♦ **un ~ de ...** (péj = imitation) a pale imitation of ...

succéder /syksede/ ► conjug 6 ◄ VT INDIR **succéder à** [+ directeur, roi] to succeed; [+ période, chose, personne] to succeed, to follow; (Jur) [+ titres, héritage] to inherit, to succeed to ♦ **~ à qn à la tête d'une entreprise** to succeed sb *ou* take over from sb at the head of a firm ♦ **des prés succédèrent aux champs de blé** cornfields were followed by meadows, cornfields gave way to meadows ♦ **le rire succéda à la peur** fear gave way to laughter

VPR **se succéder** to follow one another, to succeed one another ♦ **ils se succédèrent de père en fils** son followed father ♦ **les mois se succédèrent** month followed month ♦ **les échecs se succédèrent** one failure followed another ♦ **trois gouvernements se sont succédé en trois ans** there have been three successive governments in three years ♦ **les visites se sont succédé toute la journée dans la chambre du malade** visitors filed in and out of the patient's room all day

succès /syksɛ/ NM 1 (= réussite) [d'entreprise, roman] success ♦ **~ militaires/sportifs** military/sporting successes ♦ **félicitations pour votre ~** congratulations on your success ♦ **le ~ ne l'a pas changé** success hasn't changed him ♦ **~ d'estime** succès d'estime, praise from the critics (with poor sales) ♦ **avoir du ~ auprès des femmes** to be successful with women

2 (= livre) success, bestseller; (= chanson, disque) success, hit*; (= film, pièce) box-office success, hit* ♦ **~ de librairie** bestseller ♦ **tous ses livres ont été des ~** all his books were bestsellers, every one of his books was a success ♦ **~ commercial** commercial success ♦ **~ d'audience** success *ou* hit* with the audience(s), ratings success

3 (= conquête amoureuse) **~ (féminin)** conquest ♦ **son charme lui vaut de nombreux ~** numerous women have fallen for his charms

4 (locutions) **avec ~** successfully ♦ **avec un égal ~** equally successfully, with equal success ♦ **sans ~** unsuccessfully, without success ♦ **pour ce film, c'est le ~ assuré *ou* garanti** this film is sure to be a success ♦ **avoir du ~, être un ~** to be successful, to be a success ♦ **cette pièce a eu un grand ~ *ou* beaucoup de ~ *ou* un ~ fou*** the play was a great success *ou* was very successful *ou* was a smash hit* ♦ **ce chanteur a eu un ~ monstre* *ou* bœuf*** this singer was a big hit*

♦ **à succès** [auteur, livre] successful, bestselling ♦ **film à ~** hit film*, blockbuster* ♦ **chanson/pièce à ~** hit*, successful song/play ♦ **roman à ~** successful novel, bestseller

successeur /syksesœʀ/ NM (gén) successor

successif, -ive /syksesif, iv/ ADJ successive

succession /syksesjɔ̃/ NF 1 (= enchaînement, série) succession ♦ **la ~ des saisons** the succession *ou* sequence of the seasons ♦ **toute une ~ de visiteurs/malheurs** a whole succession *ou* series of visitors/misfortunes 2 (= transmission de pouvoir) succession; (Jur) (= transmission de biens) succession; (= patrimoine) estate, inheritance ♦ **partager une ~** to share an estate *ou* an inheritance ♦ **la ~ est ouverte** (Jur) ≈ the will is going through probate ♦ **~ vacante** estate in abeyance ♦ **par voie de ~** by right of inheritance *ou* succession ♦ **prendre la ~ de** [+ ministre, directeur] to succeed, to take over from; [+ roi] to succeed; [+ maison de commerce] to take over; → **droit[3], guerre**

successivement /syksesivmɑ̃/ ADV successively

successoral, e (mpl **-aux**) /syksesɔʀal, o/ ADJ ♦ **droits successoraux** inheritance tax

succinct, e /syksɛ̃, ɛ̃t/ ADJ [écrit] succinct; [repas] frugal ♦ **soyez ~** be brief ♦ **il a été très ~** he was very brief

succinctement /syksɛ̃tmɑ̃/ ADV [raconter] succinctly; [manger] frugally

succion /sy(k)sjɔ̃/ NF (Phys, Tech) suction; (Méd) [de plaie] sucking ♦ **bruit de ~** sucking noise

succomber /sykɔ̃be/ ► conjug 1 ◄ VI 1 (= mourir) to die, to succumb (frm) ♦ **~ à ses blessures** to die from one's injuries 2 (= être vaincu) to succumb (frm); (par tentations) to succumb, to give way ♦ **~ sous le nombre** to be overcome by numbers ♦ **~ à** [+ tentation] to succumb *ou* yield *ou* give way to; [+ promesses] to succumb to; [+ charme] to succumb to, to fall under; [+ fatigue, désespoir, sommeil] to give way to, to succumb to ♦ **~ sous le poids de qch** (littér : lit, fig) to yield *ou* give way beneath the weight of sth ♦ **ce gâteau était trop tentant, j'ai succombé !** this cake was so tempting I just couldn't resist! ♦ **la ville a succombé sous les assauts répétés de l'armée** the town fell under the repeated attacks of the army

succube /sykyb/ NM succubus

succulence /sykylɑ̃s/ NF (littér) succulence

succulent, e /sykylɑ̃, ɑ̃t/ ADJ 1 (= délicieux) [fruit, rôti] succulent; [mets, repas] delicious; [récit] juicy* 2 (Bot) [plante] succulent NF (= plante) succulent

succursale /sykyʀsal/ NF [de magasin, firme] branch; → **magasin**

sucer /syse/ ► conjug 3 ◄ VT 1 (lit) to suck ♦ **toujours à ~ des bonbons** always sucking sweets ♦ **ces pastilles se sucent** these tablets are to be sucked ♦ **~ son pouce** to suck one's thumb ♦ **ce procès lui a sucé toutes ses économies*** this lawsuit has bled him of all his savings ♦ **~ qn jusqu'à la moelle* *ou* jusqu'au dernier sou*** to suck sb dry*, to bleed sb dry* ♦ **se ~ la poire‡ *ou* la pomme‡** to neck‡, to kiss passionately ♦ **on voit bien qu'il ne suce pas de la glace !*** (hum) he really knocks it back!‡ 2 (‡ = boire) to tipple*, to booze* ♦ **cette voiture suce beaucoup** this car guzzles* a lot of petrol (Brit) *ou* gas (US) 3 *‡ (fellation) to suck off*‡; (cunnilingus) to go down on*‡

sucette /sysɛt/ NF (= *bonbon*) lollipop, lolly (*Brit*); (= *tétine*) comforter, dummy (*Brit*), pacifier (*US*) ◆ **partir en ~** * (= *se détériorer, ne pas aboutir*) to go pear-shaped *

suceur, -euse /sysœʀ, øz/ NM 1 (**insecte**) ~ sucking insect 2 [*d'aspirateur*] nozzle NM (*fig*) ◆ **~ de sang** bloodsucker NF **suceuse** (= *machine*) suction dredge

suçon * /sysɔ̃/ NM love bite * (*Brit*), hickey * (*US*) ◆ **faire un ~ à qn** to give sb a love bite (*Brit*) *ou* a hickey (*US*)

suçoter /sysɔte/ ▸ conjug 1 ◂ VT to suck

sucrage /sykʀaʒ/ NM [*de vin*] sugaring, sweetening

sucrant, e /sykʀɑ̃, ɑ̃t/ ADJ sweetening ◆ **c'est très ~** it's very sweet

sucrase /sykʀɑz/ NF sucrase

sucre /sykʀ/ NM 1 (= *substance*) sugar; (= *morceau*) lump of sugar, sugar lump ◆ **prendre deux ~s dans son café** to take two lumps of sugar *ou* two sugars in one's coffee ◆ **combien de ~s ?** how many sugars (do you take)? ◆ **fraises au ~** strawberries sprinkled with sugar ◆ **chewing-gum sans ~** sugarless *ou* sugar-free chewing gum ◆ **cet enfant n'est pas en ~ quand même !** for goodness sake, the child won't break! ◆ **être tout ~ tout miel** [*personne*] to be all sweetness and light ◆ **mon petit trésor en ~** my little honey-bun *ou* sugarplum ◆ **partie de ~** (*au Canada*) sugaring-off party; → **casser**

2 (= *unité monétaire*) sucre

COMP **sucre de betterave** beet sugar
sucre brun brown sugar
sucre candi sugar candy
sucre de canne cane sugar
sucre cristallisé (coarse) granulated sugar
sucre d'érable * (*Can*) maple sugar
sucre glace icing sugar (*Brit*), confectioners' sugar (*US*)
sucres lents complex sugars
sucre en morceaux lump *ou* cube sugar
sucre d'orge (= *substance*) barley sugar; (= *bâton*) stick of barley sugar
sucre en poudre fine granulated sugar, caster sugar (*Brit*)
sucres rapides simple sugars
sucre roux brown sugar
sucre semoule ⇒ **sucre en poudre**
sucre vanillé vanilla sugar

LE TEMPS DES SUCRES

Maple sugar and syrup production is an important traditional industry in Quebec, and the sugar harvest is a time for festivities in rural areas. The local community traditionally gets together for a celebration with music and dancing, and boiling maple sugar is thrown into the snow where it hardens into a kind of toffee known as « tire ».

sucré, e /sykʀe/ (ptp de **sucrer**) ADJ 1 [*fruit, saveur, vin*] sweet; [*jus de fruits, lait condensé*] sweetened ◆ **eau ~e** sugar water ◆ **ce thé est trop ~** this tea is too sweet, there's too much sugar in this tea ◆ **prenez-vous votre café ~ ?** do you take sugar (in your coffee)? ◆ **tasse de thé bien ~e** well-sweetened cup of tea, cup of nice sweet tea ◆ **non ~** unsweetened 2 (*péj*) [*ton*] sugary, honeyed; [*air*] sickly-sweet ◆ **elle fait sa ~e** she's turning on the charm NM ◆ **le ~ et le salé** sweet and savoury food ◆ **je préfère le ~ au salé** I prefer sweet things to savouries

sucrer /sykʀe/ ▸ conjug 1 ◂ VT 1 [*+ boisson*] to sugar, to put sugar in, to sweeten; [*+ produit alimentaire*] to sweeten ◆ **le miel sucre autant que le sucre lui-même** honey sweetens as much as sugar, honey is as good a sweetener as sugar ◆ **on peut ~ avec du miel** honey may be used as a sweetener *ou* may be used to sweeten things ◆ **sucrez à volonté** sweeten *ou* add sugar to taste ◆ **~ les fraises** ‡ to be a bit doddery *

2 (‡ = *supprimer*) ~ **son argent de poche à qn** to stop sb's pocket money ◆ **il s'est fait ~ ses heures supplémentaires** he's had his overtime money stopped ◆ **il s'est fait ~ son permis de conduire** he had his driving licence taken away ◆ **ils m'ont sucré mes vacances à la dernière minute** I was told at the last minute I couldn't take my holiday

VPR **se sucrer** 1 (* *lit* = *prendre du sucre*) to help o.s. to sugar, to have some sugar

2 (‡ = *s'enrichir*) to line one's pockets *

sucrerie /sykʀəʀi/ NF 1 (= *bonbon*) sweet (*Brit*), candy (*US*) ◆ **~s** sweets, sweet things ◆ **aimer les ~s** to have a sweet tooth, to like sweet things 2 (= *usine*) sugar house; (= *raffinerie*) sugar refinery; (*Can*) (maple) sugar house

Sucrette ® /sykʀɛt/ NF artificial sweetener

sucrier, -ière /sykʀije, ijɛʀ/ ADJ [*industrie, betterave*] sugar (*épith*); [*région*] sugar-producing NM 1 (= *récipient*) sugar basin, sugar bowl ◆ **~ (verseur)** sugar dispenser *ou* shaker 2 (= *industriel*) sugar producer

sud /syd/ NM INV 1 (= *point cardinal*) south ◆ **le vent du ~** the south wind ◆ **un vent du ~** a south(erly) wind, a southerly (*Naut*) ◆ **le vent tourne/est au ~** the wind is veering south(wards) *ou* towards the south/is blowing from the south ◆ **regarder vers le ~** *ou* **dans la direction du ~** to look south(wards) *ou* towards the south ◆ **au ~** (*situation*) in the south; (*direction*) to the south, south(wards) ◆ **au ~ de** south of, to the south of ◆ **la maison est (exposée) au ~/exposée plein ~** the house faces (the) south *ou* southwards/due south, the house looks south(wards)/due south

2 (= *régions*) south ◆ **le ~ de la France, le Sud** the South of France ◆ **l'Europe/l'Italie du Sud** Southern Europe/Italy ◆ **le Pacifique Sud** the South Pacific ◆ **les mers du Sud** the South Seas ◆ **le dialogue Nord-Sud** (*Pol*) the North-South dialogue; → **Amérique, Corée, croix**

ADJ INV [*région, partie*] southern; [*entrée, paroi*] south; [*versant, côte*] south(ern); [*côté*] south(ward); [*direction*] southward, southerly (*Mét*) ◆ **il habite (dans) la banlieue ~** he lives in the southern suburbs; → **hémisphère, pôle**

sud-africain, e (mpl **sud-africains**) /sydafʀikɛ̃, ɛn/ ADJ South African NM,F **Sud-Africain(e)** South African

sud-américain, e (mpl **sud-américains**) /sydameʀikɛ̃, ɛn/ ADJ South American NM,F **Sud-Américain(e)** South American

sudation /sydasjɔ̃/ NF sweating, sudation (*SPÉC*)

sudatoire /sydatwaʀ/ ADJ sudatory

sud-coréen, -enne (mpl **sud-coréens**) /sydkɔʀeɛ̃, ɛn/ ADJ South Korean NM,F **Sud-Coréen(ne)** South Korean

sud-est /sydɛst/ ADJ INV south-east; [*banlieue*] south-eastern; [*côte*] south-east(ern) NM south-east ◆ **le Sud-Est asiatique** South-East Asia ◆ **aller dans le Sud-Est (de la France)** to go to the south-east (of France) ◆ **au ~ de Rome** (*à l'extérieur*) south-east of Rome; (*dans la ville*) in the south-east of Rome ◆ **regarder vers le ~** to look south-east(wards) *ou* towards the southeast ◆ **en direction du ~** in a south-easterly direction ◆ **vent du** *ou* **de ~** southeasterly (wind), southeaster

sudiste /sydist/ NMF Southerner; (*Hist US*) Confederate ADJ Southern; (*Hist US*) Confederate

sudorifère /sydɔʀifɛʀ/ ADJ ⇒ **sudoripare**

sudorifique /sydɔʀifik/ ADJ, NM sudorific

sudoripare /sydɔʀipaʀ/ ADJ sudoriferous, sudoriparous ◆ **glande ~** sweat gland

sud-ouest /sydwɛst/ ADJ INV south-west; [*banlieue*] south-western; [*côte*] south-west(ern) NM southwest ◆ **aller dans le Sud-Ouest (de la France)** to go to the south-west (of France) ◆ **au ~ de Rome** (*à l'extérieur*) south-west of Rome; (*dans la ville*) in the south-west of Rome ◆ **regarder vers le ~** to look south-west(wards) *ou* towards the southwest ◆ **en direction du ~** in a south-westerly direction ◆ **vent du** *ou* **de ~** southwesterly (wind), southwester

sud-sud-est /sydsydɛst/ NM, ADJ INV south-southeast

sud-sud-ouest /sydsydwɛst/ NM, ADJ INV south-southwest

sud-vietnamien, -ienne (mpl **sud-vietnamiens**) /sydvjetnamjɛ̃, jɛn/ ADJ South Vietnamese NM,F **Sud-Vietnamien(ne)** South Vietnamese

suédé, e /sɥede/ ADJ, NM suede

Suède /sɥɛd/ NF Sweden

suède /sɥɛd/ NM (= *peau*) suede ◆ **en** *ou* **de ~** suede

suédine /sɥedin/ NF suedette

suédois, e /sɥedwa, waz/ ADJ Swedish; → **allumette, gymnastique** NM (= *langue*) Swedish NM,F **Suédois(e)** Swede

suée * /sɥe/ NF sweat ◆ **prendre** *ou* **attraper une bonne ~** to work up a good sweat ◆ **à l'idée de cette épreuve, j'en avais la ~** I was in a (cold) sweat at the thought of the test * ◆ **je dois aller le voir, quelle ~ !** I've got to go and see him – what a drag! * *ou* pain! *

suer /sɥe/ ▸ conjug 1 ◂ VI 1 (= *transpirer*) to sweat; (*fig* = *peiner*) to sweat * (*sur* over); ◆ **~ de peur** to be in a cold sweat ◆ **~ à grosses gouttes** to sweat profusely ◆ **~ sur une dissertation** to sweat over an essay *

2 (= *suinter*) [*murs*] to ooze, to sweat (*de* with)

3 (*Culin*) **faire ~** to sweat

4 (*locutions*) **faire ~ qn** (*lit*) [*médicament*] to make sb sweat ◆ **tu me fais ~** * (*fig*) you're a pain (in the neck) * *ou* a drag * ◆ **on se fait ~ ici** * it's such a drag here * ◆ **ce qu'on se fait ~ à ses cours** * his classes are such a drag * ◆ **je me suis fait ~ à le réparer** * I sweated blood to repair that ◆ **faire ~ le burnous** ‡ (*péj*) to use sweated labour, to exploit native labour

VT 1 [*+ sueur, sang*] to sweat ◆ **~ sang et eau à** *ou* **pour faire qch** (*fig*) to sweat blood to get sth done, to sweat blood over sth

2 [*+ humidité*] to ooze

3 (= *révéler, respirer*) [*+ pauvreté, misère, avarice, lâcheté*] to exude, to reek of ◆ **cet endroit sue l'ennui** this place reeks of boredom

4 († , ‡ = *danser*) **en ~ une** to shake a leg *

sueur /sɥœʀ/ NF sweat (*NonC*) ◆ **en ~** in a sweat, sweating ◆ **être en ~** to be bathed in sweat ◆ **à la ~ de son front** by the sweat of one's brow ◆ **donner des ~s froides à qn** to put sb in a cold sweat ◆ **j'en avais des ~s froides** I was in a cold sweat about it ◆ **vivre de la ~ du peuple** to live off the backs of the people

Suez /sɥɛz/ N Suez ◆ **le canal de ~** the Suez Canal ◆ **le golfe de ~** the Gulf of Suez

suffire /syfiʀ/ ▸ conjug 37 ◂ VI 1 (= *être assez*) [*somme, durée, quantité*] to be enough, to be sufficient, to suffice (*frm*) ◆ **cette explication ne (me) suffit pas** this explanation isn't enough *ou* isn't sufficient (for me) *ou* won't do ◆ **cinq hommes suffisent (pour ce travail)** five men will do (for this job) ◆ **un rien suffirait pour** *ou* **à bouleverser nos plans** it would only take the smallest thing to upset our plans; → **peine**

2 (= *satisfaire, combler*) **~ à** [*+ besoins*] to meet; [*+ personne*] to be enough for ◆ **ma femme me suffit** *ou* **suffit à mon bonheur** my wife is all I need to make me happy, my wife is enough to

make me happy ◆ **il ne suffit pas aux besoins de la famille** he does not meet the needs of his family ◆ **il ne peut ~ à tout** he can't manage (to do) everything, he can't cope with everything ◆ **les week-ends, il ne suffisait plus à servir les clients** at weekends he couldn't manage to serve all the customers by himself

3 *(locutions)* **ça suffit** that's enough, that'll do ◆ **(ça) suffit !** that's enough!, that will do! ◆ **comme ennuis, ça suffit (comme ça)** we've had enough trouble as it is thank you very much ◆ **ça ne te suffit pas de l'avoir tourmentée ?** isn't it enough for you to have tormented her? ◆ **ça suffira pour aujourd'hui** that's enough for today *ou* for one day

VB IMPERS 1 *(avec de)* **il suffit de s'inscrire pour devenir membre** all you have to do to become a member is sign up ◆ **il suffit de (la) faire réchauffer et la soupe est prête** just heat (up) the soup and it's ready (to serve) ◆ **il suffit d'un accord verbal pour conclure l'affaire** a verbal agreement is sufficient *ou* is enough *ou* will suffice *(frm)* to conclude the matter ◆ **il suffisait d'y penser** it's obvious when you think about it ◆ **il suffit d'un rien pour l'inquiéter** *(intensif)* it only takes the smallest thing to worry him, the smallest thing is enough to worry him ◆ **il suffit d'une fois : on n'est jamais trop prudent** once is enough – you can never be too careful

2 *(avec que)* **il suffit que vous leur écriviez** all you have to do is write to them ◆ **il suffit que tu me dises comment me rendre à l'aéroport** all you have to do is tell me how to get to the airport ◆ **il suffit qu'il ouvre la bouche pour que tout le monde se taise** he has only to open his mouth and everyone stops talking ◆ **il suffit qu'il soit démotivé pour faire du mauvais travail** if he feels the least bit demotivated he doesn't produce very good work

VPR **se suffire** ◆ **se ~ (à soi-même)** *[pays, personne]* to be self-sufficient ◆ **la beauté se suffit (à elle-même)** beauty is sufficient unto itself *(littér)* ◆ **ils se suffisent (l'un à l'autre)** they have each other and don't need anyone else

suffisamment /syfizamɑ̃/ ADV sufficiently, enough ◆ **~ fort/clair** sufficiently strong/clear, strong/clear enough ◆ **être ~ vêtu** to have enough clothes on ◆ **lettre ~ affranchie** letter with enough stamps on ◆ **~ de nourriture/d'argent** sufficient *ou* enough food/money ◆ **y a-t-il ~ à boire ?** is there enough *ou* sufficient to drink? ◆ **nous ne sommes pas ~ nombreux** there aren't enough of us

suffisance /syfizɑ̃s/ NF 1 *(= vanité)* self-importance, smugness 2 *(littér, †)* **avoir sa ~ de qch, avoir qch en ~** to have sth in plenty, to have a sufficiency of sth † ◆ **il y en a en ~** there is sufficient of it ◆ **des livres, il en a sa ~** † *ou* **à sa ~** he has books aplenty *ou* in abundance

suffisant, e /syfizɑ̃, ɑ̃t/ ADJ 1 *(= adéquat)* sufficient; *(Scol) [résultats]* satisfactory ◆ **c'est ~ pour qu'il se mette en colère** it's enough to make him lose his temper ◆ **je n'ai pas la place/la somme ~e** I haven't got sufficient *ou* enough room/money ◆ **75 €, c'est amplement** *ou* **plus que ~** €75 is more than enough; → **condition, grâce** 2 *(= prétentieux) [personne, ton]* self-important, smug ◆ **faire le ~** to put on airs

suffixal, e (mpl **-aux**) /syfiksal, o/ ADJ suffixal

suffixation /syfiksasjɔ̃/ NF suffixation

suffixe /syfiks/ NM suffix

suffixer /syfikse/ ► conjug 1 ◄ VT to suffix, to add a suffix to ◆ **mot suffixé** word with a suffix

suffocant, e /syfɔkɑ̃, ɑ̃t/ ADJ 1 *[fumée, chaleur]* suffocating, stifling 2 *(= étonnant)* staggering

suffocation /syfɔkasjɔ̃/ NF *(= action)* suffocation; *(= sensation)* suffocating feeling ◆ **il avait des ~s** he had fits of choking

suffoquer /syfɔke/ ► conjug 1 ◄ VI *(lit)* to choke, to suffocate, to stifle *(de* with); ◆ **~ de** *(fig) [+ rage, indignation]* to choke with VT 1 *[fumée]* to suffocate, to choke, to stifle; *[colère, joie]* to choke ◆ **les larmes la suffoquaient** she was choking with tears 2 *(= étonner) [nouvelle, comportement de qn]* to stagger ◆ **la nouvelle nous a suffoqués** we were staggered by the news

suffragant /syfʀagɑ̃/ ADJ M, NM *(Rel)* suffragan

suffrage /syfʀaʒ/ NM 1 *(Pol = voix)* vote ◆ **~s exprimés** valid votes ◆ **le parti obtiendra peu de/beaucoup de ~s** the party will poll badly/heavily, the party will get a poor/good share of the vote 2 *(= approbation) [de public, critique]* approval *(NonC)*, approbation *(NonC)* ◆ **accorder son ~ à qn/qch** to give one's approval to sb/sth ◆ **ce livre a remporté tous les ~s** this book met with universal approval ◆ **cette nouvelle voiture mérite tous les ~s** this new car deserves everyone's approval

COMP **suffrage censitaire** suffrage on the basis of property qualification
suffrage direct direct suffrage
suffrage indirect indirect suffrage
suffrage restreint restricted suffrage
suffrage universel universal suffrage *ou* franchise

suffragette /syfʀaʒɛt/ NF suffragette

suggérer /sygʒeʀe/ GRAMMAIRE ACTIVE 28.1, 42.3 ► conjug 6 ◄ VT *(gén)* to suggest; *[+ solution, projet]* to suggest, to put forward ◆ **~ une réponse à qn** to suggest a reply to sb ◆ **je lui suggérai que c'était moins facile qu'il ne pensait** I suggested to him *ou* I put it to him that it was not as easy as he thought ◆ **~ à qn une solution** to put forward *ou* suggest *ou* put a solution to sb ◆ **j'ai suggéré d'aller au cinéma/que nous allions au cinéma** I suggested going to the cinema/that we went to the cinema ◆ **elle lui a suggéré de voir un médecin** she suggested he should see a doctor ◆ **mot qui en suggère un autre** word which brings another to mind

suggestibilité /sygʒɛstibilite/ NF suggestibility

suggestible /sygʒɛstibl/ ADJ suggestible

suggestif, -ive /sygʒɛstif, iv/ ADJ *(= évocateur, indécent)* suggestive

suggestion /sygʒɛstjɔ̃/ GRAMMAIRE ACTIVE 28 NF suggestion ◆ **faire une ~** to make a suggestion

suggestionner /sygʒɛstjɔne/ ► conjug 1 ◄ VT to influence by suggestion

suggestivité /sygʒɛstivite/ NF suggestiveness

suicidaire /sɥisidɛʀ/ ADJ *(lit, fig)* suicidal NMF person with suicidal tendencies

suicide /sɥisid/ NM *(lit, fig)* suicide ◆ **c'est un** *ou* **du ~ !** *(fig)* it's suicide! ◆ **opération** *ou* **mission ~** suicide mission ◆ **attaque/commando ~** suicide attack/commando squad ◆ **~ collectif/rituel** group/ritual suicide ◆ **pousser qn au ~** to push sb to suicide ◆ **ce serait un véritable ~ politique** it would be political suicide; → **tentative**

suicidé, e /sɥiside/ (ptp de **se suicider**) ADJ who has committed suicide NM,F *(= personne)* suicide

suicider /sɥiside/ ► conjug 1 ◄ VPR **se suicider** to commit suicide VT * ◆ **ils ont suicidé le témoin** *(= tuer)* they made it look as if the witness had committed suicide

suie /sɥi/ NF soot; → **noir**

suif /sɥif/ NM tallow ◆ **~ de mouton** mutton suet ◆ **chercher du ~ à qn** *(arg Crime)* to needle sb * ◆ **il va y avoir du ~** *(arg Crime)* there's going to be trouble

sui generis /sɥiʒeneʀis/ LOC ADJ sui generis ◆ **l'odeur ~ d'un hôpital** the distinctive *ou* characteristic smell of a hospital ◆ **odeur ~** *(hum)* foul smell

suint /sɥɛ̃/ NM *[de laine]* suint

suintant, e /sɥɛ̃tɑ̃, ɑ̃t/ ADJ *[pierre, roche, mur]* oozing, sweating

suintement /sɥɛ̃tmɑ̃/ NM *[d'eau]* seepage; *[de sève]* oozing; *[de mur]* oozing, sweating; *[de plaie, ulcère]* weeping ◆ **des ~s sur le mur** moisture oozing out of the wall ◆ **le ~ des eaux entraîne des fissures** water seepage causes cracks to form

suinter /sɥɛ̃te/ ► conjug 1 ◄ VI *[eau]* to seep; *[sève]* to ooze; *[mur]* to ooze, to sweat; *[plaie]* to weep ◆ **des gouttes de pluie suintent du plafond** rainwater is seeping through the ceiling ◆ **l'humidité suintait des murs** the damp was streaming *ou* dripping off the walls

Suisse /sɥis/ NF *(= pays)* Switzerland ◆ **~ romande/allemande** *ou* **alémanique** French-speaking/German-speaking Switzerland NMF *(= personne)* Swiss ◆ **~ romand** French-speaking Swiss ◆ **~ allemand** German-speaking Swiss, Swiss German ◆ **boire/manger en ~** † *(fig)* to drink/eat alone

suisse /sɥis/ ADJ Swiss ◆ **~ romand** Swiss French ◆ **~ allemand** Swiss German NM 1 *(= bedeau)* ≈ verger 2 *[de Vatican]* Swiss Guard 3 *(= écureuil)* chipmunk

Suissesse /sɥisɛs/ NF Swiss (woman)

suite /sɥit/ GRAMMAIRE ACTIVE 44.1, 47.1 NF 1 *(= escorte)* retinue, suite

2 *(= nouvel épisode)* continuation, following episode; *(= second roman, film)* sequel; *(= rebondissement d'une affaire)* follow-up; *(= reste)* remainder, rest ◆ **voici la ~ de notre feuilleton** here is the next episode in *ou* the continuation of our serial ◆ **ce roman/film a une ~** there is a sequel to this novel/film ◆ **voici la ~ de l'affaire que nous évoquions hier** *(Presse)* here is the follow-up to *ou* further information on the item we mentioned yesterday ◆ **la ~ du film/du repas/de la lettre était moins bonne** the remainder *ou* the rest of the film/the meal/the letter was not so good ◆ **la ~ au prochain numéro** *(journal)* to be continued (in the next issue); *(* fig)* we'll talk about this later ◆ **~ et fin** concluding *ou* final episode ◆ **la ~ des événements devait lui donner raison** what followed was to prove him right ◆ **le projet n'a pas eu de ~** the project came to nothing ◆ **attendons la ~** *(d'un repas)* let's wait for the next course; *(d'un discours)* let's see what comes next; *(d'un événement)* let's (wait and) see how it turns out ◆ **lisez donc la ~** please read on ◆ **on connaît la ~** the rest is history

3 *(= aboutissement)* result ◆ **~s** *(= prolongements) [de maladie]* effects; *[d'accident]* results; *[d'affaire, incident]* consequences, repercussions ◆ **la ~ logique de qch** the obvious *ou* logical result of sth ◆ **cet incident a eu des ~s fâcheuses/n'a pas eu de ~s** the incident has had annoying consequences *ou* repercussions/has had no repercussions ◆ **il est mort des ~s de ses blessures/d'un cancer** he died as a result of his injuries/died of cancer ◆ **mourir des ~s d'un accident de cheval** to die following a riding accident

4 *(= succession, Math)* series; *(Ling)* sequence ◆ **~ de** *[de personnes, maisons]* succession *ou* string *ou* series of; *[d'événements]* succession *ou* train of ◆ **article sans ~** *(Comm)* discontinued line

5 *(frm = cohérence)* coherence ◆ **il y a beaucoup de ~ dans son raisonnement/ses réponses** his reasoning is/his replies are very coherent ◆ **ses propos n'avaient guère de ~** what he said lacked coherence *ou* consistency ◆ **travailler avec ~** to work steadily ◆ **des propos sans ~** disjointed words ◆ **il a de la ~ dans les**

idées (*réfléchi, décidé*) he's very single-minded; (*iro : entêté*) he's not easily put off; → **esprit**

6 (= *appartement*) suite

7 (*Mus*) suite ◆ ~ **instrumentale/orchestrale** instrumental/orchestral suite

8 (*locutions*) **donner ~ à** [+ *projet*] to pursue, to follow up; [+ *demande, commande, lettre*] to follow up ◆ **ils n'ont pas donné ~ à notre lettre** they have taken no action concerning our letter, they have not followed up our letter ◆ **faire ~ à** [+ *événement*] to follow; [+ *chapitre*] to follow (after); [+ *bâtiment*] to adjoin ◆ **prendre la ~ de** [+ *directeur*] to succeed, to take over from; [+ *entreprise*] to take over ◆ **entraîner qn à sa ~** (*lit*) to drag sb along behind one ◆ **entraîner qn à sa ~ dans une affaire** (*fig*) to drag sb into an affair

♦ **suite à** ◆ **(comme) ~ à votre lettre/notre entretien** further to your letter/our conversation

♦ **à la suite** (= *successivement*) one after the other ◆ **mettez-vous à la ~** (= *derrière*) join on at the back, go to *ou* join the back of the queue (*Brit*) *ou* line (*US*)

♦ **à la suite de** (*objet, personne*) behind ◆ **à la ~ de sa maladie** (= *événement*) following his illness

♦ **de suite** (* = *immédiatement*) at once ◆ **je reviens de ~*** I'll be right *ou* straight (*Brit*) back ◆ **boire trois verres de ~** (= *d'affilée*) to drink three glasses in a row *ou* one after another ◆ **pendant trois jours de ~** for three days in succession ◆ **il est venu trois jours de ~** he came three days in a row *ou* three days running ◆ **il n'arrive pas à dire trois mots de ~** he can't string two words together

♦ **par suite** consequently, therefore

♦ **par suite de** (= *à cause de*) owing to, as a result of

♦ **par la suite, dans la suite** afterwards, subsequently

suivant[1], e /sɥivɑ̃, ɑ̃t/ **ADJ** 1 (*dans le temps*) following, next; (*dans une série*) next ◆ **le mardi ~ je la revis** I saw her again the following Tuesday ◆ **vendredi et les jours ~s** Friday and the following days ◆ **le malade ~ était très atteint** the next patient was very badly affected ◆ **"voir page suivante"** "see next page"

2 (= *ci-après*) following ◆ **faites l'exercice ~** do the following exercise

NM,F 1 (= *prochain*) (*dans une série*) next (one); (*dans le temps*) following (one), next (one) ◆ **(au) ~ !** next (please)! ◆ **cette année fut mauvaise et les ~es ne le furent guère moins** that year was bad and the following ones were scarcely any better ◆ **pas jeudi prochain, le ~** not this (coming) Thursday, the one after (that) ◆ **je descends à la ~e*** I'm getting off at the next stop

2 (*littér* = *membre d'escorte*) attendant

NF suivante (*Théât*) handmaiden, lady-in-waiting; †† companion

suivant[2] /sɥivɑ̃/ **PRÉP** (= *selon*) according to ◆ **~ son habitude** as usual, as is (*ou* was) his wont ◆ **~ l'usage** according to custom ◆ **~ l'expression consacrée** as the saying goes, as they say ◆ **~ les jours/les cas** depending on the day/the circumstances ◆ **découper ~ le pointillé** cut along the dotted line ◆ **~ un axe** along an axis ◆ **~ que ...** according to whether ...

suiveur, -euse /sɥivœʀ, øz/ **ADJ** [*véhicule*] following behind (*attrib*) **NM** 1 (*Sport*) (official) follower (*of a race*) 2 (= *imitateur*) imitator ◆ **ils n'innovent pas, ce ne sont que des ~s** they don't innovate, they just follow along 3 († = *dragueur*) **elle se retourna, son ~ avait disparu** she turned round and the man who was following her had disappeared ◆ **elle va me prendre pour un ~** she'll think I'm the sort who follows women

suivi, e /sɥivi/ (ptp de **suivre**) **ADJ** 1 (= *régulier*) [*travail*] steady; [*correspondance*] regular; (= *constant*) [*qualité*] consistent; [*effort*] consistent, sustained; (*Comm*) [*demande*] constant, steady; (= *cohérent*) [*conversation, histoire, raisonnement*] coherent; [*politique*] consistent

2 [*article à la vente*] in general production (*attrib*)

3 (= *apprécié*) **très ~** [*cours*] well-attended; [*mode, recommandation*] widely adopted; [*exemple*] widely followed ◆ **le match était très ~** a lot a people watched the match ◆ **cours peu ~** poorly-attended course ◆ **mode peu ~e** fashion that has a limited following ◆ **exemple peu ~** example which is not widely followed ◆ **procès très ~** trial that is being closely followed by the public ◆ **feuilleton très ~** serial with a large following

NM (= *accompagnement*) [*de dossier, travaux, négociations*] monitoring ◆ **assurer le ~ de** [+ *affaire*] to follow through; [+ *produit en stock*] to go on stocking ◆ **il n'y a pas eu de ~** there was no follow-up ◆ **~ médical** aftercare ◆ **assurer le ~ pédagogique des élèves** to provide pupils with continuous educational support ◆ **assurer le ~ psychologique des victimes** to provide victims with counselling

suivisme /sɥivism/ **NM** (*Pol*) follow-my-leader attitude

suiviste /sɥivist/ **ADJ** [*attitude, politique*] follow-my-leader (*épith*) **NMF** person with a follow-my-leader attitude

suivre /sɥivʀ/ ▸ conjug 40 ◂ **VT** 1 (*gén*) (= *accompagner, marcher derrière, venir après*) to follow ◆ **elle le suit comme un petit chien** *ou* **un caniche** *ou* **un toutou*** she follows him around like a little dog ◆ **il me suit comme mon ombre** he follows me about like a shadow ◆ **ralentis, je ne peux pas (te) ~** slow down, I can't keep up (with you) ◆ **pars sans moi, je te suis** go on without me and I'll follow (on) ◆ **si vous voulez bien me ~** if you'll just follow me, come this way please ◆ **~ qn de près** [*garde du corps*] to stick close to sb; [*voiture, coureur*] to follow close behind sb ◆ **faire ~ qn** to have sb followed ◆ **suivez le guide !** this way, please! ◆ **son image me suit sans cesse** his image is constantly with me ◆ **cette préposition est toujours suivie de ...** this preposition is always followed by ... ◆ **il la suivit des yeux** *ou* **du regard** he followed her with his eyes, his eyes followed her ◆ **certains députés, suivez mon regard, ont ...** (*iro*) certain deputies, without mentioning any names *ou* no names mentioned, have ... ◆ **~ sa balle** (*Tennis, Golf*) to follow through ◆ **l'été suit le printemps** (*dans le temps*) summer follows spring *ou* comes after spring ◆ **le mariage sera suivi d'une réception** the wedding ceremony will be followed by a reception ◆ **le jour qui suivit son arrivée** the day following *ou* after his arrival, the day after he arrived ◆ **suivent deux mois d'intense activité** two months of intense activity will follow; → **aimer, lettre, trace**

2 (*dans une série*) to follow ◆ **la maison qui suit la mienne** the house after mine; → **jour**

3 (= *longer*) [*personne*] to follow, to keep to; [*route, itinéraire*] to follow ◆ **suivez la N7 sur 10 km** keep to *ou* go along *ou* follow the N7 for 10 km ◆ **prenez la route qui suit la Loire** take the road which goes alongside *ou* which follows the Loire ◆ **~ une piste** (*fig*) to follow up a clue ◆ **ces deux amis ont suivi des voies bien différentes** (*fig*) the two friends have gone very different ways ◆ **découpez en suivant le pointillé** cut along the dotted line ◆ **suivez les flèches** follow the arrows

4 (= *se conformer à*) [+ *exemple, mode, conseil, consigne*] to follow ◆ **~ un régime** to be on a diet ◆ **il me fait ~ un régime sévère** he has put me on a strict diet ◆ **~ son instinct** to follow one's instinct *ou* one's nose* ◆ **il suit son idée** he does things his (own) way ◆ **il se leva et chacun suivit son exemple** he stood up and everyone else followed suit ◆ **on n'a pas voulu le ~** we didn't want to follow his advice ◆ **je ne vous suivrai pas sur ce terrain** I won't follow you down that road ◆ **tout le monde vous suivra** everybody will back you up *ou* support you ◆ **la maladie/l'enquête suit son cours** the illness/the inquiry is running *ou* taking its course ◆ **laisser la justice ~ son cours** to let justice take its course ◆ **~ le mouvement** to follow the crowd ◆ **si les prix augmentent, les salaires doivent ~** if prices rise, salaries must do the same; → **marche[1], traitement**

5 (*Scol*) [+ *classe, cours*] (= *être inscrit à*) to attend, to go to; (= *être attentif à*) to follow; (= *assimiler*) [+ *programme*] to keep up with

6 (= *observer l'évolution de*) [+ *carrière de qn, affaire, match*] to follow; [+ *feuilleton*] to follow, to keep up with ◆ **~ un malade/un élève** to follow *ou* monitor the progress of a patient/a pupil ◆ **~ la messe** to follow (the) mass ◆ **elle suit de près l'actualité** she keeps abreast of *ou* up with the news ◆ **il se fait ~** *ou* **il est suivi par un médecin** he's seeing a doctor ◆ **j'ai suivi ses articles avec intérêt** I've followed his articles with interest ◆ **"à suivre"** [*feuilleton*] "to be continued" ◆ **(c'est une) affaire à ~** watch this space, it's worth keeping an eye on

7 (*Comm* = *avoir en stock*) [+ *article*] to (continue to) stock ◆ **nous ne suivons plus cet article** this is a discontinued line

8 (= *comprendre*) [+ *argument, personne, exposé*] to follow ◆ **jusqu'ici je vous suis** I'm with you *ou* I follow you so far ◆ **il parlait si vite qu'on le suivait mal** he spoke so fast he was difficult to follow ◆ **là, je ne vous suis pas très bien** I don't really follow you I'm not really with you there

9 (*Jeux*) [+ *numéro, cheval*] to follow

VI 1 [*élève*] (= *être attentif*) to pay attention ◆ **suivez avec votre voisin** share with the person sitting next to you

2 [*élève*] (= *assimiler le programme*) to keep up, to follow ◆ **elle suit bien en physique** she's keeping up well in physics ◆ **il a du mal à ~ en maths** he has trouble keeping up in maths

3 (*Cartes*) to follow ◆ **je suis** (*Poker*) I'm in, count me in

4 ◆ **faire ~ son courrier** to have one's mail forwarded ◆ **"faire suivre"** (*sur enveloppe*) "please forward"

5 (= *venir après*) to follow ◆ **lisez ce qui suit** read what follows ◆ **les enfants suivent à pied** the children are following on foot ◆ **les personnes dont les noms suivent** the following people ◆ **comme suit** as follows

VB IMPERS ◆ **il suit de ce que vous dites que ...** it follows from what you say that ...

VPR se suivre 1 (*dans une série*) to follow each other ◆ **ils se suivaient sur l'étroit sentier** [*deux personnes*] they were walking one behind the other along the narrow path; [*plusieurs personnes*] they were walking one behind the other *ou* in single file along the narrow path ◆ **leurs enfants se suivent (de près)** there's not much of an age difference between their children ◆ **trois démissions qui se suivent** three resignations in a row *ou* in close succession

2 (*dans le bon ordre*) to be in (the right) order ◆ **les pages ne se suivent pas** the pages are not in (the right) order, the pages are in the wrong order

sujet, -ette /syʒɛ, ɛt/ **ADJ** ◆ **~ à** [+ *vertige, mal de mer*] prone to; [+ *lubies, sautes d'humeur*] subject to, prone to; [+ *impôt, modification*] liable to, subject to ◆ **question sujette à controverse** *ou* **polémique** controversial issue ◆ **~ aux accidents** accident-prone ◆ **il était ~ aux accidents les plus bizarres** he used to have the strangest accidents ◆ ~ **à faire qch** liable *ou* inclined *ou* prone to do sth ◆ **il n'est pas ~ à faire des imprudences** he is not one to do anything careless ◆ ~ **à caution** *[renseignement, nouvelle]* unconfirmed; *[moralité, vie privée, honnêteté]* questionable ◆ **je vous dis ça mais c'est ~ à caution** I'm telling you that but I can't guarantee it's true

NM,F *(= gouverné)* subject

NM 1 *(= matière, question, thème)* subject *(de* for); ◆ **un excellent ~ de conversation** an excellent topic (of conversation) ◆ **revenons à notre ~** let's get back to the subject at hand ◆ **c'était devenu un ~ de plaisanterie** it had become a standing joke *ou* something to joke about ◆ **ça ferait un bon ~ de comédie** that would be a good subject *ou* theme for a comedy ◆ **bibliographie par ~s** bibliography arranged by subject ◆ **~ d'examen** examination question ◆ **quel ~ ont-ils donné ?** what did you have to write about? ◆ **distribuer les ~s** to give out the examination papers ◆ **votre dissertation est hors ~** your essay is off the point ◆ **faire du hors ~** to wander off the point; → **or¹, vif**

2 *(= motif, cause)* ~ **de mécontentement** cause *ou* grounds for dissatisfaction ◆ **il n'avait vraiment pas ~ de se mettre en colère/se plaindre** he really had no cause to lose his temper/ for complaint ◆ **il a ~ de se plaindre** he has every reason to complain ◆ **protester/réclamer sans ~** to protest/complain without good cause

3 *(= individu)* subject ◆ **le ~ parlant** *(Ling)* the speaker ◆ **les rats qui servent de ~s (d'expérience)** the rats which serve as experimental subjects ◆ **son frère est un ~ brillant/un ~ d'élite** his brother is a brilliant/an exceptionally brilliant student ◆ **un mauvais ~** *(= enfant)* a bad boy; *(= jeune homme)* a bad sort *ou* lot *(Brit)*

4 *(Ling, Mus, Philos)* subject ◆ **~ grammatical/réel/apparent** grammatical/real/apparent subject ◆ **nom/pronom ~** noun/pronoun subject

5 *(Mus, Peinture)* subject

6 *(= figurine)* figurine ◆ **des petits ~s en ivoire** small ivory figurines

7 *(Jur)* ~ **de droit** holder of a right

8 *(= à propos de)* **au ~ de** about, concerning ◆ **que sais-tu à son ~ ?** what do you know about him? ◆ **au ~ de cette fille, je peux vous dire que …** about *ou* concerning that girl, I can tell you that … ◆ **à ce ~, je voulais vous dire que …** on that subject *ou* about that*, I wanted to tell you that … ◆ **c'est à quel ~ ?** can I ask what it's about?

sujétion /syʒesjɔ̃/ **NF** 1 *(= asservissement)* subjection ◆ **maintenir un peuple dans la ~** *ou* **sous sa ~** to keep a nation in subjection ◆ **tomber sous la ~ de qn** to fall into sb's power *ou* under sb's sway ◆ **~ aux passions/au désir** *(littér) (= asservissement)* subjection to passions/to desire 2 *(= obligation, contrainte)* constraint ◆ **les enfants étaient pour elle une ~** the children were a real constraint to her *ou* were like a millstone round her neck ◆ **des habitudes qui deviennent des ~s** habits which become compulsions ◆ **indemnité de ~ spéciale** *(Scol) bonus paid to teachers working in schools in problem areas*

sulfamides /sylfamid/ **NMPL** sulpha drugs, sulphonamides *(SPÉC)*

sulfatage /sylfataʒ/ **NM** *[de vigne]* spraying (with copper sulphate *ou* sulfate *(US)*)

sulfate /sylfat/ **NM** sulphate, sulfate *(US)* ◆ ~ **de cuivre** copper sulphate

sulfaté, e /sylfate/ (ptp de **sulfater**) **ADJ** sulphated

sulfater /sylfate/ ► conjug 1 ◄ **VT** *[+ vigne]* to spray (with copper sulphate *ou* sulfate *(US)*)

sulfateuse /sylfatøz/ **NF** 1 *(Agr)* (copper sulphate *ou* sulfate *(US)*) spraying machine 2 *(arg Crime = mitraillette)* machine gun, MG*

sulfite /sylfit/ **NM** sulphite, sulfite *(US)*

sulfure /sylfyʀ/ **NM** 1 *(Chim)* sulphide, sulfide *(US)* ◆ ~ **de fer/mercure** iron/mercuric sulphide ◆ ~ **de carbone** carbon disulphide 2 *(= presse-papier)* millefiore glass paperweight

sulfuré, e /sylfyʀe/ (ptp de **sulfurer**) **ADJ** sulphurated, sulfurated *(US)*, sulphurized, sulphuretted ◆ **hydrogène ~** hydrogen sulphide *ou* sulfide *(US)*, sulphuretted *ou* sulfuretted *(US)* hydrogen

sulfurer /sylfyʀe/ ► conjug 1 ◄ **VT** to sulphurate, to sulphurize

sulfureux, -euse /sylfyʀø, øz/ **ADJ** 1 *(Chim)* sulphurous ◆ **anhydride** *ou* **gaz ~** sulphur dioxide ◆ **source sulfureuse** sulphur spring 2 *(= diabolique) [personnage, réputation]* nefarious; *[propos]* heretical; *[charme]* demonic

sulfurique /sylfyʀik/ **ADJ** sulphuric ◆ **acide ~** sulphuric acid ◆ **anhydride ~** sulphur trioxide

sulfurisé, e /sylfyʀize/ **ADJ** ◆ **papier ~** greaseproof paper

sulky /sylki/ **NM** *(Courses)* sulky

sultan /syltɑ̃/ **NM** sultan

sultanat /syltana/ **NM** sultanate

sultane /syltan/ **NF** 1 *(= épouse)* sultana 2 *(= canapé)* couch

sumac /symak/ **NM** sumach *(Brit)*, sumac *(US)*

Sumatra /symatʀa/ **N** Sumatra

sumérien, -ienne /symeʀjɛ̃, jɛn/ **ADJ** Sumerian **NM** *(= langue)* Sumerian **NM,F** **Sumérien(ne)** Sumerian

summum /sɔ(m)mɔm/ **NM** *[de gloire, civilisation]* acme, peak; *[de bêtise, hypocrisie]* height ◆ **c'est le ~ de l'horreur** it's absolutely horrific ◆ **il a atteint le ~ de sa gloire en 1985** he reached the height of his fame in 1985 ◆ **c'est un bon groupe ? – en blues, c'est le ~ !** are they a good group? – for blues, they're the best *ou* the tops* !

sumo /symo/ **NM** *(= lutteur)* sumo wrestler; *(= lutte)* sumo (wrestling)

sumotori /symotɔʀi/ **NM** sumo wrestler

sunnisme /synism/ **NM** Sunni

sunnite /synit/ **ADJ, NMF** Sunni

sup¹ * /syp/ **ADJ** (abrév de **supplémentaire**) ◆ **heures ~** overtime ◆ **faire des heures ~** to do overtime ◆ **être payé en heures ~** to be paid overtime

sup² * /syp/ **ADJ** (abrév de **supérieur**) ◆ **Sup de Co** *grande école for business students*; → **école, lettres, math(s)**

super¹ /sypɛʀ/ **NM** (abrév de **supercarburant**) four-star (petrol) *(Brit)*, extra *(US)*, premium *(US)*, super *(US)* ◆ ~ **plombé** super leaded petrol ◆ ~ **sans plomb** super unleaded (petrol)

super² * /sypɛʀ/ **ADJ INV** *(= sensationnel)* terrific*, great*, fantastic*

super- * /sypɛʀ/ **PRÉF** *(dans les mots composés à trait d'union, le préfixe reste invariable)* 1 *(avant adj)* **~cher/-chic** ultra-expensive/ultra-chic ◆ **c'est ~intéressant** it's ever so interesting ◆ **il est ~sympa** he's really nice 2 *(avant nom)* **une ~moto** a fantastic* motorbike ◆ **un ~héros** a superhero ◆ **un ~flic*** a supercop*

superbe /sypɛʀb/ **ADJ** 1 *(= splendide) [temps, journée]* superb, glorious, gorgeous; *[femme, enfant]* beautiful; *[homme]* handsome; *[maison, cheval, corps, yeux]* superb, beautiful; *[résultat, salaire, performance, vue, voix]* superb, magnificent ◆ **tu as une mine ~** you look wonderful ◆ **~ d'indifférence** *(littér)* superbly indifferent 2 *(littér = orgueilleux)* arrogant, haughty

NF *(littér)* arrogance, haughtiness ◆ **il a perdu de sa ~** he's no longer quite so high and mighty

superbement /sypɛʀbəmɑ̃/ **ADV** *(= magnifiquement)* superbly, wonderfully, beautifully ◆ **il m'a ~ ignorée** *(= orgueilleusement)* he loftily ignored me

superbénéfice /sypɛʀbenefis/ **NM** immense profit

supercalculateur /sypɛʀkalkylatœʀ/ **NM** supercomputer

supercarburant /sypɛʀkaʀbyʀɑ̃/ **NM** high-octane petrol *(Brit)*, high-octane *ou* high-test gasoline *(US)*

superchampion, -ionne /sypɛʀʃɑ̃pjɔ̃, jɔn/ **NM,F** (sporting) superstar

supercherie /sypɛʀʃəʀi/ **NF** trick, trickery *(NonC)* ◆ **il s'aperçut de la ~** he saw through the trick ◆ **user de ~s pour tromper qn** to trick sb ◆ ~ **littéraire** literary hoax *ou* fabrication

supérette /sypeʀɛt/ **NF** mini-market, superette *(US)*

superfétation /sypɛʀfetasjɔ̃/ **NF** *(littér)* superfluity

superfétatoire /sypɛʀfetatwaʀ/ **ADJ** *(littér)* superfluous, supererogatory *(littér)*

superficialité /sypɛʀfisjalite/ **NF** superficiality

superficie /sypɛʀfisi/ **NF** *(= aire)* (surface) area; *(= surface)* surface; *[de terrain]* area ◆ **couvrir une ~ de** to cover an area of ◆ **un appartement d'une ~ de 80 m²** an apartment of 80 square metres ◆ **s'en tenir à la ~ des choses** to skim the surface of things

superficiel, -ielle /sypɛʀfisjɛl/ **ADJ** *(gén)* superficial; *[idées, esprit, personne]* superficial, shallow; *[beauté]* superficial, skin-deep; *[modification]* cosmetic; *(= près de la surface) [couche de liquide]* superficial, upper; *(= fin) [couche de peinture]* thin; → **tension**

superficiellement /sypɛʀfisjɛlmɑ̃/ **ADV** superficially

superfin, e /sypɛʀfɛ̃, in/ **ADJ** *[beurre, produit]* top-quality *(épith)*; *[qualité]* top *(épith)*, superior

superflu, e /sypɛʀfly/ **ADJ** 1 *(= pas nécessaire) [précaution, travail]* unnecessary ◆ **il est ~ d'insister** there is no point (in) insisting 2 *(= en trop) [discours, détails, explications]* superfluous, redundant; *[kilos]* surplus; *[poils]* unwanted ◆ **un brin d'humour ne serait pas ~** a bit of humour wouldn't go amiss ◆ **il n'est pas ~ de rappeler que …** it's worth bearing in mind that … **NM** ◆ **le ~** *(gén)* non-essentials; *(= produits de luxe)* luxuries ◆ **distinguer le ~ de l'indispensable** to differentiate between essentials and non-essentials ◆ **maintenant, je peux m'offrir le ~** now I can afford to spend money on luxuries ◆ **débarrasser son style du ~** to pare down one's style

superfluité /sypɛʀflyite/ **NF** *(littér)* superfluity

superforme * /sypɛʀfɔʀm/ **NF** ◆ **être en ~** *(moralement)* to feel great*; *(physiquement)* to be in great shape* ◆ **c'est la ~** *(morale)* I'm *(ou* he's *etc)* feeling great*; *(physique)* I'm *(ou* he's *etc)* in great shape*

superforteresse /sypɛʀfɔʀtəʀɛs/ **NF** superfortress

super-G /sypɛʀʒe/, **super-géant** /sypɛʀʒeɑ̃/ **NM** *(Ski)* super-giant slalom

supergrand * /sypɛʀgʀɑ̃/ **NM** superpower

super-huit /sypɛʀɥit/ **ADJ INV, NM INV** super-8 ◆ **caméra ~** super-8 camera

supérieur, e /sypeʀjœʀ/ GRAMMAIRE ACTIVE 32.2

ADJ 1 *(dans l'espace, gén)* upper *(épith)*; *[planètes]* superior ◆ **dans la partie ~e du clocher** in the highest *ou* upper *ou* top part of the bell tower ◆ **la partie ~e de l'objet** the top part of the object ◆ **le feu a pris dans les étages ~s** fire broke out on the upper floors ◆ **montez à l'étage ~** go to the next floor up *ou* to the floor above, go up to the next floor ◆ **mâchoire/lèvre ~e** upper jaw/lip ◆ **le lac Supérieur** Lake Superior

2 *(dans un ordre) [vitesse]* higher, greater; *[nombre]* higher, greater, bigger; *[classes sociales]* upper *(épith)*; *[niveaux, échelons]* upper *(épith)*, topmost; *[animaux, végétaux]* higher *(épith)* ◆ **passer dans la classe ~e** *(Scol)* to go up to the next class ◆ **Père ~** *(Rel)* Father Superior ◆ **Mère ~e** *(Rel)* Mother Superior ◆ **commandement ~** *(Mil)* senior command ◆ **à l'échelon ~** on the next rung up ◆ **faire une offre ~e** *(aux enchères)* to make a higher bid ◆ **forces ~es en nombres** forces superior in number; → **cadre, enseignement, mathématique, officier**[1]

3 *(= excellent, qui prévaut) [intérêts, principe]* higher *(épith)*; *[intelligence, esprit]* superior ◆ **produit de qualité ~e** product of superior quality ◆ **des considérations d'ordre ~** considerations of a higher order

4 *(= hautain) [air, ton, regard]* superior

5 ◆ **~ à** *[nombre]* greater *ou* higher than, above; *[somme]* greater *ou* bigger than; *[production]* greater than, superior to ◆ **intelligence/qualité ~e à la moyenne** above-average *ou* higher than average intelligence/quality ◆ **il a obtenu un score nettement ~ à la moyenne nationale** he scored well above the national average ◆ **il est d'une taille ~e à la moyenne** he's of above average height ◆ **des températures ~es à 300°** temperatures in excess of *ou* higher than *ou* of more than 300° ◆ **parvenir à un niveau ~ à ...** to reach a higher level than ... ◆ **il est d'un niveau bien ~ à celui de son adversaire** he is of a far higher standard than his opponent ◆ **il se croit ~ à tout le monde** he thinks he's better than *ou* superior to everybody else ◆ **être ~ à qn (dans une hiérarchie)** to be higher up than sb (in a hierarchy), to be sb's superior ◆ **faire une offre ~e à celle de qn** *(aux enchères)* to outbid sb

NM,F *(Admin, Mil, Rel)* superior ◆ **mon ~ hiérarchique direct** my immediate superior

NM *(Univ)* ◆ **le ~** higher education

supérieurement /syperjœrmɑ̃/ ADV *[exécuter qch, dessiner]* exceptionally well ◆ **~ doué/ennuyeux** exceptionally gifted/boring

supériorité /syperjɔrite/ NF 1 *(= prééminence)* superiority ◆ **~ militaire/technologique** military/technological superiority ◆ **nous avons la ~ du nombre** we outnumber them, we are superior in number(s) ◆ **ce pays s'est révélé d'une écrasante ~ sur ses adversaires** this country has turned out to be overwhelmingly superior to its enemies 2 *(= condescendance)* superiority ◆ **air de ~** superior air, air of superiority ◆ **sourire de ~** superior smile ◆ **avoir un sentiment de ~** to feel superior; → **complexe**

super-jumbo /syperdʒəbo/ NM *(= avion)* super-jumbo

superlatif, -ive /syperlatif, iv/ ADJ superlative NM superlative ◆ **~ absolu/relatif** absolute/relative superlative ◆ **au ~** * in the superlative ◆ **il m'ennuie au ~** * I find him extremely boring

superlativement /syperlativmɑ̃/ ADV superlatively

superléger /syperleʒe/ ADJ, NM *(Sport)* light welterweight

superman /syperman/ (pl **supermans** *ou* **supermen** /sypermen/) NM superman ◆ **il aime jouer les ~s** *ou* **supermen** *(péj)* he likes to let everybody know what a great guy * he is

supermarché /sypermarʃe/ NM supermarket

supernova /sypernɔva/ (pl **supernovae** /sypernɔve/) NF supernova

superordinateur, super-ordinateur /syperɔrdinatœr/ NM supercomputer

superpétrolier /syperpetrɔlje/ NM supertanker

superphosphate /syperfɔsfat/ NM superphosphate

superposable /syperpozabl/ ADJ *(gén)* that may be superimposed, superimposable *(à* on); *[éléments de mobilier]* stacking *(épith)*

superposé, e /syperpoze/ (ptp de **superposer**) ADJ *[visions, images]* superimposed ◆ **il y avait plusieurs couches ~es** there were several layers ◆ **des blocs ~s** blocks one on top of the other; → **lit**

superposer /syperpoze/ ► conjug 1 ◄ VT 1 *(= empiler) [+ blocs, briques, éléments de mobilier]* to stack ◆ **~ des couches de peinture** to apply several layers of paint ◆ **~ les consignes aux consignes** to give one instruction after another 2 *(= faire chevaucher) [+ cartes, clichés]* to superimpose; *[+ figures géométriques]* to superpose ◆ **~ qch à** to superimpose *ou* superpose sth on VPR **se superposer** 1 *[clichés photographiques, images]* to be superimposed (on one another) 2 *(= s'ajouter) [couches de sédiments]* to be superposed; *[éléments de mobilier]* to be stackable

superposition /syperpozisjɔ̃/ NF 1 *(= action) [de blocs]* stacking; *[de cartes, clichés, visions]* superimposition; *[de figures géométriques]* superposing 2 *(Photo)* superimposition ◆ **la ~ de ces couches de sédiment** the way these strata of sediment are superposed ◆ **la ~ de plusieurs influences** the cumulative effect of several influences

superpréfet /syperprefɛ/ NM superprefect *(in charge of a region)*

superproduction /syperprɔdyksjɔ̃/ NF *(Ciné)* spectacular, blockbuster

superprofit /syperprɔfi/ NM immense profit

superpuissance /syperpɥisɑ̃s/ NF superpower

supersonique /sypersɔnik/ ADJ supersonic; → **bang** NM supersonic aircraft

superstar /syperstar/ NF superstar

superstitieusement /syperstisjøzmɑ̃/ ADV superstitiously

superstitieux, -ieuse /syperstisjø, jøz/ ADJ superstitious NM,F superstitious person

superstition /syperstisjɔ̃/ NF superstition ◆ **il a la ~ du chiffre 13** he's superstitious about the number 13

superstrat /syperstra/ NM *(Ling)* superstratum

superstructure /syperstryktyr/ NF *(gén)* superstructure

supertanker /sypertɑ̃kœr/ NM supertanker

superviser /sypervize/ ► conjug 1 ◄ VT to supervise, to oversee

superviseur /sypervizœr/ NM 1 *(= personne)* supervisor 2 *(Ordin)* supervisor

supervision /sypervizjɔ̃/ NF supervision

superwelter /syperwelter/ ADJ, NM light middleweight

superwoman /syperwuman/ (pl **superwomans** *ou* **superwomen** /syperwumen/) NF superwoman

supin /sypɛ̃/ NM supine

supinateur /sypinatœr/ ADJ supine NM *(= muscle)* supinator

supination /sypinasjɔ̃/ NF *[de main]* supination

supplanter /syplɑ̃te/ ► conjug 1 ◄ VT to supplant ◆ **le disque compact a supplanté le microsillon** the compact disc has replaced the record VPR **se supplanter** to supplant one another

suppléance /sypleɑ̃s/ NF *(= poste)* supply post *(Brit)*, substitute post *(US)*; *(= action)* temporary replacement ◆ **faire des ~s** to take supply posts, to do supply *(Brit) ou* substitute *(US)* teaching

suppléant, e /sypleɑ̃, ɑt/ ADJ *(gén)* deputy *(épith)*, substitute *(épith) (US)*; *[professeur]* supply *(épith) (Brit)*, substitute *(épith) (US)* ◆ **médecin ~** locum *(Brit)*, replacement doctor *(US)* ◆ **verbe ~** substitute verb NM,F *(= professeur)* supply *(Brit) ou* substitute *(US)* teacher; *(= juge)* deputy (judge); *(Pol)* deputy; *(= médecin)* locum *(Brit)*, replacement doctor *(US)* ◆ **pendant les vacances, on fait appel à des ~s** during the holidays we take on relief *ou* temporary staff

suppléer /syplee/ ► conjug 1 ◄ VT 1 *(= ajouter) [+ mot manquant]* to supply, to provide; *[+ somme complémentaire]* to make up, to supply 2 *(= compenser) [+ lacune]* to fill in; *[+ manque, défaut]* to make up for, to compensate for 3 *(frm = remplacer) [+ professeur]* to stand in for, to replace; *[+ juge]* to deputize for ◆ **la machine a suppléé l'homme dans ce domaine** *(littér)* men have been replaced by machines in this area VT INDIR **suppléer à** *(= compenser) [+ défaut, manque]* to make up for, to compensate for; *(= remplacer) [+ chose, personne, qualité]* to substitute for

supplément /syplemɑ̃/ NM 1 *(= surcroît)* **un ~ de travail/salaire** extra *ou* additional work/pay ◆ **avoir droit à un ~ de 50 €** to be allowed a supplement of €50 *ou* a €50 supplement, to be allowed an extra *ou* an additional €50 ◆ **demander un ~ d'information** to ask for additional *ou* further *ou* supplementary information ◆ **~ d'imposition** additional tax

2 *[de journal, dictionnaire]* supplement ◆ **~ illustré** illustrated supplement

3 *(à payer, au théâtre, au restaurant)* extra charge, supplement; *(dans le train pour prolongement de trajet)* excess fare; *(sur trains spéciaux)* supplement ◆ **~ de 1re classe** supplement for travelling 1st class, 1st-class supplement ◆ **sans ~ de prix** without additional charge *ou* surcharge ◆ **payer un ~ pour excès de bagages** to pay (for) excess luggage, to pay excess on one's luggage

◆ **en supplément** extra ◆ **le vin est en ~** wine is extra ◆ **le tableau de bord en bois est en ~** the wooden dashboard is an optional extra ◆ **ils nous l'ont facturé en ~** they charged us extra for it

supplémentaire /syplemɑ̃tɛr/ ADJ *[dépenses, crédits, retards]* additional, further *(épith)*; *[travail, vérifications]* additional, extra *(épith)*; *[trains, autobus]* relief *(épith)*; *[angle]* supplementary ◆ **lignes ~s** *(Mus)* ledger lines ◆ **accorder un délai ~** to grant an extension of the deadline, to allow additional time ◆ **faire des/10 heures ~s** to work *ou* do overtime/10 hours' overtime ◆ **les heures ~s sont bien payées** you get well paid for (doing) overtime, overtime hours are well-paid

supplétif, -ive /sypletif, iv/ ADJ additional NM *(Mil)* back-up soldier ◆ **les ~s** the back-up troops

suppliant, e /syplijɑ̃, ijɑ̃t/ ADJ *[regard, voix]* beseeching, imploring; *[personne]* imploring NM,F suppliant, supplicant

supplication /syplikasjɔ̃/ NF *(gén)* plea, entreaty; *(Rel)* supplication

supplice /syplis/ NM 1 *(= peine corporelle)* form of torture, torture *(NonC)* ◆ **le (dernier) ~** *(peine capitale)* execution, death ◆ **conduire qn au ~** to take sb to be executed ◆ **le ~ de la roue** (torture on) the wheel ◆ **le ~ du fouet** flogging, the lash ◆ **le ~ du collier** necklacing 2 *(= souffrance)* torture ◆ **~s moraux** moral tortures *ou* torments ◆ **éprouver le ~ de l'in-**

certitude to be tormented by uncertainty ◆ **cette lecture est un (vrai)** ~ **!** reading this is absolute torture!

3 *(locutions)* **être au** ~ *(appréhension)* to be in agonies *ou* on the rack; *(gêne, douleur)* to be in misery ◆ **mettre qn au** ~ to torture sb

COMP **supplice chinois** Chinese torture *(NonC)*

le supplice de la Croix the Crucifixion

supplice de Tantale *(lit)* torment of Tantalus ◆ **c'est un vrai** ~ **de Tantale** *(fig)* it's so frustrating

supplicié, e /syplisje/ (ptp de **supplicier**) NM,F victim of torture, torture victim ◆ **les corps/cris des** ~**s** the bodies/cries of the torture victims

supplicier /syplisje/ ► conjug 7 ◄ VT *(lit, fig)* to torture; *(à mort)* to torture to death

supplier /syplije/ ► conjug 7 ◄ VT to implore, to beseech *(frm)*, to entreat *(frm)* *(de faire* to do); ◆ ~ **qn à genoux** to beseech *ou* implore *ou* entreat sb on one's knees ◆ **tais-toi, je t'en supplie !** will you please be quiet! ◆ **il m'a suppliée de rester** he begged me to stay

supplique /syplik/ NF petition ◆ **présenter une** ~ **au roi** to petition the king, to bring a petition before the king

support /sypɔʀ/ NM 1 *(gén = soutien)* support; *(= béquille, pied)* prop, support; *[d'instruments de laboratoire, outils, livre]* stand 2 *(= moyen)* medium; *(= aide)* aid ◆ ~ **publicitaire** advertising medium ◆ **conférence faite à l'aide d'un** ~ **écrit/magnétique/visuel** lecture given with the help of a written text/a tape/visual aids ◆ **les différents** ~**s d'information** the different media through which information is transmitted ◆ ~ **pédagogique** teaching aid 3 *[de dessin]* support; *(Ordin) [d'information codée]* medium ◆ **passer du** ~ **papier au** ~ **informatique** to go from using paper *ou* hard copy to using computers ◆ **les chaînes d'ADN,** ~ **de l'hérédité** DNA sequences, the carriers of genetic information ◆ **le symbole est le** ~ **du concept** the symbol is the concrete expression of the concept

supportable /sypɔʀtabl/ ADJ *[douleur, température]* bearable; *[conduite]* tolerable; *(* = passable, pas trop mauvais)* tolerable, passable

supporter[1] /sypɔʀte/ GRAMMAIRE ACTIVE 34.3, 41 ► conjug 1 ◄

VT 1 *(= endurer) [+ maladie, solitude, revers]* to bear, to endure, to put up with; *[+ douleur]* to bear, to endure; *[+ conduite, ingratitude]* to tolerate, to put up with; *[+ recommandations, personne]* to put up with, to bear ◆ **il ne pouvait plus** ~ **la vie** life had become unbearable for him ◆ **il supportait leurs plaisanteries avec patience** he patiently put up with their jokes ◆ **la mort d'un être cher est difficile à** ~ the death of a loved one is hard to bear ◆ **il va falloir le** ~ **pendant toute la journée !** we're going to have to put up with him all day long! ◆ **elle supporte tout d'eux, sans jamais rien dire** she puts up with everything they do without a word ◆ **je ne supporte pas ce genre de comportement/qu'on me parle sur ce ton** I won't put up with *ou* stand for *ou* tolerate this sort of behaviour/being spoken to in that tone of voice ◆ **je ne peux pas** ~ **l'hypocrisie** I can't bear *ou* abide *ou* stand hypocrisy ◆ **je ne peux pas les** ~ I can't bear *ou* stand them ◆ **je ne supporte pas de voir ça** I can't bear seeing *ou* to see that, I can't stand seeing that ◆ **on supporte un gilet, par ce temps*** you can do with a cardigan in this weather ◆ **je pensais avoir trop chaud avec un pull, mais on le supporte*** I thought I'd be too hot with a pullover but I can do with it after all

2 *(= subir) [+ frais]* to bear; *[+ conséquences, affront, malheur]* to suffer, to endure ◆ **il m'a fait** ~ **les conséquences de son acte** he made me suffer the consequences of his action

3 *(= résister à) [+ température, conditions atmosphériques, épreuve]* to withstand ◆ **verre qui supporte la chaleur** heatproof *ou* heat-resistant glass ◆ **il a bien/mal supporté l'opération** he took the operation well/badly ◆ **il ne supporte pas l'alcool** he can't take alcohol ◆ **elle ne supporte pas la vue du sang** she can't bear *ou* stand the sight of blood *ou* seeing blood ◆ **il ne supporte pas la chaleur** he can't take *ou* stand *ou* bear the heat ◆ **je ne supporte pas les épinards** *(= je ne les aime pas)* I can't stand spinach; *(= ils me rendent malade)* spinach doesn't agree *ou* disagrees with me ◆ **lait facile à** ~ easily-digested milk ◆ **tu as de la chance de** ~ **l'ail** you're lucky being able to eat garlic ◆ **ce roman ne supporte pas l'examen** this novel does not stand up to analysis ◆ **cette règle ne supporte aucune exception** this rule admits of no exception

4 *(= servir de base à)* to support, to hold up

5 *(Ordin, Pol, Sport)* to support

VPR **se supporter** *(= se tolérer)* **ils ne peuvent pas se** ~ they can't stand *ou* bear each other

> ⚠ Au sens de 'subir' ou 'résister à', le verbe **supporter** ne se traduit pas par **to support**.

supporter[2] /sypɔʀtɛʀ/ NM, **supporteur, -trice** /sypɔʀtœʀ, tʀis/ NM,F *(Pol, Sport)* supporter

supposé, e /sypoze/ (ptp de **supposer**) ADJ *(= présumé) [nombre, total]* estimated; *[meurtrier]* alleged; *(Jur) [père]* putative; *[nom]* assumed; *(= faux) [testament, signature]* forged ◆ **l'auteur** ~ **de cet article** *(= prétendu)* the presumed *ou* alleged author of this article ◆ **un** ~ **âge d'or** a supposed *ou* so-called golden age

supposer /sypoze/ GRAMMAIRE ACTIVE 53.6 ► conjug 1 ◄ VT 1 *(à titre d'hypothèse)* to suppose, to assume ◆ **supposons une nouvelle guerre** (let's) suppose another war broke out ◆ **supposez que vous soyez malade** suppose you were ill ◆ **en supposant que, à** ~ **que** supposing (that), assuming (that) ◆ **pour les besoins de l'expérience, la pression est supposée constante** *(Sci)* for the purposes of the experiment the pressure is taken to be *ou* assumed (to be) constant ◆ **supposons une ligne A-B** let there be a line A-B

2 *(= présumer)* to suppose, to assume ◆ ~ **qn amoureux/jaloux** to imagine *ou* suppose sb to be in love/jealous ◆ **je lui suppose une grande ambition** I imagine him to have great ambition ◆ **on vous supposait malade** we thought you were ill ◆ **je ne peux que le** ~ I can only make a supposition, I can only surmise ◆ **cela laisse** ~ **que ...** it leads one to suppose that ... ◆ **je suppose que tu es contre** I assume *ou* I suppose *ou* I presume you are against it

3 *(= impliquer, présupposer)* to presuppose; *(= suggérer, laisser deviner)* to imply ◆ **la gestation suppose la fécondation** gestation presupposes fertilization ◆ **cela suppose du courage** that takes courage ◆ **cette décision suppose que les hôpitaux sont bien équipés** this decision is based on the assumption that hospitals are properly equipped

4 *(Jur) [+ testament, signature]* to forge

supposition /sypozisjɔ̃/ NF supposition, assumption ◆ **on ne peut que faire des** ~**s** we can only surmise, we can only make suppositions *ou* assumptions ◆ **je l'ignore, c'est une simple** ~ I don't know, I'm just guessing *ou* it's pure conjecture on my part ◆ **une** ~ **que ...*** supposing ...

suppositoire /sypozitwaʀ/ NM suppository

suppôt /sypo/ NM *(littér)* henchman ◆ ~ **de Satan** *ou* **du diable** fiend, hellhound ◆ **les** ~**s d'un tyran/de l'impérialisme** the lackeys of a tyrant/of imperialism

suppression /sypʀesjɔ̃/ NF 1 *(= fait d'enlever, d'abolir) [de mot, clause]* deletion, removal; *[de mur, obstacle]* removal; *[d'avantage, crédits]* withdrawal; *[de loi, taxe, peine de mort]* abolition; *[de libertés]* suppression; *[de discrimination, concurrence, pauvreté, chômage, douleur, fatigue]* elimination ◆ **la** ~ **des inégalités** the elimination *ou* abolition of inequalities ◆ **faire des** ~**s dans un texte** to make some deletions in a text ◆ **il y a eu 7 000** ~**s d'emplois** *ou* **d'effectifs** 7,000 jobs were axed *ou* shed

2 *[d'avion, train, vol]* cancellation ◆ **pour éviter la** ~ **des petites lignes de province** to prevent the closure of small regional lines

3 *[de témoin gênant]* elimination

4 *(Jur)* ~ **de part** *ou* **d'enfant** concealment of birth ◆ ~ **d'état** *depriving someone of the means to prove their civil status*

> ⚠ **suppression** se traduit rarement par le mot anglais **suppression**, qui a des emplois spécifiques.

supprimer /sypʀime/ ► conjug 1 ◄ VT 1 *(= enlever, abolir) [+ mot, clause]* to delete, to remove *(de* from); *[+ mur, obstacle]* to remove; *[+ emploi, poste]* to axe, to shed; *[+ crédits, avantage]* to withdraw; *[+ loi, taxe]* to do away with, to abolish; *[+ libertés]* to suppress; *[+ peine de mort]* to abolish; *[+ publication]* to ban; *[+ document]* to suppress; *[+ discrimination, inégalité, concurrence, pauvreté, chômage]* to do away with, to put an end to, to eliminate ◆ **ce fortifiant aide à** ~ **la fatigue** this tonic helps to banish tiredness ◆ **ce médicament supprime la douleur** this medicine is a pain-killer ◆ **on ne parviendra jamais à** ~ **la douleur** we shall never succeed in eliminating pain ◆ **cette technique supprime des opérations inutiles** this technique does away with *ou* cuts out unnecessary operations ◆ **il faut** ~ **les intermédiaires** we must cut out the middleman ◆ **l'avion supprime les distances** air travel shortens distances ◆ ~ **qch à qn** to deprive sb of sth ◆ ~ **les permissions aux soldats** to put a stop *ou* an end to the soldiers' leave ◆ **on lui a supprimé sa prime/pension** he's had his bonus/pension stopped ◆ ~ **qch de son alimentation** to cut sth out of one's diet, to eliminate sth from one's diet

2 *[+ avion, train, vol]* to cancel ◆ **la ligne a été supprimée** the line was taken out of service

3 *(= tuer) [+ témoin gênant]* to do away with, to eliminate

VPR **se supprimer** to take one's own life

> ⚠ **supprimer** se traduit rarement par **to suppress**, qui a des emplois spécifiques.

suppurant, e /sypyʀɑ̃, ɑ̃t/ ADJ suppurating

suppuration /sypyʀasjɔ̃/ NF suppuration

suppurer /sypyʀe/ ► conjug 1 ◄ VI to suppurate

supputation /sypytasjɔ̃/ NF 1 *[de dépenses, frais]* calculation, computation; *[de chances, possibilités]* calculation 2 *(frm = hypothèse)* guess, prognostication *(frm)* ◆ **ce ne sont que des** ~**s** this is just a guess

supputer /sypyte/ ► conjug 1 ◄ VT *[+ dépenses, frais]* to calculate, to compute; *[+ chances, possibilités]* to calculate ◆ **je suppute que ...** I presume that ..., my guess is that ...

supra /sypʀa/ ADV above ◆ **voir** ~ see above

supra- /sypʀa/ PRÉF supra ... ◆ **une autorité** ~**humaine** a suprahuman *ou* superhuman authority

supraconducteur, -trice /sypʀakɔ̃dyktœʀ, tʀis/ ADJ superconductive, superconducting *(épith)* NM superconductor

supraconductivité /sypʀakɔ̃dyktivite/ NF superconductivity

supraliminaire /sypʀaliminɛʀ/ **ADJ** supraliminal

supranational, e (mpl **-aux**) /sypʀanasjɔnal, o/ **ADJ** supranational

supranationalisme /sypʀanasjɔnalism/ **NM** supranationalism

supranationaliste /sypʀanasjɔnalist/ **ADJ** supranationalist

supranationalité /sypʀanasjɔnalite/ **NF** ◆ **il craint de voir l'Europe basculer dans la ~** he's afraid that Europe will end up as a supranational state

suprasegmental, e (mpl **-aux**) /sypʀasɛgmɑ̃tal, o/ **ADJ** suprasegmental

suprasensible /sypʀasɑ̃sibl/ **ADJ** suprasensitive

supraterrestre /sypʀatɛʀɛstʀ/ **ADJ** superterrestrial

suprématie /sypʀemasi/ **NF** supremacy

suprématisme /sypʀematism/ **NM** Suprematism

suprême /sypʀɛm/ **ADJ** (= *supérieur*) [*chef, autorité, cour*] supreme; (= *très grand, ultime*) [*raffinement, élégance, effort, ennui*] extreme; [*indifférence*] sublime; [*affront*] ultimate ◆ **bonheur ~, notre chambre a vue sur la mer** joy of joys, our room overlooks the sea ◆ **au ~ degré** to the highest degree ◆ **le pouvoir ~** the supreme power ◆ **le moment/l'heure ~** (= *la mort*) the moment/the hour of reckoning; → **sauce, soviet** **NM** (*Culin*) ◆ **~ de volaille** chicken supreme

suprêmement /sypʀɛmmɑ̃/ **ADV** supremely

sur[1] /syʀ/ **PRÉP** 1 (*position*) on, upon (*frm*); (= *sur le haut de*) on top of, on; (*avec mouvement*) on, onto; (= *dans*) in; (= *par-dessus*) over (= *au-dessus de*) above ◆ **il y a un sac ~ la table/une affiche ~ le mur** there's a bag on the table/a poster on the wall ◆ **mettre une annonce ~ un tableau** to put a notice (up) on a board ◆ **il a laissé tous ses papiers ~ la table** he left all his papers (lying) on the table ◆ **je n'ai pas d'argent/la lettre ~ moi** I haven't got any money on me/the letter on *ou* with me ◆ **se promener ~ la rivière** to go boating on the river ◆ **il y avait beaucoup de circulation ~ la route** there was a lot of traffic on the road ◆ **~ ma route** *ou* **mon chemin** on my way ◆ **~ les grandes/petites ondes** (*Radio*) on long/short wave ◆ **elle rangea ses chapeaux ~ l'armoire** she put her hats away on top of the wardrobe ◆ **pose ta valise ~ une chaise** put your case (down) on a chair ◆ **elle a jeté son sac ~ la table** she threw her bag onto the table ◆ **retire tes livres de ~ la table** take your books off the table ◆ **il grimpa ~ le toit** he climbed (up) onto the roof ◆ **une chambre (qui donne) ~ la rue** a room that looks out onto the street ◆ **il n'est jamais monté ~ un bateau** he's never been in *ou* on a boat ◆ **~ la place (du marché)** in the (market) square ◆ **la clé est restée ~ la porte** the key was left in the door ◆ **lire qch ~ le journal*** to read sth in the paper ◆ **chercher qch ~ une carte** to look for sth on a map ◆ **des orages sont prévus ~ l'Alsace** storms are forecast in Alsace ◆ **il a 250 € ~ son compte** he has €250 in his account ◆ **livraison gratuite ~ Paris** free delivery in *ou* within Paris ◆ **il neige ~ Paris/~ toute l'Europe** snow is falling on *ou* in Paris/over the whole of Europe, it's snowing in Paris/all over Europe ◆ **mettre du papier d'aluminium ~ un plat/un couvercle ~ une casserole** to put silver foil over a dish/a lid on a saucepan ◆ **un pont ~ la rivière** a bridge across *ou* on *ou* over the river ◆ **s'endormir ~ un livre/son travail** (*fig*) to fall asleep over a book/over *ou* at one's work ◆ **elle a acheté des poires ~ le marché** she bought some pears at the market ◆ **~ terre et ~ mer** on land and (at) sea ◆ **s'étendre ~ 3 km** to spread over 3 km ◆ **"travaux sur 5 km"** "roadworks for 5 km" ◆ **vivre les uns ~ les autres** to live on top of each other ◆ **gravure ~ bois/verre** wood/glass engraving; → **appuyer, pied, place** *etc*

2 (*direction*) to, towards ◆ **tourner ~ la droite** to turn (to the) right ◆ **l'église est ~ votre gauche** the church is on *ou* to your left ◆ **revenir ~ Paris** to return to Paris ◆ **les vols ~ Lyon** flights to Lyons ◆ **concentrer son attention ~ un problème** to concentrate on a problem, to focus one's attention on a problem ◆ **fermez bien la porte ~ vous** be sure and close the door behind *ou* after you

3 (*temps : proximité, approximation*) **il est arrivé ~ les 2 heures** he came (at) about *ou* (at) around 2 ◆ **il va ~ la quarantaine** he's getting on for (*Brit*) *ou* going on (*US*) forty ◆ **la pièce s'achève ~ une réconciliation** the play ends with a reconciliation ◆ **il est ~ le départ, il est ~ le point de partir** he's just going, he's (just) about to leave ◆ **~ le moment** *ou* **~ le coup, je n'ai pas compris** at the time *ou* at first I didn't understand ◆ **~ une période de 3 mois** over a period of 3 months ◆ **juger les résultats ~ une année** to assess the results over a year ◆ **boire du café ~ de la bière** to drink coffee on top of beer

4 (*cause*) on, by ◆ **~ invitation/commande** by invitation/order ◆ **~ présentation d'une pièce d'identité** on presentation of identification ◆ **nous l'avons nommé ~ la recommandation/les conseils de Marc** we appointed him on Marc's recommendation/advice ◆ **~ un signe/une remarque du patron, elle sortit** at the boss's signal/at a word from the boss, she left

5 (*moyen, manière*) on ◆ **ils vivent ~ son salaire/ses économies** they live on *ou* off his salary/his savings ◆ **rester ~ la défensive/ses gardes** to stay on the defensive/one's guard ◆ **travailler ~ écran** to work on screen ◆ **renseignements disponibles ~ Minitel** information available on Minitel ◆ **choisir ~ catalogue** to choose from a catalogue ◆ **chanter** *ou* **entonner qch ~ l'air de la Marseillaise** to sing sth to the tune of the Marseillaise ◆ **fantaisie ~ un air de Brahms** (*Mus*) fantasy on an air by *ou* from Brahms ◆ **~ le mode mineur** (*Mus*) in the minor key *ou* mode

6 (*matière, sujet*) on, about ◆ **conférence/renseignements ~ la Grèce/la drogue** lecture/information on *ou* about Greece/drug addiction ◆ **roman/film ~ Louis XIV** novel/film about Louis XIV ◆ **questionner** *ou* **interroger qn ~ qch** to question sb about *ou* on sth ◆ **gémir** *ou* **se lamenter ~ ses malheurs** to lament (over) *ou* bemoan one's misfortunes ◆ **être ~ un travail** to be occupied with a job, to be (in the process of) doing a job ◆ **être ~ un projet** to be working on a project ◆ **être ~ une bonne affaire/une piste/un coup*** to be onto a bargain/on a trail/in on a job* ◆ **"réductions importantes sur les chaussures"** "big discounts on shoes" ◆ **il touche une commission de 10% ~ les ventes** he gets a 10% commission on sales

7 (*rapport de proportion*) out of, in; (*prélèvement*) from; (*mesure*) by ◆ **~ douze verres, six sont ébréchés** out of twelve glasses six are chipped ◆ **un homme ~ dix** one man in (every) *ou* out of ten ◆ **neuf fois ~ dix** nine times out of ten ◆ **il a une chance ~ deux de réussir** he has a fifty-fifty chance of success ◆ **il y a une chance ~ dix pour que cela arrive** there's a one in ten chance that it will happen ◆ **il mérite 7 ~ 10** (*Scol, Univ*) he deserves 7 out of 10 ◆ **un jour/un vendredi ~ trois** every third day/Friday ◆ **il vient un jour/mercredi ~ deux** he comes every other day/Wednesday ◆ **les cotisations sont retenues ~ le salaire** contributions are deducted from salaries ◆ **la cuisine fait 2 mètres ~ 3** the kitchen is *ou* measures 2 metres by 3

8 (*accumulation*) after ◆ **faire faute ~ faute** to make one mistake after another ◆ **il a eu rhume ~ rhume** he's had one cold after another *ou* the other; → **coup**

9 (*influence, supériorité*) over, on ◆ **avoir de l'influence/de l'effet ~ qn** to have influence on *ou* over/an effect on sb ◆ **avoir des droits ~ qn/qch** to have rights over sb/to sth ◆ **cela a influé ~ sa décision** that has influenced *ou* had an influence on his decision ◆ **elle n'a aucun pouvoir ~ lui** she has no hold *ou* influence over him

LOC ADV **sur ce** (= *sur ces mots*) so saying, with this *ou* that ◆ **~ ce, il est sorti** whereupon *ou* upon which he went out ◆ **~ ce, il faut que je vous quitte** and now I must leave you

sur[2]**, e** /syʀ/ **ADJ** (= *aigre*) sour

sûr, e /syʀ/ **GRAMMAIRE ACTIVE 42.1, 43.1, 52.6, 53.6**

ADJ 1 ◆ **~ de** [+ *résultats, succès*] sure *ou* certain of; [+ *allié, réflexes, moyens*] sure of; [+ *fait, diagnostic, affirmation*] sure *ou* certain of *ou* about ◆ **il avait le moral et était ~ du succès** he was in good spirits and was sure *ou* certain *ou* confident of success ◆ **s'il s'entraîne régulièrement, il est ~ du succès** if he trains regularly he's sure of success ◆ **il est ~/il n'est pas ~ de venir** he's/he's not sure *ou* certain that he'll be able to come ◆ **il est ~ de son fait** *ou* **coup*** (*qu'il réussira*) he's sure *ou* confident he'll pull it off; (*qu'il a raison*) he's sure he's right ◆ **~ de soi** self-assured, self-confident, sure of oneself ◆ **elle n'est pas ~e d'elle(-même)** she's lacking in self-assurance *ou* self-confidence ◆ **j'en étais ~ !** I knew it!, just as I thought! ◆ **j'en suis ~ et certain** I'm positive (about it), I'm absolutely sure *ou* certain (of it) ◆ **soyez-en ~** you can depend upon it, you can be sure of it

2 (= *certain*) certain, sure ◆ **la chose est ~e** that's certain, that's for sure *ou* certain ◆ **ce** *ou* **il n'est pas ~ qu'elle aille au Maroc** it's not definite *ou* certain that she's going to Morocco ◆ **est-ce si ~ qu'il gagne ?** is he so certain *ou* sure to win? ◆ **c'est ~ et certain** that's absolutely certain ◆ **ça, c'est ~** that's for sure ◆ **ce n'est pas (si) ~*** not necessarily ◆ **c'est le plus ~ moyen de réussir** it is the surest way to succeed ◆ **ce qui est ~, c'est qu'ils ...** one thing is for sure – they ...

◆ **à coup sûr** definitely, without a doubt ◆ **à coup ~ il ne viendra pas** he definitely won't come, there's no way he'll come

◆ **pour sûr** ◆ **tenir qch pour ~** to be sure about sth ◆ **il tient pour ~ que ...** he's sure that ... ◆ **pour ~ !*** absolutely!

3 (= *sans danger*) [*quartier, rue*] safe ◆ **peu ~** unsafe ◆ **il est plus ~ de ne pas compter sur lui** it's safer not to rely on him ◆ **le plus ~ est de mettre sa voiture au garage** the safest thing is to put your car in the garage ◆ **en lieu ~** in a safe place ◆ **en mains ~es** in safe hands

4 (= *digne de confiance*) [*personne*] reliable, trustworthy; [*renseignements, diagnostic, entreprise*] reliable; [*valeurs morales, raisonnement*] sound; [*remède, moyen*] reliable, sure; [*dispositif, arme, valeurs boursières*] safe; [*investissement*] sound, safe; [*main, pied, œil*] steady; [*goût, instinct*] reliable, sound ◆ **le temps n'est pas assez ~ pour une ascension** the weather's not reliable enough to go climbing ◆ **avoir la main ~e** to have a steady hand ◆ **raisonner sur des bases peu ~es** to argue on unsound *ou* shaky premises ◆ **nous apprenons de source ~e que ...** we have been informed by a reliable source that ... ◆ **peu ~** [*allié*] unreliable, untrustworthy; [*renseignements*] unreliable; [*moyen, méthode*] unreliable, unsafe

ADV * ◆ **~ qu'il y a quelque chose qui ne tourne pas rond** there must be something wrong ◆ **tu penses qu'il viendra ? – pas ~** do you think he'll come? – I'm not so sure; → **bien, pour**

surabondamment /syʀabɔ̃damɑ̃/ ADV (*littér*) [*expliquer*] in excessive detail ◆ ~ **décoré de** overabundantly decorated with ◆ **ce thème a été ~ exploité** this theme has been dealt with more than amply ◆ ~ **informé** over-informed

surabondance /syʀabɔ̃dɑ̃s/ NF (= *quantité excessive*) overabundance, superabundance; (= *grande abondance*) profusion

surabondant, e /syʀabɔ̃dɑ̃, ɑ̃t/ ADJ (= *trop abondant*) overabundant, superabundant ◆ **recevoir un courrier ~** (= *très abondant*) to receive a huge amount of mail

surabonder /syʀabɔ̃de/ ▸ conjug 1 ◂ VI 1 [*richesses, plantes, matières premières*] to be overabundant ◆ **une station où surabondent les touristes** a resort overflowing with tourists ◆ **des circulaires où surabondent les fautes d'impression** circulars riddled *ou* littered with printing errors ◆ **un port où surabondent les tavernes** a port with an inordinate number *ou* a plethora (*frm*) of taverns 2 (*littér*) ~ **de** *ou* **en** to abound with *ou* in ◆ ~ **de richesses** to have an overabundance of riches, to have overabundant riches

suractif, -ive /syʀaktif, iv/ ADJ overactive

suractivé, e /syʀaktive/ ADJ superactivated

suractivité /syʀaktivite/ NF superactivity

suraigu, -uë /syʀegy/ ADJ very high-pitched, very shrill

surajouter /syʀaʒute/ ▸ conjug 1 ◂ VT to add ◆ **raisons auxquelles se surajoutent celles-ci** reasons to which one might add the following ◆ **ornements surajoutés** superfluous ornaments

suralimentation /syʀalimɑ̃tasjɔ̃/ NF 1 [*de personne*] (*thérapeutique*) feeding up; (*par excès*) overeating 2 [*d'animal*] fattening 3 [*de moteur*] supercharging, boosting

suralimenter /syʀalimɑ̃te/ ▸ conjug 1 ◂ VT 1 [+ *personne*] to feed up 2 (= *engraisser*) [+ *animal*] to fatten 3 [+ *moteur*] to supercharge, to boost ◆ **moteur diesel suralimenté** supercharged diesel engine VPR **se suralimenter** to overeat

suranné, e /syʀane/ ADJ [*idées, mode, beauté, style, tournure*] old-fashioned ◆ **un hôtel au charme ~** a hotel with old-fashioned charm ◆ **dans un décor délicieusement ~** in a delightfully old-world setting

surarmement /syʀaʀməmɑ̃/ NM (= *action*) stockpiling of weapons; (= *armes*) massive stock of weapons

surarmer /syʀaʀme/ ▸ conjug 1 ◂ VT (*surtout passif*) ◆ **pays surarmé** country with a massive stock of weapons

surate /syʀat/ NF ⇒ **sourate**

surbaissé, e /syʀbese/ (ptp de **surbaisser**) ADJ [*plafond*] lowered; [*voûte*] surbased; [*châssis*] underslung; [*voiture*] low-slung

surbaissement /syʀbɛsmɑ̃/ NM (*Archit*) surbasement

surbaisser /syʀbese/ ▸ conjug 1 ◂ VT [+ *plafond*] to lower; [+ *voûte*] to surbase; [+ *voiture, châssis*] to make lower

surbooké, e /syʀbuke/ ADJ [*vol, train*] overbooked ◆ **je suis ~ * en ce moment** I've got too much on at the moment

surbooker /syʀbuke/ VI [*compagnie aérienne*] to overbook

surbooking /syʀbukiŋ/ NM overbooking ◆ **les compagnies aériennes qui pratiquent le ~** airlines that overbook

surboum † * /syʀbum/ NF party

surbrillance /syʀbʀijɑ̃s/ NF (*Ordin*) ◆ **mettre qch en ~** to highlight sth ◆ **texte en ~** highlighted text

surcapacité /syʀkapasite/ NF overcapacity

surcapitalisation /syʀkapitalizasjɔ̃/ NF overcapitalization

surcharge /syʀʃaʀʒ/ NF 1 [*de véhicule*] overloading
2 (= *poids en excédent*) extra load, excess load; [*de cheval de course*] weight handicap ◆ ~ **pondérale** excess weight ◆ ~ **électrique** overload ◆ **une tonne de ~** an extra *ou* excess load of a ton ◆ **les passagers/marchandises en ~** the excess *ou* extra passengers/goods ◆ **prendre des passagers en ~** to take on excess passengers ◆ **ascenseur en ~** overloaded lift (*Brit*) *ou* elevator (*US*) ◆ **payer un supplément pour une ~ de bagages** to pay (for) excess luggage, to pay excess on one's luggage
3 (*fig*) **cela me cause une ~ de travail** it gives me extra work ◆ **la ~ des programmes scolaires** the overloaded school syllabus ◆ **il y a une ~ de détails/d'ornements** there is a surfeit *ou* an overabundance of detail/of ornamentation
4 (= *ajout manuscrit ou imprimé*) [*de document, chèque*] alteration; [*de timbre-poste*] surcharge, overprint

surcharger /syʀʃaʀʒe/ ▸ conjug 3 ◂ VT [+ *voiture, cheval, mémoire*] to overload; [+ *timbre*] to surcharge; [+ *mot écrit*] to alter; [+ *circuit électrique*] to overload; (*Écon*) [+ *marché*] to overload, to glut ◆ ~ **qn de travail/d'impôts** to overload *ou* overburden sb with work/with taxes ◆ **je suis surchargé (de travail)** I'm overloaded *ou* snowed under with work ◆ **emploi du temps surchargé** crowded timetable ◆ **programmes scolaires surchargés** overloaded syllabuses ◆ **classes surchargées** overcrowded classes ◆ **train surchargé** overcrowded train ◆ **palais surchargé de dorures** palace smothered in gilt ◆ **manuscrit surchargé de corrections** manuscript covered *ou* littered with corrections

surchauffe /syʀʃof/ NF (*Écon*) overheating; (*Tech*) superheating; (*Phys*) superheat ◆ **il y a une ~ de l'économie** the economy is overheating

surchauffé, e /syʀʃofe/ (ptp de **surchauffer**) ADJ [*pièce*] overheated; (*Phys, Tech*) superheated; (= *exalté*) overexcited ◆ **le procès s'est déroulé dans une ambiance ~e** the trial took place in a highly charged atmosphere ◆ **les esprits étaient ~s** emotions were running very high *ou* were at fever pitch

surchauffer /syʀʃofe/ ▸ conjug 1 ◂ VT [+ *pièce*] to overheat; (*Phys, Tech*) to superheat

surchoix /syʀʃwa/ ADJ INV [*viande*] prime (*épith*), top-quality; [*produit, fruit*] top-quality

surclasser /syʀklɑse/ ▸ conjug 1 ◂ VT 1 (= *surpasser*) to outclass 2 (*Trasnport*) ◆ ~ **qn** to upgrade sb's seat ◆ **ils m'ont surclassé en première** they upgraded my seat to first class, they bumped me up * to first class

surcompensation /syʀkɔ̃pɑ̃sasjɔ̃/ NF (*Psych*) overcompensation

surcomposé, e /syʀkɔ̃poze/ ADJ double-compound

surcompression /syʀkɔ̃pʀesjɔ̃/ NF [*de gaz*] supercharging

surcomprimer /syʀkɔ̃pʀime/ ▸ conjug 1 ◂ VT [+ *gaz*] to supercharge

surconsommation /syʀkɔ̃sɔmasjɔ̃/ NF overconsumption

surcontrer /syʀkɔ̃tʀe/ ▸ conjug 1 ◂ VT (*Cartes*) to redouble

surcote /syʀkɔt/ NF overvaluation

surcoter /syʀkɔte/ ▸ conjug 1 ◂ VT to overvalue

surcouper /syʀkupe/ ▸ conjug 1 ◂ VI (*Cartes*) to overtrump

surcoût /syʀku/ NM extra *ou* additional cost *ou* expenditure

surcroît /syʀkʀwa/ NM ◆ **cela lui a donné un ~ de travail/d'inquiétudes** it gave him additional *ou* extra work/worries ◆ **ça lui a valu un ~ de respect** this won him even more respect ◆ **par (un) ~ d'honnêteté/de scrupules** through an excess of honesty/of scruples, through excessive honesty/scrupulousness
◆ **de** *ou* **par surcroît** (= *de plus*) what is more, moreover ◆ **il est avare et paresseux de** *ou* **par ~** he's mean and idle into the bargain

surdéveloppé, e /syʀdevlɔpe/ ADJ overdeveloped

surdéveloppement /syʀdevlɔpmɑ̃/ NM overdevelopment

surdimensionné, e /syʀdimɑ̃sjɔne/ ADJ 1 [*objet*] oversized ◆ **le réservoir est ~ par rapport à nos besoins** the tank is far too big for our needs 2 [*investissement*] excessive; [*projet*] overambitious ◆ **les investissements sont ~s par rapport à la taille de la ville** the investments are out of proportion to the size of the town ◆ **il a un ego ~** he has an oversized ego

surdimutité /syʀdimytite/ NF deaf-and-dumbness

surdiplomé, e /syʀdiplɔme/ ADJ overqualified

surdité /syʀdite/ NF deafness ◆ ~ **verbale** word deafness

surdosage /syʀdozaʒ/ NM (*Méd*) overdosage

surdose /syʀdoz/ NF (*lit, fig*) overdose

surdoué, e /syʀdwe/ ADJ [*enfant*] gifted, exceptional (*US*) NM,F gifted *ou* exceptional (*US*) child

sureau (pl **sureaux**) /syʀo/ NM elder (tree) ◆ **baies de ~** elderberries

sureffectif /syʀefɛktif/ NM overmanning (*NonC*), overstaffing (*NonC*) ◆ **personnel en ~** excess staff

surélévation /syʀelevasjɔ̃/ NF (= *action*) raising, heightening; (= *état*) extra height

surélever /syʀel(ə)ve/ ▸ conjug 5 ◂ VT [+ *plafond, étage*] to raise, to heighten; [+ *mur*] to heighten ◆ ~ **une maison d'un étage** to heighten a house by one storey ◆ **rez-de-chaussée surélevé** raised ground floor, ground floor higher than street level

sûrement /syʀmɑ̃/ ADV 1 (= *sans risques, efficacement*) [*cacher qch, progresser*] in safety; [*attacher*] securely; [*fonctionner*] safely ◆ **l'expérience instruit plus ~ que les livres** experience is a surer teacher than books; → **lentement** 2 (= *vraisemblablement*) **il viendra ~** he's sure to come ◆ ~ **qu'il a été retenu** * he must have been held up ◆ **tu connais ~ des gens importants** you must know some important people ◆ **ça lui plaira ~** she's bound to like it, I'm sure she'll like it ◆ **il me trouve ~ trop sévère** no doubt he thinks I'm being too harsh 3 ◆ ~ **pas** (= *pas du tout*) certainly not ◆ **il n'est ~ pas très intelligent, mais ...** (= *peut-être pas*) he might not be very clever but ... ◆ **ce n'est ~ pas difficile** it can't be that difficult

surempIoi /syʀɑ̃plwa/ NM overemployment

surenchère /syʀɑ̃ʃɛʀ/ NF 1 (*sur prix fixé*) overbid; (= *enchère plus élevée*) higher bid ◆ **faire une ~ (sur)** to make a higher bid (than) ◆ **une douzaine de ~s successives firent monter le prix** a dozen bids one after the other put up the price ◆ **faire une ~ de 150 €** to bid €150 more *ou* higher (*sur* than) to bid €150 over the previous bid *ou* bidder 2 (*fig* = *exagération, excès*) **la presse, royaume de la ~** the press, where overstatement is king ◆ **faire de la ~** to try to outdo one's rivals ◆ **la ~ électorale** political one-upmanship ◆ **une ~ de violence** a build-up of violence

surenchérir /syʀɑ̃ʃeʀiʀ/ ▸ conjug 2 ◂ VI (= *offrir plus qu'un autre*) to bid higher; (= *élever son offre*) to raise one's bid; (*lors d'élections*) to try to outdo each other (*de* with); ◆ ~ **sur une offre** to bid higher than an offer, to top a bid * ◆ ~ **sur qn** to bid higher than sb, to outbid *ou* overbid sb

surenchérisseur, -euse /syʀɑ̃ʃeʀisœʀ, øz/ **NM,F** (higher) bidder

surencombré, e /syʀɑ̃kɔ̃bʀe/ **ADJ** *[rue]* overcrowded; *[lignes téléphoniques]* overloaded

surencombrement /syʀɑ̃kɔ̃bʀəmɑ̃/ **NM** *[de rue]* overcrowding; *[de lignes téléphoniques]* overloading

surendetté, e /syʀɑ̃dete/ **ADJ** over-indebted, overburdened with debt

surendettement /syʀɑ̃dɛtmɑ̃/ **NM** excessive debt ◆ **pour limiter le ~ des ménages** to reduce the chance that families will run up big debts, to stop families running up big debts

surentraînement /syʀɑ̃tʀɛnmɑ̃/ **NM** overtraining

surentraîner VT, se surentraîner VPR /syʀɑ̃tʀene/ ► conjug 1 ◄ to overtrain

suréquipement /syʀekipmɑ̃/ **NM** overequipment

suréquiper /syʀekipe/ ► conjug 1 ◄ **VT** to overequip

surestarie /syʀɛstaʀi/ **NF** *(Jur)* demurrage

surestimation /syʀɛstimasjɔ̃/ **NF** *[d'importance, forces, capacité, frais]* overestimation; *[de tableau, maison à vendre]* overvaluation ◆ **la ~ des devis est fréquente** estimates are often inflated *ou* made too high

surestimer /syʀɛstime/ ► conjug 1 ◄ **VT** *[+ importance, forces, frais]* to overestimate; *[+ tableau, maison à vendre]* to overvalue **VPR se surestimer** to overestimate one's abilities

suret, -ette /syʀɛ, ɛt/ **ADJ** *[goût]* sharp, tart

sûreté /syʀte/ **NF** 1 (= *sécurité*) safety ◆ **complot contre la ~ de l'État** plot against state security ◆ **pour plus de ~** as an extra precaution, to be on the safe side ◆ **être en ~** to be in safety, to be safe ◆ **mettre qn/qch en ~** to put sb/sth in a safe *ou* secure place ◆ **de ~** *[serrure, verrou]* safety *(épith)* ◆ **c'est une ~ supplémentaire** it's an extra precaution ◆ **20 ans de réclusion assortis d'une peine de ~ de 13 ans** a 20-year prison sentence with a minimum recommendation of 13 years

2 (= *exactitude, efficacité*) *[de renseignements, méthode]* reliability; → **cour, prudence**

3 (= *précision*) *[de coup d'œil, geste]* steadiness; *[de goût]* reliability, soundness; *[de réflexe, diagnostic]* reliability ◆ **il a une grande ~ de main** he has a very sure hand ◆ **~ d'exécution** sureness of touch

4 (= *dispositif*) safety device ◆ **mettre la ~ à une arme** to put the safety catch *ou* lock on a gun; → **cran**

5 (= *garantie*) assurance, guarantee ◆ **demander/donner des ~s à qn** to ask sb for/give sb assurances *ou* a guarantee ◆ **~ individuelle** *(Jur)* protection against unlawful detention ◆ **~ personnelle** guaranty ◆ **~ réelle** security

6 *(Police)* **la Sûreté (nationale)** the (French) criminal investigation department, ≈ the CID *(Brit)*, the FBI *(US)*

surévaluation /syʀevalɥasjɔ̃/ **NF** overvaluation

surévaluer /syʀevalɥe/ ► conjug 1 ◄ **VT** *[+ monnaie, coûts]* to overvalue; *[+ difficultés, influence]* to overestimate ◆ **l'euro est surévalué par rapport au dollar** the euro is overvalued against the dollar

surexcitable /syʀɛksitabl/ **ADJ** overexcitable

surexcitation /syʀɛksitasjɔ̃/ **NF** overexcitement

surexcité, e /syʀɛksite/ (ptp de **surexciter**) **ADJ** (= *enthousiaste, énergique*) overexcited; (= *énervé*) all worked up ◆ **il me parlait d'une voix ~e** he spoke to me in a very excited voice

surexciter /syʀɛksite/ ► conjug 1 ◄ **VT** to overexcite

surexploitation /syʀɛksplwatasjɔ̃/ **NF** *[de terre]* overexploitation; *[de main-d'œuvre]* gross exploitation

surexploiter /syʀɛksplwate/ ► conjug 1 ◄ **VT** *[+ terres, ressources]* to overexploit; *[+ main-d'œuvre]* to grossly exploit; *[+ thème, idée]* to overdo

surexposer /syʀɛkspoze/ ► conjug 1 ◄ **VT** to overexpose

surexposition /syʀɛkspozisjɔ̃/ **NF** overexposure

surf /sœʀf/ **NM** 1 (= *activité*) surfing ◆ **faire du ~** to surf, to go surfing ◆ **~ sur neige** snowboarding ◆ **faire du ~ sur neige** to snowboard, to go snowboarding 2 (= *objet*) **(planche de) ~** surfboard ◆ **~ des neiges** snowboard

surface /syʀfas/ **NF** 1 *(gén, Géom)* surface; (= *aire*) *[de champ, chambre]* surface area ◆ **faire ~** to surface ◆ **refaire ~** *(lit, fig)* to resurface ◆ **le plongeur est remonté à la ~** the diver came back up to the surface ◆ **il ne voit que la ~ des choses** he can't see below the surface ◆ **l'appartement fait 100 mètres carrés de ~** the flat has a surface area of 100 square metres ◆ **il dispose d'une ~ financière rassurante** he has a sound financial base, his financial situation is sound ◆ **avoir de la ~** * *(fig, Fin)* to have great standing

◆ **de surface** *[politesse]* superficial; *[modifications]* cosmetic; *[eaux, température]* surface *(épith)* ◆ **navire de ~** surface vessel ◆ **réseau/installations de ~** above-ground *ou* overground network/installations

◆ **en surface** *[nager, naviguer]* at the surface; *[travailler, apprendre]* superficially ◆ **tout en ~** *[personne]* superficial, shallow

2 **grande ~** (= *magasin*) hypermarket

COMP surface de but *(Ftbl)* goal area
surface de chauffe heating surface
surface corrigée *(Admin)* amended area *(calculated on the basis of amenities etc for assessing rent)*
surface habitable living space
surface porteuse *[d'aile]* aerofoil *(Brit)*, airfoil *(US)*
surface de réparation *(Ftbl)* penalty area
surface de séparation *(Phys)* interface
surface au sol floor surface
surface de sustentation ⇒ **surface porteuse**
surface utile *(Constr)* floor space
surface de vente sales area
surface de voilure sail area

surfacturation /syʀfaktyʀasjɔ̃/ **NF** *[de produit, prestations]* overbilling; *[de client]* overcharging ◆ **ils ont procédé à une ~ systématique des travaux** they systematically overcharged for the building work

surfacturer /syʀfaktyʀe/ ► conjug 1 ◄ **VT** *[+ produit, prestations]* to overbill; *[+ client]* to overcharge ◆ **il a surfacturé de 10% ses prestations** he overcharged customers by 10% for his services

surfaire /syʀfɛʀ/ ► conjug 60 ◄ **VT** *[+ réputation, auteur]* to overrate; *[+ marchandise]* to overprice

surfait, e /syʀfɛ, ɛt/ (ptp de **surfaire**) **ADJ** *[ouvrage, auteur]* overrated ◆ **c'est très ~** it's highly overrated

surfer /sœʀfe/ ► conjug 1 ◄ **VI** *(Sport)* to surf, to go surfing; *(Ordin)* to surf ◆ **~ sur Internet** to surf (on) the Internet ◆ **le Premier ministre a longtemps surfé sur la vague des opinions favorables** the Prime Minister has been riding on a wave of popularity for a long time ◆ **ces industriels surfent sur la vague écologique** these industrialists are cashing in on the ecology trend *ou* have jumped on the green bandwagon

surfeur, -euse /sœʀfœʀ, øz/ **NM,F** surfer

surfil /syʀfil/ **NM** *(Couture)* oversewing, overcasting

surfilage /syʀfilaʒ/ **NM** *(Couture)* oversewing, overcasting

surfiler /syʀfile/ ► conjug 1 ◄ **VT** *(Couture)* to oversew, to overcast

surfin, e /syʀfɛ̃, in/ **ADJ** *[beurre, produit]* top-quality *(épith)*; *[qualité]* top *(épith)*, superior

surgélation /syʀʒelasjɔ̃/ **NF** deep-freezing, fast-freezing

surgelé, e /syʀʒəle/ **ADJ** deep-frozen ◆ **produits ~s** frozen foods **NM** ◆ **les ~s** (deep-) frozen food ◆ **magasin de ~s** freezer centre

surgeler /syʀʒəle/ ► conjug 5 ◄ **VT** to deep-freeze, to fast-freeze

surgénérateur /syʀʒeneʀatœʀ/ **ADJ M, NM** ◆ **(réacteur)** ~ fast breeder (reactor)

surgeon /syʀʒɔ̃/ **NM** *(Bot)* sucker

surgir /syʀʒiʀ/ ► conjug 2 ◄ **VI** 1 *[animal, véhicule en mouvement, spectre]* to appear suddenly; *[montagne, navire]* to loom up (suddenly); *[plante, immeuble]* to shoot up, to spring up ◆ **deux hommes ont surgi de derrière un camion** two men suddenly appeared *ou* came out from behind a truck 2 *[problèmes, difficultés]* to arise, to crop up; *[dilemme]* to arise ◆ **des obstacles surgissent de toutes parts** obstacles are cropping up all over the place ◆ **cela a fait ~ plusieurs questions** this raised several questions

surgissement /syʀʒismɑ̃/ **NM** *(littér) (gen)* appearance ◆ **le ~ de l'écriture/de l'islam** the advent of writing/of Islam

surhausser /syʀose/ ► conjug 1 ◄ **VT** *(gén, Archit)* to raise

surhomme /syʀɔm/ **NM** superman

surhumain, e /syʀymɛ̃, ɛn/ **ADJ** superhuman

surimi /syʀimi/ **NM** surimi ◆ **bâtonnets de ~** crab *ou* ocean sticks

surimposé, e /syʀɛ̃poze/ (ptp de **surimposer**) **ADJ** *(Géol)* superimposed; *(Fin)* overtaxed

surimposer /syʀɛ̃poze/ ► conjug 1 ◄ **VT** *(Fin)* to overtax

surimposition /syʀɛ̃pozisjɔ̃/ **NF** 1 *(Fin)* overtaxation 2 *(Géol)* epigenesis

surimpression /syʀɛ̃pʀesjɔ̃/ **NF** *(Photo)* double exposure; *(fig) [d'idées, visions]* superimposition ◆ **en ~** superimposed ◆ **on voyait apparaître un visage en ~** a face appeared superimposed (on it)

surin †* /syʀɛ̃/ **NM** (= *couteau*) knife

Surinam, Suriname /syʀinam/ **NM** Surinam

surinamais, e /syʀinamɛ, ɛz/ **ADJ** Surinamese **NM,F Surinamais(e)** Surinamese

surinfecter (se) /syʀɛ̃fɛkte/ ► conjug 1 ◄ **VPR** to develop a secondary infection

surinfection /syʀɛ̃fɛksjɔ̃/ **NF** secondary infection

surinformation /syʀɛ̃fɔʀmasjɔ̃/ **NF** information overload ◆ **le public est victime d'une ~ quotidienne** the public are subjected to information overload every day

surinformé, e /syʀɛ̃fɔʀme/ **ADJ** *[personne]* suffering from information overload ◆ **dans notre monde ~** in today's world of information overload

surintendance /syʀɛ̃tɑ̃dɑ̃s/ **NF** *(Hist)* superintendency

surintendant /syʀɛ̃tɑ̃dɑ̃/ **NM** *(Hist)* ◆ **~ (des finances)** superintendent (of finances)

surinvestir /syʀɛ̃vɛstiʀ/ ► conjug 2 ◄ VT *(Fin)* to overinvest (*dans* in); *(Psych)* to invest too much of o.s. in

surinvestissement /syʀɛ̃vɛstismɑ̃/ NM *(Écon, Psych)* overinvestment

surir /syʀiʀ/ ► conjug 2 ◄ VI *[lait, vin]* to turn sour, to (go) sour

surjet /syʀʒɛ/ NM 1 *(Couture)* overcast seam ◆ **point de ~** overcast stitch 2 *(Chirurgie)* continuous suture

surjeter /syʀʒəte/ ► conjug 4 ◄ VT *(Couture)* to overcast

sur-le-champ /syʀləʃɑ̃/ ADV immediately, at once, right away, straightaway *(Brit)* ◆ **il a été licencié ~** he was sacked on the spot

surlendemain /syʀlɑ̃d(ə)mɛ̃/ NM ◆ **le ~ de son arrivée** two days after his arrival ◆ **il est mort le ~** he died two days later ◆ **il revint le lendemain et le ~** he came back the next day and the day after (that) ◆ **le ~ matin** two days later in the morning

surligner /syʀliɲe/ ► conjug 1 ◄ VT to highlight

surligneur /syʀliɲœʀ/ NM highlighter (pen)

surmédiatisation /syʀmedjatizasjɔ̃/ NF *[d'affaire, événement]* excessive media coverage ◆ **la ~ de l'affaire a entraîné des polémiques** the excessive coverage given to the case in the media caused controversy ◆ **il y a risque de ~** there's a danger of media overkill

surmédiatisé, e /syʀmedjatize/ ADJ *[affaire, événement]* that has received too much media exposure *ou* coverage

surmédicalisation /syʀmedikalizasjɔ̃/ NF *[de problème, cas, grossesse]* excessive medicalization; *[de population, pays]* overprovision of medical care (*de* to)

surmédicaliser /syʀmedikalize/ ► conjug 1 ◄ VT *[+ problème, cas]* to overmedicalize; *[+ population, pays]* to overprovide with medical care

surmenage /syʀmənaʒ/ NM 1 *(= action de surmener qn)* overworking, overtaxing ◆ **éviter le ~ des élèves** to avoid overworking schoolchildren *ou* pushing schoolchildren too hard 2 *(= action de se surmener)* overwork(ing) ◆ **éviter à tout prix le ~** to avoid overwork(ing) *ou* overtaxing o.s. at all costs 3 *(= état maladif)* overwork ◆ **souffrant de ~** suffering from (the effects of) overwork ◆ **le ~ intellectuel** mental fatigue ◆ **~ physique** overexertion

surmené, e /syʀməne/ (ptp de **surmener**) ADJ *(par le travail)* overworked ◆ **je suis vraiment ~ en ce moment** I've got an awful lot on my plate at the moment

surmener /syʀməne/ ► conjug 5 ◄ VT *[+ personne]* to overwork, to overtax; *[+ animal]* to overtax VPR **se surmener** *(gén)* to overwork *ou* overtax (o.s.), to push o.s. too hard; *(physiquement)* to overexert o.s.

surmoi /syʀmwa/ NM superego

surmontable /syʀmɔ̃tabl/ ADJ surmountable ◆ **obstacle difficilement ~** obstacle that is difficult to surmount *ou* overcome

surmonter /syʀmɔ̃te/ ► conjug 1 ◄ VT 1 *(= être au-dessus de)* to surmount, to top ◆ **surmonté d'un dôme/clocheton** surmounted *ou* topped by a dome/bell-turret ◆ **un clocheton surmontait l'édifice** the building was surmounted *ou* topped by a bell-turret 2 *(= vaincre) [+ obstacle, difficultés]* to overcome, to get over, to surmount; *[+ dégoût, peur]* to overcome, to get the better of, to fight down VPR **se surmonter** *[personne]* to master o.s., to control o.s. ◆ **la peur peut se ~** fear can be overcome

surmortalité /syʀmɔʀtalite/ NF comparatively high deathrate ◆ **il y a eu une ~ masculine de 12%** the deathrate was 12% higher among men

surmultiplié, e /syʀmyltiplije/ ADJ ◆ **vitesse ~e** overdrive NF **surmultipliée** overdrive ◆ **passer la ~e** *(fig)* to get a move on*, to step on it*

surnager /syʀnaʒe/ ► conjug 3 ◄ VI 1 *[huile, objet]* to float (on the surface) 2 *(fig) [sentiment, souvenir]* to linger on ◆ **tu suis en maths ? – je surnage** can you keep up in maths? – I cope ◆ **son émission surnage malgré bien des difficultés** his programme struggles on in spite of many difficulties ◆ **les rares films qui surnagent dans cette compétition** the rare films that stand out in this competition

surnatalité /syʀnatalite/ NF comparatively high birthrate

surnaturel, -elle /syʀnatyʀɛl/ ADJ *(gén)* supernatural; *(= inquiétant)* uncanny, eerie NM ◆ **le ~** the supernatural

surnom /syʀnɔ̃/ NM *(gén)* nickname; *[de roi, héros]* name ◆ **"le Courageux", ~ du roi Richard** "the Brave", the name by which King Richard was known

⚠ **surnom** ne se traduit pas par **surname**, qui a le sens de 'nom de famille'.

surnombre /syʀnɔ̃bʀ/ NM surplus ◆ **en ~** *[effectifs, personnel]* surplus *(épith)*, excess *(épith)* ◆ **nous étions en ~** *(= trop)* there were too many of us; *(= plus qu'eux)* we outnumbered them ◆ **plusieurs élèves en ~** several pupils too many ◆ **ils ont fait sortir les spectateurs en ~** they asked those without seats to leave

surnommer /syʀnɔme/ ► conjug 1 ◄ VT ◆ **~ qn le gros** to nickname sb "fatty" ◆ **~ un roi "le Fort"** to give a king the name "the Strong" ◆ **cette infirmité l'avait fait ~ "le Crapaud"** this disability had earned him the nickname of "the Toad" ◆ **le roi Richard surnommé "le Courageux"** King Richard known as *ou* named "the Brave"

surnotation /syʀnɔtasjɔ̃/ NF *(Scol)* overmarking *(Brit)*, overgrading *(US)*

surnoter /syʀnɔte/ ► conjug 1 ◄ VT *(Scol)* to overmark *(Brit)*, to overgrade *(US)*

surnuméraire /syʀnymeʀɛʀ/ ADJ, NMF supernumerary ◆ **embryons ~s** spare *ou* surplus embryos

suroffre /syʀɔfʀ/ NF *(Jur)* higher offer *ou* bid

suroît /syʀwa/ NM *(= vent)* south-wester, sou'wester; *(= chapeau)* sou'wester ◆ **vent de ~** south-westerly wind

surpassement /syʀpɑsmɑ̃/ NM *(littér)* ◆ **~ de soi** surpassing (of) oneself

surpasser /syʀpɑse/ ► conjug 1 ◄ VT 1 *(= l'emporter sur) [+ concurrent, rival]* to surpass, to outdo ◆ **~ qn en agilité/connaissances** to surpass sb in agility/knowledge ◆ **sa gloire surpassait en éclat celle de Napoléon** his glory outshone that of Napoleon 2 *(= dépasser)* to surpass ◆ **le résultat surpasse toutes les espérances** the result surpasses *ou* is beyond all our hopes VPR **se surpasser** to surpass o.s., to excel o.s. ◆ **le cuisinier s'est surpassé aujourd'hui** the cook has excelled *ou* surpassed himself today ◆ **encore un échec, décidément tu te surpasses !** *(iro)* failed again – you're really excelling *ou* surpassing yourself!

surpaye /syʀpɛj/ NF *[de salariés, marchands]* overpayment ◆ **la ~ des marchandises** paying too much for goods

surpayer /syʀpeje/ ► conjug 8 ◄ VT *[+ employé]* to overpay; *[+ marchandise]* to pay too much for

surpêche /syʀpɛʃ/ NF overfishing

surpeuplé, e /syʀpœple/ ADJ overpopulated

surpeuplement /syʀpœpləmɑ̃/ NM overpopulation

surpiquer /syʀpike/ ► conjug 1 ◄ VT to topstitch

surpiqûre /syʀpikyʀ/ NF topstitch

sur-place, surplace /syʀplas/ NM ◆ **faire du ~** *(= ne pas avancer) (à vélo)* to do a track-stand; *(en voiture) (= être immobilisé)* to be stuck; *(= avancer très lentement)* to move at a snail's pace; *[oiseau]* to hover; *(= ne pas progresser) [enquête]* to hang fire, to mark time; *[négociations]* to be getting nowhere, to stall; *[projet]* to be getting nowhere ◆ **notre économie fait du ~** our economy is stagnating

surplis /syʀpli/ NM surplice

surplomb /syʀplɔ̃/ NM overhang ◆ **en ~** overhanging

surplombant, e /syʀplɔ̃bɑ̃, ɑ̃t/ ADJ overhanging *(épith)*

surplomber /syʀplɔ̃be/ ► conjug 1 ◄ VI to overhang; *(= ne pas être d'aplomb)* to be out of plumb VT ◆ **les rochers qui surplombent la plage** the rocks which overhang the beach ◆ **le village surplombe une vallée** the village overlooks a valley

surplus /syʀply/ NM 1 *(= excédent non écoulé)* surplus *(NonC)* ◆ **vendre le ~ de son stock** to sell off one's surplus stock ◆ **avoir des marchandises en ~** to have surplus goods 2 *(= reste non utilisé)* **il me reste un ~ de clous/de papier dont je ne me suis pas servi** I've got some nails/paper left over *ou* some surplus nails/paper that I didn't use ◆ **avec le ~ (de bois), je vais essayer de me faire une bibliothèque** with what's left over (of the wood) *ou* with the leftover *ou* surplus (wood) I'm going to try to build myself a bookcase ◆ **ce sont des ~ qui restent de la guerre/de l'exposition** they're left over *ou* it's surplus from the war/the exhibition ◆ **~ américains** American army surplus 3 *(= d'ailleurs)* **au ~** moreover, what is more

surpopulation /syʀpɔpylasjɔ̃/ NF overpopulation

surprenant, e /syʀpʀənɑ̃, ɑ̃t/ ADJ surprising ◆ **il n'y a rien de ~ à cela** that's not at all surprising ◆ **cette tendance n'est guère ~e** this trend hardly comes as a surprise *ou* is hardly surprising ◆ **chose ~e, il n'a jamais répondu** surprisingly (enough), he never replied ◆ **de façon ~e** surprisingly

surprendre /syʀpʀɑ̃dʀ/ ► conjug 58 ◄ VT 1 *(= prendre sur le fait) [+ voleur]* to surprise, to catch in the act

2 *(= découvrir) [+ secret, complot]* to discover; *[+ conversation]* to overhear; *[+ regard, sourire complice]* to intercept ◆ **je crus ~ en lui de la gêne** I thought I detected signs of some embarrassment in him

3 *(= prendre au dépourvu) (par attaque) [+ ennemi]* to surprise; *(par visite inopinée) [+ amis, voisins]* to catch unawares, to catch on the hop* *(Brit)* ◆ **~ des amis chez eux** to drop in unexpectedly on friends, to pay a surprise visit to friends ◆ **espérant la ~ au bain** hoping to catch her while she was in the bath

4 *[pluie, marée, nuit]* to catch out ◆ **se laisser ~ par la marée** to be caught (out) by the tide ◆ **se laisser ~ par la pluie** to be caught in the rain ◆ **se laisser ~ par la nuit** to be overtaken by darkness

5 *(= étonner) [nouvelle, conduite]* to surprise ◆ **tu me surprends** you amaze me ◆ **cela me surprendrait fort** that would greatly surprise me ◆ **cela m'a agréablement surpris** I was pleasantly surprised ◆ **cela semble te ~** you seem *ou* look surprised ◆ **il a réussi, ce qui n'est pas pour nous ~** he succeeded, which is hardly surprising *ou* which hardly comes as a surprise ◆ **cette question a de quoi** *ou* **peut ~** this question may seem surprising

6 *(littér)* **~ la vigilance de qn** to catch sb out ◆ **~ la bonne foi de qn** to betray sb's good faith

♦ ~ **la confiance de qn** † to win sb's trust fraudulently

VPR **se surprendre** ♦ **se ~ à faire qch** to catch *ou* find o.s. doing sth

surpression /syʀpʀesjɔ̃/ NF *(gén)* extremely high pressure; *(Tech)* overpressure

surprime /syʀpʀim/ NF *(Assurances)* additional premium

surpris, e[1] /syʀpʀi, iz/ (ptp de **surprendre**) ADJ *[air, regard]* surprised ♦ ~ **de qch** surprised at sth ♦ ~ **de me voir là/que je sois encore là** surprised at seeing me there *ou* to see me there/that I was still there ♦ **il va être désagréablement** ~ he has an unpleasant surprise in store for him, he's in for an unpleasant surprise ♦ **j'ai été le premier ~ de cette victoire** this victory came as a real surprise to me ♦ **vous ne seriez pas ~ si je vous disais que ...** it wouldn't surprise you *ou* come as a surprise to you if I told you that ...

surprise[2] /syʀpʀiz/ NF [1] *(= étonnement)* surprise ♦ **regarder qn avec** ~ to look at sb with *ou* in surprise ♦ **muet de** ~ speechless with surprise ♦ **avoir la ~ de voir que ...** to be surprised to see that ... ♦ **avoir la bonne/mauvaise ~ de constater que ...** to be pleasantly/unpleasantly surprised to find that ... ♦ **à ma grande** ~ much to my surprise, to my great surprise ♦ **à la ~ générale** to everybody's surprise ♦ **avec lui, on va de ~ en ~** it's one surprise after another with him ♦ **créer la** ~ to create a stir *ou* a sensation

[2] *(= cause d'étonnement, cadeau)* surprise ♦ **avec ça, pas de (mauvaises) ~s !** you'll have no nasty *ou* unpleasant surprises with this! ♦ **il m'a apporté une petite** ~ he brought me a little surprise ♦ **quelle bonne ~ !** what a nice *ou* pleasant *ou* lovely surprise! ♦ **"la surprise du chef"** *(Culin)* "the chef's surprise"

♦ **sans surprise** ♦ **il a été réélu sans ~ avec 64% des suffrages** his re-election with 64% of the votes came as no surprise to anyone ♦ **victoire sans** ~ unsurprising victory ♦ **c'est un film/scénario sans** ~ it's a rather unexciting film/script ♦ **voyage sans** ~ uneventful *ou* unremarkable journey ♦ **prix sans** ~ (all-)inclusive price ♦ **avec cette entreprise, c'est sans** ~ you always know what you're getting with this company

♦ **par surprise** *[attaquer]* by surprise ♦ **il m'a pris par** ~ he took me by surprise, he caught me off guard *ou* unawares

[3] *(en apposition)* **attaque-~** surprise attack ♦ **échappée-~** *(Sport)* sudden breakaway ♦ **grève-~** unofficial strike ♦ **invité-~** surprise guest ♦ **visite-~** surprise visit ♦ **voyage-~** *[d'homme politique]* surprise *ou* unexpected trip *ou* visit

surprise-partie † (pl **surprises-parties**) /syʀpʀizpaʀti/ NF party

surproduction /syʀpʀɔdyksjɔ̃/ NF overproduction

surproduire /syʀpʀɔdɥiʀ/ ▸ conjug 38 ◂ VT to overproduce

surprotéger /syʀpʀɔteʒe/ ▸ conjug 6 et 3 ◂ VT to overprotect

surpuissant, e /syʀpɥisɑ̃, ɑ̃t/ ADJ *[voiture, moteur]* ultra-powerful

surqualification /syʀkalifikasjɔ̃/ NF overqualification ♦ **malgré sa ~, il a accepté le poste** despite the fact that he was overqualified, he accepted the job

surqualifié, e /syʀkalifje/ ADJ overqualified

surréalisme /syʀʀealism/ NM surrealism

surréaliste /syʀʀealist/ ADJ *[écrivain, peintre]* surrealist; *[tableau, poème]* surrealist, surrealistic; *(= bizarre)* surreal, surrealistic NMF surrealist

surréel, -elle /syʀʀeel/ ADJ surreal

surrégénérateur /syʀʀeʒeneʀatœʀ/ NM ⇒ **surgénérateur**

surrégime /syʀʀeʒim/ NM ♦ **être** *ou* **tourner en** ~ *[voiture, moteur]* to be over-revving; *[économie]* to be overheating

surrénal, e (mpl **-aux**) /sy(ʀ)ʀenal, o/ ADJ suprarenal NFPL **surrénales** ♦ **(glandes) ~es** suprarenals

surreprésentation /sy(ʀ)ʀəpʀezɑ̃tasjɔ̃/ NF *[de catégorie de personnes]* over-representation

surreprésenté, e /sy(ʀ)ʀəpʀezɑ̃te/ ADJ *[catégorie de personnes]* over-represented

sur(-)réservation /syʀʀezɛʀvasjɔ̃/ NF double booking, overbooking

surround /səʀaund/ ADJ ♦ **son** ~ surround sound

sursalaire /syʀsalɛʀ/ NM bonus, premium

sursaturé, e /syʀsatyʀe/ ADJ [1] *(Sci) [solution]* supersaturated [2] *(Écon) [marché]* saturated

sursaut /syʀso/ NM [1] *(= mouvement brusque)* start, jump ♦ **se réveiller en** ~ to wake up with a start *ou* jump ♦ **elle a eu un** ~ she gave a start, she jumped [2] *(= élan, accès)* ~ **d'énergie** (sudden) burst *ou* fit of energy ♦ **l'élève a eu un ~ au troisième trimestre** the pupil put on a spurt in the third term

sursauter /syʀsote/ ▸ conjug 1 ◂ VI to start, to jump, to give a start ♦ **faire ~ qn** to make sb jump, to give sb a start ♦ ~ **de peur** to jump with fright

surseoir /syʀswaʀ/ ▸ conjug 26 ◂ **surseoir à** VT INDIR *[+ publication, délibération]* to defer, to postpone; *[+ poursuites, jugement, sentence, exécution]* to stay ♦ ~ **à l'exécution d'un condamné** to grant a stay of execution *ou* a reprieve to a condemned man

sursis /syʀsi/ NM [1] *(Jur) [de condamnation à mort]* reprieve ♦ **peine avec ~** *ou* **assortie du** ~ suspended *ou* deferred sentence ♦ **il a eu deux ans avec** ~ he was given a two-year suspended *ou* deferred sentence ♦ ~ **à exécution** *ou* **d'exécution** stay of execution ♦ ~ **avec mise à l'épreuve** conditional discharge [2] *(Mil)* ~ **(d'incorporation)** deferment [3] *(= temps de répit)* reprieve ♦ **c'est un mort en** ~ he's a condemned man, he's living under a death sentence *ou* on borrowed time ♦ **gouvernement/entreprise en** ~ government/company living on borrowed time ♦ **demander un ~ de paiement** to ask for an extension *(on the deadline for a debt)* ♦ **on a eu un ~ de trois jours** we got three days' grace

sursitaire /syʀsitɛʀ/ ADJ *(Mil)* deferred *(épith)*; *(Jur)* with a suspended *ou* deferred sentence NM *(Mil)* deferred conscript

surtaxe /syʀtaks/ NF *(Fin)* surcharge; *[de lettre mal affranchie]* surcharge; *[d'envoi exprès]* additional charge, surcharge ♦ ~ **à l'importation** import surcharge

surtaxer /syʀtakse/ ▸ conjug 1 ◂ VT to surcharge

surtension /syʀtɑ̃sjɔ̃/ NF *(Élec)* overvoltage

surtitre /syʀtitʀ/ NM surtitle

surtitrer /syʀtitʀe/ ▸ conjug 1 ◂ VT *[+ opéra, pièce de théâtre]* to surtitle ♦ **"surtitré"** "with surtitles" ♦ **l'opéra était surtitré** the opera had surtitles

surtout[1] /syʀtu/ ADV [1] *(= avant tout, d'abord)* above all; *(= spécialement)* especially, particularly ♦ **rapide, efficace et ~ discret** quick, efficient and above all discreet ♦ **il est assez timide, ~ avec les femmes** he's quite shy, especially *ou* particularly with women ♦ **j'aime ~ les romans, mais je lis aussi de la poésie** I particularly like novels, but I also read poetry ♦ **dernièrement, j'ai ~ lu des romans** lately I've been reading mostly *ou* mainly novels ♦ **j'aime les romans, ~ les romans policiers** I like novels, especially *ou* particularly detective novels ♦ **le poulet, je l'aime ~ à la broche** I like chicken best (when it's) spit-roasted

[2] ♦ ~ **que** * especially as *ou* since

[3] *(intensif)* ~, **n'en parle pas !** don't forget, mum's the word! ♦ ~ **pas maintenant** certainly not now ♦ **je ne veux ~ pas vous déranger** the last thing I want is to disturb you, I certainly don't want to disturb you ♦ ~ **pas !** certainly not! ♦ ~ **ne vous mettez pas en frais** whatever you do, don't go to any expense ♦ **ne m'aide pas, ~ !** *(iro)* don't help me, will you!

surtout[2] /syʀtu/ NM [1] († = *manteau)* greatcoat † [2] *(= milieu de table)* centrepiece *(Brit)*, centerpiece *(US)*, epergne *(SPÉC)*

survaloriser /syʀvalɔʀize/ ▸ conjug 1 ◂ VT *[+ personne]* to overrate, to over-value; *[+ critère, fonction]* to attach too much importance to

surveillance /syʀvɛjɑ̃s/ NF [1] *(= garde) [d'enfant, élève, bagages]* watch ♦ **sous la ~ attentive de qn** under the watchful eye of sb ♦ **laisser un enfant sans** ~ to leave a child unsupervised

[2] *(Mil, Police) [de personne, maison]* surveillance; *[de frontières]* surveillance, monitoring; *[de cessez-le-feu]* monitoring, supervision ♦ ~ **aérienne** air surveillance ♦ **mission/service de** ~ surveillance mission/personnel ♦ **société de** ~ security firm ♦ **sous ~ médicale** under medical supervision ♦ **sous (étroite) ~ policière** under (close) police surveillance ♦ **placer qn/qch sous haute** ~ *(lit, fig)* to keep a close watch on sb/sth ♦ **il y aura une ~ bancaire au niveau européen** banks will be monitored at European level

♦ **en surveillance** ♦ **navire/avion en** ~ ship/plane carrying out surveillance ♦ **être/rester en ~ à l'hôpital** to be/remain under observation at the hospital

[3] *(= contrôle) [d'éducation, études, réparation, construction]* supervision; *(Scol, Univ) [d'examen]* invigilation ♦ **déjouer** *ou* **tromper la ~ de ses gardiens** to slip by *ou* evade the guards ♦ **l'enseignant qui assure la ~ de l'épreuve** the teacher invigilating

[4] *(= fait d'épier) [de personne, mouvement, proie]* watch; *(Sport)* watch ♦ **exercer une ~ continuelle/une étroite ~ sur** to keep a constant/a close watch over

COMP **surveillance à distance** remote electronic surveillance
surveillance électronique electronic surveillance; *(Méd)* electronic monitoring
surveillance vidéo video surveillance

surveillant, e /syʀvɛjɑ̃, ɑ̃t/ NM,F *[de prison]* warder *(Brit)*, guard *(US)*; *[d'usine, chantier]* supervisor, overseer; *[de magasin]* shopwalker; *(Méd)* head nurse, charge nurse; *(Scol : aux examens)* invigilator *(Brit)*, proctor *(US)* ♦ ~ **(d'étude)** supervisor ♦ ~ **général** † *(Scol)* chief supervisor ♦ ~ **d'internat** *(Scol)* dormitory supervisor, dormitory monitor *(US)* ♦ ~**e générale** *(Méd)* nursing officer, matron *(Brit)*

surveillé, e /syʀveje/ (ptp de **surveiller**) ADJ → **liberté**

surveiller /syʀveje/ ▸ conjug 1 ◂ VT [1] *(= garder) [+ enfant, élève, bagages]* to watch, to keep an eye on; *[+ prisonnier]* to keep watch over, to keep (a) watch on; *[+ malade]* to watch over, to keep watch over ♦ **les opposants au régime sont très surveillés** opponents of the regime are kept under close watch *ou* are watched very closely ♦ **ce régime politique doit être surveillé de près** this régime needs to be watched closely *ou* to be kept under close scrutiny

[2] *(= contrôler) [+ éducation, études de qn, récréation]* to supervise; *[+ réparation, construction]* to supervise, to oversee; *(Scol, Univ) [+ examen]* to invigilate ♦ **surveille la soupe** keep an eye on the soup, watch the soup ♦ **surveille la cuisson du rôti** watch the roast ♦ **je surveille**

l'heure, il ne faut pas être en retard I'm keeping an eye on the time, we mustn't be late ③ *(= défendre) [+ locaux]* to keep watch on; *[+ territoire]* to watch over, to keep watch over; *[+ frontières, espace aérien]* to monitor; *[+ cessez-le-feu]* to monitor, to supervise ◆ **l'entrée de l'aéroport est très surveillée** there is tight security at the entrance to the airport

④ *(= épier) [+ personne, mouvements, proie]* to watch; *[+ adversaire] (Mil)* to keep watch on; *(Sport)* to watch ◆ **se sentant surveillé, il partit** feeling he was being watched, he left ◆ ~ **qn de près** to keep a close eye *ou* watch on sb ◆ ~ **qn du coin de l'œil** to watch sb out the corner of one's eye

⑤ *(= être attentif à)* ~ **son langage/sa tension/sa ligne** to watch one's language/one's blood pressure/one's figure ◆ **tu devrais ~ ta santé** you should look after your health

VPR **se surveiller** to keep a check *ou* a watch on o.s. ◆ **il devrait se ~, il grossit de plus en plus** he ought to watch himself because he's getting fatter and fatter ◆ **ils sont obligés de se ~ devant les enfants** they have to watch themselves *ou* be careful in front of the children

> ⚠ **surveiller** ne se traduit pas par **to survey**, qui a le sens de 'inspecter'.

survenir /syʀvəniʀ/ ▸ conjug 22 ◂ VI *[événement]* to take place; *[incident, complications, retards]* to occur, to arise; *[personne]* to appear, to arrive (unexpectedly) ◆ **s'il survenait quelque chose de nouveau** if anything new comes up ◆ **s'il survient des complications ...** should any complications arise ...

survenue /syʀvəny/ NF *[de personne]* unexpected arrival *ou* appearance; *[de maladie]* onset; *[de mutations, symptômes]* appearance

survêt* /syʀvɛt/ NM (abrév de **survêtement**) tracksuit, sweat suit

survêtement /syʀvɛtmɑ̃/ NM *[de sportif]* tracksuit, sweat suit; *[d'alpiniste, skieur]* overgarments

survie /syʀvi/ NF *[de malade, accidenté, auteur, amitié, entreprise, mode]* survival; *(Rel : dans l'au-delà)* afterlife ◆ **ce médicament lui a donné quelques mois de ~** this drug has given him a few more months to live ◆ **une ~ de quelques jours, à quoi bon, dans son état ?** what's the use of prolonging his life for a few more days in his condition? ◆ **maintenir qn en ~** to keep sb alive artificially

♦ **de survie** *[instinct, réflexe]* survival *(épith)* ◆ **équipement/combinaison/couverture de ~** survival equipment/suit/blanket ◆ **radeau de ~** life-raft ◆ **ses chances de ~ sont importantes** he has *ou* stands a good chance of survival *ou* surviving

survirer /syʀviʀe/ ▸ conjug 1 ◂ VI *[voiture]* to oversteer

survireur, -euse /syʀviʀœʀ, øz/ ADJ ◆ **voiture survireuse** car which oversteers

survitrage /syʀvitʀaʒ/ NM double-glazing

survivance /syʀvivɑ̃s/ NF *(= vestige)* relic, survival ◆ **cette coutume est une ~ du passé** this custom is a survival *ou* relic from the past ◆ ~ **de l'âme** *(littér)* survival of the soul (after death), afterlife

survivant, e /syʀvivɑ̃, ɑ̃t/ ADJ surviving NM,F survivor ◆ **des sœurs, la ~e ...** the surviving sister ... ◆ **un ~ d'un âge révolu** a survivor from a past age

survivre /syʀvivʀ/ ▸ conjug 46 ◂ VI ① *(= continuer à vivre : lit, fig)* to survive ◆ **va-t-il ~ ?** *(après accident)* will he live? *ou* survive? ◆ **il n'avait aucune chance de ~** he had no chance of survival *ou* surviving ◆ ~ **à** *[+ accident, maladie, humiliation]* to survive ◆ **rien ne survivait de leurs anciennes coutumes** nothing survived of their old customs ② *(= vivre plus longtemps que)* ~ **à** *[personne]* to outlive; *[œuvre, idée]* to outlive, to outlast VPR **se survivre** ① *(= se perpétuer)* **se ~ dans** *[+ œuvre, enfant, souvenir]* to live on in ② *(péj) [auteur]* to outlive one's talent; *[aventurier]* to outlive one's time

survol /syʀvɔl/ NM ① *(en avion)* **le ~ de** flying over ◆ **ils interdisent le ~ de leur territoire** they won't allow anyone to fly over their territory ◆ **faire un ~ à basse altitude** to make a low flight ② *(= examen rapide) [de livre]* skimming through, skipping through; *[de question]* skimming over ◆ **après un rapide ~ de sa filmographie, nous ...** after a brief look at his filmography, we ...

survoler /syʀvɔle/ ▸ conjug 1 ◂ VT ① *(en avion)* to fly over ② *[+ livre]* to skim through, to skip through; *[+ question]* to skim over ③ *(Sport) [+ épreuve]* to sail through

survoltage /syʀvɔltaʒ/ NM *(Élec)* boosting

survolté, e /syʀvɔlte/ ADJ ① *(= surexcité) [foule]* over-excited; *[ambiance]* electric, highly charged ② *(Élec)* stepped up, boosted

sus /sy(s)/ ADV ① *(Admin)* **en ~** in addition ◆ **en ~ de** in addition to, over and above ② *(††, hum)* **courir ~ à l'ennemi** to rush upon the enemy ◆ **~ à l'ennemi !** at them! ◆ **~ au tyran !** death to the tyrant!

susceptibilité /sysɛptibilite/ NF *(= sensibilité)* touchiness *(NonC)*, sensitiveness *(NonC)* ◆ **afin de ménager** *ou* **de ne pas froisser les ~s** so as not to offend people's susceptibilities *ou* sensibilities ◆ **être d'une grande ~** to be extremely touchy, to be hypersensitive

susceptible /sysɛptibl/ ADJ ① *(= ombrageux)* touchy, sensitive ◆ **ne sois pas si ~ !** don't be so touchy *ou* sensitive!

② *(= de nature à)* ◆ **~ de** likely to ◆ **des souches de virus ~s de provoquer une épidémie** virus strains that are likely to cause an epidemic ◆ **les personnes ~s d'être infectées** the people likely to be infected ◆ **des conférences ~s de l'intéresser** lectures liable *ou* likely to be of interest to him ◆ **ce sont des documents ~s de provoquer un scandale** these documents could well cause a scandal ◆ **texte ~ d'être amélioré** *ou* **d'améliorations** text open to improvement *ou* that can be improved upon

③ *(hypothèse)* **est-il ~ de le faire ?** is he likely to do it? ◆ **il est ~ de gagner** he may well win, he is liable to win

> ⚠ Au sens de 'facilement vexé', **susceptible** ne se traduit pas par le mot anglais **susceptible**.

susciter /sysite/ ▸ conjug 1 ◂ VT ① *(= donner naissance à) [+ admiration, intérêt]* to arouse; *[+ passions, jalousies, haine]* to arouse, to incite; *[+ controverse, critiques, querelle]* to give rise to, to provoke; *[+ obstacles]* to give rise to, to create ② *(= provoquer volontairement)* to create ◆ ~ **des obstacles/ennuis à qn** to create obstacles/difficulties for sb ◆ ~ **des ennemis à qn** to make enemies for sb

suscription /syskʀipsjɔ̃/ NF *(Admin)* address

susdit, e /sysdi, dit/ ADJ *(Jur)* aforesaid

sus-dominante /sysdɔminɑ̃t/ NF submediant

sushi /suʃi/ NM sushi

susmentionné, e /sysmɑ̃sjɔne/ ADJ *(Admin)* above-mentioned, aforementioned

susnommé, e /sysnɔme/ ADJ, NM,F *(Admin, Jur)* above-named

suspect, e /syspɛ(kt), ɛkt/ ADJ ① *(= louche) [individu, conduite, colis]* suspicious ◆ **sa générosité m'est** *ou* **me paraît ~e** his generosity seems suspect *ou* suspicious to me ◆ **il est mort dans des conditions ~es** he died in suspicious circumstances

② *(= douteux) [opinion, témoignage]* suspect; *[viande, poisson]* suspect ◆ **elle était ~e aux yeux de la police** the police were suspicious of her ◆ **pensées ~es à la majorité conservatrice** thoughts which the conservative majority find suspect

③ *(= soupçonné)* **les personnes ~es** those under suspicion

④ ◆ ~ **de** suspected of ◆ **ils sont ~s de collusion avec l'ennemi** they are suspected of collusion with the enemy ◆ **Leblanc, pourtant bien peu ~ de royalisme, a proposé que ...** Leblanc, though hardly likely to be suspected of royalism, did propose that ...

NM,F suspect ◆ **principal ~** chief *ou* prime suspect

suspecter /syspɛkte/ ▸ conjug 1 ◂ VT *[+ personne]* to suspect; *[+ bonne foi, honnêteté]* to suspect, to have (one's) suspicions about, to question ◆ ~ **qn de faire qch** to suspect sb of doing sth ◆ **on le suspecte de sympathies gauchistes** he is suspected of having leftist sympathies

suspendre /syspɑ̃dʀ/ ▸ conjug 41 ◂ VT ① *(= accrocher) [+ vêtements]* to hang up; *[+ lampe, décoration]* to hang, to suspend *(à* from); *[+ hamac]* to sling (up) ◆ ~ **qch à** *[+ clou, crochet, portemanteau]* to hang sth on ◆ ~ **un lustre au plafond par une chaîne** to hang *ou* suspend a chandelier from the ceiling on *ou* by *ou* with a chain ◆ ~ **un hamac à des crochets/à deux poteaux** to sling a hammock between two hooks/between two posts

② *(= interrompre) [+ publication, combat, paiement, mouvement de grève, transactions]* to suspend; *[+ récit, négociations, relations diplomatiques]* to break off; *[+ audience, séance]* to adjourn; *[+ permis de conduire]* to suspend; *[+ jugement]* to suspend, to defer; *[+ décision]* to postpone, to defer; *[+ recherche, projet]* to suspend, to break off ◆ ~ **la cotation d'une action** *(Bourse)* to suspend a share

③ *(= destituer) [+ prélat, fonctionnaire]* to suspend; *(= mettre à pied) [+ joueur]* to suspend ◆ ~ **qn de ses fonctions** to suspend sb from office

VPR **se suspendre** ◆ **se ~ à** *[+ branche, barre]* to hang from *(par* by); ◆ **les enfants se suspendaient aux jupes de leur mère** the children were hanging onto their mother's skirt

suspendu, e /syspɑ̃dy/ (ptp de **suspendre**) ADJ ① *(= accroché)* **vêtement ~ à** garment hanging on ◆ **lustre ~ à** light hanging *ou* suspended from ◆ **benne ~e à un câble/dans le vide** skip suspended by a cable/in mid air ◆ **montre ~e à une chaîne** watch hanging on a chain ◆ **être ~ aux lèvres de qn** to be hanging on sb's every word *ou* on sb's lips ◆ **chalets ~s au-dessus d'une gorge** chalets perched *ou* suspended over a gorge; → **jardin, pont** ② *(= interrompu) [séance]* adjourned; *[jugement]* suspended, deferred; *[fonctionnaire, magistrat]* suspended ③ **voiture bien/mal ~e** car with good/poor suspension

suspens /syspɑ̃/ NM

♦ **en suspens** *(= en attente) [question, dossier, projet]* on hold; *(= dans l'incertitude)* in suspense; *(= en suspension) [poussière, flocons de neige]* in suspension ◆ **on a laissé la question en ~** the matter has been put on hold ◆ **il reste beaucoup de questions/problèmes en ~** many questions/problems remain unresolved ◆ **tenir les lecteurs en ~** to keep the reader in suspense ◆ **en ~ dans l'air** hanging *ou* suspended in the air

suspense /syspɛns, syspɑ̃s/ NM *[de film, roman]* suspense ◆ **un moment de ~** a moment's suspense ◆ **un ~ angoissant** an agonizing feeling of suspense ◆ **film à ~** suspense film, thriller

suspenseur /syspɑ̃sœʀ/ ADJ M suspensory NM suspensor

suspensif, -ive /syspɑ̃sif, iv/ ADJ (*Jur*) suspensive

suspension /syspɑ̃sjɔ̃/ NF 1 [*de vêtements*] hanging; [*de lampe, décoration*] hanging, suspending

2 (= *interruption*) [*de publication, combats, paiement, permis de conduire*] suspension; [*de récit*] breaking off; [*d'audience, séance*] adjournment ◆ **le juge a ordonné la ~ de l'audience** the judge ordered that the hearing be adjourned ◆ **il a eu un an de ~ de permis** he had his driving licence suspended for a year ◆ **la ~ des relations diplomatiques entre les deux pays** the breaking off *ou* suspension of diplomatic relations between the two countries

3 (= *fait de différer*) [*de jugement*] suspension, deferment; [*de décision*] postponement, deferment

4 [*de prélat, fonctionnaire*] suspension; [*de joueur*] suspension ◆ **prononcer la ~ de qn pour 2 ans** to suspend sb for 2 years ◆ **~ à vie** lifetime ban

5 [*de véhicule*] suspension ◆ **~ active/hydraulique** active/hydraulic suspension

6 (= *lustre*) ceiling light

7 (= *installation, système*) suspension ◆ **~ florale** hanging basket

8 (*Chim*) suspension

LOC ADJ **en suspension** [*particule, poussière*] in suspension, suspended ◆ **en ~ dans l'air** [*poussière*] hanging *ou* suspended in the air ◆ **en ~ dans l'air** *ou* **dans le vide** [*personne, câble*] hanging *ou* suspended in mid-air

COMP **suspension d'audience** adjournment
suspension des hostilités suspension of hostilities
suspension de paiement suspension of payment(s)
suspension des poursuites suspension of proceedings
suspension de séance ⇒ **suspension d'audience**

suspensoir /syspɑ̃swaʀ/ NM athletic support, jockstrap

suspicieusement /syspisjøzmɑ̃/ ADV suspiciously

suspicieux, -ieuse /syspisjø, jøz/ ADJ suspicious

suspicion /syspisjɔ̃/ NF suspicion ◆ **avoir de la ~ à l'égard de qn** to be suspicious of sb, to have one's suspicions about sb ◆ **regard plein de ~** suspicious look ◆ **~ légitime** (*Jur*) reasonable suspicion (*about the fairness of a trial*)

sustentateur, -trice /systɑ̃tatœʀ, tʀis/ ADJ (*Aviation*) lifting ◆ **surface sustentatrice** aerofoil (*Brit*), airfoil (*US*)

sustentation /systɑ̃tasjɔ̃/ NF (*Aviation*) lift ◆ **plan de ~** aerofoil (*Brit*), airfoil (*US*) ◆ **polygone** *ou* **base de ~** (*Géom*) base ◆ **train à ~ magnétique** magnetic levitation train, maglev train

sustenter /systɑ̃te/ ▸ conjug 1 ◂ VT (†= *nourrir*) to sustain ◆ **la lecture sustente l'esprit** reading nourishes the mind VPR **se sustenter** (*hum, frm*) to take sustenance (*hum, frm*)

sus-tonique /systɔnik/ ADJ (*Mus*) supertonic

susurrement /sysyʀmɑ̃/ NM [*de personne*] whisper, whispering; [*d'eau*] murmuring

susurrer /sysyʀe/ ▸ conjug 1 ◂ VTI [*personne*] to whisper; [*eau*] to murmur ◆ **il lui susurrait des mots doux à l'oreille** he whispered sweet nothings in her ear ◆ **les mauvaises langues susurrent qu'il a fait de la prison** malicious gossips are putting it about that he has been to prison ◆ **on susurre qu'il a été impliqué** it's whispered that *ou* the whisper is that he was involved

susvisé, e /sysvize/ ADJ above-mentioned, aforementioned

suture /sytyʀ/ NF (*Anat, Bot, Méd*) suture; → **point²**

suturer /sytyʀe/ ▸ conjug 1 ◂ VT to suture (*SPÉC*), to stitch up

SUV /ɛsyve/ NM (abrév de **Sport Utility Vehicle**) SUV

Suva /syva/ N Suva

suzerain, e /syz(ə)ʀɛ̃, ɛn/ NM,F suzerain, overlord ADJ suzerain

suzeraineté /syz(ə)ʀɛnte/ NF suzerainty

svastika /svastika/ NM swastika

svelte /svɛlt/ ADJ [*personne*] slender, svelte; [*édifice, silhouette*] slender, slim

sveltesse /svɛltɛs/ NF slenderness

SVP (abrév de **s'il vous plaît**) pls, please

SVT /ɛsvete/ NFPL (abrév de **sciences de la vie et de la terre**) → **science**

swahili, e /swaili/ ADJ Swahili(an) NM (= *langue*) Swahili NM,F **Swahili(e)** Swahili

swazi, e /swazi/ ADJ Swazi NM,F **Swazi(e)** Swazi

Swaziland /swazilɑ̃d/ NM Swaziland

sweat /swit, swɛt/ NM sweatshirt

sweater /switœʀ, swɛtœʀ/ NM sweater

sweat-shirt (pl **sweat-shirts**) /switʃœʀt, swɛtʃœʀt/ NM sweatshirt

sweepstake /swipstɛk/ NM sweepstake

swing /swiŋ/ NM (= *musique*) swing; (= *danse*) jive ◆ **danser le ~** to jive

swinguer* /swiŋge/ ▸ conjug 1 ◂ VI to swing* ◆ **ça swingue !** it's really swinging!*

sybarite /sibaʀit/ NMF sybarite

sybaritique /sibaʀitik/ ADJ sybaritic

sybaritisme /sibaʀitism/ NM sybaritism

sycomore /sikɔmɔʀ/ NM sycamore (tree)

sycophante /sikɔfɑ̃t/ NM (*littér* = *délateur*) informer

syllabation /si(l)labasjɔ̃/ NF syllabication, syllabification

syllabe /si(l)lab/ NF syllable ◆ **~ ouverte/fermée** open/closed syllable ◆ **~ finale/muette/accentuée** final/silent/accented *ou* stressed syllable ◆ **il n'a pas prononcé une ~** he didn't say a single word

syllabique /si(l)labik/ ADJ syllabic

syllabisme /si(l)labism/ NM syllabism

syllogisme /silɔʒism/ NM syllogism

syllogistique /silɔʒistik/ ADJ syllogistic NF syllogistics (*sg*)

sylphe /silf/ NM sylph

sylphide /silfid/ NF sylphid; (= *femme*) sylphlike creature ◆ **sa taille de ~** her sylphlike figure

sylvestre /silvɛstʀ/ ADJ forest (*épith*), silvan (*littér*); → **pin**

sylvicole /silvikɔl/ ADJ [*ouvrier, projet*] forestry (*épith*) ◆ **culture ~** tree cultivation ◆ **exploitation ~** tree farm

sylviculteur, -trice /silvikyltœʀ, tʀis/ NM,F forester

sylviculture /silvikyltyʀ/ NF forestry, silviculture (*SPÉC*)

symbiose /sɛ̃bjoz/ NF (*lit, fig*) symbiosis ◆ **en ~** in symbiosis

symbiotique /sɛ̃bjɔtik/ ADJ symbiotic

symbole /sɛ̃bɔl/ NM 1 (*gén*) symbol ◆ **une ville(-)~/des années(-)~ de la liberté** a city that has come to symbolize/years that have come to symbolize freedom ◆ **la colombe, ~ de la paix** the dove, symbol of peace 2 (*Rel*) Creed ◆ **le Symbole des apôtres** the Apostles' Creed ◆ **le ~ de saint Athanase** the Athanasian Creed

symbolique /sɛ̃bɔlik/ ADJ (*gén*) symbolic(al); (= *très modique*) [*donation, augmentation, amende*] token (*épith*), nominal; [*cotisation, contribution, dommages-intérêts*] nominal; (= *sans valeur*) [*solution*] cosmetic ◆ **c'est un geste purement ~** it's a purely symbolic gesture, it's just a token gesture ◆ **logique ~** symbolic logic; → **franc²** NF (= *science*) symbolics (*sg*); (= *système de symboles*) symbolic system ◆ **la ~ des rêves** the symbolism of dreams, dream symbolism

symboliquement /sɛ̃bɔlikmɑ̃/ ADV symbolically

symbolisation /sɛ̃bɔlizasjɔ̃/ NF symbolization

symboliser /sɛ̃bɔlize/ ▸ conjug 1 ◂ VT to symbolize

symbolisme /sɛ̃bɔlism/ NM (*gén*) symbolism; (*Littérat*) Symbolism

symboliste /sɛ̃bɔlist/ ADJ, NMF Symbolist

symétrie /simetʀi/ NF (*gén*) symmetry (*par rapport à* in relation to); ◆ **centre/axe de ~** centre/axis of symmetry

symétrique /simetʀik/ ADJ symmetrical (*de* to; *par rapport à* in relation to) NM [*de muscle, point*] symmetry NF [*de figure plane*] symmetrical figure

symétriquement /simetʀikmɑ̃/ ADV symmetrically

sympa* /sɛ̃pa/ ADJ INV (abrév de **sympathique**) [*personne, soirée, robe*] nice; [*endroit, ambiance*] nice, friendly ◆ **un type vachement ~** a really nice guy* *ou* bloke* (*Brit*) ◆ **sois ~, prête-le-moi** be a pal* and lend it to me ◆ **ce n'est pas très ~ de sa part** that's not very nice of him

sympathie /sɛ̃pati/ GRAMMAIRE ACTIVE 51.4 NF 1 (= *amitié*) liking ◆ **ressentir de la ~ à l'égard de qn** to (rather) like sb, to feel drawn to *ou* towards sb ◆ **se prendre de ~ pour qn** to take a liking to sb ◆ **j'ai beaucoup de ~ pour lui** I like him a great deal ◆ **je n'ai aucune ~ pour elle** I don't like her at all ◆ **il inspire la ~** he's very likeable, he's a likeable sort ◆ **s'attirer la ~ de qn** to win sb over ◆ **n'ayant que peu de ~ pour cette nouvelle théorie** having little time for this new theory

2 (= *affinité*) friendship ◆ **la ~ qui existe entre eux** the friendship there is between them, the affinity they feel for each other ◆ **des relations de ~ les unissaient** they were united by friendship ◆ **il n'y a guère de ~ entre ces factions/personnes** there's no love lost between these factions/people

3 (= *compassion*) sympathy; (*frm* = *condoléances*) sympathy ◆ **ce drame lui a attiré la ~ du public** the tragedy earned him the sympathy of the public ◆ **croyez à notre ~** please accept our deepest *ou* most heartfelt sympathy, you have our deepest sympathy ◆ **témoignages de ~** (*pour deuil*) expressions of sympathy

4 (= *tendance*) sympathy ◆ **on le suspecte de ~ avec le nazisme** he is suspected of having Nazi sympathies *ou* leanings ◆ **il ne cache pas ses ~s communistes** he doesn't hide his communist sympathies ◆ **ils sont en ~ avec le parti communiste** they sympathize with the communist party

> ⚠ Au sens de 'amitié' ou 'affinité', **sympathie** ne se traduit pas par le mot anglais **sympathy**.

sympathique /sɛ̃patik/ ADJ 1 (= *agréable, aimable*) [*personne*] likeable, nice; [*geste, accueil*] friendly, kindly; [*soirée, réunion, ambiance*] pleasant, friendly; [*plat*] good, nice; [*appartement*] nice, pleasant ◆ **il m'est très ~, je le trouve très ~** I like him very much, I think he's very nice ◆ **elle ne m'est pas très ~** I don't like her very much ◆ **cela me l'a rendu plutôt ~** that warmed me to him ◆ **il a une tête ~*** he has a friendly *ou* nice face ◆ **ce n'est pas un régime/une idéologie très ~** it is not a very pleasant regime/ideology [2] *(Anat)* sympathetic NM *(Anat)* ◆ **le (grand)** ~ the sympathetic nervous system

> ⚠ Au sens de 'agréable', 'aimable', **sympathique** ne se traduit pas par **sympathetic**.

sympathisant, e /sɛ̃patizɑ̃, ɑ̃t/ *(Pol)* ADJ sympathizing *(épith)* NM,F sympathizer

sympathiser /sɛ̃patize/ ► conjug 1 ◄ VI [1] *(= se prendre d'amitié)* to hit it off* *(avec* with); *(= bien s'entendre)* to get on (well) *(avec* with); ◆ **ils ont tout de suite sympathisé** they took to each other immediately, they hit it off* straight away ◆ **je suis heureux de voir qu'il sympathise avec Lucien** I'm pleased to see he gets on (well) with Lucien ◆ **ils ne sympathisent pas avec les voisins** *(= fréquenter)* they don't have much contact with *ou* much to do with* the neighbours [2] *(Pol)* ◆ **il sympathise avec l'extrême droite** he has sympathies *ou* he sympathizes with the far right

> ⚠ **sympathiser** se traduit par **to sympathize** uniquement au sens politique.

symphonie /sɛ̃fɔni/ NF *(Mus, fig)* symphony ◆ ~ **concertante** symphonia concertante

symphonique /sɛ̃fɔnik/ ADJ symphonic; → **orchestre, poème**

symphoniste /sɛ̃fɔnist/ NMF symphonist

symposium /sɛ̃pozjɔm/ NM symposium

symptomatique /sɛ̃ptɔmatik/ ADJ *(Méd)* symptomatic; *(= révélateur)* significant ◆ ~ **de** symptomatic of

symptomatiquement /sɛ̃ptɔmatikmɑ̃/ ADV symptomatically

symptomatologie /sɛ̃ptɔmatɔlɔʒi/ NF symptomatology

symptôme /sɛ̃ptom/ NM symptom

synagogue /sinagɔg/ NF synagogue

synapse /sinaps/ NF *[de neurones]* synapse, synapsis; *[de gamètes]* synapsis

synarchie /sinaʀʃi/ NF synarchy

synchro* /sɛ̃kʀo/ ADJ abrév de **synchronisé, e** NF abrév de **synchronisation**

synchrone /sɛ̃kʀon/ ADJ synchronous

synchronie /sɛ̃kʀɔni/ NF synchronic level, synchrony

synchronique /sɛ̃kʀɔnik/ ADJ *[linguistique, analyse]* synchronic; → **tableau**

synchroniquement /sɛ̃kʀɔnikmɑ̃/ ADJ synchronically

synchronisation /sɛ̃kʀɔnizasjɔ̃/ NF synchronization

synchronisé, e /sɛ̃kʀɔnize/ (ptp de **synchroniser**) ADJ synchronized

synchroniser /sɛ̃kʀɔnize/ ► conjug 1 ◄ VT to synchronize

synchroniseur /sɛ̃kʀɔnizœʀ/ NM *(Élec)* synchronizer; *[de vitesses]* synchromesh

synchroniseuse /sɛ̃kʀɔnizøz/ NF *(Ciné)* synchronizer

synchronisme /sɛ̃kʀɔnism/ NM *[d'oscillations, dates]* synchronism; *(Philos)* synchronicity ◆ **avec un ~ parfait** with perfect synchronization

synchrotron /sɛ̃kʀɔtʀɔ̃/ NM synchrotron ◆ **rayonnement** ~ synchrotron radiation

synclinal, e (mpl **-aux**) /sɛ̃klinal, o/ ADJ synclinal NM syncline

syncope /sɛ̃kɔp/ NF [1] *(= évanouissement)* blackout, fainting fit, syncope *(SPÉC)* ◆ **avoir une** ~ to have a blackout, to faint, to pass out [2] *(Mus)* syncopation [3] *(Ling)* syncope

syncopé, e /sɛ̃kɔpe/ ADJ [1] *(Littérat, Mus)* syncopated [2] (* *= stupéfait)* staggered, flabbergasted*

syncrétique /sɛ̃kʀetik/ ADJ syncretic

syncrétisme /sɛ̃kʀetism/ NM syncretism

syndic /sɛ̃dik/ NM [1] *(Jur)* receiver ◆ ~ **(d'immeuble** *ou* **de copropriété)** managing agent ◆ ~ **de faillite** *(Jur, Fin)* official assignee, trustee (in bankruptcy), judicial factor *(US)* [2] *(Hist)* syndic [3] *(Helv = maire)* mayor

syndical, e (mpl **-aux**) /sɛ̃dikal, o/ ADJ [1] *(= des syndicats)* (trade-)union, labor-union *(US)* ◆ **le mouvement** ~ the trade-union *(Brit) ou* labor-union *(US)* movement ◆ **la liberté ~e** freedom for unions ◆ **400 euros est le minimum** ~ 400 euros is the legal minimum wage ◆ **il fait le minimum** ~ *(fig)* he doesn't do any more than he has to; → **central, chambre, tarif** [2] *(= du syndic)* **conseil ~ d'un immeuble** management committee of a block of flats *(Brit) ou* of an apartment building *(US)*

syndicalisation /sɛ̃dikalizasjɔ̃/ NF unionization

syndicaliser /sɛ̃dikalize/ ► conjug 1 ◄ VT to unionize ◆ **un secteur fortement syndicalisé** a highly unionized sector

syndicalisme /sɛ̃dikalism/ NM *(= mouvement)* trade unionism; *(= activité)* (trade-)union activities; *(= doctrine politique)* syndicalism ◆ **faire du** ~ to participate in (trade-)union activities, to be a (trade-)union activist

syndicaliste /sɛ̃dikalist/ NMF *(= responsable d'un syndicat)* (trade) union official, trade unionist; *(= doctrinaire)* syndicalist ADJ *[chef]* trade-union *(épith)*; *[doctrine, idéal]* unionist *(épith)*

syndicat /sɛ̃dika/ NM [1] *[de travailleurs]* (trade) union; *[d'employeurs]* union; *[de producteurs agricoles]* union ◆ ~ **de mineurs/de journalistes** miners'/journalists' union ◆ ~ **du crime** crime syndicate

[2] *(non professionnel)* association; → **comp**

COMP **syndicat de banques** banking syndicate

syndicat de communes association of communes

syndicat financier syndicate of financiers

syndicat d'initiative tourist (information) office *ou* bureau *ou* centre

syndicat interdépartemental association of regional authorities

syndicat de locataires tenants' association

syndicat ouvrier trade union

syndicat patronal employers' syndicate, federation of employers, bosses' union*

syndicat de propriétaires *(gén)* association of property owners; *(d'un même immeuble)* householders' association

> ⚠ Au sens de 'association de travailleurs', **syndicat** ne se traduit pas par le mot anglais **syndicate**.

syndicataire /sɛ̃dikatɛʀ/ ADJ of a syndicate NMF syndicate member

syndiqué, e /sɛ̃dike/ (ptp de **syndiquer**) ADJ belonging to a (trade) union ◆ **ouvrier** ~ union member ◆ **est-il ~ ?** is he in a *ou* the union?, is he a union man *ou* member? ◆ **les travailleurs non ~s** non-union *ou* non-unionized workers NM,F union member

syndiquer /sɛ̃dike/ ► conjug 1 ◄ VT to unionize VPR **se syndiquer** *(= se grouper)* to form a trade union, to unionize; *(= adhérer)* to join a trade union

syndrome /sɛ̃dʀom/ NM syndrome ◆ ~ **chinois** China syndrome ◆ **le ~ de Down** Down's syndrome ◆ ~ **de fatigue chronique** chronic fatigue syndrome ◆ ~ **d'immunodéficience acquise** acquired immuno-deficiency syndrome ◆ ~ **prémenstruel** premenstrual syndrome ◆ ~ **respiratoire aigu sévère** severe acute respiratory syndrome ◆ ~ **de la classe économique** economy class syndrome ◆ **il souffre d'un ~ dépressif** he suffers from a depressive syndrome

synecdoque /sinɛkdɔk/ NF synecdoche

synérèse /sineʀɛz/ NF *(Ling)* synaeresis; *(Chim)* syneresis

synergie /sinɛʀʒi/ NF synergy, synergism ◆ **travailler en** ~ to work in synergy *(avec* with); ◆ **opérer des ~s entre différents services** to bring about synergies between different departments

synergique /sinɛʀʒik/ ADJ synergetic

synesthésie /sinɛstezi/ NF synaesthesia

synode /sinɔd/ NM synod

synodique /sinɔdik/ ADJ *(Astron)* synodic(al); *(Rel)* synod(ic)al

synonyme /sinɔnim/ ADJ synonymous *(de* with) NM synonym

synonymie /sinɔnimi/ NF synonymy

synonymique /sinɔnimik/ ADJ synonymic(al)

synopsis /sinɔpsis/ NF *ou* m synopsis

synoptique /sinɔptik/ ADJ synoptic ◆ **les (Évangiles) ~s** the synoptic gospels

synovial, e (mpl **-iaux**) /sinɔvjal, jo/ ADJ synovial

synovie /sinɔvi/ NF synovia; → **épanchement**

synovite /sinɔvit/ NF synovitis

syntactique /sɛ̃taktik/ ADJ ⇒ **syntaxique**

syntagmatique /sɛ̃tagmatik/ ADJ syntagmatic, phrasal NF syntagmatic analysis

syntagme /sɛ̃tagm/ NM (word) group, phrase, syntagm *(SPÉC)* ◆ ~ **adjoint** adjunctive phrase, adjunct ◆ ~ **nominal** nominal group, noun phrase ◆ ~ **verbal** verb phrase

syntaxe /sɛ̃taks/ NF *(Ling, Ordin)* syntax ◆ **erreur de** ~ syntax error

syntaxique /sɛ̃taksik/ ADJ syntactic

synthé* /sɛ̃te/ NM (abrév de **synthétiseur**) synth*

synthèse /sɛ̃tɛz/ NF synthesis ◆ **faire la ~ d'un exposé** to summarize the major points of a talk ◆ ~ **vocale/de la parole** *(Ordin)* voice/speech synthesis

◆ **de synthèse** *[drogue, molécule, produit]* synthetic; *[édulcorant]* artificial ◆ **document de** ~ *(= résumé)* summary; → **esprit, image**

synthétique /sɛ̃tetik/ ADJ [1] *[textile, fibre]* synthetic, man-made; *[résine, caoutchouc, revêtement]* synthetic ◆ **matières ~s** synthetic materials, synthetics ◆ **c'est de la fourrure** ~ it's fake fur *ou* fun fur [2] *(= artificiel) [images, voix, son]* synthetic [3] *(= qui envisage la totalité) [exposé]* that gives an overall picture (of a subject); *[ouvrage]* that takes a global perspective ◆ **avoir l'esprit** ~ to be good at synthesizing information ◆ **avoir une vision ~ des choses** to (be able to) see the overall picture ◆ **présenter un sujet de façon** ~ to give an overall picture of a subject NM ◆ **le** ~ *(= tissus)* synthetics ◆ **c'est du** ~ it's synthetic ◆ **vêtement/chaussures en** ~ garment/shoes made of synthetic material

synthétiquement /sɛ̃tetikmɑ̃/ ADV synthetically

synthétiser /sɛ̃tetize/ ► conjug 1 ◄ VT to synthetize, to synthesize

synthétiseur /sɛ̃tetizœʀ/ NM synthesizer ◆ ~ **de (la) parole** speech synthesizer

syntonie /sɛ̃tɔni/ NF *(Psych)* syntonia; *(Phys)* syntonism

syntoniser /sɛ̃tɔnize/ ► conjug 1 ◄ VT to tune

syntoniseur /sɛ̃tɔnizœʀ/ NM tuner

syphilis /sifilis/ NF syphilis

syphilitique /sifilitik/ ADJ, NMF syphilitic

syriaque /siʀjak/ ADJ Syriac *(épith)* NM *(= langue)* Syriac

Syrie /siʀi/ NF Syria

syrien, -ienne /siʀjɛ̃, jɛn/ ADJ Syrian ◆ **République arabe syrienne** Syrian Arab Republic NM,F **Syrien(ne)** Syrian

systématique /sistematik/ ADJ *[opposition, classement, esprit]* systematic; *[soutien, aide]* unconditional ◆ **opposer un refus ~ à qch** to refuse sth systematically ◆ **avec l'intention ~ de nuire** systematically intending to harm ◆ **il est trop ~** he's too dogmatic, his views are too set ◆ **chaque fois qu'elle est invitée quelque part il l'est aussi, c'est ~** every time she's invited somewhere, he's automatically invited too NF *(gén)* systematics *(sg)*; *(Bio)* taxonomy

systématiquement /sistematikmɑ̃/ ADV systematically

systématisation /sistematizasjɔ̃/ NF systematization

systématiser /sistematize/ ▸ conjug 1 ◂ VT *[+ recherches, mesures]* to systematize ◆ **il n'a pas le sens de la nuance, il systématise (tout)** he has no sense of nuance – he systematizes everything VPR **se systématiser** to become the rule

système /sistɛm/ NM 1 *(gén) (= structure)* system ◆ **~ de vie** way of life, lifestyle ◆ **entrer dans le ~** *(= institution)* to join *ou* enter the system ◆ **~ casuel** *(Ling)* case system ◆ **troubles du ~** *(Méd)* systemic disorders; → **esprit**

2 *(= moyen)* system ◆ **il connaît un ~ pour entrer sans payer** he's got a system for getting in without paying ◆ **il connaît le ~** he knows the system ◆ **le meilleur ~, c'est de se relayer** the best plan *ou* system is to take turns

3 *(locutions)* **par ~** *[agir]* in a systematic way; *[contredire]* systematically ◆ **il me tape** *ou* **court** *ou* **porte sur le ~*** he gets on my nerves* *ou* wick* *(Brit)*

COMP **système ABS** ABS
système d'alarme alarm system
système d'alimentation *(électrique)* electricity supply system; *(en eau)* water supply system
système D* resourcefulness ◆ **recourir au ~ D** to rely on one's own resources, to fend for o.s.
système décimal decimal system
système de défense *(Mil)* defence system; *(Physiol)* defence mechanism
système d'éducation education system
système d'équations system of equations
système expert expert system
système d'exploitation operating system
système de gestion de bases de données database management system
système immunitaire immune system
Système international d'unités International System of Units
système métrique metric system
système monétaire européen European monetary system
système nerveux nervous system ◆ **~ nerveux central/périphérique** central/peripheral nervous system
système pénitentiaire prison *ou* penal system
système pileux ◆ **avoir un ~ pileux très développé** to have a lot of body hair
système respiratoire respiratory system
système de santé health system
système de sécurité sociale social security system
système solaire solar system
système de traitement de l'information data-processing system

systémique /sistemik/ ADJ systemic NF systems analysis

systole /sistɔl/ NF systole

systolique /sistɔlik/ ADJ systolic

syzygie /siziʒi/ NF syzygy

T t

T, t¹ /te/ NM ① *(= lettre)* T, t ◆ **en T** *[table, immeuble]* T-shaped ◆ **bandage/antenne/équerre en T** T-bandage/-aerial/-square ② *(Méd)* **T4** T4

t² ① (abrév de **tonne**) t ② (abrév de **tome**) vol.

t' /t/ → **te, tu**

ta /ta/ ADJ POSS → **ton¹**

ta, ta, ta /tatata/ EXCL (stuff and) nonsense!, rubbish!

tabac /taba/ NM ① *(= plante, produit)* tobacco; *(= couleur)* buff, tobacco (brown); → **blague, bureau, débit** ② *(= commerce)* tobacconist's; *(= bar) café with a cigarette counter* ③ *(* : locutions)* **passer qn à ~** to beat sb up ◆ **faire un ~** to be a big hit *ou* a roaring success, to hit it big* *(US)* ◆ **quelque chose du même ~** something like that; → **passage**

◆ **coup de tabac** squall

ADJ INV buff, tobacco (brown)

COMP **tabac blond** light *ou* mild *ou* Virginia tobacco
tabac brun dark tobacco
tabac à chiquer chewing tobacco
tabac gris shag
tabac à priser snuff

tabacologie /tabakɔlɔʒi/ NF study of tobacco addiction ◆ **spécialiste de ~** specialist in tobacco addiction

tabacologue /tabakɔlɔg/ NMF specialist in tobacco addiction

tabagie /tabaʒi/ NF *(= lieu enfumé)* smoke-filled room; *(au Canada = bureau de tabac)* tobacconist's (shop) *(Brit)*, tobacco *ou* smoke shop *(US)* ◆ **ce bureau, quelle ~ !** it's really smoky in this office!

tabagique /tabaʒik/ ADJ *[consommation, publicité]* tobacco *(épith)* ◆ **dépendance ~** tobacco *ou* nicotine addiction, addiction to smoking ◆ **afin de faciliter le sevrage ~** to make it easier to give up smoking NMF chain smoker

tabagisme /tabaʒism/ NM nicotine addiction, addiction to smoking ◆ **~ passif** passive smoking ◆ **lutte contre le ~** anti-smoking campaign

tabasco ® /tabasko/ NM Tabasco (sauce) ®

tabasser* /tabase/ ► conjug 1 ◄ VT *(= passer à tabac)* ◆ **~ qn** to beat sb up ◆ **se faire ~** to get beaten up *(par by)* VPR **se tabasser** *(= se bagarrer)* to have a fight *ou* punch-up* *(Brit)*

tabatière /tabatjɛʀ/ NF ① *(= boîte)* snuffbox ◆ **~ anatomique** anatomical snuffbox ② *(= lucarne)* skylight; → **fenêtre**

T.A.B.D.T. /teabedete/ NM (abrév de **vaccin antityphoïdique et anti-paratyphoïdique A et B, antidiphtérique et tétanique**) *vaccine against typhoid, paratyphoid A and B, diphtheria and tetanus*

tabellion /tabeljɔ̃/ NM *(hum péj : = notaire)* lawyer

tabernacle /tabɛʀnakl/ NM *(Rel)* tabernacle

tablar(d) /tablaʀ/ NM *(Helv = étagère)* shelf

tablature /tablatyʀ/ NF *(Mus)* tablature

table /tabl/ NF ① *(= meuble)* table ◆ **~ de salle à manger/de cuisine/de billard** dining-room/kitchen/billiard table ◆ **~ de** *ou* **en bois/marbre** wooden/marble table ◆ **s'asseoir à la ~ des grands** to play with the big boys* *ou* in the major league *(US)*; → **dessous, carte, tennis**

② *(pour le repas)* **mettre** *ou* *(littér)* **dresser la ~** to lay *ou* set the table ◆ **débarrasser** *ou* *(littér)* **desservir la ~** to clear the table ◆ **présider la ~** to sit at the head of the table ◆ **recevoir qn à sa ~** to have sb to lunch *(ou dinner etc)* ◆ **se lever de ~** to get up from the table ◆ **quitter la ~, sortir de ~** to leave the table ◆ **~ de 12 couverts** table set for 12 ◆ **une ~ pour quatre** *(au restaurant)* a table for four ◆ **linge/vin/propos de ~** table linen/wine/talk ◆ **tenir ~ ouverte** to keep open house

◆ **à table** ◆ **être à ~** to be having a meal, to be eating ◆ **nous étions huit à ~** there were eight of us at *ou* round the table ◆ **à ~ !** come and eat!, dinner *(ou lunch etc)* is ready! ◆ **si vous voulez bien passer à ~** if you'd like to come through ◆ **se mettre à ~** to sit down to eat, to sit down at the table; *(* = avouer)* to talk, to come clean*

③ *(= tablée)* table ◆ **toute la ~ éclata de rire** everyone round the table *ou* the whole table burst out laughing ◆ **soldats et officiers mangeaient à la même ~** soldiers and officers ate at the same table

④ *(= restaurant)* restaurant ◆ **une des meilleures ~s de Lyon** one of the best restaurants in Lyons ◆ **avoir une bonne ~** to keep a good table; *[restaurant]* to serve very good food ◆ **aimer (les plaisirs de) la ~** to enjoy one's food

⑤ *(= tablette avec inscriptions)* **~ de marbre** marble tablet ◆ **les Tables de la Loi** the Tables of the Law ◆ **la Loi des Douze Tables** *(Antiq)* the Twelve Tables

⑥ *(= liste)* table ◆ **~ de logarithmes/de multiplication** log/multiplication table ◆ **~ de vérité** truth table ◆ **~ alphabétique** alphabetical table ◆ **il sait sa ~ de 8** he knows his 8 times table

⑦ *(Géol = plateau)* tableland, plateau

COMP **table à abattants** drop-leaf table
table anglaise gate-legged table
table d'architecte drawing board
table d'autel altar stone
table basse coffee table, occasional table
table de bridge card *ou* bridge table
table à cartes *(Naut)* chart house
table de chevet bedside table, night stand *ou* table *(US)*
table de communion communion table
table de conférence conference table
table de cuisson hob
table à dessin drawing board
table à digitaliser digitizer
table d'écoute wire-tapping set ◆ **mettre qn sur ~ d'écoute** to tap sb's phone
tables gigognes nest of tables
table d'harmonie sounding board
table d'honneur top table
table d'hôte table d'hôte ◆ **faire ~ d'hôte** to serve table d'hôte dinners, to serve dinner for residents
table de jeu gaming table
table de lancement launch(ing) pad
table à langer changing table
table de lecture *[de chaîne hi-fi]* turntable
table lumineuse light table
table de malade bedtable
table des matières (table of) contents
table de Mendeleïev Mendeleyev's periodic table
table de mixage mixing desk
la table des négociations the negotiating table
table de nuit ⇒ **table de chevet**
table d'opération operating table
table d'orientation viewpoint indicator
table à ouvrage worktable
table de ping-pong table-tennis table
table pliante folding table
table de Pythagore Pythagorean table
table à rallonges extending table
table rase *(Philos)* tabula rasa ◆ **faire ~ rase** to make a clean sweep *(de of)*; ◆ **on a fait ~ rase du passé** we put the past behind us
table à repasser ironing board
table ronde *(lit)* round table; *(fig)* round table, panel
la Table ronde *(Hist)* the Round Table
table roulante trolley *(Brit)*, cart *(US)*
table de survie life table
tables de tir range tables
table de toilette *(pour lavabo)* washstand; *(= coiffeuse)* dressing table
table tournante séance table
table traçante *(Ordin)* (graph) plotter
table de travail work table

tableau (pl **tableaux**) /tablo/ NM ① *(= peinture)* painting; *(= reproduction, gravure)* picture ◆ **exposition de ~x** art exhibition; → **galerie**

② *(= scène)* picture, scene ◆ **le ~ l'émut au plus haut point** he was deeply moved by the scene ◆ **un ~ tragique/idyllique** a tragic/an idyllic picture *ou* scene ◆ **le ~ changeant de la vallée du Rhône** the changing landscape of the Rhone valley

3 *(Théât)* scene ◆ **acte un, premier ~** act one, scene one

4 *(= description)* picture ◆ **un ~ de la guerre** a picture *ou* depiction of war ◆ **il m'a fait un ~ très noir de la situation** he drew a very black picture of the situation for me

5 *(Scol)* **~ (noir)** (black)board ◆ **~ blanc** (white)board ◆ **aller au ~** *(lit)* to go up to the blackboard; *(= se faire interroger)* to be asked questions *(on a school subject)*

6 *(= support mural) [de sonneries]* board; *[de fusibles]* box; *[de clés]* rack, board

7 *(= panneau)* board; *(Rail)* train indicator; *[de bateau]* escutcheon, name board ◆ **~ des départs/arrivées** departure(s)/arrival(s) board ◆ **~ des horaires** timetable

8 *(= carte, graphique)* table, chart; *(Ordin : fait par tableur)* spreadsheet ◆ **~ généalogique/chronologique** genealogical/chronological table *ou* chart ◆ **~ des conjugaisons** conjugation table, table of conjugations ◆ **présenter qch sous forme de ~** to show sth in tabular form

9 *(Admin = liste)* register, list ◆ **~ de l'ordre des avocats** ≈ register of the association of barristers ◆ **médicament au ~ A/B/C** class A/B/C drug *(according to French classification of toxicity)*

10 *(locutions)* **vous voyez (d'ici) le ~ !** you can (just) imagine! ◆ **pour compléter** *ou* **achever le ~** to cap it all ◆ **jouer** *ou* **miser sur les deux ~x** to hedge one's bets ◆ **il a gagné sur les deux/sur tous les ~x** he won on both/on all counts

COMP **tableau d'affichage** *(gén)* notice board; *(Sport)* scoreboard
tableau d'amortissement depreciation schedule
tableau d'avancement *(Admin)* promotion table
tableau de bord *[de voiture]* dashboard; *[d'avion, bateau]* instrument panel; *[d'économie]* (performance) indicators
tableau de chasse *[de chasseur]* bag; *[d'aviateur]* tally of kills; *[de séducteur]* list of conquests ◆ **ajouter qch à son ~ de chasse** to add sth to one's list of successes
tableau clinique clinical picture
tableau électronique *(gén)* electronic noticeboard; *(Sport)* electronic scoreboard
tableau d'honneur merit *ou* prize list *(Brit)*, honor roll *(US)* ◆ **être inscrit au ~ d'honneur** to appear on the merit *ou* prize list *(Brit)*, to make the honor roll *(US)* ◆ **au ~ d'honneur du sport français cette semaine, Luc Legrand ...** pride of place in French sport this week goes to Luc Legrand ...
tableau de maître masterpiece
tableau de marche schedule
tableau de service *(gén)* work notice board; *(= horaire de service)* duty roster
tableau synchronique synchronic table of events *etc*
tableau synoptique synoptic table
tableau vivant *(Théât)* tableau (vivant)

tableautin /tablotɛ̃/ NM little picture

tablée /table/ NF table *(of people)* ◆ **toute la ~ éclata de rire** the whole table *ou* everyone round the table burst out laughing

tabler /table/ ▸ conjug 1 ◂ **tabler sur** VT INDIR ◆ **~ sur qch** to count *ou* bank on sth ◆ **il avait tablé sur une baisse des taux** he had counted *ou* banked on the rates going down ◆ **table sur ton travail plutôt que sur la chance** rely on your work rather than on luck

tablette /tablɛt/ NF 1 *(= plaquette) [de chocolat]* bar; *[de médicament]* tablet; *[de chewing-gum]* stick; *[de métal]* block ◆ **~ de bouillon** stock cube 2 *(= planchette, rayon) [de lavabo, radiateur, cheminée]* shelf; *[de secrétaire]* flap ◆ **~ à glissière** pull-out flap 3 *(Archéol, Hist : pour écrire)* tablet ◆ **~ de cire/d'argile** wax/clay tablet ◆ **je vais l'inscrire sur mes ~s** *(hum)* I'll make a note of it ◆ **ce n'est pas écrit sur mes ~s** *(hum)* I have no record of it 4 *(Ordin)* tablet ◆ **~ graphique** graphic tablet

tableur /tablœʀ/ NM spreadsheet (program)

tablier /tablije/ NM 1 *(Habillement) (gén)* apron; *(pour ménage) (sans manches)* apron, pinafore; *(avec manches)* overall; *[d'écolier]* overall, smock ◆ **rendre son ~** *[domestique]* to hand *ou* give in one's notice; *[homme politique]* to resign, to step down ◆ **ça lui va comme un ~ à une vache** * *[vêtement]* it looks really weird on him; *[poste]* he's totally out of place in that job ◆ **~ de sapeur** *(Culin)* tripe in breadcrumbs 2 *[de pont]* roadway 3 *(Tech = plaque protectrice) [de cheminée]* (flue-)shutter; *[de magasin]* (iron *ou* steel) shutter; *[de machine-outil]* apron; *[de scooter]* fairing; *(entre moteur et habitacle d'un véhicule)* bulkhead

tabloïd(e) /tablɔid/ ADJ, NM tabloid

tabou, e /tabu/ ADJ taboo ◆ **sujet ~** taboo subject ◆ **une société où la sexualité reste ~(e)** a society where sexuality is still taboo NM taboo ◆ **briser un ~** to break a taboo

taboulé /tabule/ NM tabbouleh

tabouret /tabuʀɛ/ NM *(pour s'asseoir)* stool; *(pour les pieds)* footstool ◆ **~ de piano/de bar** piano/bar stool

tabulaire /tabylɛʀ/ ADJ tabular

tabulateur /tabylatœʀ/ NM tab key, tabulator

tabulation /tabylasjɔ̃/ NF tabulation ◆ **poser des ~s** to set tabs

tabulatrice /tabylatʀis/ NF tabulator *(for punched cards)*

tabuler /tabyle/ ▸ conjug 1 ◂ VT to tabulate, to tabularize, to tab

tac /tak/ NM 1 *(= bruit)* tap ◆ **le ~ ~ des mitrailleuses** the rat-a-tat(-tat) of the machine guns; → **tic-tac** 2 ◆ **il répond** *ou* **riposte du ~ au ~** he always has a ready answer ◆ **il lui a répondu du ~ au ~ que ...** he came back at him immediately *ou* quick as a flash that ...

tache /taʃ/ NF 1 *(= moucheture) [de fruit]* mark; *[de léopard]* spot; *[de plumage, pelage]* mark(ing), spot; *[de peau]* blotch, mark ◆ **les ~s des ongles** the white marks on the fingernails ◆ **faire ~** *[bâtiment, personne]* to stick out like a sore thumb

2 *(= salissure)* stain, mark ◆ **~ de graisse** greasy mark, grease stain ◆ **~ de brûlure/de suie** burn/sooty mark ◆ **des draps couverts de ~s** sheets covered in stains ◆ **sa robe n'avait pas une ~** her dress was spotless ◆ **il a fait une ~ à sa cravate** he got a stain on his tie ◆ **tu t'es fait une ~** you've got a stain on your shirt *(ou dress ou tie etc)*

3 *(littér = flétrissure)* blot, stain ◆ **c'est une ~ à sa réputation** it's a blot *ou* stain on his reputation ◆ **sans ~** *[vie, réputation]* spotless, unblemished; → **agneau, pur**

4 *(= impression visuelle)* patch, spot ◆ **le soleil parsemait la campagne de ~s d'or** the sun scattered patches of gold over the countryside ◆ **des ~s d'ombre çà et là** patches of shadow here and there

5 *(Peinture)* spot, blob ◆ **~ de couleur** patch of colour

6 *(‡ = nullité)* jerk ‡

COMP **tache d'encre** *(sur les doigts)* ink stain; *(sur le papier)* (ink) blot *ou* blotch
tache d'huile oily mark, oil stain ◆ **faire ~ d'huile** to spread, to gain ground
tache jaune (de l'œil) yellow spot (of the eye)
tache originelle *(Rel)* stain of original sin
tache de rousseur freckle ◆ **visage couvert de ~s de rousseur** freckled face, face covered in freckles
tache de sang bloodstain
tache solaire *(Astron)* sunspot
tache de son ⇒ **tache de rousseur**
tache de vin *(sur la nappe)* wine stain; *(sur la peau = envie)* strawberry mark

tâche /taʃ/ NF *(= besogne)* task, work *(NonC)*; *(= mission)* task, job; *(Ordin)* task ◆ **il a la lourde ~ de ...** he has the difficult task of ... ◆ **il a pour ~ de ...** his task is to ... ◆ **assigner une ~ à qn** to give *ou* set *(Brit)* sb a task ◆ **s'atteler à une ~** to get down to work ◆ **~ de fond** *ou* **d'arrière-plan** *(Ordin)* background task
◆ **à la tâche** *[payer]* by the piece ◆ **ouvrier à la ~** pieceworker ◆ **travail à la ~** piecework ◆ **être à la ~** to be on piecework ◆ **je ne suis pas à la ~** * I'll do it in my own good time ◆ **mourir à la ~** to die in harness

tachéomètre /takeɔmɛtʀ/ NM *(= théodolite)* tacheometer, tachymeter

tachéométrie /takeɔmetʀi/ NF tacheometry

tacher /taʃe/ ▸ conjug 1 ◂ VT 1 *[encre, vin]* to stain; *[graisse]* to mark, to stain ◆ **le café tache** coffee stains (badly) *ou* leaves a stain ◆ **taché de sang** bloodstained 2 *(littér = colorer) [+ pré, robe]* to spot, to dot; *[+ peau, fourrure]* to spot, to mark ◆ **pelage blanc taché de noir** white coat with black spots *ou* markings, white coat flecked with black 3 *(† = souiller)* to tarnish, to sully VPR **se tacher** 1 *(= se salir) [personne]* to get stains on one's clothes, to get o.s. dirty; *[nappe, tissu]* to get stained *ou* marked ◆ **tissu qui se tache facilement** fabric that stains *ou* marks easily 2 *(= s'abîmer) [fruits]* to become marked

tâcher /taʃe/ ▸ conjug 1 ◂ VT INDIR **tâcher de** *(= essayer de)* **~ de faire qch** to try *ou* endeavour *(frm)* to do sth ◆ **tâchez de venir avant samedi** try to *ou* try and come before Saturday ◆ **et tâche de ne pas recommencer !** * and make sure *ou* mind it doesn't happen again! ◆ **~ moyen de faire qch** * to try to do sth VT ◆ **tâche qu'il n'en sache rien** * make sure that he doesn't get to know about it

tâcheron /taʃ(ə)ʀɔ̃/ NM 1 *(péj)* drudge ◆ **un ~ de la littérature/politique** a literary/political drudge *ou* hack 2 *(= ouvrier) (dans le bâtiment)* jobber; *(agricole)* pieceworker

tacheter /taʃ(ə)te/ ▸ conjug 4 ◂ VT *[+ peau, fourrure]* to spot, to speckle; *[+ tissu, champ]* to spot, to dot, to fleck ◆ **pelage blanc tacheté de brun** white coat with brown spots *ou* markings, white coat flecked with brown

tachisme /taʃism/ NM *(= art abstrait)* tachisme

tachiste /taʃist/ ADJ, NMF tachiste

Tachkent /taʃkɛnt/ N Tashkent

tachycardie /takikaʀdi/ NF tachycardia

tachygraphe /takigʀaf/ NM tachograph, black box

tachymètre /takimɛtʀ/ NM tachometer

Tacite /tasit/ NM Tacitus

tacite /tasit/ ADJ tacit ◆ **par ~ reconduction** by tacit agreement

tacitement /tasitmɑ̃/ ADV tacitly ◆ **reconduit ~** renewed by tacit agreement

taciturne /tasityʀn/ ADJ taciturn, silent

tacle /takl/ NM *(Sport)* tackle ◆ **faire un ~** to make a tackle ◆ **faire un ~ à qn** to tackle sb

taco /tako/ NM *(Culin)* taco

tacot * /tako/ NM *(= voiture)* jalopy *, old rattletrap *, banger * *(Brit)*

tact /takt/ NM 1 *(= délicatesse)* tact ◆ **avoir du ~** to have tact, to be tactful ◆ **homme de ~/sans ~** tactful/tactless man ◆ **faire qch avec/sans ~** to do sth tactfully/tactlessly ◆ **manquer de**

~ to be tactless, to be lacking in tact [2] († = *toucher*) touch, tact (††)

tacticien, -ienne /taktisjɛ̃, jɛn/ NM,F tactician

tactile /taktil/ ADJ (= *physique*) tactile ◆ **écran** ~ touch screen ◆ **pavé** ~ touch pad, trackpad

tactique /taktik/ ADJ (*gén, Mil*) tactical ◆ **ils ont un jeu très** ~ they play a very tactical game NF tactics ◆ **changer de** ~ to change (one's) tactics ◆ **il y a plusieurs ~s possibles** there are several different tactics one might adopt ◆ **la ~ de l'adversaire est très simple** the opponent's tactics are very simple ◆ **ce n'est pas la meilleure ~ pour le faire céder** it's not the best way to get him to give in

tactiquement /taktikmɑ̃/ ADV tactically

TAD /teade/ NMF (abrév de **travailleur/travailleuse à domicile**) → **travailleur**

tadjik /tadʒik/ ADJ Tadzhiki NM (= *langue*) Tadzhiki NMF **Tadjik** Tadzhik, Tadjik, Tajik

Tadjikistan /tadʒikistɑ̃/ NM Tadzhikistan

tænia /tenja/ NM ⇒ **ténia**

taf, taffe * /taf/ NM (= *travail*) work ◆ **j'ai pas mal de** ~ I've got quite a bit of work

taffe * /taf/ NF [*de cigarette*] drag *, puff; [*de pipe*] puff

taffetas /tafta/ NM (= *tissu*) taffeta ◆ **robe de** ~ taffeta dress ◆ ~ **(gommé)** sticking plaster (*Brit*), bandaid ®

tag /tag/ NM (= *graffiti*) tag

Tage /taʒ/ NM ◆ **le** ~ the Tagus

tagine /taʒin/ NM ⇒ **tajine**

tagliatelles /taljatɛl/ NFPL tagliatelle (*NonC*)

taguer /tage/ ▸ conjug 1 ◂ VTI (= *faire des graffiti*) to tag

tagueur, -euse /tagœʀ, øz/ NM,F tagger

Tahiti /taiti/ NF Tahiti

tahitien, -ienne /taisjɛ̃, jɛn/ ADJ Tahitian NM,F **Tahitien(ne)** Tahitian

taïaut †† /tajo/ EXCL tallyho!

taie /tɛ/ NF [1] ◆ ~ **(d'oreiller)** pillowcase, pillowslip ◆ ~ **de traversin** bolster case [2] (*Méd*) opaque spot, leucoma (*SPÉC*)

taïga /tajga/ NF taiga

taillable /tajabl/ ADJ ◆ ~ **et corvéable (à merci)** (*Hist*) subject to tallage; [*employés, main d'œuvre*] who can be exploited at will

taillade /tajad/ NF (*dans la chair*) gash, slash; (*dans un tronc d'arbre*) gash

taillader /tajade/ ▸ conjug 1 ◂ VT to slash, to gash ◆ **se ~ les poignets** to slash one's wrists

taillanderie /tajɑ̃dʀi/ NF (= *fabrication*) edge-tool making; (= *outils*) edge-tools

taillandier /tajɑ̃dje/ NM edge-tool maker

taille[1] /taj/ NF [1] (= *hauteur*) [*de personne, cheval, objet*] height ◆ **être de petite** ~ [*personne*] to be short *ou* small; [*animal*] to be small ◆ **homme de petite** ~ short *ou* small man ◆ **les personnes de petite** ~ small people (*especially dwarves and midgets*) ◆ **homme de ~ moyenne** man of average *ou* medium height ◆ **homme de grande** ~ tall man ◆ **ils sont de la même ~, ils ont la même** ~ they're the same height ◆ **il a atteint sa ~ adulte** he's fully grown

[2] (= *grosseur, volume*) size ◆ **de petite** ~ small ◆ **de ~ moyenne** medium-sized ◆ **de grande** ~ large, big ◆ **un chien de belle** ~ quite a big *ou* large dog ◆ **le paquet est de la ~ d'une boîte à chaussures** the parcel is the size of a shoebox ◆ ~ **de mémoire** (*Ordin*) memory capacity

[3] (= *mesure*) size ◆ **les grandes/petites ~s** large/small sizes ◆ ~ **40** size 40 ◆ **"taille unique"** "one size (fits all)" ◆ **il ne reste plus de ~s moyennes** there are no medium sizes *ou* mediums left ◆ **il lui faut la ~ au-dessous/au-dessus** he needs the next size down/up, he needs one *ou* a size smaller/larger ◆ **deux ~s au-dessous/au-dessus** two sizes smaller/larger ◆ **ce pantalon n'est pas à sa** ~ these trousers aren't his size, these trousers don't fit him ◆ **avez-vous quelque chose dans ma ~ ?** do you have anything in my size? ◆ **si je trouvais quelqu'un de ma** ~ if I found someone my size ◆ **avoir la ~ mannequin** to have a perfect figure

[4] (*locutions*)

◆ **à la taille de** (= *proportionnel à*) ◆ **c'est un poste à sa** ~ it's a job which matches his capabilities ◆ **il a trouvé un adversaire à sa** ~ he's met his match

◆ **de taille** [*erreur*] serious, major; [*objet*] sizeable; [*surprise, concession, décision*] big; [*difficulté, obstacle*] huge, big ◆ **la gaffe est de ~ !** it's a major blunder! ◆ **l'enjeu est de** ~ the stakes are high ◆ **il n'est pas de** ~ (*pour une tâche*) he isn't up *ou* equal to it; (*face à un concurrent, dans la vie*) he doesn't measure up

◆ **être de taille à faire qch** to be up to doing sth, to be quite capable of doing sth

[5] (= *partie du corps*) waist; (= *partie du vêtement*) waist, waistband ◆ **elle n'a pas de** ~ she has no waist(line), she doesn't go in at the waist ◆ **avoir la ~ fine** to have a slim waist, to be slim-waisted ◆ **avoir une ~ de guêpe** to have an hour-glass figure, to have a wasp waist ◆ **avoir la ~ bien prise** to have a neat waist(line) ◆ **prendre qn par la** ~ to put one's arm round sb's waist ◆ **ils se tenaient par la** ~ they had their arms round each other's waists ◆ **avoir de l'eau jusqu'à la** ~ to be in water up to one's waist, to be waist-deep in water ◆ **robe serrée à la** ~ dress fitted at the waist ◆ **robe à ~ basse/haute** low-/high-waisted dress ◆ **pantalon (à) ~ basse** low-waisted trousers, hipsters; → **tour²**

taille[2] /taj/ NF [1] [*de pierre précieuse*] cutting; [*de pierre*] cutting, hewing; [*de bois*] carving; [*de verre*] engraving; [*de crayon*] sharpening; [*d'arbre, vigne*] pruning, cutting back; [*de haie*] trimming, clipping, cutting; [*de tissu*] cutting (out); [*de cheveux, barbe*] trimming ◆ **diamant de ~ hexagonale/en étoile** diamond with a six-sided/star-shaped cut; → **pierre** [2] (= *taillis*) ~s coppice [3] (= *tranchant*) [*d'épée, sabre*] edge ◆ **il a reçu un coup de** ~ he was hit with the sharp edge of the sword; → **frapper** [4] (= *cystotomie*) cystotomy [5] (*Hist* = *redevance*) tallage, taille [6] (*Min* = *galerie*) tunnel

taillé, e /taje/ (ptp de **tailler**) ADJ [1] (= *bâti*) **il est ~ en athlète** [*personne*] he's built like an athlete, he has an athletic build [2] (= *destiné à*) [*personne*] ~ **pour être/faire** cut out to be/do ◆ ~ **pour qch** cut out for sth [3] (= *coupé*) [*arbre*] pruned; [*haie*] clipped, trimmed; [*moustache, barbe*] trimmed ◆ **crayon ~ en pointe** pencil sharpened to a point ◆ **verre/cristal** ~ cut glass/crystal ◆ **costume bien** ~ well-cut suit ◆ **il avait les cheveux ~s en brosse** he had a crew-cut ◆ **visage ~ à la serpe** rough-hewn *ou* craggy features; → **âge**

taille-crayon (pl **taille-crayons**) /tajkʀɛjɔ̃/ NM pencil sharpener

taille-douce (pl **tailles-douces**) /tajdus/ NF (= *technique, estampe*) copperplate ◆ **gravure en** ~ copperplate engraving

taille-haie (pl **taille-haies**) /tajɛ/ NM hedge trimmer

tailler /taje/ ▸ conjug 1 ◂ VT [1] (= *couper*) [+ *pierre précieuse*] to cut; [+ *pierre*] to cut, to hew; [+ *bois*] to carve; [+ *verre*] to engrave; [+ *crayon*] to sharpen; [+ *arbre, vigne*] to prune, to cut back; [+ *haie*] to trim, to clip, to cut; [+ *tissu*] to cut (out); [+ *barbe, cheveux*] to trim ◆ ~ **qch en pointe** to cut sth to a point ◆ **bien taillé** [*haie*] neatly trimmed *ou* clipped; [*moustache*] neatly trimmed; [*crayon*] well-sharpened ◆ ~ **un if en cône** to trim *ou* clip a yew tree into a cone shape; → **serpe**

[2] (= *confectionner*) [+ *vêtement*] to make; [+ *statue*] to carve; [+ *tartines*] to cut, to slice; (*Alpinisme*) [+ *marche*] to cut ◆ **il a un rôle taillé à sa mesure** *ou* **sur mesure** the role is tailor-made for him

[3] (*locutions*) ~ **une bavette** * to have a natter * (*Brit*) *ou* a rap * (*US*) ◆ ~ **des croupières à qn** († *ou littér*) to make difficulties for sb ◆ ~ **une armée en pièces** to hack an army to pieces ◆ **il s'est fait ~ en pièces par les journalistes** the journalists tore him to pieces ◆ **il préférerait se faire ~ en pièces plutôt que de révéler son secret** he'd go through fire *ou* he'd suffer tortures rather than reveal his secret ◆ ~ **un costard** *ou* **une veste à qn** * to run sb down behind their back * ◆ **attention ! tu vas te faire ~ un short** * careful! you'll get flattened! * ◆ ~ **la route** * to hit the road *

VI [1] [*vêtement, marque*] ~ **petit/grand** to be cut on the small/large side

[2] (= *couper*) ~ **dans la chair** *ou* **dans le vif** to cut into the flesh ◆ ~ **dans les dépenses** to make cuts in expenditure

VPR **se tailler** [1] (= *se couper*) **se ~ la moustache** to trim one's moustache ◆ **elle s'est taillé une robe dans un coupon de taffetas** she made a dress for herself from a remnant of taffeta

[2] (= *se faire*) **se ~ une belle part de marché** to carve o.s. *ou* corner a large share of the market ◆ **il s'est taillé une réputation d'honnêteté/de manager** he has earned a reputation for honesty/as a manager ◆ **se ~ un beau** *ou* **franc succès** to be a great success ◆ **se ~ la part du lion** to take the lion's share ◆ **se ~ un empire/une place** to carve out an empire/a place for o.s.

[3] (* = *partir*) to beat it *, to clear off *, to split * ◆ **taille-toi !** beat it! *, clear off! * ◆ **allez, on se taille !** come on, let's split! * ◆ **il est onze heures, je me taille** it's eleven o'clock, I'm off * ◆ **j'ai envie de me ~ de cette boîte** I want to get out of this place

tailleur /tajœʀ/ NM [1] (= *couturier*) tailor ◆ ~ **pour dames** ladies' tailor [2] (= *costume*) (lady's) suit ◆ ~**-pantalon** trouser suit (*Brit*), pantsuit (*surtout US*) ◆ **un ~ Chanel** a Chanel suit [3] (*locutions*)

◆ **en tailleur** [*assis, s'asseoir*] cross-legged

COMP **tailleur de diamants** diamond-cutter
tailleur à façon bespoke tailor (*Brit*), custom tailor (*US*)
tailleur de pierre(s) stone-cutter
tailleur de verre glass engraver
tailleur de vignes vine pruner

taillis /taji/ NM copse, coppice, thicket ◆ **dans les** ~ in the copse *ou* coppice *ou* thicket

tain /tɛ̃/ NM [1] [*de miroir*] silvering ◆ **glace sans** ~ two-way mirror [2] (*Tech* = *bain*) tin bath

T'ai-pei /tajpɛ/ N Taipei, T'ai-pei

taire /tɛʀ/ ▸ conjug 54 ◂ VPR **se taire** [1] (= *être silencieux*) [*personne*] to be silent *ou* quiet; (*littér*) [*nature, forêt*] to be silent, to be still; [*vent*] to be still; [*bruit*] to disappear ◆ **les élèves se taisaient** the pupils kept *ou* were quiet *ou* silent ◆ **taisez-vous !** be quiet!, (*plus fort*) shut up! ◆ **ils ne voulaient pas se** ~ they wouldn't stop talking ◆ **les dîneurs se sont tus** the diners stopped talking, the diners fell silent ◆ **l'orchestre s'était tu** the orchestra had fallen silent *ou* was silent

[2] (= *s'abstenir de s'exprimer*) to keep quiet, to remain silent ◆ **dans ces cas il vaut mieux se** ~ in these cases it's best to keep quiet *ou* to remain silent *ou* to say nothing ◆ **il sait se** ~ he can keep a secret ◆ **se ~ sur qch** to say nothing *ou* keep quiet about sth ◆ **tais-toi !** * (= *ne m'en parle pas*) don't talk to me about it!

VT 1 *(= passer sous silence) [+ fait, vérité, raisons]* to keep silent about ◆ **une personne dont je tairai le nom** a person who shall be *ou* remain nameless ◆ ~ **la vérité, c'est déjà mentir** not telling the truth is as good as lying ◆ **il a préféré ~ le reste de l'histoire** he preferred not to reveal the rest of the story

2 *(= garder pour soi) [+ douleur, amertume]* to conceal, to keep to o.s. ◆ ~ **son chagrin** to hide one's grief

VI ◆ **faire ~** *[+ témoin gênant, opposition, récriminations]* to silence; *[+ craintes, désirs]* to suppress; *[+ scrupules, réticences]* to overcome ◆ **fais ~ les enfants** make the children keep *ou* be quiet, make the children shut up*

taiseux, -euse /tɛzø, øz/ *(Belg, Can)* **ADJ** taciturn **NM,F** taciturn person

Taiwan, Taïwan /tajwan/ **N** Taiwan

taiwanais, e, taïwanais, e /tajwanɛ, ɛz/ **ADJ** Taiwanese **NM,F** **Taiwanais(e), Taïwanais(e)** Taiwanese

tajine /taʒin/ **NM** *(= récipient)* earthenware cooking pot; *(= plat cuisiné) North African stew*

talc /talk/ **NM** *[de toilette]* talc, talcum powder; *(Chim)* talc(um)

talé, e /tale/ (ptp de **taler**) **ADJ** *[fruits]* bruised

talent[1] /talɑ̃/ **NM** 1 *(= disposition, aptitude)* talent ◆ **il a des ~s dans tous les domaines** he's multitalented ◆ **un ~ littéraire** a literary talent ◆ **il n'a pas le métier d'un professionnel mais un beau ~ d'amateur** he's not a professional but he's a talented amateur ◆ **montreznous vos ~s** * *(hum)* show us what you can do ◆ **décidément, vous avez tous les ~s !** what a talented young man *(ou* woman *etc)* you are! ◆ **ses ~s d'imitateur/d'organisateur** his talents *ou* gifts as an impersonator/as an organizer

2 ◆ **le ~** talent ◆ **avoir du ~** to have talent, to be talented ◆ **avoir beaucoup de ~** to have a great deal of talent, to be highly talented ◆ **auteur de (grand) ~** (highly) talented author

3 *(= personnes douées)* **~s** talent *(NonC)* ◆ **encourager les jeunes ~s** to encourage young talent ◆ **faire appel aux ~s disponibles** to call on (all) the available talent

4 *(iro)* **il a le ~ de se faire des ennemis** he has a talent *ou* gift for making enemies

talent[2] /talɑ̃/ **NM** *(= monnaie)* talent

talentueusement /talɑ̃tɥøzmɑ̃/ **ADV** with talent

talentueux, -euse /talɑ̃tɥø, øz/ **ADJ** talented

taler /tale/ ▸ conjug 1 ◂ **VT** *[+ fruits]* to bruise

taleth /talɛt/ **NM** ⇒ **talith**

taliban /talibɑ̃/ **ADJ** Taliban **NM** **Taliban** Taliban ◆ **les ~** the Taliban

talion /taljɔ̃/ **NM** → **loi**

talisman /talismɑ̃/ **NM** talisman

talismanique /talismanik/ **ADJ** talismanic

talith /talit/ **NM** tallith

talkie-walkie (pl **talkies-walkies**) /tokiwoki/ **NM** walkie-talkie

talle /tal/ **NF** *(Agr)* sucker

taller /tale/ ▸ conjug 1 ◂ **VI** *(Agr)* to sucker, to put out suckers

Tallin /talin/ **N** Tallin(n)

Talmud /talmyd/ **NM** ◆ **le ~** the Talmud

talmudique /talmydik/ **ADJ** Talmudic

talmudiste /talmydist/ **NMF** Talmudist

taloche /talɔʃ/ **NF** 1 *(* = gifle)* cuff, clout* *(Brit)* ◆ **flanquer une ~ à qn** to slap sb 2 *(Constr)* float

talocher /talɔʃe/ ▸ conjug 1 ◂ **VT** 1 *(* = gifler)* to cuff, to clout* *(Brit)* 2 *(Constr)* to float

talon /talɔ̃/ **NM** 1 *(Anat) [de cheval, chaussure]* heel ◆ **être sur les ~s de qn** to be hot on sb's heels ◆ **tourner les ~s** to turn on one's heel (and walk away); → **estomac, pivoter** 2 *(= croûton, bout) [de jambon, fromage]* heel; *[de pain]* crust, heel 3 *[de pipe]* spur 4 *[de chèque]* stub, counterfoil; *[de carnet à souche]* stub 5 *(Cartes)* talon 6 *(Mus) [d'archet]* heel 7 *[de ski]* tail

COMP **talon d'Achille** Achilles' heel

talons aiguilles stiletto heels

talons bottier medium heels

talons compensés wedge heels

talons hauts high heels ◆ **des chaussures à ~s hauts** high-heeled shoes, high heels

talon-minute heel bar

talons plats flat heels ◆ **chaussures à ~s plats** flat shoes, flatties* *(Brit)*, flats* *(US)*

talon rouge *(Hist)* aristocrat

talonnade /talɔnad/ **NF** *(Rugby)* heel; *(Ftbl)* back-heel

talonnage /talɔnaʒ/ **NM** heeling

talonner /talɔne/ ▸ conjug 1 ◂ **VT** 1 *(= suivre) [+ fugitifs, coureurs]* to follow (hot) on the heels of ◆ **talonné par qn** hotly pursued by sb 2 *(= harceler) [+ débiteur, entrepreneur]* to hound; *[faim]* to gnaw at 3 *(= frapper du talon) [+ cheval]* to kick, to spur on ◆ ~ **(le ballon)** *(Rugby)* to heel (the ball) **VI** *(Naut)* to touch *ou* scrape the bottom with the keel ◆ **le bateau talonne** the boat is touching the bottom

talonnette /talɔnɛt/ **NF** *[de chaussures]* heelpiece; *[de pantalon]* binding

talonneur /talɔnœʀ/ **NM** *(Rugby)* hooker

talquer /talke/ ▸ conjug 1 ◂ **VT** to put talcum powder *ou* talc on

talqueux, -euse /talkø, øz/ **ADJ** talcose

talus /taly/ **NM** 1 *[de route, voie ferrée]* embankment; *[de terrassement]* bank, embankment 2 *(Mil)* talus

COMP **talus continental** *(Géol)* continental slope

talus de déblai excavation slope

talus d'éboulis *(Géol)* scree

talus de remblai embankment slope

talweg /talvɛg/ **NM** ⇒ **thalweg**

tamago(t)chi ® /tamagɔ(t)ʃi/ **NM** tamagochi ®

tamanoir /tamanwaʀ/ **NM** anteater

tamarin /tamaʀɛ̃/ **NM** 1 *(= animal)* tamarin 2 *(= fruit)* tamarind 3 ⇒ **tamarinier** 4 ⇒ **tamaris**

tamarinier /tamaʀinje/ **NM** tamarind (tree)

tamaris /tamaʀis/, **tamarix** /tamaʀiks/ **NM** tamarisk

tambouille * /tɑ̃buj/ **NF** *(péj = nourriture)* grub‡ ◆ **faire la ~** to cook the grub‡ ◆ **ça, c'est de la bonne ~ !** that's what I call food!

tambour /tɑ̃buʀ/ **NM** 1 *(= instrument de musique)* drum; → **roulement** 2 *(= musicien)* drummer 3 *(à broder)* embroidery hoop, tambour 4 *(= porte) (sas)* tambour; *(à tourniquet)* revolving door(s) 5 *(= cylindre) [de machine à laver, treuil, roue de loterie]* drum; *[de moulinet]* spool; *[de montre]* barrel ◆ **moulinet à ~ fixe** fixed-spool reel; → **frein** 6 *(Archit) [de colonne, coupole]* drum 7 *(locutions)* ~ **battant** briskly ◆ **sans ~ ni trompette** without any fuss, unobtrusively ◆ **il est parti sans ~ ni trompette** he left quietly, he slipped away unobtrusively 8 *(Ordin)* drum ◆ ~ **magnétique** magnetic drum

COMP **tambour de basque** tambourine

tambour d'église tambour

tambour de frein brake drum

tambour plat side drum

tambour à timbre snare drum

tambour de ville *(Hist)* ≃ town crier

tambourin /tɑ̃buʀɛ̃/ **NM** *(= tambour de basque)* tambourine; *(= tambour haut et étroit)* tambourin

tambourinage /tɑ̃buʀinaʒ/ **NM** drumming *(NonC)*

tambourinaire /tɑ̃buʀinɛʀ/ **NM** *(= joueur de tambourin)* tambourin player; *(Hist) (= tambour de ville)* ≃ town crier

tambourinement /tɑ̃buʀinmɑ̃/ **NM** drumming *(NonC)*

tambouriner /tɑ̃buʀine/ ▸ conjug 1 ◂ **VI** *(avec les doigts)* to drum ◆ ~ **contre** *ou* **à/sur** to drum (one's fingers) against *ou* at/on ◆ **la pluie tambourinait sur le toit** the rain was beating down *ou* drumming on the roof ◆ ~ **à la porte** to hammer at the door **VT** 1 *(= jouer) [+ marche]* to drum *ou* beat out 2 *(† = annoncer) [+ nouvelle, décret]* to cry (out) ◆ ~ **une nouvelle** to shout a piece of news from the rooftops

tambour-major (pl **tambours-majors**) /tɑ̃buʀmaʒɔʀ/ **NM** drum major

Tamerlan /tamɛʀlɑ̃/ **NM** Tamburlaine, Tamerlane

tamil /tamil/ **ADJ, NMF** ⇒ **tamoul**

tamis /tami/ **NM** *(gén)* sieve; *(à sable)* riddle, sifter; *[de raquette] (= surface)* head; *(= cordage)* strings ◆ **raquette grand ~** largeheaded racket ◆ **passer au ~** *[+ farine, plâtre]* to sieve, to sift; *[+ sable]* to riddle, to sift; *[+ campagne, bois]* to comb, to search; *[+ personnes]* to vet thoroughly; *[+ dossier]* to sift *ou* search through ◆ ~ **moléculaire** molecular sieve

tamisage /tamizaʒ/ **NM** *[de farine, plâtre]* sifting, sieving; *[de sable]* riddling, sifting

Tamise /tamiz/ **NF** ◆ **la ~** the Thames

tamiser /tamize/ ▸ conjug 1 ◂ **VT** 1 *[+ farine, plâtre]* to sift, to sieve; *[+ sable]* to riddle, to sift ◆ **farine tamisée** sifted flour 2 *(= voiler) [+ lumière]* to filter ◆ **lumière tamisée** subdued lighting

tamoul, e /tamul/ **ADJ** Tamil **NM** *(= langue)* Tamil **NM,F** **Tamoul(e)** Tamil

tamoxifène /tamɔksifɛn/ **NM** tamoxifen

tampon /tɑ̃pɔ̃/ **NM** 1 *(pour boucher, gén)* stopper, plug; *(en bois)* plug; *(pour étendre un liquide, un vernis)* pad ◆ **rouler qch en ~** to roll sth (up) into a ball; → **vernir**

2 *(Méd) (en coton)* wad, plug; *(pour nettoyer une plaie)* swab

3 *(pour règles)* tampon

4 *(pour timbrer) (= instrument)* (rubber) stamp; *(= cachet)* stamp ◆ **le ~ de la poste** the postmark ◆ **apposer** *ou* **mettre un ~ sur qch** to stamp sth, to put a stamp on sth

5 *(Rail, fig = amortisseur)* buffer ◆ **servir de ~ entre deux personnes** to act as a buffer between two people

6 *(Chim)* **solution ~** buffer solution

ADJ INV ◆ **État/zone ~** buffer state/zone ◆ **mémoire ~** *(Ordin)* buffer (memory)

COMP **tampon buvard** blotter

tampon encreur inking-pad

tampon hygiénique tampon

tampon Jex ® Brillo pad ®

tampon à nettoyer cleaning pad

tampon à récurer scouring pad, scourer

> ⚠ **tampon** se traduit par le mot anglais **tampon** uniquement au sens de 'tampon hygiénique'.

tamponnement /tɑ̃pɔnmɑ̃/ **NM** 1 *(= collision)* collision, crash 2 *(Méd) [de plaie]* tamponade, tamponage 3 *(Tech) [de mur]* plugging

tamponner /tɑ̃pɔne/ ▸ conjug 1 ◂ **VT** 1 *(= essuyer) [+ plaie]* to mop up, to dab; *[+ yeux]* to dab (at); *[+ front]* to mop, to dab; *[+ surface à sécher, à vernir]* to dab 2 *(= heurter) [+ train, véhicule]* to ram (into), to crash into 3 *(avec un timbre)*

[+ document, lettre] to stamp ◆ **faire ~ un reçu** to have a receipt stamped 4 (Tech = percer) [+ mur] to plug, to put (wall-) plugs in **VPR se tamponner** 1 (= s'essuyer) [+ yeux] to dab; [+ front] to mop ◆ **se ~ le visage avec un coton** to dab one's face with a piece of cotton wool 2 (= se heurter) (accident) to crash into each other; (exprès) to ram each other 3 (locutions) **je m'en tamponne (le coquillard)*** I don't give a damn*

tamponneuse /tɑ̃pɔnøz/ **ADJ F** → **auto**

tamponnoir /tɑ̃pɔnwaʀ/ **NM** masonry drill bit

tam-tam (pl **tam-tams**) /tamtam/ **NM** 1 (= tambour) tomtom 2 (* = battage, tapage) fuss ◆ **faire du ~ autour de** [+ affaire, événement] to make a lot of fuss *ou* a great ballyhoo* *ou* hullaballoo* about

tan /tɑ̃/ **NM** tan (for tanning)

tancer /tɑ̃se/ ► conjug 3 ◄ **VT** (littér) to scold, to berate, to rebuke

tanche /tɑ̃ʃ/ **NF** tench

tandem /tɑ̃dɛm/ **NM** (= bicyclette) tandem; (= duo) pair, duo ◆ **travailler en ~** to work in tandem

tandis /tɑ̃di/ **tandis que LOC CONJ** (simultanéité) while, whilst (frm), as; (pour marquer le contraste, l'opposition) whereas, while, whilst (frm)

tandoori, tandouri /tɑ̃duʀi/ **NM** tandoori ◆ **poulet ~** tandoori chicken

tangage /tɑ̃gaʒ/ **NM** [de navire, avion] pitching ◆ **il y a du ~** (Naut) the boat's pitching

Tanganyika /tɑ̃ganika/ **NF** Tanganyika ◆ **le lac ~** Lake Tanganyika

tangence /tɑ̃ʒɑ̃s/ **NF** tangency

tangent, e /tɑ̃ʒɑ̃, ɑ̃t/ **ADJ** 1 (Géom) tangent, tangential ◆ **~ à** tangent *ou* tangential to 2 (* = juste) close, touch and go (attrib) ◆ **il a eu son examen mais c'était ~** he passed his exam but it was a close(-run) thing *ou* it was touch and go ◆ **le candidat était ~** the candidate was a borderline case **NF tangente** 1 (Géom) tangent 2 (fig) **prendre la ~e*** (= partir) to make off*, to make o.s. scarce; (= éluder) to dodge the issue, to wriggle out of it

tangentiel, -ielle /tɑ̃ʒɑ̃sjɛl/ **ADJ** tangential

tangentiellement /tɑ̃ʒɑ̃sjɛlmɑ̃/ **ADV** tangentially

Tanger /tɑ̃ʒe/ **N** Tangier(s)

tangerine /tɑ̃ʒ(ə)ʀin/ **NF** tangerine

tangible /tɑ̃ʒibl/ **ADJ** tangible

tangiblement /tɑ̃ʒibləmɑ̃/ **ADV** tangibly

tango /tɑ̃go/ **NM** 1 (= danse) tango ◆ **danser le ~** to tango, to do the tango 2 (= boisson) beer with grenadine 3 (= couleur) tangerine **ADJ INV** tangerine

tanguer /tɑ̃ge/ ► conjug 1 ◄ **VI** 1 [navire, avion] to pitch ◆ **l'embarcation tanguait dangereusement** the boat pitched dangerously 2 (= vaciller) to reel ◆ **tout tanguait autour de lui** (gén) everything around him was reeling; (dans une pièce) the room was spinning 3 (= tituber) to reel, to sway ◆ **des marins ivres tanguaient dans la rue** drunken sailors were reeling *ou* swaying along the street

tanière /tanjɛʀ/ **NF** [d'animal] den, lair; [de malfaiteur] lair; [de poète, solitaire] (= pièce) den; (= maison) hideaway, retreat

tanin /tanɛ̃/ **NM** tannin

tank /tɑ̃k/ **NM** tank

tanker /tɑ̃kœʀ/ **NM** tanker

tankiste /tɑ̃kist/ **NM** member of a tank crew

tannage /tanaʒ/ **NM** tanning

tannant, e /tanɑ̃, ɑ̃t/ **ADJ** 1 (* = ennuyeux) [livre, travail] boring ◆ **qu'est-ce que tu es ~ avec tes questions !** you're really getting on my nerves with all your questions! 2 (Tech) tanning

tannée /tane/ **NF** 1 (* = coups, défaite) hammering* ◆ **(se) prendre une ~** to get hammered* 2 (Tech) (spent) tanbark

tanner /tane/ ► conjug 1 ◄ **VT** 1 [+ cuir] to tan; [+ visage] to weather ◆ **visage tanné** weather-beaten face ◆ **~ le cuir à qn*** to give sb a hammering*, to tan sb's hide* 2 * **~ qn** (= harceler) to badger sb, to pester sb; (= ennuyer) to drive sb mad*, to drive sb up the wall* ◆ **ça fait des semaines qu'il me tanne pour aller voir ce film** he's been badgering *ou* pestering me for weeks to go and see that film

tannerie /tanʀi/ **NF** (= endroit) tannery; (= activité) tanning

tanneur /tanœʀ/ **NM** tanner

tannin /tanɛ̃/ **NM** ⇒ **tanin**

tannique /tanik/ **ADJ** [acide, vin] tannic

tant /tɑ̃/

ADVERBE

> Lorsque **tant** s'emploie dans des locutions figées commençant par un autre mot, telles que **si tant est que, tous tant qu'ils sont**, cherchez au premier mot.

1 = tellement

◆ **tant** + verbe so much ◆ **il mange ~ !** he eats so much! *ou* such a lot! ◆ **il l'aime ~ !** he loves her so much! ◆ **j'ai ~ marché que je suis épuisé** I've walked so much that I'm exhausted ◆ **tu m'en diras** *ou* **vous m'en direz ~ !** really! ◆ **~ va la cruche à l'eau qu'à la fin elle se casse** (Prov) people who play with fire must expect to get burnt

◆ **tant** + adjectif, participe so ◆ **il est rentré ~ le ciel était menaçant** he went home because the sky looked so overcast, the sky looked so overcast that he went home ◆ **cet enfant ~ désiré** this child they had longed for so much ◆ **le jour ~ attendu arriva** the long-awaited day arrived

◆ **tant de** + nom ou pronom singulier [+ temps, eau, argent] so much; [+ gentillesse, mauvaise foi] such, so much ◆ **fait avec ~ d'habileté** done with so much *ou* such skill ◆ **elle a ~ de sensibilité** she's so sensitive, she has such sensitivity ◆ **il a ~ de mal** *ou* **de peine à se décider** he has so much *ou* such trouble making up his mind ◆ **il gagne ~ et ~ d'argent qu'il ne sait pas quoi en faire** he earns so much money *ou* such a lot (of money) that he doesn't know what to do with it all ◆ **il y avait ~ de brouillard qu'il n'est pas parti** it was so foggy *ou* there was so much fog about that he didn't go

◆ **tant de** + nom ou pronom pluriel [+ choses, livres, arbres, gens] so many ◆ **~ de fois** so many times, so often ◆ **comme ~ d'autres** like so many others ◆ **~ de précautions semblaient suspectes** it seemed suspicious to take so many precautions ◆ **des gens comme il y en a ~** ordinary people ◆ **c'est une histoire comme il y en a ~** it's a familiar story

◆ **tant il est vrai que ...**since ..., as ... ◆ **le dialogue sera difficile, ~ il est vrai que les attentats ont altéré les relations entre les deux pays** dialogue will not be easy, as *ou* since the bombings have damaged the relationship between the two countries ◆ **il sera difficile de sauver l'entreprise, ~ il est vrai que sa situation financière est désastreuse** the financial situation is so disastrous that it will be difficult to save the company

2 quantité non précisée so much ◆ **gagner ~ par mois** to earn so much a month, to earn such-and-such an amount a month ◆ **ça coûte ~** it costs so much ◆ **il devrait donner ~ à l'un, ~ à l'autre** he should give so much to one, so much to the other ◆ **~ pour cent** so many per cent

3 comparaison = autant **les enfants, ~ filles que garçons** the children, both girls and boys *ou* girls as well as boys *ou* (both) girls and boys alike ◆ **ses œuvres ~ politiques que lyriques** both his political and his poetic works ◆ **il criait ~ qu'il pouvait** he shouted as loud as he could *ou* for all he was worth ◆ **je n'aime rien ~ que l'odeur des sous-bois** (littér) there is nothing I love more than woodland smells ◆ **ce n'est pas ~ leur maison qui me plaît que leur jardin** it's not so much their house that I like as their garden ◆ **~ que ça ?** that much?, as much as that? ◆ **pas ~ que ça** not that much ◆ **tu la paies ~ que ça ?** do you pay her that much? *ou* as much as that? ◆ **je ne l'ai pas vu ~ que ça pendant l'été** I didn't see him (all) that much during the summer

4 locutions

◆ **tant bien que mal** ◆ **ils essaient ~ bien que mal de conserver leur emploi** they're doing their best to keep their jobs ◆ **ils résistent ~ bien que mal à l'influence de la publicité** they resist the influence of advertising as best they can ◆ **il essaie, ~ bien que mal, d'égayer l'atmosphère** he's doing his best to liven things up ◆ **la centrale nucléaire continue de fonctionner ~ bien que mal** the nuclear power station is still more or less operational ◆ **la plupart survivent ~ bien que mal avec leurs économies** most of them manage to get by on what they've saved

◆ **tant et plus** ◆ **il y en a ~ et plus** [eau, argent] there is a great deal; [objets, personnes] there are a great many ◆ **il a protesté ~ et plus, mais sans résultat** he protested for all he was worth *ou* over and over again but to no avail

◆ **tant et si bien que** so much so that, to such an extent that ◆ **il a fait ~ et si bien qu'elle l'a quitté** he finally succeeded in making her leave him

◆ **tant mieux** (= à la bonne heure) good; (avec une certaine réserve) so much the better, that's fine ◆ **~ mieux pour lui** good for him

◆ **tant pis** (= ça ne fait rien) never mind, (that's) too bad; (= peu importe, qu'à cela ne tienne) (that's just) too bad ◆ **~ pis pour lui** (that's just) too bad for him ◆ **je ne peux pas venir – ~ pis pour toi !** I can't come – tough!

◆ **tant qu'à** + infinitif ◆ **~ qu'à faire, allons-y maintenant** we might *ou* may as well go now ◆ **~ qu'à faire, tu aurais pu ranger la vaisselle** you could have put away the dishes while you were at it ◆ **j'aurais préféré être mince, beau et riche, ~ qu'à faire** I would have preferred to have been slim, handsome and rich for that matter ◆ **~ qu'à faire, je préfère payer tout de suite** (since I have to pay) I might *ou* may as well pay right away ◆ **~ qu'à faire, faites-le bien** if you're going to do it, do it properly ◆ **~ qu'à marcher, allons en forêt** if we have to walk *ou* if we are walking, let's go to the woods

◆ **tant s'en faut** not by a long way, far from it, not by a long shot *ou* chalk (Brit) ◆ **il n'a pas la gentillesse de son frère, ~ s'en faut** he's not nearly as *ou* he's nothing like as nice as his brother, he's not as nice as his brother – not by a long way *ou* shot

◆ **tant soit peu** ◆ **s'il est ~ soit peu intelligent il saura s'en tirer** if he is (even) remotely intelligent *ou* if he has the slightest grain of intelligence he'll be able to get out of it ◆ **si vous craignez ~ soit peu le froid, restez chez vous** if you feel the cold at all *ou* the slightest bit, stay at home ◆ **il est un ~ soit peu prétentieux** he's ever so slightly *ou* he's just a little bit pretentious

◆ **tant que** (= aussi longtemps que) as long as ◆ **~ qu'elle aura de la fièvre, elle restera au lit** while *ou* as long as she has a temperature

she'll stay in bed ◆ ~ **que tu n'auras pas fini tes devoirs, tu resteras à la maison** you'll have to stay indoors until you've finished your homework ◆ **(tout va bien) ~ qu'on a la santé !** * (you're all right) as long as you've got your health! ◆ ~ **qu'il y a de la vie, il y a de l'espoir** *(Prov)* where there's life, there's hope *(Prov)*
(= pendant que) while ◆ ~ **que vous y êtes, achetez les deux volumes** while you are about it *ou* at it, buy both volumes ◆ ~ **que vous êtes ici, donnez-moi un coup de main** * seeing (as) *ou* since you're here, give me a hand ◆ **je veux une moto – pourquoi pas une voiture ~ que tu y es !** * I want a motorbike – why not a car while you're at it! *
◆ **en tant que** *(= comme)* as ◆ **en ~ qu'ami de la famille** as a family friend ◆ **en ~ que tel** as such

---

tantale /tɑ̃tal/ **NM** 1 *(Myth)* **Tantale** Tantalus; → **supplice** 2 *(Chim)* tantalum

tante /tɑ̃t/ **NF** *(= parente)* aunt, auntie *; (‡ *= homosexuel)* queer ‡ ◆ **la ~ Marie** Aunt *ou* Auntie * Marie ◆ **je l'ai mis chez ma ~** † * *(= au mont-de-piété)* I pawned it

tantième /tɑ̃tjɛm/ **NM** *(= pourcentage)* percentage; *(d'une copropriété)* percentage share; *(= jeton de présence)* director's percentage of profits **ADJ** ◆ **la ~ partie de qch** such (and such) a proportion of sth

tantine /tɑ̃tin/ **NF** *(langage enfantin)* auntie *

tantinet * /tɑ̃tinɛ/ **NM** ◆ **un ~ fatigant/ridicule** a tiny bit tiring/ridiculous ◆ **un ~ de** a tiny bit of

tantôt /tɑ̃to/ **ADV** 1 *(= cet après-midi)* this afternoon; (†† *= tout à l'heure)* shortly ◆ **mardi ~** † * on Tuesday afternoon 2 *(= parfois)* ~ **à pied, ~ en voiture** sometimes on foot, sometimes by car ◆ ~ **riant, ~ pleurant** *(littér)* now laughing, now crying

tantouse ‡, **tantouze** ‡ /tɑ̃tuz/ **NF** *(= homosexuel)* queer ‡

tantrique /tɑ̃tʀik/ **ADJ** Tantric

tantrisme /tɑ̃tʀism/ **NM** Tantrism

Tanzanie /tɑ̃zani/ **NF** Tanzania ◆ **la République unie de ~** the United Republic of Tanzania

tanzanien, -ienne /tɑ̃zanjɛ̃, jɛn/ **ADJ** Tanzanian **NM,F** **Tanzanien(ne)** Tanzanian

TAO /teao/ **NF** (abrév de **traduction assistée par ordinateur**) machine-aided translation

Tao /tao/ **NM** Tao

taoïsme /taoism/ **NM** Taoism

taoïste /taoist/ **ADJ, NMF** Taoist

taon /tɑ̃/ **NM** horsefly, gadfly

tapage /tapaʒ/ **NM** 1 *(= vacarme)* row, racket ◆ **faire du ~** to kick up * *ou* make a row, to make a racket 2 *(= battage)* fuss, talk ◆ **ils ont fait un tel ~ autour de cette affaire que ...** there was so much fuss made about *ou* so much talk over this affair that ... **COMP** **tapage nocturne** *(Jur)* disturbance of the peace *(at night)* ◆ **porter plainte pour ~ nocturne** to make a complaint about the noise at night

tapageur, -euse /tapaʒœʀ, øz/ **ADJ** 1 *(= bruyant) [enfant, hôtes]* noisy, rowdy 2 *(= peu discret, voyant) [élégance, toilette]* flashy, showy; *[luxe]* ostentatious ◆ **liaison tapageuse** *(= qui fait scandale)* scandalous affair ◆ **publicité tapageuse** excessive hype *

tapant, e /tapɑ̃, ɑ̃t/ **ADJ** ◆ **à 8 heures ~(es)** at 8 (o'clock) sharp, on the stroke of 8, at 8 o'clock on the dot *

tapas /tapas/ **NFPL** tapas

tape /tap/ **NF** *(= coup)* slap ◆ **il m'a donné une grande ~ dans le dos** he slapped me hard on the back ◆ **petite ~ amicale** friendly little tap

tapé, e[1] /tape/ (ptp de **taper**) **ADJ** 1 *[fruit] (= talé)* bruised; * *[personne] (= marqué par l'âge)* wizened 2 (* *= fou)* cracked *, bonkers ‡ *(Brit)*

tape-à-l'œil /tapalœj/ *(péj)* **ADJ INV** *[décoration, vêtements]* flashy, showy **NM INV** ◆ **c'est du ~** it's all show

tapecul, tape-cul (pl **tape-culs**) /tapky/ **NM** *(= voile)* jigger; (* *= balançoire)* see-saw; (* *= voiture)* rattletrap *, bone-shaker * *(Brit)*; (* *= trot assis)* close trot ◆ **faire du ~** to trot close

tapée[2] ‡ /tape/ **NF** ◆ **une ~ de, des ~s de** loads of *, masses of *

tapement /tapmɑ̃/ **NM** banging *(NonC)*, banging noise

tapenade /tap(ə)nad/ **NF** tapenade *(savoury spread made with pureed olives)*

taper /tape/ ▸ **conjug 1** ◂ **VT** 1 *(= battre) [+ tapis]* to beat; * *[+ enfant]* to slap, to smack; *(= claquer) [+ porte]* to bang, to slam ◆ ~ **le carton** * to have a game of cards
2 *(= frapper)* ~ **un coup/deux coups à la porte** to knock once/twice at the door, to give a knock/two knocks at the door ◆ ~ **un air sur le piano** *(péj)* to bang *ou* thump out a tune on the piano
3 *(à la machine, sur un ordinateur)* to type (out) ◆ **apprendre à ~ à la machine** to learn (how) to type ◆ **elle tape bien** she types well, she's a good typist ◆ **elle tape 60 mots à la minute** her typing speed is 60 words a minute ◆ **tapé à la machine** typed, typewritten ◆ **lettre tapée sur ordinateur** letter done on computer ◆ **tapez 36 15, code ...** *(sur Minitel)* type in 36 15, code ... ◆ **tape sur la touche "Retour"** hit *ou* press "Return"
4 (* *= demander de l'argent)* **il tape tous ses collègues** he scrounges * *ou* cadges *(Brit)* off all his colleagues ◆ ~ **qn de 50 €** to scrounge * *ou* cadge *(Brit)* €50 off sb
VI 1 *(= frapper)* ~ **sur un clou** to hit a nail ◆ ~ **sur la table** to bang *ou* rap on the table ◆ ~ **sur un piano** *(péj)* to bang *ou* thump away on a piano ◆ ~ **sur qn** * to thump sb ◆ ~ **sur la gueule de qn** ‡ to belt sb ‡ ◆ ~ **sur le ventre de** *ou* **à qn** * *(fig)* to be overfamiliar with sb ◆ ~ **à la porte/au mur** to knock on the door/on the wall ◆ **il tapait comme un sourd** he was thumping away for all he was worth ◆ **il tape (dur), le salaud** ‡ the bastard's got one hell of a punch ‡ ◆ ~ **dans un ballon** to kick a ball about *ou* around
2 (* *= dire du mal de)* ~ **sur qn** to run sb down *, to have a go at sb * (behind their back)
3 (* *= entamer)* ~ **dans** *[+ provisions, caisse]* to dig into *
4 *(= être fort, intense) [soleil]* to beat down; * *[vin]* to go to one's head ◆ **ça tape fort aujourd'hui !** * the sun's beating down today, it's scorching hot today
5 (‡ *= sentir mauvais)* to stink *, to pong ‡ *(Brit)*
6 *(locutions)* ~ **des pieds** to stamp one's feet ◆ ~ **des mains** to clap one's hands ◆ **se faire ~ sur les doigts** * *(fig)* to be rapped over the knuckles ◆ **il a tapé à côté** * he was wide of the mark ◆ ~ **sur les nerfs** *ou* **le système de qn** * to get on sb's nerves * *ou* wick * *(Brit)* ◆ ~ **dans l'œil de qn** * to take sb's fancy * ◆ **elle lui a tapé dans l'œil** * he took a fancy to her, she took his fancy ◆ ~ **dans le tas** * *(bagarre)* to pitch into the crowd; *(repas)* to tuck in *, to dig in *; → **mille**[1]
VPR **se taper** 1 (‡ *= prendre) [+ repas]* to put away *; *[+ corvée]* to get landed with *; *[+ importun]* to get landed * *ou* lumbered * *(Brit)* with ◆ **je me taperais bien un petit cognac** I could murder a brandy *, I'd love a brandy ◆ **on s'est tapé les 10 km à pied** we did the whole 10 km on foot ◆ **se ~ qn** *(sexuellement)* to have it off with sb ‡
2 *(locutions)* **se ~ sur les cuisses de contentement** * to slap one's thighs with satisfaction ◆ **il y a de quoi se ~ le derrière** * *ou* **le cul** ‡ **par terre** it's damned * *ou* bloody ‡ *(Brit)* ridiculous ◆ **c'est à se ~ la tête contre les murs** it's enough to drive you up the wall * ◆ **se ~ la cloche** * to feed one's face ‡, to have a blow-out * *(Brit) ou* nosh-up * *(Brit)* ◆ **il peut toujours se ~** ‡ he knows what he can do ‡ ◆ **se ~ sur le ventre** * to be buddies * *ou* pals * ◆ **il s'en tape complètement** * he couldn't give a damn ‡

tapette /tapɛt/ **NF** 1 *(= petite tape)* little tap 2 *(pour tapis)* carpet beater; *(pour mouches)* flyswatter 3 *(pour souris)* mousetrap 4 († *) **il a une bonne ~** *ou* **une de ces ~s** *(= langue)* he's a real chatterbox * 5 (‡ *= homosexuel)* poof ‡ *(Brit)*, fag ‡ *(US)*

tapeur, -euse * /tapœʀ, øz/ **NM,F** *(= emprunteur)* cadger *

tapin ‡ /tapɛ̃/ **NM** ◆ **le ~** *(= prostitution)* prostitution ◆ **faire le ~** to be on the game ‡ *(Brit)*, to hustle * *(US)*

tapiner ‡ /tapine/ ▸ **conjug 1** ◂ **VI** to be on the game ‡ *(Brit)*, to hustle * *(US)*

tapineuse ‡ /tapinøz/ **NF** streetwalker, hustler * *(US)*

tapinois /tapinwa/ **NM** ◆ **en ~** *[s'approcher]* stealthily, furtively; *[agir]* on the sly

tapioca /tapjɔka/ **NM** tapioca

tapir /tapiʀ/ **NM** *(= animal)* tapir

tapir (se) /tapiʀ/ ▸ **conjug 2** ◂ **VPR** *(= se blottir)* to crouch; *(= se cacher)* to hide away; *(= s'embusquer)* to lurk ◆ **une maison tapie au fond de la vallée** a house nestling in the bottom of the valley

tapis /tapi/ **NM** 1 *[de sol] (gén)* carpet; *(petit)* rug; *(= natte)* mat; *(dans un gymnase)* mat ◆ ~ **mécanique** machine-woven carpet ◆ **exercices au ~** *(Gym)* floor exercises; → **marchand**
2 *[de meuble]* cloth; *[de table de jeu]* baize *(NonC)*, cloth, covering ◆ **le ~ vert des tables de conférence** the green baize *ou* covering of conference tables ◆ **le ~ brûle** *(Casino)* place your stakes
3 *(= étendue)* carpet ◆ ~ **de verdure/neige** carpet of greenery/snow
4 *(locutions)* **aller au ~** to go down for the count ◆ **envoyer qn au ~** *(lit, fig)* to floor sb ◆ **mettre une entreprise au ~** to sink a company ◆ **mettre** *ou* **porter sur le ~** *[+ affaire, question]* to lay on the table, to bring up for discussion ◆ **être/revenir sur le ~** to come up/come back up for discussion
COMP **tapis à bagages** *(dans un aéroport)* carousel
tapis de bain bath mat
tapis de billard baize *(NonC)*
tapis de bombes carpet of bombs
tapis de chœur altar carpet
tapis de couloir runner
tapis de haute laine long-pile carpet
tapis d'Orient oriental carpet
tapis persan Persian carpet
tapis de prière prayer mat
tapis ras short-pile carpet
tapis rouge red carpet ◆ **dérouler le ~ rouge** to roll out the red carpet
tapis roulant *(pour colis, marchandises)* conveyor belt; *(pour piétons)* moving walkway, travelator; *(pour bagages)* carousel
tapis de selle saddlecloth
tapis de sol *(Camping)* groundsheet; *(Gym)* (exercise) mat
tapis de souris *(Ordin)* mouse mat

tapis de table table cover
tapis végétal ground cover
tapis volant magic *ou* flying carpet

tapis-brosse (pl **tapis-brosses**) / tapibʀɔs / NM doormat

tapissé, e / tapise / (ptp de **tapisser**) ADJ ◆ **~ de neige** *[sol]* carpeted with snow; *[sommet]* snow-clad, covered in snow ◆ **mur ~ de photos/d'affiches** wall covered *ou* plastered with photos/with posters ◆ **murs ~s de livres** walls lined with books ◆ **~ de lierre/de mousse** ivy-/moss-clad ◆ **carrosse ~ de velours** carriage with velvet upholstery

tapisser / tapise / ▸ conjug 1 ◂ VT 1 *[personne] (de papier peint)* to (wall)paper; *(Culin) [+ plat, moule]* to line ◆ **~ un mur/une pièce de tentures** to hang a wall/a room with drapes, to cover a wall/a room with hangings ◆ **~ un mur d'affiches/de photos** to plaster *ou* cover a wall with posters/with photos 2 *[tenture, papier]* to cover, to line; *[mousse, neige, lierre]* to carpet, to cover; *(Anat, Bot) [membranes, tissus]* to line ◆ **le lierre tapissait le mur** the wall was covered with ivy

tapisserie / tapisʀi / NF 1 *(= tenture)* tapestry; *(= papier peint)* wallpaper; *(= activité)* tapestry-making ◆ **faire ~** *[subalterne]* to stand on the sidelines; *[danseur]* to be a wallflower, to sit out ◆ **j'ai dû faire ~ pendant que ma femme dansait** I had to sit out while my wife was dancing 2 *(= broderie)* tapestry; *(= activité)* tapestrywork ◆ **faire de la ~** to do tapestry work ◆ **fauteuil recouvert de ~** tapestried armchair ◆ **pantoufles en ~** embroidered slippers ◆ **les ~s d'Aubusson/des Gobelins** the Aubusson/Gobelins tapestries; → **point²**

tapissier, -ière / tapisje, jɛʀ / NM,F *(= fabricant)* tapestry-maker; *(= commerçant)* upholsterer ◆ **~-décorateur** interior decorator

tapon† / tapɔ̃ / NM ◆ **en ~** in a ball ◆ **mettre en ~** to roll (up) into a ball

tapotement / tapɔtmɑ̃ / NM *(sur la table)* tapping *(NonC)*; *(sur le piano)* plonking *(NonC)*

tapoter / tapɔte / ▸ conjug 1 ◂ VT *[+ joue]* to pat; *[+ baromètre]* to tap ◆ **~ sa cigarette pour faire tomber la cendre** to flick (the ash off) one's cigarette VI ◆ **~ sur** *ou* **contre** to tap on; *(nerveusement)* to drum one's fingers on ◆ **~ sur un clavier d'ordinateur** to tap away at a computer keyboard

tapuscrit / tapyskʀi / NM typescript

taquet / takɛ / NM *(= coin, cale)* wedge; *(= cheville, butée)* peg; *(pour enrouler un cordage)* cleat; *[de machine à écrire]* stop ◆ **~ de tabulation** *(Ordin)* tab stop

taquin, e / takɛ̃, in / ADJ *[caractère, personne]* teasing *(épith)*; *[sourire]* mischievous, cheeky ◆ **il est très ~, c'est un ~** he's a real tease

taquiner / takine / ▸ conjug 1 ◂ VT *[personne]* to tease; *[fait, douleur]* to bother, to worry ◆ **~ le goujon** *(hum)* to do a bit of fishing ◆ **~ le cochonnet** *(hum)* to have a game of petanque ◆ **~ la muse** *(hum)* to dabble in poetry, to court the Muse *(hum)* ◆ **ils n'arrêtent pas de se ~** they're always teasing each other

taquinerie / takinʀi / NF teasing *(NonC)* ◆ **agacé par ses ~s** annoyed by his teasing

tarabiscoté, e / taʀabiskɔte / ADJ *[meuble]* (over-)ornate, fussy; *[style]* involved, (over-)ornate, fussy; *[explication]* (overly) involved

tarabuster / taʀabyste / ▸ conjug 1 ◂ VT *[personne]* to badger, to pester; *[fait, idée]* to bother, to worry ◆ **il m'a tarabusté pour que j'y aille** he badgered *ou* pestered me to go

tarama / taʀama / NM taramasalata

taratata / taʀatata / EXCL (stuff and) nonsense!, rubbish!

taraud / taʀo / NM *(Tech)* tap

taraudage / taʀodaʒ / NM *(Tech)* tapping ◆ **~ à la machine/à la main** machine-/hand-tapping

tarauder / taʀode / ▸ conjug 1 ◂ VT *(Tech) [+ plaque, écrou]* to tap; *[+ vis, boulon]* to thread; *[insecte]* to bore into; *[remords, angoisse]* to pierce ◆ **une question me taraude** there's something bothering me

taraudeur, -euse / taʀodœʀ, øz / NM,F *(= ouvrier)* tapper NF **taraudeuse** *(= machine)* tapping-machine; *(à fileter)* threader

Tarawa / taʀawa / N Tarawa

tard / taʀ / ADV *(dans la journée, dans la saison)* late ◆ **il est ~** it's late ◆ **il se fait ~** it's getting late ◆ **se coucher/travailler ~** to go to bed/work late ◆ **travailler ~ dans la nuit** to work late (on) into the night ◆ **il vint nous voir ~ dans la matinée/journée** he came to see us late in the morning *ou* in the late morning/late in the day ◆ **c'est un peu ~ pour t'excuser** it's a bit late in the day to apologize, it's a bit late to apologize now; → **jamais, mieux, tôt**

◆ **plus tard** later (on) ◆ **remettre qch à plus ~** to put sth off till later, to postpone sth ◆ **pas plus ~ qu'hier** only yesterday ◆ **pas plus ~ que la semaine dernière** just *ou* only last week, as recently as last week

◆ **au plus tard** at the latest ◆ **il vous faut arriver jeudi au plus ~** you must come on Thursday at the latest

◆ **sur le tard** *(dans la vie)* late (on) in life, late in the day *(fig) (dans la journée)* late in the day

tarder / taʀde / ▸ conjug 1 ◂ VI 1 *(= différer, traîner)* to delay ◆ **~ à entreprendre qch** to put off *ou* delay starting sth ◆ **ne tardez pas (à le faire)** don't delay, do it without delay ◆ **~ en chemin** to loiter *ou* dawdle on the way ◆ **sans (plus) ~** without (further) delay *ou* ado ◆ **pourquoi tant ~ ?** why delay it *ou* put it off so long?

2 *(= se faire attendre) [réaction, moment]* to be a long time coming; *[lettre]* to take a long time (coming), to be a long time coming ◆ **l'été tarde (à venir)** summer is a long time coming ◆ **sa réponse a trop tardé** his reply took too long

3 *(locutions)* **ça ne va pas ~** it won't be long (coming) ◆ **ça n'a pas tardé** it wasn't long (in) coming ◆ **leur réaction ne va pas ~** they won't take long to react ◆ **il est 2 heures : ils ne vont pas ~** it's 2 o'clock – they won't be long (now) ◆ **ils n'ont pas tardé à être endettés** before long they were in debt, it wasn't long before they were in debt ◆ **il n'a pas tardé à s'en apercevoir** it didn't take him long to notice, he noticed soon enough ◆ **ils n'ont pas tardé à réagir, leur réaction n'a pas tardé** they didn't take long to react ◆ **l'élève ne tarda pas à dépasser le maître** the pupil soon outstripped the teacher

4 *(= sembler long)* **le temps** *ou* **le moment me tarde d'être en vacances** I can't wait to be on holiday

VB IMPERS *(littér)* ◆ **il me tarde de le revoir/que ces travaux soient finis** I am longing *ou* I can't wait to see him again/for this work to be finished

tardif, -ive / taʀdif, iv / ADJ late; *[regrets, remords]* belated ◆ **rentrer à une heure tardive** to come home late at night ◆ **cette prise de conscience a été tardive** this realization was slow in coming

tardivement / taʀdivmɑ̃ / ADV *(= à une heure tardive) [rentrer]* late; *(= après coup, trop tard) [s'apercevoir]* belatedly

tare / taʀ / NF 1 *(= contrepoids)* tare ◆ **faire la ~** to allow for the tare 2 *(= défaut) [de personne, marchandise]* defect *(de* in, of); *[de cheval]* vice; *[de société, système]* flaw *(de* in) defect *(de* of); ◆ **~ héréditaire** *(Méd)* hereditary defect ◆ **ce n'est pas une ~ !** *(hum)* it's not a sin! *ou* crime!

taré, e / taʀe / ADJ 1 *[enfant, animal]* with a defect 2 *(péj)* **il faut être ~ pour faire cela*** *(= pervers)* you have to be sick to do that* ◆ **il est complètement ~, ce type !*** *(= fou)* that guy's completely crazy* *ou* out to lunch*! NM,F *(Méd)* degenerate ◆ **regardez-moi ce ~*** *(péj)* look at that cretin*

tarentelle / taʀɑ̃tɛl / NF tarantella

tarentule / taʀɑ̃tyl / NF tarantula

tarer / taʀe / ▸ conjug 1 ◂ VT *(Comm)* to tare, to allow for the tare

targette / taʀʒɛt / NF *(= verrou)* bolt

targuer (se) / taʀge / ▸ conjug 1 ◂ VPR *(= se vanter)* ◆ **se ~ de qch** to boast about sth ◆ **se ~ de ce que ...** to boast that ... ◆ **se ~ d'avoir fait qch** to pride o.s. on having done sth ◆ **se targuant d'y parvenir aisément ...** boasting that he would easily manage it ...

targui, e / taʀgi / ADJ Tuareg NM,F **Targui(e)** Tuareg

tarière / taʀjɛʀ / NF 1 *(Tech) (pour le bois)* auger; *(pour le sol)* drill 2 *[d'insecte]* drill, ovipositor *(SPÉC)*

tarif / taʀif / NM *(= tableau)* price list, tariff *(Brit)*; *(= prix) (gén)* rate; *(Transport)* fare ◆ **consulter/afficher le ~ des consommations** to check/put up the price list for drinks *ou* the bar tariff *(Brit)* ◆ **le ~ postal pour l'étranger/le ~ des taxis va augmenter** overseas postage rates/taxi fares are going up ◆ **payé au ~ syndical** paid according to union rates, paid the union rate ◆ **quels sont vos ~s ?** *(réparateur)* how much do you charge?; *(profession libérale)* what are your fees? ◆ **est-ce le ~ habituel ?** is this the usual *ou* going rate? ◆ **voyager à plein ~/à ~ réduit** to travel at full/at reduced fare ◆ **billet plein ~/à ~ réduit** *(Transport)* full-fare/reduced-fare ticket; *(Ciné, Théât)* full-price/reduced-price ticket ◆ **"tarifs réduits pour étudiants"** "special prices for students", "student concessions" *(Brit)* ◆ **envoyer une lettre au ~ lent** *ou* **économique** ≃ to send a letter second class, to send a letter by second-class mail *ou* post *(Brit)* ◆ **100 € d'amende/deux mois de prison, c'est le ~ !*** *(hum)* a 100-euro fine/two months' prison is what you get!

COMP **tarif de base** *(gén)* standard *ou* basic rate; *(Publicité)* open rate, transient rate *(US)*
tarif dégressif *(gén)* tapering charges; *(Publicité)* earned rate
tarif étudiant *(pour transports)* student fare; *(pour loisirs)* student concession
tarif extérieur commun *(Europe)* common external tariff
tarif jeunes *(pour transports)* youth *ou* under-26 fare
tarif de nuit night *ou* off-peak rate

tarifaire / taʀifɛʀ / ADJ *[réduction, augmentation, préférence, guerre]* tariff ◆ **conditions ~s** tariff rates ◆ **politique ~** pricing policy ◆ **harmonisation ~** harmonisation of tariffs ◆ **barrières ~s** tariff barriers

tarifer / taʀife / ▸ conjug 1 ◂ VT to fix the price *ou* rate for ◆ **marchandises tarifées** fixed-price goods

tarification / taʀifikasjɔ̃ / NF *(= action)* setting *ou* fixing of prices *(de* for); *(= prix)* prices ◆ **nouvelle ~ à compter du 23 mai** new prices as of 23 May

tarin / taʀɛ̃ / NM 1 *(* = nez)* nose, conk* *(Brit)*, snoot* *(US)* 2 *(= oiseau)* siskin

tarir / taʀiʀ / ▸ conjug 2 ◂ VI 1 *[cours d'eau, puits, ressource]* to run dry, to dry up; *[larmes]* to dry (up); *[pitié, conversation, imagination]* to dry up 2 *[personne]* **il ne tarit pas sur ce sujet** he can't stop talking about it, he's unstoppable* on that subject ◆ **il ne tarit pas d'éloges sur elle** he never stops *ou* he can't stop singing her praises VT *(= arrêter)* to dry up ◆ **~ les larmes de**

qn *(littér)* to dry sb's tears VPR **se tarir** *[source]* to run dry, to dry up; *[rentrées d'argent, imagination]* to dry up ◆ **un puits tari** a dried-up well

tarissement /taʀismɑ̃/ NM *[de cours d'eau, puits]* drying up; *[de gisement, ressource]* depletion; *[de commandes, débouchés, offre, demande]* drying up

tarmac /taʀmak/ NM tarmac *(on airstrip)*

tarot /taʀo/ NM *(= jeu)* tarot; *(= paquet de cartes)* tarot (pack)

Tarse /taʀs/ NM Tarsus

tarse /taʀs/ NM *(= partie d'un pied, d'une patte)* tarsus

tarsien, -ienne /taʀsjɛ̃, jɛn/ ADJ tarsal

Tartan ® /taʀtan/ NM *(= revêtement)* Tartan ®; *(= piste)* tartan track

tartan /taʀtɑ̃/ NM *(= tissu)* tartan

tartane /taʀtan/ NF *(Naut)* tartan

tartare /taʀtaʀ/ ADJ 1 *(Hist)* Tartar 2 *(Culin)* **sauce** ~ tartar(e) sauce; → **steak** NMF *(Hist)* ◆ **Tartare** Tartar

tarte /taʀt/ NF 1 *(Culin)* tart ◆ ~ **aux fruits/à la crème** fruit/cream tart ◆ ~ **aux pommes** apple tart ◆ ~ **Tatin** tarte Tatin, ≈ apple upside-down tart ◆ **une** ~ **à la crème** *(péj)* *(= rengaine)* a pet theme; *(= comédie)* slapstick (comedy) ◆ **c'est pas de la** ~* it's no joke*, it's no easy matter 2 *(* = gifle)* clout, clip round the ear ◆ **elle lui a filé une** ~ she slapped him in the face ADJ INV * *(= laid)* *[personne]* plain-looking; *[chaussures, vêtement]* tacky*, naff* *(Brit)*; *(= bête)* stupid, daft* *(Brit)* ◆ **j'ai l'air** ~ **dans cette robe** I look stupid in this dress

tartelette /taʀtəlɛt/ NF tartlet, tart

Tartempion * /taʀtɑ̃pjɔ̃/ NM thingumabob*, so-and-so*, what's-his (ou -her)-name ◆ **un** ~ **quelconque** someone or other

tartiflette /taʀtiflɛt/ NF *dish made with potatoes, bacon and cheese*

tartignol(l)e * /taʀtiɲɔl/ ADJ *[personne, film]* stupid, daft* *(Brit)*; *[vêtement, chaussures]* tacky*

tartine /taʀtin/ NF 1 *(= tranche)* slice ou piece of bread; *(beurrée)* slice of bread and butter; *(de confiture)* slice of bread and jam ◆ **le matin, on mange des** ~**s** in the morning we have bread and butter ◆ **tu as déjà mangé trois** ~**s, ça suffit** you've already had three slices ou three pieces of bread, that's enough ◆ **couper des tranches de pain pour faire des** ~**s** to cut (slices of) bread for buttering ◆ ~ **de miel** slice ou piece of bread and honey ◆ ~ **grillée et beurrée** piece of toast and butter 2 *(* = texte long)* **il en a mis une** ~ he wrote reams ◆ **il y a une** ~ **dans le journal à propos de ...** there's a great spread in the paper about ...

tartiner /taʀtine/ ► conjug 1 ◄ VT 1 *[+ pain]* to spread *(de* with); *[+ beurre]* to spread ◆ **pâté de foie/fromage à** ~ liver/cheese spread ◆ **pâte à** ~ spread ◆ ~ **du pain de beurre** to butter bread 2 *(fig)* **il en a tartiné plusieurs pages** * he went on about it for several pages

tartre /taʀtʀ/ NM *[de dents, tonneau]* tartar, scale; *[de chaudière, bouilloire]* scale, fur *(Brit)*

tartrique /taʀtʀik/ ADJ ◆ **acide** ~ tartaric acid

tartu(f)fe /taʀtyf/ NM (sanctimonious) hypocrite ADJ hypocritical ◆ **il est un peu tartu(f)fe** he's something of a hypocrite

tartu(f)ferie /taʀtyfʀi/ NF hypocrisy

Tarzan /taʀzɑ̃/ NM Tarzan; *(* = homme musclé)* muscleman

tas /tɑ/ NM *(= amas)* heap, pile ◆ **mettre en** ~ to make a pile of, to put into a heap, to heap ou pile up ◆ **quel gros** ~ **!** * *(= personne obèse)* what a fat lump! *

◆ **un** ou **des tas de** * *(= beaucoup de)* loads of*, heaps of*, lots of ◆ **il connaît un** ~ **de choses/gens** he knows loads* ou heaps* ou lots of things/people ◆ **il y avait tout un** ~ **de gens** there was a whole load* of people there ◆ **j'ai appris des** ~ **de choses sur lui** I found out a lot about him ◆ **il m'a raconté un** ~ **de mensonges** he told me a pack of lies ◆ ~ **de crétins !** * you load ou bunch of idiots! *

◆ **dans le tas** * ◆ **tirer dans le** ~ to fire into the crowd ◆ **foncer dans le** ~ to charge in ◆ **dans le** ~**, on en trouvera bien un qui sache conduire** we're bound to find ONE who can drive ◆ **dans le** ~**, tu trouveras bien un stylo qui marche** you're bound to find ONE pen that works ◆ **j'ai acheté des cerises, tape** ou **pioche dans le** ~ I've bought some cherries so dig in* ou tuck in* ou help yourself

◆ **sur le tas** *(= par la pratique)* ◆ **apprendre un métier sur le** ~ to learn a trade on the job ou as one goes along ◆ **il a appris/s'est formé sur le** ~ he learned/was trained on the job ◆ **formation sur le** ~ on-the-job training; → **grève**

COMP **tas de boue** * *(= voiture)* heap*, wreck*, banger* *(Brit)*

tas de charge *(Archit)* tas de charge

tas de ferraille scrapheap ◆ **cette voiture/ce vélo, c'est un vrai** ~ **de ferraille !** * that car/that bike's only fit for the scrapheap

tas de fumier dung ou manure heap

tas d'ordures rubbish *(Brit)* ou garbage *(US)* heap

Tasmanie /tasmani/ NF Tasmania

tasmanien, -ienne /tasmanjɛ̃, jɛn/ ADJ Tasmanian NM,F **Tasmanien(ne)** Tasmanian

Tasse /tas/ NM ◆ **le** ~ Tasso

tasse /tɑs/ NF cup ◆ ~ **de porcelaine** china cup ◆ ~ **à thé** teacup ◆ ~ **à café** coffee cup ◆ ~ **de thé** cup of tea ◆ **ce n'est pas ma** ~ **de thé** *(hum)* it's not my cup of tea; → **boire**

tassé, e /tɑse/ (ptp de **tasser**) ADJ 1 *(= affaissé)* *[façade, mur]* that has settled ou sunk ou subsided; *[vieillard]* shrunken ◆ ~ **sur sa chaise** slumped on his chair 2 *(= serrés)* ~**s** *[spectateurs, passagers]* packed (tight)

◆ **bien tassé** * *(= fort)* *[whisky]* stiff *(épith)*; *(= bien rempli)* *[verre]* well-filled, full to the brim *(attrib)* ◆ **café bien** ~ good strong coffee ◆ **trois kilos bien** ~**s** a good three kilos ◆ **il a 50 ans bien** ~**s** he's well into his fifties, he's well over fifty

tasseau (pl **tasseaux**) /tɑso/ NM *(= morceau de bois)* piece ou length of wood; *(= support)* bracket

tassement /tɑsmɑ̃/ NM 1 *[de sol, neige]* packing down 2 *[de mur, terrain]* settling, subsidence ◆ ~ **de la colonne (vertébrale)** compression of the spinal column 3 *(= diminution)* **le** ~ **des voix en faveur du candidat** the drop ou fall-off in votes for the candidate ◆ **un** ~ **de l'activité économique** a downturn ou a slowing down in economic activity

tasser /tɑse/ ► conjug 1 ◄ VT 1 *(= comprimer)* *[+ sol, neige]* to pack down, to tamp down; *[+ foin, paille]* to pack ◆ ~ **des vêtements dans une valise** to cram clothes into a suitcase ◆ ~ **le contenu d'une valise** to push down the contents of a case ◆ ~ **le tabac dans sa pipe** to pack ou tamp down the tobacco in one's pipe ◆ ~ **des prisonniers dans un camion** to cram ou pack prisoners into a truck

2 *(Sport)* *[+ concurrent]* to box in

VPR **se tasser** 1 *(= s'affaisser)* *[façade, mur, terrain]* to sink, to subside; *[vieillard, corps]* to shrink; *[demande]* to slow down

2 *(= se serrer)* to bunch up ◆ **on s'est tassé à dix dans la voiture** ten of us crammed into the car ◆ **tassez-vous, il y a encore de la place** bunch ou squeeze up, there's still room

3 *(* = s'arranger)* to settle down ◆ **ne vous en faites pas, ça va se** ~ don't worry – things will settle down ou iron themselves out *

4 *(* = engloutir)* *[+ petits fours, boissons]* to down*, to get through*

taste-vin /tastəvɛ̃/ NM INV (wine-)tasting cup

tata /tata/ NF 1 *(langage enfantin = tante)* auntie* 2 *(* = homosexuel)* queer*

tatami /tatami/ NM tatami

tatane * /tatan/ NF shoe

tatar, e /tataʀ/ ADJ Ta(r)tar NM *(= langue)* Ta(r)tar NM,F **Tatar(e)** Ta(r)tar

tâter /tɑte/ ► conjug 1 ◄ VT 1 *(= palper)* *[+ objet, étoffe, pouls]* to feel ◆ ~ **qch du bout des doigts** to feel ou explore sth with one's fingertips ◆ **marcher en tâtant les murs** to feel ou grope one's way along the walls

2 *(= sonder)* *[+ adversaire, concurrent]* to try (out) ◆ ~ **l'opinion** to sound ou test out opinion ◆ ~ **le terrain** to find out how the land lies, to put out feelers, to find out the lie *(Brit)* ou lay *(US)* of the land

VT INDIR **tâter de** 1 (†, *littér = goûter à)* *[+ mets]* to taste, to try

2 *(= essayer, passer par)* to sample, to try out ◆ ~ **de la prison** to sample prison life, to have a taste of prison ◆ **il a tâté de tous les métiers** he's had a go at* ou he's tried his hand at lots of jobs

VPR **se tâter** 1 *(après une chute)* to feel o.s. *(for injuries)*; *(pensant avoir perdu qch)* to feel one's pocket(s) ◆ **il se releva, se tâta : rien de cassé** he got up and felt himself but there was nothing broken

2 *(* = hésiter)* to be in *(Brit)* ou of *(US)* two minds ◆ **tu viendras ? – je ne sais pas, je me tâte** are you coming? – I don't know, I haven't made up my mind

tâte-vin /tatvɛ̃/ NM INV ⇒ **taste-vin**

tati(e) /tati/ NF *(langage enfantin)* auntie*

tatillon, -onne /tatijɔ̃, ɔn/ ADJ *[personne]* pernickety *(Brit)*, persnickety *(US)* ◆ **il est** ~**, c'est un** ~ he's very pernickety *(Brit)* ◆ **des contrôles** ~**s** overzealous checks ◆ **surveillance** ~**ne** strict supervision

tâtonnant, e /tɑtɔnɑ̃, ɑt/ ADJ *[geste, main]* groping *(épith)*; *[style]* hesitant ◆ **leurs recherches étaient** ~**es** they were feeling their way in their research

tâtonnement /tɑtɔnmɑ̃/ NM *(gén pl = essai)* trial and error *(NonC)*, experimentation *(NonC)* ◆ **après bien des** ~**s** after a lot of trial and error ◆ **procéder par** ~**(s)** to proceed by trial and error ◆ **les premiers** ~**s d'une technique** the first tentative steps in a new technique

tâtonner /tɑtɔne/ ► conjug 1 ◄ VI 1 *(pour se diriger)* to grope ou feel one's way (along), to grope along; *(pour trouver qch)* to grope ou feel around ou about 2 *(= essayer)* to grope around; *(par méthode)* to proceed by trial and error

tâtons /tɑtɔ̃/ **à tâtons** LOC ADV ◆ **avancer à** ~ *(lit)* to grope along, to grope ou feel one's way along; *(fig)* to feel one's way along ◆ **chercher qch à** ~ *(lit, fig)* to grope ou feel around for sth

tatou /tatu/ NM armadillo

tatouage /tatwaʒ/ NM *(= action)* tattooing; *(= dessin)* tattoo ◆ **son dos est couvert de** ~**s** his back is covered with ou in tattoos

tatouer /tatwe/ ► conjug 1 ◄ VT to tattoo ◆ **se faire** ~ **le dos** to have one's back tattooed ◆ **mon chat est tatoué à l'oreille** my cat has a tattoo in its ear *(for identification)*

tatoueur, -euse /tatwœʀ, øz/ NM,F tattooer

tau /to/ NM INV 1 *(= lettre grecque)* tau 2 *(Héraldique)* tau cross, Saint Anthony's cross

taudis /todi/ NM *(= logement)* hovel; *(pl)* *(Admin)* slums ◆ **ta chambre est un vrai** ~ *(en désordre)* your room's a real pigsty

taulard, -arde‡ /tolaʀ, aʀd/ NM,F convict, con‡

taule‡ /tol/ NF [1] (= prison) jail, clink‡, nick‡ (Brit) ◆ **être en ~** to be inside*, to be in the nick‡ (Brit) ◆ **aller en ~** to go down*, to get banged up‡ (Brit) ◆ **mettre** ou **foutre**‡ **qn en ~** to put sb in jail ◆ **il a fait de la ~** he's done time* ou a stretch*, he's been inside* ◆ **il a eu cinq ans de ~** he's been given a five-year stretch* ou five years in the nick‡ (Brit) [2] (= chambre) room

taulier, -ière‡ /tolje, jɛʀ/ NM,F (hotel) boss*

taupe /top/ NF [1] (= animal) mole [2] (= fourrure) moleskin; → **myope** [3] * (= espion) mole ◆ **une vieille ~** (péj) an old bag‡ ou hag [4] (arg Scol = classe) advanced maths class preparing students for the Grandes Écoles

taupin /topɛ̃/ NM [1] (= animal) click beetle, elaterida (SPÉC) [2] (arg Scol) maths student preparing for the Grandes Écoles

taupinière /topinjɛʀ/ NF (= tas) molehill; (= galeries, terrier) mole tunnel

taureau (pl **taureaux**) /tɔʀo/ NM [1] (= animal) bull ◆ **~ de combat** fighting bull ◆ **il avait une force de ~** he was as strong as an ox ◆ **une encolure** ou **un cou de ~** a bull neck ◆ **prendre le ~ par les cornes** to take the bull by the horns [2] (Astron) **le Taureau** Taurus ◆ **il est Taureau, il est (du signe) du Taureau** he's (a) Taurus; → **course**

taurillon /tɔʀijɔ̃/ NM bull-calf

taurin, e /tɔʀɛ̃, in/ ADJ bullfighting (épith)

tauromachie /tɔʀɔmaʃi/ NF bullfighting, tauromachy (SPÉC)

tauromachique /tɔʀɔmaʃik/ ADJ bullfighting (épith)

tautologie /totɔlɔʒi/ NF tautology

tautologique /totɔlɔʒik/ ADJ tautological

taux /to/ NM [1] (Fin) rate ◆ **~ actuariel (brut)** annual percentage rate ◆ **~ de base bancaire** minimum ou base ou prime (US) lending rate ◆ **~ de change** exchange rate, rate of exchange ◆ **~ court/moyen/long** short-term/medium-term/long-term rate ◆ **~ de croissance** growth rate ◆ **~ d'escompte** discount rate ◆ **~ d'intérêt** interest rate, rate of interest ◆ **~ officiel d'escompte** bank rate ◆ **~ de prêt** lending rate ◆ **~ de TVA** VAT rate ◆ **prêt à ~ zéro** interest-free loan
[2] (Stat) rate ◆ **~ de natalité/mortalité** birth/death ou mortality rate ◆ **~ de chômage** unemployment rate ◆ **~ de réussite** (à un examen) pass rate ◆ **~ d'audience** (TV) audience figures ◆ **~ d'écoute** (Radio) audience figures ◆ **~ de fréquentation** (Ciné, Théât) attendance ou audience figures
[3] (Méd, Sci = niveau, degré) [de cholestérol, sucre] level ◆ **~ de pollution/radioactivité** level of pollution/radioactivity, pollution/radioactivity level ◆ **~ d'invalidité** (Méd) degree of disability ◆ **~ de compression** [de moteur] compression ratio

tavelé, e /tav(ə)le/ (ptp de **taveler**) ADJ [fruit] marked ◆ **visage ~ de taches de son** face covered in freckles ◆ **visage ~ par la petite vérole** pockmarked face, face pitted with pockmarks

taveler /tav(ə)le/ ► conjug 4 ◄ VT [+ fruit] to mark
VPR **se taveler** [fruit] to become marked

tavelure /tav(ə)lyʀ/ NF mark (on fruit)

taverne /tavɛʀn/ NF (Hist) inn, tavern; (Can) tavern, beer parlor (Can)

tavernier, -ière /tavɛʀnje, jɛʀ/ NM,F (Hist, hum) innkeeper

taxable /taksabl/ ADJ (gén) taxable; (à la douane) liable to duty (épith), dutiable

taxation /taksasjɔ̃/ NF [1] (= imposition) [de marchandise, service, particuliers] taxing, taxation ◆ **seuil de ~** tax threshold [2] (Admin, Comm) [de valeur] fixing (the rate); [de marchandise] fixing the price; (Jur) [de dépens] taxation ◆ **~ d'office** estimation of tax(es)

taxe /taks/ NF [1] (= impôt, redevance) tax; (à la douane) duty ◆ **~s locales/municipales** local/municipal taxes ◆ **toutes ~s comprises** inclusive of tax ◆ **hors ~(s)** [boutique, article] duty-free; (sur facture) exclusive of VAT; [prix] before tax (attrib)
[2] (Admin, Comm = tarif) statutory price ◆ **vendre des marchandises à la ~/plus cher que la ~** to sell goods at/for more than the statutory price
[3] (Jur) [de dépens] taxation, assessment
COMP **taxes d'aéroport** airport tax(es)
taxe d'apprentissage apprenticeship tax (paid by French employers to finance apprenticeships)
taxe d'habitation local tax paid by residents, ≈ council tax (Brit)
taxe professionnelle local tax on businesses, ≈ business rate (Brit)
taxe de raccordement (Téléc) connection fee
taxe de séjour tourist tax
taxe à ou **sur la valeur ajoutée** ≈ sales tax, value-added tax (Brit)

taxer /takse/ ► conjug 1 ◄ VT [1] (= imposer) [+ marchandises, service] to put ou impose a tax on, to tax; (à la douane) to impose ou put duty on; [+ personne, entreprise] to tax ◆ **produits taxés à 5,5%** products taxed at 5.5% ◆ **~ qn d'office** to assess sb for tax ou taxation (purposes)
[2] (Admin, Comm) [+ valeur] to fix (the rate of); [+ marchandise] to fix the price of; (Jur) [+ dépens] to tax, to assess
[3] (‡ = voler) to pinch*, to nick‡ (Brit) ◆ **il l'a taxé au supermarché** he pinched* ou nicked‡ (Brit) it from the supermarket
[4] (* = prendre) **je peux te ~ une cigarette ?** can I pinch a cigarette? ◆ **il m'a taxé de 20 €** he got 20 euros out of me*
[5] ◆ **~ qn de qch** (= le qualifier de qch) to call sb sth; (= l'accuser de qch) to accuse sb of sth, to tax sb with sth (frm) ◆ **une méthode que l'on a taxée de charlatanisme** a method which has been referred to as charlatanism ◆ **on le taxe d'avarice** he's accused of miserliness ou of being a miser

taxi /taksi/ NM [1] (= voiture) taxi, (taxi)cab ◆ **~-brousse** bush taxi ◆ **bateau-/vélo-~** (en apposition) boat/bicycle taxi; → **chauffeur, station** [2] (* = chauffeur) cabby* (Brit), taxi ou cab driver ◆ **elle fait (le) ~** she's a cabby*, she's a taxi ou cab driver ◆ **j'en ai assez de faire le ~** (fig) I'm fed up* driving everyone around

taxidermie /taksidɛʀmi/ NF taxidermy

taxidermiste /taksidɛʀmist/ NMF taxidermist

taxi-girl (pl **taxi-girls**) /taksigœʀl/ NF (= danseuse) taxigirl

taximètre /taksimɛtʀ/ NM (taxi)meter

taxinomie /taksinɔmi/ NF taxonomy

taxinomique /taksinɔmik/ ADJ taxonomic(al)

taxinomiste /taksinɔmist/ NMF taxonomist

taxiphone ® /taksifɔn/ NM payphone, public (tele)phone

taxiway /taksiwɛ/ NM taxiway

taxonomie /taksɔnɔmi/ NF ⇒ **taxinomie**

taxonomique /taksɔnɔmik/ ADJ ⇒ **taxinomique**

taylorisation /telɔʀizasjɔ̃/ NF Taylorization

tayloriser /telɔʀize/ ► conjug 1 ◄ VT [+ production] to Taylorize ◆ **usine taylorisée** mass production factory

taylorisme /telɔʀism/ NM Taylorism

TB (abrév de **très bien**) VG

TBB /tebebe/ NM (abrév de **taux de base bancaire**) → **taux**

Tbilissi /tbilisi/ N Tbilisi

Tchad /tʃad/ NM ◆ **le ~** Chad ◆ **le lac ~** Lake Chad

tchadien, -ienne /tʃadjɛ̃, jɛn/ ADJ Chad NM,F **Tchadien(ne)** Chad

tchador /tʃadɔʀ/ NM chador

tchao /tʃao/ EXCL bye!, ciao!, cheerio! (Brit)

tchatche‡ /tʃatʃ/ NF (gén) talk; (péj) yacking* ◆ **il a une de ces ~s !** he's got the gift of the gab!*

tchatcher‡ /tʃatʃe/ ► conjug 1 ◄ VI (péj) to yack* ◆ **il ne fait que ~** he never stops yacking*, all he does is yak yak yak*

tchatcheur, -euse‡ /tʃatʃœʀ, øz/ NM,F smooth talker

tchécoslovaque /tʃekɔslɔvak/ ADJ Czechoslovak(ian) NMF **Tchécoslovaque** Czechoslovakian

Tchécoslovaquie /tʃekɔslɔvaki/ NF Czechoslovakia

Tchekhov /tʃekɔv/ NM Chek(h)ov

tchèque /tʃɛk/ ADJ Czech ◆ **la République ~** the Czech Republic NM (= langue) Czech NMF **Tchèque** Czech

Tchéquie /tʃeki/ NF ◆ **la ~** the Czech Republic

Tchernobyl /tʃɛʀnɔbil/ N Chernobyl

tchétchène /tʃetʃɛn/ ADJ Chechen NMF **Tchétchène** Chechen

Tchétchénie /tʃetʃeni/ NF Chechnya

tchin(-tchin)* /tʃin(tʃin)/ EXCL cheers!

TD /tede/ NM (abrév de **travaux dirigés**) (Univ) → **travail**[1]

TDF /tedeɛf/ NF (abrév de **Télédiffusion de France**) ≈ IBA (Brit), FCC (US)

te /tə/ PRON PERS [1] (objet direct ou indirect) you ◆ **~ l'a-t-il dit ?** did he tell you? ◆ **t'en a-t-il parlé ?** did he speak to you about it? [2] (réfléchi) yourself ◆ **si tu ~ poses des questions** if you ask yourself questions ◆ **tu t'es fait mal ?** did you hurt yourself? ◆ **comment ~ sens-tu ?** (souvent non traduit) how do you feel? ◆ **tu devrais ~ doucher** you should have a shower ◆ **va ~ laver les dents/les mains** go and brush your teeth/wash your hands

té[1] /te/ NM (= règle) T-square; (= ferrure) T(-shaped) bracket ◆ **fer en ~** T-shaped iron

té[2] /te/ EXCL (dial) well! well!, my!

TEC /teəse/ NF (abrév de **tonne équivalent charbon**) TCE

technicien, -ienne /tɛknisjɛ̃, jɛn/ NM,F technician ◆ **il est ~ en électronique** he's an electronics engineer ◆ **~ de surface** (Admin) cleaning operative ◆ **~ de (la) télévision** television technician ◆ **c'est un ~ de la politique/finance** he's a political/financial expert ou wizard

technicité /tɛknisite/ NF [de recherche, sujet, langage] technical nature; [de personne] technical skill ◆ **produit de haute ~** technically advanced ou high-tech product

technico-commercial, e (mpl **technico-commerciaux**) /tɛknikokɔmɛʀsjal, jo/ ADJ, NM,F ◆ **(agent) ~** technical salesman ◆ **(ingénieur) ~** sales engineer

Technicolor ® /tɛknikɔlɔʀ/ NM Technicolor ® ◆ **film en ~** Technicolor film, film in Technicolor

technique /tɛknik/ ADJ technical; → **contrôle, escale, incident** NF [1] (= méthode) technique ◆ **il n'a pas la (bonne) ~*** he hasn't got the knack* *ou* the right technique ◆ **c'est toute une ~ !** it's quite an art! ◆ **manquer de ~** to lack technique [2] *(= aire de la connaissance)* **la ~** technology NM *(enseignement)* ◆ **le ~** technical education, industrial arts *(US)* ◆ **il est professeur dans le ~** he's a technical teacher

techniquement /tɛknikmɑ̃/ ADV technically

techno¹ /tɛkno/ ADJ, NF *(Mus)* techno ◆ **la (musique) ~** techno (music)

techno²* /tɛkno/ NF abrév de **technologie**

technocrate /tɛknɔkʀat/ NMF technocrat

technocratie /tɛknɔkʀasi/ NF technocracy

technocratique /tɛknɔkʀatik/ ADJ technocratic

technocratisme /tɛknɔkʀatism/ NM *[de gestionnaire]* technocratic attitude; *[d'institution]* technocratic ethos

technologie /tɛknɔlɔʒi/ NF *(gén)* technology; *(Scol) subject area covering basic technological skills taught in French schools* ◆ **~ de pointe** *ou* **avancée** leading-edge *ou* advanced technology ◆ **~ de l'information** information technology ◆ **la haute ~** high technology ◆ **~ des systèmes automatisés** automated systems technology

technologique /tɛknɔlɔʒik/ ADJ technological ◆ **révolution ~** technological revolution

technologiquement /tɛknɔlɔʒikmɑ̃/ ADV technologically

technologue /tɛknɔlɔg/ NMF technologist

technophobe /tɛknɔfɔb/ NMF technophobe

technopole /tɛknɔpɔl/ NF town with high-tech industrial research and development facilities

technopôle /tɛknopol/ NM science and technology park *(with research facilities)*

technostructure /tɛknostʀyktyʀ/ NF technostructure

teck /tɛk/ NM teak

teckel /tekɛl/ NM dachshund

tectonique /tɛktɔnik/ ADJ tectonic NF tectonics *(sg)* ◆ **~ des plaques** plate tectonics

Te Deum /tedeɔm/ NM INV Te Deum

tee /ti/ NM tee ◆ **partir du ~** to tee off

tee(-)shirt /tiʃœʀt/ NM T-shirt, tee shirt

Téflon ® /teflɔ̃/ NM Teflon ®

Tegucigalpa /tegusigalpa/ N Tegucigalpa

tégument /tegymɑ̃/ NM *(Bot, Zool)* (in)tegument

Téhéran /teeʀɑ̃/ N Teheran

teigne /tɛɲ/ NF [1] *(= papillon)* moth, tinea *(SPÉC)* [2] *(= dermatose)* ringworm, tinea *(SPÉC)* [3] *(péj)* *(= homme)* bastard*‚*, swine*‚* *(Brit)*; *(= femme)* shrew, vixen ◆ **mauvais** *ou* **méchant comme une ~** as nasty as anything

teigneux, -euse /tɛɲø, øz/ ADJ *(Méd)* suffering from ringworm ◆ **il est ~** *(lit)* he has *ou* is suffering from ringworm; *(péj = pouilleux)* he's scabby*; *(péj = acariâtre)* he's very cantankerous, he's real ornery* *(US)*

teindre /tɛ̃dʀ/ ► conjug 52 ◄ VT *[+ vêtement, cheveux]* to dye; *(littér)* to tint, to tinge VPR **se teindre** [1] ◆ **se ~ (les cheveux)** to dye one's hair ◆ **se ~ la barbe/la moustache** to dye one's beard/one's moustache [2] *(littér = se colorer)* **les montagnes se teignaient de rose** the mountains took on a pink hue *ou* were tinged with pink

teint¹ /tɛ̃/ NM [1] *(= couleur de peau)* *(permanent)* complexion, colouring *(Brit)*, coloring *(US)*; *(momentané)* colour *(Brit)*, color *(US)* ◆ **avoir le ~ frais** to be looking well ◆ **~ de rose/de porcelaine** rosy/porcelain complexion [2] *(= couleur d'un tissu)* **grand ~** *[couleur]* fast; *[tissu]* colourfast *(Brit)*, colorfast *(US)* ◆ **bon ~** *[couleur]* fast; *[syndicaliste]* staunch, dyed-in-the-wool; → **fond**

teint², e¹ /tɛ̃, tɛ̃t/ (ptp de **teindre**) ADJ *[cheveux, laine]* dyed ◆ **elle est ~e** *(péj)* her hair is dyed, she dyes her hair

teinte² /tɛ̃t/ NF [1] *(= nuance)* shade, hue, tint; *(= couleur)* colour *(Brit)*, color *(US)* ◆ **pull aux ~s vives** brightly-coloured sweater [2] *(fig)* *(= léger côté)* tinge, hint ◆ **avec une ~ de tristesse dans la voix** with a tinge *ou* hint of sadness in his voice

teinté, e /tɛ̃te/ (ptp de **teinter**) ADJ *[bois]* stained; *[verre]* tinted ◆ **crème ~e** tinted day cream ◆ **table ~e acajou** mahogany-stained table ◆ **blanc ~ de rose** white with a hint of pink ◆ **discours ~ de puritanisme** speech tinged with puritanism

teinter /tɛ̃te/ ► conjug 1 ◄ VT *[+ papier, verre]* to tint; *[+ meuble, bois]* to stain ◆ **un peu d'eau teintée de vin** a little water with a hint of wine *ou* just coloured with wine VPR **se teinter** *(littér)* **se ~ d'amertume** to become tinged with bitterness ◆ **les sommets se teintèrent de pourpre** the peaks took on a purple tinge *ou* hue *ou* tint, the peaks were tinged with purple

teinture /tɛ̃tyʀ/ NF [1] *(= colorant)* dye; *(= action)* dyeing [2] *(Pharm)* tincture ◆ **~ d'arnica/d'iode** tincture of arnica/of iodine

teinturerie /tɛ̃tyʀʀi/ NF *(= métier, industrie)* dyeing; *(= magasin)* (dry) cleaner's

teinturier, -ière /tɛ̃tyʀje, jɛʀ/ NM,F *(qui nettoie)* dry cleaner; *(qui teint)* dyer

tek /tɛk/ NM ⇒ **teck**

tel, telle /tɛl/ ADJ [1] *(similitude, sg : avec nom concret)* such, like; *(avec nom abstrait)* such; *(pl)* such ◆ **une telle ignorance/réponse est inexcusable** such ignorance/such an answer is inexcusable ◆ **~ père, ~ fils** like father like son ◆ **nous n'avons pas de ~s orages en Europe** we don't get such storms *ou* storms like this in Europe ◆ **as-tu jamais rien vu de ~ ?** have you ever seen such a thing?, have you ever seen anything like it? ◆ **s'il n'est pas menteur, il passe pour ~** perhaps he isn't a liar but that's the reputation he has ◆ **il a filé ~ un zèbre** he was off like a shot ◆ **~s sont ces gens que vous croyiez honnêtes** that's what the people you thought were honest are really like ◆ **prenez telles décisions qui vous sembleront nécessaires** *(frm)* take such decisions as you deem *ou* whatever decisions you deem necessary ◆ **telles furent ses dernières paroles** those *ou* such *(frm)* were his last words ◆ **il est le patron, en tant que ~** *ou* **comme ~ il aurait dû agir** he is the boss and as such he ought to have taken action, he's the boss and in that capacity he should have acted ◆ **~ il était enfant, ~ je le retrouve** thus he was as a child, and thus he has remained ◆ **le lac ~ un miroir** *(littér)* the lake like a mirror *ou* mirror-like; → **rien**

[2] *(valeur d'indéfini)* such-and-such ◆ **~ et ~** such-and-such ◆ **venez ~ jour/à telle heure** come on such-and-such a day/at such-and-such a time ◆ **telle quantité d'arsenic peut tuer un homme et pas un autre** a given quantity of arsenic can kill one man and not another ◆ **telle ou telle personne vous dira que ...** someone *ou* somebody or other will tell you that ... ◆ **j'ai lu dans ~ ou ~ article que ...** I read in some article or other that ... ◆ **~ enfant qui se croit menacé devient agressif** any child that feels threatened will become aggressive ◆ **l'on connaît ~ bureau où ...** there's *ou* I know a certain office *ou* one office where ...

[3] *(locutions)*

♦ **tel(le) que** like, (such *ou* the same *ou* just) as; *(énumération)* like, such as ◆ **il est resté ~ que je le connaissais** he is still the same *ou* just as he used to be, he's stayed just as I remember him ◆ **un homme ~ que lui doit comprendre** a man like him *ou* such a man as he *(frm)* must understand ◆ **~ que je le connais, il ne viendra pas** if I know him, he won't come ◆ **~ que vous me voyez, je reviens d'Afrique** I'm just back from Africa ◆ **~ que vous me voyez, j'ai 72 ans** you wouldn't think it to look at me but I'm 72 ◆ **restez ~ que vous êtes** stay (just) as you are ◆ **là il se montre ~ qu'il est** now he's showing himself in his true colours *ou* as he really is ◆ **les métaux ~s que l'or, l'argent et le platine** metals like *ou* such as gold, silver and platinum ◆ **le ciel à l'occident ~ qu'un brasier** *(littér)* the western sky like a fiery furnace ◆ **laissez tous ces dossiers ~s que*** leave all those files as they are *ou* as you find them ◆ **il m'a dit : "sortez d'ici ou je vous sors", ~ que !*** he said to me "get out of here or I'll throw you out" – just like that!

♦ **tel(le) quel(le)** ◆ **il a acheté la maison telle quelle*** he bought the house (just) as it was *ou* stood ◆ **"à vendre tel quel"** *(sur objet en solde)* "sold as seen" *(Brit)*, "sold as is" *(US)*

[4] *(intensif, sg : avec nom concret)* such a; *(avec nom abstrait)* such; *(pl)* such ◆ **on n'a jamais vu une telle cohue** you've never seen such a crush ◆ **c'est une telle joie de l'entendre !** what a joy *ou* it's such a joy to hear him!

[5] *(avec conséquence)* **de telle façon** *ou* **manière** in such a way ◆ **ils ont eu de ~s ennuis avec leur voiture qu'ils l'ont vendue** they had such (a lot of) trouble *ou* so much trouble with their car that they sold it ◆ **de telle sorte que** so that ◆ **à telle(s) enseigne(s) que** so much so that; → **point¹**

PRON INDÉF ◆ **~ vous dira qu'il faut voter oui, ~ autre ...** one will tell you you must vote yes, another ... ◆ **si ~ ou ~ vous dit que ...** if somebody *ou* anybody tells you that ... ◆ **~ est pris qui croyait prendre** *(Prov)* it's the biter bit ◆ **~ qui rit vendredi, dimanche pleurera** *(Prov)* you can be laughing on Friday but crying by Sunday; → **un**

tél. (abrév de **téléphone**) tel.

télé* /tele/ NF (abrév de **télévision**) [1] *(= organisme)* TV ◆ **il travaille à la ~** he works on TV [2] *(= programmes)* TV ◆ **qu'est-ce qu'il y a à la ~ ce soir ?** what's on TV *ou* the box* *ou* telly* *(Brit)* tonight? ◆ **son mari est passé à la ~** her husband has been *ou* has appeared on TV [3] *(= poste)* TV, telly* *(Brit)* ◆ **allume la ~** turn on the TV *ou* the telly* *(Brit)* NM abrév de **téléobjectif**

téléachat /teleaʃa/ NM teleshopping *(NonC)*

téléacteur, -trice /teleaktœʀ, tʀis/ NM,F telesales operator *ou* clerk

téléalarme /telealaʀm/ NF remote alarm

télébenne /telebɛn/ NF ⇒ **télécabine**

téléboutique ® /telebutik/ NF phone shop

télécabine /telekabin/ NF cable car

télécarte ® /telekaʀt/ NF phonecard

téléchargeable /teleʃaʀʒabl/ ADJ downloadable

téléchargement /teleʃaʀʒəmɑ̃/ NM downloading

télécharger /teleʃaʀʒe/ ► conjug 3 ◄ VTI to download

télécinéma /telesinema/ NM *(= appareil)* telecine

télécommande /telekɔmɑ̃d/ NF remote control

télécommander /telekɔmɑ̃de/ ► conjug 1 ◄ VT to operate by remote control ◆ **un complot télécommandé de l'étranger** a plot masterminded from abroad

télécommunication /telekɔmynikasjɔ̃/ NF telecommunications ◆ **réseau de ~(s)** telecommunications *ou* telecoms network ◆ **les ~s sont en pleine expansion** the telecommunications industry is booming

télécoms * /telekɔm/ NFPL (abrév de **télécommunications**) ◆ **les ~** telecommunications, the telecommunications industry ◆ **ingénieur télécom(s)** telecommunications engineer

téléconférence /telekɔ̃feʀɑ̃s/ NF (= *méthode*) teleconferencing; (= *discussion*) teleconference, conference call

télécopie /telekɔpi/ NF (= *procédé*) fax; (= *document*) fax ◆ **transmettre par ~** to send by fax, to fax

télécopieur /telekɔpjœʀ/ NM fax (machine)

télédétection /teledetɛksjɔ̃/ NF remote sensing ◆ **satellite de ~** remote-sensing satellite

télédiffuser /teledifyze/ ▸ conjug 1 ◂ VT to broadcast by television

télédiffusion /teledifyzjɔ̃/ NF television broadcasting ◆ **Télédiffusion de France** *French broadcasting authority*, ≃ Independent Broadcasting Authority *(Brit)*, Federal Communications Commission *(US)*

télédistribution /teledistʀibysjɔ̃/ NF cable broadcasting

téléenseignement /teleɑ̃sɛɲmɑ̃/ NM distance learning

téléférique /telefeʀik/ NM (= *installation*) cableway; (= *cabine*) cable-car

téléfilm /telefilm/ NM television *ou* TV film, made-for-TV movie

télégénique /teleʒenik/ ADJ telegenic

télégestion /teleʒɛstjɔ̃/ NF remote management

télégramme /telegʀam/ NM telegram, wire, cable

télégraphe /telegʀaf/ NM telegraph

télégraphie /telegʀafi/ NF (= *technique*) telegraphy ◆ **~ optique** signalling ◆ **~ sans fil** † wireless telegraphy †

télégraphier /telegʀafje/ ▸ conjug 7 ◂ VT [+ *message*] to telegraph, to wire, to cable ◆ **tu devrais lui ~** you should send him a telegram *ou* wire *ou* cable, you should wire (to) him *ou* cable him

télégraphique /telegʀafik/ ADJ 1 [*poteau, fils*] telegraph *(épith)*; [*alphabet, code*] Morse *(épith)*; [*message*] telegram *(épith)*, telegraphed, telegraphic ◆ **adresse ~** telegraphic address 2 [*style, langage*] telegraphic

télégraphiste /telegʀafist/ NMF (= *technicien*) telegrapher, telegraphist; (= *messager*) telegraph boy

téléguidage /telegidaʒ/ NM remote control

téléguider /telegide/ ▸ conjug 1 ◂ VT 1 [+ *appareil*] to operate by remote control ◆ **voiture téléguidée** remote-controlled *ou* radio-controlled car ◆ **engin téléguidé** guided missile 2 (= *manipuler*) [+ *personne, organisation*] to control (from a distance); (= *diriger*) [+ *action, complot, campagne de presse*] to mastermind

téléimprimeur /teleɛ̃pʀimœʀ/ NM teleprinter

téléinformatique /teleɛ̃fɔʀmatik/ NF telecomputing, remote computing

téléjournal /teleʒuʀnal/ NM (*Helv* = *journal télévisé*) television news (bulletin)

télékinésie /telekinezi/ NF telekinesis

télémaintenance /telemɛ̃t(ə)nɑ̃s/ NF remote maintenance

télémanipulation /telemanipylasjɔ̃/ NF remote control handling

Télémaque /telemak/ NM Telemachus

télémark /telemaʀk/ NM (= *discipline*) telemark skiing; (= *virage*) telemark turn ◆ **skis ~** telemark skis

télémarketing /telemaʀketiŋ/ NM telemarketing

télématique /telematik/ ADJ [*serveur, service, réseau*] data communications *(épith)* NF computer telephone integration, CTI

télémessage /telemesaʒ/ NM text message

télémètre /telemɛtʀ/ NM *(Mil, Photo)* rangefinder

télémétrie /telemetʀi/ NF telemetry

télémétrique /telemetʀik/ ADJ telemetric(al) ◆ **appareil à visée ~** rangefinder camera

téléobjectif /teleɔbʒɛktif/ NM telephoto lens

téléologie /teleɔlɔʒi/ NF teleology

téléologique /teleɔlɔʒik/ ADJ teleologic(al)

téléopérateur, -trice /teleɔpeʀatœʀ, tʀis/ NM paging operator

téléopération /teleɔpeʀasjɔ̃/ NF ◆ **service/système de ~** paging service/system

télépaiement /telepɛmɑ̃/ NM electronic payment

télépathe /telepat/ ADJ telepathic NMF telepathist

télépathie /telepati/ NF telepathy

télépathique /telepatik/ ADJ telepathic

télépayer /telepeje/ ▸ conjug 8 ◂ VT to pay for *(via electronic payment system)*

télépéage /telepeaʒ/ NM *motorway toll system based on electronic tagging of cars*

téléphérage /telefeʀaʒ/ NM transport by cableway

téléphérique /telefeʀik/ NM ⇒ **téléférique**

téléphone /telefɔn/ GRAMMAIRE ACTIVE 54.7

NM (= *système*) telephone; (= *appareil*) (tele) phone ◆ **le ~ marche très bien dans notre pays** (= *service*) our country has an excellent telephone service ◆ **avoir le ~** to be on the (tele)phone *(Brit)*, to have a (tele)phone ◆ **donne-moi ton ~** * (= *numéro*) give me your phone number; → **abonné, numéro**

◆ **au téléphone** ◆ **demande-le-lui au ~** phone him (and ask) about it, give him a call about it ◆ **je l'ai/il est au ~** I have him/he's on the phone ◆ **j'avais Jean au ~ quand on nous a coupés** I was on the phone to Jean when we were cut off ◆ **on vous demande au ~** there's someone on the phone for you, you're wanted on the phone

◆ **par téléphone** ◆ **demande-le-lui par ~** phone him (and ask) about it, give him a call about it ◆ **tu peux me donner les renseignements par ~** you can give me the information over the phone ◆ **réserver par ~** to reserve by telephone, to make a (tele) phone booking

◆ **coup de téléphone** (phone) call ◆ **j'ai eu un coup de ~ de Richard** I had *ou* got a phone call from Richard ◆ **donner** *ou* **passer un coup de ~ à qn** to phone sb, to call sb, to give sb a call *ou* ring *(Brit)*, to ring sb up *(Brit)* ◆ **il faut que je donne un coup de ~** I've got to make a phone call ◆ **recevoir un coup de ~ (de qn)** to get a (phone) call (from sb)

COMP **téléphone arabe** bush telegraph ◆ **apprendre qch par le ~ arabe** to hear sth through the grapevine *ou* on the bush telegraph
téléphone automatique automatic telephone system
téléphone de brousse ⇒ **téléphone arabe**
téléphone à cadran dial (tele)phone
téléphone à carte (magnétique) cardphone
téléphone cellulaire cellular (tele)phone
téléphone fixe landline phone
téléphone interne internal (tele)phone
téléphone à manivelle magneto telephone
téléphone mobile mobile (tele) phone
téléphone de poche pocket (tele)phone
téléphone portable portable (tele)phone
téléphone public public (tele)phone, payphone
téléphone rose (= *service*) telephone sex line, phone sex chatline; (= *concept*) telephone sex
le téléphone rouge *(Pol)* the hot line ◆ **il l'a appelé par le ~ rouge** he called him on the hot line
téléphone sans fil cordless (tele)phone
téléphone à touches push-button (tele) phone
téléphone de voiture car phone

téléphoner /telefɔne/ GRAMMAIRE ACTIVE 54.1, 54.2 ▸ conjug 1 ◂

VT 1 [+ *message*] to give by (tele)phone ◆ **il m'a téléphoné la nouvelle** he phoned me and told me the news ◆ **téléphone-lui de venir** phone him and tell him to come ◆ **télégramme téléphoné** telegram sent by telephone

2 (* = *manipuler*) **c'était un peu téléphoné** it was a bit obvious ◆ **leur manœuvre était téléphonée** you could see what they were up to from a mile off * ◆ **ses passes/attaques sont téléphonées** *(Sport)* his passes/attacks are telegraphed

VI to (tele)phone ◆ **~ à qn** to (tele)phone sb, to call *ou* ring *(Brit)* sb (up) ◆ **où est Paul ? – il téléphone** where's Paul? – he's on the phone *ou* he's making a call ◆ **j'étais en train de ~ à Paul** I was on the phone to Paul ◆ **je téléphone beaucoup, je n'aime pas écrire** I phone people a lot *ou* I use the phone a lot as I don't like writing

VPR **se téléphoner** to (tele)phone each other

téléphonie /telefɔni/ NF telephony ◆ **~ sans fil** wireless telephony, radiotelephony ◆ **~ mobile** mobile telephony

téléphonique /telefɔnik/ ADJ telephone *(épith)*; → **appel, carte** *etc*

téléphoniquement /telefɔnikmɑ̃/ ADV by telephone, telephonically

téléphoniste /telefɔnist/ NMF [*de poste*] telephonist *(Brit)*, (telephone) operator; [*d'entreprise*] switchboard operator

téléphotographie /telefɔtɔgʀafi/ NF telephotography

téléprompteur /telepʀɔ̃ptœʀ/ NM Autocue ® *(Brit)*, Teleprompter ® *(US)*

téléprospection /telepʀɔspɛksjɔ̃/ NF telesales

téléréalité /teleʀealite/ NF reality TV ◆ **émission de ~** reality show

télescopage /telɛskɔpaʒ/ NM [*de véhicules*] concertinaing *(NonC)*; [*de trains*] telescoping *(NonC)*, concertinaing *(NonC)*

télescope /telɛskɔp/ NM telescope ◆ **~ spatial** space telescope

télescoper /telɛskɔpe/ ▸ conjug 1 ◂ VT [+ *véhicule*] to crash into; [+ *faits, idées*] to mix up, to jumble together VPR **se télescoper** [*véhicules*] to concertina; [*trains*] to telescope, to concertina; [*souvenirs*] to become confused *ou* mixed up

télescopique /telɛskɔpik/ ADJ telescopic

téléscripteur /teleskʀiptœʀ/ NM teleprinter, Teletype ® (machine)

télésecrétariat /telesəkʀetaʀja/ NM secretarial teleworking

téléservice /teleseʀvis/ NM on-line *ou* remote services

télésiège /telesjɛʒ/ NM chairlift

téléski /teleski/ NM (ski) lift, (ski) tow ◆ **~ à fourche** T-bar tow ◆ **~ à archets** T-bar lift

téléspectateur, -trice /telespɛktatœʀ, tʀis/ NM,F (television *ou* TV) viewer

télésurveillance /telesyʀvɛjɑ̃s/ NF electronic surveillance ◆ **caméra de ~** security *ou* surveillance camera

Télétel ® /teletɛl/ NM electronic telephone directory

télétexte /teletekst/ NM Teletext ®, Viewdata ®

Téléthon /teletɔ̃/ NM Telethon

télétraitement /teletʀɛtmɑ̃/ NM (*Ordin*) teleprocessing

télétransmettre /teletʀɑ̃smɛtʀ/ ▸ conjug 56 ◂ VT [*+ données*] to transmit electronically

télétransmission /teletʀɑ̃smisjɔ̃/ NF remote transmission

télétravail /teletʀavaj/ NM teleworking, telecommuting

télétravailler /teletʀavaje/ ▸ conjug 1 ◂ VI to telework, to telecommute

télétravailleur, -euse /teletʀavajœʀ, øz/ NM,F teleworker, telecommuter

Télétype ® /teletip/ NM teleprinter, Teletype ® (machine)

télévangéliste /televɑ̃ʒelist/ NMF televangelist, television *ou* TV evangelist

télévendeur, -euse /televɑ̃dœʀ, øz/ NM,F telesales operator

télévente /televɑ̃t/ NF (*= technique*) telephone selling, telesales; (*= action*) telephone sales

téléviser /televize/ ▸ conjug 1 ◂ VT to televise; → **journal**

téléviseur /televizœʀ/ NM television (set), TV (set) ◆ **~ plasma** plasma TV

télévision /televizjɔ̃/ NF 1 (*= organisme, technique*) television, TV ◆ **la ~ par satellite** satellite television *ou* TV ◆ **la ~ câblée** *ou* **par câble** cable television *ou* TV, cablevision (*US*) ◆ **~ (à) haute définition** high definition television *ou* TV, HDTV ◆ **~ 16/9ᵉ** wide-screen television ◆ **~ payante** pay television *ou* TV ◆ **il travaille pour la ~ allemande** he works for German television

2 (*= programmes*) television, TV ◆ **à la ~** on television *ou* TV ◆ **il est passé à la ~** [*personne*] he has been *ou* appeared on television *ou* TV; [*film*] it has been on television *ou* TV ◆ **regarder la ~** to watch television *ou* TV ◆ **la ~ du matin** breakfast television *ou* TV; → **carte, interactif**

3 (*= chaîne*) television channel ◆ **les ~s étrangères** foreign channels ◆ **~ privée** independent *ou* private channel

4 (*= poste*) television (set) ◆ **~ (en) noir et blanc/couleur** black-and-white/colour television

télévisuel, -elle /televizɥɛl/ ADJ television (*épith*), televisual

télex /telɛks/ NM INV telex ◆ **envoyer qch par ~** to telex sth

télexer /telɛkse/ ▸ conjug 1 ◂ VT to telex

télexiste /telɛksist/ NMF telex operator

tellement /tɛlmɑ̃/ ADV 1 (*= si*) (*avec adj ou adv*) so; (*avec compar*) so much ◆ **il est ~ gentil** he's so nice ◆ **~ mieux/plus fort/plus beau** so much better/stronger/more beautiful ◆ **j'étais ~ fatigué que je me suis couché immédiatement** I was so tired (that) I went straight to bed

2 (*= tant*) so much ◆ **~ de gens** so many people ◆ **~ de temps** so much time, so long ◆ **il a ~ insisté que ...** he insisted so much that ..., he was so insistent that ... ◆ **il travaille ~ qu'il se rend malade** he works so much *ou* hard (that) he's making himself ill

3 (*introduisant une causale = tant*) **on ne le comprend pas, ~ il parle vite** he talks so fast (that) you can't understand him ◆ **il trouve à peine le temps de dormir, ~ il travaille** he works so much *ou* hard that he hardly finds time to sleep

4 (*avec négation*)

◆ **pas tellement** ◆ **pas ~ fort/lentement** not (all) that strong/slowly, not so (very) strong/slowly ◆ **il ne travaille pas ~** he doesn't work (all) that much *ou* hard, he doesn't work so (very) much *ou* hard ◆ **tu aimes le cinéma ? – pas ~** do you like the cinema? – not (all) that much *ou* not particularly *ou* not especially

◆ **plus tellement** ◆ **on ne la voit plus ~** we don't really see (very) much of her any more ◆ **y allez-vous toujours ? – plus ~, maintenant qu'il y a le bébé** do you still go there? – not (very) much *ou* not all that much now that there's the baby ◆ **cet article n'est plus ~ demandé** this article is no longer very much in demand ◆ **ce n'est plus ~ à la mode** it's not really *ou* all that fashionable any more ◆ **cela ne se fait plus ~** people no longer do that very much

tellure /telyʀ/ NM tellurium

tellurique /telyʀik/ ADJ [*eaux, courants*] telluric; → **secousse**

téloche * /telɔʃ/ NF TV, box *, telly * (*Brit*) ◆ **à la ~** on TV, on the box * *ou* telly (*Brit*), on the (boob)tube * (*US*)

téméraire /temeʀɛʀ/ ADJ [*action, entreprise, personne*] rash, reckless, foolhardy; [*jugement*] rash ◆ **~ dans ses jugements** rash in one's judgments ◆ **courageux** *ou* **audacieux, mais pas ~ !*** (*hum*) brave maybe, but not foolhardy!

témérairement /temeʀɛʀmɑ̃/ ADV [*entreprendre*] rashly, recklessly; [*décider, juger*] rashly

témérité /temeʀite/ NF [*d'action, entreprise*] rashness, recklessness, foolhardiness; [*de jugement*] rashness; [*de personne*] (*= imprudence*) recklessness, foolhardiness, rashness; (*= audace*) temerity ◆ **avoir la ~ de faire qch** to have the temerity to do sth

témoignage /temwaɲaʒ/ NM 1 (*en justice*) (*= déclaration*) testimony (*NonC*), evidence (*NonC*); (*= faits relatés*) evidence (*NonC*) ◆ **recueillir des ~s** to gather evidence ◆ **d'après le ~ de M. Lebrun** according to Mr Lebrun's testimony *ou* evidence, according to the evidence of *ou* given by Mr Lebrun ◆ **j'étais présent lors de son ~** I was present when he gave evidence *ou* gave his testimony ◆ **ces ~s sont contradictoires** these are contradictory pieces of evidence ◆ **c'est un ~ écrasant/irrécusable** the evidence is overwhelming/incontestable ◆ **porter** *ou* **rendre ~ de qch** to testify to sth, to bear witness to sth ◆ **rendre ~ au courage de qn** to praise sb's courage; → **faux²**

2 (*= récit, rapport*) account, testimony ◆ **ce livre est un merveilleux ~ sur notre époque** this book gives a marvellous account of the age we live in

3 (*= attestation*) **~ de probité/de bonne conduite** evidence (*NonC*) *ou* proof (*NonC*) of honesty/of good conduct ◆ **invoquer le ~ de qn pour prouver sa bonne foi** to call on sb's evidence *ou* testimony to prove one's good faith ◆ **en ~ de quoi ...** in witness whereof ...

4 (*= manifestation*) expression ◆ **~ d'amitié/de reconnaissance** (*= geste*) expression *ou* gesture of friendship/of gratitude; (*= cadeau*) token *ou* mark of friendship/of gratitude ◆ **leurs ~s de sympathie nous ont touchés** we were touched by their expressions *ou* gestures of sympathy ◆ **en ~ de ma reconnaissance** as a token *ou* mark of my gratitude ◆ **le ~ émouvant de leur confiance** the touching expression of their trust

témoigner /temwaɲe/ ▸ conjug 1 ◂ VI (*Jur*) to testify ◆ **~ en faveur de qn/contre qn** to testify *ou* give evidence in sb's favour/against sb ◆ **~ en justice** to testify in court ◆ **~ de vive voix/par écrit** to give spoken/written evidence, to testify in person/in writing

VT 1 (*= attester que*) **~ que ...** to testify that ... ◆ **il a témoigné qu'il ne l'avait jamais vu** *ou* **ne l'avoir jamais vu** he testified that he had never seen him

2 (*= faire preuve de, faire paraître*) (*gén*) to show, to display; [*+ reconnaissance*] to show, to evince (*frm*) ◆ **~ un goût pour qch** to show *ou* display a taste *ou* liking for sth ◆ **~ de l'aversion à qn** to show dislike of sb

3 (*= démontrer*) **~ que ...** to show that ... ◆ **~ de qch** to show sth ◆ **son attitude témoigne qu'il est préoccupé** his behaviour shows how preoccupied he is ◆ **tout cela témoigne que les temps changent** all this shows how times change

VT INDIR **témoigner de** 1 (*= confirmer*) to testify to, to bear witness to ◆ **~ de Dieu** to bear witness to God ◆ **je peux en ~** I can testify to that, I can bear witness to that (*frm*)

2 (*= montrer*) to show ◆ **son geste témoigne de son courage** what he did shows how brave he is ◆ **cette décision témoigne de la volonté du gouvernement de négocier** this decision shows the government's wish to negotiate ◆ **comme en témoigne le courrier de nos lecteurs, ce problème préoccupe beaucoup de gens** as can be seen from our readers' letters, this problem is worrying a lot of people

témoin /temwɛ̃/ NM 1 (*gén, Jur*) (*= personne*) witness; [*de duel*] second; (*à un mariage, gén*) witness ◆ **c'est le ~ du marié** he's the best man ◆ **~ auriculaire** earwitness ◆ **~ oculaire** eyewitness ◆ **~ direct/indirect** direct/indirect witness ◆ **~ de moralité** character witness, character reference (*person*) ◆ **~ gênant** embarrassing witness ◆ **être ~ à charge/à décharge** (*Jur*) to be (a) witness for the prosecution/for the defence ◆ **être ~ de** [*+ crime, scène*] to witness, to be a witness to; [*+ la sincérité de qn*] to vouch for ◆ **prendre qn à ~ (de qch)** to call sb to witness (to sth) ◆ **parler devant ~(s)** to speak in front of witnesses ◆ **faire qch sans ~** to do sth unwitnessed ◆ **cela doit être signé devant ~** this must be signed in front of a witness ◆ **il a été entendu comme ~ dans l'affaire Lebrun** he was a witness in the Lebrun case ◆ **que Dieu m'en soit ~** as God is my witness ◆ **Dieu m'est ~ que je n'ai pas voulu le tuer** as God is my witness, I didn't mean to kill him ◆ **les Témoins de Jéhovah** Jehovah's Witnesses ◆ **ces lieux ~s de notre enfance** these places which witnessed our childhood; → **faux²**

2 (*= preuve*) evidence (*NonC*), testimony ◆ **ces ruines sont le ~ de la férocité des combats** these ruins are (the) evidence of *ou* a testimony to the fierceness of the fighting ◆ **ils sont les ~s d'une époque révolue** they are the survivors of a bygone age ◆ **la région est riche, ~ les constructions nouvelles qui se dressent partout** the region is rich – witness the new buildings going up everywhere

3 (*Sport*) baton ◆ **passer le ~** to hand on *ou* pass the baton

4 (*Géol*) outlier; [*d'excavations*] dumpling; → **butte**

5 (*Constr : posé sur une fente*) telltale

6 (*= borne*) boundary marker

7 ◆ **(lampe) ~** warning light

ADJ (*après n*) control (*épith*) ◆ **animaux/sujets ~s** control animals/subjects ◆ **appartement ~** show-flat (*Brit*), model apartment (*US*) ◆ **réalisation ~** pilot *ou* test development; → **lampe**

tempe /tɑ̃p/ NF (*Anat*) temple ◆ **avoir les ~s grisonnantes** to be going grey

tempera /tɑ̃peʀa/ **a tempera** LOC ADJ in *ou* with tempera

tempérament /tɑ̃peʀamɑ̃/ **NM** [1] *(= constitution)* constitution ◆ ~ **robuste/faible** strong/weak constitution ◆ **se tuer** *ou* **s'esquinter le ~** * to wreck one's health ◆ ~ **sanguin/lymphatique** sanguine/lymphatic constitution ◆ ~ **nerveux** nervous disposition

[2] *(= nature, caractère)* disposition, temperament, nature ◆ **elle a un ~ actif/réservé** she is of *ou* has an active/a reserved disposition ◆ ~ **romantique** romantic nature *ou* temperament ◆ **moqueur par ~** naturally given to *ou* disposed to mockery ◆ **avoir du ~** to have a strong personality ◆ **c'est un ~** he (*ou* she) has a strong personality

[3] *(= sensualité)* sexual nature ◆ **être de ~ ardent/froid** to have a passionate/cold nature ◆ **avoir du ~** to be hot-blooded *ou* highly sexed

[4] *(Comm)* **vente à ~** hire purchase *(Brit)*, installment plan *(US)* ◆ **acheter qch à ~** to buy sth on hire purchase *(Brit) ou* on an installment plan *(US)* ◆ **trop d'achats à ~ l'avaient mis dans une situation difficile** too many hire purchase commitments *(Brit) ou* too many installment purchases *(US)* had got him into a difficult situation

[5] *(Mus)* temperament

tempérance /tɑ̃peʀɑ̃s/ **NF** temperance; → **société**

tempérant, e /tɑ̃peʀɑ̃, ɑ̃t/ **ADJ** temperate

température /tɑ̃peʀatyʀ/ **NF** temperature ◆ **les ~s sont en hausse/en baisse** temperatures are rising/falling ◆ ~ **d'ébullition/de fusion** boiling/melting point ◆ ~ **absolue** *ou* **en degrés absolus** absolute temperature ◆ **lavage à basse/haute ~** low-/high-temperature wash ◆ **animaux à ~ fixe/variable** warm-blooded/cold-blooded animals ◆ **avoir** *ou* **faire de la ~** to have a temperature, to be running a temperature ◆ **prendre la ~ de** *[+ malade]* to take the temperature of; *[+ auditoire, groupe]* to sound out; → **courbe, feuille**

tempéré, e /tɑ̃peʀe/ (ptp de **tempérer**) **ADJ** *[climat, zone]* temperate; *(Mus)* tempered

tempérer /tɑ̃peʀe/ ► conjug 6 ◄ **VT** *[+ froid, rigueur du climat]* to temper; *(littér) [+ peine, douleur]* to soothe, to ease; *(littér) [+ ardeur, sévérité]* to temper

tempête /tɑ̃pɛt/ **NF** [1] *(lit)* storm, gale, tempest *(littér)* ◆ ~ **de neige** snowstorm, blizzard ◆ ~ **de sable** sandstorm; → **briquet¹, semer, souffler** [2] *(= agitation)* storm ◆ **une ~ dans un verre d'eau** a storm in a teacup *(Brit)*, a tempest in a teapot *(US)* ◆ **cela va déchaîner des ~s** that's going to raise a storm ◆ **il est resté calme dans la ~** he remained calm in the midst of the storm ◆ **les ~s de l'âme** inner turmoil [3] *(= déchaînement)* **une ~ d'applaudissements** a storm of applause, thunderous applause *(NonC)* ◆ **une ~ d'injures** a storm of abuse

tempêter /tɑ̃pete/ ► conjug 1 ◄ **VI** to rant and rave *(contre* about), to rage *(contre* against)

tempétueux, -euse /tɑ̃petɥø, øz/ **ADJ** *(littér) [région, côte]* tempestuous *(littér)*, stormy; *[vie, époque]* tempestuous, stormy, turbulent

temple /tɑ̃pl/ **NM** [1] *(Hist, littér)* temple [2] *(Rel)* (Protestant) church ◆ **l'Ordre du Temple, le Temple** the Order of the Temple

templier /tɑ̃plije/ **NM** (Knight) Templar

tempo /tɛmpo/ **NM** *(Mus)* tempo; *(= rythme)* tempo, pace

temporaire /tɑ̃pɔʀɛʀ/ **ADJ** *[personnel, mesures, crise]* temporary ◆ **nomination à titre ~** temporary appointment, appointment on a temporary basis; → **travail¹**

temporairement /tɑ̃pɔʀɛʀmɑ̃/ **ADV** temporarily

temporal, e (mpl **-aux**) /tɑ̃pɔʀal, o/ *(Anat)* **ADJ** temporal **NM** temporal (bone)

temporalité /tɑ̃pɔʀalite/ **NF** *(Ling, Philos)* temporality

temporel, -elle /tɑ̃pɔʀɛl/ **ADJ** [1] *(Rel)* (= *non spirituel)* worldly, temporal; *(= non éternel)* temporal ◆ **biens ~s** temporal *ou* worldly goods, temporals [2] *(Ling, Philos)* temporal

temporellement /tɑ̃pɔʀɛlmɑ̃/ **ADV** temporally

temporisateur, -trice /tɑ̃pɔʀizatœʀ, tʀis/ **ADJ** *[tactique]* delaying *(épith)*, stalling *(épith)*; *[effet]* delaying *(épith)* **NM,F** *(= personne)* temporizer **NM** *(Tech)* timer

temporisation /tɑ̃pɔʀizasjɔ̃/ **NF** *(= attentisme)* delaying, stalling, playing for time; *(Tech)* time delay

temporiser /tɑ̃pɔʀize/ ► conjug 1 ◄ **VI** to delay, to stall, to play for time **VT** *(Tech)* to delay

temps¹ /tɑ̃/

1 NOM MASCULIN | 2 COMPOSÉS

1 - NOM MASCULIN

[1] = passage des ans **le ~** time ◆ **le Temps** *(personnifié)* (Old) Father Time ◆ **l'usure du ~** the ravages of time ◆ **avec le ~, ça s'arrangera** things will sort themselves out in time ◆ **il faut laisser** *ou* **donner du ~ au ~** you must give these things time; → **tuer**

[2] = durée time ◆ **cela prend trop de ~** it takes (up) too much time, it's too time-consuming ◆ **la blessure mettra du ~ à guérir** the wound will take (some) time to heal ◆ **il a mis beaucoup de ~ à se préparer** he took a long time to get ready ◆ **la jeunesse n'a qu'un ~** youth doesn't last ◆ **travailler à plein ~** *ou* **à ~ plein/à ~ partiel** to work full-time/part-time ◆ **(travail à) ~ choisi** flexitime ◆ **en peu de ~** in a short time ◆ **peu de ~ avant/après Noël** shortly before/after Christmas ◆ **je l'ai vu peu de ~ après** I saw him a short time after(wards), I saw him shortly after(wards) ◆ **dans peu de ~** before (very) long ◆ **pendant ce ~(-là)** meanwhile, in the meantime ◆ **il y a beau ~ que je le sais** I've known that for a long time; → **depuis, hors, quelque**

[3] = portion de temps time ◆ **s'accorder un ~ de réflexion** to give o.s. time to think ◆ **avoir le ~ (de faire)** to have time (to do) ◆ **je n'ai pas le ~** I haven't got (the) time ◆ **je n'ai pas le ~ de le faire** I haven't got the time *ou* I can't spare the time to do it ◆ **vous avez tout votre ~** you have all the time in the world *ou* plenty of time *ou* all the time you need ◆ **avoir** *ou* **se donner** *ou* **prendre du bon ~** to enjoy o.s., to have a good time ◆ **(donnez-moi) le ~ de m'habiller et je suis à vous** just give me time *ou* a moment to get dressed and I'll be with you ◆ **faire son ~** *[soldat]* to serve one's time (in the army); *[prisonnier]* to do *ou* serve one's time ◆ **il a fait son ~** *[personnage]* he has had his day; *[objet]* it has had its day ◆ **je me suis arrêté juste le ~ de prendre un verre** I stopped just long enough for a drink *ou* to have a drink ◆ **il passe son ~ à la lecture** *ou* **à lire** he spends his time reading ◆ **passer tout son ~ à faire qch/à qch** to spends all one's time doing sth/on sth ◆ **il faut bien passer le ~** you've got to pass the time somehow ◆ **cela fait passer le ~** it passes the time ◆ **comme le ~ passe !** how time flies! ◆ **perdre du/son ~ (à faire qch)** to waste time/waste one's time (doing sth) ◆ **il n'y a pas de ~ à perdre** there's no time to lose ◆ **le ~ perdu ne se rattrape jamais** *(Prov)* time and tide wait for no man *(Prov)* ◆ **prendre le ~ de faire** to find time to do ◆ **prendre le ~ de vivre** to make time to enjoy life ◆ **prenez donc votre ~** do take your time ◆ **il a pris son ~ !** he took his time (over *ou* about it)! ◆ **le ~ presse** time is short, time presses ◆ **le ~ est compté** there's not much time left ◆ **le ~ c'est de l'argent** *(Prov)* time is money *(Prov)* → **clair, devant, plupart**

[4] = moment précis time ◆ **il est ~ de partir** it's time to go, it's time we left ◆ **il est** *ou* **il serait (grand) ~ qu'il parte** it's (high) time he went, it's time for him to go ◆ **le ~ est venu de supprimer les frontières** the time has come to abolish frontiers, it's time frontiers were abolished ◆ **ce n'est ni le ~ ni le lieu de discuter** this is neither the time nor the place for discussions ◆ **il était ~ !** *(= ce n'est pas trop tôt)* not before time!, about time too!; *(c'était juste)* it came in the nick of time! ◆ **il n'est plus ~ de se plaindre** the time for complaining is past *ou* over ◆ **il n'est que ~ de s'en préoccuper** it's high time we started worrying about it ◆ **il y a un ~ pour tout** *(Prov)* there's a right time for everything; → **chaque**

[5] = époque time, times ◆ **le ~ des moissons/des vacances** *(= saison)* harvest/holiday time ◆ **les ~ modernes** modern times ◆ **au** *ou* **du ~ où ..., dans le ~ où ..., du ~ que ...** *(littér)* in the days when ..., at the time when ... ◆ **au ~ de la marine à voile** in the days of sailing ships ◆ **ces derniers ~, ces ~ derniers** lately, recently, of late ◆ **dans les derniers ~ du colonialisme** towards the end of the colonial period ◆ **les premiers ~** at the beginning, at first, at the outset ◆ **dans les premiers ~ de la crise** at the beginning of the crisis ◆ **en ~ de guerre/paix** in wartime/peacetime ◆ **en ~ de crise** in times of crisis ◆ **en un ~ où ...** at a time when ... ◆ **en ces ~ troublés** *(actuellement)* in these troubled times; *(dans le passé)* in those troubled times ◆ **les ~ ont bien changé** times have changed ◆ **le ~ n'est plus où ...** gone are the days when ... ◆ **il fut un ~** *(frm)* **où l'on pensait que ...** time was *ou* there was a time when people thought that ... ◆ **c'était le bon ~** those were the days ◆ **dans le** *ou* **au bon vieux ~** in the good old days ◆ **quels ~ nous vivons !** what times we live in! ◆ **les ~ sont durs !** times are hard!; → **ancien, nuit, signe**

[6] = époque délimitée time(s), day(s) ◆ **du ~ de Néron** in Nero's time *ou* day, at the time of Nero ◆ **au ~ des Tudors** in Tudor times, in the days of the Tudors ◆ **de mon ~** in my day *ou* time ◆ **dans mon jeune ~** in my younger days ◆ **être de son ~** *[homme]* to be a man of his time; *[femme]* to be a woman of her time ◆ **il faut être de son ~** you have to move with the times ◆ **les jeunes de notre ~** young people today

[7] = phase **l'opération s'est déroulée en trois ~** there were three phases to the operation ◆ **dans un premier ~** at first, to start *ou* begin with ◆ **dans un deuxième ~** subsequently

[8] marquant un rythme *(Mus)* beat; *(Gym) [d'exercice, mouvement]* stage ◆ ~ **fort/faible** strong/weak beat ◆ **c'était un des ~ forts/faibles du match** it was one of the high/low points of the match ◆ ~ **frappé** *(Mus)* downbeat ◆ **trois ~** three beats to the bar ◆ **à deux/trois ~** in duple/triple time ◆ ~ **de valse** waltz time; → **deux**

[9] Ling *[de verbe]* tense ◆ ~ **simple/composé** simple/compound tense ◆ ~ **surcomposé** double-compound tense ◆ **adverbe/complément de ~** adverb/complement of time, temporal adverb/complement; → **concordance**

[10] Tech stroke ◆ **moteur à 4 ~** 4-stroke engine ◆ **un 2 ~** a 2-stroke

[11] Sport *[de coureur, concurrent]* time ◆ **le skieur a réalisé un très bon ~** the skier achieved a very good time ◆ **dans les meilleurs ~** among the best times

[12] expressions figées

◆ **à temps** in time ◆ **j'arrive à ~ !** I've come just in time!

◆ **à temps perdu** in my (*ou* your *etc*) spare time

◆ **au temps pour moi !** my mistake!

♦ **ces temps-ci** these days
♦ **dans ce temps-là, en ce temps-là** at that time
♦ **dans le temps** in the old days, in the past, formerly
♦ **dans les temps** ♦ **être dans les** ~ *(= délai)* to be within the time limit; *(= programme)* to be on schedule; *(pas en retard)* to be on time ♦ **il ne reste que 12 jours avant la fin, mais nous sommes dans les** ~ there are only 12 days left, but we're on schedule ♦ **le train part à 11h30, on est dans les** ~ the train leaves at 11.30, we're OK for time ♦ **cette commande sera livrée dans les** ~ the order will be delivered on time
♦ **de tout temps** from time immemorial, since the beginning of time
♦ **de temps à autre, de temps en temps** from time to time, now and again, every now and then
♦ **du temps que** * ♦ **du ~ que tu y es, rapporte des fruits** *(= pendant que)* while you're at it* *ou* about it*, get some fruit
♦ **en temps et en heure** in due course
♦ **en temps et lieu** in due course, at the proper time (and place)
♦ **en temps** *+ adjectif* ♦ **en** ~ **normal** *ou* **ordinaire** usually, under normal circumstances ♦ **en** ~ **opportun** at the appropriate time ♦ **en** ~ **voulu** *ou* **utile** in due time *ou* course
♦ **entre temps** ⇒ **entre-temps**
♦ **par les temps qui courent** these days, nowadays
♦ **pour un temps** for a time *ou* while
♦ **tout le temps** all the time ♦ **l'air est presque tout le** ~ **pollué** the air is polluted almost all the time ♦ **il se plaint tout le** ~ he complains all the time, he's forever complaining ♦ **je ne vis pas tout le** ~ **à Rome** I don't live in Rome all the time

2 - COMPOSÉS

temps d'accès *(Ordin)* access time
temps d'antenne airtime
temps d'arrêt pause, halt ♦ **marquer un** ~ **d'arrêt** to pause
temps astronomique mean *ou* astronomical time
temps atomique atomic time
temps de cuisson cooking time
temps différé *(Ordin)* batch mode
temps libre spare time ♦ **comment occupes-tu ton** ~ **libre** ? what do you do in your spare time?
temps mort *(Ftbl, Rugby)* injury time *(NonC)*, stoppage for injury; *(dans le commerce, le travail)* slack period; *(dans la conversation)* lull
temps de parole *(dans une émission)* air time
temps partagé *(Ordin)* time-sharing ♦ **utilisation en** ~ **partagé** *(Ordin)* time-sharing ♦ **travail à** ~ **partagé** job-sharing
temps de pose *(Photo)* exposure *ou* value index
temps de réaction reaction time
temps réel real time ♦ **ordinateur exploité en** ~ **réel** real-time computer
temps de réponse response time
temps de saignement *(Méd)* bleeding time
temps sidéral *(Astron)* sideral time
temps solaire vrai apparent *ou* real solar time
temps universel universal time

temps² /tɑ̃/ **NM** *(= conditions atmosphériques)* weather ♦ **quel** ~ **fait-il** ? what's the weather like? ♦ **il fait beau/mauvais** ~ the weather's fine/bad ♦ **le** ~ **s'est mis au beau** the weather has turned fine ♦ **le** ~ **se gâte** the weather is changing for the worse ♦ **par** ~ **pluvieux/mauvais** ~ in wet/bad weather ♦ **sortir par tous les** ~ to go out in all weathers ♦ **avec le** ~ **qu'il fait !** in this weather! ♦ **il fait un** ~ **de chien** * the weather's awful *ou* lousy* ♦ ~ **de saison** seasonable weather ♦ **il faisait un beau** ~ **sec** *(pendant une période)* it was beautiful dry weather; *(ce jour-là)* it was a lovely dry day ♦ **le** ~ **est lourd aujourd'hui** it's very humid *ou* close *(Brit)* today ♦ **prendre le** ~ **comme il vient** to take things as they come; → **air¹**

tenable /t(ə)nabl/ **ADJ** *(gén nég)* *[température, situation]* bearable; *[position]* tenable ♦ **il fait trop chaud ici, ce n'est pas** ~ it's too hot here, it's unbearable ♦ **quand ils sont ensemble, ce n'est plus** ~ when they're together it becomes *ou* they become unbearable ♦ **la situation n'est plus** ~ the situation is untenable

tenace /tənas/ **ADJ** 1 *(= persistant)* *[douleur, rhume]* stubborn, persistent; *[maladie, toux, rumeur, souvenir]* persistent; *[croyance, préjugés]* deep-seated, deep-rooted, stubborn; *[espoir, illusions]* tenacious, stubborn; *[rancune, méfiance]* lingering; *[odeur, parfum]* lingering, persistent; *[tache]* stubborn 2 *(= têtu, obstiné)* *[quémandeur]* persistent; *[chercheur]* dogged, tenacious; *[résistance, volonté]* tenacious, stubborn

ténacité /tenasite/ **NF** 1 *(= persistance)* *[de douleur, rhume]* stubbornness, persistence; *[de croyance, préjugés]* deep-seated nature, stubbornness; *[de rumeur, souvenir, odeur, parfum]* persistence; *[d'espoir, illusion]* tenacity, stubbornness 2 *(= entêtement, obstination)* *[de quémandeur]* persistence; *[de chercheur]* tenacity; *[de résistance, volonté]* tenacity, doggedness ♦ **avec** ~ persistently, tenaciously, doggedly ♦ **ils ont fait preuve de** ~ they were persistent *ou* tenacious 3 *(Tech)* tenacity, toughness

tenaille /t(ə)nɑj/ **NF** 1 *(gén pl)* *[de menuisier, bricoleur]* pliers, pincers; *[de forgeron]* tongs; *[de cordonnier]* nippers, pincers 2 *(Mil)* *[de fortification]* tenaille, tenail ♦ **prendre en** ~ *(manœuvre)* to catch in a pincer movement ♦ **mouvement de** ~ pincer movement

tenailler /tənɑje/ ▸ **conjug 1** ◂ **VT** *[remords, inquiétude]* to torture, to torment ♦ **la faim le tenaillait** hunger gnawed at him ♦ **le remords le tenaillait** he was racked with remorse ♦ **l'inquiétude le tenaillait** he was desperately worried

tenancier /tənɑ̃sje/ **NM** 1 *[de maison de jeu, hôtel, bar]* manager 2 *[de ferme]* tenant farmer; *(Hist)* *[de terre]* (feudal) tenant

tenancière /tənɑ̃sjɛʀ/ **NF** *[de maison close]* brothel-keeper, madam; *[de maison de jeu, hôtel, bar]* manageress

tenant, e /tənɑ̃, ɑt/ **ADJ** → **séance** **NM** 1 *(gén pl = partisan)* *[de doctrine]* supporter, upholder *(de* of*)* adherent *(de* to*)*; *[d'homme politique]* supporter 2 *(Sport)* *[de coupe]* holder ♦ **le** ~ **du titre** the titleholder, the reigning champion 3 *(locutions)* **les** ~**s et (les) aboutissants d'une affaire** the ins and outs of a question ♦ **d'un seul** ~ *[terrain]* all in one piece ♦ **100 hectares d'un seul** ~ 100 unbroken *ou* uninterrupted hectares 4 *(Hér)* supporter

tendance /tɑ̃dɑ̃s/ GRAMMAIRE ACTIVE 53.1

NF 1 *(= inclination, Psych)* tendency ♦ ~**s refoulées/inconscientes** repressed/unconscious tendencies ♦ **la** ~ **principale de son caractère est l'égoïsme** the chief tendency in his character *ou* his chief tendency is selfishness ♦ **manifester des** ~**s homosexuelles** to show homosexual leanings *ou* tendencies ♦ ~ **à l'exagération/à s'enivrer** tendency to exaggerate *ou* to exaggeration/to get drunk
♦ **avoir tendance à** *[+ paresse, exagération]* to have a tendency to, to tend towards ♦ **avoir** ~ **à boire/être impertinent** to have a tendency to get drunk/to be cheeky, to tend to get drunk/to be cheeky ♦ **le temps a** ~ **à se gâter vers le soir** the weather tends to deteriorate towards the evening ♦ **en période d'inflation, les prix ont** ~ **à monter** in a period of inflation, prices tend *ou* have a tendency *ou* are inclined to go up ♦ **j'aurais** ~ **à penser que ...** I'd be inclined to think that ...
2 *(= opinions)* *[de parti, politicien]* leanings, sympathies; *[de groupe artistique, artiste]* leanings; *[de livre]* drift, tenor ♦ **il est de** ~ **gauchiste/surréaliste** he has leftist/surrealist leanings ♦ **à quelle** ~ **(politique) appartient-il ?** what are his (political) leanings? *ou* sympathies? ♦ **les députés, toutes** ~**s confondues ...** deputies from across the political spectrum *ou* on all sides ...
3 *(= évolution)* *[d'art, langage, système économique ou politique]* trend ♦ ~**s démographiques** population trends ♦ ~ **à la hausse/baisse** *[de prix]* upward/downward trend, rising/falling trend; *[de température]* upward/downward trend ♦ **la récente** ~ **à la baisse des valeurs mobilières** the recent downward *ou* falling trend in stocks and shares ♦ **les** ~**s actuelles de l'opinion publique** the current trends in public opinion; → **indicateur**

ADJ ♦ **c'est très** ~ it's very trendy ♦ **le rose est très** ~ **cet été** pink is the in colour this summer

tendanciel, -ielle /tɑ̃dɑ̃sjɛl/ **ADJ** underlying

tendancieusement /tɑ̃dɑ̃sjøzmɑ̃/ **ADV** tendentiously

tendancieux, -ieuse /tɑ̃dɑ̃sjø, jøz/ **ADJ** tendentious *(frm)*, biased

tender /tɑ̃dɛʀ/ **NM** *(Rail)* tender

tendeur /tɑ̃dœʀ/ **NM** *(= dispositif)* *[de fil de fer]* wire-strainer; *[de ficelle de tente]* runner; *[de chaîne de bicyclette]* chain-adjuster; *[de porte-bagages]* bungee (cord *ou* rope) ♦ ~ **de chaussures** shoe-stretcher

tendineux, -euse /tɑ̃dinø, øz/ **ADJ** *[viande]* stringy; *(Anat)* tendinous

tendinite /tɑ̃dinit/ **NF** tendinitis *(NonC)*

tendon /tɑ̃dɔ̃/ **NM** tendon, sinew ♦ ~ **d'Achille** Achilles' tendon

tendre¹ /tɑ̃dʀ/ ▸ **conjug 41** ◂ **VT** 1 *(= raidir)* *[+ corde, câble, corde de raquette]* to tighten, to tauten; *[+ corde d'arc]* to brace, to draw tight; *[+ arc]* to bend, to draw back; *[+ ressort]* to set; *[+ muscles]* to tense; *[+ pièce de tissu]* to stretch, to pull *ou* draw tight ♦ ~ **la peau d'un tambour** to brace a drum ♦ ~ **le jarret** to flex one's leg muscles ♦ ~ **son esprit vers ...** *(littér)* to bend one's mind to ...
2 *(= installer, poser)* *[+ tapisserie, tenture]* to hang; *[+ piège]* to set ♦ ~ **une bâche sur une remorque** to pull a tarpaulin over a trailer ♦ ~ **une chaîne entre deux poteaux** to hang *ou* fasten a chain between two posts ♦ ~ **ses filets** *(lit)* to set one's nets; *(fig)* to set one's snares ♦ ~ **un piège/une embuscade (à qn)** to set a trap/an ambush (for sb)
3 *(† littér = tapisser)* ~ **une pièce de tissu** to hang a room with material ♦ ~ **une pièce de soie bleue** to line the walls of a room with blue silk
4 *(= avancer)* ~ **le cou** to crane one's neck ♦ ~ **l'oreille** to prick up one's ears ♦ ~ **la joue** to offer one's cheek ♦ ~ **l'autre joue** *(fig)* to turn the other cheek ♦ ~ **la gorge au couteau** *(fig)* to put *ou* lay one's head on the block ♦ ~ **le poing** to raise one's fist ♦ ~ **la main** *(pour attraper, mendier)* to hold out one's hand ♦ ~ **la main à qn** *(pour saluer)* to hold out one's hand to sb; *(pour aider)* to lend *ou* offer sb a helping hand; *(pour se réconcilier)* to hold out *ou* extend the hand of friendship to sb ♦ ~ **le bras** to stretch out one's arm ♦ **il me tendit les bras** he stretched out his arms to me ♦ ~ **une main secourable** to offer a helping hand ♦ ~ **le dos** *(lit, fig)* to brace oneself
5 *(= présenter, donner)* ~ **qch à qn** *[+ briquet, objet demandé]* to hold sth out to *ou* for sb; *[+ cigarette offerte, bonbon]* to offer sth to sb ♦ **il lui tendit un paquet de cigarettes** he held out a packet

of cigarettes to him ◆ **il lui tendit un bonbon/une cigarette** he offered him a sweet/a cigarette ◆ ~ **une perche à qn** *(fig)* to throw sb a line

VPR se tendre *[corde]* to become taut, to tighten; *[rapports]* to become strained

VI 1 *(= avoir tendance à)* ~ **à qch/à faire qch** to tend towards sth/to do sth ◆ **le langage tend à se simplifier** language tends to become simpler ◆ **la situation tend à s'améliorer** the situation seems to be improving ◆ **ceci tend à prouver/confirmer que ...** *(sens affaibli)* this seems *ou* tends to prove/confirm that ...

2 *(littér = viser à)* ~ **à qch/à faire** to aim at sth/to do ◆ **cette mesure tend à faciliter les échanges** this measure aims to facilitate *ou* at facilitating exchanges ◆ ~ **à** *ou* **vers la perfection** to strive towards perfection, to aim at perfection

3 *(Math)* ~ **vers l'infini** to tend towards infinity

tendre² /tɑ̃dʀ/ **ADJ** 1 *(= délicat) [peau, pierre, bois]* soft; *[haricots, viande]* tender ◆ **crayon à mine** ~ soft(-lead) pencil ◆ **un steak bien** ~ a nice tender steak ◆ **avoir la bouche** ~ *[cheval]* to be tender-mouthed ◆ **couché dans l'herbe** ~ *(littér)* lying in the sweet grass *ou* the fresh young grass ◆ ~**s bourgeons/fleurettes** *(littér)* tender shoots/little flowers ◆ **depuis sa plus** ~ **enfance** from his earliest days ◆ **dans ma** ~ **enfance** *(hum)* in my innocent childhood days ◆ ~ **comme la rosée** wonderfully tender; → **âge**

2 *(= affectueux) [ami, amitié]* loving; *[amour]* tender; *[regard, mot]* tender, loving ◆ ~ **aveu** tender confession ◆ **il la regardait d'un air** ~ he looked at her tenderly *ou* lovingly, he gave her a tender *ou* loving look ◆ **dire des mots** ~**s à qn** to say tender *ou* loving things to sb ◆ **ne pas être** ~ **pour** *ou* **avec qn** * to be hard on sb

3 *(= cher) [+ ami, époux]* dear ◆ **à mon** ~ **époux** to my dear(est) husband

4 *[couleur]* soft, delicate ◆ **rose/vert/bleu** ~ soft *ou* delicate pink/green/blue

NMF ◆ **c'est un** ~ he's tender-hearted *ou* soft-hearted ◆ **en affaires, ce n'est pas un** ~ * he's a tough businessman

tendrement /tɑ̃dʀəmɑ̃/ **ADV** *[aimer]* tenderly; *[regarder, embrasser]* tenderly, lovingly ◆ **époux** ~ **unis** loving couple

tendresse /tɑ̃dʀɛs/ **NF** 1 *(= affection)* tenderness ◆ **un geste de** ~ a tender *ou* loving gesture ◆ **privé de** ~ **maternelle** denied maternal affection ◆ **avoir** *ou* **ressentir** *ou* **éprouver de la** ~ **pour qn** to feel tenderness *ou* affection for sb 2 *(= câlineries)* ~**s** tokens of affection, tenderness *(NonC)* ◆ **combler qn de** ~**s** to overwhelm sb with tenderness *ou* with tokens of (one's) affection ◆ **mille** ~**s** *(sur lettre)* lots of love, much love 3 *(= penchant)* **n'avoir aucune** ~ **pour qn** to have no fondness for sb ◆ **il avait gardé des** ~**s royalistes** he had retained (his) royalist sympathies

tendreté /tɑ̃dʀəte/ **NF** *[de viande]* tenderness; *[de bois, métal]* softness

tendron /tɑ̃dʀɔ̃/ **NM** 1 *(Culin)* ~ **de veau** tendron of veal *(Brit)*, plate of veal *(US)* 2 *(= pousse, bourgeon)* (tender) shoot 3 *(† hum = jeune fille)* young *ou* little girl

tendu, e /tɑ̃dy/ (ptp de **tendre¹**) **ADJ** 1 *(= raide) [corde, toile]* tight, taut; *[muscles]* tensed; *[ressort]* set; *(Ling) [voyelle, prononciation]* tense ◆ **tir** ~ *(Mil)* straight shot; *(Ftbl)* straight kick ◆ **la corde est trop** ~**e/bien** ~**e** the rope is too tight *ou* taut/is taut ◆ **la corde est mal** ~**e** the rope is slack *ou* isn't tight *ou* taut enough

2 *(= appliqué) [esprit]* concentrated

3 *(= empreint de nervosité) [rapports, relations]* strained, fraught; *[personne] (gén)* tense; *(= nerveux, inquiet)* strained; *[situation]* tense, fraught; *[climat, ambiance]* tense, strained ◆ **il entra, le visage** ~ he came in looking tense ◆ **avant le match il était** ~ he was all keyed-up before the match

4 *(= en avant, pointé)* **les bras** ~**s** with arms outstretched, with outstretched arms ◆ **s'avancer la main** ~**e** to come forward with one's hand held out ◆ **la politique de la main** ~**e à l'égard de ...** a policy of friendly cooperation with ... *ou* friendly exchanges with ... ◆ **le poing** ~ with one's fist raised

5 *(= tapissé de)* ~ **de** *[+ velours, soie]* hung with ◆ **chambre** ~**e de bleu/de soie bleue** bedroom with blue hangings/blue silk hangings

ténèbres /tenɛbʀ/ **NFPL** *(littér) [de nuit, cachot]* darkness, gloom ◆ **plongé dans les** ~ plunged in darkness ◆ **s'avançant à tâtons dans les** ~ groping his way forward in the dark(ness) *ou* gloom ◆ **les** ~ **de la mort** the shades of death *(littér)* ◆ **le prince/l'empire des** ~ the prince/the world of darkness ◆ **les** ~ **de l'ignorance** the darkness of ignorance ◆ **les** ~ **de l'inconscient** the dark regions *ou* murky depths of the unconscious ◆ **une lueur au milieu des** ~ a ray of light in the darkness *ou* amidst the gloom

ténébreux, -euse /tenebʀø, øz/ **ADJ** 1 *(littér) (= obscur) [prison, forêt]* dark, gloomy; *(= mystérieux et dangereux) [intrigue, dessein]* dark *(épith)*; *(= sombre) [époque, temps]* obscure; *(= incompréhensible) [affaire, philosophie]* dark *(épith)*, mysterious 2 *(littér) [personne]* saturnine ◆ **un beau** ~ *(hum)* a man with dark, brooding good looks

Ténéré /teneʀe/ **NM** ◆ **le** ~ Ténéré

Tenerife /teneʀif/ **N** Tenerife

teneur /tənœʀ/ **NF** 1 *[de traité]* terms; *[de lettre]* content, terms; *[d'article]* content ◆ **il n'a pu révéler la** ~ **exacte de leurs entretiens** he couldn't reveal the actual content *ou* the exact nature of their conversations 2 *[de minerai]* grade, content; *[de solution]* content ◆ **de haute/faible** ~ high-/low-grade *(épith)* ◆ ~ **en cuivre/alcool/matières grasses** copper/alcohol/fat content ◆ **la forte** ~ **en fer d'un minerai** the high iron content of an ore, the high percentage of iron in an ore ◆ **la** ~ **en hémoglobine du sang** the haemoglobin content of the blood

ténia /tenja/ **NM** tapeworm, taenia *(SPÉC)*

tenir /t(ə)niʀ/
► conjug 22 ◄
GRAMMAIRE ACTIVE 53.3, 53.6

1 VERBE TRANSITIF
2 VERBE INTRANSITIF
3 VERBE TRANSITIF INDIRECT
4 VERBE TRANSITIF INDIRECT
5 VERBE IMPERSONNEL
6 VERBE PRONOMINAL

Lorsque **tenir** s'emploie dans des expressions figées telles que **tenir compagnie/compte/rigueur, tenir chaud, tenir en haleine** etc, cherchez à l'autre mot.

1 - VERBE TRANSITIF

1 avec les mains to hold ◆ **la clé qu'il tient à la main** *ou* **dans sa main** the key that he's holding *ou* that he's got in his hand ◆ **il tient son fils par la main** he's holding his son's hand ◆ **elle le tenait par le cou** *(pour l'empêcher de s'enfuir)* she had got him by the neck; *(par affection)* she had her arm around his neck

2 = maintenir dans un certain état to keep; *(maintenir dans une certaine position)* to hold, to keep ◆ ~ **les yeux fermés/les bras levés** to keep one's eyes shut/one's arms raised *ou* up ◆ **le café le tient éveillé** coffee keeps him awake ◆ **elle tient ses enfants très propres** she keeps her children very neat ◆ ~ **qch en place/en position** to hold *ou* keep sth in place/in position ◆ **ses livres sont tenus par une courroie** his books are held (together) by a strap ◆ **il m'a tenu la tête sous l'eau** he held my head under the water ◆ ~ **la porte à qn** to hold the door open for sb

3 Mus = garder *[+ note]* to hold ◆ ~ **l'accord** to stay in tune

4 = avoir, détenir *[+ voleur, maladie]* * to have, to have caught; *[+ vérité, preuve, solution]* to hold, to have ◆ **faire** ~ **qch à qn** *(littér) [+ lettre, objet]* to transmit *ou* communicate sth to sb ◆ **si je le tenais !** *(menace)* if I could get my hands *ou* lay hands on him! ◆ **nous le tenons** *(lit) (= nous l'avons attrapé)* we've got *ou* caught him; *(= il ne peut se dérober)* we've got him (where we want him) ◆ **je tiens le mot de l'énigme/la clé du mystère** I've found *ou* got the secret of the riddle/the key to the mystery ◆ **parfait, je tiens mon article/mon sujet** great, now I have my article/my subject ◆ **je tiens un de ces rhumes !** * I've got *ou* caught a nasty cold ◆ **qu'est-ce qu'il tient !** ⁑, **il en tient une bonne !** ⁑ *(= il est ivre)* he's plastered ⁑ *ou* loaded! ⁑ *(US)*; *(= il est idiot)* he's such a wally ⁑ *(Brit) ou* clot ⁑ *(Brit)*! ◆ **un tiens vaut mieux que deux tu l'auras** *(Prov)* ◆ **mieux vaut** ~ **que courir** *(Prov)* a bird in the hand is worth two in the bush *(Prov)*

5 = avoir en stock *[+ article, marchandise]* to stock

6 = avoir le contrôle de *[+ enfant, classe]* to have under control, to keep under control *ou* on a tight rein; *[+ pays]* to have under one's control ◆ **il tient (bien) sa classe** he has *ou* keeps his class (well) under control, he controls his class well ◆ **les enfants sont très tenus** the children are held very much in check *ou* are kept on a very tight rein ◆ **les soldats tiennent la plaine** the soldiers are holding the plain, the soldiers control the plain

7 = gérer *[+ hôtel, magasin]* to run, to keep; *[+ comptes, registre, maison, ménage]* to keep

8 = organiser *[+ séance, réunion, conférence]* to hold; → **langage, propos, raisonnement** *etc*

9 = occuper *[+ place, largeur]* to take up; *[+ rôle]* to fulfill; *[+ emploi]* to hold ◆ **tu tiens trop de place !** you're taking up too much room! ◆ **le camion tenait toute la largeur/la moitié de la chaussée** the lorry took up the whole width of/half the roadway ◆ **il tenait sa droite** *[automobiliste]* he was keeping to the right ◆ **elle a bien tenu son rôle de femme au foyer/de chef** she was the perfect housewife/manager ◆ **elle tient le rôle d'Ophélie** she plays the role of Ophelia, she's cast as Ophelia *ou* in the role of Ophelia

10 = contenir *[récipient]* to hold

11 = résister à, bien se comporter ~ **l'alcool** * to be able to hold *ou* take *(Brit)* one's drink ◆ ~ **la mer** *[bateau]* to be seaworthy ◆ ~ **le coup** *[personne]* to survive; *[chose] (= durer)* to last ◆ **financièrement, ils n'auraient pas tenu le coup** financially they wouldn't have survived *ou* been able to hold out ◆ **avec tout ce travail, est-ce qu'il pourra** ~ **le coup ?** with all that work will he be able to cope? ◆ **leur mariage tient le coup malgré tout** their marriage has survived *ou* lasted in spite of everything ◆ **si on danse, est-ce que la moquette tiendra le coup ?** if we dance, will the carpet stand up to it?

12 = respecter *[+ promesse]* to keep; *[+ pari]* to keep to, to honour *(Brit)*, to honor *(US)*; *(= se conformer à) [+ planning]* to keep to ◆ ~ **le rythme** to keep up (the pace)

13 = immobiliser **il m'a tenu dans son bureau pendant une heure** he kept me in his office for an hour ◆ **il est très tenu par ses affaires** he's very tied *(Brit) ou* tied up by his business ◆ **la colère le tenait** *(littér)* anger had him in its grip ◆ **l'envie me tenait de ...** *(littér)* I was filled *ou* gripped by the desire to ... ◆ **cette**

maladie le tient depuis deux mois he's had this illness for two months (now)

14 locutions

♦ **tenir qch de qn** (= *avoir reçu*) *[+ renseignement, meuble, bijou]* to have (got) sth from sb; *[+ trait physique, de caractère]* to get sth from sb ♦ **il tient cela de son père** he gets that from his father ♦ **je tiens ce renseignement d'un voisin** I have *ou* I got this information from a neighbour

♦ **tenir qn/qch pour** (= *considérer comme*) to regard sb/sth as, to consider sb/sth (as), to hold sb/sth to be *(frm)* ♦ **je le tenais pour un honnête homme** I regarded him as *ou* considered him (to be) *ou* held him to be *(frm)* an honest man ♦ **elle le tient pour responsable de l'accident** she holds him responsible *ou* considers him to be responsible for the accident ♦ ~ **pour certain** *ou* **assuré que ...** to be quite sure that ...

♦ **en tenir pour qch** (= *être partisan de*) *[+ solution]* to be keen on sth, to be in favour *(Brit) ou* favor *(US)* of sth ♦ **il en tient pour l'équipe d'Irlande** he's for the Irish team

♦ **en tenir pour qn** (= *l'aimer*) to fancy sb* *(Brit)*, to be keen on sb*, to have a crush on sb*

♦ **tiens!, tenez!** *(en donnant)* here (you are) ♦ **tiens, voilà mon frère !** *(surprise)* ah *ou* hullo, there's my brother! ♦ **tiens, tiens** well, well!, fancy that! ♦ **tenez, je vais vous expliquer** *(pour attirer l'attention)* look, I'll explain ♦ **tenez, ça m'écœure** you know, that sickens me

2 - VERBE INTRANSITIF

1 = rester en place, en position *[objet fixe, nœud]* to hold; *[objets empilés, échafaudage]* to stay up, to hold (up) ♦ **croyez-vous que le clou va** ~ **?** do you think the nail will hold? ♦ **l'armoire tient au mur** the cupboard is fixed to the wall ♦ **ce chapeau ne tient pas sur ma tête** this hat won't stay on (my head) ♦ **la branche est cassée mais elle tient encore** the branch is broken but it's still attached to the tree ♦ **il tient bien sur ses jambes** he's very steady on his legs

2 = être valable to be on ♦ **ça tient toujours, notre pique-nique ?*** is our picnic still on? ♦ **il n'y a pas de bal/match qui tienne** there's no question of going to any dance/match

3 = résister *(Mil, gén)* to hold out ♦ ~ **bon** *ou* **ferme** to stand fast *ou* firm, to hold out ♦ **il fait trop chaud, on ne tient plus ici** it's too hot - we can't stand it here any longer ♦ **il n'a pas pu** ~ **: il a protesté violemment** he couldn't contain himself and protested vehemently

4 = pouvoir être contenu dans ~ **dans** *ou* **à** *ou* **en** to fit in(to) ♦ **est-ce que la caisse tiendra en hauteur ?** will the box fit in vertically? ♦ **ils ne tiendront pas dans la pièce/la voiture** the room/the car won't hold them, they won't fit into the room/the car ♦ **à cette table, on peut** ~ **à huit** this table can seat eight, we can get eight round this table ♦ **son discours tient en quelques pages** his speech takes up just a few pages, his speech is just a few pages long ♦ **ma réponse tient en un seul mot : non** in a word, my answer is no

5 = durer *[accord, beau temps]* to hold; *[couleur]* to be fast; *[mariage]* to last; *[fleurs]* to last (well) ♦ **sa coiffure a tenu 2 jours** her hairstyle held for 2 days

3 - VERBE TRANSITIF INDIRECT

tenir à

1 = aimer, être attaché à *[+ réputation, opinion de qn]* to value, to care about; *[+ objet]* to be attached to, to be fond of; *[+ personne]* to be attached to, to be fond of, to care for ♦ **il ne tenait plus à la vie** he had lost his will to live, he no longer had any desire to live ♦ **voudriez-vous un peu de vin ? – je n'y tiens pas** would you like some wine? – not really *ou* not particularly *ou* I'm not that keen* *(Brit)*

2 = vouloir

♦ **tenir à** + *infinitif*, **tenir à ce que** + *subjonctif* to be anxious to, to be anxious that ♦ **il tient beaucoup à vous connaître** he's very anxious *ou* keen *(Brit) ou* eager to meet you ♦ **elle tenait absolument à parler** she insisted on speaking ♦ **il tient à ce que nous sachions ...** he insists *ou* is anxious that we should know ... ♦ **si vous y tenez** if you really want to, if you insist ♦ **tu viens avec nous ? – si tu y tiens** are you coming with us? – if you really want me to *ou* if you insist

3 = avoir pour cause to be due to, to stem from ♦ **ça tient au climat** it's because of the climate, it's due to the climate ♦ **à quoi tient sa popularité ?** what's the reason for his popularity? ♦ **cela tient à peu de chose, la vie d'un enfant de deux ans** a two year-old's life is precarious ♦ **le succès d'un sommet tient souvent à peu de chose** the success of a summit often depends on something quite small

4 = être contigu à to adjoin ♦ **le jardin tient à la ferme** the garden adjoins the farmhouse

4 - VERBE TRANSITIF INDIRECT

tenir de (= *ressembler à*) *[+ parent]* to take after ♦ **il tient de son père** he takes after his father ♦ **il a de qui** ~ it runs in the family ♦ **sa réussite tient du prodige** his success is something of a miracle ♦ **cela tient du comique et du tragique** there's something (both) comic and tragic about it, there are elements of both the comic and the tragic in it

5 - VERBE IMPERSONNEL

= dépendre de to depend ♦ **il ne tient qu'à vous de décider** it's up to you to decide, the decision rests with you ♦ **il ne tient qu'à elle que cela se fasse** it's up to her whether it's done ♦ **ça ne tient pas qu'à lui** it doesn't depend on him alone ♦ **à quoi cela tient-il qu'il n'écrive pas ?** how is it *ou* why is it that he doesn't write? ♦ **ça tient à peu de chose** it can easily go one way or the other

♦ **qu'à cela ne tienne** that's no problem

6 - VERBE PRONOMINAL

se tenir

1 avec les mains ou une partie du corps **il se tenait le ventre de douleur** he was clutching *ou* holding his stomach in pain ♦ **se** ~ **à qch** to hold onto sth ♦ **l'acrobate se tenait par les pieds** the acrobat hung on by his feet ♦ **ils se tenaient (par) la main** *(mutuellement)* they were holding hands *ou* holding each other by the hand ♦ **ils se tenaient par la taille/le cou** they had their arms round each other's waists/necks

2 = être dans une position, un état ou un lieu **se** ~ **debout/couché/à genoux** to be standing (up)/lying (down)/kneeling (down) *ou* on one's knees ♦ **tiens-toi droit** *ou* **bien (debout)** stand up straight; (assis) sit up (straight) ♦ **redresse-toi, tu te tiens mal** stand up straight, you're slouching ♦ **tenez-vous prêts à partir** be ready to leave ♦ **elle se tenait à sa fenêtre/dans un coin de la pièce** she was standing at her window/in a corner of the room

3 = se conduire to behave ♦ **il ne sait pas se** ~ he doesn't know how to behave ♦ **se** ~ **tranquille** to be quiet ♦ **tiens-toi tranquille** (= *sois calme*) keep still; (= *n'agis pas*) lie low ♦ **se** ~ **bien/mal** *(à table)* to have good/bad table manners; *(en société)* to behave well/badly ♦ **devant cette dame, tâche de te** ~ **comme il faut** *ou* **de bien te** ~ when you meet the lady, try to behave properly ♦ **il se tient mieux à table qu'à cheval*** *(hum)* he's a healthy eater, he's got a healthy appetite ♦ **il n'a qu'à bien se** ~ *(avertissement, bien se conduire)* he'd better behave himself; *(faire attention)* he'd better watch out

4 = avoir lieu *[réunion, séance]* to be held; *[festival]* to take place ♦ **le marché se tient là chaque semaine** the market is held there every week

5 = être cohérent *[raisonnement]* to hold together; (= *être liés, solidaires*) *[événements, faits]* to be connected *ou* interlinked ♦ **tout se tient** it's all connected

6 = se retenir *(gén nég)* **il ne peut se** ~ **de rire/critiquer** he can't help laughing/criticizing ♦ **il ne se tenait pas de joie** he couldn't contain his joy ♦ **tiens-toi bien !** wait till you hear the next bit! ♦ **tu sais combien elle a gagné ? tiens-toi bien : 3 millions !** do you know how much she won? wait for it! *ou* you won't believe it! – 3 million!; → **quatre**

7 locutions

♦ **s'en tenir à** (= *se limiter à*) to confine o.s. to, to stick to; (= *se satisfaire de*) to content o.s. with ♦ **nous nous en tiendrons là pour aujourd'hui** we'll leave it at that for today ♦ **il aimerait savoir à quoi s'en** ~ he'd like to know where he stands ♦ **je sais à quoi m'en** ~ **sur son compte** I know exactly who I'm dealing with, I know just the sort of man he is

♦ **se tenir pour** (= *se considérer comme*) ♦ **il se tient pour responsable** he holds himself responsible ♦ **il ne se tient pas pour battu** he doesn't consider himself beaten ♦ **tenez-vous-le pour dit !** *(avertissement)* you've been warned!, you won't be told again!

Tennessee /tenesi/ NM Tennessee

tennis /tenis/ NM 1 (= *sport*) tennis ♦ ~ **sur gazon** lawn tennis ♦ ~ **sur terre battue** clay-court tennis ♦ ~ **en salle** indoor tennis ♦ ~ **de table** table tennis 2 (= *terrain*) (tennis) court 3 (= *partie*) game of tennis ♦ **faire un** ~ to have a game of tennis, to play tennis NMPL (= *chaussures*) tennis shoes; *(par extension = chaussures de gym)* gym shoes, trainers *(Brit)*, sneakers *(US)*

tennisman /tenisman/ (pl **tennismen** /tenismɛn/) NM tennis player

tennistique /tenistik/ ADJ tennis *(épith)*

tenon /tənɔ̃/ NM *(Menuiserie)* tenon ♦ **assemblage à** ~ **et mortaise** mortice and tenon joint

ténor /tenɔʀ/ NM 1 *(Mus)* tenor ♦ ~ **léger** light tenor 2 *(Pol)* leading light, big name *(de* in); *(Sport)* star player, big name ADJ tenor

tenseur /tɑ̃sœʀ/ NM, ADJ M *(Anat, Math)* tensor

tensioactif, -ive /tɑ̃sjoaktif, iv/ ADJ, NM ♦ **(agent)** ~ surface-active agent

tensiomètre /tɑ̃sjɔmɛtʀ/ NM tensiometer

tension /tɑ̃sjɔ̃/ NF 1 *[de ressort, cordes de piano, muscles]* tension; *[de courroie]* tightness, tautness, tension ♦ **chaîne à** ~ **réglable** adjustable tension chain ♦ **corde de** ~ **d'une scie** tightening-cord of a saw

2 *(Phon)* (= *phase d'articulation*) attack; (= *état d'un phonème tendu*) tension, tenseness

3 *(Élec)* voltage, tension ♦ ~ **de 220 volts** tension of 220 volts ♦ **à haute/basse** ~ high-/low-voltage *ou* -tension *(épith)* ♦ **baisse** *ou* **chute de** ~ voltage drop, drop in voltage ♦ **sous** ~ live ♦ **mettre un appareil sous** ~ to switch on a piece of equipment

4 *(Méd)* ~ **nerveuse** nervous tension *ou* strain ♦ ~ **(artérielle)** blood pressure ♦ **avoir** *ou* **faire de la** ~**, avoir trop de** ~ to have high blood pressure ♦ **prendre la** ~ **de qn** to take *ou* check sb's blood pressure ♦ **baisse** *ou* **chute de** ~ sudden drop in blood pressure

5 *[de relations, situation]* tension *(de* in); ♦ ~**s sociales/ethniques/politiques** social/ethnic/political tensions ♦ ~**s inflationnistes/monétaires** inflationary/monetary pres-

sures ◆ **on note un regain de ~ dans la région** there is renewed tension in the region ◆ **~ entre deux pays/personnes** tension *ou* strained relationship between two countries/people

6 *(= concentration, effort)* **~ d'esprit** sustained mental effort ◆ **~ vers un but/idéal** *(littér)* striving *ou* straining towards a goal/an ideal

7 *(Phys) [de liquide]* tension; *[de vapeur]* pressure; *(Tech)* stress ◆ **~ superficielle** surface tension

tentaculaire /tɑ̃takylɛʀ/ **ADJ** *(= des tentacules)* tentacular ◆ **villes ~s** sprawling towns ◆ **firmes ~s** monster (international) combines

tentacule /tɑ̃takyl/ **NM** *(lit, fig)* tentacle

tentant, e /tɑ̃tɑ̃, ɑ̃t/ **ADJ** *[plat]* tempting; *[offre, projet]* tempting, attractive

tentateur, -trice /tɑ̃tatœʀ, tʀis/ **ADJ** *[beauté]* tempting, alluring, enticing; *[propos]* tempting, enticing ◆ **l'esprit ~** *(Rel)* the Tempter **NM** tempter ◆ **le Tentateur** *(Rel)* the Tempter **NF** **tentatrice** temptress

tentation /tɑ̃tasjɔ̃/ **NF** temptation ◆ **la ~ de saint Antoine** the temptation of Saint Anthony ◆ **résister à la ~** to resist temptation ◆ **succomber à la ~** to yield *ou* give in to temptation

tentative /tɑ̃tativ/ **NF** *(gén)* attempt, endeavour; *(sportive, style journalistique)* bid, attempt ◆ **de vaines ~s** vain attempts *ou* endeavours ◆ **~ d'évasion** attempt *ou* bid to escape, escape bid *ou* attempt ◆ **~ de meurtre/de suicide** *(gén)* murder/suicide attempt; *(Jur)* attempted murder/suicide ◆ **faire une ~ auprès de qn (en vue de ...)** to approach sb (with a view to ...)

tente /tɑ̃t/ **NF** *(gén)* tent ◆ **~ de camping** (camping) tent ◆ **coucher sous la ~** to sleep under canvas, to camp out ◆ **se retirer sous sa ~** *(fig)* to go and sulk in one's corner

COMP **tente de cirque** circus tent, marquee
tente(-)igloo igloo tent
tente à oxygène oxygen tent
tente de plage beach tent

tenté, e /tɑ̃te/ (ptp de **tenter**) **ADJ** ◆ **être ~ de faire/croire qch** to be tempted to do/believe sth

tente-abri (pl **tentes-abris**) /tɑ̃tabʀi/ **NF** shelter tent

tenter /tɑ̃te/ GRAMMAIRE ACTIVE 28.1 ▸ conjug 1 ◂ **VT**

1 *(= chercher à séduire) [+ personne] (gén, Rel)* to tempt ◆ **~ qn (par une offre)** to tempt sb (with an offer) ◆ **ce n'était pas cher, elle s'est laissée ~** it wasn't expensive and she let herself be tempted ◆ **se laisser ~ par une offre** to be tempted by an offer ◆ **qu'est-ce qui te tente comme gâteau ?*** what kind of cake do you feel like? *ou* do you fancy?* ◆ **un match de tennis, ça te tenterait ?** do you feel like *ou* do you fancy* *(Brit)* a game of tennis?, how about a game of tennis? ◆ **tu peux venir si ça te tente** you can come if you feel like it ◆ **c'est vraiment ~ le diable** it's really tempting fate *ou* Providence ◆ **il ne faut pas ~ le diable** don't tempt fate, don't push your luck*

2 *(= risquer) [+ expérience, démarche]* to try, to attempt ◆ **on a tout tenté pour le sauver** they tried everything to save him ◆ **on a tenté l'impossible pour le sauver** they attempted the impossible to save him ◆ **~ le tout pour le tout** to risk one's all ◆ **~ la** *ou* **sa chance** to try one's luck ◆ **~ le coup*** to have a go* *ou* a bash*, to give it a try* *ou* a whirl* ◆ **~ l'aventure** to take the plunge, to try one's luck

3 *(= essayer)* **~ de faire qch** to attempt *ou* try to do sth ◆ **je vais ~ de le convaincre** I'll try to *ou* try and convince him

tenture /tɑ̃tyʀ/ **NF** 1 *(= tapisserie)* hanging ◆ **~ murale** wall covering 2 *(= grand rideau)* hanging, curtain, drape *(US)*; *(derrière une porte)* door curtain 3 *(de deuil)* funeral hangings

tenu, e¹ /t(ə)ny/ (ptp de **tenir**) **ADJ** 1 *(= entretenu)* **bien ~** *[enfant]* well *ou* neatly turned out; *[maison]* well-kept, well looked after; *[comptes, registres]* well-kept, tidy ◆ **mal ~** *[enfant]* poorly turned out, untidy; *[maison]* poorly kept, poorly looked after; *[comptes, registres]* badly kept, untidy 2 *(= strictement surveillé)* **leurs filles sont très ~es** their daughters are kept on a tight rein *ou* are held very much in check 3 *(= obligé)* **être ~ de faire qch** to be obliged to do sth, to have to do sth ◆ **être ~ au secret professionnel** to be bound by professional secrecy; → **impossible** 4 *(Mus) [note]* held, sustained 5 *(Bourse) [valeurs]* firm, steady

ténu, e /teny/ **ADJ** *(littér)* 1 *[point, particule, fil]* fine; *[brume]* thin; *[voix]* thin, reedy 2 *[raison]* tenuous, flimsy; *[nuance, cause]* tenuous, subtle; *[souvenir, espoir]* faint

tenue² /t(ə)ny/ **NF** 1 *[de maison]* upkeep, running; *[de magasin]* running; *[de classe]* handling, control; *[de séance]* holding; *(Mus) [de note]* holding, sustaining ◆ **la ~ des livres de comptes** the book-keeping ◆ **~ fautive de la plume** wrong way of holding one's pen

2 *(= conduite)* (good) manners, good behaviour *(Brit) ou* behavior *(US)* ◆ **bonne ~ en classe/à table** good behaviour in class/at (the) table ◆ **avoir de la ~** to have good manners, to know how to behave (o.s.) ◆ **allons ! un peu de ~ !** come on, behave yourself! *ou* watch your manners!

3 *(= qualité) [de journal]* standard, quality ◆ **publication qui a de la ~** publication of a high standard, quality publication

4 *(= maintien)* posture ◆ **mauvaise ~ d'un écolier** bad posture of a schoolboy

5 *(Bourse)* performance ◆ **la bonne/mauvaise ~ du franc face au dollar** the good/poor performance of the franc against the dollar

6 *(= habillement, apparence)* dress, appearance; *(= vêtements, uniforme)* dress ◆ **leur ~ négligée** their sloppy dress *ou* appearance ◆ **en ~ négligée** wearing *ou* in casual clothes ◆ **ce n'est pas une ~ pour aller au golf !** that's no way to dress to play golf! ◆ **"tenue correcte exigée"** "strict dress code" ◆ **~ d'intérieur** indoor clothes ◆ **en ~ légère** *(d'été)* wearing *ou* in light clothing; *(osée)* scantily dressed *ou* clad ◆ **en petite ~** scantily dressed *ou* clad ◆ **en ~ d'Adam** *(ou* **d'Ève**) *(hum)* in one's birthday suit* ◆ **en grande ~** in full dress (uniform) ◆ **des touristes en ~ estivale/d'hiver** tourists in summer/winter clothes ◆ **se mettre en ~** to get dressed ◆ **être en ~** *(Mil)* to be in uniform ◆ **les policiers en ~** uniformed policemen, policemen in uniform ◆ **~ camouflée** *ou* **de camouflage/de campagne** *(Mil)* camouflage/combat dress

COMP **tenue de combat** battle dress
tenue de route road holding
tenue de service uniform
tenue de soirée formal *ou* evening dress ◆ **"tenue de soirée de rigueur"** ≃ black tie
tenue de sport sports clothes, sports gear
tenue de ville *[d'homme]* lounge suit *(Brit)*, town suit *(US)*; *[de femme]* town dress *ou* suit
tenue de vol flying gear

ténuité /tenɥite/ **NF** *(littér)* 1 *[de point, particule, fil]* fineness; *[de brume]* thinness; *[de voix]* thinness, reediness 2 *[de raison]* tenuousness, tenuity, flimsiness; *[de nuance, cause]* tenuousness, tenuity, subtlety

tenure /tənyʀ/ **NF** *(Hist, Jur)* tenure

TEP /teəpe/ **NF** (abrév de **tonne équivalent pétrole**) TOE

tequila /tekila/ **NF** tequila

ter /tɛʀ/ **ADJ** *(dans une adresse)* ◆ **il habite au 10 ~** he lives at (number) 10b **ADV** *(Mus)* three times, ter

TER /teəɛʀ/ **NM** (abrév de **train express régional**) → **train**

téraflop /teʀaflɔp/ **NM** teraflop

tératogène /teʀatɔʒɛn/ **ADJ** teratogenic

tératologie /teʀatɔlɔʒi/ **NF** teratology

tératologique /teʀatɔlɔʒik/ **ADJ** teratological

terbium /tɛʀbjɔm/ **NM** terbium

tercet /tɛʀsɛ/ **NM** *(Poésie)* tercet, triplet

térébenthine /teʀebɑ̃tin/ **NF** turpentine ◆ **nettoyer à l'essence de ~** *ou* **à la ~** to clean with turpentine *ou* turps* *(Brit) ou* turp *(US)*

térébinthe /teʀebɛ̃t/ **NM** terebinth

Tergal ® /tɛʀgal/ **NM** Terylene ®

tergiversations /tɛʀʒivɛʀsasjɔ̃/ **NFPL** prevarication, equivocation ◆ **après des semaines de ~** after weeks of prevarication ◆ **trêve de ~ !** stop beating about the bush!, stop prevaricating!

tergiverser /tɛʀʒivɛʀse/ ▸ conjug 1 ◂ **VI** to prevaricate, to equivocate, to shilly-shally ◆ **cessez donc de ~ !** stop beating about the bush!, stop prevaricating!

terme /tɛʀm/ **NM** 1 *(Ling = mot, expression)* term; *(Math, Philos = élément)* term ◆ **~ de marine/de métier** nautical/professional term ◆ **aux ~s du contrat** according to the terms of the contract ◆ **en ~s clairs/voilés/flatteurs** in clear/veiled/flattering terms ◆ **en d'autres ~s** in other words ◆ **il ne l'a pas dit en ces ~s** he didn't put it like that ◆ **il raisonne en ~s d'efficacité** he thinks in terms of efficiency ◆ **... et le ~ est faible** ... and that's putting it mildly, ... and that's an understatement ◆ **moyen ~** *(gén)* middle course; *(Logique)* middle term; → **acception, force**

2 *(= date limite)* time limit, deadline; *(littér = fin) [de vie, voyage, récit]* end ◆ **passé ce ~** after this date ◆ **se fixer un ~ pour ...** to set o.s. a time limit *ou* a deadline for ... ◆ **mettre un ~ à qch** to put an end *ou* a stop to sth

3 *(Méd)* **elle a dépassé le ~ de trois jours** she's three days overdue

4 *[de loyer] (= date)* term, date for payment; *(= période)* quarter, rental term *ou* period; *(= somme)* (quarterly) rent *(NonC)* ◆ **payer à ~ échu** to pay at the end of the rental term, to pay a quarter *ou* term in arrears ◆ **le (jour du) ~** *(= loyer)* the quarterday ◆ **il a un ~ de retard** he's one quarter *ou* one payment behind (with his rent) ◆ **devoir/payer son ~** to owe/pay one's rent

5 *(locutions)*

◆ **à + terme** ◆ **à ~** *[accouchement]* full term; *[naître]* at term; *(Bourse, Fin)* forward ◆ **être à ~** *[femme enceinte]* to be at full term ◆ **acheter/vendre à ~** to buy/sell forward ◆ **transaction à ~** *(Bourse de marchandises)* forward transaction; *(Bourse des valeurs)* settlement bargain ◆ **crédit/emprunt à court/long ~** short-term *ou* short-dated/long-term *ou* long-dated credit/loan, short/long credit/loan ◆ **arriver à ~** *[délai, mandat, contrat]* to expire; *[opération]* to reach its *ou* a conclusion; *[paiement]* to fall due ◆ **à ~, c'est ce qui arrivera** this is what will happen eventually *ou* in the long run *ou* in the end ◆ **mener qch à (son) ~** to bring sth to completion, to carry sth through (to completion) ◆ **prévisions à court/moyen/long ~** *(gén)* short-/ medium-/long-term forecasts; *(Météo)* short-/medium-/long-range forecasts ◆ **ce sera rentable à court/moyen/long ~** it will be profitable in the short/medium/long term; → **marché**

◆ **au terme de** *(= au bout de)* after ◆ **au ~ de dix jours de grève, ils sont parvenus à un accord** after ten days of strike action, they reached an agreement ◆ **arrivé au ~ de sa vie** having reached the end of his life

◆ **avant terme** *[naître, accoucher]* prematurely ◆ **bébé né/naissance avant ~** premature baby/birth ◆ **un bébé né deux mois avant ~** a baby born two months premature, a two-months premature baby

NMPL **termes** *(= relations)* terms ◆ **être en bons/mauvais ~s avec qn** to be on good *ou* friendly/bad terms with sb ◆ **ils sont dans les meilleurs ~s** they are on the best of terms

terminaison /tɛʀminɛzɔ̃/ NF *(Ling)* ending ◆ **~s nerveuses** *(Anat)* nerve endings

terminal, e (mpl **-aux**) /tɛʀminal, o/ ADJ *[élément, bourgeon, phase de maladie]* terminal ◆ **classe ~e** *(Scol)* final year, ≈ upper sixth (form) *(Brit)*, twelfth grade *(US)*, ≈ senior year *(US)* ◆ **élève de ~e** ≈ upper sixth former *(Brit)*, senior *(US)*, twelfth grader *(US)* ◆ **malade au stade ~** *ou* **en phase ~e** terminally ill patient

NM 1 *(= aérogare)* (air) terminal 2 *[de pétrole, marchandises]* terminal ◆ **~ pétrolier** oil terminal ◆ **~ maritime** shipping terminal 3 *(= ordinateur)* terminal ◆ **~ intelligent/passif** smart *ou* intelligent/dumb terminal ◆ **~ vocal** vocal terminal ◆ **~ de paiement électronique** electronic payment terminal ◆ **~ point de vente** point-of-sale *ou* POS terminal NF **terminale** *(Scol)* → **adj**

terminer /tɛʀmine/ ▸ conjug 1 ◂ VT 1 *(= clore)* *[+ débat, séance]* to bring to an end *ou* to a close, to terminate

2 *(= achever)* *[+ travail]* to finish (off), to complete; *[+ repas, temps d'exil]* to end, to finish; *[+ récit, débat]* to finish, to close, to end ◆ **il termina en nous remerciant** he finished (up *ou* off) *ou* he ended by thanking us ◆ **nous avons terminé la journée/soirée chez un ami/par une promenade** we finished off *ou* ended the day/evening at a friend's house/with a walk ◆ **~ ses jours à la campagne/à l'hôpital** to end one's days in the country/in hospital ◆ **~ un repas par un café** to finish off *ou* round off *ou* end a meal with a coffee ◆ **~ un livre par quelques conseils pratiques** to end a book with a few pieces of practical advice ◆ **en avoir terminé avec un travail** to be finished with a job ◆ **j'en ai terminé avec eux** I am *ou* have finished with them, I have done with them ◆ **pour ~ je dirais que …** in conclusion *ou* to conclude I would say that …, and finally I would say that … ◆ **j'attends qu'il termine** I'm waiting for him to finish, I'm waiting till he's finished

3 *(= former le dernier élément de)* **le café termina le repas** the meal finished *ou* ended with coffee, coffee finished off the meal ◆ **un bourgeon termine la tige** the stalk ends in a bud

VPR **se terminer** 1 *(= prendre fin)* *[rue, domaine]* to end, to terminate *(frm)*; *[affaire, repas]* to (come to an) end ◆ **les vacances se terminent demain** the holidays finish *ou* (come to an) end tomorrow ◆ **le parc se termine ici** the park ends here ◆ **ça s'est bien/mal terminé** it ended well/badly, it turned out well *ou* all right/badly (in the end) ◆ **alors ces travaux, ça se termine ?** *(gén)* well, is the work just about complete? *ou* done?; *(impatience)* when's the work going to be finished?

2 *(= s'achever sur)* **se ~ par** to end with ◆ **la thèse se termine par une bibliographie** the thesis ends with a bibliography ◆ **la soirée se termina par un jeu** the evening ended with a game ◆ **ces verbes se terminent par le suffixe "ir"** these verbs end in the suffix "ir"

3 *(= finir en)* **se ~ en** to end in ◆ **les mots qui se terminent en "ation"** words which end in "ation" ◆ **cette comédie se termine en tragédie** this comedy ends in tragedy ◆ **se ~ en pointe** to taper to a point, to end in a point

terminologie /tɛʀminɔlɔʒi/ NF terminology

terminologique /tɛʀminɔlɔʒik/ ADJ terminological

terminologue /tɛʀminɔlɔg/ NMF terminologist

terminus /tɛʀminys/ NM *[d'autobus, train]* terminus ◆ **~ ! tout le monde descend !** (last stop!) all change!

termite /tɛʀmit/ NM termite

termitière /tɛʀmitjɛʀ/ NF termites' nest

ternaire /tɛʀnɛʀ/ ADJ ternary

terne /tɛʀn/ ADJ *[teint]* lifeless, colourless *(Brit)*, colorless *(US)*; *[regard]* lifeless, lacklustre *(Brit)*, lackluster *(US)*; *[personne]* dull, drab, colourless *(Brit)*, colorless *(US)*; *[style, conversation]* dull, drab, lacklustre *(Brit)*, lackluster *(US)*; *[couleur, journée, vie]* dull, drab; *[cheveux]* dull, lifeless

terni, e /tɛʀni/ (ptp de **ternir**) ADJ *(lit, fig)* tarnished

ternir /tɛʀniʀ/ ▸ conjug 2 ◂ VT 1 *[+ métal, glace]* to tarnish 2 *[+ mémoire, honneur, réputation]* to stain, to tarnish, to sully VPR **se ternir** *[métal, glace]* to tarnish, to become tarnished; *[réputation]* to become tarnished *ou* stained

ternissement /tɛʀnismɑ̃/ NM *[de métal]* tarnishing

ternissure /tɛʀnisyʀ/ NF *(= aspect)* *[d'argenterie, métal, glace]* tarnish, tarnished condition; *(= tache)* tarnished *ou* dull spot

terrain /teʀɛ̃/ NM 1 *(= relief)* ground, terrain *(SPÉC) (littér)*; *(= sol)* soil, ground ◆ **~ caillouteux/vallonné** stony/hilly ground ◆ **~ meuble/lourd** loose/heavy soil *ou* ground ◆ **c'est un bon ~ pour la culture** it's (a) good soil for cultivation; → **accident, glissement, tout-terrain**

2 *(Ftbl, Rugby)* pitch, field; *(avec les installations)* ground; *(Courses, Golf)* course; *(Basket, Volley, Hand-ball)* court ◆ **sur le ~** on the field (*ou* on court *etc*) ◆ **disputer un match sur ~ adverse/sur son propre ~** to play an away/a home match

3 *(= étendue de terre)* land *(NonC)*; *(= parcelle)* plot (of land), piece of land; *(à bâtir)* site ◆ **~ à lotir** land for dividing into plots ◆ **"terrain à bâtir"** "site *ou* building land for sale" ◆ **une maison avec deux hectares de ~** a house with two hectares of land ◆ **le prix du ~ à Paris** the price of land in Paris

4 *(Géog, Géol : souvent pl)* formation ◆ **les ~s primaires/glaciaires** primary/glacial formations

5 *(Mil = lieu d'opérations)* terrain; *(gagné ou perdu)* ground ◆ **en ~ ennemi** on enemy ground *ou* territory ◆ **disputer le ~** *(Mil)* to fight for every inch of ground; *(fig)* to fight every inch of the way ◆ **céder/gagner/perdre du ~** *(lit, fig)* to give/gain/lose ground ◆ **céder du ~ à l'ennemi** to lose *ou* yield ground to the enemy, to fall back before the enemy ◆ **ils finiront par céder du ~** *[négociateurs]* in the end they'll make concessions ◆ **l'épidémie cède du ~ devant les efforts des médecins** the epidemic is receding before the doctors' efforts ◆ **la livre a cédé/gagné du ~** the pound has lost/gained ground *(par rapport à* against); ◆ **reconnaître le ~** *(lit)* to reconnoitre the terrain; *(fig)* to see how the land lies, to get the lie *(Brit)* *ou* lay *(US)* of the land ◆ **sonder** *ou* **tâter le ~** *(fig)* to test the ground, to put out feelers ◆ **avoir l'avantage du ~** *(lit)* to have territorial advantage; *(fig)* to have the advantage of being on (one's) home ground ◆ **préparer/déblayer le ~** to prepare/clear the ground ◆ **aller/être sur le ~** to go out into/be out in the field ◆ **de ~** *[politicien]* grass-roots ◆ **le nouveau PDG est un homme de ~** the new managing director is a practical, experienced man

6 *(= domaine)* ground ◆ **être sur son ~** to be on home ground *ou* territory ◆ **trouver un ~ d'entente** to find common ground *ou* an area of agreement ◆ **chercher un ~ favorable à la discussion** to seek an area conducive to (useful) discussion ◆ **je ne le suivrai pas sur ce ~** I can't go along with him there *ou* on that, I'm not with him on that ◆ **être en** *ou* **sur un ~ mouvant** to be on uncertain ground ◆ **être sur un ~ glissant** to be on slippery *ou* dangerous ground ◆ **le journaliste s'aventura sur un ~ brûlant** the journalist ventured onto dangerous ground *ou* brought up a highly sensitive *ou* ticklish issue ◆ **l'épidémie a trouvé un ~ très favorable chez les réfugiés** the epidemic found an ideal breeding ground amongst the refugees

7 *(Méd)* **~ allergique** conditions likely to produce allergies ◆ **il a un mauvais ~** he's quite susceptible to illness ◆ **il a un ~ arthritique** he's quite susceptible to arthritis

COMP **terrain d'atterrissage** landing ground
terrain d'aviation airfield
terrain de camping campsite, camping ground
terrain de chasse hunting ground
terrain d'exercice training ground
terrain de jeu playing field
terrain de manœuvre *(Mil)* training ground; *(= domaine)* stomping ground
terrain militaire army ground
terrain de sport sports ground
terrain de tennis tennis court
terrain de tir shooting *ou* firing range
terrain vague waste ground *(NonC)*, wasteland *(NonC)*

terra incognita /teʀaɛ̃kɔgnita/ (pl **terrae incognitae** /teʀaeɛ̃kɔgnitae/) NF *(littér)* terra incognita

terrasse /teʀas/ NF 1 *[de parc, jardin]* terrace ◆ **cultures en ~s** terrace cultivation ◆ **~ fluviale** *(Géog)* river terrace 2 *[d'appartement]* terrace; *(sur le toit)* terrace roof ◆ **toiture en ~, toit-~** flat roof 3 *[de café]* terrace, pavement (area) ◆ **j'ai aperçu Charles attablé à la ~ du Café Royal** I saw Charles sitting at the terrace of the Café Royal *ou* outside the Café Royal ◆ **à la** *ou* **en ~** outside ◆ **il refusa de me servir à la** *ou* **en ~** he refused to serve me outside 4 *(Constr = métier)* excavation work ◆ **faire de la ~** to do excavation work

terrassement /teʀasmɑ̃/ NM 1 *(= action)* excavation ◆ **travaux de ~** excavation work ◆ **engins de ~** earth-moving *ou* excavating equipment 2 *(= terres creusées)* **~s** excavations, earthworks; *[de voie ferrée]* embankments

terrasser /teʀase/ ▸ conjug 1 ◂ VT 1 *[adversaire]* to floor, to bring down; *[attaque]* to bring down; *[fatigue]* to overcome; *[émotion, nouvelle]* to overwhelm; *[maladie]* to strike down ◆ **cette maladie l'a terrassé** this illness laid him low ◆ **terrassé par une crise cardiaque** struck down *ou* felled by a heart attack 2 *(Tech)* to excavate, to dig out; *(Agr)* to dig over

terrassier /teʀasje/ NM unskilled road worker, navvy *(Brit)*

terre /tɛʀ/ NF 1 *(= planète)* earth; *(= monde)* world ◆ **la planète Terre** (the) planet Earth ◆ **sur la ~ comme au ciel** *(Rel)* on earth as it is in heaven ◆ **Dieu créa le Ciel et la Terre** God created the Heavens and the Earth, God created Heaven and Earth ◆ **il a parcouru la ~ entière** he has travelled the world over, he has travelled all over the world *ou* globe ◆ **prendre à témoin la ~ entière** to take the world as one's witness ◆ **tant qu'il y aura des hommes sur la ~** as long as there are men on (the) earth ◆ **être seul sur (la) ~** to be alone in the world ◆ **il ne faut pas s'attendre au bonheur sur (cette) ~** happiness is not to be expected in this world *ou* on this earth ◆ **redescendre** *ou* **revenir sur ~** *(fig)* to come (back) down to earth; → **remuer, sel, ventre**

2 (= *sol, surface*) ground, land; (= *matière*) earth, soil; (*pour la poterie*) clay ◆ **pipe/vase en ~** clay pipe/vase ◆ **ne t'allonge pas par ~, la ~ est humide** don't lie on the ground – it's damp, don't lie down – the ground is damp ◆ **une ~ fertile/aride** a fertile/an arid *ou* a barren soil ◆ **retourner/labourer la ~** to turn over/work the soil ◆ **travailler la ~** to work the soil *ou* land ◆ **planter un arbre en pleine ~** to plant a tree in the ground; → **chemin, motte, ver**

◆ **à/par terre** ◆ **être à ~** [*lutteur*] to be down ◆ **il ne faut pas frapper quelqu'un qui est à ~** (*lit, fig*) you shouldn't kick a man when he's down *ou* somebody when they're down ◆ **poser qch à** *ou* **par ~** to put sth (down) on the ground ◆ **jeter qch à** *ou* **par ~** to throw sth (down) on the ground, to throw sth to the ground ◆ **cela fiche** *ou* **flanque tous nos projets par ~** * that really messes up all our plans, that puts paid to all our plans (*Brit*) ◆ **mettre qn à ~** [*+ adversaire*] to beat sb hollow

◆ **en terre** ◆ **mettre qn en ~** to bury sb ◆ **mettre qch en ~** to put sth into the soil

◆ **sous terre** ◆ **cinq mètres sous ~** five metres underground ◆ **être à six pieds sous ~** (*fig*) to be six feet under, to be pushing up the daisies * ◆ **j'aurais voulu rentrer sous ~** (*de honte*) I wished the ground would swallow me up, I could have died *

3 (= *étendue, campagne*) **~(s)** land (*NonC*) ◆ **une bande** *ou* **langue de ~** a strip *ou* tongue of land ◆ **des ~s à blé** wheat-growing land ◆ **il a acheté un bout** *ou* **un lopin de ~** he's bought a piece *ou* patch *ou* plot of land ◆ **~s cultivées** cultivated land ◆ **~s en friche** *ou* **en jachère/incultes** fallow/uncultivated land

4 (*par opposition à mer*) land (*NonC*) ◆ **sur la ~ ferme** on dry land, on terra firma ◆ **apercevoir la ~** to sight land ◆ **~ !** (*Naut*) land ho! ◆ **aller à ~** (*Naut*) to go ashore ◆ **dans les ~s** inland ◆ **aller/voyager par (voie de) ~** to go/travel by land *ou* overland ◆ **toucher ~** [*navire, avion*] to land

5 (= *propriété, domaine*) land (*gén NonC*) ◆ **la ~** land ◆ **une ~** an estate ◆ **il a acheté une ~ en Normandie** he's bought an estate *ou* some land in Normandy ◆ **vivre sur/de ses ~s** to live on/off one's lands *ou* estates ◆ **se retirer sur ses ~s** to go and live on one's country estate ◆ **la ~ est un excellent investissement** land is an excellent investment

6 (= *pays, région*) land, country ◆ **sa ~ natale** his native land *ou* country ◆ **la France, ~ d'accueil** France, (the) land of welcome ◆ **~s lointaines/australes** distant/southern lands ◆ **la Terre promise** the Promised Land

7 (*Élec*) earth (*Brit*), ground (*US*) ◆ **mettre** *ou* **relier à la ~** to earth (*Brit*), to ground (*US*); → **prise²**

COMP **la Terre Adélie** the Adélie Coast, Adélie Land
terre d'asile country of refuge *ou* asylum
terre battue beaten earth ◆ **sol en ~ battue** beaten-earth floor ◆ **jouer sur ~ battue** (*Tennis*) to play on a clay court
terre brûlée ◆ **politique de la ~ brûlée** scorched earth policy
terre de bruyère heath-mould, heath-peat
terre cuite (*pour briques, tuiles*) baked clay; (*pour jattes, statuettes*) terracotta ◆ **objets en ~ cuite, ~s cuites** terracotta ware (*NonC*) ◆ **une ~ cuite** a terracotta (object)
terre d'exil land *ou* country of exile
la Terre de Feu Tierra del Fuego
terre à foulon fuller's earth
terre glaise clay
terre noire (*Géog*) chernozem
terre à potier potter's clay
terres rares (*Chim*) rare earths
la Terre sainte the Holy Land
terre de Sienne sienna
terre végétale topsoil
terres vierges virgin lands

terre à terre, terre-à-terre /tɛʀatɛʀ/ ADJ INV [*esprit*] matter-of-fact; [*personne*] down-to-earth; [*préoccupations*] mundane, workaday, prosaic

terreau /tɛʀo/ NM (soil-based) compost ◆ **~ de feuilles** leaf mould ◆ **les rumeurs trouvent ici un ~ très favorable** this is an ideal breeding ground for rumours

terre-neuvas /tɛʀnœva/ NM INV (= *bateau*) fishing boat (*for fishing off Newfoundland*); (= *marin*) fisherman, trawlerman (*who fishes off Newfoundland*)

Terre-Neuve /tɛʀnœv/ NF Newfoundland

terre-neuve /tɛʀnœv/ NM INV (= *chien*) Newfoundland terrier; (*hum* = *personne*) good Samaritan

terre-neuvien, -ienne (mpl **terre-neuviens**) /tɛʀnœvjɛ̃, jɛn/ ADJ Newfoundland (*épith*) NM,F **Terre-Neuvien(ne)** Newfoundlander

terre-neuvier (pl **terre-neuviers**) /tɛʀnœvje/ NM ⇒ **terre-neuvas**

terre-plein (pl **terre-pleins**) /tɛʀplɛ̃/ NM (*Mil*) terreplein; (*Constr*) platform ◆ **~ (central)** (*sur chaussée*) central reservation (*Brit*), median strip (*US*)

terrer /teʀe/ ▸ conjug 1 ◂ VPR **se terrer** 1 [*personne poursuivie*] to flatten o.s., to crouch down; [*criminel*] to lie low, to go to ground *ou* earth; [*personne peu sociable*] to hide (o.s.) away ◆ **terrés dans la cave pendant les bombardements** hidden *ou* buried (away) in the cellar during the bombings 2 [*lapin, renard*] (*dans son terrier*) to go to earth *ou* ground; (*contre terre*) to crouch down, to flatten itself VT (*Agr*) [*+ arbre*] to earth round *ou* up; [*+ pelouse*] to spread with soil; [*+ semis*] to earth over; (*Tech*) [*+ drap*] to full

terrestre /teʀɛstʀ/ ADJ 1 [*faune, flore, transports, habitat*] land (*épith*); [*surface, magnétisme*] earth's (*épith*), terrestrial, of earth ◆ **effectifs ~s** (*Mil*) land forces ◆ **missile ~** land-based missile; → **croûte, écorce, globe** 2 (= *d'ici-bas*) [*biens, plaisirs, vie*] earthly, terrestrial; → **paradis**

terreur /tɛʀœʀ/ NF 1 (= *peur*) terror (*gén NonC*) ◆ **avec ~** with terror *ou* dread ◆ **vaines ~s** vain *ou* empty fears ◆ **le dentiste était ma grande ~** the dentist was my greatest fear, I was terrified of the dentist ◆ **il vivait dans la ~ d'être découvert/de la police** he lived in terror of being discovered/of the police ◆ **faire régner la ~** to conduct *ou* impose a reign of terror ◆ **semer la ~** to spread terror ◆ **climat/régime de ~** climate/reign of terror 2 (= *terrorisme*) terror ◆ **la Terreur** (*Hist*) the (Reign of) Terror 3 (* *hum* = *personne*) terror ◆ **petite ~** little terror *ou* horror ◆ **jouer les ~s** to play the tough guy * ◆ **on l'appelait Joe la ~** he was known as Joe, the tough guy * ◆ **c'est la ~ de la ville** he's the terror of the town

terreux, -euse /teʀø, øz/ ADJ 1 [*goût, odeur*] earthy 2 [*semelles, chaussures*] muddy; [*mains*] grubby, soiled; [*salade*] gritty, dirty 3 [*teint*] sallow, muddy; [*ciel*] muddy, leaden, sullen

terrible /teʀibl/ ADJ 1 (= *effroyable*) [*accident, maladie, châtiment*] terrible, dreadful, awful; [*arme*] terrible

2 (= *terrifiant, féroce*) [*air, menaces*] terrible, fearsome; [*guerrier*] fearsome

3 (*intensif*) [*vent, force, pression, bruit*] terrific, tremendous; [*colère, erreur*] terrible ◆ **c'est un ~ menteur** he's a terrible *ou* an awful liar ◆ **c'est ce qu'il peut manger** he can eat an incredible amount

4 (= *affligeant, pénible*) terrible, dreadful, awful ◆ **c'est ~ d'en arriver là** it's terrible *ou* awful *ou* dreadful to come to this ◆ **le (plus) ~, c'est que ...** the (most) terrible *ou* awful thing about it is that ... ◆ **il est ~, avec sa manie de toujours vous contredire** he's got a dreadful habit of always contradicting you ◆ **c'est ~ de devoir toujours tout répéter** it's awful *ou* dreadful always having to repeat everything; → **enfant**

5 (* = *formidable*) [*film, soirée, personne*] terrific *, great *, tremendous * ◆ **ce film n'est pas ~** this film is nothing special *ou* nothing to write home about

ADV ◆ **ça marche ~** ⁑ it's working fantastically (well) * *ou* really great ⁑

terriblement /teʀibləmɑ̃/ ADV 1 (= *extrêmement*) terribly, dreadfully, awfully 2 († = *affreusement*) terribly †

terrien, -ienne /teʀjɛ̃, jɛn/ ADJ 1 (= *qui possède des terres*) landed (*épith*), landowning (*épith*) ◆ **propriétaire ~** landowner, landed proprietor 2 (= *rural*) rural, country ◆ **vertus terriennes** virtues of the soil *ou* land ◆ **avoir une vieille ascendance terrienne** to come of old country stock NM 1 (= *paysan*) man of the soil, countryman 2 (= *habitant de la Terre*) Earthman, earthling 3 (*Naut*) landsman NF **terrienne** 1 (= *paysanne*) countrywoman 2 (= *habitante de la Terre*) Earthwoman, earthling 3 (*Naut*) landswoman

terrier /tɛʀje/ NM 1 (= *tanière*) [*de lapin, taupe*] burrow, hole; [*de renard*] earth; [*de blaireau*] set 2 (= *chien*) terrier

terrifiant, e /teʀifjɑ̃, jɑ̃t/ ADJ 1 (= *effrayant*) terrifying 2 (*sens affaibli*) [*progrès, appétit*] fearsome, incredible ◆ **c'est ~ comme il a maigri/grandi !** it's frightening how much weight he's lost/how much he's grown!

terrifier /teʀifje/ ▸ conjug 7 ◂ VT to terrify

terril /teʀi(l)/ NM (coal) tip, slag heap

terrine /teʀin/ NF (= *pot*) earthenware vessel, terrine; (*Culin*) (= *récipient*) terrine; (= *pâté*) pâté, terrine ◆ **~ du chef** chef's special pâté ◆ **~ de lapin/de légumes** rabbit/vegetable terrine *ou* pâté

territoire /teʀitwaʀ/ NM territory; [*de département, commune*] area; [*d'évêque, juge*] jurisdiction ◆ **~s d'outre-mer** (French) overseas territories; → **aménagement, surveillance**

territorial, e (mpl **-iaux**) /teʀitɔʀjal, jo/ ADJ 1 [*puissance*] land (*épith*); [*intégrité, modifications*] territorial ◆ **eaux ~es** territorial waters ◆ **armée ~e** Territorial Army 2 (*Jur : opposé à personnel*) territorial NM (*Mil*) Territorial NF **territoriale** (*Mil*) Territorial Army

territorialement /teʀitɔʀjalmɑ̃/ ADV territorially ◆ **être ~ compétent** (*Jur*) to have jurisdiction

territorialité /teʀitɔʀjalite/ NF (*Jur*) territoriality

terroir /tɛʀwaʀ/ NM 1 (*Agr*) soil 2 (= *région rurale*) land ◆ **accent du ~** country *ou* rural accent ◆ **cuisine du ~** country cooking ◆ **mots du ~** words with a rural flavour ◆ **il sent son ~** [*vin*] it speaks of its place ◆ **poète du ~** poet of the land

terrorisant, e /teʀɔʀizɑ̃, ɑ̃t/ ADJ terrifying

terroriser /teʀɔʀize/ ▸ conjug 1 ◂ VT to terrorize

terrorisme /teʀɔʀism/ NM terrorism

terroriste /teʀɔʀist/ ADJ, NMF terrorist

tertiaire /tɛʀsjɛʀ/ ADJ (*Écon, Géol, Méd*) tertiary NM ◆ **le ~** (*Géol*) the Tertiary; (*Écon*) the service *ou* tertiary sector

tertiairisation /tɛʀsjɛʀizasjɔ̃/, **tertiarisation** /tɛʀsjaʀizasjɔ̃/ NF expansion *ou* development of the service sector

tertio /tɛʀsjo/ ADV third(ly)

tertre /tɛʀtʀ/ NM (= *monticule*) hillock, mound, knoll (*littér*) ◆ **~ (funéraire)** (burial) mound

tes /te/ ADJ POSS → **ton¹**

tessiture /tesityʀ/ NF [de voix] tessitura; [d'instrument] range

tesson /tesɔ̃/ NM 1 (Archéol) potsherd 2 (gén) ~ (**de bouteille**) shard (of glass), piece of broken glass ou bottle

test¹ /tɛst/ NM (gén) test • **faire passer un ~ à qn** to give sb a test • **soumettre qn à des ~s** to subject sb to tests, to test sb • **~ d'intelligence** IQ test • **~ d'orientation professionnelle** vocational ou occupational test • **~ d'aptitude/psychologique** ou **de personnalité** aptitude/personality test • **~ de grossesse/d'allergie** pregnancy/allergy test; → **dépistage** ADJ • **groupe-/région-~** test group/area

test² /tɛst/ NM (= carapace) test

test³ /tɛst/ NM ⇒ **têt**

testable /tɛstabl/ ADJ testable

testament /tɛstamɑ̃/ NM 1 (Rel) **l'Ancien/le Nouveau Testament** the Old/the New Testament 2 (Jur) will, testament (Jur) • **mourir sans ~** to die intestate ou without leaving a will • **ceci est mon ~** this is my last will and testament • **il peut faire son ~*** (hum) he can ou he'd better make out his will (hum); → **coucher, léguer** 3 (fig) [d'homme politique, artiste] legacy • **~ politique** political legacy

COMP **testament par acte public, testament authentique** *will dictated to notary in the presence of witnesses*

testament mystique *will written or dictated by testator, signed by him, and handed to notary in a sealed envelope, before witnesses*

testament olographe *will written, dated and signed by the testator*

testament secret ⇒ **testament mystique**

testamentaire /tɛstamɑ̃tɛʀ/ ADJ • **dispositions ~s** provisions of a (ou the) will • **donation ~** bequest, legacy • **héritier ~** legatee; (de biens immobiliers) devisee; → **exécuteur**

testateur /tɛstatœʀ/ NM testator, legator; (léguant des biens immobiliers) devisor

testatrice /tɛstatʀis/ NF testatrix, legator; (léguant des biens immobiliers) devisor

tester¹ /tɛste/ ▸ conjug 1 ◂ VT [+ personne, produit, connaissances] to test • **produit testé en laboratoire** laboratory-tested product • **cosmétiques non testés sur animaux** cosmetics that have not been tested on animals, non-animal-tested cosmetics • **il cherchait à ~ ma détermination** he was testing my resolve

tester² /tɛste/ ▸ conjug 1 ◂ VI (Jur) to make (out) one's will

testeur /tɛstœʀ/ NM (= personne, machine) tester

testiculaire /tɛstikylɛʀ/ ADJ testicular

testicule /tɛstikyl/ NM testicle, testis (SPÉC)

test-match (pl **test-match(e)s**) /tɛstmatʃ/ NM (Rugby) rugby international

testostérone /tɛstosteʀɔn/ NF testosterone

têt /tɛ(t)/ NM (Chim) • **~ à rôtir** roasting dish ou crucible • **~ à gaz** beehive shelf

tétanie /tetani/ NF tetany

tétanique /tetanik/ ADJ [convulsions] tetanic; [patient] tetanus (épith), suffering from tetanus (attrib)

tétanisation /tetanizasjɔ̃/ NF [de muscle] tetanization

tétaniser /tetanize/ ▸ conjug 1 ◂ VT (Méd) to tetanize • **muscle qui se tétanise** muscle that becomes tetanized • **il était tétanisé par la peur** he was paralyzed with fear • **le public était tétanisé de surprise** the audience was stunned

tétanos /tetanos/ NM (= maladie) tetanus, lockjaw; (= contraction) tetanus • **~ musculaire** ou **physiologique** tetanus (of a muscle) • **vaccin contre le ~** tetanus vaccine

têtard /tɛtaʀ/ NM tadpole

tête /tɛt/

1 NOM FÉMININ 2 COMPOSÉS

1 - NOM FÉMININ

1 Anat [de personne, animal] head; (= chevelure) hair (NonC) • **être ~ nue, n'avoir rien sur la ~** to be bareheaded, to have nothing on one's head • **avoir mal à la ~** to have a headache • **j'ai la ~ lourde** my head feels heavy • **sa ~ brune/bouclée** his brown/curly hair • **avoir la ~ sale/propre** to have dirty/clean hair • **veau à deux ~s** two-headed calf • **se tenir la ~ à deux mains** to hold one's head in one's hands • **tomber la ~ la première** to fall head-first • **c'est à se cogner** ou **se taper la ~ contre les murs** it's enough to drive you up the wall* • **j'en donnerais ma ~ à couper** I would stake my life on it • **faire une** ou **la ~ au carré à qn**‡ to smash sb's face in‡, to knock sb's block off‡ • **tenir ~ à qn/qch** to stand up to sb/sth

♦ **tête baissée** • **courir** ou **foncer ~ baissée** (lit) to rush ou charge headlong • **y aller ~ baissée** (fig) to charge in blindly • **se jeter** ou **donner ~ baissée dans** [+ entreprise, piège] to rush headlong into

♦ **la tête basse** • **marcher la ~ basse** to walk along with one's head bowed • **il est reparti la ~ basse** he left hanging his head

♦ **la tête haute** • **aller** ou **marcher la ~ haute** to walk with one's head held high, to carry one's head high • **battu aux élections, il peut néanmoins se retirer la ~ haute** although beaten in the elections he can nevertheless withdraw with his head held high

♦ **de la tête aux pieds** from head to foot ou toe, from top to toe

♦ **coup de tête** (lit) head-butt; (fig) sudden impulse • **donner un coup de ~ à qn** to head-butt sb • **donner des coups de ~ contre qch** to bang one's head against sth • **agir sur un coup de ~** to act on impulse; → **tête-à-tête**

2 = vie **mettre à prix la ~ de qn** to put a price on sb's head • **réclamer la ~ de qn** to demand sb's head • **jurer sur la ~ de qn** to swear on sb's life • **risquer sa ~** to risk one's neck • **sauver sa ~** to save one's skin ou neck • **il y va de sa ~** his life is at stake

3 = visage, expression face • **il a une ~ sympathique** he has a nice ou friendly face • **il a une ~ sinistre** he has a sinister look about him, he looks an ugly customer • **il a une bonne ~** he looks a decent sort • **quand il a appris la nouvelle il a fait une (drôle de) ~ !** he pulled a face when he heard the news!, you should have seen his face when he heard the news! • **il en fait une ~ !** what a face!, just look at his face! • **faire la ~** to sulk, to have the sulks* (Brit) • **tu as vu la ~ qu'il a !** ou **sa ~ !** have you seen his face! • **je connais cette ~-là !** I know that face! • **mettre un nom sur une ~** to put a name to a face • **il a** ou **c'est une ~ à claques*** he has got the sort of face you'd love to smack ou that just asks to be smacked • **jeter** ou **lancer à la ~ de qn que ...** to hurl in sb's face ... • **c'est à la ~ du client*** it depends on the person • **il fait son prix à la ~ du client** he charges what he feels like; → **enterrement, payer** etc

4 = personne head • **~ couronnée** crowned head • **de nouvelles ~s** new faces • **des ~s connues** familiar faces • **des ~s vont tomber** heads will roll • **avoir ses ~s*** to have one's favourites • **le repas coûtera 25 € par ~ (de pipe‡)** the meal will cost €25 a head ou €25 per person ou €25 apiece

5 = animal **20 ~s de bétail** 20 head of cattle

6 mesure head • **il a une ~/demi-~ de plus que moi** he's a head/half a head taller than me • **gagner d'une ~** (Courses) to win by a head

7 = partie supérieure [de clou, marteau] head; [d'arbre] top • **~ d'ail** head of garlic • **~ d'artichaut** artichoke head • **~ d'épingle** pinhead • **gros comme une ~ d'épingle** no bigger than a pinhead • **~ de l'humérus** head of the humerus

8 = partie antérieure [de train, procession] front, head; (Mil) [de colonne, peloton] head; (= première place) [de liste, chapitre, classe] top, head • **l'équipe conserve la ~ du classement** the team retains its lead • **prendre la ~** to take the lead • **prendre la ~ du cortège** to lead the procession, to take one's place at the head of the procession • **prendre la ~ d'un mouvement** to take over leadership of a movement, to become the leader of a movement • **prendre la ~ d'une affaire** to take over a business

♦ **à la tête de** • **à la ~ du cortège** at the head of the procession • **tué à la ~ de ses troupes** killed leading his troops ou at the head of his troops • **être à la ~ d'un mouvement/d'une affaire** (= diriger) to be at the head of a movement/of a business, to head (up) a movement/a business • **se trouver à la ~ d'une petite fortune/de deux maisons** to find o.s. the owner ou possessor of a small fortune/of two houses

♦ **en tête** • **ils sont entrés dans la ville, musique en ~** they came into the town led ou headed by the band • **on monte en ~ ou en queue ?** (Rail) shall we get on at the front or (at) the back? • **être en ~** to be in the lead ou in front • **dans les sondages, il arrive largement en ~** he's well ahead in the polls

♦ **en tête de** • **en ~ de phrase** at the beginning of the sentence • **monter dans le métro en ~ de ligne** to get on the metro at the beginning of the line • **être** ou **venir en ~ de liste** to head the list, to come at the head ou top of the list • **il arrive en ~ du scrutin** he's leading in the elections

9 = facultés mentales **avoir (toute) sa ~** to have (all) one's wits about one • **n'avoir rien dans la ~** to be empty-headed • **où ai-je la ~ ?** whatever am I thinking of? • **avoir une petite ~** to be dim-witted • **avoir** ou **être une ~ sans cervelle** ou **de linotte, être ~ en l'air** to be scatterbrained, to be a scatterbrain • **avoir de la ~** to have a good head on one's shoulders • **ce type-là, c'est une ~*** that guy's really brainy* • **c'est une ~ en maths*** he's ou she's really good at maths • **femme/homme de ~** level-headed ou capable woman/man • **avoir la ~ bien faite** to have a good mind • **avoir la ~ sur les épaules** to be level-headed • **calculer qch de ~** to work sth out in one's head • **chercher qch dans sa ~** to search one's memory for sth • **il est vieux dans sa ~** he behaves like an old man • **il est bien/mal dans sa ~*** he's at ease/not at ease with himself • **mettre** ou **fourrer* qch dans la ~ de qn** to put sth into sb's head • **se mettre dans la ~ que** (= s'imaginer) to get it into one's head that • **se mettre dans la ~ de faire qch** (= décider) to take it into one's head to do sth • **j'ai la ~ vide** my mind is a blank ou has gone blank • **avoir la ~ à ce que l'on fait** to have one's mind on what one is doing • **avoir la ~ ailleurs** to have one's mind on other matters ou elsewhere • **n'en faire qu'à sa ~** to do (exactly) as one pleases, to please o.s., to go one's own (sweet) way • **il me prend la ~‡** he drives me nuts* ou mad • **la géométrie, ça me prend la ~‡** geometry does my head in‡ • **les maths, quelle prise de ~ !*** maths does my head in!‡ • **j'y réfléchirai à ~ reposée** I'll think about it when I've got a quiet moment; → **creuser, monter¹, perdre** etc

♦ **en tête** • **je n'ai plus le chiffre/le nom en ~** I can't recall the number/the name, the number/the name has gone (clean) out of my head ◆ **avoir des projets en ~** to have plans ◆ **se mettre en ~ que** *(= s'imaginer)* to get it into one's head that ◆ **se mettre en ~ de faire qch** *(= décider)* to take it into one's head to do sth

10 = tempérament **avoir la ~ chaude/froide** to be quick- *ou* fiery-tempered/cool-headed ◆ **garder la ~ froide** to keep a cool head, to remain cool, to keep one's head ◆ **avoir la ~ dure** to be a blockhead* ◆ **avoir** *ou* **être une ~ de mule*** *ou* **de bois*** *ou* **de lard*** *ou* **de cochon*, être une ~ de pioche*** to be as stubborn as a mule, to be mulish *ou* pigheaded ◆ **avoir la ~ près du bonnet** to be quick-tempered, to have a short fuse; → **fort¹, mauvais**

11 Ftbl header ◆ **faire une ~** to head the ball

2 - COMPOSÉS

tête d'affiche *(Théât)* top of the bill ◆ **être la ~ d'affiche** to head the bill, to be top of the bill
tête de bielle big end
tête blonde* *(= enfant)* little one
tête brûlée *(= baroudeur)* desperado
tête chercheuse *(lit)* homing device; *(fig = personne)* pioneering researcher; *(= groupe)* pioneering research group ◆ **fusée à ~ chercheuse** homing rocket
tête de cuvée tête de cuvée
tête de Delco® distributor
tête d'écriture *[d'imprimante]* writing head
tête d'enregistrement recording head
tête d'injection *(Tech)* swivel
tête de lecture *[de pick-up]* pickup head; *[de magnétophone, magnétoscope]* play-back head; *(Ordin)* reading head ◆ **~ de lecture-écriture** *(Ordin)* read-write head
tête de ligne terminus, start of the line *(Rail)*
tête de liste *(Pol)* chief candidate *(in list system of voting)*
tête de lit bedhead
tête de mort *(= emblème)* death's-head; *[de pavillon]* skull and crossbones, Jolly Roger; *(= papillon)* death's-head moth; *(= fromage)* Gouda cheese
tête de nœud** prick**, dickhead**
tête nucléaire nuclear warhead
tête d'œuf *(péj)* egghead
tête pensante brains*
tête de pont *(au-delà d'un fleuve)* bridgehead; *(au-delà de la mer)* beachhead; *(fig)* bridgehead
tête de série *(Tennis)* seeded player ◆ **il était classé troisième ~ de série** he was seeded third ◆ **il est ~ de série numéro 2** he's the number 2 seed
tête de Turc whipping boy

tête-à-queue /tɛtakø/ NM INV spin ◆ **faire un ~** *[de cheval]* to turn about; *[de voiture]* to spin round

tête-à-tête /tɛtatɛt/ NM INV 1 *(= conversation)* tête-à-tête, private conversation ◆ **en ~** alone together ◆ **discussion en ~** discussion in private ◆ **on a dîné en ~** the two of us had dinner together 2 *(= service)* breakfast set for two, tea *ou* coffee set for two; *(= meuble)* tête-à-tête

tête-bêche /tɛtbɛʃ/ ADV head to foot *ou* tail ◆ **timbre ~** tête-bêche stamp

tête-de-loup (pl **têtes-de-loup**) /tɛtdəlu/ NF ceiling brush

tête-de-nègre /tɛtdənɛgʀ/ ADJ INV dark brown, chocolate brown *(Brit)* NF 1 *(Culin)* chocolate-covered meringue 2 *(= champignon)* brown boletus

tétée /tete/ NF *(= action)* sucking; *(repas, lait)* nursing, feed *(Brit)* ◆ **cinq ~s par jour** five nursings *ou* feeds *(Brit)* a day ◆ **l'heure de la ~** nursing *ou* feeding *(Brit)* time

téter /tete/ ► conjug 6 ◄ VT 1 *[+ lait]* to suck; *[+ biberon, sein]* to suck at ◆ **~ sa mère** to suck at one's mother's breast ◆ **donner à ~ à un bébé** to feed a baby (at the breast), to suckle *ou* nurse a baby 2 * *[+ pouce]* to suck; *[+ pipe]* to suck at *ou* on 3 * *[voiture]* **elle tête du 13 litres au cent** ≈ it does 20 miles to the gallon ◆ **elle tête énormément** it's a real gas-guzzler*

têtière /tɛtjɛʀ/ NF *[de cheval]* headstall; *[de siège] (en tissu, dentelle)* antimacassar; *(= repose-tête)* head rest

tétine /tetin/ NF *[de vache]* udder, dug *(SPÉC)*; *[de truie]* teat, dug *(SPÉC)*; *[de biberon]* teat *(Brit)*, nipple *(US)*; *(= sucette)* comforter, dummy *(Brit)*, pacifier *(US)*

téton /tetɔ̃/ NM 1 *(* = sein)* breast, tit** 2 *(Tech = saillie)* stud, nipple

tétrachlorure /tetʀaklɔʀyʀ/ NM tetrachloride ◆ **~ de carbone** carbon tetrachloride

tétracorde /tetʀakɔʀd/ NM tetrachord

tétraèdre /tetʀaɛdʀ/ NM tetrahedron

tétraédrique /tetʀaedʀik/ ADJ tetrahedral

tétralogie /tetʀalɔʒi/ NF tetralogy ◆ **la Tétralogie de Wagner** Wagner's Ring

tétramètre /tetʀamɛtʀ/ NM tetrameter

tétraphonie /tetʀafɔni/ NF quadraphonia

tétraphonique /tetʀafɔnik/ ADJ quadraphonic

tétraplégie /tetʀapleʒi/ NF tetraplegia

tétraplégique /tetʀapleʒik/ ADJ, NMF quadraplegic, tetraplegic

tétrapode /tetʀapɔd/ NM tetrapod

tétrarque /tetʀaʀk/ NM tetrarch

tétras /tetʀɑ(s)/ NM grouse ◆ **~-lyre** black grouse ◆ **grand ~** capercaillie

tétrasyllabe /tetʀasi(l)lab/ ADJ tetrasyllabic NM tetrasyllable

tétrasyllabique /tetʀasi(l)labik/ ADJ tetrasyllabic

têtu, e /tety/ ADJ stubborn, obstinate ◆ **~ comme une mule** *ou* **une bourrique** *ou* **un âne** as stubborn as a mule ◆ **les faits sont ~s** there's no getting away from the facts NM,F ◆ **c'est un ~** he's stubborn

teuf* /tøf/ NF party ◆ **faire la ~** to party

teuf-teuf (pl **teufs-teufs**) /tœftœf/ NM 1 *(= bruit) [de train]* puff-puff, chuff-chuff; *[de voiture]* chug-chug 2 *(* = automobile)* boneshaker, rattle-trap*; *(langage enfantin = train)* chuff-chuff, puff-puff

teuton, -onne /tøtɔ̃, ɔn/ ADJ *(Hist, péj, hum)* Teutonic NM,F **Teuton(ne)** *(Hist, hum)* Teuton ◆ **les Teutons** *(péj)* the Huns *(péj)*

teutonique /tøtɔnik/ ADJ *(Hist, péj)* Teutonic; → **chevalier**

texan, e /tɛksɑ̃, an/ ADJ Texan NM,F **Texan(e)** Texan

Texas /tɛksas/ NM Texas

tex-mex /tɛksmɛks/ ADJ *[musique, restaurant, repas]* Tex-Mex

texte /tɛkst/ NM 1 *(= partie écrite) [de contrat, livre, pièce de théâtre]* text ◆ **~ de loi** *(adopté)* law; *(en discussion)* bill ◆ **il y a des erreurs dans le ~** there are textual errors *ou* errors in the text ◆ **lire Shakespeare dans le ~ (original)** to read Shakespeare in the original (text) ◆ **"texte et illustrations de Julien Leduc"** "written and illustrated by Julien Leduc" ◆ **apprendre son ~** *(Théât)* to learn one's lines ◆ **il écrit lui-même le ~ de ses chansons** *ou* **ses ~s** he writes his own lyrics ◆ **en français dans le ~** *(lit)* in French in the original (text); *(iro)* those were the very words used ◆ **recherche en ~ intégral** *(Ordin)* full text search

2 *(= œuvre littéraire)* text; *(fragment)* passage, piece ◆ **~s choisis** selected passages ◆ **les grands ~s classiques** the great classics ◆ **expliquez ce ~ de Gide** comment on this passage *ou* prose piece from *ou* by Gide; → **explication**

3 *(Scol = énoncé) [de devoir, dissertation]* subject, topic ◆ **~ libre** free composition; → **cahier**

textile /tɛkstil/ NM 1 *(= matière)* textile ◆ **~s artificiels** man-made fibres ◆ **~s synthétiques** synthetic *ou* man-made fibres 2 *(Ind)* **le ~** the textile industry, textiles ADJ textile

texto* /tɛksto/ ADV word for word ◆ **envoyer un ~ à qn** to text sb

Texto® /tɛksto/ NM text message

textuel, -elle /tɛkstɥɛl/ ADJ 1 *(= conforme au texte) [traduction]* literal, word for word; *[copie]* exact; *[citation]* verbatim *(épith)*, exact ◆ **elle m'a dit d'aller me faire cuire un œuf : ~ !*** she told me to get lost – those were her very words! ◆ **c'est ~ !** those were his *(ou* her) very *ou* exact words! 2 *(= du texte)* textual; *[analyse, sens]* textual

textuellement /tɛkstɥɛlmɑ̃/ ADV literally, word for word, verbatim ◆ **alors il m'a dit, ~, que j'étais un imbécile** so he told me I was a fool – those were his very words ◆ **il m'a ~ rapporté ses paroles** he told me what he had said word for word

texture /tɛkstyʀ/ NF *(gén)* texture

TF1 /teɛfœ̃/ N (abrév de **Télévision française un**) *independent French television channel*

TG /teʒe/ NF (abrév de **Trésorerie générale**) → **trésorerie**

TGV /teʒeve/ NM (abrév de **train à grande vitesse**) → **train**

thaï /taj/ NM *(= langue)* Thai ADJ Thai

thaïlandais, e /tajlɑ̃dɛ, ɛz/ ADJ Thai NM,F **Thaïlandais(e)** Thai

Thaïlande /tailɑ̃d/ NF Thailand

thalamus /talamys/ NM thalamus

thalassémie /talasemi/ NF thalassemia

thalasso* /talaso/ NF abrév de **thalassothérapie**

thalassothérapie /talasoteʀapi/ NF thalassotherapy

thallium /taljɔm/ NM thallium

thalweg /talvɛg/ NM thalweg

Thanatos /tanatɔs/ NM Thanatos

thaumaturge /tomatyʀʒ/ NM miracle-worker ADJ miracle-working *(épith)*

thaumaturgie /tomatyʀʒi/ NF miracle-working, thaumaturgy *(SPÉC)*

thé /te/ NM 1 *(= feuilles séchées, boisson)* tea ◆ **~ de Chine** China tea ◆ **les ~s de Ceylan** Ceylon teas ◆ **~ vert/noir** green/black tea ◆ **~ au lait/nature** tea with milk/without milk ◆ **~ glacé** iced tea ◆ **~ au citron/au jasmin/à la menthe** lemon/jasmine/mint tea ◆ **~ à la bergamote** tea scented with bergamot, ≈ Earl Grey ◆ **faire le** *ou* **du ~** to make some tea ◆ **prendre le ~** to have tea ◆ **à l'heure du ~** at teatime; → **feuille, rose, salon** 2 *(= arbre)* tea plant 3 *(= réunion)* tea party ◆ **~ dansant** tea dance, thé-dansant 4 *(Helv = infusion)* herbal tea, tisane

théâtral, e (mpl **-aux**) /teɑtʀal, o/ ADJ 1 *[œuvre, situation]* theatrical, dramatic; *[rubrique, chronique]* stage *(épith)*, theatre *(Brit) (épith)*, theater *(US) (épith)*; *[saison]* theatre *(Brit) (épith)*, theater *(US) (épith)*; *[représentation]* stage *(épith)*, theatrical 2 *(péj) [air, personne]* theatrical, histrionic ◆ **ses attitudes ~es m'agacent** his theatricals *ou* histrionics irritate me

théâtralement /teɑtʀalmɑ̃/ ADV *(lit)* theatrically; *(péj)* histrionically

théâtralisation /teatʀalizasjɔ̃/ NF *[de roman]* dramatization ◆ **la ~ de ses discours politiques** *(péj)* the way he turns his political speeches into theatrical performances

théâtraliser /teatʀalize/ ▸ conjug 1 ◂ VT to dramatize

théâtralité /teatʀalite/ NF (littér) theatricality

théâtre /teatʀ/ NM [1] (= genre artistique) theatre (Brit), theater (US); (= ensemble de techniques) drama, theatre (Brit), theater (US); (= activité, profession) stage, theatre (Brit), theater (US) ◆ **faire du** ~ (comme acteur) to be a stage actor, to be on the stage; (comme metteur en scène) to be in the theatre ◆ **elle a fait du** ~ she has appeared on the stage, she has done some acting ◆ **elle veut faire du** ~ she wants to go on the stage ◆ **je n'aime pas le** ~ **à la télévision** I do not like televised stage dramas ou stage productions on television ◆ **c'est du** ~ **filmé** it's a filmed stage production, it's a film of the play ◆ **ce n'est pas du bon** ~ it doesn't make good theatre ◆ **technique** ou **art du** ~ stagecraft ◆ ~ **d'essai** experimental theatre ou drama ◆ **le** ~ **musical** musicals ◆ **il fait du** ~ **d'amateur** he's involved in ou he does some amateur dramatics ◆ **un roman adapté pour le** ~ a novel adapted for the stage ou the theatre; → **critique²**

[2] (= genre littéraire) drama, theatre (Brit), theater (US); (= œuvres théâtrales) plays, dramatic works, theatre (Brit), theater (US) ◆ **le** ~ **de Sheridan** Sheridan's plays ou dramatic works, the theatre of Sheridan ◆ **le** ~ **classique/élisabéthain** the classical/Elizabethan theatre, classical/Elizabethan drama ◆ **le** ~ **antique** (gén) ancient theatre; (grec) Greek theatre ◆ **le** ~ **de caractères/de situation** the theatre of character/of situation ◆ **le** ~ **de l'absurde** the theatre of the absurd ◆ **le** ~ **de boulevard** light comedies (as performed in the theatres of the Paris Boulevards); → **pièce**

[3] (= lieu, entreprise) theatre (Brit), theater (US) ◆ ~ **de rue** street theatre ◆ ~ **de marionnettes/de verdure** puppet/open-air theatre ◆ ~ **d'ombres** shadow theatre ◆ ~ **de guignol** ≈ Punch and Judy show ◆ **il ne va jamais au** ~ he never goes to the theatre, he is not a theatregoer ◆ **le** ~ **est plein ce soir** it's a full house tonight, the performance is sold out tonight

[4] (locutions)

◆ **de théâtre** ◆ **homme/femme de** ~ man/woman of the theatre ◆ **les gens de** ~ theatre people, people who work in the theatre ◆ **cours de** ~ drama lessons ◆ **accessoires/costumes/décors de** ~ stage props/costumes/sets ◆ **artifices de** ~ stage tricks ◆ **directeur de** ~ theatre ou stage director ◆ **festival de** ~ drama festival ◆ **voix/gestes de** ~ theatrical ou histrionic ou stagey* voice/gestures

◆ **coup de théâtre** (Théât) coup de théâtre; (gén) dramatic turn of events ◆ **et coup de** ~, **il a démissionné** to everybody's amazement, he resigned

[5] (péj) (= exagération) theatricals, histrionics; (= simulation) playacting ◆ **c'est du** ~ it's just playacting

[6] [d'événement, crime] scene ◆ **les Flandres ont été le** ~ **de combats sanglants** Flanders was the scene of bloody fighting ◆ **le** ~ **des opérations** (Mil) the theatre of operations ◆ **les émeutes ont eu pour** ~ **la capitale** the riots took place in the capital, the capital was the scene of the riots ou rioting

théâtreux, -euse * /teatʀø, øz/ NM,F (hum) Thespian; (péj) second-rate ou ham actor

thébaïde /tebaid/ NF (littér) solitary retreat

thébain, e /tebɛ̃, ɛn/ ADJ Theban NM,F **Thébain(e)** Theban

Thèbes /tɛb/ N Thebes

théier /teje/ NM tea plant

théière /tejɛʀ/ NF teapot

théine /tein/ NF theine

théisme /teism/ NM [1] (Rel) theism [2] (Méd) tea poisoning

théiste /teist/ ADJ theistic(al), theist NMF theist

thématique /tematik/ ADJ (gén) thematic; [voyelle] thematic; [chaîne de télévision] specialized; [exposition, supplément d'un journal] thematic, based on a theme (attrib) ◆ **index** ~ subject index NF set of themes

thème /tɛm/ NM [1] (= sujet : gén, Littérat, Mus) theme; [de débat] theme, subject ◆ **le** ~ **de composition d'un peintre** a painter's theme ◆ **ce livre propose plusieurs** ~**s de réflexion** this book raises several issues [2] (Scol = traduction) translation (into a foreign language), prose (translation) ◆ ~ **allemand/espagnol** German/Spanish prose (translation), translation into German/Spanish; → **fort²** [3] (Ling) stem, theme ◆ ~ **nominal/verbal** noun/verb stem ou theme [4] (Astrol) ~ **astral** birth chart

théocratie /teɔkʀasi/ NF theocracy

théocratique /teɔkʀatik/ ADJ theocratic

Théocrite /teɔkʀit/ NM Theocritus

théodicée /teɔdise/ NF theodicy

théodolite /teɔdɔlit/ NM theodolite

théogonie /teɔgɔni/ NF theogony

théologal, e (mpl **-aux**) /teɔlɔgal, o/ ADJ → **vertu**

théologie /teɔlɔʒi/ NF theology ◆ **études de** ~ theological studies ◆ **faire sa** ~ to study theology ou divinity

théologien, -ienne /teɔlɔʒjɛ̃, jɛn/ NM,F theologian

théologique /teɔlɔʒik/ ADJ (Rel) theological

Théophraste /teɔfʀast/ NM Theophrastus

théorbe /teɔʀb/ NM theorbo

théorème /teɔʀɛm/ NM theorem ◆ **le** ~ **d'Archimède/de Pythagore** Archimedes'/Pythagoras' theorem

théoricien, -ienne /teɔʀisjɛ̃, jɛn/ NM,F theoretician, theorist

théorie¹ /teɔʀi/ GRAMMAIRE ACTIVE 53.2 NF (= doctrine, hypothèse) theory ◆ **la** ~ **et la pratique** theory and practice ◆ **en** ~ in theory ◆ **la** ~, **c'est bien joli, mais ...** theory ou theorizing is all very well, but ... ◆ ~ **des catastrophes/du chaos/des jeux/des ensembles** catastrophe/chaos/game/set theory

théorie² /teɔʀi/ NF (littér = procession) procession, file

théorique /teɔʀik/ ADJ theoretical ◆ **c'est une liberté toute** ~ it's a purely theoretical freedom

théoriquement /teɔʀikmɑ̃/ ADV theoretically, in theory ◆ ~, **c'est vrai** in theory ou theoretically it's true

théorisation /teɔʀizasjɔ̃/ NF theorization

théoriser /teɔʀize/ ▸ conjug 1 ◂ VI to theorize (sur about) VT to theorize about

théosophe /teɔzɔf/ NMF theosophist

théosophie /teɔzɔfi/ NF theosophy

théosophique /teɔzɔfik/ ADJ theosophic

thérapeute /teʀapøt/ NMF therapist

thérapeutique /teʀapøtik/ ADJ [usage, effet, avortement] therapeutic ◆ **essais** ~**s** drug trials ◆ **les moyens** ~**s actuels** current methods of treatment NF (= branche de la médecine) therapeutics (sg); (= traitement) therapy

thérapie /teʀapi/ NF (Méd) therapy, treatment; (Psych) therapy ◆ ~ **de groupe/comportementale** group/behavioural therapy ◆ ~ **génique** gene therapy ◆ **suivre une** ~ to undergo ou have therapy

thermal, e (mpl **-aux**) /tɛʀmal, o/ ADJ [source] thermal, hot ◆ **cure** ~**e** water cure ◆ **faire une cure** ~**e** to take the waters ◆ **eaux** ~**es** hot springs ◆ **établissement** ~ hydropathic ou water-cure establishment ◆ **station** ~**e** spa ◆ **ville** ~**e** spa town

thermalisme /tɛʀmalism/ NM (= science) balneology; (= cures) water cures

thermes /tɛʀm/ NMPL (Hist) thermae; (= établissement thermal) thermal baths

thermidor /tɛʀmidɔʀ/ NM Thermidor (11th month of French Republican calendar)

thermidorien, -ienne /tɛʀmidɔʀjɛ̃, jɛn/ ADJ of the 9th Thermidor NM,F revolutionary of the 9th Thermidor

thermie /tɛʀmi/ NF (Phys) therm

thermique /tɛʀmik/ ADJ [unité, équilibre] thermal; [énergie] thermic ◆ **moteur** ~ heat engine ◆ **carte** ~ temperature map ◆ **ascendance** ~ thermal, thermal current; → **central**

thermocautère /tɛʀmɔkotɛʀ/ NM diathermy, electro-cautery

thermochimie /tɛʀmoʃimi/ NF thermochemistry

thermocouple /tɛʀmokupl/ NM thermocouple, thermoelectric couple

thermodynamique /tɛʀmodinamik/ NF thermodynamics (sg) ADJ thermodynamic(al)

thermoélectricité /tɛʀmoelɛktʀisite/ NF thermoelectricity

thermoélectrique /tɛʀmoelɛktʀik/ ADJ thermoelectric(al) ◆ **couple** ~ thermoelectric couple, thermocouple ◆ **effet** ~ thermoelectric ou Seebeck effect ◆ **pile** ~ thermopile, thermoelectric pile

thermoformage /tɛʀmofɔʀmaʒ/ NM thermal compression moulding

thermoformé, e /tɛʀmofɔʀme/ ADJ thermally moulded

thermogène /tɛʀmɔʒɛn/ ADJ → **ouate**

thermographe /tɛʀmɔgʀaf/ NM thermograph

thermographie /tɛʀmɔgʀafi/ NF thermography

thermoluminescence /tɛʀmolyminesɑ̃s/ NF thermoluminescence

thermomètre /tɛʀmɔmɛtʀ/ NM thermometer ◆ **le** ~ **affiche** ou **indique 38°** the thermometer is (standing) at ou is showing 38° ◆ **le** ~ **monte** the temperature is rising, the thermometer is showing a rise in temperature ◆ ~ **à mercure/à alcool** mercury/alcohol thermometer ◆ ~ **à maxima et minima** maximum and minimum thermometer ◆ ~ **médical** clinical thermometer ◆ **l'indice CAC 40, principal** ~ **du marché** the CAC 40 index, the main barometer of the market

thermométrie /tɛʀmɔmetʀi/ NF thermometry

thermométrique /tɛʀmɔmetʀik/ ADJ thermometric(al)

thermonucléaire /tɛʀmonykleɛʀ/ ADJ thermonuclear

thermopile /tɛʀmopil/ NF thermopile

thermoplastique /tɛʀmoplastik/ ADJ thermoplastic

thermopropulsion /tɛʀmopʀɔpylsjɔ̃/ NF thermal propulsion

Thermopyles /tɛʀmɔpil/ NFPL ◆ **les** ~ Thermopylae

thermorégulateur, -trice /tɛʀmoʀegylatœʀ, tʀis/ ADJ thermotaxic, thermoregulation (épith)

thermorégulation /tɛʀmoʀegylasjɔ̃/ NF thermotaxis, thermoregulation (épith)

thermorésistant, e /tɛʀmoʀezistɑ̃, ɑ̃t/ ADJ (gén) heat-resistant; [plastique] thermosetting

thermos® /tɛʀmos/ NM *ou* NF ◆ **(bouteille) ~** vacuum *ou* Thermos® flask *(Brit) ou* bottle *(US)*

thermoscope /tɛʀmɔskɔp/ NM thermoscope

thermosiphon /tɛʀmosifɔ̃/ NM thermosiphon

thermosphère /tɛʀmɔsfɛʀ/ NF thermosphere

thermostat /tɛʀmɔsta/ NM thermostat ◆ **préchauffez le four, ~ 7** preheat the oven to gas mark 7

thermothérapie /tɛʀmoteʀapi/ NF (deep) heat treatment, thermotherapy

thésard, e* /tezaʀ, aʀd/ NM,F PhD student

thésaurisation /tezɔʀizasjɔ̃/ NF hoarding *(of money)*; *(Écon)* building up of capital

thésauriser /tezɔʀize/ ► conjug 1 ◄ VI to hoard money VT to hoard (up)

thésauriseur, -euse /tezɔʀizœʀ, øz/ NM,F hoarder *(of money)*

thésaurus /tezɔʀys/ NM *dictionary of specialized terms*

thèse /tɛz/ NF 1 *(= doctrine)* thesis, argument ◆ **pièce/roman à ~** *play/novel expounding a philosophical or social message,* pièce/roman à thèse *(SPÉC)* 2 *(Univ)* thesis ◆ **~ de doctorat (d'État)** PhD, doctoral thesis *(Brit)*, doctoral dissertation *(US)* ◆ **~ de 3e cycle** ≃ MA *ou* MSc thesis, Master's thesis; → **soutenance, soutenir** 3 *(Philos)* thesis ◆ **~, antithèse, synthèse** thesis, antithesis, synthesis 4 *(= théorie)* theory, possibility ◆ **selon la ~ officielle, il ...** the official line is that he ... ◆ **la ~ du suicide a été écartée** suicide has been ruled out

Thésée /teze/ NM Theseus

Thessalie /tɛsali/ NF Thessaly

thessalien, -ienne /tɛsaljɛ̃, jɛn/ ADJ Thessalian NM,F **Thessalien(ne)** Thessalian

Thessalonique /tesalɔnik/ N Thessalonica

thibaude /tibod/ NF anti-slip undercarpeting *(NonC)*, carpet underlay *(NonC)* ◆ **moquette sur ~** fitted carpet *(Brit) ou* wall-to-wall carpet *(US)* with underlay

Thimbou /timbu/ N Thimbu

Thomas /tɔma/ NM Thomas ◆ **saint ~** Saint Thomas ◆ **je suis comme saint ~, je ne crois que ce que je vois** I'm a real doubting Thomas, I'll believe it when I see it, seeing is believing ◆ **saint ~ d'Aquin** (Saint) Thomas Aquinas

thomisme /tɔmism/ NM Thomism

thomiste /tɔmist/ ADJ Thomistic(al) NMF Thomist

thon /tɔ̃/ NM 1 *(= poisson)* tuna ◆ **~ blanc** long fin tuna ◆ **~ rouge** blue fin tuna ◆ **miettes de ~** flaked tuna ◆ **~ au naturel/à l'huile** tuna(-fish) in brine/in oil 2 *(✱ : péj)* lump*

thonier /tɔnje/ NM tuna boat

Thor /tɔʀ/ NM Thor

Thora, Torah /tɔʀa/ NF ◆ **la ~** the Torah

thoracique /tɔʀasik/ ADJ *[cavité, canal]* thoracic ◆ **capacité ~** respiratory *ou* vital capacity; → **cage**

thorax /tɔʀaks/ NM thorax

thorium /tɔʀjɔm/ NM thorium

Thrace /tʀas/ NF Thrace

thrène /tʀɛn/ NM threnody

thrombine /tʀɔ̃bin/ NF thrombin

thrombocyte /tʀɔ̃bɔsit/ NM thrombocyte

thrombose /tʀɔ̃boz/ NF thrombosis ◆ **~ veineuse profonde** deep vein thrombosis, DVT

Thucydide /tysidid/ NM Thucydides

Thulé /tyle/ N Thule

thulium /tyljɔm/ NM thulium

thune /tyn/ NF 1 *(† * = pièce)* 5-franc piece 2 *(✱ = argent)* **de la ~, des ~s** cash*, dosh✱ *(Brit)* ◆ **j'ai plus une ~** I'm flat *ou* stony *(Brit)* broke ◆ **il se fait pas mal de ~(s)** he makes loads of *ou* a pile of money*

thuriféraire /tyʀifeʀɛʀ/ NM *(Rel)* thurifier; *(littér)* flatterer, sycophant

thuya /tyja/ NM thuja

thym /tɛ̃/ NM thyme ◆ **~ sauvage** wild thyme

thymique /timik/ ADJ *(Méd, Psych)* thymic

thymus /timys/ NM thymus

thyroïde /tiʀɔid/ ADJ thyroid *(épith)* NF ◆ **(glande) ~** thyroid (gland)

thyroïdien, -ienne /tiʀɔidjɛ̃, jɛn/ ADJ thyroid *(épith)*

thyroxine /tiʀɔksin/ NF thyroxin

thyrse /tiʀs/ NM *(Bot, Myth)* thyrsus

tiare /tjaʀ/ NF tiara

Tibère /tibɛʀ/ NM Tiberius

Tibériade /tibeʀjad/ N ◆ **le lac de ~** Lake Tiberias, the Sea of Galilee

Tibesti /tibɛsti/ NM ◆ **le (massif du) ~** the Tibesti (Massif)

Tibet /tibɛ/ NM Tibet

tibétain, e /tibetɛ̃, ɛn/ ADJ Tibetan NM *(= langue)* Tibetan NM,F **Tibétain(e)** Tibetan

tibia /tibja/ NM *(Anat)* (= os) tibia *(SPÉC)*, shinbone; *(= partie antérieure de la jambe)* shin ◆ **donner un coup de pied dans les ~s à qn** to kick sb in the shins

Tibre /tibʀ/ NM ◆ **le ~** the Tiber

TIC /teise/ NFPL (abrév de **technologies de l'information et de la communication**) ICT

tic /tik/ NM 1 *(facial)* (facial) twitch *ou* tic; *(du corps)* twitch, mannerism, tic; *(= manie)* habit, mannerism ◆ **~ (nerveux)** nervous twitch *ou* tic ◆ **~ verbal** *ou* **de langage** verbal tic ◆ **c'est un ~ chez lui** *(manie)* it's a habit with him; *(geste)* it's a tic he has ◆ **il est plein de ~s** he never stops twitching 2 *(chez le cheval)* cribbing *(NonC)*, crib-biting *(NonC)*

ticket /tikɛ/ NM 1 *(= billet)* ticket ◆ **~ de métro/consigne/vestiaire** underground *(Brit) ou* subway *(US)*/left-luggage/cloakroom ticket 2 *(† ✱ = 10 francs)* 10-franc note 3 **j'ai le** *ou* **un ~ avec sa sœur*** I've made a hit with his sister* 4 *(Pol)* ticket

COMP **ticket d'alimentation** ≃ ration card, food stamp *(US)*

ticket de caisse sales slip *ou* receipt

ticket d'entrée (entrance) ticket ◆ **leur ~ d'entrée sur le marché européen** their ticket into the European market

ticket modérateur patient's contribution *(towards cost of medical treatment)*

ticket de quai platform ticket

ticket de rationnement ≃ ration card

ticket-repas (pl **tickets-repas**) /tikɛʀəpa/ NM luncheon voucher *(Brit)*, ≃ meal ticket *(US)*

Ticket-Restaurant® (pl **Tickets-Restaurant**) /tikɛʀɛstɔʀɑ̃/ NM ⇒ **ticket-repas**

tic-tac /tiktak/ NM INV ticking, tick-tock ◆ **faire ~** to tick, to go tick tock

tie-break (pl **tie-breaks**) /tajbʀɛk/ NM tie break ◆ **il a remporté le premier set au ~** he won the first set on *ou* in a tie-break

tiédasse /tjedas/ ADJ *(péj)* lukewarm, tepid

tiède /tjɛd/ ADJ 1 *(= refroidi) [boisson, bain] (désagréablement)* lukewarm, tepid; *(agréablement)* warm; *(= doux) [vent, saison, température]* mild, warm; *[atmosphère]* balmy ◆ **salade ~** warm salad

2 *(= sans conviction) [sentiment, foi, accueil]* lukewarm, half-hearted, tepid; *[chrétien, militant]* half-hearted, lukewarm ◆ **tu lui as proposé ? – oui, mais il était plutôt ~** did you suggest it to him? – yes, but he wasn't very enthusiastic

NMF *(péj)* lukewarm *ou* half-hearted individual ◆ **des mesures qui risquent d'effaroucher les ~s** *(Pol)* measures likely to scare the wets

ADV ◆ **elle boit son café ~** she drinks her coffee lukewarm, she doesn't like her coffee too hot ◆ **ils boivent leur bière ~** they drink their beer (luke)warm ◆ **je n'aime pas boire ~** I don't like drinking things when they're lukewarm ◆ **servir ~/à peine ~** *(dans une recette)* serve warm/just warm

tièdement /tjɛdmɑ̃/ ADV *[accueillir]* in a lukewarm way, half-heartedly ◆ **~ soutenu par son parti** with the half-hearted support of his party

tiédeur /tjedœʀ/ NF 1 *[de bain]* tepidness; *[de vent, saison, température]* mildness, warmth; *[d'atmosphère]* balminess ◆ **les premières ~s du printemps** the first warm days of spring ◆ **la ~ du vent/de la nuit** the warm wind/night air 2 *[de sentiment, foi, accueil]* lukewarmness, half-heartedness, tepidness; *[de chrétien, militant]* half-heartedness, lukewarmness ◆ **la ~ du public à l'égard du référendum** the public's lack of enthusiasm for *ou* half-hearted attitude towards the referendum

tiédir /tjediʀ/ ► conjug 2 ◄ VI 1 *(= refroidir)* to cool (down) ◆ **laisser ~ un café trop chaud** to let a cup of coffee cool down 2 *(= se réchauffer)* to grow warm(er) ◆ **faire ~ de l'eau** to warm *ou* heat up some water ◆ **dans un bol, versez le lait tiédi** pour the warmed milk into a bowl 3 *(= faiblir) [sentiment, foi, ardeur]* to cool (off) ◆ **l'enthousiasme tiédit avec le temps** enthusiasm wanes with time VT 1 *(= réchauffer)* to warm (up) 2 *(= rafraîchir)* to cool (down)

tien, tienne /tjɛ̃, tjɛn/ PRON POSS ◆ **le tien, la tienne, les tiens, les tiennes** yours; († , *Rel*) thine ◆ **ce sac n'est pas le ~** this bag is not yours, this is not your bag ◆ **mes fils sont stupides comparés aux ~s** my sons are stupid compared to yours ◆ **à la ~ne !*** your (good) health!, cheers! ◆ **tu vas faire ce travail tout seul ? - à la ~ne !** † * *(iro)* you're going to do the job all by yourself? - good luck to you!; *pour autres loc voir* **sien** NM 1 ◆ **il n'y a pas à distinguer le ~ du mien** what's mine is yours; *pour autres loc voir* **sien** 2 ◆ **les ~s** your family, your (own) folks* ◆ **toi et tous les ~s** you and yours; *pour autres loc voir* **sien** ADJ POSS † *ou hum)* ◆ **un ~ cousin** a cousin of yours

tierce¹ /tjɛʀs/ NF 1 *(Mus)* third ◆ **~ majeure/mineure** major/minor third 2 *(Cartes)* tierce ◆ **~ majeure** tierce major 3 *(Typo)* final proof 4 *(Rel)* terce 5 *(Escrime)* tierce 6 *(= unité de temps)* sixtieth of a second ADJ → **tiers**

tiercé, e /tjɛʀse/ ADJ *(Héraldique)* tiercé, tierced; → **rime** NM *French triple forecast system for horse-racing,* tierce *(Austral)* ◆ **réussir le ~ dans l'ordre/dans le désordre** *ou* **dans un ordre différent** to win on the tiercé with the right placings/without the right placings ◆ **un beau ~** a good win on the tiercé ◆ **toucher** *ou* **gagner le ~** to win the tiercé ◆ **le ~ gagnant** *(lit, fig)* the three winners, the first three

tierceron /tjɛʀsəʀɔ̃/ NM tierceron

tiers, tierce² /tjɛʀ, tjɛʀs/ ADJ third ◆ **b tierce** *(Math)* b triple dash ◆ **une tierce personne** a third party ◆ **pays ~** *(Europe)* third country ◆ **tierce épreuve** *(Typo)* final proof ◆ **~ porteur** *(Jur)* endorsee ◆ **tierce opposition** *(Jur)* opposition by third party *(to outcome of litigation)*

NM 1 *(= fraction)* third ◆ **le premier ~/les deux premiers ~ de l'année** the first third/the first two thirds of the year ◆ **j'ai lu le** *ou* **un ~/les deux ~ du livre** I have read a third/two thirds of the book ◆ **j'en suis au ~** I'm a third of the way through ◆ **les deux ~ des gens pensent que ...** the majority of people think that ... ◆ **l'article est trop long d'un ~** the article is a third too long *ou* over length, the article is too long by a third ◆ **remplissez la casserole aux deux** ~ fill the pan two-thirds full ◆ **la ville était détruite aux deux** ~ two thirds of the city was destroyed

2 *(= troisième personne)* third party *ou* person; *(= étranger, inconnu)* outsider; *(Jur)* third party ◆ **il a appris la nouvelle par un** ~ somebody else told him the news, he learnt the news through a third party ◆ **l'assurance ne couvre pas les** ~ the insurance does not cover third party risks ◆ **il se moque du** ~ **comme du quart** † he doesn't care a fig *ou* a hoot* *ou* a damn*; → **assurance**

3 *(= troisième élément)* **principe du** ~ **exclu** *(Logique)* law of excluded middle

COMP **le Tiers État** NM *(Hist)* the third estate
tiers ordre *(Rel)* third order
tiers payant direct payment by insurers *(for medical treatment)*
tiers provisionnel provisional *ou* interim payment *(of tax)*

tiers-arbitre, tiers arbitre (pl **tiers(-)arbitres**) /tjɛʀaʀbitʀ/ NM independent arbitrator

Tiers-Monde /tjɛʀmɔ̃d/ NM ◆ **le** ~ the Third World

tiers-mondisme /tjɛʀmɔ̃dism/ NM third-worldism

tiers-mondiste /tjɛʀmɔ̃dist/ ADJ *(= du Tiers-Monde)* Third-World *(épith)*; *(= en faveur du Tiers-Monde)* supporting the Third World NMF *(= spécialiste)* specialist of the Third World; *(= partisan)* supporter of the Third World

tiers-point (pl **tiers-points**) /tjɛʀpwɛ̃/ NM *(Archit)* crown; *(= lime)* saw-file

tifs* /tif/ NMPL *(gén pl)* hair

TIG /teiʒe/ NM (abrév de **travaux d'intérêt général**) → **travail**[1]

tige /tiʒ/ NF 1 *[de fleur, arbre]* stem; *[de céréales, graminées]* stalk ◆ **fleurs à longues ~s** long-stemmed flowers ◆ **(arbre de) haute/basse** ~ standard/half-standard tree ◆ ~ **aérienne/souterraine** overground/underground stem 2 *(= plant)* sapling 3 *[de colonne, plume, démarreur]* shaft; *[de botte, chaussette, bas]* leg (part); *[de chaussure]* ankle (part); *[de clé, clou]* shank; *[de pompe]* rod ◆ **chaussures à** ~ boots ◆ ~ **de métal** metal rod ◆ ~ **de culbuteur** pushrod ◆ ~ **de forage** drill pipe 4 *(†, littér) [d'arbre généalogique]* stock ◆ **faire** ~ to found a line 5 *(†, * = cigarette)* cig*, smoke*, fag* *(Brit)*

tignasse /tiɲas/ NF *(= chevelure mal peignée)* shock of hair, mop (of hair); *(* = cheveux)* hair

Tigre /tigʀ/ NM ◆ **le** ~ the Tigris

tigre /tigʀ/ NM 1 *(= animal)* tiger ◆ ~ **royal** *ou* **du Bengale** Bengal tiger 2 *(= homme cruel)* monster ◆ ~ **de papier** paper tiger ◆ **les ~s asiatiques** *(Écon)* the tiger economies, the Asian tigers

tigré, e /tigʀe/ ADJ 1 *(= tacheté)* spotted *(de* with); *[cheval]* piebald 2 *(= rayé)* striped, streaked ◆ **chat** ~ tabby (cat)

tigresse /tigʀɛs/ NF *(= animal)* tigress; *(= harpie)* tigress, hellcat*

tilbury /tilbyʀi/ NM tilbury *(type of carriage)*

tilde /tild(e)/ NM tilde

tillac /tijak/ NM *(Hist Naut)* upper deck

tilleul /tijœl/ NM *(= arbre)* lime (tree), linden (tree); *(= infusion)* lime(-blossom) tea ◆ **(vert)** ~ lime green

tilt /tilt/ NM *(Jeux)* tilt sign *ou* signal ◆ **faire** ~ *(lit)* to show tilt ◆ **ce mot a fait** ~ **dans mon esprit*** the word rang a bell ◆ **soudain, ça a fait** ~* it suddenly clicked, the penny suddenly dropped

tilter* /tilte/ ▸ conjug 1 ◂ VI *(= comprendre)* to understand, to twig*

timbale /tɛ̃bal/ NF 1 *(Mus)* kettledrum ◆ **les ~s** the timpani, the kettledrums 2 *(= gobelet)* (metal) cup *(without handle)*, (metal) tumbler 3 *(Culin) (= moule)* timbale (mould) ◆ ~ **de langouste** *(= mets)* lobster timbale

timbalier /tɛ̃balje/ NM timpanist

timbrage /tɛ̃bʀaʒ/ NM 1 *(= affranchissement) [de lettre, envoi]* stamping ◆ **dispensé de** ~ postage paid *(Brit)*, post paid *(US)* 2 *(= apposition d'un cachet) [de document, acte]* stamping; *[de lettre, envoi]* postmarking

timbre /tɛ̃bʀ/ NM 1 *(= vignette)* stamp ◆ ~ **(-poste)** (postage) stamp ◆ ~ **neuf/oblitéré** new/used stamp ◆ **marché** *ou* **Bourse aux ~s** stamp market ◆ **~s antituberculeux/anticancéreux** TB/cancer research stamps ◆ ~ **(thérapeutique)** *(Méd)* patch ◆ ~ **à la nicotine** *ou* **antitabac*** nicotine patch; → **collection**

2 *(= marque)* stamp ◆ **mettre** *ou* **apposer son** ~ **sur** to put one's stamp on, to affix one's stamp to ◆ ~ **sec/humide** embossed/ink(ed) stamp; → **droit**[3]

3 *(= instrument)* stamp ◆ ~ **de caoutchouc/de cuivre** rubber/brass stamp

4 *(Mus) [de tambour]* snares

5 *(= son) [d'instrument, voix]* timbre, tone; *[de voyelle]* timbre ◆ **avoir le** ~ **voilé** to have a muffled voice ◆ **voix qui a du** ~ sonorous *ou* resonant voice ◆ **voix sans** ~ voice lacking in resonance

6 *(= sonnette)* bell

COMP **timbre fiscal** excise *ou* revenue *ou* fiscal stamp
timbre horodateur time and date stamp
timbre de quittance receipt stamp

timbré, e /tɛ̃bʀe/ (ptp de **timbrer**) ADJ 1 *(Admin, Jur) [document, acte]* stamped, bearing a stamp *(attrib)* ◆ **"joindre une enveloppe timbrée"** "send a stamped addressed envelope" *(Brit)*, "send an sae" *(Brit)*, "send a self-addressed, stamped envelope"; → **papier** 2 *[voix]* resonant, sonorous; *[sonorité]* resonant ◆ **voix bien** ~**e** beautifully resonant voice ◆ **mal** ~ lacking in resonance 3 *(* = fou)* cracked*, nuts* NM,F *(* = fou)* loony*, nutcase*, head case*

timbre-amende (pl **timbres-amendes**) /tɛ̃bʀamɑ̃d/ NM *stamp purchased to pay a fine for a parking offence*

timbre-prime (pl **timbres-primes**) /tɛ̃bʀpʀim/ NM trading stamp

timbre-quittance (pl **timbres-quittances**) /tɛ̃bʀkitɑ̃s/ NM receipt stamp

timbrer /tɛ̃bʀe/ ▸ conjug 1 ◂ VT 1 *(= affranchir) [+ lettre, envoi]* to stamp, to put a stamp (ou stamps) on 2 *(= apposer un cachet sur) [+ document, acte]* to stamp; *[+ lettre, envoi]* to postmark ◆ **lettre timbrée de** *ou* **à Paris** letter with a Paris postmark, letter postmarked Paris

timbre-taxe (pl **timbres-taxes**) /tɛ̃bʀtaks/ NM postage-due stamp

timide /timid/ ADJ 1 *(= gauche) [personne, air, sourire, voix, amoureux]* shy, timid, bashful ◆ **ne sois pas si** ~**, approche !** don't be shy, come over here! ◆ **faussement** ~ coy ◆ **d'une voix** ~ shyly, in a shy voice ◆ **c'est un grand** ~ he's awfully shy 2 *(= hésitant) [personne, critique, réponse, tentative]* timid, timorous; *[réforme]* timid; *[politique, reprise économique]* tentative ◆ **une** ~ **amélioration de l'économie** a slight *ou* faint improvement in the economy ◆ **des mesures** ~**s** half measures ◆ **des protestations bien** ~**s** half-hearted protests ◆ **le soleil fera de** ~**s apparitions au nord** there will be intermittent sunshine in the north

timidement /timidmɑ̃/ ADV 1 *(= gauchement)* shyly, timidly ◆ **il l'a abordée** ~ he approached her shyly *ou* timidly ◆ **..., demanda-t-il** ~ ..., he asked shyly 2 *(= légèrement)* **l'activité a** ~ **repris** business has picked up slightly ◆ **la région s'ouvre** ~ **au tourisme** the region is tentatively opening up to tourism

timidité /timidite/ NF 1 *(= embarras) [de personne, air, sourire, voix, amoureux]* shyness, timidity, bashfulness ◆ **avec** ~ shyly, timidly ◆ **il n'a pas osé, par** ~ he was too shy to dare, he didn't dare, he was too shy 2 *(= faiblesse) [de personne, critique, réponse, tentative, d'entreprise]* timidity ◆ **étant donné la** ~ **de la reprise économique** given the fact that there has been only a slight *ou* faint improvement in the economy

timing /tajmiŋ/ NM timing

timon /timɔ̃/ NM *[de char]* shaft; *[de charrue]* beam; *[d'embarcation]* tiller

timonerie /timɔnʀi/ NF 1 *[de bateau] (= poste, service)* wheelhouse; *(= marins)* wheelhouse crew 2 *[de véhicule]* steering and braking systems

timonier /timɔnje/ NM 1 *(= marin)* helmsman, steersman 2 *(= cheval)* wheel-horse, wheeler

timorais, e /timɔʀɛ, ɛz/ ADJ Timorese NM,F **Timorais,e** Timorese

timoré, e /timɔʀe/ ADJ *(gén) [caractère, personne]* timorous, fearful; *(Rel, littér) [conscience]* overscrupulous

tinctorial, e (mpl **-iaux**) /tɛ̃ktɔʀjal, jo/ ADJ *[opération, produit]* tinctorial *(SPÉC)*, dyeing *(épith)* ◆ **matières** ~**es** dyestuffs ◆ **plantes** ~**es** plants used in dyeing

tinette /tinɛt/ NF *(pour la vidange)* sanitary tub ◆ **~s** *(arg Mil = toilettes)* latrines

tintamarre /tɛ̃tamaʀ/ NM racket, din, hullabaloo* ◆ **faire du** ~ to make a racket *ou* din ◆ **on a entendu un** ~ **de klaxons** we heard horns blaring

tintement /tɛ̃tmɑ̃/ NM *[de cloche]* ringing, chiming; *[de clochette]* tinkling, jingling; *[de sonnette]* ringing; *[d'objets métalliques, pièces de monnaie]* jingling, chinking; *[de verres entrechoqués]* clinking; *[de verre frotté]* ringing ◆ ~ **d'oreilles** ringing in the ears, tinnitus *(SPÉC)*

tinter /tɛ̃te/ ▸ conjug 1 ◂ VI *[cloche]* to ring, to chime; *[clochette]* to tinkle, to jingle; *[sonnette]* to ring; *[objets métalliques, pièces de monnaie]* to jingle, to chink; *[verres entrechoqués]* to clink; *[verre frotté]* to ring ◆ **faire** ~ *[+ cloche]* to ring; *[+ pièces de monnaie]* to jingle; *[+ verres]* to clink ◆ **trois coups tintèrent** the bell rang *ou* chimed three times ◆ **les oreilles me tintent** my ears are ringing, there's a ringing in my ears ◆ **les oreilles ont dû vous** ~ *(fig)* your ears must have been burning VT *[+ cloche, heure, angélus]* to ring; *[+ messe]* to ring for

tintin* /tɛ̃tɛ̃/ EXCL nothing doing!*, no way!* ◆ **faire** ~ to go without

tintinnabuler /tɛ̃tinabyle/ ▸ conjug 1 ◂ VI *(littér)* to tinkle, to tintinnabulate *(littér)*

Tintoret /tɛ̃tɔʀɛ/ NM ◆ **le** ~ Tintoretto

tintouin* /tɛ̃twɛ̃/ NM 1 *(= tracas)* bother, worry ◆ **quel** ~ **pour y aller** it was such a hassle* getting there ◆ **donner du** ~ **à qn** to give sb a lot of trouble ◆ **se donner du** ~ to go to a lot of trouble ◆ **et tout le** ~ and all the rest, and what have you* 2 *(† = bruit)* racket, din

TIP /tip/ NM (abrév de **titre interbancaire de paiement**) → **titre**

tipi /tipi/ NM te(e)pee

Tipp-Ex ® /tipɛks/ NM Tipp-Ex ® *(Brit)*, liquid paper ® *(US)*, White out ® *(US)*

ti-punch /tipɔ̃ʃ/ NM rum punch

tique /tik/ NF *(= parasite)* tick

tiquer /tike/ ▸ conjug 1 ◂ VI 1 *[personne]* to make *ou* pull *(Brit)* a face, to raise an eyebrow ◆ **il n'a**

pas tiqué he didn't bat an eyelid *ou* raise an eyebrow 2 *[cheval]* to crib(-bite), to suck wind

tiqueté, e /tik(ə)te/ ADJ *(littér)* speckled, mottled

TIR /tiʀ/ NMPL (abrév de **transports internationaux routiers**) TIR

tir /tiʀ/ NM 1 *(= discipline sportive ou militaire)* shooting ◆ **~ au pistolet/à la carabine** pistol/rifle shooting; → **stand**
2 *(= action de tirer)* firing *(NonC)* ◆ **en position de ~** in firing position ◆ **commander/déclencher le ~** to order/set off *ou* open the firing ◆ **puissance/vitesse de ~ d'une arme** fire-power/firing speed of a gun ◆ **des ~s d'exercice** practice rounds ◆ **des ~s à blanc** firing blank rounds *ou* blanks ◆ **secteur** *ou* **zone de ~ libre** free-fire zone ◆ **corriger** *ou* **rectifier** *ou* **ajuster le ~** *(lit)* to adjust one's aim; *(fig)* to make some adjustments
3 *(= manière de tirer)* firing; *(trajectoire des projectiles)* fire ◆ **arme à ~ automatique/rapide** automatic/rapid-firing gun ◆ **arme à ~ courbe/tendu** gun with curved/flat trajectory fire ◆ **~s croisés** *(lit, fig)* crossfire ◆ **être pris sous des ~s croisés** to be caught in the crossfire ◆ **~ groupé** *(lit)* grouped fire; *(fig) (= série d'attaques)* combined attack; *(= série de succès)* string of successes ◆ **un ~ groupé de mesures/films** a string of measures/films ◆ **plan/angle/ligne de ~** plane/angle/line of fire; → **table**
4 *(= feu, rafales)* fire *(NonC)* ◆ **stoppés par un ~** *ou* **des ~s de mitrailleuses/d'artillerie** halted by machine-gun/artillery fire ◆ **~s de roquettes** rocket fire ◆ **~ de harcèlement** harassing fire ◆ **~s de sommation** warning shots
5 *(Boules)* shot *(at another bowl)*; *(Ftbl)* shot ◆ **~ au but** *(gén)* shot at goal; *(de pénalité)* penalty kick ◆ **épreuve des ~s au but** penalty shoot-out
6 *(= stand)* **~ (forain)** shooting gallery, rifle range
7 *(Espace = lancement)* launch
COMP **tir d'appui** ⇒ **tir de soutien**
tir à l'arbalète crossbow archery
tir à l'arc archery
tir de barrage barrage fire; *(fig)* attack
tir au pigeon clay pigeon shooting
tir de soutien support fire

tirade /tiʀad/ NF *(Théât)* monologue, speech; *(péj)* tirade

tirage /tiʀaʒ/ NM 1 *[de chèque]* drawing; *[de vin]* drawing off; *[de carte]* taking, drawing
2 *(Photo, Typo)* printing ◆ **faire le ~ de clichés/d'une épreuve** to print negatives/a proof ◆ **~ à la main** hand-printing ◆ **un ~ sur papier glacé** a print on glazed paper ◆ **~ par contact/inversion** contact/reversal print
3 *[de journal]* circulation; *[de livre] (= nombre d'exemplaires)* (print) run; *(= édition)* edition ◆ **~ de luxe/limité** de luxe/limited edition ◆ **cet auteur réalise de gros ~s** this author's works have huge print runs *ou* are printed in great numbers ◆ **quel est le ~ de cet ouvrage ?** how many copies of this work were printed? ◆ **les gros ~s de la presse quotidienne** the high circulation figures of the daily press ◆ **magazine à faible ~** small-circulation magazine ◆ **~ de 2 000 exemplaires** run *ou* impression of 2,000 copies
4 *[de cheminée]* draught *(Brit)*, draft *(US)* ◆ **avoir du ~** to draw well, to have a good draught ◆ **cette cheminée a un bon/mauvais ~** this chimney draws well/badly
5 *(Loterie)* draw ◆ **le ~ des numéros gagnants** the draw for the winning numbers
6 *(* = désaccord)* friction ◆ **il y avait du ~ entre eux** there was some friction between them
7 *[de métaux]* drawing
COMP **tirage à part** off-print
tirage au sort drawing lots ◆ **procéder par ~ au sort** to draw lots ◆ **le gagnant sera désigné par ~ au sort** the winner will be chosen by drawing lots ◆ **le ~ au sort des équipes de football** the selection *ou* choice of the football teams by drawing lots

tiraillement /tiʀɑjmɑ̃/ NM 1 *(sur une corde)* tugging *(NonC)*, pulling *(NonC)* 2 *(= douleur) [d'intestin]* gnawing pain; *[de peau, muscles]* tightness ◆ **~s d'estomac** gnawing pains in the stomach NMPL **tiraillements** *(= conflits)* friction *(NonC)*, conflict *(NonC)*

tirailler /tiʀɑje/ ► conjug 1 ◄ VT 1 *[+ corde, moustache, manche]* to pull at, to tug at ◆ **~ qn par le bras** *ou* **la manche** to pull *ou* tug at sb's sleeve 2 *[douleurs]* to gnaw at, to stab at ◆ **douleurs qui tiraillent l'estomac** gnawing pains in the stomach ◆ **des élancements lui tiraillaient l'épaule** he had sharp *ou* shooting *ou* stabbing pains in his shoulder 3 *[doutes, remords]* to tug at, to plague, to pester; *[choix, contradictions]* to beset, to plague ◆ **être tiraillé entre plusieurs possibilités** to be torn between several possibilities ◆ **la crainte et l'ambition le tiraillaient** he was torn between fear and ambition VI *(en tous sens)* to shoot wild; *(Mil : par tir de harcèlement)* to fire at random ◆ **ça tiraillait de tous côtés dans le bois** there was firing on all sides in the wood

tirailleur /tiʀɑjœʀ/ NM 1 *(Mil, fig)* skirmisher ◆ **se déployer/avancer en ~s** to be deployed/advance as a skirmish contingent 2 *(Hist Mil : originaire des colonies)* soldier, infantryman

tiramisu /tiʀamisu/ NM tiramisu

Tirana /tiʀana/ N Tirana

tirant /tiʀɑ̃/ NM 1 *(= cordon)* (draw) string; *(= tirette) [de botte]* bootstrap; *(= partie de la tige) [de chaussure]* facing 2 *(Constr) [d'arcades]* tie-rod; *[de comble]* tie-beam ◆ **~ d'air** *[de pont]* headroom 3 *(Naut)* **~ (d'eau)** draught *(Brit)*, draft *(US)* ◆ **navire de faible ~ d'eau** ship with a shallow draught ◆ **~ avant/arrière** draught *(Brit) ou* draft *(US)* at the bows/stern ◆ **avoir six mètres de ~ (d'eau)** to draw six metres of water ◆ **~ d'air** *[de navire]* clearance height

tire[1] * /tiʀ/ NF *(= voiture)* wagon *, car ◆ **vieille ~** old rattletrap * *ou* crate * *ou* banger * *(Brit)*

tire[2] /tiʀ/ NF ◆ **vol à la ~** picking pockets ◆ **voleur à la ~** pickpocket

tire[3] /tiʀ/ NF *(Can) (= caramel)* toffee, taffy *(Can, US)*; *(= sirop d'érable)* molasses, maple candy ◆ **~ d'érable** maple toffee *ou* taffy *(Can, US)* ◆ **~ sur la neige** taffy-on-the-snow *(Can, US)*

tiré, e /tiʀe/ (ptp de **tirer**) ADJ 1 *(= tendu) [traits, visage]* drawn, haggard ◆ **avoir les traits ~s** to look drawn *ou* haggard ◆ **les cheveux ~s en arrière** with one's hair pulled back ◆ **~ à quatre épingles** impeccably *ou* well turned-out, done up *ou* dressed up to the nines * ◆ **c'est ~ par les cheveux** it's far-fetched; → **couteau** 2 *(Fin)* **la personne ~e** the drawee 3 *(= bas)* **prix ~s** rock-bottom prices NM *(Fin)* drawee; *(Mus)* down-bow NF **tirée** * *(= long trajet)* long haul, long trek ◆ **une ~e de** *(= quantité)* a load * of, heaps * *ou* tons * of COMP **tiré à part** ADJ, NM off-print

tire-au-cul * /tiʀoky/ NMF INV ⇒ **tire-au-flanc**

tire-au-flanc * /tiʀoflɑ̃/ NMF INV skiver * *(Brit)*, layabout, shirker

tire-bonde (pl **tire-bondes**) /tiʀbɔ̃d/ NM bung-drawer

tire-botte (pl **tire-bottes**) /tiʀbɔt/ NM *(pour se chausser)* boot-hook; *(pour se déchausser)* boot-jack

tire-bouchon, tirebouchon (pl **tire(-)bouchons**) /tiʀbuʃɔ̃/ NM *(= ustensile)* corkscrew; *(= mèche de cheveux)* corkscrew curl ◆ **en ~** corkscrew *(épith)* ◆ **cochon avec la queue en ~** pig with a corkscrew *ou* curly tail ◆ **avec ses chaussettes en ~** with his socks all crumpled *ou* wrinkled

tire-bouchonner, tirebouchonner /tiʀbuʃɔne/ ► conjug 1 ◄ VT *[+ mèche]* to twiddle, to twirl VI *[pantalon]* to crumple (up); *[chaussettes]* to become crumpled *ou* wrinkled ◆ **pantalon tire-bouchonné** crumpled trousers VPR **se tire-bouchonner** * *(de rire)* to fall about laughing * *(Brit)*, to be in stitches *

tire-clou (pl **tire-clous**) /tiʀklu/ NM nail puller

tire-d'aile /tiʀdɛl/ **à tire-d'aile** LOC ADV *[voler]* swiftly ◆ **passer à ~** to pass by in full flight ◆ **s'envoler à ~** to take flight in a flurry of feathers ◆ **le temps s'enfuit à ~** *(littér)* time flies past

tire-fesses * /tiʀfɛs/ NM INV *(gén, à perche)* ski tow; *(à archet)* T-bar tow

tire-fond (pl **tire-fond(s)**) /tiʀfɔ̃/ NM *(avec anneau) long screw with ring attachment; (Rail)* sleeper *(Brit) ou* tie *(US)* screw

tire-jus ‡ /tiʀʒy/ NM INV nose-wipe *, snot-rag ‡

tire-laine †† /tiʀlɛn/ NM INV footpad (††)

tire-lait (pl **tire-laits**) /tiʀlɛ/ NM breast-pump

tire-larigot * /tiʀlaʀigo/ **à tire-larigot** LOC ADV *[boire, manger]* to one's heart's content, like there's no tomorrow ◆ **il téléphone à ~** he's forever *ou* continually telephoning

tire-ligne (pl **tire-lignes**) /tiʀliɲ/ NM drawing pen

tirelire /tiʀliʀ/ NF 1 *(= récipient)* moneybox; *(en forme de cochon)* piggy bank ◆ **casser la ~** to break open the piggy bank 2 ‡ *(= estomac, ventre)* belly *, gut(s) ‡; *(= tête)* nut *, noddle *, bonce ‡ *(Brit)*; *(= visage)* face

tirer /tiʀe/ GRAMMAIRE ACTIVE 53.4 ► conjug 1 ◄
VT 1 *(= amener vers soi) [+ pièce mobile, poignée, corde]* to pull; *[+ manche, robe]* to pull down; *[+ chaussette]* to pull up ◆ **ne tire pas, ça risque de tomber/ça va l'étrangler** don't pull or it'll fall/it'll strangle him ◆ **~ les cheveux à qn** to pull sb's hair ◆ **~ l'aiguille** to ply the needle ◆ **~ qch à soi** *(lit)* to pull sth to(wards) on ◆ **~ un texte/un auteur à soi** to interpret a text/an author to suit one's own ends
2 *(pour fermer ou ouvrir) [+ rideaux]* to draw; *[+ tiroir]* to pull open; *[+ verrou] (= fermer)* to slide to, to shoot; *(= ouvrir)* to draw ◆ **tire la porte** pull the door to ◆ **as-tu tiré le verrou ?** have you bolted the door?
3 *[+ personne]* to pull ◆ **~ qn par le bras** to pull sb's arm, to pull sb by the arm ◆ **~ qn par la manche** to tug *ou* pluck sb's sleeve ◆ **~ qn de côté** *ou* **à l'écart** to draw sb aside, to take sb on one side
4 *(= remorquer) [+ véhicule, charge]* to pull, to draw; *[+ navire, remorque]* to tow; *[+ charrue]* to draw, to pull ◆ **une charrette tirée par un tracteur** a cart drawn *ou* pulled by a tractor, a tractor-drawn cart ◆ **carrosse tiré par huit chevaux** carriage drawn by eight horses; → **jambe, patte[1]**
5 *(= retirer, extraire) [+ épée, couteau]* to draw, to pull out; *[+ vin, cidre]* to draw; *[+ conclusions, morale, argument, idée, thème]* to draw; *[+ plaisir, satisfaction]* to draw, to derive *(de* from); ◆ **~ une substance d'une matière première** to extract a substance from a raw material ◆ **~ le jus d'un citron** to extract the juice from a lemon, to squeeze the juice from a lemon *ou* out of a lemon ◆ **~ un son d'un instrument** to get a sound out of *ou* draw a sound from an instrument ◆ **~ un objet d'un tiroir/d'un sac** to pull an object out of a drawer/a bag ◆ **~ de l'argent d'une activité/d'une terre** to make money from an activity/a piece of land ◆ **il a tiré 5 000 € de sa vieille voiture** he managed to get €5,000 for his old car ◆ **savoir ~ qch de la vie/d'un moment** (to know how) to get sth out of life/a moment ◆ **~ qch de qn** to obtain sth from sb, to get sth out of sb ◆ **~ de l'argent de qn** to get money out of sb ◆ **on ne peut rien en ~** *(enfant têtu)* you can't do anything with

him; *(personne qui refuse de parler)* you can't get anything out of him ◆ ~ **qn du sommeil** to arouse sb from sleep ◆ ~ **qn du lit** to get *ou* drag sb out of bed ◆ ~ **qn de son travail** to take *ou* drag sb away from his work ◆ **ce bruit le tira de sa rêverie** this noise brought him out of *ou* roused him from his daydream ◆ ~ **des larmes/gémissements à qn** to draw tears/moans from sb

6 *(= délivrer)* ~ **qn de prison/des décombres/d'une situation dangereuse** to get sb out of prison/the rubble/a dangerous situation ◆ ~ **qn du doute** to remove *ou* dispel sb's doubts ◆ ~ **qn de l'erreur** to disabuse sb ◆ ~ **qn de la misère/de l'obscurité** to rescue sb from poverty/from obscurity ◆ **il faut le ~ de là** we'll have to help him out; → **affaire, embarras**

7 *(indiquant l'origine)* ~ **son origine d'une vieille coutume** to have an old custom as its origin ◆ **mots tirés du latin** words taken *ou* derived from (the) Latin ◆ ~ **son nom de** to take one's name from ◆ **pièce tirée d'un roman** play taken from *ou* adapted from *ou* derived from a novel ◆ **on tire de l'huile des olives** oil is extracted from olives ◆ **l'opium est tiré du pavot** opium is obtained from the poppy

8 *(Jeux) [+ billet, numéro, loterie]* to draw; *[+ carte]* to take, to draw ◆ ~ **qch au sort** to draw lots for sth ◆ **qui est-ce qui donne ? on tire ?** whose deal is it? shall we pick a card? ◆ ~ **les rois** *(à l'Épiphanie)* to cut the Twelfth Night cake ◆ ~ **la fève** to win the charm; → **carte, court¹**

9 *(Photo, Typo)* to print ◆ **ce journal est tiré à 100 000 exemplaires** this paper has a circulation of 100,000 ◆ ~ **un roman à 8 000 exemplaires** to print 8,000 copies of a novel ◆ **tirons quelques épreuves de ce texte** let's run off *ou* print a few proofs of the text; → **bon², portrait**

10 *(= tracer) [+ ligne, trait]* to draw; *[+ plan]* to draw up; → aussi **plan¹**

11 *[+ coup de feu, balle]* to fire; *[+ flèche]* to shoot; *[+ boule]* to throw *(so as to hit another or the jack)*; *[+ feu d'artifice]* to set off; *[+ gibier]* to shoot ◆ **il a tiré plusieurs coups de revolver sur l'agent** he fired several shots at the policeman, he shot *ou* fired at the policeman several times ◆ ~ **le canon** to fire the cannon ◆ **la balle a été tirée avec un gros calibre** the bullet was fired from a large-bore gun ◆ **il a tiré un faisan** he shot a pheasant ◆ ~ **un coup**** *(sexuellement)* to have a bang**, to have it off**

12 *(Ftbl)* to shoot ◆ ~ **un corner/un penalty** to take a corner/a penalty

13 *[+ chèque, lettre de change]* to draw ◆ ~ **de l'argent sur son compte** to draw money out of one's account, to withdraw money from one's account ◆ **prête-moi ta carte bleue pour que j'aille ~ de l'argent** lend me your credit card so that I can go and get some money out

14 *(Naut)* ~ **6 mètres** to draw 6 metres of water; → **bord, bordée**

15 *(* = passer)* to get through ◆ **encore une heure/un mois à ~** another hour/month to get through ◆ ~ **deux ans de prison/de service** to do two years in prison *ou* a two-year stretch*/two years in the army ◆ **voilà une semaine de tirée** that's one week over with

16 *(** = voler)* to pinch*, to nick** *(Brit)* ◆ **il s'est fait ~ son blouson** he got his jacket pinched* *ou* nicked** *(Brit)*

17 *(Tech = étirer) [+ métal]* to draw

18 *(= limiter aussi bas que possible) [− délais]* to get down to an absolute minimum ◆ ~ **ses prix** to sell at rock-bottom prices

19 *(dial = traire) [+ vache]* to milk

VI 1 *(= faire feu)* to fire; *(= se servir d'une arme à feu, viser)* to shoot ◆ **il leur donna l'ordre de ~** he gave the order for them to fire ◆ **apprendre à ~** to learn to shoot ◆ ~ **à l'arbalète/à la carabine** to shoot with a crossbow/a rifle ◆ **savez-vous ~ à l'arc ?** can you use a bow (and arrow)? ◆ **le canon tirait sans arrêt** the cannon fired continuously ◆ ~ **en l'air** to fire into the air ◆ ~ **à vue** to shoot on sight ◆ ~ **à balles (réelles)/à blanc** to fire (real) bullets/blanks ◆ ~ **sans sommation** to shoot without warning ◆ **il lui a tiré dans le dos** *(lit)* he shot him in the back; *(fig)* he stabbed him in the back ◆ ~ **dans les jambes** *ou* **pattes de qn** * *(fig)* to make life difficult for sb

2 *(Ftbl etc)* to shoot, to take a shot; *(Boules)* to throw *(one boule at another or at the jack)* ◆ ~ **au but** *(gén)* to take a shot at goal, to shoot at goal; *(pénalité)* to take a penalty kick

3 *(Sports de combat)* ◆ **il tire dans la catégorie des moins de 60 kg** he's in the under 60 kg category

4 *(Presse)* ~ **à 10 000 exemplaires** to have a circulation of 10,000

5 *[cheminée, poêle]* to draw ◆ **la cheminée tire bien** the chimney draws well

6 *[moteur, voiture]* to pull ◆ **le moteur tire bien en côte** the engine pulls well on hills

7 *[points de suture, sparadrap]* to pull ◆ **le matin, j'ai la peau qui tire** my skin feels tight in the morning

8 *(locutions)* **la voiture tire à gauche** the car pulls to the left ◆ ~ **au flanc*** *ou* **au cul**** to skive* *(Brit)*, to shirk; → **conséquence, ligne¹**

◆ **tirer à sa fin** *[journée]* to be drawing to a close; *[épreuve]* to be nearly over; *[provisions]* to be nearly finished

VT INDIR **tirer sur** 1 *[+ corde, poignée]* to pull at *ou* on, to tug at ◆ ~ **sur les rênes** to pull in *ou* on the reins ◆ ~ **sur la ficelle*** *ou* **la corde*** *(fig)* to push one's luck*, to go too far, to overstep the mark

2 *(= approcher de) [+ couleur]* to border on, to verge on ◆ **il tire sur la soixantaine** he's getting on for *(Brit)* *ou* going on sixty

3 *(= faire feu sur)* to shoot at, to fire (a shot *ou* shots) at; *(= critiquer)* to criticize ◆ **il m'a tiré dessus** he shot *ou* fired at me ◆ **ils tirent sans cesse sur les médias** they're always criticizing the media ◆ **ne tirez pas sur le pianiste** *(fig)* he's *(ou I'm etc)* doing his *(ou my etc)* best ◆ **se ~ dessus** *(lit)* to shoot *ou* fire at each other; *(= se critiquer, se quereller)* to shoot each other down; → **boulet**

4 *(= aspirer) [+ pipe]* to pull at, to draw on; *[+ cigarette, cigare]* to puff at, to draw on, to take a drag at*

5 *(= prélever)* **ils tirent sur leur épargne pour maintenir leur niveau de vie** they're drawing on their savings to maintain their standard of living

VPR **se tirer** 1 ◆ **se ~ de** *(= échapper à) [+ danger, situation]* to get (o.s.) out of ◆ **il s'est tiré sans dommage de l'accident** he came out of the accident unharmed ◆ **sa voiture était en mille morceaux mais lui s'en est tiré*** his car was smashed to pieces but he escaped unharmed ◆ **il est très malade mais je crois qu'il va s'en ~** he's very ill but I think he'll pull through ◆ **la première fois il a eu un sursis mais cette fois il ne va pas s'en ~ si facilement** the first time he got a suspended sentence but he won't get off so lightly this time ◆ **il s'en est tiré avec une amende** he got off with a fine ◆ **il s'en est tiré avec une jambe cassée** he got out of it with a broken leg; → **affaire, flûte, patte¹**

2 ◆ **bien/mal se ~ de qch** *[+ tâche]* to manage *ou* handle sth well/badly, to make a good/bad job of sth ◆ **comment va-t-il se ~ de ce sujet/travail ?** how will he get on with *ou* cope with this subject/job? ◆ **les questions étaient difficiles mais il s'en est bien tiré** the questions were difficult but he managed *ou* handled them well *ou* coped very well with them ◆ **on n'a pas beaucoup d'argent mais on s'en tire** we haven't got a lot of money but we get by *ou* we manage ◆ **on s'en tire tout juste** we just scrape by, we just (about) get by

3 *(** = déguerpir)* to leave ◆ **allez, on se tire** come on, let's be off ◆ **il s'est tiré** he's gone ◆ **il s'est tiré avec la caisse** he ran off with the money

4 *(* = toucher à sa fin) [période, travail]* to be nearly over ◆ **ça se tire** the end is in sight

5 *(= être tendu) [traits, visage]* to become drawn

tiret /tiʀɛ/ **NM** *(= trait)* dash; *(† = trait d'union)* hyphen

tirette /tiʀɛt/ **NF** 1 *[de bureau, table] (pour écrire)* (writing) leaf; *(pour ranger des crayons)* (pencil) tray; *(pour soutenir un abattant)* support; *[de fermeture à glissière]* pull, tab 2 *(Belg = fermeture à glissière)* zip *(Brit)*, zipper *(US)* 3 *[de cheminée]* damper 4 *(= cordon) [de sonnette]* bell-pull; *[de rideaux]* (curtain) cord *ou* pull

tireur, -euse /tiʀœʀ, øz/ **NM,F** 1 *(avec arme à feu)* ~ **embusqué** sniper ◆ ~ **isolé** lone gunman ◆ ~ **d'élite** marksman, sharpshooter ◆ **c'est un bon ~** he's a good shot ◆ **concours ouvert aux ~s débutants et entraînés** shooting competition open to beginners and advanced classes 2 *(Boules) player who tries to dislodge the opponents' bowls* 3 *(= photographe)* printer 4 *(= escrimeur)* ~ **(d'épée** *ou* **d'armes)** swordsman, fencer 5 ◆ **tireuse** *ou* ~ **de cartes** fortune-teller **NM** *[de chèque, lettre de change]* drawer **NF** **tireuse** 1 *(= pompe)* (hand) pump ◆ **bière à la tireuse** draught beer ◆ **vin à la tireuse** wine from the barrel 2 *(Photo)* contact printer

tiroir /tiʀwaʀ/ **NM** 1 *[de table, commode]* drawer ◆ ~ **(à) secret** secret drawer ◆ **roman/pièce à ~s** novel/play made up of episodes, roman/pièce à tiroirs *(SPÉC)*; → **fond, nom** 2 *(Tech)* slide valve

tiroir-caisse (pl **tiroirs-caisses**) /tiʀwaʀkɛs/ **NM** till, cash register ◆ **pour lui, la seule chose qui compte, c'est le ~** the only thing that matters to him is profit ◆ **notre pays ne sera pas le ~ de la construction européenne** our country is not going to bankroll the construction of Europe

tisane /tizan/ **NF** *(= boisson)* herb(al) tea ◆ ~ **de tilleul/de menthe** lime(-blossom)/mint tea ◆ **c'est de la ~*** *(hum)* it's really watery

tisanière /tizanjɛʀ/ **NF** *(= pot)* teapot *(for making herbal tea)*; *(= tasse)* (large) teacup *(for herbal tea)*

tison /tizɔ̃/ **NM** brand; → **allumette, Noël**

tisonner /tizɔne/ ► conjug 1 ◄ **VT** to poke

tisonnier /tizɔnje/ **NM** poker

tissage /tisaʒ/ **NM** weaving ◆ **usine de ~** cloth *ou* weaving mill

tisser /tise/ ► conjug 1 ◄ **VT** 1 *[+ étoffe, vêtement]* to weave ◆ **l'araignée tisse sa toile** the spider spins its web ◆ **le parti continue de ~ sa toile dans la région** the party continues to spin its web in the area; → **métier** 2 *[+ liens]* to forge; *[+ réseau de relations]* to build up; *[+ intrigue]* to weave **VPR** **se tisser** *[liens]* to be forged; *[amitié, complicité]* to grow

tisserand, e /tisʀɑ̃, ɑd/ **NM,F** weaver

tisseur, -euse /tisœʀ, øz/ **NM,F** weaver

tissu /tisy/ **NM** 1 *(= étoffe)* fabric, material, cloth ◆ **c'est un ~ très délicat** it's a very delicate fabric *ou* material ◆ **acheter du ~/trois mètres de ~ pour faire une robe** to buy some material *ou* fabric/three metres of material *ou* fabric to make a dress ◆ **choisir un ~ pour faire une robe** to choose material to make a dress, to choose a dress fabric *ou* material ◆ ~ **imprimé/à fleurs** printed/floral-patterned material *ou* fabric ◆ ~ **synthétique** synthetic material *ou* fabric ◆ ~**s d'ameublement** soft furnishings ◆ **étoffe à ~ lâche/serré** loosely-/finely-woven material *ou* fabric *ou* cloth

2 *(péj)* **un ~ de mensonges/contradictions** a web *ou* tissue of lies/contradictions ◆ **un ~ d'intrigues** a web of intrigue ◆ **un ~ d'horreurs/d'obscénités/d'inepties** a catalogue of horrors/of obscenities/of blunders
3 *(Anat, Bot)* tissue ◆ **~ sanguin/osseux/cicatriciel** blood/bone/scar tissue
4 *(Sociol)* fabric ◆ **le ~ social/industriel/urbain** the social/industrial/urban fabric
COMP **tissu-éponge** NM (pl **tissus-éponge**) (terry) towelling *(NonC) (Brit) ou* toweling *(NonC) (US)*

tissulaire /tisylɛʀ/ ADJ *(Bio)* tissue *(épith)* ◆ **culture ~** tissue culture

Titan /titɑ̃/ NM Titan ◆ **les ~s** the Titans ◆ **œuvre/travail de ~** titanic work/task

titane /titan/ NM titanium

titanesque /titanɛsk/, **titanique** /titanik/ ADJ titanic

Tite-Live /titliv/ NM Livy

titi /titi/ NM ◆ **~ (parisien)** Parisian street urchin

Titien /tisjɛ̃/ NM ◆ **le ~** Titian

titillation /titijasjɔ̃/ NF *(littér, hum)* titillation

titiller /titije/ ▸ conjug 1 ◂ VT *(littér, hum) (= exciter)* to titillate; *(= chatouiller légèrement)* to tickle; *(= agacer pour provoquer)* to tease, to goad ◆ **l'envie le titillait de devenir comédien** he was quite taken with the idea of becoming an actor

titisme /titism/ NM *(Hist)* Titoism

titiste /titist/ ADJ, NMF *(Hist)* Titoist

titrage /titʀaʒ/ NM 1 *[d'alliage]* assaying; *[de solution]* titration 2 *(Ciné)* titling

titre /titʀ(ə)/ NM 1 *[d'œuvre]* title; *[de chapitre]* heading, title; *(Jur) [de code]* title; *(= manchette de journal)* headline; *(= journal)* newspaper ◆ **les (gros) ~s** the headlines ◆ **~ sur cinq colonnes à la une** five-column front page headline ◆ **~ courant** *(Typo)* running head ◆ **les principaux ~s de la presse parisienne** the major Parisian newspapers ◆ **(page de) ~** *(Typo)* title page ◆ **~ budgétaire** budgetary item
2 *(honorifique, de fonctions professionnelles)* title; *(= formule de politesse)* form of address; *(littér = nom)* title, name ◆ **~ nobiliaire** *ou* **de noblesse** title ◆ **conférer à qn le ~ de maréchal/prince** to confer the title of marshal/prince on sb ◆ **il ne mérite pas le ~ de citoyen** he doesn't deserve to be called a citizen
3 *(Sport)* title
4 *(= document)* title; *(= certificat)* certificate; *(= reçu)* receipt ◆ **~ de créance** evidence *ou* proof of debt ◆ **~ de pension** pension book ◆ **~ de propriété** title deed ◆ **~ de séjour** residence permit ◆ **~ de transport** ticket ◆ **~ de paiement** order to pay, remittance ◆ **~ universel de paiement** universal payment order ◆ **~ interbancaire de paiement** *payment slip allowing automatic withdrawal from a bank account*
5 *(Bourse, Fin)* security ◆ **acheter/vendre des ~s** to buy/sell securities *ou* stock ◆ **~s cotés/non cotés** listed/unlisted securities ◆ **~ de Bourse, ~ boursier** stock-exchange security, stock certificate ◆ **~ d'obligation** debenture (bond) ◆ **~ participatif** non-voting share *(in a public sector enterprise)* ◆ **~ au porteur** bearer bond *ou* share ◆ **~s d'État** government securities ◆ **~s nominatifs** registered securities
6 *(= preuve de capacité, diplôme) (gén)* qualification; *(Univ)* degree, qualification ◆ **~s universitaires** academic *ou* university qualifications ◆ **nommer/recruter sur ~s** to appoint/recruit according to qualifications ◆ **il a tous les ~s (nécessaires) pour enseigner** he is fully qualified *ou* he has all the necessary qualifications to teach
7 *(littér, gén pl = droit, prétentions)* **avoir des ~s à la reconnaissance de qn** to have a right to sb's gratitude ◆ **ses ~s de gloire** his claims to fame
8 *[d'or, argent, monnaie]* fineness; *[de solution]* titre ◆ **or/argent au ~** standard gold/silver ◆ **~ d'alcool** *ou* **alcoolique** alcohol content
9 *(locutions)* **à ce ~** *(= en cette qualité)* as such; *(= pour cette raison)* on this account, therefore ◆ **à quel ~ ?** on what grounds? ◆ **au même ~** in the same way ◆ **il y a droit au même ~ que les autres** he is entitled to it in the same way as the others ◆ **à aucun ~** on no account ◆ **nous ne voulons de lui à aucun ~** we don't want him on any account ◆ **à des ~s divers, à plusieurs ~s, à plus d'un ~** on several accounts, on more than one account ◆ **à double ~** on two accounts ◆ **à ~ privé/personnel** in a private/personal capacity ◆ **à ~ permanent/provisoire** on a permanent/temporary basis, permanently/provisionally ◆ **à ~ exceptionnel** *ou* **d'exception** *(dans ce cas)* exceptionally, in this exceptional case; *(dans certains cas)* in exceptional cases ◆ **à ~ d'ami/de client fidèle** as a friend/a loyal customer ◆ **à ~ gratuit** freely, free of charge ◆ **à ~ gracieux** free of *ou* without charge ◆ **à ~ lucratif** for payment ◆ **à ~ d'essai** on a trial basis ◆ **à ~ d'exemple** as an example, by way of example ◆ **à ~ onéreux** *(frm)* against payment ◆ **à ~ indicatif** for information only ◆ **il travaille à ~ de secrétaire** he works as a secretary ◆ **à ~ consultatif** *[collaborer]* in an advisory *ou* a consultative capacity ◆ **on vous donne 250 € à ~ d'indemnité** we are giving you €250 by way of indemnity *ou* as an indemnity; → **juste**
◆ **en titre** *(Admin)* titular; *(Jur) [propriétaire]* legal; *(Comm) [fournisseur]* appointed; *(hum) [maîtresse]* official ◆ **le champion du monde en ~** the world title-holder

titré, e /titʀe/ (ptp de **titrer**) ADJ 1 *(= noble) [personne]* titled; *[terres]* carrying a title *(attrib)* ◆ **l'athlète le plus ~ de ces Jeux olympiques** the athlete who has won the most medals in these Olympic Games 2 *(Tech) [liqueur]* standard

titrer /titʀe/ ▸ conjug 1 ◂ VT 1 *(gén ptp = anoblir)* to confer a title on 2 *(Chim) [+ alliage]* to assay; *[+ solution]* to titrate 3 *[+ livre, œuvre d'art]* to title; *(Ciné)* to title 4 *(Presse)* to run as a headline ◆ **~ sur 2/5 colonnes : "Défaite de la Droite"** to run a 2/5-column headline: "Defeat of the Right" 5 *[alcool, vin]* **~ 10°/38°** to be 10°/38° proof *(on the Gay Lussac scale)*, ≃ to be 17°/66° proof

titrisation /titʀizasjɔ̃/ NF securitization

titubant, e /titybɑ̃, ɑ̃t/ ADJ *[personne] (de faiblesse, fatigue)* staggering; *(d'ivresse)* staggering, reeling; *[démarche]* unsteady

tituber /titybe/ ▸ conjug 1 ◂ VI *[personne] (de faiblesse, fatigue)* to stagger (along); *(d'ivresse)* to stagger (along), to reel (along) ◆ **il avança vers nous/sortit de la cuisine en titubant** he came staggering *ou* tottering towards us/out of the kitchen, he staggered *ou* tottered towards us/out of the kitchen ◆ **nous titubions de fatigue** we were so tired that we could hardly keep upright, we were so tired we were staggering *ou* stumbling along

titulaire /titylɛʀ/ ADJ 1 *(Admin) [professeur]* with tenure ◆ **être ~** to have tenure 2 ◆ **être ~ de** *(Univ) [+ chaire]* to occupy, to hold; *(Pol) [+ portefeuille]* to hold; *[+ droit]* to be entitled to; *[+ permis, diplôme, carte, compte]* to hold, to have 3 *(Rel) [évêque]* titular *(épith)* ◆ **saint/patron ~ d'une église** (titular) saint/patron of a church NMF *(Admin) [de poste]* incumbent; *(Jur) [de droit]* person entitled (de to); *[de permis, bail, compte bancaire, carte de crédit]* holder; *[+ passeport]* holder, bearer

titularisation /titylaʀizasjɔ̃/ NF *[d'enseignant, fonctionnaire]* appointment to a permanent post; *[de professeur d'université]* granting of tenure; *[de sportif]* signing up as a full team member ◆ **sa ~ a été refusée** his application for a permanent post *ou* for tenure was refused

titulariser /titylaʀize/ ▸ conjug 1 ◂ VT *[+ enseignant, fonctionnaire]* to give a permanent appointment to; *[+ professeur d'université]* to give tenure to; *[+ sportif]* to sign up (as a full team member)

TMS /teɛmɛs/ NMPL (abrév de **troubles musculo-squelettiques**) RSI

TNT /teɛnte/ NM (abrév de **trinitrotoluène**) TNT

toast /tost/ NM 1 *(= pain grillé)* slice *ou* piece of toast ◆ **un ~ beurré** a slice *ou* piece of buttered toast 2 *(= discours)* toast ◆ **~ de bienvenue** welcoming toast ◆ **porter un ~ en l'honneur de qn** to drink (a toast) to sb, to toast sb

toasteur /tostœʀ/ NM toaster

toboggan /tɔbɔgɑ̃/ NM 1 *(= glissière, jeu)* slide; *[de piscine]* waterslide ◆ **faire du ~** *(une fois)* to go on a slide; *(plusieurs fois)* to play on a slide 2 *(= traîneau)* toboggan ◆ **faire du ~** to go tobogganing ◆ **piste de ~** toboggan run 3 *(Tech : pour manutention)* chute; *(dans avion)* emergency chute; *(= viaduc)* flyover *(Brit)*, overpass *(US)*

> ⚠ **toboggan** se traduit par le mot anglais **toboggan** uniquement au sens de 'traîneau'.

toc[1] /tɔk/ EXCL 1 *(= bruit)* **~ ~ !** knock knock!, rat-a-tat(-tat)! 2 *(* = repartie)* **et ~ !** *(en s'adressant à qn)* so there!*; *(en racontant la réaction de qn)* and serves him *(ou* her *etc)* damned *ou* jolly *(Brit)* well right!* ADJ * ◆ **il est ~ ~, celui-là !** *(= fou)* he's cracked* *ou* nuts*!, he's got a screw loose!*

toc[2] /tɔk/ NM ◆ **c'est du ~** *(= imitation, faux)* it's (a) fake; *(= camelote)* it's trash *ou* junk ◆ **en ~** *[bijou]* fake ADJ INV *(= imitation)* fake; *(= camelote)* rubbishy, trashy ◆ **ça fait ~** *(= imité, faux)* it looks fake; *(= camelote)* it looks cheap *ou* rubbishy, it's junk

TOC /tɔk/ NM (abrév de **trouble obsessionnel compulsif**) OCD, obsessive compulsive disorder

tocante* /tɔkɑ̃t/ NF watch, ticker* *(Brit)*

tocard, e* /tɔkaʀ, aʀd/ ADJ *[meubles, décor]* cheap and nasty, trashy* NM *(= personne)* dead loss*, useless twit*, washout*; *(= cheval)* (old) nag *(péj)*

toccata /tɔkata/ NF toccata

tocsin /tɔksɛ̃/ NM alarm (bell), tocsin *(littér)* ◆ **sonner le ~** to ring the alarm, to sound the tocsin *(littér)*

toge /tɔʒ/ NF 1 *(Hist)* toga ◆ **~ virile/prétexte** toga virilis/praetexta 2 *(Jur, Scol)* gown

Togo /tɔgo/ NM Togo

togolais, e /tɔgɔlɛ, ɛz/ ADJ of *ou* from Togo NM,F **Togolais(e)** native of Togo

tohu-bohu /tɔybɔy/ NM *(= désordre)* jumble, confusion; *(= agitation)* hustle (and bustle); *(= tumulte)* hubbub, commotion

toi /twa/ PRON PERS 1 *(sujet, objet)* you ◆ **~ et lui, vous êtes tous les deux aussi têtus** you're both as stubborn as one another ◆ **si j'étais ~, j'irais** if I were you *ou* in your shoes I'd go ◆ **il n'obéit qu'à ~** you are the only one he obeys, he obeys only you ◆ **il a accepté, ~ non** *ou* **pas ~** he accepted but you didn't *ou* but not you ◆ **c'est enfin ~ !** here you are at last! ◆ **qui l'a vu ? ~ ?** who saw him? did you? ◆ **~ mentir ? ce n'est pas possible** YOU tell a lie? I can't believe it ◆ **~ qui le connais bien, qu'en penses-tu ?** you know him well, so what do you think? ◆ **va devant, c'est ~ qui connais le chemin** you go first, you know the way *ou* you're the one who knows the way ◆ **~, tu n'as pas à te plaindre** you have no cause to complain ◆ **pourquoi ne le ferais-je pas, tu l'as bien fait, ~ !** why shouldn't I do it? YOU did it, didn't you? ◆ **tu l'as vu, ~ ?** did you see him?, have you seen him? ◆ **t'épouser, ~ ? jamais !** marry you? never! ◆ **~, je te connais** I know you ◆ **aide-moi, ~ !** you there* *ou* hey you*, give me a hand! ◆ **~, tu m'agaces !, tu m'agaces, ~ !** you really get on my nerves! ◆ **~, pauvre innocent, tu n'as rien compris !** you, poor fool, haven't understood a thing!, you poor fool – you haven't understood a thing!

2 *(avec vpr : souvent non traduit)* **assieds-~ !** sit down! ◆ **mets-~ là !** stand over there! ◆ **~, tais-~ !** you be quiet! ◆ **montre-~ un peu aimable !** be nice!

3 *(avec prép)* you, yourself ◆ **à ~ tout seul, tu ne peux pas le faire** you can't do it on your own *ou* by yourself ◆ **cette maison est-elle à ~ ?** does this house belong to you?, is this house yours? ◆ **tu n'as même pas une chambre à ~ tout seul ?** you don't even have a room of your own? *ou* a room to yourself? ◆ **tu ne penses qu'à ~** you only think of yourself, you think only of yourself ◆ **je compte sur ~** I'm counting on you

4 *(dans des comparaisons)* you ◆ **il me connaît mieux que ~** *(qu'il ne te connaît)* he knows me better than (he knows) you; *(que tu ne me connais)* he knows me better than you (do) ◆ **il est plus/moins fort que ~** he is stronger than/not so strong as you ◆ **il a fait comme ~** he did what you did, he did the same as you

toile /twal/ NF 1 *(= tissu) (gén)* cloth *(NonC)*; *(grossière, de chanvre)* canvas *(NonC)*; *(pour pneu)* canvas *(NonC)* ◆ **grosse ~** (rough *ou* coarse) canvas ◆ **~ de lin/de coton** linen/cotton (cloth) ◆ **en ~, de ~** *[draps]* linen; *[pantalon, blazer]* (heavy) cotton; *[sac]* canvas ◆ **en ~ tergal** in Terylene fabric ◆ **~ caoutchoutée/plastifiée** rubberized/plastic-coated cloth ◆ **relié ~** cloth bound ◆ **~ d'amiante/métallique** asbestos/metal cloth ◆ **~ imprimée** printed cotton, cotton print ◆ **reliure ~** cloth binding; → **chanson, village**

2 *(= morceau)* piece of cloth ◆ **poser qch sur une ~** to put sth on a piece of cloth ◆ **se mettre dans les ~s*** *(= draps)* to hit the hay* *ou* the sack*

3 *(Art) (= support)* canvas; *(= œuvre)* canvas, painting ◆ **il expose ses ~s chez Legrand** he exhibits his canvasses *ou* paintings at Legrand's ◆ **une ~ de maître** an old master ◆ **gâcher** *ou* **barbouiller de la ~** to daub on canvas

4 *(Naut = ensemble des voiles)* sails ◆ **faire de la/réduire la ~** to make/take in sail ◆ **navire chargé de ~s** ship under canvas, ship under full sail

5 *[d'araignée]* web ◆ **la ~ de l'araignée** the spider's web ◆ **une belle ~ d'araignée** a beautiful spider's web ◆ **le grenier est plein de ~s d'araignées** the attic is full of cobwebs

6 *(Internet)* **la Toile** the Web

7 *(* = film)* film, movie *(surtout US)* ◆ **se faire une ~** to go and see a film, to go to a movie *(surtout US)*

COMP **toile d'avion** aeroplane cloth *ou* linen
toile de bâche tarpaulin ◆ **une parka en ~ de bâche** a heavy canvas parka
toile cirée oilcloth
toile émeri emery cloth
toile de fond *(Théât)* backdrop, backcloth ◆ **un moulin avec un lac en ~ de fond** a windmill with a lake in the background ◆ **une histoire d'amour, avec en ~ de fond la guerre** a love story set against the backdrop of the war
toile goudronnée tarpaulin, tarp
toile de Jouy ≃ Liberty print
toile de jute hessian
toile à matelas ticking
toile à sac sacking, sackcloth
toile de tente *(Camping)* canvas; *(Mil)* tent sheet
toile à voile sailcloth

toilerie /twalʀi/ NF *(= fabrication)* textile manufacture *(of cotton, linen, canvas etc)*; *(= commerce)* textile trade; *(= atelier)* textile mill

toilettage /twaletaʒ/ NM *[de chien]* grooming; *[de texte de loi]* tidying up ◆ **"toilettage pour chiens", "salon de toilettage"** *(enseigne)* "grooming parlour"

toilette /twalɛt/ NF 1 *(= ablutions)* **faire sa ~** to have a wash, to get washed ◆ **être à sa ~** *(= habillage)* to be dressing, to be getting ready ◆ **faire une grande ~/une ~ rapide** *ou* **un brin de ~** to have a thorough/quick wash ◆ **faire une ~ de chat** to give o.s. a lick and a promise *ou* a cat-lick *(Brit)* ◆ **~ intime** personal hygiene ◆ **elle passe des heures à sa ~** she spends hours getting ready *ou* washing and dressing *ou* at her toilet *(frm)* ◆ **la ~ des enfants prend toujours du temps** it always takes a long time to get the children washed *ou* ready ◆ **une lotion pour la ~ de bébé** a cleansing lotion for babies ◆ **produits de ~** toiletries ◆ **j'ai oublié mes affaires de ~** I've forgotten my toothbrush and things ◆ **faire la ~ d'un mort** to lay out a corpse ◆ **la ~ d'un condamné à mort** the washing of a prisoner before execution ◆ **(table de) ~** *(pour lavabo)* washstand; *(= coiffeuse)* dressing table; → **cabinet, gant, trousse**

2 *(= nettoyage) [de voiture]* cleaning; *[de maison, monument]* facelift ◆ **faire la ~ de** *[+ voiture]* to clean; *[+ monument, maison]* to give a facelift to, to tart up* *(Brit) (hum)*; *[+ texte]* to tidy up, to polish up

3 *[d'animal]* **faire sa ~** to wash itself ◆ **faire la ~ de son chien** to groom one's dog

4 *(= habillement, parure)* clothes ◆ **en ~ de bal** wearing a ballgown ◆ **~ de mariée** wedding *ou* bridal dress *ou* gown ◆ **être en grande ~** to be (dressed) in all one's finery, to be all dressed up ◆ **aimer la ~** to like clothes ◆ **elle porte bien la ~** she wears her clothes well

5 *(= costume)* outfit ◆ **elle a changé trois fois de ~ !** she's changed her outfit *ou* clothes three times! ◆ **"nos toilettes d'été"** "summer wear *ou* outfits" ◆ **on voit déjà les ~s d'été** you can already see people in summer outfits *ou* clothes

6 *(Boucherie)* ~ **(de porc)** pig's caul

7 *(Tech) (= emballage)* reed casing

NFPL **toilettes** (= WC) toilet, bathroom *(US)*; *(publiques)* public lavatory *ou* conveniences *(Brit)*, restroom *(US)* ◆ **aller aux ~s** to go to the toilet ◆ **où sont les ~s ?** *(dans un lieu public, gén)* where's the toilet? *ou* the restroom? *(US)*; *(pour femmes)* where's the ladies' room? *ou* the ladies?* *(Brit)*; *(pour hommes)* where's the men's room? *ou* the gents?* *(Brit)*

toiletter /twalete/ ► conjug 1 ◄ VT *[+ chien, chat]* to groom; *[+ texte de loi]* to tidy up, to polish up

toiletteur, -euse /twaletœʀ, øz/ NM,F groomer ◆ **~ pour chiens** dog groomer

toi-même /twamɛm/ PRON → **même**

toise /twaz/ NF 1 *(= instrument)* height gauge ◆ **passer qn à la ~** to measure sb's height ◆ **il est passé à** *ou* **sous la ~** he had his height measured 2 *(Hist = mesure)* toise, ≃ 6 ft

toiser /twaze/ ► conjug 1 ◄ VT 1 *(= regarder avec dédain)* to look up and down, to eye scornfully ◆ **ils se toisèrent** they looked each other up and down 2 (†, *littér = évaluer*) to estimate

toison /twazɔ̃/ NF 1 *[de mouton]* fleece ◆ **la Toison d'or** the Golden Fleece 2 *(= chevelure) (épaisse)* mop; *(longue)* mane 3 *(= poils)* abundant growth

toit /twa/ NM 1 *(gén)* roof ◆ **~ de chaume/de tuiles/d'ardoises** thatched/tiled/slate roof ◆ **~ plat** *ou* **en terrasse/en pente** flat/sloping roof ◆ **habiter sous les ~s** to live in an attic flat *(Brit)* *ou* apartment *(US) (with a sloping ceiling)* ◆ **le ~ du monde** the roof of the world ◆ **voiture à ~ ouvrant** car with a sunroof ◆ **double ~** *[de tente]* fly sheet; → **crier** 2 *(= maison)* **avoir un ~** to have a roof over one's head, to have a home ◆ **chercher un ~** to look for somewhere to live ◆ **être sans ~** to have no roof over one's head, to have nowhere to call home *ou* one's own ◆ **sous le ~ de qn** under sb's roof, in sb's house ◆ **vivre sous le même ~** to live under the same roof ◆ **vivre sous le ~ paternel** to live in the paternal home ◆ **recevoir qn sous son ~** to have sb as a guest in one's house

toiture /twatyʀ/ NF roof, roofing

tokai /tɔkɛ/, **tokaï** /tɔkaj/, **tokay** /tɔkɛ/ NM Tokay

Tokyo /tɔkjo/ N Tokyo

tôlard, e ⁑ /tolaʀ, aʀd/ NM,F ⇒ **taulard**

tôle[1] /tol/ NF *(= matériau)* sheet metal *(NonC)*; *(= pièce)* steel (*ou* iron) sheet ◆ **~ d'acier/d'aluminium** sheet steel/aluminium ◆ **~ étamée** tinplate ◆ **~ galvanisée/émaillée** galvanized/enamelled iron ◆ **~ froissée** *[de voiture]* dented bodywork ◆ **~ ondulée** *(lit)* corrugated iron; *(= route)* rugged dirt track ◆ **se payer une ~** ⁑ *(= échouer)* to fall flat on one's face *(fig)*

tôle[2] ⁑ /tol/ NF ⇒ **taule**

Tolède /tɔlɛd/ N Toledo

tôlée /tole/ ADJ F ◆ **neige ~** crusted snow

tolérable /tɔleʀabl/ ADJ *[comportement, retard]* tolerable; *[douleur, attente]* tolerable, bearable ◆ **cette attitude n'est pas ~** this attitude is intolerable *ou* cannot be tolerated NM ◆ **c'est à la limite du ~** it's barely tolerable

tolérance /tɔleʀɑ̃s/ NF 1 *(= compréhension, largeur d'esprit)* tolerance *(à l'égard de, envers* toward(s)); ◆ **faire preuve de ~** to be tolerant *(à l'égard de, envers* with) 2 *(= liberté limitée)* **c'est une ~, pas un droit** it's tolerated rather than allowed as of right ◆ **il y a une ~ de 2 litres d'alcool/200 cigarettes** *(produits hors taxe)* there's an allowance of 2 litres of spirits/200 cigarettes ◆ **~ orthographique/grammaticale** permitted departure in spelling/grammar; → **maison** 3 *(Méd, Tech)* tolerance ◆ **~ aux antibiotiques** antibiotic tolerance ◆ **~ immunitaire** immunological tolerance; → **marge** 4 *(Hist, Rel)* toleration

tolérant, e /tɔleʀɑ̃, ɑ̃t/ ADJ tolerant ◆ **il est trop ~ avec ses élèves** he's too lenient *ou* easy-going with his pupils

tolérantisme /tɔleʀɑ̃tism/ NM *(Hist Rel)* tolerationism

tolérer /tɔleʀe/ ► conjug 6 ◄ VT 1 *(= ne pas sévir contre) [+ culte, pratiques, abus, infractions]* to tolerate; *(= autoriser)* to allow ◆ **ils tolèrent un excédent de bagages de 15 kg** they allow 15 kg (of) excess baggage

2 *(= supporter) [+ comportement, excentricités, personne]* to put up with, to tolerate; *[+ douleur]* to bear, to endure, to stand ◆ **ils ne s'aimaient guère : disons qu'ils se toléraient** they didn't like each other much – you could say that they put up with *ou* tolerated each other ◆ **je ne ~ai pas cette impertinence** I will not stand for *ou* put up with *ou* tolerate this impertinence ◆ **il tolérait qu'on l'appelle par son prénom** he allowed people to call him by his first name ◆ **il ne tolère pas qu'on le contredise** he won't tolerate being contradicted

3 *(Bio, Méd) [organisme]* to tolerate; *(Tech) [matériau, système]* to tolerate ◆ **il ne tolère pas l'alcool** he can't tolerate *ou* take alcohol

tôlerie /tolʀi/ NF 1 *(= fabrication)* sheet metal manufacture; *(= commerce)* sheet metal trade; *(= atelier)* sheet metal workshop 2 *(= tôles) [de voiture]* panels, coachwork *(NonC)*; *[de bateau, chaudière]* plates, steelwork *(NonC)*

tolet /tɔlɛ/ NM rowlock, thole

tôlier¹ /tolje/ NM (= industriel) sheet iron ou steel manufacturer ◆ **(ouvrier-)~** sheet metal worker ◆ **~ en voitures** panel beater

tôlier², -ière‡ /tolje, jɛʀ/ NM,F ⇒ **taulier**

tollé /tɔ(l)le/ NM general outcry ou protest ◆ **ce fut un ~ (général)** there was a general outcry

Tolstoï /tɔlstɔj/ NM Tolstoy

toluène /tɔlɥɛn/ NM toluene

TOM /tɔm/ NM (abrév de **territoire d'outre-mer**) → **territoire**

tomahawk /tɔmaok/ NM tomahawk

tomaison /tɔmɛzɔ̃/ NF volume numbering

tomate /tɔmat/ NF [1] (= plante) tomato (plant); (= fruit) tomato ◆ **~s farcies** stuffed tomatoes ◆ **~s en grappes** vine tomatoes ◆ **~s (à la) provençale** tomatoes (à la) Provençale ◆ **~s cerises/vertes** cherry/green tomatoes ◆ **il va recevoir des ~s** (fig) he'll get a hostile reception; → **rouge** [2] (= boisson) pastis with grenadine

tombal, e (mpl **tombals** ou **tombaux**) /tɔ̃bal, o/ ADJ [dalle] funerary; (littér = funèbre) tomb-like, funereal (épith) ◆ **inscription ~e** tombstone inscription; → **pierre**

tombant, e /tɔ̃bɑ̃, ɑ̃t/ ADJ [draperies] hanging (épith); [épaules] sloping (épith); [moustache, paupières] drooping (épith); [bouche] down-turned, turned down at the corners (attrib); [oreilles de chien] floppy; → **nuit**

tombe /tɔ̃b/ NF [1] (gén) grave; (avec monument) tomb; (= pierre) gravestone, tombstone ◆ **aller sur la ~ de qn** to visit sb's grave ◆ **froid comme la ~** cold as the tomb ◆ **muet ou silencieux comme la ~** (as) silent as the grave ou tomb; → **recueillir, retourner** [2] (locutions) **suivre qn dans la ~** to follow sb to the grave ◆ **descendre dans la ~** (littér) to go to one's grave; → **pied**

tombeau (pl **tombeaux**) /tɔ̃bo/ NM [1] (lit) tomb ◆ **mettre qn au ~** to commit sb to the grave, to entomb sb ◆ **mise au ~** entombment [2] (fig) (= endroit lugubre ou solitaire) grave, tomb; (= ruine) [d'espérances, amour] death (NonC); (= lieu du trépas) grave ◆ **jusqu'au ~** to the grave ◆ **descendre au ~** to go to one's grave ◆ **cette pièce est un ~** this room is like a grave ou tomb ◆ **je serai un vrai ~** (secret) my lips are sealed, I'll be as silent as the grave [3] ◆ **à ~ ouvert** at breakneck speed

tombée /tɔ̃be/ NF ◆ **(à) la ~ de la nuit** (at) nightfall ◆ **(à) la ~ du jour** (at) the close of the day

tomber¹ /tɔ̃be/

► conjug 1 ◄

1 VERBE INTRANSITIF 2 VERBE TRANSITIF

Lorsque **tomber** s'emploie dans des locutions figées telles que **tomber malade/amoureux, tomber d'accord, tomber de sommeil, tomber en désuétude,** etc, cherchez au nom ou à l'adjectif.

1 - VERBE INTRANSITIF

avec auxiliaire être

[1] de la station debout to fall (over ou down) ◆ **il est tombé et s'est cassé la jambe** he fell (over ou down) and broke his leg ◆ **le chien l'a fait ~** the dog knocked him over ou down ◆ **~ par terre** to fall down, to fall to the ground ◆ **~ de (tout) son haut** to fall ou crash ou topple to the ground, to fall headlong ◆ **se laisser ~ dans un fauteuil** to drop ou fall into an armchair ◆ **le tennis, il est tombé dedans quand il était petit** * (hum) he learnt how to play tennis almost as soon as he could walk ◆ **à ~ (par terre)** * amazing, incredible

[2] de la position verticale [arbre, bouteille, poteau] to fall (over ou down); [chaise, pile d'objets] to fall (over); [échafaudage, mur] to fall down, to collapse ◆ **faire ~** (gén) to knock down; (en renversant) to knock over

[3] d'un endroit élevé [personne, objet] to fall (down); [avion] to fall; (fig, littér = pécher) to fall ◆ **attention ! tu vas ~** careful! you'll fall ◆ **~ dans ou à l'eau** to fall into the water ◆ **~ d'un arbre** to fall from a tree, to fall out of a tree ◆ **~ d'une chaise/d'une échelle** to fall off a chair/off a ladder ◆ **~ de bicyclette/de cheval** to fall off one's bicycle/from ou off one's horse ◆ **~ à bas de son cheval** to fall from ou off one's horse ◆ **~ du cinquième étage** to fall from the fifth floor ◆ **~ de haut** (lit) to fall from a height; (fig) to come down with a bump ◆ **il est tombé sur la tête !** * he's got a screw loose *; → **ciel, lune**

[4] = se détacher [feuilles, fruits] to fall; [cheveux] to fall (out) ◆ **ramasser des fruits tombés** to pick up fruit that has fallen, to pick up windfalls ◆ **le journal tombe (des presses) à 6 heures** the paper comes off the press at 6 o'clock ◆ **la nouvelle vient de ~ à l'instant** the news has just this minute broken ◆ **un télex vient de ~** a telex has just come through ◆ **la plume me tombe des mains** the pen is falling from my hand ◆ **faire ~** (en lâchant) to drop ◆ **porte le vase sur la table sans le faire ~** carry the vase to the table without dropping it

[5] = s'abattre, descendre [eau, lumière] to fall; [neige, pluie] to fall, to come down; [brouillard] to come down ◆ **il tombe de la neige** it's snowing ◆ **qu'est-ce qu'il tombe !** * it's coming down in buckets! *, it's tipping it down * (Brit) ◆ **l'eau tombait en cascades** the water was cascading down ◆ **il tombe quelques gouttes** it's raining slightly, there are a few drops of rain (falling), it's spitting (with rain) (Brit) ou sprinkling lightly (US) ◆ **la nuit tombe** night is falling, it's getting dark ◆ **la foudre est tombée deux fois/tout près** the lightning has struck twice/nearby

[6] = baisser [fièvre] to drop; [vent] to drop, to abate, to die down; [baromètre] to fall; [jour] to draw to a close; [voix] to drop, to fall away; [prix, nombre, température] to fall, to drop (à to; de by); [colère, conversation] to die down; [exaltation, assurance, enthousiasme] to fall away ◆ **le dollar est tombé à 80 cents** the dollar has fallen ou dropped to 80 cents ◆ **les prix ne sont jamais tombés aussi bas** prices have reached a new low ou an all-time low, prices have never fallen so low ◆ **ils sont tombés bien bas** (fig) they've sunk really low ◆ **faire ~** [+ température, vent, prix] to bring down

[7] = disparaître [obstacle, objection] to disappear; [poursuites] to lapse; [record] to fall ◆ **l'as et le roi sont tombés** (Cartes) the ace and king have gone ou have been played ◆ **faire ~ les atouts** to force out the trumps

[8] = pendre, descendre [draperie, robe, chevelure] to fall, to hang; [pantalon] to hang; [moustaches] to droop; [épaules] to slope ◆ **ses cheveux lui tombaient sur les épaules** his hair fell to ou hung down to his shoulders ◆ **les rideaux tombaient jusqu'au plancher** the curtains hung down to the floor ◆ **sa jupe tombe bien** her skirt hangs nicely ou well

[9] = échoir [date, choix, sort] to fall; [verdict, sanction] to be pronounced ◆ **Pâques tombe tard cette année** Easter falls late this year ◆ **Noël tombe un mardi** Christmas falls on a Tuesday ◆ **les deux concerts tombent le même jour** the two concerts fall on the same day

[10] = arriver, se produire ◆ **il est tombé en pleine réunion/scène de ménage** he walked straight into a meeting/a domestic row ◆ **je tombe toujours aux heures de fermeture** I always manage to come at closing time ◆ **bien/mal ~** (moment) to come at the right/wrong moment; (chance) to be lucky/unlucky ◆ **ça tombe bien** that's fortunate ou convenient ◆ **ça tombe à point ou à pic** * that's perfect timing ◆ **ça ne pouvait pas mieux ~** that couldn't have come at a better time ◆ **il est vraiment bien/mal tombé avec son nouveau patron** he's really lucky/unlucky ou he's really in luck/out of luck with his new boss ◆ **si ça tombe, il viendra même pas‡** he may not even come; → **juste**

[11] = être tué [combattant] to fall

[12] = être vaincu [ville, régime, garnison] to fall ◆ **faire ~ le gouvernement** to bring down the government, to bring the government down

[13] ‡ = être arrêté to be ou get busted‡ ou nicked‡ (Brit)

[14] locutions

◆ **laisser tomber** [+ objet que l'on porte] to drop; [+ amis, activité] to drop; [+ métier] to drop, to give up, to chuck in *; [+ fiancé] to jilt, to throw over *; [+ vieux parents] to let down, to leave in the lurch ◆ **il a voulu faire du droit mais il a vite laissé ~** he wanted to do law but he soon gave it up ou dropped it ◆ **la famille nous a bien laissé ~** the family really let us down ou left us in the lurch ◆ **laisse ~ !** * (gén) forget it!; (nuance d'irritation) give it a rest! *

◆ **tomber dans** [+ état] ◆ **~ dans la misère** to become destitute ◆ **~ dans l'alcool/la drogue** to take to drinking/to drugs ◆ **~ dans le coma** to fall into a coma ◆ **son œuvre est tombée dans l'oubli** his work fell into oblivion ◆ **ce roman tombe dans le mélo/la vulgarité** the novel tends to lapse into melodrama/vulgarity ◆ **~ dans l'excès** to lapse into excess ◆ **~ dans l'excès inverse** to go to the opposite extreme ◆ **~ d'un excès dans un autre** to go from one extreme to another → **domaine, pomme, piège** etc

◆ **tomber sur** [regard] to fall ou light upon; [conversation] to come round to

(= rencontrer par hasard) [+ personne] to run ou bump into; (= trouver par hasard) [+ objet, piste, détail] to come across ou upon ◆ **j'ai eu la chance de ~ sur un spécialiste** I was lucky enough to come across a specialist ◆ **en prenant cette rue, vous tombez sur le boulevard/la gare** if you go along this street, you'll come out onto the boulevard/you'll find the station ◆ **je suis tombé sur une vieille photo** I came across ou upon an old photo; → **bec, os**

(= échoir à) ◆ **on a tiré au sort et c'est tombé sur moi** we drew straws and I was the lucky winner (iro) ◆ **et il a fallu que ça tombe sur moi !** it (just) had to be me! ◆ **il m'est tombé sur le râble‡ ou le paletot‡ ou le dos‡** he laid into me *, he went for me *

◆ **tomber dessus** * ◆ **il nous est tombé dessus le jour de Noël** he landed on us on Christmas Day * ◆ **une quantité de problèmes leur est tombée dessus** they had a whole series of problems ◆ **la maladie, ça peut vous ~ dessus n'importe quand** you can fall ill any time ◆ **quand la solitude vous tombe dessus ...** when you suddenly find yourself alone ... ◆ **je ne voulais pas d'une nouvelle relation amoureuse, ça m'est tombé dessus** I didn't want to have another love affair, it just happened ◆ **ils nous sont tombés dessus à huit contre trois** eight of them laid into the three of us‡

2 - VERBE TRANSITIF

avec auxiliaire avoir

[1] * **~ qn** (= vaincre) (Sport) to throw sb; (Pol) to beat sb ◆ **il les tombe toutes** (= séduire) he's a real ladykiller

[2] * = enlever ◆ **~ la veste** to take off one's jacket ◆ **~ le masque** to drop the mask

tomber² /tɔ̃be/ NM [1] (littér) **au ~ du jour ou de la nuit** at nightfall [2] [de vêtement, étoffe] **le ~**

de ce tissu/de cette robe the way the material/the dress hangs

tombereau (pl **tombereaux**) /tɔ̃bʀo/ NM (= *charrette*) tipcart; (= *contenu*) cartload; (*pour terrassement*) dump truck, dumper-truck ◆ **des ~x de** (*fig*) masses of

tombeur, -euse /tɔ̃bœʀ, øz/ NM,F (= *adversaire*) ◆ **le ~ du sénateur** the man who defeated the senator ◆ **la tombeuse de la championne du monde** the woman who defeated *ou* toppled the world champion NM [1] (* = *don Juan*) ladykiller, Casanova [2] (= *lutteur*) thrower

tombola /tɔ̃bɔla/ NF tombola, raffle

Tombouctou /tɔ̃buktu/ N Timbuktu

tome /tɔm/ NM (= *division*) part, book; (= *volume*) volume

tomette /tɔmɛt/ NF ⇒ **tommette**

tomme /tɔm/ NF tomme (cheese)

tommette /tɔmɛt/ NF (red, hexagonal) floor-tile

tomographie /tɔmɔgʀafi/ NF tomography

tom-pouce * /tɔmpus/ NM (= *nain*) Tom Thumb, dwarf, midget

ton[1] /tɔ̃/, **ta** /ta/ (pl **tes** /te/) ADJ POSS [1] (*possession, relation*) your; (*emphatique*) your own; († *Rel*) thy ◆ **~ fils et ta fille** your son and (your) daughter ◆ **que ta volonté soit faite** (*Rel*) Thy will be done; *pour autres loc voir* **son** [2] (*valeur affective, ironique, intensive*) **tu as de la chance d'avoir ~ samedi !** * you're lucky to have Saturday(s) off! ◆ **~ Paris est devenu très bruyant** your beloved Paris is getting very noisy ◆ **tu vas avoir ta crise de foie si tu manges ça** you'll upset your stomach if you eat that ◆ **ferme donc ta porte !** shut the door behind you!; *pour autres loc voir* **son**[1]

ton[2] /tɔ̃/ NM [1] (= *hauteur de la voix*) pitch; (= *timbre*) tone; (= *manière de parler*) tone (of voice) ◆ **~ aigu/grave** shrill/low pitch ◆ **~ nasillard** twang ◆ **d'un ~ détaché/brusque/pédant** in a detached/an abrupt/a pedantic tone (of voice) ◆ **d'un ~ sec** curtly ◆ **avec un ~ de supériorité** in a superior tone ◆ **sur le ~ de la conversation/plaisanterie** conversationally/jokingly, in a conversational/joking tone (of voice) ◆ **le ~ est à la conciliation/à la prudence** the prevailing mood is one of conciliation/of caution, conciliation/caution is the order of the day ◆ **hausser le ~** (*lit*) to raise one's voice; (= *se fâcher*) to raise one's voice; (= *durcir sa position*) to take a firmer line ◆ **les syndicats haussent le ~** the unions are taking an aggressive stand ◆ **baisser le ~** (*lit*) to lower one's voice; (*fig*) to soften *ou* moderate one's tone ◆ **baisse un peu le ~ !** pipe down! * ◆ **faire baisser le ~ à qn** (*fig*) to bring sb down a peg (or two) ◆ **les débats ont changé de ~** the tone of the debates has changed ◆ **il devra changer de ~** (*fig*) he'll have to change his tune ◆ **ne me parle pas sur ce ~ !** don't use that tone (of voice) with me!, don't you talk to me like that! ◆ **ne le prenez pas sur ce ~** don't take it like that ◆ **alors là, si vous le prenez sur ce ~** well if that's the way you're going to take it, well if you're going to take it like that ◆ **dire/répéter sur tous les ~s** to say/repeat in every possible way

[2] (*Mus* = *intervalle*) tone; [*de morceau*] key; [*d'instrument à vent*] crook; (= *hauteur d'un instrument*) pitch ◆ **le ~ de si majeur** the key of B major ◆ **passer d'un ~ à un autre** to change from one key to another ◆ **il y a un ~ majeur entre do et ré** there is a whole *ou* full tone between C and D ◆ **prendre le ~** to tune up (*de* to); ◆ **donner le ~** to give the pitch ◆ **sortir du ~** to go out of tune ◆ **il/ce n'est pas dans le ~** he/it is not in tune ◆ **le ~ est trop haut pour elle** it's set in too high a key for her, it's pitched too high for her

[3] (*Ling, Phon*) tone ◆ **langue à ~s** tone language

[4] (= *style*) tone ◆ **le ~ soutenu de son discours** the elevated tone of his speech ◆ **le bon ~** (= *manière de se comporter*) good manners, good form (*Brit*) ◆ **plaisanteries/remarques de bon ~** jokes/remarks in good taste ◆ **il est de bon ~ de ...** it's considered polite to ..., it is good manners *ou* form (*Brit*) to ... ◆ **plaisanteries de mauvais ~** tasteless jokes ◆ **être dans le ~** to fit in ◆ **il s'est vite mis dans le ~** he soon fitted in ◆ **donner le ~** to set the tone; (*en matière de mode*) to set the fashion

[5] (= *couleur, nuance*) shade, tone ◆ **être dans le ~** to tone in, to match ◆ **la ceinture n'est pas du même ~** *ou* **dans le même ~ que la robe** the belt doesn't match the dress ◆ **~s chauds** warm tones *ou* shades ◆ **~s dégradés** gradual shadings ◆ **~ sur ~** in matching tones

tonal, e (mpl **tonals**) /tɔnal/ ADJ (*Ling, Mus*) tonal

tonalité /tɔnalite/ NF [1] (*Mus*) (= *système*) tonality; (= *ton*) key; (*Phon*) [*de voyelle*] tone [2] (= *fidélité*) [*de poste, amplificateur*] tone [3] (= *timbre, qualité*) [*de voix*] tone; (*fig*) [*de texte, impression*] tone; [*de couleurs*] tonality [4] (*Téléc*) dialling tone (*Brit*), dial tone (*US*) ◆ **je n'ai pas la ~** I'm not getting the dialling tone

tondeur, -euse /tɔ̃dœʀ, øz/ NM,F (*gén*) shearer NF **tondeuse** (*à cheveux*) clippers; (*pour les moutons, pour les draps*) shears ◆ **tondeuse (à gazon)** (lawn)mower ◆ **passer la tondeuse** to mow the lawn ◆ **tondeuse à main/à moteur** hand-/motor-mower ◆ **tondeuse électrique** (*pour le gazon*) electric (lawn)mower; (*pour les cheveux*) electric clippers

tondre /tɔ̃dʀ/ ▸ conjug 41 ◂ VT [1] [+ *mouton, toison*] to shear; [+ *gazon*] to mow; [+ *haie*] to clip, to cut; [+ *caniche, poil*] to clip; [+ *cheveux*] to crop; [+ *drap, feutre*] to shear [2] (* = *couper les cheveux à*) **~ qn** to cut sb's hair; (= *escroquer*) to fleece sb; (*au jeu*) to clean sb out ◆ **je vais me faire ~** I'm going to get my hair cut really short; → **laine**

tondu, e /tɔ̃dy/ (ptp de **tondre**) ADJ [*cheveux, tête*] (closely-)cropped; [*personne*] with closely-cropped hair, close-cropped; [*pelouse, sommet*] closely-cropped; → **pelé**

Tonga /tɔ̃ga/ NM Tonga ◆ **les îles ~** Tonga

tongs /tɔ̃g/ NFPL (= *sandales*) flip-flops, thongs (*US*)

tonicité /tɔnisite/ NF [1] (*Méd*) [*de tissus*] tone, tonicity (SPÉC), tonus (SPÉC) [2] [*d'air, mer*] tonic *ou* bracing effect

tonifiant, e /tɔnifjɑ̃, jɑ̃t/ ADJ [*air*] bracing, invigorating; [*massage, lotion*] toning (*épith*), tonic (*épith*), stimulating; [*lecture, expérience*] stimulating NM tonic

tonifier /tɔnifje/ ▸ conjug 7 ◂ VT [+ *muscles*] to tone (up); [+ *esprit, personne*] to stimulate; [+ *peau*] to tone; [+ *cheveux*] to put new life into ◆ **cela tonifie l'organisme** it tones up the whole system

tonique /tɔnik/ ADJ [1] [*médicament, vin, boisson*] tonic (*épith*), fortifying; [*lotion*] toning (*épith*), tonic (*épith*) ◆ **c'est quelqu'un de très ~** (*dynamique*) he's very dynamic; (*physiquement*) he's in really good shape [2] [*air, froid*] invigorating, bracing; [*idée, expérience, lecture*] stimulating [3] (*Ling*) [*syllabe, voyelle*] tonic, accented; → **accent** NM (*Méd, fig*) tonic; (= *lotion*) toning lotion ◆ **~ du cœur** heart tonic NF (*Mus*) tonic, keynote

tonitruant, e /tɔnitʀyɑ̃, ɑ̃t/ ADJ [*voix*] thundering (*épith*), booming (*épith*)

tonitruer /tɔnitʀye/ ▸ conjug 1 ◂ VI to thunder

Tonkin /tɔ̃kɛ̃/ NM Tonkin

tonkinois, e /tɔ̃kinwa, waz/ ADJ Tonkinese NM,F **Tonkinois(e)** Tonkinese

tonnage /tɔnaʒ/ NM [*de navire*] tonnage, burden; [*de port, pays*] tonnage ◆ **~ brut/net** gross/net tonnage

tonnant, e /tɔnɑ̃, ɑ̃t/ ADJ [*voix, acclamation*] thunderous, thundering (*épith*)

tonne /tɔn/ NF [1] (= *unité de poids*) (metric) ton, tonne ◆ **une ~ de bois** a ton *ou* tonne (*Brit*) of wood ◆ **~ américaine** *ou* **courte** short *ou* net ton ◆ **~ anglaise** *ou* **longue** *ou* **forte** long *ou* gross *ou* imperial ton ◆ **~-kilomètre** ton kilometre ◆ **un navire de 10 000 ~s** a 10,000-ton *ou* -tonne (*Brit*) ship, a ship of 10,000 tons *ou* tonnes (*Brit*) ◆ **un (camion de) 5 ~s** a 5-ton truck, a 5-tonner * ◆ **~ équivalent charbon** ton coal equivalent ◆ **~ équivalent pétrole** ton oil equivalent ◆ **ses plaisanteries pèsent des ~s** his jokes are very laboured *ou* heavy-handed

[2] (* = *énorme quantité*) **des ~s de, une ~ de** tons of *, loads of * ◆ **il y en a des ~s** there are tons * *ou* loads * of them ◆ **des gens comme lui, (il n')y en a pas des ~s** you don't come across people like him every day ◆ **en faire des ~s** to overdo it, to go over the top *

[3] (*Tech* = *récipient*) tun; (*Naut* = *bouée*) tun-buoy

tonneau (pl **tonneaux**) /tɔno/ NM [1] (= *récipient*) barrel, cask; (= *contenu*) barrel(ful), cask(ful) ◆ **vin au ~** wine from the barrel *ou* cask ◆ **vieillir en ~** to age in the barrel *ou* cask ◆ **le ~ de Diogène** Diogenes' tub ◆ **le ~ des Danaïdes** (*Myth*) the Danaides' jar ◆ **c'est le ~ des Danaïdes** (= *gouffre financier*) it's a bottomless pit; (= *tâche sans fin*) it is a Sisyphean task ◆ **être du même ~** * (*péj*) to be of the same kind; → **perce** [2] (*en avion*) hesitation flick roll (*Brit*), hesitation snap roll (*US*) [3] (*en voiture*) somersault ◆ **faire un ~** to roll over, to somersault ◆ **leur voiture a fait trois ~x** their car rolled (over) *ou* somersaulted three times [4] (*Naut*) ton ◆ **~ de jauge brute** gross register ton ◆ **un bateau de 1 500 ~x** a 1,500-ton *ou* -tonne (*Brit*) ship

tonnelet /tɔnlɛ/ NM keg, (small) cask

tonnelier /tɔnəlje/ NM cooper

tonnelle /tɔnɛl/ NF (= *abri*) arbour (*Brit*), arbor (*US*), bower; (*Archit*) barrel vault ◆ **il dormait sous la ~** he was sleeping in the arbour

tonnellerie /tɔnɛlʀi/ NF cooperage

tonner /tɔne/ ▸ conjug 1 ◂ VI [1] [*canons, artillerie*] to thunder, to boom, to roar [2] [*personne*] to thunder, to rage, to inveigh (*contre* against) VB IMPERS to thunder ◆ **il tonne** it's thundering ◆ **il a tonné vers 2 heures** there was some thunder about 2 o'clock ◆ **il tonnait sans discontinuer** the thunder rumbled continuously

tonnerre /tɔnɛʀ/ NM [1] (= *détonation*) thunder; († = *foudre*) thunderbolt ◆ **j'entends le ~ qui gronde** I can hear thunder ◆ **coup de ~** thunderbolt ◆ **comme un coup de ~ dans un ciel serein** *ou* **bleu** (*fig*) like a bolt from the blue ◆ **un bruit/une voix de ~** a noise/a voice like thunder, a thunderous noise/voice ◆ **un ~ d'applaudissements** thunderous applause ◆ **le ~ des canons** the roar *ou* the thundering of the guns

[2] (* : *valeur intensive*) **du ~** terrific *, fantastic * ◆ **ça marchait du ~** it was going great guns * *ou* tremendously well ◆ **un livre du ~ de Dieu** ‡ one *ou* a hell of a book ‡, a fantastic book *

EXCL ◆ **~ !** * † ye gods! * † ◆ **mille ~s !** *, **~ de Brest !** * shiver me timbers! * † (*aussi hum*) ◆ **~ de Dieu !** ‡ hell and damnation! ‡, hell's bells! *

tonsure /tɔ̃syʀ/ NF (*Rel*) tonsure; (* = *calvitie*) bald spot *ou* patch ◆ **porter la ~** to wear the tonsure

tonsuré, e /tɔ̃syʀe/ (ptp de **tonsurer**) ADJ tonsured NM (*péj* = *moine*) monk

tonsurer /tɔ̃syʀe/ ▸ conjug 1 ◂ VT to tonsure

tonte /tɔ̃t/ NF 1 (= action) [de moutons] shearing; [de haie] clipping; [de gazon] mowing 2 (= laine) fleece 3 (= époque) shearing-time

tontine /tɔ̃tin/ NF (Fin, Jur) tontine

tonton /tɔ̃tɔ̃/ NM (langage enfantin) uncle

tonus /tɔnys/ NM 1 (Physiol) tone, tonus (SPÉC) ◆ **~ musculaire** muscle tone, muscular tonus (SPÉC) ◆ **~ nerveux** nerve tone 2 (= dynamisme) energy, dynamism; (au travail) drive ◆ **redonner du ~ à l'économie** to give the economy a boost ◆ **ce shampoing donnera du ~ à vos cheveux** this shampoo will put new life into your hair

toon* /tun/ NM cartoon character

top /tɔp/ NM 1 (= signal électrique) beep ◆ **au 4e ~ il sera midi** (Radio) at the 4th stroke it will be twelve o'clock 2 (Courses) **donner le ~ (de départ)** to give the starting signal ◆ **attention, ~, partez !** ou **~ départ !** on your marks, get set, go! 3 ◆ **~ 10/30** etc top 10 ou ten/30 ou thirty etc ◆ **le ~ 50** (Mus) the top 50 (singles), ≈ the singles charts ◆ **numéro un du ~ 50** number one in the charts 4 (* = le mieux) **c'est le (~ du) ~ !** it's the best! ◆ **être au ~** [athlète, chercheur] to be the best in one's field ◆ **être au ~ de sa forme** to be in tip-top condition ou shape, to be in great shape* ◆ **c'est ~*** (= c'est super) it's great!* ◆ **c'est pas ~*** it's nothing special
ADJ ◆ **~ secret** top secret ◆ **~ modèle** top model; [athlète, chercheur] ◆ **être au ~ niveau** to be at the top of one's field

topaze /tɔpaz/ NF topaz ◆ **~ brûlée** burnt topaz ADJ INV (= couleur) topaz ◆ **liquide ~** topaz-coloured liquid

toper /tɔpe/ ▸ conjug 1 ◂ VI ◆ **tope-là!, topez-là!** let's shake on it!, done!, you're on!*, it's a deal!*

topiaire /tɔpjɛʀ/ ADJ, NF ◆ **(art) ~** topiary

topinambour /tɔpinɑ̃buʀ/ NM Jerusalem artichoke

topique /tɔpik/ ADJ (frm) [argument, explication] pertinent; [citation] apposite; [remède, médicament] topical, local NM (Méd) topical ou local remedy; (Philos) topic NF (Philos) topics

topless* /tɔplɛs/ ADJ [bar, serveuse] topless NM ◆ **faire du ~** to go topless

topo* /tɔpo/ NM (= exposé, rapport) rundown*; (péj = laïus) spiel* ◆ **faire un ~ sur qch** to give a rundown* on sth ◆ **c'est toujours le même ~** it's always the same old story* ◆ **tu vois un peu le ~ ?** get the picture?

topographe /tɔpɔgʀaf/ NM topographer

topographie /tɔpɔgʀafi/ NF (= technique) topography; (= configuration) layout, topography; † (= description) topographical description; (= croquis) topographical plan

topographique /tɔpɔgʀafik/ ADJ topographic(al)

topographiquement /tɔpɔgʀafikmɑ̃/ ADV topographically

topoguide /tɔpɔgid/ NM topographical guide

topologie /tɔpɔlɔʒi/ NF topology

topologique /tɔpɔlɔʒik/ ADJ topologic(al)

topométrie /tɔpɔmetʀi/ NF topometry

toponyme /tɔpɔnim/ NM place name, toponym (SPÉC)

toponymie /tɔpɔnimi/ NF (= étude) toponymy (SPÉC), study of place names; (= noms de lieux) toponymy (SPÉC), place names

toponymique /tɔpɔnimik/ ADJ toponymic

toquade /tɔkad/ NF (péj) (pour qn) infatuation, crush*; (pour qch) fad, craze ◆ **avoir une ~ pour qn** to have a crush on sb*, to be infatuated with sb

toquante* /tɔkɑ̃t/ NF ⇒ **tocante**

toquard, e* /tɔkaʀ, aʀd/ ADJ, NM ⇒ **tocard, e**

toque /tɔk/ NF (en fourrure) fur hat; [de juge, jockey] cap ◆ **~ de cuisinier** chef's hat ◆ **l'une des ~s les plus renommées** (= chef cuisinier) one of the most famous chefs

toqué, e* /tɔke/ ADJ crazy*, cracked*, nuts* (attrib) ◆ **être ~ de qn** to be crazy ou mad ou nuts about sb* NM,F loony*, nutcase*, nutter* (Brit)

toquer* /tɔke/ ▸ conjug 1 ◂ VI to tap, to rap ◆ **~ (à la porte)** to tap ou rap at the door

toquer (se)* /tɔke/ ▸ conjug 1 ◂ VPR ◆ **se ~ de qn** to lose one's head over sb, to go crazy over sb* ◆ **se ~ de qch** to go crazy over sth

Tor /tɔʀ/ NM ⇒ **Thor**

Torah /tɔʀa/ NF ⇒ **Thora**

torche /tɔʀʃ/ NF 1 (= flambeau) torch ◆ **~ électrique** (electric) torch (Brit), flashlight (US) ◆ **être transformé en ~ vivante** to be turned into a human torch ◆ **se mettre en ~** (Parachutisme) to candle 2 (Ind = torchère) flare

torcher /tɔʀʃe/ ▸ conjug 1 ◂ VT 1* [+ assiette] to wipe (clean); [+ jus] to mop up 2* [+ derrière] to wipe ◆ **~ un bébé** to wipe a baby's bottom 3 (péj) [+ travail, rapport] (= produire) to toss off; (= bâcler) to make a mess of, to botch (up) ◆ **rapport/article bien torché** well-written report/article VPR **se torcher*** 1 (= s'essuyer) **se ~ (les fesses)** to wipe one's bottom 2 (= boire) **il s'est torché la bouteille de vodka** he polished off* ou downed* the bottle of vodka ◆ **il était complètement torché** (= saoul) he was completely pissed* (Brit) ou wasted* (US)

torchère /tɔʀʃɛʀ/ NF 1 [d'installation pétrolière] flare 2 (= candélabre) torchère; (= chandelier) candelabrum; (= vase) cresset

torchis /tɔʀʃi/ NM cob (for walls)

torchon /tɔʀʃɔ̃/ NM 1 (gén) cloth; (pour épousseter) duster (Brit), dustcloth (US); (à vaisselle) tea towel, dish towel ◆ **coup de ~** (= bagarre) scrap; (= épuration) clear-out ◆ **donner un coup de ~** (ménage) to give a room a dust, to flick a duster over a room; (vaisselle) to give the dishes a wipe; (épuration) to have a clear-out ◆ **le ~ brûle** (fig) there's a running battle (going on) (entre between) → **mélanger** 2 (péj) (= devoir mal présenté) mess; (= écrit sans valeur) drivel (NonC), tripe* (NonC); (= mauvais journal) rag ◆ **ce devoir est un ~** this homework is a mess

torchonner* /tɔʀʃɔne/ ▸ conjug 1 ◂ VT (péj) [+ travail] to do a rushed job on ◆ **un devoir torchonné** a slipshod ou badly done piece of homework

tordant, e* /tɔʀdɑ̃, ɑ̃t/ ADJ hilarious ◆ **il est ~** he's a scream*

tord-boyaux* † /tɔʀbwajo/ NM INV rotgut*, hooch* (US)

tordre /tɔʀdʀ/ ▸ conjug 41 ◂ VT 1 (entre ses mains) to wring; (pour essorer) to wring (out); [+ tresses] to wind; [+ brins, laine] to twist; [+ bras, poignet] to twist ◆ **"ne pas tordre"** (sur étiquette) "do not wring" ◆ **sa robe était à ~** (très mouillée) her dress was wringing wet ◆ **~ le cou à un poulet** to wring a chicken's neck ◆ **je vais lui ~ le cou*** I'll wring his neck (for him) ◆ **~ le cou à une rumeur** to put an end to ou kill a rumour ◆ **cet alcool vous tord les boyaux*** this stuff is real rot-gut* ◆ **la peur lui tordait l'estomac** his stomach was churning with fear
2 (= plier) [+ barre de fer] to twist; [+ cuiller, branche de lunette] to bend
3 (= déformer) [+ traits, visage] to contort, to twist ◆ **une joie sadique lui tordait la bouche** his mouth was twisted into a sadistic leer ◆ **la colère lui tordait le visage** his face was twisted ou contorted with anger ◆ **~ le nez (devant qch)*** to screw up one's face in disgust (at sth)
VPR **se tordre** 1 [personne] **se ~ de douleur** to be doubled up with pain ◆ **se ~ (de rire)** to be doubled up ou creased up (Brit) with laughter ◆ **c'est à se ~ (de rire) !** it's hilarious! ◆ **ça les a fait se ~ de rire** it had them in stitches* ◆ **mon estomac se tord** I've got a terrible pain in my stomach
2 [barre, poteau] to bend; [roue] to buckle, to twist; (littér) [racine, tronc] to twist round, to writhe (littér)
3 (= se faire mal à) **se ~ le pied/le poignet/la cheville** to twist one's foot/one's wrist/one's ankle ◆ **se ~ les mains (de désespoir)** to wring one's hands (in despair)

tordu, e /tɔʀdy/ (ptp de **tordre**) ADJ [nez] crooked; [jambes] bent, crooked; [tronc] twisted; [règle, barre] bent; [roue] bent, buckled, twisted; [idée] weird; [raisonnement] twisted ◆ **avoir l'esprit ~** to have a warped mind ◆ **être (complètement) ~*** to be off one's head*, to be round the bend* (Brit) ou the twist* (Brit) ◆ **il m'a fait un coup ~** he played a dirty trick on me NM,F * (= fou) loony*, nutcase*; (= crétin) twit*

tore /tɔʀ/ NM (Géom) torus; (Archit) torus, tore ◆ **~ magnétique** magnetic core ◆ **~ de ferrite** ferrite core

toréador /tɔʀeadɔʀ/ NM toreador

toréer /tɔʀee/ ▸ conjug 1 ◂ VI (ponctuellement) to fight ou work a bull; (habituellement) to be a bullfighter

torero /tɔʀeʀo/ NM bullfighter, torero

torgnole* /tɔʀɲɔl/ NF clout, wallop* ◆ **flanquer* une ~ à qn** to clout* ou wallop* sb

toril /tɔʀil/ NM bullpen

tornade /tɔʀnad/ NF tornado ◆ **entrer comme une ~** to come in like a whirlwind

toron /tɔʀɔ̃/ NM (= brin) strand

torpédo /tɔʀpedo/ NF † open tourer (Brit), open touring car (US)

torpeur /tɔʀpœʀ/ NF torpor ◆ **faire sortir** ou **tirer qn de sa ~** to bring sb out of his torpor

torpide /tɔʀpid/ ADJ (littér, Méd) torpid

torpillage /tɔʀpijaʒ/ NM (lit, fig) torpedoing

torpille /tɔʀpij/ NF 1 (Mil) (sous-marine) torpedo ◆ **~ (aérienne)** (= bombe) (aerial) torpedo 2 (= poisson) torpedo

torpiller /tɔʀpije/ ▸ conjug 1 ◂ VT (lit, fig) to torpedo

torpilleur /tɔʀpijœʀ/ NM torpedo boat

torréfacteur /tɔʀefaktœʀ/ NM 1 (= appareil) [de café, malt, cacao] roaster; [de tabac] toasting machine 2 (= commerçant) coffee merchant

torréfaction /tɔʀefaksjɔ̃/ NF [de café, malt, cacao] roasting; [de tabac] toasting

torréfier /tɔʀefje/ ▸ conjug 7 ◂ VT [+ café, malt, cacao] to roast; [+ tabac] to toast ◆ **café torréfié** roast(ed) coffee

torrent /tɔʀɑ̃/ NM 1 (= cours d'eau) stream; (tumultueux) torrent ◆ **~ de montagne** (fast-flowing) mountain stream, mountain torrent 2 (= écoulement rapide) **~ de lave** torrent ou flood of lava ◆ **~ de boue** torrent of mud ◆ **des ~s d'eau** (pluie) torrential rain; (inondation) torrents of water ◆ **il pleut à ~s** it's pouring 3 (= grande abondance) **un ~ de** [+ injures, paroles] a torrent ou stream ou flood of; [+ musique] a flood of ◆ **des ~s de** [+ fumée, lumière, larmes] streams of

torrentiel, -elle /tɔʀɑ̃sjɛl/ ADJ [eaux, régime, pluie] torrential

torride /tɔʀid/ ADJ 1 (= très chaud) [région, climat] torrid; [journée, chaleur] scorching, torrid 2 (= sensuel) [scène d'amour, ambiance] torrid

tors, torse[1] /tɔʀ, tɔʀs/ ADJ *[fil]* twisted; *[colonne]* wreathed; *[pied de verre]* twist *(épith)*; *[jambes]* crooked, bent NM *(Tech)* twist

torsade /tɔʀsad/ NF *[de fils]* twist; *(Archit)* cable moulding; *(Tricot)* cable-stitch ◆ ~ **de cheveux** twist *ou* coil of hair ◆ **en** ~ *[embrasse, cheveux]* twisted ◆ **colonne à ~s** cabled column ◆ **pull à ~s** cable(-knit *ou* -stitch) sweater; → **point²**

torsader /tɔʀsade/ ▸ conjug 1 ◂ VT *[+ frange, corde, cheveux]* to twist ◆ **colonne torsadée** cabled column ◆ **pull torsadé** cable(-knit *ou* -stitch) sweater

torse² /tɔʀs/ NM *(gén)* chest; *(Anat, Sculp)* torso ◆ ~ **nu** stripped to the waist, bare-chested ◆ **se mettre ~ nu** to strip to the waist; → **bomber¹**

torsion /tɔʀsjɔ̃/ NF *(= action)* twisting; *(Phys, Tech)* torsion ◆ **exercer sur qn une ~ du bras** to twist sb's arm back ◆ **moment de ~** torque; → **couple**

tort /tɔʀ/ GRAMMAIRE ACTIVE 29.2, 39.1, 41 NM 1 *(= action, attitude blâmable)* fault ◆ **il a un ~, c'est de trop parler** his one fault is that he talks too much ◆ **il a le ~ d'être trop jeune** the only trouble with him is that he's too young ◆ **il a eu le ~ d'être impoli avec le patron** he made the mistake of being rude to the boss ◆ **je n'ai eu qu'un seul ~, celui de t'écouter** the only mistake I made was to listen to you ◆ **ils ont tous les ~s de leur côté** the fault is entirely on their side, they are completely in the wrong ◆ **les ~s sont du côté du mari/cycliste** the fault lies with the husband/cyclist, the husband/cyclist is at fault ◆ **avoir des ~s envers qn** to have wronged sb ◆ **il n'a aucun ~** he's not at fault, he's in no way to blame ◆ **il a reconnu ses ~s** he acknowledged *ou* admitted that he had done something wrong ◆ **vous avez refusé ? c'est un ~** did you refuse? – you were wrong (to do that) *ou* you shouldn't have (done that) ◆ **tu ne le savais pas ? c'est un ~** you didn't know? – you should have *ou* that was a mistake *ou* that was unfortunate

2 *(= dommage, préjudice)* wrong ◆ **redresser un ~** to right a wrong ◆ **faire** *ou* **causer du ~ à qn, faire** *ou* **porter ~ à qn** † to harm sb, to do *ou* cause sb harm ◆ **ça ne fait de ~ à personne** it doesn't harm *ou* hurt anybody ◆ **il s'est fait du ~** he has harmed himself, he has done himself no good ◆ **cette mesure va faire du ~ aux produits laitiers** this measure will harm *ou* be harmful to *ou* be detrimental to the dairy industry ◆ **il ne me ferait pas ~ d'un centime** † he wouldn't do me out of a penny; → **redresseur**

3 *(locutions)*

◆ **avoir tort** to be wrong ◆ **il a ~ de se mettre en colère** he's wrong *ou* it's wrong of him to get angry ◆ **il n'a pas tout à fait ~ de dire que ...** he's not altogether *ou* entirely wrong in saying that ... ◆ **elle a grand** *ou* **bien ~ de le croire** she's very wrong to believe it ◆ **tu aurais bien ~ de ne pas le faire !** you'd be quite wrong not to do it! ◆ **on aurait ~ de croire que ...** it would be wrong to think *ou* believe that ...

◆ **donner tort à qn** *(= blâmer)* to lay the blame on sb, to blame sb; *(= ne pas être d'accord avec)* to disagree with sb ◆ **les statistiques donnent ~ à son rapport** statistics show *ou* prove his report to be wrong *ou* inaccurate ◆ **les événements lui ont donné ~** events proved him wrong *ou* showed that he was wrong

◆ **à tort** wrongly ◆ **soupçonner/accuser qn à ~** to suspect/accuse sb wrongly ◆ **c'est à ~ qu'on l'avait dit malade** he was wrongly *ou* mistakenly said to be ill

◆ **à tort ou à raison** rightly or wrongly

◆ **à tort et à travers** ◆ **dépenser à ~ et à travers** to spend wildly, to spend money like water ◆ **il parle à ~ et à travers** he talks a lot of rubbish*

◆ **dans+ tort** ◆ **être/se mettre/se sentir dans son ~** to be/put o.s./feel o.s. in the wrong ◆ **il venait de ma droite, j'étais dans mon ~** *[automobiliste]* he was coming from the right, I was at fault ◆ **mettre qn dans son ~** to put sb in the wrong

◆ **en tort** ◆ **être en ~** to be in the wrong *ou* at fault

torticolis /tɔʀtikɔli/ NM stiff neck, torticollis *(SPÉC)* ◆ **avoir/attraper un ~** to have/get a stiff neck

tortillard /tɔʀtijaʀ/ NM *(hum péj = train)* local train

tortillement /tɔʀtijmɑ̃/ NM *[de serpent]* writhing; *[de ver]* wriggling, squirming; *[de personne] (en dansant, en se débattant etc)* wriggling; *(d'impatience)* fidgeting, wriggling; *(d'embarras, de douleur)* squirming ◆ **elle marchait avec un léger ~ des hanches** she wiggled her hips slightly as she walked

tortiller /tɔʀtije/ ▸ conjug 1 ◂ VT *[+ corde, mouchoir]* to twist; *[+ cheveux, cravate]* to twiddle (with); *[+ moustache]* to twirl; *[+ doigts]* to twiddle ◆ **il tortillait son chapeau entre ses mains** he was fiddling with his hat VI 1 *(= remuer)* ~ **des hanches** to wiggle one's hips ◆ ~ **des fesses** *ou* **du derrière*** to wiggle one's bottom 2 *(* = tergiverser)* **il n'y a pas à ~** there's no wriggling out of it VPR **se tortiller** 1 *[serpent]* to writhe; *[ver]* to wriggle, to squirm; *[personne] (en dansant, en se débattant etc)* to wiggle; *(d'impatience)* to fidget, to wriggle; *(d'embarras, de douleur)* to squirm ◆ **se ~ comme une anguille** *ou* **un ver** to wriggle like a worm *ou* an eel, to squirm like an eel 2 *[fumée]* to curl upwards; *[racine, tige]* to curl, to writhe

tortillon /tɔʀtijɔ̃/ NM 1 *(Dessin)* stump, tortillon 2 ◆ ~ **(de papier)** twist (of paper)

tortionnaire /tɔʀsjɔnɛʀ/ NM, ADJ torturer ◆ **les militaires ~s seront jugés** the army torturers will be taken to court

tortue /tɔʀty/ NF 1 *(= animal) (terrestre)* tortoise ◆ ~ **d'eau douce** terrapin ◆ ~ **marine** *ou* **de mer** turtle; → **île** 2 *(= personne lente)* slowcoach *(Brit)*, slowpoke *(US)* ◆ **avancer comme une ~** to crawl along at a snail's pace 3 *(Hist Mil)* testudo, tortoise

tortueux, -euse /tɔʀtɥø, øz/ ADJ 1 *(= sinueux) [chemin, escalier]* winding, twisting; *[rivière]* winding 2 *(péj) [esprit]* tortuous; *[langage, discours, raisonnement]* tortuous, convoluted; *[manœuvres, conduite]* devious

torturant, e /tɔʀtyʀɑ̃, ɑ̃t/ ADJ agonizing

torture /tɔʀtyʀ/ NF *(lit)* torture *(NonC)*; *(fig)* torture *(NonC)*, torment ◆ **c'est une ~ atroce** it's an appalling form *ou* kind of torture ◆ **instruments de ~** instruments of torture ◆ **chambre** *ou* **salle de(s) ~s** torture chamber ◆ **sous la ~** under torture ◆ **cette attente fut pour elle une véritable ~** it was real torture for her to wait around like that ◆ **mettre qn à la ~** *(fig)* to torture sb, to make sb suffer

torturer /tɔʀtyʀe/ ▸ conjug 1 ◂ VT 1 *(lit) [+ prisonnier, animal]* to torture ◆ **le doute/la crainte/le remords le torturait** he was racked with *ou* by doubt/fear/remorse ◆ **la faim le torturait** hunger was gnawing at his belly ◆ **cette pensée le torturait** he was tormented by the thought 2 *(littér = dénaturer) [+ texte]* to distort, to torture *(littér)* ◆ **son visage était torturé par le chagrin** his face was twisted *ou* racked with grief ◆ **sa poésie torturée, déchirante** his tormented, heartrending poetry ◆ **c'est quelqu'un d'assez torturé** he's a tormented soul VPR **se torturer** *(= se faire du souci)* to fret, to worry o.s. sick *(pour* over); ◆ **se ~ le cerveau** *ou* **l'esprit** to rack *ou* cudgel one's brains

torve /tɔʀv/ ADJ *[regard œil]* menacing, grim

tory (pl **tories** *ou* **torys**) /tɔʀi/ ADJ, NM Tory

toscan, e /tɔskɑ̃, an/ ADJ Tuscan NM *(= dialecte)* Tuscan

Toscane /tɔskan/ NF Tuscany

tôt /to/ ADV 1 *(= de bonne heure)* early ◆ **se lever/se coucher (très) ~** to get up/go to bed (very) early ◆ **il se lève ~** he's an early riser, he gets up early ◆ **il arrive toujours ~ le jeudi** he's always early on Thursdays ◆ **venez ~ dans la matinée/soirée** come early (on) in the morning/evening *ou* in the early morning/evening ◆ ~ **dans l'année** early (on) in the year, in the early part of the year ◆ ~ **le matin, il n'est pas très lucide** he's not very clear-headed first thing (in the morning) *ou* early in the morning ◆ **il n'est pas si ~ que je croyais** it's not as early as I thought ◆ **Pâques tombe ~ cette année** Easter falls early this year; → **avenir¹**

2 *(= avant un moment déterminé, habituel ou prévu)* soon, early ◆ **il est un peu (trop) ~ pour le juger** it's a little too soon *ou* early to judge him ◆ **si tu étais venu une heure plus ~, tu l'aurais rencontré** if you'd come an hour sooner *ou* earlier you would have met him ◆ **elle m'avait téléphoné une semaine plus ~** she'd called me a week earlier ◆ **ce n'est pas trop ~ !** and about time too!*

3 *(= vite)* soon, early ◆ **si seulement vous me l'aviez dit plus ~ !** if only you'd told me sooner! *ou* earlier! ◆ **il n'était pas plus ~ parti que la voiture est tombée en panne** no sooner had he set off *ou* he had no sooner set off than the car broke down ◆ **venez le plus ~ possible** come as early *ou* as soon as you can ◆ **le plus ~ sera le mieux** the sooner the better ◆ **je ne m'attendais pas à le revoir si ~** I didn't expect to see him (again) so soon ◆ **cette soirée, je ne l'oublierai pas de si ~ !** I won't forget that party in a hurry! ◆ **une occasion pareille ne se représentera pas de si ~** you don't get an opportunity like that every day

4 *(locutions)*

◆ **avoir tôt fait de** + *infinitif* ◆ **il a eu ~ fait de s'en apercevoir !** he was quick *ou* it didn't take him long to notice it!, it wasn't long before he noticed it! ◆ **il aura ~ fait de s'en apercevoir !** it won't be long before he notices it!, it won't take him long to notice it!

◆ **au plus tôt** ◆ **il peut venir jeudi au plus ~** Thursday is the earliest *ou* soonest he can come ◆ **c'est au plus ~ en mai qu'il prendra la décision** it'll be May at the earliest that he takes *ou* he'll take the decision, he'll decide in May at the earliest ◆ **il faut qu'il vienne au plus ~** he must come as soon as possible *ou* as soon as he possibly can

◆ **tôt ou tard** sooner or later

total, e (mpl **-aux**) /tɔtal, o/ ADJ 1 *(= complet) (gén)* total, complete; *[contrôle]* complete; *[ruine, désespoir]* utter *(épith)*, total ◆ **grève ~e** all-out strike ◆ **l'arrêt ~ des hostilités** the complete *ou* total cessation of hostilities ◆ **dans la confusion la plus ~e** in utter *ou* total confusion; → **guerre**

2 *(= global) [hauteur, coût, revenu]* total ◆ **la somme ~e est plus élevée que nous ne pensions** the total (sum *ou* amount) is higher than we thought ◆ **la longueur ~e de la voiture** the overall length of the car

ADV ◆ ~, **il a tout perdu** the net result *ou* outcome was that he lost everything

NM *(= quantité)* total (number); *(= résultat)* total ◆ **le ~ s'élève à 25 €** the total amounts to €25 ◆ **le ~ de la population** the total (number of the) population ◆ ~ **général** *(Fin)* grand total ◆ **faire le ~** to work out the total ◆ **si on fait le ~, ils n'ont pas réalisé grand-chose** *(fig)* if you add it all up *ou* together they didn't achieve very much

◆ **au total** *(dans un compte)* in total; *(= finalement)* all things considered, all in all

NF totale * 1 *(Méd)* (total) hysterectomy ◆ **on lui a fait la ~e** she had her works out‡

2 ◆ **la ~e** *(= tout ce qu'on peut imaginer)* the works* ◆ **alors là, c'est la ~e !** *(= le comble)* that's the last straw!

totalement /tɔtalmɑ̃/ ADV totally

totalisateur, -trice /tɔtalizatœʀ, tʀis/ ADJ *[appareil, machine]* adding *(épith)* NM adding machine; *(Ordin)* accumulator ◆ **~ kilométrique** *[de véhicule]* kilometre counter ≈ mileometer

totalisation /tɔtalizasjɔ̃/ NF adding up, addition

totaliser /tɔtalize/ ► conjug 1 ◄ VT 1 *(= additionner)* to add up, to total, to totalize 2 *(= avoir au total)* to total, to have a total of ◆ **à eux deux ils totalisent 60 ans de service** between the two of them they have a total of 60 years' service *ou* they total 60 years' service ◆ **le candidat qui totalise le plus grand nombre de points** the candidate with the highest total *ou* who gets the highest number of points

totalitaire /tɔtalitɛʀ/ ADJ *(Pol) [régime]* totalitarian; *(Philos) [conception]* all-embracing, global

totalitarisme /tɔtalitaʀism/ NM totalitarianism

totalité /tɔtalite/ NF 1 *(gén)* **la ~ de** all of ◆ **la ~ du sable/des livres** all (of) the sand/the books ◆ **la ~ du livre/de la population** all the book/the population, the whole *ou* entire book/population ◆ **la ~ de son salaire** his whole *ou* entire salary, all of his salary ◆ **la ~ de ses biens** all of his possessions ◆ **vendu en ~ aux États-Unis** all sold to the USA ◆ **édité en ~ par Dubosc** published entirely by Dubosc ◆ **pris dans sa ~** taken as a whole *ou* in its entirety ◆ **j'en connais la quasi-~** I know virtually all of them *ou* just about all of them ◆ **la presque ~ de la population** almost the entire population 2 *(Philos)* totality

totem /tɔtɛm/ NM *(gén)* totem; *(= poteau)* totem pole

totémique /tɔtemik/ ADJ totemic

totémisme /tɔtemism/ NM totemism

toto‡ /toto/ NM *(= pou)* louse, cootie* *(US)*

totoche * /tɔtɔʃ/ NF *(= tétine)* dummy

toton /tɔtɔ̃/ NM teetotum

touage /twaʒ/ NM *(Naut)* warping, kedging

touareg, -ègue /twaʀɛg/ ADJ Tuareg NM *(= langue)* Tuareg NM,F **Touareg, Touarègue** Tuareg

toubib * /tubib/ NM doctor ◆ **elle est ~** she's a doctor ◆ **aller chez le ~** to go and see the doctor

toucan /tukɑ̃/ NM toucan

touchant[1] /tuʃɑ̃/ PRÉP *(= au sujet de)* concerning, with regard to, about

touchant[2]**, e** /tuʃɑ̃, ɑ̃t/ ADJ *(= émouvant) [histoire, lettre, situation, adieux]* touching, moving; *(= attendrissant) [geste, reconnaissance, enthousiasme]* touching ◆ **~ de naïveté/d'ignorance** touchingly naïve/ignorant

touche /tuʃ/ NF 1 *[de piano, ordinateur]* key; *[de téléphone, télécommande, lave-vaisselle]* button; *[d'instrument à corde]* fingerboard; *[de guitare]* fret ◆ **~ de fonction/programmable** *(Ordin)* function/user-defined key ◆ **~ bis** *(Téléc)* redial button

2 *(Peinture) (= tache de couleur)* touch, stroke; *(= style) [de peintre, écrivain]* touch ◆ **finesse de ~ d'un peintre/auteur** deftness of touch of a painter/an author ◆ **une ~ exotique** an exotic touch ◆ **une ~ de gaieté** a touch *ou* note of gaiety ◆ **avec une ~ d'humour** with a hint *ou* suggestion *ou* touch of humour ◆ **mettre la dernière ~** *ou* **la ~ finale à qch** to put the finishing touches to sth ◆ **par petites ~** *(= petit à petit)* little by little ◆ **il procède par petites ~s** *[peintre]* he dabs the paint on gradually ◆ **appliquez la crème par petites ~s** dab the cream on

3 *(Pêche)* bite ◆ **avoir** *ou* **faire une ~** *(lit)* to get a bite ◆ **faire une ~** * *(= séduire)* to make a hit* ◆ **avoir la ~** *, **avoir fait une ~** * to have made a hit* *(avec* with)

4 *(Escrime)* hit, touch

5 *(Sport) (= sortie)* touch; *(= ligne)* touchline; *(= remise en jeu) (Ftbl, Hand-ball)* throw-in; *(Rugby)* line-out; *(Basket)* return to play; *(Hockey)* roll-in ◆ **botter en ~** to kick into touch ◆ **envoyer** *ou* **mettre la balle en ~** to kick the ball into touch ◆ **le ballon est sorti en ~** the ball has gone into touch ◆ **coup de pied en ~** kick to touch ◆ **jouer la ~** *(Ftbl)* to play for time *(by putting the ball repeatedly into touch)* ◆ **il a trouvé la ~** *(Rugby)* he found touch ◆ **rester sur la ~** *(lit)* to stay on the bench ◆ **être mis/rester sur la ~** *(fig)* to be put/stay on the sidelines; → **juge**

6 *(* = allure)* look, appearance ◆ **quelle drôle de ~ !** what a sight!*, what does he *(ou* she *etc)* look like!* ◆ **il a une de ces ~s !** you should see the way he dresses! ◆ **il a la ~ de quelqu'un qui sort de prison** he looks as though he's just out of prison; → **pierre**

touche-à-tout /tuʃatu/ NMF INV, ADJ INV ◆ **c'est un ~, il est ~** *(= enfant)* his little fingers are *ou* he's into everything; *(= dilettante)* he dabbles in everything

touche-pipi * /tuʃpipi/ NM INV ◆ **jouer à ~** *[enfants]* to play doctors and nurses; *[adultes]* to pet*, to make out‡ *(US)*

toucher[1] /tuʃe/ ► conjug 1 ◄ VT 1 *(pour sentir, prendre, gén)* to touch; *(pour palper) [+ fruits, tissu, enflure]* to feel ◆ **il me toucha l'épaule** he touched my shoulder ◆ **"prière de ne pas toucher"** "please do not touch" ◆ **pas touche !*** hands off!* ◆ **il n'a pas touché un verre de vin depuis son accident** he hasn't touched a drop of wine since his accident ◆ **je n'avais pas touché une raquette/touché une carte depuis 6 mois** I hadn't picked up a racket/touched a pack of cards for 6 months ◆ **~ la main à qn** *(fig)* to give sb a quick handshake; → **bois, doigt**

2 *(= entrer en contact avec)* to touch ◆ **il ne faut pas que ça touche (le mur/le plafond)** it mustn't touch (the wall/the ceiling) ◆ **il lui fit ~ le sol des épaules** *(Lutte)* he got his shoulders down on the floor ◆ **l'avion toucha le sol** the plane touched down *ou* landed ◆ **au football on ne doit pas ~ le ballon (de la main)** in football you mustn't touch the ball (with your hand) *ou* you mustn't handle the ball; → **fond, terre**

3 *(= être physiquement proche de)* to adjoin ◆ **son jardin touche le nôtre** his garden (ad-) joins ours *ou* is adjacent to ours

4 *(= atteindre) (lit, fig) [+ adversaire, objectif]* to hit ◆ **il l'a touché au menton/foie** *(Boxe)* he hit him on the chin/in the stomach ◆ **il s'affaissa, touché d'une balle en plein cœur** he slumped to the ground, hit by a bullet in the heart ◆ **deux immeubles ont été touchés par l'explosion** two buildings have been hit *ou* damaged by the explosion ◆ **touché !** *(Escrime)* touché!; *(bataille navale)* hit! ◆ **il n'a pas touché une balle pendant ce match** he didn't hit a single ball throughout the match ◆ **il voudrait ~ un public plus large** *(fig)* he'd like to reach a wider audience

5 *(= contacter)* to reach, to get in touch with, to contact ◆ **où peut-on le ~ par téléphone ?** where can he be reached *ou* contacted by phone?, where can one get in touch with him by phone?

6 *(= recevoir) [+ prime, allocation, traitement]* to receive, to get; *[+ chèque]* to cash; *(Mil) [+ ration, équipement]* to draw; *(Scol) [+ fournitures]* to receive, to get ◆ **~ le tiercé/le gros lot** to win the tiercé/the jackpot ◆ **~ le chômage** * to be on the dole* ◆ **il touche une petite retraite** he gets a small pension ◆ **il touche sa pension le 10 du mois** he draws *ou* gets his pension on the 10th of the month ◆ **il est allé à la poste ~ sa pension** he went to draw (out) *ou* collect his pension at the post office ◆ **à partir du mois prochain, ils toucheront 150 € par mois** as from next month they'll get *ou* they'll be paid €150 a month ◆ **il a fini le travail mais n'a encore rien touché** he's finished the work but he hasn't been paid yet

7 *(= émouvoir) [drame, deuil]* to affect, to shake; *[scène attendrissante]* to touch, to move; *[critique, reproche]* to have an effect on ◆ **cette tragédie les a beaucoup touchés** this tragedy affected them greatly *ou* has shaken them very badly ◆ **rien ne le touche** there is nothing that can move him ◆ **votre cadeau/geste nous a vivement touchés** we were deeply touched by your gift/gesture; → **corde, vif**

8 *(= concerner)* to affect; *[affaire]* to concern ◆ **ce problème ne nous touche pas** this problem doesn't affect *ou* concern us ◆ **le chômage touche surtout les jeunes** unemployment affects the young especially ◆ **ils n'ont pas été touchés par la dévaluation** they haven't been affected *ou* hit by devaluation ◆ **une personne qui vous touche de près** someone close to you

9 *(= faire escale à) [+ port]* to put in at, to call at, to touch

VT INDIR toucher à 1 *[+ objet dangereux, drogue]* to touch; *[+ capital, économies]* to break into, to touch ◆ **n'y touche pas !** don't touch! ◆ **"prière de ne pas toucher aux objets exposés"** "please do not touch the exhibits", "kindly refrain from handling the exhibits" ◆ **~ à tout** *[enfant]* to touch everything, to fiddle with everything; *(fig) [amateur curieux]* to try one's hand at everything ◆ **elle n'a pas touché à son déjeuner/au fromage** she didn't touch her lunch/the cheese ◆ **on n'a pas touché au fromage** we haven't touched the cheese, the cheese hasn't been touched ◆ **il n'a jamais touché à un fusil** he's never handled a gun

2 *(= malmener) [+ personne]* to touch, to lay a finger on; *(= porter atteinte à) [+ réputation, légende]* to question ◆ **s'il touche à cet enfant/à ma sœur, gare à lui !** if he lays a finger on *ou* touches that child/my sister, he'd better watch out! ◆ **touche pas à ma bagnole !*** hands off my car! ◆ **~ aux intérêts d'un pays** *(Pol)* to interfere with a country's interests ◆ **la réforme touche au statut des salariés/au principe du droit d'asile** the reform affects the status of employees/the right of asylum

3 *(= modifier) [+ règlement, loi, tradition]* to meddle with; *[+ mécanisme]* to tamper with; *[+ monument, site classé]* to touch ◆ **quelqu'un a touché au moteur** someone has tampered with the engine ◆ **on peut rénover sans ~ à la façade** it's possible to renovate without touching the façade *ou* interfering with the façade ◆ **c'est parfait, n'y touche pas** it's perfect, don't change a thing

4 *(= concerner) [+ intérêts]* to affect; *[+ problème, domaine]* to touch, to have to do with ◆ **tout ce qui touche à l'enseignement** everything connected with *ou* to do with teaching

5 *(= aborder) [+ période, but]* to near, to approach; *[+ sujet, question]* to broach, to come onto ◆ **je touche ici à un problème d'ordre très général** here I am coming onto *ou* broaching a problem of a very general nature ◆ **vous touchez là à une question délicate** that is a very delicate matter you have raised *ou* broached ◆ **nous touchons au but** we're nearing our goal, our goal is in sight ◆ **l'hiver/la guerre touche à sa fin** *ou* **son terme** winter/the war is nearing its end *ou* is drawing to a

close ◆ ~ **au port** *(fig, littér)* to be within sight of home; → **air²**

6 *(= être en contact avec)* to touch; *(= être contigu à)* to border on, to adjoin; *(= confiner à)* to verge on, to border on ◆ **le jardin touche à la forêt** the garden adjoins the forest *ou* borders on the forest ◆ **cela touche à la folie/pornographie** that verges *ou* borders on madness/pornography

VPR **se toucher** 1 *(mutuellement)* to touch ◆ **leurs mains se touchèrent** their hands touched ◆ **les deux lignes se touchent** the two lines touch ◆ **nos deux jardins se touchent** our two gardens are adjacent (to each other) ◆ **les deux villes se sont tellement développées qu'elles se touchent presque** the two towns have been developed to such an extent that they almost meet ◆ **ils ont passé une nuit ensemble sans se** ~ they spent the night together without touching each other

2 ◆ **il se toucha le front** *(lit)* he touched his forehead; *(pour indiquer que qn est fou)* he screwed a finger against his temple

3 *(*, euph = se masturber)* to play with* *ou* touch o.s.

toucher² /tuʃe/ NM 1 *(= sens)* (sense of) touch 2 *(= action, manière de toucher)* touch; *(= impression produite)* feel ◆ **doux au** ~ soft to the touch ◆ **cela a le** ~ **de la soie** it feels like silk, it has the feel of silk ◆ **s'habituer à reconnaître les objets au** ~ to become used to recognizing objects by touch *ou* feel(ing) ◆ **on reconnaît la soie au** ~ you can tell silk by the feel of it 3 *(Mus)* touch 4 *(Méd)* (internal) examination ◆ ~ **rectal/vaginal** rectal/vaginal examination 5 *(Sport)* **avoir un bon** ~ **de balle** to have a nice touch

touche-touche * /tuʃtuʃ/ ADV *[trains, voitures]* ◆ **être à** ~ to be nose to tail

toucouleur /tukulœʀ/ ADJ Toucouleur, Tukulor NMF **Toucouleur** member of the Toucouleur *ou* Tukulor people

touée /twe/ NF *(Naut)* *(= câble)* warp, cable; *(= longueur de chaîne)* scope

touer /twe/ ► conjug 1 ◄ VT *(Naut)* to warp, to kedge

toueur /twœʀ/ NM warping tug

touffe /tuf/ NF *[d'herbe]* tuft, clump; *[d'arbres, buissons]* clump; *[de cheveux, poils]* tuft; *[de fleurs]* cluster, clump (de of) ◆ ~ **de lavande** lavender bush, clump of lavender

touffeur † /tufœʀ/ NF *(littér)* suffocating *ou* sweltering heat (NonC)

touffu, e /tufy/ ADJ 1 *(= épais)* *[barbe, sourcils]* bushy; *[arbres]* with thick *ou* dense foliage; *[haie]* thick, bushy; *[bois, maquis, végétation]* dense, thick 2 *[roman, style]* dense

touillage * /tujaʒ/ NM stirring

touiller * /tuje/ ► conjug 1 ◄ VT *[+ sauce, café]* to stir; *[+ salade]* to toss

touillette * /tujɛt/ NF stirrer

toujours /tuʒuʀ/ ADV 1 *(= tout le temps)* always; *(péj = sempiternellement)* forever, always, all the time ◆ **je l'avais** ~ **cru célibataire** I (had) always thought he was a bachelor ◆ **je t'aimerai** ~ I'll always love you, I'll love you forever ◆ **je déteste et détesterai** ~ **l'avion** I hate flying and always will ◆ **la vie se déroule** ~ **pareille** life goes on the same as ever ◆ **il est** ~ **à*** *ou* **en train de critiquer** he's always *ou* forever criticizing ◆ **cette rue est** ~ **encombrée** this street is always *ou* constantly jammed with traffic ◆ **les saisons** ~ **pareilles** the never-changing seasons ◆ **il n'est pas** ~ **très ponctuel** he's not always very punctual ◆ **il est** ~ **à l'heure** he's always *ou* invariably on time ◆ **il fut** ~ **modeste** he was always *ou* ever *(littér)* modest ◆ **les journaux sont** ~ **plus pessimistes** the newspapers are more and more pessimistic ◆ **les jeunes veulent** ~ **plus d'indépendance** young people want more and more *ou* still more independence ◆ **comme** ~ as ever, as always ◆ **ce sont des amis de** ~ they are lifelong friends ◆ **il est parti pour** ~ he's gone forever *ou* for good ◆ **presque** ~ almost always; → **depuis**

2 *(= encore)* still ◆ **bien qu'à la retraite il travaillait** ~ although he had retired he was still working *ou* he had kept on working ◆ **j'espère** ~ **qu'elle viendra** I keep hoping *ou* I'm still hoping she'll come ◆ **ils n'ont** ~ **pas répondu** they still haven't replied ◆ **est-ce que Paul est rentré ? – non il est** ~ **à Paris/non** ~ **pas** is Paul back? – no, he's still in Paris/no not yet *ou* no he's still not back ◆ **il est** ~ **le même/**~ **aussi désagréable** he's (still) the same as ever/(still) as unpleasant as ever

3 *(intensif)* anyway, anyhow ◆ **écrivez** ~, **il vous répondra peut-être** write anyway *ou* anyhow *ou* you may as well write – he (just) might answer you ◆ **il vient** ~ **un moment où** ... there must *ou* will come a time when ... ◆ **buvez** ~ **un verre avant de partir** at least have a drink before you go ◆ **c'est** ~ **pas toi qui l'auras*** at any rate it won't be you that gets it* ◆ **où est-elle ? – pas chez moi** ~ **!** where is she? – not at my place anyway! *ou* at any rate! ◆ **je trouverai** ~ **(bien) une excuse** I can always think up an excuse ◆ **passez à la gare, vous aurez** ~ **bien un train** go (along) to the station – you're sure *ou* bound to get a train *ou* there's bound to be a train ◆ **tu peux** ~ **courir !*** *ou* **te fouiller !**⁑ you haven't got a chance! *ou* a hope! *(Brit)* ◆ **il aime donner des conseils, mais** ~ **avec tact** he likes to give advice but he always does it tactfully ◆ **vous pouvez** ~ **crier, il n'y a personne** shout as much as you like *ou* shout by all means – there's no one about ◆ **il était peut-être là,** ~ **est-il que je ne l'ai pas vu** he may well have around, but the fact remains *ou* that doesn't alter the fact that I didn't see him ◆ **cette politique semblait raisonnable,** ~ **est-il qu'elle a échoué** the policy seemed reasonable but the fact remains it was a failure *ou* but it still failed ◆ **c'est** ~ **ça de pris*** that's something anyway, (well) at least that's something ◆ **ça peut** ~ **servir** it might come in handy some day; → **causer²**

toundra /tundʀa/ NF tundra

toupet /tupe/ NM 1 *[de cheveux]* tuft (of hair), quiff *(Brit)*; *(postiche)* toupee 2 *(* = culot)* nerve*, cheek* *(Brit)* ◆ **avoir du** ~ to have a nerve* *ou* a cheek* *(Brit)* ◆ **il avait le** ~ **de prétendre que** ... he had the nerve* *ou* cheek* *(Brit)* to make out that ... ◆ **il ne manque pas de** ~ **!** he's got a nerve!* *ou* cheek!* *(Brit)*

toupie /tupi/ NF 1 *(= jouet)* (spinning) top ◆ ~ **à musique** humming-top; → **tourner** 2 *(péj = femme désagréable)* **vieille** ~⁑ silly old trout⁑ 3 *(Tech)* *[de menuisier]* spindle moulding-machine; *[de plombier]* turn-pin; *(= bétonnière)* cement mixer

tour¹ /tuʀ/ NF 1 *(= édifice)* tower; *(Hist = machine de guerre)* siege tower; *(= immeuble très haut)* tower block, high-rise building; *(Ordin)* tower 2 *(Échecs)* castle, rook

COMP **la tour de Babel** the Tower of Babel ◆ **c'est une** ~ **de Babel** *(fig)* it's a real Tower of Babel

tour de contrôle control tower

la tour Eiffel the Eiffel Tower

tour de forage drilling rig, derrick

tour de guet watchtower, look-out tower

tour hertzienne radio mast

tour d'ivoire ivory tower ◆ **enfermé dans sa** *ou* **une** ~ **d'ivoire** shut away in an ivory tower

la tour de Londres the Tower of London

la tour de Pise the Leaning Tower of Pisa

tour² /tuʀ/

1 NOM MASCULIN — 2 COMPOSÉS

1 - NOM MASCULIN

1 [= parcours, exploration] ~ **de ville** *(pour touristes)* city tour ◆ **le** ~ **du parc prend bien une heure** it takes a good hour to walk around the park ◆ **si on faisait le** ~ **?** shall we go round (it)? *ou* walk round (it)? ◆ **faire un** ~ **d'Europe** to go on a European tour, to tour Europe ◆ **faire un** ~ **d'Europe en auto-stop** to hitch-hike around Europe ◆ **ils ont fait un** ~ **du monde en bateau** they sailed round the world ◆ **on en a vite fait le** ~ *[de lieu]* there's not much to see; *[de livre, théorie]* there isn't much to it; *[de personne]* there isn't much to him (or her *etc*)

◆ **faire le tour de** *[+ parc, pays, circuit, montagne]* to go round; *[+ magasins]* to go round, to look round; *[+ possibilités]* to explore; *[+ problème]* to consider from all angles ◆ **la route fait (tout) le** ~ **de leur propriété** the road goes (right) round their estate ◆ **faire le** ~ **du propriétaire** to look round *ou* go round *ou* over one's property ◆ **je vais te faire faire le** ~ **du propriétaire** I'll show you over *ou* round the place ◆ **faire le** ~ **du cadran** *[aiguille]* to go round the clock; *[dormeur]* to sleep (right) round the clock ◆ **faire le** ~ **du monde** to go round the world ◆ **faire le** ~ **des invités** to do the rounds of the guests ◆ **la bouteille/plaisanterie a fait le** ~ **de la table** the bottle/joke went round the table; → **repartir²**

2 [= excursion] trip, outing; *(= promenade)* *(à pied)* walk, stroll; *(en voiture)* run, drive, ride, spin*; *(en vélo)* ride; *(en bateau)* trip ◆ **allons faire un (petit)** ~ **à pied** let's go for a (short) walk *ou* stroll ◆ **faire un** ~ **de manège** *ou* **de chevaux de bois** to have a ride on a merry-go-round ◆ **faire un** ~ **en ville/sur le marché** to go for a walk round town/round the market ◆ **faire un** ~ **en Italie** to go for a trip round Italy ◆ **un** ~ **de jardin/en voiture vous fera du bien** a walk *ou* stroll round the garden/a run *ou* drive (in the car) will do you good

3 [= parcours sinueux] **la rivière fait des** ~**s et des dé**~**s** *(littér)* the river meanders along *ou* winds its way in and out, the river twists and turns (along its way)

4 [dans un ordre, une succession] turn, go ◆ **c'est votre** ~ it's your turn ◆ **à ton** ~ **(de jouer)** *(gén)* (it's) your turn *ou* go; *(Échecs, Dames)* (it's) your move ◆ **attendre/perdre son** ~ to wait/miss one's turn ◆ **prendre/passer son** ~ to take/miss one's turn *ou* go ◆ **parler à son** ~ to speak in turn ◆ **ils parleront chacun à leur** ~ they will each speak in turn ◆ **attends, tu parleras à ton** ~ wait – you'll have your turn to speak ◆ **chacun son** ~ **!** wait your turn! ◆ **nous le faisons chacun à notre** ~ *(deux personnes)* we do it in turn, we take turns at it; *(plusieurs personnes)* we take turns at it, we do it by turns ◆ **c'est au** ~ **de Marc de parler** it's Marc's turn to speak ◆ **à qui le** ~ **?** whose turn *ou* go is it?, who is next? ◆ **votre** ~ **viendra** *(lit, fig)* your turn will come; → **souvent**

◆ **à tour de rôle** alternately, in turn ◆ **ils vinrent à** ~ **de rôle nous vanter leurs mérites** they each came in turn to sing their own praises ◆ **ils sont de garde à** ~ **de rôle** they take turns being on duty

◆ **tour à tour** alternately, in turn ◆ **le temps était** ~ **à** ~ **pluvieux et ensoleillé** the weather was alternately wet and sunny ◆ **elle se sentait** ~ **à** ~ **optimiste et désespérée** she felt optimistic and despairing by turns

5 [Pol] ~ **(de scrutin)** ballot ◆ **élu au premier/second** ~ elected in the first/second round ◆ **un troisième** ~ **social** a post-election backlash (of social unrest) ◆ **ils ont été éliminés**

au premier ~ de la Coupe d'Europe *(Sport)* they were eliminated in the first round of the European Cup

6 = circonférence *[de partie du corps]* measurement; *[de tronc, colonne]* girth; *[de visage]* contour, outline; *[de surface]* circumference; *[de bouche]* outline ◆ **le ~ des yeux** *(= périphérie)* the area around the eyes ◆ **~ de tête** *(= mensuration)* head measurement; *(pour chapeau)* hat size ◆ **quel est son ~ de taille ?** what's his waist measurement?, what size waist is he? ◆ **~ de poitrine** *[d'homme]* chest measurement; *[de femme]* bust measurement ◆ **~ de hanches** hip measurement ◆ **mesurer le ~ d'une table** to measure round a table, to measure the circumference of a table ◆ **la table fait 3 mètres de ~** the table measures 3 metres round (the edge) ◆ **le tronc a 3 mètres de ~** the trunk measures 3 metres round *ou* has a girth of 3 metres

7 = rotation *[de roue, hélice]* turn, revolution; *[d'écrou, clé]* turn; *[d'axe, arbre]* revolution ◆ **l'hélice a fait deux ~s** the propeller turned *ou* revolved twice ◆ **régime de 2 000 ~s (minute)** speed of 2,000 revs *ou* revolutions per minute ◆ **donner un ~ de clé** to turn the key, to give the key a turn ◆ **battre un concurrent d'un ~ de roue** *(Cyclisme)* to beat a competitor by a wheel's turn ◆ **faire un ~/plusieurs ~s sur soi-même** to spin round once/several times (on oneself) ◆ **faire un ~ de valse** to waltz round the floor ◆ **après quelques ~s de valse** after waltzing round the floor a few times ◆ **donnez 4 ~s à la pâte** *(Culin)* roll and fold the dough 4 times, turning it as you go; → **double, quart**

◆ **à tour de bras** *[frapper, taper]* with all one's strength *ou* might; *[composer, produire]* prolifically; *[critiquer]* with a vengeance ◆ **il écrit des chansons à ~ de bras** he writes songs by the dozen, he runs off *ou* churns out songs one after the other ◆ **il prescrit des antibiotiques à ~ de bras** he hands out antibiotics like candy ◆ **l'industrie textile licenciait à ~ de bras** the textile industry was laying people off left, right and centre

8 = disque **un 33 ~s** an LP ◆ **un 45 ~s** a single ◆ **un 78 ~s** a 78

9 = tournure *[de situation, conversation]* turn, twist ◆ **~ (de phrase)** *(= expression)* turn of phrase ◆ **la situation prend un ~ dramatique/désagréable** the situation is taking a dramatic/an unpleasant turn *ou* twist ◆ **un certain ~ d'esprit** a certain turn *ou* cast of mind

10 = exercice *[d'acrobate]* feat, stunt; *[de jongleur, prestidigitateur]* trick ◆ **~ d'adresse** feat of skill, skilful trick ◆ **~s d'agilité** acrobatics ◆ **~ de cartes** card trick ◆ **et le ~ est joué !** and there you have it!, and Bob's your uncle!* *(Brit)* ◆ **c'est un ~ à prendre !** it's just a knack one picks up! ◆ **avoir plus d'un ~ dans son sac** to have more than one trick up one's sleeve

11 = duperie trick ◆ **faire** *ou* **jouer un ~ à qn** to play a trick on sb ◆ **un ~ pendable** a rotten trick ◆ **un sale ~, un ~ de cochon*** *ou* **de salaud*** a dirty *ou* lousy trick*, a mean trick ◆ **je lui réserve un ~ à ma façon !** I'll pay him back in my own way!; → **jouer**

2 – COMPOSÉS

tour de chant song recital

tour de cou *(= ruban)* choker; *(= fourrure)* fur collar; *(= mensuration)* collar measurement ◆ **faire du 39 de ~ de cou** to take a size 39 collar

tour de force *(lit)* feat of strength, tour de force *(fig)*, amazing feat

le Tour de France *(= course cycliste)* the Tour de France ◆ **le ~ de France d'un compagnon** *(Hist)* a journeyman's tour of France

tour de garde spell *ou* turn of duty ◆ **mon prochain ~ de garde est à 8 heures** my next spell *ou* turn of duty is at 8 o'clock

tour d'honneur *(Sport)* lap of honour

tour d'horizon *(fig)* (general) survey ◆ **nous avons fait un ~ d'horizon de la situation économique** we have reviewed the economic situation

tour de lit (bed) valance

tour de main *(= adresse)* dexterity ◆ **avoir/acquérir un ~ de main** to have/pick up a knack ◆ **en un ~ de main** in no time at all

tour de manivelle *(lit)* turn of the handle ◆ **le premier ~ de manivelle est prévu pour octobre** *(Ciné)* the cameras should begin rolling in October

tour de piste *(Sport)* lap; *(dans un cirque)* circuit (of the ring)

tour de reins ◆ **souffrir d'un ~ de reins** to suffer from a strained *ou* sprained back ◆ **attraper un ~ de reins** to strain one's back

tour de table *(Fin)* investor round ◆ **procéder à un ~ de table** *(dans une réunion)* to seek the views of all those present ◆ **la société immobilière a bouclé son ~ de table** the property company has finalized its capital structure

tour de vis (turn of a) screw ◆ **il faudra donner un ~ de vis** you'll have to give the screw a turn *ou* tighten the screw a bit ◆ **donner un ~ de vis monétaire** to tighten the monetary screw ◆ **donner un ~ de vis aux libertés** to clamp down on civil rights ◆ **~ de vis fiscal** tax squeeze ◆ **~ de vis militaire/politique** military/political crackdown *ou* clampdown *(à l'encontre de on)* → **chauffe, passe-passe**

LE TOUR DE FRANCE

The famous annual cycle race takes about three weeks to complete in daily stages (« étapes ») of approximately 110 miles. The leading cyclist wears a yellow jersey, the « maillot jaune ». There are a number of time trials. The route varies and is not usually confined only to France, but the race always ends on the Champs-Élysées in Paris.

tour³ /tuʀ/ **NM** 1 *(= machine)* lathe ◆ **~ de potier** potter's wheel ◆ **objet fait au ~** object turned on the lathe ◆ **travail au ~** lathe-work 2 *(= passe-plat)* hatch

tourbe /tuʀb/ **NF** peat ◆ **~ limoneuse** alluvial peat

tourbeux, -euse /tuʀbø, øz/ **ADJ** 1 *[terrain]* *(= qui contient de la tourbe)* peat *(épith)*, peaty; *(= de la nature de la tourbe)* peaty 2 *[plante]* found in peat

tourbière /tuʀbjɛʀ/ **NF** peat bog

tourbillon /tuʀbijɔ̃/ **NM** 1 *(atmosphérique)* **~ (de vent)** whirlwind ◆ **~ de fumée/sable/neige/poussière** swirl *ou* eddy of smoke/sand/snow/dust ◆ **le sable s'élevait en ~s** the sand was swirling up 2 *(dans l'eau)* eddy; *(plus important)* whirlpool ◆ **l'eau faisait des ~s** the water was making eddies 3 *(Phys)* vortex 4 *(fig)* whirl ◆ **~ de plaisirs** whirl of pleasure, giddy round of pleasure(s) ◆ **le ~ de la vie/des affaires** the hurly-burly *ou* hustle and bustle of life/of business ◆ **il regardait le ~ des danseurs** he was looking at the whirling *ou* swirling group of dancers ◆ **le pays plongea dans un ~ de violence** the country was plunged into a maelstrom of violence

tourbillonnant, e /tuʀbijɔnɑ̃, ɑ̃t/ **ADJ** *[feuilles]* swirling, eddying; *[vie]* whirlwind *(épith)*; *[jupes]* swirling

tourbillonnement /tuʀbijɔnmɑ̃/ **NM** *[de poussière, sable, feuilles mortes, flocons de neige]* whirling, swirling, eddying; *[de danseurs]* whirling, swirling, twirling; *[d'idées]* swirling, whirling

tourbillonner /tuʀbijɔne/ ► conjug 1 ◄ **VI** *[poussière, sable, feuilles mortes, flocons de neige]* to whirl, to swirl, to eddy; *[danseurs]* to whirl (round), to swirl (round), to twirl (round); *[idées]* to swirl (round), to whirl (round)

tourelle /tuʀɛl/ **NF** 1 *(= petite tour)* turret 2 *(Mil, Naut)* (gun) turret; *[de caméra]* lens turret; *[de sous-marin]* conning tower

tourière /tuʀjɛʀ/ **ADJ F, NF** ◆ **(sœur) ~** sister at the convent gate, extern sister

tourillon /tuʀijɔ̃/ **NM** *[de mécanisme]* bearing, journal; *[de canon]* trunnion; *[meuble]* dowel

tourisme /tuʀism/ **NM** 1 *(= action de voyager)* **faire du ~ en Irlande** to go touring round Ireland ◆ **faire du ~ dans Paris** *(= action de visiter)* to go sightseeing in Paris 2 *(= industrie)* **le ~** tourism, the tourist industry *ou* trade ◆ **le ~ d'hiver/d'été** winter/summer tourism, the winter/summer tourist trade ◆ **le ~ français se porte bien** the French tourist industry *ou* trade is in good shape ◆ **~ industriel** industrial tourism ◆ **~ de masse/d'affaires** mass/business tourism ◆ **~ rural** *ou* **vert** green tourism, ecotourism ◆ **~ culturel/sexuel** cultural/sex tourism ◆ **promouvoir le ~ rural** to promote tourism in rural areas ◆ **avion/voiture de ~** private plane/car ◆ **voiture (de) grand ~** GT saloon car *(Brit)*, 4-door sedan *(US)*; → **agence, office**

touriste /tuʀist/ **NMF** tourist ◆ **faire qch en ~** *(fig)* to do sth half-heartedly ◆ **il s'est présenté à l'examen en ~** he was very casual about the exam; → **classe**

touristique /tuʀistik/ **ADJ** *[itinéraire, billet, activités, saison, guide]* tourist *(épith)*; *[région, ville]* with great tourist attractions, popular with (the) tourists *(attrib)* ◆ **trop ~** touristy* ◆ **route ~** scenic route; → **menu¹**

tourment /tuʀmɑ̃/ **NM** *(littér)* *(physique)* agony; *(moral)* torment, torture *(NonC)* ◆ **les ~s de la jalousie** the torments of jealousy

tourmente /tuʀmɑ̃t/ **NF** 1 *(= tempête)* storm, gale, tempest *(littér)* 2 *(sociale, politique)* upheaval, turmoil ◆ **~ monétaire** upheaval *ou* turmoil in the currency markets ◆ **les économies européennes ont été prises dans la ~ financière asiatique** the European economies were affected by Asia's financial turmoil ◆ **sa famille a disparu dans la ~ de la guerre** her family disappeared in the upheaval caused by the war

tourmenté, e /tuʀmɑ̃te/ (ptp de **tourmenter**) **ADJ** 1 *[personne, expression, visage, esprit]* tormented, tortured 2 *[relief]* rugged; *[paysage, formes]* tortured; *[style, art]* tortured, anguished 3 *[ciel, mer]* stormy; *[vie]* stormy, turbulent ◆ **l'histoire ~e de ce pays** this country's turbulent history ◆ **nous vivons une époque ~e** we're living in troubled *ou* turbulent times

tourmenter /tuʀmɑ̃te/ ► conjug 1 ◄ **VT** 1 *[personne]* to torment ◆ **ses créanciers continuaient à le ~** his creditors continued to harass *ou* hound him ◆ **~ qn de questions** to plague *ou* harass sb with questions 2 *[douleur, rhumatismes, faim]* to rack, to torment; *[remords, doute]* to rack, to torment, to plague; *[ambition, envie, jalousie]* to torment ◆ **ce qui me tourmente dans cette affaire** what worries *ou* bothers *ou* bugs* me in this business **VPR se tourmenter** to fret, to worry (o.s.) ◆ **ne vous tourmentez pas, ce n'était pas de votre faute** don't distress *ou* worry yourself – it wasn't your fault ◆ **il se tourmente à cause de son fils** he's fretting *ou* worrying about his son

tourmenteur, -euse /tuʀmɑ̃tœʀ, øz/ **NM,F** *(littér = persécuteur)* tormentor

tourmentin /tuʀmɑ̃tɛ̃/ **NM** 1 *(Naut = foc)* storm jib 2 *(= oiseau)* stormy petrel

tournage /tuʀnaʒ/ **NM** 1 *(Ciné)* shooting ◆ **être en ~ en Italie** to be filming in Italy, to be on a shoot in Italy ◆ **c'est arrivé pendant le ~** it happened during shooting *ou* the shoot ◆ **l'équipe de ~** the film *ou* camera crew ◆ **il l'emmène sur tous ses ~s** he takes her with him on all the shoots 2 *(Menuiserie)* turning ◆ **le ~ sur bois/métal** wood-/metal-turning 3 *(Naut)* belaying cleat

tournailler * /tuʀnɑje/ ▸ conjug 1 ◂ **VI** *(péj)* to wander aimlessly ◆ **~ autour de** to hang round

tournant, e /tuʀnɑ̃, ɑ̃t/ **ADJ** 1 *[fauteuil, dispositif]* swivel *(épith)*; *[feu, scène]* revolving *(épith)*; → **grève, plaque, pont, table**
2 *[mouvement, manœuvre]* encircling *(épith)*
3 *[escalier]* spiral *(épith)*; *(littér)* *[ruelle, couloir]* winding, twisting
NM 1 *(= virage)* bend ◆ **prendre bien/mal son ~** to take a bend well/badly, to corner well/badly ◆ **cette entreprise a bien su prendre le ~** this company has managed the change *ou* switch well, this company has adapted well to the new circumstances ◆ **attendre qn au ~** * to wait for the chance to trip sb up *ou* catch sb out *(Brit)* ◆ **avoir** *ou* **rattraper qn au ~** * to get even with sb, to get one's own back on sb *(Brit)*
2 *(= changement)* turning point ◆ **~ décisif** watershed ◆ **les ~s de l'histoire/de sa vie** the turning points in history/in his life ◆ **c'est à la 50e minute qu'a eu lieu le ~ du match** the decisive *ou* turning point of the match came in the 50th minute ◆ **il arrive à un ~ de sa carrière** he's coming to a turning point in his career ◆ **au ~ du siècle** at the turn of the century ◆ **un ~ de la politique française** a watershed in French politics ◆ **marquer un ~** to be a turning point
NF **tournante** * *(= viol collectif)* gang-bang *

tourné, e[1] /tuʀne/ (ptp de **tourner**) **ADJ** 1 ◆ **bien ~** *[personne]* shapely, with a good figure; *[jambes]* shapely; *[taille]* neat, trim; *[compliment, poème, expression]* well-turned; *[article, lettre]* well-worded, well-phrased 2 ◆ **mal ~** *[article, lettre]* badly expressed *ou* phrased *ou* worded; *[expression]* unfortunate ◆ **avoir l'esprit mal ~** to have a dirty mind 3 *[lait, vin]* sour; *[poisson, viande]* off *(attrib)*, high *(attrib)*; *[fruits]* rotten, bad 4 *(Menuiserie)* *[pied, objet]* turned

tournebouler * /tuʀnəbule/ ▸ conjug 1 ◂ **VT** *[+ personne]* to put in a whirl ◆ **~ la cervelle à qn** to turn sb's head *ou* brain, to put sb's head in a whirl ◆ **il en était tourneboulé** *(mauvaise nouvelle)* he was very upset by it; *(heureuse surprise)* his head was in a whirl over it

tournebroche /tuʀnəbʀɔʃ/ **NM** roasting spit, rotisserie ◆ **poulet au ~** spit-roasted chicken

tourne-disque (pl **tourne-disques**) /tuʀnədisk/ **NM** record player

tournedos /tuʀnədo/ **NM** tournedos

tournée[2] /tuʀne/ **NF** 1 *(= tour)* *[de conférencier, artiste]* tour; *[d'inspecteur, livreur, représentant]* round ◆ **~ de conférences/théâtrale** lecture/theatre tour ◆ **~ d'inspection** round *ou* tour of inspection ◆ **partir/être en ~** *[artiste, troupe de théâtre]* to set off on/be on tour; *[livreur, représentant]* to set off on/be on one's rounds ◆ **faire une ~ électorale** to go on a campaign tour *ou* the campaign trail ◆ **faire la ~ de** *[+ magasins, musées, cafés]* to do the rounds of, to go round ◆ **faire la ~ des grands ducs** * to go out on the town *ou* on a spree ◆ **faire la ~ des popotes** * to go on a tour of inspection
2 *(= consommations)* round (of drinks) ◆ **payer une/sa ~** to buy *ou* stand a/one's round (of drinks) ◆ **c'est ma ~** it's my round ◆ **il a payé une ~ générale** he paid for drinks all round ◆ **c'est la ~ du patron** the drinks are on the house
3 (* = *raclée*) hiding, thrashing

tournemain /tuʀnəmɛ̃/ **en un tournemain** **LOC ADV** in no time at all, in the twinkling of an eye, (as) quick as a flash

tourner /tuʀne/ ▸ conjug 1 ◂ **VT** 1 *[+ manivelle, clé, poignée]* to turn; *[+ sauce]* to stir; *[+ salade]* to toss; *[+ page]* to turn (over) ◆ **tournez s.v.p** please turn over, PTO ◆ **~ et retourner** *[+ chose]* to turn over and over; *[+ pensée, problème]* to turn over and over (in one's mind), to mull over; → **dos, page**[1]**, talon**
2 *(= diriger, orienter)* *[+ appareil, tête, yeux]* to turn ◆ **elle tourna son regard** *ou* **les yeux vers la fenêtre** she turned her eyes towards the window ◆ **~ la tête à droite/à gauche** to turn one's head to the right/to the left ◆ **quand il m'a vu, il a tourné la tête** when he saw me he looked away *ou* he turned his head away ◆ **~ les pieds en dedans/en dehors** to turn one's toes *ou* feet in/out ◆ **tourne le tableau de l'autre côté/contre le mur** turn the picture the other way round/round to face the wall ◆ **~ ses pas vers** *(littér)* to wend one's way towards *(littér)* ◆ **~ ses pensées/efforts vers** to turn *ou* bend one's thoughts/efforts towards *ou* to; → **bride, casaque**
3 *(= contourner)* *(Naut)* *[+ cap]* to round; *[+ armée]* to turn, to outflank; *[+ obstacle]* to round
4 *(= éluder)* *[+ difficulté, règlement]* to get round *ou* past ◆ **~ la loi** to get round the law, to find a loophole in the law ◆ **il vient de ~ le coin de la rue** he has just turned the corner ◆ **~ la mêlée** *(Rugby)* to turn the scrum, to wheel the scrum round
5 *(frm = exprimer)* *[+ phrase, compliment]* to turn; *[+ demande, lettre]* to phrase, to express
6 *(= transformer)* **il a tourné l'incident en plaisanterie** he made light of the incident, he made a joke out of the incident ◆ **~ qn/qch en ridicule** to make sb/sth a laughing stock, to ridicule sb/sth, to hold sb/sth up to ridicule ◆ **il tourne tout à son avantage** he turns everything to his (own) advantage; → **dérision**
7 *(Ciné)* **~ une scène** *[cinéaste]* to shoot *ou* film a scene; *[acteur]* to act in *ou* do a scene ◆ **~ un film** *(= faire les prises de vues)* to shoot a film; *(= produire)* to make a film; *(= jouer)* to make *ou* do a film ◆ **ils ont dû ~ en studio** they had to do the filming in the studio; → **extérieur, silence**
8 *(= façonner)* *[+ bois, ivoire]* to turn; *[+ pot]* to throw
9 *(locutions)* **~ le cœur** *ou* **l'estomac à qn** † to turn sb's stomach, to make sb heave ◆ **~ la tête à qn** *[vin]* to go to sb's head; *[succès]* to go to *ou* turn sb's head; *[personne]* to turn sb's head
VI 1 *[manège, compteur, aiguille d'horloge]* to turn, to go round; *[disque, cylindre, roue]* to turn, to revolve; *[pièce sur un axe, clé, danseur]* to turn; *[toupie]* to spin; *[taximètre]* to tick away; *[usine, moteur]* to run ◆ **~ sur soi-même** to turn round on o.s.; *(très vite)* to spin round and round ◆ **~ comme un lion en cage** to pace angrily up and down ◆ **la grande aiguille tourne plus vite que la petite** the big hand goes round faster than the small one ◆ **l'heure tourne** time's getting on ◆ **les éléphants tournent sur la piste** the elephants move round the ring ◆ **~ comme une toupie** to spin like a top ◆ **tout d'un coup, j'ai vu tout ~** all of a sudden my head began to spin *ou* swim ◆ **usine qui tourne à plein (régime)** factory working at full capacity *ou* flat out * ◆ **la machine à laver tourne surtout la nuit** the washing machine runs mostly at night ◆ **ce représentant tourne sur Lyon** *(Comm)* this sales representative covers Lyons ◆ **son spectacle va ~ dans le Midi cet été** his show is on tour in the South of France this summer ◆ **faire ~ le moteur** to run the engine ◆ **faire ~ les tables** *(Spiritisme)* to hold seances, to do table-turning ◆ **c'est elle qui fait ~ l'affaire** she's the one who runs the business ◆ **faire ~ la tête à qn** *[compliments, succès]* to go to sb's head ◆ **ça me fait ~ la tête** *[vin]* it goes to my head; *[bruit, altitude]* it makes my head spin, it makes me dizzy *ou* giddy; → **ours, ralenti, rond, vide** *etc*
2 *(Ordin)* *[programme]* to work ◆ **arriver à faire ~ un programme** to get a program working *ou* to work ◆ **ça tourne sur quelles machines ?** which machines does it work on?, which machines is it compatible with?
3 *(= changer de direction)* *[vent, opinion]* to turn, to shift, to veer (round); *[chemin, promeneur]* to turn ◆ **la chance a tourné** his (*ou* her *etc*) luck has turned ◆ **la voiture a tourné à gauche** the car turned left *ou* turned off to the left ◆ **tournez à droite au prochain feu rouge** turn right *ou* take a right at the next traffic lights
4 *(= évoluer)* **bien ~** to turn out well ◆ **mal ~** *[farce, entreprise]* to go wrong, to turn out badly; *[personne]* to go to the dogs *, to turn out badly ◆ **ça va mal ~** no good will come of it, it'll end in trouble ◆ **si les choses avaient tourné autrement** if things had turned out *ou* gone differently ◆ **~ à l'avantage de qn** to turn to sb's advantage ◆ **le débat tournait à la polémique** the debate was becoming increasingly heated ◆ **le temps a tourné au froid/à la pluie** the weather has turned cold/rainy *ou* wet ◆ **le ciel tournait au violet** the sky was turning purple ◆ **~ au drame/au tragique** to take a dramatic/tragic turn ◆ **la discussion a tourné en** *ou* **à la bagarre** the argument turned *ou* degenerated into a fight ◆ **sa bronchite a tourné en pneumonie** his bronchitis has turned *ou* developed into pneumonia; → **bourrique**
5 *[lait]* to turn (sour); *[poisson, viande]* to go off, to go bad; *[fruits]* to go rotten *ou* bad ◆ **~ (au vinaigre)** *[vin]* to turn (vinegary) ◆ **la chaleur a fait ~ le lait** the milk's gone sour in the heat
6 *(= se relayer)* *[personnes]* to take turns
7 *(locutions)* **j'ai la tête qui tourne, la tête me tourne** my head's spinning ◆ **~ de l'œil** * to pass out, to faint; → **court**[1]**, rond** *etc*
◆ **tourner autour de** to turn *ou* go round; *[terre, roue]* to revolve *ou* go round; *[chemin]* to wind *ou* go round; *[oiseau]* to wheel *ou* circle *ou* fly round; *[mouches]* to buzz *ou* fly round; *[discussion, sujet]* to centre *ou* focus on; *(= être approximativement)* *[prix]* to be around *ou* about *(Brit)* ◆ **~ autour de la piste** to go round the track ◆ **~ autour de qn** *(péj)* *(= importuner)* to hang round sb; *(pour courtiser)* to hang round sb; *(par curiosité)* to hover round sb ◆ **un individu tourne autour de la maison depuis une heure** somebody has been hanging round outside the house for an hour ◆ **l'enquête tourne autour de ces trois suspects/de cet indice capital** the inquiry centres on *ou* around these three suspects/this vital clue ◆ **ses émissions tournent toujours autour du même sujet** his programmes are always about the same subject ◆ **le prix doit ~ autour de 10 000 €** the price must be around €10,000 *ou* the €10,000 mark *ou* in the region of €10,000 ◆ **la production tourne autour de 200 voitures par jour** production runs at around 200 cars a day; → **pot**
VPR **se tourner** ◆ **se ~ du côté de** *ou* **vers qn/qch** to turn towards sb/sth ◆ **se ~ vers qn pour lui demander de l'aide** to turn to sb for help ◆ **se ~ vers une profession/la politique/une question** to turn to a profession/to politics/to a question ◆ **une société tournée vers l'avenir** a forward-looking company ◆ **se ~ contre qn** to turn against sb ◆ **se ~ et se retourner dans son lit** to toss and turn in bed ◆ **de quelque côté que l'on se tourne** whichever way one turns ◆ **tourne-toi (de l'autre côté)** turn round *ou* the other way; → **pouce**

tournesol /tuʀnəsɔl/ **NM** 1 *(= plante)* sunflower; → **huile** 2 *(Chim)* litmus

tourneur, -euse /tuʀnœʀ, øz/ NM,F (Tech) turner ◆ ~ **sur bois/métaux** wood/metal turner ADJ → **derviche**

tournevis /tuʀnəvis/ NM screwdriver ◆ **usine** ~ screwdriver plant; → **cruciforme**

tournicoter * /tuʀnikɔte/, **tourniquer** /tuʀnike/ ▸ conjug 1 ◂ VI (péj) to wander aimlessly ◆ ~ **autour de qn** (= importuner, courtiser) to hang round sb; (par curiosité) to hover round sb

tourniquet /tuʀnikɛ/ NM [1] (= barrière) turnstile; (= porte) revolving door [2] (Tech) ~ **(hydraulique)** reaction turbine; (d'arrosage) (lawn-)sprinkler [3] (= présentoir) revolving stand [4] (Méd) tourniquet [5] (arg Mil) court-martial ◆ **passer au** ~ to come up before a court-martial

tournis /tuʀni/ NM [1] (= maladie du mouton) sturdy [2] * **avoir le** ~ to feel dizzy ou giddy ◆ **ça/il me donne le** ~ it/he makes my head spin, it/he makes me (feel) dizzy ou giddy

tournoi /tuʀnwa/ NM [1] (Hist) tournament, tourney [2] (Sport) tournament ◆ ~ **d'échecs/de tennis** chess/tennis tournament ◆ ~ **d'éloquence/d'adresse** (littér) contest of eloquence/of skill ◆ **le Tournoi des six nations** (Rugby) the Six Nations Championship ◆ **disputer** ou **faire un** ~ to play in ou enter a tournament

tournoiement /tuʀnwamɑ̃/ NM [1] [de danseurs] whirling, twirling; [d'eau, fumée] swirling, eddying, whirling; [de feuilles mortes] swirling, eddying ◆ **les ~s des danseurs** the whirling (of the) dancers ◆ **des ~s de feuilles** swirling ou eddying leaves [2] [d'oiseaux] wheeling

tournoyer /tuʀnwaje/ ▸ conjug 8 ◂ VI [danseurs] to whirl (round), to twirl (round); [eau, fumée] to swirl, to eddy; [boomerang] to spin; [papiers] to flutter around; [oiseaux] to wheel, to circle; [feuilles mortes] to swirl ou eddy around; [abeille, moustique] to fly around (in circles) ◆ **faire** ~ [danseur, canne] to twirl; [robe] to swirl ◆ **les feuilles tombaient en tournoyant** the leaves were twirling ou whirling down ◆ **la fumée s'élevait en tournoyant** the smoke spiralled up ◆ **tout s'est mis à** ~ **et je me suis évanoui** everything started to spin and I fainted

tournure /tuʀnyʀ/ NF [1] (= tour de phrase) turn of phrase; (= forme) form ◆ ~ **négative/impersonnelle** negative/impersonal form ◆ **la** ~ **précieuse de ses phrases** the affected way (in which) he phrases his sentences [2] (= apparence) **la** ~ **des événements** the turn of events ◆ **la** ~ **que prenaient les événements** the way the situation was developing, the turn events were taking ◆ **la situation a pris une mauvaise/meilleure** ~ the situation took a turn for the worse/for the better ◆ **donner une autre** ~ **à une affaire** to put a matter in a different light, to put a new face on a matter ◆ **prendre** ~ to take shape [3] ◆ ~ **d'esprit** turn ou cast of mind [4] († = allure) bearing ◆ **il a belle** ~ he carries himself well, he has a very upright bearing

tournus /tuʀnys/ NM (Helv = alternance) rota

touron /tuʀɔ̃/ NM kind of nougat

tour-opérateur (pl **tour-opérateurs**) /tuʀɔperatœʀ/ NM tour operator

tourte /tuʀt/ NF (Culin) pie ◆ ~ **à la viande/au poisson** meat/fish pie

tourteau[1] (pl **tourteaux**) /tuʀto/ NM [1] (Culin) ~ **(fromagé)** round spongecake made with fromage frais [2] (Agr) oilcake, cattle-cake

tourteau[2] (pl **tourteaux**) /tuʀto/ NM (= crabe) crab

tourtereau (pl **tourtereaux**) /tuʀtəʀo/ NM (= oiseau) young turtledove ◆ **~x** (= amoureux) lovebirds

tourterelle /tuʀtəʀɛl/ NF turtledove ◆ **gris** ~ dove ou soft grey

tourtière /tuʀtjɛʀ/ NF (à tourtes) pie tin; (à tartes) pie dish ou plate

tous → **tout**

toussailler /tusɑje/ ▸ conjug 1 ◂ VI to have a bit of a cough ◆ **arrête de** ~ ! stop coughing and spluttering like that!

Toussaint /tusɛ̃/ NF ◆ **la** ~ All Saints' Day ◆ **nous partirons en vacances à la** ~ we're going on holiday at the beginning of November ◆ **il fait un temps de** ~ it's real November weather, it's grim cold weather

> **TOUSSAINT**
>
> All Saints' Day (November 1) is a public holiday in France. It is the day when people traditionally visit cemeteries to lay heather and chrysanthemums on the graves of relatives and friends.

tousser /tuse/ ▸ conjug 1 ◂ VI [1] [personne] to cough ◆ **ne sors pas, tu tousses encore un peu** don't go out – you've still got a bit of a cough [2] [moteur] to splutter, to cough

toussotement /tusɔtmɑ̃/ NM (slight) coughing (NonC)

toussoter /tusɔte/ ▸ conjug 1 ◂ VI (Méd) to have a bit of a ou a slight cough; (pour avertir, signaler) to cough softly, to give a little cough ◆ **je l'entendais** ~ **dans la pièce à côté** I could hear him coughing in the next room ◆ **il toussote, je vais lui faire prendre du sirop** he's got a bit of a ou a slight cough – I'm going to give him some cough mixture

tout, toute /tu, tut/ (mpl **tous**, fpl **toutes**)

1 ADJECTIF QUALIFICATIF	4 ADVERBE
2 ADJECTIF INDÉFINI	5 NOM MASCULIN
3 PRONOM INDÉFINI	

Lorsque **tout** fait partie d'une expression figée telle que **à tout bout de champ, de tout repos, en tout cas, tout le temps** etc, cherchez au premier nom.

1 - ADJECTIF QUALIFICATIF

[1] [= complet, entier, total]

♦ **tout, toute** + article ou possessif ou démonstratif ◆ ~ **le,** ~**e la** all (the), the whole (of the) ◆ ~ **le reste** (all) the rest ◆ **il a** ~ **le temps/l'argent qu'il lui faut** he has all the time/the money he needs ◆ ~**e la France regardait le match** the whole of ou all France was watching the match ◆ **pendant** ~ **le voyage** during the whole (of the) trip, throughout the trip ◆ **il a plu** ~**e la nuit/**~**e une nuit** it rained all night (long) ou throughout the night/for a whole night ◆ **il a plu** ~**e cette nuit** it rained all (of) ou throughout last night ◆ **il a dépensé** ~ **son argent** he has spent all (of) his money ◆ **mange** ~**e ta viande** eat up your meat, eat all (of) your meat ◆ **il a passé** ~**es ses vacances à lire** he spent the whole of ou all (of) his holidays reading ◆ **il courait de** ~**e la vitesse de ses petites jambes** he was running as fast as his little legs would carry him

♦ **tout le monde** everybody, everyone ◆ ~ **le monde le dit/le sait** everybody says so/knows ◆ **la nature appartient à** ~ **le monde** the countryside belongs to everybody ◆ **ils veulent vivre/être comme** ~ **le monde** they want to live/be like everybody else ◆ **il ne fait jamais comme** ~ **le monde** he always has to be different

♦ **tout, toute** + nom ◆ **il a lu** ~ **Balzac** he has read the whole of ou all of Balzac ◆ **elle a visité** ~ **Londres** she has been round the whole of London ◆ **le** ~**-Londres/-Rome** the London/Rome smart set, everybody who is anybody in London/Rome ◆ **en** ~**e illégalité** quite illegally ◆ **donner** ~**e satisfaction** to give complete satisfaction, to be entirely ou completely satisfactory

[2] [= seul, unique] only ◆ **c'est** ~ **l'effet que ça lui fait** that's all the effect ou the only effect it has on him ◆ **cet enfant est** ~**e ma joie** this child is my only ou sole joy, all my joy in life lies with this child ◆ **c'est là** ~ **le problème** that's the whole problem, that's just where the problem lies ◆ ~ **le secret est dans la rapidité** the whole secret lies in speed ◆ **pour** ~ **mobilier, il avait un lit et une table** all he had in the way of furniture ou the only furniture he had was a bed and a table

2 - ADJECTIF INDÉFINI

♦ **tout, toute** + nom singulier (= n'importe quel) any, all ◆ ~**e personne susceptible de nous aider** any person ou anyone able to help us ◆ **une empreinte digitale, un cheveu,** ~ **indice qui pourrait être utile** a fingerprint, a hair, any clue that might be useful ◆ ~**e trace d'agitation a disparu** all ou any trace of agitation has gone ◆ ~ **autre (que lui) aurait deviné** anybody ou anyone (but him) would have guessed ◆ **à** ~ **âge** at any age, at all ages ◆ **pour** ~ **renseignement, téléphoner** ... for all information, ring ...

♦ **tout un chacun** everybody, everyone ◆ **comme** ~ **un chacun, il a le droit de** ... like everybody else, he has a right to ... ◆ **le fait que** ~ **un chacun puisse librement donner son avis** the fact that anybody can freely express their opinion

♦ **tous, toutes (les)** + nom pluriel (= chaque) every ◆ **tous les jours/ans/mois** every day/year/month ◆ **tous les deux jours/mois** every other ou second day/month, every two days/months ◆ **tous les 10 mètres** every 10 metres ◆ ~**es les trois heures** every three hours, at three-hourly intervals
(= l'ensemble, la totalité des) all, every ◆ ~**es les personnes que nous connaissons** all the people ou everyone ou everybody (that) we know ◆ ~**es les fois que je le vois** every time I see him ◆ **il avait** ~**es les raisons d'être mécontent** he had every reason to be ou for being displeased ◆ **tous les hommes sont mortels** all men are mortal ◆ **courir dans tous les sens** to run all over the place ◆ **film (pour) tous publics** film suitable for all audiences ◆ **des individus de** ~**es tendances/tous bords** people of all tendencies/shades of opinion ◆ **le saut en hauteur, la course, le lancer du javelot,** ~**es disciplines qui exigent** ... (frm : servant à récapituler) the high jump, running, throwing the javelin, all (of them) disciplines requiring ...

♦ **tous, toutes (les)** + numéral (= ensemble) ◆ **tous (les) deux** both (of them), the two of them, each (of them) ◆ **tous (les) trois/quatre** all three/four (of them) ◆ **ils sont arrivés tous les six hier soir** all six of them arrived last night

3 - PRONOM INDÉFINI

[1] [= l'ensemble des choses] everything, all; (sans discrimination) anything ◆ **il a** ~ **organisé** he organized everything, he organized it all ◆ **on ne peut pas** ~ **faire** you can't do everything ◆ ~ **va bien** all's (going) well, everything's fine ◆ **son travail, ses enfants,** ~ **l'exaspère** his work, the children, everything annoys him ◆ ~ **lui est bon** everything is grist to his mill (pour to); ◆ **ses enfants mangent de** ~ her children will eat anything ◆ **il vend de** ~ he sells anything and everything ◆ **il est capable de** ~ he's capable of anything ◆ **il a** ~ **pour réussir** he's got everything going for him ◆ **il**

a ~ pour plaire * *(iro)* he's got nothing going for him ♦ **il est capable d'improviser un discours sur ~ et n'importe quoi** he can improvise a speech on just about anything ♦ **il promet ~ et son contraire** he makes the wildest promises ♦ **au cours du débat, on a entendu ~ et son contraire** the discussion was a real ragbag of ideas

♦ **avoir tout de** *+ nom* ♦ **elle a ~ d'une star** she's every inch a star ♦ **avec ce chapeau, elle a ~ d'une sorcière** she looks just like a witch in that hat ♦ **ça a ~ d'un canular** it's obviously a practical joke ♦ **l'organisation a ~ d'une secte** the organization is nothing less than a sect

♦ **à tout va** * *[licencier, investir, recruter]* like mad; *[libéralisme, communication, consommation]* unbridled ♦ **à l'époque, on construisait à ~ va** at that time there were buildings going up everywhere ♦ **il répète à ~ va ce que tu lui as raconté** he's going round telling everyone what you told him

♦ **ce n'est pas tout de** *+ infinitif (= ça ne suffit pas)* ♦ **ce n'est pas ~ d'en parler** there's more to it than just talking about it ♦ **ce n'est pas ~ de faire son métier, il faut le faire bien** it's not enough just to do your job, you have to do it well

♦ **en tout** *(= au total)* in all ♦ **nous étions 16 (personnes) en ~** there were 16 of us in all ♦ **ça coûte 150 € en ~** it costs €150 in all *ou* in total ♦ **cette pratique est en ~ contraire aux droits de l'homme** *(= en tous points)* this practice is a violation of human rights in every respect ♦ **leurs programmes politiques s'opposent en ~** their political programmes clash in every way

♦ **en tout et pour tout** all in all ♦ **il lui reste trois jours/25 € en ~ et pour ~** he only has a total of three days/€25 left ♦ **j'avais une valise en ~ et pour ~** all I had was a suitcase

♦ **... et tout (et tout)** * ... and everything ♦ **j'avais préparé le dîner, fait le ménage et ~ et ~** I'd made the dinner, done the housework and everything ♦ **je lui avais expliqué et ~, mais il n'a pas compris** I'd explained and everything, but he didn't understand ♦ **avec les vacances et ~, je n'ai pas eu le temps** what with the holidays and all *, I didn't have time

♦ **être + tout** ♦ **c'est ~** that's all ♦ **ce sera ~ ?** will that be all?, (will there be) anything else? ♦ **et ce n'est pas ~ !** and that's not all!, and there's more to come! ♦ **c'est pas ~ ça** *, **mais il est tard** all this is very nice, but it's getting late ♦ **être ~ pour qn** to be everything to sb

♦ **pour tout dire** ♦ **cette idée audacieuse avait surpris et pour ~ dire n'avait pas convaincu** this daring idea surprised everybody and, to be honest, wasn't convincing ♦ **il est vaniteux, égoïste, pour ~ dire c'est un sale type** he's vain, he's selfish, in a word he's a swine

♦ **tout ce qui, tout ce que** ♦ **~ ce que je sais, c'est qu'il est parti** all I know is that he's gone ♦ **c'est ~ ce qu'il m'a dit/laissé** that's all he told me/left me ♦ **~ ce que le pays compte de sportifs/savants** all the country has in the way of sportsmen/scientists, the country's entire stock of sportsmen/scientists ♦ **est-ce que vous avez ~ ce dont vous avez besoin ?** *ou* **ce qu'il vous faut ?** have you everything *ou* all (that) you need? ♦ **ne croyez pas ~ ce qu'il raconte** don't believe everything he tells you ♦ **~ ce qui lui appartient** everything *ou* all that belongs to him ♦ **~ ce qui brille n'est pas or** *(Prov)* all that glitters is not gold *(Prov)*

♦ **tout ce qu'il y a de** *+ adjectif (= extrêmement)* most ♦ **il a été ~ ce qu'il y a de gentil/serviable** he was most kind/obliging, he couldn't have been kinder/more obliging ♦ **des gens ~ ce qu'il y a de plus distingué(s)** most distinguished people ♦ **c'était ~ ce qu'il y a de chic** it was the last word in chic *ou* the ultimate in chic

♦ **tout est là** ♦ **la persévérance, ~ est là** all that counts is perseverance, perseverance is all that matters

♦ **tous, toutes** *(= l'ensemble des personnes)* all ♦ **tous** *ou* **~es tant qu'ils** *ou* **elles sont** all of them, every single one of them ♦ **tous sont arrivés** they have all arrived ♦ **il les déteste tous** *ou* **~es** he hates them all *ou* all of them ♦ **écoutez bien tous !** listen, all of you! ♦ **tous ensemble** all together ♦ **il parle en leur nom à tous** he's speaking for them all *ou* for all of them ♦ **film pour tous** film suitable for all audiences

♦ *pronom personnel +* **tous** *ou* **toutes** ♦ **nous avons tous nos défauts** we all *ou* all of us have our faults ♦ **nous mourrons tous** we shall all die ♦ **vous ~es qui m'écoutez** all of you who are listening to me ♦ **il s'attaque à nous tous** he's attacking us all *ou* all of us

2 [locutions] **~ a une fin** there is an end to everything, everything comes to an end ♦ **~ est bien qui finit bien** all's well that ends well ♦ **~ finit par des chansons** everything ends with a song ♦ **~ de bon !** *(Helv)* all the best! ♦ **~ passe, ~ casse** nothing lasts for ever ♦ **~ vient à point à qui sait attendre** *(Prov)* everything comes to he who waits *(Prov)*

4 - ADVERBE

S'accorde en genre et en nombre devant un adjectif féminin qui commence par une consonne ou un **h** aspiré.

1 [constructions]

♦ **tout** *+ adjectif (= très)* very; *(= entièrement)* quite ♦ **il est ~ étonné** he's very *ou* most surprised ♦ **c'est une ~e jeune femme** she's a very young woman ♦ **elles étaient ~ heureuses/~es contentes** they were very *ou* extremely happy/pleased ♦ **les ~es premières années** the very first *ou* early years ♦ **c'est ~ autre chose** that's quite another matter ♦ **c'est une ~ autre histoire** that's quite another story ♦ **il a mangé sa viande ~e crue** he ate his meat quite *ou* completely raw ♦ **c'est ~ naturel** it's perfectly *ou* quite natural ♦ **~e petite, elle aimait la campagne** as a (very) small child she liked the country

♦ **tout** *+ article + nom* ♦ **c'est ~ le contraire** it's quite the opposite *ou* the very opposite ♦ **avec toi c'est ~ l'un ou ~ l'autre** there's no in between with you, you see everything in black and white

♦ **tout** *+ préposition + nom* ♦ **être ~ yeux/oreilles** to be all eyes/ears ♦ **je suis ~ ouïe !** *(hum)* I'm all ears! ♦ **~ (en) laine/coton** all wool/cotton ♦ **il était ~ à son travail** he was entirely taken up by *ou* absorbed in his work ♦ **habillé ~ en noir** dressed all in black, dressed entirely in black ♦ **un style ~ en nuances** a very subtle style, a style full of nuances ♦ **un jeu ~ en douceur** a very delicate style of play ♦ **il était ~ en sueur** he was dripping with sweat ♦ **elle était ~ en larmes** she was in floods of tears ♦ **le jardin est ~ en fleurs** the garden is a mass of flowers

♦ **tout** *+ adverbe* ♦ **~ près** *ou* **à côté** very near *ou* close ♦ **~ là-bas** right over there ♦ **~ en bas de la colline** right at the bottom of the hill ♦ **~ au fond** right at the bottom, at the very bottom ♦ **~ simplement** *ou* **bonnement** quite simply ♦ **je vois cela ~ autrement** I see it quite differently ♦ **je le sais ~ autant que toi** I know it as well as you do, I'm as aware of it as you are ♦ **j'aime ça ~ aussi peu que lui** I like that as little as he does ♦ **~ plein** * **de cartes postales** loads * of postcards ♦ **il est gentil/mignon ~ plein** * he's really very *ou* really awfully * nice/sweet

♦ **tout** *+ verbe* ♦ **tu t'es ~ sali** you've got yourself all dirty ♦ **tu as ~ sali tes habits** you've got your clothes all dirty

2 [= déjà] **~ prêt, ~ préparé** ready-made ♦ **phrases ~es faites** ready-made *ou* set *ou* standard phrases ♦ **idées ~es faites** preconceived ideas, unquestioning ideas

3 [autres locutions]

♦ **tout en** *+ participe présent (simultanéité)* ♦ **~ en marchant/travaillant** as *ou* while you walk/work, while walking/working ♦ **elle tricotait ~ en regardant la télévision** she was knitting while watching television ♦ **je suis incapable de travailler ~ en écoutant de la musique** I can't work and listen to music at the same time

(opposition) ♦ **~ en prétendant le contraire il voulait être élu** (al)though he pretended otherwise he wanted to be elected ♦ **~ en reconnaissant ses mérites je ne suis pas d'accord avec lui** (al)though *ou* even though I recognize his strengths I don't agree with him

♦ **tout** *+ nom ou adjectif +* **que** *(concession)* ♦ **~ médecin qu'il soit** even though *ou* although he's a doctor, I don't care if he's a doctor ♦ **~e malade qu'elle se prétende** however ill *ou* no matter how ill she says she is ♦ **leur appartement, ~ grand qu'il est, ne suffira pas** however large *ou* no matter how large their flat is, it won't be enough

♦ **tout à fait** quite, entirely, altogether ♦ **ce n'est pas ~ à fait la même chose** it's not quite the same thing ♦ **c'est ~ à fait faux/exact** it's quite *ou* entirely wrong/right ♦ **il est ~ à fait charmant** he's absolutely *ou* quite charming ♦ **je suis ~ à fait d'accord avec vous** I'm in complete agreement with you, I agree completely *ou* entirely with you ♦ **vous êtes d'accord ? – ~ à fait !** do you agree? – absolutely!

♦ **tout à l'heure** *(= plus tard)* later, in a short *ou* little while; *(= peu avant)* just now, a short while ago, a moment ago ♦ **je repasserai ~ à l'heure** I'll come back later ♦ **~ à l'heure tu as dit que ...** *(à l'instant)* you said just now that ...; *(il y a plus longtemps)* you said earlier that ... ♦ **à ~ à l'heure !** see you later!

♦ **tout de suite** straightaway, at once, immediately ♦ **j'ai ~ de suite compris que ...** I understood straightaway that ... ♦ **alors, tu es prêt ? – ~ de suite !** are you ready then? – just a second! ♦ **vous le voulez pour quand ? – pas ~ de suite** when do you want it for? – there's no rush ♦ **ce n'est pas pour ~ de suite** *(= ce n'est pas près d'arriver)* it won't happen overnight; *(= c'est assez improbable)* it's hardly likely to happen

5 - NOM MASCULIN

1 [= ensemble] whole ♦ **ces éléments forment un ~** these elements make up a whole ♦ **acheter/vendre/prendre le ~** to buy/sell/take the (whole) lot *ou* all of it *(ou* them) ♦ **le grand Tout** *(Rel)* the Great Whole ♦ **jouer** *ou* **tenter** *ou* **risquer le ~ pour le ~** to stake one's all

♦ **le tout + être** *(= l'essentiel)* ♦ **le ~ est qu'il parte à temps** the main *ou* most important thing is that he leaves in time ♦ **le ~ c'est de faire vite** the main thing is to be quick about it ♦ **c'est pas le ~** * **mais j'ai du travail** this is all very well but I've got work to do ♦ **ce n'est pas le ~ de s'amuser, il faut travailler** we can't just enjoy ourselves, we must get down to work

2 [dans une charade] **mon ~ est un roi de France** my whole *ou* all is a king of France

3 [locutions]

♦ **du tout** *(en réponse)* ♦ **(pas) du ~ !** not at all! ♦ **il n'y a pas de pain du ~** there's no bread at all ♦ **il n'y a plus du ~ de pain** there's no bread left at all ♦ **je n'entends/ne vois rien du ~** I can't hear/see a thing, I can't hear/see any-

thing at all ◆ **sans s'inquiéter du** ~ without worrying at all
◆ **du tout au tout** *(= complètement)* completely ◆ **il avait changé du** ~ **au** ~ he had changed completely ◆ **la situation s'est modifiée du** ~ **au** ~ the situation has completely changed

tout-à-l'égout /tutalegu/ NM INV *(= système)* mains drainage *(NonC)*; *(= tuyau)* main sewer

Toutankhamon /tutɑ̃kamɔ̃/ NM Tutankhamen, Tutankhamun

toutefois /tutfwa/ ADV however ◆ **sans** ~ **que cela les retarde** without that delaying them, however ◆ **si** ~ **il est d'accord** if he agrees, that is

tout-en-un /tutɑ̃œ̃/ ADJ INV all-in-one

toute-puissance (pl **toutes-puissances**) /tutpɥisɑ̃s/ NF omnipotence *(NonC)*

tout-fou * (pl **tout-fous**) /tufu/ ADJ M over-excited NM ◆ **il fait son** ~ he's a bit over-excited

toutim * /tutim/ NM ◆ **et (tout) le** ~ the whole caboodle * *(Brit)*, the whole kit and caboodle * *(US)*

toutou /tutu/ NM *(langage enfantin)* doggie, bow-wow *(langage enfantin)* ◆ **suivre qn/obéir à qn comme un** ~ to follow sb about/obey sb as meekly as a lamb

Tout-Paris /tupaʀi/ NM ◆ **le** ~ the Paris smart set, the tout-Paris ◆ **le** ~ **artistique assistait au vernissage** the artistic elite of Paris attended the preview of the exhibition

tout-petit (pl **tout-petits**) /tup(ə)ti/ NM toddler, tiny tot ◆ **jeu pour les** ~**s** game for the very young *ou* for toddlers *ou* tiny tots

tout-puissant, toute-puissante (mpl **tout-puissants**) /tupɥisɑ̃, tutpɥisɑ̃t/ ADJ almighty, omnipotent, all-powerful NM ◆ **le Tout-Puissant** the Almighty

tout-terrain (pl **tout-terrains**) /tuteʀɛ̃/ ADJ *[véhicule]* four-wheel drive *(épith)*, cross-country *(épith)* ◆ **vélo** ~ mountain bike ◆ **moto** ~ trail bike NM ◆ **le** ~ *(Sport) (en voiture)* cross-country racing; *(en vélo)* mountain biking; *(en moto)* trail-biking ◆ **faire du** ~ *(en voiture)* to go cross-country racing; *(en vélo)* to go mountain-biking; *(en moto)* to go trail-biking

tout(-)va /tuva/ **à tout(-)va** LOC ADV left, right and centre

tout-venant /tuv(ə)nɑ̃/ NM INV *(= charbon)* raw coal ◆ **le** ~ *(= articles, marchandises)* the run-of-the-mill *ou* ordinary stuff

toux /tu/ NF cough ◆ ~ **grasse/sèche/nerveuse** loose/dry/nervous cough; → **quinte**

toxémie /tɔksemi/ NF blood poisoning, toxaemia *(Brit)*, toxemia *(US)*

toxicité /tɔksisite/ NF toxicity

toxico * /tɔksiko/ NMF (abrév de **toxicomane**) junkie *

toxicodépendance /tɔksikodepɑ̃dɑ̃s/ NF drug-dependency

toxicodépendant, e /tɔksikodepɑ̃dɑ̃, ɑ̃t/ NM,F drug-dependent

toxicologie /tɔksikɔlɔʒi/ NF toxicology

toxicologique /tɔksikɔlɔʒik/ ADJ toxicological

toxicologue /tɔksikɔlɔg/ NMF toxicologist

toxicomane /tɔksikɔman/ ADJ drug-addicted, addicted to drugs NMF drug addict

toxicomaniaque /tɔksikɔmanjak/ ADJ *[habitude, pratique]* (drug) addiction-related

toxicomanie /tɔksikɔmani/ NF drug addiction

toxicose /tɔksikoz/ NF toxicosis

toxine /tɔksin/ NF toxin

toxique /tɔksik/ ADJ toxic ◆ **substance** ~ **pour l'organisme** substance that is toxic *ou* poisonous to the system NM toxin, poison

toxoplasme /tɔksoplasm/ NM toxoplasma

toxoplasmose /tɔksoplasmoz/ NF toxoplasmosis

TP /tepe/ NM 1 (abrév de **Trésor public**) → **trésor** 2 (abrév de **travaux pratiques**) *(Univ)* practical NF (abrév de **trésorerie principale**) → **trésorerie** NMPL (abrév de **travaux publics**) → **travail**[1]

TPE /tepeə/ NM (abrév de **terminal de paiement électronique**) EFTPOS

TPG /tepeʒe/ NM (abrév de **trésorier-payeur général**) → **trésorier**

TPV /tepeve/ NM (abrév de **terminal point de vente**) POST

trac[1] /tʀak/ NM *(Théât, en public)* stage fright; *(aux examens)* (exam) nerves ◆ **avoir le** ~ *(Théât, en public, sur le moment)* to have stage fright; *(à chaque fois)* to get stage fright; *(aux examens, sur le moment)* to be nervous; *(à chaque fois)* to get nervous, to get (an attack *ou* fit of) nerves ◆ **ficher le** ~ **à qn** * to give sb a fright, to put the wind up sb * *(Brit)*

trac[2] /tʀak/ **tout à trac** LOC ADV *[dire, demander]* right out of the blue

traçabilité /tʀasabilite/ NF traceability

traçage /tʀasaʒ/ NM 1 *[de ligne, triangle, plan, chiffre, mot]* drawing; *[de courbe de graphique]* plotting 2 *[de route, piste] (= déblaiement)* opening up; *(= balisage)* marking out 3 *(Min)* heading 4 *(Tech) [de schéma]* tracing

traçant, e /tʀasɑ̃, ɑ̃t/ ADJ 1 *[racine]* running, creeping 2 *[obus, balle]* tracer *(épith)*; → **table**

tracas /tʀaka/ NM *(littér † = embarras)* bother, upset ◆ **se donner bien du** ~ to give o.s. a great deal of trouble NMPL *(= soucis, ennuis)* worries

tracasser /tʀakase/ ▸ conjug 1 ◂ VT *(gén)* to worry, to bother; *[administration]* to harass, to bother ◆ **qu'est-ce qui te tracasse ?** what's bothering *ou* worrying *ou* bugging * you? VPR **se tracasser** *(= se faire du souci)* to worry, to fret ◆ **ne te tracasse pas pour si peu !** don't worry *ou* fret over a little thing like that!

tracasserie /tʀakasʀi/ NF *(gén pl)* harassment ◆ **les** ~**s policières dont j'ai été victime** the police harassment of which I was a victim ◆ **j'en ai assez de toutes ces** ~**s administratives !** I'm fed up with all this irritating red tape! ◆ **à la suite de cette loi, beaucoup d'étrangers ont subi des** ~**s administratives** as a result of this law many foreigners have had a lot of hassle * with bureaucracy

tracassier, -ière /tʀakasje, jɛʀ/ ADJ *[fonctionnaire, bureaucratie]* pettifogging

trace /tʀas/ NF 1 *(= empreinte) [d'animal, fugitif, pneu]* tracks ◆ **la** ~ **du renard diffère de celle de la belette** the fox's tracks differ from those of the weasel ◆ **suivre une** ~ **de blaireau** to follow some badger tracks ◆ ~**s de doigt** *(sur disque, meuble)* finger marks ◆ ~**s de pas** footprints ◆ ~**s de pneus** tyre tracks

2 *(= chemin frayé)* track, path; *(Ski)* track ◆ **s'ouvrir une** ~ **dans les broussailles** to open up a track *ou* path through the undergrowth ◆ **faire la** ~ *(Alpinisme, Ski)* to be the first to ski *(ou* walk *etc)* on new snow ◆ **on voyait leur** ~ **dans la face nord** we could see their tracks on the north face ◆ ~ **directe** *(Ski)* direct descent

3 *(= marque) [de sang]* trace; *[de brûlure, encre]* mark; *[d'outil]* mark; *[de blessure, maladie]* mark ◆ ~**s de freinage** brake marks ◆ ~**s d'effraction** signs of a break-in ◆ **il n'y avait pas de** ~ **écrite** nothing had been put down in writing ◆ **la victime portait des** ~**s de coups au visage** there were bruises on the victim's face ◆ **le corps ne présentait aucune** ~ **de violence** there were no signs of violence on the body ◆ **les** ~**s de la souffrance** *(littér)* the marks of suffering ◆ **des** ~**s de fatigue se lisaient sur son visage** his face showed signs of tiredness *ou* bore the marks of tiredness ◆ **cet incident avait laissé une** ~ **durable/profonde dans son esprit** the incident had left an indelible/a definite mark on his mind

4 *(= indice)* trace ◆ **il n'y avait pas** ~ **des documents volés/du fugitif dans l'appartement** there was no trace of the stolen documents/of the fugitive in the flat ◆ **on ne trouve pas** ~ **de cet événement dans les journaux** there's no trace of this event to be found in the papers

5 *(= vestige : gén pl) [de bataille, civilisation]* trace; *(= indice) [de bagarre]* sign ◆ **on voyait encore les** ~**s de son passage** there was still evidence that he had recently passed by ◆ **retrouver les** ~**s d'une civilisation disparue** to discover the traces *ou* signs of a lost civilisation

6 *(= quantité minime) [de poison, substance]* trace ◆ **on y a trouvé de l'albumine à l'état de** ~ traces of albumen have been found ◆ **il ne montrait nulle** ~ **de repentir/de chagrin** he showed no trace of regret/of sorrow *ou* no sign(s) of being sorry/of sorrow ◆ **sans une** ~ **d'accent étranger** without a *ou* any trace of a foreign accent ◆ **il parlait sans la moindre** ~ **d'émotion dans la voix** he spoke without the slightest trace *ou* hint of emotion in his voice

7 *(locutions)* **disparaître sans laisser de** ~**s** *[personne]* to disappear without trace; *[tache]* to disappear completely without leaving a mark ◆ **être sur les** ~**s** *ou* **la** ~ **de** *[+ fugitif]* to be on the trail of; *[+ complot, document]* to be on the track of ◆ **perdre la** ~ **d'un fugitif** to lose track of *ou* lose the trail of a fugitive ◆ **retrouver la** ~ **d'un fugitif** to pick up the trail of a fugitive again ◆ **marcher sur** *ou* **suivre les** ~**s de qn** *(fig)* to follow in sb's footsteps ◆ **suivre à la** ~ *[+ gibier, fugitif]* to track ◆ **les journalistes la suivaient à la** ~ reporters followed her wherever she went ◆ **on peut le suivre à la** ~ **!** *(iro)* you can always tell when he has been here!

tracé /tʀase/ NM 1 *(= plan) [de réseau routier ou ferroviaire, installations]* layout, plan; *[de frontière]* line ◆ **corriger le** ~ **de la frontière entre deux pays** to redraw the border between two countries 2 *(= parcours) [de ligne de chemin de fer, autoroute]* route; *[de rivière]* line, course; *[d'itinéraire]* course; *(= contour) [de côte, crête]* line 3 *(= graphisme) [de dessin, écriture]* line

tracer /tʀase/ ▸ conjug 3 ◂ VT 1 *(= dessiner) [+ ligne, triangle, plan, trait]* to draw; *[+ courbe de graphique]* to plot; *(= écrire) [+ chiffre, mot]* to write

2 *[+ frontière]* to mark out; *[+ route, piste] (= frayer)* to open up; *(= baliser)* to mark out ◆ ~ **le chemin** *ou* **la voie à qn** *(fig)* to show sb the way ◆ **son avenir est tout tracé** his future is all mapped out ◆ ~ **une frontière entre ce qui est possible et ce qui est souhaitable** to mark a boundary between what is possible and what is desirable ◆ ~ **le parcours d'une autoroute** to mark out the path of a motorway

3 *(= définir) [+ programme d'action]* to outline ◆ ~ **les grandes lignes d'un projet** to give a broad outline of a project

4 *(= retrouver l'origine de) [+ produit]* to trace the origin of

VI 1 *(* = aller vite)* to belt along *, to shift * *(Brit)* ◆ **il trace sur ses rollers/sa moto !** he really belts along * on those roller skates/on that motorbike! ◆ **allez, trace !** *ou* **que ça trace !** get a move on! *

2 *(Bot)* to creep (horizontally)

traceur, -euse /tʀasœʀ, øz/ ADJ *(Sci) [substance]* tracer *(épith)* NM *(= appareil enregistreur)* pen; *(Sci)* tracer ◆ ~ **radioactif** radioactive tracer ◆ ~ **(de courbes)** *(Ordin)* (graph) plotter ◆ ~ **de cartes** chart plotter

trachéal, e (mpl **-aux**) /trakeal, o/ ADJ tracheal

trachée /traʃe/ NF 1 (Anat) ~**(-artère)** windpipe, trachea (SPÉC) 2 (chez les arthropodes) trachea

trachéen, -enne /trakeɛ̃, ɛn/ ADJ tracheal

trachéite /trakeit/ NF tracheitis (NonC) ◆ **avoir une ~, faire de la ~** to have tracheitis

trachéotomie /trakeɔtɔmi/ NF tracheotomy

trachome /trakom/ NM trachoma

traçoir /traswar/ NM [de dessinateur, graveur] scriber; [de jardinier] drill marker

tract /trakt/ NM leaflet, handout

tractable /traktabl/ ADJ [caravane] towable

tractation /traktasjɔ̃/ NF (souvent péj) negotiation, dealings, bargaining (NonC) ◆ **après de longues ~s entre les deux partis** after long negotiations between the two parties

tracté, e /trakte/ ADJ tractor-drawn

tracter /trakte/ ▸ conjug 1 ◂ VT to tow

tracteur, -trice /traktœr, tris/ NM tractor ADJ [véhicule] towing ◆ **force tractrice** [de cours d'eau] tractive force

traction /traksjɔ̃/ NF 1 (Sci, gén = action, mouvement) traction ◆ **être en ~** to be in traction ◆ **résistance à la ~** (Sci) tensile strength ◆ **effort de ~** tensile stress ◆ **faire des ~s** (Sport) (en se suspendant) to do pull-ups; (au sol) to do push-ups ou press-ups (Brit)
2 (= mode d'entraînement d'un véhicule) traction, haulage; (Rail) traction ◆ **~ animale/mécanique** animal/mechanical traction ou haulage ◆ **à ~ animale** drawn ou hauled by animals ◆ **à ~ mécanique** mechanically drawn ◆ **~ à vapeur/électrique** steam/electric traction ◆ **~ arrière** rear-wheel drive ◆ **~ avant** (= dispositif) front-wheel drive; (= voiture) car with front-wheel drive
3 (Rail = service) **la ~** the engine and driver section ◆ **service du matériel et de la ~** mechanical and electrical engineer's department

tractopelle /traktɔpɛl/ NM backhoe

tractus /traktys/ NM (Anat) tract ◆ **~ digestif** digestive tract

tradition /tradisjɔ̃/ NF 1 (gén) tradition ◆ **la Tradition** (Rel) Tradition ◆ **la ~ orale** the oral tradition ◆ **pays de ~ catholique/musulmane** Catholic/Muslim country ◆ **il est de ~ de faire/que** (+ subj) it is a tradition ou traditional to do/that ◆ **fidèle à la ~** true to tradition ◆ **c'était bien dans la ~ française** it was very much in the French tradition ◆ **par ~** traditionally ◆ **ce pays a une longue ~ artistique/de violence** this country has a long artistic tradition/a long history of violence 2 (Jur = livraison) tradition, transfer

traditionalisme /tradisjɔnalism/ NM traditionalism

traditionaliste /tradisjɔnalist/ ADJ traditionalist(ic) NM,F traditionalist

traditionnel, -elle /tradisjɔnɛl/ ADJ [pratique, interprétation, opinion] traditional; (* = habituel) usual ◆ **sa traditionnelle robe noire*** her usual black dress

traditionnellement /tradisjɔnɛlmɑ̃/ ADV traditionally; (= habituellement) as always, as usual ◆ **~ vêtue de noir** dressed in black as always ou as is (ou was) her wont (hum) ◆ **un électorat ~ favorable à la droite** an electorate who have traditionally voted for the Right

traducteur, -trice /tradyktœr, tris/ NM,F translator ◆ **~-interprète** translator-interpreter NM (Ordin) translator

traduction /tradyksjɔ̃/ NF 1 (= action, opération, technique) translation, translating (de from; dans, en into); (Scol = exercice) translation ◆ **la ~ de ce texte a pris trois semaines** it took three weeks to translate the text ◆ **école d'interprétariat et de ~** institute of translation and interpreting ◆ **c'est une ~ assez libre** it's a fairly free translation ou rendering ◆ **une excellente ~ de Proust** an excellent translation of Proust ◆ **~ fidèle/littérale** faithful ou accurate/literal translation ◆ **~ automatique** machine ou automatic translation ◆ **~ assistée par ordinateur** machine-aided translation ◆ **~ simultanée** simultaneous translation ◆ **ce mot a plusieurs ~s différentes en anglais** this word can be translated in several different ways in English ◆ **il publie son troisième roman en ~ française** his third novel is being published in a French translation ◆ **son œuvre est disponible en ~** his work is available in translation ◆ **ce poème perd beaucoup à la ~** this poem loses a lot in translation
2 (= interprétation) [de sentiments] expression ◆ **la ~ concrète de ses promesses électorales se fait attendre** it's taking a long time for his election promises to be translated into concrete action

traduire /tradɥir/ ▸ conjug 38 ◂ VT 1 [+ mot, texte, auteur] to translate (en, dans into); ◆ **traduit de l'allemand** translated from (the) German ◆ **comment se traduit ce mot en anglais ?** how does this word translate into English?
2 (= exprimer) to convey, to render, to express; (= rendre manifeste) to be the expression of ◆ **les mots traduisent la pensée** words convey ou render ou express thought ◆ **ce tableau traduit un sentiment de désespoir** this picture conveys ou expresses a feeling of despair ◆ **sa peur se traduisait par une grande volubilité** his fear found expression in great volubility ◆ **cela s'est traduit par une baisse du pouvoir d'achat** the effect of this was a drop in buying power, it was translated into a drop in buying power
3 (Jur) **~ qn en justice/en correctionnelle** to bring sb before the courts/before the criminal court

traduisible /tradɥizibl/ ADJ translatable ◆ **ce titre est difficilement ~** this title is difficult to translate, this title does not translate easily

Trafalgar /trafalgar/ NM Trafalgar ◆ **coup de ~** underhand trick

trafic /trafik/ NM 1 (péj) (= commerce clandestin) traffic; (= activité) trafficking; († = commerce) trade (de in); ◆ **~ d'armes** arms dealing, gunrunning ◆ **faire le ou du ~ d'armes** to be engaged in arms dealing ou gunrunning ◆ **~ de stupéfiants ou de drogue** drug trafficking ◆ **faire du ~ de stupéfiants ou de drogue** [gros trafiquant] to traffic in drugs; [revendeur] to deal in drugs ◆ **~ d'enfants/de voitures volées** trafficking ou trade in children/in stolen cars
2 (= activités suspectes) dealings; (* = manigances) funny business*, goings-on* ◆ **~ d'influence** (Jur) influence peddling ◆ **il se fait ici un drôle de ~*** there's some funny business going on here*, there are some strange goings-on here*
3 (Transport) traffic ◆ **~ maritime/routier/aérien/ferroviaire** sea/road/air/rail traffic ◆ **ligne à fort ~** line carrying dense ou heavy traffic ◆ **~ (de) marchandises/(de) voyageurs** goods/passenger traffic ◆ **~ fluide/dense sur le périphérique** light/heavy traffic on the ring road ◆ **le ~ est perturbé sur la ligne 6 du métro parisien** there are delays ou problems on line 6 of the Paris metro ◆ **~ téléphonique** telephone traffic

traficoter* /trafikɔte/ ▸ conjug 1 ◂ VT 1 (= altérer) [+ vin] to doctor*; [+ moteur] to tamper ou fiddle with ◆ **~ les comptes** to fiddle ou cook* (Brit) the books 2 (= réparer) [+ serrure, transistor, robinet] to mend, to fix 3 (= faire) **qu'est-ce qu'il traficote dans la cuisine ?** what's he up to ou doing in the kitchen? VI (péj) to traffic

trafiquant, e /trafikɑ̃, ɑ̃t/ NM,F (péj) trafficker ◆ **~ de drogue** drug trafficker ◆ **~ d'armes** arms dealer, gunrunner ◆ **c'est un ~ de voitures volées** he deals in stolen cars

trafiquer /trafike/ ▸ conjug 1 ◂ VI (péj) to traffic, to trade (illicitly) ◆ **~ de son influence** to use one's influence to corrupt ends ◆ **~ de ses charmes** † (hum) to offer one's charms for sale
VT * 1 (= altérer) [+ vin] to doctor*; [+ moteur] to tamper ou fiddle with; [+ document] to tamper with; [+ chiffres] to fiddle, to doctor ◆ **compteur trafiqué** meter that has been tampered with 2 (= réparer) [+ serrure, appareil] to mend, to fix 3 (= gonfler) [+ moteur] to soup up* 4 (= manigancer) **mais qu'est-ce que tu trafiques ?** what are you up to?

tragédie /traʒedi/ NF (gén, Théât) tragedy ◆ **~ humaine/familiale** human/family tragedy ◆ **la manifestation a tourné à la ~** the demonstration ended in tragedy ◆ **ce n'est pas une ~ !*** it's not the end of the world!

tragédien /traʒedjɛ̃/ NM tragedian, tragic actor

tragédienne /traʒedjɛn/ NF tragedienne, tragic actress

tragicomédie /traʒikɔmedi/ NF (Théât, fig) tragi-comedy

tragicomique /traʒikɔmik/ ADJ (Théât, fig) tragi-comic

tragique /traʒik/ ADJ (lit, fig) tragic ◆ **ce n'est pas ~ !*** it's not the end of the world! NM 1 (= auteur) tragedian, tragic author 2 (= genre) **le ~** tragedy 3 (= caractère dramatique) [de situation] tragedy ◆ **le ~ de la condition humaine** the tragedy of the human condition ◆ **la situation tourne au ~** the situation is taking a tragic turn ◆ **prendre qch au ~** to act as if sth were a tragedy, to make a tragedy out of sth

tragiquement /traʒikmɑ̃/ ADV tragically

trahir /trair/ ▸ conjug 2 ◂ VT 1 [+ ami, patrie, cause, idéal] to betray; [+ promesse, engagement] to break ◆ **~ la confiance/les intérêts de qn** to betray sb's confidence/interests ◆ **sa rougeur l'a trahie** her blushes gave her away ou betrayed her
2 (= révéler, manifester) [+ secret, émotion] to betray, to give away ◆ **~ sa pensée** to betray ou reveal one's thoughts ◆ **son intonation trahissait sa colère** his intonation betrayed his anger
3 (= lâcher) [forces, santé] to fail ◆ **ses forces l'ont trahi** his strength failed him ◆ **ses nerfs l'ont trahi** his nerves let him down ou failed him
4 (= mal exprimer) (gén) to misrepresent; [+ vérité] to distort ◆ **ces mots ont trahi ma pensée** those words misrepresented what I had in mind ◆ **ce traducteur/cet interprète a trahi ma pièce** this translator/this performer has given a totally false rendering of my play
VPR **se trahir** to betray o.s., to give o.s. away ◆ **il s'est trahi par cette question** his question gave him away, by asking this question he gave himself away ◆ **sa peur se trahissait par un flot de paroles** his fear betrayed itself in a great flow of words

trahison /traizɔ̃/ NF (gén) betrayal, treachery (NonC); (Jur, Mil = crime) treason ◆ **il est capable des pires ~s** he is capable of the worst treachery; → **haut**

train /trɛ̃/ NM 1 (Rail) train ◆ **~ omnibus/express/rapide** slow ou stopping/fast/express train ◆ **~ express régional** local train ◆ **~ direct** fast ou non-stop train ◆ **~ à vapeur/électrique** steam/electric train ◆ **~ de marchandises/voyageurs** goods/passenger train ◆ **~ auto-couchettes** car-sleeper train, ≃ Motorail (Brit) ◆ **~s supplémentaires** extra trains

◆ **~ à supplément** fast train *(on which one has to pay a supplement)* ◆ **c'est un ~ à supplément** you have to pay a supplement on this train ◆ **le ~ de Paris/Lyon** the Paris/Lyons train ◆ **~ à grande vitesse** high-speed train ◆ **les ~s de neige** the winter-sports trains ◆ **il est dans ce ~** he's on *ou* aboard this train ◆ **mettre qn dans le ~** *ou* **au ~*** to see sb to the train, to see sb off on the train *ou* at the station ◆ **voyager par le ~, prendre le ~** to travel by rail *ou* train, to take the train ◆ **attraper/rater le ~ de 10h50** to catch/miss the 10.50 train ◆ **monter dans** *ou* **prendre le ~ en marche** *(lit)* to get on the moving train; *(fig)* to jump on *ou* climb onto the bandwagon

2 *(= allure)* pace ◆ **ralentir/accélérer le ~** to slow down/speed up, to slow/quicken the pace ◆ **aller son ~** to carry along ◆ **aller son petit ~** to go along at one's own pace ◆ **l'affaire va son petit ~** things are chugging *ou* jogging along (nicely) ◆ **aller bon ~** *[affaire, travaux]* to make good progress; *[voiture]* to go at a good pace, to make good progress; *[rumeurs]* to be rife ◆ **aller grand ~** to make brisk progress, to move along briskly ◆ **les langues des commères allaient bon ~** the old wives' tongues were wagging away *ou* were going nineteen to the dozen *(Brit)* ◆ **mener/suivre le ~** to set/follow the pace ◆ **mener grand ~** *(= dépenser beaucoup)* to live in grand style, to spend money like water ◆ **il allait à un ~ d'enfer** he was going flat out*, he was tearing along* ◆ **à un ~ de sénateur** ponderously ◆ **au ~ où il travaille** (at) the rate he's working ◆ **au** *ou* **du ~ où vont les choses, à ce ~-là** the rate things are going, at this rate; → **fond**

3 *(locutions)*

◆ **en train** ◆ **être en ~** *(= en action)* to be under way; *(= de bonne humeur)* to be in good spirits ◆ **mettre qn en ~** *(= l'égayer)* to put sb in good spirits ◆ **mettre un travail en ~** *(= le commencer)* to get a job under way *ou* started ◆ **je suis long à me mettre en ~ le matin** it takes me a long time to get going* in the morning ◆ **mise en ~** *[de travail]* starting (up), start; *(Typo)* make-ready; *(= exercices de gym)* warm-up ◆ **être/se sentir en ~** *(= en bonne santé)* to be/feel in good form *ou* shape ◆ **elle ne se sent pas très en ~** she doesn't feel too good *ou* too bright*

◆ **être en train de faire qch** to be doing sth ◆ **être en ~ de manger/regarder la télévision** to be eating/watching television ◆ **j'étais juste en ~ de manger** I was (right) in the middle of eating, I was just eating ◆ **on l'a pris en ~ de voler** he was caught stealing

4 *(= file) [de bateaux, mulets]* train, line ◆ **le ~ (des équipages)** *(Mil)* ≃ the (Army) Service Corps ◆ **~ de bois (de flottage)** timber raft ◆ **~ spatial** *(Espace)* space train

5 *(Tech = jeu)* **~ d'engrenages** train of gears ◆ **~ de pneus** set of (four) tyres

6 *(Admin = série)* batch ◆ **~ d'arrêtés/de mesures** batch of decrees/of measures ◆ **un premier ~ de réformes** a first batch *ou* set of reforms

7 *(= partie)* **~ avant/arrière** *[de véhicule]* front/rear wheel-axle unit ◆ **~ de devant** *[d'animal]* forequarters ◆ **~ de derrière** hindquarters

8 *(* = derrière)* backside*, rear (end)* ◆ **recevoir un coup de pied dans le ~** to get a kick in the pants* *ou* up the backside‡; → **filer, se magner**

COMP **train d'atterrissage** undercarriage, landing gear

train fantôme ghost train

train de maison † *(= domestiques)* household, retainers †; *(= dépenses, installation)* (household) establishment

train mixte goods and passenger train

train d'ondes wave train

train postal mail train

train sanitaire hospital train

train de sonde drilling bit and pipe

train de vie lifestyle, style of living ◆ **le ~ de vie de l'État** the government's rate of expenditure

traînailler /tʀɛnɑje/ ► conjug 1 ◄ VI 1 *(= être lent)* to dawdle, to dillydally 2 *(= vagabonder)* to loaf *ou* hang about

traînant, e /tʀɛnɑ̃, ɑ̃t/ ADJ *[voix, accent]* drawling *(épith)*; *[robe, aile]* trailing *(épith)*; *[démarche]* shuffling *(épith)*

traînard, e /tʀɛnaʀ, aʀd/ NM,F *(péj) (gén)* slowcoach* *(Brit)*, slowpoke* *(US)*; *(toujours en queue d'un groupe)* straggler

traînasser /tʀɛnase/ ► conjug 1 ◄ VI ⇒ **traînailler**

traîne /tʀɛn/ NF 1 *[de robe]* train 2 *(Pêche)* dragnet ◆ **pêche à la ~** dragnet fishing

◆ **être à la traîne** *(en remorque)* to be on tow; *(* : en retard, en arrière)* to lag behind ◆ **notre pays est à la ~ en matière de télécommunications** our country is lagging behind in telecommunications ◆ **nous sommes à la ~ par rapport aux États-Unis dans ce domaine** we are lagging behind the United States in this field

traîneau (pl **traîneaux**) /tʀɛno/ NM 1 *(= véhicule)* sleigh, sledge *(Brit)*, sled *(US)* ◆ **promenade en ~** sleigh ride 2 *(Pêche)* dragnet

traînée /tʀene/ NF 1 *(= laissée par un véhicule, un animal)* trail, tracks; *[d'humidité, sang] (sur un mur)* streak, smear; *(= bande, raie : dans le ciel, sur un tableau)* streak ◆ **~s de brouillard** wisps of fog ◆ **~ de poudre** powder trail ◆ **la nouvelle s'est répandue** *ou* **propagée comme une ~ de poudre** the news spread like wildfire 2 *(*‡, péj = femme de mauvaise vie)* slut, hussy † 3 *(Tech = force)* drag

traînement /tʀɛnmɑ̃/ NM *[de jambes, pieds]* trailing, dragging; *[de voix]* drawl

traîne-misère /tʀɛnmizɛʀ/ NM INV wretch

traîne-patins* /tʀɛnpatɛ̃/ NM INV ⇒ **traîne-savates**

traîner /tʀene/ ► conjug 1 ◄ VT 1 *(= tirer) [+ sac, objet lourd, personne]* to pull, to drag ◆ **~ un meuble à travers une pièce** to pull *ou* drag a piece of furniture across a room ◆ **~ qn par les pieds** to drag sb along by the feet ◆ **~ les pieds** *(lit)* to drag one's feet, to shuffle along; *(= hésiter)* to drag one's feet ◆ **~ la jambe** *ou* **la patte*** to limp, to hobble ◆ **elle traînait sa poupée dans la poussière** she was trailing *ou* dragging her doll through the dust ◆ **~ ses guêtres** †* to knock around* ◆ **il a traîné ses guêtres en Afrique** †* he knocked around Africa* ◆ **~ la savate** †* to bum around‡ ◆ **~ qn dans la boue** *ou* **fange** *(fig)* to drag sb *ou* sb's name through the mud ◆ **~ un boulet** *(fig)* to have a millstone round one's neck

2 *(= emmener : péj)* to drag ◆ **elle est obligée de ~ ses enfants partout** she has to trail *ou* drag her children along (with her) everywhere ◆ **il traîne toujours une vieille valise avec lui** he's always dragging *ou* lugging* an old suitcase around with him ◆ **~ de vieilles idées/des conceptions surannées** to cling to old ideas/to outdated conceptions

3 *(= subir)* **elle traîne cette bronchite depuis janvier** this bronchitis has been with her *ou* plaguing her since January ◆ **elle traîne un mauvais rhume** she's got a bad cold she can't get rid of *ou* shake off ◆ **~ une existence misérable** to drag out a wretched existence

4 *(= faire durer)* to drag out, to draw out ◆ **~ les choses en longueur** to drag things out

5 ◆ **(faire) ~** *[+ mots]* to drawl; *[+ fin de phrase]* to drag out, to drawl ◆ **(faire) ~ sa voix** to drawl

VI 1 *[personne] (= rester en arrière)* to lag *ou* trail behind; *(= aller lentement)* to dawdle; *(péj = errer)* to hang about* ◆ **~ en chemin** to dawdle on the way ◆ **~ dans les rues** to roam the streets, to hang about the streets ◆ **elle laisse ses enfants ~ dans la rue** she lets her children hang about the street(s) ◆ **il traîne pour se préparer** he dawdles when he gets dressed, he takes ages to get dressed ◆ **~ en peignoir dans la maison** to trail round *ou* hang about in one's dressing-gown in the house ◆ **~ au lit** to lounge in bed ◆ **on est en retard, il ne s'agit plus de ~** we're late – we must stop hanging around *ou* dawdling ◆ **~ dans les cafés** to hang around the cafés ◆ **après sa maladie, il a encore traîné 2 ans** after his illness he lingered on for 2 years

2 *[chose] (= être éparpillé)* to lie about *ou* around ◆ **ses livres traînent sur toutes les chaises** his books are lying about on all the chairs ◆ **ne laisse pas ~ ton argent/tes affaires** don't leave your money/your things lying about *ou* around ◆ **des histoires/idées qui traînent partout** stories/ideas that float around everywhere ◆ **elle attrape tous les microbes qui traînent** *ou* **tout ce qui traîne** she catches anything that's going

3 *(= durer trop longtemps)* to drag on ◆ **un procès qui traîne** a case which is dragging on ◆ **une maladie qui traîne** a lingering illness, an illness which drags on ◆ **la discussion a traîné en longueur** the discussion dragged on for ages *ou* dragged on and on ◆ **ça n'a pas traîné !*** that wasn't long coming! ◆ **il n'a pas traîné (à répondre)*** he was quick (with his answer), his answer wasn't long in coming, he replied immediately ◆ **ça ne ~a pas, il vous mettra tous à la porte*** he'll throw you all out before you know what's happening *ou* where you are ◆ **faire ~ qch en longueur** to drag sth out

4 *[robe, manteau]* to trail ◆ **ta ceinture/ton lacet traîne par terre** your belt/your shoelace is trailing *ou* dragging on the ground

VPR **se traîner** 1 *[personne fatiguée]* to drag o.s.; *[train, voiture]* to crawl along ◆ **on se traînait à 20 à l'heure** we were crawling along at 20 ◆ **se ~ par terre** to crawl on the ground ◆ **avec cette chaleur, on se traîne** it's all you can do to drag yourself around in this heat ◆ **elle a pu se ~ jusqu'à son fauteuil** she managed to drag *ou* haul herself (over) to her chair ◆ **je ne peux même plus me ~** I can't even drag myself about any more ◆ **se ~ aux pieds de qn** *(fig)* to grovel at sb's feet

2 *[conversation, journée, hiver]* to drag on

traîne-savates* /tʀɛnsavat/ NM INV *(= vagabond)* tramp, bum*; *(= traînard)* slowcoach *(Brit)*, slowpoke *(US)*

training /tʀeniŋ/ NM 1 *(= entraînement)* training 2 *(= chaussure)* trainer; *(= survêtement)* tracksuit top

train-train, traintrain /tʀɛ̃tʀɛ̃/ NM INV humdrum routine ◆ **le ~ de la vie quotidienne** the humdrum routine of everyday life, the daily round

traire /tʀɛʀ/ ► conjug 50 ◄ VT *[+ vache]* to milk; *[+ lait]* to draw ◆ **machine à ~** milking machine

trait /tʀɛ/ GRAMMAIRE ACTIVE 53.1

NM 1 *(= ligne) (en dessinant)* stroke; *(en soulignant, dans un graphique)* line ◆ **faire** *ou* **tirer** *ou* **tracer un ~** to draw a line ◆ **tirer un ~ sur son passé** to make a complete break with one's past, to sever all connections with one's past ◆ **tirons un ~ sur cette affaire** let's put this business behind us ◆ **ta promotion ? tu peux tirer un ~ dessus !** your promotion? you can forget about it! *ou* kiss it goodbye!* ◆ **dessin au ~** *(Art)* line drawing ◆ **le ~ est ferme** *(Art)* the line is firm ◆ **d'un ~ de plume** *(lit, fig)* with one stroke of the pen ◆ **~ de repère** reference mark ◆ **biffer qch d'un ~** to score *ou* cross sth out, to put a line through sth ◆ **les ~s d'un dessin/portrait** the lines of a drawing/portrait ◆ **dessiner qch à grands ~s** to sketch sth roughly, to make a rough sketch of sth ◆ **décrire qch à**

grands ~s to describe sth in broad outline ◆ **il l'a décrit en ~s vifs et émouvants** he drew a vivid and moving picture of it

◆ **trait pour trait** ◆ **copier** *ou* **reproduire qch ~ pour ~** to copy sth line by line, to make a line for line copy of sth ◆ **ça lui ressemble ~ pour ~** *(fig)* that's just *ou* exactly like him, that's him all over

2 *(= élément caractéristique)* feature, trait ◆ **c'est un ~ de cet auteur** this is a (characteristic) trait *ou* feature of this author ◆ **les ~s dominants d'une époque/œuvre** the dominant features of an age/a work ◆ **avoir des ~s de ressemblance avec** to have certain features in common with ◆ **il tient ce ~ de caractère de son père** this trait comes to him from his father, he gets that from his father

3 *(= acte révélateur)* **~ de générosité/courage/perfidie** act of generosity/courage/wickedness

4 *(† = projectile)* arrow, dart; *(littér = attaque malveillante)* taunt, gibe ◆ **filer** *ou* **partir comme un ~** to be off like a shot ◆ **~ mordant** biting taunt ◆ **un ~ satirique/d'ironie** a shaft of satire/of irony *(littér)* ◆ **les ~s de la calomnie** the darts of slander *(littér)*

5 *(= courroie)* trace

6 *(= traction)* **animal** *ou* **bête/cheval de ~** draught *(Brit)* *ou* draft *(US)* animal/horse

7 *(Mus)* virtuosic passage

8 *(Rel)* tract

9 *(= gorgée)* gulp, draught *(Brit)*, draft *(US)* ◆ **boire qch à longs** *ou* **grands ~s** to take big *ou* large gulps of sth

◆ **d'un trait** *[dire]* in one breath; *[boire]* in one gulp, at one go; *[dormir]* uninterruptedly, without waking

10 *(Ling)* **~ distinctif** distinctive feature

11 *(Échecs)* **avoir le ~** to have the move ◆ **en début de partie les blancs ont toujours le ~** at the start of the game white always has first move ◆ **il avait le ~** it was his move, it was his turn to move

12 *(locutions)*

◆ **avoir trait à** to relate to, to be connected with, to have to do with, to concern ◆ **tout ce qui a ~ à cette affaire** everything relating to *ou* connected with *ou* (having) to do with *ou* concerning this matter

NMPL **traits** *(= physionomie)* features ◆ **avoir des ~s fins/réguliers** to have delicate/regular features ◆ **avoir les ~s tirés/creusés** to have drawn/sunken features

COMP **trait (d'esprit)** flash *ou* shaft of wit, witticism

trait de génie brainwave, flash of inspiration *ou* genius

trait de lumière *(lit)* shaft *ou* ray of light; *(fig)* flash of inspiration, sudden revelation *(NonC)*

trait de scie cutting-line

trait d'union *(Typo)* hyphen; *(fig)* link

traitable /tʀɛtabl/ ADJ 1 *(littér) [personne]* accommodating, tractable *(frm)* 2 *[sujet, matière]* manageable

traitant, e /tʀɛtɑ̃, ɑ̃t/ ADJ 1 *[shampoing]* medicated; → **médecin** 2 *(Espionnage)* **(officier) ~** contact

traite /tʀɛt/ NF 1 *(= trafic)* **~ des Noirs** slave trade ◆ **~ des Blanches** white slave trade 2 *(Comm = billet)* draft, bill ◆ **tirer/escompter une ~** to draw/discount a draft ◆ **j'ai encore des ~s pour la voiture** I've still got payments to make on the car ◆ **j'ai encore des ~s pour la maison** I've still got mortgage payments

3 *(locutions)*

◆ **d'une (seule) traite** *[parcourir]* in one go, without stopping on the way; *[dire]* in one breath; *[boire]* in one gulp, at one go; *[dormir]* uninterruptedly, without waking

4 *[de vache]* milking ◆ **~ mécanique** machine milking ◆ **l'heure de la ~** milking time

traité /tʀete/ NM 1 *(= livre)* treatise; *(Rel = brochure)* tract 2 *(= convention)* treaty ◆ **~ de paix** peace treaty ◆ **le ~ de Versailles/Paris** the Treaty of Versailles/Paris ◆ **conclure/ratifier un ~** to conclude/ratify a treaty

traitement /tʀɛtmɑ̃/ NM 1 *(= manière d'agir)* treatment ◆ **~ de faveur** special *ou* preferential treatment ◆ **le ~ social du chômage** social measures for fighting unemployment

2 *(Méd)* treatment ◆ **suivre/prescrire un ~ douloureux** to undergo/prescribe painful treatment *ou* a painful course of treatment ◆ **~ hormonal** *(gén)* hormone therapy; *(après la ménopause)* hormone replacement therapy ◆ **~ chirurgical** surgery ◆ **~ de fond** *(lit)* long term (course of) treatment ◆ **le problème du chômage nécessite un ~ de fond** what is required is a sustained approach to tackling unemployment ◆ **~ de choc** *(lit)* intensive (course of) treatment; *(fig)* shock treatment ◆ **être en ~ (à l'hôpital)** to be having treatment (in hospital) ◆ **être sous ~** to be undergoing treatment ◆ **les nouveaux ~s de** *ou* **contre la stérilité** new ways of treating sterility ◆ **les médicaments utilisés dans le ~ du cancer** cancer drugs, drugs used in the treatment of cancer

3 *(= rémunération)* salary, wage; *(Rel)* stipend ◆ **toucher un bon ~** to get a good wage *ou* salary

4 *[de matières premières, déchets]* processing, treating

5 *(Ordin)* processing ◆ **le ~ (automatique) de l'information** *ou* **des données** (automatic) data processing ◆ **~ de texte** *(= technique)* word-processing; *(= logiciel)* word-processing package ◆ **machine** *ou* **système de ~ de texte** word processor ◆ **~ par lots** batch processing ◆ **~ d'images/du signal** image/(digital) signal processing

traiter /tʀete/ GRAMMAIRE ACTIVE 53.2 ▸ conjug 1 ◂

VT 1 *[+ personne, animal]* to treat; *(= soigner) [+ malade, maladie]* to treat ◆ **~ qn bien/mal/comme un chien** to treat sb well/badly/like a dog ◆ **~ qn d'égal à égal** to treat sb as an equal ◆ **~ qn en enfant/malade** to treat sb as *ou* like a child/an invalid ◆ **~ durement qn** to be hard on sb, to give sb a hard time ◆ **les congressistes ont été magnifiquement traités** the conference members were entertained magnificently *ou* treated royally ◆ **se faire ~ pour une affection pulmonaire** to undergo treatment for *ou* be treated for lung trouble ◆ **cette infection se traite facilement** this infection is easily treated

2 *(= qualifier)* **~ qn de fou/menteur** to call sb a fool/a liar ◆ **~ qn de tous les noms** to call sb all the names imaginable *ou* all the names under the sun ◆ **ils se sont traités de voleur(s)** they called each other thieves ◆ **je me suis fait ~ d'imbécile** they called me a fool ◆ **~ qn*** *(= l'insulter)* to call sb names

3 *(= examiner, s'occuper de) [+ question]* to treat, to deal with; *(Art) [+ thème, sujet]* to treat; *(Comm) [+ affaire]* to handle, to deal with; *(Jur) [+ dossier, plainte]* to deal with; *(Mil) [+ objectif]* to handle ◆ **il n'a pas traité le sujet** he hasn't dealt with the subject ◆ **le volume des affaires traitées a augmenté** *(Bourse)* the volume of trading has increased ◆ **le dollar se traitait à 1 € en fin de séance** the dollar was trading at €1 at the close ◆ **les valeurs qui se traitent à Paris** shares that are traded on the Paris stock exchange

4 *(Tech) [+ cuir, minerai, pétrole]* to treat, to process; *[+ déchets]* to process; *(Ordin) [+ données]* to process ◆ **non traité** untreated

5 *(Agr) [+ cultures]* to treat, to spray; *[+ aliments]* to treat ◆ **fruits non traités** unsprayed fruit

VT INDIR **traiter de** to deal with, to treat of *(frm)* ◆ **le livre/romancier traite des problèmes de la drogue** the book/novelist deals with *ou* treats of *(frm)* the problems of drugs

VI *(= négocier, parlementer)* to negotiate, to make *ou* do* a deal ◆ **~ avec qn** to negotiate *ou* deal with sb, to have dealings with sb ◆ **les pays doivent ~ entre eux** countries must deal *ou* have dealings with each other

traiteur /tʀɛtœʀ/ NM caterer; *(= épicerie)* delicatessen

traître, traîtresse /tʀɛtʀ, tʀɛtʀɛs/ ADJ 1 *[personne, allure, douceur, paroles]* treacherous ◆ **être ~ à une cause/à sa patrie** to be a traitor to a cause/to one's country, to betray a cause/one's country

2 *(= dangereux) [animal]* vicious; *[vin]* deceptive; *[escalier, virage]* treacherous ◆ **le soleil est ~ aujourd'hui** the sun is hotter than it looks today

3 *(locutions)* **il n'a pas dit un ~ mot** he didn't breathe a word

NM 1 *(gén)* traitor; *(Théât)* villain ◆ **le ~, il complotait pour m'offrir cette robe !** *(hum)* he's a sly one, he was planning to buy me this dress all along!

2 *(† = perfide)* scoundrel †

3 ◆ **prendre/attaquer qn en ~** to take/attack sb off-guard, to play an underhand trick/make an insidious attack on sb ◆ **je ne veux pas vous prendre en ~** I want to be up front with you ◆ **un coup en ~** a stab in the back

NF **traîtresse** traitress

traîtreusement /tʀɛtʀøzmɑ̃/ ADV treacherously

traîtrise /tʀetʀiz/ NF 1 *(= caractère)* treachery, treacherousness 2 *(= acte)* piece *ou* act of treachery; *(= danger)* treacherousness *(NonC)*, peril

trajectoire /tʀaʒɛktwaʀ/ NF *(gén)* trajectory; *[de projectile]* path ◆ **la ~ de la balle passa très près du cœur** the bullet passed very close to the heart ◆ **~ de vol** flight path ◆ **les deux hommes n'ont pas du tout la même ~ politique** the two men have followed very different paths in politics *ou* have pursued very different political careers

trajet /tʀaʒɛ/ NM 1 *(= distance à parcourir)* distance; *(= itinéraire)* route; *(= parcours, voyage)* trip, journey *(Brit)*; *(= par mer)* voyage ◆ **un ~ de 8 km** a distance of 8 km ◆ **le ~ aller/retour** the outward/return trip *ou* journey *(Brit)* ◆ **choisir le ~ le plus long** to choose the longest route *ou* way ◆ **elle fait à pied le court ~ de son bureau à la gare** she walks the short distance from her office to the station ◆ **il a une heure de ~ pour se rendre à son travail** it takes him an hour to get to work ◆ **elle a dû refaire le ~ en sens inverse** she had to walk *(ou drive etc)* back ◆ **faire le ~ de Paris à Lyon en voiture/train** to do the trip *ou* the journey *(Brit)* from Paris to Lyon by car/train ◆ **le ~ par mer est plus intéressant** the sea voyage *ou* crossing is more interesting ◆ **il prend l'autobus puis termine son ~ en métro** he takes the bus and goes the rest of the way on the metro ◆ **quel ~ il a parcouru depuis son dernier roman !** what a distance *ou* a long way he has come since his last novel!

2 *(Anat) [de nerf, artère]* course; *[de projectile]* path

tralala* /tʀalala/ NM *(= luxe, apprêts)* fuss *(NonC)*, frills; *(= accessoires)* fripperies ◆ **faire du ~** to make a lot of fuss ◆ **en grand ~** with all the works*, with a great deal of fuss ◆ **avec tout le ~** with all the frills *ou* trimmings ◆ **et tout le ~** and the whole kit and caboodle*, and the whole shebang* *(US)* EXCL ha ha! ◆ **~ ! j'ai gagné !** ha ha! I've won!

tram /tʀam/ NM ⇒ **tramway**

tramail (pl **tramails**) /tʀamaj/ NM trammel (net)

trame /tʀam/ NF 1 *[de tissu]* weft, woof ◆ **usé jusqu'à la ~** threadbare 2 *[de roman]* framework; *[de vie]* web 3 *(Typo = quadrillage)* screen; *(TV = lignes)* frame 4 *(Géog)* network, system ◆ **la ~ urbaine** the urban network *ou* system

tramer /tʀame/ ▸ conjug 1 ◂ VT 1 *[+ évasion, coup d'État]* to plot; *[+ complot]* to hatch, to weave ◆ **il se trame quelque chose** there's something brewing 2 *(= tisser)* to weave 3 *(Typo, Photo)* to screen ◆ **cliché tramé** halftone

traminot /tʀamino/ NM tram(way) *(Brit) ou* streetcar *(US)* worker

tramontane /tʀamɔ̃tan/ NF *(= vent)* tramontana *(cold wind from the Italian Alps)*

tramp /tʀɑ̃p/ NM *(Naut)* tramp

trampoline /tʀɑ̃pɔlin/ NM trampoline ◆ **faire du ~** to go *ou* do trampolining

tramway /tʀamwɛ/ NM *(= moyen de transport)* tram(way); *(= voiture)* tram(car) *(Brit)*, streetcar *(US)*

tranchant, e /tʀɑ̃ʃɑ̃, ɑ̃t/ ADJ 1 *[couteau, arête]* sharp ◆ **du côté ~/non ~** with the sharp *ou* cutting/blunt edge 2 *[personne, ton]* peremptory, curt NM 1 *[de couteau]* sharp *ou* cutting edge ◆ **avec le ~ de la main** with the edge of one's hand; → **double** 2 *(= instrument) [d'apiculteur]* scraper; *[de tanneur]* fleshing knife

tranche /tʀɑ̃ʃ/ NF 1 *(= portion) [de pain, jambon]* slice; *[de bacon]* rasher ◆ **~ de bœuf** beefsteak ◆ **~ de saumon** salmon steak ◆ **~ napolitaine** Neapolitan slice ◆ **en ~s** sliced, in slices ◆ **couper en ~s** to slice, to cut into slices ◆ **~ de silicium** *(Ordin)* silicon wafer ◆ **ils s'en sont payé une ~** * they had a great time *

2 *(= bord) [de livre, pièce de monnaie, planche]* edge; → **doré**

3 *(= section) (gén)* section; *(Fin) [d'actions, bons]* block, tranche; *[de crédit, prêt]* instalment; *(Admin) [de revenus]* bracket; *[d'imposition]* band, bracket ◆ **~ (d'émission)** *(Loterie)* issue ◆ **~ d'âge/de salaires** *(Admin)* age/wage bracket ◆ **~ horaire** *(TV, Radio)* (time) slot ◆ **~ de temps** period of time ◆ **~ de vie** slice of life ◆ **la première ~ des travaux** the first phase of the work

4 *(Boucherie = morceau)* ~ **grasse** silverside ◆ **bifteck dans la ~** ≃ piece of silverside steak

tranché, e¹ /tʀɑ̃ʃe/ (ptp de **trancher**) ADJ 1 *(= coupé) [pain, saumon]* sliced 2 *(= distinct) [couleurs]* clear, distinct; *[limite]* clear-cut, definite; *[opinion]* clear-cut, cut-and-dried

tranchée² /tʀɑ̃ʃe/ NF 1 *(gén, Mil = fossé)* trench; → **guerre** 2 *(Sylviculture)* cutting

tranchées /tʀɑ̃ʃe/ NFPL *(Méd)* colic, gripes, tormina *(pl) (SPÉC)* ◆ **~ utérines** after-pains

tranchefile /tʀɑ̃ʃfil/ NF *[de reliure]* headband

trancher /tʀɑ̃ʃe/ ▸ conjug 1 ◂ VT 1 *(= couper) [+ corde, nœud, lien]* to cut, to sever ◆ **~ le cou** *ou* **la tête à qn** to cut off *ou* sever sb's head ◆ **~ la gorge à qn** to cut *ou* slit sb's throat ◆ **le prisonnier s'est tranché la gorge** the prisoner slit *ou* cut his throat ◆ **la mort** *ou* **la Parque tranche le fil des jours** *(littér)* death severs *ou* the Fates sever the thread of our days; → **nœud, vif**

2 (†, *frm = mettre fin à) [+ discussion]* to conclude, to bring to a close ◆ **~ court** *ou* **net** to bring things to an abrupt conclusion ◆ **tranchons là** let's close the matter there

3 *(= résoudre) [+ question, difficulté]* to settle, to decide, to resolve; *(sans complément = décider)* to take a decision ◆ **~ un différend** to settle a disagreement ◆ **le juge a dû ~/a tranché que ...** the judge had to make a ruling/ruled that ... ◆ **il ne faut pas avoir peur de ~** you mustn't be afraid of taking decisions ◆ **le gouvernement a tranché en faveur de ce projet** the government has decided *ou* has come out in favour of this plan

VI *(= faire contraste) [couleur]* to stand out clearly *(sur, avec* against); *[trait, qualité]* to contrast strongly *ou* sharply *(sur, avec* with); ◆ **cette vallée sombre tranche sur le paysage environnant** this dark valley stands out against the surrounding countryside ◆ **la journée du dimanche a tranché sur une semaine très agitée** Sunday formed a sharp contrast to a very busy week ◆ **son silence tranchait avec** *ou* **sur l'hystérie générale** his silence was in stark contrast to the general mood of hysteria

tranchet /tʀɑ̃ʃɛ/ NM *[de bourrelier, sellier]* leather knife; *[de plombier]* hacking knife

trancheuse /tʀɑ̃ʃøz/ NF *(à bois)* cutter; *(de terrassement)* trencher; *(à pain, à jambon)* slicer

tranchoir /tʀɑ̃ʃwaʀ/ NM *(= plateau)* trencher †, platter; *(= couteau)* chopper

tranquille /tʀɑ̃kil/ ADJ 1 *(= calme) [eau, mer, air]* quiet, tranquil *(littér)*; *[sommeil]* gentle, peaceful, tranquil *(littér)*; *[vie, journée, vacances, endroit, quartier]* quiet, peaceful, tranquil *(littér)* ◆ **un coin ~** a quiet corner ◆ **un ~ bien-être l'envahissait** a feeling of quiet *ou* calm wellbeing crept over him ◆ **c'est l'heure la plus ~ de la journée** it's the quietest *ou* most peaceful time of day ◆ **aller/entrer d'un pas ~** to walk/go in calmly ◆ **ils mènent une petite vie bien ~** they have a nice quiet life

2 *(= serein) [courage, conviction]* quiet, calm ◆ **avec une ~ assurance** with quiet *ou* calm assurance

3 *(= paisible) [tempérament, personne]* quiet, placid; *[voisins, enfants, élèves]* quiet ◆ **il veut être ~** he wants to have some peace (and quiet) ◆ **rester/se tenir ~** to keep *ou* stay/be quiet ◆ **nous étions bien ~s et il a fallu qu'il nous dérange** we were having a nice quiet *ou* peaceful time and he had to come and disturb us ◆ **j'aime être ~ après le repas** I like (to have) some peace (and quiet) after my meal ◆ **ferme la porte, tu seras plus ~ pour travailler** close the door, it'll be quieter for you to work ◆ **laisser qn ~** to leave sb in peace, to give sb a bit of peace ◆ **laisser qch ~** to leave sth alone *ou* in peace ◆ **laisse-le donc ~, tu vois bien qu'il travaille/qu'il est moins fort que toi** leave him in peace *ou* let him be – you can see he's working/he's not as strong as you are ◆ **laissez-moi ~ avec vos questions** stop bothering me with your questions ◆ **il est ~ comme Baptiste** he's got nothing to worry about; → **père**

4 *(= sans souci)* **être ~** to feel *ou* be easy in one's mind ◆ **tu peux être ~** you needn't worry, you can set your mind at rest ◆ **soyez ~, tout ira bien** don't worry – everything will be all right ◆ **je ne suis pas ~ lorsqu'il est sur la route** I worry when he's out on the road ◆ **je serais plus ~ si j'avais un poste stable** I'd feel easier in my mind if I had a steady job ◆ **pouvoir dormir ~** *(lit)* to be able to sleep easy (in one's bed) ◆ **tu peux dormir ~** *(= être rassuré)* you can rest easy, you needn't worry ◆ **comme ça, nous serons ~s** that way our minds will be at rest ◆ **maintenant je peux mourir ~** now I can die in peace ◆ **il a l'esprit ~** his mind is at rest *ou* at ease ◆ **pour avoir l'esprit ~** to set one's mind at rest, to feel easy in one's mind ◆ **avoir la conscience ~** to be at peace with one's conscience, to have a clear conscience

5 *(* = certain)* **être ~ (que ...)** to be sure (that ...) ◆ **il n'ira pas, je suis ~** he won't go, I'm sure of it ◆ **tu peux être ~ que ...** you may be sure that ..., rest assured that ... ◆ **soyez ~, je me vengerai** don't (you) worry *ou* rest assured – I shall have my revenge

6 *(Pharm)* **baume ~** soothing balm ◆ **vin ~** still wine

7 *(* = facilement)* easily ◆ **il l'a fait en trois heures ~** he did it in three hours easily *ou* no trouble * ◆ **il a gagné en trois sets, ~** he won easily in three sets ◆ **tu peux y aller ~** *(= sans risque)* you can go there quite safely

⚠ Attention à ne pas traduire automatiquement **tranquille** par **tranquil**, qui est d'un registre plus soutenu.

tranquillement /tʀɑ̃kilmɑ̃/ ADV 1 *(= paisiblement) [dormir, vivre]* peacefully; *[jouer]* quietly; *(= sereinement) [affirmer, annoncer]* calmly ◆ **~ installé dans un fauteuil** sitting quietly in an armchair ◆ **il attendait ~ son tour** he calmly *ou* quietly waited his turn ◆ **on peut y aller ~, ça ne risque plus rien** * we can go ahead safely - there's no risk now 2 *(= sans se presser)* **vous pouvez y aller ~ en deux heures** you can get there easily *ou* without hurrying in two hours 3 *(= sans être dérangé) [travailler]* in peace, quietly ◆ **j'aimerais pouvoir lire ~** I'd like to have a quiet read, I'd like to read in peace *ou* quietly

tranquillisant, e /tʀɑ̃kilizɑ̃, ɑ̃t/ ADJ *[nouvelle]* reassuring; *[effet, produit]* soothing, tranquillizing NM *(Méd)* tranquillizer

tranquilliser /tʀɑ̃kilize/ ▸ conjug 1 ◂ VT ◆ **~ qn** to reassure sb, to set sb's mind at rest ◆ **je suis tranquillisé** I'm reassured *ou* relieved VPR **se tranquilliser** to set one's mind at rest ◆ **tranquillise-toi, il ne lui arrivera rien** calm down *ou* take it easy, nothing will happen to him

tranquillité /tʀɑ̃kilite/ NF 1 *[d'eau, mer]* quietness, tranquillity *(littér)*; *[de sommeil]* gentleness, peacefulness, tranquillity *(littér)*; *[de vie, journée, vacances, endroit]* quietness, peacefulness, tranquillity *(littér)*

2 *[de courage, conviction, assurance]* quietness; *[de personne]* quietness, peacefulness

3 *(= paix)* peace, tranquillity *(littér)* ◆ **en toute ~** without being bothered *ou* disturbed ◆ **ils ont cambriolé la villa en toute ~** they burgled the house without being disturbed (at all) *ou* without any disturbance ◆ **troubler la ~ publique** to disturb the peace ◆ **travailler dans la ~** to work in peace ◆ **il tient beaucoup à sa ~** all he wants is to be left in peace ◆ **je n'ai pas eu un seul moment de ~** I haven't had a moment's peace

4 *(= absence d'inquiétude)* **~ (d'esprit)** peace of mind ◆ **~ matérielle** material security ◆ **en toute ~** with complete peace of mind, free from all anxiety ◆ **vous pouvez le lui confier en toute ~** you can entrust it to him with absolute confidence

trans... /tʀɑ̃z/ PRÉF trans... ◆ **ligne trans(-)Pacifique** trans-Pacific route ◆ **réseau de communication transeuropéen** trans-European communications network ◆ **une éducation transculturelle** a cross-cultural education

transaction /tʀɑ̃zaksjɔ̃/ NF 1 *(Comm, Ordin)* transaction ◆ **~s commerciales/financières/boursières** commercial/financial/stock exchange transactions *ou* dealings 2 *(Jur = compromis)* settlement, compromise

transactionnel, -elle /tʀɑ̃zaksjɔnɛl/ ADJ *(Ordin)* transactional; *(Jur)* compromise *(épith)*, settlement *(épith)* ◆ **formule ~le** compromise formula ◆ **règlement ~** compromise settlement ◆ **analyse ~le** *(Psych)* transactional analysis

transafricain, e /tʀɑ̃zafʀikɛ̃, ɛn/ ADJ transafrican

transalpin, e /tʀɑ̃zalpɛ̃, in/ ADJ transalpine

transamazonien, -ienne /tʀɑ̃zamazɔnjɛ̃, jɛn/ ADJ trans-Amazonian ◆ **(autoroute) transamazonienne** trans-Amazonian highway

transaméricain, e /tʀɑ̃zameʀikɛ̃, ɛn/ ADJ transamerican

transaminase /tʀɑ̃zaminaz/ NF transaminase

transat /tʀɑ̃zat/ NM (abrév de **transatlantique**) *(= chaise longue)* deckchair; *(pour bébé)* bouncer chair, bouncing cradle NF (abrév de **course**

transatlantique) ◆ ~ **en solitaire** single-handed transatlantic race ◆ ~ **en double** two-man (*ou* two-woman) transatlantic race

transatlantique /tʀɑ̃zatlɑ̃tik/ ADJ transatlantic ◆ **course** ~ transatlantic race NM (*= paquebot*) transatlantic liner; (*= fauteuil*) deckchair

transbahuter * /tʀɑ̃sbayte/ ► conjug 1 ◄ VT to shift, to lug along*, to hump along* (*Brit*) VPR **se transbahuter** to traipse along*

transbordement /tʀɑ̃sbɔʀdəmɑ̃/ NM (*Naut, Rail*) [*de marchandises*] tran(s)shipment, transfer; [*de passagers*] transfer ◆ **quai de** ~ transfer dock

transborder /tʀɑ̃sbɔʀde/ ► conjug 1 ◄ VT (*Naut, Rail*) [*+ marchandises*] to tran(s)ship, to transfer; [*+ passagers*] to transfer

transbordeur /tʀɑ̃sbɔʀdœʀ/ NM ◆ **(pont)** ~ transporter bridge

transcanadien, -ienne /tʀɑ̃skanadjɛ̃, jɛn/ ADJ trans-Canada (*épith*) NF **Transcanadienne** ◆ **la Transcanadienne** the Trans-Canada highway

Transcaucasie /tʀɑ̃skokazi/ NF Transcaucasia

transcendance /tʀɑ̃sɑ̃dɑ̃s/ NF (*Philos*) transcendence, transcendency; (*littér*, †) (*= excellence*) transcendence (*littér*); (*= fait de se surpasser*) self-transcendence (*littér*)

transcendant, e /tʀɑ̃sɑ̃dɑ̃, ɑ̃t/ ADJ 1 (*littér = sublime*) [*génie, mérite*] transcendent (*littér*) ◆ **ce n'est pas** ~* [*film, livre*] it's nothing special*, it's nothing to write home about* 2 (*Philos*) transcendent(al) ◆ **être** ~ **à** to transcend 3 (*Math*) transcendental

transcendantal, e (mpl **-aux**) /tʀɑ̃sɑ̃dɑ̃tal, o/ ADJ transcendental

transcendantalisme /tʀɑ̃sɑ̃dɑ̃talism/ NM transcendentalism

transcender /tʀɑ̃sɑ̃de/ ► conjug 1 ◄ VT to transcend VPR **se transcender** to transcend o.s.

transcodage /tʀɑ̃skɔdaʒ/ NM (*Ordin*) compiling; (*TV*) transcoding

transcoder /tʀɑ̃skɔde/ ► conjug 1 ◄ VT (*Ordin*) [*+ programme*] to compile; (*TV*) to transcode

transcodeur /tʀɑ̃skɔdœʀ/ NM (*Ordin*) compiler; (*TV*) transcoder

transcontinental, e (mpl **-aux**) /tʀɑ̃skɔ̃tinɑ̃tal, o/ ADJ transcontinental

transcriptase /tʀɑ̃skʀiptɑz/ NF ◆ ~ **inverse** reverse transcriptase

transcripteur /tʀɑ̃skʀiptœʀ/ NM transcriber

transcription /tʀɑ̃skʀipsjɔ̃/ NF 1 (*= fait de copier*) copying out, transcribing, transcription 2 (*= copie*) transcript 3 (*= translittération*) transcription, transliteration ◆ ~ **en braille** braille transcription 4 (*Mus, Ling, Bio*) transcription ◆ ~ **phonétique** phonetic transcription ◆ ~ **génétique** genetic transcription

transcrire /tʀɑ̃skʀiʀ/ ► conjug 39 ◄ VT 1 (*= copier*) to copy out, to transcribe 2 (*= translittérer*) to transcribe, to transliterate 3 (*Mus, Ling, Bio*) to transcribe 4 (*= restituer*) [*+ ambiance, réalité*] to translate

transdermique /tʀɑ̃sdɛʀmik/ ADJ [*substance*] transdermal ◆ **timbre autocollant** ~ skin *ou* transdermal (*SPÉC*) patch

transdisciplinaire /tʀɑ̃sdisiplinɛʀ/ ADJ interdisciplinary

transducteur /tʀɑ̃sdyktœʀ/ NM transducer

transduction /tʀɑ̃sdyksjɔ̃/ NF (*Bio*) transduction

transe /tʀɑ̃s/ NF (*= état second*) trance ◆ **être en** ~ to be in a trance ◆ **entrer en** ~ (*lit*) to go into a trance; (*= s'énerver*) to go into a rage, to see red*

NFPL **transes** (*= affres*) agony ◆ **être dans les ~s** to be in *ou* suffer agony, to go through agony ◆ **être dans les ~s de l'attente/des examens** to be in agonies of anticipation/over the exams

transept /tʀɑ̃sɛpt/ NM transept

transférabilité /tʀɑ̃sfeʀabilite/ NF transferability

transférable /tʀɑ̃sfeʀabl/ ADJ transferable

transfèrement /tʀɑ̃sfɛʀmɑ̃/ NM [*de prisonnier*] transfer ◆ ~ **cellulaire** transfer by prison van

transférer /tʀɑ̃sfeʀe/ ► conjug 6 ◄ VT 1 [*+ fonctionnaire, assemblée, bureaux*] to transfer, to move; [*+ joueur, prisonnier*] to transfer ◆ ~ **la production dans une autre usine** to transfer *ou* switch production to another factory ◆ **nos bureaux sont transférés au 5 rue de Lyon** our offices have transferred *ou* moved to 5 rue de Lyon 2 (*Ordin, Téléc*) to transfer ◆ **faire** ~ **ses appels à un autre numéro** to have one's calls transferred to another number 3 [*+ dépouille mortelle, reliques*] to transfer, to translate (*littér*) 4 (*Fin*) [*+ capitaux*] to transfer, to move; (*Comptabilité : par virement*) to transfer 5 (*Jur*) [*+ propriété, droit*] to transfer, to convey (*SPÉC*) 6 (*Psych*) to transfer (*sur* onto)

transfert /tʀɑ̃sfɛʀ/ NM 1 [*de fonctionnaire, assemblée, bureau, prisonnier, joueur*] transfer ◆ **demander son** ~ **dans une filiale** to ask to be transferred to *ou* for a transfer to a subsidiary company ◆ **il est décédé pendant son** ~ **à l'hôpital** he died while he was being taken to hospital ◆ ~ **de technologie** transfer of technology, technology transfer ◆ ~ **d'embryon** embryo transfer

2 (*Ordin, Téléc*) transfer ◆ ~ **(électronique) de données** (electronic) data transfer ◆ ~ **d'appel** call forwarding

3 [*de dépouille mortelle, reliques*] transfer, translation (*littér*)

4 (*Fin, Comptabilité*) transfer ◆ ~ **de fonds** transfer of funds ◆ **~s sociaux** welfare transfers

5 (*Jur*) [*de propriété, droit*] transfer, conveyance

6 (*= décalcomanie*) transfer (*Brit*), decal (*US*)

7 (*Psych*) transference ◆ **faire un** ~ **sur qn** to transfer onto sb

transfiguration /tʀɑ̃sfigyʀasjɔ̃/ NF transfiguration ◆ **la Transfiguration** (*Rel*) the Transfiguration

transfigurer /tʀɑ̃sfigyʀe/ ► conjug 1 ◄ VT (*= transformer*) to transform, to transfigure (*frm*); (*Rel*) to transfigure

transfo * /tʀɑ̃sfo/ NM abrév de **transformateur**

transformable /tʀɑ̃sfɔʀmabl/ ADJ [*structure*] convertible; [*aspect*] transformable; (*Rugby*) [*essai*] convertible

transformateur, -trice /tʀɑ̃sfɔʀmatœʀ, tʀis/ ADJ [*processus*] transformation (*épith*); [*action*] transforming (*épith*) ◆ **pouvoir** ~ power to transform NM transformer

transformation /tʀɑ̃sfɔʀmasjɔ̃/ NF 1 (*= modification*) [*de personne, caractère, pays*] change; (*radicale*) transformation; [*de vêtement*] alteration; [*de larve, embryon*] transformation; [*d'énergie, matière*] conversion ◆ **travaux de** ~, **~s** alterations ◆ **subir des ~s** (*gén*) to be changed, to undergo changes; (*plus radical*) to be transformed; (*Chim, Phys*) to be converted ◆ **opérer des ~s sur qch** ⊐ change sth; (*plus radical*) to transform sth ◆ **depuis son mariage, nous assistons chez lui à une véritable** ~ since he married we've seen a real transformation in him *ou* a complete change come over him; → **industrie** 2 (*Rugby*) conversion ◆ **il a réussi la** ~ he converted the try 3 (*Géom, Math, Ling*) transformation

transformationnel, -elle /tʀɑ̃sfɔʀmasjɔnɛl/ ADJ transformational

transformer /tʀɑ̃sfɔʀme/ ► conjug 1 ◄ VT 1 (*= modifier*) [*+ personne, caractère, pays*] to change, to alter; (*= changer radicalement, améliorer*) to transform; [*+ matière première*] to convert; [*+ vêtement*] to alter, to remake ◆ **on a transformé toute la maison** we've made massive alterations to the house, we've transformed the house ◆ **on a mis du papier peint et la pièce en a été transformée** we put up wallpaper and it has completely altered the look of the room *ou* it has transformed the room ◆ **le bonheur/son mariage l'a transformé** happiness/being married has transformed him *ou* made a new man of him ◆ **rêver de** ~ **la société/les hommes** to dream of transforming society/mankind ◆ **depuis qu'il va à l'école, il est transformé** he's been a different child since he started school

2 (*= convertir*) ~ **qn/qch en** to turn sb/sth into ◆ ~ **la houille en énergie** to convert coal into energy ◆ ~ **du plomb en or** to turn *ou* change *ou* transmute lead into gold ◆ **on a transformé la grange en atelier** the barn has been converted *ou* turned *ou* made into a studio ◆ **elle a transformé leur maison en palais** she has transformed their house into a palace

3 (*Rugby*) [*+ essai*] to convert ◆ **maintenant il faut** ~ **l'essai** (*fig*) now they (*ou* we *etc*) must consolidate their (*ou* our *etc*) gains *ou* ram their (*ou* our *etc*) advantage home

4 (*Géom, Math, Ling*) to transform

VPR **se transformer** 1 (*= changer, évoluer*) [*personne, pays*] to change, to alter ◆ **la manifestation risque de se** ~ **en émeute** the demonstration could well turn into a riot

2 (*= se métamorphoser*) (*gén*) to be transformed (*en* into); [*énergie, matière*] to be converted (*en* into); ◆ **la chenille se transforme en papillon** the caterpillar turns into a butterfly ◆ **la ville s'est étonnamment transformée en deux ans** the town has been transformed over the last two years *ou* has undergone amazing changes in two years ◆ **il s'est transformé depuis qu'il a ce poste** there's been a real transformation *ou* change in him *ou* a real change has come over him since he has had this job

transformisme /tʀɑ̃sfɔʀmism/ NM transformism

transformiste /tʀɑ̃sfɔʀmist/ ADJ, NMF (*= évolutionniste*) transformist NM (*= artiste qui se change très rapidement*) quick-change artist; (*= travesti*) drag artist

transfrontalier, -ière /tʀɑ̃sfʀɔ̃talje, jɛʀ/ ADJ cross-border

transfuge /tʀɑ̃sfyʒ/ NMF (*Mil, Pol*) renegade

transfusé, e /tʀɑ̃sfyze/ (ptp de **transfuser**) ADJ [*produit*] transfused ◆ **personne ~e** person who has had a blood transfusion

transfuser /tʀɑ̃sfyze/ ► conjug 1 ◄ VT [*+ sang, liquide*] to transfuse; [*+ malade*] to give a blood transfusion to; (*fig, littér*) to transfuse (*littér*) (*à* into) to instil (*à* into) to impart (*à* to)

transfuseur /tʀɑ̃sfyzœʀ/ NM transfuser

transfusion /tʀɑ̃sfyzjɔ̃/ NF ◆ ~ **(sanguine)** (blood) transfusion ◆ **faire une** ~ **à qn** to give sb a blood transfusion ◆ **centre de** ~ **sanguine** blood transfusion centre

transfusionnel, -elle /tʀɑ̃sfyzjɔnɛl/ ADJ [*système*] blood transfusion (*épith*) ◆ **il a été contaminé par voie** ~ **le** he contracted the disease through a contaminated blood transfusion

transgène /tʀɑ̃sʒɛn/ NM transgene

transgenèse /tʀɑ̃sʒənɛz/ NF transgenesis

transgénique /tʀɑ̃sʒenik/ ADJ transgenic

transgresser /tʀɑ̃sgʀese/ ► conjug 1 ◄ VT [*+ règle, code*] to infringe, to contravene; [*+ interdit*] to defy; [*+ tabou*] to break; [*+ ordre*] to disobey, to go against, to contravene ◆ ~ **la loi** to break the law

transgresseur /tʀɑ̃sgʀesœʀ/ **NM** *(littér)* transgressor *(littér)*

transgression /tʀɑ̃sgʀesjɔ̃/ **NF** *[de règle, code]* infringement, contravention; *[d'interdit]* defiance; *[d'ordre]* disobedience, contravention; *[de tabou, loi]* breaking ◆ ~ **marine** encroachment of the sea

transhumance /tʀɑ̃zymɑ̃s/ **NF** transhumance

transhumant, e /tʀɑ̃zymɑ̃, ɑ̃t/ **ADJ** transhumant

transhumer /tʀɑ̃zyme/ ▸ conjug 1 ◂ **VTI** to move to summer pastures

transi, e /tʀɑ̃zi/ (ptp de **transir**) **ADJ** ◆ **être ~ (de froid)** to be numb with cold *ou* chilled to the bone *ou* frozen to the marrow ◆ **être ~ de peur** to be paralyzed by fear, to be transfixed *ou* numb with fear; → **amoureux**

transiger /tʀɑ̃ziʒe/ ▸ conjug 3 ◂ **VI** 1 *(dans un différend)* to compromise, to come to terms *ou* an agreement 2 *(fig)* ~ **avec sa conscience** to come to terms *ou* to a compromise with one's conscience, to make a deal with one's conscience ◆ ~ **avec le devoir** to come to a compromise with duty ◆ **ne pas ~ sur l'honneur/le devoir** to make no compromise in matters of honour/of duty ◆ **je me refuse à ~ sur ce point** I refuse to compromise on this point, I am adamant on this point

transir /tʀɑ̃ziʀ/ ▸ conjug 2 ◂ **VT** *(littér) [froid]* to chill to the bone, to freeze to the marrow; *[peur]* to paralyze, to transfix

transistor /tʀɑ̃zistɔʀ/ **NM** *(= élément, poste de radio)* transistor ◆ ~ **à effet de champ** field-effect transistor, FET

transistorisation /tʀɑ̃zistɔʀizasjɔ̃/ **NF** transistorization

transistoriser /tʀɑ̃zistɔʀize/ ▸ conjug 1 ◂ **VT** to transistorize ◆ **transistorisé** transistorized

transit /tʀɑ̃zit/ **NM** transit ◆ **en ~** *[marchandises, voyageurs]* in transit ◆ **de ~** *[document, port, zone]* transit *(épith)* ◆ **le ~ intestinal** digestion, intestinal transit *(SPÉC)* ◆ **les fibres alimentaires favorisent le ~ intestinal** high-fibre foods relieve constipation *ou* facilitate regular bowel movements

transitaire /tʀɑ̃zitɛʀ/ **ADJ** *[pays]* of transit; *[commerce]* which is done in transit **NMF** forwarding *ou* freight agent ◆ **~s en douane** customs clearance agents

transiter /tʀɑ̃zite/ ▸ conjug 1 ◂ **VT** *[+ marchandises]* to pass *ou* convey in transit **VI** to pass in transit *(par* through)

transitif, -ive /tʀɑ̃zitif, iv/ **ADJ** *(Ling, Math, Philos)* transitive

transition /tʀɑ̃zisjɔ̃/ **NF** *(gén, Art, Ciné, Mus, Sci)* transition *(vers* to, towards; *entre* between); ◆ **période/gouvernement de ~** transitional *ou* transition period/government ◆ **mesure de ~** transitional measure *ou* step ◆ **sans ~, il enchaîna avec la météo** he moved straight onto the weather forecast ◆ **une tribu passée sans ~ de l'âge de fer au vingtième siècle** a tribe who've gone straight from the Iron Age into the twentieth century ◆ **l'auteur passait sans ~ du tragique au comique** the writer switched abruptly from tragedy to comedy

transitionnel, -elle /tʀɑ̃zisjɔnɛl/ **ADJ** transitional

transitivement /tʀɑ̃zitivmɑ̃/ **ADV** transitively

transitivité /tʀɑ̃zitivite/ **NF** *(Ling, Philos)* transitivity

transitoire /tʀɑ̃zitwaʀ/ **ADJ** 1 *(= fugitif)* transitory, transient 2 *(= provisoire) [régime, mesures]* transitional, provisional; *[fonction]* interim *(épith)*, provisional ◆ **à titre ~** provisionally

transitoirement /tʀɑ̃zitwaʀmɑ̃/ **ADV** 1 *(= de manière fugitive)* transitorily, transiently 2 *(= provisoirement)* provisionally

Transjordanie /tʀɑ̃sjɔʀdani/ **NF** *(Hist)* Transjordan

translation /tʀɑ̃slasjɔ̃/ **NF** 1 *(Admin) [de tribunal, évêque]* translation *(frm)*, transfer; *(Jur) [de droit, propriété]* transfer, conveyance; *(littér) [de dépouille, cendres]* translation *(littér)*; *(Rel) [de fête]* transfer, translation *(frm)* 2 *(Géom, Sci)* translation ◆ **mouvement de ~** translatory movement ◆ **la ~ de la Terre autour du soleil** the rotation *ou* the orbit of the Earth around the Sun

translit(t)ération /tʀɑ̃sliteʀasjɔ̃/ **NF** transliteration

translit(t)érer /tʀɑ̃sliteʀe/ ▸ conjug 6 ◂ **VT** to transliterate

translocation /tʀɑ̃slɔkasjɔ̃/ **NF** *(Bio)* translocation

translucide /tʀɑ̃slysid/ **ADJ** translucent

translucidité /tʀɑ̃slysidite/ **NF** translucence, translucency

transmanche /tʀɑ̃smɑ̃ʃ/ **ADJ INV** *[liaison, trafic]* cross-Channel *(épith)*

transmetteur /tʀɑ̃smetœʀ/ **NM** *(Télec, Bio)* transmitter ◆ ~ **d'ordres** *(Naut)* speaking tube

transmettre /tʀɑ̃smɛtʀ/ GRAMMAIRE ACTIVE 48.2, 49, 50.1 ▸ conjug 56 ◂ **VT** 1 *(= léguer) [+ biens, secret, autorité]* to hand down, to pass on; *[+ qualité, recette]* to pass on ◆ **sa mère lui avait transmis le goût de la nature** his mother had passed her love of nature on to him ◆ **c'est une recette qui se transmet de mère en fille** it's a recipe that's passed down from mother to daughter ◆ **un savoir-faire que l'on se transmet de génération en génération** knowledge that is passed down from generation to generation

2 *(= transférer) [+ autorité, pouvoir]* to pass on, to hand over, to transmit *(frm)*

3 *(= communiquer) [+ message, ordre, renseignement]* to pass on; *(= faire parvenir) [+ lettre, colis]* to send on, to forward ◆ **ils se sont transmis tous les renseignements nécessaires** they exchanged all the necessary information ◆ **veuillez ~ mes amitiés à Paul** kindly give *ou* convey my best wishes to Paul ◆ **veuillez ~ mon meilleur souvenir à Paul** kindly give my regards to *ou* remember me to Paul ◆ **d'accord, je transmettrai** * OK, I'll pass on the message

4 *(Téléc) [+ signal]* to transmit, to send; *(Radio, TV) [+ émission, discours]* to broadcast ◆ ~ **sur ondes courtes** *(Téléc)* to transmit on short wave; *(Radio, TV)* to broadcast on short wave

5 *(Sport) [+ ballon]* to pass; *[+ flambeau]* to hand over, to pass on

6 *(Sci) [+ énergie, impulsion]* to transmit

7 *[+ maladie]* to pass on, to transmit *(à* to); *[+ microbe]* to transmit *(à* to); ◆ **cette maladie se transmet par contact** the disease is passed on *ou* transmitted by contact ◆ **une maladie qui se transmet sexuellement** a sexually transmitted disease, a disease transmitted by sexual contact ◆ **il risque de ~ son rhume aux autres** he may pass on his cold to the others

transmigration /tʀɑ̃smigʀasjɔ̃/ **NF** transmigration

transmigrer /tʀɑ̃smigʀe/ ▸ conjug 1 ◂ **VI** to transmigrate

transmissibilité /tʀɑ̃smisibilite/ **NF** transmissibility

transmissible /tʀɑ̃smisibl/ **ADJ** 1 *(Jur) [patrimoine, droit, caractère]* transmissible, transmittable ◆ **ce document est ~ par fax** this document can be sent by fax 2 *[maladie]* transmittable ◆ **virus ~ par voie sanguine** virus that can be transmitted by the blood; → **maladie**

transmission /tʀɑ̃smisjɔ̃/ **NF** 1 *[de biens, secret, tradition]* handing down, passing on; *[de qualité, recette]* passing on ◆ **grâce à la ~ de ce savoir de génération en génération** because this knowledge has been passed down from generation to generation

2 *[d'autorité, pouvoir]* passing on, handing over, transmission ◆ ~ **des pouvoirs** *(Pol)* handing over *ou* transfer of power

3 *[de message, ordre, renseignement]* passing on; *(= remise) [de lettre, colis]* sending on, forwarding ◆ **la ~ du savoir** transmission of knowledge ◆ ~ **des données** *(Ordin)* data transmission ◆ ~ **de pensées** thought transmission, telepathy ◆ **c'est de la ~ de pensée !** *(hum)* you *(ou* he *etc)* must be telepathic!

4 *(Téléc) [de signal]* transmission; *(Radio, TV) [d'émission, discours]* broadcasting ◆ **les ~s** *(Mil = service)* ≃ the Signals (corps)

5 *(Sport) [de ballon]* passing

6 *(Sci) [d'énergie, impulsion]* transmission ◆ **les organes de ~, la ~** *(dans moteur)* the parts of the transmission system, the transmission ◆ ~ **automatique** automatic transmission; → **arbre, courroie**

7 *[de maladie]* passing on, transmission; *[de microbe]* passing on ◆ **le mode de ~ du virus** the mode of transmission of the virus

transmuer /tʀɑ̃smɥe/ ▸ conjug 1 ◂ **VT** *(Chim, littér)* to transmute

transmutabilité /tʀɑ̃smytabilite/ **NF** transmutability

transmutation /tʀɑ̃smytasjɔ̃/ **NF** *(Chim, Phys, littér)* transmutation

transmuter /tʀɑ̃smyte/ ▸ conjug 1 ◂ **VT** ⇒ **transmuer**

transnational, e (mpl **-aux**) /tʀɑ̃snasjɔnal, o/ **ADJ** transnational

transocéanique /tʀɑ̃zɔseanik/ **ADJ** transoceanic

Transpac ® /tʀɑ̃spak/ **NM** Transpac ®

transparaître /tʀɑ̃spaʀɛtʀ/ ▸ conjug 57 ◂ **VI** to show (through) ◆ **laisser ~ un sentiment** to let an emotion show (through), to betray an emotion ◆ **il n'a rien laissé ~ de ses intentions** he gave no sign of what his intentions were

transparence /tʀɑ̃spaʀɑ̃s/ **NF** 1 *[de verre, porcelaine, papier, tissu]* transparency; *[d'eau, ciel]* transparency, limpidity; *[de regard, yeux]* limpidity, clearness; *[de teint, peau]* transparency, translucency ◆ **regarder qch par ~** to look at sth against the light ◆ **voir qch par ~** to see sth showing through ◆ **éclairé par ~** with the light shining through 2 *[d'allusion, sentiment, intentions, texte, âme, personne]* transparency; *[de négociations, comptes]* openness ◆ **réclamer la ~ du financement des partis politiques** to call for openness in the financing of political parties ◆ **société dotée de la ~ fiscale** ≃ partnership ◆ **adopter une politique de ~** to adopt a policy of openness ◆ ~ **financière** financial accountability 3 *(Ciné)* back projection

transparent, e /tʀɑ̃spaʀɑ̃, ɑ̃t/ **ADJ** 1 *(= translucide) [verre, porcelaine]* transparent; *[papier, tissu]* transparent, see-through; *[teint, peau]* transparent, translucent 2 *(= limpide) [eau, ciel]* transparent, limpid; *[regard, yeux]* limpid, clear 3 *(= clair, sans secret) [allusion, sentiment, intentions]* transparent, evident; *[négociations, comptes]* open; *[âme, personne]* transparent ◆ **nous sommes pour une gestion ~e** we favour complete openness where management is concerned ◆ **société ~e** *(Écon)* ≃ partnership **NM** 1 *(= écran)* transparent screen; *(pour rétroprojecteur)* transparency 2 *(Archit)* openwork motif 3 *(= feuille réglée)* ruled sheet *(placed under writing paper)*

transpercer /tʀɑ̃spɛʀse/ ▸ conjug 3 ◂ **VT** 1 *(gén)* to pierce; *(d'un coup d'épée)* to run through, to transfix; *(d'un coup de couteau)* to stab; *[épée, lame]* to pierce; *[balle]* to go through ◆ **transpercé de douleur** *(fig)* pierced by sorrow ◆ ~ **qn du regard** to give sb a piercing look [2] *[froid, pluie]* to go through, to pierce ◆ **malgré nos chandails, le froid nous transperçait** despite our sweaters, the cold was going *ou* cutting straight through us ◆ **la pluie avait finalement transpercé la toile de tente** the rain had finally come through *ou* penetrated the tent canvas

transpiration /tʀɑ̃spiʀasjɔ̃/ **NF** *(= processus)* perspiration, perspiring; *(Bot)* transpiration; *(= sueur)* perspiration, sweat ◆ **être en** ~ to be perspiring *ou* sweating *ou* in a sweat

transpirer /tʀɑ̃spiʀe/ ▸ conjug 1 ◂ **VI** [1] *(= suer) [personne]* to perspire, to sweat ◆ **il transpire des mains/pieds** * his hands/feet perspire *ou* sweat, he has sweaty hands/feet ◆ ~ **à grosses gouttes** to be running *ou* streaming with sweat ◆ ~ **sur un devoir** * to sweat over an exercise * [2] *[secret, projet, détails]* to come to light, to transpire ◆ **rien n'a transpiré** nothing transpired *(de* from) [3] *(Bot)* to transpire

⚠ Au sens de 'suer', **transpirer** ne se traduit pas par **to transpire**.

transplant /tʀɑ̃splɑ̃/ **NM** *(Bio)* transplant

transplantable /tʀɑ̃splɑ̃tabl/ **ADJ** transplantable

transplantation /tʀɑ̃splɑ̃tasjɔ̃/ **NF** *[d'arbre, peuple, traditions]* transplantation, transplanting; *(Méd) (= technique)* transplantation; *(= intervention)* transplant ◆ ~ **cardiaque/du rein** heart/kidney transplant

transplanté, e /tʀɑ̃splɑ̃te/ (ptp de **transplanter**) **NM,F** *(Méd) (gén)* receiver of a transplant; *(= patient à l'hôpital)* transplant patient ◆ **les ~s du cœur** people who have received heart transplants

transplanter /tʀɑ̃splɑ̃te/ ▸ conjug 1 ◂ **VT** *(Bot, Méd, fig)* to transplant ◆ **se ~ dans un pays lointain** to uproot o.s. and move to a distant country, to resettle in a distant country

transpolaire /tʀɑ̃spɔlɛʀ/ **ADJ** transpolar

transport /tʀɑ̃spɔʀ/ **NM** [1] *(à la main, à dos)* carrying; *(avec un véhicule) [de marchandises, passagers]* transport, transportation *(surtout US)* ◆ ~ **de voyageurs** transport of passengers ◆ **un car se chargera du ~ des bagages** the luggage will be taken *ou* transported by coach ◆ **pour faciliter le ~ des blessés** to facilitate the transport of the injured, to enable the injured to be moved more easily ◆ ~ **de troupes** *(Mil) (= action)* troop transportation; *(= navire, train)* troop transport ◆ ~ **de fonds** transfer of funds ◆ **endommagé pendant le** ~ damaged in transit ◆ **mode de** ~ means *ou* mode of transport ◆ **matériel/frais de** ~ transportation *ou* transport equipment/costs ◆ ~ **maritime** *ou* **par mer** shipping, sea transport ◆ ~ **maritime à la demande** tramping ◆ ~ **en ambulance** ambulance transport ◆ ~ **ferroviaire** rail transport, transport by rail ◆ ~ **aérien** *ou* **par air** *ou* **par avion** air transport ◆ **~(s) maritime(s)** sea transport ◆ **~(s) routier(s)** road haulage *ou* transport ◆ ~ **par hélicoptère** helicopter transport ◆ **entreprise de ~(s)** haulage company, trucking company (US); → **avion, moyen²**
[2] *(Tech) [d'énergie, son]* carrying
[3] *(= transfert) [de traditions, conflit]* carrying, bringing; *[de thème, idée]* carrying over, transposition
[4] *(littér = élan)* transport ◆ **(avec) des ~s de joie/d'enthousiasme** (with) transports of delight/of enthusiasm ◆ ~ **de colère** fit of rage *ou* anger ◆ **embrasser qn avec** ~ to embrace sb enthusiastically ◆ **~s amoureux** amorous transports

NMPL **transports** transport, transportation *(surtout US)* ◆ **les ~s publics** *ou* **en commun** public transport *ou* transportation (US) ◆ **prendre les ~s en commun** to use public transport ◆ **elle passe trois heures par jour dans les ~s en commun pour aller travailler** she spends three hours a day commuting to work ◆ **~s urbains** city *ou* urban transport ◆ **~s fluviaux** transport by inland waterway ◆ **mal des ~s** travel-sickness *(Brit)*, motion sickness *(US)* ◆ **médicament contre le mal des ~s** travel sickness drug *(Brit)*, anti-motion-sickness drug *(US)*

COMP **transport au cerveau** † seizure, stroke
transport de justice, transport sur les lieux *(Jur) visit by public prosecutor's office to the scene of a crime*

transportable /tʀɑ̃spɔʀtabl/ **ADJ** *[marchandise]* transportable; *[blessé, malade]* fit to be moved *(attrib)*

transportation /tʀɑ̃spɔʀtasjɔ̃/ **NF** *[de condamnés]* transportation

transporter /tʀɑ̃spɔʀte/ ▸ conjug 1 ◂ **VT** [1] *(à la main, à dos)* to carry; *(avec un véhicule) [+ marchandises, voyageurs]* to transport, to carry; *(Tech) [+ énergie, son]* to carry ◆ **le train transportait les écoliers/touristes** the train was carrying schoolchildren/tourists, the train had schoolchildren/tourists on board ◆ **le train a transporté les soldats/le matériel au camp de base** the train took *ou* transported the soldiers/the equipment to base camp ◆ **on a transporté le blessé à l'hôpital** the injured man was taken to hospital ◆ **on l'a transporté d'urgence à l'hôpital** he was rushed to hospital ◆ ~ **qch par mer** to ship sth, to transport sth by sea ◆ ~ **des marchandises par terre/train/avion** to transport goods by land/train/plane ◆ **ils ont dû ~ tout le matériel à bras** they had to move all the equipment by hand, they had to carry all the equipment ◆ **le sable/vin est transporté par péniche** the sand/wine is transported by barge ◆ **elle transportait une forte somme d'argent** she was carrying a large sum of money (on her) ◆ **ce roman nous transporte dans un autre monde/siècle** this novel transports us into another world/century ◆ **on se retrouve transporté au seizième siècle** we find ourselves transported back to the sixteenth century
[2] *(= transférer) [+ traditions, conflit]* to carry, to bring; *[+ thème, idée]* to carry over, to transpose ◆ ~ **la guerre/la maladie dans un autre pays** to carry *ou* spread war/disease into another country ◆ ~ **un fait divers à l'écran** to bring a news item to the screen ◆ **dans sa traduction, il transporte la scène à Moscou** in his translation, he shifts the scene to Moscow
[3] *(littér = exalter)* to carry away, to send into raptures ◆ ~ **qn de joie** to send sb into transports of delight *ou* into raptures ◆ **être** *ou* **se sentir transporté de joie/d'admiration** to be beside o.s. with joy/with admiration ◆ **transporté de fureur** beside o.s. with fury ◆ **cette musique m'a transporté** the music carried me away ◆ **se laisser ~ par la musique** to let o.s. be carried away by the music

VPR **se transporter** *(= se déplacer)* to go, to betake o.s. *(frm)*, to repair *(frm)* ◆ **le parquet s'est transporté sur les lieux** *(Jur)* the public prosecutor's office visited the scene of the crime ◆ **se ~ quelque part par la pensée** to let one's imagination carry one away somewhere

transporteur, -euse /tʀɑ̃spɔʀtœʀ, øz/ **ADJ** ◆ **navire ~ de marchandises en vrac** bulk carrier ◆ **(navires) ~s de pétrole/gaz/produits chimiques** oil/gas/chemical tankers ◆ **bande transporteuse** conveyor belt **NM** [1] *(= entrepreneur, entreprise)* carrier, haulage contractor, haulier *(Brit)*; *(Jur)* carrier ◆ ~ **aérien** airline company ◆ ~ **routier** road haulage contractor, road haulier *(Brit)* ◆ ~ **maritime** shipping agent *ou* company ◆ ~ **de fonds** security company *(transporting money)*, ≃ Securicor ® [2] *(Tech = appareil)* conveyor [3] *(Chim, Bio)* carrier

transposable /tʀɑ̃spozabl/ **ADJ** ◆ **roman facilement ~ à l'écran** novel that can easily be adapted for the screen *ou* that lends itself to screen adaptation ◆ **ces résultats/idées sont ~s dans d'autres domaines** these results/ideas can be applied to other areas

transposée /tʀɑ̃spoze/ **ADJ F, NF** *(Math)* ◆ **(matrice)** ~ transpose

transposer /tʀɑ̃spoze/ ▸ conjug 1 ◂ **VTI** to transpose ◆ ~ **un roman à l'écran** to adapt a novel for the screen ◆ **ils ont transposé l'action dans les années 30** they have transposed the action to the 1930s

transposition /tʀɑ̃spozisjɔ̃/ **NF** transposition ◆ **la ~ en droit français d'une directive européenne** the adaptation of a European directive to French law ◆ **la ~ d'un roman à l'écran** the adaptation of a novel for the screen

transpyrénéen, -enne /tʀɑ̃spiʀeneɛ̃, ɛn/ **ADJ** trans-Pyrenean

transrhénan, e /tʀɑ̃sʀenɑ̃, an/ **ADJ** transrhenane

transsaharien, -ienne /tʀɑ̃(s)saaʀjɛ̃, jɛn/ **ADJ** trans-Saharan

transsexualisme /tʀɑ̃(s)sɛksɥalism/ **NM** transsexualism

transsexualité /tʀɑ̃(s)sɛksɥalite/ **NF** transsexuality

transsexuel, -elle /tʀɑ̃(s)sɛksɥɛl/ **ADJ, NM,F** transsexual

transsibérien, -ienne /tʀɑ̃(s)sibeʀjɛ̃, jɛn/ **ADJ** trans-Siberian **NM** ◆ **le** ~ the Trans-Siberian Railway

transsubstantiation /tʀɑ̃(s)sypstɑ̃sjasjɔ̃/ **NF** transubstantiation

transsudation /tʀɑ̃(s)sydasjɔ̃/ **NF** transudation

transsuder /tʀɑ̃(s)syde/ ▸ conjug 1 ◂ **VI** to transude

Transvaal /tʀɑ̃sval/ **NM** ◆ **le** ~ the Transvaal

transvasement /tʀɑ̃svazmɑ̃/ **NM** decanting

transvaser /tʀɑ̃svaze/ ▸ conjug 1 ◂ **VT** to decant

transversal, e (mpl **-aux**) /tʀɑ̃svɛʀsal, o/ **ADJ** *[coupe, fibre, pièce]* cross *(épith)*, transverse *(SPÉC)*; *[chemin]* which runs across *ou* at right angles; *[vallée]* transverse; *(Naut) [cloison]* horizontal ◆ **rue ~e** side street ◆ **axe ~, (route) ~e** cross-country link, cross-country trunk road *(Brit) ou* highway *(US)* ◆ **(ligne) ~e** *(Rail) (entre deux régions)* cross-country line; *(entre deux villes)* Intercity line ◆ **moteur** ~ transverse engine ◆ **thème** ~ cross-disciplinary theme ◆ **relations ~es** lateral relations ◆ **l'organisation ~e des entreprises** horizontal management structure in companies; → **barre**

transversalement /tʀɑ̃svɛʀsalmɑ̃/ **ADV** across, crosswise, transversely *(SPÉC)*

transverse /tʀɑ̃svɛʀs/ **ADJ** *(Anat)* transverse

transvestisme /tʀɑ̃svɛstism/ **NM** ⇒ **travestisme**

transvider /tʀɑ̃svide/ ▸ conjug 1 ◂ **VT** to transfer to another container

Transylvanie /tʀɑ̃silvani/ **NF** Transylvania

trapèze /tʀapɛz/ **NM** [1] *(Géom)* trapezium *(Brit)*, trapezoid *(US)* [2] *(Sport)* trapeze ◆ ~ **volant** flying trapeze ◆ **faire du** ~ to perform on the trapeze [3] *(Anat)* **(muscle)** ~ trapezius (muscle)

trapéziste /tʀapezist/ **NMF** trapeze artist

trapézoèdre /tʀapezɔɛdʀ/ **NM** *(Minér)* trapezohedron

trapézoïdal, e (mpl **-aux**) /tʀapezɔidal, o/ **ADJ** trapezoid *(épith)*

trapézoïde /tʀapezɔid/ **ADJ, NM** ◆ **(os)** ~ trapezoid

Trappe /tʀap/ **NF** *(= monastère)* Trappist monastery; *(= ordre)* Trappist order

trappe /tʀap/ **NF** 1 *(dans le plancher)* trap door; *(Tech : d'accès, d'évacuation)* hatch; *(Théât)* trap door; *(pour parachutistes)* exit door ◆ **mettre qn à la** ~ *(fig)* to give sb the push* ◆ **passer à la** ~ *[projet]* to be written off*; *[personne]* to be given the push*, to be shown the door 2 *(= piège)* trap

trappeur /tʀapœʀ/ **NM** trapper, fur trader

trappiste /tʀapist/ **NM** Trappist (monk)

trapu, e /tʀapy/ **ADJ** 1 *[personne]* squat, stocky, thickset; *[maison]* squat 2 *(arg Scol = calé) [élève]* brainy*; *[question, problème]* tough, hard, stiff ◆ **une question ~e** a stinker* of a question, a really tough question, a poser ◆ **il est ~ en latin** he's terrific* at Latin

traque /tʀak/ **NF** *[de gibier]* tracking; *[de personne]* manhunt

traquenard /tʀaknaʀ/ **NM** *(= piège)* trap; *(fig) [de grammaire, loi]* pitfall, trap ◆ **tomber dans un** ~ to fall into a trap

traquer /tʀake/ ▸ conjug 1 ◂ **VT** *[+ gibier]* to track (down); *[+ fugitif]* to track down, to run to earth, to hunt down; *(fig, littér) [+ abus, injustice]* to hunt down; *(= harceler) [journalistes, percepteur]* to hound, to pursue ◆ **air/regard de bête traquée** look/gaze of a hunted animal ◆ **c'était maintenant un homme traqué** he was now a hunted man

traquet /tʀakɛ/ **NM** *(= oiseau)* ◆ ~ **(pâtre)** stonechat ◆ ~ **(motteux)** wheatear

traqueur, -euse /tʀakœʀ, øz/ **NM,F** *(Chasse)* tracker

trauma /tʀoma/ **NM** *(Méd, Psych)* trauma

traumatique /tʀomatik/ **ADJ** traumatic

traumatisant, e /tʀomatizɑ̃, ɑ̃t/ **ADJ** traumatic

traumatiser /tʀomatize/ ▸ conjug 1 ◂ **VT** to traumatize

traumatisme /tʀomatism/ **NM** *(physique)* injury, trauma *(SPÉC)*; *(psychologique)* trauma ◆ ~ **crânien** cranial trauma *(SPÉC)*, head injury ◆ **subir un** ~ to undergo *ou* suffer a traumatic experience ◆ **provoquer un ~ chez qn** to traumatize sb

traumatologie /tʀomatɔlɔʒi/ **NF** traumatology ◆ **service de** ~ trauma unit

traumatologique /tʀomatɔlɔʒik/ **ADJ** traumatological

traumatologiste /tʀomatɔlɔʒist(ə)/, **traumatologue** /tʀomatɔlɔg/ **NMF** trauma specialist, accident and emergency specialist

travail[1] (pl **-aux**) /tʀavaj, o/ **NM** 1 *(= labeur)* **le** ~ work ◆ ~ **intellectuel** brainwork, intellectual *ou* mental work ◆ ~ **manuel** manual work *ou* labour *(NonC)* ◆ **ce mouvement demande des semaines de** ~ it takes weeks of work to perfect this movement ◆ **il est en plein** ~ he's right in the middle of something ◆ **son ardeur au** ~ his enthusiasm for work ◆ **se mettre au** ~ to get down to work ◆ **allez, au** ~ **!** (it's) time to get down to work! ◆ **observer qn au** ~ to watch sb at work, to watch sb working ◆ **avoir du ~/beaucoup de** ~ to have (some) work/a lot of work to do ◆ **j'ai un ~ fou en ce moment** I'm up to my eyes in work at the moment*, I'm snowed under with work at the moment* ◆ **horaire/vêtements de** ~ work schedule/clothes ◆ **conditions/méthodes/groupe/déjeuner de** ~ working conditions/methods/group/lunch ◆ **le ~ c'est la santé*** work is good for you ◆ **à ~ égal, salaire égal** equal pay for equal work ◆ **améliorer la communication, c'est tout un** ~ **!** improving communications is quite a task!

2 *(= tâche)* work *(NonC)*, job; *(= ouvrage)* work *(NonC)* ◆ **c'est un ~ de spécialiste** *(difficile à faire)* it's a job for a specialist; *(bien fait)* it's the work of a specialist ◆ **je n'y touche pas : c'est le ~ de l'électricien** I'm not touching it – that's the electrician's job ◆ **fais-le tout seul, c'est ton** ~ do it yourself, it's your job ◆ **commencer/achever/interrompre un** ~ to start/complete/interrupt a piece of work *ou* a job ◆ **ce n'est pas du** ~ **!** *(= c'est mal fait)* that's shoddy work!; *(= ce n'est pas fatigant)* (do you) call that work! ◆ **et voilà le** ~ **!*** not bad, eh? ◆ **les travaux de la commission seront publiés** the committee's work *ou* deliberations *ou* findings will be published ◆ **il est l'auteur d'un gros ~ sur le romantisme** he has written a major work on romanticism ◆ **travaux scientifiques/de recherche** scientific/research work ◆ **travaux sur bois** woodwork ◆ **travaux sur métal** metalwork ◆ **les travaux de la ferme** farm work ◆ **les gros travaux, les travaux de force** the heavy work ◆ **travaux de réfection/de réparation/de construction** renovation/repair/building work ◆ **travaux de plomberie** plumbing work ◆ **travaux d'aménagement** alterations, alteration work ◆ **faire faire des travaux dans la maison** to have some work done in the house ◆ **entreprendre de grands travaux d'assainissement/d'irrigation** to undertake large-scale sanitation/irrigation work ◆ **les grands travaux présidentiels/européens** the major projects undertaken by the president/by the European Union ◆ **"pendant les travaux, le magasin restera ouvert"** "business as usual during alterations", "the shop will remain open (as usual) during alterations" ◆ **il y a des travaux (sur la chaussée)** the road is up, there are roadworks in progress ◆ **"attention ! travaux !"** "caution! work in progress!"; *(sur la route)* "roadworks *(Brit) ou* roadwork *(US)* ahead!"; → **inspecteur**

3 *(= métier, profession)* job, occupation; *(= situation)* work *(NonC)*, job, situation ◆ **le** ~ *(= activité rétribuée)* work *(NonC)* ◆ **avoir un ~ intéressant/lucratif** to have an interesting/a highly paid job ◆ **apprendre un** ~ to learn a job ◆ **être sans ~, ne pas avoir de** ~ to be out of work *ou* without a job *ou* unemployed ◆ **chercher/trouver du** ~ to look for/find work *ou* a job ◆ ~ **à mi-temps/à plein temps** part-time/full-time work ◆ ~ **temporaire** temporary job *ou* work *(NonC)* ◆ ~ **de bureau** office work ◆ ~ **d'équipe** *ou* **en équipe** team work ◆ ~ **en équipes** shift work ◆ ~ **précaire** casual labour ◆ ~ **en usine** factory work ◆ **cesser le** ~ *(dans une usine)* to stop work, to down tools ◆ **reprendre le** ~ to go back to work

4 *(Écon : opposé au capital)* labour *(Brit)*, labor *(US)* ◆ **l'exploitation du** ~ the exploitation of labour ◆ **association capital-**~ cooperation between workers and management *ou* workers and the bosses* ◆ **les revenus du** ~ earned income ◆ **le monde du** ~ the world of work

5 *(= facture)* work *(NonC)* ◆ **dentelle d'un ~ très fin** finely-worked lace ◆ **sculpture d'un ~ délicat** finely-wrought sculpture ◆ **c'est un très joli** ~ it's a very nice piece of handiwork *ou* craftsmanship *ou* work ◆ ~ **soigné** *ou* **d'artiste/d'amateur** quality/amateurish workmanship *(NonC)* ◆ **c'est du beau** *ou* **joli** ~ **!** *(iro)* nice work!* *(iro)*, well done!* *(iro)*

6 *(= façonnage) [de bois, cuir, fer]* working ◆ **le ~ de la pâte** *(Peinture)* working the paste ◆ **le ~ du marbre requiert une grande habileté** working with marble requires great skill

7 *[de machine, organe]* work ◆ ~ **musculaire** muscular effort, work of the muscles

8 *(= effet) [de gel, érosion, eaux]* work; *(= évolution) [de bois]* warp, warping; *[de vin, cidre]* working ◆ **le ~ de l'imagination/l'inconscient** the workings of the imagination/the unconscious ◆ **le ~ du temps** the work of time

9 *(Phys)* work ◆ **unité de** ~ unit of work

10 *(Méd = accouchement)* labour *(Brit)*, labor *(US)* ◆ **femme en** ~ woman in labour ◆ **le ~ n'a pas encore commencé** she hasn't gone into labour yet, labour hasn't started yet; → **salle**

COMP **travaux agricoles** agricultural *ou* farm work

travaux d'aiguille needlework

travaux d'approche *(Mil)* sapping *ou* approach works; *(fig)* initial overtures *(auprès de* to); ◆ **tu as fait des travaux d'approche auprès du patron pour ton augmentation ?** have you broached the subject of a rise with the boss?

un travail de bénédictin a painstaking task

travail à la chaîne assembly-line work

travaux des champs ⇒ **travaux agricoles**

travaux dirigés *(Univ)* tutorial (class) *(Brit)*, section (of a course) *(US)*

travail de forçat *(fig)* hard labour *(fig)* ◆ **c'est un ~ de forçat** it's hard labour

travaux forcés *(Jur)* hard labour ◆ **être condamné aux travaux forcés** (lit) to be sentenced to hard labour ◆ **dans cette entreprise c'est vraiment les travaux forcés** it's real slave labour in this company

un travail de fourmi a long, painstaking job

les travaux d'Hercule the labours of Hercules

travaux d'intérêt général *community work carried out by young people*, ≃ community service *(Brit)*

travaux manuels *(Scol)* handicrafts

travaux ménagers housework

travail au noir *(gén)* undeclared work; *(en plus d'un autre)* moonlighting

travaux pratiques *(Scol, Univ) (gén)* practical work; *(en laboratoire)* lab work *(Brit)*, lab *(US)*

travaux préparatoires *[de projet de loi]* preliminary documents

travaux publics civil engineering ◆ **ingénieur des travaux publics** civil engineer; → **entreprise**

un travail de Romain a Herculean task

travaux d'utilité collective (paid) community work *(done by the unemployed)*

travail[2] (pl **travails**) /tʀavaj/ **NM** *(= appareil)* trave

travaillé, e /tʀavaje/ (ptp de **travailler**) **ADJ** 1 *(= façonné) [bois, cuivre]* worked, wrought 2 *(= fignolé) [style, phrases]* polished, studied; *[meuble, ornement]* intricate, finely-worked ◆ **une balle très ~e** *(Tennis)* a ball with a lot of spin 3 *(= tourmenté)* ~ **par le remords/la peur/la jalousie** tormented by remorse/fear/jealousy 4 *(= ouvré)* **heures ~es** hours worked ◆ **le nombre de journées non ~es** the number of days not worked

travailler /tʀavaje/ GRAMMAIRE ACTIVE 46.2 ▸ conjug 1 ◂

VI 1 *(= faire sa besogne)* to work ◆ ~ **dur** to work hard ◆ ~ **comme un forçat/une bête de somme** to work like a galley slave/a horse *ou* a Trojan ◆ **il aime ~ au jardin** he likes working in the garden ◆ **je vais ~ un peu à la bibliothèque** I'm going to do some work in the library ◆ **faire ~ sa tête** *ou* **sa matière grise** to set one's mind *ou* the grey matter to work ◆ **va** ~ (go and) do some work ◆ **fais ~ ta tête !** get your brain working!, use your head! ◆ **faire ~ ses bras** to exercise one's arms ◆ ~ **du chapeau*** to be a bit cracked* *ou* nuts* *ou* touched* *(Brit)* ◆ ~ **pour le roi de Prusse** to receive no reward for one's pains

2 *(= exercer un métier)* to work ◆ ~ **en usine/à domicile** to work in a factory/at *ou* from home ◆ ~ **35 heures par semaine** to work *ou* do a

35-hour week ◆ ~ **dans les assurances/l'enseignement** to work in insurance/education ◆ ~ **aux pièces** to do piecework ◆ **tu pourras te l'offrir quand tu travailleras** you'll be able to buy *ou* afford it once you start work ◆ **dans ce pays on fait ~ les enfants à huit ans** in this country they put children to work at the age of eight *ou* they make children work from the age of eight ◆ **il a commencé à ~ chez Legrand hier** he started work *ou* he went to work at Legrand's yesterday ◆ **sa femme travaille** his wife goes out to work, his wife works ◆ **on finit de ~ à 17 heures** we finish *ou* stop work at 5 o'clock; → **temps**[1]

3 *(= s'exercer) [artiste, acrobate]* to practise, to train; *[boxeur]* to have a workout, to train; *[musicien]* to practise ◆ **son père le fait ~ tous les soirs** *[+ enfant]* his father makes him work every evening; → **filet**

4 *(= agir, fonctionner) [firme, argent]* to work ◆ **l'industrie travaille pour le pays** industry works for the country ◆ ~ **à perte** to work *ou* be working at a loss ◆ **faites ~ votre argent** make your money work for you ◆ **le temps travaille pour/contre eux** time is on their side/against them

5 *[métal, bois]* to warp; *[vin, cidre]* to work, to ferment; *[pâte]* to work, to rise; *(fig) [imagination]* to work

VT 1 *(= façonner) [+ matière, verre, fer]* to work, to shape ◆ ~ **la terre** to work *ou* cultivate the land ◆ ~ **la pâte** *(Culin)* to knead *ou* work the dough; *(Peinture)* to work the paste

2 *(= potasser) [+ branche, discipline]* to work at *ou* on; *[+ morceau de musique]* to work on, to practise; *[+ rôle, scène]* to work on; *(= fignoler) [+ style, phrase]* to polish up, to work on; *(Sport) [+ mouvement, coup]* to work on ◆ ~ **son anglais** to work on one's English ◆ ~ **le chant/piano** to practise singing/the piano ◆ ~ **son piano/violon** to do one's piano/violin practice ◆ ~ **une balle** *(Tennis)* to put some spin on a ball

3 *(= agir sur) [+ personne]* to work on ◆ ~ **l'opinion/les esprits** to work on public opinion/people's minds ◆ ~ **qn au corps** *(Boxe)* to punch *ou* pummel sb around the body; *(fig)* to put pressure on sb, to pressurize sb

4 *(= faire s'exercer) [+ taureau, cheval]* to work

5 *(= préoccuper) [doutes, faits]* to worry; *(= tourmenter) [douleur, fièvre]* to torment ◆ **cette idée/ce projet le travaille** this idea/this plan is very much on his mind ◆ **je lui ai menti et ça me travaille** I lied to her and it's really bothering me

VT INDIR **travailler à** *[+ livre, projet]* to work on; *[+ cause, but]* to work for; *(= s'efforcer d'obtenir)* to work towards ◆ ~ **à la perte de qn** to work towards sb's downfall, to endeavour to bring about sb's downfall

travailleur, -euse /tʀavajœʀ, øz/ **ADJ** *(= consciencieux)* hard-working, painstaking, diligent *(frm)*

NM,F 1 *(gén)* worker ◆ **un bon/mauvais ~, une bonne/mauvaise travailleuse** a good/bad worker

2 *(= personne consciencieuse)* (hard) worker

NM *(= personne exerçant un métier)* worker ◆ **les ~s** the workers, working people ◆ **les revendications des ~s** the claims made by the workers ◆ **le problème des ~s étrangers** the problem of immigrant labour *ou* workers ◆ ~ **en situation irrégulière** illegal worker

NF **travailleuse** *(= meuble)* worktable

COMP **travailleur agricole** agricultural *ou* farm worker
travailleur clandestin illegal *ou* clandestine worker
travailleur à domicile homeworker
travailleuse familiale home help
travailleur de force labourer
travailleur frontalier cross-border worker
travailleur indépendant self-employed person, freelance worker
travailleur intellectuel non-manual *ou* intellectual worker
travailleur manuel manual worker
travailleur au noir moonlighter
travailleur précaire casual worker, worker on a casual contract
travailleur saisonnier seasonal worker *ou* labourer
travailleur salarié salaried employee, employee on a permanent contract
travailleur social social worker
travailleur temporaire temporary worker

travaillisme /tʀavajism/ **NM** Labour philosophy, Labour brand of socialism

travailliste /tʀavajist/ **ADJ** Labour **NMF** Labour Party member ◆ **il est ~** he is Labour, he supports Labour ◆ **les ~s** Labour, the Labour Party

travailloter /tʀavajɔte/ ► conjug 1 ◄ **VI** *(péj)* to work a little

travée /tʀave/ **NF** 1 *(= section) [de mur, voûte, rayon, nef]* bay; *[de pont]* span 2 *(Tech = portée)* span 3 *(= rangée) [d'église, amphithéâtre]* row (of benches); *[de théâtre]* row (of seats) ◆ **les ~s du fond manifestèrent leur mécontentement** the back rows showed their displeasure

traveller /tʀavlœʀ/ **NM** abrév de **traveller's chèque** *ou* **check**

traveller's chèque, traveller's check /tʀavlœʀ(s)ʃɛk/ **NM** traveller's cheque *(Brit)*, traveler's check *(US)*

travelling /tʀavliŋ/ **NM** *(Ciné) (= dispositif)* dolly, travelling platform; *(= mouvement)* tracking ◆ ~ **avant/arrière/latéral** tracking in/out/sideways ◆ ~ **optique** zoom shots ◆ **faire un ~** to track, to dolly

travelo* /tʀavlo/ **NM** *(= travesti)* drag queen*

travers[1] /tʀavɛʀ/ **NM** *(= défaut)* failing, fault ◆ **chacun a ses petits ~** everyone has his little failings *ou* faults ◆ **tomber dans le ~ qui consiste à faire ...** to make the mistake of doing ...

travers[2] /tʀavɛʀ/ **NM** 1 *(Boucherie)* ~ **(de porc)** sparerib of pork

2 *(locutions)*

◆ **à travers** *[+ vitre, maille, trou, foule]* through; *[+ campagne, bois]* across, through ◆ **voir qn à ~ la vitre** to see sb through the window ◆ **ce n'est pas opaque, on voit à ~** it's not opaque – you can see through it ◆ **le renard est passé à ~ le grillage** the fox went through the fence ◆ **sentir le froid à ~ un manteau** to feel the cold through a coat ◆ **passer à ~ champs/bois** to go through *ou* across fields *ou* across country/through woods ◆ **la couche de glace est mince, tu risques de passer à ~** the ice is thin – you could fall through ◆ **juger qn à ~ son œuvre** to judge sb through his work ◆ **à ~ les siècles** through *ou* across the centuries ◆ **à ~ les divers rapports, on entrevoit la vérité** through the various reports we can get some idea of the truth ◆ **passer à ~ les mailles du filet** *(lit, fig)* to slip through the net

◆ **au travers** through ◆ **au ~ de** through ◆ **la palissade est délabrée : on voit au ~/le vent passe au ~** the fence is falling down and you can see (right) through/the wind comes (right) through ◆ **au ~ de ses mensonges, on devine sa peur** through his lies you can tell he's frightened ◆ **passer au ~** *(fig)* to escape ◆ **le truand est passé au ~** the criminal slipped through the net *ou* escaped ◆ **passer au ~ d'une corvée** to get out of doing a chore ◆ **tout le monde a eu la grippe mais je suis passé au ~** everyone had flu but I managed to avoid *ou* escape it

◆ **de travers** *(= pas droit)* crooked, askew ◆ **vent de ~** *(Naut)* wind on the beam ◆ **avoir la bouche/le nez de ~** to have a crooked mouth/nose ◆ **marcher de ~** *[ivrogne]* to stagger *ou* totter along ◆ **planter un clou de ~** to hammer a nail in crooked ◆ **se mettre de ~** *[véhicule]* to stop sideways on ◆ **elle a mis son chapeau de ~** she has put her hat on crooked, her hat is not on straight ◆ **il lui a jeté un regard** *ou* **il l'a regardé de ~** he looked askance at him, he gave him a funny look ◆ **il a avalé sa soupe de ~, sa soupe est passée de ~** his soup has gone down the wrong way
(= mal) ◆ **répondre de ~** to give a silly answer ◆ **comprendre de ~** to misunderstand ◆ **aller** *ou* **marcher de ~** to be going wrong ◆ **tout va de ~ chez eux en ce moment** everything is going wrong *ou* nothing is going right for them at the moment ◆ **il prend tout de ~** he takes everything the wrong way *ou* amiss

◆ **en travers** across, crosswise; *[navire]* abeam, on the beam ◆ **couper/scier en ~** to cut/saw across ◆ **se mettre en ~** *[navire]* to heave to

◆ **en travers de** across ◆ **un arbre était en ~ de la route** there was a tree lying across the road ◆ **le véhicule dérapa et se mit en ~ de la route** the vehicle skidded and stopped sideways on *ou* stopped across the road ◆ **se mettre en ~ des projets de qn** to stand in the way of sb's plans

◆ **par le travers** *[navire]* abeam, on the beam

traversable /tʀavɛʀsabl/ **ADJ** which can be crossed ◆ **rivière ~ à gué** fordable river

traverse /tʀavɛʀs/ **NF** 1 *(Rail)* sleeper *(Brit)*, tie *(US)* 2 *(= pièce, barre transversale)* strut, crosspiece 3 *(= raccourci)* **chemin de ~**, ~ † road which cuts across, shortcut

traversée /tʀavɛʀse/ **NF** 1 *[de rue, mer, pont]* crossing; *[de ville, forêt, tunnel]* going through ◆ **la ~ des Alpes/de l'Atlantique en avion** the crossing of the Alps/of the Atlantic by plane ◆ **la ~ de la ville en voiture peut prendre deux heures** driving through the town can take two hours, it can take two hours to cross the town by car ◆ **faire la ~ d'un fleuve à la nage** to swim across a river ◆ **faire la ~ de Dieppe à Newhaven** to cross from Dieppe to Newhaven

2 *(Naut = trajet)* crossing

3 *(Alpinisme) (= course)* through-route; *(= passage)* traverse ◆ **descendre en ~** *(Ski)* to traverse

COMP **traversée du désert** *[de politicien, parti, artiste]* time (spent) in the wilderness ◆ **après une ~ du désert de cinq ans, il est revenu au pouvoir** after spending five years in the political wilderness, he returned to power ◆ **et tes amours ? – c'est un peu la ~ du désert en ce moment** how's your love life? – it's non-existent at the moment

traverser /tʀavɛʀse/ ► conjug 1 ◄ **VT** 1 *[personne, véhicule] [+ rue, pont, chaîne de montagnes, mer]* to cross; *[+ ville, forêt, tunnel]* to go through ◆ ~ **une rivière à la nage** to swim across a river ◆ ~ **une rivière en bac** to take a ferry across a river, to cross a river by ferry ◆ ~ **(une rivière) à gué** to ford a river, to wade across a river ◆ **il traversa le salon à grands pas** he strode across the living room ◆ **avant de ~, assurez-vous que la chaussée est libre** before crossing, make sure that the road is clear

2 *[pont, route]* to cross, to run across; *[tunnel]* to cross under; *[barre, trait]* to run across ◆ **le fleuve/cette route traverse tout le pays** the river/this road runs *ou* cuts right across the country ◆ **ce tunnel traverse les Alpes** this tunnel crosses under the Alps ◆ **un pont traverse le Rhône en amont de Valence** a bridge crosses *ou* there is a bridge across the Rhone upstream from Valence ◆ **une cicatrice lui traversait le front** he had a scar (right) across his forehead, a scar ran right across his forehead

3 (= percer) [projectile, infiltration] to go ou come through ◆ ~ **qch de part en part** to go right through sth ◆ **les clous ont traversé la semelle** the nails have come through the sole ◆ **la pluie a traversé la tente** the rain has come through the tent ◆ **une balle lui traversa la tête** a bullet went through his head ◆ **il s'effondra, la cuisse traversée d'une balle** he collapsed, shot through the thigh ◆ **une douleur lui traversa le poignet** a pain shot through his wrist ◆ **ça ne m'a jamais traversé l'esprit** it never occurred to me ou crossed my mind

4 (= passer à travers) ~ **la foule** to make one's way through the crowd

5 (dans le temps) [+ période] to go ou live through; [+ crise] to pass ou go through, to undergo ◆ **sa gloire a traversé les siècles** his glory travelled down the ages ◆ **il a traversé une période très difficile avant de réussir** he went through a very difficult period before he succeeded

traversier, -ière /tʀavɛʀsje, jɛʀ/ ADJ 1 [rue] which runs across 2 (Naut) [navire] cutting across the bows 3 (Mus) → **flûte** NM (Can) ferryboat

traversin /tʀavɛʀsɛ̃/ NM [de lit] bolster

travertin /tʀavɛʀtɛ̃/ NM travertin(e)

travesti, e /tʀavɛsti/ (ptp de **travestir**) ADJ (= déguisé) (gén) disguised; [acteur] playing a female role; [rôle] female (played by man); → **bal** NM 1 (= acteur) actor playing a female role; (= artiste de cabaret) female impersonator, drag artist; (= homosexuel) transvestite ◆ **numéro de** ~ drag act 2 (= déguisement) fancy dress ◆ **en** ~ in fancy dress

travestir /tʀavɛstiʀ/ ▸ conjug 2 ◂ VT 1 (= déguiser) [+ personne] to dress up; [+ acteur] to cast in a female role ◆ ~ **un homme en femme** to dress a man up as a woman 2 [+ vérité, paroles] to misrepresent VPR **se travestir** (pour un bal) to put on fancy dress; (Théât) to put on a woman's costume; (pour un numéro de cabaret) to put on drag; (Psych) to dress as a woman, to cross-dress ◆ **se** ~ **en Arlequin** to dress up as Harlequin

travestisme /tʀavɛstism/ NM (Psych) transvestism

travestissement /tʀavɛstismɑ̃/ NM 1 (= action) [de personne] (gén) dressing-up; (Psych) cross-dressing; [de vérité, paroles] travesty, misrepresentation 2 (= habit) fancy dress (NonC)

traviole /tʀavjɔl/ **de traviole** * LOC ADJ, LOC ADV skew-whiff*, crooked ◆ **être/mettre de** ~ to be/put skew-whiff* ou crooked ◆ **il m'a regardé de** ~ he gave me a funny look ◆ **il comprend tout de** ~ he gets hold of the wrong end of the stick every time*, he gets in a muddle about everything ◆ **elle fait tout de** ~ she does everything wrong ◆ **tout va de** ~ **en ce moment/dans ce service** everything's going wrong these days/in this department

trayeur, -euse /tʀɛjœʀ, øz/ NM,F milker NF **trayeuse** (= machine) milking machine

trébuchant, e /tʀebyʃɑ̃, ɑ̃t/ ADJ (= chancelant) [démarche, ivrogne] tottering (épith), staggering (épith); [diction, voix] halting (épith); → **espèce**

trébucher /tʀebyʃe/ ▸ conjug 1 ◂ VI (lit, fig) to stumble ◆ **faire** ~ **qn** to trip sb up ◆ ~ **sur ou contre** [+ racine, pierre] to stumble over, to trip against; [+ mot, morceau difficile] to stumble over

trébuchet /tʀebyʃɛ/ NM 1 (= piège) bird-trap 2 (= balance) assay balance

tréfilage /tʀefilaʒ/ NM wiredrawing

tréfiler /tʀefile/ ▸ conjug 1 ◂ VT to wiredraw

tréfilerie /tʀefilʀi/ NF wireworks

tréfileur /tʀefilœʀ/ NM (= ouvrier) wireworker, wiredrawer

tréfileuse /tʀefiløz/ NF (= machine) wiredrawing machine

trèfle /tʀɛfl/ NM 1 (= plante) clover ◆ ~ **à quatre feuilles** four-leaf clover ◆ ~ **blanc/rouge** white/red clover ◆ ~ **cornu** trefoil ◆ ~ **d'eau** bogbean 2 (Cartes) clubs ◆ **jouer** ~ to play a club ou clubs ◆ **le 8 de** ~ the 8 of clubs 3 (Aut) **(carrefour en)** ~ cloverleaf (junction ou intersection) 4 (Archit) trefoil 5 (= emblème de l'Irlande) **le** ~ the shamrock ◆ **le Trèfle (irlandais)** (Rugby) the Irish team

tréflière /tʀeflijɛʀ/ NF field of clover

tréfonds /tʀefɔ̃/ NM (littér) ◆ **le** ~ **de** the inmost depths of ◆ **ébranlé jusqu'au** ~ deeply ou profoundly shaken, shaken to the core ◆ **dans le ou au** ~ **de mon cœur** deep down in my heart ◆ **dans le ou au** ~ **de son âme** in the depths of his soul

treillage /tʀɛjaʒ/ NM (sur un mur) lattice work, trellis(work); (= clôture) trellis fence ◆ ~ **en voûte** trellis archway

treillager /tʀɛjaʒe/ ▸ conjug 3 ◂ VT [+ mur] to trellis, to lattice; [+ fenêtre] to lattice ◆ **treillagé de rubans** criss-crossed with tape

treille /tʀɛj/ NF (= tonnelle) vine arbour (Brit) ou arbor (US); (= vigne) climbing vine; → **jus**

treillis¹ /tʀeji/ NM (en bois) trellis; (en métal) wire-mesh; (Constr) lattice work

treillis² /tʀeji/ NM (= tissu) canvas; (= tenue de combat) battledress, combat uniform; (= tenue d'exercice) fatigues

treize /tʀɛz/ ADJ INV, NM INV thirteen ◆ **il m'en a donné** ~ **à la douzaine** he gave me a baker's dozen ◆ **vendre des huîtres** ~ **à la douzaine** to sell oysters at thirteen for the price of twelve ◆ **le (nombre)** ~ **porte malheur** thirteen is unlucky; pour autres loc voir **six**

treizième /tʀɛzjɛm/ ADJ, NMF thirteenth ◆ ~ **mois** (de salaire) (bonus) thirteenth month's salary; pour autres loc voir **sixième**

treizièmement /tʀɛzjɛmmɑ̃/ ADV in the thirteenth place

trekking /tʀekiŋ/ NM (= activité) trekking (NonC); (= randonnée) trek ◆ **faire un** ~ to go on a trek ◆ **faire du** ~ to go trekking

tréma /tʀema/ NM dieresis ◆ **i** ~ i dieresis

trémail (pl **trémails**) /tʀemaj/ NM ⇒ **tramail**

tremblant, e /tʀɑ̃blɑ̃, ɑ̃t/ ADJ [personne, membre, main] trembling, shaking; [voix] trembling, shaky, quavering, tremulous; [lèvres] trembling; [lumière] trembling, flickering, quivering ◆ **il vint me trouver**, ~ he came looking for me in fear and trembling ◆ **il se présenta** ~ **devant son chef** he appeared trembling ou shaking before his boss ◆ ~ **de froid** shivering ou trembling with cold ◆ ~ **de peur** trembling ou shaking ou shivering with fear ◆ ~ **de colère** quivering with rage NF **tremblante** (= maladie) **la ~e (du mouton)** scrapie

tremble /tʀɑ̃bl/ NM aspen

tremblé, e /tʀɑ̃ble/ (ptp de **trembler**) ADJ 1 [écriture, dessin] shaky; [voix] trembling, shaky, tremulous, quavering (épith); [note] quavering (épith) 2 (Typo) **(filet)** ~ wavy ou waved rule

tremblement /tʀɑ̃bləmɑ̃/ NM 1 [de personne] (de froid, de fièvre) shiver, trembling (NonC), shaking (NonC); (de peur, d'indignation, de colère) trembling (NonC), shaking (NonC); (de fatigue) trembling (NonC) ◆ **un** ~ **le parcourut** a shiver ran through him ◆ **il fut saisi d'un** ~ **convulsif** he suddenly started shivering ou trembling violently ◆ **j'ai été prise de ~s incontrôlables** I was shaking ou trembling uncontrollably

2 [de feuille] trembling (NonC), fluttering (NonC); [de main] trembling (NonC), shaking (NonC); [de menton] quivering (NonC); [de paupières] fluttering (NonC); [de lèvres] trembling (NonC)

3 [de lumière, lueur] trembling (NonC), flickering (NonC), quivering (NonC); [de flamme] trembling (NonC), flickering (NonC), wavering (NonC); [de reflet] shimmering (NonC)

4 [de voix] trembling (NonC), shaking (NonC), quavering (NonC); [de son] trembling (NonC), quavering (NonC) ◆ **avec des ~s dans la voix** in a trembling ou quavering ou shaky voice

5 [de bâtiment, vitres, plancher, terre] shaking (NonC), trembling (NonC)

6 (locutions) **et tout le** ~* the whole (kit and) caboodle*

COMP **tremblement de terre** earthquake ◆ **léger** ~ **de terre** earth tremor

trembler /tʀɑ̃ble/ ▸ conjug 1 ◂ VI 1 [personne] (de froid, de fièvre) to shiver, to tremble, to shake (de with); (de peur, d'indignation, de colère) to tremble, to shake (de with); (de fatigue) to tremble (de with); ◆ **il tremblait de tout son corps ou de tous ses membres** he was shaking ou trembling all over ◆ ~ **comme une feuille** to shake ou tremble like a leaf

2 [feuille] to tremble, to flutter; [main] to tremble, to shake; [menton] to quiver; [paupières] to flutter; [lèvres] to tremble

3 [lumière, lueur] to tremble, to flicker, to quiver; [flamme] to tremble, to flicker, to waver; [reflet] to shimmer

4 [voix] to tremble, to shake, to quaver; [son] to quaver

5 [bâtiment, vitres, plancher] to shake, to tremble ◆ **faire** ~ **le sol** to make the ground tremble, to shake the ground ◆ **la terre a tremblé** the ground shook ◆ **la terre a encore tremblé en Arménie** there has been another earthquake in Armenia

6 (= avoir peur) to tremble ◆ ~ **pour qn/qch** to fear for sb/sth ◆ ~ **à la pensée ou à l'idée de qch** to tremble at the (very) thought of sth ◆ **il fait** ~ **ses subordonnés** he strikes fear (and trembling) into his subordinates, his subordinates live in dread of him ◆ **il tremble devant son patron** he lives in fear (and trembling) of his boss ◆ **il tremble de l'avoir perdu** he's terrified that he might have lost it ◆ **je tremble qu'elle ne s'en remette pas** I'm terrified she might not recover

tremblotant, e /tʀɑ̃blɔtɑ̃, ɑ̃t/ ADJ [personne, main] trembling, shaking; [voix] quavering (épith), tremulous; [flamme] trembling (épith), flickering (épith), wavering (épith); [lumière] trembling (épith), quivering (épith), flickering (épith)

tremblote * /tʀɑ̃blɔt/ NF ◆ **avoir la** ~ (de froid) to have the shivers*; (de peur) to have the jitters*; [vieillard] to have the shakes*

tremblotement /tʀɑ̃blɔtmɑ̃/ NM 1 [de personne, main] trembling (NonC), shaking (NonC) 2 [de voix] quavering (NonC), trembling (NonC) ◆ **avec un** ~ **dans sa voix** with a tremble in his voice 3 [de lumière, lueur, flamme] flickering (NonC)

trembloter /tʀɑ̃blɔte/ ▸ conjug 1 ◂ VI 1 [personne, mains] to tremble ou shake (slightly) 2 [voix] to quaver, to tremble 3 [lumière, lueur, flamme] to flicker, to waver

trémie /tʀemi/ NF 1 (Tech = entonnoir) [de concasseur, broyeur, trieuse] hopper 2 (= mangeoire) feedbox 3 (Constr) [de cheminée] hearth cavity ou space; [d'escalier] stair cavity

trémière /tʀemjɛʀ/ ADJ F → **rose**

trémolo /tʀemɔlo/ NM [d'instrument] tremolo; [de voix] quaver, tremor ◆ **avec des ~s dans la voix** with a quaver ou tremor in one's voice

trémoussement /tʀemusmɑ̃/ NM wriggling (NonC), jigging about (Brit) (NonC)

trémousser (se) /tʀemuse/ ► conjug 1 ◄ VPR *(= s'agiter)* to wriggle, to jig about *(Brit)*; *(= se déhancher)* to wiggle one's hips ♦ **se ~ sur sa chaise** to wriggle *ou* jig about *(Brit)* on one's chair ♦ **marcher en se trémoussant** to walk with a wiggle, to wiggle as one walks ♦ **dès qu'elle voit un homme elle se trémousse devant lui** as soon as she sees a man she's all over him

trempage /tʀɑ̃paʒ/ NM *[de linge, graines, semences]* soaking; *[de papier]* damping, wetting

trempe /tʀɑ̃p/ NF [1] *(Tech) [d'acier] (= processus)* quenching; *(= qualité)* temper ♦ **de bonne ~** well-tempered [2] *(fig) [de personne, âme]* calibre *(Brit)*, caliber *(US)* ♦ **un homme de sa ~** a man of his calibre *ou* of his moral fibre [3] *(Tech = trempage) [de papier]* damping, wetting; *[de peaux]* soaking [4] * *(= correction)* hiding* ♦ **flanquer une ~ à qn** to give sb a good hiding* ♦ **je lui ai filé une ~ au tennis** I thrashed* him at tennis

trempé, e /tʀɑ̃pe/ (ptp de **tremper**) ADJ [1] *(= mouillé) [vêtement, personne]* soaked, drenched ♦ **~ de sueur** bathed *ou* soaked in *ou* streaming with sweat ♦ **~ jusqu'aux os** *ou* **comme une soupe*** wet through, soaked to the skin ♦ **visage ~ de pleurs** face bathed in tears [2] *[acier, verre]* tempered ♦ **caractère bien ~** sturdy character

tremper /tʀɑ̃pe/ ► conjug 1 ◄ VT [1] *(= mouiller)* to soak, to drench ♦ **la pluie a trempé sa veste/le tapis** the rain has soaked *ou* drenched his jacket/the carpet ♦ **je me suis fait ~** I got soaked *ou* drenched

[2] *(= plonger) [+ mouchoir, plume]* to dip *(dans* into, in); *[+ pain, biscuit]* to dip, to dunk *(dans* in); ♦ **~ sa main dans l'eau** to dip one's hand in the water ♦ **il a trempé ses lèvres** he just took a sip ♦ **il n'aime pas qu'on lui trempe la tête dans l'eau** he doesn't like having his head ducked in the water

[3] *(Tech) [+ métal, lame]* to quench; → **acier**

[4] *(littér = aguerrir, fortifier) [+ personne, caractère, âme]* to steel, to strengthen

VI [1] *[tige de fleur]* to stand in water; *[linge, graines, semences]* to soak ♦ **tes manches trempent dans ton assiette !** your sleeves are trailing in your plate!

[2] ♦ **(faire) ~** *[+ linge, graines]* to soak; *[+ aliments]* to soak, to steep; *[+ papier]* to damp, to wet; *[+ tige de fleur]* to stand in water ♦ **mettre le linge à ~** to soak the washing, to put the washing to soak ♦ **faire ~ des légumes secs** to soak pulses

[3] *(fig péj = participer)* **~ dans** *[+ crime, affaire, complot]* to have a hand in, to be involved in

VPR **se tremper** *(= prendre un bain rapide)* to have a quick dip; *(= se mouiller)* to get (o.s.) soaked *ou* soaking wet, to get drenched ♦ **je ne fais que me ~** I'm just going for a quick dip

trempette /tʀɑ̃pɛt/ NF [1] *(* = baignade)* **faire ~** to have a (quick) dip [2] *(Can : Culin)* dips

tremplin /tʀɑ̃plɛ̃/ NM [1] *[de piscine]* diving-board, springboard; *[de gymnase]* springboard; *(Ski)* ski-jump [2] *(fig)* springboard ♦ **servir de ~ à qn** to be a springboard for sb ♦ **le festival est un bon ~ pour les jeunes cinéastes** the festival is a good springboard for young film-makers

trémulation /tʀemylasjɔ̃/ NF *(Méd)* tremor

trench-coat (pl **trench-coats**) /tʀɛnʃkot/ NM trench coat

trentaine /tʀɑ̃tɛn/ NF *(= âge, nombre)* about thirty, thirty or so ♦ **il a la ~** he's about thirty, he's thirty-ish ♦ **il approche de la ~** he's coming up to *ou* he's nearly thirty

trente /tʀɑ̃t/ ADJ INV, NM INV thirty ♦ **les années ~** the (nineteen) thirties; → **concile, glorieux, guerre, tour²**; *pour loc voir* **six** COMP **trente et un** *(lit, Cartes)* thirty-one ♦ **être/se mettre sur son ~ et un*** to be wearing/put on one's Sunday best *ou* one's glad rags*, to be/get all dressed up to the nines*, to be/get dressed to kill*

trente-et-quarante /tʀɑ̃tekaʀɑ̃t/ NM INV *(Jeux)* trente et quarante

trentenaire /tʀɑ̃t(ə)nɛʀ/ ADJ thirty-year ♦ **(concession) ~** thirty-year lease ♦ **(personne) ~** thirty-year-old (person)

trente-six /tʀɑ̃tsis/ ADJ INV *(lit)* thirty-six; *(* = beaucoup)* umpteen* ♦ **il y en a ~ modèles** there are umpteen* models ♦ **il n'y a pas ~ possibilités** there aren't all that many choices ♦ **faire ~ choses en même temps** *ou* **à la fois** to (try to) do too many things at once, to (try to) do a hundred things at once ♦ **j'ai ~ mille choses à faire** I've a thousand and one things to do ♦ **voir ~ chandelles** * to see stars NM INV thirty-six ♦ **tous les ~ du mois*** once in a blue moon

trente-sixième /tʀɑ̃tsizjɛm/ ADJ thirty-sixth ♦ **être dans le** *ou* **au ~ dessous** to be in the depths of depression

trentième /tʀɑ̃tjɛm/ ADJ, NMF thirtieth; *pour loc voir* **sixième**

trépan /tʀepɑ̃/ NM *(Méd)* trephine, trepan; *(Tech)* trepan

trépanation /tʀepanasjɔ̃/ NF *(Méd)* trephination, trepanation

trépané, e /tʀepane/ (ptp de **trépaner**) NM,F *(Méd)* patient who has undergone trephination *ou* trepanation ADJ ♦ **être ~** to have undergone trephination *ou* trepanation

trépaner /tʀepane/ ► conjug 1 ◄ VT *(Méd)* to trephine, to trepan

trépas /tʀepɑ/ NM *(littér)* demise, death; → **vie**

trépassé, e /tʀepɑse/ (ptp de **trépasser**) ADJ *(littér)* deceased, dead ♦ **les ~s** the departed ♦ **le jour** *ou* **la fête des Trépassés** *(Rel)* All Souls' (Day)

trépasser /tʀepɑse/ ► conjug 1 ◄ VI *(littér)* to pass away, to depart this life

trépidant, e /tʀepidɑ̃, ɑ̃t/ ADJ *[plancher]* vibrating, quivering; *[machine]* vibrating, throbbing; *[rythme]* pulsating *(épith)*, thrilling *(épith)*; *[vie]* hectic, busy

trépidation /tʀepidasjɔ̃/ NF *[de moteur, navire, train]* vibration; *(Méd)* trembling; *(fig) [de ville]* hustle and bustle

trépider /tʀepide/ ► conjug 1 ◄ VI *[plancher]* to vibrate, to reverberate; *[machine]* to vibrate, to throb

trépied /tʀepje/ NM *(gén)* tripod; *(dans l'âtre)* trivet

trépignement /tʀepiɲmɑ̃/ NM stamping (of feet) *(NonC)*

trépigner /tʀepiɲe/ ► conjug 1 ◄ VI to stamp one's feet ♦ **~ d'impatience/d'enthousiasme** to stamp (one's feet) with impatience/with enthusiasm ♦ **~ de colère** to stamp one's feet with rage, to be hopping mad*

trépointe /tʀepwɛ̃t/ NF welt

tréponème /tʀeponɛm/ NM treponema

très /tʀɛ/ ADV [1] *(avec adj)* very, most; *(devant certains ptp etc)* (very) much, greatly, highly ♦ **~ intelligent/difficile** very *ou* most intelligent/difficult ♦ **il est ~ conscient de ...** he is very much aware of ... *ou* very conscious of ... ♦ **~ admiré** greatly *ou* highly *ou* (very) much admired ♦ **~ industrialisé/automatisé** highly industrialized/automatized ♦ **c'est un garçon ~ travailleur** he's a very hard-working lad, he's a very hard worker ♦ **elle est ~ grande dame** she is very much the great lady *ou* every bit a great lady ♦ **avoir ~ peur/faim** to be very frightened/hungry ♦ **elle a été vraiment ~ aimable** she was really most *ou* very kind ♦ **c'est ~ nécessaire** it's most *ou* absolutely essential ♦ **ils sont ~ amis/~ liés** they are great friends/very close (friends) ♦ **je suis ~, ~ content** I'm very, very *ou* terribly, terribly* pleased ♦ **j'ai ~ envie de le rencontrer** I would very much like to meet him, I'm very *ou* most anxious to meet him ♦ **un jeune homme ~ comme il faut** a well brought-up young man, a very respectable young man ♦ **un hebdomadaire ~ lu dans les milieux économiques** a magazine that's widely read *ou* that's read a lot in economic circles ♦ **être ~ à la page*** *ou* **dans le vent*** to be very *ou* terribly with-it* ♦ **je ne suis jamais ~ à mon aise avec lui** I never feel very *ou* particularly *ou* terribly* comfortable with him ♦ **êtes-vous fatigué ? – ~/pas ~** are you tired? – very *ou* terribly*/not very *ou* not terribly*

[2] *(avec adv)* very ♦ **~ peu de gens** very few people ♦ **c'est ~ bien écrit/fait** it's very well written/done ♦ **il est ~ en avant/arrière** *(sur le chemin)* he is well *ou* a long way ahead/behind; *(dans une salle)* he is well forward *ou* a long way to the front/well back *ou* a long way back ♦ **~ bien, si vous insistez** all right *ou* very well, if you insist ♦ **~ bien, je vais le lui expliquer** all right *ou* fine* *ou* very good *ou* OK*, I'll explain to him ♦ **travailler le samedi ? ~ peu pour moi !** work on Saturday? not likely!* *ou* not me!; → **peu**

trésor /tʀezɔʀ/ NM [1] *(= richesses enfouies)* treasure *(NonC)*; *(Jur : trouvé)* treasure-trove; *(fig = chose, personne, vertu précieuse)* treasure ♦ **découvrir un ~** to find some treasure *ou* a treasure-trove ♦ **course** *ou* **chasse au/chercheur de ~** treasure hunt/hunter

[2] *(= petit musée)* treasure-house, treasury ♦ **le ~ de Notre-Dame** the treasure-house of Notre-Dame

[3] *(gén pl = richesses)* treasure ♦ **les ~s du Louvre/de l'océan** the treasures *ou* riches of the Louvre/of the ocean ♦ **je vais chercher dans mes ~s** *(hum)* I'll look through my treasures *ou* precious possessions

[4] *(= abondance)* **des ~s de dévouement/de patience** a wealth of devotion/of patience, boundless devotion/patience ♦ **dépenser des ~s d'ingéniosité** to exercise considerable *ou* great ingenuity

[5] *(= ouvrage)* treasury

[6] *(Admin, Fin = ressources) [de roi, État]* exchequer, finances; *[d'organisation secrète]* finances, funds ♦ **le Trésor (public)** *(= service)* the public revenue department, ≈ the Treasury *(Brit)*, the Treasury Department *(US)*; → **bon²**

[7] *(affectif)* **mon (petit) ~** my (little) treasure, my precious ♦ **tu es un ~ de m'avoir acheté ce livre** you're a (real) treasure for buying me this book

[8] *(Fin)* **~ de guerre** war chest

trésorerie /tʀezɔʀʀi/ NF [1] *(= bureaux) [d'association]* accounts department ♦ **Trésorerie (générale** *ou* **principale)** *[de Trésor public]* ≈ public revenue office [2] *(= gestion)* accounts ♦ **leur ~ est bien/mal tenue** their accounts are well/badly kept [3] *(= argent disponible)* finances, funds ♦ **difficultés** *ou* **problèmes de ~** cash shortage, cash (flow) problems, shortage of funds ♦ **~ nette** net liquid assets [4] *(= fonction de trésorier)* treasurership

trésorier, -ière /tʀezɔʀje, jɛʀ/ NM,F *(gén) [de club, association]* treasurer ♦ **~-payeur général** *(Admin)* paymaster *(for a département)* ♦ **~ d'entreprise** *(Fin)* company treasurer

tressage /tʀesaʒ/ NM [1] *[de cheveux, rubans]* plaiting, braiding; *[de paille, fil]* plaiting; *[de câble, corde, cordon]* twisting [2] *[de panier, guirlande]* weaving

tressaillement /tʀesajmɑ̃/ NM [1] *(= frémissement) (de plaisir)* thrill, quiver; *(de peur)* shudder; *(de douleur)* wince ♦ **des ~s parcoururent**

l'animal the animal twitched 2 (= sursaut) start 3 [de plancher, véhicule] shaking (NonC), vibration

tressaillir /tʀesajiʀ/ ► conjug 13 ◄ VI 1 (= frémir) (de plaisir) to thrill, to quiver; (de peur) to shudder, to shiver; (de douleur) to wince; [muscle, personne ou animal à l'agonie] to twitch ◆ **son cœur tressaillait** his heart was fluttering 2 (= sursauter) to start, to give a start ◆ **faire ~ qn** to startle sb, to make sb jump 3 [plancher, véhicule] to shake, to vibrate

tressautement /tʀesotmɑ̃/ NM (= sursaut) start, jump; (= secousses) [de voyageurs] jolting (NonC), tossing (NonC); [d'objets] shaking (NonC)

tressauter /tʀesote/ ► conjug 1 ◄ VI 1 (= sursauter) to start, to jump ◆ **faire ~ qn** to startle sb, to make sb jump 2 (= être secoué) [voyageurs] to be jolted, to be tossed about; [objets] to be shaken about, to jump about ◆ **faire ~ les voyageurs** to toss the passengers about ◆ **les tasses tressautent sur le plateau** the cups are shaking ou jumping about on the tray

tresse /tʀɛs/ NF 1 (= cheveux) plait, braid ◆ **se faire des ~s** to plait (Brit) ou braid one's hair ◆ **~s africaines** African braids 2 (= cordon) braid (NonC) 3 (Archit = motif) strapwork

tresser /tʀese/ ► conjug 1 ◄ VT 1 [+ cheveux, rubans] to plait, to braid; [+ paille, fil] to plait; [+ câble, corde, cordon] to twist ◆ **chaussures en cuir tressé** lattice-work leather shoes 2 [+ panier, guirlande] to weave ◆ **~ des couronnes** ou **des lauriers à qn** to praise ou laud sb to the skies, to sing sb's praises

tréteau (pl **tréteaux**) /tʀeto/ NM 1 (= support) trestle ◆ **table à ~x** trestle table 2 (Théât) **les ~x** the boards, the stage ◆ **monter sur les ~x** to go on the stage

treuil /tʀœj/ NM winch, windlass

treuiller /tʀœje/ ► conjug 1 ◄ VT to winch up

trêve /tʀɛv/ NF 1 (Mil, Pol) truce; (Sport) midwinter break ◆ **~ de Dieu** (Hist) truce of God ◆ **~ des confiseurs** (hum) Christmas ou New Year (political) truce 2 (= répit) respite, rest ◆ **s'accorder une ~** to allow o.s. a (moment's) respite ou a rest ◆ **faire ~ à** (littér) [+ disputes, travaux] to rest from 3 ◆ **~ de** (= assez de) **~ de plaisanteries/polémique** enough of this joking/arguing ◆ **~ de plaisanteries, tu veux vraiment te marier avec lui ?** joking apart, do you really want to marry him? 4 ◆ **sans ~** (= sans cesse) unremittingly, unceasingly, relentlessly

trévise /tʀeviz/ NF radicchio lettuce

tri /tʀi/ NM 1 (gén) sorting out; [de fiches, lettres, dossiers, linge] sorting; [de personnes] selection; [de patients à l'hôpital] triage; [de wagons] shunting, marshalling; (= calibrage) grading; (= tamisage) sifting ◆ **le ~ sélectif des ordures ménagères** the selective sorting of household waste ◆ **faire le ~ de** (gén) to sort out; [+ lettres, fiches, dossiers, linge] to sort; [+ personnes] to select; [+ wagons] to marshal; [+ déchets] to sort through; (en calibrant) to grade; (en tamisant) to sift ◆ **faire le ~ entre les rumeurs et les faits** to sift ou separate fact from rumour ◆ **quand il dit quelque chose il faut toujours faire le ~** you shouldn't believe everything he says ◆ **le chômage m'a permis de faire le ~ entre mes vrais et mes faux amis** when I became unemployed I found out who my real friends were ◆ **on a procédé à des ~s successifs pour sélectionner les meilleurs candidats** they used a series of selection procedures to sift out the best candidates

2 (Poste) sorting; (Ordin) sort, sorting ◆ **~ postal** sorting of mail ◆ **le (bureau de) ~** the sorting office

tri... /tʀi/ PRÉF tri... ◆ **triacétate** triacetate

triacide /tʀiasid/ NM triacid

triade /tʀijad/ NF triad

triage /tʀijaʒ/ NM ⇒ **tri**; → **gare¹**

trial /tʀijal/ NM motocross, scrambling (Brit) ◆ **faire du ~** to do motocross, to go scrambling (Brit); → **moto**

triangle /tʀijɑ̃gl/ NM (Géom, Mus) triangle ◆ **en ~** in a triangle ◆ **~ isocèle/équilatéral/rectangle/scalène** isosceles/equilateral/right-angled/scalene triangle ◆ **~s semblables/égaux** similar/equal triangles ◆ **~ quelconque** ordinary triangle ◆ **soit un ~ quelconque ABC** let ABC be any triangle ◆ **~ de signalisation** warning triangle ◆ **le ~ des Bermudes** the Bermuda Triangle ◆ **le Triangle d'or** the Golden Triangle ◆ **un ~ amoureux** a love triangle

triangulaire /tʀijɑ̃gylɛʀ/ ADJ [section, voile, prisme] triangular; [débat, tournoi] three-cornered ◆ **commerce** ou **trafic ~** (Hist) triangular slave trade ◆ **relation ~** triangular ou three-way relationship NF (= élection) three-cornered (election) contest ou fight

triangulation /tʀijɑ̃gylasjɔ̃/ NF triangulation

trianguler /tʀijɑ̃gyle/ ► conjug 1 ◄ VT to triangulate

trias /tʀijas/ NM (= terrain) trias ◆ **le ~** (= période) the Triassic, the Trias

triasique /tʀijazik/ ADJ Triassic

triathlète /tʀi(j)atlɛt/ NMF triathlete

triathlon /tʀi(j)atlɔ̃/ NM triathlon

triatomique /tʀiatɔmik/ ADJ triatomic

tribal, e (mpl **-aux**) /tʀibal, o/ ADJ tribal

tribalisme /tʀibalism/ NM (littér) tribalism

tribasique /tʀibazik/ ADJ tribasic

tribo-électricité /tʀiboelɛktʀisite/ NF triboelectricity

tribo-électrique /tʀiboelɛktʀik/ ADJ triboelectric

triboluminescence /tʀibolyminesɑ̃s/ NF triboluminescence

tribord /tʀibɔʀ/ NM starboard ◆ **à ~** to starboard, on the starboard side ◆ **hauban ~ arrière** aft starboard shroud

tribu /tʀiby/ NF (gén) tribe; (fig) clan ◆ **chef de ~** tribal chief ◆ **comment va la petite ~ ?*** how's the family?

tribulations /tʀibylasjɔ̃/ NFPL (littér = mésaventures) tribulations, trials, troubles

tribun /tʀibœ̃/ NM (Hist romaine) tribune; (= orateur) powerful orator; (littér = défenseur) tribune (littér)

tribunal (pl **-aux**) /tʀibynal, o/ NM 1 (lit) court ◆ **~ judiciaire/d'exception** judicial/special court ◆ **~ révolutionnaire/militaire** revolutionary/military tribunal ◆ **~ constitutionnel/international** constitutional/international court ◆ **~ fédéral** federal court ◆ **porter une affaire devant les tribunaux** to bring a case before the courts ◆ **déposer une plainte auprès des tribunaux** to instigate legal proceedings ◆ **comparaître devant un ~** to appear before a court ◆ **traduire qn devant un ~** to bring sb to court ou justice ◆ **traduire qn devant un ~ militaire** to court-martial sb ◆ **affaire renvoyée d'un ~ à l'autre** case referred from one court to another

2 (fig) **le ~ des hommes** the justice of men ◆ **être jugé par le ~ suprême** ou **de Dieu** to appear before the judgment seat of God ◆ **être condamné par le ~ de l'histoire** to be condemned by the judgment of history, to be judged and condemned by history ◆ **s'ériger en ~ du goût/des mœurs** to set o.s. up as an arbiter of (good) taste/of morals

COMP **tribunal administratif** *tribunal dealing with internal disputes in the French civil service*
tribunal arbitral arbitration court, court of arbitration
tribunal de commerce commercial court
tribunal des conflits jurisdictional court
tribunal correctionnel ≃ magistrates' court *(dealing with criminal matters)*
tribunal pour enfants juvenile court
tribunal de grande instance ≃ county court
le Tribunal de l'Inquisition the Tribunal of the Inquisition
tribunal d'instance ≃ magistrates' court *(dealing with civil matters)*
tribunal pénal international international criminal court
tribunal de police police court
tribunal de première instance † ⇒ **tribunal de grande instance**

tribune /tʀibyn/ NF 1 (pour le public) [d'église, assemblée, tribunal] gallery; [de stade, champ de courses] stand; (couverte) grandstand ◆ **~ d'honneur, ~ officielle** VIP stand ◆ **les ~s du public/de la presse** the public/press gallery ◆ **les applaudissements des ~s** applause from the stands ◆ **il avait une ~** he had a seat in the stand ◆ **~ du public** (Parl) visitors' gallery

2 (pour un orateur) platform, rostrum ◆ **monter à la ~** to mount the platform ou rostrum, to stand up to speak; (Parl = parler) to address the House, to take the floor

3 (fig = débat) forum ◆ **~ radiophonique** radio forum ◆ **offrir une ~ à la contestation** to offer a forum ou platform for protest ◆ **~ libre d'un journal** opinion column in ou of a newspaper ◆ **organiser une ~ sur un sujet d'actualité** to organize an open forum ou a free discussion on a topical issue ◆ **se présenter à l'élection pour avoir une ~ afin de faire connaître ses vues** to stand for election to give o.s. a platform from which to publicize one's views

COMP **tribune d'orgue** organ loft

> ⚠ **tribune** ne se traduit pas par le mot anglais **tribune**, qui a le sens de 'tribun'.

tribut /tʀiby/ NM (lit, fig) tribute ◆ **payer ~ au vainqueur** (= argent) to pay tribute to the conqueror ◆ **ils ont payé un lourd ~ à la maladie/guerre** disease/war has cost them dear, disease/war has taken a heavy toll (among them) ◆ **payer ~ à la nature** (littér) to go the way of all flesh, to pay the debt of nature

tributaire /tʀibytɛʀ/ ADJ 1 (= dépendant) **être ~ de** to be dependent ou reliant on 2 (Géog) **être ~ de** to be a tributary of, to flow into ◆ **rivière ~** tributary 3 (Hist = qui paie tribut) tributary ◆ **être ~ de qn** to be a tributary of sb, to pay tribute to sb

tric /tʀik/ NM ⇒ **trick**

tricard /tʀikaʀ/ NM (arg Crime) *ex-convict prohibited from entering certain French cities* ◆ **il est ~ dans le milieu du cyclisme** he's an outcast in the cycling world

tricentenaire /tʀisɑ̃t(ə)nɛʀ/ ADJ three-hundred-year-old (épith) NM tercentenary, tricentennial

tricéphale /tʀisefal/ ADJ (littér) three-headed

triceps /tʀisɛps/ ADJ, NM ◆ **(muscle) ~** triceps (muscle) ◆ **~ brachial/crural** brachial/crural triceps

triche* /tʀiʃ/ NF cheating ◆ **c'est de la ~** it's cheating ou a cheat

tricher /tʀiʃe/ ► conjug 1 ◄ VI (gén) to cheat ◆ **~ au jeu** to cheat at gambling ◆ **~ sur son âge** to lie about ou cheat over one's age ◆ **~ sur le poids/la longueur** to cheat over ou on the weight/the length, to give short weight/short measure ◆ **~ sur les prix** to cheat over the price, to overcharge ◆ **~ en affaires/en**

amour to cheat in business/in love ◆ **on a dû ~ un peu : un des murs est en contre-plaqué** we had to cheat a bit – one of the walls is plywood

tricherie /tʀiʃʀi/ NF (= *tromperie*) cheating (*NonC*) ◆ **gagner par ~** to win by cheating ◆ **c'est une ~** *ou* **de la ~** it's cheating *ou* a cheat ◆ **on s'en tire avec une petite ~** (= *astuce*) we get round the problem by cheating a bit

tricheur, -euse /tʀiʃœʀ, øz/ NM,F (*gén*) cheat; (*en affaires*) swindler, trickster, cheat

trichloréthylène /tʀiklɔʀetilɛn/ NM trichlorethylene, trichloroethylene

trichomonas /tʀikɔmɔnas/ NM trichomonad

trichrome /tʀikʀom/ ADJ (*Tech*) three-colour (*épith*) (*Brit*), three-color (*épith*) (*US*), trichromatic

trichromie /tʀikʀɔmi/ NF (*Tech*) three-colour (*Brit*) *ou* three-color (*US*) process

trick /tʀik/ NM (*Bridge*) seventh trick

tricolore /tʀikɔlɔʀ/ ADJ (*gén*) three-coloured (*Brit*), three-colored (*US*), tricolour(ed) (*frm*) (*Brit*), tricolor(ed) (*frm*) (*US*); (= *aux couleurs françaises*) red, white and blue ◆ **le drapeau ~** the (French) tricolour ◆ **le chauvinisme ~** (*fig*) French *ou* Gallic chauvinism ◆ **l'équipe ~***, **les ~s*** (*Sport*) the French team

tricorne /tʀikɔʀn/ NM three-cornered hat, tricorn(e)

tricot /tʀiko/ NM [1] (= *vêtement*) sweater, jersey, jumper (*Brit*) ◆ **~ de corps** vest (*Brit*), undershirt (*US*) ◆ **emporte des ~s** take some woollens *ou* woollies* (*Brit*) with you [2] (= *technique*) knitting (*NonC*); (= *ouvrage*) (*gén*) knitting (*NonC*); (= *articles tricotés*) knitwear (*NonC*) ◆ **faire du ~** to knit, to do some knitting ◆ **~ jacquard** Jacquard knitwear ◆ **~ plat** ordinary knitting, knitting on 2 needles ◆ **~ rond** knitting on 4 needles; → **point²** [3] (= *tissu*) knitted fabric ◆ **en ~** knitted ◆ **vêtements de ~** knitwear

tricotage /tʀikɔtaʒ/ NM knitting

tricoter /tʀikɔte/ ► conjug 1 ◄ VT [+ *vêtement, maille*] to knit ◆ **écharpe tricotée (à la) main** hand-knit(ted) scarf VI [1] (*lit*) to knit ◆ **~ serré/lâche** to be a tight/loose knitter ◆ **~ à la main** to knit by hand ◆ **~ à la machine** to machine-knit; → **aiguille, laine, machine** [2] (**fig*) [*cycliste*] to pedal fast, to twiddle* (*Brit*); [*danseur*] to prance about ◆ **~ des jambes** [*fugitif*] to run like mad*; [*danseur*] to prance about; [*bébé*] to kick its legs

tricoteur, -euse /tʀikɔtœʀ, øz/ NM,F knitter ◆ **~ de filets** netmaker NF **tricoteuse** (= *machine*) knitting machine; (= *meuble*) tricoteuse

trictrac /tʀiktʀak/ NM (*Hist*) (= *jeu*) backgammon; (= *partie*) game of backgammon; (= *plateau*) backgammon board

tricycle /tʀisikl/ NM [*d'enfant*] tricycle ◆ **faire du ~** to ride a tricycle ◆ **~ à moteur** motorized tricycle

tridactyle /tʀidaktil/ ADJ tridactyl, tridactylous

trident /tʀidɑ̃/ NM (*Myth*) trident; (*Pêche*) trident, fish-spear; (*Agr*) three-pronged fork

tridimensionnel, -elle /tʀidimɑ̃sjɔnɛl/ ADJ three-dimensional

trièdre /tʀi(j)ɛdʀ/ ADJ trihedral NM trihedron

triennal, e (mpl **-aux**) /tʀijenal, o/ ADJ [*prix, foire, élection*] triennial, three-yearly; [*charge, mandat, plan*] three-year (*épith*); [*magistrat, président*] elected *ou* appointed for three years ◆ **assolement ~** (*Agr*) three-year rotation of crops

trier /tʀije/ ► conjug 7 ◄ VT [1] (= *classer*) (*gén*) to sort out; [+ *lettres, fiches*] to sort; [+ *wagons*] to marshal; [+ *fruits*] to sort; (*en calibrant*) to grade [2] (= *sélectionner*) [+ *grains, visiteurs*] to sort out; [+ *candidats*] to select, to pick; [+ *lentilles*] to pick over; (*en tamisant*) to sift ◆ **triés sur le volet** (*fig*) hand-picked ◆ **il raconte un peu n'importe quoi, il faut ~** he talks a lot of nonsense sometimes, you have to decide what to listen to ◆ **mets ça sur la table, on va ~** (*hum*) say what you want to say and we'll decide

trieur, trieuse /tʀijœʀ, tʀijøz/ NM,F (= *personne*) sorter; (*en calibrant*) grader ◆ **~ de minerai/de légumes** ore/vegetable grader NM (= *machine*) sorter ◆ **~ de grains** grain sorter ◆ **~-calibreur** [*de fruits*] sorter; [*d'œufs*] grader, grading machine NF **trieuse** (= *machine*) sorter; [*d'ordinateur, photocopieur*] sorting machine

trifolié, e /tʀifɔlje/ ADJ trifoliate, trifoliated

trifouiller* /tʀifuje/ ► conjug 1 ◄ VT to rummage about in, to root about in VI to rummage about, to root about ◆ **il trifouillait dans le moteur** he was poking about* in the engine

triglycéride /tʀigliseʀid/ NM triglyceride

triglyphe /tʀiglif/ NM triglyph

trigo* /tʀigo/ NF (abrév de **trigonométrie**) trig*

trigonométrie /tʀigɔnɔmetʀi/ NF trigonometry

trigonométrique /tʀigɔnɔmetʀik/ ADJ trigonometric(al)

trijumeau (pl **trijumeaux**) /tʀiʒymo/ ADJ M, NM ◆ **(nerf) ~** trigeminal *ou* trifacial nerve

trilatéral, e (mpl **-aux**) /tʀilateʀal, o/ ADJ [1] (*Géom*) trilateral, three-sided [2] (*Écon*) [*accords*] tripartite ◆ **la (commission) ~e** the Trilateral Commission

trilingue /tʀilɛ̃g/ ADJ [*dictionnaire, secrétaire*] trilingual ◆ **il est ~** he's trilingual, he speaks three languages

trille /tʀij/ NM [*d'oiseau, flûte*] trill ◆ **faire des ~s** to trill

trillion /tʀiljɔ̃/ NM trillion

trilobé, e /tʀilɔbe/ ADJ [*feuille*] trilobate; [*ogive*] trefoil (*épith*)

trilogie /tʀilɔʒi/ NF trilogy

trimaran /tʀimaʀɑ̃/ NM trimaran

trimard †* /tʀimaʀ/ NM road ◆ **prendre le ~** to take to *ou* set out on the road

trimarder †* /tʀimaʀde/ ► conjug 1 ◄ VI (= *vagabonder*) to walk the roads, to be on the road VT (= *transporter*) to lug* *ou* cart* along

trimardeur, -euse †* /tʀimaʀdœʀ, øz/ NM,F (= *vagabond*) tramp, hobo (*US*)

trimbal(l)age* /tʀɛ̃balaʒ/, **trimbal(l)ement*** /tʀɛ̃balmɑ̃/ NM [*de bagages, marchandises*] carting *ou* lugging around*

trimbal(l)er /tʀɛ̃bale/ ► conjug 1 ◄ VT * [+ *bagages, marchandises*] to lug* *ou* cart* around; (*péj*) [+ *personne*] to trail along; [+ *rhume*] to carry around ◆ **ces enfants sont sans cesse trimballés du domicile de la mère à celui du père** these children are forever being dragged back and forth between their mother's home and their father's home ◆ **qu'est-ce qu'il trimballe !**** (*idiot*) he's as dumb *ou* thick (*Brit*) as they come** ◆ **qu'est-ce que je trimballe !**** (*rhume*) I've got a bloody awful cold** (*Brit*) VPR **se trimbal(l)er**** to trail along ◆ **on a dû se trimbal(l)er en voiture jusque chez eux** we had to trail over to their place in the car ◆ **il a fallu que je me trimballe jusqu'à la gare avec mes valises** I had to trail all the way to the station with my suitcases

trimer* /tʀime/ ► conjug 1 ◄ VI to slave away ◆ **faire ~ qn** to keep sb's nose to the grindstone, to drive sb hard, to keep sb hard at it*

trimestre /tʀimɛstʀ/ NM [1] (= *période*) (*gén, Comm*) quarter; (*Scol*) term ◆ **premier/second/troisième ~** (*Scol*) autumn/winter/summer term ◆ **payer par ~** to pay quarterly [2] (= *loyer*) quarter, quarter's rent; (= *frais de scolarité*) term's fees; (= *salaire*) quarter's income

trimestriel, -elle /tʀimɛstʀijɛl/ ADJ [*publication*] quarterly; [*paiement*] three-monthly, quarterly; [*fonction, charge*] three-month (*épith*), for three months (*attrib*); (*Scol*) [*bulletin, examen*] end-of-term (*épith*), termly (*épith*)

trimestriellement /tʀimɛstʀijɛlmɑ̃/ ADV [*payer*] on a quarterly *ou* three-monthly basis, every quarter, every three months; [*publier*] quarterly; (*Scol*) once a term

trimètre /tʀimɛtʀ/ NM trimeter

trimoteur /tʀimɔtœʀ/ NM three-engined aircraft

tringle /tʀɛ̃gl/ NF [1] (= *barre*) rod ◆ **~ à rideaux** curtain rod *ou* rail [2] (*Archit* = *moulure*) tenia

tringler /tʀɛ̃gle/ ► conjug 1 ◄ VT [1] (*Tech*) to mark with a line [2] (**: *sexuellement*) to lay**, to screw**, to fuck** ◆ **se faire ~** to get laid**

trinidadien, -ienne /tʀinidadjɛ̃, jɛn/ ADJ Trinidadian NM,F **Trinidadien(ne)** Trinidadian

trinitaire /tʀinitɛʀ/ ADJ, NMF (*Rel*) Trinitarian

trinité /tʀinite/ NF [1] (= *triade*) trinity ◆ **la Trinité** (= *dogme*) the Trinity; (= *fête*) Trinity Sunday ◆ **à la Trinité** on Trinity Sunday ◆ **la sainte Trinité** the Holy Trinity; → **Pâques** [2] (*Géog*) **Trinité-et-Tobago** Trinidad and Tobago ◆ **(l'île de) la Trinité** Trinidad

trinitrobenzène /tʀinitʀobɛ̃zɛn/ NM trinitrobenzene

trinitrotoluène /tʀinitʀotɔlɥɛn/ NM trinitrotoluene

trinôme /tʀinom/ NM (*Math*) trinomial

trinquer /tʀɛ̃ke/ ► conjug 1 ◄ VI [1] (= *porter un toast*) to clink glasses; (= *boire*) to drink ◆ **~ à qch** to drink to sth ◆ **~ à la santé de qn** to drink sb's health [2] (* = *être puni*) to take the rap* ◆ **il a trinqué pour les autres** he took the rap for the others* [3] (= *être endommagé*) to be damaged ◆ **c'est l'aile qui a trinqué** the wing got the worst of the damage [4] († * = *trop boire*) to booze* [5] († = *se heurter*) to knock *ou* bump into one another

trinquet /tʀɛ̃kɛ/ NM (*Naut*) foremast

trinquette /tʀɛ̃kɛt/ NF (*Naut*) fore(-topmast) staysail

trio /tʀijo/ NM (*Mus*) trio; (= *groupe*) threesome, trio ◆ **~ urbain** (*Courses*) *system of betting on three horses in any order*

triode /tʀijɔd/ NF triode

triolet /tʀijɔlɛ/ NM (*Mus*) triplet; (*Hist Littérat*) triolet

triomphal, e (mpl **-aux**) /tʀijɔ̃fal, o/ ADJ [*marche*] triumphal; [*succès*] triumphant, resounding; [*entrée, accueil, geste, air, élection*] triumphant; (*Hist romaine*) triumphal ◆ **ce chanteur a fait un retour ~ en France** this singer has made a triumphant comeback in France

triomphalement /tʀijɔ̃falmɑ̃/ ADV [*accueillir, saluer*] in triumph; [*annoncer*] triumphantly ◆ **le président a été réélu ~** the president was triumphantly re-elected

triomphalisme /tʀijɔ̃falism/ NM triumphalism ◆ **ne faisons pas de ~** let's not gloat

triomphaliste /tʀijɔ̃falist/ ADJ [*discours, slogan*] triumphalist ◆ **sur un ton ~** gloatingly, exultantly

triomphant, e /tʀijɔ̃fɑ̃, ɑ̃t/ ADJ triumphant ◆ **l'Église ~e** the Church triumphant

triomphateur, -trice /tʀijɔ̃fatœʀ, tʀis/ ADJ [*parti, nation*] triumphant NM,F (= *vainqueur*) triumphant victor NM (*Hist romaine*) triumphant general

triomphe /tʀijɔ̃f/ NM ① *(Mil, Pol, Sport, gén)* triumph ♦ **cet acquittement représente le ~ de la justice/du bon sens** this acquittal represents the triumph of *ou* is a triumph for justice/common sense ② *(Hist romaine, gén = honneurs)* triumph ♦ **en ~** in triumph ♦ **porter qn en ~** to bear *ou* carry sb in triumph, to carry sb shoulder-high (in triumph); → **arc** ③ *(= exultation)* triumph ♦ **air/cri de ~** air/cry of triumph, triumphant air/cry ④ *(= succès)* triumph ♦ **cette pièce/cet artiste a remporté** *ou* **fait un ~** this play/this artist has been *ou* had a triumphant success ♦ **ce film/livre est un vrai ~** this film/book is a triumphant success ♦ **j'ai le ~ modeste** I'm not one to boast ♦ **le public lui a fait un ~** the audience gave him an ovation

triompher /tʀijɔ̃fe/ ▸ conjug 1 ◂ VI ① *(militairement)* to triumph; *(aux élections, en sport, gén)* to triumph, to win; *[cause, raison]* to prevail, to be triumphant ♦ **faire ~ une cause** to bring *ou* give victory to a cause ♦ **ses idées ont fini par ~** his ideas eventually prevailed *ou* won the day; → **vaincre** ② *(= crier victoire)* to exult, to rejoice ③ *(= exceller)* to triumph, to excel ♦ **~ dans un rôle** *[acteur]* to give a triumphant performance in a role VT INDIR **triompher de** *[+ ennemi]* to triumph over, to vanquish; *[+ concurrent, rival]* to triumph over, to overcome; *[+ obstacle, difficulté]* to triumph over, to surmount, to overcome; *[+ peur, timidité]* to conquer, to overcome

trip* /tʀip/ NM *(arg Drogue)* trip *(arg)* ♦ **il est en plein ~, il fait un ~** he's tripping ♦ **c'est pas mon ~** *(fig)* it's not my thing* *ou* my scene* ♦ **elle est dans son ~ végétarien** she's going through a vegetarian phase at the moment

tripaille** /tʀipɑj/ NF *(péj)* guts*, innards

tripal, e* (mpl **-aux**) /tʀipal, o/ ADJ ♦ **réaction ~e** gut reaction ♦ **c'est ~** it's a gut feeling

triparti, e /tʀipaʀti/ ADJ *(= à trois éléments)* tripartite; *(Pol = à trois partis)* three-party *(épith)*

tripartisme /tʀipaʀtism/ NM three-party government

tripartite /tʀipaʀtit/ ADJ ⇒ **triparti**

tripatouillage* /tʀipatujaʒ/ NM *(péj)* ① *(= remaniement) [de texte]* fiddling about* *(de* with); *[de comptes, résultats électoraux]* fiddling* *(de* with); *[statistiques]* fiddling, juggling *(de* with) ② *(= opération malhonnête)* fiddle* ♦ **~ électoral** election rigging

tripatouiller* /tʀipatuje/ ▸ conjug 1 ◂ VT *(péj)* ① *(= remanier) [+ texte]* to fiddle about with*; *[+ comptes, résultats électoraux]* to fiddle*, to tamper with; *[+ statistiques]* to fiddle with, to massage* ② *(= tripoter) [+ objet]* to fiddle *ou* mess about with*, to toy with; *[+ moteur, moto, machine]* to tinker with*; *[+ personne]* to paw*

tripatouilleur, -euse* /tʀipatujœʀ, øz/ NM,F *(péj)* *(= touche-à-tout)* fiddler*; *(= affairiste)* grafter* *(péj)*

tripe /tʀip/ NFPL **tripes** ① *(Culin)* tripe ♦ **~s à la mode de Caen/à la lyonnaise** tripe à la mode de Caen/à la Lyonnaise ② *(* = intestins)* guts* ♦ **rendre ~s et boyaux** to be as sick as a dog* ♦ **il joue avec ses ~s** *[comédien]* he puts his heart and soul into it ♦ **ça vous prend aux ~s** it gets you right there* ♦ **c'est un spectacle qui vous remue les ~s** it's a gut-wrenching performance ♦ **il n'a vraiment pas de ~s** *(= courage)* he's got no guts* NF *(* = fibre)* ♦ **avoir la ~ républicaine/royaliste** to be a republican/a royalist through and through *ou* to the core

triper** /tʀipe/ ▸ conjug 1 ◂ VI *(Drogue)* to trip ♦ **ça/elle me fait ~** it/she blows my mind*

triperie /tʀipʀi/ NF *(= boutique)* tripe shop; *(= commerce)* tripe trade

tripette* /tʀipɛt/ NF → **valoir**

triphasé, e /tʀifɑze/ ADJ three-phase NM three-phase current

triphtongue /tʀiftɔ̃g/ NF triphthong

tripier, -ière /tʀipje, jɛʀ/ NM,F tripe butcher

triplace /tʀiplas/ ADJ, NM three-seater

triplan /tʀiplɑ̃/ NM triplane

triple /tʀipl/ ADJ ① *(= à trois éléments ou aspects)* triple; *(= trois fois plus grand)* treble, triple ♦ **le prix est ~ de ce qu'il était** the price is three times *ou* treble what it was, the price has trebled ♦ **faire qch en ~ exemplaire** to make three copies of sth, to do sth in triplicate ♦ **ce livre, je l'ai en ~** I've got three copies of this book ♦ **il faut que l'épaisseur soit ~** three thicknesses are needed, a treble thickness is needed ♦ **avec ~ couture** triple stitched ♦ **avec ~ semelle** with a three-layer sole ♦ **l'inconvénient est ~, il y a un ~ inconvénient** there are three disadvantages, the disadvantages are threefold ♦ **naissance ~** birth of triplets ♦ **prendre une ~ dose** to take three times the dose, to take a triple dose *(de* of) ② *(intensif)* **c'est un ~ idiot** he's a prize idiot ♦ **~ idiot !** you stupid idiot! *ou* fool! NM ♦ **9 est le ~ de 3** 9 is three times 3 ♦ **manger/gagner le ~ (de qn)** to eat/earn three times as much (as sb *ou* as sb does) ♦ **celui-ci pèse le ~ de l'autre** this one weighs three times as much as the other *ou* is three times *ou* treble the weight of the other ♦ **c'est le ~ du prix normal/de la distance Paris-Londres** it's three times *ou* treble the normal price/the distance between Paris and London ♦ **on a mis le ~ de temps à le faire** it took three times as long *ou* treble the time to do it COMP **la Triple Alliance** the Triple Alliance **triple saut** triple jump **triple saut périlleux** triple somersault; → **croche, entente, galop, menton**

triplé, e /tʀiple/ (ptp de **tripler**) NM ① *(Courses) [de chevaux]* treble *(betting on three different horses in three different races)* ② *(Sport) [d'athlète]* triple success; *(Ftbl)* hat trick ♦ **il a réussi un beau ~** *[athlète]* he came first in three events; *[footballeur]* he scored a hat trick ♦ **réussir le ~ dans le 4 000 mètres** *[équipe]* to win the first three places *ou* come 1st, 2nd and 3rd in the 4,000 metres NMPL **triplés** *(= bébés)* triplets; *(= garçons)* boy triplets NFPL **triplées** *(= bébés)* girl triplets

triplement /tʀipləmɑ̃/ ADV ① *(= pour trois raisons)* in three ways ② *(= à un degré triple)* trebly, three times over NM *[de prix, bénéfices, nombre]* trebling, tripling, threefold increase *(de* in); ♦ **cette politique s'est traduite par un ~ de l'endettement public** this policy has caused national debt to treble *ou* triple, this policy has brought about a threefold increase in the national debt

tripler /tʀiple/ ▸ conjug 1 ◂ VT *(gén)* to treble, to triple; *(Scol, Univ) [+ classe]* to do for the third time ♦ **il tripla la dose** he made the dose three times as big, he tripled *ou* trebled the dose ♦ **~ la longueur/l'épaisseur de qch** to treble *ou* triple the length/the thickness of sth, to make sth three times as long/thick ♦ **~ sa mise** to treble one's stake VI to triple, to treble, to increase threefold ♦ **~ de valeur/de poids/de volume** to treble in value/in weight/in volume ♦ **le chiffre d'affaires a triplé en un an** turnover has tripled *ou* trebled in a year ♦ **la population de la ville a triplé depuis la guerre** the town's population has tripled *ou* trebled since the war, there has been a threefold increase in the town's population since the war

triplette /tʀiplɛt/ NF *(Boules)* threesome

Triplex ® /tʀiplɛks/ NM *(= verre)* laminated safety glass, Triplex ® *(Brit)*

triplex /tʀiplɛks/ NM *(= appartement)* three-storey apartment *ou* flat *(Brit)*, triplex *(US)*

triploïde /tʀiplɔid/ ADJ triploid

tripode /tʀipɔd/ ADJ tripodal ♦ **mât ~** tripod (mast) NM tripod

Tripoli /tʀipɔli/ N Tripoli

triporteur /tʀipɔʀtœʀ/ NM delivery tricycle

tripot /tʀipo/ NM *(péj)* dive*, joint*

tripotage* /tʀipɔtaʒ/ NM *(péj)* ① *(= attouchements) [de personne, partie du corps]* groping*, feeling up* ② *(= manigances)* jiggery-pokery* *(NonC)* ♦ **~s électoraux** election rigging

tripotée** /tʀipɔte/ NF ① *(= correction)* belting**, hiding*, thrashing ② *(= grand nombre)* **une ~ de ...** loads* of ..., lots of ... ♦ **avoir toute une ~ d'enfants** to have a whole string of children*

tripoter* /tʀipɔte/ ▸ conjug 1 ◂ *(péj)* VT ① *[+ objet, fruit]* to fiddle with, to finger; *(machinalement) [+ montre, stylo, bouton]* to fiddle with, to play with, to toy with ♦ **se ~ le nez/la barbe** to fiddle with one's nose/one's beard ♦ **elle tripotait nerveusement ses bagues** she was playing with *ou* fiddling with her rings nervously ② *[+ personne, partie du corps]* to grope*, to feel up* ♦ **se faire ~** to be groped*, to be felt up* ♦ **se ~** to play with o.s. VI ① *(= fouiller)* to root about, to rummage about ♦ **~ dans les affaires de qn/dans un tiroir** to root about *ou* rummage about in sb's things/in a drawer ② *(= trafiquer)* to be involved in some shady business

tripoteur, -euse* /tʀipɔtœʀ, øz/ NM,F *(péj)* *(= affairiste)* shark*, shady dealer*; *(** = peloteur)* groper*

tripous, tripoux /tʀipu/ NMPL *dish (from Auvergne) made of sheep's offal*

triptyque /tʀiptik/ NM ① *(Art, Littérat)* triptych ② *(Admin = classement)* triptyque

triquard /tʀikaʀ/ NM → **tricard**

trique /tʀik/ NF cudgel ♦ **il les mène à la ~** *(fig)* he's a real slave driver ♦ **donner des coups de ~ à** to cudgel, to thrash ♦ **maigre** *ou* **sec comme un coup de ~** as skinny as a rake ♦ **avoir la ~***** to have a hard-on***

trirectangle /tʀiʀɛktɑ̃gl/ ADJ trirectangular

trirème /tʀiʀɛm/ NF trireme

trisaïeul (pl **trisaïeuls**) /tʀizajœl, ø/ NM great-great-grandfather

trisaïeule /tʀizajœl/ NF great-great-grandmother

trisannuel, -elle /tʀizanɥɛl/ ADJ *[fête, plante]* triennial

trisection /tʀisɛksjɔ̃/ NF *(Géom)* trisection

trisomie /tʀizɔmi/ NF trisomy ♦ **~ 21** Down's syndrome, trisomy 21

trisomique /tʀizɔmik/ ADJ trisomic NMF trisome ♦ **~ 21** person with Down's syndrome

trisser (se)** /tʀise/ ▸ conjug 1 ◂ VPR *(= partir)* to clear off*, to skedaddle*

trissyllabe /tʀisi(l)lab/ ADJ, NM ⇒ **trisyllabe**

trissyllabique /tʀisi(l)labik/ ADJ ⇒ **trisyllabique**

Tristan /tʀistɑ̃/ NM Tristan, Tristram ♦ **~ et Iseu(l)t** Tristan and Isolde

triste /tʀist/ ADJ ① *(= malheureux, affligé) [personne]* sad, unhappy; *[regard, sourire]* sad, sorrowful ♦ **d'un air ~** sadly, with a sad look ♦ **d'une voix ~** sadly, in a sad *ou* sorrowful voice ♦ **un enfant à l'air ~** a sad-looking *ou* an unhappy-looking child ♦ **les animaux en cage ont l'air ~** caged animals look sad *ou* miserable ♦ **être ~ à l'idée** *ou* **à la pensée de partir** to be sad at the idea *ou* thought of leaving

◆ **elle était ~ de voir partir ses enfants** she was sad to see her children go

2 (= *sombre, maussade*) *[personne]* sad, gloomy; *[pensée]* sad, depressing; *[couleur, temps, journée]* dreary, depressing, dismal; *[paysage]* bleak, dreary ◆ **il aime les chansons ~s** he likes sad *ou* melancholy songs ◆ **~ à pleurer** terribly sad ◆ **~ à mourir** *[personne, ambiance, musique]* utterly depressing ◆ **il est ~ comme un bonnet de nuit** he's as miserable as sin ◆ **son père est un homme ~** his father is a rather joyless man ◆ **avoir** *ou* **faire ~ mine** *ou* **figure** to cut a sorry figure, to look a sorry sight ◆ **faire ~ mine** *ou* **figure à qn** to give sb a cool reception, to greet sb unenthusiastically; → **vin**

3 (= *attristant, pénible*) *[nouvelle, épreuve, destin]* sad ◆ **depuis ces ~s événements** since these sad events took place ◆ **c'est une ~ nécessité** it's a painful necessity, it's sadly necessary ◆ **c'est la ~ réalité** that's the grim *ou* sad reality ◆ **il se lamente toujours sur son ~ sort** he's always bewailing his unhappy *ou* sad fate ◆ **ce furent des mois bien ~s** these were very sad *ou* unhappy months ◆ **ce pays détient le ~ record de l'alcoolisme** this country holds the unenviable record for having the highest rate of alcoholism ◆ **il aura le ~ privilège d'annoncer ...** he'll have the dubious privilege of announcing ... ◆ **c'est ~ à dire mais ...** it's sad to say but ... ◆ **~ chose que ...** it is sad that ... ◆ **depuis son accident, il est dans un ~ état** (ever) since his accident he has been in a sad *ou* sorry state ◆ **c'est pas ~ !*** (= *c'est amusant*) it's a laugh a minute!*; (= *c'est difficile*) it's really tough!*, it's no joke!*; (= *c'est la pagaille*) it's a real mess!; → **abandonner**

4 (*avant n* : *péj* = *lamentable*) **quelle ~ époque !** what sad times we live in! ◆ **une ~ réputation/affaire** a sorry reputation/business ◆ **un ~ sire** *ou* **personnage** an unsavoury *ou* dreadful individual ◆ **ses ~s résultats à l'examen** his wretched *ou* deplorable exam results

tristement /tʀistəmɑ̃/ **ADV** 1 (= *d'un air triste*) sadly, sorrowfully 2 (= *de façon lugubre*) sadly, gloomily, glumly 3 (*valeur intensive, péjorative*) sadly, regrettably ◆ **~ célèbre** notorious (*pour* for); ◆ **c'est ~ vrai** it's sad but true

tristesse /tʀistɛs/ **GRAMMAIRE ACTIVE 51.4** **NF** 1 (= *caractère, état*) *[de personne, pensée]* sadness, gloominess; *[de couleur, temps, journée]* dreariness; *[de paysage]* sadness, bleakness, dreariness ◆ **il sourit toujours avec une certaine ~** there is always a certain sadness in his smile ◆ **enclin à la ~** given to melancholy, inclined to be gloomy *ou* sad 2 (= *chagrin*) sadness (*NonC*), sorrow ◆ **avoir un accès de ~** to be overcome by sadness ◆ **les ~s de la vie** life's sorrows, the sorrows of life ◆ **c'est avec une grande ~ que nous apprenons son décès** it is with deep sadness *ou* sorrow that we have learned of his death

tristounet, -ette* /tʀistunɛ, ɛt/ **ADJ** *[temps, nouvelles]* gloomy, depressing ◆ **il avait l'air ~** he looked a bit down in the mouth* *ou* down in the dumps*

trisyllabe /tʀisi(l)lab/ **ADJ** trisyllabic **NM** trisyllable

trisyllabique /tʀisi(l)labik/ **ADJ** trisyllabic

trithérapie /tʀiteʀapi/ **NF** triple *or* combination therapy

tritium /tʀitjɔm/ **NM** tritium

Triton /tʀitɔ̃/ **NM** (*Myth*) Triton

triton[1] /tʀitɔ̃/ **NM** (= *mollusque*) triton; (= *amphibien*) newt

triton[2] /tʀitɔ̃/ **NM** (*Mus*) tritone, augmented fourth

trituration /tʀityʀasjɔ̃/ **NF** 1 (= *broyage*) grinding up, trituration (*SPÉC*) ◆ **bois de ~** wood pulp 2 *[de pâte]* pummelling, kneading 3 (= *manipulation*) manipulation

triturer /tʀityʀe/ ► conjug 1 ◄ **VT** 1 (= *broyer*) *[+ sel, médicament, fibres]* to grind up, to triturate (*SPÉC*) 2 (= *malaxer*) *[+ pâte]* to pummel, to knead ◆ **ce masseur vous triture les chairs** this masseur really pummels you 3 (= *manipuler*) *[+ objet]* to fiddle with ◆ **elle triturait nerveusement son mouchoir** she was twisting her handkerchief nervously ◆ **se ~ la cervelle*** *ou* **les méninges*** to rack *ou* cudgel one's brains*

triumvir /tʀijɔmviʀ/ **NM** triumvir

triumviral, e (mpl **-aux**) /tʀijɔmviʀal, o/ **ADJ** triumviral

triumvirat /tʀijɔmviʀa/ **NM** triumvirate

trivalence /tʀivalɑ̃s/ **NF** trivalence, trivalency

trivalent, e /tʀivalɑ̃, ɑ̃t/ **ADJ** trivalent

trivalve /tʀivalv/ **ADJ** trivalve

trivial, e (mpl **-iaux**) /tʀivjal, jo/ **ADJ** 1 (= *commun*) *[objet, acte, détail, matière]* ordinary ◆ **la réalité ~e** the mundane reality ◆ **la communication ~e** everyday communication ◆ **s'il faut entrer dans des considérations ~es** if we want to get down to the nitty gritty*, if we want to get down to brass tacks 2 (*frm*) (= *vulgaire*) *[expression]* colloquial ◆ **selon une expression ~e** to use a colloquial expression ◆ **l'image est odieusement ~e** the image is terribly undignified 3 (*Math*) trivial **NM** ◆ **le ~** the ordinary; (*plus péjoratif*) the mundane

> ⚠ **trivial** se traduit rarement par le mot anglais **trivial**, qui a le sens de 'insignifiant'.

trivialement /tʀivjalmɑ̃/ **ADV** 1 (= *banalement*) **la matière sous sa forme la plus ~ physiologique** matter at the most basically physiological level ◆ **il pense que se préoccuper ~ des maux de la société française n'est pas de son niveau** he thinks the banal task of concerning himself with the ills of French society is beneath him 2 (= *vulgairement*) *[appeler, dire]* colloquially ◆ **..., comme on l'appelle ~ ...,** as it is called colloquially

trivialité /tʀivjalite/ **NF** 1 (= *banalité*) *[d'objet, acte, détail, quotidien]* ordinariness 2 (= *vulgarité*) coarseness, crudeness 3 (= *remarque vulgaire*) coarse *ou* crude remark; (= *remarque banale*) commonplace *ou* trite remark

troc /tʀɔk/ **NM** (= *échange*) exchange; (= *système*) barter ◆ **l'économie de ~** the barter economy ◆ **faire du ~** to barter ◆ **on a fait un ~** we did a swap ◆ **le ~ de qch contre qch d'autre** bartering *ou* exchanging *ou* swapping sth for sth else

trochaïque /tʀɔkaik/ **ADJ** trochaic

trochée /tʀɔʃe/ **NM** trochee

trochlée /tʀɔkle/ **NF** trochlea

troène /tʀɔɛn/ **NM** privet

troglodyte /tʀɔglɔdit/ **NM** 1 (*Ethnol*) cave dweller; (*fig*) troglodyte 2 (= *oiseau*) wren

troglodytique /tʀɔglɔditik/ **ADJ** (*Ethnol*) troglodytic (*SPÉC*), cave-dwelling (*épith*) ◆ **habitation ~** cave dwelling, cave-dweller's settlement

trogne‡ /tʀɔɲ/ **NF** (= *visage*) mug‡, face

trognon /tʀɔɲɔ̃/ **NM** *[de fruit]* core; *[de chou]* stalk ◆ **~ de pomme** apple core ◆ **se faire avoir jusqu'au ~**‡ to be well and truly had‡ ◆ **mon petit ~*** sweetie pie* **ADJ INV** (* = *mignon*) *[enfant, objet, vêtement]* cute*, lovely

Troie /tʀwa/ **N** Troy ◆ **la guerre/le cheval de ~** the Trojan War/Horse

troïka /tʀɔika/ **NF** (*gén, Pol*) troika

trois /tʀwa/ **ADJ INV** 1 (= *nombre*) three; (= *troisième*) third ◆ **volume/acte ~** volume/act three ◆ **le ~ (janvier)** the third (of January) ◆ **Henri III** Henry the Third; *pour autres loc voir* **six** *et* **fois**

2 (= *quelques*) **je pars dans ~ minutes** I'm off in a couple of *ou* a few minutes ◆ **il n'a pas dit ~ mots** he hardly opened his mouth *ou* said a word; → **cuiller, deux**

NM INV three; (= *troisième*) third; (*Cartes, Dés*) three ◆ **c'est ~ fois rien** *[égratignure, cadeau]* it's nothing at all, it's hardly anything ◆ **ça coûte ~ fois rien** it costs next to nothing ◆ **et de ~ !** that makes three!; *pour autres loc voir* **six**

COMP **les trois coups** (*Théât*) the three knocks (*announcing beginning of play*)

les trois ordres (*Hist*) the three estates

trois quarts three-quarters ◆ **portrait de ~ quarts** three-quarter(s) portrait ◆ **j'ai fait les ~ quarts du travail** I've done three-quarters of the work ◆ **les ~ quarts des gens l'ignorent** the great majority of people *ou* most people don't know this ◆ **aux ~ quarts détruit** almost totally destroyed; → **trois-quarts, dimension, étoile, glorieux, grâce, temps[1]**

trois-deux /tʀwadø/ **NM INV** (*Mus*) three-two time

trois-huit /tʀwaɥit/ **NM INV** 1 (*Mus*) three-eight (time) 2 **faire les ~** (*au travail*) to operate three eight-hour shifts, to operate round the clock in eight-hour shifts

troisième /tʀwazjɛm/ **ADJ, NMF** third ◆ **le ~ sexe** the third sex ◆ **le ~ âge** (= *période*) retirement (years); (= *groupe social*) senior citizens ◆ **personne du ~ âge** senior citizen ◆ **~ cycle d'université** graduate school ◆ **étudiant de ~ cycle** graduate *ou* post-graduate (*Brit*) student ◆ **être** *ou* **faire le ~ larron dans une affaire** to take advantage of the other two quarrelling over something; *pour autres loc voir* **sixième** **NF** 1 (*Scol*) **(classe de) ~** fourth form *ou* year (*Brit*), 8th grade (*US*) 2 (= *vitesse*) third (gear) ◆ **en ~** in third (gear)

troisièmement /tʀwazjɛmmɑ̃/ **GRAMMAIRE ACTIVE 53.5** **ADV** third(ly), in the third place

trois-mâts /tʀwamɑ/ **NM INV** (*Naut*) three-master

trois-pièces /tʀwapjɛs/ **NM INV** (= *complet*) three-piece suit; (= *appartement*) three-room flat (*Brit*) *ou* apartment (*surtout US*)

trois-portes /tʀwapɔʀt/ **NF INV** (= *voiture*) two-door hatchback

trois-quarts /tʀwakaʀ/ **NM INV** 1 (= *manteau*) three-quarter (length) coat 2 (*Rugby*) three-quarter ◆ **il joue ~ aile** he plays wing three-quarter ◆ **~ centre** centre three-quarter ◆ **la ligne des ~** the three-quarter line 3 (= *violon*) three-quarter violin

trois-quatre /tʀwakatʀ/ **NM INV** (*Mus*) three-four time

troll /tʀɔl/ **NM** troll

trolley /tʀɔlɛ/ **NM** (= *dispositif*) trolley(-wheel); (* = *bus*) trolley bus

trolleybus /tʀɔlɛbys/ **NM** trolley bus

trombe /tʀɔ̃b/ **NF** 1 (*Météo*) waterspout ◆ **une ~ d'eau, des ~s d'eau** (= *pluie*) a cloudburst, a downpour ◆ **des ~s de lave/débris** streams *ou* torrents of lava/debris 2 ◆ **entrer/sortir/passer en ~** to sweep in/out/by like a whirlwind ◆ **démarrer en ~** *[voiture]* to take off at top speed, to roar off; (*fig*) to get off to a flying start

trombine‡ /tʀɔ̃bin/ **NF** (= *visage*) face, mug‡ (*péj*); (= *tête*) nut*

trombinoscope* /tʀɔ̃binɔskɔp/ **NM** 1 (= *photographie collective*) group photo 2 (= *annuaire de l'Assemblée nationale*) *register, with photographs, of French deputies*, ≃ rogues' gallery* of MPs (*Brit*) *ou* representatives (*US*)

tromblon /tʀɔ̃blɔ̃/ **NM** 1 (*Mil Hist*) blunderbuss; *[de fusil lance-roquettes]* grenade launcher 2 (‡ = *chapeau*) hat

trombone /tʀɔ̃bɔn/ NM 1 *(Mus)* (= *instrument*) trombone; (= *tromboniste*) trombonist, trombone (player) ◆ ~ **à coulisse/à pistons** slide/valve trombone ◆ ~ **basse** bass trombone 2 (= *agrafe*) paper clip

tromboniste /tʀɔ̃bɔnist/ NMF trombonist, trombone (player)

trompe /tʀɔ̃p/ NF 1 *(Mus)* trumpet, horn; († = *avertisseur, sirène*) horn ◆ ~ **de chasse** hunting horn ◆ ~ **de brume** fog horn; → **son²** 2 *[d'éléphant]* trunk; *[d'insecte]* proboscis; *[de tapir]* snout, proboscis *(SPÉC)*; (* = *nez*) proboscis *(hum)*, snout* 3 *(Tech)* ~ **à eau/mercure** water/mercury pump 4 *(Archit)* squinch
COMP **trompe d'Eustache** Eustachian tube
trompe de Fallope *ou* **utérine** Fallopian tube

trompe-la-mort /tʀɔ̃plamɔʀ/ NMF INV death-dodger

trompe-l'œil /tʀɔ̃plœj/ NM INV 1 *(Art)* trompe-l'œil ◆ **peinture en** ~ trompe-l'œil painting ◆ **décor en** ~ decor done in trompe-l'œil ◆ **peint en** ~ **sur un mur** painted in trompe-l'œil on a wall 2 (= *esbroufe*) eyewash *(Brit)**, hogwash *(US)* ◆ **c'est du** ~ it's all eyewash *(Brit)** *ou* hogwash *(US)*

tromper /tʀɔ̃pe/ GRAMMAIRE ACTIVE 39.1, 45.2 ► conjug 1 ◄
VT 1 (= *duper*) to deceive, to trick, to fool; (= *être infidèle à*) *[+ époux]* to be unfaithful to, to deceive, to cheat on* ◆ ~ **qn sur qch** to deceive *ou* mislead sb about *ou* over sth ◆ **on m'a trompé sur la marchandise** I was misled ◆ ~ **sa femme** to cheat on* one's wife, to be unfaithful ◆ **elle trompait son mari avec le patron** she was having an affair with her boss behind her husband's back ◆ **une femme trompée** a woman who has been deceived ◆ **cela ne trompe personne** that doesn't fool anybody ◆ **il trompe son monde** he's fooling everybody around him
2 (= *induire en erreur par accident*) *[personne]* to mislead; *[symptômes]* to deceive, to mislead ◆ **les apparences trompent** appearances are deceptive *ou* misleading ◆ **c'est ce qui vous trompe** that's where you're mistaken *ou* wrong ◆ **c'est un signe qui ne trompe pas** it's a clear *ou* an unmistakable sign
3 (= *déjouer*) *[+ poursuivants] [personne]* to elude, to escape from, to outwit; *[manœuvre]* to fool, to trick ◆ ~ **la vigilance** *ou* **surveillance de qn** *(pour entrer ou sortir)* to slip past sb's guard ◆ **il a trompé le gardien de but** *ou* **la vigilance du gardien de but** he managed to slip the ball past the goalkeeper
4 (= *décevoir*) ~ **l'attente/l'espoir de qn** to fall short of *ou* fail to come up to sb's expectations/one's hopes ◆ **être trompé dans son attente/ses espoirs** to be disappointed in one's expectations/one's hopes ◆ ~ **la faim/la soif** to stave off one's hunger/thirst ◆ **pour** ~ **le temps** to kill time, to pass the time ◆ **pour** ~ **l'ennui** *ou* **son ennui** to keep boredom at bay ◆ **pour** ~ **leur longue attente** to while away their long wait
VPR **se tromper** (= *faire erreur*) to make a mistake, to be mistaken ◆ **se** ~ **de 5 € dans un calcul** to be €5 out *(Brit)* *ou* off *(US)* in one's calculations ◆ **tout le monde peut se** ~ anybody can make a mistake ◆ **se** ~ **sur les intentions de qn** to be mistaken about sb's intentions, to misjudge *ou* mistake sb's intentions ◆ **on pourrait s'y** ~, **c'est à s'y** ~ you'd hardly know the difference ◆ **ne vous y trompez pas, il arrivera à ses fins** make no mistake, he'll get what he wants ◆ **si je ne me trompe** if I'm not mistaken, unless I'm very much mistaken
◆ **se tromper de** (= *confondre*) ◆ **se** ~ **de route/chapeau** to take the wrong road/hat ◆ **se** ~ **d'adresse** *(lit)* to get the wrong address ◆ **tu te trompes d'adresse** *ou* **de porte** *(fig)* you've come to the wrong place, you've got the wrong person ◆ **se** ~ **de jour/date** to get the day/date wrong ◆ **vous devez vous** ~ **de personne, je ne m'appelle pas Jean** you've got the wrong person *ou* you must be mistaken, I'm not called Jean

tromperie /tʀɔ̃pʀi/ NF 1 (= *duperie*) deception, deceit, trickery *(NonC)* ◆ **il y a eu** ~ **sur la marchandise** the goods are not what they were described to be 2 *(littér* = *illusion)* illusion

trompeter /tʀɔ̃pete/ ► conjug 4 ◄ VT *(péj) [+ nouvelle]* to trumpet abroad, to shout from the housetops

trompette /tʀɔ̃pɛt/ NF 1 *(Mus)* trumpet ◆ ~ **de cavalerie** bugle ◆ ~ **d'harmonie/à pistons/chromatique/naturelle** orchestral/valve/chromatic/natural trumpet ◆ ~ **basse/bouchée** bass/muted trumpet ◆ **la** ~ **du Jugement (dernier)** *(Bible)* the last Trump ◆ **la** ~ **de la Renommée** *(littér)* the Trumpet of Fame ◆ **avoir la queue en** ~ to have a turned-up tail; → **nez, tambour** 2 (= *coquillage*) trumpet shell
NM (= *trompettiste*) trumpeter, trumpet (player); *(Mil)* bugler

trompette-de-la-mort (pl **trompettes-de-la-mort**) /tʀɔ̃pɛtdəlamɔʀ/ NF (= *champignon*) horn of plenty

trompettiste /tʀɔ̃petist/ NMF trumpet player, trumpeter

trompeur, -euse /tʀɔ̃pœʀ, øz/ ADJ 1 (= *hypocrite*) *[personne, paroles, discours]* deceitful 2 (= *fallacieux*) *[distance, profondeur, virage]* deceptive ◆ **les apparences sont trompeuses** appearances are deceptive *ou* misleading NM,F deceiver ◆ **à** ~, ~ **et demi** *(Prov)* every rogue has his match

trompeusement /tʀɔ̃pøzmɑ̃/ ADV (= *hypocritement*) deceitfully; (= *faussement*) deceptively

tronc /tʀɔ̃/ NM 1 *[d'arbre]* trunk; *[de colonne]* shaft, trunk; *(Géom) [de cône, pyramide]* frustum; *(Anat) [de nerf, vaisseau]* trunk, mainstem ◆ ~ **d'arbre** tree trunk ◆ ~ **de cône/pyramide** truncated cone/pyramid 2 *(Anat* = *thorax et abdomen)* trunk; *[de cadavre mutilé]* torso 3 (= *boîte*) (collection) box ◆ **le** ~ **des pauvres** the poor box COMP **tronc commun** *(Scol)* common-core syllabus

troncation /tʀɔ̃kasjɔ̃/ NF *(Ling)* truncating; *(Ordin)* truncation ◆ **recherche par** ~ **à droite/gauche** search by truncating a word on the right/left

troncature /tʀɔ̃katyʀ/ NF *(Minér)* truncation

tronche* /tʀɔ̃ʃ/ NF (= *visage*) mug*; (= *tête*) nut*, noggin* *(US)* ◆ **faire** *ou* **tirer la** ~ *(ponctuellement)* to make a face; *(durablement)* to sulk ◆ **il a une sale** ~ he's got a nasty face, he's a nasty-looking customer* ◆ **elle a une** ~ **de cake*** she's got an ugly mug* ◆ **il lui a envoyé un coup de poing dans la** ~ he punched him in the face *ou* the kisser* ◆ **il a fait une drôle de** ~ **quand je lui ai dit ça** you should have seen the look on his face when I told him that

tronçon /tʀɔ̃sɔ̃/ NM 1 *[de tube, colonne, serpent]* section 2 *[de route, voie]* section, stretch; *[de convoi, colonne]* section; *[de phrase, texte]* part

tronconique /tʀɔ̃kɔnik/ ADJ like a flattened cone *ou* a sawn-off cone

tronçonnage /tʀɔ̃sɔnaʒ/, **tronçonnement** /tʀɔ̃sɔnmɑ̃/ NM *[de tronc]* sawing *ou* cutting up; *[de tube, barre]* cutting into sections

tronçonner /tʀɔ̃sɔne/ ► conjug 1 ◄ VT *[+ tronc]* to saw *ou* cut up; *[+ tube, barre]* to cut into sections; *(Culin)* to cut into small pieces ◆ **le film a été tronçonné en épisodes** the film was divided up into episodes

tronçonneuse /tʀɔ̃sɔnøz/ NF chain saw

trône /tʀon/ NM 1 (= *siège, fonction*) throne ◆ ~ **pontifical** papal throne ◆ **placer qn/monter sur le** ~ to put sb on/come to *ou* ascend the throne ◆ **chasser du** ~ to dethrone, to remove from the throne ◆ **le** ~ **et l'autel** King and Church 2 (* *hum* = *WC*) throne* *(hum)* ◆ **être sur le** ~ to be on the throne*

trôner /tʀone/ ► conjug 1 ◄ VI 1 *[roi, divinité]* to sit enthroned, to sit on the throne 2 (= *avoir la place d'honneur*) *[personne]* to sit enthroned; *[chose]* to sit imposingly; *(péj* = *faire l'important)* to lord it ◆ **la photo dédicacée de son joueur préféré trônait sur son bureau** the signed photograph of his favourite player had pride of place on his desk

tronquer /tʀɔ̃ke/ ► conjug 1 ◄ VT 1 (= *couper*) *[+ colonne, statue]* to truncate 2 (= *retrancher*) *[+ citation, texte]* to truncate, to shorten; *[+ détails, faits]* to abbreviate, to cut out ◆ **version tronquée** shortened *ou* truncated version

trop /tʀo/ ADV 1 *(avec vb* = *à l'excès)* too much; *(devant adv, adj)* too ◆ **beaucoup** *ou* **bien** ~ *[manger, fumer, parler]* far *ou* much too much ◆ **beaucoup** *ou* **bien** *ou* **par** *(littér)* ~ *(avec adj)* far too, much too, excessively ◆ **il a** ~ **mangé/bu** he has had too much to eat/drink, he has eaten/drunk too much ◆ **elle en a déjà bien** ~ **dit** she has said far *ou* much too much already ◆ **je suis exténué d'avoir** ~ **marché** I'm exhausted from having walked too far *ou* too much ◆ **il a** ~ **travaillé** he has worked too hard, he has done too much work ◆ **vous en demandez** ~ you're asking for too much ◆ **elle a** ~ **peu dormi** she hasn't had enough sleep, she's had too little sleep ◆ **il faut régler le problème sans** ~ **attendre** *ou* **tarder** we must solve the problem quickly *ou* without too much delay ◆ **tu as** ~ **conduit** you've been driving (for) too long ◆ **il ne faut pas** ~ **aller le voir** we mustn't go to visit him too often, we mustn't overdo the visits ◆ **en faire** ~ (= *exagérer*) to go a bit far ◆ **elle en fait toujours** ~ she always goes too far *ou* over the top ◆ **aller beaucoup** ~ **loin** to go overboard*, to go too far, to overdo it ◆ **elle en fait** ~ **pour qu'on la croie vraiment malade** she makes so much fuss it's difficult to believe she's really ill ◆ **un** ~ **grand effort l'épuiserait** too great an effort would exhaust him ◆ **des restrictions** ~ **sévères aggraveraient la situation économique** excessively severe restrictions would aggravate the economic situation ◆ **la maison est** ~ **grande pour eux** the house is too large for them ◆ **la pièce est** ~ **chauffée** the room is overheated ◆ **une** ~ **forte dose** an overdose ◆ **tu conduis bien** ~ **vite/lentement** you drive far too fast/slowly ◆ **vous êtes** ~ **(nombreux)/**~ **peu (nombreux)** there are too many/too few of you
◆ **trop de** *(quantité)* too much; *(nombre)* too many ◆ **j'ai acheté** ~ **de pain/d'oranges** I've bought too much bread/too many oranges ◆ **n'apportez pas de pain, il y en a déjà** ~ don't bring any bread – there's too much already ◆ **n'apportez pas de verres, il y en a déjà** ~ don't bring any glasses – there are too many already ◆ **s'il te reste** ~ **de dollars, vends-les moi** if you have dollars left over *ou* to spare, sell them to me ◆ **nous avons** ~ **de personnel** we are overstaffed ◆ **il y a** ~ **de monde dans la salle** the hall is overcrowded *ou* overfull, there are too many people in the hall ◆ **j'ai** ~ **de travail** I'm overworked, I've got too much work (to do) ◆ ~ **de bonté/d'égoïsme** excessive kindness/selfishness ◆ **nous n'avons pas** ~ **de place chez nous** we haven't got very much room *ou* (all) that much* room at our place ◆ **on peut le faire sans** ~ **de risques/de mal** it can be done without too much risk/difficulty ◆ **ils ne seront pas** ~ **de deux pour faire ça** it'll take at least the two of them to do it
◆ **trop ... pour** *(introduisant une conséquence, avec verbe)* too much ... to; *(devant adj, adv)* too ... to ◆ **elle a** ~ **de travail pour partir en week-end** she has too much work to go away for the weekend ◆ **il n'aura pas** ~ **de problèmes pour**

rentrer à Paris he won't have too much difficulty getting back to Paris ◆ **il se donne ~ peu de mal pour trouver du travail** he's not making enough effort to find work ◆ **le village est ~ loin pour qu'il puisse y aller à pied** the village is too far for him to walk there ◆ **il est bien ~ idiot pour comprendre** he's far too stupid *ou* too much of an idiot to understand ◆ **c'est ~ beau pour être vrai !** it's too good to be true! ◆ **les voyages à l'étranger sont ~ rares pour ne pas en profiter** trips abroad are too rare to be missed

2 *(intensif)* too ◆ **j'ai oublié mes papiers, c'est vraiment ~ bête** how stupid (of me) *ou* it's too stupid for words – I've forgotten my papers ◆ **c'est ~ drôle !** it's too funny for words!, it's hilarious!, how funny! ◆ **c'est par ~ injuste** *(littér)* it's too unfair for words ◆ **il y a vraiment par ~ de gens égoïstes** there are far too many selfish people about ◆ **il n'est pas ~ satisfait/mécontent du résultat** he's not over-pleased *ou* too satisfied *ou* too pleased/not too unhappy *ou* dissatisfied with the result ◆ **vous êtes ~ aimable** you are too *ou* most kind ◆ **cela n'a que ~ duré** it's gone on (far) too long already ◆ **je ne le sais que ~** I know only too well, I'm only too well aware of that ◆ **je ne sais ~ que faire** I am not too *ou* quite sure what to do *ou* what I should do, I don't really know what to do ◆ **cela ne va pas ~ bien** things are not going so *ou* terribly well ◆ **je n'ai pas ~ confiance en lui** I haven't much *ou* all that much* confidence in him ◆ **je n'en sais ~ rien** I don't really know ◆ **il n'aime pas ~ ça*** he doesn't like it overmuch *ou* (all) that much*, he isn't too keen *(Brit) ou* overkeen *(Brit)* (on it) ◆ **c'est ~ !, c'en est ~ !, ~ c'est ~ !** that's going too far!, enough is enough! ◆ **elle est ~, ta copine !*** your girlfriend's too much!* ◆ **c'est ~ génial !*** it's fantastic!; → **tôt**

◆ **de trop, en trop** ◆ **il y a une personne/deux personnes de ~ *ou* en ~ dans l'ascenseur** there's one person/there are two people too many in the lift ◆ **s'il y a du pain en ~, j'en emporterai** if there's any bread (left) over *ou* any bread extra *ou* any surplus bread I'll take some away ◆ **il m'a rendu 2 € de ~ *ou* en ~** he gave me back €2 too much ◆ **ces 3 € sont de ~** that's 3 euros too much ◆ **l'argent versé en ~** the excess payment ◆ **il pèse 3 kg de ~** he's 3 kg overweight ◆ **ce régime vous fait perdre les kilos en ~** this diet will help you lose those extra pounds ◆ **si je suis de ~, je peux m'en aller !** if I'm in the way *ou* not welcome I can always leave! ◆ **cette remarque est de ~** that remark is uncalled-for ◆ **un petit café ne serait pas de ~** a cup of coffee wouldn't go amiss ◆ **il a bu un verre *ou* un coup* de ~** he's had a drink *ou* one* too many ◆ **tu manges/bois de ~*** you eat/drink too much

NM excess, surplus ◆ **le ~ d'importance accordé à ...** the excessive importance attributed to ...

trope /tʀɔp/ NM *(Littérat)* trope

trophée /tʀofe/ NM trophy ◆ **~ de chasse** hunting trophy

tropical, e (mpl **-aux**) /tʀɔpikal, o/ ADJ tropical

tropicaliser /tʀɔpikalize/ ▸ conjug 1 ◂ VT *[+ matériel]* to tropicalize

tropique /tʀɔpik/ ADJ *[année]* tropical NM *(Géog = ligne)* tropic ◆ **~ du Cancer/Capricorne** tropic of Cancer/Capricorn NMPL **tropiques** *(= zone)* tropics ◆ **le soleil des ~s** the tropical sun ◆ **vivre sous les ~s** to live in the tropics

tropisme /tʀɔpism/ NM *(Bio)* tropism

troposphère /tʀɔpɔsfɛʀ/ NF troposphere

trop-perçu (pl **trop-perçus**) /tʀopɛʀsy/ NM excess payment, overpayment

trop-plein (pl **trop-pleins**) /tʀoplɛ̃/ NM 1 *(= excès d'eau) [de réservoir, barrage]* overflow; *[de vase]* excess water; *(= tuyau d'évacuation)* overflow (pipe); *(= déversoir)* overflow outlet 2 *(= excès de contenu) [de grains, terre, informations]* excess, surplus ◆ **le ~ de terre** the excess earth 3 *(fig)* **~ d'amour/d'amitié** overflowing love/friendship ◆ **~ de vie *ou* d'énergie** surplus *ou* boundless energy ◆ **déverser le ~ de son cœur/âme** to pour out one's heart/soul

troquer /tʀɔke/ ▸ conjug 1 ◂ VT *(= échanger)* to swap, to exchange; *(Comm)* to trade, to barter *(contre, pour* for); ◆ **elle a troqué son sari pour un jean** she swapped her sari for a pair of jeans

troquet* /tʀɔkɛ/ NM (small) café

trot /tʀo/ NM *[de cheval]* trot ◆ **petit/grand ~** jog/full trot ◆ **~ de manège** dressage trot ◆ **~ assis/enlevé** close/rising trot ◆ **course de ~ attelé** trotting race ◆ **course de ~ monté** *trotting race under saddle* ◆ **aller au ~** *(lit)* to trot along ◆ **vas-y, et au ~ !*** off you go, at the double *ou* and be quick about it! ◆ **partir au ~** to set off at a trot ◆ **prendre le ~** to break into a trot

trotskisme, trotskysme /tʀɔtskism/ NM Trotskyism

trotskiste, trotskyste /tʀɔtskist/ ADJ, NMF Trotskyist, Trotskyite *(péj)*

trotte* /tʀɔt/ NF ◆ **il y a *ou* ça fait une ~ (d'ici au village)** it's a fair distance (from here to the village) ◆ **on a fait une (jolie) ~** we've come a good way, we covered a good distance

trotter /tʀɔte/ ▸ conjug 1 ◂ VI 1 *[cheval, cavalier]* to trot 2 *(fig) [personne] (= marcher à petits pas)* to trot about *(ou* along); *(= marcher beaucoup)* to run around, to run hither and thither; *[souris, enfants]* to scurry (about), to scamper (about); *[bébé]* to toddle along ◆ **un air/une idée qui vous trotte dans *ou* par la tête *ou* la cervelle** a tune/an idea which keeps running through your head VPR **se trotter** * *(= se sauver)* to dash (off)

trotteur, -euse /tʀɔtœʀ, øz/ NM,F *(= cheval)* trotter, trotting horse NM 1 *(= chaussure)* flat shoe 2 *(pour apprendre à marcher)* baby-walker NF **trotteuse** *(= aiguille)* sweep *ou* second hand

trottin †† /tʀɔtɛ̃/ NM (dressmaker's) errand girl

trottinement /tʀɔtinmɑ̃/ NM *[de cheval]* jogging; *[de souris]* scurrying, scampering; *[de personne]* trotting; *[de bébé]* toddling

trottiner /tʀɔtine/ ▸ conjug 1 ◂ VI *[cheval]* to jog along; *[souris]* to scurry *ou* scamper about *ou* along; *[personne]* to trot along; *[bébé]* to toddle along

trottinette /tʀɔtinɛt/ NF *(= jouet)* (child's) scooter; *(* = voiture)* mini (car) ◆ **faire de la ~** to ride a scooter

trottoir /tʀɔtwaʀ/ NM 1 *(= accotement)* pavement *(Brit)*, sidewalk *(US)* ◆ **~ roulant** moving walkway, travelator *(Brit)* ◆ **se garer le long du ~** to park alongside the kerb ◆ **changer de ~** *(pour éviter qn)* to cross the street 2 *(péj)* **faire le ~*** to be a streetwalker *ou* a hooker*, to be on the game*̣* *(Brit)* ◆ **elle s'est retrouvée sur le ~** she ended up as a prostitute *ou* on the streets

trou /tʀu/ NM 1 *(gén, Golf)* hole; *(= terrier)* hole, burrow; *[de flûte]* (finger-)hole; *[d'aiguille]* eye ◆ **par le ~ de la serrure** through the keyhole ◆ **le ~ du souffleur** *(Théât)* the prompt box ◆ **faire un ~** *(dans le sol)* to dig *ou* make a hole; *(dans une haie)* to make a hole *ou* a gap; *(dans un mur avec une vrille)* to bore *ou* make a hole; *(en perforant : dans le cuir, papier)* to punch *ou* make a hole; *(avec des ciseaux, un couteau)* to cut a hole; *(en usant, frottant)* to wear a hole *(dans* in); ◆ **faire un ~ en un** *(Golf)* to get a hole in one ◆ **un 9/18 ~s** *(Golf)* a 9-hole/an 18-hole course ◆ **il a fait un ~ à son pantalon** *(usure)* he has (worn) a hole in his trousers; *(brûlure, acide)* he has burnt a hole in his trousers; *(déchirure)* he has torn a hole in his trousers ◆ **ses chaussettes sont pleines de ~s *ou* ont des ~s partout** his socks are in holes *ou* are full of holes ◆ **sol/rocher creusé de ~s** ground/rock pitted with holes ◆ **le ~ dans la couche d'ozone** the hole in the ozone layer

2 *(= moment de libre)* gap; *(= déficit)* deficit; *(Sport = trouée)* gap, space ◆ **un ~ (de 10 millions) dans la comptabilité** a deficit (of 10 million) in the accounts ◆ **faire le ~** *(Sport)* to break *ou* burst through ◆ **il y a des ~s dans ma collection** there are some gaps in my collection ◆ **il y a des ~s dans son témoignage** there are gaps in *ou* things missing from his account of what happened ◆ **il a des ~s en physique** there are gaps in his knowledge of physics ◆ **cela a fait un gros ~ dans ses économies** it made quite a hole in his savings ◆ **le ~ de la Sécurité sociale** the deficit in the Social Security budget ◆ **j'ai un ~ demain dans la matinée, venez me voir** I have a gap in my schedule tomorrow morning so come and see me ◆ **j'ai un ~ d'une heure** I have an hour free ◆ **j'ai eu un ~ (de mémoire)** my mind went blank ◆ **texte à ~s** *(Scol)* cloze test

3 *(Anat)* foramen ◆ **~ optique** optic foramen ◆ **~s intervertébraux** intervertebral foramina ◆ **~ vertébral** vertebral canal *ou* foramen; → **œil**

4 *(péj = localité)* place, hole* *(péj)* ◆ **ce village est un ~** this village is a real hole* *ou* dump* ◆ **il n'est jamais sorti de son ~** he has never been out of his own backyard ◆ **chercher un petit ~ pas cher** to look for a little place that's not too expensive ◆ **un ~ perdu *ou* paumé*** a dead-and-alive hole*, a god forsaken hole* *ou* dump*

5 *(locutions)* **(se) faire son ~*** to make a niche for o.s. ◆ **vivre tranquille dans son ~** to live quietly in one's little hideaway *ou* hidey-hole* *(Brit)* ◆ **mettre/être au ~*** *(= prison)* to put/be in clink*̣* *ou* in the nick *(Brit)*** ◆ **quand on sera dans le ~*** when we're dead and buried *ou* dead and gone, when we're six feet under*; → **boire**

COMP **trou d'aération** airhole, (air) vent
trou d'air air pocket
trou de balle** *(lit, fig)* arse-hole** *(Brit)*, ass-hole** *(US)*
trou du chat *(Naut)* lubber's hole
trou de cigarette cigarette burn
trou du cul** ⇒ **trou de balle**
trou d'homme manhole
trou de nez* nostril
trou noir *(Astron)* black hole ◆ **c'était le ~ noir** *(fig) (= désespoir)* I *(ou* he *etc)* was in the depths of despair
trou normand *glass of spirits, often Calvados, drunk between courses of a meal*
trou d'obus shell-hole, shell-crater
trou de souris mousehole ◆ **elle était si gênée qu'elle serait rentrée dans un ~ de souris** she was so embarrassed that she wished the ground would swallow her up
trou de ver wormhole

troubadour /tʀubaduʀ/ NM troubadour

troublant, e /tʀublɑ̃, ɑ̃t/ ADJ *(= déconcertant)* disturbing, disquieting, unsettling; *(= sexuellement provocant)* disturbing, arousing

trouble[1] /tʀubl/ ADJ 1 *[eau, vin]* unclear, cloudy, turbid *(littér)*; *[regard]* misty, dull; *[image]* blurred, misty, indistinct; *[photo]* blurred, out of focus ◆ **avoir la vue ~** to have blurred vision; → **pêcher[1]** 2 *(= équivoque) [personnage, rôle]* shady, suspicious, dubious; *[atmosphère, passé]* shady; *[affaire]* shady, murky, fishy; *[désir]* dark *(épith)*; *(= vague, pas franc) [regard]* shifty, uneasy ◆ **une période ~ de l'histoire** a murky chapter *ou* period in history ADV ◆ **voir ~** to have blurred vision, to see things dimly *ou* as if through a mist

trouble² /tʀubl/ NM [1] *(= agitation, remue-ménage)* tumult, turmoil; *(= zizanie, désunion)* discord, trouble

[2] *(= émeute)* **~s** unrest *(NonC)*, disturbances, troubles ◆ **~s politiques/sociaux** political/social unrest *(NonC) ou* disturbances *ou* upheavals ◆ **des ~s ont éclaté dans le sud du pays** rioting has broken out *ou* disturbances have broken out in the south of the country ◆ **~s à l'ordre public** disturbance *ou* breach of the peace; → **fauteur**

[3] *(= émoi affectif ou sensuel)* (inner) turmoil, agitation; *(= inquiétude, désarroi)* distress; *(= gêne, perplexité)* confusion, embarrassment ◆ **le ~ étrange qui s'empara d'elle** the strange feeling of turmoil *ou* agitation which overcame her ◆ **le ~ profond causé par ces événements traumatisants** the profound distress caused by these traumatic events ◆ **le ~ de son âme/cœur** *(littér)* the tumult *ou* turmoil in his soul/heart ◆ **le ~ de son esprit** the agitation in his mind, the turmoil his mind was in ◆ **dominer/se laisser trahir par son ~** to overcome/give o.s. away by one's confusion *ou* embarrassment ◆ **semer le ~ dans l'esprit des gens** to sow confusion in peoples' minds

[4] *(gén pl : Méd)* trouble *(NonC)*, disorder ◆ **~s physiologiques/psychiques** physiological/psychological trouble *ou* disorders ◆ **~s mentaux** mental disorders ◆ **~s respiratoires/cardiaques** respiratory/heart ailments *ou* disorders ◆ **~s du sommeil** sleeping disorders ◆ **il a des ~s de la vision** he has trouble with his (eye)sight *ou* vision ◆ **elle souffre de ~s de la mémoire** she has memory problems ◆ **~s de la personnalité** *ou* **du caractère** personality problems *ou* disorders ◆ **~s du comportement** behavioural problems ◆ **~s du langage** speech difficulties ◆ **~s musculo-squelettiques** repetitive strain injury, RSI ◆ **~ obsessionnel compulsif** *(Psych)* obsessive-compulsive disorder ◆ **ce n'est qu'un ~ passager** it's only a passing disorder

trouble-fête /tʀubləfɛt/ NMF INV spoilsport, killjoy* ◆ **jouer les ~** to be a spoilsport *ou* killjoy*

troubler /tʀuble/ ► conjug 1 ◄ VT [1] *(= perturber)* *[+ ordre]* to disturb, to disrupt; *[+ sommeil, tranquillité, silence]* to disturb; *[+ représentation, réunion]* to disrupt; *[+ jugement, raison, esprit]* to cloud; *[+ digestion]* to upset ◆ **~ l'ordre public** to disturb public order, to cause a breach of public order, to disturb the peace ◆ **en ces temps troublés** in these troubled times

[2] *[+ personne]* *(= démonter, impressionner)* to disturb, to disconcert; *(= inquiéter)* to trouble, to perturb; *(= gêner, embrouiller)* to bother, to confuse; *(= émouvoir)* to disturb, to unsettle; *(= exciter sexuellement)* to arouse ◆ **elle le regarda, toute troublée** she looked at him, all of a tremble *ou* all in a fluster ◆ **ce film/cet événement l'a profondément troublé** this film/this event has disturbed him deeply ◆ **la perspective d'un échec ne le trouble pas du tout** the prospect of failure doesn't perturb *ou* trouble him in the slightest ◆ **il y a quand même un détail qui me trouble** there's still a detail which is bothering *ou* confusing me ◆ **cesse de parler, tu me troubles (dans mes calculs)** stop talking – you're disturbing me *ou* putting me off (in my calculations) ◆ **~ un candidat** to disconcert a candidate, to put a candidate off ◆ **~ (les sens de) qn** to disturb *ou* agitate sb

[3] *(= brouiller)* *[+ eau]* to make cloudy *ou* muddy *ou* turbid *(littér)*; *[+ vin]* to cloud, to make cloudy; *[+ atmosphère]* to cloud; *[+ ciel]* to darken, to cloud; *(TV)* *[+ image]* to blur ◆ **les larmes lui troublaient la vue** tears clouded *ou* blurred her vision

VPR **se troubler** [1] *(= devenir trouble)* *[eau]* to cloud, to become cloudy *ou* muddy *ou* turbid *(littér)*; *[temps]* to become cloudy *ou* overcast; *[ciel]* to become cloudy *ou* overcast, to darken; *[lignes, images, vue]* to become blurred

[2] *(= perdre contenance)* to become flustered ◆ **il se trouble facilement lorsqu'il doit parler en public** he's easily flustered when he has to speak in public ◆ **il répondit sans se ~** he replied calmly

troué, e¹ /tʀue/ (ptp de **trouer**) ADJ ◆ **bas/sac ~** stocking/bag with a hole *ou* with holes in it ◆ **avoir une chaussette ~e** to have a hole in one's sock ◆ **ce sac est ~** this bag has a hole *ou* holes (in it) ◆ **ses chaussettes sont toutes ~es** *ou* **~es de partout** his socks are full of holes ◆ **ce seau est ~ de partout** *ou* **comme une passoire** *ou* **comme une écumoire** this bucket's like a sieve ◆ **corps ~ comme une passoire** *ou* **écumoire** body riddled with bullets ◆ **son gant ~ laissait passer son pouce** his thumb stuck *ou* poked out through a hole in his glove

trouée² /tʀue/ NF [1] *[de haie, forêt, nuages]* gap, break *(de* in); ◆ **~ de lumière** shaft of light [2] *(Mil)* breach ◆ **faire une ~** to make a breach, to break through [3] *(Géog = défilé)* gap ◆ **la ~ de Belfort** the Belfort Gap

trouer /tʀue/ ► conjug 1 ◄ VT [1] *[+ vêtement]* to make *ou* wear a hole in; *[+ ticket]* to punch (a hole in); *(= transpercer)* to pierce ◆ **il a troué son pantalon** *(avec une cigarette)* he's burnt a hole in his trousers; *(dans les ronces)* he's torn *ou* ripped a hole in his trousers; *(par usure)* he's worn a hole in his trousers ◆ **ces chaussettes se sont trouées très vite** these socks soon got holes in them ◆ **~ qch de part en part** to pierce sth through, to pierce a hole right through sth ◆ **après le bombardement, les rues étaient trouées de cratères** after the bombing, the streets were pockmarked with craters ◆ **des immeubles troués par les obus** buildings full of gaping shellholes ◆ **~ la peau à qn**‡ to put a bullet in sb ◆ **se faire ~ la peau**‡ to get a bullet in one's hide*

[2] *(fig = traverser)* *[+ silence, nuit]* to pierce ◆ **une fusée troua l'obscurité** a rocket pierced the darkness ◆ **le soleil troue les nuages** the sun's breaking through the clouds

[3] *(= parsemer : gén ptp)* to dot ◆ **la plaine trouée d'ombres** the plain dotted with shadows

troufignon †‡ /tʀufiɲɔ̃/ NM *(= derrière)* backside*, arse*‡ *(Brit)*, ass*‡ *(US)*; *(= anus)* arsehole*‡*(Brit)*, asshole*‡*(US)*

troufion * /tʀufjɔ̃/ NM soldier, squaddie* ◆ **quand j'étais ~** when I was in the army *ou* was a soldier

trouillard, e‡ /tʀujaʀ, aʀd/ *(péj)* ADJ yellow*, chicken* *(attrib)*, yellow-bellied‡ NM,F yellow-belly‡

trouille‡ /tʀuj/ NF ◆ **avoir la ~** to be scared stiff* *ou* to death ◆ **j'ai eu la ~ de ma vie** I got the fright of my life *ou* a hell of a fright* ◆ **flanquer** *ou* **ficher la ~ à qn** to scare the pants off sb*, to put the wind up sb* *(Brit)*

trouillomètre‡ /tʀujɔmɛtʀ/ NM ◆ **avoir le ~ à zéro** to be scared witless*

troupe /tʀup/ NF [1] *(Mil, Scoutisme)* troop ◆ **la ~** *(= l'armée)* the army; *(= les simples soldats)* the troops, the rank and file ◆ **les ~s** the troops ◆ **~s de choc/de débarquement** shock/landing troops ◆ **lever des ~s** to raise troops ◆ **faire intervenir la ~** to call *ou* bring in the army ◆ **réservé à la ~** reserved for the troops; → **enfant, homme** [2] *[de chanteurs, danseurs]* troupe ◆ **~ (de théâtre)** (theatre *ou* drama) company [3] *[de gens, animaux]* band, group, troop ◆ **se déplacer en ~** to go about in a band *ou* group *ou* troop

troupeau (pl **troupeaux**) /tʀupo/ NM *[de bœufs, chevaux]* *(dans un pré)* herd; *(transhumant)* drove; *[de moutons, chèvres]* flock; *[d'éléphants, buffles, girafes]* herd; *[d'oies]* gaggle; *(péj)* *[de touristes, prisonniers]* herd *(péj)* ◆ **le ~ du Seigneur** *(Rel)* the Lord's flock

troupier /tʀupje/ NM († = soldat) private ADJ → **comique**

trousse /tʀus/ NF *(= étui)* *(gén)* case, kit; *[de médecin, chirurgien]* instrument case; *[d'écolier]* pencil case *ou* wallet ◆ **~ à aiguilles** needle case ◆ **~ à couture** sewing case *ou* kit ◆ **~ de** *ou* **à maquillage** *(= mallette)* vanity case; *(= sac)* make-up bag ◆ **~ à outils** toolkit ◆ **~ à ongles** nail kit, manicure set ◆ **~ à pharmacie** *ou* **de secours** first-aid kit ◆ **~ de toilette** *ou* **de voyage** *(= sac)* toilet bag, sponge bag; *(= mallette)* travelling case, grip LOC PRÉP **aux trousses de** hot on the heels of, on the tail of ◆ **les créanciers/policiers étaient à ses ~s** the creditors/policemen were on his tail *ou* hot on his heels ◆ **avoir la police aux ~s** to have the police on one's tail *ou* hot on one's heels

trousseau (pl **trousseaux**) /tʀuso/ NM [1] ◆ **~ de clés** bunch of keys [2] *(= vêtements, linge)* *[de mariée]* trousseau; *[d'écolier]* outfit

troussequin /tʀuskɛ̃/ NM [1] *(Équitation)* cantle [2] *(= outil)* ⇒ **trusquin**

trousser /tʀuse/ ► conjug 1 ◄ VT [1] *(Culin)* *[+ volaille]* to truss [2] († = *retrousser)* *[+ robe, jupes]* to pick *ou* tuck up ◆ **se ~** to pick *ou* tuck up one's skirts [3] (†, *hum)* *[+ femme]* to tumble † [4] († *= expédier)* *[+ poème, article, discours]* to dash off, to throw together ◆ **compliment bien troussé** well-phrased compliment

trousseur † /tʀusœʀ/ NM *(hum)* ◆ **~ de jupons** womanizer, ladykiller

trou-trou (pl **trou(s)-trou(s)**) /tʀutʀu/ NM *(Tricot)* row of holes through which ribbon is passed; *(Couture)* lace trimming through which ribbon is passed ◆ **chemisier à trous-trous** openwork blouse

trouvaille /tʀuvaj/ NF *(= objet)* find; *(= idée, métaphore, procédé)* stroke of inspiration, brainwave *(Brit)*; *(= mot)* coinage ◆ **quelle est sa dernière ~ ?** *(iro)* what's his latest brainwave?

trouver /tʀuve/ GRAMMAIRE ACTIVE 33.2, 53.5 ► conjug 1 ◄

VT [1] *(en cherchant)* *[+ objet, emploi, main-d'œuvre, renseignement]* to find ◆ **je ne le trouve pas** I can't find it ◆ **où peut-on le ~ ?** where can he be found?, where is he to be found? ◆ **on lui a trouvé une place dans un lycée** he was found a place in a lycée, they found him a place *ou* a place for him in a lycée ◆ **est-ce qu'ils trouveront le chemin ?** will they find the way? *ou* their way? ◆ **~ le temps/l'énergie/le courage de faire qch** to find (the) time/the energy/the courage to do sth ◆ **comment avez-vous trouvé un secrétaire si compétent ?** how did you come by *ou* find such a competent secretary? ◆ **elle a trouvé en lui un ami sûr/un associé compétent** she has found in him a faithful friend/a competent partner ◆ **~ son maître** to find one's master

[2] *(= rencontrer par hasard)* *[+ document, information, personne]* to find, to come across; *[+ difficultés]* to meet with, to come across, to come up against; *[+ idée, plan]* to hit on ◆ **on trouve cette plante sous tous les climats humides** this plant is found *ou* is to be found in all damp climates ◆ **~ la mort (dans un accident)** to meet one's death (in an accident)

[3] *(= découvrir)* to find ◆ **~ qch cassé/vide** *(avec attribut du complément)* to find sth broken/empty ◆ **je l'ai trouvé en train de pleurer** I found him crying ◆ **je ne lui trouve aucun défaut** I can find no fault with him ◆ **mais qu'est-ce qu'elle lui trouve ?** what on earth does she see in him?

[4] ◆ **~ à** (+ *infin*) **~ à manger/boire** to find something to eat/drink ◆ **~ à se distraire/à**

s'occuper to find a way to amuse/occupy o.s., to find something to amuse/occupy o.s. with ◆ **il trouve toujours à faire dans la maison** he can always find something to do in the house ◆ **si tu trouves à te garer dans ma rue ...** if you manage to find a parking space in my street ... ◆ **elle trouvera bien à les loger quelque part** she's bound to find somewhere to put them up ◆ **il n'a rien trouvé à répondre** he couldn't think of anything to say in reply; → **redire**

5 (*= penser, juger*) to think, to find ◆ **~ que** to find *ou* think that ◆ **elle trouve qu'il fait trop chaud ici** she finds it too hot (in) here ◆ **~ qch à son goût/trop cher** to find sth to one's liking/too expensive ◆ **je trouve cela trop sucré/lourd** I find it too sweet/heavy, it's too sweet/heavy for me ◆ **il a trouvé bon de nous écrire** he saw fit to write to us ◆ **~ le temps long** to find that time passes slowly *ou* hangs heavy on one's hands ◆ **je le trouve fatigué** I think he looks tired ◆ **tu lui trouves bonne mine ?** do you think he's looking well? ◆ **comment l'as-tu trouvé ?** what did you think of him?, how did you find him? ◆ **vous la trouvez sympathique ?** do you like her?, do you think she's nice? ◆ **trouvez-vous ça normal ?** do you think that's right? ◆ **tu trouves ça drôle !, tu trouves que c'est drôle !** so you think that's funny!, so you find that funny! ◆ **vous trouvez ?** (do) you think so?

6 (*= imaginer, inventer*) [*+ solution, prétexte, moyen*] to find, to come up with ◆ **comment as-tu fait pour ~ ?** (*énigme*) how did you work it out? ◆ **j'ai trouvé !** I've got it!* ◆ **solution/explication/excuse toute trouvée** ready-made solution/explanation/excuse ◆ **c'est un sujet tout trouvé pour ta rédaction** it's an obvious topic for your essay ◆ **formule bien trouvée** clever *ou* happy phrase ◆ **tu as trouvé ça tout seul ?** (*iro*) did you work it out all by yourself? (*iro*) ◆ **où est-il allé ~ ça ?** where (on earth) did he get that idea from?, whatever gave him that idea?; → **moyen²**, **remède** *etc*

7 (*= rendre visite à*) **aller/venir ~ qn** to go/come and see sb ◆ **quand il a des ennuis, c'est moi qu'il vient ~** when he has problems, it's me he comes to

8 (*= éprouver*) **~ (du) plaisir à qch/à faire qch** to take pleasure in sth/in doing sth, to enjoy sth/doing sth ◆ **~ une consolation dans le travail** to find consolation in work *ou* in working

9 (*locutions*) **ne pas ~ ses mots** to be at a loss for words ◆ **~ le sommeil** to get to sleep, to fall asleep ◆ **il a trouvé à qui parler** he met his match ◆ **il va ~ à qui parler** he'll get more than he bargained for ◆ **cet objet n'avait pas trouvé d'amateur** no one had expressed *ou* shown any interest in the object ◆ **tu as trouvé ton bonheur dans ce bric-à-brac ?** can you find what you're after *ou* what you're looking for in this jumble? ◆ **je la trouve mauvaise !*** *ou* **saumâtre !*** I don't like it at all, I think it's a bit off* (*Brit*); → **compte, grâce, preneur** *etc*

VPR se trouver 1 (*= être dans une situation*) [*personne*] to find o.s.; [*chose*] to be ◆ **il s'est trouvé nez à nez avec Paul** he found himself face to face with Paul ◆ **la question s'est trouvée reléguée au second plan** the question went on the back burner ◆ **la voiture s'est trouvée coincée entre ...** the car was jammed between ... ◆ **nous nous trouvons dans une situation délicate** we are in a delicate situation ◆ **je me suis trouvé dans l'impossibilité de répondre** I found myself unable to reply ◆ **il se trouve dans l'impossibilité de venir** he's unable to come, he's not in a position to come ◆ **il se trouve dans l'obligation de partir** he has to *ou* is compelled to leave

2 (*= être situé*) [*personne*] to be; [*chose*] to be, to be situated ◆ **son nom ne se trouve pas sur la liste** his name isn't on *ou* doesn't appear on the list ◆ **je me trouvais près de l'entrée** I was (standing *ou* sitting *etc*) near the entrance ◆ **il ne fait pas bon se ~ dehors par ce froid** it's not pleasant to be out in this cold ◆ **la maison se trouve au coin de la rue** the house is (situated) *ou* stands on the corner of the street ◆ **où se trouve la poste ?** where is the post office? ◆ **les toilettes se trouvent près de l'entrée** the toilets are (situated) near the entrance

3 (*= pouvoir être trouvé*) **un crayon, ça se trouve facilement** you can find a pencil anywhere ◆ **ça ne se trouve pas sous le pas** *ou* **le sabot d'un cheval** it's not easy to find *ou* to come by

4 (*= se sentir*) to feel ◆ **se ~ bien** (*dans un fauteuil etc*) to be *ou* feel comfortable; (*santé*) to feel well ◆ **il se trouve mieux en montagne** he feels better in the mountains ◆ **elle se trouvait bien dans ce pays** she was happy in this country ◆ **se ~ mal** (*= s'évanouir*) to faint, to pass out ◆ **elle s'est trouvée mal à cause de la chaleur/en entendant la nouvelle** she fainted *ou* passed out in the heat/on hearing the news ◆ **se ~ bien/mal d'avoir fait qch** to be glad/to regret having done sth ◆ **il s'en est bien trouvé** he benefited from it ◆ **il s'en est mal trouvé** he lived to regret it ◆ **je me suis trouvé fin !** (*iro*) a fine *ou* right* fool I looked!

5 (*= se juger*) **il se trouve beau dans son nouveau costume** he thinks he looks good in his new suit ◆ **tu te trouves malin** *ou* **intelligent/spirituel ?** I suppose you think that's clever/funny!

6 (*exprimant la coïncidence : souvent avec infin*) **se ~ être/avoir ...** to happen to be/have ... ◆ **elles se trouvaient avoir la même robe** it turned out that they had *ou* they happened to have the same dress ◆ **pour une fois, ils se trouvaient d'accord** for once they happened to agree

7 (*= découvrir sa personnalité, son style*) **à cette époque, l'artiste ne s'était pas encore trouvé** at this time, the artist hadn't yet developed his distinctive style

VPR IMPERS se trouver

◆ **il se trouve** (*ou* **se trouvera** *etc*) + *nom* (*= il y a*) ◆ **il se trouve toujours des gens qui disent ...** *ou* **pour dire ...** there are always people *ou* you'll always find people who will say ... ◆ **il se trouvera peut-être des journalistes pour l'approuver** there'll probably be *ou* there may (well) be some journalists who approve

◆ **il se trouve** (*ou* **se trouvait** *etc*) **que** ◆ **il se trouve que c'est moi** it happens to be me, it's me as it happens ◆ **il s'est trouvé que j'étais là quand ...** I happened *ou* chanced to be there when ..., it so happened that I was there when ... ◆ **il se trouvait qu'elle avait menti** it turned out that she had been lying

◆ **si ça se trouve*** ◆ **ils sont sortis, si ça se trouve** they may well be out, they're probably out ◆ **si ça se trouve, il ne viendra pas** maybe he won't come

trouvère /tʀuvɛʀ/ **NM** trouvère (*medieval minstrel*) ◆ **Le Trouvère** (*= opéra*) Il Trovatore

troyen, -enne /tʀwajɛ̃, ɛn/ **ADJ** (*Antiq*) Trojan ◆ **(virus) ~** (*Ordin*) Trojan Horse **NM,F Troyen(ne)** (*Antiq*) Trojan

truand, e /tʀyɑ̃, ɑd/ **NM** (*= gangster*) gangster, mobster (*US*); (*= escroc*) crook **NM,F** († *= mendiant*) beggar

> ⚠ **truand** ne se traduit pas par le mot anglais **truant**, qui désigne un élève faisant l'école buissonnière.

truander* /tʀyɑ̃de/ ► conjug 1 ◄ **VT** to swindle, to do* ◆ **se faire ~** to be swindled *ou* done* **VI** to cheat

trublion /tʀyblijɔ̃/ **NM** troublemaker, agitator

truc¹ /tʀyk/ GRAMMAIRE ACTIVE 34.3 **NM** 1 (*= moyen, combine*) way, trick ◆ **il a trouvé le ~ (pour le faire)** he's got the hang* of it ◆ **il n'a pas encore compris le ~** he hasn't got the hang* of it yet ◆ **avoir le ~** to have the knack ◆ **cherche un ~ pour venir me voir** try to find some way of coming to see me ◆ **on le connaît, leur ~** we know what they're up to* *ou* playing at*, we're onto their little game* ◆ **les ~s du métier** the tricks of the trade ◆ **j'ai un ~ infaillible contre les taches** I've got just the thing for getting rid of stains, I know a great way of getting rid of stains

2 (*= tour*) [*de prestidigitateur*] trick; (*= trucage : Ciné, Théât*) trick, effect ◆ **c'est impressionnant mais ce n'est qu'un ~** it's impressive but it's only a trick *ou* an effect ◆ **il y a un ~ !** there's a trick in it!

3 (** = chose, idée*) thing ◆ **on m'a raconté un ~ extraordinaire** I've been told an extraordinary thing ◆ **j'ai pensé (à) un ~** I've thought of something, I've had a thought ◆ **il y a un tas de ~s à faire** there's a heap of things to do* ◆ **je lui ai offert un petit ~ pour son anniversaire** I gave him a little something for his birthday ◆ **il a dit un ~ dans ce style** he said something along those lines *ou* something of the sort ◆ **le ski, c'est pas mon ~** skiing isn't my thing* ◆ **la médecine/l'équitation, c'est son ~** he's really into* medicine/horseriding ◆ **chacun son ~** each to his own

4 (** = machin*) (*dont le nom échappe*) thingumajig*, thingummy*, whatsit*; (*inconnu, jamais vu*) contraption, thing, thingumajig*; (*= chose bizarre*) thing ◆ **c'est quoi, ce ~-là ?** what's that thing? *ou* thingumajig?* ◆ **méfie-toi de ces ~s-là** be careful of *ou* beware of those things

5 (*‡ = personne*) **Truc (Chouette), Machin Truc** what's-his-(*ou* her-) name*, what-d'you-call-him (*ou* -her)*

truc² /tʀyk/ **NM** (*Rail*) truck, waggon

trucage /tʀykaʒ/ **NM** ⇒ **truquage**

truchement /tʀyʃmɑ̃/ **NM** ◆ **par le ~ de qn** through (the intervention *ou* agency of) sb ◆ **par le ~ de qch** with the aid of sth

trucider* /tʀyside/ ► conjug 1 ◄ **VT** (*hum*) to knock off*, to bump off* ◆ **je vais me faire ~ si jamais j'arrive en retard !** I'll get killed* *ou* I'll get my head bitten off* if I arrive late!

trucmuche‡ /tʀykmyʃ/ **NM** 1 (*= chose*) thingumajig*, thingummy*, whatsit* 2 (*= personne*) **Trucmuche** what's-his-(*ou* her-) name*, what-d'you-call-him (*ou* -her)*

truculence /tʀykylɑ̃s/ **NF** [*de langage*] vividness, colourfulness (*Brit*), colorfulness (*US*); [*de style*] colourfulness (*Brit*), colorfulness (*US*) ◆ **la ~ de ce personnage** the liveliness *ou* verve of this character

truculent, e /tʀykylɑ̃, ɑ̃t/ **ADJ** [*langage*] vivid, colourful (*Brit*), colorful (*US*); [*style*] colourful (*Brit*), colorful (*US*); [*personnage*] colourful (*Brit*), colorful (*US*), larger-than-life (*épith*), larger than life (*attrib*)

> ⚠ **truculent** ne se traduit pas par le mot anglais **truculent**, qui a le sens de 'agressif'.

truelle /tʀyɛl/ **NF** [*de maçon*] trowel ◆ **~ à poisson** (*Culin*) fish slice

truffe /tʀyf/ **NF** 1 (*= champignon*) truffle ◆ **~ noire/blanche** black/white truffle 2 (*Culin*) **~s (au chocolat)** (chocolate) truffles 3 (*= nez*) [*de chien*] nose

truffer /tʀyfe/ ► conjug 1 ◄ **VT** 1 (*Culin*) to garnish with truffles 2 (*= remplir*) **~ qch de** to pepper sth with ◆ **truffé de citations** peppered *ou* larded with quotations ◆ **truffé de fautes** *ou* **d'erreurs** riddled with mistakes ◆ **région truffée de mines** area littered with mines

♦ **truffé de pièges** bristling with traps ♦ **pièce truffée de micros** room bristling with hidden bugging devices ♦ **film truffé d'effets spéciaux** film laden with special effects

truffier, -ière /tʀyfje, jɛʀ/ ADJ *[région]* truffle *(épith)*; *[chêne]* truffle-producing ♦ **chien** ~ truffle hound NF **truffière** truffle field

truie /tʀɥi/ NF sow

truisme /tʀyism/ NM *(littér)* truism

truite /tʀɥit/ NF trout *(inv)* ♦ ~ **saumonée** salmon trout ♦ ~ **de mer** sea trout ♦ ~ **arc-en-ciel** rainbow trout; → **bleu**

truité, e /tʀɥite/ ADJ 1 *(= tacheté) [cheval]* mottled, speckled; *[chien]* spotted, speckled 2 *(= craquelé) [porcelaine]* crackled

trumeau (pl **trumeaux**) /tʀymo/ NM 1 *(= pilier)* pier; *(entre portes, fenêtres)* pier; *(panneau ou glace)* pier glass; *[de cheminée]* overmantel 2 *(Culin)* shin of beef

truquage /tʀykaʒ/ NM 1 *[de serrure, verrou]* adapting, fixing*; *[de cartes, dés]* fixing*; *[d'élections]* rigging, fixing*; *[de combat]* fixing* 2 († = *falsification) [de dossier]* doctoring*; *[de comptes]* fiddling*; *[d'œuvre d'art, meuble]* faking 3 *(= effet spécial)* special effect ♦ **un** ~ **très réussi** a very successful effect ♦ **le** ~ **d'une scène** *(Ciné)* using special effects in a scene ♦ ~**s optiques** optical effects *ou* illusions ♦ ~**s de laboratoire** lab effects

truqué, e /tʀyke/ (ptp de **truquer**) ADJ *[élections]* rigged; *[combat]* fixed*; *[cartes, dés]* fixed* ♦ **une scène** ~**e** *(Ciné)* a scene involving special effects

truquer /tʀyke/ ▸ conjug 1 ◂ VT 1 *[+ serrure, verrou, cartes]* to fix*; *[+ dés]* to load; *[+ combat, élections]* to rig, to fix* ♦ ~ **une scène** *(Ciné)* to use special effects in a scene 2 († = *falsifier) [+ dossier]* to doctor*; *[+ comptes]* to fiddle*; *[+ œuvre d'art, meuble]* to fake

truqueur, -euse /tʀykœʀ, øz/ NM,F 1 *(= fraudeur)* cheat 2 *(Ciné)* special effects man *(ou* woman)

truquiste /tʀykist(ə)/ NM ⇒ **truqueur 2**

trusquin /tʀyskɛ̃/ NM marking gauge

trust /tʀœst/ NM *(= cartel)* trust; *(= grande entreprise)* corporation; → **antitrust**

truster /tʀœste/ ▸ conjug 1 ◂ VT *[+ secteur du marché]* to monopolize, to corner; *[+ produit]* to have the monopoly of, to monopolize; *(* = accaparer)* to monopolize ♦ **ils ont trusté les médailles aux derniers Jeux olympiques** they carried off all the medals *ou* they made a clean sweep of the medals at the last Olympic Games

trypanosome /tʀipanozom/ NM trypanosome

trypanosomiase /tʀipanozomjɑz/ NF trypanosomiasis

TSA /teɛsa/ NF (abrév de **technologie des systèmes automatisés**) → **technologie**

tsar /dzaʀ/ NM tsar, czar, tzar

tsarévitch /dzaʀevitʃ/ NM tsarevich, czarevich, tzarevich

tsarine /dzaʀin/ NF tsarina, czarina, tzarina

tsarisme /dzaʀism/ NM tsarism, czarism, tzarism

tsariste /dzaʀist/ ADJ tsarist, czarist, tzarist

tsé-tsé /tsetse/ NF ♦ **(mouche)** ~ tsetse fly

TSF † /teɛsɛf/ NF (abrév de **télégraphie sans fil**) *(= procédé)* wireless telegraphy; *(= radio)* wireless, radio; *(= poste)* wireless ♦ **à la** ~ on the radio *ou* wireless

T(-)shirt /tiʃœʀt/ NM ⇒ **tee(-)shirt**

tsigane /tsigan/ ADJ (Hungarian) gypsy *ou* gipsy, tzigane ♦ **violoniste/musique** ~ (Hungarian) gypsy violinist/music NM *(= langue)* Romany NMF **Tsigane** (Hungarian) Gypsy *ou* Gipsy, Tzigane

tsoin-tsoin*, **tsouin-tsouin*** /tswɛ̃tswɛ̃/ EXCL boom-boom!

tss-tss /tsts/ EXCL tut-tut!

TSVP (abrév de **tournez s'il vous plaît**) PTO

TTC /tetese/ (abrév de **toutes taxes comprises**) inclusive of (all) tax

TU /tey/ NM (abrév de **temps universel**) UT; → **temps¹**

tu, t'* /ty, t/ PRON PERS you *(as opposed to vous: familiar form of address)*; *(Rel)* thou ♦ **t'as* de la chance** you're lucky NM ♦ **employer le** ~ to use the "tu" form ♦ **dire** ~ **à qn** to address sb as "tu" ♦ **être à** ~ **et à toi avec qn*** to be on first-name terms with sb, to be a great pal of sb*

tuant, tuante* /tɥɑ̃, tɥɑ̃t/ ADJ *(= fatigant)* killing, exhausting; *(= énervant)* exasperating, tiresome

tub † /tœb/ NM *(= bassin)* (bath)tub; *(= bain)* bath

tuba /tyba/ NM *(Mus)* tuba; *(Sport)* snorkel, breathing tube ♦ ~ **d'orchestre** bass tuba

tubage /tybaʒ/ NM *(Méd)* intubation, cannulation

tubaire /tybɛʀ/ ADJ *(Méd)* tubal

tubard, e* /tybaʀ, aʀd/ (abrév de **tuberculeux**) *(péj)* ADJ suffering from TB NM,F TB case

tube /tyb/ NM 1 *(= tuyau) (gén, de mesure, en verre)* tube; *(de canalisation, tubulure, métallique)* pipe; *[de canon]* barrel ♦ ~ **capillaire** capillary tube ♦ ~ **à essai** test tube ♦ ~ **lance-torpilles** torpedo tube ♦ ~ **au néon** neon tube ♦ ~ **redresseur** *(Élec)* vacuum diode ♦ ~ **régulateur de potentiel** triode ♦ ~ **cathodique** cathode ray tube ♦ ~ **à vide** vacuum valve *ou* tube ♦ ~ **électronique** electronic valve *ou* tube

♦ **à pleins tubes** ♦ **marcher à pleins** ~**s** *[moteur]* to be running full throttle *ou* at maximum revs ♦ **il a mis sa chaîne hi-fi à pleins** ~**s** he turned his stereo on full blast* ♦ **délirer*** *ou* **déconner*⁎ à pleins** ~**s** to be raving mad*, to be off one's head* *ou* rocker*⁎

2 *(= emballage) [d'aspirine, dentifrice, peinture]* tube ♦ ~ **de rouge (à lèvres)** lipstick ♦ **en** ~ in a tube

3 *(Anat, Bot = conduit)* ~ **digestif** digestive tract, alimentary canal ♦ ~**s urinifères/séminaux** urinary/seminiferous tubules ♦ ~ **pollinique** pollen tube

4 *(* = chanson à succès)* hit ♦ **le** ~ **de l'été** the summer hit, the hit-song of the summer

5 *(= vêtement)* **jupe** ~ pull tube, skinny-rib (sweater *ou* jumper)

tubercule /tybɛʀkyl/ NM *(Anat, Méd)* tubercle; *(Bot)* tuber ♦ ~**s quadrijumeaux** corpora quadrigemina, quadrigeminal *ou* quadrigeminate bodies

tuberculeux, -euse /tybɛʀkylø, øz/ ADJ 1 *(Méd)* tuberculous, tubercular ♦ **être** ~ to suffer from tuberculosis *ou* TB, to have tuberculosis *ou* TB 2 *(Bot)* tuberous, tuberose NM,F tuberculosis *ou* tubercular *ou* TB patient

tuberculine /tybɛʀkylin/ NF tuberculin

tuberculinique /tybɛʀkylinik/ ADJ *[test]* tuberculinic, tuberculin

tuberculose /tybɛʀkyloz/ NF tuberculosis, TB ♦ ~ **pulmonaire** pulmonary tuberculosis ♦ ~ **osseuse** tuberculosis of the bones

tubéreux, -euse /tybeʀø, øz/ ADJ tuberous NF **tubéreuse** *(= plante)* tuberose

tubérosité /tybeʀozite/ NF *(Anat)* tuberosity

tubulaire /tybylɛʀ/ ADJ tubular

tubulé, e /tybyle/ ADJ *[plante]* tubulate; *[flacon]* tubulated

tubuleux, -euse /tybylø, øz/ ADJ tubulous, tubulate

tubulure /tybylyʀ/ NF 1 *(= tube)* pipe 2 *(Tech) (= ouverture)* tubulure ♦ ~**s** *(= tubes)* piping ♦ ~ **d'échappement/d'admission** *[de moteur]* exhaust/inlet manifold ♦ ~ **d'alimentation** feed *ou* supply pipe

TUC /tyk/ NMPL (abrév de **travaux d'utilité collective**) → **travail¹** NMF ⇒ **tucard, e**

tucard, e /tykaʀ, aʀd/ NMF, **tuciste** /tysist/ NMF (paid) community worker *(otherwise unemployed)*

tué, e /tɥe/ (ptp de **tuer**) NM,F *(dans un accident, au combat)* person killed ♦ **les** ~**s** the dead, those killed ♦ **le nombre des** ~**s sur la route ne cesse d'augmenter** the number of deaths on the road is increasing all the time ♦ **il y a eu cinq** ~**s** there were five (people) killed *ou* five dead

tue-mouche /tymuʃ/ NM INV ♦ **(amanite)** ~ *(= champignon)* fly agaric ADJ ♦ **papier** *ou* **ruban** ~**(s)** flypaper

tuer /tɥe/ ▸ conjug 1 ◂ VT 1 *[+ personne, animal]* to kill; *(à la chasse)* to shoot ♦ **tu ne tueras point** *(Bible)* thou shalt not kill ♦ ~ **qn à coups de pierre/de couteau** to stone/stab *ou* knife sb to death ♦ ~ **qn d'une balle** to shoot sb dead ♦ **l'alcool tue** alcohol can kill *ou* is a killer ♦ **la route tue des milliers de gens chaque année** thousands of people are killed on the roads every year ♦ **se faire** ~ to get killed ♦ **il était prêt à se faire** ~ **pour son pays** he was prepared to die for his country ♦ ~ **le père** *(Psych)* to kill the father ♦ **cet enfant me tuera** this child will be the death of me ♦ **il est à** ~ ! *(fig)* you *(ou* I) could kill him! ♦ **il n'a jamais tué personne !** he wouldn't hurt a fly, he's quite harmless ♦ **ça n'a jamais tué personne, ça ne va pas te** ~ it won't kill you ♦ **ça tue !*⁎** *(= c'est génial)* it's great! ♦ **quelle odeur ! ça tue les mouches à quinze pas !*** what a stink!* it's enough to kill a man at twenty paces! ♦ **un culot pareil, ça me tue !*** he's *(ou* she's *etc)* got a nerve! ♦ **ça m'a tué d'apprendre qu'ils divorçaient*** I was flabbergasted* *ou* staggered when I heard that they were getting divorced; → **poule¹, veau**

2 *(= ruiner)* to kill; *(= exténuer)* to exhaust, to wear out ♦ **la bureaucratie tue toute initiative** bureaucracy kills (off) all initiative ♦ **les supermarchés n'ont pas tué le petit commerce** supermarkets have not killed off small traders ♦ **ce rouge tue tout leur décor** this red kills (the effect of) their whole decor ♦ **ces escaliers/querelles me tuent** these stairs/quarrels will be the death of me ♦ ~ **qch dans l'œuf** to nip sth in the bud ♦ ~ **le temps** to kill time

VPR **se tuer** 1 *(l'un l'autre)* to kill each other ♦ **séparez-les, ils vont se** ~ ! pull them apart, they're going to kill each other!

2 *(soi-même, par accident)* to be killed ♦ **il s'est tué en montagne/en voiture** he was killed in a mountaineering/car accident

3 *(= se suicider)* to kill o.s. ♦ **il s'est tué d'une balle dans la tête** he put a bullet through his head, he shot himself in the head

4 *(= s'épuiser)* **se** ~ **au travail, se** ~ **à la tâche** to work o.s. to death, to kill o.s. with work ♦ **se** ~ **à répéter/expliquer qch à qn** to repeat/explain sth to sb until one is blue in the face, to wear o.s. out repeating/explaining sth to sb ♦ **je me tue à te le dire !** I've told you again and again!

tuerie /tyʀi/ NF *(= carnage)* slaughter, carnage

tue-tête /tytɛt/ **à tue-tête** LOC ADV ♦ **crier/chanter à** ~ to shout/sing at the top of one's voice, to shout/sing one's head off*

tueur, tueuse /tɥœʀ, tɥøz/ NM,F 1 *(= assassin)* killer; *(fig = personne impitoyable)* shark ◆ ~ **(à gages)** hired *ou* professional killer, contract killer, hitman* ◆ ~ **en série** serial killer 2 *(= chasseur)* ~ **de lions/d'éléphants** lion-/elephant-killer NM *(d'abattoir)* slaughterman, slaughterer

tuf /tyf/ NM *(Géol) (volcanique)* tuff; *(calcaire)* tufa

tuf(f)eau /tyfo/ NM tufa

tuilage /tɥilaʒ/ NM *[d'opérations]* overlapping

tuile /tɥil/ NF 1 *(lit)* tile ◆ ~ **creuse** *ou* **romaine** *ou* **ronde** curved tile ◆ ~ **faîtière** ridge tile ◆ ~**s mécaniques** industrial *ou* interlocking tiles ◆ **couvrir un toit de** ~**s** to tile a roof ◆ **toit de** ~**s** tiled roof ◆ ~**s de pierre/d'ardoise** stone/slate tiles ◆ **nous préférons la** ~ **à l'ardoise** we prefer tiles to slate 2 *(* = coup de malchance)* stroke *ou* piece of bad luck ◆ **quelle** ~ **!** what rotten luck!, what a pain! * ◆ **il vient de m'arriver une** ~ I've just had a piece of bad luck 3 *(Culin)* (thin sweet) biscuit *(Brit) ou* cookie *(US)*

tuiler /tɥile/ ▸ conjug 1 ◂ VT *[+ opérations]* to overlap

tuilerie /tɥilʀi/ NF *(= fabrique)* tilery; *(= four)* tilery, tile kiln

tuilier, -ière /tɥilje, jɛʀ/ ADJ tile *(épith)* NM,F tile maker *ou* manufacturer

tulipe /tylip/ NF *(= fleur)* tulip; *(= lampe)* tulip-shaped lamp ◆ **verre** ~ tulip glass

tulipier /tylipje/ NM tulip tree

tulle /tyl/ NM tulle ◆ **robe de** ~ tulle dress ◆ ~ **gras** *(Méd)* sofra-tulle

tuméfaction /tymefaksjɔ̃/ NF *(= effet)* swelling *ou* puffing up, tumefaction *(SPÉC)*; *(= partie tuméfiée)* swelling

tuméfier /tymefje/ ▸ conjug 7 ◂ VT to cause to swell, to tumefy *(SPÉC)* ◆ **visage/œil tuméfié** puffed-up *ou* swollen face/eye VPR **se tuméfier** to swell up, to puff up, to tumefy *(SPÉC)*

tumescence /tymesɑ̃s/ NF tumescence

tumescent, e /tymesɑ̃, ɑ̃t/ ADJ tumescent

tumeur /tymœʀ/ NF tumour *(Brit)*, tumor *(US) (de* of) growth *(de* in); ◆ ~ **bénigne/maligne** benign/malignant tumour ◆ ~ **au cerveau** brain tumour

tumoral, e (mpl **-aux**) /tymɔʀal, o/ ADJ tumorous, tumoral

tumorectomie /tymɔʀɛktɔmi/ NF lumpectomy

tumulte /tymylt/ NM 1 *(= bruit) [de foule]* commotion; *[de voix]* hubbub; *[d'acclamations]* thunder, tumult ◆ **un** ~ **d'applaudissements** thunderous applause, a thunder of applause ◆ **le** ~ **des flots/de l'orage** *(littér)* the tumult of the waves/of the storm ◆ **la réunion s'est achevée dans un** ~ **général** the meeting ended in uproar *ou* in pandemonium 2 *(= agitation) [d'affaires]* hurly-burly; *[de passions]* turmoil, tumult; *[de rue, ville]* hustle and bustle *(de* in, of) commotion *(de* in)

tumultueux, -euse /tymyltɥø, øz/ ADJ *[séance]* stormy, turbulent, tumultuous; *[foule]* turbulent, agitated; *(littér) [flots, bouillonnement]* turbulent; *[vie, période, jeunesse]* stormy, turbulent; *[passion]* tumultuous, turbulent

tumulus /tymylys/ NM burial mound, tumulus *(SPÉC)*, barrow *(SPÉC)*

tune /tyn/ NF ⇒ **thune**

tuner /tynɛʀ/ NM *(= amplificateur)* tuner

tungstène /tœkstɛn/ NM tungsten, wolfram

tunique /tynik/ NF 1 *[de prêtre]* tunicle, tunic; *[de femme] (droite)* tunic; *(à forme ample)* smock; *(longue)* gown 2 *(Anat)* tunic, tunica; *(Bot)* tunic ◆ ~ **de l'œil** tunica albuginea of the eye

Tunis /tynis/ N Tunis

Tunisie /tynizi/ NF Tunisia

tunisien, -ienne /tynizjɛ̃, jɛn/ ADJ 1 *(de Tunisie)* Tunisian 2 ◆ **(T-shirt)** ~ *Grandad-style T-shirt* NM,F **Tunisien(ne)** Tunisian

tunnel /tynɛl/ NM tunnel ◆ ~ **ferroviaire/routier** railway/road tunnel ◆ ~ **aérodynamique** wind tunnel ◆ **le** ~ **sous la Manche** the Channel Tunnel, the Chunnel * ◆ **voir le bout du** ~ to see (the) light at the end of the tunnel; → **effet**

tunnelier /tynəlje/ NM *(= ouvrier)* tunneller; *(= machine)* mole

TUP /typ/ NM (abrév de **titre universel de paiement**) → aussi **titre**

tuque /tyk/ NF *(Can)* woollen cap, tuque *(Can)*

turban /tyʀbɑ̃/ NM turban

turbin⁎ /tyʀbɛ̃/ NM *(= emploi)* work ◆ **aller au** ~ to go off to work ◆ **se remettre au** ~ to get back to work ◆ **après le** ~ after work

turbine /tyʀbin/ NF turbine ◆ ~ **hydraulique** water *ou* hydraulic turbine ◆ ~ **à réaction/à impulsion** reaction/impulse turbine ◆ ~ **à vapeur/à gaz** steam/gas turbine

turbiner⁎ /tyʀbine/ ▸ conjug 1 ◂ VI to graft (away)*, to slog away*, to slave away ◆ **faire** ~ **qn** to make sb work, to keep sb at it* *ou* with his nose to the grindstone*

turbo /tyʀbo/ ADJ INV 1 *[moteur, voiture]* turbo 2 *(Ordin)* ~ **pascal/C** turbo pascal/C NM *(= moteur)* turbo ◆ **mettre le** ~ * to get a move on*, to step on it* NF *(= voiture)* turbo

turbocompresseur /tyʀbokɔ̃pʀesœʀ/ NM turbocharger ◆ ~ **de suralimentation** turbosupercharger

turbodiesel /tyʀbodjezɛl/ ADJ, NM turbodiesel

turbomoteur /tyʀbomɔtœʀ/ NM turbine engine

turbopompe /tyʀbopɔ̃p/ NF turbopump, turbine-pump

turbo-prof* (pl **turbo-profs**) /tyʀbopʀɔf/ NMF *teacher commuting long distances*

turbopropulseur /tyʀbopʀɔpylsœʀ/ NM turboprop

turboréacteur /tyʀboʀeaktœʀ/ NM turbojet (engine) ◆ ~ **à double flux** bypass turbojet *ou* engine

turbot /tyʀbo/ NM turbot

turbotrain /tyʀbotʀɛ̃/ NM turbotrain

turbulence /tyʀbylɑ̃s/ NF 1 *(= dissipation)* boisterousness, unruliness 2 *(= agitation) (gén Sci)* turbulence *(NonC)* ◆ **entrer dans une zone de** ~**s** *[avion]* to go into an area of turbulence ◆ **l'euro traverse une nouvelle zone de** ~**s** the euro is going through a new period of turbulence ◆ ~**s politiques/sociales** political/social unrest

turbulent, e /tyʀbylɑ̃, ɑ̃t/ ADJ 1 *(= agité) [enfant, élève]* unruly, boisterous; *[jeunesse, foule]* unruly; *[époque]* turbulent 2 *(littér = tumultueux) [passion]* turbulent, stormy 3 *(Sci)* turbulent

turc, turque /tyʀk/ ADJ Turkish ◆ **à la turque** *(= accroupi, assis)* cross-legged; *[cabinets]* seatless; *(Mus)* alla turca NM 1 *(= personne)* **Turc** Turk ◆ **le Grand Turc** *(Hist)* the Sultan ◆ **les Jeunes Turcs** *(Hist, fig)* the Young Turks 2 *(= langue)* Turkish NF **Turque** Turkish woman

turcophone /tyʀkɔfɔn/ ADJ Turkish-speaking NMF Turkish speaker

turf /tyʀf/ NM 1 *(Sport) (= terrain)* racecourse ◆ **le** ~ *(= activité)* racing, the turf 2 *(arg Crime = prostitution)* **le** ~ streetwalking ◆ **aller au** ~ to go and walk the streets 3 *(⁎ = travail)* **aller au** ~ to go off to work

turfiste /tyʀfist/ NMF racegoer

turgescence /tyʀʒesɑ̃s/ NF turgescence

turgescent, e /tyʀʒesɑ̃, ɑ̃t/ ADJ turgescent

turgide /tyʀʒid/ ADJ *(littér)* swollen

turista* /tuʀista/ NF holiday tummy* *(Brit)*, traveler's tummy* *(US)*

turkmène /tyʀkmɛn/ ADJ Turkmen NM *(= langue)* Turkmen NMF **Turkmène** Turkmen

Turkménistan /tyʀkmenistɑ̃/ NM Turkmenistan

turlupiner* /tyʀlypine/ ▸ conjug 1 ◂ VT to bother, to worry ◆ **ce qui me turlupine** what bugs me* *ou* worries me

turlute /tyʀlyt/ NF 1 *(Can)* hummed tune 2 ⁎⁎blow-job⁎⁎ ◆ **faire une** ~ **à qn** to give sb a blow-job⁎⁎

turluter /tyʀlyte/ ▸ conjug 1 ◂ *(Can)* VT *[+ chanson]* to hum VI to hum a tune

turne* /tyʀn/ NF 1 *(† péj = logement)* digs* 2 *(Scol = chambre)* room

turpitude /tyʀpityd/ NF 1 *(caractère)* turpitude 2 *(gén pl = acte)* base act

Turquie /tyʀki/ NF Turkey

turquoise /tyʀkwaz/ NF, ADJ INV turquoise

tutélaire /tytelɛʀ/ ADJ *(littér = protecteur)* tutelary, protecting *(épith)*; *(Jur = de la tutelle)* tutelary

tutelle /tytɛl/ NF 1 *(Jur) [de mineur]* guardianship, wardship; *[d'aliéné]* guardianship ◆ **avoir la** ~ **de qn** to be sb's guardian ◆ **mettre qn en** ~ to put sb in the care of a guardian ◆ **enfant en** ~ child under guardianship ◆ **être placé sous** ~ **judiciaire** to be made a ward of court 2 *(= contrôle financier, administratif, politique)* supervision; *(= protection)* tutelage, protection ◆ ~ **administrative/de l'État** administrative/state supervision ◆ **organisme de** ~ regulator, regulating body ◆ **autorité de** ~ regulatory authority ◆ **ministère de** ~ *(Admin) ministry in charge* ◆ **régime de** ~ *(Pol)* trusteeship ◆ **territoires sous** ~ *(Pol)* trust territories ◆ **pays sous la** ~ **de l'ONU** country under UN trusteeship ◆ **mettre sous** ~ to put under supervision ◆ **la banque a été mise sous** ~ control of the bank has been put in the hands of trustees ◆ **être sous la** ~ **de qn** *(dépendant)* to be under sb's supervision; *(protégé)* to be in sb's tutelage ◆ **tenir** *ou* **garder en** ~ *[+ pays]* to hold sway over; *[+ personne]* to keep a tight rein on ◆ **exercer sa** ~ **sur** to control

tuteur, -trice /tytœʀ, tʀis/ NM,F *(Jur, fig littér = protecteur)* guardian; *(Univ)* tutor ◆ ~ **légal/testamentaire** legal/testamentary guardian ◆ ~ **ad hoc** *specially appointed guardian* NM *(Agr)* stake, support

tuteurage /tytœʀaʒ/ NM *(Agr)* staking

tuteurer /tytœʀe/ ▸ conjug 1 ◂ VT *(Agr)* to stake (up)

tutoiement /tytwamɑ̃/ NM use of (the familiar) tu *(instead of vous)*

TUTOIEMENT/VOUVOIEMENT

There are no hard-and-fast rules about when to use « tu » or « vous » to address people. Small children can be addressed as « tu », and will often reply using the « tu » form as well. In informal contexts among young people of the same age, « tu » is often used even at first meeting. Among the older generation, « vous » is standard until people know each other well; some older married couples even use the « vous » form to address their spouse. As a general rule for non-native speakers, « vous » should always be used to address adults until the other person uses « tu », or asks permission to do so.

tutorat /tytɔʀa/ NM *(Scol)* guidance; *(Univ)* tutorial system

tutoriel /tytɔrjel/ NM tutorial

tutoyer /tytwaje/ ▸ conjug 8 ◂ VT 1 (= *dire tu à*) ◆ ~ **qn** to use (the familiar) "tu" when speaking to sb, to address sb as "tu" (*instead of "vous"*) 2 (*littér* = *fréquenter*) to be on familiar *ou* intimate terms with 3 (= *frôler*) **le cheval a tutoyé l'obstacle** the horse brushed the fence ◆ **le nombre des chômeurs tutoie la barre des trois millions** unemployment is nearing the three million mark

tutsi, e /tutsi/ ADJ Tutsi NM,F **Tutsi, e** Tutsi

tutti frutti /tutifʀuti/ LOC ADJ INV [*glace*] tutti-frutti

tutti quanti /tutikwɑ̃ti/ **et tutti quanti** LOC ADV and all the rest (of them), and all that lot* *ou* crowd*

tutu /tyty/ NM tutu, ballet skirt

Tuvalu /tuvalu/ N Tuvalu

tuyau (pl **tuyaux**) /tɥijo/ NM 1 (*gén, rigide*) pipe, length of piping; (*flexible, en caoutchouc, vendu au mètre*) length of rubber tubing, rubber tubing (*NonC*); [*de pipe*] stem ◆ **il me l'a dit dans le ~ de l'oreille*** he whispered it to me

2 (*Habillement* = *pli*) flute

3 * (= *conseil*) tip; (= *renseignement*) gen* (*NonC*) ◆ **quelques ~x pour le bricoleur** a few tips for the do-it-yourself enthusiast ◆ **il nous a donné des ~x sur leurs activités/projets** he gave us some gen* on their activities/plans ◆ **~ crevé** useless tip

COMP **tuyau d'alimentation** feeder pipe
tuyau d'arrosage hosepipe, garden hose
tuyau de cheminée chimney pipe *ou* flue
tuyau de descente (*pluvial*) downpipe, fall pipe; [*de lavabo, W-C*] wastepipe
tuyau d'échappement exhaust (pipe), tailpipe
tuyau de gaz gas pipe
tuyau d'orgue (*Géol, Mus*) organ pipe
tuyau de pipe stem of a pipe ◆ **avoir les artères en ~ de pipe** to have hardened arteries
tuyau de poêle stovepipe ◆ **(chapeau en) ~ de poêle*** † stovepipe hat ◆ **quelle famille ~ de poêle !*** (*à problèmes*) what a mixed-up family!*; (*incestueuse*) everybody sleeps with everybody in that family!
tuyau de pompe pump pipe

tuyautage /tɥijɔtaʒ/ NM 1 [*de linge*] fluting, goffering 2 (* = *renseignement*) tipping off

tuyauter /tɥijɔte/ ▸ conjug 1 ◂ VT 1 [+ *linge*] to flute, to goffer ◆ **un tuyauté** a fluted frill 2 (* = *conseiller*) ~ **qn** to give sb a tip; (= *mettre au courant*) to put sb in the know*, to give sb the tip-off*

tuyauterie /tɥijɔtʀi/ NF [*de machines, canalisations*] piping (*NonC*); [*d'orgue*] pipes

tuyère /tyjɛʀ/ NF [*de turbine*] nozzle; [*de four, haut fourneau*] tuyère, twyer ◆ **~ d'éjection** exhaust *ou* propulsion nozzle

TV /teve/ NF (abrév de **télévision**) TV

TVA /tevea/ NF (abrév de **taxe sur la valeur ajoutée**) VAT

TVHD /teve'aʃde/ NF (abrév de **télévision haute définition**) HDTV

tweed /twid/ NM tweed

twin-set (pl **twin-sets**) /twinsɛt/ NM twinset

twist /twist/ NM (= *danse*) twist

twister /twiste/ ▸ conjug 1 ◂ VI (*Danse*) to twist

tympan /tɛ̃pɑ̃/ NM 1 (*Anat*) eardrum, tympanum (*SPÉC*) ◆ **bruit à vous déchirer** *ou* **crever les ~s** earsplitting noise; → **caisse** 2 (*Archit*) tympan(um) 3 (*Tech* = *pignon*) pinion

tympanique /tɛ̃panik/ ADJ (*Anat*) tympanic

tympanon /tɛ̃panɔ̃/ NM (*Mus*) dulcimer

type /tip/ NM 1 (= *modèle*) type ◆ **il y a plusieurs ~s de bicyclettes** there are several types of bicycle ◆ **une pompe du ~ B5** a pump of type B5, a type B5 pump ◆ **une pompe du ~ réglementaire** a regulation-type pump ◆ **une voiture (de) ~ break** an estate-type (*Brit*) *ou* station-wagon-type (*US*) car ◆ **"convient à tous les types de peau"** "suitable for all skin types" ◆ **certains ~s humains** certain human types ◆ **avoir le ~ oriental/nordique** to be Oriental-/Nordic-looking, to have Oriental/Nordic looks ◆ **un beau ~ de femme/d'homme** a fine specimen of womanhood/of manhood ◆ **c'est le ~ d'homme à faire cela** he's the type *ou* sort of man who would do that ◆ **plusieurs opérations de ce ~ ont déjà eu lieu** several operations of that nature *ou* kind *ou* type have already taken place ◆ **des contrats d'un ~ nouveau** new types of contract ◆ **rien ne peut justifier ce ~ de comportement** nothing can justify that kind *ou* type of behaviour ◆ **pour étudier certains ~s de comportements** to study certain behaviour patterns ◆ **ce** *ou* **il/elle n'est pas mon ~*** he/she is not my type *ou* sort

2 (= *exemple*) classic example ◆ **c'est le ~ (parfait** *ou* **même) de l'intellectuel/du vieux garçon** he's the typical intellectual/bachelor, he's a perfect *ou* classic example of the intellectual/ of the bachelor ◆ **c'est le ~ même de la machination politique** it's a classic example of political intrigue

3 (* = *individu*) guy*, chap* (*Brit*), bloke* (*Brit*); († = *individu remarquable*) character; (= *amant*) boyfriend ◆ **un sale ~** a nasty character, a nasty piece of work* ◆ **quel sale ~ !** he's such a swine* *ou* bastard*!; → **chic**

4 (*Typo*) typeface; (*Numismatique*) type

ADJ INV typical, classic; (*Stat*) standard ◆ **l'erreur/le politicien ~** the typical *ou* classic mistake/politician ◆ **l'exemple/la situation ~** the typical *ou* classic example/situation ◆ **lettre/contrat ~** standard letter/contract; → **écart**

typé, e /tipe/ (ptp de **typer**) ADJ 1 (*physiquement*) **une femme brune et très ~e** a dark-haired woman with the characteristic features of her race ◆ **elle est allemande mais pas très ~e** she's German but she doesn't look typically German *ou* doesn't have typical German looks 2 [*attitudes, goûts*] typical, characteristic ◆ **les personnages fortement ~s de la commedia dell'arte** the stock characters of the commedia dell'arte

typer /tipe/ ▸ conjug 1 ◂ VT 1 (= *caractériser*) **auteur/acteur qui type son personnage** author/actor who brings out the features of the character well ◆ **un personnage bien typé** a character well rendered as a type 2 (*Tech*) (= *marquer*) to stamp, to mark

typesse †* /tipɛs/ NF (*péj*) female* (*péj*)

typhique /tifik/ ADJ (= *du typhus*) typhous; (= *de la typhoïde*) typhic ◆ **bacille ~** typhoid bacillus NMF typhoid sufferer

typhoïde /tifɔid/ ADJ, NF ◆ **(fièvre) ~** typhoid (fever)

typhoïdique /tifɔidik/ ADJ typhic

typhon /tifɔ̃/ NM typhoon

typhus /tifys/ NM typhus (fever)

typique /tipik/ ADJ 1 (*gén, Bio*) typical (*de* of); ◆ **sa réaction est ~** his reaction is typical (of him) *ou* true to form *ou* type ◆ **un cas ~ de ...** a typical case of ... ◆ **il a encore oublié, c'est ~ !** he's forgotten again – typical! 2 † [*musique, orchestre*] Latin American

typiquement /tipikmɑ̃/ ADV typically

typo* /tipo/ NF abrév de **typographie** NM abrév de **typographe**

typographe /tipɔgʀaf/ NMF (*gén*) typographer; (= *compositeur à la main*) hand compositor

typographie /tipɔgʀafi/ NF 1 (= *procédé d'impression*) letterpress (printing); (= *opérations de composition, art*) typography 2 (= *aspect*) typography

typographique /tipɔgʀafik/ ADJ [*procédé, impression*] letterpress (*épith*); [*opérations, art*] typographic(al) ◆ **erreur** *ou* **faute ~** typographic(al) *ou* printer's error, misprint, typo* ◆ **argot ~** typographers' jargon ◆ **cet ouvrage est une réussite ~** this work is a success typographically *ou* as regards typography

typographiquement /tipɔgʀafikmɑ̃/ ADV [*imprimer*] by letter-press ◆ **livre ~ réussi** book that is a success typographically *ou* successful as regards typography

typolithographie /tipolitɔgʀafi/ NF typolithography

typologie /tipɔlɔʒi/ NF typology

typologique /tipɔlɔʒik/ ADJ typological

Tyr /tiʀ/ N Tyre

tyran /tiʀɑ̃/ NM (*lit, fig*) tyrant ◆ **c'est un ~ domestique** he's a tyrant at home

tyranneau (pl **tyranneaux**) /tiʀano/ NM (*hum, péj*) petty tyrant

tyrannie /tiʀani/ NF (*lit, fig*) tyranny ◆ **la ~ de la mode/d'un mari** the tyranny of fashion/of a husband ◆ **exercer sa ~ sur qn** to tyrannize sb, to wield one's tyrannical powers over sb

tyrannique /tiʀanik/ ADJ [*personne, régime, pouvoir*] tyrannical ◆ **il est ~ envers** *ou* **avec ses étudiants** he bullies his students

tyranniquement /tiʀanikmɑ̃/ ADV tyrannically

tyranniser /tiʀanize/ ▸ conjug 1 ◂ VT to bully, to tyrannize ◆ **un élève tyrannisé par ses camarades d'école** a pupil bullied by his classmates

tyrannosaure /tiʀanɔzɔʀ/ NM tyrannosaur, tyrannosaurus

tyrien /tiʀjɛ̃/ ADJ M ◆ **rose ~** Tyrian purple

Tyrol /tiʀɔl/ NM ◆ **le ~** the Tyrol

tyrolien, -ienne /tiʀɔljɛ̃, jɛn/ ADJ Tyrolean; → **chapeau** NM,F **Tyrolien(ne)** Tyrolean NF **tyrolienne** 1 (= *chant*) yodel, Tyrolienne ◆ **chanter des ~nes** to yodel 2 (*Alpinisme*) (= *technique*) Tyrolean traverse; (= *pont*) rope bridge

Tyrrhénienne /tiʀenjɛn/ NF → **mer**

tzar /dzaʀ/, **tzarévitch** /dzaʀevitʃ/ NM, **tzarine** /dzaʀin/ NF ⇒ **tsar, tsarévitch, tsarine**

tzigane /dzigan/ ADJ, NMF ⇒ **tsigane**

Uu

U, u /y/ NM (= *lettre*) U, u ◆ **poutre en U** U(-shaped) beam ◆ **vallée en U** U-shaped valley ◆ **disposer des tables en U** to arrange tables in a U-shape

ubac /ybak/ NM (*Géog*) north(-facing) side, ubac (*SPÉC*)

ubiquité /ybikɥite/ NF ubiquity ◆ **avoir le don d'~** to be ubiquitous, to be everywhere at once

ubuesque /ybyɛsk/ ADJ (= *grotesque*) grotesque; (*Littérat*) Ubuesque

UDF /ydeɛf/ NF (abrév de **Union pour la démocratie française**) *French centre-right political party*

UE /yə/ NF 1 (abrév de **Union européenne**) EU 2 (abrév de **unité d'enseignement**) → **unité**

UEFA /yefa/ NF (abrév de **Union of European Football Associations**) UEFA ◆ **la Coupe de l'~** the UEFA Cup

UEM /yəɛm/ NF (abrév de **Union économique et monétaire**) EMU

UEO /yəo/ NF (abrév de **Union de l'Europe occidentale**) WEU

UER † /yəɛʀ/ NF (abrév de **Unité d'enseignement et de recherche**) → **unité**

UFR /yɛfɛʀ/ NF (abrév de **Unité de formation et de recherche**) → **unité**

UHF /yaʃɛf/ NF (abrév de **ultra-high frequency**) UHF

uhlan /ylɑ̃/ NM uhlan

UHT /yaʃte/ NF (abrév de **ultra-haute température**) UHT

ukase /ukaz/ NM ⇒ **oukase**

Ukraine /ykʀɛn/ NF ◆ **l'~** the Ukraine

ukrainien, -ienne /ykʀɛnjɛ̃, jɛn/ ADJ Ukrainian NM (= *langue*) Ukrainian NM,F **Ukrainien(ne)** Ukrainian

ukulélé /jukulele/ NM ukulele

ulcération /ylseʀasjɔ̃/ NF ulceration

ulcère /ylsɛʀ/ NM ulcer ◆ **~ à l'estomac** stomach ulcer ◆ **~ variqueux** varicose ulcer

ulcérer /ylseʀe/ ▸ conjug 6 ◂ VT 1 (= *révolter*) to sicken, to appal ◆ **le verdict/cette accusation l'a ulcéré** he was outraged by *ou* appalled at the verdict/the accusation ◆ **être ulcéré (par l'attitude de qn)** to be sickened *ou* appalled (by sb's attitude) 2 (*Méd*) to ulcerate ◆ **plaie ulcérée** festering *ou* ulcerated wound

ulcéreux, -euse /ylseʀø, øz/ ADJ ulcerated, ulcerous

uléma /ylema/ NM ulema

ULM /yɛlɛm/ NM (abrév de **ultra-léger motorisé**) microlight, microlite ◆ **faire de l'~** to go microlighting

ulmaire /ylmɛʀ/ NF (= *plante*) meadowsweet

Ulster /ylstɛʀ/ NM Ulster

ultérieur, e /ylteʀjœʀ/ ADJ later ◆ **à une date ~e** at a later date ◆ **cela devrait faire l'objet de discussions ~es** this should be the subject of later *ou* future discussions ◆ **la question sera abordée dans une phase ~e (des négociations)** the question will be discussed at a later stage (of the negotiations)

ultérieurement /ylteʀjœʀmɑ̃/ ADV later

ultimatum /yltimatɔm/ NM ultimatum ◆ **envoyer** *ou* **adresser un ~ à qn** to present sb with an ultimatum

ultime /yltim/ ADJ *[étape, avertissement, réunion, hommage]* last, final; *[recours, chance]* last; *[objectif, responsabilité]* ultimate; *[tentative]* last(-ditch), final

ultra /yltʀa/ NM (= *réactionnaire*) extreme reactionary; (= *extrémiste*) extremist ◆ **Ultra (-royaliste)** (*Hist*) ultra(-royalist) PRÉF ◆ **~-chic/-long** ultra-chic/-long ◆ **~-conservateur / -nationaliste / -orthodoxe** ultra-conservative/-nationalist/-orthodox ◆ **~-court** (*gén*) ultra-short ◆ **ondes ~-courtes** (*Radio*) ultra-high frequency ◆ **~-plat** *[boîtier, montre]* slimline ◆ **~-fin** *[tranche]* wafer-thin; *[poudre, texture]* ultra-fine; *[collant, tissu]* sheer

ultra-confidentiel, -ielle /yltʀakɔ̃fidɑ̃sjɛl/ ADJ (*gén, sur un dossier*) top secret

ultra-léger, ultraléger, -ère /yltʀaleʒe, ɛʀ/ ADJ *[équipement]* ultra-light; *[cigarette]* ultra-mild; *[tissu, vêtement]* very light; → **ULM**

ultra-libéral, ultralibéral, e (mpl **-aux**) /yltʀaliberal, o/ ADJ *[idéologie, politique]* ultra-free market (*épith*); *[personne]* who advocates an ultra-free market NM,F ultra-free marketeer

ultra-libéralisme, ultralibéralisme /yltʀaliberalism/ NM doctrine of the ultra-free market

ultramicroscope /yltʀamikʀɔskɔp/ NM ultramicroscope

ultramicroscopique /yltʀamikʀɔskɔpik/ ADJ ultramicroscopic

ultramoderne /yltʀamɔdɛʀn/ ADJ (*gén*) ultra-modern; *[équipement]* high-tech, hi-tech, state-of-the-art (*épith*)

ultramontain, e /yltʀamɔ̃tɛ̃, ɛn/ (*Rel*) ADJ ultramontane NMPL ◆ **les ~s** ultramontanists, ultramontanes

ultra-rapide, ultrarapide /yltʀaʀapid/ ADJ *[bateau, ordinateur]* high-speed (*épith*) ◆ **formule ~** (*dans un restaurant*) express menu

ultrasecret, -ète /yltʀasəkʀɛ, ɛt/ ADJ top secret

ultra-sensible, ultrasensible /yltʀasɑ̃sibl/ ADJ *[appareil, balance, dossier, problème]* ultrasensitive; *[personne, peau]* hypersensitive ◆ **film** *ou* **pellicule ~** high-speed film

ultrason /yltʀasɔ̃/ NM ultrasonic sound ◆ **les ~s** ultrasound (*NonC*)

ultrasonique /yltʀasɔnik/, **ultrasonore** /yltʀasɔnɔʀ/ ADJ ultrasonic

ultraviolet, -ette /yltʀavjɔlɛ, ɛt/ ADJ ultraviolet NM ultraviolet ray ◆ **faire des séances d'~s** to have sunbed sessions

ululation /ylylasjɔ̃/ NF, **ululement** /ylylmɑ̃/ NM ⇒ **hululement**

ululer /ylyle/ ▸ conjug 1 ◂ VI ⇒ **hululer**

Ulysse /ylis/ NM Ulysses

UMTS /yɛmtees/ NM (abrév de **Universal Mobile Telecommunication System**) UMTS

un, une /œ̃, yn/

1 ARTICLE INDÉFINI	4 NOM MASCULIN INV
2 PRONOM	5 NOM FÉMININ
3 ADJECTIF	

Lorsque **un, une** s'emploient dans des locutions figées telles que **pour un rien, un de ces jours, il n'en rate pas une** etc, cherchez au nom ou au verbe.

1 – ARTICLE INDÉFINI

1 gén a, an (*devant voyelle*); (= *un, une quelconque*) some ◆ **ne venez pas ~ dimanche** don't come on a Sunday ◆ **le témoignage d'~ enfant n'est pas valable** a child's evidence *ou* the evidence of a child is not valid ◆ **~ chien sent tout de suite si quelqu'un a peur de lui** dogs know straight away when you're afraid of them ◆ **c'est l'œuvre d'~ poète** it's the work of a poet ◆ **retrouvons-nous dans ~ café** let's meet in a café ◆ **~ jour/soir il partit** one day/evening he went away ◆ **~ jour, tu comprendras** one day *ou* some day you'll understand ◆ **passez ~ soir** drop in one *ou* some evening ◆ **~e fois, il est venu avec ~ ami et ...** once he came with a friend and ...

2 avec nom abstrait **avec ~e grande sagesse/violence** with great wisdom/violence, very wisely/violently ◆ **des hommes d'~ courage sans égal** men of unparalleled courage ◆ ~

amour qui frôlait la passion a love which bordered on passion

3 avec nom propre a, an ◆ **ce n'est pas ~ Picasso** *(hum) [personne]* he's no Picasso, he's not exactly (a) Picasso; *[tableau]* it's not a Picasso ◆ **~ certain M. Legrand** a (certain) Mr Legrand, one Mr Legrand ◆ **on a élu ~ (nommé** *ou* **certain) Dupont** they've appointed a man called Dupont ◆ **c'est encore ~ Kennedy qui fait parler de lui** that's yet another Kennedy in the news ◆ **il a le talent d'~ Hugo** he has the talent of a Hugo ◆ **cet enfant sera ~ Paganini** this child will be another Paganini

4 intensif **elle a fait ~e scène !** *ou* **~e de ces scènes !** she made a dreadful scene! *ou* such a scene! ◆ **j'ai ~e faim/~e soif !** *ou* **~e de ces faims/~e de ces soifs !** I'm so hungry/ thirsty!, I'm starving/parched! ◆ **il est d'~ sale !** *ou* **d'~e saleté !** he's so dirty!, he's filthy!

2 - PRONOM

1 gén one ◆ **~ seul** (just) one ◆ **pas ~ (seul)** not one; *(emphatique)* not a single one ◆ **six contre ~** six against one ◆ **prêtez-moi ~ de vos livres** lend me one of your books ◆ **~e des trois a dû mentir** one of the three must have been lying ◆ **il est ~ des rares qui m'ont écrit** he's one of the few (people) who wrote to me ◆ **c'est ~ de ces enfants qui s'ennuient partout** he's the kind of child *ou* one of those children who gets bored wherever he goes ◆ **~ à qui je voudrais parler, c'est Jean** there's one person I'd like to speak to and that's John, one person I'd like to speak to is John ◆ **~(e) de perdu(e), dix de retrouvé(e)s** *(Prov)* there are plenty more fish in the sea

♦ **comme pas un*** ◆ **il est arrogant/bête comme pas ~** he's as arrogant/stupid as they come ◆ **elle chante/danse comme pas ~e** she's a great* singer/dancer

♦ **et d'un*** *(= voilà une chose faite, terminée)* that's one done *ou* finished *ou* out of the way

♦ **et d'une!*** *(= d'abord)* for a start! ◆ **personne ne t'a forcé de venir, et d'~e !** no one forced you to come for one thing!, for a start no one forced you to come!

♦ **un(e) à un(e), un(e) par un(e)** one by one ◆ **ajouter les œufs ~ par ~** add the eggs one by one *ou* one at a time ◆ **pris ~ par ~, ces indices ne font pas une preuve** taken individually, these clues do not constitute proof

♦ **en + un**
(= personne) ◆ **en voilà ~ qui ne se gêne pas !** well, he's got a nerve! ◆ **j'en connais ~ qui sera content !** I know someone *ou* somebody *ou* one person who'll be pleased! ◆ **il n'y en a pas eu ~ pour m'aider** nobody lifted a finger to help me
(= chose) ◆ **prête-m'en ~** lend me one (of them) ◆ **il n'en reste qu'~e** there's only one left ◆ **j'en ai vu ~ très joli, de chapeau*** I've seen a very nice hat ◆ **il m'en a raconté ~e drôle sur le directeur** *(= histoire)* he told me a really funny story about the manager; → **bon¹**

2 avec article défini **l'~ d'eux, l'~ d'entre eux** one of them ◆ **l'~e des meilleures chanteuses** one of the best singers ◆ **les ~s disent ..., les autres répondent ...** some say ..., others reply ... ◆ **l'~ après l'autre** one after the other ◆ **serrés l'~ contre l'autre** huddled together ◆ **elles étaient assises en face l'~e de l'autre** they were sitting opposite one another *ou* each other ◆ **ils sont belges l'~ et l'autre** *ou* **l'~ comme l'autre** they're both Belgian, both of them are Belgian ◆ **l'~e et l'autre solution sont acceptables** either solution is acceptable, both solutions are acceptable ◆ **malgré ce que peuvent dire les ~s et les autres** despite what some *ou* other people may say ◆ **prenez l'~ ou l'autre** take either one, take one or the other; → **ni**

♦ **l'un dans l'autre** *(= tout bien considéré)* all in all ◆ **l'~ dans l'autre il s'y retrouve** all in all he manages to break even ◆ **l'~ dans l'autre, cela fera dans les 300 €** it'll come to around €300 in all

♦ **l'un l'autre, les uns les autres** one another, each other ◆ **ils se regardaient l'~ l'autre** they looked at one another *ou* at each other ◆ **ils s'invitent régulièrement les ~s les autres** they have each other round regularly ◆ **aimez-vous les ~s les autres** *(Bible)* love one another

3 - ADJECTIF

1 numéral cardinal one ◆ **vingt/trente et ~ ans** twenty-/thirty-one years ◆ **il reviendra dans ~ an ou deux** he'll come back in a year or two ◆ **il n'y a pas ~e seule voiture dans les rues** there's not a single car in the streets ◆ **dix heures ~e (minute)** one minute past ten ◆ **sans ~ (sou)*** penniless, broke* ◆ **ils ont gagné deux à ~** *(Sport)* they won two-one ◆ **~ partout, (la) balle au centre !*** we're even!; → **fois, moins**

2 numéral ordinal **page/chapitre ~** page/chapter one ◆ **en deux mille ~** in two thousand and one

3 = formant un tout **le Dieu ~ et indivisible** the one and indivisible God

♦ **c'est tout un** it's all one, it's one and the same thing ◆ **pour moi c'est tout ~** as far as I'm concerned it amounts to the same thing

4 - NOM MASCULIN INV

= chiffre one ◆ **~ et ~ font deux** one and one are two ◆ **compter de ~ à cent** to count from one to a hundred ◆ **tu écris mal tes ~** you don't write your ones very clearly ◆ **j'ai fait deux ~** *(aux dés)* I've got two ones ◆ **il habite au 1, rue Léger** he lives at number 1, rue Léger ◆ **le cavalier ne faisait qu'~ avec son cheval** horse and rider were as one ◆ **les deux frères ne font qu'~** the two brothers are like one person

5 - NOM FÉMININ

une *(Presse)* **la ~e** the front page ◆ **cet accident fait la ~e des journaux** the accident made the front pages *ou* the headlines ◆ **la Une** *(TV)* channel one ◆ **l'addition de la ~e !** *(au restaurant)* bill for table number one please! ◆ **~e, deux ! ~e, deux !** *(Mil)* left, right! left, right! ◆ **à la ~e, à la deux, à la trois !** with a one and a two and a three! ◆ **il n'a fait ni ~e ni deux, il a accepté** he accepted without a second's hesitation *ou* like a shot ◆ **il n'a fait ni ~e ni deux et il est parti** he left there and then *ou* without further ado; → **colonne**

---

unanime /ynanim/ **ADJ** *[témoins, sentiment, vote]* unanimous ◆ **de l'avis ~ des observateurs** in the unanimous view of the observers ◆ **~s pour** *ou* **à penser que** unanimous in thinking that ◆ **la presse et les politiques sont ~s à condamner ce meurtre** the press and politicians are unanimous in condemning this murder ◆ **de manière ~** unanimously

unanimement /ynanimmɑ̃/ **ADV** unanimously, with one accord

unanimisme /ynanimism/ **NM** 1 *(= accord)* universal consensus ◆ **il dénonçait l'~ de la presse** he condemned the way in which the papers were all taking the same line 2 *(Littérat)* unanimism, unanism

unanimiste /ynanimist/ **ADJ** *[discours]* that reflects generally held beliefs ◆ **une idéologie ~** an ideology to which the majority of people subscribe **NMF** *(Littérat)* unanimist

unanimité /ynanimite/ **NF** unanimity ◆ **vote acquis à l'~** unanimous vote ◆ **ils ont voté à l'~ pour** they voted unanimously for ◆ **élu/voté à l'~** elected/voted unanimously ◆ **élu à l'~ moins une voix** elected with only one vote against *ou* with only one dissenting vote ◆ **il y a ~ pour dire que ...** the unanimous opinion is that ..., everyone agrees that ... ◆ **cette décision a fait l'~** the decision was approved unanimously ◆ **il fait l'~** there is general agreement about him ◆ **il fait l'~ contre lui** everybody disapproves of him

unau /yno/ **NM** unau, two-toed sloth

UNEDIC /ynedik/ **NF** (abrév de **Union nationale pour l'emploi dans l'industrie et le commerce**) *French national organization managing unemployment benefit schemes*

UNEF /ynɛf/ **NF** (abrév de **Union nationale des étudiants de France**) *French national students' union*

une-pièce /ynpjɛs/ **NM** ◆ **(maillot de bain) ~** one-piece swimsuit

UNESCO /ynɛsko/ **NF** (abrév de **United Nations Educational, Scientific and Cultural Organization**) UNESCO

Unetelle /yntɛl/ **NF** → **Untel**

uni¹, e /yni/ (ptp de **unir**) **ADJ** 1 *(= sans ornements) [tissu, jupe]* plain, self-coloured *(Brit)*; *[couleur]* plain, solid *(US)* ◆ **tissu de couleur ~e** plain *ou* self-coloured *(Brit)* fabric ◆ **l'imprimé et l'~** printed and plain *ou* self-coloured *(Brit)* fabrics *ou* material, prints and solids *(US)* 2 *(= soudé) [couple, amis]* close; *[famille]* close(-knit) ◆ **ils sont ~s comme les deux doigts de la main, ils sont très ~s** they're very close ◆ **ils forment un couple très ~** they're a very close couple ◆ **~s par les liens du mariage** *(frm)* joined in marriage, married ◆ **présenter un front ~ contre l'adversaire** to present a united front to the enemy ◆ **nous devons rester ~s** we must stay *ou* stand united 3 *(= uniforme, lisse) [surface]* smooth, even; *[mer]* calm, unruffled ◆ **une vie ~e et sans nuages** *(littér)* a serene, untroubled life

uni² /yni/ **NF** *(Helv)* abrév de **université**

UNICEF /ynisɛf/ **NF** *ou rare* **nm** (abrév de **United Nations Children's Fund**) *(anciennt)* (abrév de **United Nations International Children's Emergency Fund**) UNICEF

unicellulaire /yniselylɛʀ/ **ADJ** unicellular

unicité /ynisite/ **NF** uniqueness

unicolore /ynikɔlɔʀ/ **ADJ** plain, self-coloured *(Brit)*

unidimensionnel, -elle /ynidimɑ̃sjɔnɛl/ **ADJ** one-dimensional

unidirectionnel, -elle /ynidiʀɛksjɔnɛl/ **ADJ** unidirectional

unidose /ynidoz/ **ADJ** single-dose *(épith)* **NF** single dose

unième /ynjɛm/ **ADJ** ◆ **vingt/trente et ~** twenty-/thirty-first

unièmement /ynjɛmmɑ̃/ **ADV** ◆ **vingt/trente et ~** in the twenty-/thirty-first place

unificateur, -trice /ynifikatœʀ, tʀis/ **ADJ** unifying

unification /ynifikasjɔ̃/ **NF** *[de pays, système, parti]* unification ◆ **~ européenne** European unification ◆ **l'~ allemande** *ou* **de l'Allemagne** the unification of Germany ◆ **l'~ monétaire** monetary union

unifier /ynifje/ ▸ conjug 7 ◂ **VT** 1 *[+ pays, systèmes]* to unify; *[+ parti]* to unify, to unite ◆ **l'Allemagne unifiée** united *ou* unified Germany ◆ **des pays qui s'unifient lentement** countries that are slowly becoming unified 2 *[+ procédures, tarifs]* to standardize

uniforme /ynifɔʀm/ **ADJ** *[vitesse, mouvement]* regular, uniform; *[terrain, surface]* even; *[style, couleur, ciel, paysage]* uniform; *[vie, conduite]* unchanging, uniform NM uniform ◆ **être en ~** to be in uniform; *[étudiant]* to be wearing one's uniform ◆ **policier en ~** uniformed police officer ◆ **en grand ~** in dress uniform, in full regalia ◆ **endosser/quitter l'~** to join/leave the forces ◆ **servir sous l'~** to be in the army ◆ **il y avait beaucoup d'~s à ce dîner** there were a great many officers at the dinner ◆ **~ scolaire** school uniform

uniformément /ynifɔʀmemɑ̃/ ADV uniformly, regularly ◆ **le temps s'écoule ~** time goes steadily by ◆ **répartissez le caramel ~ dans le moule** spread the caramel evenly around the mould ◆ **appliquer ~ la crème** apply the cream evenly ◆ **un ciel ~ bleu/gris** a uniformly blue/grey sky ◆ **vitesse ~ accélérée** *(Phys)* uniform change of speed

uniformisation /ynifɔʀmizasjɔ̃/ NF standardization

uniformiser /ynifɔʀmize/ ► conjug 1 ◄ VT *[+ mœurs, tarifs]* to standardize; *[+ teinte]* to make uniform

uniformité /ynifɔʀmite/ NF *[de vitesse, mouvement]* regularity, uniformity, steadiness; *[de terrain, surface]* evenness; *[de style, vie, conduite, ciel, paysage]* uniformity

unijambiste /ynizɑ̃bist/ ADJ one-legged NMF one-legged man *(ou* woman)

unilatéral, e (mpl **-aux**) /ynilateʀal, o/ ADJ unilateral; → **stationnement**

unilatéralement /ynilateʀalmɑ̃/ ADV unilaterally

unilatéralisme /ynilateʀalism/ NM unilateralism

unilingue /ynilɛ̃g/ ADJ unilingual

uniment /ynimɑ̃/ ADV *(littér = uniformément)* smoothly ◆ **(tout) ~** † *(= simplement)* (quite) plainly

uninominal, e (mpl **-aux**) /yninɔminal, o/ ADJ ◆ **scrutin ~** voting for a single member *(attrib)*

union /ynjɔ̃/ NF 1 *(= alliance)* *[d'États, partis, fortunes]* union ◆ **en ~ avec** in union with ◆ **l'~ fait la force** *(Prov)* united we stand, divided we fall, strength through unity

2 *(= mariage)* union ◆ **deux enfants sont nés de cette ~** two children were born of this union

3 *(= juxtaposition)* *[d'éléments, couleurs]* combination, blending; → **trait**

4 *(= groupe)* association, union ◆ **l'Union sportive de Strasbourg** the Strasbourg sports club

COMP **union charnelle** union of the flesh
union conjugale marital union
union de consommateurs consumers' association
union douanière customs union
Union économique et monétaire Economic and Monetary Union
Union européenne European Union
Union de l'Europe occidentale Western European Union
l'union libre cohabitation
union monogame *(chez les animaux)* pair-bonding
union mystique *(Rel)* mystic union
Union des républiques socialistes soviétiques Union of Soviet Socialist Republics
union sacrée *(Hist)* union sacrée *(united front presented by the French against the enemy in 1914)* ◆ **l'~ sacrée des syndicats contre la nouvelle loi** the trade unions' united front against the new law
l'Union soviétique the Soviet Union
Union sportive sports club *ou* association

unionisme /ynjɔnism/ NM *(gén)* unionism; *(Hist)* Unionism

unioniste /ynjɔnist/ ADJ, NMF *(gén)* unionist; *(Hist)* Unionist

unipare /ynipaʀ/ ADJ uniparous

unipersonnel, -elle /ynipɛʀsɔnɛl/ ADJ *(Ling)* impersonal NM *(= verbe)* impersonal verb

unipolaire /ynipɔlɛʀ/ ADJ unipolar

unique /ynik/ GRAMMAIRE ACTIVE 32.2 ADJ 1 *(= seul)* only ◆ **mon ~ souci/espoir** my only *ou* sole *(frm) ou* one concern/hope ◆ **fils/fille ~** only son/daughter ◆ **c'est un fils/une fille ~** he's/she's an only child ◆ **système à parti ~** *(Pol)* one-party system ◆ **le candidat ~ du parti** the party's sole candidate ◆ **ce n'est pas un cas ~** this is not an isolated case ◆ **croire en un Dieu ~** to believe in one God ◆ **l'argent est son ~ sujet de préoccupation** money is the only thing he cares about ◆ **deux aspects d'un même et ~ problème** two aspects of one and the same problem ◆ **nous proposons des vols vers Strasbourg, Marseille, Lyon et Toulouse à prix ~** we offer flights to Strasbourg, Marseille, Lyon and Toulouse at a single price ◆ **"places : prix unique 10 €"** *(dans un cinéma)* "all seats €10"; → **monnaie, salaire, sens, seul**

2 *(après nom = exceptionnel)* *[livre, talent]* unique ◆ **il est/c'est ~ en son genre** he's/it's one of a kind ◆ **c'est un livre/une expérience ~ en son genre** it's a truly *ou* an absolutely unique book/experience ◆ **il se croit ~** he thinks he's unique ◆ **~ en France/en Europe** unique *ou* the only one of its kind in France/in Europe ◆ **~ au monde** quite unique ◆ **un paysage ~ au monde** a landscape that is quite unique ◆ **c'est une pièce ~** *(Art)* it's unique

3 *(* = impayable)* priceless * ◆ **il est ~ ce gars-là !** that guy's priceless! *

uniquement /ynikmɑ̃/ ADV 1 *(= exclusivement)* only, solely, exclusively ◆ **tu ne fais que du secrétariat ? – pas ~** do you only have secretarial duties? – no, that's not all I do ◆ **il était venu ~ pour me voir** he had come just to see me, he had come for the sole purpose of seeing me ◆ **il pense ~ à l'argent** he only ever thinks of money, he thinks only of money, money is all he ever thinks about 2 *(= simplement)* only, merely, just ◆ **c'était ~ par curiosité** it was only *ou* just *ou* merely out of curiosity

unir /yniʀ/ ► conjug 2 ◄ VT 1 *(= associer)* *[+ États, partis, fortunes]* to unite *(à* with); ◆ **~ ses forces** to join forces ◆ **le sentiment commun qui les unit** the shared feeling which unites them

2 *(= marier)* **~ (en mariage)** to marry ◆ **le prêtre qui les a unis** the priest who married them ◆ **ce que Dieu a uni** *(Rel)* whom God has joined together ◆ **ils ont voulu ~ leurs destinées** they wanted to get married

3 *(= juxtaposer, combiner)* *[+ couleurs, qualités]* to combine *(à* with); ◆ **il unit l'intelligence au courage** he combines intelligence with courage

4 *(= relier)* *[+ continents, villes]* to link, to join up

VPR **s'unir** 1 *(= s'associer)* *[pays, partis, fortunes]* to unite *(à, avec* with); ◆ **s'~ contre un ennemi commun** to unite against a common enemy

2 *(= se marier)* to get married ◆ **des jeunes gens qui vont s'~** a young couple who are going to be married

3 *(= s'accoupler)* **s'~ dans une étreinte fougueuse** to come together in a passionate embrace

4 *(= se combiner)* *[mots, formes, couleurs, qualités]* to combine *(à, avec* with)

unisexe /ynisɛks/ ADJ INV unisex

unisexué, e /ynisɛksɥe/ ADJ unisexual

unisson /ynisɔ̃/ NM *(Mus)* unison ◆ **à l'~** *[chanter]* in unison ◆ **répondre à l'~** to answer as one ◆ **ils ont dit à l'~ que ...** they all said that ... ◆ **les deux présidents sont à l'~ sur ce problème** the two presidents are of one mind about this problem ◆ **l'Espagne s'est mise à l'~ de ses partenaires européens** Spain has come into line with its European partners

unitaire /ynitɛʀ/ ADJ *(Comm, Math, Phys)* unitary, unit *(épith)*; *(Pol)* unitarian; *(Rel)* Unitarian ◆ **prix ~** unit price NMF *(Rel)* Unitarian

unitarien, -ienne /ynitaʀjɛ̃, jɛn/ ADJ, NM,F *(Pol)* unitarian; *(Rel)* Unitarian

unitarisme /ynitaʀism/ NM *(Pol)* unitarianism; *(Rel)* Unitarianism

unité /ynite/ NF 1 *(= cohésion)* unity ◆ **l'~ nationale** national unity ◆ **~ de vues** unity *ou* unanimity of views ◆ **l'~ d'action des syndicats** the united action of the unions ◆ **réaliser l'~ européenne** to build a united Europe ◆ **les trois ~s** *(Littérat)* the three unities ◆ **~ de lieu/de temps/d'action** unity of place/of time/of action ◆ **roman qui manque d'~** novel lacking in unity *ou* cohesion

2 *(= élément)* unit ◆ **~ de mesure/de poids** unit of measurement/of weight ◆ **~ administrative** administrative unit ◆ **~ monétaire** monetary unit ◆ **~ monétaire européenne** European monetary *ou* currency unit ◆ **~ de compte** unit of account ◆ **~ de compte européenne** European Unit of Account ◆ **~ lexicale** lexical item ◆ **la colonne des ~s** the units column ◆ **antibiotique à 100 000 ~s** antibiotic with 100,000 units ◆ **prix de vente à l'~** unit selling price, selling price per item ◆ **nous ne les vendons pas à l'~** we don't sell them singly *ou* individually

3 *(= troupe)* unit; *(= bateau)* ship ◆ **rejoindre son ~** *(Mil)* to go back to *ou* rejoin one's unit ◆ **~ mobile de police** mobile police unit ◆ **~ de combat** combat *ou* fighting unit ◆ **~ d'élite** crack unit

4 *(= établissement, service)* unit ◆ **~ de production/fabrication** production/manufacturing unit ◆ **~ de soins palliatifs** *(Méd)* care unit for the terminally ill

5 *(Univ)* **~ de formation et de recherche, ~ d'enseignement et de recherche** † university department ◆ **~ d'enseignement, ~ de valeur** † ≈ credit, course

6 *(Ordin)* **~ arithmétique et logique** arithmetic logic unit ◆ **~ centrale** mainframe, central processing unit ◆ **~ de commande** control unit ◆ **~ de (lecteur de) disquettes** disk drive unit ◆ **~ périphérique de sortie** output device

7 *(* = dix mille francs)* ten thousand francs ◆ **32 ~s** 320,000 francs

> ⚠ **unité** se traduit par **unity** uniquement au sens de 'cohésion'.

univalve /ynivalv/ ADJ univalve *(épith)*

univers /ynivɛʀ/ NM *(gén)* universe; *(= milieu, domaine)* world ◆ **dans tout l'~** throughout the world ◆ **son ~ se borne à son travail** his work is his whole world ◆ **l'~ du discours** *(Ling)* the universe of discourse ◆ **l'~ mathématique** the world of mathematics ◆ **~ virtuel** virtual world, world of virtual reality ◆ **l'~ impitoyable de la mode** the cut-throat world of fashion; → **face**

universalisation /ynivɛʀsalizasjɔ̃/ NF universalization

universaliser /ynivɛʀsalize/ ► conjug 1 ◄ VT to universalize

universalisme /ynivɛʀsalism/ NM *(Rel)* Universalism; *(Philos)* universalism

universaliste /ynivɛʀsalist/ ADJ, NMF *(Rel)* Universalist; *(Philos)* universalist

universalité /ynivɛʀsalite/ NF universality

universaux /ynivɛʀso/ NMPL ◆ **les ~ (du langage)** (language) universals ◆ **les ~** *(Philos)* the universals

universel, -elle /ynivɛʀsɛl/ ADJ 1 *(gén)* universal ◆ **esprit ~** polymath ◆ **c'est un homme ~** he's a polymath, he's a man of vast knowledge ◆ **produit de réputation universelle** world-famous product, product which is universally renowned ◆ **il a une réputation universelle d'honnêteté** he is well-known for his honesty, his honesty is universally recognized; → **exposition, légataire, suffrage** 2 *(= aux applications multiples) [outil, appareil]* universal, all-purpose *(épith)*; → **pince, remède**

universellement /yniversɛlmɑ̃/ ADV universally ◆ **des valeurs ~ partagées** universally shared values ◆ **un auteur ~ connu** an author known throughout the world ◆ **il est ~ reconnu comme le plus grand paysagiste français** he is universally recognized as the greatest French landscape artist

universitaire /yniversitɛr/ ADJ *[vie étudiante, restaurant]* university *(épith)*; *[études, milieux, carrière, diplôme]* university *(épith)*, academic; → **année, centre, cité** NMF academic

université /yniversite/ NF university ◆ **entrer à l'~** to start university ◆ **entrée à l'~** university entrance ◆ **depuis son entrée à l'~** since he started university ◆ **~ du troisième âge** university of the third age, u3a, post-retirement *ou* senior citizens' university ◆ **~ d'été** *(Univ)* summer school; *(Pol = rencontre)* party conference; *(= session de formation) summer school organized by a political party for young or potential members*

univitellin, e /ynivitelɛ̃, in/ ADJ ◆ **jumeaux ~s** identical *ou* monozygotic *(SPÉC)* twins

univocité /ynivɔsite/ NF *(Math, Philos)* univocity

univoque /ynivɔk/ ADJ *[mot]* univocal; *[relation]* one-to-one

Untel, Unetelle /œ̃tɛl, yntɛl/ NM so-and-so ◆ **Monsieur ~** Mr so-and-so

upérisation /yperizasjɔ̃/ NF ultra heat treatment

upériser /yperize/ ► conjug 1 ◄ VT to sterilize at ultrahigh temperature ◆ **upérisé** ultra heat treated ◆ **lait upérisé** UHT milk

UPF /ypeɛf/ NF (abrév de **Union pour la France**) *French political party*

uppercut /ypɛrkyt/ NM uppercut

upsilon /ypsilɔn/ NM upsilon

uranifère /yranifɛr/ ADJ uranium-bearing

uranium /yranjɔm/ NM uranium ◆ **~ appauvri/enrichi** depleted/enriched uranium

uranoscope /yranɔskɔp/ NM *(= poisson)* stargazer

Uranus /yranys/ NM *(Myth)* Uranus NF *(Astron)* Uranus

urbain, e /yrbɛ̃, ɛn/ ADJ 1 *(= de la ville) (gén)* urban; *[transports]* city *(épith)*, urban 2 *(littér = poli)* urbane

urbanisation /yrbanizasjɔ̃/ NF urbanization

urbaniser /yrbanize/ ► conjug 1 ◄ VT to urbanize ◆ **région fortement urbanisée** heavily built-up *ou* highly urbanized area ◆ **la campagne environnante s'urbanise rapidement** the surrounding countryside is quickly becoming urbanized *ou* is becoming rapidly built up; → **zone**

urbanisme /yrbanism/ NM town planning

urbaniste /yrbanist/ NMF town planner ADJ ⇒ **urbanistique**

urbanistique /yrbanistik/ ADJ *[réglementation, impératifs]* town-planning *(épith)*, urbanistic ◆ **nouvelles conceptions ~s** new concepts in town planning

urbanité /yrbanite/ NF *(= politesse)* urbanity

urbi et orbi /yrbietɔrbi/ LOC ADV *(Rel)* urbi et orbi ◆ **proclamer qch ~** *(fig)* to proclaim sth from the rooftops

urée /yre/ NF urea

urémie /yremi/ NF uraemia *(Brit)*, uremia *(US)* ◆ **faire de l'~** to get uraemia *(Brit) ou* uremia *(US)*

urémique /yremik/ ADJ uraemic *(Brit)*, uremic *(US)*

uretère /yr(ə)tɛr/ NM ureter

urétral, e (mpl **-aux**) /yretral, o/ ADJ urethral

urètre /yrɛtr/ NM urethra

urgence /yrʒɑ̃s/ NF 1 *[de décision, départ, situation]* urgency ◆ **il y a ~** it's urgent, it's a matter of (great) urgency ◆ **y a-t-il ~ à ce que nous fassions ... ?** is it urgent for us to do ...? ◆ **il n'y a pas (d')~** there's no rush, it's not urgent ◆ **c'est une ~ absolue** it's a matter of the utmost urgency ◆ **il faut le faire de toute ~** it's very *ou* extremely urgent ◆ **faire qch dans l'~** *(= très vite)* to do sth in a rush; *(= dans un état d'urgente nécessité)* to do sth urgently *ou* as a matter of urgency ◆ **affaire à traiter en première ~** question to be dealt with as a matter of the utmost urgency *ou* as (a) top priority

♦ **d'urgence** *[mesures, situation, aide]* emergency *(épith)* ◆ **procédure d'~** emergency procedure ◆ **déclencher la procédure d'extrême ~** *(Pol)* to invoke emergency powers ◆ **cela n'a aucun caractère d'~** it's not urgent ◆ **transporté d'~ à l'hôpital** rushed to hospital *(Brit)*, rushed to the hospital *(US)* ◆ **être opéré d'~** to have an emergency operation ◆ **on l'a appelé d'~** he was asked to come immediately ◆ **à envoyer d'~** to be sent immediately, for immediate dispatch ◆ **convoquer d'~ les actionnaires** to call an emergency meeting of the shareholders ◆ **faire qch d'~** to do sth urgently

2 *(= cas urgent)* emergency ◆ **service/salle des ~s** emergency department/ward, casualty department/ward *(Brit)*

urgent, e /yrʒɑ̃, ɑ̃t/ ADJ *[besoin, problème]* urgent, pressing; *[mesure, réunion]* emergency *(épith)*; *[appel, réforme]* urgent ◆ **c'est ~** it's urgent ◆ **rien d'~** nothing urgent ◆ **l'~ est de ...** the most urgent thing is to ... ◆ **il est ~ de réparer le toit** the roof is in urgent need of repair *ou* needs repairing urgently ◆ **il est ~ qu'une décision soit prise** a decision must be taken urgently *ou* as a matter of urgency ◆ **on a décidé qu'il était ~ d'attendre** *(hum)* they decided it was better to wait, they decided to hasten slowly ◆ **avoir un besoin ~ de capitaux** to need capital urgently, to be in urgent need of capital ◆ **de façon ~e** urgently

urgentissime /yrʒɑ̃tisim/ ADJ very urgent ◆ **ce n'est pas ~** it's not desperately urgent

urgentiste /yrʒɑ̃tist/ NMF (accident and) emergency physician

urger* /yrʒe/ ► conjug 3 ◄ VI ◆ **ça urge!** it's urgent! ◆ **je dois lui téléphoner mais ça urge pas** *ou* **il n'y a rien qui urge** I've got to phone him but there's no rush *ou* it's not urgent

urinaire /yrinɛr/ ADJ urinary

urinal (pl **-aux**) /yrinal, o/ NM (bed) urinal

urine /yrin/ NF urine (NonC) ◆ **sucre dans les ~s** sugar in the urine

uriner /yrine/ ► conjug 1 ◄ VI to urinate, to pass *ou* make water *(SPÉC)*

urinifère /yrinifɛr/ ADJ uriniferous

urinoir /yrinwar/ NM (public) urinal

urique /yrik/ ADJ uric

URL /yɛrɛl/ NF (abrév de **Universal Resource Locator**) URL

urne /yrn/ NF 1 *(Pol)* **~ (électorale)** ballot box ◆ **aller** *ou* **se rendre aux ~s** to vote, to go to the polls ◆ **le verdict des ~s** the result of the polls 2 *(= vase)* urn ◆ **~ funéraire** funeral urn

urogénital, e (mpl **-aux**) /yrɔʒenital, o/ ADJ urogenital

urographie /yrɔgrafi/ NF intravenous pyelogram

urologie /yrɔlɔʒi/ NF urology

urologue /yrɔlɔg/ NMF urologist

ursidés /yrside/ NMPL ursids

URSS /yrs/ NF *(Hist)* (abrév de **Union des républiques socialistes soviétiques**) USSR

URSSAF /yrsaf/ NF (abrév de **Union pour le recouvrement des cotisations de la Sécurité sociale et des allocations familiales**) *social security contribution collection agency*

ursuline /yrsylin/ NF Ursuline

urticaire /yrtikɛr/ NF nettle rash, hives, urticaria *(SPÉC)* ◆ **faire** *ou* **avoir des crises d'~** to suffer from nettle rash ◆ **donner de l'~ à qn** *(lit)* to bring sb out in a rash; *(* = insupporter)* to make sb's skin crawl

urticant, e /yrtikɑ̃, ɑ̃t/ ADJ urticant ◆ **les poils sont ~s** the hairs can cause itching

urubu /yryby/ NM buzzard

Uruguay /yrygwɛ/ NM *(= pays)* Uruguay; *(= fleuve)* Uruguay river

uruguayen, -enne /yrygwajɛ̃, ɛn/ ADJ Uruguayan NM,F **Uruguayen(ne)** Uruguayan

us /ys/ NMPL ◆ **~ (et coutumes)** customs

US /yɛs/ NF (abrév de **Union sportive**) → **union**

US(A) /yɛs(a)/ NMPL (abrév de **United States (of America)**) US(A)

usage /yzaʒ/ NM 1 *(= utilisation)* use ◆ **apprendre l'~ de la boussole** to learn how to use a compass ◆ **elle fait un ~ immodéré de parfum** she uses (far) too much *ou* an excessive amount of perfume ◆ **abîmé par l'~** damaged through constant use *ou* by heavy usage ◆ **elle nous laisse l'~ de son jardin** she lets us use her garden, she gives us *ou* allows us the use of her garden ◆ **l'~ de stupéfiants** drug use *ou* abuse ◆ **dépénaliser l'~ des drogues douces** to decriminalize (the use of) soft drugs; → **faux²**

2 *(= exercice, pratique) [de membre, langue]* use; *[de faculté]* use, power ◆ **perdre l'~ de ses yeux/membres** to lose the use of one's eyes/limbs ◆ **perdre l'~ de la parole** to lose the power of speech

3 *(= fonction, application) [d'instrument]* use ◆ **outil à ~s multiples** multi-purpose tool ◆ **document à ~ interne** document for internal use only ◆ **à ~ externe** *(Méd)* for external use (only) ◆ **à ~ unique** *[matériel stérile, seringues]* single-use ◆ **servir à divers ~s** to have several uses, to serve several purposes ◆ **moquette/pile à ~ intensif** heavy-duty carpeting/battery; → **valeur**

4 *(= coutume, habitude)* custom ◆ **un ~ qui se perd** a vanishing custom, a custom which is dying out ◆ **c'est l'~** it's the done thing, it's the custom ◆ **ce n'est pas l'~ (de)** it's not done (to), it's not the custom (to) ◆ **entrer dans l'~ (courant)** *[objet, mot]* to come into common *ou* current use; *[mœurs]* to become common practice ◆ **contraire aux ~s** contrary to common practice *ou* to custom ◆ **il n'est pas dans les ~s de la compagnie de faire cela** the company is not in the habit of doing that, it is not the usual policy of the company to do that, it is not customary for the company to do that ◆ **il était d'~** *ou* **c'était un ~ de** it was customary *ou* a custom *ou* usual to ◆ **formule d'~** set formula ◆ **après les compliments/recommandations d'~** after the usual *ou* customary compliments/recommendations

5 *(Ling)* **l'~** usage ◆ **expression consacrée par l'~** expression fixed by usage ◆ **l'~ écrit/oral** written/spoken usage ◆ **l'~ décide** (common) usage decides; → **bon¹**

6 *(littér = politesse)* **avoir de l'~** to have breeding ◆ **manquer d'~** to lack breeding, to be

lacking in the social graces ◆ **il n'a pas l'~ du monde** he lacks savoir-faire *ou* the social graces

7 *(locutions)* **à son ~ personnel, pour son propre ~** for his personal use

◆ **avoir l'usage de qch** *(= droit d'utiliser)* to have the use of sth ◆ **en aurez-vous l'~ ?** *(= occasion d'utiliser)* will you have any use for it?

◆ **faire + usage de** *[+ pouvoir, droit]* to exercise; *[+ permission, avantage, objet, thème]* to make use of; *[+ violence, force, procédé]* to use, to employ; *[+ expression]* to use ◆ **faire ~ de son arme** to use one's gun ◆ **faire (un) bon/mauvais ~ de qch** to put sth to good/bad use, to make good/bad use of sth

◆ **faire de l'usage** ◆ **ces souliers ont fait de l'~** these shoes have lasted a long time, I've *(ou* we've *etc)* had good use out of these shoes

◆ **à l'usage** ◆ **vous verrez à l'~ comme c'est utile** you'll see when you use it how useful it is ◆ **ça s'assouplira à l'~** it will soften with use ◆ **son français s'améliorera à l'~** his French will improve with practice

◆ **à l'usage de** for use of, for ◆ **notice à l'~ de** notice for (the attention of) ◆ **à l'~ des écoles** *[émission]* for schools; *[manuel]* for use in schools

◆ **en usage** *[dispositif, mot]* in use

◆ **hors d'usage** *[éclairage, installation]* out of service; *[véhicule, machine à laver]* broken down ◆ **mettre hors d'~** to put out of action

> ⚠ **usage** se traduit rarement par le mot anglais **usage**, sauf en linguistique.

usagé, e /yzaʒe/ **ADJ** *(= qui a beaucoup servi) [pneu, habits]* worn, old; *(= d'occasion)* used, second-hand; *(qui ne peut plus être utilisé) [seringue, préservatif, ticket, pile]* used ◆ **quelques ustensiles ~s** some old utensils ◆ **huiles ~es** waste oil

usager, -ère /yzaʒe, ɛʀ/ **NM,F** user ◆ **~ des transports en commun/du téléphone** public transport/telephone user ◆ **~ de la route** road user ◆ **~ de drogue** drug user ◆ **les ~s de la langue française** French (language) speakers

usant, e* /yzɑ̃, ɑ̃t/ **ADJ** *(= fatigant) [travail]* exhausting, wearing; *[personne]* tiresome, wearing ◆ **il est ~ avec ses discours** he wears *ou* tires you out with his talking

USB /yɛsbe/ **NM** (abrév de **Universal Serial Bus**) *(Ordin)* (système) USB ◆ **port/connexion ~** USB port/connection ◆ **clé ~** USB key

usé, e /yze/ (ptp de **user**) **ADJ** 1 *(= détérioré) [objet]* worn; *[vêtement, tapis]* worn, worn-out; *(Nucl Phys) [combustibles]* spent; *[personne] (= épuisé)* worn-out; *(par le stress)* burnt-out ◆ **un parti/homme politique ~ par le pouvoir** a party/politician jaded by too many years in power ◆ **~ jusqu'à la corde** threadbare; → **eau** 2 *(= banal) [thème, expression]* hackneyed, well-worn; *[plaisanterie]* well-worn

Usenet /juznɛt/ **NM** *(Ordin)* Usenet

user /yze/ ▸ conjug 1 ◂ **VT** 1 *(= détériorer) [+ outil, roches]* to wear away; *[+ vêtements]* to wear out ◆ **~ un manteau jusqu'à la corde** to wear out a coat, to wear a coat threadbare ◆ **il use deux paires de chaussures par mois** he gets through two pairs of shoes (in) a month ◆ **ils ont usé leurs fonds de culottes sur les mêmes bancs** *(hum)* they were at school together

2 *(= épuiser) [+ personne, forces]* to wear out; *[+ nerfs]* to wear down; *[+ influence]* to weaken ◆ **la maladie l'avait usé** illness had worn him out

3 *(= consommer) [+ essence, charbon]* to use, to burn; *[+ papier, huile, eau]* to use

VI *(littér)* ◆ **en ~ mal/bien avec** *ou* **à l'égard de qn** *(= se comporter)* to treat *ou* use *(littér)* sb badly/well

VT INDIR **user de** *(= utiliser) [+ pouvoir, patience, droit]* to exercise; *[+ charme, influence, liberté]* to use; *[+ autorité]* to use, to exercise; *[+ permission, avantage]* to make use of; *[+ violence, force, procédé]* to use, to employ; *[+ expression, mot]* to use; *(littér) [+ objet, thème]* to make use of ◆ **ce journaliste a usé de moyens déloyaux pour obtenir cette information** this journalist used underhand means to get this information ◆ **usant de douceur** using gentle means ◆ **il en a usé et abusé** he has used and abused it ◆ **il faut en ~ avec parcimonie** it should be used sparingly

VPR **s'user** *[tissu, vêtement, semelle]* to wear out; *[sentiments, passion]* to wear off ◆ **mon manteau s'use** my coat's showing signs of wear ◆ **elle s'use les yeux à trop lire** she's straining her eyes by reading too much ◆ **elle s'est usée au travail** she wore herself out with work ◆ **c'est ce que tout le monde s'use à lui dire** it's what everyone's been telling him all this time *ou* over and over again

> ⚠ Au sens de 'détériorer' ou 'épuiser', **user** ne se traduit pas par **to use**.

usinage /yzinaʒ/ **NM** *(= façonnage)* machining; *(= fabrication)* manufacturing

usine /yzin/ **NF** factory ◆ **un copain de l'~** *ou* **d'~** a friend from the works *ou* factory ◆ **travail en ~** factory work ◆ **ce bureau est une vraie ~ !*** this office is a hive of activity! ◆ **l'~ à rêves hollywoodienne** the Hollywood dream factory ◆ **ce pays est une véritable ~ à champions*** this country churns out one champion after the other; → **cheminée, travailler**

COMP **usine d'armement** arms *ou* armaments factory
usine d'assemblage assembly plant
usine atomique atomic energy *ou* power station, atomic plant
usine automatisée automated factory
usine d'automobiles car factory *ou* plant
usine de fabrication manufacturing plant
usine à gaz *(lit)* gasworks; *(fig)* huge labyrinthine system
usine d'incinération (d'ordures ménagères) (household waste) incineration plant
usine métallurgique ironworks
usine de montage assembly plant
usine de pâte à papier paper mill
usine de production production plant
usine de raffinage refinery
usine de retraitement (des déchets nucléaires) (nuclear waste) reprocessing plant
usine sidérurgique steelworks, steel mill
usine textile textile plant *ou* factory, mill
usine de traitement des ordures sewage works *ou* farm *ou* plant

usiner /yzine/ ▸ conjug 1 ◂ **VT** *(= façonner)* to machine; *(= fabriquer)* to manufacture **VI** * ◆ **ça usine dans le coin !** *(= travailler dur)* they're hard at it round here! *

usinier, -ière † /yzinje, jɛʀ/ **ADJ** *[vie, monde]* factory *(épith)*; *[faubourg]* industrial ◆ **bâtiments ~s** factories

usité, e /yzite/ **ADJ** in common use, common ◆ **un temps très/peu ~** a very commonly-used/a rarely-used tense ◆ **le moins ~** the least (commonly) used ◆ **ce mot n'est plus ~** this word is no longer used *ou* in use

ustensile /ystɑ̃sil/ **NM** *(gén = outil, instrument)* implement ◆ **~s*** *(= attirail)* implements, tackle *(NonC)*, gear *(NonC)* ◆ **~ (de cuisine)** (kitchen) utensil ◆ **~s de ménage** household cleaning stuff *ou* things ◆ **~s de jardinage** gardening tools *ou* implements ◆ **qu'est-ce que c'est que cet ~ ?*** what's that gadget? *ou* contraption?

usuel, -elle /yzɥɛl/ **ADJ** *[objet]* everyday *(épith)*, ordinary; *[mot, expression, vocabulaire]* everyday *(épith)* ◆ **dénomination ~le d'une plante** common name for *ou* of a plant ◆ **il est ~ de faire** it is usual to do, it is common practice to do **NM** *(= livre)* book on the open shelf ◆ **c'est un ~** it's on the open shelves

usuellement /yzɥɛlmɑ̃/ **ADV** ordinarily, commonly

usufruit /yzyfʀɥi/ **NM** usufruct ◆ **avoir l'~ de qch** to hold sth in usufruct

usufruitier, -ière /yzyfʀɥitje, jɛʀ/ **ADJ, NM,F** usufructuary

usuraire /yzyʀɛʀ/ **ADJ** *[taux, prêt]* usurious

usure[1] /yzyʀ/ **NF** *[de vêtement]* wear (and tear); *[d'objet]* wear; *[de terrain, roche]* wearing away; *[de forces, énergie]* wearing out; *(Ling) [de mot]* weakening ◆ **~ normale** fair wear and tear ◆ **résiste à l'~** wears well, hard-wearing ◆ **le tissu est devenu très brillant, c'est l'~** the material has gone all shiny because of wear ◆ **on voyait à travers le tissu à cause de l'~** the material was worn through ◆ **subir l'~ du temps** to be worn away by time ◆ **résister à l'~ du temps** to stand the test of time ◆ **c'est l'~ du pouvoir** *(Pol)* it's the wearing effect of being in power ◆ **~ de la monnaie** debasement of the currency ◆ **on l'aura à l'~ *** we'll wear him down in the end; → **guerre**

usure[2] /yzyʀ/ **NF** *(= intérêt)* usury ◆ **prêter à ~** to lend at usurious rates of interest ◆ **je te le rendrai avec ~** *(littér)* I will pay you back (with interest)

usurier, -ière /yzyʀje, jɛʀ/ **NM,F** usurer

usurpateur, -trice /yzyʀpatœʀ, tʀis/ **ADJ** *[tendance, pouvoir]* usurping *(épith)* **NM,F** usurper

usurpation /yzyʀpasjɔ̃/ **NF** *[de pouvoir, honneur, titre, nom]* usurpation; *(littér = empiètement)* encroachment

usurpatoire /yzyʀpatwaʀ/ **ADJ** usurpatory

usurper /yzyʀpe/ ▸ conjug 1 ◂ **VT** *[+ pouvoir, honneur, titre, nom, réputation]* to usurp ◆ **il a usurpé le titre de docteur en médecine** he wrongfully took *ou* assumed the title of Doctor of Medicine ◆ **sa réputation n'est pas usurpée** he well deserves his reputation **VI** *(littér)* ◆ **~ sur** *(= empiéter)* to encroach (up)on

ut /yt/ **NM** *(Mus)* C; → **clé**

Utah /yta/ **NM** Utah

utérin, e /yteʀɛ̃, in/ **ADJ** *(Anat, Jur)* uterine

utérus /yteʀys/ **NM** womb, uterus ◆ **location** *ou* **prêt d'~** womb-leasing; → **col**

utile /ytil/ **ADJ** 1 *[objet, appareil, action]* useful; *[aide, conseil]* useful, helpful *(à qn* to *ou* for sb) ◆ **livre ~ à lire** useful book to read ◆ **"adresses utiles"** "useful addresses" ◆ **cela vous sera certainement ~** that'll certainly be of use to you ◆ **veux-tu que je lui en parle ? – ce ne sera pas ~** do you want me to speak to him about it? – that won't be necessary ◆ **ça peut toujours être ~** it could always come in handy ◆ **ton parapluie m'a été bien ~ ce matin** your umbrella came in very handy (for me) this morning ◆ **j'irai – est-ce bien ~ ?** I'll go – is it really worth it *ou* is there any point ? ◆ **est-il vraiment ~ d'y aller** *ou* **que j'y aille ?** do I really need to go?, is there really any point in (my) going? ◆ **il est ~ de rappeler que ...** it's worth remembering that ... ◆ **il n'a pas jugé ~ de prévenir la police** he didn't think it was *ou* he didn't deem it necessary to tell the police, he didn't think it was worth telling the police ◆ **la vie ~ d'un bien** *(Écon)* the productive life of an asset; → **charge, temps[1], voter**

2 *[collaborateur, relation]* useful ◆ **il adore se rendre ~** he loves to make himself useful ◆ **puis-je vous être ~ ?** can I be of help?, can I do anything for you?

NM ◆ **l'~** what is useful; → **joindre**

utilement /ytilmɑ̃/ **ADV** *(= avec profit)* profitably, usefully ◆ **conseiller ~ qn** to give sb useful advice ◆ **une bibliographie vient très ~ compléter l'article** there is a very helpful bibliography at the end of the article, the article is accompanied by a very useful bibliography ◆ **ces mesures ont ~ contribué au redressement du pays** these measures were effective in putting *ou* helped put the country back on its feet

utilisable /ytilizabl/ **ADJ** usable ◆ **est-ce encore ~ ?** *[cahier, vêtement]* can it still be used?, is it still usable?; *[appareil]* is it still usable? *ou* working? ◆ **facilement ~** easy to use ◆ **ces listes incomplètes sont difficilement ~s** it's hard to use these incomplete lists ◆ **une carte de crédit ~ dans le monde entier** a credit card that can be used throughout the world

utilisateur, -trice /ytilizatœʀ, tʀis/ **NM,F** *[d'appareil]* user ◆ **~ final** end user

utilisation /ytilizasjɔ̃/ **NF** *(gén)* use; *(Culin) [de restes]* using (up) ◆ **notice d'~** instructions for use

utiliser /ytilize/ ► conjug 1 ◄ **VT** [1] *(= employer)* to use ◆ **produit facile à ~** user-friendly product, product that is easy to use ◆ **"à utiliser avant le ..."** *(sur un emballage)* "use by ..." [2] *(= tirer parti de) [+ personne]* to use; *[+ incident]* to use, to make use of; *(Culin) [+ restes]* to use (up) ◆ **savoir ~ les compétences** to know how to make the most of *ou* make use of people's abilities ◆ **~ qch au mieux** to make the most of sth, to use sth to its best advantage

> ⚠ **utiliser** se traduit rarement par **to utilize**, qui est d'un registre plus soutenu.

utilitaire /ytilitɛʀ/ **ADJ** utilitarian; → **véhicule** **NM** *(Ordin)* utility

utilitarisme /ytilitaʀism/ **NM** utilitarianism

utilitariste /ytilitaʀist/ **ADJ, NMF** *(Philos)* utilitarian

utilité /ytilite/ **NF** [1] *(= caractère utile)* usefulness; *(= utilisation possible)* use ◆ **je ne conteste pas l'~ de cet appareil** I don't deny the usefulness of this apparatus ◆ **cet outil a son ~** this tool has its uses ◆ **cet outil peut avoir son ~** this tool might come in handy *ou* useful ◆ **d'une grande ~** very useful, of great use *ou* usefulness *ou* help ◆ **ce livre ne m'est pas d'une grande ~** this book isn't much use *ou* help ◆ **de peu d'~** of little use *ou* help ◆ **d'aucune ~** (of) no use *ou* help ◆ **sans ~** useless ◆ **auras-tu l'~ de cet objet ?** can you make use of this object?, will you have any use for this object? ◆ **de quelle ~ est-ce que cela peut (bien) vous être ?** what earthly use is it to you?, what on earth can you use it for?

[2] *(= intérêt)* **reconnu** *ou* **déclaré d'~ publique** *(Jur)* state-approved

[3] *(Théât) (= rôle)* **jouer les ~s** to play small *ou* bit parts; *(fig)* to play second fiddle

utopie /ytɔpi/ **NF** [1] *(= genre, ouvrage, idéal politique)* utopia, Utopia [2] *(= idée, plan chimérique)* utopian view (*ou* idea *etc*) ◆ **~s** utopianism, utopian views *ou* ideas ◆ **ceci est une véritable ~** that's sheer utopianism ◆ **c'est de l'~ !** *(= irraisonnable)* it's just a pipedream!, it's all pie in the sky!

utopique /ytɔpik/ **ADJ** utopian, Utopian; → **socialisme**

utopisme /ytɔpism/ **NM** Utopianism

utopiste /ytɔpist/ **NMF** utopian, Utopian

UV /yve/ **NF** (abrév de **unité de valeur**) († *Univ*) → **unité** **NM** (abrév de **ultraviolet**) ultraviolet ray ◆ **filtre ~A/~B** UVA/UVB filter

uvulaire /yvylɛʀ/ **ADJ** uvular

uvule /yvyl/ **NF** *(= luette)* uvula

V v

V¹, v¹ /ve/ **NM** *(= lettre)* V, v ◆ **en V** V-shaped ◆ **moteur en V** V-engine ◆ **encolure en V** V-neck ◆ **décolleté en V** V-neckline ◆ **le V de la victoire** the victory sign, the V for victory; → **vitesse**

V², v² (abrév de **voir, voyez**) V

V³ (abrév de **volt**) V

va /va/ → **aller**

vacance /vakɑ̃s/ **NF** 1 *(Admin) [de poste]* vacancy

2 *(Jur)* ~ **de succession** abeyance of succession ◆ ~ **du pouvoir** power vacuum

NFPL vacances 1 *(gén)* holiday(s) *(Brit)*, vacation *(US)*; *(Univ)* vacation ◆ **les grandes ~s, les ~s d'été** the summer holiday(s) *(Brit)* ou vacation *(US)*; *(Univ)* the long vacation ◆ **les ~s scolaires/de Noël/d'hiver** the school/Christmas/winter holiday(s) *(Brit)* ou vacation *(US)* ◆ **~s de** ou **à la neige** winter sports holiday(s) *(Brit)* ou vacation *(US)* ◆ **~s actives** activity holiday(s) *(Brit)* ou vacation *(US)* ◆ **maison/lieu de ~s** holiday *(Brit)* ou *(US)* vacation home/spot ◆ **au moment de partir en ~s, nous ...** just as we were about to set off on (our) holiday *(Brit)* ou vacation *(US)*, we ... ◆ **aller en ~s en Angleterre** to go on holiday *(Brit)* ou vacation *(US)* to England ◆ **il n'a jamais pris de ~s** he has never taken a holiday *(Brit)* ou vacation *(US)* ◆ **prendre ses ~s en une fois** to take all one's holiday *(Brit)* ou vacation *(US)* at once ◆ **avoir droit à 5 semaines de ~s** to be entitled to 5 weeks' holiday *(Brit)* ou vacation *(US)* ◆ **j'ai besoin de ~s/de quelques jours de ~s** I need a holiday *(Brit)* ou vacation *(US)*/a few days' holiday *(Brit)* ou vacation *(US)* ◆ **il est parti ? ça va nous faire des ~s !** *(hum)* has he gone? that'll give us a break!; → **colonie, devoir**

2 *(Jur)* **~s judiciaires** recess, vacation ◆ **~s parlementaires** parliamentary recess

vacancier, -ière /vakɑ̃sje, jɛʀ/ **NM,F** holiday-maker *(Brit)*, vacationer *(US)*

vacant, e /vakɑ̃, ɑ̃t/ **ADJ** 1 *[poste, siège]* vacant; *[appartement]* unoccupied, vacant ◆ **le siège laissé ~ par sa disparition/son départ** the seat left vacant by his death/his departure 2 *(Jur) [biens, succession]* in abeyance *(attrib)*

vacarme /vakaʀm/ **NM** racket, row, din ◆ **faire du ~** to make a racket ou row ou din ◆ **il y avait un ~ de klaxons** horns were blaring ◆ **il y avait un ~ continuel de camions** trucks roared past constantly ◆ **il démarra dans un ~ assourdissant** he set off with a deafening roar

vacataire /vakatɛʀ/ **NMF** temporary replacement, stand-in; *(Univ)* part-time lecturer (on contract) ◆ **il est ~** he's on a temporary contract

vacation /vakasjɔ̃/ **NF** 1 *(= temps de travail) [d'expert, notaire, commissaire de police]* session; *[de médecin]* shift; *[d'enseignant] (= travail)* supply work; *(= honoraires)* fee; *(= vente aux enchères)* auction ◆ **faire des ~s** to work on a short-term basis ◆ **être payé à la ~** to be paid on a sessional basis 2 ◆ ~ **(radio)** radio contact time

NFPL vacations *(= vacances judiciaires)* recess, vacation

vaccin /vaksɛ̃/ **NM** *(= substance)* vaccine; *(= vaccination)* vaccination, inoculation ◆ **faire un ~ à qn** to give sb a vaccination ou an inoculation ◆ ~ **contre la grippe** flu vaccine

vaccinal, e (mpl **-aux**) /vaksinal, o/ **ADJ** *[essai, efficacité]* vaccine *(épith)* ◆ **complication ~e** complication arising from a vaccination ◆ **taux de couverture ~e** vaccination rate ◆ **campagne ~e** vaccination campaign

vaccinateur, -trice /vaksinatœʀ, tʀis/ **ADJ** vaccinating *(épith)*, inoculating *(épith)* ◆ **médecin ~** doctor specialising in vaccinations **NM,F** vaccinator, inoculator

vaccination /vaksinasjɔ̃/ **NF** vaccination, inoculation ◆ ~ **contre la rage** ou **antirabique/contre l'hépatite B** rabies/hepatitis B vaccination

vaccine /vaksin/ **NF** *(= maladie)* cowpox, vaccinia *(SPÉC)*; († *= inoculation)* inoculation of cowpox ◆ **fausse** ~ false vaccinia

vacciner /vaksine/ ► conjug 1 ◄ **VT** to vaccinate, to inoculate *(contre* against); ◆ **se faire ~** to have a vaccination ou an inoculation, to get vaccinated ou inoculated ◆ **les personnes vaccinées** the people who have been vaccinated ◆ **être vacciné contre qch** * *[+ amour, tentation, illusion]* to be cured of sth; *[+ critiques]* to be immune to sth ◆ **merci, maintenant je suis vacciné !** * thanks, I've learnt my lesson! ou I'm cured of that!; → **majeur**

vaccinostyle /vaksinostil/ **NM** scarificator

vachard, e ⁑ /vaʃaʀ, aʀd/ **ADJ** *(= méchant)* nasty, rotten *, mean

vache /vaʃ/ **NF** 1 *(= animal)* cow; *(= cuir)* cowhide ◆ ~ **laitière** dairy cow ◆ ~ **marine** sea cow ◆ **maladie de la ~ folle** mad cow disease; → **plancher¹**

2 (⁑ *péj = police*) **les ~s** the pigs ⁑, the filth ⁑; → **mort¹**

3 (⁑ *= personne méchante*) *(femme)* bitch *⁑, cow ⁑; *(homme)* swine ⁑, sod ⁑ ◆ **ah les ~s !** the bastards! *⁑; → **peau**

4 (⁑ *: intensif*) **une ~ de surprise/bagnole** a ou one hell of a surprise/car ⁑

5 *(locutions)* **comme une ~ qui regarde passer les trains** vacantly ◆ **il parle français comme une ~ espagnole** * he absolutely murders the French language ◆ **manger de la ~ enragée** to go through hard ou lean times, to have a very hard ou lean time of it ◆ **période de ~s grasses/maigres pour l'économie française** good ou prosperous/lean ou hard times for the French economy ◆ **donner des coups de pied en ~ à qn** to kick sb slyly ◆ **faire un coup en ~ à qn** to play a dirty trick on sb, to do the dirty on sb ⁑ ◆ **ah la ~ !** ⁑ *(surprise, admiration)* wow! *, blimey! ⁑ *(Brit)*; *(douleur, indignation)* hell! ⁑, damn (me)! ⁑

ADJ (* *= méchant, sévère*) rotten *, mean ◆ **il est ~** he's really rotten * ou mean, he's a (rotten) swine ⁑ ou sod ⁑ *(Brit)* ◆ **elle est ~** she's really rotten * ou mean, she's a (mean ou rotten) cow ⁑ *(Brit)* ◆ **il n'a pas été ~ avec toi** he was quite kind ou good to you ◆ **c'est ~ pour eux** it's really rotten for them *

COMP vache à eau (canvas) water bag

vache à lait (*, *péj*) cash cow, milch cow *(péj)*

vache sacrée *(lit, fig)* sacred cow

vachement * /vaʃmɑ̃/ **ADV** *(= très)* really ◆ ~ **bon/difficile** really ou damned ⁑ ou bloody ⁑ *(Brit)* good/hard ◆ **on s'est ~ dépêchés** we rushed like mad * ou hell ⁑ ◆ **ça m'a ~ aidé** it helped me no end *, it was a big help ◆ **c'est ~ important pour moi** it's really important to me ◆ **il était ~ bien, ce film !** it was a brilliant film! ◆ **il est ~ plus grand qu'elle** he's a hell of a lot bigger than she is ⁑ ◆ **il pleut ~** it's pouring (down), it's tipping it down * *(Brit)*

vacher /vaʃe/ **NM** cowherd

vachère /vaʃɛʀ/ **NF** cowgirl

vacherie /vaʃʀi/ **NF** 1 * *(= action)* dirty trick *; *(= remarque)* nasty ou bitchy ⁑ remark; *(= caractère méchant) [de personne, remarque]* meanness ◆ **faire une ~ à qn** to play a dirty * ou mean trick on sb ◆ **dire des ~s** to make nasty remarks 2 (⁑ *: intensif*) **c'est une sacrée ~, cette maladie** it's a hell of a nasty illness * ◆ **cette ~ d'appareil ne veut pas marcher** this damned ⁑ ou blasted * ou bloody ⁑ *(Brit)* machine won't work ◆ **quelle ~ de temps !** what damned ⁑ ou bloody ⁑ *(Brit)* awful weather! 3 († *= étable*) cowshed, byre

vacherin /vaʃʀɛ̃/ **NM** *(= glace)* vacherin; *(= fromage)* vacherin cheese

vachette /vaʃɛt/ **NF** 1 *(= jeune vache)* young cow 2 *(= cuir)* calfskin

vacillant, e /vasijɑ̃, ɑ̃t/ **ADJ** 1 *[jambes, démarche]* unsteady, shaky, wobbly; *[lueur, flamme]* flickering *(épith)* 2 *[santé, mémoire]* shaky, failing;

[raison] failing; [courage] wavering, faltering; [caractère] indecisive, wavering (épith)

vacillation /vasijasjɔ̃/ NF ⇒ **vacillement**

vacillement /vasijmɑ̃/ NM 1 [de personne, blessé, ivrogne] swaying; [de bébé, meuble] wobbling; [de poteau] swaying; [de flamme, lumière] flickering 2 [de résolution, courage] faltering, wavering; [de raison] failure; [de santé, mémoire] shakiness

vaciller /vasije/ ▸ conjug 1 ◂ VI 1 (= chanceler) [personne] to sway (to and fro); [blessé, ivrogne] to sway, to reel; [bébé] to wobble ◆ ~ **sur ses jambes** to be unsteady on one's legs, to sway (to and fro) ◆ **il s'avança en vacillant vers la porte** he reeled ou staggered towards the door 2 [poteau] to sway (to and fro); [meuble] to wobble ◆ **il lui semblait que les murs vacillaient autour d'elle** she felt as if the room was spinning around her 3 [flamme, lumière] to flicker 4 [résolution, courage] to falter, to waver; [raison, intelligence] to fail; [santé, mémoire] to be shaky, to be failing ◆ **il vacillait dans ses résolutions** he wavered in his resolve

va-comme-je-te-pousse /vakɔmʒtəpus/ **à la va-comme-je-te-pousse** * LOC ADV in a slapdash manner, any old how *

vacuité /vakɥite/ NF (littér = vide) vacuity (littér), emptiness; (intellectuelle, spirituelle) vacuity, vacuousness

vacuole /vakɥɔl/ NF (Bio) vacuole

vade-mecum /vademekɔm/ NM INV (littér) handbook, vade mecum

vadrouille /vadʀuj/ NF 1 (* = balade) ramble, jaunt ◆ **partir en** ~ to go on a ramble ou jaunt ◆ **être en** ~ to be out on a ramble ◆ **elle est toujours en** ~ **à l'étranger** she's always off gallivanting abroad ou around the world 2 (Can = balai) mop

vadrouiller * /vadʀuje/ ▸ conjug 1 ◂ VI to rove around ou about ◆ ~ **dans les rues de Paris** to knock * ou rove about the streets of Paris

Vaduz /vadyz/ N Vaduz

va-et-vient /vaevjɛ̃/ NM INV 1 [de personnes, véhicules] comings and goings ◆ **il y a beaucoup de** ~ **dans ce café** it's a very busy café, there are a lot of comings and goings in this café ◆ **j'en ai assez de ce** ~ **incessant dans mon bureau** I'm sick of this constant stream of people coming in and out of my office ◆ **faire le** ~ **entre** [personne, train, bus] (lit) to go to and fro ou backwards and forwards between; [bateau] to ply between ◆ **le dossier a fait le** ~ **d'un bureau à l'autre** the file has been passed backwards and forwards from one office to the other ◆ **l'interprète faisait le** ~ **entre les deux langues** the interpreter was switching back and forth between the two languages

2 [de piston, pièce] **(mouvement de)** ~ (gén) to and fro (motion), backwards and forwards motion; (verticalement) up-and-down movement

3 (Élec) (= circuit) two-way wiring (NonC) ou wiring system; (= interrupteur) two-way switch

4 (= gond) helical hinge ◆ **porte à** ~ swing door

5 (= bac) (small) ferryboat

vagabond, e /vagabɔ̃, ɔd/ ADJ [peuple, vie] wandering (épith); [imagination] roaming (épith), roving (épith), restless ◆ **son humeur** ~**e** his restless mood NM,F (péj = rôdeur) tramp, vagrant; (littér = personne qui voyage beaucoup) wanderer, vagabond

vagabondage /vagabɔ̃daʒ/ NM 1 (= errance) wandering, roaming ◆ **leurs** ~**s à travers l'Europe** their wanderings across Europe ◆ **le** ~ **de son imagination** (littér) the meanderings of his imagination 2 (Jur, péj = vie sans domicile fixe) vagrancy

vagabonder /vagabɔ̃de/ ▸ conjug 1 ◂ VI [personne] to roam, to wander; [imagination, esprit] to wander, to roam ◆ ~ **à travers l'Europe** to roam the length and breadth of Europe, to wander across Europe

vagin /vaʒɛ̃/ NM vagina

vaginal, e (mpl **-aux**) /vaʒinal, o/ ADJ vaginal; → **frottis**

vaginisme /vaʒinism/ NM vaginismus

vaginite /vaʒinit/ NF vaginitis (NonC)

vagir /vaʒiʀ/ ▸ conjug 2 ◂ VI [bébé] to wail, to cry

vagissant, e /vaʒisɑ̃, ɑ̃t/ ADJ wailing, crying

vagissement /vaʒismɑ̃/ NM wail, cry

vague[1] /vag/ ADJ 1 (= imprécis) [renseignement, geste] vague; [notion, idée] vague, hazy; [sentiment, forme] vague, indistinct; (= distrait) [air, regard] faraway (épith), vague ◆ **j'ai le** ~ **sentiment que** ... I have a vague feeling that ... ◆ **un** ~ **cousin** some distant cousin ◆ **il avait un** ~ **diplôme** he had a diploma of sorts ou some kind of (a) diploma; → **nerf, terrain**

2 (= ample) [robe, manteau] loose(-fitting)

NM 1 (littér) [de forme] vagueness, indistinctness; [de passions, sentiments] vagueness

2 ◆ **le** ~ vagueness ◆ **nous sommes dans le** ~ things are rather unclear to us ◆ **il est resté dans le** ~ he kept it all ou he remained rather vague ◆ **la police a préféré rester dans le** ~ **quant aux causes de cet incident** the police preferred not to give any details about the causes of the incident ◆ **laisser qn dans le** ~ to keep sb guessing, to keep sb in the dark ◆ **laisser qch dans le** ~ to leave sth up in the air ◆ **regarder dans le** ~ to stare into space ◆ **les yeux perdus dans le** ~ with a faraway look in his eyes ◆ ~ **à l'âme** melancholy ◆ **avoir du** ~ **à l'âme** to feel melancholic

vague[2] /vag/ NF 1 (lit) wave ◆ ~ **de fond** (lit) groundswell; (fig) groundswell of opinion ◆ **le multimédia est une** ~ **de fond qui déferle sur le monde** multimedia is a tidal wave sweeping over the world ◆ **faire des** ~**s** (lit, fig) to make waves ◆ **surtout, pas de** ~**s !** whatever you do, don't rock the boat!; → **déferlante**

2 (= déferlement) wave ◆ ~ **d'enthousiasme/de tendresse** wave ou surge of enthusiasm/of tenderness ◆ **la première** ~ **d'immigrants/de départs en vacances** the first wave of immigrants/of holiday departures ◆ ~ **d'attentats/d'arrestations** wave of bombings/of arrests ◆ ~ **de criminalité** crime wave ◆ ~ **d'assaut** (Mil) wave of assault ◆ ~ **de chaleur** heatwave ◆ ~ **de froid** cold spell ou snap; → **nouveau**

3 (= émanations) wave ◆ **une** ~ **de gaz se propagea jusqu'à nous** a smell of gas drifted ou wafted up to us

4 (= ondulation) (Archit) waved motif; [de chevelure] wave; (littér) [de blés, fougères] wave, undulation (littér) ◆ **effet de** ~ ripple effect

vaguelette /vaglɛt/ NF wavelet, ripple

vaguement /vagmɑ̃/ ADV vaguely ◆ **ils sont** ~ **parents** they're vaguely related ◆ **sourire** ~ **ironique** vaguely ou faintly ironic smile ◆ **il était** ~ **inquiet** he was slightly ou vaguely worried ◆ **à 18 ans, elle pensait** ~ **devenir professeur** when she was 18, she toyed with the idea of becoming a teacher ◆ **il était** ~ **question d'organiser une réunion** there was vague talk of planning a meeting ◆ **on entendait** ~ **parler dans le couloir** muffled voices could be heard in the corridor

vaguemestre /vagmɛstʀ/ NM army or navy officer responsible for the delivery of mail

vaguer /vage/ ▸ conjug 1 ◂ VI (littér = errer) [personne] to wander, to roam ◆ **laisser** ~ **son imagination/son regard** to let one's imagination/one's eyes wander

vahiné /vaine/ NF Tahitian woman, wahine

vaillamment /vajamɑ̃/ ADV bravely, courageously, valiantly

vaillance /vajɑ̃s/ NF (= courage) courage, bravery; (au combat) gallantry, valour (Brit), valor (US) ◆ **avec** ~ courageously, valiantly

vaillant, e /vajɑ̃, ɑ̃t/ ADJ 1 (littér = courageux) brave, courageous; (au combat) valiant, gallant ◆ **à cœur** ~ **rien d'impossible** (Prov) nothing is impossible to a willing heart (Prov) → **sou** 2 (= vigoureux) [personne] vigorous, hale and hearty, robust; [monnaie, économie] healthy ◆ **je ne me sens pas très** ~ I'm feeling a bit under the weather *, I don't feel too good

vaille que vaille /vajkəvaj/ LOC ADV → **valoir**

vain, e /vɛ̃, vɛn/ ADJ 1 (= sans fondement) [paroles, promesse] empty, hollow, vain; [craintes, espoir, plaisirs] vain, empty ◆ **pour lui la loyauté n'est pas un** ~ **mot** loyalty is not an empty word for him, the word loyalty really means something to him

2 (= frivole) [personne] shallow, superficial

3 (= infructueux) [effort, tentative, attente] vain (épith), in vain (attrib), futile, fruitless; [regrets, discussion] vain (épith), idle (épith) ◆ **son sacrifice n'aura pas été** ~ his sacrifice will not have been in vain ◆ **il est** ~ **d'essayer de** ... it is futile to try to ...

4 (littér = vaniteux) [personne] vain

LOC ADV **en vain** in vain ◆ **elle essaya en** ~ **de s'en souvenir** she tried vainly ou in vain to remember ◆ **ce ne fut pas en** ~ **que** ... it was not in vain that ... ◆ **je réessayai, mais en** ~ I tried again, but in vain ou but to no avail ◆ **invoquer le nom de Dieu en** ~ (frm) to take the Lord's name in vain

COMP **vaine pâture** (Jur) common grazing land

vaincre /vɛ̃kʀ/ ▸ conjug 42 ◂ VT 1 [+ rival, concurrent] to defeat, to beat; [+ armée, ennemi] to defeat, to vanquish (littér), to conquer ◆ **les meilleurs ont fini par** ~ the best men finally won ◆ **à** ~ **sans péril, on triomphe sans gloire** triumph without peril brings no glory ◆ **nous vaincrons** we shall overcome 2 [+ obstacle, préjugé, maladie, sentiment] to overcome; [+ chômage] to conquer ◆ **vaincu par le sommeil** overcome by sleep

vaincu, e /vɛ̃ky/ (ptp de **vaincre**) ADJ beaten, defeated, vanquished (littér) ◆ **s'avouer** ~ to admit defeat, to confess o.s. beaten ◆ **il part** ~ **d'avance** he feels he's beaten ou defeated before he begins NM,F defeated man (ou woman) ◆ **les** ~**s** the vanquished (littér), the defeated ◆ **malheur aux** ~**s !** woe to the vanquished! (littér) ◆ **mentalité/attitude de** ~ defeatist mentality/attitude

vainement /vɛnmɑ̃/ ADV vainly, in vain ◆ **j'ai** ~ **essayé de lui expliquer** I tried in vain to explain to him, I tried to explain to him (but) to no avail

vainqueur /vɛ̃kœʀ/ NM (à la guerre) victor, conqueror; (en sport) winner; [de concours, élection] winner ◆ **le** ~ **de l'Everest** the conqueror of Everest ◆ **les** ~**s de cette équipe** the conquerors of this team ◆ **les** ~**s de cette compétition** the winners in ou of this competition ◆ **accueillir qn en** ~ to welcome sb as a conquering hero ◆ **il est sorti** ~ **des élections** he emerged victorious from the election, he emerged as the winner of the election ◆ **ce film est le grand** ~ **du festival** this film scooped all the awards at the festival ADJ M victorious, triumphant

vair /vɛʀ/ NM vair (kind of fur) ◆ **la pantoufle de** ~ the glass slipper

vairon[1] /vɛʀɔ̃/ NM (= poisson) minnow

vairon[2] /vɛʀɔ̃/ ADJ M ◆ **yeux** ~**s** (cerclés de blanc) wall eyes; (de couleur différente) eyes of different colours (Brit) ou colors (US), wall eyes

vaisseau (pl **vaisseaux**) /veso/ **NM** [1] *(Naut)* vessel *(frm)*, ship ◆ ~ **amiral** flagship ◆ ~ **de guerre** warship ◆ ~ **fantôme** ghost ship ◆ ~ **spatial** spaceship; → **brûler, capitaine, enseigne, lieutenant** [2] *(Anat)* vessel ◆ ~ **sanguin/lymphatique/capillaire** blood/lymphatic/capillary vessel [3] *(Bot)* vessel ◆ **plante à ~x** vascular plant [4] *(Archit)* nave

vaisselier /vesəlje/ **NM** *(= meuble)* dresser

vaisselle /vesɛl/ **NF** *(= plats)* crockery; *(= plats à laver)* dishes; *(= lavage)* dishes, washing-up *(Brit)* ◆ ~ **de porcelaine** china ◆ ~ **de faïence** earthenware ◆ ~ **plate** (gold *ou* silver) plate ◆ **faire la ~** to do the dishes *ou* the washing-up *(Brit)*, to wash up *(Brit)* ◆ **la ~ était faite en deux minutes** the dishes were done *ou* the washing-up *(Brit)* was done in two minutes; → **eau**

VAL /val/ **NM** (abrév de **véhicule automatique léger**) automated (driverless) train

val (pl **vals** *ou* **vaux**) /val, vo/ **NM** *(gén dans noms de lieux)* valley ◆ **le Val de Loire** the Val de Loire, the Loire Valley ◆ **le Val d'Aoste** Valle d'Aosta; → **mont**

valable /valabl/ **ADJ** [1] *(= valide) [contrat, passeport]* valid ◆ **billet ~ un an** ticket valid for one year ◆ **"offre valable jusqu'au 31 mai"** "offer valid until 31 May" [2] *(= acceptable, recevable) [excuse, raison]* valid, legitimate; *[loi, critère, théorie, motif]* valid ◆ **elle n'a aucune raison ~ de le faire** she has no good *ou* valid reason for doing it ◆ **ce n'est ~ que dans certains cas** it is only valid *ou* it only holds *ou* applies in certain cases ◆ **ce que j'ai dit reste ~ dans ce cas aussi** what I said is valid *ou* applies in this case as well [3] *(= de qualité) [œuvre, solution, commentaire]* worthwhile; *[auteur, équipements]* decent; *[concurrent]* worthy; → **interlocuteur** [4] *(= rentable)* worthwhile ◆ **financièrement, ce n'est pas ~** it's not financially viable, it's not worthwhile financially

valablement /valabləmɑ̃/ **ADV** [1] *(= légitimement)* validly, legitimately ◆ **ce billet ne peut pas être ~ utilisé** this ticket isn't valid ◆ **ne pouvant ~ soutenir que ...** not being able to uphold legitimately *ou* justifiably that ... [2] *(= de façon satisfaisante)* **pour en parler ~, il faut être spécialiste** you need to be a specialist to be able to make valid comments *ou* to have anything worth saying about it

Valais /valɛ/ **NM** ◆ **le ~** Valais

valaisan, -anne /valɛzɑ̃, an/ **ADJ** of *ou* from Valais **NM,F** **Valaisan(ne)** inhabitant *ou* native of Valais

valdinguer* /valdɛ̃ge/ ▸ **conjug 1** ◂ **VI** *(= tomber)* ◆ **aller ~** *[personne]* to fall flat on one's face*, to go sprawling ◆ **les boîtes ont failli ~ (par terre)** the boxes nearly came crashing down *ou* nearly went flying* ◆ **envoyer ~ qn** *(lit)* to send sb flying; *(fig)* to tell sb to clear off* *ou* buzz off*, to send sb off with a flea in his ear* *(Brit)* ◆ **envoyer ~ qch** to send sth flying* ◆ **j'ai bien envie de tout envoyer ~ !** I'd like to jack it all in!*

valence /valɑ̃s/ **NF** *(Ling, Phys)* valency *(Brit)*, valence *(US)* ◆ **~-gramme** gramme-equivalent

valériane /valerjan/ **NF** valerian

valet /valɛ/ **NM** [1] *(= domestique)* (man) servant; *(Hist) [de seigneur]* valet; *(péj Pol)* lackey *(péj)* ◆ **premier ~ de chambre du roi** king's first valet ◆ ~ **de comédie** *(Théât)* manservant (part *ou* role) ◆ **jouer les ~s** *(Théât)* to play servant parts *ou* roles [2] *(Cartes)* jack, knave ◆ ~ **de cœur** jack *ou* knave of hearts [3] *(= cintre)* ~ **(de nuit)** valet [4] *(= outil)* ~ **(de menuisier)** (woodworker's) clamp

COMP **valet d'âtre** companion set
valet de chambre manservant, valet
valet de chiens (hunt) kennel attendant
valet d'écurie groom, stableboy, stable lad *(Brit)*
valet de ferme farmhand
valet de pied footman

valetaille /valtaj/ **NF** († *ou péj*) menials, flunkeys †

valétudinaire /valetydinɛʀ/ **ADJ, NMF** *(littér)* valetudinarian

valeur /valœʀ/ **NF** [1] *(= prix)* value, worth; *(Fin) [de devise, action]* value, price ◆ ~ **marchande** *(Comm)* market value ◆ **en ~ déclarée** *(Poste)* value declared ◆ ~ **ajoutée** added value ◆ **produits à forte ~ ajoutée** high added-value products ◆ **des activités à forte** *ou* **haute/faible ~ ajoutée** activities with high/low added value ◆ ~ **d'usage/d'échange** use/exchange value, value in use/in exchange ◆ ~ **nominale** *ou* **faciale** face *ou* nominal value, face amount *(US)* ◆ ~ **vénale** monetary value ◆ **quelle est la ~ de cet objet/de l'euro ?** what is this object/the euro worth?, what is the value of this object/the euro? ◆ **prendre/perdre de la ~** to go up/down in value, to gain/lose in value ◆ **la ~ intrinsèque de qch** the intrinsic value *ou* worth of sth ◆ **cette monnaie/cette pièce n'a plus de ~** this currency/this coin is worthless ◆ **estimer la ~ d'un terrain/d'un tableau à 100 000** € to value a piece of land/a picture at €100,000, to put the value *ou* estimate the value of a piece of land/of a picture at €100,000 ◆ **ces tableaux sont de même ~** *ou* **ont la même ~** these pictures are of equal value *ou* have the same value *ou* are worth the same amount ◆ **manuscrit d'une ~ inestimable** priceless manuscript; → **taxe**

[2] *(Bourse : gén pl = titre)* security ◆ **~s mobilières** securities, stocks and shares ◆ **~s disponibles** liquid assets ◆ **~s de premier ordre** *ou* **de tout repos** *ou* **de père de famille** gilt-edged *ou* blue-chip securities, gilts ◆ **~s de haute technologie** technology stocks; *(Internet)* Internet stocks; → **bourse, refuge, vedette**

[3] *(= qualité) [de personne, auteur]* worth, merit; *[de roman, tableau]* value, merit; *[de science, théorie]* value; *(littér = courage)* valour *(Brit)*, valor *(US)* ◆ **la ~ de cette méthode/découverte reste à prouver** the value of this method/discovery is still to be proved ◆ **estimer** *ou* **juger qn/qch à sa (juste) ~** to estimate *ou* judge sb/sth at his/its true value *ou* worth ◆ **son œuvre n'est pas sans ~** his work is not without value *ou* merit ◆ **ce meuble n'a qu'une ~ sentimentale** this piece of furniture has sentimental value only ◆ **accorder** *ou* **attacher de la ~ à qch** to value sth, to place value on sth; → **jugement**

[4] *(Jeux, Math, Mus)* value ◆ **la ~ affective/poétique/symbolique** the emotive/poetic/symbolic value ◆ ~ **absolue** *(Math)* absolute value ◆ **donnez-lui la ~ d'un verre à liqueur/d'une cuiller à café** give him the equivalent of a liqueur glass/a teaspoonful ◆ **en ~ absolue/relative, le prix des voitures a diminué** in absolute/relative terms the price of cars has gone down

[5] *(locutions)*

◆ **en valeur** ◆ **mettre en ~** *[+ bien, patrimoine, terrain]* to develop, to exploit; *[+ détail, caractéristique]* to bring out, to highlight, to emphasize; *[+ yeux, jambes]* to set off, to enhance; *[+ taille]* to emphasize; *[+ objet décoratif]* to set off, to show (off) to advantage; *[+ personne]* to show to advantage *ou* in a flattering light ◆ **se mettre en ~** to show o.s. off to advantage ◆ **ce chapeau te met en ~** that hat is very flattering *ou* becoming, that hat really suits you ◆ **son discours a mis en ~ l'importance de la culture/le rôle des syndicats** in his speech he emphasized the importance of culture/the role of the unions ◆ **mise en ~** *[de terrain, ressources naturelles, patrimoine]* development; *[de forêt]* exploitation; *[de meuble, tableau]* setting-off; *[de détail, caractéristique, mot]* emphasizing, highlighting

◆ **de valeur** *[bijou, meuble]* valuable, of value ◆ **objets de ~** valuables, articles of value ◆ **professeur/acteur de ~** teacher/actor of considerable merit

◆ **sans valeur** *[objet, témoignage]* worthless, valueless

NFPL **valeurs** *(morales, intellectuelles)* values ◆ **échelle** *ou* **hiérarchie des ~s** scale of values ◆ **système de ~s** value system ◆ **nous n'avons pas les mêmes ~s** we don't have *ou* share the same values

valeureusement /valœʀøzmɑ̃/ **ADV** *(littér)* valiantly, valorously *(littér)*

valeureux, -euse /valœʀø, øz/ **ADJ** *(littér)* valiant, valorous *(littér)*

validation /validasjɔ̃/ **NF** *[de passeport, billet]* validation; *[de document]* authentication; *[de décision]* ratification; *[de bulletin]* validation, stamping

valide /valid/ **ADJ** [1] *[personne] (= non blessé ou handicapé)* able, able-bodied; *(= en bonne santé)* fit, well *(attrib)*; *[membre]* good *(épith)* ◆ **la population ~** the able-bodied population ◆ **se sentir assez ~ pour faire** to feel fit *ou* well enough to do, to feel up to doing [2] *[billet, carte d'identité]* valid

valider /valide/ ▸ **conjug 1** ◂ **VT** *[+ passeport, billet]* to validate; *[+ document]* to authenticate; *[+ décision]* to ratify ◆ **faire ~ un bulletin** *(Jeux)* to get a coupon validated *ou* stamped ◆ **l'élection ne sera validée que si le taux de participation est suffisant** the election will only be valid if the turnout is high enough

validité /validite/ **NF** *[de billet, élection, argument, accord]* validity ◆ **quelle est la durée de ~ de votre passeport ?** how long is your passport valid for?

valise /valiz/ **NF** (suit)case, bag ◆ **faire sa ~** *ou* **ses ~s** *(lit)* to pack; *(= partir)* to pack one's bags, to pack up and leave ◆ **la ~ (diplomatique)** the diplomatic bag *ou* pouch *(US)* ◆ **avoir des ~s sous les yeux*** to have bags under one's eyes; → **boucler**

Valkyrie /valkiʀi/ **NF** Valkyrie, Walkyrie

vallée /vale/ **NF** valley ◆ ~ **suspendue/en U/glaciaire** hanging/U-shaped/glaciated valley ◆ ~ **sèche** *ou* **morte** dry valley ◆ **la ~ de la Loire/du Nil** the Loire/Nile valley ◆ **la Vallée des Rois/Reines** the Valley of the Kings/Queens ◆ **la vie est une ~ de larmes** *(littér)* life is a vale of tears *(littér)* ◆ **la ~ de la mort** *(Bible)* the valley of the shadow of death; *(Géog)* Death Valley

vallon /valɔ̃/ **NM** small valley

vallonné, e /valɔne/ **ADJ** undulating, hilly

vallonnement /valɔnmɑ̃/ **NM** undulation

valoche* /valɔʃ/ **NF** case, bag

valoir /valwaʀ/
▸ **conjug 29** ◂
GRAMMAIRE ACTIVE 28.1, 29.2

1 VERBE INTRANSITIF	3 VERBE PRONOMINAL
2 VERBE TRANSITIF	

1 - VERBE INTRANSITIF

[1] valeur marchande *[propriété, bijou]* to be worth ◆ ~ **150** € to be worth €150 ◆ **ça vaut combien ?** *(gén)* how much is it worth?; *(à un commerçant)* how much is it? ◆ ~ **de l'argent** to be worth a lot of money ◆ **ça vaut bien 400** € *(estimation)* it must easily be worth €400; *(jugement)* it's

well worth €400 ♦ ~ **cher/encore plus cher** to be worth a lot/still more; → **pesant**

♦ **à valoir** *(Comm)* to be deducted, on account ♦ **paiement/acompte à ~ sur …** payment/deposit to be deducted from … ♦ **100 € à ~ sur votre prochaine facture** €100 credit against your next bill; → **à-valoir**

♦ **faire valoir** *(= exploiter)* *[+ domaine]* to farm; *[+ titres, capitaux]* to invest profitably

2 [qualités] **que vaut cet auteur/cette émission/le nouveau maire ?** is this author/this programme/the new mayor any good? ♦ **que valent ses promesses ?** what are his promises worth? ♦ **cette pièce vaut surtout par son originalité** the chief *ou* principal merit of this play is its originality ♦ **prendre une chose pour ce qu'elle vaut** to take a thing for what it's worth ♦ **ça vaut ce que ça vaut*, mais j'ai entendu dire que …** take this for what it's worth, but I've heard that … ♦ **il a conscience de ce qu'il vaut** he's aware of his worth, he knows his (own) worth ♦ **leur fils ne vaut pas cher !** their son's no good! ♦ **il ne vaut pas la corde pour le pendre** he's not worth bothering with ♦ **sa dernière pièce ne valait pas grand-chose** his last play wasn't particularly good, his last play wasn't up to much* *(Brit)* ♦ **ce tissu/cette marchandise ne vaut rien** this material/this article is no good ♦ **votre argument ne vaut rien** your argument is worthless ♦ **cet outil ne vaut rien** this tool is useless *ou* no good *ou* no use ♦ **ce climat ne vaut rien pour les rhumatismes** this climate is no good for rheumatism ♦ **ça/il ne vaut pas tripette*** *ou* **un clou*** *ou* **un pet de lapin*** it's/he's a dead loss*; → aussi **rien**

♦ **faire valoir** *(= mettre en avant)* *[+ droit]* to assert; *[+ fait]* to emphasize; *[+ argument]* to put forward; *[+ caractéristique]* to highlight, to bring out ♦ **je lui fis ~ que …** I impressed upon him that …, I pointed out to him that … ♦ **il peut faire ~ ses droits à la retraite** he is eligible for retirement ♦ **il s'entoure de gens faibles/ignorants parce que ça le fait ~** he surrounds himself with weak/ignorant people because it makes him appear stronger/more intelligent ♦ **se faire ~** to sell o.s. ♦ **il ne sait pas se faire ~** he doesn't know how to sell himself; → aussi **faire-valoir**

♦ **valoir mieux** *(= avoir plus de qualités, être meilleur)* ♦ **tu vaux mieux que lui** you're better than he is *ou* than him ♦ **c'est un travail sans intérêt, tu vaux mieux que ça !** it's not a very good job, you're cut out *ou* made for better things! ♦ **cet endroit vaut mieux que sa réputation** this place is better than its reputation allows ♦ **ils ne valent pas mieux l'un que l'autre** they're both as bad as each other
(= être préférable) ♦ **dans ce cas, il vaut mieux refuser** *ou* **mieux vaut refuser** in that case, it's better to refuse ♦ **il vaudrait mieux que vous refusiez** you had *ou* you'd better refuse, you would *ou* you'd do better to refuse ♦ **ça vaut mieux comme ça** it's better that way ♦ **avertis-le, ça vaut mieux** I'd tell him if I were you, it would be better if you told him ♦ **il vaut mieux le prévenir** we'd *(ou* you'd *etc)* better tell him ♦ **j'aurais dû lui téléphoner – oui, il aurait mieux valu** I should have phoned him – yes, you should (have) *ou* yes, that would have been the best thing to do ♦ **je le fais tout de suite – il vaudrait mieux (pour toi) !** I'll do it straight away – you'd better! ♦ **il vaut mieux entendre ça que d'être sourd !*** what a stupid thing to say!; → aussi **mieux**

♦ **vaille que vaille** somehow ♦ **la police assurait vaille que vaille un semblant d'ordre** the police somehow managed to maintain order ♦ **pendant la révolution, les gens ont continué à vivre vaille que vaille** during the revolution people somehow managed to go on living their lives

3 [= être valable] to hold, to apply, to be valid ♦ **ceci ne vaut que dans certains cas** this only holds *ou* applies *ou* is only valid in certain cases ♦ **la décision vaut pour tout le monde** the decision applies to everyone

4 [= équivaloir à] **la campagne vaut bien la mer** the countryside is just as good *ou* is every bit as good as the seaside ♦ **une blanche vaut deux noires** *(Mus)* one minim *(Brit) ou* half note *(US)* is equivalent to two crochets *(Brit) ou* quarter notes *(US)* ♦ **un as vaut quatre points** *(Bridge)* an ace is worth four points ♦ **il vaut largement son frère** he is every bit as good as his brother ♦ **ce nouveau médicament/traitement ne vaut pas le précédent** this new medicine/treatment is not as good as *ou* isn't a patch on* *(Brit)* the previous one ♦ **cette méthode en vaut une autre** it's as good a method as any ♦ **tout ça ne vaut pas la mer/la liberté** this is all very well but it's not like the seaside/having one's freedom ♦ **rien ne vaut un bon bain chaud** there's nothing like a nice warm bath, there's nothing to beat a nice warm bath ♦ **ça ne vaut pas la réflexion qu'il m'a faite hier** you should have heard what he said to me yesterday ♦ **ça vaut pas René*, tu sais ce qu'il m'a fait ?** that's nothing on René* – do you know what he did to me?

5 [= justifier] to be worth; *(= mériter)* to deserve ♦ **Lyon vaut (bien) une visite/le déplacement** *ou* **voyage** Lyons is (well) worth a visit/the journey ♦ **une soirée pareille, ça valait le voyage*** *(hum)* it was well worth going to a party like that ♦ **ça valait bien un merci** he *(ou* they *etc)* could have said thank you ♦ **un service en vaut un autre** one good turn deserves another; → **coup, détour, peine**

2 - VERBE TRANSITIF

♦ **valoir qch à qn** *(= rapporter, procurer)* to earn sb sth ♦ **ceci lui a valu des louanges/des reproches** this earned *ou* brought him praise/criticism ♦ **les soucis/ennuis que nous a valus cette affaire !** the worry/trouble that this business has caused us! ♦ **qu'est-ce qui nous vaut l'honneur de cette visite ?** to what do we owe the honour of this visit? ♦ **l'incident lui a valu d'être accusé d'imprudence** the incident meant he was accused of carelessness ♦ **un bon rhume, c'est tout ce que ça lui a valu de sortir sous la pluie** all he got for going out in the rain was a bad cold ♦ **l'inaction ne lui vaut rien** it isn't good for him to remain inactive ♦ **ça ne lui a rien valu** it didn't do him any good

3 - VERBE PRONOMINAL

se valoir *(= être équivalents)* **ces deux candidats/méthodes se valent** there's not much to choose between the two applicants/methods, the two applicants/methods are of equal merit ♦ **aux échecs, nous nous valons** *(en bien)* we're just as good as each other at chess, we're equally good at chess; *(en mal)* we're both as bad as each other at chess ♦ **ça se vaut*** it's all the same ♦ **et pour le prix ? – ça se vaut** and pricewise? – there's hardly any difference

---

valorisable /valɔʀizabl/ ADJ *[matières, matériaux]* recyclable

valorisant, e /valɔʀizɑ̃, ɑt/ ADJ *[travail]* fulfilling ♦ **être ~ pour qn** to increase sb's self-esteem ♦ **tâches peu ~es** menial tasks ♦ **il est très attentionné avec moi, c'est très ~** he's very considerate, it makes me feel very worthwhile ♦ **c'est ~ pour des jeunes de se voir confier de telles responsabilités** being given responsibilities like these increases young people's self-respect *ou* is good for young people's self-esteem ♦ **il essaie de montrer une image ~e de sa ville** he is trying to show a positive image of his town

valorisation /valɔʀizasjɔ̃/ NF 1 *(Écon, Fin)* *(= mise en valeur)* *[de région, terrain, patrimoine]* development; *(= augmentation de la valeur)* *[de produit, monnaie, titres]* increase in value 2 *(= augmentation du mérite, du prestige)* *[de diplôme, compétences]* increased prestige; *[de profession, activité]* improved status; *[de personne]* improved self-esteem; *(Psych)* self-actualization (SPÉC) 3 *(Écol)* *[de déchets]* recovering

valoriser /valɔʀize/ ► conjug 1 ◄ VT 1 *(Écon, Fin)* *[+ région, patrimoine, capital]* to develop; *[+ produit, titre]* to increase the value of ♦ **ces aménagements vont ~ la maison** these improvements will increase the value of the house ♦ **le yen est fortement valorisé sur le marché des changes** the yen has risen sharply on the foreign exchange market 2 *(= donner plus de prestige à)* *[+ diplôme]* to increase the prestige of; *[+ personne]* to increase the standing of; *[+ profession]* to enhance the status of ♦ **pour ~ l'image de l'entreprise** to enhance the image of the company 3 *(Écol)* *[+ déchets]* to recover 4 *(= évaluer la valeur de)* *[+ entreprise]* to value
VPR **se valoriser** *[immeuble, monnaie, titres]* to increase in value; *[personne]* to increase one's standing

valse /vals/ NF 1 *(= danse, air)* waltz ♦ ~ **lente/viennoise** slow/Viennese waltz ♦ ~ **musette** waltz *(to accordion accompaniment)* 2 *(= remplacement fréquent)* **la ~ des étiquettes** *ou* **des prix** constant price rises ♦ **la ~ des ministres** *ou* **des portefeuilles** the ministerial musical chairs ♦ **~-hésitation** shilly-shallying *(NonC)*, pussyfooting* *(NonC)* ♦ **la ~ des responsables a nui à l'entreprise** the high turnover in managers has harmed the company

valser /valse/ ► conjug 1 ◄ VI 1 *(= danser)* to waltz 2 *(* : locutions)* **envoyer ~ qch/qn** to send sth/sb flying ♦ **il est allé ~ contre le mur** he went flying against the wall ♦ **faire ~ l'argent** to spend money like water, to throw money around ♦ **faire ~ les étiquettes** *ou* **les prix** to jack up* the prices ♦ **faire ~ les ministres/les employés** to play musical chairs with ministerial/staff posts

valseur, -euse /valsœʀ, øz/ NM,F *(Danse)* waltzer NFPL **valseuses** ‡ *(= testicules)* balls*‡

valve /valv/ NF valve ♦ ~ **cardiaque** heart valve

valvulaire /valvylɛʀ/ ADJ valvular

valvule /valvyl/ NF *(Anat, Tech)* valve; *(Bot)* valvule ♦ ~ **mitrale** mitral valve

vamp /vɑ̃p/ NF vamp

vamper* /vɑ̃pe/ ► conjug 1 ◄ VT to vamp

vampire /vɑ̃piʀ/ NM 1 *(= fantôme)* vampire 2 *(† = escroc)* vampire, bloodsucker 3 *(= chauve-souris)* vampire bat

vampirique /vɑ̃piʀik/ ADJ vampiric

vampiriser /vɑ̃piʀize/ ► conjug 1 ◄ VT *(lit)* to suck the blood of; *(fig)* to suck the lifeblood out of

vampirisme /vɑ̃piʀism/ NM vampirism

van[1] /vɑ̃/ NM *(= panier)* winnowing basket

van[2] /van/ NM *(= véhicule)* horse-box *(Brit)*, horse trailer *(US)*

vanadium /vanadjɔm/ NM vanadium

Vancouver /vɑ̃kuvɛʀ/ N Vancouver ♦ **l'île de ~** Vancouver Island

vandale /vɑ̃dal/ NMF vandal; *(Hist)* Vandal ADJ vandal *(épith)*; *(Hist)* Vandalic

vandaliser /vɑ̃dalize/ ► conjug 1 ◄ VT to vandalize

vandalisme /vɑ̃dalism/ NM vandalism ♦ **acte de ~** act of vandalism ♦ **c'est du ~ !** it's vandalism!

vandoise /vɑ̃dwaz/ NF dace, chub

vanesse /vanɛs/ NF vanessa

vanille /vanij/ NF *(Bot, Culin)* vanilla ◆ **crème/glace à la ~** vanilla cream/ice cream

vanillé, e /vanije/ ADJ *[sucre, thé]* vanilla *(épith)*; *[parfum]* vanilla-scented

vanillier /vanije/ NM vanilla plant

vanilline /vanilin/ NF vanillin

vanilliné, e /vaniline/ ADJ *[sucre]* flavoured with vanillin

vanité /vanite/ NF 1 *(= fatuité)* vanity ◆ **avoir la ~ de croire que ...** to be conceited enough to think that ... ◆ **il avait des petites ~s d'artiste** he had the little conceits of an artist ◆ **je le dis sans ~** I say it with all due modesty *ou* without wishing to boast ◆ **tirer ~ de** to pride o.s. on ◆ **elle n'a jamais tiré ~ de sa beauté** she has never been conceited about her beauty ◆ **blesser qn dans sa ~** to wound sb's pride ◆ **flatter la ~ de qn** to flatter sb's ego
2 *(littér) [de paroles, promesse]* emptiness, hollowness, vanity; *[de craintes, espoir, plaisirs]* vanity, emptiness; *[de personne]* shallowness, superficiality; *[d'effort, tentative, attente]* vanity, futility, fruitlessness; *[de regrets discussion]* vanity, uselessness ◆ **~, ~, tout n'est que ~** *(Bible)* vanity of vanities, all is vanity
3 *(Art)* vanitas

vaniteusement /vanitøzmɑ̃/ ADV vainly, conceitedly

vaniteux, -euse /vanitø, øz/ ADJ vain, conceited NM,F vain *ou* conceited person

vanity-case (pl **vanity-cases**) /vanitikɛz/ NM vanity case

vannage /vanaʒ/ NM *(Agr)* winnowing

vanne /van/ NF 1 *[d'écluse]* (lock) gate, sluice (gate); *[de barrage, digue]* floodgate, (sluice) gate; *[de moulin]* (weir) hatch; *[de canalisation]* gate ◆ **~ thermostatique** thermostat ◆ **ouvrir les ~s** *(fig) (= laisser passer ou s'exprimer librement)* to open the floodgates; *(* = pleurer)* to turn on the waterworks* 2 *(* = remarque)* dig*, jibe ◆ **envoyer une ~ à qn** to have a dig at sb*, to jibe at sb

vanneau (pl **vanneaux**) /vano/ NM peewit, lapwing ◆ **~ huppé** Northern lapwing

vanner /vane/ ► conjug 1 ◄ VT 1 *(Agr)* to winnow 2 *(‡ = fatiguer)* to do in*, to knacker (out)‡ *(Brit)* ◆ **je suis vanné** I'm dead-beat* *ou* knackered‡ *(Brit)*

vannerie /vanʀi/ NF *(= métier)* basketry, basketwork; *(= objets)* wickerwork, basketwork

vanneur, -euse /vanœʀ, øz/ NM,F winnower

vannier /vanje/ NM basket maker, basket worker

vantail (pl **-aux**) /vɑ̃taj, o/ NM *[de porte]* leaf; *[d'armoire]* door ◆ **porte à double ~** *ou* **à (deux) vantaux** stable door *(Brit)*, Dutch door *(US)*

vantard, e /vɑ̃taʀ, aʀd/ ADJ boastful NM,F boaster, braggart

vantardise /vɑ̃taʀdiz/ NF *(= caractère)* boastfulness; *(= action)* boasting *(NonC)*, bragging *(NonC)*; *(= propos)* boast

vanter /vɑ̃te/ ► conjug 1 ◄ VT *[+ personne]* to praise, to sing the praises of; *[+ qualité, méthode, avantage]* to speak highly of, to praise, to vaunt *(frm)* ◆ **~ la marchandise** to peddle one's wares ◆ **film dont on vante les mérites** much-praised film VPR **se vanter** 1 *(= fanfaronner)* to boast, to brag ◆ **sans (vouloir) me ~** without wishing to blow my own trumpet, without wishing to boast *ou* brag, I don't want to boast 2 *(= se targuer)* **se ~ de** to pride o.s. on ◆ **se ~ d'avoir fait qch** to pride o.s. on having done sth ◆ **il se vante de (pouvoir) faire ...** he boasts he can *ou* will do ... ◆ **il ne s'en est pas vanté** *(iro)* he kept quiet about it ◆ **il n'y a pas de quoi se ~** there's nothing to be proud of *ou* to boast about ◆ **et il s'en vante !** and he's proud of it!

Vanuatu /vanwatu/ N Vanuatu

va-nu-pieds /vanypje/ NMF INV *(péj)* tramp, beggar

vapes‡ /vap/ NFPL ◆ **tomber dans les ~** to fall into a dead faint, to pass out ◆ **être dans les ~** *(= évanoui)* to be out for the count* *ou* out cold*; *(= étourdi par un choc)* to be woozy* *ou* in a daze; *(= abruti par le travail)* to be punch-drunk *ou* in a daze; *(= distrait)* to have one's head in the clouds

vapeur /vapœʀ/ NF 1 *(littér = brouillard)* haze *(NonC)*, vapour *(Brit) (NonC)*, vapor *(US) (NonC)*
2 ◆ **~ (d'eau)** steam, (water) vapour *(Brit) ou* vapor *(US)* ◆ **~ atmosphérique** atmospheric vapour ◆ **à ~** *(Tech)* steam *(épith)* ◆ **repassage à la ~** steam-ironing ◆ **(cuit à la) ~** *(Culin)* steamed
3 *(Chim, Phys = émanation)* vapour *(Brit) (NonC)*, vapor *(US) (NonC)* ◆ **~s** *(nocives)* fumes ◆ **~s d'essence** petrol *(Brit) ou* gasoline *(US)* fumes ◆ **~ saturante** saturated vapour ◆ **~ sèche** dry steam
4 (†: *gén pl*) **~s** *(= malaises)* vapours † ◆ **avoir ses ~s** *(bouffées de chaleur)* to have hot flushes *(Brit) ou* flashes *(US)*; *(malaise)* to have the vapours †
5 *(gén pl)* **les ~s de l'ivresse/de la gloire** *(= griserie)* the heady fumes of intoxication/of glory
6 *(locutions)* **aller à toute ~** *[navire]* to sail full steam ahead; (* *fig*) to go at full speed, to go full steam ahead *(fig)* → **renverser**
NM *(= bateau)* steamship, steamer

vapo* /vapo/ NM abrév de **vaporisateur**

vaporeusement /vapɔʀøzmɑ̃/ ADV vaporously

vaporeux, -euse /vapɔʀø, øz/ ADJ *[tissu, robe]* diaphanous, gossamer *(épith) (littér)*; *(littér) [lumière, atmosphère]* hazy, misty, vaporous; *[nuage, cheveux]* gossamer *(épith) (littér)* ◆ **lointain ~** *(Art)* sfumato background

vaporisateur /vapɔʀizatœʀ/ NM *(à parfum)* spray, atomizer; *(Agr)* spray; *(Tech)* vaporizer ◆ **parfum en ~** perfume in a spray bottle *ou* in an atomizer

vaporisation /vapɔʀizasjɔ̃/ NF 1 *[de parfum, insecticide, surface]* spraying ◆ **une ~ suffit** one spray is enough 2 *(Phys)* vaporization

vaporiser /vapɔʀize/ ► conjug 1 ◄ VT 1 *[+ parfum, insecticide, surface]* to spray ◆ **vaporisez le produit sur la plaie** spray the product onto the wound 2 *(Phys)* to vaporize VPR **se vaporiser** *(Phys)* to vaporize

vaquer /vake/ ► conjug 1 ◄ VT INDIR **vaquer à** *(= s'occuper de)* to attend to, to see to ◆ **~ à ses occupations** to attend to one's affairs, to go about one's business VI 1 (†*= être vacant*) to stand *ou* be vacant 2 *(Admin = être en vacances)* to be on vacation

varan /vaʀɑ̃/ NM varanus, monitor lizard ◆ **~ de Komodo** Komodo dragon

varappe /vaʀap/ NF *(= sport)* rock-climbing; *(= ascension)* (rock) climb ◆ **faire de la ~** to go rock-climbing

varapper /vaʀape/ ► conjug 1 ◄ VI to rock-climb

varappeur, -euse /vaʀapœʀ, øz/ NM,F (rock-)climber

varech /vaʀɛk/ NM kelp, wrack

vareuse /vaʀøz/ NF *[de pêcheur, marin]* pea jacket; *(d'uniforme)* tunic; *(de ville)* jacket

variabilité /vaʀjabilite/ NF 1 *[de temps, humeur]* changeableness, variableness 2 *(Math, Sci)* variability

variable /vaʀjabl/ ADJ 1 *(= incertain) [temps]* variable, changeable, unsettled; *[humeur]* changeable, variable; *[vent]* variable ◆ **le baromètre est au ~** the barometer is at *ou* reads "change"
2 *(= susceptible de changements) [montant, allocation, part]* variable; *[dimensions, modalités, formes]* adaptable, variable; *(Math, Sci) [grandeur, quantité, facteur]* variable; *(Ling) [forme, mot]* inflectional, inflected *(épith)* ◆ **à revenu ~** *(Fin)* variable yield *(épith)* ◆ **l'effet est (très) ~ selon les individus** the effect varies (greatly) from person to person *ou* according to the individual ◆ **mot ~ en genre** word that is inflected *ou* marked for gender; → **foyer, géométrie**
3 *(au pl = varié) [résultats, réactions]* varied, varying *(épith)*
NF *(Chim, Ling, Math, Phys, Stat)* variable ◆ **~ aléatoire/continue/discrète** random/continuous/discrete variable ◆ **~ entière/numérique** *(Ordin)* integer/numeric variable

variance /vaʀjɑ̃s/ NF *(Sci)* variance

variante /vaʀjɑ̃t/ NF *(gén)* variant *(de* of) variation *(de* on); *(Ling, Littérat)* variant *(de* of)

variateur /vaʀjatœʀ/ NM ◆ **~ de vitesse** speed variator ◆ **~ (de lumière)** dimmer

variation /vaʀjasjɔ̃/ NF 1 *(= écart, changement)* variation *(de* in); ◆ **les ~s de (la) température** variations in (the) temperature, temperature variations ◆ **~s climatiques** climatic *ou* climate variations ◆ **les ~s orthographiques/phonétiques au cours des siècles/selon les régions** spelling/phonetic variations *ou* variants throughout the centuries/from region to region ◆ **les ~s du mode de vie au cours des siècles** the changes in life-style through the centuries ◆ **corrigé des ~s saisonnières** *(Écon)* seasonally adjusted, adjusted for seasonal variations ◆ **~s monétaires** currency fluctuations ◆ **~s hormonales** hormonal fluctuations ◆ **~s d'humeur** mood swings ◆ **les ~s de l'opinion** swings *ou* changes in public opinion ◆ **subir** *ou* **connaître de fortes ~s** to vary *ou* fluctuate considerably
2 *(Mus)* variation ◆ **~s pour piano** variations for piano ◆ **~s sur un thème connu** *(hum)* variations on the same old theme *ou* on a well-worn theme

varice /vaʀis/ NF *(Méd)* varicose vein, varix *(SPÉC)*; → **bas²**

varicelle /vaʀisɛl/ NF chickenpox, varicella *(SPÉC)*

varicosité /vaʀikɔzite/ NF varicosity

varié, e /vaʀje/ (ptp de **varier**) ADJ 1 *(= non monotone) [style, existence, paysage]* varied, varying *(épith)*; *[programme, menu] (= qu'on change souvent)* varying *(épith)*; *(= diversifié)* varied ◆ **un travail très ~** a very varied job ◆ **en terrain ~** *(Mil)* on irregular terrain ◆ **air ~** *(Mus)* theme with *ou* and variations 2 *(littér = non uni) [tissu, couleur]* variegated 3 *(= divers) [résultats]* various, varying *(épith)*, varied; *[produits, sujets, objets]* various ◆ **hors-d'œuvre ~s** selection of hors d'œuvres, hors d'œuvres variés ◆ **avoir recours à des arguments ~s** to use various arguments ◆ **on rencontre les opinions les plus ~es** you come across the most varied *ou* diverse opinions on the subject

varier /vaʀje/ ► conjug 7 ◄ VI 1 *(= changer)* to vary, to change ◆ **faire ~ une fonction** *(Math)* to vary a function ◆ **pour ~ un peu** for a bit of a change, for a bit of variety
2 *(= différer)* to vary ◆ **son témoignage n'a pas varié** he stuck to his story ◆ **ma réponse ne variera pas** I will not change my reply ◆ **les prix varient de 15 à 25 €/entre 15 et 25 €** prices vary from €15 to €25/between €15 and €25 ◆ **le taux peut ~ du simple au double** rates can vary by as much as 100% ◆ **les tarifs varient selon les pays** prices vary from country to country ◆ **le dosage varie en fonction de**

l'âge et du poids the dose varies according to age and weight

③ *(Ling) [mot, forme]* to be inflected ◆ **ce mot varie en genre et en nombre** this word inflects in gender and number

④ *(= changer d'opinion)* **ils varient souvent dans leurs opinions sur ...** their opinions often vary on the subject of ... ◆ **elle n'a jamais varié sur ce point** she has never changed her opinion on that

VT ① *[+ style, vie] (= changer)* to vary; *(= rendre moins monotone)* to vary, to lend *ou* give variety to ◆ **pour ~ les plaisirs** *(iro)* just for a pleasant change *(iro)* ◆ **elle variait souvent sa coiffure/le menu** she often changed her hair style/the menu

② *(= diversifier) [+ thèmes, produits]* to vary, to diversify

variété /vaʀjete/ **NF** ① *(= diversité)* variety ◆ **étonné par la grande ~ des produits/opinions** surprised at the great variety *ou* the wide range of products/opinions ◆ **aimer la ~** to like variety ◆ **~ des langues** language variety ② *(= type)* variety ◆ **il cultive exclusivement cette ~ de rose** he only grows this variety of rose ◆ **on y rencontrait toutes les ~s de criminels/de costumes** there you could find every possible variety *ou* type of criminal/of costume **NFPL variétés** *(Littérat)* miscellanies; *(Music-Hall)* variety show; *(Radio, TV = musique)* light music *(NonC)* ◆ **émission/spectacle/théâtre de ~s** variety programme/show/hall

variole /vaʀjɔl/ **NF** smallpox, variola *(SPÉC)*

variolé, e /vaʀjɔle/ **ADJ** pockmarked

varioleux, -euse /vaʀjɔlø, øz/ **ADJ** suffering from smallpox, variolous *(SPÉC)* **NM** smallpox case, patient suffering from smallpox

variolique /vaʀjɔlik/ **ADJ** smallpox *(épith)*, variolous *(SPÉC)*

variomètre /vaʀjɔmɛtʀ/ **NM** variometer

variqueux, -euse /vaʀikø, øz/ **ADJ** *[ulcère]* varicose

varlope /vaʀlɔp/ **NF** trying-plane

varloper /vaʀlɔpe/ ▸ **conjug 1** ◂ **VT** to plane (down)

Varsovie /vaʀsɔvi/ **N** Warsaw

vasculaire /vaskylɛʀ/ **ADJ** *(Anat, Bot)* vascular ◆ **système ~ sanguin** blood-vascular system

vascularisation /vaskylaʀizasjɔ̃/ **NF** *(= processus)* vascularization; *(= réseau)* vascularity

vascularisé, e /vaskylaʀize/ **ADJ** vascular

vase[1] /vɑz/ **NM** *(à fleurs, décoratif)* vase, bowl ◆ **en ~ clos** *[vivre, croître]* in isolation, cut off from the world, in seclusion; *[étudier, discuter]* behind closed doors; → **goutte**

COMP vases communicants communicating vessels

vase d'expansion expansion bottle *ou* tank

vase de nuit chamber pot

vases sacrés *(Rel)* sacred vessels

vase[2] /vɑz/ **NF** *(= boue)* silt, mud, sludge *(on riverbed)*

vasectomie /vazɛktɔmi/ **NF** vasectomy

vaseline /vaz(ə)lin/ **NF** Vaseline ®, petroleum jelly

vaseux, -euse /vɑzø, øz/ **ADJ** ① *(= boueux)* muddy, silty, sludgy ② *(* = fatigué)* in a daze ◆ **je me sens un peu ~** I'm in a bit of a daze, I feel a bit out of it * ③ * *(= confus) [raisonnement]* woolly, muddled; *[explication]* muddled; *(= médiocre) [astuce, plaisanterie]* pathetic *, lousy *

vasière /vɑzjɛʀ/ **NF** *[de marais salant]* tidal reservoir; *(= fonds vaseux)* (tidal) mud flats; *(= parc à moules)* mussel bed

vasistas /vazistɑs/ **NM** *[de porte]* (opening) window, fanlight; *[de fenêtre]* fanlight

vasoconstricteur /vazokɔ̃stʀiktœʀ/ **ADJ M** vasoconstrictor *(épith)* **NM** vasoconstrictor

vasoconstriction /vazokɔ̃stʀiksjɔ̃/ **NF** vasoconstriction

vasodilatateur /vazodilatatœʀ/ **ADJ M** vasodilator *(épith)* **NM** vasodilator

vasodilatation /vazodilatasjɔ̃/ **NF** vasodil(a-t)ation

vasomoteur, -trice /vazomɔtœʀ, tʀis/ **ADJ** vasomotor *(épith)*

vasouillard, e* /vazujaʀ, aʀd/ **ADJ** *[personne]* in a daze; *[raisonnement]* woolly, muddled; *[explication]* muddled

vasouiller* /vazuje/ ▸ **conjug 1** ◂ **VI** *[personne]* to flounder; *[opération, affaire]* to struggle along, to limp along

vasque /vask/ **NF** *(= bassin, lavabo)* basin; *(= coupe)* bowl

vassal, e (mpl **-aux**) /vasal, o/ **NM,F** *(Hist, fig)* vassal

vassaliser /vasalize/ ▸ **conjug 1** ◂ **VT** *[+ pays]* to reduce to the status of a vassal state

vassalité /vasalite/ **NF**, **vasselage** /vaslaʒ/ **NM** *(Hist, fig)* vassalage

vaste /vast/ **ADJ** ① *(= grand) [surface, bâtiment, salle]* large; *[robe, veste]* loose-fitting; *[poche]* huge; *[pantalon]* baggy ◆ **très ~** *[bâtiment, salle]* vast, huge ◆ **de par le ~ monde** throughout the whole wide world ◆ **il faudrait une salle plus ~ pour accueillir les invités** we need a much larger room to accommodate the guests

② *(= important) [organisation, réseau, mouvement, majorité]* vast, huge; *[projet, domaine, problème]* huge; *[sujet, connaissances, érudition]* vast; *[réforme]* far-reaching, sweeping; *[débat]* wide-ranging; *[campagne d'information]* massive, extensive; *[public]* very wide ◆ **à la tête d'un ~ empire industriel** at the head of a vast *ou* huge industrial empire ◆ **ils ont entamé un ~ programme de réformes** they have started a vast *ou* sweeping programme of reforms ◆ **un homme d'une ~ culture** an extremely cultured man, a man of immense learning ◆ **ce sujet est trop ~** this subject is far too wide *ou* is too vast ◆ **il a de ~s ambitions** he's extremely ambitious ◆ **pourquoi l'ont-ils fait ? – ~ question !** why did they do it? – there's no simple answer to that! ◆ **c'est une ~ rigolade *ou* plaisanterie *ou* fumisterie !** it's a huge *ou* an enormous joke!

> ⚠ **vaste** ne se traduit par le mot anglais **vast** que dans certains contextes.

va-t-en-guerre /vatɑ̃gɛʀ/ **NM INV** warmonger

Vatican /vatikɑ̃/ **NM** ◆ **le ~** the Vatican

vaticane /vatikan/ **ADJ F** *[politique, bibliothèque, grottes]* Vatican

vaticinateur, -trice /vatisinatœʀ, tʀis/ **NM,F** *(littér)* vaticinator *(frm, littér)*

vaticination /vatisinasjɔ̃/ **NF** *(littér)* vaticination *(frm, littér)* ◆ **~s** *(péj)* pompous predictions *ou* prophecies

vaticiner /vatisine/ ▸ **conjug 1** ◂ **VI** *(littér = prophétiser)* to vaticinate *(frm) (littér)*; *(péj)* to make pompous predictions *ou* prophecies

va-tout /vatu/ **NM INV** ◆ **jouer son ~** to stake *ou* risk one's all

Vaud /vo/ **NM** ◆ **le canton de ~** the canton of Vaud

vaudeville /vod(ə)vil/ **NM** vaudeville, light comedy ◆ **ça tourne au ~** it's turning into a farce

vaudevillesque /vod(ə)vilɛsk/ **ADJ** vaudeville *(épith)*; *(fig)* farcical

vaudevilliste /vod(ə)vilist/ **NM** writer of vaudeville

vaudois, e /vodwa, waz/ **ADJ** *(Hist)* Waldensian; *(Géog)* Vaudois, of *ou* from the canton of Vaud **NM,F** *(Hist)* Waldensian ◆ **Vaudois(e)** *(Géog)* Vaudois

vaudou /vodu/ **NM** ◆ **le (culte du) ~** voodoo **ADJ INV** voodoo *(épith)*

vau-l'eau /volo/ **à vau-l'eau LOC ADV** *(lit)* with the stream *ou* current ◆ **aller *ou* s'en aller à ~** *(fig)* to be on the road to ruin, to go to the dogs * ◆ **voilà tous mes projets à ~ !** there are all my plans in ruins! *ou* down the drain! *

vaurien, -ienne /voʀjɛ̃, jɛn/ **NM,F** *(= voyou)* good-for-nothing; *(= garnement)* little devil * ◆ **petit ~ !** little devil! * **NM** *(Naut)* small yacht *ou* sailing boat

vautour /votuʀ/ **NM** *(lit, fig)* vulture

vautrer (se) /votʀe/ ▸ **conjug 1** ◂ **VPR** ① *(= se rouler)* to wallow ◆ **se ~ dans** *[+ boue, vice, obscénité, oisiveté]* to wallow in ◆ **se ~ dans la fange** *(littér)* to wallow in the mire ② *(= s'avachir)* **se ~ dans un fauteuil** to loll *ou* slouch in an armchair ◆ **se ~ sur** *[+ tapis, canapé]* to sprawl on ◆ **vautré à plat ventre *ou* par terre** sprawling *ou* sprawled (flat) on the ground ◆ **vautré dans l'herbe/sur le tapis** sprawling *ou* sprawled in the grass/on the carpet ◆ **il passe ses journées vautré dans le canapé** he spends his days lounging on the sofa ③ *(* = échouer)* **se ~ à un examen** to fall flat on one's face in an exam ◆ **ils se sont vautrés aux élections** they came to grief in the elections

vauvert /vovɛʀ/ → **diable**

vaux /vo/ **NMPL** → **val**

va-vite /vavit/ **à la va-vite * LOC ADV** in a rush *ou* hurry ◆ **faire qch à la ~** to rush sth, to do sth in a rush *ou* hurry

VDQS (abrév de **vin délimité de qualité supérieure**) VDQS *(label guaranteeing quality and origin of wine)*

> **VDQS**
>
> **VDQS**, on a bottle of French wine, indicates that it contains wine from an approved regional vineyard. It is the second highest French wine classification after « AOC », and is followed by « vin de pays ». Unlike the previous categories, « vin de table » or « vin ordinaire » is table wine of unspecified origin, and is often blended. → **AOC**

veau (pl **veaux**) /vo/ **NM** ① *(= animal)* calf ◆ **~ marin** seal ◆ **le Veau d'or** *(Bible)* the golden calf ◆ **adorer le Veau d'or** to worship Mammon ◆ **tuer le ~ gras** to kill the fatted calf ◆ **~ de lait *ou* (élevé) sous la mère** suckling calf; → **pleurer** ② *(Culin)* veal ◆ **escalope/côte de ~** veal escalope/chop ◆ **foie/pied/tête de ~** calf's liver/foot/head ◆ **rôti de ~** roast veal; → **marengo** ③ *(= cuir)* calfskin; → **velours** ④ *(* : péj) (= personne)* sheep; *(= cheval)* nag *(péj)*; *(= automobile)* tank * *(péj)*

vécés* /vese/ **NMPL** ◆ **les ~** the toilet

vecteur /vɛktœʀ/ **ADJ M** *(Astron, Géom)* ◆ **rayon ~** radius vector **NM** *(Math)* vector; *(Mil = véhicule)* carrier; *(Bio) [de virus]* carrier, vector *(SPÉC)*; *(fig)* vehicle, medium ◆ **~ glissant** *(Math)* sliding vector ◆ **les médias, ~s de l'information** the media, conveyor *ou* carrier of information

vectoriel, -elle /vɛktɔʀjɛl/ **ADJ** *[espace, produit, fonction, image, ordinateur]* vector *(épith)* ◆ **calcul ~** vector analysis

vectoriser /vɛktɔʀize/ ▸ **conjug 1** ◂ **VT** *(Ordin)* to vectorize

vécu, e /veky/ (ptp de **vivre**) **ADJ** *[histoire, aventure]* real(-life) *(épith)*, true(-life) *(épith)*; *[roman]* real-life *(épith)*, based on fact *(attrib)*; *(Philos) [temps, durée]* lived ◆ **échec mal ~** failure that is hard to come to terms with ♦ **un licenciement mal ~ peut mener à une dépression** redundancy can lead to depression if the person cannot come to terms with it NM ♦ **le ~** (real-life) experience ♦ **ce que le lecteur veut, c'est du ~** what the reader wants is real-life experience ♦ **c'est une argumentation basée sur le ~** it's an argument based on actual experience ♦ **il essaie de capturer le ~ de ces SDF** he tries to capture the day-to-day life of these homeless people

vedettariat /vədetaʀja/ NM (= *état*) stardom; (= *vedettes*) stars

vedette /vədɛt/ NF 1 (= *artiste, personnage en vue*) star ♦ **les ~s de l'écran/du cinéma** screen/film stars ♦ **une ~ de la politique** a leading figure *ou* a big name in politics ♦ **joueur ~** star *ou* top player ♦ **mannequin ~** top model ♦ **présentateur ~** star presenter ♦ **produit-~** (*fig*) leading product, flagship product ♦ **l'émission ~ d'une chaîne** the flagship (programme) of a channel ♦ **valeurs** *ou* **titres ~s** (*Bourse*) leaders

2 (*Ciné, Théât* = *première place*) **avoir la ~** to top the bill, to have star billing ♦ **avoir** *ou* **tenir la ~ (de l'actualité)** (*fig*) to be in the spotlight, to make the headlines ♦ **pendant toute la soirée, il a eu la ~** (*fig*) he was in the limelight *ou* was the centre of attraction all evening ♦ **avec, en ~, Lulu** [*film, pièce*] starring Lulu; [*concert, gala*] with Lulu as top of the bill ♦ **mettre qn en ~** (*Ciné, Théât*) to give sb star billing; (*fig*) to push sb into the limelight, to put the spotlight on sb ♦ **partager la ~ avec qn** (*Ciné, Théât*) to share star billing with sb, to top the bill alongside sb; (*fig*) to share the limelight *ou* spotlight with sb ♦ **il passe en ~ américaine** he's the support (act) ♦ **ravir la ~ à qn** (*fig*) to steal the show from sb ♦ **jouer les ~s*** to act like a star

3 (= *embarcation*) launch; (*Mil*) patrol boat; (= *munie de canons*) gun boat ♦ **~ lance-torpilles** motor torpedo boat ♦ **~ lance-missiles** missile-carrying launch

4 (†† *Mil* = *guetteur*) sentinel

vedettisation /vədetizasjɔ̃/ NF ♦ **la ~ de qn** pushing sb into the limelight, putting the spotlight on sb

védique /vedik/ ADJ, NM Vedic

védisme /vedism/ NM Vedaism

végétal, e (mpl **-aux**) /veʒetal, o/ ADJ [*graisses, teintures, huiles*] vegetable (*épith*); [*biologie, histologie, fibres, cellules*] plant (*épith*); [*sol*] rich in humus; [*ornementation*] plant-like; → **règne** NM vegetable, plant

végétalien, -ienne /veʒetaljɛ̃, jɛn/ ADJ, NM,F vegan

végétalisme /veʒetalism/ NM veganism

végétarien, -ienne /veʒetaʀjɛ̃, jɛn/ ADJ, NM,F vegetarian

végétarisme /veʒetaʀism/ NM vegetarianism

végétatif, -ive /veʒetatif, iv/ ADJ (*Bot, Physiol*) vegetative ♦ **vie végétative** (*Méd*) vegetative state; (*péj*) vegetable-like existence

végétation /veʒetasjɔ̃/ NF 1 (*Bot*) vegetation 2 (*Méd*) **~s (adénoïdes)** adenoids ♦ **se faire opérer des ~s** to have one's adenoids removed *ou* out*

végéter /veʒete/ ► conjug 6 ◄ VI 1 (*péj*) [*personne*] to vegetate; [*affaire*] to stagnate 2 (*Agr*) (= *être chétif*) to grow poorly, to be stunted; († = *pousser*) to grow, to vegetate

véhémence /veemɑ̃s/ NF (*littér*) vehemence ♦ **la ~ de ses propos** the vehemence of his words ♦ **avec ~** [*protester, refuser, dénoncer*] vehemently ♦ **plaider avec ~ en faveur de** *ou* **pour qch** to make a passionate plea for sth

véhément, e /veemɑ̃, ɑ̃t/ ADJ (*littér*) vehement ♦ **d'un ton ~** vehemently

véhémentement /veemɑ̃tmɑ̃/ ADV (*littér*) vehemently

véhiculaire /veikylɛʀ/ ADJ ♦ **langue ~** lingua franca, common language

véhicule /veikyl/ NM 1 (= *moyen de transport, agent de transmission*) vehicle ♦ **~ automobile/utilitaire/industriel** motor/commercial/industrial vehicle ♦ **~ léger** light vehicle ♦ **~ spatial** spacecraft 2 (*fig*) vehicle, medium ♦ **le langage est le ~ de la pensée** language is the vehicle *ou* medium of thought 3 (*Rel*) **petit/grand ~** Hinayana/Mahayana Buddhism 4 (*Pharm*) vehicle

véhiculer /veikyle/ ► conjug 1 ◄ VT [+ *marchandises, troupes*] to convey, to transport; [+ *substance, idées*] to convey, to serve as a vehicle for; [+ *information, images*] to convey; [+ *virus*] to carry

veille /vɛj/ NF 1 (= *état*) wakefulness; (= *période*) period of wakefulness ♦ **en état de ~** in a waking state, awake ♦ **entre la ~ et le sommeil** between waking and sleeping ♦ **nuit de ~** (*sans dormir*) sleepless night

♦ **en veille** [*machine, ordinateur*] in sleep mode; [*téléphone portable*] in standby mode

2 (= *garde*) (night) watch ♦ **homme de ~** (night) watch ♦ **prendre la ~** to take one's turn on watch ♦ **nuit de ~** (*en montant la garde*) night on watch; (*auprès d'un malade*) all-night vigil ♦ **faire de la ~ technologique** to monitor technological development

3 (= *jour précédent*) **la ~** the day before ♦ **la ~ au soir** the previous evening, the night *ou* evening before ♦ **la ~ de Pâques/de l'examen** the day before Easter/the exam ♦ **la ~ de Noël/du jour de l'an** Christmas/New Year's Eve ♦ **la ~ de sa mort** on the eve of his death, on the day before his death; → **demain**

♦ **à la veille de** on the eve of ♦ **tu es à la ~ de commettre une grave injustice/une grosse erreur** you are on the brink *ou* verge of committing a grave injustice/of making a big mistake ♦ **ils étaient à la ~ d'être renvoyés/de manquer de vivres** they were on the point of being dismissed/of running out of supplies

veillée /veje/ NF 1 (= *période*) evening (*spent in company*); (= *réunion*) evening gathering *ou* meeting ♦ **faire une ~ autour d'un feu de camp** to spend the evening around a campfire ♦ **il se souvient de ces ~s d'hiver** he remembers those winter evening gatherings ♦ **~ d'armes** (*Hist*) knightly vigil ♦ **il régnait une ambiance de ~ d'armes** it felt like the night before a battle 2 [*de malade*] vigil ♦ **~ funèbre** wake, funeral vigil ♦ **~ pascale** Easter vigil ♦ **~ de prières** prayer vigil

veiller /veje/ ► conjug 1 ◄ VI 1 (= *ne pas se coucher*) to stay up, to sit up ♦ **~ tard** to stay *ou* sit up late ♦ **~ au chevet d'un malade** to sit up *ou* keep a vigil at the bedside of a sick person ♦ **~ auprès du mort** to keep watch *ou* vigil over the body

2 (= *être de garde*) to be on watch; (= *rester vigilant*) to be watchful, to be vigilant

3 (= *être en état de veille*) to be awake

4 (= *faire la veillée*) to spend the evening in company

VT [+ *mort, malade*] to watch over, to sit up with

VT INDIR 1 ♦ **~ à** [+ *intérêts, approvisionnement*] to attend to, to see to, to look after ♦ **~ au bon fonctionnement d'une machine** to make sure a machine is working properly ♦ **~ à ce que ...** to see to it that ..., to make sure that ... ♦ **veillez à ce que tout soit prêt** make sure that *ou* ensure that everything is ready ♦ **~ au grain** (*fig*) to keep an eye open for trouble *ou* problems, to look out for squalls (*fig*)

2 ♦ **~ sur** [+ *personne, santé, bonheur de qn*] to watch over, to keep a watchful eye on; [+ *trésor, lieu*] to watch over, to guard

VPR **se veiller** (*Helv*) to be careful

veilleur /vɛjœʀ/ NM 1 ♦ **~ (de nuit)** (night) watchman 2 (*Mil*) look-out

veilleuse /vɛjøz/ NF 1 (= *lampe*) night light; (*Aut*) sidelight ♦ **mettre en ~** [+ *lampe*] to dim; [+ *projet*] to put on the back burner ♦ **mettre ses phares** *ou* **se mettre en ~s** (= *allumer*) to put one's sidelights on; (= *baisser*) to switch to sidelights ♦ **mets-la en ~ !*** (= *tais-toi !*) shut your face!*, put a sock in it!* (*Brit*); (= *du calme !*) cool it!* 2 (= *flamme*) pilot light

veinard, e* /vɛnaʀ, aʀd/ ADJ lucky, jammy* (*Brit*) NM,F lucky devil* *ou* dog*, jammy so-and-so* (*Brit*)

veine /vɛn/ NF 1 (*Anat*) vein ♦ **~ coronaire/pulmonaire** coronary/pulmonary vein ♦ **~ cave** vena cava ♦ **~ porte** portal vein; → **ouvrir, saigner, sang**

2 (= *nervure*) vein; (= *filon*) [*de houille*] seam, vein; [*de minerai non ferreux*] vein; [*de minerai de fer*] lode, vein

3 (= *inspiration*) inspiration ♦ **~ poétique/dramatique** poetic/dramatic inspiration ♦ **sa ~ est tarie** his inspiration has dried up ♦ **de la même ~** in the same vein ♦ **être en ~** to be inspired ♦ **être en ~ de patience/bonté/confidences** to be in a patient/benevolent/confiding mood *ou* frame of mind

4 (* = *chance*) luck ♦ **c'est une ~** that's a bit of luck, what a bit of luck ♦ **c'est une ~ que ...** it's lucky that ... ♦ **un coup de ~** a stroke of luck ♦ **pas de ~ !** hard *ou* bad *ou* rotten* luck! ♦ **avoir de la ~** to be lucky ♦ **il n'a pas de ~** (*dans la vie*) he has no luck; (*aujourd'hui*) he's out of luck ♦ **ce type a de la ~** he's a lucky devil* *ou* dog* ♦ **avoir une ~ de cocu*** *ou* **pendu*** to have the luck of the devil* ♦ **il a eu de la ~ aux examens** he was lucky *ou* in luck at the exams, his luck was in at the exams ♦ **il n'a pas eu de ~ aux examens** he was unlucky in the exams, his luck was out at the exams ♦ **c'est bien ma ~ !** (*iro*) that's just my luck!

veiné, e /vene/ (ptp de **veiner**) ADJ 1 [*bras, peau*] veined, veiny ♦ **bras à la peau ~e** veiny arm 2 [*bois*] grained; [*marbre*] veined ♦ **marbre ~ de vert** marble with green veins, green-veined marble

veiner /vene/ ► conjug 1 ◄ VT (*aspect du bois*) to grain; (*aspect du marbre*) to vein ♦ **les stries qui veinent le marbre** the veins that can be seen in marble ♦ **les nervures qui veinent une feuille** the pattern of veins on a leaf

veineux, -euse /venø, øz/ ADJ 1 [*système, sang*] venous 2 [*bois*] grainy; [*marbre*] veined

veinotonique /venɔtɔnik/ ADJ ♦ **traitement ~** treatment using a vein tonic NM vein tonic

veinule /venyl/ NF (*Anat*) veinlet, venule (*SPÉC*); (*Bot*) venule

veinure /venyʀ/ NF [*de bois*] graining; [*de pierre*] veining ♦ **la ~ du marbre** the veins *ou* veining of the marble

vêlage /vɛlaʒ/ NM [*d'animal, iceberg*] calving

vélaire /velɛʀ/ ADJ, NF ♦ **(consonne/voyelle) ~** velar (consonant/vowel)

vélarisation /velaʀizasjɔ̃/ NF velarization

vélariser /velaʀize/ ► conjug 1 ◄ VT to velarize

Velcro ® /vɛlkʀo/ NM Velcro ® ♦ **bande/fermeture ~** Velcro strip/fastening

veld(t) /vɛlt/ NM veld(t)

vêlement /vɛlmɑ̃/ NM ⇒ **vêlage**

vêler /vele/ ► conjug 1 ◄ VI to calve

vélin /velɛ̃/ NM (= *peau*) vellum ♦ **(papier) ~** vellum (paper)

véliplanchiste /veliplɑ̃ʃist/ NMF windsurfer

vélite /velit/ NM (*Hist*) velite

velléitaire /veleitɛʀ/ ADJ irresolute, indecisive, wavering *(épith)* NMF waverer

velléité /veleite/ NF vague desire, vague impulse ◆ **ces mesures ont découragé toute ~ de changement** these measures have discouraged any thought of change ◆ **il a des ~s de carrière littéraire** he has a vague desire to take up a literary career

vélo /velo/ NM bike, cycle ◆ **~ de course** racing bike *ou* cycle, racer ◆ **~ d'appartement** exercise bike ◆ **~ tout-chemin** hybrid bike ◆ **~ tout-terrain** mountain bike ◆ **faire du ~ tout-terrain** to go mountain-biking ◆ **~-cross** *(= sport)* stunt-riding; *(= vélo)* stunt bike ◆ **faire du ~-cross** to go stunt-riding ◆ **~ couché** recumbent (bicycle) ◆ **être à** *ou* **en ~** to be on a bike ◆ **venir à** *ou* **en ~** to come by bike *ou* on a bike ◆ **il sait faire du ~** he can ride a bike ◆ **je fais beaucoup de ~** I cycle a lot, I do a lot of cycling ◆ **on va faire un peu de ~** we're going out (for a ride) on our bikes ◆ **à cinq ans, il allait déjà à ~** he could already ride a bike at five ◆ **on y va à** *ou* **en ~ ?** shall we go by bike? *ou* on our bikes?, shall we cycle there? ◆ **il a un (petit) ~ dans la tête** * he's got a screw loose *, he isn't all there *

véloce /velɔs/ ADJ *(littér)* swift, fleet *(littér)*

vélocipède †† /velɔsipɛd/ NM velocipede

vélociraptor /velɔsiʀaptɔʀ/ NM velociraptor

vélocité /velɔsite/ NF 1 *(Mus)* nimbleness, swiftness ◆ **exercices de ~** five-finger exercises 2 *(Tech)* velocity; *(littér = vitesse)* swiftness, fleetness *(littér)*

vélodrome /velodʀom/ NM velodrome

vélomoteur /velɔmɔtœʀ/ NM moped

vélomotoriste /velɔmɔtɔʀist/ NMF moped rider

véloski /veloski/ NM skibob

velours /v(ə)luʀ/ NM 1 *(= tissu)* velvet ◆ **~ de coton/de laine** cotton/wool velvet ◆ **~ côtelé** *ou* **à côtes** corduroy, cord ◆ **~ frappé** crushed velvet ◆ **il joue sur du ~** *(fig)* he's sitting pretty *; → **main** 2 *(= velouté)* velvet ◆ **le ~ de la pêche** the bloom of the peach ◆ **le ~ de sa joue** the velvety texture of her cheek, her velvet(y) cheek ◆ **voix/yeux/peau de ~** velvet(y) voice/eyes/skin ◆ **ce potage/cette crème est un vrai ~** this soup/this cream dessert is velvety-smooth ◆ **agneau/veau ~** (lambskin)/(calfskin) suede; → **œil, patte[1]**

velouté, e /vəlute/ (ptp de **velouter**) ADJ 1 *[tissu]* brushed; *(à motifs)* with a raised velvet pattern 2 *(= doux) [joues]* velvet *(épith)*, velvety, velvet-smooth; *[pêche]* velvety, downy; *[crème, potage, vin]* smooth, velvety; *[lumière, regard]* soft, mellow; *[voix]* velvet-smooth, mellow NM 1 *(= douceur) [de joues]* smoothness; *[de pêche]* smoothness, downiness; *[de lumière, regard]* softness; *[de voix]* mellowness 2 *(Culin) (= sauce)* velouté sauce; *(= potage)* velouté ◆ **~ de tomates/d'asperges** cream of tomato/asparagus soup

velouter /vəlute/ ▸ conjug 1 ◂ VT 1 *[+ papier]* to put a velvety finish on 2 *[+ joues, pêche]* to give a velvet(y) texture to; *[+ vin, crème, potage]* to make smooth; *[+ lumière, regard]* to soften, to mellow; *[+ voix]* to mellow ◆ **le duvet qui veloutait ses joues** the down that gave a velvet softness to her cheeks VPR **se velouter** *[joues, pêche]* to take on a velvety texture; *[regard]* to soften; *[voix]* to mellow

velouteux, -euse /vəlutø, øz/ ADJ velvet-like, velvety

Velpeau ® /vɛlpo/ NM → **bande[1]**

velu, e /vəly/ ADJ *[main, poitrine, homme]* hairy; *[plante]* hairy, villous *(SPÉC)*

velum, vélum /velɔm/ NM canopy

Vélux ® /velyks/ NM skylight, Velux window ®

venaison /vənɛzɔ̃/ NF venison

vénal, e (mpl **-aux**) /venal, o/ ADJ 1 *[personne]* venal, mercenary; *[activité, amour]* venal 2 *(Hist) [office]* venal; → **valeur**

vénalité /venalite/ NF venality

vendable /vɑ̃dabl/ ADJ saleable, marketable ◆ **ces produits seront difficilement ~s** these products will be difficult to sell

vendange /vɑ̃dɑ̃ʒ/ NF *(parfois pl = récolte)* wine harvest, grape harvest *ou* picking; *(= raisins récoltés)* grapes (harvested), grape crop; *(gén pl = période)* grape harvest *ou* picking (time) ◆ **pendant les ~s** during the grape harvest *ou* picking (time) ◆ **faire la ~** *ou* **les ~s** to harvest *ou* pick the grapes ◆ **~ tardive** late harvest

vendangeoir /vɑ̃dɑ̃ʒwaʀ/ NM grape-picker's basket

vendanger /vɑ̃dɑ̃ʒe/ ▸ conjug 3 ◂ VT *[+ vigne]* to gather *ou* pick *ou* harvest grapes from; *[+ raisins]* to pick, to harvest VI *(= faire la vendange)* to pick *ou* harvest the grapes; *(= presser le raisin)* to press the grapes

vendangeur, -euse /vɑ̃dɑ̃ʒœʀ, øz/ NM,F grape-picker NF **vendangeuse** *(= machine)* grape harvester; *(= plante)* aster

Vendée /vɑ̃de/ NF ◆ **la ~** the Vendée ◆ **les guerres de ~** *pro-royalist uprising in the Vendée during the French revolution*

vendéen, -enne /vɑ̃deɛ̃, ɛn/ ADJ of *ou* from the Vendée NM,F **Vendéen(ne)** inhabitant *ou* native of the Vendée

vendémiaire /vɑ̃demjɛʀ/ NM Vendémiaire *(1st month of French Republican calendar)*

venderesse /vɑ̃dʀɛs/ NF *(Jur)* vendor

vendetta /vɑ̃deta/ NF vendetta

vendeur, -euse /vɑ̃dœʀ, øz/ NM,F 1 *(dans un magasin)* shop assistant *(Brit)*, salesclerk *(US)*; *(dans un grand magasin)* sales assistant, salesman, shop assistant *(Brit)* ◆ **"cherchons 2 vendeurs, rayon librairie"** "2 sales assistants required for our book department"

2 *(= marchand)* seller, salesman ◆ **~ ambulant** street peddler ◆ **~ de journaux** newsvendor, newspaper seller ◆ **~ à domicile** door-to-door salesman; → **sauvette**

3 *(= chargé des ventes)* salesman ◆ **c'est un excellent ~** he's an excellent salesman, he has a flair for selling

4 *(Jur)* vendor, seller; *(Écon)* seller ◆ **je ne suis pas ~** I'm not selling ◆ **il serait ~** he'd be ready *ou* willing to sell ◆ **les pays ~s de cacao** the cocoa-selling countries

NF **vendeuse** 1 *(dans un magasin)* shop assistant *(Brit)*, salesclerk *(US)*; *(dans un grand magasin)* sales assistant, saleswoman, shop assistant *(Brit)*; *(jeune)* salesgirl

2 *(= marchande)* seller, saleswoman ◆ **vendeuse de glaces** ice-cream seller

ADJ *[slogan]* effective

vendre /vɑ̃dʀ/ ▸ conjug 41 ◂ VT 1 *[+ marchandise, valeurs]* to sell *(à* to*)*; ◆ **~ qch à qn** to sell sb sth, to sell sth to sb ◆ **~ au détail/au poids/au mètre/au kilo** to sell retail/by weight/by the metre/by the kilo ◆ **elle vend des foulards à 75 €** she sells scarves for *ou* at €75 ◆ **il m'a vendu un tableau 500 €** he sold me a picture for €500 ◆ **l'art de ~** salesmanship, the art of selling ◆ **elle vend cher** her prices are high, she's expensive ◆ **ces affiches publicitaires font ~** these advertising posters get things sold *ou* are boosting sales ◆ **~ qch aux enchères** to sell sth by auction ◆ **~ sa part d'une affaire** to sell (out) one's share of a business ◆ **"(maison/terrain) à vendre"** "(house/land) for sale" ◆ **~ son droit d'aînesse pour un plat de lentilles** *(Bible)* to sell one's birthright for a mess of potage; → **perte, prix** *etc*

2 *(péj) [+ droit, charge]* to sell ◆ **~ son âme/honneur** to sell one's soul/honour ◆ **~ son silence** to be paid for one's silence ◆ **il vendrait père et mère pour réussir/pour ce tableau** he would sell his grandmother to succeed/for this picture

3 *(= faire payer)* **ils nous ont vendu très cher ce droit/cet avantage** they made us pay dear *ou* dearly for this right/this advantage ◆ **~ chèrement sa vie** *ou* **sa peau** * to sell one's life *ou* one's skin dearly

4 *(* = trahir) [+ personne, complice]* to sell

5 *(locutions)* **~ la peau de l'ours (avant de l'avoir tué)** to count one's chickens (before they are hatched); → **mèche**

VPR **se vendre** 1 *[marchandise]* to sell, to be sold ◆ **se ~ à la pièce/douzaine** to be sold singly/by the dozen ◆ **ça se vend bien** it sells well ◆ **ses romans se vendent comme des petits pains** his novels are selling like hot cakes ◆ **ouvrage/auteur qui se vend bien** work/author that sells well

2 *[personne] (aussi péj)* to sell o.s. ◆ **se ~ à un parti/l'ennemi** to sell o.s. to a party/the enemy

vendredi /vɑ̃dʀədi/ NM Friday ◆ **Vendredi** *(= personnage de Robinson Crusoé)* Man Friday ◆ **c'était un ~ treize** it was Friday the thirteenth; *pour autres loc voir* **samedi**

vendu, e /vɑ̃dy/ (ptp de **vendre**) ADJ *[fonctionnaire, juge]* corrupt; → **adjuger** NM *(péj)* Judas, mercenary traitor

venelle /vənɛl/ NF alley

vénéneux, -euse /venenø, øz/ ADJ *[plante, champignon, fleur]* poisonous; *(littér) [charme, beauté]* deadly; *[idée, plaisir]* pernicious, harmful

vénérable /veneʀabl/ ADJ *(littér, hum = respectable)* venerable ◆ **(d'un âge) ~** *(hum = très vieux) [personne, chose]* venerable, ancient NM *(Rel)* Venerable; *(Franc-Maçonnerie)* Worshipful Master

vénération /veneʀasjɔ̃/ NF *(Rel)* veneration; *(gén = grande estime)* veneration, reverence ◆ **avoir de la ~ pour qn** to venerate *ou* revere sb

vénérer /veneʀe/ ▸ conjug 6 ◂ VT *(Rel)* to venerate; *(gén)* to venerate, to revere

vénère ‡ /venɛʀ/ ADJ ◆ **j'étais ~!** I was so pissed off! ‡

vénerie /vɛnʀi/ NF 1 *(= art)* venery *(SPÉC)*, hunting 2 *(= administration)* **la ~** the Hunt

vénérien, -ienne /veneʀjɛ̃, jɛn/ ADJ 1 *(Méd)* venereal; → **maladie** 2 *(†† = sexuel)* venereal †, sexual NM *(= malade)* VD patient, person with VD *ou* venereal disease

vénérologie /veneʀɔlɔʒi/ NF venereology

vénérologue /veneʀɔlɔg/ NMF venereologist

Vénétie /venesi/ NF Venetia

veneur /vənœʀ/ NM *(Hist)* huntsman, venerer † ◆ **grand ~** master of the royal hounds ◆ **sauce grand ~** grand veneur sauce *(made with redcurrant jelly and wine)*

Venezuela /venezɥela/ NM Venezuela

vénézuélien, -ienne /venezɥeljɛ̃, jɛn/ ADJ Venezuelan NM,F **Vénézuélien(ne)** Venezuelan

vengeance /vɑ̃ʒɑ̃s/ NF revenge, vengeance ◆ **soif/désir de ~** thirst/desire for revenge *ou* vengeance ◆ **tirer ~ de qch** to get revenge for sth ◆ **exercer sa ~ sur** to take (one's) revenge on ◆ **préparer sa ~ contre qn** to plan (one's) revenge on sb ◆ **crier ~** to cry out for revenge *ou* vengeance ◆ **agir par ~** to act out of revenge ◆ **assouvir une ~ personnelle** to satisfy a desire for personal revenge ◆ **de petites ~s** petty acts of revenge *ou* vengeance ◆ **la ~ divine** divine retribution *ou* vengeance ◆ **ma ~ sera terrible !** *(hum)* my revenge will be terrible! ◆ **la ~ est un plat qui se mange froid** *(Prov)* revenge is a dish best eaten cold *(Prov)*

venger /vɑ̃ʒe/ ▸ conjug 3 ◂ **VT** 1 *[+ personne, honneur, mémoire]* to avenge *(de* for) 2 *[+ injustice, affront]* to avenge ◆ **rien ne vengera cette injustice** nothing will avenge this injustice, there is no revenge for this injustice **VPR** **se venger** to avenge o.s., to take (one's) revenge *ou* vengeance ◆ **se ~ de qn** to take revenge *ou* vengeance on sb, to get one's own back on sb ◆ **se ~ de qch** to avenge o.s. for sth, to take one's revenge for sth ◆ **il l'a fait pour se ~** he did it out of revenge ◆ **je me vengerai** I shall get *ou* have *ou* take my revenge, I shall be avenged ◆ **je n'ai pas pris de fromage mais je me vengerai sur les fruits** I haven't had any cheese but I'll make up for it with the fruit

vengeur, -geresse /vɑ̃ʒœʀ, ʒ(ə)ʀɛs/ **ADJ** *[personne, geste, lettre]* vengeful **NM,F** avenger

véniel, -elle /venjɛl/ **ADJ** *[faute, oubli]* venial *(littér)*, pardonable, excusable; → **péché**

venimeux, -euse /vənimø, øz/ **ADJ** 1 *(lit) [serpent, piqûre]* venomous, poisonous 2 *[personne, voix]* venomous, vicious; *[remarque, haine]* venomous, vicious ◆ **une langue venimeuse** a poisonous *ou* venomous *ou* vicious tongue

venin /vənɛ̃/ **NM** 1 *[d'animal]* venom, poison ◆ **~ de serpent** snake venom ◆ **crochets à ~** poison fangs 2 *(fig)* venom, viciousness ◆ **jeter** *ou* **cracher son ~** to spit out one's venom ◆ **répandre son ~ contre qn** to pour out one's venom against sb ◆ **paroles pleines de ~** venomous words, words full of venom *ou* viciousness

venir /v(ə)niʀ/

▸ conjug 22 ◂

1 VERBE INTRANSITIF	3 VERBE IMPERSONNEL
2 VERBE AUXILIAIRE	4 VERBE PRONOMINAL

1 - VERBE INTRANSITIF

1 [dans l'espace] to come ◆ **je viens !** I'm coming! ◆ **venez ! venez !** come on! come on! ◆ **viens voir !** come and see! ◆ **je viens dans un instant** I'll be there in a moment ◆ **quand doit-il ~ ?** when is he coming? ◆ **comment est-il venu ? – en avion/en voiture** how did he get here? – by plane/by car ◆ **le voisin est venu** the man from next door came round *ou* called ◆ **il est venu à moi pour me demander si ...** he came to ask me if ... ◆ **il ne vient jamais aux réunions** he never comes to meetings ◆ **il vient chez nous tous les jeudis** he comes (round) to our house every Thursday ◆ **il venait sur nous l'air furieux** he bore down on us looking furious ◆ **le camion venait droit sur nous** the lorry was coming straight at us *ou* heading straight for us *ou* was bearing down on us ◆ **il vint vers moi** he came up to *ou* towards me; → **monde**

◆ **faire venir** *[+ médecin, plombier]* to send for, to call ◆ **le patron l'a fait ~ dans son bureau** the boss called him into his office ◆ **tu nous as fait ~ pour rien** you got us to come *ou* you made us come for nothing ◆ **il fait ~ son vin de Provence** he has *ou* gets his wine sent from Provence ◆ **on va prendre l'apéritif, ça les fera peut-être ~** *(hum)* let's have a drink, then they'll turn up ◆ **ferme la fenêtre, tu vas faire ~ les moustiques** shut the window or you'll attract the mosquitoes *ou* bring in the mosquitoes

◆ **venir à** *ou* **jusqu'à** + *nom (= atteindre) (vers le haut)* to come up to, to reach (up to); *(vers le bas)* to come down to, to reach (down to); *(en longueur, en superficie)* to come to, to reach ◆ **l'eau nous venait aux genoux** the water came up to our knees, we were knee-deep in water ◆ **il me vient à l'épaule** he comes up to my shoulder ◆ **la forêt vient jusqu'à la route** the forest comes right up to the road

◆ **venir de** *(provenance, cause)* to come from; *(Ling)* to derive from ◆ **ils viennent de Paris** *(en voyage)* they're coming from Paris; *(origine)* they come *ou* are from Paris ◆ **ce produit vient du Maroc** this product comes from Morocco ◆ **l'épée lui vient de son oncle** *(il l'a reçue en cadeau)* he got the sword from his uncle; *(il en a hérité)* the sword was passed down to him by his uncle ◆ **ces troubles viennent du foie** this trouble comes *ou* stems from the liver ◆ **cette substance vient d'un coquillage** this substance comes from shellfish ◆ **ceci vient de son imprudence** this is the result of his carelessness, this comes from his being careless ◆ **d'où vient que ... ?** how is it that ...?, what is the reason that ...? ◆ **de là vient que ...** the result of this is that ... ◆ **d'où vient cette hâte soudaine ?** why the hurry all of a sudden? ◆ **ça vient de ce que ...** it comes *ou* results *ou* stems from the fact that ...

2 [= se débloquer, se détacher] **j'ai tiré et la poignée est venue toute seule** I pulled the handle and it just came off in my hands ◆ **une fois que tu as mouillé le papier peint, ça vient tout seul** once you've dampened the wallpaper, it comes off all by itself

3 [= arriver, survenir] to come ◆ **quand l'aube vint** when dawn came ◆ **la nuit vient vite** night is coming (on) fast ◆ **ceci vient à point/mal à propos** this has come (along) just at the right/wrong moment ◆ **les idées ne viennent pas** I'm short of ideas ◆ **une idée m'est venue (à l'esprit)** I had an idea, something occurred to me ◆ **l'idée lui est venue de ...** it occurred to him to ... ◆ **ça ne me serait pas venu à l'idée** *ou* **à l'esprit** that would never have occurred to me *ou* entered my head, I would never have thought of that ◆ **dis le premier mot qui te vient à l'esprit** say the first word that comes into your head ◆ **le bruit est venu jusqu'à nous que ...** word has reached us *ou* come to us that ... ◆ **comment est-il venu au sport/à la religion ?** *[personne]* how did he (first) come to sport/religion? ◆ **il ne sait pas encore nager, mais ça va ~** he can't swim yet, but it'll come ◆ **ça vient ?** *(impatience)* come on! ◆ **alors ce dossier, ça vient ?** so when's that file going to be ready?, how much longer have I got to wait for that file? ◆ **et ma bière ? – ça vient !** where's my beer? – it's coming!; → **tout, voir**

4 [dans le temps, dans une série] to come ◆ **ça vient avant/après** it comes before/after ◆ **le moment viendra où ...** the time will come when ... ◆ **l'heure est venue** *ou* **le moment est venu d'agir/de changer** the time has come to act *ou* for action/to change *ou* for change ◆ **la semaine/l'année qui vient** the coming week/year ◆ **samedi qui vient** this Saturday, next Saturday; → aussi **venu**

◆ **à venir** ◆ **les années/générations à ~** the years/generations to come, future years/generations ◆ **nous le saurons dans les jours/les mois à ~** we'll know in the next few days/months

5 [= pousser] **cette plante vient bien dans un sol argileux** this plant does well in a clayey soil

6 [locutions]

◆ **en venir à** ◆ **j'en viens maintenant à votre question/à cet aspect du problème** I shall now come *ou* turn to your question/to that aspect of the problem ◆ **venons-en au fait** let's get to the point ◆ **j'en viens à la conclusion que ...** I have come to *ou* reached the conclusion that ..., I'm coming to the conclusion that ... ◆ **en ~ aux mains** *ou* **aux coups** to come to blows ◆ **où voulez-vous en ~ ?** what are you getting *ou* driving at? ◆ **j'en viens à me demander si ...** I'm beginning to wonder if ... ◆ **il en est venu à mendier** he was reduced to begging, he had to resort to begging ◆ **il en est venu à haïr ses parents** he has come to hate his parents, he has got to the stage where he hates his parents ◆ **comment les choses en sont-elles venues là ?** how did things come to this? *ou* get into this state? ◆ **il faudra bien en ~ là** that's what it'll come to in the end

◆ **y venir** ◆ **il y viendra, mais ne le brusquez pas** he'll come round to it *ou* to the idea, but don't rush him ◆ **il faudra bien qu'il y vienne** he'll just have to get used to it ◆ **et le budget ? – j'y viens** and the budget? – I'm coming *ou* getting to that ◆ **viens-y !** *(menace)* just (you) come here! ◆ **qu'il y vienne !** *(menace)* just let him come!

2 - VERBE AUXILIAIRE

◆ **venir** + *infinitif (= se déplacer pour)* ◆ **je suis venu travailler** I have come to work ◆ **il va ~ la voir** he's going to come to *ou* and see her ◆ **viens m'aider** come and help me ◆ **elle doit ~ passer une semaine chez nous** she's coming to spend a week with us ◆ **après cela ne viens pas te plaindre !** and don't (you) come and complain *ou* come complaining afterwards!

◆ **venir de** + *infinitif (passé récent)* ◆ **il vient d'arriver** he has just arrived ◆ **elle venait de se lever** she had just got up

◆ **venir à** + *infinitif* ◆ **s'il venait à mourir** if he were to die, if he should die ◆ **s'il venait à passer par là** if he should (happen *ou* chance to) go that way ◆ **quand l'eau vint à manquer** when the water started running out ◆ **vint à passer un officier** an officer happened to pass by

3 - VERBE IMPERSONNEL

1 [= arriver, survenir] **il vient beaucoup d'enfants** a lot of children are coming, there are a lot of children coming ◆ **il lui est venu des boutons*** he came out in spots ◆ **il ne lui viendrait pas à l'idée** *ou* **à l'esprit que j'ai besoin d'aide** it wouldn't occur to him *ou* enter his head *ou* cross his mind that I might need help ◆ **il m'est venu un doute** I had a doubt

2 [temps] **il vient un moment/une heure où ...** the time/the hour comes when ...

3 [éventualité] **s'il vient à pleuvoir/neiger** if it should (happen to) rain/snow

4 - VERBE PRONOMINAL

s'en venir († *ou littér = venir)* to come, to approach ◆ **il s'en venait tranquillement** he was approaching unhurriedly ◆ **il s'en vint nous voir** he came to see us

---

Venise /vəniz/ **N** Venice

vénitien, -ienne /venisjɛ̃, jɛn/ **ADJ** Venetian; → **lanterne, store** **NM,F** **Vénitien(ne)** Venetian

vent /vɑ̃/ **NM** 1 *(gén)* wind ◆ **~ du nord/d'ouest** North/West wind ◆ **le ~ du large** the sea breeze ◆ **il y a** *ou* **il fait du ~** it's windy, there's a wind blowing ◆ **le ~ tourne** *(lit, fig)* the wind is turning ◆ **un ~ d'orage** a stormy wind ◆ **un ~ à décorner les bœufs** a fierce gale, a howling wind ◆ **coup de ~** *(Naut)* gale ◆ **un coup** *ou* **une rafale de ~ a emporté son chapeau** a gust of wind blew his hat off ◆ **entrer en coup de ~** to burst in, to come bursting in ◆ **flotter/claquer au ~** to flutter/flap in the wind ◆ **elle courait cheveux au ~** she was running along with her hair streaming in the wind ◆ **observer d'où vient le ~** *(lit)* to see which way the wind blows; *(fig)* to see which way the wind blows *ou* how the land lies ◆ **j'ai senti le ~ venir** I sensed what was coming ◆ **il a senti le ~ du boulet** *(fig)* he had a narrow escape ◆ **être en plein ~** to be exposed to the wind ◆ **marché/atelier en plein** ~ outdoor market/workshop ◆ **rapide comme le** ~ swift as the wind, like the wind; → **moulin**

2 *(= tendance)* **le** ~ **est à l'optimisme** there's a (general) mood of optimism, there's optimism in the air ◆ **un** ~ **de révolte/contestation** a wind of revolt/protest ◆ **un** ~ **de panique soufflait sur les marchés financiers** a wave of panic swept the financial markets ◆ **aller dans le sens du** ~ to follow the crowd

3 *(euph, † = gaz intestinal)* wind *(NonC)* ◆ **il a des** ~**s** he has wind ◆ **lâcher un** ~ to break wind

4 *(Naut, Chasse)* **au** ~ **(de)** to windward (of) ◆ **sous le** ~ **(de)** to leeward (of) ◆ **venir au** ~ *(Naut)* to turn into the wind ◆ **chasser au** ~ *ou* **dans le** ~ to hunt upwind ◆ ~ **arrière/debout** *ou* **contraire** rear/head wind ◆ **avoir le** ~ **debout** to head into the wind ◆ **aller contre le** ~ to go into the wind ◆ **avoir le** ~ **arrière** *ou* **en poupe** to have the wind astern, to sail *ou* run before the wind ◆ **il a le** ~ **en poupe** *(fig)* he has the wind in his sails, he's on a roll* ◆ **l'entreprise a le** ~ **en poupe** the company is on a roll* ◆ **prendre le** ~ *(lit)* to test the wind; *(fig)* to test the waters ◆ **avoir bon** ~ to have a fair wind ◆ **bon** ~ **!** *(Naut)* fair journey!; *(* = fichez le camp)* good riddance!

5 *(locutions)* **les quatre** ~**s** the four winds ◆ **aux quatre** ~**s, à tous les** ~**s** to the four winds, to all (four) points of the compass ◆ **c'est du** ~* it's just hot air* ◆ **du** ~ **!** * *(= allez-vous-en)* off with you! ◆ **avoir** ~ **de** to get wind of ◆ **quel bon** ~ **vous amène ?** *(aussi hum)* what brings you here? ◆ **elle l'a fait contre** ~**s et marées** she did it against all the odds *ou* despite all the obstacles ◆ **je le ferai contre** ~**s et marées** I'll do it come hell or high water ◆ **faire du** ~ *[éventail]* to create a breeze; *(sur le feu)* to fan the flame, to blow up the fire ◆ **il fait beaucoup de** ~ **mais c'est tout** *(péj = être inefficace)* he's always busying about but he doesn't do anything ◆ **avoir du** ~ **dans les voiles*** *(= être ivre)* to be three sheets to the wind*, to be half-seas over* *(Brit)*

◆ **dans le vent** ◆ **être dans le** ~* to be trendy, to be with it* ◆ **il a mis tous ses concurrents dans le** ~ *(= les a distancés)* he left all the other competitors standing

COMP **vent coulis** draught *(Brit)*, draft *(US)*
vent solaire *(Astron)* solar wind

ventail (pl **-aux**) /vɑ̃taj, o/ NM *(= visière)* ventail

vente /vɑ̃t/ NF 1 *(= action)* sale ◆ **la** ~ **de cet article est interdite** the sale of this article is forbidden ◆ **bureau de** ~ sales office ◆ **nous n'en avons pas la** ~ we have no demand for that, we can't sell that

◆ **en vente** on sale ◆ **être en** ~ **libre** to be freely on sale ◆ **médicament en** ~ **libre** over-the-counter medicine ◆ **en** ~ **dès demain** available *ou* on sale (as) from tomorrow ◆ **en** ~ **dans toutes les pharmacies/chez votre libraire** available *ou* on sale at all chemists/at your local bookshop ◆ **tous les articles exposés sont en** ~ all (the) goods on show are for sale ◆ **mettre en** ~ *[+ produit]* to put on sale; *[+ maison, objet personnel]* to put up for sale ◆ **mise en** ~ *[de maison]* putting up for sale; *[de produit]* putting on sale ◆ **les articles en** ~ **dans ce magasin** the goods on sale in this store

2 *(Comm) (= transaction)* sale; *(= technique)* selling ◆ **avoir l'expérience de la** ~ to have sales experience, to have experience in selling ◆ **s'occuper de la** ~ *(dans une affaire)* to deal with the sales ◆ **il a un pourcentage sur les** ~**s** he gets a percentage on sales ◆ **directeur/direction/service des** ~**s** sales director/management/department

3 ◆ ~ **(aux enchères)** (auction) sale, auction ◆ **courir les** ~**s** to do the rounds of the sales *ou* auctions; → **hôtel, salle**

4 *(Bourse)* selling ◆ **la livre vaut 1,5 € à la** ~ the selling rate for (the pound) sterling is €1.5; → **terme**

COMP **vente par adjudication** sale by auction
vente ambulante *(dans les rues)* street vending *ou* peddling; *(dans un train)* trolley service
vente de charité charity sale *ou* bazaar, jumble sale
vente par correspondance mail-order selling
vente par courtage direct selling
vente directe direct selling *ou* sales
vente à distance distance selling
vente à domicile door-to-door *ou* house-to-house selling
vente judiciaire auction by order of the court
vente paroissiale church sale *ou* bazaar
vente publique public sale
vente par téléphone telephone sales, telesales, telemarketing; → **tempérament**

venté, e /vɑ̃te/ (ptp de **venter**) ADJ windswept, windy

venter /vɑ̃te/ ▸ conjug 1 ◂ VB IMPERS *(littér)* ◆ **il vente** the wind is blowing, it is windy; → **pleuvoir**

venteux, -euse /vɑ̃tø, øz/ ADJ *[lieu]* windswept, windy; *[temps]* windy

ventilateur /vɑ̃tilatœʀ/ NM *(gén)* fan; *(dans un mur, une fenêtre)* ventilator, fan; *(Ciné)* wind machine ◆ ~ **électrique** electric fan ◆ ~ **à hélice/à turbine** blade/turbine ventilator ◆ ~ **de plafond** ceiling fan; → **courroie**

ventilation /vɑ̃tilasjɔ̃/ NF 1 *(= aération)* ventilation ◆ **il y a une bonne** ~ **dans cette pièce** this room is well ventilated, this room has good ventilation 2 *(Méd)* ~ **respiratoire** respiratory ventilation ◆ ~ **artificielle/assistée** artificial/assisted ventilation 3 *(Jur = évaluation)* separate valuation; *(Comptab) [de sommes]* breaking down; *(= répartition) [de subventions, aides]* allocation, distribution ◆ **voici la** ~ **des ventes pour cette année-là** here is the breakdown of sales for that year

ventiler /vɑ̃tile/ ▸ conjug 1 ◂ VT 1 *(= aérer) [+ pièce, tunnel]* to ventilate ◆ **pièce bien/mal ventilée** well/poorly ventilated room 2 *(Méd)* to ventilate 3 *(= décomposer) [+ total, chiffre, somme]* to break down; *(Jur) [+ produit d'une vente]* to value separately; *(= répartir) [+ touristes, élèves]* to divide up (into groups) ◆ **les dépenses entre différents comptes** to spread the expenses over different accounts

ventôse /vɑ̃toz/ NM Ventôse *(6th month of French Republican calendar)*

ventouse /vɑ̃tuz/ NF 1 *(= dispositif adhésif)* suction disc, suction pad; *(pour déboucher)* plunger ◆ **faire** ~ to cling, to adhere ◆ **porte-savon à** ~ suction-grip soap holder, self-adhering soap holder; → **voiture** 2 *(Méd)* cupping glass ◆ **poser des** ~**s à qn** to place cupping glasses on sb, to cup sb 3 *[de pieuvre]* sucker 4 *(Tech = ouverture)* airhole, air-vent

ventral, e (mpl **-aux**) /vɑ̃tʀal, o/ ADJ ventral; → **parachute, rouleau**

ventre /vɑ̃tʀ/ NM 1 *(= abdomen)* stomach, belly ◆ **dormir/être étendu sur le** ~ to sleep/be lying on one's stomach *ou* front ◆ **avoir/prendre du** ~ to have/be getting rather a paunch, to have/be getting a bit of a tummy* ◆ **rentrer le** ~ to hold *ou* pull in one's stomach ◆ **passer sur le** ~ **de qn** *(fig)* to ride roughshod over sb, to walk over sb ◆ **il faudra me passer sur le** ~ **!** over my dead body!; → **danse, plat**[1]

2 *(= estomac)* stomach ◆ **se coucher le** ~ **vide** *ou* **creux** to go to bed hungry *ou* on an empty stomach ◆ **ne partez pas le** ~ **vide !** *ou* **creux !** don't leave on an empty stomach! ◆ **avoir le** ~ **plein*** to be full ◆ **avoir mal au** ~**, avoir des maux de** ~ to have stomach ache *ou* (a) tummy ache* ◆ **ça me ferait mal au** ~ **!*** *(= m'embêterait)* it would sicken me!, it would make me sick! ◆ ~ **affamé n'a point d'oreilles** *(Prov)* words are wasted on a starving man ◆ **le** ~ **de la terre** the bowels of the earth; → **œil, reconnaissance, taper**

3 *(= utérus)* womb ◆ **quand tu étais dans le** ~ **de ta mère** when you were in mummy's tummy*

4 *[d'animal]* (under)belly

5 *[de cruche, vase]* bulb, bulbous part; *[de bateau]* belly, bilge; *[d'avion]* belly; → **atterrissage**

6 *(Tech)* **faire** ~ *[mur]* to bulge; *[plafond]* to sag, to bulge

7 *(Phys) [d'onde]* antinode

8 *(locutions)* **courir** *ou* **aller** ~ **à terre** to go flat out* *ou* at top speed ◆ **galoper** ~ **à terre** to gallop flat out*, to go at full gallop ◆ **nous allons voir s'il a quelque chose dans le** ~ we'll see what he's made of, we'll see if he's got guts* ◆ **il n'a rien dans le** ~ he has no guts*, he's spineless ◆ **j'aimerais bien savoir ce qu'il a dans le** ~ *(ce qu'il pense)* I'd like to know what's going on in his mind; *(quelles sont ses qualités)* I'd like to see what he's made of ◆ **ouvrir sa montre pour voir ce qu'elle a dans le** ~* to open (up) one's watch to see what it has got inside *ou* what's inside it ◆ **le** ~ **mou de l'Europe** the soft underbelly of Europe; → **cœur**

ventrée* † /vɑ̃tʀe/ NF ◆ **une** ~ **de pâtes** a good bellyful* of pasta ◆ **on s'en est mis une bonne** ~ we pigged‡ *ou* stuffed* ourselves on it

ventre-saint-gris †† /vɑ̃tʀəsɛ̃gʀi/ EXCL gadzooks! †, zounds! †

ventriculaire /vɑ̃tʀikylɛʀ/ ADJ ventricular

ventricule /vɑ̃tʀikyl/ NM ventricle

ventrière /vɑ̃tʀijɛʀ/ NF 1 *(= sangle)* girth; *(= toile de transport)* sling 2 *(Constr)* purlin; *(Naut)* bilge block

ventriloque /vɑ̃tʀilɔk/ NMF ventriloquist ◆ **il est** ~ he can throw his voice; *(de profession)* he's a ventriloquist

ventriloquie /vɑ̃tʀilɔki/ NF ventriloquy, ventriloquism

ventripotent, e /vɑ̃tʀipɔtɑ̃, ɑ̃t/ ADJ potbellied

ventru, e /vɑ̃tʀy/ ADJ *[personne]* potbellied; *[pot, commode]* bulbous

venu, e[1] /v(ə)ny/ (ptp de **venir**) ADJ 1 *(= fondé, placé) [personne]* **être mal** ~ **de faire** to be in no position to do ◆ **elle serait mal** ~**e de se plaindre/refuser** she is in no position to complain/refuse, she should be the last to complain/refuse

2 ◆ **bien** ~ *(= à propos) [événement, question, remarque]* timely, apposite, opportune ◆ **mal** ~ *(= inopportun) [événement, question]* untimely, inapposite, inopportune ◆ **sa remarque était plutôt mal** ~**e** his remark was rather out of place *ou* uncalled-for, his remark was a bit off* ◆ **un empressement mal** ~ unseemly *ou* unfitting haste ◆ **il serait mal** ~ **de lui poser cette question** *(impers)* it would not be fitting *ou* it would be a bit out of place to ask him (that)

3 *(= développé)* **bien** ~ *[enfant]* sturdy, sturdily built; *[plante, arbre]* well-developed, fine; *[pièce, œuvre]* well-written ◆ **mal** ~ *[enfant, arbre] (= chétif)* stunted; *(= mal conformé)* malformed

4 *(= arrivé)* **tard** ~ late ◆ **tôt** ~ early ◆ **le premier/dernier** ~ the first/last to come ◆ **il n'est pas le premier** ~ *(fig)* he isn't just anybody ◆ **elle n'épousera pas le premier** ~ she won't marry the first man that comes along; → **nouveau**

venue[2] /v(ə)ny/ NF 1 *[de personne]* arrival, coming ◆ **à l'occasion de la** ~ **de la reine** *(dans le passé)* when the queen visited; *(dans le futur)* when the queen visits ◆ **il a annoncé sa ~** he announced that he was coming; → **allée** 2 *(littér = avènement)* coming ◆ **la ~ du printemps/du Christ** the coming of spring/of Christ ◆ **lors de ma ~ au monde** when I came into the world 3 *(locutions : littér)* **d'une seule ~, tout d'une ~** *[arbre]* straight-growing *(épith)* ◆ **d'une belle ~** finely *ou* beautifully developed

Vénus /venys/ **NF** *(Astron, Myth)* Venus ◆ **une ~** *(= femme)* a venus, a great beauty; → **mont**

vénus /venys/ **NF** *(= mollusque)* type of clam

vépéciste /vepesist/ **NM** *(= entreprise)* mail-order firm

vêpres /vɛpʀ/ **NFPL** vespers ◆ **sonner les ~** to ring the vespers bell

ver /vɛʀ/ **NM** *(gén)* worm; *(= larve)* grub; *[de viande, fruits, fromage]* maggot; *[de bois]* woodworm *(NonC)* ◆ **mangé** *ou* **rongé aux ~s** worm-eaten ◆ **avoir des ~s** *(Méd)* to have worms ◆ **mes poireaux ont le ~** *(Agr)* my leeks have been eaten *ou* attacked by grubs ◆ **le ~ est dans le fruit** *(fig)* the rot has already set in ◆ **tirer les ~s du nez à qn*** to worm information out of sb ◆ **se tordre** *ou* **se tortiller comme un ~** to wriggle like an eel; → **nu¹, piqué**

COMP ver blanc May beetle grub
ver d'eau caddis worm
ver luisant glow-worm
ver de sable sea slug
ver à soie silkworm
ver solitaire tapeworm ◆ **avoir/attraper le ~ solitaire** to have/get tapeworm
ver de terre *(lit)* earthworm; *(péj)* worm
ver de vase bloodworm

véracité /veʀasite/ **NF** *[de rapport, récit, témoin]* veracity *(frm)*, truthfulness; *[de déclaration, fait]* truth, veracity *(frm)*

véranda /veʀɑ̃da/ **NF** veranda(h)

verbal, e (mpl **-aux**) /vɛʀbal, o/ **ADJ** 1 *(= oral)* verbal 2 *[adjectif, locution]* verbal; *[système, forme, terminaison]* verb *(épith)*, verbal; → **groupe**

verbalement /vɛʀbalmɑ̃/ **ADV** *[dire, faire savoir]* verbally, by word of mouth; *[approuver, donner son accord]* verbally

verbalisateur /vɛʀbalizatœʀ/ **ADJ M** ◆ **l'agent ~ doit toujours ...** an officer reporting an offence must always ... ◆ **l'agent ~ a oublié de ...** the officer who reported *ou* booked* *(Brit)* me *(ou* him *etc)* forgot to ...

verbalisation /vɛʀbalizasjɔ̃/ **NF** 1 *(Police)* reporting *(by an officer) of an offence* 2 *(Psych)* verbalization

verbaliser /vɛʀbalize/ ▸ conjug 1 ◂ **VI** 1 *(Police)* **l'agent a dû ~** the officer had to report *ou* book* *(Brit)* him *(ou* me *etc)* 2 *(Psych)* to verbalize **VT** *(Psych)* to verbalize

verbalisme /vɛʀbalism/ **NM** verbalism

verbe /vɛʀb/ **NM** 1 *(Gram)* verb ◆ **~ défectif/impersonnel** defective/impersonal verb ◆ **~ transitif/intransitif** transitive/intransitive verb ◆ **~ pronominal** reflexive verb ◆ **~ actif/passif** active/passive verb, verb in the active/passive (voice) ◆ **~ d'action/d'état** action/stative verb ◆ **~ fort** strong verb ◆ **~ à particule** phrasal verb 2 *(Rel)* **le Verbe** the Word ◆ **le Verbe s'est fait chair** the Word was made flesh ◆ **le Verbe incarné** the Word incarnate 3 *(littér = mots, langage)* language, word ◆ **la magie du ~** the magic of language *ou* the word 4 *(littér = ton de voix)* tone (of voice) ◆ **avoir le ~ haut** to speak in a high and mighty tone, to sound high and mighty

verbeusement /vɛʀbøzmɑ̃/ **ADV** verbosely

verbeux, -euse /vɛʀbø, øz/ **ADJ** verbose, wordy, prolix

verbiage /vɛʀbjaʒ/ **NM** verbiage

verbicruciste /vɛʀbikʀysist/ **NMF** crossword compiler, compiler of crossword puzzles

verbosité /vɛʀbozite/ **NF** verbosity, wordiness, prolixity

verdâtre /vɛʀdɑtʀ/ **ADJ** greenish

verdeur /vɛʀdœʀ/ **NF** 1 *(= jeunesse)* vigour *(Brit)*, vigor *(US)*, vitality 2 *[de fruit]* tartness, sharpness; *[de vin]* acidity 3 *[de langage]* forthrightness

verdict /vɛʀdik(t)/ **NM** verdict ◆ **~ de culpabilité/d'acquittement** verdict of guilty/of not guilty ◆ **rendre son ~** *[tribunal]* to return its verdict ◆ **la commission a rendu son ~** the commission has returned its verdict *ou* made its decision ◆ **le ~ est tombé** *ou* **a été prononcé** the verdict was announced ◆ **il attend le ~ des critiques** he's waiting for the critics' verdict

verdier /vɛʀdje/ **NM** greenfinch

verdir /vɛʀdiʀ/ ▸ conjug 2 ◂ **VI** *[feuilles, arbres]* to turn *ou* go green; *[personne]* to turn pale, to blanch ◆ **~ de peur** to turn white with fear **VT** to turn green

verdissant, e /vɛʀdisɑ̃, ɑ̃t/ **ADJ** *(littér) [arbre, champ]* greening *(épith) (littér)*

verdoiement /vɛʀdwamɑ̃/ **NM** *(= état)* verdancy *(littér)*, greenness ◆ **le ~ des prés au printemps** *(= action)* the greening of the meadows *ou* the verdant hue taken on by the meadows in spring *(littér)*

verdoyant, e /vɛʀdwajɑ̃, ɑ̃t/ **ADJ** verdant *(littér)*, green

verdoyer /vɛʀdwaje/ ▸ conjug 8 ◂ **VI** *(= être vert)* to be verdant *(littér)* *ou* green; *(= devenir vert)* to become verdant *(littér)* *ou* green

verdure /vɛʀdyʀ/ **NF** 1 *(= végétation)* greenery *(NonC)*, verdure *(NonC) (littér)* ◆ **tapis de ~** greensward *(littér)* ◆ **rideau de ~** curtain of greenery *ou* verdure *(littér)* ◆ **tapisserie de ~** *ou* **à ~s** verdure *(tapestry)* ◆ **je vous mets un peu de ~ ?** *(pour un bouquet)* shall I put some greenery in for you?; → **théâtre** 2 *(littér = couleur)* verdure *(littér)*, greenness 3 *(= salade)* lettuce

véreux, -euse /veʀø, øz/ **ADJ** 1 *[aliment]* maggoty, worm-eaten 2 *[policier, financier]* corrupt; *[affaire]* dubious, fishy*, shady*

verge /vɛʀʒ/ **NF** 1 *(† = baguette)* stick, cane ◆ **les ~s** *(pour fouetter)* the birch ◆ **ce serait lui donner des ~s pour nous faire battre** that would be giving him a stick to beat us with ◆ **~ d'or** *(= plante)* goldenrod 2 *(Hist = insigne d'autorité) [d'huissier]* wand; *[de bedeau]* rod 3 *(Anat)* penis 4 *(Tech = tringle)* shank 5 *(Can) (= mesure)* yard *(0,914 m)*

vergé, e /vɛʀʒe/ **ADJ, NM** ◆ **(papier) ~** laid paper

vergeoise /vɛʀʒwaz/ **NF** brown sugar *(made from waste refining products)*

verger /vɛʀʒe/ **NM** orchard

vergeté, e /vɛʀʒəte/ **ADJ** *[peau]* stretch marked

vergeture /vɛʀʒətyʀ/ **NF** stretch mark

verglaçant, e /vɛʀglasɑ̃, ɑ̃t/ **ADJ** ◆ **pluie ~e** freezing rain

verglacé, e /vɛʀglase/ **ADJ** icy ◆ **les routes sont ~es** there's (black) ice on the roads, the roads are icy

verglas /vɛʀglɑ/ **NM** (black) ice *(on road etc)* ◆ **plaque de ~** icy patch, patch of black ice

vergogne /vɛʀgɔɲ/ **sans vergogne LOC ADJ, LOC ADV** *[personne, concurrence]* shameless; *[parler, agir]* shamelessly

vergue /vɛʀg/ **NF** *(Naut)* yard ◆ **grand-~** main yard ◆ **~ de misaine** foreyard ◆ **~ de hune** topsail yard

véridique /veʀidik/ **ADJ** *[récit, témoignage]* truthful, true, veracious *(frm)*; *[témoin]* truthful, veracious *(frm)*; *[repentir, douleur]* genuine, authentic

véridiquement /veʀidikmɑ̃/ **ADV** truthfully, veraciously *(frm)*

vérifiable /veʀifjabl/ **ADJ** verifiable ◆ **c'est aisément ~** it can easily be checked

vérificateur, -trice /veʀifikatœʀ, tʀis/ **ADJ** *[appareil, système]* checking *(épith)*, verifying *(épith)* **NM,F** controller, checker ◆ **~ des douanes** Customs inspector ◆ **~ des comptes** *(Fin)* auditor ◆ **~ général** *(Can)* Auditor General ◆ **~ orthographique** *ou* **d'orthographe** *(Ordin)* spellchecker, spelling checker **NF vérificatrice** *(Tech)* verifier

vérification /veʀifikasjɔ̃/ **NF** 1 *(= contrôle) [d'affirmation, fait, récit, alibi]* checking, verification; *[d'adresse, renseignement, rumeur]* checking; *[de véracité, authenticité, exactitude]* ascertaining, checking; *(Fin) [de comptes]* auditing; *[de poids, mesure, classement]* check, checking ◆ **procéder à** *ou* **effectuer plusieurs ~s** to carry out several checks ◆ **~ faite** *ou* **après ~, il se trouve que ...** on checking, we find that ... ◆ **~ d'identité** *(Police)* identity check ◆ **~ des pouvoirs** *(lors d'une assemblée générale)* check on proxies given to shareholders ◆ **~ du scrutin** *ou* **des votes** *(Pol)* scrutiny of votes ◆ **~ comptable** auditing, audit ◆ **~ fiscale** tax investigation ◆ **mission de ~** investigative mission

2 *(= confirmation)* confirmation; *[d'affirmation, fait]* establishing, confirming, proving (to be true); *[d'axiome, témoignage]* establishing, confirming; *[de soupçons, conjecture]* confirming; *[d'hypothèse, théorie]* confirming, proving (to be true)

vérifier /veʀifje/ ▸ conjug 7 ◂ **VT** 1 *(= contrôler) [+ affirmation, fait, récit, alibi]* to check, to verify; *[+ adresse, renseignement, rumeur, identité]* to check; *[+ véracité, authenticité, exactitude]* to ascertain, to check; *(Fin) [+ comptes]* to audit; *[+ poids, mesure, classement]* to check ◆ **ne vous faites pas de souci, cela a été vérifié et revérifié** don't worry – it has been checked and double-checked *ou* cross-checked ◆ **vérifie que/si la porte est bien fermée** check that/if the door's properly closed ◆ **~ ses freins/le niveau d'huile** to check one's brakes/the oil (level)

2 *(= confirmer, prouver) [+ affirmation, fait]* to establish the truth of, to confirm (the truth of), to prove to be true; *[+ axiome]* to establish *ou* confirm the truth of; *[+ témoignage]* to establish the truth *ou* veracity *(frm)* of, to confirm; *[+ soupçons, conjecture]* to bear out, to confirm; *[+ hypothèse, théorie]* to bear out, to confirm, to prove ◆ **cet accident a vérifié mes craintes** this accident has borne out *ou* confirmed my fears

VPR se vérifier *[craintes]* to be borne out, to be confirmed; *[théorie]* to be borne out, to be proved ◆ **l'adage s'est encore vérifié** the old saying has once again proved true ◆ **cette tendance se vérifie dans tous les secteurs** the tendency is clearly visible in all sectors

vérin /veʀɛ̃/ **NM** jack ◆ **~ hydraulique/pneumatique** hydraulic/pneumatic jack ◆ **monté sur ~** raised on a jack

vérisme /veʀism/ **NM** verism

vériste /veʀism/ **ADJ, NMF** verist

véritable /veʀitabl/ **ADJ** 1 *(= authentique) [argent, or, cuir, perles, larmes, colère]* real, genuine; *[ami, artiste, vocation]* real, genuine, true ◆ **l'art/l'amour ~ se reconnaît d'emblée** true art/love is immediately recognizable 2 *(= vrai, réel) [identité, raisons]* true, real; *[nom]* real ◆ **la ~ religion/joie** true religion/joy ◆ **sous son jour ~** in his true light ◆ **ça n'a pas de ~ fondement** it has no real foundation 3 *(intensif = qui mérite bien son nom)* real ◆ **un ~ coquin** an absolute *ou* a real *ou* a downright rogue ◆ **~ provocation** real *ou* downright *ou* sheer provocation ◆ **c'est une ~ folie** it's absolute *ou* sheer madness ◆ **c'est une ~ expédition/révolution** it's a real *ou* veritable *(frm)* expedition/revolution

véritablement /veritabləmɑ̃/ **ADV** really ◆ **est-il ~ fatigué/diplômé ?** is he really *ou* truly tired/qualified? ◆ **il l'a ~ fait/rencontré** he actually *ou* really did it/met him ◆ **ce n'est pas truqué : ils traversent ~ les flammes** it isn't fixed – they really *ou* genuinely do go through the flames ◆ **ce n'est pas ~ un roman/dictionnaire** it's not really *ou* exactly a novel/dictionary, it's not a real *ou* proper novel/dictionary ◆ **c'est ~ délicieux** *(intensif)* it's absolutely *ou* positively *ou* really delicious

vérité /veʀite/ GRAMMAIRE ACTIVE 53.4 **NF** 1 ◆ **la ~** *(= connaissance du vrai)* truth; *(= conformité aux faits)* the truth ◆ **nul n'est dépositaire de la ~** no one has a monopoly on (the) truth ◆ **la ~ d'un fait/principe** the truth of a fact/principle ◆ **c'est l'entière ~** it's the whole truth ◆ **c'est la ~ vraie** * it's the honest truth * ◆ **la ~ toute nue** the naked *ou* unadorned truth ◆ **son souci de (la) ~** his desire *ou* concern for (the) truth ◆ **dire la ~** to tell *ou* speak the truth ◆ **jurez de dire la ~, toute la ~, rien que la ~** *(Jur, hum)* do you swear to tell the truth, the whole truth and nothing but the truth? ◆ **la ~ dépasse souvent la fiction** truth is often stranger than fiction ◆ **la ~ sort de la bouche des enfants** *(Prov)* out of the mouths of babes and sucklings (comes forth truth) *(Prov)* ◆ **toute ~ n'est pas bonne à dire** *(Prov)* some things are better left unsaid

2 *(= sincérité, authenticité)* truthfulness, sincerity ◆ **un air/un accent de ~** an air/a note of sincerity *ou* truthfulness

3 *(= fait vrai, évidence)* truth ◆ **une ~ bien sentie** a heartfelt truth ◆ **~s éternelles/premières** eternal/first truths *ou* verities *(frm)*; → **La Palice, quatre**

4 *(= vraisemblance)* **plein de ~** *[de tableau, personnage]* very true to life

5 *(locutions)* **la ~, c'est que je n'en sais rien** the truth (of the matter) is that *ou* to tell (you) the truth I know nothing about it ◆ **l'heure** *ou* **la minute de ~** the moment of truth

◆ **en vérité** *(= en fait)* in fact, actually; *(= à dire vrai)* to tell the truth, to be honest ◆ **c'est (bien) peu de chose, en ~** it's really *ou* actually nothing very much ◆ **en ~ je vous le dis** *(Bible)* verily I say unto you

◆ **à la vérité** *(frm)* ◆ **à la ~ il préfère s'amuser que de travailler** to tell the truth *ou* to be honest he'd rather have fun than work ◆ **j'étais à la ~ loin de m'en douter** to tell the truth *ou* truth to tell I was far from suspecting it

verjus /vɛʀʒy/ **NM** verjuice

verlan /vɛʀlɑ̃/ **NM** (back) slang

> **VERLAN**
>
> **Verlan** is a particular kind of backslang that has become extremely popular among young people in France. It consists of inverting the syllables of words, and often then truncating the result to make a new word. The slang words « meuf », « keuf », « keum » and « beur » are **verlan** renderings of the words « femme », « flic », « mec » and « Arabe ». The expression « laisse béton » (« forget it ») is **verlan** for « laisse tomber », and the word **verlan** itself comes from the expression « à l'envers » (« back to front »).

vermeil, -eille /vɛʀmɛj/ **ADJ** *[tissu, objet]* vermilion, bright red; *[bouche]* ruby *(épith)*, cherry *(épith)*, ruby- *ou* cherry-red; *[teint]* rosy; → **carte** **NM** *(= métal)* vermeil ◆ **cuiller/médaille de ~** silver-gilt spoon/medal

vermicelle /vɛʀmisɛl/ **NM** *(= pâtes)* ◆ **~(s)** vermicelli, angel hair pasta *(US)* ◆ **potage au ~** vermicelli soup ◆ **~ chinois** fine rice noodles

vermiculaire /vɛʀmikylɛʀ/ **ADJ** *(Anat)* vermicular, vermiform ◆ **appendice ~** vermiform appendix ◆ **éminence ~** vermis ◆ **contraction ~** peristalsis *(NonC)*

vermiculé, e /vɛʀmikyle/ **ADJ** vermiculated

vermiculure /vɛʀmikylyʀ/ **NF** *(gén pl)* vermiculation *(NonC)*

vermiforme /vɛʀmifɔʀm/ **ADJ** vermiform

vermifuge /vɛʀmifyʒ/ **ADJ, NM** vermifuge *(SPÉC)* ◆ **poudre ~** worm powder

vermillon /vɛʀmijɔ̃/ **NM** *(= poudre)* vermilion, cinnabar ◆ **(rouge) ~** *(= couleur)* vermilion, scarlet **ADJ INV** vermilion, scarlet

vermine /vɛʀmin/ **NF** 1 *(= parasites)* vermin *(NonC)* ◆ **couvert de ~** crawling with vermin, lice-ridden 2 *(littér, péj = racaille)* vermin; (†, *péj = vaurien)* knave †, cur †

vermisseau (pl **vermisseaux**) /vɛʀmiso/ **NM** *(= ver)* small worm, vermicule *(SPÉC)*

Vermont /vɛʀmɔ̃/ **NM** Vermont

vermoulu, e /vɛʀmuly/ **ADJ** *[bois]* full of woodworm, worm-eaten; *[régime politique, institutions]* moth-eaten ◆ **cette commode est ~e** there is woodworm in this chest, this chest is full of woodworm *ou* is worm-eaten

vermoulure /vɛʀmulyʀ/ **NF** *(= traces)* woodworm *(NonC)*, worm holes

vermout(h) /vɛʀmut/ **NM** vermouth

vernaculaire /vɛʀnakylɛʀ/ **ADJ** vernacular ◆ **langue ~** vernacular

vernal, e (mpl **-aux**) /vɛʀnal, o/ **ADJ** *(Astron, Bot)* vernal

verni, e /vɛʀni/ (ptp de **vernir**) **ADJ** 1 *[bois]* varnished; *(= luisant) [feuilles]* shiny, glossy ◆ **cuir ~** patent leather ◆ **souliers ~s** patent (leather) shoes ◆ **poterie ~e** glazed earthenware 2 (* = *chanceux)* lucky, jammy ⁑ *(Brit)* ◆ **il est ~, c'est un ~** he's lucky *ou* jammy ⁑ *(Brit)*, he's a lucky devil * *ou* dog *

vernier /vɛʀnje/ **NM** vernier (scale)

vernir /vɛʀniʀ/ ► conjug 2 ◄ **VT** *[+ bois, tableau, cuir]* to varnish; *[+ poterie]* to glaze; *[+ ongles]* to put nail varnish on, to varnish ◆ **~ au tampon** *(Ébénisterie)* to French polish

vernis /vɛʀni/ **NM** 1 *[de bois, tableau, mur]* varnish; *[de poterie]* glaze ◆ **~ (à ongles)** nail varnish *ou* polish ◆ **se mettre du ~ (à ongles)** to varnish *ou* paint one's nails 2 *(= éclat)* shine, gloss 3 *(fig)* veneer *(fig)* ◆ **un ~ de culture** a veneer of culture

vernissage /vɛʀnisaʒ/ **NM** 1 *[de bois, tableau, ongles, cuir]* varnishing; *[de poterie]* glazing 2 *(= exposition)* private viewing, preview *(at an art gallery)*

vernissé, e /vɛʀnise/ (ptp de **vernisser**) **ADJ** *[poterie, tuile]* glazed; *(= luisant) [feuillage]* shiny, glossy

vernisser /vɛʀnise/ ► conjug 1 ◄ **VT** to glaze

vernisseur, -euse /vɛʀnisœʀ, øz/ **NM,F** *[de bois]* varnisher; *[de poterie]* glazer

vérole /veʀɔl/ **NF** 1 *(= variole)* → **petit** 2 (⁑ = *syphilis)* pox ⁑ ◆ **il a/il a attrapé la ~** he's got/he has caught the pox ⁑

vérolé, e ⁑ /veʀɔle/ **ADJ** 1 *(= atteint de syphilis)* pox-ridden 2 *(= mauvais) [contrat]* poxy ⁑, lousy ⁑; *(= abîmé par un virus) [fichier, disquette]* infected by a virus

véronal /veʀɔnal/ **NM** *(Pharm)* veronal

Vérone /veʀɔn/ **N** Verona

véronique /veʀɔnik/ **NF** *(= plante)* speedwell, veronica; *(Tauromachie)* veronica

verrat /veʀa/ **NM** boar

verre /vɛʀ/ **NM** 1 *(= substance)* glass ◆ **~ moulé/étiré/coulé** pressed/cast/drawn glass ◆ **cela se casse** *ou* **se brise comme du ~** it's as brittle as glass; → **laine, papier, pâte**

2 *(= objet) [de vitre, cadre]* glass; *[de lunettes]* lens ◆ **mettre qch sous ~** to put sth under glass ◆ **~ grossissant/déformant** magnifying/distorting glass ◆ **porter des ~s** to wear glasses

3 *(= récipient)* glass; *(= contenu)* glass, glassful ◆ **ajouter un ~ de lait** *(Culin)* ≈ add one cup of milk ◆ **un ~ d'eau/de bière** a glass of water/of beer ◆ **~ à bière** beer glass; → **casser, noyer², tempête**

4 *(= boisson)* drink ◆ **boire** *ou* **prendre un ~** to have a drink ◆ **payer un ~ à qn** to buy sb a drink ◆ **lever son ~** to raise one's glass ◆ **boire le ~ de l'amitié** to drink a toast to friendship ◆ **videz vos ~s !** drink up! ◆ **un petit ~** * a quick one *, a quickie * ◆ **il a bu un ~ de trop** *, **il a un ~ dans le nez** * he's had one too many * *ou* a drop too much *, he's had one over the eight * *(Brit)*

COMP **verre armé** wired glass
verre ballon balloon glass, brandy glass
verre blanc plain glass
verre cathédrale cathedral glass
verres de contact (souples/durs) (soft/hard) contact lenses
verres correcteurs corrective lenses
verre à dégustation wine-tasting glass
verre à dents tooth mug *ou* glass
verre dépoli frosted glass
verre feuilleté laminated glass
verre fumé smoked glass
verres fumés *[de lunettes]* tinted lenses
verre incassable unbreakable glass
verre de lampe lamp glass, (lamp) chimney
verre à liqueur liqueur glass ◆ **verser la valeur d'un ~ à liqueur de ...** ≈ add two tablespoons of ...
verre mesureur measuring glass
verre de montre watch glass
verre à moutarde (glass) mustard jar
verre à pied stemmed glass
verres progressifs multifocal lenses, multifocals
verre de sécurité safety glass
verre trempé toughened glass
verre à vin wineglass
verre à vitre window glass
verre à whisky whisky glass *ou* tumbler

verrerie /vɛʀʀi/ **NF** *(= usine)* glassworks *(pl inv)*, glass factory; *(= fabrication du verre)* glass-making; *(= manufacture d'objets)* glass-working; *(= objets)* glassware; *(= commerce)* glass trade *ou* industry

verrier /vɛʀje/ **NM** *(= ouvrier)* glassworker; *(= souffleur de verre)* glassblower; *(= artiste)* artist in glass ◆ **maître ~** master glazier ◆ **peintre ~** stained-glass artist **ADJ M** *[groupe, établissement]* glass-making

verrière /vɛʀjɛʀ/ **NF** 1 *(= fenêtre) [d'église, édifice]* window 2 *(= toit vitré)* glass roof 3 *(= paroi vitrée)* glass wall 4 *[d'avion]* canopy

verroterie /vɛʀɔtʀi/ **NF** ◆ **(bijoux en) ~** glass jewellery *(Brit) ou* jewelry *(US)* ◆ **un collier de ~** a necklace of glass beads

verrou /veʀu/ **NM** 1 *[de porte]* bolt ◆ **tire/pousse le ~** unbolt/bolt the door ◆ **as-tu mis le ~ ?** have you bolted the door? ◆ **~ de sécurité** *(lit)* safety *ou* security lock; *(fig)* safety net ◆ **mettre qn sous les ~s** to put sb under lock and key ◆ **être sous les ~s** to be behind bars; → **sauter** 2 *(Tech) [d'aiguillage]* facing point lock; *[de culasse]* bolt 3 *(Géol)* constriction 4 *(Mil)* stopper *(in breach)* 5 *(Ordin)* lock

verrouillage /veʀujaʒ/ **NM** 1 *(= fermeture) [de porte, fenêtre]* bolting, locking; *[de culasse]* locking ◆ **~ automatique des portes, ~ centralisé** *[de voiture]* central locking 2 *(= fait de rendre inaccessible) (Mil) [de brèche]* closing; *[de frontière]* sealing; (*Ordin*) locking ◆ **le ~ parental est recommandé pour certaines émissions/certains sites** parental locking *ou* a parental lock is recommended for certain programmes/certain sites [3] (*= muselage*) **le ~ des médias** the muzzling of the media [4] (*= dispositif*) locking mechanism

verrouiller /veʀuje/ ▸ conjug 1 ◂ **VT** [1] (*= fermer*) *[+ porte, fenêtre]* to bolt; (*à clé*) to lock; *[+ culasse]* to lock [2] (*= rendre inaccessible*) (*Mil*) *[+ brèche]* to close; *[+ frontière]* to seal; (*Ordin, TV*) to lock, to block ◆ **la police a verrouillé le quartier** the police cordoned off *ou* sealed (off) the area [3] (*= enfermer*) **ses parents le verrouillent** his parents keep him locked in ◆ **se ~ chez soi** (*fig*) to shut o.s. away at home [4] (*= bloquer*) *[+ capital, marché, processus]* to block [5] (*= contrôler*) **j'ai tout verrouillé** I've got everything under control

verrouilleur /veʀujœʀ/ **NM** (*Rugby*) last man in the line-out

verrue /veʀy/ **NF** (*lit*) wart; (*fig*) eyesore ◆ **~ plantaire** verruca ◆ **cette usine est une ~ au milieu du paysage** this factory is a blot on the landscape *ou* an eyesore in the middle of the countryside

verruqueux, -euse /veʀykø, øz/ **ADJ** warty, verrucose (*SPÉC*)

vers[1] /vɛʀ/ **PRÉP** [1] (*direction*) toward(s), to ◆ **en allant ~ Aix/la gare** going to *ou* toward(s) Aix/the station ◆ **le lieu ~ lequel il nous menait** the place he was leading us to *ou* to which he was leading us ◆ **~ la droite, la brume se levait** to *ou* toward(s) the right the mist was rising ◆ **la foule se dirigeait ~ la plage** the crowd was making for *ou* heading towards the beach ◆ **"vers la plage"** "to the beach" ◆ **elle fit un pas ~ la fenêtre** she took a step toward(s) the window ◆ **notre chambre regarde ~ le sud/la colline** our bedroom faces *ou* looks south/faces the hills *ou* looks toward(s) the hills ◆ **il tendit la main ~ la bouteille** he reached out for the bottle, he stretched out his hand toward(s) the bottle ◆ **le pays se dirige droit ~ l'abîme** the country is heading straight for disaster ◆ **c'est un pas ~ la paix/la vérité** it's a step toward(s) (establishing) peace/(finding out) the truth ◆ **"Vers une sémantique de l'anglais"** (*titre*) "Towards a Semantics of English" ◆ **traduire ~ le français/l'espagnol** to translate into French/Spanish

[2] (*= aux environs de*) around ◆ **c'est ~ Aix que nous avons eu une panne** it was (somewhere) near Aix *ou* round about Aix that we broke down ◆ **~ 2 000 mètres l'air est frais** at around the 2,000 metres mark *ou* at about 2,000 metres the air is cool

[3] (*temps : approximation*) about, around ◆ **~ quelle heure doit-il venir ?** around *ou* about what time is he due? ◆ **il est arrivé ~ 6 heures** he arrived (at) about *ou* around 6 o'clock ◆ **elle a commencé à lire ~ 6 ans** she started reading at about 6 *ou* around 6 ◆ **il était ~ (les) 3 heures quand je suis rentré** it was about *ou* around 3 when I came home ◆ **~ la fin de la soirée/de l'année** toward(s) the end of the evening/the year ◆ **~ 1900/le début du siècle** toward(s) *ou* about 1900/the turn of the century

vers[2] /vɛʀ/ **NM** [1] (*sg = ligne*) line ◆ **au 3e ~** in line 3, in the 3rd line ◆ **~ de dix syllabes, ~ décasyllabe** line of ten syllables, decasyllabic line ◆ **un ~ boiteux** a short line, a hypometric line (*SPÉC*) ◆ **je me souviens d'un ~ de Virgile** I recall a line by Virgil ◆ **réciter quelques ~** to recite a few lines of poetry [2] (*pl = poésie*) verse (*NonC*) ◆ **~ blancs/libres** blank/free verse ◆ **~ de circonstance** occasional verse ◆ **traduction en ~** verse translation ◆ **faire** *ou* **écrire des ~** to write verse, to versify (*péj*) ◆ **mettre en ~** to put into verse ◆ **il fait des ~ de temps en temps** he writes a little verse from time to time ◆ **écrire des ~ de mirliton** to write a bit of doggerel

versaillais, e /vɛʀsajɛ, ɛz/ **ADJ** from *ou* of Versailles ◆ **l'armée ~e** (*Hist*) *army which suppressed the Commune of 1871* **NM,F** **Versaillais(e)** inhabitant *ou* native of Versailles ◆ **les Versaillais** (*Hist*) *the government troops who suppressed the Commune of 1871*

Versailles /vɛʀsaj/ **N** Versailles ◆ **le château de ~** the palace of Versailles ◆ **c'est ~ !** *[appartement]* it's like a palace!, it's palatial!; *[événement, réception]* it's really spectacular!

versant /vɛʀsɑ̃/ **NM** [1] *[de vallée, toit]* side; *[de massif]* slopes ◆ **les Pyrénées ont un ~ français et un ~ espagnol** the Pyrenees have a French side and a Spanish side ◆ **le ~ nord/français de ce massif** the northern/French slopes of this range [2] *[de dossier, problème]* side, aspect

versatile /vɛʀsatil/ **ADJ** fickle, changeable, capricious

versatilité /vɛʀsatilite/ **NF** fickleness, changeability, capriciousness

verse /vɛʀs/ **à verse LOC ADV** in torrents ◆ **il pleut à ~** it's pouring down, it's coming down in torrents *ou* in buckets *

versé, e /vɛʀse/ (ptp de **verser**) **ADJ** (*= savant, expérimenté*) ◆ **~/peu ~ dans l'histoire ancienne** (well-)versed/ill-versed in ancient history ◆ **~/peu ~ dans l'art de l'escrime** (highly) skilled *ou* accomplished/unaccomplished in the art of fencing

Verseau /vɛʀso/ **NM** (*Astron*) ◆ **le ~** Aquarius, the Water-carrier ◆ **il est ~, il est (du signe) du ~** he's (an) Aquarius

versement /vɛʀsəmɑ̃/ **NM** payment; (*échelonné*) instalment, installment (*US*) ◆ **le ~ d'une somme sur un compte** the payment of a sum into an account ◆ **~ par chèque/virement** payment by cheque/credit transfer ◆ **par ~s échelonnés** in *ou* by instalments ◆ **je veux faire un ~ sur mon compte** I want to put some money into my account, I want to make a deposit into my account ◆ **le ~ de ces sommes se fera le mois prochain** these sums will be paid next month ◆ **~ en espèces** cash deposit ◆ **~ à une œuvre** donation to a charity ◆ **bulletin** *ou* **bordereau de ~** paying-in (*Brit*) *ou* deposit (*US*) slip ◆ **un premier ~** *ou* **un ~ initial de 150 €** a first *ou* an initial payment of €150

verser /vɛʀse/ ▸ conjug 1 ◂ **VT** [1] *[+ liquide, grains]* to pour, to tip (*dans* into; *sur* onto); (*= servir*) *[+ thé, café, vin]* to pour (out) (*dans* into); ◆ **~ le café dans les tasses** to pour the coffee into the cups ◆ **~ des haricots (d'un sac) dans un bocal** to pour *ou* tip beans (from a bag) into a jar ◆ **~ du vin/un verre de vin à qn** to pour sb some wine/a glass of wine ◆ **verse-lui/-toi à boire** pour him/yourself a drink ◆ **veux-tu ~ à boire/le vin s'il te plaît ?** will you pour (out) *ou* serve the drinks/the wine please?; → **huile**

[2] (*= répandre*) *[+ larmes, sang]* to shed; (*= déverser*) to pour out, to scatter (*sur* onto); ◆ **~ le sang** (*= tuer*) to shed *ou* spill blood ◆ **sans ~ une goutte de sang** without shedding *ou* spilling a drop of blood ◆ **~ un pleur/quelques pleurs** (*littér, hum*) to shed a tear/a few tears

[3] (*= classer*) **~ une pièce à un dossier** to add an item to a file

[4] (*= payer*) to pay ◆ **~ une somme à un compte** to pay a sum of money into an account, to deposit a sum of money in an account ◆ **~ des intérêts à qn** to pay sb interest ◆ **~ des arrhes** to put down *ou* pay a deposit ◆ **~ une rente à qn** to pay sb a pension

[5] (*= affecter, incorporer*) **~ qn dans** to assign *ou* attach sb to ◆ **se faire ~ dans l'infanterie** to get o.s. assigned *ou* attached to the infantry

VI [1] (*= basculer*) *[véhicule]* to overturn ◆ **il va nous faire ~ dans le fossé** he'll tip us into the ditch, we'll end up in the ditch because of him ◆ **il a déjà versé deux fois** he has already overturned twice

[2] (*= tomber dans*) **~ dans** *[+ sentimentalité, démagogie]* to lapse into

verset /vɛʀsɛ/ **NM** *[de Bible, Coran]* verse; (*= prière*) versicle; (*Littérat*) verse

verseur, -euse /vɛʀsœʀ, øz/ **ADJ** ◆ **bouchon ~** pour-through stopper ◆ **sucrier ~** sugar dispenser; → **bec NM** (*= dispositif*) pourer **NF** **verseuse** (*= cafetière*) coffeepot

versicolore /vɛʀsikɔlɔʀ/ **ADJ** versicolour (*Brit*), versicolor (*US*)

versificateur /vɛʀsifikatœʀ/ **NM** writer of verse, versifier (*péj*), rhymester (*péj*)

versification /vɛʀsifikasjɔ̃/ **NF** versification

versifier /vɛʀsifje/ ▸ conjug 7 ◂ **VT** to put into verse ◆ **une œuvre versifiée** a work put into verse **VI** to write verse, to versify (*péj*)

version /vɛʀsjɔ̃/ **NF** [1] (*Scol = traduction*) translation (*into the mother tongue*), unseen (translation) ◆ **~ grecque/anglaise** Greek/English unseen (translation), translation from Greek/English [2] (*= variante*) *[d'œuvre, texte]* version ◆ **film en ~ originale** film in the original language *ou* version ◆ **"Casablanca" en ~ originale (sous-titrée)** "Casablanca" in English (with French subtitles) ◆ **la ~ française du film** the French version of the film ◆ **film italien en ~ française** Italian film dubbed into French ◆ **~ 4 portes** (*= voiture*) 4-door model [3] (*= modèle*) model [4] (*= interprétation*) *[d'incident, faits]* version ◆ **donner sa ~ des faits** to give one's (own) version of the facts [5] (*Ordin*) version ◆ **bêta** beta version

verso /vɛʀso/ **NM** back ◆ **au ~** on the back (of the page) ◆ **"voir au verso"** "see over(leaf)"

verste /vɛʀst/ **NF** verst

versus /vɛʀsys/ **PRÉP** versus

vert, verte /vɛʀ, vɛʀt/ **ADJ** [1] (*= couleur*) green ◆ **~ de jalousie** green with envy ◆ **~ de rage** purple with rage ◆ **~ de peur** white with fear ◆ **les petits hommes ~s** (*hum*) the little green men (*hum*); → **feu**[1], **haricot, numéro, tapis** *etc*

[2] (*= pas mûr*) *[céréale, fruit]* unripe, green; *[vin]* young; (*= frais, non séché*) *[foin, bois]* green ◆ **être au régime ~** to be on a green-vegetable diet *ou* a diet of green vegetables; → **cuir**

[3] (*= alerte*) *[vieillard]* vigorous, sprightly, spry ◆ **au temps de sa ~e jeunesse** in the first bloom of his youth

[4] († *= sévère*) *[réprimande]* sharp, stiff

[5] *[propos, histoire]* spicy, saucy ◆ **elle en a vu des ~es et des pas mûres** * she has been through it, she has had a hard *ou* rough time (of it) ◆ **il en a dit des ~es (et des pas mûres)** * he came out with some pretty risqué stuff * ◆ **j'en ai entendu des ~es et des pas mûres sur son compte !** * you wouldn't believe the things I've heard about him!; → **langue**

[6] (*Agr*) **tourisme ~** country holidays ◆ **classe ~e** school camp ◆ **avoir les pouces ~s** *ou* **la main ~e** to have green fingers (*Brit*), to have a green thumb (*US*)

[7] (*= écologique*) green (*épith*) ◆ **le parti ~** (*Pol*) the Green Party ◆ **les produits ~s** green products

NM [1] (*= couleur*) green; (*Golf*) green ◆ **~ olive/pistache/émeraude** olive/pistachio/emerald(-green) ◆ **~ pomme/d'eau/bouteille** apple-/sea-/bottle-green ◆ **~ amande/mousse** almond/moss green ◆ **~ menthe** mint green ◆ **~ sapin** forest green ◆ **tu as du ~ sur ta jupe** you've got a green stain on your skirt ◆ **mettre un cheval au ~** to put a horse out to grass *ou* to pasture ◆ **se mettre au ~** (*= prendre du repos*) to take a rest *ou* a refreshing break in the country; *[gangster]* to lie low *ou* hole up for a while in the country ◆ **passer au** ~ *[voiture]* to go when the lights are on green ◆ **le feu est passé au** ~ the lights turned green; → **tendre²**

② *(Pol = écologistes)* **les Verts** the Greens

NF **verte** *(† * = absinthe)* absinth(e)

vert-de-gris /vɛʀdəgʀi/ NM INV verdigris ◆ **les** ~ *(péj) (= soldats allemands)* German soldiers *(during the Second World War)* ADJ INV grey(ish)-green

vert-de-grisé, e (mpl **vert-de-grisés**) /vɛʀdəgʀize/ ADJ coated with verdigris; *(fig)* grey(ish)-green

vertébral, e (mpl **-aux**) /vɛʀtebʀal, o/ ADJ vertebral; → **colonne**

vertébré, e /vɛʀtebʀe/ ADJ, NM vertebrate

vertèbre /vɛʀtɛbʀ/ NF vertebra ◆ **se déplacer une** ~ to slip a disc, to dislocate a vertebra *(SPÉC)* ◆ ~**s cervicales/lombaires** cervical/lumbar vertebrae

vertement /vɛʀtəmɑ̃/ ADV *[rappeler à l'ordre, répliquer]* sharply, in no uncertain terms; *[critiquer, réagir]* strongly ◆ **se faire** ~ **réprimander** to get a severe dressing-down, to be hauled over the coals

vertex /vɛʀtɛks/ NM *(Anat)* vertex

vertical, e (mpl **-aux**) /vɛʀtikal, o/ ADJ *(gén, Écon) [ligne, plan, éclairage]* vertical; *[position du corps, station]* vertical, upright; → **avion, concentration** NF **verticale** ① ◆ **la** ~**e** the vertical ◆ **à la** ~**e** *[s'élever, tomber]* vertically ◆ **falaise à la** ~**e** vertical *ou* sheer cliff ◆ **écarté de la** ~**e** off the vertical ② *(= ligne, Archit)* vertical line NM *(Astron)* vertical circle

verticalement /vɛʀtikalmɑ̃/ ADV *[monter]* vertically, straight up; *[descendre]* vertically, straight down

verticalité /vɛʀtikalite/ NF verticalness, verticality

vertige /vɛʀtiʒ/ NM ① *(= peur du vide)* **le** ~ vertigo ◆ **avoir le** ~ to suffer from vertigo, to get dizzy *ou* giddy ◆ **il eut soudain le** ~ *ou* **fut soudain pris de** ~ he suddenly felt dizzy *ou* giddy, he was suddenly overcome by vertigo ◆ **un précipice à donner le** ~ a precipice that would make you (feel) dizzy *ou* giddy ◆ **cela me donne le** ~ it makes me feel dizzy *ou* giddy, it gives me vertigo ◆ **ces chiffres donnent le** ~ these figures make your head swim *ou* spin

② *(= étourdissement)* dizzy *ou* giddy spell, dizziness *(NonC)*, giddiness *(NonC)* ◆ **avoir un** ~ to have a dizzy *ou* giddy spell *ou* turn ◆ **être pris de** ~**s** to get dizzy *ou* giddy turns *ou* spells

③ *(= exaltation)* fever ◆ **les spéculateurs étaient gagnés par ce** ~ the speculators had caught this fever ◆ **d'autres, gagnés eux aussi par le** ~ **de l'expansion ...** others, who had also been bitten by the expansion bug ... *ou* who had also caught the expansion fever ...

vertigineusement /vɛʀtiʒinøzmɑ̃/ ADV *[monter, chuter]* at a dizzying rate ◆ **les prix augmentent** ~ prices are rising at a dizzying rate, prices are rocketing *ou* are going sky-high *

vertigineux, -euse /vɛʀtiʒinø, øz/ ADJ ① *[plongée, descente]* vertiginous, breathtaking; *[précipice]* breathtakingly high; *[vitesse, hauteur]* breathtaking, dizzy *(épith)*, giddy *(épith)* ② *(= très rapide)* breathtaking ◆ **une hausse/baisse vertigineuse** a spectacular *ou* dramatic rise/fall ③ *(Méd)* vertiginous

vertigo /vɛʀtigo/ NM *(= maladie du cheval)* (blind) staggers

vertu /vɛʀty/ NF ① *(= morale)* virtue ◆ **les** ~**s bourgeoises** the bourgeois virtues ◆ **les (quatre)** ~**s cardinales** the (four) cardinal virtues ◆ ~**s théologales** theological virtues ◆ **Vertus** *(= anges)* Virtues ◆ **femme** *ou* **dame** *(hum)* **de petite** ~ † woman of easy virtue; → **nécessité, parer¹, prix**

② *(littér) (= pouvoir)* power; *(= propriété)* property; *(= courage)* courage, bravery ◆ ~ **curative/magique** healing/magic power ◆ **les** ~**s thérapeutiques du chocolat** the healing properties of chocolate ◆ **les** ~**s pédagogiques d'un débat** the educational qualities of a debate

③ *(locutions)*

◆ **en vertu de** in accordance with ◆ **en** ~ **des pouvoirs qui me sont conférés** in accordance with *ou* by virtue of the powers conferred upon me ◆ **en** ~ **de l'article 4 de la loi** in accordance *ou* compliance with article 4 of the law ◆ **en** ~ **de quoi pouvez-vous exiger ... ?** by what right can you demand ...? ◆ **en** ~ **de quoi je déclare ...** in accordance with which I declare ..., by virtue of which I declare ...

vertueusement /vɛʀtɥøzmɑ̃/ ADV virtuously

vertueux, -euse /vɛʀtɥø, øz/ ADJ virtuous

vertugadin /vɛʀtygadɛ̃/ NM *(Hist = vêtement)* farthingale

verve /vɛʀv/ NF ① *(= esprit, éloquence)* witty eloquence ◆ **être en** ~ to be in brilliant form ◆ **il nous a raconté l'entrevue avec** ~ he gave us a spirited account of the interview ② *(littér = fougue, entrain)* verve, vigour *(Brit)*, vigor *(US)*, zest ◆ **la** ~ **de son style** the vigour of his style

verveine /vɛʀvɛn/ NF *(= plante)* vervain, verbena; *(= tisane)* verbena tea; *(= liqueur)* vervain liqueur

vésical, e (mpl **-aux**) /vezikal, o/ ADJ vesical

vésicant, e /vezikɑ̃, ɑ̃t/ ADJ vesicant, vesicatory

vésicatoire /vezikatwaʀ/ ADJ, NM vesicatory

vésiculaire /vezikylɛʀ/ ADJ vesicular

vésicule /vezikyl/ NF *(Méd) (= organe)* vesicle; *(= ampoule)* blister; *(Bot)* vesicle ◆ **la** ~ **(biliaire)** the gall-bladder ◆ ~**s séminales** seminal vesicles

vésiculeux, -euse /vezikylø, øz/ ADJ ⇒ **vésiculaire**

Vespa ® /vespa/ NF Vespa ®

vespasienne /vɛspazjɛn/ NF urinal *(in the street)*

vespéral, e (mpl **-aux**) /vɛspeʀal, o/ ADJ *(littér)* evening *(épith)* NM *(Rel)* vesperal

vesse-de-loup (pl **vesses-de-loup**) /vɛsdəlu/ NF *(= champignon)* puffball

vessie /vesi/ NF bladder ◆ ~ **natatoire** swim bladder ◆ **elle veut nous faire prendre des** ~**s pour des lanternes** * she's trying to pull the wool over our eyes

Vesta /vɛsta/ NF Vesta

vestale /vɛstal/ NF *(Hist)* vestal; *(littér)* vestal, vestal virgin

veste /vɛst/ NF ① *(= habit)* jacket ◆ ~ **droite/croisée** single-/double-breasted jacket ◆ ~ **de pyjama** pyjama jacket *ou* top ◆ ~ **d'intérieur** smoking jacket ② *(* locutions)* **ramasser** *ou* **(se) prendre une** ~ *(dans une élection)* to be beaten hollow ◆ **retourner sa** ~ to change sides

vestiaire /vɛstjɛʀ/ NM ① *[de théâtre, restaurant]* cloakroom; *[de stade, piscine]* changing-room ◆ **la dame du** ~ the cloakroom attendant *ou* lady ◆ **réclamer son** ~ to collect one's things from the cloakroom ◆ **au** ~ **! au** ~ **!** * get off! ◆ **le joueur a été renvoyé au** ~ *(= expulsé)* the player was sent for an early bath ◆ **il a dû laisser sa fierté/ses convictions au** ~ he had to forget his pride/his convictions ② *(= meuble)* **(armoire-)**~ locker

vestibulaire /vɛstibylɛʀ/ ADJ vestibular

vestibule /vɛstibyl/ NM ① *[de maison]* hall; *[d'hôtel]* lobby; *[d'église]* vestibule ② *(Anat)* vestibule

vestige /vɛstiʒ/ NM *(= objet)* relic; *(= fragment)* trace; *[de coutume, splendeur, gloire]* vestige, remnant ◆ ~**s** *[de ville]* remains, vestiges; *[de civilisation, passé]* vestiges, remnants ◆ ~**s archéologiques/antiques** arch(a)eological/classical remains ◆ **les** ~**s de leur armée décimée** the remnants of their decimated army ◆ **les** ~**s de la guerre** the vestiges of war

vestimentaire /vɛstimɑ̃tɛʀ/ ADJ ◆ **modes/styles** ~**s** fashions/styles in clothing *ou* clothes ◆ **dépenses** ~**s** clothing expenditure, expenditure on clothing ◆ **élégance** ~ sartorial elegance ◆ **ses goûts** ~**s** his taste in clothes ◆ **code** ~ dress code ◆ **ces fantaisies** ~**s n'étaient pas de son goût** these eccentricities of dress were not to his taste ◆ **il se préoccupait beaucoup de détails** ~**s** he was very preoccupied with the details of his dress ◆ **sa fonction exigeait une tenue** ~ **adéquate** his position required that he dress appropriately

veston /vɛstɔ̃/ NM jacket; → **complet**

Vésuve /vezyv/ NM Vesuvius

vêtement /vɛtmɑ̃/ NM ① *(= article d'habillement)* garment, item *ou* article of clothing; *(= ensemble de vêtements, costume)* clothes, clothing *(NonC)*; *(frm = manteau, veste)* coat ◆ **le** ~ *(= industrie)* the clothing industry, the rag trade *, the garment industry *(US)* ◆ **le** ~ **masculin évolue** men's clothes are changing ◆ **c'est un** ~ **très pratique** it's a very practical garment *ou* item of clothing *ou* article of clothing

② ◆ ~**s** clothes ◆ **où ai-je mis mes** ~**s ?** where did I put my clothes? *ou* things? * ◆ **emporte des** ~**s chauds** take (some) warm clothes *ou* clothing ◆ **porter des** ~**s de sport/de ville** to wear sports/town clothes *ou* gear * ◆ **acheter des** ~**s de bébé** to buy baby garments *ou* clothes ◆ **il portait des** ~**s de tous les jours** he was wearing ordinary *ou* everyday clothes ◆ ~**s sacerdotaux** vestments ◆ ~**s de travail/de deuil** working/mourning clothes ◆ ~**s du dimanche** Sunday clothes, Sunday best *(parfois hum)*

③ *(= rayon de magasin)* **(rayon)** ~**s** clothing department ◆ ~**s pour dames** ladies' wear *(NonC)* ◆ ~**s pour hommes** menswear *(NonC)* ◆ ~**s de sport** sportswear *(NonC)* ◆ ~**s de ski** skiwear *(NonC)* ◆ ~**s de bébé** babywear *(NonC)*

④ *(= parure)* garment *(fig)* ◆ **le langage est le** ~ **de la pensée** language clothes thought

vétéran /veteʀɑ̃/ NM *(Mil)* veteran, old campaigner; *(fig)* veteran, old hand *; *(Sport)* veteran ◆ **un** ~ **de l'enseignement primaire** *(= personne expérimentée)* an old hand * at primary teaching

vétérinaire /veteʀinɛʀ/ NMF vet, veterinary surgeon *(Brit)*, veterinarian *(US)* ADJ veterinary ◆ **école** ~ veterinary college *ou* school

vététiste /vetetist/ NMF mountain biker

vétille /vetij/ NF trifle, triviality ◆ **ergoter sur des** ~**s** to quibble over trifles *ou* trivia *ou* trivialities

vétilleux, -euse /vetijø, øz/ ADJ *(littér)* quibbling, punctilious

vêtir /vetiʀ/ ► conjug 20 ◆ VT ① *(= habiller) [+ enfant, miséreux]* to clothe, to dress *(de* in) ② *(= revêtir) [+ uniforme]* to don, to put on VPR **se vêtir** to dress (o.s.) ◆ **aider qn à se** ~ to help sb (to) get dressed ◆ **les monts se vêtaient de neige** *(littér)* the mountains were clad in snow

vétiver /vetivɛʀ/ NM vetiver

veto /veto/ NM *(Pol, gén)* veto ◆ **opposer son** ~ **à qch** to veto sth ◆ **droit de** ~ right of veto ◆ **je mets mon** ~ I veto that

véto * /veto/ NMF (abrév de **vétérinaire**) vet

vêtu, e /vety/ (ptp de **vêtir**) ADJ dressed ◆ **bien/mal** ~ well-/badly-dressed ◆ **court** ~**e** short-skirted ◆ **à demi-**~ half-dressed ◆ **chaudement** ~ warmly dressed ◆ ~ **de** dressed in, wearing ◆ ~**e d'une jupe** wearing a skirt, dressed in a skirt, with a skirt on ◆ ~ **de bleu** dressed in *ou* wearing blue ◆ **toute de blanc** ~**e** dressed all in white ◆ **colline** ~**e des ors de l'automne** *(littér)* hill clad in the golden hues of autumn *(littér)*

vétuste /vetyst/ ADJ *[locaux, immeuble]* run-down, dilapidated ◆ **devenir** ~ to fall into disrepair

vétusté /vetyste/ NF *[de maison]* dilapidation ◆ **étant donné la** ~ **des installations** because the facilities are in such a bad state of repair ◆ **clause de** ~ obsolescence clause

veuf, veuve /vœf, vœv/ ADJ widowed ◆ **il est deux fois** ~ he has been twice widowed, he is a widower twice over ◆ **rester** ~**/veuve de qn** to be left sb's widower/widow NM widower NF **veuve** 1 *(gén)* widow ◆ **Madame veuve Durand** *(Jur ou vieilli)* the widow Durand ◆ **veuve de guerre** war widow 2 *(= oiseau)* whydah (bird), widow bird

veule /vøl/ ADJ spineless

veulerie /vølʀi/ NF spinelessness

veuvage /vœvaʒ/ NM *[de femme]* widowhood; *[d'homme]* widowerhood

vexant, e /vɛksɑ̃, ɑ̃t/ ADJ 1 *(= contrariant)* annoying ◆ **c'est** ~ **de ne pas pouvoir profiter de l'occasion** it's annoying *ou* a nuisance not to be able to take advantage of the opportunity 2 *(= blessant) [paroles]* hurtful *(pour* to*)*; ◆ **il s'est montré très** ~ he said some very hurtful things

vexation /vɛksasjɔ̃/ NF *(= humiliation)* humiliation ◆ **être en butte à de multiples** ~**s** to be a victim of harassment

vexatoire /vɛksatwaʀ/ ADJ *[procédés, attitude]* persecutory, hurtful ◆ **mesures** ~**s** harassment

vexer /vɛkse/ ▸ conjug 1 ◂ VT *(= offenser)* to hurt, to offend ◆ **être vexé par qch** to be hurt by sth, to be offended at sth ◆ **elle était vexée de n'avoir pas été informée** she was hurt *ou* offended that she hadn't been told ◆ **vexé comme un pou** * livid *, hopping mad * VPR **se vexer** to be hurt *(de* by*)* to be *ou* get offended *(de* at*)*; ◆ **se** ~ **facilement** *ou* **pour un rien** to be easily hurt *ou* offended

VF /veɛf/ NF (abrév de **version française**) → **version**

VHF /veaʃɛf/ (abrév de **very high frequency**) VHF

VHS /veaʃɛs/ NM (abrév de **Video Home System**) VHS ◆ **filmer en** ~ to film in VHS

via /vja/ PRÉP via

viabilisé, e /vjabilize/ ADJ *[terrain]* with services (laid on), serviced ◆ **entièrement** ~ fully serviced

viabiliser /vjabilize/ ▸ conjug 1 ◂ VT *[+ terrain]* to service

viabilité /vjabilite/ NF 1 *[de chemin]* practicability ◆ **avec/sans** ~ *[terrain]* with/without services (laid on), serviced/unserviced 2 *[d'organisme, entreprise]* viability

viable /vjabl/ ADJ viable

viaduc /vjadyk/ NM viaduct

viager, -ère /vjaʒe, ɛʀ/ ADJ *(Jur) [rente, revenus]* life *(épith)*, for life *(attrib)* ◆ **à titre** ~ for as long as one lives, for the duration of one's life NM *(= rente)* life annuity; *(= bien)* property mortgaged for a life annuity ◆ **mettre/acheter une maison en** ~ to sell/buy a house in return for a life annuity ◆ **placer son argent en** ~ to buy an annuity

Viagra ® /vjagʀa/ NM Viagra ®

viande /vjɑ̃d/ NF 1 *(gén)* meat ◆ ~ **rouge/blanche** red/white meat ◆ ~ **de boucherie** fresh meat, (butcher's) meat ◆ ~ **froide** *(lit)* cold meat(s); *(* = cadavre)* dead meat * ◆ ~ **hachée** minced meat *(Brit)*, mince *(Brit)*, ground meat *(US)*, hamburger *(US)* ◆ ~ **fraîche/séchée** fresh/dried meat ◆ ~ **de bœuf** beef ◆ ~ **de cheval** horse meat ◆ ~ **de mouton** mutton ◆ ~ **de porc** pork ◆ ~ **de veau** veal ◆ **évitez les** ~**s grasses** avoid fatty meats; → **plat²** 2 * **montrer sa** ~ to bare one's flesh ◆ **amène ta** ~ ! shift your carcass *ou* butt *(US)* over here! *; → **sac¹**

viander (se) * /vjɑ̃de/ ▸ conjug 1 ◂ VPR to smash o.s. up * *ou* get smashed up * in an accident

viatique /vjatik/ NM *(= argent)* money (for the journey); *(= provisions)* provisions (for the journey); *(Rel = communion)* viaticum ◆ **il avait pour seul** ~ **ses principes** *(littér = soutien)* the only thing he had to sustain him in life was his principles ◆ **la culture est un** ~ culture is a precious asset

vibrant, e /vibʀɑ̃, ɑ̃t/ ADJ 1 *(lit) [corde, membrane]* vibrating 2 *[son, voix]* vibrant, resonant; *(Phon) [consonne]* lateral, vibrant ◆ **voix** ~**e d'émotion** voice vibrant *ou* resonant with emotion 3 *[discours]* (powerfully) emotive; *[nature]* emotive ◆ ~ **d'émotion contenue** vibrant with suppressed emotion NF **vibrante** *(= consonne)* vibrant

vibraphone /vibʀafɔn/ NM vibraphone, vibes

vibraphoniste /vibʀafɔnist/ NMF vibraphone player, vibes player

vibrateur /vibʀatœʀ/ NM vibrator

vibratile /vibʀatil/ ADJ vibratile; → **cil**

vibration /vibʀasjɔ̃/ NF *(gén, Phys)* vibration ◆ **la** ~ **de sa voix** the vibration *ou* resonance of his voice ◆ **la** ~ **de l'air (due à la chaleur)** the heat haze

vibrato /vibʀato/ NM vibrato ◆ **jouer qch avec** ~ to play sth (with) vibrato

vibratoire /vibʀatwaʀ/ ADJ vibratory

vibrer /vibʀe/ ▸ conjug 1 ◂ VI 1 *(gén, Phys)* to vibrate; *[+ air chaud]* to shimmer ◆ **faire** ~ **qch** to cause sth to vibrate, to vibrate sth 2 *(d'émotion) [voix]* to quiver ◆ ~ **en entendant qch** to thrill to the sound of sth ◆ ~ **en écoutant Beethoven** to be stirred when listening to Beethoven ◆ **faire** ~ **qn/un auditoire** to stir *ou* thrill sb/an audience, to send a thrill through sb/an audience ◆ ~ **d'enthousiasme** to be bubbling with enthusiasm ◆ ~ **de colère** to quiver with rage; → **fibre** VT *(Tech) [+ béton]* to vibrate

vibreur /vibʀœʀ/ NM vibrator

vibrion /vibʀijɔ̃/ NM 1 *(= bacille)* vibrio ◆ **le** ~ **du choléra** vibrio cholerae 2 *(* = enfant)* fidget *

vibrionnant, e * /vibʀijɔnɑ̃, ɑ̃t/ ADJ *(hum) [personne]* buzzing with energy; *[atmosphère]* effervescent ◆ **il régnait dans la salle de rédaction une agitation** ~**e** the newsroom was buzzing with activity

vibromasseur /vibʀomasœʀ/ NM vibrator

vicaire /vikɛʀ/ NM *[de paroisse]* curate ◆ **grand** ~, ~ **général** *[d'évêque]* vicar-general ◆ ~ **apostolique** *[de pape]* vicar apostolic ◆ **le** ~ **de Jésus-Christ** the vicar of Christ

vicariat /vikaʀja/ NM curacy

vice /vis/ NM 1 *(= défaut moral, mauvais penchant)* vice ◆ **le** ~ *(= mal, débauche)* vice ◆ **le tabac est mon** ~ *(hum)* tobacco is my vice ◆ **elle travaille quinze heures par jour : c'est du** ~ **!** * it's perverted *ou* it's sheer perversion the way she works 15 hours a day like that! ◆ **vivre dans le** ~ to live a life of vice; → **oisiveté, pauvreté** 2 *(= défectuosité)* fault, defect; *(Jur)* defect ◆ ~ **de prononciation** slight speech defect ◆ ~ **de conformation** congenital malformation ◆ ~ **de construction** building fault ◆ ~ **de fabrication** manufacturing fault ◆ ~ **rédhibitoire** *(Jur)* redhibitory defect ◆ ~ **de forme** *(Jur)* technicality ◆ **cassé pour** ~ **de forme** thrown out on a technicality ◆ ~ **de procédure** procedural error ◆ ~ **caché** latent defect

vice- /vis/ PRÉF vice- ◆ ~**Premier ministre** deputy Prime Minister ◆ **le** ~**champion du monde de judo** the world's number two in judo

vice-amiral (pl **-aux**) /visamiʀal, o/ NM vice-admiral, rear admiral ◆ ~ **d'escadre** vice-admiral

vice-chancelier /visʃɑ̃səlje/ NM vice-chancellor

vice-consul /viskɔ̃syl/ NM vice-consul

vice-consulat /viskɔ̃syla/ NM vice-consulate

vicelard, e * /vis(ə)laʀ, aʀd/ ADJ *(= pervers) [air, regard, personne]* depraved; *(= rusé) [question]* trick *(épith)*; *[plan]* cunning NM,F *(= pervers)* pervert ◆ **vieux** ~ dirty old man, old lecher

vice-légat /vislega/ NM vice-legate

vice-légation /vislegasjɔ̃/ NF vice-legateship

vicennal, e (mpl **-aux**) /visenal, o/ ADJ vicennial

vice-présidence /vispʀezidɑ̃s/ NF *[de pays]* vice-presidency; *[de comité]* vice-chairmanship; *[de congrès, conseil d'administration]* vice-presidency, vice-chairmanship

vice-président /vispʀezidɑ̃/ NM,F *[de pays]* vice-president; *[de comité]* vice-chairman; *[de congrès, conseil d'administration]* vice-president, vice-chairman

vice-présidente /vispʀezidɑ̃t/ NF *[de pays]* vice-president; *[de comité]* vice-chairwoman; *[de congrès, conseil d'administration]* vice-president, vice-chairwoman

vice-reine /visʀɛn/ NF lady viceroy, vicereine

vice-roi (pl **vice-rois**) /visʀwa/ NM viceroy

vice-royauté /visʀwajote/ NF viceroyalty

vicésimal, e (mpl **-aux**) /visezimal, o/ ADJ vigesimal, vicenary

vice versa /viseveʀsa/ ADV vice versa

vichy /viʃi/ NM 1 *(= tissu)* gingham 2 ◆ **(eau de) Vichy** vichy *ou* Vichy water ◆ ~ **fraise** strawberry syrup with vichy water ◆ **carottes** ~ boiled carrots, carrots vichy ◆ **le gouvernement de Vichy** *(Hist)* the Vichy government

vichyssois, e /viʃiswa, waz/ ADJ *[gouvernement]* Vichy *(épith)*; *[population]* of Vichy

vichyste /viʃist/ ADJ *[idéologie, régime]* of the Vichy government NMF supporter of the Vichy government

vicié, e /visje/ (ptp de **vicier**) ADJ 1 *[atmosphère]* polluted, tainted; *[sang]* contaminated, tainted 2 *[rapports]* tainted; *[esprit, ambiance]* tainted, polluted 3 *(Jur) [acte juridique]* vitiated

vicier /visje/ ▸ conjug 7 ◂ VT 1 *[+ atmosphère]* to pollute, to taint; *[+ sang]* to contaminate, to taint 2 *[+ rapports]* to taint; *[+ esprit, ambiance]* to taint, to pollute 3 *(Jur) [+ élection]* to invalidate; *[+ acte juridique]* to vitiate, to invalidate

vicieusement /visjøzmɑ̃/ ADV 1 *(= sournoisement)* cunningly, slyly 2 *(= lubriquement) [regarder]* lecherously, lustfully

vicieux, -ieuse /visjø, jøz/ ADJ 1 *(= pervers) [personne, penchant]* lecherous, perverted; *[air, regard, geste]* depraved, licentious 2 *(littér = dépravé)* depraved, vicious *(littér)* 3 *(= rétif) [cheval]* restive, unruly 4 *(= sournois) [attaque, balle, coup, question]* nasty; → **cercle** 5 *(= fautif) [prononciation, expression]* incorrect, wrong

 pervert ◆ **c'est un petit** ~ he's a little lecher ◆ **un vieux** ~ a dirty old man, an old lecher

> ⚠ Sauf dans l'expression 'cercle vicieux', **vicieux** ne se traduit pas par le mot anglais **vicious**, qui a le sens de 'méchant'.

vicinal, e (mpl **-aux**) /visinal, o/ ADJ ◆ **chemin** ~ by-road, byway

vicissitudes /visisityd/ NFPL (= *infortunes*) vicissitudes; (*littér* = *variations, événements*) vicissitudes, vagaries ◆ **les** ~ **de la vie** the vicissitudes *ou* the trials and tribulations of life ◆ **il a connu bien des** ~ he has had his ups and downs

vicomte /vikɔ̃t/ NM viscount

vicomté /vikɔ̃te/ NF viscountcy, viscounty

vicomtesse /vikɔ̃tɛs/ NF viscountess

victime /viktim/ NF (*gén*) victim; [*d'accident, catastrophe*] casualty, victim; (*Jur*) aggrieved party, victim ◆ **être** ~ **de** [*+ escroc, accident, calomnie*] to be the victim of ◆ **il a été** ~ **de son imprudence/imprévoyance** he was the victim of his own imprudence/lack of foresight ◆ **il est mort,** ~ **d'une crise cardiaque** he died of a heart attack ◆ **l'incendie a fait de nombreuses** ~**s** the fire claimed many casualties *ou* victims ◆ **l'attentat n'a pas fait de** ~**s** there were no casualties *ou* no one was hurt in the bomb attack ◆ **l'entreprise est** ~ **de la concurrence/de son succès** the company is a victim of the competition/the victim of its own success ◆ ~**s de guerre** war victims ◆ **les** ~**s de la route** (*gén*) road casualties; (= *morts*) road deaths *ou* fatalities ◆ ~ **de la mode** fashion victim, fashionista *

victimisation /viktimizasjɔ̃/ NF victimization

victimiser /viktimize/ ► conjug 1 ◄ VT [*+ personne*] to victimize

victimisme /viktimism/ NM victimism

victoire /viktwaʀ/ NF (*gén*) victory; (*Sport*) win, victory ◆ ~ **aux points** (*Boxe*) win on points ◆ ~ **à la Pyrrhus** Pyrrhic victory ◆ **crier** *ou* **chanter** ~ to crow (over one's victory) ◆ **ne criez pas** ~ **trop tôt** don't count your chickens before they're hatched

Victoria /viktɔʀja/ NF Victoria ◆ **le lac** ~ Lake Victoria NM (*Géog*) Victoria

victoria /viktɔʀja/ NF (= *voiture, plante*) victoria

victorien, -ienne /viktɔʀjɛ̃, jɛn/ ADJ, NM,F Victorian

victorieusement /viktɔʀjøzmɑ̃/ ADV (*gén*) victoriously; [*combattre, résister, défendre*] successfully

victorieux, -ieuse /viktɔʀjø, jøz/ ADJ [*général, campagne, armée, parti*] victorious; [*équipe*] winning (*épith*), victorious; [*air, sourire*] triumphant ◆ **son parti est sorti** ~ **des élections** his party emerged victorious from the elections

victuailles /viktɥɑj/ NFPL food, victuals (*littér*)

vidage /vidaʒ/ NM 1 [*de récipient*] emptying 2 (* = *expulsion*) kicking out *, chucking out * 3 (*Ordin*) dump ◆ ~ **de mémoire** memory *ou* storage dump

vidame /vidam/ NM (*Hist*) vidame

vidange /vidɑ̃ʒ/ NF 1 [*de fosse, tonneau, réservoir*] emptying; [*de voiture*] oil change ◆ **entreprise de** ~ sewage disposal business ◆ **faire la** ~ (*d'une voiture*) to change the oil, to do an *ou* the oil change; → **bouchon, huile** 2 (= *matières*) ~**s** sewage 3 (= *dispositif*) [*de lavabo*] waste outlet

vidanger /vidɑ̃ʒe/ ► conjug 3 ◄ VT 1 [*+ réservoir, fosse d'aisance*] to empty 2 [*+ huile, eau*] to drain (off), to empty out

vidangeur /vidɑ̃ʒœʀ/ NM cesspool emptier

vide /vid/ ADJ 1 (*lit*) (*gén*) empty; (= *disponible*) [*appartement, siège*] empty, vacant; (*Ling*) [*élément*] empty ◆ **bouteilles** ~**s** (*Comm*) empty bottles, empties *; → **case, ensemble², estomac, main**

2 (= *sans intérêt, creux*) [*journée, heures*] empty; (= *stérile*) [*discussion, paroles, style*] empty, vacuous ◆ **sa vie était** ~ his life was empty *ou* a void ◆ **passer une journée** ~ to spend a day with nothing to do, to spend an empty day; → **tête**

3 ◆ ~ **de** empty *ou* (de)void of ◆ ~ **de sens** [*mot, expression*] meaningless, empty *ou* (de) void of (all) meaning; [*paroles*] meaningless, empty ◆ **les rues** ~**s de voitures** the streets empty of cars ◆ **elle se sentait** ~ **de tout sentiment** she felt (de)void *ou* empty of all feeling

NM 1 (= *absence d'air*) vacuum ◆ **le** ~ **absolu** an absolute vacuum ◆ **pompe à** ~ vacuum pump ◆ **faire le** ~ **dans un récipient** to create a vacuum in a container ◆ **sous** ~ under vacuum ◆ **emballé sous** ~ vacuum-packed ◆ **emballage sous** ~ vacuum packing; → **nature, tube**

2 (= *trou*) (*entre objets*) gap, empty space; (*Archit*) void ◆ ~ **sanitaire** (*Constr*) underfloor space

3 (= *abîme*) drop ◆ **le** ~ (= *l'espace*) the void ◆ **être au-dessus du** ~ to be over *ou* above a drop ◆ **tomber dans le** ~ to fall into empty space *ou* into the void ◆ **j'ai peur/je n'ai pas peur du** ~ I am/I am not afraid of heights, I have no head/I have a good head for heights

4 (= *néant*) emptiness ◆ **le** ~ **de l'existence** the emptiness of life ◆ **regarder dans le** ~ to gaze *ou* stare into space *ou* emptiness

5 (= *manque*) **un** ~ **douloureux dans son cœur** an aching void in one's heart ◆ **son départ/sa mort laisse un grand** ~ his departure/his death leaves a great void *ou* vacuum ◆ ~ **juridique** gap in the law

6 (*locutions*) **faire le** ~ **autour de soi** to isolate o.s., to drive everyone away ◆ **faire le** ~ **autour de qn** to isolate sb completely, to leave sb on his own ◆ **faire le** ~ **dans son esprit** to empty one's mind ◆ **parler dans le** ~ (*sans objet*) to talk vacuously; (*personne n'écoute*) to talk to a brick wall, to waste one's breath ◆ **repartir à** ~ [*camion*] to go off again empty ◆ **tourner à** ~ [*moteur*] to run in neutral; [*engrenage, mécanisme*] to turn without gripping; [*personne*] to be unable to think straight ◆ **la politique sociale actuelle tourne à** ~ the current social policy is not producing results; → **nettoyage, passage**

vidé, e * /vide/ (ptp de **vider**) ADJ (= *fatigué*) [*personne*] worn out, dead beat *, all in *

vidéaste /videast/ NMF video director ◆ ~ **amateur** amateur video-maker

vide-grenier (pl **vide-greniers**) /vidgʀənje/ NM garage sale *sing*

vidéo /video/ ADJ INV video ◆ **caméra/jeu/signal** ~ video camera/game/signal ◆ **images/film/bande/cassette** ~ video images/film/tape/cassette ◆ **système de surveillance** ~ video surveillance system NF video ◆ **faire de la** ~ to make videos ◆ **film disponible en** ~ film available *ou* out on video ◆ **service de** ~ **à la demande** video on demand service

vidéocassette /videokasɛt/ NF video cassette

vidéoclip /videoklip/ NM (= *chanson*) video

vidéoclub /videoklœb/ NM videoclub

vidéocommunication /videokɔmynikasjɔ̃/ NF video communication

vidéoconférence /videokɔ̃feʀɑ̃s/ NF videoconference, teleconference

vidéodisque /videodisk/ NM videodisk

vidéofréquence /videofʀekɑ̃s/ NF video frequency

vidéogramme /videɔgʀam/ NM video recording

vidéographie /videɔgʀafi/ NF videotext ◆ ~ **interactive** Videotex ®

vidéolecteur /videɔlɛktœʀ/ NM videodisk player

vidéoprojecteur /videopʀɔʒɛktœʀ/ NM video projector

vide-ordures /vidɔʀdyʀ/ NM INV rubbish chute (*Brit*), garbage chute (*US*)

vidéosurveillance /videosyʀvɛjɑ̃s/ NF video surveillance ◆ **caméra/système de** ~ video surveillance camera/system

vidéotex ® /videɔtɛks/ ADJ INV, NM INV videotex ®

vidéothèque /videɔtɛk/ NF video library

vidéotransmission /videotʀɑ̃smisjɔ̃/ NF video transmission

vide-poche (pl **vide-poches**) /vidpɔʃ/ NM (= *récipient*) tidy; (*dans voiture*) side pocket

vide-pomme (pl **vide-pommes**) /vidpɔm/ NM apple-corer

vider /vide/ ► conjug 1 ◄ VT 1 [*+ récipient, réservoir, meuble, pièce*] to empty; [*+ étang, citerne*] to empty, to drain ◆ ~ **un appartement de ses meubles** to empty *ou* clear a flat of its furniture ◆ ~ **un étang de ses poissons** to empty *ou* clear a pond of fish ◆ ~ **un tiroir sur la table/dans une corbeille** to empty a drawer (out) onto the table/into a wastebasket ◆ ~ **la corbeille** (*Ordin*) to empty the waste ◆ **ils ont vidé 3 bouteilles** (*en consommant*) they emptied *ou* drained 3 bottles ◆ **il vida son verre et partit** he emptied *ou* drained his glass and left ◆ **ils ont vidé tous les tiroirs** (*en emportant*) they cleaned out *ou* emptied all the drawers

2 [*+ contenu*] to empty (out) ◆ ~ **l'eau d'un bassin** to empty the water out of a basin ◆ **va** ~ **les ordures** go and empty (out) the rubbish ◆ ~ **des déchets dans une poubelle** to empty waste into a dustbin

3 (= *faire évacuer*) [*+ lieu*] to empty, to clear ◆ **la pluie a vidé les rues** the rain emptied *ou* cleared the streets

4 (= *quitter*) ~ **les lieux** to quit *ou* vacate the premises

5 (= *évider*) [*+ poisson, poulet*] to gut, to clean out; [*+ pomme*] to core

6 († = *régler*) [*+ querelle, affaire*] to settle

7 (*Équitation*) [*+ cavalier*] to throw ◆ ~ **les arçons/les étriers** to leave the saddle/the stirrups

8 (* = *expulser*) [*+ trouble-fête, indésirable*] to throw out, to chuck out * ◆ ~ **qn d'une réunion/d'un bistro** to throw *ou* chuck * sb out of a meeting/of a café

9 (= *épuiser*) to wear out ◆ **ce travail m'a vidé** * this work has worn me out ◆ **travail qui vous vide l'esprit** occupation that leaves you mentally drained *ou* exhausted

10 (*locutions*) ~ **son sac** * to come out with it * ◆ ~ **l'abcès** to root out the evil ◆ ~ **son cœur** to pour out one's heart

VPR **se vider** [*récipient, réservoir, bassin, salle*] to empty ◆ **les eaux sales se vident dans l'égout** the dirty water empties *ou* drains into the sewer ◆ **ce réservoir se vide dans un canal** this reservoir empties into a canal ◆ **en août, la ville se vide (de ses habitants)** in August, the town empties (of its inhabitants) ◆ **se** ~ **de son sang** to bleed to death ◆ **nos campagnes se vident** our rural areas are becoming empty of people *ou* deserted

videur /vidœʀ/ NM [*de boîte de nuit*] bouncer *

viduité /vidɥite/ NF (*Jur*) [*de femme*] widowhood, viduity (*SPÉC*); [*d'homme*] widowerhood, viduity (*SPÉC*) ◆ **délai de** ~ minimum legal period of widowhood (*ou* widowerhood)

vie /vi/

1 NOM FÉMININ 2 COMPOSÉS

1 - NOM FÉMININ

1 Bio life ♦ **la Vie** *(Rel)* the Life ♦ **le respect de la ~** respect for life ♦ **la ~ animale/végétale** animal/plant life ♦ **donner la ~** to give birth (à to); ♦ **donner/risquer sa ~ pour** to give/risk one's life for ♦ **avoir la ~ dure** *[personne, animal]* to have nine lives; *[préjugé, superstition]* to die hard ♦ **être entre la ~ et la mort** to be at death's door ♦ **avoir droit de ~ et de mort sur qn** to have the power of life and death over sb ♦ **passer de ~ à trépas** to pass on ♦ **faire passer qn de ~ à trépas** to dispatch sb into the next world ♦ **sans ~** *[personne, corps] (= mort)* lifeless; *(= évanoui)* insensible ♦ **rappeler qn à/revenir à la ~** to bring sb back to/come back to life ♦ **tôt/tard dans la ~** early/late in life ♦ **attends de connaître la ~ pour juger** wait until you know (something) about life before you pass judgment; → **fleuve, question**

♦ **en vie** alive ♦ **être en ~** to be alive ♦ **être bien en ~** to be well and truly alive, to be alive and kicking * ♦ **rester en ~** to stay *ou* remain alive ♦ **maintenir qn en ~** to keep sb alive ♦ **ce journal, ils sont fiers de l'avoir maintenu en ~** they're proud of having kept this newspaper going *ou* afloat

2 = animation life ♦ **être plein de ~** to be full of life ♦ **un film/portrait plein de ~** a lively film/portrait ♦ **donner de la ~ à qch, mettre de la ~ dans qch** to liven sth up ♦ **sa présence met de la ~ dans la maison** he brings some life *ou* a bit of life into the house, he livens the house up ♦ **sans ~** *[regard]* lifeless, listless; *[rue, quartier]* dead *(attrib)*

3 = existence life ♦ **~ sentimentale/conjugale/professionnelle** love/married/professional life ♦ **la ~ militaire** life in the services ♦ **la ~ de famille/d'étudiant** family/student life ♦ **la ~ de pêcheur** the life of a fisherman ♦ **la ~ intellectuelle à Paris** intellectual life in Paris, the intellectual life of Paris ♦ **(mode de) ~** way of life, lifestyle ♦ **dans la ~ courante** in everyday life ♦ **avoir la ~ facile** to have an easy life ♦ **une ~ difficile** *ou* **dure** a hard life ♦ **mener la ~ dure à qn** to give sb a hard time (of it), to make life hard for sb ♦ **il a** *ou* **mène une ~ sédentaire** he has a sedentary lifestyle, he leads a sedentary life ♦ **faire la ~** * † *(= se débaucher)* to live it up, to lead a life of pleasure; *(= faire une scène)* to make a scene ♦ **chaque fois, elle me fait la ~** * she goes on (and on) at me every time ♦ **il en a fait une ~ quand ...** he kicked up a real fuss * when ..., he made a real scene when ... ♦ **faire une ~ impossible à qn** to make sb's life intolerable *ou* impossible (for them) ♦ **mener joyeuse ~** to have a happy life ♦ **il poursuivit sa petite ~** he carried on with his day-to-day existence *ou* his daily affairs ♦ **elle a refait sa ~ avec lui** she made a new life with him ♦ **depuis, il a refait sa ~** since then he's started a new life ♦ **sa femme l'a quitté et il n'a jamais refait sa ~** his wife left him and he never met anyone else ♦ **il a la bonne** *ou* **belle ~** he's got it easy, he has an easy *ou* a cushy * life ♦ **c'est la belle ~ !** this is the life! ♦ **c'était la belle ~ !** those were the days! ♦ **ce n'est pas une ~ !** it's a rotten * *ou* hard life! ♦ **c'est la ~ !** that's life! ♦ **quelle ~ !** what a life! ♦ **la ~ est ainsi faite !** such is life!, that's life! ♦ **la ~ continue** life goes on; → **actif, rose, vivre¹**

4 Écon **(le coût de) la ~** the cost of living ♦ **la ~ augmente** the cost of living is rising *ou* going up ♦ **ils manifestent contre la ~ chère** they are demonstrating against the high cost of living; → **gagner, niveau**

5 = durée life(time) ♦ **il a habité ici toute sa ~** he lived here all his life ♦ **des habits qui durent une ~** clothes that last a lifetime ♦ **faire qch une fois dans sa ~** to do sth once in one's life(time) ♦ **une occasion pareille n'arrive qu'une fois dans la ~** such an opportunity happens only once in a lifetime ♦ **de ma ~** *(frm)* **je n'ai vu un homme aussi grand** never (in my life) have I seen such a tall man, I have never (in my life) seen such a tall man ♦ **tu as la ~ devant toi** you've got your whole life ahead of you; → **jamais**

♦ **à vie** for life ♦ **condamné à la prison à ~** sentenced to life imprisonment ♦ **cet accident l'a marqué à ~** this accident marked him for life ♦ **il est nommé à ~** he has a life appointment ♦ **directeur/président (nommé) à ~** life director/president, director/president for life ♦ **un emploi à ~, ça n'existe plus** there's no such thing as a job for life any more

♦ **à la vie (et) à la mort** *[amitié, fidélité]* undying *(épith)* ♦ **amis à la ~ à la mort** friends for life ♦ **entre nous, c'est à la ~ et à la mort** we have sworn eternal friendship, we are friends for life ♦ **rester fidèle à qn à la ~ à la mort** to remain faithful to sb to one's dying day

♦ **pour la vie** for life ♦ **il est infirme pour la ~** he'll be an invalid for the rest of his life ♦ **amis pour la ~** friends for life, lifelong friends ♦ **quand on est marié, c'est pour la ~** marriage is for life ♦ **quand on est bête, c'est pour la ~** once an idiot, always an idiot ♦ **à Lulu pour la ~** *(tatouage)* Lulu forever

6 = biographie life (story) ♦ **écrire/lire une ~ de qn** to write/read sb's life story ♦ **j'ai lu la ~ de Bach** I read Bach's life story *ou* the story of Bach's life ♦ **elle m'a raconté toute sa ~** she told me her whole life story, she told me the story of her life

2 - COMPOSÉS

vie de bâton de chaise riotous *ou* wild existence
vie de bohème Bohemian life *ou* lifestyle
vie de château ♦ **mener la ~ de château** to live a life of luxury
vie de garçon bachelor's life *ou* existence
vie de patachon * disorderly way of life *ou* lifestyle
vie privée private life; → **enterrer**

---

vieil /vjɛj/ **ADJ M** → **vieux**

vieillard /vjɛjaʀ/ **NM** old man ♦ **les ~s** the elderly, old people; → **asile, hospice**

vieille¹ /vjɛj/ **ADJ F, NF** → **vieux**

vieille² /vjɛj/ **NF** *(= poisson)* wrasse

vieillerie /vjɛjʀi/ **NF** *(= objet)* old-fashioned thing; *(= idée)* old *ou* stale idea ♦ **aimer les ~s** to like old *ou* old-fashioned things *ou* stuff ♦ **j'ai mal au dos – c'est la ~** * *(hum)* I've got backache – it's old age

vieillesse /vjɛjɛs/ **NF** 1 *(= période)* old age; *(= fait d'être vieux)* (old) age ♦ **mourir de ~** to die of old age ♦ **dans sa ~** in his old age; → **assurance, bâton** 2 *(= vieillards)* **la ~** the old, the elderly, the aged; → **jeunesse** 3 *[de choses]* age

vieilli, e /vjeji/ (ptp de **vieillir**) **ADJ** *(= marqué par l'âge)* aged, grown old *(attrib)*; *(= suranné) [mot, expression]* dated, old-fashioned; *(Mode) [cuir]* distressed *(épith)* ♦ **je l'ai trouvé ~** I thought he'd aged ♦ **visage prématurément ~** face that has prematurely aged

vieillir /vjejiʀ/ ▸ conjug 2 ◂ **VI** 1 *(= prendre de l'âge) [personne, maison, organe]* to grow *ou* get old; *[population]* to age ♦ **il a bien/mal vieilli** *[personne]* he has/has not aged well; *[film]* it has/has not stood the test of time, it has not/has become dated ♦ **il a vieilli dans le métier** he grew old in the job

2 *(= paraître plus vieux)* to age ♦ **il a vieilli de 10 ans en quelques jours** he aged (by) 10 years in a few days ♦ **je la trouve très vieillie** I find she has aged a lot ♦ **il ne vieillit pas** he doesn't get any older ♦ **la mort de sa femme l'a fait ~ de 20 ans** he aged 20 years when his wife died

3 *(= passer de mode)* to become (out)dated, to date ♦ **son roman a un peu/beaucoup vieilli** his novel has dated a bit/has really dated

4 *[vin, fromage]* to age ♦ **vin vieilli en cave** wine aged in the cellar ♦ **vieilli en fûts de chêne** oak-aged ♦ **j'ai fait** *ou* **laissé ~ quelques bonnes bouteilles dans ma cave** I've got some good bottles of wine maturing in the cellar

VT 1 ♦ **~ qn** *[maladie]* to put years on sb; *[coiffure, vêtement]* to make sb look older

2 *(par fausse estimation)* **~ qn** to make sb older than he (really) is ♦ **vous me vieillissez de 5 ans** you're making me out to be 5 years older than I (really) am

VPR se vieillir to make o.s. look older

vieillissant, e /vjejisɑ̃, ɑ̃t/ **ADJ** *[personne, population, société, équipement]* ageing; *[œuvre]* which is getting dated

vieillissement /vjejismɑ̃/ **NM** 1 *[de personne, population, maison, institution, équipement, matériel]* ageing ♦ **le ~ cutané** skin ageing ♦ **malgré le ~ démographique, le pays ...** despite having an ageing population, the country ... 2 *[de mot, œuvre]* fall from fashion; *[de doctrine]* decline 3 *[de vin, fromage]* ageing ♦ **~ forcé** artificial ageing

vieillot, -otte /vjɛjo, ɔt/ **ADJ** 1 *(= démodé)* antiquated, quaint 2 *(= vieux)* old-looking

vielle /vjɛl/ **NF** hurdy-gurdy

Vienne /vjɛn/ **N** *(en Autriche)* Vienna; *(en France)* Vienne

viennois, e /vjenwa, waz/ **ADJ** *(d'Autriche)* Viennese; *(de France)* of *ou* from Vienne ♦ **café/chocolat ~** coffee/hot chocolate with whipped cream; → **pain** **NM,F** **Viennois(e)** *(d'Autriche)* Viennese; *(de France)* native *ou* inhabitant of Vienne

viennoiserie /vjenwazʀi/ **NF** *sweet breads and buns such as brioches, croissants and pains au chocolat*

Vientiane /vjɛntjan/ **N** Vientiane

vierge /vjɛʀʒ/ **NF** 1 *(= pucelle)* virgin 2 *(Rel)* **la (Sainte) Vierge** the (Blessed) Virgin ♦ **la Vierge (Marie)** the Virgin (Mary) ♦ **la Vierge immaculée** the Immaculate Virgin, Immaculate Mary ♦ **une Vierge romane/gothique** *(= statue)* a Romanesque/Gothic (statue of the) Virgin; → **fil** 3 *(Astron)* **la Vierge** Virgo ♦ **il est Vierge, il est (du signe) de la Vierge** he's (a) Virgo **ADJ** 1 *[personne]* virgin *(épith)* ♦ **rester/être ~** to remain/be a virgin 2 *[ovule]* unfertilized 3 *[feuille de papier]* blank, virgin *(épith)*; *[film]* unexposed; *[bande magnétique, disquette]* blank; *[casier judiciaire]* clean; *[terre, neige]* virgin *(épith)*; *(Sport) [sommet]* unclimbed; → **huile, laine, vigne** *etc* 4 *(littér = exempt)* **~ de** free from, unsullied by ♦ **~ de tout reproche** free from (all) reproach ♦ **~ de connaissances/d'expérience** with absolutely no knowledge/experience

Vierges /vjɛʀʒ/ **NFPL** ♦ **les îles ~** the Virgin Islands

Viêtnam, Viêt Nam /vjɛtnam/ **NM** Vietnam ♦ **~ du Nord/du Sud** *(Hist)* North/South Vietnam

vietnamien, -ienne /vjɛtnamjɛ̃, jɛn/ **ADJ** Vietnamese **NM** *(= langue)* Vietnamese **NM,F** **Vietnamien(ne)** Vietnamese ♦ **Vietnamien(ne) du Nord/Sud** *(Hist)* North/South Vietnamese

vieux, vieille /vjø/, /vjɛj/ (devant nm commençant par une voyelle ou un h muet : **vieil** /vjɛj/) (mpl **vieux** /vjø/) **ADJ** 1 *(= âgé)* old ♦ **très ~** ancient, very old ♦ **un vieil homme** an old man ◆ **une vieille femme** an old woman ◆ **c'est un homme déjà** ~ he's already an old man ◆ **les vieilles gens** old people, the aged *ou* elderly ◆ **un** ~ **retraité** an old-age pensioner ◆ **il est plus** ~ **que moi** he's older than I am ◆ ~ **comme comme le monde** *ou* **Hérode** *ou* **mes robes** * *(hum)* *ou* **les chemins** as old as the hills ◆ **histoire vieille de vingt ans** story which goes back twenty years ◆ **il se fait** ~ he's getting old, he's getting on (in years); → **jour, os**

2 *(= ancien) [demeure, bijoux, meuble]* old ◆ **une belle vieille demeure** a fine old house ◆ **un vin** ~ an old wine ◆ **un pays de vieille civilisation** a country with an age-old civilization ◆ ~ **français** Old French ◆ **vieil anglais** Old English ◆ **c'est déjà** ~ **tout ça !** that's all old hat! *

3 *(= expérimenté) [marin, soldat, guide]* old, seasoned ◆ **un** ~ **loup de mer** an old sea dog; → **briscard, renard, routier**

4 *(= usé) [objet, maison, vêtement]* old ◆ **ce pull est très** ~ this sweater is ancient *ou* very old ◆ ~ **papiers** waste paper ◆ ~ **journaux** old (news)papers

5 *(avant le n) (= de longue date) [ami, habitude]* old; *[amitié]* long-standing; *(= passé) [coutumes]* old, ancient ◆ **un vieil ami** an old friend, a friend of long standing ◆ **vieille famille** old *ou* ancient family ◆ **c'est une vieille histoire** it's ancient history *ou* an old story ◆ **nous avons beaucoup de** ~ **souvenirs en commun** we share a lot of old memories ◆ **c'est la vieille question/le** ~ **problème** it's the same old question/problem ◆ **traîner un** ~ **rhume** to have a cold that is dragging on; → **date**

6 *(avant le n) (= de naguère)* old; *(= précédent)* old, former, previous ◆ **la vieille génération** the older generation ◆ **mon vieil enthousiasme** my old *ou* former *ou* previous enthusiasm ◆ **ma vieille voiture était plus confortable que la nouvelle** my old *ou* previous car was more comfortable than the one I've got now ◆ **le** ~ **Paris/Lyon** old Paris/Lyons ◆ **la vieille France/Angleterre** France/England of bygone days *ou* of yesteryear ◆ **ses vieilles craintes se réveillaient** his old fears were aroused once more; → **école, temps¹**

7 *(péj : intensif)* **vieille peau** ⁑ old bag ⁑ ◆ ~ **jeton** * old misery * ◆ **espèce de** ~ **satyre !** * you dirty old man! * ◆ **n'importe quel** ~ **bout de papier fera l'affaire** any old bit of paper will do; → **bique, chameau, chnoque** *etc*

NM 1 *(= personne)* old man ◆ **les** ~ the old *ou* aged *ou* elderly, old people ◆ **tu fais partie des** ~ **maintenant** you're one of the old folks * now ◆ **il a des manies/idées de** ~ he acts/thinks like an old man ◆ **c'est de la musique de** ~ that's music for old people ◆ **un** ~ **de la vieille** * one of the old brigade ◆ **mon** *ou* **le** ~ ⁑ *(= père)* my *ou* the old man ⁑ ◆ **ses** ~ ⁑ *(= parents)* his folks * ◆ **comment ça va, mon** ~ **?** * how are you, old boy? * *(Brit)* *ou* mate * *(Brit)* *ou* old buddy? * *(US)* ◆ **mon (petit)** ~ *, **tu vas m'expliquer ça** listen you, you're going to give me an explanation ◆ **ça, mon** ~**, c'est ton problème !** * that's your problem mate * *(Brit)* *ou* man * *(US)* ◆ **ils m'ont augmenté de 100 € – ben mon** ~ **!** *(exprimant la surprise)* they've given me a 100 euro rise – well I never!; → **petit**

2 ◆ **préférer le** ~ **au neuf** to prefer old things to new

◆ **coup de vieux** * ◆ **sa mère a pris un bon** *ou* **sacré coup de** ~ her mother has really aged ◆ **ça lui a donné un coup de** ~ *(à une personne)* it put years on him ◆ **cette nouvelle technique donne un terrible coup de** ~ **à la précédente** this new technique means the old one is now totally out of date

NF **vieille** old woman ◆ **ma** *ou* **la vieille** ⁑ *(= mère)* my *ou* the old woman ⁑ *ou* lady ⁑ ◆ **alors, ma vieille, tu viens ?** * are you coming then, old girl? *; *(hum : à un homme)* are you coming then, old man? * *ou* old chap? * *(Brit)* *ou* old boy? * *(Brit)* ◆ **comment ça va, ma vieille ?** * how are you, old girl? *; → **petit**

ADV *[vivre]* to an old age, to a ripe old age; *[s'habiller]* old ◆ **elle s'habille trop** ~ she dresses too old ◆ **ce manteau fait** ~ this coat makes you look old

COMP **vieux beau** *(péj)* ageing beau

vieille branche *(fig, archaïque ou hum)* old fruit * *(Brit)* *ou* bean * *(hum)*

le Vieux Continent the Old World

vieille fille † spinster, old maid ◆ **elle est très vieille fille** she's very old-maidish

vieille France **ADJ INV** *[personne]* with old-world values

vieux garçon † bachelor ◆ **des habitudes de** ~ **garçon** bachelor ways

la vieille garde the old guard ◆ **la vieille garde conservatrice du parti** the conservative old guard in the party

vieux jeu **ADJ INV** *[idées]* old hat *(attrib)*, outmoded; *[personne]* behind the times *(attrib)*, old-fashioned; *[vêtement]* old-fashioned, out-of-date *(épith)*, out of date *(attrib)*

vieilles lunes *(= temps passé)* olden days; *(= idées dépassées)* old-fashioned ideas

le Vieux Monde the Old World

vieil or **ADJ INV, NM** old gold

vieux rose **ADJ INV, NM** old rose

vif, vive¹ /vif, viv/ **ADJ** 1 *(= plein de vie) [enfant, personne]* lively, vivacious; *[mouvement, rythme, style]* lively, animated, brisk; *(= alerte)* sharp, quick *(attrib)*; *[imagination]* lively, keen; *[intelligence]* keen, quick ◆ **il a l'œil** *ou* **le regard** ~ he has a sharp *ou* keen eye ◆ **à l'esprit** ~ quick-witted ◆ **eau vive** (fresh) running water, flowing water; → **haie, mémoire¹**

2 *(= brusque, emporté) [personne]* sharp, brusque, quick-tempered; *[ton, propos, attitude]* sharp, brusque, curt ◆ **il s'est montré un peu** ~ **avec elle** he was rather sharp *ou* brusque *ou* curt with her ◆ **le débat prit un tour assez** ~ the discussion took on a rather acrimonious tone

3 *(= profond) [émotion]* keen *(épith)*, intense, strong; *[souvenirs]* vivid; *[impression]* vivid, intense; *[plaisirs, désir]* intense, keen *(épith)*; *[déception]* acute, keen *(épith)*, intense ◆ **j'ai le sentiment très** ~ **de l'avoir vexé** I have the distinct feeling that I've offended him

4 *(= fort, grand) [goût]* strong, distinct; *[chagrin, regret]* deep, great; *[critiques, réprobation]* strong, severe ◆ **une vive satisfaction** a great *ou* deep feeling of satisfaction, deep *ou* great satisfaction ◆ **une vive impatience** great impatience ◆ **il lui fit de** ~**s reproches** he severely reprimanded him ◆ **un** ~ **penchant pour ...** a strong liking *ou* inclination for ... ◆ **à vive allure** at a brisk pace ◆ **avec mes plus** ~**s remerciements** *(formules de politesse)* with my most profound thanks ◆ **c'est avec un** ~ **plaisir que ...** it is with very great pleasure that ...

5 *(= cru, aigu) [lumière, éclat]* bright, brilliant; *[couleur]* bright, vivid, brilliant; *[froid]* biting, bitter; *[douleur]* sharp; *[vent]* keen, biting, bitter; *[ongles, arête]* sharp ◆ **l'air** ~ **les revigorait** the bracing air revived them ◆ **rouge** ~ bright red, vivid *ou* brilliant red ◆ **il faisait un froid très** ~ it was bitterly cold

6 *(= à nu) [pierre]* bare; *[joints]* dry

7 *(† = vivant)* alive ◆ **être brûlé/enterré** ~ to be burnt/buried alive

◆ **de vive voix** *[renseigner, communiquer, remercier]* personally, in person ◆ **il vous le dira de vive voix** he'll tell you himself *ou* in person

NM 1 *(locutions)*

◆ **à vif** *[chair]* bared; *[plaie]* open ◆ **avoir les nerfs à** ~ to have frayed nerves, to be on edge

◆ **au vif** ◆ **être touché** *ou* **piqué au** ~ to be cut to the quick

◆ **dans le vif** ◆ **tailler** *ou* **couper** *ou* **trancher dans le** ~ *(lit)* to cut into the flesh; *(fig = prendre une décision)* to take drastic action ◆ **entrer dans le** ~ **du sujet** to get to the heart of the matter

◆ **sur le vif** *[peindre, décrire]* from life ◆ **scènes/photos prises sur le** ~ scenes shot/photos taken from real life ◆ **faire un reportage sur le** ~ to do a live *ou* an on-the-spot broadcast ◆ **voici quelques réactions prises sur le** ~ now for a few on-the-spot reactions

2 *(Pêche)* live bait *(NonC)* ◆ **pêcher au** ~ to fish with live bait

3 *(Jur = personne vivante)* living person ◆ **donation entre** ~**s** donation inter vivos; → **mort²**

vif-argent /vifaʀʒɑ̃/ **NM INV** *(Chim)* quicksilver ◆ **il a du** ~ **dans les veines** †, **c'est du** ~ † he is a real live wire *

vigie /viʒi/ **NF** 1 *(Naut) (= matelot)* look-out, watch; *(= poste) [de mât]* look-out post, crow's-nest; *[de proue]* look-out post ◆ **être en** ~ to be on watch 2 *(Rail)* ~ **de frein** brake cabin

vigilance /viʒilɑ̃s/ **NF** *[de personne, attention, soins]* vigilance ◆ **surveiller qn avec** ~ to keep a very close watch on sb ◆ **tromper la** ~ **de qn** to give sb the slip ◆ **rien d'important n'a échappé à leur** ~ nothing of importance escaped their notice *ou* attention ◆ **une extrême** ~ **s'impose** we *(ou* they *etc)* must be extremely vigilant ◆ **l'absorption d'alcool entraîne une baisse de la** ~ drinking alcohol affects your concentration

vigilant, e /viʒilɑ̃, ɑ̃t/ **ADJ** *[personne]* vigilant, watchful; *[attention, soins]* vigilant ◆ **essaie d'être plus** ~ **quand tu conduis** try and drive more carefully

vigile¹ /viʒil/ **NF** *(Rel)* vigil

vigile² /viʒil/ **NM** *(Hist)* watch; *(= veilleur de nuit)* (night) watchman; *[de police privée]* vigilante

Vigipirate /viʒipiʀat/ **NM** ◆ **plan** ~ *series of measures to protect the public against possible terrorist strikes*

vigne /viɲ/ **NF** 1 *(= plante)* vine ◆ **être dans les** ~**s du Seigneur** † to be in one's cups; → **cep, feuille, pied** 2 *(= vignoble)* vineyard ◆ **des champs de** ~ vineyards ◆ **la** ~ **rapporte peu** *(= activité)* wine-growing isn't very profitable ◆ **les produits de la** ~ the produce of the vineyards; → **pêche¹** **COMP** **vigne vierge** Virginia creeper

vigneau (pl **vigneaux**) /viɲo/ **NM** winkle

vigneron, -onne /viɲ(ə)ʀɔ̃, ɔn/ **NM,F** wine grower

vignette /viɲɛt/ **NF** 1 *(Art = motif)* vignette 2 *(† = illustration)* illustration 3 *(Comm = timbre)* (manufacturer's) label *ou* seal; *(sur un médicament) price label on medicines for reimbursement by Social Security* ◆ ~ **(automobile)** ≃ (road) tax disc *(Brit)*, (annual) license tag *(US)*

vignoble /viɲɔbl/ **NM** vineyard ◆ **le** ~ **français/bordelais** *(= ensemble de vignobles)* the vineyards of France/Bordeaux

vignot /viɲo/ **NM** ⇒ **vigneau**

vigogne /vigɔɲ/ **NF** *(= animal)* vicuna; *(= laine)* vicuna (wool)

vigoureusement /viguʀøzmɑ̃/ **ADV** *[taper, frotter]* vigorously, energetically; *[protester, résister]* vigorously; *[peindre, écrire]* vigorously, with vigour

vigoureux, -euse /viguʀø, øz/ **ADJ** 1 *(= robuste) [personne]* vigorous, sturdy; *[cheval]* sturdy; *[corps]* robust, vigorous; *[bras, mains]* strong, powerful; *[poignée de main]* vigorous; *[santé]* robust; *[plante]* sturdy, robust ◆ **manier la hache d'un bras** ~ to wield the axe vigorously *ou* with vigour ◆ **il est encore** ~ **pour son âge** he's still hale and hearty *ou* still vigorous for his age 2 *(= énergique) [esprit, style,* *dessin]* vigorous; *[sentiment, passion]* strong; *[résistance, protestations]* vigorous, strenuous ◆ **donner de ~ coups de poing à qch** to deal sth sturdy *ou* strong *ou* energetic blows

vigueur /vigœʀ/ **NF** 1 *[de personne]* sturdiness, vigour (Brit), vigor (US); *[de corps]* robustness, vigour (Brit), vigor (US); *[de bras, mains]* strength; *[de santé]* robustness; *[de plante]* sturdiness, robustness ◆ **dans toute la ~ de la jeunesse** in the full vigour of youth

2 *[de sentiment, passion]* strength; *[d'esprit, résistance, protestations]* vigour (Brit), vigor (US) ◆ **sans ~** without vigour ◆ **se débattre avec ~** to defend o.s. vigorously *ou* with vigour ◆ **donner de la ~ à** to invigorate ◆ **~ intellectuelle** intellectual vigour ◆ **s'exprimer/protester avec ~** to express o.s./protest vigorously

3 *[de coloris, style, dessin]* vigour (Brit), vigor (US), energy

4 *(locutions)*

◆ **en vigueur** *[loi, dispositions]* in force; *[terminologie, formule]* current, in use ◆ **entrer en ~** to come into force *ou* effect ◆ **en ~ depuis hier** in force as of *ou* from yesterday ◆ **faire entrer en ~** to bring into force *ou* effect, to implement ◆ **cesser d'être en ~** to cease to apply

VIH /veiaʃ/ **NM** (abrév de **virus de l'immunodéficience humaine**) HIV

Viking /vikiŋ/ **NM** Viking

vil, e /vil/ **ADJ** 1 *(littér = méprisable)* vile, base 2 *(† = non noble)* low(ly) 3 *(† = sans valeur) [marchandises]* worthless, cheap ◆ **métaux ~s** base metals 4 ◆ **à ~ prix** *[acheter, vendre]* at a very low price, for next to nothing

vilain, e /vilɛ̃, ɛn/ **ADJ** 1 *(= laid) [personne, visage]* ugly(-looking); *[vêtement]* ugly, unattractive; *[couleur]* nasty ◆ **elle n'est pas ~e** she's not bad-looking, she's not unattractive ◆ **le ~ petit canard** *(Littérat, fig)* the ugly duckling ◆ **150 € d'augmentation, ce n'est pas ~** a €150 pay rise – that's not bad

2 *(= mauvais) [temps]* bad, lousy*; *[odeur]* nasty, bad ◆ **il a fait ~ toute la semaine*** we've had bad *ou* lousy* weather all week

3 *(= grave, dangereux) [blessure, affaire]* nasty, bad ◆ **une ~e plaie** a nasty wound

4 *(= méchant) [action, pensée]* wicked; *[enfant, conduite]* naughty, bad ◆ **~s mots** naughty *ou* wicked words ◆ **c'est un ~ monsieur** *ou* **coco*** he's a nasty customer *ou* piece of work* ◆ **il a été ~** he was a naughty *ou* bad boy ◆ **il a été ~ au cinéma/avec sa grand-mère** he was naughty at the cinema/with his grandmother, he played up at the cinema/played his grandmother up ◆ **jouer un ~ tour à qn** to play a nasty *ou* naughty trick on sb

NM 1 *(Hist)* villein, villain

2 *(garçon = méchant)* naughty *ou* bad boy ◆ **oh le (gros) ~ !** what a naughty boy (you are)!

3 *(* : locutions)* **il va y avoir du ~, ça va tourner au ~, ça va faire du ~** things are going to get nasty, it's going to turn nasty

NF vilaine *(= méchante)* naughty *ou* bad girl ◆ **oh la (grosse) ~e !** what a naughty girl (you are)!

vilainement /vilɛnmɑ̃/ **ADV** wickedly

vilebrequin /vilbʀakɛ̃/ **NM** *(= outil)* (bit-)brace; *[de voiture]* crankshaft

vilement /vilmɑ̃/ **ADV** *(littér)* vilely, basely

vilenie /vil(ə)ni/, **vilénie** /vileni/ **NF** *(littér) (= caractère)* vileness, baseness; *(= acte)* villainy, vile *ou* base deed

vilipender /vilipɑ̃de/ ► conjug 1 ◄ **VT** *(littér)* to revile, to vilify, to inveigh against

villa /villa/ **NF** 1 *(= maison, maison de plaisance)* villa; *(= pavillon)* (detached) house ◆ **les ~s romaines** *(Antiq)* Roman villas 2 *(= impasse privée)* ≈ mews

village /vilaʒ/ **NM** *(= bourg, habitants)* village ◆ **~ de toile** tent village ◆ **~ de vacances, ~ club** holiday (Brit) *ou* vacation (US) village ◆ **~ olympique** Olympic village ◆ **le ~ global** *ou* **planétaire** the global village; → **idiot**

villageois, e /vilaʒwa, waz/ **ADJ** *[atmosphère, coutumes]* village *(épith)*, rustic *(épith)* ◆ **un air ~** a rustic air **NM** *(= résident)* villager, village resident **NF villageoise** *(= résidente)* villager, village resident

ville /vil/ **NF** 1 *(= cité, habitants)* town; *(plus importante)* city ◆ **la ~ de Paris** the city of Paris ◆ **la ~ d'Albi** the town of Albi ◆ **le plus grand cinéma de la ~** the biggest cinema in town ◆ **en ~, à la ~** in town, in the city ◆ **à la ~ comme à la scène** *(comédien)* on stage and off; *(acteur de cinéma)* on screen and off ◆ **à la ~, c'est quelqu'un de charmant** in real life he's perfectly charming ◆ **aller en ~** to go into town ◆ **habiter la ~** to live in a *(ou* the) town *ou* city ◆ **une ~ de province** a provincial town ◆ **sa ~ d'attache était Genève** Geneva was his home-base

2 *(= quartier)* **~ basse/haute** lower/upper (part of the) town ◆ **vieille ~** old (part of) town

3 *(= municipalité)* ≈ local authority, town *ou* city council ◆ **dépenses assumées par la ~** local authority spending *ou* expenditure ◆ **l'eau de la ~** tap water

4 *(= vie urbaine)* **la ~** town *ou* city life, the town *ou* city ◆ **aimer la ~** to like town *ou* city life *ou* the town *ou* city ◆ **les gens de la ~** townspeople, townsfolk, city folk ◆ **vêtements de ~** town wear *ou* clothes

COMP ville champignon mushroom town
ville d'eaux spa (town)
la Ville éternelle the Eternal City
ville forte fortified town
ville industrielle industrial town *ou* city
la Ville lumière the City of Light, Paris
ville nouvelle new town
ville ouverte open city
la Ville rose Toulouse
Ville sainte Holy City
ville satellite satellite town
ville universitaire university town *ou* city

ville-dortoir (pl **villes-dortoirs**) /vildɔʀtwaʀ/ **NF** dormitory (Brit) *ou* bedroom (US) town

villégiature /vi(l)leʒjatyʀ/ **NF** 1 *(= séjour)* holiday (Brit), vacation (US) ◆ **être en ~ quelque part** to be on holiday (Brit) *ou* vacation (US) *ou* to be holidaying (Brit) *ou* vacationing (US) somewhere ◆ **aller en ~ dans sa maison de campagne** to go for a holiday (Brit) *ou* vacation (US) *ou* to holiday (Brit) *ou* vacation (US) in one's country home 2 ◆ **(lieu de) ~** (holiday (Brit) *ou* vacation (US)) resort

villeux, -euse /vilø, øz/ **ADJ** villous

villosité /vilozite/ **NF** villus ◆ **~s** villi

Vilnius /vilnjys/ **N** Vilnius

vin /vɛ̃/ **NM** 1 *(= boisson)* wine ◆ **~ blanc/rouge/rosé** white/red/rosé wine ◆ **~ gris** pale rosé wine ◆ **~ jaune** *wine produced in the Jura region of France, similar to a light Spanish sherry* ◆ **~ mousseux/de coupage** sparkling/blended wine ◆ **~ ordinaire** *ou* **de table/de messe** ordinary *ou* table/altar *ou* communion wine ◆ **~ nouveau** new wine ◆ **grand ~, ~ fin** vintage wine ◆ **un petit ~ blanc** a nice little white wine ◆ **~ chaud** mulled wine ◆ **~ cuit** fortified wine ◆ **~ doux** sweet wine ◆ **~ délimité de qualité supérieure** *label guaranteeing quality and origin of a wine* ◆ **~ ouvert** *(Helv = en pichet)* house wine ◆ **quand le ~ est tiré, il faut le boire** *(Prov)* once the first step is taken there's no going back; → **lie, pays¹, table**

2 *(= réunion)* **~ d'honneur** reception *(where wine is served)*

3 *(= liqueur)* **~ de palme/de canne** palm/cane wine

4 *(locutions)* **être entre deux ~s** to be tipsy ◆ **avoir le ~ gai/triste** to get merry/maudlin when one drinks

vinaigre /vinɛgʀ/ **NM** 1 *(= condiment)* vinegar ◆ **~ de vin/d'alcool/de cidre/de Xérès** wine/spirit/cider/sherry vinegar; → **mère, mouche** 2 *(locutions)* **tourner au ~** to turn sour ◆ **faire ~*** to hurry up, to get a move on

vinaigrer /vinegʀe/ ► conjug 1 ◄ **VT** to season with vinegar ◆ **la salade/sauce est trop vinaigrée** there's too much vinegar on the salad/in the sauce

vinaigrerie /vinɛgʀəʀi/ **NF** *(= fabrication)* vinegar-making; *(= usine)* vinegar factory

vinaigrette /vinɛgʀɛt/ **NF** French dressing, vinaigrette, oil and vinegar dressing ◆ **tomates (en** *ou* **à la) ~** tomatoes in French dressing *ou* in oil and vinegar dressing, tomatoes (in) vinaigrette

vinaigrier /vinɛgʀije/ **NM** 1 *(= fabricant)* vinegar-maker; *(= commerçant)* vinegar dealer 2 *(= flacon)* vinegar cruet *ou* bottle

vinasse /vinas/ **NF** *(*, péj)* plonk* *(Brit) (péj)*, cheap wine; *(Tech) (= résidu)* vinasse

vindicatif, -ive /vɛ̃dikatif, iv/ **ADJ** vindictive

vindicte /vɛ̃dikt/ **NF** ◆ **~ publique** *(gén)* public condemnation; *(Jur)* prosecution and conviction ◆ **désigner qn à la ~ publique** *ou* **populaire** to expose sb to public condemnation

vineux, -euse /vinø, øz/ **ADJ** 1 *[couleur, odeur, goût]* of wine, winey; *[pêche]* wine-flavoured, that tastes win(e)y; *[haleine]* wine-laden *(épith)*, that smells of wine; *[teint]* purplish, red ◆ **d'une couleur vineuse** wine-coloured, the colour of wine ◆ **rouge ~** wine-red 2 *(= riche en alcool)* with a high alcohol content ◆ **région vineuse** rich wine-growing area

vingt /vɛ̃, vɛt en liaison et dans les nombres de 22 à 29/ **ADJ INV, NM INV** twenty ◆ **je te l'ai dit ~ fois** I've told you a hundred times ◆ **il n'avait plus son cœur/ses jambes de ~ ans** he no longer had the heart/the legs of a young man *ou* of a twenty-year-old ◆ **~ dieux ! †*** ye gods! † ◆ **il mérite ~ sur ~** he deserves full marks; *pour autres loc voir* **six, soixante**

COMP vingt-quatre heures twenty-four hours ◆ **~-quatre heures sur ~-quatre** round the clock, twenty-four hours a day
vingt et un *(= nombre)* twenty-one ◆ **le ~-et-un** *(= jeu)* pontoon, vingt-et-un, twenty-one (US)

vingtaine /vɛ̃tɛn/ **NF** ◆ **une ~** about twenty, twenty or so, (about) a score ◆ **une ~ de personnes** about twenty people, twenty people or so ◆ **un jeune homme d'une ~ d'années** a young man of around *ou* about twenty *ou* of twenty or so

vingt-deux /vɛtdø/ **ADJ INV, NM INV** twenty-two ◆ **~ ! *** watch out! ◆ **~ (voilà) les flics ! ** watch out! it's the fuzz!** ◆ **22 Long Rifle** *(= carabine)* .22 rifle, point two two rifle ◆ **la ligne des ~, les ~** *(Rugby)* the 22-metre line; → **renvoi, renvoyer**

vingtième /vɛ̃tjɛm/ **ADJ** twentieth ◆ **la ~ partie** the twentieth part ◆ **au ~ siècle** in the twentieth century **NM** twentieth, twentieth part

vinicole /vinikɔl/ **ADJ** *[industrie]* wine *(épith)*; *[région]* wine-growing *(épith)*, wine-producing *(épith)*; *[établissement]* wine-making *(épith)*

vinifère /vinifɛʀ/ **ADJ** viniferous

vinification /vinifikasjɔ̃/ **NF** *[de raisin]* wine-making (process); *[de sucres]* vinification ◆ **méthode de ~** vinification method

vinifier /vinifje/ ► conjug 7 ◄ **VT** *[+ moût]* to convert into wine

vinyle /vinil/ **NM** vinyl ◆ **il collectionne les vieux ~s** he collects old (vinyl) records ◆ **son**

album est sorti en ~ en 1959 his album came out on vinyl in 1959

vinylique /vinilik/ ADJ *[peinture]* vinyl *(épith)*

vioc‡ /vjɔk/ NMF ⇒ **vioque**

viol /vjɔl/ NM *[de personne]* rape; *[de temple]* violation, desecration ◆ **au ~ !** rape! ◆ **~ collectif** gang rape ◆ **~ conjugal** marital rape

violacé, e /vjɔlase/ (ptp de **violacer**) ADJ purplish, mauvish ◆ **rouge/rose ~** purplish red/pink NF **violacée** *(Bot)* **les ~es** the violaceae

violacer /vjɔlase/ ▸ conjug 3 ◂ VT to make *ou* turn purple *ou* mauve VPR **se violacer** to turn *ou* become purple *ou* mauve, to take on a purple hue *(littér)*

violateur, -trice /vjɔlatœʀ, tʀis/ NM,F *(= profanateur) [de tombeau]* violator, desecrator; *[de lois]* transgressor

violation /vjɔlasjɔ̃/ NF 1 *[de traité, loi]* violation, breaking; *[de constitution]* violation; *[de droit]* violation, infringement; *[de promesse]* breaking ◆ **~ du secret professionnel** *(Jur)* breach *ou* violation of professional secrecy ◆ **de nombreuses ~s de cessez-le-feu** numerous violations of the ceasefire 2 *[de temple]* violation, desecration; *[de frontières, territoire]* violation; *(littér) [de consciences]* violation ◆ **~ de domicile** *(Jur)* forcible entry *(into a person's home)* ◆ **~ de sépulture** *(Jur)* violation *ou* desecration of graves

violâtre /vjɔlɑtʀ/ ADJ purplish, mauvish

viole /vjɔl/ NF viol ◆ **~ d'amour** viola d'amore ◆ **~ de gambe** viola da gamba, bass viol

violemment /vjɔlamɑ̃/ ADV *[réagir, frapper, agresser]* violently ◆ **ces mesures ont été ~ critiquées** these measures have been severely *ou* strongly criticized ◆ **ils ont protesté ~ contre cette interdiction** they have protested vigorously *ou* strongly against this ban

violence /vjɔlɑ̃s/ NF 1 *[de personne, colère, coup, choc]* violence ◆ **~ routière** road violence ◆ **~ verbale** verbal abuse ◆ **mouvement de ~** violent impulse ◆ **répondre à la ~ par la ~** to meet violence with violence
2 *[d'odeur, parfum]* pungency; *[d'orage, vent, tempête]* violence, fierceness; *[de pluie]* violence; *[de douleur]* intensity; *[de poison]* virulence; *[d'exercice, effort]* violence, strenuousness; *[de remède]* drastic nature
3 *(= acte)* act of violence ◆ **commettre des ~s contre qn** to commit acts of violence against sb ◆ **l'enfant a subi des ~s** the child has suffered physical abuse ◆ **faire subir des ~s sexuelles à qn** to abuse sb sexually ◆ **inculpé de ~(s) à agent** found guilty of assaulting a police officer *ou* of assault on a police officer
4 *(= contrainte)* **faire ~ à qn** to do violence to sb ◆ **faire ~ à une femme** † to use a woman violently † ◆ **se faire ~** to force o.s. ◆ **faire ~ à** *[+ sentiments]* to offend, to savage, to desecrate ◆ **obtenir qch par la ~** to get sth by force; → **doux**

violent, e /vjɔlɑ̃, ɑ̃t/ ADJ 1 *(= brutal) [personne, colère, coup, choc, sport]* violent ◆ **il s'est montré ~ avec elle** he was violent with her ◆ **c'est un ~** he's a violent man; → **non, mort¹, révolution** 2 *(= intense) [odeur, parfum]* pungent, strong; *[couleur]* harsh; *[orage, vent, tempête]* violent, fierce; *[pluie]* violent; *[sentiment, passion, désir, dégoût]* violent, intense; *[douleur]* intense; *[poison]* virulent; *[exercice, effort]* violent, strenuous; *[remède]* drastic ◆ **~ besoin de s'affirmer** intense *ou* urgent need to assert o.s. ◆ **saisi d'une peur ~e** seized by a violent *ou* rabid fear ◆ **une ~e migraine** a severe migraine 3 *(* = excessif)* **c'est un peu ~ !** it's a bit much! *, that's going a bit far! *

violenter /vjɔlɑ̃te/ ▸ conjug 1 ◂ VT 1 *[+ femme]* to assault (sexually) ◆ **elle a été violentée** she has been sexually assaulted 2 *(littér) [+ texte, désir]* to do violence to, to desecrate

violer /vjɔle/ ▸ conjug 1 ◂ VT 1 *[+ traité, loi]* to violate, to break; *[+ constitution, cessez-le-feu]* to violate; *[+ droit]* to violate, to infringe; *[+ promesse, serment]* to break 2 *[+ sépulture, temple]* to violate, to desecrate; *[+ frontières, territoire]* to violate ◆ **~ le domicile de qn** to force an entry into sb's home 3 *(= abuser de) [+ personne]* to rape, to ravish † *(littér)*, to violate *(littér)* ◆ **se faire ~** to be raped 4 *(littér) [+ consciences]* to violate

violet, -ette /vjɔlɛ, ɛt/ ADJ purple, violet NM *(= couleur)* purple, violet ◆ **le ~ lui va bien** purple suits him ◆ **porter du ~** to wear purple ◆ **peindre qch en ~** to paint sth purple ◆ **un tube de ~** *(Peinture)* a tube of purple ◆ **robe d'un ~ assez pâle** pale purple dress NF **violette** *(= plante)* violet ◆ **violette odorante** sweet violet ◆ **violette de Parme** Parma violet

violeur, -euse /vjɔlœʀ, øz/ NM,F rapist

violine /vjɔlin/ ADJ dark purple, deep purple

violon /vjɔlɔ̃/ NM 1 *(= instrument d'orchestre)* violin, fiddle *; *(de violoneux)* fiddle; → **accorder, pisser** 2 *(= musicien d'orchestre)* violin, fiddle * ◆ **le premier ~** *[d'orchestre]* the leader, the first violin; *[de quatuor]* the first violin *ou* fiddle * ◆ **les premiers/seconds ~s** *(= groupe)* the first/second violins ◆ **payer les ~s (du bal)** † *(fig)* to pick up the bill *ou* tab *; → **vite** 3 (* = *prison)* cells, slammer‡, nick‡ *(Brit)* ◆ **conduire qn au ~** to take sb to the cells ◆ **passer la nuit au ~** to spend the night in the cells *ou* the slammer‡ *ou* the nick‡ *(Brit)* 4 ◆ **~ d'Ingres** (artistic) hobby

violoncelle /vjɔlɔ̃sɛl/ NM cello, violoncello *(SPÉC)*

violoncelliste /vjɔlɔ̃selist/ NMF cellist, cello player, violoncellist *(SPÉC)*

violoneux /vjɔlɔnø/ NM *(de village, péj)* fiddler *

violoniste /vjɔlɔnist/ NMF violinist, violin player

vioque‡ /vjɔk/ NMF *(= vieillard)* old person, old timer * ◆ **le ~** *(= père)* my *ou* the old man‡ ◆ **la ~** *(= mère)* my *ou* the old woman‡ *ou* lady‡ ◆ **mes ~s** my folks *

viorne /vjɔʀn/ NF *(= plante)* viburnum

VIP /veipe/ NMF (abrév de **Very Important Person**) VIP

vipère /vipɛʀ/ NF adder, viper ◆ **~ aspic** asp ◆ **cette femme est une ~** that woman's a (real) viper; → **langue, nœud**

vipereau (pl **vipereaux**) /vip(ə)ʀo/ NM young viper

vipérin, e /vipeʀɛ̃, in/ ADJ *(lit)* viperine; *(fig) [propos]* vicious, poisonous NF **vipérine** 1 *(= plante)* viper's bugloss 2 **(couleuvre) ~e** grass snake

virage /viʀaʒ/ NM 1 *(Aut = tournant)* bend ◆ **~ en épingle à cheveux** hairpin bend ◆ **~ en S** S-bend, S-curve *(US)* ◆ **"virages sur 3 km"** "bends for 3 km" ◆ **~ relevé** banked corner ◆ **accélérer dans les ~s** to accelerate round the bends *ou* curves *(US)* ◆ **cette voiture prend bien les ~s** this car corners well ◆ **il a pris son ~ trop vite** he went into *ou* took the bend *ou* curve *(US)* too fast ◆ **prendre un ~ sur les chapeaux de roues** to take a bend *ou* curve *(US)* on two wheels *ou* on one's hub caps ◆ **prendre un ~ à la corde** to hug the bend *ou* curve *(US)*
2 *(= action) [d'avion, véhicule, coureur, skieur]* turn ◆ **faire un ~ sur l'aile** *[avion]* to bank ◆ **~ parallèle** *(Ski)* parallel turn
3 *(= changement)* change in policy *ou* of direction ◆ **le ~ européen du gouvernement britannique** the British government's change of policy *ou* direction over Europe, the change in the British government's European policy ◆ **amorcer un ~ à droite** to take a turn to the right ◆ **un ~ à 180 degrés de la politique française** a U-turn in French policy ◆ **savoir prendre le ~** to adapt to meet new circumstances ◆ **l'entreprise vient de prendre un ~ stratégique** the company has just adopted a completely new strategy ◆ **le groupe a opéré un ~ vers les biotechnologies** the group has turned towards biotechnologies
4 *(= transformation) (Chim) [de papier de tournesol]* change in colour ◆ **~ à l'or/au cuivre** *(Photo)* gold/copper toning ◆ **~ d'une cuti-réaction** *(Méd)* positive reaction of a skin test

virago /viʀago/ NF virago

viral, e (mpl **-aux**) /viʀal, o/ ADJ viral

vire /viʀ/ NF *[de paroi rocheuse]* ledge

virée * /viʀe/ NF *(en voiture)* drive, ride, spin *; *(de plusieurs jours)* trip, tour; *(à pied)* walk; *(de plusieurs jours)* walking *ou* hiking tour; *(à vélo, moto)* ride; *(de plusieurs jours)* trip ◆ **faire une ~** to go for a ride *(ou* walk, drive *etc)* ◆ **faire une ~ en voiture** to go for a drive, to go for a ride *ou* spin * in the car ◆ **on a fait une ~ en Espagne** we went on a trip *ou* tour round Spain ◆ **faire une ~ dans les bars/boîtes de nuit** to go round *ou* do * the bars/nightclubs ◆ **leur ~ dans les pubs s'est mal terminée** their pub-crawl * ended badly

virelai /viʀlɛ/ NM *(Littérat)* virelay

virement /viʀmɑ̃/ NM 1 *(Fin)* **~ (bancaire)** (bank *ou* giro *(Brit)*) transfer ◆ **~ postal** postal *ou* giro *(Brit)* transfer ◆ **faire un ~ (d'un compte sur un autre)** to make a (credit) transfer (from one account to another) ◆ **j'ai fait un ~ de 1 000 € sur son compte** I transferred €1,000 to his account ◆ **~ automatique** automatic transfer ◆ **~ permanent** standing order 2 *(Naut)* **~ de bord** tacking

virer /viʀe/ ▸ conjug 1 ◂ VI 1 *(= changer de direction) [véhicule, avion, bateau]* to turn ◆ **~ sur l'aile** to bank ◆ **~ à tout vent** † *(littér)* to be as changeable as a weathercock
2 *(Naut)* **~ de bord** to tack ◆ **~ vent devant** to go about ◆ **~ vent arrière** to wear ◆ **~ sur ses amarres** to turn at anchor ◆ **~ au cabestan** to heave at the capstan
3 *(= tourner sur soi-même)* to turn (around)
4 *(= changer de couleur, d'aspect) [couleur]* to turn, to change; *(Photo) [épreuves]* to tone; *(Méd) [cuti-réaction]* to come up positive
5 *(= changer d'avis)* to take a new line ◆ **il a viré socialiste** * he's become a socialist
VT INDIR **virer à** *(= devenir)* **le bleu vire au violet** the blue is turning purple *ou* is changing to purple ◆ **~ au froid/à la pluie/au beau** *[temps]* to turn cold/rainy/fine *ou* fair ◆ **~ à l'aigre** to turn sour ◆ **l'ambiance vire au drame** things are taking a dramatic turn ◆ **le film vire à la farce** the film lapses into farce, the film turns into a farce *ou* becomes farcical ◆ **cette région a viré à droite** *(Pol)* this region has swung to the right ◆ **~ au rouge** *(Fin) [comptes, résultats]* to go *ou* slip into the red ◆ **les indicateurs (financiers) virent au rouge** indicators have dropped sharply ◆ **il a viré à l'intello** * he's become a bit of an intellectual
VT 1 *(Fin)* to transfer ◆ **~ 200 € sur** *ou* **à un compte** to transfer €200 into an account
2 * *(= expulser)* to kick out *, to chuck out *; *(= renvoyer)* to fire *, to sack * *(Brit)* ◆ **~ qn d'une réunion** to kick *ou* chuck sb out of a meeting * ◆ **se faire ~** *(= se faire expulser)* to get o.s. kicked *ou* thrown out *(de* of*)*; *(= se faire renvoyer)* to be fired *, to get the sack * *(Brit)*
3 *(* = jeter)* to chuck out *, to throw out, to get rid of ◆ **il a viré les vieux fauteuils au grenier** he's chucked * *ou* thrown the old chairs in the loft
4 *(Photo) [+ épreuve]* to tone ◆ **il a viré sa cuti(-réaction)** * *(Méd)* he gave a positive skin

test, his skin test came up positive ◆ **il a viré sa cuti** * *(fig)* he changed totally

vireux, -euse /virø, øz/ ADJ *(littér)* noxious ◆ **amanite vireuse** amanita virosa

virevoltant, e /virvɔltɑ̃, ɑ̃t/ ADJ *[danseuse]* twirling, pirouetting; *[cheval]* pirouetting; *[jupons]* twirling

virevolte /virvɔlt/ NF *[de danseuse]* twirl, pirouette; *[de cheval]* demivolt, pirouette; *(fig = volte-face)* about-turn, volte-face ◆ **les ~s élégantes de la danseuse** the elegant twirling of the dancer

virevolter /virvɔlte/ ► conjug 1 ◄ VI *[danseuse]* to twirl around, to pirouette; *[cheval]* to do a demivolt, to pirouette

Virgile /virʒil/ NM Virgil

virginal, e (mpl **-aux**) /virʒinal, o/ ADJ *(littér)* virginal, maidenly *(littér)* ◆ **d'une blancheur ~e** virgin white NM *(Mus)* virginal, virginals

Virginie /virʒini/ NF *(Géog)* Virginia ◆ **~-Occidentale** West Virginia

virginité /virʒinite/ NF 1 *(lit)* virginity, maidenhood *(littér)* ◆ **garder/perdre sa ~** to keep/lose one's virginity 2 *(fig littér) [de neige, aube, âme]* purity ◆ **il voulait rendre à ce lieu sa ~** he wished to restore this place to its untouched *ou* virgin quality ◆ **se refaire une ~** *(hum)* to restore one's image

virgule /virgyl/ NF 1 *(= ponctuation)* comma ◆ **mettre une ~** to put a comma in ◆ **sans y changer une ~** *(fig)* without changing a (single) thing, without touching a single comma ◆ **c'est exactement ce qu'il m'a dit, à la ~ près** that's exactly what he said to me, word for word ◆ **à quelques ~s près, le texte n'a pas été modifié** apart from the odd comma, the text hasn't been changed at all ◆ **moustaches en ~** curled moustache 2 *(Math)* (decimal) point ◆ **(arrondi à) 3 chiffres après la ~** (correct to) 3 decimal places ◆ **5 ~ 2** 5 point 2 ◆ **~ fixe/flottante** fixed/floating decimal (point)

viril, e /viril/ ADJ *[attributs, apparence]* male, masculine; *[attitude, courage, langage, traits]* manly, virile; *[prouesses, amant]* virile ◆ **force ~e** virile *ou* manly strength ◆ **amitiés ~es** male friendships ◆ **elle fait un peu ~** she's a bit mannish ◆ **jeu ~** *(Sport)* aggressive style; → **âge, membre, toge**

virilement /virilmɑ̃/ ADV in a manly *ou* virile way

virilisant, e /virilizɑ̃, ɑ̃t/ ADJ *[médicament]* that provokes male characteristics, virilizing

virilisation /virilizasjɔ̃/ NF *(Méd)* virilism

viriliser /virilize/ ► conjug 1 ◄ VT *(Bio)* to give male characteristics to; *(en apparence) [+ femme]* to make appear mannish *ou* masculine; *[+ homme]* to make (appear) more manly *ou* masculine

virilisme /virilism/ NM virility; *(Méd)* virilism

virilité /virilite/ NF *[d'attributs, apparence, formes]* masculinity; *[d'attitude, courage, langage, traits]* manliness, virility; *[de prouesses, amant]* virility ◆ **il se sent menacé dans sa ~** his masculinity feels threatened ◆ **manquer de ~** to be unmanly

virole /virɔl/ NF 1 *(= bague)* ferrule ◆ **couteau à ~ tournante** pocket knife with a safety catch 2 *(Tech = moule)* collar

viroler /virɔle/ ► conjug 1 ◄ VT 1 *[+ couteau, parapluie]* to ferrule, to fit with a ferrule 2 *(Tech)* to place in a collar

virologie /virɔlɔʒi/ NF virology

virologique /virɔlɔʒik/ ADJ virological

virologiste /virɔlɔʒist/, **virologue** /virɔlɔg/ NMF virologist

virose /viroz/ NF viral infection

virtualisation /virtɥalizasjɔ̃/ NF virtualization

virtualité /virtɥalite/ NF 1 *[de marché, sens, revenu]* potentiality 2 *(Philos, Phys, Ordin)* virtuality

virtuel, -elle /virtɥɛl/ ADJ 1 *(= potentiel) [candidat, marché, sens, revenu]* potential ◆ **tout cela est très ~** all that is purely theoretical 2 *(Philos, Phys, Ordin)* virtual ◆ **mémoire/réalité virtuelle** virtual memory/reality; → **image** NM *(Ordin)* ◆ **le ~** virtual reality

> ⚠ Au sens de 'potentiel', **virtuel** ne se traduit pas par **virtual**.

virtuellement /virtɥɛlmɑ̃/ ADV 1 *(littér = en puissance)* potentially 2 *(= pratiquement)* virtually ◆ **c'était ~ fini** it was virtually finished, it was as good as finished 3 *(Ordin)* **visiter ~ le Louvre** to make a virtual reality tour of the Louvre

virtuose /virtɥoz/ NMF *(Mus)* virtuoso; *(= personne douée)* master, virtuoso ◆ **~ du violon** violin virtuoso ◆ **~ de la plume/du pinceau** master of the pen/of the brush, brilliant writer/painter ADJ virtuoso

virtuosité /virtɥozite/ NF virtuosity ◆ **exercices de ~** *(Mus)* exercises in virtuosity ◆ **avec ~** masterfully ◆ **il a interprété ce morceau avec ~** he gave a virtuoso performance (of this piece), he played this piece brilliantly

virulence /virylɑ̃s/ NF 1 *(Méd)* virulence 2 *[de critique, opposition, campagne de presse]* virulence, viciousness ◆ **avec ~** virulently

virulent, e /virylɑ̃, ɑ̃t/ ADJ 1 *(Méd)* virulent 2 *[critique, opposition, déclaration, personne]* virulent, vicious

virus /virys/ NM *(Méd, Ordin)* virus ◆ **~ de la rage/du sida** rabies/AIDS virus ◆ **~ de l'immunodéficience humaine** human immunodeficiency virus ◆ **le ~ de la danse/du jeu** the dancing/gambling bug* ◆ **attraper le ~ du jeu** to be *ou* get bitten by the gambling bug*

vis /vis/ NF 1 *(gén)* screw ◆ **~ à bois** wood screw ◆ **~ à métaux** metal screw ◆ **~ à tête plate/à tête ronde** flat-headed/round-headed screw ◆ **~ à ailettes** wing nut; → **cruciforme, pas¹, serrer, tour²** 2 † **(escalier à) ~** spiral staircase

COMP **vis d'Archimède** Archimedes' screw, endless screw
vis micrométrique micrometer screw
vis platinées *[de moteur]* (contact) points
vis de pressoir press screw
vis sans fin worm screw
vis de serrage binding *ou* clamping screw

visa /viza/ NM *(= formule, sceau)* stamp; *(sur un passeport)* visa ◆ **~ d'entrée/de sortie/de transit** entry/exit/transit visa ◆ **~ touristique** *ou* **de tourisme** tourist visa ◆ **~ de censure** *(Ciné)* (censor's) certificate ◆ **~ d'exploitation** *(Ciné)* distribution number ◆ **~ pour ...** *(fig)* passport to ... ◆ **carte Visa** ® *(Fin)* Visa ® card

visage /vizaʒ/ NM 1 *(lit = figure, fig = expression, personne, aspect)* face ◆ **au ~ pâle/joufflu** pale-/chubby-faced ◆ **un ~ connu/ami** a known/friendly face ◆ **je lui trouve bon ~** he looks well (to me) ◆ **sans ~** faceless ◆ **le vrai ~ de ...** the true face of ... ◆ **un homme à deux ~s** a two-faced man ◆ **un problème aux multiples ~s** a multifaceted problem ◆ **à ~ humain** *[capitalisme, entreprise]* with a human face ◆ **le nouveau ~ du parti/pays** the new face of the party/country ◆ **donner un nouveau ~ à** *[+ ville]* to give a new look to; *[+ entreprise, parti]* to change the face of ◆ **elle changea de ~** her face *ou* expression changed ◆ **l'Europe a changé de ~** the face of Europe has changed; → **soin**

2 *(locutions)* **agir/parler à ~ découvert** to act/speak openly ◆ **faire bon ~** to put a good face on it ◆ **faire bon ~ à qn** *(littér) (= l'accueillir chaleureusement)* to give sb a warm welcome; *(avec hypocrisie)* to put on a show of friendliness for sb ◆ **montrer son vrai ~** to show one's true colours *(Brit) ou* colors *(US)*

COMP **Visage pâle** paleface

visagiste ® /vizaʒist/ NMF ◆ **(coiffeur) ~** (hair) stylist ◆ **(esthéticienne) ~** beautician

vis-à-vis /vizavi/ PRÉP 1 *(= en face de)* **~ de** opposite ◆ **~ de la gare** opposite the station
2 *(= comparé à)* **~ de** beside, next to, against ◆ **mes ennuis ne sont pas graves ~ des siens** my problems aren't serious beside *ou* next to his
3 ◆ **~ de** *(= envers)* towards, vis-à-vis; *(= à l'égard de)* as regards, with regard to, vis-à-vis ◆ **être sincère ~ de soi-même** to be frank with oneself ◆ **être méfiant ~ de ce genre d'évolution** to be wary of such developments ◆ **~ de cette proposition** with regard to this proposal ◆ **j'en ai honte ~ de lui** I'm ashamed of it in front of *ou* before him

ADV *(= face à face)* face to face ◆ **leurs maisons se font ~** their houses face *ou* are opposite each other

NM INV 1 *(= position)* **en ~** facing *ou* opposite each other ◆ **des immeubles en ~** buildings facing *ou* opposite each other ◆ **ils étaient assis en ~** they were sitting opposite each other, they were sitting face to face
2 *(= tête-à-tête)* encounter, meeting ◆ **un ~ ennuyeux** a tiresome encounter *ou* meeting
3 *(= personne faisant face)* person opposite; *(aux cartes) (= partenaire)* partner; *(= homologue)* opposite number, counterpart
4 *(= bâtiment)* **immeuble sans ~** building with an open outlook ◆ **avoir une école pour ~** to have a school opposite, to look out over a school
5 *(= canapé)* tête-à-tête

viscéral, e (mpl **-aux**) /viseral, o/ ADJ 1 *(Anat)* visceral 2 *[haine, peur, besoin]* deep-rooted, visceral *(frm)*; *[rejet]* instinctive; *[attachement]* passionate ◆ **réaction ~e** gut reaction

viscéralement /viseralmɑ̃/ ADV *[attaché]* passionately; *[hostile]* instinctively ◆ **détester ~ qch** to have a deep *ou* visceral *(frm)* loathing of sth ◆ **réagir ~ à qch** to have a gut reaction to sth ◆ **~ jaloux** pathologically jealous

viscère /viser/ NM (internal) organ ◆ **~s** intestines, entrails, viscera *(SPÉC)*

viscose /viskoz/ NF viscose

viscosité /viskozite/ NF *[de liquide]* viscosity; *[de surface gluante]* stickiness, viscosity

visée /vize/ NF 1 *(avec une arme)* taking aim *(NonC)*, aiming *(NonC)*; *(Arpentage)* sighting ◆ **pour faciliter la ~, ce fusil comporte un dispositif spécial** to help you to (take) aim *ou* to help your aim, this rifle comes equipped with a special device; → **ligne¹** 2 *(gén pl = dessein)* aim, design ◆ **avoir des ~s sur qn/qch** to have designs on sb/sth ◆ **les ~s expansionnistes d'un pays** the expansionist aims *ou* ambitions of a country ◆ **~s coupables** wicked designs

◆ **à visée** ◆ **il est contre le clonage à ~ thérapeutique** he is against therapeutic cloning *ou* cloning for therapeutic purposes ◆ **une opération à ~ médiatique** a media stunt

viser¹ /vize/ ► conjug 1 ◄ VT 1 *[+ objectif]* to aim at *ou* for; *[+ cible]* to aim at
2 *(= ambitionner) [+ effet]* to aim at; *[+ carrière]* to aim at, to set one's sights on
3 *(= concerner) [mesure]* to be aimed at, to be directed at; *[remarque]* to be aimed *ou* directed at, to be meant *ou* intended for ◆ **cette mesure vise tout le monde** this measure applies to

everyone, everyone is affected by this measure ◆ **il se sent visé** he feels he's being got at*

4 (* = *regarder*) to take a look at, to have a dekko* (*Brit*) at ◆ **vise un peu ça !** just take a look *ou* have a dekko* (*Brit*) at that!

VI 1 [*tireur*] to aim, to take aim ◆ ~ **juste** (*lit*) to aim accurately; (*fig*) not to miss the mark ◆ ~ **trop haut/trop bas** to aim (too) high/(too) low ◆ ~ **à la tête/au cœur** to aim for the head/the heart

2 (= *ambitionner*) ~ **haut/plus haut** to set one's sights high/higher, to aim high/higher

VT INDIR **viser à** (= *avoir pour but de*) ~ **à qch/à faire** to aim at sth/to do ◆ **scène qui vise à provoquer le rire** scene which sets out to raise a laugh *ou* to make people laugh ◆ **mesures qui visent à la réunification de la majorité** measures which are aimed at reuniting *ou* which aim *ou* are intended to reunite the majority

viser² /vize/ ▸ conjug 1 ◂ VT (*Admin*) [+ *passeport*] to visa; [+ *document*] to stamp ◆ **faire ~ un passeport** to have a passport visaed

viseur /vizœʀ/ NM 1 [*d'arme*] sights; [*de caméra, appareil photo*] viewfinder ◆ ~ **à cadre lumineux** (*Photo*) collimator viewfinder 2 (*Astron* = *lunette*) telescopic sight

Vishnou, Vishnu /viʃnu/ NM Vishnu

visibilité /vizibilite/ NF 1 (*gén, Sci*) visibility ◆ **bonne/mauvaise** ~ good/poor *ou* bad visibility ◆ ~ **nulle** nil *ou* zero visibility ◆ **ce pare-brise permet une très bonne** ~ this windscreen gives excellent visibility ◆ **manque de** ~ (*lit*) lack of visibility; (*fig*) lack of foresight ◆ **sans** ~ [*pilotage, virage, atterrissage*] blind (*épith*) ◆ **piloter sans** ~ to fly blind 2 (= *mise en évidence*) [*de produit, société*] visibility ◆ **une association à grande ~ médiatique** an organization with a high media profile

visible /vizibl/ ADJ 1 (= *qui peut être vu*) visible ◆ ~ **à l'œil nu/au microscope** visible to the naked eye/under a microscope; → **iceberg**

2 (= *évident, net*) [*embarras, surprise*] obvious, visible; [*amélioration, progrès*] clear, visible; [*réparation, reprise*] obvious ◆ **sa déception était** ~ his disappointment was obvious *ou* visible, you could see his disappointment *ou* that he was disappointed ◆ **il ne veut pas le faire, c'est** ~ he obviously doesn't want to, he doesn't want to, that's obvious *ou* apparent *ou* clear ◆ **il est ~ que ...** it is obvious *ou* clear that ... ◆ **nos produits ne sont pas assez ~s sur ce marché** our products aren't visible enough on the market

3 (= *en état de recevoir*) **Monsieur est-il ~ ?** is Mr X (*ou* Lord X *etc*) able to receive visitors?, is Mr X (*ou* Lord X *etc*) receiving visitors? ◆ **elle n'est pas ~ le matin** she's not at home to visitors *ou* not in to visitors in the morning

NM ◆ **le** ~ what is visible, the visible

visiblement /vizibləmɑ̃/ ADV 1 (= *manifestement*) visibly, obviously ◆ **il était ~ inquiet** he was visibly *ou* obviously worried ◆ ~**, c'est une erreur** obviously *ou* clearly it's a mistake 2 (= *de façon perceptible à l'œil*) visibly, perceptibly

visière /vizjɛʀ/ NF [*de casquette, képi*] peak; [*de casque*] visor; (*pour le soleil*) eyeshade ◆ **mettre sa main en** ~ to shade one's eyes with one's hand; → **rompre**

visioconférence /vizjokɔ̃feʀɑ̃s/ NF videoconference, teleconference

vision /vizjɔ̃/ NF 1 (= *faculté*) (eye)sight, vision; (= *perception*) vision, sight ◆ **une ~ défectueuse** defective (eye)sight *ou* vision ◆ **le mécanisme de la** ~ the mechanism of vision *ou* sight ◆ **pour faciliter la** ~ to aid (eye)sight *ou* vision ◆ ~ **nette/floue** clear/hazy vision ◆ **porter des lunettes pour la ~ de loin** to wear glasses for distance vision; → **champ¹**

2 (= *conception*) view ◆ **c'est une ~ idyllique des choses** it's an idyllic view of things ◆ **avoir une ~ globale** *ou* **d'ensemble d'un problème** to have a global view of a problem ◆ **nous partageons la même ~ des choses** we see things (in) the same way

3 (= *image, apparition, mirage*) vision ◆ **tu as des ~s** * you're seeing things

4 (= *spectacle*) sight ◆ ~ **d'horreur** horrific sight *ou* scene ◆ **après l'attentat, l'aéroport offrait une ~ d'apocalypse** after the bomb attack the airport was a scene of apocalyptic horror *ou* was like a scene from the apocalypse

visionnage /vizjɔnaʒ/ NM viewing

visionnaire /vizjɔnɛʀ/ ADJ, NMF visionary

visionner /vizjɔne/ ▸ conjug 1 ◂ VT to view

visionneuse /vizjɔnøz/ NF viewer (*for transparencies or film*)

visiophone /vizjɔfɔn/ NM videophone, viewphone

visiophonie /vizjɔfɔni/ NF video teleconferencing, video calling

Visitation /vizitasjɔ̃/ NF (*Rel*) ◆ **la** ~ the Visitation

visite /vizit/ NF 1 (= *fait de visiter*) visiting, going round ◆ **heures/jour de ~** *ou* **des ~s** (*à la prison, l'hôpital*) visiting hours/day ◆ **la ~ du château a duré deux heures** it took two hours to visit *ou* go round (*Brit*) *ou* go through (*US*) the château; → **droit³**

2 (= *tournée, inspection*) visit ◆ **au programme il y a des ~s de musée** there are museum visits on the programme ◆ ~ **accompagnée** *ou* **guidée** guided tour ◆ **ces ~s nocturnes au garde-manger** (*hum*) these nocturnal visits *ou* trips to the pantry

3 (*chez une connaissance*) visit ◆ **une courte ~** a short visit, a call ◆ **une ~ de politesse** a courtesy call *ou* visit ◆ **une ~ de remerciements** a thank-you visit ◆ **être en ~ chez qn** to be paying sb a visit, to be on a visit to sb ◆ **rendre ~ à qn** to pay sb a visit, to call on sb, to visit sb ◆ **je vais lui faire une petite** ~ I'm going to pay him a (little) visit, I'm going to call on him ◆ **rendre à qn sa** ~ to return sb's visit, to pay sb a return visit ◆ **avoir** *ou* **recevoir la ~ de qn** to have a visit from sb ◆ **vos ~s se font de plus en plus rares** you should come and visit more often ◆ **ses ~s étaient rares** he rarely visited; → **carte**

4 (= *visiteur*) visitor ◆ **nous avons des ~s** we've got visitors *ou* company *ou* guests ◆ **j'ai une ~ dans le salon** I have a visitor *ou* I have company in the lounge ◆ **nous attendons de la** ~ *ou* **des ~s** we're expecting visitors *ou* company *ou* guests ◆ **tiens, nous avons de la** ~ (*hum*) hey, we've got company *ou* guests

5 [*de chef d'État*] visit ◆ **en ~ officielle au Japon** on an official visit to Japan

6 [*de médecin hospitalier avec étudiants*] ward round ◆ ~ **(à domicile)** [*de médecin de ville*] (house)call, visit ◆ **il ne fait pas de ~s à domicile** he doesn't make housecalls ◆ ~ **de contrôle** follow-up visit ◆ **la** ~ (*chez le médecin*) (medical) consultation; (*Mil*) (*quotidienne*) sick parade; (*d'entrée*) medical (examination) (*Brit*), physical examination (*US*) ◆ **aller à la** ~ to go to the surgery (for a consultation) ◆ **passer à la ~ (médicale)** [*recrue*] to have a medical (*Brit*) *ou* physical (*US*) examination ◆ **l'heure de la ~ dans le service** the time when the doctor does his ward round(s)

7 (*de vendeur*) visit, call; (*d'expert*) inspection ◆ **j'ai reçu la ~ d'un représentant** I had a visit *ou* call from a representative, a representative called (on me)

COMP **visite du diocèse** ⇒ **visite épiscopale**
visite domiciliaire (*Jur*) house search
visite de douane customs inspection *ou* examination
visite épiscopale (*Rel*) pastoral visitation

visiter /vizite/ ▸ conjug 1 ◂ VT 1 [+ *pays, ville, site Internet*] to visit; [+ *château, musée*] to visit, to go round (*Brit*) *ou* through (*US*) ◆ ~ **une maison** (*à vendre*) to look over a house, to view a house ◆ **il me fit ~ sa maison/son laboratoire** he showed me round (*Brit*) *ou* through (*US*) his house/his laboratory ◆ **il nous a fait ~ la maison que nous envisagions d'acheter** he showed us round (*Brit*) *ou* through (*US*) *ou* over (*Brit*) the house we were thinking of buying ◆ **le monument le plus visité de Paris** the most visited site in Paris ◆ **c'est le site Internet le plus visité** it is the most frequently visited website, it is the website with the most hits

2 (*en cherchant qch*) [+ *bagages*] to examine, to inspect; [+ *boutiques*] to go round; [+ *recoins*] to search (in); [+ *armoire*] to go through, to search (in); (*Admin*) [+ *navire*] to inspect; (*hum*) [+ *coffre-fort*] to visit (*hum*), to pay a visit to (*hum*) ◆ **leur maison a été visitée plusieurs fois** (*hum*) they've been burgled *ou* they've had burglars several times

3 (*par charité*) [+ *malades, prisonniers*] to visit

4 [*médecin, représentant, inspecteur*] to visit, to call on

5 (*Rel*) to visit

6 († = *fréquenter*) [+ *voisins, connaissances*] to visit, to call on

visiteur, -euse /vizitœʀ, øz/ NM,F (*gén*) visitor ◆ **les ~s** (*Sport*) the visiting *ou* away team; → **infirmier, médical**

COMP **visiteur des douanes** customs inspector
visiteur de prison prison visitor

vison /vizɔ̃/ NM (= *animal, fourrure*) mink; (= *manteau*) mink (coat)

visonnière /vizɔnjɛʀ/ NF (*Can*) mink farm, minkery (*Can*)

visqueux, -euse /viskø, øz/ ADJ 1 [*liquide*] viscous, thick; [*pâte*] sticky, viscous; (*péj*) [*surface, objet*] sticky, goo(e)y*, viscous 2 (*fig péj*) [*personne, manière*] slimy, smarmy (*Brit*)

vissage /visaʒ/ NM screwing (on *ou* down)

visser /vise/ ▸ conjug 1 ◂ VT 1 (*au moyen de vis*) [+ *plaque, serrure*] to screw on; [+ *couvercle*] to screw down *ou* on ◆ **ce n'est pas bien vissé** it's not screwed down properly ◆ ~ **un objet sur qch** to screw an object on to sth ◆ **vissé devant la télé*** glued* to the television ◆ **il est resté vissé sur sa chaise*** he never got out of his chair ◆ **le chapeau vissé sur la tête** with his hat jammed hard *ou* tight on his head 2 (*en tournant*) [+ *couvercle, bouchon, écrou*] to screw on ◆ **ce couvercle se visse** this is a screw-on lid, this lid screws on ◆ **ce n'est pas bien vissé** [*bouchon*] it's not screwed on *ou* down properly; [*écrou*] it's not screwed down properly 3 (* = *être strict avec*) [+ *élève, subordonné*] to keep a tight rein on, to crack down on* ◆ **toi, je vais te ~ !** things are going to get tough for you around here!

visseuse /visøz/ NF screwing machine

vista /vista/ NF (*surtout Sport*) clairvoyance

Vistule /vistyl/ NF ◆ **la** ~ the Vistula

visu /vizy/ **de visu** LOC ADV with one's own eyes ◆ **s'assurer de qch de** ~ to check sth with one's own eyes *ou* for oneself

visualisation /vizɥalizasjɔ̃/ NF (*gén*) visualization; (*Ordin*) display; → **console, écran**

visualiser /vizɥalize/ ▸ conjug 1 ◂ VT (*gén*) to visualize; (*à l'écran*) to display ◆ **j'ai du mal à ~ la scène** it's hard for me to visualize what happened

visualiseur /vizɥalizœʀ/ (*Ordin*) visualizer

visuel, -elle /vizɥɛl/ ADJ (*gén*) visual ◆ **troubles ~s** eye trouble (*NonC*); → **champ¹, mémoire¹** NM,F ◆ **cet écrivain est un ~** visual images predominate in the writings of this author NM (*Ordin*) visual display unit, VDU; (*Publicité*) visual ◆ **~ graphique** graphical display unit

visuellement /vizɥɛlmɑ̃/ ADV visually

vit † /vi/ NM (*littér*) penis

vital, e (mpl **-aux**) /vital, o/ ADJ (*Bio, gén*) vital; → **centre, espace¹, minimum**

vitalisme /vitalism/ NM (*Philos*) vitalism

vitalité /vitalite/ NF [*de personne*] energy, vitality; [*d'institution, terme*] vitality ◆ **il est plein de ~** he's full of energy *ou* go *ou* vitality ◆ **la ~ de ces enfants est incroyable** it's incredible how much energy these children have

vitamine /vitamin/ NF vitamin ◆ **~ A/C** vitamin A/C ◆ **alimentation riche/pauvre en ~s** food that is rich *ou* high/low in vitamins ◆ **lait enrichi en ~s** vitamin-enriched milk, milk with added vitamins *ou* enriched with vitamins; → **carence**

vitaminé, e /vitamine/ ADJ with added vitamins

vitaminique /vitaminik/ ADJ vitamin (*épith*)

vite /vit/ ADV 1 (= *à vive allure*) [*rouler, marcher*] fast, quickly; [*progresser, avancer*] quickly, rapidly, swiftly

2 (= *rapidement*) [*travailler, se dérouler, se passer*] quickly, fast; (= *en hâte*) [*faire un travail*] quickly, in a rush *ou* hurry ◆ **ça s'est passé si ~, je n'ai rien vu** it happened so quickly *ou* fast I didn't see a thing ◆ **il travaille ~ et bien** he works quickly *ou* fast and well ◆ **vous avez fait ~ pour venir** it didn't take you long to come, you were quick getting here ◆ **ça ne va pas ~** it's slow work ◆ **fais ~ !** be quick about it!, look sharp! * ◆ **eh, pas si ~ !** hey, not so fast!, hey, hold on (a minute)! ◆ **et plus ~ que ça !** and get a move on! *, and be quick about it! ◆ **là il (y) va un peu ~** he's being a bit hasty ◆ **le temps passe ~** time flies ◆ **la police est allée ~ en besogne** * the police were quick off the mark *ou* worked fast *ou* didn't waste any time ◆ **vous allez un peu ~ en besogne** * you're going too fast, you're a bit too quick off the mark ◆ **aller plus ~ que les violons** *ou* **la musique** to jump the gun ◆ **c'est ~ dit** * (it's) easier said than done ◆ **j'aurais plus ~ fait de l'écrire moi-même** it would have been quicker if I'd written it myself

◆ **vite fait** ◆ **ça, c'est du ~ fait !** that's a rushed job!, that's been done too quickly! ◆ **elle s'est tirée ~ fait** * she was off like a shot *, she took off as quick as a flash * ◆ **il faut que tu termines ça, ~ fait (sur le gaz)** * you have to finish that, pronto * ◆ **on prend une bière, mais ~ fait (sur le gaz)** * we'll have a beer, but just a quick one * *ou* a quickie * ◆ **il l'a terminé ~ fait, bien fait** he finished it nice and quickly * ◆ **il l'a peint ~ fait, bien fait** he gave it a quick coat of paint ◆ **c'est du ~ fait, bien fait** it's a nice quick job

3 (= *bientôt*) soon, in no time ◆ **elle sera ~ arrivée/guérie** she'll soon be here/better, she'll be here/better in no time ◆ **il eut ~ fait de découvrir que ...** he soon *ou* quickly discovered that ..., in no time he discovered that ... ◆ **ce sera ~ fait** it won't take long, it won't take a moment *ou* a second ◆ **on a ~ fait de dire que ...** it's easy to say that ...

4 (= *immédiatement*) quick ◆ **lève-toi ~ !** get up quick! ◆ **va ~ voir !** go and see quick! ◆ **au plus ~** as quickly as possible ◆ **il faut le prévenir au plus ~** he must be warned as quickly *ou* as soon as possible ◆ **faites-moi ça, et ~ !** do this for me and be quick about it! ◆ **~ ! un médecin** quick! a doctor

ADJ (*style journalistique : Sport*) fast

vitellus /vitelys/ NM (*Bio*) vitellin

vitesse /vitɛs/ NF 1 (= *promptitude, hâte*) speed, quickness, rapidity

◆ **en vitesse** (= *rapidement*) quickly; (= *en hâte*) in a hurry *ou* rush ◆ **faites-moi ça en ~** do this for me quickly ◆ **faites-moi ça, et en ~ !** do this for me and be quick about it! ◆ **on va prendre un verre en ~** we'll go for a quick drink ◆ **écrire un petit mot en ~** to scribble a hasty note ◆ **j'ai préparé le déjeuner/cette conférence un peu en ~** I prepared lunch/this lecture in a bit of a hurry *ou* rush

◆ **à toute vitesse, en quatrième vitesse** at full *ou* top speed ◆ **il faut toujours tout faire en quatrième ~** everything always has to be done at top speed *ou* in a great rush ◆ **(à la nouvelle) il est arrivé en quatrième ~** *ou* **à toute ~** (on hearing the news) he came like a shot *ou* at the double

2 [*de courant, processus*] speed; [*de véhicule, projectile*] speed, velocity ◆ **aimer la ~** to love speed ◆ **à la ~ de 60 km/h** at (a speed of) 60 km/h ◆ **à quelle ~ allait-il ?, quelle ~ faisait-il ?** what speed was he going at? *ou* doing?, how fast was he going? ◆ **faire de la ~** to go *ou* drive fast ◆ **faire une ~ (moyenne) de 60** to do an average (speed) of 60 ◆ **prendre de la ~** to gather *ou* increase speed, to pick up speed ◆ **gagner** *ou* **prendre qn de ~** (*lit*) to beat sb, to outstrip sb; (*fig*) to beat sb to it, to pip sb at the post * (*Brit*), to beat sb by a nose (*US*) ◆ **entraîné par sa propre ~** carried along by his own momentum ◆ **~ de propagation/réaction/rotation** speed of propagation/reaction/rotation ◆ **à grande ~** at great speed ◆ **passer une vidéo en ~ accélérée** to fast-forward a video ◆ **faire qch à la ~ de l'éclair** to do sth with lightning speed *ou* as quick as a flash ◆ **à une ~ vertigineuse** [*conduire, avancer*] at a dizzying speed; [*augmenter, se multiplier*] at a dizzying rate ◆ **circuler à ~ réduite** to drive at reduced speed; → **course, excès, perte**

3 (*Rail*) **grande/petite ~** fast/slow goods service ◆ **expédier un colis en petite ~** to send a parcel by slow goods service ◆ **expédier un colis en grande ~** to send a parcel express

4 (= *dispositif*) gear ◆ **changer de ~** to change *ou* shift (*US*) gear ◆ **2ᵉ/4ᵉ ~** 2nd/4th gear ◆ **passer les ~s** to go *ou* run through the gears ◆ **passer la ~ supérieure** (*fig*) to quicken the pace, to shift into high gear (*US*) ◆ **une Europe à deux ~s** a two-speed Europe ◆ **société/justice à deux ~s** two-tier society/justice system; → **boîte**

5 (*locutions*) **à (la) ~ grand V** * at top speed, real fast * (*US*) ◆ **il est parti à la ~ grand V** * he shot off *, he went tearing off *, he left like a bullet from a gun

COMP **vitesse acquise** momentum
vitesse d'affichage (*Ordin*) display speed
vitesse de croisière (*lit, fig*) cruising speed
vitesse de frappe typing speed
vitesse d'impression (*Ordin*) print speed
vitesse initiale muzzle velocity
vitesse de lecture (*Ordin*) reading rate
vitesse de libération escape velocity *ou* speed
vitesse de la lumière speed of light
vitesse de pointe maximum *ou* top speed
vitesse de sédimentation sedimentation speed
vitesse du son (*lit, fig*) speed of sound
vitesse de sustentation minimum flying speed
vitesse de traitement (*Ordin*) processing speed

viticole /vitikɔl/ ADJ [*industrie*] wine (*épith*); [*région*] wine-growing (*épith*), wine-producing (*épith*); [*établissement*] wine-producing (*épith*), wine-making (*épith*) ◆ **culture ~** wine growing, viticulture (*SPÉC*)

viticulteur, -trice /vitikyltœʀ, tʀis/ NM,F wine grower, viticulturist (*SPÉC*)

viticulture /vitikyltyʀ/ NF wine growing, viticulture (*SPÉC*)

vitrage /vitʀaʒ/ NM 1 (= *action*) glazing 2 (= *vitres*) windows; (= *cloison*) glass partition; (= *toit*) glass roof ◆ **double ~** double glazing ◆ **fenêtre à double ~** double-glazed window 3 (= *rideau*) net curtain; (= *tissu*) net curtaining

vitrail (pl **-aux**) /vitʀaj, o/ NM stained-glass window, church window ◆ **l'art du ~, le ~** the art of stained-glass window making

vitre /vitʀ/ NF 1 [*de fenêtre, vitrine*] (window) pane, pane (of glass); [*de voiture*] window ◆ **poser/mastiquer une ~** to put in/putty a window pane *ou* a pane of glass ◆ **verre à ~** window glass ◆ **laver/faire les ~s** to wash/do *ou* clean the windows ◆ **appuyer son front à la ~** to press one's forehead against the window (pane) ◆ **les camions font trembler les ~s** the lorries make the window panes *ou* the windows rattle ◆ **casser une ~** to break a window (pane) ◆ **~ blindée** bullet-proof window ◆ **la ~ arrière** (*d'une voiture*) the rear window *ou* windscreen (*Brit*) *ou* windshield (*US*) ◆ **~s électriques** electric windows 2 (= *fenêtre*) **~s** windows ◆ **fermer les ~s** to close the windows

vitré, e /vitʀe/ (ptp de **vitrer**) ADJ 1 [*porte, cloison*] glass (*épith*); → **baie²** 2 (*Anat*) **corps ~** vitreous body ◆ **humeur ~e** vitreous humour NM (*Anat*) vitreous body

vitrer /vitʀe/ ► conjug 1 ◄ VT [+ *fenêtre*] to glaze, to put glass in; [+ *véranda, porte*] to put windows in, to put glass in

vitrerie /vitʀəʀi/ NF (= *activité*) glaziery, glazing; (= *marchandise*) glass

vitreux, -euse /vitʀø, øz/ ADJ 1 (*Anat*) [*humeur*] vitreous 2 (*Géol*) vitreous; → **porcelaine** 3 (*péj* = *terne, glauque*) [*yeux*] glassy, dull; [*regard*] glassy, glazed, lacklustre (*Brit*) *ou* lackluster (*US*) (*épith*); [*surface, eau*] dull

vitrier /vitʀije/ NM glazier ◆ **ton père n'est pas ~ !** * I can't see through you!

vitrification /vitʀifikasjɔ̃/ NF 1 (*Tech*) (*par fusion*) vitrification; (*par enduit*) glazing ◆ **la ~ des déchets radioactifs** vitrification of nuclear waste 2 [*de parquet*] sealing, varnishing

vitrifier /vitʀifje/ ► conjug 7 ◄ VT 1 (*Tech*) (*par fusion*) to vitrify; (*par enduit*) to glaze, to put a glaze on ◆ **déchets vitrifiés** vitrified waste 2 (= *vernir*) [+ *parquet*] to seal, to varnish VPR **se vitrifier** to vitrify

vitrine /vitʀin/ NF 1 (= *devanture*) (shop) window ◆ **en ~** in the window ◆ **la ~ du boucher/de la pâtisserie** the butcher's/ pastry *ou* cake (*Brit*) shop window ◆ **faire les ~s** to dress the windows ◆ **~ publicitaire** display case, showcase ◆ **cette exposition est la ~ de l'Europe** this exhibition is Europe's showcase ◆ **la ~ légale d'une organisation terroriste** the legal front for a terrorist organization; → **lécher** 2 (= *meuble*) (*chez soi*) display cabinet; (*au musée*) showcase, display cabinet

vitriol /vitʀijɔl/ NM (*Hist, Chim*) vitriol ◆ **une critique/un style au ~** (*fig*) a vitriolic review/ style ◆ **du ~** (*péj* = *mauvais alcool*) firewater

vitriolage /vitʀijɔlaʒ/ NM (*Tech*) vitriolization

vitrioler /vitʀijɔle/ ► conjug 1 ◄ VT 1 (*Tech*) to vitriolize, to treat with vitriol *ou* (concentrated) sulphuric acid 2 [+ *victime d'agression*] to throw acid *ou* vitriol at

vitrocéramique /vitʀoseʀamik/ NF vitreous ceramic ◆ **table de cuisson en ~** ceramic hob

vitupération /vitypeʀasjɔ̃/ NF (= *propos*) ◆ **~s** rantings and ravings, vituperations (*frm*)

vitupérer /vitypeʀe/ ► conjug 6 ◄ VI to rant and rave ◆ **~ contre qn/qch** to rail against sb/sth, to rant and rave about sb/sth VT (*littér*) to inveigh against

vivable /vivabl/ ADJ 1 * [personne] bearable ◆ **il n'est pas** ~ he's impossible to live with ◆ **ce n'est pas** ~ **!** it's intolerable! 2 [milieu, monde] fit to live in ◆ **cette maison n'est pas** ~ this house isn't fit to live in

vivace[1] /vivas/ ADJ 1 (Bot) hardy ◆ **plante** ~ (hardy) perennial 2 [préjugé] inveterate, indestructible; [haine] undying, inveterate; [souvenir] vivid; [foi] steadfast, undying; [tradition] enduring NF (= plante) perennial

vivace[2] /vivatʃe/ ADV, ADJ (Mus) vivace

vivacité /vivasite/ NF 1 (= rapidité, vie) [de personne] liveliness, vivacity; [de mouvement] liveliness, briskness; [d'intelligence] keenness; [de langue, dialogues, débat] liveliness ◆ ~ **d'esprit** quick-wittedness ◆ **avoir de la** ~ to be lively *ou* vivacious ◆ **avec** ~ [réagir, se déplacer] swiftly 2 (= brusquerie) sharpness, brusqueness ◆ **avec** ~ [critiquer, répliquer] sharply, brusquely 3 (= caractère vif) [de lumière, éclat] brightness, brilliance; [de couleur] vividness; [de froid] bitterness; [de douleur] sharpness; [de vent] keenness 4 (= intensité) [d'émotion, plaisir] keenness, intensity; [d'impression] vividness

vivandière /vivɑ̃djɛʀ/ NF (Hist) vivandière

vivant, e /vivɑ̃, ɑt/ ADJ 1 (= en vie) living, alive (attrib), live (épith) ◆ **né** ~ born alive ◆ **il est encore** ~ he's still alive *ou* living ◆ **il n'en sortira pas** ~ he won't come out of it alive ◆ **expériences sur des animaux ~s** experiments on live *ou* living animals, live animal experiments ◆ **c'est un cadavre/squelette** ~ he's a living corpse/skeleton

2 (= plein de vie) [regard, visage, enfant] lively; [ville, quartier, rue] lively, full of life (attrib); [portrait] lifelike, true to life (attrib); [dialogue, récit, film] lively; (fig) [personnage] lifelike

3 (= doué de vie) [matière, organisme] living; → **être**

4 (= constitué par des êtres vivants) [machine, témoignage, preuve] living ◆ **c'est le portrait** ~ **de sa mère** he's the (living) image of his mother; → **tableau**

5 (= en usage) [expression, croyance, influence] living ◆ **une expression encore très ~e** a phrase which is still very much alive; → **langue**

6 (Rel) **le pain** ~ the bread of life ◆ **le Dieu** ~ the living God

NM 1 (= personne, Rel) **les ~s** the living ◆ **les ~s et les morts** (gén) the living and the dead; (Bible) the quick and the dead; → **bon**[1]

2 (= vie) **de son** ~ in his (*ou* her) lifetime, while he (*ou* she) was alive

vivarium /vivaʀjɔm/ NM vivarium

vivats /viva/ NM PL cheers ◆ **il quitta la scène sous les** ~ he left the stage to the cheers of the crowd

vive[2] /viv/ EXCL ◆ ~ **le roi/la France/l'amour!** long live the king/France/love! ◆ ~ **les vacances !** three cheers for *ou* hurrah for the holidays!

vive[3] /viv/ NF (= poisson) weever

vive-eau (pl **vives-eaux**) /vivo, vivzo/ NF ◆ **(marée de)** ~ spring tide ◆ **les vives-eaux** the spring tides

vivement /vivmɑ̃/ ADV 1 (= avec brusquerie) sharply, brusquely 2 (= beaucoup) [regretter] deeply, greatly; [désirer] keenly, greatly; [affecter, ressentir, intéresser] deeply, keenly ◆ **s'intéresser ~ à** to take a keen *ou* deep interest in, to be keenly *ou* deeply interested in 3 (= avec éclat) [colorer] brilliantly, vividly; [briller] brightly, brilliantly 4 (littér = rapidement) [agir, se mouvoir] in a lively manner 5 (marque un souhait) ~ **les vacances !** I can't wait for the holidays! (Brit) *ou* for vacation! (US), roll on the holidays!* (Brit) ◆ ~ **que ce soit fini !** I'll be glad when it's all over! ◆ ~ **ce soir qu'on se couche !*** I can't wait until bedtime!, roll on bedtime!* (Brit)

viveur † /vivœʀ/ NM pleasure seeker

vivier /vivje/ NM (= étang) fishpond; (= réservoir) fish-tank; (fig) breeding ground

vivifiant, e /vivifjɑ̃, jɑ̃t/ ADJ [air, brise, promenade] invigorating, bracing; [ambiance, climat] invigorating; → **grâce**

vivifier /vivifje/ ▸ conjug 7 ◂ VT 1 [+ personne] to invigorate, to enliven; [+ sang, plante] to invigorate; (fig littér) [+ âme] to vitalize, to quicken (littér); [+ race] to vitalize, to give life to 2 (emploi absolu) **l'esprit vivifie** (Rel, littér) the spirit gives life

vivipare /vivipaʀ/ ADJ viviparous NM viviparous animal ◆ **~s** vivipara

viviparité /vivipaʀite/ NF viviparity

vivisection /viviseksjɔ̃/ NF vivisection

vivoir /vivwaʀ/ NM (Can) living room

vivoter /vivɔte/ ▸ conjug 1 ◂ VI [personne] to get by (somehow), to live from hand to mouth; [entreprise] to struggle along

vivre[1] /vivʀ/ ▸ conjug 46 ◂ VI 1 (= être vivant) to live, to be alive ◆ **il n'a vécu que quelques jours** he only lived a few days ◆ **je ne savais pas qu'il vivait encore** I didn't know he was still alive *ou* living ◆ **quand l'ambulance est arrivée, il vivait encore** he was still alive when the ambulance arrived ◆ **quand elle arriva, il avait cessé de** ~ he was dead when she arrived ◆ ~ **vieux** to live to a ripe old age, to live to a great age ◆ **il vivra centenaire** he'll live to be a hundred ◆ **les gens vivent de plus en plus vieux** people are living longer and longer ◆ **le peu de temps qu'il lui reste à** ~ the little time he has left (to live) ◆ **le colonialisme a vécu** colonialism is a thing of the past, colonialism has had its day ◆ **ce manteau a vécu*** this coat is finished *ou* has had its day ◆ **il fait bon** ~ it's good to be alive, it's a good life ◆ **qui vive ?** (Mil) who goes there? ◆ **qui vivra verra** (Prov) what will be will be (Prov) → **âme, qui-vive**

2 (= habiter) to live ◆ ~ **à Londres/en France** to live in London/in France ◆ ~ **avec qn** to live with sb ◆ **ils vivent ensemble/comme mari et femme** they live together/as husband and wife ◆ ~ **dans le passé/dans ses livres/dans la crainte** to live in the past/in one's books/in fear

3 (= se comporter) to live ◆ ~ **en paix (avec soi-même)** to be at peace (with oneself) ◆ ~ **dangereusement** to live dangerously ◆ **se laisser** ~ to live for the day, to take life *ou* each day as it comes ◆ **laissez-les** ~ **!** (= ne les tracassez pas) let them be!; (slogan anti-avortement) let them live! ◆ **être facile/difficile à** ~ to be easy/difficult to live with *ou* to get on with ◆ **ces gens-là savent** ~ [épicuriens] those people (really) know how to live; [personnes bien élevées] those people know how to behave ◆ **il faut** ~ **avec son temps** *ou* **époque** you've got to move with the times; → **apprendre**

4 (= exister) to live ◆ **on vit bien en France** life is good in France ◆ **c'est un homme qui a beaucoup vécu** he's a man who has seen a lot of life ◆ **elle ne vit plus depuis que son fils est pilote** (fig) she's been living on her nerves since her son became a pilot ◆ **il ne vit que pour sa famille** he lives only for his family; → **art, joie**

5 (= subsister) to live (de on); ◆ ~ **de laitages/de son salaire/de rentes** to live on dairy produce/on one's salary/on a private income ◆ ~ **au jour le jour** to live from day to day *ou* from hand to mouth ◆ ~ **largement** *ou* **bien** to live well ◆ **avoir (juste) de quoi** ~ to have (just) enough to live on ◆ **ils vivent très bien avec son salaire** they live very comfortably *ou* get along very well on his salary ◆ **il vit de sa peinture/musique** he earns his living by painting/with his music ◆ **travailler/écrire pour** ~ to work/write for a living ◆ **il faut bien** ~ **!** a person has to live!, you have to live! ◆ **faire** ~ **qn** [personne] to keep sb, to support sb ◆ **je n'aime pas ce métier mais il me fait** ~ I don't like this job but it pays the bills* *ou* it's a living ◆ **seul son amour pour ses enfants le fait** ~ only his love for his children keeps him going ◆ ~ **de l'air du temps** to live on air ◆ ~ **d'amour et d'eau fraîche** to live on love alone ◆ ~ **sur sa réputation** to get by on the strength of one's reputation ◆ **l'homme ne vit pas seulement de pain** (Bible) man shall not live by bread alone; → **crochet**

6 [idée, rue, paysage] to be alive ◆ **un portrait qui vit** a lively *ou* lifelike portrait, a portrait which seems alive ◆ **sa gloire vivra longtemps** his glory will live on *ou* will endure ◆ **cette idée/idéologie a vécu** this idea/ideology has had its day

VT 1 (= passer) to live, to spend ◆ ~ **des jours heureux/des heures joyeuses** to live through *ou* spend happy days/hours ◆ **il vivait un beau roman d'amour** his life was a love story come true ◆ **la vie ne vaut pas la peine d'être vécue** life isn't worth living

2 (= être mêlé à) [+ événement, guerre] to live through ◆ **nous vivons des temps troublés** we are living in *ou* through troubled times ◆ **le pays vit une période de crise** the country is going through a period of crisis

3 (= éprouver intensément) ~ **sa vie** to live one's own life, to live (one's life) as one pleases *ou* sees fit ◆ ~ **sa foi/son art** to live out one's faith/one's art ◆ ~ **l'instant/le présent** to live for the moment/the present ◆ ~ **son époque intensément** to be intensely involved in the period one lives in ◆ **il a mal vécu son divorce/son adolescence/la mort de sa mère** he had a hard time of it when he got divorced/as an adolescent/when his mother died

vivre[2] /vivʀ/ NM (littér) ◆ **le** ~ **et le couvert** bed and board ◆ **le** ~ **et le logement** board and lodging, room and board NMPL **vivres** supplies, provisions; → **couper**

vivrier, -ière /vivʀije, ijɛʀ/ ADJ food-producing (épith)

vizir /viziʀ/ NM vizier ◆ **le grand** ~ the Grand Vizier ◆ **il veut être** ~ **à la place du** ~ (hum) he wants to be top dog*

v'là* /vla/ PRÉP ⇒ **voilà**

vlan, v'lan /vlɑ̃/ EXCL wham!, bang! ◆ **et** ~ **! dans la figure** smack *ou* slap-bang in the face ◆ **et** ~ **! il est parti en claquant la porte** wham! *ou* bang! he slammed the door and left

VO /veo/ NF (abrév de **version originale**) ◆ **film en** ~ film in the original version *ou* language ◆ **en** ~ **sous-titrée** in the original version with subtitles

vocable /vɔkabl/ NM 1 (= mot) term 2 (Rel) **église sous le** ~ **de saint Pierre** church dedicated to St Peter

vocabulaire /vɔkabylɛʀ/ NM 1 [de dictionnaire] vocabulary, word list ◆ ~ **français-anglais** French-English vocabulary ◆ ~ **de la photographie** dictionary *ou* lexicon of photographic terms 2 [d'individu, groupe] (= terminologie) vocabulary ◆ ~ **technique/médical** technical/medical vocabulary ◆ ~ **actif/passif** active/passive vocabulary ◆ **enrichir son** ~ to enrich one's vocabulary ◆ **j'ai rayé ce mot de mon** ~ that word is no longer part of my vocabulary ◆ **quel** ~ **!** what language! ◆ **surveille ton** ~ **!** watch *ou* mind your language!

vocal, e (mpl **-aux**) /vɔkal, o/ ADJ [organe, musique] vocal ◆ **synthèse ~e** voice *ou* speech synthesis; → **corde, serveur**

vocalement /vɔkalmɑ̃/ ADV vocally

vocalique /vɔkalik/ ADJ vowel *(épith)*, vocalic ◆ **système** ~ vowel system

vocalisation /vɔkalizasjɔ̃/ NF *(Ling)* vocalization; *(Mus)* singing exercise

vocalise /vɔkaliz/ NF singing exercise ◆ **faire des ~s** to practise (one's) singing exercises

vocaliser /vɔkalize/ ▸ conjug 1 ◂ VT *(Ling)* to vocalize VI *(Mus)* to practise (one's) singing exercises VPR **se vocaliser** *(Ling)* to become vocalized

vocalisme /vɔkalism/ NM *(Ling)* (= *théorie)* vocalism; (= *système vocalique)* vowel system; *[de mot]* vowel pattern

vocatif /vɔkatif/ NM vocative (case)

vocation /vɔkasjɔ̃/ NF 1 *(pour un métier, une activité, Rel)* vocation, calling ◆ **avoir/ne pas avoir la** ~ to have/lack a vocation ◆ **avoir la** ~ **de l'enseignement/du théâtre** to be cut out to be a teacher *ou* for teaching/for acting *ou* the theatre ◆ ~ **artistique** artistic calling ◆ ~ **contrariée** frustrated vocation ◆ **rater sa** ~ to miss one's vocation ◆ **il a la** ~ *(hum)* it's a real vocation for him 2 (= *destin)* vocation, calling ◆ **la** ~ **maternelle de la femme** woman's maternal vocation *ou* calling ◆ **la** ~ **industrielle du Japon** the industrial calling of Japan 3 *(Admin)* **avoir** ~ **à** *ou* **pour** to have authority to

vociférateur, -trice /vɔsiferatœr, tris/ ADJ vociferous NM,F vociferator

vocifération /vɔsiferasjɔ̃/ NF cry of rage, vociferation *(frm)* ◆ **pousser des ~s** to utter cries of rage

vociférer /vɔsifere/ ▸ conjug 6 ◂ VI to utter cries of rage, to vociferate ◆ ~ **contre qn** to shout angrily at sb, to scream at sb VT *[+ insulte, ordre]* to shout (out), to scream ◆ ~ **des injures** to hurl abuse, to shout (out) *ou* scream insults

vocodeur /vɔkɔdœr/ NM vocoder

vodka /vɔdka/ NF vodka

vœu (pl **vœux**) /vø/ GRAMMAIRE ACTIVE 50 NM 1 (= *promesse)* vow ◆ **faire (le)** ~ **de faire qch** to vow to do sth, to make a vow to do sth ◆ **~x de religion** religious vows ◆ **~x de célibat** vows of celibacy ◆ **prononcer ses ~x** *(Rel)* to take one's vows ◆ ~ **de chasteté** vow of chastity ◆ **faire** ~ **de pauvreté** to take a vow of poverty 2 (= *souhait)* wish ◆ **faire un** ~ to make a wish ◆ **nous formons des ~x pour votre santé** we send our good wishes for your recovery *ou* health ◆ **tous nos ~x de prompt rétablissement** our best wishes for a speedy recovery ◆ **l'assemblée a émis le** ~ **que ...** the assembly expressed the wish *ou* its desire that ... ◆ **appeler qch de ses ~x** to hope and pray for sth ◆ **je fais le** ~ **qu'il me pardonne** I pray (that) he may forgive me ◆ **tous nos ~x (de bonheur)** all good wishes *ou* every good wish for your happiness ◆ **tous nos ~x vous accompagnent** our very best wishes go with you ◆ ~ **pieux** pious hope 3 *(au jour de l'an)* **les ~x télévisés du président de la République** the President of the Republic's televised New Year speech *ou* address ◆ **il a reçu les ~x du corps diplomatique** he received New Year's greetings from the diplomatic corps ◆ **tous nos (meilleurs** *ou* **bons) ~x de bonne et heureuse année, meilleurs ~x** best wishes for the New Year, Happy New Year; *(sur une carte)* "Season's Greetings"

vogue /vɔg/ NF 1 (= *popularité)* fashion, vogue ◆ **la** ~ **de l'informatique** the vogue for computers ◆ **connaître une** ~ **extraordinaire** to be extremely fashionable *ou* popular ◆ **être en** ~ to be in fashion *ou* vogue, to be fashionable ◆ **c'est la grande** ~ **maintenant** it's all the rage now ◆ **ce n'est plus en** ~ it's no longer fashionable, it's on the way out 2 *(dial* = *foire)* fair

voguer /vɔge/ ▸ conjug 1 ◂ VI *(littér) [embarcation, vaisseau spatial]* to sail; *(fig) [pensées]* to drift, to wander ◆ **nous voguions vers l'Amérique** we were sailing towards America ◆ **l'embarcation voguait au fil de l'eau** the boat was drifting *ou* floating along on *ou* with the current ◆ **vogue la galère !** *(hum)* come what may!

voici /vwasi/ PRÉP 1 *(pour désigner : opposé à voilà)* here is, here are, this is, these are ◆ ~ **mon bureau et voilà le vôtre** here's *ou* this is my office and there's *ou* that's yours ◆ ~ **mon frère et voilà sa femme** this is *ou* here is my brother and there's *ou* that's his wife ◆ ~ **mes parents** here are *ou* these are my parents 2 *(pour désigner : même valeur que voilà)* here is, here are, this is, these are ◆ ~ **mon frère** this is my brother ◆ ~ **le livre que vous cherchiez** here's the book you were looking for ◆ **l'homme/la maison que** ~ this (particular) man/house ◆ **M. Dupont, que** ~ Mr Dupont here ◆ **il m'a raconté l'histoire que** ~ he told me the following story 3 *(pour annoncer, introduire)* here is, here are, this is, these are ◆ ~ **le printemps/la pluie** here comes spring/the rain ◆ ~ **la fin de l'hiver** the end of winter is here ◆ **me/nous/le** *etc* ~ here I am/we are/he is *etc* ◆ **les** ~ **prêts à partir** they're ready to leave, that's them ready to leave* ◆ **nous** ~ **arrivés** here we are, we've arrived ◆ **le** ~ **qui se plaint encore** there he goes, complaining again, that's him complaining again* ◆ **me** ~ **à me ronger les sangs pendant que lui ...** *(au présent)* here am I *ou* here's me* in a terrible state while he ...; *(au passé)* there was I *ou* there was me* in a terrible state while he ... ◆ **vous voulez des preuves, en** ~ you want proof, well here you are then ◆ **nous y** ~ *(lieu)* here we are; *(question délicate)* now we're getting there ◆ ~ **qui va vous surprendre** here's something that'll surprise you ◆ ~ **qu'il se met à pleuvoir maintenant** and now it's starting to rain ◆ ~ **ce que je compte faire** this is what I'm hoping to do ◆ ~ **ce qu'il m'a dit/ce dont il s'agit** this is what he told me/what it's all about ◆ ~ **comment il faut faire** this is the way to do it, this is how it's done ◆ ~ **pourquoi je l'ai fait** this *ou* that was why I did it ◆ ~ **pourquoi je l'avais supprimé** that was why I'd eliminated it ◆ ~ **que tombe la nuit** night is falling, it's getting dark 4 *(il y a)* ~ **5 ans que je ne l'ai pas vu** it's 5 years (now) since I last saw him, I haven't seen him for the past 5 years ◆ **il est parti** ~ **une heure** he left an hour ago, it's an hour since he left ◆ ~ **bientôt 20 ans que nous sommes mariés** it'll soon be 20 years since we got married, we'll have been married 20 years soon

voie /vwa/ NF 1 (= *chemin)* way; *(Admin* = *route, rue)* road; (= *itinéraire)* route ◆ ~ **romaine/sacrée** *(Hist)* Roman/sacred way ◆ **par la** ~ **des airs** *ou* **aérienne** by air ◆ **emprunter la** ~ **maritime** to go by sea ◆ **expédier qch par** ~ **de mer** *ou* **maritime** to send sth by sea *ou* by ship, to ship sth ◆ **voyager par** ~ **de terre** *ou* **terrestre** to travel overland ◆ **~s de communication** communication routes ◆ ~ **sans issue** no through road, cul-de-sac ◆ ~ **privée** private road ◆ ~ **à double sens/à sens unique** two-way/one-way road 2 (= *partie d'une route)* lane ◆ **"travaux – passage à voie unique"** "roadworks – single-lane traffic" ◆ **route à** ~ **unique** single-lane *ou* single-track road ◆ **route à 3/4 ~s** 3-/4-lane road ◆ ~ **réservée aux autobus/aux cyclistes** bus/cycle lane ◆ ~ **à contresens** contraflow lane ◆ **une** ~ **de circulation a été mise en sens inverse sur ...** there is a contraflow system in operation on ... 3 *(Rail)* track, (railway) line ◆ **ligne à** ~ **unique/à 2 ~s** single-/double-track line ◆ **ligne à** ~ **étroite** narrow-gauge line ◆ **on répare les ~s** the line *ou* track is under repair ◆ ~ **montante/descendante** up/down line ◆ **le train est annoncé sur la** ~ **2** the train will arrive at platform 2 4 *(Anat)* **~s digestives/respiratoires/urinaires** digestive/respiratory/urinary tract ◆ **par** ~ **buccale** *ou* **orale** orally ◆ **administrer qch par** ~ **nasale/rectale** to administer sth through the nose/the rectum ◆ **évacuer qch par les ~s naturelles** to get rid of sth by the natural routes *ou* naturally ◆ **les usagers de drogues par** ~ **intraveineuse** intravenous drug users ◆ **être contaminé par** ~ **sexuelle** to be infected through sexual intercourse 5 *(fig)* way ◆ **la** ~ **du bien/mal** the path of good/evil ◆ **la** ~ **de l'honneur** the honourable course ◆ **rester dans la** ~ **du devoir** to keep to the line *ou* path of duty ◆ **entrer dans la** ~ **des aveux** to make a confession ◆ **ouvrir/tracer/montrer la** ~ to open up/mark out/show the way ◆ **préparer la** ~ **à qn/qch** to prepare *ou* pave the way for sb/sth ◆ **continuez sur cette** ~ continue in this way ◆ **il est sur la bonne** ~ he's on the right track ◆ **l'affaire est en bonne** ~ things are going well ◆ **mettre qn sur la** ~ to put sb on the right track ◆ **trouver sa** ~ to find one's way (in life) ◆ **la** ~ **est toute tracée** *(pour une personne)* his career is mapped out (for him); *(pour un projet)* the way ahead is clear ◆ **la** ~ **est libre** the way is clear *ou* open 6 (= *filière, moyen, option)* **par des ~s détournées** by devious *ou* roundabout means ◆ **par la** ~ **hiérarchique/diplomatique** through official/diplomatic channels ◆ **faire qch par (la)** ~ **légale** *ou* **par les ~s légales** to follow the proper procedures for doing sth ◆ **par** ~ **de conséquence** in consequence, as a result ◆ **annoncer qch par** ~ **de presse** to announce sth in the press ◆ **publicité par** ~ **d'affiche** poster advertising ◆ **consulter le peuple par** ~ **de référendum** to consult the people in a *ou* by referendum ◆ **recruter des cadres par** ~ **de concours/d'annonces** to recruit executives in open competition/through advertisements ◆ **proposer une troisième** ~ to suggest a third option

◆ **en voie de** ◆ **en** ~ **de réorganisation** in the process of reorganization, undergoing reorganization ◆ **en** ~ **d'exécution** in (the) process of being carried out, being carried out ◆ **en** ~ **de guérison** getting better, regaining one's health, on the road to recovery ◆ **en** ~ **de cicatrisation** (well) on the way to healing over ◆ **en** ~ **d'achèvement** (well) on the way to completion, nearing completion ◆ **elle est en** ~ **de réussir** she's on the way *ou* road to success ◆ **il est en** ~ **de perdre sa situation** he's on the way to losing his job, he's heading for dismissal

COMP **voie d'accès** access road
voie Appienne Appian Way
voie de dégagement urbain urban relief road
les voies de Dieu, les voies divines the ways of God *ou* Providence ◆ **les ~s de Dieu sont impénétrables** *ou* **insondables** God moves in mysterious ways
voie d'eau leak
voie express express way, motorway *(Brit)*, freeway *(US)*
voie de fait *(Jur)* assault (and battery) *(NonC)* ◆ ~ **de fait simple** common assault ◆ **se livrer à des ~s de fait sur qn** to assault sb, to commit an assault on sb
voie ferrée *(Rail)* railway *(Brit) ou* railroad *(US)* line
voie de garage *(Rail)* siding ◆ **mettre sur une** ~ **de garage** *[+ affaire]* to shelve; *[+ personne]* to shunt to one side ◆ **on m'a mis sur une** ~ **de garage** *(Téléc)* they put me on hold
la voie lactée the Milky Way
voies navigables waterways
voie de passage major route

les voies de la Providence ⇒ **les voies de Dieu**
la voie publique *(Admin)* the public highway
voie de raccordement slip road
voie rapide ⇒ **voie express**
voie royale *(fig)* **c'est la ~ royale vers** *ou* **pour** *(gén)* it's the pathway to; *[+ carrière, pouvoir]* it's the fast track to
les voies du Seigneur ⇒ **les voies de Dieu**

voilà /vwala/ PRÉP 1 *(pour désigner : opposé à voici)* there is, there are, that is, those are; *(même sens que voici)* here is, here are, this is, these are ◆ **voici mon bureau et ~ le vôtre** here's *ou* this is my office and there's *ou* and that's yours ◆ **voici mon frère et ~ sa femme** this is *ou* here's my brother and that's *ou* there's his wife ◆ **~ mon frère** this is *ou* here is my brother ◆ **~ le livre que vous cherchiez** *(je le tiens)* here's the book you were looking for; *(il est là-bas)* there's the book you were looking for ◆ **l'homme/la maison que ~** that man/house (there) ◆ **M. Dupont que ~** Mr Dupont there ◆ **il m'a raconté l'histoire que ~** he told me the following story
2 *(pour annoncer, introduire)* there is, there are, that is, those are ◆ **~ le printemps/la pluie** here comes spring/the rain ◆ **~ la fin de l'hiver** the end of winter is here ◆ **le ~, c'est lui** there he is, that's him ◆ **le ~ prêt à partir** he's ready to leave, that's him ready to leave* ◆ **le ~ qui se plaint encore** there he goes, complaining again, that's him complaining again* ◆ **me ~ à me ronger les sangs pendant que lui ...** *(au présent)* there am I *ou* there's me* in a terrible state while he ...; *(au passé)* there was I *ou* there was me* in a terrible state while he ... ◆ **~ ce que je compte faire** this is what I'm hoping to do ◆ **~ ce qu'il m'a dit/ce dont il s'agit** *(je viens de le dire)* that's what he told me/what it's all about; *(je vais le dire)* this is what he told me/what it's all about ◆ **~ comment il faut faire** that's how it's done ◆ **~ pourquoi je l'ai fait** that's why I did it ◆ **~ que tombe la nuit** night is falling, it's getting dark ◆ **~ qu'il se met à pleuvoir maintenant** now it's starting to rain, here comes the rain now ◆ **~ où je veux en venir** that's what I'm getting at, that's my point ◆ **nous y ~** *(lieu)* here we are; *(question délicate)* now we're getting there
3 *(pour résumer)* **... et ~ pourquoi je n'ai pas pu le faire** ... and that's why *ou* that's the reason I couldn't do it ◆ **~ ce qui fait que c'est impossible** that's what makes it impossible ◆ **~ qui est louche** that's a bit odd *ou* suspicious ◆ **~ qui s'appelle parler** that's what I call talking ◆ **~ ce que c'est (que) de ne pas obéir** that's what comes of not doing as you're told, that's what happens when you don't do as you're told
4 *(il y a)* **~ une heure que je l'attends** I've been waiting for him for an hour now, that's a whole hour I've been waiting for him now ◆ **~ 5 ans que je ne l'ai pas vu** it's 5 years since I last saw him, I haven't seen him for the past 5 years ◆ **il est parti ~ une heure** he left an hour ago, it's an hour since he left ◆ **~ bientôt 20 ans que nous sommes mariés** it'll soon be 20 years since we got married, we'll have been married 20 years soon
5 *(locutions)* **~ le hic*** that's the snag *ou* catch, there's *ou* that's the hitch ◆ **~ tout** that's all ◆ **et ~ tout** and that's all there is to it *ou* all there is to say, and that's the top and bottom of it* *(Brit)* ◆ **~ bien les Français !** how like the French!, isn't that just like the French!, that's the French all over!* ◆ **(et) ne ~-t-il pas qu'il s'avise de se déshabiller** lo and behold, he suddenly decides to get undressed!, I'm blest if he doesn't suddenly decide to get undressed! ◆ **nous ~ frais !** now we're in a mess! *ou* a nice pickle!*, that's a fine mess *ou* pickle we're in!*
◆ **en voilà** ◆ **en ~ une histoire/blague !** what a story/joke!, that's some story/joke! ◆ **en ~ un imbécile !** there's an idiot for you!, what a fool! ◆ **en ~ assez !** that's enough!, that'll do! ◆ **veux-tu de l'argent ? – en ~** do you want some money? – here's some *ou* here you are ◆ **vous voulez des preuves, en ~** you want proof, well here you are then
EXCL ◆ **~ ! j'arrive !** here I come!, there – I'm coming! ◆ **ah ! ~ ! je comprends !** oh, (so) that's it, I understand!, oh, I see! ◆ **~ autre chose !** *(incident)* that's all I need(ed)!; *(impertinence)* what a cheek!, the cheek of it! ◆ **je n'ai pas pu le faire, et ~ !** I couldn't do it and that's all there is to it! *ou* so there!* ◆ **~, je m'appelle M. Dupont et je suis votre nouvel instituteur** right (then), my name is Mr Dupont and I'm your new teacher ◆ **~, tu l'as cassé !** there (you are), you've broken it!

voilage /vwalaʒ/ NM *(= rideau)* net curtain; *(= tissu)* net *(NonC)*, netting *(NonC)*, veiling *(NonC)*; *[de chapeau, vêtement]* gauze *(NonC)*, veiling *(NonC)*

voile[1] /vwal/ NF 1 *[de bateau]* sail ◆ **~ carrée/latine** square/lateen sail ◆ **les hautes ~s** the light *ou* upper sails, the (flying) kites ◆ **les basses ~s** the lower sails ◆ **navire sous ~s** ship under sail ◆ **faire ~ vers** to sail towards ◆ **mettre à la ~** to set sail, to make way under sail ◆ **mettre toutes ~s dehors** to raise *ou* set full sail ◆ **arriver toutes ~s dehors** *(lit)* to draw near under *ou* in full sail; *(fig)* to make a grand entrance ◆ **mettre les ~s** * *(fig)* to clear off*, to scram* ◆ **marcher à ~ et à vapeur*** *[bisexuel]* to be AC/DC* *ou* bi*, to swing both ways*; → **planche, vent, vol**[1]
2 *(littér = embarcation)* sail *(inv) (littér)*, vessel
3 *(= navigation, sport)* sailing, yachting ◆ **faire de la ~** to sail, to go sailing *ou* yachting ◆ **demain on va faire de la ~** we're going sailing *ou* yachting tomorrow ◆ **faire le tour du monde à la ~** to sail round the world

voile[2] /vwal/ NM 1 *(= coiffure, vêtement)* veil ◆ **~ de deuil** (mourning) veil ◆ **~ islamique** Islamic veil ◆ **~ de mariée** bridal veil ◆ **porter le ~** to wear the veil ◆ **prendre le ~** *(Rel)* to take the veil ◆ **sa prise de ~ a eu lieu hier** she took the veil yesterday
2 *[de statue, plaque commémorative]* veil
3 *(= tissu)* net *(NonC)*, netting *(NonC)* ◆ **~ de coton/de tergal®** cotton/Terylene® net *ou* netting
4 *(fig = qui cache)* veil ◆ **le ~ de l'oubli** the veil of oblivion ◆ **sous le ~ de la franchise** under the veil *ou* a pretence of candour ◆ **le ~ de mystère qui entoure cet assassinat** the veil of mystery that surrounds this murder ◆ **jeter/tirer un ~ sur qch** to cast/draw a veil over sth ◆ **lever le ~ sur** to unveil, to lift the veil from ◆ **soulever un coin du ~** to lift a corner of the veil
5 *(fig = qui rend flou) (gén)* veil; *(sur un liquide)* cloud ◆ **~ de brume** veil of mist, veiling mist ◆ **avoir un ~ devant les yeux** to have a film before one's eyes
6 *(Photo)* fog *(NonC)* ◆ **un ~ sur la photo** a shadow on the photo
7 *(Méd)* **~ au poumon** shadow on the lung ◆ **le ~ noir/gris/rouge des aviateurs** blackout/greyout/redout
8 *(Anat)* **~ du palais** soft palate, velum
9 *[de champignon]* veil
10 *(= enregistrement du son)* warp

voilé[1]**, e**[1] /vwale/ (ptp de **voiler**[1]) ADJ 1 *[femme, statue]* veiled 2 *[termes, allusion, sens]* veiled ◆ **accusation à peine ~e** thinly disguised accusation ◆ **il fit une allusion peu ~e à ...** he made a thinly veiled reference to ... 3 *(= flou) [lumière, ciel, soleil]* hazy; *[éclat]* dimmed; *[regard]* misty; *[contour]* hazy, misty; *[photo]* fogged ◆ **les yeux ~s de larmes** his eyes misty *ou* misted (over) *ou* blurred with tears ◆ **sa voix était un peu ~e** his voice was slightly husky

voilé[2]**, e**[2] /vwale/ (ptp de **voiler**[2]) ADJ *(= tordu) [roue]* buckled; *[planche]* warped

voilement /vwalmɑ̃/ NM *(Tech) [de roue]* buckle; *[de planche]* warp

voiler[1] /vwale/ ► conjug 1 ◄ VT *(lit, fig, littér = cacher)* to veil ◆ **les larmes voilaient ses yeux** his eyes were misty with tears ◆ **un brouillard voilait les sommets** the peaks were shrouded in fog ◆ **la plaine était voilée de brume** the plain was shrouded *ou* veiled in mist ◆ **je préfère lui ~ la vérité** I prefer to shield him from the truth *ou* to conceal the truth from him VPR **se voiler** 1 *(= porter un voile)* **se ~ le visage** *[personne]* to wear a veil; *[musulmane]* to wear the veil ◆ **se ~ la face** *(fig)* to close one's eyes *(devant* to) 2 *(= devenir flou) [horizon, soleil]* to mist over; *[ciel]* to grow hazy *ou* misty; *[regard, yeux]* to mist over, to become glazed; *[voix]* to become husky

voiler[2] /vwale/ ► conjug 1 ◄ VPR **se voiler** *[roue]* to buckle; *[planche]* to warp VT *[+ roue]* to buckle; *[+ planche]* to warp

voilerie /vwalʀi/ NF sail-loft

voilette /vwalɛt/ NF (hat) veil

voilier /vwalje/ NM 1 *(= navire à voiles)* sailing ship; *(de plaisance)* sailing boat, sailboat *(US)*, yacht ◆ **grand ~** tall ship 2 *(= fabricant de voiles)* sailmaker ◆ **maître(-)~** master sailmaker 3 *(= oiseau)* long-flight bird

voilure[1] /vwalyʀ/ NF 1 *[de bateau]* sails ◆ **une ~ de 1 000 m²** 1,000 m² of sail ◆ **réduire la ~** to shorten sail ◆ **réduire sa ~** *[entreprise]* to reduce its area of activity; → **surface** 2 *[de planeur]* aerofoils ◆ **~ tournante** rotary wing 3 *[de parachute]* canopy

voilure[2] /vwalyʀ/ NF ⇒ **voilement**

voir /vwaʀ/
► conjug 30 ◄
GRAMMAIRE ACTIVE 53.2

1 VERBE TRANSITIF	4 VERBE TRANSITIF INDIRECT
2 VERBE INTRANSITIF	5 VERBE PRONOMINAL
3 LOCUTION EXCLAMATIVE	

1 – VERBE TRANSITIF

1 = percevoir par la vue to see ◆ **je vois deux arbres** I (can) see two trees ◆ **est-ce que tu le vois ?** can you see it? ◆ **je l'ai vu de mes (propres) yeux, je l'ai vu, de mes yeux vu** I saw it with my own eyes ◆ **je l'ai vu comme je vous vois** I saw him as plainly as I see you now ◆ **aller ~ un film/une exposition** to go to (see) a film/an exhibition ◆ **c'est un film à ~** it's a film worth seeing ◆ **à le ~ si joyeux/triste** seeing him look so happy/sad ◆ **à le ~, on ne lui donnerait pas 90 ans** to look at him, you wouldn't think he was 90 ◆ **vous m'en voyez ravi/navré** I'm delighted/terribly sorry about that ◆ **tu vois ce que je vois ?** do you see what I see? ◆ **~ Naples et mourir** see Naples and die ◆ **j'ai vu la mort de près** I've looked *ou* stared death in the face; → **chandelle, falloir, jour, pays**[1]
◆ **voir** + *infinitif* ◆ **nous les avons vus sauter** we saw them jump ◆ **on a vu le voleur entrer** the thief was seen going in ◆ **j'ai vu bâtir ces maisons** I saw these houses being built ◆ **je voudrais la ~ travailler plus** I'd like to see her work more
2 = être témoin de **as-tu jamais vu pareille impolitesse ?** have you ever seen *ou* did you ever see such rudeness? ◆ **il a vu deux guerres** he has lived through *ou* seen two wars ◆ **cette**

maison a vu bien des drames this house has known *ou* seen many a drama ◆ **à ~ son train de vie, elle doit être très riche** if her lifestyle is anything to go by, she must be very rich, looking *ou* to look at her lifestyle, you'd think she was very rich ◆ **je voudrais t'y ~ !** I'd like to see you try! ◆ **tu aurais dû refuser ! – j'aurais voulu t'y ~ !** you should have said no! – I'd like to see what you'd have done!; → **naître**

◆ **voir** *+ infinitif* to see ◆ **ce journal a vu son tirage augmenter** this newspaper has seen an increase in its circulation ◆ **un pays qui voit renaître le fascisme** a country which is witnessing *ou* seeing the rebirth of fascism

3 [= découvrir, constater] to see ◆ **va ~ s'il y a quelqu'un** go and see if there's anybody there ◆ **des meubles comme on en voit partout** ordinary furniture ◆ **vous verrez que ce n'est pas leur faute** you'll see that they're not to blame ◆ **il ne fera plus cette erreur – c'est à ~** he won't make the same mistake again – that remains to be seen *ou* – we'll see ◆ **nous allons bien ~ !** we'll soon find out! ◆ **(attendons,) on verra bien** we'll see, let's wait and see ◆ **voyez si elle accepte** see if she'll agree ◆ **voyez comme les prix ont augmenté** see how prices have risen ◆ **c'est ce que nous verrons !** we'll see about that! ◆ **histoire de ~, pour ~** just to see ◆ **essaie un peu, pour ~ !** *(menace)* just you try! ◆ **il n'a pas de goût, il n'y a qu'à ~ comment il s'habille** he's got no taste, just look at the way he dresses ◆ **c'est tout vu !*** that's for sure!, it's a dead cert!* ◆ **si tu me trompes, moi je vais ~ ailleurs*** *(euph)* if you're ever unfaithful to me, I'll go and find somebody else ◆ **va ~ ailleurs si j'y suis !*** get lost!*; → **falloir**

4 [= imaginer, se représenter] to see, to imagine ◆ **tu me vois aller lui dire ça/rester sans travailler ?** can you see *ou* imagine me telling him that?/not working? ◆ **je ne le vois pas** *ou* **je le vois mal habiter la banlieue** I (somehow) can't see *ou* imagine him living in the suburbs ◆ **je le verrais bien dans ce rôle** I could just see him in this role ◆ **nous ne voyons pas qu'il ait de quoi s'inquiéter** we can't see that he has any reason for worrying ◆ **voyez-vous une solution ?** can you see a solution? ◆ **je ne vois pas le problème** I don't see what the problem is ◆ **comment voyez-vous l'avenir ?** how do you see *ou* envisage the future? ◆ **je ne vois pas comment ils auraient pu gagner** I can't *ou* don't see how they could have won ◆ **tu vois, vois-tu, voyez-vous** you see ◆ **tu vois ça d'ici** you can just imagine it ◆ **il va encore protester, je vois ça d'ici** he's going to start protesting again. I can see it coming ◆ **je vois* ma sœur, elle a trois enfants et ...** take my sister, she has three children and ...; → **inconvénient, noir, rose**

5 [= examiner, étudier] *[+ problème, dossier]* to look at; *[+ leçon]* to look *ou* go over; *[+ circulaire]* to see, to read ◆ **il a encore trois malades à ~** he still has three patients to see ◆ **il faudra ~ la question de plus près** we'll have to look at *ou* into the question more closely, the question requires closer examination ◆ **il faut** *ou* **il faudra ~** we'll have to see ◆ **je verrai (ce que je dois faire)** I'll have to see, I'll think about it ◆ **voyons un peu comment tu fais** let's see how you do it

6 [= juger, concevoir] to see ◆ **c'est à vous de ~ s'il est compétent** it's up to you to see *ou* to decide whether he is competent ◆ **si elle ne revient pas travailler lundi, elle va se faire mal ~** if she doesn't come back to work on Monday, it won't look too good ◆ **il a fait ça pour se faire bien ~ de ses collègues/des autorités** he did that to impress his colleagues/to make himself popular with the authorities ◆ **façon** *ou* **manière de ~** view of things, outlook ◆ **nous n'avons pas la même façon de ~ les choses** we see things differently ◆ **voici comment on peut ~ les choses** you can look at things this way ◆ **nous ne voyons pas le problème de la même façon** we don't see *ou* view the problem in the same way, we don't take the same view of the problem ◆ **ne ~ aucun mal à ...** to see no harm in ... ◆ **~ qn comme un ami** to look upon *ou* regard sb as a friend, to consider sb a friend ◆ **il ne voit que son intérêt** he only considers his own interest; → **œil**

7 [= rencontrer] *[+ médecin, avocat]* to see ◆ **il voit le directeur ce soir** he's seeing the manager tonight ◆ **le ministre doit ~ les délégués** the minister is to see *ou* meet the delegates ◆ **on ne vous voit plus** we never see you these days, you've become quite a stranger ◆ **il la voit beaucoup** he sees a lot of her ◆ **je l'ai assez vu*** I've had (quite) enough of him* ◆ **aller ~** *[+ médecin, avocat]* to go and see; *[+ ami]* to go and see, to call on, to visit ◆ **aller ~ qn à l'hôpital** to visit sb *ou* go and see sb in hospital ◆ **passez me ~ quand vous serez à Paris** look me up *ou* call in and see me *(Brit)* when you're in Paris ◆ **je suis passé le ~** I went to see him ◆ **il vient nous ~ demain** he's coming to see us tomorrow

8 [= faire l'expérience de] **j'en ai vu d'autres !** I've seen worse! ◆ **il en a vu de dures** *ou* **de toutes les couleurs** *ou* **des vertes et des pas mûres*** he has been through the mill *ou* through some hard times, he has taken some hard knocks ◆ **en faire ~ (de dures** *ou* **de toutes les couleurs) à qn** to give sb a hard time ◆ **a-t-on jamais vu ça ?, on n'a jamais vu ça !** have you ever seen *ou* heard anything like it? ◆ **on aura tout vu !** we've seen everything now!, that beats everything! ◆ **vous n'avez encore rien vu !** you haven't seen anything yet!, you ain't seen nothing yet!*; → **autre**

9 [= comprendre] to see ◆ **je ne vois pas ce que vous voulez dire** I don't see *ou* get *ou* understand what you mean, I don't understand your meaning ◆ **elle ne voyait pas le côté drôle de l'aventure** she couldn't see *ou* appreciate the funny side of what had happened ◆ **vous aurez du mal à lui faire ~ que ...** you'll find it difficult to make him see *ou* realize that ... ◆ **je ne vois pas comment il a pu oublier** I don't see how he could forget ◆ **tu vas le faire tout de suite, vu ?*** you're going to do it straightaway, understood?

10 [*= supporter] **elle ne peut pas le ~ (en peinture)** she can't stand (the sight of) him

11 [locutions]

◆ **faire voir** *(= montrer)* to show ◆ **fais ~ !** show me!, let me have a look! ◆ **faites-moi ~ ce dessin** show me *ou* let me see the picture ◆ **va te faire ~ (ailleurs) !*** get lost!* ◆ **qu'il aille se faire ~ (chez les Grecs) !*** he can go to hell!*

◆ **voir venir** *(= attendre les événements)* to wait and see ◆ **j'ai quelques économies, ça me permettra de ~ venir*** I've got some money put by, it should be enough to see me through* ◆ **on va perdre, ça je le vois venir (gros comme une maison*)** *(= prévoir)* we're going to lose, I can see it coming (a mile off*) ◆ **je te vois venir* (avec tes gros sabots)** I can see what you're leading up to ◆ **150 € pour ce vase ? on t'a vu venir !*** *(iro)* €150 for that vase? they saw you coming!*

◆ **rien/quelque chose/pas grand-chose à voir avec** *ou* **dans** ◆ **je n'ai rien à ~ dans cette affaire** this has nothing to do with me, none of this has anything to do with me ◆ **cela n'a rien/a quelque chose à ~ avec ...** this has got nothing/something to do with ... ◆ **son nouveau film ? rien à ~ avec les précédents** his new film? it's nothing like his previous work ◆ **le résultat n'a plus grand-chose à ~ avec le projet initial** the result bears scarcely any resemblance *ou* very little relation to the initial project

2 - VERBE INTRANSITIF

1 [avec les yeux] to see ◆ **~ mal** to have trouble seeing ◆ **on voit mal ici** it's difficult to see in here ◆ **on n'y voit plus** you can't see a thing ◆ **~ trouble** to have blurred vision ◆ **il a vu grand** he planned things on a grand *ou* big scale, he thought big; → **clair, loin, rouge**

2 [*: intensif] **dites ~, vous connaissez la nouvelle ?** tell me, have you heard the news? ◆ **dis-moi ~ ...** tell me ... ◆ **essaie ~ !** just try it and see!, just you try it! ◆ **regarde ~ ce qu'il a fait !** just look what he's done!

3 - LOCUTION EXCLAMATIVE

voyons *(rappel à l'ordre)* **un peu de charité, voyons !** come (on) now, let's be charitable! ◆ **mais voyons, il n'a jamais dit ça !** oh come on, he never said that! ◆ **voyons ~ !** let's see now !

4 - VERBE TRANSITIF INDIRECT

voir à *(littér = veiller à)* to make sure that, to see (to it) that ◆ **nous verrons à vous contenter** we shall do our best *ou* our utmost to please you ◆ **il faudra ~ à ce qu'il obéisse** we must see *ou* make sure that he obeys

5 - VERBE PRONOMINAL

se voir

1 [soi-même] **se ~ dans une glace** to see oneself in a mirror ◆ **il ne s'est pas vu mourir** death caught him unawares ◆ **elle se voyait déjà célèbre** she pictured herself famous already ◆ **je me vois mal habiter** *ou* **habitant là** I can't see myself living there somehow ◆ **tu te vois faire trois heures de trajet par jour ?** can you see yourself commuting three hours every day? ◆ **il la trouve moche – il ne s'est pas vu !** he thinks she's ugly – has he looked in the mirror lately?

2 [mutuellement] to see each other ◆ **ils se voient beaucoup** they see a lot of each other ◆ **nous essaierons de nous ~ à Londres** we shall try to see each other *ou* to meet (up) in London ◆ **ils ne peuvent pas se ~*** they can't stand the sight of each other*

3 [= se trouver] **se ~ contraint de** to find o.s. forced to ◆ **je me vois dans la triste obligation de ...** sadly, I find myself obliged to ...

4 [= être visible, évident] *[tache, couleur, sentiments]* to show ◆ **la tache ne se voit pas** the stain doesn't show ◆ **il est très intelligent – ça se voit !** he's very clever – that's obvious!; → **nez**

5 [= se produire] **cela se voit tous les jours** it happens every day, it's an everyday occurrence ◆ **ça ne se voit pas tous les jours** it's not something you see every day, it's quite a rare occurrence ◆ **cela ne s'est jamais vu !** it's unheard of! ◆ **une attitude qui ne se voit que trop fréquemment** an all-too-common attitude ◆ **des attitudes/préjugés qui se voient encore chez ...** attitudes/prejudices which are still commonplace *ou* encountered in ...

6 [fonction passive] **ils se sont vu interdire l'accès du musée** they were refused admission to the museum ◆ **ces outils se sont vus relégués au grenier** these tools have been put away in the attic ◆ **je me suis vu répondre que c'était trop tard** I was told that it was too late

voire /vwaʀ/ **ADV** 1 *(frm = et même)* indeed, nay † *(littér)* ◆ **c'est révoltant, ~ même criminel** it's disgusting, indeed criminal ◆ **il faudrait attendre une semaine, ~ un mois** you would have to wait a week or even a month ◆ **ce sera difficile, ~ impossible** it'll be difficult, if not impossible 2 *(= j'en doute)* indeed? ◆ **ce n'est**

pas une manœuvre politique ? – **~ !** it isn't a political manoeuvre? – we shall see!

voirie /vwaʀi/ NF 1 *(= enlèvement des ordures)* refuse *(Brit) ou* garbage *(US)* collection; *(= dépotoir)* refuse *(Brit) ou* garbage *(US)* dump 2 *(= entretien des routes)* road *ou* highway maintenance; *(= service administratif)* roads *ou* highways department; *(= voie publique)* (public) highways ◆ **travaux de** ~ road works ◆ **les ingénieurs de la** ~ highway *ou* road engineers

voisé, e /vwaze/ ADJ *(Phon)* voiced

voisement /vwazmɑ̃/ NM *(Phon)* voicing

voisin, e /vwazɛ̃, in/ ADJ 1 *(= proche)* neighbouring *(Brit)*, neighboring *(US)*; *(= adjacent)* next ◆ **les maisons/rues ~es** the neighbouring houses/streets ◆ **il habite la maison ~e/la rue ~e** he lives in the house next door/in the next street ◆ **deux maisons ~es (l'une de l'autre)** two adjoining houses, two houses next to each other ◆ **une maison ~e de l'église** a house next to *ou* adjoining the church ◆ **ils se sont réfugiés dans des villages ~s** they took refuge in neighbouring villages ◆ **les pays ~s de la Suisse** the countries bordering on *ou* adjoining Switzerland ◆ **les années ~es de 1870** the years around 1870 ◆ **un chiffre d'affaires ~ de 2 milliards d'euros** a turnover in the region of 2 billion euros

2 *(= semblable) [idées, espèces, cas]* connected ◆ ~ **de** akin to, related to ◆ **un animal ~ du chat** an animal akin to *ou* related to the cat ◆ **dans un état ~ de la folie** in a state bordering on *ou* akin to madness

NM,F 1 *(gén)* neighbour *(Brit)*, neighbor *(US)* ◆ **nous sommes ~s** we're neighbours ◆ **nos ~s d'à côté** our next-door neighbours, the people next door ◆ **les ~s du dessus/dessous** the people (who live) above/below ◆ **nos ~s de palier** our neighbours *ou* the people who live across the landing ◆ **un de mes ~s de table** one of the people next to me at table, one of my neighbours at table ◆ **je demandai à mon ~ de me passer le sel** I asked the person (sitting) next to me *ou* my neighbour to pass me the salt ◆ **qui est ta ~e cette année ?** *(en classe)* who is sitting next to you this year? ◆ **mon ~ de dortoir/de salle** the person in the bed next to mine (in the dormitory/ward) ◆ **j'étais venu en** ~ I had dropped in as I lived nearby ◆ **nos ~s européens** our European neighbours

2 *(fig littér = prochain)* neighbour *(Brit)*, neighbor *(US)* ◆ **envier son** ~ to envy one's neighbour

voisinage /vwazinaʒ/ NM 1 *(= voisins)* neighbourhood *(Brit)*, neighborhood *(US)* ◆ **ameuter tout le** ~ to rouse the whole neighbourhood ◆ **être connu de tout le** ~ to be known throughout the neighbourhood ◆ **faire une enquête de** ~ to make inquiries in the neighbourhood ◆ **querelle/conflit de** ~ quarrel/dispute between neighbours

2 *(= relations)* **être en bon ~ avec qn, entretenir des relations de bon ~ avec qn** to be on neighbourly terms with sb

3 *(= environs)* vicinity ◆ **les villages du** ~ the villages in the vicinity, the villages round about ◆ **se trouver dans le** ~ to be in the vicinity ◆ **dans le ~ immédiat du musée** in the immediate vicinity of the museum ◆ **nous ne connaissons personne dans le** ~ we don't know anyone in the neighbourhood *ou* around here

4 *(= proximité)* proximity, closeness ◆ **le ~ de la montagne** the proximity *ou* closeness of the mountains ◆ **il n'était pas enchanté du ~ de cette usine** he wasn't very happy at having the factory so close *ou* on his doorstep

5 *(Math) [de point]* neighbourhood *(Brit)*, neighborhood *(US)*

voisiner /vwazine/ ► conjug 1 ◄ VI *(= être près de)* ◆ ~ **avec qch** to be (placed) side by side with sth

voiture /vwatyʀ/ NF 1 *(= automobile)* car, automobile *(US)* ◆ **ils sont venus en** ~ they came by car, they drove (here) ◆ **~(-)balai** *(Tour de France)* broom wagon; *(Métro)* last train ◆ **vol à la ~(-)bélier** ram-raiding ◆ **~ cellulaire** prison *ou* police van *(Brit)*, patrol *ou* police wagon *(US)* ◆ **~ de compétition** competition car ◆ **~ de course** racing car ◆ **~ décapotable** convertible ◆ **~-école** driving-school car ◆ **~ de formule un** Formula-One car ◆ **~ de grande remise** *(Admin)* hired limousine (with chauffeur) ◆ **~ de location** rental car, rented *ou* hired *(Brit)* car, hire car *(Brit)* ◆ **~ de maître** chauffeur-driven car ◆ **~ particulière** private car ◆ **~ pie** † ≈ (police) patrol car, panda car *(Brit)* ◆ **~ de place** *(Admin)* taxi cab, hackney carriage *(Brit)* ◆ **~ de police** police car ◆ **~ de pompiers** fire engine ◆ **~ publicitaire** *(Tour de France)* promoter's *ou* sponsor's back-up vehicle ◆ **~-radio** radio car ◆ **~ sans chauffeur** self-drive hire car ◆ **~ sans permis** *small car for which no driving licence is required* ◆ **~ de série** production car ◆ **~ de fonction, ~ de service, ~ de société** company car ◆ **~ de sport** sportscar ◆ **~ de tourisme** saloon *(Brit)*, sedan *(US)* ◆ **~ ventouse** illegally parked car *(exceeding the time limit for parking)*

2 *(= wagon)* carriage *(Brit)*, coach *(Brit)*, car *(US)* ◆ **~ de tête/queue** front/back carriage *(Brit) ou* coach *(Brit) ou* car *(US)* ◆ **~-bar** buffet car ◆ **~-couchette** couchette ◆ **~-lit** sleeper *(Brit)*, Pullman *(US)*, sleeping car *(US)* ◆ **~-restaurant** dining car ◆ **en ~ !** all aboard!

3 *(= véhicule attelé, poussé) (pour marchandises)* cart; *(pour voyageurs)* carriage, coach; *(pour handicapé)* wheelchair, invalid carriage *(Brit)* ◆ **~ à bras** handcart ◆ **~ à cheval** horse-drawn carriage ◆ **~ d'enfant** pram *(Brit)*, baby carriage *(US)*, perambulator *(Brit) (frm)* ◆ **~ de poste** mailcoach, stagecoach ◆ **~ des quatre saisons** costermonger's *(Brit) ou* greengrocer's *(Brit)* barrow, sidewalk vegetable barrow *(US)*; → **petit**

voiturer /vwatyʀe/ ► conjug 1 ◄ VT († † *ou hum*) *(sur un chariot)* to wheel in; (* : *en voiture)* to take in the car

voiturette /vwatyʀɛt/ NF *(d'infirme)* carriage; *(= petite auto)* little *ou* small car

voiturier /vwatyʀje/ NM (†, *Jur)* carrier, carter; *[d'hôtel, casino]* doorman *(responsible for parking clients' cars)* ◆ **"voiturier"** *(écriteau)* "valet parking"

voix /vwɑ/ NF 1 *(= sons)* voice ◆ **à ~ basse** in a low *ou* hushed voice ◆ **ils parlaient à ~ basse** they were talking in hushed *ou* low voices *ou* in undertones ◆ **à ~ haute, à haute** ~ aloud, out loud ◆ **~ de crécelle/de fausset/de gorge** shrill/falsetto/throaty voice ◆ **d'une ~ blanche** in a toneless *ou* flat voice ◆ **d'une ~ forte** in a loud voice ◆ **à haute et intelligible** ~ loud and clear ◆ **avoir de la** ~ to have a good (singing) voice ◆ **être** *ou* **rester sans** ~ to be speechless *(devant* before, at); ◆ **de la ~ et du geste** by word and gesture, with words and gestures ◆ **une ~ lui cria de monter** a voice shouted to him to come up ◆ **donner de la** ~ *(= aboyer)* to bay, to give tongue; (* *= crier)* to bawl ◆ **~ dans le champ** *ou* **in** *(Ciné, TV)* voice-in ◆ **~ hors champs** *ou* **off** *(Théât)* voice-off; *(= commentaire)* voice-over ◆ **elle commente les images en ~ off** she provides the voice-over for the pictures ◆ **la ~ des violons** the voice of the violins; → **élever, gros, portée²**

2 *(= conseil, avertissement)* **~ de la conscience/raison** voice of conscience/reason ◆ **une petite ~ m'a dit ...** something inside me said ... ◆ **se fier à la ~ d'un ami** to rely on *ou* trust to a friend's advice ◆ **la ~ du sang** the ties of blood, the call of the blood ◆ **c'est la ~ du sang qui parle** he must heed the call of his blood

3 *(= opinion)* voice; *(Pol = suffrage)* vote ◆ **la ~ du peuple** the voice of the people, vox populi ◆ **mettre qch aux** ~ to put sth to the vote ◆ **la proposition a recueilli 30** ~ the proposal received *ou* got 30 votes ◆ **demander la mise aux ~ d'une proposition** to ask for a vote on a proposal, to ask for a proposal to be put to the vote ◆ **avoir ~ consultative** to have consultative powers *ou* a consultative voice ◆ **avoir ~ prépondérante** to have a casting vote ◆ **gagner des** ~ to win votes ◆ **donner sa ~ à un candidat** to give a candidate one's vote, to vote for a candidate ◆ **le parti obtiendra peu de/beaucoup de** ~ the party will poll badly/heavily ◆ **avoir ~ au chapitre** to have a say in the matter

4 *(Mus)* voice ◆ **chanter à 2/3** ~ to sing in 2/3 parts ◆ **fugue à 3** ~ fugue in 3 voices ◆ **~ de basse/de ténor** bass/tenor (voice) ◆ **chanter d'une ~ fausse/juste** to sing out of tune/in tune ◆ **~ de tête/de poitrine** head/chest voice ◆ **être/ne pas être en** ~ to be/not to be in good voice ◆ **la ~ humaine/céleste de l'orgue** the vox humana/voix céleste on the organ

5 *(Ling)* voice ◆ **à la ~ active/passive** in the active/passive voice

vol¹ /vɔl/ NM 1 *[d'oiseau, avion] (gén)* flight ◆ **~ ramé/plané** flapping/gliding flight ◆ **faire un ~ plané** *[oiseau]* to glide through the air; *(fig = tomber)* to fall flat on one's face ◆ **~ d'essai/de nuit** trial/night flight ◆ **~ régulier/charter** scheduled/charter flight ◆ **il y a 8 heures de ~ entre ...** it's an 8-hour flight between ... ◆ **le ~ Paris-Londres** the Paris-London flight ◆ **heures/conditions de** ~ flying hours/conditions ◆ **~ habité** manned flight ◆ **~ sec** flight only ◆ **pilote qui a plusieurs centaines d'heures de** ~ pilot with several hundred hours flying time; → **haut, ravitaillement**

2 *(= ensemble d'animaux volants)* flock, flight ◆ **un ~ de perdrix** a covey *ou* flock of partridges ◆ **un ~ de canards sauvages** a flight of wild ducks ◆ **un ~ de moucherons** a cloud of gnats

3 *(locutions)* **prendre son** ~ *[oiseau]* to take wing, to fly off *ou* away; *(fig)* to take off

◆ **à vol d'oiseau** as the crow flies

◆ **au vol** ◆ **attraper qch au** ~ *[+ ballon, objet lancé]* to catch sth as it flies past, to catch sth in midair; *[+ autobus, train]* to leap onto sth as it moves off ◆ **elle a rattrapé son chapeau au** ~ she caught her hat as it went flying through the air ◆ **saisir une occasion au** ~ to leap at *ou* seize an opportunity ◆ **saisir** *ou* **cueillir une remarque/une impression au** ~ to catch a chance *ou* passing remark/impression ◆ **tirer un oiseau au** ~ to shoot (at) a bird on the wing

◆ **en (plein) vol** in (full) flight

COMP **vol libre** hang-gliding ◆ **pratiquer le ~ libre** to hang-glide, to go hang-gliding
vol relatif *(Sport)* relative work, RW *(style of free fall parachuting)*
vol à voile gliding ◆ **faire du ~ à voile** to go gliding

vol² /vɔl/ NM *(= délit)* theft ◆ **~ simple** *(Jur)* theft ◆ **~ qualifié** *ou* **aggravé** aggravated theft ◆ **~ avec violence** robbery with violence ◆ **~s de voiture** car thefts ◆ **c'est du ~ !** *(fig)* it's daylight robbery!, it's a rip-off!* ◆ **c'est du ~ organisé** *(fig)* it's a racket

COMP **vol à l'arraché** bag-snatching
vol domestique *theft committed by an employee*
vol avec effraction burglary, breaking and entering
vol à l'étalage shoplifting *(NonC)*
vol à main armée armed robbery
vol à la roulotte theft from a vehicle
vol à la tire pickpocketing *(NonC)*

volage /vɔlaʒ/ ADJ *[époux, cœur]* flighty, fickle, inconstant

volaille /vɔlɑj/ NF ◆ **une ~** a bird, a fowl ◆ **la ~** poultry ◆ **les ~s de la basse-cour** farmyard poultry ◆ **~ rôtie** roast fowl ◆ **farcir la ~ de marrons** stuff the bird with chestnuts ◆ **c'est de la ~** (= *du poulet*) it's chicken ◆ **foie/escalope de ~** chicken liver/breast

volailler, -ère /vɔlɑje, ɛʀ/ NM,F poulterer

volant¹ /vɔlɑ̃/ NM 1 *[de voiture]* steering wheel ◆ **être au ~** to be at *ou* behind the wheel ◆ **la femme au ~** women drivers ◆ **prendre le ~, se mettre au ~** to take the wheel ◆ **c'est lui qui tenait le ~** he was at *ou* behind the wheel ◆ **un brusque coup de ~** a sharp turn of the wheel ◆ **as du ~** crack *ou* ace driver 2 *(Tech = roue, régulateur)* flywheel; *(de commande)* (hand) wheel 3 *[de rideau, robe]* flounce ◆ **jupe à ~s** flounced skirt, skirt with flounces 4 *(= balle de badminton)* shuttlecock; *(= jeu)* badminton, battledore and shuttlecock † 5 *[de carnet à souches]* tear-off portion 6 *(= réserve, marge)* reserve

COMP **volant inclinable** tilt steering wheel
volant magnétique magneto
volant réglable adjustable steering wheel
volant de sécurité reserve, safeguard
volant de trésorerie cash reserve

volant², e /vɔlɑ̃, ɑ̃t/ ADJ 1 *(= qui vole)* flying ◆ **le personnel ~, les ~s** the flight *ou* flying staff; → **poisson, soucoupe, tapis** *etc* 2 *(littér = fugace) [ombre, forme]* fleeting 3 *(= mobile, transportable) [pont, camp, personnel]* flying ◆ **(brigade) ~e** *(Police)* flying squad; → **feuille**

volanté, e /vɔlɑ̃te/ ADJ *[jupe]* flounced

volapük /vɔlapyk/ NM Volapuk

volatil, e¹ /vɔlatil/ ADJ *(Bourse, Chim)* volatile; *(littér = éphémère)* evanescent, ephemeral; → **alcali**

volatile² /vɔlatil/ NM *(gén hum) (= volaille)* fowl; *(= tout oiseau)* winged *ou* feathered creature

volatilisable /vɔlatilizabl/ ADJ volatilizable

volatilisation /vɔlatilizasjɔ̃/ NF 1 *(Chim)* volatilization 2 *(= disparition)* extinguishing, obliteration

volatiliser /vɔlatilize/ ► conjug 1 ◄ VT *(Chim)* to volatilize VPR **se volatiliser** 1 *(Chim)* to volatilize 2 *(= disparaître)* to vanish (into thin air)

volatilité /vɔlatilite/ NF volatility

vol-au-vent /vɔlovɑ̃/ NM INV vol-au-vent

volcan /vɔlkɑ̃/ NM 1 *(Géog)* volcano ◆ **~ en activité/éteint** active/extinct volcano 2 *(fig) (= personne)* spitfire; *(= situation)* powder keg, volcano ◆ **nous sommes assis sur un ~** we are sitting on a powder keg *ou* a volcano

volcanique /vɔlkanik/ ADJ *(lit)* volcanic; *(fig) [tempérament]* explosive, fiery

volcanisme /vɔlkanism/ NM volcanism

volcanologie /vɔlkanɔlɔʒi/ NF vulcanology

volcanologue /vɔlkanɔlɔg/ NMF vulcanologist

volée /vɔle/ NF 1 *[d'oiseaux] (= envol, distance)* flight; *(= groupe)* flock, flight ◆ **une ~ de moineaux/corbeaux** a flock *ou* flight of sparrows/crows ◆ **s'enfuir comme une ~ de moineaux** to scatter in all directions ◆ **une ~ d'enfants** a swarm of children ◆ **prendre sa ~** *(lit)* to take wing, to fly off *ou* away; *(fig = s'affranchir)* to spread one's wings; → **haut**

2 *(en Suisse = groupe d'élèves)* (pupils in the same) year

3 *(= décharge, tir)* volley ◆ **~ de flèches** flight *ou* volley of arrows ◆ **~ d'obus** volley of shells

4 *(= suite de coups)* volley ◆ **une ~ de coups** a volley of blows ◆ **une ~ de bois vert** † *(= coups)* a volley *ou* flurry of blows; *(= réprimande)* a volley of reproaches ◆ **administrer/recevoir une bonne ~** to give/get a sound thrashing *ou* beating

5 *(Ftbl, Tennis)* volley ◆ **faire une reprise de ~** to strike the ball on the volley ◆ **~ croisée/de face/de revers** *(Tennis)* cross-court/forehand/backhand volley

6 *(Archit)* **~ de marches** flight of stairs

7 *(locutions)*

◆ **à la volée** ◆ **jeter qch à la ~** to fling sth about ◆ **semer à la ~** to sow broadcast, to broadcast ◆ **attraper la balle à la ~** to catch the ball in midair ◆ **saisir une allusion à la ~** to pick up a passing allusion

◆ **à toute volée** *[gifler, lancer]* vigorously, with full force ◆ **les cloches sonnaient à toute ~** the bells were pealing out ◆ **il referma la porte/fenêtre à toute ~** he slammed the door/window shut

voler¹ /vɔle/ ► conjug 1 ◄ VI 1 *[oiseau, avion, pilote]* to fly ◆ **vouloir ~ avant d'avoir des ailes** to want to run before one can walk ◆ **~ de ses propres ailes** to stand on one's own two feet, to fend for o.s. ◆ **on entendrait ~ une mouche** you could hear a pin drop

2 *[flèche, pierres, insultes]* to fly ◆ **~ en éclats** *[fenêtre]* to shatter; *[bâtiment]* to explode; *[mythe]* to be exploded ◆ **faire ~ en éclats** *[+ bâtiment, fenêtre]* to shatter; *[+ mythe]* to explode ◆ **~ au vent** *[neige, voile, feuille]* to fly in the wind, to float on the wind ◆ **plaisanterie qui vole bas** feeble joke ◆ **ça ne vole pas haut !** * it's pretty low-level!

3 *(= s'élancer)* **~ vers qn/dans les bras de qn** to fly to sb/into sb's arms ◆ **~ au secours de qn** to fly to sb's assistance ◆ **il lui a volé dans les plumes** * *(physiquement)* he flew at him, he laid into him *, he went for him; *(verbalement)* he went for him ◆ **se ~ dans les plumes** * to go for each other, to fly at each other

4 *(littér = passer, aller très vite) [temps]* to fly; *[embarcation, véhicule]* to fly (along) ◆ **son cheval volait/semblait ~** his horse flew (along)/seemed to fly (along)

voler² /vɔle/ ► conjug 1 ◄ VT 1 *[+ objet] (= dérober)* to steal ◆ **~ de l'argent/une idée/un baiser à qn** to steal money/an idea/a kiss from sb ◆ **on m'a volé mon stylo** somebody stole my pen, my pen has been stolen ◆ **se faire ~ ses bagages** to have one's luggage stolen ◆ **il ne l'a pas volé !** *(fig)* he asked for it!, it serves him right! ◆ **il ne l'a pas volée, cette médaille !** *(fig)* he worked hard for that medal! ◆ **qui vole un œuf vole un bœuf** *(Prov)* once a thief, always a thief *(Prov)*

2 *[+ personne] (= dépouiller)* to rob; *(= léser)* to cheat ◆ **~ les clients** to rob *ou* cheat customers ◆ **~ les clients sur le poids** to cheat customers over (the) weight, to give customers short measure ◆ **le boucher ne t'a pas volé sur le poids** the butcher gave you good weight ◆ **~ qn lors d'un partage** to cheat sb when sharing out ◆ **se sentir volé** *(lors d'un spectacle interrompu)* to feel cheated *ou* robbed ◆ **on n'est pas volé** * you get your money's worth all right *, it's good value for money

volet /vɔlɛ/ NM 1 *[de fenêtre, hublot]* shutter ◆ **~ roulant** roller shutter 2 *[d'avion]* flap ◆ **~ d'intrados/de freinage** split/brake flap ◆ **~ de courbure** *[de parachute]* flap 3 *[de capot de voiture]* bonnet flap; *[de roue à aube]* paddle ◆ **~ de carburateur** throttle valve, butterfly valve 4 *[de triptyque]* volet, wing; *[de feuillet, carte]* section; → **trier** 5 *[de trilogie, émission, plan d'action, enquête]* part ◆ **un plan de paix en trois ~s** a three-point peace plan ◆ **le ~ social du traité** the social chapter of the treaty ◆ **le ~ agricole de l'accord** the section on agriculture in the agreement

voleter /vɔl(ə)te/ ► conjug 4 ◄ VI *[oiseau]* to flutter about, to flit about; *[rubans, flocons]* to flutter

voleur, -euse /vɔlœʀ, øz/ ADJ ◆ **être ~** *(gén)* to be light-fingered, to be a (bit of a) thief; *(commerçant)* to be a cheat *ou* swindler, to be dishonest; *[d'animal]* to be a thief ◆ **~ comme une pie** thievish as a magpie NM,F *(= malfaiteur)* thief; *(= escroc, commerçant)* swindler ◆ **~ de grand chemin** highwayman ◆ **~ à l'étalage** shoplifter ◆ **~ d'enfants** † kidnapper ◆ **au ~ !** stop thief! ◆ **~ de voitures** car thief ◆ **se sauver comme un ~** to run off like a thief (in the night); → **tire²**

Volga /vɔlga/ NF Volga

volière /vɔljɛʀ/ NF *(= cage)* aviary ◆ **ce bureau est une ~** this office is a proper henhouse * *(hum)*

volige /vɔliʒ/ NF *(= toit)* lath

volitif, -ive /vɔlitif, iv/ ADJ volitional, volitive

volition /vɔlisjɔ̃/ NF volition

volley /vɔlɛ/, **volley-ball** /vɔlɛbol/ NM volleyball ◆ **~(-ball) de plage** beach volley

volleyer /vɔleje/ ► conjug 1 ◄ VI *(Tennis)* to volley

volleyeur, -euse /vɔlɛjœʀ, øz/ NM,F *(Volley)* volleyball player; *(Tennis)* volleyer

volontaire /vɔlɔ̃tɛʀ/ ADJ 1 *(= voulu) [acte, enrôlement, prisonnier]* voluntary; *[oubli]* intentional; → **engagé** 2 *(= décidé) [personne]* wilful, headstrong; *[expression, menton]* determined NMF *(Mil, gén)* volunteer ◆ **se porter ~ pour qch** to volunteer for sth ◆ **je suis ~** I volunteer ◆ **~ du service national à l'étranger** *person doing his military service as a civilian working abroad*

volontairement /vɔlɔ̃tɛʀmɑ̃/ ADV 1 *(= de son plein gré)* voluntarily, of one's own free will; *(Jur = facultativement)* voluntarily 2 *(= exprès)* intentionally, deliberately ◆ **il a dit ça ~** he said it on purpose *ou* deliberately 3 *(= d'une manière décidée)* determinedly

volontariat /vɔlɔ̃taʀja/ NM *(gén)* voluntary participation; *(Mil)* voluntary service ◆ **faire du ~** to do voluntary work ◆ **sur la base du ~** on a voluntary basis ◆ **nous faisons appel au ~ pour ce travail** we use voluntary workers *ou* volunteers for this work

volontarisme /vɔlɔ̃taʀism/ NM voluntarism

volontariste /vɔlɔ̃taʀist/ ADJ, NMF voluntarist

volonté /vɔlɔ̃te/ NF 1 *(= faculté)* will; *(= souhait, intention)* wish, will *(frm)* ◆ **manifester sa ~ de faire qch** to show one's intention of doing sth ◆ **accomplir/respecter la ~ de qn** to carry out/respect sb's wishes ◆ **la ~ générale** the general will ◆ **la ~ nationale** the will of the nation ◆ **les dernières ~s de qn** the last wishes of sb ◆ **~ de puissance** thirst for power ◆ **~ de guérir/réussir** will to recover/succeed ◆ **que ta** *ou* **votre ~ soit faite** *(Rel)* Thy will be done; → **indépendant, quatre**

2 *(= disposition)* **bonne ~** goodwill, willingness ◆ **mauvaise ~** lack of goodwill, unwillingness ◆ **il a beaucoup de bonne ~ mais peu d'aptitude** he shows great willingness but not much aptitude ◆ **il met de la bonne/mauvaise ~ à faire son travail** he goes about his work with goodwill/grudgingly, he does his work willingly/unwillingly *ou* with a good/bad grace ◆ **il fait preuve de bonne/mauvaise ~** he has a positive/negative attitude ◆ **paix sur la terre, aux hommes de bonne ~** peace on earth (and) goodwill to all men ◆ **faire appel aux bonnes ~s pour construire qch** to appeal to volunteers to construct sth ◆ **toutes les bonnes ~s sont les bienvenues** all offers of help are welcome ◆ **avec la meilleure ~ du monde** with the best will in the world

3 *(= caractère, énergie)* willpower, will ◆ **faire un effort de ~** to make an effort of will(power) ◆ **avoir de la ~** to have willpower ◆ **cette femme a une ~ de fer** this woman has an iron will *ou* a will of iron ◆ **réussir à force de ~** to succeed through sheer will(power) *ou* determination ◆ **échouer par manque de ~** to fail

through lack of will(power) *ou* determination ◆ **faire preuve de** ~ to display willpower

4 *(locutions)*

◆ **à volonté** ◆ **pain/café à volonté** "as much bread/coffee as you like *ou* want" ◆ **"sucrer à volonté"** "sweeten to taste" ◆ **vous pouvez le prendre ou le laisser à** ~ you can take it or leave it as you wish *ou* just as you like ◆ **nous avons de l'eau à** ~ we have as much water as we want, we have plenty of water ◆ **vin à** ~ **pendant le repas** as much wine as one wants *ou* unlimited wine with the meal ◆ **billet payable à** ~ *(Comm)* promissory note payable on demand ◆ **il en fait toujours à sa** ~ he always does things his own way, he always does as he pleases *ou* likes, he always suits himself

volontiers /vɔlɔ̃tje/ GRAMMAIRE ACTIVE 36.2 ADV 1 *(= avec plaisir)* gladly ◆ **je l'aiderais** ~ I would gladly *ou* willingly help him ◆ **voulez-vous dîner chez nous ?** – ~ **!** would you like to eat with us? – I'd love to *ou* with pleasure! ◆ **un autre whisky ?** – **très** *ou* **bien** ~ another whisky? – I'd love one *ou* yes please ◆ **je me serais** ~ **passé de cette corvée** I could quite happily have done without that chore ◆ **je reconnais** ~ **m'être trompé** I readily *ou* freely admit I was wrong

2 *(= habituellement)* **on croit** ~ **que ...** people often believe that ..., people are apt *ou* quite ready to believe that ... ◆ **il est** ~ **critique sur le travail des autres** he's always ready to criticize other people's work ◆ **ses œuvres sont** ~ **provocatrices** his works tend to be provocative ◆ **il lit** ~ **pendant des heures** he'll read for hours on end

volt /vɔlt/ NM volt

voltage /vɔltaʒ/ NM voltage

voltaïque /vɔltaik/ ADJ voltaic, galvanic

voltaire /vɔltɛʀ/ NM ◆ **(fauteuil)** ~ Voltaire chair

volte /vɔlt/ NF *(Équitation)* volte

volte-face /vɔltəfas/ NF INV 1 *(lit)* **faire** ~ *(= se retourner)* to turn round 2 *(= changement d'opinion)* about-turn, U-turn, volte-face *(frm)* ◆ **faire une** ~ to do an about-turn *ou* a U-turn

volter /vɔlte/ ► conjug 1 ◄ VI *(Équitation)* ◆ **faire** ~ **un cheval** to make a horse circle

voltige /vɔltiʒ/ NF *(Équitation)* trick riding ◆ ~ **(aérienne)** aerobatics, stunt flying ◆ **faire de la** ~ *(Gym)* to do acrobatics ◆ **(haute)** ~ *(Gym)* acrobatics ◆ **c'est de la (haute)** ~ **intellectuelle** it's mental gymnastics ◆ **c'était un exercice de haute** ~ **monétaire** it was an example of financial wizardry

voltiger /vɔltiʒe/ ► conjug 3 ◄ VI *[oiseaux]* to flit about, to flutter about; *[objet léger]* to flutter about

voltigeur /vɔltiʒœʀ/ NM 1 *(= acrobate)* acrobat; *(= pilote)* stunt pilot *ou* flier 2 *(Hist, Mil)* light infantryman

voltmètre /vɔltmɛtʀ/ NM voltmeter

volubile /vɔlybil/ ADJ 1 *[personne, éloquence]* voluble 2 *(Bot)* voluble

volubilis /vɔlybilis/ NM convolvulus, morning glory

volubilité /vɔlybilite/ NF volubility ◆ **parler avec** ~ to talk volubly

volucompteur ® /vɔlykɔ̃tœʀ/ NM (volume) indicator

volumateur, -trice /vɔlymatœʀ, tʀis/ ADJ *[shampoing, mousse]* that gives body to the hair

volume /vɔlym/ NM 1 *(= livre, tome)* volume 2 *(= espace, quantité)* volume ◆ ~ **moléculaire/atomique** molecular/atomic volume ◆ ~ **d'eau d'un fleuve** volume of water in a river ◆ **eau oxygénée à 20** ~**s** 20-volume hydrogen peroxide ◆ **le** ~ **des exportations/transactions** the volume of exports/trade ◆ **le marché est en baisse de 7% en** ~ the volume of the market has fallen 7% ◆ **faire du** ~ *[gros objets]* to be bulky, to take up space 3 *(= intensité) [de son]* volume ◆ ~ **de la voix/radio** volume of the voice/radio ◆ ~ **sonore** *(pour enregistrement)* sound level; *(mesure de pollution)* noise level

volumétrique /vɔlymetʀik/ ADJ volumetric

volumineux, -euse /vɔlyminø, øz/ ADJ *[catalogue, dictionnaire, dossier]* bulky, voluminous; *[courrier]* voluminous; *[paquet]* bulky

volumique /vɔlymik/ ADJ *(Phys)* ◆ **masse** ~ density ◆ **poids** ~ specific weight, weight per unit volume

volupté /vɔlypte/ NF *(sensuelle)* sensual delight, sensual *ou* voluptuous pleasure; *(morale, intellectuelle)* exquisite delight *ou* pleasure ◆ **elle s'est plongée dans son bain avec** ~ she sank luxuriously into her bath

voluptueusement /vɔlyptɥøzmɑ̃/ ADV voluptuously

voluptueux, -euse /vɔlyptɥø, øz/ ADJ voluptuous

volute /vɔlyt/ NF 1 *[de colonne, grille, escalier]* volute, scroll; *[de fumée]* curl, wreath; *[de vague]* curl ◆ **en** ~ voluted, scrolled 2 *(= mollusque)* volute

volve /vɔlv/ NF volva

vomi /vɔmi/ NM vomit

vomique /vɔmik/ ADJ F → **noix**

vomiquier /vɔmikje/ NM nux vomica *(tree)*

vomir /vɔmiʀ/ ► conjug 2 ◄ VT 1 *[+ aliments]* to vomit, to bring up; *[+ sang]* to spit, to bring up 2 *(sans compl)* to be sick, to vomit, to throw up ◆ **il a vomi partout** he was sick everywhere ◆ **ça te fera** ~ it'll make you vomit *ou* be sick ◆ **avoir envie de** ~ to feel sick ◆ **ça donne envie de** ~, **c'est à** ~ *(fig)* it makes you *ou* it's enough to make you sick, it's nauseating 3 *(fig) [+ lave, flammes]* to belch forth, to spew forth; *[+ injures, haine]* to spew out 4 *(fig = détester)* to loathe, to abhor ◆ **il vomit les intellectuels** he has a loathing for *ou* loathes intellectuals

vomissement /vɔmismɑ̃/ NM 1 *(= action)* vomiting *(NonC)* ◆ **il fut pris de** ~**s** he (suddenly) started vomiting 2 *(= matières)* vomit *(NonC)*

vomissure /vɔmisyʀ/ NF vomit *(NonC)*

vomitif, -ive /vɔmitif, iv/ ADJ, NM *(Pharm)* emetic

vorace /vɔʀas/ ADJ *[animal, personne, curiosité]* voracious ◆ **appétit** ~ voracious *ou* ravenous appetite ◆ **plantes** ~**s** plants which deplete the soil

voracement /vɔʀasmɑ̃/ ADV voraciously

voracité /vɔʀasite/ NF voracity, voraciousness

vortex /vɔʀtɛks/ NM *(littér)* vortex

vos /vo/ ADJ POSS → **votre**

Vosges /voʒ/ NFPL ◆ **les** ~ the Vosges

vosgien, -ienne /voʒjɛ̃, jɛn/ ADJ Vosges *(épith)*, of *ou* from the Vosges NM,F **Vosgien(ne)** inhabitant *ou* native of the Vosges

VOST (abrév de **version originale sous-titrée**) → **version**

votant, e /vɔtɑ̃, ɑ̃t/ NM,F voter

votation /vɔtasjɔ̃/ NF *(Helv)* voting

vote /vɔt/ NM 1 *(= approbation) [de projet de loi]* vote (de for); *[de loi, réforme]* passing; *[de crédits]* voting ◆ **après le** ~ **du budget** after the budget was voted 2 *(= suffrage, acte, opération)* vote; *(= ensemble des votants)* voters ◆ **le** ~ **électronique** e-voting ◆ **le** ~ **socialiste** Socialist voters, the Socialist vote ◆ ~ **de confiance** vote of confidence ◆ ~ **à main levée** vote by a show of hands ◆ ~ **à bulletin secret/par correspondance** secret/postal vote *ou* ballot ◆ ~ **par procuration** proxy vote ◆ ~ **direct/indirect** direct/indirect vote ◆ ~ **blanc/nul** blank/spoilt ballot paper ◆ ~ **sanction** vote of no confidence ◆ ~ **utile** tactical vote ◆ ~ **bloqué** *single vote on a bill containing several government amendments* ◆ ~ **de confiance** vote of confidence ◆ **procéder** *ou* **passer au** ~ to proceed to a vote, to take a vote; → **bulletin, bureau, droit**[3]

voter /vɔte/ ► conjug 1 ◄ VI to vote ◆ ~ **à main levée** to vote by a show of hands ◆ ~ **à droite/pour X** to vote for the right/for X ◆ ~ **libéral/à gauche** to vote Liberal/for the left ◆ ~ **utile** to vote tactically ◆ ~ **pour/contre qch** to vote for/against sth ◆ **j'ai voté contre** I voted against it ◆ ~ **sur une motion** to vote on a motion ◆ **j'ai voté blanc** I cast a blank vote VT *(= adopter) [+ projet de loi]* to vote for; *[+ loi, réforme]* to pass; *[+ crédits]* to vote ◆ ~ **la censure** to pass a vote of censure ◆ ~ **la reconduction d'une grève** to vote to continue a strike ◆ **ne pas** ~ *[+ amendement]* to vote out ◆ ~ **la mort du roi** to vote to execute the king, to vote for the king's death

votif, -ive /vɔtif, iv/ ADJ votive

votre (pl **vos**) /vɔtʀ, vo/ ADJ POSS your; *(emphatique)* your own; (†, *Rel*) thy ◆ **laissez** ~ **manteau et vos gants au vestiaire** *(à une personne)* leave your coat and gloves in the cloakroom; *(à plusieurs personnes)* leave your coats and gloves in the cloakroom ◆ **un de vos livres** one of your books, a book of yours ◆ **je vous accorde** ~ **lundi** you may have Monday off ◆ **Votre Excellence/Majesté** Your Excellency/Majesty; *pour autres loc voir* **son**[1], **ton**[1]

vôtre /votʀ/ PRON POSS ◆ **le** ~, **la** ~, **les** ~**s** yours ◆ **ce sac n'est pas le** ~ this bag isn't yours, this isn't your bag ◆ **nos enfants sont sortis avec les** ~**s** our children are out with yours

◆ **à la (bonne) vôtre!** your (good) health!, cheers! ◆ **vous voulez y aller quand même – à la (bonne)** ~ **!*** you still want to go? – rather you than me!; *pour autres loc voir* **sien**

NMF 1 ◆ **j'espère que vous y mettrez du** ~ I hope you'll pull your weight *ou* do your bit*; → aussi **sien**

2 ◆ **les** ~**s** your family, your folks* ◆ **vous et tous les** ~**s** you and all those like you, you and your kind *(péj)* ◆ **bonne année à vous et à tous les** ~**s** Happy New Year to you and yours ◆ **nous pourrons être des** ~**s ce soir** we shall be able to join your party *ou* join you tonight; → **sien**

ADJ POSS *(littér)* yours ◆ **son cœur est** ~ **depuis toujours** his (*ou* her) heart has always been yours ◆ **amicalement** ~ best wishes; → **sien**

vouer /vwe/ ► conjug 1 ◄ VT 1 *(Rel)* ~ **qn à Dieu/à la Vierge** to dedicate sb to God/to the Virgin Mary; → **savoir** 2 *(= promettre)* to vow ◆ **il lui a voué un amour éternel** he vowed his undying love to her 3 *(= consacrer)* to devote ◆ ~ **son temps à ses études** to devote one's time to one's studies ◆ **se** ~ **à une cause** to dedicate o.s. *ou* devote o.s. to a cause 4 *(gén ptp = condamner)* to doom ◆ **projet voué à l'échec** project doomed to *ou* destined for failure ◆ **famille vouée à la misère** family doomed to poverty

vouloir[1] /vulwaʀ/

► conjug 31 ◄

GRAMMAIRE ACTIVE 28.1, 30, 31, 35, 36.3

1 VERBE TRANSITIF
2 VERBE TRANSITIF INDIRECT
3 VERBE PRONOMINAL

1 – VERBE TRANSITIF

1 = exiger, être décidé à obtenir *[+ objet, augmentation, changement]* to want ◆ ~ **faire qch** to

want to do sth ♦ ~ **que qn fasse qch/que qch se fasse** to want sb to do sth/sth to be done ♦ **je veux que tu viennes tout de suite** I want you to come at once ♦ **il veut absolument venir/qu'elle parte/ce jouet** he is set on coming/on her leaving/on having that toy, he is determined to come/(that) she should leave/to have that toy ♦ **il ne veut pas y aller/qu'elle y aille** he doesn't want to go/her to go ♦ ~, **c'est pouvoir** *(Prov)* ♦ **quand on veut, on peut** *(Prov)* where there's a will there's a way *(Prov)* ♦ **qu'est-ce qu'ils veulent maintenant ?** what do they want now? ♦ **il sait ce qu'il veut** he knows what he wants ♦ **il veut sans** ~ he only half wants to ♦ **tu l'as voulu** you asked for it ♦ **tu l'auras voulu** it'll have been your own fault, you'll have brought it on yourself ♦ **elle fait de lui ce qu'elle veut** she does what she likes with him, she twists him round her little finger

♦ **en vouloir*** *(= vouloir gagner, réussir)* ♦ **il en veut** he wants to win ♦ **l'équipe de France en veut ce soir** the French team is raring to go* *ou* is out to win tonight

2 = désirer, souhaiter **voulez-vous à boire/manger ?** would you like something to drink/eat? ♦ **tu veux quelque chose à boire ?** would you like *ou* do you want something to drink? ♦ **comment voulez-vous votre poisson, frit ou poché ?** how would you like your fish – fried or poached? ♦ **je ne veux pas qu'il se croie obligé de ...** I wouldn't like *ou* I don't want him to feel obliged to ... ♦ **je voulais vous dire ...** I meant to tell you ... ♦ **il voulait partir hier mais ...** he wanted *ou* meant *ou* intended to leave yesterday but ... ♦ **il ne voulait pas vous blesser** he didn't want *ou* mean to hurt you ♦ **sans** ~ **vous vexer** no offence (meant) ♦ **qu'il le veuille ou non** whether he likes it or not ♦ **ça va comme tu veux ?*** is everything all right *ou* OK?* ♦ **veux-tu que je te dise** *ou* **raconte pourquoi ... ?** shall I tell you why ...? ♦ **que lui voulez-vous ?** what do you want with him? ♦ **qu'est-ce qu'il me veut, celui-là ?*** what does he want (from me)?

♦ **comme + vouloir** ♦ **comme tu veux (***ou* **vous voulez)** as you like *ou* wish *ou* please ♦ **bon, comme tu voudras** all right, have it your own way *ou* suit yourself ♦ **comme vous voulez, moi ça m'est égal** just as you like *ou* please *ou* wish, it makes no difference to me

♦ **si + vouloir** ♦ **si tu veux, si vous voulez** if you like, if you want (to) ♦ **oui, si on veut** *(= dans un sens, d'un côté)* yes, if you like ♦ **s'il voulait, il pourrait être ministre** if he wanted (to), he could be a minister, he could be a minister if he so desired ♦ **s'il voulait (bien) nous aider, cela gagnerait du temps** it would save time if he'd help us ♦ **s'ils veulent garder leur avance, ils ne peuvent se permettre de relâcher leur effort** if they want to keep their lead they can't afford to reduce their efforts

♦ **en veux-tu en voilà*** ♦ **il y a eu des discours en veux-tu en voilà** there were speeches galore ♦ **elle a des dettes en veux-tu en voilà** she's up to her ears *ou* eyes in debt* ♦ **on lui a proposé des stages en veux-tu en voilà** they've offered him one course after another

♦ **sans le vouloir** unintentionally, inadvertently ♦ **si je t'ai vexé, c'était sans le** ~ if I offended you it was unintentional *ou* I didn't mean to

♦ **vouloir de qch** *(avec de partitif = désirer)* ♦ **je n'en veux plus** *[+ nourriture]* I don't want any more ♦ **est-ce que tu en veux ?** *[+ gâteau]* do you want some?, would you like some?; → **verbe transitif indir**; → **bien, mal²**

3 au conditionnel **je voudrais un stylo/écrire/qu'il m'écrive** I would like a pen/to write/him to write to me ♦ **il aurait voulu être médecin mais ...** he would have liked to be a doctor *ou* he would like to have been a doctor but ... ♦ **je ne voudrais pas abuser** I don't want to impose ♦ **je voudrais/j'aurais voulu que vous voyiez sa tête !** I wish you could see/could have seen his face! ♦ **je voudrais qu'il soit plus énergique, je lui voudrais plus d'énergie** *(frm)* I wish he was a bit more energetic ♦ **je voudrais bien voir ça !** I'd like to see that!; → **voir verbe transitif 2**

4 exprimant l'impuissance **que voulez-vous, que veux-tu, qu'est-ce que vous voulez, qu'est-ce que tu veux** what can you do?, what do you expect? ♦ **que veux-tu, c'est comme ça, on n'y peut rien** what can you do? *ou* what do you expect? that's the way it is and there's nothing we can do about it ♦ **qu'est-ce que tu veux que je te dise ? j'ai perdu** what can I say? *ou* what do you want me to say? I lost

5 = consentir à **ils ne voulurent pas nous recevoir** they wouldn't see us, they weren't willing to see us ♦ **le moteur ne veut pas partir** the engine won't start ♦ **le feu n'a pas voulu prendre** the fire wouldn't light *ou* catch ♦ **il joue bien quand il veut** he plays well when he wants to *ou* has a mind to *ou* when he puts his mind to it

♦ **vouloir bien** ♦ **je veux bien le faire/qu'il vienne** *(s'il le faut vraiment)* I don't mind doing it/if he comes; *(il n'y a pas d'inconvénient)* I'm quite happy to do it/for him to come; *(enthousiaste)* I'm happy *ou* I'll be happy to do it/for him to come ♦ **je voudrais bien y aller** I'd really like *ou* I'd love to go ♦ **si tu voulais bien le faire, ça nous rendrait service** if you'd be kind enough to do it, you'd be doing us a favour ♦ **tu veux bien leur dire que ...** would you please tell them that ... ♦ **je veux bien encore un peu de café** I'd like some more coffee ♦ **encore un peu de thé ? – je veux bien** more tea? – yes, please ♦ **nous en parlerons plus tard, si vous le voulez bien** we'll talk about it later, if you don't mind ♦ **je veux bien le croire mais ...** I'd like to take his word for it but ..., I'm quite prepared to believe him but ... ♦ **moi je veux bien, mais ...** fair enough*, but ...

6 formules de politesse **voudriez-vous avoir l'obligeance** *ou* **l'amabilité de ...** would you be so kind as to ... ♦ **veuillez croire à toute ma sympathie** please accept my deepest sympathy ♦ **voulez-vous me prêter ce livre ?** will you lend me this book? ♦ **voudriez-vous fermer la fenêtre ?** would you mind closing the window? ♦ **si vous voulez bien me suivre** (come) this way, please; → **agréer**

7 à l'impératif : ordre **veux-tu (bien) te taire !** will you (please) be quiet! ♦ **veuillez quitter la pièce immédiatement** please leave the room at once ♦ **veux-tu bien arrêter !** will you please stop it!, stop it will you *ou* please!

8 = chercher à, essayer de to try ♦ **elle voulut se lever mais elle retomba** she tried to get up but she fell back ♦ **en voulant m'aider, il a fait échouer mon projet** by trying to help he ruined my plan ♦ **il veut se faire remarquer** he wants to be noticed, he's out to be noticed

9 = escompter, demander ~ **qch de qn** to want sth from sb ♦ **que voulez-vous de moi ?** what do you want from me? ♦ ~ **un certain prix de qch** to want a certain price for sth ♦ **j'en veux 150 €** I want €150 for it

10 = s'attendre à to expect ♦ **comment voulez-vous que je sache ?** how should I know?, how do you expect me to know? ♦ **avec 500 € par mois, comment veux-tu qu'elle s'en sorte ?** how do you expect her to manage on €500 a month? ♦ **il a tout, pourquoi voudriez-vous qu'il réclame ?** he's got everything so why should he complain? ♦ **que voulez-vous qu'on y fasse ?** what do you expect us (*ou* them *etc*) to do about it?

11 locutions

♦ **en vouloir à qn** to have something against sb, to have a grudge against sb ♦ **les deux frères s'en veulent à mort** the two brothers absolutely hate each other *ou* are at daggers drawn ♦ **en** ~ **à qn de qch** to hold sth against sb ♦ **il m'en veut beaucoup d'avoir fait cela** he holds a tremendous grudge against me for having done that ♦ **il m'en veut d'avoir fait rater ce projet** he holds it against me that I made the plan fail ♦ **il m'en veut de mon incompréhension** he holds the fact that I don't understand against me, he resents the fact that I don't understand ♦ **je m'en veux d'avoir accepté** I could kick myself* *ou* I'm so annoyed with myself for accepting ♦ **accepter cela ? je m'en voudrais !** accept that? not on your life! ♦ **ne m'en veuillez pas, ne m'en voulez pas*** don't hold it against me ♦ **tu ne m'en veux pas ?** no hard feelings? ♦ **je ne t'en veux pas** I'm not angry with you

♦ **en vouloir à qch** to be after sth ♦ **il en veut à son argent** he's after her money ♦ **ils en voulaient à sa vie** they wanted him dead ♦ **ils en voulaient à sa réputation** they wanted to ruin his reputation

12 = affirmer to claim ♦ **une philosophie qui veut que l'homme soit ...** a philosophy which claims that man is ... ♦ **la légende veut qu'il soit né ici** according to legend he was born here

♦ **je veux !*** ♦ **ça te dirait d'aller à la mer ? – je veux !** would you like to go to the seaside? – that would be great!* *ou* you bet!* ♦ **tu vas lui demander ? – je veux !** are you going to ask him? – you bet (I am)!

13 sujet chose = requérir to need, to require ♦ **cette plante veut un sol riche** this plant needs *ou* requires a rich soil ♦ **l'usage veut que ...** custom requires that ... ♦ **comme le veut la loi** according to the law, as the law requires ♦ **comme le veut la tradition** according to tradition

14 = faire *[destin, sort]* **le hasard voulut que ...** as luck would have it ... ♦ **le malheur a voulu qu'il prenne cette route** he had the misfortune to take this road

2 - VERBE TRANSITIF INDIRECT

vouloir de *(gén nég, interrog = accepter)* ~ **de qn/qch** to want sb/sth ♦ **on ne veut plus de lui** *ou* **on n'en veut plus au bureau** they don't want him *ou* won't have him in the office any more ♦ **je ne veux pas de lui comme chauffeur** I don't want him *ou* won't have him as a driver ♦ **voudront-ils de moi dans leur nouvelle maison ?** will they want me in their new house? ♦ **je l'accompagnerai si elle veut de moi** I'll go with her if she'll have me ♦ **elle ne veut plus de ce chapeau** she doesn't want this hat any more

3 - VERBE PRONOMINAL

se vouloir *(= vouloir être, prétendre être)* **ce journal se veut objectif** this newspaper likes to think it's *ou* is meant to be objective ♦ **son discours se veut rassurant** what he says is meant to be reassuring ♦ **cette peinture se veut réaliste** this painting is supposed to be realistic

vouloir² /vulwaʀ/ **NM** 1 *(littér = volonté)* will 2 ♦ **bon** ~ goodwill ♦ **mauvais** ~ reluctance ♦ **avec un mauvais** ~ **évident** with obvious reluctance ♦ **attendre le bon** ~ **de qn** to wait on sb's pleasure ♦ **cette décision dépend du bon** ~ **du ministre** this decision depends on the minister's goodwill

voulu, e /vuly/ (ptp de **vouloir**) **ADJ** 1 *(= requis)* required, requisite ♦ **il n'avait pas l'argent** ~ he didn't have the required *ou* requisite money *ou* the money required ♦ **au moment** ~ at the required moment ♦ **en temps** ~ in due time *ou* course ♦ **produire l'effet** ~ to produce the desired effect ♦ **le temps** ~ the time required [2] (= *volontaire*) deliberate, intentional ◆ **c'est** ~* it's done on purpose, it's intentional *ou* deliberate

vous /vu/ PRON PERS [1] (*sujet, objet*) you; (*pl de tu, toi*) you ◆ **les gens qui viennent** ~ **poser des questions** (*valeur indéfinie*) people who come asking questions *ou* who come and ask you questions ◆ ~ **avez bien répondu tous les deux** you both answered well, the two of you answered well ◆ ~ **et lui,** ~ **êtes aussi têtus l'un que l'autre** you are both as stubborn as each other ◆ **si j'étais** ~**, j'accepterais** if I were you *ou* in your shoes I'd accept ◆ **eux ont accepté,** ~ **pas** *ou* **pas** ~ they accepted but you didn't, they accepted but not you ◆ ~ **parti(s), je pourrai travailler** once you've gone *ou* with you out of the way, I'll be able to work ◆ **c'est enfin** ~**,** ~ **voilà enfin** here you are at last ◆ **qui l'a vu ?** ~ **?** who saw him? (did) you? ◆ **je** ~ **ai demandé de m'aider** I asked you to help me ◆ **elle n'obéit qu'à** ~ you're the only one *ou* ones she obeys

[2] (*emphatique : insistance, apostrophe, sujet*) you, you yourself (*sg*), you yourselves (*pl*); (*objet*) you ◆ ~ **tous écoutez-moi** listen to me all of you *ou* the lot of you* ◆ ~**,** ~ **n'avez pas à** ~ **plaindre** you have no cause to complain ◆ **pourquoi ne le ferais-je pas :** ~ **l'avez bien fait,** ~ **!** why shouldn't I do it – you did (it)! *ou* you yourself *ou* you yourselves did it! ◆ ~**, mentir ?, ce n'est pas possible** you, tell a lie? I can't believe it ◆ **alors** ~**,** ~ **ne partez pas ?** so what about you – aren't you going? ◆ ~**, aidez-moi !** you (there) *ou* hey you, give me a hand! ◆ **je** ~ **demande à** ~ **parce que je** ~ **connais** I'm asking you because I know you ◆ **je** ~ **connais,** ~ **!** I know you! ◆ ~**,** ~ **m'agacez !,** ~ **m'agacez,** ~ **!** you're getting on my nerves! ◆ ~**, je vois que** ~ **n'êtes pas bien** it's obvious to me that you're not well

[3] (*emphatique avec qui, que*) **c'est** ~ **qui avez raison** it's you who is (*ou* are) right ◆ ~ **tous qui m'écoutez** all of you listening to me ◆ **et** ~ **qui détestiez le cinéma,** ~ **avez bien changé** and (to think) you were the one who hated the cinema *ou* you used to say you hated the cinema – well you've certainly changed!

[4] (*avec prép*) you ◆ **à** ~ **quatre** ~ **pourrez le porter** with four of you *ou* between (the) four of you you'll be able to carry it ◆ **cette maison est-elle à** ~ **?** does this house belong to you?, is this house yours? ◆ ~ **n'avez même pas une chambre à** ~ **tout seul/tout seuls ?** you don't even have a room to yourself *ou* of your own/to yourselves *ou* of your own? ◆ **c'est à** ~ **de décider** it's up to you to decide ◆ **l'un de** ~ *ou* **d'entre** ~ **doit le savoir** one of you must know ◆ **de** ~ **à moi** between you and me ◆ ~ **ne pensez qu'à** ~ you think only of yourself (*ou* yourselves)

[5] (*dans comparaisons*) you ◆ **il me connaît mieux que** ~ (*mieux qu'il ne vous connaît*) he knows me better than (he knows) you; (*mieux que vous ne me connaissez*) he knows me better than you do ◆ **il est plus/moins fort que** ~ he's stronger than you/not as strong as you (are) ◆ **il a fait comme** ~ he did as *ou* what you did, he did the same as you

[6] (*avec vpr : souvent non traduit*) ~ **êtes-**~ **bien amusé(s) ?** did you have a good time? ◆ **je crois que** ~ ~ **connaissez** I believe you know each other ◆ **servez-**~ **donc** do help yourself (*ou* yourselves) ◆ **ne** ~ **disputez pas** don't fight ◆ **asseyez-**~ **donc** do sit down

NM ◆ **dire** ~ **à qn** to call sb "vous" ◆ **le** ~ **est de moins en moins employé** (the form of address) "vous" *ou* the "vous" form is used less and less frequently

vous-même (pl **vous-mêmes**) /vumɛm/ PRON → **même**

vousseau /vuso/, **voussoir** /vuswaʀ/ NM voussoir

voussure /vusyʀ/ NF (= *courbure*) arching; (= *partie cintrée*) arch; (*Archit* = *archivolte*) archivolt

voûte /vut/ NF (*Archit*) vault; (= *porche*) archway ◆ ~ **en plein cintre/d'arête** semi-circular/groined vault ◆ ~ **en ogive/en berceau** rib/barrel vault ◆ ~ **en éventail** fan-vaulting (*NonC*) ◆ **en** ~ vaulted ◆ **la** ~ **d'une caverne** the vault of a cave ◆ **une** ~ **d'arbres** (*fig*) an archway of trees; → **clé**

COMP **la voûte céleste** the vault *ou* canopy of heaven

voûte crânienne dome of the skull, vault of the cranium (*SPÉC*)

la voûte étoilée the starry vault *ou* dome

voûte du palais *ou* **palatine** roof of the mouth, hard palate

voûte plantaire arch (of the foot)

voûté, e /vute/ (ptp de **voûter**) ADJ [1] [*cave, plafond*] vaulted, arched [2] [*dos*] bent; [*personne*] stooped ◆ **être** ~**, avoir le dos** ~ to be stooped, to have a stoop

voûter /vute/ ► conjug 1 ◄ VT [1] (*Archit*) to arch, to vault [2] [*+ personne, dos*] to make stooped ◆ **la vieillesse l'a voûté** age has given him a stoop

VPR **se voûter** ◆ **il s'est voûté avec l'âge** he has become stooped with age

vouvoiement /vuvwamɑ̃/ NM addressing sb as vous, using the vous form ◆ **entre eux, le** ~ **reste de rigueur** they still address each other as "vous"; → TUTOIEMENT

vouvoyer /vuvwaje/ ► conjug 8 ◄ VT ◆ ~ **qn** to address sb as "vous", to use the "vous" form with sb; → TUTOIEMENT

vox populi /vɔkspɔpyli/ NF vox populi, voice of the people

voyage /vwajaʒ/ NM [1] (*gén*) journey, trip; (*par mer*) voyage ◆ **le** ~**, les** ~**s** travelling (*Brit*), traveling (*US*) ◆ **il aime les** ~**s** he likes travel *ou* travelling ◆ **les** ~**s le fatiguent** travelling tires him ◆ **le** ~ **l'a fatigué** the journey tired him ◆ **j'ai fait un beau** ~ I had a very nice trip ◆ **les** ~**s de Christophe Colomb** the voyages *ou* journeys of Christopher Columbus ◆ **les fatigues du** ~ the strain of the journey ◆ **il reste 3 jours de** ~ there are still 3 days' travelling left, the journey will take another 3 days (to do) ◆ **lors de notre** ~ **en Espagne** on our trip to Spain, during *ou* on our travels in Spain ◆ **frais/souvenirs de** ~ travel expenses/souvenirs ◆ ~ **aller/retour** outward/return journey ◆ ~ **d'affaires/d'agrément/d'études** business/pleasure/study *ou* field trip ◆ ~ **d'information** fact-finding trip ◆ ~ **autour du monde** round-the-world trip ◆ **faire un** ~ **autour du monde** to go round the world ◆ ~ **de noces** honeymoon ◆ ~ **organisé** *ou* **à forfait** package tour *ou* holiday (*Brit*) ◆ **le grand** ~ (*littér, euph*) the last great journey (*littér*) ◆ **faire le grand** ~ (*euph*) to pass away ◆ **les** ~**s forment la jeunesse** (*Prov*) travel broadens the mind; → **agence, bon¹, sac¹**

◆ **en voyage** ◆ **il est en** ~ he's away ◆ **il est absent, il est parti en** ~ he's away - he's gone (off) on a trip ◆ **au moment de partir en** ~ just as he (*ou I etc*) was setting off on his (*ou my etc*) journey *ou* travels

[2] (= *course*) trip, journey ◆ **faire deux** ~**s pour transporter qch** to make two trips to transport sth ◆ **j'ai dû faire le** ~ **de Grenoble une seconde fois** I had to make the trip *ou* journey from Grenoble a second time

[3] (*† Drogue*) trip

voyager /vwajaʒe/ ► conjug 3 ◄ VI to travel ◆ **j'ai voyagé en avion/par mer/en 1ᵉ classe** I travelled by air/by sea/1st class ◆ **aimer** ~ to like travelling ◆ **il a beaucoup voyagé** he has travelled widely *ou* a great deal, he has done a lot of travelling ◆ **qui veut** ~ **loin ménage sa monture** (*Prov*) he who takes it slow and steady goes a long way ◆ **cette malle a beaucoup voyagé** this trunk has travelled a great deal *ou* has done a lot of travelling ◆ **ces vins/denrées voyagent mal/bien** these wines/goods travel badly/well

voyageur, -euse /vwajaʒœʀ, øz/ NM,F (= *explorateur, vendeur*) traveller (*Brit*), traveler (*US*); (= *passager*) traveller (*Brit*), traveler (*US*), passenger ◆ **c'est un grand** ~ he travels a lot ◆ ~ **de commerce** commercial traveller, sales representative ADJ (*littér*) [*humeur, tempérament*] wayfaring (*littér*); → **commis, pigeon**

voyagiste /vwajaʒist/ NM tour operator

voyance /vwajɑ̃s/ NF clairvoyance

voyant, e /vwajɑ̃, ɑ̃t/ ADJ [*couleurs*] loud NM,F (= *illuminé*) visionary, seer; (= *personne qui voit*) sighted person ◆ **les** ~**s** the sighted NF **voyante** ◆ ~**e (extralucide)** clairvoyant NM (= *signal*) ◆ ~ **(lumineux)** (*gén*) indicator light; (*d'alerte*) (warning) light ◆ ~ **d'essence/d'huile** petrol/oil warning light

voyelle /vwajɛl/ NF vowel

voyeur, -euse /vwajœʀ, øz/ NM,F voyeur; (*qui se cache*) Peeping Tom

voyeurisme /vwajœʀism/ NM voyeurism

voyou /vwaju/ NM [1] (= *délinquant*) lout, hooligan, yobbo‡ (*Brit*) [2] (= *garnement, enfant*) rascal, brat* ◆ **espèce de petit** ~ **!** you little rascal! ADJ loutish ◆ **un air** ~ a loutish manner ◆ **il avait l'air un peu** ~ he looked like a bit of a lout

voyoucratie /vwajukʀasi/ NF thuggery ◆ **ces méthodes relèvent de la** ~ these methods are little more than thuggery

VPC /vepese/ NF (abrév de **vente par correspondance**) → **vente**

vrac /vʀak/

◆ **en vrac** LOC ADV (= *au poids, sans emballage, au détail*) loose; (= *en gros*) in bulk *ou* quantity; (= *en désordre*) in a jumble, higgledy-piggledy ◆ **acheter du vin en** ~ to buy wine in bulk ◆ **il a tout mis en** ~ **dans la valise** he jumbled everything into the case, he filled the case any old how ◆ **il a cité en** ~ **Hugo, Balzac et Baudelaire** he quoted Hugo, Balzac and Baudelaire at random ◆ **il a jeté en** ~ **quelques idées sur le papier** he jotted some ideas down on paper

vrai, vraie /vʀɛ/ GRAMMAIRE ACTIVE 53.1, 53.3

ADJ [1] (*après n* = *exact*) [*récit, fait*] true; (*Art, Littérat*) [*couleurs, personnage*] true ◆ **ce que tu dis est** ~ what you say is true *ou* right ◆ **c'est dangereux, c'est** *ou* (*frm*) **il est** ~**, mais ...** it's dangerous, it's true *ou* certainly, but ... ◆ **le tableau, tristement** ~**, que cet auteur peint de notre société** the picture, sadly only too true (to life), which this author paints of our society ◆ **tu as fini, pas** ~ **?*** you've finished, right?* *ou* haven't you? ◆ **tu veux venir aussi, pas** ~ **?*** you want to come too, right?* *ou* don't you? ◆ **c'est beau, pas** ~ **?*** it's lovely, isn't it? ◆ **c'est pas** ~ **!*** (*dénégation*) it just isn't true!; (*surprise*) I don't believe it! ◆ **c'est pas** ~ **! j'ai encore oublié mes clés !*** (*consternation*) oh no, I don't believe it! I've forgotten my keys again! ◆ **il est pas** ~**, ce type !*** that guy's unbelievable! ◆ **il n'en est pas moins** ~ **que ...** it's nonetheless *ou* nevertheless true that ... ◆ **ce n'est que trop** ~ it's only too true ◆ **et cela est si** ~ **qu'une rencontre est prévue pour demain** and to prove it a meeting has been planned for tomorrow; → **trop, vérité**

[2] (*gén avant nom* = *réel, authentique*) real ◆ **ce sont ses** ~**s cheveux** that's his own hair ◆ **une** ~**e blonde** a real *ou* genuine blonde ◆ **un** ~ **Picasso** a real *ou* genuine Picasso ◆ **son** ~ **nom c'est Charles** his real name is Charles ◆ **des bijoux en or** ~ real gold jewellery ◆ **lui c'est un cheik, un** ~ **de** ~* he's a sheik – the real thing *ou* the genuine article ◆ **un** ~ **socialiste** a true socialist; → aussi **vrai-faux**

3 *(avant nom : intensif)* real ◆ **c'est un ~ fou !** he's really *ou* completely mad! ◆ **c'est une ~e mère pour moi** she's a real mother to me ◆ **un ~ chef-d'œuvre/héros** a real masterpiece/hero

4 *(avant nom = bon)* real ◆ **c'est le ~ moyen de le faire** that's the real way to do it

5 *(Sci)* **le temps solaire ~** true solar time ◆ **le jour ~** true time

NM 1 *(= la vérité)* **le ~** the truth ◆ **il y a du ~ dans ce qu'il dit** there's some truth *ou* there's an element of truth in what he says ◆ **distinguer le ~ du faux** to distinguish truth from falsehood *ou* the true from the false ◆ **être dans le ~** to be right; → **plaider**

2 *(locutions)* **il dit ~** he's right (in what he says), it's true what he says ◆ **à ~ dire, à dire (le) ~** to tell (you) the truth, in (actual) fact, actually

◆ **en vrai** * in real life ◆ **je les ai vus en ~** I saw them in real life ◆ **comment ça se passe, en ~ ?** what actually happens ?

◆ **pour de vrai** * for real *, really, seriously ◆ **c'est pour de ~ ?** * is it for real? *, do you *(ou they etc)* really mean it?

ADV ◆ **faire ~** *[décor, perruque]* to look real *ou* like the real thing; *[peintre, artiste]* to strive for realism, to paint *(ou draw etc)* realistically ◆ **~ †, quelle honte !** oh really, how shameful!

vrai-faux, vraie-fausse (mpl **vrais-faux**) /vʀefo, vʀefos/ ADJ 1 *(délivré par une autorité)* **~ passeport/visa** false passport/visa *(issued by the state authorities to government agents etc)* 2 *(= truqué) [entretien]* faked; *[journal télévisé]* mock *(épith)*; *(= usurpateur) [chirurgien, savant]* bogus *(épith)*, phoney * *(épith)*

vraiment /vʀɛmɑ̃/ ADV 1 *(= véritablement)* really ◆ **nous voulons ~ la paix** we really do want peace ◆ **s'aiment-ils ~ ?** do they really (and truly) love each other? 2 *(intensif)* really ◆ **il est ~ idiot** he's a real idiot, he's really stupid ◆ **~, il exagère !** really, he's going too far! ◆ **je ne sais ~ pas quoi faire** I really *ou* honestly don't know what to do ◆ **oui ~, c'est dommage** yes, it's a real shame ◆ **vous trouvez ? – ah oui, ~ !** do you think so? – oh yes, definitely! 3 *(de doute)* **~ ?** really?, is that so? ◆ **il est parti – ~ ?** he has gone – (has he) really?

vraisemblable /vʀɛsɑ̃blabl/ ADJ *[hypothèse, interprétation]* likely; *[situation, intrigue]* plausible, convincing ◆ **peu ~** *[excuse, histoire]* improbable, unlikely ◆ **il est (très) ~ que ...** it's (highly *ou* most) likely *ou* probable that ...

vraisemblablement /vʀɛsɑ̃blabləmɑ̃/ ADV probably, in all likelihood *ou* probability, very likely ◆ **viendra-t-il ? – ~/~ pas** will he come? – probably/probably not ◆ **la fin, ~ proche, des hostilités** the end of hostilities, which looks imminent *ou* is likely to come very soon

vraisemblance /vʀɛsɑ̃blɑ̃s/ NF *[d'hypothèse, interprétation]* likelihood; *[de situation romanesque]* plausibility, verisimilitude ◆ **selon toute ~** in all likelihood, in all probability

vraquier /vʀakje/ NM bulk carrier

V/Réf (abrév de **votre référence**) your ref

vrille /vʀij/ NF 1 *[de plante]* tendril 2 *(= outil)* gimlet 3 *(= spirale)* spiral; *(en avion)* spin, tailspin ◆ **escalier en ~** spiral staircase ◆ **descente en ~** *(en avion)* spiral dive ◆ **descendre en ~** *(en avion)* to spiral downwards, to come down in a spin ◆ **se mettre en ~** *[avion]* to go into a tailspin ◆ **partir en ~** * *[personne]* to go crazy *; *[situation, plan]* to go pear-shaped *

vrillé, e /vʀije/ (ptp de **vriller**) ADJ *[tige]* tendrilled; *[fil]* twisted

vriller /vʀije/ ▸ conjug 1 ◂ VT to bore into, to pierce VI *[avion]* to spiral, to spin; *[fil]* to become twisted

vrombir /vʀɔ̃biʀ/ ▸ conjug 2 ◂ VI *[moteur] (régulièrement)* to throb; *(après une accélération)* to roar; *[insecte]* to buzz, to hum ◆ **faire ~ son moteur** to rev one's engine

vrombissement /vʀɔ̃bismɑ̃/ NM *[de moteur] (régulier)* humming *(NonC)*; *(après accélération)* roar; *[d'insecte]* buzzing *(NonC)*, humming *(NonC)*

vroum /vʀum/ EXCL brum! brum!

VRP /veɛʀpe/ NM (abrév de **voyageur, représentant, placier**) sales rep *; → aussi **voyageur**

vs (abrév de **versus**) vs, v

VSNE /veɛsɛnə/ NM (abrév de **volontaire du service national à l'étranger**) → **volontaire**

VSOP /veɛsɔpe/ ADJ (abrév de **very superior old pale**) VSOP

VTC /vetese/ NM (abrév de **vélo tout-chemin**) → **vélo**

VTT /vetete/ NM (abrév de **vélo tout-terrain**) → **vélo**

vu¹, vue¹ /vy/ (ptp de **voir**) ADJ 1 *(* = compris)* **c'est ~ ?** all right?, got it? *, understood? ◆ **c'est bien ~ ?** all clear? *, is that quite clear? ◆ **~ ?** OK? *, right? * ◆ **c'est tout ~** it's a foregone conclusion; → **ni**

2 *(= jugé)* **balle/passe bien ~e** well-judged ball/pass ◆ **remarque bien ~e** judicious remark ◆ **c'était bien ~ de sa part** what he said was spot-on *

3 *(= considéré)* **bien ~** *[personne]* well thought of, highly regarded ◆ **mal ~** *[personne]* poorly thought of ◆ **il est mal ~ du patron** the boss thinks poorly of him *ou* has a poor opinion of him ◆ **ici c'est bien/mal ~ de porter une cravate** it's the done thing here *ou* it's good form *(Brit)*/it's not the done thing *ou* it's bad form *(Brit)* to wear a tie here; → **déjà**

NM

◆ **au vu de** *(= étant donné, d'après) [+ sondages, résultats, rapport]* in the light of

◆ **au vu et au su de** with the full knowledge of ◆ **au ~ et au su de tous** *ou* **de tout le monde** openly and publicly

vu² /vy/ GRAMMAIRE ACTIVE 44.1 PRÉP *(gén, Jur)* in view of ◆ **~ la situation, cela valait mieux** in view of *ou* considering the situation, it was better that way ◆ **~ son humeur, il vaut mieux de rien dire** considering *ou* given his mood, it's best not to say anything

CONJ

◆ **vu que** * in view of the fact that, seeing *ou* considering that ◆ **~ qu'il était tard, nous avons abandonné la partie** seeing *ou* considering how late it was, we abandoned the game

vue² /vy/ NF 1 *(= sens)* sight, eyesight ◆ **perdre la ~** to lose one's (eye)sight ◆ **troubles de la ~** sight trouble ◆ **il a une bonne ~** he has good eyesight, his eyesight is good ◆ **il a la ~ basse** *ou* **courte** he's short-sighted *ou* near-sighted *(US)* ◆ **une politique à courte ~** a short-sighted policy ◆ **don de seconde** *ou* **double ~** gift of second sight

2 *(= regard)* **détourner la ~** to look away, to avert one's gaze ◆ **porter la ~ sur qn/qch** *(littér)* to cast one's eyes over sb/sth, to look in sb's direction/in the direction of sth ◆ **s'offrir à la ~ de tous** to present o.s. for all to see ◆ **il l'a fait à la ~ de tous** he did it in full view of everybody

3 *(= panorama)* view ◆ **de cette colline, on a une très belle ~ de la ville** there's a very good view *ou* you get a very good view of the town from this hill ◆ **avec ~ imprenable** with an open *ou* unobstructed view *ou* outlook ◆ **ces immeubles nous bouchent la ~** those buildings block our view ◆ **cette pièce a ~ sur la mer** this room looks out onto the sea ◆ **chambre avec ~ sur la montagne** room with a view of the mountains ◆ **de là, on avait une ~ de profil de la cathédrale** from there you had a side view of the cathedral ◆ **~ cavalière** *(lit)* bird's eye view; *(fig)* overview ◆ **avoir une ~ cavalière d'une situation/période** to have an overview of a situation/period; → **perte, point¹**

4 *(= spectacle)* sight ◆ **la ~ du sang l'a fait s'évanouir** the sight of the blood made him faint ◆ **à la ~ de** at the sight of ◆ **à sa ~ elle s'est mise à rougir** when she saw him she began to blush

5 *(= image)* view ◆ **des ~s de Paris** views of Paris ◆ **un film de 36 ~s** a 36-exposure film ◆ **ils nous ont montré des ~s prises pendant leurs vacances** they showed us some photos they'd taken on their holidays ◆ **~ de la ville sous la neige** view of the town in the snow; → **prise²**

6 *(= opinion)* **~s** views ◆ **exprimer ses ~s sur un sujet** to air one's views on a subject ◆ **de courtes ~s** short-sighted views; → **échange**

7 *(= conception)* view ◆ **il a une ~ pessimiste de la situation** he has a pessimistic view of the situation ◆ **donner une ~ d'ensemble** to give an overall view *ou* an overview ◆ **c'est une ~ de l'esprit** that's a purely theoretical view; → **point¹**

8 *(= projet)* **~s** plans; *(sur qn ou ses biens)* designs ◆ **la société a des ~s sur cet immeuble** the company has its eye on that building ◆ **elle a des ~s sur lui** *(pour un projet)* she has her eye on him; *(= elle veut l'épouser)* she has designs on him, she has her eye on him

9 *(Jur = fenêtre)* window

10 *(locutions)*

◆ **à vue** *[piloter, atterrir]* visually; *[atterrissage, navigation]* visual; *[payable]* at sight *ou* on demand ◆ **dépôt à ~** demand *ou* sight deposit ◆ **tirer à ~** to shoot on sight ◆ **naviguer à ~** *(lit)* to navigate visually; *(fig)* to play it by ear

◆ **à première vue** at first sight

◆ **à vue de nez** * roughly *, at a rough guess

◆ **à vue d'œil** *(= rapidement)* before one's very eyes; *(= par une estimation rapide)* at a quick glance ◆ **il maigrit à ~ d'œil** he seems to be getting thinner before our very eyes *ou* by the minute *

◆ **de vue** by sight ◆ **je le connais de ~** I know him by sight ◆ **perdre qn de ~** *(lit)* to lose sight of sb ◆ **perdre qch de ~** *(lit, fig)* to lose sight of sth ◆ **il ne faut pas perdre de ~ que ...** we mustn't lose sight of the fact that ... ◆ **perdre/ne pas perdre un ami de ~** to lose touch/keep in touch with a friend

◆ **en vue** *(lit, fig) (= proche)* in sight ◆ **(bien) en ~** *(= en évidence)* conspicuous ◆ **très/assez en ~** *(= célèbre)* very much/much in the public eye ◆ **il a mis sa pancarte bien en ~** he put his placard in a prominent *ou* a conspicuous position *ou* where everyone could see it ◆ **c'est un des hommes politiques les plus en ~** he's one of the most prominent *ou* best-known men in politics ◆ **avoir un poste en ~** to have one's sights on a job ◆ **avoir un collaborateur en ~** to have an associate in mind

◆ **en vue de** ◆ **avoir en ~ de faire** to have it in mind to do, to plan to do ◆ **il a acheté une maison en ~ de son mariage** he has bought a house with his marriage in mind ◆ **il s'entraîne en ~ de la course de dimanche/de devenir champion du monde** he's training with a view to the race on Sunday/becoming world champion ◆ **il a dit cela en ~ de le décourager** he said that with the idea of *ou* with a view to discouraging him

◆ **plein la vue** * ◆ **il lui en a mis plein la ~** * he really impressed her ◆ **il a essayé de m'en mettre plein la ~** * he really tried to impress me; → **changement, garder, tirer**

Vulcain /vylkɛ̃/ NM Vulcan

vulcain /vylkɛ̃/ NM *(= papillon)* red admiral

vulcanisation /vylkanizasjɔ̃/ NF vulcanization

vulcaniser /vylkanize/ ► conjug 1 ◄ VT to vulcanize

vulcanologie /vylkanɔlɔʒi/ NF vulcanology

vulcanologue /vylkanɔlɔg/ NMF vulcanologist

vulgaire /vylgɛʀ/ ADJ [1] *(= grossier) [langage, personne]* vulgar, coarse; *[genre, décor]* vulgar, crude ◆ **il est d'un ~ !** he's so common *ou* vulgar! [2] *(= prosaïque) [réalités, problèmes]* commonplace, everyday, mundane [3] *(= usuel, banal)* common, popular ◆ **nom ~** common *ou* popular name ◆ **langues ~s** common languages; → **latin** [4] *(littér, † = du peuple)* common ◆ **esprit ~** common mind ◆ **l'opinion ~** the common opinion [5] *(avant n = quelconque)* ordinary ◆ **~ escroc** common swindler ◆ **un ~ bout de bois** an ordinary piece of wood ◆ **de la ~ matière plastique** ordinary plastic, common or garden plastic *(Brit)*, garden-variety plastic *(US)* NM ◆ **le ~** [1] *(† ou hum = peuple)* the common herd [2] *(= vulgarité)* **tomber dans le ~** to lapse into vulgarity

vulgairement /vylgɛʀmɑ̃/ ADV [1] *(= grossièrement)* vulgarly, coarsely ◆ **j'en ai ras la casquette*, comme on dit ~** I'm fed up to the back teeth*, if you'll forgive the expression [2] *(= couramment) [dénommer]* popularly, commonly ◆ **le fruit de l'églantier, ~ appelé** *ou* **que l'on appelle ~ gratte-cul** the fruit of the wild rose, commonly known as *ou* called haws

vulgarisateur, -trice /vylgaʀizatœʀ, tʀis/ NM,F popularizer

vulgarisation /vylgaʀizasjɔ̃/ NF popularization ◆ **~ scientifique** scientific popularization ◆ **c'est un ouvrage de ~ scientifique** it's a book that makes science accessible to the layman *ou* the general public ◆ **ouvrage de ~ scientifique** popular scientific work

vulgariser /vylgaʀize/ ► conjug 1 ◄ VT [1] *[+ ouvrage]* to popularize [2] *(littér = rendre vulgaire)* to coarsen ◆ **cet accent la vulgarise** this accent makes her sound coarse

vulgarisme /vylgaʀism/ NM vulgarism

vulgarité /vylgaʀite/ NF [1] *(= grossièreté)* vulgarity, coarseness *(NonC)* ◆ **des ~s** vulgarities [2] *(littér = terre à terre)* commonplaceness, ordinariness

vulgate /vylgat/ NF vulgate

vulgum pecus* /vylgɔmpekys/ NM *(hum)* ◆ **le ~** the hoi polloi, the common herd

vulnérabilité /vylneʀabilite/ NF vulnerability

vulnérable /vylneʀabl/ ADJ *(gén, Cartes)* vulnerable

vulnéraire /vylneʀɛʀ/ NF *(= plante)* kidney vetch, ladies' fingers

vulvaire /vylvɛʀ/ ADJ *(Anat)* vulvar NF *(= plante)* stinking goosefoot

vulve /vylv/ NF vulva

vulvite /vylvit/ NF vulvitis

vumètre /vymɛtʀ/ NM recording level gauge

Vve abrév de **veuve**

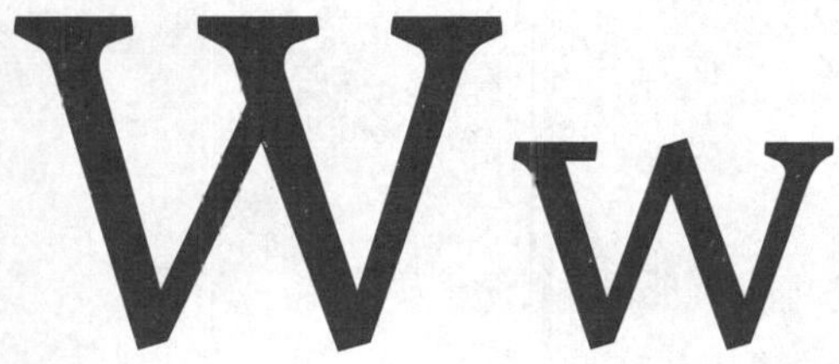

W¹, w /dubləve/ **NM** *(= lettre)* W, w

W² (abrév de **Watt**) W

wagnérien, -ienne /vagneʀjɛ̃, jɛn/ **ADJ** Wagnerian **NM,F** Wagnerian

wagon /vagɔ̃/ **NM** 1 *(Rail = véhicule)* *(de marchandises)* truck, wagon *(Brit)*, freight car *(US)*; *(de voyageurs)* carriage *(Brit)*, car *(US)* 2 *(= contenu)* truckload, wagonload ◆ **un plein ~ de marchandises** a truckful *ou* truckload of goods ◆ **il y en a tout un ~** * *(= plein)* there are stacks of them *, there's a whole pile of them *
COMP **wagon à bestiaux** cattle truck *ou* wagon
wagon frigorifique refrigerated van
wagon de marchandises goods truck, freight car *(US)*
wagon de voyageurs passenger carriage *(Brit) ou* car *(US)*

wagon-citerne (pl **wagons-citernes**) /vagɔ̃sitɛʀn/ **NM** tanker, tank wagon

wagon-couchettes (pl **wagons-couchettes**) /vagɔ̃kuʃɛt/ **NM** couchette car *ou* carriage, ≈ sleeping car

wagon-foudre (pl **wagons-foudres**) /vagɔ̃fudʀ/ **NM** (wine) tanker *ou* tank wagon

wagon-lit (pl **wagons-lits**) /vagɔ̃li/ **NM** sleeper *(Brit)*, Pullman *(US)*

wagonnet /vagɔnɛ/ **NM** small truck

wagon-poste (pl **wagons-postes**) /vagɔ̃pɔst/ **NM** mail van

wagon-réservoir (pl **wagons-réservoirs**) /vagɔ̃ʀezɛʀvwaʀ/ **NM** ⇒ **wagon-citerne**

wagon-restaurant (pl **wagons-restaurants**) /vagɔ̃ʀɛstɔʀɑ̃/ **NM** restaurant *ou* dining car

wahhabisme /waabism/ **NM** Wa(h)habism

wahhabite /waabit/ **ADJ, NMF** Wa(h)habi

Walhalla /valala/ **NM** Valhalla

Walkman ® /wɔkman/ **NM** Walkman ®, personal stereo

walkyrie /valkiʀi/ **NF** *(Myth)* Valkyrie; *(fig hum)* amazon

wallaby (pl **wallabies**) /walabi/ **NM** wallaby

wallingant, e /walɛ̃gɑ̃, ɑ̃t/ **NM,F** *(Belg péj)* Walloon separatist

Wallis-et-Futuna /walisefutuna/ **N** Wallis and Futuna Islands

wallon, -onne /walɔ̃, ɔn/ **ADJ** Walloon **NM** *(= dialecte)* Walloon **NM,F** **Wallon(ne)** Walloon

Wallonie /walɔni/ **NF** Wallonia

WAP /wap/ **NM** (abrév de **wireless access protocol**) WAP ◆ **téléphone ~** WAP phone

wapiti /wapiti/ **NM** wapiti

warning /waʀniŋ/ **NPL** *[de voiture]* hazard warning lights *(Brit)*, hazard lights *(US)*

warrant /vaʀɑ̃/ **NM** 1 *[de magasins généraux]* warrant, warehouse warrant *ou* receipt, bond warrant; *[de port]* dock *ou* deposit warrant 2 *(Bourse)* warrant

Washington /waʃiŋtɔn/ **N** *(= ville)* Washington DC **NM** *(= État)* Washington (State)

wassingue /vasɛ̃g/ **NF** floorcloth

water-closet(s) † /watɛʀklozɛt/ **NM(PL)** ⇒ **waters**

Waterloo /watɛʀlo/ **N** Waterloo ◆ **la bataille de ~** the Battle of Waterloo ◆ **il a connu son ~ quand …** he met his Waterloo when …

water-polo /watɛʀpɔlo/ **NM** water polo

waterproof /watɛʀpʀuf/ **ADJ INV** *[montre, mascara]* waterproof

waters † /watɛʀ/ **NMPL** toilet, loo * *(Brit)*, lavatory ◆ **où sont les ~ ?** where's the toilet?

waterzoï /watɛʀzɔj/ **NM** *(Belg = plat)* waterzooi *(chicken stew)*

watt /wat/ **NM** watt

wattheure /watœʀ/ **NM** watt hour

wattman † /watman/ **NM** tram driver

W-C, WC /vese/ **NMPL** (abrév de **water-closet(s)**) ⇒ **waters**

Web /wɛb/ **NM INV** ◆ **le ~** the (World Wide) Web

webcam /wɛbkam/ **NF** webcam

weber /vebɛʀ/ **NM** weber

webmaster /wɛbmastœʀ/, **webmestre** /wɛbmɛstʀ/ **NM** webmaster

webzine /wɛbzin/ **NM** webzine

week-end (pl **week-ends**) /wikɛnd/ **NM** weekend ◆ **partir en ~** to go away for the weekend ◆ **partir en ~ prolongé** to go away on *ou* for a long weekend

Weimar /vajmaʀ/ **N** Weimar ◆ **la république de ~** the Weimar Republic

Wellington /weliŋtɔn/ **N** Wellington

welter /weltɛʀ/ **NM** → **poids**

western /wɛstɛʀn/ **NM** western ◆ **~-spaghetti, ~ italien** spaghetti western

Westphalie /vɛsfali/ **NF** Westphalia

whisky (pl **whiskies**) /wiski/ **NM** *(écossais)* whisky; *(américain, irlandais)* whiskey ◆ **~ soda** whisky and soda

whist /wist/ **NM** whist

white-spirit /wajtspiʀit/ **NM** white-spirit

wifi, wi-fi /wifi/ **NM INV** (abrév de **wireless fidelity**) Wi-Fi

Wight /wait/ **N** ◆ **l'île de ~** the Isle of Wight

wigwam /wigwam/ **NM** wigwam

williams /wiljams/ **NF** ◆ **(poire) ~** Williams pear

winch /win(t)ʃ/ **NM** *(Naut)* winch

Winchester /winʃɛstɛʀ/ **NF** ◆ **(carabine) ~** Winchester (rifle)

Windhoek /windøk/ **N** Windhoek

Wisconsin /viskɔnsin/ **NM** Wisconsin

wishbone /wiʃbon/ **NM** *(Naut)* wishbone

wisigoth, e /vizigo, ɔt/ **ADJ** Visigothic **NM,F** **Wisigoth(e)** Visigoth

wisigothique /vizigɔtik/ **ADJ** Visigothic

witz * /vits/ **NM** *(Helv = plaisanterie)* joke

wolfram /vɔlfʀam/ **NM** wolfram

wolof /wɔlɔf/ **ADJ** Wolof **NM** *(= langue)* Wolof **NMF** **Wolof** Wolof

woofer /wufœʀ/ **NM** woofer

WWW /dubləvedubləvedubləve/ (abrév de **World Wide Web**) WWW

Wyoming /wajɔmiŋ/ **NM** Wyoming

wysiwyg /wiziwig/ **ADJ** (abrév de **what you see is what you get**) *(Ordin)* WYSIWYG

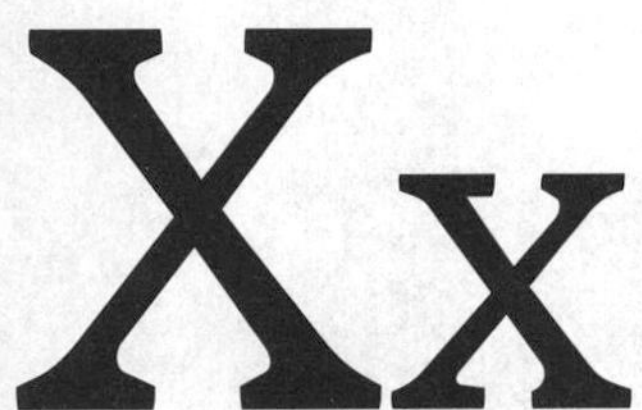

X, x /iks/ **NM** [1] *(= lettre)* X, x; *(Math)* x ◆ **chromosome X** X-chromosome ◆ **l'axe des x** *(Math)* the x axis ◆ **croisés en X** forming an x ◆ **ça fait x temps que je ne l'ai pas vu*** I haven't seen him for ages ◆ **je te l'ai dit x fois** I've told you umpteen* times ◆ **plainte contre X** *(Jur)* action against person or persons unknown ◆ **Monsieur X** Mr X ◆ **elle a accouché sous X** she gave her baby up as soon as it was born ◆ **les enfants nés sous X** children whose mothers gave them up at birth ◆ **film (classé) X** X(-rated) film, 18 film; → **rayon** [2] *(arg Univ)* **l'X** the École polytechnique ◆ **un X** a student of the École polytechnique; → POLYTECHNIQUE

Xavier /gzavje/ **NM** Xavier

xénogreffe /gzenogʀɛf/ **NF** xenograft, xenogeneic tissue graft

xénon /gzenɔ̃/ **NM** xenon

xénophobe /gzenɔfɔb/ **ADJ** xenophobic **NMF** xenophobe

xénophobie /gzenɔfɔbi/ **NF** xenophobia

Xénophon /gzenɔfɔ̃/ **NM** Xenophon

xérès /gzeʀɛs/ **NM** *(= vin)* sherry **N** **Xérès** *(= ville)* Jerez

Xerxès /gzɛʀsɛs/ **NM** Xerxes

xi /ksi/ **NM** xi

XML /iksɛmɛl/ (abrév de **Extensible Markup Language**) **NM** XML

xylographe /gzilɔgʀaf/ **NM** xylographer

xylographie /gzilɔgʀafi/ **NF** *(= technique)* xylography; *(= gravure)* xylograph

xylographique /gzilɔgʀafik/ **ADJ** xylographic

xylophage /gzilɔfaʒ/ **ADJ** *[insecte]* woodboring *(épith)* **NM** woodborer

xylophène ® /gzilɔfɛn/ **NM** wood preservative

xylophone /gzilɔfɔn/ **NM** xylophone

Yy

Y[1], y[1] /igʀɛk/ **NM** *(= lettre)* Y, y ◆ **chromosome Y** *(Bio)* Y-chromosome ◆ **l'axe des y** *(Math)* the y axis

Y[2] (abrév de **yen**) Y

y[2] /i/ **ADV** *(indiquant le lieu)* there ◆ **restez-y** stay there ◆ **nous y avons passé 2 jours** we spent 2 days there ◆ **il avait une feuille de papier et il y dessinait un bateau** he had a sheet of paper and he was drawing a ship on it ◆ **avez-vous vu le film ? – j'y vais demain** have you seen the film? – I'm going (to see it) tomorrow ◆ **les maisons étaient neuves, personne n'y avait habité** the houses were new and nobody had lived in them ◆ **la pièce est sombre, quand on y entre, on n'y voit rien** the room is dark and when you go in you can't see a thing ◆ **j'y suis, j'y reste** here I am and here I stay ◆ **ah ! j'y suis !** *(fig) (comprendre)* oh, I understand!; *(se rappeler)* oh, I remember! ◆ **vous y allez, à ce dîner ?*** are you going to that dinner then? ◆ **je suis passé le voir mais il n'y était pas** I stopped by to see him but he wasn't there; → **aller, avoir**

PRON PERS [1] *(gén se rapportant à des choses)* it ◆ **vous serez là ? – n'y comptez pas** you'll be there? – it's highly unlikely *ou* I doubt it ◆ **n'y pensez plus** forget (about) it ◆ **à votre place, je ne m'y fierais pas** if I were you I wouldn't trust it ◆ **il a plu alors que personne ne s'y attendait** it rained when no one was expecting it to ◆ **il y trouve du plaisir** he enjoys it

[2] *(locutions)* **elle s'y connaît** she knows all about it, she's an expert ◆ **il faudra vous y faire** you'll just have to get used to it ◆ **je n'y suis pour rien** it's nothing to do with me, I had no part in it ◆ **je n'y suis pour personne** I'm not in to anyone; → **avoir, comprendre, voir** *etc*

◆ **ça y est** ◆ **ça y est ! c'est fait !** that's it, it's done! ◆ **ça y est, il a cassé le verre** there you are, he's broken the glass ◆ **ça y est, il a signé le contrat** that's it, he's signed the contract ◆ **ça y est oui !, je peux parler ?** is that it then? *ou* have you finished then? can I talk now? ◆ **ça y est, tu es prêt ? – non ça n'y est pas** is that it then, are you ready? – no I'm not ◆ **ça y est pour quelque chose** it has something to do with it

[3] *(* = il)* **c'est-y pas gentil ?** *(aussi iro)* isn't it nice? ◆ **y en a qui exagèrent** some people *ou* folk go too far ◆ **du pain ? y en a pas** bread? there's none *ou* there isn't any

yacht /'jɔt/ **NM** yacht ◆ **~ de course/croisière** racing/cruising yacht

yacht-club (pl **yacht-clubs**) /'jɔtklœb/ **NM** yacht club

yachting † /'jɔtiŋ/ **NM** yachting ◆ **faire du ~** to go out on one's yacht, to go yachting

yacht(s)man † /'jɔtman/ (pl **yacht(s)men** /'jɔtmɛn/) **NM** yacht owner, yachtsman

yack /'jak/ **NM** ⇒ **yak**

Yahvé /'jave/ **NM** Yahveh

yak /'jak/ **NM** yak

yakusa /'jakuza/ **NM** yakuza

Yalta /'jalta/ **N** Yalta ◆ **la conférence/les accords de ~** the Yalta conference/agreement

Yamoussoukro /'jamusukʀo/ **N** Yamoussoukro

yang /'jɑ̃g/ **NM** yang

Yang-Tsê Kiang /'jɑ̃gtsekjɑ̃g/ **NM** Yangtze (Kiang)

yankee /'jɑ̃ki/ **ADJ, NMF** Yankee

Yaoundé /'jaunde/ **N** Yaoundé

yaourt /'jauʀt/ **NM** yog(h)urt ◆ **~ nature/maigre** natural/low-fat yog(h)urt ◆ **~ aux fruits/à la grecque** fruit/Greek yog(h)urt ◆ **~ à boire** yog(h)urt drink ◆ **~ brassé** *thick creamy yog(h)urt* ◆ **t'as du ~ dans la tête !*** you're completely daft*

yaourtière /'jauʀtjɛʀ/ **NF** yoghurt-maker

yard /'jaʀd/ **NM** yard

yatagan /'jatagɑ̃/ **NM** yataghan

yearling /'jœʀliŋ/ **NM** *(= cheval)* yearling

Yémen /'jemɛn/ **NM** ◆ **le ~** the Yemen ◆ **Nord-/Sud-~** North/South Yemen ◆ **au ~** in Yemen

yéménite /'jemenit/ **ADJ** Yemeni **NMF** **Yéménite** Yemeni

yen /'jɛn/ **NM** *(Fin)* yen

yéti /'jeti/ **NM** yeti

yeuse /'jøz/ **NF** holm oak, ilex

yeux /'jø/ pl de **œil**

yéyé, yé-yé * † /'jeje/ **ADJ INV** ◆ **musique ~** *French pop music of the 1960s* ◆ **les années ~** the sixties ◆ **la mode ~** the sixties' look **NM** ◆ **le ~** *French pop music of the 1960s* **NMF INV** *(= chanteur) French pop singer of the 1960s; (= jeune)* teenage pop fan of the 1960s

yiddish /'jidiʃ/ **ADJ, NM** Yiddish

Yi king /'jikiŋ/ **NM** I Ching

yin /'jin/ **NM** yin

ylang-ylang /ilɑ̃ilɑ̃/ **NM** ylang-ylang, ilang-ilang

yod /'jɔd/ **NM** yod

yoga /'jɔga/ **NM** yoga ◆ **faire du ~** to do yoga

yogi /'jɔgi/ **NM** yogi

yogourt, yoghourt /'jɔguʀt/ **NM** ⇒ **yaourt**

yole /'jɔl/ **NF** skiff

Yom Kippour /'jɔmkipuʀ/ **NM** Yom Kippur

yorkshire, yorkshire-terrier (pl **yorkshire-terriers**) /'jɔʀkʃœʀtɛʀje/ **NM** Yorkshire terrier, yorkie*

yougoslave /'jugɔslav/ **ADJ** Yugoslav, Yugoslavian **NMF** **Yougoslave** Yugoslav, Yugoslavian

Yougoslavie /'jugɔslavi/ **NF** Yugoslavia ◆ **la république fédérale de ~** the Federal Republic of Yugoslavia

youp /'jup/ **EXCL** hup! ◆ **allez ~, dégagez !** come on, get a move on!

youpala /'jupala/ **NM** baby bouncer

youpi /'jupi/ **EXCL** yippee

youpin, e ** /'jupɛ̃, in/ **NM,F** *(injurieux)* Yid** *(injurieux)*

yourte /'juʀt/ **NF** yurt

youyou /'juju/ **NM** *(Naut)* dinghy

yo-yo, yoyo ® /'jojo/ **NM INV** *(= jouet)* yo-yo ◆ **les mouvements de yoyo du dollar** *(Fin)* the wild fluctuations of the dollar ◆ **jouer au ~, faire le yoyo** *(fig)* to yo-yo

ypérite /ipeʀit/ **NF** mustard gas, yperite *(SPÉC)*

ytterbium /itɛʀbjɔm/ **NM** ytterbium

yttrium /itʀijɔm/ **NM** yttrium

yuan /'jyan/ **NM** yuan

yucca /'juka/ **NM** yucca

Yukon /'jykɔ̃/ **NM** ◆ **le ~** *(= fleuve)* the Yukon (River) ◆ **le (territoire du) ~** the Yukon (Territory)

yuppie (pl **yuppies**) /'jupi/ **NM** yuppie, yuppy

Zz

Z, z /zɛd/ NM (lettre) Z, z; → A¹

ZAC /zak/ NF (abrév de **zone d'aménagement concerté**) → **zone**

Zacharie /zakaʀi/ NM (= prophète) Zechariah; (= père de Jean-Baptiste) Zachariah

ZAD /zad/ NF (abrév de **zone d'aménagement différé**) → **zone**

Zagreb /ʒagʀɛb/ N Zagreb

Zaïre /zaiʀ/ NM ◆ **le** ~ († = pays) Zaire; (= fleuve) the Zaire (River)

zaïre /zaiʀ/ NM (= monnaie) zaire

zaïrois, -oise /zaiʀwa, waz/ ADJ Zairean, Zairian NM,F **Zaïrois(e)** Zairean, Zairian

zakouski /zakuski/ NMPL zakuski, zakouski

Zambèze /zɑ̃bɛz/ NM ◆ **le** ~ the Zambezi (River)

Zambie /zɑ̃bi/ NF Zambia

zambien, -ienne /zɑ̃bjɛ̃, jɛn/ ADJ Zambian NM,F **Zambien(ne)** Zambian

zanzi /zɑ̃zi/ NM dice game

Zanzibar /zɑ̃zibaʀ/ N Zanzibar

zapatiste /zapatist/ ADJ ◆ **l'armée** ~ the Zapatistas

zapper /zape/ ► conjug 1 ◄ VI (à la télévision) to channel-hop, to zap; (à la radio) to flick from one channel to the next

zappeur, -euse /zapœʀ, øz/ NM,F (TV) zapper, channel-hopper

zapping /zapiŋ/ NM (TV) zapping, channel-hopping

Zarathoustra /zaʀatustʀa/ NM Zarathustra

zarbi⁑ /zaʀbi/ ADJ (= bizarre) bizarre

zazou, e /zazu/ ADJ ◆ **la jeunesse** ~**(e)** *young jazz-swingers of the 1940s* ◆ **tenue ~e** zoot suit NM, F (parfois péj) ≃ hepcat*

zébi /zebi/ NM → **peau**

zèbre /zɛbʀ/ NM (= animal) zebra; (* = individu) guy*, bloke* (Brit) ◆ **un drôle de** ~ an oddball*, an odd bod* (Brit) ◆ **filer** *ou* **courir comme un** ~ to run like the wind

zébrer /zebʀe/ ► conjug 6 ◄ VT (lignes régulières) to stripe; (lignes irrégulières) to streak (de with); ◆ **ciel zébré d'éclairs** sky streaked with lightning ◆ **allée zébrée d'ombre et de lumière** lane dappled with light and shade

zébrure /zebʀyʀ/ NF [d'animal] stripe, streak; [de coup de fouet] weal, welt; (= éclair) streak

zébu /zeby/ NM zebu

Zélande /zelɑ̃d/ NF Zealand

zélateur, -trice /zelatœʀ, tʀis/ NM,F (gén) champion, partisan (péj), zealot (péj); (Rel) Zealot

zèle /zɛl/ NM zeal ◆ **avec** ~ zealously, with zeal ◆ **faire du** ~ (péj) to be over-zealous ◆ **faire preuve de/manquer de** ~ to show/lack enthusiasm ◆ **pas de** ~ ! don't overdo it! ◆ **pousser le** ~ **jusqu'à faire qch** to go to the extreme of doing sth, to go so far as to do sth; → **excès, grève**

zélé, e /zele/ ADJ zealous

zélote /zelɔt/ NM (Hist) Zealot

zen /zɛn/ ADJ INV (lit) Zen ◆ **jardin** ~ Zen garden ◆ **rester** ~ * (fig = serein) to remain unfazed* ◆ **c'est ~, chez lui/cette pièce !** * (fig = dépouillé) his place/this room is very minimalist! NM Zen

zénana /zenana/ NM → **peau**

zénith /zenit/ NM (lit, fig) zenith ◆ **le soleil est au** ~ *ou* **à son** ~ the sun is at its zenith *ou* height ◆ **au ~ de la gloire** at the zenith *ou* peak of glory

zénithal, e (mpl **-aux**) /zenital, o/ ADJ zenithal ◆ **éclairage** ~ overhead natural lighting

Zénon /zenɔ̃/ NM Zeno

ZEP /zɛp/ NF 1 (abrév de **zone d'éducation prioritaire**) → **zone** 2 (abrév de **zone d'environnement protégé**) → **zone**

zéphyr /zefiʀ/ NM (vent) zephyr ◆ **Zéphyr** (Myth) Zephyr(us)

zéphyrien, -ienne /zefiʀjɛ̃, jɛn/ ADJ (littér) zephyr-like (littér)

zeppelin /zɛplɛ̃/ NM zeppelin

zéro /zeʀo/ NM 1 (gén, Math) zero, nought (Brit); (compte à rebours) zero; (dans un numéro de téléphone) 0, zero (US) ◆ **les enfants de ~ à cinq ans** children up to the age of five ◆ **sur une échelle de ~ à dix** on a scale of zero *ou* nought (Brit) to ten ◆ **recommencer à ~, repartir de** *ou* **à** ~ to start from scratch again, to go back to square one ◆ **remettre à** ~ [+ compteur, chronomètre] to reset ◆ **il n'avait rien compris, j'ai dû tout reprendre à** ~ he hadn't understood a thing, I had to start all over again from scratch ◆ **tout ça, pour moi, c'est ~, je veux des preuves*** as far as I'm concerned that's worthless *ou* a waste of time – I want some proof ◆ **les avoir à** ~⁑ to be scared out of one's wits*, to be scared stiff*; → **compteur, moral, partir¹, réduire**

2 (température) freezing (point), zero (centigrade) ◆ **3 degrés au-dessus de** ~ 3 degrees above freezing (point) *ou* above zero ◆ **3 degrés au-dessous de** ~ 3 degrees below freezing (point) *ou* below zero, 3 degrees below*, minus 3 (degrees centigrade) ◆ ~ **absolu** absolute zero

3 (Rugby, Ftbl) zero, nil (Brit), nothing (US); (Tennis) love ◆ **mener par 2 jeux/sets à** ~ (Tennis) to lead (by) 2 games/sets to love ◆ ~ **à** ~ *ou* ~ **partout à la mi-temps** no score at half time ◆ **gagner par 2 (buts) à** ~ to win 2 nil (Brit) *ou* 2 nothing (US), to win by 2 goals to zero *ou* nil (Brit) *ou* nothing (US) ◆ **la France avait ~ à la mi-temps** France hadn't scored *ou* had no score by half time

4 (Scol) zero, nought (Brit) ◆ ~ **de conduite** bad mark (Brit) *ou* grade (US) for behaviour *ou* conduct ◆ ~ **pointé** (Scol) nothing, nought (Brit) (counted in the final average mark) ◆ **le gouvernement mérite un ~ pointé** the government deserves nothing out of 20 ◆ **mais en cuisine, ~ (pour la question)*** but as far as cooking goes he's (*ou* she's) useless *ou* a dead loss*

5 (* = personne) dead loss*, washout*

ADJ ◆ ~ **heure** (gén) midnight; (heure GMT) zero hour ◆ ~ **heure trente** (gén) half past midnight; (heure GMT) zero thirty hours ◆ **il a fait ~ faute** he didn't make any mistakes, he didn't make a single mistake ◆ ~ **défaut/stock** zero defect/stock ◆ **j'ai eu ~ point** I got no marks (Brit) *ou* points (US) (at all), I got zero ◆ **ça m'a coûté ~ franc ~ centime*** I got it for nothing ◆ **en ski, le risque ~ n'existe pas** in skiing there's no such thing as zero risk ◆ **taux de croissance** ~ zero growth ◆ **le point** ~ (Nucl) ground zero ◆ **l'option** ~ (Mil) the zero option

zeste /zɛst/ NM 1 [de citron, orange] peel (NonC); (en cuisine) zest (NonC), peel (NonC) ◆ **avec un ~ de citron** with a piece of lemon peel 2 (fig = pointe) [d'ironie] touch, hint ◆ **un ~ de folie/d'humour** a touch of madness/humour

zesteur /zɛstœʀ/ NM zester

zêta /(d)zɛta/ NM zeta

zeugma /zøgma/, **zeugme** /zøgm/ NM zeugma

Zeus /zøs/ NM Zeus

zézaiement /zezɛmɑ̃/ NM lisp

zézayer /zezeje/ ► conjug 8 ◄ VI to lisp

ZI /ʒɛdi/ NF (abrév de **zone industrielle**) → **zone**

zibeline /ziblin/ NF sable

zidovudine /zidɔvydin/ NF zidovudine

zieuter⁑ /zjøte/ ► conjug 1 ◄ VT (longuement) to eye; (rapidement) to have a squint at*, to have a dekko at⁑ (Brit)

zig * † /zig/ NM ⇒ **zigoto**

ziggourat /ziguʀat/ NF ziggurat, zik(k)urat

zigoto* † /zigɔto/, **zigomar*** † /zigɔmaʀ/ NM guy*, bloke* (*Brit*), chap* (*Brit*), geezer* † ◆ **c'est un drôle de** ~ he's a bit of an oddball* ◆ **faire le** ~ to mess *ou* muck (*Brit*) around

zigouiller* /ziguje/ ► conjug 1 ◄ VT to do in* ◆ **se faire** ~ to get bumped off*

zigounette* /zigunɛt/ NF (*hum ou langage enfantin*) willy* (*Brit*), peter* (*US*)

zigue* † /zig/ NM ⇒ **zig**

zigzag /zigzag/ NM zigzag ◆ **route en** ~ windy *ou* winding *ou* zigzagging road ◆ **faire des ~s** [*route*] to zigzag; [*personne*] to zigzag along ◆ **avoir fait** *ou* **eu une carrière en** ~ to have had a chequered career

zigzaguer /zigzage/ ► conjug 1 ◄ VI to zigzag (along)

Zimbabwe /zimbabwe/ NM Zimbabwe

zimbabwéen, -enne /zimbabweɛ̃, ɛn/ ADJ Zimbabwean NM,F **Zimbabwéen(ne)** Zimbabwean

zinc /zɛ̃g/ NM 1 (= *métal*) zinc 2 (* = *avion*) plane 3 (* = *comptoir*) bar, counter ◆ **boire un coup sur le** ~ to have a drink at the bar

zinguer /zɛ̃ge/ ► conjug 1 ◄ VT [+ *toiture, acier*] to coat with zinc

zingueur /zɛ̃gœʀ/ NM zinc worker ◆ **plombier-**~ plumber and zinc worker

zinnia /zinja/ NM zinnia

zinzin* /zɛ̃zɛ̃/ ADJ cracked*, nuts*, barmy* (*Brit*) NM 1 (= *fou*) nutcase*, loony* 2 (= *machin*) thingummy(jig)* (*Brit*), thingamajig (*US*), what's-it* (*Brit*) NMPL **zinzins** (*, *arg Bourse*) institutional investors

zip ® /zip/ NM zip ◆ **poche fermée par un** ~ zip(ped) pocket

zippé, e /zipe/ (ptp de **zipper**) ADJ zip-up (*épith*), with a zip

zipper /zipe/ ► conjug 1 ◄ VT [+ *vêtement*] to zip up; [+ *fichier*] to zip

zircon /ziʀkɔ̃/ NM zircon

zirconium /ziʀkɔnjɔm/ NM zirconium

zizanie /zizani/ NF ill-feeling ◆ **mettre** *ou* **semer la** ~ **dans une famille** to set a family at loggerheads, to stir up ill-feeling in a family

zizi[1]* /zizi/ NM (*hum, langage enfantin* = *pénis*) willy* (*Brit*) (*hum*), peter* (*US*) (*hum*)

zloty /zlɔti/ NM zloty

zob** /zɔb/ NM (= *pénis*) dick**, prick**, cock**

Zodiac ® /zɔdjak/ NM rubber *ou* inflatable dinghy

zodiacal, e (mpl **-aux**) /zɔdjakal, o/ ADJ [*constellation, signe*] of the zodiac; [*lumière*] zodiacal

zodiaque /zɔdjak/ NM zodiac; → **signe**

zombi(e) /zɔ̃bi/ NM zombie

zona /zona/ NM shingles (*sg*), herpes zoster (*SPÉC*) ◆ **avoir un** ~ to have shingles

zonage /zonaʒ/ NM (*Urbanisme, Ordin*) zoning

zonard, e** /zonaʀ, aʀd/ NM,F (= *marginal*) dropout*

zone /zon/ NF 1 (*gén, Sci*) zone, area; (*Transport*) travel zone ◆ ~ **d'élevage** (*Agr*) cattle-breeding area ◆ ~ **de pêche** fishing zone ◆ ~ **d'influence (d'un pays)** sphere *ou* zone of influence (of a country) ◆ **la** ~ **des combats** the combat zone ◆ ~ **de haute/basse pression** (*Météo*) area of high/low pressure ◆ ~ **franc/sterling** franc/sterling area ◆ **hors** ~ **franc** [*pays*] that does not belong to the franc area ◆ **~s A, B et C** (*Scol*) *three zones in France where schools take midterm breaks and Easter holidays at different times to avoid overcrowding in the transport system and at holiday resorts* ◆ **dans cette affaire, des ~s d'ombre subsistent encore** some aspects of this business remain very unclear ◆ **de deuxième/troisième** ~ (*fig*) second-/third-rate ◆ **arriver sur** ~ (*Mil*) to arrive at the scene of the action

2 (* = *quartiers pauvres*) **la** ~ the slum belt; (= *marginalité*) the dropout lifestyle ◆ **c'est la** ~ **!** it's the pits!* ◆ **enlève ce bric-à-brac de ton jardin, ça fait** ~* get rid of that junk in your garden, it looks like a tip*

COMP **zone d'activités** business park, enterprise zone
zone d'aménagement concerté urban development zone
zone d'aménagement différé future development zone
la zone des armées the war zone
zone artisanale industrial estate (*Brit*) *ou* park (*US*) for small businesses
zone bleue ≃ restricted parking zone *ou* area
zone dangereuse danger zone
zone démilitarisée demilitarized zone
zone de dépression *ou* **dépressionnaire** (*Météo*) trough of low pressure
zone de dialogue (*Ordin*) dialogue box
zone d'éducation prioritaire *area targeted for special help in education*
zone d'environnement protégé environmentally protected zone, ≃ SSSI (*Brit*)
zone érogène erogenous zone
zone euro Euroland
zone d'exclusion (*Mil*) exclusion zone ◆ ~ **d'exclusion aérienne** no-fly zone
zone franche free zone
zone frontalière border area *ou* zone
zone industrielle industrial estate (*Brit*) *ou* park (*US*)
zone inondable flood-risk area
zone interdite off-limits area, no-go area ◆ ~ **interdite à la navigation** area which is closed to shipping
zone libre (*Hist France*) unoccupied France ◆ **passer/se réfugier en** ~ **libre** to enter/take refuge in the unoccupied zone
zone de libre-échange free trade zone *ou* area
zone monétaire monetary zone
zone occupée occupied zone
zone piétonne *ou* **piétonnière** pedestrian precinct
zone à risque (*catastrophes naturelles*) disaster-prone area; (*criminalité*) high-risk area
zone rouge red zone
zone tampon (*Mil*) buffer zone; (*Ordin*) buffer
zone de turbulences (*en avion*) area of turbulence; (*fig*) trouble spot
zone urbaine urban area
zone à urbaniser en priorité † urban development zone

zoner /zone/ ► conjug 1 ◄ VT to zone VI ** [*marginal*] to bum around**

zoo /zo(o)/ NM zoo

zoologie /zɔɔlɔʒi/ NF zoology

zoologique /zɔɔlɔʒik/ ADJ zoological

zoologiste /zɔɔlɔʒist/, **zoologue** /zɔɔlɔg/ NMF zoologist

zoom /zum/ NM (= *objectif*) zoom lens; (= *effet*) zoom ◆ **faire un** ~ **sur** to zoom in on ◆ ~ **avant/arrière** zoom in/out ◆ **faire un** ~ **avant/arrière** to zoom in/out

zoomer /zume/ ► conjug 1 ◄ VI to zoom in (*sur* on)

zoomorphe /zɔɔmɔʀf/ ADJ zoomorphic

zoophile /zɔɔfil/ ADJ zoophilic NMF zoophilist

zoophilie /zɔɔfili/ NF (= *perversion*) zoophilia

zootechnicien, -ienne /zɔɔtɛknisjɛ̃, jɛn/ NM,F zootechnician

zootechnique /zɔɔtɛknik/ ADJ zootechnic

zoreille* /zɔʀɛj/ NMF *person from metropolitan France living in the overseas territories*

Zoroastre /zɔʀɔastʀ/ NM Zoroaster, Zarathustra

zoroastrisme /zɔʀɔastʀism/ NM Zoroastrianism, Zoroastrism

Zorro /zɔʀo/ NM Zorro ◆ **jouer les** ~* to play the hero

zou* /zu/ EXCL ◆ **(allez)** ~ **!** (= *partez*) off with you!, shoo!*; (= *dépêchez-vous*) get a move on!* ◆ **et** ~, **les voilà partis !** zoom, off they go!*

zouave /zwav/ NM Zouave, zouave ◆ **faire le** ~* to play the fool, to fool around

zouk /zuk/ NM zouk

zoulou, e /zulu/ ADJ Zulu NM (= *langue*) Zulu NM,F **Zoulou(e)** Zulu

Zoulouland /zululɑ̃d/ NM Zululand

zozo* /zozo/ NM (= *naïf*) nit(wit)*, ninny*; (= *individu*) guy, bloke (*Brit*)

zozoter* /zɔzɔte/ ► conjug 1 ◄ VI to lisp

ZUP † /zyp/ NF (abrév de **zone à urbaniser en priorité**) → **zone**

zut* /zyt/ EXCL (= *c'est embêtant*) damn!*, darn (it)!*; (= *ça suffit !*) (do) shut up!* ◆ **je te dis** ~ **!** get lost!* ◆ **je fais ce que je veux,** ~ **alors !** I'll do what I want, for goodness' sake! ◆ **et puis** ~ **à la fin ! j'abandonne !** what the heck*, I give up! ◆ **avoir un œil qui dit** ~ **à l'autre** to be cross-eyed

zwanze /zwɑ̃z/ NF (*Belg*) joke

zwanzer /zwɑ̃ze/ ► conjug 1 ◄ VI (*Belg*) to joke

zygomatique /zigɔmatik/ ADJ zygomatic ◆ **os/arcade** ~ zygomatic bone/arch NM zygomatic major (muscle) (*SPÉC*) ◆ **se dérouiller les ~s*** (*hum*) to have a good laugh

zygote /zigɔt/ NM zygote

zyklon /ziklɔ̃/ NM ◆ **(gaz)** ~, ~ **B** Zyklon B

GRAMMAIRE ACTIVE
LANGUAGE IN USE

Sommaire / Contents

LA GRAMMAIRE ACTIVE ROBERT & COLLINS

est divisée en 27 chapitres qui présentent plusieurs milliers de structures syntaxiques couvrant l'essentiel des besoins de communication entre francophones et anglophones.

Elle permet de s'exprimer directement dans la langue étrangère au lieu de procéder à la traduction à partir du mot ou de la locution, tels qu'ils figurent dans la partie dictionnaire. L'usager part ici d'un thème de réflexion ou du message qu'il cherche à communiquer et trouve dans le chapitre concerné un vaste éventail de possibilités d'expression dans la langue étrangère. De brèves indications dans sa langue maternelle, dont la fonction n'est pas de traduire mais de servir de points de repère, l'informeront sur le registre (familier ou soutenu) ou la nature (hésitante ou assurée, directe ou indirecte) du message.

Les exemples de la **Grammaire active** ont été tirés d'une très vaste base de données informatisée en langue française et en langue anglaise. Ces exemples ont été sélectionnés dans un grand nombre de sources différentes, allant de la littérature à la correspondance personnelle, en passant par les magazines, les journaux, ainsi que la langue parlée telle qu'on l'entend à la télévision et à la radio. Ils garantissent ainsi l'authenticité absolue des structures grammaticales et des expressions idiomatiques qui sont proposées.

Plusieurs centaines de mots-clés du dictionnaire sont suivis d'un renvoi vers la **Grammaire active.** Ces renvois mentionnent les numéros de chapitres concernés et avertissent l'usager qu'il trouvera dans le recueil d'expressions grammaticales des possibilités d'expression supplémentaires qui complètent l'information contenue dans les articles bilingues.

THIS "LANGUAGE IN USE" supplement

is divided into 27 topics, providing thousands of structures to facilitate self-expression and communication in French.

Using a key word in the message you wish to convey as a starting point, **Language in Use** shows you other possible ways of expressing the same message and provides you with a repertoire from which to choose the most appropriate formulation for the situation you are dealing with. The core translation which follows each phrase acts as a point of reference rather than as a direct equivalent and we have also provided guidance as to whether a phrase should be used in a familiar or formal context, whether it expresses the message directly or indirectly, or in a tentative or assertive manner.

Language in Use has been compiled using our vast linguistic databases of contemporary French and English. The examples have been selected from a wide variety of different sources: fiction and non-fiction, magazines and newspapers, business and personal correspondence, and spoken material gathered from real-life conversations and radio and television programmes. This means you can always be sure that the phrases and grammatical structures you choose are idiomatic and up-to-date.

Several hundred dictionary entries are linked to **Language in Use** by means of cross-references which show the topic number and section in **Language in Use** where that dictionary entry occurs. This linking of the main text with **Language in Use** allows you to navigate directly from a single-concept word in the dictionary to further, more diverse means of expression in context.

1 SUGGESTIONS

1.1 Making suggestions

Tentatively

- **Si je peux me permettre une suggestion** je crois qu'il faudrait …
  = if I may make a **suggestion**
- **À votre place**, je me renseignerais
  = if I were you
- **Si j'étais vous**, je resterais
  = if I were you
- **À mon avis,** il faudrait les inviter
  = in my **opinion**
- **Personnellement**, j'en parlerais à ses parents
  = **personally** (speaking)

More assertively

- **Vous pourriez** remettre cela à plus tard
  = you **could**
- **Rien ne vous empêche de** profiter des soldes
  = there's nothing to stop you
- **Essayez quand même de** lui en parler
  = still, try to
- **Vous feriez mieux de** prendre vos vacances en septembre
  = you'd do **better** to
- **Vous auriez intérêt à** prendre l'avion à Genève
  = you'd be **well-advised** to
- **Vous feriez bien d'**aller voir sur place
  = you'd do **well** to
- **N'oubliez pas de** répondre à sa lettre
  = don't **forget** to
- **Vous devriez** appeler un médecin
  = you **ought** to
- **Je propose que** nous nous mett**ions** *(subj)* au travail tout de suite
  = I **suggest** that
- **Voici mes suggestions :** présenter le projet au Conseil, …
  = my **suggestions** are (as follows):
- **Je suggère que vous** commenc**iez** *(subj)* immédiatement *(formal)*
  = I **suggest** that you

Using direct questions

- **Est-ce que vous avez songé à** faire appel à un entraîneur ?
  = have you **thought** of
- **Avez-vous pensé à** reprendre vos études ?
  = have you **thought** of
- **Que diriez-vous d'**un bon repas ?
  = what would you **say** to
- **Est-ce que cela ne vous tente pas de** partir en Italie ?
  = doesn't the **idea** of … tempt you?
- **Puis-je faire une suggestion ?** Il me semble que … *(formal)*
  = can I make a **suggestion**?

In an impersonal way

Tentatively

- **Et si** on se passait un film ? *(spoken)*
  = how about
- **Peut-être faudrait-il** discuter de ce problème
  = **perhaps** we **should**
- **Il vaudrait peut-être mieux** en rester là
  = **perhaps** it would be **better** to
- **Pourquoi ne pas** lui téléphoner ?
  = why not
- **Ce ne serait pas une mauvaise idée de** revendre la maison
  = it wouldn't be a bad **idea** to
- **On pourrait** adopter une autre méthode
  = we **could**

More assertively

- **Il serait souhaitable de** conserver cette procédure de vote
  = it would be **desirable** to
- **Il serait préférable de ne pas** trop attendre
  = it would be **preferable** not to
- **Il serait bon de** réunir le Conseil
  = it would be a good **idea** to
- **Ce serait une excellente idée de** rediffuser ce document
  = it would be an excellent **idea** to
- **Il n'y a qu'à** lui demander son avis
  = all you have to do is
- **Il conviendrait de** contacter l'entreprise dès maintenant *(formal)*
  = it would be **advisable** to

1.2 Asking for suggestions

- **Qu'est-ce que tu ferais à ma place ?**
  = what would you do if you were me?
- **Comment procéderais-tu** *or* **t'y prendrais-tu ?**
  = how would you proceed?
- **Qu'est-ce que vous proposez** pour résoudre ce problème ?
  = what do you **suggest**
- **Avez-vous une idée de** ce que l'on pourrait faire ?
  = have you any **ideas** about
- **Que fait-on dans ces cas-là ?**
  = what does one do in such cases?
- **Peut-être avez-vous une meilleure solution ?**
  = **perhaps** you have a **better solution**?

2 ADVICE

2.1 Asking for advice

- **À ma place que feriez-vous ?**
  = if you were me, what would you do?
- **Que fait-on dans ces cas-là ?**
  = what does one do in such cases?
- **Que me conseillez-vous de faire ?**
  = what do you **advise** me to do?
- **Que dois-je faire** dans l'immédiat ?
  = what do I have to do
- **J'aimerais avoir votre opinion sur** ce dossier
  = I'd like your **opinion** on
- **Quel est votre avis sur** le droit d'ingérence humanitaire ?
  = what is your **opinion** on

- **Je voudrais vous demander conseil : pensez-vous que je devrais** offrir des fleurs à notre hôtesse ?
  = I'd like your **advice**: do you think I **should**
- **Je vous serais très reconnaissant de bien vouloir me conseiller sur** la marche à suivre *(formal, written style)*
  = I **should** be most **grateful** for your **advice** on

2.2 Giving advice

- Fais comme si de rien n'était, **c'est ce que tu as de mieux à faire** *(spoken)*
  = it's the **best** thing you can do
- **Moi, je trouve que tu devrais** carrément déménager *(spoken)*
  = I **think** you **should**
- **Un conseil :** il faut découvrir cet endroit le matin quand la ville s'éveille
  = a word of **advice:**
- **Tu as (tout) intérêt à** t'y prendre aussitôt que possible
  = you'd be well-**advised** to
- Si vous vivez une passion, au moins taisez-la. **Surtout ne** la dévoilez **pas**
  = whatever you do, don't
- **Si j'ai un conseil à vous donner, c'est de** ne pas trop tarder à renvoyer ces papiers
  = if I could give you one piece of **advice**, it would be to
- **Vous auriez tort de ne pas** en profiter
  = you'd be quite **wrong** not to
- **Je trouve que tu devrais** essayer de passer ton permis de conduire
  = I **think** you **should**
- **À mon avis tu devrais** te montrer plus enthousiaste
  = in my **opinion**, you **should**
- **À votre place, je** me renseigner**ais auprès de l'association des parents d'élèves**
  = if I were you, I'd
- **Si j'étais vous, je** téléphoner**ais sans plus tarder**
  = if I were you, I'd
- **Je ne saurais trop vous recommander d'**être discret à ce sujet
  = I cannot **advise** you strongly enough to

More tentatively

- **Pourquoi ne pas** téléphoner à Martine ? Ça lui ferait plaisir
  = why not
- **Est-ce que tu as pensé à** un cours de recyclage ?
  = have you **thought** of
- **Ce ne serait pas une mauvaise idée de** partir avant l'heure de pointe
  = it wouldn't be a bad **idea** to
- **Vous feriez mieux de** vous adresser à un autre musée
  = you'd do **better** to
- Nous n'avons plus de 45 mais **vous pourriez peut-être** essayer du 44
  = **perhaps** you **could**
- **Je me demande si vous ne devriez pas** attendre quelques jours
  = I **wonder** if you **should perhaps**
- **Il est déconseillé de** se promener du côté du port après la tombée de la nuit
  = it is **inadvisable** to
- **Il serait peut-être bon de** changer de ton à défaut de changer de politique
  = **perhaps** it would be a good **idea** to
- **Il nous semble peu prudent d'**engager des fonds aussi importants dans cette affaire
  = it doesn't seem very **wise** to us
- **Il serait judicieux de** publier ce document avant la fin de l'année
  = it would be **wise** to
- **Puis-je me permettre de suggérer que** vous changi**ez** *(subj)* d'itinéraire au retour ?
  = may I **suggest** that you

2.3 Giving warnings

- **Méfiez-vous de** ces faux amis
  = **beware** of
- **Si vous ne** réservez **pas** maintenant, **vous courez le risque de** ne pas avoir de billet
  = if you don't ... you run the **risk** of
- **Tu vas avoir des ennuis** de santé **si** tu continues à fumer autant
  = you're going to have problems if
- **Je vous préviens :** interdiction de stationner entre 13 et 16 heures, sinon gare au PV
  = I am **warning** you:
- **Je vous préviens que** je ne vous accorderai pas un jour de délai
  = I **warn** you that
- **Je vous avertis que** je commence à en avoir assez de vos absences répétées
  = I **warn** you that
- **Ce serait de la folie de** s'engager dans cette direction
  = it would be madness to
- **Si vous** ne voulez pas le faire, **très bien, mais** ne venez pas vous plaindre de ce qui vous arrivera
  = if you ... (that's) fine, but

3 OFFERS

3.1 Direct offers

- **Je ferais volontiers** ce voyage avec toi
  = I'd **gladly**
- **Je suis prêt à** poursuivre le travail commencé avec lui
  = I'm **prepared** to
- **Je peux** passer vous prendre chez vous, **si vous voulez**
  = I **can** ... if you want
- **Je pourrais** venir étudier la question sur place
  = I **could**
- **N'hésitez pas à** nous poser des questions
  = don't **hesitate** to
- **Laissez-moi au moins** payer les fleurs !
  = at **least let** me

3.2 Indirect offers

- **Je serais (très) heureux de** vous rendre ce service
  = I'd be very **happy** to
- **Cela me ferait très plaisir de** vous emmener
  = it would be a **pleasure** to
- **Je ne demande pas mieux que de** participer à ce projet
  = I'd be only too **happy** to
- **Nous pourrions peut-être** déjeuner ensemble
  = **perhaps** we **could**

3.3 Using direct questions

- **Cela te dirait de** visiter la Maison Blanche ?
  = how would you **like** to
- **Et si je** pass**ais l'aspirateur ?**
  = what if I
- **Est-ce que je peux** vous renseigner ?
  = **can** I
- **Est-ce que vous voulez que j'aille** *(subj)* vous chercher un journal ?
  = do you **want** me to go
- **Voudriez-vous que** nous avanc**ions** *(subj)* la réunion ?
  = would you **like** us to
- **Puis-je** vous être utile ?
  = **can** I
- **Souhaitez-vous que nous** poursuiv**ions** *(subj)* les expériences en cours ?
  = do you **want** us to
- **Aimeriez-vous que je** m'en charge *(subj)* pour vous ?
  = would you **like** me to

4 REQUESTS

Tentatively

- **Est-ce que cela vous dérangerait beaucoup de** me céder votre place ?
  = would you **mind** awfully
- **Est-ce que cela vous ennuierait beaucoup de** me déposer chez moi ?
  = would you **mind** terribly
- **Cela me rendrait service si vous pouviez** me le prêter
  = it would be of **help** (to me) if you could
- **Cela m'arrangerait si vous pouviez** payer tout de suite
  = it would **suit** me (nicely) if you could
- **Nous aimerions** connaître vos heures d'ouverture
  = we would **like** to
- **Nous souhaiterions** clarifier quelques détails *(formal)*
  = we **wish** to
- **Puis-je vous demander de (bien vouloir)** me fournir quelques renseignements ? *(formal)*
  = **can** I **ask** you, please, to
- **Je voudrais** connaître les horaires des trains suivants
  = I'd **like** to

More assertively

- **Est-ce que vous pourriez** nous donner un mode d'emploi ?
  = **could** you
- **Est-ce que vous pouvez** nous donner un exemple de prix ?
  = **can** you
- **Je dois vous demander de** procéder à une enquête
  = I must **ask** you to
- **Nous comptons sur vous pour** terminer ce travail rapidement
  = we are **counting** on you to
- **J'insiste pour que** le rapport **soit** *(subj)* substantiel et motivé
  = I **insist** on ... being

In writing

- **Vous serait-il possible de** me dire où il faut s'adresser ?
  = **could** you **possibly**
- **Auriez-vous l'amabilité de** nous transmettre le texte ?
  = would you be so **kind** as to
- **Seriez-vous assez aimable pour** m'indiquer la marche à suivre ?
  = would you be so **kind** as to
- **Je vous remercie de bien vouloir** me faire parvenir ces renseignements
  = I would **appreciate** it if you would
- **Je vous prie de bien vouloir** attendre avant de remettre votre rapport
  = **please**
- **Je vous serais reconnaissant de bien vouloir** leur envoyer ce document
  = I would be **grateful** if you would
- **Je vous saurais gré de bien vouloir** rectifier cette erreur
  = I should be **grateful** if you would
- **Nous vous serions obligés de bien vouloir** nous faire part de vos décisions
  = we should be **obliged** if you would
- **Veuillez avoir l'obligeance de** remplir ces formulaires
  = please be so **kind** as to
- **Vous êtes prié de bien vouloir** régulariser votre situation
  = we **request** that you

5 COMPARISONS

5.1 Objective comparisons

- Cette nouvelle structure offrirait, **par comparaison avec** l'ancienne, souplesse et personnalisation de la gestion
  = by **comparison** with
- Quant au poisson, il offre, **en comparaison de** la viande, l'intérêt d'être peu gras
  = by **comparison** with
- ... un chiffre non négligeable, **comparé à** l'investissement initial
  = **compared** with
- C'est tout de même un pays riche **si on le compare à** l'ensemble du monde
  = if one **compares** it with
- Il y a des événements **bien plus** tragiques **que de** perdre une finale de Coupe d'Europe
  = **much more** ... than

- La progression, **par rapport à** l'année précédente, est importante
  = **compared** to
- Sa nouvelle maison **ressemble à** l'ancienne mais en moins grand
  = **resembles**
- **Cela fait penser à** du marbre mais en plus brillant
  = it **reminds** one of
- C'est un jardin qui peut, **par constraste avec** l'agitation environnante, évoquer ceux de Kyoto
  = when **contrasted** with
- Cet appartement donne sur un joli jardin **tandis que** *or* **alors que** l'autre donne sur une cour
  = **whereas**

5.2 Making favourable/unfavourable comparisons

- Ce vin **est de très loin supérieur à** l'autre
  = is by far **superior** to
- Ce fromage **est bien supérieur à** celui que vous venez de goûter
  = is far **superior** to
- **Je préfère** le Sud de la France **à** la Bretagne pour ce qui est du climat
  = I **prefer** ... to
- L'élève **dépasse** le maître
  = **surpasses**
- Le film **est loin d'être aussi** intéressant **que** le roman dont on l'a tiré
  = is far from being as ... as
- Cette nouvelle adaptation du roman **est loin de valoir** la version en noir et blanc réalisée en 1939
  = is a long way from **equalling**
- Les danseurs d'aujourd'hui **n'arrivent pas à la cheville de** ceux des années 30
  = can't hold a candle to

5.3 Comparing similar things

- **On a souvent comparé** Victor Hugo **à** Eugène Delacroix
  = ... has often been **compared** to ...
- La presse locale n'a pas hésité à **faire un rapprochement entre** le limogeage du ministre de la justice **et** cet assassinat
  = make the **connection** between ... and
- Le camp militaire qui se trouve à l'entrée de la ville est **comparativement** peu peuplé
  = **comparatively**
- La composition des images **rappelle** très souvent les tableaux des peintres préraphaélites anglais
  = **recalls**
- Tous les deux se sont retrouvés sur un banc d'assises, **mais la ressemblance s'arrête là**
  = but that's where the **similarity** ends
- Leurs taux de scolarisation **sont comparables à** ceux des pays développés
  = are **comparable** with
- Nous avons trouvé un fromage **qui est l'équivalent** grec **de** la mozzarella
  = which is the **equivalent** of
- Cette somme **correspond à** six mois de salaire
  = **corresponds** to
- Ces deux articles **valent pratiquement le même prix**
  = cost practically the **same**
- Un peuple qui n'a pas de mémoire n'a pas d'avenir. **Il en est de même des** formations politiques
  = the **same** is true of
- **C'est plus ou moins la même chose**
  = it's more or less the **same** thing
- **Cela revient au même**
  = it **amounts** to the **same** thing

5.4 Comparing dissimilar things

- **Ce qui distingue** notre langue **des** langues anciennes et modernes, **c'est** l'ordre et la construction de la phrase
  = what **distinguishes** ... from ... is
- **Ce qui différencie** les cafés arabica **des** robusta, **c'est** leur teneur en caféine
  = what **distinguishes** ... from ... is
- **Il n'y a aucune comparaison possible entre** l'équipement des deux armées
  = there is no possible **comparison** to be drawn between
- **On ne peut pas comparer** la situation de quelqu'un qui vit à la campagne **à** celle d'un banlieusard
  = you can't **compare** ... with
- Ces vignerons vivent de productions à faible rendement **qui n'ont rien de comparable avec** celles des Charentes
  = which are in no way **comparable** to
- Leur motivation, leur travail **ne se ressemblent vraiment en rien** mais ils ont en commun le fait d'être anglais
  = have really nothing in **common**

6 OPINION

6.1 Asking for opinions

Tentatively

- **J'aimerais connaître votre avis** *or* **votre opinion sur** ce problème
  = I'd like (to know) your **opinion** on
- **Je voudrais savoir ce que vous pensez de** son travail
  = I'd like to know what you **think** of
- **J'aimerais connaître votre réaction face à** ce brusque changement
  = I'd like (to know) your **reaction** to
- **Est-ce que vous pourriez me donner votre avis** *or* **votre opinion sur** cette émission ?
  = could you give me your **opinion** on
- **Pourriez-vous me dire ce que vous pensez de** leur politique ?
  = could you tell me what you **think** of

More directly

- **À votre avis** *or* **Selon vous**, faut-il donner plus de liberté aux jeunes ?
  = in your **opinion**
- **Est-ce que vous avez une opinion sur** la publicité ?
  = do you have any **opinion** on

- **Quelle est votre opinion sur** la situation internationale ?
  = what's your **opinion** on
- **Que pensez-vous de** sa façon d'agir ?
  = what do you **think** of

6.2 Expressing opinions

- **Il me semble que** vous vous trompez
  = I **think**
- **J'ai l'impression que** ses parents ne la comprennent pas
  = I have a **feeling**
- **Je suppose que** vous n'avez pas besoin de mes conseils
  = I **suppose**
- **J'imagine que** ce n'est pas très facile
  = I **imagine**
- **Si vous voulez mon opinion**, cette décision n'est pas raisonnable
  = if you want my **opinion**
- **Je ne peux pas m'empêcher de penser que** c'est délibéré
  = I can't help **thinking**
- **Sans vouloir vous contredire, il me semble que** nous nous rapprochons d'une solution
  = without wishing to contradict you, it **seems** to me that
- **Je dois dire que** je ne suis pas satisfait
  = I must **say** that

More directly

- **Je crains qu'il ne soit** *(subj)* trop tard maintenant
  = I **fear** that it is
- **À mon avis** il n'a pas changé
  = in my **opinion**
- **Selon moi** *or* **D'après moi** *or* **Pour moi,** il a fait une erreur
  = in my **view**
- **Personnellement**, je ne le soutiendrai pas
  = **personally**
- **En ce qui me concerne** *or* **Pour ma part** *or* **Quant à moi**, je suis content de son travail
  = as far as I am **concerned** or for my part
- **Je pense** *or* **Je crois que** ce sera possible
  = I **think** or **believe**
- **J'estime qu'**il faut reprendre cette discussion
  = I **think**
- **Je trouve que** le racisme est criminel
  = I **think**
- **Je considère que** cette réforme est une amélioration
  = I **feel**
- Il faut changer radicalement le système. **C'est du moins mon opinion**
  = at least that is my **opinion**

With more conviction

- **Je suis sûr que** nous pouvons trouver une solution
  = I am **sure**
- **Je suis certain qu'**il est tout à fait sincère
  = I am **certain**
- **Je suis persuadé qu'**il y a d'autres solutions
  = I am **convinced**
- **Je suis convaincu que** nous pouvons réussir
  = I am **convinced**

6.3 Avoiding expressing one's opinion

- **Il est difficile de** débattre de ces questions
  = it is **difficult** to
- **Je préférerais ne pas avoir à me prononcer** là-dessus
  = I'd rather not **comment**
- **Il m'est difficile de donner un avis (définitif) sur** ce point
  = I find it **difficult** to **express** a (definite) **opinion** on
- **Je n'ai pas d'opinion bien précise à** ce sujet
  = I have no definite **opinion** on
- **Je n'ai jamais vraiment réfléchi à** ce problème
  = I have never really thought about
- **Je ne me suis jamais vraiment posé la question**
  = I have never really asked myself that **question**
- **Je ne me le suis jamais demandé**
  = I have never thought about it
- **Je ne suis pas à même de dire s'**il a eu raison
  = I am not in a **position** to say whether
- **Tout dépend de** ce que vous entendez par là
  = it all **depends** on

7 LIKES, DISLIKES AND PREFERENCES

7.1 Asking what someone likes

- **Qu'est-ce que vous aimez le plus** *or* **préférez** : la mer ou la montagne ?
  = which do you **like better** or **prefer**
- **Est-ce que vous aimeriez** faire une partie de tennis cet après-midi ?
  = would you **like** to
- **Est-ce que cela vous plaît de** vivre en ville ?
  = do you **like**
- **Est-ce que cela vous plairait** *or* **ferait plaisir d'**aller à cette exposition ?
  = would you **like** to

7.2 Saying what you like

- **Cela ne me déplaît pas d'**être seule, je ne m'ennuie jamais
  = I don't **dislike**
- **J'aime que** les choses **soient** *(subj)* à leur place
  = I **like** ... to be
- **J'éprouve du plaisir à** marcher dans les vagues
  = I take **pleasure in**
- La visite de la cathédrale **m'a beaucoup plu**
  = I **liked** ... very much
- **Ce que j'aime par-dessus tout, c'est** une soirée entre amis
  = what I **like most** of all is
- **Pour moi, rien ne vaut** un grand verre d'eau fraîche pour se désaltérer
  = as far as I'm concerned, there's nothing **like**

- **Rien de tel qu'**une bonne soirée au théâtre !
  = there's nothing **like**

7.3 Saying what you dislike

- **Je n'ai aucun plaisir à** travailler dans de telles conditions
  = I don't find it at all **pleasant** to
- Sa façon d'agir **ne me plaît pas du tout**
  = I don't **like** ... at all
- **Il m'est pénible de** me trouver à côté de cet homme qui a fait tant de mal à ma famille
  = I find it hard to
- Sa façon de parler **me déplaît au plus haut point**
  = I **dislike** ... intensely
- **J'ai horreur de** la médiocrité
  = I **loathe**
- **Je ne peux pas supporter qu'**on me mente *(subj)*
  = I can't **stand**
- **Ce que je déteste le plus, c'est d'**attendre le bus sous la pluie
  = what I **hate** most is

7.4 Saying what you prefer

- **J'aime autant que** nous y all**ions** *(subj)* ensemble
  = I'd **rather**
- Les critiques ne m'émeuvent pas mais **je préférerais** les recevoir directement plutôt que de façon anonyme
  = I'd **prefer** to
- Vendredi **me conviendrait mieux** *(formal)*
  = would **suit** me **better**
- **Cela m'arrangerait que** vous ven**iez** *(subj)* plutôt vendredi
  = it would **suit me better** if
- **Je préfère** créer du nouveau **plutôt que de** modifier de l'ancien
  = I **prefer** to ... than to
- **Ce que je préfère chez** Matisse, **ce sont** ses dessins, les encres, les fusains
  = what I **like best** about ... are
- La lecture est **une de mes** activités **favorites** *or* **préférées**
  = one of my **favourite**

7.5 Expressing indifference

- Cette idée **ne m'emballe pas**
  = I'm not **thrilled** by
- **Ça m'est égal**
  = it's all the **same** to me
- **C'est comme vous voudrez**
  = as you **wish**
- Une beauté classique **me laisse froid**
  = leaves me **cold**
- **Cela n'a pas la moindre importance**
  = it doesn't **matter** in the **least**
- **Je n'ai pas de préférence**
  = I have no **preference** either way
- **Peu importe**
  = I don't **mind**

8 INTENTIONS AND DESIRES

8.1 Asking what someone intends to do

- **Qu'est-ce que vous comptez faire** pour mettre un terme à leurs difficultés ?
  = what are you **planning** to do
- **Qu'est-ce que vous envisagez de faire** pour les aider ?
  = what are you **thinking** of doing
- **Qu'allez-vous faire** dans les prochains mois ?
  = what are you going to do
- **Quelles sont vos intentions** à son égard ?
  = what do you **intend** to do
- **Avez-vous l'intention de** faire de nouvelles propositions ?
  = do you **intend** to
- **Est-ce que vous pensez** retravailler ensemble ?
  = are you **thinking** of
- **Comptez-vous** faire un reportage ?
  = are you **planning** to
- **J'aimerais savoir ce que vous comptez** obtenir
  = I would **like** to know what you **intend** to

8.2 Saying what someone intends or wants to do

Tentatively

- **Il songe à** poursuivre ses études
  = he is **thinking** of
- **J'envisage de** simplifier les procédures
  = I am **thinking** of
- **Il projette de** restaurer un vieux château
  = he is **planning** to
- **Nous nous proposons de** publier des textes intégraux de romans étrangers
  = we **intend** to
- **Nous prévoyons de** partir en voyage le mois prochain
  = we are **planning** to
- **Je voudrais** m'entretenir avec lui le plus rapidement possible
  = I would **like** to
- **J'ai l'intention de** porter plainte
  = I **intend** to

More assertively

- **Je désire** faire connaître mes opinions
  = I **wish** to
- **Je veux** monter mon propre cabinet
  = I **want** to
- **J'ai décidé de** faire appel de ce jugement
  = I have **decided** to
- **Nous sommes (bien) décidés à** prendre des décisions radicales
  = we have (definitely) made up our **minds** to
- **Il est résolu à** apporter son soutien financier
  = he is **determined** to
- **Elle a pris la résolution de** coopérer davantage
  = she has made up her **mind** to
- **Nous voulons à tout prix** trouver du travail
  = we **want** to ... at all **costs**

• **Je vais** passer quelques semaines en Albanie
= I **am going** to

8.3 Saying what someone does not intend or want to do

• **Elle n'envisage pas de** s'arrêter là
= she is not **thinking** of

• **Nous ne comptons pas** rester ici longtemps
= we don't **intend** to

• **Il n'est pas dans mes intentions de** démissionner
= it is not my **intention** to

• **Je n'ai pas l'intention** *or* **la moindre intention de** faire un effort financier
= I have no or not the slightest **intention** of

• **Nous ne voulons pas** dormir ici
= we do not **want** to

• **Je suis (bien) décidé à ne pas** me laisser faire
= I firmly **intend** not to

• **Je refuse de** mettre le nez dehors par ce froid
= I **refuse** to

• **Il n'est pas question que** je vende *(subj)* la voiture
= there is no **question** of

• **Je m'oppose formellement à ce que nous** y allions *(subj)*
= I am totally **opposed** to our

8.4 Saying what someone would like to do

• **J'ai envie d'**aller au cinéma ce soir
= I **feel like**

• **Nous aurions aimé** pouvoir le féliciter nous-mêmes
= we would have **liked** to

• **J'aimerais** écrire un livre
= I would **like** to

• **Je voudrais** réaliser un second film
= I would **like** to

• **Je voudrais que** l'entrée **soit** *(subj)* repeinte avant Noël
= I would **like** ... to be

• **Il souhaiterait** développer les contrats avec les entreprises
= he would **like** to

• **Il est à souhaiter qu'il** dispose *(subj)* de moyens suffisants
= it is to be **hoped** that he

• **Je forme le souhait que** les liens entre nos deux associations se développent *(subj)* *(formal)*
= it is my **desire** that

• **Il faut espérer que** tout se déroulera comme prévu
= it is to be **hoped** that

• **Elle rêve de** faire du cinéma
= she **dreams** of

9 PERMISSION

9.1 Asking for permission

• **Est-ce qu'on peut** *or* **peut-on fumer** dans ce bureau ?
= is smoking **allowed**?

• **Est-ce que vous accepteriez que** je vous raccompagne *(subj)* ?
= would you **allow** me to

• **Est-ce que je pourrais** me faire photographier avec vous ?
= **could** I

• **Je voulais vous demander si je pourrais** arriver un peu plus tard demain matin
= I wanted to **ask** you if I could

• **J'espère que cela ne vous ennuiera pas si** je change quelques détails dans ce compte rendu
= I hope you won't **mind** if I

• **J'aimerais bien** participer au stage, **si cela ne vous dérange pas**
= I'd like to ... if you don't **mind**

• À ce sujet, **puis-je vous demander de** m'accorder une petite entrevue ?
= **may** I **ask** you to

• **Voyez-vous un inconvénient à ce que** ces productions **soient** *(subj)* subventionnées sur fonds publics ?
= do you have any **objection** to ... being

• **Nous serait-il possible de** vous inviter à ce festival en novembre ?
= **may** we

9.2 Giving permission

• **Vous pouvez** utiliser la photocopieuse, **si vous voulez**
= you **can** ... if you want

• **Je n'y vois pas d'inconvénient**
= I have nothing **against** it

• **Je vous permets de** partir une heure plus tôt
= I'll allow you to

• **Je vous autorise à** partir plus tôt
= you have my **permission** to

• **Je vous en prie, faites comme vous jugez nécessaire**
= please do what you feel you need to

• **Je consens à ce que** vous lui en parl**iez** *(subj)* directement
= I give you my **permission** to

9.3 Refusing permission

• **Il n'en est pas question**
= there is no **question** of it

• **Vous ne pouvez pas** voir le directeur sans rendez-vous
= you can't

• **Je ne vous permets pas de** *or* **ne vous autorise pas à** photographier l'usine
= I cannot **allow** you to or give you permission to

• **Je préférerais que vous ne** lui en parl**iez** *(subj)* **pas**
= I'd prefer you not to

• **Je refuse catégoriquement de vous laisser** partir
= I absolutely **refuse** to **let** you

- **Je vous interdis formellement de** communiquer avec nos concurrents
  = I positively **forbid** you to
- **Je regrette de ne pouvoir consentir à** ce projet
  = I regret that I cannot **consent** to
- **Je m'oppose absolument à ce que nous** leur expédi**ions** *(subj)* cette commande sans garantie
  = I am totally **opposed** to our
- **Je crains d'être dans l'obligation de vous décevoir** *(formal)*
  = I am afraid I must disappoint you

9.4 Saying that permission has been granted

- **Ils le laissent** boire du café bien qu'il n'ait *(subj)* que trois ans
  = they **let** him
- **On m'a permis de** régler la machine à laver en plusieurs versements
  = they've **allowed** me to
- **Il m'a dit que je pouvais** prendre sa voiture
  = he said I **could**
- **On permet** *or* **autorise** une marge d'erreur
  = ... is **permissible**

9.5 Saying that permission has been refused

- **Défense d'entrer** *or* **Entrée interdite**
  = no entry
- **Il m'est interdit** *or* **défendu de** boire de l'alcool
  = I have been **forbidden** to
- L'alcool **m'est interdit**
  = I am **forbidden** ...
- ... le dimanche, jour où **il est défendu de** trop travailler
  = it is **forbidden** to
- Mon médecin **m'interdit de** fumer
  = **forbids** me to
- **Il est formellement interdit de** parler au conducteur
  = ... is strictly **forbidden**
- **Vous ne devez en aucun cas** ouvrir la porte
  = on no account must you

10 OBLIGATION

10.1 Saying what someone must do

- **On demande que** les patients **soient** *(subj)* à l'heure
  = ... are **requested** to be
- **Il faut que** le travail **soit** *(subj)* terminé vendredi
  = ... **must** be
- Le financement **doit être** assuré par d'autres ressources
  = ... **must** be
- **Il faut (absolument)** faire quelque chose
  = you (really) **must**
- **Il est obligatoire de** réserver pour prendre le TGV
  = ... is **obligatory**
- **Il est indispensable de** trouver d'urgence une solution
  = it is **essential** to
- **On exige que** les candidats **aient** *(subj)* de solides connaissances en algèbre
  = ... are **required** to have
- **Cela m'oblige à** *or* **me force à** venir tous les jours
  = I **have** to ... because of that
- **Vous êtes obligé de** venir
  = you **have** to
- **Je suis forcé de** partir pour Londres
  = I am **forced** to
- **Vous prendrez** deux de ces comprimés chaque matin
  = (you must) take
- **Vous devez (impérativement)** payer vos impôts pour le quinze
  = you (really) **must**
- **Il est indispensable que** vos lecteurs en **soient** *(subj)* informés
  = it is **essential** that ... are
- **Je ne peux faire autrement que d'**accepter
  = I have no **choice** but to
- **Je n'ai pas le choix**
  = I have no **choice**

More formally

- **Elle s'est trouvée obligée de** rester deux heures de plus
  = she was **obliged** to
- **Il s'est vu contraint de** suivre un traitement médical intensif
  = he was **compelled** to
- **Il me faut** leur donner les mesures de l'appartement
  = I **have** to
- **Je me vois dans l'obligation de** solliciter un nouveau prêt *(written)*
  = I am **obliged** to
- **J'ai le devoir de** *or* **Il est de mon devoir de** vous informer que votre demande a été rejetée *(written)*
  = it is my **duty** to

10.2 Enquiring if one is obliged to do something

- **Est-ce qu'on doit** consulter un spécialiste avant de suivre un régime ?
  = **must** one
- **Est-ce qu'il faut** s'en tenir à ce document ?
  = does one **have** to
- **Est-ce que j'ai vraiment besoin de** prendre un parapluie ?
  = do I really **need** to
- **Est-ce que je suis obligé** *or* **forcé de** venir avec vous ?
  = do I **have** to
- **Faut-il vraiment que je** choisisse *(subj)* un nouveau nom ?
  = do I really **have** to
- **Est-il nécessaire de** faire autant de bruit pour si peu ?
  = does one **have** to
- **Est-il obligatoire de** présenter sa carte d'identité ?
  = does one **have** to

10.3 Saying what someone is not obliged to do

- **On n'a pas besoin de** crier pour se faire entendre
  = one doesn't **have** to
- **Il n'est pas obligatoire d'**avoir ses papiers d'identité sur soi
  = it is not **compulsory** to

- **Il n'est pas nécessaire de** téléphoner pour confirmer
  = it is not **necessary** to
- **Il n'est pas indispensable de** suivre la recette traditionnelle
  = it is not **essential** to
- **Ce n'est pas la peine de** traduire tout le premier chapitre
  = it is not **worth**
- **Vous n'êtes pas obligé** *or* **forcé d'**aller voir un médecin
  = you don't **have** to
- **Je ne vous oblige pas à** y aller
  = I am not **forcing** you to
- **Ne vous sentez pas obligé de** venir la voir
  = do not feel **obliged** to
- **Je ne vous demande pas de** faire des photocopies toute la journée
  = I am not asking you to

10.4 Saying what someone must not do

- **On n'a pas le droit de** fumer dans les lieux publics
  = ... is not **allowed**
- **Il est interdit** *or* **défendu de** conduire sans permis
  = ... is **forbidden**
- **Il ne faut pas** être agressif
  = you **mustn't**
- **Nous ne tolérerons** aucun retard
  = we will not **tolerate**
- **Vous ne pouvez pas** vous absenter plus de trois jours par mois
  = you cannot
- **Je ne vous permets pas de** me parler sur ce ton
  = I will not **allow** you to
- **Je t'interdis** *or* **Je te défends d'**y aller seul
  = I **forbid** you to
- **Surtout ne** lui en parlez **pas**
  = whatever you do, do not

11 AGREEMENT

11.1 Agreeing with a statement

- **Vous avez bien** *or* **entièrement raison**
  = you are quite or absolutely **right**
- **Je suis entièrement de votre avis**
  = I **agree** with you entirely
- **Je suis entièrement d'accord** (avec vous)
  = I entirely **agree**
- Dans l'ensemble, **nous sommes d'accord avec** l'orientation du projet
  = we **agree** with
- **Nous sommes du même avis que vous sur** ce point
  = we **feel** the **same** as you on
- **Je partage votre inquiétude sur** les risques d'une guerre commerciale
  = I **share** your concern over
- **Je partage votre enthousiasme pour** les possibilités offertes par les nouvelles technologies de communication
  = I **share** your enthusiasm for
- **Je conviens que** c'est là un discours difficile
  = I **admit** that
- **Je comprends très bien que** tu **aies** *(subj)* pitié de Laura
  = I fully **understand** that
- **Je vous accorde que** les hommes politiques valent beaucoup mieux que leur image électorale
  = I **concede** that
- **Comme vous l'avez fait remarquer, il est vrai** *or* **exact que** nous n'avons pas toutes les données nécessaires
  = as you **pointed** out, it is **true** that
- **Je ne puis que vous donner raison**
  = I cannot but **agree** with you

11.2 Agreeing to a proposal

- **C'est une bonne idée**
  = it's a good **idea**
- **Je trouve que tu as raison de** prendre tes congés maintenant
  = I think you're **right** to
- **Je suis d'accord pour que vous** y all**iez** *(subj)* à pied
  = I **agree** that you should
- **J'accepte** la proposition du commissaire
  = I **accept**
- **J'accepte de** consulter un expert, comme vous l'avez suggéré
  = I **agree** to
- Votre proposition **nous plaît beaucoup**
  = we **like** ... very much
- La coopération des deux entreprises, **c'est exactement ce dont nous avons besoin**
  = is **exactly** what we need
- **Nous donnons notre accord à** la réfection des locaux
  = we **agree** to
- **Il est entendu que** la nouvelle taxe sera appliquée de façon dégressive
  = it is **agreed** that
- **Je ne manquerai pas d'**appuyer votre demande
  = I shall not **fail** to
- **Je suis heureux d'apporter mon soutien à** cette proposition
  = I am **happy** to **support**
- **Je souscris à** beaucoup de ces analyses et propositions
  = I **subscribe** to

11.3 Agreeing to a request

- **Je serai enchanté** *or* **ravi d'**aller chercher votre tante à la gare
  = I shall be **delighted** to
- La date retenue **me convient parfaitement**
  = **suits** me perfectly
- **Je suis prêt à** aller déjeuner en sa compagnie à sa sortie de prison
  = I am **prepared** to
- **Je** quitter**ai donc** l'appartement le 22, **comme vous me l'avez demandé**
  = I shall ..., then, ... as you requested
- **Il est entendu que** les négociations couvriront les questions en suspens
  = it is **agreed** that

In writing

- **J'accepte avec grand plaisir** votre aimable invitation
  = I have great **pleasure in accepting**
- **C'est avec grand plaisir que j'accepte** votre aimable invitation
  = it is with great **pleasure** that I **accept**
- Nous prenons bonne note de votre commande, **que nous honorerons dans les plus brefs délais**
  = which we will process as quickly as possible
- **Je tiens à vous assurer que je suivrai vos instructions à la lettre**
  = be **assured** that I will follow your instructions to the letter
- **Nous essayerons de nous conformer à vos désirs**
  = we shall endeavour to meet your requirements

12 DISAGREEMENT

12.1 Disagreeing with a statement

- **Je suis désolé** *or* **Je suis navré de** devoir vous contredire
  = I am **sorry** to
- **Je ne partage pas votre point de vue** là-dessus
  = I do not **share** your point of view
- **Je ne suis pas d'accord avec** cette manière de voir
  = I do not **agree** with
- **Je vois les choses (tout à fait) différemment**
  = I see things (quite) differently

More assertively

- **C'est faux**
  = it's **wrong**
- **Vous vous trompez**
  = you are **mistaken**
- **Vous faites erreur**
  = you are **mistaken**
- **Vous avez tort de** refuser
  = you are **wrong** to
- **Je rejette (totalement)** cette idée
  = I (totally) **reject**
- **Je suis contre** la violence sous toutes ses formes
  = I'm **against**
- **Je suis (catégoriquement) opposé à** une idée négative de l'Europe
  = I am (categorically) **opposed** to
- **Je ne peux pas accepter** cette condamnation globale
  = I cannot **accept**
- **Je n'admets pas que** l'on me **dise** *(subj)* pour qui je dois voter
  = I will not **allow** ... to tell
- **Je nie (catégoriquement)** l'avoir jamais rencontré
  = I (categorically) **deny**

12.2 Disagreeing with a proposal

- **Il n'est plus possible de** travailler comme avant
  = it is no longer **possible** to
- **Il est impossible de** fixer un calendrier précis
  = it is **impossible** to
- **Je ne suis pas d'accord avec** ces changements
  = I do not **agree** with
- **Je ne suis pas d'accord pour que** le problème **soit** *(subj)* posé en ces termes
  = I do not **agree** that ... should be
- **Je crains fort de ne pouvoir approuver** cette décision *(written)*
  = I am afraid I cannot **approve**

More assertively

- **Je ne peux pas accepter** des injures
  = I cannot **accept**
- **Je suis contre** le protectionnisme
  = I am **against**
- **Je suis opposé à** toute censure
  = I am **opposed** to
- **Je refuse** son licenciement
  = I **refuse** to **allow**
- **Je refuse qu'**on diffuse *(subj)* cette séquence
  = I **refuse** to **allow**
- **Il est hors de question que** je le leur **dise** *(subj)*
  = it is out of the **question** that ... should tell
- **Je mettrai mon veto à** ce projet
  = I shall **veto**

12.3 Refusing a request

Tentatively

- **Je ne pourrai malheureusement pas** jouer ce soir
  = **unfortunately**, I won't be able to
- **Il m'est difficile de** procéder à une estimation
  = I find it **difficult** to
- **Je ne suis pas en mesure de** prendre de nouveaux engagements
  = I'm not in a **position** to

More assertively

- **Il est hors de question que nous** accep**tions** *(subj)*
  = it is out of the **question** that we should
- **Je refuse de** les faire travailler pour rien
  = I **refuse** to
- **Je n'accepterai pas d'**assumer cette responsabilité
  = I will not **agree** to

In writing

- **Il m'est (vraiment) impossible de** répondre à votre demande
  = it is (really) **impossible** for me to
- **Je dois malheureusement décliner** votre invitation
  = **unfortunately**, I must **decline**
- **Nous avons le regret de vous informer que vous ne pourrez** assister au procès
  = we **regret to inform you that you will be unable** to
- **Nous regrettons de ne pouvoir** donner suite à votre requête
  = we **regret** that we are **unable** to

- **Je regrette sincèrement de ne pas être en mesure d'**apporter les garanties réclamées
  = I sincerely **regret** that I am not in a **position** to
- **Je suis au regret de ne pouvoir** appuyer votre demande
  = I **regret** that I am **unable** to

13 APPROVAL

- **Quelle excellente idée !**
  = what an **excellent** idea!
- **Vous avez bien fait de** laisser vos bagages à la consigne de la gare
  = you were **right** to
- **J'ai bien aimé** la mise en scène de la pièce
  = I **liked**
- La mise en scène de la pièce **m'a beaucoup plu**
  = I **liked** ... very much
- **J'ai beaucoup apprécié** la gentillesse avec laquelle il a proposé de nous aider
  = I greatly **appreciated**
- Je pense que cette initiative de l'administration **est une très bonne chose**
  = is a very good thing
- **Je trouve que vous avez raison de** souligner cette différence
  = I think you are **right** to
- **Je trouve que vous n'avez pas tort de** chercher à étendre la gamme de vos produits
  = I think you are not wrong in
- **Nous sommes favorables à** la création d'emplois et au développement de l'activité portuaire
  = we are **favourable** to
- **Nous sommes en faveur d'**une solution négociée
  = we are in **favour** of
- **Le plus grand mérite de** ce petit livre pratique **est de** donner pour chaque cas des adresses uti es
  = the greatest **merit** of ... is to

More formally

- Tout renfort **est le bienvenu**
  = is **welcome**
- De nombreuses voix se sont, **à juste titre**, élevées pour protester contre cette scandaleuse manipulation
  = **rightly**
- Mon voisin de table reproche **avec raison** aux meilleures maisons de servir du thé en sachet
  = **rightly**
- **On ne peut qu'admirer** l'art avec lequel Oscar Wilde a mis en scène son destin
  = one cannot but **admire**
- **J'approuve sans réserve** les mesures prises par le ministre de l'Économie
  = I **approve** unreservedly
- **Nous apportons notre soutien aux** mesures prises par le secrétaire général des Nations unies
  = we give our **support** to

14 DISAPPROVAL

- **Tu n'aurais pas dû** lui parler sur ce ton
  = you shouldn't have
- **Vous auriez mieux fait de** partir sans rien dire
  = you would have done better to
- **Je désapprouve** toute discrimination, qu'elle frappe les femmes ou les minorités
  = I **disapprove** of
- **Je trouve qu'il a eu tort d'**emprunter tant d'argent
  = I feel he was **wrong** to
- **Je condamne** quiconque s'y oppose
  = I **condemn**
- **Je ne supporte pas** une telle arrogance
  = I can't **stand**
- **Je ne comprends pas comment on peut** fermer les yeux sur ce problème
  = I don't understand how people can
- **Je déplore** son manque de sérieux
  = I **deplore**
- **Je suis profondément déçu par** son attitude désinvolte
  = I am deeply **disappointed** by
- **Je proteste contre** la façon dont nous avons été traités
  = I **protest** against
- **Je suis farouchement opposé à** ce projet
  = I am fiercely **opposed to**
- **Je suis consterné d'apprendre que** personne n'est allé vous chercher à l'aéroport
  = I am **dismayed** to hear that
- Cette idée **me déplaît profondément**
  = I **dislike** ... intensely
- **On ne peut que regretter** une telle légèreté
  = ... is only to be **regretted**
- **Il est dommage que** nul ne se **soit** *(subj)* demandé si cet organisme ne pouvait pas continuer à travailler en province
  = it is a **pity** that
- **Il est regrettable que** cet aspect essentiel de la recherche **soit** *(subj)* à ce point délaissé par l'industrie pharmaceutique
  = it is **regrettable** that
- **De quel droit** la presse s'érige-t-elle en censeur ?
  = what gives ... the right to
- La qualité de ce produit **laisse à désirer**
  = leaves a lot to be desired

15 CERTAINTY, PROBABILITY, POSSIBILITY AND CAPABILITY

15.1 Expressing certainty

In an impersonal way

- **Il est certain que** les discussions ont été longues et parfois délicates
  = it is **certain** that
- **Il est évident que** la situation est loin d'être simple
  = **evidently**

- **Il ne fait aucun doute que** les gâteaux allégés vont connaître un réel succès
  = there is no **doubt** that
- **Il est indéniable que** nous vivons une période de moindre croissance
  = it is **undeniably** true that
- **Il est incontestable que** le président **a**, en la matière, un rôle important à jouer
  = ... **unquestionably** has
- **Il faut bien reconnaître que** nous utilisons souvent les locutions sans en connaître l'histoire ou le sens exact
  = one must **recognize** that
- **Il faut bien admettre que** le texte, là encore, n'est pas très clair
  = it has to be **admitted** that
- **De toute évidence**, on pourrait dépenser moins pour soigner aussi bien
  = quite **obviously**
- **Le doute n'est plus permis :** la reprise ne se manifestera pas à temps
  = there is no longer any **doubt:**
- **Il n'y a aucun doute** : il a réussi à avoir ce qu'il voulait, mais à quel prix ...
  = there is no **doubt** about it
- **Il va sans dire que** nous vous livrerons dès que possible
  = it goes without saying that

More directly

- **Je suis sûr** *or* **certain que** le facteur est déjà passé
  = I am **sure** or **certain** that
- Je suis **sûr** *or* **certain d'**avoir rangé cette facture dans ce tiroir
  = I am **sure** or **certain** that
- **J'ai la certitude qu'**il nous a menti
  = I am **certain** that
- **Je suis persuadé qu'**un changement d'air lui ferait le plus grand bien
  = I am **convinced** that

15.2 Expressing probability

- **Il est probable que** les résultats ne seront pas affichés avant demain matin
  = **probably**
- Les résultats ne seront **probablement** pas affichés avant demain matin
  = **probably**
- **Il a dû** tomber en panne *or* Il est **sans doute** tombé en panne
  = he **must** have
- **Vous devriez** recevoir ce chèque sous peu
  = you **should**
- Ce chèque **devrait** vous parvenir sous peu
  = **should**
- **On dirait que** le temps va changer
  = it looks as though
- **Je pense** prendre quelques jours de congé la semaine prochaine
  = I am thinking of
- **Il est bien possible qu'**il n'**ait** *(subj)* jamais reçu cette lettre
  = it is quite **possible** that
- **Il se pourrait bien qu'**il y **ait** *(subj)* des retards à cause de la grève
  = it is quite **possible** that
- **Il me semble que** l'on voit moins de boucheries chevalines à Paris
  = it **strikes** me that
- Il a changé de voiture, **paraît-il** *or* **à ce qu'il paraît**
  = it **seems**
- **Tout semble indiquer qu'**il s'agit des salariés qui manifestaient hier
  = everything **seems** to indicate that

15.3 Expressing possibility

- Il s'agit **peut-être** d'une erreur
  = **perhaps**
- **Il est peut-être** déjà trop tard pour téléphoner
  = **perhaps** it's
- **Peut-être qu'il est** déjà trop tard pour téléphoner
  = **maybe** it's
- La situation **peut** changer du jour au lendemain
  = can
- **Est-il possible qu'**il **ait** *(subj)* été arrêté sans que personne n'en ait rien su ?
  = is it **possible** that
- **Il n'est pas impossible qu'**il **ait** *(subj)* changé d'avis
  = it is not **impossible** that
- **Il se peut que nous** passions *(subj)* par Paris au retour
  = we **might**
- **Il se pourrait très bien qu'il** décide *(subj)* un jour de tout quitter
  = he **may** well

15.4 Expressing capability

- **Savez-vous** vous servir de la nouvelle machine ?
  = do you know how to
- **Il sait** nager
  = he **can**
- **Je comprends** le français
  = I **understand**
- **Je vois** un grand mur blanc
  = I **can** see
- **Je peux** investir jusqu'à mille francs
  = I **can**
- **J'arrive à** aller la voir deux ou trois fois par semaine
  = I **manage** to
- **Je peux tout juste** le comprendre
  = I **can** just
- Les candidats doivent **être capables de** traduire des textes scientifiques
  = be **capable** of
- **Il m'est possible de** me libérer pour 17 heures
  = I **could**
- **Nous sommes à même de** proposer des prix très bas
  = we are in a **position** to

16 DOUBT, IMPROBABILITY, IMPOSSIBILITY AND INCAPABILITY

16.1 Expressing doubt

In an impersonal way

- **On ne sait pas exactement** ce qui se passe durant ce processus
  = we don't **know exactly**
- Les traductions récentes **ne sont pas forcément** les meilleures
  = are not **necessarily**
- **Il n'est pas sûr qu'**elle *or* **Il n'est pas certain qu'**elle **soit** *(subj)* malade
  = we don't **know** for **sure** that
- **On ne sait pas au juste** qui a inventé cette façon de s'habiller
  = we don't **know exactly**
- **Le doute subsiste quant au** nombre exact des victimes
  = some **doubt** remains as to
- **Rien ne permet de penser qu'**il **soit** *(subj)* un mafieux
  = one has no **cause** to think that ... is

More directly

- **Je ne suis pas sûr** *or* **Je ne suis pas certain qu'**il y **ait** *(subj)* du monde ce soir
  = I am not **sure** or **certain** whether
- **Je ne suis pas sûr d'**avoir *or* **Je ne suis pas certain d'**avoir raison
  = I am not **sure** or **certain** if
- **Nous nous demandons si** nous devons accepter leurs propositions
  = we **wonder** if
- **Je doute fort qu'**ils t'**aient** *(subj)* cru
  = I very much **doubt** whether
- **Je doute de** sa sincérité
  = I **question**
- **Je doute de** l'avoir jamais vu
  = I **doubt** if
- **Nous sommes encore dans l'incertitude quant à** l'application de cet accord
  = we are still **uncertain** as to

16.2 Expressing improbability

- **Cela m'étonnerait que** l'on vous réponde *(subj)*
  = it would **surprise** me if
- **Elles ne risquent pas d'**avoir le prix Nobel d'économie
  = they are not **likely** to
- Il ne changera **probablement pas** d'avis
  = **probably** not
- **Il y a peu de chances que** ce programme **soit** *(subj)* réalisé
  = there is not much **chance** of
- **Il est peu probable qu'**il **ait** *(subj)* changé d'avis
  = it is **unlikely** that
- **Il serait étonnant que** ces déclarations **soient** *(subj)* entendues
  = it would be **surprising** if
- **Il ne semble pas que** les médecins lui **aient** *(subj)* administré des calmants
  = it does not **look** as if
- **Il n'est guère probable que** les négociations aboutissent *(subj)*
  = it is hardly **likely** that
- **Il est douteux que** ma proposition **soit** *(subj)* retenue
  = it is **doubtful** whether
- **Je crains fort que** nous n'arrivions *(subj)* pas à nous entendre
  = I very much **fear** that

16.3 Expressing impossibility

- **Il n'est pas possible que** *or* **Il est impossible que** les renseignements **soient** *(subj)* faux
  = it is not **possible** that or it is **impossible** that
- **Il n'y a aucune chance que** nous terminions *(subj)* cette traduction à temps
  = there is no **chance** of
- **Nous n'avons aucune chance de** trouver un emploi
  = we have no **chance** of
- Le trajet **n'est pas faisable** en voiture
  = **cannot** be done
- **Il ne peut s'agir de** la même personne
  = it **cannot** be
- **Il m'est impossible de** m'absenter la semaine prochaine
  = it is **impossible** for me to
- **Il est absolument exclu que** nous équilibrions *(subj)* nos comptes
  = it is absolutely out of the **question** that
- **Je suis malheureusement dans l'impossibilité de** tenir mes engagements
  = unfortunately, I am **unable** to

16.4 Expressing incapability

- **Je ne peux pas** tout contrôler
  = I **cannot**
- **Il ne sait pas** présenter les plats
  = he does not **know** how to
- **Je ne sais pas comment** la décrire
  = I do not **know** how to
- **Je n'arrive pas à** *or* **Je ne parviens pas à** trouver une explication
  = I **cannot (manage** to)
- **Il est incapable de** prendre une décision
  = he is **incapable** of
- **Il n'a pas les aptitudes requises pour** ce travail
  = he does not have the necessary **aptitude** for
- **Il m'est impossible de** jouer ce rôle
  = it is **impossible** for me to
- **Je suis dans l'impossibilité de** répondre
  = I am **unable** to

17 EXPLANATIONS

17.1 Emphasizing the reason for something

- C'est un endroit à la mode **à cause du** marché aux puces qui s'y est installé
  = **because** of
- Ils ont réussi à s'en sortir **grâce à** leur dynamisme
  = **thanks** to
- Je n'en ai pas parlé **parce que** le temps me manque
  = **because**
- Je suis très inquiet **car** nous n'avons pas commencé à discuter des solutions
  = **as**
- **Comme** il se faisait tard, elle a pris un taxi
  = **as**
- Le marché des changes est délocalisé, **puisque** les échanges se font par terminaux informatiques
  = **since**
- **Étant donné qu'**il *or* **Puisqu'**il n'est pas là, je dois faire son travail à sa place
  = **given** that *or* **since**
- **Vu** *or* **Étant donné** la situation actuelle, on ne peut pas espérer d'amélioration prochaine
  = **given**
- J'ai commencé à jouer du rock à seize ans. **Voilà pourquoi** je m'implique dans ce que je joue
  = that's **why**
- **La raison de son refus** *or* **La raison pour laquelle il a refusé, c'est qu'**il doit partir ce soir
  = the **reason** for his refusal or that he refused is that
- **C'est pour cette raison que** j'ai accepté d'y aller
  = it is for this **reason** that
- C'est la hausse du dollar qui **a provoqué** cette crise
  = has **brought** about

More formally

- Il était absent **pour raisons de** santé
  = for ... **reasons**
- Le vol AF232 a été retardé **en raison des** conditions météorologiques
  = **owing** to
- Les importations ont progressé **par suite de** l'ouverture des frontières
  = as a **result** of
- **C'est grâce à** l'émission **qu'**il a pu être identifié
  = it was **thanks** to ... that
- La bataille risque de s'arrêter **faute de** munitions
  = for **lack** of
- Le drame **vient de ce qu'**elle s'est habituée à vivre au-dessus de ses moyens
  = is the **result** of
- La violence **provient de** cette mise en scène brutale
  = comes from
- Son engagement politique **tient à** une philosophie
  = **stems** from
- L'affaire **remonte à** la plainte d'un automobiliste
  = goes back to
- Le retard **est lié à** des problèmes techniques
  = is **linked** to
- **Il attribue** ce résultat **à** la flexibilité du marché du travail
  = he **attributes** ... to
- **Étant donné que** les chiffres sont approximatifs, on ne peut se fier à ces résultats
  = given that

17.2 Emphasizing the result of something

- Je dois partir ce soir ; **je ne pourrai donc pas** venir avec vous samedi
  = **so** I won't be able to
- Le débat sur ce chapitre n'est pas achevé, **si bien que** les négociations ont de sérieuses chances de se poursuivre
  = **so** much **so** that
- Les erreurs de conception se sont accumulées, **de telle sorte que** le projet a pris un sérieux retard
  = **so** much **so** that
- Le sol de cette dépression est entièrement argileux, **par conséquent** imperméable
  = **consequently**
- Cette législation **a eu pour conséquence** d'encourager les mères à rester célibataires
  = has **resulted** in
- La haine **résulte de** l'incompréhension
  = is the **result** of
- Les grèves ont été nombreuses ces derniers mois ; **il en résulte que** la production a diminué dans ce secteur
  = as a **result**

18 APOLOGIES

18.1 Apologizing for one's actions

- **Excusez-moi d'**arriver en retard
  = **sorry** I
- **Pardonnez-moi de** dire une autre banalité
  = excuse me for
- **Je suis désolé qu'**on vous **ait** *(subj)* dérangé pour rien
  = I'm **sorry**
- **Je suis vraiment navré de** ce malentendu
  = I'm really **sorry** about
- **Je regrette de** vous contredire **mais** ce mot est bien d'origine espagnole
  = I'm **sorry** to ... but
- **Je reconnais que** ce rapport contient un certain nombre de termes inutilement agressifs
  = I **admit** that
- **Je vous prie d'excuser** le décousu de cette lettre
  = please **excuse**
- **Veuillez m'excuser de** vous déranger ainsi
  = please **excuse** me for
- **Soyez assuré que** cet incident ne se reproduira pas
  = let me **assure** you that
- **Nous tenons à vous présenter nos excuses pour** les difficultés que vous avez rencontrées
  = we wish to **apologize** for

18.2 Apologizing for being unable to do something

- **Je suis vraiment désolé de ne pas pouvoir** vous fournir immédiatement ces renseignements
  = I'm really **sorry** I can't
- **Il m'est malheureusement impossible d'**arriver avant 8 heures
  = **unfortunately**, it's **impossible** for me to
- **Je regrette infiniment mais** ce document ne peut être consulté que sur place
  = I am terribly **sorry** but
- **Nous regrettons de ne pouvoir** faire suite à votre demande *(written)*
  = we **regret** that we are **unable** to
- **J'ai le regret de ne pouvoir** accepter votre aimable invitation *(written)*
  = I **regret** that I am **unable** to
- **Nous sommes au regret de** vous informer que vous ne serez pas autorisé à assister au procès *(written)*
  = we **regret** to

18.3 Admitting responsibility

- Je me rends compte que **je n'aurais jamais dû** laisser la porte ouverte
  = I should never have
- **Je reconnais que j'ai eu tort de** lui communiquer votre adresse
  = I **admit** that I was **wrong** to
- **Si seulement je ne** leur **avais pas** déjà promis que nous passerions nos vacances avec eux !
  = if only I hadn't
- **J'accepte l'entière responsabilité de** cette affaire
  = I **accept** full **responsibility** for

18.4 Disclaiming responsibility

- **Je t'assure que je n'ai pas fait exprès de** déchirer la couverture de ce livre
  = I assure you I didn't ... on **purpose**
- **J'avais cru bien faire en** expédiant immédiatement ce chèque
  = I thought I was doing the right thing by
- **J'essayais simplement de** vous éviter des problèmes
  = I was simply trying to
- **Je suis sûr que vous comprendrez les raisons qui nous ont poussés à** augmenter nos tarifs
  = I'm sure you will understand the reasons we had to
- **Je ne voulais pas vous ennuyer** avec tous ces détails
  = I didn't want to trouble you
- **Je vous assure que je ne pouvais pas faire autrement**
  = I (can) assure you I could not do otherwise
- **J'avais pourtant cru comprendre que** je pouvais me garer devant la maison
  = but I thought
- **Vous comprendrez, j'espère, que** nous ne sommes pas responsables de ce retard qui est dû à la grève de la poste
  = I trust you will understand that
- **Permettez-moi au moins de vous expliquer** ...
  = at least allow me to **explain**

19 JOB APPLICATIONS

19.1 Starting the letter

- **Je me réfère à votre annonce** parue aujourd'hui dans le Quotidien du Midi, et **vous serais reconnaissant de bien vouloir m'envoyer des renseignements plus complets** sur ce poste, ainsi qu'un dossier de candidature
  = with **reference** to your **advertisement** ... I would be **grateful** if you would send me **further information**
- **Votre annonce** parue dans La Gazette Alsacienne **a retenu toute mon attention et je me permets de poser ma candidature pour le poste d'**ingénieur que vous offrez
  = I saw your **advertisement** ... and would like to **apply** for the **post** of
- Je souhaite vivement travailler en France pendant les vacances universitaires et **vous serais très reconnaissant de me faire savoir s'il me serait possible d'obtenir un emploi** dans votre société
  = I would be most **grateful** if you could tell me if there is any **possibility** of **work**

19.2 Detailing your experience and giving your reasons for applying

- **J'ai travaillé pendant trois ans comme** secrétaire de direction pour une société parisienne **et je maîtrise** divers traitements de texte et tableurs
  = I **worked** for three years as ... and have a good command of
- **Je travaille depuis cinq ans** dans une société d'import-export de New York, **ce qui m'a permis d'acquérir une connaissance approfondie des** techniques de vente et du marché américain
  = I have been **working** for five years ..., during which time I have acquired in-depth **knowledge** of
- **Je parle couramment anglais, j'ai de bonnes connaissances en allemand et je lis le suédois**
  = I speak fluent English, good German and have a reading **knowledge** of Swedish
- **Mon salaire actuel est de ... par an et j'ai cinq semaines de congés payés**
  = my current **salary** is ... per annum with five weeks' paid leave
- **Je suis désireux de travailler en France afin de perfectionner** mes connaissances en français **et d'acquérir** une certaine expérience de l'hôtellerie
  = I **wish to work** in France in order to perfect ... and to acquire
- **Un intérêt très vif pour** le domaine des télécommunications **m'incite à poser ma candidature pour** ce poste
  = I have a **keen interest** in ..., which is why I **wish** to apply for
- **Ma formation de** comptable **et mon expérience de** la gestion des stocks **m'incitent à penser que je suis à même de vous assurer une collaboration efficace pour ce poste**
  = I believe that my **training** as ... and my **experience** in ... make me particularly **suited** to this **position**

Jane FELDON
179 Curzon Road
London N10 4EA

Service du Personnel
International Bank
18, rue La Boétie
75008 Paris

Paris, le 20 mai 2002

Messieurs[1],

Suite à votre annonce dans *The Guardian* de ce jour, je vous propose ma candidature au poste de cambiste.

Vous verrez dans mon CV ci-joint que je viens d'obtenir mon diplôme de gestion, grâce auquel j'ai pu suivre un stage de six semaines au bureau des changes de la Bradley's Bank à Londres. Je ne doute pas que cette expérience et mon excellente connaissance des langues européennes me donnent précisément le profil requis par le poste à pourvoir au sein de l'International Bank. Par ailleurs, j'envisage très sérieusement de poursuivre ma carrière dans le milieu bancaire, et ce, particulièrement en France où je pourrai mettre à profit ma connaissance du français.

N'hésitez pas à me contacter pour de plus amples renseignements. Je suis à votre disposition pour un entretien dès que vous le souhaiterez.

Je vous prie de croire, Messieurs, à l'assurance de mes salutations distinguées,

Jane Feldon

Jane Feldon

P. J. : CV

[1] *This address is appropriate if you are writing to a company. However, if you are writing to the holder of a particular post, you should write:*

Monsieur le Directeur
des Ressources humaines
International Bank
18, rue La Boétie
75008 Paris

In this case, you should begin your letter with:
Monsieur le Directeur
des Ressources humaines,
and repeat this in the closing formula instead of **Messieurs.**

If you know the name of the person, you should write:
Monsieur Jean-Bertrand Raynaud
Directeur des Ressources humaines
International Bank *etc.*

Your letter should then begin:
Monsieur, ... *or* **Madame, ...**

See sections 20 - 21 *for more information on letter writing.*

19.3 Closing the letter

- **Je serai disponible à partir de** la fin du mois d'avril
  = I will be **available** from
- **Je demeure à votre entière disposition pour toute information complémentaire**
  = I would be delighted to supply any further **information** you may require
- **Je serai heureux de vous rencontrer lors d'un entretien** à la date qui vous conviendra
  = I will be happy to **attend** an **interview**
- **Je vous remercie dès à présent de** l'attention que vous voudrez bien porter à ma candidature
  = thank you in **advance** for
- **Dans l'attente de votre réponse**, je vous prie d'agréer, Monsieur le Directeur, l'expression de mes salutations distinguées
  = I look forward to hearing from you

19.4 Asking for and giving references

- Monsieur Jean Legrand sollicite un emploi de réceptionniste dans notre hôtel et a donné votre nom comme référence. **Nous vous serions reconnaissants de bien vouloir nous faire savoir si vous le recommandez pour ce poste**
  = we should be **grateful** if you could let us know if you would **recommend** him for this **position**
- **Votre réponse sera considérée comme strictement confidentielle**
  = your reply will be treated in the strictest **confidence**
- **C'est avec grand plaisir que je vous recommande** Madame Marion Lebrun pour le poste de responsable du logement
  = I can warmly **recommend**

CURRICULUM VITAE

GASTIN Sylvie

29, rue La Quintinie
75015 Paris
01 45 33 09 85 (répondeur)
Nationalité française
26 ans, mariée, 1 enfant

FORMATION[1]

1997 : Diplôme de secrétaire bilingue, délivré par l'École de commerce de Poitiers
1996 : Licence de langues étrangères appliquées (anglais et italien), Université de Poitiers - mention bien
1992 : Baccalauréat (langues) - mention assez bien

EXPÉRIENCE PROFESSIONNELLE

depuis 10/03/99 : Adjointe au Directeur du service Exportation, Agriventes, La Rochelle
08/10/97 - 30/01/99 : Secrétaire de direction, France-Exportations, Cognac

AUTRES RENSEIGNEMENTS

Langues étrangères : anglais (courant), italien (courant), espagnol (notions)
Stage d'informatique dans le cadre de la formation continue, 1999
Nombreux voyages aux États-Unis et en Italie
Permis de conduire

[1] *People with British or American qualifications applying for jobs in a French-speaking country might use some form of wording such as* **équivalence baccalauréat** *(3 A-levels)*, **équivalence licence de lettres** *(BA Hons) etc.*

19.5 Accepting and refusing

- Je vous remercie de votre lettre du 19 mars et **serai très heureux de me rendre à vos bureaux**, avenue Parmentier, **pour un entretien** le 12 mai à 15 heures
  = I will be glad to **attend** for **interview** at your offices
- **J'ai le plaisir de vous confirmer que j'accepte le poste** d'expert-comptable que vous m'offrez
  = I have pleasure in **confirming** my **acceptance** of the **post**
- **Votre offre m'intéresse très vivement mais je souhaiterais renégocier le salaire** que vous proposez avant de donner une réponse définitive
  = I am very interested in your **offer** but I would like to **renegotiate** the salary
- **Après examen très attentif de votre offre, je me vois malheureusement dans l'obligation de la décliner**
  = after giving it very careful **consideration**, I **regret** that I must **decline** your **offer**

20 COMMERCIAL CORRESPONDENCE

20.1 Making an enquiry

- **Nous avons remarqué dans votre annonce parue dans** le numéro de février de "Campagnes de France" **que** vous produisez une gamme d'articles de pêche
  = we note from your **advertisement** in ... that
- **Nous vous serions reconnaissants de** nous adresser *or* faire parvenir une documentation complète sur cette gamme, y

LA MAISON RUSTIQUE
FABRICATION DE MOBILIER
ZONE INDUSTRIELLE DE DAMPIERRE
B.P. 531 – 17015 DAMPIERRE CEDEX
TÉL: 05 06 28 42 37

V/Réf. - HL/SA 50746
N/Réf. - MB/AL 16064
Objet : envoi de documentation

Cuisines d'hier et d'aujourd'hui
3, place du Petit-Marché
16042 Nimeuil

Dampierre, le 3 novembre 2000

Messieurs,

Nous vous remercions de votre lettre du 30 octobre, ainsi que de votre demande de renseignements concernant notre gamme de sièges de cuisine.

Nous vous prions de trouver ci-joint une documentation complète, accompagnée de nos tarifs. Toutefois, nous nous permettons d'attirer votre attention sur nos nouveaux modèles « Saintonge », qui semblent convenir particulièrement à vos besoins. Ces modèles sont actuellement offerts à des prix très avantageux.

Nous nous tenons à votre entière disposition pour toute demande de renseignements supplémentaires et vous prions d'agréer, Messieurs, l'assurance de nos sentiments dévoués.

Le Directeur commercial

Jean Leclerc

Jean Leclerc

PJ : 1 documentation complète

compris vos tarifs actuels, les remises consenties et vos délais de livraison

= we should be **grateful** if you would

20.2 Replying to an enquiry

- **Suite à votre demande, nous avons le plaisir de** vous adresser notre dernier catalogue

  = **further** to your **request**, we have **pleasure** in
- **En réponse à** votre lettre du 10 juin, **veuillez trouver ci-joint** une documentation sur notre gamme de produits ainsi que notre liste de prix qui sont fermes jusqu'au 31 août

  = in **reply** to ..., please find **enclosed**
- **Si vous désirez** des renseignements plus précis, **n'hésitez pas à nous contacter**

  = if you require ..., please do not hesitate to contact us

20.3 Placing an order

- **Je vous remercie de** votre documentation et **vous serais obligé de** m'expédier les articles suivants dans les plus brefs délais

  = **thank** you for ... I should be **grateful** if you would
- **Veuillez trouver ci-joint** un bon de commande pour 500 articles Réf PS788

  = please find **enclosed**
- **Nous espérons que vous voudrez bien** nous consentir la remise de 10 % pour grosses quantités qui figure dans vos tarifs

  = we **trust** you will
- **Cette commande tient compte de** la remise de 10 % que vous consentez sur les commandes en gros

  = this **order** takes into account

Maison Duquesnois
Porcelaine et Orfèvrerie
14 rue Montpensier–84000 Poitiers

Madame Marianne Legrand
3, chemin des Princesses
16010 Granbourg

Poitiers, le 27 mai 2001

Madame,

Nous vous remercions de votre lettre du 21 mai, qui a retenu notre meilleure attention.

Malheureusement, nous ne suivons plus le modèle qui vous intéresse, et sommes donc au regret de ne pouvoir vous satisfaire.

Nous vous prions d'agréer, Madame, l'assurance de nos sentiments respectueux.

Le Directeur

Gérard Marquet

Gérard Marquet

20.4 Delivery

- **Nous vous remercions de votre commande** en date du 10 mai **que nous exécuterons dans les plus brefs délais**
  = thank you for your order ..., which will be **dispatched** as soon as possible
- **Nous procéderons à l'expédition de votre commande dès que possible**
  = we shall **deliver** your order as soon as possible
- **Nos délais de livraison sont de** cinq semaines à partir de la date de réception de la commande
  = our **delivery** times are
- **En raison d'**une pénurie de matières premières, **nous regrettons de ne pouvoir vous livrer avant** fin avril
  = owing to ... we **regret** that we are unable to **deliver** your order before

20.5 Complaining

- **Nous n'avons pas encore reçu livraison de** la commande que nous avons passée le 20 mars dernier (voir bon de commande n° 3496)
  = we have not yet had **delivery** of
- **Nous tenons à vous signaler que** les articles que vous nous avez livrés ne sont pas de la qualité habituelle
  = we wish to draw it to your attention that
- **Malheureusement,** les marchandises ont été endommagées en transit
  = unfortunately
- Les dix articles livrés **correspondent à** la référence LS59 de votre catalogue **et non à** la référence LS58 que nous avons commandée
  = correspond to ... and not to ...

20.6 Payment

- **Veuillez trouver ci-joint notre facture** d'un montant de ... relative à cet envoi
  = please find **enclosed** our **invoice**
- **Nous vous serions reconnaissants de nous faire parvenir cette somme dans les meilleurs délais**
  = we should be **grateful** if you would **remit payment** of this **sum** at your earliest convenience
- **Vous trouverez ci-joint un chèque d'un montant de** ... en règlement de votre facture n° HM307
  = please find **enclosed** a cheque for (the **sum** of)
- **Nous vous serions obligés de nous accorder un délai de paiement de 30 jours supplémentaires**
  = we should be **obliged** if you would extend the **payment due** date by 30 days
- **J'ai été très surpris de constater que vous me facturez** chaque article 39 € **au lieu des** 35 € mentionnés dans votre catalogue
  = I was very surprised to note that you had **invoiced** me ... instead of
- **Nous regrettons de devoir vous signaler une erreur qui s'est glissée dans votre facture**
  = we regret to have to point out that there has been an error in your **invoice**

21 GENERAL CORRESPONDENCE

21.1 Starting a letter

To a friend or acquaintance

- **Je te remercie de** ta lettre qui est arrivée ce matin
  = **thanks** for
- **J'ai été très contente d'avoir de tes nouvelles**
  = it was lovely to **hear** from you
- **Je suis désolé de ne pas vous avoir répondu plus vite** : je suis actuellement débordé de travail et n'ai que peu de moments de loisirs
  = (I'm) sorry I didn't **reply** earlier
- **Voilà bien longtemps que je ne vous ai pas donné de nouvelles.** C'est pourquoi je vous envoie un petit mot rapide
  = it's been ages since I was last in touch

In formal correspondence

- **Je vous serais reconnaissant de** me faire savoir si vous avez en librairie un roman intitulé ...
  = I would be **grateful** if you would
- **Je vous prie de** m'envoyer quatre exemplaires de votre numéro 310 et je joins à cette lettre un chèque d'un montant de ...
  = **please**
- **Suite à** notre conversation téléphonique de ce matin, **je vous écris pour** vous demander de bien vouloir m'expédier ...
  = **further** to ..., I am **writing** to
- **Ayant appris que** vous organisez des stages de voile, **je vous serais reconnaissant de me faire savoir** s'il vous reste des places pour débutants début juillet
  = I believe that ... and I would be **grateful** if you would let me know

21.2 Ending a letter (before the closing formulae)

- **Embrasse** Jérôme et Laure pour moi
  = **love** to
- Paul **vous embrasse** tous les deux
  = sends his **love** to
- **Dis bonjour à** Françoise pour moi
  = say **hello** to
- **Écris-moi** si tu trouves une petite minute
  = **write** to me
- **N'oublie pas de nous donner de tes nouvelles** de temps en temps
  = don't forget to give us your news
- **N'hésitez pas à m'écrire** si je peux vous être utile
  = do not **hesitate** to **write** to me
- **Transmettez**, s'il vous plaît, **mes amitiés à** votre sœur
  = give my **regards** to
- Hélène **me charge de vous transmettre ses amitiés**
  = asked me to give you her **regards**
- **Veuillez transmettre mon meilleur souvenir à** votre mère
  = please give my best **regards** to

21.3 Enquiring about and booking accommodation

- **Je vous serais reconnaissant de bien vouloir** m'envoyer les tarifs de vos chambres
  = I would be **grateful** if you would
- **Je désirerais** retenir une chambre avec douche
  = I wish to
- **Je voudrais** retenir une chambre pour deux personnes ainsi qu'une chambre à deux lits pour mes enfants
  = I would like to
- **Veuillez me faire savoir**, par retour du courrier si possible, **si** vous avez une chambre pour une personne en demi-pension pour la semaine du 4 au 11 juillet
  = please let me know ... if
- **Veuillez m'indiquer** le montant des arrhes que je dois verser pour la réservation
  = please **advise**
- **Veuillez confirmer** par télécopie la réservation suivante : une chambre à deux lits ...
  = please **confirm**
- **Il est possible que nous** arriv**ions** *(subj)* à une heure tardive
  = we might
- **Nous devrions normalement** arriver en début de soirée
  = we should

21.4 Confirming and cancelling a booking

- **Je vous confirme par ce courrier** ma réservation
  = this is to **confirm**

- Pour des raisons indépendantes de ma volonté, **je me vois contraint d'annuler** la réservation que j'avais faite au nom de ... pour la semaine du 4 au 11 juillet
  = I am obliged to **cancel**
- **Je vous serais reconnaissant de bien vouloir reporter ma réservation du** 3 septembre **au** 7 septembre
  = I would be **grateful** if you would **change** my **booking** from ... to

22 THANKS

- **Merci de** m'avoir fait confiance
  = **thank** you for
- **C'est vraiment très gentil de votre part de** nous avoir invités
  = it is really very **kind** of you to
- **Je vous remercie de** m'avoir réservé une place
  = **thank** you for
- **Remercie-le** de ma part **pour** son accueil
  = **thank** him ... for
- **Je ne sais comment vous remercier de** votre aide
  = I don't know how to **thank** you for
- **Je vous écris pour vous remercier de tout cœur d'**avoir pensé à nous
  = I am writing to express my **heartfelt thanks** for
- **Transmettez mes remerciements à** vos collègues
  = please **thank**
- **Nous vous sommes extrêmement reconnaissants d'**être venu
  = we are extremely **grateful** to you for
- **Je vous adresse mes plus vifs remerciements pour ...**
  = my most **sincere thanks** for ...
- **Je tiens à vous exprimer notre gratitude pour** le soutien que vous nous avez apporté
  = I wish to express our **gratitude** for

23 BEST WISHES

23.1 General expressions (used on special occasions only)

- **Meilleurs vœux** + *such expressions as* "de bonheur", "à l'occasion de votre départ en retraite", "de prompt rétablissement", "de réussite", *etc*
  = **best** wishes
- **Tous mes vœux** + *such expressions as* "de bonheur", "à l'occasion de votre départ en retraite", "de prompt rétablissement", "de réussite", *etc*
  = my **best** wishes
- **Je vous présente mes meilleurs vœux** à l'occasion de
  = I send you my **best** wishes
- **Transmettez-lui tous mes vœux de ...**
  = give him my **best** wishes for ...
- **Je vous souhaite de passer d'excellentes vacances**
  = I **hope** you have an excellent holiday
- **J'espère (de tout cœur) que vous ferez bon voyage**
  = I (really) **hope** you have a good trip

23.2 Season's greetings

NB: in France cards are usually sent for New Year rather than Christmas, and may be sent in the first few weeks of January

- **Joyeux Noël et Bonne Année !**
  = **Merry Christmas** and (a) **Happy New Year!**
- **Joyeuses fêtes !**
  = **Season's** Greetings!
- **Bonne et heureuse année !**
  = **Happy New Year!**
- Paul et moi **vous adressons tous nos vœux pour la nouvelle année** *(used at New Year only)*
  = send you our **best wishes** for the **New Year**
- **Je vous présente mes meilleurs vœux pour 2002**
  = I **wish** you all the **best** for 2002

23.3 Birthday greetings

- **Bon** *or* **Joyeux anniversaire !**
  = **Happy Birthday!**
- **Je vous souhaite un bon** *or* **un (très) joyeux anniversaire**
  = I **wish** you a (very) **happy birthday**

23.4 Get well wishes

- J'ai été désolé d'apprendre que vous êtes souffrant et **vous adresse tous mes vœux de prompt rétablissement**
  = I **wish** you all the **best** for a **speedy recovery**
- **Je vous souhaite** de tout cœur **un prompt rétablissement**
  = I **wish** you a **speedy recovery**
- **J'espère** de tout cœur **que vous serez très bientôt rétabli**
  = I **hope** you will be **better** soon

23.5 Wishing someone luck

- **Je vous adresse tous mes vœux de succès** dans votre nouvelle entreprise
  = I **wish** you every **success**
- **Je vous souhaite tout le succès que vous méritez** dans votre nouvelle carrière
  = I **wish** you all the **success** you rightly deserve
- **Je te souhaite bonne chance**, de notre part à tous, pour tes examens
  = I **wish** you good **luck**

23.6 Congratulations

- **Toutes mes félicitations pour** ton succès au permis de conduire
  = my **congratulations** on
- **Je vous félicite de tout cœur pour** votre succès
  = warmest **congratulations** on
- **Je vous adresse mes plus sincères félicitations pour** la réussite de votre projet
  = my most **sincere congratulations** on
- **Je tiens à te dire combien je suis heureux que** tu aies *(subj)* obtenu ce poste
  = I want you to know how **happy** I am that

Strasbourg, le 15 mars 2002

Chère Laurence,

Un grand merci pour le livre sur les poissons d'Europe que tu m'as envoyé. C'est exactement le type d'ouvrage qu'il me fallait : il devrait m'aider énormément dans mes recherches de traductions. Je ferai en sorte de te le rendre lors de mon passage à Angers courant juin, si du moins tu n'en as pas besoin d'ici là.

Es-tu toujours d'accord pour louer un bateau cet été ? Je te donnerai bientôt un coup de fil pour en parler.

Grosses bises,

Standard opening and closing formulae

Opening Formulae	Closing Formulae
Used when the person is not personally known to you	
Monsieur, Madame,	Je vous prie de croire, (...) à l'assurance de mes salutations distinguées.
Mademoiselle,	***used by a man only*** Veuillez agréer, (...), l'expression de mes sentiments les meilleurs. ***man to woman only*** Je vous prie d'accepter, (...), l'expression de mes respectueux hommages.
Used when the person is known to you personally	
Cher Monsieur, Chère Madame, Chère Mademoiselle,	Croyez, (...), à l'expression de mes sentiments les meilleurs.

To acquaintances and friends

Opening Formulae	Closing Formulae
Still fairly formal	
Cher Monsieur, Chère Madame, Chère Mademoiselle,	Recevez, je vous prie, mes meilleures amitiés. Je vous envoie mes bien amicales pensées. Je vous adresse à tous deux mon très amical souvenir.
Fairly informal: "tu" or "vous" forms could be used	
Cher Patrick, Chère Sylvie, Chers Chantal et Jean-Claude,	Bien amicalement Cordialement Amitiés

Orléans, le 23 février 2001

Chers Sophie et Daniel,

Voilà un bon moment que nous ne nous sommes pas vus : comment allez-vous ?

Je vous écris en fait pour vous demander un renseignement. En effet, nous avons l'intention de passer une semaine dans le Vaucluse en août et je me suis rappelé l'enthousiasme avec lequel vous parliez du gîte que vous aviez loué à Carpentras deux années de suite. Pourriez-vous m'en donner les coordonnées pour que je puisse éventuellement faire une réservation ?

J'espère que tout va bien à Brest et que nous nous reverrons bientôt.

Bien amicalement,

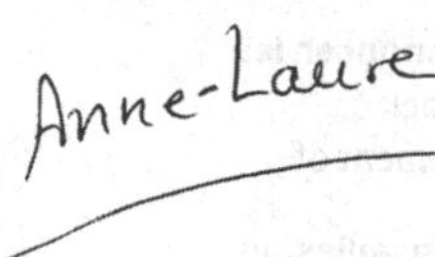

To close friends and family

OPENING FORMULAE	CLOSING FORMULAE
	"tu" or "vous" can be used, though "tu" is more likely in all these expressions.
Cher Franck, Chère tante Jacqueline, Mon cher Jean, Ma très chère Ingrid, Chers grands-parents, Mon cher cousin,	Je t'embrasse bien affectueusement Bien à toi Bien des choses à tous Bons baisers À bientôt Salut !

Writing to a firm or an institution (see also 20)

OPENING FORMULAE	CLOSING FORMULAE
Messieurs, *(to a firm)*	Je vous pr e d'agréer, (...), l'assurance de mes sentiments distingués.
Monsieur, *(to a man)*	Veuillez accepter, (...), l'expression de mes sentiments distingués.
Madame, *(to a woman)*	

To a person in an important position

OPENING FORMULAE	CLOSING FORMULAE
Very formal	
Monsieur le Directeur (*or* le Maire *etc*) Madame le Professeur (*or* le Consul *etc*)	Je vous prie d'agréer, (...) l'assurance de ma considération distinguée ***or, used by a man only :*** de mes sentiments respectueux *or* de mes sentiments dévoués.
Used only if the person is well known to you	
Cher Monsieur, Chère Madame,	Veuillez croire, (...), à l'assurance de mes sentiments les meilleurs. Je vous prie d'accepter, (...) l'expression de mes salutations distinguées. ***or, used by a man only :*** de mes sentiments distingués.
Cher collègue, Chère collègue, *(to someone in the same profession)*	***or, used by a man only :*** Croyez, (...), à l'assurance de mes sentiments les meilleurs.

- Je vous écris pour vous dire que **je me réjouis de votre succès**
  = I am **delighted** about your **success**

24 ANNOUNCEMENTS

24.1 Announcing a birth

- Claude et Anne-Marie Bernard **ont la joie de vous annoncer la naissance de** Maud, le 21 mars 2001 à Toulon
  = are **happy** to **announce** the **birth** of

- **J'ai le plaisir de t'annoncer que** Marie et Jean-Paul ont eu un petit garçon le 4 avril. Ils l'ont appelé Vincent. Tout s'est bien passé et la famille est ravie
  = I am delighted to tell you that

... and responding

- **Nous vous félicitons de l'heureuse arrivée de** Thérèse et souhaitons au bébé santé et prospérité
  = **congratulations** on the **arrival** of

- David et moi **sommes heureux d'apprendre la naissance de** Vincent et espérons faire bientôt sa connaissance
  = were delighted to learn of the **birth** of

24.2 Announcing an engagement

- Monsieur et Madame Simon **sont heureux d'annoncer les fiançailles de** leur fille Élodie avec M. Thomas Corbel
  = are pleased to **announce** the **engagement** of

- Élodie et Thomas **viennent d'annoncer leurs fiançailles.** Ils n'ont pas encore fixé la date du mariage mais nous nous réjouissons tous de leur bonheur
  = have just got **engaged**

... and responding

- **Nous nous réjouissons avec vous des fiançailles d'**Élodie et de Thomas. Transmettez tous nos vœux de bonheur aux jeunes fiancés
  = we are as delighted as you are about the **engagement** of

- **C'est avec beaucoup de joie que j'ai appris vos fiançailles avec** Thomas. Je vous adresse à tous deux mes vœux de bonheur les plus sincères
  = I was very **happy** to learn of your **engagement** to

24.3 Announcing a marriage

- Monsieur et Madame André Kervella **ont l'honneur de vous faire part du mariage de** leur fille Isabelle avec M. Christian Minguy
  = are **happy** to **announce** the **marriage** of

- **J'ai la joie de t'annoncer qu'**Isabelle et Christian **se sont mariés** samedi dernier. La cérémonie a eu lieu à l'église de Lanvéoc
  = I am pleased to tell you that ... got **married**

... and responding

- Monsieur et Madame Paul Gestin **félicitent** Monsieur et Madame André Kervella **à l'occasion du prochain mariage de** leur fille Isabelle
  = would like to **congratulate** ... on the **marriage** of ...

- **Nous présentons toutes nos félicitations aux jeunes mariés et leur souhaitons beaucoup de bonheur et de prospérité**
  = our **congratulations** and best **wishes** for happiness and prosperity to the young couple

- J'ai été très heureuse d'apprendre par ta lettre le mariage de Laetitia et de Yann. **Je leur souhaite tout le bonheur possible**
  = **I wish** them every possible **happiness**

24.4 Announcing a death

- M. et Mme Pierre Desmas et leurs enfants **ont la douleur de vous faire part du décès de** Mme Joseph Benard née Marie-Anne Chevalier
  = **regret** to **announce** the **death** of

- **Nous avons la grande tristesse de vous faire part du décès de** notre mère, survenu soudainement le 8 septembre. Le service religieux et l'inhumation ont eu lieu dans la plus stricte intimité
  = it is with deep **sorrow** that we **announce** the **death** of

- **C'est avec beaucoup de peine que je t'écris pour t'annoncer que** mon père est décédé la semaine dernière
  = I am very **sad** to have to write and tell you that

... and responding

- **J'ai été bouleversé d'apprendre** la disparition de ta sœur
  = I was terribly **upset** to hear about ...

- **Je tiens à te dire combien je pense à toi en ces moments douloureux**
  = I'd like you to know that I am **thinking** of you at this **sad** time

- Monsieur et Madame Paul Lambert **vous prient d'accepter l'expression de leur plus profonde sympathie et vous adressent leurs plus sincères condoléances à l'occasion du deuil** qui vient de vous frapper *(formal)*
  = send their deepest **sympathy** and offer you their most sincere **condolences** on your **loss**

24.5 Announcing a change of address

- **Nous vous prions de bien vouloir noter que notre nouvelle adresse sera,** à partir du 10 décembre 2001 : 10 rue Colbert, 29200 Brest
  = we wish to **inform** you that our new **address** will be

25 INVITATIONS

25.1 Formal invitations

- Madame Paul Lambert et Madame Michel Potet **recevront après la cérémonie religieuse** au Relais des Glycines, route de Marleroy, Fontanes. RSVP
  = **request** the **pleasure** of your **company** afterwards
- Les éditions Roget **ont le plaisir de vous inviter à** un cocktail à l'occasion de la sortie du premier livre de la collection Espoir, le lundi 9 août à partir de 18 h 30
  = have **pleasure** in **inviting** you to
- Monsieur et Madame André Bureau **prient Madame Labadie de leur faire le plaisir de venir dîner le** mercredi 27 octobre à 20 heures
  = **request** the **pleasure** of the **company** of Mme Labadie at dinner on
- **Pour les 20 ans de sa fille Joséphine, Madame Gérard Lamarche recevra chez elle**, le 24 novembre à partir de 19 h
  = Madame Gérard Lamarche has **pleasure** in **inviting** you to **celebrate** her daughter Josephine's 20th birthday

… and responding

- Monsieur Pierre Quentin **regrette profondément de ne pouvoir assister au** vin d'honneur organisé à l'occasion du mariage de Paul et Nathalie, d'autres obligations ne lui permettant pas de quitter Paris
  = very much **regrets** that he cannot **attend**
- Mademoiselle Charlotte Leblanc **accepte avec grand plaisir de se rendre au** cocktail organisé le 9 août par les éditions Roget
  = has great **pleasure** in **accepting** your **invitation** to
- Madame Jeanne Labadie **remercie** Monsieur et Madame André Bureau **de leur aimable invitation à** dîner **qu'elle accepte avec le plus grand plaisir/qu'elle regrette vivement de ne pouvoir accepter** en raison d'un autre engagement
  = **thanks** … for their **kind invitation**, which she is **delighted** to **accept**/deeply **regrets** she is **unable** to accept
- Monsieur Jacques Dalbret **assistera avec plaisir à** la réception organisée à l'occasion des 20 ans de Joséphine
  = will be **happy** to **attend**

25.2 Less formal invitations

- **Est-ce que cela te dirait d'**aller passer la journée à Nantes ? *(spoken)*
  = would you **like** to
- Pour fêter les fiançailles de Geneviève et de Xavier, nous organisons une réception à l'Hôtel de France, à Saint-Martin le 2 septembre à 20 heures et **serions très heureux si vous pouviez vous joindre à nous**
  = would be **delighted** if you could **join** us
- Michèle et Philippe doivent venir déjeuner dimanche prochain et **nous espérons que vous pourrez être des nôtres**
  = we **hope** you can **join** us
- Lorsque vous passerez à Lyon, **vous nous feriez très plaisir si vous pouviez nous consacrer une soirée** pour que nous dînions ensemble
  = we would be **delighted** if you could spend an evening with us
- Nous projetons de passer le mois de juillet à Montpellier et **serions très heureux de vous y accueillir** quelques jours
  = we would be very **happy** to have you

… and responding

Accepting

- **Je vous remercie de** votre aimable invitation **et me fais une joie de venir** à votre réception
  = **thank** you for … I am looking forward to coming
- **Je viendrai avec plaisir** déjeuner avec vous dimanche prochain
  = I will be **happy** to come
- Nous pensons passer le week-end de la Pentecôte à Lyon et **nous vous téléphonerons pour essayer de vous voir**
  = we will call you to see if we can meet up
- **Votre invitation** à Montpellier **nous a fait très plaisir et nous espérons passer un week-end avec vous** vers le 14 juillet
  = we were **delighted** to receive your **invitation** … and **hope** to spend a weekend with you

Declining

- **C'est très gentil à vous de m'inviter** à votre soirée de samedi, **mais je me vois malheureusement obligé de refuser**, car j'ai déjà accepté une invitation ce soir-là
  = it was very kind of you to **invite** me … but I am afraid I have to **decline**
- **J'aimerais beaucoup passer un week-end chez vous, mais malheureusement,** aucune des dates que vous me proposez ne me convient
  = I would love to spend a weekend with you but **unfortunately**
- **Malheureusement, je ne peux pas me libérer** le mois prochain. Peut-être pourrions-nous nous voir en octobre ?
  = **unfortunately**, I can't get away

26 ESSAY WRITING

26.1 The broad outline of the essay

Introductory remarks

- **Tout le monde s'accorde à penser que** le chômage est un des principaux maux de notre société. **Il convient donc d'examiner** les mesures qui pourraient être prises pour le combattre
  = everyone **agrees** that … So we should **examine**
- Peut-on lire l'œuvre d'un philosophe quand on sait qu'il a été nazi ? **Telle est la question soulevée par** l'article de …
  = such is the **question raised** by

- **Il est bien connu que** la voiture pollue. **La question est de savoir si** nous pourrions un jour nous passer de ce mode de transport
  = it is a well-known **fact** that ... The **question** is whether
- Les adolescents d'aujourd'hui ne lisent pas beaucoup. **Ceci est interprété tantôt comme** une crise passagère, **tantôt comme** un signe du déclin du message imprimé
  = some **interpret** this as ..., others as ...
- **Nous vivons dans un monde où** la paix est constamment menacée
  = we live in a world in which
- **Un problème souvent évoqué** *or* **dont il est souvent question est celui de** la corruption des milieux d'affaires
  = a much-discussed **problem** is that of
- **L'histoire nous fournit de nombreux exemples de** génies incompris à leur époque puis reconnus par la postérité
  = history provides us with countless **examples** of
- **Cette question est depuis longtemps au cœur du** débat sur l'éducation
  = this **question** has long been at the **heart** of

Developing the argument

- **La première constatation qui s'impose, c'est que** le roman va au-delà d'une simple enquête policière
  = the first **point** to note is that
- **Prenons comme point de départ** le rôle que le gouvernement a joué dans l'élaboration de ces programmes
  = **let** us take ... as a **starting point**
- **En premier lieu, examinons** ce qui fait obstacle à la paix
  = **firstly, let us examine**
- **Il serait utile d'examiner** la façon dont l'auteur a abouti à ces conclusions
  = it would be useful to **examine**
- **Il convient tout d'abord de se pencher sur** les circonstances de la parution de ce livre
  = it is worth first of all turning one's **attention** to
- **Selon l'auteur**, la psychanalyse **ne serait pas** un obstacle à la créativité
  = **according** to the author ... isn't
- **Il est significatif que** ce conflit **soit** *(subj)* le produit d'une politique africaine moderne
  = it is **significant** that ... is
- **Pour illustrer** l'association lucrative des vedettes de sport et des grandes entreprises, **il suffit de prendre un exemple**
  = in order to **illustrate** ... we only need to take an **example**
- Un second exemple **marque l'importance de** ce thème
  = **underlines** the importance of
- Un examen des origines de la laïcité **nous permettra peut-être de mieux comprendre** les bases de ce conflit
  = will perhaps **allow** us better to understand

The other side of the argument

- **Après avoir étudié** la progression de l'action, **considérons maintenant** le style
  = after **studying** ... **let** us now **consider**
- **Il faut maintenant s'interroger sur** la motivation de l'auteur dans le choix du contexte historique
  = one must now **question**
- **Venons-en maintenant à** l'analyse des retombées politiques
  = now **let** us come to
- **Ce qui vaut pour** le héros **s'applique également aux** personnages secondaires
  = what goes for ... **applies equally** to
- **Il convient maintenant d'analyser** les arguments de ceux qui préconisent une législation plus stricte
  = it is worth now **analyzing**
- Le principe de laïcité de l'enseignement est-il compatible avec le port de certains signes religieux ? **C'est ce que nous allons étudier dans la seconde partie de cette analyse**
  = ... is what we are going to study in the second part of this **analysis**
- **Plus encore que** la pollution, **c'est** le bruit qui provoque la colère de nombreux citadins
  = even more than ... it is
- **On pourrait objecter que** l'œuvre littéraire n'est pas séparable de son contexte
  = one could **object** that

The balanced view

- **Au terme de cette analyse, il faut cependant faire remarquer que** le chômage n'est pas le seul facteur en cause. **Il faudrait également examiner** ...
  = at the end of this **analysis**, it is, **however**, necessary to **point** out that ... It is **equally** necessary to **examine**
- **Mais le meilleur moyen de** limiter la pollution, **c'est encore d'**examiner comment on pourrait réduire les transports routiers
  = but the best way of ... is to
- **Enfin, il faut nous poser cette question** : la famine est-elle vraiment une fatalité ?
  = **finally,** we must ask ourselves whether

In conclusion

- **Quelles conclusions tirer de cette analyse ?**
  = what **conclusions** can be drawn from this **analysis**?
- **Le problème se résume donc à ceci :** dans un monde dominé par l'audiovisuel, le théâtre a-t-il encore une chance de survivre ?
  = the **problem**, then, **boils** down to this:
- L'expérience des dix dernières années **prouve** *or* **démontre que** le travail des organisations bénévoles n'est pas vain mais qu'il ne suffit pas
  = **proves** or **demonstrates** that
- **En dernière analyse**, c'est l'identité personnelle dans ce qu'elle a de plus secret qui est menacée
  = in the final **analysis**
- **En somme**, c'est la singularité du style qui constitue l'originalité profonde de l'auteur
  = in short
- **En définitive**, les réformateurs devraient mieux prendre en compte les leçons des expériences passées
  = when all is **said** and done

26.2 Constructing a paragraph

Assessing an idea

- **On peut avancer** plusieurs arguments différents
  = one can **put** forward
- **Plusieurs arguments viennent renforcer** cette idée
  = there are several **arguments** in **support** of
- **Examinons** les origines du problème **ainsi que** certaines des solutions suggérées
  = let us **examine** ... as well as
- **On peut noter** *or* **mentionner en passant que** l'auteur ne fait jamais allusion à ce problème
  = it may be **noted** or **mentioned** in passing that
- **Sans nous appesantir** *or* **nous attarder sur les détails, notons toutefois que** le rôle du Conseil de l'ordre a été déterminant
  = without dwelling on the details, let us **note**, **however**, that
- **Comme nous le verrons plus en détail par la suite**, ce sont surtout les personnages secondaires qui font progresser l'action
  = as we shall see in more detail later
- **Nous reviendrons plus loin sur cette question, mais signalons déjà** l'absence totale d'émotion dans ce passage
  = we shall come back to this **question** later, but let us **point** out at this stage
- **Avant d'aborder** la question du style, **mentionnons brièvement** le choix des métaphores
  = before **tackling** ... let us **mention** briefly

Establishing parallels

- **D'une part**, il y a des problèmes financiers et **d'autre part**, il y a des problèmes humains
  = on the one **hand** ... on the other (**hand**)
- Les préjugés anticommunistes **d'un côté**, anticapitalistes **de l'autre** ne sont pas morts
  = on the one **hand** ... on the other (**hand**)
- **Les premiers** disposent du pouvoir. **Les seconds** font la grève
  = the **former** ... the **latter** ...
- L'Éducation nationale fait l'objet de critiques continuelles et **il en va de même pour** la Sécurité sociale
  = the **same** is true of
- **De même que** les étudiants se demandent à quoi leurs études vont leur servir, **de même**, les professeurs s'interrogent sur leur rôle
  = in the **same** way that ... so, too ...
- **Nous ne pouvons dissocier** ce facteur **de** la décision mentionnée plus haut
  = we cannot **dissociate** ... from
- **Nous reprenons ainsi une idée suggérée antérieurement**
  = thus, we are again taking up an idea suggested earlier

Adding or detailing

- **De plus**, il s'agit là d'un progrès tout à fait remarquable
  = what is **more**
- **En outre**, il faut noter que les employés sont mal payés
  = **furthermore**
- Il faut **également** dire que le népotisme est parfois encouragé par les entreprises elles-mêmes
  = **equally**
- **Ajoutons à cela** *or* **Il faut ajouter à cela** *or* **À cela s'ajoute** un sens remarquable du détail
  = let us **add** to this or **added** to this
- **À cet égard** *or* **À ce propos**, il faut noter une détérioration dans la qualité de l'enseignement
  = in this respect or in this connection
- **De même**, on pourrait suggérer que le style de l'auteur manque d'originalité
  = by the **same token**
- **D'ailleurs**, la Russie veut croire que sa contribution permettrait de rendre le système plus efficace
  = **moreover**
- **Pour ce qui est des** personnages secondaires, ils sont, eux aussi, remarquablement vivants
  = as for the
- **En ce qui concerne** la pollution chimique, il faut reconnaître qu'elle constitue aussi un grave danger
  = as far as ... is **concerned**
- **Quant aux** émissions sportives, elles suivent toujours le même modèle précis
  = as for the
- Plusieurs catégories professionnelles ont été oubliées, **notamment** *or* **parmi lesquelles** les employés de bureaux et les réceptionnistes
  = **notably** or including
- **Ces enfants** d'origine étrangère **connaissent** parfois **de graves problèmes** de scolarité, **problèmes qui** doivent retenir toute l'attention des enseignants
  = these children ... have serious problems ..., which

Enumerating

- Différentes formules sont offertes au client : voyage à forfait **ou bien** hébergement chez l'habitant, **ou encore** demi-pension, **ou enfin** camping dans un village de vacances
  = or ... or even ... or **finally**
- Faut-il inclure dans les statistiques les handicapés ? **Ou bien** doit-on exclure les jeunes ? **Ou encore** est-il nécessaire d'analyser le mode de vie en plus des revenus ?
  = or ... or even ...
- **Du** parti communiste **à** l'extrême droite, **tous** sont d'accord pour condamner cet acte de terrorisme
  = from ... to ..., all ...
- **Parmi** ces grands auteurs, on peut citer **(tout) d'abord** Racine, **ensuite** Corneille, **enfin** Molière
  = amongst ... first (of all) ... then ... and **finally**
- **En premier lieu**, il convient d'examiner attentivement chaque offre, **puis** il faut sélectionner les plus intéressantes **et, en dernier lieu,** entrer en contact avec les différents candidats
  = in the first **instance** ... then ... and **finally**
- Ceci est dû essentiellement à trois facteurs : **premièrement**, l'originalité du projet, **deuxièmement**, la rapidité avec laquelle il a été réalisé, **troisièmement**, la faiblesse des coûts
  = **firstly** ... **secondly** ... **thirdly**

Opposing

- Nombreux sont les régimes autoritaires qui ont bénéficié à l'origine du soutien de la majorité de la population. **Néanmoins**, ces régimes ont mal vieilli
  = **nevertheless**
- Ces éléments militent en faveur de l'apparition de plusieurs conventions collectives dans les milieux sportifs. **Cependant**, chacun le pressent : les enjeux ne sont pas que sociaux
  = **however**
- **Malgré** ses airs d'enfant de chœur, cet homme fut un redoutable chef de guerre
  = **despite**
- **Malgré tout**, il est impossible de nier que le système néerlandais est coûteux
  = **despite** everything
- **En dépit de** ces maladresses, le spectacle possède un charme indéniable
  = **despite**

Introducing one's own point of view

- **À mon avis** *or* **Selon moi** *or* **D'après moi**, ce chapitre est le meilleur du livre
  = in my **opinion**
- **En ce qui me concerne** *or* **Pour ma part**, je déplore l'évolution actuelle de la politique sociale
  = as far as I am **concerned**
- **Personnellement**, ce qui me frappe le plus dans cette affaire, c'est que l'origine de ces fonds est encore inexpliquée
  = **personally**
- **Je suis d'avis que** la télévision a un effet néfaste sur l'éducation des enfants
  = I am of the **opinion** that
- **Je soutiens qu'**on n'a jamais répondu clairement aux questions posées
  = I **maintain** that
- **Je pense que** l'auteur fait ici preuve d'ironie
  = I think

Introducing someone else's point of view

- **Selon l'auteur** *or* **D'après l'auteur,** le motif principal du crime est la jalousie
  = **according** to the author
- **Comme le soulignent** les experts, il est nécessaire de réduire les coûts de production de 7 %
  = **as ... stress**
- **Comme le laisse entendre** l'auteur, certains détails n'ont pas été révélés au public
  = **as** ... gives us to understand
- Le budget du ministère est, **dit-il** *or* **affirme-t-il**, conforme aux prévisions
  = he **says** or affirms
- **Il dit/pense/croit/affirme/déclare que** ce système présente de nombreux avantages
  = he **says/thinks/believes/maintains/declares** that
- L'auteur **attire notre attention sur** l'ampleur de ce changement
  = draws our **attention** to
- **Il nous rappelle** les bouleversements qui ont suivi ce projet de loi
  = he **reminds** us of
- **Il insiste sur le fait que/souligne que/soutient que** ces rivalités internes sont la principale cause de l'échec du mouvement
  = he insists on the fact that/**stresses** that/ **maintains** that
- **Elle prétend que** ce travail ne nécessite aucune recherche
  = she **claims** that
- **Il voudrait nous faire croire que** cette rébellion n'a eu aucune conséquence grave
  = he would have us **believe** that
- **Selon la version officielle**, l'épidémie est maintenant endiguée
  = **according** to the official version

Introducing an example

- **Prenons le cas de** Louis dans "le Nœud de vipères"
  = (let us) take the **case** of
- **Il suffit de prendre pour exemple** le cinéma muet des années vingt
  = one needs only take as an **example**
- Le cas de l'agroalimentaire **en est un exemple frappant**
  = is a striking **example** of this
- L'augmentation de la délinquance **illustre bien** les conséquences de cette crise chez les jeunes
  = is a good **illustration** of

Introducing a quotation or source

- **Selon** *or* **D'après** les auteurs du rapport, "l'important n'est pas de nourrir l'Afrique mais de la faire reverdir"
  = **according** to
- "La raison du plus fort est toujours la meilleure", **constate/ affirme/observe** La Fontaine
  = **notes**/asserts/**observes**
- **Comme l'a fait remarquer** le président, "la croissance économique dépend du taux d'investissement"
  = **as** ... pointed out
- Chénier **avait écrit :** "l'art ne fait que des vers, le cœur seul est poète" et Musset **reprend la même idée lorsqu'il dit :** "Ah, frappe-toi le cœur, c'est là qu'est le génie"
  = had written: ... echoes the **same** idea when he says:
- **Selon les paroles de** Duhamel, "le romancier est l'historien du présent"
  = in the **words** of
- Dans un article récemment publié dans le journal "Le Temps", **nous trouvons cette remarque de** Gordon Thomas : "..."
  = we find this remark by
- Dans son étude sur le folklore vendéen, Jean Dumur **observe** ...
  = **observes**

Concluding

- **De toute façon**, nous sommes au pied du mur
  = in any case
- **Bref** *or* **En un mot**, il refuse de se prononcer
  = **basically** or in a **word**

- **En somme**, il faut nuancer cette affirmation
  = **in short**
- Il convient de signaler, **pour conclure**, l'exceptionnelle qualité des textes retenus
  = **in conclusion**
- **En définitive**, ce dont le monde a besoin c'est d'un style de vie et de consommation plus sobre
  = when all is **said** and done

26.3 The mechanics of the argument

Stating facts

- **Il est exact que** les trains arrivent en général à l'heure, sauf quand il gèle
  = it is **true** that
- **On constate** chez les cadres une forte motivation
  = ... is **noticeable**
- **On observe** un repli sur les valeurs sûres
  = ... can be **observed**
- **On peut noter que** l'essentiel des dépenses de santé est financé par des cotisations sociales
  = we can **see** that
- Ce mode de calcul des rémunérations **fait l'objet de** négociations entre patronat et syndicats
  = is the **object** of
- **Il s'agit d'**une mesure de défense prise face à une initiative jugée hostile
  = it is a
- **Rappelons les faits**. Victoria l'Américaine débarque à Londres en 1970 et réussit rapidement à s'imposer sur la scène musicale
  = let's **recall** the **facts**
- Le New York Times **rapporte que** l'islam est la religion qui connaît aujourd'hui la plus forte croissance aux États-Unis
  = **reports** that

Making a supposition

- Si on trouve ces fossiles à l'intérieur des terres, **on peut supposer que** jadis la mer recouvrait cette région
  = one can **assume** that
- **Il est peu probable que** la diminution de l'ensoleillement dans la région **ait** *(subj)* eu des conséquences sur la croissance des plantes
  = it is **unlikely** that
- **Il pourrait y avoir** une guerre commerciale si nous n'instaurons pas le libre accès aux marchés
  = there **could** be
- Dans les milieux diplomatiques, **on évoque la possibilité d'**un durcissement de l'embargo
  = there is **mention** of the **possibility** of
- L'ampleur des destructions **permet de penser que** d'énormes quantités d'essence ont pris feu
  = **leads** us to **think** that
- Le film **laisse supposer que** tout peut devenir spectacle
  = would have one **suppose** that

Expressing a certainty

- **Il est certain que** le chômage contribue à alimenter l'exclusion
  = it is **certain** that
- **Il est évident que** toutes les régions devront jouer leur rôle sur le plan national
  = it is **obvious** that
- La partie la plus originale de son livre réside **incontestablement** dans son analyse des arts populaires
  = **indisputably**
- Il existe **indéniablement** un art de penser, de vivre, qui est commun à toute l'Europe
  = **undoubtedly**
- **Il est indéniable que** c'est un problème
  = it cannot be **denied** that
- **Tout le monde s'accorde à penser que** le conflit est loin d'être fini
  = **everyone agrees** that
- **Il ne fait aucun doute qu'**il a du talent
  = there is no **doubt** that
- **Il est clair que** cette maison est inhabitée depuis des mois
  = **clearly**

Expressing doubt

- **Il semble que** quelqu'un a essayé d'entrer par la fenêtre
  = it **seems** that
- **Il est possible** *or* **Il se peut que** je me **sois** *(subj)* trompé
  = it is **possible** that
- **Peut-être** est-ce *or* C'est **peut-être** une meilleure idée
  = **perhaps**
- L'auteur s'est **sans doute** inspiré de contes orientaux
  = **probably**
- Les rebelles **se seraient regroupés** près de la ville, **ce qui expliquerait** la psychose de peur qui prévaut encore
  = **allegedly** regrouped ..., which would **explain**
- Chaque témoignage **remet en question** ce qui paraissait établi quelques minutes plus tôt
  = **calls** back into **question**

Conceding a point

- Écrire un texte sans la lettre "e" semble une gageure impossible. **C'est pourtant** la règle qu'il s'impose pour tout un roman
  = and yet it is
- Les héritiers ont du mal à se mettre d'accord. Ils sont **toutefois** unanimes sur un point : la propriété restera dans la famille
  = **however**
- **Bien qu'**étudiés *or* **Quoique** étudiés depuis de nombreuses années, les cyclones tropicaux comportent encore beaucoup d'inconnues
  = **though**
- **Bien que** quelques blindés **aient** *(subj)* pris position dans la ville, la situation est restée relativement calme
  = **although**
- On ne sait pas grand-chose de son enfance. **Toujours est-il qu'**il entre en apprentissage alors qu'il n'a pas quinze ans
  = the **fact** remains that
- **Quel que soit** *(subj)* le style retenu pour la mise en scène, l'atmosphère de la pièce est toujours un peu lugubre
  = **whatever**

- **On ne peut nier que** l'intrigue **soit** *(subj)* quelque peu compliquée
  = it cannot be **denied** that
- **Le moins que l'on puisse** *(subj)* **dire est qu'**entre les principales organisations professionnelles agricoles, le courant ne passait pas
  = the **least** one can say is that
- Ces faits sont **sans doute** vrais, **mais** restent quand même peu crédibles
  = no **doubt** ... but
- **Certes** un encart publicitaire coûte très cher, **mais** il permet de mieux vendre
  = **certainly** ... but
- **Tout en reconnaissant que** les grands ensembles ont permis de loger des milliers de sans-abri, **il faut néanmoins admettre que** les conditions de vie y sont souvent déplorables
  = while **recognizing** that ... one must, **however, admit** that
- La mort de ce coureur automobile, **pour** tragique **qu'**elle **soit** *(subj)*, donne à réfléchir sur ce qui pousse certains à risquer leur vie
  = ... **though** it may be
- Si on supposait depuis longtemps qu'il y avait eu corruption, **ce n'est que récemment que** les archives ont confirmé ces suppositions
  = it is only recently that

Emphasizing particular points

- **Il convient de souligner** l'importance de ces recherches
  = it is **worth stressing**
- **Il faut bien préciser que** ce produit est commercialisé depuis des années
  = it is **important** to **point** out that
- **C'est à ce niveau qu'**il faut chercher des solutions
  = it is at this level that
- **C'est une question de** temps et non pas d'argent
  = it is a **question** of
- Ce dossier délicat **met en lumière** les oppositions entre la nécessaire maîtrise des dépenses de santé et la diffusion souhaitable des innovations thérapeutiques
  = **brings** to **light**
- Peu de gens ont vu cette émission, **d'autant plus qu'**elle est passée tard le soir
  = **especially since**
- Il est important de se faire vacciner contre le tétanos, **à plus forte raison lorsque** l'on manipule régulièrement des objets rouillés
  = and all the **more so** when
- **Bien loin de** renier ses origines, il n'avait jamais rompu ses liens avec sa patrie
  = far from
- Quel choc pour les spectateurs ! **Non (pas) que** le film **soit** *(subj)* sanglant, **mais** son crescendo est redoutable
  = not that ... is ... but
- **Non seulement** les objectifs ont été atteints, **mais** ils ont été dépassés
  = not only ... but
- Ce plat délicieux, facile à préparer, économique **qui plus est**, a tout pour nous séduire
  = and **moreover**

- **J'irais même jusqu'à dire que** c'est un chef-d'œuvre
  = I would even go **so** far as to say that
- **N'oublions pas que**, sur Terre, la gravité pilote absolument tous les phénomènes
  = let us not **forget** that
- De l'enthousiasme : **voilà précisément ce qui** leur fait défaut
  = that's **precisely** what

Moderating a statement

- **Sans vouloir critiquer** cette façon de procéder, **il semble cependant qu'**une autre méthode pourrait avoir de meilleurs résultats
  = I have no wish to **criticize** ... but it **seems** that
- L'auteur a certainement raison **dans l'ensemble, mais certains détails mériteraient d'être revus**
  = ... on the **whole**, but some details require to be reviewed
- **Une mise au point serait souhaitable**
  = some clarification would be desirable
- **Sans attacher trop d'importance à ces détails, il semble pourtant qu'**une révision du texte serait utile
  = without wishing to attach too much **importance** to these details, I do **think** that
- **Il serait injuste de** reprocher à l'auteur son manque d'expérience
  = it would be unfair to
- "La sévérité de la presse est à la mesure de la démocratie." Certains philosophes **nuancent** ces propos en précisant que ...
  = **qualify**
- **Il faut néanmoins nuancer** l'affirmation selon laquelle l'Europe serait exagérément protectionniste
  = one has, **nevertheless**, to **qualify**

Indicating agreement

- Beaucoup de gens s'inquiètent de l'évolution du chômage, et **effectivement** *or* **en effet,** la situation est préoccupante
  = **indeed**
- **Il faut reconnaître que** les résultats sont décevants
  = one has to **recognize**
- Sa description de l'événement **est exacte en tous points**
  = is accurate on all **points**
- L'explication qu'il en donne **est tout à fait convaincante**
  = is totally **convincing**
- **Comme le suggère** l'auteur, il semble indispensable d'améliorer la qualité des formations et des diplômes
  = **as** ... suggests
- **Tout semble effectivement indiquer qu'**à trente ans, les surdoués ont été rattrapés par les autres
  = everything **seems** to indicate that
- **Il serait vain de le nier :** nous allons devoir faire face à une concurrence nouvelle
  = it would be pointless to **deny** it
- **Rien n'est plus vrai que** cette description de l'exil
  = there is nothing more accurate than

Indicating disagreement

Tentatively

- Je me sens tenu de **formuler quelques réserves**
  = **express** some **reservations**
- **Je formulerais quelques objections**
  = I would **express** some **objections**
- Cette affirmation **me semble contestable**
  = seems **debatable** to me
- **Bien que** son raisonnement **soit** *(subj)* intéressant, **je ne partage pas** le point de vue de l'auteur
  = **although** ... is ..., I do not **share**
- **Quand bien même** disposerait-on d'un vaccin efficace, celui-ci ne pourrait, sans grosses difficultés, être administré sur l'ensemble de la planète
  = **even if**
- À tous ceux qui critiquent la publicité, **on peut répondre** *or* **répliquer que** c'est un nouveau genre artistique
  = one can **reply** that
- **On voit mal comment** les élèves pourraient bénéficier de cette mesure
  = it is hard to **see how**

More assertively

- Cette explication **ne mérite pas d'être retenue**
  = **does not deserve to be accepted**
- Ces faits **sont en contradiction avec** la version officielle
  = **contradict**
- **Elle réfute l'argument selon lequel** la cause principale des défaillances est la fragilité financière des entreprises
  = she **refutes** the **argument** that
- L'auteur **commet une grave erreur** en laissant entendre qu'un accord avait été conclu
  = makes a serious **mistake**
- Quand on dit que la catastrophe a fait 2 000 victimes, **on est très loin de la vérité**
  = one is very far from the **truth**
- **Je m'inscris en faux** *or* **Je m'élève** *or* **Je m'insurge contre** cette version des faits
  = I **protest** against
- **Il ne saurait être question de** procéder à de nouvelles élections
  = there can be no **question** of
- **Il est impossible d'accepter** ce point de vue
  = it is **impossible** to **accept**
- **On ne saurait approuver** cette idée qui témoigne d'un manque de réflexion
  = one couldn't **approve** of

Indicating approval

- **Heureusement,** l'auteur nous précise plus loin que ce n'est pas le cas
  = **fortunately**
- **On comprend fort bien que** les jeunes **aient** *(subj)* réagi ainsi
  = it is perfectly **understandable** that
- **La meilleure solution serait effectivement de** réviser entièrement le projet
  = the best **solution** would, in fact, be to
- Les responsables de l'enquête **ont raison d'**insister sur ce point
  = are **right** to
- L'auteur souligne ce détail **à juste titre** *or* **avec raison**
  = **rightly**
- **Il était grand temps que** ces règles **soient** *(subj)* corrigées
  = it was high time that ... were
- **Enfin** un ouvrage qui traite en profondeur le problème du chômage
  = at last
- Ce livre **est le bienvenu** car il traite d'un sujet jamais abordé jusqu'ici
  = **is welcome**

Indicating disapproval

- **Il est regrettable que** l'auteur **ait** *(subj)* négligé cet aspect du problème
  = it is **regrettable** that
- **Il serait vraiment dommage qu'**une découverte aussi importante ne **soit** *(subj)* pas reconnue à sa juste valeur
  = it would be a great **pity** if
- **Malheureusement,** cette étude est très inégale
  = **unfortunately**
- **On peut s'étonner de** la rapidité avec laquelle la réforme a été appliquée
  = one may well be **surprised** at
- Les habitants **condamnent** *or* **critiquent** ce projet d'autoroute
  = **condemn** or **criticize**
- **Ils reprochent aux** autorités *or* **Ils accusent** les autorités de ne pas les avoir consultés
  = they accuse

Making a correction

- **En réalité** *or* **En fait**, il ne s'agit pas du tout d'une fiction
  = in **reality** or in actual **fact**
- **Il ne s'agit pas à proprement parler de** commerce, mais plutôt de troc
  = it is not, **strictly** speaking, a **question** of
- **Pour rétablir les faits**, je dirai que ...
  = to **re-establish** the **facts**
- Bouderaient-ils leurs pays d'accueil ? **Il semble plutôt qu'**ils les connaissent mal
  = it **seems** more **likely** that
- Dira-t-on qu'il est ambitieux ? **Le mot est faible. Aussi le qualifiera-t-on plus justement d'**arriviste
  = that's too weak a word ... **so** he would more **properly** be **called**

Indicating the reason for something

- Cette situation **résulte d'un malentendu**
  = ... is the **result** of
- **Plus qu'à** ses idées politiques, sa popularité **tient à** ses dons d'acteur
  = ... is **due** more to ... than to
- **C'est pour cette raison que** tout retour en arrière est impossible
  = it is for this **reason** that

- Le vieux château sera réparé : **en effet**, il constitue l'un des meilleurs exemples de l'architecture du XVIIe siècle
  = **because**

- On ne peut se fier à ces résultats, **étant donné que** *or* **attendu que** les chiffres sont approximatifs
  = **seeing** that

- **S'il** a accepté, **c'est** certainement **qu'**on a fait pression sur lui
  = if he ..., it is ... **because**

- **Cela expliquerait** la baisse des ventes en février
  = this would **explain**

Indicating the consequences of something

- Cette décision **a eu d'heureuses conséquences/a eu des conséquences néfastes**
  = had positive/disastrous **consequences**

- Sa nomination **a eu pour conséquence de** créer un mécontentement considérable au sein de l'organisation
  = **resulted** in

- Il était très mécontent de l'évolution de la politique salariale, **aussi a-t-il** donné sa démission
  = and **so** he

- La fermeture de l'usine **entraînera** *or* **provoquera** *or* **aura pour résultat** une augmentation du chômage dans la région
  = will **bring** about or **result** in

- Les compagnies aériennes ont augmenté leurs tarifs, **d'où** une diminution du nombre des passagers
  = **hence**

- Le nombre de postes sera réduit à trois, **ce qui implique** *or* **ce qui signifie** le départ de quatre employés
  = which **means**

- Le héros n'apparaissant pas dans ce chapitre, **il s'ensuit que** les personnages secondaires occupent le premier plan
  = it **follows** that

- **Ainsi,** la personnalité du héros se révèle beaucoup plus complexe qu'elle ne le semblait au premier abord
  = **thus**

Contrasting or comparing

- **Certains** parlent de la faillite de l'école. **À l'inverse, d'autres** proclament les progrès du système éducatif
  = some (people) .... **conversely**, others ...

- **Les uns** se proclament pour la démocratie, **les autres** vantent les bienfaits d'un régime autoritaire
  = some (people) ..., others ...

- **Il dépasse** de loin tous ses concurrents
  = he **outstrips**

- Son deuxième roman **est bien inférieur à** son premier
  = is grossly **inferior** to

- **Il n'arrive pas à la cheville de** son rival
  = ... is head and shoulders above

- **Comparée à** ses concurrents mondiaux de l'ingénierie, l'entreprise affiche désormais l'un des plus jolis bilans de la profession
  = **compared** to

- **Par rapport à** ses concurrents, cette entreprise est défavorisée
  = **compared** with

- **Il n'y a pas de comparaison possible entre** ces deux œuvres
  = there is no **possible comparison** to be drawn between

27 TELEPHONE, E-MAIL AND TEXTING

27.1 Getting a number

- **Je voudrais le 01 843 46 09 37 12, s'il vous plaît,** *(zéro un huit cent quarante-trois quarante-six zéro-neuf trente-sept douze)*
  = Could you get me 01843 46093712, please? (o-one-eight-four-three four-six-o-nine-three-seven-one-two)

- **Pourriez-vous me passer les renseignements, s'il vous plaît ?**
  = Could you give me **directory** enquiries (Brit) or **directory** assistance (US), please?

- **Je voudrais le numéro de la société Europost, 20 rue de la Marelle, à Pierrefitte**
  = Can you give me the **number** of Europost, 20 rue de la Marelle, Pierrefitte?

- **Quel est l'indicatif pour la Martinique ?**
  = What is the **code** for Martinique?

- **Comment est-ce que je peux téléphoner à l'extérieur ?**
  = How do I make an outside **call** or How do I get an outside **line**?

- **Quel numéro dois-je faire pour l'horloge parlante ?**
  = What do I **dial** to get the speaking clock?

- **Je n'ai pas trouvé le numéro dans l'annuaire**
  = It's not in the book

- **Si vous téléphonez de France en Angleterre, ne faites pas le zéro**
  = You omit the « o » when **dialling** England from France

27.2 When your number answers

- **Pourriez-vous me passer le poste 516, s'il vous plaît ?**
  = Could I have or Can you give me **extension** 516?

- **Je suis bien chez M. Lambert ?**
  = Is that Mr Lambert's **phone**?

- **Je voudrais parler à M. Wolff, s'il vous plaît** *or* **Pourrais-je parler à M. Wolff, s'il vous plaît ?**
  = Could I speak to Mr Wolff, please? or I'd like to speak to Mr Wolff, please or Is Mr Wolff there?
- **Pourriez-vous me passer le docteur Henderson, s'il vous plaît ?**
  = Could you put me through to Dr Henderson, please?
- **Qui est à l'appareil ?**
  = Who's speaking?
- **Je rappellerai dans une demi-heure**
  = I'll **call** back in half an hour
- **Pourrais-je laisser mon numéro pour qu'elle me rappelle ?**
  = Could I leave my **number** for her to call me back?
- **Je vous appelle d'une cabine téléphonique** *or* **Je téléphone d'une cabine**
  = I'm **ringing** from a callbox (Brit) or I'm calling from a pay station (US)
- **J'appelle** *or* **Je téléphone d'Angleterre**
  = I'm **phoning** from England
- **Pourriez-vous lui demander de me rappeler quand il rentrera ?**
  = Would you ask him to ring me when he gets back?

27.3 Answering the telephone

- **Allô, c'est Anne à l'appareil**
  = Hello, this is Anne speaking
- *(C'est Anne à l'appareil ?)* **Elle-même**
  = (Is that Anne?) Speaking
- **Voulez-vous laisser un message ?**
  = Would you like to leave a **message**?
- **Puis-je lui transmettre un message ?**
  = Can I take a **message**?
- **Ne quittez pas**
  = **Hold** the **line**, please
- **Je vous rappelle**
  = I'll **call** you back
- **Vous êtes en communication avec un répondeur automatique**
  = This is a **recorded message**
- **Veuillez laisser votre message après le bip sonore**
  = Please speak after the tone or after the beep

27.4 The switchboard operator speaks

- **Grand Hôtel, bonjour** *or* **à votre service**
  = Grand Hotel, can I help you?
- **Qui est à l'appareil ?**
  = Who's **calling**, please?
- **C'est de la part de qui ?**
  = Who shall I say is **calling**?
- **Est-ce que vous connaissez le numéro du poste ?**
  = Do you know his **extension number**?
- **Je vous le passe**
  = I am **connecting** you or putting you through now
- **J'ai quelqu'un en ligne de Tokyo qui demande Mme Thomas**
  = I have a **call** from Tokyo for Mrs Thomas
- **J'ai Mlle Martin à l'appareil**
  = I've got Miss Martin on the **line** for you
- **Le docteur Roberts est déjà en ligne**
  = Dr Roberts' **line** is busy
- **Désolé de vous faire attendre**
  = Sorry to keep you waiting
- **Ça ne répond pas**
  = There's no **reply**
- **Vous êtes en ligne avec le service des ventes**
  = You're through to our Sales Department

27.5 The operator speaks

- **Quel numéro demandez-vous ?**
  = What **number** do you want or What **number** are you calling?
- **D'où appelez-vous ?**
  = Where are you **calling** from?
- **Pourriez-vous répéter le numéro, s'il vous plaît ?**
  = Would you **repeat the number**, please?
- **Raccrochez et renouvelez votre appel** *or* **Raccrochez et recomposez le numéro**
  = Replace the handset and dial again
- **M. Campbell vous appelle en PCV d'Amsterdam. Est-ce que vous acceptez la communication ?**
  = There's a Mr Campbell **calling** you from Amsterdam. He wishes you to pay for the call. Will you accept it?
- **Vous êtes en ligne**
  = Go ahead, **caller**
- (Directory Enquiries) **Il n'y a pas d'abonné à ce nom**
  = (aux Renseignements) There's no listing under that name
- **Désolé, leur numéro est sur la liste rouge**
  = They're **ex-directory** (Brit) *or* **unlisted** (US)
- **Le 01 45 77 57 84 ne répond pas**
  = There's no **reply** from 01 45 77 57 84
- **Ne quittez pas**
  = Hold the line, please
- **Par suite de l'encombrement des lignes, votre appel ne peut aboutir. Veuillez rappeler ultérieurement**
  = All **lines** to Bristol are **engaged** - please try later
- **J'essaie d'obtenir votre correspondant**
  = I'm trying it for you now
- **Ça sonne**
  = It's **ringing** or **Ringing** for you now
- **La ligne est occupée**
  = The line is **engaged** (Brit) or **busy** (US)

◆ **Il n'y a pas d'abonné au numéro que vous avez demandé** *(recorded message)*
= The number you have **dialled** has not been recognized (message enregistré)

◆ **Le numéro de votre correspondant n'est plus attribué. Veuillez consulter l'annuaire ou votre centre de renseignements**
= The **number** you have **dialled** no longer exists. Please consult the **directory** *(message enregistré)*

◆ **Le numéro de votre correspondant a changé. Veuillez composer désormais le 02 33 42 21 70** *(recorded message)*
= The **number** you have **dialled** has been changed. Please **dial** 0233422170 *(message enregistré)*

◆ **Toutes les lignes de votre correspondant sont occupées. Veuillez rappeler ultérieurement** *(recorded message)*
= The **number** you are **calling** is **engaged** *(Brit) ou* **busy** *(US)*. Please try again later

27.6 Different types of call

◆ **C'est une communication locale**
= It's a local **call**

◆ **C'est une communication interurbaine**
= This is a long-distance **call**

◆ **Je voudrais appeler l'étranger**
= I want to make an international call

◆ **Je voudrais appeler Londres en PCV** (NB : system no longer exists in France)
= I want to make a **reverse** charge call to a London **number** (Brit) or I want to **call** a London number **collect** (US)

◆ **Je voudrais être réveillé à 7 h 30 demain matin?**
= I'd like an alarm **call** for 7.30 tomorrow morning

27.7 In case of difficulty

◆ **Je n'arrive pas à avoir le numéro**
= I can't get through (at all)

◆ **Leur téléphone est en dérangement**
= Their **phone** is out of **order**

◆ **On nous a coupés** *or* **La communication a été coupée**
= We were cut off

◆ **J'ai dû faire un faux numéro**
= I must have **dialled** the wrong **number**

◆ **Il y a quelqu'un d'autre sur la ligne**
= We've got a **crossed line**

◆ **J'ai appelé plusieurs fois, mais ça ne répond pas**
= I've **called** them several times with no **reply**

◆ **Vous m'avez donné un faux numéro**
= You gave me a wrong **number**

◆ **On ne m'a pas donné le bon poste** *or* **On s'est trompé de poste**
= I got the wrong **extension**

◆ **La ligne est très mauvaise**
= This is a very bad **line**

E-mail and Texting, see p. 37-38

27.8 E-mail

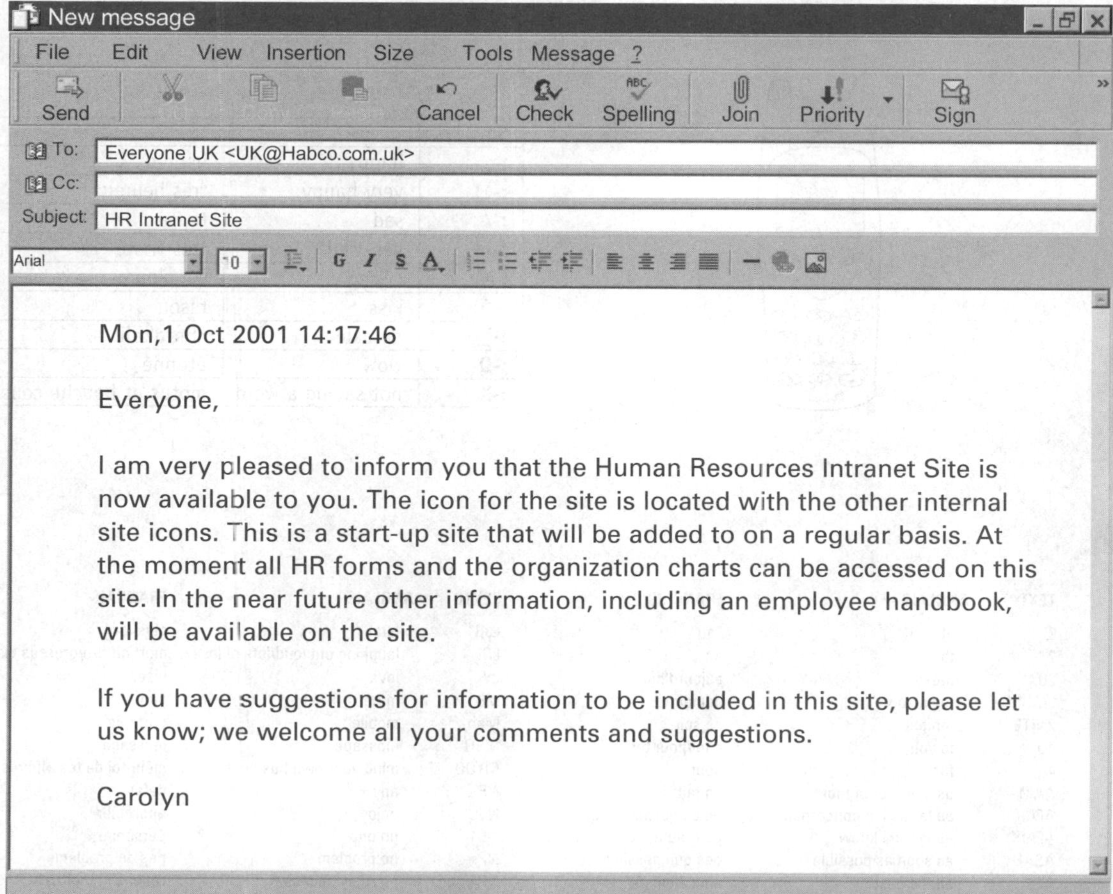

New Message	Nouveau message
File	Fichier
Edit	Edition
View	Affichage
Tools	Outils
Compose	Composer
Help	Aide
Send	Envoyer
New	Nouveau message
Reply to Sender	Répondre
Reply to All	Répondre à tous
Forward	Faire suivre
Attachment	Fichier joint
To	A
Cc	Cc
Bcc (blind carbon copy)	Copie cachée
Subject	Objet
From	De
Sent	Date

27.9 Texting

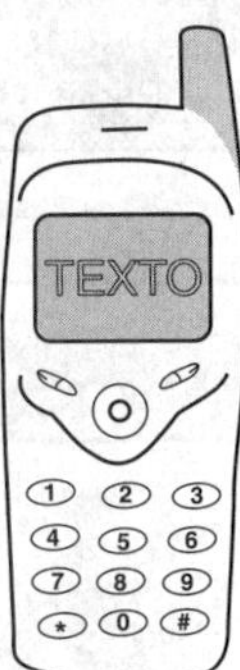

Smileys		
:-)	happy	heureux
:-))	very happy	très heureux
:-(	sad	triste
:-((	very sad	très triste
:'-(	crying	qui pleure
:-*	kiss	bisou
;-)	twinkle	clin d'œil
:-O	wow	étonné
:-X	not saying a word	motus et bouche cousue

TEXTO	ANGLAIS	FRANÇAIS
@	at	"at"
2	to	à
2DAY	today	aujourd'hui
2MORO	tomorrow	demain
2NITE	tonight	ce soir
2U	to you	à toi/pour toi
4	for	pour
AAM	as a matter of fact	en fait
AFAIC	as far as I'm concerned	en ce qui me concerne
AFAIK	as far as I know	pour autant que je sache
ASAP	as soon as possible	dès que possible
ATB	all the best	amicalement
B	be	être
B4	before	avant
BCNU	be seeing you	à plus
BRB	be right back	je reviens tout de suite
BTDT	been there done that	j'ai déjà donné
BTW	by the way	à propos
BYKT	but you knew that	mais tu le savais déjà
CID	consider it done	c'est comme si c'était fait
COZ	because	parce que
CU	see you	salut
CUL8R	see you later	à plus tard
CW2CU	can't wait to see you	j'ai hâte de te (re)voir
EZ	easy	facile
FAQ	frequently asked questions	foire aux questions
FWIW	for what it's worth	pour ce que ça vaut
FYI	for your interest /information	pour ton information
GAL	get a life	bouge-toi un peu
GBTM	get back to me	réponds-moi
GR8	great	super
GTG	got to go	il faut que j'y aille
H8	hate	la haine
HTH	hope this helps	j'espère que ça t'est utile
IAC	in any case	de toute façon
ICCL	I couldn't care less	je m'en fiche pas mal
IDK	I don't know	je ne sais pas
ILUVU	I love you	je t'aime
IMHO	in my humble opinion	à mon humble avis
IOU	I owe you	je te dois
IYKWIM	if you know what I mean	tu vois ce que je veux dire
KIT	keep in touch	donne de tes nouvelles
L8	late	tard

TEXTO	ANGLAIS	FRANÇAIS
L8R	later	plus tard
LOL	laughing out loud/lots of love	mort de rire/grosses bises
LV	love	bises
M8	mate	pote
Mob	mobile	portable
MSG	message	message
MYOB	mind your own business	mêle-toi de tes affaires
NE	any	de(s)
NJOY	enjoy	apprécier
NO1	no one	personne
NP	no problem	pas de problème
NRN	no reply necessary	réponse facultative
OIC	oh I see	ah je vois
OTT	over the top	trop
PCM	please call me	appelle-moi, s'il te plaît
PLS	please	s'il te plaît
PPL	people	les gens
R	are	es/sommes/êtes/sont
RN	right now	tout de suite
ROF	rolling on the floor	tordu de rire
RUOK	are you OK?	ça va ?
S/O	someone	quelqu'un
S/TH	something	quelque chose
SUM1	someone	quelqu'un
THX	thanks	merci
Ti2GO	time to go	il faut que j'y aille
TMB	text me back	réponds-moi par message
TTFN	ta ta for now	au revoir
TTYL	talk to you later	à plus tard
TXT	text	texte
TYVM	thank you very much	merci beaucoup
U	you	tu/toi/te/vous
V	very	très
W/O	without	sans
WAN2	want to	veux/voulons/voulez/veulent
WBS	write back soon	écris-mois vite
WIV	with	avec
WKND	weekend	le week-end
WUD	what are you doing?	qu'est-ce que tu fais ?
X	kiss	bisou
XLNT	excellent	excellent
Y	why	pourquoi
YR	your	ton/ta/tes/votre/vos

28 LA SUGGESTION

28.1 Pour faire des suggestions

- **You might like to** think it over before giving me your decision
  = **peut-être souhaitez-vous**
- **If you were to** give me the negative, **I could** get copies made
  = si vous ... je **pourrais**
- **You could** help me clear out my office, **if you don't mind**
  = vous **pourriez** ... si cela ne vous ennuie pas
- **We could** stop off in Venice for a day or two, **if you like**
  = nous **pourrions** ... si vous **voulez**
- I've got an idea — **let's organize** a surprise birthday party for Megan !
  = organisons
- **If you've no objection(s), I'll** ask them round for dinner on Sunday
  = si vous n'avez pas d'**objections**, je
- **If I were you, I'd** be very careful
  = si j'étais vous, je
- **If you ask me, you'd better** take some extra cash
  = à mon **avis**, vous feriez bien de
- **If you want my advice, I'd** steer well clear of them
  = à votre **place**, je
- **I'd be very careful not to** commit myself at this stage
  = je ferais très attention à ne pas
- **I would recommend (that) you** discuss it with him before making a decision
  = je vous **recommande** de
- **It could be in your interest to** have a word with the owner first
  = il serait **peut-être** dans votre **intérêt** de
- **There's a lot to be said for** living alone
  = a beaucoup d'**avantages**

Directement

- **I suggest that** *ou* **I'd like to suggest that** you take a long holiday
  = je **suggère** que
- **We propose that** half the fee be paid in advance, and half on completion
  = nous **proposons** que
- **It is quite important that** you develop her sense of fun and adventure
  = il est très **important** que
- I cannot put it too strongly: **you really must** see a doctor
  = il faut absolument que vous

Moins directement

- **Say you were to** approach the problem from a different angle
  = et si vous
- In these circumstances, **it might be better to** wait
  = il **vaudrait peut-être** mieux
- **It might be a good thing** *ou* **a good idea to** warn her about this
  = ce serait **peut-être** une bonne **idée** de
- **Perhaps it might be as well to** look now at the issues
  = il serait **peut-être** bon de
- **Perhaps you should** take up birdwatching
  = vous **devriez peut-être**
- **If I may make a suggestion**, a longer hemline might suit you better
  = si je **peux** me **permettre** une **suggestion**
- **Might I be allowed to offer a little advice?** — talk it over with a solicitor before you go any further
  = **puis**-je me **permettre** de vous donner un **conseil** ?
- **If I may be permitted to remind you of** one of the golden rules of journalism
  = **puis**-je me **permettre** de vous **rappeler**
- **If I might be permitted to suggest something**, installing bigger windows would make the office much brighter
  = si je **puis** me **permettre** une **suggestion**

En posant une question

- **How do you fancy** a holiday in Australia? *(familier)*
  = ça vous **tente** ...
- I was thinking of inviting her to dinner. **How about it?** *(familier)*
  = qu'est-ce que vous en **dites** ?
- **What would you say to** a trip up to town next week?
  = que **diriez**-vous de
- **Would you like to** go away on a second honeymoon?
  = **aimeriez**-vous
- **What if** you try ignoring her and see if that stops her complaining?
  = et si
- What you need is a change of scene. **Why not** go on a cruise or to a resort?
  = **pourquoi** ne pas
- **Suppose** *ou* **Supposing** you left the kids with Joe and came out with me?
  = et si
- **What do you think about** taking calcium supplements?
  = que **pensez**-vous de
- **Have you ever thought of** starting up a magazine of your own?
  = avez-vous déjà **songé** à
- **Would you care to** have lunch with me? *(soutenu)*
  = **voudriez**-vous

28.2 Pour demander des idées

- **What would you do if you were me?**
  = que feriez-vous à ma **place** ?
- **Have you any idea how I should** go about it to get the best results?
  = avez-vous une **idée** sur la façon dont je **devrais**
- I've no idea what to call our pet snake: **have you any suggestions?**
  = avez-vous des **suggestions** ?
- I can only afford to buy one of them: **which do you suggest?**
  = que feriez-vous à ma **place** ?
- **I wonder if you could suggest** where we might go for a few days?
  = je me **demande** si vous pourriez me donner une **idée** :

29 LE CONSEIL

29.1 Pour demander un conseil

- What would you do **if you were me?**
  = à ma **place**
- Would a pear tree grow in this situation? If not, **what would you recommend?**
  = que **conseilleriez**-vous
- **Do you think I ought to** tell the truth if he asks me where I've been?
  = pensez-vous que je **devrais**
- **What would you advise me to do** in the circumstances?
  = que me **conseilleriez**-vous de faire
- **Would you advise me to** seek promotion within this firm or apply for another job?
  = à votre **avis, dois-je**
- I'd like *ou* **I'd appreciate your advice on** personal pensions
  = j'aimerais avoir votre **avis** sur
- **I'd be grateful if you could advise me on** how to treat this problem
  = je vous serais **reconnaissant** si vous pouviez me donner votre avis sur

29.2 Pour donner un conseil

De manière impersonnelle

- **It might be wise** *ou* **sensible** *ou* **a good idea to** consult a specialist
  = il serait peut-être **prudent** de
- **It might be better to** think the whole thing over before making any decisions
  = il **vaudrait** peut-être mieux
- **You'd be as well to** state your position at the outset, so there is no mistake
  = vous feriez bien de
- **You would be well-advised to** invest in a pair of sunglasses if you're going to Morocco
  = vous feriez bien de
- **You'd be ill-advised to** have any dealings with this firm
  = vous auriez **tort** de
- **It would certainly be advisable to** book a table
  = il serait **prudent** de
- **It is in your interest** *ou* **your best interests to** keep your dog under control if you don't want it to be reported
  = il est dans votre **intérêt** de
- **Do be sure to** read the small print before you sign anything
  = prenez soin de
- **Try to avoid** get**ting her back up; she'll only make your life a misery**
  = essayez d'**éviter** de
- **Whatever you do, don't** drink the local schnapps
  = quoi qu'il arrive, ne ... pas

De manière plus personnelle

- **If you ask me, you'd better** take some extra cash
  = à mon **avis**, vous feriez mieux de
- **If you want my advice, I'd** steer well clear of them
  = à votre **place**, je
- **If you want my opinion, I'd** go by air to save time
  = à votre **place**, je
- **In your shoes** *ou* **If I were you, I'd** be thinking about moving on
  = à votre **place**, je
- **Take my advice** and don't rush into anything
  = suivez mon **conseil**
- **I'd be very careful not to** commit myself at this stage
  = je ferais très **attention** à ne pas
- **I think you ought to** *ou* **should** seek professional advice
  = je crois que vous **devriez**
- **My advice would be to** have nothing to do with them
  = je vous **conseillerais** de
- **I would advise you to** pay up promptly before they take you to court
  = je vous **conseille** de
- **I would advise against** call**ing in the police unless they threaten you**
  = je **déconseillerais** de
- **I would strongly advise you to** reconsider this decision
  = je vous **conseille** vivement de
- **I would urge you to** reconsider selling the property
  = je ne saurais trop vous **conseiller** de
- **Might I offer a little advice?** — talk it over with a solicitor before you go any further (*soutenu*)
  = puis-je me permettre de vous donner un **conseil** ?

29.3 Pour lancer un avertissement

- It's really none of my business but **I don't think you should** get involved
  = je ne crois pas que vous **devriez**
- **A word of caution:** watch what you say to him if you want it to remain a secret
  = un petit **conseil** :
- **I should warn you that** he's not an easy customer to deal with
  = je vous **préviens** que
- **Take care not to** burn your fingers
  = faites **attention** à ne pas
- **Make sure that** *ou* **Mind that** *ou* **See that you don't** say anything they might find offensive
  = surtout, **évitez** de
- **I'd think twice about** shar**ing a flat with the likes of him**
  = je **réfléchirais** à deux fois avant de
- **It would be sheer madness to** attempt to drive without your glasses
  = ce serait de la folie que de
- **You risk** a long delay in Amsterdam **if** you come back by that route
  = vous **risquez** ... si
- **I am afraid I must refuse**
  = je crains de devoir refuser
- **I cannot possibly comply with** this request
  = je ne peux pas accéder à
- **It is unfortunately impracticable for us** to commit ourselves at this stage
  = il nous est **malheureusement** impossible de

- In view of the proposed timescale, **I must reluctantly decline to** take part
  = je me vois **malheureusement** obligé de refuser de

30 PROPOSITIONS

De façon directe

- **I would be delighted to** help out, **if I may**
  = je serais très **heureux** de ... si vous le souhaitez
- **It would give me great pleasure to** invite your mother to dinner on Saturday
  = cela me ferait très **plaisir** de
- **We would like to offer you** the post of Sales Director
  = nous **voudrions** vous **offrir**
- **I hope you will not be offended if I offer** a contribution towards your expenses
  = j'espère que vous ne m'en **voudrez** pas **si j'offre**
- **Do let me know if I can** help in any way
  = prévenez-moi **si**
- **If we can** be of any further assistance, **please do not hesitate to** contact us *(soutenu)*
  = **si nous pouvons** ... n'hésitez pas à

En posant une question

- **Say we were to** offer you a 10 % increase plus a company car, **how would that sound?**
  = mettons que ... qu'en **dites**-vous ?
- **What if I were to** call for you in the car?
  = et **si** je
- **Could I** give you a hand with your luggage?
  = est-ce que je **peux**
- **Shall I** pick you up from work on Friday afternoon?
  = **voulez**-vous que je
- **Is there anything I can do to** help you find suitable accommodation?
  = **puis**-je
- **May** *ou* **Can I offer you** a drink?
  = **puis**-je vous **offrir**
- **Would you like me to** find out more about it for you?
  = **voulez**-vous que je
- **Would you allow me to** pay for dinner, at least?
  = me **permettez**-vous de

31 DEMANDES

- **Would you please** drop by on your way home and pick up the papers you left here?
  = **pourriez**-vous
- **Could you please** try to keep the noise down while I'm studying?
  = **pourriez**-vous
- **Would you mind** look**ing after Hannah for a couple of hours tomorrow?**
  = cela vous ennuierait-il de
- **Could I ask you to** watch out for anything suspicious in my absence?
  = **puis**-je vous demander de

À l'écrit

- **I should be grateful if you could** confirm whether it would be possible to increase my credit limit to £5000
  = je vous serais **reconnaissant** de bien **vouloir**
- **We should be glad to** receive your reply by return of post
  = nous **souhaiterions**
- **We would ask you not to** use the telephone for long-distance calls
  = nous vous **prions** de ne pas
- **You are requested to** park at the rear of the building
  = vous êtes **prié** de
- **We look forward to** receiv**ing confirmation of your order within 14 days**
  = dans l'attente de
- **Kindly inform us if** you require alternative arrangements to be made
  = **veuillez** nous faire savoir si

De façon plus indirecte

- **I would rather you didn't** breathe a word to anyone about this
  = je **préférerais** que vous ne ... pas
- **I would appreciate it if you could** let me have copies of the best photographs
  = je vous serais **reconnaissant** si vous **pouviez**
- **I was hoping that you might** find time to visit your grandmother
  = j'**espérais** que vous **pourriez**
- **I wonder whether you could** spare a few pounds till I get to the bank?
  = est-ce qu'il vous serait **possible** de
- **I hope you don't mind if I** borrow your exercise bike for half an hour
  = j'**espère** que cela ne vous ennuie pas que
- **It would be very helpful** *ou* **useful if you could** have everything ready a week in advance
  = cela me etc rendrait service si vous **pouviez**
- **If it's not too much trouble, would you** pop my suit into the dry cleaners on your way past?
  = si cela ne vous dérange pas trop, **pourriez**-vous
- **You won't forget** to lock up before you leave, **will you?**
  = vous n'oublierez pas de

32 LA COMPARAISON

32.1 Objectivement

- The streets, although wide for a Chinese city, are narrow **compared with** English streets
  = **comparé à**

- The bomb used to blow the car up was small **in** *ou* **by comparison with** those often used nowadays
  = par **rapport** à
- **In contrast to** the opulence of the Kirov, the Northern Ballet Theatre is a modest company
  = par **contraste** avec
- The loss of power because of the lower octane rating of paraffin **as opposed to** petrol is about fifteen per cent
  = par **opposition** à
- **Unlike** other loan repayments, those to the IMF cannot simply be rescheduled
  = à la **différence** de
- **If we set** the actual cost **against** our estimate, we can see how inaccurate the estimate was
  = si nous **comparons** ... à
- **Whereas** house thieves often used to make off only with video recorders, they now also tend to empty the fridge
  = alors que
- Property rights are conferred on both tenants and home owners; **the former** are common, **the latter** are private
  = les premiers ..., les seconds ...
- Anglophone Canadians have a distinctive structure to their society, which **differentiates** it **from** other anglophone societies
  = **différencie** ... de

32.2 Comparaisons favorables

- Silverlight was, indeed, **far superior to** him intellectually
  = bien **supérieur** à
- The Australians are far bigger and stronger than us — **we can't compete with** their robot-like style of play
  = nous ne pouvons pas **rivaliser** avec
- St Petersburg **has the edge over** Moscow and other central cities in availability of some foods
  = est légèrement **supérieur** à
- Michaela was astute beyond her years and altogether **in a class of her own**
  = **unique** en son genre

32.3 Comparaisons défavorables

- Joseph's amazing technicolour dreamcoat **is not a patch on** some of the jerseys now being worn by the country's leading goalkeepers
  = n'est rien à **côté** de
- The chair he sat in **was nowhere near as** comfortable **as** his own
  = était loin d'être **aussi** ... que
- The parliamentary opposition **is no match for** the government
  = ne peut pas **rivaliser** avec
- Commercially-made ice-cream **is far inferior to** the home-made variety
  = est très **inférieur** à
- The sad truth is that, as a poet, **he was never in the same class as** his friend
  = il n'a jamais pu **rivaliser** avec
- Ella doesn't rate anything that **doesn't measure up to** Shakespeare
  = n'est pas du **niveau** de
- Her brash charms **don't bear comparison with** Marlene's sultry sex appeal
  = n'est pas **comparable** à

32.4 Pour comparer deux choses semblables

- The new system costs **much the same as** the old one
  = pratiquement la **même** chose que
- When it comes to quality, **there's not much to choose between** them
  = il n'y a pas grande **différence** entre
- **There is essentially no difference between them**
  = il n'y a pas de **différence** fondamentale entre eux
- The impact was **equivalent to** 250 hydrogen bombs exploding
  = **équivalent** à
- In 1975, Spanish workers had longer hours than most Europeans but now they are **on a par with** the French
  = sur un pied d'**égalité** avec
- In Kleinian analysis, the psychoanalyst's role **corresponds to** that of mother
  = **correspond** à
- The immune system **can be likened to** a complicated electronic network
  = peut être **comparé** à
- **There was a close resemblance between** her **and** her son
  = ... et ... se **ressemblaient** beaucoup
- **It's swings and roundabouts** — what you win in one round, you lose in another
  = c'est du **pareil** au **même**

32.5 Pour opposer deux choses non comparables

- **You can't compare** bacteria levels in cooked food **with** those in raw vegetables
  = vous ne pouvez pas **comparer** ... à
- All the muffins in England **cannot compare with** her scones
  = ne sauraient être **comparés** à
- **There's no comparison between** Waddle now **and** Waddle three years ago
  = on ne peut **comparer** ... à
- His book **has little in common with** those approved by the Party
  = n'a pas grand-chose en **commun** avec
- Here we are, practically twins, except **we have nothing in common**
  = nous n'avons rien en **commun**
- The modern army **bears little resemblance to** the army of 1940
  = ne **ressemble** guère à

33 L'OPINION

33.1 Pour demander l'opinion de quelqu'un

- **What do you think of** the new Managing Director?
  = que **pensez**-vous de

- **What is your opinion on** women's rights?
  = quelle est votre **opinion** sur
- **What are your thoughts on** the way forward?
  = quel est votre **avis** sur
- **What is your attitude to** people who say there is no such thing as sexual inequality?
  = quelle est votre **attitude** à l'égard de
- **What are your own feelings about** the way the case was handled?
  = quel est votre **sentiment** sur
- **How do you see** the next stage developing?
  = à votre **avis**, comment
- **How do you view** an event like the Birmingham show in terms of the cultural life of the city?
  = comment **percevez**-vous
- **I would value your opinion on** how best to set this all up
  = je voudrais avoir votre **avis** sur
- **I'd be interested to know what your reaction is to** the latest report on food additives
  = j'aimerais connaître votre **réaction** face à

33.2 Pour exprimer son opinion

- **In my opinion**, eight years as President is enough and sometimes too much for any man to serve in that capacity
  = à mon **avis**
- **As I see it**, everything depended on Karlov being permitted to go to Finland
  = **selon** moi
- **I feel that** there is an epidemic of fear about cancer which is not helped by the regular flow of publicity about the large numbers of people who die of it
  = je **trouve** que
- **Personally, I believe** the best way to change a government is through the electoral process
  = **personnellement**, je **crois** que
- **It seems to me that** the successful designer leads the public
  = il me **semble** que
- **I am under the impression that** he is essentially a man of peace
  = j'ai l'**impression** que
- **I have an idea that** you are going to be very successful
  = j'ai **idée** que
- **I am of the opinion that** the rules should be looked at and refined
  = je suis d'**avis** que
- **I'm convinced that** we all need a new vision of the future
  = je suis **convaincu** que
- **I daresay** there are so many names that you get them mixed up once in a while
  = j'**imagine** que
- We're prepared to prosecute the company, which **to my mind** has committed a criminal offence
  = à mon **avis**
- Most parts of the black market activity, **from my point of view**, is not, strictly speaking, illegal
  = d'**après** moi
- **As far as I'm concerned**, Barnes had it coming to him
  = en ce qui me **concerne**
- It's a matter of mutual accommodation, nothing more. **That's my view of the matter**
  = telle est mon **opinion** sur la question
- **It is our belief that** to be proactive is more positive than being reactive
  = nous **croyons** que
- **If you ask me**, there's something odd going on
  = si vous voulez mon **avis**
- **If you want my opinion**, if you don't do it soon, you'll lose the opportunity altogether and you'll be sorry
  = si vous voulez mon **opinion**

33.3 Pour répondre sans exprimer d'opinion

- Would I say she had been a help? **It depends what you mean by** help
  = cela dépend de ce que vous entendez par
- It could be seen as a triumph for capitalism but **it depends on your point of view**
  = c'est une question de **point** de vue
- **It's hard** *ou* **difficult to say whether** I identify with the hippy culture or not
  = il est **difficile** de dire si
- **I'm not in a position to comment on whether** the director's accusations are well-founded
  = je ne suis pas à même de dire si
- **I'd prefer not to comment on** operational decisions taken by the service in the past
  = je préférerais ne pas me **prononcer** sur
- **I'd rather not commit myself** at this stage
  = je préférerais ne pas m'**engager**
- **I don't have any strong feelings about which of the two companies** we should use for the job
  = je n'ai pas d'**opinion** bien arrêtée sur le choix de l'entreprise
- **This isn't something I've given much thought to**
  = je n'y ai pas vraiment réfléchi
- **I know nothing about** the workings of the female mind
  = j'**ignore** tout de

34 LES GOÛTS ET PRÉFÉRENCES

34.1 Pour demander ce que quelqu'un aime

- **Would you like to** visit the castle, while you are here?
  = **aimerais**-tu
- **How would you feel about** ask**ing Simon to join us?**
  = et si on
- **What do you like** do**ing best when you're on holiday?**
  = que **préfères**-tu
- **What's your favourite** film?
  = quel est ton ... **préféré** ?
- **Which of the two** proposed options **do you prefer?**
  = entre les deux ..., lequel **préfères**-tu ?
- We could either go to Rome or stay in Florence — **which would you rather** do?
  = que **préférerais**-tu

34.2 Pour dire ce que l'on aime

- **I'm very keen on** gardening
  = j'**aime** beaucoup le
- **I'm very fond of** white geraniums and blue petunias
  = j'**adore**
- **I really enjoy** a good game of squash after work
  = j'**apprécie** vraiment
- **There's nothing I like more than** a quiet night in with a good book
  = rien de tel que
- **I have a weakness for** rich chocolate gateaux
  = j'ai un **faible** pour
- **I have a soft spot for** the rich peaty flavours of Islay malt
  = j'ai un **faible** pour

34.3 Pour dire ce que l'on n'aime pas

- Acting **isn't really my thing** — I'm better at singing
  = n'est pas mon **truc**
- Watching football on television **isn't my favourite** pastime
  = n'est pas mon ... **favori**
- Some people might find it funny but **it's not my kind of** humour
  = ce n'est pas mon **genre** de
- I enjoy playing golf but tennis is **not my cup of tea**
  = ce n'est pas ma tasse de thé
- Sitting for hours on motorways **is not my idea of fun**
  = ça ne m'amuse pas de
- The idea of walking home at 11 o'clock at night **doesn't appeal to me**
  = ne me dit rien
- **I've gone off the idea of** cycling round Holland
  = j'ai renoncé à l'idée de
- **I can't stand** *ou* **can't bear** the thought of seeing him
  = je ne **supporte** pas
- **I am not enthusiastic about** growing plants directly in greenhouse soil because of the risk of soil diseases
  = je ne suis guère **enthousiasmé** par l'idée de
- **I'm not keen on** seafood
  = je n'**aime** pas beaucoup
- **I don't like the fact that** he always gets away with not helping out
  = je n'**apprécie** pas trop le fait que
- **What I hate most is** waiting in queues for buses
  = ce que je **déteste** le plus, c'est de
- **I dislike** laziness since I'm such an energetic person myself
  = me **déplaît**
- **There's nothing I dislike more than** having to go to work in the dark
  = il n'y a rien qui me **déplaise** plus que de
- **I have a particular aversion to** the religious indoctrination of schoolchildren
  = j'ai une **aversion** particulière pour
- **I find it intolerable that** people like him should have so much power
  = je trouve **intolérable** que

34.4 Pour dire ce que l'on préfère

- **I'd prefer to** *ou* **I'd rather** wait until I have enough money to go by air
  = je **préférerais** *ou* j'**aimerais** mieux
- **I'd prefer not to** *ou* **I'd rather not** talk about it just now
  = je **préférerais** ne pas *ou* j'**aimerais** mieux ne pas
- **I'd prefer you to** *ou* **I'd rather you** put your comments in writing
  = je **préférerais** *ou* j'**aimerais** mieux que tu
- **I'd prefer you not to** *ou* **I'd rather you didn't** invite him
  = je **préférerais** *ou* j'**aimerais** mieux que tu ne ... pas
- **I like** the blue curtains **better than** *ou* **I prefer** the blue curtains **to** the red ones
  = j'**aime** mieux ... que ... *ou* je **préfère** ... à ...

34.5 Pour exprimer l'indifférence

- **It makes no odds whether you have** a million pounds or nothing, we won't judge you on your wealth
  = que vous ayez ..., ça n'a aucune importance
- **I really don't care what** you tell her as long as you tell her something
  = ce que ... m'est complètement **égal**
- **It's all the same to me whether** he comes or not
  = peu m'**importe** que
- **I don't mind at all** — let's do whatever is easiest
  = cela m'est complètement **égal**
- **It doesn't matter which** method you choose to use
  = peu **importe** le
- **I don't feel strongly about** the issue of privatization
  = ... m'est **indifférent**
- **I have no particular preference**
  = je n'ai pas de **préférence**

35 L'INTENTION ET LA VOLONTÉ

35.1 Pour demander ce que quelqu'un compte faire

- **Do you intend to** *ou* **Will you** take the job?
  = as-tu l'**intention** de
- What flight **do you intend to** take?
  = as-tu l'**intention** de
- **Did you mean to** *ou* **intend to** tell him about it, or did it just slip out?
  = avais-tu l'**intention** de
- **What do you intend to do** *ou* **What are your intentions?**
  = qu'as-tu l'**intention** de faire ?
- **What do you propose to do** with the money?
  = qu'est-ce que tu **penses** faire
- **What did you have in mind for** the rest of the programme?
  = qu'est-ce que tu avais prévu pour
- **Have you anyone in mind for** the job?
  = as-tu quelqu'un en **vue** pour

35.2 Pour exprimer ses intentions

- **We're toying with the idea of** releas**ing a compilation album**
  = nous **songeons** à
- **I'm thinking of** retir**ing next year**
  = je **pense**
- **I'm hoping to** go and see her when I'm in Paris
  = j'**espère**
- **What I have in mind is to** start a small software business
  = ce que je **pense** faire c'est de
- I studied history, **with a view to** becom**ing a politician**
  = en **vue** de
- We bought the land **in order to** farm *ou* **for the purpose of** farm**ing it**
  = **afin** de
- **We plan to** move *ou* **We are planning on** mov**ing next year**
  = nous **projetons** de
- **Our aim in** *ou* **Our object in** buy**ing the company is to** provide work for the villagers
  = le **but** que nous nous sommes fixé en ... est de
- **I aim to** reach Africa in three months
  = je **compte**

Avec plus de conviction

- **I am going to** *ou* **I intend to** sell the car as soon as possible
  = je vais *ou* j'ai l'**intention** de
- **I have made up my mind to** *ou* **I have decided to** go to Japan
  = j'ai **décidé** de
- **I intended him to** be a poet but he chose to be an accountant
  = je **voulais** qu'il
- I went to London, **intending to** visit her *ou* **with the intention of** visit**ing her, but she was away on business**
  = dans l'**intention** de
- **We have every intention of** winn**ing a sixth successive championship**
  = nous sommes **décidés** à
- **I have set my sights on** recaptur**ing the title**
  = je suis **déterminé** à
- **My overriding ambition is to** overthrow the President
  = j'ai pour principale **ambition** de
- **I resolve to** do everything in my power to bring the affair to an end
  = je suis **résolu** à

35.3 Pour exprimer ce qu'on n'a pas l'intention de faire

- **I don't mean to** offend you, but I think you're wrong
  = je ne **veux** pas
- **I don't intend to** pay unless he completes the job
  = je n'ai pas l'**intention** de
- **I have no intention of** accept**ing the post**
  = je n'ai pas du tout l'**intention** de
- **We are not thinking of** advertis**ing this post at the moment**
  = nous n'**envisageons** pas de

35.4 Pour exprimer ce que l'on désire faire

- **I'd like to** see the Sistine Chapel some day
  = j'**aimerais**
- **I want to** work abroad when I leave college
  = je **veux**
- **We want her to** be an architect when she grows up
  = nous **voulons** qu'elle
- **I'm keen to** see more students take up zoology
  = j'**aimerais** vraiment

Avec davantage d'enthousiasme

- **I'm dying to** leave and make my fortune in Paris *(familier)*
  = je meurs d'**envie** de
- **My ambition is to** go straight from being an enfant terrible to a grande dame
  = j'ai pour **ambition** de
- **I long to** go to Australia but I can't afford it
  = j'ai très **envie** de
- **I insist on** speak**ing to the manager**
  = j'**exige** de

35.5 Pour exprimer ce que l'on ne veut pas faire

- **I would prefer not to** *ou* **I would rather not** have to speak to her about this
  = j'**aimerais** mieux ne pas *ou* je **préférerais** ne pas
- **I wouldn't want to** have to change my plans just because of her
  = je n'**aimerais** pas
- **I don't want to** *ou* **I have no wish to** *ou* **I have no desire to** take the credit for something I didn't do
  = je ne **veux** pas *ou* je n'ai pas du tout l'**intention** de
- **I refuse to** be patronized by the likes of her
  = je **refuse** de

36 LA PERMISSION

36.1 Pour demander la permission de faire quelque chose

- **Can I** *ou* **Could I** borrow your car this afternoon?
  = **puis**-je *ou* **pourrais**-je
- **Can I have the go-ahead to** order the supplies?
  = est-ce que j'ai le **feu** vert pour
- **Are we allowed to** say what we're up to or is it top secret at the moment?
  = avons-nous le **droit** de
- **Would it be all right if** I arrived on Monday instead of Tuesday?
  = est-ce que cela vous **dérangerait** si
- **Would it be possible for us to** leave the car in your garage for a week?
  = est-ce qu'il nous serait **possible** de
- We leave tomorrow. **Is that all right by you?**
  = est-ce que cela vous **convient** ?

- **Do you mind if** I come to the meeting next week?
  = cela ne vous **ennuie** pas que
- **Would it bother you if** I invited him?
  = cela vous **ennuierait**-il si
- **Would you let me** come into partnership with you?
  = me **permettriez**-vous de
- **Would you have any objection to** sailing at once?
  = verriez-vous un **inconvénient** à ce que
- **With your permission, I'd like to** ask some questions
  = si vous le **permettez**, j'aimerais

Avec moins d'assurance

- **Is there any chance of** borrowing your boat while we're at the lake?
  = est-ce qu'il serait **possible** de
- **I wonder if I could possibly** use your telephone?
  = je me demande s'il serait **possible** de
- **Might I be permitted to** suggest the following ideas? *(soutenu)*
  = **puis**-je me **permettre** de
- **May I be allowed to** set the record straight? *(soutenu)*
  = est-ce qu'il m'est **permis** de

36.2 Pour donner la permission

- **You can** have anything you want
  = vous **pouvez**
- **You are allowed to** visit the museum, as long as you apply in writing to the Curator first
  = vous avez le **droit** de
- **It's all right by me if** you want to skip the Cathedral visit
  = je n'ai pas d'**objection** à ce que
- **You have my permission to** be absent for that week
  = je vous **autorise** à
- **There's nothing against her** going there with us
  = rien ne l'empêche de
- The Crown **was agreeable to** having the case called on March 23
  = **consentit** à ce que
- **I do not mind if** my letter is forwarded to the lady concerned
  = je ne vois pas d'**inconvénient** à ce que
- **You have been authorised to** use force to protect relief supply routes
  = on vous **autorise** à
- **We should be happy to allow you to** inspect the papers here *(soutenu)*
  = nous vous **autorisons volontiers** à

Avec plus d'insistance

- If you need to keep your secret, **of course you must** keep it
  = bien sûr, il faut
- **By all means** charge a reasonable consultation fee
  = n'**hésitez** pas à
- **I have no objection at all to your** quoting me in your article
  = je n'ai pas d'**objection** à ce que vous
- **We would be delighted to** have you
  = c'est avec **plaisir** que nous

36.3 Pour refuser la permission

- **You can't** *ou* **you mustn't** go anywhere near the research lab
  = vous ne **devez** pas
- **I don't want you to** see that Milner again
  = je ne **veux** pas que tu
- **I'd rather you didn't** give them my name
  = j'aimerais autant que tu ne ... pas
- **I wouldn't want you to** be asking around about them too much
  = je n'aimerais pas que tu
- **You're not allowed to** leave the ship until relieved
  = vous n'avez pas le **droit** de
- **I've been forbidden to** swim for the moment
  = on m'a **interdit** de
- **I've been forbidden** alcohol **by** my doctor
  = m'a **interdit**
- **I couldn't possibly allow you to** pay for all this
  = je ne **peux** pas vous **laisser**
- **You must not** enter the premises without the owners' authority
  = vous ne **devez** pas
- **We cannot allow** the marriage **to** take place
  = nous ne **pouvons** pas **permettre** que

De façon plus énergique

- **I absolutely forbid you to** take part in any further search
  = je vous **interdis** formellement de
- **You are forbidden to** contact my children
  = je vous **interdis** de
- Smoking **is strictly forbidden** at all times
  = il est strictement **interdit** de
- **It is strictly forbidden to** carry weapons in this country
  = il est strictement **interdit** de
- **We regret that it is not possible for you to** visit the castle at the moment, owing to the building works *(à l'écrit)*
  = nous sommes au **regret** de vous informer que vous ne pouvez pas

37 L'OBLIGATION

37.1 Pour exprimer ce que l'on est obligé de faire

- Go and see Pompeii — **it's a must!** *(familier)*
  = c'est à ne pas **manquer**
- You need to be very good, **no two ways about it** *(familier)*
  = tu n'as pas le **choix**
- **You've got to** *ou* **You have to** be back before midnight
  = vous **devez**
- **You need to** *ou* **You must** have an address in Prague before you can apply for the job
  = il **faut** que vous
- I have no choice: this is how **I must** live and I cannot do otherwise
  = je **dois**
- **He was forced to** ask his family for a loan
  = il a été **obligé** de
- Jews **are obliged to** accept the divine origin of the Law
  = sont **tenus** de

- A degree **is indispensable** for future entrants to the profession
  = est **indispensable**
- Party membership **is an essential prerequisite of** a successful career
  = est la condition **sine qua non** pour
- **It is essential to** know what the career options are before choosing a course of study
  = il est **essentiel** de
- A dog collar **is a requirement of** law
  = est **exigé** par
- Wearing the kilt **is compulsory** for all those taking part
  = est **obligatoire**
- One cannot admit defeat, **one is driven to** keep on trying
  = on est **contraint** à
- **We have no alternative but to** fight
  = nous n'avons pas le **choix**, nous **devons**
- Three passport photos **are required** *(soutenu)*
  = il **faut** fournir
- Soldiers **must not fail to** take to arms against the enemy *(soutenu)*
  = se **doivent** de
- **You will** go directly to the headmaster's office and wait for me there *(soutenu)*
  = allez

37.2 Pour savoir si l'on est obligé de faire quelque chose

- **Do I have to** *ou* **Have I got to** be home by midnight?
  = est-ce que je **dois**
- **Does one have** *ou* **need to** book in advance?
  = **faut**-il
- **Is it necessary to** look at the problem across the continent?
  = est-il **nécessaire** de
- **Ought I to** tell my colleagues?
  = **devrais**-je
- **Should I** tell my boyfriend about my fantasy to paint his face and dress him in my petticoat?
  = **devrais**-je
- **Am I meant to** *ou* **Am I expected to** *ou* **Am I supposed to** fill in this bit of the form?
  = est-ce que je suis **censé**

37.3 Pour exprimer ce que l'on n'est pas obligé de faire

- **I don't have to** *ou* **I haven't got to** be home so early now the nights are lighter
  = je ne suis pas **obligé** de
- **You don't have to** *ou* **You needn't** go there if you don't want to
  = vous n'êtes pas **obligé** de
- **You are not obliged to** *ou* **You are under no obligation to** invite him
  = rien ne vous **oblige** à
- **It is not necessary** *ou* **compulsory** *ou* **obligatory to** have a letter of acceptance but it does help
  = il n'est pas **nécessaire** de
- The Revenue **does not expect you to** pay the assessed amount
  = n'**exige** pas que vous

37.4 Pour exprimer ce que l'on ne doit pas faire

- **On no account must you** be persuaded to give up the cause
  = vous ne **devez** en aucun cas
- **You are not allowed to** sit the exam more than three times
  = on n'a pas le **droit** de
- Smoking **is not allowed** in the dining room
  = il n'est pas **permis** de
- **You mustn't** show this document to any unauthorised person
  = vous ne **devez** pas
- These are tasks **you cannot** ignore, delegate or bungle
  = que l'on ne peut pas se **permettre** de
- **You're not supposed to** *ou* **You're not meant to** use this room unless you are a club member
  = vous n'êtes pas **censé**

De façon plus énergique

- **It is forbidden to** bring cameras into the gallery
  = il est **interdit** de
- **I forbid you to** return there
  = je vous **interdis** de
- **You are forbidden to** talk to anyone while the case is being heard
  = il vous est **interdit** de
- **Smoking is forbidden** *ou* **is prohibited** *ou* **is not permitted** in the dining room
  = il est **interdit** de

38 L'ACCORD

38.1 Pour exprimer l'accord avec ce qui est dit

- **I fully agree with you** *ou* **I totally agree with you** on this point
  = je suis entièrement d'**accord** avec vous
- **We are in complete agreement** on this
  = nous sommes entièrement d'**accord**
- **I entirely take your point about** the extra vehicles needed
  = je suis entièrement de votre **avis** à propos de
- **I think we see completely eye to eye** on this issue
  = je pense que nous avons exactement le même point de vue
- **You're quite right in** point**ing at the distribution system as the main problem**
  = vous avez **raison** de
- **We share your views** on the proposed expansion of the site
  = nous **partageons** votre point de vue
- **As you have quite rightly pointed out**, we still have a long way to go
  = comme vous l'avez fait remarquer
- **I have to concede that** the results are quite eye-catching
  = je dois **reconnaître** que

- **I have no objection to this** being done
  = je n'ai pas d'**objection** à ce que
- **I agree up to a point**
  = je suis d'**accord** dans une certaine mesure

De façon familière

- Go for a drink instead of working late? **Sounds good to me!**
  = je suis **partant** !
- **That's a lovely thought**
  = comme ça serait bien !
- **I'm all for** encourag**ing a youth section in video clubs such as ours**
  = je suis tout à fait pour
- **I couldn't agree with you more**
  = je suis tout à fait d'**accord** avec vous

De façon plus soutenue

- **I am delighted to wholeheartedly endorse** your campaign
  = je suis **heureux** d'apporter mon **soutien** sans réserve à
- **Our conclusions are entirely consistent with** your findings
  = nos conclusions viennent confirmer
- Independent statistics **corroborate** those of your researcher
  = **corroborent**
- **We applaud** the group's decision to stand firm on this point
  = nous **approuvons**

38.2 Pour exprimer l'accord avec ce qui est proposé

- This certainly **seems the right way to go about it**
  = semble être la bonne façon de procéder
- **I will certainly give my backing to** such a scheme
  = je ne manquerai pas d'apporter mon **soutien** à
- **It makes sense to** enlist helping hands for the final stages
  = il semble logique de
- **We certainly welcome** this development in Stirling
  = nous nous **réjouissons** de

De façon plus familière

- **It's a great idea**
  = c'est une idée formidable
- Cruise control? **I like the sound of that**
  = ça me paraît une bonne idée
- **I'll go along with** Ted's proposal that we open the club up to women
  = je suis d'**accord** avec

De façon plus soutenue

- This solution **is most acceptable** to us
  = paraît tout à fait **acceptable**
- The proposed scheme **meets with our approval**
  = nous **approuvons**
- This is a proposal which **deserves our wholehearted support**
  = mérite pleinement notre **soutien**
- **We assent to** *ou* **We give our assent to** your plan to develop the site
  = nous donnons notre **accord** à

38.3 Pour exprimer l'accord avec ce qui est demandé

- Of course **I'll be happy to** organise it for you
  = je serai **heureux** de
- **I'll do as you suggest** and send him the documents
  = je suivrai votre **conseil**
- **There's no problem about** getting tickets for him
  = nous n'aurons aucun mal à

De façon plus soutenue

- Reputable builders **will not object to** this reasonable request
  = ne feront pas **objection** à
- **We should be delighted to** cooperate with you in this enterprise
  = nous serions **enchantés** de
- An army statement said it **would comply with** the ceasefire
  = **respecterait**
- **I consent to** the performance of such procedures as are considered necessary
  = je donne mon **assentiment** à

39 LE DÉSACCORD

39.1 Pour exprimer le désaccord avec ce qui est dit

- I'm afraid **he's quite wrong** if he's told you that vasectomies can't be reversed
  = se **trompe**
- **You're wrong in thinking that** I haven't understood
  = vous avez **tort** de penser que
- **I cannot agree with you** on this point
  = je ne suis pas du tout d'**accord** avec vous
- **We cannot accept the view that** R and D spending or rather the lack of it explains the decline of Britain
  = nous ne pouvons **accepter** l'**opinion** selon laquelle
- To say we should forget about it, no **I cannot go along with that**
  = je ne suis pas du tout d'**accord** là-dessus
- **We must agree to differ on this one**
  = nous devons reconnaître que nos **opinions divergent**
- I think **it might be better if you thought it over again**
  = il vaudrait mieux que vous reconsidériez la question

Avec plus d'insistance

- **This is most emphatically not the case**
  = cela n'est absolument pas le cas
- **I entirely reject** his contentions
  = je **rejette** absolument
- **We explicitly reject** the implication in your letter
  = nous **rejetons** catégoriquement
- **I totally disagree with** the previous two callers
  = je ne suis pas du tout d'**accord** avec

39.2 Pour exprimer le désaccord avec ce qui est proposé

Avec force

- **I'm dead against** this idea (*familier*)
  = je suis tout à fait **contre**
- **Right idea, wrong approach** (*familier*)
  = c'était une bonne idée, mais ils *etc* s'y sont mal pris
- **I will not hear of** such a thing
  = je ne veux pas entendre parler de
- **It is not feasible to** change the schedule at this late stage
  = il est **impensable** de
- This **is not a viable alternative**
  = ce n'est pas **faisable**
- Running down the street shouting "Eureka" has emotional appeal but **is the wrong approach**
  = n'est pas la bonne manière de s'y prendre

Avec moins d'insistance

- **I'm not too keen on** this idea
  = ne me **plaît** pas beaucoup
- **I don't think much of** this idea
  = je n'**aime** pas beaucoup
- **This doesn't seem to be the right way of** deal**ing with the problem**
  = cela ne semble pas être la bonne manière de
- While we are grateful for the suggestion, **we are unfortunately unable to** implement this change (*soutenu*)
  = nous ne sommes **malheureusement** pas à même de
- **I regret that I am not in a position to** accept your kind offer (*soutenu*)
  = je suis **désolé** de ne pas être en mesure de

39.3 Pour exprimer le désaccord avec ce qui est demandé

- **I wouldn't dream of** do**ing a thing like that**
  = **jamais** je ne
- I'm sorry but **I can't** do it
  = il m'est **impossible** de
- **I cannot in all conscience** leave those kids in that atmosphere
  = je ne peux pas, en conscience

Avec plus de force

- **This is quite out of the question** for the time being
  = cela est hors de **question**
- **I won't agree to** *ou* **I can't agree to** any plan that involves your brother
  = je m'**oppose** à
- **I refuse point blank to** have anything to do with this affair
  = je **refuse** net de

... et de façon plus soutenue

- **I am afraid I must refuse**
  = je crains de devoir **refuser**
- **I cannot possibly comply with** this request
  = je ne peux pas **accéder** à
- **It is impracticable for us to** commit ourselves at this stage
  = il nous est difficile de
- In view of the proposed timescale, **I must reluctantly decline to** take part
  = je me vois malheureusement obligé de **refuser** de

40 L'APPROBATION

40.1 Pour approuver ce qui a été dit

- **I couldn't agree** (with you) **more**
  = je suis entièrement de votre **avis**
- **I couldn't have put it better myself,** even if I'd tried
  = c'est **exactement** ce que j'aurais dit moi-même
- We must oppose terrorism, whatever its source. — **Hear, hear!**
  = **bravo** !
- **I endorse** his feelings regarding the situation (*soutenu*)
  = je **partage**

40.2 Pour approuver une proposition

- **It's just the job!** (*familier*)
  = c'est **exactement** ce qu'il nous faut !
- **This is just the sort of thing I wanted**
  = c'est **exactement** ce que je voulais
- **This is exactly what I had in mind** when I asked for the plan to be drawn up
  = c'est **précisément** ce que j'avais à l'esprit
- Thank you for sending the draft agenda: **I like the look of it very much**
  = il a l'air très bien
- **We are all very enthusiastic about** *ou* **very keen on** his latest set of proposals
  = nous accueillons avec **enthousiasme**
- **I shall certainly give it my backing**
  = je **soutiendrai** certainement cela
- Any game which is as clearly enjoyable as this **meets with my approval**
  = a mon **approbation**
- Skinner's plan **deserves our total support** *ou* **our wholehearted approval**
  = mérite tout notre **soutien**
- **There are considerable advantages in** the alternative method you propose
  = comporte de nombreux avantages
- **We recognize** the merits of this scheme
  = nous **reconnaissons**
- **We view** your proposal to extend the site **favourably**
  = nous voyons d'un œil **favorable**
- This project **is worthy of our attention**
  = mérite notre attention

40.3 Pour approuver une idée

- **You're quite right to** wait before making such an important decision
  = vous avez **raison** de

- **I entirely approve of** the idea
  = j'**approuve** entièrement
- **I'd certainly go along with that!**
  = je suis tout à fait pour !
- **I'm very much in favour of** that sort of thing
  = je suis vraiment pour

40.4 Pour approuver une action

- **I applaud** Noble's perceptive analysis of the problems
  = j'**approuve**
- **I have a very high opinion of** their new teaching methods
  = j'ai une très haute opinion de
- **I have a very high regard for** the work of the Crown Prosecution Service
  = je tiens en haute **estime**
- **I think very highly of** the people who have been leading thus far
  = j'ai une grande **estime** pour
- **I certainly admire** his courage in telling her exactly what he thought of her
  = j'**admire** beaucoup
- **I must congratulate you on** the professional way you handled the situation
  = je dois vous **féliciter** de

41 LA DÉSAPPROBATION

- **This doesn't seem to be the right way of** going about it
  = je ne pense pas que ce soit la bonne façon de
- **I don't think much of** what this government has done so far
  = ne me dit rien qui vaille
- **I can't say I'm pleased about** what has happened
  = je ne peux pas dire que je sois vraiment satisfait de
- As always, Britain **takes a dim view of** sex
  = voit d'un mauvais œil
- **We have a low opinion of** *ou* **poor opinion of** opportunists like him
  = nous n'avons pas une bien haute **opinion** de

Plus directement

- **I'm fed up with** having to wait so long for payments to be made
  = j'en ai **assez** de
- **I've had (just) about enough of** this whole supermodel thing
  = j'en ai vraiment **assez** de
- **I can't bear** *ou* **stand** people who smoke in restaurants
  = je ne **supporte** pas
- **He was quite wrong to** repeat what I said about her
  = il a eu **tort** de
- **I cannot approve of** *ou* **support** any sort of testing on live animals
  = je **réprouve**
- **We are opposed to** all forms of professional malpractice
  = nous nous **opposons** à
- **We condemn** any intervention which could damage race relations
  = nous **condamnons**

- **I must object to** the tag "soft porn actress"
  = je **dois protester** contre
- **I'm very unhappy about** your (idea of) going off to Turkey on your own
  = ne me **plaît** pas du tout
- **I strongly disapprove of** such behaviour
  = je **désapprouve** complètement

42 LA CERTITUDE, LA PROBABILITÉ, LA POSSIBILITÉ ET LA CAPACITÉ

42.1 La certitude

- **She was bound to** discover that you and I had talked
  = il était à prévoir qu'elle allait
- **It is inevitable that they will** get to know of our meeting
  = ils vont **inévitablement**
- **I'm sure** *ou* **certain (that)** he'll keep his word
  = je suis **sûr** que
- **I'm positive** *ou* **convinced (that)** it was your mother I saw
  = je suis **sûr et certain** que
- **We now know for certain** *ou* **for sure that** the exam papers were seen by several students before the day of the exam
  = nous savons maintenant avec **certitude** que
- **I made sure** *ou* **certain that** no one was listening to our conversation
  = je me suis **assuré** que
- From all the evidence **it is clear that** they were planning to take over
  = il est **clair** que
- **It is indisputable that** there are budgerigars in the UK that are harbouring illness
  = il est **incontestable** que
- **It is undeniable that** racial tensions in Britain have been increasing in recent years
  = il est **incontestable** que
- **There is no doubt that** the talks will be a landmark in the new political agenda
  = il ne fait aucun **doute** que
- **There can be no doubt about** the objective of the animal liberationists
  = ne fait aucun **doute**
- This crisis has demonstrated **beyond all (possible) doubt** that effective political control must be in place before the creation of such structures
  = sans le moindre **doute**
- Her pedigree **is beyond dispute** *ou* **question**
  = ne fait aucun **doute**
- **You have my absolute assurance that** this is the case
  = je peux vous **garantir** que
- **I can assure you that** I have had nothing to do with any dishonest trading
  = je peux vous **assurer** que
- **Make no mistake about it** — I will return when I have proof of your involvement
  = soyez **certain** que

42.2 La probabilité

- **There is a good** *ou* **strong chance that** they will agree to the deal
  = il y a de fortes **chances** pour que
- **It seems highly likely that** it was Bert who spilled the beans
  = il y a de fortes **chances** pour que
- **The chances** *ou* **the odds are that** he will play safe in the short term
  = il y a fort à parier que
- **The probability is that** your investment will be worth more in two years' time
  = il est fort **probable** que
- If parents tell a child that she is bright, then she will, **in all probability**, see herself as bright and behave as such
  = selon toute **probabilité**
- You will **very probably** be met at the airport by one of our men
  = très **probablement**
- **It is highly probable that** American companies will face retaliation abroad
  = il est très **probable** que
- **It is quite likely that** you will get withdrawal symptoms at first
  = il est **probable** que
- **The likelihood is that** the mood of mistrust and recrimination will intensify
  = il est très **probable** que
- The person indicted is, **in all likelihood**, going to be guilty as charged
  = selon toute **probabilité**
- **There is reason to believe that** the books were stolen from the library
  = il y a **lieu** de croire que
- **He must** know of the paintings' existence
  = il **doit**
- The talks **could very well** spill over into tomorrow
  = **pourraient** très bien
- The cheque **should** reach you by Saturday
  = devrait

42.3 La possibilité

- The situation **could** change from day to day
  = **pourrait**
- Britain **could perhaps** play a more positive role in developing policy
  = **pourrait peut-être**
- **I venture to suggest (that)** a lot of it is to do with him
  = je me permets de **suggérer** que
- **It is possible that** a premonition is triggered when a random image happens to coincide with the later event
  = il est **possible** que
- **It is conceivable that** the British economy is already in recession
  = il est **possible** que
- **It is well within the bounds of possibility that** England could be beaten
  = il est très **possible** que
- **It may be that** the whole battle will have to be fought over again
  = il se **peut** que
- **It may be (the case) that** they got your name from the voters' roll
  = il se **peut** que
- **There is an outside chance that** the locomotive may appear in the Gala
  = il existe une très faible **chance** pour que
- **There is a small chance that** your body could reject the implants
  = il y a un **risque** que

42.4 Pour exprimer ce que l'on est capable de faire

- Our Design and Print Service **can** supply envelopes and package your existing literature
  = **peut**
- Applicants must **be able to** use a word processor
  = être **capables** de
- When it came to raising the spirits of the sleep-deprived ravers at Glastonbury, Ultramarine **were more than up to the job**
  = ont vraiment été à la **hauteur** de la tâche
- **He is qualified to** teach physics
  = il a les **qualifications** requises pour

43 L'INCERTITUDE, L'IMPROBABILITÉ, L'IMPOSSIBILITÉ ET L'INCAPACITÉ

43.1 L'incertitude

- **I doubt if** *ou* **It is doubtful whether** he knows where it came from
  = je **doute** que
- **There is still some doubt surrounding** his exact whereabouts
  = le **doute** subsiste quant à
- **I have my doubts about** replacing private donations with taxpayers' cash
  = j'ai des **doutes** quant à
- **It isn't known for sure** *ou* **It isn't certain** where she is
  = on ne **sait** pas exactement
- Sometimes you stay in your room for three, four, five days at a time, **you couldn't say for sure**
  = on ne **sait** pas exactement
- It's all still up in the air — **we won't know for certain** until the end of next week
  = nous serons dans l'**incertitude**
- You're asking why I should do such an extraordinary thing and **I'm not sure** *ou* **certain that** I really know the answer
  = je ne suis pas **sûr ou certain que**
- **I'm not convinced that** you can teach people to think sideways on problems
  = je ne suis pas **convaincu** que
- **We are still in the dark about** where the letter came from
  = nous **ignorons** toujours
- **It is touch and go whether** base rates have to go up
  = il n'est pas **certain** que

◆ **I'm wondering if** I should offer to help them out?
= je me **demande** si

43.2 L'improbabilité

◆ You have **probably not** yet seen the document I am referring to
= vous n'avez **probablement** pas

◆ **It is highly improbable that**, in the past 30 years, meteor fireballs have changed the noise they have been making for billennia
= il est très peu **probable** que

◆ **It is very doubtful whether** the expedition will reach the summit
= il est peu **probable** que

◆ **In the unlikely event that** the room was bugged, the music would scramble their conversation
= si jamais

◆ **It was hardly to be expected that** the course of democratization would always run smoothly
= on ne **pouvait** guère s'attendre à ce que

43.3 L'impossibilité

◆ **There can be no** return to earlier standards
= il est **impossible** de

◆ Nowadays Carnival **cannot** happen **without** the police tell**ing us where to walk and what direction to walk in**
= ne **peut** ... sans que

◆ This is not to say that academic judgement is sacrosanct: since academic judgement is not uniform, **this cannot be the case**
= ce n'est pas **possible**

◆ **I couldn't possibly** invite George and not his wife
= je ne **pourrais** pas

◆ **The new law rules out any possibility of** exceptions
= exclut toute **possibilité** de

◆ He said **there was no question of** him representing one half of the Arab world against the other
= il n'était pas **question** que

◆ A German spokesman said **it was out of the question that** these weapons would be based in Germany
= il était hors de **question** que

◆ **There is not (even) the remotest chance that** *ou* **There is absolutely no chance that** he will succeed
= il n'y a pas la moindre **chance** que

◆ The idea of trying to govern twelve nations from one centre **is unthinkable**
= est **inconcevable**

◆ Since we had over 500 applicants, **it would be quite impossible to** interview them all
= il serait tout à fait **impossible** de

43.4 Pour exprimer ce que l'on est incapable de faire

◆ **I can't** drive, I'm afraid
= je ne **sais** pas

◆ **I don't know how to** use a word processor
= je ne **sais** pas

◆ The army **has been unable to** suppress the political violence in the area
= n'a pas **pu**

◆ The congress had shown itself **incapable of** real reform
= **incapable** de

◆ His fellow-directors **were not up** to runn**ing the business without him**
= n'étaient pas **capables** de

◆ He called all the gods to help lift the giant's leg and free Thor, but even together they **were not equal** to the task
= n'étaient pas à la **hauteur**

◆ I'm afraid the task proved (to be) **beyond his capabilities** *ou* **abilities**
= trop **difficile** pour lui

◆ I would like to leave him but sometimes I feel the effort **is beyond me**
= est au-**dessus** de mes **forces**

◆ **He simply couldn't cope with** the stresses of family life
= il ne **pouvait** pas faire face à

◆ Far too many women accept that they're **hopeless at** *ou* **no good at** manag**ing money**
= totalement **incapables** de

◆ **I'm not in a position to** say now how much substance there is in the reports
= je ne suis pas en **mesure** de

◆ **It is quite impossible for me to** describe the confusion and horror of the scene
= je suis dans l'**impossibilité** de

44 L'EXPLICATION

44.1 Donner les raisons de quelque chose

◆ He was sacked. **For the simple reason that** he just wasn't up to it any more
= pour la simple **raison** que

◆ **The reason that** we are still so obsessed by him is simply that he was the one person we had who knew what was what
= la **raison** pour laquelle

◆ He said he could not be more specific **for** security **reasons**
= pour des **raisons** de

◆ Students have been arrested recently **because of** suspected dissident activities
= en **raison** de

◆ Parliament has prevaricated, **largely because of** the unwillingness of the main opposition party to support the changes
= essentiellement en **raison** de

◆ Teachers in the eastern part of Germany are assailed by fears of mass unemployment **on account of** their communist past
= du **fait** de

◆ Morocco has announced details of the austerity package it is adopting **as a result of** pressure from the International Monetary Fund
= par **suite** de

◆ They are facing higher costs **owing to** rising inflation
= par **suite** de

◆ The full effects will be delayed **due to** factors beyond our control
= en **raison** de

◆ **Thanks to** their generosity, the charity can afford to buy new equipment
= **grâce** à

- What also had to go was the notion that some people were born superior to others **by virtue of** their skin colour
  = en **raison** de
- Tax collection was often carried out **by means of** illegal measures
  = au **moyen** de
- He shot to fame **on the strength of** a letter he had written to the Queen
  = **grâce** à
- The King and Queen's defence of old-fashioned family values has acquired a poignancy **in view of** their inability to have children
  = **vu**
- The police have put considerable pressure on the Government to toughen its stance **in the light of** recent events
  = étant **donné**
- **In the face of** this continued disagreement, the parties have asked for the polling to be postponed
  = face à
- His soldiers had so far been restraining themselves **for fear of** harm**ing civilians**
  = de **crainte** de
- Babies have died **for want of** *ou* **for lack of** proper medical attention
  = **faute** de
- I refused her a divorce, **out of** spite I suppose
  = **par**
- The warder was freed unharmed **in exchange for** the release of a colleague
  = en **échange** de
- The court had ordered his release, **on the grounds that** he had already been acquitted of most charges against him
  = sous **prétexte** que
- I am absolutely for civil disobedience **on** moral **grounds**
  = pour des **raisons**
- It is unclear why they initiated this week's attack, **given that** negotiations were underway
  = étant **donné** que
- **Seeing that** he had a police escort, the only time he could have switched containers was en route to the airport
  = étant **donné** que
- **As** these bottles are easy to come by, you can have one for each purpose
  = **comme**
- International intervention was appropriate **since** tensions had reached the point where there was talk of war
  = **puisque**
- Yet she was not deaf, **for** she started at the sound of a bell *(littér)*
  = **puisque**
- I'm naturally disappointed this is not quite enough to win on the first ballot. **So** I confirm it is my intention to let my name go forward to the second ballot
  = **donc**
- What the Party said was taken to be right, **therefore** anyone who disagreed must be wrong
  = **par conséquent**
- **Following** last weekend's rioting in central London, Conservatives say some left-wing Labour MPs were partly to blame
  = à la **suite** de
- **The thing is** that once you've retired there's no going back
  = c'est que

44.2 Pour expliquer la cause ou l'origine de quelque chose

- The serious dangers to your health **caused by** *ou* **brought about by** cigarettes are now better understood
  = **provoqué** par
- When the picture was published recently, **it gave rise to** *ou* **led to** speculation that the three were still alive and being held captive
  = cela a donné **lieu** à
- The army argues that security concerns **necessitated** the demolitions
  = rendaient ... **nécessaires**
- This lack of recognition **was at the root of** the dispute which led to their march
  = était à l'**origine** de
- **I attribute** all this mismanagement **to** the fact that the General Staff in London is practically non-existent
  = j'**attribue** ... à
- This unrest **dates from** colonial times
  = **remonte** à
- The custom **goes back to** pre-Christian days
  = **remonte** à

45 L'EXCUSE

45.1 Pour s'excuser

- **I'm really sorry**, Steve, **but** we won't be able to come on Saturday
  = je suis vraiment **désolé** ... mais
- **I'm sorry that** your time has been wasted
  = je suis **désolé** que
- **I am sorry to have to** say this to you but you're no good
  = je suis **désolé** de
- **Apologies if** I seemed obsessed with private woes last night
  = toutes mes **excuses** si
- **I must apologize for** what happened. Quite unforgivable
  = je vous prie de m'**excuser** pour
- **I owe you an apology**. I didn't think you knew what you were talking about
  = je vous dois des **excuses**
- The general back-pedalled, saying that **he had had no intention of** offend**ing the German government**
  = il n'avait aucunement l'**intention** de
- **Please forgive me for** feel**ing sorry for myself**
  = veuillez me **pardonner** de
- **Please accept our apologies** if this has caused you any inconvenience *(soutenu)*
  = nous vous prions d'accepter nos **excuses**
- **Do forgive me for** be**ing a little abrupt** *(soutenu)*
  = veuillez m'**excuser** de

45.2 Pour accepter la responsabilité de quelque chose

- **I admit** I submitted the second gun for inspection, in the knowledge that you had used my own for the killing
  = je **reconnais**
- **I have no excuse for** what happened
  = je n'ai aucune **excuse** pour
- **It is my fault that** our marriage is on the rocks
  = c'est ma **faute** si
- The Government **is not entirely to blame but neither is it innocent**
  = tout cela n'est pas entièrement la faute de ... mais il n'est pas non plus **innocent**
- **I should never have** let him rush out of the house in anger
  = je n'aurais jamais dû
- Oh, but **if only I hadn't** made Freddy try to get my bag back!
  = si seulement je n'avais pas
- I hate to admit that the old man was right, but **I made a stupid mistake**
  = je me suis grossièrement **trompé**
- **My mistake was in** fail**ing to push my concerns and convictions**
  = j'ai fait l'**erreur** de
- **My mistake was to** arrive wearing a jacket and polo-neck jumper
  = j'ai fait l'**erreur** de
- In December the markets raced ahead, and I missed out. **That was my mistake**
  = ça a été une **erreur** de ma part

45.3 Pour exprimer des regrets

- **I'm very upset about** her decision but when only one partner wants to make an effort you're fighting a losing battle
  = je suis très **contrarié** de
- **It's just a bit of a shame that**, on close inspection, the main vocalists look like Whitney Houston and Lionel Richie
  = c'est bien **dommage** que
- **I feel awful** but I couldn't stand by and watch him make a fool of himself, someone had to tell him to shut up
  = je suis vraiment **désolé**
- **I'm afraid I can't** help you very much
  = j'ai bien peur de ne pouvoir
- **It is a pity that** my profession can make money out of the misfortunes of others
  = il est **dommage** que
- **It is unfortunate that** the matter should have come to a head when the Western allies may be on the brink of military engagement
  = il est **regrettable** que
- **I very much regret that** we have been unable to reach agreement
  = suis **navré** que
- The accused **bitterly regrets** this incident and it won't happen again
  = **regrette** amèrement
- **We regret to inform you that** the post of Editor has now been filled (*style écrit*)
  = nous sommes au **regret** de vous informer que

45.4 Pour rejeter toute responsabilité

- **I didn't do it on purpose**, it just happened
  = je ne l'ai pas fait **exprès**
- Sorry, Nanna. **I didn't mean to** upset you
  = je n'avais pas l'**intention** de
- Excuse me, but **I was under the impression that** these books were being written for women
  = j'avais l'**impression** que
- **We are simply trying to** protect the interests of our horses and owners
  = nous essayons tout simplement de
- I know how this hurt you but **I had no choice**. I had to put David's life above all else
  = je n'avais pas le choix
- **We were obliged to** accept their conditions
  = nous avons été **obligés** de
- We are unhappy with 1.5 %, but under the circumstances **we have no alternative but to** accept
  = nous ne pouvons faire autrement que de
- **I had nothing to do with** the placing of any advertisement
  = je n'avais rien à voir avec
- A Charlton spokesman assured Sheffield supporters that **it was a genuine error** and there was no intention to mislead them
  = c'était vraiment une **erreur**

46 LES DEMANDES D'EMPLOI

46.1 Pour commencer la lettre

- **In reply to your advertisement** for a Trainee Manager in today's Guardian, I would be grateful if you would send me further details of the post
  = me **référant** à votre **annonce**
- **I wish to apply for the post of** bilingual correspondent, as advertised in this week's Euronews
  = je me permets de poser ma **candidature** au **poste** de
- **I am writing to ask if there is any possibility of work in your company**
  = je vous serais **reconnaissant** de me faire savoir s'il me serait possible d'obtenir un emploi dans votre **entreprise**
- **I am writing to enquire about the possibility of joining your company on work placement** for a period of 3 months
  = je vous serais **reconnaissant** de me faire savoir s'il me serait possible d'effectuer un **stage** rémunéré dans votre **entreprise**

46.2 Pour parler de son expérience professionnelle et exposer ses motivations

- **I have** three **years' experience of** office work
  = j'ai ... années d'**expérience** en
- **I am familiar with word processors**
  = je connais divers logiciels de traitement de texte
- **As well as speaking fluent** English, **I have a working knowledge of** German **and a reading knowledge of** Swedish
  = je **parle** couramment ..., possède de bonnes **connaissances** en ... et lis le

89 Short Street
Glossop
Derbys SK13 4AP

The Personnel Director
Norton Manufacturing Ltd
Sandy Lodge Industrial Estate
Northants NN10 8QT

3 February 2002

Dear Sir or Madam[1],

With reference to your advertisement in the Guardian of 2 February 2002, I wish to apply for the post of Export Manager in your company.

I am currently employed as Export Sales Executive for United Engineering Ltd. My main role is to develop our European business by establishing contact with potential new distributors and conducting market research both at home and abroad.

I believe I could successfully apply my sales and marketing skills to this post and therefore enclose my curriculum vitae for your consideration. Please do not hesitate to contact me if you require further details. I am available for interview at any time.

I look forward to hearing from you.

Yours faithfully,

Janet Lilly

Janet Lilly

1 ***Quand on ne sait pas si la personne à qui on s'adresse est un homme ou une femme, il convient d'utiliser la présentation ci-contre.***

Toutefois, si l'on connaît le nom de la personne, la présentation suivante est préférable :

Mr Leonard Easdon
ou
Mrs Emma Gault
Personnel Director
Norton Manufacturing Ltd etc.

Pour commencer votre lettre, la formule à employer est la suivante : "Dear Sir" ou "Dear Madam"

Toute lettre commençant ainsi doit se terminer par la formule "Yours faithfully" suivie de la signature. ***Pour plus de détails, voir pages 60 - 61.***

- **I am currently working in** this field
  = je **travaille** actuellement dans
- **As you will see from my CV,** I have worked in Belgium before
  = comme l'indique mon **CV**
- **Although I have no experience of** this type of work, **I have** had other holiday jobs and can supply references from my employers, if you wish
  = bien que je n'aie pas d'**expérience** dans ... j'ai
- **My current salary is** ... per annum and I have four weeks' paid leave
  = mon **salaire** actuel est de
- **I would like to change jobs** to broaden my experience
  = j'aimerais changer de **situation**
- **I would like to make better use of** my languages
  = j'aimerais **pratiquer** davantage

46.3 Pour terminer la lettre

- **I will be available from** the end of April
  = je serai **disponible** à partir de
- **I am available for interview** at any time
  = je me tiens à votre **disposition** pour un **entretien**
- **I would be glad to supply further details**
  = je me tiens à votre **disposition** pour tout complément d'**information**
- **Please do not hesitate to contact me** for further information
  = n'hésitez pas à me contacter
- **Please do not contact my current employer**
  = je vous serais **reconnaissant** de ne pas contacter mon **employeur** actuel
- **I enclose** a stamped addressed envelope for your reply
  = veuillez trouver **ci-joint**

CURRICULUM VITAE

Name: Kate Maxwell

Address: 12 Poplar Avenue, Leeds LS12 9DT, England

Telephone: 0113 246 6648

Date of Birth: 2.2.73

Marital Status: Single

Nationality: British

Qualifications[1]: Diploma in Business Management, Liverpool College of Business Studies (1997)
BA Honours in French with Hispanic Studies (Upper 2nd class), University of York (1996)
A-Levels: English (B), French (A), Spanish (A), Geography (C) (1991)
O-Levels: in 8 subjects (1989)

Employment History: Sales Assistant, Langs Bookshop, York (summer 1997)
English Assistant, Lycée Victor Hugo, Nîmes, France (1994-95)
Au Pair, Nantes, France (summer 1992)
Campsite courier, Peniscola, Spain (summer 1991)

Other Information: I enjoy reading, the cinema, skiing and amateur dramatics. I hold a clean driving licence and am a non-smoker.

References:

Mr John Jeffries	Ms Teresa González
General Reference	Department of Spanish
Langs Bookshop	University of York
York	York
YT5 2PS	YT4 3DE

1 ***Si l'on pose sa candidature à un poste à l'étranger, l'emploi de formules telles que "French equivalent of A-Levels (Baccalauréat Langues)" est conseillé.***

46.4 Comment demander et rédiger des références

- In my application for the position of German lecturer, I have been asked to provide the names of two referees and **I wondered whether you would mind if I gave your name** as one of them
  = je vous serais **reconnaissant** de me permettre de donner votre nom
- Ms Lane has applied for the post of Marketing Executive with our company and has given us your name as a reference. **We would be grateful if you would let us know whether you would recommend her for this position**
  = nous vous serions **reconnaissants** de bien vouloir nous dire si vous la **recommandez** pour ce poste
- **Your reply will be treated in the strictest confidence**
  = votre **réponse** sera considérée comme strictement confidentielle
- I have known Mr Chambers for four years in his capacity as Sales Manager and **can warmly recommend him for the position**
  = c'est avec plaisir que je vous le **recommande** pour ce poste

46.5 Pour accepter ou refuser une offre d'emploi

- Thank you for your letter of 20 March. **I will be pleased to attend for interview** at your Manchester offices on Thursday 7 April at 10am
  = je serai très heureux de me rendre à l'**entretien**
- **I would like to confirm my acceptance of** the post of Marketing Executive
  = je désire **confirmer** que j'accepte
- **I would be delighted to accept this post. However,** would it be possible to postpone my starting date until 8 May?
  = c'est avec **plaisir** que j'**accepterais** ce poste. Toutefois

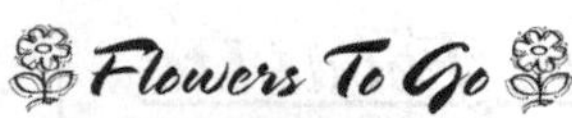

117 Rollesby Road
Beccles NR6 9DL
☎ 61 654 31 71

Ms Sharon McNeillie
41 Courthill Street
Beccles NR14 8TR

18 January 2000

Dear Ms McNeillie,

Special Offer! 5% discount on orders received in January!

Thank you for your recent enquiry. We can deliver fresh flowers anywhere in the country at very reasonable prices. Our bouquets come beautifully wrapped, with satin ribbons, attractive foil backing, a sachet of plant food and, of course, your own personalized message. For that special occasion, we can even deliver arrangements with a musical greeting, the ideal surprise gift for birthdays, weddings or Christmas!

Whatever the occasion, you will find just what you need to make it special in our latest brochure, which I have pleasure in enclosing, along with our current price list. All prices include delivery within the UK.

During the promotion, a discount of 5% will apply on all orders received before the end of January, so hurry!

We look forward to hearing from you.

Yours sincerely,

Daisy Duckworth

Daisy Duckworth
Promotions Assistant

- **I would be glad to accept your offer; however,** the salary stated is somewhat lower than what I had hoped for
  = c'est avec **plaisir** que j'**accepterais** votre **offre** ; toutefois
- Having given your offer careful thought, **I regret that I am unable to accept**
  = j'ai le **regret** de devoir la **refuser**

47 LA CORRESPONDANCE COMMERCIALE

47.1 Demandes de renseignements

- **We** see ou note from your advertisement in the latest edition of the Healthy Holiday Guide that you are offering cut-price salmon fishing holidays in Scotland, and **would be grateful if you would send us** full details of prices and dates available between 14 July and 30 August
  = nous vous serions **reconnaissants** de bien vouloir nous **envoyer**
- I read about the Association for Improvements in the Maternity Services in the NCT newsletter and would be very interested to learn more about your activities. **Please send me details of** membership
  = je vous serais **reconnaissant** de bien vouloir m'**envoyer** de plus amples **renseignements** sur
- **In response to your enquiry of** 8 March, **we have pleasure in enclosing** full details on our activity holidays in Cumbria, **together with** our price list
  = **suite à** votre lettre du ..., nous vous prions de trouver **ci-joint** ... ainsi que
- **Thank you for your enquiry about** the Association for the Conservation of Energy. **I have enclosed** a leaflet explaining our background, as well as a list of the issues we regularly campaign on. **Should you wish** to join ACE, a membership application form is also enclosed
  = nous vous **remercions** de votre demande de **renseignements** concernant ... Veuillez trouver ci-joint ... ainsi que ... Si vous désirez

Carrick Foods Ltd
Springwood Industrial estate
Alexandra Road
Sheffield S11 5GF

Ms J Chalmers
Department of English
Holyrood High School
Mirlees Road
Sheffield S19 7KL

14 April 2002

Dear Ms Chalmers,

Thank you for your letter of 7 April enquiring if it would be possible to arrange a group visit to our factory. We would of course be delighted to invite you and your pupils to take part in a guided factory tour. You will be able to observe the process from preparation through to canning, labelling and packaging of the final product ready for dispatch. Our factory manager will be available to answer pupils' questions at the end of the tour.

I would be grateful if you could confirm the date of your proposed visit, as well as the number of pupils and teachers in the party, at your earliest convenience.

Thank you once again for your interest in our company. I look forward to meeting you.

Yours sincerely,

George Whyte

George Whyte

47.2 Commandes

- **We would like to place an order for** the following items, in the sizes and quantities specified below
  = nous aimerions passer **commande** de
- **Please find enclosed our order no.** 3011 for ...
  = veuillez trouver notre **commande** n°
- **The enclosed order** is based on your current price list, assuming our usual discount of 5 % on bulk orders
  = la **commande** ci-jointe
- **I wish to order** a can of "Buzz off!" wasp repellent, as advertised in the July issue of Gardeners' Monthly **and enclose a cheque for** £2.50
  = je désire **commander** ... et vous envoie un chèque de
- **Thank you for your order of** 16 June, which will be dispatched within 30 days
  = nous vous **remercions** de votre **commande** en date du
- **We acknowledge receipt of your order no.** 3570 and advise that the goods will be dispatched within 7 working days
  = nous **accusons réception** de votre **commande** n°
- **We regret that the goods you ordered are temporarily out of stock**
  = nous **regrettons** de vous dire que les articles que vous avez **commandés** sont temporairement épuisés
- **Please allow 28 days for delivery**
  = veuillez compter un **délai** de 28 jours pour la **livraison**

47.3 Livraisons

- **Our delivery time is** 60 days from receipt of order
  = nos **délais** de **livraison** sont de

- **We await confirmation of your order**
  = nous attendons **confirmation** de votre **commande**
- **We confirm that the goods were dispatched on** 4 September
  = nous **confirmons** que les **marchandises** ont été **expédiées** le
- **We cannot accept responsibility for** goods damaged in transit
  = nous ne pouvons accepter aucune **responsabilité** pour

47.4 Pour se plaindre

- **We have not yet received** the items ordered on 22 January (our order no. 2263 refers)
  = nous n'avons pas encore reçu **livraison** de
- **We wish to draw your attention to** an error in the consignment received on 18 November
  = nous désirons vous **signaler**
- **Unfortunately**, the goods were damaged in transit
  = **malheureusement**
- **The goods received differ significantly from the description in your catalogue**
  = les articles livrés ne correspondent pas à la description qui en est donnée dans votre catalogue
- If the goods are not received by 20 October, **we shall have to cancel our order**
  = nous nous verrons contraints d'**annuler** notre **commande**

47.5 Règlement

- **The total amount outstanding is ...**
  = la **somme** qui reste à **régler** s'élève à
- **We would be grateful if you would attend to this account immediately**
  = nous vous serions reconnaissants de bien vouloir **régler** cette **somme** dans les plus brefs délais
- **Please remit payment by return**
  = veuillez nous faire parvenir ce **règlement** par retour du courrier
- Full payment **is due within** 14 working days from receipt of goods
  = est **dû** sous
- **We enclose** a cheque for ... **in settlement of your invoice no.** 2003L/58
  = veuillez trouver ci-joint ... en **règlement** de votre **facture** n°
- We must point out an error in your account and **would be grateful if you would adjust your invoice** accordingly
  = nous vous serions reconnaissants de rectifier votre **facture**
- This mistake was due to an accounting error, and **we enclose a credit note for** the sum involved
  = nous vous prions de trouver ci-joint un avoir pour
- **Thank you for your cheque** for ... in settlement of our invoice
  = nous vous remercions de votre chèque

- **We look forward to doing further business with you in the near future**
  = Nous espérons vous compter à nouveau parmi nos clients

48 LA CORRESPONDANCE GÉNÉRALE

[voir pages 60-61]
[see pages 60-61]

48.1 Pour commencer une lettre

Pour écrire à quelqu'un que l'on connaît

- **Thank you** *ou* **Thanks for your letter**, which arrived yesterday
  = **merci** pour votre **lettre**
- **It was good** *ou* **nice** *ou* **lovely to hear from you**
  = cela m'a fait plaisir d'avoir de vos **nouvelles**
- **I felt I must write a few lines** just to say hello
  = je vous **envoie** ce petit **mot**
- **I'm sorry I haven't written for so long**, and hope you'll forgive me; I've had a lot of work recently and ...
  = je suis **désolé** de ne pas vous avoir **écrit** depuis si longtemps
- **This is a difficult letter for me to write**, and I hope you will understand how I feel
  = je ne sais par où commencer cette **lettre**

Pour écrire à un organisme

- **I am writing to ask whether** you (have in) stock a book entitled ...
  = je vous **écris** pour demander si
- **Please send me** ... I enclose a cheque for ...
  = je vous prie de **m'envoyer**
- When I left your hotel last week, I think I may have left a beige raincoat in my room. **Would you kindly** let me know whether it has been found
  = je vous serais très **reconnaissant** de bien vouloir
- I have seen the details of your summer courses, and **wish to know whether** you still have any vacancies on the Beginners' Swedish course
  = je **désirerais** savoir si

48.2 Pour terminer une lettre (avant la formule de politesse)

À une connaissance

- **Gerald joins me in sending** very best wishes to you all
  = Gerald se joint à moi pour vous **adresser**
- **Irene sends her kindest regards**
  = Irene me charge de vous **transmettre** ses **amitiés**
- **Please remember me to** your wife — I hope she is well
  = mon meilleur **souvenir** à

226 Wilton Street
Leicester LE8 7SP

20th November 2002

Dear Hannah,

Sorry I haven't been in touch for a while. It's been hectic since we moved house and we're still unpacking! Anyway, it's Leah's first birthday on the 30th and I wondered if you and the kids would like to come to her party that afternoon.

We were planning to start around 4 o'clock and finish around 5.30 or so. I've invited a clown and a children's conjuror, mainly for the entertainment of the older ones. With a bit of luck, you and I might get a chance to catch up on all our news!

Drop me a line or give me a ring if you think you'll be able to make it over on the 30th. It would be lovely if you could all come!

Hoping to hear from you soon. Say hello to Danny, Paul and Jonathan for me.

Love,

Jackie

Les tableaux ci-dessous présentent quelques exemples-types de formules épistolaires.

À quelqu'un que l'on connaît personnellement

Début de lettre	Fin de lettre
	Formule habituelle
Dear Mr Brown Dear Mrs Drake Dear Mr & Mrs Charlton Dear Miss Baker Dear Ms Black Dear Dr Armstrong Dear Professor Lyons Dear Sir Gerald Dear Lady Mcleod Dear Andrew Dear Margaret	Yours sincerely **Plus amical** With all good wishes Yours sincerely With kindest regards Yours sincerely

À une connaissance, ou à un(e) ami(e)

Début de lettre	Fin de lettre
	Formule habituelle
Dear Alison Dear Annie and George Dear Uncle Eric Dear Mrs Newman Dear Mr and Mrs Jones My dear Miss Armitage	Yours sincerely **Plus amical** With best wishes Yours sincerely With kindest regards Yours sincerely With all good regards Yours sincerely **Plus familier** With best wishes Yours ever Kindest regards With best wishes As always

14 Apsley Grove
Aberdeen AB4 7LP
Scotland

14th April 2002

Dear Hélène and Michel,

I arrived back in Britain last night, just before midnight. My flight from Paris was delayed by over four hours and I was quite exhausted by the time we finally landed. Still, I have the weekend ahead to recover before going back to work on Monday!

I just wanted to thank you for all your warmth and hospitality, which made my stay with you truly unforgettable. I took hundreds of photographs, as you know, and I plan to get them developed as soon as possible and put the best ones in an album. I'll send you some, too, of course.

Remember that you're more than welcome to come and stay with me here any time. I'd be really glad to have you both and it would give me a chance to repay you for all your kindness.

Keep in touch and take care!

With love from

Sandra

Les tableaux ci-dessous présentent quelques exemples-types de formules épistolaires.

Lettres commerciales

DÉBUT DE LETTRE	FIN DE LETTRE
	Formule habituelle
à une entreprise Dear Sirs	Yours faithfully
à un homme Dear Sir	
à une femme Dear Madam	
à une personne que l'on ne connaît pas Dear Sir or Madam	

À un(e) ami(e) proche, à un(e) parent(e)

DÉBUT DE LETTRE	FIN DE LETTRE
Dear Victoria My dear Albert Dear Aunt Eleanor Dear Granny and Grandad Dear Mum and Dad My dear Elizabeth Dearest Norman My dearest Mother My dearest Dorinda My darling Augustus	**Formule habituelle** With love from Love from **Plus familier** Love to all Love from us all Yours All the best **Plus affectueusement** With much love from Lots of love from Much love, as always All my love

- If there is anything else I can do, **please don't hesitate to get in touch** again
  = n'hésitez pas à me **contacter**
- **I look forward to hearing from you**
  = j'attends votre réponse avec impatience

À un(e) ami(e)

- **Say hello to Martin for me**
  = dis **bonjour** à Martin pour moi
- **Give my warmest regards to Vincent**
  = **transmets** toutes mes **amitiés** à Vincent
- **Doreen asks me to give you her best wishes**
  = Doreen me charge de te **transmettre** ses **amitiés**
- **Do write** when you have a minute
  = **écris**-moi
- **Do let us have your news** from time to time
  = donne-nous de tes **nouvelles**
- **Hoping to hear from you before too long**
  = j'espère avoir bientôt de tes **nouvelles**
- Rhona **sends her love**/Raimond **sends his love**
  = t'**embrasse**
- **Give my love to** Daniel and Leah, and tell them how much I miss them
  = **embrasse** de ma part
- Jodie and Carla **send you a big hug**
  = t'**embrassent** très fort

48.3 L'organisation des voyages

- **Please send me details of** your prices
  = veuillez m'**adresser** le détail de
- **Please advise** availability of dates between 1 August and 30 September
  = veuillez me faire savoir
- **Please let me know by return of post if** you have one single room with bath, half board, for the week commencing 3 October
  = veuillez me faire savoir par retour du courrier si
- **I would like to book** bed-and-breakfast accommodation with you
  = je souhaite **réserver**
- **Please consider this a firm booking** and hold the room until I arrive
  = je **confirme** ma réservation
- **Please confirm the following by fax**: one single room with shower for the nights of 20-23 October 2002
  = veuillez **confirmer** par fax la **réservation** suivante:
- **I am afraid I must ask you to alter my booking from** 25 August **to** 3 September. I hope this will not cause too much inconvenience
  = je me vois obligé de vous demander de **reporter** ma **réservation** du ... au
- **I am afraid I must cancel the booking** made with you for 5 September
  = je me vois **contraint** d'**annuler**

49 LES REMERCIEMENTS

- **Please accept our sincere thanks for** all your help and support
  = recevez nos plus **sincères remerciements**
- **I am writing to thank you** *ou* **to say thank you for** allowing **me to quote your experience in my article on multiple births following fertility treatment**
  = je vous écris pour vous **remercier** de
- **We greatly appreciated** your support during our period of captivity
  = nous avons été très **sensibles** à
- Your advice and understanding **were much appreciated**
  = je vous suis très **reconnaissant** de

De façon plus familière

- Just a line to say **thanks for** the lovely book which arrived today
  = **merci** pour
- **It was really nice of you to** remember my birthday
  = c'était très **gentil** de ta part de
- **(Would you) please thank him from me**
  = **remerciez**-le pour moi
- **I can't thank you enough for** find**ing my watch**
  = je ne sais pas comment vous **remercier** d'avoir

De la part d'un groupe

- **Thank you on behalf of** the Wigtown Business Association for ...
  = au nom de ..., **merci** pour
- **We send our heartfelt thanks to** him and Olive and we hope that we shall continue to see them at future meetings of the group
  = nous adressons nos plus vifs **remerciements** à
- **I am instructed by** our committee **to tender our sincere thanks for** your assistance at our recent Valentine Social *(soutenu)*
  = je suis chargé de vous adresser nos plus **sincères remerciements** pour

À l'attention d'un groupe

- **A big thank you to** everyone involved in the show this year *(familier)*
  = un grand **merci** à
- **Please convey to everybody my warmest thanks and deepest appreciation**, and ask them to forgive me for not writing letters to each individual
  = **transmettez** à tous mes **remerciements** les plus vifs et l'expression de ma **reconnaissance**
- **We must express our appreciation to** the University of Durham Research Committee for providing a grant
  = nous sommes extrêmement **reconnaissants** à
- **I should like to extend my grateful thanks to** all the volunteers who helped make it such an enjoyable event
  = je souhaite adresser mes **remerciements** à

50 LES VŒUX

◆ NB : Dans la section suivante [...] pourrait être "a Merry Christmas and a Happy New Year", "a happy birthday", "a speedy recovery", etc.

50.1 Expressions passe-partout

◆ **I hope you have** a lovely holiday/a safe and pleasant journey/a successful trip
= je vous **souhaite**

◆ **With love and best wishes for** [...]
= meilleurs **vœux** de

◆ **With all good wishes for** [...], **from** *(+ signature)*
= (avec) tous mes **vœux** de

◆ **(Do) give my best wishes to** your mother **for** a happy and healthy retirement
= **transmettez** mes meilleurs **vœux** de ... à

◆ Len **joins me in sending you all our very best wishes for** a successful new career
= ... se joint à moi pour vous adresser nos meilleurs **vœux** de

50.2 À l'occasion de Noël et du Nouvel An

◆ NB : En G.-B. et aux U.S.A. il est traditionnel d'envoyer des cartes de vœux pour Noël et le Nouvel An avant le 25 décembre

◆ **Merry Christmas and a Happy New Year**
= **Joyeux Noël** et **Bonne Année**

◆ **With season's greetings and very best wishes from** *(+ signature)*
= **Bonnes fêtes** de fin d'**année** et meilleurs **vœux**

◆ **A Merry Christmas to you all, and best wishes for health, happiness and prosperity in the New Year**
= **Joyeux Noël** à tous et meilleurs **vœux** de santé et de prospérité pour la Nouvelle **Année**

◆ **May I send you all our very best wishes for 2002**
= nous vous présentons nos meilleurs **vœux** pour 2002

50.3 À l'occasion d'un anniversaire

◆ **All our love and best wishes on your** 21st **birthday**, from Mum, Dad, Kerry and the cats
= nous te **souhaitons** un très heureux **anniversaire** avec toute notre affection

◆ **This is to send you our fondest love and very best wishes on your eighteenth birthday, from** Aunt Alison and Uncle Paul
= nous **t'adressons** tous nos **vœux** de **bonheur** pour tes 18 ans. Bien affectueusement

◆ **Wishing you a happy birthday for next Wednesday**. See you at the party, love Hannah
= je te **souhaite** un très bon **anniversaire** pour mercredi

◆ I am writing to wish you **many happy returns (of the day)**. Hope your birthday brings you everything you wished for. Love from Grandma and Grandpa
= un très **joyeux anniversaire**

50.4 Pour envoyer des vœux de rétablissement

◆ Sorry (to hear) you're ill — **get well soon!** *(familier)*
= j'espère que tu seras bientôt **rétabli**

◆ I was very sorry to learn that you were ill, and **send you my best wishes for a speedy recovery** *(soutenu)*
= je vous adresse tous mes **vœux** de prompt **rétablissement**

50.5 Pour souhaiter bonne chance à quelqu'un

◆ NB : Dans la section suivante, [...] pourrait être "interview", "driving test", "exam", etc.

◆ I thought I'd drop you a line to send you **best wishes for your** [...]
= bonne **chance** pour ton

◆ **Good luck for your** [...]. I hope things go well for you on Friday
= bonne **chance** pour ton

◆ Sorry to hear you didn't get the job — **better luck next time!**
= je suis sûr que tu **réussiras** la prochaine fois

◆ Sorry you're leaving us. **Good luck in** your future career
= bonne **chance** pour

◆ We all wish you **the best of luck in** your new job
= bonne **chance** pour

50.6 Pour féliciter quelqu'un

Oralement

◆ You're doing a great job! **Good for you!** Keep it up!
= **bravo** !

◆ You're pregnant? **Congratulations!** When's the baby due?
= **félicitations** !

◆ You've finished the job already? **Well done!**
= **bravo** !

◆ All I can say is **well done for** complaining **and congratulations on** getting **the back-dated money**
= c'est bien d'avoir ... je vous **félicite** d'avoir

Par écrit

◆ **We all send you our love and congratulations on** such an excellent result
= nous vous adressons toutes nos **félicitations** pour

◆ This is to send you **our warmest congratulations and best wishes on** [...]
= toutes nos **félicitations** pour

◆ **Allow me to offer you my heartiest congratulations on** a well-deserved promotion
= permettez-moi de vous **féliciter** de tout cœur pour

51 LES FAIRE-PART

51.1 Comment annoncer une naissance

De façon familière

◆ Julia Archer **gave birth to** a healthy 6lb 5oz baby son, Andrew, last Monday
= a le **plaisir** de vous **annoncer** la **naissance** de

- Lisa had a baby boy, 7lb 5oz, last Saturday. **Mother and baby are both doing well**
  = La mère et l'enfant se portent bien

Officiellement

- Graham and Susan Anderson (née McDonald) **are delighted to announce the birth of** a daughter, Laura Anne, on 11th October, 2002, at the Royal Maternity Hospital, Glasgow *(dans une lettre ou un journal)*
  = ont la **joie** de vous faire part de la **naissance** de
- At the Southern General Hospital, on 1st December, 2002, **to Paul and Diane Kelly a son, John** *(dans un journal)*
  = Paul et Diane Kelly ont la **joie** d'**annoncer** la **naissance** de John

... et comment répondre

- **Congratulations (to you both) on the birth of** your son, and best wishes to Alexander for good health and happiness throughout his life
  = toutes nos **félicitations** à l'occasion de la **naissance** de
- **We were delighted to hear about the birth of** Stephanie, and send our very best wishes to all of you
  = nous avons été très **heureux** d'apprendre la **naissance** de

51.2 Comment annoncer des fiançailles

De façon familière

- **I'm sure you'll be delighted to learn that** Sally and I **got engaged** last Saturday
  = je suis sûr que tu seras **heureux** d'apprendre que ... nous nous sommes **fiancés**
- **I'm happy to be able to tell you that** James and Valerie **have** at last **become engaged**
  = je suis **heureux** de t'apprendre que ... se sont **fiancés**

Officiellement

- **It is with much pleasure that the engagement is announced between** Michael, younger son of Professor and Mrs Perkins, York, **and** Jennifer, only daughter of Dr and Mrs Campbell, Aberdeen *(dans un journal)*
  = nous avons le **plaisir** de vous annoncer les **fiançailles** de ... et de ...
- **Both families are happy to announce the engagement of** Lorna Thompson, eldest daughter of Mark and Elaine Thompson **to** Brian Gordon, only son of James and Mary Gordon *(dans un journal)*
  = les familles ... et ... sont **heureuses** de vous annoncer les **fiançailles** de ... et ...
- Mr and Mrs Levison **have much pleasure in announcing the engagement of** their daughter Marie **to** Mr David Hood, Canada *(dans un journal)*
  = ont le **plaisir** de vous annoncer les **fiançailles** de ... et ...

... et comment répondre

- **Congratulations to you both on your engagement**, and very best wishes for a long and happy life together
  = **félicitations** à tous deux pour vos **fiançailles**
- **I was delighted to hear of your engagement**, and wish you both all the best for your future together
  = j'ai été très **heureux** d'apprendre vos **fiançailles**

51.3 Comment annoncer un mariage

De façon familière

- Louise and Peter **have decided to get married** on the 4th June
  = ont décidé de se **marier**
- **I'm getting married** in June, to a wonderful man named Lester Thompson
  = je me **marie**
- **We've finally set the date for** the 19th May, 2002
  = nous avons finalement fixé la date au

Officiellement

- Mr and Mrs William Morris **are delighted to announce the marriage of** their daughter Sarah to Mr Jack Bond, in St. Francis Church, Whitley Bay, on 5th January 2002 *(dans une lettre ou un journal)*
  = sont heureux de vous annoncer le **mariage** de
- **At Netherlee Parish Church, on 1st October, 2002, by Rev. I Doherty, Alison, daughter of Ian and Mary Johnstone, Netherlee, to Derek, son of Ray and Lorraine Gilmore, Bishopbriggs** *(dans un journal)*
  = on nous prie d'annoncer le **mariage** de Mademoiselle Alison Johnstone, fille de Monsieur et Madame Ian Johnstone, avec Monsieur Derek Gilmore, fils de Monsieur et Madame Ray Gilmore, en l'église de Netherlee, le 1er octobre 2002. La cérémonie a été **célébrée** par le Révérend I. Doherty

... et comment répondre

- **Congratulations on your marriage**, and best wishes to you both for your future happiness
  = (toutes mes) **félicitations** à l'occasion de votre **mariage**
- **We were delighted to hear about your daughter's marriage to** Iain, and wish them both all the best for their future life together
  = nous avons été très heureux d'apprendre le **mariage** de votre fille et de ...

51.4 Comment annoncer un décès

Dans une lettre personnelle

- My husband **died suddenly** last year
  = ... est **mort** subitement
- **It is with great sadness that I have to tell you that** Joe's father **passed away** three weeks ago
  = c'est avec la plus grande **tristesse** que je dois t'annoncer que ... est **décédé**

Officiellement (dans un journal)

- **Suddenly**, at home, in Newcastle-upon-Tyne, on Saturday 2nd July, 2002, Alan, aged 77 years, **the beloved husband of** Helen and **loving father of** Matthew
  = ... son épouse et ... son fils ont la **douleur** de vous faire part du **décès** brutal
- Mavis Ann, wife of the late Gavin Birch, **passed away peacefully** in the Western Infirmary on 4th October 2002, aged 64 years. **No flowers, please**
  = ... s'est **éteinte** paisiblement ... Ni fleurs ni couronnes
- **It is with deep sadness that** the Fife Club **announces the death of** Mr Tom Levi, who died in hospital on May 19 after a stroke
  = c'est avec la plus profonde **tristesse** que ... vous annonce le **décès** de

... et comment répondre

- I was terribly upset to hear of Jim's death, and am writing to send you **all warmest love and deepest sympathy**
  = toute mon amitié et ma plus profonde **sympathie**
- **Deepest sympathy on the loss of** a good friend to you and all of us
  = toutes mes **condoléances** à l'occasion de la **perte** de
- My husband and I **were greatly saddened to learn of the passing of** Dr Smith, and send you and your family our most sincere condolences
  = c'est avec la plus grande **tristesse** que ... avons appris le **décès** de
- **We wish to extend our deepest sympathy on your sad loss to you and your wife**
  = nous vous adressons à votre épouse et à vous-même nos plus sincères **condoléances**

51.5 Pour annoncer un changement d'adresse

- We are moving house next week. **Our new address** as of 4 December 2002 **will be** 41 Acacia Avenue, BN7 2BT Barnton
  = notre nouvelle **adresse** ... sera

52 LES INVITATIONS

52.1 Les invitations officielles

- Mr and Mrs James Waller **request the pleasure of your company at the marriage of** their daughter Mary Elizabeth to Mr Richard Hanbury at St Mary's Church, Frampton on Saturday, 21st August, 2002 at 2 o'clock and afterwards at Moor House, Frampton
  = ont le plaisir de vous **inviter** à l'occasion du mariage de
- The Warden and Fellows of Hertford College, Oxford **request the pleasure of the company of** Miss Charlotte Young and partner **at a dinner** to mark the anniversary of the founding of the College
  = ont le plaisir de **convier** ... à un dîner
- Margaret and Gary Small **request the pleasure of your company at a reception** (ou **dinner**) to celebrate their Silver Wedding, on Saturday 12th November, 2002, at 8pm at Norton House Hotel, Edinburgh
  = ont le plaisir de vous **inviter** à une **réception** (*ou* un dîner)

... et comment répondre

- **We thank you for your kind invitation to** the marriage of your daughter Annabel on 20th November, **and have much pleasure in accepting**
  = nous vous remercions de votre aimable **invitation** au ... et nous faisons une joie d'**accepter**
- **We regret that we are unable to accept your invitation to** the marriage of your daughter on 6th May
  = nous regrettons de ne pouvoir **accepter** votre **invitation** au

52.2 Les invitations plus intimes

- **We are celebrating** Rosemary's engagement to David by holding a dinner dance at the Central Hotel on Friday 11th February, 2002, **and very much hope that you will be able to join us**
  = nous **fêtons** ... et espérons de tout cœur que vous pourrez vous **joindre** à nous
- **We** are giving a dinner party next Saturday, and **would be delighted if you and your wife could come**
  = nous serions heureux si votre femme et vous pouviez être des nôtres
- **I'm planning a** 25th **birthday party** for my nephew — **hope you'll be able to make it**
  = j'**organise** une **soirée** d'anniversaire ... j'espère que vous pourrez venir
- **I'm having a party** next week for my 18th — **come along, and bring a friend**
  = j'**organise** une **soirée** ... **joins**-toi à nous et amène un de tes amis

52.3 Invitations à se joindre à quelqu'un

- **Why don't you come down** for a weekend and let us show you Sussex?
  = pourquoi ne viendriez-vous pas
- **Would you be interested in** coming **with us to the theatre next Friday?**
  = est-ce que cela vous dirait de
- **Would you and Gordon like to come** to dinner next Saturday?
  = voulez-vous venir ... Gordon et toi ?
- **Would you be free for** lunch next Tuesday?
  = seriez-vous **libre** pour
- **Perhaps we could** meet for coffee some time next week?
  = peut-être pourrions-nous

52.4 Pour accepter une invitation

- **I'd love to** meet up with you tomorrow
  = je serais **heureux** de
- **It was good of you to invite me**, I've been longing to do something like this for ages
  = c'était très **gentil** à vous de m'**inviter**
- **Thank you for your invitation to** dinner — **I look forward to it very much**
  = **merci** pour votre **invitation** ... je me fais une joie de venir

52.5 Pour refuser une invitation

- **I'd love to come, but I'm afraid** I'm already going out that night
  = j'aimerais beaucoup venir mais **malheureusement**
- **I'm terribly sorry, but I won't be able to come to** your party
  = je suis **désolé** mais je ne pourrai pas venir à
- **I wish I could come, but unfortunately** I have something else on
  = j'aimerais pouvoir venir, mais **malheureusement**
- **Unfortunately, it's out of the question** for the moment
  = **malheureusement**, c'est impossible
- It was very kind of you to invite me to your dinner party next Saturday. **Unfortunately I will not be able to accept**
  = je ne peux **malheureusement** pas **accepter**
- **Much to our regret, we are unable to accept** (*soutenu*)
  = nous sommes au **regret** de devoir **refuser**

52.6 Sans donner de réponse précise

- **I'm not sure** what I'm doing that night, but I'll let you know either way before the end of the week
  = je ne suis pas **sûr**
- **It all depends on whether** I can get a sitter for Rosie at short notice
  = cela **dépend** : oui, si
- **I'm afraid I can't really make any definite plans** until I know when Alex will be able to take her holidays
  = je ne peux **malheureusement** pas m'**engager**
- It looks as if we might be going abroad with Jack's company in August so **I'd rather not commit myself** to a holiday yet
  = je préférerais ne pas m'**engager**

53 LA DISSERTATION

53.1 Les grandes lignes de l'argument

Pour introduire un sujet

De façon impersonnelle

- **It is often said** *ou* **asserted** *ou* **claimed that** the informing "grass" is named after the song Whispering Grass, but the tag long predates the ditty
  = on **dit** bien souvent que
- **It is a truth universally acknowledged that** the use and abuse of the Queen's English is stirring up a hornet's nest
  = tout le monde s'**accorde** à **dire** que
- **It is a truism** *ou* **a commonplace (to say) that** American accents are infinitely more glamorous than their British counterparts
  = l'**opinion** selon laquelle ... est un lieu commun
- **It is undeniably true** that Gormley helped to turn his members into far more sophisticated workers
  = il est **indéniable** que
- **It is a well-known fact that** in this age of technology, it is computer screens which are responsible for many illnesses
  = tout le monde **sait** que
- **It is sometimes forgotten that** much Christian doctrine comes from Judaism
  = on **oublie** parfois que
- **It would be naïve to suppose that** in a radically changing world these 50-year-old arrangements can survive
  = il serait **naïf** de croire que
- **It would hardly be an exaggeration to say that** the friendship of both of them with Britten was among the most creative in the composer's life
  = on peut **dire** presque sans **exagérer** que
- **It is hard to open a newspaper nowadays without reading that** TV is going to destroy reading and that electronic technology has made the written word obsolete
  = de nos jours, il est presque **impossible** d'ouvrir un journal sans lire que
- **First of all, it is important to try to understand** some of the systems and processes involved in order to create a healthier body
  = tout d'abord, il est **important** de **comprendre**
- **It is in the nature of** classics in sociological theory **to** make broad generalizations about such things as societal evolution
  = c'est un **trait caractéristique** des ... que de
- **It is often the case that** early interests lead on to a career
  = il est souvent **vrai** que

De façon personnelle

- **By way of introduction, let me** summarize the background to this question
  = en **guise** d'**introduction**, j'aimerais
- **I would like to start with** a very sweeping statement
  = je **commencerai** par
- **Before going into the issue of** criminal law, **I wish first to summarize** how Gewirth derives his principles of morality and justice
  = **avant** d'**étudier** en détail le **problème** de ... je voudrais **résumer**
- **Let us look at** what self-respect in your job actually means
  = **examinons**
- **We commonly think of** people **as** isolated individuals but, in fact, few of us ever spend more than an hour or two of our waking hours alone
  = nous **considérons généralement** ... en tant que
- **What we are mainly concerned with here is** the conflict between what the hero says and what he actually does
  = ce qui nous **préoccupe** ici, c'est
- **We live in a world in which** the word "equality" is bandied about
  = nous vivons dans un monde où

Pour évoquer des concepts ou des problèmes

- **The concept of** controll**ing disease-transmitting insects by genetic means isn't new**
  = l'**idée** de
- **The idea of** getting **rich without too much effort has universal appeal**
  = l'**idée** de
- **The question of whether** Hamlet was insane has long occupied critics
  = la **question** de **savoir** si

- Why they were successful where their predecessors had failed **is a question that has been much debated**
  = est un **problème** souvent débattu
- **One of the most striking features** *ou* **aspects of this issue** *ou* **topic** *ou* **question is** the way (in which) it arouses strong emotions
  = l'un des **aspects** les plus frappants de ce **problème**, c'est
- **There are a number of issues** on which China and Britain openly disagree
  = il existe un certain nombre de **questions**

Pour faire des généralisations

- **People** who work outside the home **tend to believe that** parenting is an easy option
  = les gens ont **tendance** à penser que
- **There's** always **a tendency for people to** exaggerate your place in the world
  = les gens ont **tendance** à
- Many gardeners **have a tendency to** anthropomorphize plants
  = ont **tendance** à
- Fate **has a propensity to** behave in the same way to people of similar nature
  = a une propension à
- **For the (vast) majority of people**, literature is a subject which is studied at school but which has no relevance to life as they know it
  = pour la **plupart** des gens
- **For most of us**, the thought of the alternative to surviving into extreme old age is worse than surviving
  = pour la **plupart** d'entre nous
- History provides **numerous examples** *ou* **instances of** misguided national heroes who did more harm than good in the long run
  = de nombreux **exemples** de

Pour être plus précis

- The Meters' work with Lee Dorsey **in particular** merits closer inspection
  = en **particulier**
- **One particular issue** raised by Narayan was, suppose Grant at the time of his conviction was old enough to be hanged, what would have happened?
  = un **problème particulier**
- **A more specific point** relates to using the instrument in figure 6.6 as a way of challenging our hidden assumptions about reality
  = un **aspect** plus **spécifique**
- **More specifically**, he accuses Western governments of continuing to supply weapons and training to the rebels
  = plus **précisément**

53.2 Pour présenter une thèse

Remarques d'ouverture

- **First of all, let us consider** the advantages of urban life
  = tout d'**abord examinons**
- **Let us begin with an examination of** the social aspects of this question
  = **commençons** par **examiner**
- **The first thing that needs to be said is that** the author is presenting a one-sided view
  = tout d'**abord**, il faut dire que
- **What should be established at the very outset is that** we are dealing with a practical rather than philosophical issue
  = la **première constatation** qui s'impose est que

Pour délimiter le débat

- In the next section, **I will pursue the question of** whether the expansion of the Dutch prison system can be explained by Box's theory
  = je **développerai** le **problème** de
- **I will then deal with the question of** whether or not the requirements for practical discourse are compatible with criminal procedure
  = je **traiterai ensuite** du **problème** de
- We must distinguish between the psychic and the spiritual, and **we shall see how** the subtle level of consciousness is the basis for the spiritual level
  = nous **verrons** comment
- **I will confine myself to** giving an account of certain decisive facts in my militant career with Sartre
  = je me **contenterai** de
- In this chapter, **I shall largely confine myself to** a consideration of those therapeutic methods that use visualization as a part of their procedures
  = j'**étudierai** essentiellement
- **We will not concern ourselves here with** the Christian legend of St James
  = nous ne nous **préoccuperons** pas ici de
- **Let us now consider** to what extent the present municipal tribunals differ from the former popular tribunals in the above-mentioned points
  = **examinons maintenant**
- **Let us now look at** the types of corporatism that theorists developed to clarify the concept
  = **abordons maintenant**

Pour exposer les problèmes

- **The main issue under discussion is** how the party should re-define itself if it is to play any future role in Hungarian politics
  = le **problème principal** est
- **A second, related problem is that** business ethics has mostly concerned itself with grand theorising
  = **problème annexe** :
- **The issue at stake here is** one of misrepresentation or cheating
  = ce dont il s'**agit** ici est
- **An important aspect of** Milton's imagery **is** the play of light and shade
  = un des **aspects** importants de ... est
- **It is worth mentioning here that** when this was first translated, the opening reference to Heidegger was entirely deleted
  = il faut **mentionner** ici que

- **Finally, there is the argument that** castrating a dog will give it a nasty streak
  = **enfin**, on peut dire que

Pour mettre un argument en doute

- In their joint statement, the two presidents use tough language to condemn violence but **is there any real substance in what's been agreed?**
  = leur accord a-t-il un contenu réel?
- This is a question which **merits close(r) examination**
  = mérite un **examen** plus attentif
- The unity of the two separate German states **raised fundamental questions for** Germany's neighbours
  = **soulevait** des **problèmes fondamentaux** pour
- The failure to protect our fellow Europeans **raises fundamental questions on** the role of the armed forces
  = **soulève** des **questions essentielles** quant à
- **This raises once again the question of** whether a government's right to secrecy should override the public's right to know
  = cela **soulève** à nouveau la **question** de savoir
- **This poses the question of** whether it is possible for equity capital to be cheap and portfolio capital to be expensive simultaneously
  = cela pose la **question** de savoir

Pour analyser les problèmes

- **It is interesting to consider why** this scheme has opened so successfully
  = il est intéressant d'**examiner** pourquoi
- **On the question of** whether civil disobedience is likely to help end the war, Chomsky is deliberately diffident
  = sur la **question** de
- **We are often faced with the choice between** our sense of duty **and** our own personal inclinations
  = nous sommes souvent contraints de faire un choix entre ... et
- **When we speak of** realism in music, **we do not at all have in mind** the illustrative bases of music
  = quand nous **parlons** de ..., nous ne **pensons** pas à
- **It is reasonable to assume that** most people living in industrialized societies are to some extent contaminated by environmental poisons
  = on peut raisonnablement **penser** que

Pour étayer un argument

- **An argument in support of** this approach **is that** it produces results
  = le fait que ... est un **argument** en **faveur** de
- **In support of his theory**, Dr Gold notes that most oil contains higher-than-atmospheric concentrations of helium-3
  = pour **appuyer** sa **théorie**
- **This is the most telling argument in favour of** an extension of the right to vote
  = c'est l'**argument** le plus éloquent en **faveur** de
- **The second reason for advocating** this course of action **is that** it benefits the community at large
  = une autre **raison de soutenir** ... est que
- **The third, more fundamental, reason for** looking **to the future is that** we need a successful market
  = la troisième **raison**, plus **essentielle**, de ... est que
- Confidence in capitalism seems to be at a post-war low. **The fundamental reason for** this contradiction seems to me quite simple
  = la **raison essentielle** de

53-3 Pour présenter une antithèse

Pour critiquer quelque chose ou pour s'y opposer

- **In actual fact, the idea of** there being a rupture between a so-called old criminology and an emergent new criminology **is somewhat misleading**
  = en **réalité**, l'**idée selon** laquelle ... est quelque peu trompeuse
- In order to argue this, I will show that Wyeth**'s position is untenable**
  = le **point** de vue de ... est **indéfendable**
- **It is claimed, however,** that the strict Leboyer method is not essential for a less traumatic birth experience
  = on **affirme cependant**
- **This need not mean that** we are destined to suffer for ever. **Indeed, the opposite may be true**
  = cela ne veut pas dire que ... il se peut même que le **contraire** soit **vrai**
- Many observers, though, **find it difficult to share his opinion that** it could mean the end of the Tamil Tigers
  = ne partagent guère son **opinion selon** laquelle
- **On the other hand**, there is a competing principle in psychotherapy that should be taken into consideration
  = d'un autre **côté**
- The judgement made **may well be true but** the evidence given to sustain it is unlikely to convince the sceptical
  = est peut-être **juste, mais**
- Reform **is all very well, but** it is pointless if the rules are not enforced
  = c'est bien joli, **mais**
- The case against the use of drugs in sport rests primarily on the argument that ... **This argument is weak, for two reasons**
  = cet **argument** manque de solidité, pour deux **raisons**
- According to one theory, the ancestors of vampire bats were fruit-eating bats. But **this idea** *ou* **argument does not hold water**
  = cette **idée** *ou* cet **argument** ne **tient** pas
- The idea **does not stand up to** historical scrutiny
  = ne **résiste** pas à
- **This view does not stand up** if we examine the known facts about John
  = ce **point** de vue ne **tient** pas
- **The trouble with the idea that** social relations are the outcome of past actions **is not that** it is wrong, **but rather that** it is uninformative
  = le **problème** que pose l'**idée selon** laquelle ... n'est pas que ... mais plutôt que

- **The difficulty with this view is that** he bases the principle on a false premise
  = là où son **point** de vue **pèche**, c'est que
- **The snag with** such speculations **is that** too much turns on one man or event
  = l'**inconvénient** que présente ... est que
- Removing healthy ovaries **is entirely unjustified in my opinion**
  = est totalement **injustifié selon** moi

Pour proposer une alternative

- **Another approach may be to** develop substances capable of blocking the effects of the insect's immune system
  = une manière **différente** d'**aborder** le **problème** serait de
- **Another way of looking at that claim is to** note that Olson's explanations require little knowledge of the society in question
  = on peut **envisager** le **problème** sous un autre **angle** en
- **However, the other side of the coin is** the fact that an improved self-image can lead to prosperity
  = cependant, il y a le **revers** de la **médaille**, à savoir que
- **It is more accurate to speak of** new criminologies rather than of a single new criminology
  = il est plus **juste** de parler de
- **Paradoxical though it may seem**, computer models of mind can be positively humanising
  = aussi **paradoxal** que cela puisse paraître

53.4 Pour présenter une synthèse

Pour évaluer les arguments exposés

- **How can we reconcile** these two apparently contradictory viewpoints?
  = comment **réconcilier**
- **On balance**, making money honestly is more profitable than making it dishonestly
  = à tout prendre
- Since vitamins are expensive, **one has to weigh up the pros and cons**
  = il faut **peser** le **pour** et le **contre**
- **The benefits of** partnership in a giant trading market will almost certainly **outweigh the disadvantages**
  = les **avantages** de ... l'emportent sur les **inconvénients**
- **The two perspectives are not mutually exclusive**
  = ces deux **points** de vue ne sont pas totalement incompatibles

Pour sélectionner un argument particulier

- Dr Meaden's theory **is the most convincing explanation**
  = est l'**explication** la plus **convaincante**
- **The truth** *ou* **fact of the matter is that** in a free society you can't turn every home into a fortress
  = la **vérité** est que
- But **the truth is that** Father Christmas has a rather mixed origin
  = la **vérité** est que
- This is an exercise that on paper might not seem to be quite in harmony, but **in actual fact** this is not the position
  = en **réalité**
- **When all is said and done, it must be acknowledged that** a purely theoretical approach to social issues is sterile
  = en **fin** de compte, il faut reconnaître que

Pour résumer les arguments

- In this chapter, **I have demonstrated** *ou* **shown that** the Cuban alternative has been undergoing considerable transformations
  = j'ai **montré** que
- **This shows how**, in the final analysis, adhering to a particular theory on crime is at best a matter of reasoned choice
  = cela **démontre** comment
- **The overall picture shows that** prison sentences were relatively frequent
  = cette vue d'ensemble **montre** que
- **To recap** *ou* **To sum up, then, (we may conclude that)** there are in effect two possible solutions to this problem
  = en **résumé**, on peut **conclure** que
- **To sum up this chapter** I will offer two examples
  = **pour résumer** ce chapitre
- **To summarize**, we have seen that the old industries in Britain had been hit after the First World War by a deteriorating international position
  = en **résumé**
- Habermas's argument, **in a nutshell**, is as follows
  = en **bref**
- But **the key to the whole argument is** a single extraordinary paragraph
  = la clé du problème ... se trouve dans
- **To round off this section** on slugs, gardeners may be interested to hear that there are three species of predatory slugs in the British Isles
  = **pour clore** cette section

Pour tirer des conclusions

- **From all this, it follows that** it is impossible to extend those kinds of security measures to all potential targets of terrorism
  = il **découle** de tout cela que
- This, of course, **leads to the logical conclusion that** those who actually produce do have a claim to the results of their efforts
  = nous amène **logiquement à conclure** que
- **There is only one logical conclusion we can reach**, which is that we ask our customers what they think of our marketing programme
  = on ne peut **aboutir** qu'à une seule **conclusion logique**
- **The inescapable conclusion is that** the criminal justice system has a hand in creating the reality we see
  = la **conclusion inéluctable** à laquelle on **aboutit** est que
- **We must conclude that** there is no solution to the problem of defining crime
  = nous devons **conclure** que
- **In conclusion**, the punishment model of deterrence is highly unsatisfactory
  = **pour conclure**

- **The upshot of all this is that** GIFT is more likely to be readily available than IVF
  = le **résultat** de tout cela est que
- **So it would appear that** ESP is not necessarily limited to the right hemisphere of the brain
  = il **semblerait** donc que
- **This only goes to show that** a good man is hard to find, be he black or white
  = cela **prouve** bien que
- **The lesson to be learned is that** the past, especially a past lived in impotence, can be enslaving
  = la leçon que l'on peut en **tirer** est que
- **At the end of the day**, the only way the drug problem will be beaten is when people are encouraged not to take it
  = en **fin** de compte
- **Ultimately, then**, these critics are significant
  = en **définitive**

53.5 Pour rédiger un paragraphe

Pour ajouter quelque chose

- **In addition**, the author does not really empathize with his hero
  = de **plus**
- This award-winning writer, **in addition to being** a critic, biographer and poet, has written 26 crime novels
  = **outre** qu'il est
- But this is only part of the picture. **Added to this** are fears that a major price increase would cause riots
  = **s'ajoute** à cela ...
- **An added** complication **is** that the characters are not aware of their relationship to one another
  = un **autre** ... est
- **Also**, there is the question of language.
  = par **ailleurs**
- **The question also arises as to** how this idea can be put into practice
  = se pose **aussi** la question de savoir
- Politicians, **as well as** academics and educationalists, tend to feel strongly about the way in which history is taught
  = **ainsi** que
- But, **over and above that**, each list contains fictitious names or addresses
  = en **plus** de cela
- **Furthermore**, ozone is, like carbon dioxide, a greenhouse gas
  = en **outre**

Pour comparer

- **Compared with** the heroine, Alison is an insipid character
  = **comparé** à
- **In comparison with** the Czech Republic, the culture of Bulgaria is less westernized
  = en **comparaison** de
- This is a high percentage for the English Midlands but low **by comparison with** some other parts of Britain
  = par **comparaison** avec
- **On the one hand**, there is no longer a Warsaw Pact threat. **On the other (hand)**, the positive changes could have negative side-effects
  = d'un **côté** ... de l'autre
- **Similarly**, a good historian is not obsessed by dates
  = de **même**
- There can only be one total at the bottom of a column of figures and **likewise** only one solution to any problem
  = **pareillement**
- What others say of us will translate into reality. **Equally**, what we affirm as true of ourselves will likewise come true
  = de **même**
- There will now be a change in the way we are regarded by our partners, and, **by the same token**, the way we regard them
  = du **même** coup
- **There is a fundamental difference between** adequate nutrient intake **and** optimum nutrient intake
  = il existe une **différence** fondamentale entre ... et

Pour relier deux éléments

- **First of all** *ou* **Firstly**, I would like to outline the benefits of the system
  = tout d'**abord**
- In music we are concerned **first and foremost** with the practical application of controlled sounds relating to the human psyche
  = en tout **premier** lieu
- **In order to understand** the conflict between the two nations, **it is first of all necessary to** know something of the history of the area
  = pour comprendre ... il faut tout d'**abord**
- **Secondly**, it might be simpler to develop chemical or even nuclear warheads for a large shell than for a missile
  = **deuxièmement**
- **In the first/second/third place**, the objectives of privatization were contradictory
  = **premièrement, deuxièmement, troisièmement**
- **Finally**, there is the argument that castrating a dog will give it a nasty streak
  = **enfin**

Pour exprimer une opinion personnelle

- **In my opinion**, the government is underestimating the scale of the epidemic
  = à mon **avis**
- **My personal opinion is that** the argument lacks depth
  = **personnellement**, je pense que
- This is a popular viewpoint, but **speaking personally**, I cannot understand it
  = **personnellement**
- **Personally**, I think that no one can appreciate ethnicity more than black or African people themselves
  = **personnellement**
- **For my part**, I cannot agree with the leadership on this question
  = pour ma **part**
- **My own view is that** what largely determines the use of non-national workers are economic factors rather than political ones
  = je **trouve** que
- **In my view**, it only perpetuates the very problem that it sets out to address
  = à mon **idée**

- Although the author argues the case for patriotism, **I feel that** he does not do it with any great personal conviction
  = je **crois** que
- **I believe that** people do understand that there can be no quick fix for Britain's economic problems
  = je **crois** que
- **It seems to me that** what we have is a political problem that needs to be solved at a political level
  = il me **semble** que
- **I would maintain that** we have made a significant effort to ensure that the results are made public
  = je **soutiens** que

Pour présenter l'opinion de quelqu'un d'autre

- **He claims** *ou* **maintains that** intelligence is conditioned by upbringing
  = il **soutient** que
- Bukharin **asserts that** all great revolutions are accompanied by destructive internal conflict
  = **affirme** que
- The communique **states that** some form of nuclear deterrent will continue to be needed for the foreseeable future
  = **affirme** que
- **What he is saying is that** the time of the highly structured political party is over
  = il **dit** que
- His admirers **would have us believe that** watching this film is more like attending a church service than having a night at the pictures
  = voudraient nous faire **croire** que
- **According to** the report, poverty creates a climate favourable to violence
  = **selon**

Pour donner un exemple

- **To take another example**: many thousands of people have been condemned to a life of sickness and pain because ...
  = pour prendre un autre **exemple**
- Let us consider, **for example** *ou* **for instance**, the problems faced by immigrants arriving in a strange country
  = par **exemple**
- His meteoric rise **is the most striking example yet of** voters' disillusionment with the record of the previous government
  = est l'**exemple** le plus frappant de
- The case of Henry Howey Robson **serves to illustrate** the courage exhibited by young men in the face of battle
  = **illustre** bien
- Just consider, **by way of illustration**, the difference in amounts accumulated if interest is paid gross, rather than having tax deducted
  = pour **illustrer**
- **A case in point is** the decision to lift the ban on contacts with the republic
  = ... est un bon **exemple**
- **Take the case of** the soldier returning from war
  = prenons le **cas de**
- **As** the Prime Minister **remarked,** the tunnel will greatly benefit us all
  = comme l'a fait **remarquer**

53.6 Les mécanismes de la discussion

Pour présenter une supposition

- They telephoned the president to put pressure on him. And **that could be interpreted as** trying to gain an unconstitutional political advantage
  = on pourrait **interpréter** cela comme
- Retail sales in Britain rose sharply last month. This was higher than expected and **could be taken to mean that** inflationary pressures remain strong
  = laisse **supposer** que
- **It might well be prudent to** find some shelter for the night rather than sleep in the van
  = il serait sans **doute** prudent de
- These substances do not remain effective for very long. This is **possibly** because they work against the insects' natural instinct to feed
  = **peut-être**
- She had become a definite security risk and **it is not beyond the bounds of possibility that** murder may have been considered
  = il n'est pas **impossible** que
- I am somewhat reassured by Mr Fraser's assertion, which **leads one to suppose that** on that subject he is in full agreement with Catholic teaching
  = nous amène à **supposer** que
- It is **probably** the case that all long heavy ships are vulnerable
  = **probablement**
- After hearing nothing from the taxman for so long, most people **might reasonably assume that** their tax affairs were in order
  = seraient en droit de **supposer** que
- **One could be forgiven for thinking that** because the substances are chemicals, they'd be easy to study
  = il serait excusable de penser que
- Thus, **I venture to suggest that** very often when visions are mentioned in the literature of occultism, self-created visualizations are meant
  = j'oserais même dire que

Pour exprimer la certitude Voir aussi 15 : La certitude

- **It is clear that** any risk to the human foetus is very low
  = il est **clair** que
- Whatever may be said about individual works, the early poetry as a whole is **indisputably** a poetry of longing
  = **indiscutablement**
- Yet, **undeniably**, this act of making it a comprehensible story does remove it one degree further from reality
  = **indéniablement**
- **There can be no doubt that** the Earth underwent a dramatic cooling which destroyed the environment and life style of these creatures
  = il ne fait aucun **doute** que
- **It is undoubtedly true that** over the years there has been a much greater emphasis on safer sex
  = il est **indéniable** que
- **As we all know**, adultery is far from uncommon
  = comme nous le savons tous

- **One thing is certain**: no one can claim that ESP has never helped make money
  = une chose est **sûre**
- **It is (quite) certain that** unless peace can be brought to this troubled land, no amount of aid will solve the long-term problems of the people
  = il est **certain** que

Pour exprimer le doute Voir aussi 16 : L'incertitude

- **It is doubtful whether**, in the present repressive climate, anyone would be brave or foolish enough to demonstrate publicly
  = il n'est pas **sûr** que
- **It remains to be seen whether** the security forces will try to intervene
  = (il) reste à savoir si
- Once in a while I think about all that textbook Nietzsche and **I wonder whether** anyone ever truly understood a word of it
  = je me **demande** si
- **I have (a few) reservations about** the book
  = j'émettrais quelques **réserves** sur
- Since it spans a spectrum of ideologies, **it is by no means certain that** it will stay together
  = il n'est pas du tout **certain** que
- **It is questionable whether** media coverage of terrorist organizations actually affects terrorism
  = il n'est pas **sûr** que
- **This raises the whole question of** exactly when men and women should retire
  = cela **soulève** la **question** de savoir
- The crisis **sets a question mark against** the Prime Minister's stated commitment to intervention
  = remet en **question**
- Both these claims are **true up to a point** and they need to be made
  = vrai dans une certaine **mesure**

Pour marquer l'accord Voir aussi 11 : L'accord

- **I agree wholeheartedly with** the opinion that smacking should be outlawed
  = je suis entièrement **d'accord** avec
- **One must acknowledge that** China's history will make change more painful
  = il faut **reconnaître** que
- **It cannot be denied that** there are similarities between these two approaches
  = il est **indéniable** que
- Courtney - **rightly in my view** - is strongly critical of the snobbery and elitism that is all too evident in these circles
  = à **juste** titre, selon moi
- Preaching was considered an important activity, **and rightly so** in a country with a high illiteracy rate
  = (et) à **juste** titre

Pour marquer le désaccord Voir aussi 12 : Le désaccord

- **I must disagree with** Gordon's article on criminality: it is dangerous to suggest that to be a criminal one must look like a criminal
  = je ne suis pas **d'accord** avec
- He was not a lovable failure but rather a difficult man who succeeded. **It is hard to agree**
  = on peut difficilement être **d'accord**
- As a former teacher **I find it hard to believe that** there is no link at all between screen violence and violence on the streets
  = il m'est difficile de croire que
- The strength of their feelings **is scarcely credible**
  = est peu **crédible**
- Her claim to have been the first to discover the phenomenon **defies credibility**
  = n'est pas **crédible**
- Nevertheless, **I remain unconvinced by** Milton
  = je ne suis toujours pas **convaincu** par
- Many do not believe that water contains anything remotely dangerous. Sadly, **this is far from the truth**
  = c'est loin d'être vrai
- To say that everyone requires the same amount of a vitamin is as stupid as saying we all have blonde hair and blue eyes. **It simply isn't true**
  = c'est complètement **faux**
- His remarks were not only highly offensive to black and other ethnic minorities but **totally inaccurate**
  = tout à fait **inexactes**
- Stomach ulcers are often associated with good living and a fast-moving lifestyle. **(But) in reality** there is no evidence to support this belief
  = (mais) en **réalité**
- This version of a political economy **does not stand up to close scrutiny**
  = ne **tient** pas lorsqu'on l'examine attentivement

Pour souligner un argument

- Nowadays, there is **clearly** less stigma attached to unmarried mothers
  = de toute **évidence**
- Evidence shows that ..., so once again **the facts speak for themselves**
  = les **faits** parlent d'eux-mêmes
- **Few will argue with the principle that** such a fund should be set up
  = on ne saurait remettre en **question** l'idée que
- Hyams **supports this claim** by looking at sentences produced by young children learning German
  = **appuie** cette affirmation
- This issue **underlines** the dangers of continuing to finance science in this way
  = **souligne**
- **The most important thing is to** reach agreement from all sides
  = le plus **important** est de
- Perhaps **the most important aspect of** cognition is the ability to manipulate symbols
  = l'aspect le plus **important** de

Pour mettre un détail en valeur

- **It would be impossible to exaggerate the importance of** these two volumes for anyone with a serious interest in the development of black gospel music
  = on ne saurait **exagérer** l'importance de

- The symbolic importance of Jerusalem for both Palestinians and Jews is almost **impossible to overemphasize**
  = on ne saurait **sous-estimer**
- **It is important to be clear that** Jesus does not identify himself with Yahweh
  = il faut bien savoir que
- **It is significant that** Mandalay seems to have become the central focus in this debate
  = le **fait** que ... est **révélateur**
- **It should not be forgotten that** many of those now in exile were close to the centre of power until only one year ago
  = il ne faut pas oublier que
- **It should be stressed that** the only way pet owners could possibly contract such a condition from their pets is by eating them
  = il faut **souligner** que
- **There is a very important point here and that is that** the accused claims that he was with Ms Martins all evening on the night of the crime
  = on trouve ici une remarque très **importante**, à savoir que
- At the beginning of his book Mr Gordon **makes a telling point**
  = fait une remarque **importante**
- Suspicion is **the chief feature of** Britain's attitude to European theatre
  = la **caractéristique** principale de
- **In order to focus attention on** Hobson's distinctive contributions to macroeconomics, these wider issues are neglected here
  = afin d'**attirer** l'**attention** sur
- These statements **are interesting in that** they illustrate different views
  = sont **intéressants** du **fait** que

54 TÉLÉPHONE, E-MAILS ET TEXTOS

54.1 Pour obtenir un numéro

- **Could you get me 01843465786, please?** *(o-one-eight-four-three-four-six-five-seven-eight-six)*
  = Je voudrais le 01 843 46 57 86, s'il vous plaît, (zéro un huit cent quarante-trois quarante-six cinquante-sept quatre-vingt six)
- **Could you give me directory enquiries** *(Brit)* *ou* **directory assistance** *(US)*, **please?**
  = Pourriez-vous me **passer** les **renseignements**, s'il vous plaît ?
- **Can you give me the number of Europost, 20 rue de la Marelle, Pierrefitte?**
  = Je voudrais le **numéro** de la société Europost, 20, rue de la Marelle, à Pierrefitte
- **What is the code for Martinique?**
  = Quel est l'**indicatif** pour la Martinique ?
- **How do I make an outside call** *ou* **How do I get an outside line?**
  = Comment est-ce que je peux **téléphoner** à l'extérieur ?
- **What do I dial to get the speaking clock?**
  = Quel **numéro** dois-je faire pour l'horloge parlante ?
- **It's not in the book**
  = Je n'ai pas trouvé le numéro dans l'**annuaire**
- **You omit the "o" when dialling England from France**
  = Si vous **téléphonez** de France en Angleterre, ne faites pas le zéro

54.2 Quand l'abonné répond

- **Could I have** *ou* **Can you give me extension 516?**
  = Pourriez-vous me passer le **poste** 516, s'il vous plaît ?
- **Is that Mr Lambert's phone?**
  = Je suis bien chez M. Lambert ?
- **Could I speak to Mr Wolff, please?** *ou* **I'd like to speak to Mr. Wolff, please**
  = Je voudrais parler à M. Wolff, s'il vous plaît *ou* Pourrais-je parler à M. Wolff, s'il vous plaît ?
- **Could you put me through to Dr Henderson, please?**
  = Pourriez-vous me **passer** le docteur Henderson, s'il vous plaît ?
- **Who's speaking?**
  = Qui est à l'**appareil** ?
- **I'll call back in half an hour**
  = Je **rappellerai** dans une demi-heure
- **Could I leave my number for her to call me back?**
  = Pourrais-je laisser mon **numéro** pour qu'elle me rappelle ?
- **I'm ringing from a callbox** *(Brit)* ou **I'm calling from a paystation** *(US)*
  = Je vous **appelle** d'une **cabine** téléphonique *ou* Je **téléphone** d'une **cabine**
- **I'm phoning from England**
  = J'appelle *ou* Je téléphone d'Angleterre
- **Would you ask him to ring me when he gets back?**
  = Pourriez-vous lui demander de me rappeler quand il rentrera ?

54.3 Pour répondre au téléphone

- **Hello, this is Anne speaking**
  = Allô, c'est Anne à l'**appareil**
- (Is that Anne?) **Speaking**
  = (C'est Anne à l'appareil ?) Elle-même
- **Would you like to leave a message?**
  = Voulez-vous laisser un **message** ?
- **Can I take a message?**
  = Puis-je lui transmettre un message ?
- **Hold the line please**
  = Ne **quittez** pas *ou* Ne raccrochez pas
- **I'll call you back**
  = Je vous rappelle
- **This is a recorded message**
  = Vous êtes en **communication** avec un répondeur automatique
- **Please speak after the tone** *ou* **after the beep**
  = Veuillez laisser votre **message** après le **bip** sonore

54.4 Le standard vous répond

- **Grand Hotel, can I help you?**
  = Grand Hôtel, bonjour *ou* à votre service

◆ **Who's calling, please?**
= Qui est à l'**appareil** ?

◆ **Who shall I say is calling?**
= C'est de la part de qui ?

◆ **Do you know his extension number?**
= Est-ce que vous connaissez son **numéro** de **poste** ?

◆ **I am connecting you** *ou* **putting you through now**
= Je vous le **passe**

◆ **I have a call from Tokyo for Mrs Thomas**
= J'ai quelqu'un en **ligne** de Tokyo qui demande Mme Thomas

◆ **I've got Miss Martin on the line for you**
= J'ai Mlle Martin à l'**appareil**

◆ **Dr Robert's line is busy**
= Le docteur Robert est déjà en ligne

◆ **Sorry to keep you waiting**
= Désolé de vous faire attendre

◆ **There's no reply**
= Ça ne **répond** pas

◆ **You're through to our Sales Department**
= Vous êtes en **ligne** avec le service des ventes

54.5 L'opérateur vous répond

◆ **What number do you want** *ou* **What number are you calling?**
= Quel **numéro** demandez-vous ?

◆ **Where are you calling from?**
= D'où **appelez**-vous ?

◆ **Would you repeat the number, please?**
= Pourriez-vous **répéter** le **numéro**, s'il vous plaît ?

◆ **Replace the handset and dial again**
= **Raccrochez** et renouvelez votre appel *ou* **Raccrochez** et recomposez le numéro

◆ **There's a Mr Campbell calling you from Amsterdam who wishes you to pay for the call. Will you accept?**
= M. Campbell vous **appelle** en **PCV** d'Amsterdam. Est-ce que vous acceptez la **communication** ?

◆ **Go ahead, caller**
= Vous êtes en **ligne**

◆ *(aux Renseignements)* **There's no listing under that name**
= (Directory Enquiries) Il n'y a pas d'**abonné** à ce nom

◆ **They're ex-directory** *(Brit) ou* **unlisted** *(US)*
= Désolé, leur **numéro** est sur la **liste** rouge

◆ **There's no reply from 01 45 77 57 84**
= Le 01 45 77 57 84 ne **répond** pas

◆ **Hold the line, please** *ou* **Please hold**
= Ne **quittez** pas

◆ **All lines to Bristol are engaged - please try later**
= Par suite de l'**encombrement** des **lignes**, votre appel ne peut aboutir. Veuillez rappeler ultérieurement

◆ **I'm trying it for you now**
= J'essaie d'obtenir votre correspondant

◆ **It's ringing for you now**
= Ça **sonne**

◆ **The line is engaged** *(Brit) ou* **busy** *(US)*
= La **ligne** est **occupée**

◆ **The number you have dialled has not been recognized** *(message enregistré)*
= Il n'y a pas d'**abonné** au **numéro** que vous avez demandé (recorded message)

◆ **The number you have dialled no longer exists. Please consult the directory** *(message enregistré)*
= Le **numéro** de votre correspondant n'est plus attribué. Veuillez consulter l'**annuaire** ou votre centre de **renseignements**

◆ **The number you have dialled has been changed. Please dial 0233 42 21 70** *(message enregistré)*
= Le **numéro** de votre correspondant a changé. Veuillez composer désormais le 02 33 42 21 70 *(recorded message)*

◆ **The number you are calling is engaged** *(Brit) ou* **busy** *(US)*. **Please try again later**
= Toutes les **lignes** de votre correspondant sont **occupées**. Veuillez **rappeler** ultérieurement *(recorded message)*

54.6 Les différents types de communication

◆ **It's a local call**
= C'est une **communication** locale

◆ **This is a long-distance call**
= C'est une **communication** interurbaine

◆ **I want to make an international call**
= Je voudrais appeler l'étranger

◆ **I want to make a reverse charge call to a London number** *(Brit) ou* **I want to call a London number collect** *(US)*
= Je voudrais **appeler** Londres en **PCV** *(NB : system no longer exists in France)*

◆ **I'd like an alarm call for 7.30 tomorrow morning**
= Je voudrais être réveillé à 7 h 30 demain

54.7 En cas de difficulté

◆ **I can't get through (at all)**
= Je n'arrive pas à avoir le **numéro**

◆ **Their phone is out of order**
= Leur **téléphone** est en **dérangement**

◆ **We were cut off**
= On nous a **coupés** *ou* La **communication** a été **coupée**

◆ **I must have dialled the wrong number**
= J'ai dû faire un faux **numéro**

◆ **We've got a crossed line**
= Il y a quelqu'un d'autre sur la **ligne**

◆ **I've called them several times with no reply**
= J'ai **appelé** plusieurs fois, mais ça ne **répond** pas

◆ **You gave me a wrong number**
= Vous m'avez donné un faux **numéro**

◆ **I got the wrong extension**
= On ne m'a pas donné le bon **poste** *ou* On s'est trompé de **poste**

◆ **This is a very bad line**
= La **ligne** est très mauvaise

54.8 E-mail

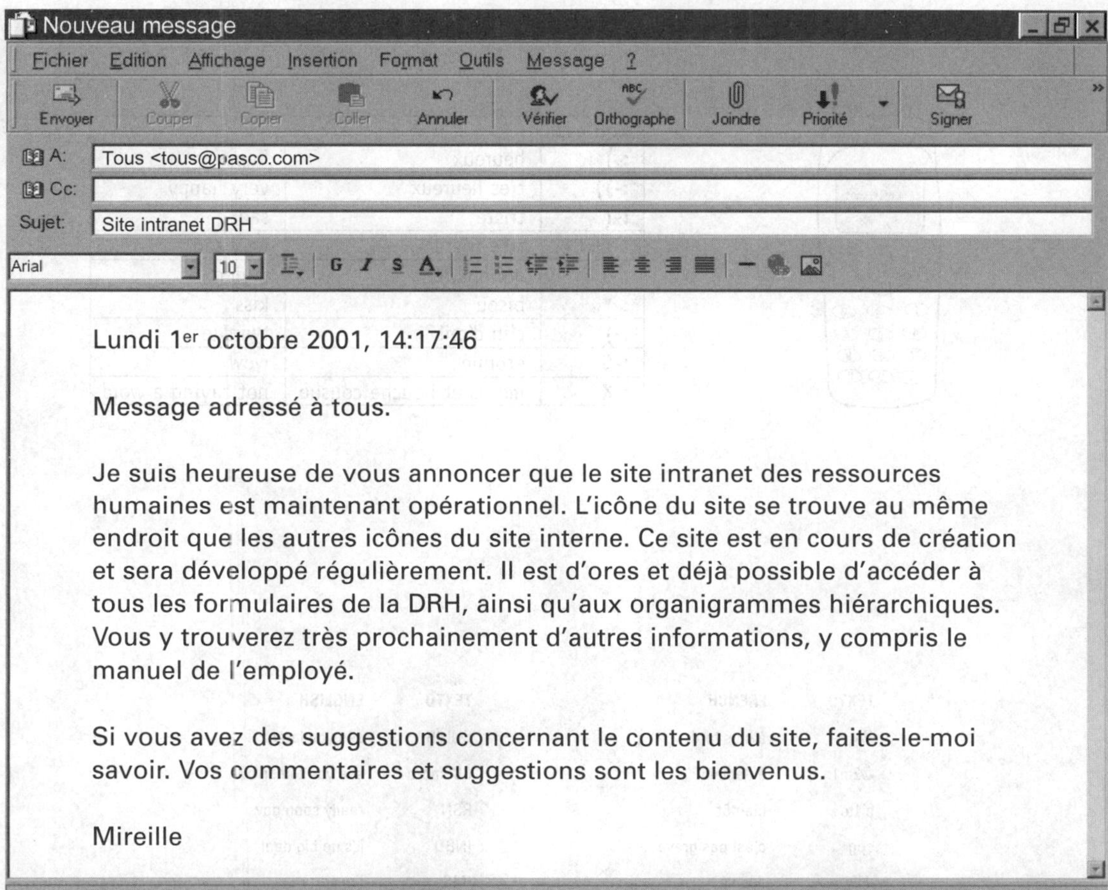
Nouveau message

Fichier Edition Affichage Insertion Format Outils Message ?

Envoyer Couper Copier Coller Annuler Vérifier Orthographe Joindre Priorité Signer

A: Tous <tous@pasco.com>

Cc:

Sujet: Site intranet DRH

Lundi 1er octobre 2001, 14:17:46

Message adressé à tous.

Je suis heureuse de vous annoncer que le site intranet des ressources humaines est maintenant opérationnel. L'icône du site se trouve au même endroit que les autres icônes du site interne. Ce site est en cours de création et sera développé régulièrement. Il est d'ores et déjà possible d'accéder à tous les formulaires de la DRH, ainsi qu'aux organigrammes hiérarchiques. Vous y trouverez très prochainement d'autres informations, y compris le manuel de l'employé.

Si vous avez des suggestions concernant le contenu du site, faites-le-moi savoir. Vos commentaires et suggestions sont les bienvenus.

Mireille

Nouveau message	New Message
Fichier	File
Edition	Edit
Affichage	View
Outils	Tools
Composer	Compose
Aide	Help
Envoyer	Send
Nouveau message	New
Répondre	Reply to Sender
Répondre à tous	Reply to All
Faire suivre	Forward
Fichier joint	Attachment
A	To
Cc	Cc
Copie cachée	Bcc (blind carbon copy)
Objet	Subject
De	From
Date	Sent

54.9 Textos

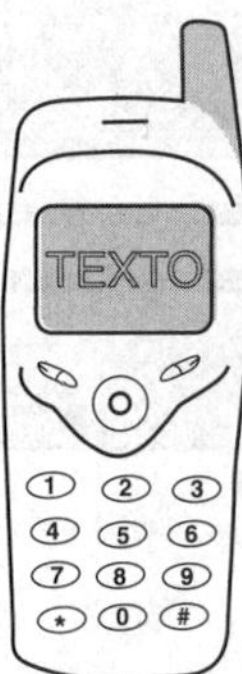

Smileys		
:-)	heureux	happy
:-))	très heureux	very happy
:-(	triste	sad
:-((	très triste	very sad
:'-(	qui pleure	crying
:-*	bisou	kiss
;-)	clin d'œil	twinkle
:-0	étonné	wow
:-X	motus et bouche cousue	not saying a word

TEXTO	FRENCH
@+	à plus tard
@2m1	à demain
bi1to	bientôt
cpg	c'est pas grave
dsl	désolé
entouK	en tout cas
G la N	j'ai la haine
je t'M	je t'aime
JMS	jamais
MDR	mort de rire
mr6	merci
MSG	message
now	maintenant
p2k	pas de quoi
parske	parce que
qqn	quelqu'un
ri1	rien
svp	s'il vous plaît
TOK	t'es OK ?
TOQP	t'es occupé ?
we	week-end
XLnt	excellent

TEXTO	ENGLISH
CUL8R	see you later
CU2moro	see you tomorrow
RSN	really soon now
INBD	it's no big deal
IMS	I'm sorry
IAC	in any case
H8	hate
NVR	never
ILUVU	I love you
ROFL	rolling on the floor laughing
Thx	thanks
Msg	message
ATM	at the moment
URW	you are welcome
COZ	because
S/O	someone
0	nothing
PLS	please
RUOK	are you ok?
RUBZ	are you busy?
Wknd	weekend
XLNT	excellent

DICTIONNAIRE ANGLAIS-FRANÇAIS

ENGLISH-FRENCH DICTIONARY

Aa

A, a[1] /eɪ/ **N** 1 *(= letter)* A, a *m* ◆ **A for Able** ≃ A comme André ◆ **to know sth from A to Z** connaître qch de A à Z ◆ **24a** *(in house numbers)* 24 bis ◆ **to get from A to B** aller d'un endroit à un autre ◆ **on the A4** *(Brit = road)* sur la (route) A4

2 *(Mus)* la *m* ; → **key**

3 *(Scol)* excellent *(de 15 à 20 sur 20)*

4 *(Elec)* (abbrev of **ampere(s)**) A

COMP A-1 ADJ super *

A2 N *(= British exam) seconde moitié des épreuves pour les A levels*

A3 (paper) N (papier *m*) A3 *m*

A4 (paper) N (papier *m*) A4 *m*

A and M college N *(US)* ≃ école *f* supérieure d'agriculture

A-bomb N bombe *f* A *or* atomique

A levels NPL *(Brit Scol)* ≃ baccalauréat *m* ◆ **to do an A level in geography** ≃ passer l'épreuve de géographie au baccalauréat

A-line dress N robe *f* trapèze *inv*

the A-list N le gratin, le dessus du panier ◆ **to be on the A-list** faire partie du gratin

A number 1 ADJ *(US)* ⇒ **A-1**

A-OK * **ADJ** super *

A-road N *(Brit)* ≃ route *f* nationale → ROADS

A-side N *[of record]* face *f* A

A-test N essai *m* nucléaire

A to Z ® **N** (pl **A to Zs**) plan *m* avec répertoire des rues ◆ **a Glasgow A to Z, an A to Z of Glasgow** un plan de Glasgow avec répertoire des rues

A LEVELS

Diplôme britannique préparé en deux ans, qui sanctionne la fin des études secondaires et permet l'accès à l'enseignement supérieur. Contrairement au baccalauréat français, dont le résultat est global, les **A levels** sont obtenus séparément dans un nombre limité de matières (trois en moyenne) choisies par le candidat. Le système d'inscription dans l'enseignement supérieur étant sélectif, les élèves cherchent à obtenir les meilleures mentions possibles afin de pouvoir choisir plus facilement leur université.

En Écosse, l'équivalent des **A levels** est le "Higher", ou "Higher Grade", qui se prépare en un an et porte sur cinq matières au maximum. → **GCSE**

a[2] /eɪ, ə/ **INDEF ART** *(before vowel or mute h: "an")* 1 un, une ◆ **a tree** un arbre ◆ **an apple** une pomme ◆ **such a hat** un tel *or* pareil chapeau ◆ **so large a country** un si grand pays

2 *(def art in French)* le, la, les ◆ **he smokes a pipe** il fume la pipe ◆ **to set an example** donner l'exemple ◆ **I've read a third of the book** j'ai lu le tiers du livre ◆ **we haven't a penny** nous n'avons pas le sou ◆ **a woman hates violence** les femmes détestent la violence

3 *(absent in French)* ◆ **she was a doctor** elle était médecin ◆ **as a soldier** en tant que soldat ◆ **my uncle, a sailor, said that ...** mon oncle, un marin *or* qui était marin, disait que ... ◆ **she's a widow** elle est veuve ◆ **what a pleasure!** quel plaisir ! ◆ **what a lovely day!** quelle belle journée ! ◆ **to make a fortune** faire fortune

4 un(e) certain(e) ◆ **I have heard of a Mr Gordon who ...** j'ai entendu parler d'un certain M. Gordon qui ...

5 le *or* la même ◆ **they are much of an age** ils sont du même âge ◆ **they are of a size** ils sont de la même grandeur

6 *(= a single)* un(e) seul(e) ◆ **to empty a glass at a draught** vider un verre d'un trait ◆ **at a blow** d'un seul coup

7 *(with abstract nouns)* du, de la, des ◆ **to make a noise/a fuss** faire du bruit/des histoires

8 ◆ **a few survivors** quelques survivants ◆ **a great many flowers** beaucoup de fleurs

9 *(= per)* ◆ **£4 a person** *or* **head** 4 livres par personne ◆ **€5 a kilo** 5 € le kilo ◆ **twice a month** deux fois par mois ◆ **twice a year** deux fois par an *or* l'an ◆ **80km an hour** 80 kilomètres-heure, 80 kilomètres à l'heure

AA /eɪ'eɪ/ **N** 1 *(Brit)* (abbrev of **Automobile Association**) *société de dépannage* 2 (abbrev of **Alcoholics Anonymous**) → **alcoholic** 3 *(US Univ)* (abbrev of **Associate in Arts**) ≃ DEUG *m* de lettres

AAA /,eɪeɪ'eɪ/ **N** 1 *(Brit)* abbrev of **Amateur Athletics Association** 2 *(US)* /'trɪpl"eɪ/ (abbrev of **American Automobile Association**) *société de dépannage*

Aachen /'ɑːxən/ **N** Aix-la-Chapelle

A & E /,eɪənd'iː/ **N** (abbrev of **Accident and Emergency**) → **accident**

aardvark /'ɑːdvɑːk/ **N** oryctérope *m*

Aaron /'eərən/ **N** Aaron *m*

AAU /,eɪeɪ'juː/ **N** *(US)* (abbrev of **Amateur Athletic Union**) *association d'athlétisme amateur*

AAUP /,eɪeɪjuː'piː/ **N** abbrev of **American Association of University Professors**

AB /eɪ'biː/ **N** 1 (abbrev of **able(-bodied) seaman**) → **able** 2 *(US)* (abbrev of **Bachelor of Arts**) **to have an ~ in French** ≃ avoir une licence de français ; → **bachelor** ; → DEGREE

ABA /,eɪbiː'eɪ/ **N** abbrev of **Amateur Boxing Association**

aback /ə'bæk/ **ADV** ◆ **to be taken** ~ être interloqué *or* décontenancé

abacus /'æbəkəs/ **N** (pl **abacuses** *or* **abaci** /'æbəsaɪ/) 1 boulier *m*, abaque *m* 2 *(Archit)* abaque *m*

abaft /ə'bɑːft/ *(Naut)* **ADV** sur *or* vers l'arrière **PREP** en arrière de, sur l'arrière de

abalone /,æbə'ləʊnɪ/ **N** ormeau *m*, haliotide *f*

abandon /ə'bændən/ **VT** 1 *(= forsake) [+ person, car]* abandonner ◆ **to ~ o.s. to** *[+ despair, pleasure]* s'abandonner à, se laisser aller à ; *[+ sleep]* s'abandonner à ◆ **to ~ o.s. to one's fate** accepter son destin 2 *[+ property, right, project, idea, principles, pretence]* renoncer à ; *[+ course of action]* abandonner, renoncer à ◆ **to ~ the attempt to do sth** renoncer à faire qch ◆ **play was ~ed** *(Sport)* le match a été interrompu *or* reporté 3 *(Jur) [+ cargo]* faire (acte de) délaissement de ◆ **to ~ ship** abandonner le navire ◆ **to ~ any claim** *(Jur)* renoncer à toute prétention
N *(NonC)* abandon *m* ◆ **to dance with ~** danser avec abandon ◆ **with (gay) ~** avec (une belle) désinvolture

abandoned /ə'bændənd/ **ADJ** 1 *(= forsaken) [person, place]* abandonné 2 *(= dissolute)* débauché 3 *(= wild) [dancing]* frénétique ; *[emotion]* éperdu

abandonment /ə'bændənmənt/ **N** abandon *m* ; *(Jur) [of action]* désistement *m* ; *[of property, right]* cession *f* ; *[of cargo]* délaissement *m*

abase /ə'beɪs/ **VT** *(= humiliate) [+ person]* mortifier, humilier ; *(= degrade) [+ person]* abaisser, avilir ; *[+ person's qualities, actions]* rabaisser, ravaler ◆ **to ~ o.s. so far as to do sth** s'abaisser *or* s'humilier jusqu'à faire qch

abasement /ə'beɪsmənt/ **N** *(= moral decay)* dégradation *f*, avilissement *m* ; *(= humiliation)* humiliation *f*, mortification *f*

abashed /ə'bæʃt/ **ADJ** confus

abate /ə'beɪt/ **VI** *[storm, emotions, pain]* s'apaiser, se calmer ; *[noise, flood]* baisser ; *[violence]* se calmer ; *[fever]* baisser, décroître ; *[wind]* se modérer ; *(Naut)* mollir ◆ **the crime wave shows no sign of abating** on n'enregistre aucune baisse du taux de criminalité **VT** *[+ tax]* baisser ; *(Jur) [+ writ]* annuler ; *[+ sentence]* remettre

abatement /ə'beɪtmənt/ **N** *(NonC, gen)* réduction *f* ◆ **~ of the levy** *(Fin)* abattement *m* sur le prélèvement ; → **noise**

abattoir /'æbətwɑːʳ/ **N** abattoir *m*

abbess /'æbɪs/ **N** abbesse *f*

abbey /'æbɪ/ **N** abbaye *f* ◆ **Westminster Abbey** l'abbaye *f* de Westminster

abbot/'æbət/ N abbé m, (Père m) supérieur m

abbr., abbrev. (abbrev of **abbreviation, abbreviated**) abrév.

abbreviate/ə'bri:vieit/ VT abréger (*to* en) raccourcir

abbreviation/ə,bri:vi'eiʃən/ N abréviation f

ABC/,eibi:'si:/ N 1 (= *alphabet*) abc m, alphabet m ◆ **it's as easy** *or* **simple as ~*** c'est simple comme bonjour 2 abbrev of **Associated British Cinemas** 3 abbrev of **Australian Broadcasting Commission** 4 (abbrev of **American Broadcasting Corporation**) ABC f NPL **ABCs** ◆ **the ~s of sth** le b.a.-ba de qch

ABD /,eibi:'di:/ N (*US Univ*) (abbrev of **all but dissertation**) *étudiant(e) n'ayant plus que sa thèse à rédiger pour compléter son doctorat* ◆ **she was still ~ after four years** au bout de quatre ans, elle n'avait toujours pas rédigé sa thèse

abdicate /'æbdikeit/ VT [+ *right*] renoncer à ; [+ *post, responsibility*] se démettre de ◆ **to ~ the throne** abdiquer VI abdiquer

abdication/,æbdi'keiʃən/ N [*of king*] abdication f, renonciation f ; [*of mandate etc*] démission f (*of* de) ; [*of right*] renonciation f (*of* à) ; désistement m (*of* de)

abdomen /'æbdəmən, æb'dəumen/ N abdomen m

abdominal /æb'dɒminl/ ADJ abdominal NPL **abdominals** abdominaux mpl

abduct/æb'dʌkt/ VT enlever, kidnapper

abduction/æb'dʌkʃən/ N enlèvement m, rapt m ; → **child**

abductor /æb'dʌktə^r^/ N 1 (= *kidnapper*) ravisseur m, -euse f 2 (*Anat*) abducteur m

abed † /ə'bed/ ADV (*liter*) au lit, couché ◆ **to lie ~** rester couché

Abel/'eibl/ N Abel m

Aberdonian/,æbə'dəuniən/ N habitant(e) m(f) *or* natif m, -ive f d'Aberdeen ADJ d'Aberdeen

aberrant/ə'berənt/ ADJ aberrant, anormal

aberration/,æbə'reiʃən/ N aberration f

abet/ə'bet/ VT encourager, soutenir ◆ **to ~ sb in a crime** aider qn à commettre un crime ; → **aid**

abetter, abettor/ə'betə^r^/ N complice mf

abeyance/ə'beiəns/ N (*NonC*) ◆ **to be in ~** [*law, custom*] ne pas être en vigueur ◆ **to fall into ~** tomber en désuétude ◆ **the question is in ~** la question reste en suspens

abhor/əb'hɔ:^r^/ VT abhorrer ; → **nature**

abhorrence /əb'hɒrəns/ N horreur f (*of* de) aversion f (*of* pour) ; ◆ **to hold in ~, have an ~ of** avoir horreur de, avoir en horreur

abhorrent/əb'hɒrənt/ ADJ odieux

abide/ə'baid/ (pret, ptp **abided** *or* **abode**) VT 1 (*neg only = tolerate*) **I can't ~ her** je ne peux pas la supporter *or* la souffrir ◆ **I can't ~ living here** je ne supporte pas de vivre ici 2 (*liter = await*) attendre VI † (= *endure*) durer ; (= *live*) demeurer

► **abide by** VT FUS [+ *rule, decision*] respecter ; [+ *consequences*] accepter, supporter ; [+ *promise*] rester *or* demeurer fidèle à ; [+ *resolve*] maintenir, s'en tenir à ◆ **they agreed to ~ by the terms of the contract** ils ont accepté de se conformer aux termes du contrat ◆ **I ~ by what I said** je maintiens ce que j'ai dit

abiding/ə'baidiŋ/ ADJ (*liter*) constant, éternel ; → **law**

Abidjan/,æbi'dʒɑ:n/ N Abidjan

ability/ə'biliti/ N 1 (*gen*) aptitude f (*to do sth* à faire qch) capacité f (*to do sth* pour faire qch) ; ◆ **people have lost confidence in the government's ~ to keep inflation in check** les gens ne croient plus que le gouvernement est capable de maîtriser l'inflation ◆ **the virus's ~ to infect the cells of the human immune system** la capacité du virus à infecter les cellules du système immunitaire humain ◆ **to have faith in sb's/one's ~** *or* **abilities** croire en qn/en soi ◆ **to the best of one's ~** *or* **abilities** de son mieux ◆ **he has the ~ to bring out the best in people** avec lui, les gens donnent le meilleur d'eux-mêmes ◆ **~ to pay** (*Fin, Jur*) solvabilité f ◆ **~ to pay tax** (*Fin, Jur*) capacité f *or* faculté f contributive

2 (*NonC = aptitude*) talent m ◆ **a person of great ~** une personne de grand talent ◆ **he has a certain artistic ~** il a un certain don *or* talent artistique ◆ **her drama teacher spotted her ~** son professeur d'art dramatique a découvert son talent

3 (*Scol etc = mental powers*) **abilities** compétences fpl

abject/'æbdʒekt/ ADJ 1 (= *wretched*) [*misery, poverty*] noir ◆ **the ~ state of sth** l'état lamentable de qch 2 (= *servile*) [*person, obedience, surrender*] servile ◆ **an ~ apology** de plates excuses fpl 3 (= *contemptible*) [*person, stupidity*] méprisable ; [*failure*] lamentable

abjectly /'æbdʒektli/ ADV [*apologize*] platement ◆ **he has ~ failed** il a lamentablement échoué ◆ **to be ~ poor** être dans une misère noire ◆ **~ miserable** profondément malheureux

abjure /əb'dʒuə^r^/ VT [+ *one's rights*] renoncer (publiquement *or* par serment) à ◆ **to ~ one's religion** abjurer sa religion, apostasier

Abkhaz /æb'kɑ:z/, **Abkhazi** /æb'kɑ:zi/ ADJ abkhaze N (pl **Abkhaz**) 1 (= *person*) Abkhaze mf 2 (= *language*) abkhaze m

Abkhazia/æb'kɑ:ziə/ N Abkhazie f

Abkhazian/æb'kɑ:ziən/ ADJ, N ⇒ **Abkhaz**

ablative /'æblətiv/ N ablatif m ◆ **in the ~** à l'ablatif ADJ ablatif COMP **ablative absolute** N ablatif m absolu

ablaze/ə'bleiz/ ADJ 1 (*lit*) en feu, en flammes ◆ **to set sth ~** mettre le feu à qch ; ◆ **to be ~** flamber 2 (*fig*) ◆ **his eyes were ~ with anger** ses yeux lançaient des éclairs ◆ **~ with light** resplendissant de lumière ◆ **the garden is ~ with colour** c'est une débauche de couleurs dans le jardin

able /'eibl/ ADJ 1 ◆ **to be ~ to do sth** (= *have means or opportunity to*) pouvoir faire qch ; (= *know how to*) savoir faire qch ; (= *be capable of*) être capable de faire qch ; (= *be in position to*) être en mesure de *or* à même de faire qch ◆ **I wasn't ~ to help him** je n'ai pas pu l'aider ◆ **I ran fast and so was ~ to catch the bus** en courant vite j'ai réussi à attraper l'autobus ◆ **he is ~ to read and write** il sait lire et écrire ◆ **~ to pay** en mesure de payer ◆ **you are better ~ to do it than he is** vous êtes mieux à même de le faire que lui ◆ **she was hardly ~ to see** (*due to darkness, fog etc*) elle arrivait à peine à voir ; (*due to poor eyesight*) elle voyait à peine

2 (= *clever*) capable, compétent ◆ **an ~ man** un homme très capable *or* très compétent ◆ **she is one of our ablest pupils** c'est une de nos meilleures élèves

3 (*Med = healthy*) sain

COMP **able-bodied** ADJ (*gen = not disabled*) valide ; (*Mil*) [*recruit*] bon pour le service

able-bodied seaman N ⇒ **able seaman**

able-minded ADJ (= *not mentally handicapped*) sain d'esprit ; (= *intelligent*) intelligent

able rating N (*Brit Naut*) matelot m breveté

able seaman N (pl **able seamen**) (*Naut*) matelot m breveté *or* de deuxième classe

ablution/ə'blu:ʃən/ N ablution f ◆ **to perform one's ~s** (*hum*) faire ses ablutions

ably /'eibli/ ADV (= *competently*) de façon très compétente ; (= *skilfully*) habilement ◆ **he was ~ assisted by his brother** son frère l'assistait avec compétence ◆ **he did it perfectly ~** il s'en est tiré d'une manière tout à fait compétente

ABM/,eibi:'em/ N (abbrev of **antiballistic missile**) → **antiballistic**

abnegate /'æbnigeit/ VT [+ *responsibility*] nier ; [+ *one's rights*] renoncer à ; [+ *one's religion*] abjurer

abnegation /,æbni'geiʃən/ N (= *denial*) reniement m, désaveu m (*of* de) ; (= *renunciation*) renoncement m (*of* à) ; (also **self-abnegation**) abnégation f

abnormal/æb'nɔ:məl/ ADJ anormal

abnormality/,æbnɔ:'mæliti/ N 1 (*gen*) anomalie f ; (= *deformity*) difformité f, malformation f ◆ **genetic abnormalities** anomalies fpl génétiques 2 (*NonC*) caractère m anormal, anormalité f

abnormally /æb'nɔ:məli/ ADV anormalement ◆ **a city with an ~ high rate of HIV infection** une ville présentant un taux anormalement élevé de séropositivité ◆ **the cells were growing ~** les cellules se développaient de manière anormale

aboard /ə'bɔ:d/ ADV 1 (= *on plane, boat*) à bord ◆ **to go ~** (s')embarquer, monter à bord ◆ **to take ~** embarquer ◆ **all ~!** (*on train, bus, car*) en voiture ! ; (*on ship*) tout le monde à bord ! 2 (= *alongside ship*) le long du bord ◆ **close ~** bord à bord PREP à bord de ◆ **~ the train/bus** dans le train/le bus ◆ **~ ship** à bord

abode /ə'bəud/ VB pret, ptp of **abide** N (*frm*) (= *home*) demeure f ◆ **place of ~** (*Jur*) domicile m ◆ **right of ~** (*Jur*) droit m de résidence ◆ **to take up one's ~** élire domicile ◆ **the ~ of the gods** le séjour des dieux ; → **fixed, humble**

abolish /ə'bɒliʃ/ VT [+ *practice, custom, slavery, apartheid, tax*] abolir ; [+ *law*] abroger, abolir

abolishment/ə'bɒliʃmənt/ N ⇒ **abolition**

abolition/,æbəu'liʃən/ N abolition f

abolitionist/,æbəu'liʃənist/ N (*Hist*) abolitionniste mf, antiesclavagiste mf

abominable /ə'bɒminəbl/ ADJ abominable COMP **the abominable snowman** N l'abominable homme m des neiges

abominably /ə'bɒminəbli/ ADV [*treat, behave, suffer*] abominablement, d'une manière abominable ◆ **~ rude/cruel** d'une grossièreté/cruauté abominable ◆ **it's ~ cold** il fait un froid de loup

abominate /ə'bɒmineit/ VT abominer, abhorrer

abomination/ə,bɒmi'neiʃən/ N abomination f ◆ **I hold him in ~** (*liter*) je l'ai en abomination, je l'abomine ◆ **this coffee is an ~*** ce café est abominable

Aboriginal/,æbə'ridʒənl/ (*in Australia*) ADJ aborigène (australien) N ⇒ **Aborigine**

aboriginal /,æbə'ridʒənl/ ADJ [*person*] autochtone, aborigène ; [*plant, animal*] aborigène N (= *person*) autochtone mf, aborigène mf ; (= *plant*) plante f aborigène ; (= *animal*) animal m aborigène

Aborigine /,æbə'ridʒini/ N (*in Australia*) Aborigène mf (australien)

abort/ə'bɔ:t/ VI (*Med, fig*) avorter ; (*Mil, Space*) échouer ; (*Comput*) abandonner VT (*Med*) faire avorter ; (*Comput*) abandonner ; [+ *mission, operation*] abandonner, interrompre ; [+ *deal, agreement, plan*] faire échouer ◆ **an ~ed coup** une tentative avortée de coup d'État, un coup d'État manqué ◆ **an ~ed attempt** une tentative avortée N (*Comput*) abandon m

abortion /ə'bɔ:ʃən/ N 1 (*Med*) (*gen*) avortement m ; (= *termination*) avortement m, interruption f volontaire de grossesse ◆ **to have an ~** (se faire) avorter 2 [*of plans, scheme, mission*] (= *abandoning*) abandon m ; (= *failure*) échec m

COMP **abortion law reform** N réforme *f* de la loi sur l'avortement
abortion pill N pilule *f* abortive

abortionist /əˈbɔːʃənɪst/ N avorteur *m*, -euse *f* ; → **backstreet**

abortive /əˈbɔːtɪv/ ADJ [1] (= *unsuccessful*) [*attempt*] avorté ; [*coup, operation, mission*] avorté, manqué ; [*plan*] qui a échoué [2] (*Med*) [*method*] abortif, d'avortement

abortively /əˈbɔːtɪvlɪ/ ADV (= *in vain*) en vain

abound /əˈbaʊnd/ VI [*fish, resources etc*] abonder ; [*river, town, area etc*] abonder (*in* en) regorger (*in* de)

about /əˈbaʊt/

> When **about** is an element in a phrasal verb, eg **bring about, come about, turn about, wander about**, look up the verb.

ADV [1] (= *approximately*) à peu près, environ ◆ **there were ~ 25 and now there are ~ 30** il y en avait environ *or* à peu près 25 et à présent il y en a une trentaine ◆ **it's ~ 11 o'clock** il est environ *or* à peu près 11 heures ◆ **~ 11 o'clock** vers 11 heures ◆ **she's ~ as old as you** elle a à peu près votre âge ◆ **that's ~ right** c'est à peu près ça ◆ **that's ~ it** *or* **all** c'est à peu près tout ◆ **it's ~ time!** * il est grand temps ! ◆ **I've had ~ enough!** * je commence à en avoir assez !
[2] (= *here and there*) ◆ **shoes lying ~** des chaussures qui traînent (çà et là) ◆ **to throw one's arms ~** gesticuler, agiter les bras en tous sens
[3] (= *near, in circulation*) par ici ◆ **he's somewhere ~** il est quelque part par ici, il est dans les parages ◆ **is anyone ~?** il y a quelqu'un ? ◆ **there was nobody ~** il n'y avait personne ◆ **there's a lot of flu ~** il y a beaucoup de cas de grippe en ce moment ◆ **there is a rumour ~ that ...** le bruit court que ... ◆ **she's up and ~ again** elle est de nouveau sur pied ◆ **you should be out and ~!** ne restez donc pas enfermé !
[4] (= *all round*) ◆ **all ~** tout autour ◆ **to glance ~** jeter un coup d'œil autour de soi
[5] (*opposite direction*) ◆ **to turn sth (the other way) ~** retourner qch ◆ **it's the other way ~** (*fig*) c'est le contraire ◆ **~ turn!, ~ face!** (*Brit Mil*) demi-tour, marche ! ◆ **to go** *or* **put ~** (*Naut*) virer de bord ; → **ready, right**
[6] (*set structures*)
◆ **to be about to do sth** aller faire qch ◆ **I was ~ to go out when ...** j'allais sortir quand ... ◆ **he was ~ to say no but changed his mind** il allait dire non, mais il a changé d'avis ◆ **I was just ~ to do it** j'étais sur le point de le faire ◆ **the film is just ~ to start** le film va commencer ◆ **I'm not ~ to tell her she's wrong!** * ce n'est pas moi qui lui dirai qu'elle se trompe !
PREP [1] (= *concerning*) au sujet de, concernant ◆ **I need to see you ~ this contract** j'ai besoin de vous voir au sujet de ce contrat ◆ **advice ~ contraception** des conseils sur la contraception ◆ **he never complains ~ his job** il ne se plaint jamais de son travail ◆ **she knows a lot ~ cars** elle s'y connaît en voitures ◆ **to tell sb ~ sth** (= *mention it*) dire qch à qn ; (= *discuss it*) dire qch à qn, parler de qch à qn ◆ **if you were gay, would you tell your boss ~ it?** si tu étais homosexuel, tu le dirais à ton patron ? ◆ **is there a problem? would you like to tell me ~ it?** il y a quelque chose qui ne va pas ? tu veux m'en parler ? ◆ **to speak ~ sth** parler de qch ◆ **he wants to talk to you – what ~?** il veut te parler – de quoi ? ◆ **I'm sorry ~ that problem with the car** je suis désolé de ces ennuis avec la voiture ◆ **I feel bad ~ having said that** je me sens coupable d'avoir dit cela ◆ **I heard nothing ~ it** je n'en ai pas entendu parler ◆ **a book ~ cats** un livre sur les chats ◆ **what's the film/book ~?** quel est le sujet du film/du livre ? ◆ **what's all this ~?** de quoi s'agit-il ? ◆ **I know what it's all ~** je sais de quoi il retourne ◆ **politics is (all) ~ compromise** la politique est une affaire de compromis ◆ **I don't know what to do ~ the cats when we go on holiday** je ne sais pas quoi faire des chats quand nous partirons en vacances ◆ **you can't let this go on: what are you going to do ~ it?** ça ne peut pas continuer comme ça, qu'est-ce que vous allez faire ? ; → **how, what**
[2] (= *near to*) près de ◆ **I dropped it (somewhere) ~ here** je l'ai laissé tomber par ici ◆ **it happened round ~ last week** ça s'est passé il y a environ une semaine
[3] (= *somewhere in*) quelque part dans ◆ **(somewhere) ~ the house** quelque part dans la maison
[4] (= *surrounding*) autour de ◆ **the countryside (round) ~ Edinburgh** la campagne autour d'Édimbourg ◆ **she had a string of pearls ~ her neck, a string of pearls hung ~ her neck** elle portait un collier de perles (autour du cou)
[5] (= *with, on sb's person*) sur ◆ **I've got it ~ me somewhere** je l'ai sur moi, quelque part ◆ **to have drugs ~ one's person** avoir de la drogue sur soi
[6] (*describing characteristics*) ◆ **there's something sinister ~ him** il a quelque chose de sinistre, il a un côté sinistre ◆ **there's something interesting ~ him** il a un côté intéressant ◆ **there's something charming ~ him** il a un certain charme ◆ **there's something odd ~ all this** il y a quelque chose qui cloche là-dedans
[7] (= *occupied with*) ◆ **what are you ~?** qu'est-ce que vous faites ? ◆ **mind what you're ~!** faites (un peu) attention ! ◆ **while we're ~ it** pendant que nous y sommes

about-face /əˈbaʊtˈfeɪs/, **about-turn** /əˈbaʊtˈtɜːn/ VI (*Mil*) faire demi-tour ; (*fig*) faire volte-face N (*Mil*) demi-tour *m* ; (*fig*) volte-face *f* ◆ **to do an ~** faire demi-tour ; (*fig*) faire volte-face

above /əˈbʌv/

> When **above** is an element in a phrasal verb, eg **get above**, look up the verb.

ADV [1] (= *overhead, higher up*) au-dessus, en haut ◆ **from ~** d'en haut ◆ **the view from ~** la vue d'en haut ◆ **the flat ~** l'appartement *m* au-dessus *or* du dessus ◆ **the powers ~** (= *of higher rank*) les autorités *fpl* supérieures ; (= *in heaven*) les puissances *fpl* célestes ◆ **orders from ~** des ordres *mpl* venant d'en haut ◆ **a warning from ~** un avertissement (venu) d'en haut
[2] (= *more*) **boys of 16 and ~** les garçons à partir de 16 ans, les garçons de 16 ans et plus ◆ **seats are available at €15 and ~** il y a des places à partir de 15 € ; → **over**
[3] (= *earlier: in book etc*) ci-dessus, plus haut ◆ **as ~** comme ci-dessus, comme plus haut ◆ **the address as ~** l'adresse *m* ci-dessus
[4] (= *upstream*) en amont, plus haut
PREP [1] (= *higher than, superior to*) au-dessus de, plus haut que ◆ **~ it** plus haut ◆ **~ the horizon** au-dessus de l'horizon ◆ **~ all (else)** par-dessus tout, surtout ◆ **he put his hands ~ his head** il a levé les mains au-dessus de sa tête ◆ **he values honesty ~ everything else** pour lui, il n'y a rien de plus important que l'honnêteté, il place l'honnêteté au-dessus de tout ; → **average**
[2] (= *more than*) plus de ◆ **children ~ seven years of age** les enfants de plus de sept ans *or* au-dessus de sept ans ◆ **it will cost ~ $10** ça coûtera plus de 10 dollars ◆ **temperatures ~ 40 degrees** des températures supérieures à 40 degrés ◆ **wage rises of 3% ~ inflation** des augmentations de salaire supérieures de 3% à l'inflation ; → **over**
[3] (= *beyond*) au-delà de ◆ **that is quite ~ me** ceci me dépasse ◆ **this book is ~ me** ce livre est trop compliqué pour moi ; → **head**
[4] (= *too proud, honest etc for*) ◆ **he is ~ such behaviour** il est incapable de se conduire ainsi ◆ **he's not ~ stealing/theft** il irait jusqu'à voler/jusqu'au vol ◆ **he's not ~ playing with the children** il ne dédaigne pas de jouer avec les enfants ◆ **they're not ~ changing the rules to suit their own purposes** ils iraient jusqu'à modifier les règles en leur faveur ◆ **he thought he was ~ failure** (*gen*) il croyait être infaillible ; (*in specific situation, task etc*) il pensait qu'il ne pouvait pas échouer ◆ **to get ~ o.s.** avoir des idées de grandeur
[5] (= *over*) ◆ **I couldn't hear what she was saying ~ the barking** les aboiements m'empêchaient d'entendre ce qu'elle disait
[6] (= *upstream from*) en amont de, plus haut que
[7] (= *north of*) au nord de, au-dessus de
ADJ mentionné ci-dessus, précité ◆ **the ~ decree** le décret précité
N ◆ **the ~ is a photo of ...** ci-dessus nous avons une photo de ... ◆ **please translate the ~** veuillez traduire ce qui se trouve au-dessus
COMP **above board** ADJ [*person, action*] régulier, correct ADV cartes sur table
above ground ADJ (*gen*) au-dessus du sol, à la surface ; [*swimming pool*] hors sol
above-mentioned ADJ susmentionné, précité
above-named ADJ susnommé

abracadabra /ˌæbrəkəˈdæbrə/ EXCL abracadabra !

abrade /əˈbreɪd/ VT user en frottant *or* par le frottement ; [+ *skin etc*] écorcher, érafler ; (*Geol*) éroder

Abraham /ˈeɪbrəhæm/ N Abraham *m*

abrasion /əˈbreɪʒən/ (*frm*) N [1] (*Med*) [*of skin*] écorchure *f* ; [*of teeth*] abrasion *f* [2] (*NonC* = *damage*) abrasion *f*

abrasive /əˈbreɪsɪv/ ADJ [1] [*substance, surface*] abrasif [2] [*person, personality, manner, speech*] caustique ; [*voice*] acerbe ; [*wit*] corrosif N abrasif *m*

abrasively /əˈbreɪsɪvlɪ/ ADV [*say, reply*] d'une voix acerbe ◆ **he was ~ aggressive** il a été d'une agressivité caustique

abreaction /ˌæbrɪˈækʃən/ N abréaction *f*

abreast /əˈbrest/ ADV [1] [*horses, vehicles, ships*] de front ; [*people*] de front, côte à côte ◆ **to walk three ~** marcher trois de front ◆ **(in) line ~** (*Naut*) en ligne de front ◆ **~ of sb/sth** (= *in line with*) à la hauteur de qn/qch ◆ **to draw ~ of sb/sth** arriver à la hauteur de qn/qch [2] (*fig*) ◆ **~ of sth** (= *aware of*) au courant de qch ◆ **to keep ~ of sth** se tenir au courant de qch ◆ **to be ~ of the times** être de son temps, marcher avec son temps

abridge /əˈbrɪdʒ/ VT [+ *book*] abréger ; [+ *article, speech*] raccourcir, abréger ; [+ *interview*] écourter ; [+ *text*] réduire

abridgement /əˈbrɪdʒmənt/ N [1] (= *shortened version*) résumé *m*, abrégé *m* [2] (*NonC*) diminution *f*, réduction *f*

abroad /əˈbrɔːd/ ADV [1] (= *in foreign country*) à l'étranger ◆ **to go/be ~** aller/être à l'étranger ◆ **news from ~** nouvelles *fpl* de l'étranger ; → **home** [2] (= *far and wide*) au loin ; (= *in all directions*) de tous côtés, dans toutes les directions ◆ **scattered ~** éparpillé de tous côtés *or* aux quatre vents ◆ **there is a rumour ~ that ...** le bruit circule *or* court que ... ; → **noise** [3] († = *out of doors*) (au) dehors, hors de chez soi

abrogate /ˈæbrəʊgeɪt/ VT (*frm*) abroger, abolir

abrogation /ˌæbrəʊˈgeɪʃən/ N (*frm*) abrogation *f*

abrupt /əˈbrʌpt/ ADJ [1] (= *sudden*) [*change, rise, fall*] soudain, brusque ; [*resignation, dismissal*] soudain ; [*movement, turn*] brusque ; [*departure*] précipité ◆ **to come to an ~ end** se terminer brusquement ◆ **to bring an ~ end to sth** mettre brusquement fin *or* un terme à qch ◆ **to come to an ~ halt** *or* **stop** s'arrêter brusquement [2] (= *brusque*) [*person, manner, comment*] abrupt [3] (= *steep*) [*hillside, precipice*] abrupt, raide

abruptly /əˈbrʌptlɪ/ **ADV** [1] (= *suddenly*) [*stop, move, turn*] brusquement [2] (= *brusquely*) [*say, ask*] abruptement [3] (= *steeply*) [*rise*] en pente raide

abruptness /əˈbrʌptnɪs/ **N** [1] (= *suddenness*) soudaineté *f* ; (= *haste*) précipitation *f* [2] (= *brusqueness*) [*of person, behaviour*] brusquerie *f* [3] (= *steepness*) ◆ **the ~ of the slope** la pente raide

ABS /ˌeɪbiːˈes/ **N** (abbrev of **anti-lock braking system**) ABS *m* **COMP** **ABS brakes** **NPL** freins *mpl* ABS

abs /æbz/ * **NPL** abdos * *mpl*

abscess /ˈæbses/ **N** abcès *m*

abscond /əbˈskɒnd/ **VI** s'enfuir, prendre la fuite (*from* de)

absconder /əbˈskɒndəʳ/ **N** fugitif *m*, -ive *f* ; (*from prison*) évadé(e) *m(f)*

absconding /əbˈskɒndɪŋ/ **ADJ** en fuite **N** fuite *f* ; [*of prisoner*] évasion *f*

abseil /ˈæbseɪl/ (*Brit*) **VI** descendre en rappel ◆ **to ~ down a cliff** descendre une falaise en rappel **N** (descente *f* en) rappel *m* ◆ **~ device** descendeur *m*

abseiling /ˈæbseɪlɪŋ/ **N** (*Brit*) (descente *f* en) rappel *m*

absence /ˈæbsəns/ **N** [1] (= *being away*) absence *f* ; [*of defendant from trial*] non-comparution *f*, défaut *m* ◆ **during/in the ~ of sb** pendant/en l'absence de qn ◆ **sentenced in his ~** (*Jur*) condamné par contumace ◆ **~ makes the heart grow fonder** (*Prov*) l'éloignement renforce les sentiments ◆ **~ without leave** absence *f* irrégulière ◆ **an ~ of three months** une absence de trois mois ; → **conspicuous, leave, unauthorized** [2] (*NonC* = *lack*) manque *m*, défaut *m* ◆ **in the ~ of accurate information** faute de données précises **COMP** **absence of mind** **N** (= *distraction*) distraction *f* ; (= *forgetfulness*) absence *f*

absent /ˈæbsənt/ **ADJ** [1] (= *away*) absent (*from* de) ; ◆ **to be** *or* **go ~ without leave** être absent sans permission ◆ **to ~ friends!** (buvons) à la santé des absents ! [2] (= *inattentive*) distrait [3] (= *lacking*) ◆ **her name was ~ from the list** son nom n'était pas sur la liste **VT** /æbˈsent/ ◆ **to ~ o.s.** s'absenter (*from* de)
COMP **absent-minded** **ADJ** [*person*] (*gen*) distrait ; (= *forgetful*) absent ; [*air, manner*] absent, distrait
absent-mindedly **ADV** (= *distractedly*) distraitement ; (= *inadvertently*) par inadvertance
absent-mindedness **N** (= *distraction*) distraction *f* ; (= *forgetfulness*) absence *f*

absentee /ˌæbsənˈtiː/ **N** absent(e) *m(f)* ; (*habitual*) absentéiste *mf*
COMP **absentee ballot** **N** (*US Pol*) vote *m* par correspondance
absentee landlord **N** propriétaire *mf* absentéiste
absentee rate **N** taux *m* d'absentéisme
absentee voter (*US*) **N** électeur *m*, -trice *f* qui vote par correspondance

absenteeism /ˌæbsənˈtiːɪzəm/ **N** absentéisme *m*

absently /ˈæbsəntlɪ/ **ADV** distraitement

absinth(e) /ˈæbsɪnθ/ **N** absinthe *f*

absolute /ˈæbsəluːt/ **ADJ** [1] (= *complete, unqualified*) [*refusal, command, majority, silence, poverty*] absolu ; (*Jur*) [*proof*] irréfutable, formel ◆ **an ~ truth** une vérité absolue ◆ **she has ~ faith** *or* **confidence in him** elle lui fait entièrement confiance ◆ **it's an ~ necessity** c'est indispensable ◆ **it's an ~ fact that ...** c'est un fait indiscutable *or* il est indiscutable que ... ◆ **in ~ terms** dans l'absolu ◆ **the divorce was made ~** le (jugement de) divorce a été prononcé [2] (*used for emphasis*) ◆ **it's an ~ scandal** c'est un véritable scandale, c'est vraiment scandaleux ◆ **that's ~ nonsense** *or* **rubbish** * c'est n'importe quoi * ◆ **it was an ~ nightmare** * c'était un vrai cauchemar ◆ **an ~ idiot** * un parfait crétin *
[3] (= *unlimited*) [*power*] absolu, souverain ; [*monarch*] absolu
[4] (*Math, Phys*) [*value*] absolu ; (*Chem*) [*alcohol*] absolu, anhydre
N absolu *m*
COMP **absolute liability** **N** (*Fin, Jur*) responsabilité *f* objective
absolute pitch **N** (*Mus*) oreille *f* absolue
absolute veto **N** veto *m* absolu
absolute zero **N** zéro *m* absolu

absolutely /ˌæbsəˈluːtlɪ/ **ADV** [1] (= *completely*) absolument ◆ **I ~ agree** je suis absolument *or* tout à fait d'accord ◆ **to be ~ right** avoir entièrement raison ◆ **to lie ~ still** rester parfaitement immobile, faire le mort ◆ **~ everything** absolument tout ◆ **it's ~ scandalous** * c'est un véritable scandale, c'est scandaleux ◆ **~!** (*expressing agreement*) absolument ! ◆ **~ not!** (*expressing disagreement*) jamais de la vie !, sûrement pas ! [2] /ˈæbsəluːtlɪ/ (*Gram*) absolument ◆ **verb used ~** verbe dans son emploi absolu

absolution /ˌæbsəˈluːʃən/ **N** absolution *f* ◆ **the Absolution** (*in liturgy*) l'absoute *f*

absolutism /ˈæbsəluːtɪzəm/ **N** (*Pol*) absolutisme *m* ; (*Rel*) prédestination *f*

absolve /əbˈzɒlv/ **VT** (*from sin, of crime*) absoudre (*from, of* de) ; (*Jur*) acquitter (*of* de) ; (*from obligation, oath*) décharger, délier (*from* de)

absorb /əbˈsɔːb/ **VT** [1] (*lit, fig*) absorber ; [+ *sound, shock*] amortir ; [+ *atmosphere of place*] s'imprégner de ; [+ *lesson*] assimiler ◆ **to ~ surplus stocks** absorber les surplus [2] **to become ~ed in one's work/in a book** s'absorber dans son travail/dans la lecture d'un livre ◆ **to be ~ed in a book** être plongé dans un livre ◆ **to be completely ~ed in one's work** être tout entier à son travail

absorbency /əbˈsɔːbənsɪ/ **N** pouvoir *m* absorbant ; (*Chem, Phys*) absorptivité *f*

absorbent /əbˈsɔːbənt/ **ADJ** absorbant **N** absorbant *m* **COMP** **absorbent cotton** **N** (*US*) coton *m* hydrophile

absorbing /əbˈsɔːbɪŋ/ **ADJ** (*lit*) absorbant ; (*fig*) [*book, film*] passionnant, captivant ; [*work*] absorbant

absorption /əbˈsɔːpʃən/ **N** [1] (*Phys, Physiol*) absorption *f* ; [*of shock*] amortissement *m* ; [*of person into group etc*] absorption *f*, intégration *f* [2] (*fig*) concentration *f* (d'esprit) ◆ **his ~ in his studies prevented him from ...** ses études l'absorbaient à tel point qu'elles l'empêchaient de ...

absquatulate * /æbˈskwɒtʃəleɪt/ **VI** se tirer *, mettre les voiles *

abstain /əbˈsteɪn/ **VI** (*gen, Rel, Pol*) s'abstenir (*from* de ; *from doing sth* de faire qch) ; (*from alcohol*) s'abstenir complètement de boire de l'alcool

abstainer /əbˈsteɪnəʳ/ **N** [1] (also **total abstainer**) ◆ **he's an ~** il ne boit jamais d'alcool [2] (*Pol*) abstentionniste *mf*

abstemious /əbˈstiːmɪəs/ **ADJ** (*frm*) [*person*] sobre, frugal ; [*meal*] frugal

abstemiousness /əbˈstiːmɪəsnɪs/ **N** (*NonC*) (*frm*) [*of person*] (*from drinking*) sobriété *f* ; (*from eating*) frugalité *f* ; [*of meal*] frugalité *f*

abstention /əbˈstenʃən/ **N** (*from voting*) abstention *f* ; (*from drinking*) abstinence *f* ◆ **400 votes with 3 ~s** 400 voix et 3 abstentions

abstinence /ˈæbstɪnəns/ **N** (*gen, Rel*) abstinence *f* (*from* de) ; (*from alcohol*) (also **total abstinence**) abstention *f* d'alcool

abstinent /ˈæbstɪnənt/ **ADJ** sobre, tempérant ; (*Rel*) abstinent

abstract /ˈæbstrækt/ **ADJ** [*idea, number, noun, art, artist*] abstrait ◆ **~ expressionism** expressionnisme *m* abstrait **N** [1] (*Philos*) abstrait *m* ; (= *idea*) abstraction *f* ◆ **in the ~** dans l'abstrait [2] (= *summary*) (*for thesis, conference*) résumé *m*, abrégé *m* ◆ **~ of accounts** (*Fin*) extrait *m* de compte [3] (= *work of art*) œuvre *f* abstraite **VT** /æbˈstrækt/ [1] (*gen, Chem* = *remove*) extraire (*from* de) [2] (= *steal*) soustraire (*sth from sb* qch à qn) dérober [3] (= *summarize*) [+ *book*] résumer

abstracted /æbˈstræktɪd/ **ADJ** [*person*] (= *absent-minded*) distrait ; (= *preoccupied*) préoccupé, absorbé

abstractedly /æbˈstræktɪdlɪ/ **ADV** distraitement

abstraction /æbˈstrækʃən/ **N** [1] (= *absent-mindedness*) distraction *f* ◆ **with an air of ~** d'un air distrait [2] (= *concept*) idée *f* abstraite, abstraction *f* [3] (= *act of removing*) extraction *f* ; (*hum* = *stealing*) appropriation *f*

abstruse /æbˈstruːs/ **ADJ** abstrus

abstruseness /æbˈstruːsnɪs/ **N** caractère *m* abstrus

absurd /əbˈsɜːd/ **ADJ** absurde ◆ **it's ~!** c'est absurde ! **N** (*Philos*) ◆ **the ~** l'absurde *m*

absurdist /əbˈsɜːdɪst/ **ADJ** [*writer*] de l'absurde ; [*humour*] absurde ; [*book, play*] fondé sur l'absurde

absurdity /əbˈsɜːdɪtɪ/ **N** absurdité *f*

absurdly /əbˈsɜːdlɪ/ **ADV** [*demand, laugh*] de façon ridicule ; [*expensive, young, rich*] ridiculement

ABTA /ˈæbtə/ **N** (abbrev of **Association of British Travel Agents**) ≈ Syndicat *m* national des agences de voyage

Abu Dhabi /ˌæbuˈdɑːbɪ/ **N** Abou Dhabi

abundance /əˈbʌndəns/ **N** (= *plenty*) abondance *f*, profusion *f* ◆ **in ~** en abondance ◆ **the sea bed yields up an ~ of food** on trouve de la nourriture en abondance au fond de la mer ◆ **he has an ~ of energy** il a de l'énergie à revendre

abundant /əˈbʌndənt/ **ADJ** abondant ◆ **there is ~ evidence that he is guilty** les preuves de sa culpabilité abondent ◆ **seals are ~ in these waters** ces eaux abondent en phoques

abundantly /əˈbʌndəntlɪ/ **ADV** abondamment, copieusement ◆ **to grow ~** pousser à foison ◆ **it was ~ clear that ...** il était tout à fait clair que ... ◆ **he made it ~ clear to me that ...** il m'a bien fait comprendre *or* m'a bien précisé que ...

abuse /əˈbjuːz/ **VT** [1] (= *misuse*) [+ *power, privilege*] abuser de [2] (*verbally*) injurier, insulter [3] (*physically*) (= *ill-treat*) malmener, maltraiter [4] [+ *person*] (*sexually*) faire subir des abus sexuels à ◆ **(sexually) ~d children** les enfants victimes d'abus sexuels **N** /əˈbjuːs/ [1] [*of power, authority*] abus *m* ◆ **the system is open to ~** le système présente des risques d'abus [2] (= *unjust practice*) abus *m* ◆ **to remedy ~s** réprimer les abus [3] (*NonC* = *curses, insults*) insultes *fpl*, injures *fpl* ; (= *ill-treatment*) (*gen*) mauvais traitements *mpl* (*of* infligés à) ; (*Sociol, Jur*) (*gen*) maltraitance *f* ; (*sexual*) abus *m* sexuel, sévices *mpl* sexuels

abuser /əˈbjuːzəʳ/ **N** [1] (*gen*) ◆ **~s of the system** les gens qui exploitent le système [2] (*Sociol, Jur, gen*) auteur *m* de sévices ; (also **sex abuser**) auteur *m* de sévices sexuels

Abu Simbel /ˌæbuˈsɪmbl/ **N** Abou Simbel

abusive /əˈbjuːsɪv/ **ADJ** [1] (= *offensive*) [*speech, words*] injurieux ◆ **to use ~ language to sb** injurier qn ◆ **he was very ~** (= *rude*) il s'est montré très grossier [2] (*Sociol, Jur*) [*parents*] qui exercent des sévices sur leurs enfants ◆ **children from an ~ home** les enfants maltraités par leurs parents [3] (= *wrongly used*) abusif, mauvais

abusively /əbˈjuːsɪvlɪ/ ADV *[refer to]* injurieusement ◆ **to shout/scream ~ at sb** crier/hurler des insultes à qn

abut /əˈbʌt/ VI ◆ **to ~ on** *or* **onto** être contigu (-guë *f*) à VT être contigu (-guë *f*) à

abutment /əˈbʌtmənt/ N *(Archit)* contrefort *m*, piédroit *m* ; *(esp on bridge)* butée *f*

abuzz /əˈbʌz/ ADJ ◆ **the office was ~ with the news** la nouvelle courait dans tout le bureau

abysmal /əˈbɪzməl/ ADJ *[taste, quality]* épouvantable, catastrophique* ; *[failure]* retentissant ◆ **the play was an ~ failure** la pièce a été un échec retentissant ◆ **his work was quite ~** son travail était tout à fait exécrable

abysmally /əˈbɪzməlɪ/ ADV *[bad, low, unsuccessful]* atrocement ; *[play]* atrocement mal ◆ **~ ignorant** d'une ignorance crasse ◆ **the government has failed ~** le gouvernement a échoué lamentablement

abyss /əˈbɪs/ N *(lit, fig)* abîme *m*, gouffre *m* ; *(in sea)* abysse *m*

Abyssinia /ˌæbɪˈsɪnɪə/ N Abyssinie *f*

Abyssinian /ˌæbɪˈsɪnɪən/ ADJ abyssinien, abyssin *(rare)* ◆ **the ~ Empire** l'empire *m* d'Éthiopie N [1] Abyssinien(ne) *m(f)* [2] (also **Abyssinian cat**) (chat *m*) abyssin *m*

AC /ˈeɪˈsiː/ N (abbrev of **alternating current**) → **alternating**

a/c N (abbrev of **account**) C, compte *m*

acacia /əˈkeɪʃə/ N acacia *m*

Acad abbrev of **academy, academic**

academe /ˈækədiːm/, **academia** /ˌækəˈdiːmɪə/ N *(NonC)* le monde universitaire

academic /ˌækəˈdemɪk/ ADJ [1] (= *of studying, colleges*) *(Univ)* universitaire ; *(Scol)* scolaire ; *[failure, progress]* scolaire ◆ **~ freedom** liberté *f* de l'enseignement

[2] (= *theoretical*) théorique, spéculatif ◆ **~ debate** discussion *f* sans portée pratique *or* toute théorique

[3] (= *scholarly*) *[style, approach]* intellectuel ◆ **a dry ~ approach** une approche aride et scolaire

[4] (= *of no practical use*) **that's all quite ~, it's an ~ question** c'est (une question) purement théorique ◆ **out of purely ~ interest** par simple curiosité

[5] *[art, portrait]* académique

[6] (= *academically able*) doué pour les études ◆ **the less ~ pupils** les élèves moins doués pour les études

N (= *university teacher*) universitaire *mf*

COMP **academic advisor** N directeur *m*, -trice *f* d'études

academic dean N *(US)* ≃ président(e) *m(f)* de faculté

academic dress N toge *f* et toque *f* de professeur *(or* d'étudiant)

academic gown N toge *f* de professeur *(or* d'étudiant)

academic officers NPL personnel *m* enseignant et cadres *mpl* administratifs

academic rank N grade *m*

academic year N année *f* universitaire

academically /ˌækəˈdemɪkəlɪ/ ADV *[competent]* sur le plan scolaire ; *[sound]* intellectuellement ◆ **~ gifted** doué pour les études ◆ **~ qualified** possédant des diplômes

academicals /ˌækəˈdemɪkəlz/ NPL toge *f* et toque *f* de professeur *(or* d'étudiant)

academician /əˌkædəˈmɪʃən/ N académicien(ne) *m(f)*

academy /əˈkædəmɪ/ N [1] (= *private college*) école *f* privée, collège *m*, pensionnat *m* ◆ **military/naval ~** école *f* militaire/navale ◆ **~ of music** conservatoire *m* ; → **police** [2] (= *society*) académie *f*, société *f* ◆ **the (Royal) Academy** l'Académie *f* royale britannique des beaux-arts ; → **French** COMP **Academy Award** N oscar *m*

acanthus /əˈkænθəs/ N (pl **acanthuses** *or* **acanthi** /əˈkænθaɪ/) acanthe *f*

ACAS, Acas /ˈeɪkæs/ N (abbrev of **Advisory, Conciliation and Arbitration Service**) *organisme d'arbitrage des conflits du travail*

acc. *(Banking)* abbrev of **account**

accede /ækˈsiːd/ VI [1] (= *agree*) ◆ **to ~ to** *[+ request]* agréer, donner suite à ; *[+ suggestion]* agréer, accepter [2] (= *gain position*) entrer en possession ◆ **to ~ to office** entrer en fonction ◆ **to ~ to the throne** monter sur le trône [3] (= *join*) adhérer, se joindre (to à)

accelerate /ækˈseləreɪt/ VT *[+ movement, growth]* accélérer ; *[+ work]* activer ; *[+ events]* précipiter, hâter ◆ **to ~ the process of reform/modernization** accélérer le processus de réformes/de modernisation VI accélérer

accelerated /ækˈseləreɪtɪd/ ADJ accéléré ◆ **~ program** *(US Univ)* cursus *m* intensif

acceleration /ækˌseləˈreɪʃən/ N accélération *f* ◆ **repayment by ~** *(Fin)* remboursement *m* par déchéance du terme COMP **acceleration clause** N *(Fin)* clause *f* d'accélération

accelerator /ækˈseləreɪtə^r^/ N *(of car, Phys, Phot)* accélérateur *m* ◆ **to step on the ~** appuyer sur l'accélérateur *or* le champignon*

accelerometer /ækˌseləˈrɒmɪtə^r^/ N accéléromètre *m*

accent /ˈæksənt/ N [1] (= *intonation, pronunciation*) accent *m* ◆ **to speak French without an ~** parler français sans accent ◆ **to have a foreign ~** avoir un accent (étranger) ◆ **she speaks with a Yorkshire ~** elle parle avec l'accent du Yorkshire ◆ **a strong French ~** un fort accent français [2] (= *stress on part of word*) accent *m* (tonique) [3] (= *written mark*) accent *m* ; → **acute** [4] *(liter* = *way of speaking)* **~s** accents *mpl*, paroles *fpl* ◆ **in ~s of rage** avec des accents de rage (dans la voix) VT /ækˈsent/ [1] (= *emphasize*) *[+ word]* accentuer, mettre l'accent sur ; *[+ syllable]* accentuer [2] (= *make prominent*) accentuer, mettre en valeur

accentuate /ækˈsentjʊeɪt/ VT (= *emphasize*) *[+ inequality, hostility, tendency]* accentuer ; *[+ physical feature]* faire ressortir ; (= *draw attention to*) attirer l'attention sur

accentuation /ækˌsentjʊˈeɪʃən/ N accentuation *f*

accept /əkˈsept/ LANGUAGE IN USE 11.2, 11.3, 12.1, 12.2, 18.3, 25 VT [1] *[+ gift, invitation, apology]* accepter ; *[+ goods]* prendre livraison de ; *[+ excuse, fact, report, findings]* admettre, accepter ; *[+ one's duty]* se soumettre à ; *[+ one's fate]* accepter, se résigner à ; *[+ task]* se charger de, accepter ; *(Comm)* *[+ bill]* accepter ◆ **I ~ that ...** je conviens que ... ◆ **it is generally** *or* **widely ~ed that ...** il est généralement admis que ... [2] (= *allow*) *[+ action, behaviour]* admettre, accepter [3] *(Med)* *[+ transplanted organ]* assimiler

acceptability /əkˌseptəˈbɪlɪtɪ/ N acceptabilité *f*

acceptable /əkˈseptəbl/ ADJ [1] (= *reasonable*) *[offer, suggestion]* acceptable *(also Ling)* ; *(morally)* *[behaviour]* admissible ◆ **I hope you will find this ~** j'espère que cela vous conviendra ◆ **if this offer is ~ to you** si la présente offre est à votre convenance [2] (= *welcome*) bienvenu, opportun ; *[gift]* qui fait plaisir ◆ **the money was most ~** l'argent était vraiment le bienvenu

acceptably /əkˈseptəblɪ/ ADV [1] (= *properly*) *[behave, treat]* de façon acceptable, d'une manière décente ; (= *sufficiently*) ◆ **~ accurate** d'une précision satisfaisante ◆ **~safe** d'un niveau de sécurité satisfaisant ◆ **noise levels were ~ low** les niveaux sonores étaient suffisamment bas pour être tolérables [2] (= *adequately*) *[play]* à peu près comme il faut, d'une manière convenable

acceptance /əkˈseptəns/ LANGUAGE IN USE 19.5 N [1] *[of invitation, gift]* acceptation *f* ; *[of proposal]* consentement *m* (of à) ; *(Comm)* *[of bill]* acceptation *f* ; *[of delivered goods]* réception *f* [2] (= *approval*) réception *f* favorable, approbation *f* ◆ **the idea met with general ~** l'idée a reçu l'approbation générale COMP **acceptance house** N banque *f* d'acceptation

acceptation /ˌæksepˈteɪʃən/ N [1] (= *meaning*) acception *f*, signification *f* [2] (= *approval*) approbation *f*

accepted /əkˈseptɪd/ ADJ accepté ; *[fact]* reconnu ; *[idea]* répandu ; *[behaviour, pronunciation]* admis ◆ **... in the ~ sense of the word ...** dans le sens usuel *or* courant du mot

acceptor /əkˈseptə^r^/ N *(Comm)* accepteur *m*

access /ˈækses/ N [1] *(NonC)* (= *way of approach*) accès *m*, abord *m* ; *(Jur)* (= *through lane etc*) droit *m* de passage ; *(into property)* droit *m* d'accès ; (= *permission to see, use*) accès *m* ◆ **easy of ~** d'accès facile, facilement accessible ◆ **~ to the house is via a narrow path** on accède à la maison par un sentier étroit ◆ **to give ~ to ...** donner accès à ... ◆ **to have ~ to sb** avoir accès auprès de qn, avoir ses entrées chez qn ◆ **to have (right of) ~ to papers** avoir accès à des documents ◆ **to have ~ to (an) education** avoir accès *or* droit à l'éducation ◆ **these children now have ~ to (an) education** ces enfants peuvent désormais bénéficier d'une scolarisation ; → **gain**

[2] (= *way of entry*) **there is another ~ to this room** cette pièce a un autre accès

[3] *(Jur: in divorce)* droit *m* de visite ◆ **he has (no) ~ to his children** il (n')a (pas) le droit de visite

[4] *(Comput)* **~ port/time** port *m*/temps *m* d'accès ; → **random**

[5] (= *sudden outburst*) *[of anger, remorse, melancholy]* accès *m* ; *[of generosity]* élan *m*

VT *(Comput)* *[+ file etc]* accéder à

COMP **access course** N *(Univ)* *cours intensif permettant aux personnes sans baccalauréat d'accéder aux études supérieures*

access provider N fournisseur *m* d'accès

access road N route *f* d'accès ; *[of motorway]* bretelle *f* d'accès *or* de raccordement ◆ **there is an ~ road for Melun** *(to motorway)* Melun est raccordé (à l'autoroute)

accessary /ækˈsesərɪ/ *(Jur)* N complice *mf* ◆ **~ before/after the fact** complice *mf* par instigation/par assistance ADJ complice *(to* de)

accessibility /ækˌsesɪˈbɪlɪtɪ/ N accessibilité *f*

accessible /ækˈsesəbl/ ADJ [1] *[place]* accessible, d'accès facile ; *[knowledge]* à la portée de tous, accessible ; *[person]* accessible, d'un abord facile [2] (= *able to be influenced*) ouvert, accessible *(to* à)

accession /ækˈseʃən/ N [1] (= *gaining of position*) accession *f* (to à) ; *(to fortune, property)* accession *f* (to à) entrée *f* en possession (to de) ; ◆ **~ (to the throne)** avènement *m* [2] (= *addition, increase*) accroissement *m*, augmentation *f* ◆ **the ~ of new members to the party** l'adhésion *f* de membres nouveaux au parti [3] (= *consent*) accord *m*, assentiment *m* ; *(to treaty, agreement)* adhésion *f* [4] *(in library, museum)* nouvelle acquisition *f* VT *[+ library book etc]* mettre au catalogue

accessorize /ækˈsesəraɪz/ VT accessoiriser

accessory /ækˈsesərɪ/ ADJ [1] (= *additional*) accessoire, auxiliaire [2] *(Jur)* ⇒ **accessary** N [1] *(gen)* accessoire *m* ◆ **car accessories** accessoires *mpl* d'automobile ◆ **toilet accessories** accessoires *mpl* de toilette [2] *(Jur)* ⇒ **accessary**

accidence /ˈæksɪdəns/ N *(Ling)* morphologie *f* flexionnelle ; *(Philos)* accident *m*

accident /ˈæksɪdənt/ N 1 *(= mishap, disaster)* accident *m* ◆ **to meet with** *or* **have an ~** avoir un accident ◆ **road ~** accident *m* de la route *or* de la circulation ◆ **~s in the home** accidents *mpl* domestiques ◆ **it's an ~ waiting to happen** *(fig)* c'est une bombe à retardement
2 *(= unforeseen event)* événement *m* fortuit, accident *m* ; *(= chance)* hasard *m*, chance *f* ◆ **it's no ~ that ...** ce n'est pas un hasard si ...
◆ **by accident** *[injure, break]* accidentellement ; *[meet, find]* par hasard
3 *(Philos)* accident *m*
COMP **Accident and Emergency Unit** N (service *m* des) urgences *fpl*
accident figures NPL statistiques *fpl* concernant les accidents
accident insurance N assurance *f* (contre les) accidents
accident prevention N *(in home, factory)* prévention *f* des accidents ; *(on roads)* prévention *f* routière
accident-prone ADJ ◆ **to be ~-prone** être sujet aux accidents, attirer les accidents
accident protection N *(on roads)* prévention *f* routière
accident statistics NPL statistiques *fpl* des accidents
Accident Unit N ⇒ **Accident and Emergency Unit**

accidental /ˌæksɪˈdentl/ ADJ 1 *(= happening by chance) [shooting, poisoning, overdose, death]* accidentel ◆ **the ~ discovery of the explosives** la découverte fortuite des explosifs ◆ **the cure was an ~ discovery** le traitement a été découvert par hasard 2 *(= of secondary importance) [effect, benefit]* secondaire, accessoire 3 *(Mus, Philos)* accidentel N *(Mus)* accident *m*
COMP **accidental damage** N *(Insurance)* accident(s) *m(pl)*
accidental injury N *(Insurance)* accident *m*

accidentally /ˌæksɪˈdentəlɪ/ ADV *[shoot, kill]* accidentellement ◆ **it was discovered quite ~** on l'a découvert par hasard ◆ **~ on purpose*** comme par hasard

acclaim /əˈkleɪm/ VT *(= applaud)* acclamer ◆ **to ~ sb king** proclamer qn roi N acclamations *fpl* ◆ **it met with great public/critical ~** cela a été salué unanimement par le public/les critiques

acclamation /ˌækləˈmeɪʃən/ N acclamation *f* ◆ **to be elected/nominated by ~** être élu/nommé par acclamation

acclimate /əˈklaɪmət/ VTI *(US)* ⇒ **acclimatize**

acclimatization /əˌklaɪmətaɪˈzeɪʃən/, **acclimation** *(US)* /ˌæklaɪˈmeɪʃən/ N *(lit)* acclimatation *f* ; *(fig: to new situation etc)* accoutumance *f* *(to à)*

acclimatize /əˈklaɪmətaɪz/, **acclimate** *(US)* /əˈklaɪmət/ VT *(lit, fig)* acclimater *(to à)* VI *(to new place, climate)* s'acclimater *(to à)* ; ◆ **to ~ to a new job** s'accoutumer *or* se faire à un nouveau travail

acclivity /əˈklɪvɪtɪ/ N montée *f*

accolade /ˈækəʊleɪd/ N accolade *f* ; *(fig)* marque *f* d'approbation ◆ **the ultimate ~** la consécration ultime

accommodate /əˈkɒmədeɪt/ VT 1 *(= provide lodging or housing for)* loger ; *(= contain) [car]* contenir ; *[house]* contenir, recevoir ◆ **the hotel/room can ~ 60 people** l'hôtel/la salle peut recevoir *or* accueillir 60 personnes 2 *(= supply)* équiper *(sb with sth* qn de qch) fournir *(sb with sth* qch à qn) ; *(= satisfy) [+ demand etc]* accéder à ◆ **to ~ sb with a loan** consentir un prêt à qn ◆ **I think we can ~ you** je crois que nous pouvons satisfaire à votre demande 3 *(= adapt) [+ plans, wishes]* accommoder, adapter *(to à)* ; ◆ **to ~ o.s. to sth** s'adapter à qch, s'accommoder à qch

accommodating /əˈkɒmədeɪtɪŋ/ ADJ *(= obliging)* obligeant ; *(= easy to deal with)* accommodant, conciliant

accommodation /əˌkɒməˈdeɪʃən/ N 1 *[of person]* logement *m* ◆ **~s** *(US)* logement *m* ◆ **"accommodation (to let)"** "appartements *or* chambres à louer" ◆ **we have no ~ available** nous n'avons pas de chambres ◆ **we have no ~ suitable for children** nous n'avons pas de chambres pour les enfants ◆ **"office accommodation to let"** "bureaux à louer" ; → **seating**
2 *(= compromise)* compromis *m* ◆ **to make** *or* **reach (an) ~ with sb** arriver à *or* trouver un compromis avec qn
3 *(Anat, Psych)* accommodation *f*
4 *(Fin)* prêt *m*, crédit *m* ◆ **to take ~** contracter un emprunt, faire un prêt
COMP **accommodation address** N adresse *f* de domiciliation
accommodation bill N *(Comm)* billet *m* or effet *m* de complaisance
accommodation bureau N agence *f* de logement
accommodation ladder N *(Naut)* échelle *f* de coupée
accommodation officer N responsable *mf* de l'hébergement
accommodation road N route *f* à usage restreint
accommodation train N *(US Rail)* (train *m*) omnibus *m*

accompaniment /əˈkʌmpənɪmənt/ N accompagnement *m*, complément *m* ; *(Mus)* accompagnement *m* ; *(Culin)* accompagnement *m*, garniture *f* ◆ **they marched to the ~ of a military band** ils ont défilé au son d'une fanfare militaire

accompanist /əˈkʌmpənɪst/ N *(Mus)* accompagnateur *m*, -trice *f*

accompany /əˈkʌmpənɪ/ VT 1 *(gen)* accompagner ◆ **accompanied by** accompagné de *or* par ◆ **cold accompanied by fever** rhume *m* accompagné de fièvre ◆ **~ing letter** lettre *f* d'accompagnement 2 *(Mus)* accompagner *(on à)*

accomplice /əˈkʌmplɪs/ N complice *mf* ◆ **to be an ~ to** *or* **in a crime** tremper dans un crime, être complice d'un crime

accomplish /əˈkʌmplɪʃ/ VT accomplir, exécuter ; *[+ task]* accomplir, achever ; *[+ desire]* réaliser ; *[+ journey]* effectuer ◆ **to ~ one's object** arriver à ses fins

accomplished /əˈkʌmplɪʃt/ ADJ *[person] (gen)* doué ; *[musician, skater etc]* accompli ; ◆ **they gave an accomplished performance** ils ont très bien joué *(or chanté etc)* ◆ **she's very ~** elle est très douée ◆ **an ~ pianist** un pianiste accompli

accomplishment /əˈkʌmplɪʃmənt/ N 1 *(= achievement)* œuvre *f* accomplie, projet *m* réalisé 2 *(= skill)* talent *m* ◆ **a woman of many ~s** une femme aux multiples talents *or* très talentueuse 3 *(NonC = completion)* ◆ **on ~ of the project** quand le projet aura été mené à bien

accord /əˈkɔːd/ VT *[+ favour, status, right, honour, privilege]* accorder *(to à)* ; *[+ respect]* témoigner ◆ **to ~ priority to** accorder la priorité à ◆ **to ~ great importance to sth** accorder beaucoup d'importance à qch ◆ **she insisted she be ~ed the same treatment as her male colleagues** elle a insisté pour avoir droit au même traitement que ses collègues masculins ◆ **he was ~ed a hero's welcome** il a été accueilli en héros VI s'accorder, concorder *(with avec)* N 1 *(NonC = agreement)* consentement *m*, accord *m* ◆ **of his own ~** de lui-même ◆ **the problem disappeared of its own ~** le problème s'est résolu tout seul ◆ **with one ~** d'un commun accord ◆ **to be in ~ with** être d'accord avec 2 *(= treaty)* traité *m*, pacte *m*

accordance /əˈkɔːdəns/ N accord *m* *(with avec)* conformité *f* *(with à)* ; ◆ **in ~ with** conformément à, suivant, en accord avec ◆ **to be in ~ with** être conforme à, correspondre à

according /əˈkɔːdɪŋ/ LANGUAGE IN USE 26.1, 26.2
ADV 1 *(gen)* ◆ **~ to** selon ◆ **~ to him they've gone** selon lui *or* d'après lui ils sont partis ◆ **classified ~ to size** classés par ordre de grandeur ◆ **everything went ~ to plan** tout s'est passé comme prévu ◆ **~ to what he says ...** d'après ce qu'il dit ... ◆ **to act ~ to the law** agir conformément à la loi 2 ◆ **~ as** selon que + *subj*, suivant que + *indic*

accordingly /əˈkɔːdɪŋlɪ/ ADV 1 *(= appropriately) [act, pay, plan]* en conséquence 2 *(= consequently)* par conséquent

accordion /əˈkɔːdɪən/ N accordéon *m*
COMP **accordion file** N *(US)* dossier *m* à soufflet
accordion pleat N pli *m* (en) accordéon

accordionist /əˈkɔːdɪənɪst/ N accordéoniste *mf*

accost /əˈkɒst/ VT accoster, aborder ; *(Jur)* accoster

account /əˈkaʊnt/ N 1 *(Comm, Fin)* compte *m* ◆ **to open an ~** ouvrir un compte ◆ **put it on my ~** *(in shop)* vous le mettrez à *or* sur mon compte ; *(in hotel)* vous le mettrez sur mon compte *or* sur ma note ◆ **to pay a sum into one's ~** *(Banking)* verser une somme à son compte ◆ **I have an ~ with them** *(at shop)* ils me font crédit ◆ **in ~ with** en compte avec ◆ **~s payable** comptes *mpl* clients, comptes *mpl* créditeurs ◆ **~s receivable** comptes *mpl* fournisseurs, effets *mpl* à recevoir ◆ **"to account rendered"** "facture non payée" ◆ **on ~** à compte ◆ **payment on ~** acompte *m*, à-valoir *m*, paiement *m* à compte ◆ **to pay £50 on ~** verser un acompte de 50 livres ◆ **cash or ~?** *(in hotel, bar)* vous payez comptant ou je le mets sur votre note ? ; *(in shop)* vous payez comptant ou je le mets sur votre compte ? ◆ **they have the Michelin ~** *(Advertising)* ce sont eux qui font la publicité de Michelin ◆ **to settle** *or* **square ~s with sb** *(fig)* régler son compte à qn ; → **bank²**, **current**, **settle²**
2 ◆ **~s** *(= calculation)* comptabilité *f*, comptes *mpl* ; *(= department)* (service *m*) comptabilité *f* ◆ **to do/keep the ~s** faire/tenir la comptabilité *or* les comptes
3 *(= report)* compte rendu *m* ◆ **to give an ~ of sth** faire le compte rendu de qch *or* un exposé sur qch ◆ **by her own ~** d'après ce qu'elle dit, d'après ses dires ◆ **by all ~s** d'après l'opinion générale, au dire de tous ◆ **he gave a good ~ of himself** *(= made a good impression)* il s'en est bien tiré, il a fait bonne impression
4 *(= importance)* ◆ **of little ~** peu important ◆ **of no ~** sans importance ◆ **your statement is of no ~ to them** ils n'attachent aucune importance *or* valeur à votre déclaration
5 *(set structures)*
◆ **on + account** ◆ **on ~ of** à cause de ◆ **on no ~**, **not on any ~** en aucun cas, sous aucun prétexte ◆ **on no ~ must you leave** vous ne devez partir sous aucun prétexte ◆ **on this** *or* **that ~** pour cette raison ◆ **on her ~** à cause d'elle ◆ **I was worried on her ~** je m'inquiétais pour elle ◆ **don't leave on my ~** ne partez pas à cause de moi
◆ **to call** *or* **hold sb to account** demander des comptes à qn ◆ **they can't be held to ~ for this** ils ne peuvent pas être tenus responsables de cela
◆ **to leave sth out of account** ne pas tenir compte de qch
◆ **to take + account of sth/sb, to take sth/sb into account** tenir compte de qch/qn ◆ **these facts must be taken into ~** ces faits doivent entrer en ligne de compte ◆ **to**

take little ~ of sth faire peu de cas de qch ◆ **to take no ~ of sth** ne pas tenir compte de qch
◆ **to turn** *or* **put sth to good account** mettre qch à profit, tirer parti de qch
VT estimer, juger ◆ **to ~ o.s. lucky** s'estimer heureux ◆ **to ~ sb (to be) innocent** considérer qn comme innocent
COMP **account book** N livre *m* de comptes
account day N *(on Stock Exchange)* terme *m*, jour *m* de liquidation
account executive N *(Advertising)* responsable *mf* du budget
account holder N *(Banking)* titulaire *mf* d'un compte
accounts department N (service *m*) comptabilité *f*
► **account for** VT FUS 1 *(= explain, justify) [+ expenses]* rendre compte de, justifier de ; *[+ one's conduct]* justifier ; *[+ circumstances]* expliquer ◆ **poor sanitation ~s for the recent outbreaks of disease** les mauvaises conditions d'hygiène expliquent les récentes épidémies ◆ **there's no ~ing for tastes** des goûts et des couleurs on ne dispute pas *(Prov)*, chacun son goût *(Prov)* ◆ **everyone is ~ed for** on n'a oublié personne ◆ **three people have not yet been ~ed for** *(after accident etc)* trois personnes n'ont pas encore été retrouvées
2 *(= represent)* représenter ◆ **this ~s for 10% of the total** ceci représente 10% du chiffre total ◆ **the Greens ~ for 10% of the vote** les Verts totalisent *or* représentent 10% des voix ◆ **this area ~s for most of the country's mineral wealth** cette région produit *or* possède la plus grande partie des ressources minières du pays
3 *(= kill, destroy: shooting etc)* tuer ; *(Fishing = catch)* attraper ◆ **he ~ed for four enemy planes** il a abattu quatre avions ennemis

accountability /əˌkaʊntəˈbɪlɪtɪ/ N responsabilité *f* ; *(financial)* responsabilité *f* financière

accountable /əˈkaʊntəbl/ ADJ responsable *(for de)* ; ◆ **to be ~ to sb for sth** être responsable de qch *or* répondre de qch devant qn ◆ **he is not ~ for his actions** *(= need not account for)* il n'a pas à répondre de ses actes ; *(= is not responsible for)* il n'est pas responsable de ses actes

accountancy /əˈkaʊntənsɪ/ N *(= subject)* comptabilité *f* ; *(= profession)* profession *f* de comptable ◆ **to study ~** faire des études de comptable *or* de comptabilité

accountant /əˈkaʊntənt/ N comptable *mf* ◆ **~'s office** agence *f* comptable

accounting /əˈkaʊntɪŋ/ N comptabilité *f*
COMP **accounting period** N exercice *m* comptable
accounting policy N politique *f* comptable
accounting practices NPL pratique *f* comptable
accounting year N ⇒ **accounting period**

accouterments /əˈkuːtərmənts/ NPL *(US)* ⇒ **accoutrements**

accoutred /əˈkuːtəd/ ADJ *(esp Mil)* équipé *(with de)*

accoutrements /əˈkuːtrəmənts/, **accouterments** *(US)* /əˈkuːtərmənts/ NPL *(Mil)* équipement *m* ; *(gen)* attirail *m*

accredit /əˈkredɪt/ VT 1 *(= credit) [+ rumour]* accréditer ◆ **to ~ sth to sb** attribuer qch à qn ◆ **he is ~ed with having discovered the site** on lui attribue la découverte de ce site 2 *[+ representative, ambassador]* accréditer *(to* auprès de*)*
→ **accredited**

accreditation /əˌkredɪˈteɪʃn/ N 1 *(US Scol, Univ)* habilitation *f* 2 ◆ **media ~** accréditation *f* presse COMP **accreditation officer** N *(US Scol)* inspecteur *m* d'académie

accredited /əˈkredɪtɪd/ ADJ *[person]* accrédité, autorisé ; *[opinion, belief]* admis, accepté ; *[agent]* accrédité ◆ **~ institution** *(Univ, Scol)* *établissement scolaire ou universitaire dont les diplômes sont reconnus par l'État* ◆ **~ representative** représentant *m* accrédité *(to* auprès de*)*

accretion /əˈkriːʃən/ N 1 *(= increase, growth)* accroissement *m* (organique) 2 *(= result of growth: Geol etc)* concrétion *f*, addition *f* ; *[of wealth etc]* accroissement *m*, accumulation *f*

accruals /əˈkruːəlz/ NPL *(Fin)* compte *m* de régularisation (du passif)

accrue /əˈkruː/ VI 1 *[money, advantages]* revenir *(to* à*)* 2 *(Fin) [interest]* courir
COMP **accrued alimony** N *(Jur)* pension *f* alimentaire due
accrued charges NPL charges *fpl* à payer
accrued expenses NPL frais *mpl* à payer
accrued income N recettes *fpl* échues
accrued interest N intérêts *mpl* courus

accumulate /əˈkjuːmjʊleɪt/ VT accumuler VI s'accumuler ◆ **to allow interest to ~** laisser courir les intérêts

accumulation /əˌkjuːmjʊˈleɪʃən/ N 1 *(NonC)* accumulation *f* 2 *(= objects accumulated)* amas *m*, tas *m*

accumulative /əˈkjuːmjʊlətɪv/ ADJ qui s'accumule ; *(Fin)* cumulatif

accumulator /əˈkjuːmjʊleɪtəʳ/ N 1 *(Elec)* accumulateur *m*, accus* *mpl* 2 *(Brit = bet)* report *m*

accuracy /ˈækjʊrəsɪ/ N *[of figures, clock]* exactitude *f* ; *[of aim, shot, story, report]* précision *f* ; *[of translation]* exactitude *f*, fidélité *f* ; *[of judgement, assessment]* justesse *f*

accurate /ˈækjʊrɪt/ ADJ *[information, figures, description]* exact ; *[typist]* bon ; *[missile]* précis ; *[measurement, clock, assessment, prediction]* juste ; *[translation, account, memory]* fidèle ; *[spelling]* correct ◆ **his father or, to be ~, his stepfather ...** son père ou, pour être exact, son beau-père ... ◆ **the newspaper is well-known for its ~ reporting** ce journal est réputé pour l'exactitude de ses informations ◆ **the tests are 90% ~** ces tests sont fiables à 90% ◆ **the scales were ~ to half a gram** la balance avait une précision de l'ordre du demi-gramme

accurately /ˈækjʊrɪtlɪ/ ADV *[reflect, report, tell]* exactement, avec exactitude ; *[calculate, predict, reproduce]* exactement ; *[describe, measure, draw]* avec précision ; *[type, spell]* correctement ; *[translate]* fidèlement

accursed /əˈkɜːst/, **accurst** /əˈkɜːst/ ADJ († *or liter*) maudit

accusal /əˈkjuːzl/ N accusation *f*

accusation /ˌækjʊˈzeɪʃən/ N accusation *f* ; *(Jur)* accusation *f*, plainte *f* ◆ **to bring an ~ against sb** *(Jur)* porter plainte *or* déposer (une) plainte contre qn

accusative /əˈkjuːzətɪv/ N accusatif *m* ◆ **in the ~** à l'accusatif ADJ accusatif

accusatory /əˈkjuːzətərɪ/ ADJ accusateur (-trice *f*)

accuse /əˈkjuːz/ VT accuser *(sb of sth* qn de qch*)* ; ◆ **they ~d him of stealing the car** *or* **of having stolen the car** ils l'ont accusé d'avoir volé la voiture ◆ **they stand ~d of murder** *(Jur)* ils sont accusés de meurtre

accused /əˈkjuːzd/ N (pl **accused**) *(Jur)* accusé(e) *m(f)*, inculpé(e) *m(f)*

accuser /əˈkjuːzəʳ/ N accusateur *m*, -trice *f*

accusing /əˈkjuːzɪŋ/ ADJ accusateur (-trice *f*)

accusingly /əˈkjuːzɪŋlɪ/ ADV d'une manière accusatrice

accustom /əˈkʌstəm/ VT habituer, accoutumer *(sb to sth* qn à qch ; *sb to doing sth* qn à faire qch*)* ; ◆ **to ~ o.s. to** s'habituer à, s'accoutumer à

accustomed /əˈkʌstəmd/ ADJ 1 *(= used)* habitué, accoutumé *(to* à ; *to do sth, to doing sth* à faire qch*)* ; ◆ **to become** *or* **get ~ to sth/to doing sth** s'habituer *or* s'accoutumer à qch/à faire qch ◆ **I am not ~ to such treatment** je n'ai pas l'habitude qu'on me traite *subj* de cette façon 2 *(= usual)* habituel, coutumier

AC/DC /ˌeɪsiːˈdiːsiː/ N (abbrev of **alternating current/direct current**) → **alternating, direct**
ADJ ◆ **he's ~** ‡ il marche à voile et à vapeur‡

ace /eɪs/ N 1 *(Cards, Dice, Dominoes)* as *m* ; *(Tennis = shot)* ace *m* ◆ **~ of diamonds** as *m* de carreau 2 *(fig)* **to have** *or* **keep an ~ up one's sleeve** avoir une carte maîtresse *or* un atout en réserve ◆ **to have the ~ in one's hand** *(Brit)* ◆ **to have an ~ in the hole** avoir un atout en réserve ◆ **to play one's ~** jouer sa meilleure carte ◆ **to hold all the ~s** avoir tous les atouts en main ◆ **as black as the ~ of spades** noir comme du charbon ◆ **to come within an ~ of sth** être à deux doigts de qch ; → **clean** 3 *(= pilot, racing driver etc)* as *m* ◆ **he's ~s*** *(US)* il est super* ADJ super* ◆ **an ~ driver** un as du volant COMP **Ace Bandage** ® N *(US)* bande *f* Velpeau ®

acerbic /əˈsɜːbɪk/ ADJ *[taste]* âpre ; *[wit, humour]* acerbe, caustique

acerbity /əˈsɜːbɪtɪ/ N âpreté *f*, aigreur *f*

acetate /ˈæsɪteɪt/ N acétate *m*

acetic /əˈsiːtɪk/ ADJ acétique ◆ **~ acid** acide *m* acétique

acetone /ˈæsɪtəʊn/ N acétone *f*

acetylene /əˈsetɪliːn/ N acétylène *m*
COMP **acetylene burner** N chalumeau *m* à acétylène
acetylene lamp N lampe *f* à acétylène
acetylene torch N ⇒ **acetylene burner**
acetylene welding N soudure *f* à l'acétylène

ache /eɪk/ VI faire mal, être douloureux ◆ **my head ~s** j'ai mal à la tête ◆ **to be aching all over** *(after exercise)* être courbaturé ; *(from illness)* avoir mal partout ◆ **it makes my heart ~** cela me brise *or* me fend le cœur ◆ **her heart ~d for them** elle souffrait pour eux ◆ **to be aching** *or* **to ~ to do sth** mourir d'envie de faire qch, brûler de faire qch N 1 *(physical)* douleur *f*, souffrance *f* ◆ **all his ~s and pains** toutes ses douleurs, tous ses maux ◆ **he's always complaining of ~s and pains** il se plaint toujours d'avoir mal partout ; → **toothache** 2 *(fig)* peine *f* ; → **heartache**

achieve /əˈtʃiːv/ VT *(gen)* accomplir, réaliser ; *[+ aim, standard]* atteindre, parvenir à ; *[+ success]* obtenir ; *[+ fame]* parvenir à ; *[+ victory]* remporter ◆ **what they have ~d** ce qu'ils ont accompli *or* réalisé ◆ **how did you ~ that?** comment est-ce que vous avez réussi à faire ça ? ◆ **to ~ something in life** arriver à quelque chose dans la vie ◆ **I feel I've really ~d something today** j'ai l'impression d'avoir fait quelque chose de valable aujourd'hui ; → **underachieve** VI *(= be successful)* réussir

achievement /əˈtʃiːvmənt/ N 1 *(= success, feat)* exploit *m*, réussite *f* 2 *(Scol)* **the level of ~** le niveau des élèves 3 *(NonC = completion)* accomplissement *m*, réalisation *f* COMP **achievement test** N *(Scol)* test *m* de niveau *(dans les écoles primaires)*

achiever /əˈtʃiːvəʳ/ N *(= successful person)* gagneur *m*, -euse *f* ◆ **high-/low-~** sujet *m* doué/peu doué

Achilles /əˈkɪliːz/ N Achille *m*
COMP **Achilles' heel** N *(fig)* talon *m* d'Achille
Achilles' tendon N *(Anat)* tendon *m* d'Achille

aching /ˈeɪkɪŋ/ ADJ douloureux, endolori ◆ **to have an ~ heart** avoir le cœur gros

achingly /ˈeɪkɪŋlɪ/ ADV *[funny, sad, beautiful]* à pleurer

achromatic /ˌeɪkrəʊˈmætɪk/ ADJ achromatique

achy* /ˈeɪkɪ/ ADJ *[legs, muscles, joints]* douloureux ◆ **I feel ~ all over** j'ai mal partout

acid /ˈæsɪd/ N 1 acide *m* 2 *(Drugs *)* acide* *m* ◆ **to drop ~ *** prendre de l'acide* 3 ◆ **Acid**

⇒ **Acid house** ADJ ① (= *sour*) acide ② (= *sharp*) *[person]* revêche ; *[voice]* aigre ; *[remark]* mordant, acide

COMP **acid drop** N bonbon *m* acidulé
acid head* N (*Drugs*) drogué(e) *m(f)* au LSD
Acid house N acid music *f*
Acid house party N acid party *f*
acid jazz N acid jazz *m*
acid-proof ADJ résistant aux acides
acid rain N pluies *fpl* acides
acid rock N (*Mus*) acid rock *m*
acid test N (*fig*) test *m* ◆ **to pass the ~ test** passer le test

acidic /əˈsɪdɪk/ ADJ acide

acidify /əˈsɪdɪfaɪ/ VT acidifier

acidity /əˈsɪdɪtɪ/ N acidité *f*

acidly /ˈæsɪdlɪ/ ADV *[say, reply]* d'un ton acide

acidulous /əˈsɪdjʊləs/ ADJ acidulé

ack-ack /ˈækˈæk/ N défense *f* contre avions, DCA *f*

COMP **ack-ack fire** N tir *m* de DCA
ack-ack guns NPL canons *mpl* antiaériens *or* de DCA

acknowledge /əkˈnɒlɪdʒ/ VT ① (= *admit*) avouer, admettre ; *[+ error]* reconnaître, avouer ◆ **to ~ sb as leader** reconnaître qn pour chef ◆ **to ~ o.s. beaten** s'avouer vaincu *or* battu ② (also **acknowledge receipt of**) *[+ letter, parcel]* accuser réception de ◆ **to ~ a gift from sb** remercier qn pour *or* d'un cadeau ③ (= *express thanks for*) *[+ person's action, services, help]* manifester sa gratitude pour, se montrer reconnaissant de ; *[+ applause, cheers]* saluer pour répondre à ④ (= *indicate recognition of*) *[+ greeting]* répondre à ◆ **I smiled at him but he didn't even ~ me** je lui ai souri mais il a fait comme s'il ne me voyait pas ◆ **he didn't even ~ my presence** il a fait comme si je n'étais pas là ◆ **to ~ a child** (*Jur*) reconnaître un enfant

acknowledged /əkˈnɒlɪdʒd/ ADJ *[leader, expert etc]* reconnu (de tous) ; *[child]* reconnu ; *[letter]* dont on a accusé réception

acknowledgement /əkˈnɒlɪdʒmənt/ N ① (*NonC*) reconnaissance *f* ; *[of one's error etc]* aveu *m* ◆ **in ~ of your help** en reconnaissance *or* en remerciement de votre aide ◆ **to raise one's arm in ~** remercier d'un geste ② *[of money]* reçu *m*, récépissé *m*, quittance *f* ; *[of letter]* accusé *m* de réception ◆ **~s** (*in preface etc*) remerciements *mpl* ◆ **to quote without ~** faire une citation sans mentionner la source COMP **acknowledgement slip** N (*Comm*) accusé *m* de réception

ACLU /ˌeɪsiːelˈjuː/ N (abbrev of **American Civil Liberties Union**) Ligue *f* des droits de l'homme

acme /ˈækmɪ/ N point *m* culminant

acne /ˈæknɪ/ N acné *f*

acolyte /ˈækəʊlaɪt/ N acolyte *m*

aconite /ˈækənaɪt/ N aconit *m*

acorn /ˈeɪkɔːn/ N gland *m* COMP **acorn cup** N cupule *f*

acoustic /əˈkuːstɪk/ ADJ acoustique ; → **coupler**

COMP **acoustic feature** N (*Phon*) trait *m* distinctif acoustique
acoustic feedback N (*Recording*) effet *m* Larsen, réaction *f* acoustique
acoustic guitar N guitare *f* acoustique
acoustic hood N (*Comput*) capot *m* insonorisant
acoustic phonetics N (*NonC*) phonétique *f* acoustique
acoustic regeneration N ⇒ **acoustic feedback**
acoustic screen N (*in office*) cloison *f* insonorisante

acoustically /əˈkuːstɪkəlɪ/ ADV *[poor, perfect]* du point de vue de l'acoustique ; *[play]* en acoustique

acoustics /əˈkuːstɪks/ N ① (*Phys: + sg vb*) acoustique *f* ② *[of room etc]* (*+ pl vb*) acoustique *f*

ACPO /ˈækpəʊ/ N (*Brit*) (abbrev of **Association of Chief Police Officers**) syndicat *m* des officiers de police

acquaint /əˈkweɪnt/ VT ① (= *inform*) ◆ **to ~ sb with sth** aviser qn de qch, renseigner qn sur qch ◆ **to ~ sb with the situation** mettre qn au courant *or* au fait de la situation ② ◆ **to be ~ed with** *[+ person, subject]* connaître ; *[+ fact]* savoir, être au courant de ◆ **to become** *or* **get ~ed with sb** faire la connaissance de qn ◆ **to become ~ed with the facts** prendre connaissance des faits ◆ **to get ~ed** faire connaissance

acquaintance /əˈkweɪntəns/ N ① (*NonC*) connaissance *f* ◆ **to make sb's ~** faire la connaissance de qn ◆ **to improve upon ~** gagner à être connu ◆ **to have some ~ with French** avoir une certaine connaissance du français, savoir un peu le français ◆ **a person of my ~** une connaissance ; → **claim** ② (= *person*) relation *f*, connaissance *f* ◆ **to have a wide circle of ~s** avoir des relations très étendues ◆ **she's an ~ of mine** je la connais un peu, c'est une de mes relations ◆ **old ~s** de vieilles connaissances *fpl*

acquaintanceship /əˈkweɪntənsʃɪp/ N relations *fpl*, cercle *m* de connaissances ◆ **a wide ~** de nombreuses relations *fpl*

acquiesce /ˌækwɪˈes/ VI acquiescer, consentir ◆ **to ~ in an opinion** se ranger à une opinion *or* à un avis ◆ **to ~ in a proposal** donner son accord *or* son assentiment à une proposition

acquiescence /ˌækwɪˈesns/ N consentement *m*, assentiment *m*

acquiescent /ˌækwɪˈesnt/ ADJ consentant

acquire /əˈkwaɪəʳ/ VT *[+ house, car, knowledge, money, fame, experience]* acquérir ; *[+ company]* acheter ; *[+ language]* apprendre ; *[+ habit]* prendre, contracter ; *[+ reputation]* se faire ◆ **to ~ a taste for sth** prendre goût à qch ◆ **she has ~d a new husband** (*hum*) elle s'est dotée d'un nouveau mari

acquired /əˈkwaɪəd/ ADJ acquis ◆ **~ characteristic** caractère *m* acquis ◆ **it's an ~ taste** on finit par aimer ça, c'est un goût qui s'acquiert COMP **acquired immune deficiency syndrome** N syndrome *m* immunodéficitaire acquis

acquirement /əˈkwaɪəmənt/ N (*NonC*) acquisition *f* (*of* de)

acquirer /əˈkwaɪərəʳ/ N acquéreur *m*

acquisition /ˌækwɪˈzɪʃən/ N acquisition *f* ; (* = *person*) recrue *f* (*to* pour) ; ◆ **~ of holdings** (*Fin*) prise *f* de participation

acquisitive /əˈkwɪzɪtɪv/ ADJ (*for money*) âpre au gain ; (= *greedy*) avide (*of* de) ; ◆ **~ instinct** instinct *m* de possession ◆ **to have an ~ nature** avoir l'instinct de possession très développé

acquisitiveness /əˈkwɪzɪtɪvnɪs/ N instinct *m* de possession, goût *m* de la propriété

acquit /əˈkwɪt/ VT ① (*Jur*) acquitter, décharger (*of* de) ② ◆ **to ~ o.s. well in battle** bien se conduire *or* se comporter au combat ◆ **it was a difficult job but he ~ted himself well** c'était une tâche difficile mais il s'en est bien tiré ③ *[+ debt]* régler, s'acquitter de

acquittal /əˈkwɪtl/ N *[of person, debt]* acquittement *m*

acre /ˈeɪkəʳ/ N ≈ demi-hectare *m*, arpent † *m*, acre *f* ◆ **he owns a few ~s in Sussex** il possède quelques hectares dans le Sussex ◆ **the rolling ~s of the estate** la vaste étendue du domaine ◆ **~s of*** (*fig*) des kilomètres et des kilomètres de ; → **god**

acreage /ˈeɪkərɪdʒ/ N aire *f*, superficie *f* ◆ **what ~ have you?** combien avez-vous d'hectares ? ◆ **to farm a large ~** cultiver *or* exploiter de grandes superficies

acrid /ˈækrɪd/ ADJ *[taste, smell]* âcre ; *[remark, style]* acerbe, mordant

Acrilan ® /ˈækrɪlæn/ N Acrilan ® *m*

acrimonious /ˌækrɪˈməʊnɪəs/ ADJ acrimonieux

acrimoniously /ˌækrɪˈməʊnɪəslɪ/ ADV avec acrimonie

acrimony /ˈækrɪmənɪ/ N acrimonie *f*

acrobat /ˈækrəbæt/ N acrobate *mf*

acrobatic /ˌækrəʊˈbætɪk/ ADJ acrobatique

acrobatics /ˌækrəʊˈbætɪks/ NPL (*lit*) acrobatie *f* ; (*fig*) acrobaties *fpl* ◆ **to do ~** (*lit*) faire des acrobaties *or* de l'acrobatie ◆ **political/linguistic ~** des acrobaties *fpl* politiques/linguistiques

acronym /ˈækrənɪm/ N acronyme *m*

Acropolis /əˈkrɒpəlɪs/ N Acropole *f*

across /əˈkrɒs/

> When **across** is an element in a phrasal verb, eg **come across, run across, stumble across**, look up the verb.

PREP ① (= *from one side to other of*) d'un côté à l'autre de ◆ **~ it** d'un côté à l'autre ◆ **a bridge ~ the river** un pont sur le fleuve ◆ **to walk ~ the road** traverser la rue

② (= *on other side of*) de l'autre côté de ◆ **~ it** de l'autre côté ◆ **he lives ~ the street (from me/him)** il habite en face (de chez moi/lui) ◆ **the shop ~ the road** le magasin d'en face, le magasin de l'autre côté de la rue ◆ **territories ~ the sea** territoires *mpl* d'outre-mer ◆ **from ~ the Channel** de l'autre côté de la Manche, d'outre-Manche

③ (= *crosswise over*) en travers de, à travers ◆ **~ it** en travers ◆ **to go ~ the fields** *or* **~ country** aller *or* prendre à travers champs ◆ **a plank ~ a door** une planche en travers d'une porte ◆ **with his arms folded ~ his chest** les bras croisés sur la poitrine

ADV (= *from one side to other*) ◆ **the river is 5km ~** le fleuve a 5 km de large ◆ **the plate is 30cm ~** l'assiette fait 30 cm de diamètre ◆ **to help sb ~** aider qn à traverser ◆ **to get sth ~** (= *make clear*) faire comprendre qch (*to sb* à qn) ; ◆ **~ from** en face de

acrostic /əˈkrɒstɪk/ N acrostiche *m*

acrylic /əˈkrɪlɪk/ ADJ, N acrylique *m* ◆ **~ paint** peinture *f* acrylique

act /ækt/ N ① (= *deed*) acte *m* ◆ **in the ~ of doing sth** en train de faire qch ◆ **caught in the ~** pris sur le fait *or* en flagrant délit

② (*Jur*) loi *f*

③ *[of play]* acte *m* ; (*in circus etc*) numéro *m* ◆ **they're a brilliant ~** (*Theat*) ils font un numéro superbe ◆ **he's a class ~*** c'est un crack* *or* un as* ◆ **it was a class ~*** (= *performance etc*) c'était génial* ◆ **she'll be a hard** *or* **tough ~ to follow** il sera difficile de l'égaler ◆ **he's just putting on an ~** il joue la comédie ◆ **it's just an ~** c'est du cinéma ◆ **to get in on the ~*** s'imposer ◆ **to get one's ~ together*** se ressaisir, se reprendre en main

VI ① (= *do sth*) agir ◆ **the government must ~ now** le gouvernement doit agir immédiatement *or* prendre des mesures immédiates ◆ **you have ~ed very generously** vous avez été très généreux ◆ **to ~ for the best** faire pour le mieux ◆ **to ~ on sb's behalf, to ~ for sb** agir au nom de qn, représenter qn ◆ **the Board, ~ing by a majority** (*Admin*) le conseil statuant à la majorité ◆ **~ing on a proposal from the Commission** (*Admin*) sur proposition de la Commission

② (= *behave*) agir, se comporter ◆ **to ~ like a fool** agir *or* se comporter comme un imbécile

3 *(Theat)* jouer ◆ **have you ever ~ed before?** avez-vous déjà fait du théâtre (*or* du cinéma) ? ◆ **she's not crying, she's only ~ing** elle ne pleure pas, elle fait semblant *or* elle joue la comédie

4 (= *serve*) servir, faire office (*as* de) ; ◆ **the table ~s as a desk** la table sert de bureau ◆ **she ~s as his assistant** elle lui sert d'assistante

5 *[medicine, chemical]* (= *have an effect*) agir (*on* sur)

VT *(Theat)* *[+ part]* jouer, tenir ◆ **to ~ Hamlet** jouer *or* tenir le rôle d'Hamlet, incarner Hamlet ◆ **to ~ the part of ...** *(Theat, fig)* tenir le rôle de ... ◆ **to ~ the fool** * *or* **~ stupid** * faire l'idiot(e)

COMP **Acts of the Apostles** NPL *(Rel)* Actes *mpl* des Apôtres
Act of Congress N loi *f* (*adoptée par le Congrès*)
act of faith N acte *m* de foi
act of God N catastrophe *f* naturelle
Act of Parliament N loi *f* (*adoptée par le Parlement*)
act of war N acte *m* de guerre

► **act on** VT FUS ⇒ **act upon**

► **act out** VT SEP *[+ event]* faire un récit mimé de ; *[+ fantasies]* vivre ; *[+ emotions]* exprimer, mimer

► **act up** * VI *[person]* se conduire mal ◆ **the car has started ~ing up** la voiture s'est mise à faire des caprices

► **act upon** VT FUS *[+ advice, suggestion]* suivre, se conformer à ; *[+ order]* exécuter ◆ **I ~ed upon your letter at once** j'ai fait le nécessaire dès que j'ai reçu votre lettre

acting /ˈæktɪŋ/ ADJ ◆ **~ headmaster** directeur *m* suppléant ◆ **~ president/head of department/police superintendent** *etc* président *m*/chef *m* de section/commissaire *m etc* par intérim N *(Cine, Theat = performance)* jeu *m*, interprétation *f* ◆ **his ~ is very good** il joue très bien ◆ **I like his ~** j'aime son jeu ◆ **he has done some ~** il a fait du théâtre (*or* du cinéma)

actinium /ækˈtɪnɪəm/ N actinium *m*

action /ˈækʃən/ N 1 *(NonC)* (= *activity*) action *f* ◆ **through** *or* **by volcanic ~** sous l'action des volcans ◆ **swift ~ is needed** il faut agir rapidement ◆ **the time has come for ~** il est temps d'agir ◆ **to take ~** agir, prendre des mesures ◆ **to go into ~** entrer en action, passer à l'action ; → **7** ◆ **to put into ~** *[+ plan]* mettre à exécution ; *[+ one's principles, a suggestion]* mettre en action *or* en pratique ; *[+ machine]* mettre en marche ◆ **to go into ~** *[person, team]* entrer en action ; *[plan]* entrer en vigueur ◆ **let's go where the ~ is** * allons là où il se passe quelque chose * ◆ **the Internet is where the ~ is nowadays** Internet, c'est là que ça se passe ◆ **they want a piece** *or* **slice of the ~** * *or* **their share of the ~** ils veulent être dans le coup *

◆ **in action** ◆ **it's interesting to see the rescue teams in ~** il est intéressant de voir les équipes de secours en action ◆ **this is democracy in ~** c'est la démocratie à l'œuvre, c'est une manifestation concrète de la démocratie

◆ **out of action** *(machine)* en panne ; *(person)* hors de combat ◆ **the lift has been out of ~ for a week** l'ascenseur est en panne depuis une semaine ◆ **to put sth out of ~** mettre qch hors d'usage *or* hors service ; *[+ machine]* détraquer ◆ **their aim was to put the enemy's runways out of ~** ils avaient pour objectif de rendre inutilisables les pistes d'atterrissage ennemies ◆ **his illness put him out of ~ for six weeks** sa maladie l'a mis hors de combat *or* hors circuit pendant six semaines

2 (= *deed*) acte *m*, action *f* ◆ **to judge sb by his ~s** juger qn sur ses actes ◆ **to suit the ~ to the word** joindre le geste à la parole ◆ **~s speak louder than words** *(Prov)* les actes sont plus éloquents que les paroles

3 (= *effect*) *[of medicine, chemical]* effet *m* ◆ **the ~ of sunlight on the skin** l'effet du soleil sur la peau

4 (= *mechanism*) mécanisme *m*, marche *f* ; *[of piano]* action *f*, mécanique *f* ; *[of clock etc]* mécanique *f*

5 *(Theat)* *[of play]* intrigue *f*, action *f* ◆ **~!** *(Cine)* action ! ◆ **the ~ (of the play) takes place in Greece** l'action (de la pièce) se passe en Grèce

6 *(Jur)* procès *m*, action *f* en justice ◆ **~ for damages/libel** procès *m or* action *f* en dommages-intérêts/en diffamation ◆ **to bring an ~ against sb** intenter une action *or* un procès contre qn, poursuivre qn en justice

7 *(Mil)* combat *m* ◆ **to go into ~** *[unit, person]* aller *or* marcher au combat ; *[army]* engager le combat ◆ **killed in ~** tombé au champ d'honneur *(frm) or* au combat ◆ **to see ~** combattre, voir le feu ; → **enemy**

NPL **actions** (= *gestures accompanying song*) **to do the ~s (to a song)** mimer les paroles (d'une chanson)

VT *(Admin)* exécuter

COMP **action committee** N comité *m* d'action
action film N film *m* d'action
action group N groupe *m* d'action
action man N (pl **action men**) aventurier *m*
action movie N *(esp US)* ⇒ **action film**
action-packed ADJ *[film]* plein d'action ; *[weekend]* bien rempli
action painting N tachisme *m*
action replay N *(Brit TV Sport)* *répétition immédiate d'une séquence* ; (= *slow-motion*) ralenti *m*
action point N décision *f*, action *f*
action stations NPL *(Mil)* postes *mpl* de combat ◆ **~ stations!** à vos postes !

actionable /ˈækʃnəbl/ ADJ *[claim]* recevable ; *[person]* passible de poursuites

activate /ˈæktɪveɪt/ VT *(gen)* activer ; (= *make radioactive*) rendre radioactif COMP **activated sludge** N boues *fpl* radioactives

activation /ˌæktɪˈveɪʃən/ N *(NonC)* activation *f*

active /ˈæktɪv/ ADJ 1 *[person, life, population]* actif ; *[mind, imagination]* vif, actif ; *[file, case]* en cours ◆ **~ volcano** volcan *m* en activité ◆ **to take an ~ part in sth** prendre une part active à qch ◆ **to be an ~ member of** *or* **be ~ in an organization** être un membre actif d'une organisation ◆ **to give ~ consideration to sth** soumettre qch à une étude attentive ◆ **we're giving ~ consideration to the idea of doing ...** nous examinons sérieusement la possibilité *or* le projet de faire ... ◆ **in ~ employment** en activité ◆ **~ childbirth** accouchement *m* sauvage *or* accroupi

2 *(Brit Mil)* ◆ **the ~ list** l'armée *f* active ◆ **to be on the ~ list** être en activité (de service)

3 *(Gram)* **~ voice** voix *f* active, actif *m* ◆ **in the ~ (voice)** à la voix active

4 *(Comm)* **~ assets** capital *m* productif ◆ **~ money** monnaie *f or* argent *m* en circulation ◆ **~ partner** partenaire *m* actif ◆ **Germany has an ~ trade balance** l'Allemagne a une balance commerciale excédentaire

COMP **active duty** N *(esp US Mil)* ⇒ **active service**
active ingredient N principe *m* actif
active service N *(Brit Mil)* service *m* actif ◆ **on ~ service** en campagne ◆ **he saw ~ service in Italy and Germany** il a servi en Italie et en Allemagne
active suspension N *[of vehicle]* suspension *f* active

actively /ˈæktɪvlɪ/ ADV *[campaign, support, promote, involve]* activement ; *[encourage, discourage]* vivement ; *[consider]* sérieusement ◆ **to be ~ seeking employment** rechercher activement un emploi

activism /ˈæktɪvɪzəm/ N activisme *m*

activist /ˈæktɪvɪst/ N activiste *mf*

activity /ækˈtɪvɪtɪ/ N 1 *(NonC)* *[of person]* activité *f* ; *[of town, port]* mouvement *m* 2 ◆ **activities** activités *fpl*, occupations *fpl* ◆ **business activities** activités *fpl* professionnelles

COMP **activity holiday** N vacances *fpl* actives, vacances *fpl* à thème
activity method N *(Scol)* méthode *f* active

actor /ˈæktəʳ/ N acteur *m*, comédien *m* ◆ **to be a good/bad ~** *(lit)* être (un) bon/mauvais acteur ; *(fig)* savoir/ne pas savoir jouer la comédie

actress /ˈæktrɪs/ N actrice *f*, comédienne *f*

actual /ˈæktjʊəl/ ADJ 1 (= *real*) *[number, cost, reason]* réel ; *[figures]* exact ◆ **there is no ~ contract** il n'y a pas vraiment *or* à proprement parler de contrat ◆ **to take an ~ example ...** pour prendre un exemple concret ... ◆ **an ~ fact** un fait réel ◆ **in ~ fact** en fait ◆ **you met an ~ film star?** * vous avez rencontré une vraie star de cinéma ? ◆ **the film used the ~ people involved as actors** pour jouer dans ce film, on a fait appel à des gens qui avaient eux-mêmes vécu les événements ◆ **~ size** grandeur *f* nature ◆ **~ size: 15cm** taille réelle : 15 cm ◆ **his ~ words were ...** les mots exacts qu'il a employés étaient ...

2 (= *proper*) ◆ **the ~ film doesn't start till 8.55** le film ne commence qu'à 20 h 55 ◆ **this is the ~ house** *(as opposed to its outbuildings)* voici la maison elle-même ; *(previously mentioned)* voici la maison en question

NPL **actuals** *(Fin)* chiffres *mpl* réels

COMP **actual bodily harm** N *(Jur)* coups *mpl* et blessures *fpl*
actual total loss N *(Insurance)* perte *f* totale absolue

> ⚠ Be careful not to translate **actual** by **actuel**, which generally means 'current' or 'topical'.

actuality /ˌæktjʊˈælɪtɪ/ N 1 *(NonC)* réalité *f* ◆ **in ~** en réalité 2 ◆ **actualities** réalités *fpl*, conditions *fpl* réelles *or* actuelles

actualize /ˈæktjʊəlaɪz/ VT réaliser ; *(Philos)* actualiser

actually /ˈæktjʊəlɪ/ ADV 1 *(gen)* en fait ; (= *truth to tell*) en fait, à vrai dire ◆ **~ I don't know him at all** en fait *or* à vrai dire je ne le connais pas du tout ◆ **his name is Smith, ~** en fait, il s'appelle Smith ◆ **the person ~ in charge is ...** la personne véritablement responsable *or* la personne responsable en fait, c'est ... ◆ **~ you were quite right** en fait *or* au fond vous aviez entièrement raison ◆ **I don't ~ feel like going** au fond je n'ai pas envie d'y aller, je n'ai pas vraiment envie d'y aller ◆ **I'm in the middle of something ~** en fait, je suis en train de faire quelque chose ◆ **~, before I forget, she asked me to give you this** au fait, avant que je n'oublie *subj or* que j'oublie *subj*, elle m'a demandé de te donner ça ◆ **I bet you've never done that!** – **~ I have** je parie que tu n'as jamais fait ça ! – en fait, si ◆ **so, you're a doctor?** – **a surgeon, ~** donc, vous êtes médecin ? – chirurgien, plutôt

2 (= *truly, even: often showing surprise*) vraiment ◆ **are you ~ going to buy it?** est-ce que tu vas vraiment l'acheter ? ◆ **if you ~ own a house** si vous êtes vraiment *or* bel et bien propriétaire d'une maison ◆ **what did he ~ say?** qu'est-ce qu'il a dit exactement *or* au juste ? ◆ **did it ~ happen?** est-ce que ça s'est vraiment *or* réellement passé ? ◆ **it's ~ taking place right now** ça se produit en ce moment même

> ⚠ Be careful not to translate **actually** by **actuellement**, which generally means 'currently'.

actuarial /ˌæktjʊˈɛərɪəl/ ADJ actuariel ◆ **~ expectation** espérance *f* mathématique ◆ **~ tables** tableaux *mpl* d'espérance de vie

actuary /'æktjʊərɪ/ N actuaire *mf*

actuate /'æktjʊeɪt/ VT [+ *device*] mettre en marche

acuity /ə'kju:ɪtɪ/ N acuité *f*

acumen /'ækjʊmen/ N flair *m*, perspicacité *f* ◆ **business** ~ sens *m* aigu des affaires

acupressure /'ækjʊpreʃə^r/ N shiatsu *m*

acupuncture /'ækjʊpʌŋktʃə^r/ N acupuncture *f*

acupuncturist /,ækjʊ'pʌŋktʃərɪst/ N acupuncteur *m*, -trice *f*

acute /ə'kju:t/ ADJ [1] (= *extreme*) [*situation, problem, shortage*] grave ; [*embarrassment*] profond ; [*anxiety, pain*] vif ◆ **to live in** ~ **poverty** vivre dans une extrême pauvreté [2] (= *keen, perceptive*) [*person*] perspicace ; [*observer, mind*] perspicace, pénétrant ; [*powers of observation*] pénétrant ; [*intelligence*] aigu (-guë *f*) ◆ **to have an** ~ **awareness of sth** être pleinement conscient de qch ◆ **to have** ~ **hearing** avoir l'oreille fine ◆ **to have an** ~ **sense of smell** avoir l'odorat très développé [3] (*Med*) [*appendicitis, leukaemia, case*] aigu (-guë *f*) ◆ ~ **beds** lits *mpl* réservés aux urgences [4] (*Ling*) ◆ **e** ~ e accent aigu
COMP **acute accent** N accent *m* aigu
acute angle N angle *m* aigu
acute-angled ADJ acutangle

acutely /ə'kju:tlɪ/ ADV [1] (= *extremely*) [*embarrassing, unhappy, difficult*] extrêmement ; [*aware, conscious*] pleinement [2] (= *strongly*) [*feel, suffer*] intensément [3] (= *perceptively*) [*observe*] avec perspicacité

acuteness /ə'kju:tnɪs/ N [1] [*of medical condition*] violence *f* [2] [*of person*] perspicacité *f* ; [*of senses*] finesse *f*

AD /eɪ'di:/ N [1] (abbrev of **Anno Domini**) ap. J-C [2] (*US Mil*) (abbrev of **active duty**) → **active**

ad* /æd/ N (abbrev of **advertisement**) (= *announcement*) annonce *f* ; (*Comm*) pub* *f* ; → **small**

A/D /eɪ'di:/ (abbrev of **analogue-digital**) → **analogue**

adage /'ædɪdʒ/ N adage *m*

Adam /'ædəm/ N Adam *m* ◆ **I don't know him from** ~* je ne le connais ni d'Ève ni d'Adam ◆ **it's as old as** ~ c'est vieux comme le monde, ça remonte au déluge COMP **Adam's apple** N pomme *f* d'Adam

adamant /'ædəmənt/ ADJ inflexible ◆ **to be** ~ **that** ... maintenir catégoriquement que ...

adamantly /'ædəməntlɪ/ ADV [*say, refuse*] catégoriquement ; [*opposed*] résolument

adapt /ə'dæpt/ VT [+ *device, room, plan, idea*] adapter (*sth to sth* qch à qch) ; ◆ **to** ~ **o.s.** s'adapter, se faire (*to* à) ; ◆ **to** ~ **a novel for television** adapter un roman pour la télévision VI s'adapter ◆ **he** ~**s easily** il s'adapte bien *or* à tout ◆ **she's very willing to** ~ elle est très accommodante

adaptability /ə,dæptə'bɪlɪtɪ/ N [*of person*] faculté *f* d'adaptation

adaptable /ə'dæptəbl/ ADJ adaptable

adaptation /,ædæp'teɪʃən/ N adaptation *f* (*of* de ; *to* à)

adapted /ə'dæptɪd/ ADV adapté (*for, to* à ; *from* de)

adapter /ə'dæptə^r/ N [1] (= *device*) adaptateur *m* ; (*Brit* = *plug*) prise *f* multiple [2] (= *person*) adaptateur *m*, -trice *f* COMP **adapter ring** N (*for camera*) bague *f* d'adaptation

adaption /ə'dæpʃən/ N ⇒ **adaptation**

adaptive /ə'dæptɪv/ ADJ [*mechanism, process*] d'adaptation ◆ **the human body is remarkably** ~ le corps humain s'adapte remarquablement bien ◆ **to have an** ~ **approach to business** avoir une grande capacité d'adaptation en affaires

adaptor /ə'dæptə^r/ N ⇒ **adapter**

ADC /,eɪdi:'si:/ N [1] (abbrev of **aide-de-camp**) → **aide** [2] (abbrev of **analogue-digital converter**) → **analogue**

ADD /,eɪdi:'di:/ N (*Med*) (abbrev of **attention deficit disorder**) → **attention**

add /æd/ LANGUAGE IN USE 26.2 VT [1] ajouter (*to* à) ; ◆ ~ **some more pepper** ajoutez encore *or* rajoutez un peu de poivre ◆ **to** ~ **insult to injury** ... (et) pour comble ... ◆ **that would be** ~**ing insult to injury** ce serait vraiment dépasser la mesure *or* aller trop loin ◆ ~**ed to which** *or* **this** ... ajoutez à cela que ... ; see also **added**
[2] [+ *figures*] additionner ; [+ *column of figures*] totaliser
[3] (= *say besides*) ajouter (*that* que) ; ◆ **there is nothing to** ~ il n'y a rien à ajouter

► **add in** VT SEP [+ *details*] inclure, ajouter ; [+ *considerations*] faire entrer en ligne de compte

► **add on**
VT SEP rajouter

► **add to** VT FUS [+ *amount, numbers*] augmenter ; [+ *anxiety, danger*] accroître, ajouter à

► **add together** VT SEP [+ *figures*] additionner ; [+ *advantages, drawbacks*] faire la somme de

► **add up**
VI [*figures, results*] se recouper ◆ **these figures don't** ~ **up (right)** *or* **won't** ~ **up** ces chiffres ne font pas le compte (exact) ◆ **it all** ~**s up*** (*fig*) tout concorde, tout s'explique ◆ **it doesn't** ~ **up*** (*fig*) cela ne rime à rien, il y a quelque chose qui cloche*
VT SEP [1] [+ *figures*] additionner ◆ **to** ~ **up a column of figures** totaliser une colonne de chiffres
[2] [+ *advantages, reasons*] faire la somme de

► **add up to** VT FUS [*figures*] s'élever à, se monter à ; (* = *mean*) signifier, se résumer à

added /'ædɪd/ ADJ [*advantage, benefit*] supplémentaire ◆ **"no added colouring/salt"** (*on packets*) "sans adjonction de colorants/de sel"
COMP **added time** N (*Sport*) temps *m* additionnel
added value N valeur *f* ajoutée

addendum /ə'dendəm/ N (pl **addenda** /ə'dendə/) addenda *m*

adder /'ædə^r/ N (= *snake*) vipère *f*

addict /'ædɪkt/ N (*to drugs*) intoxiqué(e) *m(f)*, toxicomane *mf* ; (*fig*) intoxiqué(e) *m(f)* ◆ **he's a TV/chocolate** ~ c'est un accro* de la télé/du chocolat ◆ **he's an** ~ **now** il ne peut plus s'en passer ; ◆ **gaming** ~ intoxiqué(e) *m(f)* du jeu ; → **drug, heroin** VT /ə'dɪkt/ ◆ **to** ~ **o.s. to** devenir dépendant de

addicted /ə'dɪktɪd/ ADJ adonné (*to* à) ; ◆ **to become** ~ **to** ... s'adonner à ... ◆ ~ **to drink/drugs** adonné à la boisson/aux stupéfiants ◆ **he's** ~ **to drugs** c'est un toxicomane ◆ **he's** ~ **to cigarettes** c'est un fumeur invétéré ◆ **to be** ~ **to football*** se passionner pour le football, être un mordu* *or* un fana* de football

addiction /ə'dɪkʃən/ N goût *m* (*to* pour) ; (*Med*) dépendance *f*, accoutumance *f* (*to* à) ; ◆ **this drug causes** ~ cette drogue crée une dépendance *or* un effet d'accoutumance ; → **drug**

addictive /ə'dɪktɪv/ ADJ [1] [*drug*] qui crée une dépendance *or* une accoutumance ◆ **cigarettes are highly** ~ les cigarettes créent une forte dépendance ◆ ~ **habit** dépendance *f* ◆ **people with** ~ **personalities** les gens qui deviennent facilement dépendants [2] (*fig* = *enjoyable*) ◆ **crosswords/these biscuits are** ~ les mots croisés/ces biscuits, c'est comme une drogue

adding /'ædɪŋ/ N (*NonC*) ⇒ **addition 1** COMP **adding machine** N machine *f* à calculer

Addis Ababa /'ædɪs'æbəbə/ N Addis-Abeba

addition /ə'dɪʃən/ N [1] (*Math etc*) addition *f* [2] (*to tax, income, profit*) surcroît *m* (*to* de) ; (= *fact of adding*) adjonction *f* ◆ **there's been an** ~ **to the family** la famille s'est agrandie ◆ **he is a welcome** ~ **to our team** son arrivée enrichit notre équipe ◆ **this is a welcome** ~ **to the series/collection** *etc* ceci enrichit la série/la collection *etc*
◆ **in addition** de plus, de surcroît ◆ **in** ~ **to** en plus de

additional /ə'dɪʃənl/ ADJ additionnel ; (= *extra*) supplémentaire, de plus ◆ ~ **benefits** (*Fin*) avantages *mpl* supplémentaires ◆ ~ **charge** (*Fin*) supplément *m* de prix ◆ ~ **agreement** (*Jur*) accord *m* complémentaire

additionality /ə,dɪʃə'nælɪtɪ/ N (*in EU*) additionnalité *f*

additionally /ə'dɪʃnəlɪ/ ADV [1] (= *further*) [*worry, burden*] davantage [2] (= *moreover*) en outre, de plus

additive /'ædɪtɪv/ ADJ, N additif *m* ◆ ~-**free** sans additifs

addle /'ædl/ VT (*lit*) faire pourrir ; (*fig*) embrouiller COMP **addle-headed*** ADJ écervelé, brouillon

addled /'ædld/ ADJ [*egg*] pourri ; (*fig*) [*brain*] embrouillé ; [*person*] aux idées confuses

add-on /'ædɒn/ N [1] (*Comput*) accessoire *m* [2] (*Telec*) conférence *f* à trois ADJ [1] (*Comput*) [*component, equipment, memory*] complémentaire [2] ~ **fare** (*for plane ticket*) tarif *m* complémentaire

address /ə'dres/ LANGUAGE IN USE 24.5
N [1] [*of person*] (*on letter etc*) adresse *f* ◆ **to change one's** ~ changer d'adresse *or* de domicile ◆ **he has left this** ~ il n'est plus à cette adresse ; → **name**
[2] (*Comput, Ling*) adresse *f*
[3] (= *speech*) discours *m*, allocution *f* ; → **public**
[4] (= *way of speaking*) conversation *f* ; (= *way of behaving*) abord *m*
[5] ◆ **form** *or* **manner of** ~ titre *m* (*à employer en s'adressant à qn*)
[6] († , *liter*) ~**es** cour *f*, galanterie *f* ◆ **to pay one's** ~**es to a lady** faire la cour à une dame
VT [1] (= *put address on*) [+ *envelope, parcel*] mettre *or* écrire l'adresse sur ; (= *direct*) [+ *speech, writing, complaints*] adresser (*to* à) ; ◆ **this is** ~**ed to you** [*letter etc*] ceci vous est adressé ; [*words, comments*] ceci s'adresse à vous ◆ **to** ~ **o.s. to a task** s'atteler à une tâche ◆ **to** ~ **(o.s. to) an issue** aborder un problème
[2] (= *speak to*) s'adresser à ; [+ *crowd*] haranguer ; (= *write to*) adresser un écrit à ◆ **he** ~**ed the meeting** il a pris la parole devant l'assistance ◆ **don't** ~ **me as "Colonel"** ne m'appelez pas "Colonel" ; → **chair**
COMP **address book** N carnet *m* d'adresses

addressee /,ædre'si:/ N destinataire *mf* ; (*Ling*) allocutaire *mf*

addresser /ə'dresə^r/ N expéditeur *m*, -trice *f*

addressing /ə'dresɪŋ/ N (*Comput*) adressage *m*

Addressograph ® /ə'dresəʊgrɑ:f/ N (*US*) *machine à imprimer des adresses*

addressor /ə'dresə^r/ N ⇒ **addresser**

adduce /ə'dju:s/ VT (*frm*) [+ *proof, reason*] apporter, fournir ; [+ *authority*] invoquer, citer

adductor /ə'dʌktə^r/ N (*Anat*) adducteur *m*

Adelaide /'ædəleɪd/ N Adelaïde

Aden /'eɪdn/ N Aden ◆ **the Gulf of** ~ le golfe d'Aden

adenoidal /'ædɪnɔɪdl/ ADJ adénoïde ◆ **in an** ~ **voice** en parlant du nez

adenoids /'ædɪnɔɪdz/ NPL végétations *fpl* (adénoïdes)

adept /'ædept/ N expert *m* (*in, at* en) ADJ /ə'dept/ expert (*in, at* à, en, dans ; *at doing sth* à faire qch) compétent (*in* en) ; ◆ **he's ~ with numbers** il manie bien les chiffres

adequacy /ˈædɪkwəsɪ/ N *[of reward, punishment, amount]* caractère *m* adéquat ; *[of description]* à-propos *m* ; *[of person]* compétence *f*, capacité *f* ; *(Ling)* adéquation *f*

adequate /ˈædɪkwɪt/ ADJ 1 *(gen)* adéquat ; *[amount, supply]* suffisant, adéquat ; *[tool]* adapté (*to sth* à qch) qui convient (*to sth* à qch) ; ◆ **to be ~ for sb's needs** répondre aux besoins de qn ◆ **to be ~ to the task** *[person]* être à la hauteur de la tâche ◆ **to be ~ to do sth** être adéquat pour faire qch ◆ **there are no words ~ to express my gratitude** les mots ne suffisent pas pour exprimer ma gratitude 2 *(= not outstanding) [performance, essay]* acceptable 3 *(Ling)* adéquat

adequately /ˈædɪkwɪtlɪ/ ADV de manière adéquate ◆ **I speak Turkish ~** mes connaissances en turc sont suffisantes

ADHD /ˌeɪdiːeɪtʃˈdiː/ N (abbrev of **attention deficit hyperactivity disorder**) ADHD *m*

adhere /ədˈhɪəʳ/ VI 1 *(= stick)* adhérer, coller (*to* à) 2 *(= be faithful to)* ◆ **to ~ to** *[+ party]* adhérer à, donner son adhésion à ; *[+ rule]* obéir à ; *[+ resolve]* persister dans, maintenir ◆ **the plan must be ~d to** il faut se conformer au plan

adherence /ədˈhɪərəns/ N adhésion *f* (*to* à)

adherent /ədˈhɪərənt/ N *(= sympathizer)* sympathisant(e) *m(f)*, partisan *m* ; *(= member of group)* adhérent(e) *m(f)* ; *[of religion, doctrine]* adepte *mf*

adhesion /ədˈhiːʒən/ N *(lit, Med, Tech)* adhérence *f* ; *(fig = support)* adhésion *f*

adhesive /ədˈhiːzɪv/ ADJ *[paper, label, stamp]* adhésif, collant ; *[dressing, plaster, properties]* adhésif ; → **self** N adhésif *m* COMP **adhesive tape** N *(= sticking plaster)* sparadrap *m* ; *(Stationery)* ruban *m* adhésif, scotch ® *m*

ad hoc /ˌædˈhɒk/ ADJ *[decision, solution, arrangement, measure, approach, payment]* ad hoc *inv* ◆ **~ committee** comité *m* ad hoc ◆ **on an ~ basis** ponctuellement ADV de manière ad hoc

adieu /əˈdjuː/ N, EXCL (pl **adieus** or **adieux** /əˈdjuːz/) adieu *m* ◆ **to bid sb ~** † faire ses adieux à qn

ad infinitum /ˌædɪnfɪˈnaɪtəm/ ADV à l'infini

ad interim /ˈædˈɪntərɪm/ ADV par intérim ADJ *(Jur) [judgement]* provisoire

adipose /ˈædɪpəʊs/ ADJ adipeux

adiposity /ˌædɪˈpɒsɪtɪ/ N adiposité *f*

adjacent /əˈdʒeɪsənt/ ADJ *(Math) [angle]* adjacent ; *[street, room, building]* adjacent (*to* à) ; *[territory]* limitrophe

adjectival /ˌædʒekˈtaɪvəl/ ADJ adjectif, adjectival

adjectivally /ˌædʒekˈtaɪvəlɪ/ ADV *[use]* adjectivement

adjective /ˈædʒektɪv/ N adjectif *m*

adjoin /əˈdʒɔɪn/ VT être contigu(-guë *f*) à VI se toucher, être contigu(-guë *f*)

adjoining /əˈdʒɔɪnɪŋ/ ADJ voisin, attenant ◆ **the room ~ the kitchen** la pièce à côté de *or* attenant à la cuisine ◆ **in the ~ room** dans la pièce voisine *or* d'à côté

adjourn /əˈdʒɜːn/ VT ajourner, reporter (*to, for, until* à) ; ◆ **to ~ sth until the next day** ajourner *or* remettre *or* reporter qch au lendemain ◆ **to ~ sth for a week** remettre *or* renvoyer qch à huitaine ◆ **to ~ a meeting** *(= break off)* suspendre la séance ; *(= close)* lever la séance VI 1 *(= break off)* suspendre la séance ; *(= close)* lever la séance ◆ **the meeting ~ed** on a suspendu *or* levé la séance ◆ **Parliament ~ed** *(= concluded debate)* la séance de la Chambre a été levée ; *(= interrupted debate)* la Chambre a suspendu *or* interrompu la séance ; *(= recessed)* les vacances parlementaires ont commencé 2 *(= move)* se retirer (*to* dans, à) passer (*to* à) ; ◆ **to ~ to the drawing room** passer au salon

adjournment /əˈdʒɜːnmənt/ N *[of meeting]* suspension *f*, ajournement *m* ; *[of court case]* remise *f*, renvoi *m* ◆ **to move the ~** *(Parl)* demander la clôture COMP **adjournment debate** N *(Parl)* ≈ débat *m* de clôture

adjudge /əˈdʒʌdʒ/ VT 1 *(= pronounce, declare)* déclarer ◆ **he was ~d the winner** il a été déclaré gagnant 2 *(Jur) (= pronounce)* prononcer, déclarer ; *(= decree)* décider ; *(= award) [+ costs, damages]* adjuger, accorder (*to sb* à qn) ; ◆ **to ~ sb bankrupt** déclarer qn en faillite ◆ **the court ~d that ...** le tribunal a décidé que ... ◆ **the court shall ~ costs** le tribunal statue sur les frais

adjudicate /əˈdʒuːdɪkeɪt/ VT *[+ competition]* juger ; *[+ claim]* décider VI *(frm)* se prononcer (*upon* sur)

adjudication /əˌdʒuːdɪˈkeɪʃən/ N 1 jugement *m*, décision *f* (*du juge etc*) 2 *(Jur)* **~ of bankruptcy** déclaration *f* de faillite

adjudicator /əˈdʒuːdɪkeɪtəʳ/ N juge *m* (*d'une compétition etc*)

adjunct /ˈædʒʌŋkt/ N 1 *(= thing)* accessoire *m* ; *(= person)* adjoint(e) *m(f)*, auxiliaire *mf* 2 *(Gram)* adjuvant *m* ADJ 1 *(= added, connected)* accessoire, complémentaire 2 *(= subordinate) [person]* subordonné, auxiliaire

adjure /əˈdʒʊəʳ/ VT adjurer, supplier (*sb to do sth* qn de faire qch)

adjust /əˈdʒʌst/ VT 1 *[+ height, speed, flow, tool]* ajuster, régler ; *[+ knob, lever, length of clothes]* ajuster ; *[+ machine, engine, brakes]* régler, mettre au point ; *[+ formula, plan, production, terms]* ajuster, adapter (*to* à) ; *(Admin) [+ salaries, wages, prices]* réajuster, rajuster ; *(= correct) [+ figures etc]* rectifier ; *[+ differences]* régler ; *[+ hat, tie, clothes]* rajuster ◆ **you can ~ the seat to three different heights** on peut régler *or* ajuster le siège à trois hauteurs différentes ◆ **do not ~ your set** (TV) ne changez pas le réglage de votre téléviseur ◆ **to ~ sth to meet requirements** adapter qch aux conditions requises ◆ **the terms have been ~ed in your favour** on a ajusté les conditions en votre faveur ◆ **we have ~ed all salaries upwards/downwards** nous avons réajusté tous les salaires à la hausse/à la baisse ◆ **figures ~ed for seasonal variation(s)** données corrigées des variations saisonnières ◆ **to ~ o.s. to a new situation** s'adapter à une situation nouvelle ◆ **to ~ o.s. to new demands** faire face à de nouvelles exigences

2 *(Insurance)* **to ~ a claim** régler une demande d'indemnité

VI *[person]* s'adapter (*to* à) ; *[device, machine]* se régler, s'ajuster ◆ **the seat ~s to various heights** on peut régler *or* ajuster le siège à différentes hauteurs

adjustability /əˌdʒʌstəˈbɪlɪtɪ/ N *(NonC) [of seat, lamp]* possibilité *f* de réglage

adjustable /əˈdʒʌstəbl/ ADJ *(= movable) [strap, chair, height, angle]* réglable ; *[rate]* ajustable ; *[dates, hours]* flexible ◆ **~ timetable** *(Scol, Univ)* horaire *m* aménagé COMP **adjustable spanner** N *(Brit)* clé *f* universelle

adjusted /əˈdʒʌstɪd/ ADJ *(Psych)* ◆ **badly/well/normally ~** mal/bien/normalement adapté

adjuster /əˈdʒʌstəʳ/ N expert *m* (en assurances)

adjustment /əˈdʒʌstmənt/ N *(to height, speed, knob, lever, machine, engine)* réglage *m* ; *(to clothes)* retouches *fpl* ; *(to plan, terms etc)* ajustement *m* (*to* de) ; *(to wages, prices etc)* réajustement *m*, rajustement *m* (*to* de) ; ◆ **the text needs a lot of ~** ce texte a vraiment besoin d'une mise au point ◆ **to make ~s** *(psychologically, socially)* s'adapter (*to* à) ; ◆ **"exchange flat for house – cash adjustment"** "échangerais appartement contre maison : règlement de la différence au comptant"

adjustor /əˈdʒʌstəʳ/ N ⇒ **adjuster**

adjutant /ˈædʒətənt/ N 1 *(Mil)* adjudant-major *m* 2 (also **adjutant bird**) marabout *m*

Adlerian /ædˈlɪərɪən/ ADJ de Adler

ad lib /ædˈlɪb/ ADV *[continue]* ad libitum, à volonté ; *(Mus)* ad libitum N ◆ **ad-lib** *(Theat)* improvisation(s) *f(pl)*, paroles *fpl* improvisées ; *(= witticism)* mot *m* d'esprit impromptu ADJ *[speech, performance, comment]* improvisé, impromptu VI *(Theat etc)* improviser VT (*: *gen, also Theat*) *[+ speech, joke]* improviser

Adm. 1 (abbrev of **Admiral**) Am 2 abbrev of **Admiralty**

adman * /ˈædmæn/ N (pl **-men**) publicitaire *mf*

admass /ˈædmæs/ N masse(s) *f(pl)* COMP *[culture, life]* de masse, de grande consommation

admin * /ˈædmɪn/ N abbrev of **administration 1**

administer /ədˈmɪnɪstəʳ/ VT 1 *(= manage) [+ business, company]* gérer, administrer ; *[+ sb's affairs, funds]* gérer ; *[+ property]* régir ; *[+ public affairs, department, country]* administrer 2 *(= dispense) [+ alms]* distribuer (*to* à) ; *[+ justice]* rendre, dispenser ; *[+ punishment, sacraments, medicine, drug, relief]* administrer (*to* à) ; ◆ **to ~ the law** appliquer la loi ◆ **to ~ an oath to sb** faire prêter serment à qn ◆ **the oath has been ~ed to the witness** le témoin a prêté serment COMP **administered price** N *(US)* prix *m* imposé (par le fabricant)

administrate /ədˈmɪnɪˌstreɪt/ VT gérer, administrer

administration /ədˌmɪnɪˈstreɪʃən/ N 1 *(NonC = management) [of business, company, public affairs, department, country]* administration *f* ; *[of funds]* gestion *f* ; *(= paperwork)* administration *f* ; *(Jur) [of estate, inheritance]* curatelle *f* ◆ **his new job involves a lot of ~** son nouveau poste est en grande partie administratif 2 *(esp US Pol) (= government)* gouvernement *m* ; *(= ministry)* ministère *m* ◆ **under previous ~s** sous les gouvernements précédents ◆ **the Clinton ~** l'administration Clinton 3 *(NonC) [of justice, remedy, sacrament]* administration *f* ; *[of oath]* prestation *f* COMP **administration order** N *(Jur) ordonnance instituant l'administrateur judiciaire d'une succession ab intestat*

administrative /ədˈmɪnɪstrətɪv/ ADJ *[work, post, staff]* administratif ; *[skills]* d'administrateur ; *[costs, expenses]* d'administration ◆ **~ machinery** rouages *mpl* administratifs COMP **administrative assistant** N assistant(e) *m(f)* chargé(e) des tâches administratives

administrative court N *(US Jur)* tribunal *m* administratif

administrative law N droit *m* administratif

administrative officer N employé(e) *m(f)* chargé(e) des tâches administratives

administratively /ədˈmɪnɪstrətɪvlɪ/ ADV d'un point de vue administratif

administrator /ədˈmɪnɪstreɪtəʳ/ N *[of business, public affairs etc]* administrateur *m*, -trice *f* ; *(Jur) [of estate, inheritance]* curateur *m*, -trice *f*

admirable /ˈædmərəbl/ ADJ admirable

admirably /ˈædmərəblɪ/ ADV admirablement

admiral /ˈædmərəl/ N 1 *(Naut)* amiral *m* (d'escadre) ◆ **Admiral of the Fleet** ≈ Amiral *m* de France 2 *(= butterfly)* vanesse *f*, paon-de-jour *m* ; → **red**

admiralty /ˈædmərəltɪ/ N amirauté *f* COMP **Admiralty Board** N *(Brit)* ≈ ministère *m* de la Marine

admiralty court N *(US)* tribunal *m* maritime

admiration /ˌædməˈreɪʃən/ N admiration *f* (*of, for* pour) ; ◆ **to be the ~ of ...** faire l'admiration de ...

admire /ədˈmaɪəʳ/ LANGUAGE IN USE 13 VT admirer

admirer /ədˈmaɪərəʳ/ N 1 admirateur *m*, -trice *f* 2 († = *suitor*) soupirant † *m*

admiring /ədˈmaɪərɪŋ/ ADJ admiratif

admiringly /ədˈmaɪərɪŋlɪ/ ADV avec admiration

admissibility /əd,mɪsəˈbɪlɪtɪ/ N admissibilité *f* ; (*Jur, Fin*) recevabilité *f*

admissible /ədˈmɪsəbl/ ADJ 1 (*Jur*) [*document, appeal, witness*] recevable ◆ **to rule a piece of evidence** ~ déclarer une preuve recevable ◆ ~ **as evidence/in court** recevable comme preuve/devant le tribunal 2 (= *acceptable*) [*behaviour, subject*] acceptable

admission /ədˈmɪʃən/ N 1 (= *entry*) (*to organization, university, school, hospital*) admission *f* ; (*to museum, zoo, theatre*) entrée *f* ◆ **"admission free"** "entrée gratuite" ◆ **"no admission to minors"** "entrée interdite aux mineurs" ◆ **a visa is necessary for** ~ **to this country** il faut un visa pour entrer dans ce pays ◆ ~ **to a school** admission *f* à une école ◆ **to gain** ~ **to sb** trouver accès auprès de qn ◆ **to gain** ~ **to a school/club** être admis dans une école/un club ◆ **to grant sb** ~ **to a society** admettre qn dans une association
2 (= *person admitted*) entrée *f*
3 (*Jur*) [*of evidence etc*] acceptation *f*, admission *f*
4 (= *confession*) aveu *m* ◆ **by** *or* **on one's own** ~ de son propre aveu ◆ **it's an** ~ **of guilt** en fait, c'est un aveu
COMP **admission fee** N droits *mpl* d'admission
admissions form N (*US Univ*) dossier *m* d'inscription
admissions office N (*US Univ*) service *m* des inscriptions
admissions officer N (*Univ*) responsable *mf* du service des inscriptions

admit /ədˈmɪt/ LANGUAGE IN USE 15.1, 18.1, 18.3, 26.3
VT 1 (= *let in*) [+ *person*] laisser entrer, faire entrer ; [+ *light, air*] laisser passer, laisser entrer ◆ **children not ~ted** entrée interdite aux enfants ◆ **this ticket ~s two** ce billet est valable pour deux personnes
2 (= *have space for*) [*halls, harbours etc*] contenir, (pouvoir) recevoir
3 (= *acknowledge, recognize*) reconnaître, admettre (*that* que) ; ◆ **to ~ the truth of sth** reconnaître *or* admettre que qch est vrai ◆ **he ~ted that this was the case** il a reconnu *or* admis que tel était le cas ◆ **I must ~ that ...** je dois reconnaître *or* admettre que ... ◆ **I must ~ I was wrong, I was wrong I ~** je reconnais que j'ai eu tort, j'ai eu tort, j'en conviens
4 [*criminal, wrongdoer*] avouer (*that* que) ; [+ *crime, murder etc*] reconnaître avoir commis ◆ **he ~ted stealing the books** il a reconnu avoir volé les livres ◆ **you'll never get him to ~ it** vous ne le lui ferez jamais avouer *or* reconnaître ◆ **to ~ one's guilt** reconnaître sa culpabilité, s'avouer coupable
5 [+ *claim*] faire droit à ◆ **to ~ sb's evidence** (*Jur*) admettre comme valable le témoignage de qn, prendre en considération les preuves fournies par qn
COMP **admitting office** N (*US Med*) service *m* des admissions

► **admit of** VT FUS admettre, permettre ◆ **it ~s of no delay** cela n'admet *or* ne peut souffrir aucun retard ; → **excuse**

► **admit to** VT FUS reconnaître ; [+ *crime*] reconnaître avoir commis ◆ **to ~ to a feeling of ...** avouer avoir un sentiment de ...

admittance /ədˈmɪtəns/ N droit *m* d'entrée, admission *f* (*to sth* à qch) accès *m* (*to sth* à qch ; *to sb* auprès de qn) ; ◆ **I gained ~ to the hall** on m'a laissé entrer dans la salle ◆ **I was denied** *or* **refused** ~ on m'a refusé l'entrée ◆ ~: **£5** droit d'entrée : 5 livres ◆ **"no admittance"** "accès interdit au public" ◆ **no ~ except on business** accès interdit à toute personne étrangère au service

admittedly /ədˈmɪtɪdlɪ/ ADV ◆ ~ **this is true** il faut reconnaître *or* convenir que c'est vrai ◆ **it's only a theory, ~, but ...** il est vrai que ce n'est qu'une théorie, mais ...

admixture /ədˈmɪkstʃəʳ/ N mélange *m*, incorporation *f* ◆ **X with an ~ of Y** X additionné de Y

admonish /ədˈmɒnɪʃ/ VT 1 (= *reprove*) admonester, réprimander (*for doing sth* pour avoir fait qch ; *about, for* pour, à propos de) 2 (= *warn*) avertir, prévenir (*against doing sth* de ne pas faire qch) mettre en garde (*against* contre) ; (*Jur*) avertir 3 (= *exhort*) exhorter, engager (*to do sth* à faire qch) 4 (*liter* = *remind*) **to ~ sb of a duty** † rappeler qn à un devoir

admonishment /ədˈmɒnɪʃmənt/ N (*frm*) 1 (= *rebuke*) remontrance *f*, réprimande *f* 2 (= *warning*) avertissement *m*

admonition /,ædməʊˈnɪʃən/ N 1 (= *rebuke*) remontrance *f*, admonestation *f* 2 (= *warning*) avertissement *m*, admonition *f* ; (*Jur*) avertissement *m*

ad nauseam /,ædˈnɔːsiæm/ ADV [*repeat*] ad nauseam, à satiété ; [*do*] jusqu'à saturation, à satiété ◆ **to talk ~ about sth** raconter des histoires à n'en plus finir sur qch

adnominal /,ædˈnɒmɪnl/ ADJ, N (*Ling*) adnominal *m*

ado /əˈduː/ N agitation *f* ◆ **much ~ about nothing** beaucoup de bruit pour rien ◆ **without further** *or* **more** ~ sans plus de cérémonie

adobe /əˈdəʊbɪ/ N pisé *m* COMP **adobe wall** N mur *m* en pisé

adolescence /,ædəʊˈlesns/ N adolescence *f*

adolescent /,ædəʊˈlesnt/ ADJ, N adolescent(e) *m(f)*

Adonis /əˈdəʊnɪs/ N (*Myth, fig*) Adonis *m*

adopt /əˈdɒpt/ VT 1 [+ *child*] adopter 2 [+ *idea, method*] adopter ; [+ *career*] choisir ; (*Pol*) [+ *motion*] adopter ; [+ *candidate*] choisir ; (*Jur, Admin*) [+ *wording*] retenir

adopted /əˈdɒptɪd/ ADJ [*child*] adopté ; [*country*] d'adoption, adoptif ◆ ~ **son** fils *m* adoptif ◆ ~ **daughter** fille *f* adoptive

adoption /əˈdɒpʃən/ N [*of child, country, law*] adoption *f* ; [*of career, idea, method*] choix *m* ◆ **a Londoner by** ~ un Londonien d'adoption COMP **adoption agency** N agence *f* d'adoption

adoptive /əˈdɒptɪv/ ADJ [*parent, child*] adoptif ; [*country*] d'adoption

adorable /əˈdɔːrəbl/ ADJ adorable

adorably /əˈdɔːrəblɪ/ ADV ◆ **she is ~ sweet** elle est absolument adorable ◆ **he's ~ innocent** il est d'une naïveté charmante

adoration /,ædəˈreɪʃən/ N adoration *f*

adore /əˈdɔːʳ/ VT adorer

adoring /əˈdɔːrɪŋ/ ADJ [*expression*] d'adoration ; [*eyes*] remplis d'adoration ◆ **his ~ wife** sa femme qui est en adoration devant lui

adoringly /əˈdɔːrɪŋlɪ/ ADV avec adoration

adorn /əˈdɔːn/ VT [+ *room*] orner (*with* de) ; [+ *dress*] orner, parer (*with* de) ; ◆ **to ~ o.s.** se parer

adornment /əˈdɔːnmənt/ N 1 (*in room*) ornement *m* ; (*on dress*) parure *f* 2 (NonC) décoration *f*

ADP /,eɪdiːˈpiː/ N (abbrev of **automatic data processing**) → **automatic**

adrate * /ˈædreɪt/ N tarif *m* publicitaire *or* des annonces

adrenal /əˈdriːnl/ ADJ surrénal N (also **adrenal gland**) surrénale *f*

adrenalin(e) /əˈdrenəlɪn/ N adrénaline *f* ◆ **he felt the ~(e) flowing** il a eu une poussée d'adrénaline COMP **adrenaline rush** N poussée *f* d'adrénaline

Adriatic /,eɪdrɪˈætɪk/ ADJ [*coast*] adriatique N ◆ ~ **(Sea)** (mer *f*) Adriatique *f*

adrift /əˈdrɪft/ ADV, ADJ (*Naut*) à la dérive ; (*fig*) à l'abandon ◆ **to go** ~ [*ship*] aller à la dérive ◆ **to be (all)** ~ (*fig*) divaguer ◆ **to turn sb** ~ (*fig*) laisser qn se débrouiller tout seul ◆ **to come** ~ * [*wire, connection*] se détacher ; [*plans*] tomber à l'eau ◆ **to be five points/seconds ~ of ...** (*Sport*) être cinq points/secondes derrière ...

adroit /əˈdrɔɪt/ ADJ adroit, habile

adroitly /əˈdrɔɪtlɪ/ ADV adroitement, habilement

adroitness /əˈdrɔɪtnɪs/ N adresse *f*, dextérité *f*

ADSL /,eɪdiːesˈel/ N (abbrev of **Asynchronous Digital Subscriber Line**) ADSL *m*

adspeak * /ˈædspiːk/ N style *m* *or* jargon *m* publicitaire

ADT /,eɪdiːˈtiː/ N (*US, Can*) abbrev of **Atlantic Daylight Time**

adulate /ˈædjʊleɪt/ VT aduler, flagorner

adulation /,ædjʊˈleɪʃən/ N adulation *f*

adulatory /,ædjʊˈleɪtərɪ, (US)/ ˈædʒələtɔːrɪ/ ADJ élogieux

adult /ˈædʌlt/ N adulte *mf* ◆ **~s only** (*Cine etc*) réservé aux adultes, interdit aux moins de 18 ans ADJ 1 [*person, animal*] adulte ◆ **we were very ~ about it** nous nous sommes comportés en adultes 2 [*film, book*] pour adultes (seulement)
COMP **adult classes** NPL cours *mpl* pour adultes
adult education, adult learning N enseignement *m* pour adultes
adult literacy N alphabétisation *f* des adultes

adulterate /əˈdʌltəreɪt/ VT frelater, falsifier ◆ **~d milk** lait *m* falsifié ADJ /əˈdʌltərɪt/ [*goods, wine*] falsifié, frelaté

adulteration /ə,dʌltəˈreɪʃən/ N frelatage *m*, falsification *f*

adulterer /əˈdʌltərəʳ/ N adultère *m*

adulteress /əˈdʌltərɪs/ N femme *f* adultère

adulterous /əˈdʌltərəs/ ADJ adultère

adultery /əˈdʌltərɪ/ N adultère *m*

adulthood /ˈædʌlthʊd/ N âge *m* adulte

adumbrate /ˈædʌmbreɪt/ VT esquisser, ébaucher ; [+ *event*] faire pressentir, préfigurer

ad val. /ˈædˈvæl/ ADJ, ADV (*Comm*) abbrev of **ad valorem**

ad valorem /ædvəˈlɔːrəm/ (*Comm*) ADJ, ADV ad valorem, sur la valeur

advance /ədˈvɑːns/ LANGUAGE IN USE 19.3
N 1 (= *progress, movement forward*) avance *f*, marche *f* en avant ; [*of science, ideas*] progrès *mpl* ; (*Mil*) avance *f*, progression *f* ◆ **with the ~ of (old) age** avec l'âge ◆ **to make ~s in technology** faire des progrès en technologie
◆ **in advance** [*book, warn, prepare, announce*] à l'avance ; [*thank, pay, decide*] à l'avance, d'avance ◆ **to send sb on in ~** envoyer qn en avant ◆ **$10 in ~** 10 dollars d'avance ◆ **he arrived in ~ of the others** il est arrivé en avance sur les autres ◆ **to be in ~ of one's time** être en avance sur son temps ◆ **a week in ~** une semaine à l'avance ◆ **luggage in ~** (*Rail*) bagages *mpl* enregistrés
2 (*in prices, wages*) hausse *f*, augmentation *f* (*in* de)
3 (= *sum of money*) avance *f* (*on* sur) ; ◆ **an ~ against security** une avance sur nantissement
NPL **advances** (= *overtures of friendship*) avances *fpl* ◆ **to make ~s to sb** faire des avances à qn ◆ **unwelcome ~s** avances importunes

VT 1 (= move forward) [+ date, time] avancer ; (Mil) [+ troops] avancer ; [+ work, knowledge, project] faire progresser or avancer ; [+ interest, growth] développer ; [+ cause] promouvoir ; (= promote) [+ person] élever, promouvoir (to à)
2 (= suggest, propose) [+ reason, explanation] avancer ; [+ opinion] avancer, émettre
3 (= pay on account) avancer, faire une avance de ; (= lend) prêter
4 (US Pol) [+ campaign] organiser
VI 1 (= go forward) avancer, s'avancer (on, towards vers) ; [army] avancer (on sur) ; (during a battle) [troops] se porter en avant ◆ **he ~d upon me** il est venu vers or a marché sur moi ◆ **the advancing army** l'armée f en marche
2 (= progress) [work, civilization, mankind] progresser, faire des progrès ; [person] (in rank) recevoir de l'avancement ; (Mil) monter en grade
3 (= rise) [prices] monter, augmenter
COMP **advance booking** N ◆ « **advance booking advisable** » "il est conseillé de louer les places à l'avance" ◆ **~ booking (office)** (guichet m de) location f
advance copy N [of book] exemplaire m de lancement ; [of speech] texte m distribué à l'avance (à la presse)
advance deposit N dépôt m préalable
advance factory N usine-pilote f
advance guard N (Mil) avant-garde f
advance man N (pl **advance men**) (US Pol) organisateur m (de campagne électorale)
advance notice N préavis m, avertissement m
advance party N (Mil) groupe m de reconnaissance ; (fig) éclaireurs mpl
advance payment N (Fin) paiement m anticipé or par anticipation
advance post N (Mil) poste m avancé
advance publicity N publicité f d'amorçage
advance warning N ⇒ **advance notice**

advanced /ədˈvɑːnst/ ADJ [student, society, ideas, stage] avancé ; [child] avancé, en avance ; [disease] à un stade avancé ; [level, studies, class] supérieur(e) m(f) ; [test, skill] poussé ; [design] sophistiqué ; [equipment] de pointe ◆ **~ mathematics/physics** cours m supérieur de mathématiques/physique ◆ **he is very ~ for his age** il est très avancé or très en avance pour son âge ◆ **at an ~ age** à un âge avancé ◆ **~ in years** d'un âge avancé ◆ **a man of ~ years** un homme d'âge avancé ◆ **the day/season is well ~** la journée/saison est bien avancée
COMP **advanced gas-cooled reactor** N réacteur m à gaz avancé
Advanced level N (Brit Scol) (frm) ⇒ **A levels** ; → **A**
Advanced Photo System N SING APS
advanced skills teacher N (Brit Scol) enseignant chevronné recevant un salaire relativement élevé
advanced standing N (US Univ) ◆ **to receive ~ standing** ≃ être admis par équivalence

advancement /ədˈvɑːnsmənt/ N 1 (= improvement) progrès m, avancement m 2 (= promotion) avancement m, promotion f

advantage /ədˈvɑːntɪdʒ/ N 1 avantage m ◆ **to have an ~ over sb, to have the ~ of sb** avoir un avantage sur qn ◆ **that gives you an ~ over me** cela vous donne un avantage sur moi ◆ **to get the ~ of sb** prendre l'avantage sur qn (by doing sth en faisant qch) ; ◆ **to have the ~ of numbers** avoir l'avantage du nombre (over sur) ; ◆ **to take ~ of sb** profiter de qn ; [employer etc] exploiter qn ; (sexually) abuser de qn ◆ **I took ~ of the opportunity** j'ai profité de l'occasion ◆ **to turn sth to (one's) ~** tirer parti de qch, tourner qch à son avantage ◆ **I find it to my ~** j'y trouve mon compte ◆ **it is to his ~ to do it** c'est dans son intérêt de le faire
♦ **to + best advantage** au mieux ◆ **they don't organize their investments to best ~** ils n'investissent pas leur argent au mieux or de la manière la plus avantageuse ◆ **a T-shirt in which her body is shown to its best ~** un T-shirt qui met son corps en valeur
2 (Tennis) avantage m ◆ **to play the ~ rule** (Rugby, Ftbl) laisser la règle de l'avantage
VT avantager ◆ **~d** (= privileged) privilégié

advantageous /ˌædvənˈteɪdʒəs/ ADJ avantageux (to pour)

advantageously /ˌædvənˈteɪdʒəslɪ/ ADV de façon avantageuse

advent /ˈædvənt/ N 1 venue f, avènement m 2 (Rel) **Advent** l'Avent m
COMP **Advent Calendar** N calendrier m de l'Avent
Advent Sunday N dimanche m de l'Avent

Adventist /ˈædventɪst/ N adventiste mf

adventitious /ˌædvenˈtɪʃəs/ ADJ fortuit, accidentel ; (Bot, Med) adventice

adventure /ədˈventʃəʳ/ N aventure f ◆ **to have an ~** avoir une aventure VI s'aventurer, se risquer (on dans)
COMP [story, film] d'aventures **adventure holiday** N (Brit) circuit m aventure
adventure playground N (Brit) aire f de jeux

adventurer /ədˈventʃərəʳ/ N aventurier m

adventuresome /ədˈventʃəsəm/ ADJ (US) [person] aventureux

adventuress /ədˈventʃərɪs/ N aventurière f

adventurism /ədˈventʃərɪzəm/ N aventurisme m

adventurist /ədˈventʃərɪst/ N (Pol: also **political adventurist**) aventuriste mf ; (Comm) aventurier m, -ière f ADJ (Pol) aventuriste ; (Comm) sans scrupules

adventurous /ədˈventʃərəs/ ADJ [person, journey] aventureux ; [approach, project] audacieux ◆ **the ~ spirit of the early settlers** l'esprit d'aventure or aventureux des premiers pionniers ◆ **to become more ~** devenir plus aventureux, s'enhardir

adventurously /ədˈventʃərəslɪ/ ADV aventureusement, audacieusement

adverb /ˈædvɜːb/ N adverbe m

adverbial /ədˈvɜːbɪəl/ ADJ adverbial

adverbially /ədˈvɜːbɪəlɪ/ ADV [use] adverbialement

adversarial /ˌædvəˈsɛərɪəl/ ADJ [politics] de confrontation ◆ **the ~ system** le système de débat contradictoire

adversary /ˈædvəsərɪ/ N adversaire mf

adverse /ˈædvɜːs/ ADJ [effect, reaction, consequences] négatif ; [conditions, comment, decision] défavorable ; [publicity, weather] mauvais ; [wind] contraire ◆ **~ weather conditions** conditions fpl météorologiques défavorables

adversely /ˈædvɜːslɪ/ ADV défavorablement ◆ **to affect sth ~** avoir un effet défavorable sur qch ◆ **to comment ~ on sth** faire des commentaires défavorables sur qch

adversity /ədˈvɜːsɪtɪ/ N 1 (NonC) adversité f ◆ **in ~** dans l'adversité 2 (= event) malheur m

advert[1] /ədˈvɜːt/ VI (frm) ◆ **to ~ to sth** faire référence à qch, se référer à qch

advert[2]* /ˈædvɜːt/ N (Brit) (abbrev of **advertisement**) (= announcement) annonce f (publicitaire) ; (Comm) publicité f, pub* f

advertise /ˈædvətaɪz/ VT 1 [+ goods] faire de la publicité pour ◆ **I've seen that soap ~d on television** j'ai vu une publicité pour ce savon à la télévision
2 (in newspaper etc) **to ~ a flat (for sale)** mettre or insérer une annonce pour vendre un appartement ◆ **I saw it ~d in a shop window** j'ai vu une annonce là-dessus dans une vitrine
3 (= draw attention to) afficher ◆ **don't ~ your ignorance!** inutile d'afficher votre ignorance ! ◆ **don't ~ the fact that ...** essaie de ne pas trop laisser voir que ..., ne va pas crier sur les toits que ...
VI 1 (in order to sell) faire de la publicité or de la réclame ◆ **it pays to ~** la publicité paie
2 (in order to find) chercher par voie d'annonce ◆ **to ~ for a secretary** faire paraître une annonce pour trouver une secrétaire ◆ **to ~ for sth** chercher qch par voie d'annonce

advertisement /ədˈvɜːtɪsmənt/ LANGUAGE IN USE 19.1, 20.1 N 1 (Comm) publicité f ◆ **I saw an ~ for that new car on the TV** j'ai vu une publicité pour cette nouvelle voiture à la télévision ◆ **I made tea during the ~s** j'ai fait le thé pendant la publicité ◆ **he's not a good ~ or an ~ for his school** (esp Brit) il ne donne pas une bonne image de son école 2 (private: in newspaper etc) annonce f ◆ **to put an ~ in a paper** (Brit) mettre une annonce dans un journal ◆ **I got it through an ~** je l'ai eu par or grâce à une annonce ; → **classified, small** 3 (NonC) réclame f, publicité f ; → **self**
COMP **advertisement column** N petites annonces fpl
advertisement hoarding N panneau m publicitaire

advertiser /ˈædvətaɪzəʳ/ N annonceur m

advertising /ˈædvətaɪzɪŋ/ N (= activity) publicité f ; (= advertisements) réclames fpl ◆ **a career in ~** une carrière dans la publicité
COMP [firm, work] publicitaire **advertising agency** N agence f de publicité
advertising campaign N campagne f publicitaire
advertising manager N directeur m, -trice f de la publicité
advertising medium N support m publicitaire
advertising rates NPL tarifs mpl publicitaires
advertising revenues NPL recettes fpl publicitaires
Advertising Standards Authority N (Brit) ≃ Bureau m de vérification de la publicité ; → **jingle**

advertorial /ˌædvəˈtɔːrɪəl/ N publireportage m ADJ de publireportage

advice /ədˈvaɪs/ LANGUAGE IN USE 2.1, 2.2 N (NonC) 1 conseils mpl, avis m ◆ **a piece of ~** un avis, un conseil ◆ **to seek ~ from sb** demander conseil à qn ◆ **to take medical/legal ~** consulter un médecin/un avocat ◆ **to take or follow sb's ~** suivre le(s) conseil(s) de qn ◆ **on the ~ of his doctor** sur le conseil de son médecin ◆ **against the ~ of his doctor** contre l'avis de son médecin 2 (Comm = notification) avis m ◆ **as per ~ of or from ...** suivant avis de ... ◆ **~ of dispatch** avis m d'expédition
COMP **advice column** N (Press) courrier m du cœur
advice columnist N (US) rédacteur m, -trice f de la rubrique du courrier du cœur
advice line N service m de conseil par téléphone
advice note N (Comm) avis m

advisability /ədˌvaɪzəˈbɪlɪtɪ/ N opportunité f (of sth de qch ; of doing sth de faire qch)

advisable /ədˈvaɪzəbl/ LANGUAGE IN USE 1.1 ADJ conseillé, recommandé ◆ **it is ~ to be vaccinated** il est conseillé de se faire vacciner ◆ **I do not think it ~ for you to come with me** je vous déconseille de m'accompagner

advise /ədˈvaɪz/ LANGUAGE IN USE 1, 2.1, 2.2, 21.3 VT 1 (= give advice to) conseiller, donner des conseils à (sb on or about sth qn sur or à propos de qch) ; ◆ **to ~ sb to do sth** conseiller à qn de faire qch, recommander à qn de faire qch ◆ **to ~ sb against sth** déconseiller qch à qn ◆ **to ~ sb against doing sth** conseiller à qn de ne pas faire qch 2 (= recommend) [+ course of action] recommander ◆ **I shouldn't ~ your going to see him** je ne vous conseillerais or recomman-

derais pas d'aller le voir ◆ **you would be well/ill ~d to wait** vous feriez bien/vous auriez tort d'attendre [3] (= *inform*) **to ~ sb of sth** aviser *or* informer qn de qch, faire part à qn de qch COMP
advising bank N (*Fin*) banque *f* notificatrice

advisedly /əd'vaɪzɪdlɪ/ ADV en connaissance de cause

advisement /əd'vaɪzmənt/ N (*US*) ◆ **to take sth under ~** considérer qch avec soin

adviser, advisor /əd'vaɪzəʳ/ N conseiller *m*, -ère *f* ◆ **French/maths ~** (*Scol Admin*) conseiller *m*, -ère *f* pédagogique de français/de maths ; → **educational, legal, spiritual**

advisory /əd'vaɪzərɪ/ ADJ [*group, board, role, work*] consultatif ; [*service*] de conseils ◆ **in an ~ capacity** à titre consultatif N (*esp US* = *announcement*) alerte *f*
COMP **advisory committee** N (*Pol*) comité *m* consultatif
advisory opinion N (*Jur*) avis *m* consultatif de la cour

advocacy /'ædvəkəsɪ/ N [*of cause etc*] plaidoyer *m* (*of* en faveur de)

advocate /'ædvəkɪt/ N [1] (= *upholder*) [*of cause etc*] défenseur *m*, avocat(e) *m(f)* ◆ **to be an ~ of** être partisan(e) de ◆ **to become the ~ of** se faire le champion (*or* la championne) de ; → **devil** [2] (*Scot Jur*) avocat *m* (plaidant) ; → **lord** ; → LAWYER VT /'ædvəkeɪt/ recommander, préconiser

advt (abbrev of **advertisement**) publicité *f*

adze, adz (*US*) /ædz/ N herminette *f*, doloire *f*

AEA /,eɪiː'eɪ/ N (*Brit*) (abbrev of **Atomic Energy Authority**) ≈ CEA *m*

AEC /,eɪiː'siː/ N (*US*) (abbrev of **Atomic Energy Commission**) ≈ CEA *m*

AEEU /,eɪiːiː'juː/ N (*Brit*) (abbrev of **Amalgamated Engineering and Electrical Union**) *syndicat*

Aegean /iː'dʒiːən/ ADJ égéen ◆ **~ (Sea)** (mer *f*) Égée *f* ◆ **the ~ Islands** les îles *fpl* de la mer Égée

Aegeus /iː'dʒiːəs/ N Égée *m*

aegis, egis (*US*) /'iːdʒɪs/ N égide *f* ◆ **under the ~ of ...** sous l'égide de ...

aegrotat /'aɪgrəʊ,tæt/ N (*Brit Univ*) équivalence *f* d'obtention d'un examen (*accordée à un bon étudiant malade*)

Aeneas /ɪ'niːəs/ N Énée *m*

Aeneid /ɪ'niːɪd/ N Énéide *f*

aeolian /iː'əʊlɪən/ ADJ éolien COMP **aeolian harp** N harpe *f* éolienne

Aeolus /'iːələs/ N Éole *m*

aeon /'iːən/ N temps *m* infini, période *f* incommensurable ◆ **through ~s of time** à travers des éternités

aerate /'ɛəreɪt/ VT [+ *liquid*] gazéifier ; [+ *blood*] oxygéner ; [+ *soil*] retourner ◆ **~d water** eau *f* gazeuse

aerial /'ɛərɪəl/ ADJ [1] (= *in the air*) aérien [2] (= *immaterial*) irréel, imaginaire N (*esp Brit: Telec etc*) antenne *f* ; → **indoor**
COMP **aerial cableway** N téléphérique *m*
aerial camera N appareil *m* photo pour prises de vues aériennes
aerial input N puissance *f* reçue par l'antenne
aerial ladder N (*US*) échelle *f* pivotante
aerial mast N mât *m* d'antenne
aerial photograph N photographie *f* aérienne
aerial railway N téléphérique *m*
aerial survey N levé *m* aérien
aerial tanker N ravitailleur *m* en vol

aerie /'ɛərɪ/ N (*esp US*) aire *f* (*d'aigle etc*)

aerobatics /'ɛərəʊ'bætɪks/ NPL acrobatie(s) *f(pl)* aérienne(s)

aerobic /ɛə'rəʊbɪk/ ADJ [*exercise, respiration*] aérobie (*SPEC*) ; [*workout*] d'aérobic

aerobics /ɛə'rəʊbɪks/ N (*NonC*) aérobic *f* ◆ **to do ~** faire de l'aérobic ◆ **my ~ class** mon cours d'aérobic

aerodrome /'ɛərədrəʊm/ N (*Brit*) aérodrome *m*

aerodynamic /'ɛərəʊdaɪ'næmɪk/ ADJ aérodynamique

aerodynamically /'ɛərəʊdaɪ'næmɪkəlɪ/ ADV [*efficient*] d'un point de vue aérodynamique ; [*designed, built*] de façon aérodynamique

aerodynamics /'ɛərəʊdaɪ'næmɪks/ N (*NonC*) aérodynamique *f*

aero-engine /'ɛərəʊ,endʒɪn/ N (*gen*) moteur *m* d'avion ; (= *jet engine*) réacteur *m*

aerofoil /'ɛərəʊfɔɪl/, **airfoil** /'ɛəfɔɪl/ (*US*) N [*of plane*] plan *m* de sustentation

aerogram /'ɛərəʊgræm/ N [1] (= *air letter*) aérogramme *m* [2] (= *radio telegram*) radiotélégramme *m*

aerograph /'ɛərəʊgræf/ N météorographe *m*

aerolite /'ɛərəlaɪt/ N aérolithe *m*

aeromodelling /'ɛərəʊ'mɒdlɪŋ/ N aéromodélisme *m*

aeronaut /'ɛərənɔːt/ N aéronaute *mf*

aeronautic(al) /,ɛərə'nɔːtɪk(əl)/ ADJ aéronautique COMP **aeronautic(al) engineering** N aéronautique *f*

aeronautics /,ɛərə'nɔːtɪks/ N (*NonC*) aéronautique *f*

aeroplane /'ɛərəpleɪn/ N (*Brit*) avion *m*

aerosol /'ɛərəsɒl/ N [1] (= *system*) aérosol *m* [2] (= *container, contents*) bombe *f* COMP [*insecticide, paint*] en aérosol, en bombe ; [*perfume*] en atomiseur

aerospace /'ɛərəʊspeɪs/ ADJ [*industry, project*] aérospatial

Aeschylus /'iːskələs/ N Eschyle *m*

Aesculapius /,iːskjʊ'leɪpɪəs/ N Esculape *m*

Aesop /'iːsɒp/ N Ésope *m* ◆ **~'s Fables** les fables *fpl* d'Ésope

aesthete, esthete (*US*) /'iːsθiːt/ N esthète *mf*

aesthetic(al), esthetic(al) (*US*) /iːs'θetɪk(əl)/ ADJ esthétique

aesthetically, esthetically (*US*) /iːs'θetɪkəlɪ/ ADV esthétiquement

aestheticism, estheticism (*US*) /iːs'θetɪsɪzəm/ N esthétisme *m*

aesthetics, esthetics (*US*) /iːs'θetɪks/ N (*NonC*) esthétique *f*

aether /'iːθəʳ/ N ⇒ **ether**

aetiology /,iːtɪ'ɒlədʒɪ/ N étiologie *f*

AEU /,eɪiː'juː/ N (*Brit*) (abbrev of **Amalgamated Engineering Union**) *ancien syndicat*

a.f. /eɪ'ef/ N (abbrev of **audio frequency**) audiofréquence *f*

AFA /,eɪef'eɪ/ N (*Brit*) abbrev of **Amateur Football Association**

afar /ə'fɑːʳ/ ADV (*liter*) au loin ◆ **from ~** de loin

AFB /,eɪef'biː/ N (*US Mil*) abbrev of **Air Force Base**

AFC /,eɪef'siː/ N [1] (abbrev of **Association Football Club**) AFC [2] abbrev of **automatic frequency control**

AFDC /,eɪefdiː'siː/ N (*US Admin*) abbrev of **Aid to Families with Dependent Children**

affability /,æfə'bɪlɪtɪ/ N affabilité *f*, amabilité *f*

affable /'æfəbl/ ADJ affable

affably /'æfəblɪ/ ADV avec affabilité, affablement

affair /ə'fɛəʳ/ N [1] (= *event*) affaire *f* ◆ **it was a scandalous ~** ce fut un scandale ◆ **it was an odd ~ altogether** c'était vraiment (une histoire *or* une affaire) bizarre ◆ **~ of honour** affaire *f* d'honneur ◆ **the Suez ~** l'affaire *f* de Suez
[2] (*esp Brit* = *concern*) affaire *f* ◆ **this is not her ~** ce n'est pas son affaire, cela ne la regarde pas ◆ **that's my ~** c'est mon affaire, ça ne regarde que moi ◆ **it's not your ~ what I do in the evenings** ce que je fais le soir ne te regarde pas
[3] (= *business of any kind*) **~s** affaires *fpl* ◆ **in the present state of ~s** les choses étant ce qu'elles sont, étant donné les circonstances actuelles ◆ **it was a dreadful state of ~s** la situation était épouvantable ◆ **~s of state** les affaires *fpl* d'État ◆ **to put one's ~s in order** (*business*) mettre de l'ordre dans ses affaires ; (*belongings*) mettre ses affaires en ordre ◆ **your private ~s don't concern me** votre vie privée ne m'intéresse pas ◆ **she never interferes with his business ~s** elle n'intervient jamais dans ses activités professionnelles *or* dans ses affaires ; → **current, foreign**
[4] (also **love affair**) liaison *f*, aventure *f* ◆ **to have an ~ with sb** avoir une liaison *or* une aventure avec qn ◆ **they're having an ~** ils sont amants
[5] (* = *thing*) machin *m* ◆ **that red ~ over there** ce machin rouge, là-bas

affect /ə'fekt/ VT [1] (= *have effect on*) [+ *result, experiment, numbers*] avoir un effet *or* des conséquences sur, modifier ; [+ *decision, career, the future*] influer sur ; (*Jur*) avoir une incidence sur ; (= *have detrimental effect on*) [+ *person*] atteindre, toucher ; [+ *conditions, substance, health*] détériorer ◆ **this will certainly ~ the way we approach the problem** cela va certainement influer sur la façon dont nous aborderons le problème ◆ **you mustn't let it ~ you** ne te laisse pas décourager *or* abattre par ça
[2] (= *concern*) concerner, toucher ◆ **this decision ~s all of us** cette décision nous concerne tous ◆ **it does not ~ me personally** cela ne me touche pas personnellement
[3] (*emotionally* = *move*) émouvoir, affecter ; (= *sadden*) affecter, toucher ◆ **she was deeply ~ed by the news** elle a été très affectée *or* touchée par la nouvelle
[4] [*disease*] [+ *organ, powers of recuperation*] attaquer, atteindre ; [*drug*] agir sur
[5] (= *feign*) [+ *ignorance, surprise*] affecter, feindre
[6] († = *have liking for*) affectionner ◆ **she ~s bright colours** elle a une prédilection pour *or* elle affectionne les couleurs vives
N /'æfekt/ (*Psych*) affect *m*

affectation /,æfek'teɪʃən/ N [1] (= *pretence*) affectation *f*, simulation *f* ◆ **an ~ of interest/indifference** une affectation d'intérêt/d'indifférence [2] (= *artificiality*) affectation *f*, manque *m* de naturel ◆ **her ~s annoy me** ses manières affectées *or* ses poses *fpl* m'agacent

affected /ə'fektɪd/ ADJ (= *insincere*) [*person, behaviour*] affecté, maniéré ; [*accent, clothes*] affecté ◆ **to be ~** [*person*] poser

affectedly /ə'fektɪdlɪ/ ADV avec affectation, d'une manière affectée

affecting /ə'fektɪŋ/ ADJ touchant, émouvant

affection /ə'fekʃən/ N [1] (= *fondness*) affection *f*, tendresse *f* (*for, towards* pour) ; ◆ **to win sb's ~(s)** se faire aimer de qn, gagner l'affection *or* le cœur de qn ◆ **I have a great ~ for her** j'ai beaucoup d'affection pour elle [2] (*Med*) affection *f*, maladie *f*

affectionate /ə'fekʃənɪt/ ADJ [*person, tone*] affectueux, tendre ; [*memories*] tendre ◆ **your ~ daughter** (*letter-ending*) votre fille affectionnée

affectionately /ə'fekʃənɪtlɪ/ ADV affectueusement ◆ **yours ~** (*letter-ending*) (bien) affectueusement (à vous)

affective /ə'fektɪv/ ADJ affectif (*also Ling*)

affidavit /ˌæfɪˈdeɪvɪt/ N (Jur) déclaration *f* écrite sous serment ◆ **to swear an ~ (to the effect that)** déclarer par écrit sous serment (que)

affiliate /əˈfɪlieɪt/ VT affilier (*to, with* à) ; ◆ **to ~ o.s.** s'affilier (*to, with* à) N /əˈfɪlɪət/ membre *m* affilié

affiliated /əˈfɪlieɪtɪd/ ADJ [*organisation, union, club, society*] affilié ◆ **~ company** (*Comm*) (*gen*) filiale *f* ; (*on balance sheet*) société *f* liée *or* apparentée

affiliation /əˌfɪlɪˈeɪʃən/ N 1 (*Comm etc*) affiliation *f* 2 (*Jur*) attribution *f* de paternité 3 (*= connection*) affiliation *f*, attaches *fpl*

COMP **affiliation order** N jugement *m* en constatation de paternité

affiliation proceedings NPL action *f* en recherche de paternité

affinity /əˈfɪnɪtɪ/ N 1 (*gen, Bio, Chem Ling, Math, Philos*) affinité *f* (*with, to* avec ; *between* entre) ; (*= connection, resemblance*) ressemblance *f*, rapport *m* ◆ **the ~ of one thing to another** la ressemblance d'une chose avec une autre 2 (*Jur = relationship*) affinité *f* (*to, with* avec) 3 (*= liking*) attrait *m*, attraction *f* (*with, for* pour) ; ◆ **there is a certain ~ between them** ils ont des affinités COMP **affinity card** N *carte de paiement grâce à laquelle un pourcentage des paiements est versé à une organisation caritative*

affirm /əˈfɜːm/ VT affirmer, soutenir (*that* que)

affirmation /ˌæfəˈmeɪʃən/ N affirmation *f*, assertion *f*

affirmative /əˈfɜːmətɪv/ N (*Ling*) affirmatif *m* ◆ **in the ~** à l'affirmatif ◆ **to answer in the ~** répondre affirmativement *or* par l'affirmative ADJ affirmatif ◆ **if the answer is ~** si la réponse est affirmative, si la réponse est positive

COMP **affirmative action** N mesures *fpl* de discrimination positive

AFFIRMATIVE ACTION

Ce terme désigne les mesures de discrimination positive prises aux États-Unis dans les années 1960 en faveur des femmes et des minorités ethniques. À l'instigation de l'administration Kennedy, les catégories sous-représentées ont bénéficié d'un système de quotas en matière d'emploi et pour les inscriptions universitaires. En 1972, la loi sur l'égalité de l'emploi (Equal Employment Opportunities Act) a institué une commission chargée de faire respecter ces mesures. En réaction, certains groupes majoritaires (hommes et Blancs, par exemple), qui s'estimaient lésés par cette discrimination à rebours, se sont mobilisés pour faire assouplir la politique de quotas.

affirmatively /əˈfɜːmətɪvlɪ/ ADV affirmativement

affix /əˈfɪks/ VT [*+ seal, signature*] apposer, ajouter (*to* à) ; [*+ stamp*] coller (*to* à) N /ˈæfɪks/ (*Gram*) affixe *m*

afflict /əˈflɪkt/ VT toucher ◆ **depression ~s people of all ages** la dépression touche des gens de tout âge ◆ **diabetes ~s millions of people worldwide** le diabète touche des millions de personnes dans le monde ◆ **to be ~ed by** *or* **with gout** souffrir de la goutte

affliction /əˈflɪkʃən/ N 1 (*NonC*) affliction *f*, détresse *f* ◆ **people in ~** les gens dans la détresse 2 ◆ **the ~s of old age** les misères *fpl* de la vieillesse

affluence /ˈæfluəns/ N (*= plenty*) abondance *f* ; (*= wealth*) richesse *f* ◆ **to rise to ~** parvenir à la fortune

affluent /ˈæfluənt/ ADJ (*= plentiful*) abondant ; (*= wealthy*) riche ◆ **to be ~** vivre dans l'aisance ◆ **the ~ society** la société d'abondance N (*Geog*) affluent *m*

afflux /ˈæflʌks/ N 1 (*Med*) afflux *m* 2 [*of people etc*] affluence *f*, afflux *m*

afford /əˈfɔːd/ VT 1 (*financially*) **to be able to ~ to buy sth** avoir les moyens d'acheter qch ◆ **he can well ~ a new car** il a tout à fait les moyens de s'acheter une nouvelle voiture ◆ **he couldn't ~ the £10 entrance fee** il n'avait pas les moyens *or* ne pouvait pas se payer une entrée à 10 livres ◆ **I can't ~ the prices they charge** leurs prix sont trop élevés pour moi

2 (*= allow o.s.*) se permettre ◆ **he can't ~ (to make) a mistake** il ne peut pas se permettre (de faire) une erreur ◆ **we can't ~ to lose any more customers** nous ne pouvons pas nous permettre de perdre d'autres clients ◆ **I can't ~ the time to do it** je n'ai pas le temps de le faire ; → **ill**

3 (*frm*) (*= provide*) fournir, procurer ◆ **to ~ sb great pleasure** procurer un grand plaisir à qn ◆ **this will ~ me an opportunity to say ...** ceci me fournira l'occasion de dire ... ◆ **the helmet ~s little protection in an accident** ce casque ne protège pas beaucoup en cas d'accident

affordable /əˈfɔːdəbl/ ADJ abordable ◆ **easily ~** très abordable

afforest /æˈfɒrɪst/ VT reboiser

afforestation /æˌfɒrɪsˈteɪʃən/ N boisement *m* ◆ **~ policy** politique *f* de boisement

affranchise /æˈfræntʃaɪz/ VT affranchir

affray /əˈfreɪ/ N (*= fight*) échauffourée *f*, rixe *f* ◆ **he was convicted of ~** il a été reconnu coupable de violences en réunion

affricate /ˈæfrɪˌkɪt/ N (*Phon*) affriquée *f*

affright /əˈfraɪt/ (*†, liter*) VT effrayer, terrifier N effroi *m*, épouvante *f*

affront /əˈfrʌnt/ VT 1 (*= insult*) faire un affront à, outrager 2 (*= face*) affronter, braver N affront *m*, insulte *f*

Afghan /ˈæfgæn/ ADJ afghan N 1 Afghan(e) *m(f)* 2 (*= language*) afghan *m* 3 (also **Afghan hound**) lévrier *m* afghan

Afghani /æfˈgænɪ/ ADJ afghan N 1 (*= person*) Afghan(e) *m(f)* 2 (*language*) afghan *m*

Afghanistan /æfˈgænɪstæn/ N Afghanistan *m*

aficionado /əˌfɪʃjəˈnɑːdəʊ/ N ◆ **he's an ~ of jazz** *or* **a jazz ~** c'est un fana* *or* un mordu* du jazz

afield /əˈfiːld/ ADV ◆ **far ~** [*be*] au loin ; [*go*] loin ◆ **countries further ~** pays *mpl* plus lointains ◆ **very far ~** très loin ◆ **too far ~** trop loin ◆ **to explore farther ~** pousser plus loin l'exploration ◆ **to go farther ~ for help/support** (*fig*) chercher plus loin de l'aide/un soutien

afire /əˈfaɪəʳ/ ADJ, ADV (*liter*) (*lit*) en feu, embrasé (*liter*) ; (*fig*) enflammé (*with* de)

aflame /əˈfleɪm/ (*liter*) ADJ 1 (*= on fire*) en flammes 2 (*with light, colour*) embrasé (*liter*) ◆ **to be ~ with colour** briller de vives couleurs, flamboyer 3 (*emotionally*) [*cheeks*] enflammé ◆ **she was ~ with anger/pride** elle était enflammée de colère/d'orgueil ◆ **his heart was ~ with passion** son cœur était enflammé par la passion ADV (*with light, colour*) ◆ **to set sth ~** embraser qch

AFL-CIO /ˌeɪefˈelˈsiːaɪˈəʊ/ N (abbrev of **American Federation of Labor and Congress of Industrial Organizations**) *fédération des syndicats indépendants américains*

afloat /əˈfləʊt/ ADV 1 (*= on water*) ◆ **to stay** *or* **keep ~** [*person*] garder la tête hors de l'eau ; [*object*] surnager ; [*boat*] rester à flot ◆ **to set/keep a boat ~** mettre/maintenir un bateau à flot ◆ **the largest passenger ship ~** le plus grand paquebot en exploitation 2 (*= on board ship*) sur l'eau, en mer ◆ **service ~** service *m* à bord ◆ **to serve ~** servir en mer 3 (*= solvent*) ◆ **to stay** *or* **keep ~** [*person, company*] se maintenir à flot ◆ **to set a business/scheme ~** lancer une affaire/un projet 4 (*= in circulation*) ◆ **to be ~** [*rumour*] circuler, être en circulation 5 (*Fin*) ◆ **to keep bills ~** faire circuler des effets ADJ (*Comm*) ◆ **~ price** prix *m* à flot *or* à bord

aflutter /əˈflʌtəʳ/ ADJ ◆ **to set sb's heart ~** faire battre le cœur de qn

afocal /ˈeɪˌfəʊkəl/ ADJ (*Phot*) afocal

afoot /əˈfʊt/ ADV 1 (*= in progress*) **there is something ~** il se prépare quelque chose ◆ **there is a plan ~ to demolish it** on a formé le projet *or* on envisage de le démolir 2 (*†, liter*) [*go, come*] à pied ◆ **to be ~** être sur pied

afore /əˈfɔːʳ/ CONJ (*†† or dial*) avant que de, avant que ◆ **~ he went** avant que de partir, avant qu'il ne parte

aforementioned /əˌfɔːˈmenʃənd/, **aforenamed** /əˈfɔːneɪmd/, **aforesaid** /əˈfɔːsed/ ADJ susdit, susmentionné

aforethought /əˈfɔːθɔːt/ ADJ prémédité ; → **malice**

afoul /əˈfaʊl/ ADV (*esp US*) ◆ **to run ~ of sb** se mettre qn à dos, s'attirer le mécontentement de qn ◆ **to run ~ of a ship** entrer en collision avec un bateau

afp /ˌeɪefˈpiː/ N (abbrev of **alpha-fetoprotein**) AFP *f*

afraid /əˈfreɪd/ ADJ 1 (*= frightened*) **to be ~** avoir peur ◆ **don't be ~!** n'ayez pas peur !, ne craignez rien ! ◆ **to look ~** avoir l'air effrayé ◆ **to be ~ of sb/sth** avoir peur de qn/qch, craindre qn/qch ◆ **you have nothing to be ~ of** vous n'avez aucune raison d'avoir peur ◆ **he is not ~ of hard work** il n'a pas peur de travailler dur ◆ **she's furious – I was ~ of that** elle est furieuse – c'est ce que je craignais ◆ **I am ~ of hurting him** *or* **that I might hurt him** j'ai peur *or* je crains de lui faire mal ◆ **I am ~ he will** *or* **might hurt me** je crains *or* j'ai peur qu'il (ne) me fasse mal ◆ **I am ~ to go** *or* **of going** je n'ose pas y aller, j'ai peur d'y aller ◆ **to be ~ for sb/sth** avoir peur pour qn/qch ◆ **to be ~ for one's life** craindre pour sa vie ; → **shadow**

2 (*expressing polite regret*) **I'm ~ I can't do it** je regrette *or* je suis désolé, (mais) je ne pourrai pas le faire ◆ **I am ~ I shall not be able to come** je suis désolé de ne pouvoir venir, je crains de ne pas pouvoir venir ◆ **are you going? – I'm ~ not/I'm ~ so** vous y allez ? – hélas non/hélas oui ◆ **it's a bit stuffy in here, I'm ~** je regrette *or* je suis désolé, mais on étouffe un peu ici

afresh /əˈfreʃ/ ADV de nouveau ◆ **to start ~** recommencer

Africa /ˈæfrɪkə/ N Afrique *f* ; → **south**

African /ˈæfrɪkən/ ADJ africain ; → **south** N Africain(e) *m(f)*

COMP **African-American** ADJ afro-américain N Afro-Américain(e) *m(f)*

African-Caribbean ADJ afro-antillais N Afro-Antillais(e) *m(f)*

African elephant N éléphant *m* d'Afrique

African National Congress N Congrès *m* national africain

African violet N saintpaulia *m*

Afrikaans /ˌæfrɪˈkɑːns/ N (*= language*) afrikaans *m* ADJ afrikaans

Afrikaner /ˌæfrɪˈkɑːnəʳ/ N Afrikaner *mf* ADJ afrikaner

afro /ˈæfrəʊ/ ADJ ◆ **to go ~** * s'africaniser ◆ **~ hair style** coiffure *f* afro*

COMP **Afro-American** ADJ afro-américain N Afro-Américain(e) *m(f)*

Afro-Asian ADJ afro-asiatique

Afro-Caribbean ADJ afro-antillais

aft /ɑːft/ (*Naut, Aviat*) ADV à *or* vers l'arrière ◆ **wind dead ~** vent *m* en poupe, vent *m* arrière

◆ **"lavatories aft"** "toilettes à l'arrière" ADJ *[cabin, deck, engine]* arrière

after /ˈɑːftəʳ/

When **after** is an element in a phrasal verb, eg **ask after**, **look after**, **take after**, look up the verb.

PREP 1 *(time)* après ◆ ~ **that** après cela, après ça ◆ ~ **dinner** après le dîner ; see also **comp** ◆ ~ **this date** passé cette date ◆ ~ **a week/ten minutes** au bout d'une semaine/de dix minutes ◆ **shortly** ~ **10 o'clock** peu après 10 heures ◆ **it was** ~ **2 o'clock** il était plus de 2 heures ◆ **it was 20** ~ **3** (US) il était 3 heures 20 ◆ ~ **seeing her** après l'avoir vue ◆ ~ **which he sat down** après quoi il s'est assis ◆ ~ **what has happened** après ce qui s'est passé ; → **day, hour**

2 *(order)* après ◆ **the noun comes** ~ **the verb** le substantif vient après le verbe ◆ ~ **Germany, America is Britain's second-biggest customer** l'Amérique est le plus gros client de la Grande-Bretagne après l'Allemagne ◆ ~ **you, sir** après vous, Monsieur ◆ ~ **you with the salt*** passez-moi le sel s'il vous plaît (quand vous aurez fini)

3 *(place)* ◆ **come in and shut the door** ~ **you** entrez et (re)fermez la porte (derrière vous) ◆ **he shut the door** ~ **her** il a refermé la porte derrière elle

4 *(set structures)*

◆ **after all** après tout ◆ **to succeed** ~ **all** réussir malgré *or* après tout ◆ ~ **all, no one made him go** après tout, personne ne l'a obligé à y aller ◆ ~ **all, you'd expect her to say that** évidemment, il n'est pas étonnant qu'elle dise ça ◆ **it's only two days,** ~ **all** après tout *or* au fond, ça fait seulement deux jours

◆ **after all** + *verb* ◆ ~ **all I said to him** après tout ce que je lui ai dit ◆ ~ **all I've done for you!** après tout ce que j'ai fait pour toi !, quand je pense à tout ce que j'ai fait pour toi ! ◆ ~ **all that happened, it's not surprising** avec tout ce qui est arrivé *or* quand on pense à tout ce qui est arrivé ça n'a rien d'étonnant

5 *(succession)* ◆ **day** ~ **day** jour après jour, tous les jours ◆ **(for) kilometre** ~ **kilometre** sur des kilomètres et des kilomètres ◆ **kilometre** ~ **kilometre of forest** des kilomètres et des kilomètres de forêt ◆ **you tell me lie** ~ **lie** tu me racontes mensonge sur mensonge ◆ **she gave one excuse** ~ **another** elle a avancé une excuse après l'autre ◆ **time** ~ **time** maintes (et maintes) fois ◆ **she ate three biscuits, one** ~ **the other** elle a mangé trois biscuits l'un après l'autre *or* d'affilée ◆ **they went out one** ~ **the other** *(= individually)* ils sont sortis les uns après les autres ; *(= in a line)* ils sont sortis à la file

6 *(pursuit, inquiry)* ◆ **to be** ~ **sb/sth** chercher qn/qch ; *(after loss, disappearance etc)* rechercher qn/qch ◆ **you should go** ~ **her** tu devrais essayer de la rattraper ◆ **the police are** ~ **him for this robbery** il est recherché par la police *or* la police est à ses trousses pour ce vol ◆ **she's** ~ **a green hat** elle cherche *or* voudrait un chapeau vert ◆ **what are you** ~**?** *(= want)* qu'est-ce que vous voulez *or* désirez ? ; *(= have in mind)* qu'avez-vous en tête ? ◆ **I see what he's** ~ je vois où il veut en venir ◆ **she's always** ~ **her children*** *(= nagging)* elle est toujours après ses enfants*

7 *(manner = according to)* ◆ ~ **El Greco** d'après le Greco ◆ ~ **the old style** à la vieille mode, à l'ancienne ; → **heart, name**

ADV *(place, order, time)* après, ensuite ◆ **for years** ~ pendant des années après cela ◆ **soon** ~ bientôt après ◆ **the week** ~ la semaine d'après, la semaine suivante ◆ **what comes** ~**?** qu'est-ce qui vient ensuite ?, et ensuite ?

CONJ après (que) ◆ ~ **he had closed the door, she spoke** après qu'il eut fermé la porte, elle parla ◆ ~ **he had closed the door, he spoke** après avoir fermé la porte, il a parlé

ADJ ◆ **in** ~ **years** plus tard (dans la vie), par la suite

NPL *(Brit = dessert)* ◆ ~**s*** le dessert

COMP **after-dinner drink** N digestif *m*

after-dinner speaker N orateur *m* (de fin de repas) ◆ **he's a good ~-dinner speaker** il fait de très bonnes allocutions *or* de très bons discours (de fin de repas)

after-hours drinking N consommation *f* de boissons après la fermeture des pubs (*or* du pub) ; see also **hour**

after-image N image *f* rémanente

after-lunch ADJ ◆ **to have an ~-lunch nap** faire la sieste

after-sales service N service *m* après-vente

after-school ADJ *[activities etc]* extrascolaire ◆ **~-school club** *(Brit) or* **center** *(US)* garderie *f*

after-sun ADJ *[lotion, cream]* après-soleil N *(= lotion)* lotion *f* après-soleil ; *(= cream)* crème *f* après-soleil

after-tax ADJ après impôts

after-treatment N *(Med)* soins *mpl* ; *(Tex)* apprêt *m*

afterbirth /ˈɑːftəbɜːθ/ N placenta *m*

afterburner /ˈɑːftəbɜːnəʳ/, **afterburning** /ˈɑːftəbɜːnɪŋ/ N postcombustion *f*

aftercare /ˈɑːftəkeəʳ/ N *[of convalescent]* postcure *f* ; *[of appliance, product]* entretien *m* ◆ **(prisoner)** ~ assistance *f* (aux anciens détenus)

afterdeck /ˈɑːftədek/ N *(Naut)* arrière-pont *m*, pont *m* arrière

aftereffects /ˈɑːftərɪˌfekts/ NPL *[of events etc]* suites *fpl*, répercussions *fpl* ; *[of treatment]* réaction *f* ; *[of illness]* séquelles *fpl* ; *(Psych)* after-effect *m*

afterglow /ˈɑːftəgləʊ/ N *[of setting sun]* dernières lueurs *fpl*, derniers reflets *mpl* ; *[of person] (after exercise)* sensation *f* de bien-être

afterlife /ˈɑːftəlaɪf/ N vie *f* après la mort

aftermarket /ˈɑːftəˌmɑːkɪt/ N *(for cars)* marché *m* de la rechange automobile

aftermath /ˈɑːftəmæθ/ N suites *fpl*, conséquences *fpl*, séquelles *fpl* ◆ **the** ~ **of war** le contrecoup *or* les conséquences de la guerre ◆ **in the** ~ **of the riots** à la suite des émeutes

afternoon /ˈɑːftəˈnuːn/ N après-midi *m or f* ◆ **in the** ~, ~**s*** l'après-midi ◆ **at 3 o'clock in the** ~ à 3 heures de l'après-midi ◆ **on Sunday** ~**(s)** le dimanche après-midi ◆ **every** ~ l'après-midi, chaque après-midi ◆ **on the** ~ **of 2 December** l'après-midi du 2 décembre, le 2 décembre dans l'après-midi ◆ **he will go this** ~ il ira cet après-midi ◆ **good** ~**!** *(on meeting sb)* bonjour ! ; *(on leaving sb)* au revoir ! ◆ **have a nice** ~**!** bon après-midi ! ◆ **in the early** ~ tôt dans l'après-midi ◆ **this** ~ cet après-midi ◆ **tomorrow/yesterday** ~ demain/hier après-midi ◆ **the next** *or* **following** ~ l'après-midi suivant ◆ **the** ~ **before** l'après-midi précédant ◆ **every Sunday** ~ le dimanche après-midi ◆ **one summer** ~ (par) un après-midi d'été

COMP *[lecture, class, train, meeting etc]* (de) l'après-midi **afternoon performance** N *(Theat)* matinée *f*

afternoon tea N thé *m* (de cinq heures)

afterpains /ˈɑːftəpeɪnz/ NPL tranchées *fpl* utérines

aftershave /ˈɑːftəʃeɪv/ N (lotion *f*) après-rasage *m inv*

aftershock /ˈɑːftəʃɒk/ N *[of earthquake]* réplique *f*

aftertaste /ˈɑːftəteɪst/ N *(lit, fig)* arrière-goût *m*

afterthought /ˈɑːftəθɔːt/ N pensée *f* après coup ◆ **I had an** ~ cela m'est venu après coup ◆ **I had** ~**s** *or* **an** ~ **about my decision** j'ai eu après coup des doutes sur ma décision ◆ **the window was added as an** ~ la fenêtre a été ajoutée après coup

afterward(s) /ˈɑːftəwəd(z)/ ADV après, ensuite, plus tard, par la suite

afterword /ˈɑːftəwɜːd/ N postface *f*

AG /eɪˈdʒiː/ N 1 abbrev of **Adjutant General** 2 (abbrev of **Attorney General**) → **attorney**

Aga ® /ˈɑːgə/ N *(Brit) grand fourneau de cuisine en fonte*

again /əˈgen/ ADV 1 *(= once more)* de nouveau ◆ **here we are** ~**!** nous revoilà !, nous voilà de nouveau ! ◆ **it's him** ~**!** c'est encore lui ! ◆ **he was soon well** ~ il s'est vite remis ◆ **she is home** ~ elle est rentrée chez elle, elle est de retour chez elle ◆ **what's his name** ~**?** comment s'appelle-t-il déjà ? ◆ **to begin** ~ recommencer ◆ **to see** ~ revoir

◆ **again and again, time and again** à plusieurs reprises, maintes et maintes fois ◆ **I've told you** ~ **and** ~ je te l'ai dit et répété (je ne sais combien de fois)

◆ **(all) over again** ◆ **start all over** ~ recommencez au début *or* à partir du début, reprenez au commencement ◆ **he had to count them over** ~ il a dû les recompter

◆ **as ... again** ◆ **as much** ~ deux fois autant ◆ **he is as old** ~ **as Christine** il a deux fois l'âge de Christine

2 *(with neg)* **not ...** ~ ne ... plus ◆ **I won't do it** ~ je ne le ferai plus ◆ **never** ~ jamais plus, plus jamais ◆ **I won't do it ever** ~ je ne le ferai plus jamais ◆ **never** ~**!** c'est bien la dernière fois ! ◆ **not** ~**!** encore !

3 *(emphatic = besides, moreover)* là encore, encore une fois ◆ **but there** ~ mais là encore ◆ **then** ~**, and** ~ d'autre part, d'un autre côté ◆ ~**, it is not certain that ...** et d'ailleurs *or* et encore il n'est pas sûr que ...

against /əˈgenst/ LANGUAGE IN USE 9.2, 12.1, 12.2

When **against** is an element in a phrasal verb, eg **go against**, **run up against**, **take against**, look up the verb.

PREP 1 contre ◆ **an upsurge in racism** ~ **immigrants** une montée du racisme contre les immigrants ◆ **a demonstration** ~ **the government's reforms** une manifestation contre les réformes du gouvernement ◆ **he did it** ~ **my wishes** il l'a fait contre mon gré ◆ **I've got nothing** ~ **him/it** je n'ai rien contre lui/rien contre (cela) ◆ **the weather is** ~ **us** la météo ne nous est pas favorable ◆ **to be** ~ **capital punishment** être contre la peine de mort ◆ **I'm** ~ **it** je suis contre (cela) ◆ **to be (dead)** ~ **sth** être (farouchement) opposé à qch ◆ **to hit one's head** ~ **the mantelpiece** se cogner la tête contre la cheminée ◆ **to lean** ~ **a wall** s'appuyer contre un mur *or* au mur ◆ **push the chairs right back** ~ **the wall** repoussez les chaises tout contre le mur ◆ **to work** ~ **the clock** travailler contre la montre, faire la course contre la montre *(fig)* ◆ **Tyson's fight** ~ **Bruno** le combat entre Tyson et Bruno, le combat opposant Tyson à Bruno ◆ ~ **the law** ADJ contraire à la loi ADV contrairement à la loi ◆ **there's no law** ~ **it** *(lit)* il n'y a pas de loi qui l'interdise ; *(fig)* ce n'est pas interdit ◆ **I'm** ~ **helping him at all** je ne suis pas d'avis qu'on l'aide *subj* ◆ **now we're up** ~ **it!** nous voici au pied du mur ! ◆ ~ **my will** *(= despite myself)* malgré moi, à contrecœur ; *(= despite my opposition)* contre ma volonté ; → **grain, odds, vote**

2 *(= in contrast to)* sur ◆ ~ **the light** à contre-jour ◆ **the trees stood out** ~ **the sunset** les arbres se détachaient sur le (soleil) couchant

3 *(comparison)* par rapport à ◆ **the strength of the pound** ~ **the dollar** la fermeté de la livre par rapport au dollar ◆ **the pound is down** ~ **the euro** la livre a baissé par rapport à l'euro ◆ ~ **that, it might be said ...** en revanche *or* par contre on pourrait dire ...

◆ **as against** ◆ **my rights as** ~ **his** mes droits comparés aux siens ◆ **90% of one-parent families are poor, as** ~ **22% with two parents**

90% des familles monoparentales sont pauvres, et seulement 22% des foyers où il y a deux parents ; → **over, word**
4 *(= in preparation for)* en prévision de ◆ **to have the roof repaired ~ the rainy season** faire réparer le toit en prévision de la saison des pluies

Agamemnon /ˌæɡəˈmemnən/ N Agamemnon *m*

agape /əˈɡeɪp/ ADJ, ADV bouche bée

agar(-agar) /ˌeɪɡəˈeɪɡəʳ/ N agar-agar *m*, gélose *f*

agaric /əˈɡærɪk/ N agaric *m*

agate /ˈæɡət/ N agate *f*

agave /əˈɡeɪvɪ/ N agave *m*

age /eɪdʒ/ N 1 *(= length of life)* âge *m* ◆ **what's her ~?, what ~ is she?** quel âge a-t-elle ? ◆ **when I was your ~** quand j'avais votre âge ◆ **I have a daughter your ~** *or* **the same ~ as you** j'ai une fille de votre âge ◆ **be** *or* **act your ~!** allons, sois raisonnable ! ◆ **he is ten years of ~** il a dix ans ◆ **you don't look your ~** vous ne faites pas votre âge ◆ **he's twice your ~** il a le double de votre âge ◆ **we are of an ~** nous sommes du même âge ◆ **to be under ~** *(Jur etc)* être mineur ◆ **to be of ~** être majeur ◆ **to come of ~** *(lit)* atteindre sa majorité ; *(fig) [issue, idea]* faire son chemin ◆ **the ~ of reason** l'âge *m* de raison ◆ **~ of consent** *(Jur)* âge *m* de consentement ; → **middle**
2 *(= latter part of life)* vieillesse *f*, âge *m* ◆ **the infirmities of ~** les infirmités *fpl* de la vieillesse *or* de l'âge ; → **old**
3 *(Geol etc)* âge *m* ; *(Hist, Literat)* époque *f*, siècle *m* ; → **enlightenment, stone**
4 *(gen pl) (* = long time)* **I haven't seen him for ~s** il y a une éternité que je ne l'ai vu ◆ **she stayed for ~s** *or* **for an ~** elle est restée (là) pendant une éternité *or* un temps fou
VI vieillir, prendre de l'âge ◆ **she had ~d beyond her years** elle paraissait *or* faisait maintenant plus que son âge ◆ **to ~ well** *[wine]* s'améliorer en vieillissant ; *[person]* vieillir bien ◆ **he has ~d a lot** il a beaucoup vieilli, il a pris un coup de vieux
VT 1 vieillir ◆ **her make-up really ~s her** son maquillage la vieillit beaucoup
2 *[+ wine etc]* laisser vieillir
3 *[+ accounts]* classer par antériorité *or* par ancienneté ◆ **to ~ inventories** classer *or* analyser le stock par date d'entrée
COMP d'âge **age allowance** N *(Brit Tax)* abattement *m* vieillesse
age bracket N ⇒ **age group**
age discrimination N *(US)* discrimination *f* pour raisons d'âge, âgisme *m*
age group N tranche *f* d'âge ◆ **the 40-50 ~ group** la tranche d'âge de 40 à 50 ans, les 40 à 50 ans
age limit N limite *f* d'âge
age-old ADJ séculaire, antique
age range N ◆ **children in the ~ range 12-14** les enfants (âgés) de 12 à 14 ans

aged /eɪdʒd/ ADJ 1 âgé de ◆ **a boy ~ ten** un garçon (âgé) de dix ans 2 /ˈeɪdʒɪd/ *(= old)* âgé, vieux (vieille *f*), vieil *m before vowel* NPL **the aged** les personnes *fpl* âgées ◆ **the ~ and infirm** les gens *mpl* âgés et infirmes

ageing /ˈeɪdʒɪŋ/ ADJ *[person, population, transport system]* vieillissant ; *[hairstyle etc]* qui fait paraître plus vieux (vieille *f*) N vieillissement *m*

ageism /ˈeɪdʒɪzəm/ N âgisme *m*

ageist /ˈeɪdʒɪst/ ADJ faisant preuve d'âgisme N personne *f* faisant preuve d'âgisme

ageless /ˈeɪdʒlɪs/ ADJ *[person]* sans âge ; *[beauty]* toujours jeune

agency /ˈeɪdʒənsɪ/ N 1 *(= body, organization)* agence *f*, bureau *m* ; *(Govt)* organisme *m* ◆ **they hired their nanny through an ~** ils sont passés par une agence pour trouver leur nounou ◆ **to meet sb through an ~** rencontrer qn par l'intermédiaire d'une agence ◆ **press/adoption ~** agence de presse/d'adoption ◆ **aid ~** organisation *f* humanitaire ◆ **he has the sole ~ for ...** il a l'exclusivité de ... ◆ **this garage has the Citroën ~** ce garage est le concessionnaire Citroën ; → **advertising, news, tourist**
2 *(= means)* intermédiaire *m*, entremise *f* ◆ **the matter was discussed through the ~ of a third party** ils en ont discuté par l'intermédiaire d'un tiers ◆ **a settlement was reached through the ~ of the UN** ils sont parvenus à un accord par l'entremise *or* l'intermédiaire de l'ONU ◆ **through the ~ of water** par l'action de l'eau
COMP **agency agreement** N contrat *m* de représentation
agency fee N frais *mpl* d'agence
agency nurse N infirmier *m*, -ière *f* intérimaire
agency spokes-person N porte-parole *m* de l'agence

agenda /əˈdʒendə/ N ordre *m* du jour, programme *m* ◆ **on the ~** à l'ordre du jour ◆ **to set the ~** *(fig)* donner le ton ◆ **to have an ~** *(fig)* avoir une idée en tête ◆ **they denied having a hidden ~** ils ont nié avoir des intentions cachées ◆ **what's on the ~ (for) today?** *(fig)* qu'y a-t-il au programme aujourd'hui ?

> ⚠ In French, **agenda** means 'diary'.

agent /ˈeɪdʒənt/ N 1 *(Comm) (= person)* agent *m*, concessionnaire *mf (of, for* de) ; *(= firm)* concessionnaire *m* ◆ **for Ford cars** concessionnaire *m* Ford ; → **foreign, free, special** 2 *(= thing, person, also Ling)* agent *m* ; → **chemical, principal** COMP **agent provocateur** N agent *m* provocateur

agentive /ˈeɪdʒəntɪv/ N *(Ling)* agentif *m*

agglomerate /əˈɡlɒməreɪt/ VT agglomérer VI s'agglomérer ADJ aggloméré

agglomeration /əˌɡlɒməˈreɪʃən/ N agglomération *f*

agglutinate /əˈɡluːtɪneɪt/ VT agglutiner VI s'agglutiner ADJ agglutiné ; *(Ling)* agglutinant COMP **agglutinating language** N langue *f* agglutinante

agglutination /əˌɡluːtɪˈneɪʃən/ N agglutination *f*

agglutinative /əˈɡluːtɪnətɪv/ ADJ *[substance, language]* agglutinant

aggrandize /əˈɡrændaɪz/ VT agrandir, grandir

aggrandizement /əˈɡrændɪzmənt/ N agrandissement *m* ; *[of influence]* accroissement *m*

aggravate /ˈæɡrəveɪt/ VT 1 *[+ illness]* aggraver, (faire) empirer ; *[+ quarrel, situation]* envenimer ; *[+ pain]* augmenter 2 *(= annoy)* exaspérer, agacer
COMP **aggravated assault** N *(Jur)* violences *fpl* avec voies de fait
aggravated burglary N *(Jur)* cambriolage *m* avec voies de fait

aggravating /ˈæɡrəveɪtɪŋ/ ADJ 1 *(= worsening) [circumstances]* aggravant 2 *(= annoying)* exaspérant, agaçant

aggravation /ˌæɡrəˈveɪʃən/ N 1 *(NonC = exacerbation) [of problem, situation, illness]* aggravation *f* 2 *(= annoyance)* contrariété *f* ◆ **I don't need all this ~** je pourrais me passer de toutes ces contrariétés ◆ **the ~ of having to do sth** la contrariété d'avoir à faire qch

aggregate /ˈæɡrɪɡɪt/ N 1 ensemble *m*, total *m* ◆ **in the ~** dans l'ensemble, en somme ◆ **on ~** = au total des points *(dans le groupe de sélection)* 2 *(Constr, Geol)* agrégat *m* ADJ global, total ◆ **~ value** valeur *f* totale *or* globale VT /ˈæɡrɪɡeɪt/ 1 *(= gather together)* agréger, rassembler 2 *(= amount to)* s'élever à, former un total de VI s'agréger, s'unir en un tout

aggression /əˈɡreʃən/ N *(also Psych)* agression *f* ; *(= aggressiveness)* agressivité *f* ; → **non-aggression**

aggressive /əˈɡresɪv/ ADJ *[person, behaviour, speech]* agressif ; *[salesman, ad etc]* accrocheur ; *(Mil etc) [tactics, action]* offensif ; *(Psych)* agressif

aggressively /əˈɡresɪvlɪ/ ADV agressivement

aggressiveness /əˈɡresɪvnɪs/ N agressivité *f*

aggressor /əˈɡresəʳ/ N agresseur *m*

aggrieved /əˈɡriːvd/ ADJ *(= angry)* fâché, contrarié ; *(= unhappy)* chagriné, mécontent ; → **party**

aggro* /ˈæɡrəʊ/ N *(Brit)* (abbrev of **aggravation**) *(= emotion)* agressivité *f* ; *(= physical violence)* grabuge* *m* ; *(= hassle)* embêtements *mpl* ◆ **don't give me any ~** ne fais pas d'histoires*

aghast /əˈɡɑːst/ ADJ atterré *(at* de) frappé d'horreur

agile /ˈædʒaɪl/ ADJ agile, leste

agility /əˈdʒɪlɪtɪ/ N agilité *f*, souplesse *f*

Agincourt /ˈædʒɪnˌkɔːt/ N Azincourt

aging /ˈeɪdʒɪŋ/ N, ADJ ⇒ **ageing**

agio /ˈædʒɪəʊ/ N agio *m*

agiotage /ˈædʒətɪdʒ/ N agiotage *m*

agism /ˈeɪdʒɪzəm/ N ⇒ **ageism**

agist /ˈeɪdʒɪst/ N, ADJ ⇒ **ageist**

agitate /ˈædʒɪteɪt/ VT 1 *[+ liquid]* agiter, remuer 2 *(= excite, upset)* perturber VI ◆ **to ~ for/against sth** faire campagne *or* mener une campagne en faveur de/contre qch

agitated /ˈædʒɪteɪtɪd/ ADJ inquiet (-ète *f*), agité ◆ **to be very ~** être dans tous ses états

agitatedly /ˈædʒɪteɪtɪdlɪ/ ADV avec agitation

agitation /ˌædʒɪˈteɪʃən/ N 1 *[of person]* agitation *f* ◆ **in a state of ~** agité 2 *(= social unrest)* agitation *f*, troubles *mpl* ; *(= deliberate stirring up)* campagne *f (for* pour ; *against* contre) 3 *[of liquid]* agitation *f*, mouvement *m*

agitator /ˈædʒɪteɪtəʳ/ N 1 *(= person)* agitateur *m*, -trice *f*, fauteur *m* (de troubles) 2 *(= device)* agitateur *m*

agitprop /ˈædʒɪtˌprɒp/ N agit-prop *f inv* ADJ agit-prop *inv*

aglow /əˈɡləʊ/ ADJ *[sky]* embrasé *(liter)* ; *[fire]* rougeoyant, incandescent ◆ **the rising sun sets the landscape ~** le soleil levant embrase le paysage ◆ **~ with health** rayonnant de santé ◆ **she was ~ with pride** elle rayonnait de fierté

AGM /ˌeɪdʒiːˈem/ N *(Brit)* (abbrev of **annual general meeting**) AG *f*, assemblée *f* générale

agnostic /æɡˈnɒstɪk/ ADJ, N agnostique *mf*

agnosticism /æɡˈnɒstɪsɪzəm/ N agnosticisme *m*

ago /əˈɡəʊ/ ADV ◆ **a week ~** il y a huit jours ◆ **how long ~?** il y a combien de temps (de cela) ? ◆ **a little while ~** il y a peu de temps ◆ **he died long ~** il est mort il y a longtemps, il y a longtemps qu'il est mort ◆ **he left ten minutes ~** il est sorti il y a dix minutes *or* depuis dix minutes ◆ **as long ~ as 1950** déjà en 1950, dès 1950 ◆ **no longer ~ than yesterday** pas plus tard qu'hier ; → **long**[1]

agog /əˈɡɒɡ/ ADJ en émoi ◆ **to be ~ (with excitement) about sth** être en émoi à cause de qch ◆ **to set ~** mettre en émoi ◆ **to be ~ to do sth** brûler d'envie de faire qch ◆ **~ for news** impatient d'avoir des nouvelles

agonize /ˈæɡənaɪz/ VI ◆ **to ~ over** *or* **about sth** se tourmenter à propos de qch ◆ **to ~ over how to do sth** se ronger les sangs pour savoir comment faire qch

⚠ In French, **agoniser** means 'to be dying'.

agonized /ˈægənaɪzd/ ADJ *[look]* angoissé ; *[cry, letter]* déchirant

agonizing /ˈægənaɪzɪŋ/ ADJ *[death]* atroce ; *[feeling, decision, choice]* déchirant

agonizingly /ˈægənaɪzɪŋlɪ/ ADV atrocement

agony /ˈægənɪ/ N (= *mental pain*) angoisse *f* ; (= *physical pain*) douleur *f* atroce ◆ **she remembered the ~ she had felt** elle se souvenait de l'angoisse qu'elle avait ressentie ◆ **it was ~** la douleur était atroce ◆ **death ~** agonie *f* ◆ **to be in ~** souffrir le martyre ◆ **to suffer agonies** souffrir le martyre *or* mille morts ◆ **to suffer agonies of doubt/indecision** être en proie aux affres du doute/de l'indécision ◆ **to be in an ~ of indecision** être tourmenté par l'indécision ◆ **to be in an ~ of impatience** mourir d'impatience ; → **prolong**

COMP **agony aunt** * N (Brit Press) *rédactrice de la rubrique du courrier du cœur*

agony column * N (Brit Press) courrier *m* du cœur

agony uncle * N (Brit Press) *rédacteur de la rubrique du courrier du cœur*

⚠ **agony** is only translated **agonie** when it means 'death agony'.

agoraphobia /ˌægərəˈfəʊbɪə/ N agoraphobie *f*

agoraphobic /ˌægərəˈfəʊbɪk/ ADJ agoraphobe

AGR /ˌeɪdʒiːˈɑːʳ/ N (abbrev of **advanced gas-cooled reactor**) → **advanced**

agrammatical /ˌeɪgrəˈmætɪkəl/ ADJ agrammatical

agraphia /ˌeɪˈgræfɪə/ N agraphie *f*

agrarian /əˈgreərɪən/ ADJ *[reform, laws]* agraire ◆ **Agrarian Revolution** réforme(s) *f(pl)* agraire(s) N (Pol Hist) agrarien(ne) *m(f)*

agree /əˈgriː/ LANGUAGE IN USE 11, 12, 26.1, 26.3

VT 1 (= *consent*) consentir (*to do sth* à faire qch) accepter (*to do sth* de faire qch) ; *[+ statement, report]* accepter *or* reconnaître la véracité de ◆ **he ~d to do it** il a consenti à *or* accepté de le faire

2 (= *admit*) reconnaître, admettre (*that* que) ; ◆ **I ~ (that) I was wrong** je reconnais *or* conviens que je me suis trompé

3 (= *come to an agreement*) convenir (*to do sth* de faire qch) se mettre d'accord (*to do sth* pour faire qch) ; *[+ time, price]* se mettre d'accord sur, convenir de ; (= *be of same opinion*) être d'accord (*with* avec ; *that* que) ; ◆ **everyone ~s that we should stay** tout le monde s'accorde à reconnaître que nous devrions rester ◆ **they ~d (amongst themselves) to do it** ils ont convenu de le faire, ils se sont mis d'accord *or* se sont accordés pour le faire ◆ **it was ~d** c'était convenu ◆ **to ~ to disagree** *or* **differ** en rester là, accepter que chacun reste sur ses positions ◆ **I ~ that it's difficult** je suis d'accord que c'est difficile ◆ **the delivery was three days later than ~d** la livraison a été effectuée trois jours après la date convenue ◆ **unless otherwise ~d** (Jur) sauf accord contraire, sauf convention contraire

VI 1 (= *hold same opinion*) être d'accord (*with* avec) être du même avis (*with* que) ; ◆ **I (quite) ~** je suis (tout à fait) d'accord ◆ **I don't ~ (at all)** je ne suis pas (du tout) d'accord ◆ **I ~ about trying again tomorrow** je suis d'accord avec l'idée de réessayer demain ◆ **they all ~d about how dull the play had been** tous ont été d'accord pour dire que la pièce était très ennuyeuse ◆ **she ~s with me that it is unfair** elle est d'accord avec moi pour dire que *or* elle trouve comme moi que c'est injuste ◆ **he entirely ~s with me** il est tout à fait d'accord *or* en plein accord avec moi ◆ **I can't ~ with you there** je ne suis absolument pas d'accord avec vous sur ce point ◆ **I don't ~ with children smoking** je n'admets pas que les enfants fument *subj*

2 (= *come to terms*) se mettre d'accord (*with* avec) ; (= *get on well*) s'entendre (bien), s'accorder (bien) ◆ **to ~ about** *or* **on sth** se mettre d'accord sur qch, convenir de qch ◆ **we haven't ~d about the price/about where to go** nous ne nous sommes pas mis d'accord sur le prix/sur l'endroit où aller, nous n'avons pas convenu du prix/de l'endroit où aller ◆ **they ~d as to** *or* **on how to do it/as to what it should cost** ils sont tombés *or* se sont mis d'accord sur la manière de le faire/sur le prix que cela devrait coûter

◆ **to agree to** ◆ **to ~ to a proposal** accepter une proposition, donner son consentement à une proposition ◆ **he won't ~ to that** il ne sera jamais d'accord, il n'acceptera pas ◆ **I ~ to your marriage/your marrying her** je consens à votre mariage/à ce que vous l'épousiez ◆ **he ~d to the project** il a donné son adhésion au projet

3 *[ideas, stories, assessments]* concorder, coïncider (*with* avec) ; ◆ **his explanation ~s with the facts I already knew** son explication correspond à ce que je savais déjà ◆ **these statements do not ~ with each other** ces affirmations ne concordent pas

4 (Gram) s'accorder (*with* avec ; *in* en)

5 (= *suit the health of*) **sea air ~s with invalids** l'air marin est bon pour les malades *or* réussit aux malades ◆ **the heat does not ~ with her** la chaleur l'incommode ◆ **onions don't ~ with me** les oignons ne me réussissent pas

agreeable /əˈgriːəbl/ ADJ 1 (= *pleasant, friendly*) agréable ◆ **she was always ~ to them** elle était toujours agréable avec eux 2 (*frm* = *willing*) ◆ **if you are ~, we can start immediately** si vous le voulez bien *or* si vous y consentez, nous pouvons commencer immédiatement ◆ **to be ~ to (doing) sth** consentir volontiers à (faire) qch ◆ **I am quite ~** volontiers ◆ **I am quite ~ to doing it** je le ferai très volontiers 3 (*frm* = *acceptable*) ◆ **we can start the work tomorrow, if that's ~** nous pouvons commencer le travail demain si vous n'y voyez pas d'inconvénient ◆ **is that ~ to you?** est-ce que cela vous convient ?, cela vous agrée-t-il ? (*frm*)

agreeably /əˈgriːəblɪ/ ADV *[chat, spend time]* agréablement ; *[say, smile]* aimablement ◆ **~ surprised** agréablement surpris

agreed /əˈgriːd/ LANGUAGE IN USE 11 ADJ 1 d'accord ◆ **we are ~** nous sommes d'accord (*about* au sujet de, à propos de ; *on* sur) ; ◆ **the ministers were ~** les ministres sont tombés d'accord 2 *[time, place, amount]* convenu ◆ **it's all ~** c'est tout décidé *or* convenu ◆ **as ~** comme convenu ◆ **it's ~ that ...** il est convenu que ... + *indic* ◆ **(is that) ~?** entendu ?, d'accord ? ◆ **~!** entendu !, d'accord !

agreement /əˈgriːmənt/ N 1 (= *mutual understanding*) accord *m*, harmonie *f* ◆ **to be in ~ on a subject** être d'accord sur un sujet ◆ **by (mutual) ~** (= *both thinking same*) d'un commun accord ; (*without quarrelling*) à l'amiable 2 (= *arrangement, contract*) accord *m* ; (Pol, *frm*) pacte *m* ◆ **to come to an ~** parvenir à une entente, tomber d'accord ◆ **to sign an ~** signer un accord ◆ **the Helsinki ~** les accords *mpl* d'Helsinki ; → **gentleman** 3 (Gram) accord *m*

agribusiness /ˈægrɪˌbɪznɪs/ N agro-industries *fpl*

agricultural /ˌægrɪˈkʌltʃərəl/ ADJ agricole

COMP **agricultural college** N école *f* d'agriculture

agricultural engineer N ingénieur *m* agronome

agricultural expert N expert *m* agronome

agricultural show N exposition *f* agricole

agricultural worker N travailleur *m* agricole

agriculture /ˈægrɪkʌltʃəʳ/ N agriculture *f* ◆ **Minister/Ministry of Agriculture** (Brit) ◆ **Secretary/Department of Agriculture** (US) ministre *m*/ministère *m* de l'Agriculture

agricultur(al)ist /ˌægrɪˈkʌltʃər(əl)ɪst/ N agronome *mf* ; (= *farmer*) agriculteur *m*

agrifoodstuffs /ˈægrɪˈt/ NPL agro-alimentaire *m*

agri(-)tourism /ˈægrɪˈtʊərɪzəm/ N tourisme *m* vert, agritourisme *m*

agrobiology /ˌægrəʊbaɪˈɒlədʒɪ/ N agrobiologie *f*

agrochemical /ˌægrəʊˈkemɪkəl/ ADJ agrochimique N produit *m* chimique à usage agricole ◆ **~s** *[industry]* agrochimie *f*

agro(-)forestry /əˈgrəʊˈfɒrɪstrɪ/ N agroforesterie *f*

agronomist /əˈgrɒnəmɪst/ N agronome *mf*

agronomy /əˈgrɒnəmɪ/ N agronomie *f*

aground /əˈgraʊnd/ ADV, ADJ *[ship]* échoué ◆ **to be ~** toucher le fond ◆ **to be fast ~** être bien échoué ◆ **to run ~** s'échouer, se jeter à la côte

ague †† /ˈeɪgjuː/ N (Med) fièvre *f*

ah /ɑː/ EXCL ah !

aha /ɑːˈhɑː/ EXCL ah, ah !

ahead /əˈhed/

When **ahead** is an element in a phrasal verb, eg **book ahead, draw ahead, fire ahead, go ahead**, look up the verb.

ADV 1 (*in space*) en avant, devant ◆ **stay here, I'll go on ~** restez ici, moi je vais en avant *or* devant ◆ **to get ~** (*lit, fig*) prendre de l'avance ◆ **full speed ~!** (Naut, *also fig*) en avant toute !

2 (*in classification, sport etc*) en tête ◆ **to be five points** *etc* **~** avoir une avance de cinq points *etc* ◆ **the goal put Scotland 2-1 ~** grâce à ce but, l'Écosse menait 2 à 1

3 (*in time*) *[book]* à l'avance ◆ **~ of time** *[decide, announce]* d'avance ; *[arrive, be ready]* avant l'heure, en avance ◆ **the project's ~ of schedule** le projet est plus avancé que prévu ◆ **the project's two months ~ of schedule** le projet est en avance de deux mois sur le planning *or* sur le programme prévu ◆ **~ of the meeting** avant la réunion ◆ **two hours ~ of the next car** avec deux heures d'avance sur la voiture suivante ◆ **he's two hours ~ of you** il a deux heures d'avance sur vous ◆ **clocks here are two hours ~ of clocks over there** les pendules d'ici ont deux heures d'avance sur celles de là-bas, il y a un décalage horaire de deux heures entre ici et là-bas ◆ **the months ~** les mois à venir ◆ **there are difficult times ~** l'avenir s'annonce difficile ◆ **to think** *or* **plan ~** prévoir (à l'avance) ◆ **looking** *or* **thinking ~ five years, what ...** essayez d'imaginer la situation dans cinq ans : qu'est-ce que ... ◆ **to plan ~** faire des projets ◆ **to be ~ of one's time** être en avance sur son temps ◆ **what is** *or* **lies ~** ce que l'avenir nous réserve ◆ **what is** *or* **lies ~ for him/us** ce que l'avenir lui/nous réserve

ahem /əˈhem/ EXCL hum !

ahold /əˈhəʊld/ N (*esp US*) ◆ **to get ~ of sb** (= *contact*) contacter qn, joindre qn ; (= *grab*) saisir qn ◆ **to get ~ of sth** (= *obtain*) mettre la main sur qch ; (= *grab*) saisir qch ◆ **to get ~ of o.s.** (= *pull o.s. together*) se ressaisir ; (= *control o.s.*) se maîtriser

ahoy /əˈhɔɪ/ EXCL (Naut) ohé ! ◆ **ship ~!** ohé du navire !

AI /eɪˈaɪ/ N 1 (abbrev of **artificial intelligence**) IA *f*, intelligence *f* artificielle 2 (abbrev of **artificial insemination**) IA *f*, insémination *f* artificielle 3 abbrev of **Amnesty International**

AID /ˌeɪaɪˈdiː/ N 1 (abbrev of **artificial insemination by donor**) IAD *f* 2 (US) abbrev of **Agency for International Development** 3 (US Admin) abbrev of **Aid to Families with Dependent Children**

aid /eɪd/ **N** 1 *(NonC)* *(= help)* aide *f*, assistance *f* ; *(international)* aide *f* ◆ **by** *or* **with the ~ of sb** avec l'aide de qn ◆ **by** *or* **with the ~ of sth** à l'aide de qch

◆ **in aid of** *(esp Brit)* ◆ **sale in ~ of the blind** vente *f* (de charité) au profit des aveugles ◆ **what is the meeting in ~ of?*** c'est dans quel but *or* en quel honneur*, cette réunion ?

2 *(= helper)* aide *mf*, assistant(e) *m(f)* ; *(gen pl = equipment, apparatus)* aide *f* ◆ **audio-visual ~s** supports *mpl* *or* moyens *mpl* audiovisuels ◆ **teaching ~s** outils *mpl* *or* matériel *m* pédagogique(s) ; → **deaf**

VT *[+ person]* aider ; *[+ progress, recovery]* contribuer à ◆ **to ~ one another** s'entraider, s'aider les uns les autres ◆ **to ~ sb to do sth** aider qn à faire qch ◆ **to ~ and abet (sb)** *(Jur)* être complice (de qn)

COMP **aid agency** **N** organisation *f* humanitaire

aid climbing **N** *(Climbing)* escalade *f* artificielle

aide /eɪd/ **N** aide *mf*, assistant(e) *m(f)* ; *(US Pol)* conseiller *m*, -ère *f*

COMP **aide-de-camp** **N** (pl **aides-de-camp**) aide *m* de camp

aide-mémoire **N** (pl **aides-mémoire**) mémorandum *m*

AIDS, Aids, aids /eɪdz/ **N** (abbrev of **acquired immune deficiency syndrome**) sida *m*

COMP **AIDS patient** **N** sidéen(ne) *m(f)*, malade *mf* du sida

AIDS-related **ADJ** associé au sida

AIDS-related complex **N** ARC *m*

AIDS victim **N** ⇒ **AIDS patient**

aigrette /ˈeɡret/ **N** aigrette *f*

AIH /ˌeɪaɪˈeɪtʃ/ **N** (abbrev of **artificial insemination by husband**) IAC *f*

aikido /ˈaɪkɪdəʊ/ **N** aïkido *m*

ail /eɪl/ **VT** affliger ◆ **what ~s you?** † qu'avez-vous ? **VI** être souffrant

aileron /ˈeɪlərɒn/ **N** *(of plane)* aileron *m*

ailing /ˈeɪlɪŋ/ **ADJ** souffrant ◆ **she is always ~** elle est de santé fragile, elle a une petite santé ◆ **an ~ company** une compagnie qui périclite

ailment /ˈeɪlmənt/ **N** affection *f* ◆ **all his (little) ~s** tous ses maux *mpl*

AIM /ˌeɪaɪˈem/ **N** *(Brit)* (abbrev of **Alternative Investment Market**) AIM *m*, nouveau marché *m* *(second marché de Londres)*

aim /eɪm/ **N** 1 ◆ **his ~ is bad** il vise mal ◆ **to take ~ (at sb/sth)** viser (qn/qch) ◆ **to miss one's ~** manquer la cible

2 *(= purpose)* but *m* ◆ **with the ~ of doing sth** dans le but de faire qch ◆ **her ~ is to work in London** elle a pour but de travailler à Londres ◆ **the ~ of this policy is to ...** cette politique vise à ... ◆ **the ~ of this government is to ...** le but que s'est fixé le gouvernement est de ... ◆ **his ~s are open to suspicion** ses visées *or* ses ambitions sont suspectes ◆ **political ~s** finalités *fpl* *or* buts *mpl* politiques

VT 1 *(= direct)* *[+ hosepipe, extinguisher]* pointer, diriger ; *[+ gun]* braquer *(at* sur) ; *[+ missile]* pointer *(at* sur) ; *[+ blow]* allonger, décocher *(at* à) ; *[+ remark]* diriger *(at* contre) ; ◆ **to ~ a gun at sb** braquer un revolver sur qn, viser qn avec un revolver ◆ **to ~ a stone at sb** *(= throw)* lancer une pierre sur *or* à qn ◆ **his remarks are ~ed at his father** ses remarques visent son père

2 *(= intend)* viser, aspirer *(to do sth, at doing sth* à faire qch)

VI viser ◆ **to ~ at** *(lit)* viser ; *(fig)* viser, aspirer à ; → **high**

aimless /ˈeɪmlɪs/ **ADJ** *[person, way of life]* sans but, désœuvré ; *[activity, pursuit]* qui ne mène à rien, futile

aimlessly /ˈeɪmlɪslɪ/ **ADV** *[wander, drift]* sans but ; *[chat]* à bâtons rompus

aimlessness /ˈeɪmlɪsnɪs/ **N** ◆ **a mood of ~ and despair** une sensation d'errance *(liter)* et de désespoir ◆ **his sense of ~** le sentiment qu'il éprouvait de ne pas avoir de but dans la vie

ain't‡ /eɪnt/ ⇒ **am not, is not, are not, has not, have not** ; → **be, have**

air /ɛəʳ/ **N** 1 air *m* ◆ **in the open ~** en plein air ◆ **a change of ~** un changement d'air ◆ **I need some ~!** j'ai besoin d'air ! ◆ **to go out for a breath of (fresh) ~** sortir prendre l'air ◆ **to take the ~** † prendre le frais ◆ **to throw sth (up) into the ~** jeter *or* lancer qch en l'air ◆ **the balloon rose up into the ~** le ballon s'est élevé (dans les airs) ◆ **(seen) from the ~** vu d'en haut ◆ **I can't live on ~** je ne peux pas vivre de l'air du temps ◆ **to be walking** *or* **treading on ~** être aux anges, ne pas se sentir de joie ◆ **to pull** *or* **pluck a figure out of the ~** donner un chiffre au hasard ◆ **to give sb the ~*** *(US)* *[employer]* virer* *or* renvoyer qn ; *[girlfriend etc]* plaquer‡ qn

◆ **by air** par avion ◆ **to transport sth by ~** transporter qch par avion ◆ **to go by ~** aller en avion, voyager par avion

◆ **in the air** *(fig)* ◆ **there's something in the ~** il se prépare quelque chose, il se trame quelque chose ◆ **there's a rumour in the ~ that ...** le bruit court que ... ◆ **it's still all in the ~** ce ne sont encore que des projets en l'air *or* de vagues projets ◆ **all her plans were up in the ~** *(= vague)* tous ses projets étaient vagues *or* flous ◆ **all her plans have gone up in the ~** *(= destroyed)* tous ses projets sont tombés à l'eau ◆ **he went up in the ~* when he heard the news** *(in anger)* il a bondi en apprenant la nouvelle ; *(in excitement)* il a sauté d'enthousiasme en apprenant la nouvelle ◆ **to be up in the ~ about* ...** *(= angry)* être très monté *or* très en colère à l'idée de ... ; *(= excited)* être tout en émoi *or* très excité à l'idée de ...

◆ **off (the) air** ◆ **to go off (the) ~** quitter l'antenne

◆ **on (the) air** *(Rad)* à la radio, sur les ondes, à l'antenne ; *(TV)* à l'antenne ◆ **you're on (the) ~** vous êtes à l'antenne, vous avez l'antenne ◆ **he's on (the) ~ every day** il passe tous les jours à la radio ◆ **the station is on the ~** la station émet ◆ **the programme goes** *or* **is on (the) ~ every week** l'émission passe (sur l'antenne) *or* est diffusée toutes les semaines

2 *(† = breeze)* brise *f*, léger souffle *m*

3 *(= manner)* air *m* ◆ **with an ~ of bewilderment/superiority** d'un air perplexe/supérieur ◆ **with a proud ~** d'un air fier, avec une mine hautaine ◆ **she has an ~ about her** elle a de l'allure, elle a un certain chic ◆ **to put on ~s, to give o.s. ~s** se donner de grands airs ◆ **~s and graces** minauderies *fpl* ◆ **to put on ~s and graces** minauder

4 *(Mus)* air *m*

VT 1 *[+ clothes, room, bed]* aérer

2 *[+ anger]* exhaler ; *[+ opinions]* faire connaître ; *[+ idea, proposal]* mettre sur le tapis

3 *(esp US* = broadcast)* diffuser

VI *(TV, Rad = be broadcast)* être diffusé

COMP **air alert** **N** alerte *f* aérienne

air ambulance **N** *(= plane)* avion *m* sanitaire ; *(= helicopter)* hélicoptère *m* sanitaire

air base **N** base *f* aérienne

air bed **N** *(Brit)* matelas *m* pneumatique

air brake **N** *(on truck)* frein *m* à air comprimé ; *(on plane)* frein *m* aérodynamique, aérofrein *m*

air brick **N** brique *f* évidée *or* creuse

air bridge **N** pont *m* aérien

air-brush **N** aérographe *m* **VT** *(lit)* retoucher à l'aérographe ; *(fig)* embellir

air bubble **N** *(in liquids)* bulle *f* d'air ; *(in glass, metal)* soufflure *f*

air burst **N** explosion *f* aérienne

air chamber **N** chambre *f* à air

air chief marshal **N** *(Brit)* général *m* d'armée aérienne

air commodore **N** *(Brit)* général *m* de brigade aérienne

air-con **N** ⇒ **air conditioning**

air-conditioned **ADJ** climatisé

air conditioner **N** climatiseur *m*

air conditioning **N** climatisation *f*, air *m* conditionné

air-cooled **ADJ** *[+ engine]* à refroidissement par air ; *(US *)* *[+ room]* climatisé

air corridor **N** couloir *m* aérien

air cover **N** couverture *f* aérienne

air crash **N** accident *m* d'avion

air current **N** courant *m* atmosphérique

air cushion **N** coussin *m* pneumatique ; *(Tech)* matelas *m* *or* coussin *m* d'air

air cylinder **N** bouteille *f* d'air comprimé

air disaster **N** catastrophe *f* aérienne

air display **N** meeting *m* aérien

air-dry **VT** sécher à l'air

air duct **N** conduit *m* d'aération

air express **N** *(US)* cargo *m* aérien

air ferry **N** avion *m* transbordeur

air filter **N** filtre *m* à air

air flow **N** courant *m* atmosphérique ; *(in wind tunnel)* écoulement *m* d'air

air force **N** armée *f* de l'air, aviation *f* militaire

air-force blue **ADJ** bleu gris *inv*

Air Force One **N** *(US)* l'avion *m* présidentiel

air freight **N** *(= goods)* fret *m* aérien ; *(= method)* transport *m* aérien ◆ **to send by ~ freight** expédier par voie aérienne *or* par avion

air freshener **N** désodorisant *m*

air guitar **N** *(hum)* *guitare imaginaire dont on fait semblant de jouer en écoutant de la musique*

air hole **N** trou *m* d'aération

air hostess **N** *(Brit)* hôtesse *f* de l'air

air intake **N** arrivée *f* d'air, prise *f* d'air

air lane **N** couloir *m* aérien *or* de navigation aérienne

air letter **N** aérogramme *m*

air marshal **N** général *m* de corps aérien

air mass **N** *(Weather)* masse *f* d'air

air mattress **N** matelas *m* pneumatique

air miles **NPL** miles *mpl*

air miss **N** quasi-collision *f*

air pistol **N** pistolet *m* à air comprimé

air pocket **N** trou *m* *or* poche *f* d'air

air power **N** puissance *f* aérienne

air pressure **N** pression *f* atmosphérique

air pump **N** compresseur *m*, machine *f* pneumatique

air purifier **N** purificateur *m* d'air

air rage **N** *comportement agressif de passager(s) dans un avion*

air raid **N** attaque *f* aérienne, raid *m* aérien

air-raid precautions **NPL** défense *f* passive

air-raid shelter **N** abri *m* antiaérien

air-raid warden **N** préposé(e) *m(f)* à la défense passive

air-raid warning **N** alerte *f* (aérienne)

air rifle **N** carabine *f* à air comprimé

air-sea base **N** base *f* aéronavale

air-sea missile **N** missile *m* air-mer

air-sea rescue **N** sauvetage *m* en mer *(par hélicoptère etc)*

air shaft **N** *(Min)* puits *m* d'aérage ; *(Naut)* manche *f* à vent

air show **N** *(= trade exhibition)* salon *m* de l'aéronautique ; *(= flying display)* meeting *m* aérien

air shuttle **N** navette *f* aérienne

air sock **N** manche *f* à air

air space **N** espace *m* aérien ◆ **French ~ space** l'espace *m* aérien français

air stream **N** courant *m* atmosphérique ; *(Ling)* colonne *f* d'air

air superiority **N** supériorité *f* aérienne

air suspension **N** *(in vehicle)* suspension *f* pneumatique

air terminal N aérogare *f*
air ticket N billet *m* d'avion
air time N temps *m* d'antenne
air-to-air ADJ *(Mil)* air-air *inv*, avion-avion *inv*
air-to-ground ADJ *(Mil)* air-sol *inv*
air-to-sea ADJ *(Mil)* air-mer *inv*
air-to-surface ADJ ⇒ **air-to-ground**
air traffic control N contrôle *m* du trafic aérien
air traffic controller N contrôleur *m*, -euse *f* de la navigation aérienne, aiguilleur *m* du ciel
air valve N soupape *f*
air vent N prise *f* d'air
air vice marshal N *(Brit)* général *m* de division aérienne
air waves † NPL ondes *fpl* (hertziennes) ◆ **on the ~ waves** *(= on radio)* sur les ondes

airbag /ˈɛəbæg/ N *(in vehicle)* airbag ® *m*

airborne /ˈɛəbɔːn/ ADJ *[+ troops]* aéroporté ◆ **the plane was ~** l'avion avait décollé

Airbus ® /ˈɛəbʌs/ N Airbus ® *m*

aircraft /ˈɛəkrɑːft/ N *(pl inv)* avion *m* COMP **aircraft carrier** N porte-avions *m inv*

aircraft(s)man /ˈɛəkrɑːft(s)mən/ N (pl **-men**) *(Brit)* soldat *m* de deuxième classe (de l'armée de l'air)

aircrew /ˈɛəkruː/ N équipage *m*

airdrome /ˈɛədrəʊm/ N *(US)* aérodrome *m*

airdrop /ˈɛədrɒp/ VT parachuter N parachutage *m*

Airedale /ˈɛədeɪl/ N (also **Airedale terrier**) airedale *m*

airfare /ˈɛəfɛəʳ/ N prix *m* du billet d'avion ◆ **she paid my ~** elle a payé mon billet d'avion

airfield /ˈɛəfiːld/ N terrain *m* d'aviation, (petit) aérodrome *m*

airfoil /ˈɛəfɔɪl/ N *(US)* ⇒ **aerofoil**

airframe /ˈɛəfreɪm/ N cellule *f* (d'avion)

airgun /ˈɛəgʌn/ N fusil *m* or carabine *f* à air comprimé

airhead * /ˈɛəhed/ N cruche * *f*

airily /ˈɛərɪlɪ/ ADV *[say, dismiss]* avec désinvolture

airiness /ˈɛərɪnɪs/ N ◆ **feeling of ~** impression *f* d'espace

airing /ˈɛərɪŋ/ N *(fig)* ◆ **to give an idea an ~** mettre une idée sur le tapis COMP **airing cupboard** N *(Brit)* placard-séchoir *m*

airless /ˈɛəlɪs/ ADJ 1 *[room]* privé d'air ◆ **it is ~ in here** il n'y a pas d'air ici, cela sent le renfermé ici 2 *[weather]* lourd

airlift /ˈɛəlɪft/ N pont *m* aérien VT évacuer par pont aérien

airline /ˈɛəlaɪn/ N 1 (also *airline company*) compagnie *f* aérienne 2 *(diver's)* voie *f* d'air

airliner /ˈɛəlaɪnəʳ/ N avion *m* de ligne, (avion *m*) long-courrier *m* or moyen-courrier *m*

airlock /ˈɛəlɒk/ N 1 *(in spacecraft, caisson etc)* sas *m* 2 *(in pipe)* bulle *f* d'air

airmail /ˈɛəmeɪl/ N poste *f* aérienne ◆ **by ~** par avion VT *[+ letter, parcel]* expédier par avion COMP **airmail edition** N édition *f* par avion
airmail letter N lettre *f* par avion
airmail paper N papier *m* pelure
airmail stamp, airmail sticker N étiquette *f* "par avion"

airman /ˈɛəmən/ N (pl **-men**) aviateur *m* ; *(Brit)* soldat *m* de l'armée de l'air ; *(US)* soldat *m* de première classe COMP **airman first class** N *(US)* caporal *m*

airmobile /ˈɛəməbiːl/ ADJ *(US Mil)* aéroporté

airplane /ˈɛəpleɪn/ N *(US)* avion *m*

airplay /ˈɛəpleɪ/ N *(on radio)* temps *m* de passage à l'antenne ◆ **to get a lot of ~** passer souvent à l'antenne

airport /ˈɛəpɔːt/ N aéroport *m* COMP **airport bus** N bus *m* de l'aéroport
airport lounge N salon *m* d'aéroport
airport tax(es) N(PL) taxes *fpl* d'aéroport

airscrew /ˈɛəskruː/ N *(Brit)* hélice *f*

airshed /ˈɛəʃed/ N hangar *m* (d'aviation)

airship /ˈɛəʃɪp/ N dirigeable *m*

airsick /ˈɛəsɪk/ ADJ ◆ **to be ~** avoir le mal de l'air ◆ **I get ~** je souffre du mal de l'air

airsickness /ˈɛəsɪknɪs/ N mal *m* de l'air

airspeed /ˈɛəspiːd/ N *[of aircraft]* vitesse *f* relative COMP **airspeed indicator** N badin *m*, anémomètre *m*

airstrike /ˈɛəstraɪk/ N ⇒ **air raid** ; → **air**

airstrip /ˈɛəstrɪp/ N piste *f* (d'atterrissage)

airtight /ˈɛətaɪt/ ADJ hermétique

airway /ˈɛəweɪ/ N *(= route)* voie *f* aérienne ; *(= airline company)* compagnie *f* aérienne ; *(= ventilator shaft)* conduit *m* d'air NPL **airways** voies *fpl* respiratoires

airwoman /ˈɛəwʊmən/ N (pl **-women**) aviatrice *f* ; *(in air force)* auxiliaire *f* de l'armée de l'air

airworthiness /ˈɛəwɜːðɪnɪs/ N navigabilité *f* ; → **certificate**

airworthy /ˈɛəwɜːðɪ/ ADJ en état de navigation

airy /ˈɛərɪ/ ADJ 1 *(= spacious) [room, building]* clair et spacieux 2 *(= lightweight) [fabric]* léger 3 *(= casual) [manner, gesture, wave]* désinvolte 4 *(= empty) [promise, idea]* en l'air COMP **airy-fairy** * ADJ *(Brit) [idea, person]* farfelu

aisle /aɪl/ N 1 *[of church] (central)* allée *f* centrale ; *(side)* bas-côté *m* ◆ **to take a girl up the ~** † mener une jeune fille à l'autel ◆ **to walk up the ~ with sb** *(fig)* épouser qn 2 *[of theatre, cinema, supermarket]* allée *f* ; *[of plane, train, coach]* couloir *m* ◆ **~ seat** *(on plane etc)* place *f* côté couloir

aitch /eɪtʃ/ N *(= letter)* H, h *m* ◆ **~ bone** *(Culin)* culotte *f* (de bœuf) ; → **drop**

Ajaccio /əˈʒæsjəʊ/ N Ajaccio

ajar /əˈdʒɑːʳ/ ADJ, ADV entrouvert, entrebâillé

Ajax /ˈeɪdʒæks/ N Ajax *m*

AK abbrev of **Alaska**

AKA, aka /ˌeɪkeɪˈeɪ/ (abbrev of **also known as**) alias

akimbo /əˈkɪmbəʊ/ ADJ ◆ **with arms ~** les poings sur les hanches

akin /əˈkɪn/ ADJ ◆ **~ to** *(= similar)* qui tient de, qui ressemble à, analogue à ; *(= of same family as)* parent de, apparenté à

AL, Ala. abbrev of **Alabama**

Alabama /ˌæləˈbæmə/ N Alabama *m* ◆ **in ~** en Alabama

alabaster /ˈæləbɑːstəʳ/ N albâtre *m* ADJ *(lit, fig)* d'albâtre

alacrity /əˈlækrɪtɪ/ N empressement *m* ◆ **with ~** avec empressement

Aladdin /əˈlædɪn/ N Aladin *m* COMP **Aladdin's cave** N *(fig)* caverne *f* d'Ali Baba

alarm /əˈlɑːm/ N 1 *(= warning)* alarme *f*, alerte *f* ◆ **to raise the ~** donner l'alarme or l'éveil ◆ **~s and excursions** *(Theat)* bruits *mpl* de bataille en coulisse ; *(fig)* branle-bas *m* de combat ; → **burglar, false**
2 *(NonC = fear)* inquiétude *f*, alarme *f* ◆ **to cause sb ~** mettre qn dans l'inquiétude, alarmer qn
3 ⇒ **alarm clock**
VT 1 *(= frighten) [+ person]* alarmer, éveiller des craintes chez ; *[+ animal, bird]* effaroucher, faire peur à ◆ **to become** or **be ~ed** *[person]* prendre peur, s'alarmer ; *[animal]* prendre peur, s'effaroucher
2 *(= warn)* alerter, alarmer
COMP **alarm bell** N sonnerie *f* d'alarme ◆ **the court's decision has set ~ bells ringing in government** la décision du tribunal a alerté or inquiété le gouvernement
alarm call N *(Telec)* appel *m* du service réveil ◆ **I'd like an ~ call (for 6 am)** je voudrais être réveillé (à 6 heures)
alarm clock N réveil *m*
alarm signal N signal *m* d'alarme
alarm system N système *m* d'alarme

alarming /əˈlɑːmɪŋ/ ADJ alarmant

alarmingly /əˈlɑːmɪŋlɪ/ ADV *[rise, deteriorate]* de façon alarmante ◆ **the deadline is ~ close** la date limite se rapproche de manière inquiétante ◆ **~ quickly** à une vitesse alarmante ◆ **an ~ high divorce rate** un taux de divorce qui atteint des niveaux alarmants ◆ **~, there was a sharp fall in house prices** fait alarmant, il y a eu une forte chute des prix de l'immobilier

alarmist /əˈlɑːmɪst/ ADJ, N alarmiste *mf*

alas /əˈlæs/ EXCL hélas !

Alas. abbrev of **Alaska**

Alaska /əˈlæskə/ N Alaska *m* ◆ **in ~** en Alaska ◆ **~ Highway** route *f* de l'Alaska ◆ **~ Range** chaîne *f* de l'Alaska ; → **bake**

Alaskan /əˈlæskən/ ADJ de l'Alaska N habitant(e) *m(f)* de l'Alaska

alb /ælb/ N aube *f (d'un prêtre)*

Albania /ælˈbeɪnɪə/ N Albanie *f*

Albanian /ælˈbeɪnɪən/ ADJ albanais N 1 *(= person)* Albanais(e) *m(f)* 2 *(= language)* albanais *m*

albatross /ˈælbətrɒs/ N *(also Golf)* albatros *m* ; *(= burden)* boulet *m* ◆ **to be an ~ around sb's neck** être un boulet pour qn

albeit /ɔːlˈbiːɪt/ CONJ *(frm)* bien que + *subj*

Alberta /ælˈbɜːtə/ N Alberta *m*

Albigensian /ˌælbɪˈdʒensɪən/ ADJ albigeois ◆ **the ~ Heresy** l'hérésie *f* cathare N Albigeois(e) *m(f)*

albinism /ˈælbɪnɪzəm/ N albinisme *m*

albino /ælˈbiːnəʊ/ N albinos *mf* ◆ **~ rabbit** lapin *m* albinos

Albion /ˈælbɪən/ N Albion *f*

album /ˈælbəm/ N *(= book, record etc)* album *m* COMP **album cover** N pochette *f* (de disque)

albumen, albumin /ˈælbjʊmɪn/ N *(= egg white)* albumen *m*, blanc *m* de l'œuf ; *(= endosperm)* albumen *m* ; *(Physiol)* albumine *f*

albuminous /ælˈbjuːmɪnəs/ ADJ albumineux

Alcestis /ælˈsestɪs/ N Alceste *f*

alchemical /ælˈkemɪkəl/ ADJ alchimique

alchemist /ˈælkɪmɪst/ N alchimiste *m*

alchemy /ˈælkɪmɪ/ N *(lit, fig)* alchimie *f*

alcohol /ˈælkəhɒl/ N alcool *m* COMP **alcohol abuse** N abus *m* d'alcool
alcohol abuser N alcoolique *mf*
alcohol consumption N consommation *f* d'alcool
alcohol content N *[of drink]* teneur *f* en alcool
alcohol-free ADJ sans alcool

alcoholic /ˌælkəˈhɒlɪk/ ADJ *[person]* alcoolique ; *[drink]* alcoolisé N alcoolique *mf* ◆ **Alcoholics Anonymous** Alcooliques *mpl* anonymes

alcoholism /ˈælkəhɒlɪzəm/ N alcoolisme *m*

alcopop /ˈælkəˌpɒp/ N *(Brit)* prémix *m*

alcove /ˈælkəʊv/ N *(in room)* alcôve *f* ; *(in wall)* niche *f* ; *(in garden)* tonnelle *f*, berceau *m*

aldehyde /ˈældɪhaɪd/ N aldéhyde *m*

alder /ˈɔːldəʳ/ N aulne or aune *m*

alderman /ˈɔːldəmən/ N (pl **-men**) alderman *m*, conseiller *m*, -ère *f* municipal(e) ; *(Hist)* échevin *m*

ale /eɪl/ N bière *f*, ale *f* ; → **brown, light², pale¹**

aleatoric /ˌælɪəˈtɒrɪk/ ADJ *(Mus)* aléatoire

alehouse †† /ˈeɪlˌhaʊs/ N taverne *f*

Aleppo /əˈlepəʊ/ N Alep

alert /əˈlɜːt/ N alerte *f* ◆ **to give the ~** donner l'alerte ◆ **on the ~** *(gen)* sur le qui-vive ; *(Mil)* en état d'alerte ADJ [1] *(= watchful)* vigilant [2] *(= aware)* ◆ **to be ~ to sth** avoir conscience de qch [3] *(= acute)* *[old person]* alerte ; *[child]* éveillé ◆ **to be mentally ~** avoir l'esprit vif VT alerter ; *(fig)* éveiller l'attention de (to sur) ; ◆ **we are now ~ed to the dangers** nous sommes maintenant sensibilisés aux dangers

alertly /əˈlɜːtlɪ/ ADV *[look, watch]* d'un œil alerte

alertness /əˈlɜːtnɪs/ N (NonC) [1] *(= watchfulness) [of person, animal]* vigilance *f* [2] *(= liveliness) [of person]* vivacité *f* ◆ **mental ~** vivacité *f* d'esprit

Aleutian /əˈluːʃən/ ADJ ◆ **the ~ Islands, the ~s** les (îles *fpl*) Aléoutiennes *fpl*

alevin /ˈælɪvɪn/ N alevin *m*

alewife /ˈeɪlwaɪf/ N (pl **-wives**) alose *f*

Alexander /ˌælɪgˈzɑːndəʳ/ N Alexandre *m*

Alexandria /ˌælɪgˈzɑːndrɪə/ N Alexandrie

alexandrine /ˌælɪgˈzændraɪn/ ADJ, N alexandrin *m*

ALF /ˌeɪelˈef/ N (Brit) (abbrev of **Animal Liberation Front**) *Front britannique de libération des animaux*

alfalfa /ælˈfælfə/ N luzerne *f*

alfresco /ælˈfreskəʊ/ ADJ, ADV en plein air

alga /ˈælgə/ N (pl **algae** /ˈældʒiː/) *(gen pl)* algue(s) *f(pl)*

algal /ˈælgəl/ ADJ algal

algebra /ˈældʒɪbrə/ N algèbre *f*

algebraic /ˌældʒɪˈbreɪɪk/ ADJ algébrique

Algeria /ælˈdʒɪərɪə/ N Algérie *f*

Algerian /ælˈdʒɪərɪən/ ADJ algérien N Algérien(ne) *m(f)*

Algiers /ælˈdʒɪəz/ N Alger

Algonquian /ˌælˈgɒŋkwɪən/, **Algonquin** /ælˈgɒŋkwɪn/ ADJ algonquin, algonkin

algorithm /ˈælgəˌrɪðəm/ N *(Comput, Ling)* algorithme *m*

algorithmic /ˌælgəˈrɪðmɪk/ ADJ algorithmique

Alhambra /ælˈhæmbrə/ N Alhambra *m*

alias /ˈeɪlɪəs/ ADV alias N faux nom *m*, nom *m* d'emprunt ; *[of writer]* pseudonyme *m*

Ali Baba /ˈælɪˈbɑːbɑː/ N Ali Baba *m*

alibi /ˈælɪbaɪ/ N *(Police)* alibi *m* ; (*: *gen*) excuse *f*, alibi *m (hum)* VI *(US *)* trouver des excuses *(for sth* pour expliquer qch ; *for doing sth* pour avoir fait qch) VT *(US)* ◆ **to ~ sb** * trouver des excuses à qn

Alice /ˈælɪs/ N Alice *f* ◆ **~ in Wonderland** Alice au pays des merveilles COMP **Alice band** N *(Brit)* bandeau *m (pour les cheveux)*

alien /ˈeɪlɪən/ N [1] *(from abroad)* étranger *m*, -ère *f* ◆ **resident/non-resident ~** étranger *m*, -ère *f* résident(e)/non résident(e) [2] *(from outer space)* extra-terrestre *mf* ADJ [1] *(= foreign) [forces, environment, concept]* étranger *(to sb/sth* à qn/qch) [2] *(= from outer space) [spacecraft, species, civilization]* extraterrestre ◆ **~ being** extraterrestre *mf*

alienate /ˈeɪlɪəneɪt/ VT *(also Jur)* aliéner ◆ **this has ~d all his friends** ceci (lui) a aliéné tous ses amis ◆ **she has ~d all her friends** elle s'est aliéné tous ses amis *(by doing sth* en faisant qch)

alienated /ˈeɪlɪəneɪtɪd/ ADJ *(= estranged)* étranger *(from* à) ; *(Psych)* aliéné ◆ **to become ~ from sb/sth** se détacher de qn/qch

alienation /ˌeɪlɪəˈneɪʃən/ N [1] *(= estrangement)* désaffection *f*, éloignement *m* (from de) [2] *(Jur, Psych)* aliénation *f*

alienist /ˈeɪlɪənɪst/ N aliéniste *mf*

alight¹ /əˈlaɪt/ VI *[person]* descendre (from de) ; *[bird]* se poser (on sur)

► **alight on** VT FUS *[+ fact]* apprendre par hasard ; *[+ idea]* tomber sur

alight² /əˈlaɪt/ ADJ [1] *(= lit)* ◆ **to be ~** *[candle, fire]* être allumé ; *[building]* être en feu ◆ **try and keep the fire ~** ne laissez pas éteindre le feu ◆ **to set sth ~** mettre le feu à qch ◆ **bushes ~ with fireflies** buissons *mpl* illuminés par des lucioles [2] *(= radiant)* ◆ **to be ~** *[eyes]* briller, pétiller ; *[face]* rayonner ◆ **his eyes were ~ with laughter** ses yeux pétillaient ◆ **her face was ~ with happiness** son visage rayonnait de bonheur

align /əˈlaɪn/ VT [1] aligner, mettre en ligne ; *[+ wheels]* régler le parallélisme de [2] *(Fin, Pol)* aligner (on, with sur) ; ◆ **to ~ o.s. with sb** s'aligner sur qn VI *[persons]* s'aligner *(with* sur) ; *[objects]* être alignés

alignment /əˈlaɪnmənt/ N *(lit, fig)* alignement *m* ; *(of car wheels)* parallélisme *m* ; → **non-alignment**

alike /əˈlaɪk/ ADJ ◆ **to be ~** *[people]* se ressembler, être semblables ◆ **they all look ~ to me** pour moi, ils se ressemblent tous ◆ **no two are exactly ~** il n'y en a pas deux qui soient exactement identiques ◆ **the sisters were remarkably ~ in appearance** la ressemblance physique entre les sœurs était remarquable ADV [1] *(= in the same way) [treat, speak, think, dress]* de la même façon [2] *(= equally)* ◆ **winter and summer ~** été comme hiver ◆ **the southern and northern states ~** les États du nord comme ceux du sud ; → **share**

alimentary /ˌælɪˈmentərɪ/ ADJ alimentaire ◆ **~ canal** tube *m* digestif

alimony /ˈælɪmənɪ/ N *(Jur)* pension *f* alimentaire

aliterate /eɪˈlɪtərət/ N ennemi(e) *m(f)* de la lecture ADJ antilecture

alive /əˈlaɪv/ ADJ [1] *(= living)* vivant, en vie ; *(= in existence)* au monde ◆ **to burn ~** brûler vif ◆ **to bury sb ~** enterrer qn vivant ◆ **he must be taken ~** *[prisoner]* il faut le prendre *or* capturer vivant ◆ **while ~, he ...** de son vivant, il ... ◆ **it's good to be ~** il fait bon vivre ◆ **no man ~ could do it** personne au monde ne serait capable de le faire ◆ **to do sth as well as anyone ~** faire qch aussi bien que n'importe qui ◆ **to keep sb ~** *(lit)* maintenir qn en vie ◆ **to stay ~** rester en vie, survivre ◆ **he's going to be eaten ~ by the press** la presse ne va en faire qu'une bouchée ◆ **we were eaten ~ by mosquitoes** nous avons été dévorés par les moustiques

[2] *(fig = lively)* **to bring ~** *[meeting etc]* animer ; *[past]* faire revivre ◆ **to keep ~** *[tradition]* préserver ; *[memory]* garder ◆ **to come ~** s'animer

[3] *(frm)* ◆ **~ to** sensible à ◆ **I am very ~ to the honour you do me** je suis très sensible à l'honneur que vous me faites ◆ **to be ~ to one's interests** veiller à ses intérêts ◆ **to be ~ to a danger** être conscient d'un danger

[4] *(= alert)* alerte, vif ; *(= active)* actif, plein de vie ◆ **to be ~ and kicking** * *(= living)* être bien en vie ; *(= full of energy)* être plein de vie ◆ **look ~!** * allons, remuez-vous ! *

[5] ◆ **~ with insects/tourists** *etc* grouillant d'insectes/de touristes *etc*

alkali /ˈælkəlaɪ/ N (pl **alkalis** or **alkalies**) alcali *m*

alkaline /ˈælkəlaɪn/ ADJ alcalin

alkalinity /ˌælkəˈlɪnɪtɪ/ N alcalinité *f*

alkaloid /ˈælkəlɔɪd/ N alcaloïde *m*

alkie*, **alky*** /ˈælkɪ/ N alcoolo * *mf*, poivrot(e) * *m(f)*

all /ɔːl/

1 ADJECTIVE
2 PRONOUN
3 ADVERB
4 NOUN
5 SET STRUCTURES
6 COMPOUNDS

When **all** is part of a set combination, eg **in all seriousness/probability**, **beyond all doubt**, **of all people**, look up the noun.

1 - ADJECTIVE

tout (le), toute (la), tous (les), toutes (les) ◆ **~ the time** tout le temps ◆ **~ my life** toute ma vie ◆ **~ kinds of** toutes sortes de ◆ **~ the others** tous (toutes) les autres ◆ **~ that** tout cela ◆ **~ that is irrelevant** tout cela n'a aucun rapport ◆ **he went on about loyalty and ~ that** * il parlait de loyauté et tout ça * ◆ **loss of appetite, sleepless nights and ~ that** la perte d'appétit, les nuits blanches, et tout le reste

Articles or pronouns often need to be added in French:

◆ **~ day** toute la journée ◆ **~ three** tous les trois ◆ **~ three said the same** ils ont tous les trois dit la même chose ◆ **~ three accused were found guilty of fraud** les accusés ont tous (les) trois été jugés coupables de fraude ; see also **set structures**

2 - PRONOUN

[1] [= everything] tout ◆ **~ or nothing** tout ou rien ◆ **~ is well** tout va bien ◆ **that's ~** c'est tout ◆ **you can't see ~ of Paris in a day** on ne peut pas voir tout Paris en une journée ◆ **if that's ~ it is, it's not important** si ce n'est que ça, ce n'est pas bien grave

◆ **it all** tout ◆ **he drank it ~** il a tout bu ◆ **he's seen it ~, done it ~** il a tout vu, tout fait ◆ **it ~ happened so quickly** tout s'est passé si vite

◆ **all that** *(subject of relative clause)* tout ce qui ◆ **that's ~ that matters** c'est tout ce qui importe ◆ **you can have ~ that's left** tu peux prendre tout ce qui reste

◆ **all (that)** *(object of relative clause)* tout ce que ; *(after verb taking "de")* tout ce dont ◆ **~ I want is to sleep** tout ce que je veux, c'est dormir ◆ **that is ~ he said** c'est tout ce qu'il a dit ◆ **we saw ~ there was to see** nous avons vu tout ce qu'il y avait à voir ◆ **~ I remember is ...** tout ce dont je me souviens, c'est ... ◆ **it was ~ I could do not to laugh** j'ai eu toutes les peines du monde à me retenir de rire

◆ **all of the** tout le *m*, toute la *f*, tous les *mpl*, toutes les *fpl* ◆ **~ of the work** tout le travail ◆ **~ of the cooking** toute la cuisine ◆ **~ of the cakes** tous les gâteaux

◆ **all of it** ◆ **I gave him some soup and he ate ~ of it** je lui ai donné de la soupe et il a tout mangé ◆ **I didn't read ~ of it** je ne l'ai pas lu en entier ◆ **not ~ of it was true** ce n'était pas entièrement vrai

◆ **all of them** tous *mpl*, toutes *fpl* ◆ **~ of them failed** ils ont tous échoué ◆ **I love his short stories, I've read ~ of them** j'aime beaucoup ses nouvelles, je les ai toutes lues

◆ **all of** + *number (= at least)* ◆ **it took him ~ of three hours** ça lui a pris trois bonnes heures ◆ **it weighed ~ of 30 kilos** ça pesait bien 30 kilos ◆ **exploring the village took ~ of ten minutes** *(iro = only)* la visite du village a bien dû prendre dix minutes

[2] [plural] tous *mpl*, toutes *fpl* ◆ **we ~ sat down** nous nous sommes tous assis ◆ **they've invited us ~** ils nous ont tous invités ◆ **the girls ~ knew that ...** les filles savaient toutes que ... ◆ **they ~ came with their husbands** elles sont toutes venues avec leurs maris ◆ **they were ~ broken** ils étaient tous cassés ◆ **the peaches? I've eaten them ~!** les pêches ?

je les ai toutes mangées ! ◆ **evening, ~ !*** *(greeting people)* bonsoir, tout le monde ! ; see also **each, sundry**

◆ **all who** tous ceux qui *mpl*, toutes celles qui *fpl* ◆ **~ who knew him loved him** tous ceux qui le connaissaient l'appréciaient ◆ **education should be open to ~ who want it** l'éducation devrait être accessible à tous ceux qui veulent en bénéficier

◆ **the worst/biggest/most** *etc* **of all** ◆ **this was the worst** *or* **biggest disappointment of ~** ça a été la plus grosse déception ◆ **this result was the most surprising of ~** ce résultat était le plus surprenant ◆ **best of ~, the reforms will cost nothing** et surtout, ces réformes ne coûteront rien

3 - ADVERB

[1] [= entirely] tout ◆ **she was dressed ~ in white** elle était habillée tout en blanc

When used with a feminine adjective starting with a consonant, **tout** agrees:

◆ **she came in ~ dishevelled** elle est arrivée tout ébouriffée ◆ **she went ~ red** elle est devenue toute rouge

◆ **all by oneself, all alone** tout seul ◆ **he had to do it ~ by himself** il a dû le faire tout seul ◆ **she's ~ alone** elle est toute seule ◆ **she left her daughters ~ alone in the flat** elle a laissé ses filles toutes seules dans l'appartement

[2] [in scores] ◆ **the score was two ~** *(tennis, squash)* les joueurs étaient à deux jeux *(or sets)* partout ; *(other sports)* le score était de deux à deux ◆ **what's the score? – two ~** quel est le score ? – deux partout *or* deux à deux

4 - NOUN

[= utmost] ◆ **I decided to give it my ~** j'ai décidé de donner mon maximum ◆ **he puts his ~ into every game** il s'investit complètement dans chaque match

5 - SET STRUCTURES

◆ **all along** *(= from the start)* depuis le début ; *(= the whole length of)* tout le long de ◆ **I feared that ~ along** je l'ai craint depuis le début ◆ **~ along the road** tout le long de la route

◆ **all but** *(= nearly)* presque, pratiquement ; *(= all except)* tous sauf ◆ **he is ~ but forgotten now** il est presque *or* pratiquement tombé dans l'oubli ◆ **the party won ~ but six of the seats** le parti a remporté tous les sièges sauf six ◆ **this would exclude ~ but those able to pay** cela exclurait tout le monde sauf ceux qui peuvent payer ◆ **the plant will stand ~ but the harshest winters** cette plante supportera bien le froid, à moins que l'hiver ne soit des plus rudes

◆ **all for** ◆ **to be ~ for sth** être tout à fait pour qch ◆ **I'm ~ for giving him a chance** je suis tout à fait pour lui donner une chance ◆ **I'm ~ for it** je suis tout à fait pour*

◆ **all in*** *(= exhausted)* lessivé*, crevé* ◆ **after a day's skiing I was ~ in** j'étais lessivé* *or* crevé* au bout d'une journée de ski ◆ **you look ~ in** tu as l'air lessivé* *or* crevé* ; see also **all-in**

◆ **all in all** *(= altogether)* l'un dans l'autre ◆ **we thought, all in all, it wasn't a bad idea** nous avons pensé que, l'un dans l'autre, ce n'était pas une mauvaise idée

◆ **all one** ◆ **it's ~ one** c'est du pareil au même ◆ **it's ~ one to them** c'est du pareil au même pour eux

◆ **all over** *(= everywhere)* partout ◆ **I looked for you ~ over** je vous ai cherché partout ◆ **I'm aching ~ over** j'ai mal partout ◆ **she was ~ over flour*** elle était couverte de farine, elle avait de la farine partout ◆ **~ over France** partout en France ◆ **he was trembling ~ over** il tremblait de tous ses membres ◆ **embroidered ~ over** recouvert de broderies ◆ **~ over the country** dans tout le pays ◆ **~ over the world** à travers le monde, dans le monde entier ◆ **that's him ~ over*** c'est bien lui !, on le reconnaît bien là !

◆ **to be all over** *(= finished)* être fini ◆ **it's ~ over!** c'est fini ! ◆ **it's ~ over between us** tout est fini entre nous ◆ **it'll be ~ over with him** ce sera un homme fini

◆ **to be all over sb*** *(= affectionate with)* ◆ **they were ~ over each other** ils étaient pendus au cou l'un de l'autre ◆ **when they hear about the money, they'll be ~ over you** quand ils sauront que tu as cet argent, ils ne vont plus te lâcher ◆ **Celtic were ~ over Rangers*** *(= dominating)* le Celtic a complètement dominé *or* baladé* les Rangers

◆ **all the more** ◆ **this was ~ the more surprising since ...** c'était d'autant plus surprenant que ... ◆ **~ the more so since ...** d'autant plus que ...

◆ **all the better!** tant mieux !

◆ **all too** ◆ **it was ~ too obvious he didn't mean it** on voyait bien qu'il n'en pensait rien ◆ **the evening passed ~ too quickly** la soirée a passé bien trop rapidement

◆ **all up** ◆ **it is ~ up with him*** il est fichu*

◆ **all very** ◆ **that's ~ very well but ...** c'est bien beau mais ... ◆ **it was ~ very embarrassing** c'était vraiment très gênant

◆ **and all** ◆ **the dog ate the sausage, mustard and ~** le chien a mangé la saucisse, moutarde comprise, le chien a mangé la saucisse avec la moutarde et tout* ◆ **what with the snow and ~, we didn't go** avec la neige et tout le reste, nous n'y sommes pas allés

◆ **as all that** ◆ **it's not as important/urgent as ~ that** ce n'est pas si important/urgent que ça

◆ **for all ...** *(= despite)* malgré ◆ **for ~ its beauty, the city may be losing its individuality** malgré sa beauté, la ville est peut-être en train de perdre son individualité ◆ **for ~ that** malgré tout

◆ **for all I know ...** ◆ **for ~ I know he could be right** il a peut-être raison, je n'en sais rien ◆ **for ~ I know or care, they're still living together** ils vivent peut-être encore ensemble, mais c'est le dernier de mes soucis

◆ **if ... at all** ◆ **they won't attempt it, if they have any sense at ~** ils ne vont pas essayer s'ils ont un peu de bon sens ◆ **the little grammar they learn, if they study grammar at ~** le peu de grammaire qu'ils apprennent, si tant est qu'il étudient la grammaire ◆ **very rarely if at ~** très rarement pour ne pas dire jamais ◆ **if at ~ possible** dans la mesure du possible

◆ **in all** en tout ◆ **5 people in ~ witnessed the accident** 5 personnes en tout ont vu l'accident

◆ **no ... at all** ◆ **it makes no difference at ~** ça ne fait aucune différence ◆ **I have no regrets at ~** je n'ai aucun regret, je ne regrette rien

◆ **none at all** ◆ **have you any comments? – none at ~!** vous avez des commentaires à faire ? – absolument aucun !

◆ **not ... at all** *(= not in the least)* pas ... du tout ◆ **I don't mind at ~** ça ne me gêne pas du tout ◆ **are you disappointed? – not at ~!** vous êtes déçu – pas du tout *or* pas le moins du monde ! ◆ **thank you! – not at ~!** merci ! – de rien *or* je vous en prie !

◆ **not all that** *(= not so)* ◆ **it isn't ~ that far** ce n'est pas si loin que ça

◆ **not all there** ◆ **he's not ~ there*** il lui manque une case*

6 - COMPOUNDS

all-American ADJ cent pour cent américain

all-around ADJ *(US)* → **all-round**

all clear N ◆ **~ clear (signal)** (signal *m* de) fin *f* d'alerte ◆ **~ clear!** *(= you can go through)* la voie est libre ; *(= the alert is over)* l'alerte est passée ; *(Mil)* fin d'alerte ! ◆ **to give sb the ~ clear** *(fig)* *(gen)* donner le feu vert à qn ; *(doctor to patient)* dire à qn que tout va bien

all-conquering ADJ *[hero, team]* qui triomphe de tous

all-consuming ADJ *[passion]* dévorant

all-dancing* ADJ → **all-singing, all-dancing**

all-day ADJ qui dure toute la journée

all-embracing ADJ global

all-fired* ADV *(US)* ◆ **what's so ~-fired important about it ?** qu'est-ce que ça a de si important ?

All Fools' Day N le premier avril

all found ADJ logé et nourri

all fours NPL ◆ **on ~ fours** à quatre pattes

all get-out* N *(US)* ◆ **angry as ~ get-out** vachement* en colère

All Hallows N la Toussaint

all-important ADJ de la plus haute importance, capital

all in ADJ → **set structures**

all-in ADJ *(Brit)* *[price]* net, tout compris *inv* ; *[insurance policy]* tous risques ; *(Comm)* *[tariff]* tout compris ◆ **the holiday cost £80 ~-in** *(Brit)* les vacances ont coûté 80 livres tout compris

all-inclusive ADJ *[price, rate]* tout compris *inv*, net ; *[policy]* tous risques

all-in-one N combinaison *f* ADJ ◆ **an ~-in-one outfit** une combinaison ◆ **an ~-in-one sleepsuit** une grenouillère ◆ **~-in-one shampoo and conditioner** shampooing (et baume démêlant) deux en un ◆ **~-in-one detergent and fabric conditioner** lessive *f* avec adoucissant incorporé

all-in wrestling N catch *m*

all-metal body N *[of car]* carrosserie *f* toute en tôle

all-nighter N *spectacle qui dure toute la nuit*

all-night pass N *(Mil)* permission *f* de nuit

all-night service N *(Comm etc)* permanence *f* *or* service *m* de nuit

all-night showing N *(Cine) projection ininterrompue pendant toute la nuit*

all out ADV ◆ **to go ~ out** *(physically)* y aller à fond ◆ **to go ~ out for growth/monetary union** jeter toutes ses forces dans la bataille pour la croissance/l'union monétaire

all-out effort N effort *m* maximum

all-out strike N grève *f* totale

all-out war N guerre *f* totale ◆ **an ~-out war on inflation** une guerre totale contre l'inflation

all-over ADJ (qui est) sur toute la surface

all-over pattern N *dessin or motif qui recouvre toute une surface*

all-party ADJ *(Pol)* multipartite, où tous les partis sont représentés

all-pervading, all-pervasive ADJ *[influence, presence]* qui se fait sentir partout

all-points bulletin N *(US)* message *m* à toutes les patrouilles *(on* à propos de)

all-powerful ADJ tout-puissant

all-purpose ADJ *[flour, vehicle, cleaner]* tous usages ; *[knife, spanner, glue]* universel

all-right* ADJ *(US)* ◆ **an ~-right guy** un type sûr *or* réglo*

all righty* EXCL *(US)* OK*

all-risks insurance N assurance *f* tous risques

all-round ADJ *[sportsman]* complet (-ète *f*) ; *[improvement]* général, sur toute la ligne

all-rounder N *(Cricket)* joueur *m* complet ◆ **to be a good ~-rounder** être bon en tout

All Saints' Day N (le jour de) la Toussaint

all-seater ADJ *(Brit Sport)* *[stadium, stand]* n'ayant que des places assises

all-singing, all-dancing* ADJ *(Brit fig hum)* polyvalent

All Souls' Day N le jour *or* la fête des Morts

all-star ADJ *(Theat etc)* ◆ **~-star performance, show with an ~-star cast** plateau *m* de vedettes

all-terrain bike N vélo *m* tout-terrain, VTT *m*

all-terrain vehicle N véhicule *m* tout-terrain

all-time ADJ → **all-time**

all told ADV en tout

all-weather ADJ toute saison

all-weather court N *(Tennis)* (court *m* en) quick ® *m*

all-wheel-drive N voiture *f* à quatre *(or six etc)* roues motrices

all-year-round ADJ *[sport]* que l'on pratique toute l'année ; *[resort]* ouvert toute l'année

ALL-AMERICAN

Titre honorifique décerné aux meilleurs sportifs des universités américaines, qui constituent une sorte d'équipe fictive dans leur discipline respective. Le terme désigne également l'archétype de l'Américain idéal, sain de corps et d'esprit, "bien sous tous rapports".

Allah /'ælə/ N Allah *m*

allay /ə'leɪ/ VT *[+ fears]* modérer, apaiser ; *[+ pain, thirst]* soulager, apaiser ◆ **to ~ suspicion** dissiper les soupçons

allegation /,ælɪ'geɪʃən/ N allégation *f*

allege /ə'ledʒ/ VT alléguer, prétendre *(that* que) ; ◆ **to ~ illness** prétexter *or* alléguer une maladie ◆ **he is ~d to have said that …** il aurait dit que …, on prétend qu'il a dit que …

alleged /əledʒd/ ADJ *(gen)* présumé ; *[reason]* allégué

allegedly /ə'ledʒɪdlɪ/ LANGUAGE IN USE 26.3 ADV *(esp Jur)* ◆ **the crime he had ~ committed** le crime qu'il aurait commis ◆ **~ illegal immigrants** les immigrants qui seraient en situation illégale ◆ **he's ill, ~** *(he says)* il est soi-disant malade ; *(someone says)* il est prétendument malade

allegiance /ə'liːdʒəns/ N allégeance *f (to* à) ; ◆ **the oath of ~** *(Brit)* le serment d'allégeance

allegoric(al) /,ælɪ'gɒrɪk(əl)/ ADJ allégorique

allegorically /,ælɪ'gɒrɪkəlɪ/ ADV *[interpret]* allégoriquement ; *[speak, write]* de façon allégorique

allegory /'ælɪgərɪ/ N allégorie *f*

alleluia /,ælɪ'luːjə/ EXCL alléluia !

Allen key /'ælənkiː/, **Allen wrench** *(US)* /'ælənrentʃ/ N clé *f* à six pans, clé *f* Allen

allergen /'ælədʒen/ N allergène *m*

allergenic /'ælə'dʒenɪk/ ADJ allergénique

allergic /ə'lɜːdʒɪk/ ADJ *(Med, * fig)* allergique *(to* à)

allergist /'ælədʒɪst/ N allergologue *mf*

allergy /'ælədʒɪ/ N allergie *f (to* à) ; ◆ **an ~ to dust, a dust ~** une allergie à la poussière

alleviate /ə'liːvɪeɪt/ VT *[+ pain]* soulager, calmer ; *[+ sorrow]* adoucir ; *[+ thirst]* apaiser, calmer

alleviation /ə,liːvɪ'eɪʃən/ N *(NonC) [of suffering, condition, pain]* soulagement *m* ; *[of poverty]* réduction *f* ; *[of symptoms]* atténuation *f* ; *[of sorrow]* adoucissement *m* ; *[of thirst]* apaisement *m*

alley /'ælɪ/ N *(between buildings)* ruelle *f* ; *(in garden)* allée *f* ; *(US: between counters)* passage *m* ◆ **this is right up my ~** * c'est tout à fait mon rayon * ; → **blind, bowling** COMP **alley cat** N chat *m* de gouttière ◆ **she's got the morals of an ~ cat** * elle couche à droite et à gauche *

alleyway /'ælɪweɪ/ N ruelle *f*

alliance /ə'laɪəns/ N *[of states, persons]* alliance *f* ◆ **to enter into an ~ with …** s'allier avec …

allied /'ælaɪd/ ADJ 1 *(= in league)* allié *(against sb/sth* contre qn/qch ; *to sb/sth* à qn/qch ; *with sb/sth* avec qn/qch) 2 *(= associated) [industries]* assimilé, apparenté ; *[conditions]* apparenté ; *[subjects]* connexe ◆ **lectures on subjects ~ to health** conférences *fpl* sur des sujets liés à la santé ◆ **~ products** *(Jur)* produits *mpl* assimilés *or* apparentés 3 *(= coupled)* ◆ **~ to** *or* **with sth** allié à qch ◆ **an interest rate rise ~ with a stock market slump** une augmentation des taux d'intérêts conjuguée à une chute de la Bourse 4 *(Bio)* de la même famille *or* espèce COMP **allied health professional** N *(US) médecin ou infirmière dont les prestations sont remboursées par une mutuelle*

alligator /'ælɪgeɪtə^r/ N alligator *m*

alliteration /ə,lɪtə'reɪʃən/ N allitération *f*

alliterative /ə'lɪtərətɪv/ ADJ allitératif

allocate /'æləʊkeɪt/ VT 1 *(= allot) [+ task]* allouer, attribuer *(to sb* à qn) ; *[+ money]* affecter *(to* à) 2 *(= apportion)* répartir, distribuer *(among* parmi) 3 *(Jur, Fin)* ventiler

allocation /,æləʊ'keɪʃən/ N 1 *(= allotting)* affectation *f* ; *(to individual)* attribution *f* 2 *(= apportioning)* répartition *f* 3 *(= money allocated)* part *f*, allocation *f* 4 *(Jur, Fin)* ventilation *f* ◆ **~ of overheads** ventilation *f* des frais généraux

allograph /'ælə,grɑːf/ N *(Ling)* allographe *m*

allomorph /'ælə,mɔːf/ N *(Ling)* allomorphe *m*

allopathic /,ælə'pæθɪk/ ADJ allopathique

allopathy /ə'lɒpəθɪ/ N *(NonC)* allopathie *f*

allophone /'ælə,fəʊn/ N *(Ling)* allophone *m*

allosaurus /,ælə'sɔːrəs/ N allosaure *m*

allot /ə'lɒt/ VT 1 *(= allocate)* attribuer, assigner *(sth to sb* qch à qn) ; ◆ **everyone was ~ted a piece of land** chacun a reçu un terrain en lot ◆ **to do sth in the time ~ted (to one)** faire qch dans le temps qui (vous) est imparti *or* assigné ◆ **to ~ sth to a certain use** affecter *or* destiner qch à un certain usage 2 *(= share among group)* répartir, distribuer

allotment /ə'lɒtmənt/ N 1 *(Brit = ground for cultivation)* jardin *m* ouvrier 2 *(= division of shares)* partage *m*, lotissement *m* ; *(= distribution of shares)* distribution *f*, part *f*

allotrope /'ælə,trəʊp/ N variété *f* allotropique

allottee /əlɒ'tiː/ N attributaire *mf*

allow /ə'laʊ/ LANGUAGE IN USE 9, 10.4, 12 VT 1 *(= permit)* permettre, autoriser ; *(= tolerate)* tolérer, souffrir ◆ **to ~ sb sth** permettre qch à qn ◆ **to ~ sb to do sth** permettre à qn de faire qch, autoriser qn à faire qch ◆ **to ~ sb in/out/past** *etc* permettre à qn d'entrer/de sortir/de passer *etc* ◆ **to ~ sth to happen** laisser se produire qch ◆ **to ~ o.s. to be persuaded** se laisser persuader ◆ **~ us to help you** permettez que nous vous aidions, permettez-nous de vous aider ◆ **we are not ~ed much freedom** on nous accorde peu de liberté ◆ **smoking is not ~ed** il est interdit *or* défendu de fumer ◆ **no children/dogs ~ed** interdit aux enfants/chiens ◆ **please ~ 28 days for delivery** délai de livraison : 28 jours à réception de la commande ◆ **I will not ~ such behaviour** je ne tolérerai *or* souffrirai pas une telle conduite

2 *(= grant) [+ money]* accorder, allouer ◆ **to ~ sb £30 a month** allouer *or* accorder à qn 30 livres par mois ◆ **to ~ sb a thousand pounds damages** *(Jur)* accorder à qn mille livres de dommages et intérêts ◆ **to ~ space for** prévoir *or* ménager de la place pour ◆ **to ~ sb a discount** faire bénéficier qn d'une remise, consentir une remise à qn ◆ **~ (yourself) an hour to cross the city** comptez une heure pour traverser la ville ◆ **~ 5cm for shrinkage** prévoyez 5 cm (de plus) pour le cas où le tissu rétrécirait

3 *(= agree as possible) [+ claim]* admettre

4 *(= concede)* admettre *(that* que) ; ◆ **~ing that …** en admettant que … + *subj*

► **allow for** VT FUS tenir compte de ; *[+ money spent, funds allocated] (by deduction)* déduire pour ; *(by addition)* ajouter pour ◆ **~ing for the circumstances** compte tenu des circonstances ◆ **after ~ing for his expenses** déduction faite de *or* en tenant compte de ses dépenses ◆ **we must ~ for the cost of the wood** il faut compter (avec) le prix du bois ◆ **~ing for the shrinking of the material** en tenant compte du rétrécissement du tissu *or* du fait que le tissu rétrécit ◆ **to ~ for all possibilities** parer à toute éventualité

► **allow of** VT FUS admettre, souffrir

allowable /ə'laʊəbl/ ADJ permis, admissible ; *(Tax)* déductible ◆ **~ against tax** déductible des impôts

allowance /ə'laʊəns/ N 1 *(= money given to sb)* allocation *f* ; *(for lodgings, food etc)* indemnité *f* ; *(from separated husband)* pension *f* alimentaire ; *(= salary)* appointements *mpl* ; *(= food)* ration *f* ; *(esp US = pocket money)* argent *m* de poche ◆ **he makes his mother an ~** il verse une rente *or* une pension à sa mère ◆ **his father gives him an ~ of $800 per month** son père lui verse 800 dollars par mois ◆ **rent ~** allocation *f* de logement ◆ **London ~** prime *f* de vie chère *or* indemnité *f* de résidence pour poste basé à Londres ◆ **~ in kind** prestation *f* en nature ◆ **~ for quarters** *(Mil)* indemnité *f* de logement ; → **car, clothing, family**

2 *(Comm, Fin = discount)* réduction *f* ◆ **tax ~s** sommes *fpl* déductibles

3 *(= concession)* ◆ **you must learn to make ~s** il faut savoir faire la part des choses ◆ **to make ~(s) for sb** se montrer indulgent envers qn, essayer de comprendre qn ◆ **to make ~(s) for sth** tenir compte de qch, prendre qch en considération

alloy /'ælɔɪ/ N alliage *m* VT /ə'lɔɪ/ *(Metal)* allier, faire un alliage de

COMP **alloy steel** N acier *m* allié

alloy wheels NPL roues *fpl* en alliage léger

all right /,ɔːl'raɪt/ ADJ 1 *(= satisfactory)* bien ◆ **he's ~** il est bien *or* valable * ◆ **do you like the champagne? – it's ~** aimez-vous ce champagne ? – il n'est pas mal ◆ **it's ~** ça va ; *(= don't worry)* ce n'est pas grave ◆ **is it ~ if …?** ça vous dérange si … ? ◆ **that's ~, don't worry** ce n'est pas grave ◆ **is everything ~?** tout va bien ? ◆ **it's** *or* **that's ~ by me** d'accord ◆ **see you later, ~?** à tout à l'heure, d'accord ?

2 *(= safe, well)* **to be ~** *(= healthy)* aller bien, être en bonne santé ; *(= safe)* être sain et sauf ◆ **someone should see if she's ~** quelqu'un devrait aller voir si elle va bien ◆ **the car will be ~ there overnight** la voiture ne risque rien à passer la nuit là

3 *(= well-provided)* **to be ~ for money/paper** *etc* avoir assez d'argent/de papier *etc* ◆ **we're ~ for the rest of our lives** nous sommes tranquilles *or* nous avons tout ce qu'il nous faut pour le restant de nos jours ◆ **I'm ~ Jack** * moi, je suis peinard *

EXCL *(in approval, exasperation)* ça va ! * ; *(in agreement)* d'accord ! ; *(esp US: in triumph)* bravo !

ADV 1 *(= without difficulty)* sans problème ◆ **he's getting on ~** il se débrouille pas mal ◆ **did you get home ~ last night?** tu es bien rentré chez toi, hier soir ? ◆ **I managed that ~, but I couldn't …** j'ai réussi à faire ça sans problème, mais je n'ai pas pu … ◆ **he's doing ~ for himself** il se débrouille bien

2 *(= definitely)* ◆ **he's at home ~, but he's not answering the phone** il est chez lui c'est sûr, c'est simplement qu'il ne répond pas au téléphone ◆ **you'll get the money back ~** vous serez remboursé, c'est sûr ◆ **it's warm enough ~!** il fait bien chaud, ça c'est vrai !

3 *(expressing agreement)* ◆ **can you help ? – ~, what do you want me to do ?** pouvez-vous m'aider ? – certainement, que puis-je faire pour vous ? ◆ **you say I was wrong; ~ but ...** vous dites que j'avais tort ; d'accord *or* admettons, mais ...

4 *(summoning attention)* ◆ **~, let's get started** bon, allons-y ◆ **~, who's in charge here?** bon, qui est responsable ici ?

5 *(introducing a challenge, threat)* ◆ **~, what's the joke ?** bon, qu'est-ce qu'il y a de drôle ?

all-right * /ˈɔːlˈraɪt/ ADJ *(US)* ◆ **an ~ guy** un type sûr *or* réglo *

allspice /ˈɔːlspaɪs/ N piment *m* de la Jamaïque

all-time /ˈɔːlˈtaɪm/ ADJ sans précédent, de tous les temps ◆ **he's my ~ favourite** c'est mon préféré ◆ **"Casablanca" is one of the ~ greats** *or* **great films** "Casablanca" est l'un des plus grands films de tous les temps *or* un grand classique du cinéma ◆ **he's one of the ~ greats** il fait partie des plus grands ◆ **~ record** record *m* absolu ◆ **the pound has reached an ~ low** la livre a atteint le niveau le plus bas jamais enregistré ◆ **to be at an ~ low** être au plus bas ADV ◆ **an ~ best performance** un record personnel ◆ **the ~ worst performance of that song** la pire interprétation qu'il y ait jamais eu de cette chanson ◆ **John's ~ favourite artist** l'artiste préféré de John

allude /əˈluːd/ VI ◆ **to ~ to** *[person]* faire allusion à ; *[letter etc]* avoir trait à, se rapporter à

allure /əˈljʊəʳ/ VT *(= attract)* attirer ; *(= entice)* séduire N charme *m*, attrait *m*

alluring /əˈljʊərɪŋ/ ADJ séduisant, charmant

alluringly /əˈljʊərɪŋlɪ/ ADV ◆ **to smile ~** avoir un sourire séduisant ◆ **~ mysterious** séduisant par son côté mystérieux

allusion /əˈluːʒən/ N allusion *f*

allusive /əˈluːsɪv/ ADJ allusif, qui contient une allusion

allusively /əˈluːsɪvlɪ/ ADV par allusion

alluvia /əˈluːvɪə/ NPL of **alluvium**

alluvial /əˈluːvɪəl/ ADJ *[ground]* alluvial ; *[deposit]* alluvionnaire

alluvium /əˈluːvɪəm/ N (pl **alluviums** *or* **alluvia**) alluvion *f*

ally /əˈlaɪ/ VT allier, unir *(with* avec) ; ◆ **to ~ o.s. with** s'allier avec N /ˈælaɪ/ *(gen)* allié(e) *m(f)* ; *(Pol)* allié(e) *m(f)*, coalisé(e) *m(f)* ◆ **the Allies** *(Mil Hist)* les Alliés *mpl*

alma mater /ˌælməˈmɑːtəʳ/ N alma mater *f inv*

almanac /ˈɔːlmənæk/ N almanach *m*, annuaire *m* ; → **nautical**

almighty /ɔːlˈmaɪtɪ/ ADJ 1 tout-puissant, omnipotent ◆ **Almighty God** Dieu Tout-Puissant ◆ **the ~ dollar** le dollar tout-puissant 2 (* = *tremendous) [row, scandal]* énorme ◆ **an ~ din** un vacarme de tous les diables N ◆ **the Almighty** le Tout-Puissant ADV * extrêmement, énormément

almond /ˈɑːmənd/ N amande *f* ; (also **almond tree**) amandier *m* ◆ **split ~s** amandes *fpl* effilées ; → **burnt, sugar**

COMP *[oil, paste]* d'amande **almond-eyed** ADJ aux yeux en amande

almond-shaped ADJ *[eyes etc]* en amande

almoner † /ˈɑːmənəʳ/ N *(Brit)* ◆ **(lady) ~** assistante *f* sociale *(attachée à un hôpital)*

almost /ˈɔːlməʊst/ ADV presque ◆ **I had ~ forgotten about it** j'avais presque oublié ◆ **he ~ fell/died** il a failli tomber/mourir ◆ **you're ~ there** vous y êtes presque ◆ **I can ~ do it** j'arrive presque à le faire, j'y arrive presque ◆ **~ finished/cooked/cold** presque terminé/cuit/froid ◆ **~ always** presque toujours ◆ **he's ~ certainly been murdered** il est pratiquement certain *or* très probable qu'il a été assassiné ◆ **~ a month** presque un mois, près d'un mois

alms /ɑːmz/ N aumône *f* ◆ **to give ~** faire l'aumône *or* la charité ◆ **~ box** tronc *m* des pauvres ◆ **~ house** *(Hist)* hospice *m*

aloe /ˈæləʊ/ N aloès *m* ; → **bitter** COMP **aloe vera** N *(= plant)* aloe vera *f* ; *(= extract)* (extrait *m* d')aloès *m*

aloft /əˈlɒft/ ADV (also **up aloft**) en haut, en l'air ; *(Naut)* dans la mâture ; *(hum = in heaven)* au ciel

Aloha /əˈləʊə/ N *(US)* ◆ **the ~ State** Hawaï *m*

alone /əˈləʊn/ ADJ, ADV 1 *(= by o.s.)* seul ◆ **all ~** tout(e) seul(e) ◆ **quite ~** tout à fait seul(e) ◆ **you can't do it ~** vous ne pouvez pas le faire seul ◆ **she brought up two children ~** elle a élevé deux enfants toute seule ◆ **a gunman acting ~** un bandit armé agissant seul ◆ **to go it ~** * faire cavalier seul ◆ **don't leave them ~ together** ne les laissez pas seuls ensemble ◆ **we'd never spent such a long time ~ together** nous n'avions jamais passé autant de temps seuls ensemble *or* en tête à tête ◆ **I was ~ with her/my thoughts** j'étais seul avec elle/mes pensées ◆ **I need to get her ~** il faut que je lui parle en tête-à-tête *or* entre quat'z'yeux *

♦ **let alone** encore moins ◆ **he can't read, let ~ write** il ne sait pas lire, (et) encore moins écrire ◆ **he can't afford food, let ~ clothes** il n'a pas de quoi s'acheter de la nourriture, sans parler de vêtements *or* encore moins des vêtements

2 *(= only)* seul ◆ **he ~ could tell you** lui seul pourrait vous le dire ◆ **you ~ can do it** vous êtes le seul à pouvoir le faire ◆ **we are not ~ in thinking this** nous ne sommes pas les seuls à le penser ◆ **pride ~ prevented her from giving up** seul l'orgueil l'a empêchée d'abandonner ◆ **we must have gained 100 members from this ~** nous devons avoir gagné 100 membres de plus rien qu'avec cela ◆ **man cannot live by bread ~** *(Prov)* l'homme ne vit pas seulement de pain ◆ **that charm which is hers (and hers) ~** ce charme qui lui est propre *or* qui n'appartient qu'à elle

3 *(= lonely)* seul ◆ **I feel so ~** je me sens si seul

4 *(= in peace)* **to leave** *or* **let sb ~** laisser qn tranquille, laisser qn en paix ◆ **leave** *or* **let me ~!** laisse-moi tranquille !, fiche-moi la paix ! * ◆ **leave** *or* **let him ~ to do it** laisse-le faire tout seul ◆ **leave** *or* **let the book ~!** ne touche pas au livre ! ◆ **I advise you to leave the whole business ~** je vous conseille de ne pas vous en mêler ◆ **leave** *or* **let well ~** le mieux est l'ennemi du bien *(Prov)*

along /əˈlɒŋ/

> When **along** is an element in a phrasal verb, eg **go along, play along, string along**, look up the verb.

ADV 1 **come ~!** allez venez !, venez donc ! ◆ **I'll be ~ in a moment** j'arrive tout de suite ◆ **she'll be ~ tomorrow** elle viendra demain ◆ **how is John getting ~?** et John, ça va bien ?, quelles nouvelles de John ?

2 ◆ **come ~ with me** venez avec moi ◆ **he came ~ with six others** il est venu accompagné de six autres ◆ **she escaped from the fire ~ with her baby** elle a échappé à l'incendie et son bébé aussi ◆ **bring your friend ~** amène ton ami ◆ **~ here** par là ◆ **get ~ with you!** * *(= go away)* fiche le camp ! *, décampe ! * ; *(= you can't mean it)* tu plaisantes *or* rigoles * ?

3 *(set structures)*

♦ **all along** *(space)* d'un bout à l'autre ; *(time)* depuis le début ◆ **I could see all ~ that he would refuse** je savais depuis le début qu'il allait refuser ◆ **that's what I've been saying all ~** c'est ce que je n'ai pas arrêté de dire

PREP le long de ◆ **to walk ~ the beach** se promener le long de *or* sur la plage ◆ **the railway runs ~ the beach** la ligne de chemin de fer longe la plage ◆ **the trees ~ the road** les arbres au bord de la route *or* qui bordent la route ◆ **they built houses ~ the river** ils ont construit des maisons le long de la rivière ◆ **all ~ the street** tout le long de la rue ◆ **somewhere ~ the way he lost a glove** il a perdu un gant en chemin *or* quelque part ◆ **somewhere ~ the way** *or* **the line** * **someone made a mistake** à un moment donné, quelqu'un a commis une erreur ◆ **to proceed ~ the lines suggested** agir *or* procéder conformément à la ligne d'action proposée

alongside /əˈlɒŋˈsaɪd/ PREP *(= along: also Naut)* le long de ; *(= beside)* à côté de, près de ◆ **to work ~ sb** travailler aux côtés de qn ◆ **to come ~ the quay** *(Naut)* accoster le quai ◆ **the road runs ~ the beach** la route longe la plage ◆ **to stop ~ the kerb** *[vehicle]* s'arrêter le long du trottoir ◆ **the car drew up ~ me** la voiture s'est arrêtée à côté de moi *or* à ma hauteur ADV 1 *(Naut) (ships = beside one another)* bord à bord, à couple ◆ **to come ~** accoster ◆ **to make fast ~** *(quayside)* s'amarrer à *or* au quai ; *(another vessel)* s'amarrer bord à bord, s'amarrer à *or* en couple ◆ **to pass ~ of a ship** longer un navire 2 *(people = side by side)* côte à côte

aloof /əˈluːf/ ADJ 1 *(= standoffish) [person, character]* distant ◆ **he was very ~ with me** il s'est montré très distant à mon égard ◆ **she kept very (much) ~** elle a gardé *or* conservé ses distances 2 *(= uninvolved)* ◆ **to hold o.s.** *or* **remain ~** se tenir à l'écart *(from sb/sth* de qn/qch)

aloofness /əˈluːfnɪs/ N attitude *f* distante, réserve *f*

alopecia /ˌæləʊˈpiːʃə/ N alopécie *f*

aloud /əˈlaʊd/ ADV *[read]* à haute voix, à voix haute ; *[laugh, think, wonder]* tout haut

alp /ælp/ N *(= peak)* pic *m* ; *(= mountain)* montagne *f* ; *(= pasture)* alpage *m*, alpe *f* ◆ **the Alps** les Alpes *fpl*

alpaca /ælˈpækə/ N *(= animal, wool)* alpaga *m*

alpenhorn /ˈælpənˌhɔːn/ N cor *m* des Alpes

alpenstock /ˈælpənstɒk/ N alpenstock *m*

alpha /ˈælfə/ N 1 *(= letter)* alpha *m* ◆ **~ particle** particule *f* alpha 2 *(Brit Scol, Univ)* ≃ très bien ◆ **~ plus** ≃ excellent

COMP **alpha-fetoprotein** N alpha-fœto-protéine *f*

alpha rhythm N rythme *m* alpha

alpha wave N onde *f* alpha

alphabet /ˈælfəbet/ N alphabet *m* ◆ **~ soup** *(Culin)* potage *m* aux pâtes (en forme de lettres) ; (* *fig pej*) salade *f* de sigles

alphabetic(al) /ˌælfəˈbetɪk(əl)/ ADJ alphabétique ◆ **to put in ~al order** classer par ordre alphabétique ◆ **to be in ~al order** être dans l'ordre alphabétique

alphabetically /ˌælfəˈbetɪkəlɪ/ ADV par ordre alphabétique, alphabétiquement

alphabetize /ˈælfəbətaɪz/ VT classer par ordre alphabétique

alphanumeric /ˌælfənjuːˈmerɪk/ ADJ alphanumérique

alpine /ˈælpaɪn/ ADJ *[scenery, village]* des Alpes, alpin ; *[mountain, chalet] (= in the Alps)* des Alpes ; *(= alpine-style)* alpin ; *[troops, skiing, skier]* alpin ; *[plant] (on lower slopes)* alpestre ; *(on higher slopes)* alpin ; *[meadow, pasture, climate]* alpestre N *(= plant)* plante *f* alpine COMP **alpine hut** N refuge *m* de montagne

alpinist /ˈælpɪnɪst/ N alpiniste *mf*

Al Qaeda /ælkaɪˈiːdə/ N Al-Qaida

already /ɔːlˈredɪ/ ADV déjà ◆ **(that's) enough ~!** * *(esp US: expressing impatience)* maintenant, ça suffit !

alright /ˌɔːlˈraɪt/ ADJ, ADV ⇒ **all right**

Alsace /ˈælsæs/ N Alsace *f*

Alsace-Lorraine /ˈælsæsləˈreɪn/ N Alsace-Lorraine *f*

Alsatian /æl'seɪʃən/ N [1] *(= person)* Alsacien(ne) *m(f)* [2] *(Brit:* also **Alsatian dog**) chien *m* loup, berger *m* allemand ADJ alsacien, d'Alsace

also /'ɔːlsəʊ/ ADV [1] *(= too)* aussi également ◆ **her cousin ~ came** son cousin aussi est venu *or* est venu également [2] *(= moreover)* de plus, également ◆ **~ I must explain that ...** de plus, je dois vous expliquer que ..., je dois également vous expliquer que ... COMP **also-ran** N *(Sport)* autre concurrent *m (non classé)* ; *(Racing)* cheval *m* non classé ; *(* = person)* perdant(e) *m(f)*

Alta abbrev of **Alberta**

Altamira /,æltə'mɪːrə/ N ◆ **the ~ caves** les grottes *fpl* d'Altamira

altar /'ɒltəʳ/ N *(Rel)* autel *m* ◆ **high ~** maître-autel *m* ◆ **he was sacrificed on the ~ of productivity** il a été immolé sur l'autel de la productivité

COMP **altar boy** N enfant *m* de chœur
altar cloth N nappe *f* d'autel
altar piece N retable *m*
altar rail(s) N(PL) clôture *f or* balustre *m* (du chœur) ; *(Rel)* table *f* de communion

alter /'ɒltəʳ/ VT [1] *(gen)* changer, modifier ; *(stronger)* transformer ; *(= adapt)* adapter, ajuster ; *[+ painting, poem, speech etc]* retoucher ; *(stronger)* remanier ; *[+ garment]* retoucher ; *(stronger)* transformer ◆ **to ~ one's plans** modifier *or* transformer ses projets ◆ **to ~ one's attitude** changer d'attitude (*to* envers) ; ◆ **that ~s the case** voilà qui est différent *or* qui change tout ◆ **to ~ course** *(Naut)* changer de cap *or* de route ◆ **to ~ sth for the better** changer qch en mieux, améliorer qch ◆ **to ~ sth for the worse** changer qch en mal, altérer qch [2] *(US = castrate)* châtrer, castrer VI changer ◆ **to ~ for the better** *[circumstances]* s'améliorer ; *[person, character]* changer en mieux ◆ **to ~ for the worse** *[circumstances]* empirer, s'aggraver ; *[person, character]* changer en mal

alteration /,ɒltə'reɪʃən/ N [1] *(= change) (to plan, team, rules etc)* modification *f*, changement *m* ; *(to behaviour, diet)* changement *m* ◆ **to make ~s to existing arrangements** apporter des modifications aux dispositions existantes ◆ **an ~ in the rules** une modification des règlements ◆ **to make ~s to a garment/text/painting** retoucher un vêtement/texte/tableau ◆ **textual ~s** retouches *fpl* au texte ◆ **climatic ~s** changements *mpl* climatiques ◆ **to make ~s to a team** modifier une équipe ◆ **the ~s to the house** les transformations *fpl* apportées à la maison ◆ **they're having ~s made to their house** ils font faire des travaux ◆ **"closed for alterations"** *(shop, building)* "fermé pour travaux" ◆ **~ of route** *(Naut) (deliberate)* changement *m* de route ; *(involuntary)* déroutement *m* [2] *(NonC = altering) [of structure, building]* transformation *f* ; *[of climate]* changements *mpl* ; *[of garment]* retouches *fpl* ◆ **did you see any ~ in his behaviour?** avez-vous remarqué un changement dans son comportement ? ◆ **"times and programmes are subject to alteration"** "les horaires et les programmes peuvent être modifiés"

altercation /,ɒltə'keɪʃən/ N *(frm)* altercation *f* ◆ **to have an ~** se disputer, avoir une altercation

alter ego /'æltər'iːgəʊ/ N alter ego *m* ◆ **he is my ~** c'est mon alter ego

alternate /ɒl'tɜːnɪt/ ADJ [1] *(= successive) [actions, periods, colours]* alterné ◆ **cover with ~ slices of tomato and mozzarella** recouvrir en alternant tranches de tomate et de mozzarella ◆ **a week of ~ rain and sunshine** une semaine où la pluie et le beau temps ont alterné

[2] *(= every second)* ◆ **on ~ days** un jour sur deux ◆ **he works on ~ days** il travaille un jour sur deux ◆ **they work on ~ days** *(taking turns)* ils travaillent un jour sur deux, à tour de rôle ◆ **to take ~ weeks off** être en congé une semaine sur deux ◆ **he lives ~ months in Brussels and London** il habite un mois à Bruxelles, un mois à Londres ◆ **to read ~ lines** lire une ligne sur deux

[3] *(US)* ⇒ **alternative adj**

[4] *(Bot, Math)* alterne

[5] *(Poetry)* ◆ **~ rhymes** rimes *fpl* alternées *or* croisées

N *(US)* remplaçant(e) *m(f)*, suppléant(e) *m(f)*

VT /'ɒltɜːneɪt/ faire alterner, employer alternativement *or* tour à tour ◆ **to ~ crops** alterner les cultures, pratiquer l'assolement

VI [1] *(= occur etc in turns)* alterner (*with* avec) se succéder (tour à tour)

[2] ◆ **to ~ between French and English** passer du français à l'anglais (et vice versa) ◆ **he ~s between aggression and indifference** il passe de l'agressivité à l'indifférence ◆ **in the desert the temperature ~s between boiling and freezing** dans le désert la température est tantôt torride, tantôt glaciale

[3] *(= interchange regularly)* se relayer, travailler *(or jouer etc)* en alternance

[4] *(Elec)* changer périodiquement de sens

alternately /ɒl'tɜːnɪtlɪ/ ADV tour à tour ◆ **he would ~ bully and charm people** il se montrait tour à tour tyrannique et charmant, il se montrait tantôt tyrannique, tantôt charmant ◆ **she became ~ angry and calm** elle passait de la colère au calme, et du calme à la colère ◆ **I lived ~ with my mother and my grandmother** je vivais tantôt avec ma mère, tantôt avec ma grand-mère

alternating /'ɒltəneɪtɪŋ/ ADJ alternant, en alternance ; *[movement]* alternatif ◆ **~ series** *(Math)* série *f* alternée ◆ **~ current** *(Elec)* courant *m* alternatif

alternation /,ɒltə'neɪʃən/ N alternance *f* ; *[of emotions etc]* alternatives *fpl*

alternative /ɒl'tɜːnətɪv/ ADJ [1] *(gen)* autre ; *(Philos) [proposition]* alternatif ; *(Mil) [position]* de repli ; *(Tech)* de rechange ◆ **people will be offered ~ employment where possible** d'autres emplois seront proposés lorsque cela sera possible ◆ **~ proposal** contre-proposition *f* ◆ **the only ~ method** la seule autre méthode, la seule méthode de rechange ◆ **~ route** *(for drivers)* itinéraire *m* de délestage ◆ **Alternative Vote** vote *m* alternatif

[2] *(= non-traditional)* parallèle, alternatif ; *[lifestyle]* alternatif, différent ◆ **~ school** *(US) école privée ayant adopté des méthodes nouvelles* ◆ **~ education** *(US) enseignement privé basé sur des méthodes nouvelles* ◆ **~ comedian** nouveau comique *m* ◆ **~ comedy** nouvelle comédie *f* ◆ **~ (sources of) energy** (sources *fpl* d')énergie *f* de substitution

N *(= choice) (between two)* alternative *f*, choix *m* ; *(among several)* choix *m* ; *(= solution) (only one)* alternative *f*, seule autre solution *f* ; *(one of several)* autre solution *f*, solution *f* de rechange ; *(Philos)* terme *m* d'une alternative *or* d'un dilemme ◆ **she had no ~ but to accept** elle n'avait pas d'autre solution que d'accepter, elle a été obligée d'accepter ◆ **there's no ~** il n'y a pas le choix

COMP **alternative medicine** N médecine *f* alternative *or* douce
alternative technology N les technologies *fpl* douces

alternatively /ɒl'tɜːnətɪvlɪ/ ADV autrement

alternator /'ɒltəneɪtəʳ/ N *(Brit Elec)* alternateur *m*

although /ɔːl'ðəʊ/ LANGUAGE IN USE 26.3 CONJ [1] bien que + *subj*, quoique + *subj* ◆ **~ it's raining there are 20 people here already** bien qu'il pleuve *or* malgré la pluie, il y a déjà 20 personnes ◆ **I'll do it, ~ I don't want to** je vais le faire bien que je n'en aie pas envie *or* même si je n'en ai pas envie ◆ **~ poor they were honest** ils étaient pauvres mais honnêtes, bien que pauvres, ils étaient honnêtes ◆ **~ young he knew that ...** bien qu'il fût jeune, il savait que ..., malgré sa jeunesse il savait que ... ◆ **~ he might agree to go** quand bien même il accepterait d'y aller, même s'il accepte d'y aller ◆ **the room, ~ small, was quite comfortable** la pièce était confortable, bien que petite

[2] *(= but)* mais ◆ **I don't think this is going to work, ~ it's worth a try** je ne pense pas que ça va marcher, mais ça vaut la peine d'essayer

altimeter /'æltɪmiːtəʳ/ N altimètre *m*

altitude /'æltɪtjuːd/ N *(= height above sea level)* altitude *f* ; *[of building]* hauteur *f* ◆ **~s** *(gen pl = high place)* hauteur(s) *f(pl)*, altitude *f* ◆ **it is difficult to breathe at these ~s** *or* **at this ~** il est difficile de respirer à cette altitude ◆ **~ sickness** mal *m* d'altitude *or* des montagnes

alto /'æltəʊ/ N [1] *(female voice)* contralto *m* ; *(male voice)* haute-contre *f* [2] *(= instrument)* alto *m* ADJ *(female)* de contralto ; *(male)* de haute-contre ; *(instrument)* d'alto ◆ **~ clef** clef *f* d'ut ◆ **~ saxophone/flute** saxophone *m*/flûte *f* alto

altogether /,ɔːltə'geðəʳ/ ADV [1] *(= completely) [stop, disappear]* complètement ; *[different]* tout à fait ◆ **that's another matter ~** c'est une tout autre affaire ◆ **it is ~ out of the question** il n'en est absolument pas question ◆ **you don't believe him? – no, not ~** vous ne le croyez pas ? – non, pas vraiment ◆ **such methods are not ~ satisfactory** de telles méthodes ne sont pas vraiment satisfaisantes ◆ **I'm not ~ happy about this** je n'en suis pas vraiment satisfait

[2] *(= in all)* en tout ◆ **what do I owe you ~?** je vous dois combien en tout ?, combien vous dois-je au total ? ◆ **~, he played in 44 test matches** en tout, il a joué dans 44 matchs internationaux ◆ **taken ~** à tout prendre ◆ **~, it wasn't very pleasant** ce n'était somme toute pas très agréable

N *(hum)* ◆ **in the ~*** tout nu, en costume d'Adam *(or* d'Ève)*

altoist /'æltəʊɪst/ N *(Mus)* saxophoniste *mf* alto

altruism /'æltrʊɪzəm/ N altruisme *m*

altruist /'æltrʊɪst/ N altruiste *mf*

altruistic /,æltrʊ'ɪstɪk/ ADJ altruiste

ALU /,eɪel'juː/ N *(Comput)* (abbrev of **arithmetical logic unit**) UAL *f*

alum /'æləm/ N alun *m*

alumina /ə'luːmɪnə/ N alumine *f*

aluminium /,æljʊ'mɪnɪəm/, **aluminum** (US) /ə'luːmɪnəm/ N aluminium *m*

COMP *[pot, pan etc]* en aluminium
aluminium bronze N bronze *m* d'aluminium
aluminium foil N papier *m* aluminium
aluminium oxide N oxyde *m* d'aluminium

alumna /ə'lʌmnə/ N (pl **alumnae** /ə'lʌmniː/) *(US) (Scol)* ancienne élève *f* ; *(Univ)* ancienne étudiante *f*

alumnus /ə'lʌmnəs/ N (pl **alumni** /ə'lʌmnaɪ/) *(US) (Scol)* ancien élève *m* ; *(Univ)* ancien étudiant *m*

alveolar /æl'vɪələʳ/ ADJ alvéolaire ◆ **~ ridge** alvéoles *fpl* dentaires

alveolus /æl'vɪələs/ N (pl **alveoli** /æl'vɪəlaɪ/) alvéole *f*

always /'ɔːlweɪz/ ADV toujours ◆ **he's ~ late** il est toujours en retard ◆ **I'll ~ love you** je t'aimerai toujours ◆ **I can ~ come back later** je peux toujours revenir plus tard ◆ **there's ~ tomorrow** demain, il fera jour ◆ **office ~ open** bureau *m* ouvert en permanence

◆ **as always** comme toujours

COMP **always-on** ADJ *(Comput) [Internet connection]* permanent, e

Alzheimer's (disease) /ˈæltshaɪməz(dɪˌziːz)/ N maladie *f* d'Alzheimer

AM /eɪˈem/ 1 (abbrev of **amplitude modulation**) AM ; → **modulation** 2 *(Brit Pol)* abbrev of **Assembly Member**

am¹ /æm/ → **be**

am² /eɪˈem/ ADV (abbrev of **ante meridiem**) du matin

AMA /ˌeɪemˈeɪ/ N abbrev of **American Medical Association**

amalgam /əˈmælgəm/ N amalgame *m* (*of* de, entre)

amalgamate /əˈmælgəmeɪt/ VT *[+ metals]* amalgamer ; *[+ companies, shares]* (faire) fusionner, unifier VI *[metals]* s'amalgamer ; *[companies]* fusionner, s'unifier ; *[ethnic groups]* se mélanger

amalgamation /əˌmælgəˈmeɪʃən/ N *[of organizations, businesses, schools]* fusion *f* (*into sth* en qch) ; *[of regiments]* amalgame *m* ; *[of legal systems]* unification *f* ; *[of genres, concepts]* mélange *m* ; *[of metals]* amalgamation *f* ◆ **the ~ of our regiment with ...** l'amalgame *or* le regroupement de notre régiment avec ...

amanuensis /əˌmænjʊˈensɪs/ N (pl **amanuenses** /əˌmænjʊˈensiːz/) (= *secretary, assistant*) secrétaire *mf* ; (= *copyist*) copiste *mf*

amaryllis /ˌæməˈrɪlɪs/ N amaryllis *f*

amass /əˈmæs/ VT *[+ objects]* amasser, accumuler ; *[+ fortune]* amasser

amateur /ˈæmətəʳ/ N (*also Sport*) amateur *m*
COMP *[painter, sports, player]* amateur *inv* ; *[photography etc]* d'amateur **amateur dramatics** NPL théâtre *m* amateur
amateur interest N ◆ **to have an ~ interest in sth** s'intéresser à qch en amateur
amateur status N statut *m* d'amateur

amateurish /ˈæmətərɪʃ/ ADJ (*pej*) d'amateur, de dilettante ◆ **the acting was rather ~** le jeu des acteurs n'était pas très professionnel

amateurishly /ˈæmətərɪʃlɪ/ ADV (*pej*) en amateur

amateurism /ˈæmətərɪzəm/ N amateurisme *m* (*also pej*), dilettantisme *m*

amatory /ˈæmətərɪ/ ADJ (*frm, liter*) *[feelings]* amoureux ; *[poetry]* galant ; *[letter]* d'amour

amaze /əˈmeɪz/ VT stupéfier, ébahir ◆ **you ~ me!** (*iro*) pas possible !

amazed /əˈmeɪzd/ ADJ *[person, glance, expression]* stupéfait, ébahi ◆ **to be ~ at (seeing) sth** être stupéfait de (voir) qch ◆ **I'd be ~** ça m'étonnerait

amazement /əˈmeɪzmənt/ N stupéfaction *f* ◆ **she listened in ~** elle écoutait, stupéfaite

amazing /əˈmeɪzɪŋ/ ADJ incroyable, étonnant ◆ **it's ~!** c'est incroyable !, ça alors ! ◆ **"amazing new offer"** (*Comm*) "offre sensationnelle"

amazingly /əˈmeɪzɪŋlɪ/ ADV étonnamment ◆ **she coped ~ (well)** elle s'en est étonnamment bien tirée ◆ **~ (enough), he got it right first time** chose étonnante, il a réussi du premier coup

Amazon /ˈæməzən/ N 1 (= *river*) Amazone *f* ◆ **the ~ Basin** le bassin amazonien *or* de l'Amazone ◆ **the ~ jungle/rainforest** la jungle/la forêt amazonienne 2 (*Myth*) Amazone *f* ; (*pej*) virago *f*, grande bonne femme *f*

Amazonia /ˌæməˈzəʊnɪə/ N (*Geog*) Amazonie *f*

Amazonian /ˌæməˈzəʊnɪən/ ADJ (*Geog*) amazonien

ambassador /æmˈbæsədəʳ/ N (*lit, fig*) ambassadeur *m* ◆ **the French ~ (to Italy)** l'ambassadeur *m* de France (en Italie) ◆ **~-at-large** ambassadeur *m* extraordinaire ◆ **try to be an ~ for the school** essayez de vous montrer digne de *or* d'être un bon ambassadeur de votre école

ambassadorial /æmˌbæsəˈdɔːrɪəl/ ADJ d'ambassadeur, de l'ambassadeur

ambassadorship /æmˈbæsədəʃɪp/ N fonction *f* d'ambassadeur, ambassade *f*

ambassadress † /æmˈbæsɪdrɪs/ N (*lit, fig*) ambassadrice † *f*

amber /ˈæmbəʳ/ N ambre *m* ADJ *[jewellery]* d'ambre ◆ **~-coloured** ambré ◆ **~ light** (*Brit Aut*) feu *m* orange ◆ **the lights are at ~** les feux sont à l'orange ◆ **the scheme has been given an ~ light** ce projet a reçu un feu vert provisoire

ambergris /ˈæmbəgriːs/ N ambre *m* gris

ambi... /ˈæmbɪ/ PREF ambi...

ambiance /ˈæmbɪəns/ N ⇒ **ambience**

ambidextrous /ˌæmbɪˈdekstrəs/ ADJ ambidextre

ambience /ˈæmbɪəns/ N ambiance *f*, atmosphère *f*

ambient /ˈæmbɪənt/ ADJ *[temperature, noise, humidity]* ambiant N (*Phot*) lumière *f* d'ambiance
COMP **ambient music** N musique *f* d'ambiance

ambiguity /ˌæmbɪˈgjʊɪtɪ/ N 1 (*NonC*) *[of word, phrase]* ambiguïté *f* (*also Ling*), équivoque *f* ; (*in thought, speech* = *lack of clarity*) ambiguïté *f*, obscurité *f* 2 (= *ambiguous phrase etc*) ambiguïté *f*, expression *f* ambiguë

ambiguous /æmˈbɪgjʊəs/ ADJ *[word, phrase]* ambigu (-guë *f*) (*also Ling*), équivoque ; *[thought]* obscur ; *[past]* douteux, équivoque

ambiguously /æmˈbɪgjʊəslɪ/ ADV *[say, describe]* de façon ambiguë ◆ **~ worded** exprimé en termes ambigus

ambit /ˈæmbɪt/ N *[of person]* sphère *f* d'attributions, compétence *f* ; *[of authority etc]* étendue *f*, portée *f*

ambition /æmˈbɪʃən/ N ambition *f* ◆ **it is my ~ to ...** mon ambition est de ..., j'ai l'ambition de ...

ambitious /æmˈbɪʃəs/ ADJ ambitieux ◆ **to be ~ to do sth** ambitionner de faire qch ◆ **to be ~ for sb** avoir de l'ambition pour qn ◆ **my father was very ~ for me to set up my own business** mon père avait beaucoup d'ambition pour moi et voulait que je monte ma propre affaire ◆ **to be ~ for** *or* **of** (*frm*) **sth** ambitionner qch

ambitiously /æmˈbɪʃəslɪ/ ADV ambitieusement

ambivalence /æmˈbɪvələns/ N ambivalence *f*

ambivalent /æmˈbɪvələnt/ ADJ ambivalent

amble /ˈæmbl/ VI 1 *[person]* aller *or* marcher d'un pas tranquille ◆ **to ~ in/out** *etc* entrer/sortir *etc* d'un pas tranquille ◆ **to ~ along** *[person]* aller sans se presser ◆ **he ~d up to me** il s'est avancé vers moi sans se presser 2 *[horse]* aller l'amble, ambler N 1 *[of person]* pas *m or* allure *f* tranquille 2 *[of horse]* amble *m*

ambrosia /æmˈbrəʊzɪə/ N ambroisie *f*

ambrosial /æmˈbrəʊzɪəl/ ADJ (au parfum *or* au goût) d'ambroisie

ambulance /ˈæmbjʊləns/ N ambulance *f* ; → **flying**
COMP **ambulance chaser** * N (*pej*) *avocat qui encourage les victimes d'accidents à engager des poursuites*
ambulance driver N ambulancier *m*, -ière *f*
ambulance man N (pl **ambulance men**) (= *driver*) ambulancier *m* ; (= *nurse*) infirmier *m* (d'ambulance) ; (*carrying stretcher*) brancardier *m*
ambulance nurse N infirmier *m*, -ière *f* (d'ambulance)
ambulance train N train *m* sanitaire
ambulance workers NPL ambulanciers *mpl*

> **AMBULANCE CHASER**
> Aux États-Unis, le "chasseur d'ambulances" est un avocat peu scrupuleux qui incite les victimes d'accidents à engager des poursuites afin d'obtenir des dommages et intérêts, sur lesquels il touchera une commission. Par extension, l'expression désigne quiconque cherche à tirer profit du malheur des autres.

ambulatory /ˌæmbjʊˈleɪtərɪ/ ADJ (*US Med*) ambulatoire ◆ **~ patient/care** malade *mf*/traitement *m* ambulatoire

ambush /ˈæmbʊʃ/ N embuscade *f*, guet-apens *m* ◆ **troops in ~** troupes *fpl* embusquées ◆ **to be** *or* **lie in ~** se tenir en embuscade ◆ **to be** *or* **lie in ~ for sb** tendre une embuscade à qn ; → **fall** VT (= *wait for*) tendre une embuscade à ; (= *attack*) faire tomber dans une embuscade

am-dram /ˈæmdræm/ N (abbrev of **amateur dramatics**) théâtre *m* amateur

ameba /əˈmiːbə/ N (pl **amebas, amebæ** /əˈmiːbiː/) ⇒ **amoeba**

ameliorate /əˈmiːlɪəreɪt/ VT améliorer VI s'améliorer

amelioration /əˌmiːlɪəˈreɪʃən/ N amélioration *f*

amen /ˈɑːˈmen/ EXCL (*Rel*) amen, ainsi soit-il ◆ **~ to that!** tout à fait ! N amen *m inv* ◆ **to say ~ to ..., to give one's ~ to ...** (*Rel, fig*) dire amen à ...

amenable /əˈmiːnəbl/ ADJ 1 (= *answerable*) *[person]* responsable (*to sb* envers qn ; *for sth* de qch) ; ◆ **~ to the law** responsable devant la loi 2 (= *tractable, responsive*) *[person]* maniable, souple ◆ **he is ~ to argument** c'est un homme qui est prêt à se laisser convaincre ◆ **~ to discipline** disciplinable ◆ **~ to kindness** sensible à la douceur ◆ **~ to reason** raisonnable, disposé à entendre raison 3 ◆ **~ to** (= *within the scope of*) qui relève de, du ressort de

amend /əˈmend/ VT *[+ rule]* amender, modifier ; (*Parl*) amender ; *[+ wording]* modifier ; *[+ mistake]* rectifier, corriger ; *[+ habits]* réformer VI s'amender

amendment /əˈmendmənt/ N 1 (*to rule, law, constitution*) amendement *m* (*to sth* à qch) ; ◆ **to table an ~** présenter un amendement ; → **first** 2 (*to contract*) avenant *m* (*to sth* à qch) 3 (*to letter, script, text*) modification *f* 4 (*NonC* = *changing*) *[of rule, law]* révision *f* ; *[of behaviour]* amélioration *f* ; *[of mistake]* rectification *f*

amends /əˈmendz/ NPL ◆ **to make ~** (= *apologize*) faire amende honorable ; (*by doing sth*) se racheter ◆ **to make ~ to sb for sth** dédommager qn de qch, faire réparation à qn de qch ◆ **to make ~ for an injury** (*with money*) compenser un dommage ; (*with kindness*) réparer un tort ◆ **I'll try to make ~** j'essaierai de me racheter

amenity /əˈmiːnɪtɪ/ N 1 (*gen pl*) **amenities** (= *pleasant features*) agréments *mpl* ; (= *facilities*) aménagements *mpl*, équipements *mpl* (locaux) ◆ **public amenities** (*Jur*) équipements *mpl* collectifs ◆ **houses lacking the most basic amenities** des maisons sans le moindre confort ◆ **hotels with modern amenities** des hôtels avec tout le confort moderne ◆ **social amenities such as a day nursery** des équipements sociaux, tels que les crèches de jour ◆ **local amenities will include shops and offices** les équipements locaux comprendront des magasins et des bureaux
2 (*NonC* = *pleasantness*) *[of district, climate, situation]* charme *m*, agrément *m*
NPL **amenities** † (= *courtesies*) civilités *fpl*, politesses *fpl*
COMP **amenity bed** N (*Brit Med*) *lit d'hôpital réservé aux malades qui paient un supplément*
amenity society N (*Brit*) association *f* pour la sauvegarde de l'environnement

amenorrhoea, amenorrhea (US) /ˈeɪmenəˈrɪə/ N aménorrhée f

Amerasian /ˌæməˈreɪʒən/ ADJ amérasien N Amérasien(ne) m(f)

America /əˈmerɪkə/ N Amérique f ◆ **the ~s** les Amériques fpl ; → **north, united**

American /əˈmerɪkən/ ADJ américain ; [ambassador, embassy] des États-Unis, américain ◆ **as ~ as apple pie** typiquement américain
N 1 (= person) Américain(e) m(f)
2 (* = American English) américain m ◆ **what's that in good** or **plain ~?** (US) ≈ ça veut dire quoi en bon français ?
COMP **American cheese** N (US) cheddar m américain
the American Civil War N la guerre de Sécession
the American Dream N le rêve américain
American English N anglais m américain
American football N football m américain
American Indian N Indien(ne) m(f) d'Amérique ADJ des Indiens d'Amérique
American Legion N (US) organisme d'aide aux anciens combattants ; → LEGION
American plan N (US: in hotels) (chambre f avec) pension f complète

AMERICAN DREAM

Pour beaucoup d'Américains, le "rêve américain" désigne un ensemble de valeurs et de principes inscrits dans la déclaration d'Indépendance de 1776 et qui définissent globalement une certaine conception de la vie : individualisme, ardeur au travail, égalité des chances pour tous, justice et liberté universelles. L'expression est parfois utilisée par dérision pour dénoncer le contraste entre ces idéaux et le matérialisme qui caractérise certains aspects de la vie américaine contemporaine.

Americana /əˌmerɪˈkɑːnə/ N (NonC) objets ou documents appartenant à l'héritage culturel américain

americanism /əˈmerɪkənɪzəm/ N américanisme m

Americanization /əˈmerɪkənaɪˈzeɪʃən/ N américanisation f

americanize /əˈmerɪkənaɪz/ VT américaniser

Americanized /əˈmerɪkənaɪzd/ ADJ américanisé ◆ **to become ~** s'américaniser

americium /ˌæməˈrɪsɪəm/ N américium m

Amerind /ˈæmərɪnd/ N 1 Indien(ne) m(f) d'Amérique 2 (= language) langue f amérindienne

Amerindian /ˌæməˈrɪndɪən/ ADJ amérindien(ne) N Amérindien(ne) m(f)

amethyst /ˈæmɪθɪst/ N améthyste f COMP [jewellery] d'améthyste ; [colour] violet d'améthyste inv

Amex /ˈæmeks/ N 1 ® (US) (abbrev of **American Express** ®) American Express ® f ◆ **~ card** carte f American Express ® 2 (US) (abbrev of **American Stock Exchange**) Amex f (deuxième bourse américaine)

amiability /ˌeɪmɪəˈbɪlɪtɪ/ N amabilité f, gentillesse f (to, towards envers)

amiable /ˈeɪmɪəbl/ ADJ aimable, gentil

amiably /ˈeɪmɪəblɪ/ ADV [chat] gentiment ; [say, reply] aimablement ; [nod, grin] avec amabilité

amicable /ˈæmɪkəbl/ ADJ [feeling] amical ; [relationship] amical, d'amitié ◆ **~ settlement** (Jur) arrangement m à l'amiable

amicably /ˈæmɪkəblɪ/ ADV amicalement ; (Jur) à l'amiable

amid(st) /əˈmɪd(st)/ PREP [+ shouts, trees] au milieu de ◆ **he was forced to resign ~ allegations of corruption** il a été forcé de démissionner à la suite d'accusations de corruption ◆ **... ~ reports of fresh rioting** ... tandis que l'on signale de nouvelles émeutes

amidships /əˈmɪdʃɪps/ ADV (Naut) au milieu or par le milieu du navire

amidst /əˈmɪdst/ PREP ⇒ **amid**

amino acid /əˈmiːnəʊˈæsɪd/ N acide m aminé

Amish /ˈɑːmɪʃ/ NPL ◆ **the ~** les Amish mpl ADJ Amish inv ◆ **an ~ man/woman** un/une Amish

amiss /əˈmɪs/ ADJ ◆ **there is something ~** il y a quelque chose qui cloche ◆ **have I said/done something ~?** j'ai dit/fait quelque chose qu'il ne fallait pas ? ADV 1 ◆ **to take sth ~** (= be offended) mal prendre qch 2 * ◆ **a little politeness wouldn't go** or **come ~** (= would be welcome) un peu de politesse ne ferait pas de mal ◆ **a drink wouldn't go ~** un verre ne serait pas de refus 3 (= unfavourably) ◆ **to speak ~ of sb** dire du mal de qn

amity /ˈæmɪtɪ/ N (frm) amitié f

Amman /əˈmɑːn/ N Amman

ammeter /ˈæmɪtəʳ/ N ampèremètre m

ammo * /ˈæməʊ/ N abbrev of **ammunition**

ammonia /əˈməʊnɪə/ N (gaz m) ammoniac m ; (= liquid) ammoniaque f ; → **household, liquid**

ammonium /əˈməʊnɪəm/ N ammonium m COMP **ammonium chloride** N chlorure m d'ammonium

ammunition /ˌæmjʊˈnɪʃən/ N munitions fpl ◆ **round of ~** cartouche f ◆ **this has given ~ to their critics** cela a donné des armes à leurs détracteurs
COMP **ammunition belt** N ceinturon m
ammunition dump N dépôt m de munitions
ammunition pouch N cartouchière f

amnesia /æmˈniːzɪə/ N amnésie f

amnesiac /æmˈniːzɪæk/ ADJ amnésique

amnesty /ˈæmnɪstɪ/ N amnistie f ◆ **under an ~** en vertu d'une amnistie VT amnistier COMP **Amnesty International** N Amnesty International

amnia /ˈæmnɪə/ NPL of **amnion**

amniocentesis /ˌæmnɪəʊsənˈtiːsɪs/ N (pl **amniocenteses** /ˌæmnɪəʊsənˈtiːsiːz/) amniocentèse f

amnion /ˈæmnɪən/ N (pl **amnions** or **amnia**) (Anat) amnios m

amniotic /ˌæmnɪˈɒtɪk/ ADJ (Anat) amniotique ◆ **~ fluid/cavity** liquide m/cavité f amniotique ◆ **~ sac** poche f des eaux

amoeba /əˈmiːbə/ N (pl **amoebas, amœbæ** /əˈmiːbiː/) amibe f

amoebic /əˈmiːbɪk/ ADJ amibien ◆ **~ dysentery** dysenterie f amibienne

amok /əˈmɒk/ ADV ◆ **to run ~** (= lose self-control) [person] perdre tout contrôle de soi-même ; [crowd, imagination, emotions] se déchaîner ; (= go on killing spree) être pris d'un accès de folie meurtrière ◆ **the dog ran ~ in the sheep field** le chien s'est déchaîné dans le pré des moutons ◆ **this is an example of political correctness run ~** c'est un exemple des excès du politiquement correct

among(st) /əˈmʌŋ(st)/ PREP parmi, entre ◆ **~(st) the crowd** parmi la foule ◆ **~(st) the various things he gave me, there was ...** parmi les diverses choses qu'il m'a données, il y avait ... ◆ **to count sb ~(st) one's friends** compter qn parmi or au nombre de ses amis ◆ **to be sitting ~(st) the audience** être assis au milieu des or parmi les spectateurs ◆ **divide the chocolates ~(st) you** partagez-vous les chocolats ◆ **settle it ~(st) yourselves** arrangez cela entre vous ◆ **don't quarrel ~(st) yourselves** ne vous disputez pas, pas de disputes entre vous ◆ **to be ~(st) friends** être entre amis ◆ **~(st) others, ~(st) other things** entre autres (choses) ◆ **this is ~(st) the things we must do** ceci fait partie des choses que nous avons à faire ◆ **he is ~(st) those who know** il est de ces gens qui savent, il fait partie de ceux qui savent ◆ **~(st) the French** chez les Français

amoral /eɪˈmɒrəl/ ADJ amoral

amorality /ˌeɪməˈrælɪtɪ/ N amoralité f

amorous /ˈæmərəs/ ADJ amoureux ◆ **to make ~ advances to** faire des avances à (connotations sexuelles)

amorously /ˈæmərəslɪ/ ADV amoureusement

amorphous /əˈmɔːfəs/ ADJ (also Miner) amorphe ; (fig) [personality] amorphe ; [style, ideas] informe, sans forme

amortization /əˌmɔːtaɪˈzeɪʃən/ N amortissement m

amortize /əˈmɔːtaɪz/ VT [+ debt] amortir COMP **amortized mortgage loan** N prêt m hypothécaire à remboursements périodiques

amortizement /əˈmɔːtɪzmənt/ N ⇒ **amortization**

amount /əˈmaʊnt/ LANGUAGE IN USE 5.3 N 1 (= total) montant m, total m ; (= sum of money) somme f ◆ **the ~ of a bill** le montant d'une facture ◆ **to** or **in the ~ of** (Fin, Comm) à concurrence de ◆ **debts to the ~ of $200** dettes fpl qui se montent à 200 dollars
2 (= quantity) quantité f ◆ **I have an enormous ~ of work** j'ai énormément de travail ◆ **quite an ~ of ...** beaucoup de ... ◆ **any ~ of ...** quantité de ..., énormément de ... ◆ **she's got any ~ of friends** elle a énormément or des quantités d'amis ◆ **I've got any ~ of time** j'ai tout le temps qu'il (me) faut, j'ai tout mon temps
3 (NonC = value, importance) importance f, signification f ◆ **the information is of little ~** ce renseignement n'a pas grande importance

► **amount to** VT FUS 1 (Math etc) [sums, figures, debts] s'élever à, se monter à
2 (= be equivalent to) équivaloir à ◆ **it ~s to the same thing** cela revient au même ◆ **it ~s to stealing** cela revient or équivaut à du vol ◆ **it ~s to a change in policy** cela représente un changement de politique ◆ **he will never ~ to much** il ne fera jamais grand-chose ◆ **one day he will ~ to something** un jour il sera quelqu'un

amour † /əˈmʊəʳ/ N intrigue f amoureuse †, liaison f

amour-propre /ˌæmʊəˈprɒprə/ N amour-propre m

amp /æmp/ N 1 (also **ampere**) ampère m ◆ **a 13-~ plug** une prise de 13 ampères 2 (* abbrev of **amplifier**) ampli * m 3 abbrev of **ampoule**

amperage /ˈæmpərɪdʒ/ N ampérage m

ampere /ˈæmpeəʳ/ N ampère m COMP **ampere-hour** N ampère-heure m

ampersand /ˈæmpəsænd/ N esperluette f

amphetamine /æmˈfetəmiːn/ N amphétamine f

amphibia /æmˈfɪbɪə/ NPL amphibiens mpl

amphibian /æmˈfɪbɪən/ ADJ [animal, vehicle, tank] amphibie N 1 (= animal) amphibie m 2 (Mil) (= tank) char m amphibie ; (= car) voiture f amphibie ; (= aircraft) avion m amphibie

amphibious /æmˈfɪbɪəs/ ADJ [animal, vehicle] amphibie

amphitheatre, amphitheater (US) /ˈæmfɪˌθɪətəʳ/ N (Hist, Theat, gen) amphithéâtre m ; (in mountains) cirque m

amphora /ˈæmfərə/ N (pl **amphoras** or **amphorae** /ˈæmfəˌriː/) amphore f

ample /'æmpl/ ADJ 1 *(= more than adequate)* *[space, amount, resources]* amplement suffisant *(for sb/sth* pour qn/qch) ; *[parking-space, money]* largement assez de ◆ **to have ~ evidence** *or* **proof that ...** avoir des preuves solides que ... ◆ **there are ~ grounds for believing that ...** on a tout lieu de croire que ... ◆ **there is ~ justification for his behaviour** son comportement est amplement justifié ◆ **to have ~ means** avoir de gros moyens ◆ **there'll be ~ opportunity to discuss it later** on aura largement *or* amplement l'occasion d'en discuter plus tard ◆ **to have ~ opportunities to do sth** avoir plus d'une occasion de faire qch ◆ **to have ~ reason to do sth** avoir de solides raisons de faire qch ◆ **there is ~ room for sb/sth** il y a largement la place pour qn/qch ◆ **there is ~ room for improvement** il y a encore bien du chemin *or* bien des progrès à faire ◆ **to have ~ time (to do sth)** avoir largement *or* amplement le temps (de faire qch) ◆ **to make ~ use of sth** largement utiliser qch ◆ **she was given ~ warning** elle a été suffisamment prévenue
2 *(= large) [bosom, breasts]* généreux ; *[stomach]* gros (grosse *f*) ; *[waist]* épais (épaisse *f*) ; *[garment]* ample ◆ **her ~ cleavage** son décolleté plantureux

amplification /,æmplɪfɪ'keɪʃən/ N amplification *f* ◆ **~ of previous evidence** *(Jur)* amplification *f* des offres de preuve

amplifier /'æmplɪfaɪəʳ/ N amplificateur *m*, ampli * *m*

amplify /'æmplɪfaɪ/ VT *[+ sound, movement, force]* amplifier ; *[+ instrument]* amplifier le son de ; *[+ statement, idea]* développer ; *[+ story]* amplifier

amplitude /'æmplɪtju:d/ N 1 *(Astron, Phys)* amplitude *f* ; → **modulation** 2 *[of style, thought]* ampleur *f*

amply /'æmplɪ/ ADV largement, amplement ◆ **my patience was ~ rewarded** ma patience a été largement *or* amplement récompensée

ampoule, ampule *(US)* /'æmpu:l/ N ampoule *f (pour seringue)*

ampulla /æm'pʊlə/ N (pl **ampullae** /æm'pʊli:/) *(Anat)* ampoule *f*

amputate /'æmpjʊteɪt/ VT amputer ◆ **to ~ sb's arm/leg** amputer qn du bras/de la jambe

amputation /,æmpjʊ'teɪʃən/ N amputation *f* ◆ **to carry out the ~ of a limb** pratiquer l'amputation d'un membre

amputee /,æmpjʊ'ti:/ N amputé(e) *m(f)*

Amsterdam /'æmstədæm/ N Amsterdam

Amtrak /'æmtræk/ N *(in US) société mixte de transports ferroviaires interurbains pour voyageurs*

amuck /ə'mʌk/ ADV ⇒ **amok**

amulet /'æmjʊlɪt/ N amulette *f*

amuse /ə'mju:z/ VT 1 *(= cause mirth to)* amuser, divertir 2 *(= entertain, occupy)* distraire, amuser ◆ **to ~ o.s. by doing sth** s'amuser à faire qch ◆ **to ~ o.s. with sth/sb** s'amuser avec qch/aux dépens de qn ◆ **you'll have to ~ yourselves** il va vous falloir trouver de quoi vous distraire *or* de quoi vous occuper

amused /ə'mju:zd/ ADJ *[person, look, smile, attitude]* amusé ◆ **she seemed ~ at my suggestion** ma suggestion a semblé l'amuser ◆ **I was ~ to see/hear that ...** ça m'a amusé de voir/d'entendre que ... ◆ **to keep sb ~** distraire qn ◆ **to keep o.s. ~** se distraire, s'occuper ◆ **we are not ~** *(hum)* nous ne trouvons pas cela drôle

amusedly /ə'mju:zɪdlɪ/ ADV avec amusement, d'un air amusé

amusement /ə'mju:zmənt/ N 1 *(NonC)* amusement *m*, divertissement *m* ◆ **look of ~** regard *m* amusé ◆ **to hide one's ~** dissimuler son envie de rire ◆ **to do sth for ~** faire qch pour se distraire ◆ **(much) to my ~** à mon grand amusement ◆ **there was general ~ at this** ceci a fait rire tout le monde 2 *(= diversion, pastime)* distraction *f* ◆ **~s** *(Brit: in arcade)* jeux *mpl* d'arcade ◆ **a town with plenty of ~s** une ville qui offre beaucoup de distractions
COMP **amusement arcade** N *(Brit)* galerie *f* de jeux vidéo
amusement park N *(esp Brit = fairground)* parc *m* d'attractions

amusing /ə'mju:zɪŋ/ ADJ amusant, drôle

amusingly /ə'mju:zɪŋlɪ/ ADV *[talk, write]* d'une manière amusante ◆ **the ~ named Susan Swishtail** cette femme au nom amusant de Susan Swishtail

amyl alcohol /'æmɪl,ælkəhɒl/ N alcool *m* amylique

amylase /'æmɪleɪz/ N *(Physiol)* amylase *f*

amyl nitrite /'æmɪl,naɪtraɪt/ N nitrite *m* amylique

an /æn, ən, n/ INDEF ART → **a²**

Anabaptist /,ænə'bæptɪst/ N, ADJ anabaptiste *mf*

anabolic /,ænə'bɒlɪk/ ADJ anabolique ◆ **~ steroid** stéroïde *m* anabolisant

anachronism /ə'nækrənɪzəm/ N anachronisme *m*

anachronistic /ə,nækrə'nɪstɪk/ ADJ anachronique

anacoluthon /,ænəkə'lu:θɒn/ N (pl **anacolutha** /"ænəkə'lu:θə/) anacoluthe *f*

anaconda /,ænə'kɒndə/ N eunecte *m*, anaconda *m*

Anacreon /ə'nækrɪɒn/ N Anacréon *m*

anacreontic /ə,nækrɪ'ɒntɪk/ ADJ anacréontique N poème *m* anacréontique

anaemia, anemia *(US)* /ə'ni:mɪə/ N anémie *f* ; → **pernicious**

anaemic, anemic *(US)* /ə'ni:mɪk/ N, ADJ *(Med, fig)* anémique ◆ **to become ~** s'anémier

anaerobic /,ænɛə'rəʊbɪk/ ADJ anaérobie

anaesthesia, anesthesia *(US)* /,ænɪs'θi:zɪə/ N anesthésie *f*

anaesthetic, anesthetic *(US)* /,ænɪs'θetɪk/ N anesthésique *m* ◆ **under ~** sous anesthésie ◆ **to give sb an ~** anesthésier qn ADJ anesthésique

anaesthetist, anesthetist *(US)* /æ'ni:sθɪtɪst/ N (médecin *m*) anesthésiste *mf*

anaesthetize, anesthetize *(US)* /æ'ni:sθɪtaɪz/ VT anesthésier

anaglyph /'ænəglɪf/ N anaglyphe *m*

Anaglypta ® /,ænə'glɪptə/ N papier *m* peint gaufré

anagram /'ænəgræm/ N anagramme *f*

anal /'eɪnəl/ ADJ anal ◆ **~ sex** sodomie *f* ◆ **~ retentive** qui fait une fixation au stade anal ◆ **you're so ~!** * ce que tu es maniaque !

analgesia /,ænæl'dʒi:zɪə/ N analgésie *f*

analgesic /,ænæl'dʒi:sɪk/ ADJ, N analgésique *m*

anally /'eɪnəlɪ/ ADV ◆ **~ retentive** qui fait de la fixation au stade anal

analog /'ænəlɒg/ N *(US)* ⇒ **analogue**

analogic(al) /,ænə'lɒdʒɪk(əl)/ ADJ analogique

analogous /ə'næləgəs/ ADJ analogue *(to, with* à)

analogue /'ænəlɒg/ N analogue *m* ADJ analogique
COMP **analogue device** N unité *f* analogique
analogue-digital converter N convertisseur *m* analogique-numérique
analogue watch N montre *f* à lecture analogique

analogy /ə'nælədʒɪ/ N analogie *f (between* entre ; *with* avec) ; ◆ **to argue from ~** raisonner par analogie ◆ **by ~** par analogie *(with* avec)

analysand /ə'nælɪ,sænd/ N *(Psych)* sujet *m* en analyse

analyse, analyze *(US)* /'ænəlaɪz/ LANGUAGE IN USE 26.1 VT 1 analyser, faire l'analyse de ; *(Gram) [+ sentence]* faire l'analyse logique de 2 *(Psych)* psychanalyser

analyser, analyzer *(US)* /'ænəlaɪzəʳ/ N analyseur *m* ◆ **blood/image ~** analyseur *m* de sang/d'images

analysis /ə'næləsɪs/ LANGUAGE IN USE 26.1 N (pl **analyses** /ə'nælɪsi:z/) 1 analyse *f* ; *(Gram) [of sentence]* analyse *f* logique ◆ **in the ultimate** *or* **last** *or* **final ~** en dernière analyse, finalement 2 *(Psych)* psychanalyse *f* ◆ **to be in ~** être en analyse

analyst /'ænəlɪst/ N 1 *(gen)* analyste *mf* (= *psychanalyst)* (psych)analyste *mf* ; → **news**

analytic(al) /,ænə'lɪtɪk(əl)/ ADJ analytique ◆ **~(al) mind** esprit *m* analytique ◆ **~(al) psychology** psychologie *f* analytique *or* des profondeurs

analytically /,ænə'lɪtɪkəlɪ/ ADV *[think]* d'une manière analytique ◆ **to be ~ intelligent** avoir une intelligence analytique

analyze /'ænəlaɪz/ VT *(US)* ⇒ **analyse**

analyzer /'ænəlaɪzəʳ/ N *(US)* ⇒ **analyser**

anamorphosis /,ænə'mɔ:fəsɪs/ N (pl **anamorphoses** /"ænə'mɔ:fə,si:z/) anamorphose *f*

anapaest, anapest *(US)* /'ænəpi:st/ N anapeste *m*

anaphoric /,ænə'fɒrɪk/ ADJ *(Ling)* anaphorique

anaphylactic shock /,ænəfɪ"læktɪk'ʃɒk/ N choc *m* anaphylactique

anarchic(al) /æ'nɑ:kɪk(əl)/ ADJ anarchique

anarchism /'ænəkɪzəm/ N anarchisme *m*

anarchist /'ænəkɪst/ N, ADJ anarchiste *mf*

anarchistic /,ænə'kɪstɪk/ ADJ anarchique

anarcho... /æ'nɑ:kəʊ/ PREF anarcho... ◆ **anarcho-syndicalism** anarcho-syndicalisme *m*

anarchy /'ænəkɪ/ N anarchie *f*

anastigmatic /,ænəstɪg'mætɪk/ ADJ *(Phot)* anastigmate

anathema /ə'næθɪmə/ N *(Rel, fig)* anathème *m* ◆ **the whole idea of exploiting people was ~ to him** il avait en abomination l'idée d'exploiter les gens

anathematize /ə'næθɪmətaɪz/ VT frapper d'anathème

Anatolia /,ænə'təʊlɪə/ N Anatolie *f*

Anatolian /,ænə'təʊlɪən/ ADJ anatolien N (= *person)* Anatolien(ne) *m(f)*

anatomical /,ænə'tɒmɪkəl/ ADJ anatomique

anatomically /,ænə'tɒmɪkəlɪ/ ADV *[correct, different]* d'un point de vue anatomique, anatomiquement

anatomist /ə'nætəmɪst/ N anatomiste *mf*

anatomize /ə'nætəmaɪz/ VT disséquer

anatomy /ə'nætəmɪ/ N *(Med, Sci)* anatomie *f* ; *(fig) [of country etc]* structure *f* ◆ **a delicate part of one's ~** *(hum)* une partie sensible de son anatomie ◆ **he had spots all over his ~** * il avait des boutons partout, il était couvert de boutons

ANC /,eɪen'si:/ N (abbrev of **African National Congress**) ANC *m*

ancestor /'ænsɪstəʳ/ N *(lit)* ancêtre *mf*, aïeul *m* ; *(fig)* ancêtre *mf*

ancestral /æn'sestrəl/ ADJ ancestral ◆ **~ home** demeure *f* ancestrale

ancestress † /'ænsɪstrɪs/ N aïeule *f*

ancestry /ˈænsɪstrɪ/ **N** 1 (= lineage) ascendance *f* 2 (NonC = ancestors collectively) ancêtres *mpl*, aïeux *mpl* ◆ **to trace one's** ~ constituer son arbre généalogique

anchor /ˈæŋkəʳ/ **N** ancre *f* ; (*fig*) point *m* d'ancrage ◆ **to be** *or* **ride at** ~ être à l'ancre *or* au mouillage ◆ **to come to** *or* **drop** ~ mouiller *or* jeter l'ancre ◆ **~s away!** (*Naut*) levez l'ancre ! ; (*fig*) mettons les voiles !* ; → **cast, ride, up, weigh** **VT** 1 (*Naut*) mettre à l'ancre 2 (= *tie down*) arrimer 3 (*US*) [+ *TV show*] présenter **VI** (*Naut*) mouiller, jeter l'ancre **COMP** **anchor ice** **N** glaces *fpl* de fond

anchorage /ˈæŋkərɪdʒ/ **N** (*Naut*) mouillage *m*, ancrage *m*
COMP **anchorage dues** **NPL** (*Naut*) droits *mpl* de mouillage *or* d'ancrage
anchorage point **N** (*in vehicle*) point *m* d'ancrage

anchorite /ˈæŋkəraɪt/ **N** anachorète *m*

anchorman /ˈæŋkəmæn/ **N** (pl **-men**) (*esp US*) (*Rad, TV*) présentateur *m* ; (*in team, organization*) pilier *m*, pivot *m*

anchorwoman /ˈæŋkəwʊmən/ **N** (pl **-women**) (*esp US*) (*Rad, TV*) présentatrice *f* ; (*in team, organization*) pilier *m*, pivot *m*

anchovy /ˈæntʃəvɪ/ **N** anchois *m*
COMP **anchovy paste** **N** beurre *m* d'anchois
anchovy sauce **N** sauce *f* aux anchois, anchoïade *f*

ancient /ˈeɪnʃənt/ **ADJ** 1 [*painting, document, custom*] ancien ◆ **in** ~ **days** dans les temps anciens ◆ ~ **history** histoire *f* ancienne ◆ **it's** ~ **history*** c'est de l'histoire ancienne ◆ **(scheduled as an)** ~ **monument** (*Brit*) (classé) monument *m* historique ◆ **the Ancient World** le monde *m* antique, l'Antiquité *f* ◆ **Ancient Greece** la Grèce ancienne *or* antique ◆ **the Ancient Greeks** les Grecs *mpl* de l'Antiquité ◆ ~ **Rome** la Rome antique ◆ ~ **rocks** de vieilles roches *fpl* 2 (*: *gen hum*) [*person*] très vieux (vieille *f*) ; [*clothes, object, car*] antique, antédiluvien* ◆ **this is positively** ~ cela remonte à Mathusalem *or* au déluge ◆ **he's getting pretty** ~ il se fait vieux **NPL** **the ancients** les anciens *mpl*

anciently /ˈeɪnʃəntlɪ/ **ADV** (*frm*) anciennement, autrefois

ancillary /ænˈsɪlərɪ/ **ADJ** [*service, help, forces*] auxiliaire ◆ ~ **to** subordonné à ◆ **(hospital)** ~ **workers** personnel *m* des services auxiliaires (des hôpitaux), agents *mpl* des hôpitaux ◆ ~ **staff** (*Brit Scol*) agents *mpl* (d'un établissement scolaire) ◆ ~ **costs** (*Fin, Comm*) frais *mpl* accessoires *or* annexes

and /ænd, ənd, nd, ən/ **CONJ** 1 et ◆ **a man** ~ **a woman** un homme et une femme ◆ **his table** ~ **chair** sa table et sa chaise ◆ ~ **how!*** et comment !* ◆ ~**?** et alors ? ◆ **on Saturday** ~**/or Sunday** (*Admin*) samedi et/ou dimanche ; (*gen*) samedi ou dimanche ou les deux ◆ **great artists like Monet** ~ **Picasso** de grands artistes comme Monet ou Picasso
2 (*in numbers*) **three hundred** ~ **ten** trois cent dix ◆ **two thousand** ~ **eight** deux mille huit ◆ **two pounds** ~ **six pence** deux livres (et) six pence ◆ **an hour** ~ **twenty minutes** une heure vingt (minutes) ◆ **five** ~ **three quarters** cinq trois quarts
3 (+ *infin vb*) **try** ~ **come** tâchez de venir ◆ **wait** ~ **see** on verra bien, attendez voir
4 (*repetition, continuation*) **better** ~ **better** de mieux en mieux ◆ **now** ~ **then** de temps en temps ◆ **for hours** ~ **hours** pendant des heures et des heures ◆ **I rang** ~ **rang** j'ai sonné et resonné ◆ **he talked** ~ **talked/waited** ~ **waited** il a parlé/attendu pendant des heures ◆ ~ **so on** ~ **so forth** et ainsi de suite ◆ **he goes on** ~ **on*** quand il commence il n'y a plus moyen de l'arrêter
5 (*with compar adj*) **uglier** ~ **uglier** de plus en plus laid ◆ **more** ~ **more difficult** de plus en plus difficile
6 (*with neg or implied neg*) ni ◆ **to go out without a hat** ~ **coat** sortir sans chapeau ni manteau ◆ **you can't buy** ~ **sell here** on ne peut ni acheter ni vendre ici
7 (*phrases*) **eggs** ~ **bacon** œufs *mpl* au bacon ◆ **summer** ~ **winter (alike)** été comme hiver ◆ **a carriage** ~ **pair** une voiture à deux chevaux
8 (*implying cond*) **flee** ~ **you are lost** fuyez et vous êtes perdu, si vous fuyez vous êtes perdu

Andalucia, Andalusia /ˌændəlʊˈsiːə/ **N** Andalousie *f*

Andalucian, Andalusian /ˌændəlʊˈsiːən/ **ADJ** andalou (-ouse *f*)

Andean /ˈændɪən/ **ADJ** des Andes, andin

Andes /ˈændiːz/ **N** Andes *fpl*

andiron /ˈændaɪən/ **N** chenet *m*

Andorra /ænˈdɔːrə/ **N** (principauté *f* d')Andorre *f*

Andorran /ænˈdɔːrən/ **ADJ** andorran **N** Andorran(e) *m(f)*

Andrew /ˈændruː/ **N** André *m*

androgen /ˈændrədʒən/ **N** (*Physiol*) androgène *m*

androgynous /ænˈdrɒdʒɪnəs/ **ADJ** androgyne

androgyny /ænˈdrɒdʒɪnɪ/ **N** androgynie *f*

android /ˈændrɔɪd/ **ADJ, N** androïde *m*

Andromache /ænˈdrɒməkɪ/ **N** Andromaque *f*

Andromeda /ænˈdrɒmɪdə/ **N** Andromède *f*

androsterone /ænˈdrɒstəˌrəʊn/ **N** androstérone *f*

anecdotal /ˌænɪkˈdəʊtəl/ **ADJ** [*book, speech*] plein d'anecdotes ◆ ~ **evidence suggests the treatment can be effective** dans des cas isolés, ce traitement s'est révélé efficace ◆ **there have been** ~ **reports of people being mysteriously healed** il y aurait eu quelques cas de guérisons miraculeuses

anecdote /ˈænɪkdəʊt/ **N** anecdote *f*

anemia /əˈniːmɪə/ **N** (*US*) ⇒ **anaemia**

anemic /əˈniːmɪk/ **ADJ** (*US*) ⇒ **anaemic**

anemometer /ˌænɪˈmɒmɪtəʳ/ **N** anémomètre *m*

anemone /əˈnemənɪ/ **N** anémone *f* ; → **sea**

anent /əˈnent/ **PREP** (*Scot*) concernant, à propos de

aneroid /ˈænərɔɪd/ **ADJ** anéroïde ◆ ~ **(barometer)** baromètre *m* anéroïde

anesthesia /ˌænɪsˈθiːzɪə/ **N** (*US*) ⇒ **anaesthesia**

anesthesiologist /əˌnɪsθiːzɪˈɒlədʒɪst/ **N** (*US*) (médecin *m*) anesthésiste *mf*

anesthetic /ˌænɪsˈθetɪk/ **N, ADJ** (*US*) ⇒ **anaesthetic**

anesthetist /æˈniːsθɪtɪst/ **N** (*US*) ⇒ **anaesthetist**

anesthetize /æˈniːsθɪtaɪz/ **VT** (*US*) ⇒ **anaesthetize**

aneurism, aneurysm /ˈænjʊrɪzəm/ **N** anévrisme *m*

anew /əˈnjuː/ **ADV** (*liter*) de nouveau ◆ **to be born** ~ renaître ◆ **to start life** ~ **in a fresh place** recommencer sa vie ailleurs

angel /ˈeɪndʒəl/ **N** ange *m* ; (* = *person*) ange *m*, amour *m* ; (*Theat* *) commanditaire *mf* ◆ ~ **of Darkness** ange *m* des Ténèbres ◆ **the Angel of Death** l'Ange *m* de la mort ◆ **be an** ~* **and fetch me my gloves** apporte-moi mes gants, tu seras un ange ◆ **speak** *or* **talk of** ~**s!*** quand on parle du loup (on en voit la queue) ! ◆ **to go where** ~**s fear to tread** s'aventurer en terrain dangereux ; → **fool**[1], **guardian**
COMP **angel cake** **N** ≈ gâteau *m* de Savoie
angel dust * **N** (*Drugs*) angel dust *m*, poussière *f* d'ange
angel food cake **N** (*US*) ⇒ **angel cake**
angel shark **N** ange *m* de mer
angels-on-horseback **NPL** (*Brit Culin*) huîtres bridées de lard servies sur toasts

Angeleno /ˌændʒəˈliːnəʊ/ **N** (*US*) habitant(e) *m(f)* de Los Angeles

angelfish /ˈeɪndʒəlfɪʃ/ **N** (pl **angelfish**) scalaire *m* ; (= *shark*) ange *m* de mer

angelic /ænˈdʒelɪk/ **ADJ** angélique

angelica /ænˈdʒelɪkə/ **N** angélique *f*

angelical /ænˈdʒelɪkəl/ **ADJ** angélique

angelically /ænˈdʒelɪkəlɪ/ **ADV** [*behave, sing*] comme un *or* des ange(s) ◆ **she smiled** ~ elle a eu un sourire angélique

Angelino /ˌændʒəˈliːnəʊ/ **N** ⇒ **Angeleno**

angelus /ˈændʒɪləs/ **N** (= *prayer, bell*) angélus *m*

anger /ˈæŋgəʳ/ **N** colère *f* ; (*violent*) fureur *f* ◆ **to act in** ~ agir sous l'empire *or* sous le coup de la colère, agir avec emportement ◆ **words spoken in** ~ mots prononcés sous l'empire *or* sous le coup de la colère ◆ **to move sb to** ~ mettre qn en colère ◆ **his** ~ **knew no bounds** sa colère *or* son emportement ne connut plus de bornes ◆ **in great** ~ furieux **VT** mettre en colère, irriter ; (*greatly*) rendre furieux ◆ **to be easily ~ed** se mettre facilement en colère, s'emporter facilement

angina /ænˈdʒaɪnə/ **N** angine *f* ◆ ~ **(pectoris)** angine *f* de poitrine ◆ **to have** ~ faire de l'angine de poitrine

angiogram /ˈændʒɪəʊgræm/ **N** (*Med*) angiographie *f*

angioplasty /ˈændʒɪəʊˌplæstɪ/ **N** (*Med*) angioplastie *f*

angle[1] /ˈæŋgl/ **N** 1 (*also Math*) angle *m* ◆ **at an angle** en biais (*to* par rapport à) ; ◆ **at an** ~ **of** ... formant un angle de ... ◆ **cut at an** ~ [*pipe, edge*] coupé en biseau ◆ **the building stands at an** ~ **to the street** le bâtiment fait un angle avec la rue
2 (= *aspect, point of view*) aspect *m* ◆ **the various ~s of a topic** les divers aspects *mpl* d'un sujet ◆ **to study a topic from every** ~ étudier un sujet sous toutes ses faces *or* sous tous les angles ◆ **his article has a new** ~ **on the question** son article apporte un éclairage nouveau sur la question ◆ **from the parents'** ~ du point de vue des parents ◆ **let's have your** ~ **on it*** donnez-nous votre point de vue là-dessus *or* sur la question
VT 1 * [+ *information, report*] présenter sous un certain angle ◆ **he ~d his article towards middle-class readers** il a rédigé son article à l'intention des classes moyennes *or* de façon à plaire au lecteur bourgeois
2 (*Tennis*) **to** ~ **a shot** croiser sa balle, jouer la diagonale
3 [+ *lamp etc*] régler à l'angle voulu ◆ **she ~d the lamp towards her desk** elle a dirigé la lumière (de la lampe) sur son bureau
COMP **angle bracket** **N** chevron *m*
angle iron **N** fer *m*, équerre *f*
angle of incidence **N** angle *m* d'incidence

angle[2] /ˈæŋgl/ **VI** 1 (*lit*) pêcher à la ligne ◆ **to** ~ **for trout** pêcher la truite 2 (= *try to get*) **to** ~ **for sb's attention** chercher à attirer l'attention de qn ◆ **to** ~ **for compliments** aller à la pêche aux compliments ◆ **to** ~ **for a rise in salary/for an invitation** chercher à obtenir une augmentation de salaire/à se faire inviter ◆ **she's angling for a husband** elle fait la chasse au mari, elle cherche à se caser

Anglepoise ® /ˈæŋglˌpɔɪz/ **N** (*Brit:* also **Anglepoise lamp**) lampe *f* d'architecte

angler /'æŋglə^r/ N pêcheur *m*, -euse *f* (à la ligne) ◆ ~ **(fish)** lotte *f* de mer

Angles /'æŋglz/ NPL *(Hist)* Angles *mpl*

Anglican /'æŋglɪkən/ ADJ, N anglican(e) *m(f)* ◆ **the ~ Communion** la communion *or* la communauté anglicane

Anglicanism /'æŋglɪkənɪzəm/ N anglicanisme *m*

anglicism /'æŋglɪsɪzəm/ N anglicisme *m*

anglicist /'æŋglɪsɪst/ N angliciste *mf*

anglicize /'æŋglɪsaɪz/ VT angliciser

angling /'æŋglɪŋ/ N pêche *f* (à la ligne)

Anglo * /'æŋgləʊ/ N ⇒ **Anglo-American**

Anglo- /'æŋgləʊ/ PREF anglo-

Anglo-American /'æŋgləʊə'merɪkən/ ADJ anglo-américain N *(US)* Anglo-Américain(e) *m(f) (Américain d'origine anglo-saxonne)*

Anglo-Asian /'æŋgləʊ'eɪʃn/ ADJ *britannique originaire du sous-continent indien* N *Britannique originaire du sous-continent indien*

Anglo-Catholic /'æŋgləʊ'kæθəlɪk/ ADJ, N anglo-catholique *mf*

Anglo-Catholicism /'æŋgləʊkə'θɒlɪsɪzəm/ N anglo-catholicisme *m*

Anglo-French /'æŋgləʊ'frentʃ/ ADJ franco-britannique N *(= language)* anglo-normand *m*

Anglo-Indian /'æŋgləʊ'ɪndɪən/ N *(= British person in India)* Anglais(e) *m(f)* des Indes ; *(= person of British and Indian descent)* métis(se) *m(f)* d'Anglais(e) et d'Indien(ne)

Anglo-Irish /'æŋgləʊ'aɪərɪʃ/ NPL **the Anglo-Irish** les Anglo-Irlandais *mpl* ADJ anglo-irlandais

anglophile /'æŋgləʊfaɪl/ ADJ, N anglophile *mf*

anglophobe /'æŋgləʊfəʊb/ ADJ, N anglophobe *mf*

Anglo-Saxon /'æŋgləʊ'sæksən/ ADJ anglo-saxon N 1 *(= person)* Anglo-Saxon(ne) *m(f)* 2 *(= language)* anglo-saxon *m*

ANGLO-SAXON

Langue de la famille des langues germaniques, parlée en Grande-Bretagne entre le Ve siècle et la conquête normande (1066), et dont l'anglais actuel est partiellement dérivé. Beaucoup de mots d'usage très courant, par exemple "man", "child", "eat", "love" ou "harvest" sont d'origine **anglo-saxonne**.

Angola /æŋ'gəʊlə/ N Angola *m*

Angolan /æŋ'gəʊlən/ ADJ angolais N Angolais(e) *m(f)*

angora /æŋ'gɔːrə/ N 1 *(= cat/rabbit)* (chat *m*/lapin *m*) angora *m inv* ; *(= goat)* chèvre *f* angora *inv* 2 *(= wool)* laine *f* angora *inv*, angora *m inv* ADJ *[cat, rabbit etc]* angora *inv* ; *[sweater]* (en) angora

angostura /æŋgə'stjʊərə/ N angustura *f* COMP **angostura bitters** ® N bitter *m* additionné d'angustura

angrily /'æŋgrɪlɪ/ ADV *[say, react]* avec colère ; *[leave]* en colère

angry /'æŋgrɪ/ ADJ *[person]* en colère, fâché *(with sb* contre qn ; *at sth* à cause de qch ; *about sth* à propos de qch) ; *[look]* furieux ; *[reply]* plein *or* vibrant de colère ; *(fig) [sea]* mauvais, démonté ◆ **to get ~** se fâcher, se mettre en colère ◆ **to make sb ~** mettre qn en colère ◆ **he was ~ at being dismissed** il était furieux d'avoir été renvoyé *or* qu'on l'ait renvoyé ◆ **in an ~ voice** sur le ton de la colère ◆ **you won't be ~ if I tell you?** tu ne vas pas te fâcher si je te le dis ? ◆ **this sort of thing makes me really ~** ce genre de chose me met hors de moi ◆ **there were ~ scenes when it was announced that ...** la colère de la foule a éclaté quand on a annoncé que ... ◆ **~ young man** *(Literat)* jeune homme *m* en colère ◆ **the blow left an ~ scar on his forehead** le coup lui a laissé une vilaine cicatrice au front

angst /æŋst/ N angoisse *f* existentielle

angstrom /'æŋstrəm/ N angström *or* angstrœm *m*

Anguilla /æŋ'gwɪlə/ N Anguilla *f*

anguish /'æŋgwɪʃ/ N *(mental)* angoisse *f*, anxiété *f* ; *(physical)* supplice *m* ◆ **to be in ~** *(mentally)* être dans l'angoisse *or* angoissé ; *(physically)* être au supplice, souffrir le martyre

anguished /'æŋgwɪʃt/ ADJ *(mentally)* angoissé ; *(physically)* plein de souffrance

angular /'æŋgjʊlə^r/ ADJ anguleux ; *[face]* anguleux, osseux ; *[features]* anguleux ; *[movement]* dégingandé, saccadé

aniline /'ænɪliːn/ N aniline *f* COMP **aniline dyes** NPL colorants *mpl* à base d'aniline

anima /'ænɪmə/ N *(Psych)* anima *m*

animal /'ænɪməl/ N *(lit)* animal *m* ; (* *pej = person)* brute *f* ◆ **I like ~s** j'aime les animaux *or* les bêtes ◆ **man is a social ~** l'homme est un animal sociable ◆ **the ~ in him** *(pej)* la bête en lui, son côté bestial ◆ **he's nothing but an ~** c'est une brute ◆ **there's no such ~** *(fig)* ça n'existe pas ◆ **they're two different ~s** *(fig)* ce sont deux choses complètement différentes ADJ *[instinct]* animal ◆ **~ spirits** entrain *m*, vivacité *f* ◆ **full of ~ spirits** plein d'entrain *or* de vie
COMP **animal cracker** N *(US) cracker en forme d'animal*
animal experimentation N *(NonC)* expérimentation *f* animale *or* sur les animaux
animal fat N graisse *f* animale
animal husbandry N *(NonC)* élevage *m*
the animal kingdom N le règne animal
Animal Liberation Front N *Front m britannique de libération des animaux*
animal liberationist N *militant du mouvement de libération des animaux*
animal lover N personne *f* qui aime les animaux
animal rights NPL droits *mpl* des animaux
animal rights campaigner N défenseur *m* des droits des animaux
animal sanctuary N refuge *m* pour animaux
animal testing N expérimentation *f* animale

animate /'ænɪmɪt/ ADJ *(= living)* vivant, animé ; *(Ling)* animé VT /'ænɪmeɪt/ *(= make lively) [+ discussion]* animer, rendre vivant

animated /'ænɪmeɪtɪd/ ADJ 1 *(= lively)* animé ◆ **to become ~** s'animer ◆ **the talk was growing ~** la conversation s'animait *or* s'échauffait 2 *(Cine)* animé ◆ **~ film** dessin *m* animé, film *m* d'animation

animatedly /'ænɪmeɪtɪdlɪ/ ADV avec animation ◆ **he pointed ~ at the package** tout agité, il désigna le paquet

animation /,ænɪ'meɪʃən/ N 1 *[of person]* vivacité *f*, entrain *m* ; *[of face]* animation *f* ; *[of scene, street etc]* activité *f*, animation *f* 2 *(Cine)* animation *f* ; → **suspend**

animator /'ænɪmeɪtə^r/ N *(Cine)* animateur *m*, -trice *f*

animatronics /,ænɪmə'trɒnɪks/ N *(NonC: Cine)* animatronique *f*

animism /'ænɪmɪzəm/ N animisme *m*

animist /'ænɪmɪst/ ADJ, N animiste *mf*

animosity /,ænɪ'mɒsɪtɪ/ N animosité *f (against, towards* envers)

animus /'ænɪməs/ N 1 *(NonC)* ⇒ **animosity** 2 *(Psych)* animus *m*

anise /'ænɪs/ N anis *m*

aniseed /'ænɪsiːd/ N graine *f* d'anis COMP *[flavoured]* à l'anis

anisette /,ænɪ'zet/ N anisette *f*

Anjou /ɑ̃'ʒuː/ N Anjou *m*

Ankara /'æŋkərə/ N Ankara

ankle /'æŋkl/ N cheville *f*
COMP **ankle boot** N bottine *f*
ankle bracelet N bracelet *m* de cheville
ankle-deep ADJ ◆ **he was ~-deep in water** l'eau lui montait *or* il avait de l'eau jusqu'à la cheville ◆ **the water is ~-deep** l'eau vient (jusqu')à la cheville
ankle joint N articulation *f* de la cheville
ankle sock N *(Brit)* socquette *f*
ankle strap N bride *f*

anklebone /'æŋklbəʊn/ N astragale *m*

anklet /'æŋklɪt/ N bracelet *m or* anneau *m* de cheville ; *(US)* socquette *f*

ankylosis /,æŋkɪ'ləʊsɪs/ N ankylose *f*

Ann /æn/ N Anne *f*

annalist /'ænəlɪst/ N annaliste *m*

annals /'ænəlz/ NPL annales *fpl* ◆ **unique in the ~ of ...** unique dans les annales de ...

Annam /æ'næm/ N Annam *m*

Annapurna /,ænə'pɜːnə/ N Annapurna *m*

Anne /æn/ N Anne *f* ; → **queen**

anneal /ə'niːl/ VT *[+ glass, metal]* recuire

annex /ə'neks/ VT annexer N /'æneks/ *(= building, document)* annexe *f*

annexation /,ænek'seɪʃən/ N *(= act)* annexion *f (of* de) ; *(= territory)* territoire *m* annexe

annexe /'æneks/ N ⇒ **annex noun**

Annie Oakley * /,ænɪ'əʊklɪ/ N *(US)* billet *m* de faveur

annihilate /ə'naɪəleɪt/ VT *[+ army, fleet]* anéantir ; *[+ space, time]* annihiler, supprimer ; *[+ effect]* annihiler ; *(fig: in game, argument)* écraser

annihilation /ə,naɪə'leɪʃən/ N *(Mil)* anéantissement *m* ; *(fig)* suppression *f*

anniversary /,ænɪ'vɜːsərɪ/ N *(= date, event)* anniversaire *m (of* de) ; ◆ **it's our ~** c'est l'anniversaire de notre mariage ; → **wedding** COMP **anniversary dinner** N dîner *m* commémoratif *or* anniversaire

Anno Domini /'ænəʊ'dɒmɪnaɪ/ ADV *(frm)* après Jésus-Christ ◆ **~ 1965** 1965 après J.-C.

annotate /'ænəʊteɪt/ VT annoter

annotation /,ænəʊ'teɪʃən/ N annotation *f*, note *f*

announce /ə'naʊns/ LANGUAGE IN USE 24 VT annoncer ◆ **to ~ the birth/death of ...** faire part de la naissance/du décès de ... ◆ **"I won't do it!" he ~d** "je refuse !" annonça-t-il ◆ **it is ~d from London that ...** on apprend de Londres que ...

announcement /ə'naʊnsmənt/ N *(gen)* annonce *f* ; *(esp Admin)* avis *m* ; *[of birth, marriage, death]* avis *m* ; *(privately inserted or circulated)* faire-part *m inv*

announcer /ə'naʊnsə^r/ N 1 *(Rad, TV)* présentateur *m*, -trice *f* 2 *(at airport, station)* annonceur *m*, -euse *f*

annoy /ə'nɔɪ/ VT *(= vex)* ennuyer, agacer ; *(= deliberately irritate) [+ person, animal]* agacer, énerver ; *(= inconvenience)* importuner, ennuyer ◆ **to be/get ~ed with sb** être/se mettre en colère contre qn ◆ **to be ~ed about sth** être contrarié par qch ◆ **to be ~ed about a decision** être mécontent d'une décision ◆ **to be ~ed with sb about sth** être mécontent de qn à propos de qch ◆ **to get ~ed with a machine** se mettre en colère *or* s'énerver contre une machine ◆ **don't get ~ed!** ne vous fâchez *or* énervez pas ! ◆ **I am very ~ed that he hasn't come** je suis très ennuyé *or* contrarié qu'il ne soit pas venu ◆ **I am very ~ed with him for not coming** je suis très mécontent qu'il ne soit pas venu

annoyance /əˈnɔɪəns/ N 1 (= *displeasure*) contrariété *f*, mécontentement *m* ◆ **with a look of** ~ d'un air contrarié *or* mécontent ◆ **he found to his great ~ that ...** il s'est aperçu à son grand mécontentement que ... 2 (= *cause of annoyance*) tracas *m*, ennui *m*

annoying /əˈnɔɪɪŋ/ ADJ agaçant ; (= *very irritating*) ennuyeux ◆ **the ~ thing about it is that ...** ce qui est agaçant *or* ennuyeux dans cette histoire c'est que ... ◆ **how ~!** que c'est agaçant *or* ennuyeux !

annoyingly /əˈnɔɪɪŋlɪ/ ADV [*behave*] de façon énervante *or* agaçante ◆ **she was ~ vague/cheerful** elle était si vague/gaie que c'était énervant *or* agaçant ◆ **he was ~ successful** sa réussite avait quelque chose d'énervant *or* d'agaçant

annual /ˈænjʊəl/ ADJ annuel ◆ **~ general meeting** assemblée *f* générale annuelle N 1 (= *plant*) plante *f* annuelle ; → **hardy** 2 (= *book*) publication *f* annuelle ; (*children's*) album *m* COMP **annual ring** N (*on tree*) anneau *m* de croissance, cerne *m*

annualize /ˈænjʊəlaɪz/ VT annualiser

annually /ˈænjʊəlɪ/ ADV annuellement, tous les ans ◆ **$5,000 ~** 5 000 dollars par an

annuity /əˈnjuːɪtɪ/ N (= *regular income*) rente *f* ; (*for life*) rente *f* viagère, viager *m* ; (= *investment*) viager *m* ◆ **to invest money in an ~** placer de l'argent en viager ; → **defer¹**, **life** COMP **annuity bond** N titre *m* de rente

annul /əˈnʌl/ VT [+ *law*] abroger, abolir ; [+ *decision, judgement*] casser, annuler ; [+ *marriage*] annuler

annulment /əˈnʌlmənt/ N annulation *f*

Annunciation /əˌnʌnsɪˈeɪʃən/ N Annonciation *f*

anode /ˈænəʊd/ N anode *f*

anodize /ˈænədaɪz/ VT anodiser

anodyne /ˈænəʊdaɪn/ N (*Med*) analgésique *m*, calmant *m* ; (*fig liter*) baume *m* ADJ (*Med*) antalgique, analgésique ; (*fig liter*) apaisant

anoint /əˈnɔɪnt/ VT oindre (*with* de) consacrer *or* bénir par l'onction ◆ **to ~ sb king** sacrer qn roi ◆ **the ~ed King** le roi consacré ◆ **the press have ~ed her queen of detective fiction** la presse l'a sacrée reine du roman policier

anointing /əˈnɔɪntɪŋ/ N (*Rel*) ◆ **~ of the sick** onction *f* des malades

anomalous /əˈnɒmələs/ ADJ (*Med*) anormal, irrégulier ; (*Gram*) anomal ; (*fig*) anormal

anomaly /əˈnɒməlɪ/ N anomalie *f*

anomie, anomy /ˈænəʊmɪ/ N (*NonC*) anomie *f*

anon¹ /əˈnɒn/ ADV (*archaic or hum* = *soon*) sous peu ◆ **... of which more ~** ... nous y reviendrons ◆ **see you ~** à tout à l'heure ; → **ever**

anon² /əˈnɒn/ ADJ (abbrev of **anonymous**) anonyme ◆ **"Anon"** (*at end of text*) "Anonyme"

anonymity /ˌænəˈnɪmɪtɪ/ N anonymat *m* ◆ **to preserve one's ~** garder l'anonymat ◆ **on condition of ~** [*speak*] à titre officieux, officieusement

anonymize /əˈnɒnɪmaɪz/ VT rendre anonyme

anonymous /əˈnɒnɪməs/ ADJ 1 anonyme ◆ **an ~ caller claiming to represent the group** un coup de téléphone anonyme d'une personne affirmant représenter le groupe ◆ **an ~ woman called to say that ...** une femme qui n'a pas donné son nom a appelé pour dire que ... ◆ **to remain ~** garder l'anonymat 2 impersonnel ◆ **an ~(-looking) hotel** un hôtel impersonnel ◆ **huge ~ apartment blocks** d'énormes immeubles impersonnels 3 ◆ **Overeaters/Narcotics Anonymous** Boulimiques/Toxicomanes *mpl* anonymes ; → **alcoholic, gambler**

anonymously /əˈnɒnɪməslɪ/ ADV [*send, give, publish*] anonymement ; [*speak, quote, live*] sous couvert de l'anonymat

anorak /ˈænəræk/ N (*esp Brit*) 1 (= *jacket*) anorak *m* 2 (* = *unstylish person*) ringard(e)* *m(f)*

anorectic /ˌænəˈrektɪk/ ADJ ⇒ **anorexic**

anorexia /ˌænəˈreksɪə/ N anorexie *f* ◆ **~ nervosa** anorexie *f* mentale

anorexic /ˌænəˈreksɪk/ ADJ, N anorexique *mf*

another /əˈnʌðəʳ/ ADJ 1 (= *one more*) un ... de plus, encore un ◆ **take ~ ten** prenez-en encore dix ◆ **to wait ~ hour** attendre une heure de plus *or* encore une heure ◆ **I won't wait ~ minute!** je n'attendrai pas une minute de plus ! ◆ **without ~ word** sans ajouter un mot, sans un mot de plus ◆ **~ beer?** vous reprendrez bien une bière ? ◆ **in ~ 20 years** dans 20 ans ◆ **and ~ thing ...*** (= *what's more*) et autre chose ...

2 (= *similar*) un autre, un second ◆ **there is not ~ book like it, there is not ~ such book** ce livre est unique en son genre ◆ **he will be ~ Hitler** ce sera un second *or* nouvel Hitler

3 (= *different*) un autre ◆ **that's quite ~ matter** c'est une tout autre question, c'est tout autre chose ◆ **do it ~ time** vous le ferez plus tard

PRON 1 un(e) autre, encore un(e) ◆ **in one form or ~** sous une forme ou une autre ◆ **he was opening bottles one after ~** il ouvrait des bouteilles les unes après les autres ◆ **between** *or* **what with one thing and ~*** en fin de compte ; see also **after, thing**

2 ◆ **one ~** ⇒ **each other** ; → **each**

anoxia /əˈnɒksɪə/ N anoxie *f*

anoxic /əˈnɒksɪk/ ADJ anoxique

ANSI /ˌeɪenesˈaɪ/ N (*US*) (abbrev of **American National Standards Institute**) ANSI *m*, institut *m* américain de normalisation

answer /ˈɑːnsəʳ/ N 1 (= *reply*) réponse *f* ◆ **to get** *or* **receive an ~** recevoir une réponse ◆ **to write sb an ~** répondre à qn (par écrit) ◆ **his only ~ was to shrug his shoulders** pour toute réponse il a haussé les épaules, il a répondu par un haussement d'épaules ◆ **there's no ~** (*Telec*) ça ne répond pas ◆ **I knocked but there was no ~** j'ai frappé mais il n'y a pas eu de réponse *or* mais on ne m'a pas répondu ◆ **in ~ to your letter** (*Comm*) en réponse à votre lettre ◆ **I could find no ~** je n'ai rien trouvé à répondre ◆ **she's got an ~ to everything, she's always got an ~** elle a réponse à tout ◆ **~ to a charge** (*Jur*) réponse *f* à une accusation ◆ **the ~ to my prayer** (*Rel*) l'exaucement *m* de ma prière ◆ **it's the ~ to a maiden's prayer*** (*hum*) c'est ce dont j'ai toujours rêvé ◆ **for her he was the ~ to a maiden's prayer*** (*hum*) c'était l'homme de ses rêves ◆ **there's no ~ to that!** que voulez-vous répondre à ça ? ◆ **Belgium's ~ to Sylvester Stallone** le Sylvester Stallone belge ◆ **it's the poor man's ~ to caviar** c'est le caviar du pauvre

2 (= *solution*) solution *f* ◆ **there must be an ~** il doit y avoir une solution ◆ **there is no easy ~** (*fig*) c'est un problème difficile à résoudre, il n'y a pas de réponse toute faite ◆ **he knows all the ~s** il a réponse à tout

VT 1 [+ *letter, question*] répondre à ; [+ *criticism*] répondre à ; (*sharply*) répliquer à ◆ **~ me!** répondez-moi ! ◆ **to ~ the bell** *or* **door** aller *or* venir ouvrir (la porte), aller voir qui est à la porte *or* qui est là ◆ **to ~ the bell** [*servant summoned*] répondre au coup de sonnette ◆ **to ~ the phone** répondre au téléphone ◆ **I didn't ~ a word** je n'ai rien répondu, je n'ai pas soufflé mot

2 (= *fulfil, solve*) [+ *description*] répondre à, correspondre à ; [+ *prayer*] exaucer ; [+ *problem*] résoudre ; [+ *need*] répondre à, satisfaire ◆ **it ~s the purpose** cela fait l'affaire ◆ **this machine ~s several purposes** cet appareil a plusieurs utilisations

3 (*Jur*) **to ~ a charge (of assault)** répondre d'une accusation (d'agression)

4 (*Naut*) **to ~ the helm** obéir à la barre

VI 1 (= *say, write in reply*) répondre

2 (= *succeed*) [*plan etc*] faire l'affaire, réussir

3 ◆ **he ~s to the name of "Baby Boy"** il répond au nom de "Baby Boy", il s'appelle "Baby Boy" ◆ **he ~s to that description** il répond à cette description

COMP **answer-back (code)** N indicatif *m*

answering machine N répondeur *m* (téléphonique)

answering service N permanence *f* téléphonique

► **answer back** VI, VT SEP répondre (avec impertinence) (*(to) sb* à qn) ; ◆ **don't ~ back!** ne réponds pas !

N ◆ **answer-back** → **answer**

► **answer for** VT FUS (= *be responsible for*) [+ *sb's safety etc*] répondre de ◆ **to ~ for the truth of sth** répondre de l'exactitude de qch ◆ **he has a lot to ~ for** il a bien des comptes à rendre

answerable /ˈɑːnsərəbl/ ADJ 1 (= *accountable*) [*person*] responsable (*to sb* devant qn ; *for sth* de qch) ; ◆ **I am ~ to no one** je n'ai de comptes à rendre à personne 2 (= *having an answer*) [*question*] qui admet une réponse ; [*argument*] réfutable

answerphone /ˈɑːnsəfəʊn/ N répondeur *m* (téléphonique)

ant /ænt/ N fourmi *f* ◆ **to have ~s in one's pants*** ne pas (pouvoir) tenir en place COMP **ant-heap, ant-hill** N fourmilière *f*

antacid /æntˈæsɪd/ ADJ alcalin, antiacide N (médicament *m*) alcalin *m*, antiacide *m*

antagonism /ænˈtæɡənɪzəm/ N antagonisme *m* (*between* entre) opposition *f* (*to* à) ; ◆ **to show ~ to an idea** se montrer hostile à une idée

antagonist /ænˈtæɡənɪst/ N antagoniste *mf*, adversaire *mf*

antagonistic /ænˌtæɡəˈnɪstɪk/ ADJ [*force, interest*] antagonique, antagoniste ◆ **to be ~ to sth** être opposé *or* hostile à qch ◆ **to be ~ to sb** être en opposition avec qn ◆ **two ~ ideas/decisions** deux idées/décisions antagoniques *or* antagonistes

antagonize /ænˈtæɡənaɪz/ VT [+ *person*] contrarier, se mettre à dos ◆ **I don't want to ~ him** je ne veux pas le contrarier *or* me le mettre à dos

Antarctic /æntˈɑːktɪk/ N Antarctique *m* ADJ 1 antarctique, austral 2 ⇒ **Antarctic Ocean** COMP **Antarctic Circle** N cercle *m* Antarctique **Antarctic Ocean** N océan *m* Antarctique *or* Austral

Antarctica /æntˈɑːktɪkə/ N Antarctique *m*

ante /ˈæntɪ/ N (*Cards: in poker*) première mise *f* ◆ **to raise** *or* **up the ~*** (*fig*) placer la barre plus haut VI (*Cards*) faire une première mise ; (*US** = *pay*) casquer*

► **ante up** VI (*Cards*) augmenter la mise ; (*US** = *pay*) casquer*

ante... /ˈæntɪ/ PREF anté..., anti...

anteater /ˈæntiːtəʳ/ N fourmilier *m*

antebellum /ˌæntɪˈbeləm/ ADJ (*US Hist*) d'avant la guerre de Sécession

antecedent /ˌæntɪˈsiːdənt/ ADJ antérieur (-eure *f*) (*to* à) N 1 (*Gram, Math, Philos*) antécédent *m* 2 ◆ **the ~s of sb** les antécédents de qn

antechamber /ˈæntɪˌtʃeɪmbəʳ/ N antichambre *f*

antedate /ˈæntɪˈdeɪt/ VT 1 (= *give earlier date to*) [+ *document*] antidater 2 (= *come before*) [+ *event*] précéder

antediluvian /ˈæntɪdɪˈluːvɪən/ ADJ antédiluvien ; (* *hum*) [*person, hat*] antédiluvien* (*hum*)

antelope /ˈæntɪləʊp/ N (pl **antelope** *or* **antelopes**) antilope *f*

antenatal /ˈæntɪˈneɪtl/ N (= *examination*) examen *m* prénatal ADJ prénatal ◆ ~ **clinic** service *m* de consultation prénatale ◆ **to attend an ~ clinic** aller à la consultation prénatale ◆ ~ **ward** salle *f* de surveillance prénatale

antenna /ænˈtenə/ N (pl **antennas** *or* **antennae** /ænˈteniː/) antenne *f*

antepenult /ˌæntɪpɪˈnʌlt/ N (*Ling*) antépénultième *f*

antepenultimate /ˈæntɪpɪˈnʌltɪmɪt/ ADJ antépénultième

ante-post /ˈæntɪˈpəʊst/ (*Brit Gambling*) ADJ [*bet*] engagé avant le jour de la course ◆ **the ~ favourite** le favori d'avant la course ADV ◆ **to bet ~** parier avant le jour de la course

anterior /ænˈtɪərɪəʳ/ ADJ antérieur (-eure *f*) (*to* à)

anteroom /ˈæntɪrʊm/ N antichambre *f*, vestibule *m*

anthem /ˈænθəm/ N hymne *m* ; → **national**

anther /ˈænθəʳ/ N anthère *f*

anthologist /ænˈθɒlədʒɪst/ N anthologiste *mf*

anthologize /ænˈθɒləˌdʒaɪz/ VT faire une anthologie de

anthology /ænˈθɒlədʒɪ/ N anthologie *f*

Anthony /ˈæntənɪ/ N Antoine *m*

anthraces /ˈænθrəˌsiːz/ NPL of **anthrax**

anthracite /ˈænθrəsaɪt/ N anthracite *m* ADJ ◆ ~ **(grey)** (gris) anthracite *inv*

anthrax /ˈænθræks/ N (pl **anthraces**) (= *disease, boil*) anthrax *m*

anthropoid /ˈænθrəʊpɔɪd/ ADJ, N anthropoïde *m*

anthropological /ˌænθrəpəˈlɒdʒɪkəl/ ADJ anthropologique

anthropologist /ˌænθrəˈpɒlədʒɪst/ N anthropologue *mf*

anthropology /ˌænθrəˈpɒlədʒɪ/ N anthropologie *f*

anthropometry /ˌænθrəˈpɒmɪtrɪ/ N anthropométrie *f*

anthropomorphic /ˌænθrəpəʊˈmɔːfɪk/ ADJ anthropomorphe, anthropomorphique

anthropomorphism /ˌænθrəʊpəˈmɔːfɪzəm/ N anthropomorphisme *m*

anthropomorphist /ˌænθrəpəʊˈmɔːfɪst/ ADJ, N anthropomorphiste *mf*

anthropomorphize /ˌænθrəpəʊˈmɔːfaɪz/ VT anthropomorphiser

anthropomorphous /ˌænθrəʊpəˈmɔːfəs/ ADJ anthropomorphe

anthropophagi /ˌænθrəʊˈpɒfəgaɪ/ NPL anthropophages *mpl*

anthropophagous /ˌænθrəʊˈpɒfəgəs/ ADJ anthropophage

anthropophagy /ˌænθrəʊˈpɒfədʒɪ/ N anthropophagie *f*

anthroposophical /ˌænθrəpəʊˈsɒfɪkəl/ ADJ anthroposophique

anthroposophy /ˌænθrəˈpɒsəfɪ/ N anthroposophie *f*

anti * /ˈæntɪ/ ADJ ◆ **he's rather ~** il est plutôt contre N ◆ **the ~s** ceux qui sont contre PREP ◆ **to be ~ sth** être contre qch

anti... /ˈæntɪ/ PREF anti..., contre...

anti-abortion /ˈæntɪəˈbɔːʃən/ N ◆ ~ **campaign** campagne *f* contre l'avortement

anti-abortionist /ˈæntɪəˈbɔːʃənɪst/ N adversaire *mf* de l'avortement

anti-aircraft /ˈæntɪˈeəkrɑːft/ ADJ [*gun, missile*] antiaérien ◆ ~ **defence** défense *f* contre avions, DCA *f*

anti-apartheid /ˈæntɪəˈpɑːteɪt, ˈæntɪəˈpɑːtaɪd/ ADJ anti-apartheid

anti-authority /ˈæntɪɔːˈθɒrɪtɪ/ ADJ contestataire

antibacterial /ˈæntɪbækˈtɪərɪəl/ ADJ antibactérien

antiballistic /ˈæntɪbəˈlɪstɪk/ ADJ [*missile*] antibalistique

antibiotic /ˈæntɪbaɪˈɒtɪk/ ADJ, N antibiotique *m* ◆ **to be on ~s** être sous antibiotiques

antibody /ˈæntɪˌbɒdɪ/ N anticorps *m*

Antichrist /ˈæntɪkraɪst/ N Antéchrist *m*

anti-Christian /ˈæntɪˈkrɪstɪən/ ADJ antichrétien

anticipate /ænˈtɪsɪpeɪt/ VT 1 (= *expect, foresee*) prévoir, s'attendre à ◆ **we don't ~ any trouble** nous ne prévoyons pas d'ennuis ◆ **I ~ that he will come** je m'attends à ce qu'il vienne ◆ **do you ~ that it will be easy?** pensez-vous que ce sera facile ? ◆ **I ~ seeing him tomorrow** je pense le voir demain ◆ **the attendance is larger than I ~d** je ne m'attendais pas à ce que l'assistance soit aussi nombreuse ◆ **as ~d** comme prévu

2 (= *use, deal with or get before due time*) [+ *pleasure*] savourer à l'avance ; [+ *grief, pain*] souffrir à l'avance ; [+ *success*] escompter ; [+ *wishes, objections, command, needs, request*] aller au devant de, devancer ; [+ *blow, attack, events*] anticiper ◆ **to ~ one's income/profits** anticiper sur son revenu/sur ses bénéfices

3 (= *precede*) **to ~ sb's doing sth** faire qch avant qn ◆ **they ~d Columbus' discovery of America, they ~d Columbus in discovering America** ils ont découvert l'Amérique avant Christophe Colomb

VI (= *act too soon*) agir avec précipitation ◆ **don't ~!** pas si vite !

anticipation /ænˌtɪsɪˈpeɪʃən/ N 1 (= *expectation, foreseeing*) attente *f* 2 (= *acting too soon*) précipitation *f* 3 (= *experiencing etc in advance*) [*of pleasure*] attente *f* ; [*of grief, pain*] appréhension *f* ; [*of profits, income*] jouissance *f* anticipée ◆ ~ **of sb's wishes** *etc* empressement *m* à aller au-devant des désirs *etc* de qn 4 ◆ **in ~** par anticipation, à l'avance ◆ **thanking you in ~** (*Comm*) en vous remerciant d'avance, avec mes remerciements anticipés ◆ **in ~ of a fine week** en prévision d'une semaine de beau temps ◆ **we wait with growing ~** nous attendons avec une impatience grandissante

anticipatory /ænˈtɪsɪpeɪtərɪ/ ADJ (*Phon*) régressif

anticlerical /ˈæntɪˈklerɪkl/ ADJ, N anticlérical(e) *m(f)*

anticlericalism /ˈæntɪˈklerɪkəlɪzəm/ N anticléricalisme *m*

anticlimactic /ˌæntɪklaɪˈmæktɪk/ ADJ décevant

anticlimax /ˈæntɪˈklaɪmæks/ N [*of style, thought*] chute *f* (dans le trivial) ◆ **the ceremony was an ~** la cérémonie n'a pas été à la hauteur de l'attente ◆ **what an ~!** quelle douche froide !

anticline /ˈæntɪklaɪn/ N anticlinal *m*

anticlockwise /ˈæntɪˈklɒkwaɪz/ ADJ, ADV (*Brit*) dans le sens inverse des aiguilles d'une montre ◆ **in an ~ direction** dans le sens inverse des aiguilles d'une montre

anticoagulant /ˈæntɪkəʊˈægjʊlənt/ ADJ, N anticoagulant *m*

anticonvulsant /ˌæntɪkənˈvʌlsənt/ ADJ, N antispasmodique *m*, anticonvulsivant *m*

anticorrosive /ˈæntɪkəˈrəʊsɪv/ ADJ anticorrosion *inv* N produit *m* anticorrosion *inv*

antics /ˈæntɪks/ NPL [*of child, animal*] cabrioles *fpl*, gambades *fpl* ; [*of clown*] bouffonneries *fpl*, singeries *fpl* ◆ **all his ~** (*pej*) tout le cinéma * qu'il a fait ◆ **he's up to his ~ again** il fait de nouveau des siennes *

anticyclone /ˈæntɪˈsaɪkləʊn/ N anticyclone *m*

antidandruff /ˌæntɪˈdændrʌf/ ADJ antipelliculaire

antidazzle /ˈæntɪˈdæzl/ ADJ [*glass, coating*] antireflet *f inv* ◆ ~ **headlights** phares *mpl* antiéblouissants

antidepressant /ˈæntɪdɪˈpresənt/ N antidépresseur *m* ADJ antidépresseur

anti(-)doping /ˈæntɪˈdəʊpɪŋ/ ADJ antidopage

antidotal /ˈæntɪdəʊtəl/ ADJ antivenimeux

antidote /ˈæntɪdəʊt/ N (*Med, fig*) antidote *m* (*for, to* à, contre) contrepoison *m* (*for, to* de)

antidumping /ˈæntɪˌdʌmpɪŋ/ N antidumping *m* ◆ ~ **agreement** convention *f* antidumping

anti-establishment /ˈæntɪɪsˈtæblɪʃmənt/ ADJ contestataire

antifreeze /ˈæntɪˈfriːz/ N antigel *m*

anti-friction /ˈæntɪˈfrɪkʃən/ ADJ antifriction *inv*

antigen /ˈæntɪdʒən/ N antigène *m*

antiglare /ˈæntɪgleəʳ/ ADJ ⇒ **antidazzle**

anti-globalization /ˌæntɪgləʊbəlaɪˈzeɪʃən/ N antimondialisation *f* ◆ ~ **protesters** des manifestants antimondialisation

Antigone /ænˈtɪgənɪ/ N Antigone *f*

Antigua /ænˈtiːgjʊə/ N Antigua ◆ ~ **and Barbuda** Antigua et Barbuda

antihero /ˈæntɪˌhɪərəʊ/ N (pl **antiheroes**) antihéros *m*

antiheroine /ˈæntɪˈherəʊɪn/ N antihéroïne *f*

antihistamine /ˌæntɪˈhɪstəmɪn/ N (produit *m*) antihistaminique *m*

anti-inflammatory /ˈæntɪɪnˈflæmət(ə)rɪ/ ADJ (*Med*) anti-inflammatoire

anti-inflationary /ˌæntɪɪnˈfleɪʃənərɪ/ ADJ antiinflationniste

anti-interference /ˈæntɪɪntəˈfɪərəns/ ADJ antiparasite

anti-knock /ˈæntɪˈnɒk/ N antidétonant *m*

Antilles /ænˈtɪliːz/ N ◆ **the ~** les Antilles *fpl* ◆ **the Greater/the Lesser ~** les Grandes/Petites Antilles *fpl*

antilock /ˈæntɪlɒk/ ADJ (*Aut*) ◆ ~ **braking system** système *m* antiblocage *or* ABS ◆ **anti-lock brakes** freins *mpl* ABS ◆ ~ **device** dispositif *m* antiblocage

antilogarithm /ˌæntɪˈlɒgərɪθəm/ N antilogarithme *m*

antimacassar /ˈæntɪməˈkæsəʳ/ N têtière *f*, appui-tête *m*

antimagnetic /ˈæntɪmægˈnetɪk/ ADJ antimagnétique

antimarketeer /ˈæntɪmɑːkəˈtɪəʳ/ N (*Brit Pol*) adversaire *mf* du Marché commun

antimatter /ˈæntɪˌmætəʳ/ N antimatière *f*

antimissile /ˈæntɪˈmɪsaɪl/ ADJ antimissile

antimony /ˈæntɪmənɪ/ N antimoine *m*

antinuclear /ˈæntɪˈnjuːklɪəʳ/ ADJ antinucléaire

antinuke * /ˌæntɪˈnjuːk/ ADJ antinucléaire

Antioch /ˈæntɪɒk/ N Antioche

antioxidant /ˈæntɪˈɒksɪdənt/ N antioxydant *m*

antipasto /æntɪˈpæstəʊ/ (pl **antipasti**) N antipasto *m*

antipathetic /ˌæntɪpəˈθetɪk/ ADJ antipathique (*to* à)

antipathy /æn'tɪpəθɪ/ N antipathie *f*, aversion *f* (*against, to* pour)

antipersonnel /'æntɪpɜːsə'nel/ ADJ (*Mil*) antipersonnel *inv*

antiperspirant /'æntɪ'pɜːspɪrənt/ N déodorant *m* ADJ anti(-)transpiration

antiphony /æn'tɪfənɪ/ N (*Mus*) antienne *f*

antipodean /æn,tɪpə'diən/ ADJ *d'Australie ou de Nouvelle-Zélande*

antipodes /æn'tɪpədiːz/ NPL (*esp Brit*) antipodes *mpl*

antiquarian /,æntɪ'kwɛərɪən/ ADJ d'antiquaire ◆ **~ bookseller** libraire *mf* spécialisé(e) dans le livre ancien ◆ **~ collection** collection *f* d'antiquités N 1 amateur *m* d'antiquités 2 (*Comm*) antiquaire *mf* ◆ **~'s shop** magasin *m* d'antiquités

antiquary /'æntɪkwərɪ/ N (= *collector*) collectionneur *m*, -euse *f* d'antiquités ; (= *student*) archéologue *mf* ; (*Comm*) antiquaire *mf*

antiquated /'æntɪkweɪtɪd/ ADJ [*factory, prison, industry*] vétuste ; [*machinery, equipment*] vétuste, archaïque ; [*system, practice*] archaïque ; [*idea, belief*] vieillot (-otte *f*) ; [*person*] vieux jeu *inv*

antique /æn'tiːk/ ADJ (= *very old*) [*furniture etc*] ancien ; († = *ancient*) [*civilization etc*] antique ; (* *hum*) antédiluvien * N (= *sculpture, ornament etc*) objet *m* d'art (ancien) ; (= *furniture*) meuble *m* ancien ◆ **it's a genuine ~** c'est un objet (*or* un meuble) d'époque

COMP **antique dealer** N antiquaire *mf*
antique shop N magasin *m* d'antiquités

antiqued /æn'tiːkt/ ADJ [*furniture, pine*] verni à l'ancienne ; [*finish*] à l'ancienne ; [*leather*] vieilli, patiné

antiquity /æn'tɪkwɪtɪ/ N 1 (*NonC* = *great age*) ancienneté *f* 2 (= *ancient times*) antiquité *f* ◆ **in ~** dans l'Antiquité 3 ◆ **antiquities** (= *buildings*) monuments *mpl* antiques ; (= *works of art*) objets *mpl* d'art antiques, antiquités *fpl*

anti-racism /'æntɪ'reɪsɪzəm/ N antiracisme *m*

anti-racist /'æntɪ'reɪsɪst/ ADJ antiraciste, contre le racisme

anti-religious /'æntɪrɪ'lɪdʒəs/ ADJ antireligieux

anti(-)retroviral /'æntɪretrəʊ'vaɪərəl/ N antirétroviral *m* ADJ antirétroviral, e

anti-riot /'æntɪ'raɪət/ ADJ antiémeute

anti-roll bar /'æntɪ'rəʊlbɑːʳ/ N barre *f* antiroulis, stabilisateur *m*

antirrhinum /,æntɪ'raɪnəm/ N muflier *m*, gueule-de-loup *f*

anti-rust /'æntɪ'rʌst/ ADJ [*paint, spray etc*] antirouille *inv*

antisegregationist /'æntɪsegrə'geɪʃənɪst/ ADJ, N antiségrégationniste *mf*

anti-Semite /'æntɪ'siːmaɪt/ N antisémite *mf*

anti-Semitic /'æntɪsɪ'mɪtɪk/ ADJ antisémite

anti-Semitism /'æntɪ'semɪtɪzəm/ N antisémitisme *m*

antisepsis /,æntɪ'sepsɪs/ N antisepsie *f*

antiseptic /,æntɪ'septɪk/ ADJ, N antiseptique *m*

anti-skid /'æntɪ'skɪd/ ADJ antidérapant

anti-slavery /'æntɪ'sleɪvərɪ/ ADJ antiesclavagiste

anti-smoking /'æntɪ'sməʊkɪŋ/ ADJ antitabac

antisocial /'æntɪ'səʊʃəl/ ADJ [*person*] sauvage ; [*behaviour, activity*] antisocial, asocial ; [*habit*] antisocial ◆ **he arrived at an ~ hour** il est arrivé à une heure indue ◆ **don't be ~ *, come and join us** ne sois pas si sauvage, viens nous rejoindre

antispasmodic /'æntɪspæz'mɒdɪk/ ADJ, N antispasmodique *m*

antistatic /'æntɪ'stætɪk/ ADJ antistatique

antistrike /'æntɪ'straɪk/ ADJ antigrève

antisubmarine /'æntɪ,sʌbmə'riːn/ ADJ anti-sous-marin

anti-tank /'æntɪ'tæŋk/ ADJ antichar *f inv* ◆ **~ mines** mines *fpl* antichars

anti-terrorist /'æntɪ'terərɪst/ ADJ antiterroriste

anti-theft /'æntɪ'θeft/ ADJ ◆ **~ device** (*for vehicle, bike*) antivol *m* ; (*gen*) dispositif *m* contre le vol, dispositif *m* antivol

antithesis /æn'tɪθɪsɪs/ N (pl **antitheses** /æn'tɪθɪsiːz/) 1 (= *direct opposite*) antithèse *f* (*to, of* de) 2 (= *contrast*) contraste *m* 3 (*Literat*) antithèse *f*

antithetic(al) /,æntɪ'θetɪk(əl)/ ADJ antithétique

antithetically /,æntɪ'θetɪkəlɪ/ ADV par antithèse

antitoxic /'æntɪ'tɒksɪk/ ADJ antitoxique

antitoxin /'æntɪ'tɒksɪn/ N antitoxine *f*

antitrust /'æntɪ'trʌst/ ADJ (*US*) ◆ **~ commission** commission *f* antitrust *inv* ◆ **~ law** (*esp US*) loi *f* antitrust *inv*

antivirus /,æntɪ'vaɪərəs/ ADJ [*program, software*] antivirus *inv*

antivivisection /'æntɪ,vɪvɪ'sekʃən/ N antivivisection *f*, antivivisectionnisme *m*

antivivisectionist /'æntɪ,vɪvɪ'sekʃənɪst/ N adversaire *mf* de la vivisection

antiwar /,æntɪ'wɔːʳ/ ADJ antiguerre *inv*

antiwrinkle /'æntɪ'rɪŋkl/ ADJ antirides *inv*

antler /'æntləʳ/ N bois *m* (*de cerf*) ◆ **the ~s** les bois *mpl*, la ramure ◆ **a fine set of ~s** une belle ramure

antonym /'æntənɪm/ N antonyme *m*

antonymous /æn'tɒnɪməs/ ADJ antonymique

antonymy /æn'tɒnɪmɪ/ N antonymie *f*

antsy * /'æntsɪ/ ADJ (*US*) nerveux, agité

Antwerp /'æntwɜːp/ N Anvers

anus /'eɪnəs/ N anus *m*

anvil /'ænvɪl/ N enclume *f* ◆ **forged on the ~ of ...** (*fig*) forgé sur l'enclume de ... COMP **anvil cloud** N cumulonimbus *m*

anxiety /æŋ'zaɪətɪ/ N 1 (= *concern, also Psych*) anxiété *f* ◆ **deep ~** angoisse *f* ◆ **this is a great (cause of) ~ to me** ceci m'inquiète énormément, ceci me donne énormément de soucis ◆ **~ neurosis** (*Psych*) anxiété *f* névrotique 2 (= *keen desire*) grand désir *m*, désir *m* ardent ◆ **his ~ to do well** son grand désir de réussir ◆ **in his ~ to be gone he left his pen behind** il était si pressé de partir qu'il en a oublié son stylo, dans son souci de partir au plus vite il a oublié son stylo

anxious /'æŋkʃəs/ ADJ 1 (= *worried*) [*person, face, look*] anxieux (*about sth* à propos de qch ; *about doing sth* à l'idée de faire qch) ; [*feeling*] d'anxiété ◆ **to keep an ~ eye on sb** surveiller qn d'un œil inquiet ◆ **she is ~ about my health** mon état de santé l'inquiète beaucoup 2 (= *worrying*) [*time, situation, wait*] angoissant 3 (= *eager*) ◆ **to be ~ to do sth** tenir beaucoup à faire qch ◆ **not to be very ~ to do sth** n'avoir guère envie de faire qch ◆ **to be ~ that ...** tenir beaucoup à ce que ... + *subj* ◆ **to be ~ for sth** attendre qch avec impatience ◆ **~ for praise** avide de louanges ◆ **she was ~ for him to leave** elle avait hâte qu'il s'en aille

anxiously /'æŋkʃəslɪ/ ADV 1 (= *worriedly*) [*say, ask*] anxieusement ◆ **to look ~ at sb/sth** jeter un regard anxieux à qn/qch 2 (= *eagerly*) [*wait for*] impatiemment

anxiousness /'æŋkʃəsnɪs/ N ⇒ **anxiety**

any /'enɪ/ ADJ 1 (*negative contexts* = *some*) **I haven't got ~ money/books** je n'ai pas d'argent/de livres ◆ **you haven't got ~ excuse** vous n'avez aucune excuse ◆ **this pan hasn't got ~ lid** cette casserole n'a pas de couvercle ◆ **there isn't ~ sign of life** il n'y a aucun signe de vie, il n'y a pas le moindre signe de vie ◆ **I don't see ~ reason not to allow it** je ne vois pas pourquoi cela serait défendu ◆ **without ~ difficulty (at all)** sans (la moindre) difficulté ◆ **the impossibility of giving them ~ advice** l'impossibilité de leur donner le moindre conseil ◆ **I have hardly ~ money left** il ne me reste presque plus d'argent ◆ **"no parking at any time"** "stationnement interdit 24 heures sur 24" ◆ **no animals of ~ sort are allowed** les animaux sont strictement interdits ◆ **I can't see you at ~ other time** je ne suis disponible pour vous voir qu'à ce moment-là

2 (*questions, hypotheses* = *some*) **have you got ~ butter?** avez-vous du beurre ? ◆ **did they find ~ survivors?** ont-ils trouvé des survivants ? ◆ **if you see ~ children** si vous voyez des enfants ◆ **are there ~ others?** y en a-t-il d'autres ? ◆ **is it ~ use trying?** est-ce que cela vaut la peine d'essayer ? ◆ **do you have ~ complaints?** avez-vous à vous plaindre de quelque chose ? ◆ **do you want ~ particular brand of whisky?** vous voulez une marque de whisky particulière ? ◆ **if for ~ reason you disagree** si, pour une raison ou une autre, vous n'êtes pas d'accord ◆ **if you should have ~ problems** si vous avez un problème quelconque, si vous avez des problèmes ◆ **if you have ~ money** si vous avez de l'argent ◆ **he can do it if ~ man can** si quelqu'un peut le faire, c'est bien lui ◆ **if it is in ~ way inconvenient to you** (*frm*) si cela vous cause un dérangement quel qu'il soit, si cela vous cause le moindre dérangement

3 (= *no matter which*) n'importe quel, quelconque ; (= *each and every*) tout ◆ **take ~ two points** prenez deux points quelconques ◆ **take ~ card you like** prenez n'importe quelle carte, prenez la carte que vous voulez ◆ **come at ~ time** venez à n'importe quelle heure ◆ **at ~ hour of the day (or night)** à toute heure du jour (ou de la nuit) ◆ **~ time now** d'un moment à l'autre, très bientôt ◆ **~ pupil who breaks the rules will be punished** tout élève qui enfreindra le règlement sera puni ◆ **~ actor will tell you that performing is not easy** n'importe quel acteur vous dira que ce n'est pas facile de jouer ◆ **~ other judge would have been more lenient** tout autre juge aurait été plus clément ◆ **"valid at any station in Belgium"** "valable dans toutes les gares belges" ◆ **he's not just ~ (old *) footballer** ce n'est pas n'importe quel footballeur ◆ **they're not just ~ old * shoes, they're handmade** ce ne sont pas des chaussures quelconques, elles sont faites main ◆ **they eat ~ old thing *** ils mangent n'importe quoi ; → **day, minute**[1]

4 (*phrases*) **they have ~ amount of money** ils ont énormément d'argent ◆ **we have ~ amount of time** nous avons tout le *or* notre temps ◆ **there are ~ number of ways to do it** il y a mille façons de le faire ; → **case**[1], **rate**[1], **event**

PRON 1 (*negative contexts*) **she has two brothers but I haven't got ~** elle a deux frères mais moi je n'en ai pas ◆ **I don't believe ~ of them has done it** je ne crois pas qu'aucun d'eux l'ait fait ◆ **I have hardly ~ left** il ne m'en reste presque plus

2 (*questions, hypotheses*) **have you got ~?** en avez-vous ? ◆ **if ~ of you can sing** si l'un d'entre vous *or* si quelqu'un parmi vous sait chanter ◆ **if ~ of them come out** s'il y en a parmi eux qui sortent, si quelques-uns d'entre eux sortent ◆ **if ~ of them comes out** si l'un d'entre eux sort ◆ **few, if ~, will come** il

viendra peu de gens, si tant est qu'il en vienne, il ne viendra pas grand-monde, voire personne

3 (= *no matter which*) ~ **of those pens will do** n'importe lequel de ces stylos fera l'affaire

ADV 1 (*negative contexts*) ◆ **she is not ~ more intelligent than her sister** elle n'est pas plus intelligente que sa sœur ◆ **we can't go ~ further** nous ne pouvons pas aller plus loin ◆ **I won't wait ~ longer** je n'attendrai pas plus longtemps ◆ **without ~ more discussion they left** ils sont partis sans ajouter un mot ◆ **I can't imagine things getting ~ better for the unemployed** je ne pense pas que la situation puisse s'améliorer pour les chômeurs ◆ **the room didn't look ~ too clean*** la pièce ne faisait vraiment pas propre

◆ **not ... any more** ne ... plus ◆ **I can't hear him ~ more** je ne l'entends plus ◆ **don't do it ~ more!** ne recommence pas ! ◆ **is he rich? – not ~ more** est-ce qu'il est riche ? – plus maintenant ◆ **are you still in touch? – not ~ more** êtes-vous toujours en contact ? – non, plus maintenant

2 (*questions, hypotheses, comparisons*) un peu ◆ **are you feeling ~ better?** vous sentez-vous un peu mieux ? ◆ **do you want ~ more soup?** voulez-vous encore de la soupe *or* encore un peu de soupe ? ◆ **~ colder and we'd have frozen to death** si la température avait encore baissé, nous serions morts de froid ◆ **if you see ~ more beautiful painting than this** si vous voyez jamais plus belle peinture que celle-ci ◆ **I couldn't do that ~ more than I could fly** je ne serais pas plus capable de faire cela que de voler

3 * (= *at all*) ◆ **the rope didn't help them ~** la corde ne leur a pas servi à grand-chose *or* ne leur a servi à rien du tout

anybody /ˈenɪbɒdɪ/ PRON 1 (*negative contexts = somebody*) **I can't see ~** je ne vois personne ◆ **there is hardly ~ there** il n'y a presque personne ◆ **without ~ seeing him** sans que personne (ne) le voie ◆ **it's impossible for ~ to see him today** personne ne peut le voir aujourd'hui

2 (*questions, hypotheses = somebody*) quelqu'un ◆ **was (there) ~ there?** est-ce qu'il y avait quelqu'un ? ◆ **did ~ see you?** est-ce que quelqu'un t'a vu ?, est-ce qu'on t'a vu ? ◆ **~ want my sandwich?** quelqu'un veut mon sandwich ? ◆ **if ~ can do it, he can** si quelqu'un peut le faire c'est bien lui

3 (*affirmatives = no matter who*) ~ **who wants to do it should say so now** si quelqu'un veut le faire qu'il le dise tout de suite ◆ **~ could tell you** n'importe qui pourrait vous le dire ◆ **~ would have thought he had lost** on aurait pu croire *or* on aurait cru qu'il avait perdu ◆ **bring ~ you like** amenez qui vous voudrez ◆ **~ who had heard him speak would agree** quiconque l'a entendu parler serait d'accord ◆ **~ with any sense would know that!** toute personne sensée sait ça ! ◆ **~ but Robert** n'importe qui d'autre que *or* tout autre que Robert ◆ **bring somebody to help us, ~ will do** amenez quelqu'un pour nous aider, n'importe qui fera l'affaire ◆ **he's not just ~*, he's the boss** ce n'est pas le premier venu *or* n'importe qui, c'est le patron ; → **else**

anyhow /ˈenɪhaʊ/ ADV 1 (= *in any case, at all events*) en tout cas, de toute façon ◆ **whatever you say, they'll do it** ~ vous pouvez dire ce que vous voulez, ils le feront de toute façon *or* quand même ◆ **you can try ~** vous pouvez toujours essayer

2 (* = *carelessly, haphazardly*: also **any old how**) n'importe comment ◆ **he just did it ~** il l'a fait n'importe comment ◆ **the books were all ~ on the floor** les livres étaient tous en désordre par terre

3 (= *no matter how*) ◆ **do it ~ you like** faites-le comme vous voulez ◆ **the house was locked and I couldn't get in ~** la maison était fermée à clé et je n'avais aucun moyen d'entrer ◆ **~ I do it, it always fails** de quelque façon que je m'y prenne ça ne réussit jamais

4 (*: *summing up, changing subject*) bon ◆ **~, it's time I was going** bon, il faut que j'y aille

anymore /ˌenɪˈmɔːʳ/ ADV ne ... plus ◆ **I couldn't trust him ~** je ne pouvais plus lui faire confiance ; see also **any adv**

anyone /ˈenɪwʌn/ PRON ⇒ **anybody**

anyplace* /ˈenɪpleɪs/ ADV (*US*) ⇒ **anywhere**

anyroad‡ /ˈenɪrəʊd/ ADV (*Brit*) (= *anyway*) en tout cas ◆ **~, he was in a right lather*** en tout cas, il était vachement en colère*

anything /ˈenɪθɪŋ/ PRON 1 (*negative contexts = something*) **there isn't ~ to be done** il n'y a rien à faire ◆ **there wasn't ~ in the box** il n'y avait rien dans la boîte ◆ **we haven't seen ~** nous n'avons rien vu ◆ **he won't eat meat or cheese or ~*** il ne veut manger ni viande ni fromage ni rien* ◆ **hardly ~** presque rien ◆ **without ~ happening** sans qu'il se passe *subj* rien

◆ **anything but** ◆ **this is ~ but pleasant** ceci n'a vraiment rien d'agréable ◆ **~ but!** pas du tout !, bien au contraire !

2 (*questions, hypotheses = something*) **was there ~ in the box?** est-ce qu'il y avait quelque chose dans la boîte ? ◆ **did you see ~?** avez-vous vu quelque chose ? ◆ **are you doing ~ tonight?** vous faites quelque chose ce soir ?, avez-vous quelque chose de prévu pour ce soir ? ◆ **is there ~ in this idea?** peut-on tirer quoi que ce soit de cette idée ? ◆ **can ~ be done?** y a-t-il quelque chose à faire ?, peut-on faire quelque chose ? ◆ **can't ~ be done?** n'y a-t-il rien à faire ?, ne peut-on faire quelque chose ? ◆ **have you heard ~ of her?** avez-vous de ses nouvelles ? ◆ **if ~ should happen to me** s'il m'arrivait quelque chose *or* quoi que ce soit ◆ **if I see ~ I'll tell you** si je vois quelque chose je te le dirai ◆ **he must have ~ between 15 and 20 apple trees** il doit avoir quelque chose comme 15 ou 20 pommiers; → **else**

◆ **if anything ...** ◆ **if ~ it's an improvement** ce serait plutôt une amélioration ◆ **it is, if ~, even smaller** c'est peut-être encore plus petit

3 (*with adj*) **I didn't see ~ interesting** je n'ai rien vu d'intéressant ◆ **did you see ~ interesting?** tu as vu quelque chose d'intéressant ? ◆ **is there ~ more tiring/boring than ...?** y a-t-il rien de plus fatigant/ennuyeux que ... ?

4 (= *no matter what*) **say ~ (at all)** dites n'importe quoi ◆ **take ~ you like** prenez ce que vous voudrez ◆ **~ else would disappoint her** s'il en était autrement elle serait déçue ◆ **~ else is impossible** il n'y a pas d'autre possibilité ◆ **I'll try ~ else** j'essaierai n'importe quoi d'autre ◆ **I'd give ~ to know the secret** je donnerais n'importe quoi pour connaître le secret ◆ **this isn't just ~** ce n'est pas n'importe quoi ◆ **they eat ~** (= *they're not fussy*) ils mangent de tout

◆ **like anything*** ◆ **he ran like ~** il s'est mis à courir comme un dératé* *or* un fou ◆ **she cried like ~** elle a pleuré comme une Madeleine* ◆ **we laughed like ~** on a ri comme des fous, qu'est-ce qu'on a pu rire ! ◆ **they worked like ~** ils ont travaillé d'arrache-pied *or* comme des fous* ◆ **it's raining like ~** il pleut *or* tombe des cordes*

◆ **as ... as anything*** ◆ **it's as big as ~** c'est très très grand ◆ **it was as silly as ~** c'était idiot comme tout*

anytime /ˈenɪtaɪm/ ADV ⇒ **any time** ; → **any**

anyway /ˈenɪweɪ/, **anyways*** (*US*) /ˈenɪweɪz/ ADV ⇒ **anyhow**

anywhere /ˈenɪwɛəʳ/ ADV 1 (*affirmatives*) (= *no matter where*) n'importe où, partout ◆ **I'd live ~ in France** je vivrais n'importe où en France ◆ **the oldest rock paintings ~ in North America** les peintures rupestres les plus anciennes de toute l'Amérique du Nord ◆ **there are more of this species in these waters than ~ in the world** il y a plus de représentants de cette espèce dans ces eaux que partout ailleurs dans le monde ◆ **put it down ~** pose-le n'importe où ◆ **you can find that soap ~** ce savon se trouve partout ◆ **go ~ you like** va où tu veux ◆ **~ you go it's the same (thing)** où qu'on aille c'est la même chose ◆ **~ else** partout ailleurs ◆ **miles from ~*** loin de tout ◆ **there were ~ between 200 and 300 people at the meeting** le nombre de personnes présentes à la réunion pouvait aller de 200 à 300 ◆ **the time of death could have been ~ from two to five days ago** la mort aurait pu survenir entre deux et cinq jours auparavant

2 (*negatives*) nulle part ◆ **they didn't go ~** ils ne sont allés nulle part ◆ **we haven't been ~ this summer** nous ne sommes allés nulle part cet été ◆ **this species is not to be found ~ else** cette espèce ne se trouve nulle part ailleurs ◆ **we're not going ~ in particular** nous n'allons nulle part en particulier ◆ **we can't afford to eat ~ expensive** nous ne pouvons pas nous permettre d'aller dans un restaurant cher ◆ **that had not happened ~ in human history** cela ne s'était jamais produit dans l'histoire de l'humanité ◆ **we aren't ~ near* Paris** nous sommes loin de Paris ◆ **the house isn't ~ near* big enough** la maison est loin d'être assez grande ◆ **you aren't ~ near it!*** (*guessing etc*) tu n'y es pas du tout ! ◆ **it won't get you ~** cela ne vous mènera à rien ◆ **we're not getting ~** cela ne nous mène à rien ◆ **I'm not earning any money, so I'm not going ~** je ne gagne pas d'argent, alors je ne vais nulle part ◆ **he came first and the rest didn't come ~*** (*Sport etc*) il est arrivé premier et les autres étaient loin derrière

3 (*interrogatives*) quelque part ◆ **have you seen it ~?** l'avez-vous vu quelque part ? → **else**

Anzac /ˈænzæk/ N (= *soldier*) *soldat australien ou néo-zélandais*

AOB, a.o.b. /ˌeɪəʊˈbiː/ (abbrev of **any other business**) autres sujets *mpl* à l'ordre du jour

AOCB /ˌeɪəʊsiːˈbiː/ N (abbrev of **any other competent business**) ⇒ **AOB**

AONB /ˌeɪəʊenˈbiː/ N (*Brit*) (abbrev of **Area of Outstanding Natural Beauty**) → **area**

aorist /ˈeərɪst/ N aoriste *m*

aorta /eɪˈɔːtə/ N (pl **aortas** or **aortae** /eɪˈɔːtiː/) aorte *f*

aortic /eɪˈɔːtɪk/ ADJ (*Anat*) aortique

Aosta /æˈɒstə/ N Aoste

AP /eɪˈpiː/ (abbrev of **Associated Press**) *agence de presse*

apace /əˈpeɪs/ ADV (*frm*) rapidement, vite

Apache /əˈpætʃɪ/ N (= *person*) Apache *mf*

apart /əˈpɑːt/

> When **apart** is an element in a phrasal verb, eg **fall apart**, **keep apart**, **tear apart**, **tell apart**, look up the verb.

ADV 1 (= *separated*) **houses a long way ~** maisons (fort) éloignées l'une de l'autre *or* à une grande distance l'une de l'autre ◆ **set equally ~** espacés à intervalles réguliers ◆ **their birthdays were two days ~** leurs anniversaires étaient à deux jours d'intervalle ◆ **to stand with one's feet ~** se tenir les jambes écartées ; → **class, world**

2 (= *on one side*) à part, à l'écart ◆ **to hold o.s. ~** se tenir à l'écart (*from* de) ; ◆ **joking ~** plaisanterie mise à part, blague à part* ◆ **that ~** à part cela, cela mis à part

◆ **apart from** ◆ **~ from these difficulties** en dehors de *or* à part ces difficultés, ces difficul-

tés mises à part ◆ ~ **from the fact that …** en dehors du fait que …
3 *(= separately, distinctly)* séparément ◆ **they are living ~ now** ils sont séparés maintenant ◆ **he lives ~ from his wife** il est séparé de sa femme, il n'habite plus avec sa femme ◆ **you can't tell the twins** ~ on ne peut distinguer les jumeaux l'un de l'autre ◆ **we'll have to keep those boys** ~ il va falloir séparer ces garçons
4 *(= into pieces)* en pièces, en morceaux ◆ **to take** ~ démonter, désassembler ; → **come, fall, tear**[1]

apartheid /ə'pɑːteɪt, ə'pɑːtaɪd/ N apartheid *m* ◆ **the ~ laws** la législation permettant l'apartheid

apartment /ə'pɑːtmənt/ N 1 *(esp US = flat)* appartement *m* ◆ **~ building** *or* **house** *(= block)* immeuble *m (de résidence)* ; *(= divided house)* maison *f* (divisée en appartements) 2 *(Brit)* *(= room)* pièce *f* ; *(= bedroom)* chambre *f* ◆ **a five-~ house** une maison de cinq pièces ◆ **furnished ~s** meublé *m*

apathetic /,æpə'θetɪk/ ADJ apathique

apathetically /,æpə'θetɪklɪ/ ADV avec apathie

apathy /'æpəθɪ/ N apathie *f*

APB /,eɪpiː'biː/ N *(US)* (abbrev of **all-points bulletin**) message *m* à toutes les patrouilles ◆ **to put out an** ~ envoyer un message à toutes les patrouilles

APC /eɪpiː'siː/ N (abbrev of **armoured personnel carrier**) → **armoured**

ape /eɪp/ N (grand) singe *m* ◆ **big** ~* *(pej = person)* grande brute *f* ◆ **to go** ~* *(esp US)* *(= angry)* se mettre en rogne* ; *(= excited)* s'emballer* *(over* pour) → **apeshit** VT *(pej = imitate)* singer *(pej)*

APEC /'eɪpek/ N (abbrev of **Asia Pacific Economic Cooperation**) APEC *f*, Coopération *f* économique Asie-Pacifique

Apennines /'æpənaɪnz/ NPL Apennin *m*

aperient /ə'pɪərɪənt/ ADJ, N laxatif *m*

aperitif /ə,perɪ'tiːf/ N apéritif *m*

aperture /'æpətʃjʊə^r/ N *(= hole)* trou *m*, ouverture *f* ; *(= gap)* brèche *f*, trouée *f* ; *(Phot)* ouverture *f* (du diaphragme)

apeshit** /'eɪpʃɪt/ ADJ *(esp US)* ◆ **to go** ~ *(= angry)* se mettre en rogne* ; *(= excited)* s'emballer ; → **ape**

APEX /'eɪpeks/ N 1 (abbrev of **Association of Professional, Executive, Clerical and Computer Staff**) *syndicat* 2 (also **apex**) (abbrev of **advance purchase excursion**) ~ **fare/ticket** prix *m*/billet *m* APEX

apex /'eɪpeks/ N (pl **apexes** *or* **apices**) *(Geom, Med)* sommet *m* ; *[of tongue]* apex *m*, pointe *f* ; *(fig)* sommet *m*, point *m* culminant

aphasia /æ'feɪzɪə/ N aphasie *f*

aphasic /æ'feɪzɪk/ ADJ aphasique

aphid /'eɪfɪd/ N puceron *m*

aphis /'eɪfɪs/ N (pl **aphides** /'eɪfɪdiːz/) aphidé *m*

aphonic /,eɪ'fɒnɪk/ ADJ 1 *[person]* aphone 2 *(= silent) [consonant etc]* muet

aphorism /'æfərɪzəm/ N aphorisme *m*

aphoristic /,æfə'rɪstɪk/ ADJ aphoristique

aphrodisiac /,æfrəʊ'dɪzɪæk/ ADJ, N aphrodisiaque *m*

Aphrodite /,æfrə'daɪtɪ/ N Aphrodite *f*

apiarist /'eɪpɪərɪst/ N apiculteur *m*, -trice *f*

apiary /'eɪpɪərɪ/ N rucher *m*

apices /'eɪpɪsiːz/ NPL of **apex**

apiece /ə'piːs/ ADV *(= for each person)* chacun(e), par personne ; *(= for each thing)* chacun(e), pièce *inv*

aplenty /ə'plentɪ/ ADV *(liter)* en abondance

aplomb /ə'plɒm/ N *(liter)* sang-froid *m*, assurance *f*

Apocalypse /ə'pɒkəlɪps/ N Apocalypse *f (also fig)*

apocalyptic /ə,pɒkə'lɪptɪk/ ADJ apocalyptique

apocopate /ə'pɒkəpeɪt/ VT raccourcir par apocope

apocope /ə'pɒkəpɪ/ N apocope *f*

Apocrypha /ə'pɒkrɪfə/ NPL apocryphes *mpl*

apocryphal /ə'pɒkrɪfəl/ ADJ apocryphe

apogee /'æpəʊdʒiː/ N apogée *m*

apolitical /,eɪpə'lɪtɪkəl/ ADJ apolitique

Apollo /ə'pɒləʊ/ N *(Myth)* Apollon *m* ; *(Space)* Apollo *m*

apologetic /ə,pɒlə'dʒetɪk/ ADJ *[smile, letter]* d'excuse ; *[manner, tone]* contrit ◆ **with an ~ air** d'un air contrit ◆ **to be ~ (about sth)** se montrer très contrit (au sujet de qch) ◆ **to be profusely** ~ *[person]* se confondre *or* se répandre en excuses ◆ **he didn't look in the least** ~ il n'avait du tout l'air désolé

apologetically /ə,pɒlə'dʒetɪkəlɪ/ ADV *[say, smile]* d'un air contrit, pour s'excuser

apologetics /ə,pɒlə'dʒetɪks/ N *(NonC)* apologétique *f*

apologia /,æpə'ləʊdʒɪə/ N apologie *f*

apologist /ə'pɒlədʒɪst/ N apologiste *mf (for* de)

apologize /ə'pɒlədʒaɪz/ LANGUAGE IN USE 18.1 VI s'excuser ◆ **to ~ to sb (for sth)** s'excuser (de qch) auprès de qn, faire *or* présenter des excuses à qn (pour qch) ◆ **she ~d to them for her son** elle leur a demandé d'excuser la conduite de son fils ◆ **to ~ profusely** se confondre *or* se répandre en excuses

apologue /'æpəlɒg/ N apologue *m*

apology /ə'pɒlədʒɪ/ N 1 *(= expression of regret)* excuses *fpl* ◆ **a letter of ~** une lettre d'excuses ◆ **to make an ~ for sth/for having done sth** s'excuser de qch/d'avoir fait qch, faire *or* présenter ses excuses pour qch/pour avoir fait qch ◆ **there are apologies from Mr Watt** *(for absence at meeting)* M. Watt vous prie d'excuser son absence ◆ **to send one's apologies** envoyer une lettre d'excuse, envoyer un mot d'excuse ◆ **to offer** *or* **make one's apologies** présenter ses excuses ◆ **to make no ~** *or* **apologies for sth** assumer pleinement qch
2 *(= defence: for beliefs etc)* apologie *f*
3 *(pej)* **it was an ~ for** *or* **a feeble ~ for a speech/bed** en fait de *or* comme discours/lit c'était plutôt minable* ◆ **he gave me an ~ for a smile** il m'a gratifié d'une sorte de grimace qui se voulait être un sourire ◆ **we were given an ~ for a lunch** on nous a servi un soi-disant déjeuner

apoplectic /,æpə'plektɪk/ ADJ apoplectique ◆ **~ fit** *(Med, fig)* attaque *f* d'apoplexie N apoplectique *mf*

apoplexy /'æpəpleksɪ/ N 1 († = *heart attack)* apoplexie *f* 2 *(fig = rage)* fureur *f*

apostasy /ə'pɒstəsɪ/ N apostasie *f*

apostate /ə'pɒstɪt/ ADJ, N apostat(e) *m(f)*

apostatize /ə'pɒstətaɪz/ VI apostasier

a posteriori /'eɪpɒs,terɪ'ɔːraɪ 'eɪpɒs,terɪ'ɔːrɪ/ ADJ, ADV a posteriori ◆ **~ reasoning** raisonnement *m* a posteriori

apostle /ə'pɒsl/ N *(Hist, Rel, fig)* apôtre *m* ◆ **Apostles' Creed** symbole *m* des apôtres, Credo *m* ◆ **to say the Apostles' Creed** dire le Credo COMP **apostle spoon** N *petite cuiller décorée d'une figure d'apôtre*

apostolate /ə'pɒstəleɪt/ N apostolat *m*

apostolic /,æpəs'tɒlɪk/ ADJ apostolique

apostrophe /ə'pɒstrəfɪ/ N *(Gram, Literat)* apostrophe *f*

apostrophize /ə'pɒstrəfaɪz/ VT apostropher

apothecary /ə'pɒθɪkərɪ/ N apothicaire *m*

apotheosis /ə,pɒθɪ'əʊsɪs/ N (pl **apotheoses** /ə"pɒθɪ'əʊsiːz/) 1 *(= epitome)* archétype *m* 2 *(= high point)* apothéose *f*

appal, appall *(US)* /ə'pɔːl/ VT consterner ; *(= frighten)* épouvanter ◆ **I am ~led at your behaviour** votre conduite me consterne

Appalachian /,æpə'leɪʃən/ ADJ, N ◆ **the ~ Mountains, the ~s** les (monts *mpl*) Appalaches *mpl*

appall /ə'pɔːl/ VT *(US)* ⇒ **appal**

appalling /ə'pɔːlɪŋ/ ADJ *[sight, behaviour, weather]* épouvantable ; *[suffering, crime, ignorance, poverty]* effroyable, épouvantable

appallingly /ə'pɔːlɪŋlɪ/ ADV 1 *(= badly) [behave]* de manière épouvantable 2 *(= extremely) [difficult, busy]* terriblement

apparatchik /,æpə'rætʃɪk/ N apparatchik *m*

apparatus /,æpə'reɪtəs/ N (pl **apparatus** *or* **apparatuses**) *(also Anat)* appareil *m* ; *(for filming, camping etc)* équipement *m* ; *(in laboratory etc)* instruments *mpl* ; *(in gym)* agrès *mpl* ◆ **camping** ~ équipement *m* de camping ◆ **heating** ~ appareil *m* de chauffage ◆ **~ work** *(in gym)* exercices *mpl* aux agrès ◆ **the ~ of government** l'appareil *m* d'État ◆ **critical** ~ *(Literat)* appareil *m or* apparat *m* critique

apparel /ə'pærəl/ *(Brit † or US) (liter)* N *(NonC)* habillement *m* VT vêtir

apparent /ə'pærənt/ ADJ 1 *(= seeming) [success, contradiction, interest]* apparent ◆ **the ~ coup attempt** l'apparente tentative de coup d'état 2 *(= obvious)* évident *(to sb* pour qn) ; ◆ **it is ~ that …** il est évident que … ◆ **it is ~ to me that …** il me semble évident que … ◆ **for no ~ reason** sans raison apparente ; → **heir**

apparently /ə'pærəntlɪ/ ADV apparemment ; *(= according to rumour)* à ce qu'il paraît ◆ **this is ~ the case** il semble que ce soit le cas, c'est le cas apparemment ◆ **~, they're getting a divorce** ils sont en instance de divorce, à ce qu'il paraît ◆ **I thought he was coming – ~ not** je pensais qu'il venait – apparemment non *or* il semble que non ◆ **to be ~ calm** paraître calme ◆ **an ~ harmless question** une question apparemment *or* en apparence anodine ◆ **the murders follow an ~ random pattern** ces meurtres ont apparemment été commis au hasard

apparition /,æpə'rɪʃən/ N *(= spirit, appearance)* apparition *f*

appeal /ə'piːl/ VI 1 *(= request publicly)* lancer un appel *(for sth* pour qch) ; ◆ **to ~ for the blind** lancer un appel au profit des *or* pour les aveugles ◆ **to ~ for calm** lancer un appel au calme ◆ **to ~ for funds** *(Fin)* faire un appel de fonds ◆ **he ~ed for silence** il a demandé le silence ◆ **he ~ed for tolerance** il a appelé à la tolérance ◆ **to ~ to the country** *(Pol)* en appeler au pays
2 *(= beg)* faire appel *(to* à) ; ◆ **she ~ed to his generosity** elle a fait appel à sa générosité, elle en a appelé à sa générosité ◆ **to ~ to sb for money/help** demander de l'argent/des secours à qn ◆ **I ~ to you!** je vous le demande instamment !, je vous en supplie ! → **better**[1]
3 *(Jur)* interjeter appel, se pourvoir en appel ◆ **to ~ to the supreme court** se pourvoir en cassation ◆ **to ~ against a judgement** *(Brit)* appeler d'un jugement ◆ **to ~ against a decision** *(Brit)* faire appel d'une décision
4 *(= attract)* **to ~ to sb** *[object, idea]* plaire à qn ; *[person]* plaire à qn ◆ **it doesn't ~ to me** cela ne m'intéresse pas, cela ne me dit rien* ◆ **the idea ~ed to him** cette idée l'a séduit ◆ **it ~s to the imagination** cela parle à l'imagination ◆ **does that ~?*** ça te dit ?*

VT *(Jur = appeal against)* faire appel de

N 1 *(= public call)* appel *m* ◆ ~ **to arms** appel *m* aux armes ◆ ~ **for funds** *(Comm, Fin)* appel *m* de fonds ◆ **he made a public ~ for the blind** il a lancé un appel au profit des aveugles

2 *(by individual: for help etc)* appel *m (for* à) ; *(for money)* demande *f (for* de) ; *(= supplication)* prière *f*, supplication *f* ◆ **with a look of ~** d'un air suppliant *or* implorant ◆ ~ **for help** appel *m* au secours

3 *(Jur)* appel *m*, pourvoi *m* ◆ **notice of ~** infirmation *f* ◆ **act of ~** acte *m* d'appel ◆ **with no right of ~** sans appel ◆ **acquitted on ~** acquitté en seconde instance ; → **enter, lodge, lord**

4 *(= attraction) [of person, object]* attrait *m*, charme *m* ; *[of plan, idea]* intérêt *m*

COMP **Appeal Court** **N** *(Jur)* cour *f* d'appel

appeal fund **N** fonds *m* d'aide *(constitué à partir de dons publics)*

appeal(s) tribunal **N** *(Jur)* ≈ cour *f* d'appel

appealing /əˈpiːlɪŋ/ **ADJ** *(= moving)* émouvant, attendrissant ; *[look]* pathétique ; *(= begging)* suppliant, implorant ; *(= attractive)* attirant, attachant

appealingly /əˈpiːlɪŋlɪ/ **ADV** 1 *(= charmingly)* ◆ ~ **naïve/modest** d'une charmante naïveté/modestie 2 *(= beseechingly) [look at]* d'un air implorant ; *[say]* d'un ton implorant

appear /əˈpɪəʳ/ **VI** 1 *(= become visible) [person, sun etc]* apparaître, se montrer ; *[ghost, vision]* apparaître, se manifester *(to sb* à qn)

2 *(= arrive)* arriver, se présenter ◆ **he ~ed from nowhere** il est apparu comme par miracle *or* comme par un coup de baguette magique ◆ **where did you ~ from?** d'où est-ce que tu sors ?

3 *(Jur etc)* comparaître ◆ **to ~ before a court** comparaître devant un tribunal ◆ **to ~ on a charge of ...** être jugé pour ... ◆ **to ~ for sb** plaider pour qn, représenter qn ◆ **to ~ for the defence/for the accused** plaider pour la défense/pour l'accusé ; → **fail, failure**

4 *(Theat)* **to ~ in "Hamlet"** jouer dans "Hamlet" ◆ **to ~ as Hamlet** jouer Hamlet ◆ **to ~ on TV** passer à la télévision

5 *(= be published) [magazine etc]* paraître, sortir, être publié

6 *(= seem: physical aspect)* paraître, avoir l'air ◆ **they ~ (to be) ill** ils ont l'air malades

7 *(= seem: on evidence)* paraître *(that* que *+ indic)* ; ◆ **he came then? – so it ~s** *or* **so it would ~** il est donc venu ? – il semblerait ◆ **it ~s that he did say that** il paraît qu'il a bien dit cela ; see also **8** ◆ **he got the job or so it ~s** *or* **so it would ~** il a eu le poste à ce qu'il paraît, il paraît qu'il a eu le poste ◆ **as will presently ~** comme il paraîtra par la suite, comme on le verra bientôt ◆ **it's raining! –** *(iro)* **so it ~s!** il pleut ! – on dirait ! *(iro)*

8 *(= seem: by surmise)* sembler *(that* que *gen + subj)* ; ◆ **there ~s to be a mistake** il semble qu'il y ait une erreur ◆ **it ~s he did say that** il semble avoir bien dit cela, il semble bien qu'il a dit cela ◆ **it ~s to me they are mistaken** il me semble qu'ils ont tort ◆ **how does it ~ to you?** qu'en pensez-vous ?

appearance /əˈpɪərəns/ **N** 1 *(= act)* apparition *f*, arrivée *f* ◆ **to make an ~** faire son apparition, se montrer, se présenter ◆ **to make a personal ~** apparaître en personne ◆ **to put in an ~** faire acte de présence ◆ ~ **money** cachet *m*

2 *(Jur)* ~ **before a court** comparution *f* devant un tribunal

3 *(Theat)* **since his ~ in "Hamlet"** depuis qu'il a joué dans "Hamlet" ◆ **in order of ~** par ordre d'entrée en scène ◆ **his ~ on TV** son passage à la télévision

4 *(= publication)* parution *f*

5 *(= look, aspect)* apparence *f*, aspect *m* ◆ **to have a good ~** *[person]* faire bonne figure ◆ **at first ~** au premier abord, à première vue ◆ **the ~ of the houses** l'aspect *m* des maisons ◆ **it had all the ~s of a murder** cela avait tout l'air d'un meurtre, cela ressemblait fort à un meurtre ◆ **his ~ worried us** la mine qu'il avait *or* son apparence nous a inquiétés ◆ **~s are deceptive** il ne faut pas se fier aux apparences, les apparences peuvent être trompeuses ◆ **to judge by ~s** juger sur les *or* d'après les apparences ◆ **you shouldn't judge** *or* **go by ~s** il ne faut pas se fier aux apparences ◆ **for ~s' sake, (in order) to keep up ~s** pour sauver les apparences ◆ **to** *or* **by all ~s** selon toute apparence ◆ **contrary to** *or* **against all ~s** contrairement aux apparences, contre toute apparence

appease /əˈpiːz/ **VT** apaiser, calmer

appeasement /əˈpiːzmənt/ **N** apaisement *m* ; *(Pol)* apaisement, conciliation *f*

appellant /əˈpelənt/ **N** partie *f* appelante, appelant(e) *m(f)* **ADJ** appelant

appellate /əˈpelɪt/ **ADJ** *(US Jur)* ◆ ~ **court** cour *f* d'appel ◆ ~ **jurisdiction** juridiction *f* d'appel

appellation /ˌæpeˈleɪʃən/ **N** appellation *f*, désignation *f*

append /əˈpend/ **VT** *[+ notes]* joindre, ajouter ; *[+ document]* joindre, annexer ; *[+ signature]* apposer ; *(Comput)* ajouter *(à la fin d'un fichier)*

appendage /əˈpendɪdʒ/ **N** *(frm)* appendice *m*

appendectomy /ˌæpenˈdektəmɪ/, **appendicectomy** /ˌæpendɪˈsektəmɪ/ **N** appendicectomie *f*

appendices /əˈpendɪsiːz/ **NPL** of **appendix**

appendicitis /əˌpendɪˈsaɪtɪs/ **N** appendicite *f* ◆ **to have ~** avoir une crise d'appendicite ◆ **was it ~?** c'était une appendicite ?

appendix /əˈpendɪks/ **N** (pl **appendixes** *or* **appendices**) 1 *(Anat)* appendice *m* ◆ **to have one's ~ out** se faire opérer de l'appendicite 2 *[of book]* appendice *m* ; *[of document]* annexe *f*

apperception /ˌæpəˈsepʃən/ **N** aperception *f*, appréhension *f*

appertain /ˌæpəˈteɪn/ **VI** *(= belong)* appartenir *(to* à) ; *(= form part)* faire partie *(to* de) ; *(= relate)* se rapporter *(to* à) relever *(to* de)

appetite /ˈæpɪtaɪt/ **N** 1 *(for food)* appétit *m* ◆ **he has no ~** il n'a pas d'appétit ◆ **to have a good ~** avoir bon appétit ◆ **to eat with ~** manger de bon appétit ◆ **skiing gives you an ~** le ski ouvre l'appétit 2 *(for danger, success)* goût *m* ◆ **his ~ for power** son goût du pouvoir ◆ **I have no ~ for this sort of book** je n'aime pas beaucoup ce genre de livre, je n'ai pas de goût pour ce genre de livre ◆ **the government has little ~ for tax cuts** le gouvernement n'est pas enclin à réduire les impôts ; → **spoil** **COMP** **appetite depressant, appetite suppressant** **N** coupe-faim *m inv*

appetizer /ˈæpɪtaɪzəʳ/ **N** *(= drink)* apéritif *m* ; *(= food)* amuse-gueule *m inv* ; *(US = starter)* entrée *f*

appetizing /ˈæpɪtaɪzɪŋ/ **ADJ** *(lit, fig)* appétissant

appetizingly /ˈæpɪtaɪzɪŋlɪ/ **ADV** de manière appétissante

Appian /ˈæpɪən/ **ADJ** ◆ **the ~ Way** la voie Appienne

applaud /əˈplɔːd/ **VT** *[+ person, thing]* applaudir ; *(fig) [+ decision, efforts]* applaudir à, approuver

applause /əˈplɔːz/ **N** *(NonC)* applaudissements *mpl*, acclamation *f* ◆ **to win the ~ of ...** être applaudi *or* acclamé par ... ◆ **there was loud ~** les applaudissements ont crépité ◆ **a round of ~** une salve d'applaudissements ◆ **let's have a round of ~ for Lucy!** *(Theat)* applaudissons Lucy !, un ban* pour Lucy !

apple /ˈæpl/ **N** pomme *f* ; (also **apple tree**) pommier *m* ◆ **he's/it's the ~ of my eye** je tiens à lui/j'y tiens comme à la prunelle de mes yeux ◆ ~ **of discord** pomme *f* de discorde ◆ **the (Big) Apple*** *(US)* New York ◆ **one bad** *or* **rotten ~ can spoil the whole barrel** *(Prov)* il suffit d'une brebis galeuse pour contaminer tout le troupeau ◆ **the two things are ~s and oranges** *(esp US)* on ne peut pas comparer deux choses si différentes ; → **Adam, cooking, eating**

COMP **apple blossom** **N** fleur *f* de pommier

apple brandy **N** eau-de-vie *f* de pommes

apple core **N** trognon *m* de pomme

apple fritter **N** beignet *m* aux pommes

apple-green **ADJ** vert pomme *inv*

apple orchard **N** champ *m* de pommiers, pommeraie *f*

apple pie **N** tarte *f* aux pommes

apple-pie bed **N** *(Brit)* lit *m* en portefeuille

apple-pie order **N** ◆ **in ~-pie order** parfaitement en ordre

apple sauce **N** *(Culin)* compote *f* de pommes ; *(US * fig)* bobards* *mpl*

apple tart **N** tarte *f* aux pommes ; *(individual)* tartelette *f* aux pommes

apple turnover **N** chausson *m* aux pommes

applecart /ˈæplkɑːt/ **N** → **upset**

applejack /ˈæpldʒæk/ **N** *(US)* ⇒ **apple brandy**

applet /ˈæplɪt/ **N** microprogramme *m*

appliance /əˈplaɪəns/ **N** 1 *(= device)* appareil *m* ◆ **electrical/domestic ~s** appareils *mpl* électriques/ménagers ◆ **household ~** appareil *m* électroménager 2 *(Brit:* also **fire appliance***)* voiture *f* de pompiers 3 *[of skill, knowledge]* application *f*

applicability /ˌæplɪkəˈbɪlɪtɪ/ **N** applicabilité *f*

applicable /əˈplɪkəbl/ **ADJ** applicable *(to* à)

applicant /ˈæplɪkənt/ **N** *(for job)* candidat(e) *m(f)*, postulant(e) *m(f)* ; *(Jur)* requérant(e) *m(f)* ; *(Admin: for money, assistance etc)* demandeur *m*, -euse *f*

application /ˌæplɪˈkeɪʃən/ **N** 1 *(= request)* demande *f (for* de) ; ◆ ~ **for a job** candidature *f* à un poste ◆ ~ **for membership** demande *f* d'adhésion ◆ **on ~** sur demande ◆ **to make ~ to sb for sth** s'adresser à qn pour obtenir qch ◆ **to submit an ~** faire une demande ◆ **details may be had on ~ to ...** s'adresser à ... pour tous renseignements

2 *(= act of applying)* application *f (of sth to sth* de qch à qch) ; ◆ **for external ~ only** *(Pharm)* réservé à l'usage externe

3 *(= diligence)* application *f*, attention *f*

4 *(= relevancy)* portée *f*, pertinence *f* ◆ **his arguments have no ~ to the present case** ses arguments ne s'appliquent pas au cas présent

5 *(Comput)* application *f* ; see also **comp**

COMP **application form** **N** *(gen: for benefits etc)* formulaire *m* de demande ; *(for job)* formulaire *m* de demande d'emploi ; *(for important post)* dossier *m* de candidature ; *(Univ)* dossier *m* d'inscription

application program **N** ⇒ **applications program**

application software **N** logiciel *m* d'application

applications package **N** *(Comput)* progiciel *m* d'application

applications program **N** *(Comput)* (programme *m* d')application *f*

applicator /ˈæplɪkeɪtəʳ/ **N** applicateur *m*

applied /əˈplaɪd/ **ADJ** appliqué

COMP **applied arts** **NPL** arts *mpl* appliqués

applied psychology **N** psychologie *f* appliquée

applied sciences **NPL** sciences *fpl* appliquées

appliqué /æˈpliːkeɪ/ **VT** coudre (en application) **N** *(= ornament)* application *f* ; *(= end product:* also **appliqué work***)* travail *m* d'application

apply /əˈplaɪ/ LANGUAGE IN USE 19.1, 25.1
VT 1 [+ paint, ointment, dressing] appliquer, mettre (to sur) ; ◆ **to ~ heat to sth** exposer qch à la chaleur ; (Med) traiter qch par la thermothérapie ◆ **to ~ a match to sth** mettre le feu à qch avec une allumette, allumer qch avec une allumette
2 [+ theory] appliquer (to à) mettre en pratique or en application ; [+ rule, law] appliquer (to à) ; ◆ **we can't ~ this rule to you** nous ne pouvons pas appliquer cette règle à votre cas
3 ◆ **to ~ pressure on sth** exercer une pression sur qch ◆ **to ~ pressure on sb** faire pression sur qn ◆ **to ~ the brakes** actionner les freins, freiner
4 ◆ **to ~ one's mind** or **o.s. to (doing) sth** s'appliquer à (faire) qch ◆ **to ~ one's attention to ...** porter or fixer son attention sur ...
VI s'adresser, avoir recours (to sb for sth à qn pour obtenir qch) ; ◆ **~ at the office/to the manager** adressez-vous au bureau/au directeur ; (on notice) s'adresser au bureau/au directeur ◆ **to ~ to university** faire une demande d'inscription à l'université ◆ **right to ~ to the courts against decisions by ...** (Jur) droit m de recours contre des décisions de ...

► **apply for** VT FUS [+ scholarship, grant] faire une demande de ; [+ money, assistance] demander ◆ **to ~ for a job** faire une demande d'emploi (to sb auprès de qn) poser sa candidature pour un poste ◆ **to ~ for a divorce** (Jur) formuler une demande en divorce ; → **patent**

► **apply to** VT FUS [gen] s'appliquer à ; [remarks] s'appliquer à, se rapporter à ◆ **this does not ~ to you** ceci ne s'applique pas à vous, ceci ne vous concerne pas ; → **apply vi**

appoggiatura /əˌpɒdʒəˈtʊərə/ N (pl **appoggiaturas** or **appoggiature** /əˌpɒdʒəˈtʊəreɪ/) appoggiature f

appoint /əˈpɔɪnt/ VT 1 (= fix, decide) [+ date, place] fixer 2 (= nominate) ◆ **to ~ sb (to a post)** nommer qn (à un poste) ◆ **to ~ sb manager** nommer qn directeur ◆ **to ~ a new secretary** engager une nouvelle secrétaire 3 († = ordain) prescrire, ordonner (that que + subj) décider (that que + indic)

appointed /əˈpɔɪntɪd/ ADJ [time, hour, place] convenu ; [task] fixé ; [representative, agent] attitré ◆ **at the ~ time** à l'heure convenue ; → **well²**

appointee /əpɔɪnˈtiː/ N candidat(e) m(f) retenu(e), titulaire mf du poste ; (esp US) délégué m (or ambassadeur m etc) nommé pour des raisons politiques

appointive /əˈpɔɪntɪv/ ADJ (US) [position] pourvu par nomination

appointment /əˈpɔɪntmənt/ N 1 (= arrangement to meet) rendez-vous m ; (= meeting) entrevue f ◆ **to make an ~ with sb** donner rendez-vous à qn, prendre rendez-vous avec qn ◆ **to make an ~** [two people] se donner rendez-vous ◆ **to keep an ~** aller or se rendre à un rendez-vous ◆ **I have an ~ at 10 o'clock** j'ai (un) rendez-vous à 10 heures ◆ **do you have an ~?** (to caller) vous avez (pris) rendez-vous ? ◆ **I have an ~ to see Mr Martin** j'ai rendez-vous avec M. Martin ◆ **to see sb by ~** voir qn sur rendez-vous ◆ **"viewing by appointment"** (in house-buying) "visite f sur rendez-vous" ; → **break**
2 (= selection, nomination) nomination f, désignation f (to a post à un poste) ; (= office assigned) poste m ; (= posting) affectation f ◆ **there are still several ~s to be made** il y a encore plusieurs postes à pourvoir ◆ **"by appointment to Her Majesty the Queen"** (Comm) "fournisseur de S.M. la Reine" ◆ **"appointments (vacant)"** (Press) "offres d'emploi"
COMP **appointments bureau, appointments office** N agence f or bureau m de placement

apportion /əˈpɔːʃən/ VT [+ money] répartir, partager ; [+ land, property] lotir ; [+ blame] répartir ◆ **to ~ sth to sb** assigner qch à qn

apportionment /əˈpɔːʃənmənt/ N (US Pol) répartition f des sièges (par districts)

apposite /ˈæpəzɪt/ ADJ (frm) pertinent, juste

apposition /ˌæpəˈzɪʃən/ N apposition f ◆ **in ~** en apposition

appositional /ˌæpəˈzɪʃənl/ ADJ en apposition

appraisal /əˈpreɪzəl/ N évaluation f

appraise /əˈpreɪz/ VT [+ property, jewellery] évaluer, estimer (la valeur or le coût de) ; [+ importance] évaluer, apprécier ; [+ worth] estimer, apprécier

appraiser /əˈpreɪzəʳ/ N (US) [of property, value, asset] expert m

appreciable /əˈpriːʃəbl/ ADJ appréciable, sensible

appreciably /əˈpriːʃəblɪ/ ADV sensiblement

appreciate /əˈpriːʃɪeɪt/ LANGUAGE IN USE 4, 13
VT 1 (= assess, be aware of) [+ fact, difficulty, sb's attitude] se rendre compte de, être conscient de ◆ **to ~ sth at its true value** apprécier qch à sa juste valeur ◆ **yes, I ~ that** oui, je comprends bien or je m'en rends bien compte ◆ **I fully ~ the fact that ...** je me rends parfaitement compte du fait que ... ◆ **they did not ~ the danger** ils ne se sont pas rendu compte du danger
2 (= value, esteem, like) [+ help] apprécier ; [+ music, painting, books] apprécier, goûter ; [+ person] apprécier (à sa juste valeur), faire (grand) cas de
3 (= be grateful for) être sensible à, être reconnaissant de ◆ **we do ~ your kindness/your work/what you have done** nous vous sommes très reconnaissants de votre gentillesse/du travail que vous avez fait/de ce que vous avez fait ◆ **we should ~ an early reply, an early reply would be ~d** (Comm: in letter) nous vous serions obligés de bien vouloir nous répondre dans les plus brefs délais ◆ **we deeply ~ this honour** nous sommes profondément reconnaissants de l'honneur qui nous est fait ◆ **he felt that nobody ~d him** il avait le sentiment que personne ne l'appréciait
4 (= raise in value) hausser la valeur de
VI (Fin etc) [currency] s'apprécier ; [object, property] prendre de la valeur

appreciation /əˌpriːʃɪˈeɪʃən/ N 1 (= judgement, estimation) appréciation f, évaluation f ; (Art, Literat, Mus) critique f 2 (= gratitude) reconnaissance f ◆ **she smiled her ~** elle a remercié d'un sourire ◆ **in ~ of ...** en remerciement de ... 3 (Fin) appréciation f

appreciative /əˈpriːʃɪətɪv/ ADJ 1 (= grateful) [person] reconnaissant (of sth de qch) 2 (= admiring) [person, murmur, laughter, whistle] approbateur (-trice f) ◆ **to be ~ of sb's cooking** apprécier la cuisine de qn 3 (frm = aware) ◆ **to be ~ of sth** se rendre compte de qch

appreciatively /əˈpriːʃɪətɪvlɪ/ ADV (= with pleasure) avec plaisir ; (= gratefully) avec reconnaissance

apprehend /ˌæprɪˈhend/ VT 1 (= arrest) appréhender, arrêter 2 (= fear) redouter, appréhender

apprehension /ˌæprɪˈhenʃən/ N 1 (= fear) appréhension f, inquiétude f 2 (frm = arrest) arrestation f

apprehensive /ˌæprɪˈhensɪv/ ADJ inquiet (-ète f), plein d'appréhension ◆ **to be ~ for sb** être inquiet pour qn ◆ **to be ~ about the future** avoir peur de l'avenir ◆ **he was ~ about taking the job on** il était inquiet à la perspective d'accepter ce poste ◆ **they were ~ that their request would be turned down** ils craignaient que leur requête ne soit refusée

apprehensively /ˌæprɪˈhensɪvlɪ/ ADV avec appréhension

apprentice /əˈprentɪs/ N apprenti(e) m(f) ; (Archit, Mus etc) élève mf ◆ **to place sb as an ~ to ...** mettre qn en apprentissage chez ... ◆ **plumber's/joiner's ~** apprenti m plombier/menuisier VT mettre or placer en apprentissage (to chez) placer comme élève (to chez) ; ◆ **he is ~d to a joiner/plumber** etc il est en apprentissage chez un menuisier/plombier etc ◆ **he is ~d to an architect** c'est l'élève d'un architecte
COMP **apprentice electrician** N apprenti m électricien
apprentice plumber N apprenti m plombier

apprenticeship /əˈprentɪsʃɪp/ N apprentissage m

apprise /əˈpraɪz/ VT informer (sb of sth qn de qch) ; ◆ **to be ~d of sth** être informé de or sur qch

appro * /ˈæprəʊ/ N (Brit Comm) (abbrev of **approval**) ◆ **on ~** à or sous condition, à l'essai

approach /əˈprəʊtʃ/ VI [person, vehicle] (s')approcher ; [date, season, death, war] approcher, être proche
VT 1 [+ place, person] s'approcher de ◆ **I saw him ~ing me** je l'ai vu qui s'approchait de moi
2 (= tackle) [+ problem, subject, task] aborder ◆ **it all depends on how one ~es it** tout dépend de la façon dont on aborde la question
3 (= speak to) **to ~ sb about sth** s'adresser à qn à propos de qch, aller voir qn pour qch ◆ **a man ~ed me in the street** un homme m'a abordé dans la rue ◆ **he is easy/difficult to ~** (fig) il est d'un abord facile/difficile
4 (= get near to) approcher de ◆ **we are ~ing the time when ...** le jour approche où ... ◆ **she is ~ing 30** elle approche de la trentaine, elle va sur ses 30 ans ◆ **it was ~ing midnight** il était près de or presque minuit ◆ **winds were ~ing hurricane force** le vent approchait force 12 ◆ **she spoke to him with something ~ing sarcasm** elle lui a parlé sur un ton qui frisait le sarcasme
N 1 [of person, vehicle] approche f, arrivée f ◆ **the cat fled at his ~** le chat s'est enfui à son approche ◆ **we watched his ~** nous l'avons regardé arriver
2 [of date, season, death etc] approche f ◆ **at the ~ of Easter** à l'approche de Pâques
3 (fig) approche f, démarche f ◆ **his ~ to the problem** son approche du problème, sa façon d'aborder le problème ◆ **I like his ~ (to it)** j'aime sa façon de s'y prendre ◆ **a new ~ to teaching French** une nouvelle approche de l'enseignement du français ◆ **to make ~es to sb** (gen) faire des ouvertures fpl à qn, faire des démarches fpl auprès de qn ; (amorous) faire des avances fpl à qn ◆ **to make an ~ to sb** (Comm, gen) faire une proposition à qn ◆ **he is easy/not easy of ~** (frm) il est d'un abord facile/difficile ; see also **noun 4**
4 (= access route: to town) voie f d'accès ; (Climbing) marche f d'approche ◆ **a town easy/not easy of ~** une ville d'accès facile/difficile ◆ **the ~ to the top of the hill** le chemin qui mène au sommet de la colline ◆ **the station ~** les abords mpl de la gare
5 (= approximation) ressemblance f (to à) apparence f (to de) ; ◆ **some ~ to gaiety** une certaine apparence de gaieté ◆ **this is the nearest ~ to an apology we have heard from Mr King** c'est tout ce que M. King a trouvé à dire en guise d'excuse
COMP **approach light** N (for planes) balise f
approach lights NPL (for planes) balisage m, balises fpl
approach march N (Climbing) marche f d'approche
approach road N (gen) route f d'accès ; (to

motorway) voie f de raccordement, bretelle f
approach shot N (Golf) approche f
approach stage N (in plane) phase f d'approche

approachable /ə'prəʊtʃəbl/ ADJ [place, idea, text] accessible ; [person] d'abord facile, approchable, accessible

approaching /ə'prəʊtʃɪŋ/ ADJ [crisis, death, retirement, election] prochain ; [storm, winter, date] qui approche ◆ **the ~ vehicle** le véhicule venant en sens inverse

approbation /,æprə'beɪʃən/ N approbation f ◆ **a nod of ~** un signe de tête approbateur

appropriate /ə'prəʊprɪɪt/ ADJ [time, remark] opportun ; [place, response, word, level, name] approprié ; [treatment] adapté ; [person, authority, department] compétent ◆ **to take ~ action** prendre des mesures appropriées ◆ **he is the ~ person to ask** c'est à lui qu'il faut le demander ◆ **she's a most ~ choice** c'est la personne idéale ◆ **to be ~ for sb/sth** convenir à qn/qch ◆ **what is it ~ to wear for a dinner party?** quelle est la tenue appropriée pour un dîner ? ◆ **to be ~ to sth** être approprié à qch ◆ **an outfit ~ to the job** une tenue appropriée à l'emploi ◆ **a job ~ to his talents** un emploi à la mesure de ses talents ◆ **it is ~ that ...** il est opportun que ... ◆ **it seemed ~ to end with a joke** il semblait opportun de finir par une plaisanterie ◆ **it would not be ~ for me to comment** ce n'est pas à moi de faire des commentaires
VT /ə'prəʊprieɪt/ 1 (= take for one's own use) s'approprier
2 (= set aside for special use) [+ funds] affecter (to, for à)

appropriately /ə'prəʊprɪɪtlɪ/ ADV [act, respond] comme il faut, de façon appropriée ; [dress] de façon appropriée ; [speak] avec à-propos, avec pertinence ; [called, titled] de façon appropriée ; [designed] convenablement ◆ **~ named** bien nommé ◆ **~, the winner is British** comme de juste, le gagnant est britannique

appropriateness /ə'prəʊprɪɪtnɪs/ N [of moment, decision] opportunité f ; [of remark, word] justesse f

appropriation /ə,prəʊprɪ'eɪʃən/ N (= act: also Jur) appropriation f ; (= funds assigned) dotation f ; (US Pol) crédit m budgétaire
COMP **appropriation bill** N (US Pol) projet m de loi de finances
Appropriations Committee N (US Pol) commission des finances de la Chambre des représentants (examinant les dépenses)

approval /ə'pru:vəl/ N approbation f, assentiment m ◆ **to give a nod of ~, to nod one's ~** hocher la tête en signe d'approbation ◆ **to meet with sb's ~** avoir l'approbation de qn
◆ **on approval** (Comm) à l'essai ◆ **the book will be sent to you on ~** le livre vous sera envoyé en examen gratuit

approve /ə'pru:v/ LANGUAGE IN USE 12.2, 13, 26.3 VT [+ action, publication, medicine, drug] approuver ; [+ decision] ratifier, homologuer ; [+ request] agréer ◆ **to be ~d by ...** recueillir or avoir l'approbation de ... ◆ **"read and approved"** "lu et approuvé" COMP **approved school** † N (Brit) maison f de correction †

► **approve of** VT FUS [+ behaviour, idea] approuver ; [+ person] avoir bonne opinion de ◆ **I don't ~ of his conduct** je n'approuve pas sa conduite ◆ **I don't ~ of your decision** je n'approuve pas or je désapprouve la décision que vous avez prise ◆ **she doesn't ~ of drinking/smoking** elle n'approuve pas qu'on boive/fume subj ◆ **he doesn't ~ of me** il n'a pas bonne opinion de moi ◆ **we ~ of our new neighbours** nos nouveaux voisins nous semblent tout à fait bien

approving /ə'pru:vɪŋ/ ADJ approbateur (-trice f), approbatif

approvingly /ə'pru:vɪŋlɪ/ ADV d'un air or d'un ton approbateur

approx abbrev of **approximately**

approximate /ə'prɒksɪmɪt/ ADJ [time, amount, description] approximatif ◆ **a sum ~ to what is needed** une somme voisine or proche de celle qui est requise ◆ **figures ~ to the nearest euro** chiffres mpl arrondis à l'euro près VI /ə'prɒksɪmeɪt/ être proche, se rapprocher (to de)

approximately /ə'prɒksɪmətlɪ/ ADV 1 (= about: with numbers) approximativement ◆ **we have ~ 40 pupils** nous avons approximativement 40 élèves 2 (= roughly) [true] plus ou moins ◆ **the figures were ~ correct** les chiffres étaient à peu près corrects ◆ **the word means ~ ...** en gros or grosso modo, ce mot veut dire ...

approximation /ə,prɒksɪ'meɪʃən/ N approximation f

appurtenance /ə'pɜ:tɪnəns/ N (Jur) (gen pl) ◆ **~s** installations fpl, accessoires mpl ◆ **the house and its ~s** (= outhouses etc) l'immeuble avec ses dépendances ; (= rights, privileges etc) l'immeuble avec ses circonstances et dépendances or ses appartenances

APR /,eɪpi:'ɑ:r/ N (abbrev of **annual(ized) percentage rate**) taux m annuel

après-ski /,æpreɪ'ski:/ N (= period) après-ski m

apricot /'eɪprɪkɒt/ N abricot m ; (also **apricot tree**) abricotier m
COMP **apricot jam** N confiture f d'abricots
apricot tart N tarte f aux abricots

April /'eɪprəl/ N avril m ; for phrases see **September**
COMP **April fool** N (= person) victime f d'un poisson d'avril ; (= joke) poisson m d'avril ◆ **to make an ~ fool of sb** faire un poisson d'avril à qn
April Fools' Day N le premier avril
April showers NPL ≈ giboulées fpl de mars

a priori /eɪpraɪ'ɔ:raɪ, ɑ:prɪ'ɔ:rɪ/ ADJ, ADV a priori

apron /'eɪprən/ N 1 (= garment) tablier m ◆ **tied to his mother's ~ strings** pendu aux jupes de sa mère 2 (in airport) aire f de stationnement 3 (Tech) (= protective plate) tablier m 4 (Theat: also **apron stage**) avant-scène f 5 (Phot) bande f gaufrée

apropos /,æprə'pəʊ/ (frm) ADV à propos ◆ **~, I have often wondered what happened to him** à propos, je me suis souvent demandé ce qu'il était devenu PREP ◆ **~ (of) sth** à propos de qch ADJ opportun, pertinent ◆ **it seems ~ to do that** cela semble opportun or judicieux de faire cela

APS /,eɪpi:'es/ N (abbrev of **Advanced Photo System**) APS m

apse /æps/ N abside f

APT /,eɪpi:'ti:/ N (Brit: formerly) (abbrev of **Advanced Passenger Train**) ≈ TGV m, train m à grande vitesse

apt /æpt/ ADJ 1 (= appropriate) [remark, comment, reply] juste, pertinent 2 (frm = inclined, tending) ◆ **to be ~ to do sth** avoir tendance à faire qch ◆ **he is ~ to be late** il a tendance à être en retard ◆ **one is ~ to believe that ...** (frm) on croirait volontiers que ..., on pourrait croire que ... ◆ **this is ~ to occur** il faut s'y attendre 3 (= gifted) [pupil] doué, intelligent

apt. (abbrev of **apartment**) appt

aptitude /'æptɪtju:d/ LANGUAGE IN USE 16.4 N aptitude f (for à) disposition f (for pour) ; ◆ **to have an ~ for learning** être fait pour les études ◆ **he has no ~ for languages** il n'est pas doué pour les langues ◆ **she shows great ~** elle est très douée ◆ **he has a real ~ for saying exactly the wrong thing** il a le don de dire ce qu'il ne faut pas COMP **aptitude test** N test m d'aptitude

aptly /'æptlɪ/ ADV [describe, remark] judicieusement, avec à-propos ; [called, titled] judicieusement ◆ **~, his place was taken by his wife** comme de juste, sa femme a pris sa place

aptness /'æptnɪs/ N 1 (= suitability) [of remark etc] à-propos m, justesse f 2 (= giftedness) ⇒ **aptitude**

Apulia /ə'pju:ljə/ N Pouilles fpl

aquaculture /'ækwə,kʌltʃər/ N ⇒ **aquafarming**

aquaerobics /'ækweɪ'rəʊbɪks/ N (NonC) aérobic f en piscine

aquafarming /'ækwəfɑ:mɪŋ/ N aquaculture f

aqualung /'ækwəlʌŋ/ N scaphandre m autonome

aquamarine /,ækwəmə'ri:n/ N (= stone) aigue-marine f ; (= colour) bleu vert m inv ADJ bleu-vert inv

aquanaut /'ækwənɔ:t/ N scaphandrier m, plongeur m

aquaplane /'ækwəpleɪn/ N aquaplane m VI 1 (Sport) faire de l'aquaplane 2 (Brit: while driving) faire de l'aquaplaning or de l'aquaplanage

aquaplaning /'ækwəpleɪnɪŋ/ N (Brit) aquaplaning m, aquaplanage m

aquaria /ə'kweərɪə/ NPL of **aquarium**

Aquarian /ə'kweərɪən/ N (personne née sous le signe du) Verseau m

aquarium /ə'kweərɪəm/ N (pl **aquariums** or **aquaria**) aquarium m

Aquarius /ə'kweərɪəs/ N (Astron) Verseau m ◆ **I'm (an) ~** (Astrol) je suis (du) Verseau

aquatic /ə'kwætɪk/ ADJ [animal, plant] aquatique ; [sport] nautique

aquatint /'ækwətɪnt/ N aquatinte f

aqueduct /'ækwɪdʌkt/ N (= canal) aqueduc m ; (= pipe) canalisation f d'amenée d'eau

aqueous /'eɪkwɪəs/ ADJ aqueux ◆ **~ humour** humeur f aqueuse

aquiculture /'ækwɪ,kʌltʃər, 'eɪkwɪ,kʌltʃər/ N ⇒ **aquafarming**

aquifer /'ækwɪfər/ N (Geog) aquifère m

aquiline /'ækwɪlaɪn/ ADJ [nose, profile] aquilin

Aquinas /ə'kwaɪnəs/ N ◆ **(St) Thomas ~** (saint) Thomas d'Aquin

AR abbrev of **Arkansas**

Arab /'ærəb/ N 1 (= person) Arabe mf ; → **street** 2 (= horse) cheval m arabe or anglo-arabe ADJ arabe ◆ **the ~ States** les États mpl arabes ◆ **the United ~ Emirates** les Émirats mpl arabes unis ◆ **the ~-Israeli conflict** le conflit israélo-arabe ◆ **the ~ League** la Ligue arabe

arabesque /,ærə'besk/ N arabesque f

Arabia /ə'reɪbɪə/ N Arabie f

Arabian /ə'reɪbɪən/ ADJ arabe, d'Arabie ◆ **~ Desert** désert m d'Arabie ◆ **~ Gulf** golfe m Persique ◆ **the ~ Nights** les Mille et Une Nuits fpl ◆ **~ Sea** mer f d'Arabie

Arabic /'ærəbɪk/ ADJ arabe ; → **gum²** N (= language) arabe m ◆ **written ~** l'arabe m littéral
COMP **Arabic numeral** N chiffre m arabe

Arabist /'ærəbɪst/ N (= scholar) arabisant(e) m(f) ; (= politician) pro-Arabe mf

arabization /,ærəbaɪ'zeɪʃən/ N arabisation f

arabize /'ærəbaɪz/ VT arabiser

arable /'ærəbl/ ADJ [land] arable, cultivable ; [farm] agricole
COMP **arable farmer** N cultivateur m, -trice f
arable farming N culture f

arachnid /ə'ræknɪd/ N ◆ **~s** arachnides mpl

Aramaic /,ærə'meɪk/ N araméen m

Aran /ˈærən/ **N** ◆ **the ~ Islands** les îles *fpl* d'Aran

arbiter /ˈɑːbɪtəʳ/ **N** (= *judge*) arbitre *m* ; (= *mediator*) médiateur *m*, -trice *f* ◆ **the Supreme Court is the final ~ of any dispute over constitutional rights** la Cour suprême est l'ultime arbitre en cas de litige concernant les droits constitutionnels ◆ **to be an ~ of taste/style** *etc* être une référence en matière de bon goût/de style *etc*

arbitrage /ˈɑːbɪtrɪdʒ/ **N** (*Fin*) arbitrage *m*, opération *f* d'arbitrage

arbitrager, arbitrageur /ˈɑːbɪtræˈʒɜːʳ/ **N** arbitragiste *mf*

arbitrarily /ˈɑːbɪtrərəlɪ/ **ADV** arbitrairement

arbitrary /ˈɑːbɪtrərɪ/ **ADJ** arbitraire

arbitrate /ˈɑːbɪtreɪt/ **VT** arbitrer, juger **VI** arbitrer

arbitration /ˌɑːbɪˈtreɪʃən/ **N** arbitrage *m* ◆ **to go to ~** recourir à l'arbitrage ; → **refer**
COMP **arbitration clause** **N** clause *f* compromissoire
arbitration tribunal **N** tribunal *m* arbitral

arbitrator /ˈɑːbɪtreɪtəʳ/ **N** arbitre *m*, médiateur *m*, -trice *f*

arbor /ˈɑːbəʳ/ **N** (*US*) ⇒ **arbour**

arboreal /ɑːˈbɔːrɪəl/ **ADJ** [*shape*] arborescent ; [*animal, technique*] arboricole

arboretum /ˌɑːbəˈriːtəm/ **N** (pl **arboretums** *or* **arboreta** /ˌɑːbəˈriːtə/) arboretum *m*

arbour, arbor (*US*) /ˈɑːbəʳ/ **N** tonnelle *f*, charmille † *f*

arbutus /ɑːˈbjuːtəs/ **N** arbousier *m*

ARC /ˌeɪɑːˈsiː/ **N** 1 (abbrev of **AIDS-related complex**) ARC *m* 2 (abbrev of **American Red Cross**) Croix-Rouge *f* américaine

arc /ɑːk/ **N** arc *m* **VI** 1 décrire un arc (de cercle) ◆ **the rocket ~ed down into the sea** la fusée a décrit un arc avant de retomber dans la mer 2 (*Elec*) former un arc (électrique)
COMP **arc lamp, arc light** **N** lampe *f* à arc ; (*Cine, TV*) sunlight *m*
arc welding **N** soudure *f* à l'arc

arcade /ɑːˈkeɪd/ **N** (= *series of arches*) arcade *f*, galerie *f* ; (= *shopping precinct*) passage *m*, galerie *f* marchande ; (*Brit*: also **amusement arcade**) salle *f* de jeux vidéo **COMP** **arcade game** **N** (*Brit*) jeu *m* vidéo, jeu *m* d'arcade

Arcadia /ɑːˈkeɪdɪə/ **N** Arcadie *f*

Arcadian /ɑːˈkeɪdɪən/ **ADJ** arcadien, d'Arcadie **N** Arcadien(ne) *m(f)*

Arcady /ˈɑːkədɪ/ **N** (*Poetry, Literat*) Arcadie *f*

arcane /ɑːˈkeɪn/ **ADJ** ésotérique, obscur

arch¹ /ɑːtʃ/ **N** 1 (*inside building*) arc *m*, voûte *f* ; [*of bridge, natural feature*] arche *f* 2 [*of eyebrow*] arcade *f* ; [*of foot*] cambrure *f*, voûte *f* plantaire ; → **fallen** **VI** (s')arquer **VT** arquer, cambrer ◆ **the cat ~ed his back** le chat a fait le gros dos

arch² /ɑːtʃ/ **ADJ** 1 (= *cunning*) [*glance, person*] malicieux 2 (= *superior*) [*look, remark*] condescendant

arch³ /ɑːtʃ/ **ADJ** (*gen*) grand, par excellence ◆ **an ~ traitor** un grand traître, le traître par excellence ◆ **an ~ villain** un parfait scélérat ◆ **the ~ villain** le méchant par excellence ◆ **the Prime Minister's ~-critic** le principal critique du Premier ministre **PREF** arch(i) **COMP** **arch-enemy, arch-foe** **N** ennemi *m* juré ◆ **the Arch-enemy** (*Rel*) Satan *m*

archaeological, archeological /ˌɑːkɪəˈlɒdʒɪkəl/ **ADJ** archéologique

archaeologist, archeologist /ˌɑːkɪˈɒlədʒɪst/ **N** archéologue *mf*

archaeology, archeology /ˌɑːkɪˈɒlədʒɪ/ **N** archéologie *f*

archaic /ɑːˈkeɪɪk/ **ADJ** archaïque

archaism /ˈɑːkeɪɪzəm/ **N** archaïsme *m*

archangel /ˈɑːkˌeɪndʒəl/ **N** archange *m* ◆ **the Archangel Michael** l'archange *m* Michel, saint Michel archange

archbishop /ˈɑːtʃˈbɪʃəp/ **N** archevêque *m*

archbishopric /ˈɑːtʃˈbɪʃəprɪk/ **N** archevêché *m*

archdeacon /ˈɑːtʃˈdiːkən/ **N** archidiacre *m*

archdiocese /ˈɑːtʃˈdaɪəsɪs/ **N** archidiocèse *m*

archduchess /ˈɑːtʃˈdʌtʃɪs/ **N** archiduchesse *f*

archduchy /ˈɑːtʃˈdʌtʃɪ/ **N** archiduché *m*

archduke /ˈɑːtʃˈdjuːk/ **N** archiduc *m*

arched /ɑːtʃt/ **ADJ** [*window, alcove*] cintré ; [*roof*] cintré, en voûte ; [*ceiling, doorway*] en voûte ; [*bridge*] à arches ; [*eyebrows*] voûté (*liter*) ◆ **with an ~ back** (*convex*) le dos voûté ; (*concave*) la taille cambrée, les reins cambrés

archeological /ˌɑːkɪəˈlɒdʒɪkəl/ **ADJ** (*US*) ⇒ **archaeological**

archeologist /ˌɑːkɪˈɒlədʒɪst/ **N** (*US*) ⇒ **archaeologist**

archeology /ˌɑːkɪˈɒlədʒɪ/ **N** (*US*) ⇒ **archaeology**

archer /ˈɑːtʃəʳ/ **N** archer *m*

Archers /ˈɑːtʃəz/ **NPL** (*Brit*) ◆ **The ~** *feuilleton radiophonique*

THE ARCHERS

The Archers est un feuilleton fleuve diffusé quotidiennement depuis 1951 par la BBC (Radio 4), avec un succès constant auprès des auditeurs de tous âges. Il retrace la vie d'une famille d'un village fictif, Ambridge, et de ses institutions locales, le pub et le club de cricket en particulier. Au fil des années, l'histoire s'est enrichie de thèmes plus contemporains tels que le racisme, la drogue, les familles monoparentales ou l'ordination des femmes.

archery /ˈɑːtʃərɪ/ **N** tir *m* à l'arc

archetypal /ˈɑːkɪtaɪpəl/ **ADJ** archétypal

archetypally /ˌɑːkɪˈtaɪpəlɪ/ **ADV** exemplairement

archetype /ˈɑːkɪtaɪp/ **N** archétype *m*

archetypical /ˌɑːkɪˈtɪpɪkəl/ **ADJ** ⇒ **archetypal**

Archimedes /ˌɑːkɪˈmiːdiːz/ **N** Archimède *m*

archipelago /ˌɑːkɪˈpelɪgəʊ/ **N** (pl **archipelagos** *or* **archipelagoes**) archipel *m*

archiphoneme /ˌɑːkɪˈfəʊniːm/ **N** archiphonème *m*

architect /ˈɑːkɪtekt/ **N** architecte *m* ; (*fig*) architecte *m*, artisan *m* ; → **naval**

architectonic /ˌɑːkɪtekˈtɒnɪk/ **ADJ** (*Art*) architectonique

architectural /ˌɑːkɪˈtektʃərəl/ **ADJ** architectural

architecturally /ˌɑːkɪˈtektʃərəlɪ/ **ADV** [*innovative, interesting*] du point de vue architectural ◆ **~, it represents a significant advance** du point de vue architectural, ça représente un progrès important

architecture /ˈɑːkɪtektʃəʳ/ **N** architecture *f*

architrave /ˈɑːkɪtreɪv/ **N** (*Archit*) architrave *f* ; [*of door, window*] encadrement *m*

archive /ˈɑːkaɪv/ **N** 1 (also **archives**) (= *records*) archives *fpl* ◆ **video/film ~** archives cinématographiques 2 (*Comput*) archive *f* **VT** archiver **ADJ** d'archives ◆ **~ material/film** documentation *f*/film *m* d'archives ◆ **~ file** (*Comput*) fichier *m* d'archives

archivist /ˈɑːkɪvɪst/ **N** archiviste *mf*

archly /ˈɑːtʃlɪ/ **ADV** 1 (= *cunningly*) malicieusement 2 (= *in a superior way*) avec condescendance

archness /ˈɑːtʃnɪs/ **N** malice *f*

archpriest /ˈɑːtʃˈpriːst/ **N** archiprêtre *m*

arch-rival /ˌɑːtʃˈraɪvəl/ **N** (= *person, company*) principal rival *m* ◆ **United and Liverpool are arch-rivals** United et Liverpool sont des adversaires acharnés

archway /ˈɑːtʃweɪ/ **N** voûte *f* (d'entrée), porche *m* ; (*longer*) passage *m* voûté

Arctic /ˈɑːktɪk/ **ADJ** (*Geog*) arctique ; (*fig* = *very cold*) glacial **N** ◆ **the ~ (regions)** les régions *fpl* arctiques, l'Arctique *m*
COMP **Arctic Circle** **N** cercle *m* polaire arctique
arctic fox **N** renard *m* polaire
Arctic Ocean **N** océan *m* Arctique
arctic skua **N** (*Orn*) labbe *m* parasite
arctic tern **N** (*Orn*) sterne *f* arctique

ardent /ˈɑːdənt/ **ADJ** 1 (= *enthusiastic*) [*person, opponent, feminist, desire, belief, appeal*] ardent ; [*admirer, supporter*] fervent 2 (= *passionate*) [*lover, lovemaking*] passionné

ardently /ˈɑːdəntlɪ/ **ADV** 1 (= *enthusiastically*) [*oppose, support, defend*] avec ardeur, ardemment ◆ **she's ~ socialist** c'est une fervente socialiste 2 (= *passionately*) [*kiss, respond*] passionnément

ardour, ardor (*US*) /ˈɑːdəʳ/ **N** ardeur *f*, ferveur *f*

arduous /ˈɑːdjʊəs/ **ADJ** [*work, conditions, journey, task*] ardu, difficile

arduously /ˈɑːdjʊəslɪ/ **ADV** péniblement, laborieusement

arduousness /ˈɑːdjʊəsnɪs/ **N** difficulté *f*

are /ɑːʳ, əʳ/ → **be**

area /ˈɛərɪə/ **N** 1 (= *surface measure*) superficie *f* ◆ **this field has an ~ of 2 hectares** ce champ a une superficie de 2 hectares *or* a 2 hectares de superficie
2 (= *region*) région *f* ; (*Mil, Pol*) (*large*) territoire *m* ; (*smaller*) secteur *m*, zone *f* ◆ **the London ~** la région londonienne *or* de Londres ◆ **in the whole ~** dans toute la région ; → **sterling**
3 (*fig*) [*of knowledge, enquiry*] domaine *m*, champ *m* ◆ **in this ~** dans ce domaine ◆ **the ~s of disagreement** les zones *fpl* de désaccord
4 (*Brit* = *courtyard*) courette *f* en contrebas (*sur la rue*)
5 (*with specified function*) **dining ~** (= *part of room*) coin *m* salle à manger ◆ **sleeping ~** coin *m* chambre ◆ **play/parking ~** (= *part of building, housing estate etc*) aire *f* de jeux/de stationnement
6 (*Ftbl* = *penalty area*) surface *f* de réparation
COMP **area code** **N** (*Telec*) indicatif *m* de zone
area manager **N** directeur *m* régional
area office **N** agence *f* régionale
area of outstanding natural beauty **N** site *m* naturel exceptionnel

areaway /ˈɛərɪəweɪ/ **N** (*US*) ⇒ **area 4**

arena /əˈriːnə/ **N** (*lit, fig*) arène *f* ◆ **the political ~** l'arène *f* politique ◆ **to enter the ~** (*fig*) descendre dans l'arène

aren't /ɑːnt/ ⇒ **are not, am not** ; → **be**

areola /əˈrɪələ/ **N** (pl **areolas** *or* **areolae** /əˈrɪəˌliː/) (*Anat*) aréole *f*

Argentina /ˌɑːdʒənˈtiːnə/ **N** Argentine *f*

Argentine /ˈɑːdʒəntaɪn/ **N** 1 (*Geog* †) **the ~** l'Argentine *f* ◆ **in the ~** en Argentine 2 ⇒ **Argentinian** **ADJ** argentin

Argentinean /ˌɑːdʒənˈtɪnɪən/ **ADJ** (*US*) ⇒ **Argentinian**

Argentinian /ˌɑːdʒənˈtɪnɪən/ **ADJ** argentin **N** Argentin(e) *m(f)*

argon /ˈɑːgɒn/ **N** argon *m*

Argonaut /ˈɑːgənɔːt/ N Argonaute *m*

Argos /ˈɑːgɒs/ N Argos

argosy /ˈɑːgəsɪ/ N (*liter*) galion *m*

argot /ˈɑːgəʊ/ N argot *m*

arguable /ˈɑːgjʊəbl/ ADJ discutable, contestable ◆ **it is ~ that ...** on peut soutenir que ...

arguably /ˈɑːgjʊəblɪ/ ADV ◆ **he is ~ the greatest footballer of all time** c'est sans doute le plus grand footballeur de tous les temps

argue /ˈɑːgjuː/ VI 1 (= *dispute, quarrel*) se disputer (*with sb* avec qn ; *about sth* au sujet *or* à propos de qch) ; ◆ **they are always arguing** ils se disputent tout le temps ◆ **don't ~!** pas de discussion ! ◆ **stop arguing!** (*to others arguing*) arrêtez de vous disputer ! ◆ **no one can ~ with that** personne ne peut contester cela

2 (= *debate*) argumenter (*frm*) (*against sb* contre qn ; *about sth* sur qch) ; ◆ **he ~d against going** il a donné les raisons qu'il avait de ne pas y aller ◆ **they ~d (about it) for hours** ils ont discuté (à ce sujet) pendant des heures ◆ **to ~ from sth** tirer argument de qch

3 (*Jur etc*) [*fact, evidence*] témoigner (*against sth* contre qch ; *for, in favour of sth* en faveur de qch) ; ◆ **they ~d in favour of imposing sanctions** ils ont plaidé en faveur de l'imposition de sanctions ◆ **it ~s well for him** cela parle en sa faveur

VT 1 ◆ **to ~ sb into/out of doing sth** persuader/dissuader qn de faire qch ◆ **to ~ sb into/out of a scheme** persuader/dissuader qn d'adopter un projet

2 (= *debate*) [+ *case*] discuter, débattre ◆ **a well-~d case** une argumentation solide ◆ **to ~ one's way out of a situation** se sortir d'une situation à force d'argumentation *or* d'arguments ◆ **to ~ the toss*** (*gen pej*) discuter le coup*

3 (= *show evidence of*) dénoter, indiquer ◆ **it ~s a certain lack of feeling** cela dénote *or* indique un certain manque de sensibilité

4 (= *maintain*) soutenir (*that* que) ; ◆ **she ~d that the sale of the property would be illegal** elle soutenait qu'il serait illégal de vendre la propriété ◆ **to ~ one's case** présenter ses arguments ◆ **the company has four days to ~ its case** la société a quatre jours pour présenter ses arguments ◆ **to ~ the case for sth** défendre qch, se prononcer en faveur de qch

► **argue out** VT SEP [+ *problem*] discuter *or* débattre (à fond)

argument /ˈɑːgjʊmənt/ LANGUAGE IN USE 26.2 N 1 (= *debate*) discussion *f*, débat *m* ◆ **it is beyond ~** c'est indiscutable ◆ **you've only heard one side of the ~** tu n'as entendu qu'une seule version de l'affaire *or* de l'histoire ◆ **for ~'s sake** à titre d'exemple ◆ **he is open to ~** il est prêt à écouter les arguments ◆ **it is open to ~ that ...** on peut soutenir que ...

2 (= *dispute*) dispute *f*, discussion *f* ◆ **to have an ~** se disputer (*with sb* avec qn) ; ◆ **he has had an ~ with a tree** (*hum*) il s'est bagarré* avec un arbre (*hum*)

3 (= *reasons advanced*) argument *m* ◆ **his ~ is that ...** il soutient que ..., son argument est que ... ◆ **there is a strong ~ in favour of** *or* **for doing sth** il y a de bonnes raisons pour faire qch ◆ **there is a strong ~ in favour of his resignation** il y a de bonnes raisons pour qu'il démissionne *subj* ◆ **the ~ that Europe needs Britain** le raisonnement selon lequel l'Europe a besoin de la Grande-Bretagne ; → **line**[1]

4 (= *synopsis*) sommaire *m*, argument *m*

> ⚠ When **argument** means 'discussion' or 'dispute' it is not translated by the French word **argument**.

argumentation /ˌɑːgjʊmənˈteɪʃən/ N argumentation *f*

argumentative /ˌɑːgjʊˈmentətɪv/ ADJ ergoteur, raisonneur

argy-bargy* /ˈɑːdʒɪˈbɑːdʒɪ/ N (pl **-bargies**) (*Brit*) discutailleries* *fpl* ◆ **to have an ~ (about sth)** avoir une discussion animée (à propos de qch)

aria /ˈɑːrɪə/ N aria *f*

Ariadne /ˌærɪˈædnɪ/ N Ariane *f*

Arian /ˈɛərɪən/ N Arien(ne) *m(f)* ADJ arien

Arianism /ˈɛərɪənɪzəm/ N arianisme *m*

ARIBA /əˈriːbə/ (abbrev of **Associate of the Royal Institute of British Architects**) *membre de l'institut britannique des architectes*

arid /ˈærɪd/ ADJ (*lit, fig*) aride

aridity /əˈrɪdɪtɪ/ N (*lit, fig*) aridité *f*

Aries /ˈɛəriːz/ N (*Astron*) Bélier *m* ◆ **I'm (an) ~** (*Astrol*) je suis (du) Bélier

aright /əˈraɪt/ ADV bien, correctement ◆ **did I hear ~?** ai-je bien entendu ? ◆ **to set things ~** mettre bon ordre à l'affaire

arise /əˈraɪz/ (pret **arose**, ptp **arisen**) /əˈrɪzn/ VI 1 [*difficulty*] survenir, surgir ; [*question*] se présenter, se poser ; [*cry*] s'élever ; [*problem*] se poser ◆ **if the question ~s** le cas échéant ◆ **should the need ~** en cas de besoin, si le besoin s'en fait sentir ◆ **should the occasion ~** si l'occasion se présente ◆ **doubts have ~n about the safety of this procedure** la sécurité de cette procédure a été remise en question 2 (= *result*) résulter, provenir (*from* de) 3 († , *liter*) [*person*] se lever ; [*sun*] se lever, paraître, poindre (*liter*)

aristo* /ˈærɪstəʊ/ N (*Brit*) (abbrev of **aristocrat**) aristo* *mf*

aristocracy /ˌærɪsˈtɒkrəsɪ/ N aristocratie *f*

aristocrat /ˈærɪstəkræt/ N aristocrate *mf*

aristocratic /ˌærɪstəˈkrætɪk/ ADJ aristocratique

Aristophanes /ˌærɪsˈtɒfəniːz/ N Aristophane *m*

Aristotelian /ˌærɪstəˈtiːlɪən/ ADJ aristotélicien

Aristotelianism /ˌærɪstəˈtiːlɪənɪzəm/ N aristotélisme *m*

Aristotle /ˈærɪstɒtl/ N Aristote *m*

arithmetic /əˈrɪθmətɪk/ N arithmétique *f* ADJ /ˌærɪθˈmetɪk/ arithmétique

COMP **arithmetic logic unit** N (*Comput*) unité *f* arithmétique et logique

arithmetic mean N moyenne *f* arithmétique

arithmetic progression N progression *f* arithmétique

arithmetical /ˌærɪθˈmetɪkəl/ ADJ arithmétique

arithmetician /əˌrɪθməˈtɪʃən/ N arithméticien(ne) *m(f)*

Ariz. abbrev of **Arizona**

Arizona /ˌærɪˈzəʊnə/ N Arizona *m*

ark /ɑːk/ N (*Hist*) arche *f* ◆ **Ark of the Covenant** (*Rel*) arche *f* d'alliance ◆ **it's out of the ~*** c'est vieux comme Hérode, c'est antédiluvien ; → **Noah**

Ark. abbrev of **Arkansas**

Arkansas /ˈɑːkənsɔː/ N Arkansas *m*

arm[1] /ɑːm/ N 1 (*Anat*) bras *m* ◆ **to hold sth/sb in one's ~s** tenir qch/qn dans ses bras ◆ **he had a coat over his ~** il avait un manteau sur le bras ◆ **take my ~** prenez mon bras ◆ **to give one's ~ to sb** donner le bras à qn ◆ **on her husband's ~** au bras de son mari ◆ **~ in ~** bras dessus bras dessous ◆ **to take sb in one's ~s** prendre qn dans ses bras ◆ **to put one's ~ round sb** passer son bras autour des épaules de qn ◆ **to put one's ~ round sb's waist** tenir qn par la taille ◆ **to drop one's ~s, to let one's ~s drop** *or* **fall** baisser les bras ◆ **to spread one's ~s wide (apart)** écarter les bras ◆ **with (one's) ~s outstretched, with outstretched ~s** (*to front*) les bras tendus ; (*to side*) les bras écartés ◆ **with one's ~s wide (outspread)** les bras écartés ◆ **with one's ~s by** *or* **at one's sides** les bras le long du corps ◆ **with folded ~s** les bras croisés ◆ **within ~'s reach** à portée de (la) main

◆ **at arm's length** à bout de bras ◆ **to hold sth at ~'s length** tenir qch à bout de bras ◆ **to keep sb at ~'s length** tenir qn à distance

2 (*figurative expressions*) **to welcome sb/sth with open ~s** accueillir qn/qch à bras ouverts ◆ **in the ~s of Morpheus** (*liter*) dans les bras de Morphée ◆ **a list as long as your ~*** une liste longue comme le bras* ◆ **the long ~ of the law** le bras de la justice ◆ **to have a long ~** (*fig*) avoir le bras long ◆ **to put the ~ on sb*** (*US*) (*gen*) forcer la main à qn (*to do sth* pour qu'il fasse qch) ; (= *make sb pay up*) faire cracher‡ qn ◆ **I'd give my right ~ for that/to do that*** je donnerais n'importe quoi pour ça/pour faire ça ◆ **that must have cost them an ~ and a leg*** ça a dû leur coûter les yeux de la tête*

3 [*of garment*] manche *f* ; [*of armchair*] bras *m*, accoudoir *m*

4 [*of crane, record-player*] bras *m* ; [*of spectacle frames*] branche *f*

5 [*of sea, lake, river*] bras *m* ◆ **an ~ of the sea** un bras de mer

6 [*of organization*] branche *f* ; → **fleet**[1]

COMP **arm's-length agreement** N (*Jur*) contrat *m* conclu dans les conditions normales du commerce

arm's-length price N (*Fin*) prix *m* fixé dans les conditions normales de la concurrence

arm's-length relationship N relation *f* distante

arm-twisting* N pressions *fpl* directes

arm-wrestle VI ◆ **to ~-wrestle with sb** faire un bras de fer avec qn

arm-wrestling N bras *m* de fer ◆ **an ~-wrestling match** une partie de bras de fer

arm[2] /ɑːm/ VT [+ *person, nation*] armer ◆ **to ~ o.s. with patience** s'armer de patience VI (s')armer, prendre les armes (*against* contre)

Armada /ɑːˈmɑːdə/ N Armada *f*

armadillo /ˌɑːməˈdɪləʊ/ N tatou *m*

Armageddon /ˌɑːməˈgedn/ N (*lit, fig*) Armageddon *m*

Armalite ® /ˈɑːməlaɪt/ N *fusil automatique rapide et ultraléger*

armament /ˈɑːməmənt/ N 1 (*gen pl* = *fighting strength*) force *f* de frappe 2 (*NonC* = *preparation for war*) armement *m*

armaments /ˈɑːməmənts/ NPL armement *m*

COMP **armaments depot** N dépôt *m* d'armes

armaments factory N usine *f* d'armement

armaments industry N industrie *f* d'armement

armature /ˈɑːmətjʊəʳ/ N (*gen*) armature *f* ; [*of animal*] carapace *f*

armband /ˈɑːmbænd/ N brassard *m* ; (*for swimming*) brassard *m* gonflable ; (*mourning*) brassard *m* de deuil, crêpe *m*

armchair /ˈɑːmtʃɛəʳ/ N fauteuil *m* ◆ **~ general/traveller** stratège *m*/voyageur *m* en chambre

COMP **armchair banking** N services *mpl* (bancaires) télématiques

armchair shopping N (*by post, telephone*) *achats par correspondance ou par téléphone* ; (*by computer, television*) téléachats *mpl*

armed /ɑːmd/ ADJ (*lit, fig*) armé (*with* de) ; [*missile*] muni d'une charge explosive ◆ **to go ~** (*lit*) porter une arme ◆ **to go ~ with statistics** *etc* s'armer de statistiques *etc* ◆ **~ to the teeth** armé jusqu'aux dents ◆ **~ conflict/struggle** conflit *m* armé/lutte *f* armée ◆ **the ~ forces** les forces *fpl* armées ◆ **~ neutrality** neutralité *f* armée ◆ **~ robbery** vol *m* *or* attaque *f* à main armée

-armed /ɑːmd/ ADJ *(in compounds)* 1 *(Anat)* ◆ **long-/short-armed** aux bras longs/courts 2 *(Mil)* ◆ **nuclear-/missile-armed** armé d'engins nucléaires/de missiles

Armenia /ɑːˈmiːnɪə/ N Arménie *f*

Armenian /ɑːˈmiːnɪən/ ADJ arménien N 1 *(= person)* Arménien(ne) *m(f)* 2 *(= language)* arménien *m*

armful /ˈɑːmfʊl/ N brassée *f* ◆ **in ~s** à pleins bras ◆ **he gathered up the clothes in ~s** il a ramassé les vêtements à pleins bras ◆ **he arrived with ~s of presents** il est arrivé avec des cadeaux plein les bras

armhole /ˈɑːmhəʊl/ N emmanchure *f*

armistice /ˈɑːmɪstɪs/ N armistice *m* COMP **Armistice Day** N le 11 novembre, l'Armistice *m*

armlet /ˈɑːmlɪt/ N *(= armband)* brassard *m* ; *(= bracelet)* bracelet *m*

armor /ˈɑːməʳ/ N *(US)* ⇒ **armour**

armorer /ˈɑːmərəʳ/ N *(US)* ⇒ **armourer**

armorial /ɑːˈmɔːrɪəl/ ADJ armorial ◆ **~ bearings** armoiries *fpl* N armorial *m*

armory /ˈɑːmərɪ/ N *(US)* ⇒ **armoury**

armour, armor *(US)* /ˈɑːməʳ/ N 1 *(NonC)* *[of knight]* armure *f* ◆ **in full ~** armé de pied en cap ; → **suit** 2 *(Mil)* *(NonC = armour-plating)* blindage *m* ; *(collectively)* *(= vehicles)* blindés *mpl* ; *(= forces)* forces *fpl* blindées
COMP **armour-clad** ADJ *[vehicle]* blindé ; *[ship]* cuirassé, blindé
armour-piercing ADJ *(Mil)* *[mine, gun]* antichar ; *[shell, bullet]* perforant
armour-plate N *(for vehicle)* blindage *m* ; *(for ship)* cuirasse *f*
armour-plated ADJ ⇒ **armour-clad**
armour-plating N ⇒ **armour-plate**

armoured, armored *(US)* /ˈɑːməd/ ADJ *[vehicle, division, units]* blindé
COMP **armoured car** N voiture *f* blindée
armoured personnel carrier N (véhicule *m*) blindé *m* de transport de troupes

armourer, armorer *(US)* /ˈɑːmərəʳ/ N armurier *m*

armoury, armory *(US)* /ˈɑːmərɪ/ N 1 dépôt *m* d'armes, arsenal *m* 2 *(US = arms factory)* usine *f* d'armement

armpit /ˈɑːmpɪt/ N aisselle *f* ◆ **to be up to one's ~s in water** avoir de l'eau jusqu'aux épaules

armrest /ˈɑːmrest/ N accoudoir *m*

arms /ɑːmz/ NPL 1 *(= weapons)* armes *fpl* ◆ **under ~** sous les armes ◆ **in ~** en armes ◆ **to ~!** aux armes ! ◆ **to call to ~** *[rebel leader]* appeler aux armes ; *[government]* appeler sous les drapeaux ◆ **to take up ~ against sb/sth** *(lit)* prendre les armes contre qn/qch ; *(fig)* s'insurger contre qn/qch
◆ **up in arms** ◆ **to be up in ~ against sb/the authorities** être en rébellion ouverte contre qn/les autorités ◆ **to be up in ~ against a decision** s'élever contre *or* partir en guerre contre une décision ◆ **they are up in ~ about the price of petrol** ils s'insurgent contre le prix de l'essence ◆ **she was up in ~ about it** ça l'a mise hors d'elle
2 *(Her)* armoiries *fpl*, armes *fpl* ; → **coat**
COMP **arms cache, arms dump** N cache *f* d'armes
arms control N contrôle *m* des armements
arms dealer N marchand *m* d'armes
arms dump ⇒ **arms cache**
arms embargo N embargo *m* sur les armes
arms exports N exportations *fpl* d'armes
arms factory N usine *f* d'armement
arms limitation N limitation *f* des armements
arms manufacturer N fabricant *m* d'armes
arms race N course *f* aux armements
arms sales N ventes *fpl* d'armes
arms trade N commerce *m* des armes

army /ˈɑːmɪ/ N 1 armée *f* (de terre) ◆ **to be in the ~** être dans l'armée, être militaire ◆ **to join the ~** s'engager (dans l'armée) ◆ **to go into the ~** *[professional]* s'engager dans l'armée ; *[conscript]* partir au service (militaire) ; → **occupation, territorial** 2 *(fig)* armée *f*
COMP *[life, nurse, uniform]* militaire ; *[family]* de militaires
army corps N corps *m* d'armée
army-issue ADJ *[rifle]* de l'armée ◆ **police say the grenade was ~-issue** la police dit que c'était une grenade de l'armée
Army List N annuaire *m* militaire, annuaire *m* des officiers de carrière (de l'armée de terre)
army officer N officier *m* (de l'armée de terre)
army surplus N *(NonC)* surplus *mpl* de l'armée
army-surplus ADJ *[boots, jacket etc]* des surplus de l'armée ; *[store]* de surplus (de l'armée)

aroma /əˈrəʊmə/ N arôme *m*

aromatherapist /əˈrəʊməˈθerəpɪst/ N aromathérapeute *mf*

aromatherapy /əˌrəʊməˈθerəpɪ/ N aromathérapie *f*

aromatic /ˌærəʊˈmætɪk/ ADJ aromatique N aromate *m*

arose /əˈrəʊz/ VB pt of **arise**

around /əˈraʊnd/

> When **around** is an element in a phrasal verb, eg **come around**, **move around**, **potter around**, look up the verb.

ADV 1 *(= surrounding)* autour ◆ **all ~** tout autour, de tous côtés ◆ **for miles ~** sur *or* dans un rayon de plusieurs kilomètres
2 *(= near, in circulation)* dans les parages ◆ **he is somewhere ~** il est dans les parages ◆ **you haven't seen Susan ~, have you?** vous n'auriez pas vu Susan dans les parages, par hasard ? ◆ **she'll be ~ soon** elle sera bientôt là ◆ **is he ~?** * (est-ce qu')il est là ? ◆ **there's a lot of flu ~** il y a beaucoup de cas de grippe en ce moment
◆ **to have been around** * ◆ **he's been ~** * *(travelled)* il a pas mal roulé sa bosse * ; *(experienced)* il n'est pas né d'hier *or* de la dernière pluie ◆ **it's been ~ * for more than 20 years** ça existe depuis plus de 20 ans
3 *(opposite direction)* ◆ **to turn sth (the other way) ~** retourner qch ◆ **it's the other way ~** c'est le contraire
PREP 1 *(= surrounding)* autour de ◆ **~ the fire** autour du feu ◆ **~ it** autour ◆ **the first building ~ the corner** le premier immeuble au coin de la rue ◆ **it's just ~ the corner** *(lit)* c'est juste au coin ; *(fig = very near)* c'est à deux pas (d'ici) ; *(= very soon)* ce n'est pas loin ; see also **corner**
2 *(= somewhere in)* **they are (somewhere) ~ the house** ils sont quelque part dans la maison
3 *(= approximately)* environ, à peu près ◆ **~ 2 kilos** environ *or* à peu près 2 kilos, 2 kilos environ ◆ **~ 1800** vers *or* aux alentours de 1800 ◆ **~ 10 o'clock** vers 10 heures

arousal /əˈraʊzəl/ N *(sexual)* excitation *f* (sexuelle) ; *(emotional)* éveil *m*

arouse /əˈraʊz/ VT 1 *(= awaken)* *[+ person]* réveiller, éveiller ◆ **to ~ sb from his sleep** tirer qn du sommeil 2 *(= cause)* *[+ suspicion, curiosity etc]* éveiller ; *[+ anger]* exciter, provoquer ; *[+ contempt]* susciter, provoquer 3 *(= stimulate)* stimuler, réveiller * ; *(= stir to action)* pousser à agir, secouer ◆ **that ~d him to protest** cela l'a poussé à protester

aroused /əˈraʊzd/ ADJ *(sexually)* excité

arpeggio /ɑːˈpedʒɪəʊ/ N arpège *m*

arr. 1 *(on timetable)* (abbrev of **arrives, arrival**) arr., arrivée 2 *(Mus)* (abbrev of **arranged**) adaptation de

arraign /əˈreɪn/ VT *(Jur)* traduire en justice ; *(fig)* accuser, mettre en cause

arraignment /əˈreɪnmənt/ N *(Jur)* ≈ lecture *f* de l'acte d'accusation

Arran /ˈærən/ N île *f* d'Arran

arrange /əˈreɪndʒ/ VT 1 *(= put in order)* *[+ room, clothing]* arranger ; *[+ books, objects]* ranger, mettre en ordre ; *[+ flowers]* arranger, disposer ◆ **to ~ one's hair** arranger sa coiffure ◆ **a room ~d as a play area** une pièce aménagée en espace de jeu
2 *(= decide on)* *[+ meeting]* arranger, organiser ; *[+ date]* fixer ; *[+ plans, programme]* arrêter, convenir de ; *[+ arranged marriage]* arranger ◆ **it was ~d that ...** il a été décidé *or* convenu que ... + *cond* ◆ **I have something ~d for tonight** j'ai quelque chose de prévu pour ce soir
3 *(† = settle)* *[+ dispute]* régler, arranger
4 *(Mus)* arranger, adapter ◆ **to ~ sth for violin and piano** faire un arrangement de qch pour violon et piano
VI *(= fix details)* s'arranger, prendre des *or* ses dispositions ◆ **we have ~d for the goods to be dispatched** nous avons fait le nécessaire pour que les marchandises soient expédiées ◆ **to ~ for sb's luggage to be sent up** faire monter les bagages de qn ◆ **to ~ with sb to do sth** décider avec qn de faire qch, s'entendre avec qn pour faire qch
COMP **arranged marriage** N mariage *m* arrangé

arrangement /əˈreɪndʒmənt/ N 1 *[of room, furniture]* arrangement *m*, agencement *m* ; *[of flowers, hair, clothing]* arrangement *m* ; → **flower**
2 *(= agreement)* arrangement *m* ◆ **to do sth by ~ with sb** s'entendre *or* s'arranger avec qn pour faire qch ◆ **larger sizes by ~** tailles *fpl* supérieures sur demande ◆ **price by ~** prix *m* à débattre ◆ **to come to an ~ with sb** parvenir à un arrangement avec qn, s'arranger *or* s'entendre avec qn *(to do sth* pour faire qch*)* ; ◆ **by ~ with Covent Garden** avec l'autorisation *f* de Covent Garden ; → **exceptional**
3 *(= sth decided)* arrangement *m* ◆ **~s** *(= plans, preparations)* dispositions *fpl*, préparatifs *mpl* ◆ **this ~ suited everyone** cet arrangement convenait à tous ◆ **the ~ whereby he should visit her monthly** l'arrangement selon lequel il doit aller la voir une fois par mois ◆ **I write to confirm these ~s** je vous écris pour confirmer ces dispositions ◆ **I want to change the ~s we made** je veux changer les dispositions que nous avons prises ◆ **to make ~s for a holiday** faire des préparatifs pour des vacances, organiser des vacances (à l'avance) ◆ **to make ~s for sth to be done** prendre des dispositions pour faire faire qch ◆ **can you make ~s to come tomorrow?** pouvez-vous vous arranger pour venir demain ?
4 *(Mus)* adaptation *f*, arrangement *m*

arranger /əˈreɪndʒəʳ/ N 1 *(Mus)* arrangeur *m*, -euse *f* 2 *(= organizer)* organisateur *m*, -trice *f*

arrant /ˈærənt/ ADJ *(frm)* *[fool, liar, coward]* fieffé † *before n* ; *[hypocrisy]* consommé, éhonté ◆ **his ~ stupidity** son imbécillité totale ◆ **that's the most ~ nonsense I've ever heard** je n'ai jamais rien entendu de plus absurde

array /əˈreɪ/ VT 1 *(Mil)* *[+ troops]* déployer, disposer 2 *(liter = clothe)* *[+ person]* revêtir *(in* de*)* N 1 *(Mil)* rang *m*, ordre *m* ◆ **in battle ~** en ordre de bataille 2 *[of objects]* étalage *m* ; *[of people]* assemblée *f* ◆ **an ~ of solar panels** une batterie de panneaux solaires 3 *(Math etc: also Comput)* tableau *m* ◆ **~ of figures** tableau *m* 4 *(= ceremonial dress)* habit *m* d'apparat ; *(= fine clothes)* atours *mpl* *(iro)*

arrears /əˈrɪəz/ NPL arriéré *m* ◆ **rent in ~** arriéré *m* de loyers ◆ **to get** *or* **fall into ~** accumuler des arriérés ◆ **she is three months in ~ with her rent, her rent is three months in ~** elle doit trois mois de loyer, elle a un arriéré de trois mois sur son loyer ◆ **he fell into ~ with**

his mortgage/his rent il a pris du retard dans le remboursement de son emprunt logement/dans le paiement de son loyer ◆ **to be/get in ~ with one's correspondence** avoir/prendre du retard dans sa correspondance ◆ **~ of work** travail *m* en retard

arrest /ə'rest/ VT ① *[police] [+ suspect]* arrêter, appréhender ◆ **he can't get ~ed*** *(fig)* personne ne veut de lui
② *[+ person's attention, interest]* retenir, attirer
③ *[+ growth, development, progress] (= stop)* arrêter ; *(= hinder)* entraver ; *(= retard)* retarder ◆ **measures to ~ inflation** des mesures pour arrêter l'inflation ◆ **to ~ (the course of) a disease** *(Med)* enrayer une maladie
N ① *[of person]* arrestation *f* ◆ **under ~** en état d'arrestation ; *(Mil)* aux arrêts ◆ **to put sb under ~** arrêter qn ; *(Mil)* mettre qn aux arrêts ◆ **to make an ~** procéder à une arrestation ◆ **open/close ~** *(Mil)* ≈ arrêts *mpl* simples/de rigueur
② *(Jur)* **~ of judgement** suspension *f* d'exécution d'un jugement
COMP **arrested development** N *(Med)* arrêt *m* de croissance ; *(Psych)* atrophie *f* de la personnalité
arresting officer N *(Police) policier ayant procédé à l'arrestation*
arrest warrant N mandat *m* d'arrêt

arresting /ə'restɪŋ/ ADJ *(frm = striking)* frappant, saisissant

arrhythmia /ə'rɪðmɪə/ N *(NonC)* arythmie *f*

arrival /ə'raɪvəl/ LANGUAGE IN USE 24.1 N ① *[of person, vehicle, letter, parcel]* arrivée *f* ; *(Comm) [of goods in bulk]* arrivage *m* ◆ **on ~** à l'arrivée ◆ **~s and departures** *(Rail etc)* arrivées *fpl* et départs *mpl* ② *(= consignment)* **an ~ of** un arrivage de ◆ **who was the first ~?** *(= person)* qui est arrivé le premier ? ◆ **a new ~** un nouveau venu, une nouvelle venue ; *(hum = baby)* un(e) nouveau-né(e) ◆ **the latest ~** le dernier arrivé
COMP **arrival board** N *(US)* ⇒ **arrivals board**
arrival platform N quai *m* d'arrivée
arrivals board N tableau *m* des arrivées
arrivals lounge N salon *m* d'arrivée

arrive /ə'raɪv/ VI ① *[person, vehicle, letter, goods]* arriver ◆ **to ~ at a town** arriver à *or* atteindre une ville ◆ **as soon as he ~s** dès qu'il arrivera, dès son arrivée ◆ **arriving Paris (at) 14.43** *(on timetable etc)* arrivée *f* à Paris (à) 14h43 ◆ **to ~ on the scene** *(lit) (= turn up)* arriver (sur place) ; *(fig) (= become a factor)* faire son apparition ◆ **the moment has ~d when we must go** le moment est venu pour nous de partir
② *(= succeed)* arriver, réussir ◆ **you know you've ~d when people recognise you in the street** on sait qu'on a réussi quand les gens vous reconnaissent dans la rue

▸ **arrive at** VT FUS *[+ decision, solution]* aboutir à, parvenir à ; *[+ perfection]* atteindre ◆ **to ~ at a price** *[one person]* fixer un prix ; *[two people]* se mettre d'accord sur un prix ◆ **they finally ~d at the idea of selling it** ils en sont finalement venus à l'idée de le vendre

arrogance /'ærəgəns/ N arrogance *f*, morgue *f*

arrogant /'ærəgənt/ ADJ arrogant, plein de morgue

arrogantly /'ærəgəntlɪ/ ADV *[behave, say]* avec arrogance ◆ **~ casual/careless** d'une désinvolture/insouciance arrogante

arrogate /'ærəʊgeɪt/ VT *(frm)* ① *(= claim unjustly) [+ authority, right]* revendiquer à tort, s'arroger ; *[+ victory]* s'attribuer ② *(= attribute unjustly)* attribuer injustement *(to sb* à qn)

arrow /'ærəʊ/ N *(= weapon, directional sign)* flèche *f* ◆ **to shoot** *or* **loose off an ~** décocher une flèche VT *[+ item on list etc]* cocher ; *[+ route, direction]* flécher ◆ **to ~ sth in** *(= insert)* indiquer l'emplacement de qch

arrowhead /'ærəʊhed/ N *[of arrow]* fer *m* or pointe *f* de flèche

arrowroot /'ærəʊruːt/ N *(for cooking)* arrow-root *m* ; *(= plant)* maranta *f*

arse**/ /ɑːs/ *(esp Brit)* N cul**/ *m* ◆ **shift** *or* **move your ~!** *(= move over)* bouge ton cul !**/ ; *(= hurry up)* magne-toi le cul !**/ ◆ **get (up) off your ~** *(= stand up)* lève ton cul de là**/ ; *(fig)* bouge-toi le cul**/ ◆ **he doesn't know his ~ from his elbow** il comprend rien à rien* ; → **ass², pain**
VT ◆ **I can't be ~d** j'ai la flemme*

▸ **arse about****/, **arse around****/ VI déconner**/

arsehole**/ /'ɑːshəʊl/ N *(Brit)* trou *m* du cul**/ ◆ **you ~!** trou du cul !**/

arsenal /'ɑːsɪnl/ N arsenal *m*

arsenic /'ɑːsnɪk/ N arsenic *m* COMP **arsenic poisoning** N empoisonnement *m* à l'arsenic

arsenical /ɑː'senɪkəl/ ADJ *[substance]* arsenical ◆ **~ poisoning** empoisonnement *m* à l'arsenic

arson /'ɑːsn/ N incendie *m* volontaire *or* criminel

arsonist /'ɑːsənɪst/ N *(gen)* incendiaire *mf* ; *(= maniac)* pyromane *mf*

art¹ /ɑːt/ N ① *(NonC)* art *m* ◆ **~ for ~'s sake** l'art pour l'art ◆ **to study ~** *(gen)* faire des études d'art ; *(Univ)* faire les beaux-arts ◆ **the ~s** *(= humanities)* les lettres *fpl* ; *(= plastic arts)* les arts *mpl* ; → **work**
② *(= human skill)* art *m*, habileté *f* ◆ **the ~ of embroidering/embroidery** l'art *m* de broder/de la broderie ◆ **to do sth with ~** faire qch avec art *or* habileté ◆ **~s and crafts** artisanat *m* (d'art) ; → **black, fine², state**
③ *(Univ)* **Arts** lettres *fpl* ◆ **Faculty of Arts** faculté *f* des Lettres (et Sciences humaines) ◆ **he's doing Arts** il fait des (études de) lettres ; → **bachelor, master**
④ *(= cunning)* artifice *m*, ruse *f* ◆ **to use every ~ in order to do sth** user de tous les artifices pour faire qch
COMP **art collection** N collection *f* d'œuvres d'art
art collector N collectionneur *m*, -euse *f* d'art
art college N ≈ école *f* des beaux-arts
art dealer N marchand *m* de tableaux
art deco N art *m* déco ADJ art déco *inv*
art director N *(Cine)* directeur *m*, -trice *f* artistique
art exhibition N exposition *f* (d'œuvres) d'art
art form N moyen *m* d'expression artistique
art gallery N *(= museum)* musée *m* d'art ; *(= shop)* galerie *f* (de tableaux *or* d'art)
art-house ADJ *[film, cinema]* d'art et d'essai
art nouveau N art *m* nouveau, modern style *m*
art paper N papier *m* couché
art school N ≈ école *f* des beaux-arts
Arts Council N *organisme gouvernemental britannique responsable du financement des activités culturelles*
Arts degree N *(Univ)* ≈ licence *f* ès lettres
arts student N étudiant(e) *m(f)* de *or* en lettres
art student N étudiant(e) *m(f)* des *or* en beaux-arts

art² /ɑːt/ († †, *liter:* also **thou art**) ⇒ **you are** ; → **be**

artefact /'ɑːtɪfækt/ N objet *m* (fabriqué), artefact *m*

Artemis /'ɑːtɪmɪs/ N Artémis *f*

arterial /ɑː'tɪərɪəl/ ADJ ① *(Anat)* artériel ② *(Rail)* **~ line** grande ligne *f* ◆ **~ road** route *f* or voie *f* à grande circulation, (grande) artère *f*

arteriole /ɑː'tɪərɪəʊl/ N artériole *f*

arteriosclerosis /ɑːˌtɪərɪəʊsklɪ'rəʊsɪs/ N artériosclérose *f*

artery /'ɑːtərɪ/ N *(Anat)* artère *f* ; *(fig = road)* artère *f*, route *f* or voie *f* à grande circulation

artesian well /ɑː'tiːzɪənwel/ N puits *m* artésien

artful /'ɑːtfʊl/ ADJ rusé, malin (-igne *f*) ◆ **he's an ~ one*** c'est un petit malin* ◆ **~ dodger** roublard(e)* *m(f)*

artfully /'ɑːtfəlɪ/ ADV ① *(= skilfully) [arranged, constructed, designed]* ingénieusement ② *(= cunningly)* avec ruse

artfulness /'ɑːtfʊlnɪs/ N *(= cunning)* astuce *f*, ruse *f* ; *(= skill)* adresse *f*, habileté *f*

arthritic /ɑː'θrɪtɪk/ ADJ, N arthritique *mf*

arthritis /ɑː'θraɪtɪs/ N arthrite *f* ; → **rheumatoid**

arthropod /'ɑːθrəpɒd/ N arthropode *m*

Arthurian /ɑː'θjʊərɪən/ ADJ du roi Arthur, d'Arthur ◆ **~ legend** *or* **legends** la légende du roi Arthur, le cycle d'Arthur

artic* /ɑː'tɪk/ N *(Brit Aut)* (abbrev of **articulated lorry**) → **articulate**

artichoke /'ɑːtɪtʃəʊk/ N artichaut *m* ; → **globe, Jerusalem**

article /'ɑːtɪkl/ N ① *(= object)* objet *m* ; *(Comm)* article *m*, marchandise *f* ◆ **~ of clothing** pièce *f* d'habillement ◆ **~s of clothing** vêtements *mpl* ◆ **~ of food** produit *m* or denrée *f* alimentaire ◆ **~s of value** objets *mpl* de valeur ② *(Press)* article *m* ; → **leading¹** ③ *(Jur etc) [of treaty, document]* article *m* ◆ **~s of apprenticeship** contrat *m* d'apprentissage ◆ **~ of faith** article *m* de foi ◆ **the Thirty-Nine Articles** *(Rel) les trente-neuf articles de foi de l'Église anglicane* ◆ **~s of war** *(US Mil)* code *m* de justice militaire ④ *(Gram)* article *m* ; → **definite, indefinite** VT ① *[+ apprentice] (to trade)* mettre en apprentissage (to chez) ; *(to profession)* mettre en stage *(to* chez, auprès de) ② *(Jur)* stipuler
COMP **articled clerk** N *(Brit)* avocat(e) *m(f)* stagiaire
articles of association NPL *(Jur)* statuts *mpl*

articulacy /ɑː'tɪkjʊləsɪ/ N faculté *f* d'expression

articulate /ɑː'tɪkjʊlɪt/ ADJ ① *[speech]* net, distinct ; *[thought]* clair, net ; *[person]* qui s'exprime bien, qui sait s'exprimer ② *(Anat, Bot)* articulé VT /ɑː'tɪkjʊleɪt/ ① *[+ word, sentence]* articuler ; *(fig) [+ plan, goal]* exprimer clairement ② *(Anat, Bot)* articuler VI articuler COMP **articulated lorry** N *(Brit)* semi-remorque *m*

articulately /ɑː'tɪkjʊlɪtlɪ/ ADV *(= fluently)* avec aisance ; *(= clearly)* clairement

articulation /ɑːˌtɪkjʊ'leɪʃən/ N articulation *f*

articulatory phonetics /ɑːˌtɪkjʊ'leɪtərɪ fəʊ'netɪks/ N *(NonC)* phonétique *f* articulatoire

artifact /'ɑːtɪfækt/ N ⇒ **artefact**

artifice /'ɑːtɪfɪs/ N ① *(= stratagem)* artifice *m*, ruse *f* ② *(NonC = cunning)* adresse *f*, art *m* ③ *(NonC: † = artificiality)* stratagème *m*

artificial /ˌɑːtɪ'fɪʃəl/ ADJ ① *(= synthetic) [light, flowers]* artificiel ; *[leather, jewel]* synthétique, artificiel ◆ **~ climbing** escalade *f* artificielle ◆ **~ hair** cheveux *mpl* postiches ◆ **~ arm/leg** bras *m*/jambe *f* artificiel(le) ◆ **~ limb** prothèse *f*, membre *m* artificiel ◆ **~ manure** engrais *mpl* chimiques ◆ **~ silk** soie *f* artificielle ◆ **~ teeth** fausses dents *fpl*, prothèse *f* dentaire ② *(= affected) [manner]* artificiel, affecté ; *[tears]* feint, factice ; *[smile]* forcé ; *[person]* affecté
COMP **artificial horizon** N horizon *m* artificiel
artificial insemination (by donor) N insémination *f* artificielle (par un donneur)
artificial intelligence N intelligence *f* artificielle
artificial respiration N respiration *f* artificielle

artificiality /ˌɑːtɪfɪʃɪ'ælɪtɪ/ N manque *m* de naturel

artificially /ˌɑːtɪ'fɪʃəlɪ/ ADV artificiellement

artillery /ɑː'tɪlərɪ/ N artillerie *f*

artilleryman /ɑːˈtɪlərɪmən/ **N** (pl **-men**) artilleur *m*

artisan /ˌɑːtɪˈzæn/ **N** artisan *m* ◆ **the ~s** *(collectively)* l'artisanat *m*

artisanal /ɑːˈtɪzənəl/ **ADJ** artisanal

artist /ˈɑːtɪst/ **N** artiste *mf* ; → **con³, piss, rip-off**

artiste /ɑːˈtiːst/ **N** *(esp Brit = performer)* artiste *mf* ; → **variety**

artistic /ɑːˈtɪstɪk/ **ADJ** *[talent, design, heritage, freedom]* artistique ; *[person]* qui a un sens artistique **COMP** **artistic director** **N** directeur *m*, -trice *f* artistique

artistically /ɑːˈtɪstɪkəlɪ/ **ADV** 1 *[gifted, successful]* du point de vue artistique 2 *[arranged, presented]* avec art

artistry /ˈɑːtɪstrɪ/ **N** *(NonC)* art *m*, talent *m* artistique

artless /ˈɑːtlɪs/ **ADJ** 1 *(= straightforward) [person, beauty]* naturel ; *[behaviour, comment, simplicity]* ingénu 2 *(pej = without art, skill) [object]* grossier ; *[translation]* lourd

artlessly /ˈɑːtlɪslɪ/ **ADV** ingénument

artlessness /ˈɑːtlɪsnɪs/ **N** *(NonC)* 1 *(= straightforwardness) [of person, beauty]* naturel *m* ; *[of behaviour, comment, simplicity]* ingénuité *f* 2 *(pej = lack of art, skill) [object]* grossièreté *f* ; *[translation]* lourdeur *f*

artsy* /ˈɑːtsɪ/ **ADJ** *(US)* ⇒ **arty**

artsy-craftsy* /ˈɑːtsɪˈkrɑːftsɪ/ **ADJ** *(US)* ⇒ **arty-crafty**

artsy-fartsy* /ˈɑːtsɪˈfɑːtsɪ/ **ADJ** *(US)* ⇒ **arty-farty**

artwork /ˈɑːtwɜːk/ **N** *(Publishing)* iconographie *f* ; *(= painting, sculpture)* œuvre *f* d'art ; *(US = objects)* objets *mpl* d'art

arty* /ˈɑːtɪ/, **artsy*** *(US)* **ADJ** *[person]* qui se donne le genre artiste *or* bohème ; *[clothes]* faussement bohème

arty-crafty* /ˈɑːtɪˈkrɑːftɪ/, **artsy-craftsy*** *(US)* **ADJ** *(pej) [object, style]* (exagérément) artisanal ; *[person]* qui affiche un genre artiste *or* bohème

arty-farty‡ /ˈɑːtɪˈfɑːtɪ/, **artsy-fartsy**‡ *(US)* **ADJ** *(pej) [person]* poseur ; *[book, film]* prétentieux ◆ **an ~ man/woman** un poseur/une poseuse

ARV /ˌeɪɑːˈviː/ **N** *(US Bible)* (abbrev of **American Revised Version**) *traduction américaine de la Bible*

arvee* /ɑːˈviː/ **N** *(US)* (abbrev of **recreational vehicle**) → **recreational**

arvo* /ˈɑːvəʊ/ (pl **arvos**) **N** *(Austral)* après-midi *m or f*

Aryan /ˈɛərɪən/ **N** Aryen(ne) *m(f)* **ADJ** aryen

AS /ˌeɪˈes/ 1 abbrev of **American Samoa** 2 *(US)* (abbrev of **Associate in Sciences**) ≈ titulaire *mf* d'un DEUG de sciences

as /æz, əz/

LANGUAGE IN USE 17.1, 26.2

1 CONJUNCTION
2 PREPOSITION
3 ADVERB

For set combinations in which **as** is not the first word, eg **such ... as, the same ... as, dressed/disguised as, acknowledge as**, look up the other word.

1 - CONJUNCTION

1 (= while) alors que ◆ **~ she was falling asleep she heard a noise** elle entendit un bruit alors qu'elle commençait à s'endormir ◆ **he saw the accident ~ he was going to school** il a vu l'accident en allant à l'école ◆ **another policeman has been killed ~ fighting continued this morning** un autre policier a été tué tandis que *or* alors que les combats continuaient ce matin ◆ **all the jury's eyes were upon him ~ he continued** les jurés ne le quittaient pas des yeux tandis qu'il *or* alors qu'il continuait à parler

2 (with comparative) ◆ **things will get more difficult ~ the year goes on** ça va devenir de plus en plus difficile au fur et à mesure que la fin de l'année approche ◆ **he grew deafer ~ he got older** il devenait de plus en plus sourd en vieillissant

3 (= just when) (juste) au moment où, alors que ◆ **he came in ~ I was leaving** il est arrivé (juste) au moment où je partais *or* alors que je partais

4 (= because) étant donné que, comme ◆ **~ he hasn't phoned, we don't know where he is** comme il *or* étant donné qu'il n'a pas téléphoné, nous ne savons pas où il est ◆ **patient ~ she is, she'll probably put up with it** patiente comme elle est, elle arrivera probablement à le supporter

parce que or **car** can also be used, but not at the beginning of the sentence.

◆ **this is important ~ it reduces the effectiveness of the drug** c'est important parce que *or* car cela diminue l'efficacité du médicament

5 (= though) **long ~ it was, I didn't find the journey boring** bien que le trajet ait été long, je ne me suis pas ennuyé ◆ **unlikely/amazing ~ it may seem** aussi improbable/surprenant que cela paraisse ◆ **hard ~ it is to believe, ...** aussi incroyable que cela puisse paraître, ... ◆ **(~) important ~ the president is ...** pour *or* si important que soit le président ...

6 (indicating manner) comme ◆ **do ~ you like** faites comme vous voulez ◆ **France, ~ you know, is ...** la France, comme vous le savez, est ... ◆ **~ (is) usual** comme d'habitude, comme à l'ordinaire ◆ **~ often happens** comme c'est souvent le cas ◆ **she is very gifted, ~ is her brother** elle est très douée, comme son frère ◆ **they are fine ~ they are** ils sont très bien comme ça ◆ **I'm okay ~ I am** je me trouve très bien comme ça ◆ **knowing him ~ I do, I am sure he'll refuse** le connaissant comme je le connais, je suis sûr qu'il refusera ◆ **don't tidy up, leave it ~ it is** ne range rien, laisse ça comme ça BUT **A is to B ~ C is to D** ◆ **~ A is to B so C is to D** C est à D ce que A est à B ◆ **the village, situated ~ it is near a motorway, ...** le village, étant situé non loin d'une autoroute, ...

2 - PREPOSITION

1 (= in the capacity of) comme ◆ **he works ~ a waiter** il travaille comme serveur BUT **Olivier ~ Hamlet** *(Theat)* Olivier dans le rôle de Hamlet

2 (= being) en tant que ◆ **Napoleon, ~ a statesman, was ...** Napoléon, en tant qu'homme d'État, était ... ◆ **~ a mother of five children, she is well aware ...** en tant que mère de cinq enfants, elle sait très bien ...

3 (= when) ◆ **~ a child, she was rather shy** (lorsqu'elle *or* quand elle était) enfant, elle était plutôt timide ◆ **~ a young woman, she was very interested in politics** lorsqu'elle *or* quand elle était jeune, elle s'intéressait beaucoup à la politique

3 - ADVERB

1 (= in the way) comme ◆ **you'll have it by noon ~ agreed** vous l'aurez pour midi comme convenu ◆ **he came ~ agreed** il est venu comme convenu *or* prévu ◆ **~ in all good detective stories** comme dans tout bon roman policier ◆ **"m" ~ in mother** "m" comme mère

2 (set structures)

◆ **as ... as** *(in comparisons of equality)* aussi ... que ◆ **I am ~ tall ~ you** je suis aussi grand que toi ◆ **is it ~ far ~ that?** c'est vraiment aussi loin que ça ?

◆ **as much as** autant que ◆ **you ate ~ much ~ me*** *or* **~ I did** tu as mangé autant que moi ◆ **you spend ~ much ~ me*** *or* **~ I do** tu dépenses autant que moi

◆ **twice/half** *etc* **as ...** ◆ **she's twice ~ nice ~ her sister** elle est deux fois plus gentille que sa sœur ◆ **it's half ~ expensive** ça coûte deux fois moins cher ◆ **it's twice/three times ~ expensive** ça coûte deux fois/trois fois plus cher

◆ **not as** *or* **not so ... as** pas aussi ... que ◆ **I am not so** *or* **not ~ ambitious ~ you** je ne suis pas aussi ambitieux que toi ◆ **it's not so** *or* **not ~ bad ~ all that** ce n'est pas si terrible que ça

◆ **as for** *(when changing subject)* quant à ◆ **~ for her mother ...** quant à sa mère ... ◆ **~ for that ...** *(= regarding)* pour ce qui est de ça ..., quant à cela ...

◆ **as from** *(referring to past)* depuis ; *(referring to present, future)* à partir de ◆ **~ from last Tuesday** depuis mardi dernier ◆ **~ from today/next Tuesday** à partir d'aujourd'hui/de mardi prochain

◆ **as if, as though** comme si ◆ **he was staggering ~ if** *or* **~ though he'd been drinking** il titubait comme s'il avait bu ◆ **it was ~ if** *or* **~ though he was still alive** c'était comme s'il était toujours vivant ◆ **it's not ~ if** *or* **~ though he was nice-looking** ce n'est pas comme s'il était beau garçon ◆ **~ if!*** tu parles !*

◆ **as if to** comme pour ◆ **~ if to confirm his prediction there was a loud explosion** comme pour confirmer ses prédictions on entendit une forte explosion ◆ **he looked at me ~ if to say ...** il m'a regardé avec l'air de dire ...

◆ **as it is** *(= in fact)* dans l'état actuel des choses ; *(= already)* comme ça ◆ **~ it is, it doesn't make much difference** dans l'état actuel des choses, ça ne fait pas grande différence ◆ **I've got quite enough to do ~ it is** j'ai bien assez à faire comme ça

◆ **as it were** pour ainsi dire, en quelque sorte ◆ **I have become, ~ it were, two people** je suis devenu, pour ainsi dire *or* en quelque sorte, non pas une, mais deux personnes

◆ **as of** *(from past time)* depuis ; *(from present, future time)* à partir de ; *(= up to)* jusqu'à ◆ **~ of last Tuesday** depuis mardi dernier ◆ **~ of today/next Tuesday** à partir d'aujourd'hui/de mardi prochain ◆ **~ of yesterday, the city has recorded 751 homicides this year** jusqu'à hier, la ville avait enregistré 751 meurtres cette année ◆ **the balance of your account ~ of 16 June** *(= on)* le solde de votre compte au 16 juin

◆ **as of now** pour l'instant ◆ **~ of now, I have no definite plans** pour l'instant, je ne sais pas encore ce que je vais faire

◆ **as regards** → **regard**

◆ **as such** *(= in itself)* en soi ; *(= in that capacity)* en tant que tel *or* telle, à ce titre ◆ **the work ~ such is boring but the pay is good** le travail en soi est ennuyeux mais le salaire est correct ◆ **they are the best players in the world and, ~ such, are highly paid** ce sont les meilleurs joueurs du monde et, en tant que tels *or* à ce titre, ils touchent un salaire très élevé ◆ **he was still a novice and they treated him ~ such** ce n'était qu'un débutant et ils le traitaient comme tel

◆ **not/no ... as such** pas à proprement parler, pas vraiment ◆ **I'm not a beginner ~ such** je ne suis pas à proprement parler un débutant, je ne suis pas vraiment débutant ◆ **he had no qualifications ~ such** il n'avait à proprement parler aucune qualification

◆ **as to** *(when changing subject)* quant à ◆ **~ to her mother ...** quant à sa mère ... ◆ **~ to that**

(= *regarding that*) pour ce qui est de ça, quant à cela ♦ **to question sb ~ to his intentions** (= *about*) interroger qn sur ses intentions ♦ **they should make decisions ~ to whether students need help** il faudrait qu'ils décident si les étudiants ont besoin d'aide (ou non) ♦ **he inquired ~ to what the problem was** il demanda ce qui n'allait pas
♦ **as yet** → **yet**
♦ **as you were*** (*to correct oneself*) non, je me trompe ♦ **it was in 1990 he won the trophy, ~ you were, 1992** c'est en 1990 qu'il a remporté la coupe, non, je me trompe, en 1992 ♦ **~ you were!** (*Mil*) repos !

ASA /ˌeɪesˈeɪ/ 1 (*Brit*) (abbrev of **Advertising Standards Authority**) → **advertising** 2 (*Brit*) (abbrev of **Amateur Swimming Association**) *fédération de natation* 3 (abbrev of **American Standards Association**) **100/200** ~ 100/200 ASA

ASA/BS /ˌeɪeseɪbiːˈes/ **N** abbrev of **American Standards Association/British Standard**

asap* /ˌeɪeseɪˈpiː/ (abbrev of **as soon as possible**) aussitôt que possible

asbestos /æzˈbestəs/ **N** amiante *f*, asbeste *m* **COMP asbestos mat N** plaque *f* d'amiante

asbestosis /ˌæzbesˈtəʊsɪs/ **N** asbestose *f*

ASBO /ˈæsbəʊ/**N** (*Brit*) (abbrev of **Antisocial Behaviour Order**) *décision de justice visant à empêcher une personne reconnue coupable d'incivilités de récidiver en restreignant sa liberté de mouvement ou d'action*

ascend /əˈsend/ **VI** monter, s'élever (*to* à, jusqu'à) ; (*in time*) remonter (*to* à) ; ♦ **in ~ing order** en ordre croissant **VT** [*+ ladder*] monter à ; [*+ mountain*] gravir, faire l'ascension de ; [*+ river*] remonter ; [*+ staircase*] monter ♦ **to ~ the throne** monter sur le trône **COMP ascending scale N** (*Mus*) gamme *f* ascendante *or* montante

ascendancy /əˈsendənsɪ/ **N** (= *influence*) ascendant *m*, empire *m* (*over* sur) ; (= *rise to power etc*) montée *f*, ascension *f*

ascendant /əˈsendənt/ **N** (*Astrol, fig*) ascendant *m* ♦ **to be in the ~** (*Astrol*) être à l'ascendant ♦ **his fortunes are in the ~** tout lui sourit **ADJ** (*gen*) dominant ; (*Astrol*) ascendant

ascension /əˈsenʃən/ **N** ascension *f* ♦ **the Ascension** (*Rel*) l'Ascension *f* **COMP Ascension Day N** l'Ascension *f* **Ascension Island N** l'île *f* de l'Ascension

ascensionist /əˈsenʃənɪst/ **N** ascensionniste *mf*

ascent /əˈsent/ **N** [*of mountain etc*] ascension *f* ; (*fig: in time*) retour *m* ; (*in rank*) montée *f*, avancement *m*

ascertain /ˌæsəˈteɪn/ **VT** (*gen*) établir ; [*+ person's age, name, address etc*] vérifier ♦ **to ~ that sth is true** s'assurer *or* vérifier que qch est vrai

ascertainable /ˌæsəˈteɪnəbl/ **ADJ** vérifiable

ascertainment /ˌæsəˈteɪnmənt/ **N** constatation *f*, vérification *f*

ascetic /əˈsetɪk/ **ADJ** ascétique **N** ascète *mf*

asceticism /əˈsetɪsɪzəm/ **N** ascétisme *m*

ASCII /ˈæskiː/ **N** (abbrev of **American Standard Code for Information Interchange**) ASCII *m* **COMP ASCII file N** fichier *m* ASCII

ascorbic acid /əˈskɔːbɪkˈæsɪd/ **N** acide *m* ascorbique

ascribable /əˈskraɪbəbl/ **ADJ** [*virtue, piece of work*] attribuable ; [*fault, blame*] imputable (*to* à)

ascribe /əˈskraɪb/ **VT** [*+ virtue, piece of work*] attribuer (*to* à) ; [*+ fault, blame*] imputer (*to* à)

ascription /əˈskrɪpʃən/ **N** [*of book, painting, characteristic*] attribution *f* (*to sb/sth* à qn/qch) ; [*of blame*] imputation *f* (*to sb/sth* à qn/qch)

ASEAN /ˌeɪesiːeɪˈen/ **N** (abbrev of **Association of South-East Asian Nations**) ASEAN *f*

asemantic /ˌeɪsɪˈmæntɪk/ **ADJ** asémantique

aseptic /eɪˈseptɪk/ **ADJ** aseptique ♦ **~ tank** (*Space*) cuve *f* WC

asexual /eɪˈseksjʊəl/ **ADJ** asexué ♦ **~ reproduction** reproduction *f* asexuée

asexually /eɪˈseksjʊəlɪ/ **ADV** [*reproduce*] par multiplication asexuée

ASH /æʃ/ **N** (*Brit*) (abbrev of **Action on Smoking and Health**) *comité contre le tabagisme*

ash¹ /æʃ/ **N** (*Bot: also* **ash tree**) frêne *m* ; → **mountain**

ash² /æʃ/ **N** [*of fire, coal, cigarette*] cendre *f* ♦ **~es** (*of the dead*) cendres *fpl* ♦ **to reduce sth to ~es** réduire qch en cendres ♦ **~es to ~es, dust to dust** (*Rel*) tu es poussière et tu retourneras en poussière ♦ **the Ashes** (*Cricket*) *trophée des matchs Australie-Angleterre* ; → **sackcloth** **COMP ash-bin N** (*for ashes*) cendrier *m* (*de poêle etc*) ; (*for rubbish*) poubelle *f*, boîte *f* à ordures **ash blond(e) ADJ** blond(e) cendré *inv* **ash-coloured ADJ** gris cendré *inv* **ash pan N** cendrier *m* (*de poêle etc*) **Ash Wednesday N** (*Rel*) mercredi *m* des Cendres

ashamed /əˈʃeɪmd/ **ADJ** honteux ♦ **to be** *or* **feel ~, to be ~ of o.s.** avoir honte ♦ **to be ~ of sb/sth** avoir honte de qn/qch ♦ **it's nothing to be ~ of** il n'y a aucune raison d'en avoir honte ♦ **I am ~ of her** elle me fait honte, j'ai honte d'elle ♦ **you ought to** *or* **should be ~ (of yourself)!** vous devriez avoir honte ! ♦ **to be ~ of o.s. for doing sth** avoir honte d'avoir fait qch ♦ **to be ~ about sth** avoir honte de qch ♦ **to be ~ to do sth** avoir honte de faire qch ♦ **I'm too ~ to tell anyone** j'ai trop honte pour le dire à quiconque ♦ **I've done nothing, I'm ~ to say** à ma honte je dois dire que je n'ai rien fait, c'est honteux à dire, mais je n'ai rien fait ♦ **she was ~ that she had been so nasty** elle avait honte d'avoir été aussi méchante

ashcan /ˈæʃkæn/ **N** (*US*) poubelle *f*

ashen /ˈæʃn/ **ADJ** 1 (*liter*) (= *pale*) [*face*] terreux, livide ; (= *greyish*) cendré, couleur de cendre 2 (= *of ashwood*) en (bois de) frêne

Ashkenazi /ˌæʃkəˈnɑːzɪ/ **ADJ** ashkénaze **N** ashkénaze *mf*

Ashkenazic /ˌæʃkəˈnɑːzɪk/ **ADJ** ashkénaze

ashlar /ˈæʃləʳ/ **N** pierre *f* de taille (*équarrie*)

ashman /ˈæʃmən/ **N** (pl **-men**) (*US*) éboueur *m*

ashore /əˈʃɔːʳ/ **ADV** (= *on land*) à terre ; (= *to the shore*) vers la rive, vers le rivage ♦ **to go ~** débarquer, descendre à terre ♦ **to set** *or* **put sb ~** débarquer qn ♦ **to run ~** (*Naut*) s'échouer, se jeter à la côte ♦ **to swim ~** rejoindre la rive à la nage

ashram /ˈæʃrəm/ **N** ashram *m*

ashtray /ˈæʃtreɪ/ **N** cendrier *m*

ashy /ˈæʃɪ/ **ADJ** 1 (= *ash-coloured*) cendré, couleur de cendre ; (= *pale*) terreux, livide 2 (= *covered with ashes*) couvert de cendres

Asia /ˈeɪʃə/ **N** Asie *f* **COMP Asia Minor N** Asie *f* Mineure

Asian /ˈeɪʃn/ **ADJ** 1 (= *from Asia*) asiatique ♦ **~ flu** (*Med*) grippe *f* asiatique 2 (*Brit* = *from Indian subcontinent*) *originaire du sous-continent indien*, indo-pakistanais **N** 1 (= *person from Asia*) Asiatique *mf* 2 (*Brit* = *person from Indian subcontinent*) *personne originaire du sous-continent indien*, Indo-Pakistanais(e) *m(f)* **COMP Asian-American ADJ** américain d'origine asiatique **N** Américain(e) *m(f)* d'origine asiatique

Asiatic /ˌeɪsɪˈætɪk/ **ADJ** ⇒ **Asian N** (*offensive usage*) ⇒ **Asian**

aside /əˈsaɪd/

> When **aside** is an element in a phrasal verb, eg **brush aside**, **cast aside**, **put aside**, **stand aside**, look up the verb.

ADV ♦ **joking ~** plaisanterie *or* blague* à part ♦ **~ from** (*esp US*) à part **N** (*esp Theat*) aparté *m* ♦ **to say sth in an ~** dire qch en aparté

asinine /ˈæsɪnaɪn/ **ADJ** (*frm*) sot, idiot

ask /ɑːsk/ **LANGUAGE IN USE 4, 9.1, 26.1**

VT 1 (= *inquire*) demander ♦ **to ~ sb sth** demander qch à qn ♦ **to ~ sb about sth** interroger qn *or* questionner qn au sujet de qch ♦ **to ~ (sb) a question** poser une question (à qn) ♦ **I don't know, ~ your father** je ne sais pas, demande à ton père ♦ **~ him if he has seen her** demande-lui s'il l'a vue ♦ **~ed whether this was true, he replied ...** quand on lui a demandé si c'était vrai, il a répondu ... ♦ **don't ~ me!*** allez savoir !*, est-ce que je sais (moi) !* ♦ **I ~ you!*** (*in exasperation*) je vous demande un peu !* ♦ **I'm not ~ing you!*** (= *keep quiet*) je ne te demande rien (à toi) !*

2 (= *request*) demander ♦ **to ~ sb to do sth** demander à qn de faire qch, prier qn de faire qch ♦ **to ~ that sth (should) be done** demander que qch soit fait ♦ **to ~ sb for sth** demander qch à qn ♦ **he ~ed to go on the picnic** il a demandé à se joindre *or* s'il pouvait se joindre au pique-nique ♦ **I don't ~ much from you** je ne t'en demande pas beaucoup ♦ **it's not much to ~!** ce n'est pas trop demander !, ce n'est pas grand-chose ! ♦ **that's ~ing a lot/too much!** c'est beaucoup/trop (en) demander ! ♦ **that's ~ing the impossible** c'est demander l'impossible ♦ **how much are they ~ing for it?** ils en demandent *or* veulent combien ? ♦ **he is ~ing £80,000 for the house** il demande 80 000 livres *or* veut 80 000 livres pour la maison

3 (= *invite*) inviter ♦ **to ~ sb to (come to) the theatre** inviter qn (à aller) au théâtre ♦ **to ~ sb to lunch** inviter qn à déjeuner ♦ **I was ~ed into the drawing room** on m'a prié d'entrer au salon ♦ **how about ~ing Sabine?** et si on invitait Sabine ?, et si on demandait à Sabine de venir ? ♦ **to ~ sb in/out/up** *etc* demander à qn *or* prier qn d'entrer/de sortir/de monter *etc*

VI demander ♦ **to ~ about sth** s'informer de qch, se renseigner sur qch ♦ **to ~ around** (= *make enquiries*) demander autour de soi ♦ **it's there for the ~ing*** il suffit de le demander (pour l'obtenir), on l'a comme on veut ♦ **now you're ~ing!*** est-ce que je sais (moi) !*

N (*US*) ♦ **that's a big ~*** c'est beaucoup demander

COMP asking price N (*Comm*) prix *m* de départ, prix *m* demandé au départ

► **ask after VT FUS** [*+ person*] demander des nouvelles de ♦ **to ~ after sb's health** s'informer de la santé de qn

► **ask along VT SEP** ♦ **they didn't ask me along** ils ne m'ont pas demandé de les accompagner

► **ask back VT SEP** 1 (*for a second visit*) réinviter 2 (*on a reciprocal visit*) ♦ **to ask sb back** rendre son invitation à qn 3 (*to one's home*) **to ~ sb back for coffee** inviter qn à prendre le café

► **ask for VT FUS** [*+ help, permission, money*] demander ; [*+ person*] demander à voir ♦ **he ~ed for his pen back** il a demandé (qu'on lui rende) son stylo ♦ **they are ~ing for trouble*** ils cherchent les ennuis *or* les embêtements* ♦ **she was ~ing for it!*** (= *deserved it*) elle l'a bien cherché !*, elle ne l'a pas volé !* ; → **moon**

► **ask in VT SEP** inviter à entrer ♦ **to ~ sb in for a drink** inviter qn à (entrer) prendre un verre

► **ask out VT SEP** inviter à sortir ♦ **he ~ed her out to dinner/to see a film** il l'a invitée (à dîner) au restaurant/au cinéma

► **ask over** VT SEP inviter (à la maison) ◆ **let's ~ Paul over** si on invitait Paul à venir nous voir ?

► **ask round** VT SEP inviter (à la maison)

askance /əˈskɑːns/ ADV ◆ **to look ~ at** *(= sideways)* regarder de côté ; *(= suspiciously/disapprovingly)* regarder d'un air soupçonneux/d'un œil désapprobateur ◆ **to look ~ at a suggestion** se formaliser d'une suggestion

askew /əˈskjuː/ ADJ, ADV de travers, de guingois * ◆ **something is ~** *(US fig)* il y a quelque chose qui ne tourne pas rond *

aslant /əˈslɑːnt/ ADV de travers PREP en travers de

asleep /əˈsliːp/ ADJ 1 *(= sleeping)* endormi ◆ **to be ~** dormir, être endormi ◆ **to be fast** *or* **sound ~** dormir profondément *or* à poings fermés ◆ **to fall ~** s'endormir 2 *(= numb)* *[finger etc]* engourdi

ASLEF, Aslef /ˈæzlef/ N *(Brit)* (abbrev of **Associated Society of Locomotive Engineers and Firemen**) *syndicat*

ASM /ˌeɪesˈem/ N *(Theat)* (abbrev of **assistant stage manager**) régisseur *m* adjoint

asocial /eɪˈsəʊʃəl/ ADJ asocial

asp¹ /æsp/ N *(= snake)* aspic *m*

asp² /æsp/ N *(= tree)* ⇒ **aspen**

asparagus /əsˈpærəgəs/ N *(NonC)* asperges *fpl*
COMP **asparagus fern** N asparagus *m*
asparagus spears NPL asperges *fpl*
asparagus tips NPL pointes *fpl* d'asperges

aspartame /əˈspɑːˌteɪm/ N aspartam(e) *m*

ASPCA /ˌeɪespiːsiːˈeɪ/ N (abbrev of **American Society for the Prevention of Cruelty to Animals**) *SPA américaine*

aspect /ˈæspekt/ N 1 *(= facet, element) [of question, subject etc]* aspect *m*, angle *m* ◆ **to study every ~ of a question** étudier une question sous toutes ses faces *or* tous ses aspects ◆ **seen from this ~ ...** vu sous cet angle ... 2 *(liter = appearance)* air *m*, mine *f* ◆ **of fierce ~** à la mine *or* à l'aspect féroce 3 *(= face) [of building etc]* exposition *f*, orientation *f* ◆ **the house has a southerly ~** la maison est exposée *or* orientée au midi 4 *(Gram)* aspect *m*

aspen /ˈæspən/ N tremble *m* ◆ **to shake** *or* **tremble like an ~** trembler comme une feuille

asperity /æsˈperɪtɪ/ N 1 *(NonC) [of manner, style, voice]* aspérité *f* ; *[of person]* rudesse *f* 2 *(gen pl) [of climate, weather]* rigueur(s) *f(pl)*

aspersion /əsˈpɜːʃən/ N *(untruthful)* calomnie *f* ; *(truthful)* médisance *f* ; → **cast**

asphalt /ˈæsfælt/ N asphalte *m* VT asphalter
COMP *[road]* asphalté **asphalt jungle** N jungle *f* des rues

asphyxia /æsˈfɪksɪə/ N asphyxie *f*

asphyxiate /æsˈfɪksɪeɪt/ VT asphyxier VI s'asphyxier

asphyxiation /æsˌfɪksɪˈeɪʃən/ N asphyxie *f*

aspic /ˈæspɪk/ N *(Culin)* gelée *f (pour hors-d'œuvre)* ◆ **chicken in ~** aspic *m* de volaille

aspidistra /ˌæspɪˈdɪstrə/ N aspidistra *m*

aspirant /ˈæspɪrənt/ N aspirant(e) *m(f)*, candidat(e) *m(f) (to, after* à) ADJ *[artist, poet, writer]* en herbe

aspirate /ˈæspərɪt/ N aspirée *f* ADJ aspiré ◆ **~ h** h aspiré VT /ˈæspəreɪt/ aspirer

aspiration /ˌæspəˈreɪʃən/ N *(also Ling)* aspiration *f*

aspirational /ˌæspəˈreɪʃənl/ ADJ *[person]* ambitieux ; *[product]* qui fait chic

aspirator /ˈæspəˌreɪtəʳ/ N aspirateur *m*

aspire /əsˈpaɪəʳ/ VI ◆ **to ~ after** *or* **to sth** aspirer *or* viser à qch ◆ **to ~ to do sth** aspirer à faire qch ◆ **to ~ to fame** briguer la célébrité ◆ **to ~ to a second car** ambitionner de s'acheter une deuxième voiture ◆ **we can't ~ to that** nos prétentions ne vont pas jusque-là

aspirin /ˈæsprɪn/ N (pl **aspirin** *or* **aspirins**) *(= substance)* aspirine *f* ; *(= tablet)* (comprimé *m* d')aspirine

aspiring /əsˈpaɪərɪŋ/ ADJ *[artist, poet, writer]* en herbe ; *[manager, officer]* potentiel

ass¹ /æs/ N 1 âne *m* ◆ **she-~** ânesse *f* ◆ **~'s foal** ânon *m* 2 († * *pej*) idiot(e) *m(f)*, imbécile *mf* ◆ **a silly ~** un pauvre imbécile ◆ **he is a perfect ~** il est bête comme ses pieds * ◆ **to make an ~ of o.s.** se rendre ridicule, se conduire comme un idiot *or* imbécile ◆ **don't be an ~!** *(action)* ne fais pas l'imbécile ! ; *(speech)* ne dis pas de sottises !

ass² **** /æs/ *(US)* N cul*** m* ◆ **to chew sb's ~** engueuler qn ‡ ◆ **to kiss sb's ~** lécher le cul à qn**** ◆ **kiss my ~!** va te faire foutre !**** ◆ **to work one's ~ off** bosser comme un dingue *, se casser le cul**** ◆ **my ~!** mon cul !**** ◆ **stick it** *or* **shove it up your ~!** tu peux te le foutre au cul !**** ◆ **to have one's ~ in a sling** être dans la merde ‡ ◆ **to get one's ~ in gear** se remuer le cul**** ◆ **a piece of ~** *(= sex)* une baise**** ; *(= girl)* une fille bonne à baiser**** ; → **bust²**
COMP **ass-backward** **** ADJ *(= reversed)* cul par-dessus tête * ; *(= confused)* bordélique ‡ ADV *(= in reverse)* cul par-dessus tête * ; *(= in confused manner)* de façon bordélique ‡
ass kisser **** N lèche-cul*** mf inv*
ass-wipe **** N papier *m* cul****

assail /əˈseɪl/ VT *(lit)* attaquer, assaillir ; *(fig: with questions, doubts etc)* assaillir *(with* de)

assailant /əˈseɪlənt/ N agresseur *m*, assaillant(e) *m(f)*

Assam /æˈsæm/ N Assam *m*

assassin /əˈsæsɪn/ N *(Pol)* assassin *m*

assassinate /əˈsæsɪneɪt/ VT *(Pol)* assassiner

assassination /əˌsæsɪˈneɪʃən/ N *(Pol)* assassinat *m* ◆ **~ attempt** tentative *f* d'assassinat

assault /əˈsɔːlt/ N 1 *(Mil, Climbing)* assaut *m (on* de) ; ◆ **taken by ~** emporté *or* pris d'assaut ◆ **to make an ~ on ...** donner l'assaut à ..., aller *or* monter à l'assaut de ... 2 *(Jur)* agression *f* ◆ **~ and battery** coups *mpl* et blessures *fpl*, voies *fpl* de fait ◆ **the ~ on the old lady** l'agression dont a été victime la vieille dame ◆ **~ on sb's good name** atteinte *f* à la réputation de qn ; → **aggravate, common, indecent** VT agresser ; *(Jur = attack)* se livrer à des voies de fait sur ; *(= attack sexually)* se livrer à des violences sexuelles sur, violenter ◆ **to ~ sb's sensibilities** blesser la sensibilité de qn
COMP **assault course** N *(Mil)* parcours *m* du combattant
assault rifle N fusil *m* d'assaut

assay /əˈseɪ/ N essai *m (d'un métal précieux etc)* VT 1 *[+ mineral, ore]* essayer 2 († † = *try*) essayer, tenter *(to do sth* de faire qch) COMP ~ **office** N *(US)* laboratoire *m* d'essais *(d'un hôtel des monnaies)*

assemblage /əˈsemblɪdʒ/ N 1 *[of device, machine]* assemblage *m*, montage *m* 2 *(= collection) [of things]* collection *f*, ensemble *m* ; *[of people]* assemblée *f*

assemble /əˈsembl/ VT *[+ objects, ideas]* assembler ; *[+ people]* rassembler, réunir ; *(Tech) [+ device, machine]* monter, assembler VI se réunir, se rassembler

assembler /əˈsembləʳ/ N *(Comput)* assembleur *m*

assembly /əˈsemblɪ/ N 1 *(= meeting)* assemblée *f*, réunion *f* ; *(Scol) réunion de tous les élèves de l'établissement pour la prière, les annonces etc* ◆ **the Welsh Assembly** l'assemblée galloise ◆ **the Northern Ireland ~** le parlement d'Irlande du Nord ◆ **in open ~** en séance publique ; → **unlawful**
2 *(= assembling of framework, machine)* assemblage *m*, montage *m* ; *(= whole unit)* assemblage *m* ◆ **the engine ~** le bloc moteur ; → **tail**
3 *(Mil = call)* rassemblement *m (sonnerie)*
4 *(Pol)* assemblée *f*
5 *(Comput)* assemblage *m*
COMP **assembly hall** N *(for public meetings, stage shows)* salle *f* des fêtes ; *(in school)* salle *f* de réunion
assembly language N *(Comput)* langage *m* d'assemblage
assembly line N chaîne *f* de montage
assembly plant N usine *f* de montage
assembly point N lieu *m or* point *m* de rassemblement
assembly room(s) N(PL) salle *f* de réunion ; *[of town hall]* salle *f* des fêtes
assembly shop N atelier *m* de montage

assemblyman /əˈsemblɪmən/ N (pl **-men**) *(US)* membre *m* d'une assemblée législative

assemblywoman /əˈsemblɪwʊmən/ N (pl **-women**) *(US)* membre *m* d'une assemblée législative

assent /əˈsent/ N assentiment *m*, consentement *m* ◆ **with one ~** *(two people)* d'un commun accord ; *(more than two people)* à l'unanimité ◆ **to give one's ~ to** donner son assentiment à ; → **nod, royal** VI consentir, donner son assentiment *(to* à)

assert /əˈsɜːt/ VT 1 *(= declare)* affirmer, soutenir ; *[+ one's innocence]* protester de 2 *(= maintain) [+ claim]* défendre ; *[+ one's due]* revendiquer ; *[+ one's authority]* faire respecter ◆ **to ~ o.s.** *or* **one's rights** faire valoir ses droits

assertion /əˈsɜːʃən/ N 1 *(= statement)* affirmation *f*, assertion *f* ; → **self** 2 *[of one's rights]* revendication *f*

assertive /əˈsɜːtɪv/ ADJ *[tone, voice]* assuré ; *[personality]* affirmé ◆ **~ behaviour** *or* **manner** assurance *f* ◆ **to be ~** *[person]* avoir de l'assurance, avoir confiance en soi ◆ **to become more ~** *[person]* prendre de l'assurance, s'affirmer

assertively /əˈsɜːtɪvlɪ/ ADV avec assurance

assertiveness /əˈsɜːtɪvnɪs/ N assurance *f*, confiance *f* en soi COMP **assertiveness training** N *(NonC)* stages *mpl* d'affirmation de la personnalité ◆ **~ training course** stage *m* d'affirmation de la personnalité

assess /əˈses/ VT 1 *(= estimate)* estimer, évaluer 2 *[+ payment]* fixer *or* déterminer le montant de ; *[+ income tax]* établir ; *[+ rateable property]* calculer la valeur imposable de ; *[+ damages]* fixer ; → **basis** 3 *(fig = evaluate) [+ situation]* évaluer ; *[+ time, amount]* estimer, évaluer ; *[+ candidate]* juger (la valeur de) COMP **assessed income** N revenu *m* imposable

assessable /əˈsesəbl/ ADJ imposable ◆ **~ income** (*or* **profits** *etc*) *(Fin)* assiette *f* de l'impôt

assessment /əˈsesmənt/ N 1 *(= evaluation) [of situation, effect, risk]* évaluation *f* ; *[of prospects, chances, needs]* estimation *f* ; *[of damage]* évaluation *f*, estimation *f* ◆ **he gave his ~ of the situation** il a dit ce qu'il pensait de la situation, il a donné son analyse de la situation
2 *(= appraisal) [of person]* évaluation *f* ; *(on pupil's report)* appréciation *f* des professeurs ◆ **I should be interested to hear your ~ of him** ça m'intéresserait de savoir ce que vous pensez de lui ; → **continuous, self**
3 *(Med, Psych, Sociol) [of patient, case]* examen *m* ◆ **neurological ~** diagnostic *m* neurologique
4 *(= critique) [of book, film, play]* jugement *m* ; *[of plan, policy, idea]* opinion *f*
5 *(Fin, Tax, Jur) [of finances]* estimation *f* ; *[of rateable property]* calcul *m* (de la valeur imposable) ; *[of damages]* fixation *f* ◆ **appeals against**

~s made by the taxman opposition *f* aux estimations du fisc ◆ **income** ~ évaluation *f* du revenu ◆ **tax** ~ calcul *m* de l'impôt

COMP **assessment centre** N (*for jobseekers*) centre *m* d'évaluation (*des demandeurs d'emploi*)
assessment method N (*gen*) méthode *f* d'évaluation ◆ **the ~ method** (*Educ*) le contrôle des connaissances ; (*Univ*) le contrôle continu
assessment procedure N procédure *f* d'évaluation
assessment process N processus *m* d'évaluation

assessor /əˈsesəʳ/ N 1 (*Jur*) (juge *m*) assesseur *m* 2 [*of property*] expert *m* ◆ **~ of taxes** (*US*) contrôleur *m*, -euse *f* des contributions directes 3 (*in exam*) examinateur *m*, -trice *f*, correcteur *m*, -trice *f* ; (*in sport*) juge *m*

asset /ˈæset/ N 1 bien *m* ◆ **~s** biens *mpl*, avoir *m*, capital *m* ; (*Comm, Fin, Jur*) actif *m* ◆ **~s and liabilities** actif *m* et passif *m* ◆ **their ~s amount to £1m** leur actif est d'un *or* s'élève à un million de livres ; → **liquid** 2 (= *advantage*) avantage *m*, atout *m* ◆ **he is one of our greatest ~s** c'est un de nos meilleurs éléments

COMP **asset management** N (*Fin*) gestion *f* d'actifs
asset-stripper N (*Fin*) repreneur *m* d'entreprises (en faillite)
asset-stripping N (*Fin*) dépeçage *m*
asset value N (*Fin*) valeur *f* des actifs

asseverate /əˈsevəreɪt/ VT affirmer solennellement ; [+ *one's innocence, loyalty*] protester de

asseveration /əˌsevəˈreɪʃən/ N (*frm*) affirmation *f* solennelle

asshole** /ˈæshəʊl/ N (*US lit, also fig* = *person*) trou *m* du cul**

assiduity /ˌæsɪˈdjuːɪtɪ/ N assiduité *f*, zèle *m*

assiduous /əˈsɪdjʊəs/ ADJ assidu

assiduously /əˈsɪdjʊəslɪ/ ADV [*study, work*] assidûment ◆ **to ~ avoid doing sth** prendre bien soin d'éviter de faire qch

assign /əˈsaɪn/ VT 1 (= *allot*) [+ *office*] assigner ; [+ *seat, room*] attribuer ; [+ *date*] assigner, fixer (*to sb/sth* à qn/qch) ; [+ *meaning*] donner, attribuer (*to* à) ; ◆ **to ~ sb a task** confier une tâche à qn ◆ **they cannot ~ many hours to outside jobs** ils ne peuvent pas consacrer beaucoup d'heures aux missions à l'extérieur ◆ **to ~ blame** chercher des responsables ◆ **to ~ a reason for sth** donner la raison de qch 2 (= *appoint*) [+ *person*] affecter (*to* à) ; ◆ **to ~ an FBI agent to the case** affecter un agent du FBI à l'affaire 3 (*Jur*) [+ *property, right*] céder, faire cession de (*to sb* à qn) transférer (*to sb* au nom de qn)

assignation /ˌæsɪgˈneɪʃən/ N 1 (= *appointment*) rendez-vous *m* (*souvent galant*) 2 (= *allocation*) attribution *f* ; [*of money*] allocation *f* ; [*of person, room*] affectation *f* 3 (*Jur*) cession *f*, transfert *m* (de biens)

assignee /ˌæsaɪˈniː/ N (*Jur*) cessionnaire *mf*

assignment /əˈsaɪnmənt/ N 1 (= *task*) mission *f* ; (*Scol*) devoir *m* ; (*Univ*) devoir *m* ; (= *essay*) dissertation *f* ◆ **to be on (an) ~** être en mission 2 (*NonC* = *allocation*) attribution *f* ; [*of money*] allocation *f* ; [*of person, room*] affectation *f* 3 (*Jur*) **~ of contract** cession *f* des droits et obligations découlant d'un *or* du contrat

assignor /ˌæsɪˈnɔːʳ/ N (*Jur*) cédant *m*

assimilate /əˈsɪmɪleɪt/ VT 1 (= *absorb*) [+ *food, knowledge*] assimiler 2 (= *compare*) comparer, assimiler (*to* à) rapprocher (*to* de) VI s'assimiler, être assimilé

assimilation /əˌsɪmɪˈleɪʃən/ N (= *absorption*) assimilation *f* ; (= *comparison*) assimilation *f* (*to* à) comparaison *f*, rapprochement *m* (*to* avec) ; (*Phon*) assimilation *f*

Assisi /əˈsiːzɪ/ N Assise

assist /əˈsɪst/ VT aider (*to do sth, in doing sth* à faire qch) ; ◆ **to ~ sb in/out** *etc* aider qn à entrer/sortir *etc* ◆ **to ~ one another** s'entraider ◆ **~ed by** avec le concours de VI (= *help*) aider ◆ **to ~ in (doing) sth** aider à (faire) qch N (*Sport*) action *f* qui aide un coéquipier à marquer un point

COMP **assisted passage** N (*Travel*) billet *m* subventionné
assisted place N (*Brit Scol*) *place réservée dans une école privée à un élève de milieu modeste dont les frais de scolarité sont payés par l'État*
assisted suicide N suicide *m* assisté

assistance /əˈsɪstəns/ N aide *f*, assistance *f* ◆ **to give ~ to sb** prêter assistance à qn ◆ **to come to sb's ~** venir en aide à qn, porter assistance à qn ◆ **can I be of ~?** puis-je vous aider ?, puis-je vous être utile ?

assistant /əˈsɪstənt/ N 1 (= *aid*) assistant(e) *m(f)* ◆ **foreign language ~** (*Scol*) assistant(e) *m(f)* ; (*Univ*) lecteur *m*, -trice *f*
2 (= *deputy*) adjoint(e) *m(f)*
3 (= *sales assistant*) vendeur *m*, -euse *f* ; → **shop**

COMP adjoint, sous-
assistant editor N rédacteur *m*, -trice *f* adjoint(e), assistant(e) *m(f)* de rédaction
assistant judge N (*US Jur*) juge *m* adjoint
assistant librarian N bibliothécaire *mf* adjoint(e)
assistant manager N directeur *m*, -trice *f* adjoint(e), sous-directeur *m*, -trice *f*
assistant master †, **assistant mistress** † N (*Brit Scol*) professeur *m* (*qui n'a pas la responsabilité d'une section*)
assistant priest N vicaire *m*
assistant principal N (*Scol*) directeur *m*, -trice *f* adjoint(e) ; (*in a French lycée*) censeur *m*
assistant professor N (*US Univ*) ≈ maître *m* assistant
assistant referee N (*Ftbl*) juge *m* de touche
assistant secretary N secrétaire *mf* adjoint(e), sous-secrétaire *mf*
assistant teacher N (*primary*) instituteur *m*, -trice *f* ; (*secondary*) professeur *m* (*qui n'a pas la responsabilité d'une section*)

assistantship /əˈsɪstəntʃɪp/ N (*US Univ*) poste *m* d'étudiant(e) chargé(e) de travaux dirigés

assizes /əˈsaɪzɪz/ NPL (*Jur*) assises *fpl*

assn. abbrev of **association**

assoc. abbrev of **association** *and* **associated**

associate /əˈsəʊʃɪɪt/ ADJ uni, associé ◆ **~ director** directeur *m*, -trice *f* adjoint(e) ◆ **~ judge** (*Jur*) juge *m* assesseur ◆ **Associate Justice** (*US Jur*) juge *m* de la Cour suprême ◆ **~ professor** (*US Univ*) ≈ maître *m* de conférences

N 1 (= *fellow worker*) associé(e) *m(f)*, collègue *mf* ; (*Jur*: also **associate in crime**) complice *mf* ◆ **to be ~s in an undertaking** participer conjointement à une entreprise ; → **business**
2 [*of a society*] membre *m*, associé(e) *m(f)* ; [*of learned body*] (membre *m*) correspondant *m* ◆ **~'s degree** (*US Univ*) ≈ DEUG *m*

VT /əˈsəʊʃɪeɪt/ 1 [+ *ideas, things*] associer ◆ **to ~ one thing with another** associer une chose à *or* avec une autre
2 ◆ **to be ~d with sth** être associé à qch ◆ **to ~ o.s.** *or* **be ~d with sb in an undertaking** s'associer à *or* avec qn dans une entreprise ◆ **to be ~d with a plot** tremper dans un complot ◆ **I should like to ~ myself with what has been said** je voudrais me faire l'écho de cette opinion ◆ **I don't wish to be ~d with it** je préfère que mon nom ne soit pas mêlé à ceci

VI /əˈsəʊʃɪeɪt/ ◆ **to ~ with sb** fréquenter qn, être en relations avec qn

association /əˌsəʊsɪˈeɪʃən/ N 1 (*NonC* = *connection*) association *f* (*with* avec) fréquentation *f* (*with* de) ; ◆ **in ~ with** en association avec ◆ **by ~ of ideas** par (une) association d'idées ◆ **to be guilty by ~** être incriminé (à cause de ses relations) 2 (= *organization*) association *f* ◆ **to form an ~** constituer une société ; → **freedom** 3 (= *connotation*) ◆ **full of historic ~s** portant l'empreinte du passé ◆ **this word has nasty ~s** ce mot a des connotations *fpl* désagréables COMP **association football** N (*Brit*) football *m* (association)

associative /əˈsəʊʃɪətɪv/ ADJ (*Math*) associatif ◆ **~ storage** (*Comput*) mémoire *f* associative

assonance /ˈæsənəns/ N assonance *f*

assort /əˈsɔːt/ VT classer, classifier VI [*colours etc*] s'assortir, aller bien (*with* avec)

assorted /əˈsɔːtɪd/ ADJ 1 (= *mixed*) [*shapes, styles, colours, items*] différent ◆ **in ~ sizes** dans toutes les tailles ◆ **~ wild flowers** des fleurs des champs de différentes sortes 2 (= *matched*) ◆ **an oddly ~ group** un groupe hétérogène ◆ **an strangely ~ pair** un couple qui ne semble pas bien assorti ; → **ill, well²**

assortment /əˈsɔːtmənt/ N [*of objects*] collection *f*, assortiment *m* ; [*of people*] mélange *m* ◆ **this shop has a good ~** il y a beaucoup de choix dans ce magasin, ce magasin est bien achalandé ◆ **an ~ of people/guests** des gens/des invités (très) divers

asst. abbrev of **assistant**

assuage /əˈsweɪdʒ/ VT (*liter*) [+ *hunger, desire, thirst*] assouvir ; [+ *pain*] soulager, apaiser ; [+ *anger*] apaiser ; [+ *person*] apaiser, calmer

assume /əˈsjuːm/ LANGUAGE IN USE 26.3 VT 1 (= *accept, presume, suppose*) supposer, présumer ◆ **assuming** *or* **if we ~ this to be true ...** en supposant que *or* supposons que ceci soit vrai ... ◆ **let us ~ that ...** supposons que ... + *subj* ◆ **you resigned, I ~?** vous avez démissionné, je suppose *or* présume ? ◆ **you are assuming a lot** vous faites bien des suppositions 2 (= *take on*) [+ *responsibility, burden*] assumer, endosser ; [+ *power, importance, possession*] prendre ; [+ *title, right, authority*] s'arroger, s'attribuer ; [+ *name*] adopter, prendre ; [+ *attitude*] adopter ; [+ *air*] prendre ◆ **to ~ control of sth** prendre en main la direction de qch ◆ **to ~ the role of arbiter** assumer le rôle d'arbitre ◆ **to ~ a look of innocence** prendre un air innocent ◆ **to go under an ~d name** utiliser un nom d'emprunt *or* un pseudonyme

assumption /əˈsʌmpʃən/ N 1 (= *supposition*) supposition *f*, hypothèse *f* ◆ **on the ~ that ...** en supposant que ... + *subj* ◆ **to go on the ~ that ...** présumer que ... 2 [*of power etc*] appropriation *f* ; [*of indifference*] affectation *f* 3 (*Rel*) **the Assumption** l'Assomption *f* COMP **Assumption Day** N (= *religious festival*) l'Assomption *f* ; (= *public holiday*) le 15 août

assurance /əˈʃʊərəns/ N 1 (= *certainty*) assurance *f*, conviction *f* ◆ **in the ~ that ...** avec la conviction *or* l'assurance que ... 2 (= *self-confidence*) assurance *f* 3 (= *promise*) promesse *f*, assurance *f* ◆ **you have my ~ that ...** je vous promets *or* assure que ... 4 (*Brit* = *insurance*) assurance *f* ; → **life**

assure /əˈʃʊəʳ/ LANGUAGE IN USE 11.3, 18.1 VT 1 (= *tell positively*) assurer ; (= *convince, reassure*) convaincre, assurer (*sb of sth* qn de qch) ; ◆ **it is so, I (can) ~ you** c'est vrai, je vous assure ; → **rest** 2 (= *ensure*) [+ *happiness, success*] garantir, assurer 3 (*Brit* = *insure*) assurer

assured /əˈʃʊəd/ ADJ, N assuré(e) *m(f)* (*of* de) ; ◆ **will you be ~ of a good salary?** aurez-vous l'assurance d'avoir un bon salaire ?

assuredly /əˈʃʊərɪdlɪ/ ADV assurément ◆ **most ~** sans aucun doute

Assyria /əˈsɪrɪə/ N Assyrie *f*

Assyrian /əˈsɪrɪən/ ADJ assyrien N Assyrien(ne) *m(f)*

AST /ˌeɪesˈtiː/ (*US, Can*) (abbrev of **Atlantic Standard Time**) → **Atlantic**

astatine /ˈæstətiːn/ N astate *m*

aster /ˈæstəʳ/ **N** aster *m*

asterisk /ˈæstərɪsk/ **N** astérisque *m* **VT** marquer d'un astérisque

astern /əˈstɜːn/ **ADV** *(Naut)* à l'arrière ◆ **slow ~!** (en) arrière doucement ! ◆ **to go** *or* **come ~** *(using engine)* faire machine arrière ; *(using sail)* culer ◆ **~ of** à l'arrière de

asteroid /ˈæstərɔɪd/ **N** astéroïde *m* **COMP asteroid belt N** ceinture *f* d'astéroïdes

asthma /ˈæsmə/ **N** asthme *m* ◆ **~ sufferer** asthmatique *mf*

asthmatic /æsˈmætɪk/ **ADJ, N** asthmatique *mf*

astigmatic /ˌæstɪgˈmætɪk/ **ADJ, N** astigmate *mf*

astigmatism /æsˈtɪgmətɪzəm/ **N** astigmatisme *m*

astir /əˈstɜːʳ/ **ADJ, ADV** 1 *(= excited)* agité, en émoi 2 *(† = out of bed)* debout *inv*, levé

ASTMS /ˌeɪestiːemˈes/ **N** *(Brit)* (abbrev of **Association of Scientific, Technical and Managerial Staffs**) *syndicat*

astonish /əˈstɒnɪʃ/ **VT** étonner ; *(stronger)* stupéfier ◆ **you ~ me!** *(also iro)* vous m'étonnez !

astonished /əˈstɒnɪʃt/ **ADJ** étonné, stupéfait ◆ **I am ~ that ...** cela m'étonne *or* m'ahurit que ... + *subj*

astonishing /əˈstɒnɪʃɪŋ/ **ADJ** étonnant ; *(stronger)* ahurissant, stupéfiant ◆ **that is ~, coming from them** venant d'eux, c'est ahurissant *or* étonnant ◆ **with an ~ lack of discretion** avec un incroyable manque de discrétion

astonishingly /əˈstɒnɪʃɪŋlɪ/ **ADV** étonnamment, incroyablement ◆ **~ (enough), he was right** chose étonnante, il avait raison

astonishment /əˈstɒnɪʃmənt/ **N** étonnement *m*, surprise *f* ; *(stronger)* ahurissement *m*, stupéfaction *f* ◆ **look of ~** regard *m* stupéfait ◆ **to my ~** à mon grand étonnement, à ma stupéfaction ; → **stare**

astound /əˈstaʊnd/ **VT** stupéfier, étonner, ébahir

astounded /əˈstaʊndɪd/ **ADJ** abasourdi, ébahi ◆ **I am ~** j'en reste abasourdi, je n'en crois pas mes yeux *or* mes oreilles

astounding /əˈstaʊndɪŋ/ **ADJ** stupéfiant, ahurissant

astoundingly /əˈstaʊndɪŋlɪ/ **ADV** *[good, bad, talented]* incroyablement

astrakhan /ˌæstrəˈkæn/ **N** astrakan *m* **COMP** *[coat]* d'astrakan

astral /ˈæstrəl/ **ADJ** astral **COMP astral projection N** projection *f* astrale

astray /əˈstreɪ/ **ADV** *(lit, fig)* ◆ **to go ~** s'égarer ◆ **to lead sb ~** *(fig)* détourner qn du droit chemin, dévoyer qn *(liter)*

astride /əˈstraɪd/ **ADJ, ADV** à califourchon, à cheval ◆ **to ride ~** monter à califourchon **PREP** à califourchon sur, à cheval sur

astringent /əsˈtrɪndʒənt/ **ADJ** *(Med)* astringent ; *(fig)* dur, sévère ◆ **~ lotion** lotion *f* astringente **N** *(Med)* astringent *m*

astrologer /əsˈtrɒlədʒəʳ/ **N** astrologue *mf*

astrological /ˌæstrəˈlɒdʒɪkəl/ **ADJ** astrologique **COMP astrological chart N** thème *m* astral

astrologically /ˌæstrəˈlɒdʒɪkəlɪ/ **ADV** d'un point de vue astrologique

astrologist /əˈstrɒlədʒɪst/ **N** astrologue *mf*

astrology /əsˈtrɒlədʒɪ/ **N** astrologie *f*

astronaut /ˈæstrənɔːt/ **N** astronaute *mf*

astronautic(al) /ˌæstrəʊˈnɔːtɪk(əl)/ **ADJ** astronautique

astronautics /ˌæstrəʊˈnɔːtɪks/ **N** *(NonC)* astronautique *f*

astronomer /əsˈtrɒnəməʳ/ **N** astronome *mf*

astronomical /ˌæstrəˈnɒmɪkəl/ **ADJ** 1 *(= enormous) [amount, cost, price]* astronomique ◆ **the odds against another attack were ~** une nouvelle attaque était des plus improbables 2 *(Astron) [observatory, instrument, society]* d'astronomie ; *[telescope, observation]* astronomique **COMP astronomical clock N** horloge *f* astronomique

astronomical unit N unité *f* astronomique

astronomically /ˌæstrəˈnɒmɪkəlɪ/ **ADV** 1 *(= enormously) [rise, increase]* dans des proportions astronomiques ; *[high]* effroyablement ◆ **to be ~ expensive** coûter un prix astronomique 2 *(Astron) [interesting, important]* d'un point de vue astronomique

astronomy /əsˈtrɒnəmɪ/ **N** astronomie *f*

astrophysicist /ˌæstrəʊˈfɪzɪsɪst/ **N** astrophysicien(ne) *m(f)*

astrophysics /ˌæstrəʊˈfɪzɪks/ **N** *(NonC)* astrophysique *f*

Astroturf ® /ˈæstrəʊtɜːf/ **N** gazon *m* artificiel

Asturias /æˈstʊərɪæs/ **N** Asturies *fpl*

astute /əsˈtjuːt/ **ADJ** fin, astucieux, intelligent

astutely /əsˈtjuːtlɪ/ **ADV** avec finesse, astucieusement

astuteness /əsˈtjuːtnɪs/ **N** *(NonC)* finesse *f*, astuce *f*, intelligence *f*

Asuncion /æˌsʊntsɪˈɒn/ **N** Asunción

asunder /əˈsʌndəʳ/ **ADV** *(liter) (= apart)* écartés, éloignés (l'un de l'autre) ; *(= in pieces)* en morceaux

Aswan /æsˈwɑːn/ **N** Assouan **COMP the Aswan (High) Dam N** le (haut) barrage d'Assouan

asylum /əˈsaɪləm/ **N** 1 *(NonC)* asile *m*, refuge *m* ◆ **political ~** asile *m* politique 2 † (also **lunatic asylum**) asile *m* (d'aliénés) † **COMP asylum seeker N** demandeur *m*, -euse *f* d'asile

asymmetric(al) /ˌeɪsɪˈmetrɪk(əl)/ **ADJ** asymétrique **COMP asymmetric(al) bars NPL** *(Sport)* barres *fpl* asymétriques

asymmetry /æˈsɪmətrɪ/ **N** asymétrie *f*

asymptomatic /ˌeɪsɪmptəˈmætɪk/ **ADJ** asymptomatique

asynchronous /æˈsɪŋkrənəs/ **ADJ** *(Comput)* asynchrone

AT /eɪˈtiː/ (abbrev of **alternative technology**) → **alternative**

at /æt/

> When **at** is an element in a phrasal verb, eg **look at**, look up the verb. When it is part of an expression such as **at all**, **at best** or **at first**, look up the other word.

PREP 1 *(place, position, time)* à ◆ **~ the table** à la table ◆ **~ my brother's** chez mon frère ◆ **~ home** à la maison, chez soi ◆ **to arrive ~ the house** arriver à la maison ◆ **to dry o.s. ~ the fire** se sécher devant le feu ◆ **to stand ~ the window** se tenir à *or* devant la fenêtre ◆ **~ her heels** sur ses talons ◆ **~ 10 o'clock** à 10 heures ◆ **~ a time like this** à un moment pareil ◆ **~ my time of life** à mon âge ; → **hand, sea**

2 ◆ **where are we ~ ?*** *(progress)* où en sommes-nous ? ; *(US: position)* où sommes-nous ? ◆ **this is where it's ~** * *(fashion)* c'est là que ça se passe *

3 *(activity)* **they were ~ their needlework** elles étaient en train de coudre

◆ **at it** * ◆ **while we are ~ it** pendant que nous y sommes *or* qu'on y est * ◆ **they are ~ it again!** les voilà qui recommencent !, voilà qu'ils remettent ça ! * ◆ **they are ~ it all day** ils font ça toute la journée

4 *(state, condition)* en ◆ **good/bad ~ languages** bon/mauvais en langues ; → **war**

5 *(manner)* ~ **full speed** à toute allure ◆ **~ 80km/h** à 80 km/h ◆ **he was driving ~ 80km/h** il faisait du 80 (à l'heure)

6 *(cause)* par, de ◆ **to be surprised ~ sth** être étonné de qch ◆ **annoyed ~** contrarié par ◆ **angry ~ sb** en colère contre qn ◆ **angry ~ sth** en colère à cause de qch ◆ **~ the request of ...** à la demande de ...

7 *(rate, value)* à ◆ **~ a higher rate** à un taux plus élevé ◆ **he sells them ~ 6 euros a kilo** il les vend 6 euros le kilo

8 *(* = nagging)* **she's been ~ me the whole day** elle m'a harcelé *or* tanné * toute la journée ◆ **she was on ~ her husband to buy a new car** elle harcelait *or* tannait * son mari pour qu'il achète *subj* une nouvelle voiture ◆ **he's always on ~ me** * il est toujours après moi * **N** *(= symbol : in email address)* arobase *f*

COMP at-home N réception *f (chez soi)*

at-risk register N *(Social Work) registre des enfants en risque de maltraitance*

atavism /ˈætəvɪzəm/ **N** atavisme *m*

atavistic /ˌætəˈvɪstɪk/ **ADJ** atavique

ataxia /əˈtæksɪə/ **N** ataxie *f*

ataxic /əˈtæksɪk/ **ADJ** ataxique

ATB /ˌeɪtiːˈbiː/ **N** (abbrev of **all-terrain bike**) VTT *m*

ATC /ˌeɪtiːˈsiː/ **N** *(Brit)* (abbrev of **Air Training Corps**) *préparation à l'école de l'air*

ate /et, eɪt/ **VB** pt of **eat**

Athanasian /ˌæθəˈneɪʃən/ **ADJ** ◆ **the ~ Creed** le symbole de saint Athanase

Athanasius /ˌæθəˈneɪʃəs/ **N** Athanase *m*

atheism /ˈeɪθɪɪzəm/ **N** athéisme *m*

atheist /ˈeɪθɪɪst/ **N** athée *mf*

atheistic(al) /ˌeɪθɪˈɪstɪk(əl)/ **ADJ** athée

Athena /əˈθiːnə/ **N** Athéna *f*

athenaeum /ˌæθɪˈniːəm/ **N** association *f* littéraire (*or* culturelle)

Athene /əˈθiːnɪ/ **N** ⇒ **Athena**

Athenian /əˈθiːnɪən/ **N** Athénien(ne) *m(f)* **ADJ** athénien

Athens /ˈæθɪnz/ **N** Athènes

athirst /əˈθɜːst/ **ADJ** *(liter: lit, fig)* altéré, assoiffé (*for* de)

athlete /ˈæθliːt/ **N** *(in competitions)* athlète *mf* **COMP athlete's foot N** *(Med)* mycose *f* du pied ◆ **to have ~'s foot** avoir une mycose aux pieds

athletes' village N village *m* des athlètes

athletic /æθˈletɪk/ **ADJ** 1 *(Sport) [club, association, competition]* d'athlétisme ; *[activity, achievement]* athlétique 2 *(= muscular) [person, body, build]* athlétique

COMP athletic coach N *(US Scol, Univ)* entraîneur *m* (sportif)

athletic sports NPL athlétisme *m*

athletic support(er) N suspensoir *m*

athletically /æθˈletɪkəlɪ/ **ADV** 1 *(Sport) [talented]* d'un point de vue athlétique 2 *(= agilely) [jump]* avec agilité

athleticism /æθˈletɪsɪzəm/ **N** constitution *f* athlétique

athletics /æθˈletɪks/ **N** *(NonC) (Brit)* athlétisme *m* ; *(US)* sport *m*

Athos /ˈæθɒs/ **N** ◆ **(Mount) ~** le mont Athos

athwart /əˈθwɔːt/ **ADV** en travers ; *(Naut)* par le travers **PREP** en travers de ; *(Naut)* par le travers de

atishoo /əˈtɪʃuː/ **EXCL** atchoum !

Atlantic /ətˈlæntɪk/ **ADJ** *[coast, current]* atlantique ; *[winds, island]* de l'Atlantique **N** ⇒ **Atlantic Ocean** ; → **north**

COMP Atlantic Charter N Pacte *m* atlantique

Atlantic liner N transatlantique *m*

the Atlantic Ocean N l'Atlantique *m*, l'océan *m* Atlantique

the Atlantic Provinces NPL *(Can)* les Provinces *fpl* atlantiques
Atlantic Standard Time N l'heure *f* normale de l'Atlantique

Atlanticism /ət'læntɪsɪzəm/ N *(Pol)* atlantisme *m*

Atlanticist /ət'læntɪsɪst/ ADJ, N *(Pol)* atlantiste *mf*

Atlantis /ət'læntɪs/ N Atlantide *f*

atlas /'ætləs/ N 1 (= *book*) atlas *m* 2 *(Myth)* **Atlas** Atlas *m* COMP **the Atlas Mountains** NPL (les monts *mpl* de) l'Atlas *m*

ATM /,eɪtiː'em/ N *(US)* (abbrev of **Automated Teller Machine**) GAB *m*, DAB *m*

atmosphere /'ætməsfɪəʳ/ N *(lit, Phys)* atmosphère *f* ; *(fig)* atmosphère *f*, ambiance *f* ◆ **I can't stand ~s** je ne peux pas supporter une ambiance hostile

atmospheric /,ætməs'ferɪk/ ADJ 1 *(Met, Phys)* atmosphérique 2 (= *evocative*) *[music, film, book]* évocateur (-trice *f*) COMP **atmospheric pressure** N pression *f* atmosphérique

atmospherics /,ætməs'ferɪks/ N 1 *(NonC: Rad, Telec = interference)* bruit *m* atmosphérique 2 (* = *ambience, atmosphere*) ambiance *f*, atmosphère *f*

atoll /'ætɒl/ N atoll *m*

atom /'ætəm/ N atome *m* ; *(fig)* grain *m*, parcelle *f* ◆ **smashed to ~s** réduit en miettes ◆ **not an ~ of truth** pas la moindre parcelle de vérité ◆ **if you had an ~ of sense** si tu avais un gramme *or* un atome de bon sens COMP **atom bomb** N bombe *f* atomique

atomic /ə'tɒmɪk/ ADJ atomique
COMP **atomic age** N ère *f* atomique
atomic bomb N bombe *f* atomique
atomic clock N horloge *f* atomique
atomic energy N énergie *f* atomique *or* nucléaire
Atomic Energy Authority *(in Brit)*, **Atomic Energy Commission** *(in US)* N ≈ Commissariat *m* à l'énergie atomique
atomic number N nombre *m* *or* numéro *m* atomique
atomic physicist N physicien(ne) *m(f)* nucléaire
atomic physics N physique *f* nucléaire
atomic pile N pile *f* atomique
atomic-powered ADJ (fonctionnant à l'énergie) nucléaire *or* atomique
atomic power station N centrale *f* nucléaire *or* atomique
atomic reactor N réacteur *m* nucléaire *or* atomique
atomic structure N structure *f* atomique
atomic theory N théorie *f* atomique
atomic warfare N guerre *f* nucléaire *or* atomique
atomic weapon N arme *f* atomique *or* nucléaire
atomic weight N poids *m* *or* masse *f* atomique

atomize /'ætəmaɪz/ VT pulvériser, atomiser

atomizer /'ætəmaɪzəʳ/ N atomiseur *m*

atonal /æ'təʊnl/ ADJ atonal

atonality /,eɪtəʊ'nælɪtɪ/ N atonalité *f*

atone /ə'təʊn/ VI ◆ **to ~ for** *[+ sin]* expier ; *[+ mistake]* racheter, réparer

atonement /ə'təʊnmənt/ N *(NonC, for sin, misdeed)* expiation *f* *(for sth* de qch) ; *(for mistake)* réparation *f* *(for sth* de qch) ; ◆ **in ~ for** *[+ sin, misdeed]* en expiation de ; *[+ mistake]* en réparation de ◆ **to make ~** *(for sin)* faire acte d'expiation ◆ **to make ~ for** *[+ sin, misdeed]* expier ; *[+ mistake]* réparer ◆ **he was ready to make ~ for what he'd done wrong** il était prêt à réparer le mal qu'il avait fait ; → **day**

atonic /æ'tɒnɪk/ ADJ *[syllable]* atone ; *[muscle]* atonique

atop /ə'tɒp/ ADV en haut, au sommet PREP en haut de, au sommet de

ATP /,eɪtiː'piː/ N (abbrev of **adenosine triphosphate**) ATP *m*

Atreus /'eɪtrɪəs/ N Atrée *m*

atria /'eɪtrɪə/ NPL of **atrium**

Atridae /'ætrɪdeɪ/ NPL Atrides *mpl*

atrium /'eɪtrɪəm/ N (pl **atria**) 1 *(Anat)* orifice *m* de l'oreillette 2 *(Archit)* atrium *m (couvert d'une verrière)*

atrocious /ə'trəʊʃəs/ ADJ *[crime]* atroce ; (* = *very bad) [memory, behaviour]* épouvantable ; *[weather]* épouvantable, affreux ; *[food, accent]* épouvantable, atroce

atrociously /ə'trəʊʃəslɪ/ ADV *[behave, sing, play]* de façon épouvantable, atrocement mal ◆ **~ bad** *[film, restaurant]* horriblement mauvais

atrocity /ə'trɒsɪtɪ/ N atrocité *f*

atrophy /'ætrəfɪ/ N atrophie *f* VT atrophier VI s'atrophier

att. 1 *(Comm)* abbrev of **attached** 2 abbrev of **attorney**

attaboy* /'ætəbɔɪ/ EXCL *(in encouragement)* vas-y ! ; *(in congratulation)* bravo !

attach /ə'tætʃ/ VT 1 (= *join*) *(gen)* attacher, lier ; *(to letter)* joindre ◆ **document ~ed to a letter** document *m* joint à une lettre ◆ **the ~ed letter** la lettre ci-jointe ◆ **I ~ a report from ...** *(in letter)* je joins à cette lettre un rapport de ... ◆ **to ~ conditions to sth** soumettre qch à des conditions ◆ **to ~ o.s. to a group** se joindre à un groupe, entrer dans un groupe ◆ **to be ~ed to sb/sth** (= *fond of*) être attaché à qn/qch ◆ **he's ~ed** * (= *married etc*) il n'est pas libre
2 (= *attribute*) *[+ value]* attacher, attribuer *(to* à) ; ◆ **to ~ credence to sth** ajouter foi à qch ; → **importance**
3 *(Jur)* *[+ person]* arrêter, appréhender ; *[+ goods, salary]* saisir
4 *[+ employee, troops]* affecter *(to* à) ; ◆ **he is ~ed to the Foreign Office** il est attaché au ministère des Affaires étrangères
5 *(Phys) [compound, atom]* fixer *(to* à)
VI 1 *(frm = belong)* être attribué, être imputé *(to* à) ; ◆ **no blame ~es to you** le blâme ne repose nullement sur vous ◆ **salary ~ing to a post** salaire *m* afférent à un emploi *(frm)*
2 *(Phys) [compound, atom]* se fixer

attaché /ə'tæʃeɪ/ N attaché(e) *m(f)* COMP **attaché case** N mallette *f*, attaché-case *m*

attachment /ə'tætʃmənt/ N 1 *(NonC)* fixation *f* 2 (= *accessory: for tool etc*) accessoire *m* 3 *(fig = affection)* attachement *m (to* à) affection *f (to* pour) 4 *(Jur) (on person)* arrestation *f* ; *(on goods, salary)* saisie *f (on* de) 5 (= *period of practical work, temporary transfer*) stage *m* ◆ **to be on ~** faire un stage *(to* à, auprès de, chez) 6 *(Comput)* fichier *m* joint ◆ **to send sth as an ~** envoyer qch en fichier joint

attack /ə'tæk/ N 1 attaque *f (on* contre) ; ◆ **to return to the ~** revenir à la charge ◆ **an ~ on sb's life** un attentat contre qn ; *(Jur)* un attentat à la vie de qn ◆ **to leave o.s. open to ~** *(fig)* prêter le flanc à la critique ◆ **~ is the best form of defence** le meilleur moyen de défense c'est l'attaque ◆ **to be under ~** *(Mil)* être attaqué *(from* par) ; *(fig)* être en butte aux attaques *(from* de) ; ◆ **to feel under ~** *(Psych)* se sentir agressé
2 *(Med etc)* crise *f* ◆ **asthma ~** crise *f* d'asthme ◆ **~ of nerves** crise *f* de nerfs ; → **heart**
VT 1 *[+ person]* attaquer ◆ **this idea ~s the whole structure of society** cette idée menace toute la structure de la société ◆ **to be ~ed by doubts** être assailli par des doutes
2 *[+ task, problem]* s'attaquer à ; *[+ poverty etc]* combattre
3 *(Chem) [+ metal]* attaquer
VI attaquer

COMP **attack dog** N chien *m* d'attaque

attackable /ə'tækəbl/ ADJ attaquable

attacker /ə'tækəʳ/ N *(gen)* agresseur *m* ; *(Mil)* attaquant(e) *m(f)*

attagirl* /'ætəgɜːl/ EXCL *(in encouragement)* vas-y ! ; *(in congratulation)* bravo !

attain /ə'teɪn/ VT *[+ aim, rank, age]* atteindre, parvenir à ; *[+ knowledge]* acquérir ; *[+ happiness]* atteindre à ; *[+ one's hopes]* réaliser ◆ **he's well on the way to ~ing his pilot's licence** il est en bonne voie pour obtenir sa licence de pilote VI ◆ **to ~ to** *[+ perfection]* atteindre à, toucher à ; *[+ power, prosperity]* parvenir à

attainable /ə'teɪnəbl/ ADJ accessible *(by* à), à la portée *(by* de)

attainder /ə'teɪndəʳ/ N *(Jur)* mort *f* civile ; → **bill**[1]

attainment /ə'teɪnmənt/ N 1 *(NonC) [of knowledge]* acquisition *f* ; *[of happiness]* conquête *f* ; *[of hopes]* réalisation *f* 2 *(gen pl = achievement)* réalisations *fpl*

attempt /ə'tempt/ VT essayer, tenter *(to do sth* de faire qch) ; *[+ task]* entreprendre, s'attaquer à ◆ **~ed escape/murder/theft** *etc* tentative *f* d'évasion/de meurtre/de vol *etc* ◆ **to ~ suicide** essayer *or* tenter de se suicider
N 1 tentative *f* ◆ **an ~ at escape** une tentative d'évasion ◆ **an ~ at humour** une tentative de plaisanterie ◆ **to make one's first ~** faire sa première tentative, essayer pour la première fois ◆ **to make an ~ at doing sth** *or* **to do sth** essayer de faire qch, chercher à faire qch ◆ **to be successful at the first ~** réussir du premier coup ◆ **he failed at the first ~** la première fois, il a échoué ◆ **he had to give up the ~** il lui a fallu (y) renoncer ◆ **he made no ~ to help us** il n'a rien fait pour nous aider, il n'a pas essayé de *or* cherché à nous aider ◆ **to make an ~ on the record** essayer de *or* tenter de battre le record ◆ **he made two ~s at it** il a essayé *or* tenté par deux fois de le faire ◆ **it was a good ~ on his part but ...** il a vraiment essayé mais ... ◆ **rebels were arrested in an ~ to prevent an uprising** on a arrêté des rebelles pour tenter d'empêcher une insurrection
2 (= *attack*) attentat *m* ◆ **an ~ on sb's life** un attentat contre qn

attend /ə'tend/ LANGUAGE IN USE 19.3, 19.5, 25.1
VT 1 *[+ meeting, lecture]* assister à, être à ; *[+ classes, course of studies]* suivre ; *[+ church, school]* aller à ◆ **the meeting was well ~ed** il y avait beaucoup de monde à la réunion ; see also **well**[2]
2 (= *serve, accompany*) servir, être au service de ◆ **to ~ a patient** *[doctor]* soigner un malade ◆ **~ed by a maid** servi par une *or* accompagné d'une femme de chambre ◆ **a method ~ed by great risks** une méthode qui comporte de grands risques
VI 1 (= *be present*) être présent *or* là ◆ **will you ~?** est-ce que vous y serez ?
2 (= *pay attention*) faire attention *(to* à)

▸ **attend on** † VT FUS ⇒ **attend upon**

▸ **attend to** VT FUS (= *pay attention to*) *[+ lesson, speech]* faire attention à ; *[+ advice]* prêter attention à ; (= *deal with, take care of*) s'occuper de ◆ **to ~ to a customer** s'occuper d'un client, servir un client ◆ **are you being ~ed to?** *(in shop)* est-ce qu'on s'occupe de vous ?

▸ **attend upon** † VT FUS *[+ person]* être au service de

attendance /ə'tendəns/ N 1 service *m* ◆ **to be in ~** être de service ◆ **he was in ~ on the queen** il escortait la reine ◆ **~ on a patient** *(Med)* visites *fpl* à un malade ; → **dance**
2 (= *being present*) présence *f* ◆ **regular ~ at** assiduité *f* à ◆ **in ~** présent ◆ **is my ~ necessary?** est-il nécessaire que je sois présent *or* là ?

3 (= *number of people present*) assistance *f* ◆ **a large ~** une nombreuse assistance ◆ **what was the ~ at the meeting?** combien de gens y avait-il à la réunion ?

COMP **attendance allowance** N (*Brit*) (*for councillors*) indemnité *f* d'élu ; (*for the handicapped*) *allocation pour soins constants donnée aux personnes handicapées*
attendance centre N (*Brit Jur*) ≈ centre *m* de réinsertion
attendance officer N (*Brit Scol*) *inspecteur chargé de faire respecter l'obligation scolaire*
attendance order N (*Brit*) *injonction exigeant des parents l'assiduité scolaire de leur enfant*
attendance record N ◆ **his ~ record is bad** il est souvent absent
attendance register N (= *book*) registre *m* de(s) présence(s)
attendance sheet N feuille *f* d'appel

attendant /əˈtendənt/ N 1 [*of museum etc*] gardien(ne) *m(f)* ; [*of petrol station*] pompiste *mf* ; (= *servant*) domestique *mf*, serviteur † *m*
2 (*US: in hospital*) garçon *m* de salle ; († = *doctor*) médecin *m* (de famille)
3 (= *companion, escort*) ◆ **~s** membres *mpl* de la suite (*on de*) ; ◆ **the prince and his ~s** le prince et sa suite
ADJ 1 (= *accompanying*) [*person*] qui accompagne ◆ **to be ~ on** *or* **upon sb** accompagner qn ◆ **the ~ crowd** la foule qui était présente
2 (*frm* = *associated*) ◆ **old age and its ~ ills** la vieillesse et les maux qui l'accompagnent ◆ **country life with all its ~ benefits** la vie à la campagne, avec tous les avantages qu'elle présente *or* comporte ◆ **the ~ circumstances** les circonstances *fpl* concomitantes ◆ **the ~ rise in prices** la hausse des prix correspondante ◆ **~ on** *or* **upon sth** (= *linked to*) lié à qch ; (= *due to*) dû (due *f*) à qch

attendee /əˌtenˈdiː/ N (*esp US*) participant(e) *m(f)* (*at* à)

attention /əˈtenʃən/ LANGUAGE IN USE 26.1
N 1 (*NonC* = *consideration, notice, observation*) attention *f* ◆ **may I have your ~?** puis-je avoir votre attention ? ◆ **give me your ~ for a moment** accordez-moi votre attention un instant ◆ **he gave her his full ~** il lui a accordé toute son attention ◆ **to call (sb's) ~ to sth** attirer l'attention (de qn) sur qch ◆ **to pay ~ to ...** faire *or* prêter attention à ... ◆ **to pay little/no ~ to ...** prêter peu d'attention/ne prêter aucune attention à ... ◆ **to pay special ~ to ...** faire tout particulièrement attention à ..., prêter une attention toute particulière à ... ◆ **no ~ has been paid to my advice** on n'a fait aucun cas de *or* tenu aucun compte de mes conseils ◆ **it has come to my ~ that ...** j'ai appris que ... ◆ **for the ~ of Mrs C. Montgomery** à l'attention de Mme C. Montgomery ◆ **it needs daily ~** il faut s'en occuper tous les jours ◆ **it shall have my earliest ~** (*Comm etc*) je m'en occuperai dès que possible ◆ **I was all ~** * j'étais tout oreilles ; → **attract, catch, hold**
2 (= *kindnesses*) **~s** attentions *fpl*, prévenances *fpl* ◆ **to show ~s to** avoir des égards pour ◆ **to pay one's ~s to a woman** faire la cour à *or* courtiser une femme
3 (*Mil*) garde-à-vous *m* ◆ **to stand at/come** *or* **stand to ~** être/se mettre au garde-à-vous ◆ **~!** garde-à-vous !

COMP **attention deficit disorder** N troubles *mpl* déficitaires de l'attention
attention-seeking ADJ cherchant à attirer l'attention N désir *m* d'attirer l'attention
attention span N ◆ **his ~ span is limited** il n'arrive pas à se concentrer très longtemps

attentive /əˈtentɪv/ ADJ 1 prévenant (*to sb* envers qn) empressé (*to sb* auprès de qn) ; ◆ **~ to sb's interests** soucieux des intérêts de qn ◆ **~ to detail** soucieux du détail, méticuleux 2 [*audience, spectator*] attentif (*to* à)

attentively /əˈtentɪvlɪ/ ADV attentivement, avec attention ◆ **to listen ~** écouter de toutes ses oreilles *or* attentivement

attentiveness /əˈtentɪvnɪs/ N attention *f*, prévenance *f*

attenuate /əˈtenjʊeɪt/ VT 1 [+ *statement*] atténuer, modérer 2 [+ *gas*] raréfier 3 [+ *thread, line*] affiner, amincir VI s'atténuer, diminuer
ADJ (also **attenuated**) atténué, diminué ; (*fig* = *refined*) adouci, émoussé COMP **attenuating circumstances** NPL circonstances *fpl* atténuantes

attenuation /əˌtenjʊˈeɪʃən/ N atténuation *f*, diminution *f*

attest /əˈtest/ VT 1 (= *certify*) attester (*that* que) ; (*under oath*) affirmer sous serment (*that* que) ; (= *prove*) attester, témoigner de ; (*Jur*) [+ *signature*] légaliser 2 (= *put on oath*) faire prêter serment à VI prêter serment ◆ **to ~ to sth** attester qch, témoigner de qch
COMP **attested form** N (*Ling*) forme *f* attestée
attested herd N (*Brit Agr*) cheptel *m* certifié (*comme ayant été tuberculinisé*)

attestation /ˌætesˈteɪʃən/ N attestation *f* (*that* que) ; (*Jur*) attestation *f*, témoignage *m* ; [*of signature*] légalisation *f* ; (= *taking oath*) assermentation *f*, prestation *f* de serment

attic /ˈætɪk/ N grenier *m* COMP **attic room** N mansarde *f*

Attica /ˈætɪkə/ N Attique *f*

Attila /əˈtɪlə/ N Attila *m*

attire /əˈtaɪəʳ/ (*frm*) VT vêtir, parer (*in* de) ; ◆ **to ~ o.s. in ...** se parer de ... ◆ **elegantly ~d** vêtu avec élégance N (*NonC*) vêtements *mpl*, habits *mpl* ; (*ceremonial*) tenue *f* ; (*hum*) atours *mpl* (*hum*) ◆ **in formal ~** en tenue de cérémonie

attitude /ˈætɪtjuːd/ N 1 (= *way of standing*) attitude *f*, position *f* ◆ **to strike an ~** poser, prendre une pose affectée *or* théâtrale 2 (= *way of thinking*) disposition *f*, attitude *f* ◆ **~ of mind** état *m* *or* disposition *f* d'esprit ◆ **his ~ towards me** son attitude envers moi *or* à mon égard ◆ **I don't like your ~** je n'aime pas l'attitude que vous prenez ◆ **if that's your ~** si c'est ainsi *or* si c'est comme ça * que tu le prends 3 * ◆ **sb with ~** qn de tonique ◆ **women with ~** des battantes

attitudinal /ˌætɪˈtjuːdɪnəl/ ADJ [*change, difference*] d'attitude

attitudinize /ˌætɪˈtjuːdɪnaɪz/ VI se donner des airs, adopter des attitudes affectées

attn PREP (abbrev of **(for the) attention (of)**) à l'attention de

attorney /əˈtɜːnɪ/ N 1 (*Comm, Jur* = *representative*) mandataire *mf*, représentant(e) *m(f)* ◆ **power of ~** procuration *f*, pouvoir *m* 2 (*US*: also **attorney-at-law**) avocat(e) *m(f)* ; → **district** ; → LAWYER COMP **Attorney General** N (pl **Attorneys General** *or* **Attorney Generals**) (*Brit*) ≃ Procureur Général ; (*US*) ≃ Garde *m* des Sceaux, ministre *m* de la Justice

attract /əˈtrækt/ VT 1 [*magnet etc*] attirer ◆ **to ~ sb's attention** (*fig*) attirer l'attention de qn ◆ **to ~ sb's interest** éveiller l'intérêt de qn 2 (= *charm, interest*) [*person, subject, quality*] attirer, séduire ◆ **what ~ed me to her ...** ce qui m'a attiré *or* séduit chez elle ... ◆ **I am not ~ed to her** elle ne m'attire pas ◆ **opposites ~** les contraires s'attirent

attraction /əˈtrækʃən/ N 1 (= *attractiveness*) attrait *m* ◆ **the main** *or* **chief ~ of this plan is its simplicity** l'attrait principal de ce projet est sa simplicité ◆ **one of the ~s of family life** un des charmes de la vie de famille ◆ **a charming village, with the added ~ of a beach** un village plein de charme et qui a même une plage ◆ **I don't see the ~ of camping holidays** je ne vois pas ce qu'il y a d'attrayant dans le camping ◆ **politics holds** *or* **has no ~ for me** la politique ne m'attire pas
2 (*NonC*) (= *fact of being attracted*) attirance *f* (*to* pour) ; ◆ **Phaedra's ~ for her stepson** l'attirance de Phèdre pour son beau-fils ◆ **sexual ~** attirance physique ◆ **animal ~** désir *m* animal ; → **physical**
3 (= *source of entertainment*) attraction *f* ◆ **the chief ~ of the party** la grande attraction de la soirée ◆ **local ~s include a museum of modern art** parmi les attractions de la région, il y a un musée d'art moderne ◆ **fairground ~** attraction *f* (*dans une foire*) ◆ **tourist ~** attraction *f* touristique ◆ **star ~** (*of place*) principale attraction *f* ; (*show, parade*) clou *m* ; (*sports team*) star *f* ◆ **box-office ~** (= *star*) star *f* du box-office
4 (*NonC: Phys*) attraction *f* ◆ **the ~ of gravity** l'attraction *f* universelle ◆ **the ~ between two masses** l'attraction entre deux corps

attractive /əˈtræktɪv/ ADJ 1 (= *appealing*) [*person*] séduisant, attirant ; [*personality, voice, offer*] séduisant ; [*features, object, prospect*] attrayant ; [*sound*] agréable ; [*price, salary*] intéressant, attractif ◆ **he was immensely ~ to women** les femmes le trouvaient extrêmement séduisant ◆ **the idea was ~ to her** elle trouvait cette idée séduisante 2 (*Phys*) attractif

attractively /əˈtræktɪvlɪ/ ADV [*dressed*] de façon séduisante ; [*illustrated, packaged*] de façon attrayante ; [*furnished*] agréablement ◆ **~ priced, at an ~ low price** à un prix intéressant *or* attractif ◆ **~ simple** d'une simplicité séduisante

attractiveness /əˈtræktɪvnəs/ N [*of person*] charme *m*, beauté *f* ; [*of voice, place*] charme *m* ; [*of idea, plan*] attrait *m* ◆ **physical ~** attrait *m* physique

attributable /əˈtrɪbjʊtəbl/ ADJ attribuable, imputable (*to* à)

attribute /əˈtrɪbjuːt/ LANGUAGE IN USE 17.1 VT attribuer (*sth to sb* qch à qn) ; [+ *feelings, words*] prêter, attribuer (*to sb* à qn) ; [+ *crime, fault*] imputer (*to sb* à qn) ; ◆ **they ~ his failure to his laziness** ils attribuent son échec à sa paresse, ils mettent son échec sur le compte de sa paresse N /ˈætrɪbjuːt/ 1 attribut *m* 2 (*Gram*) attribut *m*

attribution /ˌætrɪˈbjuːʃən/ N (*gen*) attribution *f* ◆ **~ of sth to a purpose** affectation *f* de qch à un but

attributive /əˈtrɪbjʊtɪv/ ADJ attributif ; (*Gram*) attributif N attribut *m* ; (*Gram*) attribut *m*

attributively /əˈtrɪbjʊtɪvlɪ/ ADV (*Gram*) comme épithète

attrition /əˈtrɪʃən/ N usure *f* (*par frottement*) ; → **war** COMP **attrition rate** N (*esp US Comm*) [*of customers*] pourcentage *m* de clients perdus ; [*of subscribers*] taux *m* de désabonnement

attune /əˈtjuːn/ VT (*lit, fig*) ◆ **to become ~d to** (= *used to*) s'habituer à ◆ **tastes ~d to mine** des goûts en accord avec les miens ◆ **to ~ o.s. to (doing) sth** s'habituer à (faire) qch ◆ **to be ~d to sb's needs** (= *listening*) être à l'écoute des besoins de qn

ATV /ˌeɪtiːˈviː/ N (*US*) (abbrev of **all-terrain vehicle**) → **all**

atypical /ˌeɪˈtɪpɪkəl/ ADJ atypique

atypically /ˌeɪˈtɪpɪkəlɪ/ ADV exceptionnellement ◆ **today, ~, he was early** exceptionnellement *or* fait inhabituel, il est arrivé en avance aujourd'hui

aubergine /ˈəʊbəʒiːn/ N (*esp Brit*) aubergine *f*

auburn /ˈɔːbən/ ADJ auburn *inv*

auction /ˈɔːkʃən/ N (vente *f* aux) enchères *fpl*, (vente *f* à la) criée *f* ◆ **to sell by ~** vendre aux enchères *or* à la criée ◆ **to put sth up for ~** mettre qch dans une vente aux enchères ;

→ **Dutch** VT (also **auction off**) vendre aux enchères *or* à la criée
COMP **auction bridge** N bridge *m* aux enchères
auction house N société *f* de vente(s) aux enchères
auction room N salle *f* des ventes
auction sale N (vente *f* aux) enchères *fpl*, vente *f* à la criée

auctioneer /ˌɔːkʃəˈnɪəʳ/ N commissaire-priseur *m*

audacious /ɔːˈdeɪʃəs/ ADJ audacieux

audaciously /ɔːˈdeɪʃəslɪ/ ADV audacieusement

audacity /ɔːˈdæsɪtɪ/ N *(NonC)* audace *f* ◆ **to have the ~ to do sth** avoir l'audace de faire qch

audibility /ˌɔːdɪˈbɪlɪtɪ/ N audibilité *f*

audible /ˈɔːdɪbl/ ADJ *(gen)* audible, perceptible ; *[words]* intelligible, distinct ◆ **she was hardly ~** on l'entendait à peine ◆ **there was ~ laughter** des rires se firent entendre

audibly /ˈɔːdɪblɪ/ ADV distinctement

audience /ˈɔːdɪəns/ N 1 *(NonC) (Theat)* spectateurs *mpl*, public *m* ; *(of speaker)* auditoire *m*, assistance *f* ; *(Mus, Rad)* auditeurs *mpl* ; *(TV)* téléspectateurs *mpl* ◆ **the whole ~ applauded** *(Theat)* toute la salle a applaudi ◆ **those in the ~** les gens dans la salle, les membres de l'assistance *or* du public ◆ **there was a big ~** les spectateurs étaient nombreux 2 *(= meeting)* audience *f* ◆ **to grant an ~ to sb** donner *or* accorder audience à qn
COMP **audience appeal** N ◆ **it's got ~ appeal** cela plaît au public
audience chamber N salle *f* d'audience
audience participation N participation *f* du public
audience rating N *(Rad, TV)* indice *m* d'écoute
audience research N *(Rad, TV)* études *fpl* d'opinion

audio /ˈɔːdɪəʊ/ ADJ acoustique N * partie *f* son ◆ **the ~'s on the blink*** il n'y a plus de son
COMP **audio book** N livre-cassette *m*
audio equipment N équipement *m* acoustique
audio frequency N audiofréquence *f*
audio recording N enregistrement *m* sonore
audio system N système *m* audio

audio- /ˈɔːdɪəʊ/ PREF audio- COMP **audio-cassette** N cassette *f* audio

audiometer /ˌɔːdɪˈɒmɪtəʳ/ N audiomètre *m*

audiotape /ˈɔːdɪəʊteɪp/ N 1 *(= tape)* bande *f* magnétique 2 *(US = cassette)* cassette *f* audio VT *(US = tape)* enregistrer sur cassette audio *or* sur bande magnétique

audiotronic /ˌɔːdɪəʊˈtrɒnɪk/ ADJ audio-électronique

audiotyping /ˈɔːdɪəʊtaɪpɪŋ/ N audiotypie *f*

audiotypist /ˈɔːdɪəʊtaɪpɪst/ N audiotypiste *mf*

audiovisual /ˌɔːdɪəʊˈvɪzjʊəl/ ADJ audiovisuel ◆ **~ aids** supports *mpl or* moyens *mpl* audiovisuels ◆ **~ methods** méthodes *fpl* audiovisuelles

audit /ˈɔːdɪt/ N audit *m*, vérification *f* des comptes VT 1 *[+ accounts]* vérifier, apurer ; *[+ company]* auditer ◆ **~ed statement of accounts** état vérifié des comptes 2 *(US Univ)* **to ~ a lecture course** assister à un cours comme auditeur libre

auditing /ˈɔːdɪtɪŋ/ N *(Fin)* ◆ **~ of accounts** audit *m or* vérification *f* des comptes

audition /ɔːˈdɪʃən/ N 1 *(Theat)* audition *f* ; *(Cine, TV)* (séance *f* d')essai *m* ◆ **to give sb an ~** *(Theat)* auditionner qn ; *(Cine)* faire faire un essai à qn 2 *(NonC: frm = power of hearing)* ouïe *f*, audition *f* VT auditionner ◆ **he was ~ed for the part** *(Theat)* on lui a fait passer une audition *or* on l'a auditionné pour le rôle ; *(Cine)* on lui a fait faire un essai pour le rôle VI *(Theat)* auditionner ◆ **he ~ed for (the part of) Hamlet** *(Theat)* il a auditionné pour le rôle de Hamlet ; *(Cine, TV)* on lui a fait faire un essai pour le rôle de Hamlet

auditor /ˈɔːdɪtəʳ/ N 1 *(= listener)* auditeur *m*, -trice *f* 2 *(Comm)* auditeur *m*, -trice *f*, vérificateur *m*, -trice *f* (des comptes) ; → **internal** 3 *(US Univ)* auditeur *m*, -trice *f* libre

auditorium /ˌɔːdɪˈtɔːrɪəm/ N (pl **auditoriums** *or* **auditoria** /ˌɔːdɪˈtɔːrɪə/) 1 auditorium *m*, salle *f* 2 *(US) (for lectures)* salle *f* de conférences ; *(for shows)* salle *f* de spectacle

auditory /ˈɔːdɪtərɪ/ ADJ auditif COMP **auditory phonetics** N *(NonC)* phonétique *f* auditive

Audubon Society /ˈɔːdəbɒnsəˈsaɪətɪ/ N *(US)* société *f* de protection de la nature

au fait /əʊˈfeɪ/ ADJ au courant, au fait (*with* de)

Augean Stables /ɔːˈdʒiːənˈsteɪblz/ NPL ◆ **the ~** les écuries *fpl* d'Augias

auger /ˈɔːgəʳ/ N *(Carpentry)* vrille *f* ; *(for ground drilling)* foreuse *f*

aught /ɔːt/ N (††, *liter = anything*) ◆ **for ~ I know** (pour) autant que je sache ◆ **for ~ I care** pour ce que cela me fait

augment /ɔːgˈment/ VT augmenter (*with, by* de) accroître ; *(Mus)* augmenter ◆ **~ed sixth/third** *(Mus)* sixte *f*/tierce *f* augmentée VI augmenter, s'accroître

augmentation /ˌɔːgmenˈteɪʃən/ N augmentation *f*, accroissement *m*

augmentative /ɔːgˈmentətɪv/ ADJ augmentatif

augur /ˈɔːgəʳ/ N augure *m* VI ◆ **to ~ well/ill** être de bon/de mauvais augure (*for* pour) VT *(= foretell)* prédire, prévoir ; *(= be an omen of)* présager ◆ **it ~s no good** cela ne présage *or* n'annonce rien de bon

augury /ˈɔːgjʊrɪ/ N *(= omen, sign)* augure *m*, présage *m* ; *(= forecast)* prédiction *f* ◆ **to take the auguries** consulter les augures

August /ˈɔːgəst/ N août *m* ; *for phrases see* **September**

august /ɔːˈgʌst/ ADJ *(frm)* auguste

Augustan /ɔːˈgʌstən/ ADJ 1 d'Auguste ◆ **the ~ Age** *(Latin Literat)* le siècle d'Auguste ; *(English Literat)* l'époque *f* néoclassique 2 ◆ **~ Confession** Confession *f* d'Augsbourg

Augustine /ɔːˈgʌstɪn/ N Augustin *m*

Augustinian /ˌɔːgəsˈtɪnɪən/ ADJ augustinien, de (l'ordre de) saint Augustin N augustin(e) *m(f)*

Augustus /ɔːˈgʌstəs/ N ◆ **(Caesar)** ~ (César) Auguste *m*

auk /ɔːk/ N pingouin *m*

Auld Lang Syne /ˌɔːldlæŋˈzaɪn/ N le bon vieux temps *(chanson écossaise chantée sur le coup de minuit à la Saint-Sylvestre)*

aunt /ɑːnt/ N tante *f* ◆ **yes ~** oui ma tante COMP **Aunt Sally** N *(Brit) (= game)* jeu *m* de massacre ; *(fig = person)* tête *f* de Turc

auntie*, **aunty*** /ˈɑːntɪ/ N tantine* *f*, tata* *f* ◆ **~ Mary** tante *f* Marie ◆ **Auntie** *(Brit hum)* la BBC

au pair /ˈəʊˈpɛə/ ADJ (also **au pair girl**) jeune fille *f* au pair N (pl **au pairs**) jeune fille *f* au pair VI ◆ **to ~ (for sb)** être au pair (chez qn)

aura /ˈɔːrə/ N (pl **auras** *or* **aurae** /ˈɔːriː/) *[of person]* aura *f* ; *[of place]* atmosphère *f*, ambiance *f* ◆ **he had an ~ of serenity about him** il respirait la sérénité ◆ **an ~ of mystery** une aura de mystère

aural /ˈɔːrəl/ ADJ 1 *(Anat)* auriculaire *(des oreilles)* 2 *(Educ)* ~ **comprehension (work)** compréhension *f* (orale) ◆ **~ comprehension (test)** exercice *m* de compréhension (orale) ◆ **~ training** *(Mus)* dictée *f* musicale

aureole /ˈɔːrɪəʊl/ N *(Art, Astron)* auréole *f*

auricle /ˈɔːrɪkl/ N *(Anat) [of ear]* pavillon *m* auriculaire, oreille *f* externe ; *[of heart]* oreillette *f*

aurochs /ˈɔːrɒks/ N (pl **aurochs**) aurochs *m*

aurora /ɔːˈrɔːrə/ N (pl **auroras** *or* **aurorae** /ɔːˈrɔːriː/) ◆ **~ borealis/australis** aurore *f* boréale/australe

auscultate /ˈɔːskəlteɪt/ VT ausculter

auscultation /ˌɔːskəlˈteɪʃən/ N auscultation *f*

auspices /ˈɔːspɪsɪz/ NPL *(all senses)* auspices *mpl* ◆ **under the ~ of ...** sous les auspices de ...

auspicious /ɔːsˈpɪʃəs/ ADJ *[start]* prometteur ; *[occasion, day, time]* propice ; *[sign]* de bon augure

auspiciously /ɔːsˈpɪʃəslɪ/ ADV favorablement, sous d'heureux auspices ◆ **to start ~** prendre un départ prometteur

Aussie* /ˈɒzɪ/ ADJ, N ⇒ **Australian**

austere /ɒsˈtɪəʳ/ ADJ *[person, building, lifestyle, beauty]* austère ; *[times, economic policy]* d'austérité

austerely /ɒsˈtɪəlɪ/ ADV avec austérité

austerity /ɒsˈterɪtɪ/ N austérité *f* ◆ **days** *or* **years of ~** période *f* d'austérité

Australasia /ˌɒstrəˈleɪzɪə/ N Australasie *f*

Australasian /ˌɒstrəˈleɪzɪən/ ADJ d'Australasie N habitant(e) *m(f) or* natif *m*, -ive *f* d'Australasie

Australia /ɒsˈtreɪlɪə/ N ◆ **(the Commonwealth of) ~** l'Australie *f*

Australian /ɒsˈtreɪlɪən/ ADJ *(gen)* australien ; *[ambassador, embassy]* d'Australie N 1 Australien(ne) *m(f)* 2 *(= language variety)* australien *m*
COMP **Australian Alps** NPL Alpes *fpl* australiennes
Australian Antarctic Territory N Antarctique *f* australienne
Australian Capital Territory N Territoire *m* fédéral de Canberra

Austria /ˈɒstrɪə/ N Autriche *f* ◆ **in ~** en Autriche

Austrian /ˈɒstrɪən/ ADJ *(gen)* autrichien ; *[ambassador, embassy]* d'Autriche N Autrichien(ne) *m(f)*

Austro- /ˈɒstrəʊ/ PREF austro- ◆ **~Hungarian** austro-hongrois

AUT /ˌeɪjuːˈtiː/ N *(Brit)* (abbrev of **Association of University Teachers**) *syndicat*

autarchy /ˈɔːtɑːkɪ/ N autocratie *f*

auteur /ɔːˈtɜːʳ/ N cinéaste-auteur *m*

authentic /ɔːˈθentɪk/ ADJ authentique ◆ **both texts shall be deemed ~** *(Jur)* les deux textes feront foi

authentically /ɔːˈθentɪkəlɪ/ ADV 1 *(= genuinely) [furnished, restored]* authentiquement ◆ **~ Chinese dishes** des plats authentiquement chinois, des plats chinois authentiques ◆ **the brass has an ~ tarnished look** l'aspect terni de ce cuivre a l'air authentique 2 *(= accurately) [describe, depict]* de façon authentique

authenticate /ɔːˈθentɪkeɪt/ VT *[+ document]* authentifier ; *[+ report]* établir l'authenticité de ; *[+ signature]* légaliser

authentication /ɔːˌθentɪˈkeɪʃən/ N *[of document]* authentification *f* ; *[of report]* confirmation *f* (de l'authenticité de)

authenticity /ˌɔːθenˈtɪsɪtɪ/ N authenticité *f*

author /ˈɔːθəʳ/ N 1 *(= writer)* écrivain *m*, auteur *m* ◆ **~'s copy** manuscrit *m* de l'auteur 2 *[of any work of art]* auteur *m*, créateur *m* ; *[of plan, trouble etc]* auteur *m* VT *(US, † Brit = be author of)* être l'auteur de

authoress /ˈɔːθərɪs/ N femme *f* écrivain

authorial /ɔːˈθɔːrɪəl/ ADJ de l'auteur

authoritarian /ˌɔːθɒrɪˈtɛərɪən/ ADJ autoritaire N partisan(e) *m(f)* de l'autorité

authoritarianism /ˌɔːθɒrɪˈtɛərɪənɪzəm/ N autoritarisme *m*

authoritative /ɔːˈθɒrɪtətɪv/ ADJ 1 *(= commanding) [person, voice, manner]* autoritaire 2 *(= reliable) [person, book, guide]* faisant autorité, digne de foi ; *[source]* sûr, autorisé ; *[survey, study, information]* sûr, digne de foi 3 *(= official) [statement]* officiel

authoritatively /ɔːˈθɒrɪtətɪvlɪ/ ADV 1 *(= commandingly) [say, nod, behave]* de façon autoritaire 2 *(= reliably) [speak, write]* avec autorité

authority /ɔːˈθɒrɪtɪ/ N 1 *(= power to give orders)* autorité *f*, pouvoir *m* ◆ **I'm in ~ here** c'est moi qui dirige ici ◆ **to be in ~ over sb** avoir autorité sur qn ◆ **those in ~** les responsables
2 *(= permission, right)* autorisation *f* (formelle) ◆ **to give sb ~ to do sth** habiliter qn à faire qch ◆ **to do sth without ~** faire qch sans autorisation ◆ **she had no ~ to do it** elle n'avait pas qualité pour le faire ◆ **on her own ~** de son propre chef, de sa propre autorité ◆ **on whose ~?** avec l'autorisation de qui ? ◆ **to speak with ~** parler avec compétence *or* autorité ◆ **to carry ~** faire autorité ◆ **I have it on good ~ that ...** je tiens de bonne source que ... ◆ **what is your ~?** sur quoi vous appuyez-vous (pour dire cela) ? ◆ **to say sth on the ~ of Plato** dire qch en invoquant l'autorité de Platon
3 *(gen pl = person or group)* **authorities** autorités *fpl*, corps *mpl* constitués, administration *f* ◆ **apply to the proper authorities** adressez-vous à qui de droit *or* aux autorités compétentes ◆ **the health authorities** les services *mpl* de la santé publique ◆ **the public/local/district authorities** les autorités *fpl* publiques/locales/régionales
4 *(= person with special knowledge)* autorité *f* (on en matière de) expert *m* (on en) ; *(= book)* autorité *f*, source *f* (autorisée) ◆ **to be an ~** *[person, book]* faire autorité (on en matière de) ; ◆ **to consult an ~** consulter un avis autorisé

authorization /ˌɔːθəraɪˈzeɪʃən/ N 1 *(= giving of authority)* autorisation *f (of, for* pour ; *to do sth* de faire qch) 2 *(= legal right)* pouvoir *m (to do sth* de faire qch)

authorize /ˈɔːθəraɪz/ VT autoriser *(sb to do sth* qn à faire qch) ; ◆ **to be ~d to do sth** avoir qualité pour faire qch, être autorisé à faire qch ◆ **~d by custom** sanctionné par l'usage

authorized /ˈɔːθəraɪzd/ ADJ *[person, signatory, overdraft]* autorisé ; *[dealer, representative, bank]* agréé ; *[signature]* social ; *[biography]* officiel ◆ **"authorized personnel only"** *(on door)* "entrée réservée au personnel" ◆ **duly ~ officer** *(Jur, Fin)* représentant *m* dûment habilité
COMP **authorized bank** N banque *f* agréée
authorized capital N *(NonC: Fin)* capital *m* social
authorized dealer N distributeur *m* agréé
authorized signature N *(Jur, Fin)* signature *f* sociale
the Authorized Version N *(Rel)* la Bible de 1611 *(autorisée par le roi Jacques I*[er]*)*

authorship /ˈɔːθəʃɪp/ N *[of book, idea etc]* paternité *f* ◆ **to establish the ~ of a book** identifier l'auteur d'un livre, établir la paternité littéraire d'un livre

autism /ˈɔːtɪzəm/ N autisme *m*

autistic /ɔːˈtɪstɪk/ ADJ autistique

auto /ˈɔːtəʊ/ *(US)* N voiture *f*, auto *f*
COMP **Auto show** N Salon *m* de l'auto
auto worker N ouvrier *m* de l'industrie automobile

auto- /ˈɔːtəʊ/ PREF auto-

autobank /ˈɔːtəʊbæŋk/ N distributeur *m* automatique de billets (de banque)

autobiographic(al) /ˈɔːtəʊˌbaɪəʊˈgræfɪk(əl)/ ADJ autobiographique

autobiography /ˌɔːtəʊbaɪˈɒgrəfɪ/ N autobiographie *f*

autocade /ˈɔːtəʊkeɪd/ N *(US)* cortège *m* d'automobiles

autocracy /ɔːˈtɒkrəsɪ/ N autocratie *f*

autocrat /ˈɔːtəʊkræt/ N autocrate *m*

autocratic /ˌɔːtəʊˈkrætɪk/ ADJ 1 *(= dictatorial) [person, style, behaviour, leadership]* autocratique 2 *(Pol) [leader, ruler]* absolu ; *[government, regime]* autocratique

autocross /ˈɔːtəʊkrɒs/ N auto-cross *m*

Autocue ® /ˈɔːtəʊkjuː/ N *(Brit TV)* téléprompteur *m*

autocycle /ˈɔːtəʊsaɪkl/ N *(small)* cyclomoteur *m* ; *(more powerful)* vélomoteur *m*

auto-da-fé /ˈɔːtəʊdɑːˈfeɪ/ N (pl **autos-da-fé** /ˈɔːtəʊdɑːˈfeɪ/) autodafé *m*

autodidact /ˈɔːtəʊˌdaɪdækt/ N *(frm)* autodidacte *mf*

autodrome /ˈɔːtəʊdrəʊm/ N autodrome *m*

autofocus /ˈɔːtəʊfəʊkəs/ N *(Phot)* autofocus *m*

autogenic /ˌɔːtəʊˈdʒenɪk/ ADJ ◆ **~ training** training *m* autogène

autogiro /ˈɔːtəʊˈdʒaɪərəʊ/ N autogire *m*

autograph /ˈɔːtəgrɑːf/ N autographe *m* VT *[+ book]* dédicacer ; *[+ other object]* signer
COMP **autograph album** N livre *m or* album *m* d'autographes
autograph hunter N collectionneur *m*, -euse *f* d'autographes

autohypnosis /ˌɔːtəʊhɪpˈnəʊsɪs/ N autohypnose *f*

autoimmune /ˌɔːtəʊɪˈmjuːn/ ADJ *[reaction, response, disease]* auto-immun

autoloading /ˈɔːtəʊləʊdɪŋ/ ADJ semi-automatique

automat /ˈɔːtəmæt/ N distributeur *m* automatique

automata /ɔːˈtɒmətə/ NPL of **automaton**

automate /ˈɔːtəmeɪt/ VT automatiser ◆ **~d teller** *(= machine)* distributeur *m* automatique de billets, guichet *m* automatique de banque

automatic /ˌɔːtəˈmætɪk/ ADJ automatique ; *[gesture]* machinal ◆ **the ~ choice** le choix naturel ◆ **he has no ~ right to ...** il n'a pas automatiquement le droit de ... ◆ **they have ~ right to French citizenship** ils ont automatiquement droit à la citoyenneté française
N *(= gun, washing machine)* automatique *m* ; *(= car)* voiture *f* à boîte *or* à transmission automatique ◆ **a Citroën ~** une Citroën à boîte *or* transmission automatique
COMP **automatic data processing** N *(Comput)* traitement *m* automatique de l'information
automatic exposure N *(Phot)* exposition *f* automatique
automatic pilot N pilote *m* automatique ◆ **on ~ pilot** *(in plane)* en pilotage *or* sur pilote automatique ◆ **to work/drive on ~ pilot** * *(fig)* travailler/conduire au radar *
automatic transmission N *(in car)* transmission *f* automatique
automatic vending machine N distributeur *m* automatique

automatically /ˌɔːtəˈmætɪkəlɪ/ ADV automatiquement ; *(without thinking)* machinalement ◆ **~ void** *(Jur)* nul de plein droit

automation /ˌɔːtəˈmeɪʃən/ N *(= technique, system, action)* automatisation *f* ; *(= state of being automated)* automation *f* ◆ **industrial ~** productique *f*

automaton /ɔːˈtɒmətən/ N (pl **automatons** *or* **automata**) automate *m*

automobile /ˈɔːtəməbiːl/ N *(esp US)* automobile *f*, auto *f*

automobilia /ˌɔːtəməʊˈbiːlɪə/ NPL accessoires *mpl* auto

automotive /ˌɔːtəˈməʊtɪv/ ADJ 1 *[industry, design]* (de l')automobile 2 *(= self-propelled)* automoteur(-trice *f*)

autonomous /ɔːˈtɒnəməs/ ADJ autonome

autonomously /ɔːˈtɒnəməslɪ/ ADV de façon autonome

autonomy /ɔːˈtɒnəmɪ/ N autonomie *f*

autonymous /ɔːˈtɒnɪməs/ ADJ autonyme

autopilot /ˈɔːtəʊpaɪlət/ N pilote *m* automatique ◆ **on ~** *(lit)* sur pilote automatique ◆ **to be on ~** * *(fig)* marcher au radar *

autopsy /ˈɔːtɒpsɪ/ N autopsie *f*

autoreverse /ˌɔːtəʊrɪˈvɜːs/ N autoreverse *m*, lecture *f* arrière automatique ◆ **a cassette deck with ~** une platine à cassettes (avec) autoreverse

autosuggestion /ˈɔːtəʊsəˈdʒestʃən/ N autosuggestion *f*

autoteller /ˈɔːtəʊteləʳ/ N distributeur *m* automatique de billets

autotimer /ˈɔːtəʊtaɪməʳ/ N *[of oven]* programmateur *m* (de four)

autumn /ˈɔːtəm/ N automne *m* ◆ **in ~** en automne ◆ **he's in the ~ of his life** il est à l'automne de sa vie
COMP d'automne, automnal *(liter)*
autumn leaves NPL *(dead)* feuilles *fpl* mortes ; *(on tree)* feuilles *fpl* d'automne

autumnal /ɔːˈtʌmnəl/ ADJ d'automne, automnal *(liter)*

auxiliary /ɔːgˈzɪlɪərɪ/ ADJ subsidiaire *(to* à) auxiliaire N 1 auxiliaire *mf* ◆ **nursing ~** infirmier *m*, -ière *f* auxiliaire, aide-soignant(e) *m(f)* ◆ **auxiliaries** *(Mil)* auxiliaires *mpl* 2 *(Gram)* (verbe *m*) auxiliaire *m*
COMP **auxiliary nurse** N aide-soignant(e) *m(f)*
auxiliary police N *(US)* corps *m* de policiers auxiliaires volontaires
auxiliary staff N *(Brit Scol)* personnel *m* auxiliaire non enseignant
auxiliary tank N *[of plane]* réservoir *m* supplémentaire
auxiliary verb N verbe *m* auxiliaire

AV /eɪˈviː/ abbrev of **audiovisual**

Av. N (abbrev of **Avenue**) av.

a.v., A/V abbrev of **ad valorem**

avail /əˈveɪl/ VT ◆ **to ~ o.s. of** *[+ opportunity]* saisir, profiter de ; *[+ right]* user de, valoir de ; *[+ service]* utiliser ◆ **to ~ o.s. of the rules of jurisdiction** *(Jur)* invoquer les règles de compétence VI († *liter*) être efficace, servir ◆ **nought ~ed** rien n'y faisait ◆ **it ~ed him nothing** cela ne lui a servi à rien N ◆ **to no ~** sans résultat, en vain ◆ **your advice was of no ~** vos conseils n'ont eu aucun effet ◆ **it is of no ~ to complain** il ne sert à rien de protester ◆ **to little ~** sans grand effet *or* résultat ◆ **it is of** *or* **to little ~** cela ne sert pas à grand-chose

availability /əˌveɪləˈbɪlɪtɪ/ N 1 *[of material, people]* disponibilité *f* 2 *(US = validity)* validité *f*

available /əˈveɪləbl/ LANGUAGE IN USE 19.3 ADJ 1 *(= obtainable) [information, product, funding, accommodation]* disponible ◆ **he is not ~ at the moment** il n'est pas disponible pour l'instant ◆ **television isn't yet ~ here** on ne dispose pas encore de la télévision ici ◆ **new treatments are becoming ~** de nouveaux traitements font leur apparition ◆ **to be ~ for sb** être à la disposition de qn ◆ **the MP was not ~ for comment yesterday** *(Press)* hier, le député ne s'est prêté à aucune déclaration ◆ **~ for hire** à louer ◆ **money ~ for spending** argent *m* disponible ◆ **a car park is ~ for the use of customers** un parking est à la disposition des clients ◆ **the guide is ~ from all good bookshops** on peut trouver ce guide dans toutes les bonnes librairies ◆ **this service is ~ in stores everywhere** tous les magasins proposent ce service ◆ **tickets are ~ from the box office** on peut se procurer des billets auprès du bureau de location ◆ **to make sth ~** rendre qch accessible ◆ **to make sth ~ to sb** mettre qch à la disposition de qn ◆ **to make o.s. ~** se rendre disponible ◆ **to use every ~ means to do sth** utiliser tous les moyens disponibles pour faire qch ◆ **the next ~ flight** le prochain vol ◆ **"other sizes/colours available"** *(Comm)* "existe également en d'autres tailles/couleurs" ◆ **in the time ~** dans le temps disponible ◆ **information ~ to patients** les informations *fpl* à la disposition des patients ◆ **benefits ~ to employees** les avantages *mpl* dont peuvent bénéficier les employés

2 *(= unattached) (person)* libre ; *(sexually)* disponible *(sexuellement)*

3 *(US Pol pej) [candidate]* honnête *before n*

avalanche /ˈævəlɑːnʃ/ **N** *(lit, fig)* avalanche *f* **VI** tomber en avalanche

COMP avalanche precautions NPL mesures *fpl* de sécurité anti-avalanche

avalanche warning N alerte *f* aux avalanches ; *(on sign)* "attention (aux) avalanches"

avant-garde /ˈævɒŋgɑːd/ **N** *(gen, Mil)* avant-garde *f* **COMP** *[dress, style]* d'avant-garde

avarice /ˈævərɪs/ **N** avarice *f*, cupidité *f*

avaricious /ˌævəˈrɪʃəs/ **ADJ** avare, cupide *(liter)*

avatar /ˈævətɑːʳ/ **N** 1 *(Rel)* avatar *m* 2 *(fig = manifestation)* incarnation *f* 3 *(Comput)* avatar *m*

avdp N abbrev of **avoirdupois**

Ave N (abbrev of **Avenue**) av.

Ave Maria /ˌɑːveɪməˈrɪə/ **N** Ave Maria *m inv*

avenge /əˈvendʒ/ **VT** *[+ person, thing]* venger ◆ **to ~ o.s.** se venger, prendre sa revanche *(on sb* sur qn)

avenger /əˈvendʒəʳ/ **N** vengeur *m*, -eresse *f*

avenging /əˈvendʒɪŋ/ **ADJ** vengeur (-eresse *f*) *(liter)*

avenue /ˈævənjuː/ **N** *(= private road)* avenue *f* ; *(= wide road in town)* avenue *f*, boulevard *m* ; *(fig)* route *f*

aver /əˈvɜːʳ/ **VT** affirmer, déclarer

average /ˈævərɪdʒ/ **N** 1 moyenne *f* ◆ **on ~** en moyenne ◆ **a rough ~** une moyenne approximative ◆ **to take an ~ of results** prendre la moyenne des résultats ◆ **above/below ~** au-dessus/en-dessous de la moyenne ◆ **to do an ~ of 70km/h** rouler à *or* faire une moyenne de 70 km/h, faire du 70 de moyenne*

2 *(Marine Insurance)* avarie *f* ◆ **to adjust the ~** répartir les avaries

ADJ *[age, wage, price]* moyen ◆ **the ~ American car owner drives 10,000 miles per year** l'automobiliste américain moyen fait 16 000 kilomètres par an ◆ **an ~ thirteen-year-old child could understand it** un enfant *or* n'importe quel enfant de treize ans comprendrait cela ◆ **$2 for a beer is ~** il faut compter en moyenne 2 dollars pour une bière ◆ **it was an ~ piece of work** c'était un travail moyen ◆ **I was only ~ academically** sur le plan des études, je ne dépassais pas la moyenne

VT 1 *(= find the average of)* établir *or* faire la moyenne de

2 *(= reach an average of)* atteindre la moyenne de ◆ **we ~ eight hours' work a day** nous travaillons en moyenne huit heures par jour ◆ **the sales ~ 200 copies a month** la vente moyenne est de 200 exemplaires par mois ◆ **we ~d 50km/h the whole way** nous avons fait 50 km/h de moyenne sur ce trajet

▸ **average out VI** ◆ **it'll average out in the end** en fin de compte ça va s'égaliser ◆ **our working hours ~ out at eight per day** nous travaillons en moyenne huit heures par jour

VT SEP faire la moyenne de

averagely /ˈævərɪdʒlɪ/ **ADV** moyennement

averager /ˈævərɪdʒəʳ/ **N** *(Marine Insurance)* répartiteur *m* d'avaries, dispatcheur *m*

averse /əˈvɜːs/ **ADJ** ennemi (*to* de) peu disposé (*to* à) ; ◆ **to be ~ to doing sth** répugner à faire qch ◆ **he is ~ to getting up early** il déteste se lever tôt ◆ **I am not ~ to an occasional drink** je n'ai rien contre un petit verre de temps à autre

aversion /əˈvɜːʃən/ **N** 1 *(NonC = strong dislike)* aversion *f* ◆ **he has an ~ to spiders** il a *or* éprouve de l'aversion pour les araignées ◆ **he has a strong ~ to work** il a horreur de travailler ◆ **I have an ~ to garlic** une chose que je déteste, c'est l'ail ◆ **he has a strong ~ to me** il ne peut pas me souffrir ◆ **I took an ~ to it** je me suis mis à détester cela ◆ **I have an ~ to him** il m'est antipathique 2 *(= object of aversion)* objet *m* d'aversion ◆ **my greatest ~ is ...** ce que je déteste le plus, c'est ... ; → **pet**[1]

avert /əˈvɜːt/ **VT** *[+ danger, accident]* prévenir, éviter ; *[+ blow]* détourner, parer ; *[+ suspicion]* écarter ; *[+ one's eyes, one's thoughts]* détourner *(from* de)

avian /ˈeɪvɪən/ **ADJ** aviaire

aviary /ˈeɪvɪərɪ/ **N** volière *f*

aviation /ˌeɪvɪˈeɪʃən/ **N** aviation *f*

COMP aviation fuel N kérosène *m*

aviation industry N aéronautique *f*

aviator /ˈeɪvɪeɪtəʳ/ **N** aviateur *m*, -trice *f* **COMP aviator glasses NPL** lunettes *fpl* sport

avid /ˈævɪd/ **ADJ** 1 *(= keen) [reader, collector, viewer]* passionné ; *[supporter, fan]* fervent 2 *(= desirous)* ◆ **~ for sth** avide de qch

avidity /əˈvɪdɪtɪ/ **N** avidité *f (for* de)

avidly /ˈævɪdlɪ/ **ADV** avidement, avec avidité

avionics /ˌeɪvɪˈɒnɪks/ **N** *(NonC) (= science)* avionique *f* ; *(pl = circuitry)* avionique *f*

avocado /ˌævəˈkɑːdəʊ/ **N** (also **avocado pear** *Brit*) avocat *m* ; *(= tree)* avocatier *m*

avocation /ˌævəʊˈkeɪʃən/ **N** 1 *(= employment)* métier *m*, profession *f* 2 *(= minor occupation)* passe-temps *m inv* favori, violon *m* d'Ingres

avocet /ˈævəset/ **N** avocette *f*

avoid /əˈvɔɪd/ **VT** *[+ person, obstacle]* éviter ; *[+ danger]* échapper à, éviter ◆ **to ~ tax** *(legally)* se soustraire à l'impôt ; *(illegally)* frauder le fisc ◆ **to ~ doing sth** éviter de faire qch ◆ **~ being seen** évitez qu'on ne vous voie ◆ **to ~ sb's eye** fuir le regard de qn ◆ **to ~ notice** échapper aux regards ◆ **I can't ~ going now** je ne peux plus faire autrement que d'y aller, je ne peux plus me dispenser d'y aller ◆ **this way we ~ London** en passant par ici nous évitons Londres ◆ **it is to be ~ed like the plague** il faut fuir cela comme la peste ; → **plague**

avoidable /əˈvɔɪdəbl/ **ADJ** évitable

avoidance /əˈvɔɪdəns/ **N** ◆ **his ~ of me** le soin qu'il met à m'éviter ◆ **his ~ of his duty** ses manquements *mpl* au devoir ◆ **tax ~** évasion *f* fiscale

avoirdupois /ˌævədəˈpɔɪz/ **N** 1 *(lit)* système *m* des poids commerciaux *(système britannique des poids et mesures)* 2 *(* = overweight)* embonpoint *m* **COMP** *conforme aux poids et mesures officiellement établis* **avoirdupois pound N** livre *f* (453,6 grammes)

avow /əˈvaʊ/ **VT** *(frm = proclaim)* déclarer, affirmer ◆ **to ~ o.s. defeated** s'avouer *or* se déclarer battu

avowal /əˈvaʊəl/ **N** *(frm)* aveu *m*

avowed /əˈvaʊd/ **ADJ** *(frm) [enemy, supporter, atheist]* déclaré ; *[aim, intention, purpose]* avoué

avowedly /əˈvaʊɪdlɪ/ **ADV** *(frm)* de son propre aveu

avuncular /əˈvʌŋkjʊləʳ/ **ADJ** avunculaire

AWACS /ˈeɪwæks/ **N** (abbrev of **Airborne Warning and Control System**) ◆ **~ plane** (avion *m*) AWACS *m*

await /əˈweɪt/ **VT** 1 *(= wait for) [+ object, event]* attendre, être dans l'attente de ; *[+ person]* attendre ◆ **parcels ~ing delivery** colis *mpl* en souffrance ◆ **long-~ed event** événement *m* longtemps attendu 2 *(= be in store for)* être réservé à, attendre ◆ **the fate that ~s us** le sort qui nous attend *or* qui nous est réservé

awake /əˈweɪk/ (pret **awoke** *or* **awaked**, ptp **awoken** *or* **awaked**) **VI** s'éveiller, se réveiller ◆ **to ~ from sleep** sortir du sommeil, s'éveiller ◆ **to ~ to one's responsibilities** prendre conscience de ses responsabilités ◆ **to ~ to the fact that ...** s'apercevoir du fait que ... ◆ **to ~ from one's illusions** revenir de ses illusions

VT 1 *(= wake) [+ person]* éveiller, réveiller

2 *(fig = arouse) [+ suspicion]* éveiller ; *[+ hope, curiosity]* éveiller, faire naître ; *[+ memories]* réveiller

ADJ 1 *(= not asleep) (before sleep)* éveillé ; *(after sleep)* réveillé ◆ **are you ~?** est-ce que tu dors ? ◆ **he was instantly ~** il s'est réveillé immédiatement ◆ **to keep sb ~** empêcher qn de dormir ◆ **to lie ~ all night** ne pas fermer l'œil de la nuit ◆ **she lies ~ at night worrying about it** ça la tracasse tellement qu'elle n'en dort plus ◆ **to shake sb ~** secouer qn pour le réveiller ◆ **to stay** *or* **keep ~** veiller ◆ **I couldn't stay** *or* **keep ~** je n'arrivais pas à rester éveillé ◆ **I don't stay ~ at night worrying about that** cela ne m'inquiète pas au point de m'empêcher de dormir ; → **wide**

2 *(= aware)* ◆ **to be ~ to sth** être conscient de qch

awaked † /əˈweɪkt/ **VB** pt, ptp of **awake**

awaken /əˈweɪkən/ **VTI** ⇒ **awake**

awakening /əˈweɪknɪŋ/ **N** *(lit, fig)* réveil *m* ◆ **a rude ~** un réveil brutal **ADJ** *[interest, passion]* naissant

award /əˈwɔːd/ **VT** *[+ prize etc]* décerner, attribuer (*to* à) ; *[+ sum of money]* allouer, attribuer (*to* à) ; *[+ dignity, honour]* conférer (*to* à) ; *[+ damages]* accorder (*to* à) **N** 1 *(= prize)* prix *m* ; *(for bravery etc)* récompense *f*, décoration *f* ; *(= scholarship)* bourse *f* 2 *(Jur = judgement)* décision *f*, sentence *f* arbitrale ; *(= sum of money)* montant *m* (*or* dommages-intérêts *mpl*) accordé(s) par le juge

COMP award ceremony, awards ceremony N cérémonie *f* de remise des prix

award-winner N *(= person)* lauréat(e) *m(f)* ; *(= work)* livre *m* (*or* film *m etc*) primé

award-winning ADJ *[person, book, film]* primé

aware /əˈweəʳ/ **ADJ** 1 *(= conscious)* conscient (*of* de) ; *(= informed)* au courant, averti (*of* de) ; ◆ **to become ~ of sth/that sth is happening** prendre conscience *or* se rendre compte de qch/que qch se passe ◆ **to be ~ of sth** être conscient de qch, avoir conscience de qch ◆ **to be ~ that something is happening** être conscient *or* avoir conscience que quelque chose se passe ◆ **I am quite ~ of it** je ne l'ignore pas, j'en ai bien conscience ◆ **as far as I am ~** autant que je sache ◆ **not that I am ~ of** pas que je sache ◆ **the management need to be made ~ of the problem** il faut que la direction prenne conscience de ce problème 2 *(= knowledgeable)* informé, avisé ◆ **politically ~** politisé ◆ **socially ~** au courant des problèmes sociaux

awareness /əˈweənɪs/ **N** *(NonC)* conscience *f* (*of* de) **COMP awareness programme N** programme *m* de sensibilisation

awash /əˈwɒʃ/ **ADJ** *(Naut)* à fleur d'eau, qui affleure ; *(= flooded)* inondé (*with* de)

away /əˈweɪ/

When **away** is an element in a phrasal verb, eg **boil away, die away, gabble away, get away**, look up the verb.

ADV 1 *(= to or at a distance)* au loin, loin ◆ **far ~** au loin, très loin ◆ **the lake is 3km ~** le lac est à 3 km (de distance) *or* à une distance de 3 km ◆ **~ back in the distance** très loin derrière (dans le lointain) ◆ **~ back in prehistoric times** dans les temps reculés de la préhistoire ◆ **~ back in 1600** il y a bien longtemps en 1600 ◆ **~ back in the 40s** il y a longtemps déjà dans les années 40 ◆ **keep the child ~ from the fire** tenez l'enfant loin *or* éloigné du feu ◆ **~ over there** là-bas au loin *or* dans le lointain, loin là-bas

2 *(= absent)* **he's ~ today** *(gen)* il est absent *or* il n'est pas là aujourd'hui ; *[businessman etc]* il est en déplacement aujourd'hui ◆ **he is ~ in London** il est (parti) à Londres ◆ **when I have to be ~** lorsque je dois m'absenter ◆ **she was ~ before I could speak** elle était partie avant que j'aie pu parler ◆ **now she's ~ with the idea that ...** * la voilà partie avec l'idée que ... ◆ **~!** hors d'ici ! ◆ **~ with you!** *(= go away)* allez-vous-en ! ◆ **get ~!***, **~ with you!*** *(disbelief)* allons ! ne dis pas de bêtises ; → **far, right, brush away, go away**

3 *(Sport)* **they're playing ~ this week** ils jouent à l'extérieur cette semaine ◆ **Chelsea are ~ to Everton on Saturday** Chelsea se déplace à Everton samedi

4 *(as intensifier)* ◆ **to be working ~** être en train de travailler ◆ **can I ask you something? – ask ~!** je peux te poser une question ? – oui, bien sûr !

COMP **away-day** N *(for training)* journée *f* de formation
away defeat N *(Sport)* défaite *f* à l'extérieur
away game, away match N *(Sport)* match *m* à l'extérieur
away team N *(Sport)* (équipe *f* des) visiteurs *mpl*, équipe *f* jouant à l'extérieur
away win N *(Sport)* victoire *f* à l'extérieur

awe /ɔː/ N *(fearful)* respect *m* mêlé de crainte ; *(admiring)* respect *m* mêlé d'admiration ◆ **to be** *or* **stand in ~ of sb** être intimidé par qn, être rempli du plus grand respect pour qn VT inspirer un respect mêlé de crainte à ◆ **in an ~d voice** d'une voix (à la fois) respectueuse et intimidée

COMP **awe-inspiring** ADJ ⇒ **awesome**
awe-struck ADJ *(= frightened)* frappé de terreur ; *(= astounded)* stupéfait

awesome /ˈɔːsəm/ ADJ *(= impressive)* impressionnant, imposant ; *(= frightening)* terrifiant ; *(esp US * = excellent)* super*, génial*

awesomely /ˈɔːsəmlɪ/ ADV *[talented, complex]* terriblement ◆ **the streets were ~ quiet** il régnait un calme impressionnant dans les rues

awful /ˈɔːfəl/ ADJ 1 affreux, terrible, atroce ◆ **he's an ~ bore** il est assommant* ◆ **what ~ weather!** quel temps affreux ! *or* de chien !* ◆ **he's got an ~ cheek!** il a un de ces culots !* *or* un fameux culot !* ◆ **how ~!** comme c'est affreux !, quelle chose affreuse ! ◆ **it was just ~** c'était vraiment affreux ◆ **his English is ~** son anglais est atroce, il parle anglais comme une vache espagnole ◆ **I feel ~** *(= ill)* je me sens vraiment mal ◆ **an ~ lot of time/money** un temps/un argent fou ◆ **there's an ~ lot of people/cars/cream** *etc* il y a énormément de monde/voitures/crème *etc* ◆ **I have an ~ lot of things to do** j'ai énormément de *or* un tas* de choses à faire ◆ **he drinks an ~ lot** il boit énormément *or* comme un trou*

2 *(= dreadful) [news, crime, accident, realization]* épouvantable, terrifiant

awfully /ˈɔːflɪ/ ADV *[good, nice, clever]* extrêmement, vraiment ; *[bad, difficult, hot, late]* terriblement ◆ **an ~ big house** une énorme maison ◆ **I'm ~ glad** je suis absolument ravi ◆ **I'm ~ sorry** je suis absolument désolé ◆ **I'm not ~ sure** je n'en suis pas vraiment sûr ◆ **I don't know her ~ well** je ne la connais pas vraiment bien *or* très bien ◆ **thanks ~** † merci infiniment ◆ **would you mind ~ (if ...)?** † est-ce que cela vous ennuierait (si ...) ?

awfulness /ˈɔːfʊlnɪs/ N horreur *f* ◆ **the ~ of it** ce qu'il y a d'affreux *or* de terrible dans cette affaire, ce que cette affaire a d'affreux *or* de terrible

awhile /əˈwaɪl/ ADV *(US)* un instant, un moment ◆ **wait ~** attendez un peu ◆ **not yet ~** pas de sitôt

awkward /ˈɔːkwəd/ ADJ 1 *(= inconvenient, difficult) [question, job, task]* difficile ; *[problem, situation, stage]* délicat ◆ **he's at an ~ age** il est à l'âge ingrat ◆ **it's ~ for me** cela m'est assez difficile, cela ne m'est pas très facile ◆ **tomorrow's ~ (for me); how about Thursday?** demain n'est pas très commode (pour moi) – que pensez-vous de jeudi ? ◆ **you've come at an ~ moment** vous tombez mal ◆ **to put sb in an ~ position** mettre qn dans une position délicate ◆ **to make things ~ for sb** rendre les choses difficiles pour qn ◆ **at an ~ time for sb** au mauvais moment pour qn ◆ **it would be ~ to postpone my trip again** il me serait difficile de reporter à nouveau mon voyage

2 *(= embarrassing) [silence]* gêné ◆ **there was an ~ moment when ...** il y a eu un moment de gêne quand ... ; → **1** ◆ **it's all a bit ~** tout ceci est un peu ennuyeux *or* gênant

3 *(= ill at ease)* ◆ **to be** *or* **feel ~ (with sb)** être mal à l'aise (avec qn) ◆ **I felt ~ about his hand on my knee** ça me gênait de sentir sa main sur mon genou ◆ **I felt ~ about touching him** ça me gênait de le toucher

4 *(= uncooperative) [person]* difficile, peu commode ◆ **he's being ~ (about it)** il fait des difficultés (à ce sujet) ◆ **to be ~ about doing sth** faire des difficultés pour faire qch ; → **customer**

5 *(= cumbersome) [object]* encombrant ; *[shape]* encombrant, malcommode ◆ **~ to carry/use** difficile à porter/utiliser

6 *(= clumsy) [person]* gauche, maladroit ; *[movement, gesture, phrase]* maladroit ; *[style]* gauche, emprunté ; *[position]* inconfortable

awkwardly /ˈɔːkwədlɪ/ ADV 1 *(= clumsily) [move, walk, express o.s., translate]* maladroitement, de façon maladroite ; *[fall]* mal ; *[lie]* dans une position inconfortable ; *[hang]* bizarrement ◆ **~ placed** mal placé 2 *(= embarrassingly)* ◆ **an ~ long silence** un long silence gêné 3 *(= embarrassedly) [say, behave, shake hands]* d'un air gêné *or* embarrassé

awkwardness /ˈɔːkwədnɪs/ N 1 *(= clumsiness)* gaucherie *f*, maladresse *f* 2 *[of situation]* côté *m* gênant *or* embarrassant 3 *(= discomfort)* embarras *m*, gêne *f*

awl /ɔːl/ N alêne *f*, poinçon *m*

awning /ˈɔːnɪŋ/ N *[of boat]* taud *m* *or* taude *f*, tente *f* ; *[of shop]* banne *f*, store *m* ; *[of hotel door]* marquise *f* ; *[of tent]* auvent *m* ; *(in garden)* vélum *m*

awoke /əˈwəʊk/ VB pt of **awake**

awoken /əˈwəʊkən/ VB ptp of **awake**

AWOL /ˈeɪwɒl/ *(Mil)* (abbrev of **absent without leave**) ◆ **to go ~** * *(fig)* disparaître de la circulation*

awry /əˈraɪ/ ADJ, ADV 1 *(= askew)* de travers, de guingois* 2 *(= wrong)* de travers ◆ **to go ~** *[plan]* s'en aller à vau-l'eau ; *[undertaking]* mal tourner

axe, ax *(US)* /æks/ N hache *f* ; *(fig: in expenditure etc)* coupe *f* claire *or* sombre ; *(Mus * = guitar)* gratte* *f* ◆ **to have an ~ to grind** prêcher pour son saint *(fig)* ◆ **I've no ~ to grind** ce n'est pas mon intérêt personnel que j'ai en vue, je ne prêche pas pour mon saint ◆ **when the ~ fell** *(fig)* quand le couperet est tombé ◆ **to get** *or* **be given the ~** *[employee]* être mis à la porte ; *[project]* être abandonné VT *[+ scheme, project]* annuler, abandonner ; *[+ jobs]* supprimer ; *[+ employees]* licencier ◆ **to ~ expenditure** réduire les dépenses, faire *or* opérer des coupes claires dans le budget COMP **axe-murderer** N assassin *m (qui tue ses victimes à la hache)*

axeman * /ˈæksmən/ N (pl **-men**) *(Mus = guitarist)* guitariste *m* ◆ **(mad) ~** tueur *m* fou *(qui se sert d'une hache)*

axes /ˈæksiːz/ NPL of **axis**

axial /ˈæksɪəl/ ADJ axial

axiom /ˈæksɪəm/ N axiome *m*

axiomatic /ˌæksɪəʊˈmætɪk/ ADJ axiomatique ; *(= clear)* évident

axis /ˈæksɪs/ N (pl **axes**) axe *m* ◆ **the Axis (Powers)** *(Hist)* les puissances *fpl* de l'Axe

axle /ˈæksl/ N *[of wheel]* axe *m* ; *[of car]* (also **axle-tree**) essieu *m* ◆ **front/rear ~** essieu *m* avant/arrière

COMP **axle-box** N *(Rail)* boîte *f* d'essieu
axle cap N chapeau *m* de roue *or* de moyeu
axle grease N graisse *f* à essieux
axle-pin N esse *f*, clavette *f* d'essieu

ay /aɪ/ N, PARTICLE ⇒ **aye**[1]

ayatollah /ˌaɪəˈtɒlə/ N ayatollah *m*

aye[1] /aɪ/ PARTICLE *(esp Scot, N Engl)* oui ◆ **~, ~ sir!** *(Naut)* oui, commandant *(or* capitaine *etc)* N oui *m* ◆ **the ~s and noes** *(in voting)* les voix *fpl* pour et contre ◆ **90 ~s and 2 noes** 90 pour et 2 contre ◆ **the ~s have it** les oui l'emportent

aye[2] † /eɪ/ ADV *(Scot)* toujours

AYH /ˌeɪwaɪˈeɪtʃ/ N *(US)* abbrev of **American Youth Hostels**

Ayurvedic /ˌaːjʊˈveɪdɪk, ˌaːjʊˈviːdɪk/ ADJ ayurvédique

AZ abbrev of **Arizona**

azalea /əˈzeɪlɪə/ N azalée *f*

Azerbaijan /ˌæzəbaɪˈdʒɑːn/ N Azerbaïdjan *m*

Azerbaijani /ˌæzəbaɪˈdʒɑːnɪ/ ADJ azerbaïdjanais N 1 Azerbaïdjanais(e) *m(f)* 2 *(= language)* Azerbaïdjanais *m*

Azeri /əˈzɛərɪ/ ADJ azéri N Azéri(e) *m(f)*

AZERTY, azerty /əˈzɜːtɪ/ ADJ ◆ **~ keyboard** clavier *m* AZERTY

azimuth /ˈæzɪməθ/ N azimut *m*

Azores /əˈzɔːz/ NPL Açores *fpl*

AZT /ˌeɪzedˈtiː/ N (abbrev of **azidothymidine**) AZT *f*

Aztec /ˈæztek/ N Aztèque *mf* ADJ aztèque

azure /ˈeɪʒəʳ/ N azur *m*

Bb

B, b /biː/ **N** [1] (*= letter*) B, b *m* ◆ **B for Baker** ≃ B comme Berthe ◆ **number 7b** (*in house numbers*) numéro *m* 7 ter [2] (*Mus*) si *m* ; → **key** [3] (*Scol*) bien, ≃ 14 sur 20 [4] (*Cine*) ◆ **B movie** *or* **picture** † *or* **film** film *m* de série B [5] [*of record*] ◆ **B side** face *f* B **COMP** **B-girl*** **N** (*US*) entraîneuse *f* (de bar)

B-road **N** (*Brit*) route *f* secondaire, route *f* départementale ; → ROADS

B2B /ˌbiːtuːˈbiː/ **ADJ** (*Comm*) (abbrev of **business-to-business**) b2b

B2C /ˌbiːtuːˈsiː/ **ADJ** (*Comm*) (abbrev of **business-to-consumer**) b2c

BA /biːˈeɪ/ **N** (*Univ*) (abbrev of **Bachelor of Arts**) ◆ **to have a ~ in French** avoir une licence de français ; → **bachelor** ; → DEGREE

BAA /ˌbiːeɪˈeɪ/ **N** (abbrev of **British Airports Authority**) → **British**

baa /bɑː/ **N** bêlement *m* ◆ **~!** bé, bê ! **VI** bêler **COMP** **baa-lamb** **N** (*baby talk*) petit agneau *m*

babble /ˈbæbl/ **N** [*of baby*] babil *m*, babillage *m* ; [*of stream*] gazouillement *m* ◆ **a ~ of voices** un brouhaha de voix **VI** [1] [*baby*] gazouiller, babiller ; [*stream*] jaser, gazouiller [2] (*= gabble*: also **babble away, babble on**) bredouiller, bafouiller* ◆ **he was babbling about his holidays** il nous débitait des histoires à n'en plus finir sur ses vacances ◆ **he was babbling about saving the rainforests** il nous débitait des banalités sur la sauvegarde des forêts tropicales **VT** (also **babble out**) bredouiller ◆ **"don't hurt me, don't hurt me!" he ~d** "ne me faites pas de mal, ne me faites pas de mal !" bredouilla-t-il ◆ **he was just babbling nonsense** il débitait des inepties

babbler /ˈbæbləʳ/ **N** bavard(e) *m(f)*

babbling /ˈbæblɪŋ/ **ADJ** [*person, baby, stream*] babillard **N** ⇒ **babble noun**

babe /beɪb/ **N** [1] (*liter*) bébé *m*, enfant *mf* en bas âge ◆ **~ in arms** enfant *mf* au berceau *or* qui vient de naître [2] (*esp US* * *= attractive woman*) jolie pépée* *f* ◆ **come on ~!** viens ma belle ! [3] (* *= inexperienced person*) innocent(e) *m(f)* ◆ **~s in the wood(s)** des jeunes gens naïfs perdus dans un monde impitoyable

babel /ˈbeɪbəl/ **N** (*= noise*) brouhaha *m* ; (*= confusion*) tohu-bohu *m* ; → **tower**

baboon /bəˈbuːn/ **N** babouin *m*

baby /ˈbeɪbɪ/ **N** [1] bébé *m* ◆ **she's just had a ~** elle vient d'avoir un bébé ◆ **the ~ of the family** le petit dernier *or* la petite dernière, le benjamin *or* la benjamine ◆ **I've known him since he was a ~** je l'ai connu tout petit *or* tout bébé ◆ **a new ~** un(e) nouveau-né(e) *m(f)* ◆ **don't be such a ~!** (*pej*) ne fais pas l'enfant ! ◆ **he was left holding the ~*** on lui a refilé le bébé* ◆ **to throw out the ~ with the bathwater** jeter le bébé avec l'eau du bain

[2] (*US* ‡) (*= girlfriend*) copine* *f*, nana‡ *f* ; (*= man*) mec‡ *m* ◆ **come on ~!** (*to woman*) viens ma belle ! ; (*to man*) viens mon gars !*

[3] (* *= special responsibility*) bébé *m* ◆ **the new system is his ~** le nouveau système est son bébé ◆ **that's not my ~** je n'ai rien à voir là-dedans

[4] (*esp US* ‡ *= thing*) petite merveille *f*

ADJ ◆ **~ vegetables/carrots/sweetcorn** mini-légumes *mpl*/-carottes *fpl*/-épis *mpl* de maïs

VT * [+ *person*] dorloter, cajoler

COMP [*clothes etc*] de bébé ; [*rabbit etc*] bébé

baby-batterer **N** bourreau *m* d'enfants

baby-battering **N** sévices *mpl* à enfant(s)

baby-blue* **ADJ** [*eyes*] bleu (*plein d'innocence*) ; [*ribbon, car*] bleu clair *inv*

baby blues* **NPL**

[1] (*= depression*) bébé blues* *m* [2] (*= eyes*) yeux *mpl* bleus (*pleins d'innocence*)

baby boom **N** baby-boom *m*

baby boomer **N** enfant *mf* du baby-boom

Baby-bouncer ® **N** Baby Bouncer ® *m*

baby boy **N** petit garçon *m*

baby brother **N** petit frère *m*

baby buggy ® **N** (*Brit*) poussette *f*

baby carriage **N** (*US*) voiture *f* d'enfant, landau *m*

baby-doll pyjamas **NPL** baby doll *m*

baby elephant **N** éléphanteau *m*

baby face **N** visage *m* poupin

baby-faced **ADJ** au visage poupin

baby food(s) **N(PL)** aliments *mpl* pour bébés

baby girl **N** petite fille *f*

baby grand **N** (also **baby grand piano**) (piano *m*) demi-queue *m*

Baby-gro ® **N** grenouillère *f*

baby linen **N** layette *f*

baby-minder **N** nourrice *f* (*qui s'occupe des enfants pendant que les parents travaillent*)

baby-scales **NPL** pèse-bébé *m*

baby seat **N** siège *m* pour bébés

baby sister **N** petite sœur *f*

baby-sit **VI** faire du baby-sitting

baby-sitter **N** baby-sitter *mf*

baby-sitting **N** garde *f* d'enfants, baby-sitting *m* ◆ **to go ~-sitting** faire du baby-sitting

baby snatcher **N** ravisseur *m*, -euse *f* d'enfant ◆ **he/she is a ~ snatcher!** * (*fig*) il/elle les prend au berceau !*

baby talk **N** langage *m* enfantin *or* de bébé

baby tooth* **N** (pl **baby teeth**) dent *f* de lait

baby-walker **N** trotteur *m*

baby wipe **N** lingette *f* (*pour bébé*)

babyhood /ˈbeɪbɪhʊd/ **N** petite enfance *f*

babyish /ˈbeɪbɪɪʃ/ **ADJ** puéril, enfantin

Babylon /ˈbæbɪlən/ **N** (*Geog, fig*) Babylone

Babylonian /ˌbæbɪˈləʊnɪən/ **ADJ** babylonien **N** Babylonien(ne) *m(f)*

baccalaureate /ˌbækəˈlɔːrɪɪt/ **N** licence *f*

baccara(t) /ˈbækərɑː/ **N** baccara *m*

bacchanal /ˈbækənæl/ **ADJ** bachique **N** (*= worshipper*) adorateur *m*, -trice *f* de Bacchus ; (*= reveller*) noceur* *m*, -euse* *f* ; (*= orgy*) orgie *f*

bacchanalia /ˌbækəˈneɪlɪə/ **N** (*= festival*) bacchanales *fpl* ; (*= orgy*) orgie *f*

bacchanalian /ˌbækəˈneɪlɪən/, **bacchic** /ˈbækɪk/ **ADJ** bachique

Bacchus /ˈbækəs/ **N** Bacchus *m*

baccy‡ /ˈbækɪ/ **N** (abbrev of **tobacco**) tabac *m*

bachelor /ˈbætʃələʳ/ **N** [1] (*= unmarried man*) célibataire *m* ; → **confirmed** [2] (*Univ*) **Bachelor of Arts/of Science/of Law** licencié(e) *m(f)* ès lettres/ès sciences/en droit ◆ **Bachelor of Education** licencié(e) *m(f)* en sciences de l'éducation ◆ **~'s degree** ≃ licence *f* ; → DEGREE [3] (*Hist*) bachelier *m* **ADJ** [*uncle, brother etc*] célibataire ; [*life, habits*] de célibataire **COMP** **bachelor flat** **N** garçonnière *f*, studio *m*

bachelor girl **N** célibataire *f*

bachelorhood /ˈbætʃələhʊd/ **N** (*gen*) vie *f* de garçon ; (*= celibacy*) célibat *m*

bacillary /bəˈsɪlərɪ/ **ADJ** bacillaire

bacillus /bəˈsɪləs/ **N** (pl **bacilli** /bəˈsɪlaɪ/) bacille *m*

back /bæk/

1 NOUN
2 ADJECTIVE
3 ADVERB
4 TRANSITIVE VERB
5 INTRANSITIVE VERB
6 COMPOUNDS
7 PHRASAL VERBS

1 - NOUN

[1] [of person, animal] dos *m* ◆ **I've got a bad ~** j'ai des problèmes de dos ◆ **to carry sb/sth on one's ~** porter qn/qch sur son dos ◆ **with one's ~ to the light** le dos à la lumière ◆ **to stand** *or* **sit with one's ~ to sb/sth** tourner le dos à qn/qch ◆ **~ to ~** (*lit, fig*) dos à dos ; see also **compounds** ◆ **to be on one's ~** (*lit*) être (étendu) sur le dos ; (* *= be ill*) être alité ◆ **behind sb's ~** (*also fig*) derrière le dos de qn ◆ **he went behind Mr Brown's ~ to the headmaster** il est allé voir le directeur derrière le dos de

M. Brown ◆ **as soon as he turns his ~, as soon as his ~ is turned** *(fig)* dès qu'il a le dos tourné ◆ **to fall on one's ~** tomber à la renverse *or* sur le dos ◆ **he stood with his ~ (up) against the wall** il était adossé au mur ◆ **I was glad to see the ~ of him** * j'étais content de le voir partir ◆ **to have one's ~ to the wall** *(lit)* être adossé au mur ; *(fig)* être le dos au mur, être acculé

◆ **to be on sb's back** * être sur le dos de qn ◆ **my boss is always on my ~** mon patron est toujours sur mon dos, j'ai sans arrêt mon patron sur le dos

◆ **to get off sb's back** * laisser qn tranquille, ficher la paix à qn * ◆ **get off my ~, will you?** laisse-moi donc tranquille à la fin !, fiche-moi la paix !

◆ **to get** *or* **put sb's back up** hérisser qn, horripiler qn ◆ **what gets my ~ up is the way he thinks he's always right** ce qui me hérisse *or* m'horripile chez lui, c'est qu'il croit qu'il a toujours raison

◆ **to live off the back of sb** exploiter qn ◆ **the rich have always lived off the ~s of the poor** les riches ont toujours exploité les pauvres

◆ **to put one's back into sth** mettre toute son énergie dans qch ◆ **put your ~ into it !*** allons, un peu de nerf !*

◆ **to turn one's back on sb/sth** *(lit, fig)* ◆ **he turned his ~ on us** il nous a tourné le dos ◆ **you can't just turn your ~ on your parents** ça ne se fait pas de tourner le dos à ses parents ◆ **he turned his ~ on the past** il a tourné la page

◆ **on the back of** *(= by means of)* en profitant de ◆ **they became immensely rich on the ~ of the property boom** ils ont fait fortune en profitant du boom immobilier

2 [of object] *[of photo, picture, dress, spoon, book]* dos *m* ; *[of chair]* dossier *m* ; *[of building]* arrière *m* ; *[of fabric]* envers *m*

◆ **at the back** *[of building]* à l'arrière, derrière ; *[of book]* à la fin ; *[of cupboard, hall, stage]* au fond ◆ **at the very ~** tout au fond ◆ **there's a car park at the ~** il y a un parking à l'arrière *or* derrière

◆ **at the back of** *[+ building]* derrière, à l'arrière de ; *[+ book]* à la fin de ; *[+ cupboard, hall, stage]* au fond de ◆ **the flour's at the ~ of the cupboard** la farine est au fond du placard ◆ **he's at the ~ of all this trouble** c'est lui qui est derrière tous ces problèmes ◆ **ambition is at the ~ of this** c'est l'ambition qui est à l'origine de tout cela ; → **beyond, mind**

◆ **in back** *(US) [of building, car]* à l'arrière, derrière ◆ **Chuck was in ~** Chuck était à l'arrière *or* derrière

◆ **in back of** *(US) [+ building, car]* à l'arrière de, derrière ◆ **in ~ of the house** à l'arrière de *or* derrière la maison

◆ **in the back** *[of car]* à l'arrière ◆ **to sit in the ~ of the car** être (assis) à l'arrière

◆ **out** *or* **round the back** * *(Brit)* derrière ◆ **the toilet's out** *or* **round the ~** les toilettes sont derrière

◆ **back to front** à l'envers, devant derrière ◆ **you've got it on ~ to front** tu l'as mis à l'envers *or* devant derrière

3 [of part of body] *[of head]* derrière *m* ; *[of hand]* dos *m*, revers *m* ◆ **the ~ of one's neck** la nuque ◆ **I know Paris like the ~ of my hand** je connais Paris comme ma poche

4 [Ftbl, Hockey *etc*] arrière *m* ◆ **right/left ~** arrière *m* droit/gauche

2 - ADJECTIVE

1 [= not front] *[wheel]* arrière *inv* ◆ **the ~ room** *[of house]* la pièce du fond ; *[of pub, restaurant]* l'arrière-salle *f*, la salle du fond ◆ **~ legs** *[of animal]* pattes *fpl* de derrière ; see also **compounds, backroom**

2 [= overdue] *[taxes]* arriéré ◆ **to owe ~ rent** devoir un arriéré de loyer

3 - ADVERB

When **back** is an element in a phrasal verb, eg **come back**, **go back**, **put back**, look up the verb.

1 [in space, time] ◆ **(stand) ~ !** reculez ! ◆ **stay well ~!** n'approchez pas ! ◆ **far ~** loin derrière ◆ **a week ~** * il y a une semaine ◆ **as far ~ as 1800** dès 1800, en 1800 déjà

When followed by a preposition, **back** is often not translated.

◆ **meanwhile, ~ in London ...** pendant ce temps-là, à Londres ... ◆ **it all started ~ in 1980** tout a commencé en 1980 ◆ **I saw her ~ in August** je l'ai vue en août ◆ **he little suspected how worried they were ~ at home** il était loin de se douter que sa famille s'inquiétait autant ◆ **the house stands ~ from the road** la maison est en retrait par rapport à la route

◆ **to go back and forth, to go back and forward** *[person]* faire des allées et venues ; *[phone calls, e-mails, letters]* être échangé

2 [= returned]

◆ **to be back** *[person]* être rentré ◆ **he's not ~ yet** il n'est pas encore rentré ◆ **I'll be ~ at six** je serai de retour *or* je rentrerai à six heures ◆ **as soon as I'm ~** dès que je serai rentré ◆ **she's now ~ at work** elle a repris le travail ◆ **the electricity is ~** l'électricité est revenue, il y a à nouveau de l'électricité ◆ **the water is ~** il y a à nouveau de l'eau ◆ **everything's ~ to normal** tout est revenu à la normale, tout est rentré dans l'ordre ; *(in fashion)* ◆ **black is ~** le noir est de nouveau à la mode

◆ **... and back** ◆ **he went to Paris and ~** il a fait le voyage de Paris aller et retour ◆ **the journey there and ~** le trajet aller et retour ◆ **you can go there and ~ in a day** tu peux faire l'aller et retour en une journée ◆ **he went to Lyons and then ~ to Paris** il est allé à Lyon, puis est rentré à Paris

3 [= reimbursed] ◆ **"full satisfaction or your money back"** "satisfait ou remboursé" ◆ **I got/want my money ~** j'ai récupéré/je veux récupérer mon argent, j'ai été/je veux être remboursé

4 - TRANSITIVE VERB

1 [= support] *[+ person, candidate, plan]* soutenir ; *[+ statement]* confirmer ◆ **they've found a witness to ~ his claim** ils ont trouvé un témoin qui confirme *or* corrobore ce qu'il a dit ; → **hilt**

2 [= accompany] *[+ singer]* accompagner

3 [= finance] *[+ person, enterprise]* financer, commanditer ; *[+ loan]* garantir ◆ **to ~ a bill** *(Fin)* endosser *or* avaliser un effet

4 [= bet on] *[+ horse, team, contestant]* parier sur, miser sur ◆ **I'm ~ing Manchester to win** je parie que Manchester va gagner ◆ **to ~ the wrong horse** *(lit, fig)* miser sur le mauvais cheval ◆ **to ~ a loser** *(lit)* miser sur un perdant ; *(fig)* miser sur le mauvais cheval ◆ **the horse was heavily ~ed** on avait beaucoup parié sur ce cheval ◆ **to ~ a horse each way** jouer un cheval gagnant et placé

5 [= reverse] *[+ vehicle]* reculer ; *[+ train]* refouler ◆ **to ~ the car in/out** entrer/sortir en marche arrière ◆ **to ~ a car round a corner** prendre un coin de rue en marche arrière ◆ **to ~ water** *or* **the oars** *(Naut)* nager à culer

6 [= attach backing to] *[+ rug, quilt]* doubler

5 - INTRANSITIVE VERB

1 [= move backwards] *[person, animal]* reculer ; *[vehicle]* reculer, faire marche arrière ◆ **to ~ in/out** *[vehicle]* entrer/sortir en marche arrière ; *[person]* entrer/sortir à reculons

2 [= change direction] tourner ◆ **during the night the south wind ~ed as predicted** au cours de la nuit le vent a tourné au nord comme prévu

6 - COMPOUNDS

back alley N ruelle *f*, venelle *f*
back benches NPL *(Brit Parl)* bancs *mpl* des députés de base ; → **backbencher**
back boiler N *(Brit)* (petite) chaudière *f (à l'arrière d'une cheminée)*
back-breaking ADJ *[work]* éreintant
back burner N ◆ **to put sth on the ~ burner** mettre qch en veilleuse *or* en attente ADJ ◆ **a ~ burner issue** un problème non urgent
back catalogue N *(Mus)* anciens enregistrements *mpl*
back-cloth N *(Brit Theat)* ⇒ **backdrop**
back-comb VT *(Brit) [+ hair]* crêper
back copy N *(Press)* ancien *or* vieux numéro *m*
the back country N *(US)* la campagne profonde
back-country ADJ *(US) [road]* de campagne ; *[expedition]* en campagne profonde
back cover N *[of book, magazine]* quatrième *f* de couverture
back door N porte *f* de derrière ◆ **to do sth by** *or* **through the ~ door** faire qch par des moyens détournés ◆ **the Government is privatizing health care through the ~ door** le gouvernement est en train de privatiser les services de santé par des moyens détournés ◆ **he got into the company by** *or* **through the ~ door** il est entré dans la société par la petite porte
back-end N *[of bus, train]* arrière *m* ◆ **~-end of the year** *(Brit)* arrière-saison *f*
back-flip N flip-flap *m*
back-formation N *(Ling)* dérivation *f* régressive
back garden N *(Brit)* jardin *m* (de derrière) ◆ **she's in the ~ garden cutting the grass** elle est dans le jardin (de derrière) en train de tondre la pelouse ◆ **they were sitting in the ~ garden** ils étaient assis dans le jardin (de derrière)
back-heel *(Ftbl)* N talonnade *f* VT ◆ **to ~-heel the ball** faire une talonnade ◆ **he ~-heeled the ball into the net** il a marqué le but d'une talonnade
back interest N *(Fin)* arriérés *mpl* d'intérêts
back issue N *[of magazine]* vieux *or* ancien numéro *m*
back-kitchen N arrière-cuisine *f*
back-line player N *(US Sport)* arrière *m*
back-lit ADJ *[stage]* éclairé de derrière *or* par l'arrière ; *(Comput) [screen]* rétro-éclairé
back lot N *(esp US) [of film studio] grand terrain à l'arrière d'un studio de cinéma*
back marker N *(Brit Sport)* dernier *m*, -ière *f*
back matter N *[of book]* appendice(s) *m(pl)*
back number N *[of newspaper etc]* vieux *or* ancien numéro *m* ◆ **to be a ~ number** *[person]* ne plus être dans le coup *
back-pack N *(Space)* appareil *m* dorsal de survie ; *(Sport)* sac *m* à dos
back-packer N routard(e) *m(f)*
back-packing N ◆ **to go ~-packing** voyager sac au dos
back pain N *(Med)* mal *m or* maux *mpl* de dos
back pass N *(Ftbl)* passe *f* en retrait
back passage N *(Brit = rectum)* rectum *m*
back pay N *(for employee)* rappel *m* de salaire *or* de traitement ; *(in armed forces)* rappel *m or* arriéré *m* de solde
back-pedal VI rétropédaler, pédaler en arrière ; *(fig = retreat)* faire marche arrière
backpedalling N *(lit)* rétropédalage *m* ; *(fig)* reculade *f*
back pocket N poche *f* arrière
back projection N rétroprojection *f*

back road N petite route f de campagne
back-scratching N (NonC) renvoi m d'ascenseur
back seat N siège m or banquette f arrière ◆ **in the ~ seat** (Aut) sur le siège arrière, sur la banquette arrière ◆ **to take a ~ seat* (to sth)** passer au second plan (par rapport à qch)
back-seat driver N ◆ **he's a ~-seat driver** il est toujours à donner des conseils (au conducteur)
back-shop N arrière-boutique f
back sight N [of rifle] cran m de mire ; (Surv) rétrovisée f
back straight N (Sport) ligne f droite (opposée à celle de l'arrivée)
back street N ruelle f ; (pej) rue f des quartiers pauvres ◆ **he grew up in the ~ streets of Leeds** il a grandi dans les quartiers pauvres de Leeds ; see also **backstreet**
back stretch N ⇒ **back straight**
back talk* N (NonC: US) ⇒ **backchat**
back-to-back ADJ dos à dos ◆ **a row of ~-to-~ houses** (Brit) une rangée de maisons adossées les unes aux autres ADV ◆ **they showed two episodes ~-to-~** ils ont passé deux épisodes de suite
back tooth N (pl **back teeth**) molaire f
back-to-the-office report N compte rendu m de mission
back-up light N (US : of car) feu m de recul, feu m de marche arrière
back vowel N voyelle f postérieure

7 - PHRASAL VERBS

► **back away** VI (se) reculer ◆ **to ~ away from** [+ problem] prendre ses distances par rapport à

► **back down** VI revenir sur sa position

► **back off** VI 1 (= draw back) reculer
2 (US *) ◆ **back off Mom, I can make my own decisions** laisse-moi tranquille, maman, je peux prendre mes propres décisions
VT FUS (= withdraw) abandonner ◆ **the union has ~ed off that demand** le syndicat a abandonné cette revendication

► **back on to** VT FUS [house etc] ◆ **the house backs on to the golf course** l'arrière de la maison donne sur le terrain de golf

► **back out** VI (lit) [person] sortir à reculons ; [car] sortir en marche arrière (of de) ; (fig) revenir sur ses engagements ◆ **at the last minute he ~ed out** à la dernière minute il a fait machine arrière
VT SEP [+ vehicle] sortir en marche arrière

► **back out of*** VT FUS [+ deal, agreement] revenir sur ; [+ duty, undertaking] se soustraire à

► **back up** VI 1 (= reverse) faire marche arrière
2 (= queue) ◆ **the traffic is backing up for miles behind the accident** l'accident a provoqué des kilomètres de bouchon
3 [water] refouler
VT SEP 1 (= support) [+ theory, claim] confirmer ; [+ person] soutenir ◆ **his colleagues ~ed him up** ses collègues l'ont soutenu ◆ **he said he had never been there and she ~ed him up** il a dit qu'il n'y était jamais allé et elle a confirmé ses dires
2 (= reverse) [+ vehicle] faire reculer
3 (Comput) [+ file] sauvegarder

backache /ˈbækeɪk/ N mal m de dos ◆ **I've got (a) ~** j'ai mal au dos

backbench /ˈbækbentʃ/ ADJ (Brit, Austral Parl) ◆ **~ MP** député m de base

backbencher /ˌbækˈbentʃəʳ/ N (Brit Parl) député m de base

BACKBENCHER

Député de la Chambre des communes qui n'occupe aucune fonction officielle, ni au gouvernement, ni dans le cabinet fantôme. Il siège donc sur les bancs du fond de la Chambre, contrairement aux « frontbenchers », membres du gouvernement ou de l'opposition, qui sont assis aux premiers rangs. Par leur position, les **backbenchers** ne sont pas tenus de suivre aussi rigoureusement les consignes de vote de leur parti. L'expression **back benches** désigne l'ensemble des **backbenchers**, toutes appartenances confondues.

backbite /ˈbækbaɪt/ VT médire de, débiner*

backbiting /ˈbækbaɪtɪŋ/ N médisance f

backboard /ˈbækbɔːd/ N (US Sport) panneau m

backbone /ˈbækbəʊn/ N 1 [of person, animal] épine f dorsale, colonne f vertébrale ; [of fish] arête f centrale ◆ **English to the ~** anglais jusqu'à la moelle (des os) 2 (fig = main part, axis) base f, ossature f ◆ **to be the ~ of an organization** être or former la base or l'ossature d'une organisation ◆ **the economic ~ of the country** la base de l'économie du pays 3 (NonC = strength of character) [of person] courage m, cran* m ; [of government, organization] fermeté f ◆ **he's got no ~** il n'a pas de cran*

backchat* /ˈbæktʃæt/ N (NonC) impertinence f

backdate /ˌbækˈdeɪt/ VT [+ cheque] antidater ◆ **increase ~d to January** augmentation f avec effet rétroactif à compter de janvier

backdoor /ˈbækdɔːʳ/ ADJ [loan, attempt etc] déguisé ; [methods] détourné

backdrop /ˈbækdrɒp/ N (Theat, fig) toile f de fond

-backed /bækt/ ADJ (in compounds) 1 (= with back) à dossier ◆ **low-backed chair** chaise f à dossier bas 2 (= with backing) doublé de ◆ **rubber-backed carpet** tapis m doublé de caoutchouc 3 (= supported by) soutenu (by par) ; ◆ **American-backed** soutenu par les américains

backer /ˈbækəʳ/ N (= supporter) partisan(e) m(f) ; (Betting) parieur m, -euse f ; (Fin) [of bill] avaliseur m ; [of firm, play, film, business venture] commanditaire m

backfire /ˈbækˈfaɪəʳ/ N (in car) (= explosion) raté m (d'allumage) ; (= noise) pétarade f ; (US: for halting a fire) contre-feu m VI 1 [car] pétarader, avoir un raté (d'allumage) ; (US = halt a fire) allumer un contre-feu 2 (fig = miscarry) [plan] avoir l'effet inverse que prévu ◆ **to ~ on sb** se retourner contre qn ◆ **his tactics could ~ (on him)** sa tactique pourrait avoir l'effet inverse or se retourner contre lui

backgammon /ˈbækˌgæmən/ N trictrac m, jacquet m

background /ˈbækgraʊnd/ N 1 [of picture, photo] arrière-plan m ; [of design] fond m ; [of music, recording] fond m sonore ◆ **on or against a blue ~** sur fond bleu ◆ **against a ~ of drums, maracas and guitars** sur fond de tambours, maracas et guitares ◆ **in the ~** [of picture, photo, design] à l'arrière-plan ; [of music, recording] en fond sonore ◆ **who's that in the ~?** qui est la personne (qu'on voit) à l'arrière-plan ? ◆ **I could hear voices in the ~** j'entendais des voix en bruit de fond ◆ **to blend or fade or disappear into the ~** se confondre avec l'arrière-plan
2 (= sidelines) arrière-plan m, second plan m ◆ **to remain in the ~** rester dans l'ombre ◆ **to keep sb in the ~** tenir qn à l'écart ◆ **their old rivalry was always there in the ~** leur vieille rivalité était toujours là, en filigrane ◆ **to be pushed into the ~** être relégué au second plan ◆ **to fade or blend into the ~** (= be sidelined) [+ person] s'effacer, disparaître de l'avant-scène ; [+ problem] passer au second plan
3 (= context, circumstances) contexte m ◆ **what is the ~ to these events?** dans quel contexte cela s'est-il passé ? ◆ **his article details the historical ~ to the crisis** son article fait l'historique de la crise ◆ **this decision was taken against a ~ of violence** cette décision a été prise dans un climat de violence ◆ **can you fill me in on the ~ to this person's case?** (doctor, social worker) pouvez-vous me rappeler les antécédents or me résumer le dossier de cette personne ? ; see also **comp**
4 (= training) formation f ◆ **my ~ is in engineering** j'ai une formation d'ingénieur ◆ **what educational ~ does she have?** qu'est-ce qu'elle a fait comme études ? ◆ **what is his professional ~?** quelle est son expérience professionnelle ?, quel est son parcours professionnel ?
5 (= origins) origines fpl, milieu m ◆ **from diverse ~s** venant d'horizons différents ◆ **what's his (family) ~?** quelles sont ses origines ?, de quel milieu est-il ? ◆ **a man from a working class ~** un homme issu d'un milieu ouvrier ◆ **he came from a conventional middle-class family ~** il venait d'une famille bourgeoise traditionnelle
COMP **background music** N musique f de fond ; (in restaurant, bar etc) musique f d'ambiance ◆ **to play sth as ~ music** passer qch en fond sonore
background noise N bruit m de fond
background paper N document m de référence or d'information
background radiation N radioactivité f naturelle
background reading N lectures fpl générales (autour du sujet)
background story N (Press) papier m d'ambiance
background studies NPL (études fpl de) culture f générale

backhand /ˈbækhænd/ ADJ [blow] en revers ; [writing] penché à gauche ◆ **~ drive** (Tennis) coup m droit de dos ◆ **~ volley/shot** coup m/volée f de revers N (Tennis) revers m

backhanded /ˌbækˈhændɪd/ ADJ 1 [shot, blow] donné du revers de la main 2 [action] déloyal ; [compliment] équivoque

backhander /ˌbækˈhændəʳ/ N (Brit) 1 (= blow) revers m 2 (* = reproof) réprimande f, semonce f 3 (* = bribe) pot-de-vin m

backing /ˈbækɪŋ/ N 1 (lit) renforcement m ; [of book] endossure f ; [of picture] entoilage m 2 (Mus) accompagnement m 3 (fig: Fin, Pol) soutien m 4 (Betting) paris mpl 5 (= movement) [of horse, cart etc] recul m ; [of boat] nage f à culer ; [of wind] changement m de direction (en sens inverse des aiguilles d'une montre)
COMP **backing group** N (Mus) groupe m (accompagnant un chanteur)
backing singer N (Mus) choriste mf
backing store N (Comput) mémoire f auxiliaire
backing vocals NPL (Mus) chœurs mpl

backlash /ˈbæklæʃ/ N [of machine] secousse f, saccade f ; [of explosion] contrecoup m, répercussion f ; (Pol, fig) réaction f brutale ◆ **there was a ~ against reforms within the party** il y a eu une réaction brutale contre les réformes au sein du parti

backless /ˈbæklɪs/ ADJ [dress etc] dos nu inv

backlist /ˈbæklɪst/ N (liste f des) ouvrages mpl disponibles or en stock

backlog /ˈbæklɒg/ N [of rent] arriéré m (de loyers) ◆ **~ of work** travail m en retard ◆ **~ of orders** (Comm) commandes fpl en carnet, commandes fpl inexécutées ◆ **~ of accumulated**

arrears *(Fin)* accumulation *f* d'arriérés de paiement

backrest /ˈbækrest/ N *[of chair]* dossier *m*

backroom /ˈbækrʊm/ N *(fig)* ◆ **the ~ boys*** *(gen)* les travailleurs *mpl* de l'ombre, ceux qui restent dans la coulisse ; *(= experts, scientists)* les chercheurs *mpl* anonymes *or* qui travaillent dans l'ombre

backshift /ˈbækʃɪft/ N *(= period)* poste *m* de nuit ; *(= workers)* équipe *f* de nuit ◆ **to be on the ~** être de l'équipe de nuit

backside /ˈbæksaɪd/ N *(= back part)* arrière *m* ; *(* = buttocks)* derrière *m*, postérieur* *m* ◆ **to sit on one's ~** * *(fig)* rester le derrière sur sa chaise*

backslapping * /ˈbæk,slæpɪŋ/ N *(fig)* (grandes) démonstrations *fpl* d'amitié

backslash /ˈbækslæʃ/ N *(Typ)* barre *f* oblique inversée

backslider /ˈbækslaɪdəʳ/ N récidiviste *mf*

backsliding /ˈbækslaɪdɪŋ/ N récidive *f*

backspace /ˈbækspeɪs/ VI revenir en arrière
COMP **backspace key** N ⇒ **backspacer**

backspacer /,bækˈspeɪsəʳ/ N touche *f* d'espacement *or* de rappel arrière

backspin /ˈbækspɪn/ N *(Tennis, Cricket etc)* coupé *m* ◆ **to give a ball ~, to put ~ on a ball** couper une balle

backstage /,bækˈsteɪdʒ/ ADV derrière la scène, dans les coulisses N coulisse(s) *f(pl)* ◆ **to go ~** aller dans les coulisses

backstairs /,bækˈsteəz/ N escalier *m* de service ; *(secret)* escalier *m* dérobé ADJ *(in servants' quarter)* *[work, activities]* des domestiques ◆ **~ gossip** *or* **rumours** *(lit)* commérages *mpl* de domestiques ; *(fig)* bruits *mpl* de couloir ◆ **~ intrigue** manigances *fpl* ◆ **the government did a ~ deal with the opposition** le gouvernement a manigancé quelque chose avec l'opposition

backstitch /ˈbækstɪtʃ/ N point *m* arrière VT, VI coudre en point arrière

backstop /ˈbækstɒp/ N *(Sport)* *(= screen, fence)* grillage *m* ; *(US Baseball * = person)* receveur *m*

backstreet /ˈbækstriːt/ ADJ *[hotel, shop]* louche
COMP **backstreet abortion** N avortement *m* clandestin *or* illégal
backstreet abortionist N faiseuse *f* d'anges, avorteur *m*, -euse *f* *(pej)*

backstroke /ˈbækstrəʊk/ N *(Swimming)* dos *m* crawlé

backswing /ˈbækswɪŋ/ N *(Sport)* swing *m* en arrière

backtrack /ˈbæktræk/ VI faire marche arrière *or* machine arrière *(fig)* ◆ **to ~ on a promise** revenir sur une promesse ◆ **to ~ home*** *(US)* retourner chez soi

backup /ˈbækʌp/ N *(= support)* appui *m*, soutien *m* *(from sb* de qn) ; *(= reserves)* réserves *fpl* ; *[of personnel, police etc]* renforts *mpl* ADJ 1 *[vehicles, supplies, weapons]* supplémentaire, de réserve ; *[pilot, personnel, policeman]* en renfort 2 *(Comput)* de sauvegarde
COMP **backup copy** N copie *f* sauvegarde
backup disk N disque *m* sauvegarde
backup file N sauvegarde *f*
backup store N mémoire *f* auxiliaire

backward /ˈbækwəd/ ADJ 1 *(= to the rear)* *[look, step]* en arrière ; *[somersault]* arrière ; *(fig)* *[step, move]* rétrograde, en arrière ◆ **~ and forward movement** mouvement *m* de va-et-vient ◆ **~ flow** contre-courant *m* ◆ **he walked out without a ~ glance** il est parti sans jeter un regard en arrière

2 *(= retarded)* *[district, nation, culture]* arriéré, peu avancé ; *[economy]* arriéré ; *[technology, equipment]* peu moderne ; † *[child]* retardé ◆ **to be socially/economically ~** être en retard *or* être arriéré sur le plan social/économique

3 *(= reluctant)* peu disposé *(in doing sth* à faire qch) ; *(= hesitant)* hésitant ◆ **he wasn't ~ in offering his opinion** il ne s'est pas fait prier pour donner son avis ◆ **he's never been ~ in coming forward** *(hum)* il n'a pas peur de se mettre en avant

ADV ⇒ **backwards**

COMP **backward-looking** ADJ *[project, attitude]* rétrograde

backwardation /ˈbækwə,deɪʃən/ N *(Stock Exchange)* report *m*

backwardness /ˈbækwədnɪs/ N 1 *[of child]* retard *m* mental ; *(Econ)* retard *m* ◆ **industrial/intellectual ~** retard *m* industriel/intellectuel 2 *(= reluctance, shyness)* réticence *f*, hésitation *f* *(in doing sth* à faire qch)

backwards /ˈbækwədz/ ADV 1 *(= towards the back)* en arrière ◆ **to fall ~** tomber en arrière *or* à la renverse ◆ **to flow ~** aller *or* couler à contre-courant ◆ **to walk ~ and forwards** marcher de long en large, aller et venir ◆ **to go ~ and forwards between two places** aller et venir *or* faire la navette entre deux endroits ; → **lean over**

2 *(= back foremost)* à rebours ◆ **to go/walk ~** aller/marcher à reculons *or* à rebours ◆ **the car moved ~ a little** la voiture a reculé un peu

3 *(= in reverse of usual way)* à l'envers, en commençant par la fin ◆ **to count ~ (from ten to one)** compter à rebours (de dix à un) ◆ **I know the poem ~** * je connais le poème sur le bout des doigts ◆ **I know this road ~** * je connais cette route comme ma poche ◆ **he's got it ~** * *(fig = misunderstood)* il a tout compris de travers

4 *(fig: in time)* en arrière, vers le passé ◆ **to look ~** jeter un regard en arrière, remonter dans le passé

5 *(= retrogressively)* en rétrogradant

backwash /ˈbækwɒʃ/ N *(Naut)* remous *m* ; *(fig)* contre-coup *m* *(from* provoqué par)

backwater /ˈbæk,wɔːtəʳ/ N *[of pool]* eau *f* stagnante ; *[of river]* bras *m* mort ; *(fig = backward place)* trou *m* perdu ; *(fig = peaceful spot)* (petit) coin *m* tranquille ◆ **to live in a ~** habiter un petit coin tranquille ; *(pej)* habiter un trou perdu

backwoods /ˈbæk,wʊdz/ NPL région *f* (forestière) inexploitée ◆ **to live in the ~** *(fig pej)* vivre dans un trou perdu

backwoodsman /ˈbæk,wʊdzmən/ N (pl **-men**) pionnier *m* ; *(fig pej)* rustre *m*

backyard /,bækˈjɑːd/ N *(Brit)* arrière-cour *f* ; *(US)* jardin *m* (de derrière) ◆ **in one's own ~** *(fig)* à sa porte

bacon /ˈbeɪkən/ N lard *m* *(généralement en tranches)*, bacon *m* ◆ **~ and eggs** œufs *mpl* au lard *or* au bacon ◆ **to bring home the ~** * *(= be breadwinner)* faire bouillir la marmite* ; *(= achieve goal)* décrocher la timbale* ; → **boil¹, save¹, streaky**
COMP **bacon fat** N gras *m* de lard
bacon rasher N tranche *f* de lard
bacon rind N couenne *f* de lard
bacon-slicer N coupe-jambon *m inv*

Baconian /beɪˈkəʊnɪən/ ADJ baconien

bacteria /bækˈtɪərɪə/ NPL of **bacterium**

bacterial /bækˈtɪərɪəl/ ADJ bactérien

bacteriological /bæk,tɪərɪəˈlɒdʒɪkəl/ ADJ bactériologique

bacteriologist /bæk,tɪərɪˈɒlədʒɪst/ N bactériologiste *mf*

bacteriology /bæk,tɪərɪˈɒlədʒɪ/ N bactériologie *f*

bacteriophage /bækˈtɪərɪə,feɪdʒ/ N bactériophage *m*

bacterium /bækˈtɪərɪəm/ N (pl **bacteria**) bactérie *f*

bad /bæd/ ADJ (compar **worse**, superl **worst**) 1 *(= wicked)* *[action, habit, behaviour]* mauvais ; *[person]* méchant ◆ **it was a ~ thing to do/to say** ce n'était pas bien de faire cela/de dire cela ◆ **it was very ~ of you to treat her like that** c'était très mal de votre part de la traiter ainsi ◆ **it's too ~ of you** ce n'est vraiment pas bien de votre part ◆ **you ~ boy!** vilain !, méchant ! ◆ **~ dog!** vilain chien ! ◆ **he's a ~ lot** *or* **sort** *or* **type*** c'est un mauvais sujet ; *(stronger)* c'est un sale type* ; → **blood, breath, language**

2 *(= inferior, poor quality)* *[workmanship]* mauvais, de mauvaise qualité ◆ **she speaks very ~ English, her English is very ~** elle parle très mal l'anglais, son anglais est très mauvais ◆ **~ quality food/material** *etc* aliments *mpl*/tissu *m etc* de mauvaise qualité ◆ **~ light stopped play** *(Cricket etc)* le match a été interrompu à cause du manque de lumière ; → **penny**

3 *(= unpleasant)* *[news, weather, smell]* mauvais ◆ **there's a ~ smell in this room** ça sent mauvais dans cette pièce ◆ **it's a ~ business** c'est une triste affaire ; see also **news**

4 *(= difficult, going badly)* **business is ~** les affaires vont mal ◆ **I didn't know things were so ~ between them** je ne savais pas que les choses allaient aussi mal entre eux ◆ **it's not so ~** ce n'est pas si mal ◆ **it's not ~ at all** ce n'est pas mal du tout ◆ **(that's) too ~!** *(unsympathetic)* tant pis ! ; *(sympathetic)* quel dommage ! ; *(indignant)* c'est un peu fort ! ◆ **how is he? – (he's) not so ~** comment va-t-il ? – (il ne va) pas trop mal ◆ **she's ill? that's very ~** elle est malade ? c'est vraiment dommage ◆ **I've had a really ~ day** j'ai eu une très mauvaise journée ◆ **I'm having a ~ hair day*** *(hair problems)* je ne sais pas quoi faire de mes cheveux aujourd'hui ; *(nightmare day)* tout va de travers pour moi aujourd'hui, c'est vraiment un jour sans* ◆ **to come to a ~ end** mal finir ◆ **she's been having a really ~ time lately** elle traverse une période très difficile ◆ **things are going from ~ to worse** les choses vont de mal en pis

5 *(= serious)* *[mistake, accident, illness]* grave ; *[sprain, wound]* sérieux ◆ **a ~ headache** un sérieux mal de tête ◆ **a ~ cold** un mauvais *or* gros rhume ◆ **a ~ case of chickenpox/flu** une mauvaise varicelle/grippe ◆ **a ~ error of judgement** une grossière erreur de jugement

6 *(= unwise)* *[idea, decision, method]* mauvais ◆ **that's not a ~ idea!** ce n'est pas une mauvaise idée ! ◆ **it was a ~ idea to invite him** c'était une mauvaise idée (que) de l'inviter ◆ **it wouldn't be a ~ thing (to do that)** ça ne ferait pas de mal (de faire cela), ce ne serait pas une mauvaise idée (de faire cela)

7 *(= unfavourable)* *[report, publicity]* mauvais ; *[opinion]* mauvais, triste ; *[result]* mauvais, malheureux ◆ **~ publicity** une mauvaise publicité

8 *(= ill)* **to feel ~** se sentir mal ◆ **to have a ~ back** *(on one occasion)* avoir mal au dos ; *(= have back problems)* avoir des problèmes de dos ◆ **to have a ~ head*** avoir mal à la tête ◆ **his ~ leg** sa mauvaise jambe, sa jambe malade

9 *(= guilty, uncomfortable)* **to feel ~ about doing sth** *(= reproach oneself)* s'en vouloir d'avoir fait qch ◆ **I feel ~ about it** je m'en veux (de l'avoir fait) ◆ **she feels very ~ about the way she treated him** elle s'en veut de l'avoir traité ainsi ◆ **I feel ~ about firing him, but there's no alternative** je m'en veux de devoir le licencier, mais je n'ai pas le choix ◆ **just get it over with and don't feel ~ about it** arrête d'hésiter, et ne te fais pas de reproches

10 *(= spoiled)* *[food]* mauvais, gâté ; *[tooth]* carié ◆ **to go ~** *[food]* se gâter, pourrir ; *[milk]* tourner ; *[bread]* moisir ; *[teeth]* se carier

11 *(= false)* *[coin, money]* faux (fausse *f*)

12 (= *harmful*) mauvais ◆ ~ **for the health/the eyes** mauvais pour la santé/les yeux ◆ **not all forms of sugar are ~ for you** toutes les formes de sucre ne sont pas mauvaises ◆ **this is ~ for you** ce n'est pas bon pour vous ◆ **can exercise be ~ for you?** l'exercice peut-il faire du mal ?, est-ce qu'il peut être mauvais de faire de l'exercice ? ◆ **it's ~ for business** c'est mauvais pour les affaires

13 (= *not skilled or talented*) ◆ **to be ~ at ...** être mauvais en ... ◆ ~ **at English/spelling** mauvais en anglais/en orthographe ◆ **I'm ~ at languages** je ne suis pas doué pour les langues ◆ **he's ~ at remembering birthdays** il n'est pas doué pour se rappeler les anniversaires

N (*NonC*) mauvais *m* ◆ **to take the good with the ~** prendre le bon avec le mauvais ◆ **he's gone to the ~** * il a mal tourné ◆ **I am 50p to the ~** * j'en suis de 50 pence * ◆ **I'm in ~** ‡ **with him** (*esp US*) je ne suis pas dans ses petits papiers *, je suis mal vu de lui

ADV ◆ **he's got it ~** * (*about hobby etc*) c'est une marotte chez lui ; (*about person*) il l'a dans la peau ‡

COMP **bad apple** N (*fig = person*) brebis *f* galeuse
bad cheque N chèque *m* sans provision
bad claim N (*Insurance*) réclamation *f* mal fondée
bad debt N créance *f* douteuse *or* irrécouvrable
bad-mannered ADJ mal élevé
bad-mouth * VT débiner *
bad-tempered ADJ [*person*] qui a mauvais caractère ; (*on one occasion*) de mauvaise humeur ; [*look, answer*] désagréable

baddie * /ˈbædɪ/ N méchant *m*

baddish /ˈbædɪʃ/ ADJ pas fameux, pas brillant

bade /bæd, beɪd/ VB pt of **bid**

badge /bædʒ/ N [*of team, association*] insigne *m* ; [*of an order, police*] plaque *f* ; (*Mil*) insigne *m* ; (*sew-on, stick-on: for jeans etc*) badge *m* ; (*Scouting*) badge *m* ; (*fig = symbol*) symbole *m*, signe *m* (distinctif) ◆ **his ~ of office** l'insigne *m* de sa fonction

badger /ˈbædʒəʳ/ N (= *animal, brush*) blaireau *m* ◆ **the Badger State** (*US*) le Wisconsin VT harceler, importuner (*with* de) ; ◆ **to ~ sb to do sth** *or* **into doing sth** harceler qn jusqu'à ce qu'il fasse qch, tanner * (la peau à) qn pour qu'il fasse qch ◆ **to ~ sth out of sb** soutirer qch à qn à force de le harceler COMP **badger baiting** N *combats où l'on force des blaireaux à se battre avec des chiens*

badinage /ˈbædɪnɑːʒ/ N (*NonC: frm*) badinage *m*

badlands /ˈbædlændz/ NPL bad-lands *fpl*

badly /ˈbædlɪ/ ADV (compar **worse**, superl **worst**)

1 (= *poorly*) [*behave, function, start, end, sleep, designed, taught, written*] mal ◆ **the project was very ~ managed** le projet a été très mal géré ◆ ~ **dressed** mal habillé ◆ **to treat sb ~, to behave ~ towards sb** mal se comporter avec qn ◆ **some people react ~ to this medicine** certaines personnes réagissent mal à ce médicament ◆ **he took it very ~** il a très mal pris la chose ◆ **to go ~** mal se passer ◆ **things aren't going too ~** ça ne se passe pas trop mal, les choses ne vont pas trop mal ◆ **things are going pretty ~ for me at the moment** tout va assez *or* plutôt mal pour moi en ce moment ◆ **to do** *or* **perform ~** [*athlete*] faire une mauvaise performance ; [*pupil, student, company, economy*] avoir de mauvais résultats ; [*political party*] (*in opinion polls*) ne pas être populaire ; (*in elections*) obtenir de mauvais résultats ◆ **the dollar is doing ~** le dollar n'est pas très fort ◆ **you did ~ out of it, you came off ~** tu n'as pas été gâté ◆ **she didn't come off too ~ in the debate** elle ne s'est pas trop mal débrouillée dans ce débat ◆ **to be ~ off** (*financially*) être dans la gêne ◆ **they're not so ~ off** (*gen*) ils ne s'en tirent pas si mal que ça ◆ **to be ~ off for sth** manquer de qch

2 (= *unfavourably*) ◆ **to speak ~ of sb** dire du mal de qn ◆ **to think ~ of sb** avoir une mauvaise opinion de qn ◆ **nobody will think ~ of you if ...** personne ne t'en voudra si ... ◆ **to reflect ~ on sb** donner une mauvaise image de qn

3 (= *seriously*) [*wound, injure*] grièvement, gravement ; [*affect*] gravement ; [*disrupt*] sérieusement, gravement ◆ **his schoolwork suffered very ~ after his mother died** son travail scolaire s'est beaucoup ressenti de la mort de sa mère ◆ **she was ~ shaken after the accident** elle a été très secouée à la suite de cet accident ◆ **they were ~ defeated** ils ont subi une sévère *or* cuisante défaite, ils ont été sévèrement battus ◆ **he was ~ beaten** (*physically*) il a reçu de très mauvais coups ◆ **to go ~ wrong** très mal tourner ◆ **something is ~ wrong with him** il ne va pas bien du tout ◆ **the ~ disabled** les grands infirmes *mfpl*, les grands invalides *mfpl*

4 [*want, need*] **to want sth ~** avoir très envie de qch ◆ **I need it ~** j'en ai absolument besoin, il me le faut absolument ◆ **I am ~ in need of advice** j'ai grand besoin de conseils ◆ **I ~ need a haircut** j'ai vraiment besoin de me faire couper les cheveux ◆ **the house ~ needs a coat of paint** la maison a sacrément besoin d'un coup de peinture *or* a besoin d'un bon coup de peinture ◆ **we need the money ~** nous avons vraiment besoin de cet argent ◆ **they will get their ~ needed medical supplies** ils vont recevoir les médicaments qui leur font cruellement défaut

badman * /ˈbæd,mæn/ N (pl **-men**) (*US*) bandit *m* ; (*in movies*) méchant *m*

badminton /ˈbædmɪntən/ N badminton *m* COMP **badminton court** N court *m* de badminton
badminton racket N raquette *f* de badminton

badness /ˈbædnɪs/ N (*NonC*) 1 (= *poor quality*) mauvaise qualité *f*, mauvais état *m* 2 (= *wickedness*) méchanceté *f*

Baffin /ˈbæfɪn/ N ◆ ~ **Bay** mer *f* *or* baie *f* de Baffin ◆ ~ **Island** terre *f* de Baffin

baffle /ˈbæfl/ VT [+ *person*] déconcerter, dérouter ; [+ *pursuers*] semer ; [+ *plot*] déjouer ; [+ *hope, expectation*] décevoir, tromper ; [+ *description, explanation*] échapper à, défier N (= *device*) déflecteur *m* ; (*in loudspeaker*) baffle *m* COMP **baffle-board, baffle-plate** N déflecteur *m* ; (*in loudspeaker*) baffle *m*

bafflement /ˈbæflmənt/ N confusion *f*

baffling /ˈbæflɪŋ/ ADJ déconcertant, déroutant

BAFTA /ˈbæftə/ N (abbrev of **British Academy of Film and Television Arts**) *Académie britannique chargée de promouvoir le cinéma et la télévision*

bag /bæg/ N 1 (*gen*) sac *m* ; ◆ **paper ~** sac *m* en papier ◆ **travel/sports/beach ~** sac *m* de voyage/sport/plage ◆ **bin** (*Brit*) *or* **garbage** (*US*) **~** sac *m* poubelle ◆ **blood ~** pochette *f* de sang ◆ **tea/coffee ~** sachet *m* de thé/café ◆ **a ~ of apples** un sac de pommes ◆ **a ~ of crisps** (*Brit*) un paquet de chips ◆ **a ~ of sweets** (*plastic sachet*) un paquet de bonbons ; (*paper bag*) un sachet de bonbons ◆ **a ~ of chips** (*Brit*) ≃ un cornet de frites ; → **gamebag, moneybag**

2 (= *sag*) poche *f* ◆ **the net must have a good ~ to it** la poche du filet doit être profonde ◆ **to have ~s under the** *or* **one's eyes** avoir des poches sous les yeux

3 (*figurative expressions*) **she was just a ~ of bones** * elle n'avait plus que la peau sur les os ◆ **it's in the ~** * c'est dans le sac * *or* dans la poche * ◆ **a mixed ~** un mélange ◆ **to pack one's ~s** (*lit*) faire ses bagages ; (*fig*) plier bagage ◆ ~ **and baggage** avec armes et bagages ◆ **the whole ~ of tricks** ‡ tout le bataclan *, tout le fourbi * ◆ **he was left holding the ~** * (*US*) il s'est retrouvé avec tout sur les bras ◆ **it's not my ~** ‡ ce n'est pas mon truc * ; → **cat**

4 (‡, *pej*) ◆ **an old ~** une vieille teigne

5 (*Hunting*) (= *amount killed*) tableau *m* de chasse ◆ **to get a good ~** faire bonne chasse, faire un beau tableau

NPL **bags** 1 ‡ (*Brit*) (= *lots*) des tas *, plein * ◆ **~s of** plein de *, des tas de *

2 **~s I go first!** ‡ (*Brit*) moi d'abord ! ◆ **~s you speak to her first!** à toi de lui parler d'abord !

VT 1 * (*Brit*) (= *grab*) s'approprier ◆ **Anne has already ~ged that seat** Anne s'est déjà approprié cette place

2 (*Hunting = kill*) tuer

3 (also **bag up**) [+ *flour, goods*] mettre en sac, ensacher

VI (also **bag out**) [*garment*] pocher

COMP **bag lady** * N clocharde *f*
bag snatcher N voleur *m*, -euse *f* à l'arraché
bag-snatching N vol *m* à l'arraché

bagatelle /ˌbægəˈtel/ N 1 (= *trifle*) bagatelle *f* 2 (*Mus*) divertissement *m* 3 (= *board game*) *sorte de flipper* 4 (*Billiards*) billard *m* anglais, billard *m* à blouses

bagel /ˈbeɪgl/ N (*Culin*) bagel *m*

bagful /ˈbægfʊl/ N sac *m* plein, plein sac *m*

baggage /ˈbægɪdʒ/ N 1 (*NonC = luggage*) bagages *mpl* ; (*Mil*) équipement *m* ; → **bag, emotional** 2 († * = *pert girl*) coquine † *f*

COMP **baggage allowance** N poids *m* de bagages autorisé
baggage car N (*esp US*) fourgon *m*
baggage check N (*US = receipt*) bulletin *m* de consigne ; (= *security check*) contrôle *m* des bagages
baggage checkroom N (*US*) consigne *f*
baggage elastic N pieuvre *f*
baggage hall N ⇒ **baggage reclaim (area)**
baggage handler N bagagiste *m*
baggage locker N (casier *m* de) consigne *f* automatique
baggage reclaim (area) N (*in airport*) livraison *f* des bagages
baggage room N consigne *f*
baggage tag N étiquette *f* à bagages
baggage train N (*Mil*) train *m* des équipages
baggage wagon N ⇒ **baggage car**

bagging /ˈbægɪŋ/ N (= *fabric*) toile *f* à sac

baggy /ˈbægɪ/ ADJ 1 (= *puffy*) gonflé, bouffant 2 [*jacket, coat*] trop ample, flottant ; (*fashionably*) ample ◆ **his trousers were ~ at the knees** son pantalon faisait des poches aux genoux

Baghdad /bægˈdæd/ N Bagdad

bagpiper /ˈbægpaɪpəʳ/ N joueur *m*, -euse *f* de cornemuse

bagpipes /ˈbægpaɪps/ NPL cornemuse *f*

baguette /bæˈget/ N baguette *f*

bah /bɑː/ EXCL bah !

Baha'i /bəˈhaɪ/ ADJ bahaï N Bahaï(e) *m(f)*

Bahama /bəˈhɑːmə/ ADJ, N ◆ **the ~ Islands, the ~s** les Bahamas *fpl*

Bahamian /bəˈheɪmɪən/ ADJ bahamien N Bahamien(ne) *m(f)*

Bahrain /bɑːˈreɪn/ N Bahreïn

Bahraini /bɑːˈreɪnɪ/ ADJ bahreïni N Bahreïni *mf*

Bahrein /bɑːˈreɪn/ N Bahreïn

Baikal /baɪˈkɑːl/ N ◆ **Lake ~** le lac Baïkal

bail¹ /beɪl/ N (*Jur*) mise *f* en liberté sous caution ; (= *sum*) caution *f* ; (= *person*) caution *f*, répondant *m* ◆ **on ~** sous caution ◆ **to free sb on ~** mettre qn en liberté provisoire sous caution ◆ **to go** *or* **stand ~ for sb** se porter *or* se rendre garant de qn ◆ **to find** ~ **for sb** fournir une caution pour qn *(pour sa mise en liberté provisoire)* ◆ **to ask for/grant/refuse** ~ demander/accorder/refuser la mise en liberté sous caution ◆ **to put up** ~ **for sb** payer la caution de qn ; → **jump, remand**

VT 1 *(Jur: also* **bail out***)* faire mettre en liberté provisoire sous caution

2 *[+ goods]* mettre en dépôt

COMP bail bandit * **N** *(Brit) condamné qui commet une infraction pendant qu'il est en liberté provisoire sous caution*

bail bond N *(US Jur) (= document)* cautionnement *m* ; *(= money)* caution *f*

bail bondsman N (pl **bail bondsmen**) *(US Jur)* garant *m (d'un condamné en liberté sous caution)*

► **bail out VT SEP** 1 ⇒ **bail¹ vt 1**

2 *(fig) (gen)* sortir d'affaire ; *(financially)* renflouer ◆ **to** ~ **o.s. out** s'en sortir

bail² /beɪl/ **N** *(Cricket)* ◆ ~**s** bâtonnets *mpl (qui couronnent le guichet)*

bail³ /beɪl/ **VT** *[+ boat]* écoper ; *[+ water]* vider **N** écope *f*

► **bail out VI** *(of aircraft)* sauter (en parachute) **VT SEP** *[+ boat]* écoper ; *[+ water]* vider

bailee /beɪ'liː/ **N** *(Jur)* dépositaire *m*

bailey /'beɪlɪ/ **N** *(= wall)* mur *m* d'enceinte ; *(= courtyard)* cour *f* intérieure ; → **old COMP**

Bailey bridge N pont *m* Bailey

bailiff /'beɪlɪf/ **N** *(Jur)* huissier *m* ; *(Brit) [of estate, lands]* régisseur *m*, intendant *m* ; *(Hist)* bailli *m*, gouverneur *m*

bailiwick /'beɪlɪwɪk/ **N** 1 *(Jur)* juridiction *f*, circonscription *f* 2 *(esp US = speciality)* domaine *m*

bailor /'beɪlə^r/ **N** *(Jur)* déposant *m*

bailout /'beɪlaʊt/ **N** *[of company]* sauvetage *m*, renflouement *m*

bain-marie /ˌbɛnmə'riː, bɛ̃mari/ **N** (pl **bains-marie**) bain-marie *m*

bairn /bɛən/ **N** *(Scot, N Engl)* enfant *mf*

bait /beɪt/ **N** *(Fishing, Hunting)* amorce *f*, appât *m* ; *(fig)* appât *m*, leurre *m* ◆ **to rise to** *or* **take** *or* **swallow the** ~ *(lit, fig)* mordre à l'hameçon **VT** 1 *[+ hook]* amorcer ; *[+ trap]* appâter, garnir d'un appât 2 *(= torment)* tourmenter ; → **bear²**

baize /beɪz/ **N** *(Snooker)* tapis *m* ◆ **(green)** ~ **door** *porte recouverte de feutre vert, généralement menant au quartier des domestiques*

bake /beɪk/ **VT** 1 *[+ food]* faire cuire au four ◆ **she ~s her own bread** elle fait son pain elle-même ◆ **to** ~ **a cake** faire (cuire) un gâteau ◆ ~**d apples** pommes *fpl* au four ; → **half** 2 *[+ pottery, bricks]* cuire (au four) ◆ **earth ~d by the sun** sol desséché *or* cuit par le soleil **VI** 1 *[bread, cakes]* cuire (au four) 2 ◆ **she ~s every Tuesday** *(bread)* elle fait du pain tous les mardis ; *(cakes)* elle fait de la pâtisserie *or* des gâteaux tous les mardis 3 *[pottery etc]* cuire ◆ **we are baking in this heat** * on cuit * *or* on grille * par cette chaleur ◆ **it's baking (hot) today!** * il fait une de ces chaleurs aujourd'hui !

COMP baked Alaska N omelette *f* norvégienne

baked beans NPL haricots *mpl* blancs à la sauce tomate

baked potato N pomme *f* de terre cuite au four

bakehouse /'beɪkhaʊs/ **N** boulangerie *f (lieu de fabrication)*

Bakelite ® /'beɪkəlaɪt/ **N** bakélite ® *f*

baker /'beɪkə^r/ **N** boulanger *m*, -ère *f* ◆ ~**'s (shop)** boulangerie *f*

COMP a baker's dozen N treize *m* à la douzaine

baker's oven N four *m* à pain

bakery /'beɪkərɪ/ **N** boulangerie(-pâtisserie) *f*

bakeware /'beɪkwɛə^r/ **N** *(NonC)* plats *mpl* et moules *mpl* à gâteaux

Bakewell tart /'beɪkwel'tɑːt/ **N** tarte *f* de Bakewell

baking /'beɪkɪŋ/ **N** 1 *(NonC = process)* cuisson *f* (au four) ◆ **after** ~ après la cuisson ◆ **use wholemeal flour in your** ~ faites votre pain *(or vos gâteaux etc)* à la farine complète ◆ **she's busy doing her** ~ elle est en train de faire son pain *(or des gâteaux etc)* 2 *(in bakery = batch of bread)* fournée *f*

COMP baking dish N plat *m* allant au four

baking powder N levure *f* chimique

baking sheet N ⇒ **baking tray**

baking soda N bicarbonate *m* de soude

baking tin N *(for cakes)* moule *m* (à gâteaux) ; *(for tarts)* moule *m* à tarte, tourtière *f*

baking tray N plaque *f* de four

baksheesh /'bækʃiːʃ/ **N** bakchich *m*

Balaclava, Balaklava /ˌbælə'klɑːvə/ **N** *(Geog)* Balaklava ◆ **balaclava (helmet)** *(Brit)* passe-montagne *m*

balalaika /ˌbælə'laɪkə/ **N** balalaïka *f*

balance /'bæləns/ **N** 1 *(NonC = equilibrium)* équilibre *m* ◆ **to keep/lose one's** ~ *(lit, fig)* garder/perdre son équilibre ◆ **off** ~ *(lit, fig)* en équilibre instable ◆ **to throw sb off** ~ *(lit)* faire perdre l'équilibre à qn ; *(fig)* déconcerter qn ◆ **the** ~ **of nature** l'équilibre *m* de la nature ◆ **to strike a** ~ trouver le juste milieu ◆ **he has no sense of** ~ il n'a aucun sens des proportions *or* de la mesure ◆ **the** ~ **of his mind was disturbed** il n'avait plus toute sa raison ◆ **a nice** ~ **of humour and pathos** un délicat dosage d'humour et de pathétique

◆ **on balance** à tout prendre, tout compte fait

2 *(= scales)* balance *f* ◆ **to be** *or* **hang in the** ~ être en jeu ◆ **his life was hanging in the** ~ *(gen)* sa vie était en jeu ; *[sick person]* il était entre la vie et la mort ◆ **to hold the** ~ faire pencher la balance ; → **spring**

3 *(Comm, Fin)* solde *m* ; (also **bank balance**) solde *m* (d'un compte) ◆ **what's my** ~**?** *(in bank)* quelle est la position de mon compte ? ◆ **credit/debit** ~ solde *m* créditeur/débiteur ◆ ~ **in hand** solde *m* créditeur ◆ ~ **carried forward** *(gen)* solde *m* à reporter ; *(on balance sheet)* report *m* à nouveau ◆ ~ **due** solde *m* débiteur ◆ **to pay off the** ~ **of an account** solder un compte ◆ **sterling** ~**s** balances *fpl* sterling

4 *(= remainder)* reste *m*

5 *[of clock, watch]* régulateur *m*, balancier *m*

VT 1 *(= maintain equilibrium of)* tenir en équilibre ; *(= place in equilibrium)* mettre *or* poser en équilibre ; *[+ wheels]* équilibrer ; *(fig)* équilibrer, compenser ◆ **I** ~**d the glass on top of the books** j'ai posé le verre en équilibre sur les livres ◆ **the seal** ~**d the ball on its nose** le phoque tenait le ballon en équilibre sur son nez ◆ **more and more women are having to** ~ **the needs of career and family** de plus en plus de femmes doivent jongler entre carrière et famille

2 *(= compare etc)* balancer, peser ; *[+ two arguments, two solutions]* comparer ◆ **this must be** ~**d against that** il faut peser le pour et le contre

3 *(= counterbalance) (in weighing, symmetrical display etc)* équilibrer ; *(in value, amount)* compenser, contrebalancer ◆ **they** ~ **each other** *[two objects] (in weighing)* ils se font contrepoids ; *(in symmetrical display)* ils s'équilibrent

4 *(Comm, Fin)* **to** ~ **an account** arrêter un compte ◆ **to** ~ **the budget** équilibrer le budget ◆ **to** ~ **the books** arrêter les comptes, dresser le bilan ◆ **to** ~ **the cash** faire la caisse

VI 1 *[two objects]* se faire contrepoids ; *[acrobat etc]* se maintenir en équilibre ; *[scales]* être en équilibre ◆ **to** ~ **on one foot** se tenir en équilibre sur un (seul) pied

2 *(Comm, Fin) [accounts]* s'équilibrer, être en équilibre

COMP balance of payments N balance *f* des paiements ◆ ~ **of payments surplus/deficit** excédent *m*/déficit *m* de la balance des paiements

balance of power N *(gen)* équilibre *m* des forces ; *(in government)* équilibre *m* des pouvoirs ◆ **the European** ~ **of power** l'équilibre *m* européen

balance of terror N équilibre *m* de la terreur

balance of trade N *(Econ)* balance *f* commerciale

balance sheet N bilan *m*

balance weight N contrepoids *m*

► **balance out VT SEP** *(fig)* contrebalancer, compenser

balanced /'bælənst/ **ADJ** *(gen)* équilibré ◆ ~ **views** vues *fpl* sensées *or* mesurées

balancing /'bælənsɪŋ/ **N** 1 *(= equilibrium)* mise *f* en équilibre, stabilisation *f* ◆ **to do a** ~ **act** *(Theat)* faire de l'équilibrisme ; *(fig)* jongler 2 *(Comm, Fin)* ~ **of accounts** règlement *m or* solde *m* des comptes ◆ ~ **of the books** balances *fpl* (mensuelles)

balcony /'bælkənɪ/ **N** 1 balcon *m* 2 *(Theat)* fauteuils *mpl or* stalles *fpl* de deuxième balcon

bald /bɔːld/ **ADJ** 1 *(gen)* chauve ; *[tyre]* lisse ◆ **as** ~ **as a coot** * *or* **an egg** * chauve comme une boule de billard * *or* comme un œuf * ◆ **to be going** ~ perdre ses cheveux, devenir chauve 2 *[style]* plat, sec (sèche *f*) ◆ **a** ~ **statement** une simple exposition de faits ◆ **a** ~ **lie** un mensonge flagrant *or* non déguisé

COMP bald eagle N aigle *m* d'Amérique

bald-headed ADJ chauve, à (la) tête chauve

bald patch N *[of person]* (petite) tonsure *f* ; *[of animal]* place *f* dépourvue de poils ; *[of carpet etc]* coin *m* dégarni *or* pelé

baldachin /'bɔːldəkən/, **baldachino** /ˌbældə'kiːnəʊ/ **N** baldaquin *m*

balderdash /'bɔːldədæʃ/ **N** balivernes *fpl*

balding /'bɔːldɪŋ/ **ADJ** qui devient chauve, atteint de calvitie naissante

baldly /'bɔːldlɪ/ **ADV** *[say, state]* abruptement

baldness /'bɔːldnɪs/ **N** *[of person]* calvitie *f* ; *[of tyre]* état *m* lisse ; *[of mountains etc]* nudité *f* ; *[of style]* platitude *f*, pauvreté *f*

baldy * /'bɔːldɪ/ **ADJ** *(= balding)* dégarni ; *(= bald)* chauve **N** tête *f* d'œuf

bale¹ /beɪl/ **N** *[of cotton, hay]* balle *f* **VT** (also **bale up**) mettre en balles

bale² /beɪl/ **VT** *(Naut)* ⇒ **bail³ vt**

► **bale out** ⇒ **bail out** ; → **bail³**

Balearic /ˌbælɪ'ærɪk/ **ADJ, N the** ~ **Islands, the** ~**s** les (îles *fpl*) Baléares *fpl*

baleful /'beɪlfʊl/ **ADJ** sinistre, menaçant ◆ **to give sb/sth a** ~ **look** regarder qn/qch d'un œil torve

balefully /'beɪlfəlɪ/ **ADV** *[look]* d'un œil torve ; *[say]* d'un ton sinistre *or* menaçant

Bali /'bɑːlɪ/ **N** Bali

Balinese /ˌbɑːlɪ'niːz/ **ADJ** balinais **N** 1 *(= person)* Balinais(e) *m(f)* 2 *(= language)* balinais *m*

balk /bɔːk/ **N** *(Agr)* terre *f* non labourée ; *(Constr) (on ceiling)* solive *f* ; *(= building timber)* bille *f* **VT** contrecarrer **VI** *[horse]* se dérober (at devant) ; ◆ **to** ~ **at doing sth** *[person]* regimber pour faire qch

Balkan /'bɔːlkən/ **ADJ, N** ◆ **the** ~**s** les Balkans *mpl* ◆ **the** ~ **States** les États *mpl* balkaniques ◆ **the** ~ **Peninsula** la péninsule Balkanique

balkanization /ˌbɔːlkənaɪ'zeɪʃən/ **N** balkanisation *f*

ball¹ /bɔːl/ **N** 1 *(gen, Cricket, Golf, Hockey, Tennis)* balle *f* ; *(inflated: Ftbl etc)* ballon *m* ; *(Billiards)* bille *f*, boule *f* ; (*Croquet*) boule *f* ◆ **as round as a ~** rond comme une boule *or* bille ◆ **behind the eight ~*** (*US fig*) dans le pétrin* ◆ **cat curled up in a ~** chat *m* couché en rond *or* pelotonné (en boule) ◆ **tennis/golf** *etc* **~** balle *f* de tennis/de golf *etc* ◆ **croquet ~** boule *f* de croquet ◆ **~ of fire, ~ lightning** (*Met*) éclair *m* en boule

2 (*fig phrases*) (*US*) ◆ **that's the way the ~ bounces !*** c'est la vie ! ◆ **to keep a lot of ~s in the air** faire plein de choses à la fois ◆ **take the ~ and run with it!** vas-y fonce !*, saisis ta chance ! ◆ **to keep the ~ rolling** (*= maintain conversation*) alimenter la conversation ; (*= maintain activity*) maintenir le mouvement ; (*= maintain interest*) soutenir l'intérêt ◆ **to start** *or* **set the ~ rolling*** lancer une affaire (*or* la conversation *etc*) ◆ **he's got the ~ at his feet** c'est à lui de saisir cette chance ◆ **the ~ is with you** *or* **in your court** (c'est) à vous de jouer ◆ **to have something on the ~*** (*US*) en avoir là-dedans* *or* dans le ciboulot‡ ◆ **to be on the ~*** (*= competent*) être à la hauteur (de la situation *or* des circonstances) ; (*= alert*) ouvrir l'œil et le bon* ◆ **he's a real ~ of fire*** il est débordant d'activité ◆ **the whole ~ of wax** (*US*) absolument tout ; → **eyeball, play, tennis**

3 [*of rifle etc*] balle *f* ◆ **~ and chain** (*lit, fig*) boulet *m* ; → **cannonball**

4 [*of wool, string*] pelote *f*, peloton *m* ◆ **to wind sth up into a ~** mettre qch en pelote

5 (*Culin*) [*of meat, fish*] boulette *f* ; [*of potato*] croquette *f*

6 (*in ball bearings*) bille *f* (de roulement)

7 (*Anat*) **~ of the foot** (partie *f* antérieure de la) plante *f* du pied ◆ **~ of the thumb** (partie *f* charnue du) pouce *m* ; → **eyeball**

NPL **balls**** 1 (*= testicles*) couilles** *fpl* ◆ **to have sb by the ~s** tenir qn par les couilles** ◆ **to break sb's ~s** casser les couilles** à qn

2 (*Brit = nonsense*) conneries** *fpl*, couillonnades** *fpl* ◆ **~s!** quelles conneries !**

3 (*Brit = courage*) **to have ~s** avoir des couilles** ◆ **to have the ~s to do sth** avoir le cran de faire qch*

VT 1 [*+ wool etc*] mettre en pelote, pelotonner

2 (***esp US = have sex with*) s'envoyer‡

VI 1 (*= form into ball*) s'agglomérer

2 (***esp US = have sex*) s'envoyer en l'air

COMP **ball-and-socket joint** N (joint *m* à) rotule *f*

ball bearings NPL roulement *m* à billes

ball boy N (*Tennis*) ramasseur *m* de balles

ball cartridge N cartouche *f* à balle

ball control N (*NonC: Ftbl, Basketball etc*) contrôle *m* du ballon

ball game N (*= sport*) jeu *m* de balle (*or* ballon) ; (*US*) (*= match*) match *m* de base-ball ◆ **it's a whole new ~ game*, it's not the same ~ game*** c'est une tout autre histoire

ball girl N (*Tennis*) ramasseuse *f* de balles

ball-point (pen) N stylo *m* (à) bille, (pointe *f*) Bic ® *m*

ball-shaped ADJ sphérique

balls-up**, **ball-up**** (*US*) N bordel‡ *m* ◆ **he made a ~s-up of the job** il a foutu le bordel‡ *or* salopé le boulot‡ ◆ **the meeting was a ~s-up** (*Brit*) la réunion a été bordélique‡

► **balls up**** VT SEP foutre la merde** *or* le bordel‡ dans ◆ **to be/get ballsed up**‡ être/se retrouver dans la merde jusqu'au cou‡

N ◆ **balls-up**** → **ball[1]**

► **ball up** VI (*Ski etc*) botter

VT SEP ** ⇒ **balls up**

ball[2] /bɔːl/ N (*= dance*) bal *m* ◆ **to give a ~** donner un bal ◆ **to open the ~** (*lit, fig*) ouvrir le bal ◆ **to have a ~*** s'amuser comme des fous, se marrer* COMP **ball gown** N robe *f* de bal

ballad /ˈbæləd/ N (*Mus*) romance *f* ; (*Literat*) ballade *f*

ballast /ˈbæləst/ N (*NonC*) 1 (*in plane, ship*) lest *m* ◆ **ship in ~** vaisseau *m* en lest ◆ **to sail in ~** être sur lest 2 (*= stone, clinker*) pierraille *f* ; (*Rail*) ballast *m* VT 1 [*+ plane, ship*] lester 2 [*+ road*] empierrer, caillouter ; [*+ railway*] ballaster

ballbreaker‡ /ˈbɔːlˌbreɪkəʳ/ N chieuse‡ *f*

ballcock /ˈbɔːlkɒk/ N robinet *m* à flotteur

ballerina /ˌbæləˈriːnə/ N ballerine *f*

ballet /ˈbæleɪ/ N 1 (*= show, work of art*) ballet *m* 2 (*NonC = type of dance*) danse *f* classique

COMP **ballet dancer** N danseur *m*, -euse *f* classique

ballet lesson N cours *m* de danse (classique)

ballet school N école *f* de danse (classique)

ballet shoe N chausson *m* de danse

ballet skirt N jupe *f* de danseuse

balletic /bæˈletɪk/ ADJ [*movement, grace, style*] de danseur de ballet

ballistic /bəˈlɪstɪk/ ADJ balistique ◆ **to go ~*** piquer une crise* COMP **ballistic missile** N engin *m* balistique

ballistics /bəˈlɪstɪks/ N (*NonC*) balistique *f*

balloon /bəˈluːn/ N 1 (*for transport*) ballon *m*, aérostat *m* ◆ **navigable/captive ~** ballon *m* dirigeable/captif ◆ **to go up in a ~** monter en ballon ◆ **the ~ went up*** (*fig*) l'affaire a éclaté ◆ **(meteorological** *or* **weather) ~** ballon-sonde *m* ; → **barrage** 2 (*= toy*) ballon *m* 3 (*for brandy: also* **balloon glass**) verre *m* ballon *inv* ; (*Chem: also* **balloon flask**) ballon *m* 4 (*in drawings, comic: for speech etc*) bulle *f* VI 1 ◆ **to go ~ing** faire une (*or* des) ascension(s) en ballon 2 (*= swell out*) gonfler, être ballonné COMP **balloon tyre** N pneu *m* ballon

balloonist /bəˈluːnɪst/ N aéronaute *mf*

ballot /ˈbælət/ N 1 (*Pol etc*) (*= paper*) bulletin *m* de vote ; (*= method of voting*) scrutin *m* ; (*= round of voting*) (tour *m* de) scrutin *m* ◆ **to vote by ~** voter par scrutin ◆ **first/second ~** premier/second tour *m* de scrutin ◆ **to take a ~** procéder à un scrutin *or* à un vote

2 (*= drawing of lots*) tirage *m* au sort

VI 1 (*Pol etc*) voter à bulletin secret ◆ **union members are currently ~ing on the offer** les membres du syndicat votent actuellement sur cette proposition (à bulletins secrets)

2 (*= draw lots*) tirer au sort ◆ **to ~ for a place on the committee** tirer au sort pour avoir un siège au comité

VT faire voter (à bulletin secret), consulter (au moyen d'un vote à bulletin secret) ◆ **the union is ~ing members on strike action** le syndicat fait voter la base (à bulletin secret) sur la décision de faire grève

COMP **ballot box** N urne *f* (électorale) ◆ **we accept the verdict of the ~ box** nous acceptons le verdict des urnes

ballot-box stuffing N (*US Pol*) bourrage *m* des urnes

ballot paper N bulletin *m* de vote

ballot rigging N (*Brit*) fraude *f* électorale

balloting /ˈbælətɪŋ/ N (*US Pol*) scrutin *m*

ballpark /ˈbɔːlpɑːk/ N (*US*) stade *m* de base-ball ◆ **to be in the (right) ~** (*fig*) [*estimates, figures*] être dans la bonne fourchette ◆ **the figures were in the ~ of our estimates** les chiffres rentraient dans la fourchette de nos premières estimations ◆ **we're in the same ~** (*in estimates, figures*) on arrive à peu près à la même somme ◆ **the two companies are not in the same ~** les deux sociétés ne sont pas comparables ADJ [*figure, estimate*] approximatif

ballplayer /ˈbɔːlˌpleɪəʳ/ N (*US*) joueur *m* de base-ball

ballroom /ˈbɔːlrʊm/ N [*of hotel*] salle *f* de danse ; [*of mansion*] salle *f* de bal COMP **ballroom dancing** N (*NonC*) danse *f* de salon

ballsy‡ /ˈbɔːlzɪ/ ADJ [*person, attempt*] gonflé*

bally †* /ˈbælɪ/ ADJ (*before n*) (*Brit*) sacré*, satané

ballyhoo* /ˌbælɪˈhuː/ N (*pej*) (*= publicity*) battage* *m*, bourrage *m* de crâne* ; (*= nonsense*) balivernes *fpl*

balm /bɑːm/ N 1 (*lit, fig*) baume *m* 2 (*= plant*) mélisse *f* officinale ; (*also* **lemon balm**) citronnelle *f*

balmy /ˈbɑːmɪ/ ADJ 1 (*liter*) (*= fragrant*) embaumé, parfumé ; (*= mild*) doux (douce *f*) ◆ **~ weather** temps doux 2 (*= like balm*) balsamique

baloney* /bəˈləʊnɪ/ N (*NonC: esp US*) balivernes *fpl*

balsa /ˈbɔːlsə/ N (*also* **balsa wood**) balsa *m*

balsam /ˈbɔːlsəm/ N 1 (*= substance*) baume *m* 2 (*= plant*) balsamine *f* 3 (*Chem*) oléorésine *f* COMP **balsam fir** N sapin *m* baumier

balsamic /bɔːlˈsæmɪk/ ADJ [*vinegar*] balsamique

balti /ˈbɔːltɪ, ˈbæltɪ/ N (*Culin*) *plat indien mijoté dans une petite poêle*

Baltic /ˈbɔːltɪk/ N ◆ **the ~** (*= sea*) la (mer) Baltique ◆ **the ~s** les pays baltes ADJ [*trade, port*] de la Baltique ◆ **the ~ Sea** la Baltique ◆ **the ~ States** les pays baltes

baluster /ˈbæləstəʳ/ N balustre *m* ◆ **~s** rampe *f* d'escalier

balustrade /ˌbæləsˈtreɪd/ N balustrade *f*

bamboo /bæmˈbuː/ N bambou *m*

COMP [*chair, fence*] de *or* en bambou

Bamboo Curtain N (*Pol*) rideau *m* de bambou

bamboo shoots NPL pousses *fpl* de bambou

bamboozle* /bæmˈbuːzl/ VT 1 (*= deceive*) embobiner* ◆ **I was ~d into believing he was a qualified doctor** on m'a embobiné* en me faisant croire que c'était un médecin qualifié 2 (*= perplex*) déboussoler* ◆ **she was quite ~d** elle ne savait plus où elle en était, elle était complètement déboussolée*

ban /bæn/ N interdit *m* ; (*Comm*) embargo *m* ◆ **to put a ~ on sth/sb's doing sth** interdire qch/à qn de faire qch VT (*gen*) interdire (*sth* qch ; *sb from doing sth* à qn de faire qch) ; (*= exclude*) [*+ person*] exclure (*from* de) ; ◆ **~ned substance** (*Sport*) substance prohibée ◆ **Ban the Bomb Campaign** campagne *f* contre la bombe atomique

banal /bəˈnɑːl/ ADJ banal, ordinaire

banality /bəˈnælɪtɪ/ N banalité *f*

banana /bəˈnɑːnə/ N (*= fruit*) banane *f* ; (*= tree*) bananier *m* ADJ ◆ **to go ~s**‡ devenir dingue* ; (*= get angry*) piquer une crise*

COMP **banana-boat** N bananier *m* (*cargo*)

banana peel N ⇒ **banana skin**

banana republic N (*pej*) république *f* bananière

banana skin N peau *f* de banane ◆ **to slip on a ~ skin** glisser sur une peau de banane

banana split N banana split *m inv*

band[1] /bænd/ N (*gen*) bande *f* ; (*narrow*) bandelette *f* ; [*of barrel*] cercle *m* ; [*of metal wheel*] bandage *m* ; (*leather*) lanière *f* ; [*of cigar*] bague *f* ; [*of hat*] ruban *m* ; (*Rad*) bande *f* ; (*= magnetic tape*) bande *f* (magnétique) ; [*of gramophone record*] plage *f* ; (*= drivebelt*) bande *f* *or* courroie *f* de transmission ; (*Educ*) tranche *f* ◆ **~s of the spectrum** bandes *fpl* du spectre ◆ **metal ~** bande *f* métallique ◆ **to vary within a narrow ~** [*figures, prices etc*] varier à l'intérieur d'une fourchette étroite ; → **elastic, frequency, rubber[1], waistband, waveband** VT [*+ tax, property*] ◆ **to be ~ed** être réparti par tranches COMP **band-saw** N (*Tech*) scie *f* à ruban

► **band together** VI se grouper ; (*= form a gang*) former une bande

band[2] /bænd/ N 1 (*= group*) bande *f*, troupe *f* 2 (*Mus*) (*gen*) orchestre *m* ; (*brass only*) fanfare *f*

♦ **members of the** ~ musiciens *mpl* ; → **brass, one-man**

bandage /ˈbændɪdʒ/ **N** (*for wound*) bande *f* ; (*Med = prepared dressing*) bandage *m*, pansement *m* ; (*blindfolding*) bandeau *m* ♦ **head swathed in ~s** tête *f* enveloppée de pansements *or* de bandages ; → **crêpe** **VT** (also **bandage up**) [*+ broken limb*] bander ; [*+ wound*] mettre un pansement *or* un bandage sur ; [*+ person*] mettre un pansement *or* un bandage à

Band-Aid ® /ˈbændeɪd/ **N** (*lit*) pansement *m* adhésif **COMP** (*fig*) [*measures*] de fortune ; [*solution*] bricolé ♦ **a ~ approach** une méthode qui tient du rafistolage

bandan(n)a /bænˈdænə/ **N** foulard *m*

B & B /ˌbiːənˈbiː/ **N** (abbrev of **bed and breakfast**) → **bed**

bandbox /ˈbændbɒks/ **N** carton *m* à chapeau(x) ♦ **he looked as if he had just stepped out of a ~** il avait l'air de sortir d'une boîte

bandeau /ˈbændəʊ/ **N** (pl **bandeaux** /ˈbændəʊz/) bandeau *m*

banderol(e) /ˈbændərɒl/ **N** (= *scroll, streamer, flag*) banderole *f*

banding /ˈbændɪŋ/ **N** 1 (*Brit*) [*of school pupils*] répartition *f* en groupes de niveaux (*dans le primaire*) 2 [*of houses*] répartition *f* par tranches

bandit /ˈbændɪt/ **N** (*lit, fig*) bandit *m* ; → **one**

banditry /ˈbændɪtrɪ/ **N** (*NonC*) banditisme *m*

bandleader /ˈbænd,liːdəʳ/, **bandmaster** /ˈbænd"mɑːstəʳ/ **N** chef *m* d'orchestre ; (*Mil etc*) chef *m* de musique *or* de fanfare

bandolier /ˌbændəˈlɪəʳ/ **N** cartouchière *f*

bandsman /ˈbændzmən/ **N** (pl **-men**) musicien *m* (d'orchestre *or* de fanfare)

bandstand /ˈbændstænd/ **N** kiosque *m* (à musique)

bandwagon /ˈbænd,wægən/ **N** (*fig*) ♦ **to jump** *or* **climb** *or* **leap on the** ~ suivre le mouvement, prendre le train en marche* ♦ **all these companies jumping on the Internet** ~ toutes ces entreprises ne font que prendre le train du Net en marche

bandwidth /ˈbændwɪdθ/ **N** (*Comput*) largeur *f* de bande

bandy¹ /ˈbændɪ/ **VT** [*+ ball, reproaches*] se renvoyer ; [*+ jokes*] échanger ♦ **to ~ blows (with sb)** échanger des coups (avec qn) ♦ **to ~ words (with sb)** discuter (avec qn)

► **bandy about, bandy around** **VT SEP** (*pej*) [*+ story, report*] faire circuler ; [*+ figures, sums*] avancer ♦ **to ~ sb's name about** parler de qn ♦ **to have one's name bandied about** faire parler de soi ♦ **his name is being bandied about in all the newspapers** il a son nom dans tous les journaux

bandy² /ˈbændɪ/ **ADJ** [*leg*] arqué **COMP** **bandy-legged** **ADJ** [*person*] bancal ; [*horse*] arqué ♦ **to be ~-legged** avoir les jambes arquées

bane /beɪn/ **N** 1 fléau *m*, peste *f* ♦ **he's/it's the ~ of my life*** il/cela m'empoisonne la vie ♦ **rain is the ~ of holiday-makers** la pluie est le fléau numéro un des vacanciers ♦ **spots can be the ~ of a teenager's life** les boutons peuvent empoisonner la vie d'un adolescent 2 (*liter*) (= *poison*) poison *m*

baneful /ˈbeɪnfʊl/ **ADJ** (*liter*) funeste, fatal ; [*poison*] mortel

banefully /ˈbeɪnfəlɪ/ **ADV** funestement

bang /bæŋ/ **N** 1 (= *noise*) [*of gun, explosives*] détonation *f*, boum *m* ; (*supersonic*) bang *m* (supersonique) ; [*of door*] claquement *m* ♦ **the door closed with a** ~ la porte a claqué ♦ **to go off with a** ~ [*fireworks*] détoner, éclater ♦ **to go with a** ~* être un franc succès ♦ **to get more ~ for the buck** *or* **more ~s for your bucks*** (*esp US*) en avoir pour son argent ♦ **to end** *or* **finish not with a ~ but a whimper** finir en queue de poisson

2 (= *blow*) coup *m* (violent)

ADV * ♦ **to go** ~ éclater ♦ ~ **in the middle** au beau milieu, en plein milieu ♦ ~ **against the wall** tout contre le mur ♦ **I ran ~ into a traffic jam** je suis tombé en plein dans un embouteillage ♦ **to hit the target ~ on** (*Brit*) frapper en plein dans la cible *or* le mille ♦ **his answer was ~ on** (*Brit*) sa réponse est tombée pile ♦ **she arrived ~ on time** (*Brit*) elle est arrivée à l'heure pile ♦ **the play's ~ up to date** cette pièce est complètement d'actualité ♦ ~ **goes my chance of promotion** je peux faire une croix sur mes chances de promotion, je peux dire adieu à mes chances de promotion ♦ ~ **goes the fantasy of retiring at 35*** on peut dire adieu au rêve de prendre sa retraite à 35 ans ; → **slap**

EXCL (*firearm*) pan ! ; (*explosion*) boum !

VT 1 frapper violemment ♦ **to ~ one's fist on the table** taper du poing sur la table, frapper la table du poing ♦ **to ~ one's head against** *or* **on sth** se cogner la tête contre *or* sur qch ♦ **talking to him is like ~ing your head against a brick wall*** autant parler à un mur que d'essayer de discuter avec lui ♦ **to ~ the door** (faire) claquer la porte ♦ **he ~ed the window shut** il a claqué la fenêtre

2 (*** = *have sex with*) baiser***

VI 1 [*door*] claquer ; (*repeatedly*) battre ; [*fireworks*] éclater ; [*gun*] détoner

2 ♦ **to ~ on** *or* **at the door** donner de grands coups dans la porte ♦ **to ~ on the table** taper du poing sur la table, frapper la table du poing

► **bang about***, **bang around*** **VI** faire du bruit *or* du potin*

► **bang away** **VI** [*guns*] tonner ; [*workman etc*] faire du vacarme

► **bang down** **VT SEP** poser *or* jeter brusquement ♦ **to ~ down the lid** rabattre violemment le couvercle ♦ **to ~ down the receiver** (*on telephone*) raccrocher brutalement

► **bang into** **VT FUS** (= *collide with*) se cogner contre, heurter ♦ **I ~ed into a table** je me suis cogné contre une table *or* j'ai heurté une table ♦ **the taxi ~ed into another car** le taxi est rentré dans *or* a percuté *or* a heurté une autre voiture

► **bang on*** **VI** continuer à laïusser* ♦ **to ~ on about sth** laïusser* sur qch

► **bang out** **VT SEP** [*+ tune*] taper

► **bang to** **VI** [*door, window*] se fermer en claquant

► **bang together** **VT SEP** [*+ objects*] cogner l'un(e) contre l'autre ♦ **I could have ~ed their heads together!*** j'en aurais pris un pour taper sur l'autre !

► **bang up*** **VT SEP** (*Brit*) [*+ prisoner*] boucler*, coffrer*

banger /ˈbæŋəʳ/ **N** (*Brit*) 1 (* = *sausage*) saucisse *f* ♦ **~s and mash** saucisses *fpl* à la purée 2 (* = *old car*) (vieux) tacot* *m*, (vieille) guimbarde *f* 3 (= *firework*) pétard *m*

Bangkok /bæŋˈkɒk/ **N** Bangkok

Bangladesh /ˌbæŋgləˈdeʃ/ **N** Bangladesh *m*

Bangladeshi /ˌbæŋgləˈdeʃɪ/ **ADJ** du Bangladesh **N** habitant(e) *m(f)* *or* natif *m*, -ive *f* du Bangladesh

bangle /ˈbæŋgl/ **N** jonc *m*, bracelet *m*

bangs /bæŋz/ **NPL** (*US* = *fringe*) frange *f* (droite)

bang-up* /ˈbæŋʌp/ **ADJ** (US) formidable, impec*

banish /ˈbænɪʃ/ **VT** [*+ person*] exiler (*from* de ; *to* en, à) bannir (*from* de) ; [*+ cares, fear*] bannir, chasser

banishment /ˈbænɪʃmənt/ **N** bannissement *m*, exil *m*

banister /ˈbænɪstəʳ/ **N** ⇒ **bannister**

banjax* /ˈbændʒæks/ **VT** (US) assommer

banjaxed* /ˈbændʒækst/ **ADJ** (*US*) nase*

banjo /ˈbændʒəʊ/ **N** (pl **banjos** *or* **banjoes**) banjo *m*

bank¹ /bæŋk/ **N** 1 (= *mound*) [*of earth, snow, flowers*] talus *m* ; (*Rail = embankment*) remblai *m* ; [*of road, racetrack*] bord *m* relevé ; (*in horse-racing*) banquette *f* irlandaise ; (= *coal face*) front *m* de taille ; (= *pithead*) carreau *m* ; [*of sand*] (*in sea, river*) banc *m* ♦ **a ~ of clouds** un amoncellement de nuages 2 (= *edge*) [*of river, lake*] bord *m*, rive *f* ; (*above water level*) berge *f* ; [*of canal*] bord *m*, berge *f* ♦ **the ~s** [*of river, lake*] le rivage ♦ **the left/right ~** (*in Paris*) la Rive gauche/droite 3 (*in flying*) virage *m* incliné *or* sur l'aile **VT** 1 (also **bank up**) [*+ road*] relever (*dans un virage*) ; [*+ river*] endiguer ; [*+ earth*] amonceler ♦ **to ~ the fire** couvrir le feu 2 ♦ **to ~ an aircraft** faire faire à un avion un virage sur l'aile **VI** 1 [*snow, clouds etc*] s'amonceler 2 [*pilot, aircraft*] virer (sur l'aile)

bank² /bæŋk/ **N** 1 (= *institution*) banque *f* ; (= *office*) agence *f* (bancaire), banque *f* ♦ ~ **of issue** banque *f* d'émission ♦ **the Bank of France** la Banque de France ♦ **the Bank of England** la Banque d'Angleterre ♦ **it's as safe as the Bank of England** ça ne court aucun risque, c'est de tout repos ; → **saving**

2 (*Betting*) banque *f* ♦ **to break the ~** faire sauter la banque

3 (*Med*) banque *f* ; → **blood, eyebank**

VT [*+ money*] mettre *or* déposer à la banque ; (*Med*) [*+ blood*] entreposer, conserver

VI ♦ **to ~ with Lloyds** avoir un compte à la Lloyds ♦ **who do you ~ with?** à quelle banque êtes-vous ?, où avez-vous votre compte bancaire ?

COMP [*cheque, credit, staff*] bancaire

bank acceptance **N** acceptation *f* bancaire

bank account **N** compte *m* bancaire, compte *m* en banque

bank balance **N** solde *m* bancaire

bank bill **N** (*US*) billet *m* de banque ; (*Brit*) effet *m* bancaire

bank-book **N** livret *m* *or* carnet *m* de banque

bank card **N** carte *f* d'identité bancaire

bank charges **NPL** (*Brit*) frais *mpl* bancaires

bank clerk **N** (*Brit*) employé(e) *m(f)* de banque

bank draft **N** traite *f* bancaire

bank employee **N** employé(e) *m(f)* de banque

Bank Giro, Bank Giro Credit **N** (*Brit*) (paiement *m* par) virement *m* bancaire

bank holiday **N** jour *m* férié

bank loan **N** crédit *m* bancaire

bank manager **N** directeur *m* d'agence (bancaire) ♦ **my ~ manager** mon banquier

bank rate **N** taux *m* d'escompte

bank robber **N** braqueur *m*, -euse *f* de banque

bank robbery **N** cambriolage *m* de banque

bank statement **N** relevé *m* de compte

bank transfer **N** ♦ **by ~ transfer** par virement bancaire ; → **job**

► **bank on** **VT FUS** (= *count on*) compter sur ♦ **I wouldn't ~ on it** il ne faut pas compter dessus

bank³ /bæŋk/ **N** 1 (= *row, tier*) [*of organ*] clavier *m* ; [*of typewriter*] rang *m* ; (*Elec*) [*of switches*] rangée *f* ♦ ~ **of oars** rangée *f* d'avirons 2 (= *rowers' bench*) banc *m* (de rameurs) **VT** (*Sport*) ♦ **double/single ~ed rowing** nage *f* à couple/en pointe

► **bank up** **VT SEP** 1 (= *arrange in tiers*) étager, disposer par étages 2 → **bank¹ vt 1**

bankable /ˈbæŋkəbl/ **ADJ** (*Comm*) bancable, négociable en banque ♦ **to be ~** [*film star etc*] être une valeur sûre

banker /ˈbæŋkəʳ/ **N** (*Betting, Fin*) banquier *m* **COMP** **banker's card** **N** carte *f* d'identité bancaire

banker's draft N traite *f* bancaire
banker's order N (*Brit*) prélèvement *m* automatique
banker's reference N références *fpl* bancaires

banking¹ /ˈbæŋkɪŋ/ N [*of aircraft*] virage *m* sur l'aile

banking² /ˈbæŋkɪŋ/ N (*Fin*) (= *transaction*) opérations *fpl* de banque *or* bancaires ; (= *profession*) profession *f* de banquier, la banque ◆ **to study** ~ faire des études bancaires
COMP **banking hours** NPL heures *fpl* d'ouverture des banques
banking house N banque *f*, établissement *m* bancaire ◆ **the big ~ houses** les grandes banques *fpl*
banking industry N secteur *m* bancaire
banking product N produit *m* bancaire
banking services NPL services *mpl* bancaires

banknote /ˈbæŋknəʊt/ N (*Brit*) billet *m* de banque

bankroll* /ˈbæŋkrəʊl/ (*esp US*) N fonds *mpl*, finances *fpl* VT financer

bankrupt /ˈbæŋkrʌpt/ N 1 (*Jur*) failli(e) *m(f)* 2 (* *fig* = *penniless person*) fauché(e)* *m(f)* ADJ 1 (*Jur*) failli ◆ **to go** ~ [*person, business*] faire faillite ◆ **to be** ~ [*person*] être en faillite ◆ **to be declared** ~ être déclaré *or* mis en faillite 2 (* *fig* = *penniless*) fauché* 3 (= *completely lacking*) ◆ **spiritually/morally** *etc* ~ dépourvu *or* dénué de spiritualité/de moralité *etc* ◆ ~ **of ideas** *etc* dépourvu *or* dénué d'idées *etc* VT 1 (*Jur*) [+ *person*] mettre en faillite 2 (* *fig*) ruiner
COMP **bankrupt's certificate** N concordat *m*
bankrupt's estate N actif *m* de la faillite

bankruptcy /ˈbæŋkrəptsɪ/ N 1 (*Jur*) faillite *f* ◆ **to file for** *or* **declare** ~ déposer son bilan, se déclarer en faillite 2 (* *fig* = *pennilessness*) ruine *f* 3 (* *fig* = *lack*) ◆ **spiritual/moral** *etc* ~ manque *m* de spiritualité/de moralité *etc*
COMP **Bankruptcy Court** N (*Brit*) ≃ tribunal *m* de commerce
bankruptcy estate N masse *f or* actif *m* de la faillite
bankruptcy petition N assignation *f* des créanciers
bankruptcy proceedings NPL procédure *f* de faillite, procédure *f* de règlement judiciaire

banner /ˈbænəʳ/ N bannière *f*, étendard *m* ; (*Rel, fig*) bannière *f* (*Comput : on web page*) bannière *f*, bandeau *m*
COMP **banner ad** N (*Comput : on web page*) bannière *f or* bandeau *m* publicitaire
banner headlines NPL (*Press*) gros titres *mpl* ◆ **in ~ headlines** en gros titres, sur cinq colonnes à la une

banning /ˈbænɪŋ/ N (= *prohibition*) [*of activity, publication, film, organization, substance*] interdiction *f* ◆ **the ~ of right-wing parties** l'interdiction *f* des partis de droite ◆ **the ~ of anti-apartheid leaders** l'interdiction *f* frappant les dirigeants du mouvement anti-apartheid ◆ **the ~ of cars from city centres** l'interdiction *f* de la circulation automobile dans les centre-villes ◆ **the ~ of three athletes from the Olympic Games** l'exclusion *f* de trois athlètes des Jeux olympiques

bannister /ˈbænɪstəʳ/ N rampe *f* (d'escalier) ◆ **to slide down the ~(s)** descendre sur la rampe

banns /bænz/ NPL bans *mpl* (*de mariage*) ◆ **to call the** ~ publier les bans

banquet /ˈbæŋkwɪt/ N (= *ceremonial dinner*) banquet *m* ; (= *lavish meal*) festin *m* VI faire un banquet, festoyer COMP **banqueting hall** N salle *f* de(s) banquet(s)

banquette /ˌbæŋˈket/ N banquette *f*

banshee /ˈbænˈʃiː/ N fée *f* (*dont les cris présagent la mort*)

bantam /ˈbæntəm/ N coq *m* nain, poule *f* naine COMP **bantam-weight** N (*Boxing*) poids *m* coq

banter /ˈbæntəʳ/ N badinage *m*, plaisanteries *fpl* VI badiner, plaisanter

bantering /ˈbæntərɪŋ/ ADJ plaisantin, badin

Bantu /ˈbæntuː/ ADJ bantou N (pl **Bantu** *or* **Bantus**) 1 (= *people*) ◆ **~(s)** Bantous *mpl* 2 (= *language*) bantou *m*

banyan /ˈbænɪən/ N banian *m*

bap /bæp/ N (*Brit Culin*) petit pain *m*

baptism /ˈbæptɪzəm/ N baptême *m* ◆ **~ of fire** baptême *m* du feu

baptismal /bæpˈtɪzməl/ ADJ de baptême
COMP **baptismal font** N fonts *mpl* baptismaux
baptismal name N nom *m* de baptême
baptismal vows NPL vœux *mpl* du baptême

baptist /ˈbæptɪst/ N 1 baptiste *m* ◆ **(Saint) John the Baptist** saint Jean-Baptiste 2 (*Rel*) **Baptist** baptiste *mf* ADJ (*Rel*) ◆ **Baptist** baptiste COMP **the Baptist Church** N l'Église *f* baptiste

baptize /bæpˈtaɪz/ VT (*Rel, fig*) baptiser

bar¹ /bɑːʳ/ N 1 (= *block, slab*) [*of metal*] barre *f* ; [*of wood*] planche *f* ; [*of gold*] lingot *m* ; [*of chocolate*] tablette *f* ◆ ~ **of soap** savonnette *f*, pain *m* de savon ◆ ~ **of gold** lingot *m* (d'or)

2 (= *rod*) [*of window, cage*] barreau *m* ; [*of grate*] barre *f* ; [*of door*] barre *f*, bâcle *f* ; (*Sport*) barre *f* ; (*Ftbl*) (= *crossbar*) barre *f* transversale ; [*of ski-lift*] perche *f* ; [*of electric fire*] résistance *f* ◆ **a two-~ electric fire** un radiateur électrique à deux résistances ◆ **to be/put sb behind (prison) ~s** être/mettre qn derrière les barreaux ; → **anti-roll bar, parallel**

3 [*of river, harbour*] barre *f*

4 (*fig* = *obstacle*) obstacle *m* ◆ **to be a ~ to progress** empêcher le *or* faire obstacle au progrès ◆ **his criminal record was a ~ to getting a job** son casier judiciaire l'empêchait de trouver du travail ; → **colour**

5 [*of light*] raie *f* ; [*of colour*] bande *f*

6 (*NonC: Jur*) (= *profession*) barreau *m* ; (*in court*) barre *f* ◆ **to call** (*Brit*) *or* **admit** (*US*) **sb to the** ~ inscrire qn au barreau ◆ **to be called** (*Brit*) *or* **admitted** (*US*) **to the** ~ s'inscrire au barreau ◆ **to read for the** ~ préparer le barreau ◆ **the prisoner at the** ~ l'accusé(e) *m(f)*

7 (= *public house*) café *m*, bar *m* ; [*of hotel, theatre*] bar *m* ; [*of station*] café *m*, bar *m* ; (*at open-air shows etc*) buvette *f* ; → **coffee, public**

8 (= *counter: for drinks*) comptoir *m* ◆ **to have a drink at the** ~ prendre un verre au comptoir ◆ **sock/hat** ~ (*Comm*) rayon *m* des chaussettes/des chapeaux ◆ **heel** ~ talon-minute *m*

9 (*Mus*) mesure *f* ; (also **bar line**) barre *f* de mesure ◆ **the opening ~s** les premières mesures *fpl* ; → **double**

10 (*Brit Mil*) barrette *f* (*portée sur le ruban d'une médaille*) ; (*US Mil*) galon *m*

11 (*Weather*) bar *m*

VT 1 (= *obstruct*) [+ *road*] barrer ◆ **to ~ sb's way** *or* **path** barrer le passage à qn, couper la route à qn ◆ **to ~ the way to progress** faire obstacle au progrès

2 (= *put bars on*) [+ *window*] munir de barreaux ◆ **to ~ the door** mettre la barre à la porte ◆ **to ~ the door against sb** (*lit, fig*) barrer la porte à qn

3 (= *exclude, prohibit*) [+ *person*] exclure (from de) ; [+ *action, thing*] défendre ◆ **to ~ sb from doing sth** interdire à qn de faire qch ◆ **many jobs were ~red to them** de nombreux emplois leur étaient interdits ◆ **they're ~red from the country/the pub** il leur est interdit d'entrer dans le pays/le bar ◆ **she ~s smoking in her house** elle défend qu'on fume *subj* chez elle ◆ **to be ~red** (*Jur*) [*contract provisions*] se prescrire ; → **hold**

4 (= *stripe*) rayer, barrer

COMP **bar billiards** N (*NonC: Brit*) billard *m* russe
bar chart N ⇒ **bar graph**
bar code N (*Comm*) code *m* à barres, code-barre *m*
bar-coded ADJ avec code à barres, avec code-barre
bar-code reader N lecteur *m* de code à barres *or* de code-barre
bar girl* N (*US*) entraîneuse *f* de bar
bar graph N graphique *m* en barres *or* en tuyaux d'orgue

bar² /bɑːʳ/ PREP sauf, à l'exception de ◆ ~ **none** sans exception ◆ ~ **one** sauf un(e) ; see also **shouting**

Barabbas /bəˈræbəs/ N Barabbas *m*

barb¹ /bɑːb/ N 1 [*of fish hook*] barbillon *m* ; [*of arrow*] barbelure *f* ; [*of feather*] barbe *f* 2 (= *cutting remark*) pique *f* ◆ **the ~s of criticism** les traits *mpl* acérés de la critique 3 (*Dress*) barbette *f* VT [+ *arrow*] garnir de barbelures, barbeler ; [+ *fish hook*] garnir de barbillons COMP **barb wire** N fil *m* de fer barbelé

barb² /bɑːb/ N (= *horse*) (cheval *m*) barbe *m*

Barbadian /bɑːˈbeɪdɪən/ ADJ barbadien N Barbadien(ne) *m(f)*

Barbados /bɑːˈbeɪdɒs/ N Barbade *f* ◆ **in** ~ à la Barbade

barbarian /bɑːˈbeərɪən/ ADJ, N (*Hist, fig*) barbare *mf*

barbaric /bɑːˈbærɪk/ ADJ (*Hist, fig*) barbare, de barbare

barbarism /ˈbɑːbərɪzəm/ N 1 (*NonC*) barbarie *f* 2 (*Ling*) barbarisme *m*

barbarity /bɑːˈbærɪtɪ/ N barbarie *f*, cruauté *f* ◆ **the barbarities of modern warfare** la barbarie *or* les atrocités *fpl* de la guerre moderne

barbarize /ˈbɑːbəraɪz/ VT 1 [+ *people*] ramener à l'état barbare 2 [+ *language*] corrompre

Barbarossa /ˌbɑːbəˈrɒsə/ N Barberousse *m*

barbarous /ˈbɑːbərəs/ ADJ (*Hist, Ling, fig*) barbare

barbarously /ˈbɑːbərəslɪ/ ADV cruellement, inhumainement

Barbary /ˈbɑːbərɪ/ N Barbarie *f*, États *mpl* barbaresques
COMP **Barbary ape** N magot *m*
the Barbary Coast N les côtes *fpl* de Barbarie
Barbary duck N canard *m* de Barbarie
Barbary horse N (cheval *m*) barbe *m*

barbecue /ˈbɑːbɪkjuː/ (vb : prp **barbecuing**) N barbecue *m* ◆ **to have a** ~ faire un barbecue VT faire cuire au barbecue
COMP **barbecue sauce** N sauce *f* barbecue
barbecue set N (grill) barbecue *m*

barbed /bɑːbd/ ADJ 1 [*arrow*] barbelé 2 (*fig*) [*words, wit*] acéré
COMP **barbed wire** N fil *m* de fer barbelé
barbed wire entanglements NPL (réseau *m* de) barbelés *mpl*
barbed wire fence N (haie *f* de fils) barbelés *mpl*

barbel /ˈbɑːbəl/ N (= *fish*) barbeau *m* ; (*smaller*) barbillon *m* ; (= *filament*) barbillon *m*

barbell /ˈbɑːbel/ N (*Sport*) barre *f* d'haltères

barber /ˈbɑːbəʳ/ N coiffeur *m* (pour hommes) ◆ **~'s** (*Brit*) salon *m* de coiffure (pour hommes) ◆ **to go to the ~'s** aller chez le coiffeur COMP **barber's pole** N enseigne *f* de coiffeur

barbershop /ˈbɑːbəʃɒp/ N 1 (*US*: = *shop*) salon *m* de coiffure (pour hommes) 2 (*Mus*) mélodies *fpl* sentimentales (*chantées en harmonie étroite*) COMP **barbershop quartet** N (*Mus*) *groupe de quatre hommes chantant en harmonie étroite*

barbican /ˈbɑːbɪkən/ N barbacane *f*

Barbie ® /ˈbɑːbɪ/ N (also **Barbie doll**) poupée *f* Barbie ®

barbitone /ˈbɑːbɪtəʊn/ N véronal *m*

barbiturate /bɑːˈbɪtjʊrɪt/ N barbiturique *m*
COMP **barbiturate poisoning** N le barbiturisme

barbituric /ˌbɑːbɪˈtjʊərɪk/ ADJ barbiturique

barbs‡ /bɑːbz/ NPL (US) barbituriques *mpl*

Barcalounger ® /ˈbɑːkəlaʊndʒəʳ/ N (US) fauteuil *m* réglable

barcarol(l)e /ˌbɑːkəˈrəʊl/ N barcarolle *f*

Barcelona /ˌbɑːsɪˈləʊnə/ N Barcelone

bard[1] /bɑːd/ N (= minstrel) (esp Celtic) barde *m* ; [of Ancient Greece] aède *m* ; (Poetry, also hum = poet) poète *m* ◆ **the Bard of Avon** le chantre d'Avon (Shakespeare)

bard[2] /bɑːd/ (Culin) N barde *f* (de lard) VT barder

bardic /ˈbɑːdɪk/ ADJ *(esp Celtic) [poetry etc]* du barde, des bardes

bare /bɛəʳ/ ADJ 1 (= naked, uncovered) *[person, skin, sword, floor etc]* nu ; *[hill, summit]* pelé ; *[countryside, tree]* dénudé, dépouillé ; (Elec) *[wire]* dénudé, à nu ◆ ~ **to the waist** nu jusqu'à la ceinture ◆ **in his ~ skin*** tout nu ◆ **he killed the wolf with his ~ hands** il a tué le loup à mains nues ◆ **to fight with ~ hands** se battre à main nue ◆ **there are ~ patches on the lawn** la pelouse est pelée par endroits ◆ **the dog had a few ~ patches on his back** le chien avait la peau du dos pelée par endroits ◆ **with his head ~** nu-tête *inv* ◆ **to sleep on ~ boards** coucher sur la dure ◆ **the ~ bones** les grandes lignes *fpl*, les lignes *fpl* essentielles ◆ **to strip sth down to the ~ bones** réduire qch à l'essentiel *or* à sa plus simple expression ; see also **comp** ◆ **she told him the ~ bones of the story** elle lui a raconté les grandes lignes *or* les lignes essentielles de l'histoire ◆ **ace/king ~** (Cards) as *m*/roi *m* sec ; → **lay**

2 (= empty, unadorned) *[garden]* dénudé ; *[wall]* nu ; *[style]* dépouillé ◆ **a room ~ of furniture** une pièce vide ◆ **a ~ cupboard** un placard vide *or* dégarni ◆ **a ~ statement of facts** un simple énoncé des faits ◆ **they only told us the ~ facts** ils ne nous ont raconté que les faits à l'état brut

3 (= absolute) **the ~ necessities (of life)** le strict nécessaire ◆ **to provide people with the ~ necessities of life** assurer aux gens le minimum vital ◆ **we're happy with the ~ necessities of life** nous nous contentons du strict minimum ◆ **the ~ essentials** le strict nécessaire ◆ **the ~ essentials of furnishing** les meubles *mpl* de base ◆ **a ~ majority** une faible majorité ◆ **the ~ minimum** le plus strict minimum

4 (= mere) **the match lasted a ~ 18 minutes** le match n'a pas duré plus de 18 minutes ◆ **sales grew at a ~ two percent a year** les ventes n'ont pas augmenté de plus de deux pour cent par an

VT mettre à nu, découvrir ; *[+ sword]* dégainer, tirer du fourreau ; *[+ electrical wire]* dénuder, mettre à nu ◆ **to ~ one's head** se découvrir ◆ **to ~ one's chest/breasts** montrer son torse/sa poitrine ◆ **to ~ one's teeth** *[person, animal]* montrer les dents (*at* à) ; ◆ **he ~d his teeth in a smile** il a grimacé un sourire ◆ **to ~ one's soul (to sb)** mettre son cœur à nu (à qn)

COMP **bare-bones** ADJ (esp US) réduit à l'essentiel *or* à sa plus simple expression
bare-knuckle ADJ *[fight]* à mains nues ; *[confrontation]* à couteaux tirés
bare owner N nu(e)-propriétaire *m(f)*
bare ownership, bare property N nue-propriété *f*

bareback /ˈbɛəbæk/ ADV à cru ◆ ~ **rider** cavalier *m*, -ière *f* qui monte à cru VI (* = *have unprotected sex*) avoir des rapports sexuels non protégés

barebacking * /ˈbɛəbækɪŋ/ N (= *unprotected sex*) rapports *mpl* sexuels non protégés

barefaced /ˌbɛəˈfeɪst/ ADJ *[lie, liar]* éhonté ◆ **it is ~ robbery** c'est un *or* du vol manifeste

barefoot(ed) /ˈbɛəfʊt(ɪd)/ ADV nu-pieds, (les) pieds nus ADJ aux pieds nus

bareheaded /ˌbɛəˈhedɪd/ ADV nu-tête *inv*, (la) tête nue ADJ nu-tête *inv* ; *[woman]* en cheveux †

barelegged /ˌbɛəˈlegd/ ADV nu-jambes, (les) jambes nues ADJ aux jambes nues

barely /ˈbɛəlɪ/ ADV 1 (= *only just*) à peine, tout juste ◆ **he can ~ read** c'est tout juste *or* à peine s'il sait lire, il sait tout juste *or* à peine lire ◆ **the temperature ~ rose above freezing** la température est à peine montée au-dessus de zéro ◆ ~ **visible/perceptible** à peine visible/perceptible ◆ **her voice was ~ audible** sa voix était à peine audible, on entendait à peine sa voix ◆ **he was ~ able to speak** il pouvait à peine parler ◆ **she was ~ conscious** elle était à peine consciente ◆ ~ **concealed** *or* **disguised resentment/contempt** une rancœur/un mépris mal dissimulé(e) ◆ **she had ~ begun to speak when ...** elle avait à peine commencé de parler lorsque ... ◆ **the car was ~ a year old** la voiture avait à peine un an ◆ ~ **half the graduates had found jobs** à peine la moitié des diplômés avaient trouvé des emplois ◆ **the truce is holding,** ~ la trêve est respectée, (mais) tout juste

2 ◆ **a ~ furnished room** (= *poorly furnished*) une pièce pauvrement meublée ; (= *scantily furnished*) une pièce très peu meublée

3 (= *plainly*) sans ambages ◆ **to state a fact ~** ne pas tourner autour du pot

bareness /ˈbɛənɪs/ N *[of person]* nudité *f* ; *[of room]* dénuement *m* ; *[of furniture]* pauvreté *f* ; *[of style]* (= *poverty*) sécheresse *f*, pauvreté *f* ; (= *simplicity*) dépouillé *m*

Barents Sea /ˈbærənts'siː/ N mer *f* de Barents

barf‡ /bɑːf/ VI (US) dégueuler‡

barfly * /ˈbɑːflaɪ/ N (US) pilier *m* de bistro(t)

bargain /ˈbɑːgɪn/ N 1 (= *transaction*) marché *m*, affaire *f* ◆ **to make** *or* **strike** *or* **drive a ~** conclure un marché (*with* avec) ; ◆ **it's a ~!*** (= *agreed*) c'est convenu *or* entendu ! ◆ **a good ~** une bonne affaire ◆ **a ~'s a ~** on ne peut pas revenir sur un marché conclu ◆ **to keep one's side of the ~** (*fig*) tenir ses engagements ; → **best, drive**

◆ **into the bargain** par-dessus le marché, en plus ◆ **... and we get paid into the ~** ... et en plus nous sommes payés

2 (= *good buy*) occasion *f* ◆ **it's a (real) ~!** c'est une véritable occasion *or* affaire !

VI 1 (= *haggle*) **to ~ with sb** marchander avec qn ◆ **to ~ over an article** marchander un article

2 (= *negotiate*) négocier (*with* avec) ; ◆ **to ~ with sb for sth** négocier qch avec qn

3 (= *count on*) **to ~ for sth** s'attendre à qch ◆ **I didn't ~ for that** je ne m'attendais pas à cela ◆ **I got more than I ~ed for** je ne m'attendais pas à cela ◆ **to ~ on sth** compter sur qch ◆ **to ~ on doing sth** penser faire qch ◆ **to ~ on sb's doing sth** s'attendre à ce que qn fasse qch

COMP **bargain basement** N coin *m* des (bonnes) affaires
bargain-hunter N personne *f* à l'affût des bonnes occasions
bargain-hunting N chasse *f* aux (bonnes) occasions
bargain offer N (Comm) offre *f* exceptionnelle ◆ **this week's ~ offer** la promotion de la semaine
bargain price N prix *m* avantageux
bargain sale N soldes *fpl*

bargaining /ˈbɑːgənɪŋ/ N marchandage *m* ◆ **that gives us more ~ power** cela nous met en position de force pour négocier ; → **collective**

COMP **bargaining chip** N ◆ **to use sth as a ~ chip** se servir de qch comme argument dans une négociation
bargaining position N position *f* de négociation ◆ **to be in a weak/strong ~ position** être en mauvaise/bonne position pour négocier
bargaining table N table *f* de négociations

barge /bɑːdʒ/ N (on river, canal) chaland *m* ; (*large*) péniche *f* ; (*with sail*) barge *f* ◆ **the admiral's ~** la vedette de l'amiral ◆ **motor ~** chaland *m* automoteur, péniche *f* automotrice ◆ **state ~** barque *f* de cérémonie

VI ◆ **he ~d through the crowd** il bousculait les gens pour passer

COMP **barge pole** N gaffe *f* ◆ **I wouldn't touch it with a ~ pole*** (Brit) (*revolting*) je n'y toucherais pas avec des pincettes ; (*risky*) je ne m'y frotterais pas

▸ **barge about, barge around** VI aller et venir comme un troupeau d'éléphants*

▸ **barge in** VI (= *enter*) faire irruption ; (= *interrupt*) interrompre la conversation ; (= *interfere*) se mêler de ce qui ne vous regarde pas

▸ **barge into** VT FUS 1 (= *knock against*) *[+ person]* rentrer dans* ; *[+ thing]* donner *or* se cogner contre ◆ **to ~ into a room** faire irruption dans une pièce, entrer sans façons dans une pièce

2 (= *interfere in*) *[+ discussion]* (*clumsily*) intervenir mal à propos dans ; (*rudely*) intervenir impoliment dans ; *[+ affair]* s'immiscer dans

▸ **barge through** VI traverser comme un ouragan

bargee /bɑːˈdʒiː/ N (Brit) batelier *m*, marinier *m*

bargeman /ˈbɑːdʒmən/ N (pl **-men**) batelier *m*, marinier *m*

baritone /ˈbærɪtəʊn/ N (= *voice, singer, instrument*) baryton *m* COMP *[voice, part]* de baryton

barium /ˈbɛərɪəm/ N baryum *m*
COMP **barium enema** N (Med) lavement *m* baryté
barium meal N (Med) (bouillie *f* de) sulfate *m* de baryum

bark[1] /bɑːk/ N *[of tree]* écorce *f* ◆ **to strip the ~ off a tree** écorcer un arbre VT *[+ tree]* écorcer ◆ **to ~ one's shins** s'écorcher *or* s'égratigner les jambes

bark[2] /bɑːk/ N *[of dog]* aboiement *m* ; *[of fox]* glapissement *m* ; (* = *cough*) toux *f* sèche ◆ **to let out a ~** (*lit*) aboyer ; (= *cough*) tousser ◆ **his ~ is worse than his bite** il fait plus de bruit que de mal, chien qui aboie ne mord pas VI *[dog]* aboyer (*at* après) ; *[fox]* glapir ; *[gun]* aboyer ; (= *speak sharply*) aboyer ; (= *cough*) tousser ◆ **to ~ at sb** aboyer après qn ◆ **to ~ up the wrong tree** faire fausse route VT ◆ **"leave me in peace!" he ~ed** "laisse-moi tranquille !" aboya-t-il

▸ **bark out** VT SEP *[+ order]* glapir

bark[3] /bɑːk/ N (*liter*) barque *f* ; (Naut) trois-mâts *m inv or* quatre-mâts *m inv* carré

barkeeper /ˈbɑːkiːpəʳ/ N (US) barman *m*, barmaid *f*

barker /ˈbɑːkəʳ/ N *[of fairground]* bonimenteur *m*, aboyeur † *m*

barking /ˈbɑːkɪŋ/ N *[of dog]* aboiement *m* ; *[of fox]* glapissement *m* ADJ (Brit *: also **barking mad**) complètement cinglé* *or* frappé‡

barley /ˈbɑːlɪ/ N orge *f* ◆ **Scotch ~** orge *m* mondé ; → **pearl** EXCL (N Engl, Scot: *in games*) pouce !
COMP **barley beer** N cervoise *f*
barley field N champ *m* d'orge

barley sugar N sucre *m* d'orge
barley water N *(esp Brit)* ≈ orgeat *m*
barley wine N *sorte de bière très forte et sucrée*

barleycorn /ˈbɑːlɪkɔːn/ N grain *m* d'orge

barm /bɑːm/ N levure *f* (de bière)

barmaid /ˈbɑːmeɪd/ N *(esp Brit)* serveuse *f* (de bar)

barman /ˈbɑːmən/ N (pl **-men**) barman *m*

Bar Mitzvah, bar mitzvah /ˌbɑːˈmɪtsvə/ N bar-mitsva *f*

barmy † * /ˈbɑːmɪ/ ADJ *(Brit)* timbré *, maboul ⁑

barn /bɑːn/ N 1 grange *f* ◆ **it's a great ~ of a house** * c'est une énorme bâtisse 2 *(US) (for horses)* écurie *f* ; *(for cattle)* étable *f*
COMP **barn dance** N *(= dance)* danse *f* campagnarde *or* paysanne ; *(= party)* bal *m* campagnard
barn dancing N *(NonC)* danse *f* campagnarde *or* paysanne
barn door N ◆ **it's as big as a ~ door** c'est gros comme une maison *
barn egg N ≈ œuf *m* de poule élevée en liberté
barn owl N chat-huant *m*

barnacle /ˈbɑːnəkl/ N 1 *(= shellfish)* bernache *f*, anatife *m* ; *(pej = person)* crampon * *m* ; *(⁑ = old sailor)* vieux loup de mer * *m* 2 (also **barnacle goose**) bernache (nonnette) *f*, bernacle *f*

barney ⁑ /ˈbɑːnɪ/ N *(Brit = quarrel)* prise *f* de bec *

barnstorm /ˈbɑːnstɔːm/ VI *(Theat)* jouer sur les tréteaux ; *(US Pol)* faire une tournée électorale (dans les circonscriptions rurales)

barnstormer /ˈbɑːnstɔːməʳ/ N *(Theat)* acteur *m* ambulant ; *(US Pol)* orateur *m* électoral

barnstorming /ˈbɑːnstɔːmɪŋ/ N *(Theat)* ≈ tournée *f* théâtrale ; *(US Pol)* tournée *f or* campagne *f* électorale (dans les circonscriptions rurales) ADJ * *[performance]* emballant

barnyard /ˈbɑːnjɑːd/ N basse-cour *f* COMP **barnyard fowl(s)** N(PL) volaille *f*

barogram /ˈbærəʊɡræm/ N barogramme *m*

barograph /ˈbærəʊɡrɑːf/ N barographe *m*

barometer /bəˈrɒmɪtəʳ/ N *(lit, fig)* baromètre *m* ◆ **the ~ is set fair** le baromètre est au beau fixe ◆ **a good ~ of public opinion** un bon baromètre de l'opinion publique ; → **aneroid**

barometric /ˌbærəʊˈmetrɪk/ ADJ barométrique

baron /ˈbærən/ N 1 *(= nobleman)* baron *m* 2 *(= magnate)* **cattle ~** magnat *m* du bétail ◆ **press/tobacco/coffee ~** magnat *m* de la presse/du tabac/du café ◆ **industrial ~** magnat *m* de l'industrie, gros industriel *m* ◆ **drug(s) ~** baron *m* de la drogue COMP **baron of beef** N double aloyau *m* de bœuf

baroness /ˈbærənɪs/ N baronne *f*

baronet /ˈbærənɪt/ N *(Brit)* baronnet *m*

baronetcy /ˈbærənɪtsɪ/ N dignité *f* de baronnet

baronial /bəˈrəʊnɪəl/ ADJ *(lit)* de baron ; *(fig)* seigneurial COMP **baronial hall** N demeure *f* seigneuriale

barony /ˈbærənɪ/ N baronnie *f*

baroque /bəˈrɒk/ ADJ, N *(Archit, Art, Mus)* baroque *m*

barque † /bɑːk/ N ⇒ **bark³**

barrack¹ /ˈbærək/ N caserne *f*, quartier *m* ; → **barracks**
COMP **barrack life** N vie *f* de caserne
barrack room N chambrée *f* ◆ **~-room language** propos *mpl* de caserne *or* de corps de garde ◆ **to be a ~-room lawyer** se promener toujours avec le code sous le bras
barrack square N cour *f* (de caserne)

barrack² /ˈbærək/ VT *(esp Brit)* chahuter, conspuer *(frm)*

barracks /ˈbærəks/ N caserne *f*, quartier *m* ◆ **cavalry ~** quartier *m* de cavalerie ◆ **in ~** à la caserne, au quartier ; → **confine, naval** COMP **barracks bag** N *(US)* sac *m (de soldat)*

barracuda /ˌbærəˈkjuːdə/ N (pl **barracuda** *or* **barracudas**) barracuda *m*

barrage /ˈbærɑːʒ/ N 1 *[of river]* barrage *m* 2 *(Mil)* tir *m* de barrage ; *(fig) [of questions, reproaches]* pluie *f* ; *[of words]* flot *m*, déluge *m* COMP **barrage balloon** N ballon *m* de barrage

barratry /ˈbærətrɪ/ N *(Marine Insurance)* baraterie *f*

barred /bɑːd/ ADJ *[window etc]* muni de barreaux

-barred /bɑːd/ ADJ *(in compounds)* ◆ **five-barred gate** barrière *f* à cinq barreaux

barrel /ˈbærəl/ N 1 *(= cask) [of wine]* tonneau *m*, fût *m* ; *[of cider]* futaille *f* ; *[of beer]* tonneau *m* ; *[of herring]* caque *f* ; *[of oil]* baril *m* ; *[of tar]* tonne *f* ; *(small)* baril *m* ◆ **to have sb over a ~** * tenir qn à sa merci ◆ **to pay cash on the ~** *(US)* payer rubis sur l'ongle ; → **biscuit, scrape** 2 *[of firearm]* canon *m* ; *[of fountain pen]* corps *m* ; *[of key]* canon *m* ; *[of lock, clock]* barillet *m* ◆ **to give sb both ~s** * *(fig)* enguirlander qn * VT *[+ wine, cider etc]* mettre en fût (*or* en futaille *etc*) VI *(US *)* foncer *, aller à toute pompe *
COMP **barrel-chested** ADJ au torse puissant
barrel-house jazz N *(US)* jazz *m* de bastringue
barrel organ N orgue *m* de Barbarie
barrel-shaped ADJ en forme de barrique *or* de tonneau ; *[person]* gros (grosse *f*) comme une barrique
barrel vault N voûte *f* en berceau

barrelhead /ˈbærəlhed/ N *(US)* ◆ **to pay cash on the ~** payer rubis sur l'ongle

barren /ˈbærən/ ADJ 1 *(†† = infertile) [woman, plant, tree]* stérile 2 *(= dry) [land, landscape]* aride 3 *(fig) [film, book]* dénué *or* dépourvu d'intérêt ; *[discussion, period of time]* stérile ; *[lifestyle]* vide de sens ; *[surroundings]* monotone ; *[style]* aride, sec (sèche *f*) ◆ **his latest book is ~ of interest** son dernier livre est dénué *or* dépourvu d'intérêt ◆ **a government ~ of new ideas** un gouvernement qui ne sait plus innover N *(esp US)* ◆ **~(s)** *(gen pl)* lande(s) *f(pl)* COMP **Barren Grounds, Barren Lands** NPL toundra *f* canadienne

barrenness /ˈbærənnɪs/ N 1 *(†† = infertility) [of woman, plant, tree, land]* stérilité *f* 2 *(= dryness) [of land, landscape]* aridité *f* 3 *(fig) [of film, book, surroundings]* manque *m* d'intérêt ; *[of lifestyle]* monotonie *f* ; *[of discussion]* stérilité *f* ; *[of style]* aridité *f*, sécheresse *f*

barrette /bəˈret/ N *(US)* barrette *f*

barricade /ˌbærɪˈkeɪd/ N barricade *f* VT *[+ street]* barricader ◆ **to ~ o.s. (in)** se barricader ◆ **police ~d them in** la police les a empêchés de sortir

barrier /ˈbærɪəʳ/ N barrière *f* ; *(Rail:* also **ticket barrier**) portillon *m* (d'accès) ; *(fig)* obstacle *m*, barrière *f (to à)* ; ◆ **age is no ~ to success** l'âge n'est pas un obstacle à la réussite ◆ **a trade ~** une barrière douanière ◆ **to put up ~s to sb/sth** dresser *or* élever des obstacles sur le chemin de qn/qch ◆ **to break down ~s** supprimer les barrières ; → **language, sound¹**
COMP **barrier contraceptive** N contraceptif *m* local
barrier cream N crème *f* protectrice
barrier method N méthode *f* de contraception locale
barrier reef N barrière *f or* récif *m* de corail ◆ **the Great Barrier Reef** la Grande Barrière (de corail *or* d'Australie)

barring /ˈbɑːrɪŋ/ PREP excepté, sauf ◆ **~ accidents** sauf accident, à moins d'accident(s) ◆ **~ the unforeseen** sauf imprévu

barrio /ˈbærɪəʊ/ N *(US)* quartier *m* latino-américain

barrister /ˈbærɪstəʳ/ N *(Brit:* also **barrister-at-law**) avocat *m* ; → LAWYER

barroom /ˈbɑːrʊm/ N *(US)* salle *f* de bar

barrow¹ /ˈbærəʊ/ N (also **wheelbarrow**) brouette *f* ; *(esp Brit:* also **coster's barrow**) voiture *f* des quatre saisons ; *(Rail:* also **luggage barrow**) diable *m* ; (also **hand barrow**) charrette *f* à bras ; *(Min)* wagonnet *m* ◆ **to wheel sth in a ~** brouetter qch COMP **barrow-boy** N marchand *m* des quatre saisons

barrow² /ˈbærəʊ/ N *(Archeol)* tumulus *m*

Bart /bɑːt/ N *(Brit)* abbrev of **baronet**

bartender /ˈbɑːˌtendəʳ/ N *(US)* barman *m*, barmaid *f*

barter /ˈbɑːtəʳ/ N échange *m*, troc *m* VT échanger, troquer (*for* contre) VI faire un échange *or* un troc
► **barter away** VT *[+ rights, liberty]* vendre ; *[+ one's honour]* faire trafic de

Bartholomew /bɑːˈθɒləmjuː/ N Barthélemy *m* ◆ **the Massacre of St ~** *(Hist)* (le massacre de) la Saint-Barthélemy

barytone /ˈbærɪtəʊn/ N *(Mus)* baryton *m (instrument)*

basal /ˈbeɪsl/ ADJ *(lit, fig)* fondamental ; *(Physiol)* basal

basalt /ˈbæsɔːlt/ N basalte *m*

bascule /ˈbæskjuːl/ N bascule *f* COMP **bascule bridge** N pont *m* à bascule

base¹ /beɪs/ N 1 *(= lowest part)* base *f*, partie *f* inférieure ; *[of column, wall, skull, brain]* base *f*, pied *m* ; *[of building]* soubassement *m* ; *[of tree, lamp]* pied *m* ; *[of statue]* socle *m* ◆ **the ~ of the spine** le coccyx
2 *(= headquarters, also Mil)* base *f* ; *[of company, organization]* siège *m* ◆ **London is my ~** je suis basé à Londres ◆ **the FBI decided to use an old cinema as their ~** le FBI a décidé d'utiliser un ancien cinéma comme base ◆ **political/electoral ~** assise *f* politique/électorale ◆ **army/air force ~** base militaire/de l'armée de l'air ◆ **to return to ~** rejoindre sa base ; → **air, naval**
3 *(= basis)* point *m* de départ ◆ **to use** *or* **take sth as one's ~** prendre qch comme point de départ ◆ **the novel takes real-life events as its ~** ce roman prend des faits réels comme point de départ
4 *(= main ingredient)* base *f*
5 *(Chem, Math, Ling)* base *f* ◆ **~ 2/10** *etc (Comput)* base 2/10 *etc*
6 *(Baseball)* base *f* ◆ **he's way off ~** * *(US)* il déraille * ◆ **to touch ~ with sb** * reprendre contact avec qn ◆ **we'll touch ~ this afternoon** * on se tient au courant *or* on s'appelle cet après-midi ◆ **I'll touch ~ with you about the schedule** * il faut qu'on parle du programme, toi et moi ◆ **to touch** *or* **cover all the ~s** *(US)* penser à tout
VT 1 *(= derive from)* baser, fonder (*on, around* sur) ; ◆ **this conclusion is ~d on an erroneous assumption** cette conclusion est fondée sur des prémisses erronées ◆ **your pension will be ~d on your existing salary** votre retraite sera fonction de votre salaire actuel ◆ **these figures are ~d on past experience of book sales** ces chiffres sont basés sur les ventes de livres enregistrées dans le passé ◆ **the novel is largely ~d on** *or* **around his experiences as a policeman** le roman se fonde en grande partie sur son expérience d'agent de police
2 *(= locate base of) [+ person, organization, job] (also Mil)* **to ~ sb/sth somewhere** baser qn/qch quelque part ◆ **the post will be ~d in London but will involve considerable travel** le poste sera basé à Londres mais il exigera de nombreux déplacements ◆ **they've decided to ~ their operation in London instead of Glasgow** ils ont choisi Londres plutôt que Glasgow comme base de leurs opérations ◆ **I am ~d in** *or* **at Glasgow** je suis basé à Glasgow, j'opère à

partir de Glasgow ◆ **the company is ~d in Glasgow** l'entreprise a son siège *or* est basée à Glasgow

COMP **base camp** N *(Climbing)* camp *m* de base
base coat N *[of paint]* première couche *f*
base form N *(Ling)* forme *f* de base
base jumping N base-jump *m*
base lending rate N *(Fin)* taux *m* de base bancaire
base line N *(Baseball)* ligne *f* des bases ; *(Surv)* base *f* ; *[of diagram]* ligne *f* zéro ; *(Tennis)* ligne *f* de fond ; *(Art)* ligne *f* de fuite
base period N *(Stat)* période *f* de référence *or* de base
base rate N *(Fin)* ⇒ **base lending rate**
base year N *(Fin)* année *f* de référence

base² /beɪs/ ADJ 1 *(= contemptible) [person, behaviour, crime, betrayal, action, motive, thoughts, emotions]* vil (vile *f*), indigne ; *[instincts]* bas (basse *f*) ; *[task]* ingrat 2 *(liter) [birth, descent]* bas (basse *f*) ◆ **of ~ descent** de basse extraction 3 *(= counterfeit) [coin]* faux (fausse *f*) 4 *(US)* ⇒ **bass¹** adj COMP **base metal** N métal *m* vil

baseball /ˈbeɪsbɔːl/ N base-ball *or* baseball *m* COMP **baseball cap** N casquette *f* de base(-)ball

BASEBALL

Sport national américain, très répandu aussi au Canada, dont certaines qualités – l'esprit de camaraderie et de compétition, par exemple – ont été popularisées par le cinéma et en viennent à symboliser l'« American way of life ».

En plus de la célèbre casquette, le base-ball est à l'origine d'un certain nombre d'expressions courantes telles que « ballpark figure » (chiffre approximatif), a « whole new ball game » (une autre histoire) ou « to get to first base » (franchir le premier obstacle).

baseboard /ˈbeɪsbɔːd/ N *(US Constr)* plinthe *f*

-based /beɪst/ ADJ *(in compounds)* ◆ **to be London-based** être basé à Londres ◆ **an oil-based economy** une économie basée sur le pétrole ◆ **sea-/land-based missile** missile *m* marin/terrestre

Basel /ˈbɑːzəl/ N Bâle

baseless /ˈbeɪslɪs/ ADJ sans fondement

baseline costs /ˌbeɪslaɪnˈkɒsts/ NPL *(Fin)* coûts *mpl* de base

basely /ˈbeɪslɪ/ ADV bassement, vilement

baseman /ˈbeɪsmən/ (pl **-men**) N *(Baseball)* gardien *m* de base

basement /ˈbeɪsmənt/ N sous-sol *m* ◆ **in the ~** au sous-sol COMP **basement flat** N appartement *m* en sous-sol

baseness /ˈbeɪsnɪs/ N 1 *[of person, behaviour, crime, betrayal]* ignominie *f* ; *[of action, motive, thoughts, instincts, emotions]* bassesse *f* 2 *(liter)* **the ~ of his birth** *or* **descent** sa basse extraction

bases¹ /ˈbeɪsiːz/ NPL of **basis**

bases² /ˈbeɪsɪz/ NPL of **base¹**

bash* /bæʃ/ N 1 coup *m* ; *(with fist)* coup *m* de poing ◆ **to give sb a ~ on the nose** donner un coup de poing sur le nez de qn ◆ **the car bumper has had a ~** le pare-chocs est cabossé *or* bosselé

2 **to have a ~ at sth/at doing sth*** s'essayer à qch/à faire qch ◆ **I'll have a ~ (at it)*, I'll give it a ~*** je vais tenter le coup ◆ **have a ~!*** vas-y, essaie !

3 († = *party*) surboum † * *f*

VT frapper, cogner ◆ **to ~ one's head against a wall** se cogner la tête contre un mur ◆ **to ~ sb on the head** assommer qn

► **bash about***, **bash around*** VT SEP *[+ person] (= hit)* flanquer* des coups à ; *(= ill-treat) [+ person]* maltraiter, rudoyer ; *[+ object]* malmener

► **bash in*** VT SEP *[+ door]* enfoncer ; *[+ hat, car]* cabosser, défoncer ; *[+ lid, cover]* défoncer ◆ **to ~ sb's head in*** défoncer le crâne de qn*

► **bash on*** VI continuer *(with sth* avec qch)

► **bash up*** VT SEP *[+ car]* bousiller* ; *(Brit) [+ person]* tabasser*

basher* /ˈbæʃəʳ/ N cogneur* *m* N *(in compounds)* ◆ **he's a queer-~*** il casse du pédé*

bashful /ˈbæʃfʊl/ ADJ timide, qui manque d'assurance

bashfully /ˈbæʃfəlɪ/ ADV d'un air embarrassé

bashfulness /ˈbæʃfʊlnɪs/ N timidité *f*

bashing* /ˈbæʃɪŋ/ N rossée* *f*, raclée* *f* ◆ **to take a ~** *[team, regiment]* prendre une raclée* *or* une dérouillée* ; *[car, carpet etc]* en prendre un (vieux *or* sacré) coup* N *(in compounds)* ◆ **union-~** dénigrement *m* systématique des syndicats ; → **Paki, queer**

BASIC, Basic /ˈbeɪsɪk/ N *(Comput)* basic *m*

basic /ˈbeɪsɪk/ ADJ 1 *(= fundamental) [difficulty, principle, problem, essentials]* fondamental ; *(= elementary) [rule]* élémentaire ◆ **the four ~ operations** *(Math)* les quatre opérations fondamentales ◆ **~ French** le français fondamental *or* de base ◆ **a ~ knowledge of Russian/electronics** une connaissance de base du russe/de l'électronique ◆ **~ research** recherche *f* fondamentale ◆ **~ vocabulary** vocabulaire *m* de base ◆ **~ English** l'anglais *m* fondamental ◆ **~ needs** besoins *mpl* essentiels

2 *(= forming starting point) [salary, working hours]* de base ◆ **a ~ suit to which one can add accessories** un petit tailleur neutre auquel on peut ajouter des accessoires ◆ **a ~ black dress** une petite robe noire

3 *(Chem)* basique ◆ **~ salt** sel *m* basique ◆ **~ slag** scorie *f* de déphosphoration

NPL **the basics** l'essentiel *m* ◆ **to get down to the ~s** en venir à l'essentiel ◆ **to get back to ~s** revenir au b.a.-ba ◆ **a new back-to-~s drive** une nouvelle campagne prônant un retour à la simplicité

COMP **basic airman** N (pl **basic airmen**) *(US)* soldat *m* de deuxième classe (de l'armée de l'air)
basic overhead expenditure N *(Fin)* frais *mpl* généraux essentiels
basic rate N *(Fin, Comm)* taux *m* de référence ◆ **~ rate of (income) tax** taux *m* de base de l'impôt sur le revenu
basic training N *(Mil)* ◆ **to do one's ~ training** faire ses classes
basic wage N salaire *m* de base

basically /ˈbeɪsɪklɪ/ LANGUAGE IN USE 26.2 ADV au fond ◆ **it's ~ simple** au fond, c'est simple ◆ **it's ~ the same** c'est pratiquement la même chose ◆ **he's ~ lazy** au fond, il est paresseux, il est fondamentalement paresseux ◆ **~, it's easy** au fond *or* en fait, c'est simple ◆ **~ we agree** nous sommes d'accord sur le fond

basil /ˈbæzl/ N *(= plant)* basilic *m*

basilica /bəˈzɪlɪkə/ N basilique *f*

basilisk /ˈbæzɪlɪsk/ N *(= mythical beast, lizard)* basilic *m*

basin /ˈbeɪsn/ N 1 *(gen)* cuvette *f*, bassine *f* ; *(for food)* bol *m* ; *(wide: for cream etc)* jatte *f* ; (also **washbasin, wash-hand basin**) lavabo *m* ; *[of lavatory]* cuvette *f* ; *[of fountain]* vasque *f* ; → **sugar** 2 *(Geog) [of river]* bassin *m* ; *(= valley)* cuvette *f* ; *(= harbour)* bassin *m* ; → **catchment, tidal**

basinful /ˈbeɪsnfʊl/ N *[of milk]* bolée *f* ; *[of water]* pleine cuvette *f* ◆ **I've had a ~*** j'en ai par-dessus la tête* *or* ras le bol* *(of de)*

basis /ˈbeɪsɪs/ N (pl **bases**) *(lit, fig)* base *f* ◆ **a possible ~ for negotiation** un éventuel point de départ pour des négociations ◆ **on that ~** dans ces conditions ◆ **on the ~ of what you've told me** d'après ce que vous m'avez dit ◆ **~ for assessing VAT** assiette *f* de la TVA

◆ **on a + basis** ◆ **on a temporary ~** temporairement ◆ **on an equal ~** sur un pied d'égalité ◆ **the shops are operated on a voluntary ~** les magasins sont tenus par des bénévoles ◆ **on a mileage ~** en fonction du kilométrage ◆ **open on a 24-hour ~** ouvert 24 heures sur 24 ◆ **paid on a daily/day-to-day/regular ~** payé à la journée/au jour le jour/régulièrement

COMP **basis point** N *(Fin)* point *m* de base

bask /bɑːsk/ VI ◆ **to ~ in the sun** *[person]* se dorer au soleil, se prélasser au soleil ; *[animal]* se prélasser au soleil ◆ **the team were ~ing in the glory of their victory** l'équipe savourait sa victoire ◆ **we can all ~ in reflected glory when our team does well** nous pouvons tous tirer fierté des succès de notre équipe ◆ **to ~ in sb's praise** savourer les éloges de qn ◆ **to ~ in sb's favour** jouir de la faveur de qn COMP **basking shark** N requin *m* pèlerin

basket /ˈbɑːskɪt/ N *(gen)* corbeille *f* ; (also **shopping basket**) *(one-handled)* panier *m* ; *(deeper, two-handled)* cabas *m* ; (also **clothes basket**) corbeille *f or* panier *m* à linge (sale) ; (also **wastepaper basket**) corbeille *f* (à papier) ; *(on person's back)* hotte *f* ; *(on donkey)* panier *m* ; *(for game, fish, oysters)* bourriche *f* ; *(Basketball)* panier *m* ; *(on ski stick)* rondelle *f* (de ski) ◆ **a ~ of currencies/products** *(Econ)* un panier de devises/produits ◆ **a ~(ful) of eggs** un panier d'œufs ◆ **to make a ~** *(Basketball)* marquer un panier ; → **laundry, luncheon, picnic, workbasket**

COMP *[handle etc]* de panier
basket case* N *(= country)* cas *m* désespéré ◆ **he's a ~ case** *(= person, crazy)* il est cinglé* ; *(= inadequate)* c'est un paumé* ; *(= nervous)* c'est un paquet de nerfs*
basket chair N chaise *f* en osier
basket maker N vannier *m*

basketball /ˈbɑːskɪtbɔːl/ N basket(-ball) *m* COMP **basketball player** N basketteur *m*, -euse *f*

basketry /ˈbɑːskɪtrɪ/ N ⇒ **basketwork**

basketweave /ˈbɑːskɪtwiːv/ N *(= cloth)* tissage *m* ; *(= cane)* tressage *m*

basketwork /ˈbɑːskɪtwɜːk/ N vannerie *f*

Basle /bɑːl/ N ⇒ **Basel**

basmati /bəzˈmætɪ/ N (also **basmati rice**) (riz *m*) basmati *m*

Basque /bæsk/ N 1 *(= person)* Basque *m*, Basque *f or* Basquaise *f* 2 *(= language)* basque *m* ADJ basque ◆ **a ~ woman** une Basque *or* Basquaise ◆ **the ~ Country** le Pays basque ◆ **the ~ Provinces** les provinces *fpl* basques

basque /bæsk/ N guêpière *f*

bas-relief /ˈbæsrɪˌliːf/ N bas-relief *m*

bass¹ /beɪs/ *(Mus)* N *(= part, singer, guitar)* basse *f* ; (also **double bass**) contrebasse *f* ; → **double** ADJ *[voice]* de basse ; *[note]* grave ; *(= low-sounding)* bas (basse *f*), grave

COMP **bass-baritone** N baryton-basse *m*
bass clarinet N clarinette *f* basse
bass clef N clef *f* de fa
bass drum N grosse caisse *f*
bass flute N flûte *f* basse
bass guitar N guitare *f* basse
bass guitarist N bassiste *mf*
bass horn N serpent *m*
bass-relief ADJ ⇒ **bas-relief**
bass strings NPL basses *fpl*
bass trombone N trombone *m* basse
bass tuba N tuba *m* d'orchestre
bass viol N viole *f* de gambe

bass² /bæs/ N *(= fish) (freshwater)* perche *f* ; *(sea)* bar *m*, loup *m*

basset /ˈbæsɪt/ N (also **basset hound**) basset *m* COMP **basset horn** N *(Mus)* cor *m* de basset

bassi /ˈbæsɪ/ NPL of **basso**

bassist /ˈbeɪsɪst/ N bassiste *mf*

bassline /ˈbeɪslaɪn/ N (ligne *f* de) basse *f*

basso continuo /ˌbæsəʊkənˈtɪnjʊəʊ/ N (pl **bassos** or **bassi continuo**) (*Mus*) basse *f* continue

bassoon /bəˈsuːn/ N basson *m* ; → **double**

bassoonist /bəˈsuːnɪst/ N basson *m*, bassoniste *mf*

basso profundo /ˌbæsəʊprəʊˈfʌndəʊ/ N (pl **bassos** or **bassi profundo**) (*Mus*) basse *f* profonde

Bass Strait /ˈbæstreɪt/ N ◆ **the** ~ le détroit de Bass

bastard /ˈbɑːstəd/ N 1 (*lit*) enfant naturel(le) *m(f)*, bâtard(e) *m(f)* 2 (*‡pej = unpleasant person*) salaud‡ *m*, salope‡ *f* 3 *‡**he's a lucky** ~! c'est un drôle de veinard !* ◆ **you old** ~! sacré vieux !* ◆ **poor** ~ pauvre type* ◆ **silly** ~! quel corniaud !* ADJ [*child*] naturel, bâtard ; [*language, dialect*] corrompu, abâtardi ; (*Typ*) [*character*] d'un autre œil ◆ ~ **title** faux-titre *m*

bastardized /ˈbɑːstədaɪzd/ ADJ [*language*] corrompu, abâtardi

bastardy /ˈbɑːstədɪ/ N (*Jur*) bâtardise *f*

baste[1] /beɪst/ VT (*Sewing*) bâtir, faufiler

baste[2] /beɪst/ VT (*Culin*) arroser

bastion /ˈbæstɪən/ N bastion *m*

Basutoland /bəˈsuːtəʊlænd/ N Bas(o)utoland *m*

bat[1] /bæt/ N (= *animal*) chauve-souris *f* ◆ **an old** ~* une vieille bique* ◆ **to have** ~**s in the belfry*** avoir une araignée au plafond* ◆ **he ran like a** ~ **out of hell*** il a couru comme un dératé ◆ **her new Ferrari goes like a** ~ **out of hell*** sa nouvelle Ferrari est un vrai bolide* ; → **blind**

bat[2] /bæt/ (*Sport etc*) N 1 (*Baseball, Cricket*) batte *f* ; (*Table Tennis*) raquette *f* ◆ **off one's own** ~ de sa propre initiative, de son propre chef ◆ **right off the** ~ (*US*) sur-le-champ ◆ **he's a good** ~ (*Baseball, Cricket*) il manie bien la batte 2 (= *blow*) coup *m* VI (*Baseball, Cricket*) ◆ **he** ~**s well but is a poor bowler** il manie bien la batte, mais n'est pas bon lanceur ◆ **Smith was** ~**ting** Smith était à la batte ◆ **to go in to** ~ **(for England)** passer à la batte (pour l'équipe anglaise) ◆ **to go (in) to** ~ **for sb*** (= *support*) intervenir en faveur de qn VT 1 [+ *ball*] frapper (*avec une batte, raquette etc*) 2 * (= *hit*) cogner*, flanquer un coup à* ◆ **to** ~ **sth around** (*US fig*) (= *discuss*) discuter de qch (à bâtons rompus)

bat[3] /bæt/ VT ◆ **he didn't** ~ **an eyelid** (*Brit*) or **an eye** (*US*) il n'a pas sourcillé or bronché ◆ **without** ~**ting an eyelid** (*Brit*) or **an eye** (*US*) sans sourciller or broncher

batch /bætʃ/ N [*of loaves*] fournée *f* ; [*of people*] groupe *m* ; [*of prisoners*] convoi *m* ; [*of recruits*] contingent *m*, fournée *f* ; [*of letters*] paquet *m* ; (*Comm*) [*of goods*] lot *m* ; [*of concrete*] gâchée *f*
COMP **batch file** N (*Comput*) fichier *m* batch
batch mode N (*Comput*) ◆ **in** ~ **mode** en temps différé
batch-process VT (*Comput*) traiter par lots
batch processing N (*Comput*) traitement *m* par lots

bated /ˈbeɪtɪd/ ADJ ◆ **with** ~ **breath** en retenant son souffle

bath /bɑːθ/ N (pl **baths** /bɑːðz/) 1 bain *m* ; (also **bath tub**) baignoire *f* ◆ **to take** or **have** (*Brit*) **a** ~ prendre un bain ◆ **to give sb a** ~ baigner qn, donner un bain à qn ◆ **while I was in my** or **the** ~ pendant que j'étais dans or que je prenais mon bain ◆ **room with (private)** ~ (*in hotel*) chambre *f* avec salle de bains (particulière) ; → **blood, eyebath, Turkish**
2 (*Chem, Phot, Tech*) bain *m* ; (*Phot = container*) cuvette *f*
NPL **baths** (*for swimming*) piscine *f* ; (*for washing*) (établissement *m* de) bains(-douches) *mpl* ; (*Hist*) thermes *mpl*
VT (*Brit*) baigner, donner un bain à
VI (*Brit*) prendre un bain
COMP **bath bomb** N sels *mpl* de bain effervescents
bath cube N sels *mpl* de bain en cube
bath oil N huile *f* pour le bain
bath pearls NPL perles *fpl* de bain
bath salts NPL sels *mpl* de bain
bath sheet N drap *m* de bain
bath towel N serviette *f* de bain

Bath bun /ˈbɑːθˌbʌn/ N (*Brit*) ≃ pain *m* aux raisins

bathchair † /ˈbɑːθtʃɛəʳ/ N fauteuil *m* roulant, voiture *f* d'infirme

bathe /beɪð/ VT (*gen, also fig*) baigner ; [+ *wound*] laver ◆ **to** ~ **one's eyes** se baigner or se bassiner les yeux ◆ **to** ~ **one's feet** prendre un bain de pieds ◆ ~**d in tears** baigné de larmes ◆ **to be** ~**d in sweat** être en nage ◆ **to** ~ **the baby** (*US*) baigner l'enfant ◆ ~**d in light** baigné or inondé de lumière VI (*Brit*) se baigner, prendre un bain (*de mer ou de rivière*) ; (*US*) prendre un bain (*dans une baignoire*) N (*Brit*) bain *m* (*de mer ou de rivière*) ◆ **an enjoyable** ~ une baignade agréable ◆ **to take** or **have a** ~ se baigner ◆ **let's go for a** ~ allons nous baigner

bather /ˈbeɪðəʳ/ N baigneur *m*, -euse *f*

bathhouse /ˈbɑːθhaʊs/ N bains *mpl* publics

bathing /ˈbeɪðɪŋ/ N bains *mpl*, baignade(s) *f(pl)* ◆ ~ **prohibited** défense de se baigner, baignade interdite ◆ **safe** ~ baignade *f* sans (aucun) danger ; → **sea**
COMP **bathing beauty** N naïade *f*
bathing cap N bonnet *m* de bain
bathing costume N (*Brit*) maillot *m* (de bain)
bathing hut N cabine *f* (de bains)
bathing machine N cabine *f* de bains roulante
bathing suit N (*esp US*) ⇒ **bathing costume**
bathing trunks NPL (*Brit*) maillot *m* or slip *m* de bain
bathing wrap N peignoir *m* (de bain), sortie *f* de bain

bathmat /ˈbɑːθmæt/ N tapis *m* de bain

bathos /ˈbeɪθɒs/ N (*Literat*) chute *f* du sublime au ridicule

bathrobe /ˈbɑːθrəʊb/ N peignoir *m* (de bain)

bathroom /ˈbɑːθrʊm/ N salle *f* de bains ◆ **to go to** or **use the** ~ (*esp US*) aller aux toilettes
COMP **bathroom cabinet** N armoire *f* de toilette
bathroom fittings NPL (= *main fixtures*) appareils *mpl* or installations *fpl* sanitaires ; (= *accessories*) accessoires *mpl* de salle de bains
bathroom scales NPL balance *f*, pèse-personne *m inv*

bathtub /ˈbɑːθtʌb/ N (*esp US*) baignoire *f* ; (*round*) tub *m*

bathwater /ˈbɑːθwɔːtəʳ/ N eau *f* du bain

bathysphere /ˈbæθɪsfɪəʳ/ N bathysphère *f*

batik /bəˈtiːk/ N batik *m*

batiste /bæˈtiːst/ N batiste *f*

batman /ˈbætmən/ N (pl **-men**) (*Brit Mil*) ordonnance *f*

baton /ˈbætən/ N (*Mil, Mus*) bâton *m*, baguette *f* ; (*Brit*) [*of policeman*] matraque *f* ; [*of French traffic policeman*] bâton *m* ; [*of relay race*] témoin *m* ◆ **to hand on** or **pass the** ~ **to sb** passer le flambeau à qn
COMP **baton charge** N charge *f* (*de police etc*) à la matraque
baton round N (*Mil*) balle *f* en plastique
baton twirler N majorette *f* (*menant un défilé*)

bats‡ /bæts/ ADJ toqué*, timbré*

batsman /ˈbætsmən/ N (pl **-men**) (*Cricket*) batteur *m*

battalion /bəˈtælɪən/ N (*Mil, fig*) bataillon *m*

batten[1] /ˈbætn/ N (*Carpentry*) latte *f* ; [*of roofing*] volige *f* ; [*of flooring*] latte *f*, planche *f* (de parquet) ; (*Naut*) latte *f* (de voile) ; (*Theat*) herse *f* VT latter ; [+ *roof*] voliger ; [+ *floor*] planchéier
► **batten down** VT SEP (*Naut*) ◆ **to batten down the hatches** fermer les écoutilles, condamner les panneaux

batten[2] /ˈbætn/ VI (= *prosper illegitimately*) s'engraisser (*on sb* aux dépens de qn ; *on sth* de qch) ; (= *feed greedily*) se gorger, se gaver (*on* de)

batter[1] /ˈbætəʳ/ N (*Culin*) (*for frying*) pâte *f* à frire ; (*for pancakes*) pâte *f* à crêpes ◆ **fried fish in** ~ poisson *m* frit (*enrobé de pâte à frire*)

batter[2] /ˈbætəʳ/ VT 1 (= *strike repeatedly*) battre, frapper ; [+ *baby*] maltraiter, martyriser ◆ **ship** ~**ed by the waves** navire *m* battu par les vagues ◆ **town** ~**ed by bombing** ville *f* ravagée or éventrée par les bombardements 2 (*Typ*) [+ *type*] endommager VI ◆ **to** ~ **at the door** cogner or frapper à la porte à coups redoublés N (*US Sport*) batteur *m*
► **batter about** VT SEP [+ *person*] rouer de coups, rosser
► **batter down** VT SEP [+ *wall*] démolir, abattre ; (*Mil*) battre en brèche
► **batter in** VT SEP [+ *door*] enfoncer, défoncer ; [+ *skull*] défoncer

battered /ˈbætəd/ ADJ 1 (= *maltreated*) battu ◆ ~ **children** enfants *mpl* battus ◆ ~ **child syndrome** syndrome *m* de l'enfant battu ◆ ~ **wife** femme *f* battue 2 (= *in poor condition*) [*hat, pan*] cabossé, bosselé ; [*face*] (*lit*) meurtri ; (*fig*) buriné ; [*furniture, house*] délabré ◆ **a** ~ **old car** une vieille bagnole cabossée*

batterer /ˈbætərəʳ/ N *personne qui bat son conjoint ou ses enfants* ; → **wife**

battering /ˈbætərɪŋ/ N ◆ **the town took a dreadful** ~ **during the war** la ville a été terriblement éprouvée pendant la guerre ◆ **he got such a** ~ on l'a roué de coups, on l'a rossé ; → **baby** COMP **battering ram** N (*Mil*) bélier *m*

battery /ˈbætərɪ/ N 1 (= *guns*) batterie *f* 2 (*Elec*) [*of torch, radio*] pile *f* ; [*of vehicle*] batterie *f* 3 (= *number of similar objects*) batterie *f* ◆ **to undergo a** ~ **of tests** subir une batterie de tests ◆ **a** ~ **of questions** une pluie or un feu nourri de questions 4 (*Agr*) batterie *f* 5 (*Jur*) voie *f* de fait ; → **assault**
COMP **battery acid** N électrolyte *m*
battery charger N chargeur *m* de batterie
battery-driven ADJ à piles ; [*car*] électrique
battery egg N œuf *m* produit en batterie
battery farm N (*Brit*) élevage *m* en batterie
battery fire N (*Mil*) tir *m* par salves
battery hen N poulet *m* d'élevage en batterie, poulet *m* de batterie
battery lead connection N (*in car*) cosse *f* de batterie
battery-operated, battery-powered ADJ à pile(s) ; [*car*] électrique
battery set N (= *radio*) poste *m* à piles

battle /ˈbætl/ N 1 (*Mil*) bataille *f*, combat *m* ◆ **to fight a** ~ se battre, lutter (*against* contre) ; ◆ **to lead an army into** ~ mener une armée au combat ◆ **the Battle of Britain** la bataille d'Angleterre ◆ **killed in** ~ tué au combat
2 (*fig*) combat *m*, lutte *f* ◆ **to have a** ~ **of wits** jouer au plus fin ◆ ~ **of wills** (partie *f* de) bras *m* de fer ◆ **life is a continual** ~ la vie est un combat perpétuel or une lutte perpétuelle ◆ **a political** ~ une lutte or un combat politique ◆ **to do** ~ **for/against** lutter pour/contre ◆ **the** ~ **against crime** la lutte contre le crime ◆ **to fight sb's** ~**s** se battre à la place de qn ◆ **we are fighting the same** ~ nous nous battons pour la même cause ◆ **that's half the** ~* c'est déjà pas mal* ◆ **getting an interview is only half the** ~ quand on obtient un entretien la partie n'est pas encore gagnée ◆ ~ **for control of**

sth/to control sth lutte *f or* combat *m* pour obtenir le contrôle de qch/pour contrôler qch ♦ **to lose/win the ~** perdre/gagner la bataille ♦ **to win the ~ but lose the war** gagner une bataille mais perdre la guerre ; → **cancer, join, losing, Nile**

VI *(lit, fig)* se battre, lutter *(against* contre ; *to do sth* pour faire qch) ; ♦ **sailors constantly battling with the elements** des marins luttant sans cesse contre les éléments

COMP **battle array** N ♦ **in ~ array** en ordre de bataille

battle-axe N *(= weapon)* hache *f* d'armes ; *(* pej = woman)* virago *f*

battle cruiser N croiseur *m* cuirassé

battle cry N cri *m* de guerre

battle dress N *(Mil)* tenue *f* de campagne *or* de combat

battle fatigue N psychose *f* traumatique *(du soldat)*

battle-hardened ADJ aguerri

battle lines NPL lignes *fpl* de combat ♦ **the ~ lines are drawn** chacun a choisi son camp

battle order N ⇒ **battle array**

battle royal N *(= quarrel)* bataille *f* en règle

battle-scarred ADJ *(lit) [troops, country]* marqué par les combats ; *(fig) [person]* marqué par la vie ; *(* hum) [furniture]* endommagé, abîmé

battle zone N zone *f* de combat

► **battle out** VT SEP ♦ **Leeds battled it out with Manchester in the final** Leeds s'est mesuré à or avec Manchester en finale ♦ **the three political parties ~d it out** les trois partis politiques se sont livré une bataille acharnée

battledore /ˈbætldɔːʳ/ N *(Sport)* raquette *f* ♦ **~ and shuttlecock** (jeu *m* de) volant *m*

battlefield /ˈbætlfiːld/, **battleground** /ˈbætlgraʊnd/ N *(Mil, fig)* champ *m* de bataille

battlements /ˈbætlmənts/ NPL *(= wall)* remparts *mpl* ; *(= crenellation)* créneaux *mpl*

battleship /ˈbætlʃɪp/ N cuirassé *m*

battleships /ˈbætlʃɪps/ N *(NonC = game)* bataille *f* navale

batty ‡ /ˈbætɪ/ ADJ *(esp Brit)* ⇒ **bats**

bauble /ˈbɔːbl/ N babiole *f*, colifichet *m* ; *[of jester]* marotte *f*

baud /bɔːd/ *(Comput)* N baud *m* COMP **baud rate** N vitesse *f* en bauds

baulk /bɔːlk/ N, VT, VI ⇒ **balk**

bauxite /ˈbɔːksaɪt/ N bauxite *f*

Bavaria /bəˈveərɪə/ N Bavière *f*

Bavarian /bəˈveərɪən/ ADJ bavarois ♦ **~ Alps** Alpes *fpl* bavaroises N Bavarois(e) *m(f)* COMP **Bavarian cream** N *(Culin)* bavaroise *f*

bawd †† /bɔːd/ N *(= prostitute)* catin † *f*

bawdiness /ˈbɔːdɪnɪs/ N paillardise *f*

bawdy /ˈbɔːdɪ/ ADJ paillard

bawdyhouse †† /ˈbɔːdɪhaʊs/ N maison *f* de tolérance ††

bawl /bɔːl/ VI 1 *(= shout)* brailler, hurler *(at* contre) 2 *(* = weep)* brailler, beugler* VT brailler, hurler

► **bawl out** VT SEP 1 ⇒ **bawl** vt 2 *(‡ = scold)* engueuler‡

bay[1] /beɪ/ N *(Geog)* baie *f* ; *(small)* anse *f* ♦ **the Bay of Biscay** le golfe de Gascogne ♦ **the Bay State** *(US)* le Massachusetts

bay[2] /beɪ/ N (also **bay tree, sweet bay**) laurier(-sauce) *m*

COMP **bay leaf** N (pl **bay leaves**) feuille *f* de laurier

bay rum N *lotion capillaire*

bay wreath N couronne *f* de laurier

bay[3] /beɪ/ N 1 *(= alcove)* renfoncement *m* ; *[of window]* baie *f* 2 *(Rail)* voie *f* d'arrêt ; → **bomb, loading, parking, sick** COMP **bay window** N bow-window *m*, bay-window *f*

bay[4] /beɪ/ N *(Hunting, fig)* ♦ **to be at ~** être aux abois ♦ **to bring to ~** acculer ♦ **to keep** *or* **hold at ~** *(fig)* tenir à distance *or* en échec VI aboyer *(at* à, après) donner de la voix ♦ **to ~ at the moon** aboyer *or* hurler à la lune ♦ **to ~ for blood** *(Brit fig)* crier vengeance ♦ **to ~ for sb's blood** *(Brit)* réclamer la tête de qn *(fig)*

bay[5] /beɪ/ ADJ *[horse]* bai N cheval *m* bai ♦ **red ~** *(= horse)* alezan *m*

Baykal /baɪˈkɑːl/ N ♦ **Lake ~** le lac Baïkal

bayonet /ˈbeɪənɪt/ N baïonnette *f* ; → **fix** VT passer à la baïonnette

COMP **bayonet bulb** N *(Elec)* ampoule *f* à baïonnette

bayonet charge N charge *f* à la baïonnette

bayonet drill N *(NonC)* ⇒ **bayonet practice**

bayonet fitting N *(Elec)* douille *f* à baïonnette

bayonet-fitting bulb N ⇒ **bayonet bulb**

bayonet point N ♦ **at ~ point** à (la pointe de) la baïonnette

bayonet practice N *(NonC)* exercices *mpl* de baïonnette

bayonet socket N *(Elec)* douille *f* à baïonnette

bayou /ˈbaɪuː/ N *(US)* bayou *m*, marécages *mpl*

bazaar /bəˈzɑːʳ/ N *(in East)* bazar *m* ; *(= large shop)* bazar *m* ; *(= sale of work)* vente *f* de charité

bazoo ‡ /bəˈzuː/ N *(US)* gueule ‡ *f*, bouche *f*

bazooka /bəˈzuːkə/ N bazooka *m*

BB /biːˈbiː/ N (abbrev of **Boys' Brigade**) → **boy** COMP **BB gun** N *(US)* carabine *f* à air comprimé

BBC /ˌbiːbiːˈsiː/ N (abbrev of **British Broadcasting Corporation**) BBC *f*

BBQ /ˌbiːbiːˈkjuː/ N abbrev of **barbecue**

BBS /ˌbiːbiːˈes/ N *(Comput)* (abbrev of **bulletin board system**) BBS *m*, babillard *m*

BC /biˈsiː/ 1 (abbrev of **Before Christ**) av. J.-C. 2 (abbrev of **British Columbia**) → **British**

BCD /ˌbiːsiːˈdiː/ N *(Comput)* (abbrev of **binary-coded decimal**) DCB *f*

BCG ® /ˌbiːsiːˈdʒiː/ N (abbrev of **bacille Calmette et Guérin**) BCG ® *m*

BD /biːˈdiː/ N 1 (abbrev of **bank draft**) → **bank**[2] 2 *(Univ)* (abbrev of **Bachelor of Divinity**) *licence de théologie*

BDD /ˌbiːdiːˈdiː/ N (abbrev of **body dysmorphic disorder**) → **body**

BDS /ˌbiːdiːˈes/ N *(Univ)* (abbrev of **Bachelor of Dental Surgery**) *diplôme de chirurgie dentaire*

BE /biːˈiː/ N *(Comm)* (abbrev of **bill of exchange**) → **bill**[1]

be /biː/

pres **am, is, are**, pret **was, were**, ptp **been**.

1 COPULATIVE VERB	4 INTRANSITIVE VERB
2 AUXILIARY VERB	5 IMPERSONAL VERB
3 MODAL VERB	6 COMPOUNDS

1 - COPULATIVE VERB

1 [joining subject and predicate] être ♦ **the sky is blue** le ciel est bleu ♦ **~ good!** sois sage ! ♦ **who is that? – it's me!** qui est-ce ? – c'est moi ! ♦ **she is English** elle est anglaise ♦ **they are friendly** ils sont sympathiques ♦ **if I were you I would refuse** à votre place *or* si j'étais vous, je refuserais ♦ **and even if it were true ...** et même si c'était vrai ...

The following translations use **ce + être** because they contain an article or possessive in French:

♦ **she is an Englishwoman** c'est une Anglaise ♦ **they are friendly people** ce sont des gens sympathiques ♦ **they are my best friends** ce sont mes meilleurs amis ♦ **it's the most expensive** c'est le plus cher

2 [with occupation] être

No article is used in French, unless the noun is qualified by an adjective.

♦ **he wants to ~ a doctor** il veut être médecin ♦ **she is a lawyer** elle est avocate ♦ **she's a well-known lawyer** c'est une avocate renommée

3 [referring to health] aller ♦ **how are you?** comment allez-vous ? ♦ **I'm better now** je vais mieux maintenant ♦ **she's none too well** elle ne va pas très bien

4 [= cost] coûter ♦ **how much is it?** combien ça coûte ? ♦ **the book is €3** le livre coûte 3 €

5 [Math = equal] faire ♦ **two and two are four** deux et deux font quatre ♦ **three times two is six** trois fois deux font six

6 [with certain adjectives: translated 'avoir'] ♦ **to ~ cold/hot/hungry/thirsty/ashamed/right/wrong** avoir froid/chaud/faim/soif/honte/raison/tort

Note how French makes the person, not the part of the body, the subject of the sentence in the following:

♦ **my feet are cold** j'ai froid aux pieds ♦ **my hands are frozen** j'ai les mains gelées

7 [with age] avoir ♦ **how old is he?** quel âge a-t-il ? ♦ **he's 25** il a vingt-cinq ans ♦ **she's about my age** elle a à peu près mon âge ♦ **he will ~ three next week** il aura trois ans la semaine prochaine ♦ **she was 40 on Sunday** elle a eu quarante ans dimanche

2 - AUXILIARY VERB

1 [in continuous tenses]

♦ **to be** + *-ing*

French does not distinguish between simple and continuous actions as much as English does.

♦ **I'm coming !** j'arrive ! ♦ **she's always complaining** elle se plaint constamment, elle est toujours en train de se plaindre ♦ **what have you been doing this week?** qu'est-ce que tu as fait cette semaine ? ♦ **what's been keeping you?** qu'est-ce qui t'a retenu ? ♦ **I have just been packing my case** je viens de faire ma valise ♦ **it's a pity you aren't coming with us – but I am coming!** c'est dommage que tu ne viennes pas avec nous – mais si, je viens ! ♦ **will you ~ seeing her tomorrow?** est-ce que vous allez la voir demain ?

être en train de + infinitive emphasizes that one is in the middle of the action:

♦ **I haven't got time, I'm cooking the dinner** je n'ai pas le temps, je suis en train de préparer le repas ♦ **I was just writing to him when he phoned** j'étais en train de lui écrire quand il m'a appelé

The imperfect tense is used for continuous action in the past.

♦ **he was driving too fast** il conduisait trop vite

♦ **have/had been** ... + **for/since**

French uses the present and imperfect where English uses the perfect and past perfect.

♦ **I've been waiting for you for an hour** je t'attends depuis une heure, ça fait une heure que je t'attends ♦ **I've been waiting for you since six o'clock** je t'attends depuis six heures ♦ **I'd been at university for six weeks when my father got ill** j'étais à l'université depuis six semaines quand mon père est tombé malade

2 in tag questions : seeking confirmation n'est-ce pas ? ◆ **he's a friend of yours, isn't he ?** c'est un ami à toi, n'est-ce pas ? ◆ **they were surprised, weren't they?** ils ont été surpris, n'est-ce pas *or* non ? ◆ **she wasn't happy, was she?** elle n'était pas heureuse, n'est-ce pas ? ◆ **so it's all done, is it ?** tout est fait, alors ? ◆ **you are not ill, are you ?** tu n'es pas malade j'espère ?

3 in tag responses ◆ **they're getting married – oh are they ?** ils vont se marier – ah bon *or* ah oui ? ◆ **he's going to complain about you – oh is he?** il va porter plainte contre toi – ah vraiment ? ◆ **she is pretty – no, she isn't** elle est jolie – non, je ne trouve pas

When answering questions, **oui** or **non** may be used alone.

◆ **he's always late, isn't he? – yes, he is** il est toujours en retard, n'est-ce pas ? – oui ◆ **is it what you expected? – no it isn't** est-ce que tu t'attendais à ça ? – non ; → **so, neither, nor**

4 in passives être ◆ **he was killed** il a été tué ◆ **he was struck by a car** il a été renversé par une voiture

The passive is used less in French than in English. It is often expressed by **on** + active verb when there is no obvious agent.

◆ **the door was shut in his face** on lui a fermé la porte au nez ◆ **it is said that ...** on dit que ...

The reflexive can express the established way of doing something.

◆ **peaches are sold by the kilo** les pêches se vendent au kilo ◆ **oysters are usually eaten raw** les huîtres se mangent généralement crues

3 - MODAL VERB

1 = will ◆ **the talks are to start tomorrow** les négociations doivent commencer demain ◆ **they are to ~ married in the summer** ils doivent se marier cet été ◆ **now the old lady has died, her house is to ~ sold** maintenant que la vieille dame est décédée, sa maison doit être mise en vente ◆ **you must work harder if you are to succeed** tu dois travailler davantage si tu veux réussir

2 = must ◆ **you are to follow these instructions exactly** tu dois suivre ces instructions scrupuleusement ◆ **you are not to touch that** tu ne dois pas y toucher ◆ **no, YOU are to do it!** non, c'est à toi de le faire ! ◆ **I am not to speak to him** on m'a défendu de lui parler ◆ **this door is not to ~ opened** cette porte ne doit pas être ouverte, il est interdit *or* défendu d'ouvrir cette porte ◆ **I wasn't to tell you his name** je ne devais pas *or* je n'étais pas supposé te dire son nom

3 = should ◆ **he is to ~ pitied** il est à plaindre ◆ **not to ~ confused with ...** à ne pas confondre avec ... ◆ **is it to ~ wondered at if ...?** faut-il s'étonner si ... ?

4 = can ◆ **these birds are to ~ found all over the world** on trouve ces oiseaux dans le monde entier ◆ **little traffic was to ~ seen** il n'y avait pas beaucoup de circulation

5 = be destined to ◆ **this was to have serious repercussions** cela devait avoir de graves répercussions ◆ **they were never to return** ils ne devaient jamais revenir

6 in conditional clauses : frm ◆ **were I to** *or* **if I were to tell him, what could he do ?** à supposer que je le lui dise, que pourrait-il faire ? ◆ **how would he react, were he to find out?** comment réagirait-il s'il venait à tout découvrir ?

◆ **were it not for ...** *(frm)* n'eût été ... ◆ **were it not for my friendship for him ...** n'eût été l'amitié que je lui porte ...

4 - INTRANSITIVE VERB

1 = exist, occur, remain, be situated être ; *(= take place)* avoir lieu ◆ **to ~ or not to ~** être ou ne pas être ◆ **he is there at the moment, but he won't ~ there much longer** il est là en ce moment mais il ne va pas rester très longtemps ◆ **there he was, sitting at the table** il était là, assis à la table ◆ **~ that as it may** quoi qu'il en soit ◆ **the match is tomorrow** le match a lieu demain ◆ **Christmas Day is on a Wednesday this year** Noël tombe un mercredi cette année ◆ **leave it as it is** laissez-le tel quel

◆ **there + be** *(= there exist(s))* il y a ◆ **there is a mouse in the room** il y a une souris dans la pièce ◆ **there are pigeons on the roof** il y a des pigeons sur le toit ◆ **there was once a castle here** autrefois, il y avait un château ici ◆ **I thought there would ~ problems** je pensais qu'il y aurait des problèmes ◆ **there must ~ an answer** il doit y avoir une solution ◆ **there being no alternative solution ...** comme il n'y a aucune autre solution ... ◆ **there is nothing more beautiful** il n'y a *or* il n'est *(liter)* rien de plus beau ◆ **there were three of us** nous étions trois ◆ **let there ~ light and there was light** que la lumière soit et la lumière fut

◆ **there's/there are** *(pointing out sth)* voilà ◆ **there's the church** voilà l'église ◆ **there are the others** voilà les autres ◆ **there's democracy for you!** *(iro)* voilà ce qu'on appelle *or* c'est ce qu'on appelle de la démocratie !

◆ **here is/are** voici ◆ **here's your key** voici ta clé ◆ **here are the tickets** voici les billets ◆ **here you are at last!** te voici enfin ! ◆ **here you are !** *(= take this)* tenez *or* tiens !

2 to a place

◆ **to have + been** ◆ **I have already been to Paris** j'ai déjà été *or* je suis déjà allé à Paris ◆ **I have been to see my aunt** je suis allé voir ma tante ◆ **the postman has already been** le facteur est déjà passé ◆ **he has been and gone** il est venu et reparti

5 - IMPERSONAL VERB

1 weather, temperature faire ◆ **it's fine/cold/dark** il fait beau/froid/nuit ◆ **it's 20 degrees in the shade** il fait 20 degrés à l'ombre ◆ **it's windy/foggy** il y a du vent/du brouillard

2 time être ◆ **it's morning** c'est le matin ◆ **it's 6 o'clock** il est 6 heures ◆ **tomorrow is Friday** demain c'est vendredi ◆ **it is 14 June today** nous sommes le 14 juin (aujourd'hui), c'est le 14 juin (aujourd'hui)

3 emphatic ◆ **it's me who does all the work** c'est moi qui fais tout le travail ◆ **it was me who decided to finish the relationship** c'est moi qui ai décidé de rompre ◆ **it was then we realised that ...** c'est alors que nous nous sommes rendu compte que ... ◆ **it was they who suggested that ...** ce sont eux qui ont suggéré que ... ◆ **it was they who had suggested that ...** c'étaient eux qui avaient suggéré que ... ◆ **how is it that you got back so early?** comment se fait-il que tu sois rentré si tôt ? ◆ **why is it that she is so popular?** pourquoi a-t-elle tant de succès ?

6 - COMPOUNDS

the be-all and end-all N le but suprême *(of de)* ; ◆ **for women today, marriage is not the be-all and end-all** pour les femmes d'aujourd'hui, le mariage n'est pas le but suprême

beach /biːtʃ/ N *[of sea]* plage *f* ; *(= shore)* grève *f* ; *[of lake]* rivage *m* ◆ **private/sandy ~** plage *f* privée/de sable VT *[+ boat]* échouer

COMP **beach ball** N ballon *m* de plage
beach buggy N buggy *m*
beach bum* N *jeune qui passe son temps à traîner sur les plages*
beach house N maison *f* en bord de plage
beach hut N cabine *f* de bain *or* de plage
beach party N fête *f* (*or* soirée *f*) sur la plage
beach towel N serviette *f* de plage
beach umbrella N parasol *m*

beachcomber /ˈbiːtʃˌkəʊməʳ/ N *(= person) (lit)* ramasseur *m* d'épaves ; *(fig = idler)* propre *mf* à rien ; *(= wave)* vague *f* déferlante

beachhead /ˈbiːtʃhed/ N *(Naut)* tête *f* de pont

beachwear /ˈbiːtʃweəʳ/ N tenue(s) *f(pl)* de plage

beacon /ˈbiːkən/ N 1 *(= danger signal)* phare *m*, signal *m* lumineux ; *(= lantern itself)* fanal *m* ; *(for ships)* balise *f* ; *(for planes)* balise *f*, phare *m* ; *(fig) (= person)* figure *f* phare ◆ **a moral ~** un guide moral ; → **Belisha beacon, radio** 2 *(Hist: on hills)* feu *m* (d'alarme) 3 *(= hill: gen in place-names)* colline *f*

COMP **beacon light** N balise *f* lumineuse
beacon school N *(Brit)* école *f* modèle

bead /biːd/ N 1 *[of glass, coral, amber etc]* perle *f* ; *[of rosary]* grain *m* ◆ **(string of) ~s** collier *m* ; → **tell** 2 *(= drop) [of dew]* perle *f* ; *[of sweat]* goutte *f* ; *(= bubble)* bulle *f* ◆ **his forehead was covered in ~s of sweat** la sueur lui perlait au front 3 *[of gun]* guidon *m* ◆ **to draw a ~ on sb/sth** viser qn/qch

beaded /ˈbiːdəd/ ADJ *[fabric, dress]* perlé, orné de perles ◆ **his forehead was ~ with sweat** la sueur perlait à son front

beading /ˈbiːdɪŋ/ N *(Carpentry)* baguette *f* ; *(Archit)* chapelet *m* ; *(Dress)* broderie *f* perlée, garniture *f* de perles

beadle /ˈbiːdl/ N *(Brit Univ)* appariteur *m*, huissier *m* ; *(Rel)* bedeau *m*

beady /ˈbiːdɪ/ ADJ ◆ **to watch sth with ~ eyes** regarder qch avec des yeux de fouine COMP **beady-eyed** ADJ *(bright-eyed)* aux yeux en boutons de bottines ; *(pej)* aux yeux de fouine

beagle /ˈbiːgl/ N beagle *m* VI chasser avec des beagles

beak /biːk/ N 1 *[of bird, turtle etc]* bec *m* ; (*: also **beaked nose**) nez *m* crochu 2 *(Brit * = judge)* juge *m* ; *(Brit Scol † * = headmaster)* protal* *m*

beaker /ˈbiːkəʳ/ N gobelet *m* ; *(wide)* coupe *f* ; *(Chem)* vase *m* à bec

beam /biːm/ N 1 *(Archit)* poutre *f* ; *(thick)* madrier *m* ; *(small)* poutrelle *f* ; → **crossbeam**

2 *(Sport: in gym)* poutre *f*

3 *[of ship] (= transverse member)* barrot *m* ; *(= greatest width)* largeur *f* ◆ **on the ~** par le travers ◆ **on the port ~** *(Naut)* à bâbord ◆ **on the starboard ~** à tribord ; → **broad**

4 *[of scales]* fléau *m* ; *[of engine]* balancier *m* ; *[of plough]* age *m* ; *[of loom]* rouleau *m*

5 *[of light, sunlight]* rayon *m*, trait *m* ; *[of lighthouse, headlight, searchlight]* faisceau *m* (lumineux) ; *(Phys)* faisceau *m* ; *(for guiding ships, planes)* chenal *m* de radioguidage ◆ **to be on/be off (the) ~** être/ne pas être dans le chenal de radioguidage ◆ **to be on (the) ~*** *(fig)* être sur la bonne voie ◆ **to be off (the) ~*** *(Brit)*, **to be off the ~*** *(US) (fig)* dérailler* ◆ **to be way off ~*** *(Brit fig)* être complètement à côté de la plaque* ; → **electron**

6 *(= smile)* sourire *m* épanoui

VI 1 (also **beam down**) *[sun]* rayonner, darder ses rayons

2 *(= smile)* ◆ **she ~ed** son visage s'est épanoui en un large sourire ◆ **at the sight of the money she ~ed at me** elle a levé vers moi un visage épanoui *or* rayonnant en voyant l'argent ◆ **her face was ~ing with joy** son visage

rayonnait de joie ◆ **~ing with pride, she showed them her ring** rayonnante de fierté, elle leur a montré sa bague

[3] *(Rad, Telec)* **soon we will be ~ing into your homes via the Astra satellite** bientôt nos émissions vous parviendront chez vous grâce au satellite Astra

[4] *(Sci Fi)* ◆ **they ~ed up to their spaceship** ils ont été téléportés dans leur vaisseau spatial

VT [1] *(Rad, Telec) [+ message]* transmettre par émission dirigée ◆ **to ~ a programme to the Arab-speaking countries** diffuser un programme à l'intention des pays de langue arabe

[2] **"welcome" she ~ed** "bienvenue" dit-elle d'un air radieux

[3] *(Sci Fi)* **aliens were ~ed down to earth** des extraterrestres ont été téléportés sur terre ◆ **he was ~ed up into the spacecraft** il a été téléporté dans le vaisseau spatial

COMP *(Naut) [sea, wind]* de travers

beam balance N balance *f* à fléau

beam compass N compas *m* à verge

beam-ends NPL *(Naut)* ◆ **on her ~-ends** couché sur le côté *or* le flanc ◆ **to be on one's ~-ends** * être dans la dèche‡ *or* dans la gêne

beaming /ˈbiːmɪŋ/ ADJ *[sun]* radieux, resplendissant ; *[smile, face]* rayonnant, radieux, épanoui

bean /biːn/ N *(Bot, Culin)* haricot *m* ; (also **green bean**) haricot *m* vert ; (also **broad bean**) fève *f* ; *[of coffee]* grain *m* ; *(US *) (= head)* tête *f*, tronche * *f* ; *(= brain)* cervelle *f* ◆ **to be full of ~s** * *(Brit)* être en pleine forme, péter le feu * ◆ **to know how many ~s make five** *(Brit)* avoir du bon sens ◆ **he doesn't know ~s about it** * *(US)* il n'y connaît absolument rien ◆ **it isn't worth a ~** * ça ne vaut pas un clou * ◆ **it doesn't amount to a hill** *or* **row of ~s** * ça ne vaut pas un clou ◆ **he hasn't a ~** * *(Brit)* il n'a pas le sou *or* un radis * ◆ **it won't cost you a ~** * ça ne vous coûtera pas un centime ◆ **hello, old ~!** †* salut mon pote ! * ; → **bake, kidney, spill¹** VT * frapper à la tête

COMP **bean counter** * N *(pej)* petit(e) comptable *mf*

bean curd N fromage *m* de soja

bean sprouts NPL ⇒ **beanshoots**

beanbag /ˈbiːnbæg/ N *(chair)* sacco *m* ; *(for throwing)* balle *f* lestée

beanery * /ˈbiːnərɪ/ N *(US)* gargote *f (pej)*

beanfeast * /ˈbiːnfiːst/, **beano** †* /ˈbiːnəʊ/ N *(Brit) (= meal)* gueuleton‡ *m* ; *(= spree)* bombe * *f*, nouba * *f*

beanpole /ˈbiːnpəʊl/ N *(lit)* perche *f* ; *(* fig)* (grande) perche * *f*

beanshoots /ˈbiːnʃuːts/ NPL *(Culin)* germes *mpl* de soja

beanstalk /ˈbiːnstɔːk/ N tige *f* de haricot

bear¹ /bɛəʳ/ (pret **bore**, ptp **borne**) VT [1] *(= carry) [+ burden, arms, message]* porter ◆ **music borne on the wind** musique *f* portée par le vent ◆ **to ~ away** emporter ◆ **to ~ back** rapporter ◆ **it is a cross he has to ~** c'est une croix qu'il doit porter ◆ **we each have our cross to ~** chacun a *or* porte sa croix ◆ **the strong current bore us towards the sea** la force du courant nous a entraînés *or* emportés vers la mer ; → **mind**

[2] *(= show) [+ inscription, mark, traces, signature]* porter ◆ **to ~ some resemblance to …** ressembler à … ◆ **to ~ no relation to …** être sans rapport avec …, n'avoir aucun rapport avec …

[3] *(= be known by) [+ name]* porter

[4] ◆ **he bore himself like a soldier** *(= carried himself)* il avait une allure de soldat ; *(= conducted himself)* il se comportait en soldat

[5] *(= feel)* avoir en soi, porter ◆ **the love/hatred he bore her** l'amour/la haine qu'il lui portait *or* qu'il avait à son égard ◆ **to ~ sb ill will** en avoir contre qn ; → **grudge**

[6] *(= bring, provide)* apporter, fournir ◆ **to ~ witness to sth** *[thing, result etc]* témoigner de qch ; *[person]* attester qch ◆ **to ~ false witness** porter un faux témoignage ◆ **to ~ sb company** † tenir compagnie à qn

[7] *(= sustain, support) [+ weight, person]* supporter ◆ **to ~ the weight of …** supporter le poids de … ◆ **to ~ comparison with …** soutenir la comparaison avec … ◆ **to ~ the expense of sth** prendre les frais de qch à sa charge ◆ **to ~ the responsibility for sth** assumer la responsabilité de qch

[8] *(= endure) [+ person]* supporter, souffrir ; *[+ event]* supporter ◆ **I cannot ~ (the sight of) that man** je ne peux pas souffrir *or* voir cet homme ◆ **he can't ~ the smell of garlic** il ne supporte pas l'odeur de l'ail ◆ **she cannot ~ being laughed at** elle ne supporte pas qu'on se moque *subj* d'elle ◆ **she can't ~ being** *or* **to be wrong** elle ne supporte pas d'avoir tort *or* de se tromper ◆ **his language will not ~ repeating** ses propos sont trop grossiers pour être rapportés ◆ **it doesn't ~ thinking about!** mieux vaut ne pas y penser ! ; → **brunt, grin**

[9] *(= produce, yield) [+ interest]* rapporter, produire ◆ **to ~ fruit** *(lit, fig)* produire des fruits ◆ **investment which ~s 5%** *(Fin)* placement *m* qui rapporte 5% ◆ **to ~ interest at 5%** *(Fin)* produire *or* rapporter un intérêt de 5%

[10] *(= give birth to)* donner naissance à, mettre au monde ◆ **she has borne him three daughters** elle lui a donné trois filles ; → **born**

[11] *(= push, press)* entraîner, porter ◆ **he was borne along by the crowd** il s'est trouvé entraîné *or* emporté par la foule

VI [1] *(= move)* se diriger ◆ **to ~ right/left** prendre sur la droite/la gauche *or* à droite/à gauche ◆ **~ towards the church** allez vers l'église ◆ **~ north at the windmill** prenez la direction nord au moulin ◆ **to ~ off** *(Naut)* virer (de bord)

[2] *[fruit, tree etc]* donner, produire

[3] *(= lean, press)* porter, appuyer *(on* sur*)* ; ◆ **he bore heavily on his stick** *(liter)* il s'appuyait lourdement sur sa canne ◆ **these taxes ~ most heavily on the poor** ces impôts pèsent plus lourdement sur les pauvres

◆ **to bring … to bear** ◆ **to bring one's energies to ~ on sth** consacrer *or* mettre toute son énergie à qch ◆ **to bring one's mind to ~ on sth** porter son attention sur qch ◆ **to bring pressure to ~ on sth** exercer une pression sur qch ◆ **to bring pressure to ~ on sb** faire pression sur qn ◆ **to bring a telescope to ~ on sth** braquer une lunette sur qch ◆ **to bring a gun to ~ on a target** pointer un canon sur un objectif

► **bear down** VI [1] *(= approach)* **to ~ down on** *[ship]* venir sur ; *[person]* foncer sur

[2] *(= press)* appuyer fermement, peser *(on* sur*)*

[3] *[woman in labour]* pousser

► **bear in (up)on** VT FUS *(pass only)* ◆ **it was gradually borne in (up)on me that …** la conviction s'est faite peu à peu en moi que …, il est apparu de plus en plus évident à mes yeux que …

► **bear on** VT FUS ⇒ **bear upon**

► **bear out** VT SEP confirmer, corroborer ◆ **to ~ sb out, to ~ out what sb says** corroborer les dires de qn, corroborer ce que qn dit ◆ **the result ~s out our suspicions** le résultat confirme nos soupçons ◆ **you will ~ me out that …** vous serez d'accord avec moi (pour dire) que …

► **bear up** VI ne pas se laisser abattre *or* décourager ◆ **he bore up well after the death of his father** il a supporté courageusement la mort de son père ◆ **~ up!** courage ! ◆ **how are you? – ~ing up!** * comment ça va ? – on fait aller *

► **bear upon** VT FUS *(= be relevant to)* se rapporter à, avoir trait à ; *(= concern)* intéresser, concerner

► **bear with** VT FUS *[+ person, sb's moods etc]* supporter patiemment ◆ **~ with me a little longer** je vous demande encore un peu de patience

bear² /bɛəʳ/ N [1] *(= animal)* ours(e) *m(f)* ◆ **he's like a ~ with a sore head** * il est d'une humeur massacrante *or* de dogue, il n'est pas à prendre avec des pincettes ◆ **the Great/the Little Bear** *(Astron)* la Grande/la Petite Ourse ; → **grizzly, koala, polar** [2] *(pej = person)* ours *m (pej)* [3] *(Stock Exchange)* baissier *m* VT *(Stock Exchange)* chercher à faire baisser VI *(Stock Exchange)* jouer à la baisse

COMP **bear-baiting** N combat *m* d'ours et de chiens

bear cub N ourson *m*

bear garden N *(fig)* pétaudière *f*

bear hug N ◆ **he gave me a big ~ hug** il m'a serré très fort dans ses bras

bear market N *(Stock Exchange)* marché *m* (orienté) à la baisse, marché *m* baissier

bear pit N fosse *f* aux ours

the Bear State N *(US)* l'Arkansas *m*

bearable /ˈbɛərəbl/ ADJ supportable, tolérable

beard /bɪəd/ N [1] barbe *f* ; *(small, pointed)* barbiche *f*, bouc *m* ◆ **to have** *or* **wear** † **a ~** porter la barbe ◆ **a man with a ~** un homme barbu *or* à barbe, un barbu [2] *[of fish, oyster]* branchie *f* ; *[of goat]* barbiche *f* ; *[of grain]* barbe *f*, arête *f* ; *[of hook etc]* barbe *f*, barbelure *f* ; *(Typ)* talus *m* VT *(= face up to)* affronter, braver ◆ **to ~ the lion in his den** aller braver le lion dans sa tanière

bearded /ˈbɪədɪd/ ADJ barbu ◆ **a ~ man** un barbu COMP **the bearded lady** N la femme à barbe

beardless /ˈbɪədlɪs/ ADJ imberbe, sans barbe ◆ **~ youth** *(fig)* (petit) jeunet *m*

bearer /ˈbɛərəʳ/ N [1] *[of letter, news, burden]* porteur *m*, -euse *f* ; *[of tradition]* tenant(e) *m(f)* ; *(at funeral)* porteur *m* ; *(= servant)* serviteur *m* [2] *[of cheque, name, title]* porteur *m* ; *[of passport]* titulaire *mf* [3] *(= fruit tree)* **a good ~** un arbre qui donne bien

COMP **bearer bond** N titre *m* au porteur

bearer cheque N chèque *m* au porteur

bearing /ˈbɛərɪŋ/ N [1] *(= relation, aspect)* relation *f*, rapport *m* ◆ **to have a** *or* **some ~ on sth** influer sur qch ◆ **to have no ~ on the subject** n'avoir aucun rapport avec le sujet

[2] *[of ship]* position *f* ◆ **to take a compass ~** prendre un relèvement au compas ◆ **to take a ship's ~s** faire le point ◆ **to take** *or* **get one's ~s** s'orienter, se repérer ◆ **to lose one's ~s** *(fig)* être désorienté, perdre le nord

[3] *(= posture, behaviour)* allure *f* ◆ **military ~** allure *f* martiale ◆ **noble ~** allure *f or* maintien *m* noble ◆ **queenly ~** port *m* de reine

[4] *(frm)* ◆ **it is beyond (all) ~** c'est absolument insupportable

[5] *(in machine)* palier *m* ; → **ball¹, main**

[6] *(Heraldry)* → **armorial**

ADJ *(in compounds)* ◆ **carbon-/oxygen-~** *etc* contenant du carbone/de l'oxygène *etc* ◆ **an interest-~ deposit account** un compte de dépôt qui rapporte des intérêts

bearish /ˈbɛərɪʃ/ ADJ [1] *[market]* à la baisse ◆ **to be ~ (on sth)** *(= speculate)* spéculer à la baisse (sur qch) [2] *[person]* bourru COMP **bearish tendency** N tendance *f* à la baisse, tendance *f* baissière

bearskin /ˈbɛəskɪn/ N *(Mil Dress)* bonnet *m* à poil COMP **bearskin rug** N tapis *m* en peau d'ours

beast /biːst/ N [1] bête *f*, animal *m* ◆ **the king of the ~s** le roi des animaux ◆ **~ of burden** bête *f* de somme *or* de charge ◆ **~ of prey** prédateur *m* ◆ **~s** *(Agr)* bétail *m*, bestiaux *mpl* ◆ **the Beast** *(Rel)* l'Antéchrist *m*, la Bête de l'Apocalypse ◆ **the mark of the Beast** la marque de la Bête ◆ **a good thriller is a rare ~ indeed** *(hum)* un bon thriller est vraiment une denrée rare ◆ **this is a very different ~ from ...** ça n'a vraiment rien à voir avec ... ; → **wild** 2 *(pej = person: cruel)* brute *f* ; *(*: disagreeable)* vache* *f*, chameau* *m* ◆ **a sex ~*** un maniaque sexuel

beastliness† /ˈbiːstlɪnɪs/ N *(NonC)* *(= act, quality)* bestialité *f* ; *[of language]* obscénité *f* ; *(* = unpleasantness)* caractère *m* infect ; *[of person]* méchanceté *f*, rosserie* *f*

beastly† /ˈbiːstlɪ/ ADJ *[person, conduct]* bestial, brutal ; *[language]* obscène ; *[food, sight]* dégoûtant, répugnant ; *(*: less strong)* infect*, abominable ; *[child, trick]* sale, vilain *both before n* ◆ **what ~ weather!*** quel temps infect !*, quel sale temps ! ◆ **it's a ~ business*** c'est une sale affaire ◆ **to be ~ to sb*** être infect* avec qn, se conduire de façon abominable avec qn ADV *(Brit *)* méchamment*, terriblement

beat /biːt/ (vb : pret **beat**, ptp **beaten**) N 1 *[of heart, pulse]* battement *m* ; *[of drums]* battement *m*, roulement *m* ; *(Acoustics)* battement *m* ◆ **to march to the ~ of the drum** marcher au (son du) tambour ◆ **80 ~s a minute** *[of heart]* 80 pulsations *fpl* par minute ; see also **drum**

2 *(Mus)* temps *m* ; *[of conductor's baton]* battement *m* (de la mesure) ; *(Jazz)* rythme *m* ◆ **strong/weak ~** *(Mus)* temps *m* fort/faible ◆ **there are three ~s to a bar** c'est une mesure à trois temps ◆ **he answered without missing a ~** il a répondu sans se démonter ◆ **she never misses a ~** *(fig)* elle a toujours une longueur d'avance

3 *[of policeman]* *(= round)* ronde *f* ; *(= area)* secteur *m* ; *[of sentry]* ronde *f* ◆ **the policeman on the ~ noticed it** l'agent l'a remarqué pendant qu'il effectuait sa ronde ◆ **we need to put more officers on the ~** il faut augmenter le nombre des policiers affectés aux rondes ◆ **policeman on the ~** îlotier *m* ◆ **that's off my ~** *(fig)* cela n'est pas de mon domaine *or* de mon rayon* ; → **offbeat**

4 *(Hunting)* battue *f*

5 ‡ *(= beatnik)* beatnik *mf*

ADJ 1 *(* : also **dead-beat**)* claqué*, crevé*

2 ‡ beatnik *inv*

VT 1 *(= strike)* *[+ person, animal]* battre, frapper ; *[+ carpet]* battre ; *[+ eggs, cream]* fouetter, battre ; *[+ metal]* battre ◆ **to ~ sth flat** aplatir qch ◆ **to ~ sb with a stick** donner des coups de bâton à qn ◆ **to ~ sb to death** battre qn à mort ◆ **she ~ the flames with her jacket** elle essayait d'étouffer les flammes avec sa veste ◆ **to ~ a drum** battre du tambour ◆ **to ~ a drum for sth*** *(US = publicize)* faire du battage* autour de qch ◆ **to ~ the retreat** *(Mil)* battre la retraite ◆ **to ~ a retreat** *(Mil, fig)* battre en retraite ◆ **~ it!**‡ fiche le camp !*, fous le camp !‡ ◆ **to ~ one's breast** *(liter: lit, fig)* se frapper la poitrine ◆ **to ~ a way through sth** se frayer un passage *or* un chemin à travers qch ◆ **to ~ the forest/the moors** *(Hunting)* battre les bois/les landes ◆ **to ~ the bushes to do sth** *(US)* se donner de la peine pour faire qch ◆ **~ing the air with its wings** battant l'air de ses ailes ◆ **the bird ~s its wings** l'oiseau bat des ailes ◆ **to ~ time** battre la mesure ◆ **to ~ the bounds** *(Brit Hist)* *marquer les limites d'une paroisse (au cours d'une procession)* ; → **dead, tattoo²**

2 *(= defeat)* battre, vaincre ◆ **the army was ~en** l'armée a été battue ◆ **to ~ sb to the top of a hill** arriver au sommet d'une colline avant qn ◆ **to ~ sb at chess** battre qn aux échecs ◆ **to ~ sb into second place** reléguer qn à la seconde place, battre qn et lui prendre la première place ◆ **to ~ sb hollow** *(Brit)* *or* **hands down** *or* **into a cocked hat** battre qn à plate(s) couture(s) ◆ **to ~ the record** battre le record ◆ **to ~ the system** contourner le système ◆ **to ~ the charge*** *or* **the rap**‡ *(US)* *[accused person]* se tirer d'affaire ◆ **to ~ sb to it** couper l'herbe sous le pied à qn, devancer qn ◆ **coffee ~s tea any day*** le café vaut tout le thé du monde ◆ **the police confess themselves ~en** la police s'avoue vaincue ◆ **this problem has got me ~en** *or* **~*** ce problème me dépasse complètement ◆ **if you can't ~ them, join them** si tu n'es pas sûr de les vaincre, mets-toi de leur côté ◆ **that ~s everything!*** ça, c'est le bouquet !*, faut le faire !* ◆ **his behaviour takes some ~ing*** il dépasse les bornes ◆ **that will take some ~ing!*** *(admiring)* pour faire mieux, il faudra se lever de bonne heure !* ◆ **that ~s me*** cela me dépasse ◆ **it ~s me how you can speak to her*** je ne comprends pas *or* ça me dépasse que tu lui adresses *subj* la parole ◆ **can you ~ that** *or* **it!*** faut le faire !*

VI 1 *[rain, wind]* battre ; *[sun]* (also **beat down**) taper*, cogner* ◆ **to ~ at the door** cogner à la porte ◆ **the rain was ~ing against the window** la pluie battait contre la vitre ◆ **the waves ~ against the cliff** les vagues battent la falaise ◆ **he doesn't ~ about the bush** il n'y va pas par quatre chemins, il ne tourne pas autour du pot ◆ **well, not to ~ about the bush, he ...** bref, il ...

2 *[heart, pulse, drum]* battre ◆ **her heart was ~ing with joy** son cœur battait *or* palpitait de joie ◆ **with ~ing heart** le cœur battant ◆ **his pulse began to ~ quicker** son pouls s'est mis à battre plus fort ◆ **they heard the drums ~ing** ils entendaient le roulement des tambours

3 *(Naut)* **to ~ (to windward)** louvoyer au plus près

COMP **Beat Generation** N beat generation *f*
beat-up* ADJ déglingué‡, bousillé*

► **beat back** VT SEP *[+ enemy, flames]* repousser

► **beat down** VI ◆ **the rain was beating down** il pleuvait à verse ◆ **the sun was ~ing down** le soleil tapait* *or* cognait* dur ; see also **beat vi 1**
VT SEP 1 *(= reduce)* *[+ prices]* faire baisser ; *[+ person]* faire baisser ses prix à ◆ **I ~ him down to £8** je l'ai fait descendre à 8 livres
2 ◆ **the rain has beaten down the wheat** la pluie a couché les blés

► **beat in** VT SEP *[+ door]* défoncer ◆ **to ~ sb's brains in**‡ défoncer le crâne à qn

► **beat off** VT SEP *[+ attack, attacker, competition]* repousser

► **beat out** VT SEP 1 *[+ fire]* étouffer ◆ **he ~ out the flames with a blanket** il a étouffé les flammes avec une couverture
2 *[+ metal]* marteler, étaler *or* amincir au marteau ◆ **to ~ one's brains out*** *(US)* se creuser la cervelle
3 ◆ **to beat out the rhythm** marquer le rythme, battre la mesure
4 *(esp US = beat)* battre

► **beat up** VT SEP *[+ eggs, cream]* fouetter, battre ; * *(fig)* *[+ person]* passer à tabac, tabasser*
VT REFL ◆ **to beat o.s. up*** culpabiliser, s'en vouloir ◆ **don't ~ yourself up about it** ne te culpabilise pas
ADJ ◆ **beat-up** * déglingué‡, bousillé*
N ◆ **beating-up** → **beating**

► **beat up on*** VT FUS *(US)* *(= hit)* tabasser* ; *(= bully)* intimider ; *(= criticize)* descendre en flammes*

beaten /ˈbiːtn/ VB ptp of **beat** ADJ 1 *[metal]* battu, martelé ; *[earth, path]* battu ◆ **~ track** chemin *m or* sentier *m* battu ◆ **off the ~ track** *(lit, fig)* hors des sentiers battus 2 *(= defeated)* battu, vaincu 3 *(= exhausted)* claqué*, crevé*
COMP **beaten-up*** ADJ déglingué‡, bousillé*

beater /ˈbiːtəʳ/ N 1 *(= gadget)* *(for carpet)* tapette *f* ; *(for eggs = whisk)* fouet *m* ; *(rotary)* batteur *m* ; *(Tex)* peigne *m* ; → **wife** 2 *(Shooting)* rabatteur *m*

beatific /ˌbiːəˈtɪfɪk/ ADJ béatifique ◆ **to wear a ~ smile** sourire aux anges, arborer un sourire béat

beatifically /ˌbiːəˈtɪfɪkəlɪ/ ADV béatement

beatification /biːˌætɪfɪˈkeɪʃən/ N béatification *f*

beatify /biːˈætɪfaɪ/ VT béatifier

beating /ˈbiːtɪŋ/ N 1 *(= punishment)* correction *f*, raclée* *f* ; *(= series of blows)* passage *m* à tabac ◆ **to give sb a ~** flanquer une correction *or* une raclée* à qn, passer qn à tabac ◆ **to get a ~** recevoir une correction *or* une raclée*, être passé à tabac 2 *(NonC)* *[of metal]* batte *f* ; *[of drums]* battement *m*, roulement *m* ; *[of carpet]* battage *m* 3 *(= defeat)* défaite *f* ◆ **to take a ~*** *(= rough time)* *[person]* en voir de toutes les couleurs*, passer un mauvais quart d'heure* ; *(Sport)* se faire battre à plate(s) couture(s), se faire piler* ◆ **the car takes a ~ on that road*** la voiture en voit de dures sur cette route ; → **beat vt 2** 4 *[of wings, heart etc]* battement *m* 5 *(Shooting)* battue *f* COMP **beating-up*** N passage *m* à tabac, raclée* *f*

beatitude /biːˈætɪtjuːd/ N béatitude *f* ◆ **the Beatitudes** les béatitudes

beatnik /ˈbiːtnɪk/ N, ADJ beatnik *mf*

beau /bəʊ/ N (pl **beaus** *or* **beaux**) *(= dandy)* élégant *m*, dandy *m* ; *(= suitor)* galant *m* ; *(US = boyfriend)* petit ami* *m*

Beaufort scale /ˈbəʊfətˌskeɪl/ N échelle *f* de Beaufort

beaut* /bjuːt/ N ◆ **what a ~!** quelle merveille !*

beauteous /ˈbjuːtɪəs/ ADJ *(liter)* ⇒ **beautiful adj**

beautician /bjuːˈtɪʃən/ N esthéticien(ne) *m(f)*, visagiste *mf*

beautiful /ˈbjuːtɪfʊl/ ADJ *[person, music, picture, clothes]* beau (belle *f*), bel *m before vowel* ; *[weather]* superbe, splendide ; *[dinner]* magnifique ◆ **really ~** de toute beauté ◆ **the ~ game** *(Brit)* le football *m* N ◆ **the ~** le beau

beautifully /ˈbjuːtɪflɪ/ ADV *[sew, drive etc]* admirablement, à la perfection ; *[quiet, empty]* merveilleusement ◆ **that will do ~** cela convient parfaitement, c'est tout à fait ce qu'il faut

beautify /ˈbjuːtɪfaɪ/ VT embellir, orner ◆ **to ~ o.s.** se faire une beauté

beauty /ˈbjuːtɪ/ N 1 *(NonC)* beauté *f* ◆ **to mar** *or* **spoil** *or* **ruin the ~ of sth** déparer qch ◆ **~ is only skin-deep** *(Prov)* la beauté est quelque chose de superficiel ◆ **~ is in the eye of the beholder** *(Prov)* la beauté est quelque chose de subjectif ◆ **the ~ of it is that*** ... *(fig)* le plus beau, c'est que ... ◆ **that's the ~ of it*** *(fig)* c'est ça qui est formidable*

2 *(= person)* beauté *f* ◆ **she is a ~** elle est d'une grande beauté, c'est une beauté ◆ **she's no ~*** ce n'est pas une beauté ◆ **Beauty and the Beast** la Belle et la Bête

3 * ◆ **his goal was a real ~** son but était vraiment superbe ◆ **isn't this car a ~!** elle est pas superbe, cette voiture ?

COMP **beauty competition, beauty contest** N concours *m* de beauté
beauty cream N crème *f* de beauté
beauty editor N rédacteur *m*, -trice *f* de la rubrique beauté
beauty pageant N *(US)* ⇒ **beauty contest**
beauty parlour N institut *m or* salon *m* de beauté
beauty preparations NPL produits *mpl* de beauté
beauty queen N reine *f* de beauté
beauty salon N ⇒ **beauty parlour**
beauty shop N *(US)* ⇒ **beauty parlour**
beauty sleep N ◆ **off you go to bed now, you need your ~ sleep** va te coucher maintenant pour être frais et dispos demain matin
beauty specialist N esthéticien(ne) *m(f)*, visagiste *mf*
beauty spot N *(on skin, natural)* grain *m* de

beauté ; *(applied)* mouche *f* ; *(in countryside)* site *m* pittoresque
beauty treatment N soins *mpl* de beauté

beaux /bəʊz/ NPL of **beau**

beaver /ˈbiːvəʳ/ N 1 (= *animal*) castor *m* ; (= *fur*) (fourrure *f* de) castor *m* ; (= *hat*) (chapeau *m* de) castor *m* ◆ **to work like a ~** travailler d'arrache-pied ; → **eager** 2 ****** *(esp US)* foufoune** *f*, chatte** *f* VI *(Brit)* ◆ **to ~ away* at sth** travailler d'arrache-pied à qch COMP *[coat, hat]* (en poil) de castor **the Beaver State** N *(US)* l'Oregon *m*

Beaverboard ® /ˈbiːvəbɔːd/ N *(Constr)* (panneau *m* d')aggloméré *m* *(de bois)*

bebop /ˈbiːbɒp/ N *(Mus)* be-bop *m*

becalm /bɪˈkɑːm/ VT ◆ **to be ~ed** *(Naut)* être encalminé ; *(fig) [economy, stock market, talks]* faire du sur-place

became /bɪˈkeɪm/ VB pt of **become**

because /bɪˈkɒz/ LANGUAGE IN USE 17.1, 26.3 CONJ parce que ◆ **I did it ~ you asked me to** je l'ai fait parce que tu me l'as demandé ◆ **I won't go out ~ it's raining** je ne sortirai pas parce qu'il pleut *or* à cause de la pluie ◆ **it's all the more surprising ~ we were not expecting it** c'est d'autant plus surprenant que nous ne nous y attendions pas ◆ **if I did it, it was ~ it had to be done** je l'ai fait parce qu'il fallait bien le faire ◆ **~ he lied, he was punished** il a été puni pour avoir menti *or* parce qu'il avait menti ◆ **we are annoyed ~ the weather is bad** nous sommes contrariés parce qu'il fait mauvais ◆ **not ~ he was offended but ~ he was angry** non qu'il fût offusqué mais parce qu'il était furieux ◆ **~ he was leaving** à cause de son départ

◆ **because of** à cause de, en raison de ◆ **~ of his age** en raison de son âge, vu son âge

bechamel /ˌbeɪʃəˈmel/ N (also **bechamel sauce**) (sauce *f*) béchamel *f*

beck[1] /bek/ N ◆ **to be at sb's ~ and call** être à l'entière disposition de qn, être constamment à la disposition de qn ◆ **to have sb at one's ~ and call** faire marcher qn à la baguette *or* au doigt et à l'œil

beck[2] /bek/ N *(N Engl)* ruisseau *m*, ru *m*

beckon /ˈbekən/ VI 1 (= *signal*) faire signe *(to sb* à qn) ; ◆ **he ~ed to her to follow him** il lui a fait signe de le suivre 2 (= *be attractive*) *[bright lights, fame]* attirer VT 1 (= *signal*) faire signe à ◆ **he ~ed me in/back/over** *etc* il m'a fait signe d'entrer/de revenir/d'approcher *etc* 2 (= *attract*) attirer

become /bɪˈkʌm/ (pret **became**, ptp **become**) VI devenir, se faire ◆ **to ~ famous** *etc* devenir célèbre *etc* ◆ **to ~ king** devenir roi ◆ **to ~ a doctor** devenir *or* se faire médecin ◆ **to ~ old** vieillir, se faire vieux ◆ **to ~ thin** maigrir ◆ **to ~ fat** grossir ◆ **to ~ accustomed to ...** s'accoutumer à ..., s'habituer à ... ◆ **to ~ interested in ...** commencer à s'intéresser à ... ◆ **to ~ known** *[person]* commencer à être connu, se faire connaître ◆ **we are fast becoming a nation of cynics** nous nous transformons rapidement en une nation de cyniques

IMPERS VB ◆ **what has ~ of him ?** qu'est-il devenu ? ◆ **I don't know what will ~ of her** je ne sais pas ce qu'elle va devenir

VT *(liter, frm)* 1 (= *suit*) aller à ◆ **her hat does not ~ her** son chapeau ne lui sied pas *(frm)*

2 (= *befit*) convenir à, être digne de ◆ **it does not ~ him to speak thus** il lui sied mal *(frm)* de parler ainsi

becoming /bɪˈkʌmɪŋ/ ADJ *[behaviour, speech]* convenable, bienséant ; *[clothes, hair style]* seyant, qui va bien ◆ **her hat is not ~** son chapeau ne lui va pas *or* n'est pas seyant

becomingly /bɪˈkʌmɪŋlɪ/ ADV 1 (= *attractively*) *[smile, blush]* de façon charmante ◆ **she was dressed ~ in black** elle était habillée en noir, ce qui lui allait fort bien 2 (= *suitably*) convenablement, d'une manière convenable

becquerel /ˌbekəˈrel/ N becquerel *m*

BEd /biːˈed/ N (abbrev of **Bachelor of Education**) → **bachelor**

bed /bed/ N 1 (= *furniture*) lit *m* ◆ **a room with two ~s** une chambre à deux lits ◆ **to book in (at a hotel) for ~ and breakfast** *(Brit)* réserver une chambre avec le petit déjeuner (à l'hôtel) ◆ **to sleep in separate ~s** faire lit à part ◆ **to make the ~** faire le lit ◆ **to turn down the ~** préparer le lit *(en repliant le haut des draps)* ◆ **to change the ~** changer les draps (du lit) ◆ **to be in ~** être couché ; *(through illness)* être alité, garder le lit ◆ **to get into ~** se coucher, se mettre au lit ◆ **before ~** avant de se coucher ◆ **to get out of ~** se lever ◆ **to get out of ~ on the wrong side, to get up (on) the wrong side of the ~*** *(US)* se lever du pied gauche ◆ **to get sb to ~** réussir à coucher qn ◆ **to put sb to ~** coucher qn ◆ **to go to ~** se coucher ◆ **to go to ~ with sb*** (= *have sex with*) coucher avec qn* ◆ **to get into ~ with sb** *(fig)* s'allier à qn ◆ **to go home to ~** rentrer se coucher ◆ **as you make your ~ so you must lie on it** *(Prov)* comme on fait son lit on se couche ; → **campbed, deathbed, feather**

2 *(liter)* **she was brought to ~ of a boy** †† elle accoucha d'un garçon

3 *(Press)* **to put a paper to ~*** mettre un journal sous presse ◆ **the paper has gone to ~*** le journal est sous presse ◆ **to put sth to ~** *(fig)* mener qch à bien

4 (= *layer*) *[of coal]* couche *f*, gisement *m* ; *[of clay]* couche *f*, lit *m* ; *[of coral]* banc *m* ; *[of ore]* gisement *m* ; *[of mortar]* bain *m* (de mortier) ; *[of oysters]* banc *m*

5 (= *base*) *[of engine]* berceau *m* ; *[of lathe]* banc *m* ; *[of machine]* base *f*, bâti *m* ; *[of truck]* plateau *m* ; *[of building]* assises *fpl* ◆ **on a ~ of lettuce/rice** sur un lit de laitue/riz

6 (= *bottom*) *[of sea]* fond *m* ; *[of river]* lit *m*

7 *(in garden) [of vegetables]* planche *f* ; *(square)* carré *m* ; *[of flowers]* parterre *m*, massif *m* ; *(strip)* platebande *f* ; *(oval, circular)* corbeille *f* ◆ **life is not a ~ of roses** la vie n'est pas une partie de plaisir ◆ **my job isn't exactly a ~ of roses*** mon travail n'est pas drôle tous les jours

VT 1 **to ~ (out) plants** repiquer des plantes

2 *[+ foundations]* asseoir ◆ **to ~ stones in mortar** cimenter *or* sceller des pierres

3 († *) *[+ woman]* coucher avec*

COMP **bed and board** N le gîte *or* le vivre et le couvert

bed and breakfast N *(gen)* chambre *f* et petit déjeuner *m*, chambre *f* d'hôte ◆ **we stayed at ~ and breakfasts** *or* **~-and-breakfast places** nous avons logé dans des chambres d'hôtes ◆ **price for ~ and breakfast** prix *m* pour la chambre et le petit déjeuner

bed bath N toilette *f* *(d'un malade)*

bed jacket N liseuse *f*

bed linen N *(NonC)* draps *mpl* de lit (et taies *fpl* d'oreillers), literie *f*

bed of nails N *(lit)* lit *m* de clous ◆ **it's a ~ of nails** *(Brit fig)* c'est extrêmement pénible

bed pad N *(waterproof)* alaise *f* ; *(for extra comfort)* molleton *m*

bed-settee N canapé-lit *m*

bed-sitting room N *(Brit)* chambre *f* meublée

bed-wetting N incontinence *f* nocturne

► **bed down** VI (= *go to bed*) (aller) se coucher ; (= *spend night*) coucher

VT *[+ children etc]* coucher

bedaub /bɪˈdɔːb/ VT barbouiller *(with* de)

bedazzle /bɪˈdæzəl/ VT éblouir

bedbug /ˈbedbʌg/ N punaise *f* des lits

bedchamber †† /ˈbedˌtʃeɪmbəʳ/ N chambre *f* à coucher

bedclothes /ˈbedkləʊðz/ NPL couvertures *fpl* et draps *mpl* (de lit)

bedcover /ˈbedkʌvəʳ/ N couvre-lit *m*, dessus-de-lit *m inv*

-bedded /ˈbedɪd/ ADJ *(in compounds)* ◆ **twin-bedded room** chambre *f* à deux lits

bedding /ˈbedɪŋ/ N literie *f* ; *(Mil)* matériel *m* de couchage ; *(for animals)* litière *f*

COMP **bedding out** N *[of plants]* repiquage *m*

bedding(-out) plants NPL plantes *fpl* à repiquer

bedeck /bɪˈdek/ VT parer, orner *(with* de) ; *(slightly pej)* attifer* *(with* de)

bedevil /bɪˈdevl/ VT (= *confuse*) *[+ issue, person]* embrouiller ; (= *torment*) *[+ person]* tourmenter, harceler

◆ **bedevilled by** ◆ **the project has been ~led by poor management** le projet a pâti d'une mauvaise gestion ◆ **he was ~led by ill health** il a été miné par des problèmes de santé ◆ **the police, ~led by corruption and low morale** la police, minée par la corruption et le découragement

bedfellow /ˈbedˌfeləʊ/ N *(lit)* ◆ **they were ~s for a night** ils ont partagé le même lit une nuit ◆ **they are strange ~s** ils forment une drôle de paire *or* un drôle de couple

bedhead /ˈbedhed/ N tête *f* de lit, chevet *m*

bedlam /ˈbedləm/ N 1 (= *uproar*) chahut *m* ◆ **the crowd went absolutely mad – it was ~** la foule est devenue complètement folle – c'était le cirque ◆ **he's causing ~ at the hotel** il fait du chahut dans l'hôtel ◆ **the room was a ~ of banging and shouting** la pièce retentissait de coups et de cris 2 *(Hist)* maison *f* de fous †

bedmate* /ˈbedmeɪt/ N ⇒ **bedfellow**

Bedouin /ˈbedʊɪn/ N (pl **Bedouin** *or* **Bedouins**) Bédouin(e) *m(f)* ADJ bédouin

bedpan /ˈbedpæn/ N bassin *m* (hygiénique)

bedpost /ˈbedpəʊst/ N colonne *f* de lit

bedraggled /bɪˈdrægld/ ADJ *[clothes, person]* débraillé ; *[hair]* embroussaillé ; (= *wet*) trempé

bedridden /ˈbedrɪdn/ ADJ alité, cloué au lit ; *(permanently)* grabataire

bedrock /ˈbedrɒk/ N *(Geol)* soubassement *m* ; *(fig)* base *f*

bedroll /ˈbedrəʊl/ N tapis *m* de couchage

bedroom /ˈbedrʊm/ N chambre *f* (à coucher) ; → **spare**

COMP **bedroom farce** N *(Theat)* comédie *f* de boulevard

bedroom scene N ≈ scène *f* d'amour

bedroom slipper N pantoufle *f*

bedroom suburb* N *(US fig)* banlieue-dortoir *f*

bedroom suite N chambre *f* à coucher *(mobilier)*

-bedroomed /ˈbedrʊmd/ ADJ *(in compounds)* ◆ **a two-/four-bedroomed house** une maison avec deux/quatre chambres ◆ **a onebedroomed flat** un (appartement) deux-pièces

Beds N abbrev of **Bedfordshire**

bedside /ˈbedsaɪd/ N chevet *m* ◆ **at his ~** à son chevet

COMP *[book, lamp]* de chevet

bedside manner N *[of doctor]* comportement *m* envers les malades ◆ **he has a good ~ manner** il sait parler à ses malades

bedside rug N descente *f* de lit

bedside table N table *f* de chevet *or* de nuit

bedsit /ˈbedsɪt/, **bedsitter** /ˈbedsɪtəʳ/ N *(Brit)* chambre *f* meublée

bedsocks /ˈbedsɒks/ NPL chaussettes *fpl* (de lit)

bedsore /ˈbedsɔːʳ/ N escarre *f*

bedspread /ˈbedspred/ N dessus-de-lit *m inv*, couvre-lit *m*

bedspring /ˈbedsprɪŋ/ **N** *(US)* *(= framework)* sommier *m* à ressorts ; *(= single spring)* ressort *m* de sommier

bedstead /ˈbedsted/ **N** châlit *m*, bois *m* de lit

bedstraw /ˈbedstrɔː/ **N** *(= plant)* gaillet *m*

bedtime /ˈbedtaɪm/ **N** heure *f* du coucher ◆ **it is ~** il est l'heure d'aller se coucher *or* d'aller au lit ◆ **his ~ is 7 o'clock** il se couche à 7 heures ◆ **it's past your ~** tu devrais être déjà couché
COMP **bedtime drink N** boisson *f* chaude *(prise avant d'aller se coucher)*
bedtime reading N ◆ **it's my favourite ~ reading** c'est ce que je préfère lire le soir, au lit
bedtime story N ◆ **to tell a child a ~ story** raconter une histoire à un enfant avant qu'il s'endorme

bee /biː/ **N** 1 abeille *f* ◆ **to have a ~ in one's bonnet*** avoir une idée fixe *(about* en ce qui concerne) avoir une marotte ◆ **they crowded round him like ~s round a honeypot** ils se pressaient autour de lui comme des mouches sur un pot de confiture ◆ **it's the ~'s knees*** c'est extra* *or* super* ◆ **he thinks he's the ~'s knees*** il se croit sorti de la cuisse de Jupiter* ; → **bumblebee, busy, queen** 2 *(esp US = meeting)* *réunion entre voisins ou voisines pour effectuer des activités en commun* ◆ **they have a sewing ~ on Thursdays** ils se réunissent pour coudre le jeudi ; → **spelling**
COMP **bee eater N** *(= bird)* guêpier *m*
bee sting N piqûre *f* d'abeille

Beeb* /biːb/ **N** *(Brit)* ◆ **the ~** la BBC

beech /biːtʃ/ **N** *(also* **beech tree***)* hêtre *m* ; *(= wood)* (bois *m* de) hêtre ; → **copper**
COMP *[hedge, chair]* de hêtre
beech grove N hêtraie *f*

beechmast /ˈbiːtʃmɑːst/ **N** *(NonC)* faînes *fpl* (tombées)

beechnut /ˈbiːtʃnʌt/ **N** faîne *f*

beechwood /ˈbiːtʃwʊd/ **N** *(= material)* (bois *m* de) hêtre *m* ; *(= group of trees)* bois *m* de hêtres

beef /biːf/ **N** 1 *(NonC)* bœuf *m* ◆ **roast ~** rôti *m* de bœuf, rosbif *m* ◆ **there's too much ~ on him**‡ il a trop de viande‡, il est trop gros ; → **bully³, corned beef** 2 *(esp US)* **what's your ~?**‡ *(= complaint)* qu'est-ce que tu as à râler ?*
VI (‡ *= complain)* rouspéter*, râler* *(about* contre)
COMP **beef cattle N** bœufs *mpl* de boucherie
beef olive N paupiette *f* de bœuf
beef sausage N ≈ saucisse *f* de Strasbourg
beef tea N bouillon *m* (de viande)

► **beef up*** **VT SEP** *[+ speech, essay]* étoffer ; *[+ team]* renforcer

beefburger /ˈbiːfˌbɜːgəʳ/ **N** ≈ hamburger *m*

beefcake* /ˈbiːfkeɪk/ **N** *(hum)* monsieur-muscles* *m*

beefeater /ˈbiːfˌiːtəʳ/ **N** *(Brit)* hallebardier *m (de la Tour de Londres)*

beefsteak /ˈbiːfsteɪk/ **N** bifteck *m*, steak *m*
COMP **beefsteak tomato N** tomate *f* à farcir

beefy* /ˈbiːfɪ/ **ADJ** 1 *(= strong)* costaud* *f inv* ; *(= fat)* bien en chair 2 *[flavour]* de bœuf

beehive /ˈbiːhaɪv/ **N** *(gen)* *(lit, fig)* ruche *f* ; *(= hair style)* choucroute* *f* **COMP** **the Beehive State N** *(US)* l'Utah *m*

beekeeper /ˈbiːˌkiːpəʳ/ **N** apiculteur *m*, -trice *f*

beekeeping /ˈbiːˌkiːpɪŋ/ **N** apiculture *f*

beeline /ˈbiːlaɪn/ **N** ◆ **in a ~** à vol d'oiseau, en ligne droite ◆ **to make a ~ for** *(= go straight to)* se diriger tout droit *or* en droite ligne vers ; *(= rush towards)* se ruer sur, filer droit sur

Beemer* /ˈbiːməʳ/ **N** BM* *f (voiture)*

been /biːn/ **VB** ptp of **be**

beep /biːp/ **N** *(esp Brit)* *[of watch]* bip *m* ; *[of answering machine]* signal *m* sonore, bip *m* (sonore) ◆ **after the ~** après le bip *or* le signal sonore **VI** faire bip **VT** ◆ **to ~ the** *or* **one's horn** klaxonner

beeper /ˈbiːpəʳ/ **N** ⇒ **bleeper**

beer /bɪəʳ/ **N** bière *f* ◆ **life's not all ~ and skittles*** *(Brit)* la vie n'est pas une partie de plaisir ; → **ginger**
COMP **beer barrel N** tonneau *m* à *or* de bière
beer belly* N bedaine* *f* (de buveur de bière)
beer bottle N canette *f* (de bière)
beer bust‡ **N** *(US)* *(= party)* soirée *f* bière *inv* ; *(= drinking spree)* soûlerie* *f* à la bière
beer can N boîte *f* de bière (vide)
beer drinker N buveur *m*, -euse *f* de bière
beer engine N pompe *f* à bière
beer garden N *(Brit)* jardin *m* attenant à un pub *(où l'on peut amener ses consommations)*
beer glass N bock *m*
beer gut* N ⇒ **beer belly**
beer pump N ⇒ **beer engine**
beer-swilling* **ADJ** *(pej)* qui s'envoie de la bière à tire-larigot*

beerfest /ˈbɪəfest/ **N** *(US)* fête *f* de la bière

beermat /ˈbɪəmæt/ **N** dessous *m* de verre, dessous *m* de bock

beery /ˈbɪərɪ/ **ADJ** *[atmosphere, room, breath]* qui sent la bière ; *[party, evening]* où la bière coule à flots ; *[person]* un peu éméché*, parti*

beeswax /ˈbiːzwæks/ **N** cire *f* d'abeille **VT** *[+ floor, furniture]* cirer, encaustiquer

beet /biːt/ **N** betterave *f* ◆ **red ~** *(US)* betterave *f* (potagère) ; → **sugar** **COMP** **beet sugar N** sucre *m* de betterave

beetle¹ /ˈbiːtl/ **N** *(gen)* scarabée *m* ; *(more technically)* coléoptère *m* ; → **black, Colorado, stag** **VI** ◆ **to ~ in/through*** *etc* entrer/traverser *etc* en vitesse

► **beetle off*** **VI** décamper, ficher le camp*

beetle² /ˈbiːtl/ **N** *(= mallet)* mailloche *f* ; *(heavier)* mouton *m*

beetling /ˈbiːtlɪŋ/ **ADJ** ◆ **~ brow** front *m* proéminent ◆ **~ cliffs** falaises *fpl* surplombantes

beetroot /ˈbiːtruːt/ **N** *(Brit)* betterave *f* (potagère *or* rouge) ◆ **to go ~*** devenir rouge comme une tomate, devenir cramoisi ◆ **~ salad** salade *f* de betterave(s)

befall /bɪˈfɔːl/ (pret **befell** /bɪˈfel/, ptp **befallen** /bɪˈfɔːlən/) *(liter: only infin and 3rd pers)* **VI** arriver ◆ **whatever may ~** quoi qu'il puisse arriver, quoi qu'il advienne **VT** arriver à, échoir à ◆ **a misfortune befell him** il lui arriva un malheur

befit /bɪˈfɪt/ **VT** *(frm)* convenir à ◆ **the luxurious ambience ~ting such an occasion** le cadre luxueux qui convient à une telle occasion ◆ **they offered him a post ~ting his experience** ils lui ont offert un poste en rapport avec *or* qui correspondait à son expérience ◆ **it ill ~s him to speak thus** il lui sied *(frm)* mal de parler ainsi ◆ **it ill ~s them to complain about this** ils sont mal placés pour s'en plaindre ◆ **he is a cautious man, as ~s a high-ranking politician** il est prudent, comme il sied à un homme politique de haut niveau

befitting /bɪˈfɪtɪŋ/ **ADJ** convenable, seyant ◆ **with ~ humility** avec l'humilité qui convient *or* qui sied *(frm)*

befog /bɪˈfɒg/ **VT** *(= puzzle)* brouiller, embrouiller ; *(= obscure)* *[+ origin, meaning]* obscurcir ◆ **she was quite ~ged** † elle était dans le brouillard le plus complet

before /bɪˈfɔːʳ/

When **before** is an element in a phrasal verb, eg **come before**, **go before**, look up the verb.

PREP 1 *(time)* avant ◆ **I got there ~ you** je suis arrivé avant vous, je vous ai devancé ◆ **that was ~ my time** *(= before I was here)* je n'étais pas encore là ; *(= before I was born)* je n'étais pas encore né ◆ **she died ~ I was born** je n'étais pas né quand elle est morte, elle est morte avant ma naissance ◆ **~ Christ** avant Jésus-Christ ◆ **the day ~ yesterday** avant-hier *m* ◆ **he came the year ~ last** il est venu il y a deux ans ◆ **the programme ~ last** l'avant-dernier programme *m* ◆ **the day ~ their departure** la veille de leur départ ◆ **two days ~ Christmas** l'avant-veille *f* de Noël ◆ **~ it, ~ now, ~ then** avant (cela *or* ça), auparavant ◆ **you should have done it ~ now** vous devriez l'avoir déjà fait ◆ **~ long** sous peu, d'ici peu ◆ **~ doing sth** avant de faire qch
2 *(order, rank)* avant ◆ **ladies ~ gentlemen** les dames avant les messieurs ◆ **~ everything** avant tout ◆ **she puts her family ~ her job** pour elle, sa famille passe avant son travail
3 *(place, position)* devant ◆ **he stood ~ me** il était (là) devant moi ◆ **~ my (very) eyes** sous mes (propres) yeux ◆ **turn left at the junction ~ the roundabout** tournez à gauche au croisement avant le rond-point ◆ **he said it ~ us all** il l'a dit en notre présence *or* devant nous tous ◆ **~ a lawyer** par-devant notaire ◆ **to appear ~ a court/a judge** comparaître devant un tribunal/un juge ◆ **he brought the case ~ the court** il a saisi le tribunal de l'affaire ◆ **the question ~ us** la question qui nous occupe ◆ **the task ~ him** la tâche qu'il a devant lui *or* qui l'attend ; → **carry**
4 *(= rather than)* plutôt que ◆ **he would die ~ betraying his country** il mourrait plutôt que de trahir sa patrie ◆ **to put death ~ dishonour** préférer la mort au déshonneur
ADV 1 *(time)* avant, auparavant ◆ **the day ~** la veille ◆ **the evening ~** la veille au soir ◆ **the week/year ~** la semaine/l'année d'avant *or* précédente ◆ **two days ~** l'avant-veille *f*, deux jours avant *or* auparavant ◆ **I have read that book ~** j'ai déjà lu ce livre ◆ **I had read it ~** je l'avais déjà lu, je l'avais lu auparavant ◆ **I said ~ that ...** j'ai déjà dit que ... ◆ **she has never met him ~** c'est la première fois qu'elle le rencontre, elle ne l'a encore jamais rencontré ◆ **it has never happened ~** c'est la première fois que cela arrive ◆ **long ~** longtemps auparavant ◆ **to continue as ~** faire comme par le passé ◆ **he should have told me ~** il aurait dû me le dire avant *or* plus tôt
2 *(order)* avant ◆ **that chapter and the one ~** ce chapitre et le précédent *or* et celui d'avant
CONJ 1 *(time)* avant de + *infin*, avant que (+ ne) + *subj* ◆ **I did it ~ going out** je l'ai fait avant de sortir ◆ **go and see him ~ he goes** allez le voir avant son départ *or* avant qu'il (ne) parte ◆ **~ I come/go/return** avant mon arrivée/mon départ/mon retour ◆ **we will need a year ~ it is finished** il nous faudra un an pour l'achever ◆ **it will be a long time ~ he comes again** il ne reviendra pas d'ici longtemps ◆ **it will be six weeks ~ the boat returns** le bateau ne reviendra pas avant six semaines ◆ **~ you could say Jack Robinson** en moins de deux, en moins de temps qu'il n'en faut pour le dire ◆ **get out ~ I call the police!** sors ou j'appelle la police ! ◆ **~ I forget, your mother phoned** avant que je n'oublie *subj or* que j'oublie *subj*, votre mère a téléphoné
2 *(= rather than)* plutôt que de + *infin* ◆ **he will die ~ he surrenders** il mourra plutôt que de se rendre
COMP **before-and-after test N** test *m* "avant-après"
before-tax ADJ *[income]* brut ; *[profit]* avant impôts

beforehand /bɪˈfɔːhænd/ **ADV** à l'avance ◆ **you must tell me ~** il faut me le dire à l'avance ◆ **to make preparations well ~** faire des préparatifs bien à l'avance

befoul /bɪˈfaʊl/ **VT** *(liter: lit, fig)* souiller *(liter)*, salir

befriend /bɪˈfrend/ **VT** *(= be friend to)* se lier d'amitié avec ; *(= help)* venir en aide à, aider

befuddle /bɪˈfʌdl/ **VT** *(= confuse)* brouiller l'esprit *or* les idées de ; *(= make tipsy)* griser, éméché ◆ **~d with drink** éméché*

beg /beg/ **VT** [1] *[+ money, alms, food]* mendier [2] *[+ favour]* solliciter, quémander ◆ **to ~ sb's pardon** demander pardon à qn ◆ **(I) ~ your pardon** *(apologizing)* je vous demande pardon ; *(not having heard)* pardon ?, vous disiez ? ◆ **to ~ (sb's) forgiveness** demander pardon (à qn) ◆ **I ~ to point out that ...** *(frm)* je me permets de (vous) faire remarquer que ..., qu'il me soit permis de faire remarquer que ... ◆ **I ~ to differ** *(frm)* permettez-moi d'être d'un autre avis, je me permets de ne pas partager cet avis ◆ **I ~ to inform you that ...** *(frm)* je tiens à *or* j'ai l'honneur *(frm)* de vous faire savoir que ... ◆ **to ~ leave to do sth** *(frm)* solliciter l'autorisation de faire qch

[3] *(= entreat)* supplier ◆ **to ~ (of) sb to do sth** supplier qn de faire qch ◆ **I ~ (of) you!** je vous en supplie !, de grâce !

[4] ◆ **to ~ the question** *(= raise the question)* poser *or* soulever la question ; *(= evade the issue)* éluder la question ; *(= assume sth already proved)* présumer la question résolue

VI [1] mendier, demander la charité ◆ **to ~ for money** mendier ◆ **to ~ for food** mendier de la nourriture ◆ **to sit up and ~** *[dog]* faire le beau ◆ **I'll have that sausage if it's going ~ging*** donne-moi cette saucisse s'il n'y a pas d'amateurs

[2] *(= entreat)* supplier ◆ **to ~ for mercy/help** demander grâce/de l'aide ; see also **vt**

► **beg off** **VI** se faire excuser *(from* de)

began /bɪˈgæn/ **VB** pt of **begin**

beget †† /bɪˈget/ (pret **begot** *or* **begat** /bɪˈgæt/, ptp **begotten**) **VT** *(lit)* engendrer ; *(fig)* engendrer, causer ◆ **the only begotten Son of the Father** le Fils unique engendré par le Père

begetter /bɪˈgetəʳ/ **N** *(frm: fig)* créateur *m*, -trice *f*

beggar /ˈbegəʳ/ **N** [1] mendiant(e) *m(f)*, mendigot(e)* *m(f)* ; *(fig = very poor person)* indigent(e) *m(f)*, pauvre *m*, -esse *f* ◆ **~s can't be choosers** *(Prov)* nécessité fait loi *(Prov)* ◆ **~'s opera** opéra *m* de quat' sous [2] *(* = fellow)* **poor ~!** pauvre diable !* ◆ **a lucky ~** un veinard* ◆ **a funny little ~** un drôle de petit bonhomme **VT** *(lit)* réduire à la mendicité ; *(fig = ruin)* mettre sur la paille, ruiner ◆ **to ~ description** défier toute description ◆ **to ~ belief** défier la raison ◆ **the arrogance of the man ~s belief** l'arrogance de cet homme défie la raison **COMP** **beggar-my-neighbour** **N** *(Cards)* bataille *f* ◆ **~-my-neighbour policy** *(Econ)* politique *f* protectionniste

beggarly /ˈbegəlɪ/ **ADJ** *[amount]* piètre, misérable ; *[existence]* misérable, sordide ; *[meal]* maigre, piètre, pauvre ; *[wage]* dérisoire, de famine

beggary /ˈbegərɪ/ **N** mendicité *f*

begging /ˈbegɪŋ/ **N** mendicité *f* ◆ **to live by ~** vivre de charité *or* d'aumône ; see also **beg** **ADJ** ◆ **~ letter** lettre *f* quémandant de l'argent **COMP** **begging bowl** **N** sébile *f* ◆ **to hold out a ~ bowl** *(fig)* tendre la main *(fig)*

begin /bɪˈgɪn/ (pret **began**, ptp **begun**) **VT** [1] *(= start) [+ work, book, song, letter]* commencer *(to do sth, doing sth* à faire qch) ; *[+ task]* entreprendre ; *[+ attack]* déclencher ◆ **to ~ a cheque book/a page** commencer un nouveau carnet de chèques/une nouvelle page ◆ **to ~ a journey** partir en voyage ◆ **he began the day with a glass of milk** il a bu un verre de lait pour bien commencer la journée ◆ **to ~ the day right** bien commencer la journée, se lever du pied droit ◆ **to ~ life as ...** débuter dans la vie comme ... ◆ **that doesn't (even) ~ to compare with ...** cela est loin d'être comparable à ..., cela n'a rien de comparable avec ... ◆ **it soon began to rain** il n'a pas tardé à pleuvoir ◆ **I'd begun to think you weren't coming** je commençais à croire que tu ne viendrais pas ◆ **to ~ sth again** recommencer qch *(to do sth* à faire qch) ; ◆ **"listen, darling" he began** "écoute, chérie" commença-t-il

[2] *(= originate, initiate) [+ discussion]* commencer, ouvrir ; *[+ conversation]* amorcer, engager ; *[+ quarrel, argument, dispute]* faire naître ; *[+ reform, movement, series of events]* déclencher ; *[+ fashion]* lancer ; *[+ custom, policy]* inaugurer ; *[+ war]* causer ; *[+ rumour]* faire naître

VI [1] commencer *(with* par) ; ◆ **let's ~!** commençons !, allons-y ! ◆ **we must ~ at once** il faut commencer *or* nous y mettre immédiatement ◆ **well, to ~ at the beginning ...** bon, commençons par le commencement ... ◆ **it's ~ning rather well/badly** cela commence plutôt bien/mal ◆ **to ~ in business** se lancer dans les affaires ◆ **before October ~s** avant le début octobre *or* le début du mois d'octobre ◆ **to ~ again** recommencer ◆ **he began afresh in a new country** il est reparti à zéro dans un nouveau pays ◆ **school ~s again on Tuesday** les cours reprennent mardi, la rentrée (des classes) est mardi ◆ **the classes ~ again soon** *(after short break)* les cours reprennent bientôt ; *(after summer break)* c'est bientôt la rentrée ◆ **~ning from Monday** à partir de lundi ◆ **he began in the sales department/as a clerk** il a débuté dans le service des ventes/comme employé de bureau ◆ **he began as a Marxist** il a commencé par être marxiste, au début *or* au départ il était marxiste ◆ **he began with the intention of writing a thesis** au début son intention était d'écrire *or* il avait l'intention d'écrire une thèse ◆ **to ~ by doing sth** commencer par faire qch ◆ **~ by putting everything away** commence par tout ranger ◆ **to ~ with sth** commencer *or* débuter par qch ◆ **~ with me!** commencez par moi ! ◆ **we only had €20 to ~ with** nous n'avions que 20 € pour commencer *or* au début ◆ **to ~ with there were only three of them but later ...** (tout) d'abord ils n'étaient que trois, mais plus tard ... ◆ **the spelling is wrong, to ~ with** d'abord, l'orthographe est fausse ◆ **~ on a new page** prenez une nouvelle page ◆ **the fields ~ where the garden ends** au bout du jardin il y a des champs

[2] *(= make a start)* **to ~ on** *[+ book]* commencer (à écrire *or* à lire) ; *[+ course of study]* commencer, entreprendre ◆ **I began on the job last week** j'ai commencé à travailler *or* j'ai débuté dans ce travail la semaine dernière

[3] *[shooting, fight, quarrel]* commencer ; *[music, noise, guns]* commencer, retentir ; *[fire]* prendre, se déclarer ; *[river]* prendre sa source ; *[road]* partir *(at* de) ; *[political party, movement, custom]* commencer, naître ◆ **that's when the trouble ~s** c'est alors *or* là que les ennuis commencent ◆ **it all began when he refused to pay** toute cette histoire a commencé *or* tout a commencé quand il a refusé de payer ◆ **since the world began** depuis le commencement du monde, depuis que le monde est monde

beginner /bɪˈgɪnəʳ/ **N** [1] *(= novice)* débutant(e) *m(f)*, novice *mf* ◆ **it's just ~'s luck** c'est la chance des débutants [2] *(= originator)* auteur *m*, cause *f*

beginning /bɪˈgɪnɪŋ/ **N** [1] *[of speech, book, film, career etc]* début *m*, commencement *m* ◆ **from the ~** dès le début, dès le commencement ◆ **from ~ to end** du début à la fin ◆ **to start again at** *or* **from the ~** recommencer depuis le début ◆ **in the ~** *(gen)* au début ; *(Bible)* au commencement ◆ **to make a ~** commencer, débuter ◆ **the ~ of the academic year** la rentrée (universitaire *or* scolaire) ◆ **the ~ of the world** le commencement *or* l'origine *f* du monde ◆ **the ~ of negotiations** l'amorce *f or* l'ouverture *f* des négociations ◆ **it was the ~ of the end for him** ce fut pour lui le commencement de la fin ◆ **since the ~ of time** depuis le commencement du monde, depuis que le monde est monde

[2] *(= origin)* origine *f*, commencement *m* ◆ **the shooting was the ~ of the rebellion** la fusillade a été à l'origine de la révolte ◆ **fascism had its ~s in Italy** le fascisme prit naissance en Italie ◆ **to come from humble ~s** *[person]* être d'origine modeste *or* d'un milieu humble

ADJ ◆ **~ learner** *or* **student** débutant(e) *m(f)*

begone †† /bɪˈgɒn/ **EXCL** *(liter)* partez !, hors d'ici ! *(liter)*

begonia /bɪˈgəʊnɪə/ **N** bégonia *m*

begot /bɪˈgɒt/ **VB** pt of **beget**

begotten /bɪˈgɒtn/ **VB** ptp of **beget**

begrimed /bɪˈgraɪmd/ **ADJ** *(liter)* noirci, sale

begrudge /bɪˈgrʌdʒ/ **VT** ⇒ **grudge vt**

begrudgingly /bɪˈgrʌdʒɪŋlɪ/ **ADV** à contrecœur, de mauvaise grâce

beguile /bɪˈgaɪl/ **VT** [1] *(= swindle)* abuser, duper ◆ **to ~ sb with promises** bercer qn de promesses, endormir qn avec des promesses ◆ **to ~ sb into doing sth** amener qn par la supercherie à faire qch [2] *(= charm)* séduire, captiver ; *(= amuse)* distraire [3] *(liter)* ◆ **to ~ the time (doing sth)** faire passer le temps (en faisant qch)

beguiling /bɪˈgaɪlɪŋ/ **ADJ** *[woman, charm]* captivant, séduisant ; *[ideas, theory]* séduisant ; *[story]* captivant

begum /ˈbeɪgəm/ **N** bégum *f*

begun /bɪˈgʌn/ **VB** ptp of **begin**

behalf /bɪˈhɑːf/ **N** ◆ **on ~ of** *(= in the interest of)* en faveur de, pour ; *(= as a representative of)* au nom de ◆ **she made an emotional appeal on her son's ~** elle a lancé un appel chargé d'émotion en faveur de son fils ◆ **he spoke on my ~** *(= to support me)* il m'a soutenu ◆ **to come on sb's ~** venir de la part de qn ◆ **on ~ of all of us, I would like to say how sorry we are** en notre nom à tous, je voudrais vous dire que nous sommes vraiment désolés ◆ **to plead on sb's ~** plaider en faveur de qn ◆ **he was worried on my ~** il s'inquiétait pour moi *or* à mon sujet

◆ **to act on behalf of sb** agir pour qn *or* pour le compte de qn ◆ **the solicitors acting on ~ of the police officers** les avocats qui agissaient pour le compte des officiers de police ◆ **she acts on ~ of clients in buying and selling shares** elle achète et vend des actions pour des clients

behave /bɪˈheɪv/ **VI** [1] *(= conduct o.s.)* se conduire, se comporter ◆ **to ~ (o.s.) well/badly** bien/mal se conduire *or* se comporter ◆ **to ~ well towards sb** bien se comporter à l'égard de *or* envers qn, bien agir envers qn ◆ **to ~ wisely** agir sagement ◆ **to ~ like an honest man** se comporter *or* se conduire en honnête homme ◆ **he was behaving strangely** il avait un comportement bizarre

[2] *(* = conduct o.s. well)* bien se tenir ; *[child]* être sage ◆ **he knows how to ~ in society** il sait se tenir dans le monde ◆ **~ (yourself)!** *(physical behaviour)* sois sage !, tiens-toi bien ! ; *(sth said)* ne dis pas n'importe quoi !

[3] *[natural entity, substance]* se comporter ; *[machine]* marcher, fonctionner ◆ **an alloy that ~s like plastic** un alliage qui se comporte comme le plastique ◆ **we are studying how electrons ~ within atoms** nous étudions le comportement des électrons à l'intérieur des atomes

behaviour, behavior (US) /bɪˈheɪvjəʳ/ **N** [1] *(= manner, bearing)* conduite *f*, comportement *m* ◆ **to be on one's best ~** * se conduire de son mieux ; *[child]* se montrer d'une sagesse exemplaire [2] *(= conduct towards others)* conduite *f*, comportement *m* *(to sb, towards sb* envers qn, à l'égard de qn) [3] *[of machines]* fonctionnement *m*

COMP **behaviour modification** **N** modification *f* du comportement

behaviour patterns NPL types *mpl* de comportement

behaviour therapy N thérapie *f* comportementale

behavioural, behavioral *(US)* /bɪ'heɪvjərəl/ ADJ 1 *[sciences, studies]* behavioriste 2 *[pattern]* de comportement ◆ ~ **problems** troubles *mpl* du comportement

behaviourism, behaviorism *(US)* /bɪ'heɪvjərɪzəm/ N behaviorisme *m*

behaviourist, behaviorist *(US)* /bɪ'heɪvjərɪst/ ADJ, N behavioriste *mf*

behead /bɪ'hed/ VT décapiter

beheading /bɪ'hedɪŋ/ N décapitation *f*

beheld /bɪ'held/ VB pt, ptp of **behold**

behemoth /bɪ'hi:mɒθ/ N *(= creature)* béhémot(h) *m* ; *(fig)* monstre *m* ingérable

behest /bɪ'hest/ N *(frm)* commandement *m*, ordre *m* ◆ **at the ~ of ...** sur l'ordre de ...

behind /bɪ'haɪnd/

> When **behind** is an element in a phrasal verb, eg **fall behind**, **lag behind**, **stay behind**, look up the verb.

ADV 1 *(= in or at the rear)* derrière, en arrière ◆ **to follow a long way ~/not far ~** suivre de loin/d'assez près ; → **fall behind**

2 *(= late)* en retard ◆ **to be ~ with one's studies/payments** être en retard dans ses études/ses paiements ◆ **to be ~ with one's work** avoir du travail en retard, être en retard dans son travail ◆ **I'm too far ~ to catch up now** j'ai pris trop de retard pour me rattraper maintenant

PREP 1 *(lit, fig = at the back of)* derrière ◆ **~ the table** derrière la table ◆ **come out from ~ the door** sortez de derrière la porte ◆ **walk close ~ me** suivez-moi de près ◆ **she closed the door ~ her** elle a fermé la porte derrière elle ◆ **an employee with seven years' service ~ her** une employée ayant sept ans d'ancienneté ◆ **~ my back** *(lit)* dans mon dos ; *(fig)* derrière mon dos, à mon insu ◆ **to put sth ~ one** *(fig)* oublier qch, refuser de penser à qch ◆ **~ the scenes** *(Theat, fig)* dans les coulisses ◆ **what is ~ this?** *(fig)* qu'y a-t-il là-dessous ? ; → **bar¹, schedule**

2 *(support)* ◆ **he has the Communists ~ him** il a les communistes derrière lui ◆ **she's the one ~ this scheme** c'est elle qui est à l'origine de ce projet ◆ **the motives ~ her decision** les motivations *fpl* profondes de sa décision

3 *(= responsible for)* **who was ~ the attack?** qui est derrière cet attentat ?, qui est le commanditaire de cet attentat ?

4 *(= less advanced than)* en retard sur, en arrière de ◆ **her son is ~ the other pupils** son fils est en retard sur les autres élèves

5 *(time)* ~ **time** en retard ◆ **to be ~ the times** être en retard sur son temps, ne pas être de son époque ◆ **their youth is far ~ them** leur jeunesse est loin derrière eux

N *(* = buttocks)* derrière *m*, postérieur * *m*

behindhand /bɪ'haɪndhænd/ ADV en retard *(with dans)*

behold /bɪ'həʊld/ (pret, ptp **beheld**) VT *(liter)* voir ◆ **~!** regardez ! ◆ **~ thy servant** voici ton serviteur ◆ **and ~ I am with you** et voici que je suis avec vous ; → **lo**

beholden /bɪ'həʊldən/ ADJ *(frm)* ◆ **to be ~** être redevable *(to sb for sth* à qn de qch)

behove /bɪ'həʊv/, **behoove** *(US)* /bɪ'hu:v/ IMPERS VT *(frm)* incomber, appartenir *(sb to do sth* à qn de faire qch) être du devoir *or* de l'intérêt *(sb to do sth* de qn de faire qch) ; ◆ **it ill ~s me/him** *etc* **to ...** il me/lui *etc* sied mal de ...

beige /beɪʒ/ ADJ, N beige *m*

Beijing /'beɪ'dʒɪŋ/ N Beijing

being /'bi:ɪŋ/ N 1 *(NonC = existence)* existence *f* ◆ **to come into ~** prendre naissance ◆ **when the world came into ~** lorsque le monde fut créé, au moment de la naissance du monde ◆ **to bring** *or* **call into ~** faire naître, susciter ◆ **to bring a plan into ~** exécuter *or* réaliser un plan ◆ **then in ~** qui existait alors 2 être *m*, créature *f* ◆ **human ~s** les êtres *mpl* humains ◆ **~s from outer space** des extraterrestres *mpl* ; → **supreme** 3 *(= essential nature)* être *m*, essence *f* ◆ **with all** *or* **every fibre of my ~** de tout mon être ◆ **I wanted to be an actress with every fibre of my ~** je désirais être actrice de tout mon être

Beirut /beɪ'ru:t/ N Beyrouth

bejewelled, bejeweled *(US)* /bɪ'dʒu:əld/ ADJ *[person]* paré de bijoux ; *[thing]* incrusté de joyaux ; *(fig) [grass]* émaillé *(with* de)

belabour, belabor *(US)* /bɪ'leɪbə^r^/ VT rouer de coups ; *(fig: with words)* invectiver

Belarus /belə'rus/ N Bélarus *m*, Biélorussie *f*

Belarussian /ˌbelə'rʌʃən/ ADJ bélarusse, biélorusse N *(= person)* Bélarusse *mf*, Biélorusse *mf*

belated /bɪ'leɪtɪd/ ADJ *[apology, greetings, measures]* tardif

belatedly /bɪ'leɪtɪdlɪ/ ADV tardivement

belay /bɪ'leɪ/ VT 1 *(Naut)* amarrer 2 *(Climbing)* assurer VI *(Climbing)* assurer N assurage *m*, assurance *f* COMP ◆ **~ing pin** N cabillot *m* (d'amarrage)

belch /beltʃ/ VI *[person]* avoir un renvoi, éructer VT (also **belch forth** *or* **out** : *liter) [volcano, gun] [+ smoke, flames]* vomir, cracher N renvoi *m*, éructation *f*

beleaguered /bɪ'li:gəd/ ADJ 1 *[city]* assiégé, investi ; *[army]* cerné 2 *(fig)* aux abois

belfry /'belfrɪ/ N beffroi *m* ; *[of church]* clocher *m*, beffroi *m* ; → **bat¹**

Belgian /'beldʒən/ ADJ *(gen)* belge, de Belgique ; *[ambassador, embassy]* de Belgique ◆ **~ French** le français de Belgique N Belge *mf* ◆ **the king of the ~s** le roi des Belges

belgicism /'beldʒɪsɪzəm/ N belgicisme *m*

Belgium /'beldʒəm/ N Belgique *f*

Belgrade /bel'greɪd/ N Belgrade

belie /bɪ'laɪ/ VT *(= fail to justify) [+ hopes]* démentir, tromper ; *(= prove false) [+ words]* donner le démenti à, démentir ; *[+ proverb]* faire mentir ; *(= misrepresent) [+ facts]* donner une fausse impression *or* idée de

belief /bɪ'li:f/ N 1 *(NonC = acceptance as true)* croyance *f (in* en, à) ; ◆ **~ in ghosts** croyance *f* aux revenants ◆ **~ in God** croyance *f* en Dieu ◆ **he has lost his ~ in God** il ne croit plus en Dieu, il a perdu la foi (en Dieu) ◆ **worthy of ~** digne de foi ◆ **it is beyond** *or* **past (all) ~** c'est incroyable, c'est à ne pas (y) croire ◆ **wealthy beyond ~** incroyablement riche

2 *(Rel) (= faith)* foi *f* ; *(= doctrine)* credo *m*

3 *(= conviction)* opinion *f*, conviction *f* ◆ **in the ~ that ...** persuadé que ..., convaincu que ... ◆ **it is my ~ that ...** je suis convaincu *or* persuadé que ... ◆ **to the best of my ~** (pour) autant que je sache ; → **strong**

4 *(NonC = trust)* confiance *f*, foi *f (in* en) ; ◆ **he has no ~ in doctors** il n'a aucune confiance dans les médecins ◆ **he has no ~ in the future** il ne croit pas en l'avenir

COMP **belief system** N système *m* de croyances

believable /bɪ'li:vəbl/ ADJ croyable

believe /bɪ'li:v/ LANGUAGE IN USE 6.2, 26.2

VT 1 *(= accept truth of) [+ statement, account, evidence, person]* croire ◆ **to ~ what sb says** croire ce que dit qn ◆ **I don't ~ a word of it** je n'en crois rien *or* pas un mot ◆ **I don't ~ it!** *(in exasperation)* ce n'est pas vrai ! ; *(in incredulity, triumph)* ce n'est pas possible *or* vrai ! ◆ **don't you ~ it!*** ne va pas croire ça ! * ◆ **and would you ~ it, he's younger than me!** et figurez-vous qu'il est plus jeune que moi ! ◆ **he could hardly ~ his eyes/ears** il en croyait à peine ses yeux/ses oreilles ◆ **if he is to be ~d** à l'en croire, s'il faut l'en croire ◆ **~ it or not, he ...** c'est incroyable, mais il ... ◆ **~ me** crois-moi, tu peux me croire ◆ **~ you me*** tu peux m'en croire ◆ **I ~ you, thousands wouldn't*** *(hum)* moi, je te crois, mais je dois être le seul !

2 *(= think)* croire ◆ **I ~ I'm right** je crois avoir raison, je crois que j'ai raison ◆ **I don't ~ he will come** je ne crois pas qu'il viendra *or* qu'il vienne ◆ **he is ~d to be ill** on le croit malade ◆ **he is ~d to have a chance of succeeding** on lui donne des chances de succès ◆ **that is ~d to be true** cela passe pour vrai ◆ **I have every reason to ~ that ...** j'ai tout lieu de croire que ... ◆ **I ~ so** je crois que oui, je le crois ◆ **I ~ not** je crois que non, je ne (le) crois pas ◆ **I don't know what to ~** je ne sais que croire *or* à quoi m'en tenir ; → **make**

VI croire ; *(Rel)* croire, avoir la foi ◆ **to ~ in** *[+ God]* croire en ; *[+ ghosts, promises, antibiotics etc]* croire à ◆ **to ~ in sb** croire en qn, avoir confiance en qn ◆ **to ~ in a method** être partisan d'une méthode ◆ **I don't ~ in doctors** je n'ai pas confiance dans les médecins ◆ **I don't ~ in letting children do what they want** je ne suis pas d'avis qu'il faille laisser les enfants faire ce qu'ils veulent

believer /bɪ'li:və^r^/ N 1 *(= advocate)* partisan(e) *m(f)* ◆ **a ~ in capital punishment** un partisan de la peine capitale ◆ **I'm a great ~ in giving rewards for achievement** je suis tout à fait partisan de récompenser la réussite ◆ **she's a firm ~ in herbal medicines** elle croit profondément aux vertus de la phytothérapie 2 *(Rel)* croyant(e) *m(f)* ◆ **to be a ~** être croyant, avoir la foi ◆ **to be a ~ in ghosts/in astrology** croire aux fantômes/à l'astrologie

Belisha beacon /bɪ'li:ʃə'bi:kən/ N lampadaire *m (à globe orange marquant un passage pour piétons)*

belittle /bɪ'lɪtl/ VT *[+ person, action, object]* déprécier, rabaisser ◆ **to ~ o.s.** se déprécier

Belize /be'li:z/ N Belize *m* ◆ **in ~** au Belize

Belizean /be'li:zɪən/ ADJ bélizien N Bélizien(ne) *m(f)*

bell¹ /bel/ N 1 *[of church, school]* cloche *f* ; (also **handbell**) clochette *f* ; *(on toy, cat's collar, clothes etc)* grelot *m* ; *(on cows)* cloche *f*, clarine *f* ; *(on goats, sheep)* clochette *f* ; *(at door)* sonnette *f* ; *(on cycle, typewriter)* timbre *m* ; *[of telephone]* sonnerie *f* ◆ **great ~** bourdon *m*, grosse cloche *f* ◆ **the first ~ for mass was ringing** le premier coup de la messe sonnait ◆ **to give sb a ~*** *(Brit = phone sb)* passer un coup de fil * à qn ◆ **there's the ~!** *(door)* on sonne !, ça sonne ! * ; *(telephone)* le téléphone (sonne) ! ◆ **~s** *(Naut)* coups *mpl* de cloche ◆ **eight ~s** huit coups *mpl* piqués ◆ **to sound four/six/eight ~s** piquer quatre/six/huit coups ◆ **~s and whistles*** accessoires *mpl* fantaisie ; → **answer, chime, ring²**

2 *[of flower]* calice *m*, clochette *f* ; *[of trumpet]* pavillon *m*

VT mettre une cloche à ◆ **to ~ the cat** *(fig)* attacher le grelot *(fig)*

COMP **bell-bottomed trousers, bell-bottoms** NPL (pantalon *m* à) pattes *fpl* d'éléphant ; *(Naut)* pantalon *m* de marine

bell buoy N bouée *f* à cloche

bell captain N *(US) chef des grooms dans un hôtel*

bell glass N cloche *f* (en verre)

bell heather N bruyère *f* cendrée

bell jar N cloche *f* (en verre)

bell pepper N *(US) (= capsicum)* poivron *m*

bell pull N *[of door]* poignée *f* de sonnette ; *[of room]* cordon *m* de sonnette

bell push N bouton *m* de sonnette

bell-ringer N sonneur *m*, carillonneur *m*

bell-ringing N art du sonneur
bell rope N (in belfry) corde f de cloche ; (in room) cordon m de sonnette
bell-shaped ADJ en forme de cloche or de clochette
bell tent N tente f conique
bell tower N clocher m

bell² /bel/ N [of stag] bramement m VI bramer

belladonna /ˌbeləˈdɒnə/ N (= plant, drug) belladone f

bellboy /ˈbelbɔɪ/ N groom m, chasseur m

belle /bel/ N beauté f, belle f ♦ **the ~ of the ball** la reine du bal

bellhop /ˈbelhɒp/ N (US) ⇒ **bellboy**

bellicose /ˈbelɪkəʊs/ ADJ (frm) belliqueux, guerrier

bellicosity /ˌbelɪˈkɒsɪtɪ/ N (frm) caractère m belliqueux

belligerence /bɪˈlɪdʒərəns/, **belligerency** /bɪˈlɪdʒərənsɪ/ N belligérance f

belligerent /bɪˈlɪdʒərənt/ N belligérant(e) m(f) ADJ [person] belliqueux ; [voice, remarks, statement, policies, mood] agressif

belligerently /bɪˈlɪdʒərəntlɪ/ ADV [say, ask, demand] sur un ton agressif ; [stare, look] d'un air belliqueux or agressif

bellow /ˈbeləʊ/ VI [animals] mugir ; [esp cow, bull] beugler, meugler ; [person] brailler, beugler* (with de) ; [wind, ocean] mugir VT (also **bellow out**) [+ song, order] brailler, hurler ; [+ blasphemies] vociférer N [of animal] mugissement m ; [of esp cow, bull] beuglement m, meuglement m ; [of person] hurlement m, beuglement* m ; [of storm, ocean] mugissement m

bellows /ˈbeləʊz/ NPL [of forge, organ] soufflerie f ; [of fire] soufflet m ♦ **a pair of ~** un soufflet

Bell's palsy /ˌbelzˈpɔːlzɪ/ N (Med) paralysie f de Bell

bellwether /ˈbelˌweðəʳ/ N (US) (= sheep) sonnailler m ; (fig) indicateur m

belly /ˈbelɪ/ N 1 (= abdomen) ventre m ; (fat) panse* f, bedaine* f ♦ **your eyes are bigger than your ~!** tu as les yeux plus grands que le ventre ! ♦ **to go ~ up*** se casser la figure*

2 [of container] panse f, ventre m ; [of violin] table f (d'harmonie) ; [of guitar] table f (d'harmonie), ventre m ; [of ship] ventre m ; [of sail] creux m

3 (Culin) ~ **of pork** poitrine f de porc

VT [wind] gonfler, enfler

VI (also **belly out**) se gonfler, s'enfler

COMP **belly button*** N nombril m
belly dance N danse f du ventre
belly dancer N danseuse f du ventre
belly flop N (Swimming) ♦ **to do a ~ flop** faire un plat
belly-landing N (in plane) atterrissage m sur le ventre ♦ **to make a ~-landing** atterrir or se poser sur le ventre
belly laugh N gros rire m (gras)
belly tank N (in plane) réservoir m de secours
belly-up* ADV ♦ **to go ~-up** (= fail) [company] se planter*, se ramasser* ; [scheme] capoter*

bellyache /ˈbelɪeɪk/ N mal m de or au ventre ♦ **to have a ~** avoir mal au ventre VI * ronchonner*, bougonner*

bellyaching* /ˈbelɪeɪkɪŋ/ N ronchonnements* mpl, bougonnements* mpl

bellyband /ˈbelɪbænd/ N sous-ventrière f

bellyful /ˈbelɪfʊl/ N [of food] ventre m plein ♦ **he'd had a ~**‡ (fig) il en avait plein le dos*, il en avait ras le bol*

belong /bɪˈlɒŋ/ VI 1 ~ **to** (= be the property of) appartenir à ♦ **this book ~s to me** ce livre m'appartient, ce livre est à moi ♦ **lands which ~ to the Crown** des terres fpl qui appartiennent à la Couronne ♦ **the lid ~s to this box** le couvercle va avec cette boîte, c'est le couvercle de cette boîte ♦ **the handwriting ~s to a male** c'est une écriture masculine or d'homme ♦ **... but the last word ~ed to Roseanne** ... mais c'est Roseanne qui a eu le dernier mot

2 (= be member, inhabitant etc) **to ~ to a society** faire partie or être membre d'une société ♦ **to ~ to a town** [native] être originaire or natif d'une ville ; [inhabitant] habiter une ville

3 (= be in right place) être à sa place ♦ **to feel that one doesn't ~** se sentir étranger ♦ **you don't ~ here** tu n'es pas à ta place ici ♦ **people need to feel they ~** les gens ont besoin de sentir qu'ils ont leur place dans la société ♦ **to ~ together** aller ensemble ♦ **socks that don't ~ together** des chaussettes dépareillées ♦ **the book ~s on this shelf** le livre va sur ce rayon ♦ **put it back where it ~s** remets-le à sa place ♦ **murder ~s under the heading of capital crimes** le meurtre rentre dans la catégorie des crimes capitaux ♦ **his attitude ~s to a bygone era** c'est une attitude d'un autre âge ♦ **the future ~s to democracy** l'avenir est dans la démocratie

4 (Jur) ♦ **this case ~ed to the Appeal Court** ce procès ressortissait à la cour d'appel

belongings /bɪˈlɒŋɪŋz/ NPL affaires fpl, possessions fpl ♦ **personal ~** objets mpl or effets mpl personnels

Belorussia /ˌbeləʊˈrʌʃə/ N ⇒ **Byelorussia**

Belorussian /ˌbeləʊˈrʌʃən/ ADJ, N ⇒ **Byelorussian**

beloved /bɪˈlʌvɪd, bɪˈlʌvd/ ADJ bien-aimé, chéri ♦ **~ by all** aimé de tous ♦ **dearly ~ brethren ...** mes bien chers frères ... N bien-aimé(e) m(f)

below /bɪˈləʊ/

> When **below** is an element in a phrasal verb, eg **go below**, look up the verb.

PREP 1 (= under) sous ; (= lower than) au-dessous de ♦ **~ the bed** sous le lit ♦ **on the bed and ~ it** sur le lit et en dessous ♦ **her skirt is well ~ her knees** sa jupe est bien au-dessous du genou ♦ **~ average/sea level** au-dessous de la moyenne/du niveau de la mer ♦ **~ freezing point** au-dessous de zéro ♦ **~ the horizon** au-dessous de l'horizon ♦ **~ the surface** sous la surface ♦ **to be ~ sb in rank** occuper un rang inférieur à qn, être au-dessous de qn

2 (river) en aval de ♦ **the Thames ~ Oxford** la Tamise en aval d'Oxford

3 (= unworthy of) **it would be ~ my dignity to speak to him** je m'abaisserais en lui parlant ♦ **he feels housework is ~ him** pour lui, faire le ménage c'est s'abaisser, il trouve que les tâches ménagères sont indignes de lui

ADV 1 (= at lower level) plus bas, en contrebas ; (= at lowest level) en bas ; (= directly underneath) au-dessous ♦ **you can see the town spread out ~** on voit la ville qui s'étale plus bas or en contrebas ♦ **the canopy of trees shades the ground ~** la voûte des arbres fait de l'ombre sur le sol au-dessous ♦ **~, we could see the valley** plus bas or en bas, on apercevait la vallée, on apercevait la vallée en contrebas ♦ **the road ~** la route en contrebas ♦ **a window with a view to the street ~** une fenêtre avec vue sur la rue en bas ♦ **lying in our bunks, she above, me ~** couchés dans nos lits superposés, elle en haut, moi en bas ♦ **several thousand feet ~** (from mountain top) plusieurs milliers de mètres plus bas ; (from aeroplane) plusieurs milliers de mètres au-dessous ♦ **down ~** plus bas, en contrebas ♦ **far ~** beaucoup plus bas, loin en contrebas ♦ **from ~** d'en bas

2 (= downstairs) en bas ♦ **she heard two men talking ~** elle a entendu deux hommes qui parlaient en bas ♦ **the floor ~** l'étage m au-dessous ♦ **they live two floors ~** ils habitent deux étages plus bas or au-dessous ♦ **the people (in the flat) ~** les gens mpl (de l'appartement) du dessous or d'en dessous* ♦ **voices from ~** des voix fpl venant d'en bas

3 (later in document) [mentioned, summarized] plus bas, ci-dessous ♦ **please write to me at the address ~** veuillez m'écrire à l'adresse ci-dessous ♦ **listed ~ are some of the books we have in stock** vous trouverez ci-dessous une liste de certains des livres que nous avons en stock ♦ **see ~** voir ci-dessous or plus bas ♦ **see the picture ~** voir l'illustration ci-dessous ♦ **as stated ~** comme indiqué ci-dessous or plus bas

4 (in hierarchy) plus bas, au-dessous

5 (on boat) en bas ♦ **to go ~** descendre

6 (expressing temperature) au-dessous ♦ **it will be extremely cold, with temperatures at zero or ~** il fera extrêmement froid, avec des températures tombant à zéro ou au-dessous ♦ **it was twenty (degrees) ~** * il faisait moins vingt

7 (liter = on earth) ♦ **here ~** ici-bas

8 (liter = in hell: also **down below**) en enfer

COMP **below stairs** ADV ♦ **life ~ stairs at Buckingham Palace** la vie des domestiques de Buckingham Palace ADJ des domestiques ♦ **the ~-stairs world of a 1920s country house** l'univers des domestiques d'une gentilhommière des années 20
below-the-line advertising N publicité f hors média

belt /belt/ N 1 (Dress, Judo, fig) ceinture f ; (Mil etc) ceinturon m, ceinture f ; (= corset) gaine f ♦ **shoulder ~** baudrier m ♦ **he has ten years' experience under his ~** * il a dix années d'expérience à son actif ♦ **blow below the ~** (Boxing, also fig) coup m bas ♦ **to hit below the ~** porter un coup bas ♦ **that was below the ~!** (fig) c'était un coup bas or un coup en traître ! ♦ **to pull in** or **tighten one's ~** (fig) se serrer la ceinture ♦ **to be a black ~ (in judo etc)** être ceinture noire (de judo etc) ♦ **to give sb the ~** (= punishment) punir qn à coups d'étrivière ; → **safety**

2 (= tract of land) région f ♦ **industrial ~** région f industrielle ♦ **the cotton ~** la région de culture du coton ; → **green**

3 (= drivebelt) courroie f

4 (US = road) route f de ceinture

5 (= region) région f

VT 1 (= thrash) administrer une correction à, donner une raclée* à ; (‡ = hit) flanquer or coller un gnon‡ à ♦ **she ~ed him (one) in the eye**‡ elle lui a flanqué or collé un gnon‡ dans l'œil

2 (US) ⇒ **belt out**

VI (esp Brit * = rush) ♦ **to ~ in/out/across** etc entrer/sortir/traverser etc à toutes jambes or à toute blinde‡ ♦ **he ~ed down the street** il a descendu or dévalé la rue à fond de train

COMP **belt-and-braces** ADJ (fig) ♦ **it was a ~-and-braces job** * on a fait ça pour se donner une marge de sécurité or pour être vraiment tranquilles
belt bag N banane f
belt pulley N poulie f de courroie ; → **conveyor**

► **belt down**‡ VT SEP (US) [+ drink] descendre‡, se taper‡

► **belt out** * VT SEP ♦ **to belt out a song** chanter une chanson à tue-tête

► **belt up** VI 1 (= put on seat belt) attacher sa ceinture

2 (Brit ‡ = be quiet) la boucler‡, la fermer‡ ♦ **~ up!** la ferme !‡, boucle-la !‡

belter * /ˈbeltəʳ/ N (= shot, kick) boulet m (de canon) ; (= match, game) super match* m ; (= party) super soirée* f ♦ **it's a ~!** (song) ça décoiffe ! ♦ **she's a ~!** (singer) elle a du coffre !

belting * /ˈbeltɪŋ/ N *(= beating)* raclée * *f* ◆ **to give sb a good ~** filer une bonne raclée * à qn

beltway /ˈbeltweɪ/ N *(US: motorway-type)* périphérique *m*

belvedere /ˌbelvɪˈdɪəʳ/ N belvédère *m*

bemoan /bɪˈməʊn/ VT pleurer, déplorer

bemuse /bɪˈmjuːz/ VT rendre perplexe

bemused /bɪˈmjuːzd/ ADJ *[person, expression, smile]* perplexe

bemusedly /bɪˈmjuːzɪdlɪ/ ADV *[stare, gaze]* d'un air perplexe ; *[say]* sur un ton perplexe

bemusement /bɪˈmjuːzmənt/ N perplexité *f*

ben /ben/ *(Scot)* N mont *m*, sommet *m* COMP **Ben Nevis** N Ben Nevis *m*

bench /bentʃ/ N [1] *(= seat) (Brit Parl)* banc *m* ; *(in tiers)* gradin *m* ; *(padded)* banquette *f* ◆ **on the ~** *(Sport)* sur le banc de touche ; → **back, Opposition**

[2] *(Jur)* **the Bench** *(= court)* la cour, le tribunal ; *(= judges collectively)* les magistrats *mpl* ◆ **to be raised to the ~** être nommé juge ◆ **to be on the ~** *(permanent office)* être juge *(or* magistrat) ; *(when in court)* siéger au tribunal ◆ **to appear before the ~** comparaître devant le tribunal ◆ **the Bench has ruled that ...** la cour a décrété que ... ; → **king**

[3] (also **workbench**) *[of factory, workshop]* établi *m* ; *[of laboratory]* paillasse *f*

VT *(US Sport* *) *[+ player]* exclure du jeu *(souvent comme pénalisation)*

COMP **bench lathe** N tour *m* à banc
bench-press VT *(Weight Lifting)* soulever
bench scientist N expérimentateur *m*, -trice *f*
bench seat N banquette *f*
bench study N étude-pilote *f*
bench vice N étau *m* d'établi

bencher /ˈbentʃəʳ/ N *(Brit Jur)* ≃ membre *m* de l'ordre des avocats ; → **backbencher**

benchmark /ˈbentʃmɑːk/ N *(= reference point)* point *m* de référence, repère *m* ; *(in surveying)* repère *m* de nivellement ; *(Comput)* jeu *m* d'essai ◆ **the 1984 bench mark** *(Stat)* l'année *f* de référence 1984 ADJ *(= benchmark price)* prix *m* de base *or* de référence ; ◆ **~ test** *(Comput)* test *m* d'évaluation de performance VT *(= compare)* comparer ◆ **to ~ against** mesurer à l'aune de

benchmarking /ˈbentʃmɑːkɪŋ/ N benchmarking *m*, étalonnage *m* concurrentiel

benchwarmer * /ˈbentʃwɔːməʳ/ N *(US Sport)* joueur *m* (médiocre) en réserve

bend /bend/ (vb : pret, ptp **bent**) N [1] *[of river]* coude *m*, détour *m* ; *[of tube, pipe]* coude *m* ; *[of arm]* pli *m*, saignée *f* ; *[of knee]* pli *m* ; *[of road]* virage *m*, coude *m* ; *(Naut = knot)* nœud *m* de jonction ◆ **there is a ~ in the road** la route fait un coude ◆ **~s for 8km** *(on road)* virages *mpl* sur 8 km ◆ **to take a ~** *[car]* prendre un virage *or* un tournant ◆ **round the ~** ⁑ *(Brit)* tombé sur la tête *, cinglé * ◆ **to drive sb round the ~** * *(Brit)* rendre qn chèvre *

[2] *(Med)* **the ~s** * la maladie des caissons

VT [1] *[+ back, body]* courber ; *[+ leg, arm]* plier ; *[+ knee, leg]* fléchir, plier ; *[+ head]* baisser, pencher ; *[+ branch]* courber, faire ployer ; *[+ light ray]* réfracter ; *[+ rail, pipe, rod, beam]* tordre, courber ; *[+ bow]* bander ; *(Naut) [+ cable]* étalinguer ; *[+ sail]* enverguer ◆ **to ~ the rules** * faire une entorse au règlement ◆ **to ~ at right angles** couder ◆ **to ~ out of shape** fausser, gauchir ◆ **to get bent out of shape** * **(about sth)** *(US)* s'énerver (à cause de qch) ◆ **to be (all) bent out of shape** * être contrarié ◆ **with her head bent over a book** la tête penchée *or* courbée sur un livre ◆ **on ~ed knee(s)** à genoux ◆ **to go down on ~ed knee (to** *or* **before sb)** s'agenouiller *or* se mettre à genoux (devant qn) ◆ **to ~ the elbow** * *(= drink)* lever le coude * ◆ **to ~ o.s. to sb's will** *(liter)* se plier à la volonté de qn ◆ **to ~ sb to one's will** *(liter)* mettre qn sous son joug ◆ **to ~ sb's ear** *(gen)* accaparer (l'attention de) qn ; (* *pej*) casser les pieds à qn * ; see also **bent¹**

[2] *(= direct)* **all eyes were bent on him** tous les regards étaient braqués sur lui ◆ **the Government bent its efforts to lowering unemployment** le gouvernement a concentré ses efforts sur la lutte contre le chômage

VI *[person]* se courber ; *[branch, instrument etc]* être courbé, plier ; *[river, road]* faire un coude, tourner ; *(fig = submit)* se soumettre, céder *(to* à) ; ◆ **to ~ backward/forward** se pencher en arrière/en avant

COMP **bend sinister** N *(Heraldry)* barre *f* de bâtardise ; → **double, hairpin**

► **bend back** VI *[wire etc]* se recourber ; *[person]* se pencher en arrière
VT SEP replier, recourber

► **bend down** VI *[person]* se courber, se baisser ; *[tree, branch]* ployer, plier
VT SEP *[+ wire]* replier, recourber ; *[+ branch]* faire ployer

► **bend over** VI *[person]* se pencher ◆ **to ~ over backwards to help sb** * se mettre en quatre pour aider qn
VT SEP replier

bender /ˈbendəʳ/ N [1] *(= tool for bending)* cintreuse *f* [2] ◆ **to go on a ~** ⁑ aller se cuiter * [3] *(= tent)* hutte *f* (improvisée) [4] ⁑ *(pej) (= homosexual)* tapette ⁑ *f*

bendy * /ˈbendɪ/ ADJ *[branch]* flexible ; *[river, road]* sinueux

beneath /bɪˈniːθ/ PREP [1] *(= under)* sous ◆ **~ the table** sous la table ◆ **to labour ~ a burden** *(liter)* ployer sous un fardeau [2] *(= lower than)* au-dessous de, sous ◆ **the town ~ the castle** la ville (située) au-dessous du château [3] *(= unworthy of)* indigne de ◆ **it is ~ my notice** cela ne mérite pas mon attention *or* que je m'y arrête *subj* ◆ **he regards the critics as ~ his notice** il se considère au-dessus des critiques ◆ **she considered it ~ her to lie** elle pensait que mentir aurait été indigne d'elle ◆ **she married ~ her** elle a fait une mésalliance ◆ **they took jobs that were far ~ them** ils ont accepté des emplois qui étaient vraiment indignes d'eux
ADV dessous, au-dessous ◆ **the flat ~** l'appartement *m* au-dessous *or* du dessous

Benedict /ˈbenɪdɪkt/ N Benoît *m*

Benedictine /ˌbenɪˈdɪktɪn/ N *(Rel)* bénédictin(e) *m(f)* ADJ *(Rel)* bénédictin

benedictine /ˌbenɪˈdɪktiːn/ N *(= liqueur)* Bénédictine *f*

benediction /ˌbenɪˈdɪkʃən/ N *(= blessing)* bénédiction *f* ; *(at table)* bénédicité *m* ; *(Rel = office)* salut *m*

benefaction /ˌbenɪˈfækʃən/ N *(= good deed)* bienfait *m* ; *(= gift)* donation *f*, don *m*

benefactor /ˈbenɪfæktəʳ/ N bienfaiteur *m*

benefactress † /ˈbenɪfæktrɪs/ N bienfaitrice *f*

benefice /ˈbenɪfɪs/ N bénéfice *m (Rel)*

beneficence /bɪˈnefɪsəns/ N [1] *(NonC = generosity)* bienfaisance *f* [2] *(= act)* acte *m or* œuvre *f* de bienfaisance

beneficent /bɪˈnefɪsənt/ ADJ *[person]* bienfaisant ; *[thing]* salutaire

beneficial /ˌbenɪˈfɪʃəl/ ADJ salutaire, bénéfique *(to* à) ; ◆ **alcohol in moderation may have a ~ effect on the heart** la consommation modérée d'alcool pourrait avoir un effet salutaire *or* bénéfique sur le cœur ◆ **exercise is most ~ when ...** l'exercice est surtout salutaire *or* bénéfique lorsque ... ◆ **~ to health** bon pour la santé ◆ **the change will be ~ to you** le changement vous fera du bien *or* vous sera salutaire
COMP **beneficial owner** N *(Jur)* usufruitier *m*, -ière *f*

beneficially /ˌbenɪˈfɪʃəlɪ/ ADV avantageusement

beneficiary /ˌbenɪˈfɪʃərɪ/ N *[of will etc]* bénéficiaire *mf*, légataire *mf* ; *[of person]* ayant droit *m* ; *[of insurance]* bénéficiaire *mf* ; *(Rel)* bénéficier *m*

benefit /ˈbenɪfɪt/ N [1] bienfait *m*, avantage *m* ◆ **it's to your ~** c'est dans votre intérêt ◆ **to be of ~ to sb** être utile à qn ◆ **I hope what I have written will be of ~ to someone who may feel the same way** j'espère que ce que j'ai écrit servira à quelqu'un qui partage mon opinion ◆ **did he get much ~ from his holiday?** est-ce que ses vacances lui ont fait du bien ? ◆ **he's beginning to feel the ~ of his stay in the country** il commence à ressentir les bienfaits de son séjour à la campagne ◆ **he had the ~ of the work I had put in** il a profité de mon travail ◆ **without the ~ of** sans l'avantage de ◆ **to give sb the ~ of the doubt** accorder à qn le bénéfice du doute ◆ **the ~s of a good education** les bienfaits d'une bonne éducation

◆ **for + benefit** ◆ **for the ~ of your health** dans l'intérêt de votre santé ◆ **a concert for the ~ of the refugees** un concert au profit des réfugiés ◆ **we're doing all this for his ~** c'est pour lui que nous faisons tout cela ◆ **he's not really hurt, he's just crying for your ~** * il ne s'est pas vraiment fait mal, il pleure juste pour attirer votre attention

[2] *(Admin = money)* allocation *f*, prestation *f* ◆ **unemployment ~** *(formerly)* allocation *f* (de) chômage ◆ **to be on ~(s)** recevoir des allocations ; → **sickness** ; → **DSS**

[3] *(= perk)* avantage *m*

[4] *(= charity performance)* représentation *f* de bienfaisance

VT faire du bien à ; *(financially)* profiter à

VI *[person]* se trouver bien *(from, by* de) ; *(financially)* gagner *(from or by doing sth* à faire qch) ; *[work, situation]* être avantagé *(from* par) ; ◆ **he will ~ from a holiday** des vacances lui feront du bien

COMP **benefit association** N *(US)* ⇒ **benefit society**
benefit club N assurance *f* mutuelle, caisse *f* de secours mutuel
benefit match N *(Sport)* match *m* au profit d'un joueur
benefit of clergy N *(= privileges)* privilège *m* du clergé ; *(= rites)* rites *mpl* de l'Église, rites *mpl* religieux ◆ **marriage without ~ of clergy** mariage non béni par l'Église
benefit performance N représentation *f* de bienfaisance
benefit society N *(US)* société *f* de prévoyance, (société *f*) mutuelle *f*

Benelux /ˈbenɪlʌks/ N Benelux *m* ◆ **the ~ countries** les pays du Benelux

benevolence /bɪˈnevələns/ N [1] *(NonC) (= kindness)* bienveillance *f* ; *(= generosity)* bienfaisance *f*, générosité *f* [2] *(= gift, act)* bienfait *m* [3] *(Hist)* don *m* forcé *(au souverain)*

benevolent /bɪˈnevələnt/ ADJ [1] *(= kind)* bienveillant *(to* envers) ; ◆ **a ~ smile** un sourire bienveillant *or* plein de bonté [2] *(= charitable) [organization, society]* de bienfaisance ◆ **~ fund** fonds *m* de secours

benevolently /bɪˈnevələntlɪ/ ADV avec bienveillance *or* bonté

BEng /biːˈendʒ/ N abbrev of **Bachelor of Engineering**

Bengal /beŋˈgɔːl/ N Bengale *m* ◆ **the Bay of ~** le golfe du Bengale
COMP **Bengal light** N feu *m* de Bengale
Bengal tiger N tigre *m* du Bengale

Bengali /beŋˈgɔːlɪ/ ADJ bengali *f inv* N [1] *(= person)* Bengali *mf* [2] *(= language)* bengali *m*

benighted /bɪˈnaɪtɪd/ ADJ [1] *(fig = uncultured) [person]* plongé dans (les ténèbres de) l'ignorance ; *[policy etc]* à courte vue, aveugle 2 († *lit*) surpris par la nuit

benign /bɪˈnaɪn/, **benignant** /bɪˈnɪgnənt/ ADJ 1 *(= kindly)* bienveillant, affable ; *(= beneficial)* bienfaisant, salutaire ; *[climate]* doux (douce *f*) 2 *(= harmless) [research, substance, process]* inoffensif 3 *(Med) [tumour]* bénin (-igne *f*) 4 ◆ **~ neglect** laisser-faire *m* ◆ **a policy of ~ neglect of the economy** une politique de laisser-faire en matière économique, une politique économique non-interventionniste ◆ **the best thing for these moors is ~ neglect** la meilleure chose qu'on puisse faire pour cette lande, c'est de la laisser en friche

benignly /bɪˈnaɪnlɪ/ ADV avec bienveillance

Benin /beˈniːn/ N Bénin *m*

Beninese /ˌbenɪˈniːz/ ADJ béninois N Béninois(e) *m(f)*

benison /ˈbenɪzn/ N bénédiction *f*

Benjamin /ˈbendʒəmɪn/ N Benjamin *m*

benny‡ /ˈbenɪ/ N *(Drugs)* (comprimé *m* de) benzédrine *f*

bent¹ /bent/ VB pt, ptp of **bend** ADJ 1 *[wire, pipe]* tordu 2 *(esp Brit* ‡ *= dishonest)* véreux, ripou* ◆ **a ~ copper** un ripou* 3 *(Brit pej* ‡ *= homosexual)* homo* 4 **to be ~ on doing sth** être résolu *or* décidé à faire qch, vouloir absolument faire qch ◆ **he is ~ on seeing me** il veut absolument me voir ◆ **he is ~ on pleasure** il ne recherche que son plaisir N 1 *(= aptitude)* dispositions *fpl*, aptitudes *fpl (for* pour) ; ◆ **to have a ~ for languages** avoir des dispositions pour les langues 2 *(= liking)* penchant *m*, goût *m* ◆ **to have a ~ for** *or* **towards sth** avoir du goût *or* un penchant pour qch ◆ **to follow one's ~** suivre son inclination *f* ◆ **of literary ~** tourné vers les lettres

bent² /bent/ N (also **bent grass**) agrostide *f*

bentwood /ˈbentwʊd/ ADJ *[furniture]* en bois courbé

benumb /bɪˈnʌm/ VT *[+ limb]* engourdir, endormir

benumbed /bɪˈnʌmd/ ADJ *(= cold) [person]* transi (de froid) ; *[fingers]* engourdi par le froid ; *(= frightened)* transi de peur ; *(= shocked)* paralysé

Benzedrine ® /ˈbenzɪdriːn/ N benzédrine *f*

benzene /ˈbenziːn/ N benzène *m*

benzine /ˈbenziːn/ N benzine *f*

benzoin¹ /ˈbenzəʊɪn/ N *(= resin)* benjoin *m* ; *(= shrub)* styrax *m* (benjoin)

benzoin² /ˈbenzəʊɪn/ N *(Chem)* benzoïne *f*

bequeath /bɪˈkwiːð/ VT *(in will)* léguer *(to* à) ; *(fig) [+ tradition]* transmettre, léguer *(to* à)

bequest /bɪˈkwest/ N legs *m*

berate /bɪˈreɪt/ VT admonester *(liter)*, réprimander

Berber /ˈbɜːbəʳ/ ADJ berbère N 1 *(= person)* Berbère *mf* 2 *(= language)* berbère *m*

bereave /bɪˈriːv/ VT 1 (pret, ptp **bereft**) *(= deprive)* priver, déposséder *(of* de) see also **bereft** 2 (pret, ptp *gen* **bereaved**) *(by death)* ravir *(sb of sb* qn à qn)

bereaved /bɪˈriːvd/ ADJ endeuillé, affligé

bereavement /bɪˈriːvmənt/ N *(= loss)* perte *f* ; *(NonC = state)* deuil *m* ◆ **a sad ~** une perte cruelle ◆ **in his ~** dans son deuil ◆ **owing to a recent ~** en raison d'un deuil récent ◆ **~ counselling** thérapie *f* du deuil

bereft /bɪˈreft/ VB pt, ptp of **bereave** ADJ *(liter)* ◆ **~ of** privé *or* démuni de ◆ **~ of hope** désespéré ◆ **he is ~ of reason** il a perdu la raison

beret /ˈbereɪ/ N béret *m*

berg* /bɜːg/ N abbrev of **iceberg**

bergamot /ˈbɜːgəmɒt/ N bergamote *f*

bergschrund /ˈberkʃrʊnt/ N *(Geol)* rimaye *f*

beriberi /ˈberɪˈberɪ/ N béribéri *m*

Bering /ˈbeɪrɪŋ/ ADJ ◆ **~ Sea/Strait** mer *f*/détroit *m* de Béring

berk‡ /bɜːk/ N *(Brit)* connard‡ *m*, connasse‡ *f*

berkelium /bɜːˈkiːlɪəm/ N berkélium *m*

Berks N abbrev of **Berkshire**

Berlin /bɜːˈlɪn/ N 1 Berlin ◆ **East/West ~** Berlin Est/Ouest 2 *(= carriage)* **berlin** berline *f* COMP **the Berlin Wall** N le mur de Berlin **Berlin wool** N laine *f* à broder

Berliner /bɜːˈlɪnəʳ/ N Berlinois(e) *m(f)*

berm /bɜːm/ N *(US)* accotement *m*, bas-côté *m*

Bermuda /bɜːˈmjuːdə/ N Bermudes *fpl* COMP **Bermuda shorts** NPL bermuda *m* **the Bermuda Triangle** N le triangle des Bermudes

Bern /bɜːn/ N Berne

Bernard /ˈbɜːnəd/ N Bernard *m*

Bernese /ˈbɜːniːz/ ADJ bernois ◆ **~ Oberland** Oberland *m* bernois N Bernois(e) *m(f)*

berry /ˈberɪ/ N baie *f* ; → **brown** VI ◆ **to go ~ing** aller cueillir des baies

berserk /bəˈsɜːk/ ADJ fou furieux (folle furieuse *f*) ◆ **to go ~** devenir fou furieux, se déchaîner

berth /bɜːθ/ N 1 *[of plane, train, ship]* couchette *f* ◆ **to find a soft ~** *(fig)* trouver une bonne planque* 2 *(Naut = place for ship)* mouillage *m*, poste *m* d'amarrage ◆ **to give a wide ~ to a ship** passer au large d'un navire ◆ **to give sb a wide ~** éviter qn, se tenir à une distance respectueuse de qn ◆ **you should give him a wide ~** vous devriez l'éviter à tout prix VI *(at anchor)* mouiller ; *(alongside)* venir à quai, accoster VT *[+ ship] (= assign place)* donner *or* assigner un poste d'amarrage à ; *(perform action)* amarrer, faire accoster

beryl /ˈberɪl/ N béryl *m*

beryllium /beˈrɪljəm/ N béryllium *m*

beseech /bɪˈsiːtʃ/ (pret, ptp **besought** *or* **beseeched**) VT *(liter)* 1 *(= ask for) [+ permission]* demander instamment, solliciter ; *[+ pardon]* implorer 2 *(= entreat)* conjurer *(liter)*, supplier *(sb to do sth* qn de faire qch)

beseeching /bɪˈsiːtʃɪŋ/ ADJ *[voice, look]* suppliant, implorant N *(NonC)* supplications *fpl*

beseechingly /bɪˈsiːtʃɪŋlɪ/ ADV d'un air *or* d'un ton suppliant ◆ **she looked ~ into his eyes** elle le regarda d'un air suppliant ◆ **"how could it happen?" I asked him, ~** "comment est-ce possible ?" lui ai-je demandé d'un ton suppliant

beset /bɪˈset/ (pret, ptp **beset**) VT *[dangers, fears]* assaillir ; *[temptations]* entourer ◆ **a path ~ with obstacles** un chemin semé d'obstacles ◆ **~ with difficulties** *[enterprise, journey]* semé de difficultés ◆ **he is ~ with difficulties** les difficultés l'assaillent (de toutes parts) ◆ **~ with** *or* **by doubts** assailli par le doute

besetting /bɪˈsetɪŋ/ ADJ ◆ **his ~ sin** son grand défaut

beside /bɪˈsaɪd/ PREP 1 *(= at the side of)* à côté de, auprès de ◆ **she sat down ~ him** elle s'est assise à côté *or* auprès de lui ◆ **~ it** à côté 2 *(= compared with)* à côté de 3 *(= except)* ◆ **~ him, no one agreed with me** à part lui, personne n'était d'accord avec moi 4 *(phrases)* **that's ~ the point** cela n'a rien à voir (avec la question) ◆ **it's quite ~ the point to suggest that ...** il est tout à fait inutile de suggérer que ... ◆ **to be ~ o.s. (with anger)*** être hors de soi ◆ **he was quite ~ himself with excitement*** il était dans un grand état d'excitation ◆ **he is ~ himself with joy*** il est transporté de joie, il ne se sent pas de joie

besides /bɪˈsaɪdz/ ADV 1 *(= in addition)* en plus, en outre *(frm)* ◆ **you'll earn money and gain valuable experience ~** tu gagneras de l'argent et en plus ça te donnera une expérience précieuse ◆ **and many more ~** et bien d'autres encore ◆ **he wrote a novel and several short stories ~** il a écrit un roman et aussi plusieurs nouvelles 2 *(= moreover)* d'ailleurs, du reste PREP 1 *(= in addition to)* en plus de, en dehors de ◆ **she has other qualities, ~ intelligence and humour** elle a d'autres qualités en plus *or* en dehors de l'intelligence et de l'humour ◆ **she has many good qualities, ~ being beautiful** non seulement elle est belle, mais en plus elle a beaucoup de qualités ◆ **there was only one person ~ him who knew her** à part lui *or* en dehors de lui, il n'y avait qu'une personne qui la connaissait ◆ **others ~ ourselves** d'autres que nous ◆ **there were three of us ~ Jacques** nous étions trois sans compter Jacques ◆ **~ this book I bought some CDs** outre ce livre, j'ai acheté des CD ◆ **~ which he was unwell** sans compter qu'il était souffrant, et en plus il était souffrant 2 *(= apart from)* sauf, sinon ◆ **no one ~ you** personne sauf vous, personne d'autre que vous ◆ **who ~ them could have done it?** qui aurait pu faire cela, sinon eux ?, qui d'autre qu'eux aurait pu le faire ◆ **who ~ yourself has a key to this room?** qui à part vous a la clé de cette pièce ?, qui d'autre que vous a la clé de cette pièce ?

besiege /bɪˈsiːdʒ/ VT 1 *[+ town]* assiéger, mettre le siège devant 2 *(fig = surround)* assaillir ◆ **~d by journalists** assailli par des journalistes 3 *(fig = pester)* assaillir, harceler *(with* de) ; ◆ **~d with questions** assailli de questions

besmear /bɪˈsmɪəʳ/ VT *(lit)* barbouiller *(with* de) ; *(fig)* salir, souiller *(liter)*

besmirch /bɪˈsmɜːtʃ/ VT ternir, entacher

besom /ˈbiːzəm/ N balai *m* de bouleau

besotted /bɪˈsɒtɪd/ ADJ 1 *(= drunk)* abruti, hébété *(with* de) 2 *(= infatuated)* entiché, fou (folle *f*) *(with* de) 3 *(= foolish)* idiot, imbécile

besought /bɪˈsɔːt/ VB pt, ptp of **beseech**

bespatter /bɪˈspætəʳ/ VT éclabousser *(with* de)

bespeak /bɪˈspiːk/ (pret **bespoke**, ptp **bespoken** *or* **bespoke**) VT 1 *(= order) [+ goods]* commander ; *[+ room, place]* retenir, réserver 2 *(= indicate)* témoigner de ; *[+ weakness, fault]* accuser

bespectacled /bɪˈspektɪkld/ ADJ à lunettes

bespoke /bɪˈspəʊk/ VB pt, ptp of **bespeak** ADJ *(Brit) [goods]* fait sur commande ; *[garments]* fait sur mesure ; *[tailor etc]* à façon ◆ **~ software** *(Comput)* logiciel *m* sur mesure

bespoken /bɪˈspəʊkən/ VB ptp of **bespeak**

besprinkle /bɪˈsprɪŋkl/ VT *(liter) (with liquid)* arroser, asperger *(with* de) ; *(with powder)* saupoudrer *(with* de) ; *(= dot with)* parsemer *(with* de)

Bess /bes/ N (dim of **Elizabeth**) ◆ **Good Queen ~** *(Brit Hist)* la reine Élisabeth (Ire)

Bessarabia /ˌbesəˈreɪbɪə/ N Bessarabie *f*

best /best/ LANGUAGE IN USE 2.2, 7.4, 23

ADJ *(superl of* **good***)* le meilleur, la meilleure ◆ **the ~ novel he's written** le meilleur roman qu'il ait écrit ◆ **the ~ pupil in the class** le meilleur élève de la classe ◆ **Belgian beer is the ~ in the world** la bière belge est la meilleure du monde *or* au monde ◆ **the ~ route to Paris** le meilleur chemin *or* itinéraire pour Paris ◆ **the ~ thing about Spain/living abroad is ...** ce qu'il y a de mieux en Espagne/quand on vit à l'étranger, c'est ... ◆ **the ~ thing about her is ...** sa plus grande qualité, c'est ... ◆ **the ~ thing to do is to wait** le mieux c'est d'attendre ◆ **the ~ years of one's life** les plus belles années de sa vie ◆ **in one's ~ clothes** vêtu de ses plus beaux vêtements ◆ **may the ~ man win!** que le meilleur gagne ! ◆ **to put one's ~ foot forward** *(in walking)* allonger le pas ; *(= do one's best)* faire de son mieux ◆ **she's his ~ girl** † * c'est sa petite amie ◆ **~ before ...** *(Comm: on product)* à consommer de préférence avant ... ◆ **to have the ~ diamond** *(Cards)* être maître à carreau ◆ **best!** *(at end of letter)* amitiés ; see also **comp** ; → **behaviour, second-best, wish**

◆ **the best part of** * *(= most of)* la plus grande partie de ◆ **for the ~ part of an hour/month** pendant près d'une heure/d'un mois ◆ **it took the ~ part of an hour** ça m'a pris une petite heure

N 1 ◆ **the ~** le mieux, le meilleur ◆ **she's the ~ in the class at maths/drawing** elle est la meilleure de la classe en maths/en dessin ◆ **to get the ~ out of sb/sth** tirer le maximum de qn/qch ◆ **to get the ~ of the bargain** *or* **of it** l'emporter, avoir le dessus ◆ **to have** *or* **get the ~ of both worlds** gagner sur les deux tableaux ◆ **the ~ there is** ce qu'il y a de mieux ◆ **to save the ~ for last** garder le meilleur pour la fin ◆ **the ~ is yet to come** il y a mieux ◆ **the ~ of it is that ...** le plus beau de l'affaire c'est que ... ◆ **the final is the ~ of three matches** *(Sport)* la finale se dispute au meilleur des trois matchs ◆ **to be the ~ of friends** être les meilleurs amis (du monde) ◆ **even the ~ of us can make mistakes** tout le monde peut se tromper ◆ **the ~ of plans can go astray** les meilleurs projets peuvent échouer ◆ **he can sing with the ~ of them** * il sait chanter comme pas un * ◆ **even at the ~ of times** même dans les circonstances les plus favorables ◆ **he's not very patient (even) at the ~ of times but ...** il n'est jamais particulièrement patient mais ...

◆ **all the best !** * *(= goodbye)* salut ! * ; *(at end of letter)* amicalement, amitiés ◆ **all the ~ to your sister** mes amitiés à ta sœur ◆ **all the ~ for your exam** bonne chance pour ton examen

◆ **at best** au mieux

◆ **do + best** ◆ **to do one's (level) ~ (to come)** faire tout son possible (pour venir) ◆ **do the ~ you can!** faites de votre mieux !, faites pour le mieux ! ◆ **it's the ~ I can do** je ne peux pas faire mieux ◆ **well, I did my ~** eh bien, j'ai fait de mon mieux

◆ **for the best** ◆ **it's (all) for the ~** c'est pour le mieux ◆ **to do sth for the ~** faire qch dans les meilleures intentions

◆ **to be at one's best** *(= on form)* être en pleine forme * *or* en train ◆ **the roses are at their ~ just now** les roses sont de toute beauté en ce moment ◆ **that is Racine at his ~** voilà du meilleur Racine

◆ **to look one's best** être resplendissant ; *[+ woman]* être en beauté ◆ **I always like to look my ~** j'aime bien être à mon avantage ◆ **she looks her ~ in blue** c'est le bleu qui l'avantage le plus

◆ **to make the best of sth** s'accommoder de qch (du mieux que l'on peut) ◆ **to make the ~ of a bad job** faire contre mauvaise fortune bon cœur ◆ **to make the ~ of one's opportunities** profiter au maximum des occasions qui se présentent

◆ **to the best of ...** ◆ **to the ~ of my ability/knowledge/recollection** autant que je puisse/que je sache/que je me souvienne ◆ **to the ~ of my (knowledge and) belief** autant que je sache ◆ **I avoided it to the ~ of my power** je l'ai évité autant que j'ai pu

2 *(= clothes)* ◆ **in one's Sunday ~** * endimanché, sur son trente et un ◆ **(to keep sth) for ~** * (garder qch) pour les grandes occasions

ADV *(superl of* **well***)* le mieux, le plus ◆ **the ~ dressed man in Paris** l'homme *m* le mieux habillé de Paris ◆ **the ~ loved actor** l'acteur *m* le plus aimé ◆ **I like apples ~** ce que je préfère, ce sont les pommes ◆ **I like strawberries ~ of all** j'aime les fraises par-dessus tout ◆ **that is the hat which suits her ~** voilà le chapeau qui lui va le mieux ◆ **I helped him as ~ I could** je l'ai aidé de mon mieux *or* du mieux que j'ai pu ◆ **he thought it ~ to accept** il a trouvé *or* jugé préférable d'accepter ◆ **do as you think ~** faites à votre idée, faites pour le mieux ◆ **you know ~** vous savez mieux que personne, c'est vous le mieux placé pour en juger, vous êtes (le) meilleur juge en la matière ◆ **you had ~ go at once** tu ferais mieux de t'en aller tout de suite ◆ **the ~-laid plans of mice and men oft go awry** même les projets les mieux élaborés peuvent échouer

VT *(= defeat, win over)* battre, l'emporter sur

COMP **best-before date** N *(Comm)* date *f* limite d'utilisation *or* de consommation

best boy N *(Cine) assistant du chef électricien ou du technicien*

best friend N meilleur(e) ami(e) *m(f)* ◆ **she is her ~ friend** c'est sa meilleure amie

best man N (pl **best men**) *(at wedding)* ≈ garçon *m* d'honneur, témoin *m*

best-selling ADJ *[+ book, writer]* à succès ; *[+ record]* qui remporte un grand succès

Best Man

Choisi parmi les amis ou les proches parents du marié, le **best man** est à la fois le témoin et le garçon d'honneur. Traditionnellement responsable du bon déroulement de la journée, il doit veiller à ce que le marié soit à l'heure et à ce que les invités soient bien accueillis. Pendant la réception, il lui revient de lire les messages de félicitations, d'annoncer les orateurs, de prononcer le discours humoristique d'usage et de porter un toast aux nouveaux mariés.

bestial /ˈbestɪəl/ ADJ *(lit, fig)* bestial

bestiality /ˌbestɪˈælɪtɪ/ N bestialité *f*

bestiary /ˈbestɪərɪ/ N bestiaire *m (recueil)*

bestir /bɪˈstɜːʳ/ VT ◆ **to ~ o.s.** se remuer, se démener, s'activer

bestow /bɪˈstəʊ/ VT *(frm)* 1 *(= grant) [+ favour, sb's hand]* accorder *(on, upon* à*)* ; *[+ title]* conférer *(on, upon* à*)* 2 *(= devote) [+ energy]* consacrer, employer *(upon* à*)* ; *[+ admiration]* accorder ◆ **to ~ friendship on sb** prendre qn en amitié ◆ **the attention ~ed on this boy** l'attention dont ce garçon est l'objet

bestowal /bɪˈstəʊəl/ N *(NonC: frm)* octroi *m*

bestraddle /bɪˈstrædl/ VT *[+ horse, bicycle]* enfourcher ; *[+ wall]* chevaucher ; *[+ chair]* se mettre à califourchon sur

bestrew /bɪˈstruː/ (pret **bestrewed**, ptp **bestrewed** *or* **bestrewn** /bɪˈstruːn/) VT *(liter)* parsemer, joncher *(with* de*)*

bestride /bɪˈstraɪd/ (pret **bestrode** /bɪˈstrəʊd/, ptp **bestridden** /bɪˈstrɪdn/) VT 1 *[+ chair]* être à cheval *or* à califourchon sur ; *[+ horse, bicycle]* enfourcher 2 *[+ brook, ditch]* enjamber

bestseller /ˌbestˈseləʳ/ N *(= book)* best-seller *m*, livre *m* à succès, succès *m* de librairie ; *(Comm) (other article)* article *m* très demandé ; *(= author)* auteur *m* à succès

bet /bet/ (pret, ptp **bet** *or* **betted**) VI parier *(against* contre ; *on* sur ; *with* avec*)* ; ◆ **to ~ 10 to 1** parier *or* miser à 10 contre 1 ◆ **to ~ on horses** parier *or* jouer aux courses ◆ **to ~ on a horse** jouer un cheval, miser sur un cheval ◆ **don't ~ on it!, I wouldn't ~ on it!** ne compte pas trop dessus

VT 1 ◆ **to ~ £10 on a horse** parier *or* miser 10 livres sur un cheval ◆ **she ~ me $10 he would refuse** elle m'a parié 10 dollars qu'il refuserait

2 **I ~ he'll come!** je te parie qu'il viendra ! ◆ **I'll ~ you anything (you like)** je te parie tout ce que tu veux ◆ **~ you won't do it** * (je te parie que) t'es pas capable de le faire * ◆ **you ~!** * un peu ! *, tu parles ! * ◆ **~ you can't!** * chiche ! * ◆ **you can ~ your boots** * *or* **your bottom dollar** * *or* **your life** * **that ...** tu peux parier tout ce que tu veux *or* parier ta chemise que ... ◆ **to ~ the ranch** *or* **farm on sb/sth** *(US fig)* tout miser sur qn/qch

N 1 *(lit)* pari *m* ◆ **to make** *or* **lay a ~ (on sth/sb)** parier (sur qch/qn), faire un pari (sur qch/qn) ◆ **to accept** *or* **take (on) a ~** accepter un pari ◆ **to win a ~** gagner un pari ◆ **place your ~s!** *(in casino)* faites vos jeux ! ◆ **want a ~?** * (qu'est-ce que) tu paries ? *

2 **this is your best ~** c'est ce que vous avez de mieux à faire ◆ **it's a good** *or* **safe ~ that she'll turn up** il est à peu près certain qu'elle viendra ◆ **Liverpool look a good** *or* **safe ~ for the championship** Liverpool a toutes les chances de gagner le championnat ◆ **all ~s are off** *(fig)* impossible de dire ce qui va se passer ; → **hedge**

beta /ˈbiːtə/ N bêta *m*

COMP **beta blocker** N *(Med, Pharm)* bêta-bloquant *m*

beta-blocking ADJ bêta-bloquant

beta carotene N bêtacarotène *m*

betake /bɪˈteɪk/ (pret **betook**, ptp **betaken** /bɪˈteɪkən/) VT ◆ **to ~ o.s. to ...** (s'en) aller à ..., se rendre à ...

betcha ⁑ /ˈbetʃə/ EXCL ◆ **(you) ~ !** un peu ! *, tu parles ! *

betel /ˈbiːtəl/ N bétel *m* COMP **betel nut** N noix *f* de bétel

Bethany /ˈbeθənɪ/ N Béthanie

bethink † /bɪˈθɪŋk/ (pret, ptp **bethought**) VT ◆ **to ~ o.s.** réfléchir, considérer ◆ **to ~ o.s. of sth/to do/that** s'aviser de qch/de faire/que

Bethlehem /ˈbeθlɪhem/ N Bethléem

bethought /bɪˈθɔːt/ VB pt, ptp of **bethink**

betide /bɪˈtaɪd/ VTI ◆ **whatever (may) ~** quoi qu'il advienne *or* arrive *subj* ; → **woe**

betimes † /bɪˈtaɪmz/ ADV *(= early)* de bonne heure, tôt ; *(= quickly)* promptement, vite ; *(= in good time)* à temps, assez tôt

betoken /bɪˈtəʊkən/ VT *(frm) (= forecast)* présager, annoncer ; *(= indicate)* dénoter, être signe de

betook /bɪˈtʊk/ VB pt of **betake**

betray /bɪˈtreɪ/ VT 1 *(= be disloyal to) [+ one's country]* trahir, être traître à ; *[+ friends]* trahir ; *[+ spouse, partner]* tromper, trahir ; *(fig) [+ hope etc]* trahir, décevoir ; *[+ ideals, principles]* trahir ◆ **he has ~ed our trust** il a trahi notre confiance, il a commis un abus de confiance 2 *(= give up treacherously) [+ person, secret]* livrer *(to* à*)* trahir ◆ **to ~ sb into enemy hands** livrer qn à l'ennemi *or* aux mains de l'ennemi 3 *(= disclose) [+ age, fears, intentions, facts, truth]* trahir, révéler ◆ **to ~ o.s.** se trahir ◆ **his speech ~ed the fact that he had been drinking** on devinait à l'écouter qu'il avait bu

betrayal /bɪˈtreɪəl/ N *[of country, ally etc]* trahison *f* ; *[of age, secret, plan]* divulgation *f* ; *[of fears, intentions]* manifestation *f* (involontaire) ; *[of facts, truth]* révélation *f* ◆ **a ~ of trust** un abus de confiance ◆ **to feel a sense of ~** se sentir trahi

betrayer /bɪˈtreɪəʳ/ N *[of country]* traître(sse) *m(f) (of* à, envers*)* ; *[of friend]* dénonciateur *m*, -trice *f (of* de*)* ; ◆ **she killed her ~** elle a tué celui qui l'avait trahie

betroth /bɪˈtrəʊð/ VT († †, *liter)* fiancer *(to* à, avec*)* promettre en mariage *(to* à*)*

betrothal /bɪˈtrəʊðəl/ N *(liter)* fiançailles *fpl (to* avec*)*

betrothed /bɪˈtrəʊðd/ ADJ, N *(pl inv: liter or hum)* fiancé(e) *m(f)*

better[1] /ˈbetəʳ/ LANGUAGE IN USE 1, 2.2, 7.1, 7.4, 23.4

ADJ (compar of **good**) meilleur ◆ **that book is ~ than this one** ce livre-là est meilleur que celui-ci ◆ **she is a ~ dancer than her sister, she is ~ at dancing than her sister** elle danse mieux que sa sœur ◆ **she is ~ at dancing than at singing** elle danse mieux qu'elle ne chante ◆ **these products are ~ for the environment** ces produits polluent moins ◆ **he's a ~ man than his brother** il est mieux que son frère ◆ **you're a ~ man than I!** tu es vraiment très fort ! ◆ **he's no ~ than a thief** c'est un voleur ni plus ni moins ◆ **she's no ~ than she should be!** † (= slightly dishonest) ce n'est pas l'honnêteté qui l'étouffe ! * ; (loose morals) elle n'est pas d'une vertu farouche ! ◆ **he is much ~ now** (in health) il va or se porte bien mieux maintenant ◆ **how are you? – much ~** comment allez-vous ? – bien mieux ◆ **to grow ~** s'améliorer ◆ **his writing is ~ since he got a new pen** son écriture est meilleure depuis qu'il a un nouveau stylo ◆ **(it's getting) ~ and ~!** (ça va) de mieux en mieux ! ◆ **that's ~!** voilà qui est mieux ! ◆ **it** or **things couldn't be ~!** ça ne pourrait pas mieux aller ! ◆ **it would be ~ to stay at home** il vaudrait mieux rester à la maison ◆ **wouldn't it be ~ to refuse?** ne vaudrait-il pas mieux refuser ? ◆ **~ not!** mieux vaut pas ! ◆ **~ not wake him!** mieux vaut ne pas le réveiller ! ◆ **it is ~ not to promise anything than to let him down** il vaut mieux ne rien promettre que de le décevoir ◆ **a ~ class of hotel** un hôtel de catégorie supérieure ◆ **he has seen ~ days** il a connu des jours meilleurs ◆ **this hat has seen ~ days** ce chapeau n'est plus de la première fraîcheur ◆ **his ~ half*** (hum) sa moitié * (hum) ◆ **his ~ nature stopped him from ...** ses bons sentiments, reprenant le dessus, l'ont empêché de ... ◆ **to appeal to sb's ~ nature** faire appel au bon cœur de qn ◆ **to go one ~ than sb** damer le pion à qn ◆ **the ~ part of a year/of 200km** etc près d'un an/de 200 km etc ◆ **to hope for ~ things** espérer mieux

◆ **to get better** ◆ **he got ~ very quickly after his illness** il s'est très vite remis de sa maladie ◆ **the weather is getting ~** le temps s'améliore ◆ **this book gets ~ towards the end** ce livre s'améliore vers la fin ◆ **his technique got ~ as he grew older** sa technique s'est affirmée avec l'âge

ADV (compar of **well**) mieux ◆ **he sings ~ than you** il chante mieux que toi ◆ **he sings ~ than he dances** il chante mieux qu'il ne danse ◆ **I like it ~ than I used to** je l'aime mieux qu'autrefois or que je ne l'aimais autrefois ◆ **~ dressed** mieux habillé ◆ **~ known** plus or mieux connu ◆ **~ known as** mieux connu sous le nom de ◆ **~ late than never** (Prov) mieux vaut tard que jamais (Prov)

◆ **better off** ◆ **they are ~ off than we are** (= richer) ils ont plus d'argent que nous ; (= more fortunate) ils sont dans une meilleure position que nous ◆ **he is ~ off at his sister's than living alone** il est mieux chez sa sœur que s'il vivait tout seul ◆ **he is ~ off where he is** il est mieux là où il est

◆ **better still** ◆ **write to her, or ~ still go and see her** écris-lui, ou mieux encore va la voir

◆ **had better** ◆ **I had ~ do it** (= must do it) il faut que je le fasse ; (= would be preferable to do it) il vaut mieux que je le fasse ◆ **hadn't you ~ speak to him?** ne vaudrait-il pas mieux que tu lui parles subj ?

◆ **the better (...)** ◆ **the ~ I know him the more I admire him** mieux je le connais plus je l'admire ◆ **the ~ to see/hear** pour mieux voir/entendre ◆ **so much the ~!** tant mieux !

◆ **all the better** ◆ **he was all the ~ for it** il s'en est trouvé mieux ◆ **it would be all the ~ for a lick of paint** un petit coup de peinture ne lui ferait pas de mal ◆ **all the ~!** tant mieux !

N [1] ◆ **it's a change for the ~** c'est une amélioration ◆ **to get the ~ of sb** triompher de qn ◆ **to get the ~ of sth** venir à bout de qch

◆ **for better or (for) worse** pour le meilleur et pour le pire ◆ **for ~ or for worse, the Net has become a truly international means of communication** qu'on s'en réjouisse ou non, il est un fait que le Net est devenu un moyen de communication vraiment international

[2] ◆ **one's ~s** ses supérieurs mpl

VT [+ sb's achievements] dépasser ; [+ record, score] améliorer ◆ **to ~ o.s.** améliorer sa condition

better[2] /ˈbetəʳ/ N (= person betting) parieur m, -euse f ; (at races) turfiste mf (qui parie sur les chevaux)

betterment /ˈbetəmənt/ N amélioration f ; (Jur) [of property] plus-value f COMP **betterment tax** N (Jur) impôt m sur les plus-values

betting /ˈbetɪŋ/ N pari(s) m(pl) ◆ **the ~ was brisk** les paris allaient bon train ◆ **what is the ~ on Omar?** quelle cote fait Omar ? ◆ **the ~ was 2 to 1 on Baby Boy** la cote était 2 contre 1 sur Baby Boy, Baby Boy avait une cote de 2 contre 1 ◆ **what's the ~ he'll leave?** combien on parie qu'il partira ? ◆ **the ~ is he won't succeed** il y a peu de chances (pour) qu'il réussisse

COMP **betting man** N (pl **betting men**) ◆ **if I were a ~ man I'd say that ...** si j'avais l'habitude de faire des paris je dirais que ...
betting news N résultats mpl des courses
betting shop N (Brit) bureau m de paris (appartenant à un bookmaker), ≃ bureau m de PMU
betting slip N (Brit) ≃ ticket m de PMU
betting tax N impôt m sur les paris

bettor /ˈbetəʳ/ N ⇒ **better**[2]

between /bɪˈtwiːn/ PREP [1] entre ◆ **sit ~ those two boys** asseyez-vous entre ces deux garçons ◆ **F comes ~ E and G** F se trouve or vient entre E et G ◆ **a captain comes ~ a lieutenant and a major** la grade de capitaine se situe entre celui de lieutenant et celui de commandant ◆ **~ 5 and 6 o'clock** entre 5 et 6 heures ◆ **~ 6 and 7 kilometres/litres** etc entre 6 et 7 kilomètres/litres etc ◆ **she is ~ 25 and 30** elle a entre 25 et 30 ans ◆ **the ferry goes ~ Dover and Calais** le ferry fait la navette entre Douvres et Calais ◆ **the four boys have five oranges ~ them** les quatre garçons ont cinq oranges en tout or à eux tous ◆ **you will have time to rest ~ flights** vous aurez le temps de vous reposer entre les deux vols ◆ **the train does not stop ~ here and London** le train est direct d'ici (à) Londres, le train ne s'arrête pas entre ici et Londres ◆ **~ now and next week we must ...** d'ici la semaine prochaine nous devons ... ◆ **no one can come ~ us** personne ne peut nous séparer ◆ **to choose ~ two cars** choisir entre deux voitures ◆ **the difference ~ them** la différence entre eux ◆ **the match ~ England and Scotland** le match entre l'Angleterre et l'Écosse ◆ **the war ~ the two countries** la guerre entre les deux pays ◆ **the distance ~ them** la distance qui les sépare (l'un de l'autre), la distance entre eux ◆ **a comparison ~ the two books** une comparaison entre les deux livres, une comparaison des deux livres ◆ **divide the sweets ~ the two children** partagez les bonbons entre les deux enfants ◆ **~ you and me, he is not very clever** entre nous, il n'est pas très intelligent ◆ **~ housework and study I have no time for going out** entre le ménage et mes études je n'ai pas le temps de sortir

[2] (indicating cooperation) **the boys managed to lift the box ~ (the two of) them** à eux deux les garçons sont arrivés à soulever la caisse ◆ **we got the letter written ~ us** à nous tous nous avons réussi à écrire la lettre ◆ **you should manage it ~ you** en vous y mettant tous ensemble, vous devriez y arriver

ADV au milieu, dans l'intervalle ◆ **her visits are few and far ~** ses visites sont très espacées or très rares

◆ **in between** ◆ **rows of trees with grass in ~** des rangées d'arbres séparées par de l'herbe ◆ **in ~ the two world wars** pendant l'entre-deux-guerres, entre les deux guerres mondiales ◆ **two flights with a four-hour wait in ~** deux vols avec une attente de quatre heures entre les deux

betweentimes /bɪˈtwiːn,taɪmz/ ADV dans l'intervalle, entre-temps

betwixt /bɪˈtwɪkst/ PREP (††, liter, dial) ⇒ **between** ADV ◆ **~ and between** entre les deux, ni l'un ni l'autre

bevel /ˈbevəl/ N [1] (= surface) surface f oblique ; (also **bevel edge**) biseau m ; (= tool: also **bevel square**) fausse équerre f VT biseauter, tailler de biais or en biseau
COMP en biseau
bevel gear N engrenage m conique
bevelled edge N bord m biseauté
bevelled mirror N glace f biseautée
bevel wheel N roue f dentée conique

beverage /ˈbevərɪdʒ/ N boisson f ; (liter, hum) breuvage m

bevvied ‡ /ˈbevɪd/ ADJ (Brit: also **bevvied up**) soûl ◆ **to get ~** se soûler la gueule ‡, se biturer ‡

bevvy ‡ /ˈbevɪ/ (Brit) N [1] (= a drink) verre m, pot * m ; (= alcohol in general) boisson f ◆ **to go for a ~** aller prendre un verre or un pot * ◆ **he fancied a few bevvies** il avait envie d'aller écluser quelques godets * ◆ **he's back on the ~** il s'est remis à picoler * [2] (= drinking session) beuverie f ◆ **to go out on the ~** aller picoler *

bevy /ˈbevɪ/ N (gen) bande f, troupe f ; [of girls, beauties] essaim m ; [of larks, quails] volée f ; [of roe deer] harde f

bewail /bɪˈweɪl/ VT [+ one's lot] se lamenter sur, déplorer ; [+ sb's death] pleurer

beware /bɪˈwɛəʳ/ LANGUAGE IN USE 2.3 VTI ◆ **to ~** prendre garde (of sb/sth à qn/qch ; of doing sth de faire qch) se méfier (of sth de qch) ; ◆ **~ of falling** prenez garde de tomber ◆ **~ of being deceived, ~ lest you are** or **lest you be deceived** (frm) prenez garde qu'on ne vous trompe subj ◆ **~ of listening to him** gardez-vous de l'écouter ◆ **~ (of) how you speak** faites attention à ce que vous dites, surveillez vos paroles ◆ **"beware of the dog"** "(attention,) chien méchant" ◆ **"beware of pickpockets"** "attention aux pickpockets" ◆ **"trespassers beware"** "défense d'entrer" ◆ **"beware of imitations"** (Comm) "méfiez-vous des contrefaçons"

bewhiskered /bɪˈwɪskəd/ ADJ (liter) barbu (or moustachu)

bewilder /bɪˈwɪldəʳ/ VT dérouter ; (stronger) abasourdir

bewildered /bɪˈwɪldəd/ ADJ [person, look] perplexe

bewildering /bɪˈwɪldərɪŋ/ ADJ déroutant, déconcertant ; (stronger) ahurissant

bewilderingly /bɪˈwɪldərɪŋlɪ/ ADV d'une façon déroutante or déconcertante ; (stronger) d'une façon ahurissante ◆ **it is ~ complicated** c'est d'un compliqué déconcertant

bewilderment /bɪˈwɪldəmənt/ N confusion f, perplexité f ; (stronger) ahurissement m

bewitch /bɪˈwɪtʃ/ VT ensorceler, enchanter ; (fig) charmer, enchanter

bewitching /bɪˈwɪtʃɪŋ/ ADJ [look, smile] enchanteur (-teresse f) ; [face, person] séduisant, ravissant

bewitchingly /bɪˈwɪtʃɪŋlɪ/ ADV d'une façon séduisante or enchanteresse ◆ **beautiful** belle à ravir

bey /beɪ/ N bey m ◆ **Hassan Bey** Hassan Bey

beyond /bɪ'jɒnd/ PREP 1 *(place)* au-delà de, de l'autre côté de ◆ ~ **the Pyrenees** au-delà des Pyrénées ◆ **you can't go ~ the barrier** vous ne pouvez pas aller au-delà de la barrière, vous ne pouvez pas dépasser la barrière ◆ ~ **the convent walls** en dehors des *or* par-delà les murs du couvent ◆ **the countries ~ the sea** les pays *mpl* au-delà des mers, les pays *mpl* d'outre-mer
2 *(in time)* plus de ◆ **she won't stay much ~ a month** elle ne restera pas beaucoup plus d'un mois ◆ ~ **next week/June** au-delà de *or* après la semaine prochaine/juin ◆ **it was ~ the middle of June** on avait dépassé la mi-juin ◆ ~ **bedtime** passé l'heure du coucher
3 *(= surpassing, exceeding)* au-dessus de ◆ **a task ~ her abilities** une tâche au-dessus de ses capacités ◆ **this work is quite ~ him** ce travail le dépasse complètement ◆ **it was ~ her to pass the exam** réussir à l'examen était au-dessus de ses forces ◆ **maths is quite ~ me** les maths, ça me dépasse* ◆ **it's ~ me why he hasn't left her** * je ne comprends pas *or* ça me dépasse* qu'il ne l'ait pas quittée ◆ ~ **my reach** hors de ma portée ◆ ~ **doubt** ADJ hors de doute, indubitable ADV à n'en pas douter, indubitablement ◆ **that is ~ human understanding** cela dépasse l'entendement humain ◆ **he is ~ caring** il ne s'en fait plus du tout ◆ ~ **repair** irréparable ◆ ~ **his means** au-dessus de ses moyens ; → **compare, grave¹, help**
4 *(with neg or interrog)* sauf, excepté ◆ **he gave her no answer ~ a grunt** il ne lui a répondu que par un grognement, pour toute réponse il a émis un grognement
ADV au-delà, plus loin, là-bas ◆ **the year 2000 and ~** l'an 2000 et au-delà ◆ **the room ~** la pièce d'après ◆ **the lands ~** les terres *fpl* lointaines
N au-delà *m* ◆ **in** *or* **at the back of ~** au diable*, en pleine cambrousse* ◆ **the great Beyond** l'au-delà

bezant /'bezənt/ N besant *m*

bezel /'bezl/ N *[of chisel]* biseau *m* ; *[of gem]* facette *f* ; *(holding gem)* chaton *m* ; *(holding watch glass)* portée *f* VT tailler en biseau

bezique /bɪ'zi:k/ N bésigue *m*

BFPO /,bi:efpi:'əʊ/ N *(Brit Mil)* abbrev of **British Forces Post Office**

bhaji /'bɑ:dʒɪ/ N (pl **bhaji**) bhaji *m (beignet indien à base de légumes)*

bhangra /'bæŋgrə/ N *musique de danse de la communauté indo-pakistanaise du Royaume-Uni, combinant rythmes pop et traditionnels*

Bhutan /bu:'tɑ:n/ N Bhoutan *m*

Bhutanese /,bu:tə'ni:z/ ADJ bhoutanais N *(= person)* Bhoutanais(e) *m(f)*

bi* /baɪ/ ADJ *(= bisexual)* bi*

bi... /baɪ/ PREF bi...

Biafra /bɪ'æfrə/ N Biafra *m*

Biafran /bɪ'æfrən/ ADJ biafrais N Biafrais(e) *m(f)*

biannual /baɪ'ænjʊəl/ ADJ semestriel

bias /'baɪəs/ N 1 *(= inclination)* tendance *f*, inclination *f (towards* à*)* penchant *m (towards* pour*)* ; *(= prejudice)* préjugé *m*, parti *m* pris *(towards* pour ; *against* contre*)* prévention *f (towards* en faveur de ; *against* contre*)* ; *(Jur)* distorsion *f* ◆ **a strong ~ towards ...** un penchant marqué pour ... ◆ **he is without ~** il n'a aucun parti pris, il est sans préjugés 2 *(Sewing)* biais *m* ◆ **cut on the ~** coupé dans le biais 3 *(Sport) [of bowls] (= weight)* poids placé à l'intérieur d'une boule ; *(= swerve)* déviation *f* VT *(= give inclination)* influencer *(towards* en faveur de ; *against* contre*)* ; *(= prejudice)* prévenir *(towards* en faveur de ; *against* contre*)* COMP **bias binding** N biais *m*

bias(s)ed /'baɪəst/ ADJ *[person, jury]* qui n'est pas impartial ; *[judgement]* qui n'est pas objectif ; *[report]* déformé, tendancieux

biathlete /baɪ'æθli:t/ N biathlète mf

bib /bɪb/ N 1 *[of child]* bavoir *m* 2 *[of apron]* bavette *f* ◆ **in her best ~ and tucker*** sur son trente et un 3 *(= fish)* tacaud *m*

Bible /'baɪbl/ N *(lit)* Bible *f* ; *(fig)* bible *f*, évangile *m* ; → **holy**
COMP **Bible-basher*** N prédicateur *m*, -trice *f* frénétique*
Bible-bashing* N ◆ **he really likes ~-bashing** il brandit sa Bible à tout va* ◆ **a ~-bashing preacher** un prêcheur qui brandit sa Bible à tout va*
the Bible Belt N *(US) les États du sud des USA, profondément protestants*
Bible class N *(Scol)* classe *f* d'instruction religieuse ; *(Rel)* catéchisme *m*
Bible college N université *f* de théologie
Bible oath N serment *m* (prêté) sur la Bible
Bible school N *(US)* cours *m* d'été d'instruction religieuse
Bible stories NPL histoires *fpl* tirées de la Bible
Bible study N étude *f* de la Bible ; *(in group)* lecture *f* commentée de la Bible
Bible-thumper* N *(pej)* ⇒ **Bible-basher**
Bible-thumping* N ⇒ **Bible-bashing**

biblical /'bɪblɪkəl/ ADJ biblique ◆ **to know sb in the ~ sense** connaître qn dans le sens biblique du terme

biblio... /'bɪblɪəʊ/ PREF biblio...

bibliographer /,bɪblɪ'ɒgrəfə^r^/ N bibliographe *mf*

bibliographic(al) /,bɪblɪəʊ'græfɪk(əl)/ ADJ bibliographique

bibliography /,bɪblɪ'ɒgrəfɪ/ N bibliographie *f*

bibliomania /,bɪblɪəʊ'meɪnɪə/ N bibliomanie *f*

bibliomaniac /,bɪblɪəʊ'meɪnɪæk/ N bibliomane *mf*

bibliophile /'bɪblɪəʊfaɪl/ N bibliophile *mf*

bibulous /'bɪbjʊləs/ ADJ adonné à la boisson ; *[look]* aviné ; *[evening, party]* bien arrosé

bicameral /baɪ'kæmərəl/ ADJ bicaméral ◆ ~ **system** bicamér(al)isme *m*

bicarb* /'baɪkɑ:b/ N (abbrev of **bicarbonate of soda**) bicarbonate *m* (de soude)

bicarbonate /baɪ'kɑ:bənɪt/ N bicarbonate *m*
COMP **bicarbonate of soda** N bicarbonate *m* de soude

bicentenary /,baɪsen'ti:nərɪ/ ADJ, N bicentenaire *m*

bicentennial /,baɪsen'tenɪəl/ ADJ, N *(US)* bicentenaire *m*

bicephalous /baɪ'sefələs/ ADJ bicéphale

biceps /'baɪseps/ N *(pl inv)* biceps *m*

bichloride /'baɪ'klɔ:raɪd/ N bichlorure *m*

bichromate /'baɪ'krəʊmɪt/ N bichromate *m*

bicker /'bɪkə^r^/ VI *(= quarrel)* se chamailler *(over, about* à propos de*)* ; ◆ **they are always ~ing** ils sont toujours à se chamailler *or* toujours en bisbille*

bickering /'bɪkərɪŋ/ N chamailleries *fpl* ADJ 1 *[person]* querelleur 2 *[stream]* murmurant ; *[flame]* tremblotant, vacillant

bickie* /'bɪkɪ/ N *(Brit)* petit gâteau *m*, biscuit *m*

bicuspid /baɪ'kʌspɪd/ ADJ bicuspide N (dent *f*) prémolaire *f*

bicycle /'baɪsɪkl/ N bicyclette *f*, vélo *m* ◆ **to ride a ~** faire de la bicyclette *or* du vélo ; → **racing**
VI † faire de la bicyclette, aller à bicyclette
COMP *[lamp, chain, wheel]* de bicyclette, de vélo
bicycle bell N sonnette *f* de bicyclette
bicycle clip N pince *f* de cycliste
bicycle kick N *(Ftbl)* coup *m* de pied retourné
bicycle pump N pompe *f* à bicyclette
bicycle rack N *(on ground)* râtelier *m* à bicyclettes ; *(on car)* porte-vélos *m inv*
bicycle rickshaw N vélo-pousse *m*
bicycle shed N abri *m* à bicyclettes
bicycle shop N magasin *m* de cycles
bicycle touring N *(Sport)* cyclotourisme *m*

bicyclist † /'baɪsɪklɪst/ N cycliste *mf*

bid /bɪd/ (pret **bade** *or* **bid**, ptp **bidden** *or* **bid**) VT
1 *(liter = command)* ordonner, enjoindre *(liter) (sb to do sth* à qn de faire qch*)* ; ◆ **he was ~den to come** on lui a ordonné de venir ◆ **do what I ~ you** fais ce que je te dis *or* t'ordonne
2 *(= say)* dire ◆ **to ~ sb good morning** dire bonjour à qn ◆ **to ~ sb welcome** souhaiter la bienvenue à qn ; → **farewell**
3 *(†† = invite)* inviter, convier
4 *(= offer) [+ amount]* offrir, faire une offre de ; *(at auction)* faire une enchère de ◆ **he is ~ding 500 euros for the painting** il fait une offre *or* une enchère de 500 euros pour ce tableau ◆ **I did not ~ (high) enough** je n'ai pas offert assez ◆ **the one that ~s most** le plus offrant
5 *(Cards)* demander ◆ **he ~ three spades** il a demandé trois piques
VI 1 *(= make an offer)* faire une offre, proposer un prix ◆ **to ~ for sth** faire une offre pour qch ; *(at auction)* faire une enchère pour qch ◆ **to ~ against sb** renchérir sur qn ◆ **to ~ on** *(US Comm) [+ contract etc]* soumissionner
2 *(phrases)* **to ~ for power/fame** viser *or* ambitionner le pouvoir/la gloire ◆ **to ~ fair to do sth** *(liter)* sembler devoir faire qch, promettre de faire qch ◆ **everything ~s fair to be successful** *(liter)* tout semble annoncer *or* promettre le succès
N 1 *(= offer)* offre *f* ; *(at auction)* enchère *f* ◆ **to make a ~ for** faire une offre pour ; *(at auction)* faire une enchère pour ◆ **a high ~** une forte enchère ◆ **a higher ~** une surenchère ◆ **to make a higher ~** surenchérir
2 *(Cards)* demande *f*, annonce *f* ◆ **to raise the ~** monter ◆ **to make no ~** *(Bridge)* passer parole ◆ **"no bid"** "parole", "passe"
3 *(= attempt)* tentative *f* ◆ **escape/suicide ~** tentative *f* d'évasion/de suicide ◆ **to make a ~ for power** tenter de s'emparer du pouvoir ◆ **to make a ~ for freedom** tenter de s'évader ◆ **he scaled the wall in a ~ for freedom** il a escaladé le mur pour tenter de s'évader ◆ **in a desperate ~ for a better life abroad** tentant désespérément de trouver une vie meilleure à l'étranger ◆ **to make a ~ to do sth** tenter de faire qch ◆ **she tried acupuncture in a ~ to stop smoking** elle a essayé l'acupuncture pour tenter d'arrêter de fumer
COMP **bid bond** N caution *f* de soumission
bid price N *(for shares)* cours *m* d'achat

biddable /'bɪdəbl/ ADJ 1 *[child]* docile, obéissant 2 *(Cards)* ~ **suit** couleur *f* demandable

bidden /'bɪdn/ VB ptp of **bid**

bidder /'bɪdə^r^/ N *(at sale)* enchérisseur *m*, offrant *m* ; *(for contract)* soumissionnaire *m* ◆ **the highest ~** le plus offrant ◆ **the lowest ~** *(for contract)* le soumissionnaire le moins cher ◆ **successful ~** *(in auction, for contract)* adjudicataire *mf* ◆ **there were no ~s** personne n'a fait d'offre

bidding /'bɪdɪŋ/ N 1 *(NonC, at sale)* enchère(s) *f(pl)* ◆ ~ **up** surenchères *fpl* ◆ ~ **was brisk** les enchères étaient vives ◆ **the ~ is closed** l'enchère est faite, c'est adjugé ◆ **to raise the ~** *(at sale)* surenchérir 2 *(NonC) (Cards)* enchères *fpl* ◆ **to open the ~** *(Bridge)* ouvrir (les enchères) 3 *(† = order)* ordre *m*, commandement *m* ◆ **at whose ~?** sur l'ordre de qui ? ◆ **I did his ~** j'ai fait ce qu'il m'a ordonné *or* demandé ◆ **at sb's ~** sur l'ordre *or* l'injonction de qn ◆ **he needed no second ~** il ne se l'est pas fait dire deux fois
COMP **bidding war** N *(Fin)* guerre *f* des enchères

biddy /'bɪdɪ/ N ◆ **old ~** vieille bonne femme *f*

bide /baɪd/ VI († or liter or dial) ⇒ **abide vi** VT 1 **to ~ one's time** se réserver, attendre son heure or le bon moment 2 († or liter or dial) ⇒ **abide vt**

bidet /ˈbiːdeɪ/ N bidet m

bidirectional /ˌbaɪdɪˈrekʃənl/ ADJ bidirectionnel

biennial /baɪˈenɪəl/ ADJ 1 (= happening every two years) biennal, bisannuel 2 (= lasting two years) biennal 3 [plant] bisannuel N (= plant) bisannuel m

bier /bɪəʳ/ N (for coffin) brancards mpl (de cercueil) ; (for corpse) bière f

biff †* /bɪf/ N coup m de poing, baffe‡ f ◆ ~! (onomatopoeia) vlan !, pan ! VT cogner sur, flanquer une baffe à* ◆ **to ~ sb on the nose** flanquer* son poing dans or sur la figure de qn

bifocal /ˈbaɪˈfəʊkəl/ ADJ bifocal, à double foyer NPL **bifocals** lunettes fpl à double foyer

bifurcate /ˈbaɪfɜːkeɪt/ VI bifurquer ADJ à deux branches

bifurcation /ˌbaɪfɜːˈkeɪʃən/ N bifurcation f, embranchement m

big /bɪɡ/ ADJ 1 (in size) [person, fruit, parcel, book] gros (grosse f) ; [person, building, tree] grand ◆ **a ~ fellow** un grand gaillard ◆ **a ~ man** un homme grand et fort ◆ **a ~ drop in share prices** une forte baisse du prix des actions ◆ **to grow ~** or **~ger** grossir ; (= taller) grandir ◆ **a ~ stick** un gros bâton ; see also **stick** ◆ **~ with child** grosse, enceinte ; → **drum**

2 (in age) grand, aîné ◆ **a ~ boy/girl** un grand garçon/une grande fille ◆ **my ~ brother** mon grand frère, mon frère aîné ◆ **to grow** or **get ~ger** grandir ◆ **to be a ~ brother to sb** servir de conseiller à qn ; see also **comp** ◆ **you're a ~ boy/girl now!** (lit, fig) tu es un grand garçon/une grande fille maintenant ! ◆ **I am ~ enough to know ...** je suis assez grand pour savoir ...

3 (= important, serious) [problem, difference, mistake] gros ; [question, issue] grand ; [step] important ; [decision] grand, important ◆ **what's the ~ hurry?** * il n'y a pas le feu !* ◆ **he's a ~ fish** * c'est un gros poisson* ◆ **he's a ~ fish** or (US) **frog in a small pond** c'est une gloire locale ◆ **boots are ~ this year** * (= fashionable) les bottes sont in‡ cette année ◆ **this is my/his ~ day** c'est le grand jour (pour moi/lui) ◆ **try and get some rest - we have a ~ day ahead of us** essaie de te reposer : nous avons une journée bien remplie devant nous ◆ **a ~ event** un événement marquant ◆ **to have ~ ideas** voir grand ◆ **but, and it's a ~ but** ... mais, car il y a un mais ... ◆ **a ~ lie** un gros mensonge ◆ **the ~ger they are, the harder they fall** plus haut ils sont arrivés, plus dure sera la chute ◆ **to do things in a ~ way** faire les choses en grand ◆ **a tragedy? that's rather a ~ word** une tragédie ? c'est un bien grand mot ; see also **way**

4 (* = grand) [words] ambitieux ◆ **~ talk** fanfaronnades fpl, grands discours mpl ◆ **to get/be too ~ for one's boots** attraper/avoir la grosse tête* ◆ **he's got a ~ head** il est crâneur*, il a la grosse tête* ◆ **he's got a ~ mouth** il ne sait pas se taire or la boucler* ◆ **why can't you keep your ~ mouth shut!** pas moyen que tu te taises !*, tu aurais mieux fait de la boucler !‡ ; see also **comp, bigmouth**

5 (= generous) grand, généreux ◆ **a heart as ~ as yours** un cœur aussi grand or aussi généreux que le vôtre ◆ **that's ~ of you!** * (iro) quelle générosité ! (iro) ◆ **to be ~ on** ‡ [+ person] adorer, être un fan* de ; [+ thing] être grand amateur or un fana* de ; see also **hand**

ADV ◆ **to talk ~** * fanfaronner, se faire mousser* ◆ **to act ~** * frimer*, faire l'important ◆ **to go over ~** ‡ avoir un succès fou or monstre* ◆ **to make it ~** * avoir un succès fou* ◆ **his speech went down ~ with his audience**‡ ses auditeurs ont été emballés* par son discours

COMP **big band** N (Mus) big band m, grand orchestre m (des années 40-50)

big bang N (Phys) big-bang or big bang m ◆ **the Big Bang** (on British Stock Exchange) le Big Bang (informatisation de la Bourse de Londres)

Big Ben N (Brit) Big Ben m

big-boned ADJ bien or fortement charpenté

Big Brother N (Pol etc) Big Brother m, l'État m omniprésent ◆ **Big Brother is watching you** on vous espionne

big bug‡ N grosse légume* f, huile* f

big business N (NonC) les grandes entreprises fpl, les grandes firmes fpl ◆ **the lottery has become ~ business** la loterie rapporte beaucoup d'argent or rapporte gros ◆ **tourism in Hong Kong is ~ business** le tourisme est un secteur florissant à Hong-Kong

big cat N fauve m, grand félin m

big cheese‡ N grosse légume* f, huile* f

the big city N la grande ville

big dipper N [of fairground] montagnes fpl russes ◆ **the Big Dipper** (US Astron) la Grande Ourse

the Big Eight N (US Univ) les grandes universités du Midwest

big end N (in car) tête f de bielle

the Big Four N (Pol) les Quatre (Grands) ; (Brit = banks) les quatre grandes banques anglaises

big game N gros gibier m ◆ **~ game hunter** chasseur m de gros gibier ◆ **~ game hunting** chasse f au gros (gibier)

big-hearted ADJ au grand cœur ◆ **to be ~-hearted** avoir bon cœur, avoir du cœur ◆ **a ~-hearted fellow** un homme de cœur

big-hitter N (Sport) frappeur m -euse f ; (fig = powerful person) poids m lourd

The Big Issue N (Brit) journal des sans-abri

big-mouthed * ADJ fort en gueule* ◆ **to be ~-mouthed** être fort en gueule*, avoir une grande gueule‡

big name * N (= authority) grand nom m ◆ **he's a ~ name in politics** (person) c'est un grand nom de la politique

big noise * N (Brit) grand ponte* m ◆ **she's a ~ noise in linguistics** c'est un grand ponte* de la linguistique

big one‡ N (US = a thousand dollars) (billet m de) mille dollars mpl

big science N la recherche scientifique à gros budget

the big screen N (Cine) le grand écran

big shot * N grand ponte* m

big-sounding ADJ [idea, plan etc] prétentieux ; [name] ronflant, pompeux

big-style → **big-time**

the Big Ten N → **the Big Eight**

big-ticket * ADJ (US) ◆ **~-ticket item** or **purchase** gros achat m

big time * N ◆ **to make the ~ time** percer

big-time * ADJ [politician, industrialist] de première catégorie ; [part, role] de premier plan ; [farming] sur une grande échelle ◆ **~-time gambler** flambeur‡ m ADV ◆ **you screwed up ~-time!** * tu as cafouillé quelque chose de bien !*

big toe N gros orteil m

big top N (= circus) cirque m ; (= main tent) grand chapiteau m

big wheel N (in fairground etc) grande roue f ; (* = important person) huile* f ; → **apple, deal¹**

bigamist /ˈbɪɡəmɪst/ N bigame mf

bigamous /ˈbɪɡəməs/ ADJ bigame

bigamy /ˈbɪɡəmɪ/ N bigamie f

Bigfoot /ˈbɪɡfʊt/ N ⇒ **Sasquatch**

biggie‡ /ˈbɪɡɪ/ N (= success) (song, record) tube* m ; (film) succès m ◆ **now it's the ~** (= anything important) maintenant, on passe aux choses sérieuses

biggish * /ˈbɪɡɪʃ/ ADJ assez or relativement grand

bighead * /ˈbɪɡhed/ N crâneur* m, -euse* f

bigheaded * /ˌbɪɡˈhedɪd/ ADJ crâneur*

bight /baɪt/ N 1 (Geog) baie f, anse f ; (larger) golfe m 2 [of rope] boucle f

bigmouth * /ˈbɪɡmaʊθ/ N grande gueule‡ f ◆ **he is just a ~** il a or c'est une grande gueule‡

bigot /ˈbɪɡət/ N 1 (Philos, Pol) fanatique mf, sectaire mf ; (Rel) bigot(e) m(f) 2 (US = racist) raciste mf

bigoted /ˈbɪɡətɪd/ ADJ 1 (Rel) bigot ; (Pol etc) [person] fanatique, sectaire ; [attitude, devotion] fanatique 2 (US = racist) raciste

bigotry /ˈbɪɡətrɪ/ N (NonC) 1 (Rel) bigoterie f ; (Philos, Pol etc) fanatisme m, sectarisme m 2 (US = racism) racisme m

bigwig‡ /ˈbɪɡwɪɡ/ N grosse légume‡ f, huile‡ f

Bihar /bɪˈhɑːʳ/ N Bihâr m

bijou /ˈbiːʒuː/ ADJ (Brit) ◆ **"bijou residence for sale"** "maison à vendre, véritable bijou"

bike /baɪk/ N (abbrev of **bicycle**) vélo m ; (= motorbike) moto f ◆ **on your ~!** * (Brit) (= go away) dégage !* ; (= no way) tu plaisantes !* VI * faire du vélo ◆ **to ~ to work** aller au travail à vélo ◆ **to ~ 10km** faire 10 km à vélo

COMP **bike lane** N piste f cyclable

bike rack N (on floor) râtelier m à bicyclettes ; (on car roof) porte-vélos m inv

bike shed N abri m à bicyclettes

bike shop N magasin m de cycles

biker * /ˈbaɪkəʳ/ N motard(e) m(f)

bikeway /ˈbaɪkweɪ/ N piste f cyclable

bikini /bɪˈkiːnɪ/ N bikini ® m

COMP **bikini bottom(s)** * N(PL) bas m de bikini ®

bikini briefs, bikini pants NPL mini-slip m

bikini line N (ligne f du) maillot ◆ **to do one's ~ line** s'épiler le maillot

bikini top N haut m de bikini ®

bikini wax N épilation f (à la cire) du maillot

bilabial /baɪˈleɪbjəl/ ADJ bilabial N bilabiale f

bilateral /baɪˈlætərəl/ ADJ bilatéral

bilaterally /baɪˈlætərəlɪ/ ADV bilatéralement

bilberry /ˈbɪlbərɪ/ N myrtille f

bile /baɪl/ N 1 (Physiol) bile f 2 (fig = anger) mauvaise humeur f 3 (Hist = choler) bile f

COMP **bile duct** N canal m biliaire

bile stone N calcul m biliaire

bilevel /baɪˈlevl/ ADJ sur or à deux niveaux

bilge /bɪldʒ/ N 1 (Naut) (= rounded part of hull) bouchain m, renflement m ; (= bottom of hold) fond m de cale, sentine f 2 (also **bilge water**) eau f de cale or de sentine 3 (‡ = nonsense) idioties fpl, foutaises‡ fpl

bilharzia /bɪlˈhɑːzɪə/, **bilharziasis** /ˌbɪlhɑːˈzaɪəsɪs/ N bilharziose f

bilingual /baɪˈlɪŋɡwəl/ ADJ bilingue

bilingualism /baɪˈlɪŋɡwəlɪzəm/ N bilinguisme m

bilious /ˈbɪlɪəs/ ADJ 1 (Med) bilieux ◆ **~ attack** crise f de foie 2 (fig) maussade, irritable

biliousness /ˈbɪlɪəsnɪs/ N (NonC: Med) affection f hépatique

bilk /bɪlk/ VT (esp US) [+ creditor] filouter, blouser* ◆ **to ~ sb's efforts** mettre des bâtons dans les roues à qn

Bill /bɪl/ N (dim of **William**) Guillaume m

bill¹ /bɪl/ N 1 (for product, work done) facture f ; (for gas etc) note f ; [of restaurant] addition f ; [of hotel] note f ◆ **have you paid the milk ~?** as-tu payé le lait ? ◆ **a pile of ~s in the post** une pile de factures dans le courrier ◆ **may I have the ~ please** l'addition (or la note) s'il vous plaît ◆ **put it on my ~ please** mettez-le sur ma note, s'il vous plaît ◆ **the factory has a high wages ~** l'usine a d'importantes sorties en salaires,

le poste salaires est élevé dans l'entreprise ; → **foot, pay, settle²**
2 *(= written statement)* état *m*, liste *f*
3 *(Comm, Fin etc)* effet *m*, traite *f* ◆ **to meet a ~** faire honneur à un effet ◆ **to draw a ~ on ...** tirer une traite sur ... ◆ **~s payable** *(Fin)* effets *mpl* à payer ◆ **~s receivable** *(Fin)* effets *mpl* à recevoir ◆ **exchequer ~** bon *m* du Trésor ; → **endorse**
4 *(US = banknote)* billet *m* (de banque) ◆ **5-dollar ~** billet *m* de 5 dollars
5 *(Parl)* projet *m* de loi ◆ **to propose/pass/throw out a ~** présenter/voter/rejeter un projet de loi ◆ **the ~ passed the Commons** *(Brit)* le projet de loi a été voté par la Chambre des communes
6 *(Jur)* plainte *f*, requête *f*
7 *(= poster, advertisement) (Theat etc)* affiche *f* ; *[of house for sale]* écriteau *m* ; *(= public notice)* placard *m* ◆ **to head** *or* **top the ~** être en vedette, être en tête d'affiche ◆ **to fit** *or* **fill the ~** *(gen)* faire l'affaire ; *(for job)* avoir le profil ◆ **we need someone with leadership qualities, and she fits the ~ perfectly** il nous faut quelqu'un qui ait des qualités de chef et elle fait tout à fait l'affaire *or* elle a le profil requis ◆ **she fits the ~ as a leader** elle a tout à fait le profil d'un chef ; → **handbill, stick**

VT 1 *[+ goods]* facturer ◆ **to ~ sb for sth** envoyer la facture de qch à qn
2 *[+ play]* mettre à l'affiche, annoncer ◆ **he is ~ed to play Hamlet** il est à l'affiche dans le rôle de Hamlet

COMP **bill of attainder** N décret *m* de confiscation de biens et de mort civile
bill of costs N état *m* de frais
bill of entry N *(Customs)* déclaration *f* d'entrée en douane
bill of exchange N *(Comm)* lettre *f* de change ◆ **foreign ~ of exchange** traite *f* sur l'étranger
bill of fare N menu *m*, carte *f* (du jour)
bill of goods N *(US)* ◆ **to sell sb a ~ of goods** * rouler * qn
bill of health N *(Naut)* patente *f* (de santé) ; → **clean**
bill of indictment N acte *m* d'accusation
bill of lading N *(Comm)* connaissement *m*
bill of quantities N *(Constr)* métré *m (devis)*
bill of rights N déclaration *f* des droits ◆ **the Bill of Rights** *(US Hist)* la Déclaration des droits
bill of sale N acte *m or* contrat *m* de vente

BILL OF RIGHTS

Ensemble des dix premiers amendements ajoutés à la Constitution américaine en 1791 et qui définissent les droits individuels des citoyens et les pouvoirs respectifs du gouvernement fédéral et des États. Ainsi le premier amendement garantit la liberté de culte et de réunion et la liberté de la presse, le second le droit au port d'armes, le sixième le droit à un procès équitable. → FIFTH AMENDMENT

bill² /bɪl/ N 1 *[of bird]* bec *m* ; → **scissor** 2 *(Geog)* promontoire *m*, bec *m* ◆ **Portland Bill** la presqu'île de Portland VI *[birds]* se becqueter ◆ **to ~ and coo** *(lit, fig)* roucouler

bill³ /bɪl/ N 1 *(= tool)* serpe *f* 2 *(Hist = weapon)* hache *f* d'armes

billboard /ˈbɪlbɔːd/ N panneau *m* d'affichage

billet¹ /ˈbɪlɪt/ N *(Mil) (= document)* billet *m* de logement ; *(= accommodation)* cantonnement *m* (chez l'habitant) ◆ **a cushy ~** * *(fig)* un fromage *, une planque * VT *(Mil)* ◆ **to ~ a soldier (on sb)** loger un soldat (chez qn), cantonner un soldat (chez qn) ◆ **to ~ soldiers on a town** cantonner des soldats dans une ville

billet² /ˈbɪlɪt/ N *[of wood etc]* billette *f (also Archit)*

billeting /ˈbɪlɪtɪŋ/ N *(Mil)* cantonnement *m*
COMP **billeting officer** N chef *m* de cantonnement

billfold /ˈbɪlfəʊld/ N *(US)* portefeuille *m*

billhook /ˈbɪlhʊk/ N serpette *f*

billiard /ˈbɪljəd/ N *(NonC)* ◆ **~s** (jeu *m* de) billard *m* ◆ **to have a game of ~s** faire une partie de billard
COMP **billiard ball** N boule *f* de billard
billiard cue N queue *f* de billard
billiard table N (table *f* de) billard *m*

billing¹ /ˈbɪlɪŋ/ N 1 *(of posters)* affichage *m* 2 *(Theat)* **to get top** *or* **star/second ~** figurer en tête d'affiche/en deuxième place à l'affiche

billing² /ˈbɪlɪŋ/ N *(lit, fig)* ◆ **~ and cooing** roucoulements *mpl*

billing³ /ˈbɪlɪŋ/ N *(Comm)* facturation *f*

Billingsgate /ˈbɪlɪŋzgeɪt/ N *ancien marché au poisson du quartier de Billingsgate à Londres*

billion /ˈbɪljən/ N (pl **billion** *or* **billions**) *(= thousand million)* milliard *m* ; *(Brit* † *= million million)* billion *m*

billionaire /ˌbɪljəˈneəʳ/ N milliardaire *mf*

billow /ˈbɪləʊ/ N *(liter)* ◆ **the ~s** les flots *mpl (liter)* VI *[sail]* se gonfler ; *[cloth]* onduler ; *[smoke]* s'élever en tourbillons *or* en volutes, tournoyer

► **billow out** VI *[sail etc]* se gonfler

billowy /ˈbɪləʊɪ/ ADJ *[sea]* houleux, agité ; *[waves]* gros (grosse *f*) ; *[sail]* gonflé (par le vent) ; *[smoke]* en (grosses) volutes

billposter /ˈbɪl,pəʊstəʳ/, **billsticker** /ˈbɪlˈstɪkəʳ/ N colleur *m* d'affiches

billy¹ /ˈbɪlɪ/ N *(US = club)* matraque *f*

billy² /ˈbɪlɪ/ N (also **billy can**) gamelle *f*

billy goat /ˈbɪlɪgəʊt/ N bouc *m* COMP **billy goat beard** N bouc *m (barbe)*

billy-ho‡, **billy-o(h)**‡ /ˈbɪlɪəʊ/ N ◆ **like billy-oh** *[laugh, run, work]* comme un fou

bimbo * /ˈbɪmbəʊ/ N (pl **bimbos**) *(pej)* ravissante idiote *f*

bimetallic /ˌbaɪmɪˈtælɪk/ ADJ bimétallique

bimetallism /baɪˈmetəlɪzəm/ N bimétallisme *m*

bimonthly /ˈbaɪˈmʌnθlɪ/ ADJ *(= twice a month)* bimensuel ; *(= every two months)* bimestriel ADV deux fois par mois, tous les deux mois

bin /bɪn/ N 1 *[of coal, corn]* coffre *m* ; *[of bread]* boîte *f* ; *(larger)* huche *f* 2 *(Brit Wine)* casier *m* (à bouteilles) 3 *(Brit:* also **rubbish bin**) boîte *f* à ordures, poubelle *f* VT *(* = throw away)* mettre *or* jeter à la poubelle
COMP **bin bag** N (grand) sac *m* poubelle
bin end N *(Wine)* fin *f* de série
bin liner N sac *m* poubelle

binary /ˈbaɪnərɪ/ ADJ binaire N *(= the binary system)* système *m* binaire ◆ **in ~** en binaire
COMP **binary code** N *(Comput)* code *m* binaire
binary form N *(Mus)* forme *f* binaire
binary notation N *(Math)* numération *f* binaire
binary number N *(Math)* nombre *m* binaire
binary star N *(Astron)* étoile *f* double
binary system N *(Math)* système *m* binaire

bind /baɪnd/ (pret, ptp **bound**) VT 1 *(= fasten) [+ thing]* attacher ; *[+ two or more things]* attacher, lier ; *[+ person, animal]* lier, attacher *(to* à) ; *[+ prisoner]* ligoter ◆ **he bound the files (together) with string** il a attaché *or* lié (ensemble) les dossiers avec une ficelle ◆ **bound hand and foot** pieds et poings liés ◆ **bound by gratitude to sb** attaché à qn par la reconnaissance ◆ **to be bound together** *[people, ideas]* être liés
2 *(= encircle)* entourer *(with* de) ceindre *(liter) (with* de) ; *(Med) [+ artery]* ligaturer ; *[+ wound]* bander
3 *[+ book]* relier ◆ **bound in calf** relié (en) veau
4 *(= oblige, pledge)* obliger, contraindre *(sb to do sth* qn à faire qch) ; ◆ **to ~ o.s. to sth/to do sth** s'engager à qch/à faire qch ◆ **to ~ sb to a promise** astreindre qn à tenir une promesse ◆ **to ~ by an oath** lier par (un) serment ◆ **to ~ sb as an apprentice (to)** mettre qn en apprentissage (chez) ; → **bound³**
5 *(= stick together) (also Chem, Phys)* lier ; *(Med) [+ bowels]* resserrer ◆ **~ the mixture with an egg** *(Culin)* lier la préparation avec un œuf
VI *[rule]* être obligatoire ; *[agreement]* engager ; *[machinery]* se coincer, se gripper ; *[brakes]* se bloquer
N 1 *(Mus)* liaison *f*
2 *(Brit * = nuisance)* ◆ **what a ~ you've got to go** quelle barbe * que tu doives partir ◆ **this meeting is a terrible ~** cette réunion me casse les pieds * ◆ **to be in a ~** être dans le pétrin *, être coincé

► **bind down** VT SEP *(fig)* obliger, contraindre, astreindre *(sb to do sth* qn à faire qch) ; ◆ **to be bound down (to do sth)** être obligé *or* contraint (de faire qch), être astreint (à faire qch)

► **bind on** VT SEP attacher *(avec une corde etc)*
VI * rouspéter *, geindre * *(about* à propos de)

► **bind over** VT SEP *(esp Brit Jur)* mettre en liberté conditionnelle ◆ **to ~ sb over to keep the peace** relaxer qn sous condition qu'il ne trouble *subj* pas l'ordre public ◆ **he was bound over for six months** on l'a relaxé sous peine de comparaître en cas de récidive dans les six mois

► **bind to** VT FUS *(Chem)* se lier à

► **bind together** VT SEP *(lit) [+ sticks]* lier ; *(fig) [+ people]* unir

► **bind up** VT SEP *[+ wound]* panser, bander ; *(fig)* lier, attacher ◆ **his money is bound up in shares** son argent est immobilisé dans des actions ◆ **your life is bound up in hers** votre existence est étroitement liée à la sienne ◆ **the future of their country is inextricably bound up with Europe** l'avenir de leur pays est inextricablement lié à celui de l'Europe ◆ **to be totally bound up with sb** se dévouer entièrement à qn ◆ **to be totally bound up with one's work** se donner corps et âme à son travail

binder /ˈbaɪndəʳ/ N 1 *(Agr) (= machine)* lieuse *f* 2 *(for papers)* classeur *m* ; → **ring¹** 3 *(Constr) (= cement, mortar)* liant *m*, agglomérant *m* 4 *(US = agreement in deal)* engagement *m*, option *f* d'achat

bindery /ˈbaɪndərɪ/ N atelier *m* de reliure

binding /ˈbaɪndɪŋ/ N 1 *[of book]* reliure *f* ; → **cloth, half** 2 *(Textiles = tape)* extrafort *m* ; → **bias** 3 *[of skis]* fixation *f* ADJ *[rule]* obligatoire ; *[agreement, promise]* qui lie, qui engage ; *[price]* ferme ◆ **to be ~ on sb** lier qn, engager qn ◆ **a promise is ~** on est lié par une promesse ◆ **~ effect** *(Jur: of agreement)* force *f* obligatoire ◆ **measure ~ on each contracting party** *(Jur)* mesure *f* exécutoire pour chaque partie contractante

bindweed /ˈbaɪndwiːd/ N liseron *m*

binge /bɪndʒ/ VI *(gen)* faire des excès ; *(on alcohol)* se soûler, boire avec frénésie ; *(on food)* manger à l'excès ; *(spending)* dépenser comme un fou ◆ **to ~ on chocolate** s'empiffrer * de chocolat ◆ **to ~ on chartreuse** se soûler à la chartreuse N ◆ **a drinking ~** une beuverie ◆ **to go on a ~** ⇒ **to binge**
COMP **binge drinker** N buveur, -euse *m/f* excessif, -ive
binge drinking N *consommation excessive d'alcool dans un laps de temps relativement court*

bingo /ˈbɪŋgəʊ/ N bingo *m* EXCL ◆ **~!** * eurêka ! *

binman /ˈbɪnmæn/ N (pl **-men**) *(= dustman)* boueux *m*, éboueur *m*

binnacle /ˈbɪnəkl/ N *(Naut)* habitacle *m*

binocular /bɪˈnɒkjʊləʳ/ ADJ binoculaire NPL **binoculars** jumelle(s) *f(pl)*

binomial /baɪˈnəʊmɪəl/ ADJ, N *(Math)* binôme *m* ◆ ~ **distribution** distribution *f* binomiale ◆ **the ~ theorem** le théorème (de binôme) de Newton

bint‡ /bɪnt/ N *(Brit)* nana‡ *f*

binuclear /baɪˈnjuːklɪəʳ/ ADJ binucléaire

bio... /ˈbaɪəʊ/ PREF bio...

biochemical /ˈbaɪəʊˈkemɪkəl/ ADJ biochimique

biochemist /ˈbaɪəʊˈkemɪst/ N biochimiste *mf*

biochemistry /ˈbaɪəʊˈkemɪstrɪ/ N biochimie *f*

biocompatible /ˈbaɪəʊkəmˈpætəbəl/ ADJ biocompatible

biodegradable /ˈbaɪəʊdɪˈgreɪdəbl/ ADJ biodégradable

biodiesel /ˈbaɪəʊˌdiːzəl/ N biodiesel *m (gasoil d'origine végétale)*

biodiversity /ˌbaɪəʊdaɪˈvɜːsətɪ/ N biodiversité *f*

biodynamic /ˌbaɪəʊdaɪˈnæmɪk/ ADJ biodynamique

bioengineering /ˌbaɪəʊˌendʒɪˈnɪərɪŋ/ N bioingénierie *f*

bioethics /ˌbaɪəʊˈeθɪks/ N *(NonC)* bioéthique *f*

biofeedback /ˌbaɪəʊˈfiːdbæk/ N biofeedback *m*

biofuel /ˈbaɪəʊfjʊəl/ N biocarburant *m*

biogenesis /ˈbaɪəʊˈdʒenɪsɪs/ N biogenèse *f*

biogenetics /ˌbaɪəʊdʒəˈnetɪks/ N biogénétique *f*

biographer /baɪˈɒgrəfəʳ/ N biographe *mf*

biographic(al) /ˌbaɪəʊˈgræfɪk(əl)/ ADJ biographique

bioinformatics /ˌbaɪəʊˌɪnfəˈmætɪks/ N bioinformatique *f*

biography /baɪˈɒgrəfɪ/ N biographie *f*

biological /ˌbaɪəˈlɒdʒɪkəl/ ADJ *(gen)* biologique ; *[detergent, washing powder]* aux enzymes

COMP **biological clock** N horloge *f* biologique
biological diversity N diversité *f* biologique
biological father N père *m* biologique
biological mother N mère *f* biologique
biological parents NPL parents *mpl* biologiques
biological warfare N guerre *f* biologique
biological weapons NPL armes *fpl* biologiques

biologically /ˌbaɪəʊˈlɒdʒɪkəlɪ/ ADV biologiquement

biologist /baɪˈɒlədʒɪst/ N biologiste *mf*

biology /baɪˈɒlədʒɪ/ N biologie *f*

biomass /ˈbaɪəʊmæs/ N biomasse *f*

biome /ˈbaɪəʊm/ N biome *m*

biomechanics /ˌbaɪəʊmɪˈkænɪks/ N *(NonC)* biomécanique *f*

biomedical /ˌbaɪəʊˈmedɪkəl/ ADJ biomédical

biometric /ˌbaɪəˈmetrɪk/ ADJ *[data, technology, device]* biométrique

biometrics /baɪəˈmetrɪks/, **biometry** /baɪˈɒmɪtrɪ/ N *(NonC)* biométrie *f*

bionic /baɪˈɒnɪk/ ADJ bionique

bionics /baɪˈɒnɪks/ N *(NonC)* bionique *f*

biophysical /ˌbaɪəʊˈfɪzɪkəl/ ADJ biophysique

biophysicist /ˌbaɪəʊˈfɪzɪsɪst/ N biophysicien(ne) *m(f)*

biophysics /ˌbaɪəʊˈfɪzɪks/ N *(NonC)* biophysique *f*

biopic* /ˈbaɪəʊˌpɪk/ N film *m* biographique

biopiracy /ˌbaɪəˈpaɪərəsɪ/ N biopiraterie *f*

biopsy /ˈbaɪɒpsɪ/ N biopsie *f*

biorhythm /ˈbaɪəʊrɪðəm/ N biorythme *m*

biosphere /ˈbaɪəsfɪəʳ/ N biosphère *f*

biosynthesis /ˌbaɪəʊˈsɪnθɪsɪs/ N biosynthèse *f*, anabolisme *m*

biosynthetic /ˌbaɪəʊˌsɪnˈθetɪk/ ADJ biosynthétique

biota /baɪˈəʊtə/ N biote *m*

biotechnology /ˌbaɪəʊtekˈnɒlədʒɪ/ N biotechnologie *f*

bioterror /ˈbaɪəʊˌterəʳ/ N bioterrorisme *m* ◆ **bioterror attack** attaque bioterroriste

bioterrorism /ˌbaɪəʊˈterərɪzm/ N bioterrorisme *m*

bioterrorist /ˌbaɪəʊˈterərɪst/ N bioterroriste *mf* ADJ *[attack, threat]* bioterroriste

biotic /baɪˈɒtɪk/ ADJ biotique

biowarfare /ˈbaɪəʊˈwɔːfeəʳ/ N guerre *f* biologique

bioweapon /ˈbaɪəʊˌwepən/ N arme *f* biologique

bipartisan /ˌbaɪˈpɑːtɪzæn/ ADJ biparti *or* bipartite ◆ ~ **politics** politique *f* qui fait l'unanimité

bipartite /baɪˈpɑːtaɪt/ ADJ *(Bio, Pol)* biparti *or* bipartite ; *(Jur) [document]* rédigé en double

biped /ˈbaɪped/ ADJ, N bipède *m*

biplane /ˈbaɪpleɪn/ N (avion *m*) biplan *m*

bipolar /baɪˈpəʊləʳ/ ADJ bipolaire ◆ ~ **disorder** *or* **illness** troubles *(mpl)* bipolaires ◆ **to be ~*** souffrir de troubles bipolaires

bipolarization /baɪˌpəʊləraɪˈzeɪʃən/ N bipolarisation *f*

bipolarize /baɪˈpəʊləraɪz/ VT bipolariser

birch /bɜːtʃ/ N (also **birch tree**) bouleau *m* ; (also **birch wood**) (bois *m* de) bouleau *m* ; *(for whipping)* verge *f*, fouet *m* ◆ **the ~** *(Jur)* la peine du fouet (avec les verges) VT fouetter

COMP de bouleau
birch plantation N boulaie *f*, plantation *f* de bouleaux

birching /ˈbɜːtʃɪŋ/ N peine *f* du fouet (avec les verges)

bird /bɜːd/ N 1 oiseau *m* ; *(Culin)* volaille *f* ◆ ~ **of ill omen** *(liter)* oiseau *m* de mauvais augure *or* de malheur ◆ **a ~ in the hand is worth two in the bush** *(Prov)* un tiens vaut mieux que deux tu l'auras *(Prov)* ◆ **~s of a feather flock together** *(Prov)* qui se ressemble s'assemble *(Prov)* ◆ **they're ~s of a feather** *(gen)* ils se ressemblent beaucoup ; *(pej)* ils sont à mettre dans le même sac ◆ **a little ~ told me*** mon petit doigt me l'a dit ◆ **the ~ has flown** *(fig)* l'oiseau s'est envolé ◆ **to give sb the ~**†* *(Theat, Sport)* huer *or* siffler qn ; *(= send sb packing)* envoyer bouler* *or* paître* qn ◆ **to get the ~**†* *(Theat)* se faire siffler *or* huer ◆ **for the ~s**‡ *(= worthless)* nul* ; *(= silly)* débile* ◆ **he'll have to be told about the ~s and the bees** *(hum)* il va falloir lui expliquer que les bébés ne naissent pas dans les choux ; → **early**

2 *(‡ = fellow)* oiseau* *m (pej)*, type* *m* ◆ **he's a queer ~** c'est un drôle d'oiseau* *or* de numéro* ◆ **he's a cunning old ~** c'est un vieux singe *or* rusé

3 *(Brit ‡ = girl)* nana* *f*, gonzesse‡ *f*

4 *(‡ = prison)* **five years' ~** cinq ans de taule‡ ◆ **to do ~** faire de la taule‡

COMP **bird bath** N vasque *f (pour les oiseaux)*
bird brain* N *(pej)* étourneau *m*, tête *f* de linotte
bird-brained* ADJ qui a une cervelle d'oiseau, écervelé
bird call N cri *m* d'oiseau
bird dog N *(US)* chien *m* de chasse *(pour le gibier à plume)*
bird fancier N aviculteur *m*, -trice *f*
bird feeder N mangeoire *f*, trémie *f*
bird flu N grippe *f* aviaire
bird-like ADJ *[eyes, features]* d'oiseau
bird nesting N ◆ **to go ~ nesting** aller dénicher les oiseaux
bird of paradise N oiseau *m* de paradis
bird of passage N *(lit, fig)* oiseau *m* de passage
bird of prey N oiseau *m* de proie
bird sanctuary N réserve *f* ornithologique
birds' eggs NPL œufs *mpl* d'oiseaux
bird's-eye view N *(fig)* vue *f* d'ensemble, vue *f* générale ◆ **a ~'s-eye view of Paris** *(from plane)* Paris vu d'avion
bird's foot N (pl **bird's foots**) *(= plant)* pied-d'oiseau *m*
bird's nest N nid *m* d'oiseau(x)
bird's-nest soup N soupe *f* aux nids d'hirondelles
bird table N *(in garden)* mangeoire *f*
bird-watcher N ornithologue *mf* amateur
bird-watching N ornithologie *f* (pratiquée en amateur) ◆ **to go ~-watching** aller observer les oiseaux

birdcage /ˈbɜːdkeɪdʒ/ N cage *f* à oiseaux ; *(large)* volière *f*

birdie /ˈbɜːdɪ/ N 1 *(baby talk)* (gentil) petit oiseau *m* ◆ **watch the ~!*** *(for photo)* le petit oiseau va sortir ! 2 *(Golf)* birdie *m* VT *(Golf)* ◆ **to ~ a hole** faire un birdie

birdlime /ˈbɜːdlaɪm/ N glu *f*

birdseed /ˈbɜːdsiːd/ N *(NonC)* graines *fpl (pour les oiseaux)*

birdsong /ˈbɜːdsɒŋ/ N chant *m* des oiseaux

biretta /bɪˈretə/ N barrette *f*

biriani /ˌbɪrɪˈɑːnɪ/ N ⇒ **biryani**

birling /ˈbɜːlɪŋ/ N *(US) sport de bûcheron, consistant à faire tourner avec les pieds, sans tomber, un tronc d'arbre flottant*

Biro ®/ˈbaɪərəʊ/ N *(Brit)* stylo *m* (à) bille, Bic ® *m*

birth /bɜːθ/ LANGUAGE IN USE 24.1

N 1 *(= being born)* naissance *f* ; (also **childbirth**) accouchement *m*, couches *fpl* ; *[of animal]* mise *f* bas ◆ **at ~** à la naissance ◆ **during the ~** pendant l'accouchement ◆ **to give ~ to** *[woman]* donner naissance à ; *[animal]* mettre bas ◆ **blind/deaf from** *or* **since ~** aveugle/sourd de naissance ◆ **the village/country of one's ~** son village/pays natal

2 *(= parentage)* naissance *f*, extraction *f* ◆ **Scottish by ~** écossais de naissance ◆ **of good ~** bien né, de bonne famille ◆ **of humble ~** de basse extraction

3 *(fig) [of movement, idea]* naissance *f*, éclosion *f* ; *[of new era]* naissance *f*, commencement *m* ; *[of trend, project]* naissance *f*, lancement *m* ; *[of phenomenon]* apparition *f*

COMP **birth certificate** N *(original)* acte *m* de naissance ; *(copy)* extrait *m* de naissance
birth control N régulation *f or* contrôle *m* des naissances ◆ **~ control pill** ⇒ **birth pill**
birth defect N défaut *m* de naissance
birth father N père *m* biologique, géniteur *m*
birth mother N mère *f* biologique, génitrice *f*
birth parents NPL parents *mpl* biologiques, géniteurs *mpl*
birth pill N pilule *f* contraceptive
birth plan N projet *m* d'accouchement
birth rate N (taux *m* de) natalité *f*

birthdate /ˈbɜːθdeɪt/ N date *f* de naissance

birthday /ˈbɜːθdeɪ/ LANGUAGE IN USE 23.3 N anniversaire *m* ◆ **what did you get for your ~?** qu'est-ce que tu as eu pour ton anniversaire ? ; → **happy**

COMP **birthday cake** N gâteau *m* d'anniversaire
birthday card N carte *f* d'anniversaire
Birthday Honours N *(Brit)* ⇒ **Honours List** ; → **honour** ; → HONOURS LIST
birthday party N ◆ **she is having a ~ party** elle a organisé une petite fête *or* une soirée pour son anniversaire
birthday present N cadeau *m* d'anniversaire
birthday suit* N *(hum)* ◆ **in one's ~ suit** en costume d'Adam *(or* d'Ève*)**, dans le plus simple appareil *(hum)*

birthing /ˈbɜːθɪŋ/ ADJ [equipment, room] d'accouchement
COMP **birthing chair** N chaise f d'accouchement
birthing pool N piscine f or bassin m d'accouchement
birthing stool N tabouret m d'accouchement

birthmark /ˈbɜːθmɑːk/ N tache f de vin

birthplace /ˈbɜːθpleɪs/ N (gen, Admin) lieu m de naissance ; (= house) maison f natale ◆ **the ~ of civilization** le berceau de la civilisation

birthright /ˈbɜːθraɪt/ N (lit) [of firstborn] droit m d'aînesse ◆ **it is the ~ of every Englishman** (fig) c'est un droit que chaque Anglais a or acquiert à sa naissance

birthstone /ˈbɜːθstəʊn/ N pierre f porte-bonheur

biryani /ˌbɪriˈɑːni/ N biriani m (plat indien à base de riz)

biscuit /ˈbɪskɪt/ N 1 (Brit) petit gâteau m sec, biscuit m ◆ **that takes the ~!**‡ ça c'est le bouquet !* ◆ **he takes the ~!**‡ il décroche le pompon !* ; → **digestive, ship, water** 2 (US) biscuit m sec ADJ (also **biscuit-coloured**) (couleur) biscuit inv, beige
COMP **biscuit barrel** N boîte f à biscuits
biscuit-firing N (Pottery) dégourdi m
biscuit ware N (Pottery) biscuit m

bisect /baɪˈsekt/ VT couper or diviser en deux ; (Math) couper en deux parties égales VI [road etc] bifurquer

bisection /baɪˈsekʃən/ N (Math) division f en deux parties égales ; [of angle] bissection f

bisector /baɪˈsektəʳ/ N (Math) bissectrice f

bisexual /ˈbaɪˈseksjʊəl/ ADJ 1 [person] bisexuel 2 [organism, animal] bisexué

bishop /ˈbɪʃəp/ N 1 (Rel) évêque m ; (as term of address) Monseigneur 2 (Chess) fou m

bishopric /ˈbɪʃəprɪk/ N (= diocese) évêché m ; (= function) épiscopat m

bismuth /ˈbɪzməθ/ N bismuth m

bison /ˈbaɪsn/ N (pl inv) bison m

bisque /bɪsk/ N (Culin, Sport) bisque f ; (Pottery) biscuit m

bissextile /bɪˈsekstaɪl/ N année f bissextile ADJ bissextile

bistable /baɪˈsteɪbl/ ADJ (Comput) bistable

bistoury /ˈbɪstʊrɪ/ N bistouri m

bistre /ˈbɪstəʳ/ ADJ, N bistre m

bistro /ˈbiːstrəʊ/ N petit restaurant m (style bistrot)

bit[1] /bɪt/ N 1 [of horse] mors m ◆ **to get or take the ~ between one's teeth** (lit, fig) prendre le mors aux dents ; → **champ**[1] 2 (= tool) mèche f ; → **brace, centre**

bit[2] /bɪt/ N 1 (= piece) [of bread] morceau m ; [of paper, string] bout m ; [of book, talk etc] passage m ; (= tiny amount) peu m ◆ **a ~ of garden** un bout de jardin, un tout petit jardin ◆ **a tiny little ~** un tout petit peu ◆ **there's a ~ of the soldier in him** il y a un peu du soldat en lui ◆ **a ~ of advice** un petit conseil ◆ **a ~ of news** une nouvelle ◆ **a ~ of luck** une chance ◆ **what a ~ of luck!** quelle chance or veine !* ◆ **in ~s and pieces** (= broken) en morceaux, en miettes ; (= dismantled) en pièces détachées ; (fig) (plan, scheme) en ruines ◆ **bring all your ~s and pieces** * apporte toutes tes petites affaires ◆ **~s and bobs*** petites affaires fpl ◆ **to come to ~s** (= break) s'en aller or tomber en morceaux ; (= dismantle) se démonter ◆ **he went to ~s*** il a craqué* ◆ **~ by ~** (= gradually) petit à petit ; (= piecemeal) par morceaux ◆ **and a ~ over** et même un peu plus ◆ **to do one's ~** fournir sa part d'effort ◆ **he's got a ~ on the side**‡ il a une maîtresse ◆ **for him, I was just a ~ on the side**‡ pour lui, je n'étais qu'une aventure

2 (phrases) **a ~** un peu ◆ **a ~ of money** un peu d'argent ◆ **it is or that is a ~ much** (= expensive) c'est un peu exagéré ! ; (= unfair) c'est un peu fort* ! ◆ **a good ~ of or quite a ~ of money** pas mal d'argent ◆ **he paid a good ~ for it** ça lui a coûté assez cher (lit) ◆ **I'm a ~/a little ~/a good ~ late** je suis un peu/un petit peu/très en retard ◆ **it's a good ~ further than we thought** c'est bien or beaucoup plus loin que nous ne pensions ◆ **a good ~ bigger** bien or beaucoup plus grand ◆ **every ~ as good as** tout aussi bon que ◆ **every ~ of the wall** le mur tout entier ◆ **he's every ~ a soldier** il est militaire jusqu'à la moelle ◆ **I'm a ~ of a socialist** je suis socialiste sur les bords* ◆ **he seems to be a ~ of an expert** il a l'air de s'y connaître (pas mal) ◆ **she's a ~ of a liar** elle est un brin or un tantinet menteuse ◆ **it was a ~ of a shock** ça (nous) a plutôt fait un choc ◆ **that's a ~ of all right**‡ c'est super* or chouette* ◆ **he's/she's a ~ of all right**‡ (= attractive) il/elle est plutôt bien balancé(e)* ◆ **not a ~** pas du tout ◆ **not a ~ of it!** pas du tout !, pas le moins du monde ! ◆ **it's not a ~ of use** cela ne sert strictement or absolument à rien ◆ **he wasn't a ~ the wiser** or **the better for it** il n'en était pas plus avancé ; → **much**

3 (of time) **after a ~** après un moment ◆ **a good** or **quite a ~** un bon bout de temps* ◆ **wait a ~** attendez un instant or un peu

4 († = coin) pièce f ; → **threepenny, two**

5 (Comput) bit m

ADJ (Theat) ◆ **~ part** petit rôle m, panne* f (Theat)

COMP **bit-map** (Comput) N 1 (NonC = mode) mode point m 2 (also **bit-map(ped) image**) image f en mode point ADJ (also **bit-mapped**) [graphics] en mode point, par points ◆ **~-map font** police f en mode point or par points
bit player* N (Theat, Cine, fig) figurant(e) m(f)

bit[3] /bɪt/ VB pt of **bite**

bitch /bɪtʃ/ N 1 (dog) chienne f ; (canines generally) femelle f ; (fox) renarde f ; (wolf) louve f ◆ **terrier ~** terrier m femelle 2 (*‡pej = woman) garce‡ f ◆ **she's a ~** elle est rosse*, c'est une garce‡ 3 ‡ ◆ **that ~ of a car** cette putain de bagnole‡ ◆ **that ~ of a job** cette saloperie de boulot‡ ◆ **it's a ~** c'est la merde‡ ◆ **life's a ~ (and then you die)** chienne de vie* 4 (esp US) **what's your ~?**‡ (= complaint) qu'est-ce que tu as à râler ?* VI (* = complain) rouspéter*, râler* ◆ **to ~ about sb** dire du mal de qn

bitching‡ /ˈbɪtʃɪŋ/ ADJ (esp US) du tonnerre

bitchy* /ˈbɪtʃɪ/ ADJ rosse*, vache* ◆ **to be ~ to sb** être vache* avec qn ◆ **he was ~ about it** il a été vache* (à ce sujet) ◆ **that was a ~ thing to do** c'était (un coup) vache*

bite /baɪt/ (vb : pret **bit**, ptp **bitten**) N 1 [of dog etc] morsure f ; [of snake, insect] piqûre f ◆ **face covered in (insect) ~s** visage couvert de piqûres d'insectes ; → **bark**[2], **fleabite**

2 (= piece bitten off) bouchée f ; (= something to eat) morceau m, quelque chose (à manger) ◆ **in two ~s** en deux bouchées ◆ **chew each ~ carefully** mâchez bien chaque bouchée ◆ **to take a ~ out of** (lit) [+ apple etc] manger une bouchée de ; (esp US fig) [+ savings, budget] faire un trou dans ◆ **to get a second** or **another ~ at the cherry, to have two ~s at the cherry** avoir une seconde chance

3 * ◆ **a ~ (to eat)** un casse-graine ◆ **I'll get a ~ on the train** je mangerai un morceau dans le train ◆ **come and have a ~** venez manger un morceau

4 (Fishing) touche f ◆ **I haven't had a ~ all day** je n'ai pas eu une seule touche aujourd'hui ◆ **got a ~?*** ça a mordu ?

5 [of sauce etc] piquant m ◆ **there's a ~ in the air** l'air est piquant ◆ **his speech didn't have much ~** son discours manquait de mordant

VT [person, animal] mordre ; [snake, insect] piquer, mordre ◆ **to ~ one's nails** se ronger les ongles ◆ **to ~ sth in two** couper qch en deux d'un coup de dents ◆ **to ~ one's lips/fingers** se mordre les lèvres/les doigts ◆ **to ~ one's tongue** (lit, fig) se mordre la langue ◆ **to ~ one's tongue** or **one's lip** (fig) tenir sa langue ◆ **it won't ~ (you)!*** (hum) ça ne mord pas !* ◆ **what's biting you?**‡ qu'est-ce que tu as à râler ?* ◆ **to ~ the bullet*** serrer les dents (fig) ◆ **to ~ the dust** (lit, fig) mordre la poussière ◆ **to ~ the hand that feeds one** cracher dans la soupe* ◆ **once bitten twice shy** (Prov) chat échaudé craint l'eau froide (Prov) ◆ **to be bitten with* the desire to do sth** mourir d'envie de faire qch ◆ **to get bitten**‡ (= be cheated) se faire avoir*, se faire rouler* ; → **biter**

VI [dog] mordre ; [fish] mordre (à l'hameçon) ; [insect] piquer ; [cold, frost, wind] mordre, pincer ; [cogs] s'engrener ; [anchor, screw] mordre ◆ **to ~ into sth** [person] mordre (dans) qch ; [acid] mordre sur qch

COMP **bite-size(d)*** ADJ (lit) [piece of food] petit ; [biscuit, chocolate bar] miniature ◆ **~-size(d) cheeses** mini-fromages mpl ◆ **~-size(d) chunks** petits morceaux mpl ◆ **cut the food into ~-size(d) chunks** coupez la nourriture en petits morceaux ◆ **~-size(d) chunks of information** informations fpl brèves de lecture aisée ◆ **classical music in ~-size(d) chunks** des extraits de musique classique

► **bite back** VI (= respond) réagir, rendre la pareille VT SEP [+ words, retort] ravaler

► **bite off** VT SEP arracher d'un coup de dent(s) ◆ **she bit off a piece of apple** elle a mordu dans la pomme ◆ **he has bitten off more than he can chew** il a eu les yeux plus grands que le ventre, il a visé trop haut ◆ **to ~ sb's head off*** rembarrer qn (brutalement)

► **bite on** VT FUS mordre

► **bite through** VT FUS [+ tongue, lip] mordre (de part en part) ; [+ string, thread] couper or casser avec les dents

biter /ˈbaɪtəʳ/ N ◆ **the ~ bit** tel est pris qui croyait prendre

biting /ˈbaɪtɪŋ/ ADJ [cold] âpre, mordant ; [winter] dur, rude ; [wind] piquant, cinglant ; (fig) [style, wit, remarks] mordant, caustique ◆ **~ irony** ironie f mordante or cinglante ◆ **~ sarcasm** sarcasme m acerbe or mordant ◆ **~ insects** insectes mpl piqueurs or voraces

bitingly /ˈbaɪtɪŋlɪ/ ADV [speak] d'un ton mordant or caustique

bitten /ˈbɪtn/ VB ptp of **bite**

bitter /ˈbɪtəʳ/ ADJ 1 [taste] amer, âpre ◆ **it was a ~ pill (to swallow)** la pilule était dure à avaler 2 [cold, weather] glacial ; [wind] glacial, cinglant ; [winter] rude, rigoureux 3 [person] amer ; [critic, criticism] acerbe ; [disappointment, reproach, tears] amer ; [fate, sorrow] pénible, cruel ; [hatred] acharné, profond ; [opposition, protest] violent ; [remorse] cuisant ; [sight, look] amer, plein d'amertume ; [suffering] âpre, cruel ; [tone] amer ◆ **to the ~ end** jusqu'au bout ◆ **his ~ enemy** son ennemi acharné ◆ **he was always a ~ enemy of corruption** il a toujours été un adversaire acharné de la corruption ◆ **I feel (very) ~ about the whole business** toute cette histoire me remplit d'amertume ◆ **~ and twisted** aigri
N 1 (Brit = beer) sorte de bière brune anglaise 2 (Pharm) amer m
NPL **bitters** (= drink) bitter m, amer m ◆ **gin and ~s** cocktail m au gin et au bitter
COMP **bitter aloes** NPL aloès m (médicinal)
bitter lemon N Schweppes ® m au citron
bitter orange N orange f amère, bigarade f

bitterly /ˈbɪtəlɪ/ ADV [regret, weep] amèrement ; [say, think] avec amertume ; [criticize, denounce, *reproach]* âprement ; *[oppose, contest, fight]* farouchement ; *[ashamed]* profondément ◆ **~ disappointed** amèrement déçu ◆ **~ jealous** atrocement jaloux ◆ **to be ~ resentful of sb's success** en vouloir amèrement à qn de son succès ◆ **opinions are ~ divided** les avis sont profondément partagés ◆ **it's ~ cold** il fait un froid de canard ◆ **on a ~ cold day** par une journée glaciale

bittern /ˈbɪtɜːn/ **N** *(= bird)* butor *m*

bitterness /ˈbɪtənɪs/ **N** *(NonC: gen)* amertume *f* ; *[of opposition etc]* violence *f*

bittersweet /ˈbɪtəswiːt/ **ADJ** *(lit, fig)* aigre-doux (-douce *f*) **N** *(= plant)* douce-amère *f* ; *(fig)* amère douceur *f*

bitty * /ˈbɪtɪ/ **ADJ** *(Brit)* décousu

bitumen /ˈbɪtjʊmɪn/ **N** bitume *m*

bituminous /bɪˈtjuːmɪnəs/ **ADJ** bitumineux

bivalent /ˈbaɪˈveɪlənt/ **ADJ** bivalent

bivalve /ˈbaɪvælv/ **ADJ, N** bivalve *m*

bivouac /ˈbɪvʊæk/ **N** bivouac *m* **VI** bivouaquer

bi-weekly /ˈbaɪˈwiːklɪ/ **ADJ** *(= twice in a week)* bihebdomadaire ; *(US = fortnightly)* bimensuel **ADV** *(= twice a week)* deux fois par semaine ; *(US = fortnightly)* tous les quinze jours

biz ‡ /bɪz/ **N** (abbrev of **business**) ◆ **it's the ~** *(= great)* c'est génial → **show**

bizarre /bɪˈzɑːʳ/ **ADJ** bizarre

bk [1] abbrev of **book** [2] abbrev of **bank**

BL /biːˈel/ [1] (abbrev of **British Library**) → **British** [2] (abbrev of **Bachelor of Law**) → **bachelor** [3] (abbrev of **bill of lading**) → **bill¹**

blab /blæb/ **VI** [1] *(= tell secret)* manger le morceau ‡ [2] *(= chatter)* jaser **VT** (also **blab out**) *[+ secret]* laisser échapper, aller raconter

blabber * /ˈblæbəʳ/ **VI** (also **blabber on**) ⇒ **blab vi 1**

blabbermouth * /ˈblæbə,maʊθ/ **N** *(pej)* grande bouche * *f*, grande gueule ‡ *f*

black /blæk/ **ADJ** [1] *[hair, clouds, smoke etc]* noir ◆ **eyes as ~ as sloes** des yeux noirs comme (du) jais, des yeux de jais ◆ **~ and blue** *(fig)* couvert de bleus ◆ **to beat sb ~ and blue** battre qn comme plâtre, rouer qn de coups ◆ **~ gold** *(= oil)* l'or *m* noir ◆ **"black tie"** *(on invitation)* "tenue de soirée exigée" ◆ **you can scream till you're ~ in the face but …** tu peux toujours t'égosiller *or* t'époumoner mais … ; see also **comp, belt, coal, jet², pitch², pot¹**

[2] (also **Black**) *[person, race, skin]* noir ; *[music, culture]* noir, black * ; *[art]* nègre ◆ **you never see a ~ face around here** on ne voit jamais de Noirs par ici ◆ **~ man** Noir *m* ◆ **~ woman** Noire *f* ◆ **~ people** les Noirs *mpl* ◆ **the Black community/population** la communauté/population noire ◆ **Black American** Noir(e) *m(f)* américain(e) ◆ **Black America** l'Amérique *f* noire ◆ **~ college** *(US Univ)* université *f* noire ◆ **~ consciousness** identité *f* noire ◆ **~ consciousness movement** mouvement *m* de revendication de l'identité noire ◆ **Black English** l'anglais *m* des Noirs américains ◆ **Black Nationalism** *(US)* mouvement *m* nationaliste noir ◆ **Black Studies** études *fpl* afro-américaines ◆ **Black Madonna** Madone *f* noire ; see also **comp**

[3] *(= dark)* noir ◆ **the sky was ~ with birds** le ciel était noir d'oiseaux ; ⇒ **pitch**

[4] *(= dirty)* noir ◆ **his hands were ~** il avait les mains noires ◆ **he was as ~ as a sweep** il était noir de la tête aux pieds ◆ **their faces were ~ with coal-dust** leurs visages étaient noircis par le charbon

[5] *(without milk) [coffee]* noir ; *[tea]* nature ◆ **to take** *or* **drink one's coffee/tea ~** boire son café/thé sans lait, ne pas mettre de lait dans son café/thé

[6] *(liter) (= wicked) [crime, action]* noir ; *[thought]* mauvais ◆ **a ~ deed** un crime, un forfait *(liter)* ◆ **he painted their conduct in the ~est colours** il a présenté leur conduite sous les couleurs les plus noires ◆ **he's not as ~ as he's painted** il n'est pas aussi mauvais qu'on le dit

[7] *(= gloomy) [thoughts, prospects]* noir ; *[grief]* intense, violent ; *[rage]* noir ; *[despair]* sombre ◆ **things are looking ~** les choses se présentent très mal ◆ **it's a ~ outlook** *or* **things are looking ~ for him** ses affaires se présentent très mal ◆ **a ~ day on the roads** une sombre journée sur les routes ◆ **it's a ~ day for England** c'est un jour (bien) triste pour l'Angleterre ; *(stronger)* c'est un jour de deuil pour l'Angleterre

[8] *(angry)* ◆ **to give sb a ~ look** lancer un regard noir à qn ◆ **I got some ~ looks from John** j'ai eu des regards noirs de la part de John, John m'a lancé des regards noirs ◆ **his face was as ~ as thunder, he looked as ~ as thunder** il avait l'air furibond

N [1] *(= colour)* noir *m*, couleur *f* noire ; *(mourning)* noir *m*, deuil *m* ◆ **dressed in ~** habillé de noir ◆ **to wear ~ for sb** porter le deuil de qn ◆ **there it is in ~ and white** c'est écrit noir sur blanc ◆ **~ and white** *(Art)* dessin *m* en noir et blanc ◆ **to swear that ~ is white** *(fig) (obstinate person)* se refuser à l'évidence, nier l'évidence ; *(liar)* mentir effrontément ◆ **to be in the ~** * *(Fin)* être créditeur ◆ **to get (back) into the ~** ne plus être à découvert ; → **lampblack**

[2] *(Snooker, Billiards)* boule *f* noire

[3] *(= person)* Noir(e) *m(f)*, Black * *mf*

[4] *(= darkness)* ténèbres *fpl*, obscurité *f* ; *(outdoors only)* nuit *f* noire

VT [1] *(= blacken)* noircir ; *[+ shoes]* cirer ◆ **to ~ one's face** se noircir le visage ◆ **to ~ sb's eye (for him)** pocher l'œil à qn

[2] *(Brit) [+ cargo, firm, goods]* boycotter

COMP **Black Africa N** Afrique *f* Noire

black art(s) N(PL) magie *f* noire, sciences *fpl* occultes

black-ball N vote *m* contre **VT** blackbouler

black bass N achigan *m*

black beetle N cafard *m*, cancrelat *m*

black books NPL ◆ **she was in his ~ books** elle n'était pas dans ses petits papiers *, elle était mal vue (de lui)

black box (recorder) N *(in plane)* boîte *f* noire ; *(= mysterious device)* boîte *f* noire

black cab N *(Brit)* taxi *m* anglais

black cap N *(= bird)* fauvette *f* à tête noire ; *(Brit Jur Hist)* bonnet *m* noir *(que mettait un juge avant de prononcer la peine de mort)*

black comedy N comédie *f* noire

Black Country N Pays *m* noir *(région industrielle des Midlands)*

Black Death N *(Hist)* peste *f* noire

black economy N économie *f* parallèle *or* souterraine

black eye N œil *m* poché *or* au beurre noir * ◆ **to give sb a ~ eye** pocher l'œil à qn

Black Forest N Forêt-Noire *f*

Black Forest gateau N forêt-noire *f*

Black Friar N frère *m* prêcheur, dominicain *m*

black frost N gel *m*

black goods N *(= boycotted)* marchandises *fpl* boycottées

black grouse N tétras-lyre *m*, coq *m* de bruyère

black-headed gull N mouette *f* rieuse

black-hearted ADJ mauvais, malfaisant

black hole N *(Astron, also fig)* trou *m* noir ◆ **the Black Hole of Calcutta** *(Brit Hist)* le cachot de Calcutta

black humour N humour *m* noir

black ice N verglas *m*

black knight N *(Comm)* chevalier *m* noir

black magic N magie *f* noire

Black Maria * **N** *(Brit)* panier *m* à salade *

black mark N *(fig)* ◆ **that gets a ~ mark** c'est zéro * ◆ **that's a ~ mark for** *or* **against him** c'est un mauvais point pour lui

black market N marché *m* noir ◆ **on the ~ market** au marché noir

black marketeer N profiteur *m*, -euse *f (vendant au marché noir)*

black mass N messe *f* noire

Black Muslim N Musulman(e) noir(e) *m(f)*, Black Muslim *mf*

black nightshade N *(= plant)* morelle *f* noire

Black Panthers NPL *(Hist)* Panthères *fpl* noires

Black Papers NPL *(Brit Scol) livres blancs sur le système éducatif*

black pepper N poivre *m* noir

Black Power (movement) N Black Power *m*, pouvoir *m* noir

the Black Prince N *(Brit Hist)* le Prince Noir

black pudding N *(Brit)* boudin *m* noir

Black Rod N *(Brit Parl) fonctionnaire rattaché à la Chambre des lords, chargé de convoquer les Communes lors de l'ouverture de la session parlementaire*

the Black Sea N la mer Noire

Black September N *(Pol)* Septembre *m* noir

black sheep N ◆ **the ~ sheep of the family** la brebis galeuse (de la famille)

black spot N (also **accident black spot** : *Brit*) point *m* noir

black-tie ADJ *[dinner, function]* habillé, en smoking ; see also **adj a**

black velvet N *cocktail de champagne et de stout*

Black Watch N *(Brit Mil)* Black Watch *mpl (régiment écossais)*

black widow (spider) N veuve *f* noire

► **black out VI** *(= faint)* s'évanouir

VT SEP [1] *(in wartime) [+ town, building]* faire le black-out dans ◆ **a power cut ~ed out the building** *(in peacetime)* une panne d'électricité a plongé l'immeuble dans l'obscurité (totale) ◆ **to ~ out the stage** *(Theat)* faire l'obscurité *or* le noir sur scène

[2] *(= censor)* censurer

blackamoor †† /ˈblækəmʊəʳ/ **N** nègre † *m*

blackberry /ˈblækbərɪ/ **N** mûre *f* ◆ **~ bush** mûrier *m*, ronce *f*

blackberrying /ˈblækbərɪɪŋ/ **N** ◆ **to go ~** aller cueillir des mûres

blackbird /ˈblækbɜːd/ **N** merle *m*

blackboard /ˈblækbɔːd/ **N** tableau *m* (noir) ◆ **~ duster** chiffon *m* ◆ **the ~ jungle** la loi de la jungle (dans les classes) ◆ **~ rubber** frottoir *m*

blackcock /ˈblækkɒk/ **N** *(= male black grouse)* tétras-lyre *m*, coq *m* de bruyère

blackcurrant /ˌblækˈkʌrənt/ **N** *(= fruit, bush)* cassis *m*

blacken /ˈblækən/ **VT** [1] *(with dirt, soot, dust)* noircir, salir ◆ **his hands were ~ed with filth** il avait les mains noires de crasse [2] *(with paint, cosmetics etc)* noircir, barbouiller de noir [3] *(with smoke, by fire)* noircir ◆ **~ed remains** restes *mpl* calcinés [4] *(fig = discredit)* salir, noircir, ternir **VI** *[sky]* noircir, s'assombrir ; *[furniture]* noircir, devenir noir

blackened /ˈblækənd/ **ADJ** *(US Culin)* noirci au gril

blackfly /ˈblækflaɪ/ **N** puceron *m* noir

blackguard † /ˈblægɑːd/ **N** canaille *f*, fripouille *f*

blackguardly † /ˈblægɑːdlɪ/ **ADJ** *[deed, person]* infâme, ignoble

blackhead /ˈblækhed/ **N** *(Med)* point *m* noir

blacking /ˈblækɪŋ/ **N** [1] *[of shoes]* cirage *m* (noir) ; *[of stoves]* pâte *f* à noircir [2] *[of goods, cargo]* boycottage *m*

blackish /ˈblækɪʃ/ **ADJ** tirant sur le noir, noirâtre *(pej)*

blackjack /ˈblækdʒæk/ **N** *(= flag)* pavillon *m* noir *(des pirates)* ; *(= drinking vessel)* pichet *m* ; *(Min)* blende *f* ; *(US = weapon)* matraque *f* ; *(Cards)* black-jack *m* ≃ vingt-et-un *m* **VT**

(= beat) matraquer ; *(= coerce)* contraindre sous la menace *(sb into doing sth* qn à faire qch*)*

blacklead /ˈblækled/ **N** mine *f* de plomb, graphite *m* **VT** *[+ stove]* frotter à la mine de plomb

blackleg /ˈblækleg/ *(Brit)* **N** jaune *m*, briseur *m* de grève **VI** briser la grève

blacklist /ˈblæklɪst/ **N** liste *f* noire **VT** *[+ person]* mettre sur la liste noire ; *[+ book]* mettre à l'index *(lit, fig)*

blackmail /ˈblækmeɪl/ **N** chantage *m* ◆ **emotional ~** chantage *m* affectif **VT** faire chanter, faire du chantage auprès de ◆ **to ~ sb into doing sth** forcer qn par le chantage à faire qch

blackmailer /ˈblækmeɪləʳ/ **N** maître-chanteur *m*

blackness /ˈblæknɪs/ **N** *[of colour, substance]* couleur *f* or teinte *f* noire, noir *m* ; *[of night]* obscurité *f*, ténèbres *fpl* ; *[of hands, face]* saleté *f*, crasse *f*

blackout /ˈblækaʊt/ **N** 1 *(= amnesia)* trou *m* de mémoire ; *(= fainting)* étourdissement *m*, évanouissement *m* ◆ **to have a ~** avoir une absence 2 *(= power cut)* panne *f* d'électricité 3 *(Theat)* obscurcissement *m* de la scène ; *(during war)* black-out *m* ; → **news**

blackshirt /ˈblækʃɜːt/ **N** *(Pol)* chemise *f* noire

blacksmith /ˈblæksmɪθ/ **N** *(shoes horses)* maréchal-ferrant *m* ; *(forges iron)* forgeron *m*

blackthorn /ˈblækθɔːn/ **N** épine *f* noire, prunellier *m*

blacktop /ˈblæktɒp/ **N** *(US)* bitume *m*

blackwater fever /ˌblækwɔːtəˈfiːvəʳ/ **N** fièvre *f* bilieuse hémoglobinurique

bladder /ˈblædəʳ/ **N** *(Anat)* vessie *f* ; *(Bot)* vésicule *f* ; *(Ftbl etc)* vessie *f (de ballon)* ; → **gall¹** **COMP** **bladder kelp, bladder wrack N** fucus *m* vésiculeux

bladderwort /ˈblædəwɜːt/ **N** utriculaire *f*

blade /bleɪd/ **N** 1 *[of knife, tool, weapon, razor]* lame *f* ; *[of chopper, guillotine]* couperet *m* ; *[of tongue]* dos *m* ; *[of oar]* plat *m*, pale *f* ; *[of spade]* fer *m* ; *[of turbine]* aube *f* ; *[of propeller]* pale *f*, aile *f* ; *[of windscreen wiper]* caoutchouc *m*, balai *m* ; *[of grass, mace]* brin *m* ; *[of cereal]* pousse *f* ; *[of leaf]* limbe *m* ◆ **wheat in the ~** blé *m* en herbe ; → **shoulder** 2 *(liter = sword)* lame *f* 3 († *= gallant)* gaillard *m* ◆ **a gay ~** un joyeux luron

-bladed /ˈbleɪdɪd/ **ADJ** *(in compounds)* ◆ **two-bladed knife** canif *m* à deux lames

blaeberry /ˈbleɪbərɪ/ **N** *(Brit)* myrtille *f*

blag* /blæg/ **VT** *(Brit)* *[+ ticket]* obtenir à l'esbroufe* *(out of or off sb* de qn*)* ; ◆ **he ~ged his way into the nightclub** il est entré dans la boîte de nuit à l'esbroufe*

blah* /blɑː/ **N** boniment *m*, blablabla* *m* ◆ **~, ~, ~** bla, bla, bla* ◆ **the ~s** *(US)* le cafard* **ADJ** *(US)* barbant*, peu attrayant

Blairite /ˈblɛəraɪt/ **N, ADJ** *(Brit Pol)* blairiste *mf*

blamable /ˈbleɪməbl/ **ADJ** blâmable

blame /bleɪm/ **VT** 1 *(= fix responsibility on)* ◆ **to ~ sb for sth, to ~ sth on sb*** rejeter la responsabilité de qch sur qn, mettre qch sur le dos de qn* ◆ **I'm not to ~** ce n'est pas ma faute ◆ **you have only yourself to ~, you have no one but yourself to ~** tu ne peux t'en prendre qu'à toi-même, tu l'auras cherché ◆ **I ~ the parents** à mon avis c'est la faute des parents, je tiens les parents pour responsables ◆ **politicians get ~d or get the ~ for everything** les hommes politiques sont tenus pour responsables de tout ◆ **she ~s her job for destroying her marriage** elle dit que c'est son travail qui a brisé son mariage ◆ **who/what is to ~** or **whom/what are we to ~ for this accident?** à qui/à quoi attribuer cet accident ? ◆ **faulty brakes were to ~** *(= deserve the blame)* cela était dû à un mauvais fonctionnement des freins ◆ **faulty brakes were ~d** *(= received the blame)* on a mis en cause le mauvais fonctionnement des freins ; → **workman**

2 *(= censure)* condamner, blâmer ◆ **to ~ sb for doing sth** reprocher à qn de faire qch ◆ **to ~ sb for sth** reprocher qch à qn ◆ **it's no use blaming your subordinates for everything** ça ne sert à rien de tenir ses subordonnés pour responsables de tous les problèmes or de tout imputer à ses subordonnés ◆ **to ~ o.s. for sth/for having done sth** se reprocher qch/d'avoir fait qch ◆ **he was greatly to ~ for doing that** il a eu grand tort de faire cela ◆ **don't ~ me if you can't keep up with your workload!** ce n'est pas ma faute si tu ne t'en sors pas avec ton travail ! ◆ **you can't ~ him for wanting to leave** vous ne pouvez lui reprocher de vouloir s'en aller ◆ **he's leaving, and you can't ~ him!** il part, et on ne peut pas lui en vouloir or on le comprend ! ◆ **you look angry – can you ~ me?** tu as l'air en colère – ça t'étonne ?

N 1 *(= responsibility)* faute *f*, responsabilité *f* ◆ **to put** or **lay** or **place** or **throw the ~ for sth on sb** rejeter la responsabilité de qch sur qn ◆ **to bear** or **take the ~ (for sth)** supporter la responsabilité (de qch)

2 *(= censure)* blâme *m*, reproches *mpl* ◆ **without ~** exempt de blâme, irréprochable

blameless /ˈbleɪmlɪs/ **ADJ** irréprochable

blamelessly /ˈbleɪmlɪslɪ/ **ADV** *[behave, live]* de façon irréprochable

blameworthy /ˈbleɪmwɜːðɪ/ **ADJ** *[action]* répréhensible ; *[person]* blâmable

blanch /blɑːntʃ/ **VT** *(gen, Agr, Culin)* blanchir ◆ **~ed almonds** amandes *fpl* (é)mondées or épluchées **VI** *[person]* blêmir

blancmange /bləˈmɒnʒ/ **N** *(esp Brit)* blanc-manger *m*

bland /blænd/ **ADJ** *[taste, food]* fade ; *[book, film]* fade, terne ; *[person, character]* terne, falot ; *[smile, expression]* terne

blandish /ˈblændɪʃ/ **VT** flatter, cajoler

blandishment /ˈblændɪʃmənt/ **N** *(gen pl)* flatterie(s) *f(pl)*

blandly /ˈblændlɪ/ **ADV** *[say, reply]* platement ; *[smile]* mollement

blank /blæŋk/ **ADJ** 1 *[paper]* blanc (blanche *f*) ; *[page]* blanc (blanche *f*), vierge ; *[map]* muet ; *[cheque]* en blanc ◆ **to give sb a ~ cheque (to do sth)** *(fig)* donner à qn carte blanche (pour faire qch) ◆ **~ cartridge** cartouche *f* à blanc ◆ **~ space** blanc *m*, (espace *m*) vide *m* ◆ **~ form** formulaire *m*, imprimé *m* (à remplir) ◆ **please leave ~** *(on form)* laisser en blanc s.v.p.

2 *(= unrelieved)* *[wall]* aveugle ; *[silence, darkness]* profond ; *[refusal, denial]* absolu, net ; *(= empty)* *[life etc]* dépourvu d'intérêt, vide ; *(= expressionless)* *[face]* sans expression ; *[look]* sans expression, vide ; *(= puzzled)* déconcerté, dérouté ◆ **to look ~** *(= expressionless)* être sans expression ; *(= puzzled)* avoir l'air interdit ◆ **a look of ~ astonishment** un regard ébahi ◆ **his mind went ~** il a eu un blanc

3 *(Poetry)* ◆ **~ verse** vers *mpl* blancs or non rimés

N 1 *(= void)* blanc *m*, (espace *m*) vide *m* ; *(fig = gap)* lacune *f*, trou *m* ◆ **she left several ~s in her answers** elle a laissé plusieurs de ses réponses en blanc ◆ **your departure has left a ~** votre départ a laissé un vide ◆ **my mind was a ~** j'avais la tête vide, j'ai eu un blanc

2 *(= form)* formulaire *m* ◆ **telegraph ~** formule *f* de télégramme

3 *[of target]* but *m* ; *(Dominoes)* blanc *m* ; *[of coin, medal, record]* flan *m* ; *[of key]* ébauche *f* ; *(= cartridge)* cartouche *f* à blanc ◆ **to draw a ~** *(fig)* *(= fail in search etc)* échouer, faire chou blanc ; *(mentally)* avoir un trou ◆ **double ~** *(Dominoes)* double blanc *m*

VT * *[+ person]* snober

► **blank out VT SEP** *[+ feeling, thought]* faire abstraction de

blanket /ˈblæŋkɪt/ **N** couverture *f* ; *[of snow etc]* couche *f* ; *[of fog]* manteau *m*, nappe *f* ; *[of smoke]* nuage *m* ◆ **born on the wrong side of the ~** † illégitime, adultérin † ; → **electric, wet** **ADJ** *[ban, condemnation]* général ; *[bombing]* intensif ; *[coverage]* complet (-ète *f*) **VT** 1 *[snow]* recouvrir ; *[fog, smoke]* recouvrir, envelopper 2 *[+ sounds]* étouffer, assourdir 3 *(Naut)* déventer

COMP **blanket bath N** toilette *f (de malade alité)* ◆ **to give sb a ~ bath** faire la toilette de qn dans son lit

blanket cover N ◆ **this insurance policy gives ~ cover** cette police d'assurances couvre tous les risques or est tous risques

blanket finish N arrivée *f* très serrée or dans un mouchoir

blanket stitch N point *m* de feston

blanket-stitch VTI border au point de feston

► **blanket out VT** noyer

blankety-blank* /ˈblæŋkɪtɪˈblæŋk/ **ADJ** *(euph)* ⇒ **blinking adj**

blankly /ˈblæŋklɪ/ **ADV** 1 *(= expressionlessly)* ◆ **to look** or **stare ~ at sb/sth** fixer qn/qch le regard vide or d'un air absent 2 *(= uncomprehendingly)* *[look at, stare at, say]* d'un air ébahi

blankness /ˈblæŋknɪs/ **N** *(NonC: in eyes, face)* air *m* mort, absence *f* d'expression ; *[of life]* vide *m*

blare /blɛəʳ/ **N** *(gen)* vacarme *m* ; *[of hooter, car horn]* bruit *m* strident ; *[of radio, music]* beuglement *m* ; *[of trumpet]* sonnerie *f* **VI** (also **blare out**) *[music, horn etc]* retentir ; *[loud voice]* trompeter, claironner ; *[radio]* beugler **VT** (also **blare out**) *[+ music]* faire retentir

blarney* /ˈblɑːnɪ/ **N** boniment* *m*, bobards* *mpl* ◆ **he's kissed the Blarney stone** c'est un beau parleur **VT** *[+ person]* enjôler, embobeliner* **VI** manier la flatterie

blasé /ˈblɑːzeɪ/ **ADJ** blasé *(about* de*)* ; ◆ **he's acting ~** il joue les blasés

blaspheme /blæsˈfiːm/ **VTI** blasphémer *(against* contre*)*

blasphemer /blæsˈfiːməʳ/ **N** blasphémateur *m*, -trice *f*

blasphemous /ˈblæsfɪməs/ **ADJ** *[person]* blasphémateur (-trice *f*) ; *[words]* blasphématoire

blasphemously /ˈblæsfɪməslɪ/ **ADV** de façon blasphématoire

blasphemy /ˈblæsfɪmɪ/ **N** blasphème *m* ◆ **to utter ~** blasphémer ◆ **it is ~ to say that** c'est blasphémer que de dire cela

blast /blɑːst/ **N** 1 *(= sound)* *[of bomb]* explosion *f* ; *[of space rocket]* grondement *m*, rugissement *m* ; *[of trumpets etc]* fanfare *f*, sonnerie *f* ; *[of whistle, car horn]* coup *m* strident ◆ **a ~ on the siren** un coup de sirène ◆ **to blow a ~ on the bugle** donner un coup de clairon ◆ **hearing those old records was a ~ from the past** * entendre ces vieux disques nous ramenait des années en arrière ◆ **a letter from Paul! what a ~ from the past!** * une lettre de Paul ! ça me ramène des années en arrière !

◆ **at full blast** ◆ **a radio on at full ~*** une radio à plein(s) tube(s)* ◆ **the heating was on at full ~*** le chauffage était au maximum

2 *(= explosion)* explosion *f* ; *(= shock wave)* *[of bomb etc]* souffle *m* ; *(= gust)* *[of furnace]* souffle *m* (d'air chaud) ◆ **~ victims** victimes *fpl* de l'explosion ◆ **~ of air/steam** jet *m* d'air/de vapeur ◆ **~ of wind** coup *m* de vent, rafale *f*

3 *(liter = wind)* → **icy**

4 *(* = fun)* fête *f*, foire *f* ◆ **to have a ~** faire la foire ◆ **it was a ~** ça a été le pied* ◆ **to get a ~ out of sth** trouver qch marrant*

VT 1 *[lightning] [+ tree]* foudroyer ; *(with explosive) [+ rocks]* faire sauter ; *(= blight) [+ plant]* détruire ; *(fig) [+ reputation, hopes, future]* anéantir, briser ; *(verbally)* attaquer à boulets rouges *or* violemment

2 *(= shoot)* ◆ **he ~ed the policeman with a shotgun** il a tiré sur le policier avec un fusil de chasse

3 *(* = criticize)* éreinter ◆ **"it's a disgrace!" he ~ed** "c'est une honte !" fulmina-t-il

4 *(= shoot out) [+ air, water]* souffler

EXCL *(Brit *)* la barbe ! * ◆ ~ **him!** il est embêtant *or* empoisonnant ! *

COMP **blast effect** **N** effet *m* de souffle

blast furnace **N** haut fourneau *m*

blast-off **N** *(Space)* lancement *m*, mise *f* à feu

► **blast away** **VI** *[music, band]* brailler ; *[gun]* retentir ◆ **to ~ away with a rifle/shotgun** *etc* tirer continuellement avec un fusil/fusil de chasse, *etc*

► **blast off** **VI** *[rocket etc]* être mis à feu ; *(US fig ‡)* partir

N ◆ **blast-off** → **blast**

► **blast out** **VI** *[music, radio]* brailler

VT SEP *[+ song, tune]* brailler

blasted /ˈblɑːstɪd/ **ADJ** 1 *[heath]* désolé, desséché ; *[tree]* foudroyé, frappé par la foudre ; *(fig) [hopes]* anéanti 2 *(‡ = annoying)* fichu * *before n* ◆ **he's a ~ nuisance** c'est un enquiquineur *, il nous enquiquine *

blasting /ˈblɑːstɪŋ/ **N** *(in mine, quarry)* minage *m* ◆ **"blasting in progress"** "attention, tir de mines" ◆ **to give sb a ~ for sth/for having done sth** attaquer violemment qn pour qch/pour avoir fait qch

blastoderm /ˈblæstəʊdɜːm/ **N** blastoderme *m*

blatancy /ˈbleɪtənsɪ/ **N** *(= flagrance)* caractère *m* flagrant, évidence *f* ; *(= showiness)* aspect *m* criard *or* voyant

blatant /ˈbleɪtənt/ **ADJ** *[injustice, lie etc]* criant, flagrant ; *[bully, social climber]* éhonté ; *[coward, thief]* fieffé ◆ **a ~ liar** un menteur éhonté, un fieffé menteur

blatantly /ˈbleɪtəntlɪ/ **ADV** *[false, untrue, unfair]* manifestement ; *[sexist, prejudiced]* ouvertement ; *[disregard, encourage]* de façon éhontée ◆ **it's ~ obvious that ...** il n'est que trop évident que ..., il est manifeste que ...

blather * /ˈblæðəʳ/ **VI** raconter *or* débiter des bêtises, parler à tort et à travers ; *(Scot * = chat)* bavarder **N** 1 *(NonC)* bêtises *fpl*, blabla * *m* ; *(Scot * = chat)* causette *f* ◆ **to have a ~** * *(Scot)* bavarder, causer 2 *(= person)* **she's a ~** * elle dit n'importe quoi, elle dit tout ce qui lui passe par la tête

blatherskite ‡ /ˈblæðəskaɪt/ **N** *(= chatterbox)* moulin *m* à paroles ; *(NonC US = nonsense)* bêtises *fpl*

blaze¹ /bleɪz/ **N** 1 *(= cheering fire)* (belle) flambée *f* ; *(= conflagration)* incendie *m* ; *(= light from fire)* lueur *f* des flammes *or* du brasier ◆ **forest ~** incendie *m* de forêt ◆ **all in a ~** en flammes

2 *(= shine) [of gems, beauty etc]* éclat *m*, splendeur *f* ◆ **~ of day** éclat *m* du jour ◆ **~ of light** torrent *m* de lumière ◆ **~ of colour** flamboiement *m* de couleur(s) ◆ **in a ~ of glory** auréolé de gloire

3 *(= outburst) [of rage, passion etc]* explosion *f*, flambée *f* ◆ **in a ~ of anger he killed her** dans le feu de la colère *or* dans une explosion de colère il l'a tuée

NPL **blazes** ‡ ◆ **go to ~s!** va te faire voir ! * ◆ **what the ~s!** qu'est-ce que ça peut bien fiche ! * ◆ **how the ~s!** comment diable ! ◆ **what the ~s have you done now?** qu'est-ce que tu as encore fichu ? * ◆ **like ~s** comme un fou *or* dingue *, furieusement ◆ **he ran like ~s** il a filé comme un zèbre ◆ **he worked like ~s** il a travaillé comme une brute *or* un dingue *

VI 1 *[fire]* flamber ; *[sun]* flamboyer, darder ses rayons

2 *[colour]* flamboyer ; *[jewel, light]* resplendir, jeter un vif éclat ; *[anger]* éclater ; *(fig)* resplendir *(with* de*)* ; ◆ **a garden blazing with colour** un jardin resplendissant de couleurs

► **blaze abroad** **VT SEP** *(liter) [+ news etc]* crier sur tous les toits

► **blaze away** **VI** *[fire etc]* flamber (toujours) ; *[soldiers, guns]* maintenir un feu nourri *(at* contre*)*

► **blaze down** **VI** *[sun]* flamboyer, darder ses rayons

► **blaze forth** **VI** *(liter) [sun]* apparaître soudain (dans tout son éclat) ; *[anger]* éclater

► **blaze out** **VI** *[sun]* apparaître soudain ; *[light]* ruisseler ; *[anger, hatred]* éclater

► **blaze up** **VI** *[fire]* s'enflammer, s'embraser *(liter)* ; *(fig) [person]* éclater, s'emporter ; *[anger]* éclater

blaze² /bleɪz/ **N** *(= mark) [of horse etc]* étoile *f* ; *[of tree]* encoche *f* **VT** *[+ tree]* faire une encoche à ◆ **to ~ a trail** *(lit)* frayer un *or* le chemin ; *(fig)* montrer la voie, faire un travail de pionnier

blazer /ˈbleɪzəʳ/ **N** blazer *m*

blazing /ˈbleɪzɪŋ/ **ADJ** 1 *[building etc]* en feu, en flammes ; *[torch]* enflammé ; *[sun]* éclatant, ardent ; *(fig) [eyes]* flamboyant, qui jette des éclairs ; *[jewel]* étincelant ; *[colour]* très vif 2 * *(= angry)* furibond, furibard *

blazon /ˈbleɪzn/ **N** *(Heraldry)* blason *m* **VT** *(Her)* blasonner ; *(fig:* also **blazon abroad, blazon forth***) [+ virtues, story]* proclamer, claironner

bldg abbrev of **building**

bleach /bliːtʃ/ **N** décolorant *m* ; *(= liquid)* eau *f* oxygénée ◆ **(household) ~** eau *f* de Javel **VT** 1 *[sun, bleach etc] [+ linen, bones, etc]* blanchir ◆ **~ing agent** produit *m* à blanchir, décolorant *m* ◆ **~ing powder** (chlorure *m*) décolorant *m* 2 *[+ hair]* décolorer, oxygéner ; *[+ jeans]* délaver ; *[+ flour]* raffiner ; *[+ paper]* blanchir ◆ **to ~ one's hair** se décolorer *or* s'oxygéner les cheveux ◆ **~ed hair** cheveux *mpl* décolorés *or* oxygénés 3 *(Phot) [+ image]* blanchir **VI** blanchir

► **bleach out** **VT SEP** *[+ colour]* enlever

bleachers /ˈbliːtʃəz/ **N** *(US)* gradins *mpl (de stade en plein soleil)*

bleak¹ /bliːk/ **N** *(= fish)* ablette *f*

bleak² /bliːk/ **ADJ** *[country, landscape]* morne, désolé ; *[room]* nu, austère ; *[weather, wind]* froid, glacial ; *(fig) [existence]* sombre, désolé ; *[prospect]* triste, morne ; *[smile]* pâle ; *[voice, tone]* monocorde, morne ◆ **it looks** *or* **things look rather ~ for him** les choses se présentent plutôt mal pour lui

bleakly /ˈbliːklɪ/ **ADV** *[look]* d'un air désolé, sombrement ; *[speak]* d'un ton morne, sombrement

bleakness /ˈbliːknɪs/ **N** *[of landscape]* aspect *m* morne *or* désolé ; *[of room, furnishings]* austérité *f* ; *[of weather]* froid *m*, rigueurs *fpl* ; *[of prospects, future]* aspect *m* sombre *or* décourageant

blearily /ˈblɪərɪlɪ/ **ADV** *[look]* avec un regard trouble

bleary /ˈblɪərɪ/ **ADJ** 1 *[eyes] (from sleep, fatigue)* trouble, voilé ; *(from illness)* chassieux ; *(from tears, wind etc)* larmoyant ◆ **~-eyed** aux yeux troubles *or* chassieux *or* larmoyants 2 *[outline]* indécis, vague

bleat /bliːt/ **VI** 1 *[sheep]* bêler ; *[goat]* bêler, chevroter 2 *[person, voice]* bêler, chevroter ; *(* = talk nonsense)* débiter des idioties, débloquer ‡ ; *(‡ = complain)* se plaindre *(about* de*)* ; ◆ **what are you ~ing about?** ‡ qu'est-ce que tu as à te lamenter ? **VT** (also **bleat out**) dire d'une voix bêlante, chevroter **N** *[of sheep]* bêlement *m* ; *[of voice, goat]* bêlement *m*, chevrotement *m*

bleb /bleb/ **N** *[of skin]* cloque *f*, ampoule *f* ; *[of glass, water]* bulle *f*

bled /bled/ **VB** pt, ptp of **bleed**

bleed /bliːd/ (pret, ptp **bled**) **VI** 1 saigner, perdre du sang ◆ **his nose is ~ing** il saigne du nez ◆ **the wound bled profusely** la plaie saignait copieusement ◆ **his heart is ~ing** *(liter)* son cœur saigne ◆ **my heart ~s for you** *(gen iro)* tu me fends le cœur *(iro)*, tu vas me faire pleurer *(iro)* ; → **death** 2 *[plant]* pleurer, perdre sa sève **VT** 1 *(Med) [+ person]* saigner, faire une saignée à ; *[+ brakes, radiator]* purger 2 *(* fig = get money from)* tirer de l'argent à, faire casquer ‡ ◆ **to ~ sb dry** *or* **white** saigner qn à blanc **N** saignement *m* ; → **nosebleed**

bleeder /ˈbliːdəʳ/ **N** 1 *(Med * = haemophiliac)* hémophile *mf* 2 *(Brit ‡)* gars * *m* ◆ **poor ~!** le pauvre gars ! * ◆ **lucky ~!** veinard ! *

bleeding /ˈbliːdɪŋ/ **N** 1 *(= taking blood from)* saignée *f* ; *(= losing blood)* saignement *m* ; *(more serious)* hémorragie *f* ◆ **~ from the nose** saignement *m* de nez ◆ **to stop the ~** arrêter l'hémorragie 2 *[of plant]* écoulement *m* de sève **ADJ** 1 *[wound]* saignant ; *[person]* qui saigne, ensanglanté ◆ **~ heart** *(pej = person)* âme *f* sensible ◆ **~-heart Liberal** *(fig, pej)* libéral(e) *m(f)* trop sentimental(e) 2 *(Brit ‡ = bloody)* maudit *before n* ◆ **that ~ car** cette maudite voiture **ADV** *(Brit ‡ = bloody)* vachement ‡, fichtrement ‡

bleep /bliːp/ **N** 1 *(Rad, TV = noise)* top *m* 2 *(* = pager)* bip *m* **VI** *[transmitter]* émettre des signaux **VT** *(using pager)* biper

bleeper /ˈbliːpəʳ/ **N** *(= pager)* bip *m*

blemish /ˈblemɪʃ/ **N** *(= defect)* défaut *m*, imperfection *f* ; *(on fruit)* tache *f* ; *(fig) (moral)* souillure *f (liter)*, tare *f* ; *(inborn)* défaut *m* ◆ **there's a ~ in this cup** cette tasse a un défaut ◆ **to find a ~ in sth** *(fig)* trouver à redire à qch ◆ **a ~ on his reputation** une tache *or* une souillure *(liter)* à sa réputation ◆ **without (a) ~** *(lit)* sans imperfection ; *(fig)* sans tache, sans souillure *(liter)* **VT** *[+ beauty etc]* gâter ; *[+ reputation, honour]* ternir, flétrir

blemished /ˈblemɪʃt/ **ADJ** *[+ fruit]* talé, meurtri, abîmé ; *[+ skin]* abîmé

blench /blentʃ/ **VI** 1 *(= flinch)* sursauter ◆ **without ~ing** sans sourciller, sans broncher 2 *(= turn pale)* pâlir *or* blêmir (de peur)

blend /blend/ **N** *(= mixture) [of tea, whisky, wine etc]* mélange *m* ; *[of colours, styles]* mariage *m* ; *[of cultures]* fusion *f* ; *[of qualities]* ensemble *m* ◆ **an excellent ~ of tea** un excellent mélange de thés, un excellent thé ◆ **Brazilian ~** *(= coffee)* café *m* du Brésil ◆ **"our own blend"** "mélange (spécial de la) maison"

VT (also **blend in**) mélanger, mêler *(with* à, avec*)* faire un mélange *(sth with sth* de qch avec qch*)* ; *[+ teas, coffees etc]* mélanger, faire un mélange de ; *[+ wines]* couper, mélanger ; *[+ qualities]* joindre, unir *(with* à*)* ; *[+ ideas]* fusionner ; *[+ colours, styles]* fondre, mêler

VI (also **blend in, blend together**) se mêler, se mélanger *(with* à, avec*)* former un mélange *(with* avec*)* se confondre *(into* en*)* ; *[voices, perfumes]* se confondre, se mêler ; *[styles]* se marier, s'allier ; *[ideas, political parties, races]* fusionner ; *[colours] (= shade into one another)* se fondre ; *(= go well together)* aller bien ensemble ◆ **the colours ~ (in) well** les couleurs vont bien ensemble

blended /ˈblendɪd/ **ADJ** ◆ **a ~ tea/wine** un mélange de thés/vins ◆ **~ whisky** du whisky blended *or* de mélange

blender /ˈblendəʳ/ **N** *(industrial)* malaxeur *m* ; *(= liquidizer)* mixer *m*

blenny /ˈblenɪ/ **N** *(= fish)* blennie *f*

bless /bles/ (pret, ptp **blest** *or* **blessed** /blest/) **VT** *[God, priest, person, fate]* bénir ◆ **God ~ the king!**

Dieu bénisse le roi ! ◆ **to be ~ed with** avoir la chance de posséder, être doté de ◆ **God did not ~ them with ...** Dieu ne leur accorda pas le bonheur d'avoir ... ◆ **Nature ~ed him with ...** la Nature l'a doué de ... ◆ **I was never ~ed with children** je n'ai jamais connu le bonheur d'avoir des enfants ◆ **she'll ~ you for this!** *(iro)* elle va te bénir ! * ◆ **~ you!** * mille fois merci !, tu es un ange ! ; *(sneezing)* à vos souhaits ! ◆ **and Paul, ~ him** *or* **~ his heart, had no idea that ...** et ce brave Paul (dans son innocence) ne savait pas que ... ◆ **~ his little heart!** qu'il est mignon ! ◆ **~ my soul!** †* mon Dieu !, Seigneur ! † ◆ **well, I'm ~ed!** * par exemple !, ça alors ! * ◆ **I'm** *or* **I'll be ~ed if I remember!** * c'est bien le diable * si je m'en souviens !

blessed /ˈblesɪd/ ADJ 1 *(Rel)* *(= holy)* béni, saint ; *(= beatified)* bienheureux ◆ **Blessed Virgin** Sainte Vierge *f* ◆ **Blessed Sacrament** Saint Sacrement *m* ◆ **~ be God!** (que) Dieu soit béni ! ◆ **the Blessed John of ...** le bienheureux Jean de ... ◆ **the Blessed Elizabeth the Good** la bienheureuse Élisabeth la Bonne 2 *(Rel, liter = happy)* bienheureux, heureux ◆ **~ are the pure in heart** bienheureux *or* heureux ceux qui ont le cœur pur ◆ **of ~ memory** d'heureuse mémoire 3 *(liter = giving joy)* *[thing]* béni ; *[person]* cher 4 *(esp Brit *: for emphasis)* sacré * *before n*, satané *before n* ◆ **that child is a ~ nuisance!** cet enfant, quelle peste *or* quel poison ! * ◆ **the whole ~ day** toute la sainte journée ◆ **every ~ evening** tous les soirs que le bon Dieu fait * NPL **the Blessed** les bienheureux *mpl*

blessedly /ˈblesɪdlɪ/ ADV *(liter)* *[cool, quiet]* merveilleusement ; *[brief]* fort heureusement

blessedness /ˈblesɪdnɪs/ N *(Rel)* béatitude *f* ; *(= happiness)* bonheur *m*, félicité *f*

blessing /ˈblesɪŋ/ N 1 *(= divine favour)* grâce *f*, faveur *f* ; *(= prayer)* bénédiction *f* ; *(at meal)* bénédicité *m* ; *(= approval)* bénédiction *f* ◆ **with God's ~ we shall succeed** nous réussirons par la grâce de Dieu ◆ **the priest pronounced the ~** le prêtre a donné la bénédiction ◆ **to ask a** *or* **the ~** *(at meal)* dire le bénédicité ◆ **the plan had his ~** * il avait donné sa bénédiction à ce projet * 2 *(= benefit)* bien *m*, bienfait *m* ◆ **the ~s of civilization** les bienfaits de la civilisation ◆ **what a ~ that the weather was fine!** quelle chance qu'il ait fait beau !, heureusement qu'il a fait beau ! ◆ **this rain has been a real ~** * cette pluie a été une vraie bénédiction * ◆ **it was a ~ in disguise** à quelque chose malheur est bon *(Prov)* → **count**[1]

blest /blest/ *(liter)* VB pt, ptp of **bless** ADJ heureux

blether /ˈbleðəʳ/ VI, N ⇒ **blather**

blew /bluː/ VB pt of **blow**[1]

blight /blaɪt/ N *[of cereals]* rouille *f*, charbon *m* ; *[of potato]* mildiou *m* ; *[of rose]* rouille *f* ; *[of fruit trees]* cloque *f* ◆ **this marriage was a ~ on his happiness** ce mariage a terni son bonheur ◆ **she's been a ~ on his life** elle a gâché son existence ◆ **what a ~ that woman is!** ‡ cette femme est un vrai fléau *or* une véritable plaie ! * ◆ **urban ~** dégradation *f* urbaine VT *[disease]* *[+ plants]* rouiller ; *[+ wheat etc]* nieller ; *[wind]* saccager ; *(fig)* *[+ hopes]* anéantir, détruire ; *[+ career, life]* gâcher, briser ; *[+ future]* gâcher

blighter †* /ˈblaɪtəʳ/ N *(Brit)* type * *m*, bonne femme *f* ◆ **a funny ~** un drôle de numéro * ◆ **silly ~** imbécile *mf* ◆ **lucky ~!** quel(le) veinard(e) * ! ◆ **you ~!** espèce de chameau ! *

Blighty †* /ˈblaɪtɪ/ N *(Brit Mil)* Angleterre *f*

blimey ‡ /ˈblaɪmɪ/ EXCL *(Brit)* mince alors ! *, merde alors ! ‡

blimp /blɪmp/ N 1 *(Brit)* **a (Colonel) Blimp** * une (vieille) culotte de peau *(pej)* 2 *(esp US = balloon)* petit dirigeable *m* de reconnaissance

blind /blaɪnd/ ADJ 1 *(= unable to see)* aveugle ◆ **a ~ man** un aveugle ◆ **a ~ boy** un garçon aveugle ◆ **to go ~** perdre la vue, devenir aveugle ◆ **the accident left him ~** cet accident l'a rendu aveugle, il a perdu la vue dans cet accident ◆ **~ in one eye** borgne ◆ **~ in the left eye** aveugle de l'œil gauche ◆ **~ from birth** aveugle de naissance ◆ **(as) ~ as a bat** myope comme une taupe ◆ **to be struck ~** être frappé de cécité ◆ **to be ~ with rage/tears** être aveuglé par la rage/par les larmes ◆ **there's none so ~ as those that won't see** *(Prov)* il n'est pire aveugle que celui qui ne veut pas voir

2 *(fig = unwilling to see)* aveugle ◆ **love is ~** l'amour est aveugle ◆ **to be ~ to sb's faults** ne pas voir les défauts de qn ◆ **to be ~ to the consequences of one's actions** ne pas se rendre compte des conséquences de ses actes ◆ **I am not ~ to that consideration** cela ne m'échappe pas ◆ **to turn a ~ eye (to sth)** fermer les yeux (sur qch) ; → **colour**

3 *(= unthinking)* *[panic, obedience]* aveugle ◆ **~ faith (in sth)** foi *f* aveugle (en qch)

4 *[flying, landing, corner, turning]* sans visibilité ◆ **on sb's ~ side** hors du champ visuel de qn

5 *(= without openings)* *[building, wall, window]* aveugle

6 *(‡: for emphasis)* ◆ **she never takes a ~ bit of notice (of sb/sth)** elle n'écoute jamais (qn/qch) ◆ **it won't make a ~ bit of difference** ça ne changera strictement rien ◆ **it's not a ~ bit of use** ça ne sert strictement à rien ◆ **nobody can do a ~ thing without her permission** on ne peut strictement rien faire sans sa permission

VT aveugler, rendre aveugle ; *[sun, light]* aveugler, éblouir ; *(fig)* aveugler, empêcher de voir ◆ **the war ~ed** les aveugles *mpl* de guerre ◆ **her love ~ed her to his faults** son amour l'aveuglait au point qu'elle ne voyait pas ses défauts ; → **science**

N 1 *[of window]* store *m* ◆ **to lower/raise the ~s** baisser/lever les stores ; → **Venetian**

2 *(= pretence)* paravent *m* ◆ **this action is only a ~** cette action n'est qu'un paravent

3 ◆ **to go on a ~** ‡ (aller) se soûler la gueule ‡

4 *(Hunting)* affût *m*

NPL **the blind** les aveugles *mpl* ◆ **it's the ~ leading the ~** c'est un aveugle qui conduit un aveugle

ADV 1 ◆ **to drive/fly ~** conduire/voler sans visibilité

2 ◆ **to bake sth ~** cuire qch à blanc

3 ◆ **to swear ~ that ...** * jurer ses grands dieux que ...

4 *(Brit)* ◆ **~ drunk** * complètement bourré *

COMP **blind alley** N *(lit, fig)* impasse *f*

blind corner N virage *m* sans visibilité

blind date N *(= meeting)* rendez-vous *m* arrangé *(avec quelqu'un qu'on ne connaît pas)* ; *(= person)* inconnu(e) *m(f)* (avec qui on a rendez-vous) ◆ **on a ~ date** lors d'un rendez-vous arrangé ◆ **to go on a ~ date** sortir avec quelqu'un qu'on ne connaît pas ◆ **to go on a ~ date with sb** aller à un rendez-vous arrangé avec qn

blind man's buff N colin-maillard *m*

blind spot N *(in eye)* tache *f* aveugle ; *(in road)* section *f* sans visibilité ; *(in car, plane)* angle *m* mort ◆ **to have a ~ spot about sth** ne rien comprendre à qch ◆ **computers are a ~ spot with me** je ne comprends rien aux ordinateurs ◆ **he has a ~ spot where she's concerned** il ne voit pas ses défauts

blind-stitch N point *m* perdu VI coudre à points perdus

blind summit N *(on road)* sommet *m* de côte à visibilité réduite

blind test N *(Marketing)* test *m* (en) aveugle

blind trust N *(Fin)* *fiduciaire qui gère la fortune de quelqu'un sans l'informer de la manière dont elle l'investit*

blinder /ˈblaɪndəʳ/ N 1 *(US)* œillère *f* 2 *(Brit)* ◆ **to play a ~** * jouer merveilleusement bien

blindfold /ˈblaɪndfəʊld/ VT bander les yeux à *or* de N bandeau *m* ADJ (also **blindfolded**) aux yeux bandés ADV (also **blindfolded**) les yeux bandés ◆ **(it's so easy) I could do it ~** (c'est si facile que) je le ferais les yeux bandés

blinding /ˈblaɪndɪŋ/ ADJ *[light]* aveuglant ; *[pain]* fulgurant

blindingly /ˈblaɪndɪŋlɪ/ ADV ◆ **it is ~ obvious** c'est d'une évidence flagrante, ça saute aux yeux

blindly /ˈblaɪndlɪ/ ADV 1 *(= unseeingly)* *[grope, stumble, shoot]* à l'aveuglette ◆ **she stared ~ at the wall** elle fixait le mur comme si elle ne le voyait pas 2 *(= unquestioningly)* *[follow, accept, obey]* aveuglément ◆ **a ~ obedient follower** un disciple inconditionnel

blindness /ˈblaɪndnɪs/ N cécité *f* ; *(fig)* aveuglement *m* *(to* devant) ; ◆ **~ to the truth** refus *m* de voir la vérité ; → **colour**

blindworm /ˈblaɪndwɜːm/ N orvet *m*

bling * /blɪŋ/, **bling-bling** * /blɪŋblɪŋ/ N *(= jewellery)* *bijoux lourds et clinquants*

blini(s) /ˈblɪnɪ(z)/ NPL blinis *mpl*

blink /blɪŋk/ N *[of eyes]* clignotement *m* (des yeux), battement *m* des paupières ; *[of sun]* (petit) rayon *m* ; *[of hope]* lueur *f* ; *(= glimpse)* coup *m* d'œil ◆ **in the ~ of an eye** en un clin d'œil ◆ **my telly's on the ~** * ma télé est détraquée VI 1 cligner des yeux ; *(= half-close eyes)* plisser les yeux 2 *[light]* vaciller VT ◆ **to ~ one's eyes** cligner des yeux ◆ **to ~ back the tears** refouler les larmes (d'un battement de paupières)

blinker /ˈblɪŋkəʳ/ N 1 *(Brit)* **~s** *(= for horse)* œillères *fpl* ; *(in car)* feux *mpl* de détresse, clignotants *mpl* ◆ **to wear ~s** *(fig)* avoir des œillères 2 (also **blinker light**) (feu *m*) clignotant *m*

blinkered /ˈblɪŋkəd/ ADJ *(Brit)* 1 *(pej = narrow-minded)* *[person, approach, attitude]* borné ; *[view]* étroit ◆ **to be ~** *[person]* avoir des œillères ◆ **to be ~ to sth, to have a ~ view of sth** *or* **approach to sth** voir qch avec des œillères 2 *[horse]* qui porte des œillères

blinking /ˈblɪŋkɪŋ/ ADJ *(Brit *)* sacré * *before n* ◆ **~ idiot** espèce *f* d'idiot N *[of eyes]* clignement *m* (d'yeux) ; *[of light]* vacillement *m*

blintz(e) /blɪnts/ N *(US Culin)* *sorte de crêpe fourrée*

blip /blɪp/ N 1 *(on radar etc)* spot *m* ; *(= beep)* bip *m* 2 *(on graph)* petite déviation *f* ; *(fig = aberration)* petite anomalie *f* (passagère)

bliss /blɪs/ N 1 *(Rel)* béatitude *f* ; *(gen)* félicité *f*, bonheur *m* suprême *or* absolu 2 *(* fig)* ◆ **what ~ to collapse into a chair !** quelle volupté de se laisser tomber dans un fauteuil ! ◆ **the concert was ~** le concert était divin ◆ **it's ~!** c'est merveilleux !, c'est divin !

► **bliss out** ‡ VT SEP *(esp US)* ◆ **to be blissed out** être au septième ciel

blissful /ˈblɪsfʊl/ ADJ *(Rel, gen)* bienheureux ; *(* = wonderful)* divin, merveilleux ◆ **to be in ~ ignorance** être dans l'ignorance la plus totale

blissfully /ˈblɪsfəlɪ/ ADV *[smile]* d'un air béat ; *[happy, quiet, ignorant, unaware]* parfaitement

blister /ˈblɪstəʳ/ N *(on skin)* ampoule *f*, cloque *f* ; *(on paintwork)* cloque *f* ; *(in glass)* bulle *f* VI *[skin]* se couvrir de cloques ; *[paintwork]* cloquer ; *[metal, glass]* former des soufflures VT *[+ paint]* faire cloquer

COMP **blister pack** N *(for pills etc)* plaquette *f* ; *(for pens, plugs etc)* blister *m*

blister-packed ADJ *[pills etc]* en plaquette ; *[pens, plugs etc]* sous blister

blistered /ˈblɪstəd/ ADJ *[skin, feet, hands]* couvert d'ampoules ; *[paintwork]* cloqué

blistering /ˈblɪstərɪŋ/ N *[of skin]* formation *f* d'ampoules ; *[of paint]* boursouflage *m* ADJ 1 *(= scorching)* *[heat]* torride ; *[day]* torride, de canicule ; [sun] brûlant ◆ **a ~ pace** or **speed** une vitesse foudroyante ② (= scathing) [attack, criticism, speech] cinglant

blithe /blaɪð/ ADJ (liter) joyeux, allègre

blithely /ˈblaɪðlɪ/ ADV allégrement

blithering * /ˈblɪðərɪŋ/ ADJ ◆ **~ idiot** crétin fini * ◆ **you ~ idiot!** espèce d'idiot !

blithesome /ˈblaɪðsəm/ ADJ ⇒ **blithe**

BLitt /biːˈlɪt/ N abbrev of **Bachelor of Literature**

blitz /blɪts/ N (= army attack) attaque f éclair inv ; (= air attack) bombardement m (aérien) ◆ **the Blitz** (Brit Hist) le Blitz ◆ **to have a ~ on sth** * s'attaquer à qch VT ① (= bomb) bombarder ◆ **~ed houses** maisons fpl bombardées ◆ **to ~ sth in a food processor** * passer qch au mixer ② (* fig = go to work on) s'attaquer à

blitzed ⁑ /blɪtst/ ADJ (= drunk) bourré ⁑

blitzkrieg /ˈblɪtskriːg/ N ① (Mil Hist) guerre f éclair ② (* fig = attack) attaque f éclair ◆ **an advertising ~** une intense campagne publicitaire

blizzard /ˈblɪzəd/ N tempête f de neige ; (in Arctic) blizzard m ; (fig) avalanche f

bloated /ˈbləʊtɪd/ ADJ ① (= swollen) [stomach, body, corpse] gonflé ; [face] bouffi ② (after eating) ◆ **to feel ~** se sentir ballonné ③ (= over-large) [bureaucracy] hypertrophié ; [budget, ego] démesuré ④ (= self-important: also **bloated with pride**) [person] gonflé d'orgueil

bloater /ˈbləʊtəʳ/ N hareng m saur or fumé

blob /blɒb/ N (= drop: gen) (grosse) goutte f ; [of ink] pâté m, tache f ; (= stain) tache f

bloc /blɒk/ N ① (Pol) bloc m ② ◆ **en ~** en bloc, en gros

block /blɒk/ N ① [of stone] bloc m ; [of wood] bille f ; [of blacksmith, butcher, executioner] billot m ; [of chocolate] tablette f ◆ **~s** (= toy) cubes mpl, jeu m de construction ◆ **a ~ of ice cream** un litre (or demi-litre etc) de glace ◆ **butcher's ~** billot m de boucher ◆ **on the ~** (US) [buy] aux enchères ; [pay] rubis sur l'ongle ◆ **to die on the ~** périr sur le billot or l'échafaud ; → **chip**

② [of buildings] pâté m (de maisons) ◆ **a ~ of flats** (Brit) un immeuble ◆ **to take a stroll round the ~** faire le tour du pâté de maisons, faire un tour dans le coin ◆ **she lived three ~s away** (US) elle habitait trois rues plus loin

③ (= part of prison, hospital etc) quartier m, pavillon m ; [of factory etc] bâtiment m

④ (= obstruction) [of traffic] embouteillage m ; [of pipe] obstruction f ; (Med, Psych) blocage m ◆ **I've got a (mental) ~ about that whole period** j'ai un trou (de mémoire), je n'ai aucun souvenir de cette période ◆ **I couldn't do it – I had a mental ~ about it** (fig: frightened etc) je n'ai pas pu le faire, c'est plus fort que moi ◆ **he's/I've got a ~** [writer] c'est le vide or blocage total ; → **roadblock**

⑤ [of tickets] série f ; [of shares] tranche f ; [of seats] groupe m

⑥ (Brit Typ) cliché m (plaque)

⑦ (also **block and tackle**) palan m, moufles mpl

⑧ (⁑ = head) caboche * f, ciboulot ⁑ m ; → **knock off**

⑨ (Brit = writing pad) bloc-notes m ; (also **artist's block**) bloc m à dessein

⑩ (Comput) sélection f

⑪ (Fin) [of shares] paquet m ; (larger) bloc m

⑫ (also **starting block**) ◆ **to be first/fast off the (starting) ~s** être le premier à/ne pas attendre pour se lancer ◆ **to be quick/slow off** or **out of the ~s** (fig) être rapide/lent à réagir or à la détente *

VT ① [+ pipe etc] boucher, bloquer ; [+ road] bloquer, barrer ; [+ harbour, wheel] bloquer ; [+ progress, traffic] entraver, gêner ; (Ftbl) [+ opponent] gêner ; [+ transaction, credit, negotiations] bloquer ; (Med) [+ pain] anesthésier, neutraliser ◆ **the leaves ~ed the drain** les feuilles mortes ont bouché or bloqué le puisard ◆ **to ~ sb's way** barrer le chemin à qn ◆ **to ~ the ball** (Sport) bloquer (la balle)

② [+ title, design] graver au fer

③ (Comput) sélectionner

VI [wheel] (se) bloquer

COMP **block association** N association f de copropriétaires (d'un immeuble)

block booking N réservation f groupée or en bloc

block capitals NPL ⇒ **block letters**

block diagram N (Comput, Geog) bloc-diagramme m ; (Elec) schéma m (de principe)

block grant N (Brit Admin) dotation f or enveloppe f gouvernementale (accordée aux autorités locales)

block letters NPL majuscules fpl, capitales fpl ◆ **in ~ letters** en majuscules

block release N (Brit Educ) système de stages de formation alternant avec l'activité professionnelle

block system N (Rail) bloc-système m, bloc m automatique à signaux lumineux

block vote N vote m groupé

block voting N (pratique f du) vote m groupé

► **block in** VT SEP (= sketch out) esquisser

► **block off** VT SEP [+ part of road etc] interdire, condamner ; (accidentally) obstruer

► **block out** VT SEP ① (= obscure) [+ view] boucher ; [+ light] empêcher de passer

② (from mind) [+ thoughts, idea] refouler, repousser

③ (= sketch) [+ scheme, design] ébaucher

► **block up** VT SEP [+ gangway] encombrer ; [+ pipe etc] bloquer, boucher ; [+ window, entrance] murer, condamner ; [+ hole] boucher, bloquer ; (Comput) [+ text] sélectionner

blockade /blɒˈkeɪd/ N (Mil) blocus m ; (fig) barrage m ◆ **under ~** en état de blocus ◆ **to break/raise the ~** forcer/lever le blocus ◆ **to run a ~** forcer un blocus VT ① (Mil) [+ town, port] bloquer, faire le blocus de ; (fig) bloquer, obstruer ② (US) [+ traffic] bloquer ; [+ street] encombrer COMP **blockade runner** N briseur m de blocus

blockage /ˈblɒkɪdʒ/ N (gen) obstruction f ; (Med) obstruction f, blocage m ; (intestinal) occlusion f ; (mental) blocage m ; (fig) bouchon m

blockbuster * /ˈblɒkˌbʌstəʳ/ N (= bomb) bombe f de gros calibre ; (= film) film m à grand succès ; (= book) best-seller m ; (= argument) argument m massue ◆ **he's a real ~** il est d'une efficacité à tout casser *

blockhead * /ˈblɒkhed/ N (pej) imbécile mf, crétin(e) * m(f)

blockhouse /ˈblɒkhaʊs/ N (Mil) casemate f, blockhaus m

blog /blɒg/(Comput) N blog m, blogue m VI bloguer sur VI bloguer

blogger /ˈblɒgəʳ/ N (Comput) bloggeur, euse * m,f

blogging /ˈblɒgɪŋ/ N (Comput)blogging m

bloke * /bləʊk/ N (Brit) type * m, mec ⁑ m

blokey * /ˈbləʊkɪ/, **blok(e)ish** * /ˈbləʊkɪʃ/ ADJ (Brit) [behaviour, activity] de mec * ; [man] macho * ◆ **a ~ sense of humour** un humour typiquement masculin

blond(e) /blɒnd/ ADJ blond N blond(e) m(f) ; → **ash², platinum** COMP **blonde bombshell** * N blonde f explosive

blood /blʌd/ N ① (NonC) sang m ◆ **to give** or **donate ~** donner son sang ◆ **the ~ rushed to his face** le sang lui est monté au visage ◆ **to beat/whip sb till the ~ comes** battre/fouetter qn jusqu'au sang ◆ **it's like trying to get ~ out of** or **from a stone** c'est comme si on parlait à un mur ◆ **his ~ ran cold** son sang s'est figé or s'est glacé dans ses veines ◆ **you make my ~ run cold** vous me donnez le frisson ◆ **it makes my ~ boil** cela me fait bouillir ◆ **my ~ was boiling** je bouillais (de rage) ◆ **his ~ is up** il est très monté ◆ **bad ~** animosité f ◆ **there is bad ~ between them** le torchon brûle (entre eux) ◆ **this firm needs new** or **fresh** or **young ~** cette maison a besoin d'un or de sang nouveau ◆ **he believes in putting ~, sweat and tears into any job he does** il se donne à fond dans tout ce qu'il fait ◆ **he's out for ~** * il cherche quelqu'un sur qui passer sa colère ◆ **to be out for** or **after sb's ~** * vouloir la peau * de qn ◆ **I've already apologized! what do you want, ~?** * je me suis déjà excusé ! qu'est-ce que tu veux, que je me mette à genoux ? ◆ **to have ~ on one's hands** (fig) avoir du sang sur les mains ◆ **to spill** or **shed ~** (in conflict, war) faire couler le sang ◆ **his ~ will be on your head** (liter) vous aurez sa mort sur la conscience ; → **cold, flesh, sweat**

② (= heredity) sang m ◆ **the ties of ~** les liens mpl du sang ◆ **~ is thicker than water** (Prov) la voix du sang est la plus forte ◆ **it's in his ~** il a cela dans le sang ◆ **of Irish ~** de sang irlandais ; → **blue**

③ († = dashing young man) petit-maître † m

④ (US ⁑ also **~ brother**) frère m

NPL **bloods** (Med) ◆ **to take ~s** faire une prise de sang

VT (Hunting) [+ hounds] acharner, donner le goût du sang à ; (fig) [+ troops] donner le baptême du feu à

COMP **blood-and-thunder** ADJ (Brit) ◆ **a ~-and-thunder speech** un discours mélodramatique ◆ **~-and-thunder novel** roman m à sensation

blood bank N (Med) banque f du sang

blood bath N (fig) bain m de sang, massacre m

blood blister N pinçon m

blood brother N frère m de sang

blood-caked ADJ couvert de sang coagulé

blood cell N cellule f sanguine ◆ **red/white ~ cell** globule m rouge/blanc

blood cholesterol (level) N cholestérolémie f

blood clot N caillot m de sang

blood corpuscle N globule m sanguin

blood count N (Med) numération f globulaire

blood donor N donneur m, -euse f de sang

blood doping N dopage m par autotransfusion

blood feud N vendetta f

blood flow N circulation f sanguine ◆ **~ flow to the brain/stomach** l'afflux m de sang au cerveau/à l'estomac

blood group N (Med) groupe m sanguin

blood grouping N (Med) recherche f du groupe sanguin

blood heat N température f du sang

blood lust N soif f de sang

blood money N prix m du sang

blood orange N (orange f) sanguine f

blood plasma N plasma m sanguin

blood poisoning N septicémie f

blood pressure N tension f (artérielle) ◆ **to have high/low ~ pressure** faire de l'hypertension/hypotension ◆ **to take sb's ~ pressure** prendre la tension de qn ◆ **his ~ pressure went up/down** (Med) sa tension a monté/a baissé ◆ **his ~ pressure shot up at the news** (fig) il a failli avoir une attaque en apprenant la nouvelle

blood product N produit m sanguin

blood pudding N (US) boudin m noir

blood-red N, ADJ rouge m sang inv

blood relation N parent(e) m(f) (par le sang)

blood sample N prélèvement m de sang ◆ **to take a ~ sample** faire une prise de sang

blood sausage N (US) ⇒ **blood pudding**

blood sports NPL sports mpl sanguinaires

blood sugar N sucre m dans le sang ◆ **~ sugar level** taux m de sucre dans le sang

blood supply N (= blood vessels) système m de circulation sanguine ; (= flow of blood) circula-

tion *f* (du sang *or* sanguine) ◆ **skin ulcers are usually caused by poor ~ supply** les ulcères sur la peau sont généralement dus à une mauvaise circulation ◆ **to increase ~ supply to the pelvis** augmenter l'afflux de sang au pelvis
blood test N *(Med)* analyse *f or* examen *m* de sang
blood transfusion N transfusion *f* sanguine
blood type N ⇒ **blood group**
blood vessel N vaisseau *m* sanguin ; → **burst**

bloodcurdling /ˈblʌdkɜːdlɪŋ/ ADJ à (vous) figer *or* tourner* le sang, qui (vous) fige le sang

bloodhound /ˈblʌdhaʊnd/ N (= *dog*) limier *m* ; (* = *detective*) détective *m*, limier *m*

bloodied /ˈblʌdɪd/ ADJ sanglant, ensanglanté ◆ **~ but unbowed** vaincu mais sa fierté intacte

bloodily /ˈblʌdɪlɪ/ ADV *[kill]* d'une manière sanglante ; *[defeat, repress]* dans le sang

bloodiness /ˈblʌdɪnɪs/ N *(lit)* état *m* sanglant

bloodless /ˈblʌdlɪs/ ADJ [1] (= *pallid*) *[face, lips]* blême, exsangue *(liter)* [2] (= *without bloodshed*) *[coup, revolution, victory]* sans effusion de sang ◆ **the Bloodless Revolution** *(Brit Hist) la révolution de 1688-89 en Angleterre*

bloodlessly /ˈblʌdlɪslɪ/ ADV sans effusion de sang

bloodletting /ˈblʌd,letɪŋ/ N *(Med)* saignée *f*

bloodline /ˈblʌdlaɪn/ N lignée *f*

bloodmobile /ˈblʌdmə,biːl/ N *(US)* centre *m* mobile de collecte du sang

bloodshed /ˈblʌdʃed/ N effusion *f* de sang, carnage *m* ◆ **without ~** sans effusion de sang

bloodshot /ˈblʌdʃɒt/ ADJ *[eyes]* injecté (de sang) ◆ **to become ~** s'injecter de sang

bloodstain /ˈblʌdsteɪn/ N tache *f* de sang

bloodstained /ˈblʌdsteɪnd/ ADJ taché de sang, ensanglanté

bloodstock /ˈblʌdstɒk/ N *(NonC)* bêtes *fpl* de race (pure) *or* de sang

bloodstone /ˈblʌdstəʊn/ N *(Miner)* héliotrope *m*

bloodstream /ˈblʌdstriːm/ N système *m* sanguin

bloodsucker /ˈblʌd,sʌkəʳ/ N *(lit, fig)* sangsue *f*

bloodthirstiness /ˈblʌd,θɜːstɪnɪs/ N *[of person, animal]* soif *f* de sang ; *[of book, story]* cruauté *f*, caractère *m* sanguinaire

bloodthirsty /ˈblʌd,θɜːstɪ/ ADJ *[+ person, animal]* assoiffé de sang, sanguinaire ; *[+ disposition, tale]* sanguinaire

bloody /ˈblʌdɪ/ ADJ [1] *(lit)* sanglant, ensanglanté ; *[battle, history]* sanglant ; (= *blood-coloured*) rouge, rouge sang *inv* ◆ **a ~ nose** un nez en sang ◆ **to give sb a ~ nose** *(in contest)* donner *or* infliger un camouflet à qn ; *(in war)* faire subir une défaite à qn ◆ **with ~ hands** les mains couvertes de sang *or* ensanglantées ◆ **a ~ sun** un soleil rouge sang

[2] *(Brit *‡)* foutu‡ *before n*, sacré* *before n* ◆ **this ~ machine won't start!** cette bon Dieu‡ de machine *or* cette foutue‡ machine refuse de démarrer ! ◆ **shut the ~ door!** (mais) nom de Dieu*‡ veux-tu fermer la porte ! ◆ **it's a ~ nuisance** ce que c'est emmerdant‡ ◆ **you ~ fool!** espèce de con !*‡ ◆ **you've got a ~ cheek** *or* **nerve!** tu charries !‡ ◆ **those ~ doctors!** ces bon Dieu‡ de médecins !, ces foutus‡ médecins ! ◆ **~ hell!** merde alors !‡ ◆ **it's a ~ miracle he wasn't killed!** c'est un sacré* miracle qu'il en ait réchappé !

[3] († * = *awful*) affreux, atroce ◆ **we had a perfectly ~ evening with them** ils nous ont fait passer une soirée (drôlement) barbante*

ADV *(Brit *‡)* vachement‡ ◆ **not ~ likely!** tu te fous de moi !‡, tu te fous de ma gueule !‡ ◆ **I've ~ (well) lost it!** je l'ai perdu nom de Dieu !‡

VT ensanglanter, souiller de sang *(liter)*

COMP **Bloody Mary** N (= *cocktail*) bloody mary *m*

bloody-minded* ADJ *(Brit)* *[person]* qui fait toujours des difficultés ; *[attitude]* buté ◆ **he's being ~-minded** il le fait pour emmerder le monde‡

bloody-mindedness* N ◆ **out of sheer ~-mindedness** (rien que) pour emmerder le monde‡

bloom /bluːm/ N [1] fleur *f* [2] *(NonC)* *[of flower, plant]* floraison *f* ; *(fig)* épanouissement *m*, floraison *f* ◆ **in ~** *[tree]* en fleurs ; *[flower]* éclos ◆ **in full ~** *[tree]* en pleine floraison ; *[flower]* épanoui ◆ **roses in full ~** roses *fpl* épanouies ◆ **to burst** *or* **come into ~** fleurir, s'épanouir ◆ **in the ~ of her youth** *(fig liter)* dans la fleur de sa jeunesse, en pleine jeunesse [3] *[of fruit, skin]* velouté *m* ◆ **the ~ had gone from her cheek** ses joues avaient perdu leurs fraîches couleurs
VI *[flower]* éclore ; *[tree]* fleurir ; *[person]* être florissant ◆ **~ing with health** resplendissant de santé

bloomer /ˈbluːməʳ/ N * bévue *f*, gaffe *f* ◆ **to make a ~** faire une gaffe, mettre les pieds dans le plat NPL **bloomers** *(Dress)* culotte *f* bouffante

blooming /ˈbluːmɪŋ/ ADJ *(Brit)* [1] *[tree]* en fleur, fleuri ; *[looks, health]* florissant [2] * ⇒ **blinking adj**

blooper‡ /ˈbluːpəʳ/ N *(esp US)* gaffe *f*

blossom /ˈblɒsəm/ N [1] *(NonC)* floraison *f*, fleur(s) *f(pl)* ◆ **a spray of ~** une petite branche fleurie, un rameau en fleur(s) ◆ **tree in ~** arbre *m* en fleur(s) ◆ **pear trees in full ~** poiriers *mpl* en pleine floraison ◆ **to come into ~** fleurir, s'épanouir ◆ **peach ~** fleur *f* de pêcher ; → **orange** [2] (= *flower*) fleur *f* VI fleurir ; *[person]* s'épanouir ◆ **to ~ (out) into** devenir

blot /blɒt/ N *[of ink]* tache *f*, pâté *m* ; *(fig)* tache *f*, souillure *f (liter)* ◆ **a ~ on his character** *or* **on his escutcheon** une tache à sa réputation ◆ **to be a ~ on the landscape** déparer le paysage VT [1] (= *spot with ink*) tacher, faire des pâtés sur ◆ **you've really ~ted your copybook*** *(Brit)* ta réputation en a pris un coup* [2] (= *dry*) *[+ ink, page]* sécher
COMP **blotting-pad** N (bloc *m*) buvard *m*
blotting-paper N (papier *m*) buvard *m*
▸ **blot out** VT SEP *[+ words]* biffer, rayer ; *[+ memories]* effacer ; *[fog etc]* *[+ view]* voiler, masquer ; *[sound]* étouffer, couvrir

blotch /blɒtʃ/ N [1] *(on skin)* (= *mark*) tache *f*, marbrure *f* ; (= *spot*) bouton *m* [2] *[of ink, colour]* tache *f* VT *[+ paper, written work]* tacher, barbouiller, faire des taches sur ◆ **~ed with** taché de, couvert de taches de

blotchy /ˈblɒtʃɪ/ ADJ *[skin, complexion]* marbré, couvert de taches *or* de marbrures ; *[drawing, written work]* couvert de taches, barbouillé

blotter /ˈblɒtəʳ/ N [1] (= *block*) (bloc *m*) buvard *m* ; (= *sheet*) buvard *m* ; (also **hand blotter**) tampon *m* buvard ; (= *desk pad*) sous-main *m inv* [2] *(US = notebook)* registre *m*

blotto‡ /ˈblɒtəʊ/ ADJ bourré‡, bituré‡

blouse /blaʊz/ N *[of woman]* corsage *m*, chemisier *m* ; *[of workman, artist, peasant]* blouse *f*, sarrau *m* ; *(US Mil)* vareuse *f*

blouson /ˈbluːzɒn/ N blouson *m*

blow¹ /bləʊ/ (vb : pret **blew**, ptp **blown**) N [1] ◆ **to give a ~** *(through mouth)* souffler ; *(through nose)* se moucher
[2] (= *wind*) coup *m* de vent, bourrasque *f*
[3] *(Drugs *)* *(Brit = marijuana)* herbe* *f* ; *(US = cocaine)* coke* *f*

VT [1] *[wind]* *[+ ship]* pousser ; *[+ leaves]* chasser, faire voler ◆ **the wind blew the ship off course** le vent a fait dévier le navire (de sa route) *or* a dérouté le navire ◆ **a gust of wind blew her hat off** un coup de vent a fait s'envoler son chapeau ◆ **the wind blew the chimney down** le vent a fait tomber *or* a renversé la cheminée ◆ **the wind blew away the clouds** le vent a chassé *or* dispersé les nuages ◆ **the wind blew the door open/shut** un coup de vent a ouvert/fermé la porte ◆ **it was ~ing a gale** le vent soufflait en tempête ◆ **it's ~ing great guns*** il fait un vent à décorner les bœufs* ; → **ill**

[2] (= *drive air into*) *[+ fire]* souffler sur ; *[+ bellows]* faire marcher ◆ **to ~ one's nose** se moucher ◆ **to ~ an egg** vider un œuf *(en soufflant dedans)* ◆ **to ~ smoke in sb's face** *(lit)* souffler la fumée à la figure de qn ; *(US fig)* induire qn en erreur ◆ **to ~ smoke up sb's ass*‡** *(US)* lécher le cul de qn*‡

[3] (= *make by blowing*) *[+ bubbles]* faire ; *[+ glass]* souffler ◆ **to ~ a kiss** envoyer un baiser ◆ **to ~ smoke rings** faire des ronds de fumée

[4] *[+ trumpet, horn]* jouer de, souffler dans ◆ **the referee blew his whistle** l'arbitre a sifflé ; see also **whistle** ◆ **to ~ one's own trumpet** *or (US)* **horn** se faire mousser*, chanter ses propres louanges ◆ **he blew the dust off the record** il a enlevé la poussière du disque en soufflant dessus

[5] *(Drugs ‡)* **to ~ grass** fumer de l'herbe

[6] (= *destroy*) *[+ safe]* faire sauter ◆ **to ~ a fuse** *(lit)* faire sauter un plomb *or* un fusible ◆ **to ~ a tyre** *[driver, vehicle]* crever ◆ **the car blew a tyre** la voiture a crevé ◆ **to ~ a gasket** *(in car)* griller* *or* casser un joint de culasse ◆ **to ~ a gasket*** *or (US)* **one's cork*** *or (US)* **one's stack*** *or* **one's top*** *or* **a fuse*** piquer une crise* ◆ **that blew the lid off the whole business*** c'est cela qui a fait découvrir le pot aux roses ◆ **the whole plan has been ~n sky-high** * tout le projet a volé en éclats ◆ **to ~ sth out of the water*** *(fig)* réduire qch à néant

[7] (‡ = *spend extravagantly*) *[+ wages, money]* claquer* ◆ **I blew $60 on a new hat** j'ai claqué* 60 dollars pour un nouveau chapeau

[8] (* = *spoil, fail*) rater, gâcher ◆ **he blew it (with her)** il a tout loupé* *or* raté (avec elle) ◆ **to ~ one's lines** *(US)* s'emmêler les pinceaux*

[9] *(esp US *‡= fellate)* tailler une pipe à‡

[10] *(phrases)* **to ~ sb's mind**‡ (= *astound*) en boucher un coin à qn*, en mettre plein la vue à qn* ◆ **to ~ the gaff**‡ *(Brit)* (= *reveal a secret*) vendre la mèche ; (= *leave*) mettre les voiles* ◆ **to ~ the gaff on sb**‡ *(Brit)* dénoncer *or* vendre qn ◆ **he realized he was ~n**‡ il a compris qu'il était grillé* ◆ **~ the expense!**‡ tant pis pour la dépense !, au diable la dépense !* ◆ **well, I'm ~ed!**‡ ça alors !*, par exemple ! ◆ **I'll be ~ed**‡ **if I'll do it!** pas question que je le fasse !, je veux être pendu si je le fais !* ◆ **~ it!*** la barbe !*, zut !*

VI [1] *[wind]* souffler ◆ **the wind was ~ing hard** le vent soufflait très fort, il faisait grand vent ◆ **the wind was ~ing from the south** le vent soufflait du sud ◆ **to see which way the wind ~s** *(fig)* regarder *or* voir de quel côté souffle le vent ◆ **she ~s hot and cold with me** avec moi elle souffle le chaud et le froid ◆ **the government has been ~ing hot and cold on the subject of peace talks** le gouvernement souffle le chaud et le froid en ce qui concerne les pourparlers de paix

[2] (= *move with wind*) **the door blew open/shut** un coup de vent a ouvert/a fermé la porte ◆ **his hat blew out of the window** son chapeau s'est envolé par la fenêtre ◆ **the question/agreement is ~ing in the wind** * la question/l'accord est dans l'air

[3] *[whistle]* retentir ; *[foghorn]* mugir ◆ **when the whistle ~s** au coup de sifflet

[4] (= *breathe out hard*) souffler ; (= *breathe hard*) *[person]* souffler, être à bout de souffle ; *[animal]* souffler ◆ **to ~ on one's fingers** souffler

dans ses doigts ◆ **to ~ on one's soup** souffler sur sa soupe ; → **puff**

5 *[whale]* souffler (par les évents)

6 *[fuse, light bulb]* sauter ; *[tyre]* éclater

7 (*‡ = leave)* filer *

EXCL * la barbe ! *, zut ! *

COMP **blow-dry** N brushing *m* VT ◆ **to ~-dry sb's hair** faire un brushing à qn

blow dryer N sèche-cheveux *m inv*

blow job *‡ N pipe *‡ *f* ◆ **to give sb a ~ job** tailler une pipe à qn *‡

blow-up N explosion *f* ; (*‡ = quarrel)* engueulade‡ *f*, prise *f* de bec * ; *(Phot *)* agrandissement *m*

► **blow away**‡ VT SEP *(esp US)* 1 (*= kill)* descendre *, flinguer‡

2 *(= defeat)* écraser, battre à plate(s) couture(s)

3 *(= surprise)* sidérer

► **blow down** VI *[tree, fence etc]* être abattu par le vent, tomber

VT SEP *[wind]* faire tomber ; *[person]* faire tomber (en soufflant)

► **blow in** VI (* *= turn up)* s'amener *, débarquer * ; *(unexpectedly)* arriver *or* débarquer * à l'improviste

VT SEP 1 *[+ door, window]* enfoncer

2 **look what the wind's ~n in!** * *(hum)* regardez qui s'amène ! *

► **blow off** VI 1 *[hat]* s'envoler

2 *(Brit ‡)* lâcher un pet, péter

VT SEP 1 *[+ hat]* emporter

2 *[+ air]* laisser échapper, lâcher ◆ **to ~ off steam** * *(fig)* se défouler *

► **blow out** VI *[light]* s'éteindre ; *[tyre]* éclater ; *[fuse]* sauter

VT SEP 1 *[+ light]* éteindre ; *[+ candle]* souffler ◆ **the storm blew itself out** la tempête a fini par s'apaiser

2 *(= puff out) [+ one's cheeks]* gonfler

3 ◆ **to blow one's brains out** se faire sauter *or* se brûler la cervelle ◆ **to ~ sb's brains out** faire sauter la cervelle à qn

4 *(esp US * = let down, reject) [+ person]* envoyer balader *, laisser tomber

N ◆ **blow-out** → **blow-out**

► **blow over** VI *[storm, dispute]* se calmer

VT SEP *[+ tree]* renverser, abattre

► **blow up** VI 1 *[bomb]* exploser, sauter ◆ **the whole thing has ~n up** *(fig)* tout a été fichu en l'air * ◆ **his allegations could ~ up in his face** ses allégations pourraient se retourner contre lui

2 *[wind]* se lever ; *[storm]* se préparer

3 (*: with anger, indignation)* exploser *, sauter au plafond * ◆ **to ~ up at sb** s'emporter contre qn, se mettre en colère contre qn

4 *(= start up) [affair, crisis]* se déclencher

VT SEP 1 *[+ mine]* (faire) exploser, faire sauter ; *[+ building, bridge]* faire sauter

2 *[+ tyre]* gonfler ◆ **~n up with pride** gonflé *or* bouffi d'orgueil ◆ **the media blew up the story** les médias ont grossi l'affaire

3 * *[+ photo]* agrandir ; *[+ event]* exagérer

4 (* *= reprimand) [+ person]* passer un (bon) savon à *

N ◆ **blow-up** → **blow**[1]

blow[2] /bləʊ/ N 1 *(lit) (= impact)* coup *m* ; *(with fist)* coup *m* de poing ◆ **to come to ~s** en venir aux mains ◆ **at one ~** du premier coup ◆ **to cushion** *or* **soften the ~** *(fig)* amortir le choc ; → **strike** 2 *(fig = sudden misfortune)* coup *m*, malheur *m* ◆ **it was a terrible ~ for them** cela a été un coup terrible pour eux COMP **blow-by-blow** ADJ *(fig)* ◆ **he gave me a ~-by-~ account** il ne m'a fait grâce d'aucun détail

blow[3] /bləʊ/ VI *(††, liter) [flowers]* fleurir, s'épanouir

blower /ˈbləʊəʳ/ N 1 *[of grate]* tablier *m or* rideau *m* de cheminée ; *[of ventilation]* ventilateur *m* (soufflant), machine *f* à vent ; *(Min)* jet *m* de grisou 2 *(Brit † ‡ = telephone)* bigophone * *m* ◆ **to get on the ~ to sb** passer un coup de bigophone‡ à qn ; → **glassblower**

blowfly /ˈbləʊflaɪ/ N mouche *f* à viande

blowgun /ˈbləʊgʌn/ N *(US)* sarbacane *f*

blowhard * /ˈbləʊhɑːd/ N *(US)* vantard(e) *m(f)*

blowhole /ˈbləʊhəʊl/ N *[of whale]* évent *m* ; *(= air vent)* évent *m*, bouche *f* d'aération ◆ **~s** *(in ingot)* soufflures *fpl*

blowlamp /ˈbləʊlæmp/ N *(Brit)* lampe *f* à souder, chalumeau *m*

-blown /bləʊn/ ADJ *(in compounds)* → **fly**', **windblown**

blow-out /ˈbləʊaʊt/ N 1 *[of tyre]* éclatement *m* ◆ **he had a ~** il a eu un pneu qui a éclaté 2 *(Elec)* **there's been a ~** les plombs ont sauté 3 *[of gas well, oil well]* jaillissement *m* 4 (*‡ = meal)* gueuleton‡ *m* ◆ **to have a ~** faire un gueuleton‡ *or* une bouffe‡

blowpipe /ˈbləʊpaɪp/ N *(= weapon)* sarbacane *f* ; *(in laboratory, industrial process)* chalumeau *m* ; *(in glass-making)* canne *f* (de souffleur), fêle *f*

blowsy /ˈblaʊzɪ/ ADJ *[woman]* débraillé

blowtorch /ˈbləʊtɔːtʃ/ N lampe *f* à souder, chalumeau *m*

blowy * /ˈbləʊɪ/ ADJ venté, venteux

blowzy /ˈblaʊzɪ/ ADJ ⇒ **blowsy**

BLT /ˌbiːelˈtiː/ N (abbrev of **bacon, lettuce and tomato**) ◆ **a ~ sandwich** un sandwich bacon, laitue, tomate

blub /blʌb/ VI *(Brit = cry)* pleurer comme un veau

blubber /ˈblʌbəʳ/ N *[of whale]* blanc *m* de baleine VI (*‡ = cry)* pleurer comme un veau ◆ **stop ~ing!** arrête de chialer ! *‡

blubbery /ˈblʌbərɪ/ ADJ *(= fat)* plein de graisse

bludgeon /ˈblʌdʒən/ N gourdin *m*, matraque *f* VT matraquer, assener un coup de gourdin *or* de matraque à ◆ **he ~ed me into doing it** *(fig)* il m'a forcé la main (pour que je le fasse)

blue /bluː/ ADJ 1 bleu ◆ **to go** *or* **turn ~** devenir bleu ◆ **~ with cold** bleu de froid ◆ **to be ~ in the face** *(lit)* avoir le visage cyanosé ◆ **you can talk till you are ~ in the face** * tu peux toujours parler ◆ **you can shout till you're ~ in the face** *, **nobody will come** tu auras beau crier *or* tu pourras crier tout ce que tu voudras *, personne ne viendra ◆ **I've told you till I'm ~ in the face** * je me tue à te le dire ◆ **once in a ~ moon** tous les trente-six du mois ◆ **the wide** *or* **wild ~ yonder** *(liter)* l'inconnu *m* ◆ **like a ~ streak** * *[run, go]* comme une flèche, au triple galop ◆ **to have a ~ fit**‡ piquer une crise * ◆ **to be in a ~ funk** avoir la frousse * *or* la trouille * ; see also **comp, black, murder, true**

2 (* *= miserable)* cafardeux, triste ◆ **to feel ~** broyer du noir, avoir le cafard

3 (* *= obscene) [talk, language]* cochon *, obscène ; *[book, film]* porno * *inv*

N 1 *(= colour)* bleu *m*, azur *m* ; → **navy, Prussian, sky**

2 *(= sky)* azur *m (liter)*, ciel *m* ◆ **to come out of the ~** *(gen)* être complètement inattendu ; *[pleasant thing]* tomber du ciel ◆ **to go off into the ~** *(= into the unknown)* partir à l'aventure ; *(= out of touch)* disparaître de la circulation * ; → **bolt**

3 *(liter = sea)* **the ~** la mer, les flots *mpl*

4 (* *= depression)* **the ~s** le cafard ◆ **to have the ~s** avoir le cafard, broyer du noir

5 *(Mus)* ◆ **the ~s** le blues

6 *(Brit Univ)* **the Dark/Light Blues** l'équipe *f* d'Oxford/de Cambridge ◆ **to get one's ~ for rugby** devenir membre de l'équipe de rugby *(surtout de l'université d'Oxford ou de Cambridge)*

◆ **he was a rowing ~ at Oxford** il faisait partie de l'équipe d'aviron de l'université d'Oxford

7 *(in washing)* bleu *m*

VT *(Brit ‡ = squander) [+ inheritance, fortune, money]* croquer *, dilapider ◆ **to ~ money on sth** dilapider de l'argent pour acheter qch

COMP **blue-arsed fly** *‡ N *(Brit)* ◆ **to run about** *or* **around like a ~-arsed fly** courir dans tous les sens, ne plus savoir où donner de la tête

blue asbestos N amiante *f* bleue

blue baby N enfant *m* bleu

Blue Beret N béret *m* bleu

blue-black ADJ noir bleuté *inv*

blue blood N sang *m* bleu *or* noble

blue-blooded ADJ de sang noble, aristocratique

blue book N *(Brit Parl)* livre *m* bleu, *publication officielle du gouvernement* ; *(US Scol etc)* cahier *m* d'examen

blue cheese N (fromage *m*) bleu *m*

blue chips, blue-chip securities NPL valeurs *fpl* de premier ordre, placements *mpl* de tout repos *or* de père de famille

blue collar worker N col *m* bleu

blue-eyed ADJ aux yeux bleus ◆ **the ~-eyed boy** *(fig)* le chouchou *, le chéri

blue fin tuna, blue fin tunny N thon *m* rouge

Blue Flag N *(on beach)* drapeau *m* bleu

the Blue Hen State N *(US)* le Delaware

blue jeans NPL blue-jean(s) *m(pl)*

blue law * N *(US) loi limitant les activités publiques le dimanche*

blue-pencil VT corriger

Blue Peter N 1 *(Naut)* pavillon *m* de partance 2 *(Brit TV) émission télévisée pour enfants*

blue riband, blue ribbon *(US)* N *(Naut)* ◆ **the ~ riband** *or* **ribbon** le ruban bleu ADJ *[event, competition]* de très haut niveau ; *[prize]* prestigieux ; *[committee, panel]* éminent

blue rinse N rinçage *m* bleuté ◆ **the ~ rinse brigade** les rombières * *fpl*

blue-rinsed ADJ *[+ hair]* aux reflets bleutés ; *[+ woman]* à la chevelure bleutée

blue shark N requin *m* bleu

blue-sky ADJ *(US) [stock, bond]* douteux ; *[project, research]* sans but pratique ◆ **~-sky laws** *lois protégeant le public contre les titres douteux*

blue tit N mésange *f* bleue

blue whale N baleine *f* bleue

BLUE PETER

Célèbre émission télévisée pour enfants dont les programmes vont du documentaire sur des sujets intéressant les enfants à la recette de cuisine et à la confection d'objets artisanaux. Les badges **Blue Peter** récompensent les spectateurs qui participent aux émissions ou se rendent utiles à la collectivité.

Bluebeard /ˈbluːbɪəd/ N Barbe-Bleue *m*

bluebell /ˈbluːbel/ N jacinthe *f* des bois ; *(Scot = harebell)* campanule *f*

blueberry /ˈbluːbərɪ/ N myrtille *f*

bluebird /ˈbluːbɜːd/ N oiseau *m* bleu

bluebottle /ˈbluːbɒtl/ N 1 mouche *f* bleue *or* à viande 2 *(= plant)* bleuet *m* 3 *(† ‡ = policeman)* poulet * *m*, flic * *m*

bluegrass /ˈbluːgrɑːs/ N *(US Bot)* pâturin *m* des champs

COMP **bluegrass music** N musique *f* bluegrass

the Bluegrass State N le Kentucky

blueish /ˈbluːɪʃ/ ADJ ⇒ **bluish**

blueness /ˈbluːnɪs/ N bleu *m*

blueprint /ˈbluːprɪnt/ N *(print, process)* bleu *m* ; *(US = Ozalid)* ozalid ® *m* ; *(fig)* plan *m*, projet *m* (for de)

bluestocking † /ˈbluːˌstɒkɪŋ/ N bas-bleu *m*

bluesy /ˈbluːzɪ/ ADJ *(Mus)* dans le style du blues

bluey * /ˈbluːɪ/ ADJ *(= bluish)* bleuté ◆ **~ green** vert bleuâtre *or* bleuté ◆ **~ grey** gris bleu N *(Austral* ✻ *= redhead)* rouquin(e) * *m(f)*

bluff¹ /blʌf/ ADJ 1 *[person]* carré, direct 2 *[cliff, coast]* à pic, escarpé N *(= headland)* promontoire *m*

bluff² /blʌf/ VI *(also Cards)* bluffer * VT 1 *[+ person]* bluffer *, donner le change à ◆ **we ~ed him into believing ...** nous l'avons si bien bluffé * qu'il a cru ... ◆ **he ~ed his way through (it)** il y est allé au culot 2 *(Cards) [+ opponent]* bluffer * N *(esp Cards)* bluff *m* ◆ **he called my ~** *(fig)* il m'a pris au mot ◆ **let's call his ~** on va le mettre au pied du mur

bluffer /ˈblʌfəʳ/ N bluffeur *m*, -euse *f*

bluish /ˈbluːɪʃ/ ADJ tirant sur le bleu ; *(pej)* bleuâtre ◆ **~ grey** gris bleuté ◆ **~ white** blanc bleuté *or* aux reflets bleus

blunder /ˈblʌndəʳ/ N *(= gaffe)* bévue *f*, gaffe * *f* ; *(= error)* faute *f*, bourde *f* ◆ **to make a ~** faire une bévue *or* une gaffe * ◆ **social ~** impair *m* VI 1 *(= make mistake)* faire une bourde *or* une faute 2 *(= move clumsily)* avancer d'un pas maladroit ◆ **to ~ in/out** *etc* entrer/sortir *etc* d'un pas maladroit ◆ **to ~ against** *or* **into sth** buter *or* se cogner contre qch ◆ **he ~ed his way through his speech** il s'est embrouillé dans son discours ◆ **to ~ into sth** *(fig)* s'engager par erreur dans qch VT *[+ affair, business]* gâcher, saboter

blunderbuss /ˈblʌndəbʌs/ N tromblon *m*, espingole *f*

blunderer /ˈblʌndərəʳ/ N gaffeur *m*, -euse *f*

blundering /ˈblʌndərɪŋ/ ADJ *[person]* gaffeur *, maladroit ; *[words, act]* maladroit, malavisé N maladresse *f*

blunt /blʌnt/ ADJ 1 *[blade, knife]* émoussé, peu tranchant ; *[pencil]* mal taillé, épointé ; *[point, needle]* émoussé, épointé ◆ **with a ~ instrument** *(Jur, Police)* avec un instrument contondant 2 *(fig = outspoken) [person]* brusque ; *[fact]* brutal ◆ **he was very ~** il n'a pas mâché ses mots VT *[+ blade, knife, point, sword]* émousser ; *[+ pencil, needle]* épointer ; *(fig) [+ palate, feelings, appetite]* émousser ; *[+ threat]* désamorcer ; *[+ impact]* atténuer, limiter ; *[+ criticism]* atténuer

bluntly /ˈblʌntlɪ/ ADV *[speak]* sans ménagements, sans mettre de gants

bluntness /ˈblʌntnɪs/ N 1 *[of blade, knife]* manque *m* de tranchant ; *[of needle, pencil]* pointe *f* émoussée 2 *(= frankness)* franc-parler *m* ; *(= brusqueness)* brusquerie *f*

blur /blɜːʳ/ N 1 *(= smear, blot)* tache *f*, bavure *f* 2 *(= vague form)* masse *f* indistincte ◆ **a ~ of colours and forms** une masse confuse de couleurs et de formes ◆ **a ~ of movement** un mouvement confus ◆ **the evening passed in a ~** la soirée a passé dans une sorte de brouillard 3 *(= mist: on mirror etc)* buée *f* VT 1 *[+ shining surface]* embuer, troubler ; *[+ writing, inscription]* estomper, effacer ; *[+ view, outline]* estomper 2 *[+ sight, judgement]* troubler, brouiller ◆ **eyes ~red with tears** yeux *mpl* voilés de larmes 3 *(fig) [+ distinction, boundary]* brouiller, rendre flou VI *[vision]* se voiler

blurb /blɜːb/ N notice *f* publicitaire ; *[of book]* (texte *m* de) présentation *f*, texte *m* de couverture (*or* au volet de jaquette)

blurred /blɜːd/ ADJ *[photo, image, outline, inscription]* flou ; *[eyesight]* troublé ◆ **to become ~** s'estomper ◆ **the issue is threatening to become ~** on risque de perdre de vue le vrai problème ◆ **class distinctions are becoming ~** les distinctions entre les classes s'estompent ◆ **his memory of what happened was rather ~** il avait un souvenir assez flou de ce qui s'était passé COMP **blurred vision** N vue *f* trouble

blurry * /ˈblɜːrɪ/ ADJ *[photo, image, outline, inscription]* flou ; *[eyesight]* troublé

blurt /blɜːt/ VT *(also* **blurt out***) [+ word]* lâcher, jeter ; *[+ information, secrets]* laisser échapper, lâcher étourdiment *or* à l'étourdie

blush /blʌʃ/ VI 1 rougir, devenir rouge *(with* de) ; ◆ **to ~ deeply** rougir très fort, devenir tout rouge ◆ **to ~ to the roots of one's hair** *or* **up to the ears** rougir jusqu'aux oreilles 2 *(fig = be ashamed)* rougir, avoir honte ◆ **I ~ for him** j'ai honte pour lui ◆ **I ~ to say so** je rougis de le dire N rougeur *f* ◆ **with a ~** en rougissant ◆ **without a ~** sans rougir ◆ **the first ~ of dawn** *(liter)* les premières rougeurs *fpl* de l'aube ◆ **the ~ of the rose** *(liter)* l'incarnat *m* de la rose *(liter)* ◆ **at the first ~** *(= at first sight)* au premier aspect, de prime abord ; → **spare**

blusher /ˈblʌʃəʳ/ N fard *m* à joues

blushing /ˈblʌʃɪŋ/ ADJ *(with shame)* le rouge au front ; *(from embarrassment)* le rouge aux joues ◆ **the ~ bride** *(hum)* la mariée rougissante

bluster /ˈblʌstəʳ/ VI 1 *[wind]* faire rage, souffler violemment *or* en rafales ; *[storm]* faire rage, se déchaîner 2 *(= rage)* tempêter, fulminer *(at sb* contre qn) ; *[boast]* fanfaronner N *(NonC = boasting)* fanfaronnade(s) *f(pl)*

blusterer /ˈblʌstərəʳ/ N fanfaron(ne) *m(f)*, bravache *m*

blustering /ˈblʌstərɪŋ/ ADJ fanfaron N *(NonC = boasting)* fanfaronnades *fpl*

blustery /ˈblʌstərɪ/ ADJ *[wind]* de tempête, qui souffle en rafales ; *[weather, day]* venteux, à bourrasques

Blu-Tack ® /ˈbluːtæk/ N pâte *f* adhésive

Blvd N (abbrev of **Boulevard**) Bd, Bld

BM /biːˈem/ N 1 (abbrev of **British Museum**) British Museum *m* 2 (abbrev of **Bachelor of Medicine**) *(= diploma) diplôme de médecine* ; *(= person) diplômé de médecine*

BMA /ˌbiːemˈeɪ/ N (abbrev of **British Medical Association**) ≃ ordre *m* des médecins

BMI /ˌbiːemˈaɪ/ N *(Med)* (abbrev of **body mass index**) IMC *m*

BMus N (abbrev of **Bachelor of Music**) diplômé(e) *m(f)* des études musicales

BMX /ˌbiːemˈeks/ N (abbrev of **bicycle motocross**) 1 *(= sport)* bicross *m* 2 (also **BMX bike**) (vélo *m* de) bicross *m*

BO * /biːˈəʊ/ 1 (abbrev of **body odour**) odeur *f* corporelle ◆ **he's got ~** il sent la transpiration 2 *(US)* abbrev of **box office**

boa /ˈbəʊə/ N *(= snake, fur or feather wrap)* boa *m* COMP **boa constrictor** N (boa *m*) constricteur *m*

Boadicea /ˌbəʊædɪˈsiːə/ N Boadicée *f*

boar /bɔːʳ/ N *(wild)* sanglier *m* ; *(= male pig)* verrat *m* ◆ **young (wild) ~** marcassin *m* ◆ **~'s head** *(Culin)* hure *f* (de sanglier) COMP **boar-hunting** N chasse *f* au sanglier

board /bɔːd/ N 1 *(= piece of wood)* planche *f* ; († *or hum = table)* table *f* ◆ **the ~s** *(Theat)* les planches *fpl*, la scène

◆ **above board** ◆ **it is all quite above ~** c'est tout ce qu'il y a de plus régulier, c'est tout à fait dans les règles

◆ **across the board** systématiquement ◆ **they cut salaries across the ~** ils ont réduit les salaires à tous les niveaux ◆ **prices fell across the ~** les prix ont chuté partout

2 *(NonC = cardboard)* carton *m NonC* ; *(= piece of board: for games)* tableau *m*

3 *(NonC = provision of meals)* pension *f* ◆ **~ and lodging** *(Brit)* (chambre *f* avec) pension *f* ◆ **full ~** *(Brit)* pension *f* complète ; → **bed, half**

4 *(= group of officials, council)* conseil *m*, comité *m* ◆ **he is on the ~ (of directors), he has a seat on the ~ (of directors)** il siège au conseil d'administration ◆ **medical ~** commission *f* médicale

5 *(NonC: on ship, plane)* bord *m*

◆ **on board** ◆ **to come (***or* **go) on ~** monter à bord, embarquer ◆ **to take goods on ~** embarquer des marchandises ◆ **on ~ the Queen Elizabeth** à bord du Queen Elizabeth ◆ **on ~ (ship)** à bord ◆ **welcome on ~!** *(fig)* bienvenue (dans notre équipe) ! ◆ **to take sth on ~** * *(= take note of)* prendre note de qch ; *(= accept responsibility for)* prendre qch sur soi ; *(= undertake)* assumer qch

◆ **to go by the board** *[plan, attempt]* échouer ; *[principles, hopes, dreams]* être abandonné ; *[business, firm]* aller à vau-l'eau

VT 1 *(= go on to) [+ ship, plane]* monter à bord de ; *(Naut) (in attack)* monter à l'abordage de, prendre à l'abordage ; *(for inspection)* arraisonner ; *[+ train, bus]* monter dans

2 *(= cover with boards)* couvrir *or* garnir de planches, planchéier

3 *(= feed, lodge)* prendre en pension *or* comme pensionnaire

VI 1 *(= lodge)* **to ~ with sb** être en pension chez qn

2 *[passengers]* embarquer ◆ **your flight is now ~ing** l'embarquement a commencé ◆ **"flight A123 is now boarding at gate 3"** "vol A123 : embarquement immédiat porte 3"

COMP *(= of board of directors) [decision etc]* du conseil d'administration

board game N jeu *m* de société *(se jouant sur un tableau)*

board meeting N réunion *f* du conseil d'administration

board of directors N conseil *m* d'administration

board of education N *(US Scol)* ≃ conseil *m* d'établissement

board of examiners N *(Scol, Univ)* jury *m* d'examen

board of governors N *(Brit Scol)* ≃ conseil *m* d'établissement *(d'un lycée ou d'un IUT)*

board of health N *(US)* service *m* municipal d'hygiène ; *(Mil)* conseil *m* de révision

board of inquiry N commission *f* d'enquête

board of managers N *(Brit Scol)* ≃ conseil *m* d'établissement *(d'une école primaire)*

board of pardons N *(US Jur)* commission *f* de remises de peine

board of parole N *(US Jur)* commission *f* de mise en liberté surveillée

board of regents N ⇒ **board of trustees**

Board of Trade N *(in Brit)* ≃ ministère *m* du Commerce

board of trade N *(US)* chambre *f* de commerce

board of trustees N *(US Univ)* ≃ conseil *m* d'université

board room N salle *f* de conférence ; *(in large organization)* salle *f* du conseil

board school N *(Hist)* école *f* communale

► **board out** VT SEP *[+ person]* mettre en pension *(with* chez)

► **board up** VT SEP *[+ door, window]* condamner (à l'aide de planches)

boarded-up /ˌbɔːdɪdˈʌp/ ADJ ◆ **a ~ window/door** une fenêtre/porte condamnée

boarder /ˈbɔːdəʳ/ N 1 pensionnaire *mf* ◆ **to take in ~s** prendre des pensionnaires 2 *(Brit Scol)* interne *mf*, pensionnaire *mf* ; → **day**

boarding /ˈbɔːdɪŋ/ N 1 *[of floor]* planchéiage *m* ; *[of fence]* planches *fpl* 2 *[of ship, plane]* embarquement *m* ; *(in attack on ship)* abordage *m* ; *(for inspection of ship)* arraisonnement *m* COMP **boarding card** N *(Brit)* carte *f* d'embarquement

boarding house N pension *f* (de famille) ; *(Scol)* internat *m* ◆ **to live at a ~ house** vivre dans une *or* en pension
boarding kennels NPL pension *f* pour chiens
boarding officer N officier *m* chargé de l'arraisonnement
boarding party N *(on ship)* section *f* d'abordage
boarding pass N ⇒ **boarding card**
boarding school N pension *f*, pensionnat *m* ◆ **to send a child to ~ school** mettre un enfant en pension ◆ **to be at ~ school** être en pension

boardwalk /'bɔːdwɔːk/ N *(US)* passage *m* en bois, trottoir *m* en planches ; *(on beach)* promenade *f* (en planches)

boarhound /'bɔːhaʊnd/ N vautre *m* ◆ **pack of ~s** vautrait *m*

boast /bəʊst/ N rodomontade *f*, fanfaronnade *f* ◆ **it was her proud ~ that she had twice travelled round the world** elle se vantait *or* s'enorgueillissait d'avoir fait le tour du monde à deux reprises ◆ **it is their ~ that no one went hungry** ils se vantent *or* s'enorgueillissent de ce que personne n'ait eu faim VI se vanter *(about, of* de) ; ◆ **without ~ing** *or* **without wishing to ~, I may say that ...** sans (vouloir) me vanter, je peux dire que ... ◆ **that's nothing to ~ about** il n'y a pas de quoi se vanter VT être fier de posséder, se glorifier d'avoir ◆ **the church ~s a fine steeple** l'église possède *or* est dotée d'un beau clocher

boaster /'bəʊstə^r^/ N vantard(e) *m(f)*, fanfaron(ne) *m(f)*

boastful /'bəʊstfʊl/ ADJ *[person, words]* fanfaron, vantard

boastfully /'bəʊstfəlɪ/ ADV en se vantant, avec forfanterie

boasting /'bəʊstɪŋ/ N vantardise *f*, fanfaronnade(s) *f(pl)*

boat /bəʊt/ N *(gen)* bateau *m* ; *(= small light boat)* embarcation *f* ; *(= ship)* navire *m*, bâtiment *m* ; *(= vessel)* vaisseau *m* ; *(= liner)* paquebot *m* ; *(= rowing-boat)* barque *f*, canot *m* ; *(= sailing-boat)* voilier *m* ; *(= barge)* chaland *m*, péniche *f* ◆ **to go by ~** prendre le bateau ◆ **to cross the ocean by ~** traverser l'océan en bateau *or* en paquebot ◆ **to take the ~ at Dover** s'embarquer à *or* prendre le bateau à Douvres ◆ **we're all in the same ~** nous sommes tous logés à la même enseigne, nous sommes tous dans la même galère ; → **burn¹, lifeboat, miss¹, rock¹**
VI ◆ **to go ~ing** aller faire une partie de canot ◆ **to ~ up/down the river** remonter/descendre la rivière en bateau
COMP **boat deck** N pont *m* des embarcations
boat hook N gaffe *f*
boat people NPL boat people *mpl*
boat race N course *f* d'aviron, régate(s) *f(pl)* ◆ **the Boat Race** la course d'aviron *(entre les universités d'Oxford et de Cambridge)*
boat-shaped ADJ en forme de bateau
boat train N train *m* (qui assure la correspondance avec le ferry)

boatbuilder /'bəʊt,bɪldə^r^/ N constructeur *m* naval *or* de bateaux

boatbuilding /'bəʊt,bɪldɪŋ/ N *(NonC)* construction *f* navale

boater /'bəʊtə^r^/ N *(= hat)* canotier *m*

boatful /'bəʊtfʊl/ N *[of goods]* cargaison *f* ; *[of people]* plein bateau *m*, cargaison *f (hum)*

boathouse /'bəʊthaʊs/ N hangar *m or* abri *m* à bateaux

boating /'bəʊtɪŋ/ N canotage *m*
COMP *[club, accident]* de canotage
boating holiday N vacances *fpl* en bateau
boating trip N excursion *f* en bateau

boatload /'bəʊtləʊd/ N *[of goods etc]* cargaison *f* ; *[of people]* plein bateau *m*, cargaison *f (hum)*

boatman /'bəʊtmən/ N (pl **-men**) *(= boat-hire proprietor)* loueur *m* de canots ; *(actually rowing)* passeur *m*

boatswain /'bəʊsn/ N maître *m* d'équipage
COMP **boatswain's chair** N sellette *f*
boatswain's mate N second maître *m*
boatswain's pipe N sifflet *m*

boatyard /'bəʊtjɑːd/ N chantier *m* naval

Bob /bɒb/ N (dim of **Robert**) Bob *m* ◆ **~'s your uncle!** * *(Brit)* le tour est joué !

bob¹ /bɒb/ VI 1 ◆ **to ~ (up and down)** *(in the air)* pendiller ; *(in water)* danser sur l'eau ◆ **to ~ for apples** *jeu consistant à essayer d'attraper avec les dents des pommes flottant sur l'eau* 2 *(= curtsy)* faire une (petite) révérence N 1 *(= curtsy)* (petite) révérence *f* ; *(= nod)* (bref) salut *m* de tête ; *(= jerky movement)* petite secousse *f*, petit coup *m* 2 *(= weight) [of pendulum]* poids *m* ; *[of plumbline]* plomb *m* ; *(= float)* bouchon *m* VI *(Fishing)* pêcher à la ligne flottante
► **bob down** VI *(= duck)* baisser la tête ; *(straight)* se baisser subitement
► **bob up** VI remonter brusquement

bob² * /bɒb/ N *(pl inv: Brit)* shilling *m* ◆ **five ~** cinq shillings *mpl* ◆ **he's not short of a ~ or two** il n'est pas à court d'argent ◆ **that must be worth a few ~!** ça doit coûter les yeux de la tête !
COMP **bob-a-job** N *(Brit) collecte organisée par les scouts en échange de petits travaux à domicile*
bob-a-job week N *(Brit) semaine de la collecte organisée par les scouts en échange de petits travaux à domicile*

bob³ /bɒb/ N *(= curl)* boucle *f* ; *(gen = short haircut)* coiffure *f* courte ; *(= haircut: chin-length all round)* coupe *f* au carré ; *(= horse's tail)* queue *f* écourtée VT *[+ hair]* couper au carré ; *[+ horse's tail]* écourter

bob⁴ /bɒb/ N *(= sleigh:* also **bobsled, bobsleigh**) bobsleigh *m*, bob *m* ; *(= runner)* patin *m*

bobbin /'bɒbɪn/ N *[of thread, wire]* bobine *f* ; *[of sewing machine]* bobine *f* ; *[of lace]* fuseau *m* COMP **bobbin lace** N dentelle *f* aux fuseaux

bobble /'bɒbl/ N 1 *(Brit = pom-pom)* pompon *m* 2 *(US * = mistake etc)* cafouillage* *m* VT *(US * = handle ineptly)* cafouiller* COMP **bobble hat** N *(Brit)* bonnet *m* à pompon

Bobby /'bɒbɪ/ N dim of **Robert**

bobby * /'bɒbɪ/ N *(= policeman)* flic* *m*

bobby-dazzler †* /,bɒbɪ'dæzlə^r^/ N *(Brit) (= object)* truc *m* sensass †* inv ; *(= girl)* jolie pépée †* *f*

bobby pin /'bɒbɪpɪn/ N *(esp US)* pince *f* à cheveux

bobbysocks, bobbysox * /'bɒbɪsɒks/ NPL *(US)* socquettes *fpl*

bobbysoxer * /'bɒbɪsɒksə^r^/ N *(US)* minette* *f* (des années 40)

bobcat /'bɒbkæt/ N *(US)* lynx *m*

bobtail /'bɒbteɪl/ N *(= tail)* queue *f* écourtée ; *(= horse/dog)* cheval *m*/chien *m* écourté

bobtailed /'bɒbteɪld/ ADJ écourté

Boche ‡ /bɒʃ/ *(pej)* N Boche* *m (pej)* ADJ boche* *(pej)*

bock /bɒk/ N *(US:* also **bock beer**) 1 *(NonC)* bière *f* bock 2 *(= glass of beer)* bock *m*

bod ‡ /bɒd/ N 1 *(Brit = person)* type* *m* ; → **oddbod** 2 *(= body)* physique *m*, corps *m*

bodacious ‡ /,bəʊ'deɪʃəs/ ADJ *(US)* fabuleux*

bode /bəʊd/ VI ◆ **to ~ well (for)** être de bon augure (pour) ◆ **it ~s ill (for)** cela est de mauvais augure (pour), cela ne présage rien de bon (pour) VT présager, augurer

bodega /bəʊ'diːgə/ N *(US)* épicerie *f* portoricaine

bodge * /bɒdʒ/ *(Brit)* VT bricoler* N (also **bodge job**) bricolage *m**

bodice /'bɒdɪs/ N 1 *[of dress]* corsage *m* ; *[of peasant's dress]* corselet *m* 2 *(= undergarment)* cache-corset *m*
COMP **bodice ripper** * N roman *m* rose sur fond historique
bodice-ripping * ADJ ◆ **~-ripping novel/film** roman *m*/film *m* rose sur fond historique

-bodied /'bɒdɪd/ ADJ *(in compounds)* → **able, full**

bodily /'bɒdɪlɪ/ ADV *[lift]* à bras-le-corps ; *[carry]* dans ses *etc* bras ◆ **the explosion flung him ~ to the ground** l'explosion l'a plaqué au sol ADJ *[need, comfort]* matériel ; *[pain]* physique ◆ **~ functions** fonctions *fpl* physiologiques ◆ **~ fluids** fluides *mpl* organiques ◆ **~ illness** troubles *mpl* physiques ◆ **~ injury** blessure *f* corporelle ◆ **~ harm** blessures *fpl* ; → **actual, grievous**

bodkin /'bɒdkɪn/ N *(= big darning needle)* aiguille *f* à repriser ; *(for threading tape)* passe-lacet *m* ; *(for leather)* alêne *f* ; *(†† = hairpin)* épingle *f* à cheveux

body /'bɒdɪ/ N 1 *[of man, animal]* corps *m* ◆ **the (human) ~** le corps (humain) ◆ **the female ~** le corps de la femme ◆ **the ~'s natural defences** la défense de l'organisme ◆ **to sell one's ~** vendre son corps ◆ **you only want me for my ~!** il n'y a que mon corps qui t'intéresse ! ◆ **a part of the ~** une partie du corps ◆ **just enough to keep ~ and soul together** juste assez pour subsister ◆ **to belong to sb ~ and soul** appartenir à qn corps et âme ; → **sound²**
2 *(= corpse)* cadavre *m*, corps *m*
3 *(= organization, entity)* organisme *m*, organe *m* ◆ **official ~** organisme *m* officiel ; → **governing, legislative, regulatory**
4 *(= main part) [of structure, of dress]* corsage *m*, corps *m* (de robe) ; *[of car]* carrosserie *f* ; *[of plane]* fuselage *m* ; *[of ship]* coque *f* ; *[of church]* nef *f* ; *[of camera]* boîtier *m* ; *[of speech, document]* fond *m*, corps *m* ◆ **in the ~ of the hall** dans la salle proprement dite
5 *(= bulk, majority)* masse *f* ◆ **the great ~ of readers** la masse des lecteurs ◆ **the main ~ of the army** le gros de l'armée
6 *(= mass, accumulation)* masse *f* ◆ **a large ~ of people** une masse de gens, une foule nombreuse ◆ **the student ~** les étudiants ◆ **~ of troops** corps *m* de troupes ◆ **a large ~ of water** une grande étendue d'eau ◆ **a strong ~ of evidence** une forte accumulation de preuves ◆ **a strong ~ of opinion was against it** une grande partie de l'opinion était contre ◆ **a large** *or* **substantial** *or* **considerable ~ of information** une importante documentation ◆ **a large ~ of literature on ...** une abondante bibliographie sur ... ◆ **in a ~** en bloc ◆ **taken in a ~** pris ensemble, dans leur ensemble
7 * *(= man)* bonhomme* *m* ; *(= woman)* bonne femme* *f* ◆ **an inquisitive old ~** une vieille fouine ◆ **a pleasant little ~** une gentille petite dame
8 *(Med, Phys etc = piece of matter)* corps *m* ◆ **heavenly ~** corps *m* céleste ; → **foreign**
9 *(NonC) [of wine, paper]* corps *m* ◆ **a white wine with some ~** un vin blanc qui a du corps ◆ **to give one's hair ~** donner du volume à ses cheveux
10 *(= garment)* body *m*
COMP **body armour** N *(NonC)* gilet *m* d'armes
body bag N housse *f* mortuaire
body belt N ceinture *f* d'haltérophilie *or* de force
body blow N *(Boxing)* coup *m* au corps ; *(fig: disappointment)* coup *m* dur
body building N culturisme *m* ◆ **~-building exercises** exercices *mpl* de culturisme *or* de musculation
body-check *(Sport)* N body-check *m (on* à) VT faire un body-check à

body clock N horloge *f* biologique
body corporate N *(Jur)* personne *f* morale
body count N ◆ **to do a ~ count** *(of those present)* compter les présents ; *(of fatalities)* compter le nombre des morts
body double N doublure *f*
body dysmorphic disorder N dysmorphophobie *f*
body fascism N *discrimination fondée sur l'apparence physique*
body fluids NPL fluides *mpl* organiques
body image N schéma *m* corporel
body language N *(lit)* langage *m* du corps ◆ **the ~ language is good between the two leaders** *(fig)* le courant passe bien entre les deux leaders
body lotion N lait *m* corporel *or* pour le corps
body mass N masse *f* corporelle
body mass index N indice *m* de masse corporelle
body mike N *(on clip)* micro *m* cravate *inv* ; *(clandestine)* micro *m* caché
body odour N odeur *f* corporelle
body part N partie *f* du corps
body piercing N piercing *m*
body politic N ◆ **the ~ politic** le corps politique
body popping N *(NonC)* smurf *m*
body repairs NPL *(for car)* travaux *mpl* de carrosserie
body repair shop N ⇒ **body shop**
body scanner N scanner *m*, scanographe *m*
body search N fouille *f* corporelle ◆ **to carry out a ~ search on sb** fouiller qn ◆ **to submit to** *or* **undergo a ~ search** se faire fouiller
body shop N *(for cars)* atelier *m* de carrosserie
body snatcher N *(Hist)* déterreur *m*, -euse *f* de cadavres
body stocking N combinaison *f* de danse
body-surf VI faire du body(-surf)
body-surfing N *(NonC)* body(-surf) *m*
body swerve N *(Sport)* écart *m* ◆ **to give sb/sth a ~ swerve** * *(fig)* éviter qn/qch ◆ **thanks, I think I'll give that a ~ swerve** non merci, je préfère éviter
body warmer N gilet *m* matelassé

bodybuilder /ˈbɒdɪˌbɪldəʳ/ N ① *(= carmaker)* carrossier *m* ; ② *(= food)* aliment *m* énergétique ; ③ *(Sport) (= person)* culturiste *mf* ; *(= apparatus)* extenseur *m*

bodyguard /ˈbɒdɪgɑːd/ N *(= person)* garde *m* du corps ; *(= group)* gardes *mpl* du corps

bodyshell /ˈbɒdɪʃel/ N *[of car]* carrosserie *f*, caisse *f*

bodysuit /ˈbɒdisuːt/ N combinaison *f*

bodywork /ˈbɒdɪwɜːk/ N *[of car]* carrosserie *f*

Boeotia /bɪˈəʊʃɪə/ N Béotie *f*

Boeotian /bɪˈəʊʃɪən/ ADJ béotien

Boer /ˈbəʊəʳ/ N Boer *mf* ◆ **the ~ War** la guerre des Boers ADJ boer *f inv*

boffin * /ˈbɒfɪn/ N *(Brit)* expert *m*

boffo ⁑ /ˈbɒfəʊ/ ADJ *(US)* sensationnel

bog /bɒg/ N ① marais *m*, marécage *m* ; *[of peat]* tourbière *f* ② *(Brit* ⁑ *= lavatory)* chiottes *⁑ *fpl* VT (also **bog down** : *gen pass) [+ cart etc]* embourber, enliser ◆ **to be** *or* **get ~ged down** *(lit, fig)* s'embourber, s'enliser *(in* dans)
COMP **bog oak** N chêne *m* des marais
bog paper ⁑ N *(Brit)* PQ ⁑ *m*
bog roll ⁑ N *(Brit) (= roll)* rouleau *m* de PQ ⁑ ; *(NonC = paper)* PQ ⁑ *m* ◆ **there's no ~ roll** il n'y a pas de PQ ⁑
bog-standard * ADJ *(Brit)* ordinaire

bogey /ˈbəʊgɪ/ N ① *(frightening)* démon *m* ; *(= bugbear)* bête *f* noire ◆ **this is a ~ for them** *(fig)* c'est leur bête noire ◆ **age is a real ~ for actresses** vieillir est la terreur des comédiennes ② *(Golf)* bogey *or* bogée *m* ③ *(⁑: in nose)* crotte *f* de nez VT *(Golf)* ◆ **to ~ a hole** faire un bogey

bogeyman /ˈbəʊgɪmæn/ N (pl **-men**) croquemitaine *m*, père *m* fouettard

boggle /ˈbɒgl/ VI ① *(= be alarmed, amazed)* être ahuri ◆ **the mind ~s!** on croit rêver ! ◆ **stories that make the mind ~** des histoires à dormir debout ② *(= hesitate)* hésiter *(at* à) reculer *(at* devant) VT *(US)* ◆ **to ~ sb's mind** époustoufler qn

boggy /ˈbɒgɪ/ ADJ *[ground]* marécageux, bourbeux, tourbeux

bogie /ˈbəʊgɪ/ N *(Rail)* bogie *m* ; *(esp Brit = trolley)* diable *m*

Bogotá /ˌbɒgəˈtɑː/ N Bogotá

bogus /ˈbəʊgəs/ ADJ faux (fausse *f*) ◆ **a ~ marriage** un mariage blanc ◆ **measures to deter ~ asylum seekers** des mesures *fpl* visant à décourager les faux demandeurs d'asile

bogy /ˈbəʊgɪ/ N ⇒ **bogey**

Bohemia /bəʊˈhiːmɪə/ N Bohême *f*

Bohemian /bəʊˈhiːmɪən/ N ① *(Geog)* Bohémien(ne) *m(f)* ② *(† = gipsy)* bohémien(ne) *m(f)* ③ *(= artist, writer etc)* bohème *mf* ADJ ① *(Geog)* bohémien ② *(† = gipsy)* bohémien ③ *[artist, surroundings]* bohème ◆ **~ life** la (vie de) bohème

Bohemianism /bəʊˈhiːmɪənɪzəm/ N (vie *f* de) bohème *f*

boho * /ˈbəʊhəʊ/ ADJ, N branché(e) * *m(f)*

boil[1] /bɔɪl/ LANGUAGE IN USE 26.1
VI ① *[water etc]* bouillir ◆ **the kettle is ~ing** l'eau bout (dans la bouilloire) ◆ **to begin to ~** se mettre à bouillir, entrer en ébullition ◆ **to ~ fast/gently** bouillir à gros bouillons/à petits bouillons ◆ **to let the kettle/the vegetables ~ dry** laisser s'évaporer complètement l'eau de la bouilloire/des légumes ◆ **the potatoes were ~ing** *(Culin)* les pommes de terre bouillaient ; → **pot**[1]
② *[sea]* bouillonner ; *(fig) [person]* bouillir *(with* de) ; ◆ **he was ~ing with rage** il bouillait (de rage) ; see also **boiling** ; → **blood**
VT ① *[+ water]* faire bouillir ; *(= bring to the boil)* amener à ébullition
② *[+ food]* (faire) cuire à l'eau, (faire) bouillir ◆ **~ed bacon** lard *m* bouilli ◆ **~ed beef** bœuf *m* bouilli, pot-au-feu *m* ◆ **~ed egg** œuf *m* à la coque ◆ **~ed ham** jambon *m* cuit ◆ **~ed potatoes** pommes *fpl* à l'anglaise *or* à l'eau ◆ **~ed sweet** *(Brit)* bonbon *m* à sucer, ≈ berlingot *m* ; → **hard, soft**
③ *[+ washing]* ◆ **to ~ the whites** faire bouillir le (linge) blanc ◆ **~ed shirt** * chemise *f* empesée
N ◆ **on the ~** *(lit)* bouillant, qui bout ; *(* fig) [situation, project]* en ébullition ◆ **off the ~** *(lit)* qui ne bout plus ; *(* fig) [situation]* en voie d'apaisement ; *[project]* au ralenti ◆ **to bring sth to the** *(Brit) or* **a** *(US)* **~** faire bouillir qch ◆ **to come to the** *(Brit) or* **a** *(US)* **~** venir à ébullition ◆ **to go off the ~** *(lit)* cesser de bouillir ; *(* fig) [person]* baisser ◆ **the situation has come to the ~** la situation a atteint le *or* son point critique ◆ **the issue has brought tempers to the ~** cette question a échauffé les esprits
COMP **boil-in-a-bag, boil-in-the-bag** ADJ que l'on cuit dans le sachet

► **boil away** VI ① *(= go on boiling)* (continuer de) bouillir
② *(= evaporate completely)* s'évaporer, se réduire (par ébullition)

► **boil down**
VI ① *(lit) [jam etc]* se réduire
② *(* fig)* revenir *(to* à) ; ◆ **it all ~s down to the same thing** tout cela revient absolument au même ◆ **all the arguments ~ down to this** tous les arguments se résument à ceci
VT SEP ① *(lit) [+ sauce etc]* faire réduire (par ébullition)
② *(* fig) [+ text]* réduire *(to* à) abréger

► **boil over** VI ① *[water]* déborder ; *[milk]* se sauver, déborder ◆ **the pot ~ed over** la casserole a débordé
② *(with rage)* bouillir *(with* de) ; ◆ **their anger ~ed over into violence** leur colère a dégénéré en violence

► **boil up** VI *(lit) [milk]* monter ◆ **anger was ~ing up in him** la moutarde lui montait au nez

boil[2] /bɔɪl/ N *(Med)* furoncle *m*, clou *m*

boiler /ˈbɔɪləʳ/ N ① *(for hot water, steam)* chaudière *f* ; *(Brit: for washing clothes)* lessiveuse *f* ; *(= pan)* casserole *f* ; → **double, potboiler** ② *(= fowl)* poule *f* à faire au pot
COMP **boiler house** N bâtiment *m* des chaudières
boiler room N *(gen)* salle *f* des chaudières ; *(Naut)* chaufferie *f*, chambre *f* de chauffe
boiler suit N *(Brit)* bleu(s) *m(pl)* (de travail *or* de chauffe)

boilermaker /ˈbɔɪləˌmeɪkəʳ/ N chaudronnier *m*

boilermaking /ˈbɔɪləˌmeɪkɪŋ/ N grosse chaudronnerie *f*

boilerman /ˈbɔɪləmæn/ N (pl **-men**) *(= person in charge of boiler)* chauffeur *m*

boiling /ˈbɔɪlɪŋ/ N *[of water etc]* ébullition *f* ADJ ① *[water, oil]* bouillant ◆ **the whole ~ lot** ⁑ *(Brit)* tout le bataclan *, tout le bazar * ◆ **it's ~ (hot) today** * il fait une chaleur terrible aujourd'hui ◆ **I'm ~ (hot)!** * je meurs de chaleur ! ② *(* fig = angry)* bouillant de colère, en rage ◆ **he is ~** il bout de colère ③ *(Culin)* ◆ **~ beef** bœuf *m* pour pot-au-feu ◆ **~ fowl** poule *f* à faire au pot ADV ◆ **~ hot** *(lit)* tout bouillant ; *(fig)* → **adj**
COMP **boiling point** N point *m* d'ébullition ◆ **at ~ point** *(fig)* en ébullition

boisterous /ˈbɔɪstərəs/ ADJ *[person, crowd, behaviour]* tapageur, turbulent ; *[game]* tumultueux ; *(fig) [wind]* furieux

boisterously /ˈbɔɪstərəslɪ/ ADV tumultueusement

boisterousness /ˈbɔɪstərəsnɪs/ N *[of person, crowd, behaviour]* gaieté *f* turbulente ; *[of game]* tumulte *m*

bold /bəʊld/ ADJ ① *(= brave) [person, action]* hardi, intrépide ◆ **to grow ~** s'enhardir ◆ **a ~ step** une démarche osée *or* audacieuse ◆ **a ~ stroke** un coup d'audace ; → **face** ② *[person, look] (= forward)* hardi, effronté *(pej)* ; *(= not shy)* assuré ◆ **to be** *or* **make so ~ as to do sth** *(frm)* avoir l'audace de faire qch ◆ **to make ~ with sth** *(frm)* prendre la liberté de se servir de qch ◆ **if I may make so ~ ...** *(frm)* si je peux me permettre de faire remarquer ... ◆ **as ~ as brass** d'une impudence peu commune, culotté * ③ *(Art, Literat = striking)* hardi, vigoureux ◆ **to bring out in ~ relief** faire ressortir vigoureusement ◆ **to paint in ~ strokes** *[artist]* avoir une touche puissante ④ *(Typ)* en grasse, gras (grasse *f*) N *(NonC: Typ)* caractères *mpl* gras ◆ **in ~** en (caractères) gras

boldly /ˈbəʊldlɪ/ ADV ① *(= bravely)* hardiment, audacieusement ② *(= confidently, not shyly) [declare, announce, claim]* avec assurance ; *[gaze]* effrontément ◆ **to smile ~** sourire avec assurance ③ *(= strikingly)* ◆ **~ patterned/checked** à grands motifs/carreaux ◆ **~ coloured** *(one colour)* de couleur voyante ; *(contrasting colours)* de couleurs voyantes

boldness /ˈbəʊldnɪs/ N ① *(= braveness, daring) [of person, action, plan, idea]* audace *f* ; *[of gaze]* audace *f*, aplomb *m* ② *[of colour, design]* vigueur *f*

bole /bəʊl/ N fût *m*, tronc *m* (d'arbre)

bolero /bəˈlɛərəʊ/ N ① *(= music, dance)* boléro *m* ② /ˈbɒlərəʊ/ (also **bolero jacket**) boléro *m*

boletus /bəʊˈliːtəs/ N (pl **boletuses** *or* **boleti** /bəʊˈliːˌtaɪ/) bolet *m*

bolide /ˈbəʊlaɪd/ N *(Astron)* bolide *m*

Bolivia /bəˈlɪvɪə/ N Bolivie *f*

Bolivian /bəˈlɪvɪən/ ADJ *(gen)* bolivien ; *[ambassador, embassy]* de Bolivie N Bolivien(ne) *m(f)*

boll /bəʊl/ N graine *f* *(du cotonnier, du lin)* COMP **boll weevil** N anthonome *m* *(du cotonnier)*

bollard /ˈbɒləd/ N *(on quay)* bitte *f* d'amarrage ; *(Brit) (on road)* borne *f*

bollix‡ /ˈbɒlɪks/ VT *(US: also* **bollix up***)* ⇒ **balls up vt sep** ; → **ball**¹

bollocking*‡ /ˈbɒləkɪŋ/ N engueulade‡ *f* ◆ **to give sb a ~** engueuler qn‡ ◆ **I got a real ~ from him** il m'a bien engueulé‡

bollocks*‡ /ˈbɒləks/ N *(Brit)* ⇒ **balls** ; → **ball**¹

Bollywood* /ˈbɒlɪwʊd/ N Bollywood *m* *(le Hollywood du cinéma indien, à Bombay)*

Bologna /bəˈləʊnjə/ N Bologne

bolognese /bɒləˈnjeɪz/ ADJ ◆ **~ sauce** sauce *f* bolognaise

boloney‡ /bəˈləʊnɪ/ N ⇒ **baloney**

Bolshevik /ˈbɒlʃəvɪk/ N Bolchevik *mf* ADJ bolchevique

Bolshevism /ˈbɒlʃəvɪzəm/ N bolchevisme *m*

Bolshevist /ˈbɒlʃəvɪst/ N, ADJ bolcheviste *mf*

bolshie*, **bolshy*** /ˈbɒlʃɪ/ *(Brit pej)* N *(Pol)* rouge *mf* ADJ *(Pol)* rouge ◆ **he's rather ~** il ne pense qu'à enquiquiner le monde*, c'est un mauvais coucheur ◆ **he turned ~** il a commencé à râler*

bolster /ˈbəʊlstəʳ/ N 1 *[of bed]* traversin *m* 2 *(Constr)* racinal *m*, sous-poutre *f* VT *(also* **bolster up***)* *[+ person, morale]* soutenir *(with* par*)*

bolt /bəʊlt/ N 1 *[of door, window]* verrou *m* ; *[of lock]* pêne *m* ; *(for nut)* boulon *m* ; *[of crossbow]* carreau *m* ; *[of rifle]* culasse *f* mobile ; *(Climbing:* also **expansion bolt***)* piton *m* à expansion ; → **shoot**

2 *[of cloth]* rouleau *m*

3 *(= lightning)* éclair *m* ◆ **it was a ~ from the blue** c'était totalement inattendu

4 *(set phrase)*

◆ **to make a bolt for ...** ◆ **he made a ~ for the door** il a fait un bond *or* a bondi vers la porte ◆ **to make a ~ for it*** filer* *or* se sauver à toutes jambes

ADV ◆ **~ upright** droit comme un piquet *or* comme un i ◆ **she sat ~ upright** *(suddenly)* elle s'est redressée d'un coup

VI 1 *(= run away) [horse]* s'emballer ; *[person]* filer*, se sauver

2 *(= move quickly)* se précipiter, foncer* ◆ **he ~ed along the corridor** il a enfilé le couloir à toutes jambes

3 *[plant]* monter

VT 1 *[+ food]* engouffrer, engloutir

2 *[+ door, window]* verrouiller, fermer au verrou ◆ **~ the door!** mettez *or* poussez le(s) verrou(s) !

3 *(Tech) [+ beams]* boulonner

4 *(US * = stop)* abandonner, laisser tomber

COMP **bolt cutters** NPL coupe-boulons *m*
bolt-hole N *(Brit) [of animal]* terrier *m*, trou *m* ; *[of person]* abri *m*, refuge *m*
bolt-on ADJ ◆ **~-on extra*** option *f* ◆ **~-on goodies** gadgets *mpl* (en option) ◆ **~-on acquisitions** *(Comm)* achats *mpl* d'entreprises déjà opérationnelles

▸ **bolt in** VI *(= rush in)* entrer comme un ouragan
VT SEP *(= lock in)* enfermer au verrou

▸ **bolt on** VT SEP *(Tech)* boulonner ; → **bolt-on**

▸ **bolt out** VI *(= rush out)* sortir comme un ouragan

bolus /ˈbəʊləs/ N (pl **boluses**) *(Med)* bol *m*

bomb /bɒm/ N 1 *(= explosive device)* bombe *f* ◆ **letter/parcel ~** lettre *f*/paquet *m* piégé(e) ◆ **the Bomb** la bombe atomique ◆ **to put a ~ under sb*** *(fig)* secouer (les puces à) qn* ◆ **his party went like a ~*** *(Brit)* sa réception a été (un succès) du tonnerre* ◆ **this car goes like a ~**‡ *(Brit)* cette bagnole est un vrai bolide* ◆ **the car cost a ~**‡ *(Brit)* la bagnole* a coûté les yeux de la tête ◆ **we made a ~*** *(fig, Brit)* on a gagné une fortune *or* un bon paquet* ; → **A, car, H**

2 *(US * = flop)* fiasco *m*, bide* *m*

VT *[+ town]* bombarder ; → **dive**¹

VI 1 *(esp US * = flop)* être un fiasco *or* un bide*

2 *(* = go quickly)* **to ~ along** foncer, bomber* ◆ **we ~ed down the road** nous avons foncé le long de la rue ◆ **we ~ed down to London** nous avons bombé* jusqu'à Londres

COMP **bomb aimer** N *(= airman)* bombardier *m*
bomb attack N attentat *m* à la bombe
bomb bay N soute *f* à bombes
bomb crater N *(Geog)* entonnoir *m*
bomb disposal N déminage *m* ◆ **~ disposal expert** démineur *m* ; *(Mil)* artificier *m* ◆ **~ disposal squad** *or* **unit** équipe *f* de déminage
bomb factory N fabrique *f* de bombes
bomb scare N alerte *f* à la bombe
bomb shelter N abri *m* (antiaérien)
bomb site N lieu *m* bombardé

▸ **bomb out** VI *(‡ = collapse)* s'effondrer
VT SEP *[+ house]* détruire par un bombardement ◆ **the family was ~ed out** la famille a dû abandonner sa maison bombardée ◆ **~ed out families** familles *fpl* sinistrées *(par un bombardement)*

bombard /bɒmˈbɑːd/ VT bombarder *(with* de*)*

bombardier /ˌbɒmbəˈdɪəʳ/ N *(= soldier)* caporal *m* d'artillerie ; *(= airman)* bombardier *m* *(aviateur)*

bombardment /bɒmˈbɑːdmənt/ N bombardement *m*

bombast /ˈbɒmbæst/ N grandiloquence *f*, boursouflure *f*

bombastic /bɒmˈbæstɪk/ ADJ *[style, person]* grandiloquent, pompeux

bombastically /bɒmˈbæstɪkəlɪ/ ADV *[speak]* avec grandiloquence, avec emphase ; *[write]* dans un style ampoulé

Bombay /bɒmˈbeɪ/ N Bombay COMP **Bombay duck** N *(Culin)* poisson *m* salé *(indien)*

bombazine /ˈbɒmbəziːn/ N bombasin *m*

bombed‡ /bɒmd/ ADJ *(esp US) (= drunk)* bourré‡ ; *(= on drugs)* défoncé‡

bomber /ˈbɒməʳ/ N *(= aircraft)* bombardier *m* ; *(terrorist)* plastiqueur *m*

COMP **bomber command** N commandement *m* tactique aérien
bomber jacket N blouson *m* d'aviateur
bomber pilot N pilote *m* de bombardier

bombing /ˈbɒmɪŋ/ N *(from plane)* bombardement *m* ; *(by terrorist)* attentat *m* à la bombe ; → **dive**¹ ADJ *[raid, mission, plane]* de bombardement

bomblet /ˈbɒmlɪt/ N mini-bombe *f*

bombproof /ˈbɒmpruːf/ ADJ 1 *(lit) [bunker etc]* à l'épreuve des bombes 2 *(* fig)* indestructible

bombshell /ˈbɒmʃel/ N 1 *(† = bomb)* obus *m* 2 *(= shock)* ◆ **to come like a ~** faire l'effet d'une bombe ◆ **the decision was a legal/political ~** cette décision a fait l'effet d'une bombe dans les milieux juridiques/politiques ◆ **this news was a ~** la nouvelle a fait l'effet d'une bombe ◆ **to drop a** *or* **one's ~** lâcher une bombe* *(fig)* ◆ **then came the ~** et puis ça a été le coup de théâtre 3 * ◆ **she's a real ~** c'est une fille canon !*

bombsight /ˈbɒmsaɪt/ N viseur *m* de bombardement

bona fide /ˈbəʊnəˈfaɪdɪ/ ADJ *[member, traveller, student etc]* authentique, vrai ; *[offer]* sérieux

bona fides /ˈbəʊnəˈfaɪdɪz/ N bonne foi *f*

bonanza /bəˈnænzə/ N *(= windfall)* aubaine *f* ; *(= boom)* boom *m* ; *(US Min)* riche filon *m* ◆ **a property/sales ~** un boom immobilier/sur les ventes ◆ **the North Sea oil ~** la manne pétrolière de la mer du Nord

COMP **the Bonanza State** N *(US)* le Montana
bonanza year N année *f* exceptionnelle

Bonaparte /ˈbəʊnəpɑːt/ N Bonaparte *m*

bonbon /ˈbɒnbɒn/ N bonbon *m*

bonce‡ /bɒns/ N *(Brit = head)* tronche‡ *f*

bond /bɒnd/ N 1 *(= agreement)* engagement *m*, contrat *m* ◆ **to enter into a ~** s'engager *(to do sth* à faire qch*)*

2 *(= link)* lien(s) *m(pl)*, attachement *m* ◆ **to break a ~ with the past** rompre les liens avec le passé ◆ **~s** *(= chains)* fers *mpl*, chaînes *fpl* ; *(fig = ties)* liens *mpl* ◆ **marriage ~s** liens *mpl* conjugaux ; → **pair**

3 *(Comm, Fin)* bon *m*, titre *m*

4 *(NonC: Comm = custody of goods)* entreposage *m* *(en attendant le paiement de la taxe)* ◆ **to put sth into ~** entreposer qch en douane ◆ **to take goods out of ~** dédouaner des marchandises

5 *(= adhesion between surfaces)* adhérence *f*

6 *(Constr)* appareil *m*

7 *(Chem)* liaison *f*

8 *(also* **bond paper***)* papier *m* à lettres de luxe

VT 1 *(Comm) [+ goods]* entreposer

2 *(= stick)* coller ; *[+ bricks]* liaisonner

3 *(Fin)* lier (par une garantie financière)

4 *(= place under bond)* placer sous caution ; *(= put up bond for)* se porter caution pour

VI 1 *(= stick together)* coller

2 *(Psych)* se lier ◆ **to ~ with one's baby** s'attacher à son bébé ◆ **we ~ed immediately** nous nous sommes tout de suite liés d'amitié, nous avons tout de suite sympathisé

COMP **bonded labour** N *(NonC: Brit)* travail *m* non rémunéré *(pour le compte d'un créancier)*
bonded warehouse N entrepôt *m* des douanes
bond market N *(Fin)* marché *m* obligataire

bondage /ˈbɒndɪdʒ/ N 1 *(lit)* esclavage *m*, servage *m* ◆ **to be in ~ to sb** *(Hist)* être le serf de qn 2 *(fig)* esclavage *m*, asservissement *m* ◆ **the ~ of dieting/heroin addiction** l'esclavage que représentent les régimes/que représente l'héroïnomanie 3 *(= sexual practice)* bondage *m* COMP *[gear, magazine]* de bondage

bondholder /ˈbɒndˌhəʊldəʳ/ N *(Fin)* porteur *m* d'obligations *or* de bons

bonding /ˈbɒndɪŋ/ N 1 *(Constr)* liaison *f* ; *[of wood, plastic etc]* collage *m* ; *(Elec)* système *m* *or* circuit *m* régulateur de tension 2 *(Psych)* formation *f* de liens affectifs ; *(in general parlance)* action *f* de sympathiser

bondsman /ˈbɒndzmən/ N (pl **-men**) *(Hist)* serf *m*, esclave *m* ; *(Jur)* garant *m*, caution *f*

bone /bəʊn/ N 1 os *m* ; *[of fish]* arête *f* ◆ **~s** *[of the dead]* ossements *mpl*, os *mpl* ; *(‡ = dice)* dés *mpl* (à jouer) ◆ **on the ~** à l'os ; ◆ **to cut costs to the ~** réduire les coûts au strict minimum ◆ **chilled** *or* **frozen to the ~** transi de froid, glacé jusqu'à la moelle (des os) ◆ **my old ~s** *(hum)* mes vieux os, ma vieille carcasse* ◆ **to have a ~ to pick with sb** avoir un compte à régler avec qn ◆ **he made no ~s about saying what he thought** il n'a pas hésité à dire ce qu'il pensait ◆ **he made no ~s about it*** il n'y est pas allé par quatre chemins *or* avec le dos de la cuiller* ◆ **there are no ~s broken** *(lit)* il n'y a rien de cassé ; *(fig)* il y a plus de peur que de mal, il n'y a rien de grave ◆ **he won't make old ~s** il ne fera pas de vieux os ◆ **that was a bit close** *or* **near to the ~** *[remark]* c'était un peu limite ◆ **to work one's fingers to the ~*** s'user au travail, s'épuiser à la tâche → **anklebone, bag, feel, skin**

2 (NonC = substance) os m ◆ **a handle (made) of ~** un manche en os
3 [of corset] baleine f
VT [+ meat, fowl] désosser ; [+ fish] ôter les arêtes de
COMP [buttons, handle etc] en os
bone-chilling ADJ à vous glacer le sang
bone china N porcelaine f tendre
bone-dry ADJ absolument sec (sèche f)
bone-idle *, **bone-lazy** * ADJ fainéant, paresseux comme une couleuvre
bone marrow N (Anat) moelle f osseuse
bone meal N engrais m (de cendres d'os)
bone of contention N pomme f de discorde
bone-shaker * N (= car) vieille guimbarde f, tacot * m ; (= dilapidated cycle) vieux clou * m
bone structure N (NonC: gen) ossature f ; [of face] ossature f de la tête
► **bone up** * VT SEP, **bone up on** * VT FUS [+ subject] bûcher *, potasser *

boned /bəʊnd/ ADJ 1 [meat] désossé ; [fish] sans arêtes 2 [corset] baleiné

bonehead * /ˈbəʊnhed/ N crétin(e) * m(f), abruti(e) * m(f)

boneheaded * /ˈbəʊn,hedɪd/ ADJ idiot, abruti *

boneless /ˈbəʊnlɪs/ ADJ [meat] désossé, sans os ; [fish] sans arêtes

boner /ˈbəʊnəʳ/ N 1 (US * = blunder) gaffe * f, bourde f ◆ **to pull a ~** faire une gaffe *, mettre les pieds dans le plat 2 (= erection) ◆ **to have a ~** **bander**

boneyard * /ˈbəʊnjɑːd/ N (US) cimetière m

bonfire /ˈbɒnfaɪəʳ/ N feu m (de joie) ; (for rubbish) feu m (de jardin) COMP **Bonfire Night** N (Brit) le 5 novembre ; → GUY FAWKES NIGHT

bong /bɒŋ/ N 1 (= sound) bong m 2 (* = pipe) bong m

bongo (drum) /ˈbɒŋgəʊ(drʌm)/ N (tambour m) bongo m

bonhomie /ˈbɒnɒmiː/ N bonhomie f

bonk /bɒŋk/ N 1 (* = hit) coup m ; (with hand) beigne * f, pain * m 2 (Brit * = sex) **to have a ~** s'envoyer en l'air * VI (Brit * = have sex) s'envoyer en l'air * VT 1 (* = hit) frapper, filer un coup à * ; (with hand also) filer une beigne * or un pain * à 2 (Brit * = have sex with) s'envoyer *, sauter * EXCL bang

bonkers * /ˈbɒŋkəz/ ADJ cinglé *, dingue *

bonking * /ˈbɒŋkɪŋ/ N (NonC: Brit) partie f de jambes en l'air *

Bonn /bɒn/ N Bonn

bonnet /ˈbɒnɪt/ N 1 (= hat) [of woman] bonnet m ; [of child] béguin m, bonnet m ; → **bee, sun** 2 (Brit: of car) capot m 3 (Archit) auvent m ; [of chimney] capuchon m 4 (Naut) bonnette f

bonny /ˈbɒnɪ/ ADJ (esp N Engl, Scot) joli, beau (belle f)

bonsai /ˈbɒnsaɪ/ N (pl inv) bonsaï m

bonus /ˈbəʊnəs/ N prime f, bonus m ; (Brit Fin) dividende m exceptionnel ; (Educ, cycle racing) bonification f ◆ ~ **of €150** 500 € de prime ◆ **as a ~** (fig) en prime ◆ **an added ~** (fig) un avantage supplémentaire ; → **incentive, no**
COMP **bonus issue** N (Fin) émission f d'actions gratuites
bonus number N (Lottery) numéro m complémentaire
bonus point N (in game, quiz etc) point m (en prime)
bonus share N action f gratuite

bony /ˈbəʊnɪ/ ADJ 1 [tissue] osseux ; [knee, person] anguleux, maigre, décharné 2 [fish] plein d'arêtes ; [meat] plein d'os

boo /buː/ EXCL hou !, peuh ! ◆ **he wouldn't say ~ to a goose** * il n'ose jamais ouvrir le bec * VT [+ actor, play] huer, siffler ◆ **to be ~ed off the stage** sortir de scène sous les huées or les sifflets VI huer N huée f

boob * /buːb/ N 1 (Brit = mistake) gaffe f ; (= silly person) ballot * m, nigaud(e) m(f) 2 (= breast) sein m, nichon * m VI (Brit) gaffer
COMP **boob job** * N ◆ **to have a ~ job** se faire refaire les seins
boob tube * N (Dress = sun top) bain m de soleil ; (US = TV set) télé f

boo-boo * /ˈbuːbuː/ N boulette * f, bourde f

booby /ˈbuːbɪ/ N nigaud(e) m(f), bêta(sse) * m(f)
COMP **booby hatch** N (Naut) écoutillon m ; (US * pej = mental hospital) cabanon * m, maison f de fous *
booby prize N prix m de consolation (décerné au dernier)
booby trap N traquenard m ; (Mil) objet m piégé
booby-trapped ADJ [car, door etc] piégé

boodle † * /ˈbuːdl/ N (= money) oseille * f, pèze * m ; (US = bribe) pot-de-vin m ◆ **the whole ~** (US) le tout, tous les trucs *

booger * /ˈbuːgəʳ/ N (US) crotte f de nez

boogeyman * /ˈbuːgɪmæn/ N (US) ⇒ **bogeyman**

boogie * /ˈbuːgɪ/ N (= dance) ◆ **to have a ~** guincher * ◆ **to go for a ~** aller guincher * or se trémousser * VI guincher * COMP **boogie-woogie** N boogie-woogie m

boohoo * /,buːˈhuː/ VI pleurnicher, brailler * EXCL ouin ! ouin !

booing /ˈbuːɪŋ/ N (NonC) huées fpl ; (Theat) sifflets mpl

book /bʊk/ N 1 livre m, bouquin * m ◆ **the (Good) Book** la Bible ; → **bank², telephone, textbook**
2 (= chapter) [of Bible etc] livre m ; [of poem] chant m ◆ **the Book of Job/Kings** etc (Bible) le livre de Job/des Rois etc
3 (also **exercise book**) cahier m ; → **notebook**
4 [of tickets, stamps, cheques etc] carnet m ◆ ~ **of matches** pochette f d'allumettes ; → **chequebook, passbook**
5 (Accounting)
◆ **the books** les comptes mpl ◆ **to keep the ~s of a firm** tenir les comptes d'une entreprise ◆ **to be on the ~s** [employee] faire partie du personnel ; [member] être inscrit ◆ **already on the ~s** [regulation] qui figure déjà dans les textes ; [member] déjà inscrit au registre ◆ **to go on the ~s** [law] entrer en vigueur
6 (Betting) **to keep a ~ on sth** prendre les paris sur qch ◆ **to make a ~** (= take bets) inscrire les paris ; (= bet) parier ◆ **to open** or **start a ~ (on sth)** ouvrir les paris (sur qch)
7 (= libretto) [of opera etc] livret m
8 (phrases) **to bring sb to ~** obliger qn à rendre des comptes ◆ **by the ~** selon les règles ◆ **to close the ~ on sth** considérer qch comme une affaire classée ◆ **to go by the ~, to stick to the ~** appliquer strictement le règlement ◆ **to be in sb's bad ~s** * être mal vu de qn ◆ **I am in his good ~s** * je suis dans ses petits papiers *, il m'a à la bonne * ◆ **in my ~** * **he's unreliable** à mon avis or d'après moi on ne peut pas se fier à lui ◆ **he knew the district like a ~** il connaissait la région comme sa poche ◆ **that's one for the ~** or **~s!** * c'est à marquer d'une pierre blanche !, il faut faire une croix à la cheminée ! ; → **suit, throw**
VT 1 (= reserve) réserver ; [+ room, table] retenir, réserver ◆ **to ~ one's seat in advance** réserver sa place à l'avance ◆ **tonight's performance is fully ~ed** (Theat) on joue à guichets fermés ce soir ◆ **the hotel is fully ~ed (until September)** l'hôtel est complet (jusqu'en septembre) ◆ **I'm ~ed for tomorrow lunch** je suis pris demain à déjeuner ◆ **to ~ sb through to Birmingham** (Rail) assurer à qn une réservation jusqu'à Birmingham ◆ **I've ~ed my holiday** j'ai fait les réservations pour mes vacances ; → **solid**
2 (Police) [+ driver etc] dresser un procès-verbal or PV * à ; (Ftbl) [+ player] montrer un carton jaune à ◆ **to be ~ed for speeding** attraper une contravention pour excès de vitesse ◆ **to be ~ed** (Ftbl) recevoir un carton jaune
3 (Comm, Fin) [+ order] inscrire, enregistrer ◆ **to ~ goods to sb's account** inscrire des marchandises au compte de qn
VI (at hotel, on arrival) se présenter à la réception ; (= reserve in advance) réserver une chambre
COMP **book club** N cercle m de lecture, club m du livre
book ends NPL serre-livres m inv
book fair N salon m du livre
book jacket N jaquette f
book-keeper N comptable mf
book-keeping N comptabilité f
book knowledge, book learning N connaissances fpl livresques
book lover N bibliophile mf
book post N tarif m livres
book review N compte rendu m de livre
book token N (Brit) bon-cadeau m (négociable en librairie), chèque-livre m
book value N (Fin) valeur f comptable
► **book in** (Brit) VI (at hotel etc, on arrival) se présenter à la réception ; (= reserve in advance) réserver une chambre
VT SEP (at reception) se présenter à la réception ; (= reserve room for) réserver une chambre pour
► **book up** (Brit) VI réserver
VT SEP retenir, réserver ◆ **the school ~ed up all the seats on the coach** l'école a réservé toutes les places dans le car ◆ **the tour is ~ed up** on ne prend plus d'inscriptions pour l'excursion ◆ **the hotel is ~ed up until September** l'hôtel est complet jusqu'en septembre ; see also **book vt 1**

bookable /ˈbʊkəbl/ ADJ (Brit) 1 [seat etc] qu'on peut réserver ◆ **seats are ~ in advance** on peut retenir ses places (à l'avance) ◆ **seats ~ from 6 June** location (des places) ouverte dès le 6 juin 2 (Sport) [offence] passible d'un avertissement

bookbinder /ˈbʊkbaɪndəʳ/ N relieur m, -euse f

bookbinding /ˈbʊkbaɪndɪŋ/ N (NonC) reliure f

bookcase /ˈbʊkkeɪs/ N bibliothèque f (meuble)

Booker Prize /ˈbʊkə,praɪz/ N (Brit) ◆ **the ~** le Booker Prize

> **BOOKER PRIZE**
>
> Prix littéraire britannique créé en 1969 par un industriel (M. Booker) pour récompenser une œuvre de fiction écrite par un romancier originaire du Royaume-Uni, d'Irlande ou du Commonwealth. La cérémonie de remise du prix est diffusée en direct à la télévision, et le choix du jury suscite souvent des controverses.

bookie * /ˈbʊkɪ/ N book * m, bookmaker m

booking /ˈbʊkɪŋ/ LANGUAGE IN USE 21.4 N 1 (esp Brit) réservation f ◆ **to make a ~** louer, réserver, faire une réservation 2 (Ftbl) **there were three ~s at the game** il y a eu trois cartons jaunes lors de ce match
COMP **booking clerk** N (Brit Rail etc) préposé(e) m(f) aux réservations
booking fee N frais mpl de location
booking office N (Brit: Rail, Theat) (bureau m de) location f

bookish /ˈbʊkɪʃ/ ADJ [person] studieux, scolaire (pej) ; [word, phrase] livresque

booklet /ˈbʊklɪt/ N brochure f, plaquette f

bookmaker /ˈbʊkmeɪkəʳ/ N bookmaker m

bookmaking /ˈbʊkmeɪkɪŋ/ N (NonC) métier m de bookmaker COMP **bookmaking firm** N bookmaker m

bookmark /ˈbʊkmɑːk/ N marque-page *m*, signet *m* ; *(Comput)* signet *m* VT *(Comput)* mettre un signet à

bookmobile /ˈbʊkməˌbiːl/ N *(US)* bibliobus *m*

bookplate /ˈbʊkpleɪt/ N ex-libris *m*

bookrest /ˈbʊkrest/ N lutrin *m*

bookseller /ˈbʊkˌseləʳ/ N libraire *mf* ; → **secondhand**

bookshelf /ˈbʊkʃelf/ N étagère *f* (à livres) ; *(in bookcase)* rayon *m* (de bibliothèque)

bookshop /ˈbʊkʃɒp/ N *(esp Brit)* librairie *f* ; → **secondhand**

bookstall /ˈbʊkstɔːl/ N *(Brit: in station, airport)* kiosque *m* à journaux ; *[of secondhand books]* étalage *m* de bouquiniste

bookstand /ˈbʊkstænd/ N *(US)* [1] *(= bookrest, lectern)* lutrin *m* [2] *(= bookstall: in station, airport)* kiosque *m* à journaux ◆ **to hit the ~s** * *[book]* sortir en librairie

bookstore /ˈbʊkstɔːʳ/ N *(esp US)* librairie *f*

bookworm /ˈbʊkwɜːm/ N *(fig)* rat *m* de bibliothèque

Boolean /ˈbuːlɪən/ ADJ booléen

boom¹ /buːm/ N [1] *(= barrier: across river etc)* barrage *m (de radeaux, de chaînes etc)*, bôme *f* [2] *[of boat]* gui *m* ; *(Tech:* also **derrick boom***)* bras *m* ; *[of crane]* flèche *f* ; *[of microphone, camera]* perche *f*, girafe *f*

boom² /buːm/ N *(= sound) [of sea, waves]* grondement *m*, mugissement *m* ; *[of wind]* mugissement *m*, hurlements *mpl* ; *[of guns, thunder]* grondement *m* ; *[of storm]* rugissement *m* ; *[of organ]* ronflement *m* ; *[of voices]* rugissement *m*, grondement *m* ◆ **sonic** ~ *(Aviat)* bang *m* supersonique VI [1] *[sea]* gronder, mugir ; *[wind]* hurler, mugir (sourdement) ; *[thunder]* gronder, rouler [2] (also **boom out**) *[organ]* ronfler ; *[guns]* tonner, gronder ; *[voice]* retentir ; *[person]* tonner, tonitruer VT ◆ **"never !" he ~ed** "jamais !" dit-il d'une voix tonitruante *or* retentissante COMP **boom box** * N *(US)* ghetto-blaster *m*

boom³ /buːm/ VI [1] *[trade]* être en expansion *or* en plein essor ◆ **business is ~ing** les affaires prospèrent

[2] *[prices]* monter en flèche

VT *(US *) [+ market, sales]* développer ; *(= publicize) [+ person, place]* promouvoir

N *(in business, transactions)* montée *f* en flèche, boom *m* ; *(for firm)* forte progression *f* ; *(for product)* popularité *f*, vogue *f* ; ◆ **a property** ~ un boom sur l'immobilier ◆ **an export** ~ un boom sur les exportations

COMP **boom and bust** ADJ ⇒ **boom-bust**

boom baby N bébé *m* du baby-boom

boom-bust ADJ *[economy, market]* en dents de scie ◆ **the ~-bust pattern of the economy in recent years** l'évolution *f* en dents de scie de l'économie ces dernières années ◆ **property is a ~-bust business** l'immobilier est un marché en dents de scie, l'immobilier connaît des hauts et des bas

boom town N ville *f* en plein développement, ville *f* champignon

boomerang /ˈbuːməræŋ/ N *(lit, fig)* boomerang *m* VI *(fig) [words, actions]* faire boomerang

booming /ˈbuːmɪŋ/ ADJ *[sound]* retentissant ; *[voice]* tonitruant, retentissant

boomlet /ˈbuːmlɪt/ N *(Econ)* expansion *f* de faible amplitude

boon /buːn/ N [1] *(= blessing)* bénédiction* *f*, aubaine *f* ◆ **it would be a ~ if he went** quelle aubaine s'il s'en allait ◆ **this new machine is a great** ~ cette nouvelle machine est une bénédiction* ◆ **it is a ~ to me** cela m'est très précieux [2] *(† † = favour)* faveur *f* COMP **boon companion** † N joyeux compère *m*, compagnon *m* de virée

boondocks * /ˈbuːndɒks/ NPL *(US)* ◆ **the** ~ le bled* *(pej)*

boondoggle ‡ /ˈbuːndɒgl/ VI *(US)* [1] *(= work uselessly)* passer son temps à des tâches secondaires [2] *(esp Pol)* créer des emplois bidon*

boonies ‡ /ˈbuːnɪz/ NPL *(US)* ⇒ **boondocks**

boor /bʊəʳ/ N *(coarse)* rustre *m* ; *(ill-mannered)* malotru(e) *m(f)*, butor *m*

boorish /ˈbʊərɪʃ/ ADJ rustre, grossier

boorishly /ˈbʊərɪʃlɪ/ ADV *[behave]* en rustre, avec grossièreté ; *[speak]* sans tact

boorishness /ˈbʊərɪʃnɪs/ N manque *m* de savoir-vivre, grossièreté *f*

boost /buːst/ VT [1] *(= increase) [+ price]* hausser, faire monter ; *[+ output, productivity]* accroître, augmenter ; *[+ sales]* stimuler, faire monter en flèche ; *[+ product]* promouvoir ; *[+ confidence etc]* renforcer ◆ **to ~ the economy** stimuler l'économie [2] *(= do publicity for) [+ person, product]* faire de la réclame *or* du battage* pour [3] *(Elec)* survolter ; *[+ car engine]* suralimenter ; *[+ spacecraft]* propulser N ◆ **to give a ~ to** *[+ economy, sales]* stimuler ; *[+ project]* relancer ◆ **to give a ~ to sb's morale** remonter le moral à qn

booster /ˈbuːstəʳ/ N *(Elec) (= device)* survolteur *m* ; *(= charge)* charge *f* d'appoint ; *(Rad)* amplificateur *m* ; *(Rail)* booster *m* ; *(Space:* also **booster rocket***)* fusée *f* de lancement, booster *m* ; *(Med:* also **booster shot, booster dose***)* (piqûre *f* de) rappel *m* ; *(US * = supporter)* supporter *m* actif *or* enthousiaste COMP **booster cushion** N *(Brit: in car)* rehausseur *m*

booster seat N *(in car)* rehausseur *m*

boot¹ /buːt/ N [1] *(gen)* botte *f* ; (also **ankle boot**) bottine *f*, boot *m* ; *[of soldier, workman etc]* (grosse) chaussure *f*, brodequin *m* ◆ **the ~ is on the other foot** *(Brit)* les rôles sont renversés ◆ **to quake** *or* **shake** *or* **tremble** *or* **shiver in one's ~s** trembler comme une feuille ◆ **to fill one's ~s with sth** *(Brit)* se remplir les poches de qch ◆ **his heart was in his ~s** il avait la mort dans l'âme ◆ **to give sb the** ~ ‡ flanquer* qn à la porte, sacquer* qn ◆ **to get** *or* **be given the** ~ ‡ être flanqué* à la porte, être sacqué* ◆ **to put the ~ in** ‡ *(Brit) (= attack physically)* rentrer dans le chou ‡ des gens ; *(fig)* enfoncer le couteau dans la plaie ◆ **to put the ~ into sb/sth** ‡ *(Brit)* débiner* *or* éreinter qn/qch ◆ **Boots** † *(Brit)* garçon *m* d'hôtel ; → **bet, big, die¹, lick**

[2] *(Brit) [of car etc]* coffre *m*, malle *f* (arrière)

VT [1] *(* = kick)* donner *or* flanquer* des coups de pied à ◆ **to ~ sb out** *(lit, fig)* flanquer* qn à la porte

[2] *(Comput:* also **boot up***)* amorcer

COMP **boot boy** * N *(Brit)* skinhead *m (qui porte des rangers)*

boot camp N *(US Mil)* camp *m* d'entraînement *(pour nouvelles recrues)*

boot-polish N cirage *m*

boot sale N *(Brit)* brocante *f*, vide-grenier *m*

bootscraper N décrottoir *m*

boot² /buːt/ N ◆ **to** ~ par-dessus le marché, en plus, de plus, par surcroît ◆ **and his insolence to** ~ sans parler de son insolence

bootblack † /ˈbuːtblæk/ N cireur *m* (de chaussures)

bootee /buːˈtiː/ N *[of baby]* petit chausson *m (tricoté)* ; *[of woman]* bottillon *m*

booth /buːð/ N *[of fair]* baraque *f* (foraine) ; *[of cinema, language laboratory, telephone etc]* cabine *f* ; *[of restaurant]* box *m* ; (also **voting booth**) isoloir *m*

bootlace /ˈbuːtleɪs/ N lacet *m* (de chaussure) ◆ **to pull o.s. up by one's (own) ~s** se faire tout seul, se hisser à la force du poignet

bootleg * /ˈbuːtleg/ VI faire de la contrebande d'alcool *or* de boissons alcoolisées VT vendre *or* importer en contrebande, fabriquer illicitement ADJ *[spirits]* de contrebande ; *[software, tape, copy, edition]* pirate N *(= illicit recording)* enregistrement *m* pirate

bootlegger ‡ /ˈbuːtlegəʳ/ N bootlegger *m*

bootless /ˈbuːtlɪs/ ADJ [1] *(= without boots)* sans bottes [2] *(liter = to no avail)* infructueux

bootlicker ‡ /ˈbuːtlɪkəʳ/ N lèche-botte* *mf inv*

bootmaker /ˈbuːtmeɪkəʳ/ N bottier *m*

bootstrap /ˈbuːtstræp/ N [1] *(lit)* tirant *m* de botte ◆ **to pull o.s. up by one's (own) ~s** se faire tout seul, se hisser à la force du poignet ◆ **he's British/a republican** *etc* **to his ~s** *(Austral)* il est britannique/républicain, *etc* jusqu'au bout des ongles [2] *(Comput)* programme *m* amorce, amorce *f*

booty /ˈbuːtɪ/ N butin *m*

booze ‡ /buːz/ N *(NonC)* boisson(s) *f(pl)* alcoolisée(s) ◆ **bring the ~** apporte à boire ◆ **I'm going to buy some ~** je vais acheter à boire ◆ **to go on the ~** se mettre à picoler ‡ ◆ **he's on the ~** il picole ‡ ◆ **he's off the ~** il ne boit plus VI picoler ‡

COMP **booze cruise** N *traversée en ferry pour acheter des boissons alcoolisées bon marché*

booze-up ‡ N *(Brit)* beuverie *f*

boozer ‡ /ˈbuːzəʳ/ N [1] *(= drunkard)* soûlard(e) ‡ *m(f)* [2] *(Brit = pub)* bistro(t)* *m*

boozy ‡ /ˈbuːzɪ/ ADJ *[person]* pochard ‡, soûlard ‡ ◆ **a ~ party** une (partie de) soûlographie*

bop¹ /bɒp/ N [1] *(Mus)* bop *m* [2] *(= dance)* **to have a ~** * guincher* VI guincher*

bop² ‡ /bɒp/ VT *(= hit)* cogner ‡, taper

► **bop off** VI *(US)* filer

bo-peep /bəʊˈpiːp/ N cache-cache *m* ◆ **Little Bo-Peep** la petite bergère *(chanson enfantine)*

boraces /ˈbɔːrəˌsiːz/ NPL of **borax**

boracic /bəˈræsɪk/ ADJ borique

borage /ˈbɒrɪdʒ/ N bourrache *f*

borax /ˈbɔːræks/ N (pl **boraxes** *or* **boraces**) borax *m*

Bordeaux /bɔːˈdəʊ/ N [1] *(Geog)* Bordeaux ◆ **native of** ~ Bordelais(e) *m(f)* [2] *(= wine)* bordeaux *m*

bordello /bɔːˈdeləʊ/ N maison *f* de tolérance

border /ˈbɔːdəʳ/ N [1] *(= edge, side) [of lake]* bord *m*, rive *f* ; *[of woods, field]* lisière *f*, bordure *f*

[2] *(Pol, Geog) (= frontier)* frontière *f* ◆ **within the ~s of Serbia** à l'intérieur des frontières de la Serbie ◆ **to escape over the ~** s'enfuir en passant la frontière ◆ **on the ~s of France** aux frontières françaises ; → **Borders**

[3] *(fig) (= boundary)* frontière *f* ◆ **beyond the borders of their homeland** au-delà des frontières de leur pays

[4] *(in garden)* bordure *f*, platebande *f* ; → **herbaceous**

[5] *(= edging) [of carpet, dress]* bord *m* ; *[of picture]* encadrement *m*, cadre *m* ◆ **black ~** *[of notepaper]* liseré *m* noir

VT [1] *[trees etc] (= line edges of)* border ; *(= surround)* entourer, encadrer

[2] ◆ **France ~s Germany** la France touche à l'Allemagne, la France et l'Allemagne ont une frontière commune

COMP *[state, post]* frontière *inv* ; *[zone, town]* frontière *inv*, frontalier ; *[search]* à la frontière

border dispute N différend *m* sur une question de frontière(s)

border guard N garde-frontière *mf*

border incident N incident *m* de frontière
bordering countries NPL pays *mpl* avoisinants *or* limitrophes
border patrol N *(US Police)* patrouille *f* frontalière
border police N police *f* de l'air et des frontières
border raid N incursion *f*
border State N État *m* frontalier
border taxes NPL taxes *fpl* douanières

► **border (up)on** VT FUS 1 *[country etc]* être limitrophe de, avoisiner ◆ **the two countries ~ (up)on one another** les deux pays ont une frontière commune *or* se touchent ◆ **his estate ~s (up)on mine** sa propriété et la mienne se touchent
2 *(fig = come near to being)* être voisin *or* proche de, frôler ◆ **to ~ (up)on insanity** être voisin de *or* frôler la folie ◆ **it ~s (up)on fanaticism** cela touche au fanatisme, cela frise le fanatisme ◆ **with a boldness ~ing (up)on insolence** avec une hardiesse qui frise l'insolence

borderer /ˈbɔːdərəʳ/ N frontalier *m*, -ière *f*

borderland /ˈbɔːdəlænd/ N région *f* limitrophe

borderline /ˈbɔːdəlaɪn/ N ligne *f* de démarcation ADJ ◆ **it's ~** c'est un cas limite ◆ **~ case** cas *m* limite

Borders /ˈbɔːdəz/ NPL *(Brit Geog)* ◆ **the ~** *la région du sud-est de l'Écosse*

bore¹ /bɔːʳ/ VT 1 *[+ hole]* percer ; *[+ well]* forer, creuser ; *[+ tunnel]* creuser, percer 2 *[+ rock]* forer VI forer, sonder ◆ **to ~ for oil** forer (le sous-sol) pour extraire du pétrole, rechercher du pétrole par sondage *or* forage N 1 (also **borehole**) trou *m* de sonde 2 *[of tube, pipe, shot, gun, wind instrument]* calibre *m* ◆ **a 12-~ shotgun, a 12-~** * un fusil de (calibre) 12

bore² /bɔːʳ/ VT ennuyer, assommer ◆ **to ~ sb rigid** *or* **stiff** *or* **stupid** *or* **silly** *or* **to death** *or* **to tears** *, **to ~ the pants off sb** ‡ pomper l'air à qn * N 1 *(= person)* raseur * *m*, -euse *f*, casse-pieds * *mf inv*, importun(e) *m(f)* ◆ **what a ~ he is!** ce qu'il peut être ennuyeux *or* raseur ! * 2 *(† * = nuisance, annoyance)* corvée *f* ◆ **it's a frightful ~** quelle barbe ! *, quelle corvée ! ◆ **what a ~ this meeting is!** quelle corvée, cette réunion !

bore³ /bɔːʳ/ VB pt of **bear¹**

bore⁴ /bɔːʳ/ N *(= tidal wave)* mascaret *m*

bored /bɔːd/ ADJ *[person]* qui s'ennuie ; *[look]* de quelqu'un qui s'ennuie ◆ **to be ~ (with doing sth)** s'ennuyer (à faire qch) ◆ **I am ~ with this work/book/film** ce travail/livre/film m'ennuie ◆ **to be ~ rigid** *or* **stiff** *or* **stupid** *or* **silly** *or* **to death** *or* **to tears** * s'ennuyer à mourir, s'emmerder ‡

boredom /ˈbɔːdəm/ N ennui *m* ◆ **his ~ with the whole proceedings** l'ennui que lui inspirait toute cette cérémonie

borehole /ˈbɔːhəʊl/ N trou *m* de sonde

borer /ˈbɔːrəʳ/ N 1 *(= tool) (for wood)* vrille *f*, foret *m* ; *(for metal cylinders)* alésoir *m* ; *(for a well, mine)* foret *m*, sonde *f* ; *(= person)* foreur *m*, perceur *m* 2 *(= insect)* insecte *m* térébrant

boric /ˈbɔːrɪk/ ADJ borique

boring¹ /ˈbɔːrɪŋ/ *(Tech)* N *[of tunnel]* percement *m* ; *[of well]* forage *m* ; *[of wood]* perçage *m* ; *[of metal]* perçage *m*, alésage *m (Tech)* COMP **boring machine** N *(gen)* perforatrice *f* ; *(for metal cylinders)* alésoir *m*

boring² /ˈbɔːrɪŋ/ ADJ *[person, place, job, life, film, book]* ennuyeux ; *[colour, taste, food]* fade ; *[clothes]* sans originalité

boringly /ˈbɔːrɪŋlɪ/ ADV *[speak, write etc]* de façon ennuyeuse ◆ **it was ~ predictable** c'était tout ce qu'il y a de plus prévisible

born /bɔːn/ ADJ 1 né ◆ **to be ~** naître ◆ **to be ~ again** renaître ; see also **comp** ◆ **~ in Paris** né à Paris ◆ **the town where he was ~** la ville où il est né, sa ville natale ◆ **Napoleon was ~ in 1769** Napoléon est né *or* naquit en 1769 ◆ **three sons ~ to her** trois fils nés d'elle ◆ **every baby ~ into the world** tout enfant qui vient au monde ◆ **when he was ~** quand il est né ◆ **she was ~ blind/deaf** elle est née aveugle/sourde, elle est aveugle/sourde de naissance ◆ **the baby was ~ dead** l'enfant était mort-né ◆ **he was ~ evil** c'est de la mauvaise graine * ◆ **he was ~ stupid** il a toujours été stupide ◆ **a Parisian ~ and bred** un Parisien de souche ◆ **he wasn't ~ yesterday** * il n'est pas né d'hier *or* de la dernière pluie ◆ **in all my ~ days** * de toute ma vie ◆ **~ of poor parents** né de parents pauvres ◆ **people ~ to riches** ceux qui naissent riches ◆ **poets are ~, not made** on naît poète, on ne le devient pas ◆ **qualities ~ in him** qualités *fpl* innées (en lui) ◆ **misfortunes ~ of war** malheurs *mpl* dus à la guerre ◆ **anger ~ of frustration** colère *f* issue de la frustration ◆ **there's one ~ every minute** * je (*or* il *etc*) tombe toujours dans le panneau * ; → **first, highborn, lowborn, newborn, silver, stillborn**
2 *(= innate)* **a ~ poet** un poète-né ◆ **a ~ actress** une actrice-née ◆ **~ fool** parfait idiot *m* ; → **loser**
COMP **born-again** ADJ ◆ **~-again Christian** évangéliste *mf* ◆ **he's a ~-again cyclist/socialist** *etc (fig = convert)* il s'est converti au cyclisme/socialisme, *etc*

-born /bɔːn/ ADJ *(in compounds)* ◆ **Chicago-born** originaire de Chicago, né à Chicago ◆ **Australian-born** originaire d'Australie, né en Australie

borne /bɔːn/ VB ptp of **bear¹**

Borneo /ˈbɔːnɪəʊ/ N Bornéo *f* ◆ **in ~** à Bornéo

boron /ˈbɔːrɒn/ N bore *m*

borough /ˈbʌrə/ N municipalité *f* ; *(in London)* arrondissement *m* ; *(Brit Parl)* circonscription *f* électorale urbaine

borrow /ˈbɒrəʊ/ VT *[+ money, word, book]* emprunter *(from* à) ; *(fig) [+ idea etc]* emprunter *(from* à) adapter *(from* de) ; ◆ **a ~ed word** un mot d'emprunt ◆ **a word ~ed from Greek** un mot emprunté au grec ◆ **to ~ trouble** *(US)* voir toujours tout en noir ◆ **~ 1** *(Math: in subtraction)* je retiens 1

borrower /ˈbɒrəʊəʳ/ N emprunteur *m*, -euse *f*

borrowing /ˈbɒrəʊɪŋ/ N *(Fin, Ling)* emprunt *m* COMP **borrowing rate** N *(Econ, Fin)* taux *m* d'intérêt des emprunts

borsch(t) /bɔːʃt/ N bortsch *or* bortch *m*

borstal † /ˈbɔːstəl/ N *(Brit Jur)* ≃ maison *f* de redressement † COMP **borstal boy** N jeune délinquant *m*

borzoi /ˈbɔːzɔɪ/ N (lévrier *m*) barzoï *m*

bosh † * /bɒʃ/ N niaiseries *fpl*

bosk /bɒsk/, **bosket** /ˈbɒskɪt/ N *(= plantation)* bosquet *m* ; *(= thicket)* fourré *m*

bos'n /ˈbəʊsn/ N ⇒ **boatswain**

Bosnia /ˈbɒznɪə/ N Bosnie *f* COMP **Bosnia-Herzegovina** N Bosnie-Herzégovine *f*

Bosnian /ˈbɒznɪən/ ADJ bosniaque N Bosniaque *mf*

bosom /ˈbʊzəm/ N *[of person]* poitrine *f*, seins *mpl* ; *[of dress]* corsage *m* ; *(fig)* sein *m*, milieu *m* ◆ **in the ~ of the family** au sein de la famille ◆ **the ~ of the earth** *(liter)* les entrailles *fpl (liter)* de la terre COMP **bosom friend** N ami(e) *m(f)* intime *or* de cœur

bosomy /ˈbʊzəmɪ/ ADJ à la poitrine généreuse

Bosphorus /ˈbɒsfərəs/, **Bosporus** /ˈbɒspərəs/ N ◆ **the ~** le Bosphore

bosquet /ˈbɒskɪt/ N ⇒ **bosk**

BOSS /bɒs/ N *(in South Africa)* abbrev of **Bureau of State Security**

boss¹ * /bɒs/ N patron(ne) *m(f)*, chef *m* ; *[of gang etc]* caïd ‡ *m* ; *(US Pol)* chef *m* (du parti) ◆ **to be one's own ~** être son propre patron ◆ **we'll have to show him who's ~** il va falloir lui montrer qui commande ici ◆ **who's the ~ round here?** qui est le chef ici ? ◆ **it's his wife who's the ~** c'est sa femme qui porte la culotte * VT *[+ person]* mener, régenter ; *[+ organization]* diriger, faire marcher ADJ *(US ‡ = terrific)* formidable, terrible *

► **boss about** *, **boss around** * VT SEP *[+ person]* mener à la baguette ◆ **I don't like being ~ed around** je n'aime pas qu'on me donne des ordres

boss² /bɒs/ N *(= knob) [of shield]* ombon *m* ; *[of vault, ceiling]* bossage *m* ; *[of machine component]* mamelon *m*, bossage *m* ; *[of propeller]* moyeu *m* COMP **boss-eyed** * ADJ ◆ **to be ~-eyed** loucher

bossa nova /ˌbɒsəˈnəʊvə/ N bossa-nova *f*

bossiness * /ˈbɒsɪnɪs/ N autoritarisme *m*

bossy * /ˈbɒsɪ/ ADJ autoritaire, tyrannique ◆ **she's very ~** elle mène tout le monde à la baguette, c'est un vrai gendarme *

Boston /ˈbɒstən/ N Boston
COMP **Boston baked beans** NPL *(US) haricots blancs cuits avec du petit salé et de la mélasse*
Boston ivy N *(US)* vigne *f* vierge

Bostonian /bɒsˈtəʊnɪən/ N Bostonien(ne) *m(f)*

bosun /ˈbəʊsn/ N ⇒ **boatswain**

botanic(al) /bəˈtænɪk(əl)/ ADJ botanique ◆ **~(al) garden(s)** jardin *m* botanique

botanical /bəˈtænɪkəl/ N *(gen pl: = medicine)* médicament *m* à base de plantes

botanist /ˈbɒtənɪst/ N botaniste *mf*

botanize /ˈbɒtənaɪz/ VI herboriser

botany /ˈbɒtənɪ/ N *(NonC)* botanique *f* COMP **botany wool** N laine *f* mérinos

botch /bɒtʃ/ VT (also **botch up**) *(= repair crudely)* rafistoler * ; *(= bungle)* bâcler, saboter ◆ **a ~ed job** * un travail bâclé *or* de cochon * N (also **botch-up**) ◆ **to make a ~ of sth** bâcler *or* saboter qch

both /bəʊθ/ ADJ les deux, l'un(e) et l'autre ◆ **~ books are his** les deux livres sont à lui, les livres sont à lui tous les deux ◆ **on ~ sides** des deux côtés, de part et d'autre ◆ **to hold sth in ~ hands** tenir qch à *or* des deux mains ◆ **you can't have it ~ ways** * il faut choisir
PRON tous (les) deux *m*, toutes (les) deux *f*, l'un(e) et l'autre *m(f)* ◆ **~ (of them) were there, they were ~ there** ils étaient là tous les deux ◆ **from ~ of us** de nous deux ◆ **~ of us agree** nous sommes d'accord tous les deux ◆ **~ alike** l'un comme l'autre
ADV ◆ **~ this and that** non seulement ceci mais aussi cela, aussi bien ceci que cela ◆ **~ you and I saw him** nous l'avons vu vous et moi, vous et moi (nous) l'avons vu ◆ **~ Paul and I came** Paul et moi sommes venus tous les deux ◆ **she was ~ laughing and crying** elle riait et pleurait à la fois ◆ **he can ~ read and write** il sait et lire et écrire

bother /ˈbɒðəʳ/ VT *(= annoy)* ennuyer ; *(= pester)* harceler ; *(= worry)* inquiéter, ennuyer ◆ **don't ~ me!** laisse-moi tranquille !, fiche-moi la paix ! *, ne viens pas m'embêter ! * ◆ **don't ~ him with your problems** ne l'embête pas * *or* ne l'ennuie pas avec tes problèmes ◆ **I'm sorry to ~ you** je m'excuse de vous déranger ◆ **does it ~ you if I smoke?** ça vous dérange si je fume ? ◆ **to ~ o.s. about sth** se tracasser au sujet de qch, se mettre martel en tête au sujet de qch ◆ **to be ~ed about sb/sth** se faire du souci *or* s'inquiéter au sujet de qn/qch ◆ **which do you prefer? – I'm not ~ed** * lequel tu préfères ? – ça m'est égal ◆ **it doesn't ~ me** * ça m'est égal ◆ **to get (all hot and) ~ed*** **(about sth)** se mettre dans tous ses états (à propos de qch) ◆ **I can't be ~ed going out** *or* **to go out** je n'ai pas le courage de sortir ◆ **are you going? – no, I can't be ~ed** tu y vas ? – non, je n'en ai pas envie *or* non, ça me casse les pieds* ◆ **his leg ~s him a lot** sa jambe le fait pas mal souffrir ◆ **~ that child!** quelle barbe ce gosse !*

VI se donner la peine (*to do sth* de faire qch) ; ◆ **please don't ~ to get up!** ne vous donnez pas la peine de vous lever ! ◆ **you needn't ~ to come** ce n'est pas la peine de venir ◆ **don't ~ about me/about my lunch** ne vous occupez pas de moi/de mon déjeuner, ne vous tracassez pas pour moi/pour mon déjeuner ◆ **I'll do it – please don't ~** je vais le faire – non ce n'est pas la peine *or* ne vous donnez pas cette peine ◆ **why ~?** à quoi bon ?

N * 1 (= *nuisance*) barbe* *f* ◆ **what a ~ it all is!** quelle barbe !*

2 (*NonC* = *problems*) ennui *m*, embêtement* *m* ◆ **she's having** *or* **she's in a spot of ~** elle a des ennuis *or* des embêtements* en ce moment ◆ **we had a spot** *or* **bit of ~ with the car** on a eu un petit embêtement* avec la voiture

3 (= *effort*) mal *m* ◆ **to go to (all) the ~ of doing sth** se donner beaucoup de mal pour faire qch ◆ **it's not worth (going to) the ~ of ...** ça ne vaut pas la peine de ... ◆ **it is no ~ (at all)** il n'y a pas de problème ◆ **he found it without any ~** il l'a trouvé sans aucune difficulté ◆ **he is no ~ to look after** il est facile à garder ◆ **save yourself a lot of ~ and have it done professionally** épargnez-vous beaucoup de mal et laissez les professionnels s'en occuper

4 (*Brit* * = *violence*) bagarre* *f*, baston‡ *m or f*

EXCL (*esp Brit* *) flûte !*, la barbe !*

botheration †* /ˌbɒðəˈreɪʃən/ EXCL flûte !*, la barbe !*

bothersome * /ˈbɒðəsəm/ ADJ ennuyeux, gênant

Bothnia /ˈbɒθnɪə/ N ◆ **Gulf of ~** golfe *m* de Botnie

Botox ® /ˈbəʊtɒks/ N Botox *m*

Botswana /bɒtˈswɑːnə/ N Botswana *m*

bottle /ˈbɒtl/ N 1 (= *container, contents*) bouteille *f* ; (also **perfume bottle**) flacon *m* ; (also **medicine bottle**) flacon *m*, fiole *f* ; (*wide-mouthed*) bocal *m* ; (*goatskin*) outre *f* ; (*of stone*) cruche *f*, cruchon *m* ; (*for beer*) canette *f* ; (also **baby's bottle**) biberon *m* ◆ **wine ~** bouteille *f* à vin ◆ **to drink a ~ of wine** boire une bouteille de vin ◆ **we'll discuss it over a ~** nous en discuterons en prenant un verre ◆ **he is too fond of the ~*** il aime trop la bouteille* ◆ **to take to the ~*** se mettre à boire *or* picoler‡ ◆ **her husband's on the ~*** son mari picole* ◆ **child brought up on the ~** enfant *m* élevé *or* nourri au biberon ; → **hot, ink**

2 (*Brit* *) **he's got a lot of ~** il a un drôle de cran* ◆ **to lose one's ~** perdre courage

VT [+ *wine*] mettre en bouteille(s) ; [+ *fruit*] mettre en bocal *or* en conserve ◆ **to ~ it**‡ se dégonfler*

COMP **bottle bank** N conteneur *m* de collecte du verre usagé

bottle blonde N (*pej*) fausse blonde *f*

bottled beer N bière *f* en canette

bottled fruit N fruits *mpl* en bocal *or* en conserve

bottled gas N gaz *m* en bouteille

bottled wine N vin *m* en bouteille(s)

bottle-feed VT nourrir au biberon

bottle glass N verre *m* à bouteilles

bottle-green N, ADJ vert *m* bouteille *inv*

bottle-opener N décapsuleur *m*, ouvre-bouteille *m*

bottle party N soirée *f* (*où chacun apporte une bouteille*)

bottle rack N porte-bouteilles *m inv*, casier *m* à bouteilles

bottle shop N (*Austral*) magasin *m* de vins et spiritueux

bottle-top N capsule *f*

bottle-washer N laveur *m*, -euse *f* de bouteilles, plongeur *m*, -euse *f* ; → **cook**

► **bottle out**‡ VI (*Brit*) se dégonfler*

► **bottle up** VT SEP (*fig*) [+ *feelings etc*] contenir, refouler

bottlebrush /ˈbɒtlbrʌʃ/ N rince-bouteille(s) *m inv* COMP **bottlebrush moustache** N moustache *f* en brosse

bottleneck /ˈbɒtlnek/ N (*lit*) goulot *m* ; (*fig*) [*road*] rétrécissement *m* de la chaussée ; [*traffic*] embouteillage *m*, bouchon *m* ; [*production etc*] goulet *m* d'étranglement

bottler /ˈbɒtləʳ/ N (= *company*) société *f* de mise en bouteille *or* d'embouteillage

bottom /ˈbɒtəm/ N 1 [*of box*] (*outside*) bas *m* ; (*inside*) fond *m* ; [*of glass, well*] fond *m* ; [*of dress, heap, page*] bas *m* ; [*of tree, hill*] pied *m* ; [*of sea, lake, river*] fond *m* ; [*of garden*] fond *m*, bas *m* ; [*of chair*] siège *m*, fond *m* ; [*of ship*] carène *f* ◆ **"bottom"** (*on label*) "bas" ◆ **at the ~ of page ten** en *or* au bas de la page dix ◆ **at the ~ of the hill** au pied *or* au bas de la colline ◆ **the name at the ~ of the list** le nom en bas de la liste ◆ **he's at the ~ of the list** (*fig*) il est en queue de liste ◆ **to be at the ~ of the heap** *or* **pile** (*fig*) être en bas de l'échelle ◆ **to be (at the) ~ of the class** être le dernier de la classe ◆ **to knock the ~ out of an argument** démolir un argument ◆ **the ~ has fallen out of the market** le marché s'est effondré ◆ **the ~ fell out of his world*** son monde s'est effondré *or* a basculé ◆ **at the ~ of the table** en bout de table, au bout de la table ◆ **the ship went to the ~** le navire a coulé ◆ **the ship touched the ~** le navire a touché le fond ◆ **to go ~ up** (= *capsize*) se renverser ◆ **the ship was floating ~ up** le navire flottait la quille en l'air

2 (= *buttocks*) derrière *m*, postérieur* *m* ◆ **~s up!**‡ cul sec !

3 (*fig* = *origin, foundation*) base *f*, origine *f* ◆ **to be at the ~ of sth** être à l'origine de qch ◆ **to get to the ~ of a mystery** aller jusqu'au fond d'un mystère ◆ **we can't get to the ~ of it** impossible de découvrir le fin fond de cette histoire *or* affaire

◆ **at bottom** au fond

ADJ [*shelf*] du bas, inférieur(e) *m(f)* ; [*step, rung etc*] premier ; [*price*] le plus bas ; [*part of garden etc*] du fond ◆ **~ dollar** dernier dollar *m* ; → **bet** ◆ **to put sth away in one's ~ drawer** (*Brit*) mettre qch de côté pour son trousseau ◆ **~ floor** [*of building*] rez-de-chaussée *m* ◆ **~ gear** (*in car*) première *f* (vitesse) ◆ **~ half** [*of box*] partie *f* inférieure ; [*of class, list*] deuxième moitié *f* ◆ **~ land** (*US*) terre *f* alluviale ◆ **~ lands** (*US*) plaine *f* alluviale ◆ **the ~ line** (= *financial result*) le résultat financier ◆ **the ~ line is that ...** le fond du problème c'est que ... ◆ **she says £95 is her ~ line** elle dit qu'elle ne descendra pas en dessous de 95 livres ◆ **the ~ right-hand corner** le coin en bas à droite ◆ **~ round** (*US Culin*) gîte *m* à la noix ; → **rock²**

COMP **bottom feeder** N (= *fish*) espèce *f* benthique ; (* *pej*) (= *person*) vautour *m*, charognard *m*

bottom-up ADJ ◆ **~-up design/information** conception *f*/information *f* ascendante ◆ **~-up planning** planification *f* de bas en haut *or* de la base au sommet, planification *f* pyramidale

► **bottom out*** VI [*figures, sales, graph*] atteindre son niveau plancher ; [*recession*] atteindre son plus bas niveau

bottomless /ˈbɒtəmlɪs/ ADJ [*pit, well*] sans fond ; [*supply*] inépuisable ◆ **he's a ~ pit*** il a un appétit d'ogre

bottommost /ˈbɒtəmməʊst/ ADJ le plus bas

bottomry /ˈbɒtəmrɪ/ N (*Marketing*) hypothèque *f* à la grosse aventure

botulism /ˈbɒtjʊlɪzəm/ N botulisme *m*

bouclé /buːˈkleɪ/ N (laine *f or* tissu *m*) bouclette *f* ADJ en laine *or* en tissu bouclette

boudoir /ˈbuːdwɑːʳ/ N boudoir *m*

bouffant /ˈbuːfɒŋ/ N (= *hairdo*) coiffure *f* bouffante ADJ [*hairdo*] bouffant

bougainvill(a)ea /ˌbuːgənˈvɪlɪə/ N bougainvillée *f*, bougainvillier *m*

bough /baʊ/ N (*liter*) rameau *m*, branche *f*

bought /bɔːt/ VB pt, ptp of **buy**

bouillon /ˈbuːjɒn/ N bouillon *m*, consommé *m* COMP **bouillon cube** N bouillon cube *m*

boulder /ˈbəʊldəʳ/ N rocher *m* (rond), grosse pierre *f* ; (*smaller*) (gros) galet *m* COMP **boulder clay** N (*Geol*) dépôt *m* (argileux) erratique

boulevard /ˈbuːləvɑːʳ/ N boulevard *m*

bounce /baʊns/ VI 1 [*ball*] rebondir ; [*person*] bondir (*into* dans ; *out of* hors de) ; ◆ **to ~ in/out etc** [*person*] entrer/sortir *etc* d'un bond ◆ **the child ~d up and down on the bed** l'enfant faisait des bonds sur le lit ◆ **the car ~d along the road** la voiture faisait des bonds sur la route ◆ **the ball ~d down the stairs** la balle a rebondi de marche en marche ◆ **to ~ off sth** [*light, sound etc*] se réverbérer sur qch ◆ **the heat/light ~d off the white walls** la chaleur/lumière se réverbérait sur les murs blancs, les murs blancs réverbéraient la chaleur/lumière

2 * [*cheque*] être sans provision, être refusé pour non-provision

3 (= *be returned*) [*e-mail message*] être retourné *or* renvoyé (à l'expéditeur)

VT 1 [+ *ball*] faire rebondir ; [+ *light, heat etc*] renvoyer, réverbérer ◆ **use a mirror to ~ light onto the subject's face** servez-vous d'un miroir pour renvoyer *or* réverbérer la lumière sur le visage du sujet ◆ **they ~ radio waves off the moon** ils émettent des ondes radio qui se réverbèrent sur la surface de la lune ◆ **to ~ one's ideas off sb*** soumettre ses idées à qn, tester ses idées sur qn* ◆ **to ~ sb into doing sth** pousser qn à faire qch

2 (‡ = *eject*) [+ *person*] vider‡, flanquer* à la porte (*out of* de)

3 * [+ *cheque*] refuser

N 1 (= *rebound*) [*of ball*] bond *m*, rebond *m*

2 (= *springiness*) ◆ **there's not much ~ in this pitch** les balles ne rebondissent pas bien sur ce terrain

3 (*NonC*) **this ball hasn't much ~ left** cette balle ne rebondit plus beaucoup ◆ **to give your hair ~** pour donner du volume à vos cheveux ◆ **he's got plenty of ~*** il a beaucoup d'allant, il est très dynamique

► **bounce back** VI se remettre très vite

bouncer /ˈbaʊnsəʳ/ N (*at pub, dance hall etc*) videur *m*

bouncing /ˈbaʊnsɪŋ/ ADJ ◆ **a beautiful ~ baby** un beau bébé qui respire la santé

bouncy /ˈbaʊnsɪ/ ADJ [*ball, mattress*] élastique ; [*hair*] vigoureux ; [*person*] dynamique, plein d'allant COMP **bouncy castle** N château *m* gonflable (*servant de trampoline géant pour enfants*)

bound¹ /baʊnd/ N (*lit, fig*) ◆ **~s** limite(s) *f(pl)*, bornes *fpl* ◆ **his ambition knows no ~s** son ambition est sans bornes ◆ **to keep within ~s** (*fig*) rester dans la juste mesure, user de modération ; (*lit*) rester dans les limites ◆ **to break ~s** (*Mil*) violer la consigne ◆ **within the ~s of probability** dans les limites du probable ◆ **within the ~s of possibility** dans la limite du possible ◆ **to go over** *or* **pass over the ~s** dépasser les bornes

◆ **out of bounds** (*place etc*) dont l'accès est interdit ; (*Scol*) interdit aux élèves ; (*Sport*) hors du terrain, sorti ◆ **it's out of ~s to soldiers** c'est interdit *or* consigné aux soldats

VT (gen pass) [+ country] borner ◆ ~**ed by** borné or limité par

bound² /baʊnd/ N bond m, saut m ◆ **at a** ~ d'un saut, d'un bond ; → **leap** VI [person] bondir, sauter ; [horse] bondir, faire un bond or des bonds ◆ **to** ~ **in/away/back** etc entrer/partir/revenir etc en bondissant or d'un bond ◆ **the horse ~ed over the fence** le cheval sauta la barrière (d'un bond)

bound³ /baʊnd/ VB pt, ptp of **bind**

ADJ 1 lié, attaché ; (Ling) [morpheme] lié ◆ ~ **hand and foot** pieds mpl et poings mpl liés ; → **earthbound, icebound, spellbound**

2 [book etc] relié ◆ ~ **in boards** cartonné

3 (= obliged) obligé ◆ **to be** ~ **by law/an oath** etc **to do sth** être tenu par la loi/un serment à faire qch ◆ **you are not** ~ **to do it** vous n'êtes pas obligé de le faire ◆ **I am** ~ **to confess** je suis forcé d'avouer ◆ **to feel** ~ **to do sth** se sentir obligé de faire qch ; → **duty, honour**

4 (= certain)

◆ **to be bound to do sth** ◆ **he's** ~ **to say no** il dira sûrement non ◆ **it is** ~ **to rain** il va sûrement pleuvoir, il ne peut pas manquer de pleuvoir ◆ **it was** ~ **to happen** cela devait arriver, c'était à prévoir

5 (= destined) ◆ ~ **for** [person] en route pour ; [parcel] à destination de ; [train] en direction de, à destination de ; [ship, plane] à destination de, en route pour ; (= about to leave) en partance pour ◆ **ship** ~ **for Australia** (before sailing) navire m en partance pour l'Australie ; (en route) navire m à destination de or en route pour l'Australie ◆ **where are you** ~ **(for)?** où allez-vous ?

-bound /baʊnd/ ADJ (in compounds) ◆ **Australia-bound** à destination de l'Australie ◆ **Paris-bound traffic** la circulation dans le sens province-Paris ; → **northbound, outward**

boundary /ˈbaʊndərɪ/ N limite f, frontière f ◆ **to score a** ~ (Cricket) envoyer une balle jusqu'aux limites du terrain

COMP **boundary changes** NPL (Brit Pol) ◆ **to make** ~ **changes** effectuer un redécoupage des circonscriptions, redécouper la carte des circonscriptions

Boundary Commission N (Brit Pol) organisme chargé du redécoupage de circonscriptions

boundary line N ligne f frontière inv or de démarcation ; (Sport: gen) limites fpl du terrain ; (Basketball) ligne f de touche

boundary-stone N borne f, pierre f de bornage (Jur)

bounden duty /ˈbaʊndənˈdjuːtɪ/ N devoir m impérieux

bounder †* /ˈbaʊndəʳ/ N (esp Brit) butor m, goujat m

boundless /ˈbaʊndlɪs/ ADJ [space] infini ; [trust] illimité ; [ambition, devotion] sans bornes

bounteous /ˈbaʊntɪəs/, **bountiful** /ˈbaʊntɪfʊl/ ADJ [harvest] abondant ; [rain] bienfaisant ; [person] généreux

bounty /ˈbaʊntɪ/ N 1 (NonC = generosity) générosité f, libéralité f 2 (= gift) don m ; (= reward) prime f

COMP **bounty-fed farmers** NPL agriculteurs mpl qui ne vivent que de subventions

bounty hunter N chasseur m de primes

bouquet /ˈbʊkeɪ/ N 1 [of flowers] bouquet m 2 [of wine] bouquet m COMP **bouquet garni** N (pl **bouquets garnis**) (Culin) bouquet garni m

Bourbon /ˈbʊəbən/ N (Hist) Bourbon m

bourbon /ˈbɜːbən/ N (US) (whisky) bourbon m

bourgeois /ˈbʊəʒwɑː/ ADJ bourgeois N (pl inv) bourgeois(e) m(f)

bourgeoisie /ˌbʊəʒwɑːˈziː/ N bourgeoisie f

bourse /bʊəs/ N (Econ) bourse f

bout /baʊt/ N 1 (= period) période f ; [of malaria etc] attaque f, accès m ◆ ~ **of rheumatism** crise f de rhumatisme ◆ ~ **of fever** accès m de fièvre ◆ **a** ~ **of bronchitis** une bronchite ◆ **a** ~ **of flu** une grippe ◆ **he's had several ~s of illness** il a été malade plusieurs fois ◆ **a** ~ **of work(ing)** une période de travail intensif ◆ **drinking** ~ beuverie f 2 (Boxing, Wrestling) combat m ; (Fencing) assaut m

boutique /buːˈtiːk/ N (= shop) boutique f (de mode ou d'objets branchés) ◆ **hat/teenage** ~ (= within a store) rayon m des chapeaux/des jeunes

bovine /ˈbəʊvaɪn/ ADJ (lit, fig) bovin ◆ ~ **spongiform encephalopathy** encéphalopathie f spongiforme bovine

bovver‡ /ˈbɒvə/ N (Brit) ◆ **bovver boy** hooligan m ◆ **bovver boots** rangers mpl

bow¹ /bəʊ/ N 1 (= weapon etc) arc m ◆ **to draw the** ~ tirer à l'arc ; → **crossbow, longbow, string** 2 (Mus) archet m 3 (= curve) [of rainbow etc] arc m ; → **saddlebow** 4 (= knot) [of ribbon etc] nœud m VI (Mus) manier l'archet

COMP **bow and arrow** N (= child's game) arc m et flèches, jeu m de tir à l'arc

bow compass N compas m à balustre

bow-legged ADJ aux jambes arquées

bow legs NPL jambes fpl arquées

bow tie N nœud m papillon

bow window N bow-window m (en arc-de-cercle)

bow² /baʊ/ N (with head) salut m ; (with body) révérence f ◆ **to make a (deep)** ~ saluer (bas) ◆ **to make a** ~ **to sb** faire un salut à qn, saluer qn ◆ **to give sb a gracious** ~ adresser un gracieux salut à qn ◆ **to make one's** ~ **(as a pianist** etc**)** (fig) faire ses débuts (de pianiste etc) ◆ **to take a** ~ saluer

VI 1 (in greeting) saluer, incliner la tête ◆ **to** ~ **to sb** saluer qn ◆ **to** ~ **and scrape** faire des courbettes ; see also **bowing²**

2 (= bend) [branch etc] (in wind) fléchir, se courber ; (under weight) ployer ; [person] se courber

3 (fig = submit) s'incliner (before, to devant ; under sous) se soumettre (before, to à ; under sous) ; ◆ **to** ~ **before the storm** laisser passer l'orage ◆ **we must** ~ **to your greater knowledge** (iro) nous devons nous incliner devant votre grand savoir ◆ **to** ~ **to sb's opinion** se soumettre à l'opinion de qn ◆ **to** ~ **to the inevitable** s'incliner devant les faits or devant l'inévitable ◆ **to** ~ **to the majority** s'incliner devant la majorité

VT courber ◆ **to** ~ **one's back** courber le dos ◆ **to** ~ **one's knee** fléchir le genou ◆ **to** ~ **one's head** pencher or courber la tête ◆ **his head was ~ed in thought** il méditait la tête penchée ◆ **to** ~ **one's consent** signifier son consentement par une inclination de tête ◆ **to** ~ **sb in/out** faire entrer/faire sortir qn en saluant ◆ **to** ~ **o.s. out** saluer pour prendre congé

► **bow down** VI (lit, fig) s'incliner (to sb devant qn)

VT SEP (lit) faire plier, courber ; (fig) écraser, briser

► **bow out** VI (fig) tirer sa révérence (fig) see also **bow²**

bow³ /baʊ/ N 1 (often pl) [of ship] avant m, proue f ◆ **in the ~s** à l'avant, en proue ◆ **on the port** ~ par bâbord devant ◆ **on the starboard** ~ par tribord devant 2 (= oarsman) nageur m de l'avant

COMP **bow doors** NPL (on ferry) porte(s) f(pl) d'étrave

bow wave N lame f or vague f d'étrave

Bow Bells /ˈbəʊˈbelz/ NPL les cloches de l'église de St-Mary-le-Bow à Londres ◆ **born within the sound of** ~ né en plein cœur de Londres ; → COCKNEY

bowdlerization /ˌbaʊdləraɪˈzeɪʃən/ N expurgation f

bowdlerize /ˈbaʊdləraɪz/ VT [+ book] expurger

bowel /ˈbaʊəl/ N (gen pl: Anat) [of person] intestin(s) m(pl) ; [of animal] boyau(x) m(pl), intestin(s) m(pl) ◆ **to empty** or **relieve one's ~s** déféquer ◆ **~s** (fig) entrailles fpl ◆ **~s of the earth** entrailles fpl de la terre ; → **move, movement**

COMP **bowel cancer** N cancer m des intestins

bowel complaint N dérangement m intestinal

bower /ˈbaʊəʳ/ N (= arbour) tonnelle f ; († †, liter = cottage) chaumière f ; [of lady] boudoir m

bowing¹ /ˈbəʊɪŋ/ N (Mus) technique f d'archet ; (marked on score) indications fpl d'archet ◆ **his** ~ **was very sensitive** il avait un coup d'archet très délicat ◆ **to mark the** ~ indiquer or introduire les coups d'archet

bowing² /ˈbaʊɪŋ/ N ◆ ~ **and scraping** salamalecs mpl, courbettes fpl ; see also **bow²**

bowl¹ /bəʊl/ N 1 (= container) (gen) bol m ; (larger) saladier m, jatte f ; (for water) cuvette f ; (for fruit) coupe f ; [of beggar] sébile f ; (US Sport) championnat m, coupe f ◆ **a** ~ **of milk** un bol de lait ◆ **a** ~ **of water** une cuvette d'eau ◆ **a** ~ **of punch** un bol de punch ; → **finger, salad, sugar** 2 [of wineglass] coupe f ; [of pipe] fourneau m ; [of spoon] creux m ; [of lamp] globe m ; [of lavatory, sink] cuvette f 3 (Geog) bassin m, cuvette f

bowl² /bəʊl/ N (Sport) boule f ◆ **(game of) ~s** (Brit) (jeu m de) boules fpl ; (in Provence) pétanque f, boules fpl ; (US = skittles) bowling m

VI 1 (Brit) jouer aux boules ; (US) jouer au bowling ; (in Provence) jouer à la pétanque ; (Cricket) lancer (la balle) (to à)

2 **to** ~ **down the street** [person, car] descendre la rue à bonne allure ◆ **to** ~ **along, to go ~ing along** [car] rouler bon train

VT 1 (Sport) [+ bowl, hoop] faire rouler ; [+ ball] lancer

2 (Cricket) [+ ball] servir ; [+ batsman] (also **bowl out**) éliminer (en lançant la balle contre les guichets)

► **bowl down** * VT SEP renverser

► **bowl out** VT SEP [+ batsman] éliminer (en lançant la balle contre les guichets)

► **bowl over** VT SEP 1 [+ ninepins] renverser, faire tomber

2 (fig) stupéfier, sidérer * ◆ **she was ~ed over by him** (= impressed) il l'a éblouie ◆ **he was ~ed over to find his wife was expecting twins** quelle émotion d'apprendre que sa femme attendait des jumeaux ◆ **I was ~ed over by the beauty of Cornwall** j'ai été émerveillé par la (beauté de la) Cornouailles ◆ **we've been ~ed over by the offers of help from the public** nous avons été stupéfaits par toutes ces propositions d'aide (émanant) du public ◆ **I was ~ed over with admiration at the way Henry performed** la performance de Henry m'a laissé muet d'admiration

bowler¹ /ˈbəʊləʳ/ N (Brit) joueur m, -euse f de boules ; (US) joueur m, -euse f de bowling ; (in Provence) joueur m, -euse f de pétanque, bouliste mf ; (Cricket) lanceur m, -euse f (de la balle)

bowler² /ˈbəʊləʳ/ N (Brit: also **bowler hat**) (chapeau m) melon m

bowline /ˈbəʊlɪn/ N (= knot) nœud m de chaise ; (= rope) bouline f

bowling /ˈbəʊlɪŋ/ N bowling m

COMP **bowling alley** N bowling m

bowling green N terrain m de boules (sur gazon)

bowling match N (Brit) concours m de boules ; (US) concours m de bowling ; (in Provence) concours m de pétanque

bowman /ˈbəʊmən/ N (pl **-men**) (Archery) archer m

bowsprit /ˈbəʊsprɪt/ N beaupré m

bowstring /ˈbəʊstrɪŋ/ N corde f

bow-wow /ˈbaʊwaʊ/ *(baby talk)* N toutou *m* EXCL /baʊˈwaʊ/ ouah, ouah !

box[1] /bɒks/ N 1 boîte *f* ; *(= crate)* caisse *f* ; (also **cardboard box**) (boîte *f* en) carton *m* ; *(= casket)* coffret *m* ; *(† = trunk)* malle *f* ; *(* = set-top box)* décodeur *m*, set-top box *f* ◆ **a ~ of matches/chocolates** une boîte d'allumettes/de chocolats ◆ **(on) the ~*** *(esp Brit = television)* (à) la télé* ◆ **to be first out of the ~ with sth** *(US)* être le premier à faire qch ◆ **to come out of the ~ with sth** *(US)* se lancer dans qch ◆ **to think outside the ~** être innovant ◆ **to be out of one's ~*** *(Brit)* *(through drink)* être pété* ; *(through drugs)* être défoncé* ; *(= crazy)* être débile* ; → **icebox, letterbox, toolbox**

2 *(for money)* caisse *f* ; *(in church)* tronc *m* ; → **strongbox**

3 *[of axle, steering]* carter *m* ; → **axle, gearbox**

4 *(Theat)* loge *f* ; *[of coachman]* siège *m* (du cocher) ; *(for jury, press)* banc *m* ; (also **witness-box**) barre *f* ; *(in stable)* box *m* ; → **horsebox, sentry, signal**

5 (also **wine box**) cubitainer ® *m*

6 *(Sport = protection)* coquille *f*

7 *(* Ftbl = penalty area)* surface *f* de réparation

8 *(Brit = road junction)* zone *f* (de carrefour) d'accès réglementé

9 *(Printing)* encadré *m*

VT mettre en boîte *or* en caisse *etc*

COMP **box calf** N box(-calf) *m*
box camera N appareil *m* (photographique) *(rudimentaire)*
boxed set N coffret *m*
box file N boîte *f* à archives
box girder N *(Constr)* poutre-caisson *f*
box junction N *(Brit)* zone *f* (de carrefour) d'accès réglementé
box kite N cerf-volant *m* cellulaire
box lunch N panier-repas *m*
box number N *(Post: in newspaper)* référence *f* d'annonce ; see also **post office**
box pleat N *(Sewing)* pli *m* creux
box spring N sommier *m* à ressorts
box stall N *(US)* box *m*

► **box in** VT SEP *[+ bath, sink]* encastrer ◆ **to feel ~ed in** se sentir confiné *or* à l'étroit ◆ **house ~ed in by tall buildings** maison *f* coincée entre de grands immeubles

► **box off** VT SEP compartimenter

► **box up** VT SEP mettre en boîte ; *(fig)* enfermer

box[2] /bɒks/ VI *(Sport)* boxer, faire de la boxe ◆ **to ~ clever** *(Brit)* bien manœuvrer VT 1 *(Sport)* boxer avec, boxer* 2 ◆ **to ~ sb's ears** chauffer les oreilles à qn, gifler *or* claquer qn, flanquer* une claque *or* une gifle à qn N ◆ **a ~ on the ear** une claque, une gifle

box[3] /bɒks/ N *(= plant)* buis *m* COMP en *or* de buis

boxboard /ˈbɒksbɔːd/ N carton *m* d'emballage

boxcar /ˈbɒkskɑːʳ/ N *(Rail)* wagon *m* (de marchandises) couvert

boxer[1] /ˈbɒksəʳ/ N *(Sport)* boxeur *m* NPL **boxers** ⇒ **boxer shorts** COMP **boxer shorts** NPL boxer-short *m*

boxer[2] /ˈbɒksəʳ/ N *(= dog)* boxer *m*

boxing /ˈbɒksɪŋ/ N boxe *f*
COMP *[gloves, match]* de boxe
boxing ring N ring *m* (de boxe)

Boxing Day /ˈbɒksɪŋdeɪ/ N *(Brit)* le lendemain de Noël

Boxing Day

Boxing Day est un jour férié en Grande-Bretagne ; il est fixé le 26 décembre, ou le 27 si Noël tombe un samedi. C'était à l'origine le jour où l'on donnait les étrennes (une « boîte de Noël » ou « Christmas box ») au facteur et aux artisans. Aujourd'hui, cette journée est surtout consacrée aux sports, au repos ou à la poursuite des festivités de Noël.

box office /ˈbɒksɒfɪs/ *(Theat)* N *(= office)* bureau *m* de location ; *(= window)* guichet *m* (de location) ◆ **this show will be good ~** ce spectacle fera recette
COMP **box-office attraction** N spectacle *m* à (grand) succès
box-office receipts NPL recette *f*
box-office success N pièce *f etc* qui fait courir les foules *or* qui fait recette ; *(= film)* succès *m* au box-office

boxroom /ˈbɒksrʊm/ N *(Brit)* débarras *m*

boxwood /ˈbɒkswʊd/ N buis *m*

boxy* /ˈbɒksɪ/ ADJ *[building]* en forme de boîte, qui ressemble à une boîte ; *[car]* en forme de caisse à savon

boy /bɔɪ/ N 1 *(= child)* garçon *m*, enfant *m* ; *(= young man)* jeune *m* (homme *m*), garçon *m* ; *(= son)* fils *m*, garçon *m* ; *(Scol)* élève *m*, garçon *m* ◆ **little ~** petit garçon *m*, garçonnet *m* ◆ **beggar ~** petit mendiant *m* ◆ **English ~** petit *or* jeune Anglais *m* ◆ **come here, my ~** viens ici mon petit *or* mon grand ◆ **bad ~!, naughty ~!** vilain ! ◆ **the Jones ~** le petit Jones ◆ **I lived here as a ~** j'habitais ici quand j'étais petit *or* enfant ◆ **he knew me from a ~** il me connaissait depuis mon (*or* son) enfance, il me connaissait depuis tout petit ◆ **~s will be ~s!** les garçons, on ne les changera jamais ! ◆ **he was as much a ~ as ever** il était toujours aussi gamin ◆ **sit down, ~s** *(Scol)* *(to small boys)* asseyez-vous, mes enfants ; *(to sixth formers etc)* asseyez-vous, messieurs *or* mes amis ; → **choirboy, day, old, page**[2]

2 *(* = fellow)* **my dear ~** mon cher (ami) ◆ **old ~** mon vieux ◆ **the old ~** *(= boss)* le patron ; *(= father)* le paternel* ◆ **a night out with the ~s** une sortie avec les copains ; → **wide**

3 *(= native servant)* boy *m*

EXCL * bigre !

COMP **boy band** N *(Brit Mus)* boys band *m*
boy-meets-girl story N *(film, novel etc)* histoire *f* romantique conventionnelle
boy racer* N *(Brit)* jeune fou *m* du volant
Boys' Brigade N *(Brit)* *organisation de scoutisme*
boy scout † N *(Catholic)* scout *m* ; *(non-Catholic)* éclaireur *m*
the boys in blue* NPL *(Brit)* les défenseurs *mpl* de l'ordre
boy soprano N soprano *m*
boy wonder* N jeune prodige *m*

boycott /ˈbɔɪkɒt/ VT *[+ person, product, place]* boycotter N boycottage *m*, boycott *m*

boyfriend /ˈbɔɪfrend/ N petit ami *m*

boyhood /ˈbɔɪhʊd/ N enfance *f*, adolescence *f*

boyish /ˈbɔɪɪʃ/ ADJ *[male's behaviour]* d'enfant, de garçon ; *[smile]* gamin ; *(pej)* enfantin, puéril (puérile *f*) ; *(= tomboyish)* *[girl]* garçonnier ; *[behaviour]* garçonnier, de garçon ◆ **he looks very ~** il fait très jeune ◆ **his ~ good looks** son air de beau garçon

boyishly /ˈbɔɪɪʃlɪ/ ADV comme un garçon ◆ **~ cut hair** cheveux *mpl* coupés à la garçonne

boyo* /ˈbɔɪəʊ/ N *(Brit dial)* gars* *m* ◆ **listen, ~** écoute, mon gars*

boysenberry /ˈbɔɪzənbərɪ/ N boysenberry *f* *(variété de mûre)*

bozo* /ˈbəʊzəʊ/ N *(esp US)* bozo* *m*, drôle de type* *m*

BP /biːˈpiː/ N abbrev of **blood pressure**

Bp abbrev of **Bishop**

bpi /ˌbiːpiːˈaɪ/ N (abbrev of **bits per inch**) bits *mpl* par pouce

bps /ˌbiːpiːˈes/ N (abbrev of **bits per second**) bits *mpl* par seconde

BR /biːˈɑːʳ/ N *(formerly)* (abbrev of **British Rail**) → **British** NPL abbrev of **bills receivable**

bra /brɑː/ N (abbrev of **brassière**) soutien-gorge *m* ◆ **half-cup ~** balconnet *m* soutien-gorge *m* pigeonnant

Brabant /brəˈbænt/ N Brabant *m*

brace /breɪs/ N 1 attache *f*, agrafe *f* ; *(Med)* appareil *m* orthopédique ; *(Constr)* entretoise *f*, étrésillon *m* ; *(US Mil *)* garde-à-vous *m* rigide ◆ **~(s)** *(for teeth)* appareil *m* dentaire *or* orthodontique ◆ **~ (and bit)** *(= tool)* vilebrequin *m* (à main)

2 *(pl inv = pair)* *[of animals, pistols]* paire *f*

3 *(Mus, Typ:* also **brace bracket***)* accolade *f*

NPL **braces** *(Brit Dress)* bretelles *fpl*

VT 1 *(= support, strengthen)* soutenir, consolider ; *[+ structure]* entretoiser, étrésillonner ; *[+ beam]* armer *(with* de*)* soutenir

2 ◆ **to ~ o.s.** *(lit)* s'arc-bouter ; *(fig)* rassembler ses forces *(to do sth* à faire qch*)* fortifier son âme *(to do sth* pour faire qch*)* ; ◆ **he ~d his leg against the door** il a bloqué la porte avec sa jambe ◆ **~ yourself for the news!** tenez-vous bien que je vous raconte *subj* la nouvelle ! *or* que je vous en dise une bien bonne !*

3 *[climate etc]* fortifier, tonifier

► **brace up** VT SEP *[+ person]* revigorer, remonter ◆ **to ~ o.s. up** rassembler ses forces *(to do sth* pour faire qch*)* ; *(by having a drink)* reprendre des forces *(hum)*
EXCL ◆ **brace up !** du courage !

bracelet /ˈbreɪslɪt/ N 1 bracelet *m* 2 **~s*** *(= handcuffs)* menottes *fpl*, bracelets *mpl* *(hum)*

bracer* /ˈbreɪsəʳ/ N *(= drink)* remontant *m*

bracing /ˈbreɪsɪŋ/ ADJ *[air, climate]* fortifiant, tonifiant ◆ **a ~ wind** un vent vivifiant

bracken /ˈbrækən/ N *(NonC)* fougère *f*

bracket /ˈbrækɪt/ N 1 *(= angled support)* support *m* ; *[of shelf]* tasseau *m*, équerre *f* ; *(Archit)* console *f*, corbeau *m*

2 *[of lamp]* fixation *f*

3 *(= small shelf)* rayon *m*, étagère *f*

4 *(Typ)* (also **round bracket**) parenthèse *f* ; (also **square bracket**) crochet *m* ; *(Mus, Typ:* also **brace bracket, curly bracket***)* accolade *f* ◆ **in ~s** entre parenthèses

5 *(fig = group)* tranche *f* ◆ **the lower/upper income ~** la tranche des petits/des gros revenus ◆ **he's in the £30,000-a-year ~** il est dans la tranche (de revenus) des 30 000 livres par an ◆ **price ~** fourchette *f* de prix ◆ **tax ~** tranche *f* d'imposition ◆ **age ~** classe *f* d'âge

VT 1 *(Typ)* *[+ sentence etc]* mettre entre parenthèses *or* entre crochets

2 *(= join by brackets)* réunir par une accolade ; *(fig:* also **bracket together***)* *[+ names, persons]* mettre dans le même groupe *or* dans la même catégorie ; *[+ candidates etc]* mettre ex æquo, accoler ; *(fig = link in one's mind)* mettre dans le même sac ◆ **~ed first** *(Scol, Sport etc)* premiers ex æquo

3 *(Mil)* *[+ target]* encadrer

COMP **bracket lamp** N applique *f*

bracketing /ˈbrækətɪŋ/ N 1 *(Gram)* parenthésage *m* 2 *(Phot)* bracketing *m* d'exposition

brackish /ˈbrækɪʃ/ ADJ *[water, taste]* saumâtre

brad /bræd/ N semence *f*, clou *m* de tapissier
COMP **brad awl** N poinçon *m*

brae /breɪ/ N *(Scot)* pente *f*, côte *f*

brag /bræg/ VI se vanter (*about, of* de) VT ◆ **to ~ that one has done sth** se vanter d'avoir fait qch N 1 (*= boast*) vantardise *f*, fanfaronnades *fpl* 2 ⇒ **braggart** 3 (*Cards*) *jeu de cartes semblable au poker*

braggart /'brægət/ N vantard(e) *m(f)*, fanfaron(ne) *m(f)*

bragging /'brægɪŋ/ N vantardise *f* (*about* à propos de)

Brahma /'brɑːmə/ N 1 (*= god*) Brahmâ *m* 2 (*US = animal*) zébu *m* américain

Brahman /'brɑːmən/ N (pl **Brahmans**) 1 (*= person*) brahmane *m* 2 ⇒ **Brahma 2**

Brahmaputra /ˌbrɑːmə'puːtrə/ N Brahmâpoutre *m*, Brahmaputra *m*

Brahmin /'brɑːmɪn/ N (pl **Brahmin** or **Brahmins**) ⇒ **Brahman 1**

braid /breɪd/ VT 1 (*esp US*) (*= plait*) tresser, natter ; (*= interweave*) entrelacer (*with* avec) 2 (*= trim with braid*) [*+ clothing, material*] galonner, soutacher N 1 (*esp US = plait of hair*) tresse *f*, natte *f* 2 (*NonC = trimming*) soutache *f*, ganse *f*, galon *m* ; (*Mil*) galon *m* ◆ **gold ~** galon *m* d'or or doré

braided /'breɪdɪd/ ADJ galonné

Braille /breɪl/ N braille *m* ADJ braille *inv*

brain /breɪn/ N 1 (*Anat*) cerveau *m* ; (*fig*) cerveau *m*, tête *f* ◆ **~s** (*Anat, Culin*) cervelle *f* ◆ **he's got that on the ~!*** il ne pense qu'à ça ! ◆ **he's got politics on the ~*** il n'a que la politique en tête ◆ **his ~ reeled** la tête lui a tourné ◆ **to beat sb's ~s out*** estourbir qn* ◆ **to blow sb's ~s out*** brûler la cervelle à qn ◆ **calves' ~** (*Culin*) cervelle *f* de veau ; → **pick, rack¹**
2 (*gen pl = intelligence*) **~s** intelligence *f* ◆ **he's got ~s** il est intelligent ◆ **he's the ~s of the family** c'est le cerveau de la famille
VT (*‡ = knock out*) [*+ person*] assommer
COMP [*disease*] du cerveau, cérébral ; [*operation*] au cerveau
brain-box* N tête* *f*, cerveau *m*
brain-child N idée *f* personnelle, invention *f* personnelle ◆ **it's his ~-child** c'est lui qui l'a inventé
brain damage N lésions *fpl* cérébrales
brain-damaged ADJ atteint de lésions cérébrales ◆ **the accident left him severely ~-damaged** l'accident a provoqué (chez lui) des lésions cérébrales
brain dead ADJ (*Med*) dans un coma dépassé ; (** = stupid*) balourd*
brain death N mort *f* cérébrale
brain drain N exode *m* or fuite *f* des cerveaux
brain fever N fièvre *f* cérébrale
brain pan N boîte *f* crânienne
brain scan N scanographie *f* du cerveau, scanner *m* cérébral
brain scanner N scanner *m*, tomodensitomètre *m*
brains trust N (*= panel of experts*) groupe *m* d'experts or de spécialistes ; (*US = advisory experts*: also **brain trust**) brain-trust *m*
brain surgeon N neurochirurgien(ne) *m(f)*
brain-teaser N casse-tête *f*
brain trust N (*US*) → **brains trust**
brain tumour N tumeur *f* au cerveau
brain wave N (*Brit = idea*) idée *f* géniale, inspiration *f*
brain waves NPL (*Psych*) ondes *fpl* cérébrales

brainless /'breɪnlɪs/ ADJ [*person*] sans cervelle, stupide ; [*idea*] stupide ◆ **to be ~** [*person*] n'avoir rien dans la tête

brainpower /'breɪnpaʊəʳ/ N intelligence *f*

brainstorm /'breɪnstɔːm/ N (*Med*) congestion *f* cérébrale ; (*Brit fig = sudden aberration*) moment *m* d'aberration ; (*US = brilliant idea*) idée *f* géniale VI faire du remue-méninges, faire du brainstorming VT explorer

brainstorming /'breɪnstɔːmɪŋ/ N remue-méninges *m*, brainstorming *m* COMP **brainstorming session** N (séance *f* de) brainstorming *m*, séance *f* de remue-méninges

brainwash /'breɪnwɒʃ/ VT faire un lavage de cerveau à ◆ **he was ~ed into believing that ...** on a réussi à lui faire croire or à lui mettre dans la tête que ...

brainwashing /'breɪnwɒʃɪŋ/ N [*of prisoners etc*] lavage *m* de cerveau ; * [*of public etc*] bourrage* *m* de crâne, intox* *f*

brainwork /'breɪnwɜːk/ N travail *m* intellectuel

brainy* /'breɪnɪ/ ADJ intelligent, doué

braise /breɪz/ VT braiser

brake¹ /breɪk/ N (*= bracken*) fougère *f* ; (*= thicket*) fourré *m*

brake² /breɪk/ N (*= vehicle*) break *m*

brake³ /breɪk/ N [*of machine, vehicle*] frein *m* ◆ **to put on** or **apply the ~s** freiner ◆ **to act as a ~ on sb's activities** mettre un frein aux activités de qn ; → **handbrake, slam on** VI freiner
COMP **brake band** N bande *f* de frein
brake block N sabot *m* or patin *m* de frein
brake disc N disque *m* de frein
brake drum N tambour *m* de frein
brake fluid N liquide *m* de freins, lockheed ® *m*
brake horsepower N puissance *f* au frein or effective
brake lever N frein *m* à main
brake light N (feu *m* de) stop *m*
brake lining N garniture *f* de frein
brake pad N plaquette *f* de frein
brake pedal N pédale *f* de frein
brake shoe N mâchoire *f* de frein
brake-van N (*Brit Rail*) fourgon *m* à frein

brakeman /'breɪkmən/ N (pl **-men**) (*US Rail*) chef *m* de train

braking /'breɪkɪŋ/ N freinage *m*
COMP **braking distance** N distance *f* de freinage
braking power N puissance *f* de freinage

bramble /'bræmbl/ N 1 (*= thorny shrub*) roncier *m*, roncière *f* 2 (*= blackberry*) (*bush*) ronce *f* des haies, mûrier *m* sauvage ; (*berry*) mûre *f* (sauvage)

brambling /'bræmblɪŋ/ N (*= bird*) pinson *m* du nord

bran /bræn/ N son *m* (*de blé*)
COMP **bran loaf** N pain *m* au son
bran mash N bran *m* or son *m* mouillé
bran tub N (*Brit*) pêche *f* miraculeuse (*jeu*)

branch /brɑːntʃ/ N 1 [*of tree, candelabra*] branche *f* ; [*of river*] bras *m*, branche *f* ; [*of mountain chain*] ramification *f* ; [*of road*] embranchement *m* ; [*of railway*] bifurcation *f*, raccordement *m* ; [*of pipe*] branchement *m* ; [*of family*] rameau *m*, branche *f* ; (*Ling*) rameau *m* ; [*of subject, science etc*] branche *f* ; (*Admin*) division *f*, section *f* ◆ **he did not belong to their ~ of the service** (*Mil*) il n'appartenait pas à leur arme ; → **olive, root**
2 (*Comm*) [*of store*] succursale *f* ; [*of company*] succursale *f*, filiale *f* ; [*of bank*] agence *f*, succursale *f* ; [*of police force*] antenne *f* ; [*of industry*] branche *f*, secteur *m*
3 (*Comput*) branchement *m*
4 (*US = stream*) ruisseau *m*
VI 1 [*tree*] se ramifier
2 [*road*] bifurquer ; [*river*] se diviser ◆ **the road ~es off the main road at ...** la route quitte la grand-route à ...
COMP **branch depot** N (*Comm*) dépôt *m* auxiliaire
branch line N (*Rail*) ligne *f* secondaire
branch manager N (*gen*) directeur *m* de succursale *etc* ; [*of bank*] directeur *m* d'agence or de succursale
branch office N succursale *f* ; [*of bank*] agence *f*, succursale *f*
branch water* N (*US*) eau *f* plate

► **branch off** VI [*road*] bifurquer

► **branch out** VI [*person, company*] étendre ses activités ◆ **the firm is ~ing out into the publishing business** la compagnie étend ses activités à l'édition

branching /'brɑːntʃɪŋ/ N (*Gram*) branchement *m*, arborescence *f* COMP **branching rules** NPL règle *f* de formation d'arbre

brand /brænd/ N 1 (*Comm = trademark*: also **brand name**) marque *f* (de fabrique) ◆ **that rum is an excellent ~** c'est une excellente marque de rhum ◆ **a ~ of chocolate** une marque de chocolat
2 (*= mark*) [*of cattle, property*] marque *f* ; [*of prisoner*] flétrissure *f* ; (*fig = stigma*) marque *f*, stigmate *m*
3 (also **branding-iron**) fer *m* à marquer
4 (*= burning wood*) tison *m* ; → **firebrand**
5 († , *liter = sword*) glaive *m* (*liter*), épée *f*
VT [*+ cattle, property*] marquer ; (*fig*) [*+ person*] cataloguer (*as* comme) ; ◆ **he was ~ed (as) a traitor** (*fig*) on l'a catalogué comme traître ◆ **to ~ sth on sb's memory** graver qch dans la mémoire de qn
COMP **brand acceptance** N (*Comm*) accueil *m* réservé à une (or la) marque
brand awareness N (*Comm*) notoriété *f* de (la) marque
branded goods NPL (*Comm*) produits *mpl* de marque
brand image N (*Comm*) image *f* de marque
branding-iron N fer *m* à marquer
brand loyalty N (*Comm*) fidélité *f* à la marque
brand-new ADJ tout neuf (toute neuve *f*), flambant neuf (neuve *f*)

brandish /'brændɪʃ/ VT brandir

brandy /'brændɪ/ N cognac *m* ◆ **~ and soda** fine *f* à l'eau ◆ **plum ~** eau-de-vie *f* de prune or de quetsche
COMP **brandy butter** N *beurre sucré et aromatisé au cognac*
brandy snap N (*Culin*) cornet *m* croquant

brash /bræʃ/ ADJ (*pej*) 1 (*= overconfident*) [*person*] effronté, culotté* ; [*behaviour, style*] impertinent 2 (*= bold*) [*colour*] criard ; [*perfume*] qui cocotte*

brashly /'bræʃlɪ/ ADV (*pej*) [*say, behave*] avec outrecuidance ◆ **to be ~ confident** or **assertive** faire preuve d'outrecuidance

brashness /'bræʃnɪs/ N (*NonC*) (*pej*) 1 (*= overconfidence*) [*of person*] outrecuidance *f* 2 (*= boldness*) [*of colour*] aspect *m* criard

Brasilia /brə'zɪljə/ N Brasilia

brass /brɑːs/ N 1 (*NonC*) cuivre *m* (jaune), laiton *m* ; → **bold**
2 (*= tablet*) plaque *f* mortuaire (en cuivre)
3 (*= object/ornament of brass*) objet *m*/ornement *m* en cuivre ◆ **to do/clean the ~(es)** faire/astiquer les cuivres ◆ **the ~** (*Mus*) les cuivres *mpl* ◆ **the (top) ~*** les huiles* *fpl*
4 (*NonC*: ‡) (*= impudence*) toupet* *m*, culot* *m* ; (*Brit = money*) pognon‡ *m*
COMP [*ornament etc*] en or de cuivre
brass band N fanfare *f*, orchestre *m* de cuivres
brassed off‡ ADJ (*Brit*) ◆ **to be ~ed off with sth** en avoir ras le bol* de qch
brass farthing* N ◆ **it's not worth a ~ farthing** cela ne vaut pas un clou* or un pet de lapin* ; → **care**
brass foundry N fonderie *f* de cuivre
brass hat* N (*Mil*) huile* *f*
brass knuckles NPL coup *m* de poing américain
brass monkey‡ N (*Brit*) ◆ **it's ~ monkey weather** or **~ monkeys, it's cold enough to freeze the balls off a ~ monkey** on se les gèle‡, on caille‡
brass neck‡ N ◆ **he's got a ~ neck** il a du toupet* or du culot*

brass plate N plaque *f* de cuivre ; *[of church]* plaque *f* mortuaire *or* commémorative
brass ring N *(US fig)* ◆ **to go** *or* **reach for the ~ ring** * essayer de décrocher la timbale *
brass rubbing N *(= action)* décalquage *m* par frottement ; *(= object)* décalque *m*
brass tacks * NPL ◆ **to get down to ~ tacks** en venir aux faits *or* aux choses sérieuses

brasserie /ˈbrɑːsərɪ/ N brasserie *f*

brassica /ˈbræsɪkə/ N crucifère *f*, brassicacée *f*

brassie /ˈbrɑːsɪ/ N *(Golf)* ⇒ **brassy noun**

brassière † /ˈbræsɪəʳ/ N soutien-gorge *m*

brassware /ˈbræswɛəʳ/ N *(NonC)* chaudronnerie *f* d'art, dinanderie *f*

brassy /ˈbrɑːsɪ/ ADJ 1 *(= yellow) [hair]* d'un blond cuivré artificiel 2 *(= harsh) [sound]* métallique ; *[voice]* claironnant ; *[laugh]* éclatant 3 *(pej = flashy) [woman]* à l'allure tapageuse 4 *(* pej = impudent) [person]* culotté * N *(Golf)* brassie *m*

brat /bræt/ N *(pej)* (sale) môme * *mf*, (sale) gosse * *mf* ◆ **all these ~s** toute cette marmaille * ◆ **one of his ~s** un de ses gosses *

Bratislava /ˌbrætɪˈslɑːvə/ N Bratislava

bratpack /ˈbrætpæk/ N jeunes loups *mpl*

bravado /brəˈvɑːdəʊ/ N (pl **bravados** *or* **bravadoes**) bravade *f*

brave /breɪv/ ADJ 1 *[person, smile, attempt, action]* courageux ◆ **to be as ~ as a lion** être courageux comme un lion, être intrépide ◆ **be ~!** du courage ! ◆ **be ~ and tell her** prends ton courage à deux mains et va lui dire ; → **face** 2 *(liter = fine)* beau (belle *f*), élégant ◆ **it's a ~ new world!** *(iro)* on n'arrête pas le progrès ! *(iro)* N 1 ◆ **the bravest of the ~** des braves parmi les braves 2 *(= Indian warrior)* guerrier *m* indien, brave *m* VT *[+ danger, person, sb's anger]* braver, affronter

► **brave out** VT SEP ◆ **to brave it out** faire face à la situation

bravely /ˈbreɪvlɪ/ ADV *[fight, struggle, try, speak, smile]* bravement ◆ **the flag was flying ~** le drapeau flottait fièrement

bravery /ˈbreɪvərɪ/ N *(NonC)* courage *m*, bravoure *f*

bravo /ˈbrɑːˈvəʊ/ EXCL, N (pl **bravoes** *or* **bravos**) bravo *m*

bravura /brəˈvʊərə/ N *(also Mus)* bravoure *f*

brawl /brɔːl/ VI se bagarrer *, se quereller N rixe *f*, bagarre *f* ◆ **drunken ~** querelle *f* d'ivrognes

brawling /ˈbrɔːlɪŋ/ ADJ bagarreur *, querelleur N rixe *f*, bagarre *f*

brawn /brɔːn/ N 1 *(Brit Culin)* fromage *m* de tête 2 *(= muscle)* muscle(s) *m(pl)* ; *(= strength)* muscle *m* ◆ **to have plenty of ~** être bien musclé, avoir du muscle ◆ **he is all ~ and no brain** *(hum)* il est tout en muscles et sans cervelle

brawny /ˈbrɔːnɪ/ ADJ *[arms]* musculeux ; *[person]* musclé

bray /breɪ/ N *[of ass]* braiment *m* ; *[of trumpet]* sonnerie *f*, son *m* éclatant VI *[ass]* braire ; *[trumpet]* sonner

braze /breɪz/ VT souder (au laiton)

brazen /ˈbreɪzn/ ADJ 1 *(pej = shameless) [person, action, attitude, lie]* effronté ◆ **I'm ~ about asking for things** je ne me gêne pas pour demander ◆ **they are ~ about their sales tactics** ils ne font pas mystère de leur stratégie de vente ◆ **a ~ hussy** une dévergondée 2 *(= made of brass)* en *or* de laiton 3 *(liter = brass-coloured) [light, sun]* cuivré 4 *(= harsh) [sound]* métallique VT ◆ **to ~ it out** crâner * COMP **brazen-faced** ADJ effronté

brazenly /ˈbreɪznlɪ/ ADV effrontément

brazier¹ /ˈbreɪzɪəʳ/ N *[of fire]* brasero *m*

brazier² /ˈbreɪzɪəʳ/ N *(= craftsman)* chaudronnier *m*

Brazil /brəˈzɪl/ N Brésil *m*

brazil /brəˈzɪl/ N (also **brazil nut**) noix *f* du Brésil

Brazilian /brəˈzɪlɪən/ ADJ brésilien, du Brésil N Brésilien(ne) *m(f)*

BRCS /ˌbiːɑːsiːˈes/ N (abbrev of **British Red Cross Society**) → **British**

breach /briːtʃ/ N 1 *(Jur etc = violation) [of agreement]* non-respect *m* ; *[of rules, order]* infraction *f* ; *[of law]* violation *f* ; *[of friendship, good manners, discipline]* manquement *m* (*of* à) ; ◆ **~ of contract** rupture *f* de contrat, inexécution *f* de contrat ◆ **a ~ of decorum** un manquement au protocole ◆ **~ of faith** déloyauté *f* ◆ **~ of the peace** atteinte *f* à l'ordre public ◆ **~ of privilege** *(US Pol)* atteinte *f* portée aux prérogatives parlementaires ◆ **~ of promise** rupture *f* de promesse de mariage ◆ **action for ~ of promise** ≈ action *f* en dommages-intérêts *(pour rupture de promesse de mariage)* ◆ **~ of professional secrecy** violation *f* du secret professionnel ◆ **~es in security** des manquements *mpl* aux règles de sécurité ◆ **~ of trust** abus *m* de confiance ◆ **players in ~ of league rules** les joueurs qui contreviennent au règlement de la ligue ◆ **we are advised that we are not in ~ of the law** on nous a fait savoir que nous ne violions pas la loi *or* que nous n'étions pas dans l'illégalité

2 *(= estrangement)* brouille *f*, désaccord *m*

3 *(= gap: in wall)* brèche *f*, trou *m* ◆ **to make a ~ in the enemy's lines** *(Mil)* percer les lignes ennemies ◆ **to make a ~ in sb's defences** entamer la résistance de qn, faire une brèche dans la défense de qn ◆ **a ~ in relations between the two countries** une rupture des relations entre les deux pays ◆ **to step into the ~** *(fig)* s'engouffrer dans la brèche

VT 1 *[+ wall]* ouvrir une brèche dans, faire une trouée dans ; *(Mil) [+ enemy lines, defences]* percer

2 **to ~ security** ne pas respecter les règles de sécurité

VI *[whale]* sauter hors de l'eau

bread /bred/ N 1 pain *m* ◆ **a loaf of ~** un pain, une miche de pain ◆ **new ~** pain *m* frais ◆ **~ fresh from the oven** du pain sortant du four ◆ **an invalid on a diet of ~ and milk** un invalide qui se nourrit de pain et de lait ◆ **to put sb on (dry) ~ and water** mettre qn au pain (sec) et à l'eau ◆ **the ~ and wine** *(Rel)* les (deux) espèces *fpl* ◆ **to break ~** *(Rel) [congregation]* recevoir la communion ; *[priest]* administrer la communion ◆ **~ and butter** du pain et du beurre ; see also **comp**

2 *(fig phrases)* **writing is his ~ and butter** sa plume est son gagne-pain, il vit de sa plume ◆ **to earn one's ~** gagner son pain *or* sa vie ◆ **to take the ~ out of sb's mouth** ôter à qn le pain de la bouche ◆ **he knows which side his ~ is buttered** il sait où est son intérêt ◆ **to throw** *or* **cast one's ~ upon the water(s)** agir de façon désintéressée ◆ **~ and circuses** du pain et des jeux ; → **brown, gingerbread, slice**

3 *(‡ = money)* fric ‡ *m*, oseille ‡ *f*

COMP **bread-and-butter** ADJ *(fig) [job etc]* alimentaire ; *(= reliable) [player etc]* sur qui l'on peut compter
bread-and-butter letter N lettre *f* de château, lettre *f* de remerciements *(pour hospitalité reçue)*
bread-and-butter pudding N pudding *m (à base de pain beurré)*
bread line N *(US)* file *f* d'attente pour la soupe populaire ◆ **to be on the ~ line** * *(Brit)* vivre en-dessous du seuil de pauvreté
bread poultice N cataplasme *m* à la mie de pain
bread pudding N pudding *or* pouding *m*
bread sauce N sauce *f* à la mie de pain

breadbasket /ˈbred,bɑːskɪt/ N corbeille *f* à pain ; *(fig) (= granary)* grenier *m* ; *(‡ = stomach)* estomac *m* ADJ *(Econ etc)* fondamental

breadbin /ˈbredbɪn/ N boîte *f* à pain ; *(larger)* huche *f* à pain

breadboard /ˈbredbɔːd/ N planche *f* à pain ; *(Comput, Elec)* montage *m* expérimental

breadbox /ˈbredbɒks/ N *(US)* ⇒ **breadbin**

breadcrumb /ˈbredkrʌm/ N miette *f* de pain ◆ **~s** *(Culin: as topping)* chapelure *f* ◆ **fried in ~s** pané

breaded /ˈbredɪd/ ADJ pané

breadfruit /ˈbredfruːt/ N (pl **breadfruit** *or* **breadfruits**) *(= tree)* arbre *m* à pain, artocarpe *m* ; *(= fruit)* fruit *m* à pain

breadknife /ˈbrednaɪf/ N (pl **-knives**) couteau *m* à pain

breadstick /ˈbredstɪk/ N gressin *m*

breadth /bretθ/ N 1 *(= width)* largeur *f* ◆ **this field is 100 metres in ~** ce champ a 100 mètres de large ; *see also* **hair's breadth** → **hair** 2 *(fig) [of mind, thought]* largeur *f* ; *[of style]* ampleur *f* ; *(Art)* largeur *f* d'exécution ; *(Mus)* jeu *m* large ◆ **~ of tone** *(Mus)* ampleur *f* du son

breadthwise /ˈbretθwaɪz/ ADV en largeur, dans la largeur

breadwinner /ˈbred,wɪnəʳ/ N soutien *m* de famille

break /breɪk/ (vb : pret **broke**, ptp **broken**) N 1 *(= interruption) (in conversation)* interruption *f*, pause *f* ; *(in TV programme)* interruption *f* ; *(in journey)* arrêt *m* ; *(Brit Scol)* récréation *f* ◆ **I need a ~** *(= few minutes)* j'ai besoin d'une pause ; *(= holiday)* j'ai besoin de vacances ; *(= change)* j'ai besoin de me changer les idées ◆ **to take a ~** *(= few minutes)* faire une pause ; *(= holiday)* prendre des vacances ; *(= change)* se changer les idées ◆ **~ cigarette** *or* **smoke** ~ pause-cigarette *f* ◆ **six hours without a ~** six heures de suite, six heures d'affilée ◆ **after the ~** *(Rad, TV = advertisements)* après la publicité ◆ **a ~ in transmission** *(Rad)* une interruption (due à un incident technique) ◆ **~ in circuit** *(Elec)* rupture *f* de circuit ◆ **a ~ in the clouds** une éclaircie ◆ **a ~ in the weather** un changement de temps ◆ **with a ~ in her voice** d'une voix entrecoupée

◆ **to make a break** ◆ **to make a ~ for it** prendre la fuite ◆ **he made a ~ for the door** il s'est élancé vers la porte

2 *(= fracture)* cassure *f*, rupture *f* ; *[of relationship]* rupture *f*, brouille *f* ◆ **he spoke of the need for a ~ with the past** il a dit qu'il fallait rompre avec le passé

3 *(liter)* **at ~ of day** au point du jour, à l'aube

4 *(* = luck, opportunity)* chance *f*, veine * *f* ◆ **to have a good/bad ~** avoir une période de veine */de déveine * ◆ **he's had all the ~s** il a eu toutes les veines * ◆ **she got her first big ~ in the Broadway play "Sarafina"** elle a percé dans "Sarafina", une pièce montée à Broadway ◆ **to give sb a ~** donner une chance à qn ◆ **give me a ~!** * *(= leave me alone)* fichez-moi la paix ! *

5 *(Sport, Snooker)* série *f* ◆ **to have a ~ of serve** *(Tennis)* prendre le service de son adversaire, faire le break

VT 1 *(= smash, fracture, tear)* casser ; *[+ skin]* écorcher ◆ **to ~ sth in two** casser qch en deux ◆ **the child has broken all his toys** l'enfant a cassé *or* brisé tous ses jouets ◆ **to ~ one's neck** se rompre *or* se casser le cou ; see also **breakneck** ◆ **I'll ~ his neck if I catch him doing that again** * *(fig)* si je l'y reprends, je lui tords le cou * ◆ **to ~ one's leg** se casser la jambe ◆ **~ a leg!** * *(Theat)* merde ! ‡ ◆ **the bone is not bro-**

ken il n'y a pas de fracture ◆ **his skin is not broken** il ne s'est pas écorché ◆ **to ~ open** *[+ door]* enfoncer, forcer ; *[+ packet]* ouvrir ; *[+ lock, safe]* fracturer, forcer ◆ **to ~ ground on a new building** *(US)* commencer la construction d'un nouveau bâtiment, commencer à construire un nouveau bâtiment ◆ **to ~ new** *or* **fresh ground** *(fig)* innover, faire œuvre de pionnier ◆ **to ~ one's back** *(lit)* se casser la colonne vertébrale ◆ **he almost broke his back trying to lift the stone** il s'est donné un tour de reins en essayant de soulever la pierre ◆ **he's ~ing his back to get the job finished in time** il s'échine à finir le travail à temps ◆ **to ~ the back of a task** *(Brit)* faire le plus dur *or* le plus gros d'une tâche ◆ **to ~ sb's heart** briser le cœur de qn ◆ **to ~ one's heart over sth** avoir le cœur brisé par qch ◆ **it ~s my heart to think that ...** cela me brise le cœur de penser que ... ; → **ball[1], barrier, bone, bread, code, ice, path[1], record, surface, wind[1]**

2 *(= fail to observe) [+ promise]* manquer à ; *[+ treaty]* violer ; *[+ commandment]* désobéir à ◆ **to ~ the law** violer la loi ◆ **to ~ a vow** rompre un serment ; → **bound[1], camp[1], cover, faith, jail, parole, rank[1], Sabbath**

3 *(= weaken) [+ courage, spirit]* abattre, briser ; *[+ strike]* briser ; *[+ horse]* dresser ; *(Mil) [+ officer]* casser ◆ **to ~ sb** *(morally)* causer la perte de qn ; *(financially)* ruiner qn ◆ **this will make or ~ him** *(financially)* cela fera sa fortune ou sa ruine ; *(morally)* cela sera son salut ou sa perte ◆ **to ~ sb of a habit** faire perdre une habitude à qn ◆ **to ~ a habit** se débarrasser *or* se défaire d'une habitude ◆ **to ~ the bank** *(Betting)* faire sauter la banque ◆ **it won't ~ the bank*** cela ne va pas te (*or* nous *or* les *etc*) ruiner

4 *(= interrupt) [+ silence, spell, fast]* rompre ; *[+ current, circuit]* couper ◆ **to ~ sb's serve** *(Tennis)* prendre le service de qn ◆ **to ~ one's journey** faire une étape (*or* des étapes)

5 *[+ fall]* amortir, adoucir

6 *[+ news]* révéler, annoncer ◆ **try to ~ it to her gently** essayez de le lui annoncer avec ménagement

VI 1 *(= fracture) (gen)* (se) casser, se briser ; *[stick, rope]* se casser, se rompre ; *[bone]* se casser, se fracturer ; *[heart]* se briser ◆ **to ~ in two** se casser en deux

2 *[clouds]* se disperser, se dissiper

3 *[storm]* éclater, se déchaîner ; *[wave]* déferler ◆ **she tried to reach the house before the storm broke** elle a essayé d'atteindre la maison avant que l'orage éclate ; → **water**

4 *[news, story]* éclater, se répandre

5 *(= weaken, change) [health]* se détériorer ; *[voice] (boy's)* muer ; *(in emotion)* se briser, s'étrangler (*with* sous le coup de) ; *[weather]* se gâter ◆ **the heat wave was ~ing** la vague de chaleur touchait à sa fin ◆ **he broke under torture** il a craqué sous la torture ◆ **his courage** *or* **spirit broke** son courage l'a abandonné

6 *(in relationship, friendship)* ◆ **to ~ with sb** rompre avec qn

7 *(Boxing)* se dégager

8 *[dawn]* poindre ; *[day]* se lever, poindre

9 *(= pause)* **we broke for lunch** nous nous sommes arrêtés *or* nous avons fait une pause pour le déjeuner

10 *(set structures)*

◆ **to break even** rentrer dans ses fonds

◆ **to break free** se libérer, se dégager

◆ **to break loose** *[person, animal]* s'échapper (*from* de) ; *[boat]* rompre ses amarres, partir à la dérive

◆ **to break with sb/sth** rompre avec qn/qch ◆ **to ~ with tradition/the past** rompre avec la tradition/avec le passé

COMP **break dancer** N smurfeur *m*, -euse *f*
break dancing N smurf *m*
break-even point N *(Comm)* seuil *m* de rentabilité
break-in N cambriolage *m*
break point N *(Tennis)* balle *f* de break ; *(Comput)* point *m* de rupture
break-up N *[of ship]* dislocation *f* ; *[of ice]* débâcle *f* ; *[of friendship]* rupture *f* ; *[of empire]* démembrement *m* ; *[of political party]* scission *f*, schisme *m*

► **break away** VI 1 *[piece of cliff, railway coach]* se détacher (*from* de) ; *[boat]* rompre ses amarres, partir à la dérive ◆ **to ~ away from a group** se séparer d'un groupe

2 *(Ftbl)* déborder ; *(Racing)* s'échapper, se détacher du peloton

VT SEP détacher (*from* de)

► **break down** VI 1 *(= fail, cease to function) [vehicle, machine]* tomber en panne ; *[health]* se détériorer ; *[argument]* s'effondrer ; *[resistance]* céder ; *[negotiations, plan]* échouer ◆ **after negotiations broke down ...** après l'échec *m or* la rupture des négociations ...

2 *(= weep)* fondre en larmes, éclater en sanglots

3 *(Chem) (= decompose)* se décomposer

VT SEP 1 *(= demolish)* démolir, mettre en morceaux ; *[+ door]* enfoncer ; *[+ opposition]* briser

2 *(= analyse) [+ accounts]* analyser, détailler ; *[+ sales figures, costs]* ventiler ; *[+ substance]* décomposer ◆ **he broke down his argument into three points** il a décomposé son raisonnement en trois points

► **break forth** VI *(liter) [light, water]* jaillir ; *[storm]* éclater

► **break in** VI 1 *(= interrupt, intrude)* interrompre ◆ **to ~ in on sb/sth** interrompre qn/qch

2 *(= enter illegally)* entrer par effraction

VT SEP 1 *[+ door]* enfoncer ; *[+ cask]* défoncer

2 *(= tame, train) [+ horse]* dresser ; *(esp US) [+ engine, car]* roder ◆ **it took a month to ~ in my new running shoes** cela a pris un mois avant que mes nouvelles chaussures de course se fassent ◆ **it will take you six months before you're broken in* (to the job)** vous mettrez six mois à vous faire au métier

N ◆ **break-in** → **break**

► **break into** VT FUS 1 *(= enter illegally) [+ house]* entrer par effraction dans ◆ **to ~ into a safe** fracturer *or* forcer un coffre-fort ◆ **to ~ into the cashbox** forcer la caisse

2 *(= use part of) [+ savings]* entamer ◆ **to ~ into a new box of sth** entamer une nouvelle boîte de qch

3 *(Comm)* **to ~ into a new market** percer sur un nouveau marché ◆ **she finally broke into films after an acclaimed singing career** elle a fini par percer au cinéma après une brillante carrière de chanteuse

4 *(= begin suddenly)* ◆ **to break into song** se mettre à chanter ◆ **she broke into a smile** elle s'est mise à sourire ◆ **he broke into a long explanation** il s'est lancé dans une longue explication ◆ **to ~ into a trot** *[horse]* prendre le trot ◆ **to ~ into a run** se mettre à courir

► **break off** VI 1 *[piece, twig]* se détacher net, se casser net

2 *(= stop)* s'arrêter (*doing sth* de faire qch) ; ◆ **he broke off in mid-sentence** il s'est arrêté au milieu d'une phrase ◆ **to ~ off from work** faire une pause

3 *(= end relationship)* rompre (*with sb* avec qn)

4 *(Snooker)* commencer la partie

VT SEP 1 *(gen)* casser, détacher ; *[+ piece of chocolate]* casser

2 *(= end, interrupt) [+ engagement, negotiations]* rompre ; *[+ habit]* rompre avec, se défaire de ; *[+ work]* interrompre, cesser

► **break out** VI 1 *[epidemic, fire]* éclater, se déclarer ; *[storm, war, argument]* éclater ◆ **to ~ out in spots** se couvrir de boutons ◆ **to ~ out into a sweat** suer, prendre une suée* ; *(from fear etc)* commencer à avoir des sueurs froides ◆ **he broke out into a stream of insults** il a déversé un chapelet d'injures

2 *(= escape)* s'échapper, s'évader (*of* de)

VT FUS *[+ champagne etc]* sortir

► **break through** VI *(Mil)* faire une percée ; *[sun]* percer les nuages

VT FUS *[+ defences, obstacles]* enfoncer, percer ◆ **to ~ through sb's reserve** faire sortir qn de sa réserve ◆ **to ~ through the crowd** se frayer un passage à travers la foule

► **break up** VI 1 *[ice]* craquer, se fêler ; *[road]* être défoncé ; *[ship in storm]* se disloquer ; *[partnership]* cesser, prendre fin ; *[health]* se détériorer ◆ **the weather is ~ing up** le temps se gâte ◆ **their marriage broke up** leur couple s'est brisé ◆ **to ~ up with sb** rompre avec qn

2 *(= disperse) [clouds, crowd, meeting]* se disperser ; *[group]* se disperser, se séparer ; *[friends]* se quitter, se séparer ◆ **the schools ~ up tomorrow** *(Brit)* les vacances (scolaires) commencent demain

3 *(US ‡ = laugh)* se tordre de rire

4 *[telephone line]* couper ◆ **you're ~ing up** je ne te capte plus

VT SEP 1 *(lit)* mettre en morceaux, morceler ; *[+ house]* démolir ; *[+ ground]* ameublir ; *[+ road]* défoncer ◆ **to ~ sth up into three pieces** casser qch en trois morceaux

2 *(fig) [+ coalition]* briser, rompre ; *[+ empire]* démembrer ◆ **to ~ up a marriage/a home** désunir un couple/les membres d'une famille ◆ **to do sth to ~ up one's day** faire qch pour faire une coupure dans la journée

3 *(= disperse) [+ crowd, meeting]* disperser ◆ **~ it up!** séparez-vous ! ; *(said by policeman)* circulez ! ◆ **police used tear gas to ~ up the demonstration** la police a utilisé du gaz lacrymogène pour disperser les manifestants

4 *(US ‡ = make laugh)* donner le fou rire à

N 1 ◆ **break-up** → **break**

2 ◆ **breaking-up** → **breaking**

breakable /ˈbreɪkəbl/ ADJ cassable, fragile NPL **breakables** objets *mpl* fragiles

breakage /ˈbreɪkɪdʒ/ N *(in chain)* rupture *f* ; *[of glass, china]* casse *f*, bris *m* ◆ **to pay for ~s** payer la casse

breakaway /ˈbreɪkəˌweɪ/ N *(separating)* séparation *f* (*from* d'avec) rupture *f* (*from* avec) ; *(Sport)* échappée *f* ; *(Boxing)* dégagement *m* ADJ *[group, movement]* séparatiste, dissident ; *(Pol) [state, region]* séparatiste

breakdown /ˈbreɪkdaʊn/ N 1 *[of machine, vehicle, electricity supply]* panne *f* 2 *[of communications etc]* rupture *f* ; *[of railway system etc]* interruption *f* (subite) de service ; *(fig) [of moral values etc]* érosion *f*, dégradation *f* 3 *(Med) (mental)* dépression *f* nerveuse ; *(physical)* effondrement *m* 4 *(= analysis)* analyse *f* ; *(into categories)* décomposition *f* (*into* en) ; *[of sales figures, costs etc]* ventilation *f* ◆ **give me a ~ of these results** faites-moi l'analyse de ces résultats 5 *(Ecol) [of matter]* décomposition *f*

COMP *[gang, service]* de dépannage
breakdown truck, breakdown van N *(Brit)* dépanneuse *f*

breaker /ˈbreɪkə^r/ N 1 *(= wave)* brisant *m* 2 *[of cars] (= person)* casseur *m* ; *(= business)* casse *f* ◆ **to send to the ~'s** *[+ ship, car]* envoyer à la casse ◆ **~'s yard** casse *f* ; → **housebreaker, lawbreaker** 3 *(= machine)* concasseur *m*, broyeur *m* ; → **icebreaker** 4 *(= CB user)* cibiste *mf*

breakfast /ˈbrekfəst/ N petit déjeuner *m* ◆ **to have ~** déjeuner, prendre le (petit) déjeuner ; → **wedding** VI déjeuner (*off, on* de)

COMP **breakfast bar** N bar *m* américain (*dans une cuisine américaine*)
breakfast cereals NPL céréales *fpl*
breakfast cloth N nappe *f* (ordinaire)

breakfast cup N déjeuner *m (tasse)*
breakfast meeting N petit déjeuner *m* d'affaires
breakfast room N salle *f* à manger *(où l'on prend le petit déjeuner)*
breakfast set N service *m* à petit déjeuner
breakfast table N ◆ **they were still sitting at the ~ table** ils étaient encore assis à la table du petit déjeuner
breakfast TV N la télévision du matin

breaking /ˈbreɪkɪŋ/ N *[of cup, chair]* bris *m* ; *[of bone, limb]* fracture *f* ; *(Jur) [of window, seals]* bris *m* ; *[of promise]* manquement *m (of* à) ; *[of treaty, law]* violation *f (of* de) ; *[of commandment]* désobéissance *f (of* à) ; *[of silence, spell]* rupture *f* ; *[of journey]* interruption *f (of* de) ADJ ◆ **~ news** dernières nouvelles *fpl*
COMP **breaking and entering** N *(Jur)* effraction *f*
breaking-point N *(of object)* point *m* de rupture ◆ **to try sb's patience to ~-point** pousser à bout la patience de qn ◆ **she has reached ~-point** elle est à bout, elle n'en peut plus ◆ **the situation has reached ~-point** *(Pol etc)* la situation a atteint le point de rupture
breaking strain, breaking stress N *(Tech)* point *m* de rupture
breaking-up N *[of school, college]* début *m* des vacances, fin *f* des cours ; *[of meeting etc]* clôture *f*, levée *f*

breakneck /ˈbreɪknek/ ADJ ◆ **at ~ speed** *[run]* à une allure folle, à fond de train ; *[drive]* à une allure folle, à tombeau ouvert

breakout /ˈbreɪkaʊt/ N évasion *f*

breakthrough /ˈbreɪkθruː/ N *(Mil)* percée *f* ; *(in research etc)* découverte *f* capitale ◆ **a major ~ in medical research** une découverte capitale dans le domaine de la recherche médicale ◆ **this summit could represent a significant ~ in improving relations between the two countries** ce sommet pourrait constituer une étape décisive dans l'amélioration des relations entre les deux pays
◆ **to make a breakthrough** ◆ **the company looks poised to make a significant ~ in China** il est pratiquement certain que cette entreprise va percer sur le marché chinois ◆ **scientists say they have made a ~ in finding the cause of this disease** les chercheurs disent qu'ils ont fait une avancée capitale dans la recherche de la cause de cette maladie

breakwater /ˈbreɪkˌwɔːtəʳ/ N brise-lames *m inv*, digue *f*

bream /briːm/ N *(pl inv)* brème *f*

breast /brest/ N 1 *(= chest) [of man, woman]* poitrine *f* ; *[of animal]* poitrine *f*, poitrail *m* ; *(Culin) [of chicken]* blanc *m* ; → **beat, clean** 2 *[of woman]* sein *m*, mamelle † *f (liter)* ; *[of man]* sein *m* ◆ **baby at the ~** enfant *mf* au sein 3 *(Min)* front *m* de taille ; → **chimney** VT 1 *(= face) [+ waves, storm, danger]* affronter 2 *[+ hill]* atteindre le sommet de ◆ **to ~ the tape** *(Sport)* franchir la ligne d'arrivée (le premier)
COMP **breast cancer** N cancer *m* du sein
breast enlargement N augmentation *f* mammaire
breast-fed ADJ nourri au sein
breast-feed VT allaiter, donner le sein à VI allaiter
breast-feeding N allaitement *m* maternel *or* au sein
breast milk N lait *m* maternel
breast-pocket N poche *f* de poitrine
breast pump N tire-lait *m inv*
breast-stroke N brasse *f* ◆ **to swim ~-stroke** nager la brasse

breastbone /ˈbrestbəʊn/ N *(Anat)* sternum *m* ; *[of bird]* bréchet *m*

breastplate /ˈbrestpleɪt/ N *(= armour)* plastron *m* (de cuirasse) ; *[of priest]* pectoral *m*

breastwork /ˈbrestwɜːk/ N *(Mil)* parapet *m* ; *(Naut)* rambarde *f*

breath /breθ/ N 1 haleine *f*, souffle *m*, respiration *f* ◆ **bad ~** mauvaise haleine *f* ◆ **to have bad ~** avoir mauvaise haleine ◆ **to get one's ~ back** *(esp Brit)* reprendre haleine, retrouver son souffle ◆ **to catch one's ~** retenir son souffle ◆ **out of ~** à bout de souffle, essoufflé, hors d'haleine ◆ **to take ~** respirer, reprendre haleine ◆ **to take a deep ~** respirer à fond ◆ **take a deep ~!** *(fig)* accroche-toi bien ! * ◆ **to take sb's ~ away** couper le souffle à qn ◆ **save your ~!** inutile de perdre *or* gaspiller ta salive ! ◆ **to be short of ~** avoir le souffle court ◆ **to gasp for ~** haleter ◆ **to stop for ~** s'arrêter pour reprendre haleine ◆ **below** *or* **beneath** *or* **under one's ~** *[say, talk]* à voix basse, tout bas ◆ **to laugh under one's ~** rire sous cape ◆ **to say sth (all) in one ~** dire qch d'un trait ◆ **it was the ~ of life to him** c'était (toute) sa vie, cela lui était aussi précieux que la vie même ◆ **his last** *or* **dying ~** son dernier soupir ◆ **with one's dying ~** en mourant ◆ **to draw one's last ~** *(liter)* rendre l'âme, rendre le dernier soupir ; → **hold, same, waste**
2 *(air in movement)* souffle *m* ◆ **there wasn't a ~ of air** il n'y avait pas un souffle d'air ◆ **to go out for a ~ of (fresh) air** sortir prendre l'air ◆ **a ~ of fresh air** *(fig)* une bouffée d'air frais ◆ **a little ~ of wind** un (léger) souffle d'air ◆ **not a ~ of scandal** pas le moindre soupçon de scandale
COMP **breath test** N alcootest ® *m*, éthylotest *m*
breath-test VT faire subir l'alcootest ® à

breathable /ˈbriːðəbl/ ADJ *[air, atmosphere]* respirable ; *[fabric, garment]* respirant

breathalyse, breathalyze *(US)* /ˈbreθəlaɪz/ VT *(esp Brit)* faire subir l'alcootest ® à

Breathalyser ®, Breathalyzer ® *(US)* /ˈbreθəlaɪzəʳ/ N alcootest ® *m*, éthylomètre *m*

breathe /briːð/ VI *[person, fabric, garment]* respirer ◆ **to ~ deeply** *or* **heavily** *(after running etc)* haleter, souffler (fort) ; *(in illness)* respirer péniblement ◆ **to ~ hard** souffler (fort), haleter ◆ **to ~ freely** *or* **again** *or* **more easily** *(fig)* (pouvoir) respirer ◆ **she is still breathing** *(= be alive)* elle respire encore ◆ **red wine should be allowed to ~ before drinking** il faut faire respirer le vin rouge avant de le boire ◆ **to ~ down sb's neck** *(fig)* talonner qn ◆ **Newcastle are breathing down Liverpool's neck at the top of the table** Newcastle talonne Liverpool en haut du classement ◆ **I've got the bank manager breathing down my neck** j'ai le directeur de la banque sur le dos
VT 1 *[+ air]* respirer ◆ **to ~ one's last (breath)** rendre le dernier soupir ◆ **to ~ air into sth** insuffler de l'air *or* souffler dans qch ◆ **to ~ new life into sb** redonner goût à la vie *or* du courage à qn ◆ **to ~ fire over** *or* **about sth** fulminer contre qch
2 *(= utter) [+ sigh]* pousser ; *[+ prayer]* murmurer ◆ **to ~ a sigh of relief** pousser un soupir de soulagement ◆ **don't ~ a word (about it)!** n'en dis rien à personne !, motus (et bouche cousue) !
3 *(Ling)* aspirer

► **breathe in** VI, VT SEP aspirer, inspirer

► **breathe out** VI, VT SEP expirer

breather * /ˈbriːðəʳ/ N 1 *(= short rest)* moment *m* de repos *or* répit ◆ **to give sb a ~** laisser souffler qn 2 *(= fresh air)* **let's go (out) for a ~** sortons prendre l'air

breathing /ˈbriːðɪŋ/ N 1 respiration *f*, souffle *m* ; *[of singer, flautist etc]* respiration *f* ◆ **heavy ~** respiration *f* bruyante 2 *(Ling)* aspiration *f* ◆ **rough/smooth ~** *(Greek Gram)* esprit *m* rude/doux
COMP **breathing apparatus** N appareil *m* respiratoire
breathing space N *(fig)* ◆ **to give sb a ~ space** donner à qn le temps de souffler *or* un moment de répit

breathless /ˈbreθlɪs/ ADJ 1 *(= out of breath) (from exertion)* essoufflé, à bout de souffle, hors d'haleine ; *(from illness)* qui a du mal à respirer ; *[voice]* essoufflé ◆ **to make sb ~** essouffler qn ◆ **~ from doing sth** essoufflé d'avoir fait qch ◆ **at a ~ pace** à une allure folle 2 *(emotionally) [excitement]* fébrile ◆ **she was ~ with excitement** elle avait le souffle coupé par l'excitation ◆ **he was ~ with anticipation** il retenait son souffle

breathlessly /ˈbreθlɪslɪ/ ADV *(lit) [say, ask]* en haletant, à bout de souffle ; *(fig) (= excitedly) [wait, watch]* en retenant son souffle

breathlessness /ˈbreθlɪsnɪs/ N difficulté *f* respiratoire

breathtaking /ˈbreθteɪkɪŋ/ ADJ époustouflant

breathtakingly /ˈbreθteɪkɪŋlɪ/ ADV ◆ **~ beautiful** d'une beauté à vous couper le souffle ◆ **~ simple** d'une simplicité stupéfiante

breathy /ˈbreθɪ/ ADJ *[voice]* voilé

bred /bred/ VB pt, ptp of **breed** ADJ *(in compounds)* ◆ **well-~** bien élevé ; → **country, ill**

breech /briːtʃ/ N 1 *[of gun]* culasse *f* 2 *(Med)* **~ (birth** *or* **delivery)** (accouchement *m* par le) siège *m* ◆ **he was a ~** * il s'est présenté par le siège VT *[+ gun]* munir d'une culasse

breechblock /ˈbriːtʃblɒk/ N bloc *m* de culasse

breechcloth /ˈbriːtʃklɒθ/ N *(US)* pagne *m (d'étoffe)*

breeches /ˈbrɪtʃɪz/ NPL ◆ **(pair of) ~** (also **knee breeches**) haut-de-chausses *m* ; (also **riding breeches**) culotte *f* (de cheval) ◆ **his wife wears the ~** c'est sa femme qui porte la culotte COMP /ˈbriːtʃɪz/ **breeches buoy** N *(Naut)* bouée-culotte *f*

breechloader /ˈbriːtʃˌləʊdəʳ/ N *(Mil)* arme *f* qui se charge par la culasse

breed /briːd/ (pret, ptp **bred**) VT *[+ animals]* élever, faire l'élevage de ; †† *[+ children]* élever ; *(fig = give rise to) [+ hatred, resentment, violence, confusion, despair]* engendrer ◆ **he ~s horses** il fait l'élevage des chevaux, il élève des chevaux ◆ **to ~ in/out a characteristic** faire acquérir/faire perdre une caractéristique *(par la sélection)* ◆ **to be bred for sth/to do sth** *[animals]* être élevé pour qch/pour faire qch ; *[people]* être conditionné pour qch/pour faire qch ; → **born, cross, familiarity** VI *[animals]* se reproduire, se multiplier ◆ **they ~ like rabbits** ils se multiplient comme des lapins N *(of animal) (= race)* race *f*, espèce *f* ; *(within race)* type *m* ; *(of plant)* espèce *f* ; *(fig)* sorte *f*, espèce *f* ; → **crossbreed, half**

breeder /ˈbriːdəʳ/ N 1 *(Phys:* also **breeder reactor)** sur(ré)générateur *m* 2 *(Agr etc = person)* éleveur *m*, -euse *f* ; → **cattle, plant, stockbreeder**

breeding /ˈbriːdɪŋ/ N 1 *(= reproduction)* reproduction *f*, procréation *f* 2 *(Agr = raising)* élevage *m* ; → **cattle** 3 *(= upbringing)* **(good) ~** (bonne) éducation *f*, bonnes manières *fpl*, savoir-vivre *m* ◆ **to lack ~** manquer de savoir-vivre *or* d'éducation 4 *(Phys)* surrégénération *f*
COMP **breeding ground** N *(lit)* zone *f* de reproduction ◆ **~ ground for revolution/germs** terrain *m* propice à la révolution/aux microbes ◆ **~ ground for talent/revolutionaries** pépinière *f* de talents/de révolutionnaires
breeding season N *[of animals]* saison *f* des amours

breeks /briːks/ NPL *(Scot)* pantalon *m*

breeze[1] /briːz/ N 1 *(= wind)* brise *f* ◆ **gentle ~** petite brise *f*, brise *f* légère ◆ **stiff ~** vent *m* frais ◆ **there is quite a ~** cela souffle ; → **sea** 2 * **it's a ~** c'est facile comme tout, c'est fastoche * ◆ **to do sth in a ~** faire qch les doigts dans le nez * VI ◆ **to ~ in/out** *etc (jauntily)* entrer/sortir *etc* d'un air dégagé ; *(briskly)* entrer/sortir *etc* en coup de vent ◆ **to ~ through sth** * faire qch les doigts dans le nez *

breeze² /ˈbriːz/ **N** (= *cinders*) cendres *fpl* (de charbon) **COMP** **breeze block** **N** (*Brit*) parpaing *m* (*de laitier*)

breezeway /ˈbriːzweɪ/ **N** (*US*) *passage couvert reliant deux bâtiments*

breezily /ˈbriːzɪlɪ/ **ADV** jovialement

breezy /ˈbriːzɪ/ **ADJ** 1 (= *windy*) [*day*] de brise ; [*place*] venteux, éventé ◆ **it's ~ today** il y a du vent aujourd'hui 2 (= *cheery*) [*person, manner*] pétulant ; [*style*] pétulant, enlevé ; [*melody*] enjoué ; [*clothes*] gai ; → **bright**

Bren carrier /ˈbren,kærɪəʳ/ **N** ⇒ **Bren gun carrier**

Bren gun /ˈbrengʌn/ **N** fusil-mitrailleur *m* **COMP** **Bren gun carrier** **N** chenillette *f* (pour fusil mitrailleur)

brent goose /,brentˈguːs/ **N** bernache *f* cravant

brethren /ˈbreðrɪn/ **NPL** 1 (††, *Rel*) frères *mpl* 2 (= *fellow members*) [*of trade union etc*] camarades *mpl*

Breton /ˈbretən/ **ADJ** breton **N** 1 Breton(ne) *m(f)* 2 (= *language*) breton *m*

breve /briːv/ **N** (*Typ*) brève *f* ; (*Mus*) double ronde *f*

brevet /ˈbrevɪt/ **N** (*esp Mil*) brevet *m*

breviary /ˈbriːvɪərɪ/ **N** bréviaire *m*

brevity /ˈbrevɪtɪ/ **N** (= *shortness*) brièveté *f* ; (= *conciseness*) concision *f* ; (= *abruptness*) [*of reply*] laconisme *m* ; [*of manner*] brusquerie *f* ◆ **~ is the soul of wit** (*Prov*) les plaisanteries les plus courtes sont les meilleures

brew /bruː/ **N** 1 [*of beer*] brassage *m* ; (= *amount brewed*) brassin *m* ; → **home** 2 [*of tea*] infusion *f* ; [*of herbs*] tisane *f* ◆ **what's this ~ * in the jug?** (*hum*) qu'est-ce que c'est que ce liquide *or* cette mixture dans la cruche ? **VT** [+ *beer*] brasser ; [+ *tea*] faire infuser, préparer ; [+ *punch*] préparer, mélanger ; (*fig*) [+ *scheme, mischief, plot*] tramer, mijoter * **VI** 1 (= *make beer*) brasser, faire de la bière 2 [*beer*] fermenter ; [*tea*] infuser ; (*fig*) [*storm*] couver, se préparer ; [*plot*] se tramer ◆ **there's trouble ~ing** il y a de l'orage dans l'air, ça va barder * ◆ **something's ~ing** il se trame quelque chose **COMP** **brew-up** * **N** (*Brit*) ◆ **let's have a ~-up** on va se faire du thé

► **brew up** **VI** 1 (*Brit* * = *make tea*) faire du thé 2 [*storm, dispute*] se préparer, couver **N** ◆ **brew-up** * → **brew**

brewer /ˈbruːəʳ/ **N** brasseur *m* **COMP** **brewer's droop** ‡ **N** (*NonC: Brit hum*) impuissance *f* (passagère) due à l'alcool ◆ **to get ~'s droop** bander mou ‡

brewery /ˈbruːərɪ/ **N** brasserie *f* (*fabrique*)

briar /ˈbraɪəʳ/ **N** ⇒ **brier**

bribe /braɪb/ **N** pot-de-vin *m* ◆ **to take a ~** se laisser corrompre *or* acheter, accepter un pot-de-vin ◆ **to offer a ~** faire une tentative de corruption, offrir un pot-de-vin ◆ **I'll give the child a sweet as a ~ to be good** je donnerai un bonbon à l'enfant pour qu'il se tienne tranquille **VT** acheter, soudoyer ; [+ *witness*] suborner ◆ **to ~ sb into silence** acheter le silence de qn ◆ **to ~ sb to do sth** soudoyer *or* corrompre qn pour qu'il fasse qch ◆ **to let o.s. be ~d** se laisser soudoyer

bribery /ˈbraɪbərɪ/ **N** corruption *f* ; (*Jur*) [*of witness*] subornation *f* ◆ **~ and corruption** (*Jur*) corruption *f* ◆ **open to ~** corruptible

bric-à-brac /ˈbrɪkəbræk/ **N** (*NonC*) bric-à-brac *m* ◆ **~ dealer** brocanteur *m*

brick /brɪk/ **N** 1 (*for building*) brique *f* ◆ **made of ~** en brique(s) ◆ **it has not damaged the ~s and mortar** ça n'a pas endommagé les murs ◆ **to put one's money into ~s and mortar** investir dans la pierre *or* l'immobilier ◆ **you can't make ~s without straw** (*Prov*) à l'impossible nul n'est tenu (*Prov*) ◆ **he came down on me like a ton of ~s!** * il m'est tombé sur le râble ! *, il m'a passé un de ces savons ! * ◆ **you might as well talk to a ~ wall** * autant parler à un mur ◆ **to run one's head against** *or* **come up against a ~ wall** se heurter à un mur ◆ **to drop a ~** * (*fig*) faire une gaffe * *or* une bourde * ; → **built, cat**

2 (*Brit* = *toy*) cube *m* (*de construction*) ◆ **box of ~s** jeu *m or* boîte *f* de construction

3 ◆ **a ~ of ice cream** une glace (*empaquetée*)

4 († * = *person*) type *m* sympa *, fille *f* sympa * ◆ **be a ~!** sois sympa * *or* chic !

COMP [*house*] en brique(s)

brick-built **ADJ** en brique(s)

brick-kiln **N** four *m* à briques

brick red **N, ADJ** (rouge *m*) brique *inv*

► **brick in** **VT SEP** ⇒ **brick up**

► **brick off** **VT SEP** [+ *area*] (em)murer

► **brick up** **VT SEP** [+ *door, window*] murer

brickbat /ˈbrɪkbæt/ **N** (*lit*) morceau *m* de brique ; (* *fig*) critique *f*

brickie * /ˈbrɪkɪ/ **N** (*Brit*) abbrev of **bricklayer**

bricklayer /ˈbrɪk,leɪəʳ/ **N** maçon *m*

bricklaying /ˈbrɪk,leɪɪŋ/ **N** (*NonC*) maçonnerie *f*

brickwork /ˈbrɪkwɜːk/ **N** briquetage *m*, brique *f*

brickworks /ˈbrɪkwɜːks/, **brickyard** /ˈbrɪkjɑːd/ **N** briqueterie *f*

bridal /ˈbraɪdl/ **ADJ** [*feast*] de noce(s) ; [*bed, chamber, procession*] nuptial ; [*bouquet*] de la mariée **COMP** **bridal gown** **N** robe *f* de mariée

bridal party **N** famille *f* et amis *mpl* de la mariée

bridal shop **N** magasin *m* de robes de mariées

bridal shower **N** (*US*) *fête en l'honneur de la future mariée*

bridal suite **N** suite *f* nuptiale

bridal veil **N** voile *m* de mariée

bridal wear **N** (*NonC*) vêtements *mpl* de mariée

bride /braɪd/ **N** (*about to be married*) (future) mariée *f* ; (*just married*) (jeune) mariée *f* ◆ **the ~ and (bride)groom** les jeunes mariés *mpl* ◆ **the ~ of Christ** (*Rel*) l'épouse *f* du Christ **COMP** **bride-to-be** **N** future mariée *f* ◆ **his ~-to-be** sa future femme, sa promise (*hum*)

bridegroom /ˈbraɪdgruːm/ **N** (*about to be married*) (futur) marié *m* ; (*just married*) (jeune) marié *m*

bridesmaid /ˈbraɪdzmeɪd/ **N** demoiselle *f* d'honneur

bridge¹ /brɪdʒ/ **N** 1 pont *m* ◆ **to build/throw a ~ across a river** construire/jeter un pont sur un fleuve ◆ **to build ~s between two communities/organizations** jeter un pont entre deux communautés/organisations ◆ **don't cross your ~s before you come to them** (*Prov*) chaque chose en son temps (*Prov*) ◆ **let's cross that ~ when we come to it** on s'occupera de ce problème-là en temps et en heure ; → **burn¹, drawbridge, footbridge**

2 (*Naut*) passerelle *f* (de commandement)

3 [*of nose*] arête *f*, dos *m* ; [*of spectacles*] arcade *f* ; [*of violin*] chevalet *m*

4 (*Dentistry*) bridge *m*

VT [+ *river*] construire *or* jeter un pont sur ◆ **to ~ a gap** (*fig*) (*in knowledge, facts*) combler une lacune (*in* dans) ; (*in budget*) combler un trou (*in* dans) ; ◆ **to ~ the gap** *or* **divide** (*between people*) combler le fossé (*between* entre)

COMP **bridge-builder** **N** (*fig*) médiateur *m*, -trice *f*

bridge-building **N** (*Mil*) pontage *m* ; (*fig*) efforts *mpl* de rapprochement

bridge² /brɪdʒ/ **N** (*Cards*) bridge *m* ◆ **to play ~** bridger, jouer au bridge ; → **auction, contract**

COMP **bridge party** **N** soirée *f or* réunion *f* de bridge

bridge player **N** bridgeur *m*, -euse *f*

bridge roll **N** petit pain *m* (brioché)

bridgehead /ˈbrɪdʒhed/ **N** (*Mil*) tête *f* de pont

bridgework /ˈbrɪdʒwɜːk/ **N** (*esp US Dentistry*) bridge *m*

bridging /ˈbrɪdʒɪŋ/ **N** (*Climbing*) opposition *f* **COMP** **bridging loan** **N** (*Brit Fin*) prêt-relais *m*

bridle /ˈbraɪdl/ **N** [*of horse*] bride *f* ; (*fig*) frein *m*, contrainte *f* **VT** [+ *horse*] brider ; [+ *one's emotions*] refréner, tenir en bride ◆ **to ~ one's tongue** se taire, tenir sa langue **VI** (*in anger*) regimber, se rebiffer ; (*in scorn*) lever le menton (*en signe de mépris*) **COMP** **bridle path** **N** piste *f* cavalière

bridleway /ˈbraɪdlweɪ/ **N** piste *f* cavalière

brief /briːf/ **ADJ** 1 (= *short*) [*period, career, visit, glimpse, moment, interval*] bref ◆ **for a ~ moment, I thought she was going to hit him** pour un (bref) instant, j'ai cru qu'elle allait le frapper

2 (= *concise*) [*description, statement*] bref ◆ **a ~ note** un mot ◆ **a ~ history** un résumé succinct ◆ **I shall be ~** je serai bref ◆ **to be ~, the same thing happened again** bref *or* en deux mots, il s'est passé la même chose

3 (= *skimpy*) [*skirt, shorts*] très court

N 1 (= *task*) mission *f* ; (*Jur*) dossier *m* ◆ **their ~ is to investigate the cause of the accident** ils ont pour mission d'enquêter sur la cause de l'accident ◆ **she has a ~ to prepare a report for 3 June** elle a été chargée de préparer un rapport pour le 3 juin ◆ **to hold a ~ for sb** (*Jur*) représenter qn en justice ◆ **I hold no ~ for those who ...** (*fig*) je ne me fais pas l'avocat *or* le défenseur de ceux qui ... ◆ **I hold no ~ for him** (*fig*) je ne prends pas sa défense ◆ **to have a watching ~ for ...** veiller aux intérêts de ... ◆ **to take a ~** (*Jur*) accepter de plaider une cause

◆ **in brief** en bref ◆ **in ~ then, do you agree?** en bref, vous êtes d'accord ? ◆ **the news in ~** les actualités en bref

2 (*Mil* = *instructions*) briefing *m* ◆ **his ~ is to ...** la tâche qui lui a été assignée consiste à ...

3 (*Brit* * = *lawyer*) avocat *m*

NPL **briefs** (= *pants*) slip *m*

VT 1 [+ *barrister*] confier une cause à

2 (= *give order to*) briefer, donner des instructions à ; (= *bring up to date*) mettre au courant (*on sth* de qch) ; ◆ **the pilots were ~ed** les pilotes ont reçu leur briefing *or* bref ◆ **we ~ our salesmen once a week** nous faisons un briefing hebdomadaire à l'intention de nos représentants

briefcase /ˈbriːfkeɪs/ **N** serviette *f* ; (*handleless*) porte-documents *m inv*

briefer /ˈbriːfəʳ/ **N** (= *spokesperson*) porte-parole *m inv*

briefing /ˈbriːfɪŋ/ **N** (*for soldiers, airmen*) briefing *m*, dernières instructions *fpl* ; (*gen*) briefing *m* ; (= *notes*) notes *fpl*

briefly /ˈbriːflɪ/ **ADV** 1 (= *for short time*) [*smile, glance, pause*] un bref instant ; [*speak, visit*] brièvement 2 (= *concisely*) [*tell, reply, describe*] en peu de mots ◆ **put ~, his argument was this** en deux mots *or* en bref, voici quel était son argument ◆ **the facts, ~, are these** en deux mots *or* en bref, les faits sont les suivants

briefness /ˈbriːfnɪs/ **N** (*NonC*) 1 (= *shortness*) [*of visit, career*] brièveté *f* ; [*of interval*] courte durée *f* 2 (= *conciseness*) [*of description, statement*] brièveté *f*

brier /ˈbraɪəʳ/ **N** 1 (= *wood*) (racine *f* de) bruyère *f* ; (*also* **brier pipe**) pipe *f* de bruyère 2 (= *wild rose*) églantier *m* ; (= *thorny bush*) ronces *fpl* ; (= *thorn*) épine *f* **COMP** **brier rose** **N** églantine *f*

brig /brɪg/ **N** (*Naut*) brick *m*

Brig. (abbrev of **brigadier**) ~ **A. Robert** le général A. Robert

brigade /brɪˈgeɪd/ N (*Mil, fig*) brigade *f* ◆ **one of the old** ~ (*fig*) un vétéran, un vieux de la vieille ; → **blue, fire, green**

brigadier /ˌbrɪgəˈdɪəʳ/ N (*Brit*) général *m* de brigade COMP **brigadier general** N (pl **brigadier generals**) (*US*) (*in army*) général *m* de brigade ; (*in airforce*) général *m* de brigade aérienne

brigand /ˈbrɪgənd/ N brigand *m*, bandit *m*

brigandage /ˈbrɪgəndɪdʒ/ N brigandage *m*

bright /braɪt/ ADJ 1 (= *vivid, shining*) [*colour, light*] vif ; [*room, water*] clair ; [*clothes, bird, flower*] (*one colour*) d'une couleur vive ; (*two or more colours*) aux couleurs vives ; [*star, eyes*] brillant ; [*metal*] luisant ◆ ~ **red/yellow/blue** rouge/jaune/bleu vif *inv* ◆ **her eyes** ~ **with excitement, she ...** les yeux brillants d'excitation, elle ...

2 [*day, weather*] radieux ; [*sunshine, sun*] éclatant ◆ **to become** ~**er** [*weather*] s'éclaircir ◆ ~ **intervals** *or* **periods** éclaircies *fpl* ◆ **the outlook is** ~**er** on prévoit une amélioration (du temps)

3 (= *clever*) [*person*] intelligent ; [*child*] éveillé, intelligent ◆ **she's as** ~ **as a button** elle est très vive d'esprit ◆ **full of** ~ **ideas** plein de bonnes idées ◆ **to have the** ~ **idea of doing sth** avoir la bonne idée de faire qch

4 (= *cheerful*) [*person, smile, voice*] jovial ◆ ~ **and breezy** [*person, manner*] décontracté et jovial

5 (= *promising*) [*future, outlook, prospects, start*] brillant ; (= *positive*) [*moment*] bon ◆ **the future looks** ~ (**for him**) l'avenir s'annonce bien (pour lui) ◆ **the outlook is** ~**er** les perspectives d'avenir sont plus prometteuses ◆ ~**er days** des jours plus heureux ◆ ~ **spot** lueur *f* d'espoir ◆ **to look on the** ~ **side** prendre les choses du bon côté ◆ **(looking) on the** ~ **side, ...** si l'on prend les choses du bon côté, ...

6 ◆ **to be (up)** ~ **and early** se lever de bon matin ◆ **to arrive** ~ **and early** arriver de bon matin

ADV (*liter*) ◆ **to shine** ~ briller

COMP **bright-eyed** ADJ [*person*] aux yeux brillants ◆ ~**-eyed idealism** idéalisme *m* fervent ◆ ~**-eyed and bushy-tailed** * en pleine forme

the bright lights NPL les lumières *fpl* de la grande ville ◆ **the** ~ **lights of New York** les lumières *fpl* de New York

bright spark * N petit(e) futé(e) * *m(f)*

bright young things NPL la génération qui monte

brighten /ˈbraɪtn/ (also **brighten up**) VT 1 (= *make cheerful*) [+ *room, spirits, person*] égayer ; [+ *conversation*] égayer, animer ; [+ *prospects, situation, future*] améliorer 2 (= *make shine*) faire briller, rendre (plus) brillant ; [+ *metal*] faire reluire ; [+ *colour*] aviver VI 1 [*weather, sky*] s'éclaircir, se dégager 2 [*eyes*] s'éclairer, s'allumer ; [*expression*] s'éclairer, s'épanouir ; [*person*] s'égayer, s'animer ; [*prospects, future*] s'améliorer, se présenter sous un meilleur jour COMP **brightening agent** N [*of washing powder*] agent *m* blanchissant

brightly /ˈbraɪtlɪ/ ADV 1 (*with light*) [*sparkle*] de mille feux ◆ **to burn** ~ [*fire, substance*] flamber ; [*light*] étinceler ◆ ~ **lit** bien éclairé 2 ◆ **the stars were shining** ~ les étoiles brillaient ; (= *vividly*) ◆ ~ **coloured** (*one colour*) d'une couleur vive ; (*two or more colours*) aux couleurs vives ◆ ~ **painted** (*one colour*) peint d'une couleur vive ; (*two or more colours*) peint avec des couleurs vives ◆ ~ **patterned** (*one colour*) avec des motifs d'une couleur vive ; (*two or more colours*) avec des motifs aux couleurs vives 3 (= *cheerfully*) [*say, answer, smile*] jovialement

brightness /ˈbraɪtnɪs/ N (*NonC*) 1 (= *vividness*) [*of colour*] vivacité *f* ; [*of clothes, fire, sunshine, eyes*] éclat *m* ; [*of star, daylight, room*] luminosité *f* ; [*of light*] intensité *f* ; [*of metal*] brillant *m* ; (*TV, Comput*) [*of screen*] luminosité *f* 2 (= *light*) lumière *f* 3 (= *cheerfulness*) [*of person, expression, tone*] vivacité *f*, jovialité *f* ; [*of smile*] éclat *m*, jovialité *f* 4 (= *intelligence*) intelligence *f* 5 (= *promise*) [*of prospects, future*] caractère *m* prometteur COMP **brightness control** N réglage *m* de la luminosité

Bright's disease /ˈbraɪtsdɪˌziːz/ N mal *m* de Bright, néphrite *f* chronique

brill[1] /brɪl/ N (pl **brill** *or* **brills**) barbue *f*

brill[2] * /brɪl/ ADJ (*Brit*) (abbrev of **brilliant**) super * *inv*

brilliance /ˈbrɪljəns/, **brilliancy** /ˈbrɪljənsɪ/ N 1 (= *splendour: lit, fig*) éclat *m*, brillant *m* 2 (= *great intelligence*) intelligence *f* supérieure

brilliant /ˈbrɪljənt/ ADJ 1 (= *clever*) [*person, mind, book, performance*] brillant ; [*idea*] génial 2 (= *successful*) [*career*] brillant ; [*future*] radieux ; [*success*] éclatant ; [*victory*] brillant, éclatant 3 (= *bright*) [*light, sunshine, colour, smile*] éclatant 4 (*Brit* * = *excellent*) génial *, super * *inv* ◆ **I'll help** – ~**!** je vais aider – super ! * ◆ **she's** ~ **with children** elle est super * avec les enfants ◆ ~ **at sth** super bon * (bonne * *f*) en qch ◆ **to be** ~ **at doing sth** être drôlement * doué pour faire qch ◆ **yoga is** ~ **for stress reduction** *or* **for reducing stress** le yoga est génial * *or* super * pour combattre le stress

brilliantine /ˈbrɪljənˌtiːn/ N brillantine *f*

brilliantly /ˈbrɪljəntlɪ/ ADV 1 (= *cleverly*) [*write, play, perform*] brillamment ; [*simple, funny*] remarquablement 2 (= *superbly*) [*succeed, work*] magnifiquement ◆ **he was** ~ **successful** il a magnifiquement réussi 3 (= *brightly*) [*lit, illuminated*] bien ; [*shine*] d'un vif éclat ◆ **to smile** ~ sourire de toutes ses dents ◆ ~ **coloured** (*one colour*) d'une couleur vive ; (*two or more colours*) aux couleurs vives ◆ **a** ~ **sunny day** une journée radieuse 4 (*Brit* * = *excellently*) ◆ **she played/drove** ~ elle a super bien * joué/conduit

Brillo ® /ˈbrɪləʊ/ N (also **Brillo pad**) tampon *m* Jex ®

brim /brɪm/ N [*of cup, hat, lake*] bord *m* ◆ **to be full to the** ~ **with sth** (*lit*) être plein à ras bord de qch ; (*fig*) déborder de qch VI déborder (*with* de) ; ◆ ~**ming with** (*lit*) plein à ras bord de ; (*fig*) débordant de

► **brim over** VI (*lit, fig*) déborder (*with* de)

brimful /ˈbrɪmˈfʊl/ ADJ (*lit*) plein à ras bord ; (*fig*) débordant (*with* de)

brimstone /ˈbrɪmstəʊn/ N soufre *m* ; → **fire**

brindle(d) /ˈbrɪndl(d)/ ADJ moucheté, tavelé

brine /braɪn/ N 1 (= *salt water*) eau *f* salée ; (*Culin*) saumure *f* 2 (*liter*) (= *sea*) mer *f*, océan *m* ; (= *sea water*) eau *f* de mer

bring /brɪŋ/ LANGUAGE IN USE 17.1, 26.3 (pret, ptp **brought**)

VT 1 [+ *person, animal, vehicle, peace*] amener ; [+ *object, news, information*] apporter ◆ **to** ~ **sb up/down/across** faire monter/faire descendre/faire traverser qn (avec soi) ◆ **to** ~ **sth up/down** monter/descendre qch ◆ **I brought him up his breakfast** je lui ai monté son petit déjeuner ; → **bacon, bed**

2 (= *cause*) amener ◆ **the hot weather** ~**s storms** le temps chaud provoque *or* amène des orages ◆ **this song brought her international fame** la chanson lui a assuré une renommée internationale ◆ **his books brought him a good income** ses livres lui rapportaient bien *or* lui étaient d'un bon rapport ◆ **to** ~ **good/bad luck** porter bonheur/malheur ◆ **to** ~ **a blush to sb's cheeks** faire rougir qn, faire monter le rouge aux joues de qn ◆ **to** ~ **tears to sb's eyes** faire venir les larmes aux yeux de qn ◆ **that brought him to the verge of insanity** cela l'a mené *or* amené au bord de la folie ◆ **to** ~ **sth (up)on o.s.** s'attirer qch ◆ **to** ~ **sb to book** faire rendre des comptes à qn ◆ **to** ~ **sth to a close** *or* **an end** mettre fin à qch ◆ **to** ~ **sb to his feet** faire lever qn ◆ **to** ~ **sb to justice** traduire qn en justice ◆ **to** ~ **sb low** abaisser qn ◆ **to** ~ **sth to sb's knowledge** signaler qch à qn, porter qch à la connaissance de qn ◆ **to** ~ **sth to mind** rappeler qch, évoquer qch ◆ **to** ~ **sth into question** (= *throw doubt on*) remettre qch en question ◆ **to** ~ **sth to pass** (*liter*) causer qch ◆ **to** ~ **sth to perfection** porter qch à la perfection ◆ **to** ~ **sth into play** *or* **line** faire jouer qch, faire entrer qch en ligne de compte ◆ **to** ~ **sb to his senses** ramener qn à la raison ◆ **to** ~ **into the world** mettre au monde ; → **bear**[1]**, head, light**[1]

3 (+ *infin* = *persuade*) amener (*sb to do sth* qn à faire qch) ; ◆ **he brought him to understand that ...** il l'a amené à comprendre que ... ◆ **I cannot** ~ **myself to speak to him** je ne peux me résoudre à lui parler

4 (*Jur*) **to** ~ **an action against sb** intenter un procès à qn ◆ **to** ~ **a charge against sb** inculper qn ◆ **the case was brought before Lord MacLeod** la cause fut entendue par Lord MacLeod ◆ **to** ~ **evidence** fournir des preuves

COMP **bring-and-buy sale** N (*Brit*) vente *f* de charité *or* de bienfaisance

► **bring about** VT SEP 1 [+ *reforms, review*] amener, provoquer ; [+ *war*] causer, provoquer ; [+ *accident*] provoquer, occasionner ; [+ *sb's ruin*] entraîner, amener

2 [+ *boat*] faire virer de bord

► **bring along** VT SEP ◆ **to bring sth along (with one)** apporter qch (avec soi) ◆ **to** ~ **sb along (with one)** amener qn (avec soi) ◆ **may I** ~ **along a friend?** est-ce que je peux amener un ami ?

► **bring back** VT SEP 1 [+ *person*] ramener ; [+ *object*] rapporter ◆ **to** ~ **a spacecraft back to earth** récupérer un vaisseau spatial ◆ **her holiday brought back her health** ses vacances lui ont rendu la santé ◆ **a rest will** ~ **him back to normal** du repos le remettra d'aplomb

2 (= *call to mind*) rappeler (à la mémoire)

► **bring down** VT SEP 1 (= *cause to fall*) abattre ; (= *cause to land*) [+ *kite etc*] ramener au sol ; [+ *plane*] faire atterrir ; (= *shoot down*) [+ *animal, bird, plane*] abattre

2 [+ *dictator, government*] faire tomber ; [+ *temperature, prices, cost of living*] faire baisser ; [+ *swelling*] réduire ; (*Math*) [+ *figure*] abaisser ◆ **his action brought down everyone's wrath upon him** son action lui a attiré *or* lui a valu la colère de tout le monde ; → **house**

► **bring forth** VT SEP (*liter*) [+ *fruit*] produire ; [+ *child*] mettre au monde ; [+ *animal*] mettre bas ; (*fig*) [+ *protests, criticism*] attirer

► **bring forward** VT SEP 1 [+ *person*] faire avancer ; [+ *chair etc*] avancer ; [+ *witness*] produire ; [+ *evidence, proof, argument*] avancer

2 (= *advance time of*) [+ *meeting*] avancer

3 (*Accounting*) [+ *figure, amount*] reporter

► **bring in** VT SEP 1 [+ *person*] faire entrer ; [+ *object*] rentrer

2 (= *introduce*) [+ *fashion*] lancer ; [+ *custom, legislation*] introduire ◆ **to** ~ **in the police/the troops** faire intervenir la police/l'armée ◆ **to** ~ **in a bill** (*Parl*) présenter *or* déposer un projet de loi

3 (*Fin*) [+ *income*] rapporter ◆ **to** ~ **in interest** rapporter des intérêts

4 (*Jur*) **to** ~ **in a verdict** [*jury*] rendre un verdict ◆ **to** ~ **in a verdict of guilty** déclarer qn coupable

► **bring off** VT SEP 1 [+ *people from wreck*] sauver

2 *[+ plan, aim, deal]* mener à bien ; *[+ attack, hoax]* réussir ◆ **he didn't manage to ~ it off** il n'a pas réussi son coup

► **bring on** VT SEP 1 *(= cause) [+ illness, quarrel]* provoquer, causer ◆ **to ~ on sb's cold** enrhumer qn

2 *(Agr etc) [+ crops, flowers]* faire pousser

3 *(Theat) [+ person]* amener ; *[+ thing]* apporter sur (la) scène

► **bring out** VT SEP 1 *[+ person]* faire sortir ; *[+ object]* sortir ; *[+ meaning]* mettre en évidence ; *[+ colour]* faire ressortir ; *[+ qualities]* faire valoir, mettre en valeur ◆ **it ~s out the best in him** c'est dans des cas comme celui-là qu'il se montre sous son meilleur jour

2 *[+ book]* publier, faire paraître ; *[+ actress, new product]* lancer

► **bring over** VT SEP 1 *[+ person]* amener ; *[+ object]* apporter

2 *(= convert) [+ person]* convertir, gagner *(to* à)

► **bring round** VT SEP 1 *(to one's house etc) [+ person]* amener, faire venir ; *[+ object]* apporter ◆ **to ~ the conversation round to football** amener la conversation sur le football

2 *[+ unconscious person]* ranimer

3 *(= convert) [+ person]* convertir, gagner *(to* à)

► **bring through** VT SEP *[+ sick person]* sauver

► **bring to** VT SEP 1 *(Naut)* arrêter, mettre en panne

2 *[+ unconscious person]* ranimer

► **bring together** VT SEP 1 *(= put in touch) [+ people]* mettre en contact, faire se rencontrer

2 *(= end quarrel between)* réconcilier

3 *[+ facts etc]* rassembler

► **bring under** VT SEP *(fig)* assujettir, soumettre

► **bring up** VT SEP 1 *[+ person]* faire monter ; *[+ object]* monter

2 *[+ child, animal]* élever ◆ **well/badly brought-up child** enfant *m* bien/mal élevé

3 *(= vomit)* vomir, rendre

4 *(= call attention to) [+ fact, allegation, problem]* mentionner ; *[+ question]* soulever ◆ **we shan't ~ it up again** nous n'en reparlerons plus

5 *(= stop) [+ person, vehicle]* (faire) arrêter ◆ **the question brought him up short** la question l'a arrêté net

6 *(Jur)* **to ~ sb up before a court** citer *or* faire comparaître qn devant un tribunal

7 ◆ **to bring up to date** *[+ accounts, correspondence etc]* mettre à jour ; *[+ method etc]* moderniser ◆ **to ~ sb up to date on sth** mettre qn au courant (des derniers développements) de qch

brink /brɪŋk/ N *(lit, fig)* bord *m* ◆ **on the ~ of sth** à deux doigts de qch, au bord de qch ◆ **on the ~ of doing sth** à deux doigts de faire qch, sur le point de faire qch

brinkmanship /ˈbrɪŋkmənʃɪp/ N stratégie *f* de la corde raide ◆ **a game of political ~ has begun at Westminster with the careers of some ministers on the line** les politiciens de Westminster ont entamé une partie de poker, où se joue la carrière de plusieurs ministres

briny /ˈbraɪnɪ/ ADJ saumâtre, salé ◆ **the ~ deep** *(liter)* la grande bleue N ◆ **the ~** †* la grande bleue

briquet(te) /brɪˈket/ N briquette *f*, aggloméré *m*

brisk /brɪsk/ ADJ 1 *[person] (= lively)* vif, animé ; *(= abrupt in manner)* brusque 2 *[movement]* vif, rapide ◆ **~ pace** allure *f* (très) vive ◆ **to take a ~ walk** marcher *or* se promener d'un bon pas ◆ **at a ~ trot** au grand trot ; → **start** 3 *[attack]* vigoureux, vivement mené ; *[trade]* actif, florissant ; *[demand]* important ◆ **business is ~** les affaires marchent (bien) ◆ **trading was ~** *(on Stock Exchange)* le marché était actif ◆ **the betting was ~** les paris allaient bon train 4 *[beer]* mousseux ; *[champagne, cider]* pétillant 5 *[air, weather, day]* frais (fraîche *f*) et vivifiant

brisket /ˈbrɪskɪt/ N poitrine *f* de bœuf

briskly /ˈbrɪsklɪ/ ADV *[move]* vivement ; *[walk]* d'un bon pas ; *[speak]* brusquement ; *[act]* sans tarder ◆ **these goods are selling ~** *(Comm etc)* ces articles se vendent (très) bien

briskness /ˈbrɪsknɪs/ N 1 *(= liveliness) [of walk, movement]* vivacité *f* ; *[of trade]* dynamisme *m* 2 *(= abruptness)* brusquerie *f*

brisling /ˈbrɪzlɪŋ/ N sprat *m*

bristle /ˈbrɪsl/ N *[of beard, brush]* poil *m* ; *[of boar]* soie *f* ; *[of plant]* poil *m* ◆ **a brush with nylon ~s** une brosse en nylon ® VI 1 *[animal hair]* se hérisser ◆ **a shirt bristling with pins** une chemise hérissée d'épingles ◆ **bristling with difficulties** hérissé de difficultés ◆ **a town bristling with police** une ville grouillante de policiers 2 *(fig) [person]* s'irriter *(at* de) se hérisser ◆ **he ~d at the suggestion** il s'est hérissé à cette suggestion COMP **bristle brush** N brosse *f* en soie de sanglier

bristly /ˈbrɪslɪ/ ADJ *[animal]* au(x) poil(s) raide(s) *or* dur(s) ; *[moustache, beard]* aux poils raides ; *[hair]* raide ; *[chin, cheek]* mal rasé ◆ **you're very ~ today** * tu piques drôlement aujourd'hui *

Bristol /ˈbrɪstəl/ N ◆ **~ Channel** canal *m* de Bristol ◆ **~ board** *(Art, Comm)* bristol *m* ; → **shipshape**

bristols ‡ /ˈbrɪstəlz/ NPL roberts ‡ *mpl*

Brit * /brɪt/ N Britannique *mf*

Britain /ˈbrɪtən/ N (also **Great Britain**) Grande-Bretagne *f* ; → GREAT BRITAIN, UNITED KINGDOM

Britannia /brɪˈtænɪə/ N Britannia *f* COMP **Britannia metal** N métal *m* anglais

Britannic /brɪˈtænɪk/ ADJ ◆ **His** *or* **Her ~ Majesty** sa Majesté britannique

britches /ˈbrɪtʃəz/ NPL ⇒ **breeches**

Briticism /ˈbrɪtɪsɪzəm/ N briticisme *m*

British /ˈbrɪtɪʃ/ ADJ britannique ; *(loosely)* anglais ; *[ambassador, embassy]* de Grande-Bretagne ◆ **~ English** l'anglais *m* britannique

NPL **the British** les Britanniques *mpl* ; *(loosely)* les Anglais *mpl*

COMP **British Airports Authority** N administration *f* des aéroports britanniques

British Antarctic Territory N Territoire *m* britannique de l'Antarctique

British Asian ADJ *britannique originaire du sous-continent indien* N *Britannique originaire du sous-continent indien*

the British Broadcasting Corporation N la BBC

British Columbia N Colombie *f* britannique

British Columbian ADJ de la Colombie britannique N habitant(e) *m(f)* de la Colombie britannique

the British Commonwealth N le Commonwealth

British Council N British Council *m (organisme chargé de promouvoir la langue et la culture britanniques dans le monde)*

British Honduras N Honduras *m* britannique

the British Isles NPL les îles *fpl* Britanniques ; → GREAT BRITAIN, UNITED KINGDOM

British Legion N *organisme d'aide aux anciens combattants ;* → LEGION

the British Library N *la bibliothèque nationale de Grande-Bretagne*

British Rail N *(formerly) chemins de fer britanniques*

British Red Cross Society N Croix *f* Rouge britannique

British Summer Time N l'heure *f* d'été britannique

British Telecom N *société britannique de télécommunications*

Britisher * /ˈbrɪtɪʃəʳ/ N *(US)* Britannique *mf* ; *(loosely)* Anglais(e) *m(f)*

Briton /ˈbrɪtən/ N 1 Britannique *mf* 2 *(Hist)* Breton(ne) *m(f)* (de Grande-Bretagne)

Britpop /ˈbrɪtpɒp/ N *musique pop britannique des années 90*

Brittany /ˈbrɪtənɪ/ N Bretagne *f*

brittle /ˈbrɪtl/ ADJ 1 *(= breakable) [twig, hair, nails]* cassant 2 *(= fragile) [agreement, peace]* fragile 3 *[person, personality]* sec (sèche *f*) ; *[laugh, voice]* crispé COMP **brittle-bone disease** N ostéogénèse *f* imparfaite

Brittonic /brɪˈtɒnɪk/ ADJ brittonique

bro ‡ /brəʊ/ N *(US)* 1 *(= friend)* pote * *m* ◆ **hi, ~!** salut, vieux * *or* mon pote * ! 2 *(= brother)* frangin * *m*

Bro. *(Rel)* abbrev of **Brother**

broach /brəʊtʃ/ VT *[+ barrel]* mettre en perce ; *[+ box, supplies]* entamer ; *[+ subject, topic]* entamer, aborder N *(Culin)* broche *f* ; *(= tool)* perçoir *m*, foret *m*

broad /brɔːd/ ADJ 1 *(= wide) [road, shoulders, smile]* large ◆ **the lake is 200 metres ~** le lac a 200 mètres de large *or* de largeur ◆ **a garden about 6 metres long and 3 metres ~** un jardin d'environ 6 mètres de long et 3 mètres de large ◆ **to grow ~er** s'élargir ◆ **to make ~er** élargir ◆ **~ in the shoulder** *[person]* large d'épaules ; *[garment]* un peu large aux épaules ; see also **comp** ◆ **~ in the beam** *[ship]* ventru ; *(*: pej) [person]* fort de l'arrière-train * ◆ **he's got a ~ back** *(fig)* il a bon dos ◆ **it's as ~ as it's long** * *(fig)* c'est du pareil au même * ◆ **a ~ expanse of lawn** une vaste étendue de pelouse ; → **-gauge**

2 *(= approximate, general) [aims, objectives, term]* général ; *[phonetic transcription]* large ◆ **the ~ outlines** les grandes lignes *fpl* ◆ **in the ~est sense of the word** au sens (le plus) large du terme ◆ **in ~ terms** grosso modo ◆ **to be in ~ agreement** être d'accord sur l'essentiel ◆ **he distinguished three ~ possibilities** il a distingué trois grandes possibilités ◆ **to paint sth with a ~ brush** *(fig)* décrire qch à grands traits ; see also **comp** ◆ **~ construction** *(US Jur)* interprétation *f* large

3 *(= wide-ranging) [category, range]* large ; *[coalition]* vaste ; *[education]* diversifié ; *[syllabus]* étendu ◆ **a ~ spectrum of opinion** un large éventail d'opinions ◆ **a film with ~ appeal** un film grand public ◆ **the agreement won ~ support in Congress** cet accord a été largement soutenu par le Congrès ◆ **to have ~ implications** avoir de vastes implications

4 *(= unsubtle) [hint]* à peine voilé ; *[humour]* grivois ; *[comedy]* grossier ; *[joke]* gras (grasse *f*)

5 *(Ling) [accent]* prononcé ◆ **to speak ~ Scots** *(accent)* parler avec un fort accent écossais ; *(dialect)* s'exprimer en dialecte écossais ◆ **to say sth in ~ Yorkshire** dire qch en dialecte du Yorkshire

6 *(= full)* ◆ **in ~ daylight** en plein jour ◆ **it was ~ daylight** il faisait grand jour

7 *(= liberal) [mind, ideas]* large, libéral

N 1 *(= widest part)* **the ~ of the back** le milieu du dos ◆ **the (Norfolk) Broads** *(Geog) les lacs et estuaires du Norfolk*

2 *(US ‡ pej) (= woman)* nana * *f* ; *(= prostitute)* putain ‡ *f*

COMP **broad-based** ADJ *[support, government]* réunissant des tendances très variées, large ; *[tax]* à assiette large

broad bean N *(esp Brit)* fève *f*

broad-brimmed ADJ *[hat]* à larges bords

broad-brush ADJ *(fig) [analysis, report]* schématique, sommaire

Broad Church N *(Rel) groupe libéral au sein de l'Église anglicane* ◆ **the Labour Party is a ~ church** le parti travailliste accueille des courants très divers

broad jump N *(US Sport)* saut *m* en longueur

broad-minded ADJ ◆ **he is ~-minded** il a les idées larges
broad-mindedness N largeur *f* d'esprit
broad-shouldered ADJ large d'épaules

broadband /ˈbrɔːdbænd/ *(Telec)* N transmission *f* à large bande ADJ à large bande

broadcast /ˈbrɔːdkɑːst/ (pret, ptp **broadcast**) VT 1 *[+ news, speech, programme] (Rad)* (radio-)diffuser, émettre ; *(TV)* téléviser, émettre ; *(fig) [+ news, rumour etc]* répandre ◆ **don't ~ it!*** *(fig)* ne va pas le crier sur les toits ! 2 *(Agr) [+ seed]* semer (à la volée) VI *(Rad, TV) [station]* émettre ; *[actor, interviewee etc]* participer à une émission ; *[interviewer]* faire une émission N *(Rad, TV)* émission *f* ◆ **live/recorded ~** émission *f* en direct/en différé ◆ **repeat ~** reprise *f*, rediffusion *f* ADJ *(Rad)* (radio)diffusé ; *(TV)* télévisé ◆ **~ account of a match** *(Rad)* reportage *m* radiodiffusé d'un match ; *(TV)* reportage *m* télévisé d'un match ◆ **~ journalism** *(TV)* journalisme *m* télévisé ; *(Rad)* journalisme *m* radio ◆ **~ satellite** satellite *m* de radiodiffusion ADV *[sow]* à la volée

broadcaster /ˈbrɔːdkɑːstəʳ/ N *(Rad, TV)* personnalité *f* de la radio *or* de la télévision

broadcasting /ˈbrɔːdkɑːstɪŋ/ N *(Rad)* radiodiffusion *f* ; *(TV)* télévision *f* ◆ **that is the end of ~ for tonight** ainsi prennent fin nos émissions de la journée ◆ **~ was interrupted** les émissions ont été interrompues ◆ **a career in ~** une carrière à la radio (*or* à la télévision)
COMP **Broadcasting House** N *siège de la BBC à Londres*
Broadcasting Standards Authority N ≈ Conseil *m* supérieur de l'audiovisuel
Broadcasting Standards Council N *(Brit)* ≈ Conseil *m* supérieur de l'audiovisuel
broadcasting station N station *f* de radio, poste *m* émetteur ; → **British**

broadcloth /ˈbrɔːdklɒθ/ N drap *m* fin *(en grande largeur)*

broaden /ˈbrɔːdn/ (also **broaden out** : *lit, fig*) VT élargir ◆ **to ~ one's outlook** élargir ses horizons VI s'élargir

broadloom /ˈbrɔːdluːm/ ADJ *[carpet]* en grande largeur

broadly /ˈbrɔːdlɪ/ ADV 1 *(= generally) [agree, accept, define]* dans les grandes lignes, d'une manière générale ; *[welcome]* généralement ; *[support]* largement ◆ **this is ~ true** c'est vrai, grosso modo ◆ **~ similar** à peu près semblable ◆ **~-based** large ◆ **~ speaking** en gros, généralement parlant 2 *[hint]* fortement 3 ◆ **to smile ~** avoir un large sourire

broadness /ˈbrɔːdnɪs/ N *[of road]* largeur *f* ; *[of joke, story]* grossièreté *f*, vulgarité *f* ; *[of accent]* caractère *m* prononcé

broadsheet /ˈbrɔːdʃiːt/ N *(Hist, Typ)* placard *m* ; *(Press) (= large-format newspaper)* journal *m* grand format ; *(= serious newspaper)* journal *m* de qualité ; → TABLOIDS, BROADSHEETS

broadside /ˈbrɔːdsaɪd/ N 1 *(= side of ship)* flanc *m* 2 *(= discharge of guns)* bordée *f* ◆ **to fire a ~** lâcher une bordée 3 *(= criticism)* attaque *f* cinglante ; *(= insults)* bordée *f* d'injures *or* d'invectives ◆ **he let him have a ~** il l'a incendié*, il l'a descendu en flammes* ADV 1 *(in ship)* ◆ **to turn ~ (on)** virer en présentant le flanc ◆ **to hit sth ~ (on)** heurter qch par le travers ◆ **to be moored ~ to sth** être amarré le long de qch 2 *(in car)* ◆ **he** *or* **his car hit me ~ (on)** il m'a heurté de côté

broadsword /ˈbrɔːdsɔːd/ N épée *f* à deux tranchants, glaive † *m*

broadways /ˈbrɔːdweɪz/, **broadwise** /ˈbrɔːdwaɪz/ ADV en largeur, dans le sens de la largeur

brocade /brəʊˈkeɪd/ N brocart *m* COMP de brocart

broccoli /ˈbrɒkəlɪ/ N brocoli *m*

brochure /ˈbrəʊʃjʊəʳ/ N *[of college, vacation course]* prospectus *m* ; *[of hotel, travel agent]* brochure *f*, dépliant *m* (touristique)

brock /brɒk/ N *(Brit: rare) (= badger)* blaireau *m*

brogue¹ /brəʊg/ N *(= shoe)* chaussure *f* de marche, richelieu *m*

brogue² /brəʊg/ N *(= accent) (Irish)* accent *m* irlandais ; *(gen)* accent *m* du terroir

broil /brɔɪl/ VT *(US Culin)* griller, faire cuire sur le gril ; *(fig)* griller* ◆ **~ing sun** soleil *m* brûlant VI *(also fig)* griller

broiler /ˈbrɔɪləʳ/ N 1 *(= fowl)* poulet *m* (à rôtir) 2 *(US = grill)* rôtisserie *f*, gril *m*
COMP **broiler house** N éleveuse *f*
broiler pan N *(US)* plateau *m* à grillades *(avec poignée)*

broiling /ˈbrɔɪlɪŋ/ ADJ *(esp US) [sun]* brûlant ; *[summer]* torride

broke /brəʊk/ VB pt of **break** ADJ 1 *(= broken)* ◆ **if it ain't ~, don't fix it*** s'il n'y a pas de gros problèmes, il ne faut rien changer 2 *(* = penniless)* à sec*, fauché* ◆ **to be dead** *or* **stony ~** être fauché (comme les blés)*, être (complètement) à sec* ◆ **to go ~** faire faillite ◆ **to go for ~** jouer le tout pour le tout, jouer le grand jeu *or* son va-tout

broken /ˈbrəʊkən/ VB ptp of **break**
ADJ 1 *(= cracked, smashed) [cup, window, branch, biscuits etc]* cassé ; *(= uneven, rugged) [ground]* accidenté ; *[road]* défoncé ; *[surface]* raboteux ; *[coastline]* dentelé ◆ **pieces of ~ glass** des éclats *mpl* de verre ◆ **pieces of ~ crockery** des morceaux *mpl* de vaisselle
2 *(Med = fractured) [neck, leg, rib, tooth, nail]* cassé ; *[bone, hand, foot]* fracturé ◆ **~ bones** fractures *fpl* ◆ **"do not use on broken skin"** "ne pas utiliser sur plaie ouverte"
3 *(= not working) [machine, phone]* détraqué ◆ **the coffee machine is ~** la machine à café est détraquée ◆ **he sounds like a ~ record** on dirait un disque rayé
4 *(fig = ruined) [body, mind]* brisé ; *[health]* délabré ; *[spirit]* abattu ◆ **to be ~ in body and mind** avoir le corps et le cœur brisés ◆ **the scandal left him a ~ man** ce scandale l'a brisé *or* a fait de lui un homme brisé ◆ **to have a ~ heart** avoir le cœur brisé ◆ **she died of a ~ heart** elle est morte de chagrin, elle est morte le cœur brisé ◆ **he is a ~ reed** on ne peut pas compter sur lui
5 *(= interrupted) [journey]* interrompu ; *[sleep] (= disturbed)* interrompu ; *(= restless)* agité ; *[voice, line]* brisé ◆ **I've had several ~ nights** j'ai eu plusieurs mauvaises nuits ◆ **a spell of ~ weather** un temps variable ◆ **~ cloud** ciel *m* couvert avec des éclaircies ◆ **~ sunshine** soleil *m* intermittent ◆ **(to speak in) ~ English/French** (parler un) mauvais anglais/français
6 *(= violated) [promise, contract, engagement]* rompu ; *[appointment]* manqué
7 *(by divorce) [marriage]* brisé ◆ **he comes from a ~ home** il vient d'un foyer désuni
COMP **broken chord** N *(Mus)* arpège *m*
broken-down ADJ *(= out of order) [car]* en panne ; *[machine]* détraqué ; *(= dilapidated) [house]* délabré
broken-hearted ADJ au cœur brisé
broken lots NPL *(Comm)* articles *mpl* dépareillés
broken numbers NPL *(Math)* fractions *fpl*
broken veins NPL couperose *f*
broken white line N ligne *f* blanche discontinue
broken-winded ADJ poussif

brokenly /ˈbrəʊkənlɪ/ ADV *[say]* d'une voix entrecoupée ; *[sob]* par à-coups

broker /ˈbrəʊkəʳ/ N 1 *(= stockbroker)* ≈ courtier *m* (en bourse), agent *m* de change 2 *(= commissioned agent)* courtier *m* ; *(in shipping)* courtier *m* maritime ◆ **wine ~** courtier *m* en vins 3 *(= secondhand dealer)* brocanteur *m* ; → **pawnbroker** VT *[+ deal, agreement]* négocier ◆ **a UN-~ed ceasefire** un cessez-le-feu négocié sous l'égide l'ONU

brokerage /ˈbrəʊkərɪdʒ/, **broking** /ˈbrəʊkɪŋ/ N *(= trade, commission)* courtage *m*

brolly* /ˈbrɒlɪ/ N *(Brit)* pépin* *m*, parapluie *m*

bromide /ˈbrəʊmaɪd/ N 1 *(Chem, Typ)* bromure *m* ; *(Med *)* bromure *m* (de potassium) ◆ **~ paper** papier *m* au (gelatino-)bromure d'argent 2 *(fig)* banalité *f* or platitude *f* euphorisante

bromine /ˈbrəʊmiːn/ N brome *m*

bronchi /ˈbrɒŋkaɪ/ NPL of **bronchus**

bronchial /ˈbrɒŋkɪəl/ ADJ *[infection]* des bronches, bronchique ◆ **~ tubes** bronches *fpl*

bronchiole /ˈbrɒŋkɪəʊl/ N bronchiole *f*

bronchitic /brɒŋˈkɪtɪk/ ADJ bronchitique

bronchitis /brɒŋˈkaɪtɪs/ N *(NonC)* bronchite *f* ◆ **to have ~** avoir *or* faire une bronchite

bronchopneumonia /ˌbrɒŋkəʊnjuːˈməʊnɪə/ N *(NonC)* bronchopneumonie *f*

bronchus /ˈbrɒŋkəs/ N (pl **bronchi**) bronche *f*

bronco /ˈbrɒŋkəʊ/ N cheval *m* semi-sauvage (de l'Ouest américain), bronco *m*

broncobuster* /ˈbrɒŋkəʊbʌstəʳ/ N *(US)* cowboy *m (qui dompte les chevaux sauvages)*

brontosaurus /ˌbrɒntəˈsɔːrəs/ N (pl **brontosauruses** or **brontosauri** /ˈbrɒntəˈsɔːraɪ/) brontosaure *m*

Bronx /brɒŋks/ N ◆ **the ~** le Bronx ◆ **~ cheer** *(US)* huées *fpl*

bronze /brɒnz/ N *(= metal, colour, work of art)* bronze *m* VI se bronzer, brunir VT *[+ metal]* bronzer ; *[+ skin]* brunir, faire bronzer
COMP en bronze ; *(= colour)* (couleur *f* de) bronze
the Bronze Age N l'âge *m* du bronze
bronze medal N médaille *f* de bronze

bronzed /brɒnzd/ ADJ *[skin, person]* bronzé

bronzer /ˈbrɒnzəʳ/ N autobronzant *m*

bronzing powder /ˈbrɒnzɪŋˌpaudəʳ/ N poudre *f* de soleil

brooch /brəʊtʃ/ N broche *f*

brood /bruːd/ N *[of birds]* couvée *f*, nichée *f* ; *[of mice]* nichée *f* ; *[of children]* progéniture *f*, nichée *f (hum)* ; *[of vipers, scoundrels]* engeance *f* ◆ **she has a great ~ of children** elle a une nombreuse progéniture ◆ **I'm going to take my ~ home*** je vais remmener ma progéniture à la maison VI *[bird]* couver ; *[storm, danger]* couver, menacer ; *[person]* broyer du noir, ruminer ◆ **to ~ on** *[person] [+ misfortune]* remâcher ; *[+ plan]* ruminer ; *[+ the past]* ressasser ◆ **to ~ over sth** *[night etc]* planer sur qch ; *[storm]* couver sur qch ; *(oppressively)* peser sur qch
COMP **brood hen** N couveuse *f*
brood mare N (jument *f*) poulinière *f*

brooding /ˈbruːdɪŋ/ ADJ 1 *(= disturbing)* troublant 2 *(= reflective)* rêveur, songeur ; *(= gloomy)* maussade, soucieux N rumination *f*

broody /ˈbruːdɪ/ ADJ 1 *[hen] (= ready to lay eggs)* prêt à pondre ; *(= ready to sit on eggs)* prêt à couver 2 *(* hum)* ◆ **to be feeling ~** *[person]* avoir envie d'avoir un enfant 3 *(= pensive)* mélancolique

brook¹ /brʊk/ N ruisseau *m*

brook² /brʊk/ VT *(liter) [+ contradiction, delay, reply]* souffrir ◆ **it ~s no argument** c'est incontestable

brooklet /ˈbrʊklɪt/ N ruisselet *m*, petit ruisseau *m*

broom /brʊm/ N 1 *(= plant)* genêt *m* 2 *(= brush)* balai *m* ◆ **a new ~ sweeps clean** *(Prov)* tout nouveau, tout beau *(Prov)* ◆ **this firm needs a new ~** cette compagnie a besoin d'un bon coup de balai *or* a besoin de sang neuf

COMP **broom closet** N (US) ⇒ **broom cupboard**
broom cupboard N (Brit) placard m à balais

broomstick /ˈbrʊmstɪk/ N manche m à balai

Bros. (Comm) (abbrev of **Brothers**) **Martin** ~ Martin Frères

broth /brɒθ/ N bouillon m

brothel /ˈbrɒθl/ N maison f close or de passe
COMP **brothel-creepers** * NPL (Brit) *chaussures d'homme en daim à semelles de crêpe*

brother /ˈbrʌðəʳ/ N 1 (gen, Rel) frère m ◆ **older/younger** ~ frère m aîné/cadet ◆ **Brother Paul** Frère Paul ; → **lay⁴** 2 (in trade unions etc) camarade m ; (US: also **soul brother**) frère m (de couleur) ADJ ◆ **his** ~ **prisoners** *etc* ceux qui sont (or étaient) prisonniers *etc* comme lui, les autres prisonniers mpl *etc* ◆ **his** ~ **officers** ses compagnons mpl d'armes
COMP **brother-in-arms** N (pl **brothers-in-arms**) (liter) frère m d'armes
brother-in-law N (pl **brothers-in-law**) beau-frère m

brotherhood /ˈbrʌðəhʊd/ N 1 (NonC) (lit) fraternité f ; (fig) fraternité f, confraternité f ◆ ~ **of man** fraternité f des hommes 2 (= association: esp Rel) confrérie f ; (US) corporation f ◆ **the Brotherhood** (Freemasonry) la franc-maçonnerie

brotherly /ˈbrʌðəlɪ/ ADJ fraternel ◆ ~ **love** l'amour m fraternel

brougham /ˈbruːəm/ N coupé m de ville

brought /brɔːt/ VB pt, ptp of **bring**

brouhaha * /ˈbruːhɑːhɑː/ N histoires * fpl

brow /braʊ/ N 1 (= forehead) front m ; (= arch above eye) arcade f sourcilière ; (also **eyebrow**) sourcil m ; → **beetling, highbrow, knit, sweat** 2 [of hill] sommet m ; [of cliff] bord m ; (Min) tour f d'extraction

browbeat /ˈbraʊbiːt/ (pret **browbeat**, ptp **browbeaten**) VT intimider, persécuter ◆ **to** ~ **sb into doing sth** forcer qn à faire qch

browbeaten /ˈbraʊbiːtn/ ADJ intimidé

brown /braʊn/ ADJ 1 brun, marron inv ; [hair] châtain ; [boots, shoes, leather] marron ◆ **light** ~ **hair** cheveux mpl châtain clair inv ◆ **light** ~ **material** étoffe f marron clair ◆ **in a** ~ **study** † plongé dans ses pensées or méditations ◆ **to go** ~ [leaves] roussir ; → **nut**
2 (= tanned) [person, skin] bronzé ◆ **to go** ~ bronzer ◆ **as** ~ **as a berry** tout bronzé
3 (= dusky-skinned) brun de peau
4 (US) **to do sth up** ~ ⁑ (fig) soigner qch dans les moindres détails
N brun m, marron m ◆ **her hair was a rich, deep** ~ ses cheveux étaient d'un beau brun foncé
VT 1 [sun] [+ skin, person] bronzer, hâler
2 (Culin) [+ meat, fish, potatoes, onions] faire dorer ; [+ sauce] faire roussir
3 (Brit) **he is ~ed off** † * il en a marre * or ras le bol ⁑
VI 1 [leaves] roussir
2 [person, skin] brunir
3 (Culin) dorer
COMP **brown ale** N *sorte de bière brune*
brown bear N ours m brun
brown belt N (Judo etc) ceinture f marron
brown bread N pain m bis
brown coal N lignite m
brown flour N farine f complète
brown goods NPL (Comm) produits mpl audiovisuels or bruns
brown-nose ⁑ N lèche-cul ⁑ m inv, lèche-bottes * mf VT lécher le cul à or de ⁑, lécher les bottes de *
brown owl N (= bird) chat-huant m ; (in Brownie Guides) cheftaine f
brown paper N papier m d'emballage, papier m Kraft
brown rice N riz m complet
brown sauce N (Brit Culin) *sauce brune relevée*
Brown Shirt N (Hist) Chemise f brune
brown sugar N cassonade f, sucre m brun

brownbag * /ˈbraʊnbæg/ VT (US) ◆ **to** ~ **it, to** ~ **one's lunch** apporter son repas (dans un sac en papier)

brownfield /ˈbraʊnfiːld/ ADJ ◆ ~ **site** ancien terrain m industriel

brownie /ˈbraʊnɪ/ N 1 (= fairy) lutin m, farfadet m 2 ◆ **Brownie (Guide)** jeannette f ◆ **to win** or **get** or **earn Brownie points** * (fig hum) obtenir des bons points 3 ◆ **Brownie** ® (= camera) brownie m kodak ® 4 (esp US = cake) brownie m (petit gâteau au chocolat)

browning /ˈbraʊnɪŋ/ N (Brit Culin) *produit préparé pour roux brun*

brownish /ˈbraʊnɪʃ/ ADJ tirant sur le brun

brownout /ˈbraʊnaʊt/ N (US) (Mil) camouflage m partiel des lumières ; (Elec) panne f partielle

brownstone /ˈbraʊnstəʊn/ N (US) (= material) grès m brun ; (= house) bâtiment m de grès brun

browse /braʊz/ VI 1 (in bookshop, library) feuilleter les livres ; (in other shops) regarder sans acheter ◆ **to** ~ **through a book** feuilleter or parcourir un livre ◆ **I'm just browsing** (in shop) je regarde seulement, merci 2 (Comput) surfer or naviguer sur le Net 3 [animal] brouter, paître VT 1 [+ animals] brouter, paître 2 (Comput) **to** ~ **the Net** surfer or naviguer sur le Net N ◆ **to have a** ~ ⇒ **to browse vi 1**

browser /ˈbraʊzəʳ/ N 1 (Comput) navigateur m 2 (in shop) **"browsers welcome"** "entrée libre"

brucellosis /ˌbruːsəˈləʊsɪs/ N brucellose f

bruise /bruːz/ VT 1 [+ person, part of body] faire un bleu à, contusionner ; [+ finger] faire un pinçon à ; [+ fruit] abîmer, taler ; [+ lettuce] froisser ◆ **to** ~ **one's foot** se faire un bleu au pied ◆ **to be ~d all over** avoir le corps or être couvert de bleus, être tout contusionné 2 (= crush) (lit) écraser, piler ; (fig) [+ ego, feelings, pride] blesser ◆ **~d heart** (liter) cœur m meurtri or blessé ◆ **~d spirit** (liter) esprit m meurtri ◆ **to feel ~d** se sentir secoué VI [fruit] se taler, s'abîmer ◆ **peaches** ~ **easily** les pêches se talent facilement ◆ **he ~s easily** il se fait facilement des bleus N (on person) bleu m, ecchymose f ; (on fruit) meurtrissure f, talure f ◆ **body covered with ~s** corps m couvert d'ecchymoses or de bleus

bruised /bruːzd/ ADJ 1 [person, body, skin, elbow etc] contusionné ◆ ~ **all over** couvert de bleus, tout contusionné 2 [fruit] meurtri, talé ; [vegetables] abîmé, meurtri 3 (fig) [ego, feelings, pride] blessé ◆ **to feel** ~ [person] être blessé

bruiser * /ˈbruːzəʳ/ N malabar * m, cogneur * m

bruising /ˈbruːzɪŋ/ N bleus mpl, contusions fpl ◆ **light** or **minor/heavy** or **severe** ~ contusions fpl légères/graves ADJ éprouvant

Brum * /brʌm/ N (Brit) Birmingham

brum * /brʊm/ EXCL (baby talk) ◆ **~, ~ !** broum, broum !

Brummie * /ˈbrʌmɪ/ N (Brit) ◆ **he's a** ~ il est de Birmingham

brunch /brʌntʃ/ N brunch m

Brunei /ˈbruːnaɪ/ N Brunei m

brunette /bruːˈnet/ N (femme f) brune f, brunette f ADJ [person, skin] brun ; [eyes] marron inv ; [hair] châtain

brunt /brʌnt/ N ◆ **the** ~ [of attack, blow] le (plus gros du) choc ; [of argument, displeasure] le poids ◆ **to bear the** ~ **of the assault** soutenir or essuyer le plus fort de l'attaque ◆ **to bear the** ~ **of the work** faire le (plus) gros du travail ◆ **to bear the** ~ **of the expense** payer le (plus) gros des frais ◆ **he bore the** ~ **of it all** c'est lui qui a porté le poids de l'affaire

bruschetta /brʊˈsketə/ N bruschetta f

brush /brʌʃ/ N 1 brosse f ; (also **paint brush**) pinceau m, brosse f ; (= broom) balai m ; (short-handled = hearth brush etc) balayette f ; (also **scrubbing brush**) brosse f (dure) ; (also **bottle brush**) goupillon m, rince-bouteilles m inv ; (also **shaving brush**) blaireau m ◆ **nail/clothes/hat** ~ brosse f à ongles/à habits/à chapeau ; → **pastry, tar¹**
2 (= act of brushing) coup m de brosse ◆ **give your coat a** ~ donne un coup de brosse à ton manteau ◆ **to give one's hair a** ~ donner un coup de brosse à ses cheveux, se brosser les cheveux
3 (= light touch) effleurement m
4 (= fox's tail) queue f
5 (NonC = undergrowth) broussailles fpl, taillis m
6 (= skirmish) accrochage m, escarmouche f ◆ **to have a** ~ **with the law** avoir des démêlés mpl avec la justice, avoir maille à partir avec la justice ◆ **to have a** ~ **with sb** (= quarrel) avoir un accrochage or une prise de bec * avec qn
7 (Elec) [of commutator] balai m ; [of dynamo] frottoir m ; (= discharge) décharge f
VT 1 [+ carpet] balayer ; [+ clothes, hair etc] brosser, donner un coup de brosse à ◆ **to** ~ **one's teeth** se brosser or se laver les dents ◆ **to** ~ **one's hair** se brosser les cheveux ◆ **hair ~ed back, ~ed-back hair** cheveux ramenés or rejetés en arrière ◆ **he ~ed the chalk off his coat** il a enlevé (à la main or à la brosse) les traces de craie qui étaient sur son manteau
2 (= touch lightly) frôler, effleurer
3 (Tech) [+ wool] gratter ◆ **~ed cotton** pilou m, finette f ◆ **~ed nylon** nylon ® m gratté
VI ◆ **to** ~ **against sb/sth** effleurer or frôler qn/qch ◆ **to** ~ **past sb/sth** frôler qn/qch en passant
COMP **brush maker** N (= manufacturer) fabricant m de brosses ; (= employee) brossier m, -ière f
brush-off * N ◆ **to give sb the ~-off** envoyer balader * qn ◆ **to get the ~-off** se faire envoyer sur les roses *
brush-stroke N coup m or trait m de pinceau
brush-up N coup m de brosse ◆ **to give one's German a ~-up** * rafraîchir ses notions d'allemand ; → **wash**

► **brush aside** VT SEP [+ argument, objections] balayer (d'un geste) ; [+ protester, objector] repousser

► **brush away** VT SEP [+ tears] essuyer ; [+ mud, dust] (on clothes) enlever à la brosse or à la main ; (on floor) balayer ; [+ insects] chasser

► **brush down** VT SEP [+ person, garment] donner un coup de brosse à ; [+ horse] brosser

► **brush off** VI ◆ **the mud brushes off easily** avec un coup de brosse la boue s'enlève facilement
VT SEP 1 [+ mud, snow] enlever (à la brosse or à coups de balai) ; [+ insect] balayer, écarter d'un geste ; [+ fluff on coat] enlever (à la brosse or à la main)
2 (= dismiss) [+ offer, challenge, threat etc] repousser
N ◆ **brush-off** * → **brush**

► **brush up** VT SEP 1 [+ crumbs, dirt] ramasser avec une brosse or à la balayette
2 [+ wool] gratter
3 (* = revise, improve) rafraîchir (ses notions de) ◆ **to** ~ **up (on) one's English** rafraîchir son anglais or ses notions d'anglais
N ◆ **brush-up** → **brush**

brushwood /ˈbrʌʃwʊd/ **N** (= *undergrowth*) broussailles *fpl*, taillis *m* ; (= *cuttings*) menu bois *m*, brindilles *fpl*

brushwork /ˈbrʌʃwɜːk/ **N** (*Art*) facture *f*

brusque /bruːsk/ **ADJ** brusque

brusquely /ˈbruːsklɪ/ **ADV** [*behave, speak*] avec brusquerie, avec rudesse

brusqueness /ˈbruːsknɪs/ **N** brusquerie *f*, rudesse *f*

Brussels /ˈbrʌslz/ **N** Bruxelles
COMP [*lace*] de Bruxelles
Brussels sprouts **NPL** (also **Brussel sprouts**) choux *mpl* de Bruxelles

brutal /ˈbruːtl/ **ADJ** 1 (= *cruel, violent*) [*person, treatment, attack, régime*] brutal ; [*film, scene*] violent 2 (= *unmitigated*) [*frankness, reality, change, reply*] brutal 3 (= *harsh*) [*winter, climate*] rude 4 (*liter* = *animal-like*) [*instincts*] animal

brutality /bruːˈtælɪtɪ/ **N** violence *f*

brutalize /ˈbruːtəlaɪz/ **VT** 1 (= *ill-treat*) brutaliser 2 (= *make brutal*) rendre brutal

brutally /ˈbruːtəlɪ/ **ADV** [*suppress, say*] brutalement ; [*murder*] sauvagement ◆ **to put it ~, ...** pour dire les choses de façon brutale, ... ◆ **~ frank** d'une franchise brutale ◆ **in a ~ competitive world** dans un monde livré à une concurrence sans merci

brute /bruːt/ **N** (= *animal*) brute *f*, bête *f* ; (= *person*) (*cruel*) brute *f*, brutal *m* ; (*coarse*) brute *f* (épaisse) ◆ **this machine is a ~!*** quelle vacherie de machine !‡ **ADJ** 1 (= *animal-like*) animal 2 [*strength, passion*] brutal ◆ **by (sheer) ~ force** par la force

brutish /ˈbruːtɪʃ/ **ADJ** (= *animal-like*) brutal

BS /biːˈes/ 1 (abbrev of **British Standard**) norme *f* britannique 2 (*US Univ*) (abbrev of **Bachelor of Science**) **to have a ~ in biology** avoir une licence de biologie ; → **bachelor** ; → DEGREE 3 abbrev of **balance sheet** 4 (abbrev of **bill of sale**) acte *m* de vente 5 (*esp US*: ‡) ⇒ **bullshit**

BSA /biːesˈeɪ/ **N** 1 (*US*) (abbrev of **Boy Scouts of America**) *scouts américains* 2 (abbrev of **Broadcasting Standards Authority**) ≈ CSA *m*

BSC /biːesˈsiː/ **N** (*Brit*) (abbrev of **Broadcasting Standards Council**) ≈ CSA *m*

BSc /biːesˈsiː/ **N** (*Univ*) (abbrev of **Bachelor of Science**) ◆ **to have a ~ in biology** avoir une licence de biologie ; → **bachelor** ; → DEGREE

BSE /biːesˈiː/ **N** (abbrev of **bovine spongiform encephalopathy**) ESB *f*

BSI /biːesˈaɪ/ **N** (*Brit*) (abbrev of **British Standards Institution**) ≈ AFNOR *f*

BST /biːesˈtiː/ **N** (abbrev of **British Summer Time**) → **British**

BT /biːˈtiː/ **N** (abbrev of **British Telecom**) → **British**

Bt abbrev of **Baronet**

BTEC /ˈbiːtek/ **N** (*Brit*) (abbrev of **Business and Technology Education Council**) 1 (= *organization*) → **business** 2 (= *diploma*) *diplôme en gestion, sciences et techniques etc*

btu /biːtiːˈjuː/ **N** (abbrev of **British thermal unit**) → **thermal**

BTW*, **btw** (* abbrev of **by the way**) → **by**

bub* /bʌb/ **N** (*US*) mec* *m*

bubble /ˈbʌbl/ **N** 1 (*gen*: also **air bubble**) bulle *f* ; (*in glass*) bulle *f*, soufflure *f* ; (*in paint*) boursouflure *f* ; (*in metal*) soufflure *f*, boursouflement *m* ◆ **to blow ~s** faire des bulles ◆ **soap ~** bulle *f* de savon ◆ **the ~ burst** (*fig*) (*gen*) le rêve s'est envolé ; (*Econ*) la chance a tourné ◆ **to burst sb's ~** faire revenir *or* redescendre qn (brutalement) sur terre
2 (*Med* = *sterile chamber*) bulle *f*
3 (= *sound*) glouglou *m*
VI 1 [*liquid*] bouillonner, dégager des bulles ; [*champagne*] pétiller ; [*gas*] barboter ; (= *gurgle*) faire glouglou, glouglouter ; 2 (* = *cry*) pleurnicher*
COMP **bubble and squeak** **N** (*Brit*) *purée aux choux et à la viande hachée*
bubble bath **N** bain *m* moussant
bubble-car **N** (*Brit*) petite voiture *f* (*à toit transparent*)
bubble company **N** (*Comm, Fin*) compagnie *f* véreuse
bubble-jet printer **N** imprimante *f* à bulles d'encre
bubble memory **N** (*Comput*) mémoire *f* à bulles
bubble pack **N** (*for pills etc*) plaquette *f* ; (*in shop: for pens, plugs etc*) blister *m*
bubble wrap **N** emballage *m* à bulles
► **bubble out** **VI** [*liquid*] sortir à gros bouillons
► **bubble over** **VI** (*lit, fig*) déborder ◆ **to ~ over with joy** déborder de joie
► **bubble under*** **VI** (*fig*) être latent, couver
► **bubble up** **VI** (*lit*) [*liquid*] monter en bouillonnant ; (*fig*) [*excitement etc*] monter

bubble-gum /ˈbʌblɡʌm/ **N** chewing-gum *m*

bubblehead‡ /ˈbʌblhed/ **N** (*esp US*: *pej*) andouille* *f*, crétin(e)* *m(f)*

bubbly /ˈbʌblɪ/ **ADJ** (*lit, fig*) pétillant **N** ‡ (= *champagne*) champagne *m*, champ‡ *m* ; (= *sparkling wine*) mousseux *m*

bubonic /bjuːˈbɒnɪk/ **ADJ** bubonique ◆ **~ plague** peste *f* bubonique

buccal /ˈbʌkl/ **ADJ** buccal

buccaneer /ˌbʌkəˈnɪəʳ/ **N** (*Hist*) boucanier *m* ; (*fig*) flibustier *m*, pirate *m*

buccaneering /ˌbʌkəˈnɪərɪŋ/ **ADJ** (*pej, fig*) aventurier, intrigant

Bucharest /ˌbuːkəˈrest/ **N** Bucarest

buck /bʌk/ **N** 1 (= *male deer, rabbit, hare etc*) mâle *m*
2 († = *dandy*) élégant *m*, dandy *m*
3 (*US* * = *dollar*) dollar *m* ◆ **to be down to one's last ~** être sur la paille ◆ **to make a ~** se faire du fric‡ ◆ **to make a few ~s on the side** se faire un peu de pognon‡ à côté, se faire un petit à-côté* ; (*at sb's expense*) se sucrer en douce* ◆ **to make a fast *or* quick ~** gagner du fric‡ facile ◆ **to get more bang for the *or* one's ~** tirer le maximum de profit de son argent
4 (* = *responsibility*) ◆ **to pass the ~** refiler* la responsabilité aux autres ◆ **the ~ stops here** la responsabilité commence ici
5 (= *sawhorse*) chevalet *m*, baudet *m* ; (*Gym*) cheval *m* d'arçons
6 ◆ **the horse gave a ~** le cheval a lancé une ruade
VI 1 [*horse*] lancer *or* décocher une ruade
2 (= *object to*) **to ~ at sth**‡ regimber devant qch
3 (*US*) **to ~ for sth*** rechercher qch
VT ◆ **to ~ the trend/system** se rebiffer contre la tendance/le système
COMP **buck-naked*** (*esp US*) **ADJ** à poil*, nu comme un ver
buck private **N** (*US Mil*) deuxième classe *m inv*
buck rabbit **N** lapin *m* mâle
buck sergeant **N** (*US Mil*) simple sergent *m*
buck's fizz **N** (= *cocktail*) mimosa *m*
buck teeth **N** ◆ **to have ~ teeth** avoir les dents en avant
buck-toothed **ADJ** qui a les dents en avant
► **buck up*** **VI** 1 (= *hurry up*) se grouiller*, se magner‡ ; (= *exert o.s.*) se remuer*, se magner‡ ◆ **~ up!** remue-toi !*, grouille-toi !*, active un peu !*
2 (= *cheer up*) se secouer* ◆ **~ up!** courage !
VT SEP 1 (= *cheer up*) [+ *person*] remonter le moral de, ravigoter*
2 ◆ **you'll have to buck up your ideas** il va falloir que tu te secoues *subj* un peu*

bucked‡ /bʌkt/ **ADJ** tout content

bucket /ˈbʌkɪt/ **N** 1 seau *m* ◆ **~ of water** seau *m* d'eau ◆ **to weep ~s*** pleurer toutes les larmes de son corps ◆ **chain of ~s** chaîne *f* de seaux ◆ **they made a chain of ~s to fight the fire** ils ont fait la chaîne pour combattre l'incendie ; → **kick, rain** 2 [*of dredger, grain elevator*] godet *m* ; [*of pump*] piston *m* ; [*of wheel*] auget *m* **VI** 1 [*rain*] ◆ **it's ~ing (down)*** ◆ **the rain is ~ing down*** il pleut à seaux, il tombe des cordes 2 (= *hurtle*) aller à fond de train
COMP **bucket elevator** **N** noria *f*, élévateur *m* à godets
bucket seat **N** (siège-)baquet *m*
bucket shop **N** (= *stockbrokers*) bureau *m* *or* maison *f* de contrepartie, bureau *m* de courtier marron ; (*for air tickets*) *organisme de vente de billets d'avion à prix réduit*

bucketful /ˈbʌkɪtfʊl/ **N** plein seau *m* ◆ **to produce/get sth by the ~*** produire/obtenir des masses* de qch

Buckeye State /ˈbʌkaɪˈsteɪt/ (*US*) **N** ◆ **the ~** l'Ohio *m*

Buck House* /ˈbʌkˌhaʊs/ **N** (*Brit*) ⇒ **Buckingham Palace**

Buckingham Palace /ˈbʌkɪŋəmˈpælɪs/ **N** palais *m* de Buckingham

buckle /ˈbʌkl/ **N** 1 [*of shoe, belt*] boucle *f* 2 (= *distortion*) [*of wheel*] voilure *f* ; [*of metal*] gauchissement *m*, flambage *m* **VT** 1 [+ *belt, shoe etc*] boucler, attacher 2 [+ *wheel*] voiler ; [+ *metal*] gauchir, fausser **VI** 1 [*belt, shoe*] se boucler, s'attacher 2 [*metal*] gauchir, se déformer ; [*wheel*] se voiler
► **buckle down*** **VI** se coller au boulot* ◆ **to ~ down to a job** s'atteler à un boulot* ◆ **~ down to it!** au boulot !*
► **buckle in** **VT SEP** (*into seat*) attacher
► **buckle on** **VT SEP** [+ *armour*] revêtir, endosser ; [+ *sword*] ceindre
► **buckle to*** **VI** s'y mettre, s'y coller*

buckra‡ /ˈbʌkrə/ **N** (*US pej*) Blanc *m*

buckram /ˈbʌkrəm/ **N** bougran *m*

Bucks **N** abbrev of **Buckinghamshire**

bucksaw /ˈbʌksɔː/ **N** scie *f* à refendre

buckshee‡ /bʌkˈʃiː/ **ADJ, ADV** (*Brit*) gratis *inv*, à l'œil*

buckshot /ˈbʌkʃɒt/ **N** chevrotine(s) *f(pl)*

buckskin /ˈbʌkskɪn/ **N** peau *f* de daim

buckthorn /ˈbʌkθɔːn/ **N** nerprun *m*, bourdaine *f*

buckwheat /ˈbʌkwiːt/ **N** sarrasin *m*, blé *m* noir

bucolic /bjuːˈkɒlɪk/ **ADJ** bucolique, pastoral **N** (*Literat*) ◆ **the Bucolics** les Bucoliques *fpl*

bud¹ /bʌd/ **N** 1 [*of tree, plant*] bourgeon *m*, œil *m* ; [*of grafting*] écusson *m* ◆ **to be in ~** bourgeonner ◆ **a poet *etc* in the ~** un poète *etc* en herbe ; → **nip¹** 2 [*of flower*] bouton *m* ◆ **in ~** en bouton ; → **rosebud** 3 (*Anat*) papille *f* ; → **taste** **VI** [*tree, plant*] bourgeonner, se couvrir de bourgeons ; [*flower*] former des boutons ; [*horns*] (commencer à) poindre *or* percer ; [*talent etc*] (commencer à) percer **VT** [+ *tree*] greffer, écussonner

bud²* /bʌd/ **N** (*esp US*) ⇒ **buddy**

Budapest /ˌbjuːdəˈpest/ **N** Budapest

Buddha /ˈbʊdə/ **N** Bouddha *m*

Buddhism /ˈbʊdɪzəm/ **N** bouddhisme *m*

Buddhist /ˈbʊdɪst/ **N** bouddhiste *mf* **ADJ** [*monk, nation*] bouddhiste ; [*religion, art, dogma*] bouddhique

budding /ˈbʌdɪŋ/ **ADJ** [*plant*] bourgeonnant ; [*flower*] en bouton ; (*fig*) [*poet etc*] en herbe ; [*passion*] naissant

buddleia /ˈbʌdlɪə/ N buddleia *m*, lilas *m* de Chine

buddy * /ˈbʌdɪ/ N *(US)* copain *m*, pote‡ *m* ; *(esp US) (of Aids sufferer)* buddy *mf (bénévole accompagnant une personne atteinte du sida)* ◆ **hi there, ~!** salut, mon pote !‡ ◆ **~ movie** *or* **film** *film qui raconte l'histoire de deux amis* COMP **buddy-buddy** * ADJ *(esp US)* ◆ **Paul and Mark are very ~-~, Paul is very ~-~ with Mark** Paul et Mark sont très copains *or* copains comme cochons

budge /bʌdʒ/ VI *(= move)* bouger ; *(fig)* changer d'avis ◆ **I will not ~ an inch** *(= move from here)* je ne bougerai pas d'ici ; *(= change my mind)* rien ne me fera changer d'avis VT faire bouger ◆ **you can't ~ him** *(fig)* il reste inébranlable, vous ne le ferez pas changer d'avis

► **budge over** *, **budge up** * VI se pousser

budgerigar /ˈbʌdʒərɪgɑːʳ/ N perruche *f*

budget /ˈbʌdʒɪt/ N *(gen, Fin)* budget *m* ; *(Parl)* budget *m*, loi *f* de finances ◆ **my ~ won't stretch** *or* **run to steak nowadays** mon budget ne me permet plus d'acheter de bifteck ◆ **to be on a tight ~** disposer d'un budget modeste

ADJ 1 *(Econ, Fin) [spending, credit]* budgétaire ◆ **~ cuts** *(Econ)* compressions *fpl* budgétaires

2 *(= cut-price) [tour, holiday, price]* pour petits budgets, économique

VI dresser *or* préparer un budget ◆ **to ~ for sth** *(Econ)* inscrire *or* porter qch au budget, budgéter qch ; *(gen)* inscrire qch à son budget

VT budgéter, budgétiser ◆ **to ~ one's time** planifier son temps ◆ **~ed balance sheet** bilan *m* provisionnel ◆ **a ~ed expense** une dépense budgétée

COMP **budget account** N *(Comm)* compte-crédit *m*

budget day N *(Parl)* jour *m* de la présentation du budget

budget deficit N *(Econ)* découvert *m* budgétaire

budget heading N *(Econ, Comm)* poste *m* budgétaire

budget plan N *(US Comm)* système *m* de crédit

budget speech N *(Parl)* discours *m* de présentation du budget

budget surplus N *(Econ)* excédent *m* budgétaire

BUDGET

Le **budget** de la nation est présenté au Parlement britannique au printemps par le chancelier de l'Échiquier qui rend publiques les prévisions du gouvernement pour l'année à venir et précise en particulier les modifications apportées à la fiscalité et au régime des prestations sociales. L'intervention du ministre est diffusée intégralement à la télévision, et les contribuables peuvent donc prendre connaissance « en direct » des augmentations frappant certains produits, essence, alcool et tabac notamment.

-budget /ˈbʌdʒɪt/ ADJ *(in compounds)* ◆ **big-budget** à gros budget ; → **low**[1]

budgetary /ˈbʌdʒɪtrɪ/ ADJ budgétaire

COMP **budgetary control** N contrôle *m* budgétaire

budgetary deficit N déficit *m* budgétaire

budgetary year N exercice *m* budgétaire

budgeting /ˈbʌdʒɪtɪŋ/ N *[of company, institution]* prévisions *fpl* budgétaires ◆ **with careful ~ ...** si l'on équilibre soigneusement le budget ...

budgie * /ˈbʌdʒɪ/ N abbrev of **budgerigar**

Buenos Aires /ˈbweɪnɒsˈaɪrɪz/ N Buenos Aires

buff[1] /bʌf/ N 1 *(= leather)* (peau *f* de) buffle *m* ; *(= colour)* (couleur *f*) chamois *m* ◆ **in the ~**‡ à poil‡ 2 *(= polishing disc)* polissoir *m* ADJ 1 (en peau) de buffle, en buffle 2 (also **buff-coloured**) (couleur) chamois *inv* ◆ **~ envelope** enveloppe *f* (en papier) bulle VT *(= polish)* polir

buff[2] * /bʌf/ N *(= enthusiast)* mordu(e) * *m(f)* ◆ **a film ~** un(e) mordu(e) * de cinéma

buffalo /ˈbʌfələʊ/ N (pl **buffalo** *or* **buffaloes**) *(= wild ox)* buffle *m*, bufflesse *f* ; *(esp in US)* bison *m* ; → **water**

buffer[1] /ˈbʌfəʳ/ N *(lit, fig)* tampon *m* ; *(Brit) (on train)* tampon *m* ; *(at terminus)* butoir *m* ; *(US) (on car)* pare-chocs *m inv* ; *(Comput)* mémoire *f* tampon VT *[+ shocks]* amortir ; *(Chem)* tamponner

COMP **buffer fund** N fonds *m* régulateur

buffer memory N *(Comput)* mémoire *f* tampon

buffer solution N *(Chem)* solution *f* tampon

buffer state N *(Pol)* état *m* tampon

buffer stock N *(Comm)* stock *m* de sécurité *or* de régularisation

buffer zone N zone *f* tampon

buffer[2] /ˈbʌfəʳ/ N *(for polishing)* polissoir *m*

buffer[3] ‡ /ˈbʌfəʳ/ N *(Brit)* ◆ **(old) ~** vieux fossile * *m*

buffet[1] /ˈbʌfɪt/ N *(= blow) (with hand)* gifle *f*, soufflet *m* ; *(with fist)* coup *m* de poing ◆ **the ~s of fate** *(fig)* les coups *mpl* du sort VT *(with hand)* frapper, souffleter ; *(with fist)* donner un coup de poing à ◆ **~ed by the waves** battu *or* ballotté par les vagues ◆ **~ed by the wind** secoué par le vent ◆ **~ed by events** *(fig)* secoué par les événements

buffet[2] /ˈbʊfeɪ/ N *(= refreshment bar, sideboard)* buffet *m* ◆ **cold ~** *(in menu)* viandes *fpl* froides

COMP **buffet car** N *(Brit Rail)* voiture-buffet *f*, buffet *m*

buffet lunch N lunch *m*

buffet supper N buffet *m* dînatoire

buffeting /ˈbʌfɪtɪŋ/ N *[of person, object]* bourrades *fpl*, coups *mpl* ; *[of wind, rain etc]* assaut *m* ◆ **to get a ~ from the waves** être ballotté (de tous côtés) par les vagues ADJ *[wind]* violent

buffing /ˈbʌfɪŋ/ N polissage *m*

buffoon /bəˈfuːn/ N bouffon *m*, pitre *m*

buffoonery /bəˈfuːnərɪ/ N *(NonC)* bouffonnerie(s) *f(pl)*

bug /bʌg/ N 1 *(= bedbug etc)* punaise *f* ; *(esp US = any insect)* insecte *m*, bestiole * *f* ◆ **big ~**‡ *(= important person)* grosse légume * *f*, huile * *f* ; → **firebug**

2 *(* = germ)* microbe *m* ◆ **he picked up a ~ on holiday** il a attrapé un microbe pendant ses vacances ◆ **the flu ~** le virus de la grippe

3 *(= defect, snag)* défaut *m*, inconvénient *m* ; *(Comput)* bogue *m*

4 *(* = hidden microphone)* micro *m* (caché)

5 *(US * = car)* petite voiture *f*, coccinelle * *f*

6 *(= enthusiasm)* **to be bitten by** *or* **get the jogging ~** * attraper le virus du jogging

7 *(US)* **a basketball ~**‡ *(= enthusiast)* un(e) mordu(e) * de basket

VT 1 * *[+ phone etc]* brancher sur table d'écoute ; *[+ room etc]* poser *or* installer des micros (cachés) dans

2 *(* = annoy)* embêter *, casser les pieds à *

COMP **bug-eyed** ADJ aux yeux exorbités

bug-hunter * N entomologiste *mf*, chasseur *m* de petites bestioles *

bug-ridden ADJ infesté de punaises

► **bug out** ‡ VI *(US)* foutre le camp‡

bugaboo /ˈbʌgəbuː/ N croquemitaine *m*, loup-garou *m*

bugbear /ˈbʌgbeəʳ/ N *(= obsession)* bête *f* noire ; *(= ogre)* croquemitaine *m*, ogre *m*

bugger /ˈbʌgəʳ/ N 1 *(† or Jur = sodomite)* pédéraste *m*

2 *(Brit *‡)* salaud‡ *m* ◆ **silly ~** pauvre con‡ *m* ◆ **to play silly ~s** déconner‡ ◆ **lucky ~** veinard‡ *m* ◆ **poor little ~** pauvre petit bonhomme * *m*

3 *(Brit)* **it's a ~** *‡ *(= difficulty, annoyance)* c'est casse-couilles *‡ *or* casse-pieds *

EXCL ◆ **~ (it** *or* **me) !** *‡ merde !‡

VT 1 *(Jur)* sodomiser

2 *(Brit *‡)* **well, I'm ~ed!** merde alors !‡ ◆ **I'll be** *or* **I'm ~ed if I'm going to do that!** je préfère plutôt crever (que de faire ça) !‡ ◆ **~ all** que dalle‡ ◆ **~ him!** il peut aller se faire foutre !*‡ ◆ **~ the consequences!** je me fous des conséquences !‡

► **bugger about** *‡, **bugger around** *‡ *(Brit)* VI glandouiller‡ ◆ **to ~ around with sth** *(= play around with)* faire le con avec qch *‡

VT SEP emmerder‡, faire chier *‡

► **bugger off** *‡ VI *(Brit)* foutre le camp‡

► **bugger up** *‡ VT SEP *(Brit)* foutre en l'air‡

buggered *‡ /ˈbʌgəd/ *(Brit)* VB pt, ptp of **bugger** ADJ *(= ruined) [machine]* foutu‡, nase * ; *(= exhausted) [person]* nase *

buggery /ˈbʌgərɪ/ N sodomie *f*

bugging /ˈbʌgɪŋ/ N utilisation *f* d'appareils d'écoute ◆ **~ device** appareil *m* d'écoute *(clandestine)*

buggy /ˈbʌgɪ/ N *(horse-drawn)* boghei *m* ; (also **beach buggy**) buggy *m* ; (also **moon buggy**) jeep ® *f* lunaire ; *(US ‡ = car)* bagnole * *f* ; (also **baby buggy**) *(Brit = pushchair)* poussette (-canne) *f* ; *(US = pram)* voiture *f* d'enfant

bughouse ‡ /ˈbʌghaʊs/ N *(US = asylum)* asile *m*, maison *f* de dingues‡

bugle /ˈbjuːgl/ N clairon *m* ◆ **~ call** sonnerie *f* de clairon

bugler /ˈbjuːgləʳ/ N (joueur *m* de) clairon *m*

bugs ‡ /bʌgz/ ADJ *(US)* cinglé *, dingue *

build /bɪld/ (vb : pret, ptp **built**) N *(= physique)* carrure *f*, charpente *f* ◆ **man of strong ~** homme *m* solidement bâti *or* charpenté ◆ **of medium ~** de corpulence moyenne ◆ **of slim ~** fluet ◆ **he's got the ~ of a wrestler** il a une carrure de catcheur, il est bâti comme un catcheur ◆ **of the same ~ as ...** de même carrure que ...

VT *[+ house, town]* bâtir, construire ; *[+ bridge, ship, machine]* construire ; *[+ temple]* bâtir, édifier ; *[+ nest]* faire, bâtir ; *(fig) [+ theory, plan]* bâtir, construire ; *[+ empire, company]* fonder, bâtir ; *(in games) [+ words, sequence]* former ◆ **the house is being built** la maison se bâtit ◆ **the architect who built the palace** l'architecte qui a bâti *or* qui a fait bâtir le palais ◆ **this car was not built for speed** cette voiture n'était pas conçue pour la vitesse ◆ **to ~ castles in the air** *or* **in Spain** faire des châteaux en Espagne ◆ **to ~ a mirror into a wall** encastrer un miroir dans un mur ◆ **house built into the hillside** maison *f* bâtie à flanc de colline ◆ **his theory is not built on facts** *(fig)* sa théorie n'est pas basée *or* construite sur des faits

VI bâtir ; *[edifice]* se bâtir ◆ **to ~ (up)on a piece of land** bâtir sur un terrain ◆ **to ~ upon sand** *(lit, fig)* bâtir sur le sable ◆ **it's a good start, something to ~ on** *(fig)* c'est une base solide sur laquelle on peut bâtir ◆ **to ~ upon sb/a promise** † *(frm)* faire fond sur qn/une promesse

► **build in** VT SEP *(lit) [+ wardrobe etc]* encastrer *(into* dans) ; *(fig) [+ safeguards]* intégrer *(into* à) see also **build vt**

ADJ ◆ **built-in** → **built**

► **build on** VT SEP *[+ room, annex]* ajouter *(to* à)

► **build up** VI *[business connection etc]* se développer ; *[pressure]* s'accumuler ; *[tension, excitement]* monter, augmenter

VT SEP 1 *(= establish) [+ reputation]* édifier, bâtir ; *[+ business]* créer, monter ; *[+ theory]* échafauder ; *(= increase) [+ production, forces]* accroître,

augmenter ; *[+ pressure]* accumuler ; *[+ tension, excitement]* augmenter, faire monter ◆ **to ~ up one's strength** prendre des forces
2 *(= cover with houses) [+ area, land]* urbaniser
3 *(fig = publicize) [+ person, reputation]* faire de la publicité pour, faire du battage * autour de
N ◆ **build-up** → **build-up**
ADJ ◆ **built-up** → **built**

builder /ˈbɪldəʳ/ N 1 *[of houses etc] (= owner of firm)* entrepreneur *m* ; *(= worker)* maçon *m* ; *[of ships, machines]* constructeur *m* ◆ **~'s labourer** ouvrier *m* du bâtiment ; → **organ** 2 *(fig)* fondateur *m*, -trice *f*, créateur *m*, -trice *f* ; → **empire**

building /ˈbɪldɪŋ/ N 1 *(= edifice)* bâtiment *m*, construction *f* ; *(imposing)* édifice *m* ; *(= habitation or offices)* immeuble *m* ; *(Jur, Insurance: in contract etc)* immeuble *m* ; → **public**
2 *(NonC)* construction *f* ◆ **the ~ of the church took seven years** il a fallu sept ans pour construire l'église ; → **body, empire**
COMP **building block** N *(= toy)* cube *m* ; *(fig)* composante *f*
building contractor N entrepreneur *m* (en bâtiment)
building industry N (industrie *f* du) bâtiment *m*
building labourer N ouvrier *m* du bâtiment
building land N terrain *m* à bâtir
building materials NPL matériaux *mpl* de construction
building permit N permis *m* de construire
building plot N (petit) terrain *m* à bâtir
buildings insurance N *(NonC)* assurance *f* sur le capital immobilier
building site N chantier *m* (de construction)
building society N *(Brit)* ≃ société *f* de crédit immobilier
building trade N ⇒ **building industry**
the building trades NPL les métiers *mpl* du bâtiment
building workers NPL ouvriers *mpl* du bâtiment
building works NPL travaux *mpl* de construction

build-up /ˈbɪldʌp/ N 1 *(= increase) [of pressure]* intensification *f* ; *[of gas]* accumulation *f* ; *(Mil) [of troops]* rassemblement *m* ; *[of production]* accroissement *m* ; *(Comm) [of stock etc]* accumulation *f* ; *[of tension, excitement]* montée *f* ◆ **arms ~** *(Mil)* accumulation *f* des armements 2 *(fig = presentation)* présentation *f* publicitaire, battage * *m* ◆ **to give sb/sth a good ~** faire une bonne publicité pour qn/qch, faire beaucoup de battage * autour de qn/qch

built /bɪlt/ VB pt, ptp of **build**
ADJ 1 *(Constr)* ◆ **~ of brick/stone** (construit) en briques/pierres ◆ **~ to last** fait pour durer ◆ **a car ~ for speed** une voiture conçue pour faire de la vitesse ◆ **Anne isn't exactly ~ for speed** * *(hum)* Anne n'est pas vraiment du genre rapide * *(hum)*
2 *[person]* ◆ **heavily** *or* **solidly ~** costaud, solidement bâti ◆ **powerfully ~** puissamment charpenté ◆ **slightly ~** fluet ◆ **to be ~ like a tank** *(Brit) [machine etc]* être tout ce qu'il y a de plus solide ◆ **he's ~ like a tank** *or* **like a brick shithouse** ** *(Brit)* c'est une véritable armoire à glace, il est superbaraqué * ; → **well²**
COMP **built-in** ADJ *[oven, wardrobe, mirror, beam]* encastré ; *(fig) [desire etc]* inné ; see also **obsolescence** ◆ **~-in cupboard** placard *m* (encastré)
built-up ADJ *(Dress) [shoulders]* rehaussé ; *[shoes]* à semelle compensée ◆ **~-up area** agglomération *f* (urbaine)

-built /bɪlt/ ADJ *(in compounds)* ◆ **pine-built house** maison *f* (construite) en bois de pin ◆ **French-built ship** navire *m* de construction française ; → **clinker**

Bukhara /bʊˈkɑːrə/ N Boukhara

bulb /bʌlb/ N 1 *[of plant]* bulbe *m*, oignon *m* ◆ **~ of garlic** tête *f* d'ail ◆ **tulip ~** bulbe *m or* oignon *m* de tulipe ◆ **~ fibre** terreau *m* enrichi (pour bulbes) 2 *(Elec)* ampoule *f* 3 *(Chem)* ballon *m* ; *[of thermometer]* cuvette *f*

bulbous /ˈbʌlbəs/ ADJ *[plant]* bulbeux ; *[nose]* gros (grosse *f*), bulbeux

Bulgar † /ˈbʌlgəʳ/ N Bulgare *mf*

Bulgaria /bʌlˈgɛərɪə/ N Bulgarie *f*

Bulgarian /bʌlˈgɛərɪən/ ADJ bulgare N 1 *(= person)* Bulgare *mf* 2 *(= language)* bulgare *m*

bulge /bʌldʒ/ N 1 *(in surface, metal)* bombement *m* ; *(in cheek)* gonflement *m* ; *(in column)* renflement *m* ; *(in jug, bottle)* panse *f*, ventre *m* ; *(in plaster)* bosse *f* ; *(in tyre)* soufflure *f*, hernie *f* ; *(in pocket, jacket)* renflement *m* ; *(Brit Mil)* saillant *m* ◆ **the Battle of the Bulge** *(Hist)* la bataille des Ardennes 2 *(= increase) [of numbers]* augmentation *f* temporaire ; *[of sales, prices, profits]* hausse *f*, poussée *f* ; *[of birth rate]* poussée *f* ◆ **the postwar ~** l'explosion *f* démographique de l'après-guerre VI (also **bulge out**) *(= swell)* se renfler, bomber ; *(= stick out)* faire *or* former saillie ; *[plaster]* être bosselé ; *[pocket, sack, cheek]* être gonflé *(with* de) ; ◆ **my address book is bulging with new numbers** mon carnet d'adresses est bourré de nouveaux numéros

bulging /ˈbʌldʒɪŋ/ ADJ 1 *(= protruding) [eyes]* globuleux ; *[muscles]* saillant ; *[stomach]* protubérant ; *[forehead, wall]* bombé 2 *(= full) [pockets, suitcase]* bourré *(with* de) ; *[wallet]* bien garni

bulgur /ˈbʌlgəʳ/ N (also **bulgur wheat**) boulgour *m*

bulimia /bəˈlɪmɪə/ N (also **bulimia nervosa**) boulimie *f*

bulimic /bəˈlɪmɪk/ ADJ boulimique

bulk /bʌlk/ N 1 *(= great size) [of thing]* grosseur *f*, grandeur *f* ; *[of person]* corpulence *f* ; *(= large volume)* masse *f*, volume *m*
◆ **in bulk** *(Comm) (= in large quantities)* en gros ; *(not prepacked)* en vrac
◆ **the bulk of** *(= most of)* la majeure partie de, la plus grande partie de, le (plus) gros de ◆ **the ~ of the working community** la plus grande partie *or* l'ensemble *m* de la population ouvrière ◆ **the ~ of the work is done** le plus gros du travail est fait
2 *(in food)* fibre *f* (végétale)
3 *(Naut)* cargaison *f* (en cale)
ADJ *[order, supplies etc]* en gros ◆ **~ mailing** mailing *m* à grande diffusion ◆ **~ mail** envois *mpl* en nombre
VI ◆ **to ~ large (in sb's life/thoughts)** occuper une place importante (dans la vie/les pensées de qn)
VT *(Customs)* estimer ◆ **to ~ a container** estimer le contenu d'un conteneur
COMP **bulk-buy** VI *[trader]* acheter en gros ; *[individual]* acheter par *or* en grosses quantités
bulk-buying N *[of trader]* achat *m* en gros ; *[of individual]* achat *m* par *or* en grosses quantités
bulk carrier N transporteur *m* de vrac
bulk transport N transport *m* en vrac

bulkhead /ˈbʌlkhed/ N *(Brit Naut)* cloison *f*

bulkiness /ˈbʌlkɪnɪs/ N *[of parcel, luggage]* grosseur *f*, volume *m* ; *[of person]* corpulence *f*

bulky /ˈbʌlkɪ/ ADJ *[parcel, suitcase]* volumineux, encombrant ; *[book]* épais (-aisse *f*) ; *[person]* gros (grosse *f*), corpulent

bull¹ /bʊl/ N 1 taureau *m* ◆ **to take** *or* **seize** *or* **grasp the ~ by the horns** prendre *or* saisir le taureau par les cornes ◆ **like a ~ in a china shop** comme un éléphant dans un magasin de porcelaine ◆ **to go at it like a ~ at a gate** * foncer tête baissée ◆ **the Bull** *(Astron)* le Taureau ; → **bull's-eye, cock, John, strong**
2 *(= male of elephant, whale etc)* mâle *m*
3 *(Stock Exchange)* haussier *m*
4 *(Mil * = cleaning, polishing)* fourbissage *m*
5 (** = nonsense) ⇒ **bullshit noun**
VT *[+ stocks, shares]* pousser à la hausse ◆ **to ~ the market** pousser les cours à la hausse
COMP *[elephant, whale etc]* mâle
bull bars NPL *(Brit: on car)* barres *fpl* antibuffles
bull calf N jeune taureau *m*, taurillon *m*
bull-dyke ** N *(pej)* gouine ** *f (pej)* aux allures de camionneur
bull market N *(Stock Exchange)* marché *m* haussier *or* à la hausse
bull neck N cou *m* de taureau
bull-necked ADJ au cou de taureau, épais (épaisse *f*) d'encolure
bull session * N *(US)* discussion *f* entre hommes
bull terrier N bull-terrier *m*

bull² /bʊl/ N *(Rel)* bulle *f*

bulldog /ˈbʊldɒg/ N bouledogue *m*
COMP *[tenacity]* à toute épreuve
bulldog breed N *(fig)* ◆ **he is one of the ~ breed** il est d'une ténacité à toute épreuve
bulldog clip N *(Brit)* pince *f* à dessin

bulldoze /ˈbʊldəʊz/ VT *(lit)* passer au bulldozer ◆ **to ~ sb into doing sth** * forcer qn à faire qch, faire pression sur qn pour qu'il fasse qch ◆ **the government ~d * the bill through parliament** le gouvernement a fait du forcing * pour que le parlement adopte *subj* le projet de loi

bulldozer /ˈbʊldəʊzəʳ/ N bulldozer *m*

bullet /ˈbʊlɪt/ N balle *f (projectile)* ◆ **to get** *or* **be given the ~** * *(Brit)* se faire virer *
COMP **bullet-headed** ADJ à (la) tête ronde
bullet hole N trou *m* de balle
bullet point N *(= dot)* point *m* centré ; *(fig)* point *m* important
bullet train N train *m* à grande vitesse *(japonais)*
bullet wound N blessure *f* par balle

bulletin /ˈbʊlɪtɪn/ N bulletin *m*, communiqué *m* ◆ **health ~** bulletin *m* de santé ; → **news**
COMP **bulletin board** N *(gen)* tableau *m* d'affichage ; *(Comput)* panneau *m* d'affichage (électronique)

bulletproof /ˈbʊlɪtpruːf/ ADJ *[garment]* pare-balles *inv* ; *[car, glass]* blindé VT blinder

bullfight /ˈbʊlfaɪt/ N course *f* de taureaux, corrida *f*

bullfighter /ˈbʊlfaɪtə/ N torero *m*

bullfighting /ˈbʊlfaɪtɪŋ/ N courses *fpl* de taureaux ; *(= art)* tauromachie *f* ◆ **~ has been banned here** les courses de taureaux sont interdites ici

bullfinch /ˈbʊlfɪntʃ/ N bouvreuil *m*

bullfrog /ˈbʊlfrɒg/ N grenouille-taureau *f*, ouaouaron *m (Can)*

bullhorn /ˈbʊlhɔːn/ N *(US)* porte-voix *m inv*, mégaphone *m*

bullion¹ /ˈbʊljən/ N *(NonC)* encaisse-or *f* ; (also **gold bullion**) or *m* en barre *or* en lingot(s) ; (also **silver bullion**) argent *m* en lingot(s)

bullion² /ˈbʊljən/ N *(= fringe)* frange *f* de cannetille

bullish /ˈbʊlɪʃ/ ADJ *(Stock Exchange)* haussier

bullock /ˈbʊlək/ N bœuf *m* ; *(young)* bouvillon *m*
COMP **bullock cart** N char *m* à bœufs

bullpen * /ˈbʊlpen/ N *(US)* 1 *(Baseball) (= area)* zone *f* d'entraînement des lanceurs ; *(= players)* lanceurs *mpl* à l'entraînement 2 *(= office)* bureau *m* paysager 3 *(= cell)* local *m* de garde à vue

bullring /ˈbʊlrɪŋ/ N arène *f (pour courses de taureaux)*

bull's-eye /ˈbʊlzaɪ/ N 1 *[of target]* mille *m*, centre *m* ◆ **to get a ~, to hit the ~** *(lit, fig)* faire mouche, mettre dans le mille [2] (= *sweet*) gros bonbon *m* à la menthe [3] (= *window*) œil-de-bœuf *m*, oculus *m* ; (*in glass*) boudine *f*

bullshit **/ˈbʊlʃɪt/ **N** connerie(s)‡ *f(pl)*, foutaise(s)‡ *f(pl)* ◆ **(that's) ~!** c'est des conneries *or* de la foutaise !‡ **VI** déconner‡, dire des conneries‡ **VT** raconter des conneries à‡

bullshitter **/ˈbʊlʃɪtəʳ/ **N** ◆ **to be a ~** raconter des conneries‡

bullwhip /ˈbʊlwɪp/ **N** fouet *m* (*à longue mèche tressée*) **VT** fouetter

bully¹ /ˈbʊlɪ/ **N** [1] tyran *m* ; (*esp Scol*) petit(e) dur(e) *m(f)*, (petite) brute *f* [2] (*Brit Hockey*: also **bully-off**) engagement *m* (du jeu) **VT** (= *persecute*) tyranniser, persécuter ; (= *treat cruelly*) malmener, brutaliser ; (= *frighten*) intimider ; (*Scol*) brutaliser, brimer ◆ **to ~ sb into doing sth** contraindre qn par la menace à faire qch **VI** être une brute

COMP **bully boy** * **N** dur *m*, brute *f*

bully-boy **ADJ** ◆ **~-boy tactics/politics** manœuvres *fpl*/politique *f* d'intimidation

► **bully off** **VI** (*Brit*) mettre la balle en jeu, engager (le jeu) **N** ◆ **bully-off** → **bully¹**

bully² ‡/ˈbʊlɪ/ **ADJ** † épatant † **EXCL** ◆ **~ for you !** t'es un chef !‡

bully³ * /ˈbʊlɪ/ **N** (*Mil*: also **bully beef**) corned-beef *m*, singe‡ *m*

bullying /ˈbʊlɪɪŋ/ **ADJ** [*person, manner*] tyrannique, brutal **N** (*psychological*) brimade(s) *f(pl)* ; (*physical*) brutalités *fpl*

bulrush /ˈbʊlrʌʃ/ **N** jonc *m*

bulwark /ˈbʊlwək/ **N** (= *rampart*) rempart *m*, fortification *f* ; (= *breakwater*) brise-lames *m inv* ; (*fig* = *defence*) rempart *m* ; (*Naut*) bastingage *m*

bum¹ * /bʌm/ (*esp US*) **N** (= *vagrant*) clodo* *m*, clochard *m* ; (= *good-for-nothing*) bon à rien *m* ◆ **to get** *or* **be given the ~'s rush**‡ être mis en quarantaine *or* à l'index ◆ **to give sb the ~'s rush**‡ mettre qn en quarantaine *or* à l'index ◆ **to live on the ~** vivre en clochard **ADJ** (= *bad*) minable*, de camelote* ; (= *false*) faux (fausse *f*) ◆ **a ~ rap**‡ une accusation bidon*, une fausse accusation ◆ **a ~ steer** un mauvais tuyau*, un tuyau crevé* ◆ **to give sb a ~ steer** refiler un mauvais tuyau *or* un tuyau crevé à qn* **VI** [1] (= *scrounge*) taper* les autres [2] (= *loaf*: also **bum about** *or* **around**) vadrouiller* **VT** [+ *money, food*] taper* ◆ **to ~ a meal/cigarette off sb** taper* qn d'un repas/d'une cigarette

bum² ‡/bʌm/ (*Brit*) **N** (= *bottom*) derrière *m*, arrière-train* *m* ◆ **to put ~s on seats** remplir les salles **COMP** **bum boy**‡ **N** (*pej*) pédale‡ *f*

bumbag /ˈbʌmbæɡ/ **N** (sac *m*) banane *f*

bumbershoot †* /ˈbʌmbəʃuːt/ **N** (*US*) pépin* *m*, parapluie *m*

bumble /ˈbʌmbl/ **VI** [1] (= *walk*) marcher en titubant *or* d'un pas chancelant ◆ **to ~ about** *or* **around (a place)** s'affairer d'une façon désordonnée (dans un endroit) ◆ **we ~d about on the computer** nous tapotions sur l'ordinateur [2] (= *speak*) bafouiller ◆ **to ~ on about sth** bafouiller *or* rabâcher qch

bumblebee /ˈbʌmblbiː/ **N** bourdon *m*

bumbling /ˈbʌmblɪŋ/ **ADJ** (= *inept*) empoté ; (= *muttering*) rabâcheur

bumboat /ˈbʌmbəʊt/ **N** canot *m* d'approvisionnement

bumf * /bʌmf/ **N** (*Brit*) (*pej* = *forms etc*) paperasses *fpl*, paperasserie *f* ; (= *toilet paper*) PQ‡ *m*

bumfreezer †* /ˈbʌmfriːzəʳ/ **N** blouson *m* court

bummer‡ /ˈbʌməʳ/ **N** [1] (*Drugs*) mauvais trip* *m* [2] (*annoying*) **you're working on Sunday? what a ~!** tu travailles dimanche ? quelle poisse !* ◆ **I had a ~ of a day** j'ai eu une journée vraiment pourrie*

bump /bʌmp/ **N** [1] (= *blow*) choc *m*, coup *m* ; (= *jolt*) cahot *m*, secousse *f* ◆ **he sat down with a ~** il s'est assis lourdement ◆ **he came down to earth with a ~*** le retour à la réalité a été brutal pour lui ◆ **the news brought us back to earth with a ~*** la nouvelle nous a brutalement rappelés à la réalité

[2] (= *lump on head, in road, Ski*) bosse *f*

[3] (= *rising air current*) (soudain) courant *m* ascendant

[4] (*Rowing*) heurt *m*

VT [*car*] [+ *another car*] heurter, tamponner ; [+ *boat*] heurter ; (*esp US* = *dislodge*) déloger ◆ **to ~ one's head/knee** se cogner la tête/le genou (*against* contre) ◆ **he was bumped from the flight** il est resté en rade* à cause du surbooking sur son vol

VI ◆ **to ~ along** cahoter, bringuebaler ◆ **to ~ down** (= *sit*) s'asseoir brusquement ◆ **the economy continues to ~ along the bottom** (*Brit*) l'économie est toujours au creux de la vague

EXCL boum !, pan !

COMP **bump-start** **VT** [+ *car*] (*by pushing*) démarrer en poussant ; (*by running down a hill*) démarrer dans une descente **N** ◆ **to give a car a ~-start** démarrer une voiture en la poussant

► **bump into** **VT FUS** [1] [*person*] butter contre, se cogner contre ; [*vehicle*] entrer en collision avec, rentrer dans*

[2] (* = *meet*) rencontrer par hasard, tomber sur*

► **bump off**‡ **VT SEP** liquider*, supprimer ; (*with gun*) descendre‡

► **bump up** **VI** ◆ **the car bumped up onto the pavement** la voiture a grimpé sur le trottoir

VT SEP * [1] (= *increase sharply*) [+ *prices, sales, points, profits*] faire grimper

[2] ◆ **he was bumped up to first class on his flight home** au retour, il a eu droit à un surclassement *or* à une place en première

► **bump up against** **VT FUS** ⇒ **bump into**

bumper /ˈbʌmpəʳ/ **N** [1] [*of car*] pare-chocs *m inv* ◆ **to be ~-to-~** être pare-chocs contre pare-chocs, être à touche-touche* [2] (= *full glass*) rasade *f*, plein verre *m* **ADJ** [*crop, issue*] exceptionnel, sensationnel

COMP **bumper car** **N** auto *f* tamponneuse

bumper sticker, bumper strip **N** autocollant *m* (*pour voiture*)

bumph * /bʌmf/ **N** ⇒ **bumf**

bumpkin /ˈbʌmpkɪn/ **N** (*pej*: also **country bumpkin**) plouc* *mf*, péquenaud‡ *m*

bumptious /ˈbʌmpʃəs/ **ADJ** suffisant, prétentieux

bumpy /ˈbʌmpɪ/ **ADJ** [*road*] bosselé, cahoteux ; [*forehead*] couvert de bosses ; [*ride*] cahoteux ; [*crossing*] agité ◆ **we had a ~ flight/drive/crossing** nous avons été très secoués *or* chahutés* pendant le vol/sur la route/pendant la traversée

bun /bʌn/ **N** [1] (*Culin*: also **bread bun**) petit pain *m* au lait ; (= *cake*) petit gâteau *m* ◆ **to have a ~ in the oven**‡ avoir un polichinelle dans le tiroir‡, être en cloque‡ [2] (= *hairstyle*) chignon *m* ◆ **she had her hair in a ~** elle portait un chignon [3] (*US* ‡) **to get a ~ on** (= *get drunk*) prendre une biture‡ ◆ **he had a ~ on** il tenait une de ces bitures !‡ **NPL** **buns** ‡ (*esp US* = *buttocks*) fesses *fpl* **COMP** **bun-fight** * **N** thé *m* (*servi pour un grand nombre de personnes*)

bunch /bʌntʃ/ **N** [1] [*of flowers, watercress, herbs*] bouquet *m* ; [*of hair*] touffe *f*, houppe *f* ; [*of bananas*] régime *m* ; [*of radishes, asparagus*] botte *f* ; [*of twigs*] poignée *f*, paquet *m* ; [*of keys*] trousseau *m* ; [*of ribbons*] nœud *m*, flot *m* ◆ **~ of flowers** bouquet *m* (de fleurs) ◆ **~ of grapes** grappe *f* de raisins ◆ **to wear one's hair in ~es** (*Brit*) porter des couettes ◆ **the pick of the ~** (*fig*) le dessus du panier ◆ **to give sb a ~ of fives**‡ envoyer* un coup de poing dans la figure de qn

[2] * [*of people*] groupe *m*, bande *f* ◆ **the best of the ~** le meilleur de la bande *or* de l'équipe* ◆ **the best of a bad ~*** le *or* les moins médiocre(s) ◆ **what a ~!** quelle équipe !*

[3] (*Sport*) [*of runners, cyclists*] peloton *m*

VT [+ *flowers*] mettre en bouquets ; [+ *vegetables, straw*] botteler, mettre en bottes

► **bunch together** **VI** se serrer, s'agglutiner

VT SEP [+ *people, things*] grouper, concentrer

► **bunch up** **VI** ◆ **don't bunch up so much, space out !** ne vous entassez pas les uns sur les autres, écartez-vous !

VT SEP [1] [+ *dress, skirt*] retrousser, trousser

[2] ◆ **they sat bunched up on the bench** ils étaient (assis) serrés sur le banc

bunco * /ˈbʊŋkəʊ/ (*US*) **N** (= *swindle*) arnaque‡ *f*, escroquerie *f* **VT** arnaquer‡, escroquer **COMP** **bunco squad** **N** ≈ brigade *f* de répression des fraudes

buncombe‡ /ˈbʌŋkəm/ **N** (*US*) ⇒ **bunkum**

bundle /ˈbʌndl/ **N** [1] [*of clothes, goods*] paquet *m*, ballot *m* ; [*of hay*] botte *f* ; [*of letters, papers*] liasse *f* ; [*of linen*] paquet *m* ; [*of firewood*] fagot *m* ; [*of sticks*] faisceau *m*, poignée *f* ◆ **he's a ~ of nerves** c'est un paquet de nerfs ◆ **he's a ~ of laughs*** (*iro*) il n'est vraiment pas marrant* ◆ **to drop one's ~*** (*Austral fig*) baisser les bras ◆ **~ (of joy)** (= *baby*) (petit) bout *m* de chou* ◆ **she's a ~ of mischief*** elle est très espiègle

[2] (‡ = *money*) **a ~** beaucoup de fric* ◆ **to make a ~** faire son beurre* ◆ **it cost a ~*** ça a coûté bonbon*, ça a coûté beaucoup de fric*

[3] (= *great deal*) beaucoup ◆ **we've learned a ~ of lessons** nous avons beaucoup appris ◆ **I don't go a ~ on it*** ça ne me botte* pas, ça ne m'emballe pas beaucoup ◆ **I don't go a ~ on him*** il ne me branche pas ce type-là*

[4] (*Comput*) lot *m*

VT [1] (also **bundle up**) empaqueter, mettre en paquet ; [+ *clothes*] faire un paquet *or* ballot de ; [+ *hay*] botteler ; [+ *papers, banknotes*] mettre en liasse ; [+ *letters*] mettre en paquet ; [+ *sticks*] mettre en faisceau

[2] (= *put hastily*) **to ~ sth into a corner** fourrer* *or* entasser qch dans un coin ◆ **to ~ sb into the house** pousser qn dans la maison sans ménagement ◆ **to ~ sb into a car** pousser qn dans une voiture (sans ménagement) ◆ **he ~d her into her winter coat** il l'a emmitouflée dans son manteau d'hiver

[3] (*Comput*) [+ *software*] intégrer

COMP **bundled software** **N** (*NonC*: *Comput*) progiciel *m*

► **bundle off** **VT SEP** [+ *person*] faire sortir (en toute hâte), pousser dehors (sans façons) ◆ **he was ~d off to Australia** on l'a expédié en Australie

► **bundle out** **VT SEP** pousser dehors (sans façons), faire sortir (en toute hâte)

► **bundle up** **VT SEP** [1] ⇒ **bundle vt 1**

[2] emmitoufler

bung /bʌŋ/ **N** [1] [*of cask*] bondon *m*, bonde *f* [2] (‡ = *bribe*) dessous-de-table *m* **VT** [1] (*esp Brit*: also **bung up**) [+ *cask*] boucher [2] (*Brit* ‡ = *throw*) balancer*

► **bung in**‡ **VT SEP** (= *include*) rajouter (par-dessus le marché)

► **bung out**‡ **VT SEP** flanquer* à la porte ; [+ *rubbish*] jeter

► **bung up** **VT SEP** [1] (= *block up*) [+ *pipe etc*] boucher, obstruer ◆ **his eyes were/his nose was ~ed up*** il avait les yeux bouffis/le nez bouché *or* pris ◆ **I'm all ~ed up*** j'ai un gros rhume (de cerveau) [2] → **bung vt 1**

bungaloid /ˈbʌŋɡəlɔɪd/ **ADJ** *(pej)* de bungalow, genre *or* style bungalow ◆ ~ **growth** extension *f* pavillonnaire

bungalow /ˈbʌŋɡələʊ/ **N** (petit) pavillon *m* *(de plain pied)* ; *(in East)* bungalow *m*

bungee /ˈbʌndʒiː/ **N** *(for securing luggage etc)* sandow *m*, tendeur *m*
COMP **bungee cord** **N** élastique *m* *(pour saut à l'élastique)*
bungee jumping **N** saut *m* à l'élastique
bungee rope **N** ⇒ **bungee cord**

bunghole /ˈbʌŋhəʊl/ **N** bonde *f*

bungle /ˈbʌŋɡl/ **VT** *[+ attempt, robbery]* rater ; *[+ piece of work]* gâcher, bousiller* ◆ **he ~d it** il s'y est mal pris, il a tout bousillé* ◆ **it was a ~d job** c'était fait n'importe comment ◆ **a ~d attempt/burglary** une tentative/un cambriolage qui a mal tourné **VI** s'y prendre mal, faire les choses n'importe comment **N** fiasco *m*, ratage *m*

bungler /ˈbʌŋɡləʳ/ **N** bousilleur* *m*, -euse* *f* ◆ **he's a ~** il bousille* tout, il est incompétent

bungling /ˈbʌŋɡlɪŋ/ **ADJ** *[person]* maladroit, incompétent ; *[attempt]* maladroit, gauche **N** *(NonC)* gâchis *m*, bousillage* *m*

bunion /ˈbʌnjən/ **N** *(Med)* oignon *m*

bunk /bʌŋk/ **N** 1 *(Naut, Rail etc = bed)* couchette *f* 2 *(Brit)* **to do a ~‡** mettre les bouts‡ *or* les voiles* 3 ‡ abbrev of **bunkum** **VI** 1 (*: also **bunk down**) coucher, camper *(dans un lit de fortune)* 2 *(Brit* ‡: also **bunk off**) mettre les bouts‡ *or* les voiles*
COMP **bunk beds** **NPL** lits *mpl* superposés
bunk-up* **N** ◆ **to give sb a ~-up** soulever qn par derrière *or* par en dessous

bunker /ˈbʌŋkəʳ/ **N** 1 *(for coal)* coffre *m* ; *(Naut)* soute *f* (à charbon *or* à mazout) 2 *(Golf)* bunker *m* ; *(fig)* obstacle *m* 3 *(Mil)* blockhaus *m*, bunker *m* ◆ **(nuclear) ~** bunker *m* *or* abri *m* antinucléaire **VT** 1 *(Naut)* *[+ coal, oil]* mettre en soute ◆ **to ~ a ship** mettre du charbon *or* du mazout en soute 2 *(Golf)* ◆ **to ~ one's shot** envoyer la balle dans un bunker ◆ **to be ~ed** *(Golf)* se trouver dans un bunker ; (‡ *fig*) se trouver face à un obstacle, se trouver dans une impasse **VI** *(Naut)* charbonner, mazouter **COMP** **bunker mentality** **N** ◆ **to have a ~ mentality** être toujours sur la défensive

bunkhouse /ˈbʌŋkhaʊs/ **N** *(esp US)* bâtiment-dortoir *m*

bunkum‡ /ˈbʌŋkəm/ **N** foutaise(s)‡ *f(pl)* ◆ **to talk ~** dire n'importe quoi, déconner‡ ◆ **that's all ~** c'est n'importe quoi, tout ça, c'est des conneries‡

bunny /ˈbʌnɪ/ **N** 1 (also **bunny rabbit**) lapin *m* ◆ **he's not a happy bunny*** il n'est pas bien dans ses baskets* 2 *(US* * *= pretty girl)* jolie fille *f* *or* nana* *f* ; (also **bunny girl**) hôtesse *f* *(dans un club Playboy)* ; → **ski, snow**

Bunsen burner /ˈbʌnsnˈbɜːnəʳ/ **N** bec *m* Bunsen

bunting¹ /ˈbʌntɪŋ/ **N** *(= bird)* bruant *m* ; → **reed**

bunting² /ˈbʌntɪŋ/ **N** *(NonC)* *(= material)* étamine *f* (à pavillon) ; *(= flags etc)* banderoles *fpl*

buoy /bɔɪ/ **N** bouée *f*, balise *f* flottante ◆ **to put down a ~** mouiller une bouée ; → **lifebuoy, mooring** **VT** *[+ waterway]* baliser ; *[+ net]* liéger
COMP **buoy rope** **N** orin *m*

► **buoy up** **VT SEP** *(lit)* maintenir à flot ; *(fig)* soutenir ◆ **they felt ~ed up by their recent successes** leurs récents succès les avaient regonflés*

buoyancy /ˈbɔɪənsɪ/ **N** 1 *[of ship, object]* flottabilité *f* ; *[of liquid]* poussée *f* 2 *(= lightheartedness)* gaieté *f*, entrain *m* 3 *(Fin)* ◆ **the ~ of the markets** la fermeté des marchés
COMP **buoyancy aid** **N** gilet *m* de sauvetage
buoyancy chamber, buoyancy tank **N** *(Naut)* caisson *m* étanche

buoyant /ˈbɔɪənt/ **ADJ** 1 *[ship, object]* capable de flotter, flottable ; *[liquid]* dans lequel les objets flottent ◆ **fresh water is not so ~ as salt water** l'eau douce ne porte pas si bien que l'eau salée 2 *(= lighthearted)* *[person]* enjoué, plein d'entrain *or* d'allant ; *[mood]* gai, optimiste ; *[step]* léger, élastique 3 *(Fin)* *[market]* soutenu, actif

buoyantly /ˈbɔɪəntlɪ/ **ADV** *[walk, float]* légèrement ; *(fig)* avec entrain

BUPA /ˈbuːpə/ **N** (abbrev of **British United Provident Association**) *association britannique d'assurance-maladie privée*

buppie* /ˈbʌpɪ/ **N** yuppie *mf* noir(e)

bur¹ /bɜːʳ/ **N** *[of plant]* bardane *f* ; (‡ *pej = person*) pot *m* de colle *(pej)* ◆ **chestnut ~** bogue *f*

bur² /bɜːʳ/ **N** *(Ling)* grasseyement *m* ◆ **to speak with a ~** grasseyer **VT** ◆ **to ~ (one's Rs)** prononcer les R grasseyés

Burberry ® /ˈbɜːbərɪ/ **N** imperméable *m* *(de la marque Burberry)*

burble /ˈbɜːbl/ **VI** 1 *[stream]* murmurer 2 *(pej)* *[person]* marmonner ◆ **what's he burbling (on) about?** qu'est-ce qu'il est encore en train de raconter ? ◆ **he ~d on about freedom** il radotait sur le thème de la liberté **VT** marmonner **N** *[of stream]* murmure *m*

burbling /ˈbɜːblɪŋ/ **N** *(NonC)* 1 *[of stream]* murmure *m* 2 *[of person]* jacassements *mpl* **ADJ** *[person]* qui n'arrête pas de jacasser

burbot /ˈbɜːbət/ **N** (pl **burbot** *or* **burbots**) lotte *f* (de rivière)

burbs*, **'burbs*** /bɜːbz/ **NPL** *(US)* (abbrev of **suburbs**) ◆ **the ~** la banlieue

burden /ˈbɜːdn/ **N** 1 *(lit)* fardeau *m*, charge *f* ; → **beast**
2 *(fig)* fardeau *m*, charge *f* ; *[of taxes, years]* poids *m* ; *[of debts]* fardeau *m* ; *(Fin, Jur = debt weighing on company's balance sheet or on an estate)* encombrement *m* ◆ **to be a ~ to ...** être un fardeau pour ... ◆ **the ~ of the expense** les frais *mpl* à charge ◆ **~ of proof** *(Jur)* charge *f* de la preuve ◆ **the ~ of proof lies** *or* **rests with him** la charge de la preuve lui incombe, il lui incombe d'en fournir la preuve ; → **tax**
3 *(Naut)* jauge *f*, tonnage *m* ◆ **ship of 4,000 tons' ~** navire *m* qui jauge 4 000 tonneaux
4 *(= chorus)* refrain *m*
5 *(= chief theme)* substance *f*, fond *m* ◆ **the ~ of their complaint** leur principal grief *or* sujet de plainte
VT *(= oppress)* accabler *(with* de) ; ◆ **to be ~ed with debt** être accablé de dettes ◆ **I don't like to ~ other people with my worries** je n'aime pas infliger (le récit de) mes soucis aux autres ◆ **to be ~ed by guilt** être tenaillé par la culpabilité, être rongé de remords ◆ **to be ~ed by regret** être accablé de regrets

burdensome /ˈbɜːdnsəm/ **ADJ** *[load]* lourd, pesant ; *[task, restriction]* pénible

burdock /ˈbɜːdɒk/ **N** bardane *f*

bureau /ˈbjʊərəʊ/ **N** (pl **bureaus** *or* **bureaux**) 1 *(esp Brit = writing desk)* bureau *m*, secrétaire *m*
2 *(US = chest of drawers)* commode *f* *(souvent à miroir)*
3 *(= office)* bureau *m* ; → **information, travel**
4 *(esp US = government department)* service *m* (gouvernemental) ◆ **federal ~** *(US)* bureau *m* fédéral
COMP **Bureau of Indian Affairs** **N** *(US)* *organisme responsable des affaires amérindiennes*
Bureau of Prisons **N** *(US)* administration *f* pénitentiaire

> **BUREAU OF INDIAN AFFAIRS**
>
> Organisme américain responsable des affaires amérindiennes. D'abord rattaché au ministère de la Guerre à sa création en 1824, il était responsable de l'administration des réserves. Aujourd'hui, il relève du ministère de l'Intérieur et a pour mission d'améliorer les conditions de vie des populations autochtones, et en particulier de leur apporter formation et assistance technique pour la gestion de leurs ressources.

bureaucracy /bjʊəˈrɒkrəsɪ/ **N** bureaucratie *f*

bureaucrat /ˈbjʊərəʊkræt/ **N** bureaucrate *mf*

bureaucratese* /ˌbjʊərəʊkræˈtiːz/ **N** jargon *m* administratif

bureaucratic /ˌbjʊərəʊˈkrætɪk/ **ADJ** bureaucratique

bureaux /ˈbjʊərəʊz/ **NPL** of **bureau**

burette /bjʊəˈret/ **N** éprouvette *f* graduée

burg* /bɜːɡ/ **N** *(US pej = town)* bled* *m*, patelin* *m*

burgeon /ˈbɜːdʒən/ **VI** *(liter)* *[flower]* (commencer à) éclore ; *[plant]* bourgeonner, se couvrir de bourgeons ; *[talent]* naître ; *[population]* être en pleine croissance ; *[trade, industry]* être en plein essor

burgeoning /ˈbɜːdʒənɪŋ/ **ADJ** *[industry, market, demand, growth, career, popularity]* en plein essor ; *[population]* en pleine croissance ; *[numbers, costs, debt]* croissant ◆ **the ~ pacifist movement** le mouvement pacifiste en plein essor ◆ **a young man with ~ talent** un jeune homme dont le talent grandit de jour en jour

burger /ˈbɜːɡəʳ/ **N** hamburger *m* **COMP** **burger bar** **N** fast-food *m* *(où l'on sert des hamburgers)*

burgess /ˈbɜːdʒɪs/ **N** 1 *(Brit Hist)* *(= citizen)* bourgeois *m*, citoyen *m* ; *(Parl)* député *m* *(représentant au Parlement d'un bourg ou d'une circonscription universitaire)* 2 *(US Hist)* député *m*

burgh /ˈbʌrə/ **N** *(Scot)* ville *f* *(possédant une charte)*

burgher /ˈbɜːɡəʳ/ **N** *(archaic or liter)* citoyen(ne) *m(f)*

burglar /ˈbɜːɡləʳ/ **N** cambrioleur *m*, -euse *f* ; → **cat**
COMP **burglar alarm** **N** (système *m* d')alarme *f*
burglar-proof **ADJ** *[house]* muni d'un système d'alarme ; *[lock]* incrochetable

burglarize /ˈbɜːɡləraɪz/ **VT** *(US)* cambrioler

burglary /ˈbɜːɡlərɪ/ **N** cambriolage *m*

burgle /ˈbɜːɡl/ **VT** cambrioler, dévaliser **VI** cambrioler

burgomaster /ˈbɜːɡəˌmɑːstəʳ/ **N** bourgmestre *m*

Burgundian /bɜːˈɡʌndɪən/ **ADJ** bourguignon, de Bourgogne **N** Bourguignon(ne) *m(f)*

Burgundy /ˈbɜːɡəndɪ/ **N** 1 *(Geog)* Bourgogne *f* 2 *(= wine)* bourgogne *m* 3 *(= colour)* **burgundy** bordeaux

burial /ˈberɪəl/ **N** *(= interment)* enterrement *m*, inhumation *f* ; *(religious)* sépulture *f* ; *(= ceremony)* funérailles *fpl*, obsèques *fpl* ; *[of hopes etc]* mort *f*, fin *f* ◆ **Christian ~** sépulture *f* chrétienne ◆ **~ at sea** funérailles *fpl* en mer
COMP **burial ground** **N** cimetière *m*
burial mound **N** tumulus *m*
burial place **N** lieu *m* de sépulture
burial service **N** office *m* des morts, service *m* funèbre
burial vault **N** tombeau *m*

burin /ˈbjʊərɪn/ **N** burin *m* (à graver)

burk‡ /bɜːk/ **N** *(Brit)* ⇒ **berk**

burke /bɜːk/ **VT** *(= suppress)* *[+ scandal]* étouffer ; *(= shelve)* *[+ question]* escamoter

Burkina-Faso /bɜːˈkiːnəˈfæsəʊ/ **N** Burkina-Faso *m*

burlap /ˈbɜːlæp/ **N** (*esp US*) toile *f* d'emballage, toile *f* à sac

burlesque /bɜːˈlesk/ **N** 1 (*= parody*) [*of book, poem etc*] parodie *f* ; [*of society, way of life*] caricature *f* 2 (*NonC: Literat*) (genre *m*) burlesque *m* 3 (*US = striptease*) revue *f* déshabillée (*souvent vulgaire*) **ADJ** [*poem etc*] burlesque ; [*description*] caricatural **VT** (*= make ridiculous*) tourner en ridicule ; (*= parody*) [*+ book, author*] parodier

burly /ˈbɜːlɪ/ **ADJ** de forte carrure, solidement charpenté ◆ **a big ~ fellow*** un grand gaillard baraqué* ◆ **a ~ policeman** un grand gaillard d'agent

Burma /ˈbɜːmə/ **N** Birmanie *f*

Burmese /bɜːˈmiːz/ **ADJ** birman, de Birmanie ◆ **the ~ Empire** l'Empire *m* birman **N** 1 (*pl inv*) Birman(e) *m(f)* 2 (*= language*) birman *m* **COMP** **Burmese cat N** (chat *m*) birman *m*

burn¹ /bɜːn/ (vb : pret, ptp **burned** *or* (*Brit*) **burnt**) **N** 1 (*Med*) brûlure *f* ◆ **cigarette ~** brûlure *f* de cigarette ; → **degree**

2 (*Space*) [*of rocket*] (durée *f* de) combustion *f*

VT 1 (*gen*) brûler ; [*+ town, building*] incendier, mettre le feu à ◆ **to ~ to a cinder** *or* **crisp** carboniser, calciner ◆ **to be ~t to death** être brûlé vif, mourir carbonisé ◆ **to be ~t alive** être brûlé vif ◆ **to be ~t at the stake** être brûlé sur le bûcher ◆ **to ~ o.s.** se brûler ◆ **to ~ one's finger** se brûler le doigt ◆ **he ~ed a hole in his coat with a cigarette** il a fait un trou à son manteau avec une cigarette ◆ **you could get your fingers ~t over this** (*fig*) vous risquez de vous brûler les doigts dans cette affaire ◆ **to get ~ed** (*fig*) se brûler les doigts ◆ **money ~s a hole in my pocket** l'argent me fond dans les mains ◆ **to ~ one's boats/one's bridges** brûler ses vaisseaux/les ponts ◆ **to ~ the candle at both ends** brûler la chandelle par les deux bouts ; → **midnight**

2 (*Culin*) [*+ meat, toast, cakes*] laisser brûler ; [*+ sauce, milk*] laisser attacher

3 [*acid*] brûler, ronger ; [*sun*] [*+ person, skin*] brûler ◆ **delicious curries which won't ~ your throat** de délicieux currys qui ne vous emporteront pas la bouche ◆ **the date was ~ed into his memory** la date se grava dans sa mémoire

VI 1 [*wood, meat, cakes etc*] brûler ; [*milk, sauce*] attacher ◆ **you left all the lights ~ing** vous avez laissé toutes les lumières allumées ◆ **her skin ~s easily** elle a la peau facilement brûlée par le soleil, elle attrape facilement des coups de soleil ◆ **my head is ~ing** j'ai la tête brûlante ◆ **his wound was ~ing** la blessure le cuisait ◆ **his face was ~ing with cold** le froid lui brûlait le visage ◆ **her face was ~ing** (*from heat, embarrassment*) elle était cramoisie

2 [*person*] (*lit*) être brûlé vif ; (*fig*) brûler (*with* de) ; ◆ **he was ~ing to get his revenge** *or* **~ing for revenge** il brûlait (du désir) de se venger ◆ **he was ~ing with ambition** il brûlait d'ambition

3 ◆ **acid ~s into metal** l'acide ronge le métal ◆ **his eyes ~ed into mine** (*romantically*) il m'a regardé avec des yeux de braise ; (*threateningly*) son regard était fixé sur moi ◆ **her words ~ed into my brain** ses paroles sont restées gravées dans ma mémoire

4 (*Space*) [*rocket*] brûler

COMP **burns unit N** (*Med*) service *m* des grands brûlés

► **burn away VI** 1 (*= go on burning*) **the fire was ~ing away** le feu flambait *or* brûlait bien

2 (*= be consumed*) se consumer

VT SEP détruire (par le feu) ; [*+ paint*] brûler (au chalumeau)

► **burn down VI** 1 [*house etc*] brûler complètement, être réduit en cendres

2 [*fire, candle*] baisser

VT SEP [*+ building*] incendier ◆ **the house was ~t down** la maison a été réduite en cendres *or* calcinée

► **burn off VT SEP** [*+ paint etc*] brûler (au chalumeau)

► **burn out VI** [*fire, candle*] s'éteindre ; [*light bulb*] griller, sauter

VT SEP 1 [*+ candle*] laisser brûler jusqu'au bout ; [*+ lamp*] griller ◆ **the candle ~t itself out** la bougie est morte ◆ **he ~t himself out** il s'est abîmé la santé

2 (*= force out by fire*) [*+ enemy troops etc*] forcer à sortir en mettant le feu ◆ **they were ~t out of house and home** un incendie a détruit leur maison avec tout ce qu'ils possédaient

► **burn up VI** 1 [*fire etc*] flamber, monter

2 [*rocket etc in atmosphere*] se volatiliser, se désintégrer

3 **to be ~ing up (with fever)** être brûlant (de fièvre)

VT SEP 1 [*+ rubbish*] brûler

2 ◆ **burned up with jealousy** mort de jalousie

3 (*US* * *= make angry*) foutre en rogne*

burn² /bɜːn/ **N** (*Scot*) ruisseau *m*

burner /ˈbɜːnəʳ/ **N** [*of gas cooker*] brûleur *m* ; [*of lamp*] bec *m* (de gaz) ; → **back, Bunsen burner, charcoal, front**

Burnham scale /ˈbɜːnəm,skeɪl/ **N** (*Brit Scol Admin*) grille *f* indiciaire des enseignants

burning /ˈbɜːnɪŋ/ **ADJ** 1 (*= on fire*) [*town, forest*] en flammes ; [*fire, candle*] allumé ; [*coals*] ardent ; [*feeling*] cuisant ◆ **the ~ bush** le buisson ardent ◆ **with a ~ face** (*from shame*) le rouge au front ; (*from embarrassment*) le rouge aux joues 2 (*fig*) [*thirst, fever*] brûlant ; [*faith*] ardent, intense ; [*indignation*] violent ; [*words*] véhément, passionné ; [*topic*] brûlant, passionnant ◆ **a ~ question** une question brûlante ◆ **it's a ~ * shame that ...** c'est une honte *or* un scandale que ... + *subj* **N** 1 ◆ **there is a smell of ~** ça sent le brûlé *or* le roussi ◆ **I could smell ~** je sentais une odeur de brûlé 2 (*= setting on fire*) incendie *m*, embrasement *m* ◆ **they ordered the ~ of the town** ils ont ordonné l'incendie de la ville, ils ont ordonné qu'on mette le feu à la ville

burnish /ˈbɜːnɪʃ/ **VT** [*+ metal*] brunir, polir ◆ **~ed hair** (beaux) cheveux *mpl* brillants ◆ **~ed skin** (belle) peau *f* dorée ◆ **~ed leaves** feuilles *fpl* aux reflets dorés ◆ **to ~ sb's image** redorer le blason de qn, rehausser l'image de qn

burnisher /ˈbɜːnɪʃəʳ/ **N** (*= person*) brunisseur *m*, -euse *f* ; (*= tool*) brunissoir *m*

burnous(e), burnoos (*US*) /bɜːˈnuːs/ **N** burnous *m*

burnout /ˈbɜːnaʊt/ **N** 1 (*Elec*) ◆ **there's been a ~** les circuits sont grillés 2 (*fig*) épuisement *m*

Burns' Night /ˈbɜːnz,naɪt/ **N** (*Brit*) *fête écossaise à la gloire du poète Robert Burns*

Burns' Night

Fête écossaise, le 25 janvier, commémorant l'anniversaire de la naissance du poète national écossais Robert Burns (1759-1796). À cette occasion, les Écossais se réunissent pour un dîner (Burns' supper) qui comprend traditionnellement du haggis, apporté au son de la cornemuse, qui se mange accompagné d'une purée de rutabagas et de pommes de terre (neeps and tatties). Après les toasts d'usage, l'assistance lit des poèmes et chante des chansons de Burns.

burnt /bɜːnt/ **VB** pt, ptp of **burn¹** **ADJ** brûlé, carbonisé ◆ **a ~ child dreads the fire** (*Prov*) chat échaudé craint l'eau froide (*Prov*) ◆ **~ smell/taste** odeur *f*/goût *m* de brûlé

COMP **burnt almond N** amande *f* grillée, praline *f*

burnt lime N chaux *f* vive

burnt offering N holocauste *m*

burnt orange ADJ orange foncé *inv*

burnt sacrifice N ⇒ **burnt offering**

burnt sienna N terre *f* de sienne *or* d'ombre brûlée

burnt sugar N caramel *m*

burnt umber N ⇒ **burnt sienna**

burp * /bɜːp/ **VI** roter*, avoir un renvoi **VT** ◆ **to ~ a baby** faire faire son rot* *or* son renvoi à un bébé **N** rot* *m*, renvoi *m* **COMP** **burp gun** ‡ **N** (*US*) (*= pistol*) pistolet *m* automatique ; (*= submachine gun*) sulfateuse* *f* (*Mil*), mitraillette *f*

burqa /bɜːkə/ **N** burqa *f or m*

burr /bɜːʳ/ **N** ⇒ **bur²**

burrow /ˈbʌrəʊ/ **N** terrier *m* **VI** [*rabbit*] creuser un terrier ; [*dog*] creuser (la terre) ◆ **to ~ under** [*person*] (*in earth*) se creuser un chemin sous ; (*under blanket*) se réfugier sous ; (*= feel around in*) fouiller sous ◆ **to ~ into the past** fouiller dans le passé **VT** creuser ◆ **to ~ one's way underground** (se) creuser (un chemin) sous terre

bursa /ˈbɜːsə/ **N** (pl **bursas** *or* **bursae** /ˈbɜːsiː/) (*Anat*) bourse *f*

bursar /ˈbɜːsəʳ/ **N** 1 (*= administrator: gen*) intendant(e) *m(f)* ; (*in private school, hospital*) économe *mf* 2 (*Brit = student*) (élève *mf*) boursier *m*, -ière *f*

bursary /ˈbɜːsərɪ/ **N** (*Brit*) bourse *f* (d'études)

bursitis /bɜːˈsaɪtɪs/ **N** hygroma *m*

burst /bɜːst/ (vb : pret, ptp **burst**) **N** [*of shell, bomb*] explosion *f*, éclatement *m* ; [*of anger, indignation*] explosion *f* ; [*of anger, laughter*] éclat *m* ; [*of affection, eloquence*] élan *m*, transport *m* ; [*of activity*] vague *f* ; [*of enthusiasm*] accès *m*, montée *f* ; [*of thunder*] coup *m* ; [*of applause*] salve *f* ; [*of flames*] jaillissement *m*, jet *m* ◆ **to put on a ~ of speed** faire une pointe de vitesse ◆ **a ~ of gunfire** une rafale (de balles)

ADJ (*Med*) ◆ **~ appendix** crise *f* d'appendicite ◆ **~ ulcer** perforation *f* d'ulcère ◆ **~ eardrum** rupture *f* du tympan ◆ **~ blood vessel** vaisseau *m* éclaté ◆ **~ pipe** (*Plumbing*) tuyau *m* éclaté

VI 1 [*shell*] éclater, faire explosion ; [*pipe, boiler*] éclater ; [*dam*] se rompre ; [*bubble, balloon, abscess*] crever ; [*tyre*] (*= blow out*) éclater ; (*= puncture*) crever ; (*Med*) [*boil, spot*] crever ; [*appendix, ulcer*] se perforer ◆ **to ~ open** [*door*] s'ouvrir violemment ; [*container*] s'éventrer ◆ **my lungs are ~ing** je suis à bout de souffle

2 **to be ~ing (at the seams*)** [*bag, room*] être plein à craquer (*with* de) ; ◆ **to fill a sack to ~ing point** remplir un sac à craquer ◆ **to be ~ing with health** déborder de santé ◆ **to be ~ing with impatience** brûler d'impatience ◆ **to be ~ing with pride** éclater d'orgueil ◆ **to be ~ing with joy** déborder de joie ◆ **I was ~ing to tell you*** je mourais d'envie de vous le dire ◆ **to be ~ing*** [*person*] avoir une envie pressante

3 (*= move etc suddenly*) se précipiter, se jeter (*into* dans ; *out of* hors de)

4 (*= begin etc suddenly*) **the horse ~ into a gallop** le cheval a pris le galop ◆ **he suddenly ~ into speech/song** il s'est mis tout d'un coup à parler/chanter ◆ **the truth ~ (in) upon him** la vérité lui a soudain sauté aux yeux ◆ **the applause ~ upon our ears** les applaudissements ont éclaté à nos oreilles ◆ **to ~ into tears** fondre en larmes ◆ **to ~ into bloom** [*flower*] s'épanouir (soudain) ◆ **to ~ into flames** prendre feu (soudain) ◆ **the sun ~ through the clouds** le soleil a percé les nuages ◆ **the oil ~ from the well** le pétrole a jailli du puits

VT [*+ balloon, bubble*] crever ; [*+ tyre*] (*= blow out*) faire éclater ; (*= puncture*) crever ; [*+ pipe*] faire sauter ◆ **to ~ open** [*+ door*] ouvrir violemment ; [*+ container*] éventrer ◆ **the river has ~ its banks** le fleuve a rompu ses digues ◆ **to ~ one's sides with laughter*** se tordre de rire

◆ **to ~ a blood vessel** *(Med)* (se) faire éclater une veine, (se) rompre un vaisseau ◆ **he almost ~ a blood vessel*** *(with anger etc)* il a failli prendre un coup de sang* *or* avoir une attaque*

► **burst forth** VI *(liter)* *[person]* sortir précipitamment ; *[sun]* surgir

► **burst in** VI entrer en trombe *or* en coup de vent, faire irruption ◆ **he ~ in (on us/them** *etc***)** il a fait irruption (chez nous/eux *etc*) ◆ **to ~ in on a conversation** interrompre brutalement une conversation

VT SEP *[+ door]* enfoncer

► **burst out** VI 1 ◆ **to burst out of a room** se précipiter hors d'une pièce, sortir d'une pièce en trombe

2 ◆ **she's bursting out of that dress** elle éclate de partout *or* elle est très boudinée* dans cette robe

3 *(in speech)* s'exclamer, s'écrier ◆ **"that's cruel!" she ~ out** "c'est cruel !" s'exclama-t-elle

4 ◆ **to burst out laughing** éclater de rire ◆ **to ~ out crying** fondre en larmes

bursting /ˈbɜːstɪŋ/ N *(Comput)* déliassage *m*

burthen †† /ˈbɜːðən/ ⇒ **burden**

burton /ˈbɜːtn/ N *(Brit)* ◆ **he's gone for a ~*** il est fichu* *or* foutu‡ ◆ **it's gone for a ~*** *(= broken)* c'est fichu* *or* foutu‡ ; *(= lost)* ça a disparu

Burundi /bəˈrʊndɪ/ N Burundi *m*

Burundian /bəˈrʊndjən/ ADJ burundais N Burundais(e) *m(f)*

bury /ˈberɪ/ VT 1 *(gen)* enterrer ; *(at funeral)* enterrer, inhumer ◆ **to ~ sb alive** enterrer qn vivant ◆ **he was buried at sea** son corps fut immergé (en haute mer) ◆ **buried by an avalanche** enseveli par une avalanche ◆ **he buried his wife on Friday** il a enterré sa femme vendredi ; → **dead**

2 *[+ treasure]* enterrer, enfouir ; *[+ quarrel]* enterrer, oublier ◆ **the dog buried a bone** le chien a enterré un os ◆ **to ~ one's head in the sand** pratiquer la politique de l'autruche ◆ **they agreed to ~ their differences** ils ont décidé d'enterrer la hache de guerre, ils ont décidé d'oublier leurs désaccords ◆ **to ~ the hatchet** *or* (US) **the tomahawk** enterrer la hache de guerre

3 *(= conceal)* enfouir, cacher ◆ **to ~ o.s. under the blankets** s'enfouir sous les couvertures ◆ **to ~ one's face in one's hands** se couvrir *or* se cacher la figure de ses mains ◆ **the bullet was buried deep in the woodwork** la balle était fichée profondément dans le bois ◆ **a village buried in the country** un village perdu en pleine campagne ◆ **she buried herself in the country** elle est allée s'enterrer à la campagne ◆ **they buried the story** ils ont enterré cette nouvelle

4 *(= engross)* plonger ◆ **to ~ one's head** *or* **o.s. in a book** se plonger dans un livre ◆ **to ~ o.s. in one's studies** se plonger dans ses études ◆ **buried in one's work** plongé *or* absorbé dans son travail ◆ **buried in thought** plongé dans une rêverie *or* dans ses pensées

5 *(= plunge)* *[+ hands, knife]* enfoncer, plonger (in dans)

► **bury away** VT SEP ◆ **to be buried away** être enterré *(fig)*

bus /bʌs/ N (pl **buses,** (US) **buses** *or* **busses**) 1 bus *m*, autobus *m* ; *(long-distance)* autocar *m*, car *m* ◆ **all ~es stop here** arrêt *m* fixe *or* obligatoire ; → **double, miss¹, trolley**

2 ‡ *(= car)* bagnole* *f* ; *(= plane)* (vieux) coucou* *m*

3 *(Comput)* bus *m*

VI 1 *(* = go by bus)* prendre l'autobus (*or* le car)

2 *(US *: in café)* travailler comme aide-serveur, desservir

VT ◆ **to ~ children to school** transporter des enfants à l'école en car ; → **bussing**

COMP **bus conductor** N receveur *m*, -euse *f* d'autobus *or* de bus

bus depot N dépôt *m* d'autobus *or* de bus

bus driver N conducteur *m*, -trice *f* d'autobus *or* de bus

bus lane N *(Brit)* voie *f* réservée aux autobus

bus pass N *(Brit)* carte *f* d'autobus *or* de bus

bus route N ◆ **the house is/is not on a ~ route** la maison est/n'est pas sur un trajet d'autobus *or* de bus

bus service N réseau *m or* service *m* d'autobus

bus shelter N Abribus ® *m*

bus station N gare *f* d'autobus ; *(for coaches)* gare *f* routière

bus stop N arrêt *m* d'autobus *or* de bus

bus ticket N ticket *m* d'autobus *or* de bus

busbar /ˈbʌsbɑːʳ/ N *(Comput)* bus *m*

busboy /ˈbʌsbɔɪ/ N *(US)* aide-serveur *m*

busby /ˈbʌzbɪ/ N *(Brit)* bonnet *m* à poil *(de soldat)*

bush¹ /bʊʃ/ N 1 *(= shrub)* buisson *m* ◆ **he had a great ~ of hair** il avait une épaisse tignasse ; → **beat, burning, rosebush** 2 *(= thicket)* taillis *m*, fourré *m* ; *(NonC = brushwood)* broussailles *fpl* ◆ **the ~** *(in Africa, Australia)* le bush ◆ **to take to the ~** partir *or* se réfugier dans la brousse

COMP **bush baby** N *(= animal)* galago *m*

bush jacket N saharienne *f*

bush-league* ADJ *(US Baseball)* de catégorie médiocre

bush leaguer* N *(US Baseball)* joueur *m* de catégorie médiocre ; *(fig)* minus *mf*

bush telegraph N *(lit)* téléphone *m* de brousse ; *(* fig)* téléphone *m* arabe

bush² /bʊʃ/ N *(= metal sleeve)* bague *f*

bushed /bʊʃt/ ADJ 1 * *(= exhausted)* flapi*, claqué* ; *(= puzzled)* ahuri 2 *(Austral)* perdu en brousse

bushel /ˈbʊʃl/ N *(Brit = measure)* boisseau *m* ; → **hide¹**

bushfighting /ˈbʊʃfaɪtɪŋ/ N guérilla *f*

bushfire /ˈbʊʃfaɪəʳ/ N feu *m* de brousse

bushing /ˈbʊʃɪŋ/ N *(esp US: = metal sleeve)* bague *f*

Bushman /ˈbʊʃmən/ N (pl **-men**) *(in South Africa)* Bochiman *m*, Bushman *m*

bushman /ˈbʊʃmən/ N (pl **-men**) *(in Australia)* broussard* *m*

bushranger /ˈbʊʃreɪndʒəʳ/ N *(in Australia)* forçat *m* réfugié dans la brousse, broussard* *m* ; *(in Canada, US)* trappeur *m*

bushwhack /ˈbʊʃwæk/ (US) VI se frayer un chemin à travers la brousse VT *(= ambush)* tendre une embuscade à

bushwhacker /ˈbʊʃwækəʳ/ N *(= frontiersman)* colon *m* de la brousse ; *(= guerilla soldier)* guérillero *m* ; *(= bandit)* bandit *m* de la brousse ; *(in Australia = lumberjack)* bûcheron *m*

bushwhacking /ˈbʊʃwækɪŋ/ N (US) ⇒ **bushfighting**

bushy /ˈbʊʃɪ/ ADJ *[land, ground]* broussailleux, couvert de buissons ; *[shrub]* épais (épaisse *f*) ; *[tree]* touffu ; *[beard, eyebrows, hair]* touffu, broussailleux

busily /ˈbɪzɪlɪ/ ADV *(= actively, eagerly)* activement ; *(pej = officiously)* avec trop de zèle ◆ **to be ~ engaged in sth/in doing sth** être très occupé *or* activement occupé à qch/à faire qch

business /ˈbɪznɪs/ N 1 *(NonC = commerce)* affaires *fpl* ◆ **it's good for ~** ça fait marcher les affaires ◆ **the ~ section** *(in newspaper)* la rubrique affaires ◆ **to do ~ with sb** faire des affaires avec qn ◆ **~ is ~** les affaires sont les affaires ◆ **his ~ is cattle rearing** il a une affaire d'élevage de bestiaux ◆ **his line of ~** sa partie ◆ **what line of ~ is he in?*** qu'est-ce qu'il fait (dans la vie) ? ◆ **the music ~** le secteur musical ◆ **to know one's ~** connaître son affaire, s'y connaître ◆ **to get down to ~** *(fig)* passer aux choses sérieuses ◆ **he means ~*** il ne plaisante pas ◆ **"business as usual"** *(lit)* "nous restons ouverts pendant les travaux" ◆ **it's ~ as usual, despite the bomb** la vie continue, en dépit de l'attentat ◆ **it's the ~!*** c'est super !* ◆ **she's the ~!*** elle est vraiment géniale !*

♦ **in + business** ◆ **to be in ~** être dans les affaires ◆ **to be in the grocery ~** être dans l'alimentation ◆ **to be in ~ for o.s.** travailler pour son propre compte, être à son compte ◆ **to set up in ~ as a butcher** *etc* s'établir (comme) boucher *etc* ◆ **young people seeking a career in ~** les jeunes qui veulent faire carrière dans les affaires ◆ **she's in the publishing ~** elle travaille dans l'édition ◆ **now we're in ~!*** *(fig)* maintenant nous sommes prêts ! ◆ **all we need is a microphone and we're in ~*** tout ce qu'il nous faut c'est un micro et le tour est joué

♦ **out of business** ◆ **to go out of ~** *[businessman]* fermer ; *[company]* cesser ses activités, fermer ◆ **to put out of ~** *[+ company, businessman]* faire fermer ◆ **this will put us out of ~** cela nous obligera à mettre la clé sous la porte

♦ **on business** ◆ **to go to Paris on ~** aller à Paris pour affaires ◆ **to be away on ~** être en déplacement pour affaires ; → **mix, nobody**

2 *(NonC = volume of trade)* **our ~ has doubled in the last year** notre chiffre d'affaires a doublé par rapport à l'année dernière ◆ **most of the shop's ~ comes from women** la clientèle du magasin est essentiellement féminine ◆ **he gets a lot of ~ from the Americans** il travaille beaucoup avec les Américains ◆ **during the ten days of the fair, ~ was excellent** pendant les dix jours de la foire, les affaires ont très bien marché ◆ **~ is good/booming** les affaires marchent bien/sont prospères ◆ **to lose ~** perdre des clients

3 *(= commercial enterprise)* commerce *m*, affaire *f* ◆ **he has a little ~ in the country** il tient un petit commerce *or* il a une petite affaire à la campagne ◆ **he owns a grocery ~** il a un commerce d'alimentation ◆ **a small ~** une petite entreprise ◆ **a family ~** une entreprise familiale

4 *(= task, duty)* affaire *f*, devoir *m* ◆ **the ~ of the day** les affaires courantes ◆ **it's all part of the day's ~** cela fait partie de la routine journalière ◆ **the ~ before the meeting** l'ordre *m* du jour de l'assemblée ◆ **we're not in the ~ of misleading the public** notre propos n'est pas de tromper le public ◆ **it's time the government got on with the ~ of dealing with inflation** il est temps que le gouvernement s'occupe sérieusement du problème de l'inflation ◆ **to make it one's ~ to do sth** se charger de faire qch ◆ **that's none of his ~** cela ne le regarde pas, ce n'est pas ses affaires ◆ **it's your ~ to do it** c'est à vous de le faire ◆ **you've no ~ to do that** ce n'est pas à vous de faire cela ◆ **I really had no ~ being there** je n'avais rien à faire dans cet endroit ◆ **that's my ~!** ça me regarde ! ◆ **my private life is my own ~** ma vie privée ne regarde que moi ◆ **mind your own ~!*** mêlez-vous de vos affaires *or* de ce qui vous regarde ! ◆ **I know my own ~** je ne veux pas me mêler de ce qui ne me regarde pas ◆ **to go about one's ~** s'occuper de ses propres affaires ◆ **to send sb about his ~** envoyer promener* qn

5 *(= difficult job)* **finding a flat is quite a ~** c'est toute une affaire de trouver un appartement ◆ **moving house is a costly ~** les déménagements sont coûteux, un déménagement entraîne des frais ◆ **parenting can be a stressful ~** cela peut être stressant d'élever des enfants

6 *(pej)* affaire *f*, histoire *f* ◆ **a wretched ~** une affaire regrettable ◆ **there's some funny ~ going on** il se passe quelque chose de louche *or* de pas catholique* ; → **bad**

7 **to do its ~** * *[animal]* faire ses besoins

COMP *[lunch, meeting, trip]* d'affaires
business accounting N comptabilité *f* d'entreprise
business activity N activité *f* industrielle et commerciale
business address N *[of individual]* adresse *f* professionnelle ; *[of company]* adresse *f* du siège social
Business and Technology Education Council N (Brit) *organisme habilité à conférer des diplômes en gestion, sciences et techniques etc*
business associate N associé(e) *m(f)* ◆ **Jones & Co are ~ associates of ours** nous sommes en relations commerciales avec Jones & Cie
business card N carte *f* de visite (professionnelle)
business centre N centre *m* des affaires
business class N classe *f* affaires
business college N école *f* de commerce
business contact N relation *f* de travail
business cycle N cycle *m* économique
business day N jour *m* ouvrable
business deal N affaire *f*
business district N centre *m* d'affaires
business end N ◆ **the ~ end of a knife** le côté opérant *or* la partie coupante d'un couteau ◆ **the ~ end of a rifle** le canon d'un fusil
business expenses NPL frais *mpl* généraux
business girl N jeune femme *f* d'affaires
business hours NPL *[of shops etc]* heures *fpl* d'ouverture, heures *fpl* d'affaires *(Can)* ; *[of offices]* heures *fpl* de bureau, heures *fpl* d'affaires *(Can)*
business letter N lettre *f* commerciale
business manager N *(in company)* directeur *m*, -trice *f* commercial(e) ; *(of sports team)* manager *m* ; *(of theatre)* directeur *m*, -trice *f*
business park N parc *m* d'activités
business people NPL hommes *mpl* et femmes *fpl* d'affaires
business plan N *[of company]* plan *m* de développement
business proposition N proposition *f*
business reply service N *(on envelope)* enveloppe *f* pré-affranchie
business school N ⇒ **business college**
business sense N ◆ **to have ~ sense** avoir le sens des affaires
business studies NPL *(Univ)* études *fpl* commerciales *or* de commerce
business suit N complet *m*, complet-veston *m*
business trip N voyage *m* d'affaires ◆ **to be on a ~ trip** être en voyage d'affaires

businesslike /ˈbɪznɪslaɪk/ ADJ *[person]* qui agit en professionnel ; *[firm, transaction]* sérieux ; *[manner, method, style]* de professionnel ; *[appearance]* sérieux ◆ **this is a very ~ knife!** * ça c'est un couteau (sérieux) ! *

businessman /ˈbɪznɪsmæn/ N (pl **-men**) homme *m* d'affaires ◆ **big ~** brasseur *m* d'affaires ◆ **he's a good ~** il a le sens des affaires

businesswoman /ˈbɪznɪsˌwʊmən/ N (pl **-women**) femme *f* d'affaires ◆ **she's a good ~** elle a le sens des affaires

busing /ˈbʌsɪŋ/ N ⇒ **bussing**

busk /bʌsk/ VI (Brit) jouer (*or* chanter) dans la rue

busker /ˈbʌskəʳ/ N (Brit) musicien(ne) *m(f)* ambulant *or* des rues

busload /ˈbʌsləʊd/ N ◆ **a ~ of children** un autobus *or* un autocar plein d'enfants ◆ **they came by the ~** *or* **in ~s** ils sont venus par cars entiers

busman /ˈbʌsmən/ N (pl **-men**) (= *driver*) conducteur *m* d'autobus ; (= *conductor*) receveur *m* ◆ **to take a ~'s holiday** se servir de ses compétences professionnelles en vacances

bussing /ˈbʌsɪŋ/ N ramassage *m* scolaire *(surtout aux USA comme mesure de déségrégation)*

bust¹ /bʌst/ N 1 *(Sculp)* buste *m* 2 *(Anat)* buste *m*, poitrine *f* COMP **bust measurement** N tour *m* de poitrine

bust² /bʌst/ ADJ 1 (* = *broken*) fichu *, foutu ‡
2 (‡ = *bankrupt*) **to go ~** faire faillite ◆ **to be ~** être fauché *, être à sec *
N 1 (‡ = *spree*) bombe * *f*, bringue * *f*
2 * (also **drugs bust**) (= *police raid*) descente *f* de police (pour saisie de drogue) ◆ **Australia's biggest ever cocaine bust** la plus grosse saisie de cocaïne jamais effectuée en Australie
3 *(US * = failure)* fiasco *m*
VT 1 ‡ ⇒ **burst vt** ◆ **to ~ a gut** *(lit)* attraper une hernie ; *(fig)* se donner un mal de chien * *(to do sth, doing sth* pour faire qch) ; ◆ **to ~ one's ass** (US) s'éreinter *, se crever le cul ‡ *(to do sth* pour faire qch) ; ◆ **I'll ~ your ass for you!** (US) je vais te casser la gueule ! ‡
2 ‡ *[police] (= break up) [+ crime ring etc]* démanteler ; (= *arrest*) *[+ person]* choper *, arrêter ; (= *raid*) *[+ place]* perquisitionner ; *(esp US) (= demote) [+ police officer]* rétrograder
3 *(US *) [+ horse]* dresser
VI * ⇒ **burst vi** ◆ **New York or ~!** New York ou rien !
COMP **bust-up** ‡ N engueulade ‡ *f* ◆ **to have a ~-up with sb** s'engueuler avec qn ‡
▸ **bust out** * VI (= *escape*) ◆ **he ~ out (of jail)** il s'est fait la malle (de la prison) *
▸ **bust up** ‡ VI *[friends]* se brouiller, rompre après une engueulade ‡ *(with sb* avec qn)
VT SEP *(fig) [+ marriage, friendship]* flanquer en l'air *
N ◆ **bust-up** ‡ → **bust²**

bustard /ˈbʌstəd/ N outarde *f*

buster ‡ /ˈbʌstəʳ/ N ◆ **hi, ~!** salut mon pote ! *

bustier /buːstɪeɪ/ N bustier *m*

bustle¹ /ˈbʌsl/ VI s'affairer, s'agiter ◆ **to ~ about** s'affairer ◆ **to ~ in/out** *etc* entrer/sortir *etc* d'un air affairé ◆ **to be bustling with** *(fig) [place, streets etc]* grouiller de ; see also **bustling**
N affairement *m*, remue-ménage *m*

bustle² /ˈbʌsl/ N *(Dress)* tournure *f*

bustling /ˈbʌslɪŋ/ ADJ *[person]* affairé ; *[place]* bruyant, agité ◆ **~ with life** plein de vie, plein d'animation, trépidant N ⇒ **bustle¹ noun**

busty * /ˈbʌstɪ/ ADJ *[woman]* forte de poitrine ◆ **she's rather ~** elle a beaucoup de poitrine, il y a du monde au balcon *

busy /ˈbɪzɪ/ LANGUAGE IN USE 27.5
ADJ 1 *[person]* (= *occupied*) occupé *(doing sth* à faire qch ; *with sth* à qch) ; (= *active*) énergique ◆ **he's ~ cooking** il est en train de faire la cuisine ◆ **he's ~ playing with the children** il est occupé à jouer avec les enfants ◆ **too ~ to do sth** trop occupé pour faire qch ◆ **he was ~ at his work** il était tout entier à *or* absorbé dans son travail ◆ **she's always ~** (= *active*) elle n'arrête pas ; (= *not free*) elle est toujours prise *or* occupée ◆ **as ~ as a bee** très occupé ◆ **she's a real ~ bee** * elle est toujours à s'activer, elle est débordante d'activité ◆ **to keep o.s. ~** trouver à s'occuper ◆ **to get ~** * s'y mettre
2 *[day]* chargé ; *[period]* de grande activité ; *[place]* plein de mouvement *or* d'animation ; *[street]* passant, animé ; *[town]* animé, grouillant d'activité ◆ **a ~ time** une période de grande activité ◆ **to keep a factory ~** fournir du travail à une usine ◆ **the shop is at its busiest in summer** c'est en été qu'il y a le plus d'affluence dans le magasin
3 *[telephone line, room etc]* occupé
VT ◆ **to ~ o.s.** s'appliquer, s'occuper *(doing sth* à faire qch ; *with sth* à qch)
N (‡ = *detective*) flic * *m*
COMP **Busy Lizzie** N impatiente *f*, impatiens *f*
busy signal N (US) tonalité *f* occupé *inv*

busybody /ˈbɪzɪˌbɒdɪ/ N fouineur *m*, -euse *f*

but /bʌt/ CONJ 1 *(coordinating)* mais ◆ **I would like to do it ~ I have no money** j'aimerais le faire, mais je n'ai pas d'argent ◆ **she was poor ~ she was honest** elle était pauvre, mais honnête
2 *(contradicting)* mais ◆ **he's not English ~ Irish** il n'est pas anglais, mais irlandais ◆ **he wasn't singing, ~ he was shouting** il ne chantait pas, plutôt il criait ◆ **poor, ~ happy** pauvre, mais heureux ◆ **she's like her sister, ~ thinner** elle ressemble à sa sœur, mais en plus mince ◆ **not once, ~ twice** pas une fois mais deux
3 *(subordinating)* **I never eat asparagus ~ I remember that evening** je ne mange jamais d'asperges sans me souvenir de cette soirée ◆ **never a day goes by ~ she complains about the weather** il ne se passe pas un jour sans qu'elle se plaigne du temps ◆ **it never rains ~ it pours** un malheur n'arrive jamais seul
4 *(set structures)*
◆ **but then** ◆ **Michael is selfish ~ then so was his father** Michael est égoïste, mais il faut dire que son père l'était aussi ◆ **he might score tonight, ~ then again, he's not been on form recently** peut-être qu'il marquera un but ce soir, mais il faut dire qu'il n'a pas la forme ces derniers temps
5 *(emphatic)* ◆ **~ that's crazy!** mais c'est insensé !
ADV seulement, ne ... que ◆ **she's ~ a child** *(liter)* ce n'est qu'une enfant ◆ **I cannot help ~ think** je suis bien obligé de penser, je ne peux m'empêcher de penser ◆ **the chocolate was placed where I couldn't help ~ see it** le chocolat était placé à un endroit où il était impossible de ne pas le voir ◆ **you can ~ try** *(to sb trying sth)* vous pouvez toujours essayer ; *(after sth has gone wrong)* ça valait quand même la peine d'essayer ◆ **if I could ~ tell you why** *(liter)* si je pouvais seulement vous dire pourquoi ◆ **she left ~ a few minutes ago** *(liter)* il n'y a que quelques minutes qu'elle est partie ◆ **Napoleon, to name ~ one, stayed here** Napoléon, pour n'en citer qu'un, a séjourné ici
PREP sauf, excepté ◆ **no one ~ me could do it** personne sauf moi ne pourrait le faire, je suis le seul à pouvoir *or* qui puisse le faire ◆ **they've all gone ~ me** ils sont tous partis sauf moi ◆ **who could do it ~ me?** qui pourrait le faire sinon moi ? ◆ **no one ~ him** personne d'autre que lui ◆ **France won all ~ two of its matches** la France a gagné tous ses matchs sauf deux ◆ **anything ~ that** tout mais pas ça ◆ **he didn't speak anything ~ Greek** il ne parlait que le grec ◆ **they gave us nothing ~ bread to eat** ils ne nous ont donné que du pain à manger ◆ **he's nothing ~ a thief** ce n'est qu'un voleur ◆ **there was nothing for it ~ to jump** il n'y avait plus qu'à sauter ◆ **the last house ~ one** l'avant-dernière maison ◆ **the next house ~ one** la deuxième maison (à partir d'ici), pas la maison voisine mais la suivante
◆ **but for** ◆ **~ for you/that I would be dead** sans vous/cela je serais mort ◆ **~ for his illness, we'd have gone on holiday** s'il n'avait pas été malade, nous serions partis en vacances ◆ **I could definitely live in Scotland, ~ for the weather** je pourrais tout à fait vivre en Écosse si le temps n'était pas si mauvais ◆ **the car park was empty ~ for a delivery van** le parking était vide, sauf pour une camionnette de livraison
N ◆ **no ~s about it!** il n'y a pas de mais (qui tienne) ! ; → **if**

butane /ˈbjuːteɪn/ N butane *m* ; *(US: for camping)* Butagaz ® *m* COMP **butane gas** N gaz *m* butane, Butagaz ® *m*

butch ‡ /bʊtʃ/ ADJ hommasse N gouine ‡ *f (hommasse)*

butcher /ˈbʊtʃəʳ/ N 1 *(for meat)* boucher *m* ◆ **at the ~'s** chez le boucher ◆ **to have a ~'s (hook)** ‡ *(Brit)* jeter un coup d'œil ; → RHYMING SLANG 2 *(US = candy etc seller)* vendeur *m* ambulant VT *[+ animal]* tuer, abattre ; *[+ person]* égorger ; *(fig)* massacrer

COMP **butcher meat** N viande *f* de boucherie
butcher's boy N garçon *m* boucher, livreur *m* *(du boucher)*
butcher's shop N boucherie *f (magasin)*
butcher's wife N (pl **butchers' wives**) bouchère *f*, femme *f* du *(or* de) boucher

butchery /ˈbʊtʃərɪ/ N 1 *(NonC)* *(lit)* abattage *m* ; *(fig)* boucherie *f*, massacre *m* 2 *(= slaughterhouse)* abattoir *m*

butler /ˈbʌtləʳ/ N maître *m* d'hôtel, majordome *m*

COMP **butler's pantry** N office *m*
butler's tray N (petit) plateau *m (de service)*

Butlins ® /ˈbʌtlɪnz/ N *(Brit)* *chaîne de villages de vacances*

BUTLINS

Chaîne de villages de vacances proposant logement, restauration et activités de loisirs pour tous les âges et toutes les bourses. Les distractions sont organisées par des animateurs vêtus d'un costume rouge et qui, pour cette raison, sont surnommés « redcoats ».

butt¹ /bʌt/ N *(for wine, rainwater etc)* (gros) tonneau *m*

butt² /bʌt/ N *(= end)* (gros) bout *m* ; *[of rifle]* crosse *f* ; *[of cigarette]* mégot *m* ; *(US* ⁑ *= cigarette)* clope* *f* ; *(US* ⁑ *= bottom)* cul*⁑ *m*

COMP **butt-cheeks**⁑ NPL fesses* *fpl*, cul*⁑ *m*
butt-naked⁑ ADJ, ADV *(esp US)* à poil⁑

butt³ /bʌt/ N *(= target)* cible *f* ; *(= earth mound)* butte *f* (de tir) ◆ **the ~s** le champ de tir, le polygone (de tir) ◆ **to be a ~ for ridicule** être un objet de risée, être en butte au ridicule ◆ **the ~ of a practical joker** la victime d'un farceur

butt⁴ /bʌt/ N coup *m* de tête ; *[of goat etc]* coup *m* de corne VT 1 *[goat]* donner un coup de corne à ; *[person]* donner un coup de tête à 2 *(= place end on)* abouter

► **butt in** VI *(= interfere)* s'immiscer dans les affaires des autres, intervenir ; *(= say sth)* dire son mot, mettre son grain de sel* ◆ **I don't want to ~ in** je ne veux pas déranger ◆ **to ~ in on sth** s'immiscer dans qch

► **butt into** VT FUS *[+ meeting, conversation]* intervenir dans, s'immiscer dans

► **butt out**⁑ VI *(US)* ◆ **to ~ out of sth** ne pas se mêler de qch ◆ **~ out!** mêle-toi de ce qui te regarde !*

butter /ˈbʌtəʳ/ N beurre *m* ◆ **he looks as if ~ wouldn't melt in his mouth** on lui donnerait le bon Dieu sans confession ; → **bread, peanut** VT *[+ bread etc]* beurrer ; *[+ vegetables]* mettre du beurre sur

COMP **butter bean** N *(Brit)* (gros) haricot *m* blanc
butter cloth N mousseline *f* à beurre, étamine *f*
butter cooler N pot *m* à (rafraîchir le) beurre
butter dish N beurrier *m*
butter icing N glaçage *m* au beurre
butter knife N (pl **butter knives**) couteau *m* à beurre
butter muslin N mousseline *f* à beurre, étamine *f* ; *(= dress material)* mousseline *f*
butter paper N papier *m* à beurre, papier *m* sulfurisé

► **butter up*** VT SEP *(esp Brit fig)* passer de la pommade* à

butterball* /ˈbʌtəbɔːl/ N *(US)* patapouf* *m*, rondouillard(e) *m(f)*

buttercup /ˈbʌtəkʌp/ N bouton *m* d'or, renoncule *f* des champs

buttered /ˈbʌtəd/ ADJ *[potatoes]* au beurre

butterfingers /ˈbʌtəˌfɪŋgəz/ N maladroit(e) *m(f)*, manche* *m* ◆ **~!** quel empoté tu fais !

butterfly /ˈbʌtəflaɪ/ N papillon *m* ◆ **to have butterflies in one's stomach*** avoir le trac* ◆ **to break a ~ on a wheel** *(Brit)* ne pas y aller avec le dos de la cuillère*

COMP **butterfly bush** N buddleia *m*
butterfly effect N effet *m* papillon
butterfly knot N nœud *m* papillon
butterfly net N filet *m* à papillons
butterfly nut N papillon *m*, écrou *m* à ailettes
butterfly stroke N brasse *f* papillon *inv*

buttermilk /ˈbʌtəmɪlk/ N babeurre *m*

butterscotch /ˈbʌtəskɒtʃ/ N caramel *m* dur (au beurre)

buttery /ˈbʌtərɪ/ ADJ *[taste]* de beurre ; *(= spread with butter)* *[bread]* beurré ; *[fingers]* couvert de beurre N *[of college, school]* dépense *f*, office *f*

buttock /ˈbʌtək/ N fesse *f* ◆ **~s** *[of person]* fesses *fpl* ; *[of animal]* croupe *f*

button /ˈbʌtn/ N 1 *[of garment, door, bell, lamp, fencing foil]* bouton *m* ◆ **chocolate ~s** pastilles *fpl* de chocolat ◆ **Buttons*** *(esp Brit: in hotel)* groom *m*, chasseur *m* ◆ **she knew which ~s to press*** **to get what she wanted** elle savait s'y prendre pour obtenir ce qu'elle voulait ◆ **to be (right) on the ~*** avoir (tout à fait) raison 2 *(Bot)* bouton *m* 3 *(US* ⁑ *= tip of chin)* pointe *f* de menton VT 1 (also **button up**) *[+ garment]* boutonner 2 ◆ **to ~ one's lip** ⁑ la fermer⁑ ◆ **~ your lip!, ~ it!** boucle-la !⁑, la ferme !⁑ VI *[garment]* se boutonner

COMP **button-down** ADJ *(lit)* *[collar]* boutonné ; *(fig = square)* conformiste
button lift N *(Ski)* téléski *m* à perche
button mushroom N (petit) champignon *m* de couche *or* de Paris
button-through ADJ *[skirt]* boutonné tout du long ◆ **~-through dress** robe *f* chemisier

buttoned-up* /ˈbʌtndˌʌp/ ADJ *[person]* coincé*

buttonhole /ˈbʌtnhəʊl/ N 1 *[of garment]* boutonnière *f* 2 *(Brit = flower)* fleur *f (portée à la boutonnière)* ◆ **to wear a ~** avoir *or* porter une fleur à sa boutonnière VT 1 *(fig)* *[+ person]* accrocher* 2 *(Sewing)* faire du point de boutonnière sur

COMP **buttonhole stitch** N *(Sewing)* point *m* de boutonnière

buttonhook /ˈbʌtnhʊk/ N tire-bouton *m*

buttress /ˈbʌtrɪs/ N *(Archit)* contrefort *m*, éperon *m* ; (also **flying buttress**) arc-boutant *m* ; *(fig)* *(= defence)* défense *f*, rempart *m* *(against* contre) ; *(= support)* pilier *m* *(of* de) VT *(Archit)* étayer ; *(fig)* *[+ argument]* étayer

butty* /ˈbʌtɪ/ N *(Brit dial)* sandwich *m*

buxom /ˈbʌksəm/ ADJ *[woman]* plantureuse

buy /baɪ/ (pret, ptp **bought**) VT 1 *(= purchase)* acheter *(sth from sb* qch à qn ; *sth for sb* qch pour *or* à qn) ; ◆ **to ~ o.s. sth** s'acheter qch ◆ **the things that money cannot ~** les choses qui ne s'achètent pas ◆ **to ~ petrol** prendre de l'essence ◆ **to ~ a train ticket** prendre un billet de train ◆ **to ~ a theatre ticket** réserver une place de théâtre ◆ **to ~ and sell goods** acheter et revendre des marchandises ◆ **to ~ a pig in a poke*** acheter chat en poche ◆ **to ~ sth cheap** acheter qch bon marché *or* pour une bouchée de pain ◆ **to ~ (one's way) into a company** *(Comm)* prendre une participation dans une entreprise ◆ **the victory was dearly bought** la victoire fut chèrement payée ◆ **I'd like to ~ you lunch** j'aimerais t'inviter à déjeuner ◆ **to ~ time** gagner du temps ◆ **£100,000 will ~ you a flat in Glasgow** avec 100 000 livres, vous pourrez vous acheter un appartement à Glasgow

2 *(= bribe)* *[+ person]* acheter, corrompre ◆ **to ~ one's way into a business** avoir recours à la corruption pour entrer dans une affaire

3 *(* = believe)* croire ◆ **he won't ~ that explanation** il n'est pas question qu'il avale* *subj* cette explication ◆ **they bought the whole story** ils ont avalé* *or* gobé* toute l'histoire ◆ **all right, I'll ~ it** (bon,) d'accord *or* je marche*

4 *(= die)* **to ~ it**⁑ *or* **~ the farm*** casser sa pipe*

N affaire *f* ◆ **that house is a good/bad ~** cette maison est une bonne/mauvaise affaire ◆ **tomatoes are a good ~ at the moment** les tomates sont bon marché en ce moment

COMP **buy-back** ADJ *[price, clause]* de rachat
buy-back option N option *f or* possibilité *f* de rachat

► **buy back** VT SEP racheter

ADJ ◆ **buy-back** → **buy**

► **buy in** VT SEP *(Brit)* *[+ goods]* s'approvisionner en, stocker ; *[+ stocks, shares]* acquérir, acheter

► **buy into** VT FUS 1 *[+ business, organization]* acheter des parts de ; *[+ industry]* investir dans 2 *(* = believe)* croire

► **buy off** VT SEP *(= bribe)* *[+ person, group]* acheter (le silence de) ◆ **policies designed to ~ off the working classes** des mesures destinées à s'attirer les votes des travailleurs

► **buy out** VT SEP *[+ business partner]* désintéresser, racheter la part de ◆ **he bought his brother out for $7,000** il a racheté la part de son frère pour 7 000 dollars ◆ **to ~ o.s. out** *(from army)* se racheter *(d'un engagement dans l'armée)*

► **buy over** VT SEP *(= bribe)* corrompre, acheter

► **buy up** VT SEP acheter tout ce qu'il y a de, rafler*

buyer /ˈbaɪəʳ/ N 1 *(gen)* acheteur *m*, -euse *f*, acquéreur *m* ◆ **house-/car-~s** les gens *mpl* qui achètent un logement/une voiture 2 *(for business, firm, shop etc)* acheteur *m*, -euse *f* (professionnel(le)) COMP **buyer's market** N marché *m* acheteur *or* à la hausse

buying /ˈbaɪɪŋ/ N achat *m*

COMP **buying group** N centrale *f* d'achat
buying power N pouvoir *m* d'achat
buying spree N ◆ **to go on a ~ spree** se mettre à dépenser sans compter, faire des folies *or* de folles dépenses

buyout /ˈbaɪaʊt/ N rachat *m* (d'entreprise) ◆ **leveraged ~** rachat *m* d'entreprise financé par l'endettement ; see also **management**

buzz /bʌz/ N 1 *[of insect]* bourdonnement *m*, vrombissement *m*

2 *[of conversation]* bourdonnement *m*, brouhaha *m* ◆ **a ~ of approval** un murmure d'approbation ◆ **slowly the ~ of conversation resumed** peu à peu le murmure des conversations a repris

3 *(* = telephone call)* coup *m* de fil* ◆ **to give sb a ~** donner *or* passer un coup de fil* à qn

4 *(Rad, Telec etc = extraneous noise)* friture *f*

5 *(* = sensation)* **driving fast gives me a ~, I get a ~ from driving fast** je prends mon pied quand je conduis vite⁑ ◆ **it gives you a ~, you get a ~ from it** *[drug]* tu t'éclates quand tu prends ça⁑

ADJ *(= trendy)* en vogue, dernier cri

VI 1 *[insect]* bourdonner, vrombir

2 *[ears]* tinter, bourdonner ◆ **my head is ~ing** j'ai des bourdonnements (dans la tête) ◆ **my head is ~ing with thoughts** j'ai la tête qui bourdonne d'idées *or* bourdonnante d'idées

3 *[hall, town]* être (tout) bourdonnant *(with* de)

VT 1 *(= call by buzzer)* *[+ person]* appeler (par interphone) ; *(US * = telephone)* donner *or* passer un coup de fil* à

2 *(in plane)* *[+ building]* raser ; *[+ other plane]* frôler

COMP **buzz bomb** N V1 *m inv*
buzz cut N coupe *f* tondeuse
buzz saw N scie *f* mécanique *or* circulaire
buzz word* N mot *m* à la mode

► **buzz about***, **buzz around*** VI s'affairer

► **buzz off** ‡ VI décamper*, foutre le camp‡

buzzard /ˈbʌzəd/ N 1 *(= falcon)* buse *f* ; *(= vulture)* urubu *m* 2 *(pej)* ◆ **old** ~ *(= man)* vieux schnock* *m* ; *(= woman)* vieille bique‡ *f*

buzzer /ˈbʌzəʳ/ N 1 *(= intercom)* interphone *m* 2 *(= factory hooter)* sirène *f*, sifflet *m* 3 *(electronic: on cooker, timer etc)* sonnerie *f*

buzzing /ˈbʌzɪŋ/ N 1 ⇒ **buzz** 2 *(in ears)* tintement *m*, bourdonnement *m* ADJ *[insect]* bourdonnant, vrombissant ; *[sound]* confus, sourd

BVDs ® /ˌbiːviːˈdiːz/ NPL *(US)* sous-vêtements *mpl* (d'homme)

b/w (abbrev of **black and white**) NB

by /baɪ/

1 PREPOSITION 3 COMPOUNDS
2 ADVERB

When **by** is the second element in a phrasal verb, eg **go by**, **put by**, **stand by**, look up the verb. When it is part of a set combination, eg **by myself**, **by the sea**, **by degrees**, **by night**, **surrounded by**, look up the other word.

1 - PREPOSITION

1 [= close to] à côté de, près de ◆ **come and sit ~ me** viens t'asseoir à côté de *or* près de moi ◆ **the house ~ the church** la maison à côté de l'église ◆ **her cousins are over there, and she's sitting ~ them** ses cousins sont là-bas et elle est assise à côté (d'eux) BUT **sitting ~ the fire** assis auprès *or* au coin du feu ◆ **I've got it ~ me** je l'ai sous la main

by it and **by them**, when **them** refers to things, are translated by **à côté** alone:

◆ **her bag was on the table and her keys right ~ it** son sac était sur la table et ses clés juste à côté

2 [= past] à côté de ◆ **he rushed ~ me without seeing me** dans sa précipitation il est passé à côté de moi sans me voir

3 [= via] par ◆ **which route did you come ~?** par où êtes-vous passés ? ◆ **I went ~ Dover** je suis passé par Douvres ◆ **~ land and (~) sea** par terre et par mer ◆ **he came in ~ the window** il est entré par la fenêtre

4 [= not later than] pour ◆ **I'll be back ~ midnight** je serai de retour pour minuit ◆ **can you do it ~ tomorrow?** pouvez-vous le faire pour demain ? ◆ **applications must be submitted ~ 21 April** les candidatures doivent nous parvenir pour le 21 avril

5 [in year, on date, on day] ◆ **~ 1990 the figure had reached ...** en 1990, ce chiffre avait atteint ... ◆ **~ 2010 the figure will have reached ...** en 2010, cette somme aura atteint ... ◆ **~ 30 September we had paid out $500** au 30 septembre nous avions payé 500 dollars ◆ **~ yesterday it was clear that ...** dès hier on savait que ..., il était déjà clair hier que ... ◆ **~ tomorrow/Tuesday, I'll be in France** demain/mardi, je serai en France ; → **now, then, time**

6 [= according to] ◆ **~ my calculations** d'après mes calculs ◆ **~ my watch it is 9 o'clock** il est 9 heures à ma montre ◆ **~ the terms of Article 1** aux termes de l'article 1

7 [* = for] ◆ **it's fine** *or* **all right ~ me** je n'ai rien contre* ◆ **if that's okay ~ you** si ça vous va

8 [margin of difference] de ◆ **wider ~ a metre** plus large d'un mètre ◆ **the bullet missed me ~ inches** la balle m'a raté de quelques centimètres ; → **far, half**

9 [dimensions] ◆ **a room three metres ~ four** une pièce de trois mètres sur quatre

10 [points of compass] ◆ **south ~ south-west** sud quart sud-ouest ◆ **south-west ~ south** sud-ouest quart sud

11 [in oaths] ◆ **"I swear by Almighty God to ..."** "je jure devant Dieu de ..." ◆ **~ heck*, there's money to be made in this business!** fichtre* ! il y a vraiment de l'argent à gagner dans cette affaire !

12 [method, means, manner] à ◆ **to do sth ~ hand/~ machine** faire qch à la main/à la machine ◆ **to sell ~ the metre/the kilo** vendre au mètre/au kilo ◆ **to pay ~ the hour** payer à l'heure ◆ **to rent a house ~ the month** louer une maison au mois

◆ **by** + *-ing* en ◆ **~ leaving early he missed the rush** en partant de bonne heure il a évité la foule ◆ **~ saving hard he managed to buy a small flat** en économisant beaucoup, il a réussi à s'acheter un petit appartement

13 [with means of transport] en ◆ **~ bus/car/taxi** en bus/voiture/taxi ◆ **~ plane/train** en avion/train ◆ **~ bicycle** à bicyclette, à vélo

14 [with agent] par ◆ **he was killed ~ lightning** il a été tué par la foudre ◆ **he had been warned ~ his neighbour** il avait été prévenu par son voisin ◆ **I was surprised ~ their reaction** j'ai été surpris par leur réaction ◆ **he had a daughter ~ his first wife** il a eu une fille de sa première femme

When there is no clear agent, the active is more natural in French:

◆ **he was disappointed ~ it** ça l'a déçu

15 [= created, written by] de ◆ **a painting ~ Van Gogh** un tableau de Van Gogh ◆ **who's it ~?** c'est de qui ?

16 [set structures]

◆ **by and by** *(= in a minute)* dans un instant ; *(= soon)* bientôt ◆ **I'll be with you ~ and ~** je suis à vous dans un instant ◆ **you'll be sorry ~ and ~** tu vas bientôt le regretter, tu ne seras pas long à le regretter ◆ **~ and ~ we heard voices** au bout d'un certain temps, nous avons entendu des voix ; see also **compounds**

◆ **by and large** globalement ◆ **~ and large, I still think this is true** globalement, je crois toujours que c'est vrai

◆ **by the way, by the by** au fait, à propos ◆ **~ the way, did you know it was Ann's birthday?** au fait *or* à propos, tu savais que c'était l'anniversaire d'Ann ?

2 - ADVERB

[= along, past] ◆ **he'll be ~ any minute** il sera là dans un instant ◆ **a train hurtled ~** un train passa à toute allure

3 - COMPOUNDS

by-and-by * N *(hum)* ◆ **in the sweet ~-and-~** un de ces jours

by-election N élection *f* (législative) partielle

by-law N *(Brit)* arrêté *m* (municipal)

by-line N *(Press)* signature *f (en tête d'un article)*

by-play N *(Theat)* jeu *m* de scène secondaire

by-product N *(lit)* sous-produit *m*, dérivé *m* ; *(fig)* sous-produit *m*, conséquence *f* (indirecte)

by-road N chemin *m* détourné, chemin *m* de traverse

by-your-leave N ◆ **without so much as a ~-your-leave** sans même demander la permission

bye[1] /baɪ/ N ◆ **by the ~** à propos, au fait
COMP **bye-election** N ⇒ **by-election** ; → **by**
bye-law N ⇒ **by-law** ; → **by**

bye[2] * /baɪ/ EXCL (abbrev of **goodbye**) au revoir ! ◆ **~ for now!** à tout à l'heure !

bye-bye * /ˈbaɪˈbaɪ/ EXCL au revoir ! N *(baby talk)* ◆ **to go to ~s** aller au dodo*, aller faire dodo*

Byelorussia /ˌbjeləʊˈrʌʃə/ N Biélorussie *f*

Byelorussian /ˌbjeləʊˈrʌʃən/ ADJ biélorusse N Biélorusse *mf*

bygone /ˈbaɪgɒn/ ADJ passé, d'autrefois ◆ **in ~ days** dans l'ancien temps, jadis N ◆ **let ~s be ~s** oublions le passé, passons l'éponge (là-dessus)

BYO /ˌbiːwaɪˈəʊ/ N *(Austral)* (abbrev of **bring your own**) *restaurant non autorisé à vendre de l'alcool où l'on peut apporter son propre vin, etc*

BYOB /ˌbiːwaɪəʊˈbiː/ (abbrev of **bring your own bottle** *or* **beer** *or* **booze**) apportez à boire

bypass /ˈbaɪpɑːs/ N 1 *(= road)* route *f or* bretelle *f* de contournement ◆ **the Carlisle ~** la route qui contourne Carlisle 2 *(Tech = pipe etc)* conduit *m* de dérivation, by-pass *m inv* 3 *(Elec)* dérivation *f*, by-pass *m inv* 4 *(Med)* pontage *m* ◆ **he's had a charisma ~*** il est totalement dépourvu de charme ◆ **he's had a humour ~*** il n'a pas le sens de l'humour VT 1 *[+ town, village]* contourner, éviter 2 *[+ source of supply, material]* éviter d'utiliser, se passer de ; *[+ part of programme, method]* omettre ; *[+ regulations]* contourner ◆ **he ~ed his foreman and went straight to see the manager** il est allé trouver le directeur sans passer par le contremaître
COMP **bypass operation** N, **bypass surgery** N *(NonC) (Med)* pontage *m*

byre /ˈbaɪəʳ/ N *(dial)* étable *f*

bystander /ˈbaɪˌstændəʳ/ N spectateur *m*, -trice *f*

byte /baɪt/ N *(Comput)* octet *m*

byway /ˈbaɪweɪ/ N chemin *m* (écarté) ; *(fig) [of subject]* élément *m* annexe ; → **highway**

byword /ˈbaɪwɜːd/ N *(Brit)* ◆ **he** *or* **his name was a ~ for meanness** son nom était devenu synonyme d'avarice

Byzantine /baɪˈzæntaɪn/ ADJ 1 *(lit)* byzantin, de Byzance 2 *(fig) (= complicated)* d'une complexité byzantine

Byzantium /baɪˈzæntɪəm/ Byzance

C c

C, c /siː/ **N** 1 *(= letter)* C, c *m* ◆ **C for Charlie** ≃ C comme Camille 2 *(Mus)* do *m*, ut *m* ; → **key, middle** 3 *(Comput)* C *m* 4 *(Scol = mark)* assez bien *(12 sur 20)* **ABBR** 1 (abbrev of **Celsius, Centigrade**) C 2 *(US etc)* abbrev of **cent** 3 abbrev of **century** 4 (abbrev of **circa**) vers 5 abbrev of **centime** 6 abbrev of **cubic**

C4 *(Brit TV)* (abbrev of **Channel 4**) → **channel**

C5 *(Brit TV)* (abbrev of **Channel 5**) → **channel**

CA¹ abbrev of **California**

CA² /siːˈeɪ/ **N** 1 (abbrev of **chartered accountant**) → **charter** 2 (abbrev of **Central America**) → **central**

C/A *(Fin)* 1 (abbrev of **capital account**) → **capital** 2 (abbrev of **current account**) → **current** 3 (abbrev of **credit account**) → **credit**

CAA /ˌsiːeɪˈeɪ/ **N** 1 *(Brit)* (abbrev of **Civil Aviation Authority**) → **civil** 2 *(US)* abbrev of **Civil Aeronautics Authority**

CAB /ˌsiːeɪˈbiː/ **N** *(Brit)* (abbrev of **Citizens' Advice Bureau**) → **citizen**

cab /kæb/ **N** 1 *(= taxi)* taxi *m* ; *(horse-drawn)* fiacre *m* ◆ **by ~** en taxi, en fiacre 2 *[of lorry, train] (= driver's cab)* cabine *f* **COMP cab rank, cab stand N** station *f* de taxis

cabal /kəˈbæl/ **N** cabale *f*

cabala /kəˈbɑːlə/ **N** ⇒ **cabbala**

cabalistic /ˌkæbəˈlɪstɪk/ **ADJ** ⇒ **cabbalistic**

cabana /kəˈbɑːnə/ **N** *(US)* cabine *f* (de plage)

cabaret /ˈkæbəreɪ/ **N** cabaret *m* ; *(= floor show)* spectacle *m* (de cabaret)

cabbage /ˈkæbɪdʒ/ **N** chou *m* ◆ **he was little more than a ~⁑ after the accident** il n'était plus qu'un légume * après l'accident
COMP cabbage lettuce N laitue *f* pommée
cabbage rose N rose *f* cent-feuilles
cabbage tree N palmiste *m*
cabbage white (butterfly) N piéride *f* du chou

cabbala /kəˈbɑːlə/ **N** cabale *f (juive)*

cabbalistic /ˌkæbəˈlɪstɪk/ **ADJ** cabalistique

cabbie*, cabby* /ˈkæbɪ/, **cabdriver** /ˈkæbˌdraɪvəʳ/ **N** *[of taxi]* chauffeur *m* (de taxi), taxi * *m* ; *[of horse-drawn cab]* cocher *m*

caber /ˈkeɪbəʳ/ **N** *(Scot Sport)* tronc *m* ◆ **to toss the ~** lancer le tronc ◆ **tossing the ~** le lancement du tronc

cabin /ˈkæbɪn/ **N** *(= hut)* cabane *f*, hutte *f* ; *[of boat]* cabine *f* ; *(Rail = signal box)* cabine *f* d'aiguillage ; *[of lorry, train] (= driver's cabin)* cabine *f* ; → **log¹**
COMP cabin boy N mousse *m*
cabin class N *(on ship)* deuxième classe *f*
cabin crew N *(on plane)* équipage *m*
cabin cruiser N cruiser *m*
cabin trunk N malle-cabine *f*

cabinet /ˈkæbɪnɪt/ **N** 1 *(= furniture)* meuble *m* (de rangement) ; *(glass-fronted)* vitrine *f* ; *(= filing cabinet)* classeur *m* ; → **medicine**
2 *(Brit Parl)* cabinet *m*, ≃ Conseil *m* des ministres ◆ **to form a ~** former un gouvernement
3 *(US Pol) organe qui conseille le Président*
COMP *(Parl) [crisis, decision, post]* ministériel
Cabinet meeting N réunion *f* du Cabinet *or* du Conseil des ministres
Cabinet minister N membre *m* du Conseil des ministres ; → **reshuffle**

> **CABINET**
>
> Au Royaume-Uni, **Cabinet** désigne l'équipe gouvernementale. Composée d'une vingtaine de ministres choisis par le Premier ministre, ce conseil soumet des projets de lois au Parlement et défend la politique gouvernementale.
>
> Aux États-Unis en revanche, le **Cabinet** est un organe purement consultatif, qui conseille le président. Ses membres n'appartiennent pas nécessairement au monde politique ; ce sont souvent de hauts fonctionnaires choisis pour leurs compétences et dont la nomination est approuvée par le Sénat. Le « kitchen cabinet » est un groupe de conseillers officieux du président.

cabinetmaker /ˈkæbɪnɪtˌmeɪkəʳ/ **N** ébéniste *m*

cabinetmaking /ˈkæbɪnɪtˌmeɪkɪŋ/ **N** ébénisterie *f*

cable /ˈkeɪbl/ **N** *(gen)* câble *m* ; *(= nautical measure)* encablure *f* ◆ **by ~** par câble ; → **overhead** **VT** *[+ news]* câbler, télégraphier *(sth to sb* qch à qn) ; *[+ city, homes]* câbler ◆ **to ~ sb** *(= send cable to)* câbler à qn
COMP cable car N téléphérique *m* ; *(on rail)* funiculaire *m*
cable-knit ADJ *[sweater]* à torsades
cable-laying N pose *f* de câbles ◆ **~-laying ship** câblier *m*
cable network N réseau *m* câblé
cable railway N funiculaire *m*
cable release N *(Phot)* déclencheur *m* souple
cable stitch N *(Knitting)* point *m* de torsade
cable television N télévision *f* par câble

cablecast /ˈkeɪblkɑːst/ *(TV)* **N** émission *f* de télévision par câble **VT** transmettre par câble

cablegram † /ˈkeɪblgræm/ **N** câblogramme † *m*

cablevision /ˈkeɪblˌvɪʒən/ **N** ⇒ **cable television** ; → **cable**

cableway /ˈkeɪblweɪ/ **N** benne *f* suspendue

cabling /ˈkeɪblɪŋ/ **N** *(NonC) (= cables)* câbles *mpl* ; *(= process)* câblage *m*

caboodle⁑ /kəˈbuːdl/ **N** ◆ **the whole ~** tout le bazar *, tout le tintouin *

caboose /kəˈbuːs/ **N** *(Brit Naut)* coquerie *f* ; *(US Rail)* fourgon *m* de queue

cabotage /ˌkæbəˈtɑːʒ/ **N** *fait de réserver le trafic intérieur aux transporteurs d'un pays*

ca' canny* /ˈkɔːˈkænɪ/ **EXCL** *(Scot)* doucement !

cacao /kəˈkɑːəʊ/ **N** *(= bean)* cacao *m* ; *(= tree)* cacaoyer *m*

cache /kæʃ/ **N** 1 *(= place)* cachette *f* ◆ **a ~ of weapons** une cache d'armes 2 *(Comput)* mémoire *f* tampon **VT** mettre dans une cachette **COMP cache memory N** *(Comput)* mémoire cache

cachepot /ˈkæʃˌpɒt, kæʃˈpəʊ/ **N** cache-pot *m*

cachet /ˈkæʃeɪ/ **N** *(all senses)* cachet *m*

cack⁑ /kæk/ **N** *(Brit lit, fig)* merde*⁑ *f* **COMP cack-handed* ADJ** *(Brit)* maladroit

cackle /ˈkækl/ **N** *[of hen]* caquet *m* ; *[of people] (= laugh)* gloussement *m* ; *(= talking)* caquetage *m*, jacasserie *f* **VI** *[hens]* caqueter ; *[people] (= laugh)* glousser ; *(= talk)* caqueter, jacasser

cacophonous /kæˈkɒfənəs/ **ADJ** cacophonique, discordant

cacophony /kæˈkɒfənɪ/ **N** cacophonie *f*

cactus /ˈkæktəs/ **N** (pl **cactuses** *or* **cacti** /ˈkæktaɪ/) cactus *m*

CAD /kæd/ **N** (abbrev of **computer-aided design**) CAO *f*

cad †* /kæd/ **N** goujat *m*, mufle *m*

cadaver /kəˈdeɪvəʳ, kəˈdɑːvəʳ/ **N** cadavre *m*

cadaverous /kəˈdævərəs/ **ADJ** *(lit, fig) [complexion]* cadavéreux ; *[appearance]* cadavérique

CADCAM /ˈkædˌkæm/ **N** (abbrev of **computer-aided design and manufacture**) CFAO *f*

caddie /ˈkædɪ/ *(Golf)* **N** caddie *or* caddy *m* **VI** ◆ **to ~ for sb** être le caddie de qn **COMP caddie car, caddie cart N** *(= trolley)* chariot *m* ; *(motorized)* chariot *m* électrique, golfette *f*

caddish †* /ˈkædɪʃ/ **ADJ** *[person]* grossier, mufle ◆ **a ~ thing to do** une muflerie

caddy¹ /ˈkædɪ/ **N** 1 (also **tea caddy**) boîte *f* à thé 2 *(US = shopping trolley)* chariot *m*, caddie ® *m*

caddy² /ˈkædɪ/ **N** ⇒ **caddie**

cadence /ˈkeɪdəns/ N (= *intonation*) modulation *f* (de la voix) ; (= *rhythm*) cadence *f*, rythme *m* ; (*Mus*) cadence *f*

cadenza /kəˈdenzə/ N (*Mus*) cadence *f*

cadet /kəˈdet/ N 1 (*Mil etc*) élève *m* officier (*d'une école militaire ou navale*) ; (*Police*) élève *mf* agent de police ; (*Scol*) *collégien qui poursuit une préparation militaire* 2 (= *younger son*) cadet *m* ADJ cadet

COMP **cadet corps** N (*in school*) peloton *m* de préparation militaire ; (*Police*) corps *m* d'élèves policiers (*de moins de 18 ans*)
cadet school N école *f* militaire

cadge * /kædʒ/ (*Brit*) VT ◆ **to ~ £10 from** *or* **off sb** taper* qn de 10 livres ◆ **to ~ a meal from** *or* **off sb** se faire payer* un repas par qn ◆ **to ~ a lift from** *or* **off sb** se faire emmener en voiture par qn

cadger /ˈkædʒəʳ/ N (*Brit*) parasite *m* ; [*of money*] tapeur* *m*, -euse* *f* ; [*of meals*] pique-assiette *mf inv*

Cadiz /kəˈdɪz/ N Cadix

cadmium /ˈkædmɪəm/ N cadmium *m*

cadre /ˈkædrɪ/ N (*Mil, Pol, fig*) cadre *m*

CAE /ˌsiːeɪˈiː/ N (abbrev of **computer-aided engineering**) IAO *f*

caecum, cecum (*US*) /ˈsiːkəm/ N (pl **caeca** /ˈsiːkə/) caecum *m*

Caesar /ˈsiːzəʳ/ N César *m* ◆ **Julius ~** Jules César *m* ◆ **~ salad** salade *f* César

Caesarea /ˌsiːzəˈrɪə/ N Césarée

Caesarean, Caesarian /siːˈzeərɪən/ ADJ césarien ◆ **~ (operation** *or* **section)** (*Med*) césarienne *f*

caesium, cesium (*US*) /ˈsiːzɪəm/ N cæsium *m*

caesura /sɪˈzjʊərə/ N (pl **caesuras** *or* **caesurae** /sɪˈzjʊəriː/) césure *f*

CAF /ˌsiːeɪˈef/ (abbrev of **cost and freight**) → **cost**

café /ˈkæfeɪ/ N (*Brit*) snack(-bar) *m*

COMP **café bar** N café *m*
café society N (*NonC*) beau monde *m*

cafeteria /ˌkæfɪˈtɪərɪə/ N (*gen*) cafétéria *f* ; (*US Scol*) cantine *f* ; (*US Univ*) restaurant *m* universitaire

cafetière /ˌkæfəˈtjeəʳ/ N cafetière *f* à piston

caff ‡ /kæf/ N ⇒ **café**

caffein(e) /ˈkæfiːn/ N caféine *f* ◆ **~(e)-free** sans caféine

caftan /ˈkæftæn/ N caf(e)tan *m*

cage /keɪdʒ/ N cage *f* ; [*of elevator*] cabine *f* ; (*Min*) cage *f* VT 1 (also **cage up**) mettre en cage, encager 2 * (= *imprison*) mettre en prison, mettre à l'ombre* COMP **cage(d) bird** N oiseau *m* en cage *or* captif

cagey * /ˈkeɪdʒɪ/ ADJ [*person*] (= *discreet*) cachottier ; (= *suspicious*) méfiant ◆ **she is ~ about her age** elle n'aime pas avouer son âge ◆ **the company was ~ about releasing its results** la compagnie était réticente à divulguer ses résultats

cagily * /ˈkeɪdʒəlɪ/ ADV avec méfiance

cagoule /kəˈguːl/ N anorak *m*, K-way ® *m*

cahoots * /kəˈhuːts/ N ◆ **to be in ~ (with)** être de mèche (avec)*

CAI /ˌsiːeɪˈaɪ/ N (abbrev of **computer-aided instruction**) EAO *m*

caiman /ˈkeɪmən/ N (pl **-mans**) caïman *m*

Cain /keɪn/ N Caïn *m* ◆ **to raise ~** * (= *make a noise*) faire un boucan de tous les diables* ; (= *make a fuss*) faire tout un scandale (*about* à propos de)

cairn /keən/ N 1 (= *pile of stones*) cairn *m* 2 (also **cairn terrier**) cairn *m*

cairngorm /ˈkeəngɔːm/ N 1 (= *stone*) quartz *m* fumé 2 ◆ **Cairngorm Mountains, Cairngorms** monts *mpl* Cairngorm

Cairo /ˈkaɪərəʊ/ N Le Caire

caisson /ˈkeɪsən/ N (*Mil, Naut*) caisson *m*

cajole /kəˈdʒəʊl/ VT cajoler ◆ **to ~ sb into doing sth** faire faire qch à qn à force de cajoleries

cajolery /kəˈdʒəʊlərɪ/ N cajoleries *fpl*

Cajun /ˈkeɪdʒən/ (*US*) ADJ cajun N Cajun *mf*

cake /keɪk/ N 1 gâteau *m* ; (= *fruit cake*) cake *m* ; (= *sponge cake*) génoise *f*, gâteau *m* de Savoie ◆ **~s and ale** (*fig*) plaisirs *mpl* ◆ **it's selling** *or* **going like hot ~s** * cela se vend comme des petits pains ◆ **it's a piece of ~** * c'est du gâteau* ◆ **he takes the ~** * à lui le pompon* ◆ **that takes the ~!** * ça, c'est le bouquet* *or* le comble ! ◆ **they want a slice of the ~, they want a fair share of the ~** ils veulent leur part du gâteau ◆ **you can't have your ~ and eat it** on ne peut pas avoir le beurre et l'argent du beurre ; → **Christmas, fish**

2 [*of chocolate*] tablette *f* ; [*of wax, tobacco*] pain *m* ◆ **~ of soap** savonnette *f*, (pain *m* de) savon *m*

VI [*mud*] sécher, former une croûte ; [*blood*] (se) coaguler

VT ◆ **mud ~d his forehead** la boue formait une croûte sur son front ; see also **caked**

COMP **cake mix** N préparation *f* pour gâteaux
cake pan N (*US*) moule *m* à gâteau
cake shop N pâtisserie *f*
cake stand N assiette *f* montée *or* à pied ; (*tiered*) serviteur *m* ; (*in shop*) présentoir *m* (à gâteaux)
cake tin N (*for storing*) boîte *f* à gâteaux ; (*Brit*) (*for baking*) moule *m* à gâteaux

caked /keɪkt/ ADJ [*blood*] coagulé ; [*mud*] séché ◆ **his clothes were ~ with** *or* **in blood/mud** ses vêtements étaient maculés de sang séché/crottés

cakewalk /ˈkeɪkwɔːk/ N (*Mus*) cake-walk *m*

CAL /ˌsiːeɪˈel/ N (abbrev of **computer-aided learning**) EAO *m*

Cal. abbrev of **California**

calabash /ˈkæləbæʃ/ N (= *fruit*) calebasse *f*, gourde *f* ; (= *tree*) calebassier *m* ; (*Mus*) calebasse *f* (*utilisée comme bongo ou maraca*)

calaboose * /ˈkæləbuːs/ N (*US*) taule‡ *f*

calabrese /ˌkæləˈbreɪzɪ/ N brocoli *m*

Calabria /kəˈlæbrɪə/ N Calabre *f*

Calabrian /kəˈlæbrɪən/ ADJ calabrais N Calabrais(e) *m(f)*

calamine /ˈkæləmaɪn/ N calamine *f* COMP **calamine lotion** N lotion *f* calmante à la calamine

calamitous /kəˈlæmɪtəs/ ADJ [*event, decision*] calamiteux ; [*person*] infortuné

calamity /kəˈlæmɪtɪ/ N calamité *f*

calcareous /kælˈkeərɪəs/ ADJ calcaire COMP **calcareous clay** N marne *f*

calcification /ˌkælsɪfɪˈkeɪʃən/ N calcification *f*

calcify /ˈkælsɪfaɪ/ VT calcifier VI se calcifier

calcination /ˌkælsɪˈneɪʃən/ N calcination *f*

calcine /ˈkælsaɪn/ VT calciner VI se calciner

calcium /ˈkælsɪəm/ N calcium *m*

COMP **calcium chloride** N chlorure *m* de calcium
calcium oxide N oxyde *m* de calcium

calculable /ˈkælkjʊləbl/ ADJ calculable

calculate /ˈkælkjʊleɪt/ VT 1 [+ *speed, weight, distance, numbers*] calculer (*also Math*) ◆ **to ~ the cost of sth** calculer le prix de qch ◆ **he ~d that he would have enough money to do it** il a calculé qu'il aurait assez d'argent pour le faire

2 (= *reckon, judge*) [+ *probability, consequence, risk*] évaluer ◆ **to ~ one's chances of escape** évaluer les chances qu'on a de s'évader

3 (*US* = *suppose*) supposer, estimer

4 (*fig*) ◆ **it is ~d to do …** (= *intended*) c'est destiné à faire … ◆ **their actions were ~d to terrify farmers into abandoning their land** leurs actions étaient destinées à terrifier les fermiers afin qu'ils abandonnent leurs terres ◆ **this was not ~d to reassure me** (= *didn't have the effect of*) cela n'était pas fait pour me rassurer ◆ **their statement was hardly ~d to deter future immigrants** leur déclaration n'était certes pas faite pour dissuader de futurs immigrants

VI (*Math*) calculer, faire des calculs

► **calculate on** VT FUS (= *reckon on*) ◆ **to ~ on doing sth** compter faire qch, avoir l'intention de faire qch ◆ **she ~d on spending three days in Glasgow** elle comptait passer trois jours à Glasgow ◆ **he is calculating on delaying the elections until spring** il a l'intention de repousser les élections jusqu'au printemps

calculated /ˈkælkjʊleɪtɪd/ ADJ [*action, decision, insult*] délibéré ◆ **a ~ gamble** *or* **risk** un risque calculé ; → **calculate**

calculating /ˈkælkjʊleɪtɪŋ/ ADJ 1 (= *scheming, unemotional*) [*person*] calculateur (-trice *f*) ◆ **to give sb a ~ look** regarder qn d'un air calculateur ◆ **his eyes were ~ and calm** son regard était calme et calculateur ◆ **a cold and ~ criminal** un criminel froid et calculateur 2 (= *cautious*) prudent, prévoyant 3 ◆ **~ machine** ⇒ **calculator 1**

calculation /ˌkælkjʊˈleɪʃən/ N 1 (*Math, fig*) calcul *m* ◆ **to make a ~** faire *or* effectuer un calcul ◆ **by my ~s** d'après mes calculs ◆ **it upset his ~s** cela a déjoué ses calculs 2 (*NonC* = *scheming*) attitude *f* calculatrice ◆ **cold, cruel ~** une attitude calculatrice, froide et cruelle

calculator /ˈkælkjʊleɪtəʳ/ N 1 (= *machine*) machine *f* à calculer, calculatrice *f* ; (*pocket*) calculatrice *f* (de poche), calculette *f* 2 (= *table of figures*) table *f*

calculus /ˈkælkjʊləs/ N (pl **calculuses** *or* **calculi** /ˈkælkjʊlaɪ/) (*Math, Med*) calcul *m* ; → **differential, integral**

Calcutta /kælˈkʌtə/ N Calcutta

caldron /ˈkɔːldrən/ N ⇒ **cauldron**

Caledonia /ˌkælɪˈdəʊnɪə/ N Calédonie *f*

Caledonian /ˌkælɪˈdəʊnɪən/ ADJ calédonien N (*liter*) Calédonien(ne) *m(f)*

calendar /ˈkæləndəʳ/ N 1 calendrier *m* 2 (= *directory*) annuaire *m* ◆ **university ~** (*Brit*) ≈ livret *m* de l'étudiant 3 (*Jur*) rôle *m* VT (= *index*) classer (*par ordre de date*) ; (= *record*) inscrire sur un calendrier

COMP **calendar month** N mois *m* calendaire
calendar year N année *f* calendaire

calends /ˈkæləndz/ NPL calendes *fpl* ◆ **at the Greek ~** (*fig*) aux calendes grecques

calf¹ /kɑːf/ N (pl **calves**) 1 (= *young cow or bull*) veau *m* ◆ **a cow in** *or* **with ~** une vache pleine ; → **fat** 2 (also **calfskin**) (cuir *m* de) veau *m*, vachette *f* ; (*for shoes, bags*) box (-calf) *m* 3 [*of elephant*] éléphanteau *m* ; [*of deer*] faon *m* ; [*of whale*] baleineau *m* ; [*of buffalo*] buffletin *m* COMP **calf love** N amour *m* juvénile

calf² /kɑːf/ N (pl **calves**) (*Anat*) mollet *m*

caliber /ˈkælɪbəʳ/ N (*US*) ⇒ **calibre**

calibrate /ˈkælɪbreɪt/ VT [+ *instrument, tool*] étalonner, calibrer ; [+ *level, amount*] calibrer

calibration /ˌkælɪˈbreɪʃən/ N étalonnage *m*, calibrage *m*

calibre, caliber (*US*) /ˈkælɪbəʳ/ N (*lit, fig*) calibre *m* ◆ **a man of his ~** un homme de cette envergure *or* de ce calibre

calico /ˈkælɪkəʊ/ N (pl **calicoes** *or* **calicos**) calicot *m* ; (*US*) indienne *f*

Calif. abbrev of **California**

California /ˌkælɪˈfɔːnɪə/ N Californie *f*

Californian /ˌkælɪˈfɔːnɪən/ ADJ californien N Californien(ne) *m(f)*

californium /ˌkælɪˈfɔːnɪəm/ N californium *m*

calipers /ˈkælɪpəz/ NPL (US) ⇒ **callipers**

caliph /ˈkeɪlɪf/ N calife *m*

calisthenics /ˌkælɪsˈθenɪks/ N (NonC) gymnastique *f* suédoise

calk¹ /kɔːk/ VT *[+ shoe, horseshoe]* munir de crampons N *[of shoe, horseshoe]* crampon *m*

calk² /kɔːk/ VT *[+ drawing, design]* décalquer, calquer

call /kɔːl/ LANGUAGE IN USE 26.3, 27

N 1 *(= shout)* appel *m*, cri *m* ◆ **within ~** à portée de (la) voix ◆ **a ~ for help** un appel au secours ; → **roll**

2 *[of bird]* cri *m* ; *[of bugle, trumpet]* sonnerie *f* ; *[of drum]* batterie *f*

3 (also **telephone call**) coup *m* de téléphone, coup *m* de fil* ◆ **to make a ~** téléphoner, passer un coup de téléphone *or* de fil* ◆ **there's a ~ for you** on te demande au téléphone, il y a un appel pour toi ◆ **I have a ~ for you from London** *[operator]* on vous appelle de Londres, j'ai un appel pour vous de Londres ◆ **I'm putting your ~ through** *[operator]* je vous mets en communication ◆ **I want to pay for the three ~s I made** je voudrais régler mes trois communications (téléphoniques) ; → **local, long¹, trunk**

4 *(= summons, invitation) (also Comput)* appel *m* ; *[of justice]* exigence *f* ; *[of conscience]* voix *f* ; *(Theat) (= actor's reminder)* appel *m* ; (also **curtain call**) rappel *m* ; *(= vocation)* vocation *f* ; *(Rel: in Presbyterian church)* nomination *f* ◆ **to have** *or* **receive a ~ to ...** *(Rel)* être nommé pasteur à ... ◆ **to be on ~** *[doctor etc]* être de garde ◆ **to give sb an early morning ~** réveiller qn de bonne heure ◆ **I'd like a ~ at 7am** j'aimerais qu'on me réveille *subj* à 7 heures ◆ **they put out a ~ for him** *(Telec, Rad etc)* on l'a fait appeler, on a lancé un appel à son intention ◆ **~ for capital** *(Fin)* appel *m* de fonds ◆ **the ~ of the unknown** l'attrait *m* de l'inconnu ◆ **the ~ of the sea** l'appel *m* du large ◆ **the ~ of duty** l'appel *m* du devoir ◆ **a ~ of nature** *(euph)* un besoin naturel

5 *(= short visit: also Med)* visite *f* ◆ **to make** *or* **pay a ~ on sb** rendre visite à qn, aller voir qn ◆ **I have several ~s to make** *(gen)* j'ai plusieurs choses à faire ; *[doctor]* j'ai plusieurs visites à faire ◆ **place** *or* **port of ~** *(Naut)* (port *m* d')escale *f* ; see also **pay**

6 *(= demand)* ◆ **there have been ~s for new security measures** on a demandé de nouvelles mesures de sécurité ◆ **there's not much ~ for these articles** ces articles ne sont pas très demandés ◆ **money repayable at** *or* **on ~/at three months'** ~ *(Fin)* argent *m* remboursable sur demande/à trois mois ◆ **I have many ~s on my time** je suis très pris *or* très occupé ◆ **the UN has too many ~s on its resources** on fait trop appel aux ressources de l'ONU ◆ **to have first ~ on sb's time** avoir la priorité dans l'emploi du temps de qn

7 *(= need)* ◆ **there is no ~ for you to worry** il n'y a pas lieu de vous inquiéter ◆ **there was** *or* **you had no ~ to say that** vous n'aviez aucune raison de dire cela, vous n'aviez pas à dire cela

8 *(Bridge)* annonce *f* ; *(Cards)* demande *f* ◆ **whose ~ is it?** à qui de parler *or* d'annoncer ? ◆ **it's your/their** *etc* **~** *(fig)* c'est à toi/eux *etc* de décider

VT 1 *[+ person]* appeler ; *(from afar)* héler ; *[+ sb's name]* appeler, crier ◆ **to ~ sb in/out/up** *etc* crier à qn d'entrer/de sortir/de monter *etc* ◆ **"hello!" he ~ed** "bonjour !" cria-t-il ◆ **let's ~ it a day!*** ça suffira pour aujourd'hui ! ◆ **we ~ed it a day* at 3 o'clock** à 3 heures, on a décidé d'arrêter ; → **shot, tune**

2 *(= give name to)* appeler ◆ **to be ~ed** s'appeler ◆ **what are you ~ed?** comment vous appelez-vous ? ◆ **they ~ each other by their surnames** ils s'appellent par leur nom de famille ◆ **to ~ sth by its proper name** désigner qch par son vrai nom ◆ **he is ~ed after his father** on lui a donné *or* il porte le nom de son père ◆ **he ~s himself a colonel** il se prétend colonel ◆ **are you ~ing me a liar?** dites tout de suite que je suis un menteur ◆ **he ~ed her a liar** il l'a traitée de menteuse ◆ **she ~s me lazy and selfish** elle dit que je suis fainéant et égoïste, elle me traite de fainéant et d'égoïste ; → **name, so, spade**

3 *(= consider)* trouver, considérer ◆ **would you ~ French a difficult language?** diriez-vous que le français est une langue difficile ? ◆ **I ~ that a shame** je trouve que c'est (vraiment) dommage ◆ **that's what I ~ rudeness** c'est ce que j'appelle de la grossièreté ◆ **shall we ~ it $10?** *(agreeing on price)* disons 10 dollars ?

4 *(= summon)* appeler, convoquer ; *(= waken)* réveiller ◆ **to ~ a doctor** appeler *or* faire venir un médecin ◆ **~ me at eight** réveillez-moi à huit heures ◆ **London ~ing** *(Rad)* ici Londres ◆ **to ~ the police/an ambulance** appeler la police/une ambulance ◆ **the fire brigade was ~ed** on a appelé les pompiers ◆ **~ me a taxi!** appelez-moi un taxi ! ◆ **to ~ a meeting** convoquer une assemblée ◆ **a meeting has been ~ed for Monday** une réunion est prévue lundi ◆ **he felt ~ed to be a teacher** sa vocation était d'enseigner ; → **case¹, duty, evidence, witness**

5 *(= telephone)* appeler ◆ **don't ~ us, we'll ~ you** ce n'est pas la peine de nous appeler, on vous appellera

6 *(Bridge)* ◆ **to ~ three spades** annoncer *or* demander trois piques ◆ **to ~ game** demander la sortie

7 *(US Sport) [+ game]* arrêter, suspendre

8 *(phrases)* → **account, arms, banns, bar¹, being, bluff², close¹**

VI 1 *[person]* appeler, crier ; *[bird]* pousser un cri ◆ **I have been ~ing for five minutes** cela fait cinq minutes que j'appelle ◆ **to ~ (out) to sb** appeler qn ; *(from afar)* héler qn

2 *(= visit:* also **call in**) passer ◆ **she ~ed (in) to see her mother** elle est passée voir sa mère ◆ **he was out when I ~ed (in)** il n'était pas là quand je suis passé chez lui ◆ **will you ~ (in) at the grocer's?** voulez-vous passer *or* vous arrêter chez l'épicier ? ◆ **to ~ (in) at a port/at Dover** *(Naut)* faire escale dans un port/à Douvres

3 *(= telephone)* appeler ◆ **who's ~ing?** c'est de la part de qui ? ◆ **to ~ in sick** téléphoner pour dire qu'on est malade

COMP **call centre** N *(Telec)* centre *m* d'appels
call girl N call-girl *f*
call-in, call-in program N *(US Rad)* émission *f* à lignes ouvertes
call letters NPL *(US Telec)* indicatif *m* (d'appel)
call loan N *(Fin)* prêt *m* exigible
call money N *(NonC: Fin)* taux *m* de l'argent au jour le jour
call number N *(US) [of library book]* cote *f*
call option N *(Stock Exchange)* option *f* d'achat
call-out charge, call-out fee N frais *mpl* de déplacement
call-over N appel *m* nominal ; *(Mil)* appel *m*
call screening N *(Telec)* filtrage *m* des appels
call sign, call signal N *(Telec)* indicatif *m* (d'appel)
call slip N *(in library)* fiche *f* de prêt
call-up N *(= military service)* appel *m* (sous les drapeaux), convocation *f* ; *[of reservists]* rappel *m* ◆ **general ~-up** *(in wartime)* mobilisation *f* générale, levée *f* en masse ◆ **to get a ~-up into a squad** *(Sport)* être sélectionné pour jouer dans une équipe
call-up papers NPL papiers *mpl* militaires
call waiting N *(Telec)* signal *m* d'appel

► **call aside** VT SEP *[+ person]* prendre à part

► **call away** VT SEP ◆ **to be called away on business** être obligé de s'absenter pour affaires ◆ **to be ~ed away from a meeting** devoir quitter une réunion

► **call back** *(Telec)*

VI rappeler

VT SEP rappeler

► **call down** VT SEP 1 *[+ curses]* appeler *(on sb* sur la tête de qn)

2 *(US * = scold)* enguirlander*, attraper

► **call for** VT FUS 1 *(= summon) [+ person]* appeler ; *[+ food, drink]* demander, commander ; *(fig) [+ courage]* exiger, nécessiter ◆ **to ~ for measures against** demander que des mesures soient prises contre ◆ **the situation ~s for a new approach** la situation nécessite *or* exige une nouvelle approche ◆ **this contract ~s for the development of ...** ce contrat prévoit le développement de ... ◆ **strict measures are ~ed for** des mesures strictes sont nécessaires, il est nécessaire de prendre des mesures strictes ◆ **such rudeness was not ~ed for** une telle grossièreté n'était pas justifiée ◆ **to ~ for sb's resignation** réclamer la démission de qn

2 *(= collect)* ◆ **I'll call for you at 6 o'clock** je passerai vous prendre à 6 heures ◆ **he ~ed for the books** il est passé chercher les livres

► **call forth** VT SEP *(liter) [+ protest]* soulever, provoquer ; *[+ remark]* provoquer

► **call in**

VI → **call**

VT SEP 1 *[+ doctor]* faire venir, appeler ; *[+ police]* appeler ◆ **he was ~ed in to lead the inquiry** on a fait appel à lui pour mener l'enquête

2 *[+ money, library books]* faire rentrer ; *[+ banknotes]* retirer de la circulation ; *[+ faulty machines etc]* rappeler ◆ **the bank ~ed in his overdraft** la banque l'a obligé à couvrir son découvert *or* à approvisionner son compte ◆ **to ~ in one's chips*** *(esp Brit fig)* utiliser son influence

► **call off**

VI se décommander

VT SEP 1 *[+ appointment, trip, wedding]* annuler ; *[+ agreement]* rompre, résilier ; *[+ match] (= cancel)* annuler ; *(= cut short)* interrompre ◆ **to ~ off a deal** résilier *or* annuler un marché ◆ **to ~ off a strike** *(before it starts)* annuler une grève ; *(after it starts)* mettre fin à une grève ◆ **they ~ed off their engagement** ils ont rompu leurs fiançailles ◆ **he ~ed off their engagement** il a rompu ses fiançailles

2 *[+ dog]* rappeler ◆ **to ~ off the dogs** *(fig)* cesser ses attaques

► **call on** VT FUS 1 *(= visit person)* rendre visite à, aller *or* passer voir ◆ **our representative will ~ on you** notre représentant passera vous voir

2 (also **call upon**) ◆ **to call on sb to do sth** *(= invite)* prier qn de faire qch ; *(= order)* mettre qn en demeure de faire qch ◆ **I now ~ on Mr Austin to speak** je laisse maintenant la parole à M. Austin ◆ **to ~ on sb for sth** demander *or* réclamer qch à qn ◆ **to ~ on God** invoquer le nom de Dieu

► **call out**

VI pousser un *or* des cri(s) ◆ **to ~ out for sth** demander qch à haute voix ◆ **to ~ out to sb** héler qn

VT SEP 1 *[+ doctor]* appeler ; *[+ troops, fire brigade, police]* faire appel à ◆ **to ~ workers out (on strike)** lancer un ordre de grève

2 *(for duel)* appeler sur le terrain

► **call over**

VT SEP appeler ◆ **he ~ed me over to see the book** il m'a appelé pour que je vienne voir le livre

N ◆ **call-over** → **call**

► **call round** VI ◆ **to call round to see sb** passer voir qn ◆ **I'll ~ round in the morning** je passerai dans la matinée

► **call up**
VT SEP 1 *(Mil)* *[+ reinforcements]* appeler ; *[+ troops]* mobiliser ; *[+ reservists]* rappeler
2 *(esp US Telec)* appeler (au téléphone), téléphoner à
3 *(= recall)* *[+ memories]* évoquer
4 *(Comput)* ◆ **to call up a file** ouvrir un fichier
N ◆ **call-up** → **call**

► **call upon** VT FUS ⇒ **call on 2**

Callanetics ® /ˌkæləˈnetɪks/ N *(NonC)* *gymnastique douce caractérisée par la répétition fréquente de légers exercices musculaires*

callbox /ˈkɔːlbɒks/ N *(Brit)* cabine *f* (téléphonique) ; *(US)* ≃ dispositif *m or* borne *f* d'urgence

callboy /ˈkɔːlbɔɪ/ N *(Theat)* avertisseur *m* ; *[of hotel]* chasseur *m*, groom *m*

caller /ˈkɔːlə^r/ LANGUAGE IN USE 27.5 N *(= visitor)* visiteur *m*, -euse *f* ; *(Brit Telec)* demandeur *m*, -euse *f* COMP **caller display, caller ID display** N affichage du numéro

calligramme, calligram *(US)* /ˈkælɪgræm/ N calligramme *m*

calligrapher /kəˈlɪgrəfə^r/ N calligraphe *mf*

calligraphic /ˌkælɪˈgræfɪk/ ADJ calligraphique

calligraphy /kəˈlɪgrəfɪ/ N calligraphie *f*

calling /ˈkɔːlɪŋ/ N 1 *(= occupation)* métier *m*, état † *m* ; *(= vocation)* vocation *f* ◆ **he is a doctor by ~** il est médecin par vocation ◆ **a man dedicated to his ~** un homme qui se consacre entièrement à son métier 2 *(NonC)* *[of meeting etc]* convocation *f* COMP **calling card** N carte *f* de visite

calliope /kəˈlaɪəpɪ/ N orgue *m* à vapeur

callipers /ˈkælɪpəz/ NPL *(Brit)* 1 *(Math)* compas *m* 2 *(Med)* *(for limb)* gouttière *f* ; *(for foot)* étrier *m* ; *(= leg-irons)* appareil *m* orthopédique

callisthenics /ˌkælɪsˈθenɪks/ N *(NonC)* ⇒ **calisthenics**

callosity /kæˈlɒsɪtɪ/ N callosité *f*

callous /ˈkæləs/ ADJ 1 *(fig)* dur, sans cœur ◆ **~ to** insensible à 2 *(Med)* calleux

calloused /ˈkæləst/ ADJ calleux

callously /ˈkæləslɪ/ ADV *[treat, behave, act, speak]* avec dureté, durement ; *[decide, suggest]* cyniquement

callousness /ˈkæləsnɪs/ N *[of person, statement]* dureté *f* ; *[of behaviour]* froideur *f*, insensibilité *f* ; *[of crime]* inhumanité *f*

callow /ˈkæləʊ/ ADJ inexpérimenté, novice ◆ **a ~ youth** un blanc-bec *

callus /ˈkæləs/ N (pl **calluses**) cal *m*, durillon *m*

callused /ˈkæləst/ ADJ ⇒ **calloused**

calm /kɑːm/ ADJ calme ◆ **the weather is ~** le temps est calme ◆ **the sea was dead ~** la mer était d'huile ◆ **to grow ~** se calmer ◆ **to keep** *or* **remain ~** garder son calme *or* sang-froid ◆ **keep ~!** du calme ! ◆ **(cool,) ~ and collected** maître (maîtresse *f*) de soi (-même) ◆ **on ~ reflection** après avoir réfléchi calmement ◆ **~(er) waters** *(lit, fig)* eaux *fpl* (plus) calmes N 1 *(= calm period)* période *f* de calme *or* de tranquillité ; *(after movement, agitation)* accalmie *f* ◆ **a dead ~** *(Naut)* un calme plat ◆ **the ~ before the storm** *(lit, fig)* le calme qui précède la tempête 2 *(= calmness)* calme *m* ; *(under stress)* calme *m*, sang-froid *m* VT calmer VI *[sea, wind]* calmir *(liter)*, se calmer

► **calm down** VI se calmer, s'apaiser ◆ **~ down!** du calme !, calmez-vous ! VT SEP *[+ person]* calmer, apaiser

calming /ˈkɑːmɪŋ/ ADJ calmant, apaisant

calmly /ˈkɑːmlɪ/ ADV calmement

calmness /ˈkɑːmnɪs/ N *[of person]* calme *m* ; *(under stress)* sang-froid *m* ; *[of sea, elements]* calme

Calor gas ® /ˈkæləgæs/ N *(Brit)* butane *m*, Butagaz ® *m*

caloric /ˈkælərɪk/ ADJ thermique N chaleur *f* COMP **caloric energy** N énergie *f* thermique

calorie /ˈkælərɪ/ N calorie *f* COMP **calorie-conscious** * ADJ ◆ **she's too ~-conscious** elle pense trop aux calories **calorie-controlled diet** N ◆ **to be on a ~-controlled diet** suivre un régime basses calories ; → **low**[1]

calorific /ˌkæləˈrɪfɪk/ ADJ calorifique COMP **calorific value** N valeur *f* calorifique

calque /kælk/ N *(also Ling)* calque *m (on* de)

calumniate /kəˈlʌmnɪeɪt/ VT calomnier

calumny /ˈkæləmnɪ/ N calomnie *f* ; *(Jur)* diffamation *f*

calvary /ˈkælvərɪ/ N *(= monument)* calvaire *m* ◆ **Calvary** le Calvaire

calve /kɑːv/ VI *[animal]* vêler, mettre bas; *[glacier]* vêler

calves /kɑːvz/ NPL of **calf**

Calvinism /ˈkælvɪnɪzəm/ N calvinisme *m*

Calvinist /ˈkælvɪnɪst/ ADJ, N calviniste *mf*

Calvinistic /ˌkælvɪˈnɪstɪk/ ADJ calviniste

calyces /ˈkeɪlɪsiːz/ NPL of **calyx**

calypso /kəˈlɪpsəʊ/ N calypso *m*

calyx /ˈkeɪlɪks/ N (pl **calyxes** *or* **calyces**) *[of flower]* calice *m*

calzone /kælˈtsəʊnɪ/ N calzone *f*, pizza *f* soufflée

CAM /kæm/ N (abbrev of **computer-aided manufacture**) FAO *f*

cam /kæm/ N 1 *(on camshaft)* came *f* 2 * (also **camshaft**) arbre *m* à cames

camaraderie /ˌkæməˈrɑːdərɪ/ N camaraderie *f*

camber /ˈkæmbə^r/ N *[of road]* profil *m*, pente *f* transversale ; *[of beam]* cambrure *f*, courbure *f* ; *[of plane wing]* courbure *f* ; *[of boat deck]* tonture *f* VT *[+ road]* bomber ; *[+ beam]* cambrer ; *[+ deck]* donner une tonture à VI *[beam]* être cambré ; *[road]* bomber, être bombé

Cambodia /kæmˈbəʊdɪə/ N Cambodge *m*

Cambodian /kæmˈbəʊdɪən/ ADJ cambodgien N 1 Cambodgien(ne) *m(f)* 2 *(= language)* khmer *m*

Cambrian /ˈkæmbrɪən/ ADJ *[period]* cambrien COMP **Cambrian Mountains** NPL monts *mpl* Cambriens

cambric /ˈkeɪmbrɪk/ N batiste *f*

Cambs abbrev of **Cambridgeshire**

camcorder /ˈkæmˌkɔːdə^r/ N caméscope *m*

came /keɪm/ VB pt of **come**

camel /ˈkæməl/ N *(gen)* chameau *m* ; (also **she-camel**) chamelle *f* ; *(= dromedary)* dromadaire *m* ; (also **racing camel**) méhari *m* ; → **straw** COMP *(in colour)* *[coat]* (de couleur) fauve *inv* **the Camel Corps** N *(Mil)* les méharistes *mpl* **camel hair, camel's hair** N poil *m* de chameau ADJ *[brush, coat]* en poil de chameau **camel train** N caravane *f* de chameaux

camellia /kəˈmiːlɪə/ N camélia *m*

cameo /ˈkæmɪəʊ/ N 1 *(= object)* camée *m* 2 *(Cine)* ◆ **~ (part** *or* **appearance)** brève apparition *f (d'une grande vedette)*

camera /ˈkæmərə/ N 1 *(stills)* appareil *m* (photographique), appareil-photo *m* ; *(film, video)* caméra *f* ◆ **on ~** filmé, enregistré ; → **aerial, capture, colour, film** 2 *(Jur)* ◆ **in ~** à huis clos COMP **camera crew** N *(Cine, TV)* équipe *f* de prise de vues **camera obscura** N chambre *f* noire *(appareil)* **camera operator** N caméraman *m* (caméramans *pl*), cameraman *m* (cameramen *pl*), cadreur *m* **camera phone** N (téléphone) *m* portable *m* appareil photo **camera-ready copy** N *(Typ)* copie *f* prête à la reproduction **camera-shy** ADJ qui déteste être pris en photo

⚠ In French, **caméra** only means a film or video camera.

cameraman /ˈkæmərəmən/ N (pl **-men**) caméraman *m* (caméramans *pl*), cadreur *m* ; *(on credits)* "prise de vue(s)"

camerawork /ˈkæmərəwɜːk/ N *(NonC)* prise *f* de vue(s)

Cameroon /ˌkæməˈruːn/ N Cameroun *m*

Cameroonian /ˌkæməˈruːnɪən/ ADJ camerounais N Camerounais(e) *m(f)*

camiknickers /ˈkæmɪˌnɪkəz/ NPL chemise-culotte *f* ; *(modern)* teddy *m*

camisole /ˈkæmɪsəʊl/ N caraco *m*

camomile /ˈkæməʊmaɪl/ N camomille *f* COMP **camomile shampoo** N shampoing *m* à la camomille **camomile tea** N (infusion *f* de) camomille *f*

camouflage /ˈkæməflɑːʒ/ N camouflage *m* VT camoufler

camp[1] /kæmp/ N 1 *(lit)* camp *m* ; *(less permanent)* campement *m* ◆ **to be in ~** camper ◆ **to go to ~** partir camper ◆ **to break ~** lever le camp ◆ **to set up ~** installer son camp ; *(fig)* s'installer ; → **concentration, foot, holiday, pitch**[1] 2 *(fig)* camp *m*, parti *m* ◆ **in the same ~** dans le même camp, du même bord ◆ **the Blair ~** les partisans de Blair, le camp de Blair VI camper ◆ **to go ~ing** partir camper COMP **camp chair** N ⇒ **camping chair** ; → **camping** **camp counsellor** N *(US Scol)* animateur *m*, -trice *f (de camp de vacances)* **camp follower** N *(fig)* sympathisant(e) *m(f)* ; *(Mil † = prostitute)* prostituée *f*, fille *f* à soldats * ; *(Mil † = civilian worker) civil accompagnant une armée* **camp ground** N ⇒ **camping ground** ; → **camping** **camp meeting** N *(US Rel)* rassemblement *m* religieux *(en campement ou sous un chapiteau)* **camp site** N ⇒ **camping site** ; → **camping** **camp stool** N ⇒ **camping stool** ; → **camping** **camp stove** N ⇒ **camping stove** ; → **camping**

► **camp out** VI camper, vivre sous la tente ◆ **we'll have to ~ out in the kitchen** * nous allons devoir camper *or* il va falloir que nous campions *subj* dans la cuisine

camp[2] * /kæmp/ ADJ 1 *(= affected)* *[person, behaviour, talk]* affecté, maniéré ; *(= overdramatic)* *[person]* cabotin ; *[gestures]* théâtral ; *(= affecting delight in bad taste)* qui aime le kitsch, qui fait parade de mauvais goût ; *(= fashionable because of poor taste)* kitsch *inv* 2 *(= effeminate)* efféminé ; *(= homosexual)* *[man]* qui fait pédé ‡ *or* tapette ‡ ; *[manners, clothes]* de pédé ‡, de tapette ‡ ◆ **to be as ~ as a row of tents** * être pédé comme un phoque ‡ N (also **high camp**) *(of manners)* affectation *f* ; *(effeminate)* manières *fpl* efféminées VT ◆ **to ~ it up** cabotiner

campaign /kæmˈpeɪn/ N *(Mil, fig)* campagne *f* ◆ **to lead** *or* **conduct** *or* **run a ~ for/against** mener une campagne *or* faire campagne pour/contre ; → **advertising, election, publicity** VI *(Mil)* faire campagne ; *(fig)* mener une *or* faire campagne *(for* pour ; *against* contre) COMP **campaign worker** N *(Pol)* membre *m* de l'état-major *(d'un candidat)*

campaigner /kæm'peɪnəʳ/ N ◆ **old** ~ (= *war veteran*) vétéran *m* ◆ **a** ~ **for/against electoral reform** un(e) militant(e) pour/contre la réforme électorale ◆ **a human rights/peace/environmental** ~ un(e) militant(e) des droits de l'homme/de la paix/de la protection de l'environnement ◆ **his qualities as a** ~ (*Pol*) ses qualités en tant que candidat en campagne (électorale)

Campania /kæm'peɪnɪə/ N Campanie *f*

campanile /ˌkæmpə'niːlɪ/ N campanile *m*

campanology /ˌkæmpə'nɒlədʒɪ/ N (*NonC*) art *m* du carillonnement

campbed /kæmp'bed/ N (*Brit*) lit *m* de camp

camper /'kæmpəʳ/ N [1] (= *person*) campeur *m*, -euse *f* [2] (*also* ~ **van**) camping-car *m*

campfire /'kæmpfaɪəʳ/ N feu *m* de camp

camphone /'kæmfəʊn/ N (téléphone *m*) portable *m* appareil photo

camphor /'kæmfəʳ/ N camphre *m*

camphorated /'kæmfəreɪtɪd/ ADJ camphré
COMP **camphorated oil** N huile *f* camphrée

camping /'kæmpɪŋ/ N camping *m* (*activité*)
COMP **camping chair** N chaise *f* de camping, chaise *f* pliante
Camping gas N (*Brit* = *gas*) butane *m* ; (*US* = *stove*) camping-gaz ® *m inv*
camping ground, camping site N (*commercialized*) (terrain *m* de) camping *m* ; (*clearing etc*) endroit *m* où camper
camping stool N pliant *m*
camping stove N réchaud *m* de camping, camping-gaz ® *m inv*
camping van N camping-car *m*, autocaravane *f* ; → **camp**[1]

campion /'kæmpɪən/ N (= *plant*) lychnis *m*

campus /'kæmpəs/ N (pl **campuses**) (*Univ*) (*gen*) campus *m* ; (= *building complex*) campus *m*, complexe *m* universitaire ; (*fig*) monde *m* universitaire ; → **off, on** COMP **campus police** N (*US Univ*) vigiles *mpl*

campy‡ /'kæmpɪ/ ADJ ⇒ **camp**[2] **adj**

CAMRA /'kæmrə/ N (*Brit*) (abbrev of **Campaign for Real Ale**) *association qui cherche à améliorer la qualité de la bière*

camshaft /'kæmʃɑːft/ N arbre *m* à cames

can[1] /kæn/ LANGUAGE IN USE 3, 4, 9.2, 15.4
MODAL AUX VB (neg **cannot**, cond, pret **could**) [1] (*indicating possibility: in neg improbability*) ◆ **the situation** ~ **change from day to day** la situation peut changer d'un jour à l'autre ◆ **it could be true** cela pourrait être vrai, il se peut que cela soit vrai ◆ **she could still decide to go** elle pourrait encore décider d'y aller ◆ **you could be making a big mistake** tu fais peut-être *or* tu es peut-être en train de faire une grosse erreur ◆ ~ **he have done it already?** est-il possible qu'il l'ait déjà fait ? ◆ **could he have done it without being seen?** est-ce qu'il aurait pu le faire *or* lui aurait-il été possible de le faire sans être vu ? ◆ ~ *or* **could you be hiding something from us?** est-il possible *or* se peut-il que vous nous cachiez *subj* quelque chose ? ◆ **he could have changed his mind without telling you** il aurait pu changer d'avis sans vous le dire ◆ **(perhaps) he could have forgotten** il a peut-être oublié ◆ **it could have been you who got hurt** cela aurait aussi bien pu être vous le blessé ◆ **you can't be serious!** (ce n'est pas possible,) vous ne parlez pas sérieusement ! ◆ **that cannot be!** † c'est impossible ! ◆ **as big/pretty** *etc* **as** ~ *or* **could be** aussi grand/joli *etc* qu'il est possible de l'être ◆ **as soon as** ~ *or* **could be** aussitôt *or* dès que possible, le plus vite possible ◆ **he can't have known about it until you told him** (il est) impossible qu'il l'ait su avant que vous (ne) lui en ayez parlé ◆ **she can't be very clever if she failed this exam** elle ne doit pas être très intelligente pour avoir été recalée à cet examen ◆ **things can't be as bad as you say they are** la situation n'est sûrement pas aussi mauvaise que tu le dis

[2] (*stressed, expressing astonishment*) **he CAN'T be dead!** ce n'est pas possible, il n'est pas mort ! ◆ **how CAN you say that?** comment pouvez-vous *or* osez-vous dire ça ? ◆ **where CAN he be?** où peut-il bien être ? ◆ **what CAN it be?** qu'est-ce que cela peut bien être ? ◆ **what COULD she have done with it?** qu'est-ce qu'elle a bien pu en faire ?

[3] (= *am etc able to*) (je) peux *etc* ◆ **he** ~ **lift the suitcase if he tries hard** il peut soulever la valise s'il fait l'effort nécessaire ◆ **help me if you** ~ aidez-moi si vous (le) pouvez ◆ **more cake? – no, I really couldn't** encore du gâteau ? – non, je n'ai vraiment plus faim ◆ **he will do what he** ~ il fera ce qu'il pourra, il fera son possible ◆ **he will help you all he** ~ il vous aidera de son mieux ◆ ~ **you come tomorrow?** pouvez-vous venir demain ? ◆ **he couldn't speak because he had a bad cold** il ne pouvait pas parler parce qu'il avait un mauvais rhume ◆ **I could have done that 20 years ago but can't now** il y a 20 ans j'aurais pu le faire mais (je ne peux) plus maintenant ◆ **he could have helped us if he'd wanted to** il aurait pu nous aider s'il l'avait voulu ◆ **he could have described it but he refused to do so** il aurait pu *or* su le décrire mais il a refusé (de le faire)

[4] (= *know how to*) (je) sais *etc* ◆ **he** ~ **read and write** il sait lire et écrire ◆ **he** ~ **speak Italian** il parle italien, il sait parler (l')italien ◆ **she could not swim** elle ne savait pas nager

[5] (*with verbs of perception*) ◆ **I** ~ **see you** je vous vois ◆ **they could hear him speak** ils l'entendaient parler ◆ ~ **you smell it?** tu le sens ? ◆ **I could see them coming in** je les voyais entrer *or* qui entraient ◆ **he could hear her shouting** il l'entendait crier

[6] (= *have the right to, have permission to*) (je) peux *etc* ◆ **you** ~ **go** vous pouvez partir ◆ ~ **I have some milk? – yes, you** ~ puis-je avoir du lait ? – mais oui, bien sûr ◆ **could I have a word with you? – yes, of course you could** est-ce que je pourrais vous parler un instant (s'il vous plaît) ? – oui bien sûr ◆ **I could have left earlier but decided to stay** j'aurais pu partir plus tôt, mais j'ai décidé de rester ◆ **I can't go out** je ne peux pas sortir, je n'ai pas le droit de sortir ◆ **I couldn't leave until the meeting ended** il m'était impossible de partir *or* je ne pouvais pas partir avant la fin de la réunion

[7] (*indicating suggestion*) ◆ **you could try telephoning him** tu pourrais (toujours) lui téléphoner ◆ **you could have been a little more polite** (*indicating reproach*) tu aurais pu être un peu plus poli ◆ **you could have told me before** tu aurais pu me le dire avant *or* plus tôt

[8] (= *be occasionally capable of*) ◆ **she** ~ **be very unpleasant** elle peut (parfois) être très désagréable ◆ **it** ~ **be very cold here** il peut faire très froid ici, il arrive qu'il fasse très froid ici

[9] (*: "could" = *want to*) ◆ **I could smack him !** je le giflerais !, je pourrais le gifler ! ◆ **I could have smacked him** je l'aurais giflé ◆ **I could have wept** j'en aurais pleuré

COMP **can-do** * ADJ (*US*) [*person, organization*] dynamique

can[2] /kæn/ N [1] (*for milk, oil, water, petrol*) bidon *m* ; (*for garbage*) boîte *f* à ordures, poubelle *f* ◆ **(to be left) to carry the** ~ * (*Brit*) payer les pots cassés

[2] [*of preserved food*] boîte *f* (de conserve) ; [*of hair spray, deodorant*] bombe *f*, aérosol *m* ◆ **a** ~ **of fruit** une boîte de fruits (en conserve) ◆ **a** ~ **of beer/cola** une canette *or* une boîte de bière/coca ◆ **meat in** ~**s** de la viande en boîte *or* en conserve ◆ **a** ~ **of worms** * un sac de nœuds * ◆ **to open a** ~ **of worms** * ouvrir la boîte de Pandore (*liter*), déclencher un sac de nœuds *

[3] (*Cine*) [*of film*] boîte *f* ◆ **it's in the** ~ * c'est dans la boîte

[4] (*US* ‡) (= *lavatory*) waters *mpl*, chiottes‡ *fpl* ; (= *buttocks*) postérieur * *m*

[5] (*US* ‡ = *jail*) taule‡ *f*, prison *f*

VT [1] [+ *food*] mettre en boîte(s) *or* en conserve ◆ ~**ned fruit/salmon** fruits *mpl*/saumon *m* en boîte *or* en conserve ◆ ~**ned food,** ~**ned goods** conserves *fpl* ◆ ~**ned heat** (*US*) méta ® *m* ◆ ~**ned music** * musique *f* enregistrée ◆ ~**ned laughter** (*Rad, TV*) rires *mpl* en conserve *or* préenregistrés ◆ **to be** ~**ned**‡ (*fig* = *drunk*) être rétamé‡ *or* rond * ◆ ~ **it!**‡ (*US*) ferme-la ! *, la ferme ! *

[2] (*US* * = *dismiss from job*) virer *, renvoyer
COMP **can opener** N ouvre-boîtes *m inv*

Canaan /'keɪnən/ N terre *f or* pays *m* de C(h)anaan

Canaanite /'keɪnənaɪt/ N C(h)ananéen(ne) *m(f)*

Canada /'kænədə/ N Canada *m*

Canadian /kə'neɪdɪən/ ADJ (*gen*) canadien ; [*ambassador, embassy*] du Canada, canadien N Canadien(ne) *m(f)* ; → **French**
COMP **Canadian elk** N orignal *m*
Canadian English N (= *language variety*) anglo-canadien *m*, anglais *m* du Canada
Canadian French N (= *language variety*) franco-canadien *m*, français *m* du Canada

canal /kə'næl/ N [1] canal *m* [2] (*Anat*) conduit *m*, canal *m* ; → **alimentary**
COMP **canal barge, canal boat** N chaland *m*, péniche *f*
the Canal Zone N (*Brit: Suez*) la zone du canal de Suez ; (*US: Panama*) la zone du canal de Panama

canalization /ˌkænəlaɪ'zeɪʃən/ N canalisation *f*

canalize /'kænəlaɪz/ VT canaliser

canapé /'kænəpeɪ/ N (*Culin*) canapé *m*

canard /kæ'nɑːd/ N canard * *m*, bobard * *m*

Canaries /kə'neərɪz/ NPL ⇒ **Canary Islands** ; → **canary**

canary /kə'neərɪ/ N [1] (= *bird*) canari *m*, serin *m* [2] (= *wine*) vin *m* des Canaries
COMP (*also* **canary yellow**) (de couleur) jaune serin *inv*, jaune canari *inv*
canary grass N alpiste *m*
the Canary Islands, the Canary Isles NPL les (îles *fpl*) Canaries *fpl*
canary seed N (= *millet*) millet *m*

canasta /kə'næstə/ N canasta *f*

Canberra /'kænbərə/ N Canberra

cancan /'kænkæn/ N (*also* **French cancan**) cancan *m*

cancel /'kænsəl/ LANGUAGE IN USE 21.4 VT [1] [+ *reservation, room booked, travel tickets, plans*] annuler ; (= *annul, revoke*) [+ *agreement, contract*] résilier, annuler ; [+ *order, arrangement, meeting, performance, debt*] annuler ; [+ *cheque*] faire opposition à ; [+ *taxi, coach or car ordered, appointment, party*] décommander, annuler ; [+ *stamp*] oblitérer ; [+ *mortgage*] lever ; [+ *decree, will*] révoquer ; [+ *application*] retirer ; [+ *ticket*] (= *punch*) poinçonner ; (= *stamp*) oblitérer [2] [+ *flight, train etc*] annuler ; (= *withdraw permanently*) supprimer [3] (*Math*) [+ *figures, amounts*] éliminer [4] (= *cross out, delete*) barrer, rayer VI [*tourist etc*] se décommander

► **cancel out** VT SEP (*Math*) [+ *noughts*] barrer ; [+ *amounts*] annuler, éliminer ; (*fig*) neutraliser ◆ **they** ~ **each other out** (*Math*) ils s'annulent ; (*fig*) ils se neutralisent

cancellation /ˌkænsə'leɪʃən/ N [*of event, order, debt, flight, train, reservation, hotel room*] annulation *f* ; [*of agreement, contract*] annulation *f*, résiliation *f* (*Jur*) ; [*of mortgage*] levée *f* ; [*of decree, will*] révocation *f* ; [*of stamp*] oblitération *f* ; [*of writing, numbers*] biffage *m* ; (*Math*) élimination *f* ◆ ~ **of a cheque** opposition *f* à un chèque ◆ ~

fee taxe f d'annulation ◆ **~s will not be accepted after ...** *(for travel, hotel)* les réservations ne peuvent être annulées après ... ; *(Theat)* les locations ne peuvent être annulées après ...

cancer /ˈkænsəʳ/ **N** 1 *(Med)* cancer *m* ; *(fig)* fléau *m* ◆ **she has ~** elle a un cancer ◆ **lung/breast ~** cancer *m* du poumon/du sein ◆ **his battle against ~** sa bataille contre le cancer 2 *(Astron)* ◆ **Cancer** le Cancer ◆ **I'm (a) Cancer** *(Astrol)* je suis (du) Cancer ; → **tropic**
COMP **cancer-causing ADJ** cancérigène
cancer patient N cancéreux *m*, -euse *f*
cancer-producing ADJ cancérigène
cancer research N cancérologie *f* ; *(in appeals, funds, charities)* recherche *f* sur *or* contre le cancer
cancer specialist N cancérologue *mf*
cancer stick‡ **N** *(Brit pej)* cigarette *f*, clope* *f*

Cancerian /kænˈsɪərɪən/ **N** ◆ **to be a ~** être (du) Cancer

cancerous /ˈkænsərəs/ **ADJ** cancéreux

candelabra /ˌkændɪˈlɑːbrə/ **N** (pl **candelabra** *or* **candelabras**) candélabre *m*

candelabrum /ˌkændɪˈlɑːbrəm/ **N** (pl **candelabrums** *or* **candelabra**) ⇒ **candelabra**

candid /ˈkændɪd/ **ADJ** *[person, smile, criticism]* franc (franche *f*), sincère ; *[report, biography]* qui ne cache rien ◆ **he gave me his ~ opinion of it** il m'a dit franchement ce qu'il en pensait ◆ **~ shots of his friends** photos prises sur le vif
COMP **Candid Camera N** (= TV programme) la Caméra cachée

⚠ **candid** is not translated by the French word **candide**, which means 'naive'.

candida /ˈkændɪdə/ **N** *(Med)* candidose *f*

candidacy /ˈkændɪdəsɪ/ **N** *(esp US)* candidature *f*

candidate /ˈkændɪdeɪt/ **N** candidat(e) *m(f)* ◆ **to stand as/be a ~** se porter/être candidat ◆ **a ~ for president** un candidat à la présidence ◆ **they are ~s for relegation** *(Ftbl)* ils risquent la relégation ◆ **the obese are prime ~s for heart disease** les obèses sont particulièrement exposés aux maladies cardiaques ◆ **A-level ~s** ≈ candidats *mpl* au baccalauréat

candidature /ˈkændɪdətʃəʳ/ **N** *(Brit)* candidature *f*

candidly /ˈkændɪdlɪ/ **ADV** *[admit, confess]* avec franchise ; *[say, reply]* avec franchise, franchement

candidness /ˈkændɪdnɪs/ **N** franchise *f*, sincérité *f*

candied /ˈkændɪd/ **ADJ** *(Culin) [whole fruit]* glacé, confit ; *[cherries, angelica etc]* confit COMP **candied peel N** écorce *f* d'orange (*or* de citron *etc*) confite

candle /ˈkændl/ **N** 1 *(wax: household, on cakes etc)* bougie *f* ; *(tallow: tall, decorative)* chandelle *f* ; *[of church]* cierge *m* ◆ **the game isn't worth the ~** le jeu n'en vaut pas la chandelle ◆ **he can't hold a ~ to his brother** il n'arrive pas à la cheville de son frère ; → **burn¹**, **Roman** 2 ⇒ **candle-power**
COMP **candle grease N** *(from household candle)* suif *m* ; *(from others)* cire *f*
candle pin N *(US)* quille *f*
candle-power N *(Elec)* ◆ **a 20 ~-power lamp** une (lampe de) 20 bougies

candlelight /ˈkændllaɪt/ **N** ◆ **by ~** à la lueur d'une bougie COMP **candlelight dinner N** dîner *m* aux chandelles

candlelit /ˈkændllɪt/ **ADJ** *[room, restaurant]* éclairé à la bougie *or* aux chandelles COMP **candlelit dinner N** dîner *m* aux chandelles

Candlemas /ˈkændlmæs/ **N** la Chandeleur

candlestick /ˈkændlstɪk/ **N** *(flat)* bougeoir *m* ; *(tall)* chandelier *m*

candlewick /ˈkændlwɪk/ **N** chenille *f* (de coton) ◆ **a ~ bedspread** un couvre-lit en chenille

candour, candor *(US)* /ˈkændəʳ/ **N** franchise *f*, sincérité *f*

C & W /ˌsiːənˈdʌbljuː/ (abbrev of **country-and-western**) → **country**

candy /ˈkændɪ/ **N** sucre *m* candi ; *(US)* bonbon(s) *m(pl)* ◆ **it's like taking ~ from a baby** c'est simple comme bonjour **VT** *[+ sugar]* faire candir ; *[+ fruit]* glacer, confire **VI** se candir, se cristalliser
COMP **candy-ass***‡ **N** *(US)* couille molle*‡ *f*
candy bar N *(US)* confiserie *f* en barre
candy-floss N *(Brit)* barbe *f* à papa
candy store N *(US)* confiserie *f* *(souvent avec papeterie et tabac)*
candy-striped ADJ à rayures multicolores
candy striper N *(US) jeune fille s'occupant d'œuvres de bienfaisance dans un hôpital*

cane /keɪn/ **N** 1 *[of bamboo etc]* canne *f* ; *(for plants)* tuteur *m* ; *(in basket- and furniture-making)* rotin *m*, jonc *m* ; → **sugar** 2 (= *walking stick*) canne *f* ; *[of officer, rider]* badine *f*, jonc *m* ; *(for punishment)* trique *f*, bâton *m* ; *(Scol)* verge *f*, baguette *f* ◆ **the schoolboy got the ~** l'écolier a reçu des coups de baguette **VT** *(gen)* donner des coups de trique *or* de bâton à ; *(Scol)* donner des coups de baguette à
COMP canné ; *[chair, furniture]* en rotin
cane sugar N *(NonC)* sucre *m* de canne

canine /ˈkænaɪn/ **ADJ** canin ◆ **~ (tooth)** *(Anat)* canine *f* COMP **canine corps N** *(US Police)* corps *m* des maîtres-chiens

caning /ˈkeɪnɪŋ/ **N** ◆ **to get a ~** *(lit)* recevoir la trique ; *(Scol)* recevoir des coups de baguette

canister /ˈkænɪstəʳ/ **N** boîte *f* ◆ **a ~ of teargas** une bombe lacrymogène

canker /ˈkæŋkəʳ/ **N** *(Med)* ulcère *m* ; *(gen syphilitic)* chancre *m* ; *(Bot, fig)* chancre *m* **VT** *(Med)* ronger COMP **canker-worm N** ver *m*

cankerous /ˈkæŋkərəs/ **ADJ** *[sore]* rongeur ; *[tissue]* chancreux

cannabis /ˈkænəbɪs/ **N** 1 (= *plant*) chanvre *m* indien 2 (= *resin*) cannabine *f* 3 (= *drug*) cannabis *m*

cannel(l)oni /ˌkænɪˈləʊnɪ/ **N** *(NonC)* cannelloni *mpl*

cannery /ˈkænərɪ/ **N** *(US)* fabrique *f* de conserves, conserverie *f*

cannibal /ˈkænɪbəl/ **ADJ, N** cannibale *mf*, anthropophage *mf*

cannibalism /ˈkænɪbəlɪzəm/ **N** cannibalisme *m*, anthropophagie *f*

cannibalistic /ˌkænɪbəˈlɪstɪk/ **ADJ** *[person, tribe]* cannibale ; *[practices]* de cannibale

cannibalization /ˌkænɪbəlaɪˈzeɪʃən/ **N** *[of machine, product]* cannibalisation *f*

cannibalize /ˈkænɪbəlaɪz/ **VT** *(Tech) [+ machine, car]* démonter pour en réutiliser les pièces ◆ **~d parts** pièces *fpl* récupérées

cannily /ˈkænɪlɪ/ **ADV** astucieusement

canning /ˈkænɪŋ/ **N** mise *f* en conserve *or* en boîte
COMP **canning factory N** fabrique *f* de conserves, conserverie *f*
canning industry N industrie *f* de la conserve, conserverie *f*

cannon /ˈkænən/ **N** (pl **cannon** *or* **cannons**) 1 *(Mil)* canon *m* ; → **water** 2 *(Tech)* canon *m* 3 *(Brit Billiards)* carambolage *m* **VI** *(Brit Billiards)* caramboler ◆ **to ~ off the red** caramboler la rouge ◆ **to ~ into** *or* **against sth** percuter qch ◆ **to ~ into** *or* **against sb** se heurter à qn
COMP **cannon fodder N** chair *f* à canon*
cannon-shot N ◆ **within ~-shot** à portée de canon

cannonade /ˌkænəˈneɪd/ **N** canonnade *f*

cannonball /ˈkænənbɔːl/ **N** boulet *m* de canon COMP **cannonball serve N** *(Tennis)* service *m* boulet de canon

cannot /ˈkænɒt/ LANGUAGE IN USE 16.3, 16.4 **NEG** of **can¹**

canny /ˈkænɪ/ **ADJ** (= *cautious*) prudent, circonspect ; (= *shrewd*) malin (-igne *f*), futé ; (= *careful with money*) regardant* *(pej)*, économe ◆ **~ answer** réponse *f* de Normand ; → **ca' canny**

canoe /kəˈnuː/ **N** *(gen)* canoë *m* ; (= *dug-out*) pirogue *f* ; *(Sport)* kayak *m* ; → **paddle** **VI** *(Sport)* faire du canoë-kayak ; *(in dug-out)* aller en pirogue

canoeing /kəˈnuːɪŋ/ **N** *(Sport)* canoë-kayak *m*

canoeist /kəˈnuːɪst/ **N** canoéiste *mf*

canon /ˈkænən/ **N** 1 *(Mus, Rel, Tech)* canon *m* ; (= *criterion*) canon *m*, critère *m* ◆ **~ of the mass** *(Rel)* canon *m* de la messe 2 *(Rel = chapter member)* chanoine *m* COMP **canon law N** *(Rel)* droit *m* canon

cañon /ˈkænjən/ **N** *(US)* ⇒ **canyon**

canonical /kəˈnɒnɪkəl/ **ADJ** *(Rel)* canonique, conforme aux canons de l'église ; *(Mus)* en canon ; (= *accepted*) autorisé, qui fait autorité ◆ **~ dress** *(Rel)* vêtements *mpl* sacerdotaux

canonization /ˌkænənaɪˈzeɪʃən/ **N** *(Rel)* canonisation *f*

canonize /ˈkænənaɪz/ **VT** *(Rel, fig)* canoniser

canoodle †* /kəˈnuːdl/ **VI** se faire des mamours*

canopied /ˈkænəpɪd/ **ADJ** *[bed]* à baldaquin

canopy /ˈkænəpɪ/ **N** *[of bed]* baldaquin *m*, ciel *m* de lit ; *[of throne etc]* dais *m* ; *[of tent etc]* marquise *f* ; *[of rain forest]* canopée *f* ; *(Archit)* baldaquin *m* ; *[of parachute]* voilure *f* ; *[of cockpit]* verrière *f* ; *(fig) [of sky, heavens]* voûte *f*

cant¹ /kænt/ **N** 1 (= *insincere talk*) paroles *fpl* hypocrites ; (= *stock phrases*) phrases *fpl* toutes faites, clichés *mpl* 2 (= *jargon*) jargon *m*, argot *m* de métier ◆ **lawyers' ~** jargon *m* juridique ; → **thief** **VI** parler avec hypocrisie *or* affectation

cant² /kænt/ **N** 1 (= *slope, steepness*) pente *f*, déclivité *f* ; (= *sloping surface*) plan *m* incliné ◆ **this wall has a definite ~** ce mur penche très nettement 2 (= *jolt*) secousse *f*, à-coup *m* **VI** (= *tilt*) pencher, s'incliner **VT** (= *tilt*) incliner, pencher ; (= *overturn*) retourner d'un coup sec

can't /kɑːnt/ (abbrev of **cannot**) → **can¹**

Cantab. (abbrev of **Cantabrigiensis**) de Cambridge

Cantabrian /kænˈteɪbrɪən/ **ADJ, N** ◆ **the ~s, the ~ Mountains** les (monts *mpl*) Cantabriques *mpl*

cantaloup(e) /ˈkæntəluːp/ **N** cantaloup *m*

cantankerous /kænˈtæŋkərəs/ **ADJ** irascible

cantata /kænˈtɑːtə/ **N** cantate *f*

canteen /kænˈtiːn/ **N** 1 (= *restaurant*) cantine *f* 2 *(Mil)* (= *flask*) bidon *m* ; (= *mess tin*) gamelle *f* 3 ◆ **a ~ of cutlery** une ménagère 4 ◆ **~ culture*** *(Brit)* esprit *m* de corps de garde

canter /ˈkæntəʳ/ **N** petit galop *m* ◆ **to go for a ~** aller faire une promenade à cheval *(au petit galop)* ◆ **to win in** *or* **at a ~*** *(Brit fig)* gagner haut la main, arriver dans un fauteuil* **VI** aller au petit galop **VT** mener *or* faire aller au petit galop

Canterbury /ˈkæntəbərɪ/ **N** Cantorbéry
COMP **Canterbury bell N** (= *plant*) campanule *f*
Canterbury Tales NPL *(Literat)* Contes *mpl* de Cantorbéry

canticle /ˈkæntɪkl/ N cantique *m*, hymne *m* ◆ **the Canticles** le cantique des cantiques

cantilever /ˈkæntɪliːvəʳ/ N *(Tech)* cantilever *m* ; *(Archit)* corbeau *m*, console *f*
COMP **cantilever beam** N poutre *f* en console
cantilever bridge N pont *m* cantilever *inv*

canting /ˈkæntɪŋ/ ADJ *(= hypocritical)* hypocrite, tartufe

cantle /ˈkæntl/ N troussequin *m*

canto /ˈkæntəʊ/ N chant *m* *(d'un poème)*

canton /ˈkæntɒn/ N *(Admin)* canton *m* VT ① *[+ land]* diviser en cantons ② *[+ soldiers]* cantonner

cantonal /ˈkæntənl/ ADJ cantonal

Cantonese /ˌkæntəˈniːz/ ADJ cantonais N ① *(pl inv = person)* Cantonais(e) *m(f)* ② *(= language)* cantonais *m* NPL **the Cantonese** les Cantonais *mpl*

cantonment /kənˈtuːnmənt/ N cantonnement *m*

cantor /ˈkæntɔːʳ/ N *(Rel)* chantre *m*

Cantuar. *(Brit Rel)* (abbrev of **Cantuariensis**) de Cantorbéry

Canuck * /kəˈnʌk/ N *(often pej)* Canadien(ne) *m(f)* français(e)

Canute /kəˈnjuːt/ N Canut *m*

canvas¹ /ˈkænvəs/ N ① *(Art, Naut, also of tent)* toile *f* ; *(Sewing)* canevas *m* ◆ **under ~** *(= in a tent)* sous la tente ; *(Naut)* sous voiles ② *(= painting)* toile *f*, tableau *m*
COMP en *or* de toile
canvas chair N chaise *f* pliante *(en toile)*
canvas shoes NPL *(gen)* chaussures *fpl* en toile ; *(rope-soled)* espadrilles *fpl*

canvas² /ˈkænvəs/ ⇒ **canvass**

canvaser /ˈkænvəsəʳ/ N *(US)* ⇒ **canvasser**

canvass /ˈkænvəs/ VT ① *(Pol) [+ district]* faire du démarchage électoral dans ; *[+ person]* solliciter la voix *or* le suffrage de ; *(US = scrutinize votes)* pointer ② *[sales rep] [+ district, customers]* prospecter ③ *(= seek support of) [+ influential person]* solliciter le soutien de ④ *(= seek opinion of) [+ person]* sonder *(on* à propos de*)* ; ◆ **to ~ opinions (on sth)** sonder l'opinion *or* faire un sondage d'opinion (sur qch) ⑤ *(= discuss) [+ matter, question]* débattre, examiner à fond VI ① *(Pol) [candidate]* faire campagne ◆ **to ~ for sb** *(Pol)* solliciter des voix pour qn ; *(gen)* faire campagne pour qn ② *[sales rep]* visiter la clientèle ; *(door to door)* faire du démarchage N ⇒ **canvassing**

canvasser, canvaser *(US)* /ˈkænvəsəʳ/ N ① *(esp Brit Pol: for support)* agent *m* électoral *(qui sollicite les voix des électeurs)* ; *(US: checking votes)* scrutateur *m*, -trice *f* ② *(= sales rep)* placier *m* ; *(door to door)* démarcheur *m* ◆ **"no canvassers"** "accès interdit aux colporteurs"

canvassing /ˈkænvəsɪŋ/ N ① *(Pol)* démarchage *m* électoral ; *(when applying for job, membership etc)* visites *fpl* de candidature ; *(US = inspection of votes)* vérification *f* des votes ② *(by sales rep)* démarchage *m*

canyon /ˈkænjən/ N canyon *m*, cañon *m*, gorge *f*

canyoning /ˈkænjənɪŋ/ N canyoning *m*

CAP /ˌsiːeɪˈpiː/ N *(Pol)* (abbrev of **Common Agricultural Policy**) PAC *f*

cap /kæp/ N ① *(= headgear) [of man, woman, boy]* casquette *f* ; *[of jockey, judge]* toque *f* ; *[of soldier]* calot *m* ; *[of sailor]* bonnet *m* ; *[of gendarme]* képi *m* ; *(= skullcap)* calotte *f* ; *[of cardinal]* barrette *f* ◆ **~ and gown** *(Univ)* costume *m* universitaire ◆ **to go ~ in hand to sb** aller quémander qch (auprès) de qn ◆ **if the ~ fits(, wear it)** il n'y a que la vérité qui blesse, qui se sent morveux (qu'il) se mouche ◆ **to set one's ~ at sb** † *[woman]* jeter son dévolu sur qn ◆ **~ and bells** marotte *f* (de bouffon) ; → **black, feather, nightcap, thinking**
② *(Brit Sport)* ◆ **he won his first England ~ against France** il a été sélectionné pour la première fois dans l'équipe d'Angleterre à l'occasion de son match contre la France ◆ **Davis has won 50 ~s for Wales** Davis compte 50 sélections dans l'équipe du pays de Galles ◆ **Elwood is the team's only new ~** Elwood est le seul nouveau joueur sélectionné dans l'équipe
③ *(= lid, cover) [of pen]* capuchon *m* ; *[of tooth]* couronne *f* ; *[of car radiator, tyre-valve]* bouchon *m* ; *(Archit)* chapiteau *m*, couronnement *m* ; *[of mushroom]* chapeau *m* ; *[of bottle] (screw-off)* bouchon *m* ; *(pry-off)* capsule *f* ; → **axle, kneecap, toecap**
④ *(= contraceptive)* diaphragme *m*
⑤ (also **percussion cap**) capsule *f* fulminante ; *(for toy gun)* amorce *f*
VT ① *(= put cover on) (gen)* couvrir d'une capsule, d'un capuchon *etc* ; *[+ bottle etc]* capsuler ; *(Mil) [+ shell]* visser la fusée de ; *(Dentistry) [+ tooth]* couronner ; → **snow**
② *[+ person]* coiffer ; *(Univ)* conférer un grade universitaire à ◆ **he was ~ped four times for England** *(Brit Sport)* il a joué quatre fois dans l'équipe d'Angleterre
③ *(= surpass, improve on) [+ sb's words]* renchérir sur ; *[+ achievements]* surpasser ◆ **he ~ped this story/quotation (with another one)** il a trouvé une histoire/une citation encore meilleure que celle-ci ◆ **to ~ it all** pour couronner le tout ◆ **that ~s it all!** * ça, c'est le bouquet * *or* le comble !
④ *(= limit) [+ spending, taxes]* imposer un plafond à, plafonner ◆ **he has the power to ~ city councils that spend excessively** il a le pouvoir d'imposer des restrictions budgétaires aux conseils municipaux qui dépensent trop ; see also **charge, rate¹**

cap. * /kæp/ N (abbrev of **capital letter**) → **capital**

capability /ˌkeɪpəˈbɪlɪtɪ/ N ① aptitude *f* *(to do sth, of doing sth* à faire qch*)* capacité *f* *(to do sth, for doing sth* de *or* à faire qch*)* ; ◆ **mental ~** aptitudes *fpl* *or* capacités *fpl* intellectuelles ◆ **within/beyond one's capabilities** dans ses/au-dessus de ses capacités ② *[of machine]* potentiel *m* ; *(Mil = range of weapons etc)* capacité *f* ◆ **NATO's nuclear capabilities** le potentiel *or* la capacité nucléaire de l'OTAN ◆ **we have the military ~ to defend the area** nous avons le potentiel *or* la capacité militaire nécessaire pour défendre cette région ◆ **they have the ~ to produce their own nuclear weapons** ils sont en mesure de produire leurs propres armements nucléaires

capable /ˈkeɪpəbl/ LANGUAGE IN USE 15.4 ADJ ① *[person]* capable *(of* de*)* ; *[event, situation]* susceptible *(of* de*)* ; ◆ **he is ~ of great warmth/tenderness** il est capable de (montrer) beaucoup de chaleur/de tendresse ◆ **he was ~ of murder** il était capable de commettre un meurtre ◆ **sports cars ~ of 150 mph** des voitures *fpl* de sport pouvant atteindre les 240 km/h ◆ **a ship ~ of carrying 650 people** un bateau pouvant transporter 650 personnes ② *(= competent)* capable

capably /ˈkeɪpəblɪ/ ADV avec compétence

capacious /kəˈpeɪʃəs/ ADJ *[hall, hotel]* vaste, d'une grande capacité ; *[container]* d'une grande contenance *or* capacité

capacitance /kəˈpæsɪtəns/ N *(Elec)* capacitance *f*

capacitor /kəˈpæsɪtəʳ/ N *(Elec)* condensateur *m*

capacity /kəˈpæsɪtɪ/ N ① *[of container]* contenance *f* ; *[of hall, hotel]* capacité *f* ◆ **filled** *or* **full to ~** *[box, suitcase]* bourré ; *[hall, bus]* comble, bondé ; *[refugee camp, hospital]* saturé ◆ **the hall has a seating ~ of 400** la salle a 400 places assises ◆ **the tank has a ~ of 100 litres** le réservoir a une capacité *or* une contenance de 100 litres ◆ **a 40,000 ~ stadium** un stade pouvant accueillir 40 000 personnes ◆ **lung ~** capacité *f* pulmonaire
② *(= capability, inclination)* capacité(s) *f(pl)*, aptitude *f* ◆ **his tremendous ~ for hard work** son énorme capacité à travailler dur ◆ **~ to do** *or* **for doing sth** capacité *f* à faire qch ◆ **mental ~** capacités *fpl* intellectuelles ◆ **capacities** capacités *fpl*
③ *(= production potential)* capacité *f* de production ; *(= output, production)* rendement *m* ◆ **to work at** *or* **(full) ~** *[factory]* fonctionner à plein rendement ◆ **I'm not working at (full) ~ today** je ne suis pas très productif aujourd'hui ◆ **we are increasing (our) ~** nous augmentons notre capacité de production ◆ **we haven't yet reached (full) ~** nous n'avons pas encore atteint notre rendement maximum ◆ **spare** *or* **excess ~** surcapacité *f* ◆ **production ~** capacité *f* de production ◆ **productive ~** capacité *f* de production ◆ **military ~** capacités *fpl* militaires ◆ **earning ~** capacité *f* à gagner de l'argent ◆ **(electricity-)generating ~** capacité *f* de production (d'électricité)
④ *(frm = position, status)* qualité *f*, titre *m* ◆ **in my ~ as a doctor** en ma qualité de médecin ◆ **in his official ~** à titre officiel ◆ **in a personal ~** à titre personnel ◆ **in an advisory ~** à titre consultatif ◆ **we must not employ him in any ~ whatsoever** il ne faut pas l'employer à quelque titre que ce soit
⑤ *(= legal power)* capacité *f* juridique *(to do sth* de faire qch*)* ; ◆ **to have the ~ to do sth** avoir capacité *or* qualité pour faire qch
COMP **capacity attendance** N ◆ **there was a ~ attendance** c'était plein *or* bondé
capacity audience N ◆ **they were hoping for a ~ audience** ils espéraient faire salle comble ◆ **the show attracted** *or* **drew ~ audiences all over Europe** le spectacle a fait salle comble dans toute l'Europe ◆ **her speech was delivered to a ~ audience** elle a prononcé son discours devant une salle comble
capacity booking N ◆ **there was ~ booking** toutes les places étaient louées *or* retenues, on jouait à guichets fermés
capacity crowd N ◆ **there was a ~ crowd** il n'y avait plus une place (de) libre ; *(Sport)* le stade était comble

caparison /kəˈpærɪsn/ *(liter)* N caparaçon *m* VT *[+ horse]* caparaçonner

cape¹ /keɪp/ N *(full length)* cape *f* ; *(half length)* pèlerine *f* ; *[of policeman, cyclist]* pèlerine *f*

cape² /keɪp/ N *(Geog)* cap *m* ; *(= high cape)* promontoire *m*
COMP **Cape Canaveral** N le Cap Canaveral
Cape Cod N le cap Cod
Cape Coloureds NPL *(in South Africa)* métis *mpl* sud-africains
Cape Horn N le cap Horn
Cape of Good Hope N le cap de Bonne-Espérance
Cape Province N province *f* du Cap
Cape Town N Le Cap
Cape Verde N Cap-Vert *m* ◆ **the Cape Verde Islands** les îles *fpl* du Cap-Vert

caped /keɪpt/ ADJ portant une cape

caper¹ /ˈkeɪpəʳ/ VI (also **caper about**) *[child, elf]* gambader (de joie) N ① *(= leap, jump)* cabriole *f*, gambade *f* ② *(fig = prank)* **~s** farces *fpl* ◆ **that was quite a ~** * ça a été une vraie partie de rigolade * ◆ **what a ~!** * *(= fuss)* quelle histoire ! ◆ **she served six months in prison for the helicopter ~** * elle a fait six mois de prison pour le coup de l'hélicoptère

caper² /ˈkeɪpəʳ/ N *(Culin)* câpre *f* ; *(= shrub)* câprier *m* COMP **caper sauce** N sauce *f* aux câpres

capercaillie, capercailzie /ˌkæpəˈkeɪlɪ/ N grand tétras *m*, grand coq *m* de bruyère

Capernaum /kəˈpɜːnɪəm/ N Capharnaüm

capeskin /ˈkeɪpskɪn/ N *(US)* peau *f* souple pour ganterie

capful /ˈkæpfʊl/ N (= *measure of liquid*) ◆ **one ~ to four litres of water** un bouchon (plein) pour quatre litres d'eau

capillary /kəˈpɪlərɪ/ ADJ, N (*Bio, Bot*) capillaire *m*

capital /ˈkæpɪtl/ ADJ 1 (= *essential, important*) capital ◆ **of ~ importance** d'une importance capitale
2 (= *chief, principal*) capital, principal
3 ◆ **~ letter** majuscule *f*, capitale *f* ◆ **~ A, B** *etc* A, B *etc* majuscule ◆ **Art/Life with a ~ A/L** l'Art/la Vie avec un grand A/V
4 (*Jur*) capital
5 († * = *splendid*) épatant *, fameux *
N 1 (also **capital city**) capitale *f*
2 (also **capital letter**) majuscule *f*, capitale *f*
3 (= *money and property*) capital *m* (en espèces et en nature) ; (= *money only*) capital *m*, capitaux *mpl* ◆ **~ invested** mise *f* de fonds ◆ **~ and labour** le capital et la main-d'œuvre ◆ **to make ~ out of** (*fig*) tirer parti *or* profit de ; → **working**
4 (*Archit*) chapiteau *m*
COMP **capital account** N (*Fin, Econ*) compte *m* capital
capital allowances NPL déductions *fpl* fiscales pour investissements
capital assets NPL actif *m* immobilisé
capital city N capitale *f*
capital cost N coût *m* d'investissement
capital equipment N (*NonC*) biens *mpl* d'équipement
capital expenditure N dépenses *fpl* d'investissement
capital gains NPL augmentation *f* de capital, plus-values *fpl* (en capital)
capital gains tax N impôt *m* sur les plus-values (en capital)
capital goods NPL biens *mpl* d'équipement
capital intensive ADJ [*industry etc*] (à forte intensité) capitalistique
capital levy N prélèvement *m* *or* impôt *m* sur le capital
capital offence N crime *m* capital
capital punishment N peine *f* capitale, peine *f* de mort
capital reserves NPL réserves *fpl* et provisions *fpl*
capital sentence N condamnation *f* à mort
capital ship N (*Naut*) grosse unité *f* de guerre
capital stock N capital *m* social
capital sum N capital *m*
capital transactions NPL transactions *fpl* en capital
capital transfer tax N (*Brit*) impôt *m* sur le transfert des capitaux

capitalism /ˈkæpɪtəlɪzəm/ N capitalisme *m*

capitalist /ˈkæpɪtəlɪst/ ADJ, N capitaliste *mf*

capitalistic /ˌkæpɪtəˈlɪstɪk/ ADJ capitaliste

capitalization /kəˌpɪtəlaɪˈzeɪʃən/ N capitalisation *f*

capitalize /kəˈpɪtəlaɪz/ VT 1 (*Fin*) [+ *property, plant*] capitaliser ; [+ *company*] constituer le capital social de (*par émission d'actions*) ; (*fig*) capitaliser sur, tirer profit *or* parti de ◆ **over-/under-~d** (*Fin*) sur-/sous-capitalisé 2 (*Typ* = *put into capitals*) mettre en majuscule(s) VI (*fig*) ◆ **to ~ on** [+ *circumstances, information*] exploiter, tirer profit de ; [+ *public ignorance, sb's naivety*] exploiter ; [+ *talents, one's image*] tirer parti de ; (*financially*) monnayer

capitation /ˌkæpɪˈteɪʃən/ N (*Fin*: also **capitation tax**) capitation *f* COMP **capitation allowance** N (*Brit Scol*) dotation *f* forfaitaire par élève (*accordée à un établissement*)

Capitol /ˈkæpɪtl/ N ◆ **the ~** (*US*) le Capitole (*siège du Congrès américain*) ; (*Roman Hist*) le Capitole

capitulate /kəˈpɪtjʊleɪt/ VI (*Mil, fig*) capituler

capitulation /kəˌpɪtjʊˈleɪʃən/ N 1 (*Mil, fig*) capitulation *f* 2 (= *summary*) récapitulation *f*, sommaire *m* 3 (*Jur*) **~s** capitulation *f*

capo /ˈkæpəʊ/ N (*US*) capo *m*

capon /ˈkeɪpən/ N chapon *m*

cappuccino /ˌkæpʊˈtʃiːnəʊ/ N cappuccino *m*

Capri /kəˈpriː/ N Capri *f* ◆ **in ~** à Capri

caprice /kəˈpriːs/ N 1 (= *change of mood*) saute *f* d'humeur ; (= *whim*) caprice *m* 2 (*Mus*) capriccio *m*

capricious /kəˈprɪʃəs/ ADJ capricieux, fantasque

capriciously /kəˈprɪʃəslɪ/ ADV capricieusement

Capricorn /ˈkæprɪkɔːn/ N (*Astron, Geog*) Capricorne *m* ◆ **I'm (a) ~** (*Astrol*) je suis (du) Capricorne ; → **tropic**

caps /kæps/ NPL (abbrev of **capital letters**) → **capital**

capsicum /ˈkæpsɪkəm/ N poivron *m*

capsize /kæpˈsaɪz/ VI se renverser ; (*Naut*) chavirer VT renverser ; (*Naut*) faire chavirer

capstan /ˈkæpstən/ N (*Naut*) cabestan *m* COMP **capstan lathe** N (*Brit*) tour *m* revolver

capsule /ˈkæpsjuːl/ N (*all senses*) capsule *f* ADJ [*description, résumé*] succinct

Capt. N (*Mil*) (abbrev of **Captain**) ◆ **~ P. Martin** (*on envelope*) le Capitaine P. Martin

captain /ˈkæptɪn/ N (*Army, US Airforce*) capitaine *m* ; (*Navy*) capitaine *m* (de vaisseau) ; [*of Merchant Navy*] capitaine *m* ; (*Sport*) capitaine *m* (d'équipe) ; (*US Police*: also **precinct captain**) ≈ commissaire *m* (de police) de quartier ◆ **school ~** (*Brit*) élève (*des classes terminales*) *chargé d'un certain nombre de responsabilités* ◆ **~ of industry** capitaine *m* d'industrie VT (*Sport*) [+ *team*] être le capitaine de ; (*Mil, Naut*) commander ; (*fig*) diriger

captaincy /ˈkæptənsɪ/ N (*Mil*) grade *m* de capitaine ; (*Sport*) capitanat *m* ◆ **to get one's ~** (*Mil*) être promu *or* passer capitaine ◆ **during his ~ (of the team)** (*Sport*) quand il était capitaine (de l'équipe)

caption /ˈkæpʃən/ N 1 (*Press*) (= *heading*) sous-titre *m* ; (*under illustration*) légende *f* 2 (*Cine*) sous-titre *m* VT [+ *illustration*] légender, mettre une légende à ; (*Cine*) sous-titrer

captious /ˈkæpʃəs/ ADJ (*liter*) [*person*] chicanier, vétilleux (*liter*) ; [*remark*] critique

captivate /ˈkæptɪveɪt/ VT captiver, fasciner

captivating /ˈkæptɪveɪtɪŋ/ ADJ captivant

captive /ˈkæptɪv/ N captif *m*, -ive *f* ◆ **to take sb ~** faire qn prisonnier ◆ **to hold sb ~** garder qn en captivité ; (*fig*) captiver qn, tenir qn sous le charme ADJ [*person*] prisonnier ; [*animal, bird, balloon, customer*] captif ◆ **a ~ audience** un public captif ◆ **to be ~ to sth** (*fig*) être prisonnier de qch
COMP **captive-bred** ADJ élevé en captivité
captive breeding N reproduction *f* en captivité
captive market N (*Comm*) marché *m* captif

captivity /kæpˈtɪvɪtɪ/ N captivité *f* ◆ **in ~** en captivité

captor /ˈkæptəʳ/ N (*unlawful*) ravisseur *m* ; (*lawful*) personne *f* qui capture

capture /ˈkæptʃəʳ/ VT [+ *animal, soldier*] capturer ; [+ *escapee*] reprendre ; [+ *city*] prendre, s'emparer de ; (*fig*) [+ *attention*] capter ; [+ *interest*] gagner ; (*Art*) reproduire, rendre ◆ **they have ~d a large part of that market** ils ont conquis une grande partie de ce marché ◆ **to ~ sth on camera/film** photographier/filmer qch N [*of town, treasure, escapee*] capture *f*

capuchin /ˈkæpjʊʃɪn/ N 1 cape *f* (*avec capuchon*) 2 (*Rel*) **Capuchin** capucin(e) *m(f)*

car /kɑːʳ/ N 1 (= *automobile*) voiture *f* ; → **racing, saloon, sports**
2 (*US Rail*) wagon *m*, voiture *f* ; → **dine, freight**
3 (also **tramcar**) (voiture *f* de) tramway *m*, tram *m*
4 [*of lift, elevator*] cabine *f* (d'ascenseur)
5 [*of airship*] nacelle *f*
COMP [*wheel, door, seat, tyre etc*] de voiture ; [*travel etc*] en voiture
car alarm N alarme *f* de voiture, alarme *f* auto
car allowance N indemnité *f* de déplacement (en voiture)
car bomb N voiture *f* piégée
car bomber N auteur *m* d'un attentat à la voiture piégée
car bombing N attentat *m* à la voiture piégée
car boot N (*Brit*) coffre *m*
car-boot sale N (*Brit*) brocante *f*, vide-grenier *m*
car chase N course-poursuite *f* (en voiture)
car coat N manteau *m* court
car crime N (*NonC*) (*Brit*) délits *mpl* commis sur des véhicules
car dealer N concessionnaire *mf* automobile
car expenses NPL frais *mpl* de déplacement (en voiture)
car-fare N (*US*) prix *m* du trajet (en bus)
car-ferry N [*of sea*] ferry(-boat) *m* ; [*of river, small channel*] bac *m* (pour voitures)
car hire N location *f* de voitures ◆ **~ hire company** société *f* de location de voitures
car industry N industrie *f* automobile
car insurance N assurance *f* automobile
car journey N voyage *m* en voiture ; (*shorter*) trajet *m* en voiture
car keys NPL clés *fpl* de voiture
car licence N vignette *f* (auto)
car maintenance N mécanique *f* auto ◆ **~ maintenance classes** cours *fpl* de mécanique auto
car-maker, car manufacturer N constructeur *m* automobile
car number N numéro *m* d'immatriculation
car park N (*Brit*) parking *m*, parc *m* de stationnement
car part N (*Brit*) pièce *f* détachée (de voiture)
car phone N téléphone *m* de voiture
car-pool N 1 (= *people sharing car trips*) groupe *m* de covoiturage 2 (= *cars owned by organisation*) (parc *m* de) voitures *fpl* de service
car radio N autoradio *m*
car rental N location *f* de voitures
car rug N plaid *m*
car-sharing N covoiturage *m*
car sick ADJ ◆ **to be ~ sick** être malade en voiture, avoir le mal de la route
car sickness N mal *m* des transports
car sleeper N (*Rail*) train *m* autos-couchettes
car stereo N autoradio *m*
car thief N (*Brit*) voleur *m* de voitures
car transporter N (= *lorry*) camion *m* transportant des automobiles ; (= *train*) wagon *m* transportant des automobiles
car wash N (= *action*) lavage *m* de voitures ; (= *place*) portique *m* de lavage automatique
car-worker N ouvrier *m*, -ière *f* de l'industrie automobile

CAR-BOOT SALE, GARAGE SALE

Type de brocante très populaire en Grande-Bretagne, où chacun vide sa cave ou son grenier. Les articles sont présentés dans des coffres de voitures et la vente a souvent lieu sur un parking ou dans un champ. Les brocanteurs d'un jour doivent s'acquitter d'une petite contribution pour participer à la vente.

Aux États-Unis et en Australie, les ventes de ce genre s'appellent **garage sales** ou **yard sales**.

Caracas /kəˈrækəs/ N Caracas

carafe /kəˈræf/ N carafe *f* ; *(small)* carafon *m*

caramel /ˈkærəməl/ N caramel *m* ◆ **~ cream** crème *f* (au) caramel

caramelize /ˈkærəməlaɪz/ VT caraméliser VI se caraméliser

carapace /ˈkærəpeɪs/ N carapace *f*

carat /ˈkærət/ N carat *m* ◆ **24 ~ gold** or *m* à 24 carats

caravan /ˈkærəvæn/ N 1 *(Brit: towed behind car)* caravane *f* ; *[of gipsy]* roulotte *f* ; *(= group: in desert etc)* caravane *f* VI ◆ **to go ~ning** faire du caravaning COMP **caravan site** N *[of tourists]* camping *m* pour caravanes ; *[of gipsies]* campement *m*

caravanette /ˌkærəvəˈnet/ N *(Brit)* auto-camping *f*, voiture-camping *f*

caravanserai /ˌkærəˈvænsəraɪ/, **caravansary** /ˈkærəˈvænsərɪ/ N caravansérail *m*

caravel /kærəˈvel/ N *(Naut)* caravelle *f*

caraway /ˈkærəweɪ/ N carvi *m* COMP **caraway seeds** NPL graines *fpl* de carvi

carb* /kɑːb/ N *(= carbohydrate)* glucide *m* ◆ **a low-carb diet** un régime pauvre en glucides

carbide /ˈkɑːbaɪd/ N carbure *m*

carbine /ˈkɑːbaɪn/ N carabine *f*

carbohydrate /ˈkɑːbəʊˈhaɪdreɪt/ N hydrate *m* de carbone ◆ **~s** *(in diets etc)* farineux *mpl*, féculents *mpl*

carbolic /kɑːˈbɒlɪk/ ADJ phéniqué
COMP **carbolic acid** N phénol *m*
carbolic soap N savon *m* au crésol, crésyl ® *m*

carbon /ˈkɑːbən/ N *(Chem)* carbone *m* ; *(Art, Elec)* charbon *m* ; *(= paper, copy)* carbone *m*
COMP **carbon-14 dating** N ⇒ **carbon dating**
carbon copy N *[of typing etc]* carbone *m* ; *(fig)* réplique *f* ADJ *(fig)* identique
carbon credit N droit *m* d'émission de gaz carbonique
carbon-date VT dater au carbone 14
carbon dating N datation *f* au carbone 14
carbon dioxide N gaz *m* carbonique
carbon fibre N fibre *f* de carbone
carbon microphone N microphone *m* à charbon
carbon monoxide N oxyde *m* de carbone
carbon paper N (papier *m*) carbone *m*
carbon ribbon N ruban *m* de machine à écrire
carbon tissue N ⇒ **carbon paper**

carbonaceous /ˌkɑːbəˈneɪʃəs/ ADJ charbonneux ; *(Chem)* carboné

carbonate /ˈkɑːbənɪt/ N carbonate *m*

carbonated /ˈkɑːbəneɪtɪd/ ADJ *[water, drink]* gazeux

carbonic /kɑːˈbɒnɪk/ ADJ carbonique

carboniferous /ˌkɑːbəˈnɪfərəs/ ADJ carbonifère

carbonization /ˌkɑːbənaɪˈzeɪʃən/ N carbonisation *f*

carbonize /ˈkɑːbənaɪz/ VT carboniser

carbonless paper /ˌkɑːbənlɪsˈpeɪpəʳ/ N papier *m* autocopiant

carborne /ˈkɑːbɔːn/ ADJ *(US)* transporté en voiture

Carborundum ® /ˌkɑːbəˈrʌndəm/ N carborundum ® *m*, siliciure *m* de carbone

carboy /ˈkɑːbɔɪ/ N bonbonne *f*

carbuncle /ˈkɑːbʌŋkl/ N 1 *(= jewel)* escarboucle *f* 2 *(Med)* furoncle *m*

carburation /ˌkɑːbjʊˈreɪʃən/ N carburation *f*

carburettor, carburetor *(US)* /ˌkɑːbjʊˈretəʳ/ N carburateur *m*

carcass /ˈkɑːkəs/ N 1 *[of animal]* carcasse *f*, cadavre *m* ; *(Butchery)* carcasse *f* ; *(= human corpse)* cadavre *m* ; *(hum, iro = body)* carcasse *f* ◆ **chicken ~** os *mpl* de poulet 2 *[of vehicle, boat, machine]* carcasse *f*

carcinogen /kɑːˈsɪnədʒen/ N substance *f* cancérigène *or* cancérogène

carcinogenic /ˌkɑːsɪnəˈdʒenɪk/ N ⇒ **carcinogen** ADJ cancérigène *or* cancérogène

carcinoma /ˌkɑːsɪˈnəʊmə/ N (pl **carcinomas** *or* **carcinomata** /ˈkɑːsɪˈnəʊmətə/) carcinome *m*

card[1] /kɑːd/ N 1 *(gen)* carte *f* ; (also **playing card**) carte *f* (à jouer) ; (also **postcard**) carte *f* (postale) ; (also **index card**) fiche *f* ; (also **member's card**) carte *f* de membre *or* d'adhérent ; (also **press card**) carte *f* de presse ; (also **visiting card**) carte *f* (de visite) ; (also **invitation card**) carton *m or* carte *f* d'invitation ; *(at dance, races)* programme *m* ; *(= piece of cardboard)* (morceau *m* de) carton *m* ◆ **identity ~** carte *f* d'identité ◆ **game of ~s** partie *f* de cartes ◆ **to play ~s** jouer aux cartes ◆ **high/low ~** haute/basse carte *f* ; → **court, face, scorecard, trump**[1]

2 *(fig phrases)* **to hold all the ~s** avoir tous les atouts (dans son jeu *or* en main) ◆ **to put** *or* **lay one's ~s on the table** jouer cartes sur table ◆ **to have a ~ up one's sleeve** avoir un atout dans sa manche ◆ **to play** *or* **keep one's ~s close to one's chest, to play** *or* **keep one's ~s close to the vest** *(US)* cacher son jeu ◆ **to throw in the ~s** abandonner la partie ◆ **it's on the ~s** *or* *(US)* **in the ~s that ...*** il y a de grandes chances (pour) que ... *+ subj* ◆ **to get one's ~s** †* *(Brit Ind etc)* être mis à la porte, être licencié ◆ **to ask for one's ~s** *(Brit Ind etc)* demander son compte ◆ **he's (quite) a ~!** †* c'est un rigolo !* ; → **play**

VT 1 *(= put on cards)* ficher, mettre sur fiches

2 *(US)* **to ~ sb*** *(= check sb's identity)* contrôler l'identité de qn

COMP **card-carrying member** N membre *m*, adhérent(e) *m(f)*
card catalogue N catalogue *m*, fichier *m* *(de bibliothèque etc)*
card game N *(= bridge, whist etc)* jeu *m* de cartes ; *(= game of cards)* partie *f* de cartes
card-holder N *[of political party, organization etc]* membre *m*, adhérent(e) *m(f)* ; *[of library]* lecteur *m*, -trice *f* ; *[of restaurant etc]* détenteur *m*, -trice *f* de carte de fidélité ; *[of credit cards]* titulaire *mf* d'une carte (*or* de cartes) de crédit
card hopper N *(Comput)* magasin *m* d'alimentation
card index N fichier *m*
card-index VT ficher, mettre sur fiches
card player N joueur *m*, -euse *f* de cartes
card punch N perforatrice *f* de cartes
card reader N *(Comput)* lecteur *m* de cartes
card stacker N *(Comput)* case *f* de réception
card table N table *f* de jeu *or* à jouer
card trick N tour *m* de cartes
card vote N vote *m* sur carte *(même nombre de voix que d'adhérents représentés)*

card[2] /kɑːd/ *(Tech)* N carde *f* VT *[+ wool, cotton]* carder

cardamom /ˈkɑːdəməm/ N cardamome *f*

cardboard /ˈkɑːdbɔːd/ N carton *m* NonC ADJ *[bookcover]* cartonné ; *[doll]* de *or* en carton ◆ **~ box** (boîte *f* en) carton *m* ◆ **~ cutout** *(lit)* figurine *f* de carton à découper ; *(fig)* homme *m* de paille ◆ **~ city*** *endroit de la ville où dorment les sans-abri* ◆ **he sleeps in ~ city*** il dort sous les ponts, c'est un SDF

carder /ˈkɑːdəʳ/ N *(for textiles)* cardeuse *f*

cardiac /ˈkɑːdɪæk/ ADJ cardiaque COMP **cardiac arrest** N arrêt *m* du cœur

cardie* /ˈkɑːdɪ/ N abbrev of **cardigan**

cardigan /ˈkɑːdɪgən/ N cardigan *m*, gilet *m* (de laine)

cardinal /ˈkɑːdɪnl/ ADJ *[number, point, vowel]* cardinal ◆ **the four ~ virtues** les quatre vertus *fpl* cardinales ◆ **of ~ importance/significance** d'une importance/portée capitale N *(Rel)* cardinal *m* ; → **college**
COMP **cardinal red** N, ADJ rouge cardinal *inv*, pourpre
cardinal sin N *(Rel, fig)* péché *m* capital

cardio... /ˈkɑːdɪəʊ/ PREF cardio- ◆ **cardiovascular** cardiovasculaire

cardiogram /ˈkɑːdɪəgræm/ N cardiogramme *m*

cardiograph /ˈkɑːdɪəgrɑːf/ N cardiographe *m*

cardiography /ˌkɑːdɪˈɒgrəfɪ/ N cardiographie *f*

cardiological /ˌkɑːdɪəˈlɒdʒɪkəl/ ADJ cardiologique

cardiologist /ˌkɑːdɪˈɒlədʒɪst/ N cardiologue *mf*

cardiology /ˌkɑːdɪˈɒlədʒɪ/ N cardiologie *f*

cardphone /ˈkɑːdfəʊn/ N téléphone *m* à carte

cardsharp /ˈkɑːdʃɑːp/, **cardsharper** /ˈkɑːdʃɑːpəʳ/ N tricheur *m*, -euse *f* *(professionnel)*

cardy /ˈkɑːdɪ/ N abbrev of **cardigan**

care /keəʳ/ N 1 *(= attention, heed)* attention *f*, soin *m* ◆ **with the greatest ~** avec le plus grand soin ◆ **the house has been restored with loving ~** la maison a été restaurée avec un soin tout particulier *or* avec le plus grand soin ◆ **children need tough discipline and loving ~** les enfants ont besoin d'une discipline rigoureuse, de soins et d'affection ◆ **"(handle) with care"** *(on parcels)* "fragile" ◆ **it got broken despite all our ~** ça s'est cassé bien que nous y ayons fait très attention ◆ **have a ~!** † prenez garde ! ◆ **convicted of driving without due ~ and attention** *(Jur)* condamné pour conduite dangereuse

♦ **care of, in care of** *(US)* *(on letters)* chez, aux bons soins de

♦ **to take + care** faire attention ◆ **take ~ not to catch cold, take ~ that you don't catch cold** faites attention de *or* à ne pas prendre froid ◆ **take ~!** *(as warning)* (fais) attention ! ; *(as good wishes)* fais bien attention (à toi) ! ◆ **you should take more ~ with** *or* **over your work** vous devriez apporter plus d'attention *or* plus de soin à votre travail ◆ **he took ~ to explain why ...** il a pris soin d'expliquer pourquoi ... ; see also **tender**[3]

2 *(= charge, responsibility)* garde *f* ◆ **he was left in his aunt's ~** on l'a laissé à la garde de sa tante ◆ **to be in ~ of sb** *(frm)* être sous la garde *or* la surveillance de qn ◆ **he is in (the) ~ of Dr Harrison** c'est le docteur Harrison qui le soigne ◆ **the four children in her ~** les quatre enfants dont elle a la responsabilité ◆ **I leave** *or* **put it in your ~** je vous le confie

♦ **to take + care of** *[+ book, details, arrangements]* s'occuper de, se charger de ; *[+ valuables]* garder ; *[+ person, animal]* prendre soin de, s'occuper de ◆ **to take good ~ of sb** bien s'occuper de qn ◆ **to take good ~ of sth** prendre grand soin de qch ◆ **you should take more** *or* **better ~ of yourself** tu devrais faire plus attention (à ta santé) ◆ **I'll take ~ of him!** *(threateningly)* je vais m'occuper de lui ! ◆ **I'll take ~ of that** je vais m'en occuper ◆ **he can take ~ of himself*** il peut *or* sait se débrouiller* tout seul ◆ **that can take ~ of itself*** cela s'arrangera tout seul

3 *(= anxiety)* souci *m* ◆ **he hasn't a ~ in the world** il n'a pas le moindre souci ◆ **full of ~s, full of ~** † accablé de soucis ◆ **the ~s of State** les responsabilités *fpl* de l'État

4 *(Med)* soins *mpl* ◆ **medical** *or* **clinical ~** soins *mpl* médicaux ◆ **nursing ~** soins *mpl* aux malades ◆ **palliative ~** soins *mpl* palliatifs ◆ **primary (health) ~** soins *mpl* médicaux de base *or* élémentaires ◆ **~ in the community** *soins en dehors du milieu hospitalier* ; see also **child, health, intensive**

5 *(for vulnerable children)* **to put** *or* **take a child into (council) ~** ≈ mettre un enfant à la DDASS ◆ **to be in ~** ≈ être à la DDASS ◆ **to be/be put in foster ~** être/être placé en famille d'accueil

VI 1 ◆ **he really ~s** c'est vraiment important pour lui ◆ **I don't ~!, as if I ~d!** * ça m'est égal !, je m'en moque !, je m'en fiche !* ◆ **what do I ~?** * qu'est-ce que ça peut me faire ? ◆ **for all I ~** * pour ce que cela me fait ◆ **I couldn't ~ less** * **what people say** je me fiche pas mal * de ce que les gens peuvent dire ◆ **he doesn't ~ a damn**‡ *or* **two hoots** * *or* **a brass farthing** * il s'en fiche * comme de l'an quarante *or* de sa première chemise ◆ **who ~s!**‡ qu'est-ce que ça peut bien faire ! ; → **naught**

◆ **to care about sb/sth** *(= feel interest, anxiety, sorrow for)* se soucier de qn/qch ; *(= be interested in)* s'intéresser à qn/qch ◆ **money is all he ~s about** il n'y a que l'argent qui l'intéresse *subj* ◆ **to ~ deeply about sth** être profondément concerné par qch ◆ **to ~ deeply about sb** être profondément attaché à qn ◆ **she doesn't ~ about that** elle se soucie peu de cela, elle se moque *or* elle se fiche * de ça

2 *(= like)* aimer ◆ **would you ~ to take off your coat?** voulez-vous retirer votre manteau ? ◆ **I shouldn't ~ to meet him** je n'aimerais pas le rencontrer, ça ne me dirait rien de le rencontrer ◆ **I don't much ~ for it** cela ne me dit rien ◆ **I don't ~ for him** il ne me plaît pas tellement *or* beaucoup ◆ **would you ~ for a cup of tea?** voulez-vous (prendre) une tasse de thé ? ◆ **thank you, I don't ~ for tea** merci, je n'aime pas le thé ◆ **would you ~ for a walk?** voulez-vous faire une promenade ?

COMP **care assistant** N *(Brit)* aide-soignant(e) *m(f)*
care home N ≈ foyer *m* de la DDASS
care label N *(on garment)* instructions *fpl* de lavage
care order N *(Brit Jur, Social Work)* ordre *m* de placement à l'assistance publique
care plan N *(Med, Soc Work)* projet *m* de soins
care-worker N travailleur *m*, -euse *f* social(e) ; → **child, health**

► **care for** VT FUS *[+ invalid]* soigner ; *[+ child]* s'occuper de ◆ **well-~d for** *[invalid]* qu'on soigne bien ; *[child]* dont on s'occupe bien ; *[hands, hair]* soigné ; *[garden]* bien entretenu ; *[house]* bien tenu

careen /kəˈriːn/ VT *(Naut) [+ ship]* caréner, mettre *or* abattre en carène VI *(Naut)* donner de la bande *(de façon dangereuse)*

career /kəˈrɪəʳ/ N 1 *(= profession, occupation)* carrière *f*, profession *f* ◆ **journalism is his ~** il fait carrière dans le journalisme ◆ **he is making a ~ (for himself) in advertising** il est en train de faire carrière dans la publicité

2 *(= life, development, progress)* vie *f*, carrière *f* ◆ **he studied the ~s of the great** il a étudié la vie des grands hommes ◆ **his university ~** sa carrière universitaire

3 *(= movement)* **in full ~** en pleine course

VI (also **career along**) aller à toute vitesse *or* à toute allure ◆ **to ~ up/down** *etc* monter/descendre *etc* à toute allure

COMP *[soldier, diplomat]* de carrière
career break N *(to look after one's children)* congé *m* parental ; *(for further education)* congé *m* de formation
career girl N jeune femme *f* ambitieuse ◆ **she's a ~ girl** elle s'intéresse avant tout à sa carrière, elle est très ambitieuse
career move N changement *m* d'emploi, étape *f* dans un plan de carrière ◆ **a good/bad ~ move** *(= decision, also hum)* une bonne/mauvaise décision sur le plan professionnel
career prospects NPL possibilités *fpl* d'avancement, débouchés *mpl*
careers advisor, careers counselor *(US)* N conseiller *m*, -ère *f* d'orientation professionnelle
careers guidance N *(Brit)* orientation *f* professionnelle
careers office N centre *m* d'orientation professionnelle
careers officer, careers teacher N *(Brit Scol)* ⇒ **careers advisor**
career woman N femme *f* qui s'intéresse avant tout à sa carrière

careerism /kəˈrɪərɪzəm/ N carriérisme *m*

careerist /kəˈrɪərɪst/ N *(pej)* carriériste *mf (pej)*

carefree /ˈkɛəfriː/ ADJ sans souci, insouciant

careful /ˈkɛəfʊl/ ADJ 1 *(= painstaking) [writer, worker]* consciencieux, soigneux ; *[work]* soigné ; *[planning, study, examination]* minutieux ◆ **managing your workload takes ~ planning** gérer sa charge de travail demande une organisation minutieuse ◆ **we have made a ~ study of the report** nous avons étudié le rapport soigneusement, nous avons procédé à une étude minutieuse du rapport ◆ **after giving this problem ~ thought, I believe ...** après avoir longuement réfléchi à ce problème, je pense que ... ◆ **long hair needs ~ attention** les cheveux longs demandent beaucoup de soin ◆ **after ~ consideration of the facts ...** après avoir soigneusement examiné les faits ..., après un examen minutieux des faits ...

2 *(= cautious)* prudent ; *(= acting with care)* soigneux ◆ **(be) ~!** (fais) attention ! ◆ **she's very ~ about what she eats** elle fait très attention à ce qu'elle mange ◆ **be ~ with the glasses** fais attention aux verres ◆ **be ~ of the dog** (faites) attention au chien ◆ **be ~ what you do/say to him** faites attention à ce que vous faites/vous lui dites ◆ **~ on those stairs!** faites attention à ces escaliers ! ◆ **be ~ (that) he doesn't hear you** faites attention à ce qu'il ne vous entende pas ◆ **be ~ to shut the door** n'oubliez pas de fermer la porte ◆ **he was ~ to point out that ...** il a pris soin de faire remarquer que ... ◆ **be ~ not to drop it, be ~ (that) you don't drop it** faites attention à ne pas le laisser tomber ◆ **he was ~ not to offend them** il a pris soin de ne pas les offenser ◆ **we have to be very ~ not to be seen** nous devons faire bien attention de ne pas être vus ◆ **you can't be too ~** *(gen)* on n'est jamais trop prudent ◆ **if we are not ~ we're going to lose this election** si nous ne faisons pas attention, nous allons perdre les élections

3 *(= rather miserly)* économe ; *(pej)* regardant ◆ **he is very ~ with (his) money** il est très regardant

carefully /ˈkɛəfəlɪ/ ADV 1 *(= painstakingly) [look at, consider, plan, write, place, explain]* soigneusement, avec soin ; *[listen, read]* attentivement 2 *(= cautiously) [drive, choose]* prudemment, avec précaution ; *[reply]* avec circonspection ◆ **we must go ~ here** *(fig)* il faut nous montrer prudents

carefulness /ˈkɛəfʊlnɪs/ N soin *m*, attention *f*

caregiver /ˈkɛəˌgɪvəʳ/ N ⇒ **carer**

careless /ˈkɛəlɪs/ ADJ 1 *(= taking little care)* négligent, insouciant *(of* de) ; *(= done without care) [action]* inconsidéré, irréfléchi ; *[work]* bâclé ◆ **to be ~ in sth** se montrer négligent dans qch ◆ **it was ~ of her to do that** elle a fait preuve de négligence en faisant cela ◆ **how ~ of me!** comme j'ai été négligent ! ◆ **~ driver** conducteur *m* négligent ◆ **convicted of ~ driving** condamné pour conduite dangereuse ◆ **~ mistake** faute *f* d'inattention ◆ **his spelling is ~** il ne fait pas attention à son orthographe 2 *(= carefree)* sans souci, insouciant

carelessly /ˈkɛəlɪslɪ/ ADV 1 *(= inattentively, thoughtlessly) [leave, discard, place, handle, allow]* négligemment 2 *(= casually) [say]* avec insouciance ; *[throw, toss]* négligemment ◆ **a shirt ~ open at the neck** une chemise au col négligemment ouvert

carelessness /ˈkɛəlɪsnɪs/ N *(NonC)* négligence *f* ◆ **the ~ of his work** le peu de soin qu'il apporte *(or* a apporté) à son travail

carer /ˈkɛərəʳ/ N *(professional)* travailleur *m* social ; *(Brit) (= relative, friend) personne qui s'occupe d'un proche dépendant*

caress /kəˈres/ N caresse *f* VT caresser

caret /ˈkærət/ N *(Typ)* lambda *m (signe d'insertion)*

caretaker /ˈkɛəˌteɪkəʳ/ N *(Brit)* gardien(ne) *m(f)* (d'immeuble), concierge *mf* ◆ **~ government/president** gouvernement *m*/président(e) *m(f)* intérimaire

careworn /ˈkɛəwɔːn/ ADJ rongé par les soucis

cargo /ˈkɑːgəʊ/ N (pl **cargoes** *or* **cargos**) cargaison *f*, chargement *m*
COMP **cargo boat** N cargo *m*
cargo plane N avion-cargo *m*

carhop /ˈkɑːhɒp/ N *(US) (serving food)* serveur *m*, -euse *f (dans un restaurant drive-in)* ; *(parking cars)* gardien *m* de parking *(qui gare les voitures)*

Carib /ˈkærɪb/ ADJ caraïbe N Caraïbe *mf*

Caribbean /ˌkærɪˈbiːən, *(esp US)* kəˈrɪbiən/ ADJ caribéen, des Caraïbes ◆ **a ~ island** une île des Caraïbes ◆ **the ~ (Sea)** la mer des Antilles *or* des Caraïbes ◆ **the ~ Islands** les petites Antilles *fpl*

caribou /ˈkærɪbuː/ N (pl **caribous** *or* **caribou**) caribou *m*

caricature /ˈkærɪkətjʊəʳ/ N 1 *(Art, fig)* caricature *f* 2 *(NonC)* (art *m* de la) caricature *f* VT *(Art, fig)* caricaturer

caricaturist /ˌkærɪkəˈtjʊərɪst/ N caricaturiste *mf*

CARICOM /ˈkærɪˌkɒm/ N abbrev of **Caribbean Community and Common Market**

caries /ˈkɛəriːz/ N *(pl inv)* carie *f*

carillon /kəˈrɪljən/ N carillon *m*

caring /ˈkɛərɪŋ/ ADJ *[parent]* aimant ; *[teacher]* bienveillant ◆ **we want a ~ society** nous voulons une société à visage humain ◆ **the ~ professions** les professions *fpl* à vocation sociale ◆ **a child needs a ~ environment** un enfant a besoin d'être entouré d'affection

carious /ˈkɛərɪəs/ ADJ carié, gâté

carjacker /ˈkɑːˌdʒækəʳ/ N pirate *m* de la route

carjacking /ˈkɑːˌdʒækɪŋ/ N piraterie *f* sur la route

carload /ˈkɑːləʊd/ N *[of books etc]* voiturée *f* ◆ **a ~ of people** une voiture pleine de gens

Carmelite /ˈkɑːməlaɪt/ ADJ, N carmélite *f*

carminative /ˈkɑːmɪnətɪv/ ADJ *(Med)* carminatif

carmine /ˈkɑːmaɪn/ ADJ, N carmin *m*

carnage /ˈkɑːnɪdʒ/ N carnage *m*

carnal /ˈkɑːnl/ ADJ *(liter)* charnel † COMP **carnal knowledge** N *(Jur)* acte *m* or union *f* charnel(le) ◆ **to have ~ knowledge of sb** connaître qn charnellement

carnally /ˈkɑːnlɪ/ ADV *[desire]* charnellement

carnation /kɑːˈneɪʃən/ N *(= plant)* œillet *m* ADJ *(= pink)* rose ; *(= red)* incarnat

carnet /ˈkɑːneɪ/ N *(Jur, Comm)* passavant *m*

carnival /ˈkɑːnɪvəl/ N carnaval *m* ; *(US = fair)* fête *f* foraine COMP *[hat, procession]* de carnaval

carnivora /kɑːˈnɪvərə/ NPL *(Zool)* carnivores *mpl*

carnivore /ˈkɑːnɪvɔːʳ/ N 1 carnivore *m* 2 (*: *hum = non-vegetarian)* carnivore *m*, amateur *m* de viande

carnivorous /kɑːˈnɪvərəs/ ADJ *[animal, plant]* carnivore ◆ **~ guests will enjoy the excellent game** les amateurs de viande ne seront pas déçus par le gibier

carny‡ /ˈkɑːnɪ/ N *(US) (= carnival)* foire *f*, fête *f* foraine ; *(= person)* forain *m*

carob /ˈkærəb/ N ◆ ~ **(powder)** (poudre *f* de) caroube *f* COMP **carob tree** N caroubier *m*

carol /ˈkærəl/ N (= *song*) chant *m* joyeux ; (also **Christmas carol**) chant *m* de Noël ◆ **~-singers** *groupe de gens qui chantent des chants de Noël* VI (*liter*) chanter joyeusement ; [*birds*] chanter ; [*small birds*] gazouiller

caroller /ˈkærələʳ/ N chanteur *m*, -euse *f*

carom /ˈkærəm/ (*Billiards*) N carambolage *m* VI caramboler

carotene /ˈkærətiːn/ N carotène *m*

carotid /kəˈrɒtɪd/ N carotide *f* ADJ carotidien COMP **carotid artery** N carotide *f*

carousal /kəˈraʊzəl/ N beuverie *f*, ribote † *f*

carouse /kəˈraʊz/ VI faire ribote †

carousel /ˌkæruːˈsel/ N ① (*esp US* = *merry-go-round*) manège *m* (*de chevaux de bois etc*) ② (*Phot: for slides*) magasin *m or* panier *m* circulaire (pour diapositives) ③ (*at airport: for luggage*) carrousel *m*, tapis *m* roulant à bagages

carp¹ /kɑːp/ N (pl **carp** *or* **carps**) (= *fish*) carpe *f*

carp² /kɑːp/ VI critiquer ◆ **to ~ at** [+ *person*] critiquer, blâmer ; [+ *thing, action*] trouver à redire à

carpal /ˈkɑːpl/ ADJ (*Anat*) carpien COMP **carpal tunnel syndrome** N (*Med*) syndrome *m* du canal carpien

Carpathians /kɑːˈpeɪθɪənz/ NPL ◆ **the ~** les Carpates *fpl*

carpel /ˈkɑːpl/ N (*Bot*) carpelle *m*

Carpentaria /ˌkɑːpənˈteərɪə/ N ◆ **Gulf of ~** golfe *m* de Carpentarie

carpenter /ˈkɑːpɪntəʳ/ N charpentier *m* ; (= *joiner*) menuisier *m* VI (*in building*) faire de la charpenterie ; [*joiner*] faire de la menuiserie

carpentry /ˈkɑːpɪntrɪ/ N (*NonC*) charpenterie *f* ; (= *joinery*) menuiserie *f*

carpet /ˈkɑːpɪt/ N tapis *m* ; (*fitted*) moquette *f* ◆ **to be on the ~** * (*fig*) [*subject*] être sur le tapis ; [*person scolded*] être sur la sellette ; → **fitted, red, sweep** VT ① [+ *floor*] recouvrir d'un tapis ; (*with fitted carpet*) recouvrir d'une moquette, moquetter ◆ **a garden ~ed with flowers** un jardin tapissé de fleurs ② († * = *scold*) [+ *person*] houspiller
COMP **carpet bombing** N (*Mil*) bombardement *m* intensif
carpet slippers NPL pantoufles *fpl*
carpet sweeper N balai *m* mécanique
carpet tile N dalle *f* de moquette

carpetbagger * /ˈkɑːpɪtbægəʳ/ N (*US*) (*Pol*) candidat(e) *m(f)* parachuté(e) ; (*Fin*) opportuniste *mf* (*qui cherche à profiter financièrement du changement de statut d'une société de crédit immobilier*) ; (*Hist*) carpetbagger *m*

carpeting /ˈkɑːpɪtɪŋ/ N (*NonC*) moquette *f* ; → **wall**

carpi /ˈkɑːpaɪ/ NPL of **carpus**

carping /ˈkɑːpɪŋ/ ADJ [*person*] chicanier, qui trouve à redire à tout ; [*manner*] chicanier ; [*criticism*] mesquin ; [*voice*] malveillant N chicanerie *f*, critique *f* (malveillante)

carport /ˈkɑːpɔːt/ N auvent *m* (pour voiture)

carpus /ˈkɑːpəs/ N (pl **carpi**) (*Anat*) carpe *m*

carrel(l) /ˈkærəl/ N box *m* (*dans une bibliothèque*)

carriage /ˈkærɪdʒ/ N ① (*horse-drawn*) voiture *f* (de maître), équipage *m* ◆ **~ and pair/four** voiture *f or* équipage *m* à deux/quatre chevaux ② (*Brit Rail*) voiture *f*, wagon *m* (de voyageurs) ③ (*NonC: Brit Comm* = *conveyance of goods*) transport *m*, factage *m* ◆ **~ forward** (en) port dû ◆ **~ free** franco de port ◆ **~ paid** (en) port payé ④ [*of typewriter*] chariot *m* ; [*cf printing press*] train *m* ; (*Mil:* also **gun-carriage**) affût *m* ⑤ [*of person*] (= *bearing*) maintien *m*, port *m*
COMP **carriage clock** N pendulette *f*
carriage drive N allée *f* (pour voitures), grande allée *f*
carriage return N (*Typ*) retour *m* (du) chariot
carriage trade N (*Comm*) clientèle *f* riche, grosse clientèle *f*

carriageway /ˈkærɪdʒweɪ/ N (*Brit*) chaussée *f* ; → **dual**

carrier /ˈkærɪəʳ/ N ① (*Comm*) (= *company*) entreprise *f* de transports ; (= *passenger airline*) compagnie *f* aérienne ; (= *truck owner etc*) entrepreneur *m* de transports, transporteur *m*, camionneur *m* ◆ **by ~** (= *by road*) par la route, par camion ; (= *by rail*) par chemin de fer ◆ **express ~** messageries *fpl* ② (*for luggage: on car, cycle etc*) porte-bagages *m inv* ; (= *bag*) sac *m* (en plastique) ③ (*Med* = *person*) porteur *m*, -euse *f* ④ (also **aircraft carrier**) porte-avions *m inv* ; (also **troop carrier**) (= *plane*) appareil *m* transporteur (de troupes) ; (= *ship*) transport *m*
COMP **carrier bag** N (*Brit*) sac *m* (en plastique)
carrier pigeon N pigeon *m* voyageur

carrion /ˈkærɪən/ N (*NonC*) charogne *f*
COMP **carrion crow** N corneille *f* noire
carrion feeder N charognard *m*
carrion flesh N charogne *f*

carrot /ˈkærət/ N (*lit, fig*) carotte *f* ◆ **to dangle a ~ in front of sb, to offer sb a ~** (*fig*) tendre une carotte à qn
COMP **carrot and stick** ADJ (*fig*) alternant la carotte et le bâton
carrot cake N gâteau *m* à la carotte
carrot-top N (*: *hum* = *redhead*) rouquin(e) * *m(f)* ◆ **~-tops** (*Culin*) fanes *fpl*

carroty /ˈkærətɪ/ ADJ [*hair*] carotte *inv*, roux (rousse *f*)

carrousel /ˌkærəˈsel/ N (*US*) ⇒ **carousel**

carry /ˈkærɪ/ VT ① (= *bear, transport*) [*person*] porter ; [*vehicle*] transporter ; [+ *goods, heavy loads*] transporter ; [+ *message, news*] porter ◆ **she was ~ing the child in her arms** elle portait l'enfant dans ses bras ◆ **this ship carries coal/passengers** ce bateau transporte du charbon/des passagers ◆ **this coach carries 30 people** ce car peut transporter 30 personnes ◆ **he carried the plates through to the kitchen** il a emporté les assiettes à la cuisine ◆ **as fast as his legs could ~ him** à toutes jambes ◆ **the sea carried the boat westward** la mer a emporté le bateau vers l'ouest ◆ **to ~ sth in one's head** connaître qch par cœur ◆ **he carried his audience with him** il a enthousiasmé son auditoire, il a emporté la conviction de son auditoire ◆ **enough food to ~ us through the winter** assez de provisions pour nous durer *or* nous faire * tout l'hiver ; → **can², coal, torch**

② (= *have on one's person*) [+ *identity card, documents*] porter *or* avoir (sur soi) ; [+ *matches, cigarettes, money*] avoir (sur soi) ; [+ *umbrella, gun, sword*] porter

③ [+ *disease*] être porteur de ◆ **people ~ing the AIDS virus** des porteurs *mpl* du virus du sida

④ (= *have, be provided with*) [+ *label, tag*] porter, être muni de ; [+ *warning, notice*] comporter ◆ **it carries a five-year guarantee** c'est garanti cinq ans

⑤ (= *involve, lead to, entail*) avoir comme conséquence(s), produire ; [+ *consequences*] entraîner ; [+ *risk*] comporter ◆ **this job carries a lot of responsibility** ce travail comporte beaucoup de responsabilités ◆ **it also carries extra pay** cela comporte aussi un supplément de salaire ◆ **this offence carries a penalty of £100** ce délit est passible d'une amende de 100 livres ◆ **a crime which carries the death penalty** un crime passible de la peine de mort ◆ **to ~ a crop** donner *or* produire une récolte ◆ **to ~ authority** faire autorité ; → **conviction, interest, mortgage, weight**

⑥ (= *support*) [*pillar etc*] supporter, soutenir, porter ◆ **the ship was ~ing too much canvas** *or* **sail** le navire portait trop de toile

⑦ (*Comm*) [+ *goods, stock*] stocker, vendre ◆ **we don't ~ that article** nous ne faisons pas cet article

⑧ (*Tech*) [*pipe*] [+ *water, oil*] amener ; [*wire*] [+ *sound*] conduire

⑨ (= *extend*) faire passer ◆ **they carried the pipes under the street** ils ont fait passer les tuyaux sous la rue ◆ **to ~ sth too far** *or* **to excess** (*fig*) pousser qch trop loin ◆ **this basic theme is carried through the book** ce thème fondamental se retrouve tout au long du livre

⑩ (= *win*) gagner, remporter ; [+ *enemy's position*] emporter d'assaut ◆ **to ~ the day** gagner (la partie), l'emporter ; (*Mil*) être vainqueur ◆ **to ~ all** *or* **everything before one** marcher en vainqueur, l'emporter sur tous les tableaux ◆ **he carried his point** il a eu gain de cause ◆ **the motion/bill was carried (by 302 votes to 197)** la motion/le projet de loi a été voté(e) (par 302 voix contre 197) ◆ **he will ~ Ohio** (*US Pol*) [*presidential candidate*] il va l'emporter dans l'Ohio

⑪ ◆ **to ~ o.s.** (*physical*) se tenir ; (*behaviour*) se comporter, se conduire ◆ **she carries herself very well** elle se tient très bien ◆ **he carries himself like a soldier** il a le port d'un militaire ◆ **he carries himself with dignity** il a un maintien fort digne ◆ **he carried his head erect** il tenait la tête bien droite

⑫ [*newspaper etc*] [+ *story, details*] rapporter ◆ **all the papers carried (the story of) the murder** l'histoire du meurtre était dans tous les journaux, tous les journaux ont parlé du meurtre ◆ **the papers all carried a photograph of the explosion** dans tous les journaux on trouvait une photo de l'explosion

⑬ (*Math*) retenir ◆ **… and ~ three** … et je retiens trois

⑭ (*Med*) [+ *child*] attendre ◆ **when she was ~ing her third son** quand elle était enceinte de *or* quand elle attendait son troisième fils

VI [*voice, sound*] porter

COMP **carry-on** * N (*pej*) histoires * *fpl* ◆ **what a ~-on (about nothing)!** * que d'histoires (pour rien) ! *
carry-out ADJ [*meal etc*] à emporter N (= *food*) snack *m* à emporter ; (= *drink*) boisson *f* à emporter

► **carry away** VT SEP ① (*lit*) [+ *sick or injured person*] emporter ; [+ *thing*] emporter, enlever ; [*tide, wind*] emporter
② (*fig*) transporter ◆ **he was carried away by his friend's enthusiasm** il a été transporté par l'enthousiasme de son ami ◆ **to get carried away by sth** * s'emballer * pour qch ◆ **don't get carried away!** * ne t'emballe pas ! *, du calme ! ◆ **I got carried away** * (*with excitement etc*) je me suis laissé emporter (by par) ; (*forgetting time*) je n'ai pas vu passer l'heure

► **carry back** VT SEP (*lit*) [+ *things*] rapporter ; (*fig*) reporter ; (*Fin*) reporter (*sur comptes antérieurs*) ◆ **the music carried me back to my youth** la musique m'a reporté à l'époque de ma jeunesse

► **carry forward** VT SEP (*Accounting, gen*) reporter (*to* à) ; ◆ **carried forward** à reporter

► **carry off** VT SEP ① (*lit*) [+ *thing*] emporter, enlever ; (= *kidnap*) enlever, ravir
② (*fig*) [+ *prizes, honours*] remporter ◆ **to ~ it off well** bien s'en tirer ◆ **to ~ it off** * réussir (son coup)
③ (*euph*) ◆ **he was carried off by pneumonia** il a été emporté par une pneumonie

► **carry on** VI ① (= *continue*) continuer (*doing sth* à *or* de faire qch) ; ◆ **~ on!** continuez ! ◆ **~ on with your work!** continuez votre travail ! ◆ **if you ~ on like that …** si tu continues comme ça …
② (* = *make a scene*) faire une scène, faire des histoires ◆ **you do ~ on!** tu en fais des histoi-

res ! ♦ **don't ~ on so!** ne fais (donc) pas tant d'histoires *or* toute une scène ! *

3 *(= have an affair)* **to be ~ing on with sb** * avoir une liaison avec qn

VT SEP 1 *(= conduct) [+ business, trade]* faire marcher, diriger ; *[+ correspondence]* entretenir ; *[+ conversation]* soutenir ; *[+ negotiations]* mener

2 *(= continue) [+ business, conversation]* continuer, poursuivre ; *[+ tradition]* entretenir, continuer

VT FUS ♦ **he carried on a passionate affair with Mrs Gilbert** il avait une liaison passionnée avec Mme Gilbert

N ♦ **carry-on** * → **carry**

► **carry out** VT SEP 1 *(lit) [+ thing, sick or injured person, meal]* emporter ♦ **the current carried him out (to sea)** le courant l'a entraîné vers le large

2 *(fig = put into action) [+ plan]* exécuter, mettre en œuvre ; *[+ order]* exécuter ; *[+ idea, threat]* mettre à exécution, donner suite à ; *[+ obligation]* s'acquitter de ; *[+ experiment]* se livrer à, effectuer ; *[+ search, investigation, inquiry]* mener, procéder à, conduire ; *[+ reform]* effectuer, mettre en œuvre ; *[+ the law, regulations]* appliquer ♦ **to ~ out one's duty** faire son devoir ♦ **to ~ out one's duties** s'acquitter de ses fonctions ♦ **to ~ out a promise** respecter *or* tenir une promesse

► **carry over** VT SEP 1 *(lit)* faire passer du côté opposé, faire traverser

2 *(from one page to the other)* reporter ; *(Accounting, Stock Exchange)* reporter ♦ **to ~ over stock from one season to the next** *(in shop)* stocker des marchandises d'une saison à l'autre

► **carry through** VT SEP *[+ plan]* mener à bonne fin, exécuter ; *[+ person]* soutenir dans l'épreuve ♦ **his courage carried him through** son courage lui a permis de surmonter l'épreuve

► **carry up** VT SEP monter

carryall /ˈkærɪɔːl/ N *(US)* (sac *m*) fourre-tout *m inv*

carrycot /ˈkærɪkɒt/ N *(Brit) (gen)* porte-bébé *m* ; *(wicker)* moïse *m*

carrying-on /ˈkærɪɪŋˈɒn/ N 1 *(NonC) [of work, business etc]* continuation *f* 2 *(often pl: pej)* **carryings-on** * façons *fpl* de se conduire *or* de faire

cart /kɑːt/ N *(horse-drawn)* charrette *f* ; (also **tip-cart**) tombereau *m* ; (also **hand cart**) voiture *f* à bras ; *(US: for luggage, shopping)* chariot *m* ♦ **to put the ~ before the horse** mettre la charrue avant les bœufs VT *[+ goods] (in van, truck)* transporter (par camion), camionner ; *(in cart)* charroyer, charrier ; (* : also **cart about, cart around**) *[+ shopping, books]* trimballer *, coltiner

COMP **cart horse** N cheval *m* de trait

cart track N chemin *m* rural *or* de terre

► **cart away, cart off** VT SEP *[+ goods]* emporter ; *[+ garbage]* ramasser

cartage /ˈkɑːtɪdʒ/ N *(in van, truck)* camionnage *m*, transport *m* ; *(in cart)* charroi *m*

carte blanche /ˌkɑːtˈblɑːntʃ/ N *(NonC)* carte *f* blanche ♦ **to give sb ~ to do sth** donner carte blanche à qn pour faire qch

cartel /kɑːˈtel/ N cartel *m*

carter /ˈkɑːtəʳ/ N charretier *m*

Cartesian /kɑːˈtiːzɪən/ ADJ, N cartésien(ne) *m(f)*

Cartesianism /kɑːˈtiːzɪənɪzəm/ N cartésianisme *m*

Carthage /ˈkɑːθɪdʒ/ N Carthage

Carthaginian /ˌkɑːθəˈdʒɪnɪən/ N *(Rel)* Carthaginois *m* ADJ carthaginois

Carthusian /kɑːˈθjuːzɪən/ ADJ de(s) chartreux ♦ **a ~ monk** un chartreux N chartreux *m*, -euse *f*

cartilage /ˈkɑːtɪlɪdʒ/ N cartilage *m*

cartload /ˈkɑːtləʊd/ N charretée *f*

cartographer /kɑːˈtɒɡrəfəʳ/ N cartographe *mf*

cartographic(al) /ˌkɑːtəˈɡræfɪk(l)/ ADJ cartographique

cartography /kɑːˈtɒɡrəfɪ/ N cartographie *f*

cartomancy /ˈkɑːtəmænsɪ/ N cartomancie *f*

carton /ˈkɑːtən/ N *(for yogurt, cream)* pot *m* (en carton) ; *(for milk, squash)* carton *m*, brick *m* ; *(for ice cream)* boîte *f (en carton)* ; *(for cigarettes)* cartouche *f*

cartoon /kɑːˈtuːn/ N *[of newspaper etc]* dessin *m* (humoristique) ; *(Cine, TV)* dessin *m* animé ; *(Art = sketch)* carton *m* ♦ **~ strip** *(esp Brit)* bande *f* dessinée VT caricaturer, ridiculiser *(par un dessin humoristique)*

cartoonist /ˌkɑːˈtuːnɪst/ N *[of newspaper etc]* caricaturiste *mf*, dessinateur *m*, -trice *f* humoristique ; *(Cine, TV)* dessinateur *m*, -trice *f* de dessins animés, animateur *m*, -trice *f*

cartridge /ˈkɑːtrɪdʒ/ N *[of rifle etc]* cartouche *f* ; *[of cannon]* gargousse *f* ; *[of stylus]* cellule *f* ; *[of recording tape, typewriter or printer ribbon, pen]* cartouche *f* ; *[of camera]* chargeur *m* ; *(Comput)* chargeur *m*, cartouche *f*

COMP **cartridge belt** N *(= belt)* (ceinture-)cartouchière *f* ; *(= strip)* bande *f* (de mitrailleuse)

cartridge case N *[of rifle]* douille *f*, étui *m* (de cartouche) ; *[of cannon]* douille *f*

cartridge clip N chargeur *m* (d'arme à feu)

cartridge paper N papier *m* à cartouche, papier *m* fort

cartridge player N lecteur *m* de cartouche

cartwheel /ˈkɑːtwiːl/ N *(lit)* roue *f* de charrette ♦ **to do** *or* **turn a ~** faire la roue

cartwright /ˈkɑːtraɪt/ N charron *m*

carve /kɑːv/ VT tailler ; *(= sculpt)* sculpter ; *(= chisel)* ciseler ; *(Culin)* découper ♦ **~d out of** *or* **in wood/ivory** en bois/ivoire sculpté ♦ **~d in(to) the wood/the stone** sculpté dans le bois/la pierre ♦ **to ~ one's initials on** *or* **in sth** graver ses initiales sur qch ♦ **to ~ one's way through sth** se frayer un chemin à travers qch à coups de hache (*or* d'épée *etc*) ♦ **to ~ a road through the jungle** percer une route à travers la jungle ♦ **to ~ a niche for o.s., to ~ o.s. a niche** se faire une place ♦ **to ~ o.s. a career (as)** faire carrière (comme) ; see also **stone**

COMP **carve-up** * N *(fig) [of inheritance]* partage *m* ; *[of estate, country]* morcellement *m*

► **carve out** VT SEP *[+ piece of wood]* découper *(from* dans) ; *[+ piece of land]* prendre *(from* à) ; *[+ statue, figure]* sculpter, tailler ; *(fig) [+ reputation, market share, role]* se tailler ♦ **to ~ out a career (for o.s.) (as)** faire carrière (comme)

► **carve up** VT SEP 1 *[+ meat]* découper ; *(fig) [+ country]* morceler

2 *(* = disfigure) [+ person]* amocher ‡ à coups de couteau ; * *[+ sb's face]* taillader, balafrer

3 *(‡ fig) [+ play, performer]* massacrer *, éreinter ; *[+ candidate, opponent]* tailler en pièces

N ♦ **carve-up** * → **carve**

carver /ˈkɑːvəʳ/ N 1 *(Culin = knife)* couteau *m* à découper ♦ **~s** service *m* à découper 2 *(= person)* personne *f* qui découpe 3 *(Brit = chair)* chaise *f* de salle à manger avec accoudoirs

carvery /ˈkɑːvərɪ/ N grill *m*

carving /ˈkɑːvɪŋ/ N 1 *(Art)* sculpture *f* 2 *(NonC: Culin)* découpage *m* COMP **carving knife** N (pl **carving knives**) couteau *m* à découper

caryatid /ˌkærɪˈætɪd/ N (pl **caryatids** *or* **caryatides** /ˈˌkærɪˈætɪˌdiːz/) cariatide *f*

Casablanca /ˌkæsəˈblæŋkə/ N Casablanca

Casanova /ˌkæsəˈnəʊvə/ N *(also fig)* Casanova *m*

cascade /kæsˈkeɪd/ N cascade *f* ; *(fig) [of ribbons, silks, lace]* flot *m* ; *[of sparks]* pluie *f* VI tomber en cascade

cascara /kæsˈkɑːrə/ N *(Pharm)* cascara sagrada *f*

case¹ /keɪs/ LANGUAGE IN USE 26.2

N 1 *(= fact, eventuality, example)* cas *m* ♦ **is it the ~ that ...?** est-il vrai que ... ? ♦ **that's not the ~** ce n'est pas le cas ♦ **if that's the ~** en ce cas, dans ce cas-là ♦ **as is the ~ here** comme c'est le cas ici ♦ **that** *or* **such** *(frm)* **being the ~** par conséquent ♦ **in such a ~** en pareil cas ♦ **if such is the ~** *(now)* si tel est le cas ; *(= if it happens)* le cas échéant, en pareil cas ♦ **put the ~ that ...** admettons que ... + *subj* ♦ **as the ~ may be** selon le cas ♦ **it's a clear ~ of sexual harassment** c'est un cas flagrant de harcèlement sexuel ♦ **in this ~** dans ce cas ♦ **in that ~** dans ce cas-là ♦ **in no ~** en aucun cas ♦ **in the present ~** dans le cas présent ♦ **as in the ~ of ...** comme dans le cas de ... ♦ **in the ~ in point** en l'occurrence ♦ **here is a ~ in point** en voici un bon exemple, en voici un exemple typique ♦ **in your ~** dans votre cas ♦ **in most ~s** dans la plupart des cas ♦ **in nine ~s out of ten** neuf fois sur dix ♦ **a difficult ~** un cas difficile

♦ **in case** ♦ **in ~ he comes** au cas où *or* pour le cas où il viendrait ♦ **I'm supposed to be in charge here, in ~ you've forgotten!** * je suis censé commander ici, au cas où vous l'auriez oublié ! ♦ **she's nervous about something, in ~ you didn't notice** il y a quelque chose qui la rend nerveuse, au cas où vous ne l'auriez pas remarqué ♦ **in ~ of** en cas de ♦ **(just) in ~** à tout hasard, au cas où *

♦ **in any case** en tout cas, de toute façon

2 *(Med etc)* cas *m* ♦ **six ~s of pneumonia** six cas de pneumonie ♦ **the most serious ~s were sent to hospital** les cas les plus graves *or* les malades les plus atteints ont été envoyés à l'hôpital ♦ **it's a hopeless ~** son cas est désespéré ♦ **he's a hopeless ~** *(fig)* c'est un cas pathologique * ♦ **he's a hard ~** * c'est un dur * ♦ **she's a real ~!** * c'est un cas * *or* un sacré numéro * (celle-là) ! ♦ **to be on sb's ~** ‡ enquiquiner * qn ♦ **to get on sb's ~** ‡ prendre la tête à qn * ♦ **get off my ~!** ‡ lâche-moi les baskets ! ‡, ne me prends pas la tête ! *

3 *(Jur)* affaire *f*, procès *m* ♦ **he's a suspect in the ~** c'est un suspect dans cette affaire *or* ce procès ♦ **to try a ~** juger une affaire ♦ **to win one's ~** *(Jur)* gagner son procès ; *(fig)* avoir gain de cause ♦ **the ~ for the defendant** *or* **defence** les arguments *mpl* en faveur de l'accusé, les arguments *mpl* de la défense ♦ **the ~ for the prosecution** les arguments *mpl* contre l'accusé, les arguments *mpl* de l'accusation ♦ **there is no ~ against ...** il n'y a pas lieu à poursuites contre ... ♦ **he's working on the Gibson ~** il s'occupe de l'affaire Gibson ♦ **~ before the Court** affaire *f* portée devant le tribunal ♦ **his ~ was called today** son affaire est venue aujourd'hui devant le tribunal ♦ **to take a ~ to the High Court** saisir le tribunal de grande instance d'une affaire

4 *(= argument, reasoning)* arguments *mpl* ♦ **to make out one's ~** présenter ses arguments ♦ **to make a ~ for sth** plaider en faveur de qch ♦ **to make (out) a good ~ for sth** réunir *or* présenter de bons arguments en faveur de qch ♦ **to make out a good ~ for doing sth** bien expliquer pourquoi il faudrait faire qch ♦ **there is a strong ~ for/against compulsory vaccination** il y a *or* aurait beaucoup à dire en faveur de la/contre la vaccination obligatoire ♦ **there's a ~ for saying that ...** on peut à raison *or* légitimement dire que ... ♦ **there's a ~ for refusing to sign the contract** il y a des arguments *or* des raisons pour refuser de signer le contrat ♦ **that is my ~** voilà mes arguments ♦ **a ~ of conscience** un cas de conscience ♦ **to have a good/strong ~** avoir de bons/solides arguments

5 *(Gram)* cas *m* ♦ **the nominative ~** le nominatif ♦ **the accusative ~** l'accusatif *m*

COMP **case conference** N *(Med, Social Work) réunion de spécialistes pour parler d'un patient ou d'un cas social*
case file N *(Jur, Med, Social Work)* dossier *m*
case grammar N *(Gram)* grammaire *f* des cas
case history N *(Social Work)* passé *m* du *(or* d'un) cas social ; *(Med) (= past facts)* antécédents *mpl* médicaux ; *(= past and present development)* évolution *f* de la maladie
case law N *(NonC: Jur)* droit *m* jurisprudentiel
case load N *(Social Work)* dossiers *mpl (confiés à un assistant social)* ◆ **to have a heavy ~ load** avoir beaucoup de dossiers à traiter
case notes NPL *(Jur, Med, Social Work)* (notes *fpl* pour l'établissement d'un) dossier *m*
case papers NPL *(Jur, Med, Social Work)* pièces *fpl* du dossier
case study N étude *f* de cas ◆ **~ study method** *(US Univ)* méthode *f* des cas
case system N *(Gram)* système *m* casuel
case work N *(Social Work)* travail *m* avec des cas (sociaux) individuels
case worker N *(Social Work)* ≈ assistant(e) social(e)

case[2] /keɪs/ N 1 *(Brit = suitcase)* valise *f* ; *(= packing case)* caisse *f* ; *(= crate: for bottles etc)* caisse *f* ; *(for peaches, lettuce, oysters etc)* cageot *m* ; *(= box)* boîte *f* ; *(= chest)* coffre *m* ; *(for goods on display)* vitrine *f* ; *(for jewels)* coffret *m* ; *(for watch, pen, necklace etc)* écrin *m* ; *(for camera, binoculars etc)* étui *m* ; *(= covering)* enveloppe *f* ; *(Bookbinding)* couverture *f* ; *(= casing of machine)* boîte *f* ; *(in car engine)* carter *m* ◆ **violin/umbrella** *etc* **~** étui *m* à violon/parapluie *etc* ; → **bookcase, pillowcase**

2 *(Typ)* casse *f* ; → **lower[1], upper**

VT 1 mettre dans une caisse *or* un cageot *etc*, mettre en boîte

2 ◆ **to ~ the joint*** *[burglars etc]* surveiller la maison *etc (avant un mauvais coup)*

COMP **cased edition** N *(of book)* édition *f* sous coffret
case-harden VT *(Metal)* cémenter ; *(fig)* endurcir
case knife N (pl **case knives**) *(US)* couteau *m* à gaine
case-sensitive ADJ *(Comput)* sensible à la casse

casebook /'keɪsbʊk/ N *(Social Work)* comptes rendus *mpl or* rapports *mpl* de cas sociaux *(réunis dans un registre)*

casement /'keɪsmənt/ N *(= window)* fenêtre *f* (à battants), croisée *f* ; *(= frame)* battant *m* de fenêtre ; *(liter)* fenêtre *f*

cash /kæʃ/ N *(NonC)* 1 *(= notes and coins)* espèces *fpl*, argent *m* ◆ **how much ~ is there in the till?** combien d'argent y a-t-il dans la caisse ? ◆ **I want to be paid in ~ and not by cheque** je veux être payé en espèces et non par chèque ◆ **to pay in ~** payer en argent comptant *or* en espèces ◆ **~ or charge?** *(esp US: in shop)* vous payez en espèces ou par carte ? ◆ **to take the ~ to the bank** porter l'argent à la banque ◆ **ready ~** (argent *m*) liquide *m* ◆ **how much do you have in (ready) ~?** combien avez-vous en liquide ? ; → **hard, petty, spot**

2 ◆ **~ down** *(= immediate payment)* argent *m* comptant ◆ **to pay ~ (down)** payer comptant *or* cash* ◆ **discount for ~** escompte *m or* remise *f* au comptant ◆ **~ with order** payable à la commande ◆ **~ on delivery** paiement *m* à la livraison, livraison *f* contre espèces *or* contre remboursement ◆ **~ on shipment** comptant *m* à l'expédition

3 *(* = money in general)* argent *m*, sous* *mpl* ◆ **how much ~ have you got?** combien d'argent as-tu ?, qu'est-ce que tu as comme argent ? ◆ **I have no ~** je n'ai pas un sou *or* un rond* ◆ **to be short of ~** être à court d'argent ◆ **I am out of ~** je suis à sec*, je n'ai plus de sous*

VT *[+ cheque]* encaisser, toucher ◆ **to ~ sb a cheque** donner à qn de l'argent contre un chèque ; *[bank]* payer un chèque à qn ◆ **to ~ a bill** encaisser une facture

COMP *(gen) [problems, calculations etc]* d'argent
cash account N compte *m* de caisse
cash advance N *(Fin)* crédit *m* de caisse
cash-and-carry N libre-service *m* de gros, cash and carry *m inv* ADJ *[goods, business]* de gros, de cash and carry
cash bar N bar *m* payant *(à une réception)*
cash card N carte *f* bancaire *(permettant le retrait d'argent aux distributeurs de billets)*
cash cow* N *(Comm)* mine *f* d'or *(fig)*
cash crop N culture *f* de rapport *or* commerciale
cash dealings NPL transactions *fpl* immédiates
cash deficit N déficit *m or* découvert *m* de trésorerie
cash desk N *[of shop, restaurant]* caisse *f* ; *[of cinema, theatre]* guichet *m*
cash discount N escompte *m or* remise *f* au comptant
cash dispenser N distributeur *m* (automatique) de billets
cash economy N économie *f* monétaire
cash flow N marge *f* brute d'autofinancement, cash-flow *m* ◆ **~ flow problems** difficultés *fpl* de trésorerie
cash holdings NPL avoirs *mpl* en caisse *or* en numéraire
cash income N revenu *m* monétaire
cash in hand N espèces *fpl* en caisse, encaisse *f* ADV ◆ **$100, ~ in hand** 100 dollars, de la main à la main
cash machine N *(US)* ⇒ **cash dispenser**
cash offer N offre *f* d'achat avec paiement comptant ◆ **he made me a ~ offer** il m'a offert de l'argent
cash payment N paiement *m* comptant, versement *m* en espèces
cash point N *(in shop)* caisse *f* ; *(Brit = cash dispenser)* distributeur *m* (automatique) de billets
cash price N prix *m* (au) comptant
cash prize N prix *m* en espèces
cash receipts NPL recettes *fpl* de caisse
cash reduction N ⇒ **cash discount**
cash register N caisse *f* (enregistreuse)
cash reserves NPL liquidités *fpl*
cash sale N vente *f* (au) comptant
cash squeeze N *(Econ)* restrictions *fpl* de crédit
cash terms NPL conditions *fpl* au comptant
cash transaction N affaire *f or* opération *f* au comptant

► **cash in** VT SEP *[+ bonds, savings certificates]* réaliser, se faire rembourser

► **cash in on*** VT FUS tirer profit de

► **cash up** VI *(Brit)* faire sa caisse

cashback /'kæʃbæk/ N 1 *(= discount)* remise *f* 2 *(at supermarket etc) retrait d'espèces à la caisse d'un magasin*

cashbook /'kæʃbʊk/ N livre *m* de caisse

cashbox /'kæʃbɒks/ N caisse *f*

cashew /kæ'ʃuː/ N anacardier *m* ; (also **cashew nut**) noix *f* de cajou

cashier[1] /kæ'ʃɪəʳ/ N *(Comm, Banking)* caissier *m*, -ière *f*

COMP **cashier's check** N *(US)* chèque *m* de banque
cashier's desk N *(US)* caisse *f*

cashier[2] /kæ'ʃɪəʳ/ VT *(Mil)* casser ; *(gen)* renvoyer, congédier

cashless /'kæʃlɪs/ ADJ ◆ **the ~ society** *or* **economy** la société sans argent *(où l'on ne paie plus qu'en argent électronique)*

cashmere /kæʃ'mɪəʳ/ N cachemire *m* COMP de *or* en cachemire

casing /'keɪsɪŋ/ N *(gen)* revêtement *m*, enveloppe *f* ; *[of door, window]* chambranle *m* ; *[of tyre]* chape *f* ; *[of oil well]* cuvelage *m*

casino /kə'siːnəʊ/ N casino *m*

cask /kɑːsk/ N *(gen)* tonneau *m*, fût *m* ; *(large)* pièce *f*, barrique *f* ; *(small)* baril *m* ◆ **wine in ~** vin *m* en fût

casket /'kɑːskɪt/ N *[of jewels etc]* coffret *m*, boîte *f* ; *(esp US = coffin)* cercueil *m*

Caspian /'kæspɪən/ ADJ ◆ **the ~ Sea** la mer Caspienne

Cassandra /kə'sændrə/ N *(Myth, fig)* Cassandre *f*

cassava /kə'sɑːvə/ N *(= plant)* manioc *m* ; *(= flour)* farine *f* de manioc

casserole /'kæsərəʊl/ N *(Brit Culin = utensil)* cocotte *f* ; *(= food)* ragoût *m* VT *[+ meat]* (faire) cuire en *or* à la cocotte COMP **casserole dish** N cocotte *f*

⚠ **casserole** is not translated by the French word **casserole**, which means 'saucepan'.

cassette /kæ'set/ N *(Recording)* cassette *f* ; *(Phot)* recharge *f*

COMP **cassette deck** N platine *f* (à) cassettes
cassette player N lecteur *m* de cassettes
cassette recorder N magnétophone *m* à cassettes

cassis /kæ'siːs/ N cassis *m*

cassock /'kæsək/ N soutane *f*

cassowary /'kæsəweərɪ/ N casoar *m*

cast /kɑːst/ (vb : pret, ptp **cast**) N 1 *(= throw) [of dice, net]* coup *m* ; *(Fishing)* lancer *m*

2 *(Art, Tech = act of casting metal)* coulage *m*, coulée *f*

3 *(= mould)* moule *m* ; *(in plaster, metal etc)* moulage *m* ; *[of medallion etc]* empreinte *f* ◆ **to have one's leg in a ~** *(Med)* avoir une jambe dans le plâtre ◆ **~ of features** *(fig)* traits *mpl* (du visage) ◆ **~ of mind** *or* **thought** mentalité *f*, tournure *f* d'esprit ◆ **a man of quite a different ~** un homme d'une tout autre trempe ; → **plaster**

4 *(Theat) (= allocation of parts)* distribution *f* ; *(= actors collectively)* acteurs *mpl* ◆ **~ (and credits)** *(Cine, TV)* générique *m* ◆ **~ list** *(Theat etc)* distribution *f* ◆ **he was in the ~ of Evita** il a joué dans Evita

5 *[of snake]* dépouille *f* ; *[of worm]* déjections *fpl*

6 *(Med = squint)* strabisme *m* ◆ **to have a ~ in one eye** avoir un œil qui louche, loucher d'un œil

VT 1 *(= throw) [+ dice]* jeter ; *[+ net, fishing line, stone]* lancer, jeter ◆ **to ~ anchor** *(Naut)* jeter l'ancre, mouiller (l'ancre) ◆ **to ~ sb into jail** jeter qn en prison ◆ **to ~ sb's horoscope** tirer *or* dresser l'horoscope de qn ◆ **to ~ o.s. on sb's mercy** *(liter)* s'en remettre à la clémence *(liter)* de qn, remettre son sort entre les mains de qn ◆ **to ~ a vote** voter ◆ **to ~ aspersions on sth/sb** dénigrer qch/qn ◆ **to ~ the blame on sb** rejeter la responsabilité sur qn ◆ **to ~ doubt on sth** jeter un doute sur qch ◆ **to ~ a look at sth** jeter un regard sur qch ◆ **to ~ a shadow on** *or* **over sb/sth** *(lit)* projeter une ombre sur qn/qch ; *(fig)* jeter une ombre sur qn/qch ◆ **to ~ a light on sth** *(lit)* éclairer qch ◆ **to ~ one's eye(s) round a room** promener ses regards sur une pièce, balayer une pièce du regard ◆ **to ~ one's eye(s) in the direction of ...** porter les yeux *or* son regard du côté de ... ◆ **to ~ a critical eye on sth** considérer qch d'un œil critique ◆ **to ~ a greedy eye** *or* **greedy eyes on sth** dévorer qch des yeux ; → **die[2], light[1], lot[2], spell[1]**

2 *(= shed)* ◆ **to ~ its skin** *[snake]* muer ◆ **to ~ a shoe** *[horse]* perdre un fer

3 *(Art, Tech) [+ plaster]* couler ; *[+ metal]* couler, fondre ; *[+ statue]* mouler ; → **mould[1], stone**

4 *[+ play, film]* distribuer les rôles de ◆ **he was ~ as Hamlet** *or* **for the part of Hamlet** on lui a donné le rôle de Hamlet
5 *(= describe)* étiqueter, cataloguer ◆ **to ~ o.s. as** se présenter comme
VI *(Fishing)* lancer sa ligne
COMP **cast-iron** N fonte *f* ADJ de *or* en fonte ; *(fig) [will, constitution]* de fer ; *[excuse, alibi]* inattaquable, (en) béton* ; *[case]* solide
cast-off clothes, cast-offs NPL vêtements *mpl* dont on ne veut plus ; *(pej)* vieilles nippes* *fpl* *or* frusques* *fpl* ◆ **the ~-offs from society** les laissés *mpl* pour compte (de la société)

► **cast about, cast around** VI ◆ **to cast about for sth** chercher qch ◆ **she has been ~ing around for a good excuse to ...** elle cherche une bonne excuse pour ... ◆ **to ~ about for how to do/how to reply** chercher le moyen de faire/la façon de répondre

► **cast aside** VT SEP rejeter, mettre de côté ; *(fig) [+ person]* rejeter, abandonner ; *[+ object]* abandonner, se défaire de

► **cast away** VT SEP rejeter ; *(fig)* se défaire de ◆ **to be ~ away** *(Naut)* être naufragé

► **cast back** VI *(fig, liter)* revenir *(to* à)
VT SEP ◆ **to cast one's thoughts back** se reporter en arrière

► **cast down** VT SEP *[+ object]* jeter par terre ; *[+ eyes]* baisser ; *[+ weapons]* déposer, mettre bas ◆ **to be ~ down** *(fig, liter)* être abattu

► **cast in** VI, VT SEP ◆ **to cast in (one's lot) with sb** partager le sort de qn

► **cast off** VI *(Naut)* larguer les amarres, appareiller ; *(Knitting)* rabattre les mailles
VT SEP *(Naut)* larguer les amarres de ; *(Knitting)* arrêter ; *[+ bonds, chains] (lit)* se défaire de, se libérer de ; *(fig)* s'affranchir de ◆ **~ off eight stitches at the beginning of the next row** *(Knitting)* rabattez huit mailles au début du prochain rang
N ◆ **cast-off** ADJ → **cast**

► **cast on** *(Knitting)* VI monter les mailles
VT SEP *[+ stitch, sleeve]* monter ◆ **~ on 159 stitches** montez 159 mailles

► **cast out** VT SEP *(liter)* chasser

► **cast up** VT SEP 1 *(lit)* lancer en l'air ◆ **to ~ one's eyes up** lever les yeux au ciel
2 ◆ **the ship was cast up on a beach** le navire s'est échoué sur une plage ◆ **~ up by the sea** rejeté par la mer
3 *(Math)* calculer
4 *(fig = reproach)* **to ~ sth up to** *or* **at sb** reprocher qch à qn

castanets /ˌkæstəˈnets/ NPL castagnettes *fpl*

castaway /ˈkɑːstəweɪ/ N naufragé(e) *m(f)* ; *(fig: from society etc)* réprouvé(e) *m(f)*, paria *m*

caste /kɑːst/ N caste *f*, classe *f* sociale ◆ **to lose ~** déroger, déchoir
COMP **caste mark** N *(in India)* signe *m* de (la) caste ; *(fig)* signe *m* distinctif (d'un groupe)
caste system N système *m* des castes

castellated /ˈkæstəleɪtɪd/ ADJ *(Archit)* crénelé, de style féodal COMP **castellated nut** N *(Tech)* écrou *m* crénelé

caster /ˈkɑːstəʳ/ N 1 *(= sifter)* saupoudroir *m* 2 *(= wheel)* roulette *f*
COMP **caster angle** N *[of car]* angle *m* de chasse
caster sugar N *(Brit)* sucre *m* en poudre

castigate /ˈkæstɪgeɪt/ VT *[+ person]* châtier *(liter)*, corriger ; *[+ book etc]* éreinter ; *[+ theory, vice]* fustiger *(liter)*

castigation /ˌkæstɪˈgeɪʃən/ N *[of person]* châtiment *m*, correction *f* ; *[of book etc]* éreintement *m*

Castile /kæˈstiːl/ N Castille *f*

Castilian /kæsˈtɪlɪən/ ADJ castillan N 1 Castillan(e) *m(f)* 2 *(= language)* espagnol *m*, castillan *m*

casting /ˈkɑːstɪŋ/ N *(NonC = act of throwing)* lancer *m*, lancement *m* ; *(Tech) (= act)* fonte *f*, coulée *f* ; *(= object)* pièce *f* fondue ; *(Art)* moulage *m* ; *(Theat)* distribution *f* ; *(Cine)* casting *m*
COMP **casting couch** N ◆ **she got the role on the ~ couch** elle a couché pour avoir ce rôle
casting director N *(Theat)* responsable *mf* de la distribution ; *(Cine)* directeur *m*, -trice *f* du casting
casting vote N voix *f* prépondérante ◆ **to have a** *or* **the ~ vote** avoir voix prépondérante

castle /ˈkɑːsl/ N 1 château *m* (fort) ; → **build** 2 *(Chess)* tour *f* VI *(Chess)* roquer

castling /ˈkɑːslɪŋ/ N *(Chess)* roque *f*

castor¹ /ˈkɑːstəʳ/ N ⇒ **caster**

castor² /ˈkɑːstəʳ/ N 1 *(= beaver)* castor *m* 2 *(Med)* castoréum *m*
COMP **castor oil** N huile *f* de ricin
castor oil plant N ricin *m*

castrate /kæsˈtreɪt/ VT *[+ animal, man]* châtrer, castrer ; *(fig) [+ personality]* émasculer ; *[+ text, film, book]* expurger

castration /kæsˈtreɪʃən/ N castration *f*

castrato /kæsˈtrɑːtəʊ/ N (pl **castrato** *or* **castrati** /kæsˈtrɑːtiː/) castrat *m*

Castroism /ˈkæstrəʊɪzəm/ N *(Pol)* castrisme *m*

Castroist /ˈkæstrəʊɪst/ ADJ, N *(Pol)* castriste *mf*

casual /ˈkæʒjʊl/ ADJ 1 *(= nonchalant) [person, manner, attitude, tone, glance, wave]* désinvolte ; *[chat, conversation]* informel ◆ **he tried to sound ~** il a essayé de parler avec désinvolture ◆ **to the ~ eye** *or* **observer** pour le simple observateur ◆ **he ran a ~ eye down the page** il a négligemment parcouru la page ◆ **to be ~ about sth** *(pej)* prendre qch à la légère *or* avec désinvolture ◆ **her ~ attitude (to safety/discipline)** la désinvolture dont elle fait preuve (en matière de sécurité/discipline)
2 *(= occasional) [drinker, drug use, relationship]* occasionnel ; *[sexual partner]* occasionnel ◆ **a ~ acquaintance** une (simple) connaissance ◆ **a ~ affair** une passade, une aventure ◆ **~ contact** contacts *mpl* ordinaires ◆ **~ drug users** les consommateurs *mpl* (de drogue) occasionnels ◆ **~ sex** rapports *mpl* sexuels occasionnels ◆ **to have ~ sex** faire l'amour au hasard d'une rencontre
3 *(= by chance) [remark, comment]* fait en passant ; *[meeting, encounter]* fortuit ; *[spark]* accidentel ; *[visitor, caller]* de passage
4 *(= informal) [clothes, shoes]* sport *inv*, décontracté ◆ **~ wear** vêtements *mpl* sport *inv*, tenue *f* décontractée
5 *(= temporary) [work, employment, job, labour]* temporaire ; *[farm worker] (daily)* journalier ; *(seasonally)* saisonnier ◆ **~ labourer** *(on building site)* ouvrier *m* sans travail fixe ; *(on farm, daily)* journalier *m*, -ière *f* ; *(seasonally)* saisonnier *m*, -ière *f* ◆ **on a ~ basis** à titre temporaire
N 1 ◆ **~s** *(= clothes)* vêtements *mpl* sport *inv* ; *(= shoes)* chaussures *fpl* sport *inv*
2 *(= worker) (in office)* employé(e) *m(f)* temporaire ; *(in factory)* ouvrier *m*, -ière *f* temporaire

casualize /ˈkæʒjʊlaɪz/ VT précariser

casually /ˈkæʒjʊlɪ/ ADV 1 *(= nonchalantly) [mention, say, ask, walk, lean]* avec désinvolture 2 *(= accidentally)* par hasard 3 *(= informally) [dress]* de façon décontractée, décontracté* *inv*

casualness /ˈkæʒjʊlnɪs/ N *[of speech, manner]* désinvolture *f* ; *[of dress]* style *m* décontracté

casualty /ˈkæʒjʊltɪ/ N 1 *(Mil) (= dead)* mort(e) *m(f)* ; *(= wounded)* blessé(e) *m(f)* ◆ **casualties** les morts *mpl* et blessés *mpl* ; *(= dead)* les pertes *fpl* 2 *(= accident victim)* accidenté(e) *m(f)*, victime *f* ; *(= accident)* accident *m*
COMP **casualty department** N service *m* des urgences
casualty list N *(in war)* état *m* des pertes ; *(after accident)* liste *f* des victimes
casualty ward N salle *f* des urgences

casuist /ˈkæzjʊɪst/ N casuiste *mf*

casuistry /ˈkæzjʊɪstrɪ/ N *(NonC)* casuistique *f* ; *(instance of this)* arguments *mpl* de casuiste

CAT N 1 /ˌsiːeɪˈtiː/ (abbrev of **computer-aided teaching**) EAO *m* 2 /kæt/ (abbrev of **computerized axial tomography**) scanographie *f*, tomodensitométrie *f*, scanner* *m*
COMP **CAT scan** N scanographie *f*, tomodensitométrie *f*, scanner* *m* ◆ **to have a ~ scan** se faire faire une scanographie *or* un scanner*
CAT scanner N tomodensitomètre *m*, scanner* *m*

cat /kæt/ N 1 chat *m* ; *(specifically female)* chatte *f* ; *(= species)* félin *m* ; *(* pej = woman)* mégère *f* ◆ **the big ~s** les fauves *mpl* ; → **tabby, tom**
2 ⇒ **cat-o'-nine-tails**
3 *(phrases)* **to let the ~ out of the bag** vendre la mèche ◆ **the ~'s out of the bag** ce n'est plus un secret maintenant ◆ **to look like the ~ that got the cream** *(esp Brit) or* **that ate the canary** avoir l'air content de soi ◆ **to wait for the ~ to jump, to wait to see which way the ~ jumps** attendre pour voir d'où vient le vent ◆ **(has the) ~ got your tongue?** * tu as perdu ta langue ? ◆ **to fight** *or* **be at each other like ~ and dog** *(lit)* se battre comme des chiffonniers ; *(fig)* être *or* s'entendre comme chien et chat ◆ **to fight like Kilkenny ~s** *(† Brit)* se battre comme des chiffonniers ◆ **he doesn't have a ~ in hell's chance of winning** il n'a pas l'ombre d'une chance de gagner ◆ **a ~ may look at a king** *(Prov)* un chien regarde bien un évêque *(Prov)* ◆ **to be like a ~ on a hot tin roof** *or* **a ~ on hot bricks** être sur des charbons ardents ◆ **when** *or* **while the ~'s away the mice will play** *(Prov)* quand le chat n'est pas là, les souris dansent ◆ **that set the ~ among the pigeons** ça a été le pavé dans la mare ◆ **he thinks he's the ~'s whiskers** *or* **the ~'s miaow*** il se prend pour le nombril du monde* ◆ **to be a bag of ~s*** *(Ir)* être d'une humeur massacrante *or* de chien *(pej)* ◆ **look what the ~ dragged in** *or* **brought in!*** *(pej)* regarde donc un peu qui pointe son nez ! ◆ **you look like something the ~ dragged in** *or* **brought in!*** *(pej)* non mais regarde à quoi tu ressembles ! ; see also **comp** ; → **bell¹, grin, rain, room, skin**
4 *(US* ‡*)* *(= man)* gars* *m*, type* *m* ; *(= woman)* gonzesse‡ *f*, nana* *f* ◆ **cool ~** type *m* (*or* nana *f*) cool*
5 ◆ **~s and dogs** *(= dodgy shares)* actions *fpl* et obligations *fpl* de valeur douteuse ; *(= less popular goods)* articles *mpl* peu demandés
6 *(* = catalytic converter)* pot *m* catalytique
COMP **cat-and-mouse** N, ADJ *(fig)* ◆ **to play (at) ~-and-mouse with sb, to play a ~-and-mouse game with sb** jouer au chat et à la souris avec qn
cat-basket N *(for carrying)* panier *m* pour chat ; *(for sleeping)* corbeille *f* pour chat
cat burglar N monte-en-l'air* *m inv*
cat door N chatière *f*
cat fight* N *(esp US: between women)* crêpage *m* de chignon*
cat flap N ⇒ **cat door**
cat-lick* N toilette *f* de chat, brin *m* de toilette ◆ **to give o.s. a ~-lick** faire une toilette de chat *or* un brin de toilette
cat litter N litière *f* (pour chats)
cat-o'-nine-tails N *(pl inv)* martinet *m*, chat-à-neuf-queues *m*
cat's-cradle N (jeu *m* des) figures *fpl (que l'on forme entre ses doigts avec de la ficelle)*
cat's-eye N *(= gemstone)* œil-de-chat *m* ; *(Brit: on road)* (clou *m* à) catadioptre *m*, cataphote® *m*

cat's-paw N dupe *f (qui tire les marrons du feu)*
cat's-whisker N *(Rad)* chercheur *m* (du détecteur à galène)

cataclysm /ˈkætəklɪzəm/ N cataclysme *m*

cataclysmic /ˌkætəˈklɪzmɪk/ ADJ cataclysmique

catacombs /ˈkætəkuːmz/ NPL catacombes *fpl*

catafalque /ˈkætəfælk/ N catafalque *m*

Catalan /ˈkætəˌlæn/ N Catalan(e) *m(f)* ; *(= language)* catalan *m* ADJ catalan

catalepsy /ˈkætəlepsɪ/ N catalepsie *f*

cataleptic /ˌkætəˈleptɪk/ ADJ cataleptique

catalogue, catalog *(US)* /ˈkætəlɒg/ N *(gen)* catalogue *m* ; *(in library)* fichier *m* ; *(US Univ etc = brochure)* brochure *f (d'un établissement d'enseignement supérieur)* VT cataloguer

Catalonia /ˌkætəˈləʊnɪə/ N Catalogne *f*

catalysis /kəˈtæləsɪs/ N (pl **catalyses** /kəˈtæləˌsiːz/) catalyse *f*

catalyst /ˈkætəlɪst/ N *(Chem, fig)* catalyseur *m*

catalytic /ˌkætəˈlɪtɪk/ ADJ *(Tech)* catalytique ; *(fig) [person]* qui agit comme un catalyseur ; *[role]* de catalyseur COMP **catalytic converter** N *(Aut)* pot *m* catalytique

catalyze /ˈkætəlaɪz/ VT *(US Chem, fig)* catalyser

catamaran /ˌkætəməˈræn/ N catamaran *m*

cataphoric /ˌkætəˈfɒrɪk/ ADJ *(Ling)* cataphorique

catapult /ˈkætəpʌlt/ N *(Brit = slingshot)* lance-pierre(s) *m inv* ; *(= war machine, device on aircraft carrier)* catapulte *f* VT catapulter
COMP **catapult-launched** ADJ catapulté
catapult launching N catapultage *m*

cataract /ˈkætərækt/ N 1 *(= waterfall)* cataracte *f* 2 *(in eye)* cataracte *f*

catarrh /kəˈtɑːʳ/ N rhume *m* (chronique), catarrhe *m*

catarrhal /kəˈtɑːrəl/ ADJ catarrheux

catastrophe /kəˈtæstrəfɪ/ N catastrophe *f*

catastrophic /ˌkætəˈstrɒfɪk/ ADJ catastrophique

catastrophically /ˌkætəˈstrɒfɪklɪ/ ADV de façon catastrophique ◆ **~ inept** d'une ineptie catastrophique ◆ **to go ~ wrong** tourner à la catastrophe ◆ **supplies were at ~ low levels** les vivres étaient tombés à un niveau catastrophique

catatonia /ˌkætəˈtəʊnɪə/ N *(NonC)* catatonie *f*

catatonic /ˌkætəˈtɒnɪk/ ADJ catatonique

catbird /ˈkætbɜːd/ N *(US)* ◆ **to be (sitting) in the ~ seat** * être en position de force

catcall /ˈkætkɔːl/ N sifflet *m* VI siffler

catch /kætʃ/ (vb : pret, ptp **caught**) N 1 *(= act, thing caught)* prise *f*, capture *f* ; *(Fishing) (= several fish)* prise *f* ; *(= one fish)* prise *f* ◆ **good ~!** *(Sport)* bien rattrapé ! ◆ **the fisherman lost his whole ~** le pêcheur a perdu toute sa pêche ◆ **he's a good ~** * *(as husband)* c'est un beau parti

2 *(* = concealed drawback)* attrape *f*, entourloupette* *f* ◆ **there must be a ~ (in it)** il y a anguille sous roche ◆ **where's the ~?** qu'est-ce qui se cache là-dessous ?

3 *[of buckle]* ardillon *m* ; *(Brit: on door)* loquet *m* ; *[of latch]* mentonnet *m* ; *[of wheel]* cliquet *m* ; *(Brit: on window)* loqueteau *m*

4 *(fig)* ◆ **with a ~ in one's voice** d'une voix entrecoupée

5 *(Mus)* canon *m*

6 *(= ballgame)* jeu *m* de balle ; *(= tag)* (jeu *m* du) chat *m*

VT 1 *[+ ball]* attraper ; *[+ object]* attraper, saisir ; *[+ fish, mice, thief]* attraper ◆ **to ~ an animal in a trap** prendre un animal dans un piège *or* au piège ◆ **to ~ sb by the arm, to ~ sb's arm** prendre qn par le bras ◆ **to be caught between two people/alternatives** être pris entre deux personnes/possibilités ◆ **a toaster with a tray to ~ the breadcrumbs** un grille-pain avec un plateau pour ramasser les miettes de pain ◆ **you can usually ~ me (in) around noon** * en général on peut me trouver vers midi ◆ **I dialled her number hoping to ~ her before she went to work** je lui ai téléphoné en espérant l'avoir * *or* la joindre avant qu'elle (ne) parte au travail ◆ **hello Adrienne, glad I caught you** * bonjour Adrienne, je suis content de te trouver *or* que tu sois là ◆ **can I ring you back? you've caught me at a bad time** je peux vous rappeler ? je suis occupé en ce moment ◆ **(I'll) ~ you later!** * à plus ! *, à plus tard ! ; → **crab¹, sun**

2 *(= take by surprise)* surprendre ◆ **to ~ sb doing sth** surprendre qn à faire qch ◆ **to be caught unprepared** être pris au dépourvu ◆ **to ~ sb by surprise** prendre qn à l'improviste ◆ **to be caught cold** *(esp Brit Sport)* être pris au dépourvu ◆ **she caught herself dreaming of Spain** elle se surprit à rêver de l'Espagne ◆ **I caught myself feeling sorry for them** je me suis surpris à les plaindre ◆ **if I ~ them at it!** * si je les y prends ! ◆ **if I ~ you at it again!** * que je t'y reprenne ! ◆ **(you won't) ~ me doing that again!** * (il n'y a) pas de danger que je recommence *subj* !, c'est bien la dernière fois que je le fais ! ◆ **to ~ sb in the act** prendre qn sur le fait *or* en flagrant délit ◆ **we were caught in a storm** nous avons été pris dans *or* surpris par un orage ◆ **to get caught by sb** se faire *or* se laisser attraper par qn

3 *[+ bus, train etc] (= be in time for)* attraper ; *(= get on board)* prendre ◆ **he didn't ~ his train** il a manqué son train ◆ **to ~ the post** arriver à temps pour la levée ◆ **he caught the ferry to France** *(= go by)* il a pris le ferry pour aller en France ◆ **did you ~ the news/that film last night?** (TV) tu as vu *or* pu voir les informations/ce film hier soir ?

4 *(= trap)* **I caught my skirt on the branch, the branch caught my skirt** ma jupe s'est accrochée à la branche ◆ **I caught my skirt in the door, the door caught my skirt** ma jupe s'est prise dans la porte ◆ **the top of the lorry caught the bridge** le haut du camion a accroché le pont ◆ **she caught him with her elbow** elle lui a donné un coup de coude (sans le faire exprès) ◆ **to ~ one's foot in sth** se prendre le pied dans qch

5 *(= understand, hear)* saisir, comprendre ◆ **to ~ the meaning of sth** saisir le sens de qch ◆ **I didn't ~ what he said** je n'ai pas saisi ce qu'il a dit

6 *[+ flavour]* sentir, discerner ◆ **to ~ the sound of sth** percevoir le bruit de qch

7 *(Med) [+ disease]* attraper ◆ **to ~ a cold** attraper un rhume ◆ **to ~ cold** attraper *or* prendre froid ◆ **to ~ one's death of cold** *, **to ~ one's death** * attraper la crève *

8 *(phrases)* **to ~ sb's attention** *or* **eye** attirer l'attention de qn ◆ **to ~ the chairman's eye** obtenir la parole ◆ **to ~ the Speaker's eye** *(Brit Parl)* obtenir la parole *(à la Chambre des communes)* ◆ **to be caught between envy and admiration** osciller entre l'envie et l'admiration ◆ **to ~ sb a blow** donner un coup à qn ◆ **she caught him one** *or* **caught him a blow on the nose** * elle lui a flanqué * un coup sur le nez ◆ **to ~ the light** accrocher la lumière ◆ **his speech caught the mood of the assembly** son discours traduisait *or* reflétait l'humeur de l'assemblée ◆ **to ~ sb with his** (*or* **her** *etc*) **pants** *or* **trousers down** *(fig)* surprendre qn dans une situation embarrassante ◆ **you'll ~ it!** * tu vas écoper ! * ◆ **he caught it all right!** * qu'est-ce qu'il a pris ! * ◆ **to ~ sb on the wrong foot, to ~ sb off balance** *(lit)* prendre qn à contre-pied ; *(fig)* prendre qn au dépourvu ; → **breath, fire, glimpse, likeness, nap¹, sight**

VI 1 *[fire, wood, ice]* prendre ; *(Culin)* attacher

2 *[lock]* fermer

3 ◆ **her dress caught in the door/on a nail** sa robe s'est prise dans la porte/s'est accrochée à un clou

COMP **catch 22** * N ◆ **it's a ~ 22 situation** il n'y a pas moyen de s'en sortir, c'est une situation inextricable
catch-all N fourre-tout *m inv (fig)* ADJ *[regulation, clause etc]* général, fourre-tout *inv* ◆ **~-all phrase** expression *f* passe-partout *inv*
catch-as-catch-can N catch *m*
catch phrase N *(constantly repeated)* rengaine *f* ; *(= vivid, striking phrase)* accroche *f*, slogan *m* accrocheur
catch question N colle * *f*
catch-up * N ◆ **to play ~-up** *[losing player, team]* essayer de revenir à la marque ; *(fig)* essayer de rattraper son retard

► **catch at** VT FUS *[+ object]* (essayer d')attraper

► **catch on** VI 1 *(= become popular) [fashion]* se répandre ; *[song]* devenir populaire, marcher
2 *(= understand)* saisir, comprendre *(to sth* qch)

► **catch out** VT SEP *(esp Brit) (= catch napping)* prendre en défaut ; *(= catch in the act)* prendre sur le fait ◆ **to ~ sb out in a lie** surprendre qn en train de mentir, prendre qn à mentir ◆ **to be caught out (by sth)** être pris par surprise (par qch) ◆ **he'll get caught out some day** un beau jour il se fera prendre

► **catch up** VI 1 se rattraper, combler son retard ; *(with studies)* se rattraper, se remettre au niveau ; *(with news, gossip)* se remettre au courant ◆ **to ~ up on** *or* **with one's work** se (re)mettre à jour dans son travail ◆ **to ~ up on one's sleep** rattraper *or* combler son retard de sommeil ◆ **to ~ up on** *or* **with sb** *(going in the same direction)* rattraper qn, rejoindre qn ; *(in work etc)* rattraper qn ◆ **the police caught up with him in Vienna** la police l'a attrapé à Vienne ◆ **the truth/illness has finally caught up with him** la vérité/la maladie a fini par le rattraper

2 ◆ **to be** *or* **get caught up in sth** *(in net etc)* être pris dans qch ; *(fig) (in activity, campaign etc)* être pris dans qch ; *(in sb's enthusiasm etc)* être gagné par qch ; *(in sb's ideas etc)* être emballé par qch ; *(in circumstances etc)* être prisonnier de qch ; *(in scandal)* être mêlé à qch

VT SEP 1 *[+ person]* rattraper

2 *(= interrupt) [+ person]* interrompre, couper la parole à

3 *(= pick up quickly)* ramasser vivement

4 *[+ hair]* relever ; *[+ curtain]* retenir

catcher /ˈkætʃəʳ/ N 1 *(Baseball)* attrapeur *m* 2 → **mole¹, rat** COMP **catcher's mitt** N gant *m* de baseball

catching * /ˈkætʃɪŋ/ ADJ *[disease]* contagieux ; *(fig) [laughter, enthusiasm]* contagieux, communicatif ; *[habit, mannerism]* contagieux

catchment /ˈkætʃmənt/ N captage *m* COMP **catchment area** N *(Brit Geog:* also **catchment basin**) bassin *m* hydrographique ; *[of hospital]* circonscription *f* hospitalière ; *[of school]* secteur *m* de recrutement scolaire

catchpenny /ˈkætʃˌpenɪ/ *(pej)* ADJ clinquant, accrocheur

catchup /ˈkætʃəp/ N *(US)* ⇒ **ketchup**

catchword /ˈkætʃwɜːd/ N *(= slogan)* slogan *m* ; *(Pol)* mot *m* d'ordre, slogan *m* ; *(Printing) [of foot of page]* réclame *f* ; *[of top of page]* mot-vedette *m* ; *(Theat = cue)* réplique *f*

catchy * /ˈkætʃɪ/ ADJ *[tune]* entraînant ; *[title, name, slogan]* accrocheur

catechism /ˈkætɪkɪzəm/ N catéchisme *m*

catechist /ˈkætɪkɪst/ N catéchiste *mf*

catechize /ˈkætɪkaɪz/ **VT** *(Rel)* catéchiser ; *(fig)* *(= teach)* instruire *(par questions et réponses)* ; *(= examine)* interroger, questionner

categoric(al) /ˌkætɪˈgɒrɪk(əl)/ **ADJ** catégorique

categorically /ˌkætɪˈgɒrɪkəlɪ/ **ADV** catégoriquement

categorization /ˌkætɪgəraɪˈzeɪʃən/ **N** catégorisation *f*

categorize /ˈkætɪgəraɪz/ **VT** classer par catégories

category /ˈkætɪgərɪ/ **N** catégorie *f* **COMP** **Category A prisoner N** *(Brit)* *détenu condamné pour meurtre, vol à main armée ou terrorisme*

cater /ˈkeɪtəʳ/ **VI** *(= provide food)* s'occuper de la nourriture, préparer un *or* des repas *(for* pour) ; ◆ **to ~ for** *(Brit) or* **to** *(US)* *(sb's needs)* pourvoir à ; *(sb's tastes)* satisfaire ◆ **this magazine ~s for all ages** ce magazine s'adresse à tous les âges ◆ **the playgroup ~s mainly for 3- and 4-year-olds** cette garderie est destinée essentiellement aux enfants de 3 et 4 ans

cater-corner(ed) /ˌkeɪtəˈkɔːnəʳ(d)/ **ADV** *(US)* en diagonale *(from, to* par rapport à)

caterer /ˈkeɪtərəʳ/ **N** *(providing meals)* traiteur *m* ; *(providing supplies)* fournisseur *m (en alimentation)*

catering /ˈkeɪtərɪŋ/ **N** *(providing meals)* restauration *f* ; *(providing supplies)* approvisionnement *m*, ravitaillement *m* ◆ **the ~ for our reception was done by Smith and Lee** nous avons pris Smith and Lee comme traiteur pour notre réception

COMP **catering industry N** industrie *f* de la restauration

catering manager N intendant(e) *m(f)*

catering school N école *f* hôtelière

catering trade N restauration *f*

caterpillar /ˈkætəpɪləʳ/ **N** *(= grub, vehicle track)* chenille *f*

COMP *[vehicle, wheel]* à chenilles

Caterpillar track ® **N** chenille *f*

Caterpillar tractor ® **N** autochenille *f*

caterwaul /ˈkætəwɔːl/ **VI** 1 *(lit) [cat]* miauler 2 *(* fig) [person]* brailler, pousser des braillements **N** 1 *(lit) [of cat]* miaulement *m* 2 *(fig) [of person]* braillements *mpl*, hurlements *mpl*

caterwauling /ˈkætəwɔːlɪŋ/ **N** *[of cat]* miaulement *m* ; *[of music]* cacophonie *f* ; *[of person]* braillements *mpl*, hurlements *mpl*

catfight /ˈkætfaɪt/ **N** crêpage *m* de chignon

catfish /ˈkætfɪʃ/ **N** (pl **catfish** *or* **catfishes**) poisson-chat *m*

catfood /ˈkætfuːd/ **N** nourriture *f* pour chats

catgut /ˈkætgʌt/ **N** *(Mus, Sport)* boyau *m* (de chat) ; *(Med)* catgut *m*

Cath. abbrev of **Cathedral**

Cathar /ˈkæθəʳ/ **N** (pl **Cathars** *or* **Cathari** /ˈkæθərɪ/) Cathare *mf* **ADJ** cathare

catharsis /kəˈθɑːsɪs/ **N** (pl **catharses** /kəˈθɑːsɪs/) *(Literat, Psych)* catharsis *f*

cathartic /kəˈθɑːtɪk/ **ADJ** *(Literat, Med, Psych)* cathartique **N** *(Med)* purgatif *m*, cathartique *m*

Cathay /kæˈθeɪ/ **N** Cathay *m*

cathedral /kəˈθiːdrəl/ **N** cathédrale *f*

COMP **cathedral church N** cathédrale *f*

cathedral city N évêché *m*, ville *f* épiscopale

Catherine /ˈkæθərɪn/ **N** Catherine *f* ◆ **~ the Great** *(Hist)* la Grande Catherine, Catherine la Grande **COMP** **Catherine wheel N** *(= firework)* soleil *m*

catheter /ˈkæθɪtəʳ/ **N** cathéter *m*

catheterize /ˈkæθɪtəˌraɪz/ **VT** *[+ bladder, person]* sonder

cathiodermie /ˌkæθɪəʊˈdɜːmɪ/ **N** ionophorèse *f*

cathode /ˈkæθəʊd/ **N** cathode *f*

COMP *[ray]* cathodique

cathode ray tube N tube *m* cathodique

catholic /ˈkæθəlɪk/ **ADJ** 1 *(Rel)* ◆ **Catholic** catholique 2 *(= varied, all-embracing) [tastes, person]* éclectique ; *(= universal)* universel ◆ **to be ~ in one's tastes** avoir des goûts éclectiques **N** ◆ **Catholic** catholique *mf*

COMP **the Catholic Church N** l'Église *f* catholique

Catholic school N école *f* catholique

Catholicism /kəˈθɒlɪsɪzəm/ **N** catholicisme *m*

cathouse ‡ /ˈkæthaʊs/ **N** *(US)* bordel ‡ *m*

cation /ˈkætaɪən/ **N** *(Chem)* cation *m*

catkin /ˈkætkɪn/ **N** chaton *m*

catlike /ˈkætlaɪk/ **ADJ** félin **ADV** comme un chat

catmint /ˈkætmɪnt/ **N** herbe *f* aux chats

catnap * /ˈkætnæp/ **VI** sommeiller, faire un (petit) somme **N** (petit) somme *m* ◆ **to take a ~** sommeiller, faire un (petit) somme

catnip /ˈkætnɪp/ **N** *(US)* ⇒ **catmint**

Cato /ˈkeɪtəʊ/ **N** Caton *m*

catsuit /ˈkætsuːt/ **N** combinaison-pantalon *f*

catsup /ˈkætsəp/ **N** *(US)* ketchup *m*

cattery /ˈkætərɪ/ **N** pension *f* pour chats

cattiness * /ˈkætɪnɪs/ **N** méchanceté *f*, rosserie * *f*

cattle /ˈkætl/ **N** bétail *m* ◆ **the prisoners were treated like ~** les prisonniers étaient traités comme du bétail ◆ **a herd of ~** un troupeau de bovins ◆ **"cattle crossing"** "passage *m* de troupeaux" ; → **head**

COMP **cattle breeder N** éleveur *m* (de bétail)

cattle breeding N élevage *m* (de bétail)

cattle drive N *(US)* déplacement *m* de bétail

cattle grid *(Brit)*, **cattle guard** *(US)* **N** *grille à même la route permettant aux voitures mais non au bétail de passer*

cattle market N foire *f or* marché *m* aux bestiaux

cattle plague N peste *f* bovine

cattle raising N ⇒ **cattle breeding**

cattle shed N étable *f*

cattle show N concours *m* agricole

cattle truck N *(= lorry)* fourgon *m* à bestiaux ; *(Brit: on train)* fourgon *m or* wagon *m* à bestiaux

cattleman /ˈkætlmən/ **N** (pl **-men**) vacher *m*, bouvier *m*

catty * /ˈkætɪ/ **ADJ** *(pej) [person, gossip, criticism]* rosse *, vache * ◆ **~ remark** vacherie * *f* ◆ **to be ~ about sb/sth** dire des vacheries * sur qn/qch

catty-corner(ed) /ˌkætɪˈkɔːnəʳ(d)/ **ADV** *(US)* ⇒ **cater-corner(ed)**

Catullus /kəˈtʌləs/ **N** Catulle *m*

CATV /ˌsiːeɪtiːˈviː/ **N** (abbrev of **community antenna television**) → **community**

catwalk /ˈkætwɔːk/ **N** *(Constr, Theat)* passerelle *f* ; *(Fashion)* podium *m* ◆ **the models on the ~** les mannequins *mpl* du défilé

Caucasia /kɔːˈkeɪzɪə/ **N** Caucase *m*

Caucasian /kɔːˈkeɪzɪən/ **ADJ** *(= of Caucasia)* caucasien ; *(= white)* blanc (blanche *f*) **N** *(= person from Caucasia)* Caucasien(ne) *m(f)* ; *(= White)* Blanc *m*, Blanche *f*

caucasoid /ˈkɔːkəsɔɪd/ **ADJ** de race blanche *or* caucasique **N** Blanc *m*, Blanche *f*

Caucasus /ˈkɔːkəsəs/ **N** ◆ **the ~** le Caucase

caucus /ˈkɔːkəs/ **N** (pl **caucuses**) *(US)* *(= committee)* comité *m* électoral ; *(= meeting)* réunion *f* du comité électoral ; *(Brit pej)* coterie *f* politique

caudal /ˈkɔːdl/ **ADJ** caudal

caught /kɔːt/ **VB** pt, ptp of **catch**

caul /kɔːl/ **N** *(Anat)* coiffe *f* ◆ **to be born with a ~** naître coiffé *(Lit)*

cauldron /ˈkɔːldrən/ **N** chaudron *m* ◆ **a ~ of intrigue/ethnic strife** un foyer d'intrigues/de conflit ethnique

cauliflower /ˈkɒlɪflaʊəʳ/ **N** chou-fleur *m*

COMP **cauliflower cheese N** *(Culin)* chou-fleur *m* au gratin

cauliflower ear * **N** oreille *f* en feuille de chou

caulk /kɔːk/ **VT** *(Naut)* calfater

causal /ˈkɔːzəl/ **ADJ** causal ; *(Gram)* causal, causatif ◆ **~ link** lien *m* causal

causality /kɔːˈzælɪtɪ/ **N** causalité *f*

causally /ˈkɔːzəlɪ/ **ADV** causalement ◆ **to be ~ related** avoir un lien *or* une relation de cause à effet

causation /kɔːˈzeɪʃən/ **N** 1 *(= causing)* causalité *f* 2 *(= cause-effect relation)* relation *f* de cause à effet

causative /ˈkɔːzətɪv/ **ADJ** causal ; *(Gram)* causal, causatif ◆ **~ of** *(frm)* (qui est) cause de **N** *(Gram)* mot *m* causal *or* causatif

cause /kɔːz/ LANGUAGE IN USE 16.1

N 1 *(gen, also Philos)* cause *f* ; *(= reason)* cause *f*, raison *f*, motif *m* ◆ **~ and effect** la cause et l'effet *m* ◆ **the relation of ~ and effect** la relation de cause à effet ◆ **the ~ of his failure** la cause de son échec ◆ **to be the ~ of sth** être cause de qch, causer qch ◆ **~ of action** *(Jur)* fondement *m* (d'une action en justice) ◆ **~ of loss** *(Jur)* fait *m* générateur du sinistre ◆ **she has no ~ to be angry** elle n'a aucune raison de se fâcher ◆ **there's no ~ for anxiety** il n'y a pas lieu de s'inquiéter *or* de raison de s'inquiéter *or* de quoi s'inquiéter ◆ **with (good) ~** à juste titre ◆ **not without ~** non sans raison ◆ **without ~** sans cause *or* raison *or* motif ◆ **without good ~** sans raison *or* cause *or* motif valable ◆ **~ for complaint** sujet *m* de plainte

2 *(= purpose)* cause *f*, parti *m* ◆ **to make common ~ with sb** *(frm)* faire cause commune avec qn ◆ **to work in a good ~** travailler pour la *or* une bonne cause ◆ **it's all in a good ~** * c'est pour une bonne cause ; → **lost**

3 *(Jur)* cause *f* ◆ **to plead sb's ~** plaider la cause de qn ◆ **~ list** rôle *m* des audiences

VT causer, occasionner ◆ **to ~ damage/an accident** causer des dégâts/un accident ◆ **to ~ grief to sb** causer du chagrin à qn ◆ **to ~ trouble** causer des ennuis ◆ **to ~ trouble to sb** causer des ennuis à qn ◆ **I don't want to ~ you any trouble** je ne veux pas vous déranger ◆ **to ~ sb to do sth** faire faire qch à qn ◆ **to ~ sth to be done** faire faire qch

'cause * /kɒz, kəz/ **CONJ** ⇒ **because**

causeway /ˈkɔːzweɪ/ **N** chaussée *f*

caustic /ˈkɔːstɪk/ **ADJ** *(Chem, fig)* caustique ◆ **~ remark** remarque *f* caustique **N** substance *f* caustique, caustique *m* **COMP** **caustic soda N** soude *f* caustique

caustically /ˈkɔːstɪklɪ/ **ADV** *[say, describe]* de façon caustique ◆ **to be ~ funny** *[person]* avoir un humour caustique ; *[book]* être d'un humour caustique

cauterize /ˈkɔːtəraɪz/ **VT** cautériser

cautery /ˈkɔːtərɪ/ **N** cautère *m*

caution /ˈkɔːʃən/ **N** 1 *(NonC = circumspection)* prudence *f*, circonspection *f* ◆ **proceed with ~** *(gen)* agissez avec prudence *or* circonspection ; *(in vehicle)* avancez lentement

2 *(= warning)* avertissement *m (de la police)* ; *(= rebuke)* réprimande *f* ◆ **"caution"** *(on label)* "attention" ◆ **he got off with a ~** il s'en est tiré avec une réprimande

3 († * = *rascal)* numéro * *m*, phénomène * *m*

VT avertir, donner un avertissement à ; *(Brit Police: on charging suspect)* mettre en garde *(un suspect que toute déclaration de sa part peut être rete-*

nue contre lui) ◆ **to ~ sb against sth** mettre qn en garde contre qch ◆ **to ~ sb against doing sth** déconseiller à qn de faire qch
COMP **caution money** N *(Jur)* cautionnement *m*

⚠ **caution** is not translated by the French word **caution**, whose meanings include 'guarantee', 'deposit' and 'support'.

cautionary /ˈkɔːʃənərɪ/ ADJ (servant) d'avertissement ; *(Jur)* donné en garantie ◆ **a ~ tale** un récit édifiant
cautious /ˈkɔːʃəs/ ADJ *[person, welcome, response, optimism]* prudent, circonspect
cautiously /ˈkɔːʃəslɪ/ ADV *[move]* avec précaution ; *[say, react]* prudemment, avec prudence ; *[welcome, accept]* avec circonspection ◆ **~ optimistic** d'un optimisme prudent
cautiousness /ˈkɔːʃəsnɪs/ N circonspection *f*
cavalcade /ˌkævəlˈkeɪd/ N cavalcade *f* VI cavalcader
cavalier /ˌkævəˈlɪəʳ/ N *(gen, Mil)* cavalier *m* ; *(Brit Hist)* royaliste *m (partisan de Charles Ier et de Charles II)* ADJ 1 *(Brit Hist)* royaliste 2 *[person, behaviour, attitude]* cavalier
cavalierly /ˌkævəˈlɪəlɪ/ ADV cavalièrement
cavalry /ˈkævəlrɪ/ N cavalerie *f* ; → **household**
COMP **cavalry charge** N charge *f* de cavalerie
cavalry officer N officier *m* de cavalerie
cavalry twill N drap *m* sergé pour culotte de cheval, tricotine *f*
cavalryman /ˈkævəlrɪmən/ N (pl **-men**) cavalier *m*
cave¹ /keɪv/ N caverne *f*, grotte *f* VI ◆ **to go caving** faire de la spéléologie
COMP **cave dweller** N *(in prehistory)* homme *m* des cavernes ; *(in historical times)* troglodyte *mf*
cave-in N *[of floor, building]* effondrement *m*, affaissement *m* ; *(* = defeat, surrender)* effondrement *m*
cave painting N peinture *f* rupestre
caving-in N ⇒ **cave-in**
► **cave in** VI 1 *[floor, building]* s'effondrer, s'affaisser ; *[wall, beam]* céder 2 *(* = yield)* se dégonfler*, caner* N ◆ **cave-in, caving-in** → **cave**
cave² †* /ˈkeɪvɪ/ EXCL *(Brit Scol)* ◆ **~!** pet pet !*, vingt-deux !‡ ◆ **to keep ~** faire le guet
caveat /ˈkævɪæt/ N *(gen)* avertissement *m* ; *(Jur)* notification *f* d'opposition ◆ **~ emptor** sans garantie du fournisseur, aux risques de l'acheteur
caveman /ˈkeɪvmæn/ N (pl **-men**) homme *m* des cavernes
caver /ˈkeɪvəʳ/ N spéléologue *mf*
cavern /ˈkævən/ N caverne *f*
cavernous /ˈkævənəs/ ADJ *[room, building, space etc]* énorme ; *[eyes]* cave *(liter)*, enfoncé ; *[mouth]* immense ; *[voice, laugh]* caverneux ; *[yawn]* profond
caviar(e) /ˈkævɪɑːʳ/ N caviar *m*
cavil /ˈkævɪl/ VI ergoter, chicaner *(about, at* sur)
caving /ˈkeɪvɪŋ/ N spéléologie *f*
cavity /ˈkævɪtɪ/ N *(gen)* cavité *f* ; *(Med: in rotten tooth)* carie *f* ; *(Phon)* orifice *m* ◆ **to have cavities (in one's teeth)** avoir des caries COMP **cavity wall** N mur *m* creux ◆ **~ wall insulation** isolation *f* des murs creux
cavort * /kəˈvɔːt/ VI *(= jump about) [children]* s'ébattre ◆ **while you were ~ing (around) in Paris ...** pendant que tu prenais du bon temps à Paris ... ◆ **they were ~ing (around) in the pool** ils faisaient les fous dans la piscine
cavortings /kəˈvɔːtɪŋz/ NPL ébats *mpl*
cavy /ˈkeɪvɪ/ N *(= guinea pig)* cobaye *m*, cochon *m* d'Inde
caw /kɔː/ VI croasser N croassement *m*
cawing /ˈkɔːɪŋ/ N *(NonC)* croassement *m*
cay /keɪ/ N *(= sandbank)* banc *m* de sable ; *(= coral reef)* récif *m* or banc *m* de corail
Cayenne /ˈkeɪen/ N (also **Cayenne pepper**) (poivre *m* de) Cayenne *m*
cayman /ˈkeɪmən/ N (pl **-mans**) 1 caïman *m* 2 ◆ **the Cayman Islands** les îles *fpl* Caïmans
CB /siːˈbiː/ ABBR 1 (abbrev of **Citizens' Band Radio**) *(= activity)* CB *f* ; *(= set)* poste *m* de CB 2 *(Mil)* (abbrev of **confined to barracks**) → **confined** 3 (abbrev of **Companion (of the Order) of the Bath**) *titre honorifique* COMP **CB user** N cibiste *mf*
CBE /ˌsiːbiːˈiː/ N (abbrev of **Companion (of the Order) of the British Empire**) *titre honorifique*
CBI /ˌsiːbiːˈaɪ/ N (abbrev of **Confederation of British Industry**) *conseil du patronat en Grande-Bretagne*
CBS /ˌsiːbiːˈes/ N abbrev of **Columbia Broadcasting System**
CC /siːˈsiː/ *(in Brit: formerly)* (abbrev of **County Council**) → **county**
cc /siːˈsiː/ 1 (abbrev of **cubic centimetre(s)**) cm³ 2 (abbrev of **carbon copy, carbon copies**) → **carbon**
CCTV /ˌsiːsiːtiːˈviː/ N (abbrev of **closed-circuit television**) → **closed**
CD /siːˈdiː/ N 1 (abbrev of **compact disc**) CD *m* 2 (abbrev of **Corps Diplomatique**) CD *m* 3 (abbrev of **Civil Defence**) → **civil** 4 *(US)* (abbrev of **Congressional District**) → **congressional**
COMP **CD burner** N graveur *m* de CD
CD player N platine *f* laser
CD-writer N graveur *m* de CD
CDC /ˌsiːdiːˈsiː/ N *(US)* (abbrev of **Center for Disease Control and Prevention**) → **centre** ; → CENTERS FOR DISEASE CONTROL
CD-I ® /ˌsiːdiːˈaɪ/ N (abbrev of **compact disc interactive**) CD-I *m*, disque *m* compact interactif
Cdr. *(Mil)* (abbrev of **Commander**) ~ **J. Thomas** *(on envelope)* le commandant J. Thomas
CD-ROM /ˌsiːdiːˈrɒm/ N (abbrev of **compact disc read-only memory**) CD-ROM *m*, cédérom *m*
COMP **CD-ROM drive** N lecteur *m* (de) CD-ROM
CDT /ˌsiːdiːˈtiː/ N 1 *(US)* (abbrev of **Central Daylight Time**) → **central** 2 *(Brit Scol)* (abbrev of **Craft, Design and Technology**) EMT *f*
CDTV /ˌsiːdiːtiːˈviː/ N *(NonC)* (abbrev of **compact disc television**) télévision *f* interactive
CDV /ˌsiːdiːˈviː/, **CD-video** /ˈˌsiːdiːˈvɪdɪəʊ/ N (abbrev of **compact disc video**) CD-V *m*, vidéodisque *m* compact
CE /siːˈiː/ N (abbrev of **Church of England**) → **church**
cease /siːs/ VI *[activity, noise etc]* cesser, s'arrêter ◆ **to ~ from work** cesser le travail ◆ **to ~ from doing sth, to ~ to do sth** cesser *or* arrêter de faire qch ◆ **I never ~ to be amazed by people's generosity** la générosité des gens ne cesse de m'étonner VT *[+ work, activity]* cesser, arrêter ◆ **to ~ doing sth** cesser *or* arrêter de faire qch ◆ **to ~ fire** *(Mil)* cesser le feu ◆ **to ~ trading** *(Comm)* fermer, cesser ses activités N ◆ **without ~** sans cesse
ceasefire /ˈsiːsfaɪəʳ/ N *(Mil)* cessez-le-feu *m inv*
ceaseless /ˈsiːslɪs/ ADJ incessant, continuel
ceaselessly /ˈsiːslɪslɪ/ ADV sans arrêt, sans cesse
cecum /ˈsiːkəm/ N (pl **ceca**) *(US)* ⇒ **caecum**
cedar /ˈsiːdəʳ/ N cèdre *m* ◆ **~ of Lebanon** cèdre *m* du Liban COMP de *or* en cèdre **cedar wood** N (bois *m* de) cèdre *m*
cede /siːd/ VT céder
cedilla /sɪˈdɪlə/ N cédille *f* ◆ **"c" ~** "c" cédille
Ceefax ® /ˈsiːfæks/ N télétexte ® *m (de la BBC)*
ceilidh /ˈkeɪlɪ/ N *bal folklorique écossais ou irlandais*
ceiling /ˈsiːlɪŋ/ N plafond *m* ◆ **to fix a ~ for** *or* **put a ~ on prices/wages** fixer un plafond pour les prix/salaires ◆ **to hit the ~**‡ *(= get angry)* sortir de ses gonds, piquer une crise* ; *[prices]* crever le plafond ◆ **prices have reached their ~ at 160 pence** les prix plafonnent à 160 pence
COMP *[lamp, fan, covering]* de plafond ; *(fig) [rate, charge]* plafond *inv*
ceiling decoration N décoration *f* de plafond
ceiling price N prix *m* plafond *inv*
celadon /ˈseləˌdɒn/ N *(= porcelain)* céladon
celandine /ˈseləndaɪn/ N chélidoine *f*
celeb‡ /səˈleb/ N célébrité *f*, vedette *f*
celebrant /ˈselɪbrənt/ N célébrant *m*, officiant *m*
celebrate /ˈselɪbreɪt/ LANGUAGE IN USE 25.1 VT *[+ person]* célébrer, glorifier ; *[+ event]* célébrer, fêter ◆ **to ~ the anniversary of sth** commémorer qch ◆ **to ~ mass** *(Rel)* célébrer la messe VI 1 *(Rel)* célébrer (l'office) 2 faire la fête ◆ **let's ~!** * il faut fêter ça ! ; *(with drink)* il faut arroser ça !*
celebrated /ˈselɪbreɪtɪd/ ADJ *(= famous)* célèbre
celebration /ˌselɪˈbreɪʃən/ N 1 (also **celebrations**) fête(s) *f(pl)* ; *(at Christmas, for family event etc)* fête *f*, festivités *fpl* ; *(public event)* cérémonies *fpl*, fête(s) *f(pl)* ◆ **we must have a ~!** il faut fêter ça ! ◆ **to join in the ~s** participer à la fête *or* aux festivités ◆ **the victory ~s** les cérémonies marquant la victoire 2 *(NonC = act of celebrating) [of event] (also Rel)* célébration *f* ; *[of past event]* commémoration *f* ; *[of sb's virtues etc]* éloge *m*, louange *f* ◆ **in ~ of** *(victory etc)* pour fêter *or* célébrer ; *(past victory etc)* pour commémorer ; *(sb's achievements)* pour célébrer COMP *[dinner, outing etc]* de fête ; *(for past event)* commémoratif
celebratory /ˌselɪˈbreɪtərɪ/ ADJ de célébration ◆ **how about a ~ drink?** et si on prenait un verre pour fêter ça ?
celebrity /sɪˈlebrɪtɪ/ N *(= fame, famous person)* célébrité *f*
celeriac /səˈlerɪæk/ N céleri(-rave) *m*
celerity /sɪˈlerɪtɪ/ N *(liter)* célérité *f*
celery /ˈselərɪ/ N céleri *m* (ordinaire *or* à côtes) ◆ **a bunch** *or* **head of ~** un pied de céleri ◆ **a stick of ~** une branche de céleri COMP *[seeds, salt]* de céleri
celesta /sɪˈlestə/ N célesta *m*
celestial /sɪˈlestɪəl/ ADJ *(lit, fig)* céleste
celiac /ˈsiːlɪˌæk/ ADJ *(esp US)* ⇒ **coeliac**
celibacy /ˈselɪbəsɪ/ N célibat *m*
celibate /ˈselɪbɪt/ ADJ, N *(= unmarried) [priest, nun]* célibataire *mf* ; *(= sexually inactive)* chaste
cell /sel/ N 1 *(gen, Bot, Phot, Telec)* cellule *f* ; *(Elec)* élément *m (de pile)* ◆ **to form a ~** *(Pol)* créer une cellule 2 *(Police etc)* cellule *f* ◆ **he spent the night in the ~s** il a passé la nuit au poste *or* en cellule ; → **condemn**
COMP **cell culture** N *(Bio)* culture *f* de cellules
cell wall N *(Bio)* paroi *f* cellulaire
cellar /ˈseləʳ/ N 1 *(for wine, coal)* cave *f* ; *(for food etc)* cellier *m* ◆ **in the ~** à la cave 2 *(= store for wine)* cave *f* (à vins) ◆ **he keeps an excellent ~** il a une excellente cave ; → **coal, saltcellar**
cellist /ˈtʃelɪst/ N violoncelliste *mf*
cellmate /ˈselmeɪt/ N compagnon *m*, compagne *f* de cellule
cello /ˈtʃeləʊ/ N violoncelle *m* COMP de violoncelle
Cellophane ® /ˈseləfeɪn/ N cellophane ® *f*
cellphone /ˈselfəʊn/ N téléphone *m* cellulaire

cellular /'seljʊləʳ/ ADJ [1] *(Anat, Bio etc)* cellulaire [2] *[blanket]* en cellular
COMP **cellular phone** N ⇒ **cellular telephone**
cellular radio N *(Rad)* radio *f* cellulaire
cellular telephone N téléphone *m* cellulaire

cellulite /'seljʊˌlaɪt/ N cellulite *f (gonflement)*

cellulitis /ˌseljʊ'laɪtɪs/ N cellulite *f (inflammation)*

Celluloid ® /'seljʊlɔɪd/ N celluloïd *m* COMP en celluloïd

cellulose /'seljʊləʊs/ N cellulose *f*
COMP cellulosique, en *or* de cellulose
cellulose acetate N acétate *m* de cellulose
cellulose varnish N vernis *m* cellulosique

Celsius /'selsɪəs/ ADJ Celsius *inv* ◆ **degrees** ~ degrés *mpl* Celsius

Celt /kelt, selt/ N Celte *mf*

Celtic /'keltɪk, 'seltɪk/ ADJ celtique, celte N *(= language)* celtique *m*

cembalo /'tʃembələʊ/ N (pl **cembalos** *or* **cembali** /'tʃembəlɪ/) *(Mus)* clavecin *m*

cement /sə'ment/ N [1] *(Constr, fig)* ciment *m* [2] *(Chem, Dentistry)* amalgame *m* [3] ⇒ **cementum**
VT *(Constr, fig)* cimenter ; *(Chem)* cémenter ; *(Dentistry)* obturer COMP **cement mixer** N bétonnière *f*, bétonneuse *f*

cementation /ˌsiːmen'teɪʃən/ N *(Constr, fig)* cimentation *f* ; *[of metals]* cémentation *f*

cementum /sɪ'mentəm/ N *(Anat)* cément *m*

cemetery /'semɪtrɪ/ N cimetière *m*

cenotaph /'senətɑːf/ N cénotaphe *m*

censer /'sensəʳ/ N encensoir *m*

censor /'sensəʳ/ N censeur *m* VT censurer

censorious /sen'sɔːrɪəs/ ADJ *[person, comments]* critique, sévère

censorship /'sensəʃɪp/ N (NonC) *(= censoring)* censure *f* ; *(= function of censor)* censorat *m*

censurable /'senʃərəbl/ ADJ blâmable, critiquable

censure /'senʃəʳ/ VT *(publicly)* réprimander publiquement ; *(= blame)* critiquer N critique *f*, blâme *m* COMP **censure motion** N motion *f* de censure ; → **vote**

census /'sensəs/ N (pl **censuses**) recensement *m* ◆ **to take a ~ of the population** faire le recensement de la population ◆ **the increase between ~es** l'augmentation *f* intercensitaire
COMP **census enumerator, census taker** (US) N agent *m* recenseur

cent /sent/ N [1] ◆ **per** ~ pour cent [2] *(= coin)* cent *m* ; *(= unit of euro)* cent *m*, centime *m* d'euro ◆ **I haven't a ~** * je n'ai pas un centime *or* rond *

cent. [1] abbrev of **centigrade** [2] abbrev of **central** [3] abbrev of **century**

centaur /'sentɔːʳ/ N centaure *m*

centenarian /ˌsentɪ'nɛərɪən/ ADJ, N centenaire *mf*

centenary /sen'tiːnərɪ/ *(esp Brit)* ADJ centenaire N *(= anniversary)* centenaire *m* ; *(= century)* siècle *m* ◆ **he has just passed his** ~ il vient de fêter son centième anniversaire *or* son centenaire COMP **centenary celebrations** NPL fêtes *fpl* du centenaire

centennial /sen'tenɪəl/ *(esp US)* ADJ *(= 100 years old)* centenaire, séculaire ; *(= every 100 years)* séculaire *(frm)* N centenaire *m*, centième anniversaire *m* COMP **the Centennial State** N (US) Colorado *m*

center /'sentəʳ/ N (US) ⇒ **centre**

centesimal /sen'tesɪməl/ ADJ centésimal

centigrade /'sentɪgreɪd/ ADJ *[thermometer, scale]* centigrade ; *[degree]* centigrade, Celsius *inv*

centigramme, centigram (US) /'sentɪgræm/ N centigramme *m*

centilitre, centiliter (US) /'sentɪˌliːtəʳ/ N centilitre *m*

centimetre, centimeter (US) /'sentɪˌmiːtəʳ/ N centimètre *m*

centipede /'sentɪpiːd/ N mille-pattes *m inv*

central /'sentrəl/ ADJ *[courtyard, committee, control, command, idea, character]* central ; *[location]* central, proche du centre ; *[flat, house, office]* proche du centre ; *[planning]* centralisé ; *[aim, fact, role]* essentiel ◆ ~ **London/Poland** le centre de Londres/de la Pologne ◆ **of ~ importance** d'une importance capitale ◆ **to be ~ to sth** jouer un rôle essentiel dans qch, être au centre de qch
N (US) central *m* téléphonique
COMP **Central African** ADJ centrafricain
Central African Republic N République *f* centrafricaine
Central America N Amérique *f* centrale
Central American ADJ d'Amérique centrale N habitant(e) *m(f)* d'Amérique centrale
Central Asia N Asie *f* centrale
Central Asian ADJ d'Asie centrale
central bank N banque *f* centrale
central casting N (NonC: *esp US Cine)* service *m* du casting *(d'un studio de cinéma)* ◆ **straight out of ~ casting** *(fig)* caricatural
Central Committee N *(Pol)* comité *m* central
Central Daylight Time N (US) heure *f* d'été du Centre *(des États-Unis)*
Central Europe N Europe *f* centrale
Central European ADJ d'Europe centrale N habitant(e) *m(f)* d'Europe centrale
Central European Time N *(Geog)* heure *f* d'Europe centrale
central government N pouvoir *m* central
central heating N chauffage *m* central
central locking N *[of car]* verrouillage *m* centralisé
central locking device N *[of car]* condamnation *f* électromagnétique des serrures
central nervous system N système *m* nerveux central
central processing unit N *(Comput)* unité *f* centrale
central reservation N *(Brit) [of road, motorway]* terre-plein *m* central
Central Standard Time N (US) heure *f* normale du Centre *(des États-Unis)*

centralism /'sentrəlɪzəm/ N *(Pol)* centralisme *m*

centralist /'sentrəlɪst/ ADJ, N *(Pol)* centraliste *mf*

centrality /sen'trælɪtɪ/ N *(= central role)* rôle *m* central ◆ **the ~ of rice to their economy** le rôle central du riz dans leur économie ◆ **the ~ of the hotel's location is ideal** *(= central location)* ce qui est idéal, c'est que l'hôtel est situé dans le centre-ville

centralization /ˌsentrəlaɪ'zeɪʃən/ N centralisation *f*

centralize /'sentrəlaɪz/ VT centraliser VI se centraliser, être centralisé

centrally /'sentrəlɪ/ ADV [1] *(= in middle) [positioned, placed]* au centre [2] *(= near city centre) [located, situated]* dans le centre ◆ **very ~ situated** situé tout près du centre ◆ **he lives** ~ il habite dans le centre *or* près du centre [3] *(= primarily)* ◆ **to be ~ important** être d'une importance capitale, occuper une place centrale ◆ **the novel is ~ concerned with the subject of unhappiness** la tristesse est le motif central de ce roman [4] *(Admin, Pol) [organize]* de façon centralisée ◆ ~ **based** centralisé ◆ ~ **planned economy** économie *f* dirigée *or* centralisée COMP **centrally heated** ADJ équipé du chauffage central ◆ **the house is ~ heated** la maison a le chauffage central

centre, center (US) /'sentəʳ/ N [1] *(gen, Comput)* centre *m* ◆ **the ~ of the target** le centre de la cible, le mille ◆ **in the** ~ au centre ◆ ~ **of attraction** *(lit)* centre *m* d'attraction ; *(fig)* point *m* de mire ◆ **she was the ~ of attention** *or* **interest** elle a été le centre d'attention *or* d'intérêt ◆ **she likes to be the ~ of attention** elle aime être le point de mire ◆ **the man at the ~ of the controversy** l'homme au cœur de la controverse ◆ **a ~ of industry/commerce** un centre industriel/commercial ◆ **a party of the** ~ *(Pol)* un parti du centre ; → **city, nerve, town**
[2] *(= place for specific activity)* centre *m* ◆ **adult education** ~ centre *m* d'enseignement (postscolaire) pour adultes ◆ **law/business consultancy** ~ boutique *f* de droit/de gestion ; → **civic, community, job**
VT *(gen, Comput)* centrer ◆ **to ~ the ball** *(Ftbl)* centrer ◆ **the fighting has been ~d around the capital** les combats se sont concentrés autour de la capitale ◆ **the silk industry was ~d in Valencia** l'industrie de la soie était concentrée à Valence ◆ **to be ~d** *(mentally)* être équilibré
VI [1] *[thoughts, hatred]* se concentrer *(on, in sur)* ; *[problem, discussion]* tourner *(on autour de)*
[2] *(Archery)* frapper au centre
COMP *[row etc]* central
Center for Disease Control and Prevention N (US) *organisme de santé publique*
centre armrest N *(in car, bus, train)* accoudoir *m* central
centre bit N *[of drill]* mèche *f*, foret *m*, mèche *f* anglaise
centre court N *(Tennis)* court *m* central
centre-forward N *(Sport)* avant-centre *m*
centre-half N *(Sport)* demi-centre *m*
centre of gravity N centre *m* de gravité
centre parties NPL *(Pol)* partis *mpl* du centre
centre spread N *(Advertising)* pages *fpl* centrales
centre-stage N *(lit, fig)* ◆ **to take ~-stage** occuper le devant de la scène
centre three-quarter N *(Sport)* trois-quarts *m* centre
centre vowel N *(Phon)* voyelle *f* centrale

CENTERS FOR DISEASE CONTROL

Les **Centers for Disease Control and Prevention** (ou **CDC**) sont un organisme américain de santé publique dont le siège se trouve à Atlanta, en Géorgie. Son rôle est d'élaborer des règlements sanitaires et des normes de sécurité, de collecter et d'analyser les informations relatives à la santé publique et d'organiser la prévention des maladies transmissibles. Il doit son renom international au rôle de pionnier qu'il a joué dans la détection du virus HIV et dans l'identification de ses modes de transmission.

centreboard /'sentəbɔːd/ N *(Naut)* dérive *f*

-centred /'sentəd/ ADJ *(in compounds)* basé sur

centrefold /'sentəfəʊld/ N *(Press)* double page *f* (détachable) ; *(= pin-up picture)* photo *f* de pin up *(au milieu d'un magazine)*

centrepiece /'sentəpiːs/ N [1] *(= key feature, event)* **the ~ of the town** le joyau de la ville ◆ **the ~ of their campaign strategy** le pivot *or* la clé de voûte de leur stratégie électorale ◆ **the ~ of the summit will be the signing of a treaty** le moment le plus important du sommet sera la signature du traité [2] *[of table]* milieu *m* de table

centrifugal /sentrɪ'fjuːgəl/ ADJ centrifuge COMP **centrifugal force** N force *f* centrifuge

centrifuge /'sentrɪfjuːʒ/ N centrifugeur *m*, centrifugeuse *f* VT centrifuger

centripetal /sen'trɪpɪtl/ ADJ centripète COMP **centripetal force** N force *f* centripète

centrism /'sentrɪzəm/ N centrisme *m*

centrist /ˈsentrɪst/ ADJ, N centriste *mf*

centurion /senˈtjʊərɪən/ N centurion *m*

century /ˈsentjʊrɪ/ N 1 siècle *m* ◆ **several centuries ago** il y a plusieurs siècles ◆ **in the twentieth** ~ au vingtième siècle 2 *(Mil Hist)* centurie *f* 3 *(Cricket)* cent courses *fpl*
COMP **centuries-old** ADJ séculaire, vieux (vieille *f*) de plusieurs siècles
century note ✻ N *(US)* billet *m* de cent dollars

CEO /ˌsiːiːˈəʊ/ N (abbrev of **chief executive officer**) → **chief**

cephalic /sɪˈfælɪk/ ADJ céphalique

ceramic /sɪˈræmɪk/ ADJ *[art]* céramique ; *[cup, vase]* en céramique N 1 *(NonC)* céramique *f* 2 (objet *m* en) céramique *f* COMP **ceramic hob** N table *f* de cuisson en vitrocéramique

Cerberus /ˈsɜːbərəs/ N Cerbère *m*

cereal /ˈsɪərɪəl/ N *(= plant)* céréale *f* ; *(= grain)* grain *m* *(de céréale)* ◆ **baby** ~ Blédine ® *f* ◆ **breakfast** ~ céréale *f* ADJ de céréale(s)

cerebellum /ˌserɪˈbeləm/ N (pl **cerebellums** or **cerebella** /ˌserɪˈbelə/) cervelet *m*

cerebra /ˈserɪbrə/ NPL of **cerebrum**

cerebral /ˈserɪbrəl/ ADJ cérébral
COMP **cerebral death** N mort *f* cérébrale
cerebral palsy N paralysie *f* cérébrale

cerebration /ˌserɪˈbreɪʃən/ N *(frm)* cogitation *f*

cerebrum /ˈserɪbrəm/ N (pl **cerebrums** or **cerebra**) *(Anat)* cerveau *m*

ceremonial /ˌserɪˈməʊnɪəl/ ADJ *[rite]* cérémoniel ; *[dress]* de cérémonie ; *(US)* *[office, post]* honorifique N cérémonial *m NonC* ; *(Rel)* cérémonial *m*, rituel *m*

ceremonially /ˌserɪˈməʊnɪəlɪ/ ADV selon le cérémonial d'usage

ceremonious /ˌserɪˈməʊnɪəs/ ADJ solennel ; *(slightly pej)* cérémonieux

ceremoniously /ˌserɪˈməʊnɪəslɪ/ ADV solennellement, avec cérémonie ; *(slightly pej)* cérémonieusement

ceremony /ˈserɪmənɪ/ N 1 *(= event)* cérémonie *f* ; → **master** 2 *(NonC)* cérémonies *fpl*, façons *fpl* ◆ **to stand on** ~ faire des cérémonies, faire des manières ◆ **with** ~ cérémonieusement ◆ **without** ~ sans cérémonie(s)

cerise /səˈriːz/ ADJ (de) couleur cerise, cerise *inv*

cerium /ˈsɪərɪəm/ N cérium *m*

cert ✻ /sɜːt/ N *(Brit)* certitude *f* ◆ **it's a dead** ~ ça ne fait pas un pli *, c'est couru * ◆ **he's a (dead)** ~ **for the job** il est sûr et certain de décrocher le poste *

cert. 1 abbrev of **certificate** 2 abbrev of **certified**

certain /ˈsɜːtən/ LANGUAGE IN USE 6.2, 15.1, 16.1, 26.3
ADJ 1 *(= sure)* certain ◆ **to be** or **feel** ~ **(about** or **of sth)** être certain (de qch) ◆ **are you absolutely** ~ **(about** or **of that)?** en es-tu absolument certain ? ◆ **you don't sound very** ~ tu n'en as pas l'air très sûr ◆ ~ **of oneself** sûr de soi ◆ **to be** ~ **that ...** être certain que ... ◆ **be** ~ **to go!** allez-y sans faute ! ◆ **I am not** ~ **who/why/when/how ...** je ne sais pas avec certitude qui/pourquoi/quand/comment ... ◆ **we are not** ~ **what is happening** nous ne sommes pas certains de *or* nous ne savons pas au juste ce qui se passe
◆ **to make certain** ◆ **to make** ~ **that ...** *(= check, ensure)* s'assurer que ... ◆ **to make** ~ **of sth** *(= get facts about)* s'assurer de qch ; *(= be sure of getting)* s'assurer qch
◆ **for certain** *(= definitely)* ◆ **he's up to something, that's for** ~ il manigance quelque chose, c'est une certitude *or* c'est sûr et certain ◆ **he'll do it for** ~ il le fera, c'est certain ◆ **to know sth for** ~ savoir qch avec certitude ◆ **to know for** ~ **that ...** avoir la certitude que ... ◆ **to know for** ~ **what/where ...** savoir avec certitude ce qui *or* que/où ... ◆ **we know for** ~ **of ten fatalities** nous savons avec certitude qu'il y a au moins dix victimes ◆ **I don't know for** ~, **I can't say for** ~ je n'en suis pas certain *or* sûr ◆ **I can't say for** ~ **that ...** je ne peux pas affirmer que ...
2 *(= assured, guaranteed)* *[defeat, success, victory, death]* certain *after n* ◆ **nothing's** ~ **in this world** il n'y a rien de certain dans ce monde ◆ **one thing is** ~ **...** une chose est certaine ... ◆ **he's a** ~ **winner/loser** il est sûr de gagner/perdre ◆ **there's** ~ **to be strong opposition to these proposals** ces propositions se heurteront certainement à une forte opposition ◆ **he is** ~ **to come** il viendra sans aucun doute ◆ **it is** ~ **that ...** il est certain que ... ◆ **he was 99%** ~ **of winning** il était à 99% certain de gagner ◆ **to my** ~ **knowledge, she has never been there** je sais pertinemment qu'elle n'y est jamais allée
3 *(= particular)* *[person, matter, place, manner, type]* certain *before n* ◆ **of a** ~ **age** d'un certain âge ◆ **in** ~ **circumstances** dans certaines circonstances ◆ **on a** ~ **day in spring** un certain jour de printemps ◆ **there is a** ~ **knack to doing it** il faut un certain coup de main pour le faire ◆ **a** ~ **Mrs Wendy Smith** une certaine Mme Wendy Smith ◆ **a** ~ **number of people** un certain nombre de personnes ◆ **at** ~ **times** à certains moments
4 *(= slight)* *[impatience, bitterness, courage]* certain *before n* ◆ **to a** ~ **extent** *or* **degree** dans une certaine mesure
PRON certains ◆ ~ **of our members have not paid** certains *or* quelques uns de nos membres n'ont pas payé

certainly /ˈsɜːtənlɪ/ LANGUAGE IN USE 26.3 ADV 1 *(= undoubtedly)* certainement, assurément ◆ **it is** ~ **true that ...** on ne peut pas nier que ... + *subj or indic* ◆ **your answer is almost** ~ **right** il est presque certain que votre réponse est juste
2 *(= definitely)* ◆ **it** ~ **impressed me** cela m'a vraiment impressionné ◆ **I shall** ~ **be there** j'y serai sans faute, je ne manquerai pas d'y être ◆ **such groups most** ~ **exist** il est absolument certain que de tels groupes existent, de tels groupes existent, c'est une certitude
3 *(expressing agreement)* certainement ◆ **wouldn't you agree? – oh,** ~ vous ne croyez pas ? – oh si, bien sûr ◆ **had you forgotten? –** ~ **not** vous aviez oublié ? – certainement pas
4 *(expressing willingness)* certainement, bien sûr ◆ **could you help me? –** ~ pourriez-vous m'aider ? – certainement *or* bien sûr
5 *(= granted)* certes ◆ ~, **she has potential, but ...** certes, elle a des capacités mais ...

certainty /ˈsɜːtəntɪ/ N 1 *(= fact, quality)* certitude *f* ◆ **for a** ~ à coup sûr, sans aucun doute ◆ **to bet on a** ~ parier en étant sûr de gagner ◆ **she is a** ~ **for the gold medal** elle est pratiquement sûre de gagner la médaille d'or ◆ **his success is a** ~ son succès est certain *or* ne fait aucun doute ◆ **that reunification will eventually happen is a** ~ il ne fait aucun doute que la réunification finira par se faire ◆ **it is a moral** ~ c'est une certitude morale ◆ **faced with the** ~ **of disaster ...** face à un désastre inévitable ... ◆ **there are no certainties in modern Europe** il n'y a aucune certitude dans l'Europe moderne ◆ **there is too little** ~ **about the future** l'avenir est trop incertain ◆ **they cannot plan for the future with any degree of** ~ il y a trop d'incertitude, ils ne peuvent pas faire de projets d'avenir
2 *(NonC = conviction)* certitude *f*, conviction *f* ◆ **to say sth with some** ~ affirmer qch avec assurance

certifiable /ˌsɜːtɪˈfaɪəbl/ ADJ 1 *[fact, statement]* qu'on peut certifier 2 *(* = mad)* bon à enfermer

certifiably /ˌsɜːtɪˈfaɪəblɪ/ ADV ◆ ~ **safe** conforme aux normes de sécurité ◆ ~ **mad** * *or* **insane** * bon à enfermer

certificate /səˈtɪfɪkɪt/ N 1 *(= legal document)* certificat *m*, acte *m* ◆ ~ **of airworthiness**, ~ **of seaworthiness** certificat *m* de navigabilité ◆ ~ **of origin/value** *(Comm)* certificat *m* d'origine/de valeur ◆ ~ **of posting** récépissé *m* ◆ **birth** ~ acte *m* or extrait *m* de naissance ; → **death, marriage** 2 *(= academic document)* diplôme *m* ; *(for skilled or semi-skilled work)* qualification *f* professionnelle ◆ **Certificate of Secondary Education** *(Brit Scol: formerly)* ≃ brevet *m* (d'études du premier cycle) *(dans une seule matière)* ; → **teacher**

certificated /səˈtɪfɪkeɪtɪd/ ADJ diplômé

certification /ˌsɜːtɪfɪˈkeɪʃən/ N 1 *(NonC)* certification *f*, authentification *f* 2 *(= document)* certificat *m*

certify /ˈsɜːtɪfaɪ/ VT 1 certifier, attester *(that* que) ; ◆ **certified as a true copy** *(Jur)* certifié conforme ◆ **to** ~ **sb (insane)** *(Psych)* déclarer qn atteint d'aliénation mentale ◆ **she was certified dead** elle a été déclarée morte ◆ **the painting has been certified (as) genuine** le tableau a été authentifié 2 *(Fin)* *[+ cheque]* certifier 3 *(Comm)* *[+ goods]* garantir ◆ **to send by certified mail** *(US Post)* ≃ envoyer avec accusé de réception VI ◆ **to** ~ **to sth** attester qch
COMP **certified milk** N *(US) lait soumis aux contrôles d'hygiène réglementaires*
certified public accountant N *(US)* expert-comptable *mf*, comptable *mf* agréé(e) *(Can)*
certified teacher N *(US Scol)* professeur *m* diplômé

certitude /ˈsɜːtɪtjuːd/ N certitude *f*, conviction *f* absolue

cerulean /sɪˈruːlɪən/ ADJ *(liter)* bleu ciel *inv*, azuré

cerumen /sɪˈruːmen/ N cérumen *m*

ceruminous /sɪˈruːmɪnəs/ ADJ cérumineux

cervical /ˈsɜːvɪkəl/ ADJ cervical
COMP **cervical cancer** N cancer *m* du col de l'utérus
cervical smear N frottis *m* vaginal

cervix /ˈsɜːvɪks/ N (pl **cervixes** or **cervices** /səˈvaɪsiːz/) col *m* de l'utérus

cesium /ˈsiːzɪəm/ N *(esp US)* ⇒ **caesium**

cessation /seˈseɪʃən/ N cessation *f* ◆ ~ **of hostilities** cessation *f* des hostilités

cession /ˈseʃən/ N cession *f* ◆ **act of** ~ acte *m* de cession

cesspit /ˈsespɪt/ N fosse *f* d'aisance ; *(fig)* cloaque *m*

cesspool /ˈsespuːl/ N ⇒ **cesspit**

CET /ˌsiːiːˈtiː/ (abbrev of **Central European Time**) → **central**

cetacean /sɪˈteɪʃɪən/ ADJ, N cétacé *m*

Ceylon /sɪˈlɒn/ N *(formerly)* *(= island)* Ceylan *f* ; *(= state)* Ceylan *m* ◆ **in** ~ à Ceylan

Ceylonese /sɪlɒˈniːz/ *(formerly)* ADJ ceylanais N Ceylanais(e) *m(f)*

cf (abbrev of **confer**) cf

c/f *(Fin)* (abbrev of **carried forward**) → **carry forward**

CFC /ˌsiːefˈsiː/ N (abbrev of **chlorofluorocarbon**) CFC *m*

CFE /ˌsiːefˈiː/ N *(Brit)* (abbrev of **college of further education**) → **college** NPL (abbrev of **Conventional Forces in Europe**) FCE *fpl*

CFS /ˌsiːefˈes/ N (abbrev of **chronic fatigue syndrome**) → **chronic**

CG /siːˈdʒiː/ abbrev of **coastguard**

cg (abbrev of **centigram(me)(s)**) cg

CGA /ˌsiːdʒiːˈeɪ/ N (abbrev of **colour graphics adaptor**) → **colour**
COMP **CGA card** N carte *f* graphique CGA
CGA monitor N moniteur *m* CGA

CGI /ˌsiːdʒiːˈaɪ/ N (abbrev of **computer-generated imagery**) images *fpl* générées par ordinateur

CGT /ˌsiːdʒiːˈtiː/ N (abbrev of **capital gains tax**) → **capital**

CH (abbrev of **Companion of Honour**) *titre honorifique*

Ch. abbrev of **chapter**

c.h. (abbrev of **central heating**) → **central**

cha-cha /ˈtʃɑːtʃɑː/ N *(Mus)* cha-cha-cha *m*

Chad /tʃæd/ N Tchad *m* ◆ **Lake ~** le lac Tchad ADJ tchadien

chador /ˈtʃʌdəʳ/ N tchador *m*

chafe /tʃeɪf/ VT 1 *(= rub against)* frotter contre ; *(= irritate)* irriter ◆ **his shirt ~d his neck** sa chemise frottait contre son cou *or* lui irritait le cou ◆ **his neck was ~d** il avait le cou irrité 2 *(= wear out) [+ collar, cuffs, rope]* user (en frottant) ; *(Naut)* raguer 3 *(= rub)* frotter, frictionner ◆ **she ~d the child's hands to warm them** elle a frotté *or* frictionné les mains de l'enfant pour les réchauffer VI s'user ; *[rope]* raguer ◆ **his wrists ~d against the ropes binding them** ses poignets frottaient contre les cordes qui les entravaient ◆ **to ~ at sth** *(fig)* s'irriter de qch ◆ **he ~d at having to take orders from her** cela l'irritait de recevoir des ordres d'elle ◆ **to ~ at the bit** ronger son frein ◆ **he ~d against these restrictions** ces restrictions l'irritaient

chaff¹ /tʃɑːf/ N *(NonC: Agr) [of grain]* balle *f* ; *(= cut straw)* menue paille *f* ; → **wheat** VT *[+ straw]* hacher

chaff² /tʃɑːf/ N *(NonC = banter)* taquinerie *f* VT taquiner

chaffinch /ˈtʃæfɪntʃ/ N pinson *m*

chafing dish /ˈtʃeɪfɪŋdɪʃ/ N poêlon *m* (de table)

chagrin /ˈʃægrɪn/ N *(= deception)* déception *f*, dépit *m* ; *(= annoyance)* contrariété *f* ◆ **much to my ~** à ma grande déception VT *(frm) (= deceive)* dépiter, décevoir ; *(= annoy)* contrarier

chain /tʃeɪn/ N 1 *(gen, also ornamental)* chaîne *f* ◆ **~s** *(= fetters)* chaînes *fpl* ◆ **~ of office** *[of mayor]* chaîne *f (insigne de la fonction de maire)* ◆ **to keep a dog on a ~** tenir un chien à l'attache ◆ **in ~s** enchaîné ◆ **(snow) ~s** *(for car)* chaînes *fpl* (à neige) ◆ **to pull the ~** *[of lavatory]* tirer la chasse (d'eau) *or* la chaîne ; → **ball¹, bicycle**

2 *[of mountains, atoms etc]* chaîne *f* ; *(fig) [of ideas]* enchaînement *m* ; *[of events]* série *f*, suite *f* ◆ **~ of shops** chaîne *f* de magasins ◆ **to make a ~** *[people]* faire la chaîne ; → **bucket**

3 *(Tech) (for measuring)* chaîne *f* d'arpenteur ; *(= measure)* chaînée *f*

VT *(lit, fig)* enchaîner ; *[+ door]* mettre la chaîne à ◆ **he was ~ed to the wall** il était enchaîné au mur

COMP **chain gang** N chaîne *f* de forçats

chain letter N lettre *f* faisant partie d'une chaîne ◆ **~ letters** chaîne *f* (de lettres)

chain lightning N éclairs *mpl* en zigzag

chain-link fence N grillage *m*

chain mail N *(NonC)* cotte *f* de mailles

chain of command N *(Mil)* voies *fpl* hiérarchiques

chain reaction N *(Phys, fig)* réaction *f* en chaîne

chain saw N tronçonneuse *f*

chain-smoke VI fumer cigarette sur cigarette

chain smoker N grand(e) *or* gros(se) fumeur *m*, -euse *f*

chain stitch N *(Sewing)* (point *m* de) chaînette *f*

chain store N grand magasin *m* à succursales multiples

► **chain down** VT SEP enchaîner

► **chain up** VT SEP *[+ animal]* mettre à l'attache

chair /tʃɛəʳ/ N 1 chaise *f* ; *(= armchair)* fauteuil *m* ; *(= seat)* siège *m* ; *(Univ)* chaire *f* ; *(= wheelchair)* fauteuil *m* roulant ; *(US = electric chair)* chaise *f* (électrique) ◆ **to take a ~** s'asseoir ◆ **dentist's ~** fauteuil *m* de dentiste ◆ **to hold the ~ of French** *(Univ)* être titulaire de *or* avoir la chaire de français ◆ **to go to the ~** *(US)* passer à la chaise (électrique) ; → **deck, easy, highchair** 2 *(at meeting etc = function)* fauteuil *m* présidentiel, présidence *f* ◆ **to take the ~, to be in the ~** présider ◆ **to address the ~** s'adresser au président ◆ **~! ~!** à l'ordre ! 3 *(Admin)* ⇒ **chairman, chairwoman** VT 1 *(Admin) [+ meeting]* présider 2 *[+ hero]* porter en triomphe COMP **chair back** N dossier *m* (de chaise)

chairlift /ˈtʃɛəlɪft/ N télésiège *m*

chairman /ˈtʃɛəmən/ N (pl **-men**) président *m (d'un comité etc)* ◆ **Mr Chairman** Monsieur le Président ◆ **Madam Chairman** Madame la Présidente ◆ **~ and chief executive officer** président-directeur *m* général, P.D.G. *m* ◆ **Chairman Mao** le président Mao

chairmanship /ˈtʃɛəmənʃɪp/ N présidence *f (d'un comité etc)* ◆ **under the ~ of ...** sous la présidence de ...

chairperson /ˈtʃɛə,pɜːsn/ N président(e) *m(f)*

chairwarmer‡ /ˈtʃɛə,wɔːməʳ/ N *(US)* rond-de-cuir *m* (paresseux)

chairwoman /ˈtʃɛəwʊmən/ N (pl **-women**) présidente *f*

chaise /ʃeɪz/ N cabriolet *m*

chaise longue /ˈʃeɪzˈlɒŋ/ N (pl **chaise longues**) méridienne *f*

> ⚠ **chaise longue** in French means 'deckchair'.

chakra /ˈtʃækrə/ N *(Rel)* chakra *m*

chalet /ˈʃæleɪ/ N *(gen)* chalet *m* ; *[of motel]* bungalow *m*

chalice /ˈtʃælɪs/ N *(Rel)* calice *m* ; *(liter = wine cup)* coupe *f*

chalk /tʃɔːk/ N *(NonC)* craie *f* ◆ **a piece of ~** une craie, un morceau de craie ◆ **they're as different as ~ and cheese** *(Brit)* c'est le jour et la nuit ◆ **by a long ~** *(Brit)* de loin ◆ **the biggest by a long ~** de loin le plus grand ◆ **did he win? – not by a long ~** est-ce qu'il a gagné ? – non, loin de là *or* loin s'en faut ; → **French**

VT *(= write with chalk)* écrire à la craie ; *(= rub with chalk)* frotter de craie ; *[+ billiard cue]* mettre du bleu sur ; *[+ luggage]* marquer à la craie

COMP **chalk board** N *(US)* tableau *m* (noir)

chalk dust N poussière *f* de craie

chalk talk N *(US)* conférence *f* illustrée au tableau noir

► **chalk out** VT SEP *(lit) [+ pattern]* esquisser, tracer (à la craie) ; *(fig) [+ project]* esquisser ; *[+ plan of action]* tracer

► **chalk up** VT SEP 1 ◆ **chalk it up** mettez-le sur mon ardoise *or* compte ◆ **he ~ed it up to experience** il l'a mis au compte de l'expérience

2 *[+ achievement, victory]* remporter

chalkface /ˈtʃɔːkfeɪs/ N *(NonC: Brit Scol: hum)* ◆ **at the ~** en classe

chalkpit /ˈtʃɔːkpɪt/ N carrière *f* de craie

chalky /ˈtʃɔːkɪ/ ADJ *[soil]* crayeux, calcaire ; *[water]* calcaire ; *[complexion]* crayeux, blafard

challenge /ˈtʃælɪndʒ/ N 1 *(= difficult task)* défi *m* ◆ **the government's first ~ is to get the economy going** le premier défi qu'aura à relever le gouvernement est la relance économique ◆ **he sees the job as a great ~** il considère ce travail comme un véritable défi ◆ **the ~ of the 21st century** le défi du 21ᵉ siècle ◆ **to issue** *or* **put out a ~** lancer un défi ◆ **to take up the ~** relever le défi ◆ **I need the ~ of new ideas** j'ai besoin de nouvelles idées qui me stimulent

◆ **challenge for sth** *[of competitor, candidate]* ◆ **Hunter's ~ for the party leadership** la tentative de Hunter pour prendre la tête du parti ◆ **how did he finance his ~ for the presidency?** comment a-t-il financé sa candidature à la présidence ?

◆ **to rise to the challenge** se montrer à la hauteur

◆ **to be** *or* **pose a challenge to sb** *or* **sth** ◆ **a general strike is a political ~ to any government** les grèves générales sont un problème politique pour quelque gouvernement que ce soit ◆ **fundamentalists started to pose a serious ~ to the ruling establishment** les fondamentalistes commençaient à poser un sérieux problème à la classe dirigeante ◆ **it was a ~ to his skill** c'était un défi à son savoir-faire ◆ **the situation poses a serious ~ to the country's political system** la situation représente un sérieux défi pour le système politique national ◆ **this action is a ~ to authority** c'est un acte qui défie l'autorité

2 *(by sentry)* sommation *f*

3 *(Jur) [of juror, jury]* récusation *f*

VT 1 *(= compete against) (Sport)* jouer contre ◆ **she is challenging him in elections called for May 17** elle sera son adversaire aux élections du 17 mai ◆ **in the hope of challenging the company's supremacy** dans l'espoir de disputer à cette entreprise sa position de leader ◆ **to ~ sb to a game** proposer à qn de faire une partie ◆ **to ~ sb to a duel** provoquer qn en duel

◆ **to challenge sb to do sth** mettre qn au défi de faire qch

◆ **to challenge sb for sth** *[+ position]* disputer qch à qn

2 *(= question)* demander des explications à ◆ **when the editor was ~d, he said ...** lorsqu'on lui a demandé des explications, le rédacteur a dit que ...

◆ **to challenge sb over** *or* **about sth** demander des explications à qn au sujet de qch ◆ **he was ~d over the absence of women on the committee** on lui a demandé des explications sur l'absence de femmes dans le comité

3 *(= call into question) [+ statement, idea]* contester ◆ **this view is ~d by conservationists** ce point de vue est contesté par les défenseurs de l'environnement ◆ **to ~ sb's authority to do sth** contester à qn le droit de faire qch

4 *(= question authority of) [+ person]* défier ◆ **she would never dare to ~ him** elle n'oserait jamais le défier

5 *(= tax)* demander un effort à ◆ **the job didn't ~ me** ce travail ne me demandait aucun effort

6 *[police]* interpeller ; *[sentry]* faire une sommation à

7 *(Jur) [+ juror, jury]* récuser

-challenged /ˈtʃælɪndʒd/ ADJ 1 *(esp US euph)* ◆ **visually-challenged** malvoyant ◆ **physically-challenged** handicapé 2 *(hum)* ◆ **vertically-challenged** de petite taille ◆ **intellectually-challenged** limité intellectuellement

challenger /ˈtʃælɪndʒəʳ/ N *(Sport, Pol, also fig)* adversaire *mf*, challenger *m* ◆ **she received more votes than her ~** elle a obtenu plus de voix que son adversaire *or* challenger

challenging /ˈtʃælɪndʒɪŋ/ ADJ *[look, tone]* de défi ; *[remark, speech]* provocateur (-trice *f*) ; *[job, work]* difficile, qui représente un challenge ; *[book]* stimulant ◆ **he found himself in a ~ situation** il s'est trouvé là devant une gageure ◆ **this is a very ~ situation** cette situation est une véritable gageure

challengingly /ˈtʃælɪndʒɪŋlɪ/ ADV 1 *(= defiantly) [say, announce]* avec un air de défi ◆ **to look ~ at sb** lancer un regard de défi à qn 2 *(= demandingly)* ◆ **~ difficult** difficile mais stimulant

chamber /ˈtʃeɪmbəʳ/ N 1 *(†, frm = room)* salle *f*, pièce *f* ; (also **bedchamber**) chambre *f*

2 *(= hall)* chambre *f* ◆ **the Upper/Lower Chamber** *(Parl)* la Chambre haute/basse ; → **audience, second¹**

3 [of revolver] chambre f ; (Anat) cavité f ◆ **the ~s of the eye** les chambres fpl de l'œil

NPL **chambers** (Brit) 1 († = lodgings) logement m, appartement m ; [of bachelor] garçonnière † f 2 [of barrister, judge, magistrate] cabinet m ; [of solicitor] étude f ◆ **to hear a case in ~s** (Jur) ≃ juger un cas en référé

COMP **chamber concert** N concert m de musique de chambre
chamber music N musique f de chambre
Chamber of Commerce N Chambre f de commerce
the Chamber of Deputies N la Chambre des députés
Chamber of Horrors N cabinet m des horreurs
Chamber of Trade N Chambre f des métiers
chamber orchestra N orchestre m (de musique) de chambre
chamber pot N pot m de chambre, vase m de nuit †

chamberlain /ˈtʃeɪmbəlɪn/ N chambellan m ; → **lord**

chambermaid /ˈtʃeɪmbəmeɪd/ N femme f de chambre

chambray /ˈtʃæmbreɪ/ N (US) batiste f

chameleon /kəˈmiːlɪən/ N caméléon m ◆ **he's a real ~** fig c'est un véritable caméléon

chamfer /ˈtʃæmfəʳ/ N (= bevel) chanfrein m ; (= groove) cannelure f VT chanfreiner, canneler

chammy * /ˈʃæmɪ/ N ⇒ **chamois**

chamois /ˈʃæmwɑː/ N (pl inv) 1 (= animal) chamois m 2 /ˈʃæmɪ/ (also **chamois cloth**) chamois m COMP **chamois leather** N peau f de chamois

chamomile /ˈkæməʊmaɪl/ N ⇒ **camomile**

champ¹ /tʃæmp/ VI mâchonner ◆ **to ~ at the bit** (lit, fig) ronger son frein VT mâchonner

champ² * /tʃæmp/ N champion(ne) m(f)

champagne /ʃæmˈpeɪn/ N 1 (= wine) champagne m 2 (Geog) ◆ **Champagne** Champagne f COMP (also **champagne-coloured**) champagne inv
champagne cup N cocktail m au champagne
champagne glass N (wide) coupe f à champagne ; (tall and narrow) flûte f à champagne
champagne lifestyle N grand train m de vie
champagne socialist N ◆ **to be a ~ socialist** appartenir à la gauche caviar

champers * /ˈʃæmpəz/ N (NonC) champ* m, champagne m

champion /ˈtʃæmpjən/ N 1 champion(ne) m(f), défenseur m ◆ **the ~ of free speech** le champion de la liberté d'expression 2 (Sport = person, animal) champion(ne) m(f) ◆ **world ~** champion(ne) m(f) du monde ◆ **boxing ~** champion m de boxe ◆ **skiing ~** champion(ne) m(f) de ski ◆ **Champions' League** (Ftbl) Ligue des champions ADJ 1 [show animal] champion ◆ **~ swimmer/skier** etc champion(ne) m(f) de natation/de ski etc 2 (dial = excellent) [meal, holiday, film] du tonnerre* ◆ **that's ~!** c'est super !*, c'est champion !* VT [+ person] prendre fait et cause pour ; [+ action, cause, sb's decision] se faire le champion de, défendre

championship /ˈtʃæmpjənʃɪp/ N 1 (Sport) championnat m ◆ **world ~** championnat m du monde ◆ **boxing ~** championnat m de boxe ◆ **world boxing ~** championnat m du monde de boxe 2 (NonC) [of cause etc] défense f

chance /tʃɑːns/ LANGUAGE IN USE 16.2, 16.3

N 1 (= luck) hasard m ◆ **(totally) by ~, by (sheer) ~** (tout à fait) par hasard, par (pur) hasard ; (= fortunately) par chance ◆ **have you a pen on you by (any) ~?** auriez-vous par hasard un stylo sur vous ? ◆ **it was not (by) ~ that he came** ce n'est pas par hasard qu'il est venu, ce n'est pas un hasard s'il est venu ◆ **to trust (o.s.) to ~** s'en remettre au hasard ◆ **a game of ~** un jeu de hasard ◆ **to leave things to ~** laisser faire le hasard ◆ **he left nothing to ~** il n'a rien laissé au hasard

2 (= possibility) chance(s) f(pl), possibilité f ◆ **to stand a ~ (of doing sth)** avoir une bonne chance (de faire qch) ◆ **to stand no ~ (of doing sth)** ne pas avoir la moindre chance (de faire qch) ◆ **he hasn't much ~** or **doesn't stand much ~ of winning** il n'a pas beaucoup de chances de gagner ◆ **he's still in with a ~** il a encore une petite chance ◆ **on the ~ that you might return** dans le cas or au cas où vous reviendriez ◆ **I went there on the ~ of seeing him** j'y suis allé dans l'espoir de le voir ◆ **the ~s are that ...** il y a de grandes chances que ... + subj, il est très possible que ... + subj ◆ **the ~s are against that happening** il y a peu de chances pour que cela arrive subj ◆ **the ~s are against him** il y a peu de chances pour qu'il réussisse ◆ **there is little ~ of his coming** il est peu probable qu'il vienne ◆ **you'll have to take a ~ on his coming** tu verras bien s'il vient ou non ◆ **he's taking no ~s** il ne veut rien laisser au hasard, il ne veut prendre aucun risque ◆ **that's a ~ we'll have to take** c'est un risque que nous allons devoir prendre or que nous devons courir ◆ **no ~!***, **not a ~!*** pas de danger !*, jamais ! ; → **off**

3 (= opportunity) occasion f ◆ **I had the ~ to go** or **of going** j'ai eu l'occasion d'y aller, l'occasion m'a été donnée d'y aller ◆ **if there's a ~ of buying it** s'il y a une possibilité d'achat ◆ **to lose a ~** laisser passer une occasion ◆ **she was waiting for her ~** elle attendait son heure ◆ **she was waiting for her ~ to speak** elle attendait or guettait l'occasion de parler ◆ **now's your ~!** (in conversation, traffic etc) vas-y ! ; (in career etc) saute sur l'occasion !, à toi de jouer ! ◆ **this is his big ~** c'est le grand moment pour lui ◆ **give him another ~** laisse-lui encore une chance ◆ **he has had every ~** il a eu toutes les chances ◆ **he never had a ~ in life** il n'a jamais eu sa chance dans la vie ◆ **give me a ~ to show you what I can do** donnez-moi la possibilité de vous montrer ce que je sais faire ◆ **you'll have your ~** (= your turn will come) votre tour viendra

ADJ de hasard, accidentel ◆ **a ~ companion** un compagnon rencontré par hasard ◆ **a ~ discovery** une découverte accidentelle ◆ **a ~ meeting** une rencontre de hasard or fortuite

VT 1 (= risk) [+ rejection, fine] risquer, courir le risque de ◆ **to ~ doing sth** se risquer à faire qch, prendre le risque de faire qch ◆ **I'll go round without phoning and ~ finding him there** je vais passer chez lui sans téléphoner en espérant l'y trouver ◆ **I want to see her alone but I'll have to ~ finding her husband there** je voudrais la voir seule, mais il faut que je prenne le risque que son mari soit là ◆ **I'll ~ it!** * je vais risquer le coup !* ◆ **to ~ one's arm** * risquer le tout (pour le tout) ◆ **to ~ one's luck** tenter or courir sa chance

2 (frm = happen) ◆ **to ~ to do sth** faire qch par hasard ◆ **I ~d to hear his name** j'ai entendu son nom par hasard, il s'est trouvé que j'ai entendu son nom ◆ **it ~d that I was there** il s'est trouvé que j'étais là

► **chance upon** VT FUS (frm) [+ person] rencontrer par hasard ; [+ thing] trouver par hasard

chancel /ˈtʃɑːnsəl/ N chœur m (d'une église) COMP **chancel screen** N clôture f du chœur, jubé m

chancellery /ˈtʃɑːnsələrɪ/ N chancellerie f

chancellor /ˈtʃɑːnsələʳ/ N (Hist, Jur, Pol) chancelier m ; (Brit Univ) président(e) m(f) honoraire ; (US Univ) président(e) m(f) d'université COMP **Chancellor of the Exchequer** N (Brit) chancelier m de l'Échiquier, ≃ ministre m des Finances ; → **lord** ; → TREASURY

chancellorship /ˈtʃɑːnsələʃɪp/ N fonctions fpl de chancelier

chancer * /ˈtʃɑːnsəʳ/ N arnaqueur* m, -euse* f ; (= child) loustic* m

chancery /ˈtʃɑːnsərɪ/ N 1 (Brit, Jur) cour f de la chancellerie (une des cinq divisions de la Haute Cour de justice anglaise) ◆ **ward in ~** pupille mf (sous tutelle judiciaire) 2 (US) ⇒ **chancellery** 3 (US: also **court of chancery**) ≃ cour f d'équité or de la chancellerie

chancre /ˈʃæŋkəʳ/ N (Med) chancre m

chancy * /ˈtʃɑːnsɪ/ ADJ (= risky) risqué, hasardeux ; (= doubtful) aléatoire, problématique

chandelier /ˌʃændəˈlɪəʳ/ N lustre m

chandler /ˈtʃɑːndləʳ/ N ◆ **(ship's) ~** shipchandler m, marchand m de fournitures pour bateaux

change /tʃeɪndʒ/ LANGUAGE IN USE 21.4

N 1 (= alteration) changement m (from, in de ; into en) ; ◆ **a ~ for the better** un changement en mieux, une amélioration ◆ **a ~ for the worse** un changement en mal ◆ **~ in the weather** changement m de temps ◆ **~ in public opinion** revirement m de l'opinion publique ◆ **~ in attitudes** changement m d'attitude, évolution f des attitudes ◆ **a ~ in government policy** un changement dans la politique du gouvernement ◆ **(just) for a ~** pour changer un peu ◆ **by way of a ~** histoire de changer* ◆ **to make a ~ in sth** changer qch ◆ **to make a ~ of direction** (fig) changer son fusil d'épaule (fig) ◆ **to have a ~ of heart** changer d'avis ◆ **it makes a ~** ça change un peu ◆ **it will be a nice ~** cela nous fera un changement, voilà qui nous changera agréablement ! ; (iro) ça nous changera ! (iro) ◆ **a picnic will be** or **make a nice ~ from being stuck indoors** un pique-nique nous changera de rester toujours enfermé à l'intérieur ◆ **the ~ (of life)** le retour d'âge, la ménopause

2 (= substitution) changement m ◆ **~ of address** changement m d'adresse ◆ **~ of air** changement m d'air ◆ **a ~ of air will do us good** un changement d'air or changer d'air nous fera du bien ◆ **he brought a ~ of clothes** il a apporté des vêtements de rechange ◆ **I need a ~ of clothes** il faut que je me change subj ◆ **~ of scene** (Theat, fig) changement m de décor ◆ **~ of horses** relais m ◆ **~ of job** changement m de travail or de poste

3 (NonC) changement m, variété f ◆ **she likes ~** elle aime le changement or la variété ◆ **political ~** changement m politique

4 (NonC = money) monnaie f ◆ **small ~** petite monnaie f ◆ **can you give me ~ for this note/of £5?** pouvez-vous me faire la monnaie de ce billet/de 5 livres ? ◆ **keep the ~** gardez la monnaie ◆ **"no change given"** "faites l'appoint" ◆ **you don't get much ~ from a fiver these days** aujourd'hui il ne reste jamais grand-chose d'un billet de cinq livres ◆ **you won't get much ~ out of him*** tu perds ton temps avec lui

5 ◆ **the Change** (= the Stock Exchange) la Bourse ◆ **on the Change** en Bourse

VT 1 (by substitution) changer de ◆ **to ~ (one's) clothes** changer de vêtements, se changer ◆ **to ~ one's shirt/skirt** etc changer de chemise/jupe etc ◆ **to ~ one's address** changer d'adresse ◆ **to ~ the baby/his nappy** changer le bébé/ses couches ◆ **to ~ hands** (= one's grip) changer de main ; [goods, property, money] changer de mains ◆ **to ~ the scene** (Theat) changer le décor ◆ **to ~ trains/stations/buses** changer de train/de gare/d'autobus ◆ **to ~ one's name/seat** changer de nom/place ◆ **to ~ one's opinion** or **mind** changer d'avis ◆ **to ~ sb's mind (about sth)** faire changer qn d'avis (à propos de qch) ; → **bed, colour, gear, guard, subject, track, tune, wheel**

[2] *(= exchange)* échanger (X *for* Y X contre Y) ; ◆ **to ~ places (with sb)** *(lit)* changer de place (avec qn) ◆ **I wouldn't like to ~ places with you** *(fig)* je n'aimerais pas être à votre place ◆ **to ~ sides** *or* **ends** *(Tennis)* changer de côté ; *(Ftbl etc)* changer de camp ◆ **to ~ sides** *(fig: in argument etc)* changer de camp
[3] *[+ banknote, coin]* faire la monnaie de, changer ; *[+ foreign currency]* changer *(into* en)
[4] *(= alter, modify, transform)* changer, transformer (X *into* Y X en Y) ; ◆ **the witch ~d him into a cat** la sorcière l'a changé en chat ◆ **drugs ~d him into a person we didn't recognize** les drogues l'ont changé au point qu'on ne le reconnaissait plus ◆ **this has ~d my ideas** cela m'a fait changer d'idée ◆ **success has greatly ~d her** la réussite l'a complètement transformée
VI [1] *(= become different)* changer, se transformer ◆ **you've ~d a lot!** tu as beaucoup changé ! ◆ **he will never ~** il ne changera jamais, on ne le changera pas ◆ **his mood ~d from resignation to rage** il est passé de la résignation à la fureur ◆ **the prince ~d into a swan** le prince s'est changé en cygne ◆ **the water had ~d to ice** l'eau s'était changée en glace
[2] *(= change clothes)* se changer ◆ **I must ~ at once** je dois me changer tout de suite, il faut que je me change *subj* tout de suite ◆ **she ~d into an old skirt** elle s'est changée et a mis une vieille jupe
[3] *(on bus, plane, train journey)* changer ◆ **you must ~ at Edinburgh** vous devez changer à Édimbourg ◆ **all ~!** tout le monde descend !
[4] *[moon]* entrer dans une nouvelle phase
COMP **change machine** N distributeur *m* de monnaie
change purse N (US) porte-monnaie *m inv*
► **change around** VT SEP changer de place
► **change down** VI *(Brit: in car gears)* rétrograder
► **change over**
VI *(gen)* passer *(from* de ; *to* à) ; *[two people]* faire l'échange ; *(Sport = change ends) (Tennis)* changer de côté ; *(Ftbl etc)* changer de camp
► **change round** VT SEP ⇒ **change around**
► **change up** VI *(Brit: in car gears)* passer la vitesse supérieure

changeability /ˌtʃeɪndʒəˈbɪlɪtɪ/ N *[of circumstances, weather]* variabilité *f*

changeable /ˈtʃeɪndʒəbl/ ADJ *[person]* changeant, inconstant ; *[character]* versatile, changeant ; *[colour]* changeant ; *[weather, wind, circumstances]* variable

changeless /ˈtʃeɪndʒlɪs/ ADJ *[rite]* immuable, invariable ; *[person]* constant ; *[character]* inaltérable

changeling /ˈtʃeɪndʒlɪŋ/ N enfant *mf* changé(e) *(substitué à un enfant volé)*

changeover /ˈtʃeɪndʒəʊvəʳ/ N changement *m*, passage *m* ; *(NonC: Mil) [of guard]* relève *f* ◆ **the ~ from dictatorship to democracy** le passage de la dictature à la démocratie

changing /ˈtʃeɪndʒɪŋ/ ADJ *[wind, prices, interest rates]* variable, changeant ; *[expression]* mobile ; *[social attitudes, principles]* qui change, qui évolue ◆ **a ~ society** une société en mutation
N *(NonC)* acte *m* de (se) changer, changement *m* ◆ **the ~ of the guard** la relève de la garde
COMP **changing-room** N *(Brit Sport)* vestiaire *m*

channel /ˈtʃænl/ N [1] *(= bed of river etc)* lit *m* ; *(= navigable passage)* chenal *m* ; *(between two land masses)* bras *m* de mer ; *(for irrigation, small)* rigole *f* ; *(wider)* canal *m* ; *(in street)* caniveau *m* ; *(= duct)* conduit *m* ◆ **the (English) Channel** la Manche
[2] *(= groove in surface)* rainure *f* ; *(Archit)* cannelure *f*
[3] *(TV)* chaîne *f*
[4] *(Customs)* ◆ **red/green ~** file *f* marchandises à déclarer/rien à déclarer
[5] *(fig)* direction *f* ◆ **he directed the conversation into a new ~** il a orienté la conversation dans une nouvelle direction ◆ **~ of communication** voie *f* de communication ◆ **the government used all the diplomatic ~s available** le gouvernement a utilisé toutes les voies diplomatiques possibles ◆ **they applied for asylum through the official ~s** ils ont fait une demande d'asile par voie officielle ◆ **to go through the usual ~s** *(Admin)* suivre la filière (habituelle)
[6] *(Comput)* canal *m*
VT [1] *(= make channels in: for irrigation)* creuser des rigoles (*or* des canaux) dans ; *[+ street]* pourvoir d'un *or* de caniveau(x) ◆ **the river ~led its way towards ...** la rivière a creusé son lit vers ...
[2] *(fig) [+ crowd]* canaliser *(into* vers) ; *[+ energies, efforts, resources]* canaliser, diriger *(towards, into* vers) ; *[+ information]* canaliser *(into, towards* vers) concentrer *(into, towards* dans)
[3] *(Archit)* canneler
COMP **Channel ferry** N *(Brit)* ferry *m* transmanche *inv*
channel-hop VI *(Brit TV)* zapper *
channel-hopping N *(Brit TV)* zapping * *m*
Channel Islander N habitant(e) *m(f)* des îles Anglo-Normandes
the Channel Islands, the Channel Isles NPL *(Geog)* les îles *fpl* Anglo-Normandes
channel-surf VI *(US)* ⇒ **channel-hop**
channel-surfing N *(US)* ⇒ **channel-hopping**
the Channel tunnel N le tunnel sous la Manche
► **channel off** VT SEP *(lit) [+ water]* capter ; *(fig) [+ energy, resources]* canaliser

chant /tʃɑːnt/ N *(Mus)* chant *m* (lent), mélopée *f* ; *(Rel Mus)* psalmodie *f* ; *[of crowd, demonstrators, audience etc]* chant *m* scandé VT *(= sing)* chanter lentement ; *(= recite)* réciter ; *(Rel)* psalmodier ; *[crowd, demonstrators etc]* scander, crier sur l'air des lampions VI chanter ; *(Rel)* psalmodier ; *[crowd, demonstrators etc]* scander des slogans

chantey /ˈʃæntɪ/ N (US) chanson *f* de marin

Chanukah /ˈhɑːnəkə/ N Hanoukka *f*

chaos /ˈkeɪɒs/ N chaos *m* COMP **chaos theory** N théorie *f* du chaos

chaotic /keɪˈɒtɪk/ ADJ chaotique

chaotically /keɪˈɒtɪklɪ/ ADV de façon chaotique ◆ **he's ~ untidy/disorganized** il est effroyablement désordonné/désorganisé

chap[1] /tʃæp/ N *(Med)* gerçure *f*, crevasse *f* VI se gercer, se crevasser VT gercer, crevasser COMP **Chap Stick** ® N pommade *f* rosat *or* pour les lèvres

chap[2] /tʃæp/ N ⇒ **chop**[2]

chap[3] * /tʃæp/ N *(= man)* gars * *m* ◆ **old ~** *(term of address)* mon vieux * ◆ **he was a young ~** c'était un jeune gars * ◆ **a nice ~** un chic type *, un bon gars * ◆ **the poor old ~** le pauvre vieux * ◆ **poor little ~** pauvre petit *m* ◆ **he's very deaf, poor ~** il est très sourd, le pauvre garçon *or* le pauvre vieux * ◆ **be a good ~ and say nothing** † sois gentil, ne dis rien

chapat(t)i /tʃəˈpætɪ, tʃəˈpɑːtɪ/ N (pl **chapat(t)i** *or* **chapat(t)is** *or* **chapat(t)ies**) chapati *m*

chapel /ˈtʃæpəl/ N [1] chapelle *f* ; → **lady** [2] *(= nonconformist church)* église *f* (non conformiste) ◆ **a ~ family** une famille non conformiste [3] *[of print union]* section *f* syndicale *(dans l'édition)*
COMP **chapel of ease** N (église *f*) succursale *f*
chapel of rest N chapelle *f* ardente

chaperon(e) /ˈʃæpərəʊn/ N chaperon *m* ◆ **she was the ~(e)** elle faisait office de chaperon VT chaperonner

chaplain /ˈtʃæplɪn/ N *(in armed forces, prison, school, hospital)* aumônier *m* ; *(to nobleman)* chapelain *m*

chaplaincy /ˈtʃæplənsɪ/ N [1] *(= building, room)* aumônerie *f* [2] *(NonC = work) (in armed forces, prison, school, hospital)* aumônerie *f* ; *(for nobleman)* chapellenie *f*

chaplet /ˈtʃæplɪt/ N *[of flowers]* guirlande *f*, chapelet *m* ; *(Archit, Rel)* chapelet *m*

chappy ‡ /ˈtʃæpɪ/ N ⇒ **chap**[3]

chaps /tʃæps/ NPL (US) jambières *fpl* de cuir *(portées par les cow-boys)*

chapter /ˈtʃæptəʳ/ N [1] *[of book]* chapitre *m* ◆ **in ~ four** au chapitre quatre ◆ **to give** *or* **quote ~ and verse** citer ses références *or* ses autorités [2] *(Rel)* chapitre *m* [3] *(fig = period)* chapitre *m*, épisode *m* ◆ **a ~ of accidents** une succession de mésaventures, une kyrielle de malheurs ◆ **this ~ is now closed** ce chapitre est maintenant clos [4] *(= branch of society, club, organization etc)* branche *f*, section *f* COMP **chapter room** N *(Rel)* salle *f* capitulaire *or* du chapitre

chapterhouse /ˈtʃæptəhaʊs/ N *(Rel)* chapitre *m (lieu)*

char[1] /tʃɑːʳ/ VT *(= burn black)* carboniser VI être carbonisé

char[2] † * /tʃɑːʳ/ *(Brit)* N *(= charwoman)* femme *f* de ménage VI *(also* **go out charring)** faire des ménages

char[3] † * /tʃɑːʳ/ N (Brit = *tea)* thé *m*

char[4] /tʃɑːʳ/ N *(= fish)* omble *m*

char-à-banc † /ˈʃærəbæŋ/ N *(Brit)* (auto)car *m (décapotable)*

character /ˈkærɪktəʳ/ N [1] *(= temperament, disposition) [of person]* caractère *m*, tempérament *m* ◆ **he has the same ~ as his brother** il a le même caractère que son frère ◆ **it's very much in ~ (for him)** c'est bien de lui, cela lui ressemble tout à fait ◆ **that was not in ~ (for him)** cela ne lui ressemblait pas, ce n'était pas dans son caractère
[2] *(= nature) [of country, village]* caractère *m* ; *[of book, film]* caractère *m*, nature *f* ◆ **the state farms were semi-military in ~** les fermes d'État étaient de nature quasi-militaire ◆ **he stressed the global ~ of the modern economy** il a mis l'accent sur le caractère international de l'économie moderne
[3] *(NonC = strength, energy, determination etc)* caractère *m* ◆ **to have ~** avoir du caractère ◆ **it takes ~ to say such a thing** il faut avoir du caractère pour dire une chose pareille ; see also **strength**
[4] *(= outstanding individual)* personnage *m* ; (* *= original person)* numéro * *m*, phénomène * *m* ◆ **he's quite a ~!** * c'est un sacré numéro * *or* un phénomène ! * ◆ **he's a queer** *or* **an odd ~** c'est un curieux personnage
[5] réputation *f* ◆ **of good/bad ~** de bonne/mauvaise réputation, qui a une bonne/qui a mauvaise réputation ◆ **evidence of good ~** *(Jur)* preuve *f* de moralité
[6] *(= testimonial)* références *fpl*
[7] *(Literat)* personnage *m* ; *(Theat)* personnage *m*, rôle *m* ◆ **one of Shakespeare's ~s** un des personnages de Shakespeare ◆ **he played the ~ of Hamlet** il a joué (le rôle de) Hamlet
[8] *(Typ)* caractère *m*, signe *m* ◆ **Gothic ~s** caractères *mpl* gothiques
[9] *(Comput)* caractère *m* ◆ **~s per inch** caractères *mpl* par pouce ◆ **~s per second** caractères/seconde *mpl*
COMP **character actor** N acteur *m* de genre
character actress N actrice *f* de genre
character assassination N diffamation *f*
character-building ADJ qui forme le caractère
character comedy N comédie *f* de caractère

character part N rôle *m* de composition
character reference N certificat *m* de (bonne) moralité
character set N *(Typ)* chasse *f* (de caractères) ; *(Comput)* jeu *m* de caractères
character sketch N portrait *m* or description *f* rapide
character space N *(Typ)* espace *f*
character string N *(Comput)* chaîne *f* de caractères
character witness N *(Jur)* témoin *m* de moralité

characterful /ˈkærɪktəfʊl/ ADJ *[place, building]* de caractère, qui a du cachet

characteristic /ˌkærɪktəˈrɪstɪk/ ADJ caractéristique ♦ **with (his) ~ enthusiasm** avec l'enthousiasme qui le caractérise N *(gen, Math)* caractéristique *f*

characteristically /ˌkærɪktəˈrɪstɪkəlɪ/ ADV ♦ **he was ~ laconic** comme à son habitude, il a été laconique ♦ **she proposed a ~ brilliant solution** elle a proposé une excellente solution, comme à son habitude ♦ **he replied in ~ robust style** il a répondu dans ce style robuste qui le caractérise ♦ **~, she refused** comme on pouvait s'y attendre, elle a refusé

characterization /ˌkærɪktəraɪˈzeɪʃən/ N *(gen)* caractérisation *f* ; *(by playwright, novelist etc)* manière *f* de camper les personnages ; *(by actor)* interprétation *f* ♦ **~ in Dickens** la manière dont Dickens campe ses personnages

characterize /ˈkærɪktəraɪz/ VT 1 (= *be typical of*) caractériser, être caractéristique de ; *(Literat)* camper un (or des) personnage(s)
♦ **to be characterized by** se caractériser par ♦ **the election campaign was ~d by violence** la campagne électorale s'est caractérisée par une atmosphère de violence
2 (= *describe*) qualifier ♦ **both companies have ~d the talks as friendly** les deux entreprises ont qualifié les discussions d'"amicales"

characterless /ˈkærɪktəlɪs/ ADJ sans caractère, fade

charade /ʃəˈrɑːd/ N 1 *(fig)* comédie *f* 2 (= *game*) **~s** charades *fpl* en action

charbroiled /ˈtʃɑːbrɔɪld/ ADJ *(US)* ⇒ **chargrilled**

charcoal /ˈtʃɑːkəʊl/ N charbon *m* de bois
COMP *[drawing, sketch]* au charbon ; (= *colour:* also **charcoal-grey**) gris foncé *inv*, (gris) anthracite *inv*
charcoal burner N (= *person*) charbonnier *m* ; (= *stove*) réchaud *m* à charbon de bois

chard /tʃɑːd/ N (also **Swiss chard**) bettes *fpl*, blettes *fpl*

charge /tʃɑːdʒ/

1 NOUN	4 COMPOUNDS
2 TRANSITIVE VERB	5 PHRASAL VERBS
3 INTRANSITIVE VERB	

1 - NOUN

1 [Jur] inculpation *f*, chef *m* d'accusation ♦ **what is the ~?** quelle est le chef d'accusation ? ♦ **the ~ was murder** il était (or j'étais *etc*) inculpé de meurtre ♦ **the ~ was read** on a lu l'acte *m* d'accusation ♦ **no ~ was brought against him** il n'y a pas eu de poursuites (judiciaires), il n'a pas été poursuivi or inculpé ♦ **the ~ was dropped** l'inculpation a été retirée, on a cessé les poursuites ♦ **to press ~s (against sb)** engager des poursuites (contre qn) ♦ **to bring** or **lay a ~ against sb** porter plainte or déposer une plainte contre qn ♦ **to give sb in ~** remettre qn à la police ♦ **they were convicted on all three ~s** ils ont été reconnus coupables pour les trois chefs d'accusation ♦ **to be on a murder ~** être inculpé de meurtre ♦ **he was arrested on a ~ of murder** il a été arrêté sous l'inculpation de meurtre ♦ **to be on a ~** *[soldier]* être aux arrêts

2 [= accusation] accusation *f* (*of* de) ; ♦ **he denied** or **repudiated these ~s** il a repoussé or rejeté ces accusations ♦ **there were many ~s of cruelty** on les (or nous *etc*) a fréquemment accusés de cruauté ♦ **the ~s made against him** les accusations *fpl* or les charges *fpl* portées contre lui ♦ **~s that he had betrayed his friends** des accusations selon lesquelles il aurait trahi ses amis

3 [= attack] *(esp Mil)* charge *f*, attaque *f* ; *[of police, bull]* charge *f* ♦ **the police made three ~s into the crowd** la police a chargé la foule par trois fois ♦ **to sound the ~** *(Mil)* sonner la charge ; → **baton, bayonet**

4 [= fee] prix *m* ♦ **what's the ~?** ça coûte combien ?, ça revient à combien ? ♦ **is there a ~?** faut-il payer ?, y a-t-il quelque chose à payer ? ♦ **at a ~ of ...** pour ..., moyennant ... ♦ **for a small ~, we can supply ...** pour un prix modique, nous pouvons fournir ... ♦ **there's no ~ for this, no ~ is made for this** c'est gratuit ♦ **there is an extra** or **additional ~ for ...** il y a un supplément (à payer) pour ... ♦ **to make a ~ for sth** facturer qch ♦ **he made no ~ for mending it** il n'a pas facturé la réparation, il n'a rien pris pour la réparation ♦ **he made a ~ of £20 for doing it** il a facturé 20 livres pour le faire ♦ **~ for admission** droit *m* d'entrée ♦ **"no charge for admission"** "entrée libre" ♦ **~ for delivery** *(Comm)* frais *mpl* de port ; → **bank², delivery, free, reverse**

5 [= responsibility] **I've been given ~ of this class** on m'a donné la responsabilité or la charge de cette classe ♦ **the patients in** or **under her ~** les malades *mpl* dont elle a la charge
♦ **in charge** ♦ **who's in ~ here?** qui est le or la responsable ? ♦ **look, I'm in ~ here!** c'est moi qui commande ici ! ♦ **the person in ~** le or la responsable ♦ **I left him in ~** je lui ai laissé la charge de tout
♦ **in charge of** ♦ **to be in ~ of** *[+ firm, department]* diriger, être à la tête de ; *[+ ship, plane]* commander ; *[+ operation, project]* diriger, être responsable de ; *[+ children, animals]* s'occuper de, avoir la charge de ♦ **a few months later, he was in ~ of the shop** au bout de quelques mois, il dirigeait le magasin ♦ **he's in ~ of the shop when I'm out** c'est lui qui s'occupe du magasin or qui surveille le magasin lorsque je m'absente ♦ **while in ~ of a motor vehicle, he ...** alors qu'il était au volant d'un véhicule, il ... ♦ **to put sb in ~ of** *[+ firm, department, operation, project]* confier à qn la direction de ; *[+ ship, plane]* confier à qn le commandement de ; *[+ children, animals]* confier aux soins or à la garde de qn ♦ **to put sb in ~ of doing sth** charger qn de faire qch
♦ **to take charge** *(in firm, project etc)* prendre or assurer la direction (*of* de) ; *(in ship, plane)* prendre or assurer le commandement (*of* de) ; ♦ **he took ~ of the situation at once** il a immédiatement pris la situation en main ♦ **will you take ~ of the children while I'm away?** est-ce que tu veux bien te charger des enfants pendant mon absence ?

6 [= person or thing cared for] ♦ **she took her ~s for a walk** elle a emmené les personnes dont elle avait la charge en promenade

7 [Rel] (= *priest's parish*) cure *f* ♦ **the priest's ~s** (= *parishioners*) les ouailles *fpl* du curé

8 [= financial burden] charge *f*, fardeau *m* (*on* pour) ; ♦ **to be a ~ on ...** constituer une charge or un fardeau pour ...

9 [= instructions: frm] recommandation *f*, instruction *f* ♦ **to have strict ~ to do sth** avoir reçu l'ordre formel de faire qch ♦ **the judge's ~ to the jury** *(Jur)* les recommandations données aux jurés par le juge

10 [Elec, Phys] charge *f* ♦ **to put a battery on ~** mettre une batterie en charge ♦ **there is no ~ left in the battery** la batterie est déchargée or à plat ♦ **an electrical ~** une charge électrique ♦ **it still gives me a ~*** *(fig)* ça me fait toujours de l'effet

11 [of firearm, rocket] charge *f* ; → **depth**

12 [Heraldry] meuble *m*

2 - TRANSITIVE VERB

1 [= accuse] *(gen)* accuser ; *(Jur)* inculper ♦ **to find sb guilty/not guilty as ~d** déclarer qn coupable/non coupable ♦ **he ~d that some companies had infringed the regulations** *(US)* il a allégué que certaines compagnies avaient enfreint le règlement
♦ **to charge sb with** *(gen)* accuser qn de ; *(Jur)* inculper qn de ♦ **to ~ sb with doing** or **having done sth** accuser qn d'avoir fait qch ♦ **he was ~d with murder/with stealing a car** *(Jur)* il a été inculpé de meurtre/de vol de voiture ; see also **transitive verb 6**

2 [= attack] *[troops]* charger, attaquer ; *[police, bull]* charger

3 [in payment] *[+ person]* facturer à ; *[+ amount]* facturer (*for* pour) ; ♦ **to ~ a commission** facturer une commission ♦ **to ~ £100 a day** facturer 100 livres par jour ♦ **to ~ a fair price** facturer or prendre un prix raisonnable ♦ **to ~ sb a fee of £200** facturer 200 livres à qn
♦ **to charge sb for sth** ♦ **I ~d him £20 for this table** je lui ai facturé 20 livres pour cette table, je lui ai fait payer cette table 20 livres ♦ **how much do you ~ for mending shoes?** combien prenez-vous pour réparer des chaussures ? ♦ **to ~ sb too much for sth** faire payer qch trop cher à qn ♦ **I won't ~ you for that** je ne vous facturerai or compterai rien pour cela

4 [= record as debt: also **charge up**] mettre sur le compte, porter au compte or au débit (*to sb* de qn) ; ♦ **to ~ a book** *(US: in library)* inscrire un livre au registre du prêt ; → **cash**
♦ **to charge sth to sb** ♦ **~ all these purchases to my account** mettez tous ces achats sur mon compte ♦ **I can ~ it to the company** je peux le faire payer or rembourser par la société

5 [+ firearm, battery] *(also Phys)* charger

6 [= command: frm] ♦ **to ~ sb to do sth** ordonner à qn or sommer qn de faire qch ♦ **to ~ sb with sth** confier qch à qn

3 - INTRANSITIVE VERB

1 [= rush] se précipiter, foncer ♦ **to ~ in/out** entrer/sortir en coup de vent ♦ **to ~ up/down** grimper/descendre à toute vitesse ♦ **to ~ through** passer en coup de vent ; → **charge off**

2 [Mil] ♦ **to ~ (down) on the enemy** fondre or foncer sur l'ennemi

3 [battery] se (re)charger, être en charge

4 - COMPOUNDS

charge account N *(Comm)* compte *m*
charge-cap VT *(Brit)* fixer un plafond aux impôts locaux à
charge capping N *(Brit)* plafonnement *m* des impôts locaux
charge card N *(Brit Comm)* carte *f* de paiement
charge hand N *(Brit)* sous-chef *m* d'équipe
charge nurse N *(Brit)* infirmier *m*, -ière *f* en chef *(responsable d'une salle ou d'un pavillon)*
charge sheet N *(Brit Police)* ≃ procès-verbal *m*

5 - PHRASAL VERBS

► **charge down** VT SEP *(Rugby)* ♦ **to charge a kick down** contrer un coup de pied ; see also **charge intransitive verb**

► **charge off** 1 VI partir en courant
2 VT SEP *(Comm)* *[+ machine]* amortir ♦ **they ~d off drilling costs as business expenses** ils ont

imputé les coûts de forage à l'exploitation ◆ **to ~ off an expense** passer une dépense en charge

► **charge up** VI [battery] se (re)charger, être en charge
2 VT SEP [+ firearm, battery] (also Phys) charger

chargeable /'tʃɑːdʒəbl/ ADJ 1 (Jur) [crime, offence] passible de poursuites ◆ **~ with sth** [person] passible de poursuites pour qch 2 (= payable) [fee] à payer ◆ **a late entry fee of $20 is ~** il y a un supplément de 20 dollars à payer pour les inscriptions en retard ◆ **fees ~ by the solicitor** honoraires mpl qu'il faut payer à l'avocat ◆ **the lowest lending rates ~ by UK banks** les taux les plus bas pratiqués par les banques du Royaume-Uni 3 (= assignable) [expenses] (to tax office) déductible ; (to employer) à la charge de l'employeur ◆ **~ to sb** à facturer à qn, à porter au compte de qn ◆ **~ to an account** imputable sur un compte 4 (= taxable) [asset] imposable

charged /tʃɑːdʒd/ ADJ 1 (Elec) [particles] chargé 2 (fig) **~ with emotion, emotionally ~** plein d'émotion ◆ **a highly ~ atmosphere** une atmosphère très tendue

chargé d'affaires /ˌʃɑːʒeɪdæ'feəʳ/ N (pl **chargés d'affaires**) chargé m d'affaires

charger /'tʃɑːdʒəʳ/ N 1 [of battery, firearm] chargeur m 2 (Mil = horse) cheval m (de combat)

chargrilled /'tʃɑːˌgrɪld/ ADJ (Brit Culin) grillé au feu de bois

charily /'tʃeərɪlɪ/ ADV prudemment, avec prudence or circonspection

chariot /'tʃærɪət/ N char m

charioteer /ˌtʃærɪə'tɪəʳ/ N conducteur m de char, aurige m

charisma /kæ'rɪzmə/ N (Rel, fig) charisme m

charismatic /ˌkærɪz'mætɪk/ ADJ 1 (= fascinating) [person, personality, charm] charismatique 2 (Rel) [church, movement] charismatique ◆ **~ Christian** charismatique mf

charitable /'tʃærɪtəbl/ ADJ 1 (= helping the needy) [organization, foundation, institution] caritatif ; [donation] à une œuvre d'intérêt public ◆ **~ work** bonnes œuvres fpl ◆ **to have ~ status** avoir le statut d'organisation caritative 2 (= kindly) [person, thought, deed, gesture] charitable (to sb envers qn) ; ◆ **to take a ~ view of sth** être indulgent pour qch

charitably /'tʃærɪtəblɪ/ ADV charitablement

charity /'tʃærɪtɪ/ N 1 (NonC) charité f ◆ **for ~'s sake, out of ~** par (pure) charité ◆ **~ begins at home** (Prov) charité bien ordonnée commence par soi-même (Prov) ◆ **sister of Charity** (Rel) sœur f de charité ; → **cold, faith** 2 (= charitable action) acte m de charité, action f charitable 3 (NonC = alms) charité f, aumône f ◆ **to live on ~** vivre d'aumônes ◆ **to collect for ~** faire une collecte pour une œuvre (charitable) ◆ **the proceeds go to ~** les fonds recueillis sont versés à des œuvres 4 (= charitable society) fondation f or institution f caritative, œuvre f de bienfaisance
COMP **charity sale** N vente f de charité or de bienfaisance
charity shop N boutique vendant des articles d'occasion au profit d'une organisation caritative
charity toss N (Basketball) lancer m franc

charlady /'tʃɑːleɪdɪ/ N (Brit) femme f de ménage

charlatan /'ʃɑːlətən/ N charlatan m ADJ charlatanesque

Charlemagne /'ʃɑːləmeɪn/ N Charlemagne m

Charles /tʃɑːlz/ N Charles m

charleston /'tʃɑːlstən/ N charleston m

charley horse* /'tʃɑːlɪhɔːs/ N (US) crampe f, spasme m

Charlie /'tʃɑːlɪ/ N ◆ **he must have looked a proper ~!*** (Brit) il a dû avoir l'air fin or malin ! * ◆ **I felt a right ~!*** (Brit) j'ai vraiment eu l'air idiot ! ◆ **~ Chaplin** (as film character) Charlot m

charlie* /'tʃɑːlɪ/ N (Drugs = cocaine) coke* f

charlotte /'ʃɑːlət/ N (Culin) charlotte f ◆ **apple ~** charlotte f aux pommes

charm /tʃɑːm/ N 1 (= attractiveness) charme m, attrait m ◆ **a lady's ~s** les charmes d'une dame ◆ **to have a lot of ~** avoir beaucoup de charme ◆ **to fall victim to sb's ~s** succomber aux charmes de qn
2 (= spell) charme m, enchantement m ◆ **to hold sb under a ~** tenir qn sous le charme ◆ **it works like a ~** * ça marche à merveille ◆ **the plan worked like a ~** * tout s'est déroulé exactement comme prévu
3 (for bracelet) breloque f ; (= amulet) charme m, amulette f
VT (= attract, please) charmer, enchanter ; (= cast spell on) enchanter, ensorceler ; [+ snakes] charmer ◆ **to have or lead a ~ed life** être béni des dieux ◆ **to ~ sth out of sb** obtenir qch de qn par le charme or en lui faisant du charme ◆ **to ~ one's way somewhere** s'introduire quelque part grâce à son charme ◆ **to ~ one's way out of a situation** se sortir d'une situation grâce à son charme ◆ **he could ~ the birds off or out of the trees** il sait vraiment y faire
COMP **charm bracelet** N bracelet m à breloques
charmed circle N ◆ **they seemed part of a ~ed circle** ils semblaient comme protégés par un enchantement
charm offensive N offensive f de charme
charm price N prix m psychologique
charm school N cours m de maintien

charmer /'tʃɑːməʳ/ N charmeur m, -euse f ; → **snake**

charming /'tʃɑːmɪŋ/ ADJ (also iro) charmant

charmingly /'tʃɑːmɪŋlɪ/ ADV [behave, smile] d'une façon charmante ◆ **~ naive/simple** d'une naïveté/simplicité charmante

charmless /'tʃɑːmlɪs/ ADJ dénué de charme

charnel-house † /'tʃɑːnlhaʊs/ N ossuaire m, charnier m

charr /tʃɑːʳ/ N ⇒ **char⁴**

chart /tʃɑːt/ N 1 (= map) carte f (marine)
2 (= graph) graphique m ; (= diagram) diagramme m ; (= table) tableau m ; (Med) courbe f ◆ **temperature ~** (= sheet) feuille f de température ; (= line) courbe f de température
3 (Mus) ◆ **the ~s** le Top 50, le hit-parade, le palmarès de la chanson ◆ **in the ~s** au Top 50 or au hit-parade ◆ **to reach the ~s** figurer au Top 50 or au hit-parade ◆ **to top the ~s** être en tête des meilleures ventes or du Top 50 or du hit-parade
VT 1 (= draw on map) [+ route, journey] porter sur la carte
2 (on graph) [+ sales, profits, results] faire le graphique or la courbe de ◆ **this graph ~s the progress made last year** ce graphique montre les progrès accomplis l'an dernier
3 (fig = plan) organiser, planifier
COMP **chart topper** N (Mus) ≈ numéro m 1 du Top 50
chart-topping ADJ qui vient en tête des meilleures ventes or du Top 50

charter /'tʃɑːtəʳ/ N 1 (= document) charte f ; [of society, organization] statuts mpl, acte m constitutif ◆ **the Charter of the United Nations** la Charte des Nations unies ◆ **it's a muggers' ~** (fig) c'est un encouragement pour les agresseurs ; → **citizen**
2 (NonC) [of boat, plane, coach, train etc] affrètement m ◆ **on ~** sous contrat d'affrètement
3 (also **charter flight**) (vol m) charter m
VT 1 accorder une charte à, accorder un privilège (par une charte) à
2 [+ plane etc] affréter
COMP **chartered accountant** N (Brit, Can) expert-comptable mf, comptable mf agréé(e) (Can)
chartered company N société f privilégiée
chartered society N compagnie f à charte
chartered surveyor N expert m immobilier
charter flight N (vol m) charter m ◆ **to take a ~ flight to Rome** aller à Rome en charter
charter member N (US) membre m fondateur
charter party N (Jur) charte-partie f
charter plane N (avion m) charter m
charter train N train m charter

charterer /'tʃɑːtərəʳ/ N affréteur m

Chartist /'tʃɑːtɪst/ N (Hist) ◆ **the ~s** les chartistes mpl

charwoman † /'tʃɑːˌwʊmən/ N (pl **-women**) femme f de ménage

chary /'tʃeərɪ/ ADJ 1 (= cautious) prudent, circonspect ◆ **to be ~ of doing sth** hésiter à faire qch 2 (= stingy) pingre, ladre † (also liter) (of de) ; ◆ **he is ~ of praise** il est avare de compliments

chase¹ /tʃeɪs/ N (= action) chasse f, poursuite f ; (Racing = steeple-chase) steeple m ◆ **a high-speed car ~** une course-poursuite en voiture ◆ **the ~ for the championship** (Sport) la course au titre (de champion) ◆ **to give ~ (to sb)** donner la chasse (à qn), se lancer à la poursuite (de qn) ◆ **US fighters gave ~ to two enemy planes** des chasseurs américains ont donné la chasse à or se sont lancés à la poursuite de deux avions ennemis ◆ **they ran out and the police gave ~** ils sont sortis en courant et la police leur a donné la chasse or s'est lancée à leur poursuite ◆ **in ~ of** à la poursuite de ◆ **the ~** (Sport) la chasse (à courre) ; (= huntsmen) la chasse, les chasseurs mpl ; → **paper, steeplechase, wild**
VT poursuivre, donner la chasse à ; [+ success, women, job etc] courir après ◆ **he ~d him down the hill** il l'a poursuivi jusqu'au bas de la colline ◆ **she ~d the thief for 100 metres** elle a poursuivi le voleur sur 100 mètres ◆ **2,000 unemployed people chasing five jobs** 2 000 chômeurs qui se disputent cinq emplois ◆ **to ~ the dragon*** (Drugs) fumer de l'héroïne
VI 1 (lit, fig) ◆ **to ~ after sb** courir après qn
2 (= rush) ◆ **to ~ up/down/out etc** monter/descendre/sortir etc au grand galop ◆ **to ~ about, to ~ here and there** (Brit) courir à droite et à gauche

► **chase away** VI * filer*, se tirer*
VT SEP [+ person, animal] chasser, faire partir

► **chase down** VT SEP 1 (= track down) retrouver
2 (US = catch) rattraper

► **chase off** ⇒ **chase away**

► **chase up*** VT SEP [+ information] rechercher ; [+ sth already asked for] réclamer ◆ **to ~ sb up for sth** relancer qn pour qch ◆ **I'll ~ it up for you** (= hurry things along) je vais essayer d'activer les choses

chase² /tʃeɪs/ VT (Tech) [+ diamond] sertir, enchâsser (in dans) ; [+ silver] ciseler ; [+ metal] repousser ; [+ screw] fileter

chaser /'tʃeɪsəʳ/ N 1 (= pursuer) poursuivant m 2 (= engraver) graveur m sur métaux ; (= lathe tool) peigne m (à fileter) 3 (* = drink) verre pris pour en faire descendre un autre

chasm /'kæzəm/ N (lit, fig) gouffre m, abîme m

chassis /'ʃæsɪ/ N (pl **chassis** /'ʃæsɪz/) [of car] châssis m ; [of plane] train m d'atterrissage ; (US* = body) châssis* m

chaste /tʃeɪst/ ADJ [person] chaste, pur ; [style] sobre

chastely /ˈtʃeɪstlɪ/ ADV [behave] chastement ; [dress] avec sobriété, simplement

chasten /ˈtʃeɪsn/ VT (= punish) châtier, corriger ; (= subdue) assagir, calmer ; (= rebuke) réprimander

chastened /ˈtʃeɪsnd/ ADJ [person] assagi, calmé ; [style] châtié

chasteness /ˈtʃeɪstnɪs/ N (NonC) [1] (sexual) [of person, relationship] chasteté f [2] (frm = simplicity) [of style] sobriété f

chastening /ˈtʃeɪsnɪŋ/ ADJ [thought] qui fait réfléchir (à deux fois) ◆ **the accident had a ~ effect on him** l'accident l'a fait réfléchir

chastise /tʃæsˈtaɪz/ VT (= scold) réprimander ; (= punish) punir, châtier ; (= beat) battre, corriger

chastisement /ˈtʃæstɪzmənt/ N (NonC) [1] (= criticism) condamnation f, fustigation f (liter) [2] († = punishment) châtiment m

chastity /ˈtʃæstɪtɪ/ N chasteté f COMP **chastity belt** N ceinture f de chasteté

chasuble /ˈtʃæzjʊbl/ N chasuble f

chat /tʃæt/ N (NonC) bavardage m ; (= casual conversation) brin m de conversation or de causette* ; (Internet) participation f à un forum de discussion ◆ **to have a ~** bavarder un peu, faire un brin de conversation or de causette* ◆ **I must have a ~ with him about this** il faut que je lui en parle or que je lui en touche un mot VI bavarder, causer (with, to avec) ; (Internet) chatter

COMP **chat room** N (on the Web) forum m de discussion

chat show N (Brit TV) causerie f télévisée

chat-up line N (Brit) ◆ **that's his usual ~-up line** c'est son entrée en matière habituelle pour draguer*

► **chat up*** VT SEP (Brit) baratiner*, faire du plat* à

chatline /ˈtʃætlaɪn/ N (for dating) ≈ téléphone m rose

chattel /ˈtʃætl/ NPL **chattels** (gen) biens mpl, possessions fpl ; (Jur) biens meubles mpl ◆ **with all his goods and ~s** avec tout ce qu'il possède (or possédait etc) COMP **chattel mortgage** N (Jur, Fin) nantissement m de biens meubles

chatter /ˈtʃætəʳ/ VI bavarder, jacasser (pej) ; [children, monkeys] jacasser ; [birds] jacasser, jaser ◆ **his teeth were ~ing** il claquait des dents N [of person] bavardage m ; [of birds, children, monkeys] jacassement m ; [of teeth] claquement m

chatterbox* /ˈtʃætəbɒks/, **chatterer** /ˈtʃætərəʳ/ N moulin m à paroles*, bavard(e) m(f) ◆ **to be a ~** être bavard comme une pie

chattering /ˈtʃætərɪŋ/ N bavardage m COMP **the chattering classes*** NPL (Brit esp pej) les intellos* mpl

chatty* /ˈtʃætɪ/ ADJ [person] bavard ; [style] familier, qui reste au niveau du bavardage ; [letter] plein de bavardages ◆ **she was a regular Chatty Cathy*** (US) c'était un vrai moulin à paroles*

Chaucerian /tʃɔːˈsɪərɪən/ ADJ de Chaucer, chaucérien

chauffeur /ˈʃəʊfəʳ/ N chauffeur m (de maître) VT ◆ **to ~ sb around** or **about** servir de chauffeur à qn COMP **chauffeur-driven car** N voiture f avec chauffeur

chauvinism /ˈʃəʊvɪnɪzəm/ N (gen) chauvinisme m ; (= male chauvinism) machisme m, phallocratie f

chauvinist /ˈʃəʊvɪnɪst/ N (= male chauvinist) phallocrate m, machiste m ; (= jingoist) chauvin(e) m(f) ADJ (= male chauvinist) phallocrate, machiste ; (= jingoistic) chauvin ◆ **male ~ pig** phallocrate m

chauvinistic /ˌʃəʊvɪˈnɪstɪk/ ADJ (= male chauvinistic) machiste, phallocrate ; (= jingoistic) chauvin

chav‡ /tʃæv/ N (Brit) caillera‡ mf

chaw /tʃɔː/ (dial) ⇒ **chew**

cheap /tʃiːp/ ADJ [1] (= inexpensive) [goods, services, housing, café, price, labour] bon marché inv ; [rate, fare] réduit ; [loan, credit] à faible taux d'intérêt ; [currency, pound, dollar] déprécié ◆ **~er** meilleur marché inv, moins cher (chère f) ◆ **it's 10 pence ~er** ça coûte 10 pence de moins ◆ **a ~ electrician** un électricien pas cher ◆ **the ~est seats are around £15** les places les moins chères sont autour de 15 livres ◆ **calls cost 36p per minute ~ rate** (Telec) les appels coûtent 36 pence la minute en tarif réduit ◆ **~ edition** (Printing) édition f populaire or bon marché ◆ **it was going ~*** cela se vendait à bas prix ◆ **it is ~er to buy than to rent** cela revient moins cher d'acheter que de louer ◆ **to be ~ to run** ne pas revenir cher à l'emploi ◆ **these cars are very ~ to produce** la production de ces voitures est très bon marché ◆ **quality doesn't come ~** la qualité se paie ◆ **it's ~ at the price*** [goods, services] à ce prix-là, c'est bon marché ; [freedom] ce n'est pas cher payé ◆ **~ and cheerful*** pas cher et sans prétentions ◆ **human life is ~ in wartime** la vie humaine ne vaut pas grand-chose en temps de guerre ; → **dirt**

[2] (pej = poor-quality) [wine, material, brand, copy, imitation, perfume, seat] bon marché ; [cut of meat] de qualité inférieure ; [jewellery] de pacotille ; [hotel, café] de second ordre ◆ **~ and nasty*** [wine, plastic] minable et bon marché

[3] (pej) ◆ **on the ~*** [buy, employ] au rabais ; [decorate] à bas prix ◆ **it was a bad idea, done on the ~** c'était une mauvaise idée, réalisée avec de petits moyens

[4] (pej = unworthy) [remark, question, opportunism, sensationalism] de bas étage ; [joke, jibe, trick, ploy, gimmick, woman] facile ; [behaviour, attitude] minable ◆ **to feel ~** se sentir minable ◆ **to look ~** [person] avoir l'air minable ; [clothes, make-up] faire bon marché ◆ **to make o.s. ~** s'avilir ◆ **~ thrills** sensations fpl fortes

ADV [buy] (= inexpensively) bon marché ; (= cut-price) au rabais

COMP **cheap shot** N coup m bas

cheapen /ˈtʃiːpən/ VT baisser le prix de ; (fig) déprécier ◆ **to ~ o.s.** se déprécier, s'abaisser VI baisser, devenir moins cher

cheapie‡ /ˈtʃiːpɪ/ ADJ pas cher N (= ticket/meal etc) billet m/repas m etc pas cher

cheapjack /ˈtʃiːpdʒæk/ ADJ de mauvaise qualité

cheaply /ˈtʃiːplɪ/ ADV [buy, sell] bon marché ; [borrow, produce, decorate, furnish, eat] à bon marché ; [live] à peu de frais ; [available] à moindre prix ◆ **two can live as ~ as one** (Prov) ≈ quand il y en a pour l'un, il y en a pour l'autre

cheapness /ˈtʃiːpnɪs/ N (lit) bas prix m

cheapo* /ˈtʃiːpəʊ/ ADJ bon marché

cheapshot /ˈtʃiːpʃɒt/ VT (US) débiner*, dénigrer

cheapskate* /ˈtʃiːpskeɪt/ N radin* mf, avare mf

cheat /tʃiːt/ VT (= deceive) tromper, duper ; (= defraud) frauder ; (= swindle) escroquer ; (fig) [+ time etc] tromper ◆ **to ~ sb at cards** tricher aux cartes en jouant avec qn ◆ **to ~ sb out of sth** escroquer qch à qn ◆ **to ~ sb into doing sth** faire faire qch à qn en le trompant ◆ **to feel ~ed** (= swindled) se sentir floué ; (= betrayed) se sentir trahi VI (at cards, games) tricher (at à) ; (= defraud) frauder ◆ **to ~ on sb*** (= be unfaithful to) tromper qn N (also **cheater** : US) [1] (= person) tricheur m, -euse f [2] (= deception) tricherie f, triche* f ◆ **it's a bit of a ~ to use ready-prepared meals** c'est un peu de la triche d'utiliser des plats cuisinés

cheater /ˈtʃiːtəʳ/ N (US) ⇒ **cheat**

cheating /ˈtʃiːtɪŋ/ N (NonC, at cards, games) tricherie f ; (= deceit) tromperie f ; (= fraud) fraude f ; (= swindle) escroquerie f ADJ tricheur

Chechen /ˈtʃetʃən/ N (pl **Chechen** or **Chechens**) (= person) Tchétchène mf ADJ tchétchène

Chechenia /tʃeˈtʃenɪə/, **Chechnya** /ˈtʃetʃnɪə/ N Tchétchénie f

check[1] /tʃek/ N (US) ⇒ **cheque**

check[2] /tʃek/ N [1] (= setback) [of movement] arrêt m brusque ; (Mil) échec m, revers m ◆ **to hold** or **keep in ~** (gen) [+ emotions etc] contenir, maîtriser ; (Mil) tenir en échec ◆ **to put a ~ on** mettre un frein à ◆ **to act as a ~ upon** constituer un frein à ◆ **~s and balances** (Pol) freins mpl et contrepoids mpl

[2] (= examination) [of papers, passport, ticket] contrôle m ; [of luggage] vérification f ; (at factory door) pointage m ◆ **to make a ~ on** contrôler ◆ **to keep a ~ on** surveiller ◆ **~!*** (US = OK) d'accord !, OK !*

[3] (Chess) échec m ◆ **in ~** en échec ◆ **~!** échec au roi !

[4] (US) [of left luggage] ticket m de consigne ; (Theat) ticket m de vestiaire ; [of restaurant] addition f

VT [1] (also **check out**) (= examine, verify) [+ accounts, figures, statement, quality etc] vérifier ; [+ tickets, passports] contrôler ; (= mark off) pointer, faire le pointage de ; (= tick off) cocher ◆ **to ~ a copy against the original** comparer une copie à l'original, collationner une copie avec l'original ◆ **I'll have to ~ whether** or **if there's an age limit** il faudra que je vérifie s'il y a une limite d'âge

[2] [+ baggage to be loaded] enregistrer

[3] (‡ : also **check out** = look at) mater*, viser* ◆ **~ his shoes!** vise (un peu) or mate un peu ses chaussures !

[4] (= stop) [+ enemy] arrêter ; [+ advance] enrayer ; (= restrain) [+ excitement] refréner, contenir ; [+ anger] maîtriser, réprimer ◆ **he was going to protest, but she ~ed him** il allait protester, mais elle l'a retenu ◆ **to ~ o.s.** se contrôler, se retenir ◆ **it is hoped that sex education will help ~ the spread of AIDS** on espère que l'éducation sexuelle aidera à enrayer la progression du sida

[5] (= rebuke) réprimander

[6] (Chess) faire échec à

[7] (US) [+ coats] (in cloakroom) mettre au vestiaire ; (Rail) [+ luggage] (= register) faire enregistrer ; [+ left luggage] mettre à la consigne

VI [1] ◆ **is Matthew there ? – hold on, I'll just ~** est-ce que Matthew est là ? – attends, je vais voir

[2] (= pause) s'arrêter (momentanément)

[3] (also **check out** = confirm each other) [figures, stories] correspondre, s'accorder

COMP **check-in** N (at airport) enregistrement m (des bagages) ◆ **your ~-in time is half-an-hour before departure** présentez-vous à l'enregistrement des bagages une demi-heure avant le départ

check-out N (Comm) caisse f (dans un libre-service)

check-out time N (in hotel) heure f limite d'occupation

► **check in** VI (in hotel) (= arrive) arriver ; (= register) remplir une fiche (d'hôtel) ; (at airport) se présenter à l'enregistrement

VT SEP faire remplir une fiche (d'hôtel) à ; (at airport) enregistrer

N ◆ **check-in** → **check[2]**

► **check off** VT SEP pointer, cocher

► **check on** VT FUS *[+ information, time etc]* vérifier ◆ **to ~ on sb** voir ce que fait qn ◆ **just go and ~ on the baby** va jeter un coup d'œil sur le bébé

► **check out** VI [1] *(from hotel)* régler sa note
[2] → **check[2] vi 3**
[3] *(‡ euph = die)* passer l'arme à gauche‡, mourir
VT SEP [1] → **check[2] vt 1**
[2] *(* = look at)* jeter un œil à *
[3] *[+ luggage]* retirer ; *[+ person]* contrôler la sortie de ; *[+ hotel guest]* faire payer sa note à
N ◆ **check-out** → **check[2]**

► **check over** VT SEP examiner, vérifier

► **check up** VI se renseigner, vérifier ◆ **to ~ up on sth** vérifier qch ◆ **to ~ up on sb** se renseigner sur qn

CHECKS AND BALANCES

Dans le système politique américain, les « freins et contrepoids » sont des mécanismes qui tendent à garantir l'équilibre des pouvoirs par une stricte séparation entre l'exécutif, le législatif et le judiciaire, et à empêcher la domination d'un de ces pouvoirs sur les autres. Dans l'esprit des auteurs de la Constitution, la liberté est assurée par le fait qu'il est toujours possible de contester les pouvoirs du président, du Congrès, des tribunaux ou de l'administration des États.

check[3] /tʃek/ N *(gen pl)* ◆ **~s** *(= pattern)* carreaux *mpl*, damier *m* ; *(= cloth)* tissu *m* à carreaux ◆ **broken ~** pied-de-poule *m* COMP ⇒ **checked**

checkbook /ˈtʃekbʊk/ N *(US)* carnet *m* de chèques, chéquier *m*

checked /tʃekt/ ADJ [1] *[tablecloth, suit, pattern]* à carreaux [2] *(Phon) [vowel]* entravé

checker /ˈtʃekəʳ/ N [1] *(= examiner)* ◆ **fact ~** vérificateur *m*, -trice *f* ◆ **work ~** contrôleur *m*, -euse *f* du travail ; → **grammar, spell[3]** [2] *(US) (in supermarket)* caissier *m*, -ière *f* ; *(in cloakroom)* préposé(e) *m(f)* au vestiaire

checkerboard /ˈtʃekəbɔːd/ N *(US) (Chess)* échiquier *m* ; *(Checkers)* damier *m* COMP **checkerboard pattern** N motif *m* à damiers

Checker cab ® /ˈtʃekəˌkæb/ N *(US) ancien modèle de taxi américain à damier*

checkered /ˈtʃekəd/ ADJ *(US)* ⇒ **chequered**

checkers /ˈtʃekəz/ NPL *(US)* jeu *m* de dames

checking /ˈtʃekɪŋ/ N *(NonC) [of equipment, system, facts, exam paper, document]* vérification *f* ; *[of ticket, passport]* contrôle *m* ; *(Med)* examen *m* médical ◆ **to do some ~ on sb/sth** effectuer des vérifications sur qn/qch
COMP **checking account** N *(US Fin)* compte *m* courant
checking deposit N dépôt *m* à vue

checklist /ˈtʃeklɪst/ N check-list *f*, liste *f* de contrôle

checkmate /ˈtʃekmeɪt/ N *(Chess)* (échec *m* et) mat *m* ; *(fig)* échec *m* total, fiasco *m* VT *(Chess)* mettre (échec et) mat ; *(fig) [+ person]* coincer *, faire échec à ; *[+ plans etc]* déjouer

checkpoint /ˈtʃekpɔɪnt/ N *(at border, in motor rally)* (poste *m* de) contrôle *m* COMP **Checkpoint Charlie** N Checkpoint *m* Charlie

checkroom /ˈtʃekrʊm/ N *(US = cloakroom)* vestiaire *m*

checkup /ˈtʃekʌp/ N *(gen)* contrôle *m*, vérification *f* ; *(Med)* bilan *m* de santé, check-up *m* ◆ **to go for** *or* **have a ~** *(Med)* se faire faire un bilan (de santé)

cheddar /ˈtʃedəʳ/ N (fromage *m* de) cheddar *m*

cheek /tʃiːk/ N [1] *(= part of face)* joue *f* ◆ **~ by jowl** côte à côte ◆ **~ by jowl with** tout près de ◆ **to dance ~ to ~** danser joue contre joue ◆ **to turn the other ~** tendre l'autre joue ; → **tongue** [2] *(= buttock)* fesse *f* [3] *(= impudence)* effronterie *f*, toupet * *m*, culot * *m* ◆ **to have the ~ to do sth** * avoir le toupet * *or* le culot * de faire qch ◆ **what (a) ~!** * ◆ **of all the ~!** * quel culot ! *, quel toupet ! * ◆ **the ~ of it!** * ce toupet ! * VT *(Brit *) [+ person]* être insolent avec, narguer

cheekbone /ˈtʃiːkbəʊn/ N pommette *f*

cheekily /ˈtʃiːkɪlɪ/ ADV *(Brit) [say]* avec insolence ; *[grin]* d'un air effronté

cheekiness /ˈtʃiːkɪnɪs/ N effronterie *f*, toupet * *m*, culot * *m*

cheeky /ˈtʃiːkɪ/ ADJ *[child]* effronté, insolent ; *[remark]* impertinent ◆ **~ child** petit(e) effronté(e) *m(f)* ◆ **(you) ~ monkey!** * quel toupet ! *

cheep /tʃiːp/ N *[of bird]* piaulement *m* ; *[of mouse]* couinement *m* ◆ **cheep, cheep!** cui-cui ! VI *[bird]* piauler ; *[mouse]* couiner

cheer /tʃɪəʳ/ N [1] ◆ **~s** acclamations *fpl*, applaudissements *mpl*, hourras *mpl*, bravos *mpl* ◆ **to give three ~s for** acclamer ◆ **three ~s for ...!** un ban pour ... !, hourra pour ... ! ◆ **three ~s!** hourra ! ◆ **the children gave a loud ~** les enfants ont poussé des acclamations ◆ **~s!** * *(esp Brit) (= your health!)* à la vôtre ! * *(or à la tienne ! *)* ; *(= goodbye)* salut !, tchao ! * ; *(= thanks)* merci !
[2] *(† = cheerfulness)* gaieté *f*, joie *f* ◆ **words of ~** paroles *fpl* d'encouragement ◆ **be of good ~!** prenez courage !
[3] *(†† = food etc)* chère † *f* ◆ **good ~** bonne chère
VT [1] (also **cheer up**) *[+ person]* remonter le moral à, réconforter ; *[+ room]* égayer
[2] *(= applaud)* acclamer, applaudir
VI applaudir, pousser des vivats *or* des hourras

► **cheer on** VT SEP *[+ person, team]* encourager

► **cheer up** VI *(= be gladdened)* s'égayer, se dérider ; *(= be comforted)* prendre courage, prendre espoir ◆ **~ up!** courage !
VT SEP ⇒ **cheer vt 1**

cheerful /ˈtʃɪəfʊl/ ADJ *[person]* joyeux, gai ; *[mood, colour, occasion, place, atmosphere]* gai ; *[smile, expression, voice, conversation]* enjoué ; *[news, prospect, outlook, belief]* réjouissant ◆ **to be ~ about sth** se réjouir de qch ◆ **to sound ~** avoir l'air réjoui ; → **cheap**

cheerfully /ˈtʃɪəfəlɪ/ ADV [1] *(= happily) [smile, say, greet]* joyeusement, gaiement [2] *(= enthusiastically) [work]* avec enthousiasme ◆ **she went ~ off to work** elle partit gaiement au travail [3] *(= blithely) [ignore]* allégrement [4] *(= gladly)* ◆ **I could ~ strangle him** * je l'étranglerais avec joie

cheerfulness /ˈtʃɪəfʊlnɪs/ N *[of person]* bonne humeur *f*, gaieté *f* ; *[of smile, conversation, place]* gaieté *f*

cheerily /ˈtʃɪərɪlɪ/ ADV gaiement, avec entrain

cheering /ˈtʃɪərɪŋ/ N *(NonC)* acclamations *fpl*, hourras *mpl* ADJ *[news, sight]* réconfortant, réjouissant

cheerio‡ /ˈtʃɪərɪˈəʊ/ EXCL *(esp Brit)* [1] *(= goodbye)* salut ! *, tchao ! * [2] *(† = your health)* à la vôtre *(or à la tienne)* !

cheerleader /ˈtʃɪəliːdəʳ/ N *(Sport)* pom-pom girl *f* ; *(fig)* meneur *m*, -euse *f (qui œuvre pour une cause, une personnalité politique)*

cheerless /ˈtʃɪəlɪs/ ADJ *[person, thing]* morne, triste

cheery /ˈtʃɪərɪ/ ADJ gai, joyeux

cheese /tʃiːz/ N fromage *m* ◆ **Dutch ~** fromage *m* de Hollande ◆ **"say cheese!"** *(for photograph)* "un petit sourire !" ◆ **big ~** * gros bonnet *m* ; → **cottage, cream, lemon** VT [1] *(Brit ‡)* ◆ **to be ~d (off)** en avoir marre * ◆ **to be ~d off with sth** en avoir marre de qch * [2] *(US)* ◆ **~ it!** ‡ *(= look out)* vingt-deux ! ‡ ; *(= run away)* tire-toi ! ‡
COMP *[sandwich]* au fromage
cheese and wine (party) N ≈ buffet *m* campagnard
cheese dip N *sauce au fromage dans laquelle on trempe des légumes etc en bâtonnets*
cheese dish N ⇒ **cheeseboard**
cheese straw N allumette *f* au fromage
cheese wire N fil *m* à couper le beurre

cheeseboard /ˈtʃiːzbɔːd/ N *(= dish)* plateau *m* à fromage(s) ; *(with cheeses on it)* plateau *m* de fromages

cheeseburger /ˈtʃiːzˌbɜːgəʳ/ N hamburger *m* au fromage, cheeseburger *m*

cheesecake /ˈtʃiːzkeɪk/ N *(NonC) (Culin)* cheesecake *m*, ≈ gâteau *m* au fromage blanc ; *(* fig)* photo *f* (de fille) déshabillée

cheesecloth /ˈtʃiːzklɒθ/ N *(for cheese)* étamine *f*, mousseline *f* à fromage ; *(for clothes)* toile *f* à beurre

cheeseparing /ˈtʃiːzˌpeərɪŋ/ N économie(s) *f(pl)* de bouts de chandelles ADJ *[person]* pingre, qui fait des économies de bouts de chandelles ; *[attitude, action]* mesquin

cheesy /ˈtʃiːzɪ/ ADJ [1] *(lit)* qui a un goût de fromage, qui sent le fromage [2] *(‡ = naff)* moche *, ringard * [3] * *[grin]* large [4] *(‡ = banal)* rebattu

cheetah /ˈtʃiːtə/ N guépard *m*

chef /ʃef/ N chef *m* (de cuisine)

chef d'œuvre /ʃeɪˈdɜːvrə/ N (pl **chefs d'œuvre**) chef-d'œuvre *m*

cheiromancer /ˈkaɪərəmænsəʳ/ N ⇒ **chiromancer**

cheiromancy /ˈkaɪərəmænsɪ/ N ⇒ **chiromancy**

Chekhov /ˈtʃekɒf/ N Tchekhov *m*

Chelsea Pensioner /ˌtʃelsɪˈpenʃənəʳ/ N *(Brit) ancien combattant résidant au "Chelsea Royal Hospital"*

chemical /ˈkemɪkəl/ ADJ chimique N *(gen pl)* produit *m* chimique
COMP **chemical agent** N agent *m* chimique
chemical castration N castration *f* chimique
chemical engineer N ingénieur *m* en génie chimique
chemical engineering N génie *m* chimique
chemical toilet N toilettes *fpl* chimiques
chemical warfare N guerre *f* chimique
chemical weapons NPL armes *fpl* chimiques

chemically /ˈkemɪkəlɪ/ ADV chimiquement

chemise /ʃəˈmiːz/ N *(= undergarment)* chemise *f (de femme)* ; *(= dress)* robe-chemisier *f*

chemist /ˈkemɪst/ N [1] *(= researcher etc)* chimiste *mf* [2] *(Brit = pharmacist)* pharmacien(ne) *m(f)* ◆ **~'s (shop)** pharmacie *f*

chemistry /ˈkemɪstrɪ/ N chimie *f* ◆ **they work so well together because the ~ is right** ils travaillent très bien ensemble parce que le courant passe
COMP *[laboratory, lesson, teacher]* de chimie
chemistry set N panoplie *f* de chimiste

chemo * /ˈkiːməʊ/ N (abbrev of **chemotherapy**) chimio * *f*

chemotherapy /ˌkeməʊˈθerəpɪ/ N chimiothérapie *f*

chenille /ʃəˈniːl/ N *(= fabric)* chenille *f*

Chennai /tʃɪˈnaɪ/ N Chennai *(nouveau nom de Madras)*

cheque, check (US) /tʃek/ N chèque *m* ◆ **~ for £10** chèque *m* de 10 livres ◆ **~ to** *or* **in the amount of $10** chèque *m* de 10 dollars ◆ **to pay by ~** payer par chèque ◆ **to cross a ~** *(Brit)* barrer un chèque ◆ **bad** *or* **dud** * *or* **rubber** * **~** chèque *m* sans provision *or* en bois *
COMP **cheque account** N compte-chèque *m*

cheque card N (*Brit*) carte *f* d'identité bancaire ; → **traveller**

chequebook /'tʃekbʊk/ N carnet *m* de chèques, chéquier *m* COMP **chequebook journalism** N (*pej*) *pratique qui consiste à payer des sommes considérables pour obtenir les confidences exclusives de personnes impliquées dans une affaire*

chequered, checkered (*US*) /'tʃekəd/ ADJ 1 (= *varied*) [*history, career, past*] en dents de scie 2 (= *checked*) [*tablecloth, dress, shirt, pattern*] à carreaux ♦ ~ **floor** *or* **tiles** carrelage *m* COMP **chequered flag** N (*Motor Racing*) drapeau *m* à damier

chequers /'tʃekəz/ N jeu *m* de dames

cherish /'tʃerɪʃ/ VT [+ *person*] chérir, aimer ; [+ *feelings, opinion*] entretenir ; [+ *hope, illusions*] nourrir, caresser ; [+ *memory*] chérir

cherished /'tʃerɪʃt/ ADJ [*dream, belief, ambition, memory*] cher ♦ **a ~ memory of mine** un souvenir qui m'est cher

Chernobyl /tʃɜː'nəʊbl/ N Tchernobyl

Cherokee /'tʃerəkiː/ N (= *person*) Cherokee *mf*

cheroot /ʃə'ruːt/ N petit cigare *m*

cherry /'tʃerɪ/ N 1 (= *fruit*) cerise *f* ; (also **cherry tree**) cerisier *m* ♦ **wild** ~ (= *fruit*) merise *f* ; (= *tree*) merisier *m* ; → **bite** 2 (‡ = *virginity*) ♦ **to take sb's** ~ dépuceler qn ♦ **to lose one's** ~ se faire dépuceler *

COMP (= *colour*) (rouge) cerise *inv* ; (*liter*) [*lips*] vermeil ; (*Culin*) [*pie, tart*] aux cerises

cherry blossom N (*NonC*) fleurs *fpl* de cerisier

cherry bomb N (*US*) pétard *m* (*rond et rouge*)

cherry brandy N cherry *m*, liqueur *f* de cerise

cherry orchard N cerisaie *f*

cherry-pick VT trier sur le volet

cherry picker N (= *vehicle*) grue *f* à nacelle

cherry-red ADJ (rouge) cerise *inv*

cherry tomato N tomate *f* cerise

cherub /'tʃerəb/ N 1 (pl **cherubs**) chérubin *m*, petit ange *m* 2 (pl **cherubim** /'tʃerəbɪm/) (*Rel*) chérubin *m*

cherubic /tʃe'ruːbɪk/ ADJ angélique

chervil /'tʃɜːvɪl/ N cerfeuil *m*

Ches. abbrev of **Cheshire**

Cheshire cat /,tʃeʃə'kæt/ N → **grin**

chess /tʃes/ N échecs *mpl*

COMP **chess piece** N ⇒ **chessman**

chess set N jeu *m* d'échecs

chessboard /'tʃesbɔːd/ N échiquier *m*

chessman /'tʃesmæn/ N (pl **-men**) pièce *f* (de jeu d'échecs)

chessplayer /'tʃes,pleɪəʳ/ N joueur *m*, -euse *f* d'échecs

chest¹ /tʃest/ N (= *box*) coffre *m*, caisse *f* ; (= *tea chest*) caisse *f* ; → **medicine, toolchest**

COMP **chest freezer** N congélateur-bahut *m*

chest of drawers N commode *f*

chest² /tʃest/ N (*Anat*) poitrine *f*, cage *f* thoracique (*Med frm*) ♦ **to have a weak** ~ être faible des bronches ♦ **to get something off one's** ~ * dire ce que l'on a sur le cœur

COMP **chest cold** N inflammation *f* des voies respiratoires

chest expander N extenseur *m* (*pour développer les pectoraux*)

chest infection N infection *f* des voies respiratoires

chest pain N (*NonC*) ⇒ **chest pains**

chest pains NPL douleurs *fpl* de poitrine

chest specialist N spécialiste *mf* des voies respiratoires

chesterfield /'tʃestəfiːld/ N canapé *m*, chesterfield *m*

chestnut /'tʃesnʌt/ N 1 (= *fruit*) châtaigne *f* ; (*Culin*) châtaigne *f*, marron *m* ♦ **to pull sb's ~s out of the fire** tirer les marrons du feu pour qn ; → **horse, Spanish, sweet** 2 (also **chestnut tree**) châtaignier *m*, marronnier *m* 3 (= *horse*) alezan *m* 4 (*pej*) ♦ **(old)** ~ * (= *story*) vieille histoire *f* rabâchée ; (= *joke*) vieille blague * *f* usée ADJ (also **chestnut-brown**) châtain ♦ ~ **hair** cheveux *mpl* châtains COMP **chestnut horse** N (cheval *m*) alezan *m*

chesty /'tʃestɪ/ ADJ (*Brit*) [*person*] fragile de la poitrine ; [*cough*] de poitrine

Chetnik /'tʃetnɪk/ N (*Pol, Hist*) tchetnik *m*

cheval glass /ʃə'vælglɑːs/ N psyché *f* (*glace*)

chevron /'ʃevrən/ N chevron *m*

chew /tʃuː/ VT [+ *food*] mâcher, mastiquer ; [+ *betel, coca etc*] chiquer ; [+ *pencil*] mâchonner, mordiller ; [+ *lip*] mordiller ♦ **to ~ tobacco** chiquer ♦ **to ~ the cud** (*lit, fig*) ruminer ♦ **to ~ the fat**‡ tailler le bout de gras *, tailler une bavette * N 1 (= *action*) mastication *f* 2 (*Brit* = *sweet*) bonbon *m* ; [*of tobacco*] chique *f* COMP **chewing gum** N chewing-gum *m*

► **chew on** VT FUS (*fig*) [+ *facts, problem*] tourner et retourner

► **chew out** VT SEP engueuler

► **chew over** VT SEP [+ *problem etc*] (= *think over*) tourner et retourner ; (= *discuss*) discuter de

► **chew up** VT SEP mâchonner, mâchouiller *

chewy /'tʃuːɪ/ ADJ [*food*] difficile à mâcher ♦ **a ~ wine** un vin corsé et généreux COMP **chewy toffee** N caramel *m* mou

Cheyenne /ʃaɪ'æn/ N (= *person*) Cheyenne *mf*

chi /kaɪ/ N (= *letter*) chi *m*

chiaroscuro /kɪ,ɑːrəs'kʊərəʊ/ N clair-obscur *m*

chiasma /kaɪ'æzmə/ N (pl **chiasmas** or **chiasmata** /kaɪ'æzmətə/) (*Anat*) chiasma *m*, chiasme *m*

chic /ʃiːk/ ADJ chic *inv*, élégant N chic *m*, élégance *f*

chicanery /ʃɪ'keɪnərɪ/ N (= *legal trickery*) chicane *f* ; (= *false argument*) chicane *f*, chicanerie *f*

Chicano /tʃɪ'kɑːnəʊ/ N (*US*) Mexicain(e) *m(f)* américain(e), Chicano *mf*

chichi * /'ʃiː,ʃiː/ ADJ trop recherché

chick /tʃɪk/ N 1 (= *chicken*) poussin *m* ; (= *nestling*) oisillon *m* ; → **day** 2 (‡ = *child*) poulet * *m*, coco * *m* ♦ **come here ~!** viens ici mon coco *or* mon petit poulet ! 3 (‡ = *girl*) pépée‡ *f*, poulette‡ *f*

COMP **chick flick** * N *film destiné au public féminin ou particulièrement apprécié par celui-ci*

chick lit * N *genre romanesque décrivant des jeunes femmes actives et leur vie sentimentale*

chickadee /'tʃɪkə,diː/ N mésange *f* à tête noire

chicken /'tʃɪkɪn/ N poulet(te) *m(f)* ; (*very young*) poussin *m* ; (*Culin*) poulet *m* ♦ **you're a big ~ at times!** (*pej*) quelle poule mouillée tu fais parfois ! * ♦ **to run around like a headless** ~ *or* **like a ~ with its head cut off** courir dans tous les sens, ne pas savoir où donner de la tête ♦ **which came first, the ~ or the egg?** qui vient en premier, l'œuf ou la poule ? ♦ **it's a ~ and egg situation** * c'est la vieille histoire de l'œuf et de la poule ♦ **don't count your ~s (before they're hatched)** il ne faut pas vendre la peau de l'ours (avant de l'avoir tué) → **spring**

ADJ (* *pej* = *cowardly*) froussard * ♦ **to play** ~ jouer au premier qui se dégonfle * ♦ **he's too ~ to try it** il est trop dégonflé * pour essayer

COMP **chicken farmer** N éleveur *m* de poules *or* de volailles, volailleur *m*

chicken farming N élevage *m* avicole *or* de volailles *or* de poules

chicken-fried steak N steak pané et poêlé

chicken-hearted ADJ peureux

chicken liver N foie(s) *m(pl)* de volaille

chicken run N poulailler *m*

chicken wire N grillage *m*

► **chicken out**‡ VI se dégonfler * ♦ **he ~ed out of his exams** au moment de ses examens, il s'est dégonflé * ♦ **he ~ed out of asking her to dinner** il s'est dégonflé * au moment de l'inviter à dîner

chickenfeed /'tʃɪkɪnfiːd/ N 1 (*lit*) nourriture *f* pour volaille 2 (*esp US* * = *insignificant sum*) somme *f* dérisoire, bagatelle *f*

chickenpox /'tʃɪkɪnpɒks/ N varicelle *f*

chickenshit *‡ /'tʃɪkɪnʃɪt/ (*US*) N 1 (= *coward*) dégonflé(e)‡ *m(f)* 2 (*NonC* = *worthless*) ♦ **to be ~** être de la merde *‡ ADJ 1 (= *cowardly*) dégonflé‡ 2 (= *worthless*) de merde *‡

chickpea /'tʃɪkpiː/ N pois *m* chiche

chickweed /'tʃɪkwiːd/ N mouron *m* blanc *or* des oiseaux

chicory /'tʃɪkərɪ/ N (*for coffee*) chicorée *f* ; (= *endive*) endive *f* ; (= *frisée*) chicorée *f* frisée

chide /tʃaɪd/ (pret **chided** or **chid** /tʃɪd/, ptp **chided** or **chidden** /'tʃɪdn/) VT gronder, réprimander

chief /tʃiːf/ N 1 [*of organization, tribe*] chef *m* ♦ **too many ~s and not enough Indians** * trop de chefs et pas assez d'exécutants ; → **commander, editor, lord**

2 (* = *boss*) patron *m* ♦ **yes, ~!** oui, chef *or* patron !

ADJ principal

COMP **chief assistant** N premier assistant *m*

chief constable N (*Brit Police*) ≈ directeur *m* (de police)

chief education officer N (*Scol*) ≈ recteur *m* d'académie

chief engineer N (*Naut*) ingénieur *m* en chef

Chief Executive N (*Brit: in local government*) directeur *m* ; (*US Pol*) chef *m* de l'Exécutif, président *m* des États-Unis

chief executive officer N (*Ind, Comm*) directeur *m* général

chief inspector N (*gen*) inspecteur *m* principal *or* en chef ; (*Brit Police*) commandant *m* (des gardiens de la paix)

chief inspector of schools N (*Brit Scol*) ≈ inspecteur *m* général

chief master sergeant N (*US Airforce*) major *m*

chief of police N ≈ préfet *m* de police

chief of staff N (*Mil*) chef *m* d'état-major ♦ **(White House) Chief of Staff** (*US*) secrétaire *mf* général (de la Maison-Blanche)

chief of state N chef *m* d'État

chief operating officer N président,e *m,f*

chief petty officer N (*Naut*) ≈ maître *m*

chief priest N archiprêtre *m*

chief rabbi N grand rabbin *m*

Chief Secretary (to the Treasury) N (*Brit Pol*) ≈ ministre *m* délégué au budget

chief state school officer N (*US Scol*) ≈ recteur *m* d'académie

chief superintendent N (*Brit Police*) ≈ commissaire *m* divisionnaire

chief technician N (*gen*) technicien *m* en chef ; (*Mil*) sergent *m* (de l'armée de l'air)

chief town N chef-lieu *m*

chief warrant officer N (*Mil*) adjudant *m* chef

chief whip N (*Brit Parl*) *chef des parlementaires responsable de la discipline de vote* ; → **lord**

Chief Whip

En Grande-Bretagne, le parti gouvernemental et celui de l'opposition ont chacun leur **Chief Whip**, qui est le responsable de la discipline du parti à la Chambre des communes. Il tient les députés informés des activités parlementaires et fait remonter l'opinion des députés jusqu'à la direction du parti. Il veille également à ce que les députés participent aux scrutins importants ; son rôle est donc particulièrement décisif lorsque le gouvernement ne dispose que d'une faible majorité aux Communes.

chiefly /ˈtʃiːflɪ/ ADV principalement, surtout

chieftain /ˈtʃiːftən/ N chef m *(de clan, de tribu)*

chiffchaff /ˈtʃɪfˌtʃæf/ N pouillot m véloce

chiffon /ˈʃɪfɒn/ N mousseline f de soie ADJ *[dress]* en mousseline (de soie)

chignon /ˈʃiːnjɔːŋ/ N chignon m

Chihuahua /tʃɪˈwɑːwɑː/ N chihuahua m

chilblain /ˈtʃɪlbleɪn/ N engelure f

child /tʃaɪld/ (pl **children** /ˈtʃɪldrən/) N 1 enfant mf ◆ **when still a ~, he ...** tout enfant, il ... ◆ **don't be such a ~** ne fais pas l'enfant ◆ **she has three children** elle a trois enfants ◆ **children's publishing** l'édition f jeunesse ◆ **to be with ~** † être enceinte

2 *(fig)* produit m, fruit m ◆ **the ~ of his imagination** le produit *or* le fruit de son imagination ; → **brain**

COMP *[labour]* des enfants ; *[psychology, psychiatry]* de l'enfant, infantile ; *[psychologist, psychiatrist]* pour enfants

child abduction N *(Jur)* enlèvement m d'enfant

child abuse N *(gen)* maltraitance f d'enfant(s) ; *(sexual)* abus m sexuel sur enfant, sévices mpl sexuels infligés à enfant

child abuser N *(gen)* auteur m de sévices sur enfant(s) ; *(sexual)* auteur m de sévices sexuels *or* d'abus sexuels sur enfant(s)

child battering N mauvais traitements mpl à enfant, maltraitance f d'enfant(s)

child benefit N *(Brit)* ≃ allocations fpl familiales

child care N protection f infantile *or* de l'enfance, assistance f à l'enfance

child-care center N *(US)* crèche f, garderie f

child-care worker N travailleur m, -euse f social(e) *(s'occupant d'enfants)*

child guidance N soutien m psychopédagogique ◆ **~ guidance centre** *or* **clinic** centre m psychopédagogique

child lock N *[of door]* (serrure f de) sécurité f enfants

child molester † N auteur m de sévices sexuels *or* d'abus sexuels sur enfant(s)

child prodigy N enfant mf prodige

Child Protection Register N *(Brit) registre des enfants en danger selon les services locaux de la protection de l'enfance*

child sex abuser N *(gen)* auteur m de sévices sexuels *or* abus sexuels sur enfants

child's play N *(fig)* ◆ **it's ~'s play** c'est enfantin, c'est un jeu d'enfant *(to sb* pour qn)

Child Support Agency N *(Brit) organisme chargé de faire respecter le paiement des pensions alimentaires chez les couples divorcés* ; → **DSS**

child welfare N protection f de l'enfance ◆ **Child Welfare Centre** centre m *or* service m de protection de l'enfance

childbearing /ˈtʃaɪldˌbeərɪŋ/ N *(NonC)* maternité f ◆ **constant ~** grossesses fpl répétées ◆ **of ~ age** en âge d'avoir des enfants

childbed /ˈtʃaɪldbed/ N ◆ **in ~** en couches

childbirth /ˈtʃaɪldbɜːθ/ N accouchement m ◆ **in ~** en couches

childhood /ˈtʃaɪldhʊd/ N enfance f ◆ **in his ~ he ...** tout enfant il ... ; → **second**[1]

childish /ˈtʃaɪldɪʃ/ ADJ 1 *[behaviour]* puéril (puérile f) ◆ **~ reaction** réaction f puérile ◆ **don't be so ~** ne fais pas l'enfant ◆ **he was very ~ about it** il s'est montré très puéril à ce sujet 2 *[ailment, disease]* infantile ◆ **~ games** jeux mpl d'enfant

childishly /ˈtʃaɪldɪʃlɪ/ ADV *(pej) [say, behave, act]* puérilement, d'une manière puérile ◆ **~ simple** simple comme bonjour, d'une simplicité enfantine

childishness /ˈtʃaɪldɪʃnɪs/ N *(slightly pej)* puérilité f, enfantillage m

childless /ˈtʃaɪldlɪs/ ADJ sans enfants

childlike /ˈtʃaɪldlaɪk/ ADJ d'enfant, enfantin

Childline ® /ˈtʃaɪldˌlaɪn/ N ≈ SOS Enfants en péril *(numéro de téléphone mis à la disposition des enfants maltraités)*

childminder /ˈtʃaɪldˌmaɪndəʳ/ N *(Brit)* assistante f maternelle, nourrice f

childminding /ˈtʃaɪldˌmaɪndɪŋ/ N *(Brit)* garde f d'enfants (en bas âge)

childproof /ˈtʃaɪldpruːf/ ADJ *[door etc]* sans danger pour les enfants ◆ **~ (door) lock** (serrure f de) sécurité f enfants ◆ **the house is ~** * *(= safe)* la maison est sans danger pour les enfants ; *(= cannot be damaged)* les enfants ne peuvent rien abîmer dans la maison

children /ˈtʃɪldrən/ NPL of **child** ; → **home**

Chile /ˈtʃɪlɪ/ N Chili m

Chilean /ˈtʃɪlɪən/ ADJ chilien N Chilien(ne) m(f)

chili /ˈtʃɪlɪ/ N (pl **chilies**) piment m (rouge)

COMP **chili con carne** N chili con carne m

chili powder N piment m (rouge) en poudre, poudre f de piment (rouge)

chill /tʃɪl/ N 1 *(lit)* fraîcheur f, froid m ◆ **there's a ~ in the air** il fait assez frais *or* un peu froid ◆ **to take the ~ off** *[+ wine]* chambrer ; *[+ water, room]* réchauffer un peu

2 *(fig)* froid m, froideur f ◆ **to cast a ~ over** jeter un froid sur ◆ **there was a certain ~ in the way she looked at me** il y avait une certaine froideur dans sa façon de me regarder ◆ **it sent a ~ down my spine** j'en ai eu un frisson dans le dos ◆ **he felt a certain ~ as he remembered ...** il a eu un *or* le frisson en se rappelant ...

3 *(Med)* refroidissement m ◆ **to catch a ~** prendre froid, attraper un refroidissement

ADJ *(liter)* frais (fraîche f), froid ; *(fig)* froid, glacial

VT 1 *(lit) [+ person]* faire frissonner, donner froid à ; *[+ wine, melon]* (faire) rafraîchir ; *[+ champagne]* frapper ; *[+ meat]* réfrigérer ; *[+ dessert]* mettre au frais ; *[+ plant]* geler ; *[+ casting, metal]* tremper en coquille ◆ **to be ~ed to the bone** *or* **marrow** être transi

2 *(fig) [+ enthusiasm]* refroidir ◆ **to ~ sb's blood** glacer le sang de qn ; → **spine**

VI 1 *[wine]* rafraîchir 2 ⇒ **chill out**

COMP **chill cabinet** N *(Brit)* vitrine f réfrigérante

chill-out * ADJ *[music]* relaxant ◆ **~-out room** *(in rave club)* salle f de repos *(dans une boîte de nuit)*

► **chill out** * VI se relaxer, décompresser * ◆ **~ out** relax ! *

chiller * /ˈtʃɪləʳ/ N *(= film)* film m d'épouvante ; *(= book)* roman m d'épouvante COMP **chiller cabinet** N ⇒ **chill cabinet**

chilli /ˈtʃɪlɪ/ N ⇒ **chili**

chilliness /ˈtʃɪlɪnɪs/ N *(= cold)* froid m ; *(= coolness)* fraîcheur f ; *(fig)* froideur f

chilling /ˈtʃɪlɪŋ/ ADJ 1 *(= frightening) [effect, reminder, story, sight, prospect, sound, look, thought]* effrayant, qui fait froid dans le dos ; → **bone, spine** 2 *(= freezing) [wind]* glacial

chillingly /ˈtʃɪlɪŋlɪ/ ADV *[say, describe]* d'une façon qui fait froid dans le dos ◆ **the voice was ~ familiar** la voix était familière et cela faisait froid dans le dos

chillness /ˈtʃɪlnɪs/ N ⇒ **chilliness**

chilly /ˈtʃɪlɪ/ ADJ 1 * *[weather, wind, air, water, room]* froid ; *[day, afternoon]* frais (fraîche f) ◆ **to be** *or* **feel ~** *[person]* avoir froid ◆ **it's ~ today** il fait frais aujourd'hui 2 *(= unfriendly) [person, manner, look, smile, response, reception]* froid ; *[relationship]* distant

chime /tʃaɪm/ N carillon m ◆ **to ring the ~s** carillonner ◆ **a ~ of bells** un carillon ◆ **door ~s** carillon m de porte VI *[bells, voices]* carillonner ; *[clock]* sonner VT *[+ bells, hours]* sonner

► **chime in** VI *(fig) [person] (in agreement, approval)* suivre le mouvement ◆ **he ~d in with another complaint** il a suivi le mouvement, et il s'est plaint à son tour ◆ **"why?" Bob ~d in** "pourquoi ?" répéta Bob

chimera /kaɪˈmɪərə/ N *(liter)* chimère f

chimerical /kaɪˈmerɪkəl/ ADJ chimérique

chimney /ˈtʃɪmnɪ/ N *(Archit, Geog, Naut, Sport)* cheminée f ; *[of lamp]* verre m

COMP **chimney breast** N *(Brit)* manteau m de (la) cheminée

chimney-climbing N *(Climbing)* ramonage m

chimney corner N coin m du feu

chimney pot N tuyau m de cheminée

chimney-pot hat * N (chapeau m) tuyau m de poêle *

chimney stack N *(Brit = group of chimneys)* souche f de cheminée ; *[of factory]* tuyau m de cheminée

chimney sweep N ramoneur m

chimneypiece /ˈtʃɪmnɪpiːs/ N *(Brit)* (dessus m *or* tablette f de) cheminée f

chimp * /tʃɪmp/ N ⇒ **chimpanzee**

chimpanzee /ˌtʃɪmpænˈziː/ N chimpanzé m

chin /tʃɪn/ N menton m ◆ **to keep one's ~ up** * tenir bon, tenir le coup * ◆ **(keep your) ~ up!** * courage !, du cran ! * ◆ **to take it on the ~** * encaisser * ; → **double** VI *(US* *)* bavarder

COMP **chin-chin !** † * EXCL tchin-tchin ! *

chin job * N lifting m du menton ◆ **to have a ~ job** se faire rectifier le menton

chinning bar N *(Sport)* barre f fixe

chin-up N *(Sport)* ◆ **to do ~-ups** faire des tractions à la barre fixe

China /ˈtʃaɪnə/ N Chine f

COMP **China Sea** N mer f de Chine

China tea N thé m de Chine

china /ˈtʃaɪnə/ N 1 *(NonC = material, dishes)* porcelaine f ◆ **a piece of ~** une porcelaine ; → **bone** 2 *(‡ = friend)* poteau * m

COMP *[cup, plate, figure etc]* de *or* en porcelaine

china cabinet N dressoir m

china clay N kaolin m

china industry N industrie f de la porcelaine

Chinaman † /ˈtʃaɪnəmən/ N (pl **-men**) Chinois m

Chinatown /ˈtʃaɪnətaʊn/ N quartier m chinois

chinaware /ˈtʃaɪnəweəʳ/ N *(NonC)* (objets mpl de) porcelaine f

chinchilla /tʃɪnˈtʃɪlə/ N chinchilla m COMP **chinchilla coat** N manteau m de chinchilla

Chinese /tʃaɪˈniːz/ ADJ *(gen)* chinois ; *[ambassador, embassy]* de Chine ; *[teacher]* de chinois N 1 *(pl inv)* Chinois(e) m(f) 2 *(= language)* chinois m 3 *(* : also **Chinese meal**)* (repas m) chinois m ; *(* : also **Chinese restaurant**)* (restaurant m) chinois m NPL **the Chinese** les Chinois mpl

COMP **Chinese burn** * N torture f indienne

Chinese cabbage N ⇒ **Chinese leaves**

Chinese gooseberry † N kiwi m

Chinese lantern N lanterne f vénitienne

Chinese leaves NPL chou m chinois

Chinese puzzle N casse-tête m inv chinois

Chinese whispers NPL *(Brit) (= game)* jeu m du téléphone ; *(fig = garbled messages)* téléphone m arabe

Chinese white N, ADJ blanc m de zinc

Chink *‡ /tʃɪŋk/ N *(pej)* Chin(e)toque ‡ mf *(pej)*

chink[1] /tʃɪŋk/ N *(= slit, hole) [of wall]* fente f, fissure f ; *[of door]* entrebâillement m ◆ **the ~ in the armour** le défaut de la cuirasse

chink[2] /tʃɪŋk/ N *(= sound)* tintement m *(de verres, de pièces de monnaie)* VT faire tinter VI tinter

chinless /ˈtʃɪnlɪs/ ADJ *(lit)* qui a le menton fuyant ; *(fig = feeble)* mou (molle f) COMP **chinless wonder** * N *(Brit)* (aristo m) chiffe f molle *

chinos /ˈtʃiːnəʊz/ NPL chinos mpl

chinstrap /ˈtʃɪnstræp/ **N** *[of helmet etc]* jugulaire *f*

chintz /tʃɪnts/ **N** chintz *m* **COMP** **chintz curtains** **NPL** rideaux *mpl* de chintz

chintzy /ˈtʃɪntsɪ/ **ADJ** 1 *[style]* rustique 2 *(US * = mean)* moche *, mesquin

chinwag * /ˈtʃɪnwæg/ **N** causerie *f* ◆ **to have a ~ (with sb)** tailler une bavette * *or* papoter (avec qn)

chip /tʃɪp/ **N** 1 *(gen)* fragment *m* ; *[of wood]* copeau *m*, éclat *m* ; *[of glass, stone]* éclat *m* ; *(Elec)* microplaquette *f* ◆ **he's/she's a ~ off the old block** * c'est bien le fils/la fille de son père ◆ **to have a ~ on one's shoulder** être aigri ◆ **to have a ~ on one's shoulder because ...** n'avoir jamais digéré * le fait que ... ; → **polystyrene**

2 *(Culin) (Brit)* frite *f* ; *(US)* (also **potato chip**) chips *f* ◆ **would you like some ~s?** *(Brit)* tu veux des frites ? ; *(US)* tu veux des chips ? ◆ **egg and ~s** œuf-frites ◆ **steak and ~s** steak-frites

3 *(Comput)* puce *f*

4 *(= break) [of stone, crockery, glass]* ébréchure *f* ; *[of furniture]* écornure *f* ◆ **this cup has a ~** cette tasse est ébréchée

5 *(Poker etc)* jeton *m*, fiche *f* ◆ **to cash in one's ~s** * *(fig)* passer l'arme à gauche * ◆ **he's had his ~s** * il est cuit * *or* fichu * ◆ **when the ~s are down** * dans les moments cruciaux ◆ **in the ~s** * *(US)* plein aux as *

6 *(Golf:* also **chip shot***)* coup *m* coché

VT 1 *(= damage) [+ cup, plate]* ébrécher ; *[+ furniture]* écorner ; *[+ varnish, paint]* écailler ; *[+ stone]* écorner, enlever un éclat de ◆ **to ~ wood** faire des copeaux ◆ **the chicken ~ped the shell open** le poussin a cassé sa coquille

2 *(Brit) [+ vegetables]* couper en lamelles

3 *(= cut deliberately)* tailler

4 *(Golf)* ◆ **to ~ the ball** cocher

VI *[cup, plate]* s'ébrécher ; *[furniture]* s'écorner ; *[varnish, paint]* s'écailler

COMP **chip and PIN** **N** système *m* d'identification par carte à puce et code confidentiel

chip and PIN card **N** carte à puce électronique

chip basket **N** *(Brit)* panier *m* à frites

chip pan **N** *(Brit)* friteuse *f*

chip shop **N** *(Brit)* friterie *f*

► **chip at** **VT FUS** 1 *[+ rock, wood, ice]* tailler petit à petit

2 *(* = make fun of)* se ficher de *

► **chip away** **VI** *[paint, etc]* s'écailler ◆ **to ~ away at** *[+ rock, wood, ice]* tailler petit à petit ; *[+ sb's authority, lands]* grignoter, réduire petit à petit ; *[+ law, decision]* réduire petit à petit la portée de

VT SEP *[+ paint etc]* enlever *or* décaper petit à petit *(au couteau etc)*

► **chip in** **VI** 1 *(= interrupt)* dire son mot, mettre son grain de sel *

2 *(* = contribute)* contribuer, souscrire *(à une collecte etc)* ◆ **he ~ped in with 2 euros** il y est allé de (ses) 2 euros *

► **chip off** ⇒ **chip away**

chipboard /ˈtʃɪpbɔːd/ **N** *(US)* carton *m* ; *(Brit)* panneau *m* de particules, aggloméré *m*

chipmunk /ˈtʃɪpmʌŋk/ **N** tamia *m*, suisse *m (Can)*

chipolata /ˌtʃɪpəˈlɑːtə/ **N** *(Brit)* chipolata *f*

chipped /tʃɪpt/ **ADJ** *[cup, bone, tooth]* ébréché ; *[enamel, step, windowsill]* abîmé ; *[paint, nail varnish]* écaillé **COMP** **chipped potatoes** **N** (pommes *fpl* de terre) frites *fpl*

Chippendale /ˈtʃɪpəndeɪl/ **ADJ** *[chair]* chippendale *inv*

chipper * /ˈtʃɪpəʳ/ **ADJ** *(= happy)* joyeux, gai ; *(= smart)* chic *inv*

chippings /ˈtʃɪpɪŋz/ **NPL** gravillons *mpl* ◆ **"loose chippings"** "attention gravillons"

chippy * /ˈtʃɪpɪ/ **N** *(Brit)* 1 friterie *f* 2 *(Brit = carpenter)* menuisier *m* **ADJ** aigri

chiromancer /ˈkaɪərəmænsəʳ/ **N** chiromancien(ne) *m(f)*

chiromancy /ˈkaɪərəmænsɪ/ **N** chiromancie *f*

chiropodist /kɪˈrɒpədɪst/ **N** *(Brit)* pédicure *mf*

chiropody /kɪˈrɒpədɪ/ **N** *(Brit) (= science)* podologie *f* ; *(= treatment)* soins *mpl* du pied, traitement *m* des maladies des pieds

chiropractic /ˈkaɪərəpræktɪk/ **N** *(NonC)* chiropraxie *or* chiropractie *f*

chiropractor /ˈkaɪərəpræktəʳ/ **N** chiropracteur *m*

chirp /tʃɜːp/ **VI** *[birds]* pépier, gazouiller ; *[crickets]* chanter, striduler *(liter)* ; *(* fig) [person]* pépier, couiner * *(pej)* **N** *[of birds]* pépiement *m*, gazouillis *m* ; *[of crickets]* chant *m*, stridulation *f*

chirpy * /ˈtʃɜːpɪ/ **ADJ** *[person]* gai, de bonne humeur ; *[voice, mood]* gai

chirrup /ˈtʃɪrəp/ ⇒ **chirp**

chisel /ˈtʃɪzl/ **N** *[of carpenter, sculptor, silversmith]* ciseau *m* ; *[of stonemason]* burin *m* ; *(= blunt chisel)* matoir *m* ; *(= hollow chisel)* gouge *f* ; *(= mortise chisel)* bédane *m* ; *(= roughing-out chisel)* ébauchoir *m* ; → **cold** **VT** 1 ciseler ; *(Engraving)* buriner 2 *(* = swindle) [+ thing]* resquiller ; *[+ person]* rouler *, posséder *

chiselled /ˈtʃɪzld/ **ADJ** *[features]* buriné ◆ **finely ~ features** traits *mpl* finement ciselés

chiseller *, **chiseler** * *(US)* /ˈtʃɪzləʳ/ **N** *(= crook)* escroc *m*, filou *m* ; *(= scrounger)* resquilleur *m*, -euse *f*

chit[1] /tʃɪt/ **N** ◆ **she's a mere ~ of a girl** ce n'est qu'une gosse * *or* une gamine *

chit[2] /tʃɪt/ **N** *(gen)* bulletin *m* de livraison ; *(= receipt)* reçu *m* ; *(= note)* note *f*

chitchat * /ˈtʃɪttʃæt/ **N** bavardage *m*

chitterlings /ˈtʃɪtəlɪŋz/ **NPL** tripes *fpl* (de porc)

chitty /ˈtʃɪtɪ/ **N** ⇒ **chit**[2]

chiv * /tʃɪv/ **N** surin * *m*, couteau *m*

chivalresque /ʃɪvəlˈresk/, **chivalric** /ʃɪˈvælrɪk/ **ADJ** chevaleresque

chivalrous /ˈʃɪvəlrəs/ **ADJ** *(= courteous)* chevaleresque ; *(= gallant)* galant

chivalrously /ˈʃɪvəlrəslɪ/ **ADV** de façon chevaleresque

chivalry /ˈʃɪvəlrɪ/ **N** 1 chevalerie *f* ◆ **the rules/the age of ~** les règles *fpl*/l'âge *m* de la chevalerie ◆ **the age of ~ is not dead** *(iro)* on sait encore être galant aujourd'hui 2 *(= quality)* qualités *fpl* chevaleresques ; *(= gallantry)* galanterie *f* 3 *(collective: Hist = knights)* chevalerie *f*

chives /tʃaɪvz/ **NPL** ciboulette *f*

chiv(v)y * /ˈtʃɪvɪ/ **VT** *(Brit)* 1 (also **chiv(v)y along**) *[+ person, animal]* chasser, pourchasser 2 *(= pester)* ne pas laisser la paix à ◆ **she chiv(v)ied him into writing the letter** elle l'a harcelé jusqu'à ce qu'il écrive la lettre

► **chiv(v)y up** * **VT SEP** *[+ person]* faire activer

chlamydia /kləˈmɪdɪə/ **N** *(Med)* chlamydia *f*

chloral /ˈklɔːrəl/ **N** chloral *m*

chlorate /ˈklɔːreɪt/ **N** chlorate *m*

chloric /ˈklɔːrɪk/ **ADJ** chlorique **COMP** **chloric acid** **N** acide *m* chlorique

chloride /ˈklɔːraɪd/ **N** chlorure *m* **COMP** **chloride of lime** **N** chlorure *m* de chaux

chlorinate /ˈklɒrɪneɪt/ **VT** *[+ water]* chlorer, javelliser ; *(Chem)* chlorurer

chlorination /ˌklɒrɪˈneɪʃən/ **N** *[of water]* javellisation *f*

chlorine /ˈklɔːriːn/ **N** chlore *m*

chlorofluorocarbon /ˌklɔːrəˈfluərəʊˈkɑːbən/ **N** chlorofluorocarbone *m*

chloroform /ˈklɒrəfɔːm/ **N** chloroforme *m* **VT** chloroformer

chlorophyll /ˈklɒrəfɪl/ **N** chlorophylle *f*

chloroplast /ˈklɔːrəʊˌplæst/ **N** chloroplaste *m*

choc * /tʃɒk/ **N** abbrev of **chocolate** **COMP** **choc-ice** **N** esquimau ® *m*

chocaholic * /ˌtʃɒkəˈhɒlɪk/ **N** accro * *mf* du chocolat

chock /tʃɒk/ **N** *[of wheel]* cale *f* ; *[of barrel]* cale *f*, chantier *m* ; *(Naut)* chantier *m*, cale *f* **VT** *[+ wheel]* caler ; *(Naut)* mettre sur le chantier *or* sur cales **COMP** **chock-a-block** *, **chock-full** * **ADJ** *[basket, pan, box]* plein à ras bord *(with, of* de) ; *[room]* plein à craquer *(with, of* de), comble ; *[town]* bondé

chocker * /ˈtʃɒkəʳ/ **ADJ** ⇒ **chock-a-block** ; → **chock**

chocolate /ˈtʃɒklɪt/ **N** chocolat *m* ◆ **(drinking) ~** chocolat *m* ◆ **a ~** un chocolat, une crotte de chocolat ; → **dessert, milk, plain**

COMP *(= made of chocolate)* en chocolat ; *(= containing, flavoured with chocolate)* (au) chocolat, chocolaté ; *(= colour:* also **chocolate brown***)* chocolat *inv*

chocolate bar **N** barre *f* de *or* au chocolat

chocolate biscuit **N** biscuit *m* au chocolat

chocolate-box **ADJ** *[landscape, village]* de carte postale

chocolate chip cookie **N** biscuit *m* aux pépites de chocolat

chocolate drop **N** pastille *f* au chocolat

chocolate eclair **N** éclair *m* au chocolat

choice /tʃɔɪs/ LANGUAGE IN USE 10.1

N 1 *(= act or possibility of choosing)* choix *m* ◆ **to make a ~** faire un choix, choisir ◆ **to make** *or* **take one's ~** faire son choix ◆ **to have no ~** ne pas avoir le choix ◆ **be careful in your ~** faites attention en choisissant ◆ **he didn't have a free ~** il n'a pas été libre de choisir ◆ **to have a very wide ~** avoir l'embarras du choix ◆ **he had no ~ but to obey** il ne pouvait qu'obéir ◆ **from** *or* **for ~** de *or* par préférence ◆ **he did it from ~** il l'a fait de son plein gré, il a choisi de le faire ◆ **the house of your (own) ~** la maison de votre choix ◆ **the drug/weapon of ~** la drogue/l'arme favorite *or* de choix ◆ **it's your ~!** * c'est ton problème ! * ; → **Hobson's choice**

2 *(= thing or person chosen)* choix *m* ◆ **this book would be my ~** c'est ce livre que je choisirais

3 *(= variety to choose from)* choix *m*, variété *f* ◆ **a wide ~ of dresses** un grand choix de robes

ADJ 1 *[goods, fruit]* de choix ◆ **choicest** de premier choix

2 *[word, phrase] (= well-chosen)* bien choisi

choir /ˈkwaɪəʳ/ **N** 1 *(Mus)* chœur *m*, chorale *f* ; *(Rel)* chœur *m*, maîtrise *f* ◆ **to sing in the ~** faire partie du chœur *or* de la chorale, chanter dans la maîtrise 2 *(Archit, Rel)* chœur *m* **VTI** chanter en chœur

COMP **choir organ** **N** petit orgue *m* ; *(= keyboard)* positif *m*

choir practice **N** ◆ **to go to ~ practice** aller à la chorale

choir school **N** maîtrise *f*, manécanterie *f (rattachée à une cathédrale)*

choir-stall **N** stalle *f* (du chœur)

choirboy /ˈkwaɪəbɔɪ/ **N** *(Rel)* enfant *m* de chœur

choirgirl /ˈkwaɪəgɜːl/ **N** *(Rel)* enfant *f* de chœur

choirmaster /ˈkwaɪəˌmɑːstəʳ/ **N** *(Mus)* chef *m* de(s) chœur(s) ; *(Rel)* maître *m* de chapelle

choke /tʃəʊk/ **VT** 1 *[+ person, voice, breathing]* étrangler ◆ **the fumes ~d her** la fumée l'a fait suffoquer ◆ **to ~ the life out of sb** étrangler qn ◆ **in a voice ~d with sobs** d'une voix étranglée par les sanglots

2 *(fig)* *[+ fire]* étouffer ; *[+ pipe, tube]* boucher, engorger ◆ **flowers ~d by weeds** fleurs *fpl* étouffées par les mauvaises herbes ◆ **street ~d with traffic** rue *f* engorgée *or* embouteillée

VI 1 étouffer, s'étrangler ◆ **to ~ to death** mourir étouffé ◆ **he ~d on some bread** il s'est étranglé en avalant un morceau de pain de travers ◆ **she ~d on a fish bone** elle s'est étranglée avec une arête ◆ **she was choking with anger** la rage l'étouffait, elle étouffait de rage ◆ **he was choking with laughter** il s'étranglait de rire

2 *(*: esp US = crack under pressure)* craquer *

N *[of engine]* starter *m* ; *(= inductor coil)* bobine *f* de réactance, inductance *f* de protection

COMP **choke chain** N collier *m* étrangleur

► **choke back** VT SEP *[+ feelings]* réprimer, contenir ; *[+ tears]* refouler ; *[+ words]* ravaler

► **choke down** VT SEP *[+ rage]* contenir ; *[+ sobs]* ravaler, étouffer

► **choke off** * VT SEP *(fig)* *[+ suggestions etc]* étouffer (dans l'œuf) ; *[+ discussion]* empêcher ◆ **raising taxes could ~ off the recovery** une augmentation des impôts pourrait empêcher la reprise

► **choke up** VI s'engorger, se boucher

VT SEP *[+ pipe, drain]* engorger, boucher

choked /tʃəʊkt/ ADJ 1 *(= strangled)* étranglé ◆ **in a ~ voice** d'une voix étranglée ◆ **~ with emotion** d'une voix étranglée par l'émotion 2 *(Brit *)* *(= moved)* (très) ému ; *(= angry)* (très) vexé *or* contrarié ◆ **I still feel ~ about him leaving** je n'ai pas encore encaissé * *or* digéré * qu'il soit parti

choker /ˈtʃəʊkəʳ/ N 1 *(= scarf)* foulard *m*, écharpe *f* ; *(= collar)* col *m* droit ; *(= necklace)* collier *m* (de chien) 2 ‡ ◆ **what a ~ !** c'est difficile à encaisser * *or* digérer * ! ◆ **losing at Wembley was a ~!** on n'a pas encaissé * *or* digéré * d'avoir perdu à Wembley !

choking /ˈtʃəʊkɪŋ/ N *(Med)* suffocation *f* ADJ *[fumes, dust]* étouffant

cholera /ˈkɒlərə/ N choléra *m* COMP *[epidemic]* de choléra ; *[victim, symptoms]* du choléra

choleric /ˈkɒlərɪk/ ADJ colérique, coléreux

cholesterol /kəˈlestəˌrɒl/ N cholestérol *m*

chomp * /tʃɒmp/ VTI mâcher bruyamment ◆ **to ~ (away) on** *or* **at sth** dévorer qch à belles dents

Chomskyan /ˈtʃɒmskɪən/ ADJ chomskien, de Chomsky

choo-choo /ˈtʃuːtʃuː/ N *(baby talk)* train *m*, tchou-tchou *m* *(baby talk)*

choose /tʃuːz/ (pret **chose**, ptp **chosen**) VT 1 *(= select)* choisir ; *(= elect)* élire ◆ **which will you ~?** lequel choisirez-vous ? ◆ **they chose a president** ils ont élu un président ◆ **he was chosen (as) leader** ils l'ont pris pour chef ◆ **the Chosen (People)** le peuple élu ◆ **the chosen (few)** les (quelques) élus *mpl* ◆ **there is little** *or* **not much to ~ between them** il n'y a guère de différence entre eux ◆ **there is nothing to ~ between them** ils se valent ; *(pej)* ils ne valent pas mieux l'un que l'autre ◆ **in a few (well-)chosen words** en quelques mots choisis

2 *(= opt)* décider, juger bon *(to do sth* de faire qch) vouloir *(to do sth* faire qch) ; ◆ **he chose not to speak** il a jugé bon de se taire, il a préféré se taire ◆ **I didn't ~ to do so** *(= decided not to)* j'ai décidé de ne pas le faire ; *(= did it unwillingly)* je ne l'ai pas fait de mon propre gré

VI choisir ◆ **as you ~** comme vous voulez *or* l'entendez, à votre gré ◆ **if you ~** si cela vous dit ◆ **to ~ between/among** faire un choix entre/parmi ◆ **there's not much to ~ from** il n'y a pas tellement de choix

choos(e)y * /ˈtʃuːzɪ/ ADJ *[person]* difficile (à satisfaire) ◆ **I'm not choos(e)y** je ne suis pas difficile ◆ **you can't be choos(e)y in your position** votre situation ne vous permet pas de faire la fine bouche ◆ **I'm choos(e)y about the people I go out with** je ne sors pas avec n'importe qui

chop¹ /tʃɒp/ N 1 *(Culin)* côtelette *f* ◆ **mutton/pork ~** côtelette *f* de mouton/de porc ; → **loin**

2 *(= blow)* coup *m* (de hache *etc*) ◆ **you're (the) next for the ~** * *(Brit)* tu es le prochain à y passer * ◆ **to get the ~** * *(Brit)* *[employee]* se faire sacquer * *or* virer * ; *[project]* être annulé

3 *(Tennis)* volée *f* coupée *or* arrêtée

VT 1 couper ◆ **to ~ wood** couper du bois ◆ **to ~ one's way through sth** se frayer un chemin (à coups de hache) à travers qch ◆ **to ~ a project** * *(fig)* *(= cancel)* annuler un projet ; *(= reduce costs, bills)* faire des coupes sombres dans, réduire à la portion congrue

2 *[+ meat, vegetables]* hacher

3 *(Sport)* *[+ ball]* couper

COMP **chop-chop** ‡ EXCL au trot ! *, et que ça saute ! * ADV fissa ‡

chopping block N billot *m*

chopping board N planche *f* à hacher

chopping knife N (pl **chopping knives**) hachoir *m* *(couteau)*

chop suey N chop suey *m*

► **chop at** VT FUS *[+ person etc]* essayer de frapper ; *(with axe)* *[+ wood]* tailler

► **chop down** VT SEP *[+ tree]* abattre

► **chop off** VT SEP trancher, couper ◆ **they ~ped off his head** on lui a tranché la tête

► **chop up** VT SEP hacher, couper en morceaux

chop² /tʃɒp/ VI 1 *(Naut)* *[wind]* varier ; *[waves]* clapoter 2 *(Brit fig)* **to ~ and change** changer constamment d'avis ◆ **he's always ~ping and changing** c'est une vraie girouette, il ne sait pas ce qu'il veut VT *(pej)* ◆ **to ~ logic** ergoter, discutailler

chop³ ‡ /tʃɒp/ N *(= food)* bouffe ‡ *f*

chophouse /ˈtʃɒphaʊs/ N (petit) restaurant *m*, gargote *f* *(pej)*

chopper /ˈtʃɒpəʳ/ N 1 *(for cutting)* couperet *m*, hachoir *m* ; *(Agr)* coupe-racines *m inv* 2 *(* = helicopter)* hélico * *m*, hélicoptère *m* ; *(US * = motorcycle)* chopper *m* ; *(Brit = cycle)* vélo *m* à haut guidon VI *(US ‡ = go by helicopter)* se rendre en hélicoptère *(to à)*

choppers ‡ /ˈtʃɒpəz/ NPL *(= teeth)* ratiches ‡ *fpl* ; *(= false teeth)* râtelier * *m*

choppy /ˈtʃɒpɪ/ ADJ *[lake]* clapoteux ; *[sea]* agité ; *[wind]* variable

chops /tʃɒps/ NPL *(= jaws)* *[of animal]* mâchoires *fpl* ; *(= cheeks)* joues *fpl* ; *[of animals]* bajoues *fpl* ; *(Tech)* *[of vice]* mâchoires *fpl* ; → **lick**

chopsticks /ˈtʃɒpstɪks/ NPL baguettes *fpl* *(pour manger)*

choral /ˈkɔːrəl/ ADJ choral, chanté en chœur COMP **choral society** N chorale *f*

chorale /kɒˈrɑːl/ N choral *m*

chord /kɔːd/ N *(Anat, Geom: also of harp etc)* corde *f* ; *(Mus)* accord *m* ◆ **to strike** *or* **touch a ~, to touch the right ~** *(fig)* toucher la corde sensible ; → **vocal**

COMP **chord change** N changement *m* d'accord

chord progression N suite *f* d'accords

chore /tʃɔːʳ/ N *(everyday)* travail *m* de routine ; *(unpleasant)* corvée *f* ◆ **the ~s** les tâches *fpl* ménagères ◆ **to do the ~s** faire le ménage

choreograph /ˈkɒrɪəˌgrɑːf/ VT 1 chorégraphier 2 *(fig = stage)* monter, mettre en scène *(fig)*

choreographer /ˌkɒrɪˈɒgrəfəʳ/ N chorégraphe *mf*

choreographic /ˌkɒrɪəʊˈgræfɪk/ ADJ chorégraphique

choreography /ˌkɒrɪˈɒgrəfɪ/ N chorégraphie *f*

chorister /ˈkɒrɪstəʳ/ N *(Rel)* choriste *mf*

chortle /ˈtʃɔːtl/ VI glousser ◆ **he was chortling over the newspaper** la lecture du journal le faisait glousser N gloussement *m*

chorus /ˈkɔːrəs/ N (pl **choruses**) 1 *(Mus, Theat = song, singers, speakers)* chœur *m* ◆ **in ~** en chœur ◆ **she's in the ~** *(at concert)* elle chante dans le chœur ; *(Theat)* elle fait partie de la troupe ◆ **a ~ of praise/objections** un concert de louanges/protestations 2 *(= part of song)* refrain *m* ◆ **to join in the ~** *[one person]* reprendre le refrain ; *[several people]* reprendre le refrain en chœur VT *[+ song]* chanter *or* réciter en chœur ; *[+ verse]* réciter en chœur ◆ **"yes," they ~ed** "oui" répondirent-ils en chœur

COMP **chorus girl** N *(Theat)* girl *f*

chorus line N *(Theat: in musical)* chœurs *mpl*

chose /tʃəʊz/ VB pt of **choose**

chosen /ˈtʃəʊzn/ VB (ptp of **choose**) → **choose** vt 1

chough /tʃʌf/ N crave *m* à bec rouge

choux /ʃuː/ N *(Culin:* also **choux pastry**) pâte *f* à choux

chow¹ /tʃaʊ/ N *(= dog)* chow-chow *m*

chow² ‡ /tʃaʊ/ N *(esp US = food)* bouffe ‡ *f*, boustifaille ‡ *f*

► **chow down** * VI *(esp US)* manger, bouffer * ◆ **to ~ down on sth** bouffer * qch

chowder /ˈtʃaʊdəʳ/ N soupe *f* épaisse de palourdes ; → **clam**

chow mein /tʃaʊˈmeɪn/ N chow mein *m*, nouilles *fpl* sautées

Chrimbo ‡ /ˈkrɪmbəʊ/ N *(Brit)* ⇒ **Christmas**

Chrissake(s) ‡ /ˈkraɪseɪk(s)/ N *(esp US)* ◆ **for ~(s)** nom de Dieu ‡

Christ /kraɪst/ N le Christ, Jésus-Christ EXCL ◆ **~ !** ‡ nom de Dieu ! ‡, Bon Dieu (de Bon Dieu) ! ‡ ◆ **~ (only) knows!** Dieu seul le sait ! *

COMP **the Christ Child** N l'enfant *m* Jésus

Christadelphian /ˌkrɪstəˈdelfɪən/ ADJ, N christadelphe *mf*

christen /ˈkrɪsn/ VT *(Rel, also Naut)* baptiser ; *(gen)* *(= name)* appeler, nommer ; *(= nickname)* surnommer ; *(= use for first time)* étrenner ◆ **to ~ sb after ...** donner à qn le nom de ... ◆ **he was ~ed Robert but everyone calls him Bob** son nom de baptême est Robert mais tout le monde l'appelle Bob

Christendom /ˈkrɪsndəm/ N chrétienté *f*

christening /ˈkrɪsnɪŋ/ N baptême *m* COMP **christening robe** N robe *f* de baptême

Christian /ˈkrɪstɪən/ ADJ *(lit)* chrétien ; *(fig)* charitable, compatissant ◆ **the ~ era** l'ère *f* chrétienne ◆ **early ~** paléochrétien N chrétien(ne) *m(f)* ◆ **to become a ~** se faire chrétien

COMP **Christian Democrat** N démocrate-chrétienne *m(f)*

Christian Democratic ADJ démocrate-chrétien

Christian name N prénom *m*, nom *m* de baptême ◆ **my ~ name is Julie** je m'appelle Julie, mon prénom est Julie

Christian Science N science *f* chrétienne

Christian Scientist N scientiste *mf* chrétien(ne)

christiania /ˌkrɪstɪˈɑːnɪə/ N *(Ski)* christiania *m*

Christianity /ˌkrɪstɪˈænɪtɪ/ N *(= faith, religion)* christianisme *m* ; *(= character)* caractère *m* *or* qualité *f* du chrétien ◆ **his ~ did not prevent him from ...** le fait d'être chrétien ne l'a pas empêché de ...

Christianize /ˈkrɪstɪənaɪz/ VT christianiser

christie /ˈkrɪstɪ/ N *(Ski)* christiania *m*

Christlike /ˈkraɪstlaɪk/ ADJ qui ressemble *or* semblable au Christ ◆ **he had a ~ forbearance** il avait une patience d'ange

Christmas /ˈkrɪsməs/ LANGUAGE IN USE 23.2
N Noël *m* ◆ **at ~** à Noël ◆ **the week before ~** la semaine précédant Noël ◆ **for ~** pour Noël ◆ **she spent ~ with us** elle a passé (la) Noël chez nous ◆ **it's as if ~ had come early!** *(fig)* c'est comme si c'était Noël ! ◆ **I thought all my ~es had come at once** pour moi c'était Noël avant l'heure !, c'est comme si tous mes vœux étaient exaucés ! ; → **father, happy, merry**
COMP *[visit, gift]* de Noël
Christmas box **N** *(Brit)* étrennes *fpl (offertes à Noël)*
Christmas cake **N** gâteau *m* de Noël *(gros cake décoré au sucre glace)*
Christmas card **N** carte *f* de Noël
Christmas carol **N** chant *m* de Noël, noël *m* ; *(Rel)* cantique *m* de Noël
Christmas Day **N** le jour de Noël
Christmas Eve **N** la veille de Noël
Christmas Island **N** l'île *f* Christmas
Christmas party **N** fête *f* de Noël
Christmas present **N** cadeau *m* de Noël
Christmas pudding **N** *(esp Brit)* (plum-) pudding *m (pudding traditionnel de Noël)*
Christmas rose **N** rose *f* de Noël
Christmas stocking **N** ◆ **I got it in my ~ stocking** ≈ je l'ai trouvé dans mon soulier *or* dans la cheminée *or* sous l'arbre (de Noël)
Christmas time **N** la période de Noël *or* des fêtes ◆ **at ~ time** à Noël
Christmas tree **N** arbre *m* de Noël

Christmassy * /ˈkrɪsməsɪ/ **ADJ** *[atmosphere]* de Noël ◆ **the town is looking very ~** la ville a un air de fête pour Noël

Christopher /ˈkrɪstəfəʳ/ **N** Christophe *m*

christy /ˈkrɪstɪ/ **N** *(Ski)* ⇒ **christie**

chromatic /krəˈmætɪk/ **ADJ** *(Art, Mus)* chromatique
COMP **chromatic printing** **N** impression *f* polychrome
chromatic scale **N** gamme *f* chromatique

chromatics /krəˈmætɪks/ **N** *(NonC)* science *f* des couleurs

chromatography /ˌkrəʊməˈtɒɡrəfɪ/ **N** chromatographie *f*

chrome /krəʊm/ **N** chrome *m*
COMP *[fittings etc]* chromé
chrome dioxide **N** dioxyde *m* de chrome
chrome lacquer **N** laque *f or* peinture *f* laquée (à base de chrome)
chrome steel **N** acier *m* chromé
chrome yellow **N** jaune *m* de chrome

chromium /ˈkrəʊmɪəm/ **N** chrome *m*
COMP **chromium-plated** **ADJ** chromé
chromium-plating **N** chromage *m*

chromosomal /ˌkrəʊməˈsəʊml/ **ADJ** *(Bio)* chromosomique

chromosome /ˈkrəʊməsəʊm/ **N** chromosome *m*

chronic /ˈkrɒnɪk/ **ADJ** ① *(= lasting, severe) [illness, depression, pain, problem, shortage, unemployment]* chronique ② *(= inveterate) [smoker, liar, alcoholism, alcoholic]* invétéré, incorrigible ; *[worrier, idealist]* incorrigible ③ *(Brit * = terrible) [film, singing, food]* nul ; *[weather]* dégueulasse*, pourri*
COMP **chronic fatigue syndrome** **N** syndrome *m* de fatigue chronique

chronically /ˈkrɒnɪkəlɪ/ **ADV** ① *(Med)* ◆ **to be ~ sick/depressed** souffrir de maladie/dépression chronique ◆ **the ~ ill** *or* **sick** les malades *mpl* chroniques ② *(= extremely) [tired, overworked, overloaded, underfunded]* terriblement ◆ **~ jealous** en proie à une jalousie chronique ◆ **~ overcrowded** (extrêmement) surpeuplé

chronicle /ˈkrɒnɪkl/ **N** chronique *f* ◆ **(the Book of) Chronicles** *(Bible)* le livre des Chroniques ◆ **a ~ of disasters** une succession de catastrophes **VT** faire la chronique de, enregistrer au jour le jour

chronicler /ˈkrɒnɪkləʳ/ **N** chroniqueur *m*

chronological /ˌkrɒnəˈlɒdʒɪkəl/ **ADJ** chronologique ◆ **~ age** âge *m* réel ◆ **in ~ order** par ordre chronologique

chronologically /ˌkrɒnəˈlɒdʒɪkəlɪ/ **ADV** chronologiquement

chronology /krəˈnɒlədʒɪ/ **N** chronologie *f*

chronometer /krəˈnɒmɪtəʳ/ **N** chronomètre *m*

chrysalis /ˈkrɪsəlɪs/ **N** (pl **chrysalises** /ˈkrɪsəlɪsɪz/) chrysalide *f*

chrysanthemum /krɪˈsænθəməm/, **chrysanth** * /krɪˈsænθ/ **N** chrysanthème *m*

chub /tʃʌb/ **N** (pl **chub** or **chubs**) chevesne *m*, chevaine *m*

Chubb lock ® /ˈtʃʌblɒk/ **N** *(Brit) serrure incrochetable*

chubby /ˈtʃʌbɪ/ **ADJ** *[person, arm]* potelé ◆ **~-cheeked, ~-faced** joufflu

chuck[1] /tʃʌk/ **VT** ① *(* = throw)* lancer, jeter ; *(in bin)* balancer* ② *(⁑ = give up) [+ job, hobby]* lâcher, laisser tomber* ; *[+ boyfriend, girlfriend]* plaquer⁑, laisser tomber* ◆ **~ it!** assez !, ça va !*, laisse tomber !* ③ ◆ **he ~ed her under the chin** il lui a caressé le menton **N** ① ◆ **to give sb a ~ under the chin** caresser le menton à qn ② ◆ **to give sb the ~** ⁑ balancer qn* ◆ **he got the ~** ⁑ *(from job)* il s'est fait virer* ◆ **she gave him the ~** ⁑ *(from relationship)* elle l'a plaqué*

► **chuck away** * **VT SEP** *(= throw out) [+ old clothes, books]* balancer* ; *(= waste) [+ money]* jeter par les fenêtres ; *[+ opportunity]* laisser passer

► **chuck in** ⁑ **VT SEP** *[+ job, hobby]* lâcher, laisser tomber *

► **chuck out** * **VT SEP** *[+ useless article, old clothes, books]* balancer* ; *[+ person]* vider*, sortir*

► **chuck up** ⁑ **VT SEP** ① *[+ job, hobby]* lâcher, laisser tomber* ② *(= vomit)* dégueuler⁑, vomir

chuck[2] /tʃʌk/ **N** *(= tool)* mandrin *m* **VT** *(= fix in a chuck)* fixer sur un mandrin

chuck[3] /tʃʌk/ **N** (also **chuck steak**) morceau *m* dans le paleron

chucker-out * /ˈtʃʌkərˈaʊt/ **N** *(Brit)* videur* *m*

chuckle /ˈtʃʌkl/ **N** gloussement *m*, petit rire *m* ◆ **we had a good ~ over it** ça nous a bien fait rire **VI** rire *(over, at* de*)*, glousser

chuffed ⁑ /tʃʌft/ **ADJ** *(Brit)* vachement⁑ content *(about* de*)* ; ◆ **he was quite ~ about it** il était vachement⁑ content

chug /tʃʌɡ/ **N** *[of machine]* souffle *m* ; *[of car, railway engine]* teuf-teuf *m* **VI** *[machine]* souffler ; *[car]* haleter, faire teuf-teuf

► **chug along** **VI** *[car, train]* avancer en haletant *or* en faisant teuf-teuf

chug-a-lug ⁑ /ˈtʃʌɡəlʌɡ/ **VT** *(US)* boire d'un trait

chukka, chukker /ˈtʃʌkəʳ/ **N** *(Polo)* période *f (de 7,5 minutes)*

chum †* /tʃʌm/ **N** copain* *m*, copine* *f* **VI** *(= share lodgings)* crécher ensemble⁑

► **chum up** * **VI** fraterniser *(with* avec*)*

chummy * /ˈtʃʌmɪ/ **ADJ** sociable, (très) liant ◆ **she is very ~ with him** elle est très copine avec lui*

chump /tʃʌmp/ **N** ① * *(= fool)* ballot* *m*, crétin(e)* *m(f)* ② *(⁑ = head)* citron* *m*, caboche* *f* ◆ **he's off his ~** il est timbré* *or* toqué*, il a perdu la boule* ③ *(Culin)* **~ chop** côte *f* de mouton

chunder ⁑ /ˈtʃʌndəʳ/ **VI** *(esp Austral)* dégueuler⁑

chunk /tʃʌŋk/ **N** *[of wood, metal, dough]* gros morceau *m* ; *[of bread]* quignon *m*

chunky /ˈtʃʌŋkɪ/ **ADJ** *[person]* trapu ; *[jumper, cardigan, shoes, jewellery]* gros (grosse *f*) ◆ **~ pieces of meat** de gros morceaux de viande

Chunnel * /ˈtʃʌnəl/ **N** (abbrev of **Channel Tunnel**) → **channel**

chunter * /ˈtʃʌntəʳ/ **VI** *(Brit)* (also **chunter on**) bougonner*

church /tʃɜːtʃ/ **N** ① *(= building)* église *f* ; *[of French Protestants]* église *f*, temple *m*
② *(NonC)* **to go to ~** *(for service, gen)* aller à l'église *f* ; *[Catholic]* aller à la messe ; *[Protestant]* aller au temple ◆ **he doesn't go to ~ any more** il ne va plus à l'église ◆ **to be in ~** être à l'église *or* à la messe ◆ **after ~** après l'office ; *(for Catholics)* après la messe
③ *(= whole body of Christians)* **the Church** l'Église *f* ◆ **the Church Militant** l'Église *f* militante
④ *(= denomination)* **the Church of England** l'Église *f* anglicane ◆ **the Church of Rome** l'Église *f* catholique ◆ **the Church of Scotland/Ireland** l'Église *f* d'Écosse/d'Irlande ; → **high**
⑤ *(= religious orders)* **Church** ordres *mpl* ◆ **he has gone into the Church** il est entré dans les ordres
VT *(Rel)* faire assister à une messe
COMP **Church Fathers** **NPL** Pères *mpl* de l'Église
church hall **N** salle *f* paroissiale
church owl **N** chouette *f* des clochers, effraie *f*
church school **N** *(Brit)* école *f* confessionnelle
church service **N** office *m*
church wedding **N** ◆ **they want a ~ wedding** ils veulent se marier à l'église

churchgoer /ˈtʃɜːtʃɡəʊəʳ/ **N** pratiquant(e) *m(f)*

Churchillian /tʃəˈtʃɪlɪən/ **ADJ** churchillien

churching /ˈtʃɜːtʃɪŋ/ **N** *(Rel)* ◆ **the ~ of women** la messe de relevailles

churchman /ˈtʃɜːtʃmən/ **N** (pl **-men**) *(= clergy)* ecclésiastique *m* ◆ **he is/is not a good ~** *(= churchgoer)* il est/n'est pas pratiquant

churchwarden /ˌtʃɜːtʃˈwɔːdn/ **N** ① *(= person)* bedeau *m*, marguillier *m* ② *(= pipe) longue pipe en terre*

churchy * /ˈtʃɜːtʃɪ/ **ADJ** *(pej) [person]* bigot ◆ **a ~ person** une grenouille de bénitier* *(pej)*

churchyard /ˈtʃɜːtʃjɑːd/ **N** cimetière *m (autour d'une église)*

churl /tʃɜːl/ **N** ① † *(= ill-mannered person)* rustre *m*, malotru *m* ; *(= bad-tempered person)* ronchon *m*, personne *f* revêche ② *(Hist)* manant † *m*

churlish /ˈtʃɜːlɪʃ/ **ADJ** *[person, behaviour] (= rude)* grossier ; *(= surly)* revêche ◆ **it would be ~ to complain** il serait malvenu de se plaindre

churlishly /ˈtʃɜːlɪʃlɪ/ **ADV** *[say, refuse] (= rudely)* grossièrement ; *(= surlily)* d'un ton revêche

churlishness /ˈtʃɜːlɪʃnɪs/ **N** *(= bad manners)* grossièreté *f* ; *(= bad temper)* mauvaise humeur *f*

churn /tʃɜːn/ **N** baratte *f* ; *(Brit = milk can)* bidon *m* **VT** ① *[+ butter]* baratter ② (also **churn up**) *[+ water]* faire bouillonner ◆ **to ~ sb up** * *(fig)* retourner* qn ③ *[+ engine]* faire tourner **VI** *[water, sea]* bouillonner ◆ **his stomach was ~ing** *(feeling sick)* il avait l'estomac barbouillé ; *(from nerves)* son cœur se serra

► **churn out** **VT SEP** *[+ objects]* débiter ; *[+ essays, letters, books]* produire à la chaîne, pondre en série*

► **churn up** **VT SEP** ⇒ **churn vt 2**

chute /ʃuːt/ **N** ① glissière *f* ; → **coal, refuse[2]** ② *(in river)* rapide *m* ③ * ⇒ **parachute** ④ *(Sport, for toboggans)* piste *f* ; *(Brit = children's slide)* toboggan *m*

chutney /ˈtʃʌtnɪ/ **N** condiment *m (à base de fruits)* ◆ **apple/tomato ~** condiment *m* à la pomme/à la tomate

chutzpa(h) ⁑ /ˈxʊtspə/ **N** *(US)* culot* *m*

chyme /kaɪm/ **N** chyme *m*

CI (abbrev of **Channel Islands**) → **channel**

CIA /ˌsiːaɪ'eɪ/ N (US) (abbrev of **Central Intelligence Agency**) CIA *f*

ciao /tʃaʊ/ INTERJ tchao !, salut ! *

cicada /sɪ'kɑːdə/ N (pl **cicadas** or **cicadae** /sɪ'kɑːdiː/) cigale *f*

cicatrix /'sɪkətrɪks/ (pl **cicatrices** /ˌsɪkə'traɪsiːz/) N *(Med)* cicatrice *f*

cicatrize /'sɪkəˌtraɪz/ VI *(Med)* (se) cicatriser

Cicero /'sɪsərəʊ/ N Cicéron *m*

cicerone /ˌtʃɪtʃə'rəʊnɪ/ N (pl **cicerones** or **ciceroni** /ˌtʃɪtʃə'rəʊnɪ/) cicérone *m*

Ciceronian /ˌsɪsə'rəʊnɪən/ ADJ cicéronien

CID /ˌsiːaɪ'diː/ ABBR *(Brit)* abbrev of **Criminal Investigation Department** ≃ PJ *f*, police *f* judiciaire
COMP *[operation, team etc]* de la PJ
CID man (pl **CID men**), **CID officer** N ≃ inspecteur *m* de police judiciaire *or* de la PJ

cider /'saɪdəʳ/ N cidre *m*
COMP **cider-apple** N pomme *f* à cidre
cider-press N pressoir *m* à cidre
cider vinegar N vinaigre *m* de cidre

CIF, c.i.f. /ˌsiːaɪ'ef/ (abbrev of **cost, insurance, freight**) CAF

cig * /sɪg/ N *(esp Brit)* ⇒ **ciggie**

cigar /sɪ'gɑːʳ/ N 1 cigare *m* 2 *(esp US)* ◆ **close but no ~ !** pas mal mais ce n'est pas ça *or* la bonne réponse !
COMP *[box etc]* à cigares
cigar case N étui *m* à cigares, porte-cigares *m inv*
cigar holder N fume-cigare *m inv*
cigar lighter N *(in car)* allume-cigare *m inv*
cigar-shaped ADJ en forme de cigare

cigarette /ˌsɪgə'ret/ N cigarette *f*
COMP *[box etc]* à cigarettes
cigarette ash N cendre *f* de cigarette
cigarette butt N ⇒ **cigarette end**
cigarette card N *carte avec des publicités ou des jeux, dans les paquets de cigarettes*
cigarette case N étui *m* à cigarettes, porte-cigarettes *m inv*
cigarette end N mégot *m*
cigarette holder N fume-cigarette *m inv*
cigarette lighter N *(gen)* briquet *m* ; *(in car)* allume-cigare *m inv*
cigarette machine N distributeur *m* de paquets de cigarettes
cigarette paper N papier *m* à cigarettes

ciggie *, **ciggy** * /'sɪgɪ/ N *(Brit)* clope * *f*, tige * *f*

ciliary /'sɪlɪərɪ/ ADJ ciliaire

CIM /ˌsiːaɪ'em/ N *(Comput)* (abbrev of **computer-integrated manufacturing**) FIO *f*

C.-in-C. (abbrev of **Commander-in-Chief**) → **commander**

cinch /sɪntʃ/ N 1 *(US = saddle girth)* sous-ventrière *f*, sangle *f* (de selle) 2 ◆ **it's a ~** ⁑ *(= certain)* c'est du tout cuit *, c'est du gâteau * ; *(= easy)* c'est l'enfance de l'art VT 1 *[+ horse]* sangler ; *[+ saddle]* attacher par une sangle (de selle) 2 *(fig) [+ success]* rendre sûr, assurer

cinder /'sɪndəʳ/ N cendre *f* ◆ **~s** *(= burnt coal)* cendres *fpl* (de charbon) ; *[of furnace, volcano]* scories *fpl* ◆ **to rake out the ~s** racler les cendres (du foyer) ◆ **burnt to a ~** réduit en cendres
COMP **cinder block** N *(US)* parpaing *m*
cinder track N (piste *f*) cendrée *f*

Cinderella /ˌsɪndə'relə/ N Cendrillon *f* ◆ **the ~ of sciences** la Cendrillon des sciences

Cinders * /'sɪndəz/ N *(= Cinderella)* Cendrillon *f*

cineaste /'sɪnɪæst/ N cinéphile *mf*

cine-camera /'sɪnɪˌkæmərə/ N *(Brit)* caméra *f*

cine-film /'sɪnɪfɪlm/ N *(Brit)* film *m*

cinema /'sɪnəmə/ *(esp Brit)* N cinéma *m* ◆ **to go to the ~** aller au cinéma
COMP **cinema complex** N complexe *m* or cinéma *m* multisalle(s)
cinema-going N fréquentation *f* des cinémas ADJ ◆ **the ~-going public** le public qui fréquente les cinémas

cinemagoer /'sɪnəməˌgəʊəʳ/ N *(gen) personne qui fréquente les cinémas* ; *(= film enthusiast)* cinéphile *mf*

Cinemascope ® /'sɪnəməskəʊp/ N cinémascope ® *m*

cinematic /ˌsɪnɪ'mætɪk/ ADJ filmique

cinematograph /ˌsɪnɪ'mætəgrɑːf/ N *(Brit)* cinématographe *m*

cinematographer /ˌsɪnɪmə'tɒgrəfəʳ/ N directeur *m* de la photo

cinematography /ˌsɪnɪmə'tɒgrəfɪ/ N cinématographie *f*

cine projector /'sɪnɪprəˌdʒektəʳ/ N *(Brit)* projecteur *m* de cinéma

Cinerama ® /ˌsɪnə'rɑːmə/ N Cinérama ® *m*

cinerary /'sɪnərərɪ/ ADJ cinéraire

cinnabar /'sɪnəbɑːʳ/ N cinabre *m*

cinnamon /'sɪnəmən/ N cannelle *f* COMP *[cake, biscuit]* à la cannelle ; *(in colour)* cannelle *inv*

Cinque /sɪŋk/ ADJ *(Brit Hist)* ◆ **the ~ Ports** les Cinq Ports *mpl (ancienne confédération des cinq ports du Kent et du Sussex)*

cipher /'saɪfəʳ/ N 1 *(= secret writing)* chiffre *m*, code *m* secret ◆ **in ~** en chiffre, en code 2 *(= message)* message *m* chiffré *or* codé 3 *(= Arabic numeral)* chiffre *m (arabe)* ; *(= zero)* zéro *m* ◆ **he's a mere ~** ce n'est qu'un chiffre 4 *(= monogram)* chiffre *m*, monogramme *m* VT *[+ calculations, communications]* chiffrer

circa /'sɜːkə/ PREP circa, vers

circadian /sɜː'keɪdɪən/ ADJ circadien

circle /'sɜːkl/ N 1 *(= shape)* cercle *m* ; *[of hills, houses, vehicles]* cercle *m* ; *[of mountains]* cirque *m* ; *(Gym)* soleil *m* ; *(Astron = orbit)* orbite *f* ◆ **to stand in a ~** faire (un) cercle, se tenir en cercle ◆ **to draw a ~** tracer un cercle ◆ **to have ~s around** *or* **under one's eyes** avoir des cernes ◆ **to come full ~** revenir à son point de départ ◆ **they were going** *or* **running round in ~s** *(fig)* ils tournaient en rond ; → **wheel**
2 *(= group of persons)* cercle *m*, groupe *m* ◆ **a close ~ of friends** un cercle d'amis proches ◆ **an inner ~ of advisers** un groupe de proches conseillers ◆ **in political/financial ~s** dans les milieux *mpl* politiques/financiers ◆ **in some ~s** dans certains milieux
3 *(Brit Theat)* balcon *m*
VT 1 *(= go round outside of sth)* contourner ; *(= keep moving round sth)* tourner autour de ; *(liter = encircle)* entourer, encercler
2 *(= draw circle round)* entourer
VI *[birds]* faire *or* décrire des cercles ; *[aircraft]* tourner (en rond) ◆ **the cyclists ~d round him** les cyclistes ont tourné autour de lui
► **circle about, circle (a)round** VI faire *or* décrire des cercles, tourner

circlet /'sɜːklɪt/ N petit cercle *m* ; *[of hair]* bandeau *m* ; *[of arm]* brassard *m* ; *[of finger]* anneau *m*

circuit /'sɜːkɪt/ N 1 *(= lap)* tour *m*, circuit *m* ◆ **to make a ~ of a room/a garden** faire le tour d'une pièce/d'un jardin ◆ **I did several ~s of the area to find a parking space** j'ai dû faire le tour du quartier plusieurs fois pour *or* avant de trouver une place où me garer
2 *(Cine, Theat: houses visited by same company)* tournée *f* ; *(houses owned by same owner)* groupe *m*
3 *(Sport = series of races, matches etc)* circuit *m* ◆ **the tennis ~** le circuit du tennis ◆ **the Scottish cathedrals ~** *(Tourism)* le circuit des cathédrales d'Écosse
4 *(Elec)* circuit *m* ; → **closed, short**
5 *(esp Brit Sport = track)* circuit *m*, parcours *m* ; *(Athletics)* piste *f* ◆ **ten laps of the ~** *(Racing)* dix tours du circuit ; *(Athletics)* dix tours de la piste
6 *(Brit Jur) (= journey)* tournée *f (des juges d'assises)* ; *(= district)* circonscription *f* (judiciaire) ◆ **he is on the eastern ~** il fait la tournée de l'est
COMP **circuit board** N *(Comput)* circuit *m* imprimé
circuit breaker N *(Elec)* disjoncteur *m*
circuit court N *(Jur)* tribunal *m* itinérant
circuit judge N *(Jur)* juge *m(f)* itinérant(e)
circuit training N *(Sport)* entraînement *m (selon un programme préétabli)*

circuitous /sɜː'kjʊɪtəs/ ADJ *[route, road]* tortueux ; *[journey]* plein de détours ; *[means]* détourné ; *[method]* indirect, détourné

circuitously /sɜː'kjʊɪtəslɪ/ ADV *(lit) [approach, reach]* en faisant des détours ; *(fig) [speak]* de façon contournée

circuitry /'sɜːkɪtrɪ/ N *(Elec)* circuits *mpl*

circular /'sɜːkjʊləʳ/ ADJ *[outline, saw, ticket]* circulaire ◆ **~ tour** voyage *m* circulaire, circuit *m* N *(= printed advertisement etc)* prospectus *m* ; (also **circular letter**) circulaire *f*

circularity /ˌsɜːkjʊ'lærɪtɪ/ N circularité *f*

circularize /'sɜːkjʊləraɪz/ VT *[+ person, firm]* envoyer des circulaires *or* des prospectus à

circulate /'sɜːkjʊleɪt/ VI *(gen)* circuler ; *(at party etc)* se mêler aux invités *or* à la fête VT *[+ object, bottle]* faire circuler ; *[+ news, rumour]* propager ; *[+ document] (from person to person)* faire circuler ; *(= send out)* diffuser
COMP **circulating decimal** N *(Math)* fraction *f* périodique
circulating library N bibliobus *m*
circulating medium N monnaie *f* d'échange

circulation /ˌsɜːkjʊ'leɪʃən/ N *(NonC) (Anat, Bot, Fin, Med)* circulation *f* ; *[of news, rumour]* propagation *f* ; *[of newspaper etc]* tirage *m* ◆ **a magazine with a ~ of 10,000** un magazine qui tire à 10 000 exemplaires ◆ **he has poor ~** *(Med)* il a une mauvaise circulation ◆ **in ~** *(Fin)* en circulation ◆ **to put into ~** *(Fin)* mettre en circulation ◆ **to take out of** *or* **withdraw from ~** *(Fin)* retirer de la circulation ◆ **he's now back in ~** * il est à nouveau dans le circuit * ◆ **to be out of ~** * *[person]* avoir disparu de la circulation * ; → **drop out** COMP **circulation manager** N *(Press)* directeur *m* du service de la diffusion

circulatory /ˌsɜːkjʊ'leɪtərɪ/ ADJ circulatoire

circumcise /'sɜːkəmsaɪz/ VT *[+ male]* circoncire ; *[+ female]* exciser

circumcision /ˌsɜːkəm'sɪʒən/ N *[of male]* circoncision *f* ; *[of female]* excision *f* ◆ **the Circumcision** *(Rel)* (la fête de) la Circoncision

circumference /sə'kʌmfərəns/ N circonférence *f*

circumflex /'sɜːkəmfleks/ ADJ circonflexe N accent *m* circonflexe

circumlocution /ˌsɜːkəmlə'kjuːʃən/ N circonlocution *f*

circumlunar /ˌsɜːkəm'luːnəʳ/ ADJ autour de la lune ◆ **~ flight** vol *m* autour de la lune

circumnavigate /ˌsɜːkəm'nævɪgeɪt/ VT *[+ cape]* doubler, contourner ◆ **to ~ the globe** faire le tour du monde en bateau

circumnavigation /'sɜːkəmˌnævɪ'geɪʃən/ N circumnavigation *f*

circumscribe /'sɜːkəmskraɪb/ VT *(gen)* circonscrire ; *[+ powers]* limiter

circumspect /'sɜːkəmspekt/ ADJ circonspect *(about sth* à l'égard de qch *or* sur qch) ; ◆ **to be ~ in one's behaviour** faire preuve de circonspection ◆ **to be ~ in one's language** s'exprimer avec circonspection

circumspection /ˌsɜːkəm'spekʃən/ N circonspection *f*

circumspectly /ˈsɜːkəmspektlɪ/ ADV avec circonspection

circumstance /ˈsɜːkəmstəns/ N 1 circonstance *f* ; *(= fact, detail)* circonstance *f*, détail *m* ◆ **in** *or* **under the present ~s** dans les circonstances actuelles, vu l'état des choses ◆ **in** *or* **under no ~s** en aucun cas *or* en aucune circonstance ◆ **under similar ~s** en pareil cas, en *or* dans de pareilles circonstances ◆ **to take the ~s into account** tenir compte des circonstances ◆ **a victim of ~** une victime des circonstances ; → **attenuate, extenuate, pomp**
2 *(= financial condition)* **~s** situation *f* financière *or* pécuniaire ◆ **in easy ~s** dans l'aisance, à l'aise ◆ **in poor ~s** gêné, dans la gêne ◆ **what are his ~s?** quelle est sa situation financière *or* pécuniaire ? ◆ **if our ~s allow it** si nos moyens nous le permettent

circumstantial /ˌsɜːkəmˈstænʃəl/ ADJ 1 *(Jur)* *[case]* fondé sur des présomptions ◆ **~ evidence** présomptions *fpl*, preuves *fpl* indirectes ◆ **much of the evidence is ~** il s'agit surtout de présomptions 2 *(= detailed) [account, report, description]* détaillé, circonstancié 3 *(= anecdotal) [reasons, factors, detail]* anecdotique

circumstantiate /ˌsɜːkəmˈstænʃɪeɪt/ VT *(frm)* *[+ evidence]* confirmer en donnant des détails sur ; *[+ event]* donner des détails circonstanciés sur

circumvent /ˌsɜːkəmˈvent/ VT *[+ person]* circonvenir ; *[+ law, regulations, rule]* tourner ; *[+ sb's plan, project]* faire échouer

circumvention /ˌsɜːkəmˈvenʃən/ N *[of plan, project]* mise *f* en échec ◆ **the ~ of the guard/rule proved easy** circonvenir le garde/tourner le règlement s'avéra facile

circus /ˈsɜːkəs/ N (pl **circuses**) 1 *(Hist, Theat)* cirque *m* 2 *(in town)* rond-point *m* COMP *[animal, clown]* de cirque

cirrhosis /sɪˈrəʊsɪs/ N cirrhose *f*

cirrus /ˈsɪrəs/ N (pl **cirri** /ˈsɪraɪ/) 1 *(= cloud)* cirrus *m* 2 *(Bot)* vrille *f*

CIS /ˌsiːaɪˈes/ N (abbrev of **Commonwealth of Independent States**) CEI *f*

cissy /ˈsɪsɪ/ N ⇒ **sissy**

Cistercian /sɪsˈtɜːʃən/ N cistercien(ne) *m(f)* ADJ cistercien ◆ **~ Order** ordre *m* de Cîteaux ◆ **a ~ monk** un cistercien

cistern /ˈsɪstən/ N citerne *f* ; *[of lavatory]* réservoir *m* de la chasse d'eau ; *[of barometer]* cuvette *f*

citadel /ˈsɪtədl/ N citadelle *f*

citation /saɪˈteɪʃən/ N *(gen, US Jur, Mil)* citation *f*

cite /saɪt/ VT *(gen, Jur, Mil)* citer ; *(Sport = sanction)* sanctionner ◆ **to ~ as an example** citer en exemple ◆ **to ~ sb to appear** *(Jur)* citer qn ; → **dispatch**

citified /ˈsɪtɪˌfaɪd/ ADJ *(pej)* qui a pris les manières de la ville

citizen /ˈsɪtɪzn/ N *[of town]* habitant(e) *m(f)* ; *[of state]* citoyen(ne) *m(f)* ; *(Admin)* ressortissant(e) *m(f)* ; *(Hist)* bourgeois(e) *m(f)* ; *(= townsman)* citadin(e) *m(f)* ◆ **the ~s of Paris** les habitants *mpl* de Paris, les Parisiens *mpl* ◆ **French ~** citoyen(ne) *m(f)* français(e) ; *(when abroad)* ressortissant *m* français ◆ **~ of the world** citoyen *m* du monde ; → **fellow**
COMP **Citizens' Advice Bureau** N centre *m* d'information sur les droits des citoyens
citizen's arrest N *arrestation effectuée par un simple citoyen conformément au droit coutumier* ◆ **to make a ~'s arrest** *effectuer une arrestation, en tant que particulier, conformément au droit coutumier*
Citizen's Band Radio N CB *f*, bande *f* de fréquences publique
Citizen's Charter N *(Brit)* *charte mise en place par le gouvernement britannique en 1991 et visant à améliorer la qualité des services publics*

CITIZENS' ADVICE BUREAU

Les **Citizens' Advice Bureaux** ont été créés en 1939 pour diffuser auprès de la population britannique la réglementation applicable en temps de guerre. Transformés par la suite en organismes d'assistance gratuite, ils dispensent des conseils sur tout problème concernant l'endettement des ménages, le logement, l'assurance maladie, les services sociaux ou les droits du consommateur. Le service, financé par des fonds publics, emploie dans ses nombreuses antennes locales des cadres salariés qui forment et gèrent un volant de personnels bénévoles.

citizenry /ˈsɪtɪznrɪ/ N *(esp US)* ◆ **the ~** l'ensemble *m* des citoyens

citizenship /ˈsɪtɪznʃɪp/ N citoyenneté *f* ◆ **~ papers** *(US)* déclaration *f* de naturalisation

citrate /ˈsɪtreɪt/ N citrate *m*

citric /ˈsɪtrɪk/ ADJ citrique COMP **citric acid** N acide *m* citrique

citron /ˈsɪtrən/ N *(= fruit)* cédrat *m* ; *(= tree)* cédratier *m*

citronella /ˌsɪtrəˈnelə/ N *(= grass)* citronnelle *f* ; *(= oil)* (huile *f* de) citronnelle *f*

citrus /ˈsɪtrəs/ N (pl **citruses**) *(= tree)* citrus *m* ; *(= fruit)* agrume *m*

city /ˈsɪtɪ/ N 1 *(gen)* (grande) ville *f* ◆ **the ~** *(= population)* la ville ◆ **large cities like Leeds** les grandes villes comme Leeds ◆ **life in the modern ~** la vie dans les villes modernes
2 *(Brit)* **the City** la City *(centre financier à Londres)* ◆ **he's (something) in the City*** il travaille dans la City
COMP *[streets]* de la ville ; *[offices, authorities]* municipal ; *(Brit Press) [editor, page, news]* financier
City and Guilds (examination) N *(Brit)* certificat *m* d'aptitude professionnelle
city centre N centre *m* de la ville, centre-ville *m*
city college N *(US Univ)* université *f (financée par la ville)*
city councilman N *(US)* (pl **city councilmen**) conseiller *m* municipal
city desk N *(Brit)* antenne *f* financière ; *(US)* antenne *f* locale
city dweller N citadin(e) *m(f)*
city editor N *(Brit)* responsable *mf* de la rubrique financière *(dans un journal)* ; *(US)* rédacteur *m* en chef (pour les nouvelles locales)
city fathers NPL édiles *mpl*
city hall N *(lit)* mairie *f* ; *(in large towns)* hôtel *m* de ville ; *(US fig = city authorities)* administration *f* municipale
city manager N *(US)* administrateur *m* communal *(payé par une municipalité et faisant fonction de maire)*
city planner N *(US)* urbaniste *mf*
city planning N *(US)* urbanisme *m*
city police N *(US)* police *f* municipale
city slicker* N citadin(e) *m(f)* sophistiqué(e)
city-state N cité *f*
city technology college N *(Brit)* établissement *m* d'enseignement technologique

CITY NICKNAMES

Si l'on sait que « The Big Apple » désigne la ville de New York (« apple » est en réalité un terme d'argot signifiant « grande ville »), on connaît moins les surnoms donnés aux autres grandes villes américaines. Chicago est surnommée « Windy City » à cause des rafales soufflant du lac Michigan. La Nouvelle-Orléans doit son sobriquet de « Big Easy » à son style de vie décontracté, et l'industrie automobile a donné à Detroit son surnom de « Motown ».
D'autres villes sont familièrement désignées par leurs initiales : « LA » pour Los Angeles, « Big D » pour Dallas, ou par des diminutifs : « Vegas » pour Las Vegas, « Frisco » pour San Francisco, « Philly » pour Philadelphie.

cityfied /ˈsɪtɪˌfaɪd/ ADJ *(pej)* ⇒ **citified**

cityscape /ˈsɪtɪskeɪp/ N paysage *m or* panorama *m* urbain

civet /ˈsɪvɪt/ N *(= animal, substance)* civette *f*

civic /ˈsɪvɪk/ ADJ *[pride, duty, rights, movement]* civique ; *[authorities, administration, building]* municipal ; *[life]* des citoyens ◆ **~ event/reception** cérémonie *f*/réception *f* officielle locale ◆ **~ leader** notable *m*
COMP **civic centre** N *(Brit)* centre *m* administratif (municipal)
civic hall N salle *f* municipale
civic society N *(= local organization)* association *f* culturelle *(organisant des manifestations à caractère régional)* ; *(= civilized values)* valeurs *fpl* civiques

civics /ˈsɪvɪks/ N instruction *f* civique

civies* /ˈsɪvɪz/ NPL *(US)* ⇒ **civvies** ; → **civvy**

civil /ˈsɪvl/ ADJ 1 *(= civic or non-military)* civil ◆ **~ commotion** émeute *f* ◆ **~ divorce** *divorce non reconnu par l'église* ◆ **~ marriage** mariage *m* civil ◆ **~ wedding** mariage *m* civil ◆ **to have a ~ wedding** se marier civilement
2 *(= polite)* civil, poli ◆ **that's very ~ of you** vous êtes bien aimable ; → **tongue**
COMP **Civil Aviation Authority** N *(Brit)* ≃ Direction *f* générale de l'aviation civile
civil defence N défense *f* passive
civil disobedience N désobéissance *f* civile ◆ **~ disobedience campaign** campagne *f* de désobéissance civile
civil engineer N ingénieur *m* civil
civil engineering N génie *m* civil
civil law N *(= system)* code *m* civil ; *(= study)* droit *m* civil
civil liberties NPL libertés *fpl* civiques
civil list N *(Brit)* liste *f* civile *(allouée à la famille royale)*
civil rights NPL droits *mpl* civils ◆ **~ rights activist** *or* **campaigner** militant(e) *m(f)* pour les droits civils ◆ **~ rights group** groupe *m* d'action pour les droits civils ◆ **~ rights leader** chef *m* de file du mouvement pour les droits civils ◆ **~ rights movement** mouvement *m* pour les droits civils
civil servant N fonctionnaire *mf*
civil service N fonction *f* publique administration *f* ◆ **~ service examination** concours *m* d'entrée dans la fonction publique ◆ **~ service recruitment** recrutement *m* de(s) fonctionnaires
Civil Service Commission N commission *f* de recrutement dans la fonction publique
civil war N guerre *f* civile ◆ **the (American) Civil War** la guerre de Sécession ; see also **Spanish**

civilian /sɪˈvɪlɪən/ N civil(e) *m(f)* *(opposé à militaire)* ADJ civil

civility /sɪˈvɪlɪtɪ/ N courtoisie *f*, civilité † *f* ◆ **civilities** civilités *fpl*

civilization /ˌsɪvɪlaɪˈzeɪʃən/ N civilisation *f*

civilize /ˈsɪvɪlaɪz/ VT civiliser

civilized /ˈsɪvɪlaɪzd/ ADJ 1 *(= socially advanced) [society, country, world, people]* civilisé ; *[values]* de civilisation ◆ **to become ~** se civiliser 2 *(= refined) [person, behaviour, conversation, place, meal]* raffiné ; *[time of day]* (tout à fait) convenable ◆ **I know we disagree, but we could at least be ~ about it** je sais que nous ne sommes pas d'accord, mais nous pourrions au moins essayer de rester aimables

civilizing /ˈsɪvɪlaɪzɪŋ/ ADJ civilisateur (-trice *f*)

civilly /ˈsɪvɪlɪ/ ADV poliment

civism /ˈsɪvɪzəm/ N civisme *m*

civvy* /'sɪvɪ/ (abbrev of **civilian**) NPL **civvies** vêtements *mpl* civils ◆ **in civvies** (habillé) en civil *or* en bourgeois* COMP **civvy street** N (*Brit*) vie *f* civile ◆ **to be in ~ street** être civil *or* pékin*

CJD /,siːdʒeɪ'diː/ N (abbrev of **Creutzfeldt-Jakob disease**) MCJ *f* ◆ **(new) variant ~** (nouvelle) variante de MCJ

cl (abbrev of **centilitre(s)**) cl

clack /klæk/ N claquement *m* ; [*of pump etc*] clapet *m* ; (*fig = talk*) jacasserie *f*, caquet *m* VI claquer ; (*fig*) jacasser ◆ **this will set tongues ~ing** cela va faire jaser

clad /klæd/ ADJ habillé, vêtu (*in* de) ; ◆ **~ with** (*liter = covered with*) revêtu de

cladding /'klædɪŋ/ N [*of building*] habillage *m*, revêtement *m* ; [*of nuclear reactor*] gainage *m* ◆ **timber** *or* **wood(en)** ~ bardage *m*

claim /kleɪm/ LANGUAGE IN USE 26.2

VT 1 (*= demand*) réclamer (*from sb* à qn) ; [*+ right, privilege*] revendiquer ; [*+ sb's attention*] demander, solliciter ◆ **to ~ diplomatic immunity** invoquer l'immunité diplomatique ◆ **to ~ the right to decide** revendiquer le droit de décider ◆ **the group which ~ed responsibility for the attack** le groupe qui a revendiqué l'attentat ◆ **no one has yet ~ed responsibility for the explosion** l'explosion n'a pas encore été revendiquée ◆ **to ~ damages** réclamer des dommages et intérêts ◆ **an avalanche has ~ed the lives of three skiers** une avalanche a coûté la vie à trois skieurs, trois skieurs ont trouvé la mort dans une avalanche ◆ **heart disease ~s thousands of lives** *or* **victims a year** les maladies cardiovasculaires font des milliers de victimes par an ◆ **to ~ a title** (*Sport*) remporter un titre ; → **credit**

2 (*= profess*) prétendre, déclarer ◆ **to ~ acquaintance with sb** prétendre connaître qn ◆ **they ~ a 100% success rate** ils déclarent que le taux de réussite est de 100% ◆ **he ~s to have seen you** *or* **(that) he's seen you** il prétend *or* déclare vous avoir vu, il déclare qu'il vous a vu ◆ **both armies ~ed the victory** les deux armées ont revendiqué la victoire

VI faire une demande d'indemnité ◆ **to ~ on (the** *or* **one's) insurance** faire jouer son assurance ◆ **to ~ for damages** demander des dommages-intérêts

N 1 (*= act of claiming*) revendication *f*, réclamation *f* ◆ **to lay ~ to** prétendre à, avoir des prétentions à ◆ **there are many ~s on my time** je suis très pris ◆ **there are many ~s on my purse** j'ai beaucoup de frais, mes moyens sont fortement mis à contribution ◆ **that's a big ~ to make!** la *or* cette prétention est de taille ! ◆ **his ~ that he acted legally** son affirmation selon laquelle il aurait agi dans les limites de la loi

2 (*= formal application*) (*Insurance*) ≈ déclaration *f* de sinistre, demande *f* d'indemnité ; (*Social Security*) demande *f* de prestations sociales ◆ **the ~s were all paid** (*Insurance*) les dommages ont été intégralement payés *or* réglés ◆ **to put in a ~** (*gen*) faire une réclamation ; (*Insurance*) faire une déclaration de sinistre *or* une demande d'indemnité ◆ **they put in a ~ for a 3% pay rise** ils ont demandé une augmentation de 3% ◆ **a ~ for an extra 3%** une demande d'augmentation de 3% ◆ **benefit ~** demande *f* de prestations sociales ; → **outstanding, wage**

3 (*= right*) droit *m*, titre *m* ◆ **~ to ownership** titre *m* de propriété ◆ **he renounced his ~ to the throne** il a renoncé à toute prétention à la couronne *or* à faire valoir ses droits à la couronne ◆ **~s to** *or* **on sb's friendship** droits *mpl* à l'amitié de qn ◆ **its only ~ to fame is ...** son seul titre de gloire est ... ◆ **what is his particular ~ to fame?** à quel titre est-il connu ? ◆ **he is a busy man, with many ~s on his time** c'est un homme très occupé, dont l'emploi du temps est très chargé

4 (*Min etc*) concession *f* ; → **stake**

COMP **claim form** N (*Admin*) (*for benefit*) (formulaire *m* de) demande *f* ; (*for expenses*) (feuille *f* pour) note *f* de frais

claims adjuster N (*Insurance*) agent *m* général d'assurances

claimant /'kleɪmənt/ N (*Brit*) [*of social benefits*] demandeur *m*, -euse *f* ; (*Jur, Insurance*) requérant(e) *m(f)* ; [*of throne*] prétendant(e) *m(f)* (*to* à) ; ◆ **benefit ~** demandeur *m* (-euse *f*) de prestations sociales

clairvoyance /klɛə'vɔɪəns/ N voyance *f*, (don *m* de) double vue *f*

clairvoyant(e) /klɛə'vɔɪənt/ N voyant(e) *m(f)*, extralucide *mf* ADJ doué de double vue

clam /klæm/ N 1 (*= shellfish*) palourde *f*, clam *m* 2 (*US* ‡) dollar *m* COMP **clam chowder** N (*Culin*) soupe *f* de palourdes

► **clam up*** VI la boucler‡, la fermer‡ ◆ **to ~ up like an oyster** se fermer comme une huître ◆ **he ~med up on me** il l'a bouclée‡, il ne m'a plus dit un mot là-dessus

clambake /'klæmbeɪk/ N (*US*) 1 (*Culin*) barbecue *m* de fruits de mer 2 (*= party*) réunion *f* à la bonne franquette

clamber /'klæmbəʳ/ VI grimper (*en s'aidant des mains ou en rampant*), se hisser (avec difficulté) ◆ **to ~ up a hill** gravir péniblement une colline ◆ **to ~ over a wall** escalader un mur N escalade *f*

clammy /'klæmɪ/ ADJ [*skin, hands, handshake, clothes, sheets*] moite ; [*weather*] lourd ◆ **~ with sweat/fear** moite de sueur/peur

clamor /'klæməʳ/ (*US*) ⇒ **clamour**

clamorous /'klæmərəs/ ADJ 1 (*= noisy*) [*voice, noise*] tonitruant ; [*crowd*] bruyant ◆ **~ applause** tonnerre *m* d'applaudissements 2 (*= vehement*) [*demand, campaign*] véhément

clamour, clamor (*US*) /'klæməʳ/ N (*= shouts*) clameur *f*, cris *mpl* ; (*= angry cries*) vociférations *fpl* ; (*= demands*) revendications *fpl or* réclamations *fpl* bruyantes VI pousser des cris ◆ **to ~ against sth/sb** vociférer contre qch/qn ◆ **to ~ for sth/sb** (*= shout*) demander qch/qn à grands cris ; (*= demand*) réclamer qch/qn à cor et à cri

clamp¹ /klæmp/ N (*gen*) attache *f*, pince *f* ; (*bigger*) crampon *m* ; (*Med*) clamp *m* ; (also **ring clamp**) collier *m* de serrage ; (*Carpentry*) valet *m* (d'établi) ; (*Archit*) agrafe *f* ; [*of china*] agrafe *f* ; (*for parked car*) sabot *m* de Denver ; (*Elec*) serre-fils *m inv* ; (*Naut*) serre-câbles *m inv* VT 1 (*= put clamp on*) serrer, attacher ; [*+ stones, china*] agrafer ; [*+ wheel, car*] mettre un sabot à ◆ **to ~ sth to sth** fixer qch à qch 2 ◆ **to ~ shut** *or* **together** [*+ teeth*] serrer 3 * [*+ embargo, curfew*] imposer (*on* sur)

► **clamp down on*** VT FUS [*+ person*] prendre des mesures autoritaires contre ; [*+ inflation, expenditure*] mettre un frein à ; [*+ the press, the opposition*] bâillonner N ◆ **clampdown** → **clampdown**

► **clamp together** VT SEP serrer ensemble

clamp² /klæmp/ N [*of bricks*] tas *m*, pile *f* ; [*of potatoes*] silo *m* VT entasser

clampdown /'klæmpdaʊn/ N (*gen*) répression *f* (*on sth* de qch ; *on sb* contre qn) ; ◆ **a ~ on terrorists** la répression *or* des mesures répressives contre les terroristes ◆ **a ~ on arms sales** un renforcement des restrictions sur la vente d'armes

clan /klæn/ N clan *m* (écossais) ; (*fig*) famille *f*

clandestine /klæn'destɪn/ ADJ clandestin

clang /klæŋ/ N bruit *m or* son *m* métallique ; (*louder*) fracas *m* métallique VI émettre un son métallique ◆ **the gate ~ed shut** la grille s'est refermée bruyamment *or* avec un bruit métallique

clanger* /'klæŋəʳ/ N (*Brit*) gaffe *f* ◆ **to drop a ~** faire une gaffe, gaffer lourdement

clangor /'klæŋgəʳ/ N (*US*) ⇒ **clangour**

clangorous /'klæŋgərəs/ ADJ [*noise*] métallique

clangour, clangor (*US*) /'klæŋgəʳ/ N vacarme *m* ; (*metallic*) son *m or* bruit *m* métallique

clank /klæŋk/ N cliquetis *m*, bruit *m* métallique (*de chaînes etc*) VI cliqueter, émettre un son métallique VT faire cliqueter

clannish /'klænɪʃ/ ADJ (*slightly pej = exclusive, unwelcoming*) [*group*] fermé ; [*person*] qui a l'esprit de clan *or* de clique

clansman /'klænzmən/ (pl **-men**), **clanswoman** /'klænz,wʊmən/ (pl **-women**) N (*in Scotland*) membre *m* d'un clan (écossais)

clap¹ /klæp/ N (*= sound*) claquement *m*, bruit *m* sec ; [*of hands*] battement *m* ; (*= action*) tape *f* ; (*= applause*) applaudissements *mpl* ◆ **a ~ on the back** une tape dans le dos ◆ **to give the dog a ~** (*Scot = stroke*) caresser le chien ◆ **a ~ of thunder** un coup de tonnerre ◆ **he got a good ~** il a été très applaudi

VT 1 (*= applaud*) applaudir ◆ **to ~ one's hands** battre des mains ◆ **to ~ sb on the back/the shoulder** donner à qn une tape dans le dos/sur l'épaule ◆ **to ~ a dog** (*Scot = stroke*) caresser un chien ◆ **he ~ped his hand over my mouth** il a mis *or* plaqué sa main sur ma bouche

2 (*= put, set*) ◆ **to ~ sb in irons** jeter qn aux fers ◆ **to ~ sb into prison** jeter qn en prison ◆ **to ~ eyes on** voir ◆ **to ~ hands on sb** prendre qn sur le fait

VI taper *or* frapper dans ses mains ; (*= applaud*) applaudir

► **clap on** VT SEP ◆ **to clap on one's hat** enfoncer son chapeau sur sa tête ◆ **to ~ on sail** (*Naut*) mettre toutes voiles dehors

► **clap to** VTI claquer

clap²*‡ /klæp/ N (*= disease*) ◆ **the ~** la chtouille‡, la chaude-pisse‡

clapboard /'klæpbɔːd/ N bardeau *m*

clapped-out‡ /'klæptaʊt/ ADJ (*Brit*) [*person, horse*] au bout du rouleau* ; [*car, train*] pourri* ; [*TV, washing machine*] fichu*, nase*

clapper /'klæpəʳ/ N [*of bell*] battant *m* ◆ **to go like the ~s‡** (*Brit*) aller à toute blinde‡

clapperboard /'klæpə,bɔːd/ N clap *m*, claquette *f*

clapping /'klæpɪŋ/ N applaudissements *mpl*

claptrap* /'klæptræp/ N boniment* *m*, baratin* *m*

claque /klæk/ N (*Theat*) claque *f*

Clare /klɛəʳ/ N Claire *f* ◆ **the Poor ~s** (*Rel*) clarisses *fpl*, Pauvres Dames *fpl*

claret /'klærət/ N (vin *m* de) bordeaux *m* (rouge) ADJ (also **claret-coloured**) bordeaux *inv*

clarification /,klærɪfɪ'keɪʃən/ N (*gen*) clarification *f*, éclaircissement *m* ; [*of wine*] collage *m* ◆ **request for ~** (*Jur*) demande *f* d'éclaircissement

clarified /'klærɪfaɪd/ ADJ [*butter, stock, wine, sugar*] clarifié

clarify /'klærɪfaɪ/ VT [*+ sugar, butter, wine*] clarifier ; (*fig*) [*+ situation*] éclaircir, clarifier VI se clarifier ; (*fig*) s'éclaircir

clarinet /,klærɪ'net/ N clarinette *f*

clarinettist /,klærɪ'netɪst/ N clarinettiste *mf*

clarion /'klærɪən/ (*liter*) N clairon *m* VT (*frm*) ◆ **to ~ (forth)** claironner COMP **clarion call** N appel *m* de clairon

clarity /'klærɪtɪ/ N clarté *f*, précision *f* ◆ **for the sake of ~** pour plus de clarté

clash /klæʃ/ VI 1 (= bang noisily) [swords, metallic objects] s'entrechoquer ; [cymbals] résonner
2 (= do battle) [armies, teams] s'affronter ◆ **to ~ with sb** affronter qn ◆ **rioters ~ed with the police in the main square** les émeutiers ont affronté la police sur la grand-place, il y a eu des affrontements entre les émeutiers et la police sur la grand-place ◆ **the two parties ~ over ...** les deux partis sont en désaccord total à propos de ...
3 (= conflict) [interests] se heurter, être incompatible or en contradiction (with avec) ; [personalities] être incompatible (with avec) ; [colours] jurer, détonner (with avec)
4 (= coincide) [two events, invitations etc] tomber en même temps (or le même jour etc) ◆ **the dates ~** les deux événements (or rencontres etc) tombent le même jour
VT [+ metallic objects] entrechoquer bruyamment ; [+ cymbals] faire résonner ◆ **to ~ the gears** faire grincer les vitesses
N 1 (= sound) choc m or fracas m métallique ◆ **a ~ of cymbals** un coup de cymbales
2 [of armies, weapons] choc m, heurt m ; (between people, parties) désaccord m ; (with police, troops) affrontement m, échauffourée f ◆ **during a ~ with the police** au cours d'un affrontement or d'une échauffourée avec la police ◆ **~es between police and demonstrators** des heurts mpl entre la police et les manifestants ◆ **I don't want a ~ with him about it** je ne veux pas me disputer avec lui à ce sujet ◆ **to have a (verbal) ~ with sb** avoir un accrochage * avec qn
3 [of interests] conflit m ◆ **a ~ of personalities** une incompatibilité de caractères
4 ◆ **a ~ of colours** des couleurs qui détonnent
5 [of dates, events, invitations] coïncidence f fâcheuse

clasp /klɑːsp/ N 1 [of brooch, necklace, purse] fermoir m ; [of belt] boucle f 2 (NonC: in one's arms, of a hand) étreinte f VT étreindre, serrer ◆ **to ~ sb's hand** serrer la main de qn ◆ **to ~ one's hands (together)** joindre les mains ◆ **with ~ed hands** les mains jointes ◆ **to ~ sb in one's arms/to one's heart** serrer qn dans ses bras/sur son cœur COMP **clasp knife** N (pl **clasp knives**) grand couteau m pliant

class /klɑːs/ N 1 (= group, division) classe f, catégorie f ; (Bot, Ling, Mil, Sociol, Zool etc) classe f ; (Naut) [of ship] type m ; (in Lloyd's Register) cote f ◆ **he's not in the same ~ as his brother** (fig) il n'arrive pas à la cheville de son frère ◆ **these books are just not in the same ~** il n'y a pas de comparaison (possible) entre ces livres ◆ **in a ~ by itself, in a ~ of its own** hors concours, unique ◆ **they are in a ~ apart** ils sont tout à fait à part ◆ **a good ~ (of) hotel** un très bon hôtel, un hôtel de très bonne classe ◆ **the ruling ~** la classe dirigeante ◆ **what ~ of degree did he get?** (Brit Univ) quelle mention a-t-il obtenue (à sa licence) ? ◆ **first ~ honours in history** ≈ licence f d'histoire avec mention très bien ; → **middle, working**
2 (= lesson) classe f, cours m ; (= students, pupils) classe f ; (US = year) promotion f scolaire ◆ **to give** or **take a ~** faire un cours ◆ **to attend a ~** suivre un cours ◆ **the French ~** la classe or le cours de français ◆ **an evening ~** un cours du soir ◆ **the ~ of 1990** (US) la promotion or la promo * de 1990
3 (NonC: *) (= distinction, elegance) classe f, ◆ **to have ~** avoir de la classe
VT classer, classifier ; (Naut Insurance) coter ◆ **he was ~ed with the servants** il était assimilé aux domestiques
ADJ (= classy) de grande classe
COMP **class action** N (Jur) ◆ **~ actions** actions fpl de groupe ◆ **~ action suit** recours m collectif en justice
class bias N (Sociol) préjugés mpl de classe
class-conscious ADJ [person] conscient des distinctions sociales ; (pej = snobbish) [person, attitude] snob inv
class consciousness N conscience f de classe
class distinction N distinction f sociale
class list N (Scol) liste f des élèves
class mark, class number N (Brit: in library) cote f
class president N (US) ≃ chef m de classe
class rank N (US Scol, Univ) numéro m de sortie
class roll N ⇒ **class list**
class society N (Pol) société f de classes
class struggle N lutte f des classes
class system N système m de classes
class teacher N (Brit Scol) professeur m principal
class war(fare) N ⇒ **class struggle**

classic /ˈklæsɪk/ ADJ (gen) classique ◆ **it was ~ *** c'était le coup classique * N (= author, work) classique m ; (Racing) classique f ◆ **it is a ~ of its kind** (fig) c'est un classique du genre COMP **classic car** N voiture f ancienne

classical /ˈklæsɪkəl/ ADJ [pianist, economist, Greece, Latin] classique ; [Greek] de l'époque classique ; [album, CD] de musique classique ◆ **~ times** antiquité f gréco-latine ◆ **~ scholar** spécialiste mf en lettres classiques COMP **classical music** N (NonC) musique f classique, classique m

classically /ˈklæsɪkəlɪ/ ADV 1 (Mus, Dancing) ◆ **to be ~ trained** avoir reçu une formation classique ◆ **a ~ trained pianist/dancer** un pianiste/danseur de formation classique 2 (Hist, Art) ◆ **a ~ proportioned building** un bâtiment aux proportions classiques ◆ **a ~ inspired church** une église d'inspiration classique ◆ **a ~ shaped vase** un vase de forme classique or aux formes classiques 3 (= traditionally) ◆ **~ beautiful/elegant** d'une beauté/élégance classique 4 (= typically) typiquement ◆ **~ English** typiquement anglais ◆ **~, overweight people underestimate how much they eat** on constate généralement que les personnes qui ont des kilos en trop sous-estiment la quantité de nourriture qu'elles absorbent

classicism /ˈklæsɪsɪzəm/ N classicisme m

classicist /ˈklæsɪsɪst/ N spécialiste mf de lettres classiques ; (esp Archit) partisan(e) m(f) du classicisme

classics /ˈklæsɪks/ N lettres fpl classiques ◆ **to study ~** faire des études de lettres classiques

classifiable /ˈklæsɪfaɪəbl/ ADJ qu'on peut classifier

classification /ˌklæsɪfɪˈkeɪʃən/ N classification f

classified /ˈklæsɪfaɪd/ ADJ 1 classifié 2 (Admin = secret etc) [document] classé secret (classée secrète f) ◆ **~ information** renseignements mpl (classés) secrets ◆ **this is ~ information** ces informations sont (classées) secrètes
COMP **classified ad** *, **classified advertisement** N (Press) petite annonce f
classified results NPL (Brit Sport) résultats mpl sportifs complets
classified section N (Press) (rubrique f des) petites annonces fpl

classify /ˈklæsɪfaɪ/ VT 1 classer, classifier 2 (Admin = restrict circulation of) classer secret

classism /ˈklɑːsɪzəm/ N (NonC) discrimination f sociale or de classe

classless /ˈklɑːslɪs/ ADJ [society] sans classes ; [person] qui n'appartient à aucune classe ; [accent] standard

classmate /ˈklɑːsmeɪt/ N (Brit) camarade mf de classe ; (US) camarade mf de promotion (or de classe)

classroom /ˈklɑːsrʊm/ N (salle f de) classe f COMP **classroom assistant** N = assistant m d'éducation (en école primaire)

classy * /ˈklɑːsɪ/ ADJ [person] classe inv * ; [hotel, restaurant] classe inv *, chic inv ; [area, neighbourhood, clothes, car] chic inv ; [watch, image] de luxe ; [performance, album, film] de grande classe ◆ **her flat looks very ~** son appartement fait très classe * or très chic

clatter /ˈklætəʳ/ N (= noise) cliquetis m ; (louder) fracas m ◆ **the ~ of cutlery** le bruit or cliquetis de couverts entrechoqués VI (= rattle) [heels, keys, typewriter, chains] cliqueter ; (= bang) [large falling object, cymbals] résonner ◆ **to ~ in/out/away** etc entrer/sortir/partir etc bruyamment VT choquer or entrechoquer bruyamment

clause /klɔːz/ N 1 (Gram) membre m de phrase, proposition f ◆ **principal/subordinate ~** proposition f principale/subordonnée 2 (Jur) [of contract, law, treaty] clause f ; [of will] disposition f ; → **saving**

claustrophobia /ˌklɔːstrəˈfəʊbɪə/ N claustrophobie f ; (fig) atmosphère f oppressante

claustrophobic /ˌklɔːstrəˈfəʊbɪk/ ADJ [person] claustrophobe ; [feeling] de claustrophobie ; [room] où l'on se sent claustrophobe ; [atmosphere] oppressant ; [film, thriller] à l'atmosphère oppressante ◆ **to feel ~** [person] avoir une sensation de claustrophobie ◆ **the house felt too ~** on se sentait trop à l'étroit dans la maison N claustrophobe mf

clavichord /ˈklævɪkɔːd/ N clavicorde m

clavicle /ˈklævɪkl/ N clavicule f

claw /klɔː/ N 1 [of cat, lion, small bird etc] griffe f ; [of bird of prey] serre f ; [of lobster etc] pince f ◆ **to get one's ~s into sb** * tenir qn entre ses griffes ◆ **to get one's ~s on sth** * mettre le grappin sur qch * ◆ **get your ~s off (that)!** * bas les pattes ! * 2 (Tech) [of bench] valet m ; [of hammer] pied-de-biche m VT (= scratch) griffer ; (= rip) déchirer or labourer avec ses griffes ; [bird of prey] déchirer or labourer avec ses serres ; (= clutch) agripper, serrer ◆ **to ~ one's way to the top** se hisser en haut de l'échelle COMP **claw hammer** N marteau m fendu, marteau m à pied-de-biche

► **claw at** VT FUS [+ object] essayer de s'agripper à ; [+ person] essayer de griffer

► **claw back** VT SEP (Econ) récupérer

clawback /ˈklɔːbæk/ N (Econ) récupération f

clay /kleɪ/ N argile f, (terre f) glaise f ; (Tennis) terre f battue ◆ **potter's ~** argile f (à potier) ◆ **to play on ~** (Tennis) jouer sur terre battue ; → **china**
COMP **clay court** N (Tennis) court m de terre battue
clay pigeon N pigeon m d'argile or de ball-trap ; (US fig) victime f or cible f facile ◆ **~ pigeon shooting** ball-trap m
clay pipe N pipe f en terre
clay pit N argilière f, glaisière f
clay-with-flints N (Geol) argile f à silex

clayey /ˈkleɪɪ/ ADJ argileux, glaiseux

claymore /ˈkleɪmɔːʳ/ N claymore f

clean /kliːn/ ADJ 1 (= not dirty, having clean habits) propre ; (= non-polluting) [fuel, vehicle, power-station, energy] propre ; [process] non polluant ◆ **to keep sth ~** garder qch propre ◆ **to keep o.s. ~** se laver ◆ **he washed the floor ~** il a bien nettoyé or lavé le sol ◆ **the rain washed it ~** la pluie l'a entièrement nettoyé ◆ **the rain washed the car ~ of mud** la pluie a fait partir or a lavé toute la boue de la voiture ◆ **to wipe sth ~** bien essuyer qch ◆ **to have ~ hands** (lit, fig) avoir les mains propres ◆ **to be washed ~ of sin** être lavé de tout péché ◆ **as ~ as a new pin** or **as a whistle** propre comme un sou neuf ; see also **pin noun**
2 (= blank) [sheet of paper] vierge ; (= untarnished) [image, reputation] sans tache ◆ **the doctor gave him a ~ bill of health** le médecin l'a trouvé en parfait état de santé ◆ **~ bill of lading** (Comm) connaissement m net or sans

réserves ◆ ~ **record** *(Jur)* casier *m* (judiciaire) vierge ◆ **to have a ~ sheet** *(Ftbl)* n'avoir encaissé aucun but ◆ **let me have a ~ copy of your report** donnez-moi une copie propre de votre rapport ◆ **to have a ~ (driving) licence** ≈ avoir tous ses points sur son permis ◆ **she has had a ~ licence for 25 years** elle n'a commis aucune contravention grave en 25 ans ◆ **to make a ~ breast of it** décharger sa conscience, dire ce qu'on a sur la conscience

3 *(= pure, smooth) [smell, taste, profile]* pur ; *[look, sound, edge, stroke, shape]* net ; *[curve]* élégant ◆ **this car has very ~ lines** cette voiture a des lignes très pures ◆ **a ~ cut** une coupure nette *or* franche

4 *(= efficient, trouble-free) [operation, job]* sans bavures ◆ **~ getaway** fuite *f* sans encombre

5 *(= clear, uninterrupted) [shot]* direct ◆ **~ leap** saut *m* sans toucher (l'obstacle) ◆ **a ~ ace** *(Tennis)* un as ◆ **~ break** *(Med)* fracture *f* simple ; *(fig)* rupture *f* définitive ◆ **to make a ~ break** *(fig)* tourner la page ◆ **to make a ~ break with the past** rompre définitivement avec le passé ◆ **~ break (divorce)** *(Jur) divorce à la suite duquel les époux, grâce à un versement unique, ne se doivent plus rien* ◆ **~ sweep** grand chelem *m (fig)* ◆ **to make a ~ sweep** réussir le grand chelem ◆ **the first club to make a ~ sweep of all three trophies** le premier club à remporter les trois trophées

6 *(= ritually pure) [animal]* pur

7 *(= not radioactive) [area, person, object]* propre

8 *(* = innocent of wrongdoing)* ◆ **to be ~** *(gen)* n'avoir rien à se reprocher ◆ **he's been ~ for six months** *[criminal]* ça fait six mois qu'il se tient à carreau *

9 *(* = not in possession of drugs, weapon, stolen property)* ◆ **to be ~** n'avoir rien sur soi ◆ **his room was ~** il n'y avait rien dans sa chambre, on n'a rien trouvé dans sa chambre

10 * *(= off drugs)* clean *inv* ; *(= off alcohol)* qui ne touche plus à l'alcool

ADV * ◆ **to cut ~ through sth** couper qch de part en part ◆ **the chain saw cut his fingers ~ off** la tronçonneuse lui a coupé les doigts tout net ◆ **it broke off ~, it broke off as ~ as a whistle** ça a cassé net ◆ **the bullet went ~ through his forehead** la balle lui a transpercé le front tout net ◆ **the car went ~ through the hedge** la voiture est carrément passée à travers la haie ◆ **the fish jumped ~ out of the net** le poisson a sauté carrément hors du filet ◆ **he jumped ~ over the fence** il a sauté la barrière sans la toucher ◆ **the thief got ~ away** le voleur s'est enfui sans encombre ◆ **I ~ forgot** j'ai complètement oublié

◆ **to come clean** *(= confess: gen)* tout déballer * ; *[criminal]* se mettre à table * ◆ **to come ~ about sth** tout déballer * sur qch ◆ **he came ~ about it** il a lâché le morceau *, il a tout déballé *

N ◆ **to give sth a good ~(up)** bien nettoyer qch

VT *[+ clothes, room, fish]* nettoyer ; *[+ vegetables]* laver ; *[+ blackboard]* essuyer ◆ **to ~ one's teeth** se laver les dents ◆ **to ~ one's nails** se nettoyer les ongles ◆ **to ~ one's face** se débarbouiller, se laver la figure ◆ **to ~ the windows** faire les vitres ; → **dry**

VI 1 *(= do housework)* faire le ménage

2 *(= be cleaned)* se nettoyer ◆ **that floor ~s easily** ce plancher se nettoie facilement *or* est facile à nettoyer

COMP **clean-and-jerk** N *(Weightlifting)* épaulé-jeté *m*

clean-cut ADJ bien délimité, net, clair ; *[person]* à l'allure soignée

clean-limbed ADJ bien proportionné, bien découplé

clean-living ADJ décent, honnête

clean-out N nettoyage *m* à fond

clean room N *(in factory)* salle *f* blanche

clean-shaven ADJ sans barbe ni moustache ; *(= close-shaven)* rasé de près

► **clean off** VT SEP *[+ writing] (from blackboard)* essuyer ; *(from wall)* enlever

► **clean out** VT SEP *[+ drawer, box]* nettoyer à fond ; *[+ cupboard, room]* nettoyer *or* faire à fond ; *(* fig = leave penniless etc) [+ person]* nettoyer * ◆ **the hotel bill ~ed me out** * la note de l'hôtel m'a nettoyé * *or* m'a mis à sec * ◆ **he was ~ed out** * il était fauché *or* à sec * ◆ **the burglars had ~ed out the whole house** * les cambrioleurs avaient complètement vidé la maison

N ◆ **clean-out** → **clean**

► **clean up** VI 1 tout nettoyer, mettre de l'ordre ◆ **she had to ~ up after the children's visit** elle a dû tout remettre en ordre après la visite des enfants ◆ **to ~ up after sb** nettoyer après qn

2 *(* fig = make profit)* faire son beurre * ◆ **he ~ed up on that sale** * cette vente lui a rapporté gros, il a touché un joli paquet * sur cette vente

VT 1 *[+ room, mess, person]* nettoyer ◆ **to ~ o.s. up** se laver, se débarbouiller

2 *(fig)* remettre de l'ordre dans les affaires de, épurer ◆ **to ~ up one's act** * acheter une conduite *, s'amender ◆ **the new mayor ~ed up the city** le nouveau maire a remis de l'ordre dans la ville ◆ **they are trying to ~ up television** ils essaient d'épurer la télévision

cleaner /ˈkliːnəʳ/ N 1 *(= woman) (in home)* femme *f* de ménage ; *(in office, school)* femme *f* de service ; *(in hospital)* fille *f* de salle ; *(= man)* agent *m* de service, ouvrier *m* nettoyeur 2 *(Comm)* teinturier *m*, -ière *f* ; *(= device)* appareil *m* de nettoyage ; *(= household cleaner)* produit *m* d'entretien ; *(= stain-remover)* détachant *m* ◆ **the ~'s shop** la teinturerie ◆ **he took his coat to the ~'s** il a donné son pardessus à nettoyer *or* au teinturier ◆ **to take sb to the ~'s** * *(fig)* plumer * qn ; → **dry, vacuum**

cleaning /ˈkliːnɪŋ/ N nettoyage *m* ; *(= housework)* ménage *m* ; → **spring**

COMP **cleaning fluid** N *(for stains)* détachant *m* (liquide)

cleaning lady, cleaning woman N femme *f* de ménage

cleanliness /ˈklenlɪnɪs/ N propreté *f*, habitude *f* de la propreté ◆ **~ is next to godliness** *(Prov)* la propreté du corps est parente de la propreté de l'âme

cleanly¹ /ˈkliːnlɪ/ ADV 1 *(= smoothly) [cut]* de façon bien nette 2 *(= fairly) [play, fight]* dans les règles ; *(fig)* loyalement 3 *(= skilfully) [strike, hit, catch]* avec précision 4 *(= without polluting) [burn]* proprement

cleanly² /ˈklenlɪ/ *(liter)* ADJ *[person, animal]* propre

cleanness /ˈkliːnnɪs/ N propreté *f*

cleanse /klenz/ VT nettoyer ; *[+ ditch, drain etc]* curer ; *(Bible = cure)* guérir ; *(fig) [+ person]* laver *(of de)* ; *(Rel) [+ soul etc]* purifier ; *(Pol = ethnically cleanse)* nettoyer, procéder à un nettoyage ethnique de ◆ **to ~ the blood** *(Med)* dépurer le sang

cleanser /ˈklenzəʳ/ N *(= detergent)* détersif *m*, détergent *m* ; *(for complexion)* démaquillant *m*

cleansing /ˈklenzɪŋ/ ADJ *(for complexion)* démaquillant ; *(fig)* purifiant ◆ **~ cream/lotion** crème *f*/lotion *f* démaquillante ◆ **~ milk** lait *m* démaquillant ◆ **~ department** service *m* de voirie N nettoyage *m*

cleanup /ˈkliːnʌp/ N 1 *[of room]* nettoyage *m* ; *[of person]* débarbouillage *m* ; *(fig)* épuration *f*, assainissement *m* ◆ **to give o.s. a ~** se laver, se débarbouiller ; see also **clean noun** 2 *(* fig)* profit *m* ◆ **he made a good ~ from that business** il a fait son beurre dans cette affaire *, cette affaire lui a rapporté gros

clear /klɪəʳ/

1 ADJECTIVE	5 INTRANSITIVE VERB
2 NOUN	6 COMPOUNDS
3 ADVERB	7 PHRASAL VERBS
4 TRANSITIVE VERB	

1 – ADJECTIVE

1 = lucid, definite *[message, motive, proof, explanation, reasoning, style]* clair ; *[commitment]* évident ; *[mind, thought, thinking]* lucide ◆ **they are faced with ~ alternatives** ils sont confrontés à des possibilités *or* solutions bien distinctes ◆ **a ~ case of homicide** un cas évident d'homicide ◆ **~ indication** signe *m* manifeste *or* certain ◆ **to have a ~ head** avoir les idées claires ◆ **to be a ~ thinker** être un esprit lucide ◆ **you'll do as I say, is that ~?** tu vas faire ce que je te dis, c'est clair ? ◆ **as ~ as day** clair comme le jour *or* comme de l'eau de roche ◆ **as ~ as mud** * *(iro)* clair comme de l'encre ; → **crystal**

◆ **to get sth clear** bien comprendre qch ◆ **I think I've got it pretty ~** ça me paraît tout à fait clair ◆ **now let's get this ~ ...** maintenant, que les choses soient bien claires ...

◆ **to make sth clear** bien faire comprendre qch ◆ **to make it ~ (to sb) that ...** bien faire comprendre (à qn) que ... ◆ **I wish to make it ~ that ...** je tiens à préciser que ...

◆ **to be/seem clear (to sb)** ◆ **it's ~ to me that ...** pour moi, il est clair que ... ◆ **it was ~ that ...** il était clair que ... ◆ **the matter is ~ to me** pour moi, l'affaire est claire ◆ **it's not ~ whether ...** on ne sait pas avec certitude si ... ◆ **it all seems ~ enough to me** tout cela me semble *or* paraît assez clair

◆ **to become clear (to sb)** ◆ **now it becomes ~ to me** maintenant, j'y vois (plus) clair ◆ **the matter became ~ to me** l'affaire m'a semblé *or* m'est apparue plus claire ◆ **it became ~ that ...** il était de plus en plus clair *or* évident que ... ◆ **it becomes ~ to me that ...** il me semble *or* paraît de plus en plus clair que ... ◆ **it became ~ to me that ...** j'ai fini par comprendre que ...

2 = understandable *[person]* clair

◆ **to make o.s. clear** se faire bien comprendre ◆ **do I make myself ~?** me suis-je bien fait comprendre ?

3 = sure *[person]* ◆ **if you are not ~ about anything, ask me** s'il y a quelque chose qui ne vous paraît *or* semble pas clair, dites-le-moi ◆ **it is important to be ~ about what the author is saying here** il est important de bien comprendre ce que l'auteur dit ici ◆ **I want to be quite ~ on this point** je veux que les choses soient bien claires ◆ **I'm not ~ whether you agree or not** je ne suis pas sûr de comprendre si vous êtes d'accord ou pas

4 = distinct *[handwriting, footprint, picture, voice, tone, majority]* net ◆ **as ~ as a bell** *[sound]* parfaitement clair ; *[voice]* limpide

5 = transparent *[plastic, glass, gel]* transparent ; *[honey]* liquide ; *[water, air]* limpide ◆ **a ~ soup** un bouillon

6 = pure in sound *[voice, tone]* clair

7 = bright *[light, colour]* vif ◆ **~ blue eyes** des yeux *mpl* bleus limpides ◆ **her eyes were ~ and steady** ses yeux étaient clairs et ne cillaient pas

8 = unobstructed *[road, runway]* dégagé, libre ; *[area, view]* dégagé ; *[space]* libre ; *[route]* sans obstacles ◆ **all exits must be kept ~** toutes les sorties doivent rester dégagées ◆ **she keeps her desk ~ of clutter** son bureau n'est jamais

en désordre ◆ **to get a ~ look at sb/sth** apercevoir qn/qch distinctement ; → **all, coast**

9 = cloudless ◆ **the weather was ~** le temps était clair ◆ **a ~ sky** un ciel dégagé ◆ **on a ~ day** par temps clair ◆ **the days were warm and ~** les journées étaient chaudes et le ciel dégagé

10 = unblemished *[skin]* sans taches, immaculé ; *[complexion]* frais (fraîche *f*)

11 = not guilty *[conscience]* tranquille ◆ **my conscience is ~, I have a ~ conscience** j'ai la conscience tranquille ◆ **he left with a ~ conscience** il est parti la conscience tranquille

12 = without commitments *[afternoon, morning, diary]* libre

13 = complete *[day, week]* plein ◆ **that gives us four ~ days to finish the job** ça nous donne quatre jours pleins pour finir le travail

14 = after deductions net *inv* ◆ **I'll make a ~ hundred from the deal** je tirerai cent livres net de la transaction ◆ **a ~ profit** un bénéfice net

15 = away from ◆ **raise the jack until the wheel is ~ of the ground** actionnez le cric jusqu'à ce que la roue ne touche plus le sol ◆ **as soon as he was ~ of the terminal building ...** dès qu'il fut sorti de l'aérogare ...

16 Brit Sport *(= ahead of)* ◆ **to be 7 metres/seconds/points ~ of sb** avoir 7 mètres/secondes/points d'avance sur qn

17 Phon *[vowel]* clair

2 - NOUN

◆ **in clear** en clair ◆ **to send a message in ~** envoyer un message en clair

◆ **to be in the clear*** *(= above suspicion)* être au-dessus de tout soupçon ; *(= no longer suspected)* être blanchi de tout soupçon ; *(= out of debt)* être libre de toutes dettes ; *(= out of danger)* être hors de danger

3 - ADVERB

1 = distinctly → **loud**

2 = completely ◆ **the thief got ~ away** le voleur s'est enfui sans encombre

3 = away ◆ **to steer** *or* **keep** *or* **stay ~ of sb/sth** éviter qn/qch ; → **jump, pull, stand, steer²**

◆ **to get clear of sth** *(= go away from)* s'éloigner *or* s'écarter de qch ; *(= rid o.s. of)* se débarrasser de qch ◆ **it will be easier once we get ~ of winter** cela sera plus facile une fois l'hiver passé

4 = net ◆ **he'll get £250 ~** il aura 250 livres net

5 esp US ◆ **~ to sth** *(= as far as)* jusqu'à qch ◆ **they went ~ to Mexico** ils sont allés jusqu'au Mexique

4 - TRANSITIVE VERB

1 = clarify *[+ liquid]* clarifier ; *[+ wine]* coller, clarifier ; *[+ skin]* purifier ; *[+ complexion]* éclaircir ; *(Med) [+ blood]* dépurer, purifier ; *(fig) [+ situation, account]* éclaircir, clarifier ◆ **to ~ the air** aérer ; *(fig)* détendre l'atmosphère ◆ **to ~ one's head** s'éclaircir les idées

2 = remove obstacles *etc* from *[+ canal, path, road, railway line]* dégager, déblayer ; *[+ lungs, chest, airway]* dégager ; *[+ pipe]* déboucher ; *[+ land]* défricher ; *[+ computer screen]* effacer ; *(fig) [+ one's conscience]* décharger ; *[+ doubts]* dissiper ◆ **to ~ sth of rubbish** déblayer qch ◆ **to ~ one's throat** s'éclaircir la voix ◆ **to ~ a room** *(of people)* faire évacuer une salle ; *(of things)* débarrasser une salle ◆ **the box is ~ed twice a day** *(Post)* la levée a lieu deux fois par jour ◆ **to ~ a way** *or* **a path through** (se) frayer un passage à travers ◆ **~ the way!** circulez !, dégagez !* ◆ **to ~ the way for ...** *(lit)* faire place à ..., libérer le passage pour ... ◆ **to ~ the way for further discussions** préparer *or* déblayer le terrain pour des négociations ultérieures ◆ **to ~ the ball** *(Ftbl)* dégager le ballon ; → **court, deck, ground¹, table**

3 = find innocent *[+ person]* innocenter, disculper *(of* de) ; ◆ **he was ~ed of the murder charge** il a été disculpé du meurtre dont on l'accusait ◆ **he will easily ~ himself** il se disculpera facilement, il prouvera facilement son innocence ◆ **to ~ sb of suspicion** laver qn de tout soupçon

4 = authorize ◆ **you will have to be ~ed by our security department** il faudra que nos services de sécurité vous donnent leur feu vert

◆ **to clear sth with sb** ◆ **we've ~ed it with him before beginning** nous avons obtenu son accord avant de commencer ◆ **you must ~ the project with the manager** il faut que le directeur donne *subj* le feu vert à votre projet

5 = get past *or* over sauter par-dessus, franchir ; *[+ obstacle]* franchir ; *[+ rocks]* éviter ; *[+ harbour]* quitter ◆ **the horse ~ed the gate by 10cm** le cheval a sauté *or* a franchi la barrière avec 10 cm de marge ◆ **the car just ~ed the lamppost** la voiture a évité le réverbère de justesse ◆ **raise the car till the wheel ~s the ground** soulevez la voiture jusqu'à ce que la roue ne touche *subj* plus le sol ◆ **the boat just ~ed the bottom** le bateau a tout juste réussi à passer sans toucher le fond

6 Fin, Comm *[+ cheque]* compenser ; *[+ account]* solder, liquider ; *[+ debt]* s'acquitter de ; *[+ profit]* gagner net ; *(Comm) [+ goods]* liquider ; *(Customs) [+ goods]* dédouaner ; *[+ port dues]* acquitter ; *[+ ship]* expédier ◆ **"half price to clear"** *(Comm)* "soldé à moitié prix pour liquider" ◆ **I've ~ed £100 on this business** cette affaire m'a rapporté 100 livres net *or* tous frais payés

5 - INTRANSITIVE VERB

1 = brighten, improve *[weather]* s'éclaircir ; *[sky]* se dégager ; *[fog]* se dissiper ; *[face, expression]* s'éclairer ; *[complexion]* s'éclaircir ; *[skin]* devenir plus sain ◆ **his brow ~ed** son visage s'est éclairé

2 Naut *[ship]* prendre la mer

6 - COMPOUNDS

clear-cut ADJ *[outline, shape]* net, précis, nettement défini ; *[attitude, proposal, situation]* précis, clair ; *[problem, division]* précis ◆ **~-cut features** traits *mpl* nets *or* bien dessinés

clear-headed ADJ lucide

clear-headedness N lucidité *f*

clear-out N rangement *m* complet

clear round N *(Horse-riding)* parcours *m* sans faute, sans faute *m inv* ◆ **to do a ~ round** faire un sans-faute

clear-sighted ADJ *[person]* clairvoyant, lucide ; *[plan]* lucide

clear-sightedness N *[of person]* clairvoyance *f* ; *[of plan]* réalisme *m*

clear-up rate N ◆ **the ~-up rate for murders** le taux de meurtres résolus

7 - PHRASAL VERBS

► **clear away** VI 1 *[mist etc]* se dissiper 2 *(= clear the table)* débarrasser, desservir VT SEP enlever, retirer ◆ **to ~ away the dishes** desservir, débarrasser (la table)

► **clear off** VI * filer*, décamper ◆ **~ off!** fichez le camp !*, filez !* VT SEP 1 *(= get rid of)* se débarrasser de ; *[+ debts]* s'acquitter de ; *(Comm) [+ stock]* liquider ; *[+ goods]* solder ◆ **to ~ off arrears of work** rattraper le retard dans son travail 2 *(= remove) [+ things on table etc]* enlever

► **clear out** VI * ⇒ **clear off** VI VT SEP *[+ cupboard]* vider ; *[+ room]* nettoyer, débarrasser ; *[+ unwanted objects]* enlever, jeter ◆ **he ~ed everyone out of the room** il a fait évacuer la pièce ◆ **he ~ed everything out of the room** il a débarrassé la pièce

► **clear up** VI 1 *[weather]* s'éclaircir, se lever ◆ **I think it will ~ up** je pense que ça va se lever 2 *[illness, spots]* disparaître ◆ **his skin has ~ed up** sa peau est devenue nette 3 *(= tidy)* ranger, faire des rangements VT SEP 1 *[+ mystery]* éclaircir, résoudre ; *[+ matter, subject]* éclaircir, tirer au clair 2 *(= tidy) [+ room]* ranger, mettre en ordre ; *[+ books, toys]* ranger

clearance /ˈklɪərəns/ N 1 *(NonC) [of road, path]* déblaiement *m*, dégagement *m* ; *[of land, bomb site]* déblaiement *m* ; *[of room, court]* évacuation *f* ; *[of litter, objects, rubbish]* enlèvement *m* ; (also **stock clearance**) soldes *mpl*, liquidation *f* (du stock)

2 *[of boat, car etc]* dégagement *m*, espace *m* libre ◆ **2 metre ~** espace *m* de 2 mètres ◆ **how much ~ is there between my car and yours?** je suis à combien de votre voiture ?

3 *[of cheque]* compensation *f* ; *(Customs)* dédouanement *m* ; *(= permission etc)* autorisation *f*, permis *m (de publier etc)* ◆ **~ outwards/inwards** *(Naut)* permis *m* de sortie/d'entrée ◆ **the dispatch was sent to the Foreign Office for ~** la dépêche a été soumise au ministère des Affaires étrangères pour contrôle ◆ **to give (sb) ~ for takeoff** donner (à qn) l'autorisation de décoller

4 *(Ftbl)* dégagement *m*

COMP **clearance certificate** N *(for ship)* congé *m* de navigation, lettre *f* de mer

clearance sale N liquidation *f*

clearing /ˈklɪərɪŋ/ N 1 *(in forest)* clairière *f* 2 *(NonC) [of liquid]* clarification *f* ; *[of wine]* collage *m* ; *[of bowels]* purge *f* ; *[of blood]* dépuration *f* 3 *(NonC = tidying, unblocking) [of room, cupboard, passage]* dégagement *m*, désencombrement *m* ; *[of litter, objects, rubbish]* enlèvement *m* ; *[of land]* défrichement *m* ; *[of pipe etc]* débouchage *m* ; *[of road]* dégagement *m*, déblaiement *m* ; *[of room, court]* évacuation *f* 4 *(Jur) [of accused]* disculpation *f* 5 *[of cheque]* compensation *f* ; *[of account]* liquidation *f* ; *[of debt]* acquittement *m*

COMP **clearing bank** N *(Brit)* banque *f* (appartenant à une chambre de compensation)

clearing house N *(Banking)* chambre *f* de compensation ; *(fig: for documents etc)* bureau *m* central

clearly /ˈklɪəlɪ/ LANGUAGE IN USE 26.3 ADV 1 *(= lucidly) [define, explain, express o.s., think, remember, understand]* clairement 2 *(= explicitly) [forbidden]* explicitement 3 *(= distinctly) [see]* clairement, nettement ; *[speak]* distinctement ; *[hear]* distinctement, nettement ; *[label, write]* clairement, lisiblement ; *[visible]* bien, nettement ; *[audible]* nettement 4 *(= obviously) [intelligent, worried, upset, overjoyed]* manifestement ◆ **he ~ believes that ...** il croit manifestement que ... ◆ **he was ~ not expecting us** manifestement, il ne nous attendait pas ◆ **~, we must find a solution quickly** il est évident que nous devons trouver une solution rapidement

clearness /ˈklɪənɪs/ N 1 *[of air, liquid]* transparence *f*, limpidité *f* ; *[of glass]* transparence *f* 2 *[of sound, sight, print, thought etc]* clarté *f*, netteté *f*

clearway /ˈklɪəweɪ/ N *(Brit)* route *f* à stationnement interdit

cleat /kliːt/ N *(Carpentry)* tasseau *m* ; *(on boat)* taquet *m* ; *(on shoe)* clou *m*

cleavage /ˈkliːvɪdʒ/ N *(lit) (Chem, Geol)* clivage *m* ; *(Bio) [of cell]* division *f* ; *(between breasts)* décolleté *m* ; *(fig) [of opinion]* division *f*, clivage *m*

cleave¹ /kliːv/ (pret **cleft** *or* **clove**, ptp **cleft** *or* **cloven**) VT *(gen liter)* fendre ; *(Chem, Geol)* cliver ; *(Bio, also fig)* diviser VI se fendre ; *(Chem, Geol)* se cliver ; *(Bio)* se diviser ◆ **to ~ through the waves** fendre les vagues

cleave² /kliːv/ (pret, ptp **cleaved**) VI (*liter*) (= *stick*) coller, adhérer (*to* à) ; (*fig*) s'attacher, rester attaché *or* fidèle (*to* à)

cleaver /ˈkliːvəʳ/ N fendoir *m*, couperet *m*

clef /klef/ N (*Mus*) clé *or* clef *f* (*signe*) ; → **bass¹, treble**

cleft /kleft/ VB pt, ptp of **cleave¹** ADJ fendu ; [*stick*] fourchu ◆ **to be in a ~ stick** se trouver *or* être dans une impasse ◆ **~ palate** (*Anat*) palais *m* fendu ◆ **a ~ chin** un menton creusé d'un sillon vertical ◆ **~ sentence** (*Gram*) phrase *f* clivée N (*in rock*) crevasse *f*, fissure *f* ; (*in chin*) sillon *m*

cleg /kleg/ N taon *m*

clematis /ˈklemətɪs/ N clématite *f*

clemency /ˈklemənsɪ/ N [*of person*] clémence *f* (*towards* envers) ; [*of weather etc*] douceur *f*, clémence *f*

clement /ˈklemənt/ ADJ [*person*] clément (*towards* envers) ; [*weather*] doux (douce *f*), clément

clementine /ˈkleməntaɪn/ N clémentine *f*

clench /klentʃ/ VT 1 ◆ **to ~ sth (in one's hands)** empoigner *or* serrer qch dans ses mains ◆ **to ~ one's fists/teeth** serrer les poings/les dents 2 ⇒ **clinch vt** N ⇒ **clinch noun 1**

Cleopatra /ˌkliːəˈpætrə/ N Cléopâtre *f* COMP **Cleopatra's needle** N l'obélisque *m* de Cléopâtre

clerestory /ˈklɪəstɔːrɪ/ N (*Archit*) claire-voie *f*, clair-étage *m*

clergy /ˈklɜːdʒɪ/ N clergé *m*

clergyman /ˈklɜːdʒɪmən/ N ecclésiastique *m* ; (*Protestant*) pasteur *m* ; (*Roman Catholic*) prêtre *m*, curé *m*

clergywoman /ˈklɜːdʒɪˌwʊmən/ N (pl **-women**) femme *f* pasteur

cleric /ˈklerɪk/ N ecclésiastique *m*

clerical /ˈklerɪkəl/ ADJ 1 [*job, work, staff*] de bureau ; [*position, skills*] administratif ◆ **~ error** (*in book-keeping*) erreur *f* d'écriture ; (*in documentation*) erreur *f* administrative ◆ **~ worker** employé(e) *m(f)* de bureau 2 (*Rel*) [*life, training*] clérical COMP **clerical collar** N col *m* d'ecclésiastique

clericalism /ˈklerɪkəlɪzəm/ N cléricalisme *m*

clerihew /ˈklerɪhjuː/ N petit poème *m* humoristique (*pseudo-biographique*)

clerk /klɑːk, (US) klɜːrk/ N 1 (*in office*) employé(e) *m(f)* de bureau ; (*Jur*) clerc *m* ◆ **bank ~** employé(e) *m(f)* de banque ◆ **desk ~** (*in hotel*) réceptionniste *mf* ◆ **Clerk of the Court** (*Jur*) greffier *m* (du tribunal) ; → **head, town** 2 †† (*Rel*) ecclésiastique *m* ; (= *scholar*) clerc † *m*, savant *m* 3 (*US = shop assistant*) vendeur *m*, -euse *f* 4 (*Brit Constr*) ~ **of works** conducteur *m* de travaux VI 1 (*US Jur*) **to ~ for a judge** être assistant(e) *m(f)* stagiaire d'un juge 2 (*US Comm*) travailler comme vendeur/vendeuse

clerkship /ˈklɑːkʃɪp, (US) ˈklɜːrkʃɪp/ N fonctions *fpl* d'employé de bureau ; (*Med*) stage *m*

clever /ˈklevəʳ/ ADJ 1 (= *intelligent*) [*person, face, eyes*] intelligent ◆ **~ girl!** quelle fille intelligente tu fais ! 2 (= *skilful*) [*craftsman*] habile, adroit ; [*sportsman*] habile ; [*piece of work*] astucieux, ingénieux ; (*Sport*) [*shot, pass, header*] bien pensé ◆ **~ at doing sth** habile à faire qch, doué pour faire qch ◆ **~ with one's hands** habile *or* adroit de ses mains 3 (= *astute*) [*plan, trick, idea, accounting, advertising, explanation*] astucieux ; [*technique*] astucieux, ingénieux ; [*invention, gadget, design, approach*] ingénieux ; [*person*] malin (-igne *f*) ; [*book, film*] astucieusement construit ; [*joke*] fin ◆ **~ clogs** or **Dick*** (*Brit pej*) petit malin, petite maligne ◆ **don't be** *or* **get ~ with me!*** ne fais pas le malin avec moi ! ; → **half** COMP **clever-clever*** ADJ (*pej*) un peu trop futé

cleverly /ˈklevəlɪ/ ADV (*with vb*) 1 (= *intelligently*) intelligemment 2 (= *skilfully*) ingénieusement ◆ **~ designed** d'une conception ingénieuse 3 (*often pej = astutely*) [*plan, disguise*] astucieusement ; [*construct*] d'une façon ingénieuse

cleverness /ˈklevənɪs/ N (*NonC*) 1 (= *intelligence*) [*of person, face, eyes*] intelligence *f* 2 (= *skill*) [*of craftsman*] habileté *f*, adresse *f* (*at sth* à qch) ; [*of sportsman*] habileté *f* ; [*of piece of work*] ingéniosité *f* ; (*Sport*) [*of shot, pass, header*] intelligence *f* 3 (= *astuteness*) [*of person, plan, trick, accounting, advertising*] astuce *f* ; [*of technique, idea, invention, design, solution, scheme, script*] ingéniosité *f* ; [*of book, film, argument, story*] construction *f* astucieuse ; [*of joke*] finesse *f*

clew /kluː/ N (*US*) ⇒ **clue**

cliché /ˈkliːʃeɪ/ N cliché *m*, expression *f* or phrase *f* toute faite

clichéd /ˈkliːʃeɪd/ ADJ rebattu, galvaudé

click /klɪk/ N déclic *m*, petit bruit *m* sec ; [*of tongue*] claquement *m* ; [*of wheel*] cliquet *m* ; (*Phon*) clic *m* VI 1 faire un bruit sec, cliqueter ◆ **the door ~ed shut** la porte s'est refermée avec un déclic ◆ **the part ~ed into place** la pièce s'est mise en place *or* s'est enclenchée avec un déclic ◆ **suddenly it ~ed*** (*fig*) tout à coup ça a fait tilt* ◆ **to ~ with sb*** (= *hit it off*) se découvrir des atomes crochus* avec qn 2 (* = *be successful*) [*product, invention*] bien marcher VT ◆ **to ~ one's heels** claquer des talons ◆ **to ~ one's tongue** faire claquer sa langue ◆ **she ~ed the shelf back into place** elle a remis l'étagère en place avec un déclic

► **click on** VT FUS (*Comput*) cliquer sur

clickable /ˈklɪkəbl/ ADJ (*Comput*) [*icon, image*] cliquable

clicking /ˈklɪkɪŋ/ N cliquetis *m*

client /ˈklaɪənt/ N client(e) *m(f)* COMP **client state** N (*Pol*) pays *m* satellite

clientele /ˌkliːɑːnˈtel/ N (*Comm*) clientèle *f* ; (*Theat*) habitués *mpl*

cliff /klɪf/ N [*of seashore*] falaise *f* ; [*of mountains*] escarpement *m* ; (*Climbing*) à-pic *m* COMP **cliff-dweller** N (*lit*) troglodyte *mf* ; (*US*) habitant(e) *m(f)* de gratte-ciel

cliffhanger* /ˈklɪfˌhæŋəʳ/ N récit *m* (*or* situation *f etc*) à suspense ; (= *moment of suspense*) moment *m* d'angoisse

cliffhanging* /ˈklɪfˌhæŋɪŋ/ ADJ tendu, à suspense ◆ **~ vote*** vote *m* à suspense

clifftop /ˈklɪftɒp/ N ◆ **a ~** le sommet d'une falaise ADJ [*walk, setting*] sur le sommet d'une falaise

climacteric /klaɪˈmæktərɪk/ N climatère *m* ; (*esp US Med*) ménopause *f* ADJ climatérique ; (*fig*) crucial, dangereux

climactic /klaɪˈmæktɪk/ ADJ ◆ **it was a ~ moment** ça a été un moment-clé *or* un moment décisif ◆ **the ~ scene of the film, where Joan is burned at the stake** la scène la plus forte du film, où Jeanne est brûlée sur le bûcher

climate /ˈklaɪmɪt/ N climat *m* ◆ **the ~ of opinion** (les courants *mpl* de) l'opinion *f* COMP **climate change** N changement *m* climatique

climatic /klaɪˈmætɪk/ ADJ climatique

climatologist /ˌklaɪməˈtɒlədʒɪst/ N climatologue *mf*, climatologiste *mf*

climatology /ˌklaɪməˈtɒlədʒɪ/ N climatologie *f*

climax /ˈklaɪmæks/ N 1 (= *high point*) point *m* culminant, apogée *m* ◆ **the ~ of his political career** l'apogée *m* de sa vie politique ◆ **to come to a ~** atteindre son paroxysme ◆ **to build** *or* **work up to a ~** [*events*] atteindre un paroxysme ; [*orator*] parachever son discours ◆ **the tournament is building up to a tremendous ~** le tournoi s'achemine vers une conclusion palpitante ◆ **this brought matters to a ~** cela a porté l'affaire à son paroxysme, cela a porté les événements à leur point culminant ◆ **a firework display brought the festival to a fitting ~** le festival se conclut en beauté sur un feu d'artifice 2 (= *orgasm*) orgasme *m* ◆ **to bring sb to ~** faire jouir qn VT ◆ **this performance ~ed a season of staggering success for Bailey** cette prestation a marqué le point culminant d'une saison extraordinaire pour Bailey ◆ **the reception was ~ed by a brilliant display of fireworks** la réception s'est conclue *or* terminée en beauté sur un magnifique feu d'artifice VI 1 (= *reach high point*) ◆ **I felt the novel ~ed a little too quickly** j'ai trouvé que l'on atteignait un peu vite le point culminant du roman ◆ **a busy schedule of matches which ~ed with victory in the Heineken Trophy** une rapide succession de matches qui s'est conclue *or* terminée en beauté avec une victoire dans le Heineken Trophy 2 (= *reach orgasm, orgasm*) jouir

climb /klaɪm/ VT (*also* **climb up**) [+ *stairs, steps, slope*] monter, grimper ; [+ *hill*] grimper, escalader ; [+ *tree*] grimper dans *or* sur ; [+ *ladder*] grimper à, monter sur ; [+ *rope*] monter à ; [+ *cliff, wall*] escalader ; [+ *mountain*] gravir, faire l'ascension de ◆ **the record ~ed three places** le disque a gagné trois places (au hit-parade) ◆ **shares ~ed three points** les actions ont augmenté de trois points ◆ **to be ~ing the wall** (= *crazy*) être dingue VI 1 (*lit, fig: also* **climb up**) monter, grimper ; [*aircraft, rocket*] monter, prendre de l'altitude ; [*sun*] monter ; [*prices, shares, costs*] augmenter ; (*Sport*) escalader, grimper ; (*also* **rock-climb**) varapper 2 ◆ **to ~ down a tree** descendre d'un arbre ◆ **to ~ down a mountain** descendre d'une montagne, effectuer la descente d'une montagne ◆ **to ~ over a wall/an obstacle** escalader un mur/un obstacle ◆ **to ~ into an aircraft/a boat** monter *or* grimper à bord d'un avion/bateau ◆ **to ~ out of a hole** se hisser hors d'un trou ◆ **to ~ to power** accéder au pouvoir N [*of hill*] montée *f*, côte *f* ; (*Climbing*) ascension *f* ; [*of aircraft*] montée *f*, ascension *f* COMP **climb-down*** N reculade *f*, dérobade *f*

► **climb down** VI 1 (*lit: from tree, wall*) descendre ; (*Climbing*) descendre, effectuer une descente 2 (* = *abandon one's position*) en rabattre N ◆ **climb-down** * → **climb**

► **climb up** VT, VI → **climb**

climber /ˈklaɪməʳ/ N (= *person*) grimpeur *m*, -euse *f* ; (= *mountaineer*) alpiniste *mf*, ascensionniste *mf* ; (*fig pej: also* **social climber**) arriviste *mf* (*pej*) ; (= *plant*) plante *f* grimpante ; (*also* **rock-climber**) varappeur *m*, -euse *f*

climbing /ˈklaɪmɪŋ/ ADJ [*person, bird*] grimpeur ; [*plant*] grimpant ; [*plane, sun*] ascendant N montée *f*, escalade *f* ; (*Sport*) alpinisme *m* ; (*also* **rock-climbing**) varappe *f* ; (*fig pej: also* **social climbing**) arrivisme *m* (*pej*) ◆ **to go ~** (= *mountaineering*) faire de l'alpinisme ; (= *rock-climbing*) faire de la varappe COMP **climbing boot** N chaussure *f* de montagne **climbing frame** N cage *f* à poules **climbing irons** NPL crampons *mpl* **climbing speed** N (*Aviat*) vitesse *f* ascensionnelle

clime /klaɪm/ N (*liter*) (= *climate*) climat *m* ; (= *country*) contrée *f* ◆ **in sunnier ~s** sous des cieux plus cléments

clinch /klɪntʃ/ VT (*also* **clench**) (*Tech*) [+ *nail, rivet*] river ; (*Naut*) étalinguer ; (*fig*) [+ *argument*] mettre un point final à ; [+ *bargain*] conclure ◆ **to ~ the deal** conclure l'affaire ◆ **to**

~ an agreement sceller un pacte ◆ **that ~es it** comme ça c'est réglé, ça coupe court à tout * VI (Boxing) combattre corps à corps N 1 (Tech) rivetage m ; (Naut) étalingure f 2 (Boxing) corps-à-corps m ◆ **to get into a ~** s'accrocher * 3 (* = embrace) étreinte f ◆ **in a ~** enlacés

clincher * /ˈklɪntʃəʳ/ ADJ argument m décisif

clinching /ˈklɪntʃɪŋ/ ADJ convaincant, concluant

cline /klaɪn/ N cline m

cling /klɪŋ/ (pret, ptp **clung**) VI 1 (= hold tight) se cramponner, s'accrocher (to à) ; ◆ **to ~ together, to ~ to one another** se tenir étroitement enlacés, se cramponner l'un à l'autre ◆ **despite the opposition of all he clung to his opinion** il s'est cramponné à or a maintenu son opinion envers et contre tous ◆ **to ~ to a belief** se raccrocher à une croyance ◆ **to ~ to the belief that ...** se raccrocher à la notion que ... 2 (= stick) adhérer, (se) coller (to à) ; [clothes] coller ◆ **to ~ together, to ~ to one another** rester or être collés l'un à l'autre

Clingfilm ®, **clingfilm** /ˈklɪŋfɪlm/ N film m alimentaire (transparent), Scellofrais ® m

clinging /ˈklɪŋɪŋ/ ADJ 1 (pej = overdependent) [person] collant, crampon inv * 2 [material, garment] collant, moulant 3 [smell] tenace COMP **clinging vine** * N (US) pot m de colle *

clingwrap /ˈklɪŋræp/ N ⇒ **Clingfilm**

clingy * /ˈklɪŋɪ/ ADJ 1 (pej = overdependent) [person] collant, crampon * inv 2 [material, garment] collant, moulant

clinic /ˈklɪnɪk/ N (= private nursing home, consultant's teaching session) clinique f ; (= health centre) centre m médicosocial or d'hygiène sociale ; (also **outpatients' clinic**) service m de consultation (externe), dispensaire m (municipal)

clinical /ˈklɪnɪkəl/ ADJ 1 (Med) [test, research, practice, medicine] clinique ; [waste] médical 2 (fig pej = dispassionate) [person, attitude, tone, term] froidement objectif ; [detachment] froid 3 (pej = austere) [room, building, decor, style] austère, froid ; [colour] froid
COMP **clinical depression** N dépression f (nerveuse)
clinical psychologist N psychologue mf clinicien(ne)
clinical psychology N psychologie f clinique
clinical thermometer N thermomètre m médical
clinical trial N essai m clinique

clinically /ˈklɪnɪkəlɪ/ ADV 1 (Med) [prove] cliniquement ◆ **~ dead** cliniquement mort ◆ **to be ~ insane** être fou au sens médical du terme, être un malade mental ◆ **to be ~ depressed** souffrir de dépression (nerveuse), faire de la dépression (nerveuse) 2 (= dispassionately) [say] d'un ton froidement objectif, avec une froide objectivité

clinician /klɪˈnɪʃən/ N clinicien(ne) m(f)

clink[1] /klɪŋk/ VT faire tinter ◆ **to ~ glasses with sb** trinquer avec qn VI tinter, résonner N tintement m (de verres etc)

clink[2] * /klɪŋk/ N (= prison) taule * f, bloc * m ◆ **in ~** en taule *

clinker /ˈklɪŋkəʳ/ N 1 (= burnt out coal) mâchefer m, scories fpl 2 (= paving material) brique f vitrifiée 3 (US * = mistake) (Mus) pavé m ; (gen) couac m ; (= failed film, play etc) four * m, bide * m
COMP **clinker-built** ADJ (Naut) (bordé) à clins

clip[1] /klɪp/ N (for papers) trombone m ; (for tube) collier m, bague f ; (also **cartridge clip**) chargeur m ; (= brooch) clip m VT 1 [+ papers] attacher (avec un trombone) ◆ **to ~ a brooch on one's dress** fixer une broche sur sa robe 2 (US) **to ~ * the customers** estamper * les clients
COMP **clip art** N (NonC: Comput) images fpl numériques insérables
clip-clop N ◆ **the ~-clop of hooves** les claquements mpl de sabots
clip frame N sous-verre m
clip-on ADJ avec clip ◆ **~-on sunglasses** lunettes de soleil que l'on fixe sur ses lunettes de vue

► **clip on** VT SEP [+ brooch] fixer ; [+ document etc] attacher (avec un trombone) ADJ ◆ **clip-on** → **clip**[1]

► **clip together** VT SEP attacher

clip[2] /klɪp/ VT 1 (= cut, snip) couper (avec des ciseaux) ; [+ hedge] tailler ; [+ sheep, dog] tondre ; [+ ticket] poinçonner ; [+ article from newspaper] découper ; [+ hair] couper ; [+ wings] rogner, couper ◆ **to ~ sb's wings** rogner les ailes à qn
2 (* = hit) donner une baffe à * ; (= collide with) accrocher ◆ **I ~ped him on the jaw** * je lui ai envoyé le poing dans la mâchoire * ◆ **to ~ sb's heels** cogner dans les pieds de qn
3 (= reduce time) **to ~ a few seconds off a record** améliorer un record de quelques secondes
N 1 ◆ **to give sth a ~** ⇒ **to clip sth** → **vt 1**
2 (Cine, Rad) court extrait m ; (TV) clip m
3 (* = blow) taloche * f, marron * m ◆ **to give sb a ~ round the ear** filer une claque à qn *
4 (US) **at a ~** à toute vitesse
COMP **clip joint** * N (pej) boîte f où l'on se fait tondre or fusiller * ◆ **that's a real ~ joint** c'est vraiment le coup de fusil dans cette boîte *

clipboard /ˈklɪpbɔːd/ N (gen) écritoire f à pince ; (Comput) bloc-notes m, presse-papiers m inv

clipped /klɪpt/ ADJ [tone, voice] sec (sèche f) ◆ **he has a ~ way of speaking** il avale ses mots or les syllabes (en parlant) ◆ **in a ~ voice** d'un ton sec

clipper /ˈklɪpəʳ/ N (= plane, ship) clipper m NPL **clippers** (= tool) tondeuse f ; → **hair, hedge, nail**

clippie † * /ˈklɪpɪ/ N (Brit = conductress) receveuse f

clipping /ˈklɪpɪŋ/ N 1 [of newspaper etc] coupure f de presse or de journal 2 ◆ **~s** [of grass, hedge] chutes fpl ; [of nails] bouts mpl d'ongles (qu'on a coupés)

clique /kliːk/ N (pej) coterie f (pej), clique * f

cliquey /ˈkliːkɪ/, **cliquish** /ˈkliːkɪʃ/ ADJ (pej) exclusif, qui a l'esprit de clique or de chapelle

cliquishness /ˈkliːkɪʃnɪs/ N (pej) esprit m de clique or de chapelle

clit ** /klɪt/ N clitoris m

clitoral /ˈklɪtərəl/ ADJ clitoridien

clitoridectomy /ˌklɪtərɪˈdektəmɪ/ N clitoridectomie f

clitoris /ˈklɪtərɪs/ N clitoris m

Cllr (Brit) abbrev of **Councillor**

cloak /kləʊk/ N grande cape f ; [of shepherd etc] houppelande f ◆ **as a ~ for sth** pour cacher or masquer qch ◆ **a ~ of mist** une nappe de brouillard ◆ **under the ~ of darkness** sous le manteau or le voile de la nuit VT (fig) masquer, cacher ; (= dress) revêtir d'un manteau ◆ **~ed with respectability/mystery** empreint de respectabilité/de mystère COMP **cloak-and-dagger** ADJ clandestin ◆ **the ~-and-dagger boys** * les membres mpl du service secret, les barbouzes * fpl ◆ **a ~-and-dagger story** un roman d'espionnage

cloakroom /ˈkləʊkrʊm/ N 1 [of coats etc] vestiaire m ; (Brit = left luggage) consigne f ◆ **to put or leave in the ~** [+ clothes] mettre or déposer au vestiaire ; [+ luggage] mettre à la consigne 2 (Brit = toilet) (public) toilettes fpl ; (in house) cabinets mpl
COMP **cloakroom attendant** N (in theatre) préposé(e) m(f) au vestiaire
cloakroom ticket N (for clothes) numéro m de vestiaire ; (for luggage) bulletin m de consigne

clobber * /ˈklɒbəʳ/ N (NonC: Brit = belongings) barda * m VT (= hit) tabasser * ; (fig) frapper de plein fouet ◆ **to be ~ed by the rise in interest rates** être mis à mal par la hausse des taux d'intérêt

cloche /klɒʃ/ N (Agr, Dress) cloche f

clock /klɒk/ N 1 (large) horloge f ; (smaller) pendule f ◆ **it's midday by the church ~** il est midi à l'horloge de or au clocher de l'église ◆ **it lasted two hours by the ~** cela a duré deux heures d'horloge ◆ **to keep one's eyes on the ~, to watch the ~** surveiller l'heure ◆ **they're watching the premises round the ~** ils surveillent les locaux vingt-quatre heures sur vingt-quatre ◆ **to work round the ~** travailler vingt-quatre heures d'affilée ; (fig) travailler sans relâche ◆ **to work against the ~** travailler contre la montre ◆ **to do sth by the ~ or according to the ~** faire qch en respectant l'horaire ◆ **to put the ~(s) back/forward** retarder/avancer l'horloge ◆ **to put or turn the ~ back** (fig) revenir en arrière ◆ **you can't put the ~ back** ce qui est fait est fait ◆ **this decision will put the ~ back 50 years** cette décision va nous ramener 50 ans en arrière ; → **grandfather, o'clock, sleep**
2 * (= meter) [of taxi] compteur m, taximètre m ; (= milometer) ≈ compteur m (kilométrique) ◆ **there were 50,000 miles on the ~** la voiture avait 80 000 kilomètres au compteur
3 (Comput) horloge f
VT 1 (Sport) [+ runner] chronométrer ◆ **he ~ed four minutes for the 1,500 metres** il a fait le 1 500 mètres en quatre minutes
2 (Brit) **he ~ed him one** * (= hit) il lui a collé un pain * or un marron *
3 (Brit * = notice) voir
4 **to ~ a car** * (= tamper with) trafiquer * le compteur d'une voiture
COMP **clock card** N (for clocking in) carte f de pointage
clock-golf N jeu m de l'horloge
clock-radio N radio-réveil m
clock repairer N horloger m réparateur
clock-tower N clocher m
clock-watcher N (pej) ◆ **he's a terrible ~-watcher** il ne fait que guetter l'heure de sortie, il a les yeux fixés sur la pendule
clock-watching N ◆ **to be guilty of ~-watching** passer son temps à surveiller les aiguilles de la pendule

► **clock in** VI (at work) pointer (à l'arrivée) VT SEP ◆ **he clocked in three hours' work** il a fait trois heures de travail

► **clock off** VI (from work) pointer (à la sortie)

► **clock on** VI ⇒ **clock in vi**

► **clock out** VI ⇒ **clock off**

► **clock up** VT SEP 1 ⇒ **clock in vt sep**
2 **he ~ed up 250 miles** (in car) il a fait 250 miles au compteur

clockface /ˈklɒkfeɪs/ N cadran m (d'une horloge)

clockmaker /ˈklɒkˌmeɪkəʳ/ N horloger m, -ère f

clockwise /ˈklɒkwaɪz/ ADV, ADJ dans le sens des aiguilles d'une montre

clockwork /ˈklɒkwɜːk/ N (= mechanism) [of clock] mouvement m (d'horloge) ; [of toy etc] mécanisme m, rouages mpl ◆ **to go or run like ~** (fig) aller comme sur des roulettes ; → **regular**
COMP [toy, train, car] mécanique ; (fig) précis, régulier
clockwork precision N ◆ **with ~ precision** avec la précision d'une horloge

clod /klɒd/ N 1 [of earth etc] motte f (de terre etc) 2 (* pej) balourd(e) * m(f)

clodhopper * /ˈklɒdˌhɒpəʳ/ N (pej) (= person) lourdingue * m ; (= shoe) godillot * m, croquenot * m

clodhopping* /ˈklɒd,hɒpɪŋ/ ADJ *[person]* lourdingue* ◆ ~ **shoes** *or* **boots** godillots* *mpl*, croquenots* *mpl*

clog /klɒg/ N (= *shoe*) *(wooden)* sabot *m* ; *(with wooden soles)* socque *m*, galoche † *f* VT (also **clog up**) *[+ pores, arteries, lungs]* obstruer ; *[+ pipe]* boucher, encrasser ; *[+ streets, system]* congestionner ◆ **~ged with traffic** congestionné, embouteillé VI (also **clog up**) *[pipe etc]* se boucher, s'encrasser

cloister /ˈklɔɪstəʳ/ N *(Archit, Rel)* cloître *m* VT *(Rel)* cloîtrer ◆ **to lead a ~ed life** mener une vie monacale *or* de cloître

clone /kləʊn/ N *(also Comput)* clone *m* VT cloner

cloning /ˈkləʊnɪŋ/ N clonage *m*

clonk /klɒnk/ N (= *sound*) bruit *m* sourd VI (= *make sound*) émettre un bruit sourd

close¹ /kləʊs/ ADJ 1 (= *near*) proche ◆ **an agreement seems ~** il semble qu'on s'approche d'un accord ◆ **in ~ proximity to sb/sth** dans le voisinage immédiat de qn/qch ◆ **at ~ quarters** de très près ◆ **to shoot sb at ~ range** tirer sur qn à bout portant ◆ **to have a ~ shave** *(lit)* se (faire) raser de près ◆ **it was a ~ shave*** *or* **thing*** *or* **call*** je l'ai (*or* il l'a *etc*) échappé belle ◆ **the house is ~ to the shops** la maison est près *or* proche des magasins ◆ **his birthday is ~ to mine** son anniversaire est proche du mien ◆ **she was very ~ to her brother** *(in age)* il y avait très peu de différence d'âge entre son frère et elle ; *(in friendship)* elle était très proche de son frère ; see also **3** ◆ **to be ~ to success** être près de réussir ◆ **to be very ~ to success** être à deux doigts de réussir ◆ **to be ~ to starvation** être au bord de la famine ◆ **to be ~ to tears** être au bord des larmes ◆ **to be ~ to doing sth** être à deux doigts de faire qch ◆ **to be too close to call** *[results]* être très serré ; → **bone, comfort, home**

2 (= *similar*) **~ to** proche de ◆ **it was something ~ to obsession** cela tenait de l'obsession ◆ **she felt something ~ to loathing for the man** elle éprouvait un sentiment proche de la haine pour cet homme ◆ **she regarded him with something that was ~ to fear** elle le regardait avec une sorte de peur ◆ **her desire was ~r to passion than love** son désir tenait plus de la passion que de l'amour

3 (= *intimate*) *[friend, relative, partner, adviser]* proche ; *[relationship]* profond ; *[cooperation, ties, links, connection]* étroit ; *[friendship]* intime ; *[resemblance]* fort ◆ **she is very ~ to her brother** elle est très proche de son frère ◆ **we are very ~** nous sommes très proches ◆ **a ~ circle of friends** un cercle d'amis proches ◆ **to be in/keep in ~ contact with sb** être/rester en contact étroit avec qn ◆ **to be/feel ~ to sb** être/se sentir proche de qn ◆ **a source ~ to the president** une source proche du président

4 (= *careful*) *[examination, inspection, study]* attentif ; *[questioning, reasoning]* serré ; *[investigation, enquiry, checking]* minutieux ; *[translation]* fidèle ; *[account]* détaillé ; *[argument]* précis ◆ **to pay ~ attention to sth** faire bien attention à qch ◆ **the children were paying ~ attention to the teacher** les enfants écoutaient le professeur avec beaucoup d'attention ◆ **to be (kept) in ~ confinement** être sous bonne garde ◆ **(up)on ~r inspection** *or* **examination** après un examen plus minutieux ◆ **to have a ~r look at sth** regarder qch de plus près ◆ **to keep sb/sth under ~ surveillance, to keep a ~ eye** *or* **watch on sb/sth** surveiller qn/qch de près

5 (= *dense*) *[handwriting, ranks]* serré ; *[grain, texture]* fin ◆ **I find it difficult to read such ~ print** j'ai du mal à lire un texte si serré ◆ **in ~ formation** *or* **order** en formation serrée

6 (= *decided by a small amount*) *[election, contest, race, finish]* serré

7 (= *stuffy*) *[room]* mal aéré ; *[atmosphere, air]* lourd ◆ **it's very ~ in here** ça manque d'air ici ◆ **it's very ~ today** (= *humid*) il fait très lourd aujourd'hui

8 (= *secretive*) ◆ **to be ~ (about sth)** *[person]* rester secret (quant à qch)

9 *[vowel]* fermé

ADV 1 ◆ **~ to sb/sth** près de qn/qch ◆ **sit ~ up to me** assieds-toi tout près de moi ◆ **~ against the wall** tout contre le mur ◆ **~ behind (sb/sth)** juste derrière (qn/qch) ◆ **he followed ~ behind me** il me suivait de près ◆ **~ by (sb/sth)** tout près (de qn/qch) ◆ **to get ~ (to sb/sth)** s'approcher (de qn/qch) ◆ **to get ~r (to sb/sth)** se rapprocher (de qn/qch) ◆ **to be ~ at hand** *or* **to hand** *[object]* être à portée de main ; *[place]* être à proximité ; *[date, event]* être proche ◆ **to hold sb ~** serrer qn dans ses bras ◆ **shut ~, ~ shut** hermétiquement fermé *or* clos ◆ **their two heads were ~ together** leurs deux têtes étaient tout près l'une de l'autre ◆ **the tables were pushed ~ together** on a rapproché les tables ◆ **to come ~r together** se rapprocher ◆ **to look at sth ~ to** *or* **up** regarder qch de très près

2 ◆ **~ to** *or* **on** (= *almost*) près de ◆ **~ to** *or* **on ten thousand pounds** près de dix mille livres ◆ **he is ~ on 60** il a près de 60 ans ◆ **it's ~ on midnight** il est près de minuit

N (= *enclosure*) clos *m* ; *[of cathedral]* enceinte *f* ; *(Scot = alleyway)* passage *m*, couloir *m*

COMP **close combat** N *(gen)* corps à corps *m*, close-combat *m (SPEC)*

close company N *(Brit Fin) société dont le nombre d'actionnaires est limité*

close-cropped ADJ *[hair]* (coupé) ras ; *[grass]* ras

close-fisted ADJ avare, grippe-sou *inv*, pingre

close-fitting ADJ *[clothes]* ajusté, près du corps

close-grained ADJ *[wood]* au grain serré

close-harmony singing N chant *m* dans une tessiture restreinte *or* rapprochée *or* réduite

close-knit ADJ *[group, community]* très uni

close-mouthed ADJ taciturne, peu bavard

close-run ADJ ◆ **~-run race** course *f* très serrée ◆ **it was a ~-run thing** ils sont arrivés dans un mouchoir

close-set ADJ *[eyes]* rapprochés

close-shaven ADJ rasé de près

close-up N gros plan *m* ◆ **in ~-up** en gros plan

close² /kləʊz/ N (= *end*) fin *f*, conclusion *f* ◆ **to come to a ~** se terminer, prendre fin ◆ **to draw to a ~** tirer à sa fin ◆ **to draw sth** *or* **bring sth to a ~** mettre fin à qch ◆ **the ~ of (the) day** *(liter)* la tombée du jour ◆ **towards the ~ of the century** vers la fin du siècle

VT 1 (= *shut*) fermer ; *[+ eyes, door, factory, shop]* fermer ; *[+ pipe, tube, opening]* boucher ; *[+ road]* barrer ◆ **road ~d to traffic** route *f* interdite à la circulation ◆ **to ~ one's mind to new ideas** fermer son esprit à toute idée nouvelle ; → **ear¹, eye**

2 (= *bring to an end*) *[+ proceedings, discussion]* mettre fin à, clore ; *(Fin) [+ account]* arrêter, clore ; *[+ bargain]* conclure ◆ **to ~ the meeting** lever la séance

3 (= *bring together*) serrer, rapprocher ◆ **to ~ the gap between two objects** réduire l'intervalle entre deux objets ◆ **to ~ the gap between ...** *(fig)* combler le fossé entre ... ◆ **Britain is closing the gap on** *or* **with Japan** la Grande-Bretagne comble son retard sur le Japon ◆ **to ~ ranks** *(Mil, also fig)* serrer les rangs

4 *[+ electrical circuit]* fermer

VI 1 *[door, box, lid, drawer]* fermer, se fermer ; *[museum, theatre, shop]* fermer ◆ **the door ~d** la porte s'est fermée ◆ **the door/box ~s badly** la porte/la boîte ferme mal ◆ **the shop ~s at 6 o'clock** le magasin ferme à 18 heures ◆ **the shop ~s on Sundays** le magasin est fermé le dimanche ◆ **his eyes ~d** ses yeux se fermèrent ◆ **his fingers ~d around the pencil** ses doigts se sont refermés sur le crayon

2 (= *end*) *[session]* se terminer, prendre fin ; *[speaker]* terminer, finir ◆ **the meeting ~d abruptly** la séance a pris fin *or* s'est terminée brusquement ◆ **he ~d with an appeal to their generosity** il a terminé par un appel à leur générosité ◆ **shares ~d at 120p** les actions étaient cotées à *or* valaient 120 pence en clôture

COMP **close-down** N *[of shop, business etc]* fermeture *f* (définitive) ; *(Brit Rad, TV)* fin *f* des émissions

close-out sale N *(US)* liquidation *f* avant fermeture

close season N *(Brit) (Hunting)* période *f* de fermeture de la chasse ; *(Fishing)* période *f* de fermeture de la pêche ; *(Ftbl)* intersaison *f*

► **close down** VI *[business, shop]* fermer (définitivement) ; *(Brit Rad, TV)* terminer les émissions

VT SEP 1 *[+ shop, business]* fermer (définitivement)

2 *(Ftbl) [+ player]* marquer à la culotte

N ◆ **close-down** → **close²**

► **close in** VI *[hunters etc]* se rapprocher, approcher ; *[evening, darkness, night]* tomber ; *[fog]* descendre ◆ **the days are closing in** les jours raccourcissent (de plus en plus) ◆ **to ~ in on sb** (= *approach*) s'approcher *or* se rapprocher de qn ; *(in race, pursuit)* rattraper qn ◆ **the police are closing in on the killer** *(lit)* (= *approaching*) la police resserre son étau autour du meurtrier ; *(fig)* (= *nearer to finding*) le filet de la police se resserre autour du meurtrier

VT SEP clôturer, enclore

► **close off** VT SEP *[+ room]* condamner ; *[+ road etc]* barrer

► **close on** VT FUS 1 (= *get nearer to: in race, achievement etc*) rattraper

2 *(US)* ⇒ **close in on** ; → **close in vi**

► **close out** VT SEP *(US Comm) [+ stock]* liquider (avant fermeture)

► **close up** VI *[people in line etc]* se rapprocher, se serrer ; *(Mil)* serrer les rangs ; *[wound]* se refermer

VT SEP *[+ house, shop]* fermer (complètement) ; *[+ pipe, tube, opening]* fermer, obturer, boucher ; *[+ wound]* refermer, recoudre

► **close with** VT FUS 1 (= *strike bargain with*) conclure un marché avec, tomber d'accord avec

2 (= *agree to*) *[+ offer, conditions]* accepter

closed /kləʊzd/ ADJ *[door, eyes]* fermé, clos ; *[road]* barré ; *[pipe, opening etc]* bouché, obturé ; *[class, economy]* fermé ; *(Ling) [syllable]* couvert ◆ **"closed"** *(notice, gen)* "fermé" ; *(Theat)* "relâche" ◆ **the shop is ~ (now)** le magasin est fermé (maintenant) ◆ **the shop is ~ on Sundays** le magasin ferme le dimanche ◆ **to find the door ~** *(lit, fig)* trouver porte close ◆ **to have a ~ mind** avoir l'esprit étroit ◆ **~ session** *(Jur)* huis *m* clos ◆ **maths is a ~ book to me*** je ne comprends rien aux maths ◆ **behind ~ doors** *(fig)* à l'abri des indiscrets ◆ **~ staff hospital** *(US) hôpital où des médecins agréés peuvent traiter leurs propres malades*

COMP **closed-circuit television** N télévision *f* en circuit fermé

closed company N *(Brit Fin) société dont le nombre d'actionnaires est limité*

closed-door ADJ *[meeting, session]* à huis clos

closed primary N *(US Pol) élection primaire réservée aux membres d'un parti*

closed season N *(US) (Hunting)* période *f* de fermeture de la chasse ; *(Fishing)* période *f* de fermeture de la pêche

closed set N *(Math)* ensemble *m* fermé

closed shop N *atelier or organisation qui n'admet*

que des travailleurs syndiqués ◆ **the unions insisted on a ~-shop policy** les syndicats ont exigé l'exclusion des travailleurs non syndiqués

closely /ˈkləʊslɪ/ ADV 1 *(= strongly) [linked, connected, associated]* étroitement ; *[resemble]* beaucoup ◆ **we are ~ related** nous sommes proches parents ◆ **fruits ~ related to the orange** des fruits *mpl* très proches de l'orange ◆ **~ identified with sth** étroitement associé à qch ◆ **~ involved with a campaign/project** étroitement associé à une campagne/un projet ◆ **to become ~ involved with sb** *(romantically)* se lier intimement à qn ◆ **a ~ knit community** une communauté très unie

2 *(= carefully) [look at, study]* de près ; *[listen]* attentivement ◆ **to monitor sth ~** suivre qch de près ◆ **to question sb ~** presser qn de questions ◆ **a ~ guarded secret/prisoner** un secret/prisonnier bien gardé

3 *(= tightly)* ◆ **he held her ~ to him** il la serrait *or* la tenait serrée (tout) contre lui ◆ **they crowded more ~ around the television** ils se sont pressés davantage autour de la télévision ◆ **~ followed by sb/sth** suivi de près par qn/qch ◆ **to stick ~ to the subject** rester près du sujet

4 *(= densely)* ◆ **~ typed** aux caractères serrés ◆ **~ written** à l'écriture serrée

5 *(= intimately)* ◆ **to work ~ with sb** travailler en étroite collaboration avec qn

6 *(= keenly) [fought, contested]* âprement

closeness /ˈkləʊsnɪs/ N 1 *[of cloth, weave]* texture *f or* contexture *f* serrée ; *[of friendship]* solidité *f* ; *[of translation, reproduction]* fidélité *f* ; *[of examination, interrogation, study]* minutie *f*, rigueur *f* ; *[of reasoning]* logique *f* ; *[of pursuit]* vigueur *f* ; *[of pursuers]* proximité *f* ◆ **~ of blood relationship** proche degré *m* de parenté ◆ **the ~ of the resemblance** la grande ressemblance 2 *(= proximity)* proximité *f* 3 *[of weather, atmosphere]* lourdeur *f* ; *[of room]* manque *m* d'air 4 *(= stinginess)* avarice *f*

closet /ˈklɒzɪt/ N 1 *(US = cupboard)* armoire *f*, placard *m* ; *(for hanging clothes)* penderie *f* 2 *(esp US = small room)* cabinet *m* (de travail), (petit) bureau *m* 3 (also **water closet**) cabinets *mpl*, waters *mpl* 4 *(fig)* **to come out of the ~*** se montrer au grand jour VT *(gen pass)* enfermer *(dans un cabinet de travail etc)* ◆ **he was ~ed with his father for several hours** son père et lui sont restés enfermés plusieurs heures à discuter ◆ **she ~ed herself (away) in her bedroom** elle s'est cloîtrée dans sa chambre ADJ *(* fig = secret)* honteux, qui n'ose pas s'avouer ◆ **a ~ homosexual** un(e) homosexuel(le) refoulé(e) *or* qui ne s'assume pas ◆ **he's a ~ fascist** c'est un fasciste refoulé *or* un crypto-fasciste

closing /ˈkləʊzɪŋ/ N (NonC) *[of factory, house, shop]* fermeture *f* ; *[of meeting]* clôture *f* ; *(Fin)* clôture *f* ADJ 1 *(= final)* final, dernier ◆ **~ remarks** observations *fpl* finales ◆ **~ speech** discours *m* de clôture ◆ **~ price** *(on Stock Exchange)* cours *m* en clôture 2 *(= concluding) [speech, ceremony]* de clôture ◆ **~ date** *(for applications)* date *f* limite de dépôt ; *(Fin, Jur)* date de réalisation (d'une opération) ◆ **~ time** *(Brit)* heure *f* de fermeture *(d'un magasin, d'un café etc)* ◆ **when is ~ time?** à quelle heure fermez-vous ? ◆ **"closing time!"** "on ferme !" ; → **early**
COMP **closing-down sale** N *(Brit Comm)* liquidation *f* totale *(avant fermeture définitive)*
closing-out sale N *(US)* ⇒ **close-out sale** ; → **close²**

closure /ˈkləʊʒəʳ/ N 1 *[of factory, business]* fermeture *f* ; → **lane** 2 *(Parl)* clôture *f* ◆ **to move the ~** *(Parl)* demander la clôture ◆ **~ rule** *(US Pol)* règlement *m* limitant le temps de parole 3 ◆ **to get or achieve ~** *(on deal)* conclure ; *(on past)* tourner la page

clot /klɒt/ N 1 *[of blood, milk]* caillot *m* ◆ **a ~ in the lung/on the brain** une embolie pulmonaire/cérébrale ◆ **a ~ in the leg** une thrombose à la jambe 2 *(Brit ‡ pej = person)* ballot* *m*, cruche* *f* VT *[+ blood]* coaguler VI *[blood]* (se) coaguler COMP **clotted cream** N *(Brit) sorte de crème fraîche épaisse*

cloth /klɒθ/ N 1 (NonC) tissu *m*, étoffe *f* ; *[of linen, cotton]* toile *f* ; *[of wool]* drap *m* ; *(Bookbinding)* toile *f* ; *(Naut)* toile *f*, voile *f* ◆ **bound in ~** *[book]* relié (en) toile ◆ **~ of gold** drap *m* d'or ; → **oilcloth** 2 *(= tablecloth)* nappe *f* ; *(= duster)* chiffon *m*, linge *m* ; → **dishcloth, tea** 3 *(Rel)* **the ~** *(collective)* le clergé ◆ **out of respect for his ~** par respect pour son sacerdoce
COMP *(= made of cloth)* de *or* en tissu, de *or* en étoffe
cloth-binding N *[of books]* reliure *f* (en) toile
cloth-bound ADJ *[book]* relié (en) toile
cloth cap N *(Brit)* casquette *f* (d'ouvrier)
cloth-eared‡ ADJ *(= deaf)* sourdingue‡, dur de la feuille‡
cloth ears‡ N ◆ **wake up ~ ears!** hé ! tu es sourd ou quoi ?*

clothe /kləʊð/ VT habiller, vêtir *(in, with* de) ; *(fig)* revêtir, couvrir *(in, with* de)

clothes /kləʊðz/ NPL 1 vêtements *mpl*, habits *mpl* ◆ **with one's ~ on** (tout) habillé ◆ **with one's ~ off** déshabillé ◆ **to put on one's ~** s'habiller ◆ **to take off one's ~** se déshabiller ; → **plain**

2 (also **bedclothes**) draps *mpl* et couvertures *fpl*
COMP **clothes basket** N panier *m* à linge
clothes brush N brosse *f* à habits
clothes drier, clothes dryer N séchoir *m* (à linge), sèche-linge *m*
clothes hanger N cintre *m*
clothes horse N séchoir *m* (à linge) ; *(fig)* mannequin *m* ◆ **she's just a ~ horse*** *(US)* à part la mode, rien ne l'intéresse
clothes line N corde *f* (à linge)
clothes moth N mite *f*
clothes peg N *(Brit)* pince *f* à linge
clothes pole, clothes prop N perche *f or* support *m* pour corde à linge
clothes rack N *(in shop)* portant *m* de vêtements
clothes rope N ⇒ **clothes line**
clothes shop N magasin *m* de vêtements
clothes tree N *(US)* portemanteau *m*

clothespin /ˈkləʊðzpɪn/ N *(US, Scot)* ⇒ **clothes peg** ; → **clothes**

clothier /ˈkləʊðɪəʳ/ N *(= clothes seller)* marchand *m* (de vêtements) de confection ; *(= cloth dealer, maker)* drapier *m*

clothing /ˈkləʊðɪŋ/ N (NonC) 1 *(= clothes)* vêtements *mpl* ◆ **an article of ~** un vêtement, une pièce d'habillement 2 *(= act of clothing)* habillage *m* ; *[of monks, nuns]* prise *f* d'habit ; *(= providing with clothes)* habillement *m* COMP **clothing allowance** N indemnité *f* vestimentaire

cloture /ˈkləʊtʃəʳ/ *(US Pol)* N clôture *f* COMP **cloture rule** N règlement *m* limitant le temps de parole

cloud /klaʊd/ N 1 *(in sky)* nuage *m*, nuée *f (liter)* ; *[of smoke, dust etc]* nuage *m* ; *[of insects, arrows etc]* nuée *f* ; *[of gas]* nappe *f* ◆ **to have one's head in the ~s** être dans les nuages *or* dans la lune ◆ **to be on ~ nine*** être aux anges *or* au septième ciel* ◆ **every ~ has a silver lining** *(Prov)* à quelque chose malheur est bon *(Prov)* ◆ **under a ~** *(fig) (= under suspicion)* en butte aux soupçons ; *(= in disgrace)* en disgrâce

2 *(= cloudiness) [of liquid]* nuage *m* ; *[of mirror]* buée *f* ; *[of marble]* tache *f* noire
VT *[+ liquid]* rendre trouble ; *[+ mirror]* embuer ; *[+ prospects, career]* assombrir ; *[+ reputation]* ternir ◆ **a ~ed sky** un ciel couvert *or* nuageux ◆ **a ~ed expression** *or* **face** un air sombre *or* attristé ◆ **a ~ed mind** un esprit obscurci ◆ **to ~ the issue** embrouiller les choses
VI (also **cloud over**) *[sky]* se couvrir (de nuages), s'obscurcir ; *(fig) [face, expression]* s'assombrir, se rembrunir
COMP **cloud cover** N couche *f* de nuages
cloud-cuckoo-land N ◆ **she lives in ~-cuckoo-land** elle plane complètement, elle n'a pas les pieds sur terre

cloudberry /ˈklaʊdbərɪ/ N *baie jaune, de la famille de la framboise*

cloudburst /ˈklaʊdbɜːst/ N grosse averse *f*

cloudiness /ˈklaʊdɪnɪs/ N *[of sky]* état *m or* aspect *m* nuageux ; *[of liquid]* aspect *m* trouble ; *[of mirror]* buée *f*

cloudless /ˈklaʊdlɪs/ ADJ *(lit, fig)* sans nuages

cloudy /ˈklaʊdɪ/ ADJ *[sky]* nuageux, couvert ; *[liquid]* trouble ; *[diamond etc]* taché, nuageux ; *[leather]* marbré ; *(fig) [ideas]* nébuleux, embrumé *(fig)* ◆ **it was ~, it was a ~ day** le temps était couvert

clout /klaʊt/ N 1 *(= blow)* coup *m* de poing *(or* de canne *etc)* 2 *(* = influence)* influence *f*, poids *m* ◆ **he's got** *or* **he carries** *or* **he wields a lot of ~** c'est un homme de poids 3 *(dial) (= cloth)* chiffon *m* ; *(= garment)* vêtement *m* VT *[+ object]* frapper ; *[+ person]* donner un coup de poing *(or* de canne *etc)* à

clove¹ /kləʊv/ N clou *m* de girofle ◆ **oil of ~s** essence *f* de girofle ◆ **~ of garlic** gousse *f* d'ail

clove² /kləʊv/ VB pt of **cleave¹** COMP **clove hitch** N *(= knot)* demi-clé *f*

cloven /ˈkləʊvn/ VB ptp of **cleave¹**
COMP **cloven-footed** ADJ *[animal]* aux sabots fendus ; *[devil]* aux pieds fourchus
cloven hoof N *[of animal]* sabot *m* fendu ; *[of devil]* pied *m* fourchu

clover /ˈkləʊvəʳ/ N trèfle *m* ◆ **to be in ~*** être *or* vivre comme un coq en pâte ; → **four**

cloverleaf /ˈkləʊvəliːf/ N *(= leaf)* feuille *f* de trèfle ; *(= road intersection)* (croisement *m* en) trèfle *m*

clown /klaʊn/ N *[of circus etc]* clown *m* ; *(Theat)* bouffon *m* ; *(fig) (= funny person)* clown *m*, pitre *m* ; *(= idiot)* imbécile *m* VI *(fig:* also **clown about, clown around**) faire le clown *or* le pitre

clowning /ˈklaʊnɪŋ/ N (NonC) pitreries *fpl*, singeries *fpl*

clownish /ˈklaʊnɪʃ/ ADJ *[person, behaviour, sense of humour]* clownesque

cloy /klɔɪ/ VT écœurer *(with* de) VI perdre son charme

cloying /ˈklɔɪɪŋ/ ADJ *(lit)* écœurant ; *(fig)* sirupeux

cloyingly /ˈklɔɪɪŋlɪ/ ADV ◆ **~ sentimental** d'une sentimentalité écœurante, dégoulinant de sentimentalité

cloze test /ˈkləʊz,test/ N texte *m* à trous *or* blancs

club /klʌb/ N 1 *(social, sports)* club *m* ◆ **tennis ~** club *m* de tennis ◆ **sports/drama ~** club *m* sportif/de théâtre ◆ **yacht ~** yacht-club *m*, club *m* nautique ◆ **literary ~** cercle *m* littéraire ◆ **he is dining at his ~** il dîne à son club *or* à son cercle ◆ **join the ~!*** *(fig)* tu n'es pas le *or* la seul(e) ! ◆ **to be in the ~**‡ *(Brit = pregnant)* être en cloque‡ ; → **benefit, youth**

2 (also **night club**) boîte *f* de nuit, boîte* *f* ◆ **the ~ scene** le monde des boîtes de nuit ◆ **London's ~ scene** la nuit londonienne

3 *(= weapon) (gen)* massue *f*, gourdin *m* ; *(= truncheon)* matraque *f* ; (also **golf club**) club *m* ; → **Indian**

4 *(Cards)* trèfle *m* ◆ **~s** trèfles *mpl* ◆ **the ace of ~s** l'as *m* de trèfle ◆ **the six of ~s** le six de trèfle ◆ **he played a ~** il a joué (un *or* du) trèfle ◆ **~s**

are trumps atout trèfle ◆ **a low/high** ~ un petit/gros trèfle ◆ **have you any ~s?** avez-vous du trèfle ? ◆ **I haven't any ~s** je n'ai pas de trèfle ◆ **three tricks in ~s** trois levées à trèfle
VT *[+ person]* frapper avec un gourdin *or* une massue ; *(with truncheon)* matraquer ◆ **to ~ sb with a rifle** frapper qn à coups de crosse ◆ **they ~ the baby seals to death** ils tuent les bébés phoques à coups de massue *or* gourdin
VI ◆ **to go ~bing** sortir en boîte *
COMP *[premises, secretary etc]* du club
club car N *(US Rail)* wagon-restaurant *m*
club chair N fauteuil *m* club *inv*
club class N classe *f* club
club foot N (pl **club feet**) pied-bot *m*
club-footed ADJ pied bot *inv*
club member N membre *m* d'un club
club sandwich N club sandwich *m*, ≃ sandwich *m* mixte
club soda N *(US)* eau *f* de seltz
club steak N *(US)* (bifteck *m* pris dans la) queue *f* de filet
club subscription N cotisation *f* (à un club)

► **club together** VI *(esp Brit)* se cotiser ◆ **to ~ together to buy sth** se cotiser pour acheter qch

clubbable * /ˈklʌbəbl/ ADJ sociable

clubber * /ˈklʌbəʳ/ N *(Brit)* noctambule *mf*, habitué(e) *m(f)* des boîtes de nuit

clubbing * /ˈklʌbɪŋ/ N *(Brit)* sorties *fpl* en boîte * ◆ **to go** ~ sortir en boîte *

clubhouse /ˈklʌbhaʊs/ N *(Sport)* pavillon *m*, club-house *m*

clubland /ˈklʌblænd/ N *(NonC)* 1 *(esp Brit: for nightclubs)* le monde des boîtes de nuit 2 *(Brit: for gentlemen's clubs) quartier des clubs chics à Londres*

clubman /ˈklʌbmən/ N (pl **-men**) membre *m* d'un club ; *(= man about town)* homme *m* du monde, mondain *m* ◆ **he is not a** ~ il n'est pas homme à fréquenter les clubs *or* les cercles

clubroom /ˈklʌbrʊm/ N salle *f* de club *or* de réunion

cluck /klʌk/ VI *[hens, people]* glousser N gloussement *m*

clue, clew *(US)* /kluː/ N *(gen)* indication *f*, indice *m* ; *(in crime)* indice *m* ; *(in crossword)* définition *f* ◆ **the killer left behind few ~s as to his identity** le meurtrier n'a laissé que peu d'indices sur son identité ◆ **he gave few ~s about when he intends to leave** il n'a pas donné beaucoup d'indications sur le moment de son départ ◆ **have the police found any ~s as to who killed him?** la police a-t-elle trouvé des indices quant à l'identité du meurtrier ? ◆ **to find the ~ to sth** découvrir *or* trouver la clé de qch ◆ **they may have found the ~ to the cause of this disease** ils ont peut-être découvert *or* trouvé la cause de cette maladie ◆ **the condition of your cat's fur can be a ~ to his state of health** l'aspect du pelage de votre chat peut être une indication de son état de santé ◆ **a person's record collection is often a big ~ to their character** la collection de disques d'une personne en dit souvent long sur son caractère ◆ **my hesitation gave her the ~ to what I was thinking about** mon hésitation lui a permis de deviner à quoi je pensais ◆ **the outside of the building gives little ~ to what goes on inside** il est difficile de deviner, quand on voit l'extérieur du bâtiment, ce qui s'y passe à l'intérieur ◆ **give me a ~!** mets-moi sur la voie ! ◆ **I'll give you a ~** je vais te mettre sur la voie, je vais te donner un indice ◆ **I haven't a ~!** * *(fig)* je n'en ai pas la moindre idée !, aucune idée ! * ◆ **he hasn't a ~ what he's going to do about it** * il n'a pas la moindre idée de ce qu'il va faire à ce sujet ◆ **you haven't got a ~ what I'm talking about, have you?** * tu n'as pas la moindre idée de ce que je raconte, n'est-ce pas ? ◆ **I haven't got a ~ where she's gone** * je n'ai pas la moindre idée de l'endroit où elle est allée, je ne sais pas du tout où elle est allée

► **clue in** ‡ VT SEP mettre au courant *or* au parfum * *(on or about sth* à propos de qch)

► **clue up** ‡ VT SEP mettre au parfum * *(on* de) ; ◆ **to be ~d up** être au parfum * ◆ **to get ~d up about** *or* **on sth** se renseigner sur qch ◆ **he's pretty ~d up on the current political situation** il est assez au courant de la situation politique actuelle

clueless * /ˈkluːlɪs/ ADJ ◆ **he's** ~ il ne sait rien de rien *

clump¹ /klʌmp/ N *[of shrubs]* massif *m* ; *[of trees]* bouquet *m* ; *[of flowers]* touffe *f* ; *(larger)* massif *m* ; *[of grass]* touffe *f* VT ◆ ~ **(together)** rassembler

clump² /klʌmp/ N *(= noise)* bruit *m* de pas lourd(s) *or* pesant(s) VI (also **clump about**) marcher d'un pas lourd *or* pesant

clumpy /ˈklʌmpɪ/ ADJ ◆ ~ **shoes** godillots * *mpl*, croquenots * *mpl*

clumsily /ˈklʌmzɪlɪ/ ADV *(= inelegantly)* gauchement, maladroitement ; *(= tactlessly)* sans tact

clumsiness /ˈklʌmzɪnɪs/ N *[of person, action]* gaucherie *f*, maladresse *f* ; *[of tool etc]* incommodité *f*, caractère *m* peu pratique ; *[of shape, form]* lourdeur *f* ; *(fig = tactlessness) [of person, remark]* maladresse *f*, manque *m* de tact *or* de discrétion

clumsy /ˈklʌmzɪ/ ADJ *[person, action]* gauche, maladroit ; *[tool etc]* incommode, peu pratique ; *[shape, form]* lourd, disgracieux ; *[painting, forgery]* maladroit ; *(fig = tactless) [person, apology, remark]* maladroit ; *[style]* gauche, lourd

clung /klʌŋ/ VB pt, ptp of **cling**

Cluniac /ˈkluːnɪæk/ ADJ, N clunisien *m*

clunk /klʌŋk/ N 1 *(= sound)* bruit *m* sourd 2 *(US* ‡ *= stupid person)* pauvre imbécile *mf* VI *(= make sound)* faire un bruit sourd

clunker ‡ /ˈklʌŋkəʳ/ N *(US = old car)* guimbarde * *f*

clunky * /ˈklʌŋkɪ/ ADJ *[vehicle]* bringuebalant ◆ **a ~ old car** une vieille guimbarde ◆ ~ **shoes** godillots * *mpl*

cluster /ˈklʌstəʳ/ N *[of flowers, blossom, fruit]* grappe *f* ; *[of bananas]* régime *m* ; *[of trees]* bouquet *m* ; *[of bees]* essaim *m* ; *[of people]* (petit) groupe *m*, rassemblement *m* ; *[of houses, islands]* groupe *m* ; *[of stars]* amas *m* ; *(Ling)* groupe *m*, agglomérat *m* ◆ **a sapphire set in a ~ of diamonds** un saphir entouré de brillants VI *[people]* se rassembler, se grouper *(around* autour de) ; *[flowers, blossom, fruit]* être rassemblé (en grappe *or* en bouquet) *(around* autour de)
COMP **cluster bomb** N bombe *f* à fragmentation
cluster pack N *(Comm)* emballage *m* groupé, pack *m*

clutch /klʌtʃ/ N 1 *(= action)* étreinte *f*, prise *f* 2 *[of car]* embrayage *m* ; (also **clutch pedal**) pédale *f* d'embrayage ◆ **to let in the** ~ débrayer ◆ **to let out the** ~ embrayer ◆ ~ **play** garde *f* d'embrayage 3 *[of chickens, eggs]* couvée *f* ◆ **a ~ of** *(fig) [+ prizes etc]* un lot de ; *[+ people, companies]* une poignée de 4 *(fig)* ◆ **to fall into sb's/sth's ~es** tomber entre les griffes de qn/qch ◆ **to get out of sb's/sth's ~es** se tirer des griffes *or* des pattes de qn/qch 5 *(US* ‡ *= crisis)* crise *f* VT *(= grasp)* empoigner, saisir ; *(= hold tightly)* serrer fort ; *(= hold on to)* se cramponner à VI 1 *(= cling)* ◆ **to ~ at** *(lit)* se cramponner à, s'agripper à ; *(fig) [+ hope, idea, chance]* se cramponner à, se raccrocher à ◆ **to ~ at a straw** *or* **at straws** se raccrocher à n'importe quoi 2 *(US)* embrayer
COMP **clutch bag** N pochette *f*
clutch plate N disque *m* d'embrayage

clutter /ˈklʌtəʳ/ N 1 *(NonC = disorder, confusion)* désordre *m*, pagaïe * *f* ◆ **in a** ~ en désordre 2 *(= objects lying about)* fouillis *m*, pagaille * *f*, pagaïe * *f* ◆ **the ~ of bottles and crockery in the kitchen** le fouillis de bouteilles et de vaisselle dans la cuisine VT (also **clutter up** : *lit, fig)* encombrer *(with* de)

Clytemnestra /ˌklaɪtɪmˈnestrə/ N Clytemnestre *f*

cm abbrev of **centimetre(s)**

Cmdr *(Mil)* abbrev of **Commander**

CND /ˌsiːenˈdiː/ N *(in Brit)* (abbrev of **Campaign for Nuclear Disarmament**) *mouvement pour le désarmement nucléaire*

CNN /ˌsiːenˈen/ N (abbrev of **Cable News Network**) CNN *f*

CO /siːˈəʊ/ 1 *(Mil)* (abbrev of **Commanding Officer**) → **commanding** 2 *(Brit Admin)* (abbrev of **Commonwealth Office**) ministère *m* des Affaires étrangères et du Commonwealth 3 (abbrev of **conscientious objector**) → **conscientious** 4 abbrev of **Colorado**

Co. 1 *(Comm)* (abbrev of **company**) Cie ◆ **Joe and ~ * are coming** Joe et compagnie *or* et sa bande * vont venir 2 abbrev of **County**

c/o /ˈkeərəv/ (abbrev of **care of**) chez, aux bons soins de

coach /kəʊtʃ/ N 1 *(horse-drawn)* carrosse *m* ; *(= stagecoach)* diligence *f*, coche *m* ; *(Brit = bus)* car *m*, autocar *m* ; *(Brit) [of train]* voiture *f*, wagon *m* ◆ ~ **and four** carrosse *m* à quatre chevaux 2 *(= tutor)* répétiteur *m*, -trice *f* ; *(Sport: gen)* entraîneur *m* ; *(Ski)* moniteur *m*, -trice *f* VT donner des cours particuliers à ; *(Sport)* entraîner ◆ **to ~ sb for an exam** préparer qn à un examen ◆ **he had been ~ed in what to say** on lui avait fait répéter ce qu'il aurait à dire
COMP **coach building** N *(Brit)* carrosserie *f* *(construction)*
coach class N *(US) (= economy class)* classe *f* économique
coach driver N *(Brit)* chauffeur *m*, -euse *f* de car
coach operator N *(Brit)* compagnie *f* d'autocars
coach park N *(Brit)* parking *m* pour autocars
coach party N groupe *m* voyageant en car
coach station N *(Brit)* gare *f* routière
coach trip N *(Brit)* excursion *f* en car

coachbuilder /ˈkəʊtʃˌbɪldəʳ/ N *(Brit)* carrossier *m*

coaching /ˈkəʊtʃɪŋ/ N *(Sport)* entraînement *m* ; *(Scol)* cours *mpl* particuliers

coachload /ˈkəʊtʃləʊd/ N *(Brit)* ◆ **a ~ of tourists** un car plein de touristes

coachman /ˈkəʊtʃmən/ N (pl **-men**) cocher *m*

coachwork /ˈkəʊtʃwɜːk/ N *(NonC: Brit)* carrosserie *f*

coadjutant /kəʊˈædʒʊtənt/ N assistant(e) *m(f)*, aide *mf*

coagulant /kəʊˈægjʊlənt/ N coagulant *m*

coagulate /kəʊˈægjʊleɪt/ VT coaguler VI se coaguler

coagulation /kəʊˌægjʊˈleɪʃən/ N coagulation *f*

coal /kəʊl/ N charbon *m* ◆ **a piece of** ~ un morceau de charbon ◆ **as black as** ~ noir comme du charbon ◆ **to be on hot ~s** être sur des charbons ardents ◆ **it's like carrying** *or* **taking ~s to Newcastle** c'est comme porter de l'eau à la rivière † ; → **heap, soft**
VT fournir *or* ravitailler en charbon ◆ **to ~ ship** *(Naut)* charbonner
VI *(Naut)* charbonner
COMP *[fire]* de charbon ; *[box, shed]* à charbon
coal basin N bassin *m* houiller
coal-black ADJ noir comme du charbon

Coal Board N (Brit: formerly) ≃ Charbonnages mpl
coal-burning ADJ à charbon, qui marche au charbon
coal cellar N cave f à charbon
coal chute N goulotte f à charbon
coal cutter N haveur m
coal depot N dépôt m de charbon
coal face N front m de taille
coal fire N feu m de charbon or de cheminée
coal-fired power station N centrale f thermique or électrique au charbon
coal gas N gaz m (de houille)
coal hod N seau m à charbon
coal hole N petite cave f à charbon
coal industry N industrie f houillère or charbonnière, charbonnages mpl
coaling station N dépôt m de charbon
coal measures NPL (Geol) gisements mpl houillers
coal merchant N charbonnier m, marchand m de charbon
coal mine N houillère f, mine f de charbon
coal miner N mineur m
coal mining N charbonnage m
coal oil N (US) pétrole m lampant, kérosène m
coal pit N ⇒ **coal mine**
coal scuttle N seau m à charbon
coal strike N grève f des mineurs
coal tar N coaltar m, goudron m de houille
coal tit N (= bird) mésange f noire
coal yard N dépôt m de charbon

coaldust /ˈkəʊldʌst/ N poussier m, poussière f de charbon

coalesce /ˌkəʊəˈles/ VI (lit, fig) s'unir, se fondre

coalescence /ˌkəʊəˈlesəns/ N (lit, fig) fusion f, union f

coalfield /ˈkəʊlfiːld/ N gisement m de houille

coalfish /ˈkəʊlfɪʃ/ N (pl **coalfish** or **coalfishes**) lieu m noir, colin m

coalition /ˌkəʊəˈlɪʃən/ N coalition f COMP **coalition government** N (Pol) gouvernement m de coalition

coalman /ˈkəʊlmən/ N (pl **-men**) 1 (= merchant) charbonnier m, marchand m de charbon 2 (= delivery man) charbonnier m

coarse /kɔːs/ ADJ 1 (in texture) [fabric, feathers, fur, features, grass, gravel, powder] grossier ; [face] aux traits grossiers ◆ ~ **cloth** drap m grossier ◆ ~ **linen** grosse toile f ◆ ~ **salt** gros sel m ◆ ~ **sand** sable m à gros grains, gros sable m ◆ ~ **sandpaper** papier m de verre à gros grain ◆ ~ **skin** peau f rêche ◆ ~ **weave** texture f grossière 2 (= common) ordinaire, grossier ◆ ~ **red wine** gros rouge m 3 (pej) (= uncouth) [person] grossier ; [manners] grossier, vulgaire ; (= indecent) [language, joke] grossier, cru ; [laugh] gros (grosse f), gras (grasse f) ; [accent] commun, vulgaire
COMP **coarse fishing** N pêche f à la ligne (pour poissons autres que le saumon et la truite)
coarse-grained ADJ à gros grain
coarse-grain salt N gros sel m

coarsely /ˈkɔːslɪ/ ADV 1 (= in large pieces) [chop, grate, grind] grossièrement ◆ ~ **woven cloth** tissu m de texture grossière 2 (= uncouthly, vulgarly) [speak] d'une voix or d'un ton vulgaire ; [laugh] grassement, vulgairement ; [say] grossièrement, vulgairement ; [behave] vulgairement

coarsen /ˈkɔːsn/ VI [voice] s'érailler ; [features] s'épaissir ; [laugh, language] devenir vulgaire VT [+ voice] érailler ; [+ features] épaissir

coarseness /ˈkɔːsnɪs/ N (NonC) 1 (in texture) [of grain, sand] grossièreté f ; [of material] grossièreté f, rudesse f ; [of skin] rugosité f ; [of grass] rigidité f 2 (= vulgarity) [of person, behaviour, language, laugh, accent] vulgarité f

coast /kəʊst/ N côte f ; (= coastline) littoral m ◆ **from** ~ **to** ~ (in US, Britain) d'est en ouest ◆ **the** ~ **is clear** la voie or le champ est libre VI 1 ◆ **to** ~ **along/down** [motorist, cyclist] avancer/descendre en roue libre ◆ **to** ~ **along** (fig) (= encounter few problems) avancer (sans problèmes) ; (= take things easy) se la couler douce* ◆ **to** ~ **through** (fig) passer sans difficultés 2 (Naut) caboter

coastal /ˈkəʊstəl/ ADJ [defence, state] côtier ◆ ~ **navigation** navigation f côtière ◆ ~ **traffic** navigation f côtière, cabotage m

coaster /ˈkəʊstəʳ/ N 1 (Naut) caboteur m 2 (= drip mat) dessous m de verre or de bouteille ; (= wine tray) présentoir m à bouteilles ; → **roller**
COMP **coaster brake** N (US) [of cycle] frein m à rétropédalage

coastguard /ˈkəʊstˌgɑːd/ N 1 (= service) ≃ gendarmerie f maritime 2 (= person) membre m de la gendarmerie maritime ; (Hist) garde-côte m
COMP **coastguard station** N (bureau m de la) gendarmerie f maritime
coastguard vessel N (vedette f) garde-côte m

coastguard(s)man /ˈkəʊstˌgɑːd(z)mən/ N (pl **-men**) (esp US) ⇒ **coastguard noun 2**

coastline /ˈkəʊstlaɪn/ N littoral m

coat /kəʊt/ N 1 (gen) manteau m ; (also **overcoat, topcoat**) pardessus m ◆ **winter** ~ manteau m d'hiver or pour l'hiver ◆ **to cut one's** ~ **according to one's cloth** vivre selon ses moyens ; → **housecoat, morning, sport**
2 [of animal] pelage m, livrée f ; [of horse] robe f ◆ **winter** ~ pelage m d'hiver
3 (= covering) [of paint, tar etc] couche f ; [of plastic] enveloppe f ; → **base¹, topcoat**
VT [dust, frost, conditioner, plastic] (re)couvrir ; [person] (with glue, paste, ointment) enduire ; (with chocolate) enrober ; (with breadcrumbs etc) paner ; (with egg, batter) tremper (with dans) ; ◆ **to** ~ **the wall with paint** passer une couche de peinture sur le mur, enduire le mur de peinture ◆ **his tongue was ~ed** (Med) il avait la langue chargée ◆ **~ed lens** (Phot) objectif m traité
COMP **coat hanger** N cintre m
coat of arms N (Her) blason m, armoiries fpl, écu m
coat of mail N cotte f de mailles
coat rack N ⇒ **coatstand**
coat-tails NPL queue f de pie (habit) ◆ **to be hanging on sb's ~-tails** être pendu aux basques de qn ◆ **to ride on sb's ~-tails** (US Pol) se faire élire dans le sillage de qn

-coated /ˈkəʊtɪd/ ADJ (in compounds) recouvert de ◆ **chocolate-coated** enrobé de chocolat

coating /ˈkəʊtɪŋ/ N (gen) couche f ; (on saucepan etc) revêtement m

coatstand /ˈkəʊtstænd/ N portemanteau m

co-author /ˈkəʊˌɔːθəʳ/ N coauteur m VT [+ book, play, report] cosigner

coax /kəʊks/ VT amadouer ◆ **to** ~ **sb into/out of doing sth** amener qn à faire qch/à ne pas faire qch en l'amadouant ◆ **to** ~ **sth out of sb** obtenir qch de qn en l'amadouant

coaxial /kəʊˈæksɪəl/ ADJ (gen, Geom, Elec) coaxial
COMP **coaxial cable** N (TV) câble m coaxial

coaxing /ˈkəʊksɪŋ/ N câlineries fpl, cajolerie(s) f(pl) ADJ enjôleur, câlin

coaxingly /ˈkəʊksɪŋlɪ/ ADV [speak, ask] d'une manière câline, d'un ton enjôleur ; [look] d'un air câlin or enjôleur

cob /kɒb/ N (= swan) cygne m mâle ; (= horse) cob m ; (also **cob-nut**) grosse noisette f ; (Brit: also **cob loaf**) miche f (de pain) ; [of maize] épi m (de maïs) ; → **corn¹**

cobalt /ˈkəʊbɒlt/ N cobalt m ◆ ~ **60** cobalt m 60, cobalt m radioactif ◆ ~ **blue** bleu m de cobalt ◆ ~ **bomb** bombe f au cobalt

cobber‡ /ˈkɒbəʳ/ N (Austral) pote‡ m

cobble /ˈkɒbl/ VT ◆ **to** ~ **together** [+ object, figures] bricoler* ; [+ solution, agreement] bricoler*, concocter* N ⇒ **cobblestone**

cobbled /ˈkɒbld/ ADJ ◆ ~ **street** rue f pavée

cobbler /ˈkɒbləʳ/ N 1 cordonnier m ◆ **~'s wax** poix f de cordonnier 2 (US Culin) tourte f aux fruits 3 (US = drink) (sorte f de) punch m (glacé) 4 (Brit) **that's a load of ~s!**‡ (= nonsense) c'est de la connerie !‡

cobblestone /ˈkɒblstəʊn/ N pavé m rond

COBOL, Cobol /ˈkəʊbɔːl/ N (Comput) COBOL m

cobra /ˈkəʊbrə/ N cobra m

cobweb /ˈkɒbweb/ N toile f d'araignée ◆ **to blow** or **clear away the ~s** (fig) remettre les idées en place

cobwebbed /ˈkɒbwebd/ ADJ couvert de toiles d'araignée

coca /ˈkəʊkə/ N 1 (= shrub) coca m or f 2 (NonC = dried leaves) coca f

cocaine /kəˈkeɪn/ N cocaïne f ◆ ~ **addict** cocaïnomane mf ◆ ~ **addiction** cocaïnomanie f

coccus /ˈkɒkəs/ N (pl **cocci** /ˈkɒksaɪ/) coccidie f

coccyx /ˈkɒksɪks/ N (pl **coccyges** /kɒkˈsaɪdʒiːz/) coccyx m

co-chairman /ˈkəʊˌtʃeəmən/ N (pl **-men**) coprésident(e) m(f)

co-chairmanship /kəʊˈtʃeəmənˌʃɪp/ N coprésidence f

Cochin China /ˌkəʊtʃɪnˈtʃaɪnə/ N Cochinchine f

cochineal /ˈkɒtʃɪniːl/ N (= insect) cochenille f ; (= colouring) colorant m rouge

cochlea /ˈkɒklɪə/ N (pl **cochleae** /ˈkɒklɪˌiː/) (Anat) limaçon m

cochlear /ˈkɒklɪəʳ/ ADJ cochléaire

cock /kɒk/ N 1 (esp Brit = rooster) coq m ; (= male bird) (oiseau m) mâle m ◆ **he thinks he's the** ~ **of the walk** il est vaniteux comme un paon ; → **fighting, gamecock, weather**
2 (= tap) robinet m
3 [of rifle] chien m ◆ **at full** ~ armé ◆ **at half** ~ au cran de repos ; see also **half**
4 [of hay] meulon m ; [of corn, oats] moyette f
5 (*‡= penis) bite*‡f
VT 1 [+ gun] armer
2 ◆ **to** ~ **one's ears** (lit) dresser les oreilles ; (fig) dresser l'oreille ◆ **to** ~ **one's eye at ...** jeter un regard interrogateur à ... ◆ **to** ~ **a snook at ...*** (Brit) faire la nique à ...
COMP [bird] mâle
cock-a-doodle-doo EXCL cocorico !
cock-a-hoop ADJ fier comme Artaban ADV d'un air triomphant
cock-a-leekie soup N (Scot) potage à la volaille et aux poireaux
cock-and-bull story N (pej) histoire f à dormir debout
cock lobster N homard m (mâle)
cock sparrow N moineau m (mâle)
cock-teaser*‡ N allumeuse‡ f
cock-up‡ N (Brit) foirade* f, couille‡ f ◆ **there's been a ~-up** il y a eu une couille‡ ◆ **he made a ~-up of the job** il a salopé le boulot‡ ◆ **the meeting was a ~-up** la réunion a complètement foiré*

► **cock up**‡ (Brit) VT SEP saloper‡ ; [+ exam] foirer‡
VI merder‡, foirer‡
N ◆ **cock-up** → **cock**

cockade /kɒˈkeɪd/ N cocarde f

Cockaigne /kɒˈkeɪn/ N ◆ **(the land of)** ~ le pays de Cocagne

cockamamie* /ˌkɒkəˈmeɪmɪ/ ADJ (US) farfelu

cockatoo /ˌkɒkəˈtuː/ N cacatoès m

cockchafer /ˈkɒkˌtʃeɪfəʳ/ N hanneton m

cockcrow /ˈkɒkkrəʊ/ N ◆ **at ~** au chant du coq, à l'aube

cocked /kɒkt/ ADJ ◆ **~ hat** chapeau *m* à cornes ; *(two points)* bicorne *m* ; *(three points)* tricorne *m* ◆ **to knock** *or* **beat sb into a ~ hat*** battre qn à plate(s) couture(s)

cocker /ˈkɒkəʳ/ N (also **cocker spaniel**) cocker *m*

cockerel /ˈkɒkərəl/ N jeune coq *m*

cockeyed* /ˌkɒkˈaɪd/ ADJ *(= cross-eyed)* qui louche ; *(= crooked)* de travers, de traviole* ; *(= mad, absurd)* qui ne tient pas debout, dingue* ; *(= drunk)* soûl*, schlass‡ *inv*

cockfight /ˈkɒkfaɪt/ N combat *m* de coqs

cockfighting /ˈkɒkˌfaɪtɪŋ/ N combats *mpl* de coqs

cockieleekie soup /ˌkɒkɪliːkɪˈsuːp/ N ⇒ **cock-a-leekie soup** ; → **cock**

cockily /ˈkɒkɪlɪ/ ADV avec impudence *or* effronterie

cockiness /ˈkɒkɪnɪs/ N impudence *f*, effronterie *f*

cockle /ˈkɒkl/ N *(= shellfish)* coque *f* ◆ **it warmed the ~s of his heart** *(† or hum)* cela lui a réchauffé le cœur

cockleshell /ˈkɒklʃel/ N *(= shellfish)* (coquille *f* de) coque *f* ; *(= boat)* petit canot *m*, coquille *f* de noix

cockney /ˈkɒknɪ/ N 1 *(= person)* cockney *mf* ; → RHYMING SLANG 2 *(= dialect)* cockney *m* ADJ cockney, londonien

> **COCKNEY**
>
> Les véritables **cockneys** sont les personnes nées à portée du son des Bow Bells, c'est-à-dire des cloches de l'église de Sainte-Mary-le-Bow dans la City, mais on y inclut tous les habitants de l'est londonien. Le mot désigne aussi le parler des habitants de ces quartiers et, par extension, n'importe quel accent, argot ou parler populaire londonien. → RHYMING SLANG

cockpit /ˈkɒkpɪt/ N *[of aircraft]* poste *m* de pilotage, cockpit *m* ; *[of yacht, racing car]* cockpit *m* ; *(for cockfighting)* arène *f* ; *(fig)* arènes *fpl* COMP **cockpit voice recorder** N enregistreur *m* de vol

cockroach /ˈkɒkrəʊtʃ/ N cafard *m*, blatte *f*

cockscomb /ˈkɒkskəʊm/ N 1 *[of cockerel]* crête *f* (de coq) 2 *(= plant)* crête-de-coq *f* 3 *(† = dandy)* fat *m*, poseur *m*, muscadin † *m*

cocksucker**‡ /ˈkɒkˌsʌkəʳ/ N enfoiré**‡ *m*, enculé**‡ *m*

cocksure /ˈkɒkʃʊəʳ/ ADJ *(pej)* (trop) sûr de soi, outrecuidant

cocktail /ˈkɒkteɪl/ N *(lit, fig)* cocktail *m* (boisson) ◆ **fruit ~** salade *f* de fruits ◆ **prawn ~** *(Brit)*, **shrimp ~** *(US)* coupe *f* or cocktail de crevettes ; → **Molotov**

COMP **cocktail bar** N bar *m* américain, cocktail-bar *m*
cocktail cabinet N meuble *m* bar
cocktail dress N robe *f* de cocktail
cocktail lounge N bar *m* *(de luxe, dans un hôtel)*
cocktail onion N petit oignon *m* *(au vinaigre)*
cocktail party N cocktail *m*
cocktail sausage N petite saucisse *f* *(pour l'apéritif)*
cocktail shaker N shaker *m*
cocktail stick N pique *f* (à apéritif)
cocktail waitress N *(US)* serveuse *f* *(de bar)*

cocky* /ˈkɒkɪ/ ADJ *(pej)* effronté, impudent

cocoa /ˈkəʊkəʊ/ N *(= drink)* chocolat *m* ; *(= powder)* cacao *m*
COMP **cocoa bean** N fève *f* de cacao
cocoa butter N beurre *m* de cacao

coconut /ˈkəʊkənʌt/ N noix *f* de coco
COMP **coconut ice** N *(NonC)* *confiserie à la noix de coco*
coconut matting N tapis *m* de coco
coconut oil N huile *f* de (noix de) coco
coconut palm N cocotier *m*
coconut shy N jeu *m* de massacre
coconut tree N cocotier *m*

cocoon /kəˈkuːn/ N cocon *m* ◆ **wrapped in a ~ of blankets** emmitouflé dans des couvertures VT *(fig)* *[+ object]* envelopper avec soin ; *[+ child]* couver ◆ **~ed from** *(fig)* à l'abri de ◆ **~ed in the bosom of one's family** bien à l'abri au sein de sa famille

COD /ˌsiːəʊˈdiː/ 1 *(Brit)* (abbrev of **cash on delivery**) → **cash** 2 *(US)* (abbrev of **collect on delivery**) → **collect²**

cod /kɒd/ N (pl **cod** or **cods**) *(= fish)* morue *f* ; *(Culin: fresh)* morue *f* fraîche, cabillaud *m* ◆ **dried ~** merluche *f* ADJ *(Brit *)* *(= not genuine)* faux (fausse *f*), prétendu ; *(= assumed)* *[accent]* faux (fausse *f*)
COMP **cod-liver oil** N huile *f* de foie de morue
the Cod War N *(Brit)* la guerre de la morue

coda /ˈkəʊdə/ N épilogue *m* ; *(Mus)* coda *f*

coddle /ˈkɒdl/ VT 1 *[+ child, invalid]* dorloter, choyer 2 *(Culin)* *[+ eggs]* cuire à feu doux au bain-marie

code /kəʊd/ LANGUAGE IN USE 27.1
N code *m* ◆ **~ of behaviour/of honour** code *m* de conduite/de l'honneur ◆ **in ~** en code ◆ **to dial a ~** *(to access service)* taper un code ; *(area code)* taper un indicatif ◆ **what's the ~ for Germany?** quel est l'indicatif de l'Allemagne ? ◆ **to break a secret ~** déchiffrer *or* décrypter un code secret ; → **highway, Morse, penal, zip**
VT coder
COMP **code dating** N *(Comm)* inscription *f* de date codée *(sur les denrées périssables)*
code letter N lettre *f* *(employée dans un code)*
code name N nom *m* de code
code-name VT ◆ **an operation ~-named "Condor"** une opération qui a pour nom de code "Condor"
code number N *(gen)* numéro *m* de code ; *(= access code)* code *m* d'accès ; *(Telec = dialling code)* indicatif *m* ; *(Tax)* *code numérique désignant chaque tranche d'imposition*
code of conduct N code *m* de conduite
code of ethics N *(gen)* code *m* (d')éthique ; *[of profession]* (code *m* de) déontologie *f*
code of practice N *(gen)* déontologie *f* ; *(= set of rules)* règlements *mpl* et usages *mpl*
code word N *(lit)* mot *m* de passe ; *(fig: Pol)* mot *m* codé

coded /ˈkəʊdɪd/ ADJ 1 *(= in code)* *[message, instructions]* codé ◆ **in ~ form** codé, sous forme de code ◆ **a ~ telephone warning** un avertissement téléphonique codé 2 *(= indirect)* *[criticism, attack, reference]* voilé ◆ **in ~ language** en termes voilés, à mots couverts 3 *(Telec)* *[signal]* codé

codeine /ˈkəʊdiːn/ N codéine *f*

co-dependent /ˌkəʊdɪˈpendənt/ *(esp US Psych)* N codépendant(e) *m(f)* ADJ codépendant

codex /ˈkəʊdeks/ N (pl **codices**) manuscrit *m* (ancien)

codfish /ˈkɒdfɪʃ/ N (pl **codfish** or **codfishes**) morue *f*

codger‡ /ˈkɒdʒəʳ/ N ◆ **old ~** drôle de vieux bonhomme *m*

codices /ˈkɒdɪsiːz/ NPL of **codex**

codicil /ˈkɒdɪsɪl/ N codicille *m*

codify /ˈkəʊdɪfaɪ/ VT codifier

coding /ˈkəʊdɪŋ/ N *(NonC)* *[of telegram, message]* encodage *m* ; *(Comput)* codage *m* ; → **tax** COMP **coding sheet** N *(Comput)* feuille *f* de programmation

codpiece /ˈkɒdˌpiːs/ N braguette *f* *(portée aux xve et xvie siècles)*

co-driver /ˈkəʊdraɪvəʳ/ N *(in race)* copilote *m* ; *[of lorry, bus]* deuxième chauffeur *m*

codswallop‡ /ˈkɒdzwɒləp/ N *(NonC: Brit)* bobards* *mpl*, foutaises‡ *fpl*

coed* /ˈkəʊˈed/ ADJ abbrev of **coeducational** N *(US)* étudiante *f* *(dans un établissement mixte)*

co-edit /ˌkəʊˈedɪt/ VT *[+ book]* coéditer

co-edition /ˌkəʊɪˈdɪʃən/ N coédition *f*

coeducation /ˈkəʊˌedjʊˈkeɪʃən/ N éducation *f* mixte

coeducational /ˈkəʊˌedjʊˈkeɪʃənl/ ADJ *[school, teaching]* mixte

coefficient /ˌkəʊɪˈfɪʃənt/ N coefficient *m*

coeliac /ˈsiːlɪˌæk/ ADJ cœliaque ◆ **~ disease** cœlialgie *f*

coequal /ˌkəʊˈiːkwəl/ ADJ, N égal(e) *m(f)*

coerce /kəʊˈɜːs/ VT contraindre ◆ **to ~ sb into doing sth** contraindre qn à faire qch

coercion /kəʊˈɜːʃən/ N contrainte *f*, coercition *f*

coercive /kəʊˈɜːsɪv/ ADJ coercitif

coeval /kəʊˈiːvəl/ ADJ contemporain (*with* de) du même âge (*with* que) N contemporain(e) *m(f)*

coexist /ˈkəʊɪgˈzɪst/ VI coexister (*with* avec)

coexistence /ˈkəʊɪgˈzɪstəns/ N coexistence *f* ; → **peaceful**

coexistent /ˈkəʊɪgˈzɪstənt/ ADJ coexistant (*with* avec)

coextensive /ˈkəʊɪkˈstensɪv/ ADV ◆ **~ with** *(in space)* de même étendue que ; *(in time)* de même durée que

C of C (abbrev of **Chamber of Commerce**) → **chamber**

C of E /ˌsiːəˈviː/ N *(Brit)* (abbrev of **Church of England**) → **church**

coffee /ˈkɒfɪ/ N café *m* ◆ **a cup of ~** une tasse de café ◆ **one** *or* **a ~** un café ◆ **black ~** café *m* noir ◆ **white ~** *(Brit)*, **~ with milk** *(US)* *(gen)* café *m* au lait ◆ **a white ~** *(Brit)*, **a ~ with milk** *(US)* *(in café: when ordering)* un café-crème
COMP *(= coffee flavoured)* au café ; *(= coffee coloured)* *(dark)* couleur café *inv* ; *(light)* café au lait *inv*
coffee bar N *(Brit)* café *m*, cafétéria *f*
coffee bean N grain *m* de café
coffee break N pause-café *f*
coffee cake N *(Brit: coffee-flavoured)* moka *m* *(au café)* ; *(US: served with coffee)* gâteau *m* *(que l'on sert avec le café)*
coffee-coloured ADJ *(dark)* couleur café *inv* ; *(light)* couleur café au lait *inv*
coffee cup N tasse *f* à café
coffee filter N filtre *m* à café
coffee grounds NPL marc *m* de café
coffee house N *(Hist)* café *m* *(au 18e siècle)*
coffee machine N *(in café etc)* percolateur *m* ; *(= vending machine)* machine *f* à café
coffee-maker N *(electric)* cafetière *f* électrique ; *(non-electric)* cafetière *f*
coffee mill N moulin *m* à café
coffee morning N *(gen)* *réunion de femmes qui se retrouvent pour bavarder autour d'une tasse de café* ; *(for fund-raising)* vente *f* de charité *(où l'on sert le café)*
coffee percolator N ⇒ **coffee-maker**
coffee service, coffee set N service *m* à café
coffee shop N *(= restaurant)* cafétéria *f* ; *(= shop)* brûlerie *f*
coffee spoon N cuiller *f* à café
coffee table N table *f* basse
coffee table book N beau livre *m* *(grand format)*
coffee tree N caféier *m*
coffee whitener N succédané *m* de lait

coffeepot /ˈkɒfɪpɒt/ N cafetière *f*

coffer /ˈkɒfəʳ/ N 1 coffre *m*, caisse *f* ; (*fig*) ◆ **~s** (= *funds*) coffres *mpl* ◆ **the ~s (of State)** les coffres *mpl* de l'État 2 (*Hydraulics*) caisson *m* 3 (*also* **coffer dam**) batardeau *m*

coffin /ˈkɒfɪn/ N cercueil *m*, bière *f* ◆ **~ nail** † (* = *cigarette*) sèche* *f* COMP **coffin dodger*** N (*hum*) vieux débris *m*

C of I /ˌsiːəvˈaɪ/ N (*Brit*) (abbrev of **Church of Ireland**) → **church**

C of S /ˌsiːəvˈes/ N 1 (*Brit*) (abbrev of **Church of Scotland**) → **church** 2 (*Mil*) (abbrev of **Chief of Staff**) → **chief**

cog /kɒg/ N (= *tooth*) dent *f* (d'engrenage) ; (= *wheel*) roue *f* dentée ◆ **he's only a ~ in the wheel** *or* **machine** il n'est qu'un rouage (de la machine) ◆ **a system of ~s** un engrenage

cogency /ˈkəʊdʒənsɪ/ N [*of argument etc*] puissance *f*, force *f*

cogent /ˈkəʊdʒənt/ ADJ (= *compelling*) irrésistible ; (= *convincing*) puissant, convaincant ; (= *relevant*) pertinent, (fait) à-propos

cogently /ˈkəʊdʒəntlɪ/ ADV (*frm*) [*argue, speak, express*] de façon convaincante

cogitate /ˈkɒdʒɪteɪt/ VI méditer, réfléchir ((*up*)*on* sur) ; (*hum*) cogiter ((*up*)*on* sur) VT [+ *scheme*] méditer

cogitation /ˌkɒdʒɪˈteɪʃən/ N (*NonC*) réflexion *f* ; (*hum*) cogitations *fpl*

cognac /ˈkɒnjæk/ N cognac *m*

cognate /ˈkɒgneɪt/ ADJ apparenté, analogue (*with* à) de même origine *or* source (*with* que) ; (*Ling*) [*word, language*] apparenté ; (*Jur*) parent N (*Ling*) mot *m* apparenté ; (*Jur*) cognat *m*, parent *m* proche

cognition /kɒgˈnɪʃən/ N (*NonC*) connaissance *f* ; (*Philos*) cognition *f*

cognitive /ˈkɒgnɪtɪv/ ADJ cognitif COMP **cognitive meaning** N (*Ling*) sens *m* cognitif **cognitive psychology** N psychologie *f* cognitive **cognitive therapy** N thérapie *f* cognitive

cognizance /ˈkɒgnɪzəns/ N 1 (*Jur, gen: frm*) connaissance *f* ◆ **to take/have ~ of ...** prendre/avoir connaissance de ... ◆ **this is outside his ~** ceci n'est pas de sa compétence ◆ **this case falls within the ~ of the court** (*Jur*) cette affaire est de la compétence du tribunal 2 (*Her*) emblème *m*

cognizant /ˈkɒgnɪzənt/ ADJ (*frm*) instruit, ayant connaissance (*of* de) ; (*Jur*) compétent (*of* pour)

cognomen /kɒgˈnəʊmen/ N (pl **cognomens** *or* **cognomina** /kɒgˈnɒmɪnə/) (= *surname*) nom *m* de famille ; (= *nickname*) surnom *m*

cognoscenti /ˌkɒgnəˈʃentɪ, kɒnjəʊˈʃentɪ/ NPL ◆ **the ~** les spécialistes, les connaisseurs

cogwheel /ˈkɒgwiːl/ N roue *f* dentée

cohabit /kəʊˈhæbɪt/ VI cohabiter (*with* avec)

cohabitant /kəʊˈhæbɪtənt/ N ⇒ **cohabitee**

cohabitation /ˌkəʊhæbɪˈteɪʃən/ N cohabitation *f*

cohabitee /ˌkəʊhæbɪˈtiː/, **cohabiter** /kəʊˈhæbɪtəʳ/ N (*Admin*) concubin(e) *m(f)*

coheir /ˈkəʊˈɛəʳ/ N cohéritier *m*

coheiress /ˈkəʊˈɛərɪs/ N cohéritière *f*

cohere /kəʊˈhɪəʳ/ VI 1 (*fig*) être cohérent, se tenir 2 (*lit* = *stick*) adhérer

coherence /kəʊˈhɪərəns/ N 1 (*fig*) cohérence *f* 2 (*lit*) adhérence *f*

coherent /kəʊˈhɪərənt/ ADJ cohérent ◆ **incapable of ~ speech** incapable de s'exprimer de façon cohérente

coherently /kəʊˈhɪərəntlɪ/ ADV de façon cohérente

cohesion /kəʊˈhiːʒən/ N cohésion *f*

cohesive /kəʊˈhiːsɪv/ ADJ cohésif

cohort /ˈkəʊhɔːt/ N (*gen, Mil*) cohorte *f* ; (*pej* = *supporter*) acolyte *m*

COI /ˌsiːəʊˈaɪ/ N (*Brit*) (abbrev of **Central Office of Information**) *service d'information gouvernemental*

coif /kɔɪf/ N (= *headdress*) coiffe *f* ; (= *skullcap*) calotte *f*

coiffed /kɔɪfd/ ADJ (*frm*) coiffé

coiffure /kwɒˈfjʊəʳ/ N (*frm*) coiffure *f*

coiffured /kwɒˈfjʊəd/ ADJ (*frm*) ⇒ **coiffed**

coil /kɔɪl/ VT [+ *rope*] enrouler ; [+ *hair*] enrouler, torsader ; (*Elec*) [+ *wire*] embobiner ; (*Naut*) glèner ◆ **the snake ~ed itself (up)** le serpent s'est lové VI [*river*] onduler, serpenter ; [*rope*] s'enrouler (*round, about* autour de) ; [*snake*] se lover N 1 (= *loops, roll*) [*of rope, wire*] rouleau *m* ; (*Naut*) glène *f* ; [*of hair*] rouleau *m* ; (*at back of head*) chignon *m* ; (*over ears*) macaron *m* 2 (*one loop*) spire *f* ; [*of cable*] tour *m* ; [*of hair*] boucle *f* ; [*of snake, smoke*] anneau *m* 3 (*Elec*) bobine *f* ; (*one loop*) spire *f* 4 (*Med*) **the ~*** (= *contraceptive*) le stérilet COMP **coil spring** N ressort *m* hélicoïdal

coin /kɔɪn/ N 1 pièce *f* de monnaie ◆ **a 10p ~** une pièce de 10 pence ; → **toss** 2 (*NonC*) monnaie *f* ◆ **current ~** monnaie *f* courante ◆ **in (the) ~ of the realm** (*frm*) en espèces (sonnantes et trébuchantes) ◆ **to pay sb back in his own ~** (*liter*) rendre à qn la monnaie de sa pièce VT 1 [+ *money, medal*] frapper ◆ **he is ~ing money** *or* **it (in)** (*fig*) il fait des affaires en or 2 (*fig*) [+ *word, phrase*] inventer ◆ **to ~ a phrase ...** (*hum iro*) si je peux m'exprimer ainsi ... COMP **coin box** N (= *phone box*) cabine *f* téléphonique (à pièces) ; (= *part of vending machine*) caisse *f* **coin-operated** ADJ automatique ◆ **~-operated laundry** (*abbr: coin-op*) laverie *f* automatique

coinage /ˈkɔɪnɪdʒ/ N (*NonC*) 1 (= *coins*) monnaie *f* ; (= *system*) système *m* monétaire 2 (= *act*) [*of money*] frappe *f* ; (*fig*) [*of word etc*] création *f*, invention *f*

coincide /ˌkəʊɪnˈsaɪd/ VI coïncider (*with* avec)

coincidence /kəʊˈɪnsɪdəns/ N coïncidence *f*

coincident /kəʊˈɪnsɪdənt/ ADJ (*frm*) identique (*with* à)

coincidental /kəʊˌɪnsɪˈdentl/ ADJ fortuit ◆ **it's entirely ~** c'est une pure coïncidence

coincidentally /kəʊˌɪnsɪˈdentlɪ/ ADV par coïncidence ◆ **quite** *or* **purely ~** par pure coïncidence

coinsurance /ˌkəʊɪnˈʃʊərəns/ N (*US Med*) *assurance dont les cotisations sont payées pour moitié par l'entreprise*

coir /ˈkɔɪəʳ/ N coco *m*, coir *m* COMP **coir matting** N (*NonC*) tapis *m* de coco

coital /ˈkɔɪtəl/ ADJ coïtal

coitus /ˈkɔɪtəs/ N coït *m* COMP **coitus interruptus** N coït *m* interrompu ◆ **to practise ~ interruptus** pratiquer le coït interrompu

Coke ® /kəʊk/ N coca ® *m*

coke[1] /kəʊk/ N coke *m* COMP **coke oven** N four *m* à coke

coke[2] * /kəʊk/ N (= *drug*) coco *f*, coke *f*

Col. (*Mil*) (abbrev of **Colonel**) ◆ **T. Richard** (*on envelope*) le Colonel T. Richard

col. 1 abbrev of **column** 2 abbrev of **colour**

COLA /ˈkəʊlə/ N (*US Fin*) (abbrev of **cost-of-living adjustment**) → **cost**

cola[1] /ˈkəʊlə/ N cola *or* kola *m* COMP **cola nut** N noix *f* de cola

cola[2] /ˈkəʊlə/ NPL of **colon**

colander /ˈkʌləndəʳ/ N passoire *f*

cold /kəʊld/ LANGUAGE IN USE 7.5

ADJ 1 [*day, drink, meal, meat, metal, water*] froid ◆ **to be as ~ as ice** [*object*] être froid comme de la glace ; [*room*] être glacial ; [*person*] être glacé jusqu'aux os ◆ **it's a ~ morning/day** il fait froid ce matin/aujourd'hui ◆ **I'm ~** j'ai froid ◆ **I'm freezing ~** je suis gelé ◆ **my feet are ~** j'ai froid aux pieds ◆ **to get ~ feet (about doing sth)** hésiter (à faire qch) ◆ **to get ~** [*weather, room*] se refroidir ; [*food*] refroidir ; [*person*] commencer à avoir froid ◆ **you're getting ~er!** (*in guessing games*) tu refroidis ! ◆ **a ~ colour** une couleur froide ◆ **~ steel** (= *weapon*) arme *f* blanche ◆ **the scent is ~** la piste a disparu (*also fig*) ◆ **that's ~ comfort** ce n'est pas tellement réconfortant *or* rassurant, c'est une maigre consolation ◆ **to be in a ~ sweat (about)*** avoir des sueurs froides (au sujet de) ◆ **that brought him out in a ~ sweat** cela lui a donné des sueurs froides ◆ **to pour** *or* **throw ~ water on** [+ *optimism, hopes*] refroidir ◆ **he poured ~ water on my idea** sa réaction devant mon idée m'a refroidi ◆ **a ~ reception** un accueil froid ◆ **to be ~ to sb** se montrer froid envers qn ◆ **that leaves me ~*** ça ne me fait ni chaud ni froid, cela me laisse froid ◆ **in ~ blood** de sang-froid ◆ **he's a ~ fish!*** qu'est-ce qu'il est froid ! ; see also **comp, blow**[1], **icy, light**

2 (* = *unconscious*) ◆ **to be out ~** être dans les pommes* ◆ **it knocked him (out) ~** ça l'a mis KO

N 1 (*in temperature*) froid *m* ◆ **don't go out in this ~!** ne sors pas par ce froid ! ◆ **to come in out of** *or* **from the ~** se mettre à l'abri ; (*fig*) rentrer en grâce ◆ **to be left out in the ~** (*fig*) rester en plan* ; → **feel**

2 (*Med*) rhume *m* ◆ **~ in the head/on the chest** rhume de cerveau/de poitrine ◆ **a heavy** *or* **bad ~** un gros *or* mauvais rhume ◆ **to have a ~** être enrhumé ◆ **to get a ~** s'enrhumer, attraper un rhume ◆ **to take ~** prendre froid

ADV (*US* *) (= *completely*) absolument ; (= *unexpectedly*) de façon totalement inattendue ◆ **to know sth ~** connaître qch à fond *or* sur le bout des doigts

COMP **cold-blooded** ADJ [*animal*] à sang froid ; (*fig*) [*person*] insensible, sans pitié ; [*murder, attack*] commis de sang-froid ◆ **to be ~-blooded about sth** (*fig*) faire qch sans aucune pitié
cold-bloodedly ADV de sang-froid
cold call N (*Comm*) (*on phone*) appel *m* de démarchage ; (= *visit*) démarchage *m* (à domicile)
cold calling N (*Comm*) (*on phone*) démarchage *m* téléphonique ; (= *visit*) démarchage *m* (à domicile)
cold chisel N ciseau *m* à froid
cold cream N crème *f* de beauté
cold cuts NPL (*Culin*) ≈ assiette *f* anglaise
cold frame N (*for plants*) châssis *m* de couches
cold front N (= *weather front*) front *m* froid
cold fusion N (*Phys*) fusion *f* froide
cold-hearted ADJ impitoyable, sans pitié
cold meat N charcuterie *f*
cold-pressed ADJ pressé à froid
cold room N chambre *f* froide *or* frigorifique
cold shoulder* N ◆ **to give sb the ~ shoulder, to turn a ~ shoulder on** *or* **to sb** (*US*) snober qn, battre froid à qn
cold-shoulder VT ◆ **to ~-shoulder sb** ⇒ **to give sb the cold shoulder**
cold snap N (= *weather*) coup *m* de froid, vague *f* de froid de courte durée
cold sore N bouton *m* de fièvre
cold start, cold starting (*US*) N (*in car*) démarrage *m* à froid
cold storage N conservation *f* par le froid ◆ **to put into ~ storage** [+ *food*] mettre en chambre froide ; [+ *fur coat*] mettre en garde ; (*fig*) [+ *idea, book, scheme*] mettre de côté *or* en attente
cold store N entrepôt *m* frigorifique
cold turkey* N (*Drugs*) manque *m* ADJ ◆ **to go ~ turkey** (= *stop*) arrêter la drogue d'un seul coup ; (= *suffer withdrawal symptoms*) être en manque*

the cold war N (*Pol*) la guerre froide
cold warrior N (*Pol*) partisan(e) *m(f)* de la guerre froide
cold wave N (*= weather*) vague *f* de froid ; (*Hairdressing*) minivague *f*
cold-weather payment N (*Brit*) *allocation supplémentaire aux retraités et personnes à faibles revenus en période de grand froid*

coldly /ˈkəʊldlɪ/ ADV [*look, say*] froidement ; [*behave*] avec froideur

coldness /ˈkəʊldnɪs/ N (*lit, fig*) froideur *f*

coleslaw /ˈkəʊlslɔː/ N salade *f* de chou cru

coley /ˈkəʊlɪ/ N lieu noir *m*, colin *m*

colic /ˈkɒlɪk/ N coliques *fpl*

colicky /ˈkɒlɪkɪ/ ADJ [*baby*] qui souffre de coliques ; [*pain*] dû à des coliques ; (*fig*) [*disposition*] grincheux

Coliseum /ˌkɒlɪˈsiːəm/ N Colisée *m*

colitis /kɒˈlaɪtɪs/ N colite *f*

collaborate /kəˈlæbəreɪt/ VI (*also pej*) collaborer ♦ **to ~ with sb on** *or* **in sth** collaborer avec qn à qch

collaboration /kəˌlæbəˈreɪʃən/ N (*also pej*) collaboration *f* (*in* à) ; (*= piece of work*) œuvre *f* produite en commun

collaborationist /kəˌlæbəˈreɪʃənɪst/ N collaborationniste *mf*

collaborative /kəˈlæbərətɪv/ ADJ fait en collaboration, commun

collaboratively /kəˈlæbərətɪvlɪ/ ADV [*work*] en collaboration (*with* avec)

collaborator /kəˈlæbəreɪtə^r^/ N (*gen*) collaborateur *m*, -trice *f* ; (*pej: in World War II*) collaborateur *m*, -trice *f*, collabo* *mf*

collage /kɒˈlɑːʒ/ N (*Art*) collage *m*

collagen /ˈkɒlədʒən/ N (*Bio*) collagène *m*

collapsar /kəˈlæpsə^r^/ N (*Astron*) trou *m* noir

collapse /kəˈlæps/ VI 1 [*person, building, roof, floor, bridge, scaffolding*] s'écrouler, s'effondrer ; [*balloon*] se dégonfler ; [*beam*] s'affaisser ; (*fig*) [*one's health*] se délabrer ; [*government*] s'écrouler ; [*coalition*] se disloquer ; [*business, communism, defences, market, prices, system*] s'effondrer ; [*civilization, society, institution*] s'effondrer, s'écrouler ; [*plan, scheme*] s'écrouler, tomber à l'eau ; [*company*] faire faillite ; [*talks, legal case, trial*] échouer ; [*agreement*] tomber à l'eau ; [*marriage*] se solder par un échec ; (**: with laughter*) être écroulé de rire ♦ **he ~d at work and was taken to hospital** il a eu un grave malaise à son travail et on l'a emmené à l'hôpital ♦ **she ~d onto her bed, exhausted** elle s'est écroulée *or* effondrée sur son lit, épuisée ♦ **his lung ~d** (*Med*) il a fait un collapsus pulmonaire ♦ **~d lung** (*Med*) collapsus *m* pulmonaire
2 (*lit: fold for storage etc*) [*table, chairs*] se plier
VT 1 [*+ table, chair*] plier
2 (*fig*) [*+ paragraphs, items*] réduire, comprimer
N [*of person, building, roof, bridge, scaffolding*] écroulement *m*, effondrement *m* ; [*of beam*] affaissement *m* ; [*of lung*] collapsus *m* ; [*of health*] délabrement *m* ; [*of government*] chute *f* ; [*of coalition*] dislocation *f* ; [*of company*] faillite *f* ; [*of business, communism, defences, market, prices, system*] effondrement *m* ; [*of talks, agreement, marriage, legal case, trial*] échec *m* ; [*of civilization, empire, plan, scheme*] effondrement *m*, écroulement *m* ♦ **the country faces economic ~** le pays risque l'effondrement de son économie ♦ **a 90% ~ in profits** une chute des profits de 90% ♦ **this led to a ~ in confidence in the economy** cela a eu pour effet de détruire la confiance dans l'économie ♦ **the ~ in demand for cars** l'effondrement de la demande de voitures

collapsible /kəˈlæpsəbl/ ADJ [*table, chair, umbrella*] pliant

collar /ˈkɒlə^r^/ N (*attached: on garment*) col *m* ; (*separate, for men*) faux-col *m* ; (*for women*) col *m*, collerette *f* ; (*for dogs, horses etc*) collier *m* ; (*= part of animal's neck*) collier *m* ; (*Culin*) [*of beef, mutton etc*] collier *m* ; (*Tech: on pipe etc*) bague *f* ♦ **to get hold of sb by the ~** saisir qn au collet ; → **blue, white** VT 1 * [*+ person*] (*lit*) mettre la main au collet de ; [*+ book, object*] faire main basse sur ♦ **I managed to ~ her for long enough to talk about ...** j'ai réussi à la coincer* assez longtemps pour pouvoir lui parler de ... 2 (*Tech*) [*+ pipe etc*] baguer COMP **collar button** N (*US*) bouton *m* de col

collarbone /ˈkɒləbəʊn/ N clavicule *f*

collarstud /ˈkɒləstʌd/ N (*Brit*) bouton *m* de col

collate /kɒˈleɪt/ VT 1 (*= gather*) réunir, rassembler 2 (*= compare*) collationner (*with* avec) 3 (*Rel*) nommer (*to* à)

collateral /kɒˈlætərəl/ ADJ 1 (*= parallel*) parallèle ; [*fact, phenomenon*] concomitant ; (*Jur, Med*) collatéral 2 (*= subordinate*) secondaire, accessoire ; (*Fin*) subsidiaire ♦ **~ security** (*Fin*) nantissement *m* 3 (*Mil*) **~ damage** dommages *mpl* collatéraux N 1 (*Fin*) nantissement *m* ♦ **securities lodged as ~** titres *mpl* remis en nantissement 2 (*Jur*) collatéral(e) *m(f)*

collateralize /kɒˈlætərəlaɪz/ VT garantir par nantissement

collation /kəˈleɪʃən/ N 1 (*= gathering*) collecte *f* 2 (*= comparison*) collationnement *m*

colleague /ˈkɒliːg/ N collègue *mf*

collect[1] /ˈkɒlekt/ N (*Rel*) collecte *f* (*prière*)

collect[2] /kəˈlekt/ LANGUAGE IN USE 27.6
VT 1 (*= gather together, assemble*) [*+ valuables, wealth*] accumuler, amasser ; [*+ facts, information, documents*] rassembler, recueillir ; [*+ evidence, proof*] rassembler ♦ **the ~ed works of Shakespeare** les œuvres *fpl* complètes de Shakespeare ♦ **she ~ed (together) a group of volunteers** elle a réuni un groupe de volontaires ♦ **the dam ~s the water from the mountains** le barrage retient l'eau des montagnes ♦ **to ~ paper for recycling** mettre le papier de côté pour le recycler ♦ **to ~ one's wits** rassembler ses esprits ♦ **to ~ o.s.** (*= regain control of o.s.*) se reprendre ; (*= reflect quietly*) se recueillir ♦ **to ~ one's thoughts** se recueillir, se concentrer
2 (*= pick up*) ramasser ♦ **the children ~ed (up) the books for the teacher** les enfants ont ramassé les livres pour le professeur ♦ **these vases ~ the dust** ces vases attirent la poussière
3 (*= obtain*) [*+ money, subscriptions, signatures*] recueillir ; [*+ taxes, dues, fines*] percevoir ; [*+ rents*] encaisser, toucher ♦ **~ on delivery** (*US*) paiement *m* à la livraison, livraison *f* contre remboursement ♦ **she ~ed the prize for best writer** elle a reçu le prix du meilleur écrivain
4 (*= take official possession of*) [*bus or railway company*] [*+ luggage etc*] venir chercher (à domicile) ; [*ticket collector*] [*+ tickets*] ramasser ♦ **to ~ letters** (*Brit Post*) faire la levée du courrier ♦ **the rubbish is ~ed twice a week** les ordures sont ramassées deux fois par semaine ♦ **the firm ~s the empty bottles** la compagnie récupère les bouteilles vides ♦ **to ~ goods/an order** (*Comm*) retirer des marchandises/une commande
5 (*as hobby*) [*+ stamps, antiques, coins*] collectionner, faire collection de ♦ **she ~s* poets/lame ducks** *etc* (*fig*) elle collectionne* les poètes/canards boiteux *etc*
6 (*= call for*) [*+ person*] aller chercher, (passer) prendre ♦ **I'll ~ you in the car/at 8 o'clock** j'irai vous chercher *or* je passerai vous prendre en voiture/à 8 heures ♦ **to ~ one's mail/one's keys** *etc* (passer) prendre son courrier/ses clés *etc* ♦ **I'll come and ~ the book this evening** je passerai prendre le livre ce soir ♦ **the bus ~s the children each morning** l'autobus ramasse les enfants tous les matins
VI 1 [*people*] se rassembler, se réunir ; [*things*] s'amasser, s'entasser ; [*dust, water*] s'accumuler ♦ **a crowd had ~ed outside the building** une foule s'était rassemblée devant le bâtiment
2 (*for charity*) ♦ **to ~ for the injured** faire la quête *or* quêter pour les blessés
3 (*⁎ = make money*) se faire du fric⁎ ♦ **he really ~ed on that deal** il s'est fait un sacré paquet de fric⁎ sur cette affaire
ADV (*US Telec*) ♦ **to call ~** téléphoner en PCV
COMP **collect call** N (*US Telec*) communication *f* en PCV

collectable /kəˈlektəbl/ ADJ ♦ **a ~ antique** *or* **item** une pièce de collection

collected /kəˈlektɪd/ ADJ serein

collection /kəˈlekʃən/ N 1 (*= group*) [*of records, coins, stamps, paintings*] collection *f* ♦ **winter/summer ~** (*Fashion*) collection *f* d'hiver/d'été
2 (*= anthology*) [*of stories, essays, songs*] recueil *m*
3 ♦ **a ~ of buildings/people** (*= a number of*) un ensemble de bâtiments/personnes ♦ **there was a ~ of books on the table** il y avait un assortiment de livres sur la table
4 (*= pick-up*) [*of goods, refuse*] ramassage *m* ♦ **your curtains are ready for ~** vos rideaux sont prêts, vous pouvez venir les chercher
5 (*Brit Post*) [*of mail*] levée *f*
6 [*of money*] (*for charity*) collecte *f* ; (*in church*) quête *f* ♦ **to take the ~** faire la quête ♦ **to take a ~ (for sb/sth)** faire une collecte (au profit de qn/qch *or* pour qn/qch)
7 (*NonC = act of gathering*) [*of taxes*] perception *f*, collecte *f*, levée *f* ; [*of rents*] encaissement *m* ; [*of information, signatures*] collecte *f*
COMP **collection box** N (*Rel*) tronc *m*
collection charges NPL (*Fin, Comm*) frais *mpl* d'encaissement
collection plate N (*Rel*) plateau *m* pour la quête
collection tin N ⇒ **collection box**

collective /kəˈlektɪv/ ADJ collectif N coopérative *f*
COMP **collective bargaining** N (négociations *fpl* pour une) convention *f* collective de travail
collective noun N collectif *m*
collective unconscious N inconscient *m* collectif

collectively /kəˈlektɪvlɪ/ ADV collectivement

collectivism /kəˈlektɪvɪzəm/ N collectivisme *m*

collectivist /kəˈlektɪvɪst/ ADJ, N collectiviste *mf*

collectivization /kəˌlektɪvaɪˈzeɪʃən/ N collectivisation *f*

collectivize /kəˈlektɪvaɪz/ VT collectiviser

collector /kəˈlektə^r^/ N [*of taxes*] percepteur *m* ; [*of dues*] receveur *m* ; [*of rent, cash*] encaisseur *m* ; [*of stamps, coins etc*] collectionneur *m*, -euse *f* ♦ **ticket ~** contrôleur *m*, -euse *f* COMP **collector's item** N pièce *f* de collection

colleen /ˈkɒliːn/ N jeune Irlandaise *f* ; (*in Ireland*) jeune fille *f*

college /ˈkɒlɪdʒ/ N 1 (*= institution for higher education*) établissement *m* d'enseignement supérieur ; (*for professional training*) école *f* professionnelle, collège *m* technique ; (*= university*) université *f* ♦ **College of Advanced Technology** (*Brit*) ≃ IUT *m*, Institut *m* universitaire de technologie ♦ **~ of agriculture** institut *m* agronomique ♦ **~ of art** école *f* des beaux-arts ♦ **~ of domestic science** école *f* *or* centre *m* d'enseignement ménager ♦ **College of Education** (*Brit*) ≃ IUFM *m*, institut *m* universitaire de formation des maîtres ♦ **College of Further Education** (*Brit*) centre *m* de formation continue ♦ **~ of music** conservatoire *m* de musique ♦ **to go to ~** (*gen*) faire des études supérieures ;

(*specifically university*) aller à l'université ◆ ~ **catalog(ue)** (*US Univ*) livret *m* de l'étudiant ◆ ~ **staff** corps *m* enseignant ; → **naval, teacher**

2 (*within a university*) (*Brit*) collège *m* ; (*US*) faculté *f*

3 (= *club*) société *f* ; (= *learned society*) académie *f* ◆ **College of Physicians/Surgeons** Académie *f* de médecine/de chirurgie ◆ **the College of Cardinals** le Sacré Collège ; → **electoral**

COMP **college-bound** ADJ (*US Scol*) ◆ **~-bound student** élève *mf* qui se destine aux études universitaires ◆ **~-bound program** programme *m* de préparation aux études universitaires

COLLEGE

Terme désignant de façon générale un établissement d'enseignement supérieur, le plus souvent une université. En Grande-Bretagne, un **college** peut aussi bien enseigner les arts plastiques ou la musique que préparer des brevets de technicien supérieur en coiffure ou en secrétariat.

Certaines universités, dont Oxford et Cambridge, sont organisées en **colleges**, qui sont responsables de l'organisation de l'enseignement ; la délivrance des diplômes reste la prérogative des universités.

Aux États-Unis, les universités sont administrativement divisées en **colleges**, qui correspondent à des facultés, par exemple « **College** of Arts and Sciences » et « **College** of Medicine ». Les « junior **colleges** » ou « community **colleges** » sont des établissements de premier cycle universitaire, qui assurent également la formation continue des adultes salariés. Les diplômes de troisième cycle universitaire sont décernés par une « graduate school ». → DEGREE, OXBRIDGE

collegial /kə'liːdʒɪəl/ ADJ collégial

collegiate /kə'liːdʒɪɪt/ ADJ [*life*] de collège ; (*Can*) [*studies*] secondaire COMP **collegiate church** N collégiale *f*

collide /kə'laɪd/ VI 1 (*lit*) [*vehicles, trains, planes*] entrer en collision, se heurter ; [*people*] se heurter ◆ **to ~ with** [*vehicle, train, plane*] entrer en collision avec, heurter ; [*person*] heurter ; (*Naut*) aborder 2 (*fig*) se heurter (*with* à) entrer en conflit (*with* avec)

collie /'kɒlɪ/ N colley *m*

collier /'kɒlɪəʳ/ N 1 (= *miner*) mineur *m* 2 (= *ship*) charbonnier *m*

colliery /'kɒlɪərɪ/ N (*Brit*) houillère *f*, mine *f* (de charbon)

collimator /'kɒlɪˌmeɪtəʳ/ N collimateur *m* COMP **collimator viewfinder** N (*Phot*) viseur *m* à cadre lumineux

collision /kə'lɪʒən/ N 1 (*lit*) collision *f*, heurt *m* ; (*Rail*) collision *f* ; (*Naut*) abordage *m* ◆ **to come into ~ with** [+ *car, train*] entrer en collision avec, heurter ; [+ *boat*] aborder 2 (*fig*) conflit *m*, opposition *f*

COMP **collision course** N ◆ **to be on a ~ course** (*Naut etc*) être sur une route de collision ; (*fig*) aller au-devant de l'affrontement (*with* avec)
collision damage waiver N (*Insurance*) *clause d'exclusion des dommages dus à une collision, donnant droit à une réduction des frais de contrat*

collocate /'kɒləkət/ (*Ling*) N cooccurrent *m* VI /'kɒləkeɪt/ [*words*] être cooccurrents ◆ **to ~ with ...** être le cooccurrent de ...

collocation /ˌkɒlə'keɪʃən/ N (*Ling*) collocation *f*

colloquial /kə'ləʊkwɪəl/ ADJ familier

colloquialism /kə'ləʊkwɪəlɪzəm/ N expression *f* familière

colloquially /kə'ləʊkwɪəlɪ/ ADV familièrement, dans le langage parlé

colloquium /kə'ləʊkwɪəm/ N (pl **colloquiums** *or* **colloquia** /kə'ləʊkwɪə/) colloque *m*

colloquy /'kɒləkwɪ/ N colloque *m*, conversation *f*

collude /kə'luːd/ VI s'associer (*dans une affaire louche*)

collusion /kə'luːʒən/ N collusion *f* ◆ **in ~ with ...** en complicité avec ..., de connivence avec ...

collusive /kə'luːsɪv/ ADJ (*frm pej*) collusoire (*frm*)

collywobbles* /'kɒlɪˌwɒblz/ NPL ◆ **to have the ~** (= *be scared*) avoir la frousse* *or* la trouille* ; (= *have stomach trouble*) avoir la chiasse*

Colo. abbrev of **Colorado**

Cologne /kə'ləʊn/ N 1 Cologne 2 ◆ **(eau de) ~** eau *f* de Cologne

Colombia /kə'lɒmbɪə/ N Colombie *f*

Colombian /kə'lɒmbɪən/ ADJ colombien N Colombien(ne) *m(f)*

colon[1] /'kəʊlən/ N (pl **colons** *or* **cola**) (*Anat*) côlon *m*

colon[2] /'kəʊlən/ N (pl **colons**) (*Gram*) deux-points *m inv*

colonel /'kɜːnl/ N colonel *m* ◆ **Colonel Smith** le colonel Smith ; (*on envelope*) le Colonel Smith

colonial /kə'ləʊnɪəl/ ADJ 1 colonial 2 [*house*] en style du 18e siècle, style 18e ; → **House** N colonial(e) *m(f)* COMP **Colonial Office** N ministère *m* des Colonies

colonialism /kə'ləʊnɪəlɪzəm/ N colonialisme *m*

colonialist /kə'ləʊnɪəlɪst/ ADJ, N colonialiste *mf*

colonic /kəʊ'lɒnɪk/ ADJ du côlon COMP **colonic irrigation** N lavage *m* de l'intestin

colonist /'kɒlənɪst/ N colon *m* (*habitant etc d'une colonie*)

colonization /ˌkɒlənaɪ'zeɪʃən/ N colonisation *f*

colonize /'kɒlənaɪz/ VT coloniser

colonized /'kɒlənaɪzd/ ADJ colonisé

colonnade /ˌkɒlə'neɪd/ N colonnade *f*

colony /'kɒlənɪ/ N (*all senses*) colonie *f* ; → **leper**

colophon /'kɒləfən/ N (= *emblem*) logotype *m*, colophon *m* ; (= *end text in book*) achevé *m* d'imprimer ; (= *end text in manuscript*) colophon *m*

color (*etc*) /'kʌləʳ/ (*US*) ⇒ **colour**

Colorado /ˌkɒlə'rɑːdəʊ/ N (= *state*) Colorado *m* ◆ **in ~** dans le Colorado COMP **Colorado beetle** N doryphore *m*

colorant /'kʌlərənt/ N (*US*) ⇒ **colourant**

coloration /ˌkʌlə'reɪʃən/ N coloration *f*, coloris *m* ; → **protective**

coloratura /ˌkɒlərə'tʊərə/ N colorature *f* ADJ [*voice, part*] de colorature

colorcast /'kʌləkɑːst/ N émission *f* en couleurs VT retransmettre en couleurs

colossal /kə'lɒsl/ ADJ (*lit, fig*) colossal

colossally /kə'lɒsəlɪ/ ADV [*expensive, destructive*] effroyablement ; [*improve, increase*] de façon phénoménale ◆ **~ powerful** d'une puissance colossale

colossi /kə'lɒsaɪ/ NPL of **colossus**

Colossians /kə'lɒʃənz/ N Colossiens *mpl*

colossus /kə'lɒsəs/ N (pl **colossi** *or* **colossuses**) colosse *m* ◆ **the Colossus of Rhodes** le Colosse de Rhodes

colostomy /kə'lɒstəmɪ/ N colostomie *f* COMP **colostomy bag** N poche *f* pour colostomie

colostrum /kə'lɒstrəm/ N colostrum *m*

colour, color (*US*) /'kʌləʳ/ N 1 (= *hue*) couleur *f* ◆ **what ~ is it?** de quelle couleur est-ce ? ◆ **there's not enough ~ in it** cela manque de couleur ◆ **to change ~** changer de couleur ◆ **to take the ~ out of sth** décolorer qch ; → **primary**

2 (*fig*) **the ~ of a newspaper** la couleur *or* les opinions *fpl* d'un journal ◆ **let's see the ~ of your money*** fais voir la couleur de ton fric* ◆ **a symphony/a poem full of ~** une symphonie pleine/un poème plein de couleur ◆ **to give** *or* **lend ~ to a tale** colorer un récit ◆ **to give a false ~ to sth** présenter qch sous un faux jour, dénaturer qch ◆ **under (the) ~ of ...** sous prétexte *or* couleur de ...

3 (= *complexion*) teint *m*, couleur *f* (*du visage*) ◆ **to change ~** changer de couleur *or* de visage ◆ **to lose (one's) ~** pâlir, perdre ses couleurs ◆ **to get one's ~ back** reprendre des couleurs ◆ **he looks an unhealthy ~** il a très mauvaise mine ◆ **he had gone a funny ~** il avait pris une couleur bizarre ◆ **to have a high ~** être rougeaud ; → **off**

4 (*Art*) (= *pigment*) matière *f* colorante, couleur *f* ; (= *paint*) peinture *f* ; (= *dye*) teinture *f* ; (= *shades, tones*) coloris *m*, couleur *f* ◆ **to paint sth in bright/dark ~s** (*lit*) peindre qch de couleurs vives/sombres ; (*fig*) peindre qch sous de belles couleurs/sous des couleurs sombres ◆ **to see sth in its true ~s** voir qch sous son vrai jour ; see also **colours npl** ; → **local, watercolour**

5 [*of race*] couleur *f* ◆ **his ~ counted against him** sa couleur jouait contre lui ◆ **it is not a question of ~** ce n'est pas une question de race ◆ **people of ~** † gens *mpl* de couleur

NPL **colours** (= *symbol of allegiance*) couleurs *fpl* (*d'un club, d'un parti etc*) ; (*Mil*) couleurs *fpl*, drapeau *m* ; (*Naut*) couleurs *fpl*, pavillon *m* ◆ **to get** *or* **win one's ~s** (*Sport*) être sélectionné pour (faire partie de) l'équipe ◆ **to salute the ~s** saluer le drapeau ◆ **to fight with the ~s** combattre sous les drapeaux ◆ **to stick to one's ~s** rester fidèle à ses principes *or* à ce qu'on a dit ◆ **he showed his true ~s when he said ...** il s'est révélé tel qu'il est vraiment quand il a dit ... ; → **flying, nail, troop**

VT 1 (*lit*) (= *give colour to*) colorer, donner de la couleur à ; (*with paint*) peindre ; (*with crayons etc*) colorier ; (= *dye*) teindre ; (= *tint*) teinter ◆ **to ~ sth red** colorer (*or* colorier *etc*) qch en rouge ◆ **to ~ (in) a picture** colorier une image

2 (*fig*) [+ *story, description*] colorer ; [+ *facts*] (= *misrepresent*) fausser ; (= *exaggerate*) exagérer ; see also **coloured adj 2**

VI [*thing*] se colorer ; [*person*] rougir

COMP **color line** N (*US*) ⇒ **colour bar**
colour bar N (*Brit*) discrimination *f* raciale
colour-blind ADJ daltonien ; (*fig* = *non-discriminatory*) sans discrimination raciale
colour blindness N daltonisme *m*, achromatopsie *f*
colour camera N (*TV*) caméra *f* couleur *inv*
colour code N code *m* couleurs
colour-code VT codifier par couleurs
colour film N (*for camera*) pellicule *f* couleur(s) ; (*for movie camera; in cinema*) film *m* en couleur(s)
colour filter N (*Phot*) filtre *m* coloré
colour photograph N photo *f* en couleur(s)
colour photography N photographie *f* en couleur(s)
colour printer N imprimante *f* couleur
colour scheme N combinaison *f* de(s) couleurs ◆ **to choose a ~ scheme** assortir les couleurs *or* les tons
colour sergeant N (*Brit Mil*) ≈ sergent-chef *m*
colour slide N diapositive *f* en couleur(s)
colour supplement N (*Brit Press*) supplément *m* illustré
colour television N télévision *f* en couleur(s)

colourant /'kʌlərənt/ N (*Brit*) colorant *m*

coloured, colored (*US*) /'kʌləd/ ADJ 1 (= *not black or white*) [*glass, water*] coloré ; [*chalk, pencil,* *bead]* de couleur ; *[picture, photo, television]* en couleur(s) ; *[fabric, garment]* de couleur ; *[drawing]* colorié ◆ **to be ~ pink/blue** être coloré en rose/en bleu ◆ **brightly ~** aux couleurs vives ◆ **coffee-~** couleur café *inv* ◆ **gold-~** doré ◆ **mauve-~** (de couleur) mauve ◆ **muddy-~** couleur de boue ◆ **a straw-~ hat** un chapeau couleur paille [2] *(= exaggerated)* ◆ **a highly ~ tale** un récit enjolivé [3] † *[person]* de couleur [4] *(in South Africa) [person]* métis (métisse *f*) NPL **coloureds** † *(US, Brit)* personnes *fpl* de couleur ; *(in South Africa)* métis *mpl* ; → **cape²**

colourfast, colorfast *(US)* /ˈkʌlərfɑːst/ ADJ grand teint *inv*

colourful, colorful *(US)* /ˈkʌləfʊl/ ADJ [1] *(= bright) [flowers, clothes, poster, design]* aux couleurs vives [2] *(= exciting) [story, account, history, character, figure]* pittoresque, haut en couleur [3] *(euph = immoral) [past, career, background]* mouvementé [4] *(euph = vulgar) [language]* très libre

colourfully, colorfully *(US)* /ˈkʌləfəlɪ/ ADV [1] *(= brightly) [dressed, painted, decorated]* de couleurs vives [2] *(= excitingly) [describe]* dans un style pittoresque *or* haut en couleur [3] *(euph = vulgarly) [swear, call]* d'une manière expressive

colouring, coloring *(US)* /ˈkʌlərɪŋ/ N [1] *(= complexion)* teint *m* ◆ **high ~** teint *m* coloré [2] *(NonC)* coloration *f* ; *[of drawings etc]* coloriage *m* ; *(fig) [of news, facts etc]* travestissement *m*, dénaturation *f* [3] *(= hue)* coloris *m*, coloration *f* [4] *(in food)* colorant *m* (alimentaire) COMP **colouring book** N album *m* à colorier

colourist, colorist *(US)* /ˈkʌlərɪst/ N *(Art, Hairdressing)* coloriste *mf* ; *(Printing)* chromiste *mf*

colourization, colorization *(US)* /ˌkʌləraɪˈzeɪʃən/ N *(Cine)* colorisation *f*

colourize, colorize *(US)* /ˈkʌləraɪz/ VT *(Cine)* coloriser

colourless, colorless *(US)* /ˈkʌləlɪs/ ADJ *(lit)* sans couleur, incolore ; *(fig)* terne, fade

colourway /ˈkʌləweɪ/ N *(Brit)* coloris *m*

colt /kəʊlt/ N [1] *(= horse)* poulain *m* ; *(fig = a youth)* petit jeune *m (pej)*, novice *m* [2] ◆ **Colt** ® *(= pistol)* colt *m*

coltish /ˈkɒltɪʃ/ ADJ *(= frisky)* guilleret, folâtre ; *(= inexperienced)* jeunet, inexpérimenté

coltsfoot /ˈkəʊltsfʊt/ N (pl **coltsfoots**) *(= plant)* pas-d'âne *m inv*, tussilage *m*

Columbia /kəˈlʌmbɪə/ N *(US)* ◆ **(District of) ~** (le district fédéral de) Columbia ; → **British**

Columbine /ˈkɒləmbaɪn/ N *(Theat)* Colombine *f*

columbine /ˈkɒləmbaɪn/ N ancolie *f*

Columbus /kəˈlʌmbəs/ N ◆ **(Christopher) ~** Christophe Colomb *m* COMP **Columbus Day** N *(US) jour férié le deuxième lundi d'octobre, commémorant la découverte de l'Amérique par Christophe Colomb*

column /ˈkɒləm/ N *(all senses)* colonne *f* ; → **fifth** COMP **column inch** N *dans un journal, espace de 2,5 centimètres sur la largeur d'une colonne*

columnist /ˈkɒləmnɪst/ N *(Press)* chroniqueur *m*, échotier *m*, -ière *f*

coma /ˈkəʊmə/ N coma *m* ◆ **in a ~** dans le coma

comatose /ˈkəʊmətəʊs/ ADJ comateux

comb /kəʊm/ N [1] peigne *m* ; *(large-toothed)* démêloir *m* ◆ **to run a ~ through one's hair, to give one's hair a ~** se donner un coup de peigne, se peigner [2] *(for horse)* étrille *f* ; *(Tech: for wool etc)* peigne *m*, carde *f* ; *(Elec)* balai *m* [3] *[of fowl]* crête *f* ; *[of helmet]* cimier *m* [4] *(= honeycomb)* rayon *m* de miel VT [1] peigner ; *[+ wool, fabric]* peigner, carder ; *[+ horse]* étriller ◆ **to ~ one's hair** se peigner ◆ **to ~ sb's hair** peigner qn [2] *(fig = search) [+ area, hills, town]* fouiller, ratisser ◆ **he ~ed (through) the papers looking for evidence** il a dépouillé le dossier à la recherche d'une preuve COMP **comb-over** * N *(pej) mèche rabattue sur un crâne chauve*

► **comb out** VT SEP *[+ hair]* peigner, démêler ◆ **they ~ed out the useless members of the staff** on a passé le personnel au peigne fin et éliminé les incapables

combat /ˈkɒmbæt/ N combat *m* ; → **close¹, unarmed** VT combattre, lutter contre COMP **combat car** N (véhicule *m*) blindé *m* léger de campagne
combat duty N ◆ **on ~ duty** en service commandé
combat fatigue N psychose *f* traumatique *(du soldat)*
combat jacket N veste *f* de treillis
combat knife N (pl **combat knives**) poignard *m*
combat neurosis N ⇒ **combat fatigue**
combat-ready ADJ prêt à combattre *or* au combat
combat troops NPL troupes *fpl* de combat
combat trousers NPL treillis *m*
combat zone N zone *f* de combat

combatant /ˈkɒmbətənt/ ADJ, N combattant(e) *m(f)*

combative /ˈkɒmbətɪv/ ADJ combatif

combe /kuːm/ N ⇒ **coomb**

combination /ˌkɒmbɪˈneɪʃən/ N *(gen, Chem, Math: also of lock)* combinaison *f* ; *[of people]* association *f*, coalition *f* ; *[of events]* concours *m* ; *[of interests]* coalition *f* ◆ **(motorcycle) ~** *(Brit)* side-car *m* NPL **combinations** (= *undergarment*) combinaison-culotte *f* (de femme) COMP **combination lock** N serrure *f* à combinaison
combination sandwich N *(US)* gros sandwich *m* mixte
combination therapy N thérapie *f* combinée

combine /kəmˈbaɪn/ VT combiner *(with* avec) joindre *(with* à) ; *(Chem)* combiner ◆ **he ~d generosity with discretion** il alliait la générosité à la discrétion ◆ **they ~d forces/efforts** ils ont uni *or* joint leurs forces/efforts ◆ **to ~ business with pleasure** mélanger le travail et l'agrément, joindre l'utile à l'agréable VI s'unir, s'associer ; *[parties]* fusionner ; *[workers]* s'associer ; *(Chem)* se combiner ; *(fig)* se liguer *(against* contre) ; *[events]* concourir *(to do sth* à faire qch) N /ˈkɒmbaɪn/ [1] association *f* ; *(Comm, Fin)* trust *m*, cartel *m* ; *(Jur)* corporation *f* [2] (also **combine harvester**) moissonneuse-batteuse *f* COMP **combining form** N *(Ling)* élément *m* de mot

combined /kəmˈbaɪnd/ ADJ [1] *(= mixed)* ◆ **~ with** conjugué à *or* avec [2] *(= joint) [efforts]* conjugué, combiné [3] *(= total) [salaries]* joint ◆ **~ assets** capital *m* commun ◆ **their ~ wealth** leurs fortunes réunies [4] ◆ **~ clock and radio** radio-réveil *m* COMP **combined forces** NPL *(Mil)* forces *f* alliées
combined honours N *(Brit Univ)* ◆ **to do ~ honours** faire un double cursus
combined operation N *(Mil)* opération *f* combinée

combo ‡ /ˈkɒmbəʊ/ N *(Mus)* petite formation *f* musicale

combustible /kəmˈbʌstɪbl/ ADJ *[material]* combustible ; *(fig) [situation, atmosphere]* explosif, critique

combustion /kəmˈbʌstʃən/ N combustion *f* ; → **internal, spontaneous** COMP **combustion chamber** N chambre *f* d'explosion

come /kʌm/

vb : pret **came**, ptp **come**

1 INTRANSITIVE VERB	4 COMPOUNDS
2 TRANSITIVE VERB	5 PHRASAL VERBS
3 NOUN	

1 - INTRANSITIVE VERB

[1] venir ; *(= arrive)* venir, arriver ◆ **~ here** venez ici ◆ **no one has ~** personne n'est venu ◆ **~ and see me soon, ~ see me soon**(US) venez me voir bientôt ◆ **he has ~ to mend the television** il est venu réparer la télévision ◆ **the time will ~ when ...** un jour viendra où ..., il viendra un temps où ... ◆ **he has ~ a long way** *(lit)* il est venu de loin ; *(fig = made great progress)* il a fait du chemin ◆ **help came in time** les secours sont arrivés à temps ◆ **when did he ~?** quand est-il arrivé ? ◆ **to ~ home** rentrer (chez soi *or* à la maison) ◆ **coming!** j'arrive ! ◆ **~, ~!, ~ now!** allons !, voyons ! ◆ **when your turn ~s** quand ce sera (à) votre tour, quand votre tour viendra ◆ **she is coming * six** elle va sur ses six ans, elle va avoir six ans ◆ **she had it coming to her *** elle l'a *or* l'avait (bien) cherché ◆ **he got what was coming to him** il n'a eu que ce qu'il méritait ◆ **~ again?** ‡ comment ?, pardon ? ◆ **I don't know whether I'm coming or going** je ne sais plus où donner de la tête

◆ **to come** + *preposition* ◆ **you go on, I'll ~ after (you)** allez-y, je vous suis ◆ **the rain came closely after the thunderclap** la pluie a suivi de près le coup de tonnerre ◆ **it came as a shock to him** cela lui a fait un choc ◆ **it came as a surprise to him** cela l'a (beaucoup) surpris ◆ **to ~ before sb/sth** venir avant qn/qch ◆ **to ~ before a judge** *(Jur) [accused]* comparaître devant un juge ; *[case]* être entendu par un juge ◆ **to ~ behind sb/sth** suivre qn/qch ◆ **to ~ between two people** *(fig = cause trouble)* (venir) se mettre entre deux personnes ◆ **to ~ for sb/sth** venir chercher *or* venir prendre qn/qch ◆ **he has ~ from Edinburgh** il est venu d'Édimbourg ◆ **he has just ~ from Edinburgh** il arrive d'Édimbourg ◆ **to ~ from** *(fig = originate from) [person]* venir de, être originaire *or* natif de ; *[object, commodity]* provenir *or* venir de ◆ **he ~s from a very poor family** il vient *or* il est issu d'une famille très pauvre ◆ **I know where you're coming from** * *(fig)* je te comprends ◆ **it came into my head that ...** il m'est venu à l'esprit que ... ◆ **to ~ into sight** apparaître, devenir visible ◆ **they came to a town** ils sont arrivés à une ville, ils ont atteint une ville ◆ **to ~ to a decision** parvenir à *or* prendre une décision ◆ **to ~ to an end** toucher à sa fin ◆ **to ~ to the throne** monter sur le trône ◆ **so it has ~ to this!** nous en sommes donc là ! ◆ **if it ~s to that, you shouldn't have done it either** à ce compte-là *or* à ce moment-là * tu n'aurais pas dû le faire non plus ◆ **if it ~s to that, why did you go?** dans ce cas-là *or* à ce moment-là, pourquoi y es-tu allé ? ◆ **when it ~s to mathematics, no one can beat her** pour ce qui est des mathématiques, elle est imbattable ◆ **~ with me** venez avec moi ; → **agreement, bloom, blossom, blow², effect, grief**

◆ **to come** + *-ing* ◆ **to ~ running/shouting** *etc* arriver en courant/en criant *etc* ◆ **to ~ hurrying in** arriver en toute hâte

◆ **to come** + *infinitive (= be finally in a position to)* en venir à, finir par ◆ **I have ~ to believe him** j'en suis venu à le croire ◆ **he came to admit he was wrong** il a fini par reconnaître qu'il avait tort ◆ **now I ~ to think of it** réflexion faite, quand j'y songe ◆ **it came to pass that ...** *(liter)* il advint que ... *(liter)*

◆ **to come** + *adverb/adjective* ◆ **to ~ apart** *(= come off)* se détacher ; *(= come unstuck)* se décoller ; *(= fall to pieces)* tomber en morceaux ◆ **it**

came apart in my hands ça s'est cassé tout seul ◆ **all the other candidates came far behind** tous les autres candidats sont arrivés loin derrière ◆ **everything came right in the end** tout s'est arrangé à la fin ◆ **his dreams came true** ses rêves se sont réalisés ◆ **to ~ undone** se défaire, se dénouer ; → **clean, loose, naturally, unstick**

◆ **to come and go** aller et venir ◆ **they were coming and going all day** ils n'ont fait qu'aller et venir toute la journée ◆ **the pain ~s and goes** la douleur est intermittente

◆ **... to come** ◆ **the life to ~** la vie future ◆ **the years to ~** les années *fpl* à venir ◆ **in time to ~** à l'avenir

◆ **come** *+ day, month* ◆ **I've known him for three years ~ January** cela fera trois ans en janvier que je le connais ◆ **she will be six ~ August** elle aura six ans au mois d'août *or* en août ◆ **a week ~ Monday** il y aura huit jours lundi

2 = have one's place venir, se trouver, être placé ◆ **May ~s before June** mai vient avant *or* précède juin ◆ **July ~s after June** juillet vient après *or* suit juin ◆ **this passage ~s on page 10** ce passage se trouve à la page 10 ◆ **the adjective must ~ before the noun** l'adjectif doit être placé devant *or* précéder le substantif ◆ **a princess ~s before a duchess** une princesse prend le pas *or* a la préséance sur une duchesse ◆ **to ~ first/second** *(in race)* arriver premier/deuxième ; *(in exam)* être classé premier/deuxième

3 = happen arriver *(to* à*)* se produire ◆ **no harm will ~ to him** il ne lui arrivera rien de mal ◆ **economic recovery came slowly** la reprise économique a été lente ◆ **how do you ~ to be so late?** comment se fait-il que vous soyez si en retard ? ◆ **~ what may** quoi qu'il arrive *subj*

◆ **to come of sth** ◆ **nothing came of it** il n'en est rien résulté ◆ **that's what ~s of not doing as you're told!** voilà ce que c'est que de désobéir !, voilà ce qui arrive quand on désobéit ! ◆ **no good will ~ of it** ça ne mènera à rien de bon, il n'en sortira rien de bon

◆ **how come ?*** comment ça se fait ?* ◆ **how ~ you can't find it?*** comment se fait-il que tu n'arrives *subj* pas à le trouver ?

4 = be available ◆ **this dress ~s in three sizes** cette robe existe *or* se fait en trois tailles ◆ **she's as clever as they ~*** elle est futée comme pas une* ◆ **how do you like your tea? – as it ~s** comment voulez-vous votre thé ? – peu importe *or* ça m'est égal

5 ‡ = reach orgasm jouir

2 - TRANSITIVE VERB

‡ ◆ **that's coming it a bit strong !** faut pas pousser !*, ça, c'est un peu fort ! ; → **innocent**

3 - NOUN

‡ = semen foutre‡ *m*

4 - COMPOUNDS

come-at-able* ADJ accessible

come-hither* ADJ ◆ **she gave him a ~-hither look** elle lui a lancé un regard aguichant

come-on* N *(gen = lure)* attrape-nigaud *m*, truc* *m* ◆ **to give sb the ~-on** *(sexual)* provoquer qn, allumer* qn

come-to-bed eyes* NPL ◆ **she has ~-to-bed eyes** elle a un regard provocant *or* aguicheur

5 - PHRASAL VERBS

► **come about** VI 1 *(impers = happen)* se faire *impers + que + subj*, arriver, se produire ◆ **how does it ~ about that you are here?** comment se fait-il que vous soyez ici ? ◆ **this is why it came about** voilà pourquoi c'est arrivé *or* cela s'est produit 2 *(Naut) [wind]* tourner, changer de direction

► **come across** VI 1 *(= cross)* traverser 2 ◆ **he comes across as an honest man** il donne l'impression d'être un honnête homme ◆ **his speech came across very well** son discours a fait bonne impression ◆ **his speech came across very badly** son discours n'a pas fait d'effet *or* n'a pas passé la rampe ◆ **despite his attempts to hide them, his true feelings came across quite clearly** malgré ses efforts pour les cacher, ses vrais sentiments se faisaient sentir clairement 3 *(US * = keep promise etc)* s'exécuter, tenir parole VT FUS *(= find or meet by chance) [+ thing]* trouver par hasard, tomber sur ; *[+ person]* rencontrer par hasard, tomber sur ◆ **if you ~ across my watch ...** si vous tombez sur ma montre ...

► **come across with*** VT FUS *[+ money]* se fendre de*, y aller de ; *[+ information]* donner, vendre ◆ **he came across with £10** il s'est fendu* de 10 livres ◆ **the criminal came across with the names of his accomplices** le criminel a donné* ses complices

► **come along** VI 1 *(imper only)* ~ **along!** *(impatiently)* allons *or* voyons, dépêchez-vous ! ; *(in friendly tone)* (allez,) venez ! 2 *(= accompany)* venir, suivre ◆ **could my sister ~ along as well?** est-ce que ma sœur peut venir aussi ? ◆ **why don't you ~ along?** pourquoi ne viendrais-tu pas ? ◆ **~ along with me** venez avec moi, suivez-moi 3 *(= arrive by chance)* ◆ **it was lucky you came along** c'est une chance que vous soyiez venu ◆ **he waited a long time for the perfect job to ~ along** il a attendu longtemps avant que l'emploi idéal ne se présente *subj* 4 *(= progress)* avancer, faire des progrès ; *[plants, children]* pousser ; *[plans]* avancer ◆ **he's coming along in French** il fait des progrès en français ◆ **how is your broken arm? – it's coming along quite well** comment va votre bras cassé ? – il *or* ça se remet bien ◆ **my book isn't coming along at all well** mon livre n'avance pas bien

► **come around** VI ⇒ **come round**

► **come at** VT FUS attaquer ◆ **he came at me with an axe** il s'est jeté sur moi en brandissant une hache

► **come away** VI 1 *(= leave)* partir, s'en aller ◆ **she had to ~ away before the end** elle a dû partir avant la fin ◆ **~ away from there!** sors de là !, écarte-toi de là ! 2 *(= become detached) [button etc]* se détacher, partir ◆ **it came away in my hands** cela m'est resté dans les mains

► **come back** VI *[person]* revenir ; *[fashion]* revenir à la mode ◆ **he came back two hours later** il est revenu deux heures plus tard ◆ **he came back strongly into the game** *(Sport)* il est revenu en force dans le jeu ◆ **to ~ back from injury/defeat** faire son come-back après une blessure/défaite ◆ **I asked her to ~ back with me** je lui ai demandé de me raccompagner ◆ **to ~ back to what I was saying ...** pour en revenir à ce que je disais ... ◆ **I'll ~ back to you on that one*** nous en reparlerons (plus tard) ◆ **his face/name is coming back to me** son visage/son nom me revient (à la mémoire *or* à l'esprit)

► **come back with** VT FUS répondre par ◆ **when accused, he came back with a counteraccusation** quand on l'a accusé, il a répondu par une contre-accusation

► **come by** VI passer (par là) ◆ **he came by yesterday and told us** il est venu *or* passé (par là) hier et nous l'a raconté VT FUS *(= obtain) [+ object]* obtenir, se procurer ; *[+ idea, opinion]* se faire ◆ **how did you ~ by that book?** comment vous êtes-vous procuré ce livre ?

► **come down** VI 1 *(from ladder, stairs)* descendre *(from* de*)* ; *(from mountain)* descendre, faire la descente *(from* de*)* ; *[aircraft]* descendre ◆ **~ down from there at once!** descends de là tout de suite ! ◆ **to ~ down in the world** *(fig)* descendre dans l'échelle sociale, déchoir ◆ **her hair ~s down to her shoulders** ses cheveux lui descendent jusqu'aux épaules *or* lui tombent sur les épaules ◆ **to ~ down (strongly) for** *or* **in favour of** *or* **on the side of sth** *(fig)* prendre (fermement) position en faveur de qch ◆ **he came down on the side of the President** il s'est rangé du côté du président, il a pris parti pour le président 2 ◆ **the problem comes down to money** le problème se résume à *or* se réduit à une question d'argent ◆ **it all ~s down to the fact that people are very dependent on their cars** tout le problème réside dans le fait que les gens ne peuvent pas se passer de leurs voitures ◆ **when it ~s down to it, are we really free to speak our mind?** au fond, sommes-nous vraiment libres de dire ce que nous pensons ? 3 *[buildings etc] (= be demolished)* être démoli, être abattu ; *(= fall down)* s'écrouler 4 *(= drop) [prices]* baisser ◆ **if you buy three, the price ~s down to £2** si vous en achetez trois, le prix est ramené à 2 livres 5 *(= be transmitted) [tradition etc]* être transmis (de père en fils)

► **come down on** VT FUS 1 *(= punish)* punir ; *(= rebuke)* s'en prendre à ◆ **he came down on me like a ton of bricks*** il m'est tombé dessus à bras raccourcis 2 ◆ **they came down on me*** for a subscription ils m'ont mis le grappin dessus* pour que je souscrive

► **come down with** VT FUS 1 *(= become ill from)* attraper ◆ **to ~ down with flu** attraper une grippe 2 *(* = pay out)* allonger‡

► **come forward** VI se présenter (*as* comme) ◆ **several witnesses have ~ forward** plusieurs personnes se sont présentées comme témoins ◆ **who will ~ forward as a candidate?** qui va se présenter comme candidat *or* se porter candidat ? ◆ **after the burglary, her neighbours came forward with help/money** après le cambriolage, ses voisins ont offert de l'aider/lui ont offert de l'argent ◆ **to ~ forward with a suggestion** faire une suggestion ◆ **to ~ forward with an answer** suggérer une réponse

► **come in** VI 1 *[person]* entrer ; *[train, plane etc]* arriver ; *[tide]* monter ◆ **reports are now coming in of a terrorist attack** des informations nous parviennent selon lesquelles il y aurait eu un attentat terroriste ◆ **when** *or* **where do I ~ in?** *(fig)* quand est-ce que j'entre en jeu, moi ? ◆ **where does your brother ~ in?** *(fig) (= how is he involved?)* qu'est-ce que ton frère a à voir là-dedans ? ; *(= what's to be done with him?)* qu'est-ce qu'on fait de ton frère là-dedans ?, qu'est-ce que ton frère devient là-dedans ? ◆ **this is where we came in!** *(fig)* nous sommes revenus à la case départ ! 2 *[fashion]* devenir à la mode 3 *(in a race)* arriver ◆ **he came in fourth** il est arrivé quatrième ◆ **he came in first in geography** *(Scol)* il a eu la meilleure note en géographie, il a été premier en géographie 4 *(Pol = be elected to power)* être élu, arriver au pouvoir ◆ **the socialists came in at the last election** les socialistes sont arrivés au pouvoir aux dernières élections 5 ◆ **he has £20,000 coming in every year** il touche *or* encaisse 20 000 livres chaque année ◆ **if I'm not working my pay won't be coming in** si je ne travaille pas, je ne toucherai pas ma paie ◆ **we have no money coming in at the moment** nous n'avons aucune rentrée d'argent en ce moment 6 ◆ **to come in handy** *or* **useful** avoir son utilité, venir à propos ◆ **to ~ in handy** *or* **useful for sth** servir à qch, être commode pour qch

► **come in for** VT FUS *(= receive) [+ criticism]* être l'objet de, subir, être en butte à ; *[+ reproach]* subir ; *[+ praise]* recevoir

► **come into** VT FUS 1 *(= inherit)* hériter de, entrer en possession de ◆ **to ~ into some money** *(gen)* recevoir une somme d'argent ; *(by inheritance)* hériter (d'une somme d'argent) ◆ **to ~ into one's own** se réaliser, trouver sa voie [2] *(= play a role)* ◆ **logic doesn't really come into it** la logique n'a pas grand-chose à voir là-dedans

► **come near to** VT FUS ◆ **to come near to doing sth** faillir faire qch, être à deux doigts de faire ◆ **I came near to telling her everything** pour un peu je lui aurais tout dit, j'étais à deux doigts de tout lui dire ◆ **he came near to (committing) suicide** il a été à deux doigts de se suicider

► **come off** VI [1] *[button]* se détacher, se découdre ; *[stains, marks]* s'enlever, partir [2] *(= take place)* avoir lieu, se produire ◆ **her wedding did not ~ off after all** son mariage n'a finalement pas eu lieu [3] *(= succeed) [plan]* se réaliser ; *[attempt, experiment]* réussir [4] *(= acquit o.s.)* s'en tirer, s'en sortir ◆ **he came off well by comparison with his brother** il s'en est très bien tiré en comparaison de son frère ◆ **to ~ off best** gagner [5] *(Theat) [actor]* sortir de scène ; *[play]* s'arrêter, cesser d'être donné [6] *(‡ = reach orgasm)* venir‡, jouir VT FUS [1] ◆ **a button came off his coat** un bouton s'est détaché *or* décousu de son manteau ◆ **he came off his bike** il est tombé de son vélo ◆ **to ~ off the gold standard** *(Fin)* abandonner l'étalon-or [2] *[+ drugs, medication]* arrêter [3] ◆ **come off it!** * et puis quoi encore ?, à d'autres !

► **come on** VI [1] *(= follow)* suivre ; *(= continue to advance)* continuer d'avancer [2] *(imper only)* ~ **on, try again!** allons *or* allez, encore un effort ! [3] *(= progress, develop)* faire des progrès, avancer ◆ **how are your lettuces/plans coming on?** où en sont vos laitues/vos projets ? ◆ **my lettuces are coming on nicely** mes laitues poussent bien ◆ **my plans are coming on nicely** mes plans avancent ◆ **how are the children? – they are coming on** comment vont les enfants ? – ils poussent bien *or* ça pousse !* [4] *(= start) [night]* tomber ; *[illness]* se déclarer ; *[storm]* survenir, éclater ; *[seasons]* arriver ◆ **it came on to rain, the rain came on** il s'est mis à pleuvoir ◆ **I feel a cold coming on** je sens que je m'enrhume [5] *(= arise for discussion or judgement) [subject]* être soulevé, être mis sur le tapis ; *[question]* être posé ◆ **his case ~s on this afternoon** *(Jur)* son affaire viendra devant le juge cet après-midi [6] *[actor]* entrer en scène ; *[play]* être joué *or* donné ◆ **"Hamlet" is coming on next week** on donne "Hamlet" la semaine prochaine [7] *(US fig)* **he came on quite sincere** il a donné l'impression d'être tout à fait sincère ◆ **he came on as a fine man** il a fait l'effet d'être un homme bien VT FUS ⇒ **come upon**

► **come on to** VT FUS [1] *(= start discussing) [+ question, topic, issue]* aborder ◆ **I'll ~ on to that in a moment** j'aborderai cela dans un moment [2] *(sexually)* ◆ **to come on to sb*** draguer qn*

► **come out** VI [1] *(gen)* sortir *(of* de) ; *[sun, stars]* paraître, se montrer ; *[flower]* pousser, sortir ; *[spots, rash]* sortir ; *[secret, news]* être divulgué *or* révélé ; *[truth]* se faire jour ; *[book, magazine]* paraître, sortir, être publié ; *[film]* sortir ; *(Scol etc: in exams)* se classer ; *[qualities]* se manifester, se révéler, se faire remarquer ; *[stain]* s'en aller, partir ; *[dye, colour] (= run)* déteindre ; *(= fade)* passer, se faner ; *(Math) [problem]* se résoudre ; *[division etc]* tomber juste ◆ **he came out third in French** il s'est classé *or* il est troisième en français [2] ◆ **to come out well** être réussi ◆ **this photo didn't ~ out well** cette photo n'a rien donné *or* n'est pas réussie ◆ **the photo came out well** la photo est réussie *or* est très bonne ◆ **you always ~ out well in photos** tu es toujours très bien sur les photos, tu es très photogénique [3] *(with preposition)* ◆ **the total comes out at** *or* **to 500** le total s'élève à 500 ◆ **to ~ out in a rash** *(Med)* avoir une éruption ◆ **to ~ out for/against sth** *(fig)* se déclarer ouvertement pour/contre qch, prendre position pour/contre qch ◆ **to ~ out of o.s.** *or* **one's shell** sortir de sa coquille *or* réserve *(fig)* [4] *(Brit:* also **to come out on strike**) se mettre en grève, faire grève [5] (also **to come out of the closet**) *[homosexual]* se déclarer ouvertement homosexuel, faire son coming-out ◆ **she came out as a lesbian** elle s'est ouvertement déclarée lesbienne [6] *(= go into society)* faire ses débuts dans le monde [7] *(= result from)* ~ **out of** être né de

► **come out with*** VT FUS *(= say)* sortir*, dire ◆ **you never know what she's going to ~ out with next** on ne sait jamais ce qu'elle va sortir* *or* dire ◆ ~ **out with it!** dis ce que tu as à dire !, accouche !‡

► **come over** VI [1] *(lit)* venir ◆ **he came over to England for a few months** il est venu passer quelques mois en Angleterre ◆ **his family came over with the Normans** sa famille s'est installée ici du temps des Normands ◆ **he came over to our side** *(fig)* il est passé de notre côté ◆ **he came over to our way of thinking** il s'est rangé à notre avis [2] *(* = feel suddenly)* **to ~ over giddy** *or* **funny** se sentir mal tout d'un coup, se sentir tout chose* ◆ **she came over faint** elle a failli s'évanouir *or* tourner de l'œil* ◆ **she came over all shy** tout à coup la timidité la saisit *or* elle fut prise de timidité [3] *(= make impression)* **he came over well in his speech** son discours l'a bien mis en valeur ◆ **his speech came over well** son discours a fait bonne impression ◆ **he came over as a fine politician** il a donné l'impression d'être un bon homme politique VT FUS *[influences, feelings] [+ person]* saisir, s'emparer de ◆ **a feeling of shyness came over her** la timidité la saisit, elle fut saisie de timidité ◆ **a sudden change came over him** un changement soudain s'est fait jour en lui ◆ **I don't know what came over her to speak like that!** je ne sais pas ce qui lui a pris de parler comme ça ! ◆ **what's ~ over you?** qu'est-ce qui vous prend ?

► **come round** VI [1] faire le tour *or* un détour ◆ **the road was blocked and we had to ~ round by the farm** la route était bloquée et nous avons dû faire un détour par la ferme [2] *(= drop in)* venir, passer ◆ **do ~ round and see me one evening** passez me voir un de ces soirs [3] *(= recur regularly)* revenir périodiquement ◆ **your birthday will soon ~ round again** ce sera bientôt à nouveau ton anniversaire [4] *(= change one's mind)* changer d'avis ◆ **perhaps in time she will ~ round** peut-être qu'elle changera d'avis avec le temps ◆ **he came round to our way of thinking in the end** il a fini par se ranger à notre avis [5] *(= regain consciousness)* revenir à soi, reprendre connaissance ; *(= get better)* se rétablir, se remettre *(after* de) [6] *(= throw off bad mood etc)* se radoucir, redevenir aimable ◆ **leave her alone, she'll soon ~ round** laissez-la tranquille, elle reviendra bientôt à d'autres sentiments [7] *[boat]* venir au vent

► **come through** VI [1] *(= cope)* s'en tirer, s'en sortir [2] *(= arrive)* ◆ **reports of fighting are coming through** on raconte qu'il y a des combats ◆ **his divorce has ~ through** son divorce a été prononcé ◆ **the call came through** *(Telec)* on a reçu *or* eu la communication [3] ◆ **what came through most was her enthusiasm for the project** ce qui ressortait surtout *or* ce qui était frappant, c'était son enthousiasme pour le projet [4] ◆ **she came through for us** elle nous a donné satisfaction ◆ **they came through on their promises** ils ont respecté leurs promesses, ils ont tenu parole VT FUS *(= survive) [+ illness, danger, war]* survivre à

► **come through with** VT FUS *(US)* ⇒ **come up with**

► **come to** VI [1] *(= regain consciousness)* revenir à soi, reprendre connaissance [2] *(Naut = stop)* s'arrêter VT FUS *[cost, sum]* revenir à, se monter à ◆ **how much does it ~ to?** cela fait combien ?, cela se monte à combien ? ◆ **it ~s to £20** ça fait 20 livres en tout ◆ **it ~s to much less per metre if you buy a lot** cela revient beaucoup moins cher le mètre si vous en achetez beaucoup ◆ **it ~s to the same thing** *(fig)* ça revient au même *or* à la même chose ◆ **he will never ~ to much** *(fig)* il ne sera *or* fera jamais grand-chose

► **come together** VI *(= assemble)* se rassembler ; *(= meet)* se rencontrer ◆ **to ~ together again** *(fig)* se réconcilier

► **come under** VT FUS [1] *(= be subjected to) [+ sb's influence, domination]* tomber sous, subir ; *[+ attack, criticism]* être l'objet de, essuyer [2] *(= be classified under)* être classé sous ◆ **that ~s under "towns"** c'est classé *or* cela se trouve sous la rubrique "villes" ◆ **this ~s under another department** *(Admin, Comm)* c'est du ressort *or* de la compétence d'un autre service

► **come up** VI [1] monter ◆ **do you ~ up to York often?** est-ce que vous venez *or* montez souvent à York ? ◆ **he came up to me** il s'est approché de moi, il est venu vers moi ◆ **he came up to me with a smile** il m'a abordé en souriant ◆ **he came up to Oxford last year** *(Brit)* il est entré à (l'université d')Oxford l'année dernière ◆ **"coming up!"** *(in restaurant)* "ça marche !"* ◆ **he has ~ up in the world** *(fig)* il a grimpé les échelons [2] *(Jur) [accused]* comparaître *(before* devant) ; *[case]* être entendu *(before* par) [3] *[plant]* sortir, pointer ◆ **the tulips haven't ~ up yet** les tulipes ne sont pas encore sorties [4] *[sun]* se lever [5] *(= arise) [matter for discussion]* être soulevé, être mis sur le tapis ; *[question]* se poser, être soulevé ◆ **the question of a subsidy came up** la question d'une subvention s'est posée *or* a été soulevée ◆ **I'm afraid something's ~ up** malheureusement j'ai un empêchement [6] *[job, vacancy]* se présenter

► **come up against** VT FUS se heurter à *or* contre *(fig)* ◆ **he came up against total opposition to his plans** il s'est heurté à une opposition radicale à ses projets ◆ **to ~ up against sb** entrer en conflit avec qn

► **come upon** VT FUS *(= find or meet by chance) [+ object]* trouver par hasard, tomber sur ; *[+ person]* rencontrer par hasard, tomber sur

► **come up to** VT FUS [1] *(= reach up to)* s'élever jusqu'à, arriver à ◆ **the water came up to his knees** l'eau lui montait *or* arrivait jusqu'aux genoux ◆ **my son ~s up to my shoulder** mon fils m'arrive à l'épaule ◆ **it's just coming up to five minutes to six** il est presque six heures moins cinq [2] *(= equal)* répondre à ◆ **to ~ up to sb's hopes** réaliser les *or* répondre aux espoirs de qn ◆ **his work has not ~ up to our expectations** son travail n'a pas répondu à notre attente

► **come up with** VT FUS *[+ object, money, funds]* fournir ; *[+ idea, plan]* proposer, suggérer ◆ **she ~s up with some good ideas** elle propose *or* suggère de bonnes idées

---

comeback /ˈkʌmbæk/ N *(Theat etc)* retour *m* ; *(= response)* réplique *f* ; *(= redress)* recours *m* ◆ **to make** *or* **stage a ~** *[fashion]* revenir ; *[politician]* revenir sur la scène politique ; *[entertainer]* faire un come-back ◆ **to have no ~** n'avoir aucun recours

Comecon /ˈkɒmɪˌkɒn/ N *(formerly)* (abbrev of **Council for Mutual Economic Aid**) COMECON *m*

comedian /kəˈmiːdɪən/ N [1] *(Theat) [of variety]* comique *m* ; *[of plays]* comédien *m* ; *(stand-up)* humoriste *mf* ; *(fig)* comique *m* [2] *(†† = author)* auteur *m* de comédies

comedic /kəˈmiːdɪk/ ADJ *(frm) [moment, incident, performer]* de comédie

comedienne /kə,miːdɪ'en/ N *(Theat) [of variety]* actrice *f* comique ; *[of plays]* comédienne *f* *(stand-up)* humoriste *f*

comedown* /'kʌmdaʊn/ N dégringolade* *f*, déchéance *f* ◆ **it was rather a ~ for him to have to work for his brother** c'était assez humiliant pour lui de devoir travailler pour son frère

comedy /'kɒmɪdɪ/ N *(= play: also fig)* comédie *f* ; *(NonC = style of play)* la comédie, le genre comique ◆ **"The Comedy of Errors"** "La Comédie des Méprises" ◆ **~ of manners** comédie *f* de mœurs ◆ **high ~** haute comédie *f* ◆ **low ~** farce *f* ◆ **cut (out) the ~!*** *(fig)* pas de comédie ! ; → **musical**

comeliness /'kʌmlɪnɪs/ N *(liter)* beauté *f*

comely /'kʌmlɪ/ ADJ *(liter = beautiful)* beau (belle *f*) ; *(†† = proper)* bienséant

comer /'kʌməʳ/ N arrivant(e) *m(f)* ◆ **open to all ~s** ouvert à tous ◆ **they decided to give the job to the first ~** ils ont décidé d'offrir le poste au premier candidat qui se présenterait ; → **latecomer, newcomer**

comestible † /kə'mestɪbl/ ADJ comestible N *(gen pl)* ◆ **~s** denrées *fpl* comestibles, comestibles *mpl*

comet /'kɒmɪt/ N comète *f*

comeuppance* /,kʌm'ʌpəns/ N ◆ **to get one's ~** avoir ce qu'on mérite ◆ **at last he's got his ~** il a finalement eu ce qu'il méritait ◆ **he got his ~!** il ne l'a pas volé !*, il l'a bien cherché !

comfit /'kʌmfɪt/ N dragée *f*

comfort /'kʌmfət/ N ① *(= well-being)* confort *m*, bien-être *m* ◆ **he has always been used to ~** il a toujours eu tout le *or* son confort ◆ **to live in ~** vivre dans l'aisance *or* à l'aise ◆ **~s** *(= material goods)* aises *fpl*, commodités *fpl* (de la vie) ◆ **every (modern) ~** tout le confort moderne ◆ **he likes his ~s** il aime ses aises ◆ **he has never lacked ~s** il n'a jamais manqué des choses matérielles

② *(= consolation)* consolation *f*, réconfort *m* ◆ **to take ~ from sth** trouver du réconfort *or* une consolation dans qch ◆ **your presence is/you are a great ~ to me** votre présence est/vous êtes pour moi d'un grand réconfort ◆ **if it's any ~ to you** si ça peut te consoler ◆ **it is a ~ to know that ...** c'est un soulagement *or* c'est consolant de savoir que ... ◆ **to take ~ from the fact that/from the knowledge that ...** trouver rassurant le fait que/de savoir que ... ; → **cold**

③ *(= peace of mind)* **too close for ~** dangereusement près

VT *(= console)* consoler ; *(bring relief to)* soulager ; *(†† = hearten)* réconforter, encourager

COMP **comfort eating** N suralimentation *f* par compensation

comfort station N *(US euph)* toilette(s) *f(pl)*

comfort zone N zone *f* de confort

comfortable /'kʌmfətəbl/ ADJ ① *[chair, clothes, room, journey, life, position, majority]* confortable ; *[temperature]* agréable ◆ **to be a ~ winner of sth** remporter qch haut la main

② *(= physically at ease)* ◆ **are you ~ there ?** vous êtes bien ? ◆ **would you prefer to sit here? – no thanks, I'm quite ~ where I am** préféreriez-vous vous asseoir là ? – non merci, je me trouve très bien ici ◆ **to feel ~** se sentir bien ◆ **you don't look very ~** vous n'avez pas l'air bien installé ◆ **to make o.s. ~** *(in armchair etc)* s'installer confortablement ; *(= make o.s. at home)* se mettre à l'aise ◆ **to be ~** *(Med)* être dans un état satisfaisant

③ *(= mentally at ease) [person]* à l'aise ◆ **I'm not ~ at formal dinners** je ne suis pas à l'aise dans les dîners protocolaires ◆ **to be** *or* **feel ~ doing sth** être à l'aise pour faire qch ◆ **to feel ~ with sb/sth** être à l'aise avec qn/qch ◆ **I am not very ~ about it** cela me met mal à l'aise

④ *(financially) [person, family]* aisé ◆ **to have a ~ income** avoir des revenus confortables ◆ **he is in ~ circumstances** il est (financièrement) à l'aise

⑤ *(= undemanding) [job]* de tout repos

⑥ *(= kindly)* ◆ **she was a ~ grandmotherly woman** c'était une femme avec qui on se sentait à l'aise, comme on peut l'être avec une grand-mère

⑦ *(= comforting) [belief]* rassurant

comfortably /'kʌmfətəblɪ/ ADV ① *(physically) [sit, settle, sleep]* confortablement ◆ **~ furnished** confortablement meublé ② *(financially) [live]* à l'aise, confortablement ◆ **to be ~ off** être (financièrement) à l'aise ③ *(= easily) [manage, win, fit, afford]* sans difficulté

comforter /'kʌmfətəʳ/ N ① *(= person)* consolateur *m*, -trice *f* *(liter)* ② *(= scarf)* cache-nez *m* *inv* ; *(= dummy-teat)* tétine *f*, sucette *f* ③ *(US = quilt)* édredon *m*

comforting /'kʌmfətɪŋ/ ADJ *[words, thoughts, feeling]* réconfortant ; *[voice]* apaisant ◆ **it is ~ to think that ...** il est réconfortant de penser que ...

comfortless /'kʌmfətlɪs/ ADJ *[room]* sans confort ; *[person]* désolé, triste ; *[thought, prospect]* peu réconfortant, triste

comfrey /'kʌmfrɪ/ N consoude *f*

comfy* /'kʌmfɪ/ ADJ *[chair, room etc]* confortable ◆ **are you ~?** êtes-vous bien ?

comic /'kɒmɪk/ ADJ comique, amusant ; *(Theat)* comique, de la comédie N ① *(= person)* (acteur *m*) comique *m*, actrice *f* comique ② *(esp Brit = magazine)* comic *m* ◆ **the ~s** *(within newspaper etc)* les bandes *fpl* dessinées

COMP **comic book** N *(esp US)* magazine *m* de bandes dessinées *or* de BD*

comic opera N opéra *m* comique

comic relief N *(Theat)* intervalle *m* comique ; *(fig)* moment *m* de détente (comique)

comic strip N bande *f* dessinée, BD* *f*

comic verse N poésie *f* humoristique

comical /'kɒmɪkəl/ ADJ cocasse, comique

comically /'kɒmɪkəlɪ/ ADV *[say, behave]* comiquement, de façon comique ◆ **~ naive** d'une naïveté comique

coming /'kʌmɪŋ/ N ① arrivée *f*, venue *f* ◆ **~ and going** va-et-vient *m* ◆ **~s and goings** allées *fpl* et venues *fpl* ◆ **~ away/back/down/in/out** *etc* départ *m*/retour *m*/descente *f*/entrée *f*/sortie *f* *etc* ② *(Rel)* avènement *m* ; → **second**[1] ADJ ① *(= approaching) [weeks, months, years]* à venir, prochain *before n* ; *[election, battle]* prochain *before n*, futur *after n* ; *[revolution]* prochain *before n*, futur *after n*, qui se prépare (*or* préparait) ◆ **the ~ year** l'année *f* à venir, l'année *f* prochaine ◆ **~ generations** les générations *fpl* à venir *or* futures ② *(= promising)* ◆ **a ~ politician** un homme politique d'avenir ; → **up** ③ *(= becoming significant)* ◆ **it's the ~ thing** * c'est le truc* qui devient à la mode COMP **coming of age** N passage *m* à l'âge adulte

Comintern /'kɒmɪn,tɜːn/ N Komintern *m*

comity /'kɒmɪtɪ/ N courtoisie *f* ◆ **~ of nations** *(Jur)* courtoisie *f* internationale

comm. ① abbrev of **commerce** ② abbrev of **commercial** ③ abbrev of **committee**

comma /'kɒmə/ N ① *(Gram)* virgule *f* ; → **inverted** ② *(Mus)* comma *m*

command /kə'mɑːnd/ VT ① *(= order)* ordonner, donner l'ordre *(sb to do sth* à qn de faire qch) ; ◆ **to ~ that ...** ordonner *or* donner l'ordre que ... + *subj* ◆ **to ~ sth to be done** donner l'ordre de (faire) faire qch

② *(= be in control of) [+ army, ship]* commander ; *[+ passions, instincts]* maîtriser, dominer

③ *(= be in position to use) [+ money, services, resources]* disposer de, avoir à sa disposition

④ *(= deserve and get) [+ respect]* commander ; *[+ support]* obtenir, inspirer ◆ **to ~ attention** forcer l'attention ◆ **that ~s a high price** cela se vend très cher

⑤ *[place, building] (= overlook)* avoir vue sur, donner sur ; *(= overlook and control)* commander, dominer

VI *(= be in command) (Mil, Naut)* commander, avoir le commandement ; *(gen)* commander ; *(= order)* commander, donner un ordre

N ① *(= order)* ordre *m* ; *(Mil)* commandement *m* ; *(Comput)* commande *f* ◆ **at** *or* **by the ~ of ...** sur l'ordre de ... ◆ **at the word of ~** au commandement

② *(NonC: Mil = power, authority)* commandement *m* ◆ **to be in ~ of ...** être à la tête de ..., avoir sous ses ordres ... ◆ **to have/take ~ of ...** avoir/prendre le commandement de ... ◆ **under the ~ of ...** sous le commandement *or* les ordres de ... ◆ **who's in ~ here?** *(gen)* qui est-ce qui commande ici ? ; → **second**[1]

③ *(Mil) (= troops)* troupes *fpl* ; *(= district)* région *f* militaire ; *(= military authority)* commandement *m* ; → **high**

④ *(fig = possession, mastery)* maîtrise *f*, possession *f* ◆ **~ of the seas** maîtrise *f* des mers ◆ **he has a ~ of three foreign languages** il possède trois langues étrangères ◆ **his ~ of English** sa maîtrise de l'anglais ◆ **to have sth at one's ~** avoir qch à sa disposition ◆ **all the money at my ~** tout l'argent à ma disposition *or* dont je peux disposer ◆ **to be at sb's ~** être à la disposition de qn, être prêt à obéir à qn ◆ **to be in full ~ of one's faculties** être en pleine possession de ses moyens

COMP **command and control** N *(Mil)* commandement *m*

command economy N économie *f* planifiée

command key N *(Comput)* touche *f* de commande

command language N *(Comput)* ordres *mpl* de gestion

command line N *(Comput)* ligne *f* de commande

command module N *(Space)* module *m* de commande

command performance N *(Theat)* ≈ représentation *f* de gala *(à la requête du souverain)*

command post N *(Mil)* poste *m* de commandement

commandant /'kɒmən,dænt/ N *(Mil)* commandant *m* *(d'un camp militaire, d'une place forte etc)*

commandeer /,kɒmən'dɪəʳ/ VT réquisitionner

commander /kə'mɑːndəʳ/ N ① *(gen)* chef *m* ; *(Mil)* commandant *m* ; *(Naut)* capitaine *m* de frégate ; *(Brit Police)* ≈ commissaire *m* (de police) divisionnaire, divisionnaire *m* ; → **lieutenant, wing** ② *[of order of chivalry]* commandeur *m* COMP **commander in chief** N (pl **commanders in chief**) *(Mil)* commandant *m* en chef, généralissime *m*

commanding /kə'mɑːndɪŋ/ ADJ ① *(= powerful)* ◆ **to be in a ~ position** être en position de force ◆ **to have a ~ lead** avoir une avance respectable ② *(= authoritative) [person, voice, manner, look, air]* plein d'autorité ; *[tone]* de commandement, plein d'autorité ③ *(= overlooking)* ◆ **the house offers a ~ view of the capital** depuis la maison, on domine la capitale ◆ **the castle stands in a ~ position overlooking the lake** le château domine le lac COMP **commanding officer** N *(Mil)* commandant *m*

commandingly /kə'mɑːndɪŋlɪ/ ADV *[behave]* de manière imposante ; *[speak]* d'un ton imposant

commandment /kə'mɑːndmənt/ N commandement *m* *(de Dieu ou de l'Église)* ◆ **the Ten Commandments** les dix commandements *mpl*, le décalogue *(frm)*

commando /kəˈmɑːndəʊ/ **N** (pl **commandos** *or* **commandoes**) *(all senses)* commando *m*

commemorate /kəˈmeməreɪt/ **VT** commémorer

commemoration /kəˌmeməˈreɪʃən/ **N** commémoration *f*

commemorative /kəˈmemərətɪv/ **ADJ** commémoratif

commence /kəˈmens/ **VTI** commencer *(to do sth, doing sth* à faire qch) ; ◆ **to ~ proceedings against ...** *(Jur)* former un recours contre ... *(devant une juridiction)*

commencement /kəˈmensmənt/ **N** [1] commencement *m*, début *m* ; *[of law]* date *f* d'entrée en vigueur [2] *(Univ: Cambridge, Dublin, US)* remise *f* des diplômes

commend /kəˈmend/ **VT** *(= praise)* louer, faire l'éloge de ; *(= recommend)* recommander, conseiller ; *(= entrust)* confier *(to* à) remettre *(to* aux soins de) ; ◆ **to ~ o.s. to** *[person]* se recommander à ; *[idea, project]* être du goût de ◆ **his scheme did not ~ itself to the public** son projet n'a pas été du goût du public ◆ **his scheme has little to ~ it** son projet n'a pas grand-chose qui le fasse recommander ◆ **~ me to Mr White** † *(frm)* présentez mes respects à M. White *(frm)*, rappelez-moi au bon souvenir de M. White ◆ **to ~ one's soul to God** recommander son âme à Dieu

commendable /kəˈmendəbl/ **ADJ** louable

commendably /kəˈmendəblɪ/ **ADV** *[behave]* de façon louable ◆ **~ restrained** d'une retenue louable ◆ **his speech was ~ short** son discours avait le mérite d'être bref

commendation /ˌkɒmenˈdeɪʃən/ **N** [1] *(= praise)* éloges *mpl (for sth* pour qch) [2] *(= recommendation)* recommandation *f* [3] *(= award)* récompense *f (for sth* pour qch) [4] *(NonC:* † *= entrusting)* remise *f (to sb* à qn, aux soins de qn)

commensurable /kəˈmenʃərəbl/ **ADJ** commensurable *(with, to* avec)

commensurate /kəˈmenʃərɪt/ **ADJ** *(= of equal extent)* de même mesure *(with* que) ; *(Math)* coétendu *(with* à) de même mesure *(with* que) ; *(= proportionate)* proportionné *(with, to* à)

comment /ˈkɒment/ **LANGUAGE IN USE 6.3** **N** *(spoken, written)* commentaire *m*, remarque *f* ; *(written)* annotation *f* ◆ **his action went** *or* **passed without ~** son action n'a donné lieu à aucun commentaire ◆ **he let it pass without ~** il ne l'a pas relevé ◆ **"no comment"** *(Press)* "je n'ai rien à dire" ◆ **he passed a sarcastic ~** il a fait une observation *or* une remarque sarcastique ◆ **put your ~s in the margin** inscrivez vos commentaires dans la marge ◆ **teacher's ~s** *(Scol: on report)* appréciations *fpl* du professeur **VT** *[+ text]* commenter ◆ **he ~ed that ...** il a remarqué que ..., il a fait la remarque que ... **VI** faire des commentaires ◆ **to ~ on sth** commenter qch, faire des commentaires sur qch

commentary /ˈkɒməntərɪ/ **N** *(= remarks)* commentaire *m*, observation *f* ; *(Rad, TV: on news, events)* commentaire *m* ; *(Sport)* reportage *m* ; → **running** **COMP** **commentary box** **N** *(Sport)* cabine *f* de reportage

commentate /ˈkɒmenteɪt/ **VI** *(Rad, TV)* faire un reportage *(on* sur) **VT** *(Rad, TV) [+ match]* commenter

commentator /ˈkɒmenteɪtəʳ/ **N** [1] *(Rad, TV)* reporter *m* [2] *(on texts etc)* commentateur *m*, -trice *f*

commerce /ˈkɒmɜːs/ **N** [1] *(Comm)* commerce *m*, affaires *fpl* ◆ **he is in ~** il est dans le commerce *or* dans les affaires ◆ **Secretary/Department of Commerce** *(US)* ≈ ministre *m*/ministère *m* du Commerce ; → **chamber** [2] *(fig = intercourse, dealings)* relations *fpl*, rapports *mpl*

commercial /kəˈmɜːʃəl/ **ADJ** *[dealings, art, attaché, radio, TV]* commercial ; *[world]* du commerce ; *[value]* marchand, commercial ; *[district]* commerçant ◆ **to produce sth on a ~ scale** fabriquer *or* produire qch à une échelle industrielle ◆ **Christmas has become very ~** les fêtes de Noël sont devenues une affaire commerciale ; → **establishment**

N *(Rad, TV)* publicité *f*, spot *m* publicitaire

COMP **commercial artist** **N** dessinateur *m* de publicité créateur *m*, -trice *f* publicitaire

commercial bank **N** banque *f* commerciale *or* de commerce

commercial break **N** *(TV, Rad)* page *f* de publicité

commercial college **N** école *f* de commerce

commercial law **N** droit *m* commercial

commercial traveller **N** voyageur *m or* représentant *m* de commerce, commis-voyageur † *m*

commercial vehicle **N** véhicule *m* utilitaire

commercialese /kəˌmɜːʃəˈliːz/ **N** jargon *m* commercial

commercialism /kəˈmɜːʃəlɪzəm/ **N** *(NonC, attitude)* mercantilisme *m (pej)*, esprit *m* commerçant ; *(on large scale)* affairisme *m (pej)* ; *(= business practice)* (pratique *f* du) commerce *m*, (pratique *f* des) affaires *fpl*

commercialization /kəˌmɜːʃəlaɪˈzeɪʃən/ **N** commercialisation *f*

commercialize /kəˈmɜːʃəlaɪz/ **VT** commercialiser

commercialized /kəˈmɜːʃəlaɪzd/ **ADJ** *(pej)* commercial

commercially /kəˈmɜːʃəlɪ/ **ADV** [1] *(= financially) [viable, competitive]* commercialement ◆ **to be ~ minded** avoir le sens des affaires [2] *(= on a large scale) [produce]* à échelle commerciale [3] *(= publicly) [available]* dans le commerce

commie * /ˈkɒmɪ/ **ADJ, N** *(pej)* (abbrev of **communist**) coco * *mf (pej)*

commis chef /ˈkɒmɪʃef/ **N** commis *m* de cuisine

commiserate /kəˈmɪzəreɪt/ **VI** *(= show commiseration)* témoigner de la sympathie *(with* à) ; *(= feel commiseration)* éprouver de la commisération *(with* pour) ; ◆ **I do ~ with you** je compatis ◆ **I went to ~ with him on his exam results** je suis allé m'apitoyer avec lui sur ses résultats d'examen

commiseration /kəˌmɪzəˈreɪʃən/ **N** commisération *f*

commissar † /ˈkɒmɪsɑːʳ/ **N** commissaire *m* du peuple *(en URSS etc)*

commissariat /ˌkɒmɪˈsɛərɪət/ **N** *(Mil)* intendance *f* ; *(Admin, Pol)* commissariat *m* ; *(= food supply)* ravitaillement *m*

commissary /ˈkɒmɪsərɪ/ **N** [1] *(US Mil etc = shop)* intendance *f* [2] *(US Mil = officer)* intendant *m* [3] *(US Cine)* restaurant *m* du studio [4] *(= representative)* représentant *m* ; *(Rel) [of bishop]* délégué *m (d'un évêque)*

commission /kəˈmɪʃən/ **N** [1] *(gen)* ordres *mpl*, instructions *fpl* ; *(to artist etc)* commande *f* ◆ **he gave the artist a ~** il a passé une commande à l'artiste

[2] *(Comm)* commission *f*, courtage *m* ◆ **on a ~ basis** à la commission ◆ **he gets 10% ~** il reçoit une commission de 10%

[3] *(= errand)* commission *f*

[4] *(NonC) [of crime etc]* perpétration *f (Jur or liter)*

[5] *(= official warrant)* pouvoir *m*, mandat *m* ; *(Mil)* brevet *m* ◆ **to get one's ~** être nommé officier ◆ **to give up one's ~** démissionner

[6] *(NonC = delegation of authority etc)* délégation *f* de pouvoir *or* d'autorité, mandat *m*

[7] *(= body of people)* commission *f*, comité *m* ; → **royal**

[8] *(NonC: Naut)* armement *m (d'un navire)* ◆ **to put in ~** armer ◆ **to take out of ~** désarmer ◆ **in ~** en armement, en service ◆ **out of ~** *(Naut)* hors de service ; *(Naut = in reserve)* en réserve ; *(gen = not in working order)* hors service

VT [1] donner pouvoir *or* mission à, déléguer ◆ **he was ~ed to inquire into ...** il a été chargé de faire une enquête sur ...

[2] *[+ artist]* passer une commande à ; *[+ book, painting, article]* commander, commanditer ◆ **this work was ~ed by the town council** cette œuvre a été commandée *or* commanditée par le conseil municipal

[3] *[+ officer in armed forces]* nommer à un commandement ◆ **he was ~ed in 1990** il a été nommé officier en 1990 ◆ **he was ~ed sub-lieutenant** il a été nommé *or* promu au grade de sous-lieutenant

[4] *[+ ship]* mettre en service, armer

COMP **commission agent** **N** *(= bookmaker)* bookmaker *m* ; *(Comm)* courtier *m*

commissioned officer **N** officier in armed forces *m*

Commission for Racial Equality **N** *(Brit)* *commission pour l'égalité des races* ; → **EOC, EEOC**

commissioning editor **N** responsable *mf* de publication

commission of inquiry **N** commission *f* d'enquête

commissionaire /kəˌmɪʃəˈnɛəʳ/ **N** *(Brit, Can)* commissionnaire *m (d'un hôtel etc)*, portier *m*

commissioner /kəˈmɪʃənəʳ/ **N** membre *m* d'une commission, commissaire *m* ; *(Brit Police)* ≈ préfet *m* de police ; *(US Police)* (commissaire *m*) divisionnaire *m* ; → **high, lord** **COMP** **commissioner for oaths** **N** *(Jur) officier ayant qualité pour recevoir les déclarations sous serment*

commissioner of education **N** *(US Scol, Univ)* ≈ recteur *m*, doyen *m*

Commissioner of Official Languages **N** *(Can)* Commissaire *m* aux langues officielles

commit /kəˈmɪt/ **VT** [1] *[+ crime, sacrilege]* commettre ; *[+ mistake]* commettre, faire ◆ **to ~ hara-kiri** faire hara-kiri ◆ **to ~ perjury** se parjurer ; *(Jur)* faire un faux serment ◆ **to ~ suicide** se suicider

[2] *(= consign) [+ letter etc]* confier *(to* à) remettre *(to* à la garde de, aux soins de) ; *[+ person] (gen)* confier *(to* à) ; *(for mental health reasons)* faire interner ◆ **to ~ sb to sb's care** confier qn à la garde de qn ◆ **to ~ sb (to prison)** *(Jur)* faire incarcérer qn ◆ **to ~ sb for trial** *(Jur)* mettre qn en accusation ◆ **to ~ sth to writing** *or* **to paper** consigner *or* coucher qch par écrit ◆ **to ~ sth to the flames** *(liter)* livrer qch aux flammes ◆ **to ~ sth to memory** apprendre qch par cœur

[3] *(Parl) [+ bill]* renvoyer à une commission

[4] ◆ **to ~ o.s.** s'engager *(to sth* à qch ; *to doing sth* à faire qch) ; ◆ **to be ~ted to a policy** s'être engagé à poursuivre une politique ◆ **I'm afraid I'm ~ted** je regrette, je me suis déjà engagé

VI ◆ **to ~ to sth/sb** s'engager à qch/envers qn

COMP **committing magistrate** **N** *(US Jur)* juge *m* d'instruction

commitment /kəˈmɪtmənt/ **N** [1] *(gen)* engagement *m* ; *(= responsibility, obligation)* charges *fpl*, responsabilité(s) *f(pl)* ; *(Comm, Fin)* engagement *m* financier ◆ **"without commitment"** *(Comm)* "sans obligation d'achat" ◆ **teaching ~s** (heures *fpl* d')enseignement *m* ◆ **he has heavy teaching ~s** il a un enseignement chargé ◆ **to have a ~ to another firm** *(Comm etc)* avoir des obligations envers une autre société [2] *(Jur:* also **commitment order**) mandat *m* de dépôt [3] *(Parl) [of bill]* renvoi *m* à une commission **COMP** **commitment fee** **N** *(Fin)* commission *f* d'engagement

committal /kəˈmɪtl/ **N** [1] *(NonC)* remise *f (to* à, aux soins de) ; *(to prison)* incarcération *f*, emprisonnement *m* ; *(for mental health reasons)* internement *m* ; (= *burial*) mise *f* en terre ◆ ~ **for trial** mise *f* en accusation [2] (*NonC*) [*of crime etc*] perpétration *f* (*Jur, liter*) [3] (*Parl*) ⇒ **committment 3**

COMP **committal order** N (*Jur*) mandat *m* de dépôt

committal proceedings NPL ≈ mise *f* en accusation

committed /kəˈmɪtɪd/ ADJ [*writer*] engagé ; [*Christian etc*] convaincu ; [*parent*] dévoué, attentif ◆ **a ~ supporter** un ardent défenseur, un adepte convaincu

committee /kəˈmɪtɪ/ N commission *f*, comité *m* ; (*Parl*) commission *f* ◆ **to be** *or* **sit on a ~** faire partie d'une commission *or* d'un comité ; → **management**

COMP **committee meeting** N réunion *f* de commission *or* de comité

committee member N membre *m* d'une commission *or* d'un comité

committee of inquiry N (*Parl*) commission *f* d'enquête

Committee of the Whole N (*US Pol*) *séance de commission étendue à la chambre entière*

committee stage N (*Brit Parl*) *étape de discussion d'un projet de loi en commission*

committeeman /kəˈmɪtɪmæn/ N (pl **-men**) (*esp US*) [1] (= *member of committee*) membre *m* d'un comité [2] (*Pol*) *responsable d'un parti pour une circonscription électorale*

committeewoman /kəˈmɪtɪwʊmən/ N (pl **-women**) (*esp US*) [1] (= *member of committee*) membre *m* d'un comité [2] (*Pol*) *responsable d'un parti pour une circonscription électorale*

commode /kəˈməʊd/ N [1] (= *chest of drawers*) commode *f* [2] (also **night-commode**) chaise *f* percée

commodious /kəˈməʊdɪəs/ ADJ spacieux, vaste

commodity /kəˈmɒdɪtɪ/ N produit *m* de base, matière *f* première ; (= *consumer goods*) produit *m*, article *m* ; (= *food*) denrée *f* ◆ **staple commodities** produits *mpl* de base ◆ **household commodities** articles *mpl* de ménage ◆ **dollar commodities** matières *fpl* premières négociées en dollars

COMP **commodity exchange** N bourse *f* du commerce *or* des marchandises

commodity loan N financement *m* de marchandises gagées

commodity markets NPL bourse *f* de marchandises

commodity-producing countries NPL pays *mpl* de production primaire

commodity trade N négoce *m* de matières premières

commodore /ˈkɒmədɔːʳ/ N (*Mil*) contre-amiral *m* ; (*Naut*) commodore *m* ; [*of yacht club*] président *m* ; [*of shipping line*] doyen *m* (*des capitaines*)

common /ˈkɒmən/ LANGUAGE IN USE 5.4

ADJ [1] (= *not unusual*) courant, fréquent ; [*plant*] commun ◆ **a ~ name** un nom courant ◆ **this is a ~ problem** c'est un problème qui se pose souvent ◆ **it's quite ~** c'est très courant, ça n'a rien d'extraordinaire ◆ **it's a ~ experience** cela arrive à tout le monde, c'est une chose qui arrive à tout le monde ◆ **a ~ occurrence** une chose fréquente *or* répandue ◆ **in ~ parlance** dans le langage courant ◆ **is this ~ practice?** cela se fait couramment ? ◆ **this is an increasingly ~ practice** cela se fait de plus en plus ◆ **a ~ sight** un spectacle familier ◆ **~ or garden** (*esp Brit*) [*plant*] commun ◆ **he's just a ~ or garden office boy** il n'est qu'un vulgaire *or* simple garçon de bureau ◆ **the ~ or garden variety** le modèle standard *or* ordinaire ◆ **the Book of Common Prayer** (*Rel*) *le livre du rituel anglican*

[2] (= *used by or affecting many*) [*interest, cause, language*] commun ◆ **to make ~ cause with sb** faire cause commune avec qn ◆ **by ~ consent** d'un commun accord ◆ **~ ground** point *m* commun, terrain *m* d'entente ◆ **there is no ~ ground for negotiations** il n'y a aucun terrain d'entente pour (entreprendre) des négociations ◆ **it's ~ knowledge that ...** chacun sait que ..., il est de notoriété publique que ... ◆ **the ~ belief that ...** l'idée largement répandue que ... ◆ **~ ownership** copropriété *f* ◆ **~ prostitute** (*Admin, Jur*) prostituée *f* ◆ **~ wall** mur *m* mitoyen

◆ **common to** ◆ **it's something ~ to all young children** c'est quelque chose qui se trouve chez tous les jeunes enfants ◆ **a belief ~ to Jews and Christians** une croyance partagée par les juifs et les chrétiens

◆ **in common** en commun ◆ **they have nothing in ~** ils n'ont rien de commun ◆ **in ~ with** en commun avec ◆ **to hold in ~** partager

[3] (= *ordinary*) commun, ordinaire ◆ **the ~ man** l'homme *m* du commun *or* du peuple ◆ **the ~ people** le peuple, les gens *mpl* du commun (*pej*) ◆ **the ~ herd** (*pej*) la plèbe, la populace (*pej*) ◆ **the ~ run of mankind** le commun des hommes *or* des mortels ◆ **out of the ~ run** hors du commun, exceptionnel

[4] (= *basic*) **it is only ~ courtesy to apologise** la politesse la plus élémentaire veut qu'on s'excuse *subj* ◆ **a ~ soldier** un simple soldat

[5] (= *vulgar*) [*accent, clothes, person*] commun, vulgaire ◆ **they're as ~ as muck** * ils sont d'un vulgaire !

[6] (*Math*) commun ◆ **~ denominator/factor** dénominateur *m*/facteur *m* commun ◆ **~ multiple** commun multiple *m* ; see also **low¹**

[7] (*Gram*) [*gender*] non marqué ; [*noun*] commun

[8] (*Mus*) ◆ **~ time** *or* **measure** (= *duple*) mesure *f* à deux temps ; (= *quadruple*) mesure *f* à quatre temps ◆ **~ chord** accord *m* parfait

N (*land*) terrain *m* communal ◆ **right of ~** (*Jur*) [*of land*] communauté *f* de jouissance ; [*of property*] droit *m* de servitude

COMP **Common Agricultural Policy** N politique *f* agricole commune

common area charges NPL (*US*) charges *fpl* locatives

common assault N (*Jur*) voie *f* de fait simple

common carrier N transporteur *m* (public), entreprise *f* de transport public

the common cold N le rhume

common core, common-core syllabus N (*Educ*) tronc *m* commun

common crab N dormeur *m*, tourteau *m*

common currency N (*NonC*) ◆ **to be ~ currency** [*idea, story*] être généralement admis ◆ **to become ~ currency** se répandre

Common Entrance N (*Brit Scol*) *examen d'entrée dans l'enseignement privé*

common gull N goéland *m* cendré

common land N terrain *m* communal

common law N le droit coutumier

common-law ADJ ◆ **~-law wife** concubine *f* ◆ **~-law marriage** concubinage *m*

common lodging house N hospice *m*, asile *m* de nuit

the Common Market N le Marché commun

common market N (= *free trade organization*) organisation *f* de libre-échange, marché *m* commun (*entre pays quelconques*)

common room N (*Brit*) salle *f* commune ; (= *staffroom*) salle *f* des professeurs

common salt N sel *m* (ordinaire)

common stock N (*US Stock Exchange*) actions *fpl* cotées en Bourse

commonality /ˌkɒməˈnælɪtɪ/ N [1] [*of manufactured products*] standardisation *f* ◆ **we are looking for commonalities** nous cherchons à utiliser des composants communs à plusieurs produits [2] (= *thing in common*) point *m* commun ◆ **our commonalities** ce que nous avons en commun

commoner /ˈkɒmənəʳ/ N (= *not noble*) roturier *m*, -ière *f* ; (*at Oxford Univ etc*) étudiant(e) *m(f)* non boursier (-ière) ; (*Brit Jur: with common land rights*) personne *f* qui a droit de vaine pâture

commonly /ˈkɒmənlɪ/ ADV [1] (= *frequently*) [*use, occur, prescribe*] fréquemment ; [*called*] couramment ◆ **more ~ known as ...** plus connu sous le nom de ... ◆ **eating disorders are more ~ found among women students** on constate que les troubles alimentaires sont plus fréquents chez les étudiantes ◆ **such a shrub is not ~ found in this country** cet arbuste n'est pas commun dans ce pays ◆ **it is ~ the case that ...** il est fréquent que ... + *subj* [2] (= *generally*) [*accept, associate, think, believe*] généralement ◆ **it is ~ believed that ...** on croit généralement que ... ◆ **the ~ held view** l'opinion *f* généralement répandue [3] (*pej* = *vulgarly*) [*behave, speak, dress*] vulgairement, d'une façon vulgaire *or* commune

commonness /ˈkɒmənnɪs/ N (*NonC*) (= *frequency*) fréquence *f* ; (= *ordinariness*) caractère *m* commun *or* ordinaire, banalité *f* (*pej*) ; (= *universality*) caractère *m* général *or* universel ; (= *vulgarity*) vulgarité *f*

commonplace /ˈkɒmənpleɪs/ ADJ banal, commun, ordinaire ◆ **such things are ~** de telles choses sont courantes *or* sont monnaie courante N lieu *m* commun, banalité *f*

commons /ˈkɒmənz/ NPL [1] ◆ **the ~** le peuple, le tiers état ◆ **the Commons** (*Parl*) les Communes *fpl* ; → **house** [2] (= *food*) nourriture *f* (*partagée en commun*) ◆ **to be on short ~** faire maigre chère, être réduit à la portion congrue

commonsense /ˈkɒmənˈsens/ N sens *m* commun, bon sens *m* ADJ [*approach, view, precaution, solution*] plein de bon sens

commonsensical /ˌkɒmənˈsensɪkl/ ADJ plein de bon sens

commonweal /ˈkɒmənˌwiːl/ N (= *general good*) bien *m* public ; (= *people*) État *m*

commonwealth /ˈkɒmənwelθ/ N [1] ◆ **the (British) Commonwealth (of Nations)** le Commonwealth ◆ **Minister** *or* **Secretary of State for Commonwealth Affairs** (*Brit*) ministre *m* du Commonwealth

[2] (*Brit Hist*) **the Commonwealth** la république de Cromwell

[3] †† ⇒ **commonweal**

[4] ◆ **the Commonwealth of Australia/Puerto Rico** *etc* le Commonwealth d'Australie/de Porto-Rico *etc* ◆ **Commonwealth of Independent States** Communauté *f* des États indépendants

COMP **Commonwealth Games** NPL Jeux *mpl* du Commonwealth

COMMONWEALTH

Le **Commonwealth**, ou **Commonwealth of Nations**, est une communauté d'États souverains (en général d'anciens territoires britanniques) qui compte une cinquantaine de membres, parmi lesquels le Royaume-Uni, l'Australie, le Canada, l'Inde, la Jamaïque, le Kenya, la Nouvelle-Zélande et la République sud-africaine. Tous ces pays reconnaissent le souverain britannique comme chef du **Commonwealth** et se réunissent lors de conférences annuelles pour débattre de questions d'ordre politique ou économique. Chaque État membre est représenté dans les autres pays du **Commonwealth** par un Haut-Commissariat (High Commission) qui fait fonction d'ambassade.

commotion /kəˈməʊʃən/ N [1] (= *noise*) **to make a ~** faire du tapage ◆ **what a ~!** quel brouhaha *or* vacarme ! [2] (= *upheaval*) **to cause a ~** semer la perturbation ◆ **what a ~!** quel cirque ! ◆ **to be in a state of ~** [*crowd*] être agité ; [*town*] être en émoi [3] (*Pol* = *uprising*) insurrection *f*, troubles *mpl* ; → **civil**

comms /kɒms/ (abbrev of **communications**) NPL communication *f* ADJ *[software, package, program]* de communication

communal /'kɒmjuːnl/ ADJ *(= of whole community) [profit, good]* communautaire, de la communauté ; *(= shared)* commun ◆ **a ~ bathroom** une salle de bains commune ◆ **~ life** la vie collective

communally /'kɒmjuːnəlɪ/ ADV en commun ; *[agree, decide]* en commun, collectivement ; *[live]* en communauté

commune /kə'mjuːn/ VI [1] converser intimement, avoir un entretien à cœur ouvert *(with* avec) ; ◆ **to ~ with nature** communier avec la nature [2] *(US Rel)* communier N /'kɒmjuːn/ [1] *(= group of people living together)* communauté *f* ◆ **to live in a ~** vivre en communauté [2] *(= administrative division)* commune *f* [3] *(French Hist)* **the Commune** la Commune

communicable /kə'mjuːnɪkəbl/ ADJ communicable ; *(Med)* transmissible

communicant /kə'mjuːnɪkənt/ N [1] *(Rel)* communiant(e) *m(f)* [2] *(= informant)* informateur *m*, -trice *f* ADJ [1] qui communique (avec), communicant [2] *(Rel)* **~ member** fidèle *mf*, pratiquant(e) *m(f)*

communicate /kə'mjuːnɪkeɪt/ VT [1] *[+ news etc]* communiquer, transmettre ; *[+ illness]* transmettre *(to* à) ; *[+ feelings, enthusiasm]* communiquer, faire partager [2] *(Rel)* donner la communion à VI [1] communiquer *(with* avec) ; ◆ **to ~ with sb by letter/by telephone** communiquer avec qn par lettre/par téléphone ◆ **I no longer ~ with him** je n'ai plus aucun contact avec lui [2] *[rooms]* communiquer ◆ **communicating rooms** des pièces *fpl* qui communiquent *or* communicantes [3] *(Rel)* communier, recevoir la communion

communication /kə,mjuːnɪ'keɪʃən/ N [1] *(NonC)* communication *f* ◆ **to be in ~ with sb** être en contact *or* relations avec qn ◆ **to be in radio ~ with sb** communiquer avec qn par radio ◆ **there is/has been no ~ between them** il n'y a/n'y a eu aucun contact entre eux

[2] *(= message transmitted)* communication *f*

[3] *(= roads, railways, telegraph lines etc)* **~s** communications *fpl* ; *(Mil)* liaison *f*, communications *fpl*

COMP **communication cord** N *(Brit Rail)* sonnette *f* d'alarme
communication gap N manque *m or* absence *f* de communication
communication line N *(Mil etc)* ligne *f* de communication
communication science N sciences *fpl* de la communication
communication skills NPL techniques *fpl* de communication
communications satellite N satellite *m* de communication
communications zone N (zone *f* des) arrières *mpl*

communicative /kə'mjuːnɪkətɪv/ ADJ [1] *(= talkative)* communicatif, expansif [2] *[difficulties etc]* de communication ◆ **~ competence** compétence *f* à la communication

communicator /kə'mjuːnɪkeɪtə^r/ N communicateur *m*, -trice *f*

communion /kə'mjuːnɪən/ N *(gen)* communion *f* ; *(Rel) (= religious group)* communion *f* ; *(= denomination)* confession *f* ; (also **Holy Communion**) communion *f* ◆ **a ~ of interests** des intérêts *mpl* en commun ◆ **to make one's ~** communier ◆ **to make one's Easter ~** faire ses pâques ◆ **to take ~** recevoir la communion

COMP **communion rail** N *(Rel)* balustre *m* du chœur *(où l'on vient communier)*
communion service N office *m* de communion
communion table N sainte table *f*

communiqué /kə'mjuːnɪkeɪ/ N communiqué *m*

communism /'kɒmjʊnɪzəm/ N communisme *m*

communist /'kɒmjʊnɪst/ ADJ, N communiste *mf* ◆ **the Communist Manifesto** le Manifeste communiste

communistic /,kɒmjʊ'nɪstɪk/ ADJ communisant

community /kə'mjuːnɪtɪ/ N [1] *(= group)* communauté *f* ◆ **the black ~** la communauté noire ◆ **a ~ of nuns** une communauté de religieuses ◆ **~ leaders** les chefs de file de la communauté ◆ **the French ~ in Edinburgh** la colonie française d'Édimbourg ◆ **the business ~** le monde des affaires ◆ **the student ~** les étudiants *mpl*, le monde étudiant ◆ **for the good of the ~** pour le bien de la collectivité

[2] *(= local people)* **leaders in the ~** les leaders de la population locale ◆ **the Prime Minister wants to involve the ~ in decision-making** le Premier ministre veut impliquer la population dans la prise de décision

[3] *(= area, place)* **councillors discussed the high levels of unemployment in their ~** les conseillers municipaux ont parlé des taux de chômage élevés dans leurs quartiers ◆ **40 miles from the remote ~ where he lives** à 64 kilomètres du village isolé où il habite ◆ **they don't live in the ~, so they don't know the people** ils ne vivent pas sur place, alors ils ne connaissent pas les gens ◆ **handicapped people are helped to live in the ~** on aide les handicapés à vivre de manière indépendante ◆ **we have helped the people in this ~** nous avons aidé les gens autour de nous

[4] *(= solidarity)* **a real feeling of ~ exists in this building** il existe un vrai sentiment de communauté dans cet immeuble ◆ **~ of interests** communauté *f* d'intérêts

[5] *(Pol = EU)* **the Community** la Communauté

COMP **community antenna distribution** N câblodistribution *f*
community antenna television N télévision *f* par câble
community association N *(Brit)* association *f* de quartier *(reconnue d'utilité publique)*
Community bodies NPL *(Pol)* instances *fpl* communautaires
Community budget N *(Pol)* budget *m* communautaire
community care N *(NonC: Brit Social Work = home care)* service *m* d'aide à domicile ; (also **community care programme**) *programme visant à déléguer la responsabilité de l'État aux collectivités locales en matière d'aide sociale*
community centre N foyer *m* municipal, ≃ MJC *f*
community charge N *(Brit Pol: formerly) ancien impôt local, fondé sur le principe de la capitation*
community chest N *(US)* fonds *m* commun
community college N *(US Univ)* centre *m* universitaire (de premier cycle)
community correctional center N *(US)* centre *m* de détention
community education N *(Brit)* cours *mpl* organisés par les municipalités
community health centre N centre *m* médico-social
community home N *(Brit)*
[1] [a] *(= children's home)* ≃ foyer *m* de la DDASS ◆ **he grew up in a ~ home** il a grandi à la DDASS [2] *(for young offenders)* centre *m* d'éducation surveillée
community hospital N *(US Med)* hôpital *m* communal
community life N *(Social Work)* vie *f* associative
community medicine N médecine *f* générale
community policeman N (pl **community policemen**) *(Brit)* ≃ îlotier *m*
community policing N ≃ îlotage *m*
community property N *(US Jur)* communauté *f* des biens entre époux
Community regulations NPL *(Pol)* règlements *mpl* communautaires
community school N *(Brit) école servant de maison de la culture*
community service N *(Jur)* travaux *mpl* d'intérêt général
community singing N chants *mpl* en chœur *(improvisés)*
community spirit N sens *m or* esprit *m* communautaire
community worker N animateur *m*, -trice *f* socioculturel(le)

> ⚠ Be cautious about translating **community** by **communauté**.

communize /'kɒmjuːnaɪz/ VT [1] *(= impose communism on)* imposer le communisme à [2] *[+ land, factories, peoples]* collectiviser

commutability /kə,mjuːtə'bɪlɪtɪ/ N interchangeabilité *f*, permutabilité *f* ; *(Jur)* commuabilité *f*

commutable /kə'mjuːtəbl/ ADJ [1] *(= exchangeable)* interchangeable, permutable [2] *(Jur) [sentence]* commuable *(to* en) [3] ◆ **within ~ distance** à une distance que l'on peut facilement parcourir tous les jours

commutation /,kɒmjʊ'teɪʃən/ N [1] *(= exchange)* échange *m*, substitution *f* ; *(Fin)* échange *m* ; *(Elec, Jur)* commutation *f* [2] *(Jur)* **~ of punishment** commutation *f* de peine [3] *(US)* trajet *m* journalier COMP **commutation ticket** N carte *f* d'abonnement

commutative /kə'mjuːtətɪv/ ADJ *(Math)* ◆ **~ laws** lois *fpl* commutatives

commutator /'kɒmjʊ,teɪtə/ N commutateur *m*

commute /kə'mjuːt/ VT [1] *(= exchange)* substituer *(into* à) échanger *(for, into* pour, contre, avec) ; *(Elec)* commuer [2] *(Jur)* commuer *(into* en) ; ◆ **~d sentence** *(Jur)* sentence *f* commuée VI faire un *or* le trajet régulier, faire la navette *(between* entre ; *from* de) N *(= single journey)* trajet *m* quotidien

commuter /kə'mjuːtə^r/ N banlieusard(e) *m(f) (qui fait un trajet régulier pour se rendre à son travail)*, navetteur *m*, -euse *f* ◆ **I work in London but I'm a ~** je travaille à Londres mais je fais la navette tous les jours

COMP **the commuter belt** N *(Brit)* la grande banlieue
commuter train N train *m* de banlieue

commuting /kə'mjuːtɪŋ/ N *(NonC)* migrations *fpl* quotidiennes, trajets *mpl* réguliers, migrations *fpl* pendulaires *(SPEC)* ◆ **~ every day is hell!** faire la navette tous les jours, c'est l'enfer !

Comoro /'kɒmə,rəʊ/ N ◆ **the ~ Islands, the ~s** les Comores *fpl*

compact /kəm'pækt/ ADJ *(lit) (in size)* compact ; *(fig) (= concise) [style]* concis, condensé ◆ **a ~ mass** une masse compacte ◆ **the house is very ~** la maison n'a pas de place perdue VT *(gen pass) (lit)* rendre compact, resserrer ; *(fig)* condenser ◆ **~ed of** †† composé de N /'kɒmpækt/ [1] *(= agreement)* contrat *m*, convention *f* ; *(informal)* entente *f* [2] (also **powder compact**) poudrier *m* [3] *(US:* also **compact car**) (voiture *f*) compacte *f*, voiture *f* de faible encombrement [4] (also **compact camera**) (appareil-photo *m*) compact *m*

COMP **compact disc** N disque *m* compact
compact disc player N lecteur *m* de CD, platine *f* laser
compact video disc N compact-disc *m* vidéo

compactly /kəm'pæktlɪ/ ADV *(lit) [store, fold up]* de façon compacte ; *(fig) [write]* dans un style concis, d'une manière concise ◆ **~ built** *[car]* d'une facture compacte, compact ; *[person]* trapu

compactness /kəm'pæktnɪs/ N (NonC) (*lit: in size*) [*of room, building, computer, equipment*] compacité *f* ; (*fig* = *conciseness*) [*of style, writing*] concision *f*

companion /kəm'pænjən/ N 1 compagnon *m*, compagne *f* ; (also **lady companion**) dame *f* de compagnie ; (*in order of knighthood*) compagnon *m* ◆ **travelling ~s** compagnons *mpl* de voyage ◆ **~s in arms/in misfortune** compagnons *mpl* d'armes/d'infortune 2 (= *one of pair of objects*) pendant *m* (*to* à) 3 (= *handbook*) manuel *m* ◆ **a ~ to literature** un manuel de littérature
COMP **companion hatch** N ⇒ **companionway**
companion ladder N (*Navy*) échelle *f* ; (*Merchant Navy*) escalier *m*
companion piece N pendant *m* (*to* à)
companion volume N volume *m* qui va de pair (*to* avec) autre volume *m*

companionable /kəm'pænjənəbl/ ADJ [*person*] de compagnie agréable ; [*evening, group*] sympathique ◆ **to sit in ~ silence** être assis dans un silence complice

companionship /kəm'pænjənʃɪp/ N (NonC) 1 (= *friendliness*) **I enjoy the ~ at the club** j'apprécie la camaraderie *or* l'esprit cordial du cercle 2 (= *company*) compagnie *f* ◆ **she keeps a cat for ~** elle a un chat, ça lui fait une compagnie

companionway /kəm'pænjənweɪ/ N (*Naut*) escalier *m* menant aux cabines ; [*of small vessel*] escalier *m* ; (*in yacht*) (also **companion hatch**) capot *m* (d'escalier)

company /'kʌmpənɪ/ LANGUAGE IN USE 25.1
N 1 compagnie *f* ◆ **to keep sb ~** tenir compagnie à qn ◆ **to keep ~ with** fréquenter ◆ **to part ~ with** se séparer de ◆ **in ~** en public *or* société ◆ **in ~ with** en compagnie de ◆ **he's good ~** on ne s'ennuie pas avec lui ◆ **he's bad ~** il n'est pas d'une compagnie très agréable ◆ **she keeps a cat, it's ~ for her** elle a un chat, ça lui fait une compagnie ; → **two**
2 (= *guests*) compagnie *f* ◆ **we are expecting ~** nous attendons des visites *or* des invités ◆ **we've got ~** nous avons de la visite* ◆ **to be in good ~** (*lit, fig*) être en bonne compagnie ; → **present**
3 (= *companions*) compagnie *f*, fréquentation *f* ◆ **to keep** *or* **get into good/bad ~** avoir de bonnes/mauvaises fréquentations ◆ **she is no(t) fit ~ for your sister** ce n'est pas une compagnie *or* une fréquentation pour votre sœur ◆ **a man is known by the ~ he keeps** (*Prov*) dis-moi qui tu hantes, je te dirai qui tu es (*Prov*)
4 (*Comm, Fin*) entreprise *f*, société *f*, compagnie *f* ◆ **Smith & Company** Smith et Compagnie ◆ **shipping ~** compagnie *f* de navigation ◆ **the Company*** (*US* = *CIA*) la CIA ◆ **... and ~*** (*also pej*) ... et compagnie ; → **affiliate, holding**
5 (= *group*) compagnie *f* ; [*of actors*] troupe *f*, compagnie *f* ◆ **National Theatre Company** la troupe du Théâtre National ◆ **ship's ~** (*Naut*) équipage *m*
6 (*Mil*) compagnie *f*
COMP **Companies Act** N (*Jur*) loi *f* sur les sociétés
company car N voiture *f* de fonction
company commander N (*Mil*) capitaine *m* (de compagnie)
company director N directeur *m* général
company doctor N médecin *m* du travail
company law N droit *m* des sociétés
company lawyer N (*Jur*) avocat *m* d'entreprise ; (*working within company*) juriste *m*
company man N (pl **company men**) employé *m* dévoué ◆ **he's a real ~ man** il a vraiment l'esprit maison
company manners* NPL (*Brit*) belles manières *fpl*
company policy N politique *f* de l'entreprise
company secretary N (*Brit Comm*) secrétaire *m* général
company sergeant-major N (*Mil*) adjudant *m*
company time N temps *m* de travail
company union N (*US*) syndicat *m* maison

comparability /ˌkɒmpərə'bɪlətɪ/ N comparabilité *f* ◆ **pay ~** alignement *m* des salaires (*sur ceux d'autres secteurs industriels*)

comparable /'kɒmpərəbl/ LANGUAGE IN USE 5.3, 5.4 ADJ comparable (*with, to* à) ; ◆ **the two things are not ~** il n'y a pas de comparaison possible entre ces deux choses

comparably /'kɒmpərəblɪ/ ADV ◆ **~ sized buildings** des bâtiments ayant des dimensions comparables ◆ **~ qualified students** des étudiants possédant des qualifications comparables

comparative /kəm'pærətɪv/ ADJ 1 (= *relative*) [*ease, safety, peace, silence, freedom, cost*] relatif ◆ **he's a ~ stranger (to me)** je le connais relativement peu ◆ **to be a ~ newcomer/beginner** être relativement nouveau/débutant 2 (*involving comparison*) [*study, analysis, method*] comparatif ; [*literature, religion, linguistics, law, data*] comparé ◆ **~ form** (*Gram*) comparatif *m* ◆ **~ mythologist** spécialiste *mf* de mythologie comparée N (*Gram*) comparatif *m* ◆ **in the ~** au comparatif

comparatively /kəm'pærətɪvlɪ/ LANGUAGE IN USE 5.3 ADV 1 (= *relatively*) relativement 2 (*involving comparison*) comparativement

compare /kəm'pɛəʳ/ LANGUAGE IN USE 5.1, 5.3, 5.4, 26.3
VT comparer (*with* à, avec) ; ◆ **~ the first letter with the second** comparez la première lettre à *or* avec la seconde ◆ **~d to** *or* **with ...** comparé à ... ◆ **to ~ notes with sb** (*fig*) échanger ses impressions *or* ses vues avec qn ◆ **the poet ~d her eyes to stars** le poète compara ses yeux à des étoiles ◆ **the book ~s and contrasts the North and South Poles** ce livre compare les pôles Nord et Sud et met en évidence leurs différences
VI être comparable (*with* à) ; ◆ **how do the cars ~ for speed?** quelles sont les vitesses respectives des voitures ? ◆ **how do the prices ~?** est-ce que les prix sont comparables ? ◆ **it doesn't** *or* **can't ~ with the previous one** il n'y a aucune comparaison avec le précédent ◆ **he can't ~ with you** il n'y a pas de comparaison (possible) entre vous et lui ◆ **it ~s very favourably** cela soutient la comparaison
N ◆ **beyond** *or* **without** *or* **past ~** ADV incomparablement ADJ sans comparaison possible

comparison /kəm'pærɪsn/ LANGUAGE IN USE 5.1, 5.4, 26.3 N 1 comparaison *f* (*with* avec ; *to* à) ; ◆ **in ~ with** *or* **to ..., by ~ with ...** par comparaison avec ..., par rapport à ... ◆ **by** *or* **in ~** par comparaison ◆ **for ~** pour comparaison ◆ **to make a ~** faire une comparaison ◆ **to stand** *or* **bear ~ (with)** soutenir la comparaison (avec) ◆ **there's no ~** ça ne se compare pas 2 (*Gram*) comparaison *f* ◆ **degrees of ~** degrés *mpl* de comparaison COMP **comparison test** N essai *m* comparatif

compartment /kəm'pɑːtmənt/ N compartiment *m* ; → **freezer, glove**

compartmentalize /ˌkɒmpɑːt'mentəlaɪz/ VT compartimenter

compass /'kʌmpəs/ N 1 boussole *f* ; (*Naut*) compas *m* ; → **point** 2 (*Math*) **~es, a pair of ~es** compas *m* 3 (*fig*) (= *extent*) étendue *f* ; (= *reach*) portée *f* ; (= *scope*) rayon *m*, champ *m* ; (*Mus*) [*of voice*] étendue *f*, portée *f* ◆ **within the ~ of sth** dans les limites de qch ◆ **within the ~ of sb** dans les possibilités de qn ◆ **to be within the ~ of a committee** relever des compétences d'un comité ; → **narrow** VT (= *go round*) faire le tour de ; (= *surround*) encercler, entourer
COMP **compass card** N (*Naut*) rose *f* des vents
compass course N route *f* magnétique
compass rose N ⇒ **compass card**

compassion /kəm'pæʃən/ N compassion *f*

compassionate /kəm'pæʃənət/ ADJ compatissant ◆ **on ~ grounds** pour raisons de convenance personnelle *or* de famille COMP **compassionate leave** N (*Mil*) permission *f* exceptionnelle (*pour raisons de famille*)

compassionately /kəm'pæʃənətlɪ/ ADV [*look, say*] avec compassion ; [*release*] par compassion

compatibility /kəmˌpætə'bɪlɪtɪ/ N compatibilité *f* (*with* avec)

compatible /kəm'pætɪbl/ ADJ 1 [*people*] fait pour s'entendre ◆ **a ~ board of directors** un conseil d'administration sans problèmes de compatibilité d'humeur ◆ **to be ~ with sb** bien s'entendre avec qn 2 (= *reconcilable*) [*ideas, aims, interests*] (*also Comput, Telec*) compatible (*with sth* avec qch) ; ◆ **an IBM-~ computer** un ordinateur compatible IBM N (*Comput*) compatible *m* ◆ **an IBM-~** un compatible IBM

compatibly /kəm'pætɪblɪ/ ADV de façon compatible

compatriot /kəm'pætrɪət/ N compatriote *mf*

compel /kəm'pel/ LANGUAGE IN USE 10.1 VT 1 [*+ person*] (*physically*) contraindre, obliger ; (*legally, morally*) obliger ; (*psychologically*) pousser ◆ **to be ~led to do sth** (*physically*) être contraint *or* obligé de faire qch ; (*psychologically*) se sentir poussé à faire qch, éprouver l'envie profonde *or* irrésistible de faire qch ◆ **to feel morally ~led to do sth** se sentir moralement obligé *or* tenu de faire qch 2 [*+ admiration etc*] imposer, forcer ◆ **to ~ obedience/respect from sb** imposer l'obéissance/le respect à qn

compelling /kəm'pelɪŋ/ ADJ 1 (= *convincing*) [*argument*] irréfutable ; [*evidence*] incontestable ; [*reason, need*] impérieux ◆ **to make a ~ case for sth** réunir des arguments irréfutables en faveur de qch ◆ **to have a ~ interest in doing sth** avoir le plus grand intérêt à faire qch 2 (= *riveting*) [*story, account, film, book*] fascinant ◆ **his new novel makes ~ reading** son nouveau roman est passionnant

compellingly /kəm'pelɪŋlɪ/ ADV [*write, tell*] d'une manière fascinante ; [*persuasive, attractive*] irrésistiblement

compendia /kəm'pendɪə/ NPL of **compendium**

compendious /kəm'pendɪəs/ ADJ concis

compendium /kəm'pendɪəm/ N (pl **compendiums** *or* **compendia**) 1 (= *summary*) abrégé *m* 2 (*Brit*) **~ of games** boîte *f* de jeux

compensate /'kɒmpənseɪt/ VI compenser (*by* en) ; ◆ **to ~ for sth** compenser qch VT (= *indemnify*) dédommager, indemniser (*for* de) ; (= *pay*) rémunérer (*for* pour) ; (*in weight, strength etc*) compenser, contrebalancer ; (*Tech*) compenser, neutraliser

compensation /ˌkɒmpən'seɪʃən/ N (= *indemnity*) (*gen, Psych*) compensation *f* ; (*financial*) dédommagement *m*, indemnisation *f* ; (= *payment*) rémunération *f* ; (*in weight, strength etc*) contrepoids *m* ; (*Tech*) compensation *f*, neutralisation *f* ◆ **in ~** (*financial*) en dédommagement
COMP **Compensation Fund** N (*Stock Exchange*) caisse *f* de garantie

compensatory /ˌkɒmpən'seɪtərɪ/ ADJ (*gen*) compensateur (-trice *f*) ◆ **~ levy** (*Econ: of EU*) prélèvement *m* compensatoire

compère /'kɒmpɛəʳ/ (*Brit*) N animateur *m*, -trice *f* VT [*+ show*] animer, présenter

compete /kəm'piːt/ VI 1 (*gen*) rivaliser ◆ **his poetry can't ~ with Eliot's** sa poésie ne peut pas rivaliser avec celle d'Eliot ◆ **we can't ~ with their financial resources** vu leurs ressources financières, il nous est impossible de rivaliser avec eux ◆ **to ~ with sb for a prize** disputer un prix à qn ◆ **they will ~ for the history prize** ils se disputeront le prix d'histoire

◆ **to be competing** être en lice ◆ **ten students were competing for six places** dix candidats étaient en lice pour six places ◆ **2300 candidates are competing for 486 seats** il y a 2300 candidats en lice pour 486 sièges ◆ **who's competing?** qui s'est présenté ? ◆ **there were only four people competing** il n'y avait que quatre concurrents

2 *(Comm)* être en concurrence ◆ **to ~ for a contract** être en concurrence pour obtenir un contrat ◆ **there are six firms competing for a share in the market** six entreprises se font concurrence pour une part du marché ◆ **they are forced to ~ with the multinationals** ils sont obligés d'entrer en concurrence *or* en compétition avec les multinationales

3 *(Sport)* concourir *(against sb* avec qn ; *for sth* pour (obtenir) qch ; *to do sth* pour faire qch) ; ◆ **to ~ in a race** participer à une course ◆ **he's competing against world-class athletes** il concourt avec *or* il est en compétition avec des athlètes de réputation mondiale ◆ **there were only four teams/runners competing** il n'y avait que quatre équipes/coureurs sur les rangs

4 *[animals, plants]* être en concurrence

competence /ˈkɒmpɪtəns/ N 1 *(gen, Ling)* compétence *f (for* pour ; *in* en) 2 *(Jur)* compétence *f* ◆ **within the ~ of the court** de la compétence du tribunal

competency /ˈkɒmpɪtənsɪ/ N 1 ⇒ **competence** 2 *(= money, means)* aisance *f*, moyens *mpl*

competent /ˈkɒmpɪtənt/ ADJ 1 *(= proficient) [person]* compétent *(at sth* dans qch ; *to do sth* pour faire qch) ; ◆ **to be ~ at** *or* **in maths** être compétent en mathématiques ◆ **to feel ~ to do sth** se sentir compétent pour *or* capable de faire qch 2 *(= satisfactory) [work, performance]* satisfaisant ◆ **to do a ~ job** faire un travail satisfaisant ◆ **a ~ knowledge of the language** une connaissance suffisante de la langue 3 *(Jur) [court]* compétent ; *[evidence]* admissible, recevable ; *[person]* habile ; → **court**

competently /ˈkɒmpɪtəntlɪ/ ADV *[handle, perform, play] (= proficiently)* avec compétence, de façon compétente ; *(= satisfactorily)* suffisamment bien, assez bien

competing /kəmˈpiːtɪŋ/ ADJ contradictoire, en concurrence ◆ **~ interests** intérêts *mpl* contradictoires

competition /ˌkɒmpɪˈtɪʃən/ N 1 *(NonC)* compétition *f*, rivalité *f (for* pour) ; *(Comm)* concurrence *f* ◆ **unfair ~** concurrence *f or* compétition *f* déloyale ◆ **there was keen ~ for it** on se l'est âprement disputé, il y a eu beaucoup de concurrence pour l'avoir ◆ **in ~ with** en concurrence avec

2 *(= event, game)* concours *m (for* pour) ; *(Sport)* compétition *f* ; *(= car race)* course *f* ◆ **to go in for a ~** se présenter à un concours ◆ **beauty/swimming ~** concours *m* de beauté/de natation ◆ **I won it in a newspaper ~** je l'ai gagné en faisant un concours dans le journal ◆ **to choose by ~** choisir au concours

3 *(NonC = competitors) (gen)* concurrence *f* ; *(Sport)* autres concurrents *mpl* ◆ **he was waiting to see what the ~ would be like** il attendait de voir qui lui ferait concurrence *or* qui seraient ses rivaux

COMP **competition car** N voiture *f* de compétition

competitive /kəmˈpetɪtɪv/ ADJ 1 *(Comm) [society, system]* compétitif ; *[market, prices, rates]* compétitif, concurrentiel ; *[product]* concurrentiel ◆ **to gain a ~ advantage** *or* **edge (over sb)** obtenir un avantage concurrentiel (sur qn) 2 *(= ambitious) [person]* qui a (*or* avait) l'esprit de compétition ◆ **I'm a very ~ person** j'ai un esprit de compétition très développé 3 *(Sport) [spirit, tennis, match]* de compétition ◆ **his ~ ability** sa capacité à être compétitif ◆ **to gain a ~ advantage** *or* **edge (over sb)** avoir un avantage dans la compétition (sur qn) 4 *(Educ) [entry, selection]* par concours ◆ **~ examination** concours *m* COMP **competitive bidding, competitive tendering** N appel *m* d'offres

competitively /kəmˈpetɪtɪvlɪ/ ADV 1 *(Comm)* ◆ **both models are ~ priced** les deux modèles sont à des prix compétitifs ◆ **a very ~ priced car** une voiture à prix très compétitif 2 *(in competitions)* en compétition, en lice ◆ **I stopped playing ~ in 1995** j'ai arrêté la compétition en 1995

competitiveness /kəmˈpetətɪvnɪs/ N compétitivité *f*

competitor /kəmˈpetɪtə^r^/ N *(also Comm)* concurrent(e) *m(f)*

compilation /ˌkɒmpɪˈleɪʃən/ N compilation *f*

compile /kəmˈpaɪl/ VT *(gen, Comput)* compiler ; *[+ dictionary]* élaborer ; *[+ list, catalogue, inventory]* dresser

compiler /kəmˈpaɪlə^r^/ N *(gen)* compilateur *m*, -trice *f* ; *[of dictionary]* rédacteur *m*, -trice *f* ; *(Comput)* compilateur *m*

complacence /kəmˈpleɪsəns/, **complacency** /kəmˈpleɪsnsɪ/ N contentement *m* de soi, suffisance *f*

complacent /kəmˈpleɪsənt/ ADJ *(= self-satisfied)* content de soi, suffisant ◆ **he's so ~!** il est tellement suffisant ! ◆ **we are confident, but not ~** nous sommes confiants, mais nous restons prudents ◆ **to be ~ about sth** *(= unconcerned)* sous-estimer qch ◆ **we cannot afford to be ~ about the huge task which faces us** nous ne pouvons pas nous permettre de sous-estimer l'ampleur de la tâche qui nous attend

complacently /kəmˈpleɪsəntlɪ/ ADV avec suffisance

complain /kəmˈpleɪn/ VI 1 se plaindre *(of, about* de) ; ◆ **to ~ that ...** se plaindre que ... + *subj or indic or* de ce que ... + *indic* ◆ **how are you? – I can't ~** * comment vas-tu ? – je ne peux pas me plaindre 2 *(= make a complaint)* formuler une plainte *or* une réclamation *(against* contre) se plaindre ◆ **you should ~ to the manager** vous devriez vous plaindre au directeur ◆ **to ~ to the court of justice** *(Jur)* saisir la Cour de justice

complainant /kəmˈpleɪnənt/ N *(Jur)* plaignant(e) *m(f)*, demandeur *m*, -deresse *f*

complaint /kəmˈpleɪnt/ N 1 *(= expression of discontent)* plainte *f* ; *(= reason for complaint)* grief *m*, sujet *m* de plainte ; *(Jur)* plainte *f* ; *(Comm)* réclamation *f* ◆ **~s department** *(Comm)* service *m* des réclamations ◆ **don't listen to his ~s** n'écoutez pas ses plaintes *or* ses récriminations ◆ **I have no ~(s), I have no cause for ~** je n'ai aucun sujet *or* motif de plainte, je n'ai pas lieu de me plaindre ◆ **to make a ~** *(Comm)* se plaindre *(about* de) faire une réclamation ◆ **to lodge** *or* **lay a ~ against ...** *(Jur)* porter plainte contre ... ; → **police** 2 *(Med)* maladie *f*, affection *f* ◆ **what is his ~?** de quoi souffre-t-il ?, de quoi se plaint-il ? ◆ **a heart ~** une maladie de cœur ◆ **bowel ~** affection *f* intestinale

complaisance /kəmˈpleɪzəns/ N complaisance *f*, obligeance *f*

complaisant /kəmˈpleɪzənt/ ADJ complaisant, obligeant

-complected /kəmˈplektɪd/ ADJ *(in compounds) (US)* ⇒ **-complexioned**

complement /ˈkɒmplɪmənt/ N *(gen, Gram, Math)* complément *m* ; *[of staff etc]* personnel *m*, effectif *m* ◆ **with full ~** au grand complet VT /ˈkɒmplɪment/ compléter, être le complément de

complementary /ˌkɒmplɪˈmentərɪ/ ADJ *(gen, Math)* complémentaire COMP **complementary medicine** N médecine *f* parallèle *or* douce

complete /kəmˈpliːt/ ADJ 1 *(= whole) [list, set]* complet (-ète *f*) ◆ **the ~ works of Shakespeare** les œuvres *fpl* complètes de Shakespeare ◆ **no garden is ~ without a bed of roses** sans un parterre de rosiers, un jardin est incomplet

2 ◆ **~ with sth** *(= also having)* avec qch ◆ **a large hotel ~ with swimming pool** un grand hôtel avec piscine ◆ **a house ~ with furniture** une maison meublée ◆ **to come ~ with sth** être pourvu de qch

3 *(= entire)* tout *inv* entier ◆ **a ~ tenement block was burnt to the ground** un immeuble entier a été démoli par les flammes, un immeuble a été complètement démoli par les flammes

4 *(= finished) [work]* achevé ◆ **the task is now ~** la tâche est accomplie

5 *(= total, full) [change, surprise, disaster, failure]* complet (-ète *f*) ; *[lack]* total ; *[approval]* entier ; *[idiot, liar]* fini ◆ **in ~ agreement** en parfait accord ◆ **in ~ contrast to sb/sth** à l'opposé de qn/qch, contrairement à qn/qch ◆ **to take ~ control of sth** prendre le contrôle complet de qch ◆ **at last her happiness was ~** enfin son bonheur était complet ◆ **he is the ~ opposite of me** il est tout le contraire de moi ◆ **to my ~ satisfaction** à mon entière satisfaction ◆ **she's a ~ bitch** ‡ c'est une vraie peau de vache‡

6 *(= accomplished)* ◆ **he is the ~ film-maker/footballer** † c'est le parfait cinéaste/footballeur

VT 1 *(= finish) [+ collection]* compléter ; *[+ piece of work]* achever, terminer ◆ **and to ~ his happiness/misfortune** et pour comble de bonheur/d'infortune ◆ **and just to ~ things** et pour couronner le tout ◆ **to ~ an order** exécuter une commande

2 *(= fill in) [+ form, questionnaire]* remplir

completely /kəmˈpliːtlɪ/ ADV totalement, complètement ◆ **~ and utterly** totalement ◆ **almost ~** presque entièrement

completeness /kəmˈpliːtnɪs/ N caractère *m* complet ; *[of report, study]* exhaustivité *f* ◆ **at varying stages of ~** à différents stades d'achèvement

completion /kəmˈpliːʃən/ N *[of work]* achèvement *m* ; *[of happiness, misfortune]* comble *m* ; *(Jur) [of contract, sale]* exécution *f* ◆ **near ~** près d'être achevé ◆ **payment on ~ of contract** paiement *m* à la signature du contrat COMP **completion date** N *(Jur) (for work)* date *f* d'achèvement (des travaux) ; *(in house-buying)* date *f* d'exécution du contrat

completist /kəmˈpliːtɪst/ N collectionneur *m*, -euse *f (qui cherche à avoir une collection complète)*

complex /ˈkɒmpleks/ ADJ complexe N 1 complexe *m* ◆ **industrial/mining ~** complexe *m* industriel/minier ◆ **housing ~** (ensemble *m* de) résidences *fpl* ; *(high rise)* grand ensemble *m* ; → **cinema** 2 *(Psych)* complexe *m* ◆ **he's got a ~ about it** ça lui a donné un complexe, il en fait (tout) un complexe ; → **guilt, inferiority**

complexion /kəmˈplekʃən/ N *[of face]* teint *m* ; *(fig)* caractère *m*, aspect *m* ◆ **that puts a new** *or* **different ~ on the whole affair** l'affaire se présente maintenant sous un tout autre aspect *or* jour

-complexioned /kəmˈplekʃənd/ ADJ *(in compounds)* ◆ **dark-complexioned** de *or* au teint mat, mat de teint ◆ **fair-complexioned** de *or* au teint clair, clair de teint

complexity /kəm'pleksɪtɪ/ N complexité *f*

compliance /kəm'plaɪəns/ N (NonC) 1 *(= acceptance)* acquiescement *m (with à)* ; *(= conformity)* conformité *f (with avec)* ; ◆ **in ~ with ...** conformément à ..., en accord avec ... 2 *(= submission)* basse complaisance *f*, servilité *f* COMP **compliance lawyer, compliance officer** N conseiller *m* fiscal

compliant /kəm'plaɪənt/ ADJ *[person]* accommodant ; *[child]* docile ◆ **to be ~ with** être conforme à ; *[person]* se conformer à

complicate /'kɒmplɪkeɪt/ VT compliquer *(with de)* ; *(= muddle)* embrouiller ◆ **that ~s matters** cela complique les choses ◆ **she always ~s things** elle complique toujours tout, elle se crée des problèmes

complicated /'kɒmplɪkeɪtɪd/ ADJ *(= involved)* compliqué, complexe ; *(= muddled)* embrouillé

complication /,kɒmplɪ'keɪʃən/ N *(gen, Med)* complication *f*

complicit /kəm'plɪsɪt/ ADJ 1 *(= knowing) [look, wink, silence]* complice 2 *(= involved)* ◆ **~ in sth** complice de qch ◆ **he was ~ in allowing it to happen** il a été complice en laissant la chose se produire

complicity /kəm'plɪsɪtɪ/ N complicité *f (in dans)*

compliment /'kɒmplɪmənt/ N 1 compliment *m* ◆ **to pay sb a ~** faire *or* adresser un compliment à qn ◆ **to return the ~** *(fig)* retourner le compliment, renvoyer l'ascenseur 2 *(frm)* **~s** compliments *mpl*, respects *mpl*, hommages *mpl (frm)* ◆ **give him my ~s** faites-lui mes compliments ◆ **(I wish you) the ~s of the season** (je vous présente) tous mes vœux ◆ **with the ~s of Mr Green** avec les hommages *or* les compliments de M. Green ◆ **"with compliments"** "avec nos compliments" VT /'kɒmplɪment/ complimenter, féliciter *(on de)* faire des compliments à *(on de, sur)* COMP **compliments slip** N *(Comm)* ≈ papillon *m* (avec les bons compliments de l'expéditeur)

complimentary /,kɒmplɪ'mentərɪ/ ADJ 1 *(= flattering) [person]* élogieux ; *[remark]* élogieux, flatteur ◆ **to be ~ about sb/sth** faire des compliments sur qn/qch 2 *(= free) [ticket, drink]* gratuit ◆ **~ copy** exemplaire *m* offert à titre gracieux

complin(e) /'kɒmplɪn/ N *(Rel)* complies *fpl*

comply /kəm'plaɪ/ VI 1 *[person]* obtempérer
◆ **to comply with** ◆ **to ~ with the rules** observer *or* respecter le règlement ◆ **to ~ with sb's wishes** se conformer aux désirs de qn ◆ **to ~ with a request** faire droit à une requête, accéder à une demande ◆ **to ~ with a clause** observer *or* respecter une disposition
2 *[equipment, object] (to specifications etc)* être conforme *(with à)*

component /kəm'pəʊnənt/ ADJ composant, constituant ◆ **the ~ parts** les parties *fpl* constituantes N *(gen, also Econ)* élément *m* ; *(Chem)* composant *m* ; *[of machine, car]* pièce *f* ◆ **~s factory** usine *f* de pièces détachées

componential /,kɒmpə'nenʃəl/ ADJ componentiel ◆ **~ analysis** *(Ling)* analyse *f* componentielle

comport /kəm'pɔːt/ VT ◆ **to ~ o.s.** se comporter, se conduire VI convenir *(with à)* s'accorder *(with avec)*

comportment /kəm'pɔːtmənt/ N comportement *m*, conduite *f*

compose /kəm'pəʊz/ VT
1 *[+ written text, music]* composer
2 *(= constitute)* composer
◆ **to be composed of** se composer de ◆ **the force would be ~d of troops from NATO countries** cette force se composerait de troupes des pays de l'OTAN
3 *(= calm)* ◆ **to ~ o.s.** se calmer ◆ **to ~ one's features** composer son visage ◆ **to ~ one's thoughts** mettre de l'ordre dans ses pensées
4 *(= typeset)* composer

composed /kəm'pəʊzd/ ADJ calme, posé

composedly /kəm'pəʊzɪdlɪ/ ADV calmement, posément

composer /kəm'pəʊzəʳ/ N *(Mus)* compositeur *m*, -trice *f*

composite /'kɒmpəzɪt/ ADJ *(gen, Archit, Phot)* composite ; *(Bot, Math)* composé N *(Archit)* (ordre *m*) composite *m* ; *(Bot)* composée *f*, composacée *f*
COMP **composite school** N *(Can)* école *f* polyvalente
composite vote N vote *m* groupé

composition /,kɒmpə'zɪʃən/ N 1 *(= act of composing)* composition *f* ◆ **music/verse of her own ~** de la musique/des vers de sa composition
2 *(= thing composed)* composition *f*, œuvre *f* ; *(Scol = essay)* rédaction *f* ◆ **one of her most famous ~s** une de ses œuvres les plus célèbres
3 *(= parts composing whole)* composition *f*, constitution *f* ; *(= mixture of substances)* composition *f (of de)* ; ◆ **to study the ~ of a substance** étudier la constitution d'une substance
4 *(Gram) [of sentence]* construction *f* ; *[of word]* composition *f*
5 *(= temperament, make-up)* nature *f*, constitution *f* intellectuelle (*or* morale)
6 *(Jur)* accommodement *m*, compromis *m*, arrangement *m (avec un créancier)* ◆ **to come to a ~** *(frm)* venir à composition *(frm)*, arriver à une entente *or* un accord
COMP *[substance]* synthétique **composition rubber** N caoutchouc *m* synthétique

compositional /,kɒmpə'zɪʃənl/ ADJ *[style]* de composition ; *[skills, tools]* de compositeur

compositor /kəm'pɒzɪtəʳ/ N *(Typ)* compositeur *m*, -trice *f*

compos mentis /'kɒmpɒs'mentɪs/ ADJ sain d'esprit

compost /'kɒmpɒst/ N compost *m* VT composter COMP **compost heap** N tas *m* de compost

composure /kəm'pəʊʒəʳ/ N calme *m*, sang-froid *m* ◆ **to lose (one's) ~** *(gen)* perdre contenance ; *(= get angry)* perdre son sang-froid

compote /'kɒmpəʊt/ N compote *f* ; *(US = dish)* compotier *m*

compound /'kɒmpaʊnd/ N 1 *(Chem)* composé *m (of de)* ; *(Gram)* (mot *m*) composé *m* ; 2 *(= enclosed area)* enclos *m*, enceinte *f* ADJ *(Chem)* composé, combiné ; *(Math) [number, fraction]* complexe ; *(Med) [fracture]* compliqué ; *(Tech) [engine]* compound *inv* ; *(Gram) [tense, word]* composé ; *[sentence]* complexe ◆ **~ time** *(Mus)* la mesure composée VT /kəm'paʊnd/ 1 *(Chem, Pharm) [+ mixture]* composer *(of de)* ; *[+ ingredients]* combiner, mélanger ; *(fig) [+ problem, difficulties]* aggraver 2 *(Jur etc) [+ debt, quarrel]* régler à l'amiable, arranger par des concessions mutuelles ◆ **to ~ a felony** composer *or* pactiser (avec un criminel) VI /kəm'paʊnd/ *(Jur etc)* composer, transiger *(with avec ; for au sujet de, pour)* s'arranger à l'amiable *(with avec ; for au sujet de)* ; ◆ **to ~ with one's creditors** s'arranger à l'amiable *or* composer avec ses créanciers

compounding /'kɒmpaʊndɪŋ/ N *(Ling)* composition *f*

comprehend /,kɒmprɪ'hend/ VT 1 *(= understand)* comprendre, saisir 2 *(= include)* comprendre, englober VI comprendre

comprehending /,kɒmprɪ'hendɪŋ/ ADJ compréhensif

comprehensibility /,kɒmprɪhensə'bɪlətɪ/ N intelligibilité *f*

comprehensible /,kɒmprɪ'hensəbl/ ADJ compréhensible

comprehensibly /,kɒmprɪ'hensəblɪ/ ADV de façon compréhensible *or* intelligible

comprehension /,kɒmprɪ'henʃn/ N 1 *(= understanding)* compréhension *f*, entendement *m* ◆ **that is beyond my ~** cela dépasse ma compréhension *or* mon entendement 2 *(Scol)* exercice *m* de compréhension 3 *(= inclusion)* inclusion *f*

comprehensive /,kɒmprɪ'hensɪv/ ADJ 1 *(= broad, inclusive) [description, report, review, survey]* détaillé, complet (-ète *f*) ; *[knowledge]* vaste, étendu ; *[planning]* global ◆ **~ measures** mesures *fpl* d'ensemble ◆ **~ insurance (policy)** *(Insurance)* assurance *f* tous risques
2 *(Brit Scol) [education, system]* polyvalent ◆ **~ school** établissement *m* polyvalent d'enseignement secondaire ◆ **to go ~** abandonner les critères sélectifs d'entrée
N ⇒ **comprehensive school**

COMPREHENSIVE SCHOOL

Créées dans les années 60 par le gouvernement travailliste de l'époque, les **comprehensive schools** sont des établissements polyvalents d'enseignement secondaire conçus pour accueillir tous les élèves sans distinction et leur offrir des chances égales, par opposition au système sélectif des « grammar schools ». La majorité des enfants britanniques fréquentent aujourd'hui une **comprehensive school**, mais les « grammar schools » n'ont pas toutes disparu.

comprehensively /,kɒmprɪ'hensɪvlɪ/ ADV complètement ◆ **we were ~ beaten** nous avons été battus à plate couture ◆ **to be ~ insured** avoir une assurance tous risques

compress /kəm'pres/ VT *[+ substance]* comprimer ; *[+ essay, facts]* condenser, concentrer ; *(Comput) [+ data]* compresser ◆ **~ed air** air *m* comprimé VI *(gen)* se comprimer ; *[gas]* se condenser N /'kɒmpres/ compresse *f*

compression /kəm'preʃən/ N *(gen, Comput)* compression *f*
COMP **compression pistol** N ensemble *m* pistolet compresseur
compression ratio N *(Aut)* taux *m* de compression

compressor /kəm'presəʳ/ N compresseur *m*
COMP **compressor program** N *(Comput)* programme *m* de compression
compressor unit N groupe *m* compresseur

comprise /kəm'praɪz/ VT 1 *(= include)* comprendre, être composé de ◆ **to be ~d of** se composer de 2 *(= make up)* constituer ◆ **women ~ 80% of the workforce** les femmes constituent 80% de l'effectif

compromise /'kɒmprəmaɪz/ N compromis *m* ◆ **to come to** *or* **reach a ~** aboutir à un compromis ◆ **to agree to a ~** accepter un compromis VI transiger *(over sur)* aboutir à *or* accepter un compromis VT *[+ reputation, safety, security, plan]* compromettre ◆ **to ~ o.s.** se compromettre
COMP **compromise decision** N décision *f* de compromis
compromise solution N solution *f* de compromis

compromising /'kɒmprəmaɪzɪŋ/ ADJ compromettant

Comptometer ® /,kɒmp'tɒmɪtəʳ/ N machine *f* comptable COMP **Comptometer operator** N mécanographe *mf*

comptroller /kən'trəʊləʳ/ N *(Admin, Fin)* contrôleur *m*, -euse *f* (des finances) COMP

Comptroller General N *(US Jur, Pol)* ≈ président *m* de la Cour des comptes

compulsion /kəmˈpʌlʃən/ N contrainte *f* ◆ **under** ~ de force, sous la contrainte ◆ **you are under no** ~ vous n'êtes nullement obligé, rien ne vous force

compulsive /kəmˈpʌlsɪv/ ADJ 1 *(= habitual)* ◆ **to be a ~ gambler/liar** être un joueur/menteur invétéré ◆ **to be a ~ eater** ne pas pouvoir s'empêcher de manger, être boulimique 2 *(Psych) [behaviour, desire, need]* compulsif ; → **obsessive** 3 *(= irresistible) [reading]* fascinant ◆ **the programme was ~ viewing** l'émission était fascinante

compulsively /kəmˈpʌlsɪvlɪ/ ADV 1 *[lie]* compulsivement ; *[behave, gamble, talk]* d'une façon compulsive ◆ **to eat** ~ être boulimique ◆ **she is ~ tidy** elle est tellement ordonnée que cela tourne à l'obsession 2 *(= irresistibly)* ◆ ~ **readable** d'une lecture fascinante ◆ **the series is ~ watchable** ce feuilleton est fascinant, on n'arrive pas à décrocher de ce feuilleton

compulsorily /kəmˈpʌlsərɪlɪ/ ADV *[purchased, retired]* d'office

compulsory /kəmˈpʌlsərɪ/ LANGUAGE IN USE 10.3
ADJ 1 *(= obligatory) [education, test, school subject, military service]* obligatoire ; *[retirement]* obligatoire, d'office ; *[redundancies]* d'office 2 *(= compelling) [powers]* coercitif N **the compulsories** NPL *(Skating)* les figures *fpl* imposées
COMP **compulsory liquidation** N *(Fin)* liquidation *f* forcée
compulsory purchase (order) N *(Brit)* (ordre *m* d')expropriation *f (pour cause d'utilité publique)*

compunction /kəmˈpʌŋkʃən/ N remords *m*, scrupule *m* ; *(Rel)* componction *f* ◆ **without the slightest** *or* **the least** ~ sans le moindre scrupule *or* remords ◆ **he had no ~ about doing it** il n'a eu aucun scrupule à le faire

computation /ˌkɒmpjʊˈteɪʃən/ N 1 *(gen)* calcul *m* 2 *(NonC)* estimation *f*, évaluation *f (of* de)

computational /ˌkɒmpjʊˈteɪʃənl/ ADJ statistique, quantitatif COMP **computational linguistics** N *(NonC)* linguistique *f* computationnelle

compute /kəmˈpjuːt/ VT calculer ◆ **to ~ sth at ...** évaluer *or* estimer qch à ...

computer /kəmˈpjuːtəʳ/ N 1 *(electronic)* ordinateur *m* ; *(mechanical)* calculatrice *f* ◆ **he is in ~s** il est dans l'informatique ◆ **on** ~ sur ordinateur ◆ **to do sth by** ~ faire qch sur ordinateur ; → **digital, personal**
2 *(= person)* calculateur *m*, -trice *f*
COMP **the computer age** N l'ère *f* informatique *or* de l'ordinateur
computer agency N bureau *m* d'informatique
computer-aided ADJ assisté par ordinateur
computer-aided design N conception *f* assistée par ordinateur
computer-assisted ADJ ⇒ **computer-aided**
computer code N code *m* machine
computer crime N *(= illegal activities)* criminalité *f* informatique ; *(= illegal act)* délit *m* informatique
computer dating service N club *m* de rencontres sélectionnées par ordinateur
computer error N erreur *f* informatique
computer game N jeu *m* électronique
computer-generated ADJ *[graphics]* généré par ordinateur ; *[image]* de synthèse
computer graphics N *(NonC) (= field)* infographie *f* ; *(= pictures)* images *fpl* de synthèse
computer-integrated manufacturing N fabrication *f* assistée par ordinateur
computer language N langage *m* de programmation, langage *m* machine
computer literacy N compétence *f* (en) informatique
computer-literate ADJ initié à l'informatique
computer model N modèle *m* informatique
computer nerd ‡ N *(pej)* cinglé(e)* *m(f)* d'informatique
computer operator N opérateur *m*, -trice *f*
computer peripheral N périphérique *m* d'ordinateur
computer printout N listage *m or* listing *m* d'ordinateur
computer program N programme *m* informatique
computer programmer N programmeur *m*, -euse *f*
computer programming N programmation *f*
computer science N informatique *f*
computer scientist N informaticien(ne) *m(f)*
computer studies NPL l'informatique *f*
computer system N système *m* informatique
computer typesetting N composition *f* informatique
computer virus N virus *m* informatique

computerese * /kəmˌpjuːtəˈriːz/ N jargon *m* informatique

computerist /kəmˈpjuːtərɪst/ N *(US)* informaticien(ne) *m(f)*

computerization /kəmˌpjuːtəraɪˈzeɪʃən/ N informatisation *f*

computerize /kəmˈpjuːtəraɪz/ VT informatiser COMP **computerized axial tomography** N scanographie *f*, tomodensitométrie *f*

computing /kəmˈpjuːtɪŋ/ N informatique *f* COMP *[service, facility, problem]* informatique ; *[course, department]* d'informatique

comrade /ˈkɒmreɪd/ N camarade *mf* COMP **comrade-in-arms** N compagnon *m* d'armes

comradely /ˈkɒmreɪdlɪ/ ADJ amical

comradeship /ˈkɒmreɪdʃɪp/ N camaraderie *f*

Comsat ® /ˈkɒmsæt/ N *(US)* abbrev of **Communications Satellite Corporation**

con¹ /kɒn/ VT 1 *(† = study)* apprendre par cœur 2 *(Naut)* gouverner ; *(US Naut)* piloter

con² /kɒn/ PREP, N contre *m* ; → **pro¹**

con³ * /kɒn/ VT arnaquer*, escroquer ◆ **to ~ sb into doing sth** amener qn à faire qch en l'abusant *or* en le dupant ◆ **I've been ~ned!** on m'a eu !*, je me suis fait avoir !* ◆ **he ~ned his way into the building** il est entré dans l'immeuble par ruse N 1 ◆ **it was all a big** ~ *(= empty boasting etc)* tout ça c'était de la frime* ; *(= swindle)* c'était une vaste escroquerie *or* arnaque* 2 (‡ abbrev of **convict**) taulard ‡ *m*
COMP **con artist** * N arnaqueur* *m*
con game * N ⇒ **con trick**
con man * N (pl **con men**) escroc *m*
con trick * N escroquerie *f*

Con. N *(Brit)* 1 abbrev of **Conservative** 2 abbrev of **constable**

conc. N (abbrev of **concessions**) ◆ **admission £5 (~ £4)** entrée 5 livres (tarif réduit 4 livres)

concatenate /kɒnˈkætɪˌneɪt/ VT enchaîner

concatenation /kɒnˌkætɪˈneɪʃən/ N *[of circumstances]* enchaînement *m* ; *(Ling, Comput)* concaténation *f*

concave /ˈkɒnˈkeɪv/ ADJ concave

concavity /kɒnˈkævɪtɪ/ N concavité *f*

conceal /kənˈsiːl/ VT *(= hide) [+ object]* cacher, dissimuler ; *(= keep secret) [+ news, event]* garder *or* tenir secret ; *[+ emotions, thoughts]* dissimuler ◆ **to ~ sth from sb** cacher qch à qn ◆ **to ~ the fact that ...** dissimuler le fait que ... ◆ **~ed lighting** éclairage *m* indirect ◆ **~ed turning** *or* **road** intersection *f* cachée

concealment /kənˈsiːlmənt/ N *(NonC)* dissimulation *f* ; *(Jur) [of criminal]* recel *m* ; *[of background, knowledge, truth, facts]* occultation *f* ; *(= place of concealment)* cachette *f*

concede /kənˈsiːd/ LANGUAGE IN USE 11.1 VT *[+ privilege]* concéder, accorder ; *[+ point]* concéder ; *(Sport) [+ match]* concéder ◆ **to ~ that ...** concéder *or* reconnaître que ... ◆ **to ~ victory** s'avouer vaincu VI céder

conceit /kənˈsiːt/ N 1 *(NonC = pride)* vanité *f*, suffisance *f* 2 *(= witty expression)* trait *m* d'esprit, expression *f* brillante ◆ **he is wise in his own ~** *(liter)* il se croit très sage ◆ **~s** *(Literat)* concetti *mpl*

conceited /kənˈsiːtɪd/ ADJ vaniteux, suffisant

conceitedly /kənˈsiːtɪdlɪ/ ADV *[say]* avec suffisance ◆ **I don't mean that** ~ je ne dis pas cela par vanité

conceivable /kənˈsiːvəbl/ ADJ concevable, imaginable ◆ **it is hardly ~ that ...** il est à peine concevable que ... *+ subj*

conceivably /kənˈsiːvəblɪ/ ADV de façon concevable, en théorie ◆ **she may ~ be right** il est concevable *or* il se peut bien qu'elle ait raison

conceive /kənˈsiːv/ VT *[+ child, idea, plan]* concevoir ◆ **to ~ a hatred/love for sb/sth** concevoir de la haine/de l'amour pour qn/qch ◆ **I cannot ~ why he wants to do it** je ne comprends vraiment pas pourquoi il veut le faire VI *[woman]* ◆ **unable to** ~ qui ne peut pas avoir d'enfants ◆ **to ~ of** concevoir, avoir le concept de ◆ **I cannot ~ of anything better** je ne conçois rien de mieux ◆ **I cannot ~ of a better way to do it** je ne conçois pas de meilleur moyen de le faire

concelebrant /kənˈselɪˌbrənt/ N *(Rel)* concélébrant *m*

concentrate /ˈkɒnsəntreɪt/ VT *[+ attention]* concentrer *(on* sur) ; *[+ hopes]* reporter *(on* sur) ; *[+ supplies]* concentrer, rassembler ; *(Chem, Mil)* concentrer ◆ **it ~s the mind** cela fait réfléchir
VI 1 *(= direct thoughts, efforts etc)* se concentrer, concentrer *or* fixer son attention *(on* sur) ; ◆ **to ~ on doing sth** s'appliquer à faire qch ◆ **I just can't ~!** je n'arrive pas à me concentrer ! ◆ **try to ~ a little more** essaie de te concentrer un peu plus *or* de faire un peu plus attention ◆ **~ on getting yourself a job** essaie avant tout de *or* occupe-toi d'abord de te trouver du travail ◆ **~ on getting well** occupe-toi d'abord de ta santé ◆ **the terrorists ~d on the outlying farms** les terroristes ont concentré leurs attaques sur les fermes isolées ◆ **today I shall ~ on the 16th century** *(giving speech etc)* aujourd'hui je traiterai en particulier le 16e siècle
2 *(= converge) [troops, people]* se concentrer, converger ◆ **the crowds began to ~ round the palace** la foule a commencé à se concentrer *or* à se rassembler autour du palais
ADJ, N *(Chem)* concentré *m*

concentrated /ˈkɒnsəntreɪtɪd/ ADJ 1 *[liquid, substance]* concentré ◆ **in a ~ form** sous une forme concentrée 2 *(= focused) [effort]* intense ; *[attack]* en règle

concentration /ˌkɒnsənˈtreɪʃən/ N concentration *f* COMP **concentration camp** N camp *m* de concentration

concentric /kənˈsentrɪk/ ADJ concentrique

concept /ˈkɒnsept/ N notion *f*, idée *f* ; *(Philos, Marketing etc)* concept *m* COMP **concept album** N *(Mus)* album *m* concept

conception /kənˈsepʃən/ N idée *f*, conception *f* ; *(Med)* conception *f* ◆ **he has not the slightest ~ of teamwork** il n'a pas la moindre idée de ce qu'est le travail en équipe ◆ **a new ~ of democracy** une nouvelle conception de la démocratie ; → **immaculate**

conceptual /kənˈseptjʊəl/ ADJ conceptuel COMP **conceptual art** N art *m* conceptuel

conceptualize /kənˈseptjʊəˌlaɪz/ VT concevoir, conceptualiser

conceptually /kənˈseptjʊəlɪ/ ADV du point de vue conceptuel

concern /kənˈsɜːn/ LANGUAGE IN USE 6.2, 26.2

VT 1 (= *trouble, worry*) inquiéter ◆ **to be ~ed by sth** s'inquiéter de qch, être inquiet de qch ◆ **what ~s me is that ...** ce qui me préoccupe, c'est que ... ; see also **concerned**

2 (= *interest*) intéresser, importer à ◆ **all that ~s me is his health** ce qui m'importe, c'est qu'il soit en bonne santé ◆ **these considerations do not ~ us here** ces considérations ne nous intéressent pas ici ◆ **to ~ o.s. in** *or* **with** s'occuper de, s'intéresser à ◆ **we are ~ed only with facts** nous ne nous occupons que des faits

3 (= *affect*) concerner ; (= *be the business of*) regarder, être l'affaire de ◆ **that doesn't ~ you** cela ne vous regarde pas, ce n'est pas votre affaire ◆ **to whom it may ~** (*frm*) à qui de droit ◆ **as ~s ...** en ce qui concerne ... ◆ **where we are ~ed** en ce qui nous concerne

◆ **as far as + concerned** ◆ **as far as I'm ~ed there is blame on both sides** à mon avis, ils ne sont innocents ni l'un ni l'autre ◆ **as far as he is ~ed** en ce qui le concerne, quant à lui ◆ **as far as starting a family is ~ed, the trend is ...** pour ce qui est de faire des enfants, la tendance est ...

◆ **noun/pronoun + concerned** ◆ **the persons ~ed** les intéressés *mpl* ◆ **those most closely ~ed** les personnes les plus touchées ◆ **the department ~ed** (= *in question*) le service en question *or* dont il s'agit ; (= *relevant*) le service compétent

4 (= *be about*) [*report etc*] se rapporter à

N 1 (= *anxiety*) inquiétude *f* ; (*stronger*) anxiété *f* ◆ **they have expressed ~ about the situation** ils se sont dits inquiets de la situation ◆ **there is growing public ~ over the situation** les gens sont de plus en plus inquiets de cette situation, devant cette situation, l'inquiétude du public est croissante ◆ **he was filled with ~** il était très soucieux *or* préoccupé ◆ **a look of ~** un regard inquiet ◆ **it is of great ~ to us (that)** c'est un grand souci pour nous (que) ◆ **this is a matter of great ~ to us** c'est une question qui nous préoccupe beaucoup ◆ **there is no cause for ~** il n'y a pas lieu de s'inquiéter ◆ **there is ~ that there would be an increase in drug addiction** on craint qu'il n'y ait une augmentation des cas de toxicomanie

2 (= *interest*) préoccupation *f* ◆ **the ~s of local people** les préoccupations des gens d'ici ◆ **the electorate's main ~ is with the economy** les électeurs se préoccupent avant tout de l'état de l'économie, les électeurs s'intéressent surtout à l'état de l'économie ◆ **excessive ~ about healthy eating** l'obsession de se nourrir sainement ◆ **it is of no ~ to him** cela n'a aucun intérêt pour lui

3 (= *solicitude*) sollicitude *f* ◆ **I did it out of ~ for you** je l'ai fait par égard pour toi

4 (= *business*) affaire *f* ; (= *responsibility*) responsabilité *f* ◆ **it's no ~ of his** ce n'est pas son affaire, cela ne le regarde pas ◆ **what ~ is it of yours?** en quoi est-ce que cela vous regarde ?

5 (Comm: also **business concern**) entreprise *f*, affaire *f* ; → **going**

> ⚠ Be cautious about translating **to concern** by **concerner**.

concerned /kənˈsɜːnd/ ADJ 1 (= *worried*) [*parent, neighbour, look*] préoccupé, inquiet (-ète *f*) (*for sb/sth* pour qn/qch) ; ◆ **to be ~ about sb** se faire du souci pour qn ◆ **to be ~ about sth** être inquiet de qch ◆ **to be ~ that ...** être inquiet que ... + *subj* ◆ **I am ~ to hear that ...** j'apprends avec inquiétude que ... ; see also **concern** 2 (= *keen*) ◆ **to be ~ to do sth** tenir à faire qch ◆ **they are more ~ to save face than to ...** ils se soucient davantage de ne pas perdre la face que de ...

concerning /kənˈsɜːnɪŋ/ PREP concernant, en ce qui concerne

concert /ˈkɒnsət/ N 1 (*Mus*) concert *m* ◆ **in ~** en concert 2 [*of voices etc*] unisson *m*, chœur *m* ◆ **in ~** à l'unisson, en chœur 3 (*fig*) ◆ **a ~ of colours** une harmonie de couleurs ◆ **in ~ with** de concert avec VT /kənˈsɜːt/ concerter, arranger (ensemble)

COMP [*ticket, date*] de concert **concert grand** N piano *m* de concert
concert hall N salle *f* de concert
concert party N (*Mus*) concert *m* populaire (*donné en plein air ou dans une salle des fêtes*)
concert performer N concertiste *mf*
concert pianist N pianiste *mf* de concert
concert pitch N (*Mus*) diapason *m* (de concert) ◆ **at ~ pitch** (*fig* = *on top form*) au maximum *or* à l'apogée de sa forme
concert tour N tournée *f* de concerts

concerted /kənˈsɜːtɪd/ ADJ concerté

concertgoer /ˈkɒnsətgəʊə^r^/ N amateur *m* de concerts, personne *f* allant régulièrement au concert

concertina /ˌkɒnsəˈtiːnə/ N concertina *m* VI ◆ **the vehicles ~ed into each other** les véhicules se sont emboutis *or* télescopés (les uns les autres) COMP **concertina crash** N (= *car accident*) carambolage *m*

concertmaster /ˈkɒnsətmɑːstə^r^/ N (*US*) premier violon *m*

concerto /kənˈtʃeətəʊ/ N (pl **concertos** *or* **concerti** /kənˈtʃeətiː/) concerto *m* (*for* pour)

concession /kənˈseʃən/ N (*gen, Jur*) concession *f* ; (*Comm*) réduction *f*

concessionaire /kənˌseʃəˈneə^r^/ N concessionnaire *mf*

concessionary /kənˈseʃənərɪ/ ADJ (*Fin, Jur etc*) concessionnaire ; (*Comm*) [*ticket, fare*] à prix réduit ◆ **~ aid** aide *f* libérale N concessionnaire *mf*

concessioner /kənˈseʃənə^r^/ N (*US*) ⇒ **concessionaire**

conch /kɒntʃ/ N (pl **conchs** *or* **conches**) (= *shell, Anat*) conque *f* ; (*Archit*) voûte *f* semi-circulaire, (voûte *f* d')abside *f*

concha /ˈkɒŋkə/ N (pl **conchae** /ˈkɒŋkiː/) (*Anat*) conque *f*

conchology /kɒŋˈkɒlədʒɪ/ N conchyliologie *f*

conciliate /kənˈsɪlɪeɪt/ VT 1 (= *appease*) apaiser ; (= *win over*) se concilier (l'appui de) 2 (= *reconcile*) [+ *opposing views or factions, extremes*] concilier

conciliation /kənˌsɪlɪˈeɪʃən/ N (*NonC*) 1 (*in politics, industrial relations*) conciliation *f* 2 (= *appeasement*) [*of person*] apaisement *m* 3 (= *resolution*) [*of dispute, differences*] règlement *m* COMP **conciliation board** N (*Ind*) conseil *m* d'arbitrage
conciliation service N (*gen*) service *m* de conciliation ; (*in industrial relations*) service *m* de règlement amiable

conciliator /kənˈsɪlɪˌeɪtə^r^/ N conciliateur *m*, -trice *f* ; (*Ind*) médiateur *m*

conciliatory /kənˈsɪlɪətərɪ/ ADJ [*person, tone, gesture, mood, statement*] conciliant ; [*spirit*] de conciliation ; [*procedure*] conciliatoire

concise /kənˈsaɪs/ ADJ (= *short*) concis ; (= *shortened*) abrégé

concisely /kənˈsaɪslɪ/ ADV de façon concise

conciseness /kənˈsaɪsnɪs/, **concision** /kənˈsɪʒən/ N concision *f*

conclave /ˈkɒnkleɪv/ N (*Rel*) conclave *m* ; (*fig*) assemblée *f* (secrète), réunion *f* (privée) ◆ **in ~** (*fig*) en réunion privée

conclude /kənˈkluːd/ VT 1 (= *end*) [+ *business, agenda*] conclure, terminer ◆ **"to be concluded"** (*in magazine*) "suite et fin au prochain numéro" ; (*in TV programme*) "suite et fin au prochain épisode" 2 (= *arrange*) [+ *treaty*] conclure, aboutir à 3 (= *infer*) conclure, déduire (*from* de ; *that* que) 4 (*US* = *decide*) décider (*to do sth* de faire qch) VI (= *end*) [*things, events*] se terminer, s'achever (*with* par, sur) ; [*person*] conclure ◆ **to ~ I must say ...** pour conclure *or* en conclusion je dois dire ...

concluding /kənˈkluːdɪŋ/ ADJ final

conclusion /kənˈkluːʒən/ LANGUAGE IN USE 26.1, 26.2 N 1 (= *end*) conclusion *f*, fin *f* ◆ **in ~** pour conclure, finalement, en conclusion ◆ **to bring to a ~** mener à sa conclusion *or* à terme 2 (= *settling*) [*of treaty etc*] conclusion *f* 3 (= *opinion, decision*) conclusion *f*, déduction *f* ◆ **to come to the ~ that ...** conclure que ... ◆ **to draw a ~ from ...** tirer une conclusion de ... ◆ **this leads one to the ~ that ...** ceci amène à conclure que ... ; → **foregone, jump** 4 (*Philos*) conclusion *f* 5 ◆ **to try ~s with sb** se mesurer avec *or* contre qn

conclusive /kənˈkluːsɪv/ ADJ concluant, probant

conclusively /kənˈkluːsɪvlɪ/ ADV de façon concluante *or* probante

concoct /kənˈkɒkt/ VT (*lit, fig*) concocter

concoction /kənˈkɒkʃən/ N mélange *m*, préparation *f*

concomitant /kənˈkɒmɪtənt/ ADJ concomitant N événement *m* concomitant

concord /ˈkɒŋkɔːd/ N 1 concorde *f*, harmonie *f* ◆ **in complete ~** en parfaite harmonie 2 (*Gram*) accord *m* ◆ **to be in ~ with ...** s'accorder avec ... 3 (*Mus*) accord *m*

concordance /kənˈkɔːdəns/ N 1 (= *agreement*) accord *m* 2 (= *index*) index *m* ; (*Bible, Ling*) concordance *f*

concordant /kənˈkɔːdənt/ ADJ concordant, s'accordant (*with* avec)

concordat /kɒnˈkɔːdæt/ N concordat *m*

Concorde /ˈkɒnkɔːd/ N (= *plane*) Concorde *m* ◆ **in ~** en Concorde

concourse /ˈkɒŋkɔːs/ N 1 (*in building, station*) hall *m* ; (*in pedestrian precinct*) parvis *m*, piazza *f* ; (*US: in a park*) carrefour *m* ; (*US* = *street*) cours *m*, boulevard *m* 2 [*of people, vehicles*] affluence *f*

concrete /ˈkɒnkriːt/ ADJ 1 [*floor, wall, steps*] en béton ; [*block*] de béton 2 (= *definite, not abstract*) concret (-ète *f*) N 1 béton *m* ◆ **nothing is yet set** *or* **embedded in ~** rien n'est encore arrêté *or* décidé ; → **prestressed, reinforce** 2 (*Philos*) **the ~** le concret VT bétonner
COMP **concrete jungle** N jungle *f* de béton
concrete mixer N bétonneuse *f*

concretion /kənˈkriːʃən/ N concrétion *f*

concubine /ˈkɒŋkjʊbaɪn/ N concubine *f*

concupiscence /kənˈkjuːpɪsəns/ N (*frm*) concupiscence *f*

concupiscent /kənˈkjuːpɪsənt/ ADJ (*frm*) concupiscent

concur /kənˈkɜː^r^/ VI 1 (= *agree*) [*person*] être d'accord, s'entendre (*with sb* avec qn ; *in sth* sur *or* au sujet de qch) ; [*opinions*] converger 2 (= *happen together*) coïncider, arriver en même temps ; (= *contribute*) concourir (*to* à) ; ◆ **everything ~red to bring about this result** tout a concouru à produire ce résultat

concurrence /kənˈkʌrəns/ N (*frm*) 1 (= *consent*) accord *m* 2 (= *coincidence*) coïncidence *f* ◆ **a ~ of events** une coïncidence, un concours de circonstances 3 (= *consensus*) ◆ **a ~ of opinion** une convergence de vues

concurrent /kənˈkʌrənt/ ADJ 1 (= *occurring at same time*) concomitant, simultané ◆ **~ with**

her acting career, she managed to … parallèlement à sa carrière d'actrice, elle a réussi à … ◆ **~ with** en même temps que ◆ **he was given ~ sentences totalling 24 years** il a été condamné à 24 ans de prison par confusion des peines 2 *(frm = acting together)* concerté 3 *(frm = in agreement) [views etc]* concordant 4 *(Math, Tech)* concourant

concurrently /kən'kʌrəntlɪ/ ADV simultanément

concuss /kən'kʌs/ VT 1 *(Med: gen pass)* commotionner ◆ **to be ~ed** être commotionné 2 *(= shake)* secouer violemment, ébranler

concussion /kən'kʌʃən/ N 1 *(Med)* commotion *f* (cérébrale) 2 *(= shaking)* ébranlement *m*, secousse *f*

condemn /kən'dem/ LANGUAGE IN USE 14, 26.3 VT 1 *(gen, Jur, Med, fig)* condamner *(to* à*)* ; ◆ **to ~ sb to death** condamner qn à mort ◆ **the ~ed man** le condamné ◆ **the ~ed cell** la cellule des condamnés 2 *[+ building]* déclarer inhabitable, condamner ; *(Mil, Tech) [+ materials]* réformer, déclarer inutilisable

condemnation /ˌkɒndem'neɪʃən/ N *(gen, Jur, fig)* condamnation *f* ; *(US Jur) [of property]* expropriation *f* pour cause d'utilité publique ◆ **the murder drew unanimous ~ from the press** l'assassinat a été unanimement condamné par la presse

condemnatory /kəndem'neɪtərɪ/ ADJ réprobateur (-trice *f*)

condensation /ˌkɒnden'seɪʃən/ N condensation *f*

condense /kən'dens/ VT condenser, concentrer ; *[+ gas]* condenser ; *[+ rays]* concentrer ; *(fig)* condenser, résumer ◆ **~d book** livre *m* condensé VI se condenser, se concentrer COMP **condensed milk** N lait *m* concentré

condenser /kən'densə^r^/ N *(Elec, Tech)* condensateur *m* ; *[of gas]* condenseur *m* ; *[of light]* condensateur *m*

condescend /ˌkɒndɪ'send/ VI 1 condescendre *(to do sth* à faire qch*)* daigner *(to do sth* faire qch*)* ; ◆ **to ~ to sb** se montrer condescendant envers *or* à l'égard de qn 2 *(= stoop to)* s'abaisser *(to* à*)* descendre *(to* à, jusqu'à*)*

condescending /ˌkɒndɪ'sendɪŋ/ ADJ condescendant *(to or towards sb* avec qn*)* ; ◆ **in a ~ way** avec condescendance

condescendingly /ˌkɒndɪ'sendɪŋlɪ/ ADV avec condescendance

condescension /ˌkɒndɪ'senʃən/ N condescendance *f*

condign /kən'daɪn/ ADJ *(= fitting)* adéquat, proportionné ; *(= deserved)* mérité

condiment /'kɒndɪmənt/ N condiment *m*

condition /kən'dɪʃən/ N 1 *(= determining factor)* condition *f* ◆ **~ of sale** condition *f* de vente ◆ **~ of a contract** *(Jur)* condition *f* d'un contrat ◆ **he made the ~ that no one should accompany him** il a stipulé que personne ne devait l'accompagner ◆ **on this ~** à cette condition ◆ **I'll lend you my car on ~ that** *or (US)* **on the ~ that you don't damage it** je vous prête ma voiture à condition que vous ne l'abîmiez *subj* pas ◆ **you can go on holiday on ~ that** *or (US)* **on the ~ that you pass your exam** tu partiras en vacances à condition de réussir ton examen ; → **term**

2 *(= circumstance)* condition *f* ◆ **under** *or* **in the present ~s** dans les conditions *or* circonstances actuelles ◆ **working/living ~s** conditions *fpl* de travail/de vie ◆ **weather ~s** conditions *fpl* météorologiques ◆ **the human ~** la condition humaine

3 *(NonC = state, nature)* état *m*, condition *f* ◆ **physical/mental ~** état *m* physique/mental ◆ **in ~** *[thing]* en bon état ; *[person]* en forme, en bonne condition physique ◆ **in good ~** en bon état ◆ **it's out of ~** c'est en mauvais état ◆ **he's out of ~** il n'est pas en forme ◆ **she was in no ~** *or* **was not in a ~** *or* **not in any ~ to go out** elle n'était pas en état de sortir ◆ **she is in an interesting ~** * *(euph)* elle est dans une position intéressante †

4 *(NonC: frm = social position)* position *f*, situation *f*

VT 1 *(= determine)* déterminer, conditionner ◆ **his standard of living is ~ed by his income** son niveau de vie dépend de ses revenus

2 *(= bring into good condition) [+ animal]* mettre en forme ; *[+ thing]* remettre en bon état ; *[+ hair, skin]* traiter ; → **air**

3 *(Psych, fig) [+ person, animal]* provoquer un réflexe conditionné chez, conditionner ; *(by propaganda) [+ person]* conditionner ◆ **he was ~ed into believing that …** il a été conditionné à croire que … ◆ **~ed reflex** réflexe *m* conditionné ◆ **~ed response** réaction *f* conditionnée

conditional /kən'dɪʃənl/ ADJ 1 *(gen) [offer, acceptance, support, ceasefire]* conditionnel ◆ **to be ~ (up)on sth** dépendre de qch ◆ **his appointment is ~ (up)on his passing his exams** il sera nommé à condition qu'il soit reçu à ses examens 2 *(Gram)* conditionnel N *(Gram)* conditionnel *m* ◆ **in the ~** au conditionnel COMP **conditional access** N *(TV)* accès *m* limité aux abonnés
conditional discharge N *(Brit Jur)* condamnation *f* avec sursis ◆ **a one-year ~ discharge** un an de prison avec sursis

conditionally /kən'dɪʃnəlɪ/ ADV *[agree]* sous condition, à certaines conditions ◆ **she said yes, ~** elle a dit oui, mais à certaines conditions

conditioner /kən'dɪʃənə^r^/ N *(for hair)* après-shampooing *m* ; *(for skin)* crème *f* traitante ; → **fabric**

conditioning /kən'dɪʃənɪŋ/ N *(Psych)* conditionnement *m* ; *[of hair]* traitement *m* ADJ traitant

condo /'kɒndəʊ/ N *(US)* (abbrev of **condominium unit**) → **condominium**

condole /kən'dəʊl/ VI exprimer *or* présenter ses condoléances *(with sb* à qn*)*

condolence /kən'dəʊləns/ LANGUAGE IN USE 24.4 N ◆ **~s** condoléances *fpl* ◆ **to offer one's ~s to sb** présenter ses condoléances à qn ◆ **message/letter of ~** message *m*/lettre *f* de condoléances ◆ **book of ~(s)** registre *m* de condoléances

condom /'kɒndəm/ N préservatif *m*

condominium /ˌkɒndə'mɪnɪəm/ N (pl **condominiums**) 1 condominium *m* 2 *(US) (= ownership)* copropriété *f* ; *(= building)* immeuble *m* (en copropriété) ; *(= rooms)* appartement *m* (dans un immeuble en copropriété) COMP **condominium unit** N appartement *m* en copropriété ; → HOUSE

condonation /ˌkɒndəʊ'neɪʃən/ N *(Fin)* remise *f* d'une dette

condone /kən'dəʊn/ VT *(= tolerate)* admettre, laisser faire ; *(= overlook)* fermer les yeux sur ; *(= forgive)* pardonner ◆ **we cannot ~ that kind of behaviour** nous ne pouvons pas admettre ce genre de comportement, nous ne pouvons pas laisser faire cela ◆ **to ~ adultery** *(Jur)* ≈ pardonner un adultère ◆ **to ~ a student** *(Educ)* repêcher un étudiant ◆ **to ~ a student's exam results** remonter les notes d'un étudiant

condor /'kɒndɔː^r^/ N condor *m*

conduce /kən'djuːs/ VI ◆ **to ~ to** conduire à, provoquer

conducive /kən'djuːsɪv/ ADJ ◆ **~ to** propice à *or* favorable à ◆ **to be ~ to** prédisposer à

conduct /'kɒndʌkt/ N 1 *(= behaviour)* conduite *f*, comportement *m* ◆ **good/bad ~** bonne/mauvaise conduite *f or* tenue *f* ◆ **his ~ towards me** son attitude avec moi, son comportement envers moi ; → **disorderly**

2 *(= leading)* conduite *f* ; → **safe**

VT /kən'dʌkt/ 1 *(= lead)* conduire, mener ◆ **he ~ed me round the gardens** il m'a fait faire le tour des jardins ◆ **~ed visit** visite *f* guidée

2 *(= direct, manage)* diriger ◆ **to ~ one's business** diriger ses affaires ◆ **to ~ an orchestra** diriger un orchestre ◆ **to ~ an inquiry** *(Jur)* conduire *or* mener une enquête ◆ **to ~ sb's case** *(Jur)* assurer la défense de qn

3 ◆ **to ~ o.s.** se conduire, se comporter

4 *(Elec, Phys) [+ heat etc]* conduire, être conducteur *m*, -trice *f* de

COMP **conducted tour** N *(Brit)* excursion *f* accompagnée, voyage *m* organisé ; *[of building]* visite *f* guidée
conduct mark N *(Scol)* avertissement *m*
conduct report N *(Scol)* rapport *m* *(sur la conduite d'un élève)*
conduct sheet N *(Mil)* feuille *f or* certificat *m* de conduite

conductance /kən'dʌktəns/ N *(Elec, Phys)* conductance *f*

conduction /kən'dʌkʃən/ N *(Elec, Phys)* conduction *f*

conductive /kən'dʌktɪv/ ADJ *(Elec, Phys)* conducteur (-trice *f*)

conductivity /ˌkɒndʌk'tɪvɪtɪ/ N *(Elec, Phys)* conductivité *f*

conductor /kən'dʌktə^r^/ N 1 *(= leader)* conducteur *m*, chef *m* ; *(Mus) [of orchestra]* chef *m* d'orchestre ; *[of choir]* chef *m* de chœur 2 *[of bus]* receveur *m* ; *(US Rail)* chef *m* de train 3 *(Phys)* (corps *m*) conducteur *m* ; → **lightning**

conductress /kən'dʌktrɪs/ N receveuse *f*

conduit /'kɒndɪt/ N 1 *(for water)* conduite *f* d'eau, canalisation *f* ; *(for cables)* gaine *f* 2 *(= person)* intermédiaire *mf*

condyle /'kɒndɪl/ N *(Anat)* condyle *m*

cone /kəʊn/ N *(gen)* cône *m* ; *(= road cone)* cône *m* de signalisation ; *[of tree]* cône *m* ; *[of pine tree]* pomme *f* ; *[of ice cream]* cornet *m*

► **cone off** VT SEP *[+ road]* placer des cônes de signalisation sur

coney /'kəʊnɪ/ N ⇒ **cony**

confab * /'kɒnfæb/ N (brin *m* de) causette * *f*

confabulate /kən'fæbjʊleɪt/ VI s'entretenir, deviser

confabulation /kənˌfæbjʊ'leɪʃən/ N conciliabule *m*, conversation *f*

confection /kən'fekʃən/ N 1 *(Culin) (= sweet)* sucrerie *f*, friandise *f* ; *(= cake)* gâteau *m*, pâtisserie *f* ; *(= dessert)* dessert *m* (sucré) ; *(Dress)* vêtement *m* de confection 2 *(= action, process)* confection *f*

confectioner /kən'fekʃənə^r^/ N *(= sweet-maker)* confiseur *m*, -euse *f* ; *(= cakemaker)* pâtissier *m*, -ière *f* ◆ **~'s (shop)** confiserie *f* (-pâtisserie *f*) COMP **confectioner's sugar** N *(US)* sucre *m* glace

confectionery /kən'fekʃənərɪ/ N *(= sweets)* confiserie *f* ; *(Brit = cakes etc)* pâtisserie *f* COMP **confectionery sugar** N *(US)* sucre *m* glace

confederacy /kən'fedərəsɪ/ N 1 *(Pol = group of states)* confédération *f* ◆ **the Confederacy** *(US Hist)* les États *mpl* confédérés 2 *(= conspiracy)* conspiration *f*

confederate /kən'fedərɪt/ ADJ 1 confédéré 2 *(US Hist)* **Confederate** confédéré N 1 confédéré(e) *m(f)* ; *(in criminal act)* complice *mf* 2 *(US Hist)* **Confederate** Confédéré *m* VT /kən'fedəreɪt/ confédérer VI se confédérer

confederation /kənˌfedəˈreɪʃən/ N confédération *f*

confer /kənˈfɜːʳ/ VT conférer, accorder (*on* à) ; ◆ **to ~ a title** conférer un titre ◆ **to ~ a degree (on)** (*at ceremony*) remettre un diplôme (à) VI conférer, s'entretenir (*with sb* avec qn ; *on or about sth* de qch)

conferee /ˌkɒnfɜːˈriː/ N (*at congress*) congressiste *mf*

conference /ˈkɒnfərəns/ N (*= meeting, Pol*) conférence *f*, congrès *m* ; (*especially academic*) congrès *m*, colloque *m* (*on* sur) ; (*= discussion*) conférence *f*, consultation *f* ◆ **to be in ~** être en conférence ◆ **(the) ~ decided ...** les participants à la conférence *or* les congressistes ont décidé ... ; → **press**

COMP **conference call** N (*Telec*) audioconférence *f*, téléconférence *f*

conference centre N (*= town*) ville *f* de congrès ; (*= building*) palais *m* des congrès ; (*in institution*) centre *m* de conférences

conference committee N (*US Pol*) *commission interparlementaire de compromis sur les projets de loi*

conference member N congressiste *mf*

conference room N salle *f* de conférences

conference table N (*lit, fig*) table *f* de conférence

conferencing /ˈkɒnfərənsɪŋ/ N (*Telec*) ◆ **~ (facility)** possibilité *f* de réunion-téléphone

conferment /kənˈfɜːmənt/ N (*Univ*) [*of degree*] remise *f* (de diplômes) ; [*of title, favour*] octroi *m*

confess /kənˈfes/ VT 1 [*+ crime*] avouer, confesser ; [*+ mistake*] reconnaître, avouer ◆ **he ~ed that he had stolen the money** il a avoué qu'il avait volé l'argent ◆ **to ~ (to) a liking for sth** reconnaître qu'on aime qch ◆ **she ~ed herself guilty/ignorant of ...** elle a confessé qu'elle était coupable/ignorante de ... 2 (*Rel*) [*+ faith*] confesser, proclamer ; [*+ sins*] confesser, se confesser de ; [*+ penitent*] confesser VI 1 avouer, passer aux aveux ◆ **to ~ to** [*+ crime*] avouer, confesser ; [*+ mistake*] reconnaître, avouer ◆ **to ~ to having done sth** avouer *or* reconnaître avoir fait qch ; see also **vt** 2 (*Rel*) se confesser

confessedly /kənˈfesɪdlɪ/ ADV (*= generally admitted*) de l'aveu de tous ; (*= on one's own admission*) de son propre aveu ◆ **a ~ terrorist group** un groupe terroriste qui se revendique comme tel

confession /kənˈfeʃən/ N 1 (*= admission of guilt*) [*of mistake, crime*] aveu *m* ; (*Jur*) aveux *mpl* ◆ **to make a full ~** faire des aveux complets 2 (*Rel*) confession *f* ◆ **to go to ~** aller se confesser ◆ **to hear sb's ~** confesser qn ◆ **to make one's ~** se confesser ◆ **to make a ~ (of faith)** faire une confession (de foi) ◆ **general ~** confession *f* générale ◆ **to be of the Protestant ~** (*= denomination*) être de confession protestante ◆ **"Confessions of a Taxi Driver"** (*as title of book, article etc*) "les Confessions d'un chauffeur de taxi"

confessional /kənˈfeʃənl/ (*Rel*) N confessionnal *m* ◆ **under the seal of the ~** sous le secret de la confession ADJ confessionnel

confessor /kənˈfesəʳ/ N (*Rel*) confesseur *m* ; (*= confidant*) confident(e) *m(f)*

confetti /kənˈfetiː/ N (*NonC*) confettis *mpl*

confidant /ˌkɒnfɪˈdænt/ N confident *m*

confidante /ˌkɒnfɪˈdænt/ N confidente *f*

confide /kənˈfaɪd/ VT 1 [*+ object, person, job, secret*] confier (*to sb* à qn) ; ◆ **to ~ sth to sb's care** confier qch à la garde *or* aux soins de qn ◆ **to ~ secrets to sb** confier des secrets à qn 2 avouer en confidence ◆ **she ~d to me that ...** elle m'a avoué en confidence que ..., elle m'a confié que ...

► **confide in** VT FUS 1 (*= tell secrets to*) s'ouvrir à, se confier à ◆ **to ~ in sb about sth** confier qch à qn ◆ **to ~ in sb about what one is going to do** révéler à qn ce qu'on va faire 2 (*= have confidence in*) [*+ sb's ability*] se fier à, avoir confiance en ◆ **you can ~ in me** vous pouvez me faire confiance

confidence /ˈkɒnfɪdəns/ LANGUAGE IN USE 19.4

N 1 (*= trust, hope*) confiance *f* ◆ **to have ~ in sb/sth** avoir confiance en qn/qch, faire confiance à qn/qch ◆ **to put one's ~ in sb/sth** mettre sa confiance en qn/qch ◆ **to have every ~ in sb/sth** faire totalement confiance à qn/qch, avoir pleine confiance en qn/en *or* dans qch ◆ **to have ~ in the future** faire confiance à l'avenir ◆ **I have every ~ that he will come back** je suis sûr *or* certain qu'il reviendra ◆ **motion of no ~** (*Pol etc*) motion *f* de censure ; → **vote**

2 (*= self-confidence*) confiance *f* en soi, assurance *f* ◆ **he lacks ~** il manque d'assurance

3 (*NonC*) confidence *f* ◆ **to take sb into one's ~** faire des confidences à qn, se confier à qn ◆ **he told me that in ~** il me l'a dit en confidence *or* confidentiellement ; → **strict**

4 (*= private communication*) confidence *f* ◆ **they exchanged ~s** ils ont échangé des confidences

COMP **confidence game** N abus *m* de confiance, escroquerie *f*

confidence man N (pl **confidence men**) escroc *m*

confidence trick N ⇒ **confidence game**

confidence trickster N ⇒ **confidence man**

confident /ˈkɒnfɪdənt/ ADJ 1 (*= self-assured*) [*person*] sûr de soi, assuré ; [*manner, smile, prediction*] confiant ; [*performance*] plein d'assurance ; [*reply*] assuré ◆ **to be in (a) ~ mood** être confiant 2 (*= sure*) ◆ **to be ~ of sth** [*person*] être sûr de qch ◆ **to be ~ of success** être sûr de réussir ◆ **to be** *or* **feel ~ about sth** avoir confiance en qch ◆ **to be ~ that ...** être sûr que ...

confidential /ˌkɒnfɪˈdenʃəl/ ADJ 1 (*= secret*) [*information, document, advice, discussion, tone*] confidentiel ◆ **he became very ~** il a pris un ton très confidentiel ◆ **to say sth in a ~ whisper** chuchoter qch d'un ton confidentiel ◆ **in a ~ tone** sur le ton de la confidence 2 (*= trusted*) [*servant, clerk*] de confiance COMP **confidential secretary** N secrétaire *mf* particulier (-ière *f*)

confidentiality /ˌkɒnfɪˌdenʃɪˈælɪtɪ/ N confidentialité *f*

confidentially /ˌkɒnfɪˈdenʃəlɪ/ ADV 1 (*= privately*) [*discuss*] confidentiellement ◆ **to write ~ to sb** envoyer une lettre confidentielle à qn ◆ **all information will be treated ~** tous les renseignements resteront confidentiels 2 (*= confidingly*) [*speak, whisper*] sur le ton de la confidence ◆ **~, I don't like him at all** (*= between ourselves*) tout à fait entre nous, je ne l'aime pas du tout

confidently /ˈkɒnfɪdəntlɪ/ ADV [*predict, assert*] avec beaucoup d'assurance ; [*expect*] en toute confiance ; [*stride, walk*] d'un pas assuré ; [*smile*] d'un air assuré ; [*speak*] avec assurance

confiding /kənˈfaɪdɪŋ/ ADJ confiant

confidingly /kənˈfaɪdɪŋlɪ/ ADV [*say, speak*] sur un ton de confidence ◆ **he leaned towards her ~** il s'est penché vers elle comme pour lui faire une confidence

configuration /kənˌfɪgjʊˈreɪʃən/ N (*gen, Ling, Comput*) configuration *f*

configure /kənˈfɪgə/ VT (*gen, Comput*) configurer

confine /kənˈfaɪn/ VT 1 (*= imprison*) emprisonner, enfermer ; (*= shut up*) confiner, enfermer (*in* dans) ; ◆ **to ~ a bird in a cage** enfermer un oiseau dans une cage ◆ **to be ~d to the house/to one's room/to bed** être obligé de rester chez soi/de garder la chambre/de garder le lit ◆ **to ~ sb to barracks** (*Mil*) consigner qn 2 (*= limit*) [*+ remarks*] limiter ◆ **to ~ o.s. to doing sth** se borner à faire qch ◆ **to ~ o.s. to generalities** s'en tenir à des généralités ◆ **the damage is ~d to the back of the car** seul l'arrière de la voiture est endommagé NPL **confines** /ˈkɒnfaɪnz/ (*lit, fig*) limites *fpl* ◆ **within the ~s of ...** dans les limites de ...

confined /kənˈfaɪnd/ ADJ [*atmosphere, air*] confiné ◆ **in a ~ space** dans un espace restreint *or* réduit ◆ **~ to barracks/base** (*Mil*) consigné ◆ **to be ~** † (*in childbirth*) accoucher, être en couches

confinement /kənˈfaɪnmənt/ N (*Med* †) couches *fpl* ; (*= imprisonment*) détention *f*, incarcération *f* (*Jur*) ◆ **~ to barracks** (*Mil*) consigne *f* au quartier ◆ **to get ten days' ~ to barracks** (*Mil*) attraper dix jours de consigne ◆ **~ to bed** alitement *m* ◆ **~ to one's room/the house** obligation *f* de garder la chambre/de rester chez soi ; → **close¹**

confirm /kənˈfɜːm/ LANGUAGE IN USE 19.5, 21.3, 21.4

VT 1 [*+ statement, claim, theory, report, news, suspicion*] confirmer, corroborer ; [*+ arrangement, reservation*] confirmer (*with sb* auprès de qn) ; [*+ authority*] (r)affermir, consolider ; [*+ one's resolve*] fortifier, raffermir ; [*+ treaty, appointment*] ratifier ; (*Jur*) [*+ decision*] entériner, homologuer ; [*+ election*] valider ◆ **to ~ sth to sb** confirmer qch à qn ◆ **to ~ sb in an opinion** confirmer *or* fortifier qn dans une opinion ◆ **to be ~ed in one's opinion** voir son opinion confirmée ◆ **his new play ~s him as a leading playwright** sa nouvelle pièce le confirme dans sa position de grand auteur dramatique ◆ **we ~ receipt of your letter** nous avons bien reçu votre courrier, nous accusons réception de votre courrier 2 (*Rel*) confirmer

confirmation /ˌkɒnfəˈmeɪʃən/ N 1 [*of statement, claim, theory, suspicion, arrangement, appointment*] confirmation *f* ; [*of treaty*] ratification *f* ; (*Jur*) entérinement *m* ◆ **she looked at me for ~** (*confidently*) elle m'interrogea du regard pour (avoir) confirmation ◆ **the ~ of** *or* **for a booking** la confirmation d'une réservation ◆ **"subject to confirmation"** " à confirmer " ◆ **that's subject to ~** cela reste à confirmer ◆ **all timings are subject to ~ when booking** tous les horaires doivent être confirmés lors des réservations 2 (*Rel*) confirmation *f*

confirmed /kənˈfɜːmd/ ADJ 1 (*= inveterate*) [*non-smoker, meat-eater, atheist*] convaincu ; [*bachelor*] endurci ◆ **I am a ~ admirer of ...** je suis un fervent admirateur de ... 2 (*= definite*) [*booking, reservation*] confirmé

COMP **confirmed credit** N crédit *m* confirmé

confirmed letter of credit N lettre *f* de crédit confirmée

confiscate /ˈkɒnfɪskeɪt/ VT confisquer (*sth from sb* qch à qn)

confiscation /ˌkɒnfɪsˈkeɪʃən/ N confiscation *f*

confit /ˈkɒnfiː/ N confit *m* ◆ **~ of duck** confit de canard

conflagration /ˌkɒnfləˈgreɪʃən/ N incendie *m*, sinistre *m* ; (*fig*) conflagration *f*

conflate /kənˈfleɪt/ VT assembler, réunir

conflation /kənˈfleɪʃən/ N assemblage *m*, réunion *f*

conflict /ˈkɒnflɪkt/ N conflit *m*, lutte *f* ; (*= quarrel*) dispute *f* ; (*Mil*) conflit *m*, combat *m* ; (*Jur*) conflit *m* ; (*fig*) [*of interests, ideas, opinions*] conflit *m* ◆ **armed ~** (*Mil*) conflit *m* armé ◆ **to be in ~ (with)** être en conflit (avec) ◆ **to come into ~ with ...** entrer en conflit *or* en lutte avec ... ◆ **a great deal of ~** un conflit considérable

VI /kənˈflɪkt/ 1 être en conflit (*with* avec) ; ◆ **the interests of pedestrians ~ with those of motorists** les intérêts des piétons sont en conflit avec ceux des automobilistes ◆ **these countries' interests ~** les intérêts de ces deux pays sont contradictoires, il y a conflit d'intérêts entre ces deux pays

2 *[opinions, ideas]* s'opposer, se heurter ; *[dates]* coïncider ◆ **that ~s with what he told me** ceci est en contradiction avec *or* contredit ce qu'il m'a raconté

conflicting /kən'flɪktɪŋ/ ADJ *(= incompatible) [views, opinions, demands, evidence]* contradictoire ; *(= divided) [emotions, loyalties]* conflictuel

confluence /'kɒnflʊəns/ N *[of rivers] (= place)* confluent *m* ; *(= act)* confluence *f* ; *(fig = crowd)* foule *f*, assemblée *f*

conform /kən'fɔːm/ VI 1 se conformer *(to, with* à) ; *[actions, sayings]* être en conformité *(to* avec) 2 *(gen, Rel)* être conformiste *mf*

conformable /kən'fɔːməbl/ ADJ 1 conforme *(to* à) 2 *(= in agreement with)* en conformité, en accord *(to* avec) 3 *(= submissive)* docile, accommodant

conformation /,kɒnfə'meɪʃən/ N conformation *f*, structure *f*

conformism /kən'fɔːmɪzəm/ N conformisme *m*

conformist /kən'fɔːmɪst/ ADJ, N *(gen, Rel)* conformiste *mf*

conformity /kən'fɔːmɪtɪ/ N *(= likeness)* conformité *f* ; *(= conformism)* conformisme *m* ; *(Rel) adhésion à la religion conformiste* ◆ **in ~ with** conformément à

confound /kən'faʊnd/ VT *(= perplex)* déconcerter ; *(frm = defeat) [+ enemy, plans]* confondre *(frm)* ; *(= mix up)* confondre *(A with B* A avec B) prendre *(A with B* A pour B) ; ◆ **~ it!*** la barbe ! * ◆ **~ him!*** qu'il aille au diable !, (que) le diable l'emporte ! † ◆ **it's a ~ed nuisance!*** c'est la barbe !*, quelle barbe !*

confront /kən'frʌnt/ VT 1 *(= bring face to face)* confronter *(with* avec) mettre en présence *(with* de) ; ◆ **the police ~ed the accused with the witnesses** la police a confronté l'accusé avec les témoins ◆ **the police ~ed the accused with the evidence** la police a présenté les preuves à l'accusé ◆ **she decided to ~ him with what she'd learnt** elle a décidé de lui dire ce qu'elle avait appris ◆ **to ~ two witnesses** confronter deux témoins (entre eux)

2 *[+ enemy, danger]* affronter, faire face à ; *(= defy)* affronter, défier ◆ **the problems which ~ us** les problèmes auxquels nous sommes confrontés ◆ **to be ~ed with money problems** être confronté à des problèmes d'argent ◆ **they are forced to ~ fundamental moral problems** ils sont forcés de faire face à des problèmes fondamentaux de morale ◆ **the candidates ~ed each other during a televised debate** les candidats se sont affrontés lors d'un débat télévisé

confrontation /,kɒnfrən'teɪʃən/ N 1 *(military)* affrontement *m* ; *(in human relationships)* conflit *m*, affrontement *m* 2 *(= act of confronting)* confrontation *f (of sb with sth* de qn à *or* avec qch)

confrontational /,kɒnfrən'teɪʃənəl/ ADJ *(gen)* conflictuel ◆ **to be ~** *[person]* être agressif, rechercher la confrontation

Confucian /kən'fjuːʃən/ ADJ confucéen N confucianiste *mf*

Confucianism /kən'fjuːʃənɪzəm/ N confucianisme *m*

Confucius /kən'fjuːʃəs/ N Confucius *m*

confuse /kən'fjuːz/ VT 1 *(= throw into disorder) [+ opponent]* confondre ; *[+ plans]* semer le désordre dans, bouleverser ; *(= perplex)* jeter dans la perplexité ; *(= embarrass)* embarrasser ; *(= disconcert)* troubler ; *(= mix up) [+ person]* embrouiller ; *[+ ideas]* embrouiller, brouiller ; *[+ memory]* brouiller ◆ **you're just confusing me** tu ne fais que m'embrouiller (les idées) ◆ **to ~ the issue** compliquer *or* embrouiller les choses 2 ◆ **to ~ A with B** confondre A avec B, prendre A pour B ◆ **to ~ two problems** confondre deux problèmes

confused /kən'fjuːzd/ ADJ *[person] (= muddled)* désorienté ; *(= perplexed)* déconcerté ; *(= embarrassed)* confus, embarrassé ; *[opponent]* confondu ; *[mind]* embrouillé, confus ; *[sounds, voices]* confus, indistinct ; *[memories]* confus, vague ; *[ideas, situation]* confus, embrouillé ◆ **to have a ~ idea** avoir une vague idée ◆ **to get ~** *(= muddled up)* ne plus savoir où on en est, s'y perdre ; *(= embarrassed)* se troubler

confusedly /kən'fjuːzɪdlɪ/ ADV 1 *(= in bewilderment) [shake one's head]* avec perplexité 2 *(= in disorder)* confusément

confusing /kən'fjuːzɪŋ/ ADJ déroutant ◆ **it's all very ~** on ne s'y retrouve plus, on s'y perd

confusingly /kən'fjuːzɪŋlɪ/ ADV *[do, write, say]* d'une manière qui prête à confusion ◆ **the two names are ~ similar** la similitude des deux noms prête à confusion

confusion /kən'fjuːʒən/ N *(= disorder, muddle)* confusion *f*, désordre *m* ; *(= embarrassment)* confusion *f*, trouble *m* ; *(= mixing up)* confusion *f (of X with Y* de X avec Y) ; ◆ **he was in a state of ~** la confusion régnait dans son esprit, il avait l'esprit troublé ◆ **the books lay about in ~** les livres étaient en désordre *or* pêle-mêle ; → **throw**

confute /kən'fjuːt/ VT *[+ person]* démontrer l'erreur de ; *[+ notion]* réfuter

conga /'kɒŋgə/ N *(= dance)* conga *f*

congeal /kən'dʒiːl/ VI *[fat, grease, oil]* (se) figer ; *[milk]* (se) cailler ; *[blood]* se coaguler ; *[paint]* sécher VT *[+ fat, grease, oil]* faire figer ; *[+ milk]* faire cailler ; *[+ blood]* coaguler

congenial /kən'dʒiːnɪəl/ ADJ *(frm) [atmosphere, environment, work, place]* agréable *(to sb* pour qn) ; *[person]* sympathique, agréable ◆ **to be in ~ company** être en agréable compagnie ◆ **he found few people ~ to him** il trouvait peu de gens à son goût

congenital /kən'dʒenɪtl/ ADJ *[dislike, aversion, mistrust] (also Med)* congénital ; *[liar]* de naissance

congenitally /kən'dʒenɪtəlɪ/ ADV *[lazy, suspicious etc] (also Med)* de naissance

conger /'kɒŋgəʳ/ N (also **conger eel**) congre *m*, anguille *f* de roche

congested /kən'dʒestɪd/ ADJ 1 *(= busy) [place]* congestionné ; *[telephone lines]* surchargé ◆ **~ traffic** encombrements *mpl* ◆ **~ with traffic** embouteillé 2 *(Med = blocked) [nose]* bouché ; *[lungs]* congestionné ◆ **I feel very ~** j'ai vraiment les bronches prises

congestion /kən'dʒestʃən/ N *[of town, countryside]* surpeuplement *m* ; *[of street, traffic]* encombrement *m*, embouteillage *m* ; *(Med)* congestion *f* COMP **congestion charge** N taxe *f* embouteillage *(système de péage électronique urbain instauré pour réduire la circulation automobile)*

congestive /kən'dʒestɪv/ ADJ *(Med)* congestif

conglomerate /kən'glɒməreɪt/ VT conglomérer *(frm)*, agglomérer VI s'agglomérer ADJ /kən'glɒmərɪt/ congloméré *(also Geol)*, aggloméré N *(gen, Econ, Geol)* conglomérat *m*

conglomeration /kən,glɒmə'reɪʃən/ N *(= group) [of objects]* assemblage *m* (hétéroclite) ; *[of houses]* agglomération *f*

Congo /'kɒŋgəʊ/ N *(= country, river)* Congo *m* ◆ **the Democratic/People's Republic of the ~** la République démocratique/populaire du Congo ◆ **~-Kinshasa** Congo-Kinshasa *m* ◆ **~-Brazzaville** Congo-Brazzaville *m*

Congolese /,kɒŋgəʊ'liːz/ ADJ congolais N *(pl inv)* Congolais(e) *m(f)*

congrats* /kən'græts/ EXCL bravo !

congratulate /kən'grætjʊleɪt/ LANGUAGE IN USE 24.3 VT féliciter, complimenter *(sb on sth* qn de qch ; *sb on doing sth* qn d'avoir fait qch) ; ◆ **to ~ o.s. on sth/on doing sth** se féliciter de qch/d'avoir fait qch ◆ **we would like to ~ you on your engagement** nous vous présentons toutes nos félicitations à l'occasion de vos fiançailles

congratulations /kən,grætjʊ'leɪʃənz/ LANGUAGE IN USE 23.6, 24.1, 24.3 NPL félicitations *fpl*, compliments *mpl* ◆ **~!** toutes mes félicitations ! ◆ **~ on your success/engagement** (toutes mes) félicitations pour votre succès/à l'occasion de vos fiançailles

congratulatory /kən'grætjʊlətərɪ/ ADJ *[telegram, letter, message, speech]* de félicitations ◆ **to give sb a ~ handshake** féliciter qn en lui serrant la main

congregate /'kɒŋgrɪgeɪt/ VI se rassembler, se réunir *(round* autour de ; *at* à) VT rassembler, réunir

congregation /,kɒŋgrɪ'geɪʃən/ N rassemblement *m*, assemblée *f* ; *(Rel) [of worshippers]* assemblée *f* (des fidèles), assistance *f* ; *[of cardinals, monks etc]* congrégation *f* ; *(Univ) [of professors]* assemblée *f* générale

congregational /,kɒŋgrɪ'geɪʃnl/ ADJ *[minister]* de l'Église congrégationaliste ; *[prayer]* prononcé par l'ensemble des fidèles ◆ **the Congregational Church** l'Église *f* congrégationaliste

Congregationalist /,kɒŋgrɪ'geɪʃənəˈlɪst/ ADJ, N congrégationaliste *mf*

congress /'kɒŋgres/ N 1 congrès *m* ◆ **education ~** congrès *m* de l'enseignement ; → **trade** 2 *(US Pol)* **Congress** Congrès *m* ; *(= session)* session *f* du Congrès COMP **congress member** N congressiste *mf*

congressional /kɒŋ'greʃənl/ ADJ 1 d'un congrès 2 *(Pol)* **Congressional** *(in US, India)* du Congrès ◆ **Congressional Directory** annuaire *m* du Congrès ◆ **Congressional district** circonscription *f* d'un Représentant ◆ **Congressional Record** Journal *m* Officiel du Congrès

congressman /'kɒŋgresmən/ *(US Pol)* N (pl **-men**) membre *m* du Congrès, ≃ député *m* ◆ **Congressman J. Smith said that ...** le député J. Smith a dit que ... COMP **congressman-at-large** N *représentant non attaché à une circonscription électorale*

congressperson /'kɒŋgres,pɜːsən/ N *(US Pol)* membre *m* du Congrès, ≃ député *m*

congresswoman /'kɒŋgres,wʊmən/ N (pl **-women**) *(US Pol)* membre *m* du Congrès, député *m*

congruence /'kɒŋgrʊəns/ N *(Math)* congruence *f* ; *(fig)* conformité *f*

congruent /'kɒŋgrʊənt/ ADJ en accord *or* harmonie *(with* avec) ; *(Math) [number]* congru *(with* à) ; *[triangle]* isométrique

congruity /kɒŋ'gruːɪtɪ/ N convenance *f*

congruous /'kɒŋgrʊəs/ ADJ qui s'accorde, en harmonie *(to, with* avec) ; *(Rel)* congru

conic(al) /'kɒnɪk(əl)/ ADJ (de forme) conique

conifer /'kɒnɪfəʳ/ N conifère *m*

coniferous /kə'nɪfərəs/ ADJ *[tree]* conifère ; *[forest]* de conifères

conjectural /kən'dʒektʃərəl/ ADJ conjectural

conjecture /kən'dʒektʃəʳ/ VT conjecturer VI conjecturer, faire des conjectures N conjecture *f*

conjoin /kən'dʒɔɪn/ *(frm)* VT lier, unir ◆ **~ed twins** (enfants *mpl*) siamois *mpl* VI s'unir

conjoint /'kɒn'dʒɔɪnt/ ADJ *(frm) [therapy, counselling]* de couple

conjointly /'kɒn'dʒɔɪntlɪ/ ADV conjointement

conjugal /'kɒndʒʊgəl/ ADJ *[state, rights, happiness]* conjugal

conjugate /'kɒndʒʊgeɪt/ (*Bio, Gram*) VT conjuguer VI se conjuguer

conjugation /,kɒndʒʊ'geɪʃən/ N conjugaison *f*

conjunct /kən'dʒʌŋkt/ ADJ conjoint

conjunction /kən'dʒʌŋkʃən/ N (*Astron, Gram*) conjonction *f* ◆ **in ~ with** conjointement avec

conjunctiva /,kɒndʒʌŋk'taɪvə/ N (pl **conjunctivas** *or* **conjunctivae** /"kɒndʒʌŋk'taɪviː/) (*Anat*) conjonctive *f*

conjunctive /kən'dʒʌŋktɪv/ ADJ (*Anat, Gram*) conjonctif

conjunctivitis /kən,dʒʌŋktɪ'vaɪtɪs/ N conjonctivite *f* ◆ **to have ~** avoir de la conjonctivite

conjuncture /kən'dʒʌŋktʃəʳ/ N conjoncture *f*

conjure /kən'dʒʊəʳ/ VT [1] (= *appeal to*) conjurer (*liter*) (*sb to do sth* qn de faire qch) [2] /'kʌndʒəʳ/ faire apparaître (*par la prestidigitation*) ◆ **he ~d a rabbit from his hat** il a fait sortir un lapin de son chapeau VI /'kʌndʒəʳ/ faire des tours de passe-passe ; (= *juggle*) jongler (*with* avec) ; (*fig*) jongler (*with* avec) ; ◆ **a name to ~ with** un nom prestigieux

► **conjure away** VT SEP faire disparaître (comme par magie)

► **conjure up** VT SEP [+ *ghosts, spirits*] faire apparaître ; [+ *memories*] évoquer, rappeler ; [+ *meal*] préparer à partir de (trois fois) rien ◆ **to ~ up visions of ...** évoquer ...

conjurer /'kʌndʒərəʳ/ N prestidigitateur *m*, -trice *f*

conjuring /'kʌndʒərɪŋ/ N prestidigitation *f* COMP **conjuring trick** N tour *m* de passe-passe *or* de prestidigitation

conjuror /'kʌndʒərəʳ/ N ⇒ **conjurer**

conk‡ /kɒŋk/ N (*Brit* = *nose*) pif‡ *m*, blair‡ *m* ; (*US* = *head*) caboche‡ *f* VT (*US*) frapper sur la caboche‡ COMP **conk-out**‡ N (*US*) panne *f* mécanique

► **conk out*** VI [*person*] (= *tire*) s'écrouler de fatigue ; [*engine, machine*] tomber en rade

conker* /'kɒŋkəʳ/ N (*Brit*) marron *m*

Conn. abbrev of **Connecticut**

connect /kə'nekt/ LANGUAGE IN USE 27.4

VT [1] (= *join: gen*) [*person*] [+ *machine*] connecter (*to* à) ; [+ *plug*] brancher (*to* sur) ; (*Tech*) [+ *pinions*] embrayer ; [+ *wheels*] engrener ; [+ *pipes, drains*] raccorder (*to* à) ; [+ *shafts etc*] articuler, conjuguer ; (*Elec*) [+ *two objects*] raccorder, connecter ◆ **to ~ sth to the mains** brancher qch sur le secteur ◆ **to ~ sth to earth** (*Elec*) mettre qch à la terre *or* à la masse ◆ **we haven't been ~ed yet** (*to water, electricity etc services*) nous ne sommes pas encore reliés *or* branchés, nous n'avons pas encore l'eau (*or* l'électricité *etc*)

[2] (*Telec*) [+ *caller*] mettre en communication (*with sb* avec qn) ; [+ *telephone*] brancher ◆ **we're trying to ~ you** nous essayons d'obtenir votre communication ◆ **I'm ~ing you now** vous êtes en ligne, vous avez votre communication ◆ **~ed by telephone** [*person, place*] relié par téléphone (*to, with* à)

[3] (= *associate*) associer (*with, to* à) ; ◆ **I always ~ Paris with springtime** j'associe toujours Paris au printemps ◆ **I'd never have ~ed them** je n'aurais jamais fait le rapport entre eux ; see also **connected**

[4] (= *form link between*) [*road, railway*] relier (*with, to* à) ; [*rope etc*] relier, rattacher (*with, to* à) ; ◆ **the city is ~ed to the sea by a canal** la ville est reliée à la mer par un canal

VI [1] (= *be joined*) [*two rooms*] être relié, communiquer ; [*two parts, wires etc*] être connectés *or* raccordés

[2] [*coach, train, plane*] assurer la correspondance (*with* avec) ; ◆ **this train ~s with the Rome express** ce train assure la correspondance avec l'express de Rome

[3] (* = *hit*) **to ~ with the ball** [*golf club etc*] frapper la balle ◆ **my fist ~ed with his jaw*** je l'ai touché à la mâchoire

[4] [*two people*] se comprendre ◆ **to ~ with sb** communiquer avec qn

connected /kə'nektɪd/ ADJ

[1] (*gen*) lié ◆ **these matters are not ~ at all** ces affaires n'ont aucun lien *or* rapport entre elles ◆ **these two things are ~ in my mind** les deux sont liés dans mon esprit ◆ **to be ~ with** (= *be related to*) être allié à, être parent de ; (= *have dealings with*) être en contact *or* en relation avec ; (= *have a bearing on*) se rattacher à, avoir rapport à ◆ **people ~ with education** ceux qui ont quelque chose à voir avec le monde de l'éducation ◆ **he is ~ with many big firms** il a des contacts avec beaucoup de grandes entreprises, il est en relation avec beaucoup de grandes entreprises ◆ **his departure is not ~ with the murder** son départ n'a aucun rapport *or* n'a rien à voir avec le meurtre ◆ **he's very well ~** (= *of good family*) il est de très bonne famille, il est très bien apparenté ; (= *of influential family*) sa famille a des relations ; see also **connect**

[2] [*languages*] affin (*frm*), connexe ; (*Bot, Jur*) connexe ; (*fig*) [*argument*] logique ; [*talk, oration*] suivi ◆ **(closely) ~ professions** des professions *fpl* connexes ◆ **a (properly) ~ sentence** une phrase correctement construite ◆ **~ speech** (*Ling*) la chaîne parlée

Connecticut /kə'netɪkət/ N Connecticut *m* ◆ **in ~** dans le Connecticut

connecting /kə'nektɪŋ/ ADJ [*rooms*] communicant ; [*parts, wires*] raccordé, connecté ◆ **bedroom with ~ bathroom** chambre *f* avec salle de bains attenante

COMP **connecting flight** N (vol *m* de) correspondance *f*

connecting rod N (*US Aut*) bielle *f*

connection /kə'nekʃən/ LANGUAGE IN USE 5.3

N [1] (= *association*) rapport *m*, lien *m* (*with or to* avec ; *between* entre) ; (= *relationship*) rapports *mpl*, relations *fpl* (*with or to* avec ; *between* entre) ; ◆ **this has no ~ with what he did** ceci n'a aucun rapport avec ce qu'il a fait ◆ **to form a ~ with sb** établir des relations *or* des rapports avec qn ◆ **to break off a ~ (with sb)** rompre les relations *or* les rapports (avec qn) ◆ **to build up a ~ with a firm** établir des relations d'affaires avec une entreprise ◆ **to have no further ~ with sb/sth** ne plus avoir aucun contact avec qn/qch ◆ **in ~ with sth** à propos de qch ◆ **in this** *or* **that ~** (*frm*) à ce sujet, à ce propos ◆ **in another ~** (*frm*) dans un autre contexte

[2] (= *associate*) ◆ **a business ~ of mine, one of my business ~s** une de mes relations d'affaires ◆ **to have important ~s** avoir des relations (importantes) ◆ **to have criminal ~s** avoir des relations *or* des contacts dans le milieu

[3] (= *kinship*) parenté *f* ; (= *relative*) parent(e) *m(f)* ◆ **~s** famille *f* ◆ **there is some family ~ between them** ils ont un lien de parenté ◆ **he is a distant ~** c'est un parent éloigné ◆ **she is a ~ of mine** c'est une de mes parentes

[4] (*Transport*) (= *link*) liaison *f* ; (= *train, bus, plane*) correspondance *f* (*with* avec) ; ◆ **to miss one's ~** rater la correspondance

[5] (*Elec*) raccordement *m*, branchement *m* ; → **loose**

[6] (*Telec*) (= *link*) liaison *f* ; (= *act of connecting*) (*for call*) branchement *m* ; (= *installing*) raccordement *m* ◆ **a telephone/radio/satellite ~** une liaison téléphonique/radio/par satellite ◆ **to break the ~** couper la communication

[7] (*Tech* = *joint*) raccord *m*

[8] (*Drugs* ‡) filière *f*

COMP **connection charge, connection fee** N (*Telec*) frais *mpl* de raccordement

connective /kə'nektɪv/ ADJ (*gen, Gram, Anat*) conjonctif N (*Gram, Logic*) conjonction *f* COMP **connective tissue** N (*Bio*) tissu *m* conjonctif

connectivity /,kɒnek'tɪvɪtɪ/ N (*Comput*) connectivité *f*

connector /kə'nektəʳ/ N (*gen*) raccord *m*, connecteur *m* ; (*Elec*) pince *f* de bout, pince *f* de courant

connexion /kə'nekʃən/ N ⇒ **connection**

conning tower /'kɒnɪŋ,taʊəʳ/ N [*of submarine*] kiosque *m* ; [*of warship*] centre *m* opérationnel

conniption* /kə'nɪpʃən/ N (*US:* also **conniptions**) accès *m* de colère *or* de rage

connivance /kə'naɪvəns/ N connivence *f*, accord *m* tacite ◆ **this was done with her ~/in ~ with her** cela s'est fait avec sa connivence *or* son accord tacite/de connivence avec elle

connive /kə'naɪv/ VI ◆ **to ~ at** (= *pretend not to notice*) fermer les yeux sur ; (= *aid and abet*) être de connivence dans, être complice de ◆ **to ~ (with sb) in sth/in doing sth** être de connivence (avec qn) dans qch/pour faire qch

conniving /kə'naɪvɪŋ/ (*pej*) ADJ intrigant N (*NonC*) machinations *fpl*, intrigues *fpl*

connoisseur /,kɒnə'sɜːʳ/ N connaisseur *m*, -euse *f* (*of* de, en)

connotation /,kɒnəʊ'teɪʃən/ N (*Ling, Philos*) connotation *f* ; (*Logic*) implication *f*

connotative /'kɒnə,teɪtɪv/ ADJ [*meaning*] connotatif

connote /kɒ'nəʊt/ VT évoquer, suggérer ; (*Ling, Philos*) connoter

connubial /kə'njuːbɪəl/ ADJ conjugal

conquer /'kɒŋkəʳ/ VT [+ *enemy, mountain, illness*] vaincre ; [+ *nation, country*] conquérir ; [+ *fear, obsession*] surmonter, vaincre ; [+ *one's feelings*] dominer ; [+ *one's audience*] subjuguer

conquering /'kɒŋkərɪŋ/ ADJ victorieux

conqueror /'kɒŋkərəʳ/ N (*Mil*) conquérant *m* ; [*of mountain etc*] vainqueur *m* ; → **William**

conquest /'kɒŋkwest/ N conquête *f* ◆ **to make a ~*** faire une conquête ◆ **she's his latest ~*** c'est sa dernière conquête*

conquistador /kɒn'kwɪstədɔːʳ/ N (*Hist*) conquistador *m*

Cons. (*Brit*) abbrev of **Conservative**

consanguinity /,kɒnsæŋ'gwɪnɪtɪ/ N consanguinité *f*

conscience /'kɒnʃəns/ N conscience *f* ◆ **to have a clear** *or* **an easy ~** avoir bonne conscience, avoir la conscience tranquille ◆ **he left with a clear ~** il est parti la conscience tranquille ◆ **he has a bad** *or* **guilty ~** il a mauvaise conscience, il n'a pas la conscience tranquille ◆ **to have sth on one's ~** avoir qch sur la conscience ◆ **in (all) ~** en conscience ◆ **for ~' sake** par acquit de conscience ◆ **upon my ~, I swear ...** (*frm*) en mon âme et conscience, je jure ... ◆ **to make sth a matter of ~** faire de qch un cas de conscience

COMP **conscience clause** N (*Jur*) clause *f* de conscience

conscience money N don *m* d'argent (*pour racheter une faute*)

conscience-stricken ADJ pris de remords

conscientious /,kɒnʃɪ'enʃəs/ ADJ [1] [*person, worker, piece of work*] consciencieux [2] [*scruple, objection*] de conscience ◆ **~ objector** objecteur *m* de conscience

conscientiously /,kɒnʃɪ'enʃəslɪ/ ADV consciencieusement

conscientiousness /,kɒnʃɪ'enʃəsnɪs/ N conscience *f*

conscious /'kɒnʃəs/ ADJ [1] (*Med, Psych, Philos*) [*person, memory, mind, thought, prejudice*] conscient ◆ **to become ~** [*person*] revenir à soi, reprendre connaissance ◆ **below the level of ~**

awareness au-dessous du seuil de conscience ◆ **on a ~ level** à un niveau conscient
2 *(= aware)* ◆ **~ of sth** conscient de qch ◆ **to become ~ of sth** prendre conscience de qch, se rendre compte de qch ◆ **she became ~ of him looking at her** elle prit conscience du fait qu'il la regardait, elle se rendit compte qu'il la regardait ◆ **to be ~ of doing sth** avoir conscience de faire qch ◆ **to be ~ that ...** être conscient du fait que ... ◆ **to become ~ that ...** se rendre compte que ...
3 *(after adv)* ◆ **politically ~** politisé ◆ **environmentally ~** sensibilisé aux problèmes de l'environnement ; see also **-conscious**
4 *(= deliberate) [effort, choice, insult]* délibéré ◆ **to make a ~ decision to do sth** prendre délibérément la décision de faire qch ◆ **~ humour** humour *m* voulu
5 *(= clearly felt)* ◆ **... he said, with ~ guilt/superiority** ... dit-il, conscient de sa culpabilité/supériorité
N *(Psych)* conscient *m*

-conscious /ˈkɒnʃəs/ SUF ◆ **to be health-/price-/image-conscious** faire attention à sa santé/au prix des choses/à son image ◆ **to be security-conscious** être sensibilisé aux problèmes de sécurité

consciously /ˈkɒnʃəslɪ/ ADV 1 *(= with full awareness) [remember, think]* consciemment ◆ **to be ~ aware of sth** avoir pleinement conscience de qch 2 *(= deliberately) [hurt, mislead, deceive]* sciemment

consciousness /ˈkɒnʃəsnɪs/ N 1 *(Med)* connaissance *f* ◆ **to lose ~** perdre connaissance ◆ **to regain ~** revenir à soi, reprendre connaissance 2 *(Philos)* conscience *f* 3 *(= awareness)* conscience *f* *(of* de) sentiment *m* *(of* de) ; ◆ **the ~ that he was being watched prevented him from ...** le sentiment qu'on le regardait l'empêchait de ... COMP **consciousness-raising** N sensibilisation *f* ◆ **~-raising is a priority** il nous faut d'abord faire prendre conscience aux gens

conscript /kənˈskrɪpt/ VT *[+ troops]* enrôler, appeler sous les drapeaux ◆ **we were ~ed to help with the dishes** *(fig, hum)* nous avons été embauchés pour aider à faire la vaisselle ; see also **conscripted** N /ˈkɒnskrɪpt/ *(Brit)* conscrit *m*, appelé *m* ADJ *[army]* d'appelés

conscripted /kənˈskrɪptɪd/ ADJ *[troops]* enrôlé ; *[workers, labourers]* enrôlé de force

conscription /kənˈskrɪpʃən/ N conscription *f*

consecrate /ˈkɒnsɪkreɪt/ VT *[+ church, ground]* consacrer ; *[+ bishop]* consacrer, sacrer ; *(fig) [+ custom, one's life]* consacrer *(to* à) ; ◆ **he was ~d bishop** il a été sacré *or* consacré évêque

consecration /ˌkɒnsɪˈkreɪʃən/ N *(NonC) [of church, cathedral, one's life]* consécration *f* *(to sth* à qch) ; *[of bishop, pope]* consécration *f*, sacre *m*

consecutive /kənˈsekjʊtɪv/ ADJ 1 consécutif ◆ **on four ~ days** pendant quatre jours consécutifs *or* de suite 2 *(Gram) [clause]* consécutif

consecutively /kənˈsekjʊtɪvlɪ/ ADV consécutivement ◆ **he won two prizes ~** il a gagné consécutivement *or* coup sur coup deux prix ◆ **... the sentences to be served ~** *(Jur)* ... avec cumul de peines

consensual /kənˈsensjʊəl/ ADJ *(Jur, Physiol)* consensuel

consensus /kənˈsensəs/ N consensus *m*, accord *m* général ◆ **~ of opinion** consensus *m* d'opinion ◆ **what is the ~?** quelle est l'opinion générale ? ADJ *[decision, view]* collectif

consent /kənˈsent/ LANGUAGE IN USE 9.3 VI consentir *(to sth* à qch ; *to do sth* à faire qch) ; *(= to request)* accéder *(to sth* à qch) ; ◆ **between ~ing adults** *(Jur)* entre adultes consentants N consentement *m*, assentiment *m* ◆ **to refuse one's ~ to sth** refuser son consentement *or* assentiment à qch ◆ **by common ~** de l'aveu de tous *or* de tout le monde, de l'opinion de tous ◆ **by mutual ~** *(= general agreement)* d'un commun accord ; *(= private arrangement)* de gré à gré, à l'amiable ◆ **divorce by (mutual) ~** divorce *m* par consentement mutuel ◆ **age of ~** *(Jur)* âge *m* légal *(pour avoir des relations sexuelles)* ; → **silence** COMP **consent form** N *(Med)* autorisation *f* d'opérer

consentient /kənˈsenʃɪənt/ ADJ *(frm)* d'accord, en accord *(with* avec)

consequence /ˈkɒnsɪkwəns/ LANGUAGE IN USE 26.3 N 1 *(= result, effect)* conséquence *f*, suites *fpl* ◆ **in ~** par conséquent ◆ **in ~ of which** par suite de quoi ◆ **as a ~ of sth** en conséquence de qch ◆ **to take** *or* **face** *or* **suffer the ~s** accepter *or* supporter les conséquences *(of* de) 2 *(NonC = importance)* importance *f*, conséquence *f* ◆ **it's of no ~** cela ne tire pas à conséquence, cela n'a aucune importance ◆ **a man of no ~** un homme de peu d'importance *or* de peu de poids ◆ **he's of no ~** lui, il ne compte pas

consequent /ˈkɒnsɪkwənt/ ADJ *(= following)* consécutif *(on* à) ; *(= resulting)* résultant *(on* de) ; ◆ **the loss of harvest ~ upon the flooding** la perte de la moisson résultant des *or* causée par les inondations

consequential /ˌkɒnsɪˈkwenʃəl/ ADJ 1 consécutif, conséquent *(to* à) ; ◆ **~ damages** *(Jur)* dommages-intérêts *mpl* indirects 2 *(pej) [person]* suffisant, arrogant

consequently /ˈkɒnsɪkwəntlɪ/ LANGUAGE IN USE 17.2 ADV ◆ **~, he has been able to ...** c'est pourquoi il a pu ... ◆ **he has ~ been able to ...** il a donc pu ... ◆ **he didn't have enough money: ~, he was unable to ...** il n'avait pas assez d'argent : par conséquent, il n'a pas pu ... ◆ **who, ~, did as little as possible** qui, en conséquence, en a fait le moins possible

conservancy /kənˈsɜːvənsɪ/ N 1 *(Brit: commission controlling forests, ports etc)* ≃ Office *m* des eaux et forêts 2 ⇒ **conservation**

conservation /ˌkɒnsəˈveɪʃən/ N sauvegarde *f*, protection *f* ; *(Phys)* conservation *f* ◆ **energy ~** économies *fpl* d'énergie COMP **conservation area** N *(Brit)* secteur *m* sauvegardé

conservationist /ˌkɒnsəˈveɪʃənɪst/ N défenseur *m* de l'environnement, écologiste *mf*

conservatism /kənˈsɜːvətɪzəm/ N conservatisme *m*

conservative /kənˈsɜːvətɪv/ ADJ 1 conservateur (-trice *f*) ◆ **the Conservative Party** *(Pol)* le parti conservateur ◆ **Conservative and Unionist Party** parti *m* conservateur et unioniste 2 *(= moderate) [assessment]* modeste ; *(= conventional) [clothes, appearance, style, behaviour]* classique, conventionnel ◆ **at a ~ estimate** au bas mot N *(Pol)* conservateur *m*, -trice *f*

conservatively /kənˈsɜːvətɪvlɪ/ ADV *[dressed]* classique *inv*, d'une manière conventionnelle ◆ **the cost of the operation is ~ estimated at £500** le coût de l'opération est estimé au bas mot à 500 livres

conservatoire /kənˈsɜːvətwɑːʳ/ N *(Mus)* conservatoire *m*

conservator /ˈkɒnsəˌveɪtəʳ/ N *(gen)* conservateur *m* ; *(US Jur)* tuteur *m* *(d'un incapable)*

conservatorship /ˈkɒnsəveɪtəˌʃɪp/ N *(US Jur)* tutelle *f*

conservatory /kənˈsɜːvətrɪ/ N 1 *(= greenhouse)* jardin *m* d'hiver *(attenante à une maison)* 2 *(= school)* conservatoire *m*

conserve /kənˈsɜːv/ VT conserver, préserver ; *[+ one's resources, one's strength]* ménager ; *[+ energy, electricity, supplies]* économiser N *(Culin)* confiture *f*, conserve *f* (de fruits)

consider /kənˈsɪdəʳ/ LANGUAGE IN USE 26.1 VT 1 *(= think about) [+ problem, possibility]* considérer, examiner ; *[+ question, matter, subject]* réfléchir à ◆ **I had not ~ed taking it with me** je n'avais pas envisagé de l'emporter ◆ **everything** *or* **all things ~ed** tout bien considéré, tout compte fait ◆ **it is my ~ed opinion that ...** après avoir mûrement réfléchi je pense que ... ◆ **he is being ~ed for the post** on songe à lui pour le poste
2 *(= take into account) [+ facts]* prendre en considération ; *[+ person's feelings]* avoir égard à, ménager ; *[+ cost, difficulties, dangers]* tenir compte de, considérer ◆ **when one ~s that ...** quand on considère *or* pense que ...
3 *(= be of the opinion)* considérer, tenir ◆ **she ~s him very mean** elle le considère comme très avare ◆ **to ~ sb responsible** tenir qn pour responsable ◆ **to ~ o.s. happy** s'estimer heureux ◆ **~ yourself lucky*** estimez-vous heureux ◆ **~ yourself dismissed** considérez-vous comme renvoyé ◆ **I ~ that we should have done it** je considère que *or* à mon avis nous aurions dû le faire ◆ **~ it (as) done** considérez que c'est chose faite ◆ **I ~ it an honour to help you** je m'estime honoré de (pouvoir) vous aider

considerable /kənˈsɪdərəbl/ ADJ *[number, size, amount, influence, success, damage]* considérable ◆ **to face ~ difficulties** être confronté à des difficultés considérables *or* à de grosses difficultés ◆ **we had ~ difficulty in finding you** nous avons eu beaucoup de mal à vous trouver ◆ **to a ~ extent** dans une large mesure ◆ **I've been living in England for a ~ time** je vis en Angleterre depuis longtemps

considerably /kənˈsɪdərəblɪ/ ADV considérablement

considerate /kənˈsɪdərɪt/ ADJ prévenant *(towards* envers) attentionné

considerately /kənˈsɪdərɪtlɪ/ ADV *[behave, say]* gentiment

consideration /kənˌsɪdəˈreɪʃən/ LANGUAGE IN USE 19.5 N 1 *(NonC = thoughtfulness)* considération *f*, égard *m* ◆ **out of ~ for ...** par égard pour ... ◆ **to show ~ for sb's feelings** ménager les susceptibilités de qn ◆ **show some ~!** aie un peu plus d'égards !
2 *(NonC = careful thought)* considération *f* ◆ **under ~** à l'examen, à l'étude ◆ **the matter is under ~** l'affaire est à l'examen *or* à l'étude ◆ **to take sth into ~** prendre qch en considération, tenir compte de qch ◆ **taking everything into ~ ...** tout bien considéré *or* pesé ... ◆ **he left it out of ~** il n'en a pas tenu compte, il n'a pas pris cela en considération ◆ **in ~ of** en considération de, eu égard à ◆ **after due ~** après mûre réflexion ◆ **please give my suggestion your careful ~** je vous prie d'apporter toute votre attention à ma suggestion ◆ **he said there should be careful ~ of the future role of the BBC** il a dit qu'il faudrait réfléchir sérieusement au futur rôle de la BBC
3 *(= factor to be taken into account)* préoccupation *f*, considération *f* ; *(= motive)* motif *m* ◆ **money is the first ~** il faut considérer d'abord *or* en premier lieu la question d'argent ◆ **many ~s have made me decide that ...** plusieurs considérations m'ont amené à décider que ... ◆ **it's of no ~** cela n'a aucune importance ◆ **money is no ~** l'argent n'entre pas en ligne de compte ◆ **his age was an important ~** son âge constituait un facteur important
4 *(= reward, payment)* rétribution *f*, rémunération *f* ◆ **to do sth for a ~** faire qch moyennant finance *or* contre espèces ◆ **for a good and valuable ~** *(Jur, Fin)* ≃ moyennant contrepartie valable

considering /kənˈsɪdərɪŋ/ PREP vu, étant donné ◆ **~ the circumstances** vu *or* étant donné les circonstances CONJ vu que, étant donné que ◆ **~ she has no money** vu que *or* étant donné qu'elle n'a pas d'argent ADV tout compte fait, en fin de compte ◆ **he played very well, ~** il a très bien joué, tout compte fait *or* en fin de compte

consign /kən'saɪn/ **VT** 1 *(= hand over) [+ person, thing]* confier, remettre ◆ **to ~ a child to sb's care** confier un enfant aux soins de qn 2 *(= send) [+ goods]* expédier *(to sb* à qn, à l'adresse de qn)

consignee /ˌkɒnsaɪ'niː/ **N** consignataire *mf*

consigner /kən'saɪnəʳ/ **N** ⇒ **consignor**

consignment /kən'saɪnmənt/ **N** 1 *(NonC)* envoi *m*, expédition *f* ◆ **goods for ~ abroad** marchandises *fpl* à destination de l'étranger 2 *(= quantity of goods) (incoming)* arrivage *m* ; *(outgoing)* envoi *m* **COMP consignment note N** *(Brit Comm)* bordereau *m* d'expédition

consignor /kən'saɪnəʳ/ **N** expéditeur *m*, -trice *f (de marchandises)*, consignateur *m*, -trice *f*

consist /kən'sɪst/ **VI** 1 *(= be composed)* se composer *(of* de) consister *(of* en) ; ◆ **what does the house ~ of?** en quoi consiste la maison ?, de quoi la maison est-elle composée ? 2 *(= have as its essence)* consister *(in doing sth* à faire qch ; *in sth* dans qch) ; ◆ **his happiness ~s in helping others** son bonheur consiste à aider autrui

consistency /kən'sɪstənsɪ/ **N** 1 *(= texture)* consistance *f* 2 *(fig) [of actions, argument, behaviour]* cohérence *f*, uniformité *f* ◆ **to lack ~** *(fig)* manquer de logique

consistent /kən'sɪstənt/ **ADJ** *[policy, approach]* cohérent ; *[support, opposition]* constant ◆ **French policy has not been ~ throughout Africa** la politique de la France en Afrique a été peu cohérente ◆ **his ~ support for free trade** son soutien constant en faveur du libre échange ◆ **he's the team's most ~ player** c'est le joueur le plus régulier de l'équipe ◆ **a ~ pattern of response** des réactions homogènes ◆ **to be ~ with** *(= in agreement with)* être compatible *or* en accord avec ; *(= compatible with) [injury etc]* correspondre à

consistently /kən'sɪstəntlɪ/ **ADV** 1 *(= unfailingly) [good, bad]* invariablement ◆ **to be ~ successful** réussir invariablement ◆ **you have ~ failed to meet the deadlines** vous avez constamment dépassé les délais 2 *(= logically)* avec logique 3 *(= in agreement)* conformément *(with sth* à qch)

consolation /ˌkɒnsə'leɪʃən/ **N** consolation *f*, réconfort *m* ◆ **if it's any ~ to you ...** si ça peut te consoler ... **COMP consolation prize N** prix *m* de consolation

consolatory /kən'sɒlətərɪ/ **ADJ** consolant, réconfortant

console¹ /kən'səʊl/ **VT** consoler *(sb for sth* qn de qch)

console² /'kɒnsəʊl/ **N** 1 *[of organ, language lab]* console *f* ; *(Comput)* console *f* ; *[of aircraft]* tableau *m* de bord, commandes *fpl* 2 *(= radio cabinet)* meuble *m* de hi-fi 3 *(Archit)* console *f* **COMP console game N** jeu *m* de console

consolidate /kən'sɒlɪdeɪt/ **VT** 1 *(= make strong) [+ one's position]* consolider ◆ **the government is trying to ~ voter support ahead of the election** le gouvernement essaie de consolider son électorat avant l'élection 2 *(Comm, Fin = unite) [+ businesses]* réunir ; *[+ loan, funds, annuities]* consolider **VI** se consolider, s'affermir **COMP consolidated balance sheet N** bilan *m* consolidé
consolidated deliveries NPL livraisons *fpl* groupées
consolidated fund N ≈ fonds *mpl* consolidés
consolidated laws NPL *(Jur)* codification *f* (des lois)
consolidated school district N *(US Scol)* secteur *m* scolaire élargi

consolidation /kənˌsɒlɪ'deɪʃən/ **N** *(NonC)* 1 *(= strengthening) [of power, democracy, nation, one's position]* consolidation *f* 2 *(Comm = amalgamation) [of companies, divisions]* fusion *f* 3 *(Fin) [of balance sheet]* consolidation *f* **COMP Consolidation Act N** *(Jur)* codification *f*

consoling /kən'səʊlɪŋ/ **ADJ** consolant

consols /'kɒnsɒlz/ **NPL** *(Brit Fin)* consolidés *mpl*

consonance /'kɒnsənəns/ **N** *[of sounds]* consonance *f*, accord *m* ; *[of ideas]* accord *m*, communion *f*

consonant /'kɒnsənənt/ **N** consonne *f* **ADJ** *(frm)* en accord *(with* avec) ◆ **behaviour ~ with one's beliefs** comportement *m* qui s'accorde avec ses croyances
COMP consonant cluster N groupe *m* consonantique
consonant shift N mutation *f* consonantique

consonantal /ˌkɒnsə'næntl/ **ADJ** consonantique

consort /'kɒnsɔːt/ **N** 1 *(†† = spouse)* époux *m*, épouse *f* 2 (also **prince consort**) (prince *m*) consort *m* 3 *[of musicians, instruments]* ensemble *m* 4 *(Naut)* conserve *f* ◆ **in ~** de conserve **VI** /kən'sɔːt/ *(frm)* 1 *(= associate)* **to ~ with sb** fréquenter qn, frayer avec qn 2 *(= be consistent) [behaviour]* s'accorder *(with* avec)

consortium /kən'sɔːtɪəm/ **N** (pl **consortia** /kən'sɔːtɪə/) consortium *m*

conspectus /kən'spektəs/ **N** vue *f* générale

conspicuous /kən'spɪkjʊəs/ **ADJ** 1 *(= attracting attention) [person, behaviour, clothes]* peu discret (-ète *f*), que l'on remarque ◆ **to be ~** se remarquer ◆ **to be ~ for sth** se faire remarquer par qch ◆ **to feel ~** sentir que l'on attire les regards ◆ **to look ~, to make o.s. ~** se faire remarquer ◆ **to be ~ by one's absence** briller par son absence 2 *(= noticeable) [success, failure]* manifeste, flagrant ; *[absence, lack]* manifeste, notable ; *[change]* visible, évident ; *[gallantry, bravery]* remarquable **COMP conspicuous consumption N** *(Sociol)* consommation *f* ostentatoire

conspicuously /kən'spɪkjʊəslɪ/ **ADV** 1 *(= so as to attract attention) [behave]* avec ostentation 2 *(= noticeably) [silent]* ostensiblement ; *[uneasy]* visiblement, manifestement ◆ **to be ~ successful** réussir visiblement *or* manifestement ◆ **to be ~ lacking in sth** manquer visiblement *or* manifestement de qch ◆ **to be ~ absent** briller par son absence ◆ **the government has ~ failed to intervene** la non-intervention du gouvernement a été remarquée

conspiracy /kən'spɪrəsɪ/ **N** 1 *(= plot)* conspiration *f*, complot *m* ◆ **a ~ of silence** une conspiration du silence 2 *(NonC: Jur)* **(criminal) ~** ≈ association *f* de malfaiteurs ◆ **~ to defraud** *etc* complot *m* d'escroquerie *etc* **COMP conspiracy theory N** thèse *f* du complot

conspirator /kən'spɪrətəʳ/ **N** conspirateur *m*, -trice *f*, conjuré(e) *m(f)*

conspiratorial /kənˌspɪrə'tɔːrɪəl/ **ADJ** *[whisper, smile, wink, nod, activity]* de conspirateur ; *[group, meeting]* de conspirateurs ◆ **in a ~ manner** *or* **way** avec un air de conspirateur ◆ **to be ~** avoir l'air de conspirer *or* comploter ◆ **they were ~ about getting her birthday present** ils complotaient pour lui faire un cadeau d'anniversaire

conspiratorially /kənˌspɪrə'tɔːrɪəlɪ/ **ADV** *[behave, smile]* d'un air conspirateur ; *[say, whisper]* sur le ton de la conspiration, avec un air de conspirateur

conspire /kən'spaɪəʳ/ **VI** 1 *[people]* conspirer *(against* contre) ; ◆ **to ~ to do sth** comploter de *or* se mettre d'accord pour faire qch 2 *[events]* conspirer, concourir *(to do sth* à faire qch) **VT** † comploter, méditer

constable /'kʌnstəbl/ **N** *(Brit:* also **police constable**) *(in town)* agent *m* de police, gardien *m* de la paix ; *(in country)* gendarme *m* ◆ **"yes, Constable"** "oui, monsieur l'agent" ; → **chief, special**

constabulary /kən'stæbjʊlərɪ/ **COLLECTIVE N** *(Brit) (in town)* (la) police en uniforme ; *(in country)* (la) gendarmerie ; → **royal**

Constance /'kɒnstəns/ **N** ◆ **Lake ~** le lac de Constance

constancy /'kɒnstənsɪ/ **N** *(= firmness)* constance *f*, fermeté *f* ; *[of feelings, love]* constance *f* ; *[of temperature etc]* invariabilité *f*, constance *f*

constant /'kɒnstənt/ **ADJ** 1 *(= occurring often) [quarrels, interruptions]* incessant, continuel, perpétuel 2 *(= unchanging) [love]* constant ; *[friend]* fidèle, loyal **N** *(Math, Phys)* constante *f*

Constantine /'kɒnstənˌtaɪn/ **N** Constantin *m*

Constantinople /ˌkɒnstæntɪ'nəʊpl/ **N** Constantinople

constantly /'kɒnstəntlɪ/ **ADV** constamment, continuellement ◆ **~ evolving** en évolution constante

constellation /ˌkɒnstə'leɪʃən/ **N** constellation *f*

consternation /ˌkɒnstə'neɪʃən/ **N** consternation *f* ◆ **filled with ~** frappé de consternation, consterné ◆ **there was general ~** la consternation était générale

constipate /'kɒnstɪpeɪt/ **VT** constiper

constipated /'kɒnstɪpeɪtɪd/ **ADJ** *(lit, fig)* constipé

constipation /ˌkɒnstɪ'peɪʃən/ **N** constipation *f*

constituency /kən'stɪtjʊənsɪ/ **N** 1 *(Pol) (= place)* circonscription *f* électorale ; *(= people)* électeurs *mpl* (d'une circonscription) 2 *(= group)* **a powerful political ~** une force politique puissante ◆ **Mr Jackson had a natural ~ among American Blacks** M. Jackson trouvait un appui politique naturel chez les Noirs américains **COMP constituency party N** section *f* locale (du parti)

constituent /kən'stɪtjʊənt/ **ADJ** *[part, element]* constituant, constitutif ◆ **~ assembly** *(Pol)* assemblée *f* constituante ◆ **~ power** pouvoir *m* constituant **N** 1 *(Pol)* électeur *m*, -trice *f (de la circonscription d'un député)* ◆ **one of my ~s wrote to me ...** quelqu'un dans ma circonscription m'a écrit ... ◆ **he was talking to one of his ~s** il parlait à un habitant *or* un électeur de sa circonscription 2 *(= part, element)* élément *m* constitutif ; *(Ling)* constituant *m* ◆ **~ analysis** *(Ling)* analyse *f* en constituants immédiats

constitute /'kɒnstɪtjuːt/ **VT** 1 *(= appoint) [+ government, assembly]* constituer ; *[+ people]* désigner ◆ **to be ~d** être constitué ◆ **to ~ sb leader of the group** désigner qn (comme) chef du groupe 2 *(= establish) [+ organization]* monter, établir ; *[+ committee]* constituer 3 *(= amount to, make up)* faire, constituer ◆ **these parts ~ a whole** toutes ces parties font *or* constituent un tout ◆ **that ~s a lie** cela constitue un mensonge ◆ **it ~s a threat to our sales** ceci représente une menace pour nos ventes ◆ **so ~d that ...** fait de telle façon que ..., ainsi fait que ...

constitution /ˌkɒnstɪ'tjuːʃən/ **N** 1 *(Pol)* constitution *f* ◆ **under the French ~** selon *or* d'après la constitution française ◆ **the Constitution State** le Connecticut 2 *[of person]* constitution *f* ◆ **to have a strong/weak** *or* **poor ~** avoir une robuste/chétive constitution ◆ **iron ~** santé *f* de fer 3 *(= structure)* composition *f*, constitution *f (of* de)

CONSTITUTION

Contrairement à la France ou aux États-Unis, la Grande-Bretagne n'a pas de constitution écrite à proprement parler. Le droit constitutionnel britannique se compose donc d'un ensemble de textes épars qui peut être amendé ou complété par le Parlement.

constitutional /ˌkɒnstɪˈtjuːʃənl/ ADJ 1 *(Pol, Univ) [reform, amendment]* de la constitution ; *[change, crisis, law]* constitutionnel ; *[monarch]* soumis à une constitution ◆ ~ **lawyer** spécialiste *mf* du droit constitutionnel ◆ **we have a ~ right to demonstrate** de par la constitution, nous avons le droit de manifester ◆ **the ~ head of state is the Queen** le chef de l'État est, de par la constitution, la reine 2 *[weakness, tendency]* constitutionnel 3 *(frm = inherent) [optimism, envy]* inhérent N *(hum)* ◆ **to go for a ~** * faire sa petite promenade *or* son petit tour
COMP **constitutional monarch** N souverain(e) *m(f)* d'une monarchie constitutionnelle
constitutional monarchy N monarchie *f* constitutionnelle

constitutionality /ˌkɒnstɪtjuːʃəˈnælɪtɪ/ N constitutionnalité *f*

constitutionally /ˌkɒnstɪˈtjuːʃənəlɪ/ ADV 1 *(Pol, Univ = legally) [act]* conformément à la constitution ; *[protected, guaranteed]* par la constitution 2 *(= physically)* ◆ ~ **frail** de faible constitution 3 *(= inherently) [incapable, reserved]* par nature, de nature

constitutive /ˈkɒnstɪtjuːtɪv/ ADJ constitutif

constrain /kənˈstreɪn/ VT 1 *(= compel)* contraindre *(sb to do sth* qn à faire qch) ; ◆ **I find myself ~ed to write to you** je me vois dans la nécessité de vous écrire ◆ **to be/feel ~ed to do sth** être/se sentir contraint *or* obligé de faire qch 2 *(= limit)* limiter 3 *(= restrict) [+ liberty, person]* contraindre ◆ **women often feel ~ed by family commitments** les femmes trouvent souvent contraignantes les responsabilités familiales

constrained /kənˈstreɪnd/ ADJ 1 *(= awkward) [smile, expression]* contraint ; *[voice, silence]* gêné ; *[atmosphere]* de gêne 2 *(= limited) [resources, budget]* limité

constraint /kənˈstreɪnt/ N contrainte *f* ◆ **financial ~s** contraintes financières ◆ **lack of water is the main ~ on development** la pénurie d'eau est la principale entrave au développement ◆ **to speak freely and without ~** parler librement et sans contrainte ◆ **the ~s placed upon us** les contraintes auxquelles nous sommes soumis

constrict /kənˈstrɪkt/ VT *(gen)* resserrer ; *(= tighten) [+ muscle etc]* serrer ; *(= hamper) [+ movements]* gêner ; *(fig) [convention etc]* limiter

constricted /kənˈstrɪktɪd/ ADJ 1 *(= narrow, limited) [artery]* rétréci ; *[throat]* serré ; *[breathing]* gêné ; *[space]* réduit, restreint ; *[freedom]* restreint ; *[movement]* limité ◆ **to feel ~ (by sth)** *(lit)* se sentir à l'étroit (dans qch) ; *(fig) (by convention etc)* se sentir limité (par qch) 2 *(Phon)* constrictif

constricting /kənˈstrɪktɪŋ/ ADJ *[garment]* gênant, étriqué ; *[ideology]* étroit ; *(fig)* restreignant

constriction /kənˈstrɪkʃən/ N *(esp Med)* constriction *f*, resserrement *m*, étranglement *m*

constrictive /kənˈstrɪktɪv/ ADJ ⇒ **constricting**

construct /kənˈstrʌkt/ VT construire N /ˈkɒnstrʌkt/ *(Philos, Psych)* construction *f* mentale ; *(= machine etc)* construction *f*

construction /kənˈstrʌkʃən/ N 1 *[of roads, buildings]* construction *f* ◆ **in course of ~, under ~** en construction 2 *(= building, structure)* construction *f*, bâtiment *m* 3 *(= interpretation)* interprétation *f* ◆ **to put a wrong ~ on sb's words** mal interpréter *or* interpréter à contresens les paroles de qn 4 *(Gram)* construction *f*
COMP **construction engineer** N ingénieur *m* des travaux publics et des bâtiments
construction site N chantier *m*
construction worker N ouvrier *m* du bâtiment

constructional /kənˈstrʌkʃənl/ ADJ de construction ◆ ~ **engineering** construction *f* mécanique

constructive /kənˈstrʌktɪv/ ADJ constructif
COMP **constructive dismissal** N démission *f* forcée

constructively /kənˈstrʌktɪvlɪ/ ADV d'une manière constructive

constructivism /kənˈstrʌktɪvɪzəm/ N constructivisme *m*

constructivist /kənˈstrʌktɪvɪst/ ADJ constructiviste N constructiviste *mf*

constructor /kənˈstrʌktəʳ/ N constructeur *m*, -trice *f* ; *(of ships)* ingénieur *m* des constructions navales

construe /kənˈstruː/ VT 1 *(gen = interpret meaning of)* interpréter ◆ **her silence was ~d as consent** son silence a été interprété comme *or* pris pour un assentiment ◆ **this was ~d as a step forward in the negotiations** cela a été interprété comme un pas en avant dans les négociations ◆ **his words were wrongly ~d** ses paroles ont été mal comprises, on a interprété ses paroles à contresens 2 *(Gram = parse etc) [+ sentence]* analyser, décomposer ; *[+ Latin etc text]* analyser 3 *(= explain) [+ poem, passage]* expliquer VI *(Gram)* s'analyser grammaticalement ◆ **the sentence will not ~** la phrase n'a pas de construction

consul /ˈkɒnsəl/ N consul *m* COMP **consul general** N (pl **consuls general**) consul *m* général

consular /ˈkɒnsjʊləʳ/ ADJ consulaire ◆ ~ **section** service *m* consulaire

consulate /ˈkɒnsjʊlɪt/ N consulat *m* COMP **consulate general** N consulat *m* général

consulship /ˈkɒnsəlʃɪp/ N poste *m* *or* charge *f* de consul

consult /kənˈsʌlt/ VT 1 *[+ book, person, doctor]* consulter *(about* sur, au sujet de) 2 *(= show consideration for) [+ person's feelings]* avoir égard à, prendre en considération ; *[+ one's own interests]* consulter VI consulter, être en consultation *(with* avec) ; ◆ **to ~ together over sth** se consulter sur *or* au sujet de qch
COMP **consulting engineer** N ingénieur-conseil *m*
consulting hours NPL *(Brit Med)* heures *fpl* de consultation
consulting room N *(Brit esp Med)* cabinet *m* de consultation

consultancy /kənˈsʌltənsɪ/ N *(= company, group)* cabinet-conseil *m* ◆ ~ **(service)** service *m* d'expertise *or* de consultants

consultant /kənˈsʌltənt/ N *(gen)* consultant *m*, expert-conseil *m* ; *(Brit Med)* médecin *m* consultant, spécialiste *m* ◆ **he acts as ~ to the firm** il est expert-conseil auprès de la compagnie ; → **management**
COMP **consultant engineer** N ingénieur-conseil *m*, ingénieur *m* consultant
consultant physician N médecin-chef *m*, chef *m* de service
consultant psychiatrist N (médecin-)chef *m* de service psychiatrique

consultation /ˌkɒnsəlˈteɪʃən/ N 1 *(NonC)* consultation *f* ◆ **in ~ with** en consultation avec 2 *(meeting)* consultation *f* ◆ **to hold a ~** conférer *(about* de), délibérer *(about* sur)

consultative /kənˈsʌltətɪv/ ADJ consultatif ◆ **in a ~ capacity** dans un rôle consultatif

consumable /kənˈsjuːməbl/ ADJ *(Econ etc)* de consommation ◆ ~ **goods** biens *mpl* *or* produits *mpl* de consommation

consumables /kənˈsjuːməblz/ NPL *(Econ etc)* produits *mpl* de consommation ; *(Comput)* consommables *mpl*

consume /kənˈsjuːm/ VT *[+ food, drink]* consommer ; *[+ supplies, resources]* consommer, dissiper ; *[engine fuel]* brûler, consommer ; *[fire] [+ buildings]* consumer, dévorer ◆ **to be ~d with grief** *(fig)* se consumer de chagrin ◆ **to be ~d with desire** brûler de désir ◆ **to be ~d with jealousy** être rongé par la jalousie

consumer /kənˈsjuːməʳ/ N *(gen)* consommateur *m*, -trice *f* ; *(= user)* abonné(e) *m(f)* ◆ **gas etc ~** abonné(e) *m(f)* au gaz *etc*
COMP **consumer behaviour** N comportement *m* du consommateur
consumer credit N crédit *m* à la consommation
consumer demand N demande *f* de consommation *or* des consommateurs
consumer durables NPL biens *mpl* durables
consumer electronics N *(NonC)* électronique *f* grand public
consumer goods NPL biens *mpl* de consommation
consumer group N association *f* de consommateurs
consumer price index N *(US)* indice *m* des prix à la consommation, indice *m* des prix de détail
consumer protection N défense *f* du consommateur ◆ **Secretary of State for** *or* **Minister of Consumer Protection** *(Brit)* ministre *m* chargé de la Défense des consommateurs, ≃ secrétaire *m* d'État à la Consommation ◆ **Department** *or* **Ministry of Consumer Protection** ministère *m* chargé de la Défense des consommateurs, ≃ secrétariat *m* d'État à la Consommation
consumer research N études *fpl* de marchés
consumer resistance N résistance *f* du consommateur
consumer sampling N enquête *f* auprès des consommateurs
the Consumers' Association N *(in Brit) association britannique de défense des consommateurs*
consumer society N société *f* de consommation
consumer spending N *(NonC)* dépenses *fpl* de consommation
consumer watchdog N organisme *m* de protection des consommateurs

consumerism /kənˈsjuːməˌrɪzəm/ N 1 *(= consumer protection)* défense *f* du consommateur, consumérisme *m* 2 *(Econ = policy)* consumérisme *m* ◆ **Western ~** la société de consommation occidentale

consumerist /kənˈsjuːməˌrɪst/ N consumériste *mf*, défenseur *m* des consommateurs

consuming /kənˈsjuːmɪŋ/ ADJ *[desire, passion]* dévorant, brûlant

consummate /kənˈsʌmɪt/ ADJ consommé, achevé VT /ˈkɒnsʌmeɪt/ consommer

consummately /kənˈsʌmɪtlɪ/ ADV *[acted, executed]* à la perfection ; *[professional, skilful]* éminemment

consummation /ˌkɒnsʌˈmeɪʃən/ N *[of union, esp marriage]* consommation *f* ; *[of art form]* perfection *f* ; *[of one's desires, ambitions]* couronnement *m*, apogée *m*

consumption /kənˈsʌmpʃən/ N *(NonC)* 1 *[of food, fuel]* consommation *f* ◆ **not fit for human ~** *(lit)* non comestible ; (* *pej*) pas mangeable, immangeable 2 *(Med* † *= tuberculosis)* consomption *f* (pulmonaire) †, phtisie † *f*

consumptive † /kənˈsʌmptɪv/ ADJ, N phtisique † *mf*, tuberculeux *m*, -euse *f*

cont. abbrev of **continued**

contact /ˈkɒntækt/ N 1 *(communicating)* contact *m* ◆ **to be in/come into/get into ~ with sb** être/entrer/se mettre en contact *or* rapport avec qn ◆ **to make ~ (with sb)** prendre contact (avec qn) ◆ **we've lost ~ (with him)** nous avons perdu contact (avec lui) ◆ **we have**

had no ~ with him for six months nous sommes sans contact avec lui depuis six mois ◆ **I seem to make no ~ with him** je n'arrive pas à communiquer avec lui ◆ **~ with the net** *(Volleyball)* faute *f* de filet

[2] *(= touching) (Elec)* contact *m* ◆ **point of ~** point *m* de contact *or* de tangence ◆ **to make/ break the ~** établir/couper le contact ◆ **~!** *(said by pilot)* contact !

[3] *(= person in secret service etc)* agent *m* de liaison ; *(= acquaintance)* connaissance *f*, relation *f* ◆ **he has some ~s in Paris** il a des relations à Paris, il connaît des gens *or* il est en relation avec des gens à Paris ◆ **a business ~** une relation de travail

[4] *(Med)* contaminateur *m* possible, contact *m*

[5] ⇒ **contact lens**

VT *[+ person]* se mettre en contact *or* en rapport avec, contacter ◆ **we'll ~ you soon** nous nous mettrons en rapport avec vous sous peu

COMP *[adhesive etc]* de contact

contact breaker N *(Elec)* interrupteur *m*, rupteur *m*

contact cement N ciment *m* de contact

contact centre *(Brit)*, **contact center** *(US)*, centre *m* de contact

contact details NPL coordonnées *fpl*

contact lens N verre *m* de contact, lentille *f* (cornéenne)

contact man N (pl **contact men**) *(Comm)* agent *m* de liaison

contact number N ◆ **could you give me your ~ number?** pourriez-vous me laisser un numéro de téléphone où je puisse vous joindre ?

contact print N *(Phot)* (épreuve *f* par) contact *m*

contact sport N sport *m* de contact

contagion /kənˈteɪdʒən/ N contagion *f*

contagious /kənˈteɪdʒəs/ ADJ *[disease, person, sense of humour, enthusiasm, laugh]* contagieux

contain /kənˈteɪn/ VT [1] *(= hold) [box, bottle, envelope etc]* contenir ; *[book, letter, newspaper]* contenir, renfermer ◆ **sea water ~s a lot of salt** l'eau de mer contient beaucoup de sel *or* a une forte teneur en sel ◆ **the room will ~ 70 people** la salle peut contenir 70 personnes ; → **self** [2] *(= hold back, control) [+ one's emotions, anger]* contenir, maîtriser ◆ **he couldn't ~ himself for joy** il ne se sentait pas de joie ◆ **to ~ the enemy forces** *(Mil)* contenir les troupes ennemies [3] *(Math)* être divisible par

contained /kənˈteɪnd/ ADJ *(emotionally)* réservé

container /kənˈteɪnəʳ/ N [1] *(= goods transport)* conteneur *m* [2] *(= jug, box etc)* récipient *m* ; *(for plants)* godet *m* ; *(for food)* barquette *f*

COMP *[of train, ship]* porte-conteneurs *inv*

container dock N dock *m* pour la manutention de conteneurs

container line N *(Naut)* ligne *f* transconteneurs

container port N port *m* à conteneurs

container terminal N terminal *m* (à conteneurs)

container transport N transport *m* par conteneurs

containerization /kənˌteɪnəraɪˈzeɪʃən/ N conteneurisation *f*

containerize /kənˈteɪnəraɪz/ VT mettre en conteneurs, conteneuriser

containment /kənˈteɪnmənt/ N *(Pol)* endiguement *m*

contaminant /kənˈtæmɪnənt/ N polluant *m*

contaminate /kənˈtæmɪneɪt/ VT *(lit, fig)* contaminer, souiller ; *[radioactivity]* contaminer ◆ **~d air** air *m* vicié *or* contaminé

contamination /kənˌtæmɪˈneɪʃən/ N *(NonC)* contamination *f*

contango /kənˈtæŋgəʊ/ N *(Brit)* report *m*

contd. abbrev of **continued**

contemplate /ˈkɒntempleɪt/ VT [1] *(= plan, consider) [+ action, purchase]* envisager ◆ **to ~ doing sth** envisager de *or* se proposer de faire qch ◆ **I don't ~ a refusal from him** je ne m'attends pas à *or* je n'envisage pas un refus de sa part [2] *(= look at)* contempler, considérer avec attention

contemplation /ˌkɒntemˈpleɪʃən/ N *(NonC)* [1] *(= deep thought)* contemplation *f*, méditation *f* ◆ **deep in ~** plongé dans de profondes méditations [2] *(= act of looking)* contemplation *f* [3] *(= expectation)* prévision *f* ◆ **in ~ of their arrival** en prévision de leur arrivée

contemplative /kənˈtemplətɪv/ ADJ [1] *(= thoughtful) [person]* songeur, pensif ; *[mood]* contemplatif ; *[walk]* méditatif [2] *(Rel) [life, order, prayer]* contemplatif N *(Rel)* contemplatif *m*, -ive *f*

contemplatively /kənˈtemplətɪvlɪ/ ADV *[look, stare, say]* d'un air pensif

contemporaneous /kənˌtempəˈreɪnɪəs/ ADJ contemporain *(with* de)

contemporaneously /kənˌtempəˈreɪnɪəslɪ/ ADV à la même époque *(with* que)

contemporary /kənˈtempərərɪ/ ADJ *(= of the same period)* contemporain *(with* de) de la même époque *(with* que) ; *(= modern)* contemporain, moderne ◆ **Dickens and ~ writers** Dickens et les écrivains contemporains *or* de son époque ◆ **he's bought an 18th century house and is looking for ~ furniture** il a acheté une maison du 18ᵉ siècle et il cherche des meubles d'époque ◆ **a ~ narrative** un récit de l'époque ◆ **I like ~ art** j'aime l'art contemporain *or* moderne ◆ **it's all very ~** c'est tout ce qu'il y a de plus moderne N contemporain(e) *m(f)*

contempt /kənˈtempt/ N mépris *m* ◆ **to hold in ~** mépriser, avoir du mépris pour ◆ **in ~ of danger** au mépris *or* en dépit du danger ◆ **it's beneath ~** c'est tout ce qu'il y a de plus méprisable, c'est au-dessous de tout ◆ **~ of court** *(Jur)* outrage *m* à la Cour

contemptible /kənˈtemptəbl/ ADJ méprisable, indigne

contemptuous /kənˈtemptjʊəs/ ADJ *[person, manner]* dédaigneux, méprisant ; *[dismissal, disregard, look, laugh, remark]* méprisant ; *[gesture]* de mépris ◆ **to be ~ of sb/sth** avoir du mépris pour qn/qch

contemptuously /kənˈtemptjʊəslɪ/ ADV avec mépris, dédaigneusement

contend /kənˈtend/ VI [1] *(assert)* prétendre *(that* que) [2] ◆ **to ~ with** combattre, lutter contre ◆ **to ~ with sb for sth** disputer qch à qn ◆ **to ~ with sb over sth** se disputer *or* se battre avec qn au sujet de qch ◆ **they had to ~ with very bad weather conditions** ils ont dû faire face à des conditions météorologiques déplorables ◆ **we have many problems to ~ with** nous sommes aux prises avec de nombreux problèmes ◆ **he has a lot to ~ with** il a pas mal de problèmes à résoudre ◆ **I should not like to have to ~ with him** je ne voudrais pas avoir affaire à lui ◆ **you'll have me to ~ with** vous aurez affaire à moi [3] ◆ **to ~ for** *[+ title, medal, prize]* se battre pour ; *[+ support, supremacy]* lutter pour

contender /kənˈtendəʳ/ N prétendant(e) *m(f)* *(for* à) ; *(in contest, competition, race)* concurrent(e) *m(f)* ; *(in election, for a job)* candidat *m* ◆ **presidential ~** candidat *m* à l'élection présidentielle

contending /kənˈtendɪŋ/ ADJ opposé, ennemi

content¹ /kənˈtent/ ADJ content, satisfait ◆ **to be ~ with sth** se contenter *or* s'accommoder de qch ◆ **she is quite ~ to stay there** elle ne demande pas mieux que de rester là N contentement *m*, satisfaction *f* ; → **heart** VT *[+ person]* contenter, satisfaire ◆ **to ~ o.s. with doing sth** se contenter de *or* se borner à faire qch

content² /ˈkɒntent/ N [1] ◆ **~s** *(= thing contained)* contenu *m* ; *(= amount contained)* contenu *m*, contenance *f* ; *[of house etc] (gen)* contenu *m* ; *(Insurance)* biens *mpl* mobiliers ◆ **(table of) ~s** *[of book]* table *f* des matières [2] *(NonC) [of book, play, film]* contenu *m (also Ling)* ; *[of official document]* teneur *f* ; *[of metal]* teneur *f*, titre *m* ◆ **what do you think of the ~ of the article?** que pensez-vous du contenu *or* du fond de l'article ? ◆ **oranges have a high vitamin C ~** les oranges sont riches en vitamine C *or* ont une haute teneur en vitamine C ◆ **gold ~** teneur *f* en or ◆ **the play lacks ~** la pièce est mince *or* manque de profondeur

COMP **content provider** N fournisseur *m* de contenus

contents insurance N *(NonC)* assurance *f* sur le contenu de l'habitation

contented /kənˈtentɪd/ ADJ content, satisfait *(with* de)

contentedly /kənˈtentɪdlɪ/ ADV avec contentement ◆ **to smile ~** avoir un sourire de contentement

contentedness /kənˈtentɪdnɪs/ N contentement *m*, satisfaction *f*

contention /kənˈtenʃən/ N [1] *(= dispute)* dispute *f* ; → **bone** [2] *(= argument, point argued)* assertion *f*, affirmation *f* ◆ **it is my ~ that ...** je soutiens que ...

contentious /kənˈtenʃəs/ ADJ [1] *(= controversial) [issue, question]* controversé, litigieux ; *[view, proposal]* controversé [2] *(= argumentative) [person]* querelleur

contentment /kənˈtentmənt/ N contentement *m*, satisfaction *f*

conterminous /ˌkɒnˈtɜːmɪnəs/ ADJ *(frm = contiguous) [county, country]* limitrophe *(with,* to de) ; *[estate, house, garden]* adjacent, attenant *(with, to* à)

contest /kənˈtest/ VT [1] *(= argue, debate) [+ question, matter, result]* contester, discuter ; *(Jur) [+ judgement]* attaquer ◆ **to ~ sb's right to do sth** contester à qn le droit de faire qch ◆ **to ~ a will** *(Jur)* attaquer *or* contester un testament [2] *(= compete for)* disputer ◆ **to ~ a seat** *(Parl)* disputer un siège ◆ **to ~ an election** *(Pol)* disputer une élection VI se disputer *(with, against* avec) contester N /ˈkɒntest/ *(= struggle) (lit, fig)* combat *m*, lutte *f (with* avec, contre ; *between* entre) ; *(Sport)* lutte *f* ; *(Boxing, Wrestling)* combat *m*, rencontre *f* ; *(= competition)* concours *m* ◆ **beauty ~** concours *m* de beauté ◆ **~ of wills/personalities** lutte *f* entre des volontés/des personnalités différentes ◆ **the mayoral ~** (la lutte pour) l'élection du maire

contestant /kənˈtestənt/ N [1] *(for prize, reward)* concurrent(e) *m(f)* [2] *(in fight)* adversaire *mf*

contestation /ˌkɒntesˈteɪʃən/ N contestation *f*

context /ˈkɒntekst/ N contexte *m* ◆ **in/out of ~** dans le/hors contexte ◆ **to put sth in(to) ~** mettre qch en contexte ◆ **to see sth in ~** regarder qch dans son contexte ◆ **~ of situation** *(Ling)* situation *f* de discours COMP **context-sensitive** ADJ *(Comput)* contextuel

contextual /kɒnˈtekstjʊəl/ ADJ contextuel, d'après le contexte

contextualize /kɒnˈtekstjʊəlaɪz/ VT remettre *or* replacer dans son contexte

contiguity /kɒntɪˈgjuːɪtɪ/ N contiguïté *f*

contiguous /kənˈtɪgjʊəs/ ADJ contigu (-guë *f*) ◆ **~ to** contigu à *or* avec, attenant à ◆ **the two fields are ~** les deux champs se touchent *or* sont contigus

continence /ˈkɒntɪnəns/ N continence *f*

continent¹ /ˈkɒntɪnənt/ ADJ *(= chaste)* chaste ; *(= self-controlled)* continent † ; *(Med)* qui n'est pas incontinent

continent² /ˈkɒntɪnənt/ N (*Geog*) continent *m* ◆ **the Continent** (*Brit*) l'Europe *f* continentale ◆ **the Continent of Europe** le continent européen ◆ **on the Continent** (*Brit*) en Europe (*continentale*)

continental /ˌkɒntɪˈnentl/ ADJ continental ◆ **~ climate** climat *m* continental N (*Brit*) Européen(ne) *m(f)* (continental(e))
COMP **continental breakfast** N petit déjeuner *m* continental
continental crust N croûte *f* continentale
continental drift N dérive *f* des continents
continental quilt N (*Brit*) couette *f*
continental shelf N plate-forme *f* continentale, plateau *m* continental
continental shields NPL aires *fpl* continentales

contingency /kənˈtɪndʒənsɪ/ N 1 éventualité *f*, événement *m* imprévu *or* inattendu ◆ **in a ~, should a ~ arise** en cas d'imprévu ◆ **to provide for all contingencies** parer à toute éventualité 2 (*Stat*) contingence *f*
COMP **contingency fee** N (*US Jur*) *honoraires versés par un client à son avocat seulement s'il gagne son procès*
contingency fund N caisse *f* de prévoyance
contingency planning N mise *f* sur pied de plans d'urgence
contingency plans NPL plans *mpl* d'urgence
contingency reserve N (*Fin*) fonds *mpl* de prévoyance
contingency sample N (*Space*) échantillon *m* lunaire (*prélevé dès l'alunissage*)

contingent /kənˈtɪndʒənt/ ADJ contingent ◆ **to be ~ upon sth** dépendre de qch, être subordonné à qch N (*gen, also Mil*) contingent *m*

continua /kənˈtɪnjʊə/ NPL of **continuum**

continual /kənˈtɪnjʊəl/ ADJ continuel

continually /kənˈtɪnjʊəlɪ/ ADV continuellement, sans cesse

continuance /kənˈtɪnjʊəns/ N (= *duration*) durée *f* ; (= *continuation*) continuation *f* ; [*of human race etc*] perpétuation *f*, continuité *f*

continuant /kənˈtɪnjʊənt/ N (*Phon*) continue *f*

continuation /kənˌtɪnjʊˈeɪʃən/ N 1 (*no interruption*) continuation *f* 2 (*after interruption*) reprise *f* ◆ **the ~ of work after the holidays** la reprise du travail après les vacances 3 [*of serial story*] suite *f*

continue /kənˈtɪnjuː/ VT continuer (*to do sth or doing sth* à *or* de faire qch) ; [+ *piece of work*] continuer, poursuivre ; [+ *tradition*] perpétuer, maintenir ; [+ *policy*] maintenir ; (*after interruption*) [+ *conversation, work*] reprendre ◆ **to be ~d** [*serial story etc*] à suivre ◆ **~d on page 10** suite page 10 ◆ **to ~ (on) one's way** continuer *or* poursuivre son chemin ; (*after pause*) se remettre en marche ◆ **"and so", he ~d** "et ainsi", reprit-il *or* poursuivit-il
VI 1 (= *go on*) [*road, weather, celebrations*] continuer ; (*after interruption*) reprendre ; [*investigations, efforts, incidents*] se poursuivre ◆ **his speech ~d until 3am** son discours s'est prolongé jusqu'à 3 heures du matin ◆ **sales ~ to be affected by the recession** les ventes continuent d'être affectées par la récession
◆ **to continue with sth** continuer qch ◆ **he ~d with his story/his work/his reading** il a continué son histoire/son travail/sa lecture
2 (= *remain*) **to ~ in one's job** continuer à faire le même travail ◆ **she ~d as his secretary** elle est restée sa secrétaire ◆ **this ~s to be one of the main problems** ceci continue d'être *or* demeure un des principaux problèmes

continued /kənˈtɪnjuːd/ ADJ [*efforts*] soutenu ; [*presence, growth, success*] constant ◆ **the ~ existence of the system of white minority domination** la permanence du système de suprématie de la minorité blanche ◆ **the government's ~ support for the coalition** le soutien indéfectible du gouvernement à la coalition

continuing /kənˈtɪnjuɪŋ/ ADJ [*argument*] ininterrompu ; [*correspondence*] soutenu ◆ **~ education** formation *f* permanente *or* continue

continuity /ˌkɒntɪnˈjuːɪtɪ/ N (*gen, Cine, Rad*) continuité *f*
COMP **continuity announcer** N (*TV, Rad*) speaker(ine) *m(f)* annonçant la suite des émissions
continuity girl N (*Cine, TV*) script-girl *f*, script *f*

continuo /kənˈtɪnjʊˌəʊ/ N (*Mus*) basse *f* continue

continuous /kənˈtɪnjʊəs/ ADJ 1 continu ◆ **~ assessment** (*Scol, Univ*) contrôle *m* continu des connaissances ◆ **~ performance** (*Cine*) spectacle *m* permanent ◆ **~ paper** *or* **stationery** (*Comput*) papier *m* en continu 2 (*Gram*) [*aspect*] imperfectif ; [*tense*] progressif ◆ **in the present/past ~** à la forme progressive du présent/du passé

continuously /kənˈtɪnjʊəslɪ/ ADV 1 (= *uninterruptedly*) sans interruption 2 (= *repeatedly*) continuellement, sans arrêt

continuum /kənˈtɪnjʊəm/ N (pl **continuums** *or* **continua**) continuum *m* ◆ **cost ~** échelle *f* *or* éventail *m* des coûts ◆ **human development from fertilisation onwards is a ~** le développement humain est une évolution continue qui débute avec la fécondation

contort /kənˈtɔːt/ VT 1 [+ *one's features, limbs*] tordre, contorsionner ◆ **a face ~ed by pain** un visage tordu *or* contorsionné par la douleur 2 (*fig*) [+ *sb's words, story*] déformer, fausser

contortion /kənˈtɔːʃən/ N [*of esp acrobat*] contorsion *f* ; [*of features*] torsion *f*, crispation *f*

contortionist /kənˈtɔːʃənɪst/ N contorsionniste *mf*

contour /ˈkɒntʊəʳ/ N contour *m*, profil *m* VT ◆ **to ~ a map** tracer les courbes de niveau sur une carte
COMP **contour flying** N vol *m* à très basse altitude
contour line N courbe *f* de niveau
contour map N carte *f* avec courbes de niveau

contoured /ˈkɒntʊəd/ ADJ [*shape, lines*] sinueux ◆ **a comfortably ~ seat** un siège bien galbé

contra /ˈkɒntrə/ N (*Pol*) contra *f*

contraband /ˈkɒntrəbænd/ N contrebande *f*
COMP [*goods*] de contrebande

contrabass /ˌkɒntrəˈbeɪs/ N contrebasse *f*

contrabassoon /ˌkɒntrəbəˈsuːn/ N contrebasson *m*

contraception /ˌkɒntrəˈsepʃən/ N contraception *f*

contraceptive /ˌkɒntrəˈseptɪv/ N contraceptif *m* ADJ [*device, measures*] contraceptif, anticonceptionnel

contract /ˈkɒntrækt/ N 1 (= *agreement*) contrat *m* ; (*US Comm* = *tender*) adjudication *f* ◆ **marriage ~** contrat *m* de mariage ◆ **to enter into a ~ with sb for sth** passer un contrat avec qn pour qch ◆ **to put work out to ~** sous-traiter un travail ◆ **by ~** par contrat, contractuellement ◆ **under ~ (to)** sous contrat (avec) ◆ **on ~** [*work*] sur contrat ◆ **to be on ~** avoir un contrat ◆ **~ for services** (*Jur*) contrat *m* de louage d'ouvrage ◆ **there's a ~ out on** *or* **for him** * (*fig: by killer*) on a engagé un tueur pour le descendre * ; → **breach**
2 (also **contract bridge**) (bridge *m*) contrat *m*
VT /kənˈtrækt/ 1 [+ *debts, illness*] contracter ; [+ *habits, vices*] prendre, contracter
2 [+ *alliance*] contracter
3 (= *commit*) ◆ **to ~ to do sth** s'engager (par contrat) à faire qch ◆ **to ~ with sb to do sth** passer un contrat avec qn pour faire qch
4 [+ *metal, muscle etc*] contracter
5 (*Ling*) [+ *word, phrase*] contracter (*to* en) ; ◆ **~ed form** forme *f* contractée
VI /kənˈtrækt/ 1 [*metal, muscles*] se contracter
2 (*Comm*) s'engager (par contrat) ◆ **he has ~ed for the building of the motorway** il a un contrat pour la construction de l'autoroute
COMP **contract bargaining** N (*Jur*) négociations *fpl* salariales
contracting parties NPL contractants *mpl*
contracting party N partie *f* contractante
contract killer N tueur *m* à gages
contract killing N meurtre *m* commis par un tueur à gages
contract law N (*NonC*) droit *m* contractuel
contract price N prix *m* forfaitaire
contract work N travail *m* à forfait
► **contract in** VI s'engager (par contrat)
► **contract out** VI (*Brit*) se dégager (*of* de) se soustraire (*of* à) ; ◆ **to ~ out of a pension scheme** cesser de cotiser à une caisse de retraite
VT SEP [+ *work etc*] sous-traiter (*to sb* à qn)

contractile /kənˈtræktaɪl/ ADJ contractile

contraction /kənˈtrækʃən/ N 1 (*NonC*) [*of metal etc*] contraction *f* 2 (*Med*) contraction *f* 3 (*Ling*) forme *f* contractée, contraction *f* ◆ **"can't" is a ~ of "cannot"** "can't" est une forme contractée *or* une contraction de "cannot" 4 (= *acquiring*) ◆ **~ of debts** endettement *m*

contractionary /kənˈtrækʃənərɪ/ ADJ (*Econ*) ◆ **~ pressure** poussée *f* récessionniste ◆ **~ policy** politique *f* d'austérité

contractor /kənˈtræktəʳ/ N 1 (*Comm*) entrepreneur *m* ◆ **army ~** fournisseur *m* de l'armée ; → **building** 2 (*Jur*) partie *f* contractante

contractual /kənˈtræktʃʊəl/ ADJ contractuel

contractually /kənˈtræktʃʊəlɪ/ ADV par contrat ◆ **~, we have to ...** d'après le contrat, nous devons ...

contradict /ˌkɒntrəˈdɪkt/ LANGUAGE IN USE 26.3 VT 1 (= *deny truth of*) [+ *person, statement*] contredire ◆ **don't ~!** ne (me) contredis pas ! 2 (= *be contrary to*) [+ *statement, event*] contredire, démentir ◆ **his actions ~ed his words** ses actions démentaient ses paroles

contradiction /ˌkɒntrəˈdɪkʃən/ N contradiction *f*, démenti *m* ◆ **to be in ~ with ...** être en contradiction avec ..., donner un démenti à ... ◆ **a ~ in terms** une contradiction dans les termes

contradictory /ˌkɒntrəˈdɪktərɪ/ ADJ contradictoire, opposé (*to* à)

contradistinction /ˌkɒntrədɪsˈtɪŋkʃən/ N contraste *m*, opposition *f* ◆ **in ~ to ...** en contraste avec ..., par opposition à ...

contraflow /ˈkɒntrəˌfləʊ/ ADJ (*Brit*) ◆ **~ lane** voie *f* à contresens ◆ **there is a ~ system in operation on ...** une voie a été mise en sens inverse sur ... ◆ **~ (bus) lane** couloir *m* (d'autobus) à contre-courant

contraindicated /ˌkɒntrəˈɪndɪˌkeɪtɪd/ ADJ (*Med*) contre-indiqué

contraindication /ˌkɒntrəˌɪndɪˈkeɪʃən/ N (*Med*) contre-indication *f*

contralto /kənˈtræltəʊ/ N (pl **contraltos** *or* **contralti** /kənˈtræltɪ/) (= *voice, person*) contralto *m* ADJ [*voice, part*] de contralto ; [*aria*] pour contralto

contraption * /kənˈtræpʃən/ N bidule * *m*, truc * *m*

contrapuntal /ˌkɒntrəˈpʌntl/ ADJ en contrepoint, contrapuntique

contrarian /kənˈtreərɪən/ ADJ, N anticonformiste *mf*

contrarily /kənˈtreərɪlɪ/ ADV 1 (= *from contrariness*) par esprit de contradiction 2 (= *on the contrary*) au contraire

contrariness /kənˈtreərɪnɪs/ N esprit *m* de contradiction, esprit *m* contrariant

contrariwise /ˈkɒntrərɪˌwaɪz/ ADV 1 *(= on the contrary)* au contraire, par contre 2 *(= in opposite direction)* en sens opposé

contrary /ˈkɒntrərɪ/ ADJ 1 *(= opposing)* *[idea, opinion, evidence, information, wind]* contraire *(to sth* à qch) ; *[direction]* opposé *(to sth* à qch)

♦ **contrary to** ♦ **it was ~ to public interest** c'était contraire à l'intérêt du public ♦ **~ to nature** contre nature ♦ **to run ~ to sth** aller à l'encontre de qch

2 /kənˈtreərɪ/ *(pej = unreasonable)* *[person, attitude]* contrariant

ADV ♦ **~ to sth** contrairement à qch

N ♦ **the ~** le contraire ♦ **I think the ~ is true** je pense que c'est le contraire ♦ **on the ~** au contraire ♦ **quite the ~!** bien au contraire ! ♦ **come tomorrow unless you hear to the ~** venez demain sauf avis contraire *or* sauf contrordre ♦ **I have nothing to say to the ~** je n'ai rien à redire ♦ **a statement to the ~** une déclaration affirmant le contraire ♦ **there is considerable evidence to the ~** il y a énormément de preuves du contraire

contrast /kənˈtrɑːst/ LANGUAGE IN USE 5.1

VT mettre en opposition, opposer ♦ **the film ~s the attitudes of two different social groups** le film oppose *or* met en opposition les attitudes de deux groupes sociaux différents ♦ **he ~ed the present situation with last year's crisis** il a souligné le contraste entre la situation actuelle et la crise de l'année dernière ♦ **the ideas of the management as ~ed with those of employees** les idées de la direction par opposition à celles des employés ♦ **the atmosphere was relaxed, especially when ~ed with the situation a year ago** l'atmosphère était détendue, surtout comparée à ce qu'elle était l'année dernière ; → **compare**

VI contraster *(with* avec) ; ♦ **to ~ strongly** *[colour]* contraster fortement *(with* avec) trancher *(with* sur) ; ♦ **his statement ~ed starkly with the Prime Minister's own words** il y avait un contraste évident entre sa déclaration et les paroles du Premier ministre

N /ˈkɒntrɑːst/ contraste *m* *(between* entre) ; ♦ **the weather in Florida was quite a ~ to what we'd been used to** le temps en Floride était très différent de ce qu'on avait l'habitude d'avoir ♦ **the peaceful garden provides a welcome ~ to the busy streets nearby** la tranquillité du jardin contraste agréablement avec l'agitation des rues alentour ♦ **to adjust the ~** *(TV)* régler le contraste ♦ **to stand out in ~** *(in landscapes, photographs)* se détacher *(to* de, sur) ressortir *(to* sur, contre) ; *[colours]* contraster *(to* avec) trancher *(to* sur)

♦ **in** *or* **by contrast, by way of contrast** *(= on the other hand)* en revanche ♦ **in** *or* **by ~, the Times devotes a whole column to the incident** en revanche, le Times consacre une colonne entière à l'incident

♦ **in + contrast to** ♦ **in ~ to Christian theology, ...** à la différence de la théologie chrétienne, ... ♦ **this is** *or* **stands in stark ~ to what he had said previously** ceci se démarque fortement de ce qu'il avait dit précédemment

COMP **contrast medium** N *(Med)* substance *f* de contraste

> ⚠ When it has an object the verb **to contrast** is not translated by **contraster**.

contrasting /kənˈtrɑːstɪŋ/ ADJ très différent, contrasté ♦ **two ~ views** deux points de vue contrastés

contrastive /kənˈtrɑːstɪv/ ADJ contrastif

contravene /ˌkɒntrəˈviːn/ VT 1 *[+ law]* enfreindre, contrevenir à *(frm)* 2 *[+ sb's freedom]* nier, s'opposer à ; *[+ myth]* contredire

contravention /ˌkɒntrəˈvenʃən/ N infraction *f* *(of* à) ; ♦ **in ~ of the rules** en violation des règles, en dérogation aux règles

contretemps /ˈkɒntrətɒm/ N *(pl inv)* 1 *(= mishap)* contretemps *m* 2 *(= disagreement)* malentendu *m*

contribute /kənˈtrɪbjuːt/ VT *[+ money]* contribuer, cotiser ♦ **he has ~d £5** il a offert *or* donné 5 livres ♦ **to ~ an article to a newspaper** écrire un article pour un journal ♦ **his presence didn't ~ much to the success of the evening** sa présence n'a guère contribué au succès de la soirée VI ♦ **to ~ to** contribuer à ♦ **he ~d to the success of the venture** il a contribué à assurer le succès de l'affaire ♦ **to ~ to a discussion** prendre part *or* participer à une discussion ♦ **to ~ to a newspaper** collaborer à un journal ♦ **it all ~d to the muddle** tout cela a contribué au désordre

contribution /ˌkɒntrɪˈbjuːʃən/ N *[of money, goods etc]* contribution *f* ; *(Social Security)* cotisation *f* ; *(to publication)* article *m* ; ♦ **employee's ~** cotisation *f* salariale ♦ **employer's ~** cotisation *f* patronale → DSS

contributor /kənˈtrɪbjʊtəʳ/ N *(to publication)* collaborateur *m*, -trice *f* ; *[of money, goods]* donateur *m*, -trice *f*

contributory /kənˈtrɪbjʊtərɪ/ ADJ 1 *(= partly responsible)* *[cause, reason]* accessoire ♦ **a ~ factor in sth** un des facteurs responsables de qch ♦ **to be ~ to sth** contribuer à qch 2 *[pension scheme, fund]* contributif COMP **contributory negligence** N *(Jur)* faute *f* de la victime

contrite /ˈkɒntraɪt/ ADJ penaud, contrit

contritely /kənˈtraɪtlɪ/ ADV d'un air penaud *or* contrit

contrition /kənˈtrɪʃən/ N contrition *f*

contrivance /kənˈtraɪvəns/ N *(= tool, machine etc)* appareil *m*, machine *f* ; *(= scheme)* invention *f*, combinaison *f* ♦ **it is beyond his ~** il n'en est pas capable

contrive /kənˈtraɪv/ VT 1 *(= invent, design)* *[+ plan, scheme]* combiner, inventer ♦ **to ~ a means of doing sth** trouver un moyen pour faire qch 2 *(= manage)* ♦ **to ~ to do sth** s'arranger pour faire qch, trouver (le) moyen de faire qch ♦ **can you ~ to be here at 3 o'clock?** est-ce que vous pouvez vous arranger pour être ici à 3 heures ? ♦ **he ~d to make matters worse** il a trouvé moyen d'aggraver les choses

contrived /kənˈtraɪvd/ ADJ forcé, qui manque de naturel

control /kənˈtrəʊl/ N 1 *(NonC)* *(= authority, power to restrain)* autorité *f* ; *(= regulating)* *[of traffic]* réglementation *f* ; *[of aircraft]* contrôle *m* ; *[of pests]* élimination *f*, suppression *f* ♦ **border ~s** contrôles *mpl* à la frontière ♦ **passport ~** contrôle *m* des passeports ♦ **the ~ of disease/forest fires** la lutte contre la maladie/les incendies de forêt ♦ **~ of the seas** *(Pol)* maîtrise *f* des mers ♦ **he has no ~ over his children** il n'a aucune autorité sur ses enfants ♦ **to keep ~ (of o.s.)** se contrôler ♦ **to lose ~ (of o.s.)** perdre le contrôle de soi ♦ **to lose ~ of a vehicle/situation** perdre le contrôle d'un véhicule/d'une situation, ne plus être maître d'un véhicule/d'une situation ♦ **circumstances beyond our ~** circonstances *fpl* indépendantes de notre volonté ♦ **his ~ of the ball is not very good** *(Sport)* il ne contrôle pas très bien le ballon ; → **birth, self**

♦ **in control** ♦ **to be in ~ of a vehicle/situation** être maître d'un véhicule/d'une situation ♦ **who is in ~ here?** qui *or* quel est le responsable ici ?

♦ **out of control** ♦ **inflation is out of ~** l'inflation est galopante ♦ **the fire burned out of ~** l'incendie n'a pas pu être maîtrisé ♦ **the children are quite out of ~** les enfants sont déchaînés

♦ **under (...) control** ♦ **to have a vehicle/situation under ~** être maître d'un véhicule/d'une situation ♦ **to keep a dog under ~** se faire obéir d'un chien ♦ **to have a horse under ~** (savoir) maîtriser un cheval ♦ **to bring** *or* **get under ~** *[+ fire]* maîtriser ; *[+ situation]* dominer ; *[+ gangsters, terrorists, children, dog]* maîtriser ; *[+ inflation]* maîtriser, juguler ♦ **the situation is under ~** on a *or* on tient la situation bien en main ♦ **everything's under ~** tout est en ordre ♦ **under French ~** sous contrôle français ♦ **under government ~** sous contrôle gouvernemental

2 ♦ **~s** *[of train, car, ship, aircraft]* commandes *fpl* ; *[of radio, TV]* boutons *mpl* de commande ♦ **to be at the ~s** *(Rail etc)* être aux commandes ♦ **volume/tone ~** *(Rad, TV)* réglage *m* de volume/de sonorité

3 ♦ **price ~s** le contrôle des prix

4 *(Phys, Psych etc = standard of comparison)* cas *m* témoin

5 *(Comput)* ♦ **"control W"** "contrôle W"

VT *[+ emotions]* maîtriser, dominer ; *[+ child, animal]* se faire obéir de ; *[+ car]* avoir *or* garder la maîtrise de ; *[+ crowd]* contenir ; *[+ organization, business]* diriger, être à la tête de ; *[+ expenditure]* régler ; *[+ prices, wages]* juguler ; *[+ immigration]* contrôler ; *[+ inflation, unemployment]* maîtriser, juguler ; *[+ a market]* dominer ♦ **to ~ o.s.** se contrôler, se maîtriser, rester maître de soi ♦ **~ yourself!** maîtrisez-vous ! ♦ **she can't ~ the children** elle n'a aucune autorité sur les enfants ♦ **to ~ traffic** régler la circulation ♦ **to ~ a disease** enrayer une maladie ♦ **to ~ the spread of malaria** enrayer la progression du paludisme ♦ **to ~ the ball** *(Sport)* contrôler le ballon ; see also **controlled**

COMP **control case** N *(Med, Psych etc)* cas *m* témoin

control column N *[of plane]* manche *m* à balai

control experiment N expérience *f* de contrôle

control freak * N *(pej)* personne *f* qui veut tout régenter

control group N *(in experiment, survey)* groupe *m* témoin

control key N *(Comput)* touche *f* contrôle

control knob N bouton *m* de commande *or* de réglage

control panel N *[of aircraft, ship]* tableau *m* de bord ; *[of TV, computer]* pupitre *m* de commande

control point N poste *m* de contrôle

control room N *(of ship)* poste *m* de commande ; *(for military operation)* salle *f* de commande ; *(in radio, TV studio)* régie *f*

control tower N *(in airport)* tour *f* de contrôle

control unit N *(Comput)* unité *f* de commande

controllable /kənˈtrəʊləbl/ ADJ *[child, animal]* discipliné ; *[expenditure, inflation, imports, immigration]* maîtrisable ; *[disease]* qui peut être enrayé

controlled /kənˈtrəʊld/ ADJ *[emotion]* contenu ♦ **he was very ~** il se dominait très bien ♦ **... he said in a ~ voice** ... dit-il en se contrôlant *or* en se dominant ♦ **~ economy** *(Econ)* économie *f* dirigée *or* planifiée COMP **controlled drug, controlled substance** N substance *f* inscrite au tableau

-controlled /kənˌtrəʊld/ ADJ *(in compounds)* ♦ **a Labour-controlled council** un conseil municipal à majorité travailliste ♦ **a government-controlled organisation** une organisation sous contrôle gouvernemental ♦ **computer-controlled equipment** outillage *m* commandé par ordinateur ♦ **radio-controlled car** voiture *f* télécommandée

controller /kənˈtrəʊləʳ/ N 1 *[of accounts etc]* contrôleur *m*, -euse *f*, vérificateur *m*, -trice *f* 2 *(= comptroller)* contrôleur *m*, -euse *f* (des finances) 3 *(= device)* appareil *m* de contrôle

controlling /kənˈtrəʊlɪŋ/ ADJ *[factor]* déterminant ♦ **~ interest** *(Fin)* participation *f* majoritaire

controversial /ˌkɒntrəˈvɜːʃəl/ ADJ *[person, theory, decision, proposal, speech]* controversé ; *[issue]* controversé, sujet à controverse ; *[action]* sujet à controverse

controversially /ˌkɒntrəˈvɜːʃəlɪ/ ADV de façon controversée

controversy /kənˈtrɒvəsɪ/ N controverse *f*, polémique *f* ; *(Jur, Fin)* différend *m* ◆ **there was a lot of ~ about it** ça a provoqué *or* soulevé beaucoup de controverses, ça a été très contesté *or* discuté ◆ **to cause ~** provoquer *or* soulever une controverse ◆ **they were having a great ~** ils étaient au milieu d'une grande polémique

controvert /ˈkɒntrəvɜːt/ VT disputer, controverser

contumacious /ˌkɒntjʊˈmeɪʃəs/ ADJ rebelle, insoumis, récalcitrant

contumacy /ˈkɒntjʊməsɪ/ N *(= resistance)* résistance *f*, opposition *f* ; *(= rebelliousness)* désobéissance *f*, insoumission *f* ; *(Jur)* contumace *f*

contumelious /ˌkɒntjʊˈmiːlɪəs/ ADJ *(liter)* insolent, méprisant

contumely /ˈkɒntju(ː)mlɪ/ N *(liter)* mépris *m*

contusion /kənˈtjuːʒən/ N contusion *f*

conundrum /kəˈnʌndrəm/ N devinette *f*, énigme *f* ; *(fig)* énigme *f*

conurbation /ˌkɒnɜːˈbeɪʃən/ N *(Brit)* conurbation *f*

convalesce /ˌkɒnvəˈles/ VI relever de maladie, se remettre (d'une maladie) ◆ **to be convalescing** être en convalescence

convalescence /ˌkɒnvəˈlesəns/ N convalescence *f*

convalescent /ˌkɒnvəˈlesənt/ N convalescent(e) *m(f)* ADJ convalescent ◆ **~ home** maison *f* de convalescence *or* de repos

convection /kənˈvekʃən/ N convection *f* COMP *[heating]* à convection

convector /kənˈvektəʳ/ N (also **convector heater**) radiateur *m* (à convection)

convene /kənˈviːn/ VT convoquer VI se réunir, s'assembler ; see also **convening**

convener /kənˈviːnəʳ/ N *(Brit Ind) [of union]* responsable *mf* des délégués syndicaux ; *[of other committee]* président(e) *m(f)*

convenience /kənˈviːnɪəns/ N [1] *(NonC) (= suitability, comfort)* commodité *f* ◆ **the ~ of a modern flat** la commodité d'un appartement moderne ◆ **I doubt the ~ of an office in the suburbs** je ne suis pas sûr qu'un bureau en banlieue soit pratique ◆ **for ~(s) sake** par souci de commodité ◆ **at your earliest ~** *(Comm)* dans les meilleurs délais ◆ **to find sth to one's ~** trouver qch à sa convenance ◆ **do it at your own ~** faites-le quand cela vous conviendra ; → **marriage**

[2] ◆ **~s** commodités *fpl* ◆ **the house has all modern ~s** la maison a tout le confort moderne

[3] *(Brit euph)* toilettes *fpl*, W.-C. *mpl* ; → **public**

COMP **convenience foods** NPL aliments *mpl* tout préparés ; *(complete dishes)* plats *mpl* cuisinés

convenience goods NPL produits *mpl* de grande consommation *or* de consommation courante

convenience market, convenience store N *(US)* commerce *m* de proximité, dépanneur *m (Can)*

convenient /kənˈviːnɪənt/ ADJ *[tool, place]* commode ◆ **if it is ~ (to you)** si vous n'y voyez pas d'inconvénient, si cela ne vous dérange pas ◆ **will it be ~ for you to come tomorrow?** est-ce que cela vous arrange *or* vous convient de venir demain ? ◆ **what would be a ~ time for you?** quelle heure vous conviendrait ? ◆ **is it ~ to see him now?** est-il possible de le voir tout de suite ? ◆ **it is not a very ~ time** le moment n'est pas très bien choisi ◆ **we were looking for a ~ place to stop** nous cherchions un endroit convenable *or* un bon endroit où nous arrêter ◆ **his cousin's death was very ~ for him** la mort de son cousin l'a bien arrangé *or* est tombée au bon moment pour lui ◆ **the house is ~ for** *or* **to shops and buses** la maison est bien située, à proximité des magasins et des lignes d'autobus ◆ **he put it down on a ~ chair** il l'a posé sur une chaise qui se trouvait (là) à portée

conveniently /kənˈviːnɪəntlɪ/ ADV [1] *(= handily) [located, situated]* de façon pratique, de façon commode ◆ **~ situated for the shops** bien situé pour les magasins ◆ **to be ~ close** *or* **near to sth** être commodément situé à proximité de qch [2] *(iro = deliberately) [forget, ignore, overlook]* fort à propos ◆ **he ~ forgot to post the letter** comme par hasard, il a oublié de poster la lettre

convening /kənˈviːnɪŋ/ ADJ ◆ **~ authority** autorité *f* habilitée à *or* chargée de convoquer ◆ **~ country** pays *m* hôte N convocation *f*

convenor /kənˈviːnəʳ/ N ⇒ **convener**

convent /ˈkɒnvənt/ N couvent *m* ◆ **to go into a ~** entrer au couvent COMP **convent school** N couvent *m*

conventicle /kənˈventɪkl/ N conventicule *m*

convention /kənˈvenʃən/ N *(= meeting, agreement, rule)* convention *f* ; *(= accepted behaviour)* usage *m*, convenances *fpl* ; *(= conference, fair)* salon *m* ◆ **according to ~** selon l'usage, selon les convenances ◆ **there is a ~ that ladies do not dine here** l'usage veut que les dames ne dînent pas ici ◆ **stamp collectors' ~** salon *m* de la philatélie COMP **convention centre** N palais *m* des congrès

conventional /kənˈvenʃənl/ ADJ [1] *(= unoriginal) [person, organization, life, clothes]* conformiste ; *[behaviour, tastes, opinions, expression]* conventionnel [2] *(= traditional) [method, approach]* conventionnel ; *[argument, belief, product, values]* traditionnel, classique ◆ **in the ~ sense** au sens classique du terme [3] *(= not nuclear) [war, weapon]* conventionnel

COMP **Conventional Forces in Europe** NPL Forces *fpl* conventionnelles en Europe

conventional medicine N médecine *f* traditionnelle

conventional wisdom N sagesse *f* populaire ◆ **~ wisdom has it that ...** selon la sagesse populaire, ...

conventionality /kənˌvenʃəˈnælɪtɪ/ N *[of person, clothes]* conformisme *m* ; *[of behaviour, remarks]* banalité *f*

conventionally /kənˈvenʃənəlɪ/ ADV *(= according to accepted norms)* d'une manière conventionnelle, conventionnellement ; *(= by agreement)* par convention, conventionnellement ◆ **~ armed** doté d'armes conventionnelles

conventioneer /kənˌvenʃəˈnɪəʳ/ N *(esp US Pol)* délégué(e) *m(f)* à la convention d'un parti

converge /kənˈvɜːdʒ/ VI converger *(on* sur)

convergence /kənˈvɜːdʒəns/ N convergence *f* ◆ **~ criteria** *(in EU)* critères *mpl* de convergence

convergent /kənˈvɜːdʒənt/, **converging** /kənˈvɜːdʒɪŋ/ ADJ convergent ◆ **~ thinking** raisonnement *m* convergent

conversant /kənˈvɜːsənt/ ADJ ◆ **to be ~ with** *[+ car, machinery]* s'y connaître en ; *[+ language, science, laws, customs]* connaître ; *[+ facts]* être au courant de ◆ **I am ~ with what he said** je suis au courant de ce qu'il a dit ◆ **I am not ~ with nuclear physics** je ne comprends rien à la physique nucléaire ◆ **I am not ~ with sports cars** je ne m'y connais pas en voitures de sport

conversation /ˌkɒnvəˈseɪʃən/ N conversation *f*, entretien *m* ◆ **to have a ~ with sb** avoir une conversation *or* un entretien avec qn, s'entretenir avec qn ◆ **I have had several ~s with him** j'ai eu plusieurs entretiens *or* conversations avec lui ◆ **to be in ~ with ...** s'entretenir avec ..., être en conversation avec ... ◆ **they were deep in ~** ils étaient en grande conversation ◆ **what was your ~ about?** de quoi parliez-vous ? ◆ **she has no ~** elle n'a aucune conversation ◆ **to make ~** faire (la) conversation

COMP **conversation piece** N [1] *(something interesting)* **her hat was a real ~ piece** son chapeau a fait beaucoup jaser [2] *(Art)* tableau *m* de genre, scène *f* d'intérieur **conversation stopper** N ◆ **that was a (real) ~ stopper** cela a arrêté net la conversation, cela a jeté un froid

conversational /ˌkɒnvəˈseɪʃənl/ ADJ [1] *[style]* de conversation ; *[person]* qui a la conversation facile ◆ **his tone was ~, he spoke in a ~ tone** *or* **voice** il parlait sur le ton de la conversation ◆ **to adopt a ~ manner** se mettre à parler sur le ton de la conversation ◆ **a ~ gambit** *(starting)* une astuce pour engager la conversation ; *(continuing)* une astuce pour alimenter la conversation ◆ **her ~ skills are limited to the weather** ses talents en matière de conversation se limitent à parler du temps ◆ **his ~ ability** *or* **powers** son don de la conversation ◆ **to learn ~ German** apprendre l'allemand de la conversation courante ◆ **classes in ~ German** des cours *mpl* de conversation allemande [2] *(Comput)* conversationnel

conversationalist /ˌkɒnvəˈseɪʃnəlɪst/ N causeur *m*, -euse *f* ◆ **she's a great ~** elle a de la conversation, elle brille dans la conversation

conversationally /ˌkɒnvəˈseɪʃnəlɪ/ ADV *[speak, write, describe]* sur le ton de la conversation ◆ **"nice day" she said ~** "il fait beau" dit-elle en cherchant à engager la conversation

converse[1] /kənˈvɜːs/ VI converser ◆ **to ~ with sb about sth** s'entretenir avec qn de qch

converse[2] /ˈkɒnvɜːs/ ADJ *(= opposite, contrary) [statement]* contraire, inverse ; *(Math, Philos)* inverse ; *[proposition]* inverse, réciproque N *[of statement]* contraire *m*, inverse *m* ; *(Math, Philos)* inverse *m*

conversely /kɒnˈvɜːslɪ/ LANGUAGE IN USE 26.3 ADV inversement

conversion /kənˈvɜːʃən/ N *(NonC)* conversion *f* ; *(Rugby)* transformation *f* ◆ **the ~ of salt water into drinking water** la conversion *or* la transformation d'eau salée en eau potable ◆ **the ~ of an old house into flats** l'aménagement *m or* l'agencement *m* d'une vieille maison en appartements ◆ **improper ~ of funds** détournement *m* de fonds, malversations *fpl* ◆ **his ~ to Catholicism** sa conversion au catholicisme COMP **conversion table** N table *f* de conversion

convert /ˈkɒnvɜːt/ N converti(e) *m(f)* ◆ **to become a ~ to ...** se convertir à ... VT /kənˈvɜːt/ [1] *(= transform)* transformer *(into* en) ; *(Rel etc)* convertir *(to* à) ; ◆ **to ~ pounds into euros** convertir des livres en euros ◆ **to ~ a try** *(Rugby)* transformer un essai ◆ **he has ~ed me to his way of thinking** il m'a converti *or* amené à sa façon de penser [2] *(= make alterations to) [+ house]* aménager, agencer *(into* en) ; ◆ **they have ~ed one of the rooms into a bathroom** ils ont aménagé une des pièces en salle de bains

converted /kənˈvɜːtɪd/ ADJ *[barn, chapel, loft]* aménagé ; → **preach**

converter /kənˈvɜːtəʳ/ N *(Elec, Metal)* convertisseur *m* ; *(Rad)* changeur *m* de fréquence

convertibility /kənˌvɜːtəˈbɪlɪtɪ/ N convertibilité *f*

convertible /kən'vɜːtəbl/ ADJ *(gen)* convertible *(into en)* ; ◆ ~ **into** ... *(room, building)* aménageable en ... N *(= car)* (voiture *f*) décapotable *f*

convertor /kən'vɜːtəʳ/ N ⇒ **converter**

convex /'kɒn'veks/ ADJ convexe

convexity /kɒn'veksɪtɪ/ N convexité *f*

convey /kən'veɪ/ VT *[+ goods, passengers]* transporter ; *[pipeline etc]* amener ; *[+ sound]* transmettre ; *(Jur) [+ property]* transférer, transmettre *(to* à) ; *[+ message, opinion, idea]* communiquer *(to* à) ; *[+ order, thanks]* transmettre *(to* à) ; ◆ **to** ~ **to sb that** ... faire savoir à qn que ... ◆ **I couldn't** ~ **my meaning to him** je n'ai pas pu lui communiquer ma pensée *or* me faire comprendre de lui ◆ **would you** ~ **my congratulations to him?** voudriez-vous lui transmettre mes félicitations ? ◆ **words cannot** ~ **how I feel** les paroles ne peuvent traduire ce que je ressens ◆ **the name ~s nothing to me** le nom ne me dit rien ◆ **what does this music** ~ **to you?** qu'est-ce que cette musique évoque pour vous ?

conveyance /kən'veɪəns/ N [1] *(NonC)* transport *m* ◆ ~ **of goods** transport *m* de marchandises ◆ **means of** ~ moyens *mpl* de transport [2] *(= vehicle)* voiture *f*, véhicule *m* [3] *(Jur) [of property]* transmission *f*, transfert *m*, cession *f* ; *(= document)* acte *m* translatif *(de propriété)*, acte *m* de cession

conveyancer /kən'veɪənsəʳ/ N rédacteur *m* d'actes translatifs de propriété

conveyancing /kən'veɪənsɪŋ/ N *(Jur) (= procedure)* procédure *f* translative (de propriété) ; *(= operation)* rédaction *f* d'actes translatifs

conveyor /kən'veɪəʳ/ N transporteur *m*, convoyeur *m* COMP **conveyor belt** N convoyeur *m*, tapis *m* roulant

convict /'kɒnvɪkt/ N prisonnier *m*, détenu *m* VT /kən'vɪkt/ *(Jur) [+ person]* déclarer *or* reconnaître coupable ◆ **he was ~ed** il a été déclaré *or* reconnu coupable ◆ **to** ~ **sb of a crime** reconnaître qn coupable d'un crime ◆ **he is a ~ed criminal/murderer** il a été jugé *or* reconnu *(frm)* coupable de crime/meurtre VI /kən'vɪkt/ *[jury]* rendre un verdict de culpabilité

conviction /kən'vɪkʃən/ N [1] *(Jur)* condamnation *f* ◆ **there were 12 ~s for drunkenness** 12 personnes ont été condamnées pour ivresse ; → **previous, record** [2] *(NonC = persuasion, belief)* persuasion *f*, conviction *f* ◆ **to be open to** ~ être ouvert à la persuasion ◆ **to carry** ~ être convaincant ◆ **his explanation lacked** ~ son explication manquait de conviction *or* n'était pas très convaincante [3] *(= belief)* conviction *f* ◆ **the** ~ **that** ... la conviction selon laquelle ... ; → **courage**

convince /kən'vɪns/ LANGUAGE IN USE 6.2, 15.1 VT convaincre, persuader *(sb of sth* qn de qch) ; ◆ **he ~d her that she should leave** il l'a persuadée de partir, il l'a convaincue qu'elle devait partir ◆ **I am ~d he won't do it** je suis persuadé *or* convaincu qu'il ne le fera pas ◆ **a ~d Christian** un chrétien convaincu

convincing /kən'vɪnsɪŋ/ LANGUAGE IN USE 26.3 ADJ [1] *(= persuasive) [argument, evidence, performance, picture]* convaincant ; *[person]* convaincant, persuasif ◆ **he was** ~ **as Richard III** il était convaincant dans le rôle de Richard III [2] *(= decisive) [win, victory, lead]* net ◆ **to be a** ~ **winner of a race** gagner une course haut la main

convincingly /kən'vɪnsɪŋlɪ/ ADV [1] *(= persuasively) [speak, argue, demonstrate]* de façon convaincante [2] *(= decisively) [win, beat]* haut la main

convivial /kən'vɪvɪəl/ ADJ *[person]* de bonne compagnie ; *[mood, atmosphere, occasion]* convivial ◆ **in** ~ **company** en agréable compagnie

conviviality /kən,vɪvɪ'ælɪtɪ/ N convivialité *f*

convocation /,kɒnvə'keɪʃən/ N *(= act)* convocation *f* ; *(= assembly)* assemblée *f*, réunion *f* ; *(Rel)* assemblée *f*, synode *m* ; *(US Educ)* cérémonie *f* de remise des diplômes

convoke /kən'vəʊk/ VT convoquer

convoluted /'kɒnvəluːtɪd/ ADJ [1] *(pej = tortuous) [argument, reasoning, sentence, plot]* alambiqué [2] *(= coiling) [pattern]* en volutes ; *[shape, object]* enroulé

convolution /,kɒnvə'luːʃən/ N circonvolution *f* NPL **convolutions** *[of plot]* méandres *mpl* ◆ **the ~s of this theory** la complexité infinie de cette théorie

convolvulus /kən'vɒlvjʊləs/ N (pl **convolvuluses** *or* **convolvuli** /kən'vɒlvjʊ,laɪ/) *(= flower)* volubilis *m* ; *(= weed)* liseron *m*

convoy /'kɒnvɔɪ/ N *[of ships, vehicles]* convoi *m* ◆ **in** ~ en convoi VT convoyer, escorter *(to* à)

convulse /kən'vʌls/ VT ébranler, bouleverser ◆ **a land ~d by war** un pays bouleversé par la guerre ◆ **a land ~d by earthquakes** un pays ébranlé par des tremblements de terre ◆ **to be ~d (with laughter)** se tordre de rire ◆ **a face ~d with pain** un visage décomposé *or* contracté par la douleur

convulsion /kən'vʌlʃən/ N [1] *(Med)* convulsion *f* ◆ **to have ~s** avoir des convulsions ◆ **to go into ~s of laughter** se tordre de rire [2] *(= violent disturbance) [of land]* bouleversement *m*, convulsion *f* ; *[of sea]* violente agitation *f*

convulsive /kən'vʌlsɪv/ ADJ convulsif

convulsively /kən'vʌlsɪvlɪ/ ADV convulsivement

cony /'kəʊnɪ/ N *(US)* lapin *m* ; (also **cony skin**) peau *f* de lapin

COO /,siːəʊ'əʊ/ N abbrev of **chief operating officer** → **chief**

coo¹ /kuː/ VTI *[doves etc]* roucouler ; *[baby]* gazouiller ; → **bill²** N roucoulement *m*, roucoulade *f*

coo² * /kuː/ EXCL *(Brit)* ça alors ! *

co-occur /,kəʊə'kɜːʳ/ VI figurer simultanément, être cooccurrent(s) *(with avec)*

co-occurrence /,kəʊə'kʌrəns/ N cooccurrence *f*

cooing /'kuːɪŋ/ N *[of doves]* roucoulement *m*, roucoulade *f* ; *[of baby]* gazouillement *m*

cook /kʊk/ N cuisinier *m*, -ière *f* ◆ **she is a good** ~ elle est bonne cuisinière ◆ **to be head** *or* **chief** ~ **and bottle-washer** * servir de bonne à tout faire, être le factotum VT [1] *[+ food]* (faire) cuire ◆ **~ed breakfast** petit déjeuner *m* complet à l'anglaise ◆ **~ed meat** viande *f* froide ◆ **~ed meat(s)** *(Comm)* ≃ charcuterie *f* ◆ **to** ~ **sb's goose** * mettre qn dans le pétrin * [2] *(Brit* * *= falsify) [+ accounts]* truquer, maquiller ◆ **to** ~ **the books** * truquer les comptes VI *[food]* cuire ; *[person]* faire la cuisine, cuisiner ◆ **she ~s well** elle fait bien la cuisine, elle cuisine bien ◆ **what's ~ing?** * *(fig)* qu'est-ce qui se passe ?
COMP **cook-chill foods** NPL plats *mpl* cuisinés
cook-off N *(US)* concours *m* de cuisine

► **cook up** * VT SEP *[+ story, excuse]* inventer, fabriquer

cookbook /'kʊkbʊk/ N livre *m* de cuisine

cooker /'kʊkəʳ/ N [1] *(Brit)* cuisinière *f (fourneau)* ; → **gas** [2] *(= apple)* pomme *f* à cuire

cookery /'kʊkərɪ/ N *(gen, also school etc subject)* cuisine *f (activité)* ◆ ~ **book** *(Brit)* livre *m* de cuisine ◆ ~ **teacher** professeur *m* d'enseignement ménager

cookhouse /'kʊkhaʊs/ N *(Mil, Naut)* cuisine *f*

cookie /'kʊkɪ/ N [1] *(Culin) (US)* petit gâteau *m* (sec) ; *(Brit)* cookie *m* ◆ **that's the way the** ~ **crumbles!** * c'est la vie ! ◆ **to be caught with one's hand in the** ~ **jar** *(esp US)* être pris sur le fait [2] *(* * *= person)* type * *m* ; *(US = girl)* jolie fille *f* ◆ **a smart** ~ un petit malin, une petite maligne ◆ **tough** ~ dur(e) *m(f)* à cuire [3] *(Comput)* cookie *m* ADJ (* *fig*) sans originalité COMP
cookie cutter N *(US)* forme *f* à biscuits

cooking /'kʊkɪŋ/ N cuisine *f (activité)* ◆ **plain/French** ~ cuisine *f* bourgeoise/française
COMP *[utensils]* de cuisine ; *[apples, chocolate]* à cuire
cooking film N film *m* alimentaire
cooking foil N papier *m* d'aluminium, papier *m* alu *
cooking salt N *(NonC)* gros sel *m*, sel *m* de cuisine
cooking time N temps *m* de cuisson

cookout /'kʊkaʊt/ N *(US)* barbecue *m*

cooktop /'kʊktɒp/ N *(esp US)* plaque *f* de cuisson

cookware /'kʊkwɛəʳ/ N batterie *f* de cuisine

cool /kuːl/ ADJ [1] *(in temperature)* frais (fraîche *f*) ◆ **it is** ~ *(Weather)* il fait frais ◆ **it's getting** *or* **turning ~(er)** *(Weather)* il commence à faire frais, ça se rafraîchit ◆ **to get** ~ *[person]* se rafraîchir ◆ **to feel** ~ *[person]* ne pas avoir trop chaud ◆ **I feel quite** ~ **now** j'ai bien moins chaud maintenant ◆ **to keep** ~ *[person]* éviter d'avoir chaud ◆ **it helps you (to) keep** ~ ça vous empêche d'avoir chaud ◆ **to keep sth** ~ tenir qch au frais ◆ **"keep in a cool place"** "tenir au frais", "conserver dans un endroit frais" ◆ **"store in a cool, dark place"** "conserver au frais et à l'abri de la lumière" ◆ **"serve cool, not cold"** "servir frais mais non glacé" ◆ **his forehead is much ~er now** il a le front beaucoup moins chaud maintenant
[2] *(= light) [clothing, shirt, dress]* léger ◆ **to slip into something** ~ passer quelque chose de plus léger
[3] *(= pale) [colour, blue, green]* rafraîchissant
[4] *(= calm) [person, manner, composure, action, tone, voice]* calme ◆ **the police's** ~ **handling of the riots** le calme avec lequel la police a fait face aux émeutes ◆ **to keep a** ~ **head** garder la tête froide ◆ **to keep** *or* **stay** ~ garder son calme ◆ **keep** *or* **stay ~!** du calme !
[5] *(= audacious) [behaviour]* d'une décontraction insolente ◆ **to be a** ~ **customer** * ne pas avoir froid aux yeux ◆ **as** ~ **as you please** *[person]* parfaitement décontracté
[6] *(= unfriendly) [person, relations]* froid *(with or towards sb* avec qn) ; ◆ ~ **and calculating** froid et calculateur ◆ **to get a** ~ **welcome/reception** être fraîchement accueilli/reçu ◆ **the idea met with a** ~ **response** cette idée a été accueillie avec indifférence *or* n'a guère suscité d'enthousiasme
[7] ◆ **to be (as)** ~ **as a cucumber** *(= calm, audacious)* être d'un calme olympien
[8] *(* = trendy)* cool * *inv* ◆ **computers are** ~ les ordinateurs, c'est cool * ◆ **he acts ~, but he's really very insecure** il agit de façon calme et détendue mais en fait il n'est pas du tout sûr de lui ◆ **to look** ~ avoir l'air cool *
[9] *(* = excellent)* super * *inv*, génial *
[10] *(* * *= acceptable)* ◆ **that's** ~**!** ça c'est cool ! * ◆ **don't worry: it's** ~ t'inquiète pas : c'est cool *
[11] *(= not upset)* ◆ **to be** ~ **(about sth)** * * *[person]* rester cool * (à propos de qch)
[12] *(= full)* ◆ **he earns a** ~ **£40,000 a year** * * il se fait * la coquette somme de 40 000 livres par an
[13] *(Mus) [jazz]* cool * *inv*
ADV → **play**
N [1] fraîcheur *f*, frais *m* ◆ **in the** ~ **of the evening** dans la fraîcheur du soir ◆ **to keep sth in the** ~ tenir qch au frais
[2] * * **keep your ~!** t'énerve pas ! * ◆ **he lost his** ~ *(= panicked)* il a paniqué * ; *(= got angry)* il s'est fichu en rogne *

VT 1 [+ air] rafraîchir, refroidir ◆ **to ~ one's heels** faire le pied de grue, poireauter* ◆ **to leave sb to ~ his heels** faire attendre qn, faire poireauter* qn
2 ◆ **~ it!** ‡ t'énerve pas !*, panique pas !*
VI (also **cool down**) [air, liquid] (se) rafraîchir, refroidir
COMP **cool bag** N sac m isotherme
cool box N glacière f
cool-headed ADJ calme, imperturbable
► **cool down** VI (lit) refroidir ; (fig) [anger] se calmer, s'apaiser ; [critical situation] se détendre ; * [person] se calmer ◆ **let the situation ~ down!** attendez que la situation se détende or que les choses se calment subj !
VT SEP (= make colder) faire refroidir ; (= make calmer) calmer
► **cool off** VI (= lose enthusiasm) perdre son enthousiasme, se calmer ; (= change one's affections) se refroidir (towards sb à l'égard de qn, envers qn) ; (= become less angry) se calmer, s'apaiser

coolant /'ku:lənt/ N liquide m de refroidissement

cooler /'ku:ləʳ/ N 1 (for food) glacière f 2 (Prison *) taule‡ f ◆ **in the ~** en taule‡ ◆ **to get put in the ~** se faire mettre au frais* or à l'ombre* 3 (= drink) boisson à base de vin, de jus de fruit et d'eau gazeuse

coolie /'ku:lı/ N coolie m

cooling /'ku:lıŋ/ ADJ [drink, swim, breeze] rafraîchissant N (in engine) refroidissement m
COMP **cooling fan** N ventilateur m
cooling-off period N (for buyer) délai m de réflexion
cooling process N refroidissement m
cooling rack N grille f à gâteaux
cooling system N circuit m de refroidissement
cooling tower N tour f de refroidissement

coolly /'ku:lı/ ADV 1 (= calmly) calmement 2 (= in unfriendly way) froidement 3 (= unenthusiastically) froidement, fraîchement 4 (= audaciously) avec une décontraction insolente

coolness /'ku:lnıs/ N [of water, air, weather] fraîcheur f ; [of welcome] froideur f ; (= calmness) sang-froid m, impassibilité f, flegme m ; (= impudence) toupet* m, culot* m

coomb /ku:m/ N petite vallée f, combe f

coon /ku:n/ N 1 abbrev of **raccoon** 2 (*‡ pej = Negro) nègre*‡ m, négresse*‡ f

coop /ku:p/ N (also **hen coop**) poulailler m, cage f à poules ◆ **to fly the ~** * se défiler* VT [+ hens] faire rentrer dans le poulailler
► **coop up** VT SEP [+ person] claquemurer, cloîtrer, enfermer

co-op /'kəʊ'ɒp/ N 1 (= shop) (abbrev of **cooperative**) coopérative f, coop* f 2 (US) (abbrev of **cooperative apartment**) → **cooperative** 3 (US Univ) (abbrev of **cooperative**) coopérative f étudiante

cooper /'ku:pəʳ/ N tonnelier m

cooperage /'ku:pərıdʒ/ N tonnellerie f

cooperate /kəʊ'ɒpəreıt/ VI collaborer (with sb avec qn ; in sth à qch ; to do sth pour faire qch) coopérer ◆ **I hope he'll ~** j'espère qu'il va se montrer coopératif or qu'il va coopérer

cooperation /kəʊ,ɒpə'reıʃən/ N coopération f ◆ **in ~ with ..., with the ~ of ...** en coopération avec ..., avec la coopération or le concours de ... ◆ **international judicial ~** (Jur) entraide f judiciaire internationale

cooperative /kəʊ'ɒpərətıv/ ADJ [person, firm, attitude] coopératif ◆ **~ apartment** (US) appartement m en copropriété ◆ **~ society** (Brit Comm etc) coopérative f, société f coopérative or mutuelle ◆ **Cooperative Commonwealth Federation** (Can Pol) parti m social démocratique (Can) N coopérative f

cooperatively /kəʊ'ɒpərətıvlı/ ADV (= jointly) en coopération ; (= obligingly) obligeamment

coopt /kəʊ'ɒpt/ VT [+ person] (= get help of) s'assurer les services de ; (= cause to join sth) coopter (on to à) ; [+ slogan, policy] récupérer ◆ **~ed member** membre m coopté

cooption /kəʊ'ɒpʃən/ N cooptation f

coordinate /kəʊ'ɔ:dınıt/ ADJ (gen, Gram, Math) coordonné ◆ **~ geometry** géométrie f analytique N (gen, Math, on map) coordonnée f NPL **coordinates** (Dress) ensemble m (coordonné), coordonnés mpl VT /kəʊ'ɔ:dıneıt/ coordonner (X with Y X à Y) ; ◆ **coordinating committee** comité m de coordination ◆ **coordinating conjunction** (Ling) conjonction f de coordination

coordinated /kəʊ'ɔ:dıneıtıd/ ADJ 1 (= organized) [action, effort, approach, operation] coordonné, concerté 2 (physically) [person] qui a une bonne coordination ; [hands, limbs] aux mouvements coordonnés ; [movements] coordonné ◆ **to be badly ~** [person] avoir une mauvaise coordination 3 (= matching) [clothes, designs] coordonné ◆ **colour ~** [clothes] aux couleurs assorties

coordination /kəʊ,ɔ:dı'neıʃən/ N coordination f ◆ **in ~ with ...** en coordination avec ...

coordinator /kəʊ'ɔ:dıneıtəʳ/ N coordinateur m, -trice f

coot /ku:t/ N 1 (= bird) foulque f ; → **bald** 2 (= fool) ◆ **old ~** ‡ vieux chnoque* m

co-owner /'kəʊ'əʊnəʳ/ N copropriétaire mf

co-ownership /,kəʊ'əʊnəʃıp/ N copropriété f

cop * /kɒp/ N 1 (= policeman) flic‡ m, poulet‡ m ◆ **to play at ~s and robbers** jouer aux gendarmes et aux voleurs 2 (Brit) **it's not much ~, it's no great ~** ça ne vaut pas grand-chose or tripette VT (Brit = arrest, catch) pincer*, piquer* ; (= steal) piquer*, faucher ; (= obtain) obtenir ◆ **to ~ hold of** (Brit) prendre ◆ **to ~ it** (Brit) écoper*, trinquer‡ ◆ **to ~ a plea**‡ (US) plaider coupable (pour une charge mineure, afin d'en éviter une plus grave)
COMP **cop-out**‡ N (= excuse) excuse f bidon* ; (= act) échappatoire f
cop-shop * N (Brit) maison f Poulaga*, poste m (de police)
► **cop off** * VT FUS (Brit) ◆ **to cop off with sb** * (= get off with) emballer* qn
► **cop out**‡ VI se défiler*

copacetic * /,kəʊpə'setık/ ADJ (US) formidable

copartner /'kəʊ'pɑ:tnəʳ/ N coassocié(e) m(f), coparticipant(e) m(f)

copartnership /'kəʊ'pɑ:tnəʃıp/ N (Fin) société f en nom collectif ; (gen) coassociation f, coparticipation f ◆ **to go into ~ with ...** entrer en coassociation avec ...

cope[1] /kəʊp/ N (Dress Rel) chape f

cope[2] /kəʊp/ VI se débrouiller, s'en sortir ◆ **can you ~?** vous vous en sortirez ?, vous vous débrouillerez ? ◆ **how are you coping without a secretary?** comment vous débrouillez-vous sans secrétaire ? ◆ **he's coping pretty well** il s'en tire or se débrouille pas mal ◆ **I can ~ in Spanish** je me débrouille en espagnol ◆ **she just can't ~ any more** (= she's overworked etc) elle ne s'en sort plus ; (= work is too difficult for her) elle n'est plus du tout dans la course*, elle est complètement dépassée
► **cope with** VT FUS 1 (= deal with, handle) [+ task, person] se charger de, s'occuper de ; [+ situation] faire face à ; [+ difficulties, problems] (= tackle) affronter ; (= solve) venir à bout de ◆ **they ~ with 500 applications a day** 500 formulaires leur passent entre les mains chaque jour ◆ **you get the tickets, I'll ~ with the luggage** toi tu vas chercher les billets, moi je m'occupe or je me charge des bagages ◆ **I'll ~ with him** je m'occupe or je me charge de lui ◆ **he's got a lot to ~ with** (work) il a du pain sur la planche ; (problems) il a pas mal de problèmes à résoudre
2 (= manage) [+ child, work] s'en sortir avec ◆ **I just can't ~ with my son** je ne sais plus quoi faire avec mon fils, je ne m'en sors plus avec mon fils ◆ **we can't ~ with all this work** avec tout ce travail nous ne pouvons plus en sortir

Copenhagen /,kəʊpn'heıgən/ N Copenhague

Copernican /kəʊ'pɜ:nıkən/ ADJ copernicien

Copernicus /kə'pɜ:nıkəs/ N Copernic m

copestone /'kəʊpstəʊn/ N (Archit) couronnement m ; [of wall] chaperon m ; (fig) [of career etc] couronnement m, point m culminant

copier /'kɒpıəʳ/ N machine f à photocopier

co-pilot /'kəʊ'paılət/ N (Aviat) copilote m, pilote m auxiliaire

coping /'kəʊpıŋ/ N chaperon m COMP **coping stone** N ⇒ **copestone**

copious /'kəʊpıəs/ ADJ [quantities] grand ; [amount] ample, abondant ; [notes] abondant ; [writer, letter] prolixe

copiously /'kəʊpıəslı/ ADV [bleed, sweat] abondamment ; [write] longuement ; [cry] à chaudes larmes ◆ **to water a plant ~** arroser une plante copieusement or abondamment ◆ **~ illustrated** abondamment illustré

copper /'kɒpəʳ/ N 1 (NonC) cuivre m 2 (Brit = money) **~s** la petite monnaie ◆ **I gave the beggar a ~** j'ai donné une petite pièce au mendiant 3 (Stock Exchange) **~s** les cuprifères mpl 4 (= washtub) lessiveuse f 5 (Brit * = policeman) flic‡ m, poulet‡ m ◆ **~'s nark** indic* m, mouchard m
COMP [mine] de cuivre ; [bracelet] de or en cuivre
copper beech N hêtre m pourpre
copper-bottomed ADJ [saucepan] avec un fond en cuivre ; [investment] sûr
copper-coloured ADJ cuivré
copper sulphate N sulfate m de cuivre
copper wire N fil m de cuivre

copperhead /'kɒpəhed/ N (US = snake) vipère f cuivrée

copperplate /'kɒpəpleıt/ (in engraving) N planche f (de cuivre) gravée ADJ sur cuivre, en taille-douce ◆ **~ handwriting** écriture f moulée, belle ronde f

coppersmith /'kɒpəsmıθ/ N artisan m en chaudronnerie d'art

coppery /'kɒpərı/ ADJ cuivré

coppice /'kɒpıs/ N taillis m, boqueteau m VT [+ tree] élaguer, émonder

copra /'kɒprə/ N copra m

co-presidency /kəʊ'prezıdənsı/ N coprésidence f

co-president /kəʊ'prezıdənt/ N coprésident(e) m(f)

co-processor /kəʊ'prəʊsesəʳ/ N (Comput) coprocesseur m

co-produce /,kəʊprə'dju:s/ VT [+ film, album] coproduire

co-production /,kəʊprə'dʌkʃən/ N coproduction f

copse /kɒps/ N ⇒ **coppice**

Copt /kɒpt/ N Copte mf

'copter * /'kɒptəʳ/ N (abbrev of **helicopter**) hélico* m

coptic /'kɒptık/ ADJ copte ◆ **the Coptic Church** l'Église f copte

copula /'kɒpjʊlə/ N (pl **copulas** or **copulae** /'kɒpjʊ,li:/) (Gram) copule f

copulate /'kɒpjʊleıt/ VI copuler

copulation /,kɒpjʊ'leıʃən/ N copulation f

copulative /'kɒpjʊlətıv/ ADJ (Gram) copulatif

copy /'kɒpı/ N 1 (= duplicate) [of painting etc] copie f, reproduction f ; [of letter, document, memo] copie *f*, double *m* ; *(Phot) [of print]* épreuve *f* ◆ **to take** *or* **make a ~ of sth** faire une copie de qch ; → **carbon, fair**[1]

[2] *(= one of series) [of book]* exemplaire *m* ; *[of magazine, newspaper]* exemplaire *m*, numéro *m* ; → **author, presentation**

[3] *(NonC = text written) (Press)* copie *f* ; *(for advertisement)* message *m*, texte *m* ◆ **it gave him ~ for several articles** cela lui a fourni la matière de *or* un sujet pour plusieurs articles ◆ **that's always good ~** ça fait toujours de la très bonne copie ◆ **the murder will make good ~** le meurtre fera de l'excellente copie ◆ **the journalist handed in his ~** le journaliste a remis son article *or* papier* ◆ **they are short of ~** ils sont en mal de copie*

[4] *(Comput)* copie *f*

VT [1] (also **copy down, copy out**) *[+ letter, passage from book]* copier

[2] *(= imitate) [+ person, gestures]* copier, imiter

[3] *(Scol etc)* copier ◆ **to ~ sb's work** copier sur qn ◆ **he copied in the exam** il a copié à l'examen

[4] *(Comput)* copier ◆ **to ~ sth to a disk** copier qch sur une disquette

[5] *(Rad, Telec *)* copier

[6] *(= send a copy to)* envoyer une copie à

COMP **copy and paste** *(Comput)* N copier-coller *m* VT copier-coller

copy-edit VT corriger

copy editor N *(Press)* secrétaire *mf* de rédaction ; *[of book]* secrétaire *mf* d'édition

copy machine N photocopieuse *f*

copy press N presse *f* à copier

copybook /ˈkɒpɪbʊk/ N cahier *m* ; → **blot** ADJ *(= trite)* banal ; *(= ideal, excellent)* modèle

copyboy /ˈkɒpɪbɔɪ/ N *(Press)* grouillot *m* de rédaction

copycat* /ˈkɒpɪkæt/ N copieur *m*, -ieuse *f* ADJ *[crime]* inspiré par un autre

copying /ˈkɒpɪɪŋ/ N ◆ **he was disqualified from the exam for ~** il a été recalé à l'examen pour avoir copié COMP **copying ink** N encre *f* à copier

copyist /ˈkɒpɪɪst/ N copiste *mf*, scribe *m*

copyreader /ˈkɒpɪriːdəʳ/ N correcteur-rédacteur *m*, correctrice-rédactrice *f*

copyright /ˈkɒpɪraɪt/ N droit *m* d'auteur, copyright *m* ◆ **~ reserved** tous droits (de reproduction) réservés ◆ **out of ~** dans le domaine public VT *[+ book]* obtenir les droits exclusifs sur *or* le copyright de

copywriter /ˈkɒpɪraɪtəʳ/ N rédacteur *m*, -trice *f* publicitaire

coquetry /ˈkɒkɪtrɪ/ N coquetterie *f*

coquette /kəˈket/ N coquette *f*

coquettish /kəˈketɪʃ/ ADJ *[woman]* coquet ; *[look, smile, behaviour]* plein de coquetterie

coquettishly /kəˈketɪʃlɪ/ ADV avec coquetterie

cor‡ /kɔːʳ/ EXCL *(Brit:* also **cor blimey**) mince alors !*

coracle /ˈkɒrəkl/ N coracle *m*, canot *m* (d'osier)

coral /ˈkɒrəl/ N corail *m*

COMP *[necklace]* de corail ; *[island]* corallien ; (also **coralcoloured**) (couleur) corail *inv*

coral lips NPL *(liter)* ◆ **her ~ lips** ses lèvres de corail

coral reef N récif *m* corallien

Coral Sea N mer *f* de Corail

cor anglais /ˈkɔːrˈɑːŋgleɪ/ N (pl **cors anglais** /ˈkɔːzˈɑːŋgleɪ/) cor *m* anglais

corbel /ˈkɔːbəl/ N corbeau *m*

cord /kɔːd/ N [1] *[of curtains, pyjamas]* cordon *m* ; *[of windows]* corde *f* ; *[of parcel]* ficelle *f* ; (also **umbilical cord**) cordon *m* ombilical ; → **communication, sash**[2]**, spinal, vocal** [2] *(NonC: Tex)* ⇒ **corduroy** *(Elec)* cordon *m* NPL **cords** pantalon *m* en velours côtelé VT *(= tie)* corder

COMP *[trousers, skirt, jacket]* en velours côtelé

cord carpet N tapis *m* de corde

cordage /ˈkɔːdɪdʒ/ N *(NonC)* cordages *mpl*

corded /ˈkɔːdɪd/ ADJ *[fabric]* côtelé

cordial /ˈkɔːdɪəl/ ADJ [1] *(= friendly) [person, tone, relationship, atmosphere, visit]* cordial [2] *(= strong)* ◆ **to have a ~ dislike for sb/sth** détester qn/qch cordialement N *(Brit)* cordial *m*

cordiality /ˌkɔːdɪˈælɪtɪ/ N cordialité *f*

cordially /ˈkɔːdɪəlɪ/ ADV cordialement ◆ **I ~ detest him** je le déteste cordialement

cordite /ˈkɔːdaɪt/ N cordite *f*

cordless /ˈkɔːdlɪs/ ADJ à piles, fonctionnant sur piles ◆ **~ phone** téléphone *m* sans fil

cordon /ˈkɔːdn/ N *(all senses)* cordon *m* VT (also **cordon off**) *[+ crowd]* contenir *(au moyen d'un cordon de sécurité)* ; *[+ area]* mettre en place un cordon de sécurité autour de

COMP **cordon bleu** ADJ cordon bleu

cordon sanitaire N *(Med, Pol)* cordon *m* sanitaire

corduroy /ˈkɔːdərɔɪ/ N velours *m* côtelé NPL **corduroys** pantalon *m* en velours côtelé COMP *[trousers, jacket]* en velours côtelé ; *(US) [road]* de rondins

CORE /kɔːʳ/ N *(US)* (abbrev of **Congress of Racial Equality**) *défense des droits des Noirs*

core /kɔːʳ/ N *[of fruit]* trognon *m* ; *[of magnet, earth]* noyau *m* ; *[of cable]* âme *f*, noyau *m* ; *[of atom]* noyau *m* ; *[of nuclear reactor]* cœur *m* ; *(Comput:* also **core memory**) mémoire *f* centrale ; *(fig) [of problem etc]* cœur *m*, essentiel *m* ◆ **apple ~** trognon *m* de pomme ◆ **the earth's ~** le noyau terrestre ◆ **~ sample** *(Geol)* carotte *f* ◆ **he is rotten to the ~** il est pourri jusqu'à la moelle ◆ **English to the ~** anglais jusqu'au bout des ongles ; → **hard** VT *[+ fruit]* enlever le trognon *or* le cœur de

COMP *[issue, assumption, subject]* fondamental

core business N activité *f* principale

core curriculum N *(Scol, Univ)* tronc *m* commun

core subject N *(Scol, Univ)* matière *f* principale

core time N plage *f* fixe

co-religionist /ˈkəʊrɪˈlɪdʒənɪst/ N coreligionnaire *mf*

corer /ˈkɔːrəʳ/ N *(Culin)* vide-pomme *m*

co-respondent /ˈkəʊrɪsˈpɒndənt/ N *(Jur)* codéfendeur *m*, -deresse *f (dans une affaire d'adultère)*

Corfu /kɔːˈfuː/ N Corfou *f*

corgi /ˈkɔːgɪ/ N corgi *m*

coriander /ˌkɒrɪˈændəʳ/ N coriandre *f*

Corinth /ˈkɒrɪnθ/ N Corinthe COMP **Corinth Canal** N le canal de Corinthe

Corinthian /kəˈrɪnθɪən/ ADJ corinthien N Corinthien(ne) *m(f)*

Coriolanus /ˈkɒrɪəˈleɪnəs/ N Coriolan *m*

cork /kɔːk/ N [1] *(NonC)* liège *m* [2] *(in bottle etc)* bouchon *m* ◆ **to pull the ~ out of a bottle** déboucher une bouteille [3] *(Fishing:* also **cork float**) bouchon *m* flotteur VT (also **cork up**) *[+ bottle]* boucher

COMP *[mat, tiles, flooring]* de liège

cork oak N ⇒ **cork tree**

cork-tipped ADJ à bout de liège

cork tree N chêne-liège *m*

corkage /ˈkɔːkɪdʒ/ N droit *m* de bouchon *(payé par le client qui apporte dans un restaurant une bouteille achetée ailleurs)*

corked /kɔːkt/ ADJ *[wine]* qui sent le bouchon

corker †* /ˈkɔːkəʳ/ N *(= lie)* mensonge *m* de taille, gros mensonge *m* ; *(= story)* histoire *f* fumante* ; *(Sport) (= shot, stroke)* coup *m* fumant* ; *(= player)* crack* *m* ; *(= girl)* beau brin* *m* (de fille)

corking †* /ˈkɔːkɪŋ/ ADJ *(Brit)* épatant †*, fameux*

corkscrew /ˈkɔːkskruː/ N tire-bouchon *m* COMP **corkscrew curls** NPL anglaises *fpl (boucles)*

corm /kɔːm/ N bulbe *m (de crocus etc)*

cormorant /ˈkɔːmərənt/ N cormoran *m*

Corn. *(Brit)* abbrev of **Cornwall**

corn[1] /kɔːn/ N [1] *(= seed)* grain *m (de céréale)* [2] *(Brit)* blé *m* ; *(US)* maïs *m* ◆ **~ on the cob** épis *mpl* de maïs [3] *(US = whiskey)* bourbon *m* [4] * *(= sentimentality)* sentimentalité *f* vieillotte *or* bébête ; *(= humour)* humour *m* bébête

COMP **corn bread** N *(US)* pain *m* de maïs

corn crops NPL céréales *fpl*

corn dog N *(US Culin)* saucisse *f* en beignet

corn dolly N *(Brit)* poupée *f* de paille

corn exchange N halle *f* au blé

corn-fed ADJ *[chicken]* de grain

corn liquor N *(US)* eau-de-vie *f* à base de maïs *(de fabrication artisanale)*

corn meal N farine *f* de maïs

corn oil N huile *f* de maïs

corn pone N *(NonC: US)* pain *m* de maïs

corn poppy N coquelicot *m*

corn salad N doucette *f*

corn whiskey N *(US)* whisky *m* de maïs, bourbon *m*

corn[2] /kɔːn/ N *(Med)* cor *m* ◆ **to tread on sb's ~s** *(Brit fig)* toucher qn à l'endroit sensible, blesser qn dans son amour-propre ◆ **~ plaster** *(Med)* pansement *m* pour cor

cornball‡ /ˈkɔːnbɔːl/ *(US)* N ◆ **to be a ~** *[person]* être très fleur bleue ADJ cucul (la praline)*

corncob /ˈkɔːnkɒb/ N *(US)* épi *m* de maïs

Corncracker State /ˌkɔːnkrækəˈsteɪt/ N ◆ **the ~** le Kentucky

corncrake /ˈkɔːnkreɪk/ N *(Orn)* râle *m* des genêts

corncrib /ˈkɔːnkrɪb/ N *(US Agr)* séchoir *m* à maïs

cornea /ˈkɔːnɪə/ N (pl **corneas** *or* **corneae** /ˈkɔːnɪˌiː/) cornée *f*

corneal /ˈkɔːnɪəl/ ADJ cornéen ◆ **~ lenses** lentilles *fpl* cornéennes, verres *mpl* cornéens

corned beef /ˈkɔːndˈbiːf/ N corned-beef *m*

cornelian /kɔːˈniːlɪən/ N cornaline *f*

corner /ˈkɔːnəʳ/ N [1] *(= angle) [of page, field, eye, mouth, room, boxing ring]* coin *m* ; *[of street, box, table]* coin *m*, angle *m* ; *[of road]* tournant *m*, virage *m* ; *(Climbing)* dièdre *m* ; *(Ftbl)* corner *m*, coup *m* de pied de coin ◆ **to look at sb out of the ~ of one's eye** regarder qn du coin de l'œil ◆ **to put a child in the ~** mettre un enfant au coin ◆ **to drive** *or* **force sb into a ~** *(lit)* pousser qn dans un coin ; *(fig)* acculer qn ◆ **to be in a (tight) ~** *(fig)* être dans le pétrin, être dans une situation difficile ◆ **you'll find the church round the ~** vous trouverez l'église juste après le coin ◆ **the little shop around the ~** la petite boutique du coin ◆ **it's just round the ~** *(= very near)* c'est à deux pas d'ici ◆ **Christmas is just around the ~** Noël n'est pas loin ◆ **the domestic robot is just around the ~** le robot domestique, c'est pour demain ◆ **to take a ~** *(in car)* prendre un tournant ; *(Ftbl)* faire un corner ◆ **to cut a ~** *(in car)* prendre un virage à la corde ◆ **to cut ~s** *(fig)* prendre des raccourcis *(fig)* ◆ **to cut ~s (on sth)** *(financially)* rogner sur les coûts (de qch) ◆ **to turn the ~** *(lit)* tourner au *or* le coin de la rue ; *(fig)* passer le moment critique ; *[patient]* passer le cap

[2] *(= cranny, place)* ◆ **in every ~ of the garden** dans tout le jardin ◆ **treasures hidden in odd ~s** des trésors *mpl* cachés dans des recoins ◆ **in every ~ of the house** dans tous les recoins de la maison ◆ **in every ~ of Europe** dans toute l'Europe

[3] *(fig = position)* **to fight one's ~** défendre sa position *or* son point de vue

4 (= *market*) **to make a ~ in wheat** accaparer le marché du blé
5 (*Boxing = person*) soigneur *m*
VT [+ *hunted animal*] acculer ; (*fig = catch to speak to etc*) coincer* ◆ **she ~ed me in the hall** elle m'a coincé* dans l'entrée ◆ **he's got you ~ed** (*fig*) il t'a coincé*, il t'a mis au pied du mur ◆ **to ~ the market** accaparer le marché
VI (*in car*) prendre un virage
COMP **corner cupboard** N placard *m* d'angle
corner flag N (*Ftbl*) piquet *m* de corner ; (*in roadway*) dalle *f* de coin
the corner house N la maison du coin, la maison qui fait l'angle (de la rue)
corner kick N (*Ftbl*) corner *m*
corner seat N (*gen*) siège *m* d'angle ; (*in train*) (place *f* de) coin *m*
corner shop N (*Brit*) magasin *m* or boutique *f* du coin
corner store N (*US*) ⇒ **corner shop**

cornering /'kɔːnərɪŋ/ N 1 (*in car*) amorce *f* du virage 2 (*of market*) accaparement *m*, monopolisation *f*

cornerstone /'kɔːnəstəʊn/ N (*lit, fig*) pierre *f* angulaire ; (= *foundation stone*) première pierre *f*

cornerways fold /'kɔːnəweɪz'fəʊld/ N pli *m* en triangle

cornet /'kɔːnɪt/ N 1 (*Mus*) cornet *m* (à pistons) ◆ **~ player** cornettiste *mf* 2 (*Brit*) [*of sweets etc*] cornet *m* ; [*of ice cream*] cornet *m* (de glace)

cornfield /'kɔːnfiːld/ N (*Brit*) champ *m* de blé ; (*US*) champ *m* de maïs

cornflakes /'kɔːnfleɪks/ NPL pétales *mpl* de maïs, corn-flakes *mpl*

cornflour /'kɔːnflaʊəʳ/ N (*Brit*) farine *f* de maïs, maïzena ® *f*

cornflower /'kɔːnflaʊəʳ/ **N** bleuet *m*, barbeau *m* **ADJ** (also **cornflower blue**) bleu vif *inv*, bleu barbeau *inv*

cornice /'kɔːnɪs/ N corniche *f*

corniche /'kɔːniːʃ, kɔː'niːʃ/ N (also **corniche road**) corniche *f*

Cornish /'kɔːnɪʃ/ **ADJ** de Cornouailles, cornouaillais **N** (= *language*) cornique *m* **COMP** **Cornish pasty** N chausson à la viande avec des pommes de terre et des carottes

Cornishman /'kɔːnɪʃmən/ N (pl **-men**) natif *m* de Cornouailles

Cornishwoman /'kɔːnɪʃwʊmən/ N (pl **-women**) native *f* de Cornouailles

cornstarch /'kɔːnstɑːtʃ/ N (*US*) farine *f* de maïs, maïzena ® *f*

cornucopia /kɔːnjʊ'kəʊpɪə/ N corne *f* d'abondance

Cornwall /'kɔːnwəl/ N Cornouailles *f* ◆ **in ~** en Cornouailles

corny* /'kɔːnɪ/ ADJ [*joke*] rebattu, éculé ; [*film, novel*] (*sentimental*) à l'eau de rose ; (*obvious*) bateau* *inv* ; [*song*] sentimental ◆ **the ~ line "do you come here often?"** la phrase bateau* "vous venez souvent ici ?" ◆ **I know it sounds ~, but ...** je sais que ça a l'air idiot mais ...

corolla /kə'rɒlə/ N corolle *f*

corollary /kə'rɒlərɪ/ N corollaire *m*

corona /kə'rəʊnə/ N (pl **coronas** or **coronae** /kə'rəʊniː/) (*Anat, Astron*) couronne *f* ; (*Elec*) couronne *f* électrique ; (*Archit*) larmier *m*

coronary /'kɒrənərɪ/ **ADJ** (*Anat*) coronaire ◆ **~ bypass** pontage *m* coronarien ◆ **~ care unit** unité *f* de soins coronariens ◆ **~ heart disease** maladie *f* coronarienne ◆ **~ thrombosis** infarctus *m* du myocarde, thrombose *f* coronarienne **N** (= *heart attack*) infarctus *m*

coronation /,kɒrə'neɪʃən/ **N** (= *ceremony*) couronnement *m* ; (= *actual crowning*) sacre *m*
COMP [*ceremony, oath, robe*] du sacre ; [*day*] du couronnement
coronation chicken N poulet froid sauce mayonnaise au curry

coroner /'kɒrənəʳ/ N coroner *m* (*officiel chargé de déterminer les causes d'un décès*) ◆ **~'s inquest** enquête *f* judiciaire (*menée par le coroner*) ◆ **~'s jury** jury *m* (*siégeant avec le coroner*)

coronet /'kɒrənɪt/ N [*of duke etc*] couronne *f* ; [*of lady*] diadème *m*

Corp, corp abbrev of **corporation**

corpora /'kɔːpərə/ NPL of **corpus**

corporal¹ /'kɔːpərəl/ N [*of infantry, RAF*] caporal-chef *m* ; [*of cavalry etc*] brigadier-chef *m* ◆ **Corporal Smith** (*on envelope etc*) le Caporal-Chef Smith

corporal² /'kɔːpərəl/ ADJ corporel ◆ **~ punishment** châtiment *m* corporel

corporate /'kɔːpərɪt/ **ADJ** 1 (*Comm*) (= *of a business*) [*executive, culture, restructuring, sponsorship, planning etc*] d'entreprise ; [*finance, image, identity, logo, jet*] de l'entreprise ; (= *of business in general*) [*affairs, debt, earnings etc*] des entreprises ◆ **~ America** l'Amérique *f* des entreprises ◆ **~ clients** or **customers** entreprises *fpl* clientes ◆ **the ~ world** le monde de l'entreprise ◆ **~ crime** la criminalité d'entreprise
2 (= *joint*) [*decision, responsibility*] collectif ; [*objective*] commun ; [*action, ownership*] en commun
COMP **corporate body** N personne *f* morale
corporate bond N (*US*) (*local*) obligation *f* municipale ; (*private*) obligation *f* émise par une société privée
corporate governance N gouvernance *f* or gouvernement *m* d'entreprise
corporate headquarters NPL siège *m* social
corporate hospitality N *soirées, déjeuners, etc aux frais d'une entreprise*
corporate institution N *institution fonctionnant comme une entreprise*
corporate killing N (*Jur*) homicide *m* involontaire (*dont est accusé un chef d'entreprise pour décès par négligence d'un de ses employés*)
corporate ladder N ◆ **to move up the ~ ladder** monter dans la hiérarchie d'une entreprise
corporate law N droit *m* des entreprises
corporate lawyer N juriste *mf* spécialisé(e) dans le droit des entreprises ; (*working for corporation*) avocat(e) *m(f)* d'entreprise ; (= *specialist in corporate law*) juriste *mf* d'entreprise
corporate name N raison *f* sociale
corporate property N biens *mpl* sociaux
corporate raider N raider *m*
corporate sponsor N gros sponsor *m*
corporate stock N actions *fpl*
corporate takeover N OPA *f*
corporate tax N impôt *m* sur les sociétés

corporately /'kɔːpərɪtlɪ/ ADV ◆ **to be ~ owned** appartenir à une entreprise (*or* des entreprises)

corporation /,kɔːpə'reɪʃən/ **N** 1 (*Brit*) [*of town*] conseil *m* municipal ◆ **the Mayor and Corporation** le corps municipal, la municipalité 2 (= *firm*) société *f* commerciale ; (*US*) société *f* à responsabilité limitée, compagnie *f* commerciale 3 (*Brit* *) bedaine* *f*, brioche* *f* ◆ **he's developed quite a ~** il a pris une sacrée brioche*
COMP (*Brit*) [*school, property*] de la ville, municipal
corporation lawyer N (*working for corporation*) avocat(e) *m(f)* d'entreprise ; (= *specialist in corporation law*) juriste *mf* d'entreprise
corporation tax N (*Brit*) impôt *m* sur les sociétés

corporatism /'kɔːpərətɪzəm/ N corporatisme *m*

corporatist /'kɔːpərətɪst/ ADJ corporatiste

corporeal /kɔː'pɔːrɪəl/ ADJ corporel, physique

corps /kɔːʳ/ **N** (pl **corps** /kɔːz/) corps *m* ; → **army, diplomatic** **COMP** **corps de ballet** N corps *m* de ballet

corpse /kɔːps/ N cadavre *m*, corps *m*

corpulence /'kɔːpjʊləns/ N corpulence *f*, embonpoint *m*

corpulent /'kɔːpjʊlənt/ ADJ corpulent

corpus /'kɔːpəs/ N (pl **corpuses** or **corpora** /'kɔːpərə/) (*Literat*) corpus *m*, recueil *m* ; (*Ling*) corpus *m* ; (*Fin*) capital *m* ◆ **Corpus Christi** (*Rel*) la Fête-Dieu

corpuscle /'kɔːpʌsl/ N 1 (*Anat, Bio*) corpuscule *m* ◆ **(blood) ~** globule *m* sanguin ◆ **red/white ~s** globules *mpl* rouges/blancs 2 (*Phys*) électron *m*

corral /kə'rɑːl/ (*US*) **N** corral *m* **VT** [+ *cattle*] enfermer dans un corral ; (* *fig*) [+ *people, support*] réunir

correct /kə'rekt/ **ADJ** 1 (= *right*) [*answer, number, term, estimate, information*] correct ; [*suspicions*] bien fondé ◆ **that's ~!** (*confirming guess*) exactement ! ; (*confirming right answer*) c'est juste *or* exact ! ◆ **"correct money** or **change only"** (*in buses etc*) "vous êtes prié de faire l'appoint" ◆ **in the ~ order** dans le bon ordre ◆ **to prove ~** s'avérer juste ◆ **have you the ~ time?** avez-vous l'heure exacte ? ◆ **at the ~ time** au bon moment ◆ **it is ~ to say that ...** il est juste de dire que ... ◆ **it is not ~ to say that ...** (*rationally*) il est inexact de dire que ... ; (*fair*) il n'est pas juste de dire que ... ; (*morally*) il n'est pas correct de dire que ...
2 **to be ~** [*person*] avoir raison ◆ **you are quite ~** vous avez parfaitement raison ◆ **he was ~ in his estimates** ses estimations étaient justes ◆ **he is ~ in his assessment of the situation** son évaluation de la situation est juste ◆ **to be ~ in doing sth** avoir raison de faire qch ◆ **to be ~ to do sth** avoir raison de faire qch ◆ **he was quite ~ to do it** il a eu tout à fait raison de le faire
3 (= *appropriate*) [*object, method, decision, size, speed, temperature*] bon ◆ **in the ~ place** au bon endroit ◆ **the ~ use of sth** le bon usage de qch ◆ **the ~ weight for your height and build** le bon poids pour votre taille et votre corpulence
4 (= *proper*) [*behaviour*] correct ; [*manners*] correct, convenable ; [*etiquette, form of address*] convenable ; [*person*] comme il faut ◆ **~ dress must be worn** une tenue correcte est exigée ◆ **it's the ~ thing to do** c'est l'usage, c'est ce qui se fait ◆ **socially ~** admis en société
VT 1 [+ *piece of work, text, error*] corriger ; (*Typ*) [+ *proofs*] corriger ◆ **to ~ sb's punctuation/spelling** corriger la ponctuation/l'orthographe de qn ◆ **he asked her to ~ his English** il lui a demandé de corriger son anglais
2 [+ *person*] reprendre, corriger ◆ **to ~ o.s.** se reprendre, se corriger ◆ **~ me if I'm wrong** reprenez-moi or corrigez-moi si je me trompe ◆ **I stand ~ed** je reconnais mon erreur
3 (= *rectify*) [+ *problem*] arranger ; [+ *eyesight*] corriger ; [+ *imbalance*] redresser
4 (†† = *punish*) réprimander, reprendre
COMP **correcting fluid** N liquide *m* correcteur

correction /kə'rekʃən/ **N** 1 (*NonC*) [*of proofs, essay*] correction *f* ; [*of error*] correction *f*, rectification *f* ◆ **I am open to ~, but ...** corrigez-moi si je me trompe, mais ... 2 [*of school work, proof, text, manuscript*] correction *f* ◆ **a page covered with ~s** une page couverte de corrections 3 (†† = *punishment*) correction *f*, châtiment *m* ◆ **house of ~** maison *f* de correction †
COMP **correction fluid** N liquide *m* correcteur
correction tape N ruban *m* correcteur

correctional /kə'rekʃənəl/ (*US*) **ADJ** [*system*] pénitentiaire
COMP **correctional facility** N établissement *m* pénitentiaire
correctional officer N gardien(ne) *m(f)* de prison

corrective /kəˈrektɪv/ ADJ *[action]* rectificatif ; *(Jur, Med) [measures, training]* de rééducation, correctif ◆ **~ surgery** *(Med)* chirurgie *f* réparatrice N correctif *m*

correctly /kəˈrektlɪ/ ADV 1 *(= accurately, in right way) [predict]* avec justesse, correctement ; *[answer, pronounce, cook, perform]* correctement ◆ **if I understand you ~** si je vous ai bien compris ◆ **if I remember ~** si je me souviens bien 2 *(= respectably, decently) [behave]* correctement, convenablement

correctness /kəˈrektnɪs/ N *(NonC)* 1 *(= rightness, appropriateness) [of decision, action, statement, calculation, spelling]* justesse *f* 2 *(= propriety) [of person, behaviour, manners, dress]* correction *f* ◆ **to treat sb with polite ~** traiter qn avec une correction polie

Correggio /kəˈredʒəʊ/ N le Corrège

correlate /ˈkɒrɪleɪt/ VI correspondre *(with* à) être en corrélation *(with* avec) VT mettre en corrélation, corréler *(with* avec)

correlation /ˌkɒrɪˈleɪʃən/ N corrélation *f*

correlative /kɒˈrelətɪv/ N corrélatif *m* ADJ corrélatif

correspond /ˌkɒrɪsˈpɒnd/ LANGUAGE IN USE 5.3 VI 1 *(= agree)* correspondre *(with* à) s'accorder *(with* avec) ; ◆ **that does not ~ with what he said** cela ne correspond pas à ce qu'il a dit 2 *(= be similar, equivalent)* correspondre *(to* à) être l'équivalent *(to* de) ; ◆ **this ~s to what she was doing last year** ceci est semblable *or* correspond à ce qu'elle faisait l'année dernière ◆ **his job ~s roughly to mine** son poste équivaut à peu près au mien *or* est à peu près l'équivalent du mien 3 *(= exchange letters)* correspondre *(with* avec) ; ◆ **they ~** ils s'écrivent, ils correspondent

correspondence /ˌkɒrɪsˈpɒndəns/ N 1 *(= similarity, agreement)* correspondance *f (between* entre ; *with* avec) 2 *(= letter-writing)* correspondance *f* ◆ **to be in ~ with sb** entretenir une *or* être en correspondance avec qn ◆ **to read one's ~** lire son courrier *or* sa correspondance

COMP **correspondence card** N carte-lettre *f*
correspondence college N établissement *m* d'enseignement par correspondance
correspondence column N *(Press)* courrier *m* des lecteurs
correspondence course N cours *m* par correspondance

correspondent /ˌkɒrɪsˈpɒndənt/ N *(gen, Comm, Press, Banking)* correspondant(e) *m(f)* ◆ **foreign/sports ~** correspondant étranger/sportif ; → **special**

corresponding /ˌkɒrɪsˈpɒndɪŋ/ ADJ correspondant ◆ **~ to ...** conforme à ... ◆ **a ~ period** une période analogue ◆ **the ~ period** la période correspondante

correspondingly /ˌkɒrɪsˈpɒndɪŋlɪ/ ADV 1 *(= proportionately)* proportionnellement 2 *(= as a result)* en conséquence

corridor /ˈkɒrɪdɔːʳ/ N couloir *m*, corridor *m* ◆ **~ train** *(Brit)* train *m* à couloir ◆ **the ~s of power** les allées *fpl* du pouvoir

corroborate /kəˈrɒbəreɪt/ VT corroborer, confirmer

corroboration /kəˌrɒbəˈreɪʃən/ N confirmation *f*, corroboration *f* ◆ **in ~ of ...** à l'appui de ..., en confirmation de ...

corroborative /kəˈrɒbərətɪv/ ADJ qui corrobore *(or* corroborait *etc)*

corrode /kəˈrəʊd/ VT *(lit, fig)* corroder, ronger VI *[metals]* se corroder

corroded /kəˈrəʊdɪd/ ADJ corrodé

corrosion /kəˈrəʊʒən/ N corrosion *f*

corrosive /kəˈrəʊzɪv/ ADJ *(Chem)* corrosif ; *(fig) (= harmful) [effect, influence, power, emotion]* destructeur (-trice *f*) N corrosif *m*

corrugated /ˈkɒrəgeɪtɪd/ ADJ *[tin, steel, surface]* ondulé ; *[roof]* en tôle ondulée ; *[brow, face]* ridé

COMP **corrugated cardboard** N carton *m* ondulé
corrugated iron N tôle *f* ondulée
corrugated paper N papier *m* ondulé

corrupt /kəˈrʌpt/ ADJ 1 *(= dishonest)* corrompu ; *(= depraved)* dépravé ; *[practice]* malhonnête ◆ **~ practices** *(= dishonesty)* tractations *fpl* malhonnêtes ; *(= bribery etc)* trafic *m* d'influence, malversations *fpl* 2 *[data, text, language]* corrompu 3 *(liter = putrid) [flesh, corpse]* putride VT *(dishonesty)* corrompre ; *(immorality)* dépraver ; *(Comput)* corrompre VI corrompre

corruptible /kəˈrʌptəbl/ ADJ corruptible

corruption /kəˈrʌpʃən/ N 1 *(NonC: moral) [of person, morals]* corruption *f* ◆ **police ~** corruption *f* de la police 2 *(Ling)* ◆ **"jean" is a ~ of "Genoa"** "jean" est une déformation de "Gênes" 3 *(NonC: liter = putrefaction)* décomposition *f*, putréfaction *f* COMP **the corruption of minors** N *(Jur)* le détournement de mineur(s)

corsage /kɔːˈsɑːʒ/ N *(= bodice)* corsage *m* ; *(= flowers)* petit bouquet *m (de fleurs porté au corsage)*

corsair /ˈkɔːseəʳ/ N *(= ship, pirate)* corsaire *m*, pirate *m*

cors anglais /ˈkɔːzˈɑːŋgleɪ/ NPL of **cor anglais**

corset /ˈkɔːsɪt/ N *(Dress:* also **corsets)** corset *m* ; *(lightweight)* gaine *f* ; *(Med)* corset *m*

corseted /ˈkɔːsɪtɪd/ ADJ corseté

Corsica /ˈkɔːsɪkə/ N Corse *f*

Corsican /ˈkɔːsɪkən/ ADJ corse N Corse *mf*

cortège /kɔːˈteɪʒ/ N cortège *m*

cortex /ˈkɔːteks/ N (pl **cortices** /ˈkɔːtɪsiːz/) *(Bot)* cortex *m*, écorce *f* ; *(Anat)* cortex *m*

corticoids /ˈkɔːtɪkɔɪdz/, **corticosteroids** /ˌkɔːtɪkəʊˈstɪərɔɪdz/ NPL corticoïdes *mpl*

cortisone /ˈkɔːtɪzəʊn/ N cortisone *f*

corundum /kəˈrʌndəm/ N corindon *m*

coruscate /ˈkɒrəskeɪt/ VI briller, scintiller

coruscating /ˈkɒrəskeɪtɪŋ/ ADJ brillant, scintillant

corvette /kɔːˈvet/ N *(Naut)* corvette *f*

COS /ˌsiːəʊˈes/ (abbrev of **cash on shipment**) → **cash**

cos[1] /kɒs/ N *(Brit:* also **cos lettuce**) (laitue *f*) romaine *f*

cos[2] /kɒs/ N abbrev of **cosine**

cos[3] * /kɒz/ CONJ parce que

cosh /kɒʃ/ *(Brit)* VT * taper sur, cogner* sur N gourdin *m*, matraque *f* ◆ **to be under the ~** * *(Brit)* être en difficulté

cosignatory /ˈkəʊˈsɪgnətərɪ/ N cosignataire *mf*

cosily, cozily (US) /ˈkəʊzɪlɪ/ ADV *[furnished]* confortablement ; *[settled]* douillettement

cosine /ˈkəʊsaɪn/ N cosinus *m*

cosiness, coziness (US) /ˈkəʊzɪnɪs/ N *(NonC)* 1 *(= warmth) [of room, pub]* atmosphère *f* douillette 2 *(= intimacy) [of evening, chat, dinner]* intimité *f* ◆ **the ~ of the atmosphere** l'atmosphère *f* douillette 3 *(pej = convenience) [of relationship]* complicité *f*, connivence *f*

cosmetic /kɒzˈmetɪk/ ADJ *[surgery]* plastique, esthétique ; *[preparation]* cosmétique ; *(fig)* superficiel, symbolique N cosmétique *m*, produit *m* de beauté

cosmetician /kɒzmeˈtɪʃən/ N *(= chemist)* cosmétologue *mf* ; *(= beautician)* esthéticien(ne) *m(f)*

cosmic /ˈkɒzmɪk/ ADJ *(lit)* cosmique ; *(fig)* immense, incommensurable ◆ **~ dust/rays** poussière *f*/rayons *mpl* cosmique(s)

cosmogony /kɒzˈmɒgənɪ/ N cosmogonie *f*

cosmographer /kɒzˈmɒgrəfəʳ/ N cosmographe *mf*

cosmography /kɒzˈmɒgrəfɪ/ N cosmographie *f*

cosmological /ˌkɒzməʊˈlɒdʒɪkəl/ ADJ cosmologique

cosmology /kɒzˈmɒlədʒɪ/ N cosmologie *f*

cosmonaut /ˈkɒzmənɔːt/ N cosmonaute *mf*

cosmopolitan /ˌkɒzməˈpɒlɪtən/ ADJ, N cosmopolite *mf*

cosmos /ˈkɒzmɒs/ N cosmos *m*

co-sponsor /ˈkəʊˈspɒnsəʳ/ N *(Advertising)* commanditaire *m* associé

Cossack /ˈkɒsæk/ N cosaque *m*

cosset /ˈkɒsɪt/ VT dorloter, choyer

cossie * /ˈkɒzɪ/ N *(Brit, Austral)* maillot *m* (de bain)

cost /kɒst/ LANGUAGE IN USE 8.2

VT (pret, ptp **cost**) 1 *(lit, fig)* coûter ◆ **how much does the dress ~?** combien coûte la robe ? ◆ **how much** *or* **what will it ~ to have it repaired?** combien est-ce que cela coûtera de le faire réparer ? ◆ **what does it ~ to get in?** quel est le prix d'entrée ? ◆ **it ~ him a lot of money** cela lui a coûté cher ◆ **it ~s him £22 a week** cela lui revient à *or* lui coûte 22 livres par semaine, il en a pour 22 livres par semaine ◆ **it ~s too much** cela coûte trop cher, c'est trop cher ◆ **it ~s the earth** * ça coûte les yeux de la tête ◆ **it ~ him an arm and a leg** * ça lui a coûté les yeux de la tête ◆ **I know what it ~ him to apologize** je sais ce qu'il lui en a coûté de s'excuser ◆ **it ~ her dear** cela lui a coûté cher ◆ **it ~ him his job** cela lui a coûté son emploi ◆ **it ~ him a great effort** cela lui a coûté *or* demandé un gros effort ◆ **it ~ him a lot of trouble** cela lui a causé beaucoup d'ennuis ◆ **it will ~ you your life** il vous en coûtera la vie ◆ **it'll** *or* **that'll ~ you!** * tu vas le sentir passer ! ◆ **politeness ~s very little** il ne coûte rien d'être poli ◆ **whatever it ~s** *(fig)* coûte que coûte

2 (pret, ptp **costed**) *(Comm = set price for) [+ article]* établir le prix de revient de ; *[+ piece of work]* évaluer le coût de ◆ **the job was ~ed at £2,000** le devis pour (l'exécution de) ces travaux s'est monté à 2 000 livres

N coût *m* ◆ **the ~ of repairs** le coût des réparations ◆ **~, insurance and freight** coût *m* assurance *f* et fret *m* ◆ **to cut the ~ of borrowing** *(Fin)* réduire le loyer de l'argent ◆ **to bear the ~ of ...** *(lit)* faire face aux frais *mpl or* aux dépenses *fpl* de ... ; *(fig)* faire les frais de ... ◆ **at great ~** *(lit, fig)* à grands frais ◆ **at little ~** à peu de frais ◆ **at little ~ to himself** *(fig)* sans que cela lui coûte *subj* beaucoup ◆ **at ~ (price)** au prix coûtant ◆ **at the ~ of his life/health** au prix de sa vie/santé ◆ **to my ~** *(fig)* à mes dépens ◆ **at all ~s, at any ~** *(fig)* coûte que coûte, à tout prix ; → **count**[1]

NPL **costs** *(Jur)* dépens *mpl*, frais *mpl* judiciaires ◆ **to be ordered to pay ~s** *(Jur)* être condamné aux dépens

COMP **cost accountant** N analyste *mf* de coûts
cost accounting N *(NonC)* comptabilité *f* analytique *or* d'exploitation
cost analysis N analyse *f* des coûts
cost-benefit analysis N analyse *f* coûts-bénéfices
cost centre N centre *m* de coût(s)
cost conscious ADJ qui fait attention à ses dépenses
cost control N contrôle *m* des dépenses

cost-cutting N compression *f or* réduction *f* des coûts ◆ **~-cutting plan** *etc* plan *m etc* de réduction des coûts
cost-effective ADJ rentable, d'un bon rapport coût-performance *or* coût-efficacité
cost-effectiveness N rentabilité *f*, rapport *m* coût-performance *or* coût-efficacité
cost estimate N devis *m*, estimation *f* des coûts
cost-in-use N coûts *mpl* d'utilisation
cost of living N coût *m* de la vie ◆ **~-of-living adjustment** augmentation *f* indexée sur le coût de la vie ◆ **~-of-living allowance** indemnité *f* de vie chère ◆ **~-of-living increase** rattrapage *m* pour cherté de la vie ◆ **~-of-living index** index *m* du coût de la vie
cost-plus N prix *m* de revient majoré du pourcentage contractuel ◆ **on a ~-plus basis** à des coûts majorés
cost price N *(Brit)* prix *m* coûtant *or* de revient
► **cost out** VT SEP *[+ project]* évaluer le coût de

co-star /ˈkəʊstɑːʳ/ *(Cine, Theat)* N partenaire *mf* VI partager l'affiche *(with* avec) ; ◆ **"co-starring X"** "avec X"

Costa Rica /ˈkɒstəˈriːkə/ N Costa Rica *m*

Costa Rican /ˈkɒstəˈriːkən/ ADJ costaricain(e), costaricien N Costaricain(e) *m(f)*, Costaricien(ne) *m(f)*

coster /ˈkɒstəʳ/, **costermonger** /ˈkɒstə,mʌŋgəʳ/ N *(Brit)* marchand(e) *m(f)* des quatre saisons

costing /ˈkɒstɪŋ/ N estimation *f* du prix de revient

costive /ˈkɒstɪv/ ADJ constipé

costliness /ˈkɒstlɪnɪs/ N *(= value)* (grande) valeur *f* ; *(= high price)* cherté *f*

costly /ˈkɒstlɪ/ ADJ *(gen)* coûteux ; *[furs, jewels]* de grande valeur, précieux ◆ **a ~ business** une affaire coûteuse

costume /ˈkɒstjuːm/ N 1 *(gen)* costume *m* ◆ **national ~** costume *m* national ◆ **in ~** *(= fancy dress)* déguisé 2 († *= lady's suit)* tailleur *m*
COMP **costume ball** N bal *m* masqué
costume drama N *(= film/play etc)* pièce *f*/film *m etc* en costume d'époque ; *(genre) (Theat/Cine etc)* théâtre *m*/cinéma *m etc* en costume d'époque
costume jewellery N bijoux *mpl* (de) fantaisie
costume piece N ⇒ **costume drama**
costume play N pièce *f* en costume d'époque

costumier /kɒsˈtjuːmɪəʳ/, **costumer** *(esp US)* /kɒsˈtjuːməʳ/ N costumier *m*, -ière *f*

cosy, cozy *(US)* /ˈkəʊzɪ/ ADJ 1 *(= warm) [flat, home, room]* douillet, cosy ; *[restaurant]* confortable ◆ **nights in front of a ~ fire** des soirées agréables au coin du feu ◆ **to be ~** *[person]* être bien ◆ **it is ~ in here** on est bien ici 2 *(= friendly) [atmosphere, evening, chat, dinner]* intime 3 *(pej = convenient) [arrangement, deal, relationship]* commode N *(= tea cosy)* couvre-théière *m* ; *(= egg cosy)* couvre-œuf *m* VI ◆ **to ~ up to sb**⁑ caresser qn dans le sens du poil *

cot /kɒt/ N *(Brit: child's)* lit *m* d'enfant, petit lit *m* ; *(US = folding bed)* lit *m* de camp COMP **cot death** N mort *f* subite du nourrisson

Cote d'Ivoire /,kəʊtdiˈvwɑːr/ N ◆ **(the) ~** la Côte-d'Ivoire

coterie /ˈkəʊtərɪ/ N coterie *f*, cénacle *m*

cotillion /kəˈtɪljən/ N cotillon *m*, quadrille *m*

cottage /ˈkɒtɪdʒ/ N petite maison *f* (à la campagne), cottage *m* ; *(thatched)* chaumière *f* ; *(holiday home)* villa *f*
COMP **cottage cheese** N fromage *m* blanc (égoutté), cottage *m* (cheese)
cottage flat N *(Brit) appartement dans une maison en regroupant quatre en copropriété*
cottage hospital N *(Brit)* petit hôpital *m*
cottage industry N *(working at home)* industrie *f* familiale ; *(= informally organized industry)* industrie *f* artisanale
cottage loaf N *(Brit)* miche *f* de pain
cottage pie N *(Brit)* ≃ hachis *m* Parmentier

cottager /ˈkɒtɪdʒəʳ/ N *(Brit)* paysan(ne) *m(f)* ; *(US)* propriétaire *mf* de maison de vacances

cottaging * /ˈkɒtɪdʒɪŋ/ N *(Brit) rencontres homosexuelles dans des toilettes publiques*

cottar, cotter¹ /ˈkɒtəʳ/ N *(Scot)* paysan(ne) *m(f)*

cotton /ˈkɒtn/ N *(NonC) (= plant, fabric)* coton *m* ; *(Brit = sewing thread)* fil *m* (de coton) ; → **absorbent, gin**
COMP *[shirt, dress]* de coton
cotton batting N *(US)* ouate *f*
the cotton belt N le Sud cotonnier *(Alabama, Géorgie, Mississippi)*
cotton bud N *(Brit)* coton-tige ® *m*
cotton cake N tourteau *m* de coton
cotton candy N *(US)* barbe *f* à papa
cotton goods NPL cotonnades *fpl*
cotton grass N linaigrette *f*, lin *m* des marais
cotton industry N industrie *f* cotonnière *or* du coton
cotton lace N dentelle *f* de coton
cotton mill N filature *f* de coton
cotton-picking ADJ *(US pej)* sale * *before n*, sacré *before n*
the Cotton State N l'Alabama *m*
cotton waste N déchets *mpl* de coton, coton *m* d'essuyage
cotton wool N *(Brit)* ouate *f* ◆ **absorbent ~ wool** ouate *f or* coton *m* hydrophile ◆ **to bring up a child in ~ wool** élever un enfant dans du coton ◆ **my legs felt like ~ wool** * j'avais les jambes en coton
cotton yarn N fil *m* de coton
► **cotton on** * VI *(Brit)* piger * ◆ **to ~ on to sth** piger * qch, saisir qch
► **cotton to**⁑ VT FUS *[+ person]* avoir à la bonne⁑ ; *[+ plan, suggestion]* apprécier, approuver ◆ **I don't ~ to it much** je ne suis pas tellement pour *, ça ne me botte pas tellement⁑

cottonseed oil /ˈkɒtnsiːdˈɔɪl/ N huile *f* de coton

cottontail /ˈkɒtnteɪl/ N *(US)* lapin *m*

cottonwood /ˈkɒtnwʊd/ N *(US)* peuplier *m* de Virginie

cotyledon /,kɒtɪˈliːdən/ N cotylédon *m*

couch /kaʊtʃ/ N 1 *(= settee)* canapé *m*, divan *m*, sofa *m* ; *[of doctor]* lit *m* ; *[of psychoanalyst]* divan *m* ; *(liter = bed)* couche *f (liter)* ◆ **to be on the ~** * *(US fig)* être en analyse 2 *(= couch grass)* chiendent *m* VT formuler, exprimer ◆ **request ~ed in insolent language** requête *f* formulée *or* exprimée en des termes insolents ◆ **request ~ed in the following terms** demande *f* ainsi rédigée VI *[animal] (= lie asleep)* être allongé *or* couché ; *(= ready to spring)* s'embusquer
COMP **couch grass** N chiendent *m*
couch potato * N mollasson *m (qui passe son temps devant la télé)*

couchette /kuːˈʃet/ N *(Rail etc)* couchette *f*

cougar /ˈkuːgəʳ/ N couguar *m*

cough /kɒf/ N toux *f* ◆ **he has a bad ~** il a une mauvaise toux, il tousse beaucoup ◆ **he has a bit of a ~** il tousse un peu ◆ **to give a warning ~** tousser en guise d'avertissement VI 1 tousser 2 *(* = confess)* parler ◆ **to ~ on** *or* **to sth** avouer qch
COMP **cough drop** N pastille *f* pour la toux
cough mixture N sirop *m* pour la toux, (sirop *m*) antitussif *m*
cough sweet N pastille *f* pour la toux
cough syrup N ⇒ **cough mixture**
► **cough up** VT SEP 1 *(lit)* expectorer, cracher en toussant 2 *(* fig) [+ money]* cracher *

coughing /ˈkɒfɪŋ/ N toux *f* ◆ **to hear ~** entendre tousser ◆ **~ fit** quinte *f* de toux

could /kʊd/ LANGUAGE IN USE 1.1, 2.2, 3.1, 4, 9.1, 26.3 VB pt, cond of **can¹**

couldn't /ˈkʊdnt/ ⇒ **could not** ; → **can¹**

could've /ˈkʊdəv/ ⇒ **could have** ; → **can¹**

coulee /ˈkuːleɪ/ N *(US)* ravine *f*

coulis /ˈkuːliː/ N *(Culin)* coulis *m*

couloir /ˈkuːlwɑːʳ/ N *(Climbing)* couloir *m*

coulomb /ˈkuːlɒm/ N coulomb *m*

council /ˈkaʊnsl/ N conseil *m*, assemblée *f* ◆ **~ of war** conseil *m* de guerre ◆ **city** *or* **town ~** conseil *m* municipal ◆ **they decided in ~ that ...** l'assemblée a décidé que ... ◆ **the Security Council of the UN** le conseil de Sécurité des Nations Unies ; → **lord, parish, privy**
COMP **council chamber** N *(Brit)* salle *f* du conseil municipal
council estate N *(Brit)* cité *f* (de logements sociaux *or* de HLM)
council flat N *(Brit)* appartement *m*/maison *f* loué(e) à la municipalité, ≃ HLM *m or f*
council house N *(Brit)* maison *f* louée à la municipalité, ≃ HLM *m or f*
council housing N *(Brit)* logements *mpl* sociaux
council housing estate N ⇒ **council estate**
the Council of Economic Advisors N *(US)* les Conseillers *mpl* économiques (du Président)
Council of Europe N Conseil *m* de l'Europe
Council of Ministers N *(Pol)* Conseil *m* des ministres
council school N *(Brit)* école *f* publique
council tax N *(Brit)* impôts *mpl* locaux
council tenant N *(Brit)* locataire *mf* d'un logement social

councillor /ˈkaʊnsləʳ/ N conseiller *m*, -ère *f*, membre *m* d'un conseil ◆ **Councillor X** *(form of address)* Monsieur le conseiller municipal X, Madame la conseillère municipale X ; → **privy, town**

councilman /ˈkaʊnsɪlmæn/ N (pl **-men**) *(US)* conseiller *m*

councilwoman /ˈkaʊnsɪlwʊmən/ N (pl **-women**) *(US)* conseillère *f*

counsel /ˈkaʊnsəl/ N 1 *(NonC)* conseil *m* ◆ **to take ~ with sb** prendre conseil de qn, consulter qn ◆ **to keep one's own ~** garder ses pensées pour soi, ne rien dévoiler de ses pensées 2 *(pl inv: Jur)* avocat(e) *m(f)* ◆ **~ for the defence** *(Brit)* (avocat *m* de la) défense *f* ◆ **~ for the prosecution** *(Brit)* avocat *m* du ministère public ◆ **King's** *or* **Queen's Counsel** avocat *m* de la couronne *(qui peut néanmoins plaider pour des particuliers)* ; → **defending, prosecuting** VT *(frm, liter)* recommander, conseiller *(sb to do sth* à qn de faire qch) ; ◆ **to ~ caution** recommander *or* conseiller la prudence

counselling, counseling *(US)* /ˈkaʊnsəlɪŋ/ N *(gen = advice)* conseils *mpl* ; *(Psych, Social Work)* assistance *f* socio-psychologique ; *(Brit Scol)* aide *f* psychopédagogique ◆ **he needs ~** *(= therapy)* il a besoin de suivre une thérapie COMP **counseling service** N *(US Univ)* service *m* d'orientation et d'assistance universitaire

counsellor, counselor *(US)* /ˈkaʊnsləʳ/ N 1 *(gen)* conseiller *m*, -ère *f* ; *(Psych, Social Work)* conseiller *m*, -ère *f* socio-psychologique ; *(US Educ)* conseiller *m*, -ère *f* d'orientation 2 *(Ir, US: also* **counsellor-at-law)** avocat *m*

count¹ /kaʊnt/ LANGUAGE IN USE 4
N 1 compte *m* ; *[of votes at election]* dépouillement *m* ◆ **to make a ~** faire un compte ◆ **at the last ~** *(gen)* la dernière fois qu'on a compté ; *(Admin)* au dernier recensement ◆ **to be out for the ~, to take the ~** *(Boxing)* être (mis) knock-out, aller au tapis pour le compte ◆ **to be out for the ~** * *(fig) (= unconscious)* être KO *, avoir son compte * ; *(= asleep)* avoir son compte * ◆ **I'll come and look for you after a ~**

of ten je compte jusqu'à dix et je viens te chercher ◆ **to keep (a) ~ of ...** tenir le compte de ... ◆ **to take no ~ of ...** (*fig*) ne pas tenir compte de ...

◆ **to lose count** ◆ **every time you interrupt you make me lose ~** chaque fois que tu m'interromps je perds le fil ◆ **I've lost ~** je ne sais plus où j'en suis ◆ **I've lost ~ of the number of times I've told you** je ne sais plus combien de fois je te l'ai dit ◆ **he lost ~ of the tickets he had sold** il ne savait plus combien de billets il avait vendus

2 (*Jur*) chef *m* d'accusation ◆ **guilty on three ~s** reconnu coupable pour trois chefs d'accusation

3 (*= respect, point of view*) ◆ **you're wrong on both ~s** tu te trompes doublement ◆ **the movie is unique on several ~s** c'est un film unique à plusieurs égards ◆ **a magnificent book on all ~s** un livre magnifique à tous points de vue

VT 1 (*= add up*) compter ◆ **to ~ the votes** (*Admin, Pol*) compter les bulletins ◆ **to ~ noses*** (*US*) compter les présents ◆ **to ~ sheep** compter les moutons ◆ **to ~ the cost** (*lit*) calculer la dépense ; (*fig*) faire le bilan ◆ **without ~ing the cost** (*lit, fig*) sans compter ◆ **(you must) ~ your blessings** estimez-vous heureux ◆ **don't ~ your chickens (before they're hatched)** (*Prov*) il ne faut pas vendre la peau de l'ours (avant de l'avoir tué) (*Prov*) → **stand**

2 (*= include*) compter ◆ **ten people not ~ing the children** dix personnes sans compter les enfants ◆ **three more ~ing Charles** trois de plus, en comptant Charles ◆ **to ~ sb among one's friends** compter qn parmi ses amis

3 (*= consider*) tenir, estimer ◆ **to ~ sb as dead** tenir qn pour mort ◆ **we must ~ ourselves fortunate** *or* **lucky (men)** nous devons nous estimer heureux ◆ **I ~ it an honour to (be able to) help you** je m'estime honoré de pouvoir vous aider

VI 1 compter ◆ **can he ~?** est-ce qu'il sait compter ? ◆ **~ing from tonight** à compter de ce soir ◆ **~ing from the left** à partir de la gauche

2 (*= be considered*) compter ◆ **you ~ among my best friends** vous comptez parmi *or* au nombre de mes meilleurs amis ◆ **two children ~ as one adult** deux enfants comptent pour un adulte ◆ **that doesn't ~** cela ne compte pas

3 (*= have importance*) compter ◆ **every minute ~s** chaque minute compte ◆ **that ~s for nothing** cela ne compte pas, cela compte pour du beurre* ◆ **he ~s for a lot in that firm** il joue un rôle important dans cette compagnie ◆ **a university degree ~s for very little nowadays** de nos jours un diplôme universitaire n'a pas beaucoup de valeur *or* ne pèse pas lourd*

COMP **count noun** N nom *m* comptable

► **count against** VT FUS desservir ◆ **his lack of experience ~s against him** son inexpérience le dessert *or* joue contre lui

► **count down** VI faire le compte à rebours

► **count in*** VT SEP compter ◆ **to ~ sb in on a plan** inclure qn dans un projet ◆ **you can ~ me in!** je suis de la partie !

► **count on** VT FUS ⇒ **count upon**

► **count out** VT SEP 1 (*Boxing*) **to be ~ed out** être mis knock-out, être envoyé *or* aller au tapis pour le compte

2 [*+ money*] compter pièce par pièce ; [*+ small objects*] compter, dénombrer

3 (*= exclude*) ◆ **you can count me out of*** this business ne comptez pas sur moi dans cette affaire

4 (*Parl etc*) **to ~ out a meeting** ajourner une séance (*le quorum n'étant pas atteint*) ◆ **to ~ out the House** (*Brit*) ajourner la séance (*du Parlement*)

► **count towards** VT FUS ◆ **these contributions will count towards your pension** ces cotisations compteront pour *or* seront prises en compte pour votre retraite

► **count up** VT SEP compter

► **count upon** VT FUS compter (sur) ◆ **I'm ~ing upon you** je compte sur vous ◆ **to ~ upon doing sth** compter faire qch

count[2] /kaʊnt/ N (*= nobleman*) comte *m*

countability /ˌkaʊntəˈbɪlɪtɪ/ N (*Ling = fact of being countable*) fait *m* d'être comptable ◆ **the problem of ~** le problème de savoir si un (*or* le *etc*) substantif est comptable ou non

countable /ˈkaʊntəbl/ ADJ (*Gram*) ◆ **~ noun** nom *m* comptable

countdown /ˈkaʊntdaʊn/ N compte *m* à rebours

countenance /ˈkaʊntɪnəns/ N 1 (*liter = face*) (expression *f* du) visage *m*, figure *f* ; (*= expression*) mine *f* ; (*= composure*) contenance *f* ◆ **out of ~** décontenancé ◆ **to keep one's ~** faire bonne contenance, ne pas se laisser décontenancer 2 (*frm = approval*) **to give ~ to** [*+ person*] encourager ; [*+ plan*] favoriser ; [*+ rumour, piece of news*] accréditer VT approuver, admettre (*sth* qch ; *sb's doing sth* que qn fasse qch)

counter[1] /ˈkaʊntəʳ/ N 1 (*in shop, canteen*) comptoir *m* ; (*= position: in bank, post office etc*) guichet *m* ; (*in pub*) comptoir *m*, zinc* *m* ◆ **the girl behind the ~** (*in shop*) la vendeuse ; (*in pub*) la serveuse ◆ **available over the ~** [*medicine*] vendu sans ordonnance ◆ **to buy/sell medicines over the ~** acheter/vendre des médicaments sans ordonnance ; see also **over-the-counter** ◆ **to buy/sell sth under the ~** acheter/vendre qch sous le manteau ; see also **under-the-counter** 2 (*= disc*) jeton *m* 3 (*= measuring, counting device*) compteur *m* ; → **Geiger counter**

COMP **counter hand** N (*in shop*) vendeur *m*, -euse *f* ; (*in snack bar*) serveur *m*, -euse *f*

counter staff N (*NonC, in bank*) caissiers *mpl*, -ières *fpl*, guichetiers *mpl* ; (*in shop*) vendeurs *mpl*, -euses *fpl*

counter[2] /ˈkaʊntəʳ/ ADV ◆ **~ to sb's wishes** à l'encontre des *or* contrairement aux souhaits de qn ◆ **~ to sb's orders** contrairement aux ordres de qn ◆ **to run ~ to sth** aller à l'encontre de qch ADJ ◆ **~ to sth** contraire à qch N ◆ **to be a ~ to sth** contrebalancer qch VT [*+ remark*] répliquer à (*by, with* par) ; [*+ decision, order*] aller à l'encontre de, s'opposer à ; [*+ plan*] contrecarrer, contrarier ; [*+ blow*] parer VI (*fig*) riposter, répliquer ; (*Boxing, Fencing etc*) contrer ◆ **he ~ed with a right** il a contré d'une droite

counteract /ˌkaʊntərˈækt/ VT neutraliser, contrebalancer

counter-argument /ˈkaʊntərˌɑːgjʊmənt/ N contre-argument *m*

counterattack /ˈkaʊntərəˌtæk/ (*Mil, fig*) N contre-attaque *f* VTI contre-attaquer

counterattraction /ˈkaʊntərəˌtrækʃən/ N attraction *f* concurrente, spectacle *m* rival

counterbalance /ˈkaʊntəˌbæləns/ N contrepoids *m* VT contrebalancer, faire contrepoids à

counterbid /ˈkaʊntəˌbɪd/ N surenchère *f*, suroffre *f*

counterblast /ˈkaʊntəblɑːst/ N réfutation *f* or démenti *m* énergique

countercharge /ˈkaʊntətʃɑːdʒ/ N (*Jur*) contre-accusation *f*

countercheck /ˈkaʊntətʃek/ N deuxième contrôle *m* or vérification *f* VT revérifier

counterclaim /ˈkaʊntəkleɪm/ N (*Jur*) demande *f* reconventionnelle ◆ **to bring a ~** introduire une demande reconventionnelle

counterclockwise /ˌkaʊntəˈklɒkwaɪz/ ADV, ADJ (*US*) dans le sens inverse des aiguilles d'une montre

counterculture /ˈkaʊntəˌkʌltʃəʳ/ N contre-culture *f*

counterespionage /ˌkaʊntərˈespɪəˌnɑːʒ/ N contre-espionnage *m*

counterexample /ˈkaʊntərɪgˌzɑːmpəl/ N contre-exemple *m*

counterfeit /ˈkaʊntəfɪt/ ADJ faux (fausse *f*) ◆ **~ coin/money** fausse pièce *f*/monnaie *f* N faux *m*, contrefaçon *f* VT [*+ banknote, signature*] contrefaire ◆ **to ~ money** fabriquer de la fausse monnaie

counterfoil /ˈkaʊntəfɔɪl/ N (*Brit*) [*of cheque etc*] talon *m*, souche *f*

counter-gambit /ˈkaʊntəgæmbɪt/ N contre-gambit *m*

counter-inflationary /ˌkaʊntərɪnˈfleɪʃənrɪ/ ADJ (*Brit Econ*) anti-inflationniste

counterinsurgency /ˌkaʊntərɪnˈsɜːdʒənsɪ/ N contre-insurrection *f*

counterinsurgent /ˌkaʊntərɪnˈsɜːdʒənt/ N contre-insurgé(e) *m(f)*

counterintelligence /ˌkaʊntərɪnˈtelɪdʒəns/ N contre-espionnage *m*

counterintuitive /ˌkaʊntərɪnˈtjuːɪtɪv/ ADJ contraire à l'intuition

counterirritant /ˌkaʊntərˈɪrɪtənt/ N (*Med*) révulsif *m*

counterman /ˈkaʊntəmæn/ N (pl **-men**) (*US*) serveur *m*

countermand /ˈkaʊntəmɑːnd/ VT [*+ order*] annuler ◆ **unless ~ed** sauf contrordre

countermeasure /ˈkaʊntəmeʒəʳ/ N contre-mesure *f*

countermove /ˈkaʊntəmuːv/ N (*Mil*) contre-attaque *f*, riposte *f*

counteroffensive /ˈkaʊntərəfensɪv/ N (*Mil*) contre-offensive *f*

counteroffer /ˈkaʊntərˌɒfəʳ/ N contre-offre *f*, contre-proposition *f*

counter-order /ˈkaʊntəˌrɔːdəʳ/ N contrordre *m*

counterpane /ˈkaʊntəpeɪn/ N dessus-de-lit *m inv*, couvre-lit *m* ; (*quilted*) courtepointe *f*

counterpart /ˈkaʊntəpɑːt/ N [*of document etc*] (*= duplicate*) double *m*, contrepartie *f* ; (*= equivalent*) équivalent *m* ; [*of person*] homologue *mf*

counterplea /ˈkaʊntəpliː/ N réplique *f*

counterpoint /ˈkaʊntəpɔɪnt/ N (*Mus*) contrepoint *m* VT (*fig*) contraster avec

counterpoise /ˈkaʊntəpɔɪz/ N (*= weight, force*) contrepoids *m* ; (*= equilibrium*) équilibre *m* ◆ **in ~** en équilibre VT contrebalancer, faire contrepoids à

counterproductive /ˌkaʊntəprəˈdʌktɪv/ ADJ contre-productif

counter-proposal /ˌkaʊntəprəˈpəʊzəl/ N contre-proposition *f*

Counter-Reformation /ˌkaʊntəˌrefəˈmeɪʃən/ N (*Hist*) Contre-Réforme *f*

counter-revolution /ˌkaʊntəˌrevəˈluːʃən/ N contre-révolution *f*

counter-revolutionary /ˌkaʊntəˌrevəˈluːʃənrɪ/ ADJ, N contre-révolutionnaire *mf*

counter-shot /ˈkaʊntəʃɒt/ N (*Cine*) contre-champ *m*

countersign /ˈkaʊntəsaɪn/ VT contresigner N mot *m* de passe *or* d'ordre

countersink /ˈkaʊntəsɪŋk/ VT [*+ hole*] fraiser ; [*+ screw*] noyer

counter-stroke /ˈkaʊntəstrəʊk/ N (*lit, fig*) retour *m* offensif

countersunk /ˈkaʊntəsʌŋk/ ADJ fraisé

countertenor /ˌkaʊntəˈtenəʳ/ N *(Mus)* *(= singer)* haute-contre *m* ; *(= voice)* haute-contre *f*

counter(-)terrorism /ˌkaʊntəˈterərɪzm/ N antiterrorisme *m* ◆ ~ **official/agent** responsable/agent de l'antiterrorisme

counter-terrorist /ˌkaʊntəˈterərɪst/ ADJ antiterroriste

countertop /ˈkaʊntətɒp/ N *(US)* plan *m* de travail

counter-turn /ˈkaʊntətɜːn/ N *(Ski)* contre-virage *m*

countervailing /ˈkaʊntəveɪlɪŋ/ ADJ *(Fin)* ◆ ~ **duties** droits *mpl* compensatoires

counterweight /ˈkaʊntəweɪt/ N contrepoids *m*

countess /ˈkaʊntɪs/ N comtesse *f*

counting /ˈkaʊntɪŋ/ N *(= school subject)* calcul *m* COMP **counting house** † N *(Brit)* salle *f* or immeuble *m* des comptables

countless /ˈkaʊntlɪs/ ADJ innombrable, sans nombre ◆ **on** ~ **occasions** en d'innombrables occasions ◆ ~ **millions of ...** des millions et des millions de ...

countrified /ˈkʌntrɪfaɪd/ ADJ rustique, campagnard

country /ˈkʌntrɪ/ N 1 pays *m* ◆ **the different countries of the world** les divers pays *mpl* du monde ◆ **the** ~ **wants peace** le pays désire la paix ◆ **to go to the** ~ *(Brit Pol)* appeler le pays aux urnes

2 *(= native land)* patrie *f*, pays *m* ◆ **to die for one's** ~ mourir pour son pays ; → **old**

3 *(NonC: as opposed to town)* campagne *f* ◆ **in the** ~ à la campagne ◆ **the** ~ **round the town** les environs *mpl* de la ville ◆ **the surrounding** ~ la campagne environnante ◆ **to live off the** ~ *(gen)* vivre de la terre ; *(Mil)* vivre sur le pays

4 *(NonC = region)* pays *m*, région *f* ◆ **there is some lovely** ~ **to the north** il y a de beaux paysages *mpl* dans le nord ◆ **mountainous** ~ région *f* montagneuse ◆ **this is good fishing** ~ c'est une bonne région pour la pêche ◆ **this is unknown** ~ **to me** *(lit)* je ne connais pas la région ; *(fig)* je suis en terrain inconnu ; → **open**

COMP *[lifestyle]* campagnard, de (la) campagne
country-and-western N *(Mus)* musique *f* country (and western)
country-born ADJ né à la campagne
country-bred ADJ élevé à la campagne
country bumpkin N *(pej)* péquenaud(e)* *m(f)* *(pej)*, cul-terreux* *m* *(pej)*
country club N club *m* de loisirs *(à la campagne)*
the country code N *(Brit)* les us *mpl* et coutumes *fpl* de la campagne
country cottage N cottage *m*, petite maison *f* (à la campagne) ; *[of weekenders]* maison *f* de campagne
country cousin N *(fig)* cousin(e) *m(f)* de province
country dance *(NonC)*, **country dancing** N danse *f* folklorique ◆ **to go** ~ **dancing** danser (des danses folkloriques)
country dweller N campagnard(e) *m(f)*, habitant(e) *m(f)* de la campagne
country folk NPL gens *mpl* de la campagne, campagnards *mpl*
country gentleman N (pl **country gentlemen**) gentilhomme *m* campagnard
country house N manoir *m*, (petit) château *m*
country life N vie *f* à la campagne, vie *f* campagnarde
country mile* N *(US)* ◆ **to miss sth by a** ~ **mile** manquer qch de beaucoup
country music N *(NonC)* (musique *f*) country *m*
country park N *(Brit)* parc *m* naturel
country people N *(NonC)* campagnards *mpl*, gens *mpl* de la campagne
country road N petite route *f* (de campagne)
country seat N manoir *m*, gentilhommière *f*

countryman /ˈkʌntrɪmæn/ N (pl **-men**) (also **fellow countryman**) compatriote *m*, concitoyen *m* ; *(opposed to town dweller)* habitant *m* de la campagne, campagnard *m*

countryside /ˈkʌntrɪsaɪd/ N ◆ **the** ~ la campagne COMP **the Countryside Commission** N *(Brit)* *organisme chargé de la protection du milieu rural*

countrywide /ˈkʌntrɪwaɪd/ ADJ à l'échelle nationale

countrywoman /ˈkʌntrɪwʊmən/ N (pl **-women**) (also **fellow countrywoman**) compatriote *f*, concitoyenne *f* ; *(opposed to town dweller)* habitante *f* de la campagne, campagnarde *f*

county /ˈkaʊntɪ/ N 1 comté *m* *(division administrative)*, ≈ département *m* ; → **home** 2 *(= people)* habitants *mpl* d'un comté ◆ **the** ~ *(Brit)* *(= nobility etc)* l'aristocratie *f* terrienne *(du comté)* ADJ *(Brit)* *[voice, accent]* aristocratique ◆ **he's very** ~ il est *or* fait très aristocratie terrienne

COMP **county agent** N *(US)* ingénieur-agronome *m*
county clerk N *(US Admin)* ≈ sous-préfet *m*
county council N *(in Brit: formerly)* ≈ conseil *m* régional
county court N ≈ tribunal *m* de grande instance
county cricket N *(Brit)* *le cricket disputé entre les comtés*
county family N *(Brit)* vieille famille *f*
county jail N *(US)* → **county prison**
county police N *(US)* police *f* régionale, ≈ gendarmerie *f*
county prison N centrale *f*
county seat N *(US)* ⇒ **county town**
county town N chef-lieu *m*

coup /kuː/ N (beau) coup *m* *(fig)* *(Pol)* coup *m* d'État

coupé /ˈkuːpeɪ/ N *(= car)* coupé *m*

couple /ˈkʌpl/ N couple *m* ◆ **the young (married)** ~ les jeunes mariés, le jeune couple ◆ **a** ~ **of** deux ◆ **I've seen him a** ~ **of times** je l'ai vu deux ou trois fois ◆ **I did it in a** ~ **of hours** je l'ai fait en deux heures environ ◆ **we had a** ~* **in the bar** nous avons pris un verre ou deux au bar ◆ **when he's had a** ~* **he begins to sing** après un ou deux verres, il se met à chanter ; → **first** VT 1 (also **couple up**) *[+ railway carriages]* atteler, (ac)coupler ; *[+ ideas, names]* associer 2 ◆ **~d with** ajouté à ◆ **~d with the fact that ...** venant en plus du fait que ... VI *(= mate)* s'accoupler

coupledom /ˈkʌpldəm/ N la vie de couple

coupler /ˈkʌpləʳ/ N *(Comput)* coupleur *m* ; *(US Rail)* attelage *m* ◆ **acoustic** ~ *(Comput)* coupleur *m* acoustique

couplet /ˈkʌplɪt/ N distique *m*

coupling /ˈkʌplɪŋ/ N 1 *(NonC)* *(= combination)* association *f* 2 *(= device)* *(Rail)* attelage *m* ; *(Elec)* couplage *m* 3 *(= sexual intercourse)* accouplement *m*

coupon /ˈkuːpɒn/ N *(= money-off voucher)* bon *m* de réduction ; *(= form in newspaper, magazine)* bulletin-réponse *m* ; *(for rationed product)* ticket *m* or carte *f* de rationnement ; *[of cigarette packets etc]* bon *m*, vignette *f* ; → **international**

courage /ˈkʌrɪdʒ/ N courage *m* ◆ **I haven't the** ~ **to refuse** je n'ai pas le courage de refuser ◆ **to take/lose** ~ prendre/perdre courage ◆ **to take** ~ **from sth** être encouragé par qch ◆ **to have the** ~ **of one's convictions** avoir le courage de ses opinions ◆ **to take one's** ~ **in both hands** prendre son courage à deux mains ; → **Dutch, pluck up**

courageous /kəˈreɪdʒəs/ ADJ courageux

courageously /kəˈreɪdʒəslɪ/ ADV courageusement

courgette /kʊəˈʒet/ N *(Brit)* courgette *f*

courier /ˈkʊrɪəʳ/ N 1 *(= messenger)* *(gen)* messager *m* ; *(Mil)* courrier *m* ; *[of urgent mail]* coursier *m*, -ière *f* 2 *(= tourist guide)* guide *m* VT *(= send)* envoyer par coursier COMP **courier service** N messagerie *f*

> ⚠ **courier** is only translated by the French word **courrier** in the military sense. The commonest sense of **courrier** is 'mail'.

course /kɔːs/ N 1

◆ **of course** bien sûr, bien entendu ◆ **did he do it? – of ~!/of ~ not!** est-ce qu'il l'a fait ? – bien sûr *or* bien entendu !/bien sûr que non ! ◆ **may I take it? – of ~!** est-ce que je peux le prendre ? – bien sûr *or* mais oui ! ◆ **do you mind? – of ~ not!** ça vous dérange ? – bien sûr que non ! ◆ **do you love him? – of ~ I do!/of ~ I don't!** tu l'aimes ? – bien sûr (que je l'aime) !/bien sûr que non ! ◆ **of ~ I won't do it!** je ne vais pas faire ça, bien sûr ! ◆ **he denied it; nobody believed him of** ~ il l'a nié ; bien sûr, personne ne l'a cru ◆ **you'll come on Saturday of** ~ vous viendrez samedi bien sûr

2 *(= duration, process)* *[of life, events, time, disease]* cours *m* ◆ **in the normal/ordinary ~ of things** *or* **events** en temps normal/ordinaire

◆ **in the course of** au cours de ◆ **in the ~ of the conversation** au cours de la conversation ◆ **in the ~ of the next few months** au cours des prochains mois ◆ **in the ~ of time** avec le temps ◆ **in the ~ of the week** dans le courant de la semaine ; → **due, matter**

3 *(= direction, way, route)* *[of river, war]* cours *m* ; *[of ship]* route *f* ; *[of planet]* trajectoire *f*, orbite *f* ◆ **to keep** *or* **hold one's** ~ poursuivre sa route ◆ **to hold (one's)** ~ *(at sea)* garder le cap ◆ **on** ~ *[rocket]* sur la bonne trajectoire ◆ **on ~ for** *(lit)* en route pour ◆ **the team is on ~ for a place in the finals** l'équipe est bien partie pour une qualification en finale ◆ **to set ~ for** *(at sea)* mettre le cap sur ◆ **to change** ~ *(at sea, fig)* changer de cap ◆ **to change the ~ of history** changer le cours de l'histoire ◆ **to get back on** ~ *[ship]* reprendre son cap ◆ **to go off** ~ *(ship, aircraft)* dévier de son cap ; *(fig)* faire fausse route ◆ **to let sth take its** ~ laisser qch suivre son cours ◆ **to let events run their** ~ laisser les événements suivre leur cours ◆ **the affair/the illness has run its** ~ l'affaire/la maladie a suivi son cours ; → **middle**

4 *(= option)* solution *f* ◆ **we have no other ~ but to ...** nous n'avons pas d'autre solution que de ... ◆ **the best ~ would be to leave at once** la meilleure solution serait de partir immédiatement ◆ **there are several ~s open to us** plusieurs possibilités s'offrent à nous ◆ **what ~ do you suggest?** quel parti (nous) conseillez-vous de prendre ? ◆ **let him take his own** ~ laissez-le agir à sa guise *or* comme bon lui semble ◆ **to take a certain ~ of action** adopter une certaine ligne de conduite

5 *(Scol, Univ)* cours *m* ; *(non-academic)* stage *m* ◆ **he did a three-year computing** ~ il a fait trois ans d'études en informatique ◆ **the firm sent me on a two-week computing** ~ mon entreprise m'a envoyé en stage d'informatique pendant deux semaines ◆ **a summer English** ~ un stage d'anglais d'été ◆ **to do a French** ~ suivre des cours de français ◆ **a creative writing** ~ un cours (*or* un stage) de création littéraire ◆ **the people on the ~ are really nice** les gens du cours (*or* du stage) sont vraiment sympathiques ◆ **he gave a ~ of lectures on Proust** il a donné une série de conférences sur Proust ◆ **I have bought part two of the German** ~ j'ai acheté la deuxième partie de la méthode *or* du cours d'allemand ; → **correspondence, foundation, refresher, sandwich**

6 (*Sport*) (*gen*) parcours *m* ; (*Golf etc*) terrain *m* ; → **assault, golf, racecourse, stay**[1]

7 [*of meal*] plat *m* ◆ **first** ~ entrée *f* ◆ **three-/four-~ meal** repas *m* de trois/quatre plats ; → **main**

8 (*Med*) [*of injections*] série *f* ◆ **~ of pills** traitement *m* à base de comprimés ◆ **~ of treatment** traitement *m*

9 (*Constr*) assise *f* (*de briques etc*) ; → **damp**

NPL **courses** (*Naut*) basses voiles *fpl*

VI 1 [*water*] couler à flots ◆ **tears ~d down her cheeks** les larmes ruisselaient sur ses joues ◆ **it sent the blood coursing through his veins** cela lui fouetta le sang

2 (*Sport*) chasser (le lièvre)

VT (*Sport*) [+ *hare*] courir, chasser

COMP **course of study** N (*Scol*) programme *m* scolaire ; (*Univ*) cursus *m* universitaire

course work N (*NonC: Univ*) (= *assessment*) contrôle *m* continu ; (= *work*) devoirs *mpl* (*comptant pour le contrôle continu*)

coursebook /ˈkɔːsbʊk/ N (*Scol*) manuel *m*

courser /ˈkɔːsəʳ/ N (= *person*) chasseur *m* (*gén de lièvres*) ; (= *dog*) chien *m* courant ; (*liter*) (= *horse*) coursier *m* (*liter*)

coursing /ˈkɔːsɪŋ/ N (*Sport*) chasse *f* au lièvre

court /kɔːt/ N 1 (*Jur*) cour *f*, tribunal *m* ◆ **tell the ~ what you heard** dites à la cour ce que vous avez entendu ◆ **to settle a case out of ~** arranger une affaire à l'amiable ◆ **to rule sth out of ~** déclarer qch inadmissible ◆ **to take sb to ~ over** *or* **about sth** poursuivre qn en justice pour qch, intenter un procès contre qn pour qch ◆ **he was brought before the ~s several times** il est passé plusieurs fois en jugement ◆ **to clear the ~** (*Jur*) faire évacuer la salle ◆ **to give sb a day in ~*** (*esp US fig*) donner à qn l'occasion de s'expliquer *or* de se faire entendre ; → **high, law**

2 [*of monarch*] cour *f* (royale) ◆ **the Court of St James** la cour de Saint-James ◆ **to be at ~** (*for short time*) être à la cour ; (*for long time*) faire partie de la cour ◆ **to hold ~** (*fig*) être entouré de sa cour

3 ◆ **to pay ~ to a woman** † faire sa *or* la cour à une femme

4 (*Tennis*) court *m* ; (*Basketball*) terrain *m* ◆ **they've been on ~ for two hours** (*Tennis*) cela fait deux heures qu'ils sont sur le court *or* qu'ils jouent

5 (*also* **courtyard**) cour *f* ; (= *passage between houses*) ruelle *f*, venelle *f*

VT [+ *woman*] faire la *or* sa cour à, courtiser ; [+ *sb's favour*] solliciter, rechercher ; [+ *danger, defeat*] aller au-devant de, s'exposer à

VI ◆ **they are ~ing** † ils sortent ensemble ◆ **are you ~ing?** † tu as un petit copain* (*or* une petite amie*) ?

COMP **court card** N (*esp Brit*) figure *f* (*de jeu de cartes*)

court case N procès *m*, affaire *f*

court circular N bulletin *m* quotidien de la cour

court correspondent N (*Brit Press*) correspondant(e) *m(f)* chargé(e) des affaires royales

courting couple † N couple *m* d'amoureux

court of appeal (*Brit*), **court of appeals** (*US*) N cour *f* d'appel

Court of Claims N (*US*) *tribunal fédéral chargé de régler les réclamations contre l'État*

court of competent jurisdiction N tribunal *m* compétent

court of inquiry N commission *f* d'enquête

Court of International Trade N (*US*) *tribunal de commerce international*

court of justice N cour *f* de justice

court of last resort N (*US*) tribunal *m* jugeant en dernier ressort

Court of Session N (*Scot*) cour *f* de cassation

court order N (*Jur*) ordonnance *f* du (*or* d'un) tribunal

court record N (*US Jur*) compte rendu *m* d'audience

court reporter N (*Jur*) greffier *m*, -ière *f* ; (*Brit Press*) ⇒ **court correspondent**

court room N ⇒ **courtroom**

court shoe N (*Brit*) escarpin *m*

Courtelle ® /kɔːˈtel/ N Courtelle ® *m*

courteous /ˈkɜːtɪəs/ ADJ courtois (*towards* envers)

courteously /ˈkɜːtɪəslɪ/ ADV courtoisement

courtesan /ˌkɔːtɪˈzæn/ N courtisane *f*

courtesy /ˈkɜːtɪsɪ/ N courtoisie *f* ◆ **you might have had the ~ to explain yourself** vous auriez pu avoir la courtoisie de vous expliquer ◆ **will you do me the ~ of reading it?** auriez-vous l'obligeance de le lire ? ◆ **an exchange of courtesies** un échange de politesses

◆ **courtesy of** ◆ **two glasses of champagne, ~ of the restaurant** deux verres de champagne offerts par la direction ◆ **illustrations by ~ of the National Gallery** illustrations reproduites avec l'aimable autorisation de la National Gallery

COMP **courtesy bus** N navette *f* gratuite

courtesy call N (= *visit*) visite *f* de politesse ; (*euph* = *cold call*) démarchage *m* téléphonique

courtesy car N *voiture gracieusement mise à la disposition d'un client* ; (*provided by insurance company, garage etc*) véhicule *m* de remplacement

courtesy card N (*US*) carte *f* privilège (*utilisable dans les hôtels, banques etc*)

courtesy coach N (*Brit*) ⇒ **courtesy bus**

courtesy light N (*in car*) plafonnier *m*

courtesy title N titre *m* de courtoisie

courtesy visit N ⇒ **courtesy call**

courthouse /ˈkɔːthaʊs/ N palais *m* de justice, tribunal *m*

courtier /ˈkɔːtɪəʳ/ N courtisan *m*, dame *f* de la cour

courtly /ˈkɔːtlɪ/ ADJ élégant, raffiné COMP **courtly love** N (*Hist, Literat*) amour *m* courtois

court martial /ˈkɔːtˈmɑːʃəl/ N (*pl* **courts martial** *or* **court martials**) (*Mil*) cour *f* martiale ◆ **to be tried by ~** passer en cour *f* martiale VT ◆ **court-martial** traduire *or* faire passer en conseil de guerre

courtroom /ˈkɔːtruːm/ N salle *f* d'audience ◆ **~ drama** (*Cine, TV*) drame *m* judiciaire

courtship /ˈkɔːtʃɪp/ N ◆ **his ~ of her** la cour qu'il lui fait (*or* faisait *etc*) ◆ **during their ~** au temps où ils sortaient ensemble COMP **courtship display** N [*of birds, animals*] parade *f* nuptiale

courtyard /ˈkɔːtjɑːd/ N cour *f* (*de maison, de château*)

couscous /ˈkuːskuːs/ N couscous *m*

cousin /ˈkʌzn/ N cousin(e) *m(f)* ; → **country, first**

couth* /kuːθ/ ADJ raffiné N bonnes manières *fpl*

couture /kuːˈtjʊə/ N (*NonC*) haute couture *f*

couturier /kuːˈtʊərɪeɪ/ N grand couturier *m*

cove[1] /kəʊv/ N (*Geog*) crique *f*, anse *f* ; (= *cavern*) caverne *f* naturelle ; (*US*) vallon *m* encaissé

cove[2]‡ /kəʊv/ N (*Brit* = *fellow*) mec‡ *m*

coven /ˈkʌvən/ N assemblée *f* de sorcières

covenant /ˈkʌvɪnənt/ N (*gen*) convention *f*, engagement *m* formel ; (*Brit Fin*) engagement *m* contractuel ; (*Jewish Hist*) alliance *f* ◆ **the Covenant** (*Scot Hist*) le Covenant (*de 1638*) ; → **deed** VT s'engager (*to do sth* à faire qch) convenir (*to do sth de faire qch*) ; ◆ **to ~ (to pay) £100 per annum to a charity** (*Fin*) s'engager par contrat à verser 100 livres par an à une œuvre VI convenir (*with sb for sth* de qch avec qn)

covenanter /ˈkʌvɪnəntəʳ/ N (*Scot Hist*) covenantaire *mf* (*adhérent au Covenant de 1638*)

Coventry /ˈkɒvəntrɪ/ N Coventry ◆ **to send sb to ~** (*Brit*) mettre qn en quarantaine

cover /ˈkʌvəʳ/

1 NOUN	3 COMPOUNDS
2 TRANSITIVE VERB	4 PHRASAL VERBS

1 – NOUN

1 [for protection] [*of table*] nappe *f* ; [*of umbrella*] fourreau *m*, étui *m* ; (*over furniture, typewriter*) housse *f* ; (*over merchandise, vehicle etc*) bâche *f* ; [*of lens*] bouchon *m* ; [*of book*] couverture *f* ; (= *lid*) couvercle *m* ; (= *envelope*) enveloppe *f* ◆ **to read a book from ~ to ~** lire un livre de la première à la dernière page ◆ **under separate ~** (*Comm*) sous pli séparé ; → **first, loose, plain**

2 [for bed, bedcover] dessus-de-lit *m inv* ◆ **the ~s** (= *bedclothes*) les couvertures *fpl*

3 [= shelter] abri *m* ; (*Hunting: for game*) fourré *m*, abri *m* ; (*Mil etc* = *covering fire*) feu *m* de couverture *or* de protection ◆ **there was no ~ for miles around** (*Mil, gen*) il n'y avait aucun abri à des kilomètres à la ronde ◆ **he was looking for some ~** il cherchait un abri

◆ **to break cover** [*animal*] débusquer ; [*hunted person*] sortir à découvert

◆ **to give sb cover** ◆ **the trees gave him ~** (= *hid him*) les arbres le cachaient ; (= *sheltered him*) les arbres l'abritaient ◆ **give me ~!** (*to soldier etc*) couvrez-moi !

◆ **to run for cover** courir se mettre à l'abri ◆ **critics within his own party are already running for ~** c'est déjà le sauve-qui-peut général parmi ses détracteurs à l'intérieur de son propre parti

◆ **to take cover** (= *hide*) se cacher ; (*Mil*) se mettre à couvert ; (= *shelter*) s'abriter, se mettre à l'abri ◆ **to take ~ from the rain/the bombing** se mettre à l'abri *or* s'abriter de la pluie/des bombes ◆ **to take ~ from enemy fire** (*Mil*) se mettre à l'abri du feu ennemi

◆ **under cover** à l'abri, à couvert ◆ **to get under ~** se mettre à l'abri *or* à couvert ◆ **under ~ of darkness** à la faveur de la nuit ◆ **under ~ of diplomacy** sous couvert de diplomatie ; → **undercover**

4 [Fin] couverture *f*, provision *f* ◆ **to operate without ~** opérer à découvert

5 [Brit Insurance] couverture *f*, garantie *f* (d'assurances) (*against* contre) ; ◆ **~ for a building against fire** *etc* couverture *f or* garantie *f* d'un immeuble contre l'incendie *etc* ◆ **full ~** garantie *f* totale *or* tous risques ◆ **fire ~** assurance-incendie *f* ◆ **they've got no (insurance) ~ for** *or* **on this** ils ne sont pas assurés pour *or* contre cela ◆ **we must extend our (insurance) ~** nous devons augmenter le montant de notre garantie (d'assurances) ◆ **the (insurance) ~ ends on 5 July** le contrat d'assurances *or* la police d'assurances expire le 5 juillet

6 [in espionage etc] fausse identité *f*, couverture *f* ◆ **what's your ~?** quelle est votre couverture ? ◆ **to blow sb's ~** démasquer qn ◆ **the conference was merely a ~ for an illegal political gathering** en fait, la conférence servait de couverture à un rassemblement politique illégal

7 [for meal] couvert *m* ◆ **~s laid for six** une table de six couverts

8 [= cover version] reprise *f*

2 – TRANSITIVE VERB

1 [+ objet, person] couvrir (*with* de) ; ◆ **snow ~s the ground** la neige recouvre le sol ◆ **ground ~ed with leaves** sol *m* couvert de feuilles ◆ **he**

~ed the paper with scribbles il a couvert la page de gribouillages ◆ **the car ~ed us in mud** la voiture nous a couverts de boue ◆ **to ~ one's eyes** *(when crying)* se couvrir les yeux ; *(against sun etc)* se protéger les yeux ◆ **to ~ one's face with one's hands** se couvrir le visage des mains ◆ **to be ~ed in** *or* **with snow/dust/chocolate** être couvert de neige/de poussière/de chocolat ◆ **~ed with confusion** confus ◆ **to ~ o.s. with ridicule** se couvrir de ridicule ◆ **to ~ o.s. with glory** se couvrir de gloire

2 [+ book, chair] recouvrir, couvrir (*with* de)

3 [= hide] *[+ feelings, facts]* dissimuler, cacher ; *[+ noise]* couvrir ◆ **to ~ (up) one's tracks** *(lit)* effacer ses traces ; *(fig)* brouiller les pistes *or* les cartes

4 [= protect] *[+ person]* couvrir, protéger ◆ **the soldiers ~ed our retreat** les soldats ont couvert notre retraite ◆ **he only said that to ~ himself** il n'a dit cela que pour se couvrir ◆ **to ~ one's back** *or* **rear** *or* **ass**** se couvrir

5 [Insurance] couvrir ◆ **the house is ~ed against fire** *etc* l'immeuble est couvert contre l'incendie *etc* ◆ **it doesn't ~ you for** *or* **against flood damage** vous n'êtes pas couvert contre les dégâts des eaux ◆ **it ~s (for) fire only** cela ne couvre que l'incendie ◆ **what does your travel insurance ~ you for?** contre quoi êtes-vous couvert avec votre assurance voyage ?

6 [= point gun at] *[+ person]* braquer un revolver sur, braquer* ◆ **to keep sb ~ed** tenir qn sous la menace d'un revolver ◆ **I've got you ~ed!** ne bougez pas ou je tire !

7 [Sport] *[+ opponent]* marquer

8 [+ distance] parcourir, couvrir ◆ **we ~ed 8km in two hours** nous avons parcouru *or* couvert 8 km en deux heures ◆ **we ~ed 300 miles on just one tank of petrol** nous avons fait 300 miles avec un seul plein d'essence ◆ **to ~ a lot of ground** *(travelling)* faire beaucoup de chemin ; *(= deal with many subjects)* traiter un large éventail de questions ; *(= do large amount of work)* faire du bon travail

9 [= be sufficient for] couvrir ◆ **£50 will ~ everything** 50 livres suffiront (à couvrir toutes les dépenses) ◆ **in order to ~ the monthly payments** pour faire face aux mensualités ◆ **to ~ one's costs** *or* **expenses** rentrer dans ses frais ◆ **to ~ a deficit/a loss** combler un déficit/une perte

10 [= take in, include] englober, comprendre ◆ **his work ~s many different fields** son travail englobe de nombreux domaines ◆ **goods ~ed by this invoice** les marchandises faisant l'objet de cette facture ◆ **in order to ~ all possibilities** pour parer à toute éventualité

11 [= deal with] traiter ◆ **the book ~s the subject thoroughly** le livre traite le sujet à fond ◆ **the article ~s the 18th century** l'article traite tout le 18e siècle ◆ **his speech ~ed most of the points raised** dans son discours il a traité la plupart des points en question ◆ **such factories will not be ~ed by this report** ce rapport ne traitera pas de ces usines ◆ **no law ~s a situation like that** aucune loi ne prévoit une telle situation

12 [Press etc] *[+ news, story, scandal]* assurer la couverture de ; *[+ lawsuit]* faire le compte rendu de ◆ **he was sent to ~ the riots** on l'a envoyé assurer le reportage des émeutes ◆ **all the newspapers ~ed the story** les journaux ont tous parlé de l'affaire

13 [Mus] reprendre ◆ **to ~ a song** reprendre une chanson

14 [= inseminate] *[animal]* couvrir

3 - COMPOUNDS

cover charge N *(in restaurant)* couvert *m*
covered market N marché *m* couvert
covered wagon N chariot *m* couvert *or* bâché
cover letter N *(US)* ⇒ **covering letter** ; → **covering**
cover-mounted ADJ *[cassette, CD]* donné en prime ; → **covermount**
cover note N *(Brit Insurance)* attestation *f* provisoire d'assurance
cover price N *[of newspaper, magazine]* prix *m* de vente (au numéro) ; *[of book]* prix *m* conseillé
cover story N *(Press)* article *m* principal ; *(in espionage etc)* couverture *f* ◆ **our ~ story this week** en couverture cette semaine
cover-up N ◆ **there's been a ~-up** on a tenté d'étouffer l'affaire
cover version N *(Mus)* reprise *f*

4 - PHRASAL VERBS

► **cover for** VT FUS 1 *(= protect) [+ person]* couvrir, protéger ; *(Insurance) [+ risk]* couvrir ◆ **why would she ~ for him if he's trying to kill her?** pourquoi voudrait-elle le couvrir *or* le protéger s'il cherche à la tuer ?
2 *(= stand in for)* remplacer

► **cover in** VT SEP *[+ trench, grave]* remplir

► **cover over** VT SEP recouvrir

► **cover up** VI 1 se couvrir ◆ **it's cold, ~ up warmly** il fait froid, couvre-toi chaudement
2 ◆ **to cover up for sb** couvrir qn, protéger qn
VT SEP 1 *[+ object]* recouvrir, envelopper ; *[+ child]* couvrir
2 *(= hide) [+ truth, facts]* dissimuler, cacher ; *[+ affair]* étouffer ; → **cover transitive verb 3**

coverage /ˈkʌvərɪdʒ/ N 1 *(Press, Rad, TV)* reportage *m* ◆ **to give full ~ to an event** assurer la couverture complète d'un événement, traiter à fond un événement ◆ **the match got nationwide ~** le match a été retransmis *or* diffusé dans tout le pays ◆ **it got full-page ~ in the main dailies** les principaux quotidiens y ont consacré une page entière 2 *(Insurance)* couverture *f*

coveralls /ˈkʌvərɔːlz/ NPL bleu(s) *m(pl)* de travail, salopette *f*

covergirl /ˈkʌvəgɜːl/ N cover-girl *f*

covering /ˈkʌvərɪŋ/ N *(= wrapping etc)* couverture *f*, enveloppe *f* ; *(= layer) [of snow, dust etc]* couche *f*
COMP **covering fire** N *(Mil)* feu *m* de protection *or* de couverture
covering letter N *(Brit)* lettre *f* explicative

coverlet /ˈkʌvəlɪt/ N dessus-de-lit *m inv*, couvre-lit *m* ; *(quilted)* courtepointe *f*

covermount /ˈkʌvəmaʊnt/ N *CD, vidéo etc donné avec un magazine*

covert /ˈkʌvət/ ADJ *[threat]* voilé, caché ; *[attack]* indirect ; *[glance]* furtif, dérobé ; *[operation, action, surveillance]* clandestin ; *[homosexuality]* refoulé N *(Hunting)* fourré *m*, couvert *m* ; *(= animal's hiding place)* gîte *m*, terrier *m*

covertly /ˈkʌvətlɪ/ ADV *(gen)* en secret ; *[watch]* à la dérobée ◆ **to film sb ~** filmer qn à son insu

covet /ˈkʌvɪt/ VT *(frm)* convoiter

covetous /ˈkʌvɪtəs/ ADJ *(frm) [person, attitude, nature]* avide ; *[look]* de convoitise ◆ **to cast ~ eyes on sth** regarder qch avec convoitise

covetously /ˈkʌvɪtəslɪ/ ADV *(frm)* avec convoitise

covetousness /ˈkʌvɪtəsnɪs/ N *(frm)* convoitise *f*

covey /ˈkʌvɪ/ N compagnie *f (de perdrix)*

cow[1] /kaʊ/ N 1 vache *f* ; *(= female) [of elephant etc]* femelle *f* ; *(= female buffalo etc)* buffle *m etc* femelle ◆ **till the ~s come home*** jusqu'à la saint-glinglin* *or* jusqu'à perpète* 2 *(** pej = woman)* vache* *f*, chameau* *m* ◆ **she's a cheeky ~** elle est sacrément* culottée ◆ **you're a lazy ~!** tu es une sacrée* fainéante ! ◆ **that nosey ~** cette sacrée* fouineuse ◆ **silly** *or* **stupid ~!** pauvre conne !**
COMP **cow college*** N *(US) (= provincial college)* boîte *f* dans un trou perdu* ; *(= agricultural college)* école *f* d'agriculture
cow parsley N cerfeuil *m* sauvage

cow[2] /kaʊ/ VT *[+ person]* effrayer, intimider ◆ **a ~ed look** un air de chien battu

coward /ˈkaʊəd/ N lâche *mf*, poltron(ne) *m(f)*

cowardice /ˈkaʊədɪs/, **cowardliness** /ˈkaʊədlɪnɪs/ N lâcheté *f*

cowardly /ˈkaʊədlɪ/ ADJ *[person]* lâche, poltron ; *[action, words]* lâche

cowbell /ˈkaʊbel/ N cloche *f* de *or* à vache

cowboy /ˈkaʊbɔɪ/ N cow-boy *m* ; *(Brit * pej)* fumiste *m* ◆ **to play ~s and Indians** jouer aux cow-boys et aux Indiens ADJ *(Brit * pej)* pas sérieux, fumiste
COMP **cowboy boots** NPL santiags* *mpl*
cowboy hat N chapeau *m* de cow-boy, feutre *m* à larges bords

cowcatcher /ˈkaʊkætʃəʳ/ N *(Rail)* chasse-pierres *m inv*

cower /ˈkaʊəʳ/ VI (also **cower down**) se tapir, se recroqueviller ◆ **to ~ before sb** *(fig)* trembler devant qn

cowgirl /ˈkaʊgɜːl/ N vachère *f* à cheval

cowherd /ˈkaʊhɜːd/ N vacher *m*, -ère *f*, bouvier *m*, -ière *f*

cowhide /ˈkaʊhaɪd/ N *(= skin)* peau *f or* cuir *m* de vache ; *(US = whip)* fouet *m* (à lanière de cuir) VT *(US)* fouetter (avec une lanière de cuir)

cowl /kaʊl/ N 1 *(= hood)* capuchon *m (de moine)* ◆ **~ neck(line)** col *m* boule 2 *[of chimney]* capuchon *m*

cowlick /ˈkaʊlɪk/ N épi *m*

cowling /ˈkaʊlɪŋ/ N capotage *m*

cowman /ˈkaʊmən/ N (pl **-men**) *(Brit)* ⇒ **cowherd**

co-worker /ˈkəʊˈwɜːkəʳ/ N collègue *mf*, camarade *mf* (de travail)

cowpat /ˈkaʊpæt/ N bouse *f* (de vache)

cowpea /ˈkaʊpiː/ N *(US)* dolique *m or* dolic *m*

cowpoke /ˈkaʊpəʊk/ N *(US)* cowboy *m*

cowpox /ˈkaʊpɒks/ N vaccine *f*, cow-pox *m* ◆ **~ vaccine** vaccin *m* antivariolique

cowpuncher* /ˈkaʊpʌntʃəʳ/ N *(US)* ⇒ **cowboy**

cowrie, cowry /ˈkaʊrɪ/ N cauri *m*

cowshed /ˈkaʊʃed/ N étable *f*

cowslip /ˈkaʊslɪp/ N coucou *m*, primevère *f* ; *(US = marsh marigold)* populage *m*

cowtown /ˈkaʊtaʊn/ N *(US pej)* bled* *m*, patelin* *m*

cox /kɒks/ N *(Rowing)* barreur *m* VT *(Rowing) [+ boat]* barrer, gouverner ◆ **~ed four** quatre *m* barré, quatre *m* avec barreur VI *(Rowing)* barrer

coxcomb † /ˈkɒkskəʊm/ N fat † *m*

coxless /ˈkɒkslɪs/ ADJ *(Rowing)* ◆ **~ four** quatre *m* sans barreur

coxswain /ˈkɒksn/ N *(Rowing)* barreur *m* ; *(Naut)* patron *m*

coy /kɔɪ/ ADJ 1 *(= demure) [person, look, smile]* faussement timide ◆ **to go (all) ~*** faire la sainte nitouche *(pej)* 2 *(= evasive) [person]* évasif (*about sth* à propos de qch) ; ◆ **they maintained a ~ refusal to disclose his name** ils ont continué à se montrer évasifs lorsqu'on leur demandait de révéler son nom 3 *(= twee) [picture, rhyme]* mièvre

coyly /ˈkɔɪlɪ/ ADV 1 *(= demurely) [describe]* par euphémisme ◆ **to look at/smile ~** regarder/sourire avec une fausse timidité, regarder/sourire avec un air de sainte nitouche *(pej)* 2 *(= evasively) [say, answer, refuse]* évasivement

coyness /ˈkɔɪnɪs/ N (NonC) [1] (= *demureness*) *[of person]* fausse timidité *f* [2] (= *evasiveness*) *[of person, film, book]* réserve *f* (*about sth* quant à qch) [3] (= *tweeness*) *[of picture, rhyme]* mièvrerie *f*

coyote /kɔɪˈəʊtɪ/ N coyote *m* ◆ **the Coyote State** le Dakota du Sud

coypu /ˈkɔɪpuː/ N (pl **coypus** or **coypu**) coypou *m*, ragondin *m*

cozily /ˈkəʊzɪlɪ/ ADV (US) ⇒ **cosily**

cozy /ˈkəʊzɪ/ (US) ⇒ **cosy**

cozzie * /ˈkɒzɪ/ N (*Brit, Austral*) ⇒ **cossie**

CP /siːˈpiː/ N [1] abbrev of **Cape Province** [2] abbrev of **Communist Party**

c/p (abbrev of **carriage paid**) → **carriage**

CPA /ˌsiːpiːˈeɪ/ N (*US Fin*) (abbrev of **certified public accountant**) → **certify**

CPI /ˌsiːpiːˈaɪ/ N (US) (abbrev of **Consumer Price Index**) → **consumer**

cpi /ˌsiːpiːˈaɪ/ (*Comput*) (abbrev of **characters per inch**) CCPP *mpl*

Cpl (*Mil*) abbrev of **corporal**

CP/M /ˌsiːpiːˈem/ (abbrev of **Control Program for Microprocessors**) CP/M *m*

CPO /ˌsiːpiːˈəʊ/ N (*Naut*) (abbrev of **chief petty officer**) → **chief**

CPR /ˌsiːpiːˈɑːʳ/ N (abbrev of **cardiopulmonary resuscitation**) réanimation *f* cardiopulmonaire, respiration *f* artificielle

cps /ˌsiːpiːˈes/ (*Comput*) [1] (abbrev of **characters per second**) → **character** [2] (abbrev of **cycles per second**) cycles *mpl* par seconde

CPU /ˌsiːpiːˈjuː/ N (*Comput*) (abbrev of **central processing unit**) UC *f*

cr. [1] abbrev of **credit** [2] abbrev of **creditor**

crab¹ /kræb/ N [1] (= *crustacean*) crabe *m* ◆ **~ stick** bâtonnet *m* de surimi ◆ **to catch a ~** (*Rowing*) plonger la rame trop profond [2] (*Tech*) *[of crane]* chariot *m* [3] (also **crab louse**) morpion *m* [4] (*Climbing*) mousqueton *m*

crab² /kræb/ N (also **crabapple**) pomme *f* sauvage ; (also **crab(apple) tree**) pommier *m* sauvage

crab³ /kræb/ VT (US ‡ = *spoil*) gâcher ◆ **to ~ sb's act** gâcher les effets de qn ◆ **to ~ a deal** faire rater* une affaire VI (US ‡ = *complain*) rouspéter* (*about* à cause de)

crabbed /ˈkræbd/ ADJ *[person]* revêche, grincheux ◆ **in a ~ hand, in ~ writing** en pattes de mouche

crabby /ˈkræbɪ/ ADJ *[person]* revêche, grincheux

crabmeat /ˈkræbmiːt/ N chair *f* de crabe

crabwise /ˈkræbˌwaɪz/ ADV en crabe

crack /kræk/ N [1] (= *split, slit*) fente *f*, fissure *f* ; (*in glass, mirror, pottery, bone etc*) fêlure *f* ; (*in wall*) lézarde *f*, crevasse *f* ; (*in ground, skin*) crevasse *f* ; (*Climbing*) fissure *f* ; (*in paint, varnish*) craquelure *f* ◆ **through the ~ in the door** (= *slight opening*) par l'entrebâillement de la porte ◆ **leave the window open a ~** laissez la fenêtre entrouverte ◆ **to paper over the ~s** masquer les problèmes ◆ **at the ~ of dawn** au point du jour, aux aurores*

[2] (= *noise*) *[of twigs]* craquement *m* ; *[of whip]* claquement *m* ; *[of rifle]* coup *m* (sec), détonation *f* ◆ **a ~ of thunder** un coup de tonnerre ◆ **the ~ of doom** la trompette du Jugement dernier

[3] (= *sharp blow*) **to give sb a ~ on the head** asséner à qn un grand coup sur la tête

[4] (* = *joke etc*) plaisanterie *f* ◆ **that was a ~ at your brother** ça, c'était pour votre frère ◆ **that was a nasty** or **mean ~ he made** c'est une vacherie‡ ce qu'il a dit là, c'était vache* or rosse* de dire ça

[5] (* = *try*) **to have a ~ at doing sth** essayer (un coup*) de faire qch ◆ **to have a ~ at sth** se lancer dans qch, tenter le coup* sur qch ◆ **I'll have a ~ at it** je vais essayer (un coup*) ; → **fair¹**

[6] (*esp Ir*) ambiance *f* ◆ **tourists come to Ireland for the ~** les touristes viennent en Irlande pour l'ambiance

[7] (= *drug*) ⇒ **crack cocaine**

VT [1] *[+ pottery, glass, bone]* fêler ; *[+ wall]* lézarder, crevasser ; *[+ ground]* crevasser ; *[+ nut etc]* casser ◆ **to ~ one's skull** se fendre le crâne ◆ **to ~ sb over the head** assommer qn ◆ **to ~ a safe*** percer un coffre-fort ◆ **to ~ a market*** (*US Comm*) réussir à s'implanter sur un marché ◆ **to ~ (open) a bottle*** ouvrir or déboucher une bouteille ◆ **to ~ a book*** (US) ouvrir un livre (pour l'étudier)

[2] *[+ petroleum etc]* craquer, traiter par craquage

[3] *[+ whip]* faire claquer ◆ **to ~ one's finger joints** faire craquer ses doigts

[4] * ◆ **to ~ a joke** raconter une blague ◆ **to ~ jokes** blaguer*

[5] *[+ code etc]* déchiffrer ; *[+ spy network]* démanteler ◆ **to ~ a case** *[detective, police]* résoudre une affaire ◆ **I think I've ~ed it!** je crois que j'ai trouvé !

VI [1] *[pottery, glass]* se fêler ; *[ground]* se crevasser, se craqueler ; *[wall]* se fendiller, se lézarder ; *[skin]* se crevasser ; (*from cold*) se gercer ; *[ice]* se craqueler

[2] *[whip]* claquer ; *[dry wood]* craquer ◆ **we heard the pistol ~** nous avons entendu le coup de pistolet

[3] *[voice]* se casser ; *[boy's voice]* muer

[4] (*Brit* *) **to get ~ing** s'y mettre, se mettre au boulot* ◆ **let's get ~ing!** allons-y !, au boulot !* ◆ **get ~ing!** magne-toi !‡, grouille-toi !‡

[5] *[person]* (*from overwork, pressure etc*) craquer*

ADJ *[sportsman, sportswoman]* de première classe, fameux* ◆ **a ~ tennis player/skier** un as or un crack du tennis/du ski ◆ **a ~ shot** un bon or excellent fusil ; (*Mil, Police etc*) un tireur d'élite

COMP **crack-brained** ADJ (*pej*) *[person, plan]* cinglé* ◆ **a ~-brained idea** une idée saugrenue or loufoque*

crack cocaine N crack *m*

crack house N crack-house *f*

crack-jaw* ADJ impossible à prononcer, imprononçable ◆ **~-jaw name** nom *m* à coucher dehors*

crack-up* N *[of plan, organization]* effondrement *m*, écroulement *m* ; *[of person]* (*physical*) effondrement *m* ; (*mental*) dépression *f* nerveuse ; (US) (= *accident*) *[of vehicle]* collision *f*, accident *m* ; *[of plane]* accident *m* (d'avion)

► **crack down on** VT FUS *[+ person]* sévir contre ; *[+ expenditure, sb's actions]* mettre un frein à

► **crack on** * VI (*Brit*) s'y mettre*

► **crack up*** VI [1] (*physically*) ne pas tenir le coup ; (*mentally*) craquer* ◆ **I must be ~ing up!** (*hum*) ça ne tourne plus rond chez moi !*

[2] (US) *[vehicle]* s'écraser ; *[plane]* s'écraser (au sol)

[3] *[person]* (*with laughter*) se tordre de rire, éclater de rire

VT SEP [1] (= *praise*) *[+ person, quality, action, thing]* vanter, louer ; *[+ method]* prôner ◆ **he's not all he's ~ed up to be*** il n'est pas aussi sensationnel qu'on le dit or prétend

[2] (US = *crash*) *[+ vehicle]* emboutir ; *[+ plane]* faire s'écraser

N ◆ **crack-up** → **crack**

crackdown /ˈkrækdaʊn/ N ◆ **~ on** mesures *fpl* énergiques contre, mesures *fpl* de répression contre

cracked /krækt/ ADJ [1] (= *damaged*) *[cup, window, mirror, tooth, bone, rib]* fêlé ; *[sink, plaster, paintwork, glaze, rubber]* craquelé ; *[wall, ceiling]* lézardé, fissuré ; *[lips, skin]* gercé ; (*stronger*) crevassé [2] (= *unsteady*) *[voice]* cassé ◆ **~ note** (*Mus*) couac *m* [3] (* = *mad*) *[person]* toqué*, timbré*

COMP **cracked wheat** N blé *m* concassé

cracker /ˈkrækəʳ/ N [1] (= *biscuit*) cracker *m*, biscuit *m* salé [2] (= *firework*) pétard *m* [3] (*Brit: at parties etc:* also **Christmas cracker**) diablotin *m* [4] (*Brit*) ◆ **to be a ~*** (= *excellent*) être super* ; (= *very funny*) être impayable* [5] (US) pauvre blanc *m* (du Sud)

COMP **cracker-barrel** ADJ (US) ≃ du café du commerce

the Cracker State N la Géorgie

crackers‡ /ˈkrækəz/ ADJ (*Brit*) cinglé*, dingue‡

crackhead‡ /ˈkrækhed/ N accro‡ *mf* du crack

cracking /ˈkrækɪŋ/ N (NonC) [1] *[of petroleum]* craquage *m*, cracking *m* [2] (= *cracks: in paint, varnish etc*) craquelure *f* ADJ [1] (*Brit*) ◆ **a ~ speed** or **pace** un train d'enfer* [2] (*Brit* *) ⇒ **cracking good** ADV (*Brit* *) ◆ **~ good** vachement* bon ◆ **his book's a ~ good read** son livre est vachement* bon ◆ **he tells a ~ good yarn** il en raconte de vachement* bonnes

crackle /ˈkrækl/ VI *[twigs burning]* crépiter ; *[sth frying]* grésiller N [1] (= *noise*) *[of wood]* crépitement *m*, craquement *m* ; *[of food]* grésillement *m* ; (*on telephone etc*) crépitement(s) *m(pl)*, friture* *f* [2] *[of china, porcelain etc]* craquelure *f*

COMP **crackle china** N porcelaine *f* craquelée

crackling /ˈkræklɪŋ/ N [1] (= *sound*) crépitement *m* ; (*Rad*) friture* *f* NonC [2] (*Culin*) couenne *f* rissolée (*de rôti de porc*)

crackly /ˈkræklɪ/ ADJ ◆ **a ~ sound** un crépitement, un grésillement ◆ **the line is ~** il y a de la friture* sur la ligne

cracknel /ˈkræknl/ N (= *biscuit*) craquelin *m* ; (= *toffee*) nougatine *f*

crackpot* /ˈkrækpɒt/ (*pej*) N (= *person*) tordu(e)* *m(f)*, cinglé(e)* *m(f)* ADJ *[idea]* tordu

cracksman* /ˈkræksmən/ N (pl **-men**) (* = *burglar*) cambrioleur *m*, casseur* *m*

Cracow /ˈkrækaʊ/ N Cracovie

cradle /ˈkreɪdl/ N [1] (*lit, fig*) berceau *m* ◆ **from the ~ to the grave** du berceau à la tombe ◆ **the ~ of civilization** le berceau de la civilisation ◆ **to rob the ~*** (*fig*) les prendre au berceau* [2] (*Naut* = *framework*) ber *m* ; (*Constr*) nacelle *f*, pont *m* volant ; *[of telephone]* support *m* ; (*Med*) arceau *m* VT ◆ **to ~ a child (in one's arms)** bercer un enfant (dans ses bras) ◆ **she ~d the vase in her hands** elle tenait délicatement le vase entre ses mains ◆ **he ~d the telephone under his chin** il maintenait le téléphone sous son menton

COMP **cradle cap** N (*Med*) croûte *f* de lait

cradle snatcher* N (*pej*) ◆ **she's a ~ snatcher** elle les prend au berceau*

cradlesong /ˈkreɪdlsɒŋ/ N berceuse *f*

craft /krɑːft/ N [1] (= *skill*) art *m*, métier *m* ; (= *job, occupation*) métier *m*, profession *f* (*généralement de type artisanal*) ; (*NonC: Scol* = *subject*) travaux *mpl* manuels ; → **art¹**, **needlecraft** [2] (= *tradesmen's guild*) corps *m* de métier, corporation *f* [3] (*pl inv*) (= *boat*) embarcation *f*, petit bateau *m* ; (= *plane*) appareil *m* ; → **aircraft**, **spacecraft** [4] (*NonC* = *cunning*) astuce *f*, ruse *f* (*pej*) ◆ **by ~** par ruse ◆ **his ~ in doing that** l'astuce dont il a fait preuve en le faisant VT ◆ **beautifully ~ed** *[vase, poem]* réalisé avec art

COMP **craft fair** N exposition-vente *f* d'artisanat

craft union N fédération *f*

craftily /ˈkrɑːftɪlɪ/ ADV avec ruse

craftiness /ˈkrɑːftɪnɪs/ N astuce *f*, finesse *f*, ruse *f* (*pej*)

craftsman /ˈkrɑːftsmən/ N (pl **-men**) artisan *m* ; (*fig* = *musician etc*) artiste *m*

craftsmanship /ˈkrɑːftsmənʃɪp/ **N** (*NonC*) connaissance *f* d'un métier ; (*= artistry*) art *m* ◆ **what ~!** quel travail ! ◆ **a superb piece of ~** un *or* du travail superbe

craftsperson /ˈkrɑːftspɜːsən/ **N** (pl **-people**) artisan(e) *m(f)* ; (*fig = musician etc*) artiste *mf*

craftswoman /ˈkrɑːftswʊmən/ **N** (pl **-women**) artisane *f* ; (*fig = musician etc*) artiste *f*

crafty /ˈkrɑːftɪ/ **ADJ** malin (-igne *f*), rusé (*pej*) ◆ **he's a ~ one*** c'est un malin ◆ **a ~ little gadget*** un petit gadget astucieux ◆ **that was a ~ move*** *or* **a ~ thing to do** c'était un coup très astucieux

crag /kræg/ **N** rocher *m* escarpé *or* à pic ; (*Climbing*) école *f* d'escalade

craggy /ˈkrægɪ/ **ADJ** 1 (*Geog*) [*mountain*] escarpé, à pic ; [*cliff, outcrop*] à pic 2 (*= strong-featured*) [*face, features*] taillé à la serpe

craic /kræk/ **N** ⇒ **crack**

cram /kræm/ **VT** 1 [*+ object*] fourrer (*into* dans) ; ◆ **to ~ books into a case** fourrer des livres dans une valise, bourrer une valise de livres ◆ **we can ~ in another book** nous pouvons encore faire de la place pour un autre livre *or* y faire tenir un autre livre ◆ **to ~ food into one's mouth** enfourner* de la nourriture ◆ **we can't ~ any more people into the hall/the bus** on ne peut plus faire entrer personne dans la salle/l'autobus ◆ **we were all ~med into one room** nous étions tous entassés dans une seule pièce ◆ **he ~med his hat (down) over his eyes** il a enfoncé son chapeau sur ses yeux

2 [*+ place*] bourrer (*with* de) ; ◆ **a shop ~med with good things** un magasin qui regorge de bonnes choses ◆ **a drawer ~med with letters** un tiroir bourré de lettres ◆ **to ~ sb with food** bourrer *or* gaver qn de nourriture ◆ **to ~ o.s. with food** se bourrer *or* se gaver de nourriture ◆ **he has his head ~med with odd ideas** il a la tête bourrée *or* farcie d'idées bizarres

3 (*Scol*) [*+ pupil*] chauffer*, faire bachoter

VI 1 [*people*] s'entasser ◆ **they all ~med into the kitchen** tout le monde s'est entassé dans la cuisine

2 ◆ **to ~ for an exam** bachoter, préparer un examen

COMP **cram-full** **ADJ** [*room, bus*] bondé ; [*case*] bourré (*of* de)

crammer /ˈkræməʳ/ **N** (*slightly pej*) (*= tutor*) répétiteur *m*, -trice *f* (*qui fait faire du bachotage*) ; (*= student*) bachoteur *m*, -euse *f* ; (*= book*) précis *m*, aide-mémoire *m inv* ; (also **crammer's** *= school*) boîte *f* à bac *or* à bachot*

cramp[1] /kræmp/ **N** (*Med*) crampe *f* ◆ **to have ~ in one's leg** avoir une crampe à la jambe ; → **writer** **VT** (*= hinder*) [*+ person*] gêner, entraver ◆ **to ~ sb's progress** gêner *or* entraver les progrès de qn ◆ **to ~ sb's style*** priver qn de ses moyens ◆ **your presence is ~ing my style*** tu me fais perdre mes moyens

cramp[2] /kræmp/ **N** (*Constr, Tech*) agrafe *f*, crampon *m*, happe *f* **VT** [*+ stones*] cramponner

cramped /kræmpt/ **ADJ** 1 (*= not spacious*) [*flat, room, accommodation*] exigu (-guë *f*) ; [*coach, train, plane*] où l'on est (*or* était) à l'étroit ; [*space*] restreint ◆ **to live in ~ quarters** *or* **conditions** être logé à l'étroit ◆ **it was ~ in the cockpit** on était à l'étroit dans le cockpit ◆ **to be ~ (for space)** [*people*] être à l'étroit ◆ **the museum is ~ for space** le musée manque de place 2 (*= squashed*) [*handwriting*] en pattes de mouche 3 (*= stiff*) [*muscle, limb*] raide

crampon /ˈkræmpən/ **N** (*Climbing, Constr*) crampon *m* **COMP** **crampon technique** **N** (*Climbing*) cramponnage *m*

cramponning /ˈkræmpənɪŋ/ **N** (*Climbing*) cramponnage *m*

cranberry /ˈkrænbərɪ/ **N** (*Bot*) canneberge *f* **COMP** **cranberry sauce** **N** ◆ **turkey with ~ sauce** dinde *f* aux canneberges

crane /kreɪn/ **N** (*= bird, machine*) grue *f* **VT** ◆ **to ~ one's neck** tendre le cou **COMP** **crane driver, crane operator** **N** grutier *m*, -ière *f*

► **crane forward** **VI** tendre le cou (*pour voir etc*)

cranefly /ˈkreɪnflaɪ/ **N** tipule *f*

cranesbill /ˈkreɪnzbɪl/ **N** (*= plant*) géranium *m*

crania /ˈkreɪnɪə/ **NPL** of **cranium**

cranial /ˈkreɪnɪəl/ **ADJ** crânien

cranium /ˈkreɪnɪəm/ **N** (pl **craniums** *or* **crania**) crâne *m*, boîte *f* crânienne

crank[1]* /kræŋk/ **N** (*Brit = person*) excentrique *mf*, loufoque* *mf* ◆ **a religious ~** un fanatique religieux

crank[2] /kræŋk/ **N** (*= handle*) manivelle *f* **VT** (also **crank up**) [*+ car*] faire partir à la manivelle ; [*+ cine-camera, gramophone etc*] remonter (à la manivelle) ; [*+ barrel organ*] tourner la manivelle de

► **crank out** **VT** produire (avec effort)

crankcase /ˈkræŋkkeɪs/ **N** carter *m*

crankpin /ˈkræŋkpɪn/ **N** maneton *m*

crankshaft /ˈkræŋkʃɑːft/ **N** vilebrequin *m*

cranky* /ˈkræŋkɪ/ **ADJ** (*= eccentric*) excentrique, loufoque* ; (*US = bad-tempered*) revêche, grincheux

cranny /ˈkrænɪ/ **N** (petite) faille *f*, fissure *f*, fente *f* ; → **nook**

crap‡ /kræp/ **N** (*= excrement*) merde*‡ *f* ; (*= nonsense*) conneries‡ *fpl* ; (*= junk*) merde*‡ *f*, saloperie‡ *f* ◆ **the film was ~** le film était merdique*‡ **ADJ** ⇒ **crappy** **VI** chier*‡

► **crap out**‡ **VI** (*US = chicken out*) se dégonfler*

crape /kreɪp/ **N** 1 ⇒ **crêpe** 2 (*for mourning*) crêpe *m* (*de deuil*) ◆ **~ band** brassard *m* (de deuil)

crapehanger‡ /ˈkreɪpˌhæŋəʳ/ **N** (*US*) rabat-joie *m inv*

crappy‡ /ˈkræpɪ/ **ADJ** merdique‡

craps /kræps/ **N** (*US*) jeu *m* de dés (*sorte de zanzi ou de passe anglaise*) ◆ **to shoot ~** jouer aux dés

crapshooter /ˈkræpʃuːtəʳ/ **N** joueur *m*, -euse *f* de dés

crapulous /ˈkræpjʊləs/ **ADJ** crapuleux

crash[1] /kræʃ/ **N** 1 (*= noise*) fracas *m* ◆ **a ~ of thunder** un coup de tonnerre ◆ **a sudden ~ of dishes** un soudain fracas d'assiettes cassées ◆ **~, bang, wallop!*** badaboum !, patatras !

2 (*= accident*) [*of car*] collision *f*, accident *m* ; [*of aeroplane*] accident *m* (d'avion) ◆ **in a car/plane ~** dans un accident de voiture/d'avion ◆ **we had a ~ on the way here** nous avons eu un accident en venant ici

3 (*= failure*) [*of company, firm*] faillite *f* ; [*of Stock Exchange*] krach *m*

ADV ◆ **he went ~ into the tree** il est allé se jeter *or* se fracasser contre l'arbre

VI 1 [*aeroplane*] s'écraser (au sol) ; [*vehicle*] avoir un accident ; [*two vehicles*] se percuter, entrer en collision ◆ **the cars ~ed at the junction** les voitures se sont percutées *or* sont entrées en collision au croisement ◆ **to ~ into sth** rentrer dans qch*, percuter qch ◆ **the plate ~ed to the ground** l'assiette s'est fracassée par terre ◆ **the car ~ed through the gate** la voiture a enfoncé la barrière

2 [*bank, firm*] faire faillite ◆ **the stock market ~ed** les cours de la Bourse se sont effondrés

3 (‡ *= sleep*) pieuter‡, crécher‡ ◆ **can I ~ at your place for a few days?** est-ce que je peux pieuter‡ chez toi pendant quelques jours ? ◆ **to ~ at sb's place** pieuter‡ *or* crécher‡ chez qn

4 (*Comput*) tomber en panne

VT 1 [*+ car*] avoir une collision *or* un accident avec ◆ **he ~ed the car through the barrier** il a enfoncé la barrière (avec la voiture) ◆ **he ~ed the car into a tree** il a percuté un arbre (avec la voiture) ◆ **he ~ed the plane** il s'est écrasé (au sol) ◆ **to ~ the gears** faire grincer le changement de vitesse

2 ‡ **to ~ a party** s'incruster dans une fête ◆ **to ~ a market** (*US Comm*) pénétrer en force sur un marché

COMP **crash barrier** **N** (*Brit*) glissière *f* de sécurité
crash course **N** cours *m* intensif
crash diet **N** régime *m* draconien
crash helmet **N** casque *m* de protection
crash-land **VI** faire un atterrissage forcé **VT** poser en catastrophe
crash landing **N** atterrissage *m* forcé
crash programme **N** programme *m* intensif
crash test **N** test *m* de résistance aux chocs
crash test dummy **N** mannequin *m* utilisé dans les tests de résistance aux chocs

► **crash down, crash in** **VI** [*roof etc*] s'effondrer (avec fracas)

► **crash out**‡ **VI** (*= fall asleep etc*) tomber raide **VT SEP** ◆ **to be crashed out** roupiller*

crash[2] /kræʃ/ **N** (*= fabric*) grosse toile *f*

crashing † /ˈkræʃɪŋ/ **ADJ** ◆ **a ~ bore** un raseur de première*

crashingly † /ˈkræʃɪŋlɪ/ **ADV** [*boring*] terriblement

crashpad‡ /ˈkræʃpæd/ **N** piaule‡ *f* de dépannage

crass /kræs/ **ADJ** [*comment, behaviour, mistake, film, person*] grossier ; [*joke*] lourd ; [*stupidity, ignorance*] crasse

crassly /ˈkræslɪ/ **ADV** grossièrement

crassness /ˈkræsnɪs/ **N** grossièreté *f*

crate /kreɪt/ **N** 1 [*of fruit*] cageot *m* ; [*of bottles*] caisse *f* (à claire-voie) ; (*esp Naut*) caisse *f* 2 (‡ *= aeroplane*) zinc* *m* ; (‡ *= car*) bagnole* *f* **VT** (also **crate up**) [*+ goods*] mettre en cageot(s) *or* en caisse(s)

crater /ˈkreɪtəʳ/ **N** [*of volcano, moon*] cratère *m* ◆ **bomb ~** entonnoir *m* ◆ **shell ~** trou *m* d'obus, entonnoir

cravat(e) /krəˈvæt/ **N** cravate *f*, foulard *m* (*noué autour du cou*)

crave /kreɪv/ **VT** 1 [*+ drink, tobacco etc*] avoir un besoin maladif *or* physiologique de ; [*+ chocolate, sweet things*] être accro* à ; [*+ attention*] solliciter ; [*+ recognition, fame*] avoir soif de ◆ **to ~ publicity** avoir besoin de la reconnaissance publique ◆ **to ~ affection** avoir grand besoin *or* soif d'affection 2 (*frm*) **to ~ permission** solliciter humblement l'autorisation ◆ **he ~d permission to leave** il supplia qu'on lui accorde la permission de partir ◆ **may I ~ leave to …?** je sollicite humblement l'autorisation de … ◆ **to ~ sb's pardon** implorer le pardon de qn **VI** ◆ **~ for** [*+ drink, tobacco etc*] avoir un besoin maladif *or* physiologique de ; [*+ chocolate, sweet things*] être accro* à ; [*+ attention*] solliciter ◆ **to ~ for affection** avoir grand besoin *or* soif d'affection

craven /ˈkreɪvən/ **ADJ, N** (*liter*) lâche *mf*, poltron(ne) *m(f)*

cravenly /ˈkreɪvənlɪ/ **ADV** (*liter*) lâchement

craving /ˈkreɪvɪŋ/ **N** (*for drink, drugs, tobacco*) besoin *m* (maladif *or* physiologique) (*for* de) ; (*for affection*) grand besoin *m*, soif *f* (*for* de) ; (*for freedom*) désir *m* insatiable (*for* de)

craw /krɔː/ **N** [*of bird*] jabot *m* ; [*of animal*] estomac *m* ◆ **it sticks in my ~** cela me reste en travers de la gorge

crawfish /ˈkrɔːfɪʃ/ **N** (pl **crawfish** *or* **crawfishes**) (*esp US*) ⇒ **crayfish** **VI** (*US* ‡ *fig*) se défiler*, faire marche arrière

crawl /krɔːl/ N 1 *[of vehicle]* allure *f* très ralentie ◆ **we had to go at a ~ through the main streets** nous avons dû avancer au pas dans les rues principales
2 *(Swimming)* crawl *m* ◆ **to do the ~** nager le crawl, crawler
VI 1 *[animals]* ramper, se glisser ; *[person]* se traîner, ramper ◆ **to ~ in/out** *etc* entrer/sortir *etc* en rampant *or* à quatre pattes ◆ **to ~ on one's hands and knees** aller à quatre pattes ◆ **the child has begun to ~ (around)** l'enfant commence à ramper ◆ **to ~ to sb** *(fig)* s'aplatir devant qn *, lécher les bottes de *or* à qn * ◆ **the fly ~ed up the wall/along the table** la mouche a grimpé le long du mur/a avancé sur la table ◆ **to make sb's skin ~** donner la chair de poule à qn ◆ **to ~ with vermin** grouiller de vermine ◆ **the street is ~ing * with policemen** la rue grouille d'agents de police ; see also **crawling**
2 *[vehicle]* avancer au pas *or* pare-chocs contre pare-chocs
COMP **crawl space** N *(US) (under ground floor)* vide *m* sanitaire ; *(under roof)* vide *m* de comble

crawler /ˈkrɔːləʳ/ N 1 *(* = person)* lécheur * *m*, -euse * *f*, lèche-bottes * *mf inv* 2 *(= vehicle)* véhicule *m* lent COMP **crawler lane** N *(Brit Aut)* file *f or* voie *f* pour véhicules lents

crawling /ˈkrɔːlɪŋ/ ADJ *[insect, movement]* rampant ◆ **a baby at the ~ stage** un bébé qui rampe ; see also **crawl**

crayfish /ˈkreɪfɪʃ/ N (pl **crayfish** or **crayfishes**) *(freshwater)* écrevisse *f* ; *(saltwater, large)* langouste *f* ; *(small)* langoustine *f*

crayon /ˈkreɪən/ N *(= coloured pencil)* crayon *m* (de couleur) ; *(Art = pencil, chalk etc)* pastel *m* ; *(Art = drawing)* crayon *m*, pastel *m* VT crayonner, dessiner au crayon ; *(Art)* colorier au crayon *or* au pastel

craze /kreɪz/ N engouement *m* (for pour) VT 1 *(= make mad)* rendre fou 2 *[+ glaze, pottery]* craqueler ; *[+ windscreen]* étoiler VI *[glaze, pottery]* craqueler ; *[windscreen]* s'étoiler

crazed /kreɪzd/ ADJ 1 *(= mad)* affolé, rendu fou (folle *f*) (with de) 2 *[glaze, pottery]* craquelé ; *[windscreen]* étoilé

crazily /ˈkreɪzɪlɪ/ ADV *[shout, gesticulate]* comme un fou ; *[skid, bounce, whirl, tilt]* follement ◆ **~ jealous/extravagant** follement jaloux/extravagant

craziness /ˈkreɪzɪnɪs/ N folie *f*

crazy /ˈkreɪzɪ/ ADJ 1 *(= mad)* fou (folle *f*) ◆ **to go ~** devenir fou ◆ **to be ~ with worry** être fou d'inquiétude ◆ **it's enough to drive you ~** c'est à vous rendre fou *or* dingue * ◆ **it was a ~ idea** c'était une idée folle ◆ **you were ~ to want to go there** tu étais fou *or* dingue * de vouloir y aller, c'était de la folie de vouloir y aller
◆ **like crazy** * comme un fou *or* une folle
2 *(* = enthusiastic)* fou (folle *f*), fana * *f inv (about sb/sth* de qn/qch) ; ◆ **I'm not ~ about it** ça ne m'emballe * pas ◆ **he's ~ about her** il est fou d'elle
3 *(fig) [price, height etc]* incroyable ; *(US = excellent)* terrible *, formidable ◆ **the tower leant at a ~ angle** la tour penchait d'une façon menaçante *or* inquiétante
COMP **crazy bone** N *(US)* petit juif * *m (partie du coude)*
crazy golf N *(NonC: Brit)* minigolf *m*
crazy house * N *(US)* cabanon * *m*, asile *m* d'aliénés
crazy paving N dallage *m* irrégulier *(en pierres plates)*
crazy quilt N *(US)* édredon *m* (piqué) en patchwork, courtepointe *f* en patchwork

CRE /ˌsiːɑːrˈiː/ N *(Brit)* (abbrev of **Commission for Racial Equality**) → **commission** ; → **EOC**, **EEOC**

creak /kriːk/ VI *[door hinge, floorboard, bed, bedsprings]* grincer ; *[shoes, joints]* craquer N *[of floorboard, door, hinge, bedsprings]* grincement *m* ; *[of shoes, leather, wood, bones]* craquement *m* ◆ **the door opened with a ~** la porte s'ouvrit en grinçant

creaky /ˈkriːkɪ/ ADJ 1 *(= noisy) [floorboard, stair, door, hinge]* grinçant ; *[shoes]* qui crisse 2 *(= old) [system, film, play, equipment]* vieillot ; *[body, legs]* usé

cream /kriːm/ N 1 crème *f* ◆ **single/double ~** *(Brit)* crème *f* fraîche liquide/épaisse ◆ **to take the ~ off the milk** écrémer le lait ◆ **the ~ of the crop** *(fig) (= people)* le dessus du panier ; *(= things)* le nec plus ultra ◆ **the ~ of society** la crème *or* la fine fleur de la société ◆ **chocolate ~** chocolat *m* fourré (à la crème) ◆ **vanilla ~** *(= dessert)* crème *f* à la vanille ; *(= biscuit)* biscuit *m* fourré à la vanille ; → **clot**
2 *(= face cream, shoe cream)* crème *f* ; → **cold**, **foundation**
ADJ *(= cream-coloured)* crème *inv* ; *(= made with cream) [cake]* à la crème
VT 1 *[+ milk]* écrémer
2 *(Culin) [+ butter]* battre ◆ **to ~ (together) sugar and butter** travailler le beurre en crème avec le sucre
3 *(US * fig) [+ enemy, opposing team]* rosser *, rétamer ; *[+ car]* bousiller *
COMP **cream cheese** N fromage *m* frais à tartiner
cream cracker N *(Brit)* cracker *m*
creamed potatoes N purée *f* de pommes de terre
cream jug N *(Brit)* pot *m* à crème
cream of tartar N crème *f* de tartre
cream of tomato soup N crème *f* de tomates
cream puff N chou *m* à la crème
cream soda N boisson *f* gazeuse à la vanille
cream tea N *(Brit) goûter où l'on sert du thé et des scones avec de la crème et de la confiture*
► **cream off** VT SEP *(fig) [+ best talents, part of profits]* prélever, écrémer

creamer /ˈkriːməʳ/ N 1 *(= to separate cream)* écrémeuse *f* 2 *(= milk substitute)* succédané *m* de lait 3 *(= pitcher)* pot *m* à crème

creamery /ˈkriːmərɪ/ N 1 *(on farm)* laiterie *f* ; *(= butter factory)* laiterie *f*, coopérative *f* laitière 2 *(= small shop)* crémerie *f*

creamy /ˈkriːmɪ/ ADJ crémeux ; *[complexion]* crème *inv*, crémeux ◆ **~ white/yellow** blanc/jaune crème *inv*

crease /kriːs/ N *(made intentionally, in material, paper)* pli *m*, pliure *f* ; *(in trouser legs, skirt etc)* pli *m* ; *(made accidentally)* faux pli *m*, pli *m* ; *(on face)* ride *f* VT *(= crumple) (accidentally)* froisser, chiffonner ; *(intentionally)* plisser VI se froisser, se chiffonner ◆ **his face ~d with laughter** le rire a plissé son visage COMP **crease-resistant** ADJ infroissable
► **crease up** VT SEP 1 *(= crumple)* froisser, chiffonner 2 *(Brit * = amuse)* faire mourir de rire VI 1 *(= crumple)* se froisser, se chiffonner 2 *(Brit * = laugh)* être plié en quatre

create /kriːˈeɪt/ VT *(gen)* créer ; *[+ new fashion]* lancer, créer ; *[+ work of art, character, role]* créer ; *[+ impression]* produire, faire ; *(Comput) [+ file]* créer ; *[+ problem, difficulty]* créer, susciter ; *[+ noise, din]* faire ◆ **to ~ a sensation** faire sensation ◆ **two posts have been ~d** il y a eu deux créations de poste, deux postes ont été créés ◆ **he was ~d baron** il a été fait baron VI *(Brit * = fuss)* faire une scène, faire un foin *

creation /kriːˈeɪʃən/ N 1 *(NonC)* création *f* ◆ **since the ~** *or* **the Creation** depuis la création du monde 2 *(Art, Dress)* création *f* ◆ **the latest ~s from Paris** les toutes dernières créations de Paris

creationism /kriːˈeɪʃənɪzəm/ N créationnisme *m*

creationist /kriːˈeɪʃənɪst/ ADJ, N créationniste *mf*

creative /kriːˈeɪtɪv/ ADJ 1 *(= imaginative) [person, talent, skill, activity, atmosphere]* créatif ; *[mind]* créatif, créateur (-trice *f*) ; *[energy, power]* créateur (-trice *f*) ; *[process]* de création ◆ **~ toys** *(Educ)* jouets *mpl* créatifs *or* d'éveil 2 *(= original) [person]* inventif ; *[solution]* ingénieux ; *[design]* novateur (-trice *f*) ◆ **the ~ use of language** l'utilisation créative du langage ◆ **with a little ~ thinking you can find a solution** avec un peu d'imagination, vous trouverez une solution
COMP **creative accounting** N *(pej)* manipulation *f* des chiffres
creative writing N création *f* littéraire

creatively /kriːˈeɪtɪvlɪ/ ADV de façon créative

creativity /ˌkriːeɪˈtɪvɪtɪ/ N créativité *f*

creator /kriˈeɪtəʳ/ N créateur *m*, -trice *f*

creature /ˈkriːtʃəʳ/ N *(gen, also fig)* créature *f* ; *(= animal)* bête *f*, animal *m* ; *(= human)* être *m*, créature *f* ◆ **dumb ~s** les bêtes *fpl* ◆ **the ~s of the deep** les animaux *mpl* marins ◆ **she's a poor/lovely ~** c'est une pauvre/ravissante créature ◆ **to be a ~ of habit** avoir ses (petites) habitudes ◆ **they were all his ~s** *(fig pej)* tous étaient ses créatures ; → **habit** COMP **creature comforts** NPL confort *m* matériel ◆ **he likes his ~ comforts** il aime son petit confort

crèche /kreɪʃ/ N *(Brit) (up to 3 years old)* crèche *f* ; *(after 3 years old)* (halte-)garderie *f*

cred * /kred/ N *(NonC)* crédibilité *f* ; see also **street cred**

credence /ˈkriːdəns/ N croyance *f*, foi *f* ◆ **to give** *or* **lend ~ to** ajouter foi à

credentials /krɪˈdenʃəlz/ NPL *(= identifying papers)* pièce *f* d'identité ; *[of diplomat]* lettres *fpl* de créance ; *(= references)* références *fpl* ◆ **to have good ~** avoir de bonnes références

credibility /ˌkredəˈbɪlɪtɪ/ N crédibilité *f* ◆ **to lose ~** perdre sa crédibilité
COMP **credibility gap** N manque *m* de crédibilité
credibility rating N ◆ **his ~ rating is not very high** sa crédibilité est très entamée

credible /ˈkredɪbl/ ADJ crédible ◆ **it is scarcely ~ that ...** on a du mal à croire que ...

credibly /ˈkredɪblɪ/ ADV de façon crédible

credit /ˈkredɪt/ N 1 *(Banking, Comm, Fin)* crédit *m* ; *(Accounting)* crédit *m*, avoir *m* ◆ **to give sb ~** faire crédit à qn ◆ **"no credit"** "la maison ne fait pas crédit" ◆ **to buy/sell on ~** acheter/vendre à crédit ◆ **in ~** *(account)* approvisionné ◆ **am I in ~?** est-ce que mon compte est approvisionné ?
2 *(= loan)* prêt *m* ◆ **they're prepared to offer extensive ~s** ils sont disposés à fournir des prêts très importants ◆ **Japan provided billions in ~s to Russia** le Japon a prêté des milliards à la Russie ◆ **to get ~** trouver des fonds
3 *(morally)* honneur *m* ◆ **to his ~ we must point out that ...** il faut faire remarquer à son honneur *or* à son crédit que ... ◆ **it is to his ~** c'est tout à son honneur ◆ **he is a ~ to his family** il fait honneur à sa famille, il est l'honneur de sa famille ◆ **the only people to emerge with any ~** les seuls à s'en sortir à leur honneur ◆ **to give sb ~ for his generosity** reconnaître la générosité de qn ◆ **to give sb ~ for doing sth** reconnaître que qn a fait qch ◆ **to claim** *or* **take (the) ~ for sth** s'attribuer le mérite de qch ◆ **it does you ~** cela est tout à votre honneur, cela vous fait grand honneur ◆ **~ where ~'s due** il faut rendre à César ce qui appartient à César ◆ **on the ~ side, he's very good to his mother** il faut dire à sa décharge qu'il est très gentil avec sa mère
4 *(Scol)* unité *f* d'enseignement *or* de valeur, UV *f*

5 *(= belief, acceptance)* **to give ~ to** *[+ person]* ajouter foi à ; *[+ event]* donner foi à, accréditer ◆ **I gave him ~ for more sense** je lui supposais *or* croyais plus de bon sens ◆ **to gain ~ with** s'accréditer auprès de ◆ **his ~ with the electorate** son crédit auprès des électeurs
NPL **credits** *(Cine)* générique *m*
VT 1 *(= believe)* *[+ rumour, news]* croire ◆ **I could hardly ~ it** je n'arrivais pas à le croire ◆ **you wouldn't ~ it** vous ne le croiriez pas
2 *(gen)* ◆ **to ~ sb/sth with certain powers/qualities** reconnaître à qn/qch certains pouvoirs/certaines qualités ◆ **to be ~ed with having done ...** passer pour avoir fait ... ◆ **I ~ed him with more sense** je lui croyais *or* supposais plus de bon sens ◆ **it is ~ed with (having) magical powers** on lui attribue des pouvoirs magiques
3 *(Banking)* **to ~ £50 to sb** *or* **to sb's account, to ~ sb** *or* **sb's account with £50** créditer (le compte de) qn de 50 livres, porter 50 livres au crédit de qn
COMP **credit account** N compte *m* créditeur
credit agency N établissement *m or* agence *f* de crédit
credit arrangements NPL accords *mpl* de crédit
credit balance N *(Banking)* solde *m* créditeur
credit bureau N *(US)* ⇒ **credit agency**
credit card N carte *f* de crédit
credit charges NPL coût *m* du crédit
credit check N vérification *f* de solvabilité ◆ **to run a ~ check on sb** vérifier la solvabilité de qn
credit control N *(= action)* encadrement *m* de crédit ; *(= department)* (service *m* de l')encadrement *m* du crédit
credit entry N *(Fin)* inscription *f or* écriture *f* au crédit
credit facilities NPL *(Banking)* ligne *f* de crédit ; *(Comm: to buyer)* facilités *fpl* de paiement *or* de crédit
credit hour N *(US Scol, Univ)* ≈ unité *f* de valeur
credit limit N limite *f or* plafond *m* de crédit
credit line N *(Banking)* ligne *f* de crédit ; *(Cine)* mention *f* au générique ; *(in book)* mention *f* de la source
credit note N *(Brit)* avoir *m*
credit rating N indice *m* de solvabilité
credit reference agency N agence *f* de notation financière *or* de rating
credit risk N ◆ **to be a good/poor ~ risk** présenter peu de risques de crédit/un certain risque de crédit
credit sales NPL ventes *fpl* à crédit
credit side N *(Accounting, also fig)* ◆ **on the ~ side** à l'actif
credit slip N *(US)* ⇒ **credit note**
credit squeeze N restrictions *fpl* de crédit
credit terms NPL conditions *fpl* de crédit
credit titles NPL *(Cine)* générique *m*
credit transfer N transfert *m*, virement *m*
credit union N *(US)* société *f* de crédit mutuel

creditable /ˈkredɪtəbl/ ADJ honorable

creditably /ˈkredɪtəblɪ/ ADV *[behave, perform, play]* honorablement

creditor /ˈkredɪtəʳ/ N créancier *m*, -ière *f* COMP **creditor nation** N pays *m* créditeur

creditworthiness /ˈkredɪtwɜːðɪnɪs/ N solvabilité *f*, capacité *f* d'emprunt

creditworthy /ˈkredɪtwɜːðɪ/ ADJ solvable

credo /ˈkreɪdəʊ/ N credo *m*

credulity /krɪˈdjuːlɪtɪ/ N crédulité *f*

credulous /ˈkredjʊləs/ ADJ crédule

credulously /ˈkredjʊləslɪ/ ADV avec crédulité

creed /kriːd/ N credo *m* ◆ **the Creed** *(Rel)* le Credo

creek /kriːk/ N 1 *(esp Brit = inlet)* crique *f*, anse *f* ◆ **to be up the ~ (without a paddle)*** *(= be wrong)* se fourrer le doigt dans l'œil (jusqu'au coude)* ; *(= be in trouble)* être dans le pétrin 2 *(US = stream)* ruisseau *m*, petit cours *m* d'eau

creel /kriːl/ N panier *m* de pêche

creep /kriːp/ (pret, ptp **crept**) VI *[animal, person, plant]* ramper ; *(= move silently)* se glisser ◆ **to ~ between** se faufiler entre ◆ **to ~ in/out/away** *[person]* entrer/sortir/s'éloigner à pas de loup ; *[animal]* entrer/sortir/s'éloigner sans un bruit ◆ **to ~ about/along on tiptoe** marcher/avancer sur la pointe des pieds ◆ **to ~ up on sb** *[person]* s'approcher de qn à pas de loup ; *[old age etc]* prendre qn par surprise ◆ **old age is ~ing on** on se fait vieux* ◆ **the traffic crept along** les voitures avançaient au pas ◆ **an error crept into it** une erreur s'y est glissée ◆ **a feeling of peace crept over me** un sentiment de paix me gagnait peu à peu *or* commençait à me gagner N 1 ◆ **it gives me the ~s** * cela me donne la chair de poule, cela me fait froid dans le dos 2 *(pej = person)* sale type * *m*

creeper /ˈkriːpəʳ/ N 1 *(= plant)* plante *f* rampante ; → **Virginia** 2 *(US)* **~s** barboteuse *f* 3 *(* = person)* lécheur* *m*, -euse* *f*, lèche-bottes* *mf inv*

creeping /ˈkriːpɪŋ/ ADJ 1 *(Bot) [plant]* rampant 2 *(= gradual) [process, inflation, privatization]* rampant ; *[change]* larvé COMP **creeping paralysis** N *(Med)* paralysie *f* progressive

creepy /ˈkriːpɪ/ ADJ *[story, place, feeling]* qui donne la chair de poule COMP **creepy-crawly** * ADJ qui donne la chair de poule N (pl **creepy-crawlies**) petite bestiole *f*

cremate /krɪˈmeɪt/ VT incinérer

cremation /krɪˈmeɪʃən/ N crémation *f*, incinération *f*

crematorium /ˌkreməˈtɔːrɪəm/ (pl **crematoriums** *or* **crematoria** /ˌkreməˈtɔːrɪə/), **crematory** *(US)* /ˈkreməˌtɔːrɪ/ N *(= place)* crématorium *m*, crématoire *m* ; *(= furnace)* four *m* crématoire

crème de la crème /ˈkremdəlɑːˈkrem/ N ◆ **the ~** le dessus du panier, le gratin *

crème fraîche /ˌkremˈfreʃ/ N crème *f* fraîche

crenellated /ˈkrenɪleɪtɪd/ ADJ crénelé, à créneaux

crenellations /ˌkrenɪˈleɪʃənz/ NPL créneaux *mpl*

creole /ˈkriːəʊl/ ADJ créole N ◆ **Creole** Créole *mf* COMP **the Creole State** N la Louisiane

creosote /ˈkrɪəsəʊt/ N créosote *f* VT créosoter

crêpe /kreɪp/ N 1 *(= fabric)* crêpe *m* 2 *(Culin)* crêpe *f*
COMP **crêpe bandage** N bande *f* Velpeau ®
crêpe paper N papier *m* crêpon
crêpe shoes, crêpe-soled shoes NPL chaussures *fpl* à semelles de crêpe

crept /krept/ VB pt, ptp of **creep**

crepuscular /krɪˈpʌskjʊləʳ/ ADJ crépusculaire

crescendo /krɪˈʃendəʊ/ N (pl **crescendos** *or* **crescendi** /krɪˈʃendɪ/) *(Mus, fig)* crescendo *m inv* VI *(Mus)* faire un crescendo

crescent /ˈkresnt/ N 1 croissant *m* ◆ **the Crescent** *(Islamic faith etc)* le Croissant 2 *(= street)* rue *f (en arc de cercle)*
COMP **crescent moon** N croissant *m* de lune
crescent roll N *(Culin)* croissant *m*
crescent-shaped ADJ en (forme de) croissant

cress /kres/ N cresson *m* ; → **mustard, watercress**

crest /krest/ N *[of bird, wave, mountain]* crête *f* ; *[of helmet]* cimier *m* ; *(= long ridge)* arête *f* ; *[of road]* haut *m* de côte, sommet *m* de côte ; *(above coat of arms, shield)* timbre *m* ; *(on seal etc)* armoiries *fpl* ◆ **the family ~** les armoiries *fpl* familiales ◆ **he is on the ~ of the wave** *(= successful)* tout lui réussit en ce moment VT *[+ wave, hill]* franchir la crête de ◆ **~ed notepaper** papier *m* à lettres armorié ◆ **~ed tit** mésange *f* huppée

crestfallen /ˈkrestˌfɔːlən/ ADJ *[person]* déconfit ◆ **to look ~** avoir l'air penaud

cretaceous /krɪˈteɪʃəs/ ADJ crétacé ◆ **the Cretaceous (period)** *(Geol)* le crétacé

Cretan /ˈkriːtən/ ADJ crétois N Crétois(e) *m(f)*

Crete /kriːt/ N Crète *f* ◆ **in ~** en Crète

cretin /ˈkretɪn/ N crétin(e) *m(f)*

cretinism /ˈkretɪnɪzəm/ N *(Med)* crétinisme *m*

cretinous * /ˈkretɪnəs/ ADJ *(Med pej)* crétin

cretonne /kreˈtɒn/ N cretonne *f*

Creutzfeldt-Jakob disease /ˌkrɔɪtsfeltˈjækɒbdɪˌziːz/ N *(NonC)* maladie *f* de Creutzfeldt-Jakob

crevasse /krɪˈvæs/ N *(Geol, Climbing)* crevasse *f*

crevice /ˈkrevɪs/ N *(in rock)* fissure *f* ; *(in wall)* lézarde *f*

crew[1] /kruː/ N *(Aviat, Naut)* équipage *m* ; *(Cine, Rowing etc)* équipe *f* ; *(= group, gang)* bande *f*, équipe *f* ◆ **what a ~!*** *(pej)* tu parles d'une équipe !*, quelle engeance ! VI *(Sailing)* ◆ **to ~ for sb** être l'équipier de qn ◆ **would you like me to ~ for you?** voulez-vous de moi comme équipier ? VT *[+ yacht]* armer
COMP **crew cut** N ◆ **to have a ~ cut** avoir les cheveux en brosse
crew-neck sweater N pull *m* ras du cou, ras-du-cou *m inv*

crew[2] /kruː/ VB pt of **crow**[2]

crewel /ˈkruːɪl/ N *(= yarn)* laine *f* à tapisserie ; *(= work)* tapisserie *f* sur canevas

crewman /ˈkruːmən/ N (pl **-men**) *(TV etc)* équipier *m*

crib /krɪb/ N 1 *(Brit: for infant)* berceau *m* ; *(US: for toddler)* lit *m* d'enfant ; *(Rel)* crèche *f* 2 *(= manger)* mangeoire *f*, râtelier *m* 3 *(= plagiarism)* plagiat *m*, copiage *m* ; *(Scol)* antisèche * *f* VT *(Scol)* copier, pomper * ◆ **to ~ sb's work** copier le travail de qn, copier *or* pomper * sur qn VI copier ◆ **to ~ from a friend** copier sur un camarade ◆ **he had ~bed from Shakespeare** il avait plagié Shakespeare COMP **crib death** N *(US)* mort *f* subite du nourrisson

cribbage /ˈkrɪbɪdʒ/ N *jeu de cartes*

crick /krɪk/ N crampe *f* ◆ **~ in the neck** torticolis *m* ◆ **~ in the back** tour *m* de reins VT ◆ **to ~ one's neck** attraper un torticolis ◆ **to ~ one's back** se faire un tour de reins

cricket[1] /ˈkrɪkɪt/ N *(= insect)* grillon *m*, cricri * *m inv*

cricket[2] /ˈkrɪkɪt/ N *(Sport)* cricket *m* ◆ **that's not ~** *(fig)* cela ne se fait pas, ce n'est pas correct
COMP *[ball, bat, match, pitch]* de cricket

CRICKET

Le **cricket** est souvent considéré comme un sport typiquement anglais, bien qu'il soit pratiqué dans toute la Grande-Bretagne et dans beaucoup de pays du Commonwealth. C'est surtout un sport d'été, dans lequel deux équipes de onze joueurs s'affrontent selon des règles assez complexes.

Comme le base-ball aux États-Unis, ce sport a fourni à la langue courante un certain nombre d'expressions imagées, parmi lesquelles « a sticky wicket » (une situation difficile) ; « to knock someone for six » (démolir qn) ; « to be stumped » (sécher) et le fameux « it's not **cricket** » (cela ne se fait pas, ce n'est pas correct).

cricketer /ˈkrɪkɪtəʳ/ N joueur *m*, -euse *f* de cricket

cricketing /ˈkrɪkɪtɪŋ/ ADJ ◆ **England's ~ heroes** les héros du cricket anglais ◆ **his ~ career** sa carrière de joueur de cricket

crier /ˈkraɪəʳ/ N crieur *m* ; *[of law courts]* huissier *m* ; → **town**

crikey * /ˈkraɪkɪ/ EXCL *(Brit)* mince (alors) !

crime /kraɪm/ N crime *m* ◆ **minor ~** délit *m* ◆ **the scene of the ~** le lieu du crime ◆ **a ~ against humanity** un crime contre l'humanité ◆ **perjury is a serious ~** un faux témoignage est un délit grave ◆ **~ and punishment** le crime et le châtiment ◆ **a life of ~** une vie de criminel ◆ **~ is on the increase/decrease** la criminalité augmente/diminue ◆ **~ doesn't pay** le crime ne paye pas ◆ **it's a ~ to make him do it** * c'est un crime de le forcer à le faire ; → **organized**
COMP **crime fighting** N *(NonC)* lutte *f* contre la criminalité
crime-fighting ADJ *[plan, strategy, group]* de lutte contre la criminalité
crime of passion N crime *m* passionnel
crime prevention N prévention *f* de la criminalité
crime prevention officer N policier *m* chargé de la prévention de la criminalité
crime spree N série *f* de délits ◆ **to go on a ~ spree** multiplier les délits
Crime Squad N brigade *f* criminelle
crime wave N vague *f* de criminalité
crime writer N auteur *m* de romans policiers

Crimea /kraɪˈmɪə/ N ◆ **the ~** la Crimée

Crimean /kraɪˈmɪən/ ADJ, N ◆ **the ~ (War)** la guerre de Crimée

criminal /ˈkrɪmɪnl/ N criminel *m*, -elle *f*
ADJ *[action, motive, law]* criminel ◆ **a ~ waste of resources** un gaspillage criminel (des ressources) ◆ **it's ~ * to stay indoors today** c'est un crime de rester enfermé aujourd'hui ; → **conspiracy**
COMP **criminal assault** N *(Jur)* agression *f* criminelle, voie *f* de fait
criminal code N code *m* pénal
criminal conversation N *(US Jur)* adultère *m* *(de la femme)*
criminal court N cour *f* d'assises
criminal damage N *(NonC: Jur)* dégradations *fpl* volontaires
criminal investigation N enquête *f* criminelle
the Criminal Investigation Department N *(in Brit)* la police judiciaire, la PJ
criminal justice system N *(Jur)* justice *f* pénale
criminal law N droit *m* pénal *or* criminel
criminal lawyer N pénaliste *m*, avocat *m* au criminel
criminal negligence N *(NonC: Jur)* négligence *f* coupable *or* criminelle
criminal offence N délit *m* ◆ **it's a ~ offence to do that** c'est un crime puni par la loi de faire cela
criminal proceedings NPL *(Jur)* ◆ **to take ~ proceedings against sb** poursuivre qn au pénal
criminal record N casier *m* judiciaire ◆ **he hasn't got a ~ record** il a un casier judiciaire vierge
the Criminal Records Office N *(in Brit)* l'identité *f* judiciaire

criminality /krɪmɪˈnælɪtɪ/ N criminalité *f*

criminalization /ˌkrɪmɪnəlaɪˈzeɪʃən/ N criminalisation *f*

criminalize /ˈkrɪmɪnəlaɪz/ VT criminaliser

criminally /ˈkrɪmɪnəlɪ/ ADV 1 *(Jur) [liable, responsible]* pénalement ◆ **to be ~ negligent** faire preuve de négligence coupable *or* criminelle ◆ **the ~ insane** les psychopathes *mpl* 2 *(= scandalously) [underpaid]* scandaleusement ◆ **~ irresponsible** d'une irresponsabilité criminelle ◆ **a ~ wasteful use of resources** un gaspillage criminel (des ressources)

criminologist /ˌkrɪmɪˈnɒlədʒɪst/ N criminologiste *mf*, criminologue *mf*

criminology /ˌkrɪmɪˈnɒlədʒɪ/ N criminologie *f*

crimp /krɪmp/ VT 1 *[+ hair]* crêper, friser ; *[+ pastry]* pincer 2 *(US = hinder)* gêner, entraver
N *(US = person)* raseur *m*, -euse *f* ◆ **to put a ~ in ...** mettre obstacle à ..., mettre des bâtons dans les roues de ...

crimped /krɪmpt/ ADJ *[fabric etc]* plissé, froncé ; *[hair]* crêpé

Crimplene ® /ˈkrɪmpliːn/ N ≈ crêpe *m* polyester

crimson /ˈkrɪmzn/ ADJ, N cramoisi *m*

cringe /krɪndʒ/ VI *(= shrink back)* avoir un mouvement de recul, reculer *(from* devant*)* ; *(fig = humble o.s.)* ramper, s'humilier *(before* devant*)* ; ◆ **the very thought of it makes me ~** * *(with embarrassment)* rien que d'y penser j'ai envie de rentrer sous terre COMP **cringe-making** ✱ ADJ *(Brit)* qui donne des boutons, qui fait grincer les dents

cringing /ˈkrɪndʒɪŋ/ ADJ *[bow, attitude, person]* servile

crinkle /ˈkrɪŋkl/ VT *[+ paper]* froisser, chiffonner VI se froisser N fronce *f*, pli *m* COMP **crinkle-cut** ADJ *(Brit) [chips, crisps]* dentelé

crinkled /ˈkrɪŋkld/ ADJ *[leaf, paper, clothes]* froissé ; *[face, head]* plein de rides

crinkly /ˈkrɪŋklɪ/ ADJ *[hair]* crépu, crêpelé ; *[skin, face, eyes]* plissé ; *[paper]* gaufré

crinoline /ˈkrɪnəlɪn/ N crinoline *f*

cripple /ˈkrɪpl/ N *(= lame)* estropié(e) *m(f)*, boiteux *m*, -euse *f* ; *(= disabled)* infirme *mf*, invalide *mf* ; *(from accident, war)* invalide *mf* ; *(= maimed)* mutilé(e) *m(f)* ◆ **he's an emotional ~** il est complètement bloqué sur le plan affectif VT 1 estropier 2 *(fig) [+ ship, plane]* désemparer ; *[strikes etc] [+ production, exports etc]* paralyser ; *[+ person]* inhiber, bloquer ◆ **activities ~d by lack of funds** activités paralysées par le manque de fonds

crippled /ˈkrɪpld/ ADJ 1 *(= physically disabled) [person] (gen)* infirme ; *(through mutilation)* estropié ; *[leg, hand]* estropié ◆ **the bomb blast left her ~** l'explosion l'a rendue infirme ◆ **~ for life** handicapé à vie ◆ **~ with arthritis** perclus d'arthrite 2 *(psychologically)* ◆ **~ with shyness** perclus de timidité ◆ **emotionally ~** bloqué sur le plan affectif 3 *(= stricken) [aircraft, ship]* désemparé 4 *(= dysfunctional) [society, economy, organization]* handicapé ◆ **~ with debt** écrasé de dettes NPL **the crippled** les estropiés *mpl*

crippling /ˈkrɪplɪŋ/ ADJ 1 *[disease, illness, injury]* invalidant 2 *(fig) [pain, inflation, strike, effect]* paralysant ; *[guilt, depression]* qui paralyse ; *[tax, debt, cost]* écrasant ◆ **a ~ blow** un coup dur

crisis /ˈkraɪsɪs/ N (pl **crises** /ˈkraɪsiːz/) crise *f* ◆ **to come to a ~, to reach ~ point** *or* **a ~** atteindre un point critique ◆ **to solve a ~** dénouer *or* résoudre une crise ◆ **we've got a ~ on our hands** nous avons un problème urgent, nous sommes dans une situation critique ◆ **the first oil ~** le premier choc pétrolier, la première crise du pétrole
COMP **crisis centre** N *(for large-scale disaster)* cellule *f* de crise ; *(for personal help)* centre *m* d'aide ; *(for battered women)* association *f* d'aide d'urgence
crisis management N *(NonC)* gestion *f* de crise

crisp /krɪsp/ ADJ 1 *(= crunchy) [apple, salad]* croquant ; *[biscuit, pastry, bacon]* croustillant ; *[snow]* qui crisse ; *[leaves]* craquant 2 *[shirt, suit, cotton, linen]* tout propre, impeccable 3 *(= refreshing) [air]* vif, piquant ; *[weather]* tonifiant ; *[day, morning]* frais (fraîche *f*) et piquant(e) ; *[wine, sherry]* gouleyant, coulant 4 *(= clear) [picture, image]* net et précis ; *[shape]* épuré ; *[voice, sound]* clair ; *[style]* précis 5 *(= succinct) [writing, style]* épuré ; *[phrase]* vif ; *[statement, speech]* concis 6 *(= brisk) [tone, voice, comment]* sec (sèche *f*) 7 *(= tight) [curls]* serré N *(Brit)* ◆ **(potato) ~s** (pommes) chips *fpl* ◆ **packet of ~s** sachet *m or* paquet *m* de chips VT *(Culin:* also **crisp up***) (with crispy topping)* faire gratiner ; *[+ chicken etc]* faire dorer

crispbread /ˈkrɪspbred/ N pain *m* scandinave

crisper /ˈkrɪspəʳ/ N *(= salad crisper)* bac *m* à légumes

Crispin /ˈkrɪspɪn/ N Crépin *m*

crisply /ˈkrɪsplɪ/ ADV 1 *(Culin)* ◆ **~ fried** *or* **grilled** croustillant 2 *(= stiffly)* ◆ **~ pressed** *or* **ironed** parfaitement repassé 3 *(= briskly) [say, reply]* sèchement

crispness /ˈkrɪspnɪs/ N 1 *(= crunchiness) [of biscuit etc]* craquant *m* 2 *(= freshness) [of air, weather]* fraîcheur *f*, piquant *m* 3 *(= succinctness) [of style]* précision *f*, tranchant *m*

crispy /ˈkrɪspɪ/ ADJ croquant, croustillant ◆ **~ noodles** nouilles *fpl* sautées ◆ **~ pancakes** crêpes *fpl* croustillantes

criss-cross /ˈkrɪskrɒs/ ADJ *[lines]* entrecroisés ; *(in muddle)* enchevêtré ◆ **in a ~ pattern** en croisillons N entrecroisement *m*, enchevêtrement *m* VT entrecroiser *(by* de*)* VI *[lines]* s'entrecroiser ADV formant (un) réseau

crit * /krɪt/ N *[of play, book etc]* papier * *m*, critique *f*

criterion /kraɪˈtɪərɪən/ N (pl **criterions** *or* **criteria** /kraɪˈtɪərɪə/) critère *m*

critic /ˈkrɪtɪk/ N *[of books, painting, music, films etc]* critique *m* ; *(= faultfinder)* critique *m*, détracteur *m*, -trice *f* ◆ **film ~** *(Press)* critique *m* de cinéma ◆ **he's a strong ~ of the government** il est très critique à l'égard du gouvernement ◆ **he is a constant ~ of the government** il ne cesse de critiquer le gouvernement ◆ **his wife is his most severe ~** sa femme est son plus sévère critique

critical /ˈkrɪtɪkəl/ ADJ 1 *(= important) [factor, element, issue]* crucial *(for or to* pour*)* ; ◆ **it was ~ for him to gain their support** il était crucial pour lui d'obtenir leur soutien
2 *(= decisive) [moment, point, time]* critique, crucial ; *[situation, state]* critique ◆ **at a ~ stage** dans une phase critique ◆ **of ~ importance** d'une importance décisive
3 *(Med) [patient]* dans un état critique ◆ **in a ~ condition, on the ~ list** dans un état critique ◆ **to be off the ~ list** être dans un état stable
4 *(= censorious) [person, attitude, speech, report]* critique *(of sb/sth* à l'égard de qn/qch*)* ; ◆ **~ remark** critique *f*
5 *(Art, Literat, Mus, Theat) [study, writings, edition]* critique ◆ **to meet with ~ acclaim** *or* **praise** être salué par la critique ◆ **to be a ~ success** connaître un succès critique
6 *(Phys)* ◆ **to go ~** atteindre le seuil critique
COMP **critical angle** N *(Flying, Optics)* angle *m* critique
critical mass N *(Phys)* masse *f* critique ; *(fig)* point *m* critique ◆ **to reach (a) ~ mass** *(Phys)* atteindre une masse critique ; *(fig)* atteindre un point critique
critical path N chemin *m* critique
critical path analysis N analyse *f* du chemin critique
critical path method N méthode *f* du chemin critique
critical temperature N *(Phys)* température *f* critique

critically /ˈkrɪtɪkəlɪ/ ADV 1 *(= crucially)* ◆ **to be ~ important** être d'une importance capitale ◆ **a ~ important moment** un moment critique ◆ **the success of the project is ~ dependent**

on his contribution sa contribution est d'une importance capitale pour la réussite du projet ◆ **to be (running) ~ low on sth** manquer sérieusement de qch ◆ **books are in ~ short supply** on manque sérieusement de livres 2 *(Med) [ill, injured]* gravement 3 *(= censoriously) [speak, say]* sévèrement 4 *(= analytically) [study, examine, watch]* d'un œil critique 5 *(= by critics)* ◆ **~ acclaimed** salué par la critique

criticism /ˈkrɪtɪsɪzəm/ N critique *f* ◆ **the decision is open to ~** cette décision prête le flanc à la critique *or* est critiquable

criticize /ˈkrɪtɪsaɪz/ LANGUAGE IN USE 26.3 VT 1 *(= assess) [+ book etc]* critiquer, faire la critique de 2 *(= find fault with) [+ behaviour, person]* critiquer ◆ **I don't want to ~, but ...** je ne veux pas avoir l'air de critiquer, mais ...

critique /krɪˈtiːk/ N critique *f*

critter‡ /ˈkrɪtəʳ/ N *(US)* créature *f* ; *(= animal)* bête *f*, bestiole *f*

croak /krəʊk/ VI 1 *[frog]* coasser ; *[raven]* croasser ; *[person] (gen)* parler d'une voix rauque ; *(due to sore throat)* parler d'une voix enrouée ; (* *= grumble)* maugréer, ronchonner 2 (‡ *= die)* claquer*, crever* VT *(gen)* dire d'une voix rauque ; *(due to sore throat)* dire d'une voix enrouée ◆ **"help" he ~ed feebly** "au secours" appela-t-il d'une voix rauque N *[of frog]* coassement *m* ; *[of raven]* croassement *m* ◆ **his voice was a mere ~** il ne proférait que des sons rauques

croaky /ˈkrəʊkɪ/ ADJ *[voice] (gen)* rauque ; *(due to sore throat)* enroué

Croat /ˈkrəʊæt/ N Croate *mf*

Croatia /krəʊˈeɪʃɪə/ N Croatie *f*

Croatian /krəʊˈeɪʃɪən/ ADJ croate

crochet /ˈkrəʊʃeɪ/ N *(NonC:* also **crochet work***)* (travail *m* au) crochet *m* VT *[+ garment]* faire au crochet VI faire du crochet COMP **crochet hook** N crochet *m*

crock /krɒk/ N 1 *(= pot)* cruche *f*, pot *m* de terre ◆ **~s** *(= broken pieces)* débris *mpl* de faïence ◆ **the ~s*** la vaisselle 2 * *(= horse)* vieille rosse *f*, cheval *m* fourbu ; *(esp Brit = car)* vieille bagnole* *f*, vieux clou* *m* ; *(Sport = injured player)* joueur *m*, -euse *f* amoché(e)* ◆ **he's an old ~** c'est un croulant*

crocked‡ /krɒkt/ ADJ *(US)* bourré*

crockery /ˈkrɒkərɪ/ N *(NonC: Brit) (= cups, saucers, plates)* vaisselle *f* ; *(= earthenware)* poterie *f*, faïence *f*

crocodile /ˈkrɒkədaɪl/ N 1 crocodile *m* 2 *(Brit Scol)* cortège *m* en rangs (par deux) ◆ **to walk in a ~** aller deux par deux
COMP *[shoes, handbag]* en crocodile, en croco*
crocodile clip N pince *f* crocodile
crocodile tears NPL larmes *fpl* de crocodile

crocus /ˈkrəʊkəs/ N (pl **crocuses**) crocus *m*

Croesus /ˈkriːsəs/ N Crésus *m* ◆ **as rich as ~** riche comme Crésus

croft /krɒft/ N petite exploitation *f* agricole

crofter /ˈkrɒftəʳ/ N petit exploitant *m* agricole

crofting /ˈkrɒftɪŋ/ N *organisation de l'agriculture en petites exploitations*

croissant /ˈkwæsɒŋ/ N croissant *m*

Cromwellian /krɒmˈwelɪən/ ADJ de Cromwell

crone /krəʊn/ N vieille ratatinée* *f*, vieille bique *f*

crony* /ˈkrəʊnɪ/ N copain* *m*, copine* *f*

cronyism* /ˈkrəʊnɪɪzəm/ N copinage* *m*

crook /krʊk/ N 1 *[of shepherd]* houlette *f* ; *[of bishop]* crosse *f* ; *(Mus) [of brass instrument]* ton *m* de rechange 2 *[of road]* angle *m* ; *[of river]* coude *m* 3 (* *= thief)* escroc *m*, filou *m* VT *[+ one's finger]* courber, recourber ; *[+ one's arm]* plier ADJ *(Austral)* 1 *(= sick)* malade ; *(= injured)* blessé 2 * *(= crooked)* malhonnête, roublard*

crooked /ˈkrʊkɪd/ ADJ 1 *(= bent, askew) [line, stick, back]* tordu ; *[nose, tooth, picture, tie]* de travers ; *[street]* tortueux ◆ **to give a ~ smile** sourire du coin des lèvres ◆ **a ~ old man** un vieillard tout tordu 2 (* *= dishonest) [person, business]* véreux ; *[deal, method]* malhonnête ADV * de travers, de traviole*

crookedly /ˈkrʊkɪdlɪ/ ADV *[smile, grin]* du coin des lèvres ; *[hang]* de travers

crookedness /ˈkrʊkɪdnɪs/ N *(= dishonesty)* malhonnêteté *f* ; *[of features]* manque *m* de symétrie

croon /kruːn/ VTI *(= sing softly)* chantonner, fredonner ; *(in show business)* chanter *(en crooner)*

crooner /ˈkruːnəʳ/ N chanteur *m*, -euse *f* de charme, crooner *m*

crooning /ˈkruːnɪŋ/ N *(NonC)* la chanson de charme

crop /krɒp/ N 1 *(= produce)* produit *m* agricole, culture *f* ; *(= amount produced)* récolte *f* ; *(of fruit etc)* récolte *f*, cueillette *f* ; *(of cereals)* moisson *f* ; *(fig) [of problems, questions]* série *f* ; *(fig) [of people]* fournée *f* ◆ **the ~s** *(at harvest time)* la récolte ◆ **one of the basic ~s** l'une des cultures de base ◆ **we had a good ~ of strawberries** la récolte *or* la cueillette des fraises a été bonne ◆ **to get the ~s in** rentrer les récoltes *or* la moisson
2 *[of bird]* jabot *m*
3 *[of whip]* manche *m* ; (also **riding crop**) cravache *f*
4 *(Hairdressing)* **to give sb a (close) ~** couper ras les cheveux de qn ◆ **Eton ~** cheveux *mpl* à la garçonne
VT 1 *[animals grass]* brouter, paître
2 *[+ tail]* écourter ; *[+ hair]* tondre ◆ **~ped hair** cheveux *mpl* coupés ras
3 *(Phot)* recadrer
VI *[land]* donner *or* fournir une récolte
COMP **crop circle** N cercle *m* dans les blés
crop dusting N ⇒ **crop spraying**
crop rotation N assolement *m*, rotation *f* des cultures
crop sprayer N *(= device)* pulvérisateur *m* ; *(= plane)* avion-pulvérisateur *m*
crop spraying N *(NonC)* pulvérisation *f* des cultures
crop top N T-shirt (court et ajusté)

► **crop out** VI *(Geol)* affleurer

► **crop up** VI 1 *[questions, problems]* survenir, se présenter ◆ **the subject ~ped up during the conversation** le sujet a été amené *or* mis sur le tapis au cours de la conversation ◆ **something's ~ped up and I can't come** j'ai un contre-temps, je ne pourrai pas venir ◆ **he was ready for anything that might ~ up** il était prêt à toute éventualité
2 *(Geol)* affleurer

cropper* /ˈkrɒpəʳ/ N *(lit, fig)* ◆ **to come a ~** *(= fall)* se casser la figure* ; *(= fail in attempt)* se planter* ; *(in exam)* se faire coller* *or* étendre

cropping /ˈkrɒpɪŋ/ N *(Phot)* recadrage *m*

croquet /ˈkrəʊkeɪ/ N croquet *m*
COMP **croquet hoop** N arceau *m* de croquet
croquet mallet N maillet *m* de croquet

croquette /krəʊˈket/ N croquette *f* ◆ **potato ~** croquette *f* de pommes de terre

crosier /ˈkrəʊʒəʳ/ N *[of bishop]* crosse *f*

cross /krɒs/ LANGUAGE IN USE 27.7
N 1 *(= mark, emblem)* croix *f* ◆ **to mark/sign with a ~** marquer/signer d'une croix ◆ **the iron ~** la croix de fer ◆ **the Cross** *(Rel)* la Croix ; → **bear¹, market, red, sign**
2 *(= mix of breeds)* hybride *m* ◆ **~ between two different breeds** mélange *m* or croisement *m* de deux races différentes, hybride *m* ◆ **it's a ~ between a novel and a poem** cela tient du roman et du poème ◆ **a ~ between a laugh and a bark** un bruit qui tient du rire et de l'aboiement
3 *(NonC) [of material]* biais *m* ◆ **to cut material on the ~** *(Sewing)* couper du tissu dans le biais ◆ **a skirt cut on the ~** une jupe en biais ◆ **line drawn on the ~** ligne tracée en biais *or* en diagonale
4 *(Sport)* centre *m* ◆ **to hit a ~ to sb** centrer sur qn, envoyer un centre sur qn
ADJ 1 *(= angry) [person]* en colère ◆ **to be ~ with sb** être fâché *or* en colère contre qn ◆ **it makes me ~ when ...** cela me met en colère quand ... ◆ **to get ~ with sb** se mettre en colère *or* se fâcher contre qn ◆ **don't be ~ with me** ne m'en veuillez pas, il ne faut pas m'en vouloir ◆ **they haven't had a ~ word in ten years** ils ne se sont pas disputés une seule fois en dix ans
2 *(= traverse, diagonal)* transversal, diagonal
VT 1 *[+ room, street, sea, continent, river, bridge]* traverser ; *[+ threshold, fence, ditch]* franchir ◆ **the bridge ~es the river here** c'est ici que le pont franchit *or* enjambe la rivière ◆ **it ~ed my mind that ...** il m'est venu à l'esprit que ... ◆ **they have clearly ~ed the boundary into terrorism** ils ont manifestement basculé dans le terrorisme ◆ **a smile ~ed her lips** un sourire se dessina sur ses lèvres ; → **bridge¹, floor, line¹, path¹**
2 ◆ **to ~ one's arms/legs** croiser les bras/les jambes ◆ **the lines are ~ed, we've got a ~ed line** *(Brit Telec)* il y a un problème sur la ligne ◆ **they've got their lines ~ed*** *(fig)* il y a un malentendu quelque part ; → **finger, sword**
3 *(Rel)* **to ~ o.s.** se signer, faire le signe de la croix ◆ **~ my heart (and hope to die)!*** croix de bois, croix de fer(, si je mens je vais en enfer) !*
4 ◆ **to ~ a "t"** barrer un "t" ; → **cheque, palm¹**
5 *[+ person] (= anger)* contrarier ; *(= thwart)* contrecarrer les projets de ; *[+ plans]* contrecarrer ◆ **~ed in love** malheureux en amour
6 *[+ animals, plants]* croiser *(with* avec*)* ; ◆ **to ~ two animals/plants** croiser *or* métisser deux animaux/plantes
VI 1 (also **cross over**) **he ~ed from one side of the room to the other to speak to me** il a traversé la pièce pour venir me parler ◆ **to ~ from one place to another** passer d'un endroit à un autre ◆ **to ~ from Newhaven to Dieppe** faire la traversée de Newhaven à Dieppe
2 *[roads, paths]* se croiser, se rencontrer ; *[letters, people]* se croiser
COMP **cross-border** ADJ transfrontalier
cross-Channel ferry N ferry *m* qui traverse la Manche
cross-check N contre-épreuve *f*, recoupement *m* VT *[+ facts]* vérifier par recoupement *or* contre-épreuve VI vérifier par recoupement
cross-compiler N *(Comput)* compilateur *m* croisé
cross-country ADJ à travers champs ◆ **~-country race** *or* **running** cross(-country) *m* ◆ **~-country skier** skieur *m* de fond *or* de randonnée ◆ **~-country skiing** ski *m* de fond *or* de randonnée
cross-court ADJ *(Tennis) [drive, shot, forehand]* croisé
cross-cultural ADJ interculturel
cross-current N contre-courant *m*
cross-curricular ADJ *[approach etc]* pluridisciplinaire
cross-cut chisel N bédane *m*
cross-disciplinary ADJ interdisciplinaire
cross-dress VI se travestir
cross-dresser N travesti(e) *m(f)*
cross-dressing N *(NonC = transvestism)* transvestisme *m*, travestisme *m*
cross-examination N *(esp Jur)* contre-interrogatoire *m*
cross-examine VT *(Jur)* faire subir un contre-

interrogatoire à ; *(gen)* interroger *or* questionner (de façon serrée)

cross-eyed ADJ qui louche, bigleux* ◆ **to be ~-eyed** loucher, avoir un œil qui dit zut* *or* merde‡ à l'autre

cross-fertilize VT *(Bot)* croiser, faire un croisement de

cross-grained ADJ *[wood]* à fibres irrégulières ; *[person]* acariâtre, atrabilaire

cross hairs NPL *[of telescope, gun]* réticule *m*

cross holdings NPL *Stock Exchange* participations *fpl* croisées

cross-legged ADV *[sit]* en tailleur

cross-match VT *[+ blood]* tester la compatibilité de

cross-party ADJ *(Brit Pol) [talks]* entre partis, interpartis ; *[support]* de plusieurs partis ; *[committee]* composé de membres de différents partis

cross-ply ADJ *[tyres]* à carcasse diagonale

cross-pollination N pollinisation *f* croisée

cross-posting N *(Comput)* diffusions *fpl* multiples ◆ **with apologies for ~-posting** veuillez nous excuser pour les diffusions multiples

cross-purposes NPL ◆ **to be at ~-purposes with sb** *(= misunderstand)* comprendre qn de travers ; *(= disagree)* être en désaccord avec qn ◆ **I think we are at ~-purposes** je crois qu'il y a malentendu, nous nous sommes mal compris ◆ **we were talking at ~-purposes** notre conversation tournait autour d'un quiproquo

cross-question VT faire subir un interrogatoire à

cross-refer VT renvoyer *(to* à)

cross-reference N renvoi *m*, référence *f (to* à) VT renvoyer

cross section N *(Bio etc)* coupe *f* transversale *[population etc]* échantillon *m*

cross-stitch N point *m* de croix VT coudre *or* broder au point de croix

cross swell N houle *f* traversière

cross-town ADJ *(US) [bus]* qui traverse la ville

cross trainers NPL *(= shoes)* chaussures *fpl* de cross-training

cross-training N *(Sport)* cross-training *m*

cross volley N *(Tennis)* volée *f* croisée

cross-vote VI *(Pol)* voter contre son parti

► **cross off** VT SEP *[+ item on list]* barrer, rayer ; *[+ person]* radier *(from* de) ; ◆ **to ~ sb off a list** radier qn d'une liste

► **cross out** VT SEP *[+ word]* barrer, rayer

► **cross over** VI traverser ; see also **cross vi 1**

crossbar /ˈkrɒsbɑːʳ/ N *(Rugby etc)* barre *f* transversale ; *[of bicycle]* barre *f*

crossbeam /ˈkrɒsbiːm/ N traverse *f*

crossbencher /ˈkrɒsˌbentʃəʳ/ N député *m* non inscrit

crossbill /ˈkrɒsbɪl/ N bec-croisé *m*

crossbones /ˈkrɒsbəʊnz/ NPL → **skull**

crossbow /ˈkrɒsbəʊ/ N arbalète *f* COMP **crossbow archery** N tir *m* à l'arbalète

crossbred /ˈkrɒsbred/ VB pt, ptp of **crossbreed** ADJ, N métis(se) *m(f)*

crossbreed /ˈkrɒsbriːd/ N *(= animal)* hybride *m*, métis(se) *m(f)* ; *(* pej = person)* sang-mêlé *mf inv*, métis(se) *m(f)* VT (pret, ptp **crossbred**) croiser, métisser

crosse /krɒs/ N *(in lacrosse)* crosse *f*

crossfire /ˈkrɒsfaɪəʳ/ N *(Mil)* feux *mpl* croisés ◆ **exposed to ~** *(Mil)* pris entre deux feux ◆ **caught in a ~ of questions** pris dans un feu roulant de questions

crosshatch /ˈkrɒshætʃ/ VT hachurer

crosshatching /ˈkrɒsˌhætʃɪŋ/ N hachures *fpl*

crossing /ˈkrɒsɪŋ/ N 1 *(esp by sea)* traversée *f* ◆ **the ~ of the line** le passage de l'équateur *or* de la ligne 2 *(= road junction)* croisement *m*, carrefour *m* ; (also **pedestrian crossing**) passage *m* clouté ; *(Rail:* also **level crossing**) passage *m* à niveau ◆ **cross at the ~** *(on road)* traversez sur le passage clouté *or* dans les clous* ; → **zebra**

COMP **crossing guard** N *(US)* ⇒ **crossing patrol**

crossing patrol N *(Brit:* also **school crossing patrol**) contractuel(le) *m(f) (chargé(e) de faire traverser la rue aux enfants)*

crossing point N point *m* de passage ; *[of river]* gué *m*

crossly /ˈkrɒslɪ/ ADV avec (mauvaise) humeur

crossover /ˈkrɒsəʊvəʳ/ N *[of roads]* (croisement *m* par) pont *m* routier ; *(Rail)* voie *f* de croisement ; *(Mus, Literat, Art)* mélange *m* de genres ◆ **a jazz-rap ~** un mélange de jazz et de rap COMP **crossover bodice** N *(Dress)* corsage *m* croisé

crosspatch */ˈkrɒspætʃ/ N grincheux *m*, -euse *f*, grognon(ne) *m(f)*

crosspiece /ˈkrɒspiːs/ N traverse *f*

crossroads /ˈkrɒsrəʊdz/ NPL *(lit)* croisement *m*, carrefour *m* ; *(fig)* carrefour *m*

crosstalk /ˈkrɒstɔːk/ N *(Rad, Telec)* diaphonie *f* ; *(Brit = conversation)* joutes *fpl* oratoires

crosstie /ˈkrɒstaɪ/ N *(US)* traverse *f* (de voie ferrée)

crosswalk /ˈkrɒswɔːk/ N *(US)* passage *m* clouté

crossway /ˈkrɒsweɪ/ N *(US)* croisement *m*

crosswind /ˈkrɒswɪnd/ N vent *m* de travers

crosswise /ˈkrɒswaɪz/ ADV *(= in shape of cross)* en croix ; *(= across)* en travers ; *(= diagonally)* en diagonale

crossword /ˈkrɒswɜːd/ N (also **crossword puzzle**) mots *mpl* croisés

crotch /krɒtʃ/ N *[of body, tree]* fourche *f* ; *[of garment]* entrejambes *m inv* ◆ **a kick in the ~** un coup de pied entre les jambes

crotchet /ˈkrɒtʃɪt/ N *(Brit Mus)* noire *f*

crotchety /ˈkrɒtʃɪtɪ/ ADJ grognon, grincheux

crouch /kraʊtʃ/ VI (also **crouch down**) *[person, animal] (gen)* s'accroupir ; *(= snuggle)* se tapir ; *(before springing)* se ramasser N position *f* accroupie

croup¹ /kruːp/ N *(Med)* croup *m*

croup² /kruːp/ N *[of horse]* croupe *f*

croupier /ˈkruːpɪeɪ/ N croupier *m*

crouton /ˈkruːtɒn/ N croûton *m*

crow¹ /krəʊ/ N corbeau *m* ◆ **as the ~ flies** à vol d'oiseau, en ligne droite ◆ **to make sb eat ~*** *(US)* faire rentrer les paroles dans la gorge à qn ◆ **to eat ~*** *(US)* faire de plates excuses ; → **carrion**

COMP **Crow Jim**‡ N racisme *m* contre les Blancs, racisme *m* inversé

crow's feet NPL pattes *fpl* d'oie *(rides)*

crow's-nest N *(on ship)* nid *m* de pie

crow² /krəʊ/ N *[of cock]* chant *m* (du *or* d'un coq), cocorico *m* ; *[of baby]* gazouillis *m* ; *(= triumphant cry)* cri *m* de triomphe VI 1 (pret **crowed** *or* **crew**, ptp **crowed**) *[cock]* chanter 2 (pret, ptp **crowed**) *[baby]* gazouiller ; *[victor]* chanter victoire ◆ **he ~ed with delight** il poussait des cris de triomphe ◆ **it's nothing to ~ about** il n'y a pas de quoi pavoiser

► **crow over** VT FUS ◆ **to crow over sb** se vanter d'avoir triomphé de qn, chanter sa victoire sur qn

crowbar /ˈkrəʊbɑːʳ/ N (pince *f* à) levier *m*

crowd /kraʊd/ N 1 foule *f* ; *(disorderly)* cohue *f* ◆ **in ~s** en foule ◆ **to get lost in the ~** se perdre dans la foule ◆ **a large ~** *or* **large ~s had gathered** une foule immense s'était assemblée ◆ **there was quite a ~** il y avait beaucoup de monde, il y avait foule ◆ **how big was the ~?** est-ce qu'il y avait beaucoup de monde ? ◆ **there was quite a ~ at the concert/at the match** il y avait du monde au concert/au match ◆ **the ~** *(Cine, Theat = actors)* les figurants *mpl* ◆ **that would pass in a ~*** *(fig)* ça peut passer si on n'y regarde pas de trop près, en courant vite on n'y verrait que du feu* ◆ **~s of** *or* **a whole ~ of books/people** des masses* de livres/de gens

2 *(NonC = people in general)* **the ~** la foule, la masse du peuple ◆ **to follow** *or* **go with the ~** suivre la foule *or* le mouvement

3 *(* = group, circle)* bande *f*, clique *f* ◆ **I don't like that ~ at all** je n'aime pas du tout cette bande ◆ **he's one of our ~** il fait partie de notre groupe *or* bande ◆ **the usual ~** la bande habituelle

VI ◆ **they ~ed into the small room** ils se sont entassés dans la petite pièce ◆ **don't all ~ together** ne vous serrez donc pas comme ça ◆ **to ~ through the gates** passer en foule par le portail ◆ **they ~ed round to see ...** ils ont fait cercle *or* se sont attroupés pour voir ... ◆ **they ~ed round him** ils se pressaient autour de lui ◆ **they ~ed up against him** ils l'ont bousculé ◆ **to ~ down/in/up** *etc* descendre/entrer/monter *etc* en foule

VT *(= push) [+ objects]* entasser *(into* dans) ; *(= jostle) [+ person]* bousculer ◆ **pedestrians ~ed the streets** les piétons se pressaient dans les rues ◆ **he was ~ed off the pavement** la cohue l'a forcé à descendre du trottoir ◆ **don't ~ me** ne poussez pas, arrêtez de me bousculer ◆ **the houses are ~ed together** les maisons sont les unes sur les autres ◆ **a room ~ed with children** une pièce pleine d'enfants ◆ **house ~ed with furniture** maison *f* encombrée de meubles ◆ **a house ~ed with guests** une maison pleine d'invités ◆ **a week ~ed with incidents** une semaine riche en incidents ◆ **memory ~ed with facts** mémoire *f* bourrée de faits ◆ **to ~ on sail** *(Naut)* mettre toutes voiles dehors ; → **crowded**

COMP **crowd control** N *(NonC)* ◆ **~ control was becoming difficult** il devenait difficile de contenir *or* contrôler la foule ◆ **expert in ~ control** spécialiste *mf* du service d'ordre

crowd-pleaser N ◆ **to be a ~-pleaser** plaire aux foules

crowd-puller * N grosse attraction *f* ◆ **to be a real ~-puller** attirer les foules

crowd scene N *(Cine, Theat)* scène *f* de foule

crowd trouble N *(NonC)* mouvements *mpl* de foule

► **crowd out** VT SEP ◆ **the place was crowded out** l'endroit était bondé ◆ **we shall be ~ed out** la cohue nous empêchera d'entrer ◆ **this article was ~ed out of yesterday's edition** cet article n'a pas pu être inséré dans l'édition d'hier faute de place ◆ **he's really ~ing me out*** il me colle aux fesses‡

crowded /ˈkraʊdɪd/ ADJ 1 *(= filled with people) [room, street, train, beach]* plein de monde, bondé ◆ **the shops are too ~** il y a trop de monde dans les magasins ◆ **it's getting ~ in there, the place is getting ~** il commence à y avoir trop de monde ◆ **the people live ~ together in insanitary conditions** les gens vivent les uns sur les autres dans des conditions insalubres ◆ **~ with people** plein de monde 2 *(= overpopulated) [city, area]* surpeuplé ; *[conditions]* de surpeuplement ◆ **it is a very ~ profession** c'est une filière très encombrée 3 *(= packed with things) [place]* plein à craquer ◆ **a room ~ with furniture** une pièce pleine de meubles 4 *(= busy) [agenda, day]* chargé ; *[life]* bien rempli

crowfoot /ˈkrəʊfʊt/ N (pl **crowfoots**) 1 *(= plant)* renoncule *f* ; 2 *(for ship's awning)* araignée *f* ; 3 *(= spiked ball)* chausse-trappe *m*

crowing /ˈkrəʊɪŋ/ N *[of cockerel]* chant *m* (du coq), cocorico *m* ; *(fig = boasting)* vantardise *f*

crown /kraʊn/ N 1 *(lit, fig)* couronne *f* ◆ **~ of roses/thorns** couronne *f* de roses/d'épines ◆ **to wear the ~** *(fig)* porter la couronne ◆ **to succeed to the ~** monter sur le trône ◆ **the**

Crown (*Jur*) la Couronne, ≃ le ministère public ◆ **the law officers of the Crown** les conseillers *mpl* juridiques de la Couronne

[2] (= *coin*) couronne *f* (*ancienne pièce valant cinq shillings*)

[3] (= *top part*) [*of hill*] sommet *m*, faîte *m* ; [*of tree*] cime *f* ; [*of roof*] faîte *m* ; [*of arch*] clé *f* ; [*of tooth*] couronne *f* ; [*of hat*] fond *m* ; [*of anchor*] diamant *m* ; (*fig* = *climax, completion*) couronnement *m* ◆ **the ~ (of the head)** le sommet de la tête ◆ **the ~ of the road** le milieu de la route

[4] (= *size of paper*) couronne *f* (*format 0,37 sur 0,47 m*)

VT couronner (*with* de) ; [*draughts*] damer ; [+ *tooth*] couronner ; (* = *hit*) flanquer* un coup sur la tête à ◆ **he was ~ed king** il fut couronné roi ◆ **all the ~ed heads of Europe** toutes les têtes couronnées d'Europe ◆ **work ~ed with success** travail *m* couronné de succès ◆ **the hill is ~ed with trees** la colline est couronnée d'arbres ◆ **to ~ it all* it began to snow** pour comble (de malheur) *or* pour couronner le tout il s'est mis à neiger ◆ **that ~s it all!*** il ne manquait plus que ça !

COMP (*Brit Jur*) [*witness, evidence etc*] à charge

Crown Agent N (*Brit Pol*) ≃ délégué(e) *m(f)* du ministère de la Coopération

crown colony N (*Brit*) colonie *f* de la couronne

Crown court N (*Jur*) Cour *f* d'assises (*en Angleterre et au Pays de Galles*)

crown estate N domaine *m* de la couronne

crown green bowling N (*NonC: Brit*) *jeu de boules sur un terrain légèrement surélevé en son milieu*

crown jewels NPL joyaux *mpl* de la couronne ; (‡ *hum* = *male genitals*) bijoux *mpl* de famille* (*hum*)

crown lands NPL terres *fpl* domaniales

crown law N droit *m* pénal

crown prince N prince *m* héritier

crown princess N princesse *f* héritière

Crown Prosecution Service N (*Brit*) ≃ Ministère *m* public (*qui décide si les affaires doivent être portées devant les tribunaux*)

crown prosecutor N ≃ procureur *m* de la République

crown wheel N (*Brit: in gears*) grande couronne *f* ◆ **~ wheel and pinion** couple *m* conique

crowning /ˈkraʊnɪŋ/ N [1] (= *ceremony*) couronnement *m* ADJ [*achievement, moment*] suprême ◆ **his ~ glory** son plus grand triomphe ◆ **her hair was her ~ glory** sa chevelure faisait sa fierté

cruces /ˈkruːsiːz/ NPL of **crux**

crucial /ˈkruːʃəl/ ADJ [*issue, factor, decision, vote, difference*] crucial ; [*moment, stage, time*] crucial, critique ◆ **~ to** *or* **for sb/sth** crucial pour qn/qch ◆ **it is ~ that ...** il est essentiel *or* capital que ... + *subj* ◆ **to play a ~ role in sth** jouer un rôle capital dans qch

crucially /ˈkruːʃəlɪ/ ADV [*influence, affect*] d'une manière décisive ◆ **~ important** d'une importance cruciale ◆ **the success of the project is ~ dependent on** *or* **depends ~ on his contribution** sa contribution est d'une importance capitale pour la réussite du projet

crucible /ˈkruːsɪbl/ N [1] (*lit*) creuset *m* [2] (*fig*) (= *melting pot*) creuset *m* ; (= *test*) (dure) épreuve *f*

crucifix /ˈkruːsɪfɪks/ N crucifix *m* ; (*at roadside*) calvaire *m*

crucifixion /ˌkruːsɪˈfɪkʃən/ N crucifiement *m* ◆ **the Crucifixion** (*Rel*) la crucifixion, la mise en croix

cruciform /ˈkruːsɪfɔːm/ ADJ cruciforme

crucify /ˈkruːsɪfaɪ/ VT (*lit*) crucifier, mettre en croix ; (*fig*) crucifier, mettre au pilori ◆ **to ~ the flesh** (*Rel*) mortifier la chair ◆ **he'll ~ me* when he finds out!** il va m'étrangler quand il saura !

crud‡ /krʌd/ N [1] (= *filth*) saloperies‡ *fpl*, saletés *fpl* ; (= *person*) salaud‡ *m*, ordure‡ *f* ◆ **the ~** (= *illness*) la crève‡ [2] (= *residue*) résidu *m*

cruddy‡ /ˈkrʌdɪ/ ADJ dégueulasse‡

crude /kruːd/ ADJ [1] (= *vulgar*) [*person, behaviour, language, joke, attempt*] grossier [2] (= *rudimentary*) [*device, weapon, hut*] rudimentaire ; [*furniture, shelter, housing*] rudimentaire, sommaire ; [*drawing*] schématique ◆ **a ~ form** *or* **kind of ...** une forme grossière de ... ◆ **a ~ method of doing sth** un moyen rudimentaire de faire qch [3] (= *garish*) [*light, colour*] cru [4] (= *not refined*) [*materials*] brut ; [*sugar*] non raffiné N (also **crude oil**) brut *m* ; → **heavy**

COMP **crude oil** N (pétrole *m*) brut *m*

crude steel N acier *m* brut

crudely /ˈkruːdlɪ/ ADV [1] (= *approximately*) [*divide, express, explain*] sommairement [2] (= *primitively*) [*carved, constructed, drawn*] grossièrement, de façon rudimentaire [3] (= *coarsely*) [*speak, behave*] grossièrement ◆ **to put it ~** pour dire les choses crûment

crudeness /ˈkruːdnɪs/ N [*of system, method*] caractère *m* rudimentaire ; (= *vulgarity*) vulgarité *f*, grossièreté *f*

crudités /ˈkruːdɪteɪz/ NPL crudités *fpl*

crudity /ˈkruːdɪtɪ/ N ⇒ **crudeness**

cruel /ˈkrʊəl/ ADJ cruel (*to sb* avec qn) ; ◆ **it was a ~ blow to his pride** sa fierté en a pris un coup*, cela a porté un coup sévère à son orgueil ◆ **you have to be ~ to be kind** (*Prov*) qui aime bien châtie bien (*Prov*)

cruelly /ˈkrʊəlɪ/ ADV cruellement

cruelty /ˈkrʊəltɪ/ N cruauté *f* (*to* envers) ; (*Jur*) sévices *mpl* ◆ **prosecuted for ~ to his wife** poursuivi pour sévices sur sa femme ◆ **divorce on the grounds of ~** divorce *m* pour sévices ◆ **mental ~** cruauté *f* mentale ; → **prevention**

COMP **cruelty-free** ADJ non testé sur les animaux

cruet /ˈkruːɪt/ N [1] (*Brit*: also **cruet set, cruet stand**) service *m* à condiments, garniture *f* de table (pour condiments) [2] (*US* = *small bottle*) petit flacon *m* (*pour l'huile ou le vinaigre*) [3] (*Rel*) burette *f*

cruise /kruːz/ VI [1] [*fleet, ship*] croiser ◆ **they are cruising in the Pacific** (*Naut*) ils croisent dans le Pacifique ; [*tourists*] ils sont en croisière dans le Pacifique

[2] [*cars*] rouler ; [*aircraft*] voler ◆ **the car was cruising (along) at 80km/h** la voiture faisait 80 km/h sans effort ◆ **we were cruising along the road when suddenly ...** nous roulions tranquillement quand tout à coup ... ◆ **to ~ to victory** remporter la victoire haut la main

[3] [*taxi, patrol car*] marauder, faire la maraude ◆ **a cruising taxi** un taxi en maraude

[4] (* = *look for pick-up*) draguer*

N [1] (*Naut*) croisière *f* ◆ **to go on a ~** partir en croisière, faire une croisière

[2] (also **cruise missile**) missile *m* de croisière ◆ **a campaign against ~** une campagne contre les missiles de croisière

COMP **cruise control** N contrôle *m* (de vitesse)

cruise missile N missile *m* de croisière

cruising range N [*of aircraft*] autonomie *f* de vol

cruising speed N vitesse *f* *or* régime *m* de croisière

cruising yacht N yacht *m* de croisière

cruiser /ˈkruːzəʳ/ N (= *warship*) croiseur *m* ; (= *cabin cruiser*) yacht *m* de croisière ; → **battle**

COMP **cruiser weight** N (*Boxing*) poids *m* milourd

cruller /ˈkrʌləʳ/ N (*US*) beignet *m*

crumb /krʌm/ N miette *f* ; (*NonC: inside of loaf*) mie *f* ; (*fig*) miette *f*, brin *m* ; [*of information*] miettes *fpl*, fragments *mpl* ◆ **a ~ of comfort** un brin de réconfort ◆ **~s!*** ça alors !, zut !*

crumble /ˈkrʌmbl/ VT [+ *bread*] émietter ; [+ *plaster*] effriter ; [+ *earth, rocks*] (faire s')ébouler VI [*buildings etc*] tomber en ruines, se désagréger ; [*plaster*] s'effriter ; [*earth, rocks*] s'ébouler ; [*bread*] s'émietter ; (*fig*) [*hopes, economy etc*] s'effondrer, s'écrouler ; (*fig*) [*person*] se laisser abattre ; → **cookie** N (*Brit Culin*) crumble *m*

crumbly /ˈkrʌmblɪ/ ADJ friable N (* = *old person*) vieux croulant* *m*

crummy*, **crumby*** /ˈkrʌmɪ/ ADJ [1] [*hotel, town, job, film*] minable* ◆ **what a ~ thing to do!** c'est un coup minable !*, c'est vraiment mesquin de faire ça ! [2] (= *ill*) ◆ **to feel ~** ne pas avoir la pêche*, être patraque* [3] (= *guilty*) **to feel ~ about doing sth** se sentir minable* de faire qch

crump /krʌmp/ N éclatement *m* (*d'un obus*) ; (*Mil* * = *shell*) obus *m*

crumpet /ˈkrʌmpɪt/ N (*esp Brit Culin*) petite crêpe *f* épaisse ◆ **a bit of ~**‡ (*Brit fig*) une belle nana*

crumple /ˈkrʌmpl/ VT froisser, friper ; (also **crumple up**) chiffonner ◆ **he ~d the paper (up) into a ball** il a fait une boule de la feuille de papier VI se froisser, se chiffonner, se friper ◆ **her features ~d when she heard the bad news** son visage s'est décomposé quand elle a appris la mauvaise nouvelle COMP **crumple zone** N [*of car*] structure *f* déformable

crunch /krʌntʃ/ VT [1] (*with teeth*) croquer ◆ **to ~ an apple/a biscuit** croquer une pomme/un biscuit [2] (*underfoot*) écraser, faire craquer [3] ◆ **to ~ numbers** [*computer*] traiter des chiffres à grande vitesse ◆ **he doesn't want to spend his life ~ing numbers** il ne veut pas passer le reste de sa vie penché sur des chiffres VI ◆ **he ~ed across the gravel** il a traversé en faisant craquer le gravier sous ses pas N [1] (= *sound of teeth*) coup *m* de dents ; [*of broken glass, gravel etc*] craquement *m*, crissement *m* [2] (* *fig*) **the ~** (= *moment of reckoning*) l'instant *m* critique ◆ **here's the ~** c'est le moment crucial ◆ **when it comes to the ~ he ...** dans une situation critique *or* au moment crucial, il ...

► **crunch up** VT SEP broyer

crunchy /ˈkrʌntʃɪ/ ADJ [*foods, peanut butter, texture*] croquant ; [*gravel, snow*] qui crisse

crupper /ˈkrʌpəʳ/ N [*of harness*] croupière *f* ; (= *hindquarters*) croupe *f*

crusade /kruːˈseɪd/ N (*Hist, also fig*) croisade *f* VI (*fig*) partir en croisade (*against* contre ; *for* pour) ; (*Hist*) partir pour la *or* en croisade

crusader /kruːˈseɪdəʳ/ N (*Hist*) croisé *m* ; (*fig*) champion *m* (*for* de ; *against* en guerre contre) militant(e) *m(f)* (*for* en faveur de ; *against* en guerre contre) ; ◆ **the ~s for peace/against the bomb** ceux qui militent pour la paix/contre la bombe

crush /krʌʃ/ N [1] (= *crowd*) foule *f*, cohue *f* ◆ **there was a great ~ to get in** c'était la bousculade pour entrer ◆ **there was a terrible ~ at the concert** il y avait une vraie cohue au concert ◆ **he was lost in the ~** il était perdu dans la foule *or* la cohue

[2] ◆ **to have a ~ on sb** * avoir le béguin* pour qn

[3] (*Brit* = *drink*) jus *m* de fruit ◆ **orange ~** orange *f* pressée

VT [1] (= *compress*) [+ *stones, old cars*] écraser, broyer ; [+ *ice*] piler ; [+ *grapes*] écraser, presser ; [+ *ore*] bocarder ◆ **to ~ to a pulp** réduire en pulpe

[2] (= *crumple*) [+ *clothes*] froisser ◆ **to ~ clothes into a bag** fourrer *or* bourrer des vêtements dans une valise ◆ **to ~ objects into a suitcase** tasser *or* entasser des objets dans une valise ◆ **we were very ~ed in the car** nous étions très tassés dans la voiture

③ *(= overwhelm) [+ enemy]* écraser, accabler ; *[+ opponent in argument, country]* écraser ; *[+ revolution]* écraser, réprimer ; *[+ hope]* détruire ; *(= snub)* remettre à sa place, rabrouer

VI ① se presser, se serrer ◆ **they ~ed round him** ils se pressaient autour de lui ◆ **they ~ed into the car** ils se sont entassés *or* tassés dans la voiture ◆ **to ~ (one's way) into/through** *etc* se frayer un chemin dans/à travers *etc*

② *[clothes]* se froisser

COMP **crush bar** N *[of theatre]* bar *m* du foyer
crush barrier N *(Brit)* barrière *f* de sécurité
crushed velvet N panne *f* de velours
crush-resistant ADJ infroissable

► **crush out** VT SEP *[+ juice etc]* presser, exprimer ; *[+ cigarette end]* écraser, éteindre

crusher /ˈkrʌʃəʳ/ N *(= machine)* broyeur *m*, concasseur *m*

crushing /ˈkrʌʃɪŋ/ ADJ *[defeat, victory]* écrasant ; *[news]* accablant ; *[blow, disappointment]* terrible ; *[remark, reply]* cinglant ◆ **a ~ burden of debt** des dettes *fpl* écrasantes

crushingly /ˈkrʌʃɪŋlɪ/ ADV *(= humiliatingly) [say]* d'un ton cinglant ; *(= extremely) [bad, dull, boring]* terriblement

crust /krʌst/ N *(on bread, pie, snow)* croûte *f* ; *(= piece of crust)* croûton *m*, croûte *f* ; *(Med: on wound, sore)* croûte *f*, escarre *f* ; *[of wine]* dépôt *m (de tanin)* ◆ **there were only a few ~s to eat** pour toute nourriture il n'y avait que quelques croûtes de pain ◆ **a thin ~ of ice** une fine couche de glace ◆ **the earth's ~** *(Geol)* la croûte terrestre ; → **earn, upper** VT ◆ **frost ~ing the windscreen** le givre recouvrant le pare-brise ◆ **~ed snow** neige *f* croûtée ◆ **~ed with mud** *etc* couvert d'une croûte de boue *etc*

crustacean /krʌsˈteɪʃən/ ADJ, N crustacé *m*

crusty /ˈkrʌstɪ/ ADJ *[loaf, roll]* croustillant ; *(* fig) [old man]* hargneux, bourru N *(* = scruffy youth)* jeune *mf* crado *

crutch /krʌtʃ/ N ① *(= support)* soutien *m*, support *m* ; *(Med)* béquille *f* ; *(Archit)* étançon *m* ; *(Naut)* support *m* (de gui) ◆ **he gets about on ~es** il marche avec des béquilles ◆ **alcohol is a ~ for him** l'alcool lui sert de soutien ② *(Anat = crotch)* fourche *f* ; *[of trousers etc]* entre-jambes *m inv*

crux /krʌks/ N (pl **cruxes** *or* **cruces** /ˈkruːsiːz/) ① point *m* crucial ; *[of problem]* cœur *m*, centre *m* ◆ **the ~ of the matter** le cœur du sujet, l'essentiel *m* ② *(Climbing)* passage-clé *m*

cry /kraɪ/ N ① *(= loud shout)* cri *m* ; *[of hounds]* aboiements *mpl*, voix *f* ◆ **to give a ~** pousser un cri ◆ **he gave a ~ for help** il a crié *or* appelé au secours ◆ **he heard a ~ for help** il a entendu crier au secours ◆ **the cries of the victims** les cris *mpl* des victimes ◆ **there was a great ~ against the rise in prices** *(fig)* la hausse des prix a déclenché un tollé

◆ **in full cry** ◆ **the pack was in full ~** *(Hunting)* toute la meute donnait de la voix ◆ **the crowd was in full ~ after the thief** la foule poursuivait le voleur en criant à pleine voix ◆ **they are in full ~ against the Prime Minister** ils s'acharnent sur *or* contre le Premier ministre ◆ **the newspapers are in full ~ over the scandal** les journaux font des gorges chaudes de ce scandale

② *(= watchword)* slogan *m* ◆ **"votes for women" was their ~** leur slogan *or* leur cri de guerre était "le vote pour les femmes" ; → **battle, war**

③ *(= weep)* **she had a good ~** * elle a pleuré un bon coup *

VT ① *(= shout out)* crier ◆ **"here I am" he cried** "me voici" s'écria-t-il *or* cria-t-il ◆ **"go away", he cried to me** "allez-vous-en", me cria-t-il ◆ **to ~ mercy** crier grâce ◆ **to ~ shame** crier au scandale ◆ **to ~ shame on sb/sth** crier haro sur qn/qch ◆ **to ~ wolf** crier au loup

② ◆ **to ~ o.s. to sleep** s'endormir à force de pleurer ◆ **to ~ one's eyes** *or* **one's heart out** pleurer toutes les larmes de son corps

VI ① *(= weep)* pleurer *(about, for, over* sur) ; ◆ **to ~ with rage** pleurer de rage ◆ **to laugh till one cries** pleurer de rire, rire aux larmes ◆ **to ~ for sth** pleurer pour avoir qch ◆ **I'll give him something to ~ for!** * *(fig)* je vais lui apprendre à pleurnicher ! ◆ **it's no use ~ing over spilt milk** *(Prov)* ce qui est fait est fait ; → **shoulder**

② *(= call out) [person, animal, bird]* pousser un cri *or* des cris ◆ **the baby cried at birth** l'enfant a poussé un cri *or* a crié en naissant ◆ **he cried (out) with pain** il a poussé un cri de douleur ◆ **to ~ for help** appeler à l'aide, crier au secours ◆ **to ~ for mercy** demander miséricorde, implorer la pitié ◆ **the starving crowd cried for bread** la foule affamée réclama du pain ◆ **to ~ foul** crier à l'injustice, crier au scandale

③ *[hunting dogs]* donner de la voix, aboyer

► **cry down** * VT SEP *(= decry)* décrier

► **cry off** *(Brit)* VI *(from meeting)* se décommander ; *(from promise)* se dédire ◆ **I'm ~ing off!** je ne veux plus rien savoir !

VT FUS *(= cancel) [+ arrangement, deal]* annuler ; *(= withdraw from) [+ meeting]* décommander

► **cry out** VI *(inadvertently)* pousser un cri ; *(deliberately)* s'écrier ◆ **he cried out with joy** il a poussé un cri de joie ◆ **to ~ out to sb** appeler qn en criant, crier pour appeler qn ◆ **to ~ out for sth** demander *or* réclamer qch à grands cris ◆ **for ~ing out loud!** * pour l'amour de Dieu ! ◆ **that floor is just ~ing out to be washed** * ce plancher a vraiment besoin d'être lavé ◆ **the door is ~ing out for a coat of paint** * la porte a bien besoin d'une couche de peinture

► **cry out against** VT FUS protester contre

► **cry up** * VT SEP *(= praise)* vanter, exalter ◆ **he's not all he's cried up to be** il n'est pas à la hauteur de sa réputation, il n'est pas aussi formidable * qu'on le dit

crybaby /ˈkraɪbeɪbɪ/ N *(pej)* pleurnicheur *m*, -euse *f*

crying /ˈkraɪɪŋ/ ADJ *(lit)* pleurant, qui pleure ; *(fig)* criant, flagrant ◆ **~ injustice** injustice *f* criante *or* flagrante ◆ **~ need for sth** besoin pressant *or* urgent de qch ◆ **it's a ~ shame** c'est une honte, c'est honteux N *(= shouts)* cris *mpl* ; *(= weeping)* larmes *fpl*, pleurs *mpl*

cryobiology /ˌkraɪəʊbaɪˈblɒdʒɪ/ N cryobiologie *f*

cryogenic /ˌkraɪəˈdʒenɪk/ ADJ cryogénique

cryogenics /ˌkraɪəˈdʒenɪks/ N (NonC) cryogénie *f*

cryonic /kraɪˈɒnɪk/ ADJ cryonique

cryonics /kraɪˈɒnɪks/ N (NonC) cryonique *f*

cryosurgery /ˌkraɪəʊˈsɜːdʒərɪ/ N cryochirurgie *f*

crypt /krɪpt/ N crypte *f*

cryptic /ˈkrɪptɪk/ ADJ *(= secret)* secret (-ète *f*) ; *(= mysterious)* sibyllin, énigmatique ; *(= terse)* laconique

cryptically /ˈkrɪptɪkəlɪ/ ADV *(= mysteriously)* énigmatiquement ; *(= tersely)* laconiquement

crypto- /ˈkrɪptəʊ/ PREF crypto- ◆ **~communist** *etc* cryptocommuniste *etc*

cryptogram /ˈkrɪptəʊgræm/ N cryptogramme *m*

cryptographer /krɪpˈtɒgrəfəʳ/ N cryptographe *mf*

cryptographic(al) /ˌkrɪptəʊˈgræfɪk(əl)/ ADJ cryptographique

cryptography /krɪpˈtɒgrəfɪ/ N cryptographie *f*

crystal /ˈkrɪstl/ N ① (NonC) cristal *m* ; → **rock²** ② *(Chem, Min)* cristal *m* ◆ **salt ~s** cristaux *mpl* de sel ③ *(US = watch glass)* verre *m* de montre ④ *(Rad)* galène *f*

COMP *(lit) [vase]* de cristal ; *(fig) [waters, lake]* cristallin, de cristal *(fig, liter)*
crystal ball N boule *f* de cristal
crystal-clear ADJ clair comme le jour *or* comme de l'eau de roche
crystal-gazer N voyant(e) *m(f) (qui lit dans une boule de cristal)*
crystal-gazing N (l'art *m* de la) voyance *f* ; *(fig)* prédictions *fpl*, prophéties *fpl*
crystal set N *(Rad)* poste *m* à galène

crystalline /ˈkrɪstəlaɪn/ ADJ cristallin, clair *or* pur comme le cristal ◆ **~ lens** *(Opt)* cristallin *m*

crystallize /ˈkrɪstəlaɪz/ VI *(lit, fig)* se cristalliser

VT cristalliser ; *[+ sugar]* (faire) cuire au cassé

COMP **crystallized fruits** NPL fruits *mpl* confits *or* candis

crystallography /ˌkrɪstəˈlɒgrəfɪ/ N cristallographie *f*

CSA /ˌsiːesˈeɪ/ N *(Brit)* (abbrev of **Child Support Agency**) → **child**

CSC /ˌsiːesˈsiː/ N (abbrev of **Civil Service Commission**) → **civil**

CSE /ˌsiːesˈiː/ N *(Brit)* (abbrev of **Certificate of Secondary Education**) ≈ BEPC *m*

CSEU /ˌsiːesiːˈjuː/ N *(Brit)* (abbrev of **Confederation of Shipbuilding and Engineering Unions**) *syndicat*

CS gas /ˌsiːesˈgæs/ N *(Brit)* gaz *m* CS

CST /ˌsiːesˈtiː/ N *(US)* (abbrev of **Central Standard Time**) → **central**

CSU /ˌsiːesˈjuː/ N *(Brit)* (abbrev of **Civil Service Union**) *syndicat*

CT abbrev of **Connecticut**

ct ① abbrev of **carat** ② abbrev of **cent**

CTT /ˌsiːtiːˈtiː/ N *(Brit)* (abbrev of **capital transfer tax**) → **capital**

cub /kʌb/ N ① *[of animal]* petit(e) *m(f)* ; *(* = youth)* gosse *m*, petit morveux *m (pej)* ; → **bear², fox, wolf** ② (also **cub scout**) louveteau *m (scout)*

COMP **cub master** N *(Scouting)* chef *m*
cub mistress N cheftaine *f*
cub reporter N *(Press)* jeune reporter *m*

Cuba /ˈkjuːbə/ N Cuba *f or m* ◆ **in ~** à Cuba

Cuban /ˈkjuːbən/ ADJ cubain N Cubain(e) *m(f)*

cubbyhole /ˈkʌbɪhəʊl/ N *(= cupboard)* débarras *m*, cagibi *m* ; *(= poky room)* cagibi *m*

cube /kjuːb/ N *(gen, Culin, Math)* cube *m* ; → **soup, stock** VT *(Math)* cuber ; *(Culin)* couper en cubes *or* en dés COMP **cube root** N *(Math)* racine *f* cubique

cubic /ˈkjuːbɪk/ ADJ *(of shape, volume)* cubique ; *(of measures)* cube ◆ **~ capacity** volume *m* ◆ **~ centimetre** centimètre *m* cube ◆ **~ content** contenance *f* cubique ◆ **~ measure** mesure *f* de volume ◆ **~ metre** mètre *m* cube ◆ **~ equation** *(Math)* équation *f* du troisième degré

cubicle /ˈkjuːbɪkəl/ N *[of hospital, dormitory]* box *m*, alcôve *f* ; *[of swimming baths]* cabine *f*

cubism /ˈkjuːbɪzəm/ N cubisme *m*

cubist /ˈkjuːbɪst/ ADJ, N cubiste *mf*

cubit /ˈkjuːbɪt/ N *(Bible)* coudée *f*

cuckold † /ˈkʌkəld/ N (mari *m*) cocu * *m* VT tromper, cocufier *

cuckoo /ˈkʊkuː/ N *(= bird)* coucou *m* ADJ *(* = mad)* piqué *, toqué * ◆ **to go ~** * perdre la boule *

COMP **cuckoo clock** N coucou *m (pendule)*
cuckoo spit N *(on plant)* crachat *m* de coucou

cuckoopint /ˈkʊkuːpaɪnt/ N *(Bot)* pied-de-veau *m*

cucumber /ˈkjuːkʌmbəʳ/ N concombre *m* ; → **cool** COMP *[sandwich]* au concombre

cud /kʌd/ N → **chew vt**

cuddle /ˈkʌdl/ **N** câlin *m* ◆ **to have a ~** (se) faire (un) câlin* ◆ **to give sb a ~** faire un câlin* à qn **VT** câliner **VI** s'enlacer

► **cuddle down** **VI** *[child in bed]* se pelotonner ◆ **~ down now!** maintenant allonge-toi (et dors) !

► **cuddle up** **VI** se pelotonner (*to, against* contre)

cuddly /ˈkʌdlɪ/ **ADJ** *[child]* caressant, câlin ; *[animal]* qui donne envie de le caresser ; *[teddy bear, doll]* doux (douce *f*), qu'on a envie de câliner ◆ **~ toy** (jouet *m* en) peluche *f*

cudgel /ˈkʌdʒəl/ **N** gourdin *m*, trique *f* ◆ **to take up the ~s for** *or* **on behalf of ...** prendre fait et cause pour ... **VT** frapper à coups de trique ◆ **to ~ one's brains** se creuser la cervelle *or* la tête (*for* pour)

cue /kjuː/ **N** 1 *(Theat)* *(verbal)* réplique *f* *(indiquant à un acteur qu'il doit parler)* ; *(action)* signal *m* ; *(Mus)* signal *m* d'entrée ; *(Rad, TV)* signal *m* ◆ **to give sb his ~** *(Theat)* donner la réplique à qn ; *(fig)* faire un signal à qn ◆ **to take one's ~** *(Theat)* entamer sa réplique ◆ **X's exit was the ~ for Y's entrance** *(Theat)* la sortie d'X donnait à Y le signal de son entrée ◆ **to take one's ~ from sb** *(fig)* emboîter le pas à qn *(fig)* ◆ **that was my ~ to ...** *(fig)* c'était mon signal pour ... 2 *(Billiards etc)* queue *f* de billard **VT** *(Cine, Rad, Theat etc)* donner la réplique à **COMP** **cue ball** **N** *(Billiards etc)* bille *f* du joueur

► **cue in** **VT SEP** *(Rad, TV)* donner le signal à ; *(Theat)* donner la réplique à ◆ **to ~ sb in on sth** *(fig)* mettre qn au courant de qch

cuesta /ˈkwestə/ **N** *(Geog, Geol)* cuesta *f*

cuff /kʌf/ **N** 1 *(gen)* poignet *m* ; *[of shirt]* manchette *f* ; *[of coat]* parement *m* ; *(US)* *[of trousers]* revers *m inv*

◆ **off the cuff** à l'improviste, au pied levé ◆ **to speak off the ~** improviser ; see also **off**

◆ **on the cuff*** *(US)* ◆ **to buy on the ~** acheter à crédit

2 *(= blow)* gifle *f*, calotte* *f*

NPL **cuffs** * *(= handcuffs)* menottes *fpl*

VT *(= strike)* gifler, calotter*

cufflink /ˈkʌflɪŋk/ **N** bouton *m* de manchette

cu.in. abbrev of **cubic inch(es)**

cuisine /kwɪˈziːn/ **N** cuisine *f* ◆ **French/oriental ~** la cuisine française/orientale

cul-de-sac /ˈkʌldəˌsæk/ **N** (pl **culs-de-sac** *or* **cul-de-sacs**) *(esp Brit)* cul-de-sac *m*, impasse *f* ◆ **"cul-de-sac"** *(road sign)* "voie sans issue"

culinary /ˈkʌlɪnərɪ/ **ADJ** culinaire

cull /kʌl/ **VT** 1 *(= take samples from)* sélectionner 2 *(= remove inferior items, animals etc)* éliminer, supprimer ; *[+ seals, deer etc]* abattre 3 *(= pick)* *[+ flowers, fruit]* cueillir **N** 1 *(= killing)* abattage *m* ; → **seal¹** 2 *(= animal)* animal *m* à éliminer (dans une portée)

culling /ˈkʌlɪŋ/ **N** *(NonC)* ◆ **seal/deer ~** réduction *f* de la population de phoques/cervidés

culminate /ˈkʌlmɪneɪt/ **VI** ◆ **to ~ in sth** *(= end in)* finir *or* se terminer par qch ; *(= lead to)* mener à qch ◆ **it ~d in his throwing her out** pour finir, il l'a mise à la porte

culminating /ˈkʌlmɪneɪtɪŋ/ **ADJ** culminant ◆ **~ point** point *m* culminant, sommet *m*

culmination /ˌkʌlmɪˈneɪʃən/ **N** *(Astron)* culmination *f* ; *(fig)* *[of success, career]* apogée *m* ; *[of disturbance, quarrel]* point *m* culminant

culotte(s) /kjuːˈlɒt(s)/ **N(PL)** jupe-culotte *f*

culpability /ˌkʌlpəˈbɪlɪtɪ/ **N** culpabilité *f*

culpable /ˈkʌlpəbl/ **ADJ** coupable (*of* de) blâmable ◆ **~ homicide** *(Jur)* homicide *m* volontaire ; *(Scot)* homicide *m* sans préméditation ◆ **~ negligence** *(Jur)* négligence *f* coupable

culprit /ˈkʌlprɪt/ **N** coupable *mf*

cult /kʌlt/ **N** *(Rel, fig)* culte *m* (*of* de) ; ◆ **he made a ~ of cleanliness** il avait le culte de la propreté

COMP **cult figure** **N** objet *m* d'un culte, idole *f* ◆ **he has become a ~ figure** *(fig)* il est devenu l'objet d'un véritable culte *or* une véritable idole

cult film **N** film-culte *m*

cult following **N** ◆ **a film/book/group with a ~ following** un film-/livre-/groupe-culte

cult movie **N** ⇒ **cult film**

cultivable /ˈkʌltɪvəbl/ **ADJ** cultivable

cultivar /ˈkʌltɪˌvɑːʳ/ **N** variété *f* cultivée

cultivate /ˈkʌltɪveɪt/ **VT** *(lit, fig)* cultiver ◆ **to ~ the mind** se cultiver (l'esprit)

cultivated /ˈkʌltɪveɪtɪd/ **ADJ** *[land, person]* cultivé ; *[voice]* distingué ◆ **~ pearls** perles *fpl* de culture

cultivation /ˌkʌltɪˈveɪʃən/ **N** culture *f* ◆ **fields under ~** cultures *fpl* ◆ **out of ~** en friche, inculte

cultivator /ˈkʌltɪveɪtəʳ/ **N** *(= person)* cultivateur *m*, -trice *f* ; *(= machine)* cultivateur *m* ; *(power-driven)* motoculteur *m*

cultural /ˈkʌltʃərəl/ **ADJ** 1 *[background, activities]* culturel ◆ **~ attaché** attaché *m* culturel ◆ **~ environment** environnement *m* *or* milieu *m* culturel ◆ **~ integration** acculturation *f* ◆ **the Cultural Revolution** la Révolution Culturelle 2 *(Agr)* de culture

culturally /ˈkʌltʃərəlɪ/ **ADV** culturellement

culture /ˈkʌltʃəʳ/ **N** 1 *(= education, refinement)* culture *f* ◆ **physical ~** † la culture physique ◆ **a woman of no ~** une femme sans aucune culture *or* complètement inculte 2 *[of country, society, organization]* culture *f* ◆ **French ~** la culture française ◆ **a ~ of dependency, a dependency ~** *(Pol)* une culture fondée sur l'assistanat 3 *(Agr)* culture *f* ; *[of bees]* apiculture *f* ; *[of fish]* pisciculture *f* ; *[of farm animals]* élevage *m* 4 *(Bio, Med)* culture *f* **VT** *(Bio)* cultiver

COMP *[tube]* à culture

culture-fair test **N** *examen conçu pour ne pas défavoriser les minorités ethniques*

culture fluid **N** *(Bio)* bouillon *m* de culture

culture-free test **N** ⇒ **culture-fair test**

culture gap **N** fossé *m* culturel

culture medium **N** *(Bio)* milieu *m* de culture

culture shock **N** choc *m* culturel

culture vulture * **N** *(hum)* fana* *mf* de culture

cultured /ˈkʌltʃəd/ **ADJ** cultivé ◆ **~ pearl** perle *f* de culture

culvert /ˈkʌlvət/ **N** caniveau *m*

cum** /kʌm/ **N** sperme *m*, foutre** *m*

-cum- /kʌm/ **PREP** ◆ **a carpenter-cum-painter** un charpentier-peintre ◆ **a secretary-cum-chauffeur** une secrétaire qui fait office de chauffeur ◆ **a dining room-cum-living room** une salle à manger-salon

cumbersome /ˈkʌmbəsəm/, **cumbrous** /ˈkʌmbrəs/ **ADJ** *(= bulky)* encombrant, embarrassant ; *(= heavy)* lourd, pesant

cumin /ˈkʌmɪn/ **N** cumin *m*

cum laude /kʊm ˈlaʊdeɪ/ **ADJ** *(Univ)* avec mention *(obtention d'un diplôme, d'un titre)*

cummerbund /ˈkʌməbʌnd/ **N** ceinture *f* *(de smoking)*

cumulative /ˈkjuːmjʊlətɪv/ **ADJ** cumulatif ◆ **~ evidence** *(Jur)* preuve *f* par accumulation de témoignages ◆ **~ interest** *(Fin)* intérêt *m* cumulatif ◆ **~ voting** vote *m* plural

cumulatively /ˈkjuːmjʊlətɪvlɪ/ **ADV** cumulativement

cumuli /ˈkjuːmjəˌlaɪ/ **NPL** of **cumulus**

cumulonimbus /ˌkjuːmjələʊˈnɪmbəs/ **N** cumulonimbus *m inv*

cumulus /ˈkjuːmjələs/ **N** (pl **cumuli** /ˈkjuːmjəˌlaɪ/) cumulus *m*

cuneiform /ˈkjuːnɪfɔːm/ **ADJ** cunéiforme **N** écriture *f* cunéiforme

cunnilingus /ˌkʌnɪˈlɪŋgəs/ **N** cunnilingus *m*

cunning /ˈkʌnɪŋ/ **N** finesse *f*, astuce *f* ; *(pej)* ruse *f*, fourberie *f* ; († † *= skill*) habileté *f*, adresse *f* **ADJ** astucieux, malin (-igne *f*) ; *(pej)* rusé, fourbe ◆ **a ~ little gadget*** un petit truc astucieux*

cunningly /ˈkʌnɪŋlɪ/ **ADV** 1 *(= cleverly)* *[disguised, camouflaged, concealed]* avec astuce, astucieusement ; *[contrived, designed, positioned, placed]* astucieusement 2 *(pej = deceitfully)* *[speak]* d'une manière fourbe ; *[say]* avec fourberie ; *[look at]* d'un air fourbe

cunt** /kʌnt/ **N** 1 *(= genitals)* con** *m*, chatte** *f* 2 *(= person)* salaud** *m*, salope** *f*

cup /kʌp/ **N** 1 tasse *f* ; *(= goblet)* coupe *f* ; *(= cupful)* tasse *f*, coupe *f* ◆ **~ of tea** tasse *f* de thé ◆ **he drank four ~s** *or* **~fuls** il (en) a bu quatre tasses ◆ **one ~** *or* **~ful of sugar/flour** *etc* *(Culin)* une tasse de sucre/farine *etc* ◆ **cider/champagne ~** cocktail *m* au cidre/au champagne ◆ **he was in his ~s** † il était dans les vignes du Seigneur, il avait un verre dans le nez* ◆ **that's just his ~ of tea*** c'est son truc* ◆ **that's not my ~ of tea*** ce n'est pas ma tasse de thé* *or* mon truc* ◆ **it isn't everyone's ~ of tea*** ça ne plaît pas à tout le monde ◆ **his ~ of happiness was full** *(liter)* il jouissait d'un bonheur sans mélange *or* nuage ◆ **to drain the ~ of sorrow** *(liter)* boire le calice jusqu'à la lie ; → **coffee, slip**

2 *(Tech)* godet *m* ; *[of flower]* corolle *f* ; *(Rel: also* **communion cup***)* calice *m* ; *(Brit Sport etc = prize competition)* coupe *f* ; *(Geog)* cuvette *f* ; *(Anat)* *[of bone]* cavité *f* articulaire, glène *f* ; *(Med Hist = cupping glass)* ventouse *f* ; *[of brassière]* bonnet *m* *(de soutien-gorge)* ; → **world**

VT 1 ◆ **to ~ one's hands** faire une coupe avec ses deux mains ◆ **to ~ one's hands round sth** mettre ses mains autour de qch ◆ **to ~ one's hands round one's ear/one's mouth** mettre ses mains en cornet/en porte-voix

2 *(Med Hist)* appliquer des ventouses sur

3 *(Golf)* **to ~ the ball** faire un divot

COMP **cup bearer** **N** échanson *m*

cup final **N** *(Brit Ftbl)* finale *f* de la coupe

cup size **N** *[of bra]* profondeur *f* de bonnet

cup-tie **N** *(Brit Ftbl)* match *m* de coupe *or* comptant pour la coupe

cupboard /ˈkʌbəd/ **N** *(esp Brit)* placard *m* ; → **skeleton** **COMP** **cupboard love** **N** *(Brit)* amour *m* intéressé

cupcake /ˈkʌpkeɪk/ **N** *(Culin)* petit gâteau *m*

cupful /ˈkʌpfʊl/ **N** (contenu *m* d'une) tasse *f* ; → **cup**

Cupid /ˈkjuːpɪd/ **N** *(Myth)* Cupidon *m* ; *(Art = cherub)* amour *m* ◆ **~'s darts** les flèches *fpl* de Cupidon

cupidity /kjuːˈpɪdɪtɪ/ **N** *(frm)* cupidité *f*

cupola /ˈkjuːpələ/ **N** 1 *(Archit)* *(= dome)* coupole *f*, dôme *m* ; *(US = lantern, belfry)* belvédère *m* 2 *(Naut)* coupole *f* 3 *(Metal)* cubilot *m*

cuppa* /ˈkʌpə/ **N** *(Brit)* tasse *f* de thé

cupric /ˈkjuːprɪk/ **ADJ** cuprique ◆ **~ oxide** oxyde *m* de cuivre

cur /kɜːʳ/ **N** 1 *(pej = dog)* sale chien *m*, sale cabot* *m* 2 (* *pej = man*) malotru *m*, mufle* *m*, rustre *m*

curable /ˈkjʊərəbl/ **ADJ** guérissable, curable

curacy /ˈkjʊərəsɪ/ **N** vicariat *m*

curare /kjʊəˈrɑːrɪ/ **N** curare *m*

curate¹ /ˈkjʊərɪt/ **N** vicaire *m* ◆ **it's like the ~'s egg** *(Brit)* il y a du bon et du mauvais

curate² /kjʊəˈreɪt/ **VT** *(= organize)* *[+ exhibition]* organiser

curative /ˈkjʊərətɪv/ **ADJ** curatif

curator /kjʊəˈreɪtəʳ/ N ① *[of museum etc]* conservateur *m* ② *(Scot Jur)* curateur *m (d'un aliéné or d'un mineur)*

curatorial /ˌkjʊərəˈtɔːrɪəl/ ADJ *[expertise, career]* de conservateur ; *[policy]* en matière de conservation ◆ **the museum's ~ team** l'équipe qui administre le musée

curb /kɜːb/ N ① *[of harness]* gourmette *f* ; *(fig)* frein *m* ; *(on trade etc)* restriction *f* ◆ **to put a ~ on sth** *(fig)* mettre un frein à qch ② *(US: at roadside)* bord *m* du trottoir VT *(US) [+ horse]* mettre un mors à ; *(fig) [+ impatience, passion]* refréner, contenir ; *[+ expenditure]* réduire, restreindre
COMP **curb bit** N mors *m*
curb chain N gourmette *f*
curb crawler N *(US)* conducteur *m* qui accoste les femmes sur le trottoir
curb crawling N *(US)* drague* *f* en voiture
curb market N *(US Stock Exchange)* marché *m* hors-cote
curb reins NPL rênes *fpl* de filet
curb roof N *(Archit)* comble *m* brisé
curb service N *(US)* service *m* au volant (dans un restaurant drive-in)
curb weight N *(US: of vehicle)* poids *m* à vide

curbstone /ˈkɜːbstəʊn/ N *(US)* pavé *m (pour bordure de trottoir)* COMP **curbstone market** N *(US Stock Exchange)* marché *m* hors-cote

curd /kɜːd/ N *(gen pl)* ◆ **~(s)** lait *m* caillé ; → **lemon** COMP **curd cheese** N ≈ fromage *m* blanc

curdle /ˈkɜːdl/ VT *[+ milk]* cailler ; *[+ mayonnaise]* faire tomber ◆ **it was enough to ~ the blood** c'était à vous glacer le sang VI *[milk]* se cailler ; *[mayonnaise]* tomber ◆ **his blood ~d** son sang s'est figé ◆ **it made my blood ~** cela m'a glacé le sang

cure /kjʊəʳ/ VT ① *(Med) [+ disease, patient]* guérir *(of* de) ; *(fig) [+ poverty]* éliminer ; *[+ unfairness]* éliminer, remédier à ◆ **to ~ an injustice** réparer une injustice ◆ **to ~ an evil** remédier à un mal ◆ **to be ~d (of sth)** guérir (de qch) ◆ **to ~ a child of a bad habit** faire perdre une mauvaise habitude à un enfant ◆ **to ~ o.s. of smoking** se déshabituer du tabac, se guérir de l'habitude de fumer ◆ **what can't be ~d must be endured** *(Prov)* il faut savoir accepter l'inévitable ② *[+ meat, fish] (= salt)* saler ; *(= smoke)* fumer ; *(= dry)* sécher N ① *(Med) (= remedy)* remède *m* ; *(= recovery)* guérison *f* ◆ **to take** *or* **follow a ~** faire une cure ◆ **past** *or* **beyond ~** *[person]* inguérissable, incurable ; *[state, injustice, evil]* irrémédiable, irréparable ; → **prevention, rest** ② *(Rel)* cure *f* ◆ **~ of souls** charge *f* d'âmes COMP **cure-all** N panacée *f*

cured /kjʊəd/ ADJ *(Culin) (= salted)* salé ; *(= smoked)* fumé ; *(= dried)* séché

curfew /ˈkɜːfjuː/ N couvre-feu *m* ◆ **to impose a/lift the ~** décréter/lever le couvre-feu

curie /ˈkjʊərɪ/ N *(Phys)* curie *m*

curing /ˈkjʊərɪŋ/ N *(by salting)* salaison *f* ; *(by smoking)* fumaison *f* ; *(by drying)* séchage *m*

curio /ˈkjʊərɪəʊ/ N bibelot *m*, curiosité *f*

curiosity /ˌkjʊərɪˈɒsɪtɪ/ N ① *(NonC = inquisitiveness)* curiosité *f (about* de) ; ◆ **out of ~** par curiosité ◆ **~ killed the cat** *(Prov)* la curiosité est un vilain défaut *(Prov)* ② *(= rare thing)* curiosité *f*, rareté *f* COMP **curiosity shop** N magasin *m* de brocante *or* de curiosités

curious /ˈkjʊərɪəs/ ADJ ① *(also pej)* curieux *(also pej)* ◆ **I'm ~ to know what he did** je suis *or* serais curieux de savoir ce qu'il a fait ◆ **I'm ~ about him** il m'intrigue ◆ **why do you ask? – I'm just ~** pourquoi vous me demandez ça ? – par curiosité, c'est tout ② *(= strange)* curieux ◆ **it is ~ that .../how ...** c'est curieux que ... *+ subj*/comme ...

curiously /ˈkjʊərɪəslɪ/ ADV ① *(= inquisitively) [ask]* d'un ton inquisiteur ② *(= oddly) [silent, reticent]* curieusement ◆ **~ shaped** d'une forme curieuse ◆ **~, he didn't object** curieusement, il n'a pas émis d'objection

curium /ˈkjʊərɪəm/ N curium *m*

curl /kɜːl/ N ① *[of hair]* boucle *f* (de cheveux) ② *(gen)* courbe *f* ; *[of smoke]* spirale *f*, volute *f* ; *[of waves]* ondulation *f* ◆ **with a ~ of the lip** *(fig)* avec une moue méprisante
VT *[+ hair] (loosely)* (faire) boucler ; *(tightly)* friser ◆ **she ~s her hair** elle frise *or* boucle ses cheveux ◆ **he ~ed his lip in disdain** il a eu une moue dédaigneuse ◆ **the dog ~ed its lip menacingly** le chien a retroussé ses babines d'un air menaçant
VI ① *[hair] (loosely)* boucler ; *(tightly)* friser ◆ **it's enough to make your hair ~*** *(fig)* c'est à vous faire dresser les cheveux sur la tête ◆ **his lip ~ed disdainfully** il a eu une moue dédaigneuse ◆ **the dog's lip ~ed menacingly** le chien a retroussé ses babines d'un air menaçant
② *[person, animal]* ⇒ **curl up**
COMP **curling irons, curling tongs** NPL fer *m* à friser
curl paper N papillote *f*

► **curl up** VI s'enrouler ; *[person]* se pelotonner ; *(*: from shame etc)* rentrer sous terre ; *[cat]* se mettre en boule, se pelotonner ; *[dog]* se coucher en rond ; *[leaves]* se recroqueviller ; *[paper]* se recourber, se replier ; *[corners]* se corner ; *[stale bread]* se racornir ◆ **he lay ~ed up on the floor** il était couché en boule par terre ◆ **to ~ up with laughter** se tordre de rire ◆ **the smoke ~ed up** la fumée montait en volutes *or* en spirales
VT SEP enrouler ◆ **to ~ o.s. up** *[person]* se pelotonner ; *[cat]* se mettre en boule, se pelotonner ; *[dog]* se coucher en rond

curler /ˈkɜːləʳ/ N ① *[of hair]* rouleau *m*, bigoudi *m* ② *(Sport)* joueur *m*, -euse *f* de curling

curlew /ˈkɜːljuː/ N courlis *m*

curlicue /ˈkɜːlɪkjuː/ N *[of handwriting]* fioriture *f* ; *[of skating]* figure *f (de patinage)*

curling /ˈkɜːlɪŋ/ N *(Sport)* curling *m*

curly /ˈkɜːlɪ/ ADJ *[hair] (loosely)* bouclé ; *(tightly)* frisé ◆ **~ eyelashes** cils *mpl* recourbés
COMP **curly bracket** N accolade *f*
curly-haired, curly-headed ADJ aux cheveux bouclés *or* frisés
curly lettuce N laitue *f* frisée

curmudgeon /kɜːˈmʌdʒən/ N *(= miser)* harpagon *m*, grippe-sou* *m* ; *(= surly person)* grincheux *m*

curmudgeonly /kɜːˈmʌdʒənlɪ/ ADJ *(= miserly)* grippe-sou ; *(= surly)* grincheux

currant /ˈkʌrənt/ N ① *(= fruit)* groseille *f* ; (also **currant bush**) groseillier *m* ; → **blackcurrant, redcurrant** ② *(= dried fruit)* raisin *m* de Corinthe
COMP **currant bun** N petit pain *m* aux raisins
currant loaf N pain *m* aux raisins

currency /ˈkʌrənsɪ/ N ① *(Fin)* monnaie *f*, devise *f* ; *(= money)* argent *m* ◆ **the ~ is threatened** la monnaie est en danger ◆ **this coin is no longer legal ~** cette pièce n'a plus cours (légal) ◆ **foreign ~** devise *f or* monnaie *f* étrangère ◆ **I have no Chinese ~** je n'ai pas d'argent chinois ; → **hard, paper**
② *(= acceptance, prevalence)* cours *m*, circulation *f* ◆ **to gain ~** se répandre, s'accréditer ◆ **to give ~ to** accréditer ◆ **such words have short ~** de tels mots n'ont pas cours longtemps ◆ **this coin is no longer in ~** cette pièce n'est plus en circulation
COMP **currency exemptions** NPL *(Fin, Jur)* dispenses *fpl* en matière de réglementation des changes
currency market N *(Fin)* place *f* financière
currency note N billet *m* de banque
currency rate N cours *m* des devises
currency restrictions NPL contrôle *m* des changes
currency snake N serpent *m* monétaire
currency trader N cambiste *mf*
currency trading N opérations *fpl* de change
currency unit N unité *f* monétaire

current /ˈkʌrənt/ ADJ ① *(= present) [situation, fashion, tendency, popularity, job]* actuel ◆ **the system in ~ use** le système utilisé actuellement ◆ **at the ~ rate of exchange** au cours actuel du change ◆ **~ events** événements *mpl* actuels, actualité *f NonC* ◆ **~ issue** *(Press)* dernier numéro *m* ◆ **~ month/year/week** mois *m*/année *f*/semaine *f* en cours ◆ **her ~ boyfriend** son copain* *or* petit ami du moment
② *(= widely accepted or used) [opinion]* courant, commun ; *[word, phrase, price]* courant, en cours ◆ **to be ~** *[phrase, expression]* être accepté *or* courant
N *[of air, water]* courant *m (also Elec)* ; *(fig) [of events etc]* cours *m*, tendance *f* ; *[of opinions]* tendance *f* ◆ **to go with the ~** *(lit, fig)* suivre le courant ◆ **to drift with the ~** *(lit)* se laisser aller au fil de l'eau ; *(fig)* aller selon le vent ◆ **to go against the ~** *(lit)* remonter le courant ; *(fig)* aller à contre-courant ; → **alternating, direct**
COMP **current account** N *(Brit)* compte *m* courant
current affairs NPL questions *fpl or* problèmes *mpl* d'actualité, actualité *f NonC*
current assets NPL actif *m* de roulement
current cost accounting N comptabilité *f* en coûts actuels
current expenditure N dépenses *fpl* courantes
current liabilities NPL passif *m* exigible *or* dettes *fpl* exigibles à court terme
current yield N *(Stock Exchange)* taux *m* de rendement courant, taux *m* actuariel

⚠ Be cautious about translating the adjective **current** by **courant**, which does not mean 'present-day'.

currently /ˈkʌrəntlɪ/ ADV actuellement, à présent

curriculum /kəˈrɪkjʊləm/ N (pl **curriculums** *or* **curricula** /kəˈrɪkjʊlə/) programme *m* scolaire ◆ **the one compulsory foreign language on the ~** la seule langue étrangère obligatoire au programme ◆ **the history ~** le programme d'histoire
COMP **curriculum coordinator** N responsable *mf* des programmes scolaires
curriculum council N *(US Scol)* ≈ service *m* des programmes scolaires
curriculum vitae N (pl **curricula vitae**) *(Brit)* curriculum vitae *m*, CV *m*

curried /ˈkʌrɪd/ ADJ au curry

curry¹ /ˈkʌrɪ/ *(Culin)* N curry *or* cari *m* ◆ **beef ~** curry *m* de bœuf VT accommoder au curry COMP **curry powder** N (poudre *f* de) curry *m*

curry² /ˈkʌrɪ/ VT *[+ horse]* étriller ; *[+ leather]* corroyer ◆ **to ~ favour with sb** chercher à gagner la faveur de qn COMP **curry-comb** N étrille *f* VT étriller

curse /kɜːs/ N ① *(= malediction, spell)* malédiction *f* ◆ **a ~ on him!** † maudit soit-il ! † ◆ **to call down** *or* **put** *or* **lay a ~ on sb** maudire qn ② *(= swearword)* juron *m*, imprécation *f* ◆ **~s!*** zut !* ③ *(fig = bane)* fléau *m*, calamité *f* ◆ **the ~ of drunkenness** le fléau de l'ivrognerie ◆ **she has the ~*** *(= menstruation)* elle a ses règles VT maudire ◆ **~ the child!*** maudit enfant ! ◆ **to be ~d with** *(fig)* être affligé de VI *(= swear)* jurer, sacrer

cursed* /ˈkɜːsɪd/ ADJ sacré*, maudit, satané *all before n*

cursive /ˈkɜːsɪv/ ADJ cursif N (écriture *f*) cursive *f*

cursor /ˈkɜːsəʳ/ N *(Comput)* curseur *m*

cursorily /ˈkɜːsərɪlɪ/ ADV en vitesse, à la hâte *(pej)*

cursory /ˈkɜːsərɪ/ ADJ *(= superficial)* superficiel ; *(= hasty)* hâtif ◆ **to give a ~ glance at** *[+ person, object]* jeter un coup d'œil à ; *[+ book, essay, letter]* lire en diagonale *

curt /kɜːt/ ADJ *[person, manner]* brusque, sec (sèche *f*), cassant ; *[explanation, question]* brusque, sec (sèche *f*) ◆ **in a ~ voice** d'un ton cassant ◆ **with a ~ nod** avec un bref signe de tête

curtail /kɜːˈteɪl/ VT *[+ account]* écourter, raccourcir, tronquer ; *[+ proceedings, visit]* écourter ; *[+ period of time]* écourter, raccourcir ; *[+ wages]* rogner, réduire ; *[+ expenses]* restreindre, réduire

curtailment /kɜːˈteɪlmənt/ N *(NonC) (frm)* 1 *(= reduction) [of money, aid]* réduction *f* 2 *(= restriction) [of sb's power, freedom]* limitation *f* 3 *(= shortening) [of visit]* raccourcissement *m*

curtain /ˈkɜːtn/ N 1 *(gen)* rideau *m* ; *(fig)* rideau *m*, voile *m* ◆ **to draw** *or* **pull the ~s** tirer les rideaux ◆ **to open/close the ~s** ouvrir/fermer les rideaux ◆ **~ of fire** *(Mil)* rideau *m* de feu ◆ **it was ~s for him**⁑ il était fichu* *or* foutu⁑ ; → **iron, safety**

2 *(Theat)* rideau *m* ; *(= time when curtain rises or falls)* lever *m or* baisser *m* de rideau ; (also **curtain call**) rappel *m* ◆ **she took three ~s** elle a été rappelée trois fois ◆ **the last** *or* **final ~** le dernier rappel ◆ **to drop the ~** baisser le rideau ◆ **the ~ drops** le rideau tombe

VT *[+ window]* garnir de rideaux

COMP **curtain hook** N crochet *m* de rideau
curtain pole N tringle *f* à rideaux
curtain raiser N *(Theat, also fig)* lever *m* de rideau
curtain ring N anneau *m* de rideau
curtain rod N tringle *f* à rideaux
curtain-up N *(Theat)* lever *m* du rideau
curtain wall N *(Constr)* mur *m* rideau

► **curtain off** VT SEP *[+ room]* diviser par un *or* des rideau(x) ; *[+ bed, kitchen area]* cacher derrière un *or* des rideau(x)

curtly /ˈkɜːtlɪ/ ADV avec brusquerie, sèchement, d'un ton cassant

curtness /ˈkɜːtnɪs/ N brusquerie *f*, sécheresse *f*

curtsey, curtsy /ˈkɜːtsɪ/ N révérence *f* ◆ **to make** *or* **drop a ~** faire une révérence VI faire une révérence *(to* à)

curvaceous* /kɜːˈveɪʃəs/ ADJ *[woman]* bien balancée*, bien roulée*

curvature /ˈkɜːvətʃəʳ/ N courbure *f* ; *(Med)* déviation *f* ◆ **~ of the spine** déviation *f* de la colonne vertébrale, scoliose *f* ◆ **the ~ of space/the earth** la courbure de l'espace/de la terre

curve /kɜːv/ N *(gen)* courbe *f* ; *[of arch]* voussure *f* ; *[of beam]* cambrure *f* ; *[of graph]* courbe *f* ◆ **~ in the road** courbe *f*, tournant *m*, virage *m* ◆ **a woman's ~s*** les rondeurs *fpl* d'une femme VT courber ; *(Archit) [+ arch, roof]* cintrer VI *[line, surface, beam]* se courber, s'infléchir ; *[road etc]* faire une courbe, être en courbe ◆ **the road ~s down into the valley** la route descend en courbe dans la vallée ◆ **the river ~s round the town** la rivière fait un méandre autour de la ville

curveball /ˈkɜːvbɔːl/ N 1 *(US Baseball)* balle *f* à effet 2 *(= tricky problem)* colle* *f*

curved /kɜːvd/ ADJ *(gen)* courbe ; *[edge of table etc]* arrondi ; *[road]* en courbe ; *(= convex)* convexe

curvet /kɜːˈvet/ *(Horse-riding)* N courbette *f* VI faire une courbette

curvilinear /ˌkɜːvɪˈlɪnɪəʳ/ ADJ curviligne

curvy* /ˈkɜːvɪ/ ADJ *[girl, body]* bien roulé* ; *(gen)* courbe

cushion /ˈkʊʃən/ N 1 coussin *m* ◆ **on a ~ of air** sur un coussin d'air ; → **pincushion** 2 *(Billiards)* bande *f* ◆ **a stroke off the ~** un doublé

VT *[+ sofa]* mettre des coussins à ; *[+ seat]* rembourrer ; *(fig) [+ shock]* amortir ; *(Fin) [+ losses]* atténuer ◆ **to ~ sb's fall** amortir la chute de qn ◆ **to ~ sb against sth** *(fig)* protéger qn contre qch ◆ **to ~ one's savings against inflation** mettre ses économies à l'abri de l'inflation

cushy⁑ /ˈkʊʃɪ/ ADJ *(Brit)* pépère⁑, tranquille ◆ **a ~ job** une bonne planque⁑, un boulot pépère⁑ ◆ **to have a ~ time** se la couler douce* ; → **billet¹**

cusp /kʌsp/ N *(Bot) [of tooth]* cuspide *f* ; *[of moon]* corne *f*

cuspidor /ˈkʌspɪdɔːʳ/ N *(US)* crachoir *m*

cuss* /kʌs/ *(US)* ⇒ **curse** N 1 *(= oath)* juron *m* ◆ **he's not worth a tinker's ~** il ne vaut pas un pet de lapin* 2 *(gen pej = person)* type* *m*, bonne femme *f (gen pej)* ◆ **he's a queer ~** c'est un drôle de type* VI jurer

cussed* /ˈkʌsɪd/ ADJ entêté, têtu comme une mule*

cussedness* /ˈkʌsɪdnɪs/ N esprit *m* contrariant *or* de contradiction ◆ **out of sheer ~** par pur esprit de contradiction

cussword* /ˈkʌswɜːd/ N *(US)* gros mot *m*

custard /ˈkʌstəd/ N *(pouring)* crème *f* anglaise ; *(set)* crème *f* renversée

COMP **custard apple** N *(= fruits)* pomme *f* cannelle, anone *f*
custard cream, custard cream biscuit N biscuit *m* fourré
custard pie N tarte *f* à la crème
custard powder N crème *f* anglaise en poudre
custard tart N flan *m*

custodial /kʌsˈtəʊdɪəl/ ADJ 1 *(Jur) [parent]* à qui est attribué la garde des enfants ◆ **~ sentence** peine *f* privative de liberté 2 *[of museum etc]* **~ staff** personnel *m* de surveillance

custodian /kʌsˈtəʊdɪən/ N *[of building]* concierge *mf*, gardien(ne) *m(f)* ; *[of museum]* conservateur *m*, -trice *f* ; *[of tradition etc]* gardien(ne) *m(f)*, protecteur *m*, -trice *f*

custody /ˈkʌstədɪ/ N 1 *(Jur etc)* garde *f* ◆ **in safe ~** sous bonne garde ◆ **the child is in the ~ of his aunt** l'enfant est sous la garde de sa tante ◆ **after the divorce she was given ~ of the children** *(Jur)* après le divorce elle a obtenu la garde des enfants 2 *(gen)* garde *f* à vue ; *(= imprisonment)* emprisonnement *m*, captivité *f* ; (also **police custody**) *(for short period)* garde *f* à vue ; *(before trial)* détention *f* provisoire ◆ **in ~** en détention provisoire ◆ **to be kept in (police) ~** être mis en garde à vue ◆ **to take sb into ~** mettre qn en état d'arrestation ◆ **to give sb into ~** remettre qn aux mains de la police ; → **protective, remand**

custom /ˈkʌstəm/ N 1 *(= tradition, convention)* coutume *f*, usage *m* ; *(= habit)* coutume *f*, habitude *f* ◆ **as ~ has it** selon la coutume, selon les us et coutumes ◆ **it was his ~ to rest each morning** il avait coutume *or* il avait l'habitude de se reposer chaque matin 2 *(NonC: Brit Comm)* clientèle *f* ◆ **the grocer wanted to get her ~** l'épicier voulait la compter parmi ses clients ◆ **he has lost a lot of ~** il a perdu beaucoup de clients ◆ **he took his ~ elsewhere** il est allé se fournir ailleurs 3 *(Jur)* coutume *f*, droit *m* coutumier ; → **customs** ADJ *(= custom-made)* personnalisé

COMP **custom-built** ADJ *(Comm)* fait sur commande
custom car N voiture *f* faite sur commande
custom-made ADJ *(Comm) [clothes]* (fait) sur mesure ; *(other goods)* fait sur commande

customarily /ˈkʌstəmərɪlɪ/ ADV habituellement, ordinairement

customary /ˈkʌstəmərɪ/ ADJ *(gen)* habituel, coutumier ◆ **it is ~ (to do that)** c'est la coutume ◆ **it is ~ to thank the host** la coutume veut que l'on remercie *subj* l'hôte ◆ **it is ~ for the children to be present** la coutume veut que les enfants soient présents COMP **customary tenant** N *(Jur)* tenancier *m* censitaire

customer /ˈkʌstəməʳ/ N 1 *(Comm)* client(e) *m(f)* 2 *(esp Brit *)* type* *m*, individu *m (pej)* ◆ **he's an awkward ~** il n'est pas commode ◆ **queer ~** drôle de type* *or* d'individu ◆ **ugly ~** sale type* *m or* individu *m*

COMP **customer appeal** N facteur *m* de séduction du client
customer base N clientèle *f*
customer profile N profil *m* du consommateur
customer services NPL service *m* clientèle *or* clients

customize /ˈkʌstəmaɪz/ VT fabriquer (*or* construire *or* arranger *etc*) sur commande

customized /ˈkʌstəmaɪzd/ ADJ *[software, service]* sur mesure

customs /ˈkʌstəmz/ N 1 *(sg or pl = authorities, place)* douane *f* ◆ **to go through (the) ~** passer la douane ◆ **at** *or* **in the ~** à la douane 2 *(pl = duty payable)* droits *mpl* de douane

COMP *[regulations, receipt etc]* de la douane
Customs and Excise N *(Brit)* douanes *fpl*
customs border patrol N brigade *f* volante des services de douane
customs clearance N dédouanement *m*
customs declaration N déclaration *f* en douane
customs duty N droit(s) *m(pl)* de douane
customs house N (poste *m or* bureaux *mpl* de) douane *f*
customs inspection N visite *f* douanière *or* de douane
customs officer N douanier *m*, -ière *f*
customs post N ⇒ **customs house**
customs service N service *m* des douanes
customs shed N poste *m* de douane
customs union N union *f* douanière

cut /kʌt/ (vb : pret, ptp **cut**) N 1 *(= stroke)* coup *m* ; *(= mark, slit, wound)* coupure *f* ; *(= notch)* entaille *f* ; *(Med)* incision *f* ◆ **saw ~** trait *m* de scie ◆ **a deep ~ in the leg** une profonde entaille à la jambe ◆ **he had a ~ on his chin from shaving** il s'était coupé au menton en se rasant ◆ **he was treated for minor ~s and bruises** on l'a soigné pour des petites coupures et des contusions ◆ **make the ~ a bit lower** coupe un peu en dessous ; → **short**

2 *(fig)* **the ~ and thrust of politics** les estocades *fpl* de la politique ◆ **that remark was a ~ at me** cette remarque était une pierre dans mon jardin *or* une pique contre moi ◆ **the unkindest ~ of all** le coup le plus perfide ◆ **he is a ~ above (the others)*** il vaut mieux que les autres, il est supérieur aux autres ◆ **that's a ~ above him*** ça le dépasse

3 *[of cards]* coupe *f*

4 *(= reduction: gen, esp Econ)* réduction *f*, diminution *f* ◆ **tax ~s** réductions *fpl* d'impôts ◆ **staff ~s** réductions *fpl* des effectifs, compressions *fpl* de personnel ◆ **the ~s** les compressions *fpl* budgétaires ◆ **drastic ~s** *(Econ)* coupes *fpl* claires ◆ **power** *or* **electricity ~** coupure *f* de courant

♦ **a cut in** une réduction *or* diminution de ◆ **a 1% ~ in interest rates** une réduction *or* une diminution de 1% des taux d'intérêt ◆ **to take a ~ in salary** subir une diminution *or* réduction de salaire

♦ **cuts in** ◆ **the ~s in defence** *or* **the defence budget** la réduction du budget de la défense ◆ **to make ~s in a book/play** faire des coupures dans un livre/une pièce

5 *[of meat] (= piece)* morceau *m* ◆ **use a cheap ~ such as spare rib chops** utilisez un bas morceau tel que le travers

6 *(* = share)* part *f* ◆ **they all want a ~ of the profits** ils veulent tous leur part du gâteau* *(fig)* ◆ **there won't be much left once the lawyers have taken their ~** il ne restera pas

grand-chose une fois que les avocats auront pris leur part

7 *[of clothes]* coupe *f* ; *[of jewel]* taille *f* ◆ **I like the ~ of this coat** j'aime la coupe de ce manteau ; → **jib**

8 *(= haircut)* coupe *f* ◆ **~ and blow-dry** coupe et brushing

9 *(Comput)* ~ **and paste** couper-coller *m*

10 *(US Typ = block)* cliché *m*

11 *(Cine, TV) (= edit)* coupure *f* ; *(= transition)* passage *m (from* de ; *to* à)

12 *(US *: from school etc)* absence *f* injustifiée

ADJ *[flowers, grass]* coupé ◆ **he had a ~ finger/hand** il avait une coupure au doigt/à la main, il s'était coupé au doigt/à la main ◆ **a ~ lip** une lèvre coupée ◆ **well-~ coat** manteau *m* bien coupé *or* de bonne coupe

◆ **cut and dried** *(= clear-cut)* simple ; *(= definite)* définitif ◆ **things are not as ~ and dried as some people would like** les choses ne sont pas aussi simples que certains le voudraient ◆ **research findings on this matter are not ~-and-dried** les résultats des recherches sur ce sujet ne sont pas définitifs

VT 1 couper ; *[+ joint of meat, tobacco]* découper ; *(= slice)* découper en tranches ; *(= notch)* encocher ; *(Med) [+ abscess]* inciser ◆ **to ~ in half/in three** *etc* couper en deux/en trois *etc* ◆ **she ~ the cake in six** elle a coupé le gâteau en six ◆ **to ~ in(to) pieces** couper en morceaux ◆ **to ~ to pieces** *[+ army, opponent]* tailler en pièces ◆ **to ~ one's finger** se couper le doigt *or* au doigt ◆ **to ~ o.s. (shaving)** se couper (en se rasant) ◆ **to ~ sb's throat** couper la gorge à qn, égorger qn ◆ **he is ~ting his own throat** *(fig)* il prépare sa propre ruine *(fig)* ; → **corner, dash, dead, figure, fine², Gordian, ground¹, ice, loss, mustard, tooth**

◆ **to cut + open** ◆ **to ~ sth open** *(with knife)* ouvrir qch au *or* avec un couteau ; *(with scissors)* ouvrir qch avec des ciseaux ◆ **he ~ his arm open on a nail** il s'est ouvert le bras sur un clou ◆ **he ~ his head open** il s'est ouvert le crâne ◆ **to ~ sb free** *(from bonds)* délivrer qn en coupant ses liens ; *(from wreckage)* dégager qn (d'un véhicule)

◆ **to cut + short** ◆ **to ~ sth short** *(fig)* abréger qch, couper court à qch ◆ **to ~ a visit short** écourter une visite ◆ **to ~ sb short** couper la parole à qn ◆ **to ~ a long story short, he came** bref, il est venu

◆ **to cut and paste** *(Comput)* couper-coller ◆ **~ and paste these lines of text into your file** coupez-collez ces lignes de texte dans votre fichier

2 *(fig = wound, hurt) [+ person]* blesser (profondément), affecter ◆ **the wind ~ his face** le vent lui coupait le visage ; → **heart, quick**

3 *(= shape)* couper, tailler ; *[+ steps]* tailler ; *[+ channel]* creuser, percer ; *[+ figure, statue]* sculpter *(out of* dans) ; *(= engrave)* graver ; *[+ jewel, key, glass, crystal]* tailler ; *[+ screw]* fileter ; *[+ dress]* couper ◆ **to ~ a hole in sth** faire un trou dans qch ◆ **to ~ one's way through the crowd/forest** se frayer un chemin à travers la foule/les bois ; → **coat, record**

4 *(= mow, clip, trim) [+ hedge, trees]* tailler ; *[+ corn, hay]* faucher ; *[+ lawn]* tondre ◆ **to ~ one's nails/hair** se couper les ongles/les cheveux ◆ **to have** *or* **get one's hair ~** se faire couper les cheveux

5 *(esp US = not attend) [+ class, school etc]* manquer, sécher* ; *[+ appointment]* manquer exprès

6 *(= cross, intersect)* couper, croiser, traverser ; *(Math)* couper ◆ **the path ~s the road here** le sentier coupe la route à cet endroit

7 *(= reduce) [+ profits, wages]* réduire, diminuer ; *[+ text, book, play]* réduire, faire des coupures dans ◆ **to ~ costs** réduire les coûts ◆ **to ~ prices** réduire les prix, vendre à prix réduit *or* au rabais ◆ **to ~ spending by 35%** réduire *or* diminuer les dépenses de 35% ◆ **we ~ the journey time by half** nous avons réduit de moitié la durée du trajet ◆ **he ~ 30 seconds off the record, he ~ the record by 30 seconds** *(Sport)* il a amélioré le record de 30 secondes

8 *(= stop)* couper ◆ **to ~ electricity supplies** couper l'électricité ◆ **~ the euphemisms and just tell me what's happened!** * arrête de tourner autour du pot et dis-moi simplement ce qui s'est passé ! ◆ **~ the crap!**‡ *(esp US)* arrête tes conneries !‡, assez bavardé comme ça ! *

9 *[+ cards]* couper

10 *(Sport)* ◆ **to ~ the ball** couper la balle

11 *(Cine etc = edit) [+ film]* monter

12 *(= dilute) [+ drug]* couper ; *[+ grease, sweetness]* atténuer

13 *(* = conclude)* ◆ **to ~ a deal** passer un marché

14 ◆ **to ~ it** * *(= be good enough)* être à la hauteur ◆ **he couldn't ~ it as a singer** comme chanteur il n'était pas à la hauteur

VI 1 *[person, knife etc]* couper ◆ **this knife ~s well** ce couteau coupe bien ◆ **he ~ into the cake** il a fait une entaille dans le gâteau, il a entamé le gâteau ◆ **~ along the dotted line** découper suivant le pointillé ◆ **his sword ~ through the air** son épée fendit l'air ◆ **the boat ~ through the waves** le bateau fendait l'eau ◆ **this ~s across all I have learnt** *(fig)* ceci va à l'encontre de tout ce que j'ai appris ◆ **to ~ and run** * mettre les bouts‡, filer* ◆ **to ~ to the chase** * en venir à l'essentiel ◆ **~ to the chase!** * abrège ! * ; → **loose**

◆ **to cut both ways** être à double tranchant ◆ **what you say ~s both ways** ce que vous dites est à double tranchant ◆ **that argument ~s both ways** c'est un argument à double tranchant

2 *[material]* se couper ◆ **paper ~s easily** le papier se coupe facilement ◆ **this piece will ~ into four** ce morceau peut se couper en quatre

3 *(Math)* se couper ◆ **lines A and B ~ at point C** les lignes A et B se coupent au point C

4 *(= take short route)* ◆ **~ across the fields and you'll soon be there** coupez à travers champs et vous serez bientôt arrivé ◆ **to ~ across country** couper à travers champs ◆ **if you ~ through the lane you'll save time** si vous coupez *or* passez par la ruelle vous gagnerez du temps

5 *(Cine, TV)* **they ~ from the street to the shop scene** ils passent de la rue à la scène du magasin ◆ **~!** coupez !

6 *(Cards)* couper ◆ **to ~ for deal** tirer pour la donne

COMP **cut glass** N *(NonC)* cristal *m* taillé ADJ de *or* en cristal taillé

cut-price ADJ *[goods, ticket]* à prix réduit, au rabais ; *[manufacturer, shopkeeper]* qui vend à prix réduits ◆ **~-price shop** *or* **store** magasin *m* à prix réduits ADV *[buy, get]* à prix réduit

cut prices NPL prix *mpl* réduits

cut-rate ADJ *(Brit)* ⇒ **cut-price**

cut-throat † N *(= murderer)* assassin *m* ADJ ◆ **~-throat competition** concurrence *f* acharnée ◆ **~-throat game** *(Cards)* partie *f* à trois ◆ **~-throat razor** *(Brit)* rasoir *m* à main *or* de coiffeur

cut tobacco N tabac *m* découpé

cut up * ADJ *(Brit = upset)* affligé ; *(US = funny)* rigolo * (-ote * *f*)

► **cut across** VT FUS *[problem, issue]* toucher ◆ **this problem ~s across all ages** ce problème touche toutes les tranches d'âge

► **cut along** VI s'en aller, filer*

► **cut away** VT SEP *[+ branch]* élaguer ; *[+ unwanted part]* enlever (en coupant)

► **cut back** VT SEP *[+ plants, shrubs]* élaguer, tailler ; *(fig* : also **cut back on**) *[+ production, expenditure]* réduire, diminuer

VI revenir (sur ses pas) ◆ **he ~ back to the village and gave his pursuers the slip** il est revenu au village par un raccourci et a semé ses poursuivants

► **cut down** VT SEP 1 *[+ tree]* couper, abattre ; *[+ corn]* faucher ; *[+ person] (by sword etc)* abattre *(d'un coup d'épée etc)* ; *(fig: through illness etc)* terrasser ◆ **~ down by pneumonia** terrassé par la *or* une pneumonie

2 *(= reduce) [+ expenses, pollution]* réduire ; *[+ article, essay]* couper ; *[+ clothes] (gen)* rapetisser, diminuer ◆ **to ~ sb down to size** * *(fig)* remettre qn à sa place

► **cut down on** VT FUS *[+ food]* manger moins de ; *[+ alcohol]* boire moins de ; *[+ cigarettes]* fumer moins de ; *[+ expenditure, costs]* réduire ◆ **you should ~ down on drink** vous devriez boire moins

► **cut in** VI *(into conversation)* se mêler à la conversation ; *(while driving)* se rabattre ◆ **to ~ in on sb** *(while driving)* faire une queue de poisson à qn ; *(= interrupt)* couper la parole à qn ◆ **to ~ in on the market** s'infiltrer sur le marché

VT SEP ◆ **to cut sb in on** *or* **into a deal** * intéresser qn à une affaire

► **cut off** VI *(† * = leave)* filer*

VT SEP 1 *[+ piece of cloth, cheese, meat, bread]* couper *(from* dans) ; *[+ limbs]* amputer, couper ◆ **to ~ off sb's head** trancher la tête de *or* à qn, décapiter qn ◆ **to ~ off one's nose to spite one's face** scier la branche sur laquelle on est assis *(par dépit)*

2 *(= disconnect) [+ telephone caller, telephone, car engine, gas, electricity]* couper ◆ **our water supply has been ~ off** on nous a coupé l'eau ◆ **we were ~ off** *(Telec)* nous avons été coupés ◆ **to ~ sb off in the middle of a sentence** interrompre qn au milieu d'une phrase ◆ **to ~ off sb's supplies** *(of food, money etc)* couper les vivres à qn

3 *(= isolate)* isoler *(sb from sth* qn de qch) ; ◆ **to ~ o.s. off from** rompre ses liens avec ◆ **he feels very ~ off in the country** il se sent très isolé à la campagne ◆ **town ~ off by floods** ville *f* isolée par des inondations ◆ **to ~ off the enemy's retreat** *(Mil)* couper la retraite à l'ennemi ◆ **to ~ sb off with a shilling** *(fig)* déshériter qn

► **cut out** VI 1 *[engine]* caler

2 *(‡ = leave)* filer*, se tailler‡

VT SEP 1 *[+ picture, article]* découper *(of, from* de) ; *[+ statue, figure]* sculpter, tailler *(of* dans) ; *[+ coat]* couper, tailler *(of, from* dans) ; *(Phot)* détourer ◆ **to ~ out a path through the jungle** se frayer un chemin à travers la jungle ◆ **to be ~ out for sth** *(fig)* avoir des dispositions pour qch ◆ **he's not ~ out for** *or* **to be a doctor** il n'est pas fait pour être médecin, il n'a pas l'étoffe d'un médecin ◆ **he had his work ~ out (for him)** *(= plenty to do)* il avait du pain sur la planche ◆ **you'll have your work ~ out to get there on time** vous n'avez pas de temps à perdre si vous voulez y arriver à l'heure ◆ **you'll have your work ~ out to persuade him to come** vous aurez du mal à le persuader de venir

2 *(fig) [+ rival]* supplanter

3 *(= remove)* enlever, ôter ; *[+ intermediary, middleman]* supprimer ; *[+ light]* empêcher de passer ; *[+ unnecessary details]* élaguer ◆ **to ~ sb out of one's will** déshériter qn ◆ **~ it out!** * *(fig)* ça suffit !*, ça va comme ça !* ◆ **~ out the talking!** *(fig)* assez bavardé !, vous avez fini de bavarder ? ◆ **~ out the noise!** *(fig)* arrêtez ce bruit !, moins de bruit ! ◆ **you can ~ out the tears for a start!** * *(fig)* et pour commencer, arrête de pleurnicher !

4 *(= give up) [+ tobacco]* supprimer ◆ **to ~ out smoking/drinking** arrêter de fumer/boire

► **cut up** VI 1 *(Brit)* **to ~ up rough** * se mettre en rogne * *or* en boule *

2 (US = clown around) faire le pitre
VT SEP 1 [+ wood, food] couper ; [+ meat] (= carve) découper ; (= chop up) hacher ; (fig) [+ enemy, army] tailler en pièces, anéantir
2 [+ other driver] faire une queue de poisson à ◆ **he was crossing from lane to lane, ~ting everyone up** il passait d'une file à l'autre, faisant des queues de poisson à tout le monde
3 (Brit *: pass only) **to be ~ up about sth** (= hurt) être affecté or démoralisé par qch ; (= annoyed) être très embêté par qch * ◆ **he's very ~ up** il n'a plus le moral * ◆ **he was very ~ up by the death of his son** la mort de son fils l'a beaucoup affecté
ADJ ◆ **cut-up** * → **cut**

cutaneous /kjuːˈteɪnɪəs/ ADJ cutané

cutaway /ˈkʌtəweɪ/ N (also **cutaway drawing** or **sketch**) (dessin m) écorché m

cutback /ˈkʌtbæk/ N (= reduction) [of expenditure, production] réduction f, diminution f (in de) ; [of staff] compressions fpl (in de) ; (Cine = flashback) flash-back m (to sur) ; ◆ **drastic ~s** (Econ etc) coupes fpl claires

cute * /kjuːt/ ADJ 1 (= attractive) mignon 2 (esp US = clever) malin (-igne f), futé ◆ **don't try and be ~ (with me)!** ne fais pas le malin !

cutely * /ˈkjuːtlɪ/ ADV 1 (= attractively) [smile, blush, pose] avec coquetterie 2 (US = cleverly) astucieusement

cutesy * /ˈkjuːtsɪ/ ADJ (esp US: pej) [person, painting, clothes] mièvre

cuticle /ˈkjuːtɪkl/ N (= skin) épiderme m ; [of fingernails] petites peaux fpl, envie f ; (Bot) cuticule f COMP **cuticle remover** N repousse-peaux m

cutie * /ˈkjuːtɪ/ N (esp US) (= girl) jolie fille f ; (= boy) beau mec * m ; (= shrewd person) malin m, -igne f ; (= shrewd action) beau coup m COMP **cutie pie** * N (esp US) mignon(ne) m(f) ◆ **she's a real ~ pie** elle est vraiment mignonne

cutlass /ˈkʌtləs/ N (Naut) coutelas m, sabre m d'abordage

cutler /ˈkʌtləʳ/ N coutelier m

cutlery /ˈkʌtlərɪ/ N 1 (Brit = knives, forks, spoons etc) couverts mpl ; → **canteen** 2 (= knives, daggers etc: also trade) coutellerie f COMP **cutlery drawer** N tiroir m des couverts

cutlet /ˈkʌtlɪt/ N 1 (gen) côtelette f ; [of veal] escalope f 2 (US = croquette of meat, chicken etc) croquette f

cutoff /ˈkʌtɒf/ N (= short cut) raccourci m ; (Tech = stopping) arrêt m NPL **cutoffs** jeans mpl coupés
COMP **cutoff date** N date f limite
cutoff device N (also **automatic cutoff device**) système m d'arrêt (automatique)
cutoff point N (in age etc) limite f ; (in time) dernier délai m
cutoff switch N interrupteur m

cutout /ˈkʌtaʊt/ N 1 [of electrical circuit] disjoncteur m, coupe-circuit m inv ; (for car exhaust) échappement m libre 2 (= figure of wood or paper) découpage m ◆ **his characters are just cardboard ~s** ses personnages manquent d'épaisseur

cutter /ˈkʌtəʳ/ N 1 (= person) [of clothes] coupeur m, -euse f ; [of stones, jewels] tailleur m ; [of films] monteur m, -euse f 2 (= tool) coupoir m, couteau m ◆ **(pair of) ~s** (for metal etc) pinces fpl coupantes ; → **bolt** 3 (= sailing boat) cotre m, cutter m ; (= motor boat) vedette f ; [of coastguards] garde-côte m ; [of warship] canot m 4 (US = sleigh) traîneau m

cutting /ˈkʌtɪŋ/ N 1 (NonC) coupe f ; [of diamond] taille f ; [of film] montage m ; [of trees] coupe f, abattage m
2 (for road, railway) tranchée f
3 (= piece cut off) [of newspaper] coupure f ; [of cloth] coupon m ; (Agr) bouture f ; [of vine] marcotte f
4 (= reduction) [of prices, expenditure] réduction f, diminution f
ADJ 1 [knife] coupant, tranchant ◆ **~ pliers** pinces fpl coupantes ◆ **the ~ edge** (lit) le tranchant ◆ **to be at the ~ edge of scientific research** être à la pointe de la recherche scientifique ◆ **to give sb a ~ edge** (commercially) donner à qn un avantage concurrentiel; see also **comp**
2 (fig) [wind] glacial, cinglant ; [rain] cinglant ; [cold] piquant, glacial ; [words] blessant, cinglant ; [remark] mordant, blessant ◆ **~ tongue** langue f acérée
COMP **cutting board** N planche f à découper
cutting-edge ADJ [technology, research, design] de pointe
cutting-out scissors NPL (Sewing) ciseaux mpl de couturière
cutting room N (Cine) salle f de montage ◆ **to end up on the ~ room floor** (fig) finir au panier

cuttlebone /ˈkʌtlbəʊn/ N os m de seiche

cuttlefish /ˈkʌtlfɪʃ/ N (pl **cuttlefish** or **cuttlefishes**) seiche f

CV /siːˈviː/ N (abbrev of **curriculum vitae**) → **curriculum**

CWO /ˌsiːdʌbljuːˈəʊ/ 1 (abbrev of **cash with order**) → **cash** 2 (abbrev of **chief warrant officer**) → **chief**

cwt abbrev of **hundredweight(s)**

cyanide /ˈsaɪənaɪd/ N cyanure m ◆ **~ of potassium** cyanure m de potassium

cyanose /ˈsaɪənəʊz/ N cyanose f

cyanosed /ˈsaɪənəʊzd/ ADJ cyanosé

cyber... /ˈsaɪbə/ PREF cyber...

cybercafé /ˈsaɪbəˌkæfeɪ/ N cybercafé m

cybercrime /ˈsaɪbəkraɪm/ N cybercrime f

cybernaut /ˈsaɪbənɔːt/ N cybernaute mf

cybernetic /ˌsaɪbəˈnetɪk/ ADJ cybernétique

cybernetics /ˌsaɪbəˈnetɪks/ N (NonC) cybernétique f

cyberpet /ˈsaɪbəpet/ N Tamagotchi ® m

cyberpunk /ˈsaɪbəpʌŋk/ N (Literat) (= writing) cyberpunk m ; (= writer) cyberpunk mf

cybersex /ˈsaɪbəseks/ N (NonC) cybersexe m

cyberspace /ˈsaɪbəspeɪs/ N cyberespace m

cybersquatter /ˈsaɪbəskwɒtəʳ/ N cybersquatter m

cybersquatting /ˈsaɪbəskwɒtɪŋ/ N cybersquatting m

cyberterrorism /ˈsaɪbəˌterərɪzəm/ N cyberterrorisme m

cyborg /ˈsaɪbɔːg/ N cyborg m

cyclamate /ˈsaɪkləˌmeɪt, ˈsɪklə"meɪt/ N cyclamate m

cyclamen /ˈsɪkləmən/ N cyclamen m

cycle /ˈsaɪkl/ N 1 vélo m, bicyclette f 2 (also **menstrual cycle**) cycle m (menstruel) 3 [of poems, seasons etc] cycle m VI faire du vélo, faire de la bicyclette ◆ **he ~s to school** il va à l'école à bicyclette or à vélo or en vélo
COMP [lamp, chain, wheel] de vélo or bicyclette ; [race] cycliste
cycle clip N pince f à vélo
cycle lane N (Brit) piste f cyclable
cycle path N piste f cyclable
cycle pump N pompe f à vélo
cycle rack N (on floor) râtelier m à bicyclettes ; (on car roof) porte-vélos m inv
cycle shed N abri m à bicyclettes
cycle shop N magasin m de cycles
cycle track N (= lane) piste f cyclable ; (Sport) vélodrome m

cycler /ˈsaɪkləʳ/ N (US) ⇒ **cyclist**

cycleway /ˈsaɪklweɪ/ N (Brit) piste f cyclable

cyclic(al) /ˈsaɪklɪk(əl)/ ADJ cyclique

cycling /ˈsaɪklɪŋ/ N cyclisme m ◆ **to do a lot of ~** (gen) faire beaucoup de bicyclette or de vélo ; (Sport) faire beaucoup de cyclisme
COMP de bicyclette
cycling clothes NPL tenue f de cycliste
cycling holiday N ◆ **to go on a ~ holiday** faire du cyclotourisme
cycling shorts NPL ◆ **(pair of) ~ shorts** (short m de) cycliste m
cycling tour N circuit m à bicyclette
cycling track N vélodrome m

cyclist /ˈsaɪklɪst/ N cycliste mf ; → **racing**

cyclone /ˈsaɪkləʊn/ N cyclone m COMP **cyclone cellar** N (US) abri m anticyclone

Cyclops /ˈsaɪklɒps/ N (pl **Cyclopses** or **Cyclopes** /saɪˈkləʊpiːz/) cyclope m

cyclorama /ˌsaɪkləˈrɑːmə/ N (also Cine) cyclorama m

cyclostyle /ˈsaɪkləstaɪl/ N machine f à polycopier (à stencils) VT polycopier

cyclothymia /ˌsaɪkləʊˈθaɪmɪə/ N cyclothymie f

cyclothymic /ˌsaɪkləʊˈθaɪmɪk/ ADJ, N cyclothymique mf

cyclotron /ˈsaɪklətrɒn/ N cyclotron m

cygnet /ˈsɪgnɪt/ N jeune cygne m

cylinder /ˈsɪlɪndəʳ/ N 1 (gen) cylindre m ◆ **a six-~ car** une six-cylindres ◆ **to be firing on all four ~s** (fig) marcher or fonctionner à pleins gaz * or tubes * ◆ **he's only firing on two ~s** (fig) il débloque * complètement 2 [of typewriter] rouleau m ; [of clock, gun] barillet m
COMP **cylinder block** N (in engine) bloc-cylindres m
cylinder capacity N cylindrée f
cylinder head N culasse f ◆ **to take off the ~ head** déculasser
cylinder head gasket N joint m de culasse
cylinder vacuum cleaner N aspirateur-traîneau m

cylindrical /sɪˈlɪndrɪkəl/ ADJ cylindrique

cymbal /ˈsɪmbəl/ N cymbale f

cynic /ˈsɪnɪk/ N (gen, Philos) cynique mf ADJ ⇒ **cynical**

cynical /ˈsɪnɪkəl/ ADJ (gen, Philos) cynique ◆ **a ~ foul** (Sport) de l'antijeu m flagrant

cynically /ˈsɪnɪklɪ/ ADV cyniquement

cynicism /ˈsɪnɪsɪzəm/ N (gen, Philos) cynisme m ◆ **~s** remarques fpl cyniques, sarcasmes mpl

cynosure /ˈsaɪnəʃʊəʳ/ N (also **cynosure of every eye**) point m de mire, centre m d'attraction

CYO /ˌsiːwaɪˈəʊ/ N (in US) (abbrev of **Catholic Youth Organization**) mouvement catholique

cypher /ˈsaɪfəʳ/ N ⇒ **cipher**

cypress /ˈsaɪprɪs/ N cyprès m

Cypriot /ˈsɪprɪət/ ADJ chypriote or cypriote ◆ **Greek/Turkish ~** chypriote grec (grecque f)/turc (turque f) N Chypriote or Cypriote mf ◆ **Greek/Turkish ~** Chypriote mf grec (grecque)/turc (turque)

Cyprus /ˈsaɪprəs/ N Chypre f ◆ **in ~** à Chypre

Cyrillic /sɪˈrɪlɪk/ ADJ cyrillique

cyst /sɪst/ N (= growth) kyste m ; (= protective membrane) sac m (membraneux)

cystic fibrosis /ˈsɪstɪkˌfaɪˈbrəʊsɪs/ N mucoviscidose f

cystitis /sɪsˈtaɪtɪs/ N cystite f

cytological /ˌsaɪtəˈlɒdʒɪkəl/ ADJ cytologique

cytology /saɪˈtɒlədʒɪ/ N cytologie f

CZ /siːˈzed/ (US Geog) (abbrev of **Canal Zone**) → **canal**

czar /zɑːʳ/ N 1 (= ruler) tsar *m* 2 (Pol) ◆ **alcohol/tobacco ~** *responsable de la lutte contre l'alcoolisme/le tabagisme*

czarevitch /ˈzɑːrəvɪtʃ/ N tsarévitch *m*

czarina /zɑːˈriːnə/ N tsarina *f*

czarism /ˈzɑːrɪzəm/ N tsarisme *m*

czarist /ˈzɑːrɪst/ N, ADJ tsariste *mf*

Czech /tʃek/ ADJ *(gen)* tchèque ; *[ambassador, embassy]* de la République tchèque ; *[teacher]* de tchèque N 1 Tchèque *mf* 2 *(= language)* tchèque *m* COMP **the Czech Republic** N la République tchèque

Czechoslovak /tʃekəʊˈsləʊvæk/ ADJ tchécoslovaque N Tchécoslovaque *mf*

Czechoslovakia /tʃekəʊsləˈvækɪə/ N Tchécoslovaquie *f*

Czechoslovakian /tʃekəʊsləˈvækɪən/ ⇒ **Czechoslovak**

Dd

D, d /diː/ N 1 (= letter) D, d *m* ◆ **D for dog, D for David** *(US)* ≃ D comme Denise ◆ **(in) 3D** *(Cine etc)* (en) 3D 2 *(Mus)* ré *m* ; → **key** 3 *(Scol = mark)* passable *(10 sur 20)* 4 *(Brit †)* abbrev of **penny** 5 abbrev of **died** 6 *(US)* abbrev of **Democrat(ic)**
COMP **D and C** * N *(Med)* (abbrev of **dilation and curettage**) → **dilation**
D-day N *(Mil, fig)* le jour J

DA /diːˈeɪ/ N 1 *(US Jur)* (abbrev of **District Attorney**) → **district** 2 (* abbrev of **duck's arse**) *(= haircut) coupe où les cheveux descendent en pointe sur la nuque*

dab¹ /dæb/ N 1 ◆ **a ~ of** un petit peu de ◆ **a ~ of glue** une goutte de colle ◆ **to give sth a ~ of paint** donner un petit coup *or* une petite touche de peinture à qch 2 *(esp Brit) (= fingerprints)* **~s**‡ empreintes *fpl* digitales VT tamponner ◆ **to ~ one's eyes** se tamponner les yeux ◆ **to ~ paint on** *or* **onto sth** peindre qch par petites touches ◆ **to ~ iodine on a wound** tamponner une blessure de teinture d'iode

► **dab at** VT FUS ◆ **to dab at a stain** tamponner une tache ◆ **to ~ at one's mouth/eyes** se tamponner la bouche/les yeux

► **dab off** VT SEP enlever (en tamponnant)

► **dab on** VT SEP appliquer *or* mettre par petites touches

dab² /dæb/ N *(= fish)* limande *f*

dab³ /dæb/ ADJ *(Brit)* ◆ **to be a ~ hand** * **at sth/at doing sth** être doué en qch/pour faire qch

dabble /ˈdæbl/ VT ◆ **to ~ one's hands/feet in the water** tremper ses mains/ses pieds dans l'eau VI *(fig)* ◆ **to ~ in** *or* **with** *[+ music, theatre, journalism, drugs, cocaine]* tâter de ◆ **to ~ in stocks and shares** *or* **on the Stock Exchange** boursicoter ◆ **to ~ in politics/acting** tâter de la politique/du théâtre (*or* du cinéma) ◆ **she ~d with the idea of going into acting** elle a pensé un moment devenir actrice

dabbler /ˈdæbləʳ/ N *(pej)* amateur *m*

dabchick /ˈdæbtʃɪk/ N petit grèbe *m*

Dacca /ˈdækə/ N Dacca

dace /deɪs/ N (pl **dace** *or* **daces**) vandoise *f*

dacha /ˈdætʃə/ N datcha *f*

dachshund /ˈdækshʊnd/ N teckel *m*

Dacron ® /ˈdækrɒn/ N dacron ® *m*

dactyl /ˈdæktɪl/ N dactyle *m*

dactylic /dækˈtɪlɪk/ ADJ dactylique

dad /dæd/ N * papa *m*, père *m* ◆ **hello ~!** bonjour, papa ! ◆ **he's an electrician and his ~'s a plumber** il est électricien et son père est plombier COMP **Dad's army** N *(hum)* l'armée *f* de (grand-)papa *(hum)*

Dada /ˈdɑːdɑː/ N Dada *m* COMP *[school, movement]* dada *inv*, dadaïste

Dadaism /ˈdɑːdɑːɪzəm/ N dadaïsme *m*

Dadaist /ˈdɑːdɑːɪst/ ADJ, N dadaïste *mf*

daddy /ˈdædɪ/ N * papa *m* COMP **daddy-longlegs** N (pl inv) *(Brit = cranefly)* tipule *f* ; *(US, Can = harvestman)* faucheur *m*, faucheux *m*

dado /ˈdeɪdəʊ/ N (pl **dadoes** *or* **dados**) plinthe *f* COMP **dado rail** N lambris *m* d'appui

Daedalus /ˈdiːdələs/ N Dédale *m*

daemon /ˈdiːmən/ N démon *m*

daff * /dæf/ N *(Brit)* jonquille *f*

daffodil /ˈdæfədɪl/ N jonquille *f* COMP **daffodil yellow** N, ADJ (jaune *m*) jonquille *m inv*

daffy‡ /ˈdæfɪ/ ADJ loufoque *

daft * /dɑːft/ ADJ *(esp Brit) [person]* dingue *, cinglé * ; *[idea, behaviour]* loufoque * ◆ **that was a ~ thing to do** c'était pas très malin * ◆ **have you gone ~?** ça va pas la tête ? * ◆ **I'll get the bus – don't be ~, I'll give you a lift!** je vais prendre le bus – ne dis pas de bêtises, je te ramène ! ◆ **to be ~ about sb/sth** * être fou de qn/qch ◆ **he's ~ in the head** ‡ il est cinglé * ◆ **~ as a brush** * complètement dingue * *or* cinglé *

dagger /ˈdægəʳ/ N 1 poignard *m* ; *(shorter)* dague *f* ◆ **to be at ~s drawn with sb** être à couteaux tirés avec qn ◆ **to look ~s at sb** lancer des regards furieux *or* meurtriers à qn, fusiller *or* foudroyer qn du regard 2 *(Typ)* croix *f*

dago‡ /ˈdeɪgəʊ/ N (pl **dagos** *or* **dagoes**) *(pej)* métèque *m (pej)*

daguerreotype /dəˈgerəʊtaɪp/ N daguerréotype *m*

dahlia /ˈdeɪlɪə/ N dahlia *m*

Dáil Éireann /dɔɪlˈeərən/ N *Chambre des députés de la république d'Irlande*

daily /ˈdeɪlɪ/ ADV quotidiennement, tous les jours ◆ **the office is open ~** le bureau est ouvert tous les jours ◆ **twice ~** deux fois par jour ADJ quotidien ; *[wage, charge]* journalier ◆ **~ consumption** consommation *f* quotidienne ◆ **~ life** la vie de tous les jours ◆ **our ~ bread** *(Rel)* notre pain *m* quotidien ◆ **~ paper** quotidien *m* ; → **recommend** N 1 *(= newspaper)* quotidien *m* 2 *(Brit *: also* **daily help, daily woman**) femme *f* de ménage

daimon /ˈdaɪmɒn/ N ⇒ **daemon**

daintily /ˈdeɪntɪlɪ/ ADV *[eat, hold]* délicatement ; *[walk]* d'un pas gracieux ◆ **~ served** servi avec raffinement

daintiness /ˈdeɪntɪnɪs/ N délicatesse *f*

dainty /ˈdeɪntɪ/ ADJ 1 *(= delicate) [hands, object, food]* délicat 2 *(= fussy)* **to be a ~ eater** être difficile sur la nourriture N mets *m* délicat

daiquiri /ˈdaɪkərɪ/ N daïquiri *m*

dairy /ˈdeərɪ/ N *(on farm)* laiterie *f* ; *(= shop)* crémerie *f*
COMP *[cow, farm]* laitier
dairy butter N beurre *m* fermier
dairy farming N industrie *f* laitière
dairy herd N troupeau *m* de vaches laitières
dairy ice cream N crème *f* glacée
dairy produce N *(NonC)* produits *mpl* laitiers

dairymaid /ˈdeərɪmeɪd/ N fille *f* de laiterie

dairyman /ˈdeərɪmən/ N (pl **-men**) *(on farm)* employé *m* de laiterie ; *(in shop)* crémier *m*

dais /ˈdeɪɪs/ N estrade *f*

daisy /ˈdeɪzɪ/ N 1 *(= flower)* pâquerette *f* ; *(cultivated)* marguerite *f* ; → **fresh, push up** 2 *(US)* ⇒ **daisy ham**
COMP **daisy chain** N guirlande *f or* collier *m* de pâquerettes ; *(fig)* série *f*, chapelet *m*
daisy ham N *(US)* jambon *m* fumé désossé

daisywheel /ˈdeɪzɪwiːl/ N *(Comput)* marguerite *f* COMP **daisywheel printer** N imprimante *f* à marguerite

Dakar /ˈdækəʳ/ N Dakar

Dakota /dəˈkəʊtə/ N Dakota *m* ◆ **North/South ~** Dakota *m* du Nord/du Sud

dal, dhal /dɑːl/ N *(Culin)* dhal *m*

Dalai Lama /ˈdælaɪˈlɑːmə/ N dalaï-lama *m*

dale /deɪl/ N *(N Engl, also liter)* vallée *f*, vallon *m* ◆ **the (Yorkshire) Dales** *région vallonnée du nord de l'Angleterre*

dalliance /ˈdælɪəns/ N 1 *(liter = affair)* badinage *m* (amoureux) 2 *(= involvement with sth)* flirt *m* ◆ **his brief ~ with politics** son bref flirt avec la politique

dally /ˈdælɪ/ VI *(= dawdle)* lambiner *, lanterner *(over sth* dans *or* sur qch) ◆ **to ~ with an idea** caresser une idée ◆ **to ~ with sb** † badiner (amoureusement) avec qn

Dalmatian /dælˈmeɪʃən/ N *(Geog)* Dalmate *mf* ; (also **dalmatian**) *(= dog)* dalmatien *m* ADJ dalmate

dalmatic /dælˈmætɪk/ N dalmatique *f*

daltonism /ˈdɔːltənɪzəm/ N daltonisme *m*

dam¹ /dæm/ N 1 *(= wall) [of river]* barrage *m* (de retenue), digue *f* ; *[of lake]* barrage *m* (de retenue) 2 *(= water)* réservoir *m*, lac *m* de retenue VT 1 (also **dam up**) *[+ river]* endiguer ; *[+ lake]* construire un barrage sur ◆ **to ~ the waters of the Nile** faire *or* construire un barrage pour contenir les eaux du Nil ② *[+ flow of words, oaths]* endiguer

dam² /dæm/ **N** *(= animal)* mère *f*

dam³ ‡ /dæm/ **ADJ, ADV** ① ⇒ **damn adj, adv** ② *(US)* **~ Yankee** sale * Yankee *or* Nordiste

damage /'dæmɪdʒ/ **N** ① *(NonC: physical)* dégâts *mpl*, dommage(s) *m(pl)* ◆ **environmental ~** dégâts *mpl or* dommages *mpl* causés à l'environnement ◆ **bomb ~** dégâts *mpl or* dommages *mpl* causés par une bombe *or* par un bombardement ◆ **earthquake/fire ~** dégâts *mpl or* dommages *mpl* causés par un tremblement de terre/un incendie ◆ **water ~** dégâts *mpl* des eaux ◆ **~ to property** dégâts *mpl* matériels ◆ **~ to the building** dégâts *mpl or* dommages *mpl* subis par le bâtiment ◆ **~ to the ozone layer** détérioration *f* de la couche d'ozone ◆ **to make good the ~** réparer les dégâts *or* les dommages ◆ **liver/tissue ~** lésions *fpl* au foie/des tissus ◆ **kidney ~** lésions *fpl* rénales ◆ **~ to the heart** lésions *fpl* cardiaques ◆ **~ to your health** effets *mpl* néfastes pour votre santé ◆ **to do** *or* **cause ~** causer *or* provoquer des dégâts *or* dommages ◆ **the storm/vandals caused £50,000 worth of ~** la tempête a provoqué/les vandales ont provoqué des dégâts *or* des dommages s'élevant à 50 000 livres ◆ **the bomb did a lot of ~** la bombe a fait de gros dégâts, la bombe a causé des dommages importants ◆ **not much ~ was done to the car/the house** la voiture/la maison n'a pas subi de gros dégâts *or* dommages ◆ **to cause ~ to sth** ⇒ **to damage sth** ; see also **vt** ; → **brain, structural**

② *(NonC: fig)* préjudice *m* (*to* à) tort *m* (*to* à) ◆ **there was considerable ~ to the local economy** cela a fait énormément de tort à l'économie locale ◆ **have you thought about the possible ~ to your child's education?** avez-vous pensé aux conséquences négatives que cela pourrait avoir pour l'éducation de votre enfant ? ◆ **to do** *or* **cause ~** *[person, gossip, scandal]* faire des dégâts ◆ **to do** *or* **cause ~ to** *[+ person]* faire du tort à ; *[+ reputation, relationship, confidence, country, economy]* nuire à, porter atteinte à ◆ **that has done ~ to our cause** cela a fait du tort *or* porté préjudice à notre cause ◆ **there's no ~ done** il n'y a pas de mal ◆ **the ~ is done (now)** le mal est fait ◆ **what's the ~?** * *(= how much is it?)* à combien s'élève la douloureuse ? * ; → **storm**

NPL damages *(Jur)* dommages *mpl* et intérêts *mpl*, dommages-intérêts *mpl* ◆ **liable for ~s** tenu de verser des dommages et intérêts ◆ **war ~s** dommages *mpl or* indemnités *fpl* de guerre ; → **sue**

VT ① *(physically) [+ object, goods, crops, eyesight]* abîmer ; *[+ ozone layer]* endommager ; *[+ environment]* porter atteinte à ◆ **to ~ the liver/ligaments** *etc* abîmer le foie/les ligaments *etc* ◆ **~d goods** marchandises *fpl* endommagées ◆ **to ~ property** causer *or* provoquer des dégâts matériels

② *[+ reputation, relationship, country, economy, confidence, image]* nuire à, porter atteinte à ; *[+ cause, objectives, person]* faire du tort à ◆ **to ~ one's chances** compromettre ses chances ◆ **(emotionally) ~d children** enfants *mpl* traumatisés

COMP damage limitation **N** ◆ **it's too late for ~ limitation** il est trop tard pour essayer de limiter les dégâts

damage-limitation exercise **N** opération *f* visant à limiter les dégâts

damage survey **N** *(Insurance)* expertise *f* d'avarie

damageable /'dæmɪdʒəbl/ **ADJ** dommageable

damaging /'dæmɪdʒɪŋ/ **ADJ** préjudiciable (*to* pour), nuisible (*to* à) ; *(Jur)* préjudiciable

Damascus /də'mɑːskəs/ **N** Damas ◆ **it proved to be his road to ~** c'est là qu'il a trouvé son chemin de Damas

damask /'dæməsk/ **N** ① *(= cloth) [of silk]* damas *m*, soie *f* damassée ; *[of linen]* (linge *m*) damassé *m* ② ◆ **~ (steel)** (acier *m*) damasquiné *m* **ADJ** *[cloth]* damassé **COMP damask rose** **N** rose *f* de Damas

dame /deɪm/ **N** ① *(esp Brit:* †*, liter or hum)* dame *f* ◆ **the ~** *(Brit Theat)* rôle féminin de farce bouffonne joué par un homme ② *(in British titles)* **Dame** titre porté par une femme décorée d'un ordre de chevalerie ③ *(US* ‡*)* fille *f*, nana ‡ *f*

COMP Dame Fortune **N** *(*†*, liter)* Dame Fortune *f*

dame school **N** *(Hist)* école *f* enfantine, petit cours *m* privé

damfool ‡ /'dæm'fuːl/ **ADJ** *(Brit)* crétin, fichu * ◆ **that was a ~ thing to do** c'était vraiment une connerie ‡ ◆ **you and your ~ questions!** toi et tes fichues * questions ! ◆ **that ~ waiter** ce crétin de garçon, ce fichu * garçon

dammit ‡ /'dæmɪt/ **EXCL** bon sang ! *, merde ! ‡ ◆ **it weighs 2 kilos as near as ~** *(Brit)* ça pèse 2 kilos à un poil * près

damn /dæm/ **EXCL** (‡ : also **damn it !**) bon sang ! *, merde ! ‡

VT ① *(Rel)* damner ; *[+ book]* condamner, éreinter ◆ **he has already ~ed himself in her eyes** il s'est déjà discrédité à ses yeux ◆ **to ~ sb/sth with faint praise** se montrer peu élogieux envers qn/qch

② *(= swear at)* pester contre, maudire

③ ‡ **~ him!** qu'il aille au diable ! ◆ **~ you!** va te faire voir ! ‡ ◆ **~ it!** merde ! ‡, bordel ! ‡ ◆ **shut up, ~ you** *or* **~ it!** tais-toi, merde *or* bordel ! ‡ ◆ **well I'll be** *or* **I'm ~ed!** ça c'est trop fort ! ◆ **I'll be** *or* **I'm ~ed if ...** je veux bien être pendu si ..., que le diable m'emporte si ... ◆ **~ this machine!** au diable cette machine !, il y en a marre de cette machine ! *

N ‡ ◆ **I don't care** *or* **give a ~** je m'en fous ‡ pas mal ◆ **he just doesn't give a ~ about anything** il se fout ‡ de tout ◆ **he doesn't give a ~ for** *or* **about anyone** il se fout ‡ complètement des autres ; see also **give**

ADJ ‡ sacré *, fichu * ◆ **those ~ keys** ces sacrées * clés ◆ **you ~ fool!** espèce de crétin ! * ◆ **it's a ~ nuisance!** c'est vachement * embêtant ! ◆ **it's one ~ thing after another** ça n'arrête pas ! * ◆ **I don't know a ~ thing about it** je n'en sais foutre ‡ rien

ADV ‡ ① *(= extremely)* sacrément *, rudement * ◆ **it's a ~ good wine!** il est sacrément * bon, ce vin ! ◆ **~ right!** et comment !

② *(Brit)* sacrément *, rudement * ◆ **you know ~ well** tu sais très bien ◆ **I ~ near died** j'ai failli crever * ◆ **~ all** que dalle ‡ ◆ **can you see anything? – ~ all!** tu vois quelque chose ? – que dalle ! ‡ ◆ **~ well** carrément ◆ **he ~ well insulted me!** il m'a carrément injurié ! ◆ **I should ~ well think so!** j'espère bien !

damnable * /'dæmnəbl/ **ADJ** détestable, fichu *

damnably † * /'dæmnəblɪ/ **ADV** sacrément *

damnation /dæm'neɪʃən/ **N** *(Rel)* damnation *f* **EXCL** ‡ enfer et damnation ! *(hum)*, misère !

damned /dæmd/ **ADJ** ① *[soul]* damné, maudit ② ‡ → **damn adj** **ADV** ‡ → **damn adv** **NPL the damned** *(Rel, liter)* les damnés *mpl*

damnedest * /'dæmdɪst/ **N** ◆ **to do one's ~ to help** faire son possible pour aider *or* se démener * **ADJ** ◆ **he's the ~** † **eccentric** il est d'une excentricité folle * *or* renversante *

damnfool ‡ /'dæm'fuːl/ **ADJ** ⇒ **damfool**

damning /'dæmɪŋ/ **ADJ** *[report, evidence]* accablant ◆ **his speech was a ~ indictment of ...** son discours était un réquisitoire accablant contre ...

Damocles /'dæməkliːz/ **N** ◆ **the Sword of ~** l'épée *f* de Damoclès

damp /dæmp/ **ADJ** *[clothes, cloth, place, weather, heat, skin, hair]* humide ; *(with sweat) [skin, palm]* moite ◆ **a ~ patch** une tache d'humidité ◆ **a ~ squib** *(Brit)* un pétard mouillé **N** ① *[of atmosphere, walls]* humidité *f* ② *(Min)* (also **choke damp**) mofette *f* ; (also **fire damp**) grisou *m* **VT** ① *[+ a cloth, ironing]* humecter ② *[+ sounds]* amortir, étouffer ; *(Mus)* étouffer ; *[+ fire]* couvrir ③ *[+ enthusiasm, courage, ardour]* refroidir ◆ **to ~ sb's spirits** décourager qn ◆ **to ~ sb's appetite** faire passer l'envie de manger à qn

COMP damp course **N** *(Brit Constr)* couche *f* d'étanchéité

damp-dry **ADJ** prêt à repasser *(encore humide)*

damp-proof **ADJ** imperméabilisé

damp-proof course **N** ⇒ **damp course**

► **damp down** **VT SEP** *[+ leaves, plant, fabric]* humecter ; *[+ fire]* couvrir ; *(fig) [+ crisis etc]* dédramatiser ; *[+ consumption, demand]* freiner, réduire

dampen /'dæmpən/ **VT** ⇒ **damp vt 1, 3**

damper /'dæmpəʳ/, **dampener** *(US)* /'dæmpənəʳ/ **N** ① *[of chimney]* registre *m* ② (* *= depressing event)* douche *f* (froide) ◆ **his presence put a ~ on things** sa présence a fait l'effet d'une douche froide ◆ **the rain had put a ~ on the demonstrations/their picnic** la pluie avait quelque peu découragé les manifestants/gâché leur pique-nique ③ *[of piano]* étouffoir *m* ④ *(= shock absorber, electrical device)* amortisseur *m* ⑤ *(for stamps, envelopes)* mouilleur *m*

dampish /'dæmpɪʃ/ **ADJ** un peu humide

damply /'dæmplɪ/ **ADV** ① *(= wetly)* **his shirt clung ~ to him** sa chemise mouillée lui collait au corps ② *(= unenthusiastically)* sans grand enthousiasme

dampness /'dæmpnɪs/ **N** humidité *f* ; *(= sweatiness)* moiteur *f*

damsel †† /'dæmzəl/ **N** *(liter, also hum)* demoiselle *f* ◆ **~ in distress** damoiselle *f* en détresse

damselfly /'dæmzəlflaɪ/ **N** demoiselle *f*, libellule *f*

damson /'dæmzən/ **N** *(= fruit)* prune *f* de Damas ; *(= tree)* prunier *m* de Damas

dan /dæn/ **N** *(Sport)* dan *m*

dance /dɑːns/ **N** ① *(= movement)* danse *f* ◆ **modern** *or* **contemporary ~** danse *f* moderne *or* contemporaine ◆ **to study ~** étudier la danse ◆ **may I have the next ~?** voudriez-vous m'accorder la prochaine danse ? ◆ **to lead sb a (merry) ~** *(Brit)* donner du fil à retordre à qn ◆ **the Dance of Death** la danse macabre ; → **folk, sequence**

② *(= social gathering)* bal *m*, soirée *f* dansante

VT *[+ waltz, tango etc]* danser ◆ **to ~ a step** exécuter un pas de danse ◆ **she ~d (the role of) Coppelia** elle a dansé (le rôle de) Coppélia ◆ **to ~ attendance on sb** être aux petits soins pour qn

VI *[person, leaves in wind, boat on waves, eyes]* danser ◆ **to ~ about, to ~ up and down** *(fig)* gambader, sautiller ◆ **the child ~d away** *or* **off** l'enfant s'est éloigné en gambadant *or* en sautillant ◆ **to ~ in/out** *etc* entrer/sortir *etc* joyeusement ◆ **to ~ for** *or* **with joy** sauter de joie ◆ **to ~ with impatience/rage** trépigner d'impatience/de colère ◆ **to ~ to the music** danser sur la musique ◆ **to ~ to sb's tune** *(fig)* faire les quatre volontés de qn

COMP *[class, teacher, partner]* de danse

dance band **N** orchestre *m* (de danse)

dance floor **N** piste *f* (de danse)

dance hall **N** dancing *m*

dance hostess **N** entraîneuse *f*

dance music **N** dance music *f*

dance programme **N** carnet *m* de bal

dance studio **N** cours *m* de danse

dancer /'dɑːnsəʳ/ **N** danseur *m*, -euse *f*

dancing /'dɑːnsɪŋ/ **N** *(NonC)* danse *f* ◆ **there will be ~** on dansera

COMP *[teacher, school]* de danse

dancing girl **N** danseuse *f*

dancing partner N cavalier *m*, -ière *f*, partenaire *mf*
dancing shoes NPL *[of men]* escarpins *mpl* ; *[of women]* souliers *mpl* de bal ; *(for ballet)* chaussons *mpl* de danse

dandelion /ˈdændɪlaɪən/ N pissenlit *m*, dent-de-lion *f*

dander †* /ˈdændəʳ/ N ◆ **to get sb's ~ up** mettre qn en boule* ◆ **to have one's ~ up** être hors de soi *or* en rogne*

dandified /ˈdændɪfaɪd/ ADJ *[arrogance, ways]* de dandy ; *[person]* qui a une allure de dandy

dandle /ˈdændl/ VT *[+ child]* *(on knees)* faire sauter sur ses genoux ; *(in arms)* bercer dans ses bras, câliner

dandruff /ˈdændrəf/ N *(NonC)* pellicules *fpl* *(du cuir chevelu)* COMP **dandruff shampoo** N shampooing *m* antipelliculaire

dandy /ˈdændɪ/ N dandy *m* ADJ * épatant*

Dane /deɪn/ N 1 Danois(e) *m(f)* 2 → **great**

dang * /dæŋ/ ADJ, ADV *(euph)* ⇒ **damn**

danger /ˈdeɪndʒəʳ/ N danger *m* ◆ **the ~s of smoking/drink-driving** les dangers *mpl* du tabac/de la conduite en état d'ivresse ◆ **there is a ~** *or* **some ~ in doing that** il est dangereux de faire cela ◆ **there's no ~ in doing that** il n'est pas dangereux de faire cela ◆ **"danger keep out"** "danger : défense d'entrer" ◆ **there is a ~ of fire** il y a un risque d'incendie ◆ **signal at ~** *(Rail)* signal à l'arrêt ◆ **there was no ~ that she would be recognized** *or* **of her being recognized** elle ne courait aucun risque d'être reconnue ◆ **to be a ~ to sb/sth** être un danger pour qn/qch ◆ **he's a ~ to himself** il risque de se faire du mal ◆ **there's no ~ of that** *(lit)* il n'y a pas le moindre danger *or* risque ; *(iro)* il n'y a pas de danger, aucune chance
◆ **in + danger** ◆ **to be in ~** être en danger ◆ **to put sb/sth in ~** mettre qn/qch en danger ◆ **he was in little ~** il ne courait pas grand risque ◆ **in ~ of invasion/extinction** menacé d'invasion/de disparition ◆ **he was in ~ of losing his job/falling** il risquait de perdre sa place/de tomber ◆ **he's in no ~, he's not in any ~** il ne risque rien ; *(Med)* ses jours ne sont pas en danger
◆ **out of danger** hors de danger
COMP **danger area** N ⇒ **danger zone**
danger list N *(Med)* ◆ **to be on the ~ list** être dans un état critique *or* très grave ◆ **to be off the ~ list** être hors de danger
danger money N prime *f* de risque
danger point N point *m* critique, cote *f* d'alerte ◆ **to reach ~ point** atteindre la cote d'alerte *or* le point critique
danger signal N signal *m* d'alarme
danger zone N zone *f* dangereuse

dangerous /ˈdeɪndʒrəs/ ADJ dangereux ; *(Med)* *[operation]* risqué *(for, to pour)* ◆ **it's ~ to do that** c'est dangereux de faire ça ◆ **the car was ~ to drive** cette voiture était dangereuse à conduire ; → **ground**[1] COMP **dangerous driving** N conduite *f* dangereuse

dangerously /ˈdeɪndʒrəslɪ/ ADV dangereusement ◆ **~ close to the fire** dangereusement près du feu ◆ **~ ill** gravement malade ◆ **food supplies were ~ low** les vivres commençaient sérieusement à manquer ◆ **he came ~ close to admitting it** il a été à deux doigts de l'admettre ◆ **the date is getting ~ close** la date fatidique approche ◆ **to live ~** vivre dangereusement

dangle /ˈdæŋgl/ VT 1 *[+ object on string]* balancer, suspendre ; *[+ arm, leg]* laisser pendre, balancer 2 *(fig)* *[+ prospect, offer]* faire miroiter *(before sb* à qn) VI *[object on string]* pendre, pendiller ; *[arms, legs]* pendre, (se) balancer ◆ **with arms dangling** les bras ballants ◆ **with legs dangling** les jambes pendantes

Daniel /ˈdænjəl/ N Daniel *m*

Danish /ˈdeɪnɪʃ/ ADJ *(gen)* danois ; *[ambassador, embassy]* du Danemark ; *[teacher]* de danois N 1 *(= language)* danois *m* 2 ⇒ **Danish pastry**
NPL **the Danish** les Danois *mpl*
COMP **Danish blue (cheese)** N bleu *m* (du Danemark)
Danish pastry N feuilleté *m* (fourré aux fruits *etc*) ; *(with raisins)* pain *m* aux raisins

dank /dæŋk/ ADJ *[air, weather, dungeon]* froid et humide

Dante /ˈdæntɪ/ N Dante *m*

Dantean /ˈdæntɪən/, **Dantesque** /dænˈtesk/ ADJ dantesque

Danube /ˈdænjuːb/ N Danube *m*

Danzig /ˈdænsɪg/ N Danzig *or* Dantzig

Daphne /ˈdæfnɪ/ N 1 *(= name)* Daphné *f* 2 *(= plant)* **daphne** lauréole *f*, laurier *m* des bois

daphnia /ˈdæfnɪə/ N daphnie *f*

dapper /ˈdæpəʳ/ ADJ fringant, sémillant

dapple /ˈdæpl/ VT tacheter COMP **dapple grey** N *(= colour)* gris *m* pommelé ; *(= horse)* cheval *m* pommelé

dappled /ˈdæpld/ ADJ *[surface, horse]* tacheté ; *[sky]* pommelé ; *[shade]* avec des taches de lumière

DAR /ˌdiːeɪˈɑːʳ/ NPL *(US)* (abbrev of **Daughters of the American Revolution**) *club de descendantes des combattants de la Révolution américaine*

Darby /ˈdɑːbɪ/ N ◆ **~ and Joan** ≈ Philémon et Baucis ◆ **~ and Joan club** *(Brit)* cercle *m* pour couples du troisième âge

Dardanelles /ˌdɑːdəˈnelz/ N ◆ **the ~** les Dardanelles *fpl*

dare /deəʳ/ VT, MODAL AUX VB 1 oser *(do sth, to do sth* faire qch) ◆ **he ~ not** *or* **daren't climb that tree** il n'ose pas grimper à cet arbre ◆ **he ~d not do it, he didn't ~ (to) do it** il n'a pas osé le faire ◆ **~ you do it?** oserez-vous le faire ? ◆ **how ~ you say such things?** comment osez-vous dire des choses pareilles ? ◆ **how ~ you!** vous osez !, comment osez-vous ? ◆ **don't ~ say that!** je vous défends de dire cela ! ◆ **don't you ~!** ne t'avise pas de faire ça ! ◆ **I daren't!** je n'ose pas ! ◆ **the show was, ~ I say it, dull** le spectacle était, si je puis me permettre, ennuyeux ◆ **who ~s wins** ≈ qui ne risque rien n'a rien
2 ◆ **I ~ say he'll come** il viendra sans doute, il est probable qu'il viendra ◆ **I ~ say you're tired after your journey** vous êtes sans doute fatigué *or* j'imagine que vous êtes fatigué après votre voyage ◆ **he is very sorry – I ~ say!** *(iro)* il le regrette beaucoup – encore heureux *or* j'espère bien !
3 *(= face the risk of)* *[+ danger, death]* affronter, braver
4 *(= challenge)* **to ~ sb to do sth** défier qn de faire qch, mettre qn au défi de faire qch ◆ **(I) ~ you!** chiche !*
N défi *m* ◆ **to do sth for a ~** faire qch pour relever un défi

daredevil /ˈdeədevl/ N casse-cou *m inv*, tête *f* brûlée ADJ *[behaviour]* de casse-cou ; *[adventure]* fou (folle *f*), audacieux

daresay /deəˈseɪ/ VT *(esp Brit)* ◆ **I ~** ⇒ **I dare say** ; → **dare vt 2**

Dar es Salaam /ˌdɑːressəˈlɑːm/ N Dar es Salaam

daring /ˈdeərɪŋ/ ADJ 1 *(= courageous)* *[person, attempt]* audacieux 2 *(= risqué)* *[dress, opinion, novel]* osé N audace *f*, hardiesse *f*

daringly /ˈdeərɪŋlɪ/ ADV *[say, suggest]* avec audace ◆ **~, she remarked that ...** elle a observé avec audace que ... ◆ **a ~ low-cut dress** une robe au décolleté audacieux

dark /dɑːk/ ADJ 1 *(= lacking light)* *[place, night]* sombre ; *(= unlit)* dans l'obscurité ◆ **it's ~** il fait nuit *or* noir ◆ **it's getting ~** il commence à faire nuit ◆ **to grow ~(er)** s'assombrir, s'obscurcir ◆ **the ~ side of the moon** la face cachée de la lune ◆ **it's as ~ as pitch** *or* **night** il fait noir comme dans un four ◆ **the whole house was ~** la maison était plongée dans l'obscurité ◆ **to go ~** être plongé dans l'obscurité
2 *[colour, clothes]* foncé, sombre ◆ **~ blue/green** *etc* bleu/vert *etc* foncé *inv* ◆ **~ brown hair** cheveux *mpl* châtain foncé *inv* ; see also **blue**
3 *[complexion]* mat ; *[skin]* foncé ; *[hair]* brun ; *[eyes]* sombre ◆ **she's very ~** elle est très brune ◆ **she has a ~ complexion** elle a le teint mat ◆ **she has ~ hair** elle est brune, elle a les cheveux bruns
4 *(= sinister)* *[hint]* sinistre ◆ **~ hints were dropped about a possible prosecution** on a fait planer la menace d'éventuelles poursuites judiciaires ◆ **I got some ~ looks from Janet** Janet m'a jeté un regard noir, Janet me regardait d'un œil noir ◆ **a ~ secret** un lourd secret ◆ **~ threats** de sourdes menaces *fpl* ◆ **~ deeds** de mauvaises actions *fpl* ◆ **the ~ side of sth** la face cachée de qch
5 *(= gloomy, bleak)* *[thoughts, mood]* sombre, noir ◆ **these are ~ days for the steel industry** c'est une époque sombre pour l'industrie sidérurgique ◆ **to think ~ thoughts** broyer du noir ◆ **to look on the ~ side of things** tout voir en noir
6 *(= mysterious)* mystérieux ◆ **~est Africa** † le fin fond de l'Afrique ◆ **to keep sth ~*** tenir *or* garder qch secret ◆ **keep it ~!** motus et bouche cousue !
7 *(Phon)* sombre
8 *(Theat = closed)* fermé
N 1 *(= absence of light)* obscurité *f*, noir *m* ◆ **after ~** la nuit venue, après la tombée de la nuit ◆ **until ~** jusqu'à (la tombée de) la nuit ◆ **to be afraid of the ~** avoir peur du noir ◆ **she was sitting in the ~** elle était assise dans le noir
2 *(fig)* **I am quite in the ~ about it** je suis tout à fait dans le noir là-dessus, j'ignore tout de cette histoire ◆ **he has kept** *or* **left me in the ~ about what he wants to do** il m'a laissé dans l'ignorance *or* il ne m'a donné aucun renseignement sur ce qu'il veut faire ◆ **to work in the ~** travailler à l'aveuglette ; → **shot**
COMP **dark age** N *(fig)* période *f* sombre
the Dark Ages NPL l'âge *m* des ténèbres
dark chocolate N chocolat *m* noir *or* à croquer
dark-complexioned ADJ brun, basané
the Dark Continent N le continent noir
dark-eyed ADJ aux yeux noirs
dark glasses NPL lunettes *fpl* noires
dark-haired ADJ aux cheveux bruns
dark horse N *(gen)* quantité *f* inconnue ; *(US Pol)* candidat *m* inattendu
dark matter N *(Astron)* matière *f* noire
dark-skinned ADJ *[person]* brun (de peau), à peau brune ; *[race]* de couleur

darken /ˈdɑːkən/ VT 1 *(lit: in brightness, colour)* *[+ room, landscape]* obscurcir, assombrir ; *[+ sky]* assombrir ; *[+ sun]* obscurcir, voiler ; *[+ colour]* foncer ; *[+ complexion]* brunir ◆ **a ~ed house/room/street** une maison/pièce/rue sombre ◆ **to ~ one's hair** se foncer les cheveux ◆ **never ~ my door again!** *(† or hum)* ne remets plus les pieds chez moi ! 2 *(fig)* *[+ future]* assombrir ; *[+ prospects, atmosphere]* assombrir VI 1 *[sky]* s'assombrir ; *[room]* s'obscurcir ; *[colours]* foncer 2 *(fig)* *[atmosphere]* s'assombrir ◆ **his face/features ~ed with annoyance** son visage/sa mine s'est rembruni(e) (sous l'effet de la contrariété) ◆ **his eyes ~ed** son regard s'est assombri ◆ **his mood ~ed** il s'est rembruni

darkie **/ˈdɑːkɪ/ N *(pej)* moricaud(e)** *m(f)* *(pej)*, nègre** *m* *(pej)*, négresse** *f* *(pej)*

darkish /ˈdɑːkɪʃ/ ADJ *[colour]* assez sombre ; *[complexion]* plutôt mat ; *[person]* plutôt brun

◆ **a ~ blue/green** *etc* un bleu/vert *etc* plutôt foncé *inv*

darkly /ˈdɑːklɪ/ ADV sinistrement ◆ **"we'll see", he said** ~ "on verra", dit-il d'un ton sinistre ◆ **the newspapers hinted ~ at conspiracies** les journaux ont fait des allusions inquiétantes à des complots ◆ ~ **comic** plein d'humour noir ◆ ~ **handsome** à la beauté ténébreuse ◆ **a ~ handsome man** un beau brun ténébreux

darkness /ˈdɑːknɪs/ N (NonC) 1 *[of night, room]* *(also fig)* obscurité *f*, ténèbres *fpl* ◆ **in total** *or* **utter** ~ dans une obscurité complète *or* totale ◆ **the house was in** ~ la maison était plongée dans l'obscurité ◆ **the powers** *or* **forces of** ~ les forces *fpl* des ténèbres ; → **prince** 2 *[of colour]* teinte *f* foncée ; *[of face, skin]* couleur *f* basanée

darkroom /ˈdɑːkrʊm/ N *(Phot)* chambre *f* noire

darky**/ˈdɑːkɪ/ N *(pej)* ⇒ **darkie**

darling /ˈdɑːlɪŋ/ N bien-aimé(e) † *m(f)*, favori(te) *m(f)* ◆ **the ~ of ...** la coqueluche de ... ◆ **a mother's ~** un(e) chouchou(te)* ◆ **she's a little** ~ c'est un amour, elle est adorable ◆ **come here, (my)** ~ viens (mon) chéri *or* mon amour ; *(to child)* viens (mon) chéri *or* mon petit chou ◆ **be a ~ * and bring me my glasses** apporte-moi mes lunettes, tu seras un ange ◆ **she was a perfect ~ about it*** elle a été un ange *or* vraiment sympa* ADJ *[child]* chéri, bien-aimé † ; *(liter)* *[wish]* le plus cher ◆ **a ~ little place*** un petit coin ravissant *or* adorable

darn¹ /dɑːn/ VT *[+ socks]* repriser ; *[+ clothes etc]* raccommoder N reprise *f*

darn²* /dɑːn/, **darned*** /dɑːnd/ *(esp US)* *(euph)* ⇒ **damn, damned**

darnel /ˈdɑːnl/ N ivraie *f*, ray-grass *m*

darning /ˈdɑːnɪŋ/ N 1 (NonC) raccommodage *m*, reprise *f* 2 *(= things to be darned)* raccommodage *m*, linge *m* *or* vêtements *mpl* à raccommoder

COMP **darning needle** N aiguille *f* à repriser
darning stitch N point *m* de reprise
darning wool N laine *f* à repriser

dart /dɑːt/ N 1 *(= movement)* ◆ **to make a sudden ~ at ...** se précipiter sur ...
2 *(Sport)* fléchette *f* ◆ **a game of ~s** une partie de fléchettes ◆ **I like (playing) ~s** j'aime jouer aux fléchettes
3 *(= weapon)* flèche *f*
4 *(fig)* ◆ **... he said with a ~ of spite** ... dit-il avec une pointe de malveillance ◆ **a ~ of pain went through him** il ressentit une vive douleur ; → **Cupid, paper**
5 *(Sewing)* pince *f*
VI se précipiter, s'élancer *(at sur)* ◆ **to ~ in/out** *etc* entrer/sortir *etc* en coup de vent ◆ **the snake's tongue ~ed out** le serpent dardait sa langue ◆ **her eyes ~ed round the room** elle jetait des regards furtifs autour de la pièce ◆ **his eyes ~ed about nervously** il lançait des regards nerveux autour de lui
VT ◆ **the snake ~ed its tongue out** le serpent dardait sa langue ◆ **she ~ed a glance at him, she ~ed him a glance** elle lui décocha un regard, elle darda *(liter)* un regard sur lui ◆ **she ~ed a glance at her watch** elle jeta un coup d'œil (furtif) à sa montre

dartboard /ˈdɑːtbɔːd/ N cible *f* *(de jeu de fléchettes)*

Darwinian /dɑːˈwɪnɪən/ ADJ darwinien

Darwinism /ˈdɑːwɪnɪzəm/ N darwinisme *m*

dash /dæʃ/ N 1 *(= sudden rush)* mouvement *m* brusque *(en avant)*, élan *m* ; *[of crowd]* ruée *f* ◆ **there was a ~ for the door** tout le monde se précipita *or* se rua vers la porte ◆ **there was a mad/last-minute ~ to get the Christmas shopping done** il y a eu une ruée effrénée/de dernière minute dans les magasins pour acheter des cadeaux de Noël ◆ **to make a ~ for/towards ...** se précipiter sur/vers ... ◆ **to make a ~ for freedom** saisir l'occasion de s'enfuir ◆ **he made a ~ for it*** il a pris ses jambes à son cou
2 *(= small amount)* *[of wine, oil, milk, water]* goutte *f* ; *[of spirits]* doigt *m*, goutte *f* ; *[of pepper, nutmeg]* pincée *f* ; *[of mustard]* pointe *f* ; *[of vinegar, lemon]* filet *m* ◆ **a ~ of soda** un peu d'eau de Seltz ◆ **cushions can add a ~ of colour to the room** les coussins peuvent apporter une touche de couleur à la pièce ◆ **her character adds a ~ of glamour to the story** son personnage apporte un peu de glamour à l'histoire
3 *(= flair, style)* panache *m* ◆ **to cut a ~** faire de l'effet ◆ **people with more ~ than cash** des gens qui ont plus de goût que de sous
4 *(= punctuation mark)* tiret *m*
5 *(in Morse code)* trait *m*
6 *[of car]* → **dashboard**
7 *(Sport)* ◆ **the 100 metre ~** † le 100 mètres
VT 1 *(liter = throw violently)* jeter *or* lancer violemment ◆ **to ~ sth to pieces** casser qch en mille morceaux ◆ **to ~ sth down** *or* **to the ground** jeter qch par terre ◆ **to ~ one's head against sth** se cogner la tête contre qch ◆ **the ship was ~ed against a rock** le navire a été précipité contre un écueil
2 *(fig)* *[+ spirits]* abattre ; *[+ person]* démoraliser ◆ **to ~ sb's hopes (to the ground)** anéantir les espoirs de qn
VI 1 *(= rush)* se précipiter ◆ **to ~ away/back/up** *etc* s'en aller/revenir/monter *etc* à toute allure *or* en coup de vent ◆ **to ~ into a room** se précipiter dans une pièce ◆ **I have to** *or* **must ~** * il faut que je file* *subj*
2 *(= crash)* ◆ **to ~ against sth** *[waves]* se briser contre qch ; *[car, bird, object]* se heurter à qch
EXCL († * *euph*) ⇒ **damn** ◆ ~ **(it)!**, ~ **it all!** zut alors !*, flûte !*

► **dash off** VI partir précipitamment
VT SEP *[+ letter etc]* faire en vitesse

dashboard /ˈdæʃbɔːd/ N *[of car]* tableau *m* de bord

dashed* /dæʃt/ ADJ, ADV *(euph)* ⇒ **damned** ; → **damn adj, adv**

dashiki /dɑːˈʃiːkɪ/ N tunique *f* africaine

dashing /ˈdæʃɪŋ/ ADJ fringant ◆ **to cut a ~ figure** avoir fière allure

dashingly /ˈdæʃɪŋlɪ/ ADV *[perform]* avec brio

dastardly /ˈdæstədlɪ/ ADJ († *or liter*) *[person, action]* ignoble

DAT /diːeɪˈtiː/ N (abbrev of **digital audio tape**) DAT *m*

data /ˈdeɪtə/ NPL of **datum** *(often with sg vb)* données *fpl* VT *(US *)* *[+ person etc]* ficher
COMP *(Comput)* *[input, sorting etc]* de(s) données
data bank N banque *f* de données
data capture N saisie *f* des données
data carrier N support *m* d'informations *or* de données
data collection N collecte *f* de données
data dictionary N dictionnaire *m* de données
data directory N répertoire *m* de données
data file N fichier *m* informatisé *or* de données
data link N liaison *f* de transmission
data preparation N préparation *f* des données
data processing N traitement *m* des données
data processor N *(= machine)* machine *f* de traitement de données ; *(= person)* informaticien(ne) *m(f)*
data protection N protection *f* des données
data protection act N ≈ loi *f* informatique et libertés
data security N sécurité *f* des informations
data transmission N transmission *f* de données

database /ˈdeɪtəbeɪs/ N base *f* de données
COMP **database management** N gestion *f* de (base de) données
database management system N système *m* de gestion de (base de) données
database manager N *(= software)* logiciel *m* de gestion de base de données ; *(= person)* gestionnaire *mf* de base de données

Datapost ® /ˈdeɪtəpəʊst/ N *(Brit Post)* ◆ **by ~** en express, ≈ par Chronopost ®

datcha /ˈdætʃə/ N ⇒ **dacha**

date¹ /deɪt/ N 1 *(= time of some event)* date *f* ◆ **what is today's ~?, what is the ~ today?** quelle est la date aujourd'hui ?, nous sommes le combien aujourd'hui ? ◆ **what ~ is he coming (on)?** quel jour arrive-t-il ? ◆ **what ~ is your birthday?** quelle est la date de votre anniversaire ? ◆ **what ~ is Easter this year?** quelle est la date de Pâques cette année ? ◆ **what is the ~ of this letter?** de quand est cette lettre ? ◆ **departure/delivery** *etc* ~ date *f* de départ/de livraison *etc* ◆ **there is speculation about a June election** ~ on parle de juin pour les élections ◆ **to fix** *or* **set a ~ (for sth)** fixer une date *or* convenir d'une date (pour qch) ◆ **have they set a ~ yet?** *(for wedding)* ont-ils déjà fixé la date du mariage ?

◆ **out of date** ◆ **to be out of ~** *[document]* ne plus être applicable ; *[person]* ne pas être de son temps *or* à la page ◆ **he's very out of ~** il n'est vraiment pas de son temps *or* à la page ◆ **to be out of ~ in one's ideas** avoir des idées complètement dépassées ; see also **out**

◆ **to date** ◆ **to ~ we have accomplished nothing** à ce jour *or* jusqu'à présent nous n'avons rien accompli ◆ **this is her best novel to ~** c'est le meilleur roman qu'elle ait jamais écrit

◆ **up to date** *[document]* à jour ; *[building]* moderne, au goût du jour ; *[person]* moderne, à la page ◆ **to be up to ~ in one's work** être à jour dans son travail ◆ **to bring up to ~** *[+ accounts, correspondence etc]* mettre à jour ; *[+ method etc]* moderniser ◆ **to bring sb up to ~** mettre qn au courant *(about sth* de qch) see also **up**

2 *(Jur)* quantième *m* (du mois)
3 *[of coins, medals etc]* millésime *m*
4 *(= appointment)* rendez-vous *m* ; *(= person)* petit(e) ami(e) *m(f)* ◆ **to have a ~ with sb** *(with boyfriend, girlfriend)* avoir rendez-vous avec qn ◆ **they made a ~ for 8 o'clock** ils ont fixé un rendez-vous pour 8 heures ◆ **I've got a lunch ~ today** je déjeune avec quelqu'un aujourd'hui ◆ **have you got a ~ for tonight?** *(= appointment)* as-tu (un) rendez-vous ce soir ? ; *(= person)* tu as quelqu'un avec qui sortir ce soir ? ◆ **he's my ~ for this evening** je sors avec lui ce soir ; → **blind**
5 *(= pop concert)* concert *m* ◆ **they're playing three ~s in Britain** ils donnent trois concerts en Grande-Bretagne ◆ **the band's UK tour ~s** les dates de la tournée du groupe au Royaume-Uni
VT 1 *[+ letter]* dater ; *[+ ticket, voucher]* dater ; *(with machine)* composter ◆ **a cheque/letter ~d 7 August** un chèque/une lettre daté(e) du 7 août ◆ **a coin ~d 1390** une pièce datée de 1390
2 *(= establish date of)* **the manuscript has been ~d at around 3,000 years old/1,000 BC** on estime que le manuscrit a 3 000 ans/remonte à 1 000 ans avant Jésus-Christ ◆ **his taste in ties certainly ~s him** son goût en matière de cravates trahit son âge ◆ **the hairstyles really ~ this film** les coupes de cheveux démodées montrent que le film ne date pas d'hier ; → **carbon**
3 *(esp US = go out with)* sortir avec
VI 1 ◆ **to ~ from, to ~ back to** dater de, remonter à
2 *(= become old-fashioned)* *[clothes, expressions etc]* dater

3 (esp US) **they're dating** (= go out with sb) ils sortent ensemble ◆ **she has started dating** elle commence à sortir avec des garçons

COMP **date book** N (US) agenda *m*

date line N (Geog) ligne *f* de changement de date *or* de changement de jour ; (Press) date *f* (d'une dépêche)

date of birth N date *f* de naissance

date rape N viol commis par une connaissance (lors d'un rendez-vous)

date-rape VT ◆ **she was ~-raped** elle a été violée par une connaissance (lors d'un rendez-vous)

date stamp N [of library etc] tampon *m* (encreur) (pour dater un livre etc), dateur *m* ; (Post) tampon *m or* cachet *m* (de la poste) ; (for cancelling) oblitérateur *m* ; (= postmark) cachet *m* de la poste

date-stamp VT [+ library book] tamponner ; [+ letter, document] (gen) apposer le cachet de la date sur ; (Post) apposer le cachet de la poste sur ; (= cancel) [+ stamp] oblitérer

date² /deɪt/ N (= fruit) datte *f* ; (= tree: also **date palm**) dattier *m*

dated /'deɪtɪd/ ADJ [book, film etc] démodé ; [word, language, expression] vieilli ; [idea, humour] désuet (-ète *f*)

dateless /'deɪtlɪs/ ADJ hors du temps

dating /'deɪtɪŋ/ N (Archeol) datation *f* COMP **dating agency** N agence *f* de rencontres

dative /'deɪtɪv/ (Ling) N datif *m* ◆ **in the ~** au datif ADJ ◆ **~ case** (cas *m*) datif *m* ◆ **~ ending** flexion *f* du datif

datum /'deɪtəm/ N (pl **data**) donnée *f* ; → **data**

DATV /diːeɪtiː'viː/ N (abbrev of **digitally assisted television**) télévision *f* numérique

daub /dɔːb/ VT (pej) (with paint, make-up) barbouiller (with de) ; (with clay, grease) enduire, barbouiller (with de) N 1 (Constr) enduit *m* 2 (pej = bad picture) croûte* *f*, barbouillage *m*

daughter /'dɔːtəʳ/ N (lit, fig) fille *f* COMP **daughter-in-law** N (pl **daughters-in-law**) belle-fille *f*

daughterboard /'dɔːtəbɔːd/ N (Comput) carte *f* fille

daunt /dɔːnt/ VT décourager ◆ **nothing ~ed, he continued** il a continué sans se (laisser) démonter

daunting /'dɔːntɪŋ/ ADJ intimidant ◆ **it's a ~ prospect** c'est décourageant

dauntless /'dɔːntlɪs/ ADJ [person, courage] intrépide

dauntlessly /'dɔːntlɪslɪ/ ADV avec intrépidité

dauphin /'dɔːfɪn/ N (Hist) Dauphin *m*

davenport /'dævnpɔːt/ N 1 (esp US = sofa) canapé *m* 2 (Brit = desk) secrétaire *m*

David /'deɪvɪd/ N David *m*

davit /'dævɪt/ N (Naut) bossoir *m*

Davy Jones' locker /,deɪvɪdʒəʊnz'lɒkəʳ/ N (Naut) ◆ **to go to ~** se noyer

Davy lamp /'deɪvɪlæmp/ N (Min) lampe *f* de sécurité

dawdle /'dɔːdl/ VI (also **dawdle about, dawdle around**) (= walk slowly, stroll) flâner ; (= go too slowly) traîner, lambiner* ◆ **to ~ on the way** s'amuser en chemin ◆ **to ~ over one's work** traînasser sur son travail

dawdler /'dɔːdləʳ/ N traînard(e) *m(f)*, lambin(e) *m(f)*

dawdling /'dɔːdlɪŋ/ ADJ traînard N flânerie *f*

dawn /dɔːn/ N 1 aube *f*, aurore *f* ◆ **at ~** à l'aube, au point du jour ◆ **from ~ to dusk** de l'aube au crépuscule, du matin au soir ◆ **it was the ~ of another day** c'était l'aube d'un nouveau jour

2 (NonC) [of civilization] aube *f* ; [of an idea, hope] naissance *f*

VI 1 [day] se lever ◆ **the day ~ed bright and clear** l'aube parut, lumineuse et claire ◆ **the day ~ed rainy** le jour s'est levé sous la pluie, il pleuvait au lever du jour ◆ **the day will ~ when ...** un jour viendra où ...

2 (fig) [era, new society] naître, se faire jour ; [hope] luire ◆ **an idea ~ed upon him** une idée lui est venue à l'esprit ◆ **the truth ~ed upon her** elle a commencé à entrevoir la vérité ◆ **it suddenly ~ed on him that no one would know** il lui vint tout à coup à l'esprit que personne ne saurait ◆ **suddenly the light ~ed on him** soudain, ça a fait tilt*

COMP **dawn chorus** N (Brit) concert *m* (matinal) des oiseaux

dawn raid N (Stock Exchange) tentative *f* d'OPA surprise, raid *m* ◆ **the police made a ~ raid on his house** la police a fait une descente chez lui à l'aube

dawn raider N (Stock Exchange) raider *m*

dawning /'dɔːnɪŋ/ ADJ [day, hope] naissant, croissant N ⇒ **dawn**

day /deɪ/ N 1 (= unit of time: 24 hours) jour *m* ◆ **three ~s ago** il y a trois jours ◆ **to do sth in three ~s** faire qch en trois jours, mettre trois jours à faire qch ◆ **he's coming in three ~s** *or* **three ~s' time** il vient dans trois jours ◆ **twice a ~** deux fois par jour ◆ **this ~ week** (Brit) aujourd'hui en huit ◆ **what ~ is it today?** quel jour sommes-nous aujourd'hui ? ◆ **what ~ of the month is it?** le combien sommes-nous ? ◆ **she arrived (on) the ~ they left** elle est arrivée le jour de leur départ ◆ **on that ~** ce jour-là ◆ **on a ~ like this** un jour comme aujourd'hui ◆ **on the following ~** le lendemain ◆ **two years ago to the ~** il y a deux ans jour pour jour *or* exactement ◆ **to this ~** à ce jour, jusqu'à aujourd'hui ◆ **the ~ before yesterday** avant-hier ◆ **the ~ before/two ~s before her birthday** la veille/l'avant-veille de son anniversaire ◆ **the ~ after, the following ~** le lendemain ◆ **two ~s after her birthday** le surlendemain de son anniversaire, deux jours après son anniversaire ◆ **the ~ after tomorrow** après-demain ◆ **from that ~ onwards** *or* **on** dès lors, à partir de ce jour(-là) ◆ **from this ~ forth** (frm) désormais, dorénavant ◆ **he will come any ~ now** il va venir d'un jour à l'autre ◆ **every ~** tous les jours ◆ **every other ~** tous les deux jours ◆ **one ~ we saw the king** un (beau) jour, nous avons vu le roi ◆ **one ~ she will come** un jour (ou l'autre) elle viendra ◆ **one of these ~s** un de ces jours ◆ **~ after ~** jour après jour ◆ **for ~s on end** pendant des jours et des jours ◆ **for ~s at a time** pendant des jours entiers ◆ **~ by ~** jour après jour ◆ **in ~ out** jour après jour ◆ **the other ~** l'autre jour, il y a quelques jours ◆ **it's been one of those ~s** ça a été une de ces journées où tout va de travers *or* où rien ne va ◆ **this ~ of all ~s** ce jour entre tous ◆ **some ~** un jour, un de ces jours ◆ **I remember it to this (very) ~** je m'en souviens encore aujourd'hui ◆ **he's fifty if he's a ~*** il a cinquante ans bien sonnés* ◆ **as of ~ one*, from ~ one*, on ~ one*** dès le premier jour ◆ **on the ~** (= in the event) le moment venu ◆ **that'll be the ~!** j'aimerais voir ça ! ◆ **the ~ he gets married (is the ~) I'll eat my hat!** le jour où il se mariera, les poules auront des dents ! ◆ **let's make a ~ of it and ...** profitons de la journée pour ... ◆ **to live from ~ to ~** vivre au jour le jour ◆ **(it's best to) take it one ~ at a time** à chaque jour suffit sa peine (Prov) ◆ **I'm just taking things one ~ at a time** je vis au jour le jour ; → **Christmas, Easter, judg(e)ment, reckoning**

2 (= daylight hours) jour *m*, journée *f* ◆ **during the ~** pendant la journée ◆ **to work all ~** travailler toute la journée ◆ **to travel by ~** voyager de jour ◆ **to work ~ and night** travailler jour et nuit ◆ **the ~ is done** (liter) le jour baisse, le jour tire à sa fin ◆ **one summer's ~** un jour d'été ◆ **on a wet ~** par une journée pluvieuse ◆ **to have a ~ out** faire une sortie ◆ **to carry** *or* **win the ~** (Mil, fig) remporter la victoire ◆ **to lose the ~** (Mil, fig) perdre la bataille ◆ **(as) clear** *or* **plain as ~** clair comme de l'eau de roche ; → **break, court, fine², good, late, time**

3 (= working hours) journée *f* ◆ **paid by the ~** payé à la journée ◆ **I've done a full ~'s work** (lit) j'ai fait ma journée (de travail) ; (fig) j'ai eu une journée bien remplie ◆ **it's all in a ~'s work!** ça fait partie de la routine !, ça n'a rien d'extraordinaire ! ◆ **to work an eight-hour ~** travailler huit heures par jour ◆ **to take/get a ~ off** prendre/avoir un jour de congé ◆ **it's my ~ off** c'est mon jour de congé ; → **call, off, rest, working**

4 (period of time: often pl) époque *f*, temps *m* ◆ **these ~s, at the present ~** à l'heure actuelle, de nos jours ◆ **in this ~ and age** par les temps qui courent ◆ **in ~s to come** à l'avenir ◆ **in his working ~s** au temps *or* à l'époque où il travaillait ◆ **in his younger ~s** quand il était plus jeune ◆ **in the ~s of Queen Victoria, in Queen Victoria's ~** du temps de *or* sous le règne de la reine Victoria ◆ **in Napoleon's ~** à l'époque *or* du temps de Napoléon ◆ **in those ~s** à l'époque ◆ **famous in her ~** célèbre à son époque ◆ **in the good old ~s** au *or* dans le bon vieux temps ◆ **in ~s gone by** autrefois, jadis ◆ **those were the ~s!** c'était le bon vieux temps ! ◆ **those were sad ~s** c'était une époque sombre ◆ **the happiest ~s of my life** les jours les plus heureux *or* la période la plus heureuse de ma vie ◆ **to end one's ~s in misery** finir ses jours dans la misère ◆ **that has had its ~** (= old-fashioned) cela est passé de mode ; (= worn out) cela a fait son temps ◆ **his ~ will come** son jour viendra ◆ **during the early ~s of the war** au début de la guerre ◆ **it's early ~s (yet)** (= too early to say) c'est un peu tôt pour le dire ; (= there's still time) on n'en est encore qu'au début ; → **dog, olden**

COMP **day bed** N (US) banquette-lit *f*

day boarder N (Brit Scol) demi-pensionnaire *mf*

day boy N (Brit Scol) externe *m*

day centre N (Brit) centre *m* d'accueil

day girl N (Brit Scol) externe *f*

Day-Glo ® ADJ fluorescent

day job N travail *m* principal ◆ **don't give up the ~ job** (hum) chacun son métier, les vaches seront bien gardées

day labourer N journalier *m*, ouvrier *m* à la journée

day letter N (US) ≃ télégramme-lettre *m*

day nurse N infirmier *m*, -ière *f* de jour

day nursery N (public) ≃ garderie *f*, crèche *f* ; (room in private house) pièce *f* réservée aux enfants, nursery *f*

the Day of Atonement N (Jewish Rel) le Grand pardon, le jour du Pardon

the day of judgement N (Rel) le jour du jugement dernier

the day of reckoning N (Rel) le jour du jugement dernier ◆ **the ~ of reckoning will come** (fig) un jour, il faudra rendre des comptes

day-old ADJ [bread] de la veille ; (= yesterday's) d'hier ◆ **~-old chick** poussin *m* d'un jour

day-pass N (for library, museum, train etc) carte *f* d'abonnement valable pour une journée ; (Ski) forfait *m* d'une journée

day pupil N (Brit Scol) externe *mf*

day release N (Brit) ◆ **~ release course** ≃ cours *m* professionnel à temps partiel ◆ **to be on ~ release** faire un stage (de formation) à temps partiel

day return (ticket) N (Brit Rail) (billet *m*) aller et retour *m* (valable pour la journée)

day room N (in hospital etc) salle *f* de séjour commune

day school N externat *m* ◆ **to go to ~ school** être externe

day shift N *(= workers)* équipe *f or* poste *m* de jour ◆ **to be on ~ shift, to work ~ shift** travailler de jour, être de jour

day-ticket N *(Ski)* ⇒ **day-pass**

day-to-day ADJ *[occurrence, routine]* quotidien ◆ **on a ~-to-~ basis** au jour le jour

day trader N *(Stock Exchange)* opérateur *m* au jour le jour, day trader *m*

day trading N *(Stock Exchange)* opérations *fpl* boursières au jour le jour, day trading *m*

day trip N excursion *f* (d'une journée) ◆ **to go on a ~ trip to Calais** faire une excursion (d'une journée) à Calais

day-tripper N excursionniste *mf*

daybook /ˈdeɪbʊk/ N *(Comm)* main *f* courante, brouillard *m*

daybreak /ˈdeɪbreɪk/ N point *m* du jour, aube *f* ◆ **at ~** au point du jour, à l'aube

daycare /ˈdeɪkeəʳ/ N *(for children)* garderie *f* ; *(for old or disabled people) soins dans des centres d'accueil de jour*

COMP **daycare centre** N *(for children)* ≈ garderie *f* ; *(for old or disabled people)* établissement *m* de jour, centre *m* d'accueil de jour

daycare worker N *(US)* animateur *m*, -trice *f*

daydream /ˈdeɪdriːm/ N rêverie *f*, rêvasserie *f* VI rêvasser, rêver (tout éveillé)

daylight /ˈdeɪlaɪt/ N 1 ⇒ **daybreak** 2 (lumière *f* du) jour *m* ◆ **in (the) ~** à la lumière du jour, au grand jour ◆ **it's still ~** il fait encore jour ◆ **I'm beginning to see ~*** *(= understand)* je commence à y voir clair ; *(= see the end appear)* je commence à voir le bout du tunnel ◆ **to beat** *or* **knock** *or* **thrash the (living) ~s out of sb**‡ *(= beat up)* rosser* qn, tabasser‡ qn ; *(= knock out)* mettre qn KO ◆ **to scare** *or* **frighten the (living) ~s out of sb**‡ flanquer une peur bleue *or* la frousse* à qn ; → **broad**

COMP *[attack]* de jour

daylight robbery* N *(Brit)* ◆ **it's ~ robbery** c'est de l'arnaque‡

daylight-saving time N *(US)* heure *f* d'été

daylong /ˈdeɪ,lɒŋ/ ADJ qui dure toute la journée ◆ **we had a ~ meeting** notre réunion a duré toute la journée

daytime /ˈdeɪtaɪm/ N jour *m*, journée *f* ◆ **in the ~** de jour, pendant la journée ADJ de jour

daze /deɪz/ N *(after blow)* étourdissement *m* ; *(at news)* stupéfaction *f*, ahurissement *m* ; *(from drug)* hébétement *m* ◆ **in a ~** *(after blow)* étourdi ; *(at news)* stupéfait, médusé ; *(from drug)* hébété VT *[drug]* hébéter ; *[blow]* étourdir ; *[news etc]* abasourdir, méduser

dazed /deɪzd/ ADJ hébété ◆ **to feel ~** ⇒ **to be in a daze** ; → **daze**

dazzle /ˈdæzl/ VT *(lit)* éblouir, aveugler ; *(fig)* éblouir ◆ **to ~ sb's eyes** éblouir qn N lumière *f* aveuglante, éclat *m* ◆ **blinded by the ~ of the car's headlights** ébloui par les phares de la voiture

dazzling /ˈdæzlɪŋ/ ADJ *(lit, fig)* éblouissant ◆ **a ~ display of agility** une démonstration d'agilité éblouissante

dazzlingly /ˈdæzlɪŋlɪ/ ADV *[shine]* de manière éblouissante ◆ **~ beautiful** d'une beauté éblouissante

dB (abbrev of **decibel**) dB

DBMS /diːbiːemˈes/ N (abbrev of **database management system**) SGBD *m*

DBS /diːbiːˈes/ N 1 (abbrev of **direct broadcasting by satellite**) → **direct** 2 (abbrev of **direct broadcasting satellite**) → **direct**

DC /diːˈsiː/ 1 (abbrev of **direct current**) → **direct** 2 (abbrev of **District of Columbia**) DC ; → DISTRICT OF COLUMBIA

DCI /,diːsiːˈaɪ/ N *(Brit)* (abbrev of **Detective Chief Inspector**) → **detective**

DD 1 *(Univ)* (abbrev of **Doctor of Divinity**) *docteur en théologie* 2 *(Comm, Fin)* (abbrev of **direct debit**) → **direct** 3 *(US Mil)* (abbrev of **dishonourable discharge**) → **dishonourable**

dd *(Comm)* 1 (abbrev of **delivered**) livré 2 (abbrev of **dated**) en date du ... 3 (abbrev of **demand draft**) → **demand**

DDT /diːdiːˈtiː/ N (abbrev of **dichlorodiphenyltrichloroethane**) DDT *m*

DE, De abbrev of **Delaware**

DEA /diːiːˈeɪ/ N *(US)* (abbrev of **Drug Enforcement Administration**) ≈ Brigade *f* des stupéfiants

deacon /ˈdiːkən/ N diacre *m* ◆ **~'s bench** *(US)* siège *m* à deux places (de style colonial)

deaconess /ˈdiːkənes/ N diaconesse *f*

deactivate /diːˈæktɪveɪt/ VT désactiver

dead /ded/ ADJ 1 *[person, animal, plant]* mort ◆ **~ or alive** mort ou vif ◆ **more ~ than alive** plus mort que vif ◆ **~ and buried** *or* **gone** *(lit, fig)* mort et enterré ◆ **to drop down ~, to fall (stone) ~** tomber (raide) mort ◆ **as ~ as a dodo** *or* **a doornail** *or* **mutton** tout ce qu'il y a de plus mort ◆ **to wait for a ~ man's shoes*** attendre que quelqu'un veuille bien mourir (pour prendre sa place) ◆ **will he do it? – over my ~ body!*** il le fera ? – il faudra d'abord qu'il me passe *subj* sur le corps ! ◆ **to flog** *(Brit) or* **beat** *(US)* **a ~ horse** s'acharner inutilement, perdre sa peine et son temps ◆ **~ men tell no tales** *(Prov)* les morts ne parlent pas ◆ **he's/it's a ~ duck*** il/c'est fichu* *or* foutu‡ ◆ **~ in the water*** fichu* ◆ **to leave sb for ~** laisser qn pour mort ◆ **he was found to be ~ on arrival** *(at hospital)* les médecins n'ont pu que constater le décès ◆ **I wouldn't be seen ~ wearing that hat** *or* **in that hat!*** je ne porterais ce chapeau pour rien au monde ! ◆ **I wouldn't be seen ~ with him!** * pour rien au monde je ne voudrais être vu avec lui ! ◆ **I wouldn't be seen ~ in that pub!** * il est hors de question que je mette les pieds* dans ce bar ! ◆ **you're ~ meat!**‡ *(esp US)* t'es un homme mort ! * *(fig)* see also **comp** ; → **drop, strike**

2 *[limbs]* engourdi ◆ **my fingers are ~** j'ai les doigts gourds ◆ **he's ~ from the neck up*** il n'a rien dans le ciboulot‡ ◆ **he was ~ to the world*** *(= asleep)* il dormait comme une souche ; *(= drunk)* il était ivre mort

3 *(fig) [custom]* tombé en désuétude ; *[fire]* mort, éteint ; *[cigarette]* éteint ; *[battery]* à plat ; *[town]* mort, triste ; *[sound]* sourd, feutré ◆ **~ language** langue *f* morte ◆ **the line is ~** *(Telec)* il n'y a pas de tonalité ◆ **the line's gone ~** la ligne est coupée ◆ **the engine's ~** le moteur est en panne

4 *(= absolute, exact)* **~ calm** calme plat ◆ **to hit sth (in the) ~ centre** frapper qch au beau milieu *or* en plein milieu ◆ **it's a ~ cert**‡ **that he'll come** il viendra à coup sûr, sûr qu'il viendra* ◆ **this horse is a ~ cert**‡ ce cheval va gagner, c'est sûr ◆ **in ~ earnest** avec le plus grand sérieux, très sérieusement ◆ **he's in ~ earnest** il ne plaisante pas ◆ **on a ~ level with** exactement au même niveau que ◆ **a ~ loss** *(Comm)* une perte sèche ; *(* = person)* un bon à rien ◆ **that idea was a ~ loss*** cette idée n'a absolument rien donné ◆ **this knife is a ~ loss*** ce couteau ne vaut rien ◆ **I'm a ~ loss at sports*** je suis nul en sport ◆ **to be a ~ shot** être un tireur d'élite ◆ **~ silence** silence *m* de mort ◆ **he's the ~ spit of his father*** c'est son père tout craché ◆ **to come to a ~ stop** s'arrêter net *or* pile

ADV *(Brit = exactly, completely)* absolument, complètement ◆ **~ ahead** tout droit ◆ **~ broke*** fauché (comme les blés)* ◆ **to be ~ certain*** **about sth** être sûr et certain de qch*, être absolument certain *or* convaincu de qch ◆ **to be ~ against*** **sth** être farouchement opposé à qch ◆ **your guess was ~ on*** tu as deviné juste ◆ **she was** *or* **her shot was ~ on target*** elle a mis dans le mille ◆ **~ drunk*** ivre mort ◆ **it's ~ easy** *or* **simple*** c'est simple comme bonjour*, il n'y a rien de plus facile *or* simple ◆ **to be/arrive ~ on time** être/arriver juste à l'heure *or* à l'heure pile ◆ **it was ~ lucky*** c'était un coup de pot monstre‡ ◆ **she's ~ right** * elle a tout à fait raison ◆ **~ slow** *(as instruction) (on road)* roulez au pas ; *(at sea)* en avant lentement ◆ **to go ~ slow** aller aussi lentement que possible ◆ **to stop ~** s'arrêter net *or* pile ◆ **to cut sb ~** faire semblant de ne pas voir *or* reconnaître qn ◆ **she cut me ~** elle a fait comme si elle ne me voyait pas ◆ **~ tired** éreinté, crevé* ◆ **he went ~ white** il est devenu pâle comme un mort ; → **stop**

N ◆ **at ~ of night, in the ~ of night** au cœur de *or* au plus profond de la nuit ◆ **in the ~ of winter** au plus fort de l'hiver, au cœur de l'hiver ◆ **to come back** *or* **rise from the ~** *(fig)* refaire surface

NPL **the dead** les morts *mpl* ◆ **office** *or* **service for the ~** *(Rel)* office *m* des morts *or* funèbre

COMP **dead account** N *(Fin)* compte *m* dormant *or* inactif

dead-and-alive ADJ *[town]* triste, mort ◆ **a ~-and-alive little place** un trou* perdu

dead ball N *(Ftbl, Rugby)* ballon *m* mort

dead-ball line N *(Rugby)* ligne *f* du ballon mort

dead-beat* N *(= lazy person)* chiffe *f* molle ; *(US)* parasite *m*, pique-assiette *mf inv* ADJ crevé*, claqué*

dead centre N *(Tech)* point *m* mort

dead end N *(lit, fig)* impasse *f* ◆ **to come to a ~ end** *(fig)* être dans l'impasse

dead-end ADJ ◆ **a ~-end job** un travail sans perspective d'avenir

dead hand N ◆ **the ~ hand of the state/bureaucracy** la mainmise *or* le carcan de État/de la bureaucratie ◆ **to shrug off the ~ hand of communism** se débarrasser de ce poids mort qu'est le communisme

dead-head VT enlever les fleurs fanées de ; see also **deadhead**

dead heat N ◆ **the race was a ~ heat** ils sont arrivés ex æquo ; *(Racing)* la course s'est terminée par un dead-heat

dead leg* N *(Med, Sport)* jambe *f* insensible *(à la suite d'un traumatisme musculaire)* ; *(= person)* poids *m* mort

dead letter N *(Post)* lettre *f* tombée au rebut ; * *(= useless thing)* chose *f* du passé ◆ **to become a ~ letter**

[law, agreement] tomber en désuétude, devenir lettre morte

dead-letter office N *(Post)* bureau *m* des rebuts

dead march N marche *f* funèbre

dead matter N matière *f* inanimée ; *(Typ)* composition *f* à distribuer

dead men* NPL *(fig = empty bottles)* bouteilles *fpl* vides, cadavres* *mpl*

dead-nettle N ortie *f* blanche

dead reckoning N *(Naut)* estime *f* ◆ **by ~ reckoning** à l'estime

the Dead Sea N la mer Morte

the Dead Sea Scrolls NPL les manuscrits *mpl* de la mer Morte

dead season N *(Comm, Press)* morte-saison *f*

dead set* N ◆ **to make a ~ set at sth** s'acharner comme un beau diable pour avoir qch ◆ **to make a ~ set at sb** chercher à mettre le grappin sur qn* ADJ ◆ **to be ~ set on doing sth** tenir mordicus à faire qch ◆ **to be ~ set against sth** être farouchement opposé à qch

dead soldiers* NPL *(US = bottles)* bouteilles *fpl* vides, cadavres* *mpl*

dead stock N invendu(s) *m(pl)*, rossignols* *mpl*

dead weight N poids *m* mort *or* inerte ; *(Naut)* charge *f or* port *m* en lourd

Dead White European Male N *(esp US) homme célèbre qui devrait sa réputation à son appartenance au sexe masculin et à la race blanche*

dead wire N *(Elec)* fil *m* sans courant

deaden /ˈdedn/ VT [+ shock, blow] amortir ; [+ feeling] émousser ; [+ sound] assourdir ; [+ passions] étouffer ; [+ pain] calmer ; [+ nerve] endormir

deadening /ˈdednɪŋ/ N [of emotions, spirit] engourdissement m ADJ abrutissant ◆ **it has a ~ effect on creativity** ça tue la créativité

deadhead* /ˈdedhed/ (US) N 1 (= person using free ticket) (on train) personne f possédant un titre de transport gratuit ; (at theatre) personne f possédant un billet de faveur 2 (= stupid person) nullité f 3 (= empty truck/train etc) camion m/train m etc roulant à vide ADJ [truck etc] roulant à vide

deadline /ˈdedlaɪn/ N 1 (= time-limit) date f (or heure f) limite, dernière limite f ◆ **to work to a ~** avoir un délai à respecter ◆ **he was working to a 6 o'clock ~** son travail devait être terminé à 6 heures, dernière limite 2 (US) (= boundary) limite f (qu'il est interdit de franchir)

deadliness /ˈdedlɪnɪs/ N [of poison] caractère m mortel or fatal ; [of aim] précision f infaillible

deadlock /ˈdedlɒk/ N impasse f ◆ **to reach (a) ~** aboutir à une impasse ◆ **to be at (a) ~** être dans l'impasse, être au point mort

deadly /ˈdedlɪ/ ADJ 1 (= lethal) [blow, poison, disease, enemy, combination] mortel (to pour) ; [weapon, attack] meurtrier ◆ **to play a ~ game** jouer un jeu dangereux ◆ **the seven ~ sins** les sept péchés capitaux ◆ **the female of the species is deadlier** or **more ~ than the male** (Prov) la femme est plus dangereuse que l'homme ◆ **assault with a ~ weapon** (US Jur) attaque f à main armée

2 (= devastating) [accuracy, logic] implacable ; [wit] mordant ◆ **a ~ silence** un silence de mort ◆ **in ~ silence** dans un silence de mort ◆ **to use ~ force (against sb)** (Police, Mil) utiliser la force (contre qn) ◆ **the police were authorized to use ~ force against the demonstrators** la police a reçu l'autorisation de tirer sur les manifestants ◆ **I am in ~ earnest** je suis on ne peut plus sérieux ◆ **he spoke in ~ earnest** il était on ne peut plus sérieux, il parlait le plus sérieusement du monde

3 (* = boring) mortel*

ADV ◆ **~ dull** mortellement ennuyeux ◆ **~ pale** d'une pâleur mortelle, pâle comme la mort ◆ **it's/I'm ~ serious** c'est/je suis on ne peut plus sérieux

COMP **deadly nightshade** N belladone f

deadness /ˈdednɪs/ N [of limbs] engourdissement m ◆ **the ~ of his eyes** son regard vide

deadpan /ˈdedpæn/ ADJ [face] de marbre ; [humour] pince-sans-rire inv ◆ **"good heavens" he said, ~** "mon Dieu" dit-il, pince-sans-rire

deadwood /ˈdedwʊd/ N (lit, fig) bois m mort ◆ **to get rid of the ~** (fig: in office, company etc) élaguer, dégraisser

deaf /def/ ADJ 1 (lit) sourd ◆ **~ in one ear** sourd d'une oreille ◆ **~ as a (door)post** sourd comme un pot ◆ **there's** or **there are none so ~ as those who will not hear** (Prov) il n'est pire sourd que celui qui ne veut pas entendre (Prov) 2 (fig = unwilling to listen) sourd, insensible (to à) ◆ **to be ~ to sth** rester sourd à qch ◆ **to turn a ~ ear to sth** faire la sourde oreille à qch ◆ **her pleas fell on ~ ears** ses appels n'ont pas été entendus NPL **the deaf** les sourds mpl

COMP **deaf aid** N appareil m acoustique, audiophone m, sonotone ® m

deaf-and-dumb ADJ sourd-muet ◆ **~-and-dumb alphabet** alphabet m des sourds et muets

deaf-mute N sourd(e)-muet(te) m(f)

deafen /ˈdefn/ VT (lit) rendre sourd ; (fig) assourdir, rendre sourd

deafening /ˈdefnɪŋ/ ADJ (lit, fig) assourdissant ◆ **a ~ silence** un silence pesant or assourdissant

deafness /ˈdefnɪs/ N surdité f

deal¹ /diːl/ (vb : pret, ptp **dealt**) N 1 (NonC) **a good** or **great ~ of, a ~ of** † (= large amount) beaucoup de ◆ **to have a great ~ to do** avoir beaucoup à faire, avoir beaucoup de choses à faire ◆ **a good ~ of the work is done** une bonne partie du travail est terminée ◆ **that's saying a good ~** ce n'est pas peu dire ◆ **there's a good ~ of truth in what he says** il y a du vrai dans ce qu'il dit ◆ **to think a great ~ of sb** avoir beaucoup d'estime pour qn ◆ **to mean a great ~ to sb** compter beaucoup pour qn

2 (adv phrases) ◆ **a good ~** (= significantly) [easier, further, longer, higher, older, happier, stronger etc] beaucoup, nettement ◆ **she's a good ~ cleverer than her brother** elle est beaucoup or nettement plus intelligente que son frère ◆ **she's a good ~ better today** elle va beaucoup or nettement mieux aujourd'hui ◆ **to learn/change/travel a great ~** beaucoup apprendre/changer/voyager ◆ **we have discussed this a great ~** nous en avons beaucoup parlé ◆ **he talks a great ~** il parle beaucoup ◆ **we have already achieved a great ~** nous avons déjà beaucoup accompli ◆ **it says a great ~ for him (that ...)** c'est tout à son honneur (que ...)

3 (= agreement) marché m, affaire f ; (pej) coup m ; (also **business deal**) affaire f, marché m ; (on Stock Exchange) opération f, transaction f ◆ **to do a ~ with sb** (gen) conclure un marché avec qn ; (Comm etc) faire or passer un marché avec qn, faire (une) affaire avec qn ◆ **we might do a ~?** on pourrait (peut-être) s'arranger ? ◆ **(it's a) ~!*** d'accord !, marché conclu ! ◆ **no ~!*** rien à faire ! ◆ **a done ~** une affaire réglée ◆ **he got a very bad ~ from them** (= treatment) ils ne l'ont pas bien traité ◆ **he got a very bad ~ on that car** (Comm) il a fait une très mauvaise affaire en achetant cette voiture ◆ **the agreement is likely to be a bad ~ for consumers** cet accord risque d'être une mauvaise affaire pour les consommateurs ◆ **a new ~** (Pol etc) un programme de réformes ; → **fair¹, raw**

4 (* iro) ◆ **big ~!** la belle affaire !, tu parles !* ◆ **it's no big ~** qu'est-ce que ça peut faire ? ◆ **the delay is no big ~** le retard n'a aucune importance ◆ **don't make such a big ~ out of it!** n'en fais pas toute une histoire or tout un plat !*

5 (Cards) donne f, distribution f ◆ **it's your ~** à vous la donne, à vous de distribuer or donner

VT 1 (also **deal out**) [+ cards] donner, distribuer

2 ◆ **to ~ sb a blow** (physically) porter or assener un coup à qn ◆ **this dealt a blow to individual freedom** cela a porté un coup aux libertés individuelles

3 * [+ drugs] revendre, dealer*

VI 1 [business, firm] ◆ **this company has been ~ing for 80 years** cette société est en activité depuis 80 ans ◆ **to ~ on the Stock Exchange** faire or conclure des opérations de bourse ◆ **to ~ in wood/property** etc être dans le commerce du bois/dans l'immobilier etc

2 (= traffic: in drugs) revendre de la drogue, dealer* ◆ **the police suspect him of ~ing (in drugs)** la police le soupçonne de revendre de la drogue or de dealer* ◆ **to ~ in stolen property** revendre des objets volés ◆ **to ~ in pornography** faire le commerce de la pornographie

3 (fig) **they ~ in terror/human misery** leur fonds de commerce, c'est la terreur/la misère humaine ◆ **drug-pushers who ~ in death** ces dealers qui sont des marchands de mort ◆ **we ~ in facts, not speculation** nous nous intéressons aux faits, pas aux suppositions

4 (Cards) donner, distribuer

► **deal out** VT SEP [+ gifts, money] distribuer, répartir (between entre) ◆ **to ~ out justice** rendre (la) justice ; → **deal¹ vt 1**

► **deal with** VT FUS 1 (= have to do with) [+ person] avoir affaire à ; (esp Comm) traiter avec ◆ **teachers who have to ~ with very young children** les enseignants qui ont affaire à de très jeunes enfants ◆ **employees ~ing with the public** les employés qui sont en contact avec le public or qui ont affaire au public ◆ **they refused to ~ with him because of this** ils ont refusé de traiter avec lui or d'avoir affaire à lui à cause de cela ◆ **he's not very easy to ~ with** il n'est pas commode

2 (= be responsible for) [+ person] s'occuper de ; [+ task, problem] se charger de, s'occuper de ; (= take action as regards) [+ person, problem] s'occuper de, prendre des mesures concernant ◆ **I'll ~ with it/him** je me charge de cela/lui ◆ **I can ~ with that alone** je peux m'en occuper tout seul ◆ **in view of the situation he had to ~ with** vu la situation qu'il avait sur les bras ◆ **he dealt with the problem very well** il a très bien résolu le problème ◆ **you naughty boy, I'll ~ with you later!** vilain garçon, tu vas avoir affaire à moi tout à l'heure ! ◆ **the headmaster dealt with the culprits individually** le directeur s'est occupé des coupables un par un ◆ **the committee ~s with questions such as ...** le comité s'occupe de questions telles que ... ◆ **the police officer ~ing with crime prevention** l'agent chargé de la prévention des crimes ◆ **to know how to ~ with sb** (= treat) savoir s'y prendre avec qn ◆ **they dealt with him very fairly** ils ont été très corrects avec lui ◆ **you must ~ with them firmly** il faut vous montrer fermes à leur égard ◆ **the firm ~s with over 1,000 orders every week** l'entreprise traite plus de 1 000 commandes par semaine

3 (= be concerned with, cover) [book, film etc] traiter de ; [speaker] parler de ◆ **the next chapter ~s with ...** le chapitre suivant traite de ... ◆ **I shall now ~ with ...** je vais maintenant vous parler de ...

4 (= cope with) supporter ◆ **to ~ with stress** combattre le stress ◆ **to ~ with the fear of AIDS** faire face à la peur du sida

5 (= come to terms with) accepter ◆ **look, just ~ with it!*** il faut que tu te fasses une raison !

6 (= buy from or sell to) **a list of the suppliers our company ~s with** une liste des fournisseurs de notre société ◆ **I won't ~ with that firm again** je ne m'adresserai plus à cette société ◆ **I always ~ with the same butcher** je me sers or me fournis toujours chez le même boucher

deal² /diːl/ N bois m blanc

dealer /ˈdiːləʳ/ N 1 (= vendor) (gen) marchand m (in de) négociant m (in en) ; (= wholesaler) stockiste m, fournisseur m (en gros) (in de) ; (Stock Exchange) opérateur m ◆ **arms ~** marchand m d'armes ◆ **Citroën ~** concessionnaire mf Citroën ; → **double, secondhand** 2 (Cards) donneur m 3 (Drugs) dealer* m

dealership /ˈdiːləʃɪp/ N (Comm) concession f ◆ **~ network** réseau m de concessionnaires

dealing /ˈdiːlɪŋ/ N 1 (NonC) (also **dealing out**) distribution f ; [of cards] donne f 2 (Stock Exchange) opérations fpl, transactions fpl ; → **wheel** COMP **dealing room** N (Stock Exchange) salle f des transactions or des opérations

dealings /ˈdiːlɪŋz/ NPL (= relations) relations fpl (with sb avec qn) ; (= transactions) transactions fpl (in sth en qch) ; (= trafficking) trafic m (in sth de qch)

dealmaker /ˈdiːl,meɪkəʳ/ N (on Stock Exchange) opérateur m, -trice f

dealt /delt/ VB pt, ptp of **deal¹**

dean /diːn/ N (Rel, fig) doyen m ; (Univ) doyen m ◆ **~'s list** (US Univ) liste f des meilleurs étudiants

deanery /ˈdiːnərɪ/ N (Univ) résidence f du doyen ; (Rel) doyenné m

deanship /ˈdiːnʃɪp/ N décanat m

dear /dɪəʳ/ ADJ 1 (= loved) [person, animal] cher ; (= precious) [object] cher, précieux ; (= lovable) adorable ; [child] mignon, adorable ◆ **she is very ~ to me** elle m'est très chère ◆ **a ~ friend of mine** un de mes meilleurs amis, un de mes amis les plus chers ◆ **to hold sb/sth ~** chérir qn/qch ◆ **all that he holds ~** tout ce qui lui est cher ◆ **his ~est wish** (liter) son plus cher désir, son souhait le plus cher ◆ **what a ~ child!** quel amour d'enfant ! ◆ **what a ~ little dress!** †* quelle ravissante or mignonne petite robe ! ; → **departed**

2 (in letter-writing) cher ◆ **Dear Daddy** Cher Papa ◆ **My ~ Anne** Ma chère Anne ◆ **Dear Alice and Robert** Chère Alice, cher Robert, Chers Alice et Robert ◆ **Dearest Paul** Bien cher Paul ◆ **Dear Mr Smith** Cher Monsieur ◆ **Dear Mr & Mrs Smith** Cher Monsieur, chère Madame ◆ **Dear Sir** Monsieur ◆ **Dear Sirs** Messieurs ◆ **Dear Sir or Madam** Madame, Monsieur ◆ **Dear John letter** * lettre f de rupture

3 (= expensive) [prices, goods] cher, coûteux ; [price] élevé ; [shop] cher ◆ **to get ~er** [goods] augmenter, renchérir ; [prices] augmenter

EXCL (surprise: also **dear dear!, dear me!**) mon Dieu !, vraiment ! ; (regret: also **oh dear!**) oh là là !, oh mon Dieu !

N cher m, chère f ◆ **my ~** mon ami(e), mon cher ami, ma chère amie ; (to child) mon petit ◆ **poor ~** (to child) pauvre petit, pauvre chou* ; (to woman) ma pauvre ◆ **your mother is a ~*** votre mère est un amour ◆ **give it to me, there's a ~!*** sois gentil, donne-le-moi !, donne-le-moi, tu seras (bien) gentil ! ; see also **dearest**

ADV [buy, pay, sell] cher

dearest /ˈdɪərɪst/ N (= darling) chéri(e) m(f)

dearie †* /ˈdɪərɪ/ (esp Brit) N mon petit chéri, ma petite chérie EXCL ◆ **~ me!** Grand Dieu !, Dieu du ciel !

dearly /ˈdɪəlɪ/ ADV 1 (= very much) [love] profondément ◆ **"Dearly beloved ..."** (Rel) "Mes bien chers frères ..." ◆ **Joan Smith, ~ beloved wife of Peter** Joan Smith, épouse bien-aimée de Peter ◆ **I would ~ love to marry** j'aimerais tellement me marier ◆ **I ~ hope I will meet him one day** j'espère vivement le rencontrer un jour ; → **departed** 2 (fig = at great cost) **he paid ~ for his success** il l'a payé cher, son succès, son succès lui a coûté cher ◆ **~ bought** chèrement payé

dearness /ˈdɪənɪs/ N 1 (= expensiveness) cherté f 2 (= lovableness) **your ~ to me** la tendresse que j'ai pour vous

dearth /dɜːθ/ N [of food] disette f ; [of money, resources, water] pénurie f ; [of ideas etc] stérilité f, pauvreté f ◆ **there is no ~ of young men** les jeunes gens ne manquent pas

deary †* /ˈdɪərɪ/ ⇒ **dearie**

death /deθ/ LANGUAGE IN USE 24.4

N mort f, décès m (Jur) (frm) ; [of plans, hopes] effondrement m, anéantissement m ◆ **~ by suffocation/drowning/hanging** etc mort f par suffocation/noyade/pendaison etc ◆ **he jumped/fell to his ~** il a sauté/est tombé et s'est tué ◆ **at the time of his ~** au moment de sa mort ◆ **till ~ do us part** jusqu'à ce que la mort nous sépare ◆ **to be in at the ~** (fig) assister au dénouement (d'une affaire) ◆ **to be at ~'s door** être à (l'article de) la mort ◆ **in ~, as in life, he was courageous** devant la mort, comme de son vivant, il s'est montré courageux ◆ **it will be the ~ of him** * (lit) il le paiera de sa vie ◆ **smoking will be the ~ of him** * le tabac le tuera ◆ **he'll be the ~ of me!** * (fig) il me tuera ! (fig) ◆ **to look/feel like ~ warmed up** * or (US) **warmed over** * avoir l'air/se sentir complètement nase* ; → **catch, dance**

◆ **to death** ◆ **he was stabbed to ~** il est mort poignardé ◆ **to starve/freeze to ~** mourir de faim/de froid ◆ **to bleed to ~** se vider de son sang ◆ **to be burnt to ~** mourir carbonisé ◆ **he drank himself to ~** c'est la boisson qui l'a tué ◆ **to sentence sb to ~** condamner qn à mort ◆ **to put sb to ~** mettre qn à mort, exécuter qn ◆ **I'm starved/frozen to ~** * je suis mort de faim/de froid ◆ **to be bored to ~** * s'ennuyer à mourir ◆ **I'm sick to ~** * or **tired to ~** * **of all this** j'en ai ras le bol de* or j'en ai marre* de tout ça ◆ **to be scared/worried to ~** être mort de peur/d'inquiétude ; → **do¹**

◆ **to the death** ◆ **to fight to the ~** lutter jusqu'à la mort ◆ **a fight to the ~** une lutte à mort

COMP **death benefit** N (Insurance) capital-décès m

death camp N camp m de la mort
death cell N cellule f de condamné à mort
death certificate N certificat m or acte m de décès
death-dealing ADJ mortel
death duties NPL (Brit) ⇒ **death duty**
death duty N (Brit: formerly) droits mpl de succession
death grant N allocation f de décès
death house N (US) (in jail) ⇒ **death row**
death knell N → **knell**
death march N marche f funèbre
death mask N masque m mortuaire
death metal N (Mus) death metal m
death penalty N (Jur) peine f de mort
death rate N (taux m de) mortalité f
death rattle N râle m (d'agonie)
death ray N rayon m de la mort, rayon m qui tue
death roll N liste f des morts
death row N (US: in jail) le couloir de la mort ◆ **he's on ~ row** il a été condamné à mort
death sentence N (lit) condamnation f à mort ; (fig) arrêt m de mort
death's-head N tête f de mort
death's-head moth N (sphinx m) tête f de mort
death squad N escadron m de la mort
death taxes NPL (US) ⇒ **death duty**
death threat N menace f de mort
death throes NPL affres fpl (liter) de la mort, agonie f ; (fig) agonie f ◆ **in one's ~ throes** dans les affres (liter) de la mort, à l'agonie
death toll N nombre m des victimes, bilan m
death warrant N (Jur) ordre m d'exécution ◆ **to sign the ~ warrant of a project** condamner un projet, signer la condamnation d'un projet ◆ **to sign sb's/one's own ~ warrant** (fig) signer l'arrêt de mort de qn/son propre arrêt de mort
death wish N (Psych) désir m de mort ; (fig) attitude f suicidaire

deathbed /ˈdeθbed/ N lit m de mort ◆ **to repent on one's ~** se repentir sur son lit de mort

COMP **deathbed confession** N ◆ **he made a ~ confession** il s'est confessé sur son lit de mort
deathbed scene N (Theat) ◆ **this is a ~ scene** la scène se passe au chevet du mourant

deathblow /ˈdeθbləʊ/ N (lit, fig) coup m mortel or fatal

deathless /ˈdeθlɪs/ ADJ immortel, éternel ◆ **~ prose** (iro) prose f impérissable

deathlike /ˈdeθlaɪk/ ADJ semblable à la mort, de mort

deathly /ˈdeθlɪ/ ADJ [pallor] cadavérique ◆ **a ~ hush** or **silence** un silence de mort ADV ◆ **~ pale** pâle comme la mort, d'une pâleur mortelle

deathtrap * /ˈdeθtræp/ N (= vehicle, building etc) piège m à rats (fig) ◆ **that corner is a real ~** ce virage est extrêmement dangereux

deb * /deb/ N abbrev of **debutante**

debacle, débâcle /deɪˈbɑːkl/ N fiasco m ; (Mil) débâcle f

debag ‡ /diːˈbæg/ VT (Brit) déculotter

debar /dɪˈbɑːʳ/ VT (from club, competition) exclure (from de) ◆ **to ~ sb from doing sth** interdire or défendre à qn de faire qch

debark /dɪˈbɑːk/ VTI (US) débarquer

debarkation /ˌdiːbɑːˈkeɪʃən/ N (US) débarquement m

debarment /dɪˈbɑːmənt/ N exclusion f (from de)

debase /dɪˈbeɪs/ VT 1 [+ person] avilir, ravaler ◆ **to ~ o.s.** s'avilir or se ravaler (by doing sth en faisant qch) 2 (= reduce in value or quality) [+ word, object] dégrader ; [+ metal] altérer ; [+ coinage] déprécier, dévaloriser

debasement /dɪˈbeɪsmənt/ N [of people] rabaissement m ; [of language, values] dégradation f ; [of culture] dévalorisation f ; [of currency] dévalorisation f, dépréciation f

debatable /dɪˈbeɪtəbl/ LANGUAGE IN USE 26.3 ADJ discutable, contestable ◆ **it's a ~ point** c'est discutable or contestable ◆ **it is ~ whether ...** on est en droit de se demander si ...

debate /dɪˈbeɪt/ VT [+ question] discuter, débattre ◆ **much ~d** [+ subject, theme etc] très discuté ◆ **he was debating what to do** il se demandait ce qu'il devait faire VI discuter (with avec ; about sur) ◆ **he was debating with himself whether to refuse or not** il se demandait s'il refuserait ou non, il s'interrogeait pour savoir s'il refuserait ou non N discussion f, débat m ; (Parl) débat(s) m(pl) ; (esp in debating society) conférence f or débat m contradictoire ◆ **to hold long ~s** discuter longuement ◆ **after much ~** après de longues discussions ◆ **the ~ was on** or **about ...** la discussion portait sur ... ◆ **the death penalty was under ~** on délibérait sur la peine de mort ◆ **to be in ~** [fact, statement] être controversé

debater /dɪˈbeɪtəʳ/ N débatteur m ◆ **he is a keen ~** il adore les débats

debating /dɪˈbeɪtɪŋ/ N art m de la discussion ◆ **~ society** société f de conférences or débats contradictoires

debauch /dɪˈbɔːtʃ/ VT [+ person] débaucher, corrompre ; [+ morals] corrompre ; [+ woman] séduire N débauche f

debauched /dɪˈbɔːtʃd/ ADJ [person] débauché ; [society] dépravé ; [lifestyle] de débauché

debauchee /ˌdebɔːˈtʃiː/ N débauché(e) m(f)

debaucher /dɪˈbɔːtʃəʳ/ N [of person, taste, morals] corrupteur m, -trice f ; [of woman] séducteur m

debauchery /dɪˈbɔːtʃərɪ/ N (NonC) débauche f

debenture /dɪˈbentʃəʳ/ N (Customs) certificat m de drawback ; (Fin) obligation f, bon m ◆ **the conversion of ~s into equity** (Fin) la conversion d'obligations en actions

COMP **debenture bond** N titre m d'obligation
debenture holder N obligataire mf
debenture stock N obligations fpl sans garantie

debilitate /dɪˈbɪlɪteɪt/ VT débiliter

debilitated /dɪˈbɪlɪteɪtɪd/ ADJ (lit, fig) affaibli

debilitating /dɪˈbɪlɪteɪtɪŋ/ ADJ 1 (Med) [disease, climate, atmosphere] débilitant 2 (fig) qui mine, qui sape ◆ **the country has suffered years of ~ poverty and war** pendant des années, ce pays a été miné par la pauvreté et la guerre

debility /dɪˈbɪlɪtɪ/ N (Med) débilité f, extrême faiblesse f

debit /ˈdebɪt/ N (Comm) débit m VT ◆ **to ~ sb's account with a sum, to ~ a sum against sb's**

account débiter le compte de qn d'une somme ◆ **to ~ sb with a sum, to ~ a sum to sb** porter une somme au débit de qn, débiter qn d'une somme
COMP **debit account** N compte *m* débiteur
debit balance N solde *m* débiteur
debit card N carte *f* de paiement
debit entry N inscription *f or* écriture *f* au débit
debit side N ◆ **on the ~ side** au débit ◆ **on the ~ side there is the bad weather** parmi les points négatifs, il y a le mauvais temps

debonair /ˌdebəˈneəʳ/ ADJ d'une élégance nonchalante

debone /diːˈbəʊn/ VT *[+ meat]* désosser ; *[+ fish]* désosser, ôter les arêtes de

debouch /dɪˈbaʊtʃ/ *(Geog, Mil)* VI déboucher N débouché *m*

debrief /ˌdiːˈbriːf/ VT *(Mil etc) [+ patrol, astronaut, spy] faire faire un compte rendu (de fin de mission) à,* débriefer ; *[+ freed hostages etc]* recueillir le témoignage de ◆ **to be ~ed** *(Mil)* faire un compte rendu oral

debriefing /ˌdiːˈbriːfɪŋ/ N *[soldier, diplomat, astronaut]* compte rendu *m* de mission, débriefing *m* ; *[freed hostage]* débriefing *m*

debris /ˈdebriː/ N *(gen)* débris *mpl* ; *[of building]* décombres *mpl* ; *(Geol)* roches *fpl* détritiques

debt /det/ N 1 *(= payment owed)* dette *f*, créance *f* ◆ **bad ~s** créances *fpl* irrécouvrables ◆ **~ of honour** dette *f* d'honneur ◆ **outstanding ~** créance *f* à recouvrer ◆ **to be in ~** avoir des dettes, être endetté ◆ **to be in ~ to sb** devoir de l'argent à qn ◆ **I am £500 in ~** j'ai 500 livres de dettes ◆ **to be out of sb's ~** être quitte envers qn ◆ **to get** *or* **run into ~** faire des dettes, s'endetter ◆ **to get out of ~** s'acquitter de ses dettes ◆ **to be out of ~** ne plus avoir de dettes
2 *(= gratitude owed)* ◆ **to be in sb's ~** être redevable à qn ◆ **I am greatly in your ~** je vous suis très redevable ◆ **to repay a ~** acquitter une dette ; → **eye, national**
COMP **debt burden** N endettement *m*
debt collection agency N agence *f* de recouvrement de créances
debt collector N agent *m* de recouvrement de créances
debt consolidation N consolidation *f* de la dette
debt crisis N crise *f* de la dette
debt forgiveness N effacement *m* de la dette
debt relief N allégement *m* de la dette
debt rescheduling N rééchelonnement *m* de la dette
debt-ridden ADJ criblé de dettes

debtor /ˈdetəʳ/ N débiteur *m*, -trice *f*

debug /diːˈbʌg/ VT 1 *(Comput)* déboguer 2 *(= remove microphones from) [+ room etc]* enlever les micros cachés dans

debugging /diːˈbʌgɪŋ/ N *(Comput)* suppression *f* des bogues *(of* dans*)* débogage *m*

debunk* /ˌdiːˈbʌŋk/ VT *[+ hero]* déboulonner* ; *[+ myth, concept]* démythifier ; *[+ system, institution]* discréditer

début /ˈdeɪbjuː/ N *(Theat)* début *m* ; *(in society)* entrée *f* dans le monde ◆ **he made his ~ as a pianist** il a débuté comme pianiste VI faire ses débuts

débutante /ˈdebjuːtɑːnt/ N débutante *f*

Dec. abbrev of **December**

dec. abbrev of **deceased**

decade /ˈdekeɪd/ N 1 *(= ten years)* décennie *f* ◆ **the 1990s were described as the ~ of democracy** on a qualifié les années 90 de décennie de la démocratie ◆ **almost a ~ ago** il y a presque dix ans ◆ **~s ago** il y a des dizaines d'années ◆ **he lived there for almost three ~s** il y a vécu pendant près de trente ans ◆ **the past four ~s** ces quarante dernières années 2 *[of rosary]* dizaine *f*

> ⚠ The word **décade** is sometimes used in French to mean "ten years", but this is regarded as incorrect.

decadence /ˈdekədəns/ N décadence *f*

decadent /ˈdekədənt/ ADJ décadent N *(Literat)* décadent *m*

decaf(f)* /ˈdiːkæf/ N déca* *m* ADJ ◆ **~(f) coffee** déca* *m* ◆ **~(f) tea** thé *m* déthéiné

decaffeinate /ˌdiːˈkæfɪneɪt/ VT décaféiner

decaffeinated /ˌdiːˈkæfɪneɪtɪd/ ADJ *[coffee]* décaféiné ; *[tea]* déthéiné

decagramme, decagram (US) /ˈdekəgræm/ N décagramme *m*

decal /dɪˈkæl/ N *(US)* décalcomanie *f*

decalcification /ˈdiːˌkælsɪfɪˈkeɪʃən/ N décalcification *f*

decalcify /ˌdiːˈkælsɪfaɪ/ VT décalcifier

decalitre, decaliter (US) /ˈdekaˌliːtəʳ/ N décalitre *m*

Decalogue /ˈdekəlɒg/ N décalogue *m*

decametre, decameter (US) /ˈdekaˌmiːtəʳ/ N décamètre *m*

decamp /dɪˈkæmp/ VI 1 * décamper, ficher le camp* 2 *(Mil)* lever le camp

decant /dɪˈkænt/ VT 1 *[+ wine]* décanter ◆ **he ~ed the solution into another container** il a transvasé la solution 2 *(fig = rehouse)* reloger

decanter /dɪˈkæntəʳ/ N carafe *f* ; *(small)* carafon *m*

decapitate /dɪˈkæpɪteɪt/ VT décapiter

decapitation /dɪˌkæpɪˈteɪʃən/ N décapitation *f*

decapod /ˈdekəpɒd/ N décapode *m*

decarbonization /ˈdiːˌkɑːbənaɪˈzeɪʃən/ N *[of engine]* décalaminage *m* ; *[of steel]* décarburation *f*

decarbonize /ˌdiːˈkɑːbənaɪz/ VT *[+ engine]* décalaminer ; *[+ steel]* décarburer

decartelize /diːˈkɑːtəlaɪz/ VT décartelliser

decasualization /ˌdɪkæʒjʊlaɪˈzeɪʃən/ N *(US)* *octroi d'un poste fixe au personnel temporaire*

decasualize /ˌdɪˈkæʒjʊˈlaɪz/ VT *(US)* octroyer un poste fixe à

decathlete /dɪˈkæθliːt/ N décathlonien *m*

decathlon /dɪˈkæθlən/ N décathlon *m*

decay /dɪˈkeɪ/ VI 1 *(= go bad, rot) [food]* pourrir, se gâter ; *[vegetation, wood]* pourrir ; *[corpse, flesh]* se décomposer, pourrir ; *[cloth, fabric]* moisir
2 *(= disintegrate) [building]* se délabrer, tomber en ruine ; *[stone]* s'effriter
3 *(Dentistry) [tooth]* se carier
4 *(Phys) [radioactive particle]* se désintégrer
5 *(fig) [civilization]* décliner ; *[city, district]* se délabrer ; *[infrastructure, system]* tomber en ruine
VT 1 *[+ food, wood]* faire pourrir
2 *(Dentistry) [+ tooth]* carier
N 1 *[of food, vegetation, wood]* pourriture *f*
2 *(Dentistry)* (also **tooth** *or* **dental decay**) carie *f* (dentaire) ◆ **to have** *or* **suffer from tooth ~** avoir des caries
3 *(Archit) [of building, stone]* délabrement *m* ◆ **to fall into ~** tomber en ruine, se délabrer
4 *(Phys) [of radioactive particle]* désintégration *f*
5 *(fig) [of civilization]* décadence *f*, déclin *m* ; *[of infrastructure, system, organization, region, city]* déclin *m* ◆ **social/industrial/economic ~** déclin *m* social/industriel/économique ◆ **moral ~** déchéance *f* morale

decayed /dɪˈkeɪd/ ADJ 1 *(= rotten) [wood]* pourri ; *[tooth]* carié ; *[corpse]* décomposé ; *[building]* délabré 2 *(fig) [civilization, nobility]* décadent ; *[health]* chancelant ; *[beauty]* fané 3 *(Phys)* désintégré

decaying /dɪˈkeɪɪŋ/ ADJ 1 *[wood, vegetation]* pourrissant ; *[food]* en train de s'avarier ; *[tooth]* qui se carie ; *[corpse, flesh]* en décomposition ; *[building]* en état de délabrement ; *[stone]* qui s'effrite 2 *(fig) [civilization, district]* sur le déclin ; *[infrastructure]* qui se dégrade

decease /dɪˈsiːs/ *(Admin, frm)* N décès *m* VI décéder

deceased /dɪˈsiːst/ *(Admin, frm)* ADJ décédé, défunt ◆ **John Brown ~** feu John Brown N ◆ **the ~** le défunt, la défunte

deceit /dɪˈsiːt/ N 1 escroquerie *f*, tromperie *f* 2 *(NonC)* ⇒ **deceitfulness**

deceitful /dɪˈsiːtfʊl/ ADJ *[person, behaviour, manner]* fourbe, déloyal

deceitfully /dɪˈsiːtfəlɪ/ ADV trompeusement

deceitfulness /dɪˈsiːtfʊlnɪs/ N fausseté *f*, duplicité *f*

deceive /dɪˈsiːv/ VT tromper, duper ; *[+ spouse, partner]* tromper ◆ **to ~ sb into doing sth** amener qn à faire qch (en le trompant) ◆ **he ~d me into thinking that he had bought it** il m'a (faussement) fait croire qu'il l'avait acheté ◆ **I thought my eyes were deceiving me** je n'en croyais pas mes yeux ◆ **to be ~d by appearances** être trompé par *or* se tromper sur les apparences ◆ **to ~ o.s. (about sth)** se faire des illusions (à propos de qch) ◆ **don't be ~d!** ne vous y trompez pas !, ne vous méprenez pas ! ◆ **don't be ~d by his air of authority, he knows nothing about it** ne vous méprenez pas sur son air d'autorité, il n'y connaît rien VI tromper, être trompeur ◆ **appearances ~** *(Prov)* les apparences sont trompeuses

> ⚠ In French **décevoir** means 'to disappoint'.

deceiver /dɪˈsiːvəʳ/ N escroc *m*, imposteur *m*

decelerate /diːˈseləreɪt/ VI décélérer

deceleration /ˈdiːˌseləˈreɪʃən/ N décélération *f*

December /dɪˈsembəʳ/ N décembre *m* ; *for phrases see* **September**

decency /ˈdiːsənsɪ/ N 1 *(NonC) [of dress, conversation]* décence *f*, bienséance *f* ; *[of person]* pudeur *f* ◆ **to have a sense of ~** avoir de la pudeur 2 *(= good manners)* convenances *fpl* ◆ **to observe the decencies** observer *or* respecter les convenances ◆ **common ~** la simple politesse, le simple savoir-vivre ◆ **for the sake of ~** par convenance, pour garder les convenances ◆ **to have the ~ to do sth** avoir la décence de faire qch ◆ **you can't in all ~ do that** tu ne peux pas décemment faire ça ◆ **sheer human ~ requires that ...** le respect de la personne humaine exige que ... 3 *(* = niceness)* gentillesse *f*

decent /ˈdiːsənt/ ADJ 1 *(= respectable) [person]* convenable, honnête, bien* *inv* ; *[house, shoes]* convenable ; *(= seemly) [language, behaviour, dress]* décent, bienséant ◆ **no ~ person would do it** jamais une personne convenable ne ferait cela, quelqu'un de bien* ne ferait jamais cela ◆ **to do the ~ thing (by sb)** agir comme il se doit (à l'égard de qn) ◆ **are you ~?*** *(= dressed)* es-tu présentable ?
2 *(* = kind, pleasant) [person]* bon, brave ◆ **a ~ sort of fellow** un bon *or* brave garçon, un type bien* ◆ **it was ~ of him** c'était chic* de sa part
3 *(* = adequate)* correct ◆ **there isn't even a ~ shop in the village** il n'y a même pas un magasin correct dans le village ◆ **I could do with a ~ meal/night's sleep** un bon repas/une bonne nuit de sommeil ne me ferait pas de mal
4 *(US * = wonderful)* formidable, terrible*

decently /ˈdiːsəntlɪ/ ADV 1 *(= properly, honourably)* décemment, convenablement ◆ **~ paid/housed** correctement *or* convenablement payé/logé ◆ **you can't ~ ask him that** vous ne pouvez pas décemment lui demander cela 2 *(= respectably) [dress]* convenablement ; *[live, bury sb]* d'une façon décente ; *[behave]* décemment, avec bienséance ◆ **they married as soon as they ~ could** ils se sont mariés dès que la décence l'a permis 3 (* *= kindly*) gentiment ◆ **he very ~ lent me some money** il m'a très gentiment prêté de l'argent

decentralization /diːˌsentrəlaɪˈzeɪʃən/ N décentralisation *f*

decentralize /diːˈsentrəlaɪz/ VT décentraliser

deception /dɪˈsepʃən/ N 1 (NonC) *(= deceitfulness)* tromperie *f*, duperie *f* ; *(= being deceived)* illusion *f*, erreur *f* ◆ **he is incapable of ~** il est incapable de tromper qui que ce soit ◆ **to obtain money by ~** obtenir de l'argent par des moyens frauduleux 2 *(= deceitful act)* supercherie *f*

⚠ In French, **déception** means 'disappointment'.

deceptive /dɪˈseptɪv/ ADJ trompeur ; → **appearance**

deceptively /dɪˈseptɪvlɪ/ ADV ◆ **it looks ~ simple** c'est plus compliqué qu'il n'y paraît ◆ **the wine was ~ strong** le vin était plus fort qu'il n'y paraissait ◆ **he has a ~ gentle manner** il semble d'un naturel doux mais il ne faut pas s'y fier

deceptiveness /dɪˈseptɪvnɪs/ N caractère *m* trompeur *or* illusoire

decibel /ˈdesɪbel/ N décibel *m*

decide /dɪˈsaɪd/ LANGUAGE IN USE 8.2

VT 1 *(= make up one's mind)* se décider *(to do sth* à faire qch) décider *(to do sth* de faire qch) se résoudre *(to do sth* à faire qch) ◆ **I ~d to go** *or* **that I would go** je me suis décidé à y aller, j'ai décidé d'y aller ◆ **I'm trying to ~ whether to go** j'essaie de décider si je dois y aller ◆ **what made you ~ to go?** qu'est-ce qui vous a décidé à y aller ? ◆ **it has been ~d that ...** on a décidé *or* il a été décidé que ... ◆ **she's ~d she hates golf** elle a décidé qu'elle déteste le golf ◆ **she's ~d she'd hate golf** elle a décidé qu'elle détesterait le golf

2 *(= settle) [+ question]* décider, trancher ; *[+ quarrel]* décider, arbitrer ; *[+ piece of business]* régler ; *[+ difference of opinion]* juger ; *[+ sb's fate, future]* décider de ◆ **to ~ a case** *(Jur)* statuer sur un cas

3 *(= cause to make up one's mind)* décider, déterminer *(sb to do sth* qn à faire qch)

VI se décider ◆ **you must ~** il vous faut prendre une décision, il faut vous décider ◆ **to ~ for sth** se décider pour qch *or* en faveur de qch ◆ **to ~ against sth** se décider contre qch ; *[judge, arbitrator, committee]* ◆ **to ~ for/against sb** donner raison/tort à qn ◆ **to ~ in favour of sb** donner gain de cause à qn

▸ **decide (up)on** VT FUS *[+ thing, course of action]* se décider pour, choisir (finalement) ◆ **to ~ (up)on doing sth** se décider à faire qch

decided /dɪˈsaɪdɪd/ ADJ 1 *(= distinct) [advantage, improvement]* net ◆ **a ~ lack of ...** un manque flagrant de ... 2 *(= categorical) [opinions]* arrêté ◆ **he's a man of very ~ opinions** c'est un homme aux opinions très arrêtées, il a des opinions très arrêtées

decidedly /dɪˈsaɪdɪdlɪ/ ADV 1 *(= distinctly)* **~ conservative/French** résolument conservateur/français ◆ **~ odd/unpleasant** franchement bizarre/désagréable ◆ **~ different** vraiment très différent ◆ **~ better/more expensive** nettement mieux/plus cher 2 *(= resolutely) [say, act]* résolument, fermement

decider /dɪˈsaɪdəʳ/ N *(esp Brit) (= goal)* but *m* décisif ; *(= point)* point *m* décisif ; *(= factor)* facteur *m* décisif ◆ **the ~** *(= game)* la belle

deciding /dɪˈsaɪdɪŋ/ ADJ *[factor, game, point]* décisif

deciduous /dɪˈsɪdjʊəs/ ADJ *[tree]* à feuilles caduques ; *[leaves, antlers]* caduc (-uque *f*)

decilitre, deciliter (US) /ˈdesɪˌliːtəʳ/ N décilitre *m*

decimal /ˈdesɪməl/ ADJ *[number, system, coinage]* décimal ◆ **~ fraction** fraction *f* décimale ◆ **to three ~ places** (jusqu')à la troisième décimale ◆ **~ point** virgule *f* (*de fraction décimale*) ; → **fixed, floating** N décimale *f* ◆ **~s** le calcul décimal, la notation décimale ; → **recurring**

decimalization /ˌdesɪməlaɪˈzeɪʃən/ N décimalisation *f*

decimalize /ˈdesɪməlaɪz/ VT décimaliser

decimate /ˈdesɪmeɪt/ VT *(lit, fig)* décimer

decimation /ˌdesɪˈmeɪʃən/ N décimation *f*

decimetre, decimeter (US) /ˈdesɪˌmiːtəʳ/ N décimètre *m*

decipher /dɪˈsaɪfəʳ/ VT déchiffrer

decipherable /dɪˈsaɪfərəbl/ ADJ déchiffrable

decision /dɪˈsɪʒən/ N 1 *(= act of deciding)* décision *f* ; *(Jur)* jugement *m*, arrêt *m* ◆ **to come to a ~** arriver à *or* prendre une décision ◆ **his ~ is final** sa décision est irrévocable *or* sans appel ◆ **to give a ~ on a case** *(Jur)* statuer sur un cas 2 (NonC) décision *f* ◆ **with ~** *[act]* d'un air décidé *or* résolu ; *[say]* d'un ton décidé *or* résolu ◆ **a look of ~** un air décidé *or* résolu

COMP **decision-maker** N décideur *m*, -euse *f*, décisionnaire *mf*

decision-making N ◆ **he's good at ~-making** il sait prendre des décisions

decision table N *(Comput)* table *f* de décision

decisive /dɪˈsaɪsɪv/ ADJ 1 *(= conclusive) [battle, step, moment, role]* décisif ◆ **the ~ factor** le facteur décisif 2 *(= resolute) [person]* décidé, ferme ; *[manner, attitude]* décidé, résolu ; *[answer]* ferme ◆ **he's very ~** c'est quelqu'un qui sait prendre des décisions

decisively /dɪˈsaɪsɪvlɪ/ ADV 1 *(= conclusively) [defeat, reject, influence]* de manière décisive 2 *(= resolutely) [speak]* de manière résolue, avec fermeté ; *[act]* avec décision

decisiveness /dɪˈsaɪsɪvnɪs/ N (NonC) *(= character)* esprit *m* de décision ; *(= manner)* air *m* décidé

deck /dek/ N 1 *[of boat, ship]* pont *m* ◆ **to go up on ~** monter sur le pont ◆ **below ~s** sous le pont, en bas ◆ **between ~s** dans l'entrepont ◆ **to clear the ~s (for action)** se mettre en branle-bas (de combat) ; *(fig)* tout déblayer ◆ **on ~** *(US fig)* prêt à l'action ◆ **to hit the ~** * se casser la gueule * ; → **afterdeck, flight¹, hand**

2 *(US: = verandah)* véranda *f* ; *(covered)* porche *m*

3 *[of vehicle]* plateforme *f* ◆ **top ~, upper ~** *[of bus]* impériale *f* ; *[of jumbo jet]* étage *m*

4 (US: also **deck of cards**) jeu *m* de cartes ◆ **he's not playing with a full ~ *, he's playing with a loaded** *or* **stacked ~** * *(fig)* il ne joue pas franc jeu *or* cartes sur table ◆ **he's not playing with a full ~** * *(fig = not very bright)* il n'est pas très futé

5 (also **mixing deck**) table *f* de mixage ; (also **cassette deck**) platine *f* cassettes ; (also **record deck**) platine *f* disques ; see also **cassette**

VT 1 (also **deck out**) *[+ person, room etc]* parer *(with* de) ◆ **she was ~ed out in her Sunday best** elle s'était mise sur son trente et un, elle s'était endimanchée

2 (*‡ = knock down*) flanquer * par terre

COMP **deck cabin** N cabine *f* (de pont)

deck cargo N pontée *f*

deck chair N chaise *f* longue, transat * *m*, transatlantique *m*

deck hand N matelot *m*

-decker /ˈdekəʳ/ N *(in compounds)* ◆ **a single-decker** *(= bus)* un autobus sans impériale ◆ **a three-decker** *(= ship)* un vaisseau à trois ponts, un trois-ponts ; → **double**

deckhouse /ˈdekhaʊs/ N rouf *m*

decking /ˈdekɪŋ/ N revêtement *m* de sol d'extérieur en bois

deckle /ˈdekl/ N (also **deckle edge**) barbes *fpl*

COMP **deckle-edged** ADJ *[paper]* non ébarbé

declaim /dɪˈkleɪm/ VTI déclamer *(against* contre)

declamation /ˌdekləˈmeɪʃən/ N déclamation *f*

declamatory /dɪˈklæmətərɪ/ ADJ déclamatoire

declaration /ˌdekləˈreɪʃən/ N *[of intentions, taxes, goods at Customs]* déclaration *f* ; *(Cards)* annonce *f*

COMP **Declaration of Independence** N *(US Hist)* Déclaration *f* d'indépendance

declaration of love N déclaration *f* d'amour

declaration of war N déclaration *f* de guerre

declarative /dɪˈklærətɪv/ ADJ *(Gram)* déclaratif, assertif

declaratory /dɪˈklærətərɪ/ ADJ *(Jur)* ◆ **~ judgement** jugement *m* déclaratoire

declare /dɪˈkleəʳ/ LANGUAGE IN USE 26.2 VT 1 *[+ intentions, love, war, hostilities]* (also *Fin etc*) *[+ income]* déclarer ; *[+ results]* proclamer ◆ **have you anything to ~?** *(Customs)* avez-vous quelque chose à déclarer ? ◆ **to ~ o.s.** *[suitor]* faire sa déclaration, se déclarer ◆ **to ~ war (on ...)** déclarer la guerre (à ...) ◆ **to ~ a state of emergency** déclarer l'état d'urgence 2 *(= assert)* déclarer *(that* que) ◆ **to ~ o.s. for** *or* **in favour of/against** se déclarer *or* se prononcer en faveur de/contre ◆ **to ~ sb president/bankrupt** déclarer qn président/en faillite VI 1 ◆ **well I (do) ~!** † * (ça) par exemple ! 2 *(US Pol) [presidential candidate]* annoncer sa candidature

declared /dɪˈkleəd/ ADJ *[intention]* déclaré, avoué ◆ **he's a ~ homosexual** il ne cache pas son homosexualité

declaredly /dɪˈkleərɪdlɪ/ ADV ouvertement

declarer /dɪˈkleərəʳ/ N *(Cards)* déclarant(e) *m(f)*

declassify /diːˈklæsɪfaɪ/ VT *[+ information, document]* déclassifier

declension /dɪˈklenʃən/ N *(Gram)* déclinaison *f* ◆ **first/second ~** première/deuxième déclinaison *f*

declinable /dɪˈklaɪnəbl/ ADJ *(Gram)* déclinable

declination /ˌdeklɪˈneɪʃən/ N *(Astron)* déclinaison *f*

decline /dɪˈklaɪn/ LANGUAGE IN USE 12.3, 19.5, 25.2

N *[of day, life]* déclin *m* ; *[of empire]* déclin *m*, décadence *f* ◆ **to be in ~** *[nation, economy, industry]* être en déclin ; *[population, number]* être en baisse ◆ **to fall** *or* **go into a ~** dépérir

◆ **decline in** *(numbers, sales, standards)* baisse *f* de ◆ **a rapid ~ in popularity** une rapide baisse de popularité ◆ **a ~ in standards** une baisse de qualité

◆ **to be on the decline** *[prices]* être en baisse, baisser ; *[fame, health]* décliner ◆ **cases of real poverty are on the ~** les cas d'indigence réelle sont de moins en moins fréquents *or* sont en diminution

VT 1 *(gen)* refuser *(to do sth* de faire qch) ; *[+ invitation, offer, honour]* décliner ; *[+ responsibility]* décliner, rejeter ◆ **he ~d to do it** il a refusé (poliment) de le faire ◆ **he offered me a lift but I ~d** il a proposé de m'emmener mais j'ai refusé ◆ **to ~ a jurisdiction** *(Jur)* se déclarer incompétent

2 *(Gram)* décliner

VI 1 *[health, influence]* décliner ; *[empire]* tomber en décadence ; *[prices]* baisser, être en baisse ; *[business]* péricliter, décliner ◆ **to ~ in importance** perdre de l'importance
2 *(= slope)* s'incliner, descendre
3 *[sun]* décliner, se coucher ; *[day]* tirer à sa fin, décliner
4 *(Gram)* se décliner

declining /dɪˈklaɪnɪŋ/ **ADJ** *[sales, standards, popularity]* en baisse ◆ **he's in ~ health** sa santé décline peu à peu ◆ **a ~ industry** une industrie sur le déclin ◆ **in his ~ years** au déclin de sa vie ◆ **she spent her ~ years in Devon** elle a passé ses dernières années dans le Devon **N** 1 *[of invitation]* refus *m* 2 *[of empire]* décadence *f* 3 *(Gram)* déclinaison *f*

declivity /dɪˈklɪvɪtɪ/ **N** déclivité *f*, pente *f*

declutch /ˈdiːˈklʌtʃ/ **VI** débrayer ; → **double**

decoction /dɪˈkɒkʃən/ **N** décoction *f*

decode /ˈdiːˈkəʊd/ **VT** 1 *(Telec, TV)* décoder, traduire (en clair) 2 *(Comput, Ling)* décoder 3 *(fig = understand, explain)* décoder

decoder /diːˈkəʊdəʳ/ **N** *(Comput, Telec, TV)* décodeur *m*

decoding /diːˈkəʊdɪŋ/ **N** *(Comput, Telec, TV, Ling)* décodage *m*

decoke /diːˈkəʊk/ *(Brit)* **VT** *[+ engine]* décalaminer **N** /ˈdiːkəʊk/ décalaminage *m*

decollate /dɪˈkɒleɪt/ **VT** *(Comput)* déliasser

décolletage /deɪˈkɒltɑːʒ/ **N** décolletage *m*, décolleté *m*

décolleté /deɪˈkɒlteɪ/ **ADJ** décolleté **N** ⇒ **décolletage**

decolonization /diːˌkɒlənaɪˈzeɪʃən/ **N** décolonisation *f*

decolonize /diːˈkɒləˌnaɪz/ **VT** décoloniser

decommission /ˌdiːkəˈmɪʃən/ **VT** 1 *[+ nuclear power station]* déclasser 2 *[+ warship, aircraft]* retirer de la circulation

decommissioning /diːkəˈmɪʃənɪŋ/ **N** *[of arms]* mise *f* hors service; *[of power station]* déclassement *m*

decompartmentalization /ˌdiːkɒmpɑːtˌmentəlaɪˈzeɪʃən/ **N** *(Sociol)* décloisonnement *m*

decompartmentalize /ˌdiːkɒmpɑːˈmentəlaɪz/ **VT** *(Sociol)* décloisonner

decompose /ˌdiːkəmˈpəʊz/ **VT** décomposer **VI** se décomposer

decomposition /ˌdiːkɒmpəˈzɪʃən/ **N** décomposition *f*

decompress /ˌdiːkəmˈpres/ **VT** décompresser

decompression /ˌdiːkəmˈpreʃən/ **N** *(Med, Phys, Tech)* décompression *f*
COMP **decompression chamber N** chambre *f* de décompression
decompression illness, decompression sickness N maladie *f* des caissons

decongestant /ˌdiːkənˈdʒestənt/ **ADJ, N** décongestif *m*

deconsecrate /ˌdiːˈkɒnsɪkreɪt/ **VT** séculariser

deconstruct /ˌdiːkənˈstrʌkt/ **VT** *(Literat)* déconstruire

deconstruction /ˌdiːkənˈstrʌkʃən/ **N** *(Literat)* déconstruction *f*

decontaminate /ˌdiːkənˈtæmɪneɪt/ **VT** décontaminer

decontamination /ˈdiːkənˌtæmɪˈneɪʃən/ **N** décontamination *f*

decontextualize /ˌdiːkənˈtekstjʊəlaɪz/ **VT** isoler de son contexte

decontrol /ˌdiːkənˈtrəʊl/ *(esp US)* **VT** *(Admin, Comm)* déréglementer ◆ **to ~ (the price of) oil** libérer le prix du pétrole **N** *[of price]* libération *f*

décor /ˈdeɪkɔːʳ/ **N** décor *m*

decorate /ˈdekəreɪt/ **VT** 1 *(= prettify)* orner, décorer *(with* de) ; *[+ cake]* décorer ◆ **to ~ with flags** pavoiser 2 *[+ room, house] (= paint)* peindre ; *(= wallpaper)* tapisser 3 *(= award medal to)* décorer, médailler ◆ **he was ~d for gallantry** il a été décoré pour sa bravoure **VI** *(= paint etc)* peindre (et tapisser)

> ⚠ When it means painting and decorating, **to decorate** is not translated by **décorer**.

decorating /ˈdekəreɪtɪŋ/ **N** 1 (also **painting and decorating**) décoration *f* intérieure ◆ **they are doing some ~** ils sont en train de refaire les peintures 2 *[of cake etc]* décoration *f*

decoration /ˌdekəˈreɪʃən/ **N** 1 *(NonC) [of cake]* décoration *f* ; *[of hat]* ornementation *f* ; *[of room] (= act)* décoration *f* (intérieure) ; *(= state)* décoration *f*, décor *m* ; *[of town]* décoration *f* ; *(with flags)* pavoisement *m* 2 *(= ornament) [of hat]* ornement *m* ; *(in streets)* décoration *f* ◆ **Christmas ~s** décorations *fpl* de Noël 3 *(Mil)* décoration *f*, médaille *f*

decorative /ˈdekərətɪv/ **ADJ** décoratif **COMP** **decorative art N** arts *mpl* décoratifs

decorator /ˈdekəreɪtəʳ/ **N** *(= designer)* décorateur *m*, -trice *f*, ensemblier *m* ; *(esp Brit*: also **painter and decorator**) peintre *m* décorateur

decorous /ˈdekərəs/ **ADJ** convenable, bienséant ◆ **try to be ~ at all times** essayez toujours de respecter les convenances

decorously /ˈdekərəslɪ/ **ADV** de façon convenable

decorum /dɪˈkɔːrəm/ **N** décorum *m*, bienséance *f* ◆ **with ~** avec bienséance, comme il faut ◆ **a breach of ~** une inconvenance ◆ **to have a sense of ~** avoir le sens des convenances

decouple /diːˈkʌpl/ **VT** découpler

decoy /ˈdiːkɔɪ/ **N** *(= bird) (live)* appeau *m*, chanterelle *f* ; *(artificial)* leurre *m* ; *(= animal)* proie *f* (servant d'appât) ; *(= person)* compère *m* ◆ **police ~** policier *m* en civil *(servant à attirer un criminel dans une souricière)* **VT** /dɪˈkɔɪ/ *(with live decoy)* attirer avec un appeau *or* une chanterelle ; *(with artificial decoy)* attirer avec un leurre ; → **noun** ; *(also fig)* attirer dans un piège ◆ **to ~ sb into doing sth** faire faire qch à qn en le leurrant **COMP** **decoy duck N** *(lit)* appeau *m*, chanterelle *f* ; *(fig)* compère *m*

decrease /diːˈkriːs/ **VI** *[amount, numbers, supplies, birth rate, population]* diminuer, décroître ; *[power]* s'affaiblir ; *[strength, intensity]* s'affaiblir, décroître ; *[price, value]* baisser ; *[enthusiasm]* se calmer, se refroidir ; *(Knitting)* diminuer **VT** diminuer, réduire **N** /ˈdiːkriːs/ *[of amount, supplies]* diminution *f*, amoindrissement *m* (in de) ; *[of numbers]* diminution *f*, décroissance *f* (in de) ; *[of birth rate, population]* diminution *f* (in de) ; *[of power]* affaiblissement *m* (in de) ; *[of strength, intensity]* diminution *f*, décroissance *f* (in de) ; *[of price, value]* baisse *f* (in de) ; *[of enthusiasm]* baisse *f*, refroidissement *m* (in de) ◆ **~ in speed** ralentissement *m* ◆ **~ in strength** affaiblissement *m*

decreasing /diːˈkriːsɪŋ/ **ADJ** *[amount, quantity, value, sales, numbers, statistic]* en baisse ; *[intensity]* décroissant ; *[strength]* déclinant ◆ **a ~ population** une baisse de la démographie, une population en baisse

decreasingly /diːˈkriːsɪŋlɪ/ **ADV** de moins en moins

decree /dɪˈkriː/ **N** *(Pol, Rel)* décret *m* ; *[of tribunal]* arrêt *m*, jugement *m* ; *(municipal)* arrêté *m* ◆ **by royal/government ~** par décret du roi/du gouvernement ◆ **~ absolute** *(divorce)* jugement *m* définitif (de divorce) ◆ **~ nisi** jugement *m* provisoire (de divorce) **VT** *(gen, also Pol, Rel)* décréter *(that* que + *indic)* ; *(Jur)* ordonner *(that* que + *subj)* ; *[mayor, council etc]* arrêter *(that* que + *indic)* ◆ **to ~ an end to ...** *(frm)* décréter la fin de ...

decrepit /dɪˈkrepɪt/ **ADJ** *[object, building]* délabré ; * *[person]* décrépit, décati *

decrepitude /dɪˈkrepɪtjuːd/ **N** 1 *(= dilapidation) [of building, place]* délabrement *m* ; *[of system]* vétusté *f*, décrépitude *f* 2 *(= infirmity)* décrépitude *f*

decretal /dɪˈkriːtl/ **N** décrétale *f*

decriminalization /ˌdiːkrɪmɪnəlaɪˈzeɪʃən/ **N** dépénalisation *f*

decriminalize /diːˈkrɪmɪnəlaɪz/ **VT** dépénaliser

decry /dɪˈkraɪ/ **VT** décrier, dénigrer

decrypt /diːˈkrɪpt/ **VT** *(Comput, Telec)* décrypter, déchiffrer

decumulation /ˌdɪkjuːmjʊˈleɪʃən/ **N** *[of capital]* réduction *f*, diminution *f* ; *[of stocks]* contraction *f*, réduction *f* ◆ **stock ~** déstockage *m*

dedicate /ˈdedɪkeɪt/ **VT** 1 *(= devote) [+ time, one's life]* consacrer *(to sth* à qch ; *to doing sth* à faire qch) ; *[+ resources, money]* allouer *(to sth* à qch ; *to doing sth* pour faire qch) ◆ **to ~ o.s. to sth/to doing sth** se consacrer à qch/à faire qch 2 *(as mark of respect, affection etc) [+ building, memorial, book, film, award]* dédier *(to* à) ◆ **to ~ a song to sb** *[singer]* dédier une chanson à qn ; *[disc jockey]* passer une chanson à la demande de qn ◆ **they ~d the statue to the memory of ...** ils ont dédié cette statue à la mémoire de ... ◆ **"this thesis is dedicated to my parents"** "je dédie cette thèse à mes parents" 3 *(Rel = consecrate) [+ church, shrine]* consacrer

dedicated /ˈdedɪkeɪtɪd/ **ADJ** 1 *(= devoted) [person]* dévoué ; *[work, attitude]* sérieux ◆ **a ~ traveller** un voyageur enthousiaste ◆ **a ~ socialist** un socialiste convaincu ◆ **a ~ follower of fashion** un fervent adepte de la mode ◆ **to be ~ to sth** *[person]* tenir beaucoup à qch ; *[organization]* se consacrer à qch ◆ **as a party we are ~ to social change** notre parti a pour vocation de promouvoir le changement social ◆ **as a party we are ~ to achieving social equality** notre parti œuvre en faveur de l'établissement de l'égalité sociale ◆ **we are ~ to making banking more convenient for our customers** nous faisons tout notre possible pour faciliter les formalités bancaires à nos clients
2 ◆ **~ to** *(= given over to)* consacré à ◆ **a museum ~ to Napoleon** un musée consacré à Napoléon ◆ **a charity ~ to famine relief** une association caritative ayant pour but de combattre la famine
3 *(= bearing a dedication) [copy of book etc]* dédicacé
4 *(= specialized) [word processor]* dédié

dedicatee /ˌdedɪkəˈtiː/ **N** dédicataire *mf*

dedication /ˌdedɪˈkeɪʃən/ **N** 1 *[of church]* dédicace *f*, consécration *f* 2 *(in book, on radio)* dédicace *f* ◆ **to write a ~ in a book** dédicacer un livre ◆ **the ~ reads: "to Emma, with love from Harry"** le livre est dédicacé "à Emma, avec tout mon amour, Harry" ◆ **if you want a ~ just write in** *(Rad)* si vous voulez faire une dédicace, écrivez-nous 3 *(quality = devotion)* dévouement *m*

deduce /dɪˈdjuːs/ **VT** déduire, conclure *(from* de ; *that* que)

deducible /dɪˈdjuːsɪbl/ **ADJ** ◆ **~ from** que l'on peut déduire *or* inférer de

deduct /dɪˈdʌkt/ **VT** *[+ amount]* déduire, retrancher *(from* de) ; *[+ numbers]* retrancher, soustraire *(from* de) ; *[+ tax]* retenir, prélever *(from* sur) ◆ **to ~ something from the price** faire une réduction sur le prix ◆ **to ~ sth for expenses** retenir qch pour les frais ◆ **to ~ 5% from the wages** faire une retenue de *or* prélever 5% sur les salaires ◆ **after ~ing 5%** déduction faite de 5%

deductible /dɪ'dʌktəbl/ ADJ à déduire (*from* de) ; (*Tax*) [*expenses*] déductible N (*US Insurance*) franchise *f* ◆ **a 50 dollar ~** une franchise de 50 dollars

deduction /dɪ'dʌkʃən/ N 1 (= *sth deducted*) déduction *f* (*from* de) ; (*from wage*) retenue *f*, prélèvement *m* (*from* sur) 2 (= *sth deduced*) déduction *f* 3 (*NonC* = *deductive reasoning*) raisonnement *m* déductif

deductive /dɪ'dʌktɪv/ ADJ déductif

deed /diːd/ N 1 (= *action*) action *f*, acte *m* ◆ **brave ~** haut fait *m*, exploit *m* ◆ **good ~(s)** bonne(s) action(s) *f(pl)* ◆ **to do one's good ~ for the day** (*hum*) faire sa B.A. quotidienne ; → **word** 2 ◆ **in ~** de fait ◆ **master in ~ if not in name** maître de fait sinon de nom 3 (*Jur*) acte *m* notarié, contrat *m* ◆ **~ of covenant** *or* **gift** (acte *m* de) donation *f* ◆ **~ of partnership** contrat *m* de société VT (*US Jur*) transférer par acte notarié

COMP **deed box** N coffre *m* *or* mallette *f* pour documents (officiels)
deed poll N ◆ **to change one's name by ~ poll** ≈ changer de nom officiellement

deejay* /'diːˌdʒeɪ/ N disc-jockey *m*

deem /diːm/ VT ◆ **to ~ it prudent to do sth** juger prudent de faire qch ◆ **to be ~ed worthy of (doing) sth** être jugé digne de (faire) qch ◆ **he was ~ed too ill to leave the hospital** on a décidé qu'il était trop malade pour quitter l'hôpital ◆ **military intervention was not ~ed necessary** on a jugé qu'une intervention militaire n'était pas nécessaire

deep /diːp/ ADJ 1 [*water, hole, wound, cut, wrinkle*] profond ; [*mud, snow, carpet*] épais (-aisse *f*) ; [*pan, bowl, container*] à hauts bords ◆ **the lake/pond was 4 metres ~** le lac/l'étang avait 4 mètres de profondeur ◆ **the water was 2 metres ~** la profondeur de l'eau était de 2 mètres ◆ **the snow lay ~** il y avait une épaisse couche de neige ◆ **the streets were 2 feet ~ in snow** les rues étaient sous 60 cm *or* étaient recouvertes de 60 cm de neige ◆ **he was ankle-/thigh-~ in water** l'eau lui arrivait aux chevilles/aux cuisses ◆ **to be in ~ water(s)** (*fig*) avoir de gros ennuis, être en mauvaise posture
2 [*edge, border*] large, haut ; [*shelf, cupboard*] large, profond ◆ **a plot of ground 15 metres ~** un terrain qui s'étend sur 15 mètres ◆ **the spectators stood ten ~** il y avait dix rangées de spectateurs ◆ **a line of policemen three ~** trois rangées de policiers ◆ **a line of cars parked three ~** des voitures garées sur trois rangées
3 [*sound, voice, tones*] grave ◆ **the animal gave a ~ growl** l'animal a émis un grognement sourd
4 [*colour*] profond ; [*darkness*] profond, total ◆ **~ blue/green/yellow** bleu/vert/jaune profond *inv*
5 [*breath, sigh*] profond ◆ **~ breathing** respiration *f* profonde ; (= *exercises*) exercices *mpl* respiratoires ◆ **to take a ~ breath** respirer profondément
6 [*sorrow, relief*] profond, intense ; [*concern, interest*] vif ; [*admiration, respect, divisions, differences, sleep, relaxation, recession*] profond ; [*mystery*] profond, total ◆ **our ~est feelings** nos sentiments les plus profonds ◆ **to gain a ~er understanding of sth** parvenir à mieux comprendre qch ◆ **to gain a ~er understanding of o.s.** parvenir à mieux se connaître ; → **breath, mourning**
7 [*writer, thinker, book*] profond ◆ **the film is not intended to be ~ and meaningful** le film ne cherche pas à être profond ◆ **I'm not looking for a ~ and meaningful relationship** je ne recherche pas une relation sérieuse
8 (*in location*) **~ in the forest/in enemy territory** au cœur de la forêt/du territoire ennemi
9 (= *absorbed, implicated*) ◆ **~ in thought/in a book** plongé *or* absorbé dans ses pensées/dans un livre ◆ **she was ~ in conversation (with him)** elle était en pleine conversation (avec lui) ◆ **~ in debt** criblé de dettes ◆ **the country is ~ in recession** le pays est en pleine récession
10 (*Sport*) [*shot, volley, pass, cross*] long (longue *f*)
11 (*Gram*) **~ structure** structure *f* profonde ◆ **~ grammar** grammaire *f* profonde
ADV profondément ◆ **to go ~ into the forest** pénétrer profondément *or* très avant dans la forêt ◆ **to bury sth ~ underground** enfouir qch profondément dans le sol ◆ **it makes its burrow ~ underground** il creuse son terrier très profond ◆ **don't go in too ~ if you can't swim** ne va pas trop loin si tu ne sais pas nager ◆ **to thrust one's hands ~ in one's pockets** enfoncer ses mains dans ses poches ◆ **to talk/read** *etc* **~ into the night** parler/lire *etc* jusque tard dans la nuit ◆ **to drink ~** boire à longs traits ◆ **to breathe ~** respirer profondément ◆ **to gaze ~ into sb's eyes** regarder qn au fond des yeux, plonger son regard dans celui de qn ◆ **to go** *or* **run ~** [*divisions, crisis, tendency*] être profond ; [*problems*] être grave, remonter à loin ; [*passions, feelings*] être exacerbé ; [*racism, prejudice, memories*] être bien enraciné ◆ **the difference between them goes** *or* **runs ~** il y a une profonde différence entre eux ◆ **their family roots run ~** leur famille remonte à loin ◆ **he's in (it) pretty ~*** (*in relationship, plot*) il s'est engagé à fond ; (*in conspiracy, illegal activity*) il est dedans jusqu'au cou ◆ **~ down she still mistrusted him** en son for intérieur, elle se méfiait encore de lui ◆ **she seems abrupt, but ~ down she's kind** sous son air *or* son extérieur brusque, c'est quelqu'un de gentil ; → **dig, knee, skin, still**^{2}
N 1 (*liter* = *sea, ocean*) **the ~** (les grands fonds *mpl* de) l'océan *m*, les grandes profondeurs *fpl*
2 (= *depths*) **in the ~ of winter** au plus fort *or* au cœur de l'hiver

COMP **deep-chested** ADJ [*person*] large de poitrine ; [*animal*] à large poitrail
deep-discount bond N (*Fin*) obligation *f* à forte décote
deep-dyed ADJ (*fig*) invétéré
the deep end N [*of swimming pool*] le grand bain ◆ **to go off (at) the ~ end*** (*fig: excited, angry*) se mettre dans tous ses états ◆ **to go in** *or* **jump in at the ~ end** (*esp Brit fig*) foncer tête baissée ◆ **to throw sb in at the ~ end*** (*fig*) mettre tout de suite qn dans le bain
deep-fat fryer N friteuse *f*
deep freeze, deep freezer (*US*) N congélateur *m* ◆ **to put sth in the ~ freeze** mettre qch au congélateur ◆ **in ~ freeze** congelé ◆ **to put sth into ~ freeze** congeler qch
deep freeze VT congeler
deep-freezing N congélation *f* ; (*in food production*) surgélation *f*
deep-frozen foods NPL aliments *mpl* surgelés
deep-fry VT faire frire
deep fryer N ⇒ **deep-fat fryer**
deep kissing N (*NonC*) baisers *mpl* profonds
deep-pan pizza N pizza *f* à pâte épaisse
deep-rooted ADJ [*affection, prejudice*] profond, profondément enraciné, vivace ; [*habit*] invétéré, ancré ; [*tree*] aux racines profondes
deep-sea ADJ [*animal, plant*] pélagique, abyssal ; [*current*] pélagique
deep-sea diver N plongeur *m* sous-marin
deep-sea diving N plongée *f* sous-marine
deep-sea fisherman N (pl **deep-sea fishermen**) pêcheur *m* hauturier *or* de haute mer
deep-sea fishing N pêche *f* hauturière
deep-seated ADJ [*prejudice, dislike*] profond, profondément enraciné ; [*conviction*] fermement ancré ◆ **~-seated cough** toux *f* bronchique *or* caverneuse
deep-set ADJ [*eyes*] très enfoncé, creux, cave ; [*window*] profondément encastré
deep-six⁑ VT (*US*) (= *throw out*) balancer⁑ ; (= *kill*) liquider⁑
the Deep South N (*US Geog*) le Sud profond (des États-Unis)
deep space N espace *m* intersidéral *or* interstellaire
deep vein thrombosis N thrombose *f* veineuse profonde

deepen /'diːpən/ VT [+ *relationship, knowledge*] approfondir ; [+ *gloom, recession*] aggraver VI [*crisis, recession*] s'aggraver ; [*voice*] devenir plus grave ; [*water*] devenir plus profond ; [*snow*] devenir plus épais ; [*relationship*] devenir plus profond ; [*knowledge*] s'approfondir ; [*darkness*] s'épaissir

deepening /'diːpənɪŋ/ ADJ [*crisis, gloom, depression*] qui s'aggrave ; [*friendship, understanding*] de plus en plus profond ; [*wrinkles*] qui se creuse N intensification *f*

deepfreeze /'diːpfriːz/ N ⇒ **deep comp**

deeply /'diːplɪ/ ADV 1 [*cut, sleep, breathe, love, think, regret*] profondément ; [*dig*] profond ; [*drink*] à grands *or* longs traits ◆ **to blush ~** rougir jusqu'aux oreilles ◆ **~ embedded** profondément incrusté ◆ **to sigh ~** pousser un gros soupir ◆ **to look ~ into sb's eyes** regarder qn au fond des yeux, plonger son regard dans celui de qn 2 [*shocked, divided, sceptical, religious, unhappy, hurt*] profondément ; [*concerned, troubled, unpopular*] extrêmement ; [*grateful*] infiniment ◆ **~ tanned** très bronzé ◆ **~ in debt** criblé de dettes

deer /dɪəʳ/ N (pl **deer** *or* **deers**) cerf *m*, biche *f* ; (also **red deer**) cerf *m* ; (also **fallow deer**) daim *m* ; (also **roe deer**) chevreuil *m* ◆ **certain types of ~** certains types de cervidés ◆ **look at those ~!** regardez ces cerfs (*or* ces biches) !

deerhound /'dɪəhaʊnd/ N limier *m*

deerskin /'dɪəskɪn/ N peau *f* de daim

deerstalker /'dɪəˌstɔːkəʳ/ N (= *hat*) casquette *f* à la Sherlock Holmes ; (= *hunter*) chasseur *m* de cerfs

deerstalking /'dɪəˌstɔːkɪŋ/ N chasse *f* au cerf (*à pied*)

de-escalate /diː'eskəleɪt/ VT [+ *tension*] faire baisser, diminuer ; [+ *situation*] détendre, décrisper

de-escalation /diːˌeskə'leɪʃən/ N (*Mil, Pol*) désescalade *f* ; (*in industrial relations*) décrispation *f*

deface /dɪ'feɪs/ VT dégrader

de facto /deɪ'fæktəʊ/ ADJ, ADV de fait, de facto N (*Austral*) concubin(e) *m(f)*

defamation /ˌdefə'meɪʃən/ N (also **defamation of character**) diffamation *f*

defamatory /dɪ'fæmətərɪ/ ADJ diffamatoire

defame /dɪ'feɪm/ VT diffamer

default /dɪ'fɔːlt/ N 1 (*Jur*) (= *failure to appear*) (*in civil cases*) défaut *m*, non-comparution *f* ; (*in criminal cases*) contumace *f* ; (= *failure to meet financial obligation*) défaillance *f*, manquement *m* ◆ **judgement by ~** jugement *m* par contumace *or* par défaut ◆ **to be in ~ of payment** [*company*] être en (situation de) cessation de paiement
2 ◆ **by ~** ◆ **we must not let it go by ~** ne laissons pas échapper l'occasion (faute d'avoir agi) ◆ **they won the election by ~** ils ont remporté l'élection en l'absence d'autres candidats sérieux ◆ **he got the job by ~** il a eu le poste en l'absence d'autres candidats (valables) ◆ **match won by ~** match gagné par forfait
3 (= *lack, absence*) manque *m*, carence *f* ◆ **in ~ of** à défaut de, faute de
4 (*Fin*) cessation *f* de paiements
5 (*Comput*) position *f* par défaut ◆ **~ option/value** option *f*/valeur *f* par défaut
VT (*Jur*) condamner par défaut *or* par contumace, rendre un jugement par défaut contre

VI [1] *(Jur)* faire défaut, être en état de contumace
[2] *(gen, Fin)* manquer à ses engagements
[3] *(Comput)* **to** ◆ **to a value** prendre une valeur par défaut ◆ **it ~s to drive C** ça se positionne par défaut sur le disque C

defaulter /dɪˈfɔːltəʳ/ N [1] *(= offender)* délinquant(e) *m(f)* ; *(Mil, Naut)* soldat *m* (or marin *m*) en infraction ; *(Mil, Naut: undergoing punishment)* consigné *m* [2] *(Fin)* défaillant(e) *m(f)*, débiteur *m*, -trice *f* défaillant(e) ; *(= defaulting tenant)* locataire *mf* qui ne paie pas son loyer

defaulting /dɪˈfɔːltɪŋ/ ADJ *[client, purchaser, tenant, witness]* défaillant

defeat /dɪˈfiːt/ N *(= act, state) [of army, team]* défaite *f* ; *[of project, ambition]* échec *m*, insuccès *m* ; *[of legal case, appeal]* rejet *m* VT *[+ opponent, army]* vaincre, battre ; *[+ team]* battre ; *[+ hopes]* frustrer, ruiner ; *[+ ambitions, plans, efforts, attempts]* faire échouer ; *(Parl) [+ government, opposition]* mettre en minorité ; *[+ bill, amendment]* rejeter ◆ **~ed in his attempts to ...** n'ayant pas réussi à ... ◆ **to ~ one's own ends** or **object** aller à l'encontre du but que l'on s'est (or s'était *etc*) proposé ◆ **that plan will ~ its own ends** ce plan sera autodestructeur

defeated /dɪˈfiːtɪd/ ADJ *[army]* vaincu ; *[team, player]* perdant

defeatism /dɪˈfiːtɪzəm/ N défaitisme *m*

defeatist /dɪˈfiːtɪst/ ADJ, N défaitiste *mf*

defecate /ˈdefəkeɪt/ VTI déféquer

defecation /ˌdefəˈkeɪʃən/ N défécation *f*

defect /ˈdiːfekt/ N *(gen)* défaut *m* ; *(in workmanship)* défaut *m*, malfaçon *f* ◆ **physical ~** défaut *m* physique ◆ **hearing/sight ~** défaut *m* de l'ouïe/de la vue ◆ **speech ~** défaut *m* de prononciation ◆ **mental ~** anomalie *f* or déficience *f* mentale ◆ **moral ~** défaut *m* ; → **latent** VI /dɪˈfekt/ *(Pol)* faire défection ◆ **to ~ from one country to another** s'enfuir d'un pays pour aller dans un autre *(pour raisons politiques)* ◆ **to ~ to the West/to another party/to the enemy** passer à l'Ouest/à un autre parti/à l'ennemi

defection /dɪˈfekʃən/ N *(Pol)* défection *f* ; *(Rel)* apostasie *f* ◆ **his ~ to the East was in all the papers** quand il est passé à l'Est, tous les journaux en ont parlé ◆ **after his ~ from Russia, he lost contact with his family** quand il s'est enfui de Russie, il a perdu contact avec sa famille

defective /dɪˈfektɪv/ ADJ *[goods, machine, work, reasoning, sight, hearing, gene]* défectueux ; *[chromosome]* anormal ; *(Gram) [verb]* défectif ◆ **to be born with a ~ heart** naître avec une malformation cardiaque ◆ **~ workmanship** malfaçons *fpl* ; → **mental, mentally** N *(Med)* déficient(e) *m(f)* ; *(Gram)* verbe *m* défectif

defector /dɪˈfektəʳ/ N *(Pol)* transfuge *mf* ; *(Rel)* apostat *m*

defence, defense (US) /dɪˈfens/ N [1] *(NonC)* défense *f* ; *[of action, belief]* justification *f* ; *(Physiol, Psych, Sport)* défense *f* ◆ **to play in ~** *(Sport)* jouer en défense ◆ **in ~ of** à la défense de, pour défendre ◆ **Secretary of State for** or **Minister of Defence** *(Brit)*, **Secretary of Defense** (US) ministre *m* de la Défense ◆ **Department** or **Ministry of Defence** *(Brit)*, **Department of Defense** (US) ministère *m* de la Défense ; → **civil, self**
[2] *(= means of defence)* défense *f* ◆ **~s** *(gen, also Mil = weapons etc)* moyens *mpl* de défense ; *(Mil = constructions)* ouvrages *mpl* défensifs ◆ **the body's ~s against disease** les défenses *fpl* de l'organisme contre la maladie ◆ **as a ~ against** pour se défendre contre ◆ **she put up** or **made a spirited ~ of her government's policies** elle a défendu la politique de son gouvernement avec fougue ◆ **Smith made a successful ~ of her title** *(Sport)* Smith a réussi à conserver son titre ◆ **to come to sb's ~** défendre qn ◆ **his conduct needs no ~** sa conduite n'a pas à être justifiée ◆ **in his ~ I will say that ...** pour sa défense *or* à sa décharge je dirai que ...
[3] *(Jur)* défense *f* ◆ **in his ~** pour sa défense, à sa décharge ◆ **witness for the ~** témoin *m* à décharge ◆ **the case for the ~** la défense
[4] *[of argument, decision]* justification *f* ; *(Univ) [of thesis]* soutenance *f*
COMP *(gen)* de défense ; *[industry, manufacturer etc]* travaillant pour la défense nationale ; *[product, contract]* destiné à la défense nationale
defence counsel N avocat *m* de la défense
defence expenditure N dépenses *fpl* militaires
defence forces NPL *(Mil)* forces *fpl* défensives, défense *f*
defence mechanism N *(Physiol)* système *m* de défense ; *(Psych)* défenses *fpl*

defenceless, defenseless (US) /dɪˈfenslɪs/ ADJ sans défense *(against* contre) ◆ **he is quite ~** il est incapable de se défendre, il est sans défense

defend /dɪˈfend/ VT [1] *(gen, Sport)* défendre ◆ **to ~ o.s.** se défendre ◆ **to ~ one's (own) interests** défendre ses (propres) intérêts [2] *(= justify)* justifier ; *(= attempt to justify)* essayer de justifier ◆ **how can he possibly ~ the way he's behaved towards her?** comment peut-il justifier la manière dont il s'est comporté avec elle ? ◆ **they ~ed their actions** ils ont justifié leurs actions, ils se sont justifiés ◆ **Smith successfully ~ed her title** *(Sport)* Smith a réussi à conserver son titre ◆ **to ~ a thesis** *(Univ)* soutenir une thèse VI *(Sport, gen)* défendre ; *(= play in defence)* être en défense ◆ **they ~ed very well** ils ont très bien défendu ◆ **to ~ against sb** *[champion]* défendre son titre contre qn, remettre son titre en jeu contre qn ; → **defending**

defendant /dɪˈfendənt/ N *(Jur)* défendeur *m*, -deresse *f* ; *(on appeal)* intimé(e) *m(f)* ; *(in criminal case)* prévenu(e) *m(f)* ; *(in assizes court)* accusé(e) *m(f)*

defender /dɪˈfendəʳ/ N défenseur *m* ; *(Sport) [of record]* détenteur *m*, -trice *f* ; *[of title]* tenant(e) *m(f)* ◆ **~ of the faith** *(Brit Hist)* défenseur *m* de la foi

defending /dɪˈfendɪŋ/ ADJ ◆ **the ~ champion** le tenant du titre ◆ **~ counsel** *(Jur)* avocat *m* de la défense

defense /dɪˈfens/ N (US) ⇒ **defence**

defensible /dɪˈfensɪbl/ ADJ défendable

defensive /dɪˈfensɪv/ ADJ défensif ◆ **he's so ~!** il est toujours sur la défensive ! N défensive *f* ◆ **to be on the ~** être sur la défensive ◆ **to put sb/go on the ~** mettre qn/se mettre sur la défensive

defensively /dɪˈfensɪvlɪ/ ADV *[speak]* sur la défensive ; *[play]* défensivement

defensiveness /dɪˈfensɪvnɪs/ N ◆ **his ~ (when we talk about ...)** sa façon d'être sur la défensive (chaque fois que nous parlons de ...)

defer¹ /dɪˈfɜːʳ/ VT [1] *[+ journey, meeting]* remettre à plus tard, reporter ; *[+ business]* remettre à plus tard ; *[+ payment, decision, judgement]* remettre à plus tard, différer ◆ **our meeting was ~red until 22 May** notre réunion a été reportée au 22 mai ◆ **to ~ making a decision/paying one's taxes** différer une décision/le paiement de ses impôts, remettre une décision/le paiement de ses impôts à plus tard [2] *(Mil)* **to ~ sb's call-up** accorder un sursis d'appel *or* d'incorporation à qn ◆ **to ~ sb on medical grounds** accorder un sursis d'appel *or* d'incorporation à qn pour raisons médicales
COMP **deferred annuity** N rente *f* à paiement différé
deferred liabilities NPL dettes *fpl* à moyen et long terme
deferred payment N paiement *m* échelonné

defer² /dɪˈfɜːʳ/ VI *(= submit)* ◆ **to ~ to sb** déférer *(frm)* à qn, s'incliner devant qn ◆ **to ~ to sb's knowledge** s'en remettre aux connaissances de qn ◆ **to ~ to California jurisdiction** *(Jur)* accepter la compétence des tribunaux californiens

deference /ˈdefərəns/ N déférence *f*, égards *mpl* *(to* pour) ◆ **in ~ to, out of ~ for** par déférence *or* égards pour ◆ **with all due ~ to you** avec tout le respect que je vous dois, sauf votre respect

deferential /ˌdefəˈrenʃəl/ ADJ *[person, attitude]* respectueux, plein de déférence ; *[tone]* de déférence ◆ **to be ~ to sb** se montrer plein de déférence pour *or* envers qn

deferentially /ˌdefəˈrenʃəlɪ/ ADV avec déférence

deferment /dɪˈfɜːmənt/ N *[of payment, tax]* report *m* ; *(Mil)* sursis *m* d'appel *or* d'incorporation ◆ **he was given ~ from military service** on lui a accordé un sursis d'appel *or* d'incorporation ◆ **draft ~** *(US Mil)* sursis *m* d'appel, sursis *m* d'incorporation

deferral /dɪˈferəl/ N ⇒ **deferment**

defiance /dɪˈfaɪəns/ N défi *m* ◆ **a gesture/act of ~** un geste/acte de défi ◆ **a ~ of our authority** un défi à notre autorité ◆ **his ~ of my orders caused an accident** en bravant mes ordres *or* en refusant d'obéir à mes ordres, il a causé un accident ◆ **he will have to answer in court for his ~ of the curfew** il devra comparaître en justice pour n'avoir pas respecté le couvre-feu ◆ **in ~ of** *[+ the law, instructions]* au mépris de ; *[+ person]* au mépris des ordres de

defiant /dɪˈfaɪənt/ ADJ *[reply, statement]* provocant ; *[attitude, tone, gesture, look]* de défi ; *[person]* rebelle ◆ **the team is in ~ mood** l'équipe est prête à relever le défi ◆ **to be ~ of sth** défier qch

defiantly /dɪˈfaɪəntlɪ/ ADV *[speak]* d'un ton de défi ; *[reply, stare]* d'un air de défi ; *[behave]* avec une attitude de défi

defibrillator /diːˈfɪbrɪleɪtəʳ/ N défibrillateur *m*

deficiency /dɪˈfɪʃənsɪ/ N [1] *(= lack) [of goods]* manque *m*, insuffisance *f* (of de) ; *(Med) [of iron, calcium, vitamins etc]* carence *f* (of en) ◆ **nutritional** or **dietary ~** carence *f* alimentaire *or* nutritionnelle ; → **mental, vitamin** [2] *(Med = failure to function properly) [of organ, immune system]* insuffisance *f* [3] *(= flaw) (in character, system)* faille *f*, faiblesse *f* ; *(in construction, machine)* imperfection *f* ; *(in service)* faiblesse *f* ◆ **his deficiencies as an administrator** ses points *mpl* faibles en tant qu'administrateur [4] *(Fin)* déficit *m*
COMP **deficiency disease** N maladie *f* de carence *or* carentielle
deficiency payment N paiement *m* différentiel

deficient /dɪˈfɪʃənt/ ADJ *(= inadequate, defective)* défectueux ; *(= insufficient)* insuffisant ◆ **to be ~ in sth** manquer de qch ◆ **his diet is ~ in fruit and vegetables** il ne mange pas assez de fruits et de légumes

deficit /ˈdefɪsɪt/ N déficit *m* ◆ **in ~** en déficit

defile¹ /ˈdiːfaɪl/ N *(= procession: place)* défilé *m* VI /dɪˈfaɪl/ *(= march in file)* défiler

defile² /dɪˈfaɪl/ VT *(lit, fig = pollute)* souiller *(liter)*, salir ; *(= desecrate)* profaner

defilement /dɪˈfaɪlmənt/ N *(lit, fig = pollution)* souillure *f (liter)* ; *(= desecration)* profanation *f*

definable /dɪˈfaɪnəbl/ ADJ définissable

define /dɪˈfaɪn/ VT [1] *(= describe, characterize) [+ word, feeling, attitude]* définir ; *[+ responsibilities, conditions]* définir, déterminer ; *[+ functions]* définir ; *[+ boundaries, powers, duties]* délimiter, définir ; *[+ problem]* délimiter, cerner ◆ **an agreement that ~s how much they are**

paid un accord qui détermine le niveau des salaires ◆ **the legislation does not ~ what exactly is meant by the term "depression"** la loi ne précise pas exactement ce que recouvre le terme "dépression" ◆ **she doesn't ~ herself as a feminist** elle ne se définit pas comme une féministe ◆ **how would you ~ yourself politically?** comment vous définiriez-vous *or* où vous situez-vous d'un point de vue politique ? [2] *(= outline)* dessiner *or* dégager (les formes de) ◆ **the tower was clearly ~d against the sky** la tour se détachait nettement sur le ciel

definite /ˈdefɪnɪt/ ADJ [1] *(= fixed, certain) [plan]* précis ; *[intention, order, sale]* ferme ◆ **is that ~?** c'est certain *or* sûr ? ◆ **have you got a ~ date for the wedding?** avez-vous décidé de la date du mariage ? ◆ **12 August is ~ for the trip** le voyage aura lieu le 12 août, c'est sûr ◆ **nothing ~** rien de précis [2] *(= distinct, appreciable) [impression, feeling, increase]* net ; *[advantage]* certain ◆ **a ~ improvement** une nette amélioration ◆ **it's a ~ possibility** c'est tout à fait possible [3] *(= positive, emphatic) [person, tone]* catégorique ; *[manner]* ferme ; *[views]* arrêté ◆ **to be ~ about sth** être catégorique à propos de qch [4] *(Gram)* **past ~ (tense)** prétérit *m*
COMP **definite article** N *(Gram)* article *m* défini
definite integral N *(Math)* intégrale *f* définie

definitely /ˈdefɪnɪtlɪ/ ADV [1] *(expressing an intention) [decide, agree, say]* de manière définitive ◆ **is he ~ coming?** est-il sûr *or* certain qu'il va venir ? ◆ **I'm ~ going to get in touch with them** j'ai la ferme intention de les contacter ◆ **probably next week, but not ~** sans doute la semaine prochaine, mais rien n'est encore décidé *or* mais sous toute réserve [2] *(expressing an opinion)* vraiment ◆ **you ~ need a holiday** tu as vraiment besoin de vacances ◆ **she's ~ more intelligent than her brother** elle est plus intelligente que son frère, c'est sûr, elle est indéniablement plus intelligente que son frère ◆ **~ not** certainement pas ◆ **~!** *(= I agree)* absolument !, tout à fait ! [3] *(= emphatically) [deny, refuse, say]* catégoriquement

definition /ˌdefɪˈnɪʃən/ N [1] *[of word, concept]* définition *f* ◆ **by ~** par définition [2] *[of powers, boundaries, duties]* délimitation *f* [3] *(Phot, TV)* définition *f*

definitive /dɪˈfɪnɪtɪv/ ADJ [1] *(= definite) [answer, refusal etc]* définitif [2] *(= authoritative) [map, authority etc]* de référence, qui fait autorité

definitively /dɪˈfɪnɪtɪvlɪ/ ADV de façon absolue

deflate /diːˈfleɪt/ VT [1] *[+ tyre]* dégonfler ◆ **~d tyre** pneu *m* dégonflé *or* à plat [2] *(Fin)* **to ~ the currency** provoquer une déflation monétaire [3] * *[+ person]* démonter, rabattre le caquet à VI se dégonfler

deflated /diːˈfleɪtɪd/ ADJ [1] *(= flat) [tyre]* dégonflé, à plat [2] *(= downcast)* découragé

deflation /diːˈfleɪʃən/ N [1] *(Econ)* déflation *f* [2] *[of tyre, ball]* dégonflement *m*

deflationary /diːˈfleɪʃənərɪ/ ADJ *[measures, policy]* déflationniste

deflationist /diːˈfleɪʃənɪst/ ADJ déflationniste

deflator /diːˈfleɪtəʳ/ N déflateur *m*, mesure *f* déflationniste

deflect /dɪˈflekt/ VT *[+ ball, projectile]* faire dévier ; *[+ stream]* détourner ; *[+ light]* défléchir, dévier ; *[+ person]* détourner *(from* de) VI dévier ; *[magnetic needle]* décliner

deflection /dɪˈflekʃən/ N *[of projectile]* déviation *f* ; *[of light]* déflexion *f*, déviation *f* ; *[of magnetic needle]* déclinaison *f* (magnétique), déviation *f*

deflector /dɪˈflektəʳ/ N déflecteur *m*

defloration /ˌdiːflɔːˈreɪʃən/ N *(lit, fig)* défloration *f*

deflower /diːˈflaʊəʳ/ VT [1] *(liter) [+ girl]* déflorer [2] *[+ plant]* défleurir

defoliant /diːˈfəʊlɪənt/ N défoliant *m*

defoliate /diːˈfəʊlɪeɪt/ VT défolier

defoliation /ˌdiːfəʊlɪˈeɪʃən/ N défoliation *f*

deforest /diːˈfɒrɪst/ VT déboiser

deforestation /diːˌfɒrɪstˈeɪʃən/ N déboisement *m*

deform /dɪˈfɔːm/ VT *[gen]* déformer ; *(Tech) [+ machine part, metal component]* fausser

deformation /ˌdiːfɔːˈmeɪʃən/ N déformation *f*

deformed /dɪˈfɔːmd/ ADJ *[person, limb, bones, body]* difforme ; *[mind, structure]* déformé, tordu

deformity /dɪˈfɔːmɪtɪ/ N *[of body]* difformité *f* ; *[of mind]* déformation *f*

DEFRA /ˈdefrə/ N *(Brit)* (abbrev of **Department for Environment, Food and Rural Affairs**) ministère *m* de l'Agriculture

defraud /dɪˈfrɔːd/ VT *[+ state]* frauder ; *[+ person]* escroquer ◆ **to ~ sb of sth** escroquer qch à qn, frustrer qn de qch *(Jur)* ; → **conspiracy**

defrauder /dɪˈfrɔːdəʳ/ N fraudeur *m*, -euse *f*

defray /dɪˈfreɪ/ VT *[+ expenses]* payer, rembourser ; *[+ cost]* couvrir ◆ **to ~ sb's expenses** défrayer qn, rembourser ses frais à qn

defrayal /dɪˈfreɪəl/, **defrayment** /dɪˈfreɪmənt/ N paiement *m or* remboursement *m* des frais

defrock /diːˈfrɒk/ VT défroquer

defrost /diːˈfrɒst/ VT *[+ refrigerator, windscreen]* dégivrer ; *[+ meat, vegetables]* décongeler VI *[fridge]* se dégivrer ; *[frozen food]* se décongeler

defroster /diːˈfrɒstəʳ/ N *(in car)* dégivreur *m* ; *(US = demister)* dispositif *m* antibuée

deft /deft/ ADJ habile, adroit

deftly /ˈdeftlɪ/ ADV adroitement

deftness /ˈdeftnɪs/ N adresse *f*, dextérité *f*

defunct /dɪˈfʌŋkt/ ADJ *[organization, company, publication]* défunt *before n*, ancien ; *[practice]* révolu ; *[policy, tradition]* dépassé ; *[factory]* désaffecté ◆ **the ~ Soviet Union** l'ex-Union soviétique ◆ **the special relationship between Russia and Cuba is now ~** la relation privilégiée entre la Russie et Cuba n'existe plus *or* est révolue N *(frm)* ◆ **the ~** le défunt, la défunte

defuse /diːˈfjuːz/ VT *[+ bomb]* désamorcer ◆ **to ~ the situation** désamorcer la situation

defy /dɪˈfaɪ/ VT [1] *(= disobey) [+ law, authority, convention]* défier ; *[+ person]* désobéir à ; *[+ orders]* désobéir à, braver ; *[+ curfew]* ne pas respecter ; *(= stand up to) [+ person]* défier ◆ **she was bold enough to stand up and ~ him** elle a osé le défier ◆ **she defied him and spoke publicly about her ordeal** elle lui a désobéi en parlant ouvertement de son épreuve ◆ **to ~ death** *(= face without fear)* braver la mort ; *(= narrowly escape)* frôler *or* échapper de justesse à la mort ◆ **the virus has defied all attempts to find a vaccine** jusqu'à maintenant, ce virus a résisté à tous les efforts qu'on a fait pour trouver un vaccin

[2] *(= contradict, go beyond) [+ logic]* défier ◆ **to ~ gravity** défier les lois de la gravité ◆ **it defies description** cela défie toute description ◆ **that defies belief!** cela dépasse l'entendement !, c'est incroyable !

[3] *(= challenge)* **to ~ sb to do sth** défier qn de faire qch, mettre qn au défi de faire qch

[4] *(liter)* **to ~ one's age** *or* **the years** ne pas faire son âge

degeneracy /dɪˈdʒenərəsɪ/ N dégénérescence *f*

degenerate /dɪˈdʒenəreɪt/ VI *[people]* dégénérer *(into* en) s'abâtardir ; *[situation]* dégénérer ◆ **the situation ~d into civil war/rioting/violence** la situation a dégénéré en guerre civile/en émeutes/dans la violence ◆ **the demonstration ~d into violence** la manifestation a dégénéré (dans la violence) ◆ **the election campaign has ~d into farce** la campagne électorale a tourné à la farce ADJ /dɪˈdʒenərɪt/ dégénéré N /dɪˈdʒenərɪt/ dégénéré(e) *m(f)*

degeneration /dɪˌdʒenəˈreɪʃən/ N *[of mind, body, morals, people]* dégénérescence *f*

degenerative /dɪˈdʒenərətɪv/ ADJ dégénératif

degradable /dɪˈgreɪdəbl/ ADJ dégradable

degradation /ˌdegrəˈdeɪʃən/ N [1] *(= process of worsening: Chem, Geol, Mil, Phys)* dégradation *f* ; *[of person]* déchéance *f* ; *[of character]* avilissement *m* ◆ **environmental ~** dégradation *f* de l'environnement [2] *(= debasement)* déchéance *f*, avilissement *m* ; *(= humiliation)* humiliation *f* ◆ **the moral ~ of our society** la déchéance morale de notre société ◆ **the ~ of prison life** le caractère dégradant de la vie carcérale ◆ **sexual ~** avilissement *m* sexuel ◆ **the ~ of having to accept charity** l'humiliation d'avoir à accepter la charité ◆ **the ~s she had been forced to suffer** les humiliations qu'elle avait été obligée de subir

degrade /dɪˈgreɪd/ VT [1] *(= debase)* avilir, dégrader *(liter)* ◆ **he felt ~d** il se sentait avili *or* dégradé ◆ **he ~d himself by accepting it** il s'est avili *or* dégradé en l'acceptant ◆ **I wouldn't ~ myself by doing that** je n'irais pas m'avilir *or* m'abaisser à faire cela [2] *(Chem, Geol, Phys)* dégrader; *[+ environnement]* dégrader [3] *[+ official]* dégrader ; *(Mil) [+ officer]* dégrader, casser; *[+ military capability]* réduire VI *(= break down)* se dégrader

degrading /dɪˈgreɪdɪŋ/ ADJ dégradant *(to* pour)

degree /dɪˈgriː/ N [1] *(Geog, Math)* degré *m* ◆ **angle of 90 ~s** angle *m* de 90 degrés ◆ **40 ~s east of Greenwich** à 40 degrés de longitude est (de Greenwich) ◆ **20 ~s of latitude** 20 degrés de latitude ◆ **a 180-~ turn** *(fig)* un virage à 180 degrés

[2] *[of temperature]* degré *m* ◆ **it was 35 ~s in the shade** il faisait 35 (degrés) à l'ombre ◆ **he's got a temperature of 39 ~s** il a 39 de fièvre

[3] *(= amount)* degré *m* ◆ **some ~** *or* **a (certain) ~ of independence/optimism/freedom** un certain degré d'indépendance/d'optimisme/de liberté ◆ **with varying ~s of success** avec plus ou moins de succès ◆ **a fairly high ~ of error** d'assez nombreuses erreurs, un taux d'erreurs assez élevé ◆ **a considerable ~ of doubt** des doutes considérables ◆ **his ~ of commitment was low** il ne se sentait pas vraiment engagé à fond ◆ **I couldn't summon up the least ~ of enthusiasm for his idea** je n'arrivais pas à éprouver le moindre enthousiasme pour son idée ◆ **to do sth by ~s** faire qch petit à petit ◆ **to some ~, to a (certain) ~** dans une certaine mesure ◆ **he possesses to a high ~ the art of putting people at their ease** il possède au plus haut degré l'art de mettre les gens à l'aise ◆ **the departments are independent to a very high ~** les services sont, dans une large mesure, indépendants ◆ **to such a ~ that ...** à (un) tel point que ...

[4] *(Med)* ◆ **first-/second-/third-~ burns** brûlures *fpl* au premier/deuxième/troisième degré ; see also **third**

[5] *(US Jur)* ◆ **first-~ murder, murder in the first ~** assassinat *m*, meurtre *m* avec préméditation ◆ **second-~ murder, murder in the second ~** meurtre *m* (sans préméditation)

[6] *(Univ)* diplôme *m* (universitaire), titre *m* universitaire ◆ **first ~** ≃ licence *f* ◆ **higher ~** *(= master's)* ≃ maîtrise *f* ; *(= doctorate)* ≃ doctorat *m* ◆ **~ in** licence *f* de ◆ **I'm taking a science ~** *or* **a ~ in science** je fais une licence de sciences ◆ **he got his ~** il a eu son diplôme ◆ **he got his ~ in geography** il a eu sa licence de géographie ; → **honorary**

[7] *(Gram)* degré *m* ◆ **three ~s of comparison** trois degrés de comparaison

[8] *(liter = position in society)* rang *m* ◆ **of high ~** de haut rang ◆ **of low ~** de rang inférieur

9 *(in genealogy)* ◆ **~s of kinship** degrés *mpl* de parenté

COMP **degree ceremony** N *(Brit Univ)* cérémonie *f* de remise des diplômes

degree course N *(Brit Univ)* ◆ **to do a ~ course (in)** faire une licence (de) ◆ **the ~ course consists of ...** le cursus (universitaire) consiste en ...

degree mill N *(US pej)* usine *f* à diplômes

DEGREE

Dans les systèmes universitaires britannique et américain, le premier titre universitaire (obtenu après trois ou quatre années d'études supérieures) est le « bachelor's **degree** », qui permet à l'étudiant en lettres de devenir « Bachelor of Arts » (« BA » en Grande-Bretagne, « AB » aux États-Unis) et à l'étudiant en sciences ou en sciences humaines d'être un « Bachelor of Science » (« BSc » en Grande-Bretagne, « BS » aux États-Unis). L'année suivante débouche sur les diplômes de « Master of Arts » (« MA ») et de « Master of Science » (« MSc » en Grande-Bretagne, « MS » aux États-Unis).

degressive /dɪˈgresɪv/ ADJ *[taxation]* dégressif

dehumanization /diːˌhjuːmənaɪˈzeɪʃən/ N déshumanisation *f*

dehumanize /diːˈhjuːmənaɪz/ VT déshumaniser

dehumanizing /diːˈhjuːmənaɪzɪŋ/ ADJ déshumanisant

dehumidifier /ˌdiːhjuːˈmɪdɪfaɪəʳ/ N *(= machine)* déshumidificateur *m*

dehumidify /ˌdiːhjuːˈmɪdɪfaɪ/ VT déshumidifier

dehydrate /ˌdiːhaɪˈdreɪt/ VT déshydrater

dehydrated /ˌdiːhaɪˈdreɪtɪd/ ADJ *[person, skin, vegetables]* déshydraté ; *[milk, eggs]* en poudre

dehydration /ˌdiːhaɪˈdreɪʃən/ N déshydratation *f*

de-ice /ˈdiːˈaɪs/ VT *[+ car, plane]* dégivrer

de-icer /ˈdiːˈaɪsəʳ/ N *(for car, plane)* dégivreur *m*

de-icing /ˈdiːˈaɪsɪŋ/ N *[of car, plane]* dégivrage *m*

COMP **de-icing fluid** N antigel *m*

deictic /ˈdaɪktɪk/ N *(Ling)* déictique *m*

deification /ˌdiːɪfɪˈkeɪʃən/ N déification *f*

deify /ˈdiːɪfaɪ/ VT déifier, diviniser

deign /deɪn/ VT daigner *(to do sth* faire qch*)* condescendre *(to do sth* à faire qch*)*

de-indexation /ˌdiːɪndekˈseɪʃən/ N désindexation *f*

deism /ˈdiːɪzəm/ N déisme *m*

deist /ˈdiːɪst/ N déiste *mf*

deity /ˈdiːɪtɪ/ N 1 *(Myth, Rel)* divinité *f*, déité *f (liter)* ◆ **the Deity** Dieu *m* 2 *(NonC)* divinité *f*

deixis /ˈdaɪksɪs/ N *(Ling)* deixis *f*

déjà vu /ˌdeɪʒɑːˈvuː/ N déjà(-)vu *m* ◆ **I had a feeling** *or* **a sense of ~** j'avais une impression de déjà(-)vu

dejected /dɪˈdʒektɪd/ ADJ abattu, découragé ◆ **to become** *or* **get ~** se décourager, se laisser abattre

dejectedly /dɪˈdʒektɪdlɪ/ ADV *[say, talk]* d'un ton abattu ; *[look]* d'un air abattu

dejection /dɪˈdʒekʃən/ N abattement *m*, découragement *m*

de jure /ˌdeɪˈdʒʊərɪ/ ADJ, ADV de jure

dekko‡ /ˈdekəʊ/ N *(Brit)* petit coup *m* d'œil ◆ **let's have a ~** fais voir ça, on va (y) jeter un œil*

Del. abbrev of **Delaware**

Delaware /ˈdeləˌwɛəʳ/ N Delaware *m* ◆ **in ~** dans le Delaware

delay /dɪˈleɪ/ VT 1 *(= postpone) [+ action, event]* retarder, différer ; *[+ payment]* différer ◆ **~ed effect** effet *m* à retardement ◆ **to ~ doing sth** tarder à faire qch, remettre qch à plus tard

2 *(= keep waiting, hold up) [+ person, traffic]* retarder, retenir ; *[+ train, plane]* retarder ◆ **I don't want to ~ you** je ne veux pas vous retenir *or* retarder

VI s'attarder *(in doing sth* en faisant qch*)* ◆ **don't ~!** dépêchez-vous !

N retard *m* ◆ **after two or three ~s** après deux ou trois arrêts ◆ **there will be ~s to trains on the London-Brighton line** on prévoit des retards sur la ligne Londres-Brighton ◆ **there will be ~s to traffic** il y aura des ralentissements (de la circulation), la circulation sera ralentie ◆ **"delays possible (until Dec 2001)"** *(on road sign)* "ralentissements possibles (jusqu'en décembre 2001)" ◆ **with as little ~ as possible** dans les plus brefs délais ◆ **there's no time for ~** il n'y a pas de temps à perdre ◆ **without ~** sans délai ◆ **without further ~** sans plus tarder *or* attendre ◆ **they arrived with an hour's ~** ils sont arrivés avec une heure de retard

COMP **delayed-action** ADJ *[bomb, fuse]* à retardement

delayed-action shutter N *(Phot)* obturateur *m* à retardement

⚠ **delay** is rarely translated by **délai**, which usually means 'time allowed'.

delaying /dɪˈleɪɪŋ/ ADJ *[action]* dilatoire, qui retarde ◆ **~ tactics** moyens *mpl* dilatoires

delectable /dɪˈlektəbl/ ADJ *(liter or hum) [food, drink]* délectable *(liter or hum)* ◆ **the ~ Miss Campbell** la délicieuse Mlle Campbell

delectation /ˌdiːlekˈteɪʃən/ N délectation *f*

delegate /ˈdelɪgeɪt/ VT *[+ authority, power]* déléguer *(to* à*)* ◆ **to ~ responsibility** déléguer les responsabilités ◆ **to ~ sb to do sth** déléguer qn pour faire qch VI déléguer ses responsabilités

N /ˈdelɪgɪt/ délégué(e) *m(f) (to* à*)* ◆ **~ to a congress** congressiste *mf*

delegation /ˌdelɪˈgeɪʃən/ N 1 *(NonC) [of power]* délégation *f* ; *[of person]* nomination *f*, désignation *f (as comme)* 2 *(= group of delegates)* délégation *f*

delete /dɪˈliːt/ VT *(gen)* effacer *(from* de*)* ; *(= score out)* barrer, rayer *(from* de*)* ; *(Gram, Comput)* supprimer, effacer ◆ **"delete where inapplicable"** *(on forms etc)* "rayer les mentions inutiles"

deleterious /ˌdelɪˈtɪərɪəs/ ADJ *[effect, influence]* nuisible, délétère *(to* à*)* ; *[gas]* délétère

deletion /dɪˈliːʃən/ N 1 *(NonC)* effacement *m* 2 *(= thing deleted)* rature *f*

delft /delft/ N faïence *f* de Delft COMP **Delft blue** N *(= colour)* bleu *m* (de) faïence

Delhi /ˈdelɪ/ N Delhi COMP **Delhi belly*** N turista* *f*, maladie *f* du touriste

deli* /ˈdelɪ/ N (abbrev of **delicatessen**) épicerie *f* fine, traiteur *m*

deliberate /dɪˈlɪbərɪt/ ADJ 1 *(= intentional) [action, insult, lie]* délibéré ◆ **it wasn't ~** ce n'était pas fait exprès 2 *(= cautious, thoughtful) [action, decision]* bien pesé, mûrement réfléchi ; *[character, judgement]* réfléchi, circonspect ; *(= slow, purposeful) [air, voice]* décidé ; *[manner, walk]* mesuré, posé VI /dɪˈlɪbəreɪt/ 1 *(= think)* délibérer, réfléchir *(upon* sur*)* 2 *(= discuss)* délibérer, tenir conseil ; *[jury]* délibérer ◆ **the jury ~d over their verdict** le jury a délibéré VT /dɪˈlɪbəreɪt/ 1 *(= study)* considérer, examiner 2 *(= discuss)* délibérer sur, débattre ◆ **The jury will begin deliberating the case today** le jury va commencer ses délibérations *or* à délibérer aujourd'hui ◆ **I was deliberating whether or not to tell her** j'étais en train de me demander si je devais le lui dire

deliberately /dɪˈlɪbərɪtlɪ/ ADV 1 *(= on purpose)* délibérément ◆ **I didn't do it ~** je ne l'ai pas fait exprès ◆ **~ vague** délibérément vague 2 *(= purposefully)* posément

deliberation /dɪˌlɪbəˈreɪʃən/ N 1 *(= consideration)* délibération *f*, réflexion *f* ◆ **after due** *or* **careful ~** après mûre réflexion 2 *(= discussion: gen pl)* **~s** débats *mpl* ; *[of jury]* délibérations *fpl* ◆ **the EC Foreign Ministers' ~s** le débat entre les ministres des Affaires étrangères de la Communauté européenne 3 *(= slowness)* mesure *f* ◆ **with ~** posément

deliberative /dɪˈlɪbərətɪv/ ADJ *[assembly, body]* délibérante

delicacy /ˈdelɪkəsɪ/ N 1 *(NonC)* délicatesse *f* ; *(= fragility)* fragilité *f*, délicatesse *f* ◆ **a matter of some ~** une affaire assez délicate 2 *(= special dish)* mets *m* délicat ◆ **a great ~** un mets très délicat

delicate /ˈdelɪkɪt/ ADJ 1 *(= fine, subtle) [object, movement, colour, flavour, touch]* délicat 2 *(= easily damaged, not robust) [china, skin, fabric, person, health]* fragile, délicat ◆ **in a ~ condition** († *= pregnant)* dans une position intéressante † 3 *(= touchy, tricky) [situation, negotiations]* délicat 4 *(= sensitive) [instrument, sense]* délicat ; *[compass]* sensible

delicately /ˈdelɪkɪtlɪ/ ADV 1 *(= subtly, daintily)* délicatement ◆ **~ flavoured** délicatement parfumé 2 *(= tactfully)* avec tact *or* délicatesse ◆ **~ worded** formulé avec tact *or* délicatesse

delicatessen /ˌdelɪkəˈtesn/ N *(= shop)* épicerie *f* fine, traiteur *m*

delicious /dɪˈlɪʃəs/ ADJ délicieux

deliciously /dɪˈlɪʃəslɪ/ ADV *(lit, fig)* délicieusement ◆ **~ creamy** délicieusement crémeux ◆ **~ ironic** d'une ironie délicieuse

delight /dɪˈlaɪt/ N 1 *(= intense pleasure)* grand plaisir *m*, joie *f* ◆ **to my ~** à *or* pour ma plus grande joie ◆ **to take (a) ~ in sth/in doing sth** prendre grand plaisir à qch/à faire qch ◆ **with ~** *(gen)* avec joie ; *(more sensual) [taste, smell]* avec délices ◆ **to give ~** charmer

2 *(= source of pleasure: often pl)* délice *m*, joie *f* ◆ **she is the ~ of her mother** elle fait la joie de sa mère ◆ **this book is an absolute ~** ce livre est vraiment merveilleux ◆ **a ~ to the eyes** un régal *or* un plaisir pour les yeux ◆ **he's a ~ to watch** il fait plaisir à voir ◆ **the ~s of life in the open air** les charmes *or* les délices *(liter)* de la vie en plein air

VT *[+ person]* enchanter, ravir ; → **delighted**

VI prendre plaisir *(in sth* à qch ; *in doing sth* à faire qch*)* se délecter *(in sth* de qch ; *in doing sth* à faire qch*)* ◆ **she ~s in him/it** il/cela lui donne beaucoup de joie ◆ **they ~ed in the scandal** ils se sont délectés du scandale

delighted /dɪˈlaɪtɪd/ LANGUAGE IN USE 11.3, 23.6, 25.1, 25.2 ADJ ravi, enchanté *(with, at, by* de, par ; *to do sth* de faire qch ; *that* que + *subj)* ◆ **absolutely ~!** tout à fait ravi ! ◆ **~ to meet you!** enchanté (de faire votre connaissance) ! ◆ **will you go? – (I shall be) ~** voulez-vous y aller ? – avec grand plaisir *or* très volontiers

delightedly /dɪˈlaɪtɪdlɪ/ ADV avec ravissement

delightful /dɪˈlaɪtfʊl/ ADJ charmant ◆ **it's ~ to ...** c'est merveilleux de ...

delightfully /dɪˈlaɪtfəlɪ/ ADV *[friendly, vague]* délicieusement ; *[arranged, decorated]* d'une façon ravissante ; *[smile, behave]* de façon charmante

Delilah /dɪˈlaɪlə/ N Dalila *f*

delimit /diːˈlɪmɪt/ VT délimiter

delimitation /ˌdiːlɪmɪˈteɪʃən/ N délimitation *f*

delineate /dɪˈlɪnɪeɪt/ VT 1 *(= describe) [+ character]* représenter, dépeindre ; *[+ plan etc] (= present)* présenter ; *(in more detail)* énoncer en détail ; (*with diagram etc*) représenter graphiquement [2] (*= define*) [*+ border, area*] définir ◆ **the frontier between the two nations is still not clearly ~d** la frontière entre les deux nations n'est pas encore bien définie ◆ **mountains clearly ~d** montagnes *fpl* qui se détachent clairement à l'horizon

delineation /dɪ,lɪnɪ'eɪʃən/ N [*of outline*] dessin *m*, tracé *m* ; [*of plan*] présentation *f* (détaillée) ; [*of character*] description *f*, peinture *f*

delinquency /dɪ'lɪŋkwənsɪ/ N [1] (*NonC*) délinquance *f* ; → **juvenile** [2] (*= act of delinquency*) faute *f*, délit *m* [3] (*US Fin = failure to pay*) défaillance *f*, défaut *m* de paiement

delinquent /dɪ'lɪŋkwənt/ ADJ [1] délinquant ; → **juvenile** [2] (*US Fin*) [*debtor*] défaillant ; [*payment*] arriéré, impayé, échu N [1] délinquant(e) *m(f)* ; (*fig*) coupable *mf*, fautif *m*, -ive *f* [2] (*US Fin*) défaillant(e) *m(f)*

deliquescence /,delɪ'kwesəns/ N déliquescence *f*

delirious /dɪ'lɪrɪəs/ ADJ [1] (*Med*) délirant ◆ **to be ~** délirer [2] (*fig = ecstatic*) ◆ **to be ~ (with joy)** délirer de joie, être ivre de joie ; [*crowd*] être en délire

deliriously /dɪ'lɪrɪəslɪ/ ADV [1] (*fig = ecstatically*) avec une joie délirante ◆ **~ happy** fou de joie [2] (*Med*) **to rave ~ about sth** délirer en parlant de qch

delirium /dɪ'lɪrɪəm/ N (pl **delirium** or **deliria** /dɪ'lɪrɪə/) (*Med, fig*) délire *m* ◆ **bout of ~** accès *m* de délire ◆ **~ tremens** delirium *m* tremens

delist /di:'lɪst/ VT [*+ security on Stock Exchange*] radier du registre (des valeurs cotées en Bourse)

deliver /dɪ'lɪvəʳ/ LANGUAGE IN USE 20.4

VT [1] (*= take*) remettre (*to* à) ; [*+ letters etc*] distribuer (*à domicile*) ; [*+ goods*] livrer ◆ **to ~ a message to sb** remettre un message à qn ◆ **milk is ~ed each day** le lait est livré tous les jours ◆ **"we deliver daily"** (*Comm*) "livraisons quotidiennes" ◆ **"delivered free"** "livraison gratuite" ◆ **I will ~ the children to school tomorrow** j'emmènerai les enfants à l'école demain ◆ **to ~ a child (over) into sb's care** confier un enfant aux soins de qn ◆ **to ~ the goods*** (*fig*) être à la hauteur

[2] (*= rescue*) délivrer, sauver (*sb from sth* qn de qch) ◆ **~ us from evil** délivrez-nous du mal

[3] (*= utter*) [*+ speech, sermon*] prononcer ◆ **to ~ an ultimatum** lancer un ultimatum ◆ **to ~ o.s. of an opinion** (*frm*) émettre une opinion

[4] (*Med*) [*+ baby*] mettre au monde ; [*+ woman*] (faire) accoucher ◆ **to be ~ed of a son** (*frm*) accoucher d'un fils

[5] (*= hand over*: also **deliver over, deliver up**) remettre, transmettre ◆ **to ~ a town (up or over) into the hands of the enemy** livrer une ville à l'ennemi ; → **stand**

[6] [*+ blow*] porter, assener

VI (** = do what is expected*) [*person, nation, government etc*] être à la hauteur (*on sth* quant à qch) ◆ **the match promised great things but didn't ~** le match promettait beaucoup mais n'a pas été à la hauteur (de ce qu'on en attendait)

⚠ **to deliver** is rarely translated by the French word **délivrer**.

deliverance /dɪ'lɪvərəns/ N [1] (*NonC*) délivrance *f*, libération *f* (*from* de) [2] (*= statement of opinion*) déclaration *f* (formelle) ; (*Jur*) prononcé *m* (du jugement)

deliverer /dɪ'lɪvərəʳ/ N [1] (*= saviour*) sauveur *m*, libérateur *m*, -trice *f* [2] (*Comm*) livreur *m*

delivery /dɪ'lɪvərɪ/ LANGUAGE IN USE 20.4, 20.5

N [1] [*of goods*] livraison *f* ; [*of parcels*] remise *f*, livraison *f* ; [*of letters*] distribution *f* ◆ **to take ~ of** prendre livraison de ◆ **to pay on ~** payer à la or sur livraison ◆ **payable on ~** payable à la livraison ◆ **price on ~** (*gen*) prix *m* à la livraison ; (*of car*) prix *m* clés en main ; → **charge, free**

[2] (*Med*) accouchement *m*

[3] (*NonC*) [*of speaker*] débit *m*, élocution *f* ; [*of speech*] débit *m* ◆ **his speech was interesting but his ~ dreary** son discours était intéressant mais son débit monotone

COMP **delivery charge** N frais *mpl* de port
delivery man N (pl **delivery men**) livreur *m*
delivery note N bulletin *m* de livraison
delivery order N bon *m* de livraison
delivery room N (*Med*) salle *f* d'accouchement
delivery service N service *m* de livraison
delivery time N délai *m* de livraison
delivery truck (*esp US*), **delivery van** N camionnette *f* de livraison

dell /del/ N vallon *m*

delouse /'di:'laʊs/ VT [*+ person, animal*] épouiller ; [*+ object*] ôter les poux de

Delphi /'delfaɪ/ N Delphes

Delphic /'delfɪk/ ADJ [*oracle*] de Delphes ; (*fig liter*) obscur

delphinium /del'fɪnɪəm/ N (pl **delphiniums** or **delphinia** /del'fɪnɪə/) pied-d'alouette *m*, delphinium *m*

delta /'deltə/ N delta *m* COMP **delta-winged** ADJ [*plane*] à ailes (en) delta

deltoid /'deltɔɪd/ ADJ, N deltoïde *m*

delude /dɪ'lu:d/ VT tromper (*with* par) induire en erreur (*with* par) ◆ **to ~ sb into thinking that ...** amener qn à penser que ..., faire croire à qn que ... ◆ **to ~ o.s.** se faire des illusions, se bercer d'illusions ◆ **to ~ o.s. that ...** s'imaginer que ... ◆ **we mustn't ~ ourselves that ...** il ne faut pas s'imaginer que ...

deluded /dɪ'lu:dɪd/ ADJ ◆ **to be ~** être victime d'illusions, être bercé d'illusions

deluding /dɪ'lu:dɪŋ/ ADJ trompeur, illusoire

deluge /'delju:dʒ/ N (*lit*) déluge *m*, inondation *f* ; (*fig*) déluge *m* ◆ **the Deluge** le déluge ◆ **a ~ of rain** une pluie diluvienne ◆ **a ~ of protests** un déluge de protestations ◆ **a ~ of letters** une avalanche de lettres VT (*lit, fig*) inonder, submerger (*with* de)

delusion /dɪ'lu:ʒən/ N (*= false belief*) illusion *f* ; (*Psych*) délire *m* ◆ **to suffer from ~s** se faire des illusions ; (*Psych*) avoir des crises de délire ◆ **to be (labouring) under a ~** être victime d'une illusion, être le jouet d'une illusion ◆ **he seems to be labouring under the ~ that I have already asked him this question** on dirait qu'il croit que je lui ai déjà posé la question ◆ **~s of grandeur** folie *f* des grandeurs

delusional /,dɪ'lu:ʒənəl/ ADJ délirant ◆ **~ jealousy** jalousie *f* délirante

delusive /dɪ'lu:sɪv/ ADJ trompeur, illusoire

delusiveness /dɪ'lu:sɪvnɪs/ N caractère *m* trompeur or illusoire

delusory /dɪ'lu:sərɪ/ ADJ trompeur, illusoire

de luxe /dɪ'lʌks/ ADJ de luxe ◆ **a ~ flat** un appartement (de) grand standing ◆ **~ model** (*car, machine*) modèle *m* (de) grand luxe, modèle *m* de luxe

delve /delv/ VI [1] (*into book, sb's past*) fouiller (*into* dans) ◆ **to ~ into a subject** creuser or approfondir un sujet ◆ **to ~ into the past** fouiller dans le passé [2] (*in drawer etc*) fouiller (*into* dans) ◆ **to ~ into one's pockets** (*lit*) fouiller dans ses poches ; (*fig*) mettre la main au portefeuille [3] (*= dig*) creuser (*into* dans) ; (*with spade*) bêcher

Dem. (*US Pol*) N abbrev of **Democrat** ADJ abbrev of **Democratic**

demagnetize /,di:'mægnɪtaɪz/ VT démagnétiser

demagog /'deməgɒg/ N (*US*) ⇒ **demagogue**

demagogic /,demə'gɒgɪk/ ADJ démagogique

demagogue, demagog (*US*) /'deməgɒg/ N démagogue *mf*

demagoguery /,demə'gɒgərɪ/ N démagogie *f*

demagogy /'deməgɒgɪ/ N démagogie *f*

de-man /,di:'mæn/ VT [1] (*Brit Ind = reduce manpower*) réduire or dégraisser les effectifs de [2] (*= deprive of virility*) déviriliser

demand /dɪ'mɑ:nd/ VT [*+ money, explanation, help*] exiger, réclamer (*from, of* de) ; [*+ higher pay etc*] revendiquer, réclamer ◆ **to ~ an apology** exiger des excuses ◆ **to ~ to do sth** exiger de faire qch ◆ **he ~s to be obeyed** il exige qu'on lui obéisse ◆ **he ~s that you leave at once** il exige que vous partiez *subj* tout de suite ◆ **a question/situation that ~s our attention** une question/une situation qui réclame or demande notre attention ◆ **« what do you expect me to do about it? » she ~ed** « que voulez-vous que j'y fasse ? », demanda-t-elle

N [1] [*of person*] exigence(s) *f(pl)*, demande *f* ; [*of duty, problem, situation*] exigence(s) *fpl* ; (*= claim*) (*for better pay etc*) revendication *f*, réclamation *f* ; (*for help, money*) demande *f* ◆ **to feed a baby on ~** allaiter un bébé quand il le demande ◆ **payable on ~** payable sur demande or sur présentation ◆ **final ~ (for payment)** dernier avertissement *m* (d'avoir à payer) ◆ **to make ~s on sb** exiger beaucoup de qn or de la part de qn ◆ **you make too great ~s on my patience** vous abusez de ma patience ◆ **the ~s of the case** les nécessités *fpl* du cas ◆ **I have many ~s on my time** je suis très pris, mon temps est très pris

[2] (*NonC: Comm, Econ*) demande *f* ◆ **~ for this product is growing** ce produit est de plus en plus demandé ◆ **to create a ~ for a product** créer la demande pour un produit ◆ **do you stock suede hats? – no, there's no ~ for them** avez-vous des chapeaux en daim ? – non, il n'y a pas de demande ; → **supply¹**

[3] ◆ **to be in (great) ~** être très demandé

COMP **demand bill, demand draft** N (*Fin*) bon *m* or effet *m* à vue
demand feeding N allaitement *m* à la demande
demand liabilities NPL engagements *mpl* à vue
demand management N (*Econ*) contrôle *m* (gouvernemental) de la demande
demand note N ⇒ **demand bill**

⚠ **to demand** is rarely translated by **demander**, which simply means 'to ask'.

demanding /dɪ'mɑ:ndɪŋ/ ADJ [1] [*boss, customer*] exigeant ◆ **new services to meet the needs of ever more ~ customers** de nouveaux services destinés à satisfaire les besoins de clients toujours plus exigeants

[2] [*job, responsibility*] **he can no longer cope with his ~ job** il ne peut plus faire face aux exigences de son travail ◆ **his working life was ~** son travail l'accaparait ◆ **she has two ~ children** elle a deux enfants qui l'accaparent

[3] (*= taxing*) difficile ; [*schedule*] éprouvant ◆ **students doing ~ courses** les étudiants qui font des études difficiles ◆ **a very ~ sport such as squash** un sport très éprouvant tel que le squash ◆ **physically ~** physiquement éprouvant, qui demande beaucoup de résistance physique ◆ **intellectually ~** qui demande un gros effort intellectuel ◆ **working with children can be emotionally ~** travailler avec des enfants peut être très éprouvant sur le plan émotionnel

de-manning /,di:'mænɪŋ/ N (*Brit*) licenciements *mpl*, réduction *f* des effectifs

demarcate /ˈdiːmɑːkeɪt/ VT délimiter

demarcation /ˌdiːmɑːˈkeɪʃən/ **N** démarcation *f*, délimitation *f*
COMP **demarcation dispute** N conflit *m* d'attributions
demarcation line N ligne *f* de démarcation

demarche /ˈdeɪmɑːʃ/ N démarche *f*, mesure *f*

dematerialize /ˌdiːməˈtɪərɪəlaɪz/ VI se dématérialiser

demean /dɪˈmiːn/ VT *[+ person]* rabaisser, humilier ; *[+ cause]* dévaloriser ; *[+ thing]* rabaisser ◆ **to ~ o.s.** s'abaisser *(by doing sth* à faire qch)

demeaning /dɪˈmiːnɪŋ/ ADJ dégradant *(to* pour) humiliant *(to* pour)

demeanour, demeanor *(US)* /dɪˈmiːnəʳ/ N *(= behaviour)* comportement *m*, conduite *f* ; *(= bearing)* maintien *m*

demented /dɪˈmentɪd/ ADJ ① *(* = crazy)* fou (folle *f*) ② *(Med)* dément ◆ **to become ~** sombrer dans la démence

dementedly /dɪˈmentɪdlɪ/ ADV comme un fou (*or* une folle)

dementia /dɪˈmenʃɪə/ **N** démence *f* ; → **senile**
COMP **dementia praecox** N démence *f* précoce

demerara /ˌdeməˈreərə/ N *(Brit:* also **demerara sugar**) sucre *m* roux (cristallisé), cassonade *f*

demerge /ˌdiːˈmɜːdʒ/ VT *(Brit) [+ company]* scinder

demerger /ˌdiːˈmɜːdʒəʳ/ N *(Brit)* scission *f*

demerit /diːˈmerɪt/ N démérite *m* ◆ **~ (point)** *(US Scol)* avertissement *m*, blâme *m*

demesne /dɪˈmeɪn/ N domaine *m*, terre *f* ; *(Jur)* possession *f* ◆ **to hold sth in ~** *(Jur)* posséder qch en toute propriété

demi... /ˈdemɪ/ PREF demi- ◆ **demigod** demi-dieu *m*

demijohn /ˈdemɪdʒɒn/ N dame-jeanne *f*, bonbonne *f*

demilitarization /ˈdiːˌmɪlɪtəraɪˈzeɪʃən/ N démilitarisation *f*

demilitarize /diːˈmɪlɪtəraɪz/ **VT** démilitariser
COMP **demilitarized zone** N zone *f* démilitarisée

de-mining /ˌdiːˈmaɪnɪŋ/ N *(= removing landmines)* déminage *m*

demise /dɪˈmaɪz/ **N** ① *(frm, hum = death)* décès *m*, mort *f* ; *(fig) [of institution, custom etc]* mort *f*, fin *f* ② *(Jur) (by legacy)* cession *f or* transfert *m* par legs, transfert *m* par testament ; *(by lease)* transfert *m* par bail ◆ **~ of the Crown** transmission *f* de la Couronne *(par décès ou abdication)*
VT *(Jur) [+ estate]* léguer ; *[+ the Crown, sovereignty]* transmettre

demisemiquaver /ˈdemɪsemɪˌkweɪvəʳ/ N *(Brit)* triple croche *f*

demist /diːˈmɪst/ VT désembuer

demister /diːˈmɪstəʳ/ N *(Brit: in car)* dispositif *m* antibuée

demisting /diːˈmɪstɪŋ/ N désembuage *m*

demitasse /ˈdemɪtæs/ N *(US) (= cup)* tasse *f* (à moka) ; *(= drink)* (tasse *f* de) café *m* noir

demo* /ˈdeməʊ/ N ① *(Brit)* (abbrev of **demonstration**) manif* *f* ② *(US)* ⇒ **demonstration model** ; → **demonstration** ③ *(US)* ⇒ **demolition worker** ; → **demolition** ④ ⇒ **demonstration record** ; → **demonstration**

demob* /ˈdiːˈmɒb/ VT, N *(Brit)* abbrev of **demobilize, demobilization**

demobilization /ˈdiːˌməʊbɪlaɪˈzeɪʃən/ N démobilisation *f*

demobilize /diːˈməʊbɪlaɪz/ VT démobiliser

democracy /dɪˈmɒkrəsɪ/ N démocratie *f* ◆ **they are working towards ~** ils sont en train de se démocratiser ; → **people**

Democrat /ˈdeməkræt/ N ① *(Brit Pol)* (libéral) démocrate *mf* ② *(US Pol)* démocrate *mf*

democrat /ˈdeməkræt/ N démocrate *mf*

democratic /ˌdeməˈkrætɪk/ ADJ ① *(Pol) [institution, organization, spirit]* démocratique ② *(US Pol)* ◆ **Democratic** démocrate ◆ **the Democratic Party** le parti démocrate ◆ **the Democratic Republic of ...** la République démocratique de ... ; see also **Christian, liberal, social** ③ *(= egalitarian) [boss, management style, atmosphere]* démocratique, non directif

democratically /ˌdeməˈkrætɪkəlɪ/ ADV démocratiquement ◆ **~ elected** démocratiquement élu ◆ **to be ~ minded** être démocratique

democratization /dɪˌmɒkrətaɪˈzeɪʃən/ N démocratisation *f*

democratize /dɪˈmɒkrətaɪz/ **VT** démocratiser
VI se démocratiser

demographer /dɪˈmɒgrəfəʳ/ N démographe *mf*

demographic /ˌdeməˈgræfɪk/ **ADJ** démographique **N** tranche *f* de population

demographics /ˌdeməˈgræfɪks/ NPL données *fpl* démographiques ; *[of market]* profil *m* démographique ◆ **the ~ of housing demand** les données démographiques concernant la demande de logement

demography /dɪˈmɒgrəfɪ/ N démographie *f*

demolish /dɪˈmɒlɪʃ/ VT *[+ building]* démolir, abattre ; *[+ fortifications]* démanteler ; *(fig) [+ theory]* démolir, détruire ; * *[+ cake]* liquider*, dire deux mots à*

demolisher /dɪˈmɒlɪʃəʳ/ N *(lit, fig)* démolisseur *m*

demolition /ˌdeməˈlɪʃən/ **N** démolition *f*
COMP **demolition area** N ⇒ **demolition zone**
demolition squad N équipe *f* de démolition
demolition work N (travail *m* de) démolition *f*
demolition worker N démolisseur *m*
demolition zone N zone *f* de démolition

demon /ˈdiːmən/ N *(all senses)* démon *m* ◆ **the old ~s of hate and prejudice** les vieux démons que sont la haine et les préjugés ◆ **his private ~s** ses démons intérieurs ◆ **the ~ drink** l'alcool *m* ◆ **to be a ~ for work** être un bourreau de travail ◆ **a ~ driver** *(skilful)* un as* du volant ; *(dangerous)* un conducteur pris de folie ◆ **he's a ~ squash player** *etc* il joue au squash *etc* comme un dieu

demonetization /diːˌmʌnɪtaɪˈzeɪʃən/ N démonétisation *f*

demonetize /diːˈmʌnɪtaɪz/ VT démonétiser

demoniac /dɪˈməʊnɪæk/ ADJ, N démoniaque *mf*

demoniacal /ˌdiːməʊˈnaɪəkəl/ ADJ démoniaque, diabolique ◆ **~ possession** possession *f* diabolique

demonic /diːˈmɒnɪk, dɪˈmɒnɪk/ ADJ démoniaque, diabolique

demonize /ˈdiːmənaɪz/ VT diaboliser

demonology /ˌdiːməˈnɒlədʒɪ/ N démonologie *f*

demonstrable /ˈdemənstrəbl/ ADJ démontrable

demonstrably /ˈdemənstrəblɪ/ ADV manifestement

demonstrate /ˈdemənstreɪt/ LANGUAGE IN USE 26.1 **VT** ① *(= show) [+ truth, need]* démontrer, prouver ◆ **to ~ that ...** démontrer *or* prouver que ... ② *(= display)* faire la preuve de, prouver ◆ **he was anxious to ~ his commitment to democracy** il voulait faire la preuve de *or* prouver son attachement à la démocratie ◆ **he ~d great skill** il a fait preuve de beaucoup d'adresse ③ *[+ appliance]* faire une démonstration de ; *[+ system]* expliquer, décrire ◆ **to ~ how sth works** montrer le fonctionnement de qch, faire une démonstration de qch ◆ **to ~ how to do sth** montrer comment faire qch **VI** *(= protest)* manifester, faire *or* organiser une manifestation *(for* pour ; *in favour of* en faveur de ; *against* contre)

demonstration /ˌdemənˈstreɪʃən/ **N** ① *(= protest)* manifestation *f* ◆ **to hold a ~** manifester, faire *or* organiser une manifestation ② *(= instructions)* démonstration *f* ◆ **to give a ~ (of)** faire une démonstration (de) ③ *(= proof)* preuve *f* ◆ **a ~ of their sincerity** une preuve de sincérité de leur part ④ *[of love, support]* manifestations *fpl*
COMP *[car, lecture, tape, diskette]* de démonstration
demonstration model N modèle *m* de démonstration

> ⚠ When **demonstration** means 'protest' or 'proof', it is not translated by the French word **démonstration**.

demonstrative /dɪˈmɒnstrətɪv/ ADJ *[behaviour, person]* démonstratif, expansif ; *(Gram, Math, Philos)* démonstratif

demonstrator /ˈdemənstreɪtəʳ/ N ① *(= person) (Comm)* démonstrateur *m*, -trice *f* ; *(Educ)* préparateur *m*, -trice *f* ; *(on protest march)* manifestant(e) *m(f)* ② *(= appliance)* appareil *m* (*or* article *m*) de démonstration ; *(= car)* voiture *f* de démonstration

demoralization /dɪˌmɒrəlaɪˈzeɪʃən/ N démoralisation *f*

demoralize /dɪˈmɒrəlaɪz/ VT démoraliser ◆ **to become ~d** perdre courage, être démoralisé

demoralizing /dɪˈmɒrəlaɪzɪŋ/ ADJ démoralisant

demote /dɪˈməʊt/ VT *(also Mil)* rétrograder

demotic /dɪˈmɒtɪk/ **ADJ** ① *(= of the people)* populaire ② *(Ling)* démotique **N** démotique *f*

demotion /dɪˈməʊʃən/ N rétrogradation *f*

demotivate /ˌdiːˈməʊtɪveɪt/ VT démotiver

demulcent /dɪˈmʌlsənt/ ADJ, N *(Med)* émollient *m*, adoucissant *m*

demur /dɪˈmɜːʳ/ **VI** rechigner *(at sth* devant qch ; *at doing sth* à faire qch) ; *(Jur)* opposer une exception **N** réserve *f*, objection *f* ◆ **without ~** sans hésiter, sans faire de difficultés

demure /dɪˈmjʊəʳ/ ADJ *[smile, look, girl]* modeste, sage ; *[child]* très sage ◆ **a ~ hat** un petit chapeau bien sage

demurely /dɪˈmjʊəlɪ/ ADV *(= modestly) [smile, move]* d'un air modeste *or* sage ; *[speak]* d'un ton modeste ; *[behave]* sagement, de façon modeste ◆ **~ dressed (in)** sagement habillé (de)

demureness /dɪˈmjʊənɪs/ N *(= modesty) [of person]* air *m* sage ; *[of clothes]* allure *f* sage ; *(pej) (= coyness)* modestie *f* affectée

demurrage /dɪˈmʌrɪdʒ/ N *(Jur)* surestarie *f* ◆ **goods in ~** marchandises *fpl* en souffrance (sur le quai)

demurrer /dɪˈmʌrəʳ/ N *(Jur)* = exception *f* péremptoire

demutualize /diːˌmjuːtjʊːəlaɪz/ VI se démutualiser

demystification /diːˌmɪstɪfɪˈkeɪʃən/ N démystification *f*

demystify /diːˈmɪstɪˌfaɪ/ VT démystifier

demythification /diːˌmɪθɪfɪˈkeɪʃən/ N démythification *f*

demythify /diːˈmɪθɪˌfaɪ/ VT démythifier

den /den/ **N** ① *[of lion, tiger]* tanière *f*, antre *m* ; *[of thieves]* repaire *m*, antre *m* ◆ **the lion's ~** *(lit, fig)* l'antre *m* du lion ◆ **~ of iniquity** *or* **vice** lieu *m* de perdition *or* de débauche ; → **gambling, opium** ② *(= room, study)* antre *m*

► **den up*** VI *(US)* se retirer dans sa piaule*

denationalization /diːˌnæʃnəlaɪˈzeɪʃən/ N dénationalisation *f*

denationalize /diːˈnæʃnəlaɪz/ VT dénationaliser

denature /ˌdiːˈneɪtʃəʳ/ VT dénaturer

dengue /ˈdeŋɡɪ/ N dengue *f*

deniability /dɪˌnaɪəˈbɪlɪtɪ/ N *(NonC)* possibilité *f* de démenti

deniable /dɪˈnaɪəbl/ ADJ *(Pol)* ◆ **~ operation** *opération confidentielle dont les commanditaires déclineront toute responsabilité*

denial /dɪˈnaɪəl/ N ① *[of rights, truth]* dénégation *f* ; *[of report, accusation]* démenti *m* ; *[of guilt]* dénégation *f* ; *[of authority]* rejet *m* ◆ **~ of justice** déni *m* (de justice) ◆ **~ of self** abnégation *f* ◆ **he met the accusation with a flat ~** il a nié catégoriquement l'accusation ◆ **to issue a ~** publier un démenti ② *(= refusal)* ◆ **the ~ of visas to aid workers** le refus d'accorder un visa aux membres d'organisations humanitaires ③ *(Psych)* dénégation *f*, déni *m* ◆ **AIDS will not be stopped by inertia and ~** on n'arrêtera pas le sida par l'immobilisme et le déni ◆ **to be in ~** être dans le déni ◆ **to be in ~ about sth** refuser d'admettre qch ④ ◆ **Peter's ~ of Christ** le reniement du Christ par Pierre

denier /ˈdenɪəʳ/ N ① *(= weight)* denier *m* ◆ **25 ~ stockings** bas *mpl* 25 deniers ② *(= coin)* denier *m*

denigrate /ˈdenɪɡreɪt/ VT dénigrer, discréditer

denigration /ˌdenɪˈɡreɪʃən/ N dénigrement *m*

denim /ˈdenɪm/ N *(for jeans, skirts etc)* (toile *f* de) jean *m* ; *(heavier: for uniforms, overalls etc)* treillis *m* NPL **denims** *(= jeans)* blue-jean *m*, jean *m* ; *(= workman's overalls)* bleus *mpl* de travail

denizen /ˈdenɪzn/ N ① *(= inhabitant)* habitant(e) *m(f)* ◆ **~s of the forest** habitants *mpl* or hôtes *mpl (liter)* des forêts ② *(Brit Jur)* étranger *m*, -ère *f* (ayant droit de cité) ③ *(= naturalized plant/animal)* plante *f*/animal *m* acclimaté(e)

Denmark /ˈdenmɑːk/ N Danemark *m*

denominate /dɪˈnɒmɪneɪt/ VT dénommer

denomination /dɪˌnɒmɪˈneɪʃən/ N ① *(= group)* groupe *m*, catégorie *f* ; *(Rel)* confession *f* ; *[of money]* valeur *f* ; *[of weight, measure]* unité *f* ② *(NonC)* dénomination *f*, appellation *f*

denominational /dɪˌnɒmɪˈneɪʃənl/ ADJ *(Rel)* confessionnel

COMP **denominational college** N *(US)* université *f* confessionnelle
denominational school N *(US)* école *f* libre or confessionnelle

denominative /dɪˈnɒmɪnətɪv/ ADJ, N dénominatif *m*

denominator /dɪˈnɒmɪneɪtəʳ/ N dénominateur *m* ; → **common**

denotation /ˌdiːnəʊˈteɪʃən/ N ① *(NonC, gen, also Ling, Philos)* dénotation *f* ; *(= meaning)* signification *f* ② *(= symbol)* indices *mpl*, signes *mpl*

denotative /dɪˈnəʊtətɪv/ ADJ *(Ling)* dénotatif

denote /dɪˈnəʊt/ VT ① *(= indicate)* indiquer ; *(Philos, Ling)* dénoter ◆ **red hair was thought to ~ a fiery temperament** on pensait que les cheveux roux indiquaient un tempérament fougueux ◆ **the agreement seems to ~ a virtual surrender** l'accord semble signifier une quasi capitulation ② *(= mean)* signifier ; *(= refer to)* désigner ; *(= represent)* représenter ◆ **in this diagram, "np" ~s net profit** dans ce diagramme, "np" signifie le bénéfice net ◆ **in medieval England, the word "drab" ~d a type of woollen cloth** au Moyen-Age en Angleterre, le mot "drab" désignait une sorte de drap de laine

denouement, dénouement /deɪˈnuːmɑ̃/ N dénouement *m*

denounce /dɪˈnaʊns/ VT *[+ person, treaty, act]* dénoncer *(to à)* ◆ **to ~ sb as an impostor** accuser publiquement qn d'imposture

denouncement /dɪˈnaʊnsmənt/ N ⇒ **denunciation**

denouncer /dɪˈnaʊnsəʳ/ N dénonciateur *m*, -trice *f*

dense /dens/ ADJ ① *(lit, fig: also Phys) [fog, crowd, vegetation, prose etc]* dense ② *(* = stupid)* bouché*

densely /ˈdenslɪ/ ADV ◆ **~ populated** densément peuplé, à forte densité démographique ◆ **~ packed** plein à craquer ◆ **~ wooded** très boisé

denseness /ˈdensnɪs/ N ① *(gen)* densité *f* ② *(* = stupidity)* stupidité *f*

densitometer /ˌdensɪˈtɒmɪtəʳ/ N densimètre *m*

density /ˈdensɪtɪ/ N densité *f* ◆ **double/high/single ~ diskette** disquette *f* double/haute/simple densité

dent /dent/ N *(in wood)* entaille *f* ; *(in metal)* bosse *f*, bosselure *f* ◆ **to have a ~ in the bumper** avoir le pare-chocs bosselé or cabossé ◆ **to make a ~ in** *(fig) [+ savings, budget]* faire un trou dans ; *[+ sb's enthusiasm, confidence]* ébranler VT *[+ hat]* cabosser ; *[+ car]* bosseler, cabosser ; *[+ wood]* entailler

dental /ˈdentl/ ADJ ① *[treatment, school]* dentaire ② *(Ling)* dental N *(Ling)* dentale *f*

COMP **dental floss** N fil *m* dentaire
dental hygiene N hygiène *f* dentaire
dental hygienist N hygiéniste *mf* dentaire
dental nurse N assistant(e) *m(f)* de dentiste
dental plaque N plaque *f* dentaire
dental receptionist N réceptionniste *mf* dans un cabinet dentaire
dental surgeon N chirurgien *m* dentiste
dental surgery N cabinet *m* dentaire or de dentiste
dental technician N mécanicien(ne) *m(f)* dentiste

dentifrice /ˈdentɪfrɪs/ N dentifrice *m*

dentine /ˈdentiːn/ N dentine *f*

dentist /ˈdentɪst/ N dentiste *mf* ◆ **~'s chair** fauteuil *m* de dentiste ◆ **~'s surgery** cabinet *m* dentaire or de dentiste ◆ **to go to the ~('s)** aller chez le dentiste

dentistry /ˈdentɪstrɪ/ N dentisterie *f* ◆ **to study ~** faire des études dentaires, faire l'école dentaire

dentition /denˈtɪʃən/ N dentition *f*

denture(s) /ˈdentʃəʳ(ʃəz)/ N(PL) dentier *m*

denude /dɪˈnjuːd/ VT *(lit, fig)* dénuder, dépouiller ◆ **~d landscape** paysage *m* nu or dépouillé ◆ **area ~d of trees** région *f* dépouillée d'arbres

denunciation /dɪˌnʌnsɪˈeɪʃən/ N *[of person]* dénonciation *f* ; *(in public)* accusation *f* publique, condamnation *f* ; *[of action]* dénonciation *f* ; *[of treaty]* dénonciation *f*

denunciator /dɪˈnʌnsɪeɪtəʳ/ N dénonciateur *m*, -trice *f*

Denver boot /ˌdenvəˈbuːt/ N sabot *m* (de Denver)

deny /dɪˈnaɪ/ LANGUAGE IN USE 12.1, 26.3 VT ① *(= repudiate)* nier *(doing sth* avoir fait qch ; *that* que + *indic or subj)* ; *[+ fact, accusation]* nier, refuser d'admettre ; *[+ sb's authority]* rejeter ◆ **he denies murder** il nie avoir commis un meurtre ◆ **she denies any involvement in the kidnapping** elle nie toute participation à l'enlèvement ◆ **to ~ all responsibility for sth** nier toute responsabilité dans qch ◆ **she denies any knowledge of ...** elle affirme ne rien savoir de ... ◆ **there is no ~ing it** c'est indéniable ◆ **I'm not ~ing the truth of it** je ne nie pas que ce soit vrai

② *(= refuse to give)* **to ~ sb sth** refuser qch à qn, priver qn de qch ◆ **he was denied admittance** on lui a refusé l'entrée ◆ **they were denied victory in the 89th minute** ils ont été privés de la victoire à la 89e minute ◆ **to ~ sb access to sth** refuser à qn l'accès à qch ◆ **to ~ o.s. cigarettes** se priver de cigarettes ◆ **to ~ sb the right to do sth** refuser or dénier à qn le droit de faire qch

③ *(= disown) [+ leader, religion]* renier

deodorant /diːˈəʊdərənt/ ADJ, N *(gen)* déodorant *m* ; *(= air-freshener)* désodorisant *m*

deodorize /diːˈəʊdəraɪz/ VT désodoriser

deontologist /ˌdiːɒnˈtɒlədʒɪst/ N déontologue *mf*

deontology /ˌdiːɒnˈtɒlədʒɪ/ N déontologie *f*

deoxidize /diːˈɒksɪdaɪz/ VT désoxyder

deoxygenate /ˌdiːˈɒksɪdʒəneɪt/ VT désoxygéner

deoxyribonucleic acid /diːˌɒksɪˈraɪbəʊnjuːˈkleɪɪk ˌæsɪd/ N acide *m* désoxyribonucléique

dep. (abbrev of **departs, departure**) *(on timetable)* dép., départ

depart /dɪˈpɑːt/ VI ① *(= go away) [person]* partir, s'en aller ; *[bus, plane, train etc]* partir ◆ **to ~ from a city** quitter une ville ◆ **to be about to ~** être sur le or son départ ② *(fig)* **to ~ from** *(gen)* s'écarter de ; *[+ a principle, the truth]* faire une entorse à VT ① *(in travel information)* ◆ **"departing London at 12.40"** *(on timetable etc)* "départ de Londres (à) 12.40" ◆ **a week in Majorca, ~ing Gatwick May 7** une semaine à Majorque, départ de Gatwick le 7 mai ② ◆ **to ~ this world** or **this life** *(liter)* quitter ce monde, trépasser *(liter)*

departed /dɪˈpɑːtɪd/ ADJ ① *(liter = dead)* défunt ◆ **the ~ leader** le chef défunt, le défunt chef ② *(= bygone) [glory, happiness]* passé ; *[friends]* disparu N *(liter)* ◆ **the ~** le défunt, la défunte, les défunts *mpl* ◆ **the dear(ly) ~** le cher disparu, la chère disparue, les chers disparus *mpl*

department /dɪˈpɑːtmənt/ N *(in office, firm)* service *m* ; *[of shop, store]* rayon *m* ; *(Scol)* section *f* ; *(Univ)* ≃ UFR *f (unité de formation et de recherche)*, département *m* ; (also **government department**) ministère *m*, département *m* ; *(French Admin)* département *m* ; *(fig = field of activity)* domaine *m*, rayon *m* ◆ **he works in the sales ~** il travaille au service des ventes ◆ **in all the ~s of public service** dans tous les services publics ◆ **the shoe ~** *(in shop)* le rayon des chaussures ◆ **the French Department** *(Scol)* la section de français ; *(Univ)* l'UFR *f* or le département de français ◆ **gardening is my wife's ~*** le jardinage, c'est le rayon de ma femme ; → **head, state**

COMP **department chairman** N (pl **department chairmen**) *(Univ)* ≃ directeur *m*, -trice *f* d'UFR
Department for Education and Skills N *(Brit)* ministère *m* de l'Éducation et du Travail
department head N ⇒ **department chairman**
Department of Health N *(Brit)* ministère *m* de la Santé
Department of Social Security N *(Brit: formerly)* ≃ Sécurité *f* sociale
department store N grand magasin *m*
Department of Work and Pensions *(Brit)* ≃ Sécurité *f* sociale

departmental /ˌdiːpɑːtˈmentl/ ADJ ① *(gen)* du département ; *(in office, firm)* du service ◆ **a ~ meeting** une réunion du département (or du service) ◆ **the ~ budget** le budget du département (or du service) ◆ **~ manager** or **head** chef *m* de service ② *(= of a French area)* départemental

departmentalization /ˌdiːpɑːtˌmentəlaɪˈzeɪʃən/ N organisation *f* en départements

departmentalize /ˌdiːpɑːtˈmentəˌlaɪz/ VT organiser en départements

departure /dɪˈpɑːtʃəʳ/ N ① *(from place) [of person, vehicle]* départ *m* ; *(from job)* départ *m*, démission *f* ◆ **on the point of ~** sur le point de partir, sur le départ ; → **arrival**

[2] *(from custom, principle)* dérogation *f*, entorse *f* *(from* à) ; *(from law)* manquement *m (from* à) ◆ **a ~ from the norm** une exception ◆ **a ~ from the truth** une entorse à la vérité
[3] *(= change of course, action)* changement *m* de direction, virage *m* ; *(Comm = new type of goods)* nouveauté *f*, innovation *f* ◆ **it's a new ~ in biochemistry** c'est une nouvelle voie qui s'ouvre en *or* pour la biochimie
[4] *(liter = death)* trépas *m (liter)*
COMP *[preparations etc]* de départ
departure board N tableau *m* des départs
departure gate N porte *f* d'embarquement
departure lounge N salle *f* d'embarquement
departure platform N quai *m* (de départ)
departure signal N signal *m* de départ
departure tax N taxe *f* d'aéroport
departure time N heure *f* de départ

depend /dɪ'pend/ LANGUAGE IN USE 6.3 IMPERS VI dépendre *(on sb/sth* de qn/qch) ◆ **it all ~s, that ~s** cela dépend, c'est selon* ◆ **it ~s on you whether he comes or not** cela dépend de vous *or* il ne tient qu'à vous qu'il vienne ou non ◆ **it ~s (on) whether he will do it or not** cela dépend s'il veut le faire ou non ◆ **it ~s (on) what you mean** cela dépend de ce que vous voulez dire
◆ **depending on** ◆ **~ing on the weather** selon le temps ◆ **~ing on where you live** selon l'endroit où vous habitez ◆ **~ing on what happens tomorrow ...** selon ce qui se passera demain ...
► **depend (up)on** VT FUS [1] *(= count on)* compter sur ; *(= be completely reliant on)* se reposer sur ◆ **you can always ~ (up)on him** on peut toujours compter sur lui ◆ **he ~s (up)on her for everything** il se repose sur elle pour tout ◆ **you may ~ (up)on his coming** vous pouvez compter qu'il viendra *or* compter sur sa venue ◆ **I'm ~ing (up)on you to tell me what he wants** je compte sur vous pour savoir ce qu'il veut ◆ **you can ~ (up)on it** soyez-en sûr, je vous le promets *or* garantis ◆ **you can ~ (up)on it that he'll forget again** tu peux être sûr (et certain) qu'il va encore oublier
[2] *(= need support or help from)* dépendre de ◆ **he ~s (up)on his father for pocket money** il dépend de son père pour son argent de poche ◆ **I'm ~ing (up)on you for moral support** votre appui moral m'est indispensable ◆ **your success ~s (up)on your efforts** votre succès dépendra de vos efforts

dependability /dɪ,pendə'bɪlɪtɪ/ N *[of machine, person]* fiabilité *f* ◆ **he is well-known for his ~** tout le monde sait qu'il est très fiable

dependable /dɪ'pendəbl/ ADJ fiable ◆ **he is not ~** il n'est pas fiable, on ne peut pas compter sur lui

dependably /dɪ'pendəblɪ/ ADV de façon fiable

dependance /dɪ'pendəns/ N ⇒ **dependence**

dependant /dɪ'pendənt/ N personne *f* à charge ◆ **he had many ~s** il avait de nombreuses personnes à (sa) charge

dependence /dɪ'pendəns/ N [1] *(= state of depending:* also **dependency)** dépendance *f (on* à, à l'égard de, envers) sujétion *f (on* à) ◆ **~ on one's parents** dépendance *f* à l'égard de *or* envers ses parents ◆ **~ on drugs** (état *m* de) dépendance *f* à l'égard de la drogue [2] ◆ **the ~ of success upon effort** le rapport entre le succès et l'effort fourni

dependency /dɪ'pendənsɪ/ N [1] ⇒ **dependence 1** [2] *(Ling)* dépendance *f* [3] *(= country)* dépendance *f*, colonie *f*
COMP **dependency allowance** N *(Jur)* indemnité *f* pour charges de famille
dependency grammar N *(Ling)* grammaire *f* dépendancielle

dependent /dɪ'pendənt/ ADJ [1] *(= reliant) [person]* dépendant *(on* de) ◆ **to be (heavily) ~ on sth** dépendre (beaucoup *or* fortement) de qch ◆ **to be ~ on sb to do sth** dépendre de qn pour faire qch ◆ **drug-~, chemically ~** *(on illegal drugs)* toxicomane ; *(on medical drugs)* en état de dépendance aux médicaments ◆ **insulin-~** insulinodépendant
[2] *(financially) [child, relative]* à charge ◆ **families with ~ children** les familles ayant des enfants à charge ◆ **to be financially ~ on sb** dépendre financièrement de qn
[3] *(= contingent)* **to be ~ on** *or* **upon sth** dépendre de qch ◆ **the results are ~ upon which programme you follow** les résultats dépendent du programme que vous suivez
[4] *(Gram) [clause]* subordonné
[5] *(Math)* dépendant ◆ **~ variable** variable *f* dépendante
N ⇒ **dependant**

depersonalize /diː'pɜːsənəlaɪz/ VT dépersonnaliser

depict /dɪ'pɪkt/ VT *(in words)* dépeindre, décrire ; *(in picture)* représenter ◆ **surprise was ~ed on his face** la surprise se lisait sur son visage, son visage exprimait la surprise

depiction /dɪ'pɪkʃən/ N *(pictorial)* représentation *f* ; *(written)* description *f* ◆ **the artist's ~ of war as a roaring lion** la représentation de la guerre par l'artiste sous la forme d'un lion rugissant ◆ **the ~ of socialists as Utopian dreamers** l'image de rêveurs utopistes que l'on donne des socialistes

depilate /'depɪleɪt/ VT épiler

depilatory /dɪ'pɪlətərɪ/ ADJ, N dépilatoire *m*

deplane /,diː'pleɪn/ VI débarquer *(d'un avion)*

deplenish /dɪ'plenɪʃ/ VT *(= reduce)* dégarnir ; *(= empty)* vider

deplete /dɪ'pliːt/ VT [1] *(= reduce) [+ supplies, funds]* réduire ; *[+ strength]* diminuer, réduire ; *(= exhaust) [+ supplies, strength]* épuiser ◆ **our stock is very ~d** *(Comm)* nos stocks sont très bas ◆ **the regiment was greatly ~d** *(Mil) (by cuts etc)* l'effectif du régiment était très réduit ; *(by war, sickness)* le régiment a été décimé ◆ **numbers were greatly ~d** les effectifs étaient très réduits [2] *(Med)* décongestionner
COMP **depleted uranium** N uranium *m* appauvri

depletion /dɪ'pliːʃən/ N *[of resources, nutrients]* diminution *f* ; *(Med)* déplétion *f* ; *[of funds]* réduction *f* ; → **ozone**

deplorable /dɪ'plɔːrəbl/ ADJ déplorable, lamentable

deplorably /dɪ'plɔːrəblɪ/ ADV *(with vb) [behave]* de façon déplorable ; *(with adj)* déplorablement ◆ **ours is a ~ materialistic society** notre société est d'un matérialisme déplorable ◆ **~, he refused to take action** il a refusé d'agir, ce qui est déplorable

deplore /dɪ'plɔːʳ/ LANGUAGE IN USE 14 VT déplorer, regretter vivement ◆ **to ~ the fact that ...** déplorer le fait que ... + *indic*, regretter vivement que ... + *subj*

deploy /dɪ'plɔɪ/ VT *(Mil) [+ missiles, ships, tanks, troops etc]* déployer ; *(gen) [+ resources, equipment]* faire usage de, utiliser ; *[+ staff]* utiliser (les services de) ; *[+ skills, talents]* déployer, faire preuve de VI *(Mil)* être déployé

deployment /dɪ'plɔɪmənt/ N *(Mil)* déploiement *m* ; *(fig)* usage *m*, utilisation *f* ; → **rapid**

depolarization /'diː,pəʊləraɪ'zeɪʃən/ N dépolarisation *f*

depolarize /diː'pəʊləraɪz/ VT dépolariser

depoliticize /,diːpə'lɪtɪsaɪz/ VT dépolitiser

depopulate /,diː'pɒpjʊleɪt/ VT dépeupler ◆ **to become ~d** se dépeupler

depopulation /'diː,pɒpjʊ'leɪʃən/ N dépopulation *f*, dépeuplement *m* ◆ **rural ~** dépeuplement *m* des campagnes

deport /dɪ'pɔːt/ VT [1] *(= expel)* expulser *(from* de) ; *(= transport)* déporter *(from* de ; *to* à) ; *(Hist) [+ prisoner]* déporter [2] *(= behave)* **to ~ o.s.** † se comporter, se conduire

deportation /,diːpɔː'teɪʃən/ N expulsion *f* ; *(Hist)* déportation *f* ; *(Jur)* COMP **deportation order** N arrêt *m* d'expulsion

deportee /,diːpɔː'tiː/ N déporté(e) *m(f)*

deportment /dɪ'pɔːtmənt/ N maintien *m*, tenue *f* ◆ **~ lessons** leçons *fpl* de maintien

depose /dɪ'pəʊz/ VT *[+ king]* déposer, détrôner ; *[+ official]* destituer VTI *(Jur)* déposer, attester par déposition

deposit /dɪ'pɒzɪt/ VT [1] *(= put down) [+ parcel etc]* déposer, poser
[2] *(in bank account) [+ money]* verser, déposer ; *[+ cheque]* déposer ; *(for safekeeping) [+ money, valuables]* déposer, laisser *or* mettre en dépôt *(with sb* chez qn) ◆ **I ~ed £200 in my account** j'ai versé 200 livres à *or* sur mon compte, j'ai déposé 200 livres sur mon compte ◆ **I ~ed a cheque in my account** j'ai déposé un chèque sur mon compte ◆ **to ~ valuables in** *or* **with the bank** déposer des objets de valeur à la banque, laisser des objets de valeur en dépôt à la banque
[3] *(Geol)* déposer, former un dépôt de
N [1] *(in bank)* dépôt *m* ◆ **to make a ~ of £50** déposer *or* verser 50 livres
[2] *(= part payment) (on goods, holiday)* arrhes *fpl*, acompte *m* ; *(on house purchase)* acompte *m* ; *(in hire purchase = down payment)* premier versement *m* ; *(in hiring goods, renting accommodation: against damage etc)* caution *f* ; *(on bottle, container)* consigne *f* ; *(Brit Pol)* cautionnement *m* électoral ◆ **to leave a ~ of £40** *or* **a £40 ~ on a washing machine** verser 40 livres d'arrhes *or* d'acompte sur un lave-linge ◆ **to pay a 5% ~** *or* **a ~ of 5% on a property** verser 5% d'acompte sur une propriété ◆ **a small ~ will secure any goods** *(Comm)* on peut faire mettre tout article de côté moyennant (le versement d')un petit acompte ◆ **to lose one's ~** *(Brit Pol)* perdre son cautionnement *(en obtenant un très faible score)*
[3] *(in wine, Chem, Geol)* dépôt *m* ; *[of mineral, oil]* gisement *m* ◆ **fat/cholesterol ~s** *(Anat)* dépôt *m* graisseux/de cholestérol ◆ **calcium ~s** calcifications *fpl* ◆ **to form a ~** se déposer
COMP **deposit account** N *(Brit)* compte *m* sur livret
deposit bank N banque *f* de dépôt
deposit loan N prêt *m* en nantissement
deposit slip N bulletin *m* de versement

depositary /dɪ'pɒzɪtərɪ/ N [1] *(= person)* dépositaire *mf* [2] ⇒ **depository**

deposition /,diːpə'zɪʃən/ N [1] *(NonC) [of king, official]* déposition *f* [2] *(Jur)* déposition *f* sous serment, témoignage *m*

depositor /dɪ'pɒzɪtəʳ/ N déposant(e) *m(f)*

depository /dɪ'pɒzɪtərɪ/ N dépôt *m*, entrepôt *m*

depot /'depəʊ/ N [1] *(Mil)* dépôt *m* [2] *(= warehouse)* dépôt *m*, entrepôt *m* ◆ **coal ~** dépôt *m or* entrepôt *m* de charbon [3] *(= railway station)* gare *f* ; *(= bus station)* dépôt *m* COMP **depot ship** N (navire *m*) ravitailleur *m*

depravation /,deprə'veɪʃən/ N dépravation *f*, corruption *f*

deprave /dɪ'preɪv/ VT dépraver, corrompre

depraved /dɪ'preɪvd/ ADJ dépravé, perverti ◆ **to become ~** se dépraver

depravity /dɪ'prævɪtɪ/ N dépravation *f*, perversion *f*

deprecate /'deprɪkeɪt/ VT *[+ action, behaviour]* désapprouver, s'élever contre

deprecating /ˈdeprɪkeɪtɪŋ/ ADJ *(= disapproving)* désapprobateur (-trice *f*) ; *(= condescending)* condescendant ; *(= modest)* modeste

deprecatingly /ˈdeprɪkeɪtɪŋlɪ/ ADV *(= disparagingly)* avec désapprobation ; *(= condescendingly)* avec condescendance ; *(= modestly)* avec modestie

deprecatory /ˈdeprɪkətərɪ/ ADJ ⇒ **deprecating**

depreciate /dɪˈpriːʃɪeɪt/ VT *(Fin) [+ property, currency]* déprécier, dévaloriser ; *(= write off asset investment)* amortir ◆ **to ~ sth by 25% a year** amortir qch de 25% *or* à un rythme de 25% par an VI *(Fin, fig)* se déprécier, se dévaloriser ◆ **most cars ~ heavily in the first year** la plupart des voitures se déprécient beaucoup *or* perdent beaucoup de leur valeur la première année

depreciation /dɪˌpriːʃɪˈeɪʃən/ N *[of property, car]* dépréciation *f*, perte *f* de valeur ; *[of currency]* dépréciation *f*, dévalorisation *f* ; *(Comm, Econ) [of goods]* moins-value *f* ; *(= writing off) [of asset, investment]* amortissement *m* ; *(fig) [of talent etc]* dépréciation *f*, dénigrement *m*

depredation /ˌdeprɪˈdeɪʃən/ N *(gen pl)* déprédation(s) *f(pl)*, ravage(s) *m(pl)*

depress /dɪˈpres/ VT 1 *[+ person]* déprimer 2 *[+ lever]* abaisser 3 *[+ status]* réduire ; *[+ trade]* réduire, (faire) diminuer ; *[+ the market, prices]* faire baisser

depressant /dɪˈpresnt/ ADJ, N *(Med)* dépresseur *m*

depressed /dɪˈprest/ ADJ 1 *[person]* déprimé *(about* à cause de) ◆ **to feel ~** être *or* se sentir déprimé ◆ **to get ~** se laisser abattre ◆ **to become ~** faire une dépression ◆ **clinically ~** qui souffre de dépression 2 *[region, market, economy]* déprimé ; *[industry]* en déclin ; *[share price]* bas (basse *f*) 3 *(= sunken)* déprimé

depressing /dɪˈpresɪŋ/ ADJ déprimant, décourageant ◆ **I find it very ~** je trouve cela très déprimant *or* décourageant

depressingly /dɪˈpresɪŋlɪ/ ADV ◆ **~ obvious** d'une évidence déprimante ◆ **~ familiar/predictable** tellement familier/prévisible que c'en est déprimant ◆ **~, the new drug is no more effective than the previous one** malheureusement, ce nouveau médicament n'est pas plus efficace que le précédent

depression /dɪˈpreʃən/ N 1 *(NonC) (Med)* dépression *f* (nerveuse), état *m* dépressif ◆ **to suffer from ~** *(Med)* souffrir de dépression, faire de la dépression ◆ **to be in a bit of a ~** *(gen)* être déprimé ◆ **her ~ at this news** son découragement en apprenant la nouvelle 2 *(Econ)* dépression *f* ◆ **the Depression** *(Hist)* la Grande dépression ◆ **the country's economy was in a state of ~** l'économie du pays était en pleine dépression 3 *(Geog)* dépression *f* ; *(Weather)* dépression *f* (atmosphérique) ◆ **a deep/shallow or weak ~** une forte/faible dépression 4 *(= hollow: in ground)* creux *m*

depressive /dɪˈpresɪv/ ADJ, N *(Med)* dépressif *m*, -ive *f*

depressurization /dɪˌpreʃəraɪˈzeɪʃən/ N dépressurisation *f*

depressurize /dɪˈpreʃəˌraɪz/ VT *(Phys etc)* dépressuriser ; *(fig) (= take strain off) [+ person]* faciliter la vie à

deprivation /ˌdeprɪˈveɪʃən/ N *(= act, state)* privation *f* ; *(= loss)* perte *f* ; *(Psych)* carence *f* affective ◆ **~ of office** *(Jur)* destitution *f* de fonction ; → **maternal**

deprive /dɪˈpraɪv/ VT *(of sleep, food, company)* priver *(of* de) ; *(of right)* priver, déposséder *(of* de) ; *(of asset)* ôter *(of* à) enlever *(of* à) ◆ **to be ~d of sth/sb** être privé de qch/qn ◆ **to ~ o.s. of ...** se priver de ...

deprived /dɪˈpraɪvd/ ADJ *[area, background, child]* défavorisé

deprogramme, deprogram (US) /diːˈprəʊgræm/ VT *[+ person]* déconditionner

dept abbrev of **department**

depth /depθ/ N 1 *(= deepness) [of water, hole, shelf, cupboard]* profondeur *f* ; *[of snow]* épaisseur *f* ; *[of edge, border]* largeur *f* ◆ **at a ~ of 3 metres** à 3 mètres de profondeur, par 3 mètres de fond ◆ **the water is 3 metres in ~** l'eau a 3 mètres de profondeur, il y a 3 mètres de fond ◆ **to get out of one's ~** *(lit, fig)* perdre pied ◆ **don't go out of your ~** *(in swimming pool etc)* ne va pas là où tu n'as pas pied ◆ **I'm completely out of my ~** *(fig)* je nage complètement*, je suis complètement dépassé*

2 *(= lowness) [of voice, tone]* registre *m* grave

3 *(= intensity) [of colour]* intensité *f* ◆ **in the ~ of winter** au plus fort *or* au cœur de l'hiver ◆ **wine with an excellent ~ of flavour** vin *m* qui a une belle complexité ◆ **cheese with an excellent ~ of flavour** fromage *m* bien affiné

4 *(= strength, profundity) [of knowledge, feeling, sorrow, relief]* profondeur *f* ◆ **a great ~ of feeling** une grande profondeur de sentiment ◆ **he had no idea of the ~ of feeling against him** il ne se rendait pas compte du ressentiment qu'il suscitait ◆ **she has a tremendous breadth and ~ of knowledge** ses connaissances sont extrêmement étendues et approfondies ◆ **this illustrated the ~ of concern among young people for the elderly** cela a montré à quel point les jeunes gens se souciaient des personnes âgées ◆ **politicians acknowledge the ~ of public interest in the environment** les hommes politiques se rendent compte à quel point le public s'intéresse à l'environnement ◆ **there was little emotional ~ to their relationship** leurs sentiments l'un pour l'autre n'étaient pas très profonds ◆ **to have intellectual ~** *[book, film]* être profond ; *[person]* être (un esprit) profond ◆ **to lack intellectual ~** manquer de profondeur ◆ **he has no ~ of character** il manque de caractère ◆ **in ~** en profondeur ◆ **to interview sb in ~** faire une interview en profondeur de qn ; see also **in**

5 *(Phot)* ◆ **~ of field** profondeur *f* de champ ◆ **~ of focus** distance *f* focale

NPL **depths** 1 *(= deep place)* ◆ **the ~s of the ocean** les profondeurs *fpl* océaniques ◆ **from the ~s of the earth** des profondeurs *fpl or* des entrailles *fpl* de la terre ◆ **in the ~s of the forest** au plus profond *or* au cœur de la forêt

2 *(fig)* fond *m* ◆ **to be in the ~s of despair** toucher le fond du désespoir ◆ **the country is in the ~s of recession** le pays est plongé dans une profonde récession ◆ **to sink to new ~s of depravity** tomber encore plus bas dans la perversité ◆ **in the ~s of winter** au plus fort *or* au cœur de l'hiver ◆ **in the ~s of night** au milieu *or* au plus profond de la nuit ◆ **I would never sink to such ~s as to do that** je ne tomberais jamais assez bas pour faire cela

COMP **depth charge** N grenade *f* sous-marine

depth psychology N psychologie *f* des profondeurs

deputation /ˌdepjʊˈteɪʃən/ N délégation *f*, députation *f*

depute /dɪˈpjuːt/ VT *[+ power, authority]* déléguer ; *[+ person]* députer, déléguer *(sb to do sth* qn pour faire qch)

deputize /ˈdepjʊtaɪz/ VI assurer l'intérim ◆ **to ~ for sb** *(on particular occasion)* remplacer qn VT députer *(sb to do sth* qn pour faire qch)

deputy /ˈdepjʊtɪ/ N 1 *(= second in command)* adjoint(e) *m(f)* ; *(= replacement)* remplaçant(e) *m(f)*, suppléant(e) *m(f)* ; *(in business)* fondé *m* de pouvoir 2 *(= member of deputation)* délégué(e) *m(f)* 3 *(French Pol)* député *m* 4 *(US)* shérif *m* adjoint ADJ adjoint

COMP **deputy chairman** N (pl **deputy chairmen**) vice-président *m*

deputy director N sous-directeur *m*, -trice *f*

deputy head N *(Scol) (gen)* directeur *m*, -trice *f* adjoint(e) ; *(of lycée)* censeur *m*

deputy headmaster, deputy headmistress N *(Scol)* ⇒ **deputy head**

deputy judge N juge *m* suppléant

deputy mayor N maire *m* adjoint

Deputy Secretary N *(US)* ministre *m* adjoint

deputy sheriff N *(US)* ⇒ **deputy noun 4**

derail /dɪˈreɪl/ VT *[+ train]* faire dérailler ; *[+ plan, negotiations]* faire avorter VI dérailler

derailleur /dəˈreɪljəʳ/ N dérailleur *m* ◆ **to have ~ gears** être muni d'un dérailleur

derailment /dɪˈreɪlmənt/ N déraillement *m*

derange /dɪˈreɪndʒ/ VT 1 *[+ plan]* déranger, troubler ; *[+ machine]* dérégler 2 *(Med)* déranger (le cerveau de), aliéner

deranged /dɪˈreɪndʒd/ ADJ dérangé ◆ **to be (mentally) ~** avoir le cerveau dérangé

derangement /dɪˈreɪndʒmənt/ N 1 *(Med)* aliénation *f* mentale 2 *[of machine]* dérèglement *m*

derate /diːˈreɪt/ VT *(Tax) [+ land, property]* dégrever

derby /ˈdɑːbɪ, (US) ˈdɜːbɪ/ N 1 *(Sport)* **local ~** match *m* entre équipes voisines ◆ **the Derby** *(Brit Racing)* le Derby (d'Epsom) 2 *(US)* **~ (hat)** (chapeau *m*) melon *m*

Derbys. abbrev of **Derbyshire**

deregulate /dɪˈregjʊˌleɪt/ VT *[+ prices]* libérer ; *[+ transport system]* déréglementer

deregulation /dɪˌregjʊˈleɪʃən/ N *[of prices]* libération *f* ; *[of transport system]* déréglementation *f*

derelict /ˈderɪlɪkt/ ADJ 1 *(= abandoned)* abandonné ; *(= ruined)* (tombé) en ruines 2 *(frm = neglectful of duty)* négligent N 1 *(Naut)* navire *m* abandonné *(en mer)* 2 *[person]* épave *f* (humaine)

dereliction /ˌderɪˈlɪkʃən/ N *[of property]* état *m* d'abandon ; *[of person]* délaissement *m* COMP **dereliction of duty** N négligence *f* (dans le service), manquement *m* au devoir

derestricted /ˌdiːrɪˈstrɪktɪd/ ADJ *(Brit) [road, area]* sans limitation de vitesse

deride /dɪˈraɪd/ VT rire de, tourner en ridicule

derision /dɪˈrɪʒən/ N dérision *f* ◆ **object of ~** objet *m* de dérision *or* de risée

derisive /dɪˈraɪsɪv/ ADJ 1 *[smile, person]* moqueur, railleur 2 *[amount, offer]* dérisoire

derisively /dɪˈraɪsɪvlɪ/ ADV *[speak]* d'un ton moqueur ◆ **he laughed ~** il eut un petit rire moqueur ◆ **known ~ as "Dumbo"** connu sous le sobriquet de "Dumbo"

derisory /dɪˈraɪsərɪ/ ADJ 1 *[amount, offer]* dérisoire 2 *[smile, person]* moqueur, railleur

derivation /ˌderɪˈveɪʃən/ N dérivation *f*

derivative /dɪˈrɪvətɪv/ ADJ 1 *(Chem, Ling, Math)* dérivé 2 *(= not original) [literary work etc]* peu original N *(Chem, Ling)* dérivé *m* ; *(Math)* dérivée *f* ; *(Fin)* produit *m* dérivé

NPL **derivatives** *(Fin)* produits *mpl* dérivés

COMP **derivatives market** N marché *m* des produits dérivés

derivatives trading N transactions *fpl* sur produits dérivés

derive /dɪˈraɪv/ VT *[+ profit, satisfaction]* tirer *(from* de) trouver *(from* dans) ; *[+ comfort, ideas]* puiser *(from* dans) ; *[+ name, origins]* tenir *(from* de) ; *[+ word]* (faire) dériver *(from* de) ◆ **to ~ one's happiness from ...** devoir son bonheur à ..., trouver son bonheur dans ... ◆ **to be ~d from** → vi VI ◆ **to ~ from** (also **be derived from**) dériver de, provenir de, venir de ; *[power, fortune]* provenir de ; *[idea]* avoir sa source *or* ses origines dans ; *[word]* dériver de ◆ **it all ~s from the fact that ...** tout cela tient au fait que *or* provient du fait que ...

dermatitis /ˌdɜːməˈtaɪtɪs/ N dermatite *f*, dermite *f*

dermatologist /ˌdɜːməˈtɒlədʒɪst/ N dermatologue *mf*, dermatologiste *mf*

dermatology /ˌdɜːməˈtɒlədʒɪ/ N dermatologie *f*

dermis /ˈdɜːmɪs/ N derme *m*

derogate /ˈderəgeɪt/ VI ◆ **to ~ from** porter atteinte à ◆ **without derogating from his authority/his merits** sans rien enlever à *or* sans vouloir diminuer son autorité/ses mérites ◆ **to ~ from one's position** *(liter)* déroger (à son rang) *(liter)*

derogation /ˌderəˈgeɪʃən/ N [1] *(= reduction)* atteinte *f* (*from, of* à) ◆ **a ~ of sovereignty** une atteinte à la souveraineté [2] *(Pol = temporary exception from law)* report *m* d'application (*from* de)

derogatory /dɪˈrɒgətərɪ/ ADJ *[remark]* désobligeant (*of, to* à) dénigrant

derrick /ˈderɪk/ N *(= lifting device, crane)* mât *m* de charge ; *(above oil well)* derrick *m*

derring-do †† /ˈderɪŋˈduː/ N bravoure *f* ◆ **deeds of ~** hauts faits *mpl*, prouesses *fpl*

derringer /ˈderɪndʒəʳ/ N *(US)* pistolet *m* (court et à gros calibre), Derringer *m*

derv /dɜːv/ N *(Brit = fuel)* gasoil *m*

dervish /ˈdɜːvɪʃ/ N derviche *m*

desalinate /diːˈsælɪneɪt/ VT dessaler

desalination /diːˌsælɪˈneɪʃən/ N dessalement *m* COMP **desalination plant** N usine *f* de dessalement

descale /diːˈskeɪl/ VT détartrer COMP **descaling agent, descaling product** N (produit *m*) détartrant *m*

descant /ˈdeskænt/ N déchant *m* ◆ **to sing ~** chanter une partie du déchant

descend /dɪˈsend/ VI [1] *(= go down, come down) [person, vehicle, road, hill etc]* descendre (*from* de) ; *[rain, snow]* tomber ◆ **in ~ing order of importance** par ordre d'importance décroissante ◆ **to ~ into** *[+ alcoholism, madness, chaos, anarchy]* sombrer dans ◆ **gloom ~ed (up)on him** il s'est assombri ◆ **silence ~ed (up)on us** le silence se fit

[2] *(by ancestry)* descendre, être issu (*from* de) ; *[plan, event etc]* tirer son origine (*from* de) ◆ **his family ~s from William the Conqueror** sa famille descend de Guillaume le Conquérant

[3] *(= pass by inheritance) [property, customs, rights]* passer (par héritage) (*from* de ; *to* à)

[4] *(= attack or arrive suddenly: Mil, fig)* faire une descente (*on* sur) ◆ **the moment the news was out, reporters ~ed** dès que la nouvelle a été connue, les reporters ont afflué (sur les lieux) ◆ **to ~ (up)on sb** tomber sur qn ◆ **to ~ (up)on a town** *[reporters, journalists, tourists, army]* envahir une ville ◆ **to ~ (up)on a building** *[reporters, journalists, tourists]* se précipiter *or* affluer vers un bâtiment ; *[army, police]* faire une descente dans un bâtiment ◆ **visitors ~ed upon us** des gens sont arrivés (chez nous) sans crier gare

[5] *(= lower o.s. to)* ◆ **to ~ to lies** *or* **to lying** s'abaisser à mentir ◆ **I'd never ~ to that level** je ne m'abaisserais pas ainsi

VT [1] *[+ stairs]* descendre

[2] ◆ **to be ~ed from** *[+ species]* descendre de ; *[+ person]* descendre de, être issu de

descendant /dɪˈsendənt/ N descendant(e) *m(f)*

descendeur /desɑːnˈdɜːʳ/ N *(Climbing)* descendeur *m*

descendible /dɪˈsendəbl/ ADJ *(Jur)* transmissible

descent /dɪˈsent/ N [1] *(= going down) [of person]* descente *f* (*into* dans) ; *(fig: into crime etc)* chute *f* ; *(Flying, Sport)* descente *f* ; *[of hill]* descente *f*, pente *f* ◆ **the street made a sharp ~** la rue était très en pente *or* descendait en pente très raide ◆ **we began the steep ~ into the valley** nous avons entamé la descente en pente raide vers la vallée ◆ **~ by parachute** descente *f* en parachute ◆ **to prevent the country's ~ into civil war** pour empêcher le pays de sombrer dans la guerre civile

[2] *(= ancestry)* origine *f*, famille *f* ◆ **of African ~** d'origine africaine ◆ **of noble ~** de noble extraction ◆ **to trace one's ~ back to ...** faire remonter sa famille à ...

[3] *[of property, customs etc]* transmission *f* (par héritage) (*to* à)

[4] *(Mil etc = attack)* descente *f*, irruption *f* ◆ **to make a ~ on the enemy camp** faire une descente sur *or* faire irruption dans le camp ennemi ◆ **to make a ~ on the enemy** faire une descente sur l'ennemi

descramble /diːˈskræmbl/ VT *(Telec)* désembrouiller ; *(TV)* décoder, décrypter ◆ **~d programme** émission *f* en clair

descrambler /diːˈskræmbləʳ/ N *(TV)* décodeur *m*

describe /dɪsˈkraɪb/ VT [1] *[+ scene, person]* décrire ◆ **~ what it is like** racontez *or* dites comment c'est ◆ **~ him for us** décrivez-le-nous ◆ **which cannot be ~d** indescriptible, qu'on ne saurait décrire ◆ **~ how you made it** décrivez comment vous l'avez fait [2] *(= represent)* décrire, représenter (*as* comme) ◆ **the article ~s him as an eccentric** l'article le décrit *or* le représente comme un personnage excentrique ◆ **he ~s himself as a doctor** il se présente comme médecin ◆ **she ~s herself as ordinary** elle se présente *or* se décrit comme quelqu'un d'ordinaire [3] *(Math)* décrire

description /dɪsˈkrɪpʃən/ N [1] *[of person, scene, object, event, situation]* description *f* ; *(Police)* signalement *m* ◆ **to give an accurate/lively ~** faire *or* donner une description exacte/vivante ◆ **he gave a ~ of what happened/how he had escaped** il a décrit ce qui s'était passé/la façon dont il s'était évadé ◆ **police have issued a ~ of the man they are looking for** la police a diffusé le signalement de l'homme qu'elle recherche ◆ **do you know anyone of this ~?** *(gen)* connaissez-vous quelqu'un qui ressemble à cette description ? ; *(Police)* connaissez-vous quelqu'un qui réponde à ce signalement ? ◆ **beyond** *or* **past ~** indescriptible, qu'on ne saurait décrire ; → **answer, beggar, defy, fit[1], job**

[2] *(= sort)* sorte *f* ◆ **people/vehicles of every ~** *or* **of all ~s** des gens/des véhicules de toutes sortes ◆ **food of every ~** *or* **of all ~s** toutes sortes d'aliments ◆ **he's a poet of some ~** c'est une sorte de poète ◆ **I need a bag of some ~** il me faut un sac, n'importe lequel

descriptive /dɪsˈkrɪptɪv/ ADJ descriptif ◆ **~ geometry/linguistics** géométrie *f*/linguistique *f* descriptive ◆ **her ~ powers are so great that ...** elle possède un tel art de la description que ...

descriptively /dɪsˈkrɪptɪvlɪ/ ADV ◆ **the nickname "abominable snowman" is not so much ~ accurate as evocative** "l'abominable homme des neiges" n'est pas tant une description fidèle qu'un surnom évocateur ◆ **linguists try to study language ~, not prescriptively** les linguistes essaient d'étudier le langage d'un point de vue descriptif et non pas normatif ◆ **a cliff known ~ as "the Black Ladders"** une falaise connue sous le nom pittoresque de "Échelles noires"

descry /dɪsˈkraɪ/ VT discerner, distinguer

desecrate /ˈdesɪkreɪt/ VT *[+ shrine, memory]* profaner, souiller *(liter)*

desecration /ˌdesɪˈkreɪʃən/ N profanation *f*

deseed /diːˈsiːd/ VT *[+ fruit]* épépiner

desegregate /diːˈsegrɪgeɪt/ VT abolir *or* supprimer la ségrégation raciale dans ◆ **~d schools** écoles *fpl* où la ségrégation raciale n'est plus pratiquée

desegregation /ˈdiːˌsegrɪˈgeɪʃən/ N déségrégation *f*

deselect /ˌdiːsɪˈlekt/ VT *(Brit Pol) [+ candidate]* ne pas resélectionner ; *(Comput)* désélectionner

desensitize /ˌdiːˈsensɪtaɪz/ VT désensibiliser

desert[1] /ˈdezət/ N *(lit, fig)* désert *m*

COMP *[region, climate, animal, plant]* désertique

desert boot N chaussure *f* montante *(en daim et à lacets)*

desert island N île *f* déserte

desert rat N *(= animal)* gerboise *f*

the Desert Rats * NPL les Rats *mpl* du désert *(forces britanniques en Libye pendant la Seconde Guerre mondiale, ou au Koweït pendant la guerre du Golfe)*

desert[2] /dɪˈzɜːt/ VT *[+ post, people, land]* déserter, abandonner ; *[+ cause, party]* déserter ; *[+ spouse, family]* abandonner ; *[+ friend]* délaisser ◆ **his courage ~ed him** son courage l'a abandonné VI *(Mil)* déserter ; *(from one's party)* faire défection ◆ **to ~ to the enemy** passer à l'ennemi

deserted /dɪˈzɜːtɪd/ ADJ *[road, place]* désert ; *[wife etc]* abandonné

deserter /dɪˈzɜːtəʳ/ N *(Mil)* déserteur *m* ; *(to the enemy)* transfuge *m*

desertification /dɪˌzɜːtɪfɪˈkeɪʃən/ N désertification *f*

desertion /dɪˈzɜːʃən/ N [1] *(Mil)* désertion *f* [2] *(by supporters, friends)* désertion *f* (*by* de) [3] *(by husband, mother etc)* abandon *m* du domicile

deserts /dɪˈzɜːts/ NPL dû *m*, ce que l'on mérite ; *(= reward)* récompense *f* méritée ; *(= punishment)* châtiment *m* mérité ◆ **according to his ~** selon ses mérites ◆ **to get one's (just) ~** avoir *or* recevoir ce que l'on mérite

deserve /dɪˈzɜːv/ VT *[person]* mériter, être digne de ; *[object, suggestion]* mériter ◆ **he ~s to win** il mérite de gagner ◆ **he ~s to be pitied** il mérite qu'on le plaigne, il est digne de pitié ◆ **he ~s more money** il mérite plus d'argent ◆ **he got what he ~d** il n'a eu que ce qu'il méritait ◆ **the idea ~s consideration** l'idée mérite réflexion ◆ **a ~d holiday** des vacances bien méritées ; → **well[2]** VI [1] ◆ **deserving of** → **deserving** [2] *(frm)* **to ~ well of one's country** bien mériter de la patrie *(liter)*

deservedly /dɪˈzɜːvɪdlɪ/ ADV ◆ **the film was a flop, and ~ so** ce film a fait un flop* mérité ◆ **~, she was awarded an Oscar** elle a reçu un Oscar bien mérité ◆ **she told him off, and ~ so** elle l'a grondé, à juste titre

deserving /dɪˈzɜːvɪŋ/ ADJ *[person]* méritant ; *[action, cause]* méritoire, louable ◆ **she's a ~ case** c'est une personne méritante ◆ **the ~ poor** les pauvres *mpl* méritants ◆ **to be ~ of respect** être digne de respect ◆ **to be ~ of support/help/recognition** mériter d'être soutenu/aidé/reconnu ◆ **a matter ~ of our careful attention** une affaire qui mérite toute notre attention ◆ **he has committed crimes ~ of punishment** il a commis des crimes pour lesquels il mérite d'être puni

deshabille /ˌdezəˈbiːl/ N ⇒ **dishabille**

desiccant /ˈdesɪkənt/ N siccatif *m*

desiccate /ˈdesɪkeɪt/ VT dessécher, sécher COMP **desiccated coconut** N noix *f* de coco séchée

desiccation /ˌdesɪˈkeɪʃən/ N dessiccation *f*

desiderata /dɪˌzɪdəˈrɑːtə/ NPL desiderata *mpl*

design /dɪˈzaɪn/ N [1] *(= process, art) (for furniture, housing)* design *m* ; *(for clothing)* stylisme *m* ◆ **industrial ~** l'esthétique *f* *or* la création industrielle ◆ **he has a flair for ~** il est doué pour le design

[2] *(= way in which sth is planned and made) [of building, book]* plan *m*, conception *f* (*of* de) ; *[of clothes]* style *m*, ligne *f* (*of* de) ; *[of car, machine*

etc] conception *f* ; (= *look*) esthétique *f*, design *m* ◆ **the ~ was faulty** la conception était défectueuse, c'était mal conçu ◆ **the ~ of the apartment facilitates …** le plan de l'appartement facilite … ◆ **the general ~ of "Paradise Lost"** le plan général *or* l'architecture *f* du "Paradis perdu" ◆ **a dress in this summer's latest ~** une robe dans le style de cet été ◆ **the ~ of the car allows …** la conception de la voiture *or* la façon dont la voiture est conçue permet … ◆ **the grand** *or* **overall ~** le plan d'ensemble ◆ **this is a very practical ~** c'est conçu de façon très pratique ◆ **these shoes are not of (a) very practical ~** ces chaussures ne sont pas très pratiques

3 (= *plan drawn in detail*) [*of building, machine, car etc*] plan *m*, dessin *m* (*of, for* de) ; [*of dress, hat*] croquis *m*, dessin *m* (*of, for* de) ; (= *preliminary sketch*) ébauche *f*, étude *f* (*for* de) ◆ **have you seen the ~s for the new theatre?** avez-vous vu les plans du nouveau théâtre ?

4 (= *ornamental pattern*) motif *m*, dessin *m* (*on* sur) ◆ **the ~ on the material/the cups** le dessin *or* le motif du tissu/des tasses ◆ **a leaf ~** un motif de feuille(s)

5 (= *completed model*) modèle *m* ◆ **a new ~ of car** un nouveau modèle de voiture ◆ **the dress is an exclusive ~ by …** cette robe est un modèle exclusif de …

6 (= *intention*) intention *f*, dessein *m* ◆ **his ~s became obvious when …** ses intentions *or* ses desseins sont devenu(e)s manifestes quand … ◆ **to conceive a ~ to do sth** former le projet *or* le dessein de faire qch ◆ **imperialist ~s against their country** les visées impérialistes sur leur pays

◆ **by design** (= *deliberately*) délibérément, à dessein ◆ **whether by ~ or accident he arrived just at the right moment** que ce soit à dessein *or* délibérément ou par hasard, il est arrivé juste au bon moment ◆ **truly important events often occur not by ~ but by accident** les événements vraiment importants sont souvent le fruit du hasard plutôt que d'une volonté précise

◆ **to have + designs** ◆ **to have ~s on sb/sth** avoir des visées sur qn/qch ◆ **to have evil ~s on sb/sth** nourrir de noirs desseins à l'encontre de qn/qch ◆ **we believe they have aggressive ~s on our country** nous pensons qu'ils ont l'intention d'attaquer notre pays

VT 1 (= *think out*) [+ *object, car, model, building*] concevoir ; [+ *scheme*] élaborer ◆ **well-~ed** bien conçu

◆ **designed as** ◆ **room ~ed as a study** pièce conçue comme cabinet de travail ◆ **the legislation is ~ed as a consumer protection measure** cette loi vise à protéger les consommateurs

◆ **designed for** ◆ **car seats ~ed for maximum safety** des sièges *mpl* de voiture conçus pour une sécurité maximale ◆ **software ~ed for use with a PC** un logiciel conçu pour être utilisé sur un PC ◆ **to be ~ed for sb** (= *aimed at particular person*) s'adresser à qn ◆ **a course ~ed for foreign students** un cours s'adressant aux étudiants étrangers

◆ **designed to** ◆ **to be ~ed to do sth** (= *be made for purpose*) être fait *or* conçu pour faire qch ; (= *be aimed at sth*) être destiné à faire qch, viser à faire qch ◆ **~ed to hold wine** fait *or* conçu pour contenir du vin ◆ **clothes that are ~ed to appeal to young people** des vêtements qui sont conçus pour plaire aux jeunes ◆ **a peace plan ~ed to end the civil war** un plan de paix visant *or* destiné à mettre fin à la guerre civile

2 (= *draw on paper*) [+ *object, building*] concevoir, dessiner ; [+ *dress, hat*] créer, dessiner

COMP **design award** N prix *m* de la meilleure conception *or* du meilleur dessin
design engineer N ingénieur *m* concepteur
design fault N défaut *m* de conception
design office N bureau *m* d'études

designate /ˈdezɪgneɪt/ VT 1 (= *indicate, appoint*) [+ *person, thing*] désigner (*as* comme ; *to sth* à qch ; *to do sth* pour faire qch) ◆ **he was ~d to take charge of the operations** on l'a désigné comme responsable des opérations ◆ **these posts ~ the boundary between …** ces poteaux montrent la frontière entre … 2 (= *entitle*) [+ *person, thing*] désigner ◆ **this area was ~d a priority development region** cette région a été classée zone de développement prioritaire
ADJ /ˈdezɪgnɪt/ désigné ◆ **the chairman ~** le président désigné COMP **designated driver** N (*for insurance*) conducteur *m* attitré ◆ **you either take a cab or you use a ~d driver** soit on prend un taxi, soit on désigne un conducteur qui ne boira pas

designation /ˌdezɪgˈneɪʃən/ N (*gen*) désignation *f* ◆ **~ of origin** (*Jur, Comm*) appellation *f* d'origine

designedly /dɪˈzaɪnɪdlɪ/ ADV à dessein, exprès

designer /dɪˈzaɪnəʳ/ N (= *architect, artist*) dessinateur *m*, -trice *f*, créateur *m*, -trice *f* ; (*industrial, commercial*) concepteur-projeteur *m* ; (*esp Advertising*) créatif *m* ; (*for furniture etc*) designer *m* ; (*for clothes*) styliste *mf* ; (*very famous*) grand couturier *m* ; (*Cine, Theat*) décorateur *m*, -trice *f* ; → **industrial**
COMP [*jeans, gloves, scarves etc*] haute couture ; (= *fashionable*) [*lager, mineral water*] branché*
designer baby N bébé *m* sur mesure
designer drug N (= *synthetic narcotic*) drogue *f* de synthèse
designer stubble N barbe *f* de trois jours (*d'un négligé savamment entretenu*)

designing /dɪˈzaɪnɪŋ/ ADJ (= *scheming*) intrigant ; (= *crafty*) rusé

desirability /dɪˌzaɪərəˈbɪlɪtɪ/ N [*of action, measures*] charme *m*, attrait *m* ; [*of person*] charmes *mpl*, sex-appeal *m* ◆ **the ~ of doing sth** l'opportunité de faire qch

desirable /dɪˈzaɪərəbl/ LANGUAGE IN USE 1.1, 8.4 ADJ [*position*] enviable ; [*offer*] tentant, séduisant ; [*person*] désirable, séduisant ; [*action, progress*] désirable, souhaitable ◆ **it is ~ that …** il est désirable *or* souhaitable que … + *subj* ◆ **~ residence for sale** belle propriété à vendre

desirably /dɪˈzaɪərəblɪ/ ADV ◆ **this property is ~ located** cette propriété est située dans un lieu très prisé *or* coté ◆ **rugby was thought of as ~ aggressive** on considérait que le rugby faisait appel à une agressivité salutaire

desire /dɪˈzaɪəʳ/ LANGUAGE IN USE 8.4 N désir *m* (*for* de ; *to do sth* de faire qch) ; (*sexual*) désir *m* ◆ **a ~ for peace** un désir (ardent) de paix ◆ **it is my ~ that …** c'est mon désir que … + *subj* ◆ **I have no ~** *or* **I haven't the least ~ to do it** je n'ai nullement envie de le faire VT 1 (= *want*) désirer (*to do sth* faire qch ; *that* que + *subj*) ◆ **if ~d** (*in instructions, recipes etc*) si vous le désirez ◆ **his work leaves much** *or* **a lot/something to be ~d** son travail laisse beaucoup à désirer/laisse à désirer ◆ **cut the fabric to the ~d length** coupez la longueur voulue de tissu ◆ **the ~d effect/outcome** *or* **result** l'effet *m*/le résultat voulu 2 (*frm* = *request*) prier (*sb to do sth* qn de faire qch)

desirous /dɪˈzaɪərəs/ ADJ désireux (*of* de) ◆ **to be ~ of sth/of doing sth** désirer qch/faire qch

desist /dɪˈzɪst/ VI cesser, s'arrêter (*from doing sth* de faire qch) ◆ **to ~ from sth** cesser qch ; (*Jur*) se désister de qch ◆ **to ~ from criticism** renoncer à *or* cesser de critiquer ◆ **to ~ from one's efforts** abandonner ses efforts

desk /desk/ N 1 (*for pupil*) pupitre *m* ; (*for teacher*) bureau *m*, chaire *f* ; (*in office, home*) bureau *m* ; (*bureau-type*) secrétaire *m* ; (*Mus*) pupitre *m* ; → **roll**
2 (*Brit: in shop, restaurant*) caisse *f* ; (*in hotel, at airport*) réception *f* ◆ **ask at the ~** demandez à la caisse (*or* à la réception) ◆ **the ~** (*Press*) le secrétariat de rédaction ◆ **the news/city ~** (*Press*) le service des informations/financier ◆ **he's on the West African ~** (*Foreign Office, State Department*) il est à la direction des affaires ouest-africaines ; → **cash desk**
COMP **desk blotter** N sous-main *m inv*
desk-bound ADJ sédentaire
desk clerk N (*US*) réceptionniste *mf*
desk diary N agenda *m* de bureau
desk job N travail *m* de bureau ◆ **he's got a ~ job** il a un travail de bureau
desk lamp N lampe *f* de bureau
desk pad N bloc *m* de bureau, bloc-notes *m*
desk study N (*Brit fig: Econ etc*) étude *f* sur documents

deskill /dɪˈskɪl/ VT déqualifier

deskilling /dɪˈskɪlɪŋ/ N déqualification *f*

deskside computer /ˈdesksaɪdkəmˈpjuːtəʳ/ N ordinateur *m* tour

desktop /ˈdesktɒp/ ADJ [*model, computer*] de table, de bureau N (*Comput*) bureau *m* COMP **desktop publishing** N publication *f* assistée par ordinateur, microédition *f*

desolate /ˈdesəlɪt/ ADJ 1 (= *deserted*) [*place*] désolé ; [*landscape*] désert ; [*beauty*] sauvage 2 [*person*] (= *grief-stricken*) désespéré ; (= *lost*) perdu ◆ **he was ~ without her** il était perdu sans elle ◆ **to feel ~** se sentir perdu VT /ˈdesəleɪt/ [+ *country*] désoler, ravager ; [+ *person*] désoler, affliger

desolately /ˈdesəlɪtlɪ/ ADV [*say etc*] d'un air désespéré

desolation /ˌdesəˈleɪʃən/ N 1 (= *grief*) abattement *m*, affliction *f* ; (= *friendlessness*) solitude *f* ; [*of landscape*] aspect *m* désert, solitude *f* 2 [*of country*] (*by war*) désolation *f* (*liter*), dévastation *f*

despair /dɪsˈpeəʳ/ N 1 (*NonC*) désespoir *m* (*about, at, over* au sujet de ; *at having done* d'avoir fait) ◆ **to be in ~** être au désespoir, être désespéré ◆ **in ~, he tried to kill himself** de désespoir il a tenté de se suicider ◆ **to drive sb to ~** réduire qn au désespoir, désespérer qn 2 (= *cause of despair*) désespoir *m* ◆ **this child is the ~ of his parents** cet enfant fait *or* est le désespoir de ses parents VI (se) désespérer, perdre l'espoir ◆ **don't ~!** ne te désespère pas ! ◆ **to ~ of (doing) sth** désespérer de (faire) qch ◆ **I ~ for the future of our planet** je suis pessimiste quant à l'avenir de la planète ◆ **they ~ed of** *or* **for his life** (*liter*) on désespérait de le sauver

despairing /dɪsˈpeərɪŋ/ ADJ [*person*] désespéré ; [*look, gesture*] de désespoir, désespéré

despairingly /dɪsˈpeərɪŋlɪ/ ADV [*say, agree, answer*] d'un ton désespéré ; [*think*] avec désespoir ; [*shake one's head*] de façon désespérée ◆ **to sigh ~** pousser un soupir de désespoir ◆ **Emma looked ~ at Vanessa** Emma jeta à Vanessa un regard désespéré ◆ **~, she waited for him to phone** elle attendait désespérément qu'il téléphone

despatch /dɪsˈpætʃ/ N ⇒ **dispatch**

desperado /ˌdespəˈrɑːdəʊ/ N (pl **desperado(e)s**) desperado *m*

desperate /ˈdespərɪt/ ADJ 1 [*situation, attempt, act, struggle*] désespéré ; [*criminal*] prêt à tout, capable de tout ◆ **he's a ~ man** il est prêt à tout *or* capable de tout ◆ **there was no sign of my taxi and I was getting ~** mon taxi n'arrivait pas et je devenais fou ◆ **to resort to ~ measures** recourir à des mesures désespérées ◆ **to do something ~** commettre un acte désespéré ◆ **I was ~ to see my children again** je voulais à tout prix revoir mes enfants ◆ **both countries are ~ to avoid war** les deux pays veulent à tout prix éviter la guerre ◆ **to be ~ for sb to do sth** vouloir à tout prix que qn fasse qch ◆ **I'm ~*** (*for the lavatory*) j'ai une envie pressante* 2 (* = *very bad*) épouvantable

desperately /ˈdespərɪtlɪ/ ADV [1] *[struggle, regret]* désespérément ; *[say, look]* avec désespoir [2] *(= appallingly) [hard, poor]* extrêmement ; *[unhappy, worried, cold]* terriblement ◆ **~ shy** d'une timidité maladive ◆ **it's ~ hard work** c'est un travail extrêmement pénible ◆ **to be ~ ill** être très gravement malade ◆ **to be ~ short of sth** manquer cruellement de qch [3] *(* = very)* ◆ **I'm not ~ happy about it** ça ne me plaît pas trop ◆ **I'm not ~ keen** ça ne me dit pas grand-chose ◆ **are you hungry? – not ~** as-tu faim ? – pas trop

desperation /ˌdespəˈreɪʃən/ N *(NonC)* [1] *(= state)* désespoir *m* ◆ **to be in ~** être au désespoir ◆ **to drive sb to ~** pousser qn à bout ◆ **in ~ she kicked the door** ne sachant plus quoi faire, elle a donné un coup de pied dans la porte ◆ **in sheer ~** en désespoir de cause [2] *(= recklessness)* désespoir *m*, rage *f* du désespoir ◆ **to fight with ~** combattre avec la rage du désespoir

despicable /dɪsˈpɪkəbl/ ADJ *[action, person]* ignoble, abject, méprisable

despicably /dɪsˈpɪkəblɪ/ ADV *[behave]* ignoblement, d'une façon ignoble ◆ **that was a ~ cruel thing to say** c'était ignoble et cruel de dire une chose pareille ◆ **that is ~ underhand behaviour!** ce comportement sournois est ignoble !

despise /dɪsˈpaɪz/ VT *[+ danger, person]* mépriser ◆ **to ~ sb for sth/for having done sth** mépriser qn pour qch/pour avoir fait qch ◆ **to ~ o.s. for sth/for doing sth** avoir honte de qch/d'avoir fait qch

despisingly /dɪsˈpaɪzɪŋlɪ/ ADV avec mépris, dédaigneusement

despite /dɪsˈpaɪt/ LANGUAGE IN USE 26.2 PREP malgré, en dépit de ◆ **~ our objecting to this, they decided ...** bien que nous ayons fait des objections *or* malgré nos objections, ils ont décidé ... ◆ **Stephen, ~ himself, had to admit that ...** Stephen dut admettre, bien malgré lui, que ... N *(liter)* dépit *m*

despoil /dɪsˈpɔɪl/ VT *(liter) [+ person]* dépouiller, spolier *(of* de*)* ; *[+ country]* piller

despoiler /dɪsˈpɔɪləʳ/ N *(liter)* spoliateur *m*, -trice *f*

despoiling /dɪsˈpɔɪlɪŋ/ N spoliation *f*

despondence /dɪsˈpɒndəns/, **despondency** /dɪsˈpɒndənsɪ/ N découragement *m*, abattement *m*

despondent /dɪsˈpɒndənt/ ADJ découragé, déprimé *(about* par*)*

despondently /dɪsˈpɒndəntlɪ/ ADV *(with vb) [speak]* d'un ton découragé ◆ **out-of-work actors trudging ~ from one audition to the next** des acteurs au chômage qui se traînent, complètement découragés, d'une audition à l'autre

despot /ˈdespɒt/ N despote *m*

despotic /desˈpɒtɪk/ ADJ despotique

despotically /desˈpɒtɪkəlɪ/ ADV *[behave]* d'une manière despotique, despotiquement ; *[govern]* despotiquement, en despote

despotism /ˈdespətɪzəm/ N despotisme *m*

des res /dezˈrez/ N (abbrev of **desirable residence**) → **desirable**

dessert /dɪˈzɜːt/ N dessert *m*
COMP **dessert apple** N pomme *f* à couteau
dessert chocolate N chocolat *m* à croquer
dessert plate N assiette *f* à dessert
dessert wine N vin *m* de dessert

dessertspoon /dɪˈzɜːtspuːn/ N *(Brit)* cuiller *f* à dessert

destabilization /diːˌsteɪbɪlaɪˈzeɪʃən/ N déstabilisation *f*

destabilize /diːˈsteɪbɪˌlaɪz/ VT *(Pol) [+ regime etc]* déstabiliser

de-Stalinization /diːˌstɑːlɪnaɪˈzeɪʃən/ N déstalinisation *f*

de-Stalinize /diːˈstɑːlɪˌnaɪz/ VT déstaliniser

destination /ˌdestɪˈneɪʃən/ N destination *f*

destine /ˈdestɪn/ VT *[+ person, object]* destiner *(for* à*)*

destined /ˈdestɪnd/ ADJ [1] *(by fate)* destiné *(to* à*)* ◆ **they were ~ to meet again later** ils étaient destinés à se rencontrer plus tard ◆ **I was ~ never to see them again** je devais ne plus jamais les revoir ◆ **~ for greatness** promis à un grand avenir ◆ **at the ~ hour** *(liter)* à l'heure fixée par le destin [2] *(= heading for)* **~ for London** à destination de Londres ◆ **a letter ~ for her** une lettre qui lui est *(or* était *etc)* destinée

destiny /ˈdestɪnɪ/ N destin *m*, destinée *f* ◆ **Destiny** le destin ◆ **the destinies of France during this period** le destin de la France pendant cette période ◆ **it was his ~ to die in battle** il était écrit qu'il devait mourir au combat ◆ **a man of ~** un homme promis à une grande destinée

destitute /ˈdestɪtjuːt/ ADJ [1] *(= poverty-stricken)* indigent, sans ressources ◆ **to be utterly ~** être dans le dénuement le plus complet [2] *(= lacking)* dépourvu, dénué *(of* de*)* NPL **the destitute** les indigents *mpl*

destitution /ˌdestɪˈtjuːʃən/ N dénuement *m*, indigence *f*, misère *f* noire

de-stress * /diːˈstres/ VI, VT déstresser *

destroy /dɪsˈtrɔɪ/ VT [1] *(= spoil completely) [+ building, town, forest, document]* détruire ◆ **~ed by bombing** détruit par bombardement ◆ **the village was ~ed by fire** le village a été détruit par le feu [2] *(= kill) [+ enemy]* détruire, anéantir ; *[+ population]* détruire, exterminer ; *[+ dangerous animal, injured horse]* abattre ; *[+ cat, dog]* supprimer, faire piquer ◆ **to ~ o.s.** se suicider, se tuer [3] *(= put an end to) [+ reputation, mood, beauty, influence, faith]* détruire ; *[+ hope, love]* anéantir, détruire ; *(= spoil)* gâcher

destroyer /dɪsˈtrɔɪəʳ/ N [1] *(Naut)* contre-torpilleur *m*, destroyer *m* [2] *(= person)* destructeur *m*, -trice *f* ; *(= murderer)* meurtrier *m*, -ière *f*
COMP **destroyer escort** N escorteur *m*

destruct /dɪsˈtrʌkt/ VT *[+ missile]* détruire volontairement VI être détruit volontairement N destruction *f* volontaire
COMP **destruct button** N télécommande *f* de destruction
destruct mechanism N mécanisme *m* de destruction

destructible /dɪsˈtrʌktəbl/ ADJ destructible

destruction /dɪsˈtrʌkʃən/ N [1] *(NonC = act) [of town, building]* destruction *f* ; *[of enemy]* destruction *f*, anéantissement *m* ; *[of people, insects]* destruction *f*, extermination *f* ; *[of documents]* destruction *f* ; *[of reputation, hope]* destruction *f*, ruine *f* ; *[of character, soul]* ruine *f*, perte *f* ◆ **~ by fire** destruction *f* par un incendie *or* par le feu [2] *(NonC = damage) (from fire)* dégâts *mpl* ; *(from war)* ravages *mpl* ◆ **a scene of utter ~ met our eyes** nous avions devant les yeux un spectacle de dévastation totale

destructive /dɪsˈtrʌktɪv/ ADJ *(= damaging) [person, behaviour, effect, emotion, comment]* destructeur (-trice *f*) ; *[power, force]* destructeur (-trice *f*), destructif ◆ **he's very ~** *[child]* il casse tout ◆ **environmentally ~ projects** des projets *mpl* destructeurs pour l'environnement ◆ **to be ~ of the environment** détruire l'environnement

destructively /dɪsˈtrʌktɪvlɪ/ ADV de façon destructrice ◆ **any power can be used creatively or ~** tout pouvoir peut être utilisé de façon créative ou destructrice

destructiveness /dɪsˈtrʌktɪvnɪs/ N *[of fire, war, criticism etc]* caractère *m or* effet *m* destructeur ; *[of child etc]* penchant *m* destructeur

destructor /dɪsˈtrʌktəʳ/ N *(Brit:* also **refuse destructor***)* incinérateur *m* (à ordures)

desuetude /dɪˈsjʊɪtjuːd/ N *(liter)* désuétude *f*

desultorily /ˈdesəltərɪlɪ/ ADV *[say, look for]* sans conviction ; *[wander around]* sans but précis ◆ **to talk** *or* **chat ~** échanger des propos décousus

desultory /ˈdesəltərɪ/ ADJ *[reading]* décousu, sans suite ; *[performance]* décousu ; *[attempt]* peu suivi, peu soutenu ; *[firing, contact, applause]* irrégulier ◆ **to have a ~ conversation** échanger des propos décousus

det. abbrev of **detective**

detach /dɪˈtætʃ/ VT *[+ hook, rope, cart]* détacher, séparer *(from* de*)* ◆ **to ~ o.s. from a group** se détacher d'un groupe ◆ **a section became ~ed from ...** une section s'est détachée de ... ◆ **troops were ~ed to protect the town** on a envoyé un détachement de troupes pour protéger la ville ; see also **detached**

detachable /dɪˈtætʃəbl/ ADJ *[part of machine, section of document]* détachable *(from* de*)* ; *[collar, lining]* amovible COMP **detachable lens** N *(Phot)* objectif *m* mobile

detached /dɪˈtætʃt/ ADJ [1] *(= separate) [part, section]* détaché, séparé ◆ **~ from the world of racing** coupé du monde des courses ◆ **~ from reality** coupé de la réalité [2] *(= unbiased) [opinion]* neutre, objectif ; *(= unemotional) [manner]* détaché, indifférent ◆ **he seemed very ~ about it** il semblait ne pas du tout se sentir concerné
COMP **detached house** N *(Brit)* maison *f* individuelle (entourée d'un jardin), pavillon *m*
detached retina N décollement *m* de la rétine

detachment /dɪˈtætʃmənt/ N [1] *(NonC) [of part, section etc]* séparation *f (from* de*)* ◆ **~ of the retina** *(Med)* décollement *m* de la rétine [2] *(NonC: fig) (in manner)* détachement *m*, indifférence *f* ; *(towards pleasure, friends)* indifférence *f (towards* à, à l'égard de*)* [3] *(Mil)* détachement *m*

detail /ˈdiːteɪl/ N [1] *(also Archit, Art)* détail *m* ; *(= information on sth wanted)* renseignement *m* ◆ **in ~** en détail ◆ **in great ~** dans les moindres détails ◆ **his attention to ~** l'attention qu'il porte aux détails ◆ **to go into ~(s)** entrer dans les détails ◆ **in every ~ it resembles ...** ça ressemble dans le moindre détail à ... ◆ **the model is perfect in every ~** la maquette est parfaite dans les moindres détails ◆ **but that's a minor ~!** ce n'est qu'un (petit) détail !
[2] *(Mil)* détachement *m*
NPL **details** *(gen)* renseignements *mpl* ; *(= personal facts)* coordonnées *fpl* ◆ **let me take down the ~s** je vais noter les renseignements nécessaires ◆ **please send me ~s of ...** veuillez m'envoyer des renseignements sur *or* concernant ... ◆ **she took down my ~s** elle a noté mes coordonnées
VT [1] *[+ reason, fact, plan, progress]* exposer en détail ; *[+ story, event]* raconter en détail ; *[+ items, objects]* énumérer, détailler ◆ **a letter ~ing the reasons for his resignation** une lettre énumérant les raisons de sa démission ◆ **a report ~ing the events leading up to the riots** un rapport où sont détaillés les événements qui ont conduit aux émeutes
[2] *(Mil) [+ troops]* affecter *(for* à ; *to do sth* à *or* pour faire qch*)* détacher, désigner *(for* pour ; *to do sth* pour faire qch*)*
COMP **detail drawing** N *(by architect, draughtsman)* épure *f*

detailed /ˈdiːteɪld/ ADJ détaillé ; *[investigation, examination]* minutieux ◆ **the police made a ~ search of the scene of the crime** la police a minutieusement fouillé le lieu du crime *or* à passé le lieu du crime au peigne fin

detain /dɪˈteɪn/ VT 1 *(= keep back)* retenir ◆ **he has been ~ed at the office** il a été retenu au bureau ◆ **I don't want to ~ you any longer** je ne veux pas vous retarder *or* retenir plus longtemps 2 *(in captivity)* détenir ; *(Scol)* mettre en retenue, consigner

detainee /ˌdiːteɪˈniː/ N détenu(e) *m(f)* ; *(political)* prisonnier *m* politique

detect /dɪˈtekt/ VT *(= perceive presence of) [+ substance, gas]* détecter, découvrir ; *[+ explosive]* découvrir ; *[+ disease]* dépister ; *[+ sadness]* déceler ; *(= see or hear)* distinguer, discerner ◆ **they ~ed traces of poison in the body** on a découvert des traces de poison dans le cadavre ◆ **I thought I could ~ a note of sarcasm in his voice** j'avais cru déceler une note sarcastique dans sa voix ◆ **I could just ~ his pulse** je sentais tout juste son pouls

detectable /dɪˈtektəbl/ ADJ détectable, décelable ; → **detect**

detection /dɪˈtekʃən/ N *[of criminal, secret]* découverte *f* ; *[of gas, mines]* détection *f* ; *(Med)* dépistage *m* ◆ **the ~ of crime** la chasse aux criminels ◆ **the bloodstains led to the ~ of the criminal** les taches de sang ont mené à la découverte du criminel ◆ **to escape ~** *[criminal]* échapper aux recherches ; *[mistake]* passer inaperçu

detective /dɪˈtektɪv/ N policier *m* (en civil) ; (also **private detective**) détective *m* (privé)
COMP **detective chief inspector** N *(Brit)* ≃ inspecteur *m* divisionnaire (de police)
detective chief superintendent N *(Brit)* ≃ commissaire *m* divisionnaire (de police)
detective constable N *(Brit)* ≃ inspecteur *m* de police
detective device N dispositif *m* de détection *or* de dépistage
detective inspector N *(Brit)* ≃ inspecteur *m* principal (de police)
detective sergeant N *(Brit)* ≃ inspecteur(-chef) *m* (de police)
detective story N roman *m* policier, polar* *m*
detective superintendent N *(Brit)* ≃ commissaire *m* (de police)
detective work N *(lit, fig)* investigations *fpl* ◆ **a bit of ~ work** quelques investigations

detector /dɪˈtektəʳ/ N *(= device, person)* détecteur *m* ; → **lie², mine²** COMP **detector van** N *(Brit TV)* camion *m* de détection radiogoniométrique

detente /deɪˈtɑːnt/ N détente *f (Pol)*

detention /dɪˈtenʃən/ N *(= captivity) [of criminal, spy]* détention *f* ; *(Mil)* arrêts *mpl* ; *(Scol)* retenue *f*, consigne *f* ◆ **to give a pupil two hours' ~** donner à un élève deux heures de retenue *or* de consigne ; → **preventive**
COMP **detention centre** N *(for immigrants)* centre *m* de rétention
detention home N *(US)* ⇒ **detention centre**

deter /dɪˈtɜːʳ/ VT *(= prevent)* empêcher *(from doing sth* de faire qch) ; *(= discourage)* décourager *(from doing sth* de faire qch) dissuader *(from doing sth* de faire qch) ; *[+ attack]* prévenir ; *[+ enemy]* dissuader ◆ **...to ~ convicted hooligans from travelling abroad** ...pour empêcher les hooligans déjà condamnés d'aller à l'étranger ◆ **this could ~ investors** cela pourrait décourager les investisseurs potentiels ◆ **the facts showed that criminals were not ~red by the experience of imprisonment** l'expérience de la prison n'avait pas d'effet dissuasif sur les délinquants ◆ **I was ~red by the cost** le coût m'a fait reculer ◆ **don't let the weather ~ you** *(= prevent)* ne vous laissez pas arrêter par le temps

detergent /dɪˈtɜːdʒənt/ ADJ, N détersif *m*, détergent *m*

deteriorate /dɪˈtɪərɪəreɪt/ VI *[material]* se détériorer, s'abîmer ; *[situation]* se dégrader ; *[species, morals]* dégénérer ; *[one's health, relationships, weather]* se détériorer ◆ **his schoolwork is deteriorating** il y a un fléchissement dans son travail scolaire VT *[+ material, machine]* détériorer, abîmer

deterioration /dɪˌtɪərɪəˈreɪʃən/ N *[of goods, weather, friendship]* détérioration *f* ; *[of situation, relations]* dégradation *f* ; *[of species]* dégénération *f* ; *(in morality)* dégénérescence *f* ; *(in taste, art)* déchéance *f*, décadence *f*

determinable /dɪˈtɜːmɪnəbl/ ADJ 1 *[quantity]* déterminable 2 *(Jur)* résoluble

determinant /dɪˈtɜːmɪnənt/ ADJ, N déterminant *m*

determinate /dɪˈtɜːmɪnɪt/ ADJ *(= fixed)* déterminé

determination /dɪˌtɜːmɪˈneɪʃən/ N *(NonC)* 1 *(= firmness of purpose)* détermination *f*, résolution *f (to do sth* de faire qch) ◆ **an air of ~** un air résolu 2 *(gen, Math etc)* détermination *f* ; *[of frontiers]* délimitation *f*

determinative /dɪˈtɜːmɪnətɪv/ ADJ déterminant ; *(Gram)* déterminatif N facteur *m* déterminant ; *(Gram)* déterminant *m*

determine /dɪˈtɜːmɪn/ VT 1 *(= settle, fix) [+ conditions, policy, date]* fixer, déterminer ; *[+ price]* fixer, régler ; *[+ frontier]* délimiter ; *[+ cause, nature, meaning]* déterminer, établir ; *[+ sb's character, future]* décider de, déterminer ; *(Jur) [+ contract]* résoudre 2 *(= resolve)* décider *(to do sth* de faire qch) se déterminer, se résoudre *(to do sth* à faire qch) ; *(= cause to decide) [+ person]* décider, amener *(to do sth* à faire qch)

► **determine (up)on** VT FUS décider de, résoudre de *(doing sth* faire qch) ; *[+ course of action]* se résoudre à ; *[+ alternative]* choisir

determined /dɪˈtɜːmɪnd/ LANGUAGE IN USE 8.2 ADJ 1 *[person, appearance]* résolu, déterminé ◆ **to make ~ efforts** *or* **a ~ attempt to do sth** faire un gros effort pour faire qch ◆ **to be ~ to do sth** être bien décidé à faire qch ◆ **to be ~ that ...** être bien décidé à ce que ... + *subj* 2 *[quantity]* déterminé, établi

determinedly /dɪˈtɜːmɪndlɪ/ ADV *[say]* d'un ton déterminé *or* résolu ; *[try]* résolument ; *[walk, stride]* d'un pas (ferme et) résolu ◆ **~ optimistic** résolument optimiste ◆ **~ cheerful** d'une gaieté inébranlable

determiner /dɪˈtɜːmɪnəʳ/ N *(Gram)* déterminant *m*

determining /dɪˈtɜːmɪnɪŋ/ ADJ déterminant

determinism /dɪˈtɜːmɪnɪzəm/ N déterminisme *m*

determinist /dɪˈtɜːmɪnɪst/ ADJ, N déterministe *mf*

deterministic /dɪˌtɜːmɪˈnɪstɪk/ ADJ déterministe

deterrence /dɪˈterəns/ N force *f* de dissuasion

deterrent /dɪˈterənt/ N ◆ **they believe capital punishment is a ~** ils pensent que la peine capitale est dissuasive ◆ **alarms are supposed to be a ~, but people don't use them** les alarmes sont censées avoir un effet dissuasif, mais les gens ne les utilisent pas ◆ **to act as a ~** *[penalty]* avoir un effet dissuasif ; → **nuclear, ultimate** ADJ dissuasif

detest /dɪˈtest/ VT détester ◆ **to ~ doing sth** détester faire qch, avoir horreur de faire qch ◆ **I ~ that sort of thing!** j'ai horreur de ce genre de chose !

detestable /dɪˈtestəbl/ ADJ détestable, odieux

detestably /dɪˈtestəblɪ/ ADV *[rude]* odieusement, horriblement ; *[ugly]* horriblement

detestation /ˌdiːtesˈteɪʃən/ N 1 *(NonC)* haine *f* 2 *(= object of hatred)* abomination *f*, chose *f* détestable

dethrone /diːˈθrəʊn/ VT détrôner

dethronement /diːˈθrəʊnmənt/ N déposition *f (d'un souverain)*

detonate /ˈdetəneɪt/ VI détoner VT faire détoner *or* exploser

detonation /ˌdetəˈneɪʃən/ N détonation *f*, explosion *f*

detonator /ˈdetəneɪtəʳ/ N détonateur *m*, amorce *f*, capsule *f* fulminante ; *(Rail)* pétard *m*

detour /ˈdiːˌtʊəʳ/ N détour *m* ; *(for traffic)* déviation *f* VI faire un détour VT *(US) [+ traffic]* dévier

detox* /diːˈtɒks/ abbrev of **detoxicate, detoxication, detoxification, detoxify**

detoxicate /diːˈtɒksɪkeɪt/ VT désintoxiquer

detoxi(fi)cation /diːˌtɒksɪ(fɪ)ˈkeɪʃən/ N désintoxication *f*
COMP **detoxi(fi)cation centre** N centre *m* de désintoxication
detoxi(fi)cation programme N cure *f* de désintoxication

detoxify /diːˈtɒksɪfaɪ/ VT ⇒ **detoxicate**

detract /dɪˈtrækt/ VI ◆ **to ~ from** *[+ quality, merit]* diminuer ◆ **these criticisms do not ~ from the overall value of the text** ces critiques ne diminuent pas *or* n'enlèvent rien à la qualité globale du texte ◆ **they feared the revelations would ~ from their election campaign** ils craignaient que ces révélations ne nuisent à leur campagne électorale ◆ **it ~s from the pleasure of walking** cela diminue le plaisir de se promener

detraction /dɪˈtrækʃən/ N détraction *f*

detractor /dɪˈtræktəʳ/ N détracteur *m*, -trice *f*, critique *m*

detrain /diːˈtreɪn/ VT débarquer *(d'un train)* VI *[troops]* débarquer *(d'un train)* ; *[passengers]* descendre *(d'un train)*

detriment /ˈdetrɪmənt/ N *(= handicap)* handicap *m* ◆ **my qualifications proved to be a ~ rather than an asset** mes diplômes se sont avérés être un handicap plutôt qu'un atout ◆ **to the ~ of** au détriment de, au préjudice de ◆ **this policy ultimately worked to his own ~** cette politique a fini par lui porter préjudice ◆ **without ~ to** sans porter préjudice à ◆ **that is no ~ to ...** cela ne nuit en rien à ...

detrimental /ˌdetrɪˈmentl/ ADJ nuisible ◆ **to be ~ for sb/sth, to have a ~ effect on sb/sth** être nuisible *or* préjudiciable à qn/qch, nuire à qn/qch ◆ **to be ~ to sth** nuire à qch ◆ **this could be ~ in its effect, this could have a ~ effect** cela pourrait avoir un effet néfaste

detritus /dɪˈtraɪtəs/ N *(Geol)* roches *fpl* détritiques, pierraille *f* ; *(fig)* détritus *m*

detumescent /ˌdiːtjʊˈmesnt/ ADJ *(frm)* détumescent

deuce¹ /djuːs/ N 1 *(Cards, Dice etc)* deux *m* 2 *(Tennis)* égalité *f* ◆ **to be at ~** être à égalité

deuce² †* /djuːs/ N *(euph)* ⇒ **devil noun 3**

deuced †* /ˈdjuːsɪd/ ADJ satané *before n*, sacré* *before n* ADV diablement † ◆ **what ~ bad weather!** quel sale temps !

deuterium /djuːˈtɪərɪəm/ N deutérium *m* COMP **deuterium oxide** N eau *f* lourde

Deuteronomy /ˌdjuːtəˈrɒnəmɪ/ N le Deutéronome

Deutschmark /ˈdɔɪtʃmɑːk/, **Deutsche Mark** /ˌdɔɪtʃəˈmɑːk/ N mark *m*

devaluate /diːˈvæljʊeɪt/ VT ⇒ **devalue**

devaluation /ˌdɪvæljʊˈeɪʃən/ N dévaluation *f*

devalue /ˈdiːˈvæljuː/ VT *(Fin, fig)* dévaluer

devastate /ˈdevəsteɪt/ VT *[+ town, land]* dévaster, ravager ; *[+ opponent, opposition]* anéantir ; *(fig) [+ person]* terrasser, foudroyer ◆ **he was absolutely ~d when he heard the news** cette nouvelle lui a porté un coup terrible

devastating /ˈdevəsteɪtɪŋ/ ADJ *[war, attack, wind, storm, effect]* dévastateur (-trice *f*) ; *[consequence, result, loss]* désastreux *(to, for* pour) ; *[grief]* profond ; *[news, reply]* accablant ; *[logic]* implacable ; *[wit, charm]* irrésistible ◆ **to have a ~ effect (on sb/sth)** avoir un effet dévastateur (sur qn/qch) ◆ **with** *or* **to ~ effect** avec un effet dévastateur ◆ **(to deal) a ~ blow (to sth)** (porter) un coup fatal (à qch)

devastatingly /ˈdevəsteɪtɪŋlɪ/ ADV ◆ **~ funny** irrésistiblement drôle ◆ **a ~ attractive woman** une femme au charme ravageur ◆ **~ effective** d'une efficacité foudroyante ◆ **to be ~ successful** avoir un succès foudroyant ◆ **the German guns were ~ accurate** les canons allemands étaient terriblement précis ◆ **a ~ frank appraisal** une évaluation d'une franchise implacable

devastation /ˌdevəˈsteɪʃən/ N dévastation *f*

develop /dɪˈveləp/ VT 1 *[+ mind, body]* développer, former ; *[+ argument, thesis, business, market]* développer ; *(Math, Phot)* développer ; see also **developed**

2 *[+ region]* exploiter, mettre en valeur ; *(= change and improve)* aménager *(as* en) ◆ **this land is to be ~ed** *(= built on)* on va construire *or* bâtir sur ce terrain ; see also **developed**

3 *(= acquire, get) [+ tic, boil, cold]* attraper ; *[+ symptoms, signs]* présenter ; *[+ bad back]* commencer à souffrir de ; *[+ habit, disease]* contracter ◆ **to ~ a taste for sth** prendre goût à qch ◆ **to ~ a talent for sth** faire preuve de talent pour qch ◆ **to ~ a tendency to** manifester une tendance à

VI *[person, embryo, tendency, town, region]* se développer ; *[disease]* se déclarer ; *[talent]* s'épanouir ; *[friendship]* s'établir ; *[jealousy]* s'installer ; *(Phot) [negative, print, image]* se développer ; *[story, plotline]* se développer ; *[event, situation]* se produire ◆ **a crack was ~ing in the wall** le mur se lézardait ◆ **to ~ into** devenir

developed /dɪˈveləpt/ ADJ 1 *[economy, country]* développé ◆ **highly ~** *[ideas, theories]* mûrement pensé ; *[sense of humour, sense of the absurd]* très développé 2 *[breasts]* développé ; *[girl]* formé

developer /dɪˈveləpəʳ/ N 1 (also **property developer**) promoteur *m* (de construction) 2 *(Phot)* révélateur *m*

developing /dɪˈveləpɪŋ/ ADJ *[crisis, storm]* qui se prépare ; *[country]* en voie de développement ; *[industry]* en expansion N 1 ⇒ **development noun 1** 2 *(Phot)* développement *m* ◆ **"developing and printing"** "développement et tirage", "travaux photographiques"

COMP **developing bath** N *(Phot)* (bain *m*) révélateur *m*

developing tank N *(Phot)* cuve *f* à développement

development /dɪˈveləpmənt/ N 1 *(NonC = growth, progress) [of person, body]* développement *m* ; *[of mind]* développement *m*, formation *f* ; *[of idea]* évolution *f* ; *[of region]* exploitation *f*, mise *f* en valeur ; *[of site]* mise *f* en exploitation ; *[of technique, technology]* mise *f* au point ; *[of industry]* développement *m*, expansion *f* ◆ **at every stage in his ~** à chaque stade de son développement ◆ **economic ~** développement *m* économique ◆ **product ~** développement *m* de produits ◆ **business ~** *(= creation of new businesses)* création *f* d'entreprise(s) ◆ **to promote business ~** promouvoir la création d'entreprise(s) ◆ **business ~ advice** *(= building of existing business)* aide *f* au développement de l'entreprise ◆ **career ~** évolution *f* professionnelle

2 *(NonC = unfolding, exposition) [of subject, theme]* développement *m*, exposé *m* ; *[of idea]* développement *m* ; *[of plot, story]* déroulement *m*, développement *m*

3 *(NonC: Math, Mus, Phot)* développement *m*

4 *(NonC: Med) [of disease] (= onset)* développement *m*, apparition *f* ; *(= progression)* développement *m* ◆ **this has been linked with the ~ of breast cancer** cela a été associé au développement *or* à l'apparition du cancer du sein

5 *(esp Press = event)* fait *m* nouveau ◆ **a new ~** des développements *mpl* ◆ **there have been no (new) ~s** il n'y a pas de changements *or* nouveaux développements ◆ **the latest ~** les derniers développements ◆ **to await ~s** attendre la suite des événements ◆ **an unexpected** *or* **a surprise ~** un rebondissement

6 *(= advance)* progrès *m* ◆ **recent ~s in the treatment of skin cancer** les progrès récents *or* les récents développements en matière de traitement du cancer de la peau

7 *(Constr = building complex)* zone *f* aménagée ◆ **an industrial ~** une zone industrielle ◆ **housing** *or* **residential ~** *[of houses]* lotissement *m* ; *[of blocks of flats]* cité *f* ◆ **shopping ~** centre *m* commercial ◆ **office ~** immeuble(s) *m(pl)* de bureaux

COMP **development area** N *(Brit)* zone *f* à urbaniser en priorité, ZUP *f*

development bank N banque *f* de développement

development company N société *f* d'exploitation

development grant N aide *f* au développement

development period N *[of project, company]* phase *f* de démarrage

development planning N planification *f* du développement

developmental /dɪˌveləpˈmentl/ ADJ de croissance

deviance /ˈdiːvɪəns/, **deviancy** /ˈdiːvɪənsɪ/ N *(gen, also Psych)* déviance *f (from* de)

deviant /ˈdiːvɪənt/ ADJ *[behaviour]* déviant ; *[development]* anormal ; *(sexually)* perverti ; *(Ling) [sentence, form]* déviant N déviant(e) *m(f)*

deviate /ˈdiːvɪeɪt/ VI 1 *(from truth, former statement etc)* dévier, s'écarter *(from* de) ◆ **to ~ from the norm** s'écarter de la norme 2 *[ship, plane, projectile]* dévier

deviation /ˌdiːvɪˈeɪʃən/ N 1 *(= straying) (from principle, disciple, custom)* manquement *m (from* à) ; *(from course, trajectory: also Pol)* déviation *f (from* de) ; *(from law, instructions)* dérogation *f (from* à) ; *(from social norm)* déviance *f (from* de) ◆ **there have been many ~s from the general rule** on s'est fréquemment écarté de la règle générale ◆ **~ from the norm** écart *m* par rapport à la norme 2 *(sexual)* déviation *f* 3 *(Math)* déviation *f* ◆ **standard ~** écart type *m*

deviationism /ˌdiːvɪˈeɪʃənɪzəm/ N déviationnisme *m*

deviationist /ˌdiːvɪˈeɪʃənɪst/ ADJ, N déviationniste *mf*

device /dɪˈvaɪs/ N 1 *(= gadget)* appareil *m* ; *(= mechanism)* mécanisme *m (for* pour) ; *(Comput)* dispositif *m* ; → **safety** 2 *(= scheme, plan)* moyen *m (to do sth* de faire qch) ◆ **to leave sb to his own ~s** laisser qn se débrouiller ◆ **left to his own ~s, he'd never have finished** tout seul *or* livré à lui-même, il n'aurait jamais fini 3 *(Literat)* procédé *m* ◆ **plot** *or* **narrative ~** procédé *m* narratif 4 *(Her = emblem)* devise *f*, emblème *m* 5 (also **explosive device**) engin *m* (explosif) ◆ **nuclear ~** engin *m* nucléaire

devil /ˈdevl/ N 1 *(= evil spirit)* diable *m*, démon *m* ◆ **the Devil** le Diable, Satan *m*

2 * **poor ~!** pauvre diable ! ◆ **he's a little ~!** c'est un petit démon ! ◆ **he's a nice little ~** c'est un bon petit diable ◆ **he's a stubborn/handsome** *etc* **~** il est sacrément* entêté/beau *etc* ◆ **you little ~!** petit monstre, va ! ◆ **go on, be a ~!*** *(hum)* vas-y, vis dangereusement !

3 († *‡: as intensifier)* **he had the ~ of a job to find it** il a eu toutes les peines du monde *or* un mal fou à le trouver ◆ **the ~ of a wind** un vent du diable *or* de tous les diables ◆ **it's a ~ of a job to get him to understand** c'est toute une affaire pour le faire comprendre ◆ **why the ~ didn't you say so?** pourquoi diable ne l'as-tu pas dit ? ◆ **how the ~ would I know?** comment voulez-vous que je (le) sache ? ◆ **where the ~ is he?** où diable peut-il bien être ? ◆ **what the ~ are you doing?** mais enfin qu'est-ce que tu fabriques ?* ◆ **who the ~ are you?** qui diable êtes-vous ? ◆ **the ~ take it!** au diable ! ◆ **to work/run/shout** *etc* **like the ~** travailler/courir/crier *etc* comme un fou ◆ **there will be the ~ to pay (if/when ...)** cela va faire du grabuge* (si/quand ...), ça va barder* (si/quand ...)

4 *(phrases)* **to be between the ~ and the deep blue sea** avoir le choix entre la peste et le choléra ◆ **the ~ finds work for idle hands (to do)** *(Prov)* l'oisiveté est la mère de tous les vices *(Prov)* ◆ **(every man for himself and) the ~ take the hindmost** *(Prov)* sauve qui peut ◆ **go to the ~!‡** va te faire voir !*, va te faire cuire un œuf !* ◆ **speak** *or* **talk of the ~ (and he appears)!** *(hum)* quand on parle du loup (on en voit la queue) ! ◆ **to play** *or* **be the ~'s advocate** se faire l'avocat du diable ◆ **(to) give the ~ his due ...** pour être honnête, il faut reconnaître que ... ◆ **he has the luck of the ~*** *or* **the ~'s own luck*** il a une veine insolente *or* une veine de cocu‡ ◆ **better the ~ you know (than the ~ you don't)** *(Prov)* mieux vaut un danger que l'on connaît qu'un danger que l'on ne connaît pas

5 (also **printer's devil**) apprenti *m* imprimeur ; *(= hack writer)* nègre* *m (d'un écrivain etc)* ; *(Jur)* ≃ avocat *m* stagiaire

VI ◆ **to ~ for sb** *(Literat etc)* servir de nègre* à qn ; *(Jur)* ≃ faire office d'avocat stagiaire auprès de qn

VT 1 *(Culin) [+ kidneys]* (faire) griller au poivre et à la moutarde ◆ **~led** *(Brit) or* **~ed** *(US)* **egg** œuf *m* à la diable

2 *(US * = nag)* harceler *(verbalement)*

COMP **devil-may-care** ADJ insouciant, je-m'en-foutiste*

devil's food cake N *(US) gâteau au chocolat*

Devil's Island N l'île *f* du Diable

devils-on-horseback NPL *(Culin) pruneaux entourés de lard servis sur toast*

devilfish /ˈdevlfɪʃ/ N (pl **devilfish** *or* **devilfishes**) *(= manta)* mante *f*

devilish /ˈdevlɪʃ/ ADJ *[idea, act, invention, cunning]* diabolique ADV († * *= very)* diablement*, rudement* ◆ **it's ~ cold** il fait un froid du diable *or* de canard*

devilishly /ˈdevlɪʃlɪ/ ADV 1 *(= wickedly)* **she grinned/laughed ~** elle eut un sourire/un rire diabolique ◆ **~ cunning/handsome/clever** d'une astuce/beauté/intelligence diabolique 2 *(* = extremely)* ⇒ **devilish adv**

devilishness /ˈdevlɪʃnɪs/ N *[of invention]* caractère *m* diabolique ; *[of behaviour]* méchanceté *f* diabolique

devilment /ˈdevlmənt/ N *(NonC) (= mischief)* diablerie *f*, espièglerie *f* ; *(= spite)* méchanceté *f*, malice *f* ◆ **a piece of ~** une espièglerie ◆ **for ~** par pure malice *or* méchanceté

devilry /ˈdevlrɪ/, **deviltry** *(US)* /ˈdevltrɪ/ N 1 *(= daring)* (folle) témérité *f* ; *(= mischief)* diablerie *f*, espièglerie *f* ; *(= wickedness)* méchanceté *f* (diabolique) 2 *(= black magic)* magie *f* noire, maléfices *mpl*

devious /ˈdiːvɪəs/ ADJ 1 *(= sly) [means]* détourné ; *[person, behaviour]* retors, sournois ;

[mind] retors, tortueux 2 *(= tortuous)* *[route]* détourné

deviously /ˈdiːvɪəslɪ/ ADV *[act, behave]* de manière sournoise, sournoisement

deviousness /ˈdiːvɪəsnɪs/ N *[of person]* fourberie *f*, sournoiserie *f* ; *[of scheme, method]* complexité(s) *f(pl)*

devise /dɪˈvaɪz/ VT *[+ scheme, style]* imaginer, concevoir ; *[+ plotline]* imaginer ; *(Jur)* léguer ◆ **of his own devising** de son invention N *(Jur)* legs *m* (de biens immobiliers)

devisee /dɪvaɪˈziː/ N *(Jur)* légataire *mf (qui reçoit des biens immobiliers)*

deviser /dɪˈvaɪzəʳ/ N *[of scheme, plan]* inventeur *m*, -trice *f*, auteur *m*

devisor /dɪˈvaɪzəʳ/ N *(Jur)* testateur *m*, -trice *f (qui lègue des biens immobiliers)*

devitalization /diːˌvaɪtəlaɪˈzeɪʃən/ N *(gen)* affaiblissement *m* ; *[tooth]* dévitalisation *f*

devitalize /diːˈvaɪtəlaɪz/ VT affaiblir ; *[+ tooth]* dévitaliser

devoice /diːˈvɔɪs/ VT *(Phon)* assourdir

devoiced /diːˈvɔɪst/ ADJ *(Phon)* *[consonant]* dévoisé

devoicing /diːˈvɔɪsɪŋ/ N *(Phon)* dévoisement *m*

devoid /dɪˈvɔɪd/ ADJ *(frm)* ◆ ~ **of** *[ornament, charm, talent, qualities, imagination]* dépourvu de ; *[scruples, compassion, good sense, humour, interest, meaning]* dénué de

devolution /ˌdiːvəˈluːʃən/ N *[of power, authority]* délégation *f* ; *(Jur)* *[of property]* transmission *f*, dévolution *f* ; *(Pol etc)* décentralisation *f* ; *(Bio)* dégénérescence *f*

devolve /dɪˈvɒlv/ VI 1 *(frm)* *[duty, responsibility]* incomber *(on, upon* à) ; *(by chance)* échoir *(on, upon* à) ◆ **it ~d on** *or* **upon me to take the final decision** c'est à moi qu'il incombait de prendre la décision définitive ◆ **the cost of the operation ~s upon the patient** le coût de l'opération est à la charge du patient 2 *(Jur)* *[property]* passer *(on, upon* à) être transmis *(on, upon* à) 3 *(= secede)* devenir autonome, faire sécession 4 *(= dissolve)* ◆ **the union ~d into a looser confederation of states** l'union s'est scindée *or* s'est fractionnée en une confédération d'États plus indépendants VT *[+ power, responsibility, authority]* déléguer *(on, upon* à) ◆ **to ~ power away from central government** déléguer le pouvoir du gouvernement central ◆ **a ~d government** un gouvernement décentralisé

Devonian /dəˈvəʊnɪən/ ADJ *(Geol)* *[period]* dévonien

devote /dɪˈvəʊt/ VT *[+ time, life, book, magazine]* consacrer *(to* à) ; *[+ resources]* affecter *(to* à) consacrer *(to* à) ◆ **to ~ o.s. to** *[+ a cause]* se vouer à, se consacrer à ; *[+ pleasure]* se livrer à ; *[+ study, hobby]* s'adonner à, se consacrer à, se livrer à ◆ **the money ~d to education** l'argent consacré à l'éducation ◆ **two chapters ~d to his childhood** deux chapitres consacrés à son enfance

devoted /dɪˈvəʊtɪd/ ADJ 1 *(= loyal)* *[husband, mother, friend]* dévoué ; *[friendship]* solide, profond ; *[follower]* fidèle ◆ ~ **care** dévouement *m* ◆ **to be a ~ admirer of sb/sth** être un fervent admirateur de qn/qch ◆ **Joyce is a ~ Star Trek fan** Joyce est une inconditionnelle de Star Trek ◆ **to be ~ to sb** être dévoué à qn ◆ **to be ~ to sth** être fidèle à qch ◆ **they are ~ to one another** ils sont très attachés l'un à l'autre 2 ◆ ~ **to** *(= concerned with)* consacré à ◆ **a museum ~ to ecology** un musée consacré à l'écologie

devotedly /dɪˈvəʊtɪdlɪ/ ADV avec dévouement

devotee /ˌdevəʊˈtiː/ N *[of doctrine, theory]* partisan(e) *m(f)* ; *[of religion]* adepte *mf* ; *[of sport, music, poetry]* passionné(e) *m(f)*

devotion /dɪˈvəʊʃən/ N *(NonC, to duty)* dévouement *m (to* à) ; *(to friend)* dévouement *m (to* à, envers) (profond) attachement *m (to* pour) ; *(to work)* dévouement *m (to* à) ardeur *f (to* pour, à) ; *(Rel)* dévotion *f*, piété *f* ◆ **with great ~** avec un grand dévouement NPL **devotions** *(Rel)* dévotions *fpl*, prières *fpl*

devotional /dɪˈvəʊʃənl/ ADJ *[book]* de dévotion, de piété ; *[attitude]* de prière, pieux

devour /dɪˈvaʊəʳ/ VT 1 *[+ food]* dévorer, engloutir ; *(fig)* *[+ book]* dévorer ; *[+ money]* engloutir, dévorer ◆ **to ~ sb/sth with one's eyes** dévorer qn/qch des yeux 2 *[fire]* dévorer, consumer ◆ **~ed by jealousy** dévoré de jalousie

devouring /dɪˈvaʊərɪŋ/ ADJ *[hunger, passion]* dévorant ; *[zeal]* ardent ; *[enthusiasm]* débordant

devout /dɪˈvaʊt/ ADJ 1 *(= pious)* *[person]* pieux, dévot ; *[faith, Christianity, Catholicism etc]* dévot ; *[prayer, attention, hope]* fervent 2 *(fig = committed)* *[supporter, opponent]* fervent

devoutly /dɪˈvaʊtlɪ/ ADV 1 *(= fervently)* *[hope, believe, wish]* sincèrement 2 *(= piously)* avec dévotion ◆ **the islanders are ~ religious** les habitants de l'île sont profondément religieux ◆ **he was a ~ Christian prince** c'était un prince chrétien très pieux

DEW, dew[1] /djuː/ ABBR *(US)* abbrev of **distant early warning** COMP **DEW line** N DEW *f (système de radars)*

dew[2] /djuː/ N rosée *f* ; → **mountain**

dewclaw /ˈdjuːklɔː/ N ergot *m*

dewdrop /ˈdjuːdrɒp/ N goutte *f* de rosée

dewlap /ˈdjuːlæp/ N *[of cow, person]* fanon *m*

dewpoint /ˈdjuːpɔɪnt/ N point *m* de rosée *or* de condensation

dewpond /ˈdjuːpɒnd/ N mare *f (alimentée par la condensation)*

dewy /ˈdjuːɪ/ ADJ *[grass]* couvert de *or* humide de rosée ◆ ~ **lips** *(liter)* lèvres *fpl* fraîches COMP **dewy-eyed** ADJ *(= innocent)* aux grands yeux ingénus ; *(= credulous)* trop naïf (naïve *f*)

dex * /deks/ N *(Drugs)* Dexédrine ® *f*

Dexedrine ® /ˈdeksɪdriːn/ N Dexédrine ® *f*

dexie * /ˈdeksɪ/ N *(Drugs)* comprimé *m* de Dexédrine ®

dexterity /deksˈterɪtɪ/ N *(intellectual)* habileté *f* ; *(manual, physical)* dextérité *f*, adresse *f* ◆ ~ **in doing sth** habileté *or* dextérité à faire qch, adresse avec laquelle on fait qch ◆ **a feat of ~** un tour d'adresse ◆ **verbal ~** éloquence *f*

dexterous /ˈdekstrəs/ ADJ *[person]* adroit, habile ; *[movement]* adroit, agile ◆ **by the ~ use of** par l'habile emploi de

dexterously /ˈdekstrəslɪ/ ADV adroitement, habilement

dextrin /ˈdekstrɪn/ N dextrine *f*

dextrose /ˈdekstrəʊs/ N dextrose *m*

dextrous(ly) /ˈdekstrəs(lɪ)/ ⇒ **dexterous(ly)**

DF (abbrev of **direction finder**) → **direction**

DFC /ˌdiːefˈsiː/ N (abbrev of **Distinguished Flying Cross**) *médaille décernée aux aviateurs militaires*

DfES /ˌdiːefiːˈes/ N *(Brit)* (abbrev of **Department for Education and Skills**) → **department**

DG 1 (abbrev of **director general**) → **director** 2 (abbrev of **Deo gratias**) par la grâce de Dieu

dg (abbrev of **decigram(s)**) dg *m*

DH /diːˈeɪtʃ/ N *(Brit)* (abbrev of **Department of Health**) → **department**

dhal /dɑːl/ N → **dal**

dhoti /ˈdəʊtɪ/ N dhotî *m*

dhow /daʊ/ N boutre *m (voilier arabe)*

DHSS /ˌdiːeɪtʃesˈes/ N *(Brit)* *(formerly)* (abbrev of **Department of Health and Social Security**) → **health**

DI /diːˈaɪ/ N 1 (abbrev of **Donor Insemination**) → **donor** 2 *(Brit Police)* (abbrev of **Detective Inspector**) → **detective**

diabetes /ˌdaɪəˈbiːtiːz/ N diabète *m* ◆ **to have ~** être diabétique, avoir du diabète

diabetic /ˌdaɪəˈbetɪk/ N diabétique *mf* ADJ 1 *(= person)* diabétique 2 *(= for diabetics)* *[chocolate, dessert, jam etc]* pour diabétiques

diabolic /ˌdaɪəˈbɒlɪk/ ADJ ⇒ **diabolical 1**

diabolical /ˌdaɪəˈbɒlɪkəl/ ADJ 1 *[act, invention, plan, power]* diabolique, infernal, satanique ; *[laugh, smile]* satanique, diabolique 2 *(* = dreadful)* *[child]* infernal * ; *[weather]* atroce *, épouvantable

diabolically /ˌdaɪəˈbɒlɪkəlɪ/ ADV 1 *(* = horribly)* *[hot, difficult]* horriblement 2 *(= wickedly)* diaboliquement ◆ ~ **clever** d'une astuce diabolique ◆ **she grinned/laughed** ~ elle eut un sourire/rire diabolique 3 *(* = very badly)* *[drive, sing, cook etc]* horriblement mal

diachronic /ˌdaɪəˈkrɒnɪk/ ADJ diachronique

diacid /daɪˈæsɪd/ N biacide *m*, diacide *m*

diacritic /ˌdaɪəˈkrɪtɪk/ ADJ diacritique N signe *m* diacritique

diacritical /ˌdaɪəˈkrɪtɪkəl/ ADJ diacritique

diadem /ˈdaɪədem/ N *(lit, fig)* diadème *m*

diaeresis, dieresis *(US)* /daɪˈerɪsɪs/ N (pl **diaereses, diereses** *(US)* /daɪˈerɪˌsiːz/) *(Ling)* diérèse *f* ; *(Typ)* *(= symbol)* tréma *m*

diagnose /ˈdaɪəgnəʊz/ VT *(Med, fig)* diagnostiquer ◆ **his illness was ~d as bronchitis** on a diagnostiqué une bronchite

diagnosis /ˌdaɪəgˈnəʊsɪs/ N (pl **diagnoses** /ˌdaɪəgˈnəʊsiːz/) *(Med, fig)* diagnostic *m* ; *(Bio, Bot)* diagnose *f*

diagnostic /ˌdaɪəgˈnɒstɪk/ ADJ diagnostique ◆ ~ **program** *(Comput)* programme *m* de diagnostic

diagnostician /ˌdaɪəgnɒsˈtɪʃən/ N diagnostiqueur *m*

diagnostics /ˌdaɪəgˈnɒstɪks/ N *(NonC: Comput etc)* diagnostic *m*

diagonal /daɪˈægənl/ ADJ diagonal N diagonale *f*

diagonally /daɪˈægənəlɪ/ ADV *(with vb)* *[write, cross, cut, fold]* en diagonale ; *[park]* en épi ◆ **the car was struck ~ by a lorry** la voiture a été prise en écharpe par un camion ◆ **a sash worn ~ across the chest** une grande écharpe portée en travers de la poitrine ◆ **the bank is ~ opposite the church, on the right/left** par rapport à l'église, la banque est de l'autre côté de la rue, sur la droite/gauche

diagram /ˈdaɪəgræm/ N *(gen)* diagramme *m*, schéma *m* ; *(Math)* diagramme *m*, figure *f* ◆ **as shown in the ~** comme le montre le diagramme *or* le schéma

diagrammatic /ˌdaɪəgrəˈmætɪk/ ADJ schématique

dial /ˈdaɪəl/ LANGUAGE IN USE 27 N cadran *m* ; → **sundial** VT *(Telec)* *[+ number]* faire, composer ◆ **you must ~ 336 12 95** il faut faire *or* composer le 336 12 95 ◆ **to ~ 999** *(Brit)* ≈ appeler police-secours ◆ **to ~ a wrong number** faire un faux *or* mauvais numéro ◆ **to ~ direct** appeler par l'automatique ◆ **can I ~ London from here?** est-ce que d'ici je peux avoir Londres par l'automatique ? ◆ **Dial-a-pizza** *service de livraison de pizzas à domicile*

COMP **dial code** N *(US Telec)* indicatif *m*

dial tone N *(US Telec)* tonalité *f*

dial-up service N *(Comput)* service *m* de télétraitement

dial. abbrev of **dialect**

dialect /ˈdaɪəlekt/ N *(regional)* dialecte *m*, parler *m* ; *(local, rural)* patois *m* ◆ **the Norman ~** le dialecte normand, les parlers *mpl* normands ◆ **in ~** en dialecte, en patois ◆ **social-class ~** sociolecte *m*
COMP *[word]* dialectal
dialect atlas N atlas *m* linguistique
dialect survey N étude *f* de dialectologie

dialectal /ˌdaɪəˈlektl/ ADJ dialectal

dialectical /ˌdaɪəˈlektɪkəl/ ADJ dialectique COMP
dialectical materialism N matérialisme *m* dialectique

dialectician /ˌdaɪəlekˈtɪʃən/ N dialecticien(ne) *m(f)*

dialectics /ˌdaɪəˈlektɪks/ N *(NonC)* dialectique *f*

dialectology /ˌdaɪəlekˈtɒlədʒɪ/ N *(NonC)* dialectologie *f*

dialling, dialing *(US)* /ˈdaɪəlɪŋ/ N *(Telec)* composition *f* d'un numéro (de téléphone)
COMP **dialling code** N *(Brit)* indicatif *m*
dialling tone N *(Brit)* tonalité *f*

dialogue, dialog *(US)* /ˈdaɪəlɒg/ N *(lit, fig)* dialogue *m* COMP **dialogue box, dialog box** *(US)* N *(Comput)* boîte *f* de dialogue

dialysis /daɪˈæləsɪs/ N (pl **dialyses** /daɪˈælɪˌsiːz/) dialyse *f* COMP **dialysis machine** N rein *m* artificiel

diamanté /ˌdaɪəˈmæntɪ/ N strass *m* ADJ *[brooch etc]* en strass

diameter /daɪˈæmɪtəʳ/ N diamètre *m* ◆ **the circle is one metre in ~** le cercle a un mètre de diamètre

diametrical /ˌdaɪəˈmetrɪkəl/ ADJ *(Math, fig)* diamétral

diametrically /ˌdaɪəˈmetrɪkəlɪ/ ADV 1 **~ opposed** *or* **opposite** diamétralement opposé *(to* à) 2 *(Math)* diamétralement

diamond /ˈdaɪəmənd/ N 1 *(= stone)* diamant *m* ; → **rough** 2 *(= shape, figure)* losange *m* 3 *(Cards)* carreau *m* ◆ **the ace/six of ~s** l'as/le six de carreau ; → **club** 4 *(Baseball)* diamant *m*, terrain *m* (de base-ball)
COMP *[clip, ring]* de diamant(s)
diamond-cutting N taille *f* du diamant
diamond district N ◆ **the ~ district of New York/Amsterdam** le quartier des diamantaires à New York/Amsterdam
diamond drill N foreuse *f* à pointe de diamant
diamond jubilee N (célébration *f* du) soixantième anniversaire *m (d'un événement)*
diamond merchant N diamantaire *m*
diamond necklace N rivière *f* de diamants
diamond-shaped ADJ en losange
diamond wedding N noces *fpl* de diamant

diamorphine /ˌdaɪəˈmɔːfiːn/ N diamorphine *f*

Diana /daɪˈænə/ N Diane *f*

diapason /ˌdaɪəˈpeɪzən/ N diapason *m* ◆ **open/stopped ~** *(of organ)* diapason *m* large/étroit

diaper /ˈdaɪəpəʳ/ N *(US)* couche *f (de bébé)* COMP **diaper service** N service *m* de couches à domicile

diaphanous /daɪˈæfənəs/ ADJ *(liter)* diaphane

diaphoretic /ˌdaɪəfəˈretɪk/ ADJ, N *(Med)* diaphorétique *m*

diaphragm /ˈdaɪəfræm/ N *(all senses)* diaphragme *m*

diarist /ˈdaɪərɪst/ N *[of personal events]* auteur *m* d'un journal intime ; *[of contemporary events]* mémorialiste *mf*, chroniqueur *m*

diarrhoea, diarrhea *(US)* /ˌdaɪəˈriːə/ N diarrhée *f* ◆ **to have ~** avoir la diarrhée *or* la colique

diarrhoeal, diarrheal *(US)* /ˌdaɪəˈrɪəl/ ADJ diarrhéique

diary /ˈdaɪərɪ/ N *(= record of events)* journal *m* (intime) ; *(for engagements)* agenda *m* ◆ **to keep a ~** tenir un journal ◆ **I've got it in my ~** je l'ai noté sur mon agenda

diaspora /daɪˈæspərə/ N diaspora *f*

diastole /daɪˈæstəlɪ/ N diastole *f*

diatonic /ˌdaɪəˈtɒnɪk/ ADJ diatonique

diatribe /ˈdaɪətraɪb/ N diatribe *f (against* contre)

dibasic /ˌdaɪˈbeɪsɪk/ ADJ bibasique, dibasique

dibber /ˈdɪbəʳ/ N *(esp Brit)* ⇒ **dibble**

dibble /ˈdɪbl/ N plantoir *m* VT repiquer

dibs /dɪbz/ NPL 1 *(= game)* osselets *mpl* ; *(Cards) (= counters)* jetons *mpl* 2 *(Brit † ‡ = money)* fric‡ *m* 3 *(US: ‡)* **to have ~ on sth** avoir des droits sur qch ◆ **~ on the cookies!** prems'‡ pour les petits gâteaux !

dice /daɪs/ N *(pl inv)* dé *m* ◆ **to play ~** jouer aux dés ◆ **no ~!‡** *(esp US) (fig)* pas question ! ; → **load** VI jouer aux dés ◆ **he was dicing with death** il jouait avec la mort VT *[+ vegetables]* couper en dés *or* en cubes

dicey* /ˈdaɪsɪ/ ADJ *(Brit)* risqué ◆ **it's ~, it's a ~ business** c'est bien risqué

dichotomy /dɪˈkɒtəmɪ/ N dichotomie *f*

Dick /dɪk/ N (dim of **Richard**) Richard *m*

dick /dɪk/ N 1 *(‡ = detective)* détective *m* ; → **clever, private** 2 *(*‡ = penis)* bite*‡ *f*

dickens †* /ˈdɪkɪnz/ N *(euph)* ⇒ **devil**

Dickensian /dɪˈkenzɪən/ ADJ à la Dickens

dicker /ˈdɪkəʳ/ VI *(US)* marchander

dickey /ˈdɪkɪ/ N * *[of shirt]* faux plastron *m (de chemise)*
COMP **dickey bird*** N *(baby talk)* petit zoziau *m (baby talk)* ◆ **watch the ~ bird!** *(Phot)* le petit oiseau va sortir ! ◆ **not a ~ bird** * que dalle‡ ◆ **I won't say a ~ bird about it** * je n'en piperai pas mot
dickey-bow* N *(= bow tie)* nœud *m* pap*
dickey seat N *(Brit)* strapontin *m* ; *(in car)* spider *m*

dickhead*‡ /ˈdɪkhed/ N tête *f* de nœud*‡

dicky¹ /ˈdɪkɪ/ ⇒ **dickey**

dicky²* /ˈdɪkɪ/ ADJ *(Brit) [person]* patraque*, pas solide* ; *[health, heart]* qui flanche*, pas solide* ; *[situation]* pas sûr*, pas solide*

dicta /ˈdɪktə/ NPL of **dictum**

Dictaphone ® /ˈdɪktəfəʊn/ N dictaphone ® *m* ◆ **~ typist** dactylo *f* qui travaille au dictaphone ®

dictate /dɪkˈteɪt/ VT 1 *[+ letter, passage]* dicter *(to* à) 2 *(= demand, impose) [+ terms, conditions]* dicter, imposer ◆ **his action was ~d by circumstances** il a agi comme le lui dictaient les circonstances ◆ **reason/common sense ~s that ...** la raison/le bon sens veut que ... VI 1 dicter ◆ **she spent the morning dictating to her secretary** elle a passé la matinée à dicter des lettres (*or* des rapports *etc*) à sa secrétaire 2 *(= order about)* ◆ **to ~ to sb** imposer sa volonté à qn, régenter qn ◆ **I won't be ~d to!** je n'ai pas d'ordres à recevoir ! N /ˈdɪkteɪt/ *(gen pl)* ◆ **~s** ordre(s) *m(pl)*, précepte(s) *m(pl) (de la raison etc)* ◆ **the ~s of conscience** la voix de la conscience

dictation /dɪkˈteɪʃən/ N *(in school, office etc)* dictée *f* ◆ **to write to sb's ~** écrire sous la dictée de qn

dictator /dɪkˈteɪtəʳ/ N *(fig, Pol)* dictateur *m*

dictatorial /ˌdɪktəˈtɔːrɪəl/ ADJ *(lit, fig) [person]* tyrannique ; *[régime, powers]* dictatorial

dictatorially /ˌdɪktəˈtɔːrɪəlɪ/ ADV *(fig, Pol)* autoritairement, dictatorialement, en dictateur

dictatorship /dɪkˈteɪtəʃɪp/ N *(fig, Pol)* dictature *f*

diction /ˈdɪkʃən/ N 1 *(Literat = style)* style *m*, langage *m* ◆ **poetic ~** langage *m* poétique 2 *(= pronunciation)* diction *f*, élocution *f* ◆ **his ~ is very good** il a une très bonne diction

dictionary /ˈdɪkʃənrɪ/ N dictionnaire *m* ◆ **to look up a word in a ~** chercher un mot dans un dictionnaire ◆ **it's not in the ~** ce n'est pas dans le dictionnaire ◆ **French ~** dictionnaire *m* de français ◆ **English-French ~** dictionnaire *m* anglais-français ◆ **monolingual/bilingual ~** dictionnaire *m* monolingue/bilingue
COMP **dictionary definition** N définition *f* de dictionnaire ◆ **the ~ definition of "art"** le mot "art" tel qu'on le définit dans le dictionnaire
dictionary-maker N *(= person)* lexicographe *mf*
dictionary-making N lexicographie *f*

dictum /ˈdɪktəm/ N (pl **dictums** *or* **dicta**) *(= maxim)* dicton *m*, maxime *f* ; *(= pronouncement)* proposition *f*, affirmation *f* ; *(Jur)* principe *m*

did /dɪd/ VB pt of **do¹**

didactic /dɪˈdæktɪk/ ADJ didactique

didactically /dɪˈdæktɪkəlɪ/ ADV *[speak]* sur un ton didactique ; *[write]* de façon didactique

diddle* /ˈdɪdl/ VT *(Brit = cheat) [+ person]* rouler (dans la farine)*, escroquer ◆ **you've been ~d** tu t'es fait rouler* *or* avoir* ◆ **to ~ sb out of sth, to ~ sth out of sb** carotter* qch à qn

diddler‡ /ˈdɪdləʳ/ N *(Brit)* carotteur* *m*, -euse* *f*, escroc *m*

diddly(-squat)‡ /ˈdɪdlɪ(ˈskwɒt)/ N *(US)* ◆ **you don't know ~(-squat) (about that)** t'y connais que dalle‡ ◆ **that doesn't mean ~(-squat) (to me)** (pour moi,) c'est du vent tout ça ◆ **their promises mean ~(-squat)** leurs promesses ne sont que du vent

didgeridoo /ˌdɪdʒərɪˈduː/ N didgeridoo *m (instrument de musique australien)*

didn't /ˈdɪdənt/ ⇒ **did not ;** → **do¹**

Dido /ˈdaɪdəʊ/ N Didon *f*

die¹ /daɪ/ VI 1 *[person]* mourir, décéder *(frm)* ; *[animal, plant]* mourir, crever ; *[engine, motor]* caler, s'arrêter ◆ **he ~d in hospital** il est mort *or* décédé à l'hôpital ◆ **to be dying** être en train de mourir ; *(= nearly dead)* être à l'article de la mort ◆ **doctors told him he was dying and had only a year to live** les médecins lui ont dit qu'il était condamné et qu'il n'avait plus qu'un an à vivre ◆ **they were left to ~** on les a laissés mourir ◆ **to ~ for one's country/beliefs** mourir pour son pays/ses idées ◆ **Christ ~d for us/for our sins** le Seigneur est mort pour nous/pour expier nos péchés ◆ **to ~ by one's own hand** *(frm)* se suicider, mettre fin à ses jours ◆ **to ~ with one's boots on*** mourir debout ◆ **he ~d a hero** il est mort en héros ◆ **he ~d a pauper** il est mort dans la misère ◆ **he ~d happy** *or* **a happy man** *(= died in peace)* il est mort en paix, il est mort heureux ◆ **to ~ like a dog** † mourir comme un chien ◆ **never say ~!** * il ne faut jamais désespérer ! ◆ **you only ~ once** on ne meurt qu'une fois ◆ **I'd rather** *or* **sooner ~!** *(fig)* plutôt mourir ! ◆ **I nearly** *or* **could have ~d!** *(lit)* j'ai failli mourir ! ; *(* fig: of embarrassment)* j'étais mort de honte ! ◆ **I want to ~!** *(lit) (pain, depression etc)* je voudrais mourir *or* être mort ! ; *(embarrassment)* je suis mort de honte ! ◆ **he'd ~ for her** il donnerait sa vie pour elle ◆ **I'd ~ for a body/car** *etc* **like that!** je ferais n'importe quoi pour avoir un corps/une voiture *etc* comme celui-là/celle-là ! ◆ **a body/car** *etc* **to ~ for** * un corps/une voiture de rêve ◆ **it's to ~ for!**‡ ça me fait craquer ! *

◆ **to die of/from** ◆ **to ~ of** *or* **from cancer/AIDS/malaria** mourir du cancer/du sida/de la malaria ◆ **to ~ of hunger/cold** mourir de faim/froid ◆ **to ~ from one's injuries** mourir des suites de ses blessures ◆ **to ~ of a broken heart** mourir de chagrin *or* de tristesse ◆ **I almost ~d of shame/fright** j'étais mort de honte/peur ◆ **we nearly ~d of boredom** on s'ennuyait à mourir

◆ **to be dying to do sth*** mourir d'envie de faire qch
◆ **to be dying for sth*** avoir une envie folle de qch ◆ **I'm dying for a cigarette/a cup of coffee** j'ai une envie folle de fumer une cigarette/de boire une tasse de café ◆ **I was dying for a pee*** j'avais très envie de faire pipi* ◆ **she was dying for him to kiss her** elle n'attendait qu'une chose : qu'il l'embrasse *subj* ; → **natural**
2 * *[performer]* faire un bide * *or* un four
3 *(fig = die out) [fire, love, memory]* s'éteindre, mourir ; *[custom, language]* mourir, disparaître ; *[sound]* s'éteindre ◆ **her smile ~d on her lips** son sourire s'est évanoui *or* a disparu ◆ **her words ~d on her lips** *(liter)* elle est restée bouche bée ◆ **the secret ~d with him** il a emporté le secret dans la tombe ◆ **to ~ hard** *[tradition, attitude, prejudice]* avoir la vie dure ◆ **old habits ~ hard** *(Prov)* les vieilles habitudes ont la vie dure
VT ◆ **to ~ a natural/violent death** mourir de mort naturelle/de mort violente ◆ **to ~ a slow *or* lingering death** mourir d'une mort lente ◆ **to ~ a painful death** mourir dans la souffrance ◆ **to ~ the death** *[person]* faire un bide* ; *[idea, plan]* tomber à l'eau ◆ **he ~d the death** * *(fig)* il aurait voulu rentrer sous terre ; *(Theat) [performer]* il a fait un bide* *or* un four ◆ **to ~ a thousand deaths** *(liter)* être au supplice, souffrir mille morts
► **die away** VI *[sound, voice, laughter]* s'éteindre ; *[breeze, wind]* tomber ◆ **his footsteps ~d away** le bruit de ses pas s'est éteint
► **die back** VI *[plant]* perdre ses feuilles et sa tige
► **die down** VI *[emotion, protest]* se calmer, s'apaiser ; *[wind]* tomber, se calmer ; *[fire] (in blazing building)* diminuer, s'apaiser ; *(in grate etc)* baisser, tomber ; *[noise]* diminuer ; *[applause]* se taire ; *[violence, conflict]* s'atténuer ◆ **the fuss quickly ~d down** l'agitation est vite retombée
► **die off** VI mourir *or* être emportés les uns après les autres
► **die out** VI *[species, race, family]* disparaître ; *[custom, language, skill, technique]* disparaître, se perdre ◆ **to be dying out** *[species, race, tribe]* être en voie d'extinction ; *[custom, language, skill]* être en train de disparaître *or* de se perdre

die² /daɪ/ N 1 (pl **dice** /daɪs/) dé *m* ◆ **the ~ is cast** le sort en est jeté, les dés sont jetés ◆ **as straight as a ~** *(Brit) (person)* franc comme l'or ; *(street, tree trunk)* droit comme un i ; → **dice** 2 (pl **dies**) *(in minting)* coin *m* ; *(in manufacturing)* matrice *f* ◆ **stamping ~** étampe *f*
COMP **die-cast** ADJ moulé sous pression VT mouler sous pression
die-casting N moulage *m* *or* coulage *m* sous pression
die-sinker N graveur *m* de matrices
die-stamp VT graver

dièdre /di'edər/ N *(Climbing)* dièdre *m*

diehard /'daɪhɑːd/ N *(= one who resists to the last)* jusqu'au-boutiste *mf* ; *(= opponent of change)* conservateur *m*, -trice *f* (à tout crin) ; *(= obstinate politician etc)* dur(e) *m(f)* à cuire*, réactionnaire *mf* ADJ intransigeant, inébranlable ; *(Pol)* réactionnaire

dielectric /,daɪɪ'lektrɪk/ ADJ, N diélectrique *m*

dieresis /daɪ'erɪsɪs/ N *(US)* ⇒ **diaeresis**

diesel /'diːzəl/ N 1 *(= fuel)* gazole *m*, diesel *m* 2 *(= car)* (voiture *f*) diesel *m*
COMP **diesel-electric** ADJ diesel-électrique
diesel engine N *(in vehicle)* moteur *m* diesel ; *(= locomotive)* motrice *f*
diesel fuel, diesel oil N gasoil *m*, diesel *m*
diesel train N autorail *m*

diestock /'daɪstɒk/ N *(= frame)* cage *f* (de filière à peignes) ; *(= tool)* filière *f* à main

diet¹ /'daɪət/ N 1 *(= restricted food)* régime *m* ◆ **to be/go on a ~** être/se mettre au régime ◆ **he's on a special ~** il suit un régime spécial ◆ **a high/low-protein ~** un régime à haute/basse teneur en protéines
2 *(= customary food)* alimentation *f*, régime *m* alimentaire ◆ **a healthy ~** une alimentation saine ◆ **as soon as I returned to my normal ~** dès que j'ai repris mon régime alimentaire habituel ◆ **to live on a (constant) ~ of** *(lit)* vivre *or* se nourrir de ◆ **she lives on a constant ~ of TV soap operas** *(fig)* elle passe son temps à regarder des feuilletons à la télévision ◆ **for years they have fed us a staple ~ of propaganda** cela fait des années qu'ils nous assènent leur propagande ◆ **children who are fed a relentless ~ of violence on TV** des enfants qui regardent sans arrêt des images violentes à la télévision
VI suivre un régime
VT mettre au régime
COMP **diet drink** N *(low calorie)* boisson *f* basses calories *or* light *inv* ; *(for special or restricted diet)* boisson *f* diététique
diet foods *(low calorie)* N aliments *mpl* basses calories ; *(for special or restricted diet)* aliments *mpl* diététiques

diet² /'daɪət/ N *(esp Pol)* diète *f*

dietary /'daɪətərɪ/ ADJ *[habit, change]* alimentaire ; *[advice]* de diététique COMP **dietary fibre** N cellulose *f* végétale, fibres *fpl* alimentaires

dieter /'daɪətər/ N personne *f* qui suit un régime ◆ **she's a keen ~** elle est souvent au régime

dietetic /,daɪə'tetɪk/ ADJ diététique

dietetics /,daɪə'tetɪks/ N *(NonC)* diététique *f*

dietician /,daɪə'tɪʃən/ N diététicien(ne) *m(f)*

differ /'dɪfər/ VI 1 *(= be different)* différer, se distinguer *(from* de) ◆ **the herring gull ~s from the common gull in the colour of its legs** le goéland argenté se distingue du goéland cendré par la couleur de ses pattes 2 *(= disagree)* ne pas être d'accord, ne pas s'entendre *(from sb* avec qn ; *on or about sth* sur qch) ◆ **the two points of view do not ~ much** les deux points de vue ne se distinguent guère l'un de l'autre *or* ne sont pas très différents l'un de l'autre ◆ **they ~ in their approach to the problem** ils diffèrent en *or* sur leur manière d'appréhender le problème ◆ **I beg to ~** permettez-moi de ne pas partager cette opinion *or* de ne pas être de votre avis ◆ **the texts ~** les textes ne s'accordent pas ◆ **to ~ from the rules** *(Jur)* déroger aux règles ; → **agree**

difference /'dɪfrəns/ N 1 *(= dissimilarity)* différence *f* (in de ; *between* entre) ◆ **that makes a big ~ to me** c'est très important pour moi, ça ne m'est pas du tout égal, cela compte beaucoup pour moi ◆ **to make a ~ in sb/sth** changer qn/qch ◆ **that makes all the ~** voilà qui change tout ◆ **what ~ does it make?, what's the ~?** quelle différence (cela fait-il) ? ◆ **what ~ does it make if ...?** qu'est-ce que cela peut faire que ... + *subj* ?, quelle importance cela a-t-il si ... + *indic* ? ◆ **it makes no ~** peu importe, cela ne change rien (à l'affaire) ◆ **it makes no ~ to me** cela m'est égal, ça ne (me) fait rien ◆ **for all the ~ it makes** pour ce que cela change *or* peut changer ◆ **it makes no ~ what colour/how expensive your car is** peu importe la couleur/le prix de votre voiture ◆ **same ~!** * c'est du pareil au même !*, c'est kif-kif !* ◆ **with this ~, that ...** à la différence que ..., à ceci près que ... ◆ **a car with a ~** une voiture pas comme les autres* ◆ **test-drive a Jaguar and feel the ~!** essayez une Jaguar et vivez la différence ! ; → **know**
2 *(= quarrel)* différend *m* ◆ **they are seeking to resolve their ~s** ils tentent de résoudre leurs différends ◆ **~ of opinion** différence *f* *or* divergence *f* d'opinions
3 *(Math)* différence *f* (in de ; *between* entre) ◆ **to pay the ~** payer la différence ; → **split**

different /'dɪfrənt/ ADJ 1 *(= not the same)* différent *(from, to, (US) than* de) ; *(= other)* autre ◆ **completely ~** totalement différent, tout autre ◆ **completely ~ from** totalement différent de ◆ **he wore a ~ tie each day** il portait chaque jour une cravate différente ◆ **go and put on a ~ tie** va mettre une autre cravate ◆ **if he'd gone to university things might have been ~** s'il était allé à l'université les choses auraient peut-être été différentes ◆ **I feel a ~ person** je me sens revivre, je me sens tout autre ◆ **let's do something ~** faisons quelque chose de différent ◆ **he wants to be ~** il veut se singulariser ◆ **~ strokes for ~ folks*** *(US)* chacun son truc*
◆ **quite + different** ◆ **quite a ~ way of doing it** une tout autre manière de le faire ◆ **that's quite a ~ matter** ça c'est une autre affaire, c'est tout autre chose ◆ **she's quite ~ from what you think** elle n'est pas du tout ce que vous croyez
2 *(= various)* différent, divers ; *(= several)* plusieurs ◆ **~ people had noticed this** plusieurs personnes l'avaient remarqué ◆ **in the ~ countries I've visited** dans les différents *or* divers pays que j'ai visités
3 *(= unusual)* original ◆ **recipes for interesting, ~ dishes** des recettes de plats intéressants et originaux ◆ **what do you think of my shirt? – well, it's ~ ...** que penses-tu de ma chemise ? – eh bien, elle est originale ...
ADV (tout) autrement ◆ **if it had happened to them, I'm sure they would think ~** si cela leur était arrivé, je suis sûr qu'ils penseraient tout autrement ◆ **she believes this, but I know ~** c'est ce qu'elle croit mais je sais qu'il n'en est rien *or* qu'il en va tout autrement ◆ **children behave like that because they don't know any ~*** les enfants se comportent ainsi parce qu'ils ignorent que ça ne se fait pas ◆ **to me things seemed normal because I didn't know any ~*** les choses me semblaient normales car je ne savais pas que ça pouvait être différent

differential /,dɪfə'renʃəl/ ADJ différentiel N *(Math)* différentielle *f* ; *(esp Brit) (in pay)* écart *m* salarial ; *(in vehicle engine)* différentiel *m*
COMP **differential calculus** N *(Math)* calcul *m* différentiel
differential equation N équation *f* différentielle
differential gear N (engrenage *m*) différentiel *m*
differential housing N boîtier *m* de différentiel
differential operator N opérateur *m* différentiel
differential pricing N *(Econ)* tarification *f* différentielle

differentially /,dɪfə'renʃəlɪ/ ADV *(Tech)* par action différentielle

differentiate /,dɪfə'renʃɪeɪt/ VI faire la différence *or* la distinction *(between* entre) ◆ **he cannot ~ between red and green** il ne fait pas la différence entre le rouge et le vert, il ne distingue pas le rouge du vert ◆ **in his article he ~s between ...** dans son article, il fait la distinction entre ... ◆ **we must ~ between the meanings of this term** il nous faut différencier les sens de ce mot VT *[+ people, things]* différencier, distinguer *(from* de) ; *(Math)* différentier, calculer la différentielle de ◆ **this is what ~s the two brothers** c'est ce qui différencie les deux frères ◆ **this is what ~s one candidate from another** c'est ce qui distingue *or* différencie les candidats

differentiation /,dɪfərenʃɪ'eɪʃən/ N différenciation *f* ; *(Math)* différentiation *f*

differently /'dɪfrəntlɪ/ ADV 1 différemment *(from* de) ◆ **she was never treated ~ from the**

men on ne l'a jamais traitée différemment des hommes ◆ **he thinks ~ from you** *(= has different mentality)* il ne pense pas comme vous ; *(= disagrees)* il n'est pas de votre avis ◆ **we all react ~ to stress** nous réagissons tous différemment face au stress, nous avons tous des réactions différentes face au stress ◆ **if only things had turned out ~!** si seulement les choses s'étaient passées différemment ! 2 ◆ **~ coloured/shaped** *(= of various colours/shapes)* de différentes couleurs/formes ; *(= having other colours/shapes)* de couleurs différentes/aux formes différentes 3 *(in politically correct language)* ◆ **~ abled** *(= physically handicapped)* handicapé

difficult /ˈdɪfɪkəlt/ LANGUAGE IN USE 6.3, 12.3 ADJ 1 *[problem, situation, decision, task, writer]* difficile ◆ **there's nothing ~ about it** ça n'a rien de difficile ◆ **it's ~ being a man today** c'est difficile d'être un homme aujourd'hui ◆ **this work is ~ to do** ce travail est difficile à faire ◆ **it's ~ to do that** c'est difficile de faire ça ◆ **it is ~ to deny that ...** il est difficile de nier que *+ indic* ... ◆ **he finds it ~ to apologize** cela lui coûte de s'excuser, il a du mal à s'excuser ◆ **to find it ~ to do sth** avoir du mal à faire qch ◆ **the climate makes it ~ to grow crops** le climat rend les cultures difficiles ◆ **his injury makes it ~ (for him) to get around** il se déplace difficilement à cause de sa blessure ◆ **he's ~ to get on with** il est difficile à vivre ◆ **it is ~ to see what they could have done** on voit mal ce qu'ils auraient pu faire ◆ **the ~ thing is knowing** *or* **to know where to start** le (plus) difficile *or* dur est de savoir par où commencer

2 *(= awkward, uncooperative) [person, child]* difficile ◆ **come on now, don't be ~!** allez, ne crée pas de problèmes !

difficulty /ˈdɪfɪkəltɪ/ N difficulté *f* ◆ **with/without ~** avec/sans difficulté *or* peine ◆ **it's feasible, but with ~** c'est faisable, mais ce sera difficile ◆ **she has ~ (in) walking** elle marche avec difficulté, elle a de la difficulté à marcher ◆ **slight ~ (in) breathing** un peu de gêne dans la respiration ◆ **we had some ~ finding him** on a eu du mal à le trouver ◆ **the ~ is (in) choosing** le difficile *or* la difficulté c'est de choisir ◆ **to make difficulties for sb** créer des difficultés à qn ◆ **without meeting any difficulties** sans rencontrer d'obstacles *or* la moindre difficulté, sans accrocs ◆ **to get into ~** *or* **difficulties** se trouver en difficulté ◆ **to get into all sorts of difficulties** se trouver plongé dans toutes sortes d'ennuis ◆ **to get o.s. into ~** se créer des ennuis ◆ **to get out of a ~** se tirer d'affaire *or* d'embarras ◆ **I am in ~** j'ai des difficultés, j'ai des problèmes ◆ **to be in (financial) difficulties** être dans l'embarras, avoir des ennuis d'argent ◆ **he was in ~** *or* **difficulties over the rent** il était en difficulté pour son loyer ◆ **he was working under great difficulties** il travaillait dans des conditions très difficiles ◆ **I can see no ~ in what you suggest** je ne vois aucun obstacle à ce que vous suggérez ◆ **he's having ~** *or* **difficulties with his wife/his car/his job** il a des ennuis *or* des problèmes avec sa femme/avec sa voiture/dans son travail

diffidence /ˈdɪfɪdəns/ N manque *m* de confiance en soi, manque *m* d'assurance

diffident /ˈdɪfɪdənt/ ADJ *[person]* qui manque de confiance *or* d'assurance ; *[smile]* embarrassé ◆ **to be ~ about doing sth** hésiter à faire qch (par modestie *or* timidité)

diffidently /ˈdɪfɪdəntlɪ/ ADV *[speak, ask]* d'un ton mal assuré ; *[behave]* avec timidité

diffract /dɪˈfrækt/ VT diffracter

diffraction /dɪˈfrækʃən/ N diffraction *f* ◆ **~ grating** réseau *m* de diffraction

diffuse /dɪˈfjuːz/ VT *[+ light, heat, perfume, news]* diffuser, répandre ◆ **~d lighting** éclairage *m* indirect VI *[light, heat, perfume, news]* se diffuser, se répandre ADJ /dɪˈfjuːs/ *[light, thought]* diffus ; *[style, writer]* prolixe, diffus

diffuseness /dɪˈfjuːsnɪs/ N 1 *[of light, thought]* qualité *f* diffuse 2 *[of style, writer]* prolixité *f*

diffuser /dɪˈfjuːzəʳ/ N *(for light, hair dryer)* diffuseur *m*

diffusion /dɪˈfjuːʒən/ N diffusion *f*

dig /dɪg/ (vb : pret, ptp **dug**) N 1 *(with hand/elbow)* coup *m* de poing/de coude ◆ **to give sb a ~ in the ribs** donner un coup de coude dans les côtes de qn

2 *(= sly comment)* pique *f* ◆ **to have** *or* **take a ~ at sb** envoyer *or* lancer une pique à qn ◆ **was that a ~ at me?** cette pique m'était destinée ?

3 *(with spade)* coup *m* de bêche

4 *(Archeol)* fouilles *fpl* ◆ **to go on a ~** aller faire des fouilles

VT 1 *[+ ground] (gen)* creuser ; *(with spade)* bêcher ; *[+ grave, trench, hole]* creuser ; *[+ tunnel]* creuser, percer ; *[+ potatoes etc]* arracher ◆ **they dug their way out of prison** ils se sont évadés de prison en creusant un tunnel ◆ **to ~ one's own grave** *(lit, fig)* creuser sa propre tombe

2 *(= thrust) [+ fork, pencil etc]* enfoncer *(sth into sth* qch dans qch) ◆ **to ~ sb in the ribs** donner un coup de coude dans les côtes de qn

3 *(esp US* ‡) *(= understand)* piger* ; *(= take notice of)* viser* ◆ **you ~?** tu piges ?* ◆ **~ that guy!** vise un peu ce mec !* ◆ **I ~ that!** *(= enjoy)* ça me botte !* ◆ **I don't ~ football** le football ne me dit rien *or* me laisse froid

VI 1 *[dog, pig]* fouiller, fouir ; *[person]* creuser *(into dans)* ; *(Tech)* fouiller ; *(Archeol)* faire des fouilles ◆ **to ~ for minerals** creuser pour extraire du minerai

2 *(fig)* ◆ **to ~ in one's pockets for sth** *(searching for sth)* fouiller dans ses poches pour trouver qch ◆ **to ~ into one's pockets** *or* **purse** *(= spend money) (for oneself)* piocher dans ses économies ; *(to help other people)* mettre la main au porte-monnaie ◆ **to ~ deep** *(= search hard)* mener une enquête approfondie ; *(= try hard) [athlete etc]* puiser dans ses réserves ; *(= give generously)* mettre la main au porte-monnaie ◆ **to ~ into the past** fouiller dans le passé

► **dig in** VI 1 *(Mil)* se retrancher ; *(fig)* être fin prêt ◆ **the pickets are ~ging in for a long strike** les piquets de grève se préparent à un conflit prolongé

2 *(* = eat)* attaquer* ◆ **~ in!** allez-y, attaquez ! ◆ **let's ~ in!** allez, on attaque !

VT SEP 1 *(into ground) [+ compost, manure]* mélanger à la terre, enterrer

2 *(= push, thrust in) [+ blade, knife]* enfoncer ◆ **to ~ one's heels in** *(fig)* se braquer, se buter ◆ **to ~ the knife in** *(fig)* remuer le couteau dans la plaie

► **dig into** VT FUS *[+ sb's past]* fouiller dans ; *(* = eat) [+ food]* attaquer*

► **dig out** VT SEP *[+ tree, plant]* déterrer ; *[+ animal]* déloger ; *(fig) [+ facts, information]* déterrer, dénicher ◆ **to ~ sb out of the snow/rubble** sortir qn de la neige/des décombres ◆ **where did he ~ out* that old hat?** où a-t-il été pêcher* *or* dénicher ce vieux chapeau ?

► **dig over** VT SEP *[+ earth]* retourner ; *[+ garden]* bêcher, retourner

► **dig up** VT SEP *[+ weeds, vegetables]* arracher ; *[+ treasure, body]* déterrer ; *[+ earth]* retourner ; *[+ garden]* bêcher, retourner ; *(fig) [+ fact, solution, idea]* déterrer, dénicher

digest /daɪˈdʒest/ VT *[+ food, idea]* digérer, assimiler ; *[+ insult]* digérer* ◆ **this kind of food is not easy to ~** *or* **easily ~ed** ce genre de nourriture est un peu indigeste VI digérer N /ˈdaɪdʒest/ *(= summary) [of book, facts]* sommaire *m*, résumé *m* ; *(= magazine)* digest *m* ; *(Jur)* digeste *m* ◆ **in ~ form** en abrégé

digester /daɪˈdʒestəʳ/ N digesteur *m*

digestible /dɪˈdʒestəbl/ ADJ *(lit, fig)* facile à digérer, digeste

digestion /dɪˈdʒestʃən/ N *(Anat, Chem, fig)* digestion *f*

digestive /dɪˈdʒestɪv/ ADJ digestif N *(Brit:* also **digestive biscuit**) ≃ (sorte *f* de) sablé *m* ; → **juice**

COMP **digestive system** N système *m* digestif
digestive tract N appareil *m* digestif

digger /ˈdɪgəʳ/ N 1 *(= machine)* excavatrice *f*, pelleteuse *f* 2 *(= miner)* ouvrier mineur *m* ; *(= navvy)* terrassier *m* 3 *(‡ = Australian)* Australien *m* ; *(‡ = New-Zealander)* Néo-Zélandais *m* 4 ** (Mil Hist) soldat australien ou néo-zélandais de la première guerre mondiale* ; → **gold**

digging /ˈdɪgɪŋ/ N *(NonC, with spade)* bêchage *m* ; *[of hole etc]* forage *m* ; *(Min)* creusement *m*, excavation *f* NPL **diggings** *(Min)* placer *m* ; *(Archeol)* fouilles *fpl*

digicam /ˈdɪdʒɪkæm/ N caméra *f* numérique

digit /ˈdɪdʒɪt/ N 1 *(Math)* chiffre *m* ◆ **double-/triple-~** à deux/trois chiffres 2 *(= finger)* doigt *m* ; *(= toe)* orteil *m* 3 *(Astron)* doigt *m*

digital /ˈdɪdʒɪtəl/ ADJ 1 *[radio, readout, recording]* numérique ; *[tape, recorder]* audionumérique ; *[clock, watch]* à affichage numérique 2 *(Anat)* digital

COMP **digital audio tape** N bande *f* audionumérique *or* DAT
digital camera N appareil *m* (photo) numérique
digital compact cassette N cassette *f* compacte numérique
digital pen N stylo *m* numérique
digital radio N radio *f* numérique
digital television N télévision *f* numérique

digitalin /ˌdɪdʒɪˈteɪlɪn/ N digitaline *f*

digitalis /ˌdɪdʒɪˈteɪlɪs/ N *(= plant)* digitale *f* ; *(= substance)* digitaline *f*

digitally /ˈdɪdʒɪtəlɪ/ ADV *(Audio, Mus) [record, transmit etc]* en numérique ◆ **~ remastered** mixé en numérique ◆ **"digitally remastered (version)"** *(on CD cover)* "remix numérique", "mixage numérique"

digitize /ˈdɪdʒɪtaɪz/ VT *(Comput)* digitaliser, numériser

digitizer /ˌdɪdʒɪtaɪzəʳ/ N *(Comput)* digitaliseur *m*, convertisseur *m* numérique

diglossia /daɪˈglɒsɪə/ N diglossie *f*

diglossic /daɪˈglɒsɪk/ ADJ diglossique

dignified /ˈdɪgnɪfaɪd/ ADJ *[person, manner]* plein de dignité, digne ; *[silence]* digne ◆ **a ~ old lady** une vieille dame très digne ◆ **he is very ~** il a beaucoup de dignité ◆ **she made a ~ exit** elle est sortie, très digne

dignify /ˈdɪgnɪfaɪ/ VT donner de la dignité à ◆ **to ~ sth/sb with the name of ...** gratifier qch/qn du nom de ... ◆ **I refuse to ~ that ridiculous comment with an answer** je ne m'abaisserai pas à répondre à cette remarque ridicule

dignitary /ˈdɪgnɪtərɪ/ N dignitaire *m*

dignity /ˈdɪgnɪtɪ/ N 1 *(NonC) [of person, occasion, character, manner]* dignité *f* ◆ **he thinks that's beneath his ~** il se croit au-dessus de ça ◆ **it would be beneath his ~ to do such a thing** il s'abaisserait en faisant une chose pareille ◆ **to stand on one's ~** prendre de grands airs ◆ **to (be allowed to) die with ~** (se voir accorder le droit de) mourir dignement *or* dans la dignité 2 *(= high rank)* dignité *f*, haut rang *m* ; *(= title)* titre *m*, dignité *f*

digress /daɪˈgres/ VI faire une digression ◆ **to ~ from** s'écarter *or* s'éloigner de ◆ **... but I ~ ...** mais je m'écarte du sujet

digression /daɪˈgreʃən/ N digression *f* ◆ **this by way of** ~ ceci (soit) dit en passant

digressive /daɪˈgresɪv/ ADJ digressif

digs †* /dɪgz/ NPL (Brit) (= *lodgings*) chambre *f* meublée (*avec ou sans pension*) ◆ **I'm looking for** ~ je cherche une chambre meublée à louer ◆ **to be in** ~ loger en garni †

dihedral /daɪˈhiːdrəl/ ADJ, N dièdre *m*

dike /daɪk/ N ⇒ **dyke 1**

diktat /ˈdɪktɑːt/ N diktat *m*

dilapidated /dɪˈlæpɪdeɪtɪd/ ADJ [*building, fence*] délabré ; [*vehicle*] en mauvais état ; [*book*] en mauvais état, abîmé ◆ **in a ~ state** [*building*] très délabré

dilapidation /dɪˌlæpɪˈdeɪʃən/ N [*of buildings*] délabrement *m*, dégradation *f* ; (*Jur: gen pl*) détérioration *f* (*causée par un locataire*) ; (*Geol*) dégradation *f*

dilate /daɪˈleɪt/ VT dilater ◆ **to ~ the cervix** dilater le col (de l'utérus) ◆ **to be 3cm ~d** (*in labour*) être dilaté de 3 cm VI 1 se dilater 2 (= *talk at length*) **to ~ (up)on sth** s'étendre sur qch, raconter qch en détail

dilation /daɪˈleɪʃən/ N dilatation *f* COMP **dilation and curettage** N (*Med*) curetage *m*

dilatoriness /ˈdɪlətərɪnɪs/ N lenteur *f* (*in doing sth* à faire qch) caractère *m* dilatoire

dilatory /ˈdɪlətərɪ/ ADJ [*person*] traînard, lent ; [*action, policy*] dilatoire ◆ **they were very ~ about it** ils ont fait traîner les choses (en longueur) COMP **dilatory motion** N (*Pol*) manœuvre *f* dilatoire

dildo /ˈdɪldəʊ/ N godemiché *m*

dilemma /daɪˈlemə/ N dilemme *m* ◆ **to be in a ~, to be on the horns of a ~** être face à *or* devant un dilemme

dilettante /ˌdɪlɪˈtæntɪ/ N (pl **dilettantes** *or* **dilettanti** /ˌdɪlɪˈtæntɪ/) dilettante *mf* COMP de dilettante

dilettantism /ˌdɪlɪˈtæntɪzəm/ N dilettantisme *m*

diligence /ˈdɪlɪdʒəns/ N zèle *m*, diligence *f* (*frm*) ◆ **his ~ in his work** le zèle *or* la diligence (*frm*) dont il fait preuve dans son travail ◆ **to work with ~** faire preuve d'assiduité dans son travail

diligent /ˈdɪlɪdʒənt/ ADJ [*student, worker, work*] appliqué ; [*search*] minutieux ◆ **to be ~ in doing sth** faire qch avec zèle *or* diligence (*frm*)

diligently /ˈdɪlɪdʒəntlɪ/ ADV avec zèle *or* diligence (*frm*)

dill /dɪl/ N aneth *m*, fenouil *m* bâtard

dilly * /ˈdɪlɪ/ N (US) ◆ **it's/he's a ~** c'est/il est sensationnel * *or* vachement * bien ◆ **we had a ~ of a storm** nous avons eu une sacrée * tempête ◆ **it's a ~** (*of problem*) c'est un casse-tête

dillydally /ˈdɪlɪdælɪ/ VI (= *dawdle*) lanterner, lambiner * ; (= *fritter time away*) musarder ; (= *vacillate*) tergiverser, atermoyer

dillydallying /ˈdɪlɪdælɪɪŋ/ N (= *vacillation*) tergiversation(s) *f(pl)* ◆ **no ~!** (= *dawdling*) ne traînez pas !

dilute /daɪˈluːt/ VT [*+ liquid*] diluer ; [*+ wine*] couper ; [*+ sauce*] délayer, allonger ; (*Pharm*) diluer ; (*fig*) diluer, édulcorer ◆ **"dilute to taste"** "à diluer selon votre goût" ADJ [*liquid*] coupé, dilué ; (*fig*) dilué, édulcoré

diluter /daɪˈluːtəʳ/ N diluant *m*

dilution /daɪˈluːʃən/ N dilution *f* ; [*of wine, milk*] coupage *m*, mouillage *m* ; (*fig*) édulcoration *f*

dim /dɪm/ ADJ 1 (= *not bright*) [*light, lamp*] faible ; [*room, place*] sombre ; (*fig*) [*prospects, outlook*] sombre

2 (= *vague*) [*shape, outline*] vague, imprécis ; [*recollection, memory*] vague ; → **view**

3 (*liter*) [*eyes, sight*] faible ◆ **Elijah's eyes were growing ~** la vue d'Élie baissait

4 (*Brit* * = *stupid*) bouché *

VT 1 (= *turn down*) [*+ light*] réduire, baisser ; [*+ lamp*] mettre en veilleuse ; [*+ sb's sight*] brouiller, troubler ◆ **to ~ the lights** (*Theat*) baisser les lumières ◆ **to ~ the headlights** (*US Aut*) se mettre en code(s)

2 (= *make dull*) [*+ colours, metals, beauty*] ternir ; [*+ sound*] assourdir ; [*+ memory, outline*] effacer, estomper ; [*+ mind, senses*] affaiblir ; [*+ glory*] ternir

VI (also **grow dim**) 1 [*light*] baisser, décliner ; [*sight*] baisser, se troubler

2 [*metal, beauty, glory*] se ternir ; [*colours*] devenir terne ; [*outlines, memory*] s'effacer, s'estomper

COMP **dim-out** N (*US*) black-out *m* partiel

dim-sighted ADJ à la vue basse

dim-witted * ADJ crétin *, idiot ◆ **a ~-witted * mechanic** un crétin * de mécanicien

▸ **dim out** (US) VT SEP [*+ city*] plonger dans un black-out partiel

N ◆ **dim-out** → **dim**

dimbo * /ˈdɪmbəʊ/ N (*Brit*) (*man*) ballot * *m* ; (*woman*) godiche * *f*

dime /daɪm/ N (pièce *f* de) dix cents ◆ **it's not worth a ~** * (*US*) cela ne vaut pas un clou * *or* un radis * ◆ **they're a ~ a dozen** * (*fig*) il y en a *or* on en trouve à la pelle *

COMP **dime novel** N (*US*) roman *m* de gare, roman *m* de quatre sous

dime store N (*in US*) ≈ Prisunic ® *m*

dimension /daɪˈmenʃən/ N (= *size, extension in space*) dimension *f* ; (*Archit, Geom*) dimension *f*, cote *f* ; (*fig*) (= *scope, extent*) [*of problem, epidemic*] étendue *f*

diminish /dɪˈmɪnɪʃ/ VT [*+ strength, power*] amoindrir ; [*+ effect*] diminuer, atténuer ; [*+ numbers, cost, speed*] réduire ; [*+ enthusiasm, optimism*] tempérer ; (*Mus*) diminuer VI diminuer ; [*effect*] s'atténuer

diminished /dɪˈmɪnɪʃt/ ADJ 1 [*strength, power*] amoindri ; [*value, budget, capacity, cost, numbers, staff, resources, supply*] réduit ; [*enthusiasm, optimism*] tempéré ; [*reputation*] terni ◆ **a ~ staff** un personnel réduit 2 (*Mus*) [*interval, fifth, seventh*] diminué COMP **diminished responsibility** N (*Jur*) responsabilité *f* atténuée

diminishing /dɪˈmɪnɪʃɪŋ/ ADJ [*amount, importance*] qui diminue, qui va en diminuant ; [*strength, power*] qui s'amoindrit ; [*resources, supply*] qui s'amenuise ; [*numbers, value, cost*] en baisse ; [*effect*] qui s'atténue ◆ **~ scale** (*Art*) échelle *f* fuyante *or* de perspective ◆ **law of ~ returns** loi *f* des rendements décroissants N diminution *f*

diminuendo /dɪˌmɪnjʊˈendəʊ/ N diminuendo *m inv* VI faire un diminuendo

diminution /ˌdɪmɪˈnjuːʃən/ N [*of value*] baisse *f*, diminution *f* ; [*of speed*] réduction *f* ; [*of strength, enthusiasm*] diminution *f*, affaiblissement *m* (*in de*) ; [*of temperature*] baisse *f*, abaissement *m* (*in de*) ; [*of authority*] baisse *f* (*in de*) ; (*Mus*) diminution *f*

diminutive /dɪˈmɪnjʊtɪv/ ADJ 1 [*person, object*] tout petit, minuscule ; [*house, garden*] tout petit, exigu (-guë *f*), minuscule 2 (*Ling* = *shortened*) diminutif N (*Ling*) diminutif *m*

dimity /ˈdɪmɪtɪ/ N basin *m*

dimly /ˈdɪmlɪ/ ADV 1 (= *not brightly*) [*shine*] faiblement ◆ **~ lit** mal éclairé 2 (= *vaguely*) [*see, hear, recollect*] vaguement ◆ **the hills were ~ visible through the mist** on apercevait confusément les collines dans la brume ◆ **I was ~ aware that someone was talking to me** j'étais vaguement conscient que quelqu'un me parlait ◆ **she was ~ aware of Gavin's voice** elle entendait vaguement la voix de Gavin

COMP **dimly-remembered** ADJ dont on se souvient mal

dimmer /ˈdɪməʳ/ N 1 (*Elec*: also **dimmer switch**) variateur *m* (de lumière) 2 (*US*) (= *headlights*) ◆ **~s** phares *mpl* code *inv*, codes *mpl* ; (= *parking lights*) feux *mpl* de position

dimming /ˈdɪmɪŋ/ N 1 [*of light*] affaiblissement *m*, atténuation *f* ; [*of mirror, reputation*] ternissement *m* 2 (*US*) [*of headlights*] mise *f* en code(s)

dimness /ˈdɪmnɪs/ N 1 [*of light, sight*] faiblesse *f* ; [*of room, forest*] obscurité *f* ; [*of outline, memory*] flou *m* ; [*of colour, metal*] aspect *m* terne ; [*of intelligence*] faiblesse *f* 2 (* = *stupidity*) stupidité *f*

dimorphism /ˌdaɪˈmɔːfɪzəm/ N dimorphisme *m*

dimple /ˈdɪmpl/ N (*in chin, cheek*) fossette *f* (*on sur*) ; (*in water*) ride *f* VI [*water*] se rider ◆ **she ~d, her cheeks ~d** ses joues se creusèrent de deux fossettes VT ◆ **the wind ~d the water** le vent ridait la surface de l'eau

dimpled /ˈdɪmpld/ ADJ [*cheek, chin*] à fossette

dim sum, Dim Sum /dɪmˈsʌm/ N dim sum *m*

dimwit ‡ /ˈdɪmwɪt/ N imbécile *mf*, crétin(e) * *m(f)*

DIN /dɪn/ N (abbrev of **Deutsche Industrie Normen**) DIN

din /dɪn/ N vacarme *m*, chahut *m* ◆ **the ~ of battle** le fracas de la bataille ◆ **to make** *or* **kick up a ~** * faire du boucan * VT ◆ **to ~ sth into sb** rebattre les oreilles à qn de qch ◆ **she ~ned it into the child that he mustn't speak to strangers** elle répétait sans cesse à l'enfant qu'il ne devait pas parler à des inconnus

dinar /ˈdiːnɑː/ N dinar *m*

din-dins /ˈdɪndɪnz/ N (*Brit: baby talk*) miam-miam *m* (*baby talk*) ◆ **it's time for ~, your ~ is ready** c'est l'heure de faire miam-miam

dine /daɪn/ VI dîner (*off, on* de) ◆ **they ~d off** *or* **on a chicken** ils ont dîné d'un poulet VT inviter à dîner ; → **wine**

COMP **dining car** N (*Brit Rail*) wagon-restaurant *m*

dining hall N réfectoire *m*, salle *f* à manger

dining room N salle *f* à manger ; (*in hotel*) salle *f* de restaurant

dining room suite N salle *f* à manger (*meubles*)

dining room table, dining table N table *f* de salle à manger

▸ **dine in** VI dîner à la maison *or* chez soi

▸ **dine out** VI dîner en ville *or* au restaurant ◆ **he ~d out on that story for a long time afterwards** il a resservi cette histoire trente-six fois par la suite

diner /ˈdaɪnəʳ/ N 1 (= *person*) dîneur *m*, -euse *f* 2 (*Rail*) wagon-restaurant *m* 3 (*US*) petit restaurant *m*

dinero ‡ /dɪˈneərəʊ/ N (*US*) pognon * *m*, fric * *m*

dinette /daɪˈnet/ N coin-repas *m* ; → **kitchen**

ding-a-ling /ˈdɪŋəˈlɪŋ/ N 1 [*of bell, telephone*] dring dring *m* 2 (*US* ‡ = *fool*) cloche * *f*

dingbat ‡ /ˈdɪŋˌbæt/ N (*US*) imbécile *mf*, andouille * *f*

ding-dong /ˈdɪŋˈdɒŋ/ N 1 (= *noise*) ding dong *m* 2 (* = *quarrel*) prise *f* de bec ADJ * [*fight*] acharné, dans les règles (*fig*) ADV ding dong

dinghy /ˈdɪŋgɪ/ N youyou *m*, petit canot *m* ; (*collapsible*) canot *m* pneumatique ; (also **sailing dinghy**) dériveur *m*

dinginess /ˈdɪndʒɪnɪs/ N aspect *m* minable * *or* miteux

dingo /ˈdɪŋgəʊ/ N (pl **dingoes**) dingo *m*

dingus ‡ /ˈdɪŋgəs/ N (*US*) truc * *m*, machin * *m*

dingy /ˈdɪndʒɪ/ ADJ miteux

dink * /dɪŋk/ N (*US baby talk* = *penis*) zizi * *m*

dinkie * /ˈdɪŋkɪ/ (abbrev of **double income no kids**) N ◆ **~s** jeune(s) couple(s) *m(pl)* salarié(s) sans enfant ≃ couple(s) *m(pl)* yuppie(s) ADJ *[attitude, lifestyle]* ≃ de yuppie

dinkum * /ˈdɪŋkəm/ ADJ *(Austral)* ◆ **he's a (fair) ~ Aussie** il est australien jusqu'au bout des ongles ◆ **fair ~!** *(= seriously!)* sans blague ! *

dinky * /ˈdɪŋkɪ/ ADJ 1 *(Brit)* mignon, gentil 2 *(US pej)* de rien du tout

dinner /ˈdɪnəʳ/ N *(= evening meal)* dîner *m* ; *(= lunch)* déjeuner *m* ; *(for dog, cat)* pâtée *f* ◆ **have you given the dog his ~?** tu as donné à manger au chien ? ◆ **he was having his ~** *(in evening)* il était en train de dîner ; *(at lunch)* il était en train de déjeuner ◆ **to be at ~** † être en train de dîner ◆ **we're having people to ~** nous avons du monde à dîner ◆ **~'s ready!** le dîner est prêt !, à table ! ◆ **we had a good ~** nous avons bien dîné *(or* déjeuné) ◆ **to go out to ~** dîner au restaurant ; *(at friends)* dîner chez des amis ◆ **a formal ~** un dîner officiel, un grand dîner ◆ **to be done like a ~** * *(Austral: in contest etc)* prendre une déculottée *

COMP **dinner bell** N ◆ **the ~ bell has gone** on a sonné (pour) le dîner
dinner-dance N dîner *m* dansant
dinner duty N *(Scol)* service *m* de réfectoire ◆ **to do ~ duty, to be on ~ duty** *(Scol)* être de service *or* de surveillance au réfectoire
dinner jacket N *(Brit)* smoking *m*
dinner knife N (pl **dinner knives**) grand couteau *m*
dinner lady N *(Brit Scol)* femme *f* de service *(à la cantine)*
dinner money N *(Brit Scol)* argent *m* pour la cantine
dinner party N dîner *m (sur invitation)* ◆ **to give a ~ party** avoir du monde à dîner, donner un dîner
dinner plate N (grande) assiette *f*
dinner roll N petit pain *m*
dinner service N service *m* de table
dinner table N ◆ **at the ~ table** pendant le dîner *(or* déjeuner), au dîner *(or* déjeuner)
dinner theater N *(US)* cabaret *m*, café-théâtre *m*
dinner time N ◆ **at ~ time** à l'heure du dîner *(or* déjeuner) ◆ **it's ~ time** c'est l'heure du *or* de dîner *(or* déjeuner)
dinner trolley, dinner wagon N table *f* roulante

dinnertime /ˈdɪnətaɪm/ N ⇒ **dinner time** ; → **dinner**

dinnerware /ˈdɪnəwɛəʳ/ N *(US)* vaisselle *f* ◆ **~ set** service *m* de table

dino * /ˈdaɪnəʊ/ N ⇒ **dinosaur**

dinosaur /ˈdaɪnəsɔːʳ/ N dinosaure *m*

dint /dɪnt/ N 1 ⇒ **dent** 2 ◆ **by ~ of (doing) sth** à force de (faire) qch VT ⇒ **dent**

diocesan /daɪˈɒsɪsən/ ADJ diocésain N (évêque *m*) diocésain *m*

diocese /ˈdaɪəsɪs/ N diocèse *m*

diode /ˈdaɪəʊd/ N diode *f*

dioptre, diopter *(US)* /daɪˈɒptəʳ/ N dioptrie *f*

diorama /daɪəˈrɑːmə/ N diorama *m*

dioxide /daɪˈɒksaɪd/ N bioxyde *m*, dioxyde *m*

dioxin /daɪˈɒksɪn/ N dioxine *f*

DIP /dɪp/ N *(Comput)* abbrev of **Dual-In-Line Package** COMP **DIP switch** N commutateur *m* en boîtier DIP

dip /dɪp/ VT 1 *(into liquid) [+ pen, hand, fingers, toes, clothes]* tremper *(into* dans) ; *[+ spoon]* plonger *(into* dans) ; *(Tech)* tremper, décaper ; *[+ candle]* fabriquer ◆ **to ~ a brush into paint** tremper un pinceau dans de la peinture ◆ **she ~ped her hand into the bag** elle a plongé sa main dans le sac ◆ **walnuts ~ped in chocolate** noix *fpl* enrobées de chocolat ◆ **~ the meat in flour** farinez la viande ◆ **to ~ a** *or* **one's toe in the water** *(fig)* s'aventurer prudemment
2 *[+ sheep]* traiter contre les parasites
3 *(= bend) [+ one's head]* incliner
4 *(Brit)* **to ~ one's headlights** se mettre en code(s)
5 ◆ **to ~ one's flag** *(Naut)* saluer avec le pavillon
VI *[ground]* descendre, s'incliner ; *[road]* descendre ; *[temperature, pointer on scale]* baisser ; *[prices]* fléchir, baisser ; *[boat, raft]* tanguer, piquer du nez * ◆ **the sun ~ped below the horizon** le soleil a disparu à l'horizon ◆ **sales ~ped (by) 6% last month** les ventes ont fléchi *or* baissé de 6% le mois dernier
◆ **to dip into sth** ◆ **she ~ped into her handbag for money** elle a cherché de l'argent dans son sac à main ◆ **to ~ into one's savings** puiser dans ses économies ◆ **to ~ into a book** feuilleter un livre
N 1 (*: *in sea etc)* baignade *f*, bain *m (de mer etc)* ◆ **to have a (quick) ~** faire trempette *
2 *(Agr: for treating animals)* bain *m* parasiticide
3 *(in ground)* déclivité *f* ; *(Geol)* pendage *m* ; *(in prices, figures, unemployment, support, enthusiasm)* fléchissement *m* ; *(in temperature)* baisse *f* ; *(Phys)* (also **angle of dip**) inclinaison *f* magnétique ◆ **share prices have recovered after a slight ~ yesterday** les cours des actions sont remontés après un léger fléchissement hier ◆ **an after-lunch ~ in concentration** une baisse de concentration après le déjeuner
4 *(Culin)* sauce *f* froide *(dans laquelle on trempe des crudités, des chips)* ◆ **avocado ~** purée *f* *or* mousse *f* d'avocat, guacamole *m* ◆ **hot cheese ~** fondue *f* savoyarde *or* au fromage
5 → **lucky**
COMP **dip needle** N aiguille *f* aimantée (de boussole)
dipped headlights NPL codes *mpl*, feux *mpl* de croisement ◆ **to drive on ~ped headlights** rouler en code(s)
dipping needle N ⇒ **dip needle**
dip switch N *(in car)* basculeur *m* de phares

Dip. abbrev of **diploma**

Dip Ed /ˈdɪped/ N *(Brit Univ)* (abbrev of **Diploma in Education**) *diplôme d'enseignement*

diphtheria /dɪfˈθɪərɪə/ N diphtérie *f* COMP **diphtheria vaccine** N vaccin *m* antidiphtérique

diphthong /ˈdɪfθɒŋ/ N diphtongue *f*

diphthongize /ˈdɪfθɒŋaɪz/ VT diphtonguer VI se diphtonguer

diplodocus /dɪˈplɒdəkəs/ N diplodocus *m*

diploid /ˈdɪplɔɪd/ ADJ diploïde

diploma /dɪˈpləʊmə/ N diplôme *m* ◆ **teacher's/nurse's ~** diplôme *m* d'enseignement/d'infirmière ◆ **to hold** *or* **have a ~ in ...** être diplômé de *or* en ...

diplomacy /dɪˈpləʊməsɪ/ N *(Pol, fig)* diplomatie *f* ◆ **to use ~** *(fig)* user de diplomatie

diplomat /ˈdɪpləmæt/ N *(Pol)* diplomate *m*, femme *f* diplomate ; *(fig)* diplomate *mf*

diplomatic /ˌdɪpləˈmætɪk/ ADJ 1 *[mission, relations]* diplomatique 2 *(fig = tactful) [person]* diplomate ; *[action, behaviour]* diplomatique, plein de tact ; *[answer]* diplomatique, habile ◆ **to be ~ in dealing with sth** s'occuper de qch avec tact *or* en usant de diplomatie
COMP **diplomatic bag** N valise *f* diplomatique
diplomatic corps N corps *m* diplomatique
diplomatic immunity N immunité *f* diplomatique
diplomatic pouch N ⇒ **diplomatic bag**
diplomatic service N diplomatie *f*, service *m* diplomatique
diplomatic shuttle N navette *f* diplomatique

diplomatically /ˌdɪpləˈmætɪkəlɪ/ ADV 1 *(= tactfully)* avec diplomatie, diplomatiquement ◆ **~, he refrained from mentioning the divorce** il a fait preuve de diplomatie en s'abstenant de mentionner le divorce 2 *(Pol = by diplomacy)* diplomatiquement ; *[isolated, active etc]* sur le plan diplomatique ◆ **~, the Franco-German alliance has proved unshakeable** sur le plan diplomatique, l'alliance franco-allemande s'est avérée inébranlable

diplomatist /dɪˈpləʊmətɪst/ N ⇒ **diplomat**

dipole /ˈdaɪˌpəʊl/ ADJ, N dipôle *m*

dipper /ˈdɪpəʳ/ N 1 *(= bird)* cincle *m* (plongeur) 2 *(= ladle)* louche *f* 3 *(for headlamps)* basculeur *m* (de phares) 4 *(US Astron)* **the Big** *or* **Great Dipper** la Grande Ourse ◆ **the Little Dipper** la Petite Ourse ; see also **big**

dippy * /ˈdɪpɪ/ ADJ toqué *

dipso * /ˈdɪpsəʊ/ N (abbrev of **dipsomaniac**) soûlard(e) * *m(f)*

dipsomania /ˌdɪpsəʊˈmeɪnɪə/ N *(Med)* dipsomanie *f*

dipsomaniac /ˌdɪpsəʊˈmeɪnɪæk/ N *(Med)* dipsomane *mf*

dipstick /ˈdɪpstɪk/ N jauge *f (de niveau d'huile)*

diptera /ˈdɪptərə/ NPL diptères *mpl*

dipterous /ˈdɪptərəs/ ADJ diptère

dir. abbrev of **director**

dire /ˈdaɪəʳ/ ADJ 1 *(= desperate, appalling) [situation, consequences, effects]* désastreux ; *[warning, prediction, threat]* sinistre ; *[poverty]* extrême ◆ **(in) ~ poverty** (dans) la misère ◆ **to do sth from** *or* **out of ~ necessity** faire qch par nécessité ◆ **to be in ~ need of sth** avoir terriblement besoin de qch ◆ **to be in ~ straits** être dans une situation désastreuse 2 (* *= awful)* nul *

direct /dɪˈrekt/ LANGUAGE IN USE 27
ADJ 1 *(= without detour) [flight, road, route, train]* direct
◆ **direct hit** *(Sport)* coup *m* (en plein) dans le mille ; *(Mil)* coup *m* au but, tir *m* de plein fouet ◆ **to score** *or* **make a ~ hit** mettre dans le mille ◆ **the building took** *or* **received** *or* **suffered a ~ hit** le bâtiment a été touché de plein fouet
2 *(= immediate) [cause, result]* direct, immédiat ; *[contact, control, responsibility, access, talks, negotiations]* direct ; *[danger]* immédiat, imminent ◆ **this has a ~ effect on the environment** cela a un impact direct sur l'environnement ◆ **the army is under his ~ control** l'armée est sous son contrôle direct ◆ **the two companies are in ~ competition (with each other)** ces deux sociétés sont en concurrence directe ◆ **to have ~ access to sth** avoir directement accès à qch ◆ **to come into** *or* **be in ~ contact with ...** être *or* entrer en contact direct avec ... ◆ **he had no ~ involvement in economic policy** il ne s'occupait pas directement de politique économique ◆ **keep away from ~ heat** éviter l'exposition directe à la chaleur ◆ **"keep out of direct sunlight"** "ne pas exposer directement à la lumière du soleil" ◆ **to be a ~ descendant of sb, to be descended in a ~ line from sb** descendre en droite ligne *or* en ligne directe de qn
3 *(= straightforward, not evasive) [person, character, answer]* franc (franche *f*), direct ; *[question]* direct ; *(= outright) [refusal]* catégorique, absolu ; *(= explicit) [attack, reference, link]* direct ; *[evidence]* tangible ◆ **there has been no ~ challenge to the chairman** le directeur n'a pas été ouvertement contesté ◆ **this is the most ~ challenge yet to UN authority** jusqu'à maintenant, l'autorité des Nations unies n'avait jamais été aussi directement remise en cause
VT 1 *(= address, aim) [+ remark, question, abuse, letter]* adresser *(to* à) ; *[+ threat]* proférer *(at* contre) ; *[+ efforts]* orienter *(towards* vers) ◆ **to ~**

sb's attention to attirer l'attention de qn sur ◆ **to ~ one's attention to sth** concentrer *or* reporter son attention sur qch ◆ **the violence was ~ed against the police** les actes de violence étaient dirigés contre la police ◆ **she ~ed an angry glance at him** elle lui a jeté un regard noir ◆ **don't ~ your anger at me** ne vous en prenez pas à moi ◆ **he ~ed his energies to winning the election** il a tout fait pour remporter l'élection ◆ **we need to ~ more money into research** il faut que nous affections davantage d'argent à la recherche ◆ **a policy ~ed towards improving public transport** une politique ayant pour but d'améliorer *or* visant à améliorer les transports publics ◆ **I ~ed the extinguisher at the fire** j'ai pointé *or* dirigé l'extincteur vers le feu

2 *(= show the way to)*

◆ **to direct sb** *(to a place)* indiquer le chemin à qn ◆ **he ~ed me to the town hall** il m'a indiqué le chemin de la mairie

3 *(= control) [+ sb's work]* diriger ; *[+ business]* diriger, gérer ; *[+ movements]* guider ; *[+ play]* mettre en scène ; *[+ film, programme]* réaliser ; *[+ group of actors]* diriger ◆ **Chris will ~ day-to-day operations** Chris dirigera les opérations courantes

4 *(= instruct)* ordonner *(sb to do sth* à qn de faire qch) ; ◆ **the bishop ~ed the faithful to stay at home** l'évêque a ordonné aux fidèles de rester chez eux ◆ **the judge ~ed the jury to find the accused not guilty** le juge imposa au jury un verdict d'acquittement ◆ **~ed verdict** *(US Jur) verdict rendu par le jury sur la recommandation du juge*

◆ **to direct that sth be done** ordonner que qch soit fait ◆ **the judge ~ed that this remark be deleted from the record** le juge a ordonné que cette remarque soit retirée du procès-verbal

◆ **as directed** ◆ **he did it as ~ed** il l'a fait comme on le lui avait dit *or* comme on l'en avait chargé ◆ **"to be taken as directed"** *(on medicines)* "respecter les doses prescrites" ◆ **"to be taken as directed by your doctor"** "se conformer à la prescription du médecin"

VI ◆ **who is ~ing ?** *(Theat)* qui est le metteur en scène ? ; *(Cine, Rad, TV)* qui est le réalisateur ?

ADV *[go, write]* directement ◆ **to fly ~ from Glasgow to Paris** prendre un vol direct de Glasgow à Paris

COMP **direct access** N *(Comput)* accès *m* direct
direct action N *(for social change etc)* action *f* directe
direct addressing N *(Comput)* adressage *m* direct
direct broadcasting by satellite N diffusion *f* en direct par satellite
direct broadcasting satellite N satellite *m* de diffusion directe
direct current N *(Elec)* courant *m* continu
direct debit N *(Comm, Fin)* prélèvement *m* automatique
direct dialling N composition *f* directe *(des numéros de téléphone)*
direct discourse N *(US)* ⇒ **direct speech**
direct grant school N *(Brit: formerly) établissement scolaire sous contrat avec l'État*
direct mail N publipostage *m*
direct marketing N marketing *m* direct
the direct method N *(Educ)* la méthode directe, l'immersion *f* linguistique
direct motion N *(Astron)* mouvement *m* direct
direct object N *(Gram)* complément *m* d'objet direct
direct rule N *(Pol)* administration *f* directe *(par le pouvoir central)*
direct sales NPL ⇒ **direct selling**
direct selling N vente *f* directe
direct speech N *(Gram)* discours *m or* style *m* direct
direct tax N impôt *m* direct
direct taxation N *(NonC)* imposition *f* directe

direction /dɪˈrekʃən/ N 1 *(= way)* direction *f*, sens *m* ; *(fig)* direction *f*, voie *f* ◆ **in every ~** dans toutes les directions, en tous sens ◆ **in the wrong/right ~** *(lit)* dans le mauvais/bon sens, dans la mauvaise/bonne direction ; *(fig)* sur la mauvaise/bonne voie ◆ **it's a move** *or* **step in the right ~** c'est un pas dans la bonne direction ◆ **in the opposite ~** en sens inverse ◆ **in the ~ of ...** dans la direction de ..., en direction de ... ◆ **what ~ did he go in?** quelle direction a-t-il prise ? ; → **sense**

2 *(= management)* direction *f*, administration *f* ◆ **under the ~ of ...** sous la direction de ..., sous la conduite de ...

3 *(Theat)* mise *f* en scène ; *(Cine, Rad, TV)* réalisation *f* ◆ **"under the direction of ..."** *(Theat)* "mise en scène de ..." ; *(Cine, Rad, TV)* "réalisation de ..."

4 *(= instruction)* instruction *f*, indication *f* ◆ **~s for use** mode *m* d'emploi ; → **stage**

NPL **directions** *(showing the way)* ◆ **to ask for ~s** demander son chemin ◆ **to give sb ~s** indiquer le chemin à qn ◆ **he gave us wrong ~s** il nous a indiqué le mauvais chemin

COMP **direction finder** N radiogoniomètre *m*
direction finding N radiogoniométrie *f*
direction indicator N *(in vehicle)* clignotant *m*

directional /dɪˈrekʃənl/ ADJ directionnel

directionless /dɪˈrekʃənlɪs/ ADJ *[person]* sans but ; *[activity]* qui ne mène nulle part

directive /dɪˈrektɪv/ N directive *f*, instruction *f*

directly /dɪˈrektlɪ/ ADV 1 *(= straight) [go, affect, communicate, pay]* directement ◆ **~ involved/responsible** directement impliqué/responsable ◆ **the two murders are not ~ related** ces deux meurtres n'ont pas de rapport direct ◆ **to be ~ descended from sb** descendre en droite ligne *or* en ligne directe de qn ◆ **to come ~ to the point** aller droit au but

2 *(= frankly) [speak, ask]* directement

3 *(= completely, exactly) [opposed]* diamétralement, directement ◆ **~ contrary to** diamétralement opposé à, exactement contraire à ◆ **~ opposite points of view** des points de vue diamétralement opposés ◆ **the bus stops ~ opposite** le bus s'arrête juste en face ◆ **~ opposite the railway station** juste en face de la gare ◆ **if a planet is at opposition, it is ~ opposite the sun** si une planète est en opposition, elle est directement à l'opposé du soleil

4 *(Brit = immediately, very soon)* tout de suite ◆ **~ after supper** tout de suite après le dîner ◆ **she'll be here ~** elle arrive tout de suite

CONJ *(esp Brit)* aussitôt que, dès que ◆ **he'll come ~ he's ready** il viendra dès qu'il sera prêt

directness /dɪˈrektnɪs/ N *[of character, reply]* franchise *f* ; *[of person]* franchise *f*, franc-parler *m* ; *[of attack, question]* caractère *m* direct ◆ **the ~ of his refusal** son refus catégorique ◆ **to speak with great ~** parler en toute franchise

director /dɪˈrektəʳ/ N 1 *(= person) (Brit) [of company]* directeur *m*, -trice *f*, administrateur *m*, -trice *f* ; *[of institution]* directeur *m*, -trice *f* ; *(Theat)* metteur *m* en scène ; *(Cine, Rad, TV)* réalisateur *m*, -trice *f* ; *(Rel)* directeur *m* de conscience ◆ **~ general** directeur *m* général ; → **board, managing, stage** 2 *(= device)* guide *m*

COMP **director of admissions** N *(US Univ etc)* responsable *mf* du service des inscriptions
Director of Education N *(Brit)* ≃ recteur *m* d'académie
director of music N *(Mil)* chef *m* de musique
Director of Public Prosecutions N *(Brit Jur)* ≃ procureur *m* général
director of studies N *(Univ) (for course)* directeur *m*, -trice *f* d'études ; *(for thesis)* directeur *m*, -trice *f* de thèse
director's chair N fauteuil *m* de metteur en scène
director's cut N *(Cine)* version *f* du réalisateur, version *f* longue

directorate /dɪˈrektərɪt/ N *(= board of directors)* conseil *m* d'administration

directorial /ˌdɪrekˈtɔːrɪəl/ ADJ directorial, de directeur

directorship /dɪˈrektəʃɪp/ N *(= job)* direction *f* ; *(= position)* poste *m* de directeur

directory /dɪˈrektərɪ/ LANGUAGE IN USE 27.1 N 1 *[of addresses]* répertoire *m* (d'adresses) ; (also **street directory**) guide *m* des rues ; *(Telec)* annuaire *m* (des téléphones) ; *(Comm)* annuaire *m* du commerce ; *(Comput)* répertoire *m* (de dossiers) 2 *(Hist)* **Directory** Directoire *m*

COMP **directory assistance** N *(US)* ⇒ **directory inquiries**
directory inquiries NPL *(Brit Telec)* (service *m* des) renseignements *mpl*

directrix /dɪˈrektrɪks/ N *(Math)* (ligne *f*) directrice *f*

direful /ˈdaɪəfʊl/ ADJ sinistre, menaçant

dirge /dɜːdʒ/ N *(lit)* hymne *m or* chant *m* funèbre ; *(fig)* chant *m* lugubre

dirigible /ˈdɪrɪdʒəbl/ ADJ, N dirigeable *m*

dirk /dɜːk/ N *(Scot)* dague *f*, poignard *m*

dirndl /ˈdɜːndəl/ ADJ, N ◆ **~ (skirt)** large jupe *f* froncée

dirt /dɜːt/ N 1 *(on skin, clothes, objects)* saleté *f*, crasse *f* ; *(= earth)* terre *f* ; *(= mud)* boue *f* ; *(= excrement)* crotte *f* ; *(in industrial process)* impuretés *fpl*, corps *mpl* étrangers ; *(on machine, in engine)* encrassement *m* ◆ **covered with ~** *(gen)* très sale, couvert de crasse ; *[clothes, shoes, mudguards]* couvert de boue, tout crotté ◆ **a layer of ~** une couche de saleté *or* de crasse ◆ **dog ~** crotte *f* de chien ◆ **to eat ~*** *(= apologise)* faire ses excuses les plus plates, ramper ◆ **to treat sb like ~*** traiter qn comme un chien ◆ **to do the ~ on sb*, to do sb ~*** *(US)* faire une vacherie‡ à qn

2 *(= obscenity)* obscénité *f*

3 *(* = scandal)* cancans *mpl*, ragots* *mpl* ◆ **to dig up ~ on sb*, to dig the ~ on sb*** *(Brit)* essayer de salir (la réputation de) qn ◆ **to dish the ~* (on sb)** *(esp Brit)* colporter des ragots* (sur qn) ◆ **what's the ~ on ...?*** qu'est-ce qu'on raconte sur ... ?

COMP **dirt bike** N moto *f* tout-terrain *(de 50 cm³)*
dirt-cheap* ADV *[buy]* pour rien, pour une bouchée de pain ADJ très bon marché *inv* ◆ **it was ~-cheap*** c'était donné
dirt farmer N *(US)* petit fermier *m*
dirt-poor* ADJ miséreux
dirt road N chemin *m* non macadamisé
dirt track N *(gen)* piste *f* ; *(Sport)* cendrée *f*
dirt track racing N courses *fpl* motocyclistes *or* de motos sur cendrée

dirtily /ˈdɜːtɪlɪ/ ADV *[eat, live]* salement, malproprement ; *(fig) [act, behave]* bassement ; *[play, fight]* déloyalement

dirtiness /ˈdɜːtɪnɪs/ N saleté *f*

dirty /ˈdɜːtɪ/ ADJ 1 *(= soiled, unhygienic) [object, place, person, habit]* sale ; *[job, work]* salissant ; *[hypodermic needle]* usagé ; *[plug, contact]* encrassé ◆ **to get ~** se salir ◆ **to get sth ~** salir qch ◆ **to get one's hands ~** *(lit, fig)* se salir les mains ◆ **to do** *or* **wash one's ~ linen** *or* **laundry in public, to do one's ~ washing in public** laver son linge sale en public ◆ **let's not wash our ~ linen** *or* **laundry in public** il vaut mieux laver son linge sale en famille

2 *[colour]* **a ~ brown/grey** un marron/gris sale ◆ **the morning light was ~ grey** la lumière du matin était d'un gris sale

3 *(= smutty) [book, film, joke, story, magazine, picture]* cochon* ; *[language]* grossier ◆ **a ~ word** *(lit, fig)* un gros mot ◆ **"communist" was a ~ word for them** "communiste" était presque

une injure pour eux ◆ **he's got a ~ mind** il a l'esprit mal tourné

4 *(= unpleasant, underhand)* sale *before n* ◆ **politics is a ~ business** la politique est un sale métier ◆ **it's a ~ job, but someone's got to do it** c'est un sale boulot, mais il faut bien que quelqu'un le fasse ◆ **~ money** argent *m* sale ◆ **it was a very ~ election** les coups bas n'ont pas manqué dans cette élection ◆ **to give sb a ~ look** regarder qn de travers ◆ **~ pool*** *(US)* tour *m* de cochon * ◆ **you ~ rat!** * sale type ! * ◆ **that was a ~ trick** c'était un sale tour *or* un tour de cochon * ◆ **~ weather** sale temps *m* ◆ **to do sb's ~ work (for them)** faire le sale boulot * de qn ◆ **there's been some ~ work here!** il y a quelque chose de pas catholique * là-dessous ! ; → **hand**

ADV 1 *(* = unfairly)* ◆ **to play ~** faire des coups en vache * ◆ **to fight ~** donner des coups en vache *

2 *(= smuttily)* ◆ **to talk ~** * dire des cochonneries

3 *(intensifier)* ◆ **a ~ great tractor** * un vachement gros tracteur *

VT *[+ hands, clothes, reputation]* salir ; *[+ machine]* encrasser ◆ **he's never had to ~ his hands to make a living** il n'a jamais eu à retrousser ses manches pour gagner sa vie

N *(Brit)* ◆ **to do the ~ on sb*** faire une vacherie * à qn, jouer un tour de cochon * à qn

COMP **dirty bomb** N bombe *f* radiologique
dirty-faced ADJ à *or* qui a la figure sale
dirty-minded ADJ à *or* qui a l'esprit mal tourné
dirty old man * N (pl **dirty old men**) vieux cochon * *m*
dirty weekend * N week-end *m* coquin

disability /ˌdɪsəˈbɪlɪtɪ/ N 1 *(NonC, physical)* invalidité *f*, incapacité *f* ; *(mental)* incapacité *f* ◆ **complete/partial ~** incapacité *f* totale/partielle 2 *(= infirmity)* infirmité *f* ; *(= handicap)* désavantage *m*, handicap *m* ◆ **his ~ made him eligible for a pension** son infirmité lui donnait droit à une pension ◆ **people with disabilities** les personnes handicapées

COMP **disability living allowance** N allocation *f* d'invalidité
disability pension N pension *f* d'invalidité

disable /dɪsˈeɪbl/ VT *[illness, accident, injury]* rendre infirme ; *(= maim)* estropier, mutiler ; *[+ tank, gun]* mettre hors de combat ; *[+ ship]* *(gen)* avarier, mettre hors d'état ; *(by enemy action)* mettre hors de combat ; *(Jur) (= make/pronounce incapable)* rendre/prononcer inhabile *(from doing sth* à faire qch)

disabled /dɪsˈeɪbld/ ADJ 1 *(permanently)* handicapé ; *(esp Admin = unable to work)* invalide ; *(= paralyzed)* estropié ; *(= maimed)* mutilé ; *(Mil)* mis hors de combat ◆ **~ ex-servicemen** mutilés *mpl or* invalides *mpl* de guerre ◆ **severely/partially ~** souffrant d'un handicap sévère/léger 2 *(Naut)* ◆ **to be ~** *[ship]* avoir des avaries, être immobilisé pour cause d'avaries ; *[propeller]* être bloqué 3 *(Jur)* incapable *(from* de) inhabile *(from* à) NPL **the disabled** les handicapés *mpl* ◆ **the severely ~** les personnes *fpl* souffrant d'un handicap sévère ◆ **the war ~** les mutilés *mpl or* les invalides *mpl* de guerre

disablement /dɪsˈeɪblmənt/ N invalidité *f*
COMP **disablement benefit** N allocation *f* d'invalidité
disablement insurance N assurance *f* invalidité
disablement pension N pension *f* d'invalidité

disabuse /ˌdɪsəˈbjuːz/ VT *(frm)* désenchanter ◆ **to ~ sb of sth** détromper qn de qch

disadvantage /ˌdɪsədˈvɑːntɪdʒ/ N 1 *(NonC)* désavantage *m*, inconvénient *m* ◆ **to be at a ~** être défavorisé ◆ **you've got me at a ~** vous avez l'avantage sur moi ◆ **to catch sb at a ~** surprendre qn en position de faiblesse ◆ **to put sb at a ~** désavantager *or* défavoriser qn, mettre qn en position de faiblesse 2 *(= prejudice, injury)* préjudice *m*, désavantage *m* ; *(Comm = loss)* perte *f* ◆ **it would be *or* work to your ~ to be seen with him** cela vous porterait préjudice *or* vous ferait du tort si on vous voyait avec lui VT désavantager, défavoriser

disadvantaged /ˌdɪsədˈvɑːntɪdʒd/ ADJ défavorisé ◆ **educationally/socially/economically ~** défavorisé sur le plan scolaire/social/économique NPL **the disadvantaged** les classes *fpl* défavorisées ; *(economically)* les économiquement faibles *mpl*

disadvantageous /ˌdɪsædvɑːnˈteɪdʒəs/ ADJ désavantageux, défavorable *(to* à)

disadvantageously /ˌdɪsædvɑːnˈteɪdʒəslɪ/ ADV d'une manière désavantageuse, désavantageusement

disaffected /ˌdɪsəˈfektɪd/ ADJ *(= discontented)* mécontent, mal disposé

disaffection /ˌdɪsəˈfekʃən/ N désaffection *f*, mécontentement *m*

disagree /ˌdɪsəˈgriː/ VI 1 *(= be of different opinion)* ne pas être d'accord *(with* avec ; *on, about* sur) ne pas être du même avis *(with* que ; *on, about* sur) se trouver *or* être en désaccord *(with* avec ; *on, about* sur) ◆ **I ~** je ne suis pas de cet avis, je ne suis pas d'accord ◆ **I ~ completely with you** je ne suis pas du tout d'accord avec vous *or* pas du tout de votre avis ◆ **they always ~ (with each other)** ils ne sont jamais du même avis *or* d'accord ; *(always quarrelling)* ils sont incapables de s'entendre ◆ **to ~ with the suggestion that ...** être contre la suggestion que ... ◆ **she ~s with everything he has done** elle se trouve en désaccord avec tout ce qu'il a fait

2 *(= be different) [explanations, reports, sets of figures]* ne pas concorder *(with* avec) ◆ **the witnesses' statements ~** les déclarations des témoins ne concordent pas

3 ◆ **to ~ with sb** * *[climate, food]* ne pas convenir *or* réussir à qn ◆ **mutton ~s with him** il ne digère pas le mouton, le mouton ne lui réussit pas ◆ **the mutton ~d with him** il a mal digéré le mouton, le mouton n'est pas bien passé *

disagreeable /ˌdɪsəˈgriːəbl/ ADJ désagréable

disagreeableness /ˌdɪsəˈgriːəblnɪs/ N *[of work, experience]* nature *f* désagréable *or* fâcheuse ; *[of person]* mauvaise humeur *f*, maussaderie *f*, attitude *f or* manière(s) *f(pl)* désagréable(s)

disagreeably /ˌdɪsəˈgriːəblɪ/ ADV désagréablement ◆ **~ pungent** d'une âcreté désagréable

disagreement /ˌdɪsəˈgriːmənt/ N 1 *(of opinion, also between accounts etc)* différence *f* 2 *(= quarrel)* désaccord *m*, différend *m* ◆ **to have a ~ with sb (about sth)** avoir un différend avec qn (à propos de qch) ◆ **to be in ~ (over sth)** *[people]* être en désaccord (sur qch)

disallow /ˌdɪsəˈlaʊ/ VT *(gen)* rejeter ; *(Sport) [+ goal etc]* refuser ; *(Jur)* débouter, rejeter

disambiguate /ˌdɪsæmˈbɪgjʊˌeɪt/ VT désambiguïser

disambiguation /ˌdɪsæmˌbɪgjʊˈeɪʃən/ N désambiguïsation *f*

disappear /ˌdɪsəˈpɪəʳ/ VI *[person, vehicle, lost object, snow, objection]* disparaître ; *[custom]* disparaître, tomber en désuétude ; *[memory]* disparaître, s'effacer ; *[difficulties]* disparaître, s'aplanir ; *(Ling) [sound]* s'amuïr ◆ **he ~ed from view *or* sight** on l'a perdu de vue ◆ **the ship ~ed over the horizon** le navire a disparu à l'horizon ◆ **to make sth ~** faire disparaître qch ; *[conjurer]* escamoter qch ◆ **to do a ~ing trick*** *(fig)* s'éclipser, s'esquiver VT *(Pol *) [+ dissident]* faire disparaître

disappearance /ˌdɪsəˈpɪərəns/ N disparition *f* ; *(Ling) [of sound]* amuïssement *m*

disappeared /ˌdɪsəˈpɪəd/ NPL *(Pol)* ◆ **the ~** les disparus *mpl*

disappoint /ˌdɪsəˈpɔɪnt/ VT 1 *(= let down) [+ person]* décevoir ; *(after promising)* manquer à sa parole envers ◆ **he couldn't ~ Claire by not going to her party** il ne pouvait pas manquer à sa parole en n'allant pas à la soirée de Claire ◆ **he promised to meet me but ~ed me several times** il m'avait promis de me rencontrer mais il m'a fait faux bond plusieurs fois 2 *(= confound) [+ expectations, hope]* décevoir

disappointed /ˌdɪsəˈpɔɪntɪd/ LANGUAGE IN USE 14
ADJ *[person, hope, ambition]* déçu ◆ **to be ~ that ...** être déçu que ... + *subj* ◆ **to be ~ to find/learn** *etc* être déçu de trouver/d'apprendre *etc* ◆ **to be ~ by *or* with sth** être déçu par qch ◆ **he was ~ with her reply** sa réponse l'a déçu ◆ **to be ~ at having to do sth** être déçu de devoir faire qch ◆ **we were ~ at not seeing her *or* not to see her** nous avons été déçus de ne pas la voir ◆ **to be ~ in sb/sth** être déçu par qn/qch ◆ **I'm (very) ~ in you** tu me déçois (beaucoup) ◆ **to be ~ in one's hopes/in love** être déçu dans ses espoirs/en amour

disappointing /ˌdɪsəˈpɔɪntɪŋ/ ADJ décevant ◆ **how ~!** quelle déception !, comme c'est décevant !

disappointingly /ˌdɪsəˈpɔɪntɪŋlɪ/ ADV ◆ **progress has been ~ slow** les progrès ont été d'une lenteur décevante ◆ **the house was ~ small** la taille de la maison était décevante ◆ **the number of new jobs created was ~ low** le nombre de nouveaux emplois créés était décevant ◆ **the boat performed ~** le bateau s'est comporté de manière décevante ◆ **~, he couldn't come** à notre grande déception *or* à la grande déception de tous, il n'a pas pu venir ◆ **~ for his parents/teachers, he failed all his exams** à la grande déception de ses parents/professeurs, il a échoué à tous ses examens

disappointment /ˌdɪsəˈpɔɪntmənt/ N 1 *(NonC)* déception *f* ◆ **to my great ~** à ma grande déception 2 *(= setback, source of disappointment)* déception *f*, déboires *mpl* ◆ **after a series of ~s** après une succession de déboires ◆ **~s in love** déboires *mpl* amoureux ◆ **he/that was a great ~ to me** il/cela a été une grosse déception pour moi, il/cela m'a beaucoup déçu

disapprobation *(liter)* /ˌdɪsæprəˈbeɪʃən/, **disapproval** /ˌdɪsəˈpruːvəl/ N désapprobation *f* ◆ **murmur *etc* of ~** murmure *m etc* désapprobateur *or* de désapprobation ◆ **to show one's ~ of sb/sth** marquer sa désapprobation à l'égard de qn/qch ◆ **the crowd were loud in their ~** la foule désapprouva bruyamment

disapprove /ˌdɪsəˈpruːv/ LANGUAGE IN USE 14 VI ◆ **to ~ of sb/sth** désapprouver qn/qch ◆ **to ~ of sb('s) doing sth** désapprouver *or* trouver mauvais que qn fasse qch ◆ **your mother would ~** ta mère n'approuverait pas ◆ **he entirely ~s of drink** il est tout à fait contre la boisson VT *[+ action, event]* désapprouver

disapproving /ˌdɪsəˈpruːvɪŋ/ ADJ *[expression, look]* désapprobateur (-trice *f*) ◆ **she seemed ~** elle avait l'air de désapprouver ◆ **Giles announced to his ~ mother that he would be marrying Kay** Giles a annoncé à sa mère, qui était contre, qu'il se mariait avec Kay ◆ **to be ~ of sb/sth** désapprouver qn/qch ◆ **to make ~ noises** *(fig)* manifester sa désapprobation

disapprovingly /ˌdɪsəˈpruːvɪŋlɪ/ ADV *[look, behave]* d'un air désapprobateur ; *[speak]* d'un ton désapprobateur

disarm /dɪsˈɑːm/ VTI *(also fig)* désarmer

disarmament /dɪsˈɑːməmənt/ N désarmement *m* COMP **disarmament talks** NPL conférence *f* sur le désarmement

disarmer /dɪsˈɑːməʳ/ N ◆ **(nuclear)** ~ partisan(e) *m(f)* du désarmement nucléaire

disarming /dɪsˈɑːmɪŋ/ N *(Mil)* désarmement *m* ADJ *[smile]* désarmant

disarmingly /dɪsˈɑːmɪŋlɪ/ ADV *[smile, admit]* de façon désarmante ◆ ~ **modest/frank/simple** d'une modestie/franchise/simplicité désarmante

disarrange /ˌdɪsəˈreɪndʒ/ VT déranger, mettre en désordre

disarranged /ˌdɪsəˈreɪndʒd/ ADJ *[bed]* défait ; *[hair, clothes]* en désordre

disarray /ˌdɪsəˈreɪ/ N *(frm)* désordre *m*, confusion *f* ◆ **the troops were in (complete)** ~ le désordre *or* la confusion régnait parmi les troupes, les troupes étaient en déroute ◆ **a political party in** ~ un parti politique en plein désarroi *or* en proie au désarroi ◆ **she was** *or* **her clothes were in** ~ ses vêtements étaient en désordre ◆ **to fall into** ~ sombrer dans le chaos

disassemble /ˌdɪsəˈsembl/ VT désassembler, démonter

disassociate /ˌdɪsəˈsəʊʃɪeɪt/ VT ⇒ **dissociate**

disassociation /ˌdɪsəsəʊsɪˈeɪʃən/ N ⇒ **dissociation**

disaster /dɪˈzɑːstəʳ/ N *(gen, also fig)* désastre *m*, catastrophe *f* ; *(from natural causes)* catastrophe *f*, sinistre *m* ◆ **air** ~ catastrophe *f* aérienne ◆ **the Madrid airport** ~ la catastrophe de l'aéroport de Madrid ◆ **an environmental** ~ une catastrophe écologique ◆ **a financial/political** ~ un désastre financier/politique ◆ **at the scene of the** ~ sur les lieux du désastre *or* de la catastrophe ◆ **to be heading** *or* **headed for** ~ courir au désastre ◆ **their marriage/her hairstyle was a** ~* leur couple/sa coiffure était une catastrophe* *or* un (vrai) désastre

COMP **disaster area** N *(lit)* région *f* sinistrée ◆ **a (walking)** ~ **area*** *(fig)* une catastrophe (ambulante)*
disaster fund N collecte *f* au profit des sinistrés ◆ **earthquake** ~ **fund** collecte *f* au profit des victimes du tremblement de terre
disaster movie N film *m* catastrophe
disaster victim N sinistré(e) *m(f)*, victime *f* de la catastrophe

disastrous /dɪˈzɑːstrəs/ ADJ désastreux *(for* pour) ◆ **with** ~ **consequences** avec des conséquences désastreuses

disastrously /dɪˈzɑːstrəslɪ/ ADV de manière désastreuse ◆ **the match started** ~ **for the French** le match a commencé de manière désastreuse pour les Français ◆ **the Socialists fared** ~ **in the elections** les socialistes ont obtenu des résultats désastreux aux élections ◆ ~ **low/high prices** des prix dramatiquement bas/élevés ◆ **to go** ~ **wrong** tourner à la catastrophe ◆ **to get it** ~ **wrong** faire une erreur monumentale

disavow /ˌdɪsəˈvaʊ/ VT *(frm)* *[+ one's words, opinions]* désavouer, renier ; *[+ faith, duties]* renier

disavowal /ˌdɪsəˈvaʊəl/ N *(frm)* *[of one's words, opinions]* désaveu *m* ; *[of faith, duties]* reniement *m*

disband /dɪsˈbænd/ VT *[+ army, corporation, club]* disperser VI *[army]* se disperser ; *[organization]* se dissoudre

disbar /dɪsˈbɑːʳ/ VT *[+ barrister]* radier de l'ordre des avocats ◆ **to be ~red** se faire radier de l'ordre des avocats

disbarment /dɪsˈbɑːmənt/ N *(Jur)* radiation *f* de l'ordre des avocats

disbelief /ˌdɪsbəˈliːf/ N incrédulité *f* ◆ **in** ~ avec incrédulité

disbelieve /ˌdɪsbəˈliːv/ VT *[+ person]* ne pas croire ; *[+ news etc]* ne pas croire à VI *(also Rel)* ne pas croire *(in* à)

disbeliever /ˌdɪsbəˈliːvəʳ/ N *(also Rel)* incrédule *mf*

disbelieving /ˌdɪsbəˈliːvɪŋ/ ADJ incrédule

disbud /dɪsˈbʌd/ VT ébourgeonner

disburden /dɪsˈbɜːdn/ VT *(lit, fig)* décharger, débarrasser *(of* de) ; *(= relieve)* soulager ◆ **to** ~ **one's conscience** se décharger la conscience

disburse /dɪsˈbɜːs/ VTI *(frm)* débourser, décaisser

disbursement /dɪsˈbɜːsmənt/ N *(frm)* *(= paying out)* déboursement *m*, décaissement *m* ; *(= money paid)* débours *mpl*

disc /dɪsk/ N 1 *(also of moon etc)* disque *m* 2 *(Anat)* disque *m* (intervertébral) ; → **slip** 3 *(Mil:* also **identity disc**) plaque *f* d'identité 4 *(= gramophone record)* disque *m*

COMP **disc brakes** NPL freins *mpl* à disque
disc camera N appareil *m* photo à disque
disc film N film *m* disque
disc harrow N pulvériseur *m*
disc jockey N disc-jockey *m*, animateur *m*, -trice *f*
disc shutter N *(Cine)* *[of projector]* obturateur *m* à disque

discard /dɪsˈkɑːd/ VT 1 *(= get rid of)* se débarrasser de ; *(= throw out)* jeter ; *[+ jacket etc]* se débarrasser de ; *[+ idea, plan]* renoncer à, abandonner ; *[+ rocket, part of spacecraft]* larguer 2 *(Bridge etc)* se défausser de, défausser ; *(Cribbage)* écarter ◆ **he was ~ing clubs** il se défaussait à trèfle ◆ **he ~ed the three of hearts** il s'est défaussé du trois de cœur VI *(Bridge etc)* se défausser ; *(Cribbage)* écarter N /ˈdɪskɑːd/ 1 *(Bridge)* défausse *f* ; *(Cribbage)* écart *m* 2 *(from manufacturing process)* pièce *f* de rebut, déchet *m*

discern /dɪˈsɜːn/ VT *[+ person, object, difference]* discerner, distinguer, percevoir ; *[+ feelings]* discerner

discernible /dɪˈsɜːnəbl/ ADJ *[object]* visible ; *[likeness, fault]* perceptible, sensible

discernibly /dɪˈsɜːnəblɪ/ ADV sensiblement

discerning /dɪˈsɜːnɪŋ/ ADJ *[person]* judicieux, sagace, doué de discernement ; *[taste]* délicat ; *[look]* clairvoyant, perspicace

discernment /dɪˈsɜːnmənt/ N *(fig)* discernement *m*, pénétration *f*

discharge /dɪsˈtʃɑːdʒ/ VT 1 *[ship]* *[+ cargo]* décharger ; *[ship, bus etc]* *[+ passengers]* débarquer
2 *[+ liquid]* déverser ; *(Elec)* décharger ; *[factory, chimney, pipe]* *[+ gas]* dégager, émettre ; *[+ liquid, pollutants, sewage]* déverser ◆ **the factory was discharging toxic gas into the atmosphere** l'usine rejetait des gaz toxiques dans l'atmosphère ◆ **the pipe was discharging sewage into the sea** le tuyau déversait les eaux usées dans la mer
3 *(Med)* *[wound]* *[+ mucus, blood]* laisser écouler ◆ **to** ~ **pus** suppurer
4 *[+ employee]* renvoyer, congédier ; *[+ soldier]* rendre à la vie civile ; *(for health reasons)* réformer ; *[+ prisoner]* libérer, élargir *(Jur)* ; *[+ jury]* congédier ; *[+ accused]* relaxer ; *[+ bankrupt]* réhabiliter ; *[+ patient]* *(from hospital)* renvoyer (guéri) de l'hôpital ◆ **to** ~ **o.s.** *(from hospital)* signer sa décharge
5 *[+ gun]* décharger, faire partir ; *[+ arrow]* décocher
6 *[+ debt, bill]* acquitter, régler
7 *(frm = fulfil)* *[+ obligation, duty]* remplir, s'acquitter de ; *[+ function]* remplir ; *[+ responsibilities]* exercer
VI *[wound]* suinter
N /ˈdɪstʃɑːdʒ/ 1 *(NonC)* *[of cargo]* déchargement *m* ; *(Elec)* décharge *f* ; *[of weapon]* décharge *f* ; *[of liquid]* écoulement *m*
2 *(Med)* *(gen)* suintement *m* ; *(vaginal)* pertes *fpl* (blanches) ; *[of pus]* suppuration *f* ◆ **nipple** ~ écoulement *m* mammaire
3 *[of employee]* renvoi *m* ; *[of prisoner]* libération *f*, élargissement *m* *(Jur)* ; *[of patient]* renvoi *m* ◆ **the soldier got his** ~ **yesterday** le soldat a été libéré hier
4 *(frm = fulfilment)* **the** ~ **of one's duty** *(gen)* l'accomplissement *m* de son devoir ◆ **the** ~ **of one's duties** *(official tasks)* l'exercice *m* de ses fonctions
5 *[of debt]* acquittement *m*

disci /ˈdɪskaɪ/ NPL of **discus**

disciple /dɪˈsaɪpl/ N disciple *m*

disciplinarian /ˌdɪsɪplɪˈneərɪən/ N personne *f* stricte en matière de discipline

disciplinary /ˈdɪsɪplɪnərɪ/ ADJ *(gen)* disciplinaire ◆ **a** ~ **offence** une faute passible de mesures disciplinaires ◆ ~ **matters/problems** questions *fpl*/problèmes *mpl* de discipline ◆ **to take** ~ **action** prendre des mesures disciplinaires

discipline /ˈdɪsɪplɪn/ N 1 *(NonC)* discipline *f* ◆ **to keep** ~ maintenir la discipline 2 *(= branch of knowledge)* discipline *f*, matière *f* VT *(= control)* *[+ person]* discipliner ; *[+ mind]* former, discipliner ; *(= punish)* punir ◆ **to** ~ **o.s. to do sth** s'astreindre à faire qch

disciplined /ˈdɪsɪplɪnd/ ADJ *[person, group]* discipliné ; *(= methodical)* méthodique

disclaim /dɪsˈkleɪm/ VT 1 *[+ news, statement]* démentir ; *[+ responsibility]* rejeter, nier ; *[+ authorship]* nier ; *[+ paternity]* désavouer ◆ **to** ~ **all knowledge of sth** nier toute connaissance de qch 2 *(Jur)* se désister de, renoncer à

disclaimer /dɪsˈkleɪməʳ/ N 1 *(= denial)* démenti *m* ; *(Jur)* désistement *m* *(of* de) renonciation *f* *(of* à) ◆ **to issue a** ~ publier un démenti 2 *(= exclusion clause)* décharge *f* (de responsabilité)

disclose /dɪsˈkləʊz/ VT *[+ secret]* divulguer, dévoiler ; *[+ news]* divulguer ; *[+ intentions]* dévoiler ; *[+ contents of envelope, box etc]* dévoiler, montrer COMP **disclosing agent** N *(Dentistry)* révélateur *m* de plaque dentaire

disclosure /dɪsˈkləʊʒəʳ/ N 1 *(NonC, by newspaper etc)* divulgation *f*, révélation *f* ; *(by individual to press etc)* communication *f* (de renseignements) *(to* à) 2 *(= fact etc revealed)* révélation *f*

disco* /ˈdɪskəʊ/ N (abbrev of **discotheque**) disco *m* COMP **disco dancing** N disco *m*

discography /dɪsˈkɒgrəfɪ/ N discographie *f*

discolour, discolor (US) /dɪsˈkʌləʳ/ VT *(= spoil colour of, fade: gen)* décolorer ; *[+ white material, teeth]* jaunir VI *(gen)* se décolorer ; *[white material, teeth]* jaunir ; *[mirror]* se ternir

discolouration, discoloration *(esp US)* /dɪsˌkʌləˈreɪʃən/ N décoloration *f*

discombobulate /ˌdɪskəmˈbɒbjʊˈleɪt/ VT *(esp US)* *[+ plans]* chambouler* ; *[+ person]* déconcerter

discomfit /dɪsˈkʌmfɪt/ VT *(= disappoint)* décevoir, tromper les espoirs de ; *(= confuse)* déconcerter, décontenancer, confondre

discomfiture /dɪsˈkʌmfɪtʃəʳ/ N *(= disappointment)* déconvenue *f* ; *(= confusion)* embarras *m*, déconfiture* *f*

discomfort /dɪsˈkʌmfət/ N 1 *(NonC: physical, mental)* gêne *f* ; *(stronger)* malaise *m* ◆ **I feel some** ~ **from it but not real pain** ça me gêne mais ça ne me fait pas vraiment mal ◆ **much to my** ~**, he announced he would accompany me** à mon grand embarras, il a annoncé qu'il m'accompagnerait 2 *(= uncomfortable thing)* désagrément *m* ◆ **the ~s of camping in wet weather** les désagréments *mpl* du camping par temps de pluie

discomposure /ˌdɪskəmˈpəʊʒəʳ/ N trouble *m*, confusion *f*

disconcert /ˌdɪskənˈsɜːt/ VT déconcerter, décontenancer

disconcerting /ˌdɪskənˈsɜːtɪŋ/ ADJ déconcertant, troublant, déroutant

disconcertingly /ˌdɪskənˈsɜːtɪŋlɪ/ ADV d'une manière déconcertante ◆ **~, I found I rather liked him** j'ai été surpris de me rendre compte que je l'aimais bien ◆ **the policemen's faces were ~ young** les policiers étaient d'une jeunesse déconcertante

disconnect /ˌdɪskəˈnekt/ VT *[+ electrical apparatus, pipe]* débrancher ; *[+ railway carriages]* décrocher ; *(= cut off) [+ gas, electricity, water supply, telephone]* couper ◆ **we've been ~ed** *(Telec) (for non-payment etc)* on nous a coupé le téléphone ; *(in mid-conversation)* nous avons été coupés ◆ **to be/feel ~ed from reality** être/se sentir coupé de la réalité ◆ **their proposal is ~ed from scientific reality** leur proposition n'est fondée sur aucune réalité scientifique

disconnected /ˌdɪskəˈnektɪd/ ADJ *[speech]* décousu ; *[thoughts]* sans suite ; *[facts, events]* sans rapport

disconnection /ˌdɪskʌˈnekʃən/ N *(Telec)* suspension *f* de ligne ; *[of gas, electricity]* coupure *f*

disconsolate /dɪsˈkɒnsəlɪt/ ADJ inconsolable

disconsolately /dɪsˈkɒnsəlɪtlɪ/ ADV 1 *(= dejectedly)* d'un air abattu ◆ **"I'm bored", he said ~** "je m'ennuie" dit-il d'un air abattu 2 *(= inconsolably) [trudge, wander]* l'air inconsolable ◆ **"there's no point going on", she said ~** "ça ne sert à rien de continuer" dit-elle inconsolable ◆ **she wept ~** elle pleurait, inconsolable

discontent /ˌdɪskənˈtent/ N mécontentement *m* ; *(Pol)* malaise *m* (social) ◆ **cause of ~** grief *m*

discontented /ˌdɪskənˈtentɪd/ ADJ mécontent *(with, about* de)

discontentedly /ˌdɪskənˈtentɪdlɪ/ ADV d'un air mécontent

discontentment /ˌdɪskənˈtentmənt/ N mécontentement *m*

discontinuance /ˌdɪskənˈtɪnjʊəns/, **discontinuation** /ˈdɪskənˌtɪnjʊˈeɪʃən/ N *(gen)* interruption *f* ; *[of production etc]* arrêt *m*

discontinue /ˌdɪskənˈtɪnjuː/ VT *(gen)* cesser ; *[+ product] (= stop manufacture of)* arrêter la production de ; *(= stop sales of)* ne plus vendre ; *[+ service]* supprimer ; *(Jur) [+ case, legal proceedings]* abandonner ; *(Med) [+ treatment]* arrêter ◆ **to ~ one's subscription to a newspaper** résilier son abonnement à un journal ◆ **a ~d line** *(Comm)* une série *or* un article qui ne se fait plus ◆ **"discontinued"** *(on sale article)* "fin de série"

discontinuity /ˌdɪskɒntɪˈnjuːɪtɪ/ N *(gen, Math)* discontinuité *f* ; *(Geol)* zone *f* de discontinuité

discontinuous /ˌdɪskənˈtɪnjʊəs/ ADJ discontinu *(also Ling)*

discord /ˈdɪskɔːd/ N 1 discorde *f*, dissension *f* ◆ **civil ~** dissensions *fpl* civiles 2 *(Mus)* dissonance *f*

discordant /dɪsˈkɔːdənt/ ADJ 1 *[opinions]* incompatible ; *[sounds, colours]* discordant 2 *(Mus)* dissonant

discotheque /ˈdɪskəʊtek/ N discothèque *f (dancing)*

discount /ˈdɪskaʊnt/ N escompte *m* ; *(on article)* remise *f*, rabais *m* ; *(rebate on transaction not shown on invoice)* ristourne *f* ; *(Stock Exchange* : also **share discount**) décote *f* ; *(in forward markets)* déport *m* ◆ **to give a ~** faire une remise *(on* sur) ◆ **to buy at a ~** acheter au rabais ◆ **~ for cash** escompte *m* au comptant ◆ **at a ~** *(Fin)* en perte, au-dessous du pair ; *(in forward markets)* avec un déport ; *(fig)* mal coté ◆ **a ~ of 25% below the nominal value of the shares** une décote de 25% par rapport à la valeur nominale de l'action

VT /dɪsˈkaʊnt/ *[+ sum of money]* faire une remise de, escompter ; *[+ bill, note]* prendre à l'escompte, escompter ; *(fig)* ne pas tenir compte de ◆ **I ~ half of what he says** je divise par deux tout ce qu'il dit

COMP **discount house** N magasin *m* de vente au rabais
discount rate N taux *m* d'escompte
discount store N ⇒ **discount house**

discounter /dɪsˈkaʊntəʳ/ N *(Fin, Banking)* escompteur *m* ; *(= store)* magasin *m* discount

discourage /dɪsˈkʌrɪdʒ/ VT 1 *(= dishearten)* décourager, abattre ◆ **to become ~d** se laisser décourager *or* rebuter, se laisser aller au découragement ◆ **he isn't easily ~d** il ne se décourage pas facilement 2 *(= advise against)* décourager, (essayer de) dissuader *(sb from sth/from doing sth* qn de qch/de faire qch) 3 *[+ suggestion]* déconseiller ; *[+ offer of friendship]* repousser ◆ **she ~d his advances** elle a repoussé *or* découragé ses avances

discouragement /dɪsˈkʌrɪdʒmənt/ N *(= act)* désapprobation *f (of* de) ; *(= depression)* découragement *m*, abattement *m*

discouraging /dɪsˈkʌrɪdʒɪŋ/ ADJ décourageant, démoralisant

discourse /ˈdɪskɔːs/ N 1 discours *m* ; *(written)* dissertation *f*, traité *m* 2 †† conversation *f* VI /dɪsˈkɔːs/ *(= hold forth)* discourir *((up)on* sur) traiter *((up)on* de) COMP **discourse analysis** N analyse *f* du discours

discourteous /dɪsˈkɜːtɪəs/ ADJ impoli, peu courtois, discourtois *(towards* envers, avec)

discourteously /dɪsˈkɜːtɪəslɪ/ ADV de façon discourtoise

discourteousness /dɪsˈkɜːtɪəsnɪs/, **discourtesy** /dɪsˈkɜːtɪsɪ/ N incivilité *f*, manque *m* de courtoisie *(towards* envers, avec)

discover /dɪsˈkʌvəʳ/ VT *[+ country, planet, treasure, reason, cause, secret, person hiding]* découvrir ; *[+ mistake, loss]* s'apercevoir de, se rendre compte de ; *(after search) [+ house, book]* dénicher ◆ **to ~ that...** *(= find out)* apprendre que ... ; *(= notice)* s'apercevoir que ... ; *(= understand)* comprendre que ...

discoverer /dɪsˈkʌvərəʳ/ N ◆ **the ~ of America/penicillin** celui qui a découvert l'Amérique/la pénicilline, le découvreur de l'Amérique/la pénicilline

discovery /dɪsˈkʌvərɪ/ N 1 *(NonC) [of fact, place, person]* découverte *f* ◆ **it led to the ~ of penicillin** cela a conduit à la découverte de la pénicilline ; → **voyage** 2 *(= happy find)* trouvaille *f* 3 *(Jur)* **~ of documents** communication *f* des pièces du dossier avant l'audience 4 *(Scol: subject)* activités *fpl* d'éveil ◆ **to learn through ~** apprendre par des activités d'éveil

discredit /dɪsˈkredɪt/ VT *(= cast slur on)* discréditer, déconsidérer ; *(= disbelieve)* ne pas croire, mettre en doute N discrédit *m*, déconsidération *f* ◆ **to bring ~ upon sb** jeter le discrédit sur qn ◆ **without any ~ to you** sans que cela vous nuise en rien ◆ **to be a ~ to ...** être une honte pour ..., faire honte à ... ◆ **to be to sb's ~** discréditer qn

discreditable /dɪsˈkredɪtəbl/ ADJ peu honorable, indigne, déshonorant

discredited /dɪsˈkredɪtɪd/ ADJ discrédité

discreet /dɪsˈkriːt/ ADJ *[person, action, presence, silence, decor, colour]* discret (-ète *f*) *(about* sur) ◆ **at a ~ distance** à distance respectueuse

discreetly /dɪsˈkriːtlɪ/ ADV *[speak, behave]* discrètement ; *[dress]* avec sobriété ◆ **~, she said nothing until her visitor had left** par discrétion, elle n'a rien dit avant le départ de son visiteur

discrepancy /dɪsˈkrepənsɪ/ N *(= difference)* différence *f* ; *(between versions, opinions)* divergence *f* ; *(between numbers)* écart *m* ◆ **the ~ between press and radio reports** la différence *or* la divergence entre la version des journaux et celle de la radio ◆ **discrepancies in pay rates** les écarts de salaire

discrete /dɪsˈkriːt/ ADJ à part, individuel ; *(Math, Med)* discret (-ète *f*) ◆ **herbal medicine does not treat mind and body as ~ entities** la médecine par les plantes ne traite pas l'esprit et le corps comme des éléments à part *or* individuels

discretion /dɪsˈkreʃən/ N 1 *(= tact)* discrétion *f* ; *(= prudence)* discrétion *f*, sagesse *f* ◆ **~ is the better part of valour** *(Prov)* prudence est mère de sûreté *(Prov)* 2 *(= freedom of decision)* discrétion *f* ◆ **to leave sth to sb's ~** laisser qch à la discrétion de qn ◆ **use your own ~** faites comme bon vous semblera, c'est à vous de juger ◆ **at the ~ of the judge/the chairman** *etc* **it is possible to ...** c'est au juge/au président *etc* de décider s'il est possible de ... ◆ **the age of ~** l'âge *m* de raison ◆ **to reach the age of ~** atteindre l'âge de raison

discretionary /dɪsˈkreʃənərɪ/ ADJ *[powers]* discrétionnaire ◆ **the new system of ~ pay awards for teachers** le nouveau système de primes accordées aux enseignants à la discrétion des établissements

discriminant /dɪsˈkrɪmɪnənt/ N *(Math)* discriminant *m*

discriminate /dɪsˈkrɪmɪneɪt/ VI 1 *(= make unfair distinction)* introduire une discrimination *(against* contre ; *in favour of* en faveur de) ◆ **to be ~d against** être victime d'une discrimination 2 *(= be discerning)* ◆ **the public should ~** le public ne devrait pas accepter n'importe quoi *or* devrait exercer son sens critique ◆ **he is unable to ~** il est incapable d'exercer son sens critique VT distinguer *(from* de) discriminer *(liter) (from* de)

discriminating /dɪsˈkrɪmɪneɪtɪŋ/ ADJ 1 *(= discerning) [person, audience, clientele]* plein de discernement, averti ; *[palate]* exercé ; *[judgement, mind]* perspicace ◆ **he's not very ~** *(about books, TV)* il manque d'esprit critique ; *(about food)* il n'a pas un goût très fin 2 *[tariff, tax]* différentiel

discrimination /dɪsˌkrɪmɪˈneɪʃən/ N 1 *(= prejudice)* discrimination *f (against* contre ; *in favour of* en faveur de) ◆ **religious ~** discrimination *f* religieuse *or* d'ordre religieux ; → **racial, sex** 2 *(= distinction)* distinction *f (between* entre) séparation *f* 3 *(NonC = judgement)* discernement *m*

discriminatory /dɪsˈkrɪmɪnətərɪ/ ADJ discriminatoire

discursive /dɪsˈkɜːsɪv/, **discursory** /dɪsˈkɜːsərɪ/ ADJ discursif, décousu *(pej)*

discus /ˈdɪskəs/ N (pl **discuses** *or* **disci**) disque *m* COMP **discus thrower** N lanceur *m* de disque, discobole *m (Hist)*

discuss /dɪsˈkʌs/ VT *(= examine in detail)* discuter, examiner ; *(= talk about) [+ problem, project, price]* discuter ; *[+ topic]* discuter de *or* sur, débattre de ◆ **we were ~ing him** nous parlions de lui ◆ **I ~ed it with him** j'en ai discuté avec lui ◆ **I won't ~ it any further** je ne veux plus en parler

discussant /dɪsˈkʌsənt/ N *(US)* participant(e) *m(f) (à une discussion etc)*

discussion /dɪsˈkʌʃən/ N discussion *f*, débat *m (of, about* sur, au sujet de) ◆ **under ~** en discussion ◆ **a subject for ~** un sujet de discussion

COMP **discussion document** N avant-projet *m*
discussion forum N *(Comput)* forum *m* de discussion
discussion group N groupe *m* de discussion
discussion paper N ⇒ **discussion document**

disdain /dɪsˈdeɪn/ VT dédaigner *(to do sth* de faire qch) N dédain *m*, mépris *m* ◆ **in ~** avec dédain ◆ **to treat sb/sth with ~** traiter qn/qch avec mépris

disdainful /dɪsˈdeɪnfʊl/ ADJ *[person]* dédaigneux ; *[tone, look]* dédaigneux, de dédain

disdainfully /dɪsˈdeɪnfəlɪ/ ADV avec dédain, dédaigneusement

disease /dɪˈziːz/ N maladie *f* ; → **heart, occupational, venereal, virus**

diseased /dɪˈziːzd/ ADJ malade

diseconomy /ˌdɪsɪˈkɒnəmɪ/ N déséconomie *f*

disembark /ˌdɪsɪmˈbɑːk/ VTI débarquer

disembarkation /ˌdɪsembɑːˈkeɪʃən/ N débarquement *m*

disembodied /ˌdɪsɪmˈbɒdɪd/ ADJ désincarné

disembowel /ˌdɪsɪmˈbaʊəl/ VT éventrer, éviscérer, étriper *

disempower /ˌdɪsemˈpaʊəʳ/ VT déresponsabiliser

disenchant /ˌdɪsɪnˈtʃɑːnt/ VT désabuser, désenchanter, désillusionner

disenchantment /ˌdɪsɪnˈtʃɑːntmənt/ N désenchantement *m*, désillusion *f*

disencumber /ˌdɪsɪnˈkʌmbəʳ/ VT *[+ mortgage]* payer ; *[+ property]* déshypothéquer

disenfranchise /ˌdɪsɪnˈfræntʃaɪz/ VT ⇒ **disfranchise**

disengage /ˌdɪsɪnˈgeɪdʒ/ VT *[+ object, hand]* dégager, libérer *(from* de) ; *(Tech) [+ machine]* déclencher, débrayer ◆ **to ~ o.s. from** se dégager de ◆ **to ~ the clutch** débrayer VI *(Fencing)* dégager (le fer) ; *(Tech)* se déclencher

disengaged /ˌdɪsɪnˈgeɪdʒd/ ADJ libre, inoccupé ; *(Tech)* débrayé

disengagement /ˌdɪsɪnˈgeɪdʒmənt/ N *(Pol)* désengagement *m*

disentangle /ˌdɪsɪnˈtæŋgl/ VT *[+ wool, problem, mystery]* débrouiller, démêler ; *[+ plot]* dénouer ◆ **to ~ o.s. from** *(lit, fig)* se dépêtrer de, se sortir de VI se démêler

disequilibrium /ˌdɪsekwɪˈlɪbrɪəm/ N instabilité *f*

disestablish /ˌdɪsɪsˈtæblɪʃ/ VT séparer de l'État ◆ **to ~ the Church** séparer l'Église de l'État

disestablishment /ˌdɪsɪsˈtæblɪʃmənt/ N séparation *f* (de l'Église et de l'État)

disfavour, disfavor (US) /dɪsˈfeɪvəʳ/ N désapprobation *f*, défaveur *f* ◆ **to fall into ~** tomber en défaveur ◆ **to fall into ~ with sb** tomber en défaveur auprès de qn ◆ **to be in ~ with sb** être mal vu de qn ◆ **to look with ~ on sth** regarder qch avec désapprobation ◆ **to look with ~ on sb** désapprouver qn VT 1 (= *dislike*) désapprouver 2 (US = *disadvantage*) être défavorable à, défavoriser

disfigure /dɪsˈfɪgəʳ/ VT *[+ face]* défigurer ; *[+ scenery]* défigurer, déparer

disfigured /dɪsˈfɪgəd/ ADJ défiguré (*by* par)

disfigurement /dɪsˈfɪgəmənt/ N défigurement *m*, enlaidissement *m*

disfranchise /dɪsˈfræntʃaɪz/ VT *[+ person]* priver du droit électoral ; *[+ town]* priver de ses droits de représentation

disgorge /dɪsˈgɔːdʒ/ VT *[+ food]* dégorger, rendre ; *[+ contents, passengers]* déverser VI *[river]* se dégorger, se décharger

disgrace /dɪsˈgreɪs/ N 1 *(NonC)* (= *dishonour*) honte *f*, déshonneur *m* ; (= *disfavour*) disgrâce *f*, défaveur *f* ◆ **there is no ~ in doing that** il n'y a aucune honte à faire cela ◆ **to be in ~** *[public figure, politician]* être en disgrâce ; *[child, dog]* être en pénitence ◆ **to bring ~ on sb** déshonorer qn

2 (= *cause of shame*) honte *f* ◆ **it's a ~!** c'est une honte !, c'est honteux ! ◆ **it's a ~ to our country** c'est une honte pour *or* cela déshonore notre pays ◆ **she's a ~ to her family** c'est la honte de sa famille ◆ **you're a ~!** tu devrais avoir honte de toi !

VT *[+ family]* faire honte à ; *[+ name, country]* déshonorer, couvrir de honte *or* d'opprobre *(liter)* ◆ **don't ~ us** ne nous fais pas honte ◆ **to ~ o.s.** se couvrir de honte ◆ **he ~d himself by losing his temper** il s'est couvert de honte en se mettant en colère ◆ **to be ~d** *[officer, politician]* être disgracié

disgraceful /dɪsˈgreɪsfʊl/ ADJ scandaleux, honteux

disgracefully /dɪsˈgreɪsfəlɪ/ ADV *[behave]* de manière scandaleuse ; (= *bad, badly etc*) scandaleusement ◆ **~ low wages** des salaires *mpl* scandaleusement bas ◆ **~ badly paid** scandaleusement mal payé

disgruntled /dɪsˈgrʌntld/ ADJ *[person]* (= *discontented*) mécontent *(about, with* de) ; (= *in bad temper*) de mauvaise humeur, mécontent *(about, with* à cause de) ; *[expression]* maussade, renfrogné

disguise /dɪsˈgaɪz/ VT *[+ person]* déguiser *(as* en) ; *[+ mistake, voice]* déguiser, camoufler ; *[+ facts, feelings]* dissimuler ◆ **to ~ o.s. as a woman** se déguiser en femme ◆ **to be ~d as a woman** être déguisé en femme ◆ **there is no disguising the fact that ...** on ne peut pas se dissimuler que ..., il faut avouer que ... N *(lit)* déguisement *m* ; *(fig)* masque *m* ; *(NonC)* artifice *m* ◆ **a novel about secrecy and ~** un roman sur le secret et l'artifice ◆ **his attitude was just a ~ for his true feelings** son attitude n'était qu'un masque qui cachait ses véritables sentiments ◆ **often bright colour is just a ~ for bad painting** les couleurs vives ne sont souvent qu'un moyen de masquer la mauvaise qualité de l'œuvre ◆ **in ~** *(lit, fig)* déguisé ◆ **in the ~ of ...** déguisé en ...

disgust /dɪsˈgʌst/ N dégoût *m*, répugnance *f* *(for, at* pour) ◆ **he left in ~** il est parti dégoûté *or* écœuré ◆ **to his ~ they left** il était écœuré de les voir partir ◆ **to my ~ he refused to do it** il a refusé et cela m'a dégoûté VT dégoûter, écœurer ; (= *infuriate*) dégoûter, révolter

disgusted /dɪsˈgʌstɪd/ ADJ dégoûté, écœuré *(at* de, par)

disgustedly /dɪsˈgʌstɪdlɪ/ ADV *[look at]* avec dégoût, d'un air dégoûté ◆ **"you really are pathetic", he said ~** "tu es vraiment minable", dit-il écœuré *or* dégoûté

disgusting /dɪsˈgʌstɪŋ/ ADJ 1 (= *revolting*) *[food, habit, behaviour, toilet, person]* dégoûtant ; *[taste, smell]* répugnant, infect ◆ **it looks ~** ça a l'air dégoûtant ◆ **it tastes ~** c'est dégoûtant *or* infect ◆ **it smells ~** ça pue 2 (= *obscene*) dégoûtant 3 (* = *disgraceful*) dégoûtant ◆ **~!** c'est dégoûtant ! ◆ **you're ~!** tu es dégoûtant ! ◆ **I think it's ~ that we have to pay** je trouve ça dégoûtant qu'on doive payer ◆ **I think it's ~ how much money they've got** je trouve (que c'est) dégoûtant qu'ils aient tant d'argent

disgustingly /dɪsˈgʌstɪŋlɪ/ ADV d'une manière dégoûtante ◆ **~ dirty** d'une saleté répugnante

dish /dɪʃ/ N 1 (= *serving plate*) plat *m* ; (= *dinner plate*) assiette *f* ; *(in laboratory etc)* récipient *m* ◆ **vegetable ~** plat *m* à légumes, légumier *m* ◆ **the ~es** la vaisselle ◆ **to do the ~es** faire la vaisselle ◆ **to clear away the breakfast ~es** débarrasser la table du petit déjeuner

2 (= *food*) plat *m*, mets *m (frm)* ◆ **fish/pasta/vegetable ~** plat *m* de poisson/de pâtes/de légumes ◆ **this is not my ~** * *(US fig)* ce n'est pas mon truc *

3 (also **dish aerial, dish antenna**) → **comp**

4 (* *fig* = *attractive person*) *(man)* beau mec * *m* ; *(woman)* belle nana * *f* ◆ **she's quite a ~** c'est vraiment une belle nana *

VT 1 *[+ food, meal]* mettre dans un plat ◆ **to ~ the dirt (on sb)** * colporter des ragots * (sur qn)

2 * *[+ opponent]* enfoncer *, écraser ; *[+ sb's chances, hopes]* flanquer par terre *

COMP **dish aerial, dish antenna** (US) N antenne *f* parabolique, parabole *f*

► **dish out** VT SEP *[+ food]* servir ; * *(fig) [+ money, sweets, books etc]* distribuer ; *[+ punishment]* administrer ◆ **to ~ out a hiding to sb** * flanquer * une correction à qn ◆ **to ~ it out to sb** * *(fig)* (= *smack etc*) flanquer * une correction à qn ; *(verbally)* passer un savon * à qn

► **dish up** VT SEP 1 *[+ food, meal]* servir, verser dans un plat ◆ **the meal was ready to ~ up** le repas était prêt à servir

2 * *[+ facts, statistics]* resservir

dishabille /ˌdɪsəˈbiːl/ N *(frm)* déshabillé *m*, négligé † *m* ◆ **in ~** en déshabillé, en négligé

disharmony /dɪsˈhɑːmənɪ/ N désaccord *m*, manque *m* d'harmonie

dishcloth /ˈdɪʃklɒθ/ N *(for washing)* lavette *f* ; *(for drying)* torchon *m* (à vaisselle)

dishearten /dɪsˈhɑːtn/ VT décourager, abattre, démoraliser ◆ **don't be ~ed** ne vous laissez pas décourager *or* abattre

disheartening /dɪsˈhɑːtnɪŋ/ ADJ décourageant, démoralisant

dishevelled /dɪˈʃevəld/ ADJ (= *ruffled*) *[person]* échevelé, ébouriffé ; *[hair]* ébouriffé ; *[clothes]* en désordre ; (= *scruffy*) *[person]* débraillé

dishmop /ˈdɪʃmɒp/ N lavette *f*

dishoard /dɪsˈhɔːd/ VT *[+ money]* déthésauriser, remettre en circulation

dishonest /dɪsˈɒnɪst/ ADJ (= *unscrupulous*) malhonnête ; (= *insincere*) déloyal, de mauvaise foi ◆ **to be ~ with sb** être de mauvaise foi avec qn, être malhonnête avec qn

dishonestly /dɪsˈɒnɪstlɪ/ ADV *[behave]* malhonnêtement ; *[obtain]* par des moyens malhonnêtes

dishonesty /dɪsˈɒnɪstɪ/ N (= *unscrupulousness*) malhonnêteté *f* ; (= *insincerity*) mauvaise foi *f*

dishonour /dɪsˈɒnəʳ/ N déshonneur *m* VT 1 *[+ family]* déshonorer, porter atteinte à l'honneur de ; *[+ woman]* déshonorer 2 *[+ bill, cheque]* refuser d'honorer ◆ **a ~ed cheque** un chèque impayé *or* non honoré

dishonourable /dɪsˈɒnərəbl/ ADJ *[person]* sans honneur ; *[act, behaviour]* déshonorant COMP **dishonourable discharge** N *(Mil) exclusion de l'armée pour conduite déshonorante*

dishonourably /dɪsˈɒnərəblɪ/ ADV de façon déshonorante ◆ **to be ~ discharged** *(Mil) être exclu de l'armée pour conduite déshonorante*

dishpan /ˈdɪʃpæn/ N (US) bassine *f* (à vaisselle)

dishrack /ˈdɪʃræk/ N égouttoir *m* (à vaisselle)

dishrag /ˈdɪʃræg/ N lavette *f*

dishtowel /ˈdɪʃtaʊəl/ N (US) torchon *m* (à vaisselle)

dishwasher /ˈdɪʃwɒʃəʳ/ N 1 (= *machine*) lave-vaisselle *m inv* 2 (= *washer-up*) laveur *m*, -euse *f* de vaisselle ; *(in restaurant)* plongeur *m*, -euse *f* ◆ **to work as a ~** travailler à la plonge

dishwater /ˈdɪʃwɔːtəʳ/ N eau *f* de vaisselle ◆ **this coffee's like** *or* **as weak as ~** * c'est du jus de chaussettes * *or* de la lavasse * ce café ; → **dull**

dishy ‡ /ˈdɪʃɪ/ ADJ *(Brit) [person]* sexy *

disillusion /ˌdɪsɪˈluːʒən/ VT désillusionner, désabuser ◆ **to be ~ed** être désabusé *or* désenchanté ◆ **to be ~ed with sth** être déçu par qch ◆ **voters were ~ed with the slow pace of change** les électeurs étaient déçus par la lenteur des changements ◆ **to grow ~ed** perdre ses illusions N désillusion *f*, désenchantement *m*

disillusionment /ˌdɪsɪˈluːʒənmənt/ N ⇒ **disillusion noun**

disincentive /ˌdɪsɪnˈsentɪv/ N ◆ **it's a real ~** cela a un effet dissuasif *or* de dissuasion ◆ **this is a ~ to work** cela n'incite pas à travailler *or* au travail ADJ dissuasif

disinclination /ˌdɪsɪnklɪˈneɪʃən/ N manque *m* d'enthousiasme (*to do sth* à faire qch ; *for sth* pour qch)

disinclined /ˌdɪsɪnˈklaɪnd/ ADJ peu disposé, peu porté, peu enclin (*for* à ; *to do sth* à faire qch)

disinfect /ˌdɪsɪnˈfekt/ VT désinfecter

disinfectant /ˌdɪsɪnˈfektənt/ ADJ, N désinfectant *m*

disinfection /ˌdɪsɪnˈfekʃən/ N désinfection *f*

disinflation /ˌdɪsɪnˈfleɪʃən/ N déflation *f*

disinflationary /ˌdɪsɪnˈfleɪʃənərɪ/ ADJ de déflation, déflationniste

disinformation /ˌdɪsɪnfəˈmeɪʃən/ N désinformation *f*

disingenuous /ˌdɪsɪnˈdʒenjʊəs/ ADJ fourbe

disingenuously /ˌdɪsɪnˈdʒenjʊəslɪ/ ADV (*frm*) avec fourberie

disingenuousness /ˌdɪsɪnˈdʒenjʊəsnɪs/ N fourberie *f*

disinherit /ˌdɪsɪnˈherɪt/ VT déshériter

disintegrate /dɪsˈɪntɪgreɪt/ VI se désintégrer, se désagréger ; (*Phys*) se désintégrer VT désintégrer, désagréger ; (*Phys*) désintégrer

disintegration /dɪsˌɪntɪˈgreɪʃən/ N désintégration *f*, désagrégation *f* ; (*Phys*) désintégration *f*

disinter /ˌdɪsɪnˈtɜːʳ/ VT déterrer, exhumer

disinterest /dɪsˈɪntrɪst/ N 1 (*= impartiality*) désintéressement *m* 2 (** = lack of interest*) indifférence *f*

disinterested /dɪsˈɪntrɪstɪd/ ADJ 1 (*= impartial*) désintéressé 2 (** = uninterested*) indifférent

disinterestedly /dɪsˈɪntrɪstɪdlɪ/ ADV 1 (*= impartially*) de façon désintéressée 2 (** = uninterestedly*) avec indifférence

disinterestedness /dɪsˈɪntrɪstɪdnɪs/ N 1 (*= impartiality*) désintéressement *m* 2 (** = lack of interest*) indifférence *f*

disinterment /ˌdɪsɪnˈtɜːmənt/ N déterrement *m*, exhumation *f*

disintoxicate /ˌdɪsɪnˈtɒksɪkeɪt/ VT désintoxiquer

disintoxication /ˌdɪsɪnˌtɒksɪˈkeɪʃən/ N désintoxication *f*

disinvest /ˌdɪsɪnˈvest/ VI désinvestir (*from* de)

disinvestment /ˌdɪsɪnˈvestmənt/ N désinvestissement *m* (*from* de)

disjoint /dɪsˈdʒɔɪnt/ ADJ (*Math*) disjoint

disjointed /dɪsˈdʒɔɪntɪd/ ADJ [*film, lecture, style, conversation, sentence, thoughts*] décousu, incohérent

disjunction /dɪsˈdʒʌŋkʃən/ N disjonction *f*

disjunctive /dɪsˈdʒʌŋktɪv/ ADJ disjonctif COMP
disjunctive pronoun N forme *f* disjointe du pronom

disk /dɪsk/ N 1 (*esp US*) ⇒ **disc** 2 (*Comput*) disque *m* ◆ **on ~** sur disque ; → **double, floppy, hard**
COMP **disk capacity** N (*Comput*) capacité *f* du disque
disk drive N lecteur *m* de disques
disk pack N unité *f* de disques
disk space N (*Comput*) espace *m* disque

diskette /dɪsˈket/ N (*Comput*) disquette *f*

dislike /dɪsˈlaɪk/ LANGUAGE IN USE 14, 7.2, 7.3 VT [*+ person, thing*] ne pas aimer ◆ **to ~ doing sth** ne pas aimer faire qch ◆ **I don't ~ it** cela ne me déplaît pas ◆ **I ~ her** elle me déplaît ◆ **I ~ this intensely** j'ai cela en horreur N antipathie *f* ◆ **his ~ of sb** l'antipathie qu'il éprouve pour qn ◆ **his ~ of sth** son aversion pour qch ◆ **one's likes and ~s** ce que l'on aime et ce que l'on n'aime pas ◆ **to take a ~ to sb/sth** prendre qn/qch en grippe ◆ **to take an instant ~ to sb/sth** prendre tout de suite qn/qch en grippe

dislocate /ˈdɪsləʊkeɪt/ VT 1 [*+ limb etc*] [*person*] se disloquer, se démettre, se luxer ; [*fall, accident*] disloquer, démettre, luxer 2 (*fig*) [*+ traffic, business*] désorganiser ; [*+ plans, timetable*] bouleverser

dislocation /ˌdɪsləʊˈkeɪʃən/ N 1 (*Med*) dislocation *f*, déboîtement *m*, luxation *f* ◆ **congenital ~** luxation *f* congénitale 2 (*= disruption: of life, society*) bouleversement *m*

dislodge /dɪsˈlɒdʒ/ VT [*+ object*] déplacer ; [*+ enemy*] déloger ; [*+ dictator*] chasser (*from* de)

disloyal /dɪsˈlɔɪəl/ ADJ [*person, behaviour*] déloyal (*to* envers)

disloyalty /dɪsˈlɔɪəltɪ/ N déloyauté *f*, infidélité *f*

dismal /ˈdɪzməl/ ADJ 1 (*= dreary*) [*place, building*] lugubre ; [*thought, prospects*] sombre ; [*weather*] maussade ◆ **the ~ science** (*= economics*) la science funeste 2 (** = awful*) lamentable ◆ **a ~ failure** un échec lamentable

dismally /ˈdɪzməlɪ/ ADV * [*fail, perform*] lamentablement

dismantle /dɪsˈmæntl/ VT [*+ machine, furniture*] démonter ; [*+ company, department*] démanteler (*also Mil*)

dismantling /dɪsˈmæntəlɪŋ/ N [*of company, department*] démantèlement *m*

dismast /dɪsˈmɑːst/ VT démâter

dismay /dɪsˈmeɪ/ LANGUAGE IN USE 14 N consternation *f*, désarroi *m* ◆ **to my ~** à ma grande consternation ◆ **in ~** d'un air consterné VT consterner

dismayed /dɪsˈmeɪd/ ADJ [*person*] consterné (*by* par)

dismember /dɪsˈmembəʳ/ VT (*lit, fig*) démembrer

dismemberment /dɪsˈmembəmənt/ N démembrement *m*

dismiss /dɪsˈmɪs/ VT 1 [*+ employee*] renvoyer, licencier ; [*+ official, officer*] destituer, casser ; [*+ class, visitors*] laisser partir, congédier ; [*+ assembly*] dissoudre ; [*+ troops*] faire rompre les rangs à ◆ **to be ~ed (from) the service** (*Mil*) être renvoyé de l'armée *or* rayé des cadres ◆ **~!** (*Mil*) rompez (les rangs) ! ◆ **class ~!** (*Scol*) le cours est terminé ! 2 [*+ thought, possibility, suggestion, objection*] écarter ; [*+ request*] rejeter 3 (*gen*) [*+ sb's appeal, claim*] rejeter ; (*Jur*) [*+ accused*] relaxer ; [*+ jury*] congédier ◆ **to ~ sb's appeal** (*Jur*) débouter qn de son appel ◆ **to ~ a case** rendre une fin de non-recevoir ◆ **to ~ a charge** rendre un arrêt de *or* une ordonnance de non-lieu

dismissal /dɪsˈmɪsəl/ N 1 [*of employee*] licenciement *m*, renvoi *m* ; [*of civil servant*] destitution *f*, révocation *f* ◆ **unfair** *or* **wrongful ~** licenciement *m* abusif 2 (*= permission to leave*) congé *m* ◆ **he made a gesture of ~** il a fait un geste pour les (*or* nous *etc*) congédier 3 (*= brushing aside*) rebuffade *f* ◆ **I was annoyed by his curt ~ of my objections** cette façon qu'il a eue d'écarter sèchement mes objections m'a agacé 4 (*Jur*) [*of appeal*] rejet *m* ; [*of jury*] congédiement *m* ◆ **the ~ of the charges against him** le non-lieu dont il a bénéficié

dismissive /dɪsˈmɪsɪv/ ADJ (*= disdainful*) dédaigneux

dismissively /dɪsˈmɪsɪvlɪ/ ADV 1 (*= disdainfully*) [*speak*] d'un ton dédaigneux, avec dédain ; [*wave, nod, shrug, laugh*] avec dédain ; [*describe, refer to*] dédaigneusement, avec dédain 2 (*sending sb away*) **he nodded ~ at the butler** d'un signe de tête, il congédia le maître d'hôtel ◆ **"thank you sergeant, that will be all", she said ~** "merci, sergent, ce sera tout", dit-elle, et sur ces mots, elle le congédia

dismount /dɪsˈmaʊnt/ VI descendre (*from* de) mettre pied à terre VT [*+ rider*] démonter, désarçonner ; [*+ troops, gun, machine*] démonter (*from* de)

Disneyfy /ˈdɪznɪfaɪ/ VT (*pej*) disneyfier

disobedience /ˌdɪsəˈbiːdɪəns/ N (*NonC*) désobéissance *f*, insoumission *f* (*to* à) ◆ **an act of ~** une désobéissance

disobedient /ˌdɪsəˈbiːdɪənt/ ADJ [*child*] désobéissant (*to* à) ◆ **he has been ~** il a été désobéissant, il a désobéi

disobey /ˌdɪsəˈbeɪ/ VT [*+ parents, officer*] désobéir à, s'opposer à ; [*+ law*] enfreindre, violer

disobliging /ˌdɪsəˈblaɪdʒɪŋ/ ADJ (*frm*) désobligeant

disorder /dɪsˈɔːdəʳ/ N 1 (*NonC*) (*= untidiness*) [*of room, plans etc*] désordre *m* ◆ **to throw sth into ~** semer *or* jeter le désordre dans qch ◆ **in ~** en désordre ◆ **to retreat in ~** (*Mil*) être en déroute 2 (*NonC: Pol etc = unrest*) troubles *mpl* 3 (*Med*) troubles *mpl* ◆ **kidney/stomach/mental ~** troubles *mpl* rénaux/gastriques/psychiques ◆ **speech/sleep/personality ~** troubles *mpl* de l'élocution/du sommeil/de la personnalité ◆ **eating ~** troubles *mpl* du comportement alimentaire ◆ **skin ~** maladie *f* de la peau VT [*+ room*] mettre en désordre ; (*Med*) troubler, déranger

disordered /dɪsˈɔːdəd/ ADJ 1 (*= untidy, disorderly*) [*room, hair*] en désordre ; [*life*] désordonné 2 (*= deranged*) [*mind*] dérangé ; [*imagination*] désordonné ◆ **mentally ~** atteint de troubles mentaux

disorderly /dɪsˈɔːdəlɪ/ ADJ 1 (*= untidy*) [*room*] en désordre ; [*mind*] confus 2 (*= unruly*) [*person, crowd, meeting*] agité ; [*behaviour*] désordonné, indiscipliné ; → **drunk**
COMP **disorderly conduct** N (*Jur*) trouble *m* à l'ordre public ◆ **the marchers were charged with ~ conduct** les manifestants ont été inculpés de trouble à l'ordre public
disorderly house N (*Jur*) (*= brothel*) maison *f* close ; (*= gambling den*) maison *f* de jeu, tripot *m*

disorganization /dɪsˌɔːgənaɪˈzeɪʃən/ N désorganisation *f*

disorganize /dɪsˈɔːgənaɪz/ VT désorganiser, déranger

disorganized /dɪsˈɔːgənaɪzd/ ADJ [*person*] désorganisé ; [*room*] mal rangé, en désordre

disorient /dɪsˈɔːrɪent/ VT désorienter

disorientate /dɪsˈɔːrɪənteɪt/ VT désorienter

disorientation /dɪsˈɔːrɪənˈteɪʃən/ N désorientation *f*

disown /dɪsˈəʊn/ VT [*+ child, country, opinion, document*] désavouer, renier ; [*+ debt, signature*] nier, renier

disparage /dɪsˈpærɪdʒ/ VT (*frm*) décrier, déprécier

disparagement /dɪsˈpærɪdʒmənt/ N (*frm*) dénigrement *m*, dépréciation *f*

disparaging /dɪsˈpærɪdʒɪŋ/ ADJ (*frm*) désobligeant, (plutôt) méprisant (*to* pour) ◆ **to be ~ about** faire des remarques désobligeantes *or* peu flatteuses sur

disparagingly /dɪsˈpærɪdʒɪŋlɪ/ ADV (*frm*) d'une manière méprisante

disparate /ˈdɪspərɪt/ ADJ disparate

disparity /dɪsˈpærɪtɪ/ N disparité *f*, inégalité *f*, écart *m*

dispassionate /dɪsˈpæʃənɪt/ ADJ (*= unemotional*) calme, froid ; (*= unbiased*) impartial, objectif

dispassionately /dɪsˈpæʃənɪtlɪ/ ADV (*= unemotionally*) sans émotion ; (*= unbiasedly*) sans parti pris, impartialement

dispatch /dɪsˈpætʃ/ LANGUAGE IN USE 20.4 VT 1 (= send) [+ letter, goods] expédier, envoyer ; [+ messenger] dépêcher ; (Mil) [+ troops] envoyer, faire partir ; [+ convoy] mettre en route ; (fig) [+ food, drink] expédier 2 (= finish off) [+ job] expédier, en finir avec ; (= kill) (euph) [+ person, animal] tuer, abattre N 1 [of letter, messenger, telegram etc] envoi m, expédition f • **date of ~** date f d'expédition • **office of ~** bureau m d'origine 2 (= official report: also Mil) dépêche f ; (Press) dépêche f (de presse) • **mentioned** or **cited in ~es** (Mil) cité à l'ordre du jour 3 (= promptness) promptitude f
COMP **dispatch box** N (Brit Parl) ≃ tribune f (d'où parlent les membres du gouvernement) ; (= case) valise f officielle (à documents)
dispatch case N serviette f, porte-documents m inv
dispatch documents NPL (Comm) documents mpl d'expédition
dispatch rider N estafette f

dispatcher /dɪsˈpætʃəʳ/ N expéditeur m, -trice f

dispel /dɪsˈpel/ VT dissiper, chasser

dispensable /dɪsˈpensəbl/ ADJ dont on peut se passer ; (Rel) dispensable

dispensary /dɪsˈpensərɪ/ N (Brit) (in hospital) pharmacie f ; (in chemist's) officine f ; (= clinic) dispensaire m

dispensation /ˌdɪspenˈseɪʃən/ N 1 (= handing out) [of food] distribution f ; [of justice, charity] exercice m, pratique f 2 (= exemption) (gen, Jur, Rel) dispense f (from de) ; (Univ, Scol: from exam etc) dispense f, dérogation f

dispense /dɪsˈpens/ VT 1 [person] [+ food] distribuer ; [+ charity] pratiquer ; [+ justice, sacrament] administrer ; [+ hospitality] offrir ; [machine] [+ product] distribuer • **to ~ alms** faire l'aumône (to sb à qn) 2 [+ medicine, prescription] délivrer 3 (also Rel = exempt) dispenser (sb from sth/from doing sth qn de qch/de faire qch) COMP **dispensing chemist** N (= person) pharmacien(ne) m(f) ; (= shop) pharmacie f

► **dispense with** VT FUS (= do without) se passer de ; (= make unnecessary) rendre superflu

dispenser /dɪsˈpensəʳ/ N (Brit) (= person) pharmacien(ne) m(f) ; (= device) distributeur m

dispersal /dɪsˈpɜːsəl/ N dispersion f

dispersant /dɪsˈpɜːsənt/ N (Chem) dispersant m

disperse /dɪsˈpɜːs/ VT [+ crowd, mist] disperser ; [+ clouds] dissiper ; [+ demonstrators, protesters, demonstration] disperser ; [+ seeds] disséminer, disperser ; [+ heat] répandre ; [+ knowledge] répandre, propager ; (Chem, Opt) décomposer VI [crowd, journalists, demonstrators, protesters] se disperser ; [fog, cloud, smoke] se dissiper ; [chemicals, oil] se propager ; [pain, tension] se dissiper

dispersion /dɪsˈpɜːʃən/ N (also Phys) dispersion f • **the Dispersion** (Hist) la dispersion des Juifs, la diaspora

dispirit /dɪsˈpɪrɪt/ VT décourager, déprimer, abattre

dispirited /dɪsˈpɪrɪtɪd/ ADJ découragé, déprimé, abattu

dispiritedly /dɪsˈpɪrɪtɪdlɪ/ ADV avec découragement, d'un air découragé • **~, they turned round and went home** découragés, ils ont fait demi-tour et sont rentrés chez eux

dispiriting /dɪsˈpɪrɪtɪŋ/ ADJ décourageant, désolant

displace /dɪsˈpleɪs/ VT 1 (= move out of place) [+ refugees] déplacer ; [+ furniture] déplacer, changer de place 2 (= deprive of office) [+ officer] destituer ; [+ official] déplacer ; (= replace) supplanter, remplacer 3 (Naut, Phys) [+ water] déplacer COMP **displaced person** N personne f déplacée

displacement /dɪsˈpleɪsmənt/ N 1 (= replacement) remplacement m 2 [of people, population] déplacement m 3 (Math, Phys, Naut, Med) déplacement m ; (Geol) rejet m (horizontal)
COMP **displacement activity** N (in animals) activité f de substitution ; (Psych) déplacement m
displacement tonnage N (Naut) déplacement m

display /dɪsˈpleɪ/ VT 1 (= show) [+ object] montrer ; (pej: ostentatiously) exhiber (pej) • **she ~ed the letter she had received from the President** elle a montré or brandi la lettre qu'elle avait reçue du président
2 (= set out visibly) exposer ; [+ goods for sale] exposer, mettre à l'étalage ; [+ items in exhibition] exposer ; [+ notice, results, poster] afficher • **she bought a cabinet to ~ her china collection in** elle a acheté une vitrine pour y exposer sa collection de porcelaines
3 (= give evidence of) [+ courage, interest, ignorance] faire preuve de ; (pej) faire étalage de, exhiber
4 (Comput) visualiser ; [electronic device, watch etc] afficher
VI [bird] parader ; [peacock] faire la roue
N 1 (pej: ostentatious) étalage m ; [of goods for sale, items in exhibition] exposition f ; [of food products, wealth] étalage m ; [of notices, results, posters] affichage m ; [of courage, interest, emotion etc] manifestation f ; [of unity, support] manifestation f, démonstration f ; [of strength, loyalty] démonstration f • **a ~ of force** une démonstration de force • **to make a great ~ of learning** (pej) faire étalage de son érudition • **she was not given to public ~s of affection** elle n'avait pas pour habitude de prodiguer son affection en public • **to be embarrassed by public ~s of affection** être gêné par des démonstrations publiques d'affection • **a fine ~ of paintings/china** une belle exposition de tableaux/de porcelaines • **the ~ of fruit** (in shop window) l'étalage m de fruits, les fruits mpl à l'étalage
♦ **on display** exposé • **to put sth on ~** exposer qch • **to go on (public) ~** être exposé
2 (= group, arrangement) arrangement m
3 (= event, ceremony) **~ of gymnastics/dancing** etc spectacle m de gymnastique/de danse etc • **military ~** parade f militaire • **a dazzling ~ of fireworks lit up the sky** d'éblouissants feux d'artifice ont illuminé le ciel ; see also **air, firework**
4 (on screen) affichage m
5 (also **courtship display, mating display**) parade f
COMP (Comm) [goods] d'étalage
display advertising N (Press) placards mpl (publicitaires)
display cabinet, display case N vitrine f (meuble)
display pack N (dummy) emballage m de démonstration ; (attractive) emballage m de luxe
display panel N écran m d'affichage
display unit N (= screen) écran m de visualisation
display window N étalage m, vitrine f (de magasin)

displease /dɪsˈpliːz/ VT mécontenter, contrarier

displeased /dɪsˈpliːzd/ ADJ • **~ at** or **with** mécontent de

displeasing /dɪsˈpliːzɪŋ/ ADJ désagréable (to à) déplaisant (to pour) • **to be ~ to sb** déplaire à qn

displeasure /dɪsˈpleʒəʳ/ N mécontentement m, déplaisir m • **to incur sb's ~** provoquer le mécontentement de qn • **to my great ~** à mon grand mécontentement or déplaisir

disport /dɪsˈpɔːt/ VT • **to ~ o.s.** s'amuser, s'ébattre, folâtrer

disposable /dɪsˈpəʊzəbl/ ADJ 1 [razor, syringe etc] jetable • **today's ~ society** notre société du tout-jetable 2 (* fig = unimportant, ephemeral) sans importance • **people should not be treated as if they were ~** on ne devrait pas traiter les gens comme s'il étaient des objets facilement remplaçables or comme s'ils n'avaient aucune importance 3 (= available) [time, money] disponible NPL **disposables** (= containers) emballages m perdus or à jeter ; (= bottles) verre m perdu ; (= nappies) couches fpl à jeter, couches-culottes fpl COMP **disposable income** N revenu(s) m(pl) disponible(s)

disposal /dɪsˈpəʊzəl/ N 1 (NonC) [of rubbish] (= collection) enlèvement m ; (= destruction) destruction f ; [of goods for sale] vente f ; (Jur) [of property] disposition f, cession f ; → **bomb, refuse²** 2 (= arrangement) [of ornaments, furniture] disposition f, arrangement m ; [of troops] disposition f 3 (= control) [of resources, funds, personnel] disposition f • **the means at one's ~** les moyens dont on dispose • **to put o.s./be at sb's ~** se mettre/être à la disposition de qn COMP **disposal unit** N broyeur m d'ordures

dispose /dɪsˈpəʊz/ VT 1 (= arrange) [+ papers, ornaments] disposer, arranger ; [+ troops] disposer ; [+ forces] déployer • **man proposes, God ~s** (Prov) l'homme propose, Dieu dispose (Prov)
2 (= influence, encourage) disposer (sb to do sth qn à faire qch) • **this does not ~ me to like him** (frm) cela ne me rend pas bien disposé à son égard

► **dispose of** VT FUS 1 (= get rid of) [+ sth no longer wanted or used] se débarrasser de, se défaire de ; (by selling) vendre ; [+ workers, staff] congédier, renvoyer ; [+ rubbish] [householder etc] jeter, se débarrasser de ; (= destroy) détruire ; [+ chemical, industrial waste etc] éliminer ; [shop] [+ stock] écouler, vendre ; [+ body] se débarrasser de • **how did the murderer ~ of the body?** comment le meurtrier s'est-il débarrassé du corps ?
2 (* fig = kill) liquider* ; (Jur) [+ property] aliéner
3 (= deal with) [+ bomb] désamorcer ; [+ question, problem, business] expédier ; [+ one's opponent, opposing team] régler son compte à ; [+ meal] liquider*, expédier
4 (= control) [+ time, money] disposer de ; (= settle) [+ sb's fate] décider de

> ⚠ The commonest sense of **to dispose of** is not translated by **disposer de**, which means 'to have at one's disposal'.

disposed /dɪsˈpəʊzd/ ADJ 1 (frm) **to be ~ to do sth** être disposé à faire qch 2 **to be well-~ towards sb/sth** être bien disposé envers qn/qch • **to be favourably** or **kindly ~ to(wards) sb/sth** être bien disposé à l'égard de qn/qch ; see also **ill-disposed** 3 (frm = arranged, distributed) [objects, people] disposé

disposition /ˌdɪspəˈzɪʃən/ N 1 (= temperament) naturel m, caractère m, tempérament m 2 (= readiness) inclination f (to do sth à faire qch) 3 (= arrangement) [of ornaments etc] disposition f, arrangement m ; [of troops] disposition f 4 (Jur) [of money, property] distribution f

dispossess /ˌdɪspəˈzes/ VT déposséder, priver (of de) ; (Jur) exproprier

dispossession /ˌdɪspəˈzeʃən/ N dépossession f ; (Jur) expropriation f

disproportion /ˌdɪsprəˈpɔːʃən/ N disproportion f

disproportionate /ˌdɪsprəˈpɔːʃnɪt/ ADJ disproportionné (to par rapport à)

disproportionately /ˌdɪsprəˈpɔːʃnɪtlɪ/ ADV [react, suffer] de manière disproportionnée • **~ small** d'une petitesse disproportionnée • **~ large numbers of blind people are unemployed** un nombre disproportionné d'aveugles sont au chômage

disprove /dɪsˈpruːv/ VT établir *or* démontrer la fausseté de, réfuter

disputable /dɪsˈpjuːtəbl/ ADJ discutable, contestable

disputably /dɪsˈpjuːtəblɪ/ ADV de manière contestable

disputant /dɪsˈpjuːtənt/ N *(US Jur)* ◆ **the ~s** les parties *fpl* en litige

disputation /ˌdɪspjuːˈteɪʃən/ N [1] *(= argument)* débat *m*, controverse *f*, discussion *f* [2] († *= formal debate)* dispute † *f*

disputatious /ˌdɪspjuːˈteɪʃəs/ ADJ *(frm)* raisonneur *(liter)*

dispute /dɪsˈpjuːt/ N [1] *(NonC) (= controversy)* discussion *f* ◆ **beyond** ~ ADJ incontestable ADV incontestablement ◆ **without** ~ sans conteste ◆ **there is some** ~ **about why he did it/what he's earning** on n'est pas d'accord sur ses motifs/le montant de son salaire ◆ **there is some** ~ **about which horse won** il y a contestation sur le gagnant ◆ **in** *or* **under** ~ *[matter]* en discussion ; *[territory, facts, figures]* contesté ; *(Jur)* en litige ◆ **a statement open to** ~ une affirmation sujette à caution, une affirmation contestable ◆ **it is open to** ~ **whether he knew** on peut se demander s'il savait

[2] *(= quarrel)* dispute *f* ; *(= argument)* discussion *f*, débat *m* ; *(Jur)* litige *m*

[3] *(Ind, Pol)* conflit *m* ◆ **to have a** ~ **with sb (about sth)** se disputer avec qn (à propos de qch) ◆ **industrial** ~ conflit *m* social ◆ **the miners'/postal workers'** ~ le conflit des mineurs/des employés des postes ◆ **the transport/Post Office** ~ le conflit dans les transports/dans les services postaux ◆ **the United Shipping Company** ~ le conflit chez United Shipping ◆ **wages** ~ conflit *m* salarial *or* sur les salaires

VT [1] *(= cast doubt on) [+ statement, claim]* contester, mettre en doute ; *(Jur) [+ will]* attaquer, contester ◆ **I do not** ~ **the fact that ...** je ne conteste pas (le fait) que ... + *subj*

[2] *(= debate) [+ question, subject]* discuter, débattre

[3] *(= try to win) [+ victory, possession]* disputer *(with sb* à qn)

disputed /dɪsˈpjuːtɪd/ ADJ *[decision]* contesté, en discussion ; *[territory, fact]* contesté ; *(Jur)* en litige

disqualification /dɪsˌkwɒlɪfɪˈkeɪʃən/ N [1] *(gen)* disqualification *f (also Sport)*, exclusion *f (from* de) ◆ **his lack of experience is not a** ~ son manque d'expérience n'est pas rédhibitoire [2] *(Jur)* incapacité *f* ◆ **his** ~ **(from driving)** le retrait de son permis (de conduire)

disqualify /dɪsˈkwɒlɪfaɪ/ VT [1] *(= debar)* rendre inapte *(from sth* à qch ; *from doing sth* à faire qch) ; *(Jur)* rendre inhabile *(from sth* à qch ; *from doing sth* à faire qch) ; *(Sport)* disqualifier [2] **to** ~ **sb from driving** retirer à qn son *or* le permis de conduire ◆ **he was disqualified for speeding** on lui a retiré son permis pour excès de vitesse ◆ **he was accused of driving while disqualified** il a été accusé d'avoir conduit alors qu'on lui avait retiré son permis [3] *(= incapacitate)* rendre incapable, mettre hors d'état *(from doing sth* de faire qch) ◆ **his lack of experience does not** ~ **him** son manque d'expérience n'est pas rédhibitoire

disquiet /dɪsˈkwaɪət/ VT inquiéter, troubler ◆ **to be ~ed about** s'inquiéter de N *(NonC)* inquiétude *f*, trouble *m* ; *(= unrest)* agitation *f*

disquieting /dɪsˈkwaɪətɪŋ/ ADJ inquiétant, alarmant, troublant

disquietude /dɪsˈkwaɪɪtjuːd/ N *(NonC)* inquiétude *f*, trouble *m*

disquisition /ˌdɪskwɪˈzɪʃən/ N *(= treatise)* traité *m*, dissertation *f*, étude *f (on* sur) ; *(= discourse)* communication *f (on* sur) ; *(= investigation)* étude *f* approfondie *(on* de)

disregard /ˌdɪsrɪˈgɑːd/ VT *[+ fact, difficulty, remark]* ne tenir aucun compte de, ne pas s'occuper de ; *[+ danger]* mépriser, ne pas faire attention à ; *[+ feelings]* négliger, faire peu de cas de ; *[+ authority, rules, duty]* méconnaître, passer outre à N *[of difficulty, comments, feelings]* indifférence *f (for* à) ; *[of danger]* mépris *m (for* de) ; *[of money]* mépris *m*, dédain *m (for* de) ; *[of safety]* négligence *f (for* en ce qui concerne) ; *[of rule, law]* désobéissance *f (for* à) non-observation *f (for* de)

disrepair /ˌdɪsrɪˈpɛəʳ/ N *(NonC)* mauvais état *m*, délabrement *m* ◆ **in (a state of)** ~ *[building]* délabré ; *[road]* en mauvais état ◆ **to fall into** ~ *[building]* tomber en ruines, se délabrer ; *[road]* se dégrader

disreputable /dɪsˈrepjʊtəbl/ ADJ [1] *(= shady, dishonorable) [establishment, area, person]* peu recommandable, louche* ; *[behaviour]* déshonorant [2] (* *= shabby)* miteux

disreputably /dɪsˈrepjʊtəblɪ/ ADV *[behave]* d'une manière peu honorable ; *[dress]* minablement*

disrepute /ˌdɪsrɪˈpjuːt/ N discrédit *m*, déshonneur *m* ◆ **to bring sth into** ~ jeter le discrédit sur qch ◆ **to fall into** ~ tomber en discrédit

disrespect /ˌdɪsrɪsˈpekt/ N manque *m* de respect, irrespect *m* ◆ **no** ~ **(to ...)** avec tout le respect que je dois (à ...) ◆ **to show** ~ **to sb/sth** manquer de respect envers qn/qch VT manquer de respect envers

disrespectful /ˌdɪsrɪsˈpektfʊl/ ADJ irrespectueux, irrévérencieux (to envers) ◆ **to be** ~ **to sb/sth** manquer de respect envers qn/qch, se montrer irrespectueux envers qn/qch

disrespectfully /ˌdɪsrɪsˈpektfəlɪ/ ADV de façon irrespectueuse ◆ **to treat sb** ~ manquer de respect à qn ◆ **he was treated** ~ on lui a manqué de respect

disrobe /dɪsˈrəʊb/ VI se dévêtir, enlever ses vêtements ; *(= undress)* se déshabiller VT enlever les vêtements (de cérémonie) à, dévêtir, déshabiller

disrupt /dɪsˈrʌpt/ VT *[+ peace, relations, train service]* perturber ; *[+ conversation]* interrompre ; *[+ plans]* déranger ; *(stronger)* mettre *or* semer la confusion dans ; *[+ communications]* couper, interrompre

disruption /dɪsˈrʌpʃən/ N perturbation *f*

disruptive /dɪsˈrʌptɪv/ ADJ [1] *[child, behaviour]* perturbateur (-trice *f*) ◆ **to be a** ~ **influence** avoir une influence perturbatrice ◆ **such a move would be very** ~ **to the local economy** une telle mesure perturberait beaucoup l'économie régionale ◆ **these changes can be very** ~ **to a small company** ces changements peuvent avoir des effets très perturbateurs sur une petite entreprise [2] *(Elec)* disruptif COMP **disruptive action** N action *f* perturbatrice

diss ‡ /dɪs/ VT *(US = treat with contempt)* se payer la tête de*

dissatisfaction /ˌdɪssætɪsˈfækʃən/ N mécontentement *m*, insatisfaction *f* ◆ **growing/widespread** ~ mécontentement *m* croissant/général *(at, with* devant, provoqué par)

dissatisfied /ˌdɪsˈsætɪsfaɪd/ ADJ mécontent, peu satisfait *(with* de)

dissect /dɪˈsekt/ VT *[+ animal, plant, truth]* disséquer ; *[+ book, article]* éplucher

dissected /dɪˈsektɪd/ ADJ *(leaf)* découpé

dissection /dɪˈsekʃən/ N *(Anat, Bot, fig)* dissection *f*

dissemble /dɪˈsembl/ VT *(= conceal)* dissimuler ; *(= feign)* feindre, simuler VI *(in speech)* dissimuler *or* déguiser sa pensée ; *(in behaviour)* agir avec dissimulation

disseminate /dɪˈsemɪneɪt/ VT disséminer, semer COMP **disseminated cancer** N *(Med)* cancer *m* généralisé **disseminated sclerosis** N *(Med)* sclérose *f* en plaques

dissemination /dɪˌsemɪˈneɪʃən/ N *[of seeds]* dissémination *f* ; *[of ideas]* dissémination *f*, propagation *f*

dissension /dɪˈsenʃən/ N dissension *f*, discorde *f*

dissent /dɪˈsent/ VI différer (d'opinion *or* de sentiment) *(from sb* de qn) ; *(Rel)* être en dissidence, être dissident N dissentiment *m*, différence *f* d'opinion ; *(Rel)* dissidence *f*

dissenter /dɪˈsentəʳ/ N *(esp Rel)* dissident(e) *m(f)*

dissentient /dɪˈsenʃɪənt/ ADJ dissident, opposé N dissident(e) *m(f)*, opposant(e) *m(f)*

dissenting /dɪˈsentɪŋ/ ADJ *[voice]* dissident ◆ **a long** ~ **tradition** une longue tradition de dissidence ◆ ~ **opinion** *(US Jur)* avis *m* minoritaire de l'un des juges *(divergeant sur des questions de fond)*

dissertation /ˌdɪsəˈteɪʃən/ N [1] *(written)* mémoire *m (on* sur) ; *(spoken)* exposé *m (on* sur) [2] *(Univ) (Brit)* mémoire *m* ; *(US)* thèse *f* (de doctorat)

disservice /dɪsˈsɜːvɪs/ N mauvais service *m* ◆ **to do sb/sth a** ~ *(= be unhelpful to)* rendre un mauvais service à qn/qch, desservir qn/qch ; *(= be unfair to)* faire du tort à qn/qch

dissidence /ˈdɪsɪdəns/ N dissidence *f (also Pol)*, désaccord *m*, divergence *f* d'opinion

dissident /ˈdɪsɪdənt/ ADJ, N dissident(e) *m(f)*

dissimilar /dɪˈsɪmɪləʳ/ ADJ dissemblable *(to* à) différent *(to* de)

dissimilarity /ˌdɪsɪmɪˈlærɪtɪ/ N différence *f*, dissemblance *f (between* entre)

dissimulate /dɪˈsɪmjʊleɪt/ VTI dissimuler

dissimulation /dɪˌsɪmjʊˈleɪʃən/ N dissimulation *f*

dissipate /ˈdɪsɪpeɪt/ VT *[+ fog, clouds, fears, suspicions]* dissiper ; *[+ hopes]* anéantir ; *[+ energy, efforts]* disperser, gaspiller ; *[+ fortune]* dissiper, dilapider VI se dissiper

dissipated /ˈdɪsɪpeɪtɪd/ ADJ *[person]* débauché, qui mène une vie dissipée ; *[activity]* dépravé ; *[life, behaviour]* dissipé, dissolu ; *[appearance]* de débauché ◆ **to lead a** ~ **life** mener une vie dissipée *or* dissolue, vivre dans la dissipation *(liter)*

dissipation /ˌdɪsɪˈpeɪʃən/ N *[of clouds, fears]* dissipation *f* ; *[of energy, efforts]* gaspillage *m* ; *[of fortune]* dilapidation *f* ; *(= debauchery)* dissipation *f*, débauche *f*

dissociate /dɪˈsəʊʃɪeɪt/ LANGUAGE IN USE 26.2 VT dissocier, séparer *(from* de) ; *(Chem, Psych)* dissocier ◆ **to** ~ **o.s. from** se dissocier de, se désolidariser de

dissociation /dɪˌsəʊsɪˈeɪʃən/ N *(all senses)* dissociation *f*

dissoluble /dɪˈsɒljʊbl/ ADJ soluble

dissolute /ˈdɪsəluːt/ ADJ *[person]* débauché, dissolu *(liter)* ; *[way of life]* dissolu, déréglé, de débauche

dissolution /ˌdɪsəˈluːʃən/ N *(all senses)* dissolution *f*

dissolvable /dɪˈzɒlvəbl/ ADJ soluble *(in* dans)

dissolve /dɪˈzɒlv/ VT [1] *[water etc] [+ substance]* dissoudre *(in* dans) ; *[person] [+ chemical etc]* faire dissoudre *(in* dans) ; *(Culin) [+ sugar etc]* faire fondre *(in* dans) [2] *[+ alliance, marriage, assembly]* dissoudre VI [1] *(Chem)* se dissoudre ; *(Culin)* fondre [2] *(fig) [hopes, fears]* disparaître, s'évanouir ; *(Jur, Pol)* se dissoudre ◆ **to** ~ **into thin air** s'en aller *or* partir en fumée ◆ **to** ~ **into tears** fondre en larmes [3] *(Cine)* se fondre

N (Cine, TV) fondu m (enchaîné) ◆ ~ **in/out** ouverture f/fermeture f en fondu

dissolvent /dɪˈzɒlvənt/ **ADJ** dissolvant **N** dissolvant m, solvant m

dissonance /ˈdɪsənəns/ **N** dissonance f, discordance f

dissonant /ˈdɪsənənt/ **ADJ** dissonant, discordant

dissuade /dɪˈsweɪd/ **VT** dissuader (sb from doing sth qn de faire qch) détourner (sb from sth qn de qch)

dissuasion /dɪˈsweɪʒən/ **N** dissuasion f

dissuasive /dɪˈsweɪsɪv/ **ADJ** (gen) dissuasif ; [voice, person] qui cherche à dissuader ; [powers] de dissuasion

distaff /ˈdɪstɑːf/ **N** quenouille f ◆ **on the ~ side** (fig) du côté maternel or des femmes

distance /ˈdɪstəns/ **N** 1 (in space) distance f (between entre) ◆ **what ~ is it from London?** c'est à quelle distance de Londres ? ◆ **what ~ is it from here to London?** nous sommes à combien de kilomètres de Londres ? ◆ **it's a good ~** c'est assez loin ◆ **a short ~ away** à une faible distance ◆ **it's no ~** c'est à deux pas, c'est tout près ◆ **to cover the ~ in two hours** franchir or parcourir la distance en deux heures ◆ **at an equal ~ from each other** à égale distance l'un de l'autre ◆ **at a ~** assez loin, à quelque distance ◆ **at a ~ of 2 metres** à une distance de 2 mètres ◆ **the ~ between the boys/the houses/the towns** la distance qui sépare les garçons/les maisons/les villes ◆ **the ~ between the eyes/rails/posts** l'écartement m des yeux/des rails/des poteaux ◆ **from a ~** de loin ◆ **seen from a ~** vu de loin ◆ **to go part of the ~ alone** faire une partie du trajet seul ◆ **to go or last the ~** (Sport, fig) tenir la distance ; → **long¹, middle** ◆ **in the ~** au loin, dans le lointain ◆ **it's within walking/cycling ~** on peut y aller à pied/en vélo ; → **spitting**
2 (in time) intervalle m ◆ **from a ~ of 40 years, I can look back on it and say ...** 40 ans plus tard or 40 ans après, je peux y repenser et dire ...
3 (in rank etc) distance f ◆ **to keep sb at a ~** tenir qn à distance ◆ **to keep one's ~ (from sb/sth)** garder ses distances (par rapport à qn/qch)
VT (Sport etc) distancer ◆ **to ~ o.s. from sth** (fig) se distancier de qch
COMP distance learning N téléenseignement m
distance race N (Sport) (also **long-distance race**) épreuve f de fond
distance teaching N enseignement m à distance, téléenseignement m

distancing /ˈdɪstənsɪŋ/ **N** distanciation f

distant /ˈdɪstənt/ **ADJ** 1 (in space, time) lointain ◆ **there was a ~ view of the church** on apercevait l'église au loin ◆ **the nearest hospital was 200km ~** l'hôpital le plus proche était à 200 km ◆ **the school is 2km ~ from the church** l'école est à 2 km (de distance) de l'église ◆ **a ~ memory** un lointain souvenir ◆ **in the ~ future/past** dans un avenir/un passé lointain ◆ **in the not too or very ~ future** dans un avenir assez proche 2 [connection] lointain ; [resemblance] vague ; [cousin, relative, relationship] éloigné 3 (= distracted) [person, manner] distrait ◆ **there was a ~ look in her eyes** elle avait un regard distrait 4 (= cool, reserved) [person, manner] distant **COMP distant early warning line N** (US Mil) ligne f DEW (système de radars)

distantly /ˈdɪstəntlɪ/ **ADV** 1 (= in the distance) [hear] dans le lointain, au loin ◆ **~, she heard the front door bell ring** elle entendit au loin qu'on sonnait à la porte d'entrée ◆ **the sound of a flute was ~ audible** on entendait au loin le son d'une flûte ◆ **she was ~ aware of Gavin's voice** elle entendait vaguement la voix de Gavin 2 [resemble] vaguement, un peu ◆ **I am ~ related to her** c'est une parente éloignée, nous sommes vaguement apparentés ◆ **the lion and the domestic cat are ~ related** le lion et le chat domestique ont des ancêtres communs 3 (= absently) [nod, smile] d'un air distrait 4 (= in a reserved way) [speak] d'un ton distant ◆ **to smile/behave ~** avoir un sourire distant/une attitude distante

distaste /dɪsˈteɪst/ **N** dégoût m, répugnance f (for pour)

distasteful /dɪsˈteɪstfʊl/ **ADJ** déplaisant, désagréable ◆ **to be ~ to sb** déplaire à qn

distastefully /dɪsˈteɪstfʊlɪ/ **ADV** [look at] d'un air dégoûté

distemper¹ /dɪsˈtempəʳ/ **N** (= paint) détrempe f **VT** peindre à la détrempe ◆ **~ed walls** murs mpl peints à la détrempe

distemper² /dɪsˈtempəʳ/ **N** (= disease) maladie f des jeunes chiens or de Carré

distend /dɪsˈtend/ **VT** (gen) ballonner ; (with gas) distendre **VI** (gen) se distendre ; (with gas) se ballonner

distension /dɪsˈtenʃən/ **N** distension f, dilatation f

distich /ˈdɪstɪk/ **N** distique m

distil, distill (US) /dɪsˈtɪl/ **VT** 1 [+ alcohol] distiller ; [+ essential oil] extraire 2 (= derive) **the new book was ~led from more than 200 conversations** ce nouveau livre est le résultat de plus de 200 conversations ◆ **the ~led wisdom of centuries** le concentré de plusieurs siècles de bon sens ◆ **to ~ into** condenser en, ramener à 3 (= drip slowly) laisser couler goutte à goutte **VI** se distiller, couler goutte à goutte **COMP distilled water N** eau f déminéralisée

distillate /ˈdɪstɪlɪt/ **N** distillat m

distillation /ˌdɪstɪˈleɪʃən/ **N** distillation f

distiller /dɪsˈtɪləʳ/ **N** distillateur m

distillery /dɪsˈtɪlərɪ/ **N** distillerie f

distinct /dɪsˈtɪŋkt/ **ADJ** 1 (= definite) [impression, preference, likeness, advantage, disadvantage] net before n ; [increase, progress] sensible, net before n ; [possibility] réel ◆ **there was a ~ lack of enthusiasm for that idea** il y avait un net manque d'enthousiasme pour cette idée
2 (= different, separate) distinct (from de)
◆ **as distinct from** par opposition à, contrairement à
3 (= clear) [silhouette, voice, memory] distinct

distinction /dɪsˈtɪŋkʃən/ **N** 1 (= difference) distinction f, différence f ; (= act of keeping apart) distinction f (of ... from de ... et de ; between entre) ◆ **to draw or make a ~ between two things** faire la or une distinction entre deux choses 2 (NonC) (= pre-eminence) distinction f, mérite m ; (= refinement) distinction f ◆ **to win ~** se distinguer, acquérir une or de la réputation ◆ **a pianist of ~** un pianiste réputé or de renom ◆ **she has great ~** elle est d'une grande distinction 3 (Univ etc) **he got a ~ in French** il a été reçu en français avec mention très bien

distinctive /dɪsˈtɪŋktɪv/ **ADJ** 1 (= idiosyncratic) caractéristique 2 (= differentiating: also Ling) distinctif ◆ **to be ~ of or to sth** caractériser qch

distinctively /dɪsˈtɪŋktɪvlɪ/ **ADV** ◆ **~ English/masculine** etc typiquement anglais/masculin etc ◆ **~ dressed** habillé de façon originale ◆ **~ patterned** au motif caractéristique ◆ **to be ~ different from sth** se démarquer nettement de qch

distinctiveness /dɪsˈtɪŋktɪvnɪs/ **N** caractère m distinctif

distinctly /dɪsˈtɪŋktlɪ/ **ADV** 1 (with vb = clearly) [speak, hear, see] distinctement ; [remember] clairement 2 (with adj = decidedly) particulièrement ◆ **it is ~ possible** c'est très possible, c'est une réelle possibilité ◆ **~ different/better** nettement différent/mieux

distinguish /dɪsˈtɪŋgwɪʃ/ **LANGUAGE IN USE 5.4** **VT** 1 (= discern) [+ landmark] distinguer, apercevoir ; [+ change] discerner, percevoir 2 [+ object, series, person] (= make different) distinguer (from de) ; (= characterize) caractériser ◆ **to ~ o.s.** se distinguer (as comme, en tant que) ◆ **you've really ~ed yourself!** (also iro) tu t'es vraiment distingué ! (also iro) ; see also **distinguished, distinguishing** **VI** ◆ **to ~ between A and B** distinguer or faire la distinction entre A et B, distinguer A de B

distinguishable /dɪsˈtɪŋgwɪʃəbl/ **ADJ** 1 (= distinct) ◆ **to be ~ from sth (by sth)** se distinguer de qch (par qch) ◆ **the two political parties are now barely ~ (from each other)** maintenant, les deux partis politiques se distinguent à peine (l'un de l'autre) ◆ **to be ~ by sth** être reconnaissable à qch, se reconnaître à qch ◆ **easily or readily ~** facile à distinguer 2 (= discernible) [shape, words, outline] perceptible

distinguished /dɪsˈtɪŋgwɪʃt/ **ADJ** 1 (= elegant, sophisticated) [person, appearance] distingué ◆ **to look ~** avoir l'air distingué 2 (= eminent) [pianist, scholar] distingué ; [career, history] brillant ◆ **in ~ company** en illustre compagnie ◆ **20 years of ~ service** 20 ans de bons et loyaux services ◆ **~ for his bravery** remarquable par or remarqué pour son courage ◆ **~ service professor** (US Univ) professeur m à titre personnel
COMP Distinguished Flying Cross N médaille décernée aux aviateurs militaires
distinguished-looking ADJ à l'air distingué
Distinguished Service Cross N médaille militaire
Distinguished Service Medal N médaille militaire
Distinguished Service Order N (Brit) médaille militaire

distinguishing /dɪsˈtɪŋgwɪʃɪŋ/ **ADJ** distinctif, caractéristique ◆ **~ mark** caractéristique f ; (on passport) signe m particulier

distort /dɪsˈtɔːt/ **VT** (physically) déformer, altérer ; (fig) [+ truth] défigurer, déformer ; [+ text] déformer ; [+ judgement] fausser ; [+ words, facts] dénaturer, déformer **VI** [face] se crisper

distorted /dɪsˈtɔːtɪd/ **ADJ** 1 [object, image, sound] déformé ◆ **his face was ~ with rage** ses traits étaient déformés par la colère 2 (= biased) [report, impression] faux (fausse f) ◆ **a ~ version of the events** une version déformée des événements 3 (= perverted) [morality, sexuality] dévoyé

distortion /dɪsˈtɔːʃən/ **N** (gen, Elec, Med, Opt) distorsion f ; [of tree etc] déformation f ; [of features] distorsion f, altération f ; [of shape, facts, text] déformation f, altération f ◆ **by ~ of the facts** en dénaturant les faits

distract /dɪsˈtrækt/ **VT** [+ person] distraire, déconcentrer ; (= interrupt) déranger ◆ **the noise ~ed her from working** le bruit la distrayait de son travail ◆ **the noise was ~ing him** le bruit le déconcentrait or l'empêchait de se concentrer ◆ **she's busy, you mustn't ~ her** elle est occupée, il ne faut pas la déranger ◆ **to ~ sb's attention** détourner l'attention de qn

distracted /dɪsˈtræktɪd/ **ADJ** 1 (= worried) éperdu, égaré ; (= inattentive) distrait ; [look] égaré, affolé ◆ **she seemed curiously ~** elle semblait étrangement distraite ◆ **~ with worry** etc fou d'anxiété etc ◆ **she was quite ~** elle était dans tous ses états ◆ **to drive sb ~** rendre qn fou 2 († = mad) fou (folle f)

distractedly /dɪsˈtræktɪdlɪ/ **ADV** 1 (= absently) [speak] d'un ton distrait, distraitement ; [behave] éperdument, distraitement 2 (liter = wildly) [behave, run] comme un fou (or une folle) ; [speak] d'un air affolé ; [weep] éperdument ◆ ~, **he ran his hands through his hair** il se passa la main dans les cheveux, l'air affolé

distracting /dɪsˈtræktɪŋ/ ADJ gênant, qui empêche de se concentrer

distraction /dɪsˈtrækʃən/ N [1] *(NonC = lack of attention)* distraction *f*, inattention *f* [2] *(= interruption: to work etc)* interruption *f* [3] *(= entertainment)* divertissement *m*, distraction *f* [4] *(NonC = madness)* affolement *m* ◆ **to love sb to** ~ aimer qn à la folie ◆ **to drive sb to** ~ rendre qn fou

distrain /dɪsˈtreɪn/ VI *(Jur)* ◆ **to ~ upon sb's goods** saisir les biens de qn, opérer la saisie des biens de qn

distrainee /ˌdɪstreɪˈniː/ N *(Jur)* saisi *m*

distrainor /dɪsˈtreɪnəʳ/ N *(Jur)* saisissant *m*

distraint /dɪsˈtreɪnt/ N *(Jur)* saisie *f*, saisie-exécution *f (sur les meubles d'un débiteur)*

distraught /dɪsˈtrɔːt/ ADJ éperdu *(with, from* de*)* égaré, affolé

distress /dɪsˈtres/ N [1] *(physical)* douleur *f* ; *(mental)* détresse *f*, affliction *f (liter)* ◆ **to be in great** ~ *(physical)* souffrir beaucoup ; *(mental)* être bouleversé, être (plongé) dans l'affliction ◆ **to be in great ~ over sth** être bouleversé *or* profondément affligé de qch ◆ **to cause ~ to** causer une grande peine *or* douleur à [2] *(= poverty)* détresse *f* ◆ **in** ~ dans la détresse [3] *(= danger)* péril *m*, détresse *f* ◆ **a ship in** ~ un navire en perdition ◆ **a plane in** ~ un avion en détresse ◆ **a damsel in** ~ une demoiselle en détresse [4] *(Jur)* saisie *f* VT affliger, peiner

COMP **distress rocket** N fusée *f* de détresse
distress sale N vente *f* de biens saisis
distress signal N signal *m* de détresse

distressed /dɪsˈtrest/ ADJ [1] *(= upset)* affligé, peiné *(by* par, de*)* ◆ **she was very** ~ elle était bouleversée [2] *(† = poverty-stricken)* **in ~ circumstances** dans la détresse *or* la misère ◆ **~ gentlewomen** dames *fpl* de bonne famille dans le besoin [3] *[clothing]* (artificiellement) vieilli ; *[furniture]* patiné

distressful /dɪsˈtresfʊl/ ADJ ⇒ **distressing**

distressing /dɪsˈtresɪŋ/ ADJ *[situation, experience]* pénible ; *[poverty, inadequacy]* lamentable

distressingly /dɪsˈtresɪŋlɪ/ ADV ◆ **the trapped animal howled** ~ les cris de l'animal pris au piège étaient déchirants ◆ **~, it took him over an hour to die** chose horrible, il a mis plus d'une heure à mourir ◆ **a ~ high/low percentage** un pourcentage tristement élevé/bas ◆ **she looked ~ thin** sa maigreur faisait peine à voir ◆ **the solution is ~ simple/obvious** la solution est d'une simplicité/évidence désespérante

distributary /dɪsˈtrɪbjʊtərɪ/ N *(Geog)* défluent *m* ADJ de distribution

distribute /dɪsˈtrɪbjuːt/ VT *[+ leaflets, prizes, food]* distribuer ; *[+ dividends, load, weight]* répartir ; *[+ goods, films, books]* distribuer ; *[+ information]* fournir ◆ **~ the almonds over the top of the cake** étaler les amandes sur le dessus du gâteau

distributed /dɪsˈtrɪbjuːtɪd/ ADJ ◆ **widely** ~ *[animal, plant]* très répandu ◆ **unevenly** ~ inégalement réparti

distribution /ˌdɪstrɪˈbjuːʃən/ N [1] *[of food, supplies, newspaper]* distribution *f (also Comm, Ling, Econ)* [2] *[of resources, wealth, power]* répartition *f* ◆ **weight/heat** ~ répartition *f* du poids/de la chaleur ◆ **geographical** ~ répartition *f or* distribution *f* géographique ◆ **the ~ of wealth** la répartition *or* distribution des richesses COMP **distribution network** N réseau *m* de distribution

distributional /ˌdɪstrɪˈbjuːʃənəl/ ADJ *(Comm)* de distribution ; *(Ling)* distributionnel

distributive /dɪsˈtrɪbjʊtɪv/ ADJ *(Comm, Gram, Philos etc)* distributif ◆ **the ~ trades** *(Econ)* le secteur de la distribution N *(Gram)* pronom *m or* adjectif *m* distributif

distributor /dɪsˈtrɪbjʊtəʳ/ N [1] *[of goods, books, films]* distributeur *m* [2] *(Tech = device)* distributeur *m* ; *(in vehicle)* delco ® *m*

COMP **distributor cap** N tête *f* de delco ®
distributor network N réseau *m* de distributeurs

distributorship /dɪsˈtrɪbjʊtəʃɪp/ N *(Comm)* [1] *(= company)* distributeur *m* [2] *(= right to supply)* contrat *m* de distribution

district /ˈdɪstrɪkt/ N *(of a country)* région *f* ; *(in town)* quartier *m* ; *(= administrative area)* district *m* ; *(in Paris, Lyon and Marseille)* arrondissement *m* ; *(US Pol)* circonscription *f* électorale *(or administrative)* ; → **electoral, postal**

COMP **district attorney** N *(US Jur)* représentant *m* du ministère public; ≃ procureur *m* de la République
district commissioner N *(Brit)* commissaire *m*
district council N *(Brit: local government)* ≃ conseil *m* général
district court N *(US Jur)* cour *f* fédérale (de grande instance)
district heating N ≃ chauffage *m* urbain
district manager N directeur *m* régional
district nurse N infirmière *f* visiteuse *or* à domicile
District of Columbia N *(US)* district *m* (fédéral) de Columbia

DISTRICT OF COLUMBIA

Le **District of Columbia** (ou **DC**) est un territoire autonome de 180 km², qui n'a pas le statut d'État mais où s'étend la capitale fédérale, Washington (ou Washington **DC**), et qui contient donc les grandes institutions politiques des États-Unis et, en particulier, la Maison-Blanche et le Capitole.

distrust /dɪsˈtrʌst/ VT se méfier de, se défier de N méfiance *f* ◆ **to have an instinctive/profound ~ of sb/sth** éprouver une méfiance instinctive/une profonde méfiance à l'égard de qn/qch

distrustful /dɪsˈtrʌstfʊl/ ADJ méfiant, qui se méfie *(of* de*)*

disturb /dɪsˈtɜːb/ VT [1] *(= inconvenience) [+ person]* déranger ◆ **sorry to ~ you** excusez-moi de vous déranger ◆ **"(please) do not disturb"** "(prière de) ne pas déranger" [2] *(= trouble) [+ person]* troubler, inquiéter ◆ **the news ~ed him greatly** la nouvelle l'a beaucoup troublé [3] *(= interrupt) [+ silence, balance]* rompre ; *[+ sleep, rest]* troubler [4] *(= disarrange) [+ waters, sediment, atmosphere]* troubler ; *[+ papers, evidence]* déranger

disturbance /dɪsˈtɜːbəns/ N [1] *(political, social)* troubles *mpl*, émeute *f* ; *(in house, street)* bruit *m*, tapage *m* ◆ **to cause a** ~ faire du bruit *or* du tapage ◆ **~ of the peace** atteinte *f* à l'ordre public [2] *(NonC) [of routine, papers]* dérangement *m* ; *[of liquid]* agitation *f* ; *[of air, atmosphere]* perturbation *f* [3] *(NonC = alarm, uneasiness)* trouble *m* (d'esprit), perturbation *f* (de l'esprit)

disturbed /dɪsˈtɜːbd/ ADJ [1] *(Psych)* perturbé ◆ **emotionally/mentally** ~ présentant des troubles affectifs/mentaux [2] *(= concerned)* inquiet (-ète *f*) *(about* au sujet de ; *at, by* par*)* [3] *(= unsettled) [childhood, period, night, sleep]* troublé ; *[background]* perturbé

disturbing /dɪsˈtɜːbɪŋ/ ADJ *(= alarming)* inquiétant, troublant ; *(= distracting)* gênant, ennuyeux

disturbingly /dɪsˈtɜːbɪŋlɪ/ ADV ◆ **a ~ high number/percentage** un nombre/pourcentage inquiétant ◆ **~, the data suggests that ...** chose inquiétante, les données suggèrent que ...

disunite /ˌdɪsjuːˈnaɪt/ VT désunir

disunity /dɪsˈjuːnɪtɪ/ N désunion *f*

disuse /dɪsˈjuːs/ N désuétude *f* ◆ **to fall into** ~ tomber en désuétude

disused /dɪsˈjuːzd/ ADJ *[building]* désaffecté, abandonné

disyllabic /ˌdɪsɪˈlæbɪk/ ADJ dissyllabe, dissyllabique

ditch /dɪtʃ/ N [1] *(by roadside, between fields etc)* fossé *m* ; *(for irrigation)* rigole *f* [2] *(Flying)* **the** ~ * la baille * ; → **last¹** VT [1] *(* = get rid of) [+ lover]* plaquer *, laisser tomber * ; *[+ car etc]* abandonner ◆ **to ~ a plane** faire un amerrissage forcé [2] *(US *) [+ class]* sécher *

ditcher /ˈdɪtʃəʳ/ N terrassier *m*

ditching /ˈdɪtʃɪŋ/ N [1] *(= making ditches)* creusement *m* de fossés ◆ **hedging and** ~ entretien *m* des haies et fossés [2] *[of plane]* amerrissage *m* forcé

ditchwater /ˈdɪtʃwɔːtəʳ/ N → **dull**

dither * /ˈdɪðəʳ/ *(esp Brit)* N ◆ **to be in a ~, to be all of a** ~ être dans tous ses états VI hésiter, se tâter ◆ **to ~ over a decision** se tâter pour prendre une décision ◆ **stop ~ing and get on with it!** arrête de te poser des questions *or* de tergiverser et fais-le !

▸ **dither about** *, **dither around** * VI tergiverser

ditherer * /ˈdɪðərəʳ/ N *(Brit)* indécis(e) *m(f)* ◆ **don't be such a ~!** ne sois pas si indécis !

dithery * /ˈdɪðərɪ/ ADJ *(pej)* indécis, qui tourne autour du pot

ditsy * /ˈdɪtsɪ/ ADJ *(esp US)* ⇒ **ditzy**

ditto /ˈdɪtəʊ/ ADV idem ◆ **restaurants are expensive here, and ~ the cinemas** *or* **the cinemas** ~ les restaurants sont chers ici et les cinémas idem * COMP **ditto mark, ditto sign** N guillemets *mpl* de répétition

ditty /ˈdɪtɪ/ N chansonnette *f*

ditz * /dɪts/ N *(US, Austral)* écervelé(e) *mf*

ditzy * /ˈdɪtsɪ/ ADJ *(esp US)* évaporé

diuresis /ˌdaɪjʊˈriːsɪs/ N diurèse *f*

diuretic /ˌdaɪjʊəˈretɪk/ ADJ, N diurétique *m*

diurnal /daɪˈɜːnl/ ADJ *(Astron, Bot)* diurne N *(Rel)* diurnal *m*

diva /ˈdiːvə/ N (pl **divas** *or* **dive**) diva *f*

divan /dɪˈvæn/ N divan *m* COMP **divan bed** N *(Brit)* divan-lit *m*

dive¹ /daɪv/ N [1] *[of swimmer, goalkeeper]* plongeon *m* ; *[of submarine, deep-sea diver etc]* plongée *f* ; *[of aircraft]* piqué *m* ◆ **to make a** ~ *(fig)* foncer (tête baissée) ◆ **to go into a** ~ *[profits, sales etc]* dégringoler, plonger ◆ **to take a** ~ * *(Ftbl)* faire du chiqué *
[2] *(* = disreputable club, café etc)* bouge *m*

VI [1] *[diver etc]* plonger, faire un plongeon ; *[submarine]* plonger ; *[aircraft]* piquer ◆ **he ~d in head first** il a piqué une tête dans l'eau ◆ **to ~ for pearls** pêcher des perles
[2] *(= plunge)* ◆ **to ~ in/out** *etc* entrer/sortir *etc* tête baissée ◆ **he ~d for the exit** il a foncé (tête baissée) vers la sortie ◆ **he ~d into the crowd** il a plongé dans la foule ◆ **he ~d under the table** il s'est jeté sous la table ◆ **to ~ for cover** se précipiter pour se mettre à l'abri ◆ **the keeper ~d for the ball** *(Ftbl)* le gardien de but a plongé pour bloquer le ballon ◆ **to ~ into one's pocket** plonger la main dans sa poche

COMP **dive-bomb** VT bombarder en piqué
dive bomber N bombardier *m (qui bombarde en piqué)*

dive bombing N bombardement *m* en piqué

► **dive in** VI 1 *[diver]* plonger
2 *(= start to eat)* ~ **in!**‡ attaquez ! *

dive² /ˈdiːvɪ/ NPL of **diva**

diver /ˈdaɪvəʳ/ N 1 *(= person)* plongeur *m* ; (also **deep-sea diver**) scaphandrier *m* ; → **scuba, skin** 2 *(= bird)* plongeon *m*, plongeur *m*

diverge /daɪˈvɜːdʒ/ VI *[lines, paths, opinions, explanations]* diverger

divergence /daɪˈvɜːdʒəns/ N divergence *f*

divergent /daɪˈvɜːdʒənt/ ADJ divergent COMP
divergent thinking N raisonnement *m* divergent

divers /ˈdaɪvɜːz/ ADJ *(liter)* divers, plusieurs

diverse /daɪˈvɜːs/ ADJ divers

diversification /daɪˌvɜːsɪfɪˈkeɪʃən/ N diversification *f*

diversify /daɪˈvɜːsɪfaɪ/ VT diversifier, varier VI *[farmer, businessman]* diversifier ses activités

diversion /daɪˈvɜːʃən/ N 1 *(Brit = redirecting) [of traffic]* déviation *f* ; *[of stream]* dérivation *f*, détournement *m* ; *[of ship] (gen)* déroutement *m* ; *[of profits]* détournement *m* 2 *(= temporary route)* déviation *f* 3 *(= relaxation)* divertissement *m*, distraction *f* ◆ **it's a ~ from work** cela change *or* distrait du travail 4 *(Mil etc)* diversion *f* ◆ **to create a ~** *(= distract attention)* faire diversion ; *(Mil)* opérer une diversion

diversionary /daɪˈvɜːʃnərɪ/ ADJ *(also Mil)* de diversion ◆ ~ **tactics** manœuvres *fpl* de diversion

diversity /daɪˈvɜːsɪtɪ/ N diversité *f*

divert /daɪˈvɜːt/ VT 1 *(= redirect) [+ stream]* détourner ; *[+ train, plane, ship]* dérouter ; *(Brit) [+ traffic]* dévier ; *[+ attention, eyes]* détourner ; *[+ conversation]* détourner ; *[+ blow]* écarter ; *[+ phone call]* transférer 2 *(= amuse)* divertir, amuser ◆ **to ~ o.s.** se distraire, se divertir

diverting /daɪˈvɜːtɪŋ/ ADJ divertissant, amusant

divest /daɪˈvest/ VT *(of clothes, weapons)* dévêtir, dépouiller *(of* de) ; *(of rights, property)* dépouiller, priver *(of* de) ; *[+ room]* dégarnir

divide /dɪˈvaɪd/ VT 1 *(= separate)* séparer *(from* de) ◆ **the Pyrenees ~ France from Spain** les Pyrénées séparent la France de l'Espagne
2 *(= split)* (also **divide up**) *(gen)* diviser *(into* en ; *among, between* entre) ; *[+ people]* répartir ; *[+ money, work]* diviser, partager, répartir ; *[+ property, kingdom]* diviser, démembrer, morceler ; *[+ house]* diviser, partager *(into* en) ; *[+ apple, room]* diviser, couper *(into* en) ; *[+ one's time, attention]* partager *(between* entre) ◆ **they ~d it (amongst themselves)** ils se le sont partagé
3 *(Math)* diviser ◆ **to ~ 36 by 6, to ~ 6 into 36** diviser 36 par 6
4 *(= cause disagreement among) [+ friends, political parties etc]* diviser ◆ ~ **and rule** *or* **conquer** *(Brit)* (politique *f* consistant à) diviser pour mieux régner
5 *(Brit Parl)* **to ~ the House** faire voter la Chambre
VI 1 *[river]* se diviser ; *[road]* bifurquer
2 (also **divide up**) *[people]* se répartir ; *(Bio) [cells etc]* se diviser
3 *(Math)* être divisible *(by* par)
4 *(Brit Parl)* **the House ~d** la Chambre a procédé au vote *or* a voté
N 1 *(= division, bar)* fossé *m* ◆ **to bridge the ~ between ...** combler le fossé entre ... ◆ **the racial/social/cultural ~** le fossé racial/social/culturel ◆ **to cross the great ~** *(= die)* passer de vie à trépas
2 *(Geog)* ligne *f* de partage des eaux ◆ **the Great Divide** *(in US)* la ligne de partage des montagnes Rocheuses

► **divide off** VI se séparer *(from* de)
VT SEP séparer *(from* de)

► **divide out** VT SEP répartir, distribuer *(among* entre)

► **divide up** VI ⇒ **divide vi 2**
VT SEP ⇒ **divide vt 2**

divided /dɪˈvaɪdɪd/ ADJ 1 *(= in two parts)* divisé 2 *(Bot) [leaf]* découpé 3 *(= disunited, in disagreement) [people, country]* divisé *(on, over* sur) ; *[opinion]* partagé *(on, over sur)* ◆ **to have** *or* **suffer from ~ loyalties** être déchiré ◆ **opinion is** *or* **opinions are ~ on** *or* **over that** les avis sont partagés sur ce point ◆ **opinions are ~ on what to do/on how long it will take (to do it)** les avis sont partagés quant à ce qu'il convient de faire/quant au temps que cela prendra ◆ **I feel ~ (in my own mind)** je suis *or* je me sens partagé
COMP **divided highway** N *(US)* (route *f* à) quatre voies *f inv* ; → ROADS
divided skirt N jupe-culotte *f*

dividend /ˈdɪvɪdend/ N *(Fin, Math)* dividende *m* ; → **pay**

divider /dɪˈvaɪdəʳ/ N 1 ◆ **~s** compas *m* à pointes sèches 2 → **room**

dividing /dɪˈvaɪdɪŋ/ ADJ *[wall, fence]* mitoyen COMP **dividing line** N ligne *f* de démarcation

divination /ˌdɪvɪˈneɪʃən/ N divination *f*

divine¹ /dɪˈvaɪn/ ADJ *(Rel, fig)* divin ◆ **Divine Providence** la divine Providence ◆ **(the) ~ right of kings** *(Hist)* le droit divin, la monarchie de droit divin ◆ **by ~ right** en vertu de droit divin ◆ ~ **service/office** *(Rel)* service *m*/office *m* divin ◆ **darling you look simply ~!** * chérie, tu es absolument divine ! ◆ **the mousse tasted absolutely ~!** * la mousse était absolument divine ! N ecclésiastique *m*, théologien *m*

divine² /dɪˈvaɪn/ VT 1 *(= foretell) [+ the future]* présager, prédire 2 *(= make out) [+ sb's intentions]* deviner, pressentir 3 *(= search for)* ◆ **to ~ for water** *etc* chercher à découvrir une source *etc* à l'aide de baguettes COMP **divining rod** N baguette *f* de sourcier

divinely /dɪˈvaɪnlɪ/ ADV 1 *(Rel)* ~ **inspired** divinement inspiré ◆ ~ **ordained/sanctioned** décrété/sanctionné par la volonté divine 2 *(† = wonderfully)* divinement ◆ **your friend waltzes ~** votre ami valse divinement ◆ ~ **handsome** divinement beau ◆ ~ **happy** aux anges

diviner /dɪˈvaɪnəʳ/ N *[of future]* devin *m*, devineresse *f* ; *[of water]* radiesthésiste *mf*

diving /ˈdaɪvɪŋ/ N 1 *(underwater)* plongée *f* sous-marine ; *(= skill)* art *m* du plongeur ; *(= trade)* métier *m* de plongeur sous-marin ; → **scuba, skin** 2 *(from diving board)* plongeon *m* ◆ **platform high ~** *(Sport)* plongeon *m* de haut vol
COMP **diving bell** N cloche *f* à plongeur
diving board N plongeoir *m* ; *(= springboard)* tremplin *m*
diving suit N scaphandre *m*

divining /dɪˈvaɪnɪŋ/ N divination *f* à l'aide de baguettes (*or* d'un pendule), rhabdomancie *f*

divinity /dɪˈvɪnɪtɪ/ N 1 *(quality = god)* divinité *f* ◆ **the Divinity** la Divinité 2 *(= theology)* théologie *f*

divisible /dɪˈvɪzəbl/ ADJ divisible *(by* par)

division /dɪˈvɪʒən/ N 1 *(= act, state)* division *f*, séparation *f (into* en) ; *(= sharing)* partage *m*, répartition *f*, distribution *f (between, among* entre) ; *(Bot, Math)* division *f* ◆ ~ **of labour** division *f* du travail ◆ **the ~ of Germany into two states in 1949** la division de l'Allemagne en deux États en 1949 ◆ **the ~ of responsibilities between national forces and the UN** la répartition *or* le partage des responsabilités entre les forces nationales et les forces des Nations unies ◆ **in two votes last year the Unionist ~ of opinion was roughly 50-50** lors de deux élections organisées l'an passé, les unionistes étaient répartis en deux camps plus ou moins égaux ; → **long¹, short, simple**
2 *(= section: gen, Admin, Comm, Mil, Naut)* division *f* ; *(= category)* classe *f*, catégorie *f*, section *f* ; *(Ftbl etc)* division *f* ; *(in box, case)* division *f*, compartiment *m* ◆ **the bank's European ~** la division européenne de la banque ◆ **the sales ~** le département des ventes ◆ **several armoured** *or* **tank ~s** plusieurs divisions *fpl* blindées
3 *(= divider)* séparation *f* ; *(in room)* cloison *f*
4 *(fig: between social classes etc)* fossé *m* ◆ **the deep ~s within the socialist movement** les profondes divisions qui règnent au sein du mouvement socialiste
5 *(= dividing line: lit, fig)* division *f*
6 *(NonC = discord)* division *f*, désaccord *m*
7 *(Brit Parl)* **to call a ~** passer au vote ◆ **to call for a ~** demander la mise aux voix ◆ **the ~ took place at midnight** la Chambre a procédé au vote à minuit ◆ **to carry a ~** avoir la majorité des voix
COMP **division bell** N *(Brit Parl) sonnerie qui annonce la mise aux voix*
division sign N *(Math)* signe *m* de division

divisional /dɪˈvɪʒənl/ ADJ divisionnaire
COMP **divisional coin** N monnaie *f* divisionnaire
Divisional Court N *(Brit Jur) juridiction supérieure composée d'au moins deux juges statuant en appel*

divisive /dɪˈvaɪsɪv/ ADJ ◆ **to be ~** diviser l'opinion ◆ **abortion is a ~ issue** l'avortement est une question qui divise l'opinion ◆ **her enemies saw her policies as ~** ses ennemis considéraient que sa politique était source de discorde

divisiveness /dɪˈvaɪsɪvnɪs/ N ◆ **the ~ of this decision** les dissensions causées par cette décision

divisor /dɪˈvaɪzəʳ/ N *(Math)* diviseur *m*

divorce /dɪˈvɔːs/ N *(Jur, fig)* divorce *m (from* d'avec, avec) ◆ **to get a ~ from** obtenir le divorce d'avec VT *(Jur)* divorcer de *or* d'avec ; *(fig)* séparer *(from* de) ◆ **she ~d her husband** elle a divorcé de *or* d'avec son mari ◆ **one cannot ~ this case from ...** *(fig)* on ne peut pas séparer ce cas de ... VI divorcer
COMP **divorce court** N ≈ tribunal *m* de grande instance
divorce proceedings NPL procédure *f* de divorce ◆ **to start ~ proceedings** entamer une procédure de divorce, demander le divorce
divorce settlement N *(mutually agreed)* règlement *m* de divorce ; *(imposed by court)* jugement *m* de divorce

divorcé /dɪˈvɔːseɪ/ N divorcé *m*

divorced /dɪˈvɔːst/ ADJ *(Jur)* divorcé *(from* d'avec)

divorcee /dɪˌvɔːˈsiː/ N divorcé(e) *m(f)*

divot /ˈdɪvɪt/ N *(esp Golf)* motte *f* de gazon

divulge /daɪˈvʌldʒ/ VT divulguer, révéler

divvy¹ /ˈdɪvɪ/ N *(Brit *)* abbrev of **dividend** VT (also **divvy up**) ‡ partager

divvy²‡ /ˈdɪvɪ/ N *(Brit)* imbécile *mf*

Diwali /dɪˈwɑːlɪ/ N Dipavali *m*

Dixie /ˈdɪksɪ/ N *(US)* les États *mpl* du Sud ◆ **the Heart of ~** l'Alabama *m* ◆ **I'm not just whistling ~** * ce ne sont pas des paroles en l'air, je ne plaisante pas
COMP *(US)* du Sud
Dixie cup ® N *(US)* gobelet *m* en carton
Dixie Democrat N *(US Pol)* démocrate *mf* du Sud

DIXIE

Surnom donné aux onze États du sud des États-Unis qui constituaient la Confédération pendant la guerre de Sécession : Alabama, Arkansas, Géorgie, Floride, Louisiane, Mississippi, Caroline du Nord, Caroline du Sud, Tennessee, Texas et Virginie. L'adjectif **Dixie** est employé pour caractériser ces États et leurs habitants : on dira ainsi que Scarlett O'Hara est l'exemple de la féminité **Dixie**.

dixie * /'dɪksɪ/ N (*Brit Mil:* also **dixie can**) gamelle *f*

Dixieland /'dɪksɪlænd/ N ⇒ **Dixie** COMP **Dixieland jazz** N le (jazz) Dixieland

DIY /,diːaɪ'waɪ/ (*Brit*) (abbrev of **do-it-yourself**) N bricolage *m* ADJ [*shop*] de bricolage ; [*job*] à faire soi-même ; [*divorce*] dont on s'occupe soi-même ◆ **~ mosaics** mosaïque à faire soi-même

dizzily /'dɪzɪlɪ/ ADV 1 (= *giddily*) [*walk, sway, slump*] en proie au vertige ; [*rise, fall, spin, swirl*] vertigineusement ◆ **her head was spinning ~** la tête lui tournait follement 2 (= *in a scatterbrained way*) étourdiment ; (= *in a silly way*) bêtement

dizziness /'dɪzɪnɪs/ N (= *state*) vertige(s) *m(pl)* ◆ **an attack of ~** des vertiges ◆ **to be overcome by ~** être pris de vertiges

dizzy /'dɪzɪ/ ADJ 1 [*person*] (*from illness, hunger etc*) pris de vertiges *or* d'étourdissements ; (*from vertigo*) pris de vertige ◆ **to feel ~** avoir le vertige, avoir la tête qui tourne ◆ **he was so ~ he couldn't move** (*from illness, hunger etc*) il était pris de tels vertiges *or* étourdissements qu'il ne pouvait plus avancer ; (*from vertigo*) il avait tellement le vertige qu'il ne pouvait plus avancer ◆ **it makes me ~** (*lit, fig*) cela me donne le vertige, j'en ai la tête qui tourne ◆ **he was ~ from the exertion** l'effort lui faisait tourner la tête ◆ **he was ~ with success** le succès l'avait grisé ◆ **she was ~ with grief** elle était hébétée de douleur

2 [*height, speed, rise in price*] vertigineux

3 [*person*] (= *scatterbrained*) étourdi, écervelé ; (= *silly*) bête ◆ **a ~ blonde** une blonde évaporée

VT (= *disorientate, confuse*) [+ *person*] étourdir, donner le vertige à ◆ **to be dizzied by success** être grisé par le succès

COMP **a dizzy spell** N un vertige, un étourdissement

DJ /'diː'dʒeɪ/ N (abbrev of **disc jockey**) → **disc**

Djakarta /dʒə'kɑːtə/ N ⇒ **Jakarta**

Djibouti /dʒɪ'buːtɪ/ N Djibouti ◆ **in ~** à Djibouti

djinn /dʒɪn/ N djinn *m*

dl (abbrev of **decilitre(s)**) dl

DLit(t) /diː'lɪt/ N (abbrev of **Doctor of Literature** *and* **Doctor of Letters**) *doctorat ès Lettres*

DM N (abbrev of **Deutschmark**) DM *m*

dm (abbrev of **decimetre(s)**) dm

D-mark /diː'mɑːk/ N (abbrev of **Deutschmark**) mark *m*

DMus N (abbrev of **Doctor of Music**) *doctorat de musique*

DMZ N (abbrev of **Demilitarized Zone**) → **demilitarize**

DNA /,diːen'eɪ/ N (*Med*) (abbrev of **deoxyribonucleic acid**) ADN *m*

COMP **DNA fingerprinting, DNA profiling** N analyse *f* de l'empreinte génétique
DNA sequence N séquence *f* d'ADN
DNA test N test *m* ADN
DNA testing N tests *mpl* ADN

Dnieper /'dniːpəʳ/ N Dniepr *m*

D-notice /'diːnəʊtɪs/ N (*Brit Govt*) *consigne officielle à la presse de ne pas publier certaines informations relatives à la sécurité nationale*

DNR /,diːen'ɑːʳ/ (*Med*) (abbrev of **do not resuscitate**) ne pas ranimer

do¹ /duː/

vb : 3rd pers sg pres **does**, pret **did**, ptp **done**

1 AUXILIARY VERB	4 NOUN
2 TRANSITIVE VERB	5 PLURAL NOUN
3 INTRANSITIVE VERB	6 PHRASAL VERBS

1 - AUXILIARY VERB

1

There is no equivalent in French to the use of **do** in questions, negative statements and negative commands.

◆ **~ you understand?** (est-ce que) vous comprenez ?, comprenez-vous ? ◆ **I do not** *or* **don't understand** je ne comprends pas ◆ **didn't you like it?** tu n'as pas aimé ça ? ◆ **don't worry!** ne t'en fais pas !

2 [in tag questions : seeking confirmation] n'est-ce pas ◆ **you know him, don't you?** vous le connaissez, n'est-ce pas ? ◆ **you do agree, don't you?** vous êtes d'accord, n'est-ce pas ?, vous êtes bien d'accord ? ◆ **she said that, didn't she?** elle a bien dit ça, n'est-ce pas ?, c'est bien ce qu'elle a dit ?

The tag is sometimes not translated.

◆ **he didn't go, did he?** il n'y est pas allé (, n'est-ce pas) ? ◆ **he didn't agree, did he?** il n'était pas d'accord(, n'est-ce pas) ? ◆ **(so) you know him, ~ you?** (*conveying interest, surprise, indignation etc*) alors comme ça vous le connaissez ? ◆ **she said that, did she?** alors comme ça elle a dit ça ?, ah oui ? elle a dit ça ?

3 [in tag responses] ◆ **they speak French – oh, ~ they ?** ils parlent français – ah oui *or* ah bon ? ◆ **he wanted £1,000 for it – did he really?** il en demandait 1 000 livres – vraiment *or* non ? ◆ **who broke the mirror? – I did** qui est-ce qui a cassé la glace ? – (c'est) moi ◆ **may I come in? – please ~!** puis-je entrer ? – je t'en prie *or* je vous en prie ! ◆ **shall I ring her again? – no, don't!** est-ce que je la rappelle ? – ah non *or* surtout pas ! ◆ **I'll tell him – don't!** je vais le lui dire – surtout pas !

oui or **non** alone are often used to answer questions.

◆ **~ you see them often? – yes, I ~** vous les voyez souvent ? – oui ◆ **did you see him? – no I didn't** est-ce que tu l'as vu ? – non

4 [substitute for another verb] faire ◆ **he's always saying he'll stop smoking, but he never does** il dit toujours qu'il va s'arrêter de fumer mais il ne le fait pas ◆ **she always says she'll come but she never does** elle dit toujours qu'elle viendra mais elle n'en fait rien *or* mais elle ne vient jamais ◆ **you drive faster than I ~** tu conduis plus vite que moi ◆ **I like this colour, don't you?** j'aime bien cette couleur, pas toi ? ◆ **they said he would object and indeed he did** on a dit qu'il s'y opposerait et c'est bien ce qui s'est passé *or* et c'est bien ce qu'il a fait

5 [encouraging, inviting] ◆ **DO come !** venez donc ! ◆ **DO tell him that ...** dites-lui bien que ...

6 [used for emphasis] ◆ **I DO wish I could come with you** je voudrais tant pouvoir vous accompagner ◆ **but I DO like pasta!** mais si j'aime bien les pâtes ! ◆ **I am sure he never said that – he DID say it** je suis sûr qu'il n'a jamais dit ça – je t'assure que si *or* mais si, il l'a dit ! ◆ **so you DO know them!** alors comme ça tu les connais !

2 - TRANSITIVE VERB

1 faire ◆ **what are you doing in the bathroom?** qu'est-ce que tu fais dans la salle de bains ? ◆ **what do you ~ (for a living)?** que faites-vous dans la vie ? ◆ **I don't know what to ~** je ne sais pas quoi faire ◆ **I don't know how she does it** je ne sais pas comment elle fait ◆ **the work is being done by a local builder** c'est un entrepreneur du coin qui fait les travaux ◆ **I've only done three pages** je n'ai fait que trois pages ◆ **we only ~ one make of gloves** nous ne faisons qu'une marque de gants ◆ **are you doing anything this evening?** vous faites quelque chose ce soir ?, êtes-vous pris ce soir ? ◆ **the car was doing 100mph** la voiture faisait du 160 km/h ◆ **we did London to Edinburgh in eight hours** nous avons fait (le trajet) Londres-Édimbourg en huit heures ◆ **we've done 200km since 2 o'clock** nous avons fait 200 km depuis 2 heures cet après-midi ◆ **to ~ the sights** faire du tourisme ◆ **to ~ six years (in jail)** faire six ans de prison ◆ **to ~ again** refaire ◆ **it's all got to be done again** tout est à refaire *or* à recommencer ◆ **now you've done it !** c'est malin ! ◆ **that's done it !** * (*dismay*) c'est foutu !‡ ; (*satisfaction*) (voilà) ça y est !

Some **do + noun** combinations require a more specific French verb.

◆ **to ~ the flowers** arranger les fleurs ◆ **to ~ one's hair** se coiffer ◆ **to ~ a play** (= *put on*) monter une pièce ◆ **to ~ nine subjects** étudier neuf matières ◆ **to ~ one's teeth** se laver *or* se brosser les dents

♦ **to do** + *person* (= *study*) ◆ **to ~ an author** faire *or* étudier un auteur ◆ **we're doing Orwell this term** on fait *or* étudie Orwell ce trimestre ◆ **the barber said he'd ~ me next** (= *attend to*) le coiffeur a dit qu'il me prendrait après ◆ **I'll ~ you‡ if I get hold of you!** (= *hurt*) attends un peu que je t'attrape !, tu auras affaire à moi si je t'attrape ! ◆ **she does the worried mother very convincingly** (= *act*) elle est très convaincante quand elle joue les mères inquiètes ◆ **he does his maths teacher to perfection** (= *imitate*) il imite son professeur de maths à la perfection ◆ **they ~ you very well at that restaurant** (= *serve*) on mange rudement* bien dans ce restaurant ◆ **to ~ sb to death** (= *kill*) tuer qn

2 [= finish] ◆ **to get done with sth** en finir avec qch ◆ **have you done moaning?*** tu as fini de te plaindre ? ◆ **when all's said and done** au bout du compte, en fin de compte

3 [Culin] (= *cook*) faire ; (= *peel*) éplucher ; (= *prepare*) faire, préparer ◆ **I'll ~ some pasta** je vais faire des pâtes ◆ **how do you like your steak done ?** comment voulez-vous votre bifteck ? ◆ **I like steak well done** j'aime le bifteck bien cuit

4 [Brit * = cheat] ◆ **he realized they'd done him** il s'aperçut qu'il s'était fait avoir* ◆ **to be done** se faire avoir* ◆ **you've been done!** tu t'es fait avoir !*, on t'a eu *or* refait !* ◆ **he was afraid he'd be done** il avait peur de se faire avoir

5 [= suffice, suit] aller à ◆ **will a kilo ~ you?** un kilo, ça ira ? ◆ **that will ~ me nicely** ça ira très bien

6 [= take] [+ *cocaine, heroin*] prendre

4 [set structures]

♦ **to do** + *preposition* ◆ **there's nothing I can ~ about it** je ne peux rien y faire ◆ **he's been badly done by** on s'est très mal conduit avec lui ◆ **what are we going to ~ for money?** comment allons-nous faire pour trouver de l'argent ? ◆ **what can I ~ for you?** qu'est-ce que je peux faire pour vous ?, en quoi puis-je vous aider ? ◆ **could you ~ something for me?** est-ce que tu peux me rendre un service ? ◆ **I**

could see what the stress was doing to him je voyais qu'il était très stressé ◆ **what are you doing to that poor cat?** qu'est-ce que tu es en train de faire à ce pauvre chat ? ◆ **this theme has been done to death** c'est un sujet rebattu ◆ **what have you done with my gloves?** qu'as-tu fait de mes gants ? ◆ **what are you doing with yourself these days?** qu'est-ce que tu deviens ? ◆ **he didn't know what to ~ with himself** il ne savait pas quoi faire de sa peau* ◆ **what am I going to ~ with you?** qu'est-ce que je vais bien pouvoir faire de toi ?

3 - INTRANSITIVE VERB

1 = act faire, agir ◆ **~ as your friends ~** faites comme vos amis ◆ **~ as I say** fais ce que je dis ◆ **he did well by his mother** il a bien agi *or* il s'est bien comporté envers sa mère ◆ **he did well to take advice** il a bien fait de prendre conseil ◆ **you would ~ well to rest more** vous feriez bien de vous reposer davantage ◆ **he did right** il a bien fait ◆ **he did right to go** il a bien fait d'y aller BUT **she was up and doing at 6 o'clock** elle était sur pied dès 6 heures du matin ◆ **do as you would be done by** *(Prov)* ne faites pas aux autres ce que vous ne voudriez pas qu'on vous fasse

♦ **nothing doing*** ◆ **there's nothing doing in this town** il ne se passe jamais rien dans cette ville ◆ **nothing doing!** *(refusing)* pas question !* ; *(reporting lack of success)* pas moyen !*

♦ **to have + to do with** *(= to be connected with)* ◆ **what has that got to ~ with it ?** et alors, qu'est-ce que ça a à voir ? ◆ **that has nothing to ~ with it!** cela n'a rien à voir !, cela n'a aucun rapport ! ◆ **they say crime has nothing to ~ with unemployment** ils prétendent que la criminalité n'a rien à voir *or* n'a aucun rapport avec le chômage ◆ **this debate has to ~ with the cost of living** ce débat porte sur le coût de la vie ◆ **that's got a lot to ~ with it!** ça y est pour beaucoup ! ◆ **money has a lot to ~ with it** l'argent y est pour beaucoup ◆ **his business activities have nothing to ~ with how much I earn** ses affaires n'ont rien à voir avec ce que je gagne ◆ **that has nothing to ~ with you!** ça ne vous regarde pas ! ◆ **I won't have anything to ~ with it** je ne veux pas m'en mêler ◆ **a doctor has to ~ with all kinds of people** un médecin a affaire à toutes sortes de gens

2 = get on aller, marcher ; *(as regards health)* se porter ◆ **how are you doing?** comment ça va ? ◆ **how's he doing?** comment va-t-il ? ◆ **the patient is doing better now** le malade va *or* se porte mieux ◆ **he's doing well at school** il a de bons résultats à l'école, il marche bien* en classe ◆ **he** *or* **his business is doing well** ses affaires vont *or* marchent bien ◆ **hi, what's doing?*** salut, comment ça va ? ◆ **the patient is doing very well** le malade est en très bonne voie ; *(on being introduced)* ◆ **how ~ you ~?** enchanté *or* très heureux (de faire votre connaissance) ◆ **the roses are doing well this year** les roses sont belles cette année

3 = finish finir, terminer ◆ **have you done?** vous avez terminé ?, ça y est ?

♦ **to have done with** ◆ **I've done with all that nonsense** je ne veux plus entendre parler de ces bêtises ◆ **have you done with that book?** vous n'avez plus besoin de ce livre ?, vous avez fini avec ce livre ?

4 = suit, be convenient aller, faire l'affaire ◆ **this room will ~** cette chambre fera l'affaire ◆ **that will ~ for the moment** ça ira pour le moment ◆ **that will never ~ !** il n'en est pas question ! ◆ **it doesn't ~ to tell him what you think of him** ce n'est pas une bonne idée de lui dire ce qu'on pense de lui ◆ **this coat will ~ for** *or* **as a blanket** ce manteau peut servir de couverture

5 = be sufficient suffire ◆ **three bottles of wine should ~** trois bouteilles de vin devraient suffire, trois bouteilles de vin, ça devrait aller ◆ **can you lend me some money? – will £10 ~?** peux-tu me prêter de l'argent ? – dix livres, ça te suffira *or* ça ira ? ◆ **that will ~!** ça suffira !, ça ira !

6 † = do housework faire le ménage ◆ **the woman who does for me** la personne qui fait mon ménage, ma femme de ménage

4 - NOUN

1 * *esp Brit* fête *f* ◆ **they had a big ~ for their twenty-fifth anniversary** ils ont fait une grande fête pour leur vingt-cinquième anniversaire de mariage

2 * Brit = swindle escroquerie *f* ◆ **the whole business was a real ~ from start to finish** toute l'affaire n'a été qu'une escroquerie du début jusqu'à la fin

3 * = state of affairs ◆ **it's a poor ~ !** c'est plutôt minable !*

5 - PLURAL NOUN

dos

1 ◆ **the dos and don'ts** ce qu'il faut faire ou ne pas faire

2 ◆ **fair dos !*** il faut être juste !

6 - PHRASAL VERBS

► **do away with** VT FUS 1 *(= get rid of)* *[+ law, controls]* abolir ; *[+ nuclear weapons]* démanteler ; *[+ subsidies]* supprimer ; *[+ building]* démolir ◆ **this will ~ away with the need for a UN presence** cela rendra la présence des Nations unies superflue

2 *(* = kill)* *[+ person]* liquider*, supprimer ◆ **to ~ away with o.s.** se suicider

► **do down*** VT SEP *(Brit)* *[+ person]* dénigrer ◆ **she's always doing herself down** il faut toujours qu'elle se déprécie *or* se rabaisse

► **do for*** VT FUS *[+ person]* *(= kill)* liquider*, supprimer ; *(= ruin)* *[+ hopes, chances, project]* ficher* *or* foutre** en l'air, bousiller* ◆ **he's/it's done for** il est/c'est fichu* *or* foutu** ; see also **do¹**

► **do in**** VT SEP 1 *(= kill)* buter**, liquider*

2 ◆ **it does my head in** ça me prend la tête*

3 *(gen pass = exhaust)* épuiser ◆ **to be** *or* **feel done in** être claqué* *or* épuisé

► **do out** VT SEP *(Brit)* *[+ room]* *(= clean)* nettoyer à fond ; *(= decorate)* refaire

► **do out of*** VT SEP ◆ **to ~ sb out of £100** arnaquer* qn de 100 livres, refaire* qn de 100 livres ◆ **to ~ sb out of a job** piquer son travail à qn

► **do over** VT SEP 1 *(US * = redo)* refaire

2 *(Brit **)* *[+ person]* *(= beat up)* tabasser*, passer à tabac* ; *[+ room, house]* *(= ransack)* fouiller de fond en comble, mettre sens dessus dessous ◆ **the door was open: they had done the place over** la porte était ouverte : ils avaient fouillé la maison de fond en comble *or* ils avaient mis la maison sens dessus dessous

3 *(= redecorate)* *[+ house]* refaire

► **do up** VI *[dress, jacket]* se fermer

VT SEP 1 *(= fasten)* *[+ buttons]* boutonner ; *[+ zip]* fermer, remonter ; *[+ dress]* fermer ; *[+ shoes]* lacer

2 *(= parcel together)* *[+ goods]* emballer, empaqueter ◆ **to ~ sth up in a parcel** emballer *or* empaqueter qch ◆ **to ~ up a parcel** faire un paquet

3 * *(= renovate)* *[+ house, room]* remettre à neuf, refaire ; *(= dress)* arranger ◆ **she was done up in a bizarre outfit** elle était bizarrement affublée ◆ **to ~ o.s. up** se faire beau (belle *f*)

► **do with*** VT FUS 1 ◆ **I could ~ with a cup of tea** je prendrais bien une tasse de thé ◆ **the house could ~ with a coat of paint** la maison a besoin d'un bon coup de peinture

2 *(= tolerate)* supporter ◆ **I can't ~ with** *or* **be doing with whining children** je ne peux pas supporter les enfants qui pleurnichent

► **do without** VT FUS se passer de ◆ **you'll have to ~ without then!** alors il faudra bien que tu t'en passes *subj* ! ◆ **I can ~ without your advice!** je vous dispense de vos conseils ! ◆ **I could have done without that!** je m'en serais très bien passé !

do² /dəʊ/ N *(Mus)* do *m*

do. (abbrev of **ditto**) id, idem

DOA /ˌdiːəʊˈeɪ/ (abbrev of **dead on arrival**) → **dead**

doable* /ˈduːəbl/ ADJ faisable

DOB (abbrev of **date of birth**) → **date¹**

Doberman /ˈdəʊbəmən/ N (also **Doberman pinscher**) doberman *m*

doc* /dɒk/ N *(US)* (abbrev of **doctor**) docteur *m*, toubib* *m* ◆ **yes ~** oui docteur

docile /ˈdəʊsaɪl/ ADJ docile, maniable

docilely /ˈdəʊsaɪlɪ/ ADV docilement

docility /dəʊˈsɪlɪtɪ/ N docilité *f*, soumission *f*

dock¹ /dɒk/ N *(for berthing)* bassin *m*, dock *m* ; *(for loading, unloading, repair)* dock *m* ◆ **my car is in ~*** *(Brit fig)* ma voiture est en réparation ; → **dry, graving dock** VT *[+ ship]* mettre à quai ; *[+ spacecraft]* amarrer, arrimer VI 1 *(Naut)* arriver *or* se mettre à quai ◆ **the ship has ~ed** le bateau est à quai 2 *(Space)* *[two spacecraft]* s'arrimer (*with* à) ◆ **the shuttle ~ed with the space station** la navette s'est arrimée à la station spatiale

COMP **dock house** N bureaux *mpl* des docks
dock labourer N docker *m*, débardeur *m*
dock strike N grève *f* des dockers
dock-worker N ⇒ **dock labourer**

dock² /dɒk/ N *(Brit Jur)* banc *m* des accusés ◆ **"prisoner in the dock"** "accusé" ◆ **in the ~** *(lit)* au banc des accusés ◆ **to be in the ~** *(fig)* être sur la sellette, être au banc des accusés

dock³ /dɒk/ VT 1 *[+ dog, horse]* écourter ; *[+ tail]* couper 2 *(Brit)* *[+ wages]* faire une retenue sur ◆ **to ~ £25 off sb's wages** retenir 25 livres sur le salaire de qn ◆ **he had his wages ~ed for repeated lateness** on lui a fait une retenue sur son salaire à cause de ses retards répétés ◆ **to ~ a soldier of two days' pay/leave** supprimer deux jours de solde/de permission à un soldat ◆ **the club was ~ed six points for cheating** *(Sport)* on a enlevé six points au club pour avoir triché

dock⁴ /dɒk/ N *(= plant)* patience *f*

docker /ˈdɒkəʳ/ N *(Brit)* docker *m*, débardeur *m*

docket /ˈdɒkɪt/ N 1 *(= paper: on document, parcel etc)* étiquette *f*, fiche *f* *(indiquant le contenu d'un paquet etc)* 2 *(Jur)* *(= register)* registre *m* des jugements rendus ; *(esp US)* *(= list of cases)* rôle *m* des causes ; *(= abstract of letters patent)* table *f* des matières, index *m* 3 *(Brit Customs = certificate)* récépissé *m* de douane, certificat *m* de paiement des droits de douane VT 1 *[+ contents]* résumer ; *(Jur)* *[+ judgement]* enregistrer *or* consigner sommairement ; *(fig)* *[+ information etc]* consigner, prendre note de 2 *[+ packet, document]* faire une fiche pour, étiqueter

docking /ˈdɒkɪŋ/ N *(Space)* arrimage *m*, amarrage *m*

dockland /ˈdɒklənd/ N *(Brit)* ◆ **the ~** le quartier des docks, les docks *mpl*

dockside /ˈdɒkˌsaɪd/ N docks *mpl*

dockwalloper* /ˈdɒkˌwɒləpəʳ/ N *(US)* ⇒ **dock labourer**

dockyard /'dɒkjɑːd/ **N** chantier *m* naval ; → **naval**

doctor /'dɒktəʳ/ **N** 1 *(Med)* médecin *m*, docteur *m* ◆ **he/she is a ~** il/elle est médecin *or* docteur ◆ **you should see a ~** tu devrais aller chez le médecin (or) chez le docteur ◆ **a woman ~** une femme médecin ◆ **who is your ~?** qui est votre docteur ?, qui est votre médecin traitant ? ◆ **Doctor Allan** le docteur Allan, Monsieur *(or* Madame) le docteur Allan ◆ **yes ~** oui docteur ◆ **to send for the ~** faire venir le médecin *or* le docteur ◆ **to go to the ~'s** aller chez le docteur ◆ **to be under the ~ * (for sth)** suivre un traitement (contre qch) ◆ **~'s line** *or* **note** *(Brit)*, **~'s excuse** *(US) (Scol etc)* dispense *f* ◆ **at the ~'s** chez le médecin ◆ **~'s office** *(US)* cabinet *m* médical ◆ **it's just what the ~ ordered** * *(fig hum)* c'est exactement ce qu'il me *(or* te *etc)* fallait ; → **Dr**

2 *(Univ etc)* docteur *m* ◆ **~'s degree** doctorat *m* ◆ **Doctor of Law/of Science** *etc* docteur *m* en droit/ès sciences *etc* ◆ **Doctor of Philosophy** ≃ titulaire *m* d'un doctorat d'État ; → **medicine**

VT 1 *[+ sick person]* soigner

2 *(Brit* * *= castrate) [+ cat etc]* couper, châtrer

3 *(* pej = mend)* rafistoler * *(pej)*

4 *(= tamper with) [+ wine]* trafiquer *, frelater ; *[+ food]* trafiquer * ; *[+ text, document, figures, accounts]* tripatouiller *

doctoral /'dɒktərəl/ **ADJ** *[student]* de doctorat ◆ **he did his ~ research at Cambridge** il a fait les recherches pour son doctorat à Cambridge

COMP **doctoral dissertation** **N** *(US)* ⇒ **doctoral thesis**

doctoral thesis **N** *(Univ)* thèse *f* de doctorat

doctorate /'dɒktərɪt/ **N** doctorat *m* ◆ **~ in science/in philosophy** doctorat *m* ès sciences/en philosophie

doctrinaire /,dɒktrɪ'nɛəʳ/ **ADJ, N** doctrinaire *mf*

doctrinal /dɒk'traɪnl/ **ADJ** doctrinal

doctrine /'dɒktrɪn/ **N** doctrine *f*

docudrama /,dɒkjʊ'drɑːmə/ **N** *(TV etc)* docudrame *m*

document /'dɒkjʊmənt/ **N** *(gen, also Comput)* document *m* ◆ **the ~s relating to a case** le dossier d'une affaire ◆ **official ~** document *m* officiel ; *(Jur)* acte *m* authentique public ◆ **judicial ~** *(Jur)* acte *m* judiciaire

VT /'dɒkjʊment/ 1 *(= record)* consigner ; *(= describe)* décrire ◆ **each accidental injury is ~ed** chaque blessure accidentelle est consignée ◆ **a bestseller ~ing his achievements** un bestseller qui décrit ses exploits ◆ **there is no ~ed case of someone being infected in this way** il n'existe aucun cas connu d'infection par ce biais ◆ **complaints must be ~ed** *(Jur)* les plaintes doivent être accompagnées de pièces justificatives

◆ **well-documented** *[case, report]* solidement documenté ◆ **there are well ~ed reports of ...** il existe des témoignages solidement documentés selon lesquels ...

◆ **to be well documented** être attesté par de nombreuses sources ◆ **the effects of smoking have been well ~ed** les effets du tabac ont été attestés par de nombreuses sources ◆ **it is well ~ed that olive oil helps reduce cholesterol levels** de nombreuses recherches tendent à prouver que l'huile d'olive contribue à réduire le taux de cholestérol

2 *[+ ship]* munir des papiers nécessaires

COMP **document case** **N** porte-documents *m inv*

document imaging **N** *reproduction de document sous forme d'image*

document reader **N** *(Comput)* lecteur *m* de documents

> ⚠ **to document** is not translated by **documenter**, except in the case of 'well-documented' (see above).

documentarian /,dɒkjʊmən'tæriən/ **N** *(esp US)* documentariste *mf*

documentary /,dɒkjʊ'mentərɪ/ **ADJ** documentaire **N** *(Cine, TV)* (film *m*) documentaire *m*

COMP **documentary evidence** **N** *(Jur)* documents *mpl*, preuve *f* documentaire *or* par écrit

documentary letter of credit **N** crédit *m* documentaire

documentation /,dɒkjʊmen'teɪʃən/ **N** documentation *f* ; *(Comm)* documents *mpl* (à fournir *etc*)

docu-soap /'dɒkjʊ'səʊp/ **N** feuilleton-documentaire *m*

DOD /,diːəʊ'diː/ **N** *(US)* (abbrev of **Department of Defense**) → **defence**

do-dad * /'duːdæd/ **N** ⇒ **doodah**

dodder /'dɒdəʳ/ **VI** ne pas tenir sur ses jambes ; *(fig)* tergiverser, atermoyer

dodderer * /'dɒdərəʳ/ **N** vieux *(or* vieille *f)* gaga *, croulant(e) * *m(f)*, gâteux *m*, -euse *f*

doddering /'dɒdərɪŋ/, **doddery** /'dɒdərɪ/ **ADJ** *(= trembling)* branlant ; *(= senile)* gâteux

doddle * /'dɒdəl/ **N** *(Brit)* ◆ **it's a ~** c'est simple comme bonjour *, c'est du gâteau *

Dodecanese /,dəʊdɪkə'niːz/ **N** Dodécanèse *m*

dodge /dɒdʒ/ **N** 1 *(= movement)* mouvement *m* de côté ; *(Boxing, Ftbl)* esquive *f*

2 *(Brit* *) *(= trick)* tour *m*, truc * *m* ; *(= ingenious scheme)* combine * *f*, truc * *m* ◆ **he's up to all the ~s** il connaît (toutes) les ficelles ◆ **I've got a good ~ for making money** j'ai une bonne combine * pour gagner de l'argent ; → **tax**

VT *[+ blow, ball]* esquiver ; *[+ pursuer]* échapper à ; *(fig = avoid ingeniously) [+ question, difficulty]* esquiver, éluder ; *[+ tax]* éviter de payer ; *(= shirk) [+ work, duty]* esquiver ◆ **he ~d the issue** il a éludé la question ◆ **I managed to ~ him before he saw me** j'ai réussi à m'esquiver avant qu'il ne me voie

VI faire un saut de côté *or* un brusque détour ; *(Boxing, Fencing)* esquiver ; *(Ftbl, Rugby)* faire une feinte de corps, feinter ◆ **to ~ out of sight** *or* **out of the way** s'esquiver ◆ **to ~ behind a tree** disparaître derrière un arbre ◆ **to ~ through the traffic/the trees** se faufiler entre les voitures/les arbres ◆ **he saw the police and ~d round the back (of the house)** il a vu les agents et s'est esquivé (en faisant le tour de la maison) par derrière

▸ **dodge about** **VI** aller et venir, remuer

dodgems /'dɒdʒəmz/ **NPL** *(Brit)* autos *fpl* tamponneuses

dodger /'dɒdʒəʳ/ **N** 1 *(* = trickster)* roublard(e) * *m(f)*, finaud(e) *m(f)* ; *(= shirker)* tire-au-flanc *m inv* ; → **artful** 2 *(Naut)* toile *f* de passerelle de commandement 3 *(US = handbill)* prospectus *m*

dodgy * /'dɒdʒɪ/ **ADJ** 1 *(Brit = uncertain, tricky) [situation, plan, finances, weather]* douteux ; *[health]* précaire ◆ **he's got a ~ back/heart** *etc* il a des problèmes de dos/de cœur *etc*, son dos/cœur *etc* lui joue des tours ◆ **her health is ~, she's in ~ health** sa santé lui joue des tours, elle n'a pas la santé * 2 *(= dubious, suspicious) [person, deal, district]* louche *

dodo /'dəʊdəʊ/ **N** (pl **dodos** or **dodoes**) dronte *m*, dodo *m* ; → **dead**

DOE /,diːəʊ'iː/ **N** 1 *(Brit)* (abbrev of **Department of the Environment**) → **environment** 2 *(US)* (abbrev of **Department of Energy**) → **energy**

doe /dəʊ/ **N** (pl **does** or **doe**) 1 *(= deer)* biche *f* 2 *(= rabbit)* lapine *f* ; *(= hare)* hase *f* ◆ **~-eyed** *[person]* aux yeux de biche ; *[look]* de biche

doer /'duː(ː)əʳ/ **N** 1 *(= author of deed)* auteur *m* de l'action ◆ **~s of good deeds often go unrewarded** ceux qui font le bien ne sont pas souvent récompensés 2 *(= active person)* personne *f* efficace *or* dynamique ◆ **he's a ~, not a thinker** il préfère l'action à la réflexion

does /dʌz/ → **do¹**

doeskin /'dəʊskɪn/ **N** peau *f* de daim

doesn't /'dʌznt/ ⇒ **does not** ; → **do¹**

doff /dɒf/ **VT** († , *hum) [+ garment, hat]* ôter, enlever

dog /dɒg/ **N** 1 *(= animal)* chien *m* ; *(specifically female)* chienne *f* ◆ **it's a real ~'s dinner** * *or* **breakfast** * c'est le bordel ‡ ◆ **he's all done up like a ~'s dinner** * regarde comme il est attifé *, il est attifé * n'importe comment ◆ **to lead a ~'s life** mener une vie de chien ◆ **it's a ~'s life** c'est une vie de chien ◆ **the ~s** * *(Brit Sport)* les courses *fpl* de lévriers ◆ **to go to the ~s** * *(fig) [person]* gâcher sa vie, mal tourner ; *[institution, business]* aller à vau-l'eau, péricliter ◆ **to throw sb to the ~s** *(fig)* abandonner qn à son sort ◆ **every ~ has his day** *(Prov)* à chacun vient sa chance, à chacun son heure de gloire ◆ **he hasn't a ~'s chance** * il n'a pas la moindre chance (de réussir) ◆ **it's (a case of) ~ eat ~** c'est un cas où les loups se mangent entre eux ◆ **give a ~ a bad name (and hang him)** *(Prov)* qui veut noyer son chien l'accuse de la rage *(Prov)* ◆ **to put on the ~** ‡ *(US)* faire de l'épate * ◆ **this is a real ~** * *(= very bad)* c'est nul * ◆ **it's the ~'s bollocks** *‡ *(Brit)* c'est génial * ; → **cat, hair**

2 *(= male) [of fox etc]* mâle *m*

3 * **lucky ~** veinard(e) * *m(f)* ◆ **dirty ~** sale type * *m* ◆ **sly ~** (petit) malin *m*, (petite) maligne *f*

4 *(‡ = unattractive woman)* cageot ‡ *m*, boudin * *m*

5 ◆ **the ~ (and bone)** ‡ *(= phone)* téléphone *m*, bigophone * *m* ◆ **to get on the ~** téléphoner

6 *(Tech) (= clamp)* crampon *m* ; *(= pawl)* cliquet *m*

VT 1 *(= follow closely) [+ person]* suivre (de près) ◆ **he ~s my footsteps** il marche sur mes talons, il ne me lâche pas d'une semelle

2 *(= harass)* harceler ◆ **~ged by ill fortune** poursuivi par la malchance

COMP **dog and pony show** **N** *(US fig) spectacle fait pour impressionner*

dog basket **N** panier *m* pour chien

dog biscuit **N** biscuit *m* pour chien

dog breeder **N** éleveur *m*, -euse *f* de chiens

dog collar **N** *(lit)* collier *m* de chien ; *(hum: clergyman's)* col *m* de pasteur, (faux) col *m* d'ecclésiastique

dog days **NPL** canicule *f*

dog-eared **ADJ** écorné

dog dirt **N** crottes *fpl* de chien

dog-end * **N** mégot *m* ◆ **they epitomize the ~-end of the British music scene** ils incarnent tout ce qu'il y a de plus médiocre sur la scène musicale britannique **ADJ** minable *

dog fancier **N** *(= connoisseur)* cynophile *mf* ; *(= breeder)* éleveur *m*, -euse *f* de chiens

dog fox **N** renard *m* (mâle)

dog guard **N** *(in car)* barrière *f* pour chien *(à l'arrière d'une voiture)*

dog handler **N** *(Police etc)* maître-chien *m*

dog Latin * **N** latin *m* de cuisine

dog licence **N** *redevance payable par les propriétaires de chiens*

dog mess **N** ⇒ **dog dirt**

dog paddle **N** nage *f* en chien **VI** nager en chien

dog rose **N** *(= flower)* églantine *f* ; *(= bush)* églantier *m*

the Dog Star **N** Sirius *m*

dog tag* N *(US Mil)* plaque *f* d'identification *(portée par les militaires)*
dog-tired* ADJ claqué*, crevé*
dog track N piste *f* (de course de lévriers)
dog wolf N loup *m*

dogcart /'dɒgkɑːt/ N charrette *f* anglaise, dog-cart *m*

doge /dəʊdʒ/ N doge *m*

dogfight /'dɒgfaɪt/ N *(lit)* combat *m* de chiens ; *(between planes)* combat *m* entre avions de chasse ; *(between people)* bagarre *f*

dogfish /'dɒgfɪʃ/ N (pl **dogfish** *or* **dogfishes**) chien *m* de mer, roussette *f*

dogfood /'dɒgfuːd/ N nourriture *f* pour chiens

dogged /'dɒgɪd/ ADJ *[person, character]* tenace ; *[courage, determination, persistence, refusal]* obstiné ; *[resistance, battle]* acharné

doggedly /'dɒgɪdlɪ/ ADV *[say, fight]* avec ténacité ; *[refuse]* obstinément ◆ ~ **determined** résolu envers et contre tout ◆ **he is ~ loyal** il fait preuve d'une loyauté à toute épreuve ◆ **he was ~ optimistic** il était résolument optimiste

doggedness /'dɒgɪdnɪs/ N obstination *f*, ténacité *f*

Dogger Bank /'dɒgəbæŋk/ N Dogger Bank *m*

doggerel /'dɒgərəl/ N vers *mpl* de mirliton

doggie /'dɒgɪ/ N ⇒ **doggy noun**

doggo* /'dɒgəʊ/ ADV *(Brit)* ◆ **to lie ~** se tenir coi (coite *f*); *[fugitive, criminal]* se terrer

doggone(d)* /ˌdɒg'gɒn(d)/ ADJ *(US euph)* ⇒ **damn, damned**

doggy* /'dɒgɪ/ N *(baby talk)* toutou* *m* *(baby talk)* ADJ *[smell]* de chien mouillé ◆ **she is a very ~ woman** elle a la folie des chiens ◆ **I'm not really a ~ person** je n'aime pas trop les chiens COMP **doggy bag*** N *petit sac pour emporter les restes après un repas au restaurant*
doggy fashion* ADV *[have sex]* en levrette
doggy paddle* N nage *f* en chien VI nager en chien
doggy style* ADV ⇒ **doggy fashion**

doghouse /'dɒghaʊs/ N *(US)* chenil *m*, niche *f* à chien ◆ **he is in the ~*** *(fig)* il n'est pas en odeur de sainteté

dogie /'dəʊgɪ/ N *(US)* veau *m* sans mère

dogleg /'dɒgleg/ N *(in road etc)* coude *m*, angle *m* abrupt ADJ *[turn, bend]* en coude, en épingle à cheveux

doglike /'dɒglaɪk/ ADJ *[appearance]* canin ; *[devotion, fidelity]* inconditionnel

dogma /'dɒgmə/ N (pl **dogmas** *or* **dogmata** /'dɒgmətə/) dogme *m*

dogmatic /dɒg'mætɪk/ ADJ dogmatique ◆ **to be very ~ about sth** être très dogmatique sur qch

dogmatically /dɒg'mætɪkəlɪ/ ADV *[speak, write, argue]* sur un ton dogmatique ; *[follow rule, apply principle]* dogmatiquement, d'une manière dogmatique

dogmatism /'dɒgmətɪzəm/ N dogmatisme *m*

dogmatist /'dɒgmətɪst/ N dogmatique *mf*

dogmatize /'dɒgmətaɪz/ VI dogmatiser

do-gooder /ˌduː'gʊdəʳ/ N bonne âme *f (iro)*

dogsbody* /'dɒgzbɒdɪ/ N *(Brit)* ◆ **she's the general ~** c'est la bonne à tout faire

dogshow /'dɒgʃəʊ/ N exposition *f* canine

dogtrot /'dɒgtrɒt/ N petit trot *m* ; *(US = passageway)* passage *m* couvert

dogwatch /'dɒgwɒtʃ/ N *(Naut)* petit quart *m*, quart *m* de deux heures

dogwood /'dɒgwʊd/ N cornouiller *m*

doh /dəʊ/ N *(Mus)* do *m*

doily /'dɔɪlɪ/ N *(under plate)* napperon *m* ; *(on plate)* dessus *m* d'assiette

doing /'duːɪŋ/ N *(NonC)* ◆ **this is your ~** c'est vous qui avez fait cela ◆ **it was none of my ~** je n'y suis pour rien, ce n'est pas moi qui l'ai fait ◆ **that takes some ~** ce n'est pas facile *or* commode, (il) faut le faire !* NPL **doings** 1 faits *mpl* et gestes *mpl* 2 *(Brit* ‡ *= thingummy)* **~s** machin* *m*, truc* *m* ◆ **that ~s over there** ce machin* là-bas

do-it-yourself /'duːɪtjə'self/ N bricolage *m* ADJ 1 *[shop]* de bricolage ◆ ~ **enthusiast** bricoleur *m*, -euse *f* ◆ ~ **kit** kit *m* (prêt-à-monter) 2 *(fig) [divorce, conveyancing, will]* dont on s'occupe soi-même *(sans employer les services d'un professionnel)*

do-it-yourselfer* /ˌduːɪtjɔː'selfəʳ/ N bricoleur *m*, -euse *f*

dojo /'dəʊdʒəʊ/ N dojo *m*

Dolby ® /'dɒlbɪ/ N Dolby ® *m*

doldrums /'dɒldrəmz/ NPL *(= area)* zone *f* des calmes équatoriaux ; *(= weather)* calme *m* équatorial ◆ **to be in the ~** *[person]* avoir le cafard*, broyer du noir ; *[business]* être dans le marasme ◆ **to come out of the ~** *[person]* reprendre le dessus ; *[business]* sortir du marasme

dole /dəʊl/ N allocation *f* *or* indemnité *f* de chômage ◆ **to go/be on the ~** *(Brit)* s'inscrire/être au chômage ◆ **how much do you get a week on the ~?** combien touche-t-on d'allocation *or* d'indemnités de chômage par semaine ? COMP **dole queue** N *(Brit)* ◆ **the ~ queues are lengthening** le nombre de chômeurs augmente

▸ **dole out** VT SEP distribuer *or* accorder au compte-gouttes

doleful /'dəʊlfʊl/ ADJ *[person, face]* triste; *[expression, voice]* dolent *(liter)*, plaintif ; *[song]* plaintif ◆ **a ~ prospect** une triste perspective

dolefully /'dəʊlfəlɪ/ ADV d'un air malheureux

dolichocephalic /'dɒlɪkəʊse'fælɪk/ ADJ dolichocéphale

doll /dɒl/ N 1 poupée *f* ◆ **to play with a ~** *or* **~s** jouer à la poupée 2 *(esp US* ‡ *= girl)* nana‡ *f*, pépée †‡ *f* ; *(= pretty girl)* poupée* *f* ◆ **he's/she's a ~** *(= attractive person)* il/elle est chou*, il/elle est adorable ◆ **you're a ~ to help me*** *(US)* tu es un ange de m'aider
COMP **doll buggy, doll carriage** N *(US)* landau *m* de poupée
doll's house N maison *f* de poupée
doll's pram N landau *m* de poupée

▸ **doll up**‡ VT SEP *[+ person, thing]* bichonner ◆ **to ~ o.s. up, to get ~ed up** se faire (tout) beau* *(or* (toute) belle*), se bichonner ◆ **all ~ed up** sur son trente et un *(for* pour) ◆ **she was ~ed up for the party** elle s'était mise sur son trente et un pour la soirée

dollar /'dɒləʳ/ N dollar *m* ◆ **it's ~s to doughnuts that ...*** *(US)* c'est couru d'avance* que ... ; → **half, sixty**
COMP **dollar area** N zone *f* dollar
dollar bill N billet *m* d'un dollar
dollar diplomacy N diplomatie *f* à coups de dollars
dollar gap N déficit *m* de la balance dollar
dollar rate N cours *m* du dollar
dollar sign N signe *m* du dollar

dollop /'dɒləp/ N *[of butter, cheese etc]* gros *or* bon morceau *m* ; *[of cream, jam etc]* bonne cuillerée *f*

dolly /dɒlɪ/ N 1 *(*: baby talk = doll)* poupée *f* 2 *(for washing clothes)* agitateur *m* 3 *(= wheeled frame)* chariot *m* ; *(Cine, TV)* chariot *m*, travelling *m (dispositif)* ; *(Rail = truck)* plate-forme *f* ADJ *(Sport * = easy)* facile VI *(Cine, TV)* ◆ **to ~ the camera in/out** avancer/reculer la caméra COMP **dolly bird**‡ N *(Brit)* jolie nana‡ *f*, poupée* *f*
dolly tub N *(for washing)* baquet *m* à lessive ; *(Min)* cuve *f* à rincer

dolman /'dɒlmən/ N dolman *m* COMP **dolman sleeve** N (sorte *f* de) manche *f* kimono *inv*

dolmen /'dɒlmen/ N dolmen *m*

dolomite /'dɒləmaɪt/ N dolomite *f*, dolomie *f* ◆ **the Dolomites** *(Geog)* les Dolomites *fpl*

dolphin /'dɒlfɪn/ N dauphin *m*

dolphinarium /ˌdɒlfɪ'nɛərɪəm/ N aquarium *m* pour dauphins savants

dolt /dəʊlt/ N balourd(e) *m(f)*

doltish /'dəʊltɪʃ/ ADJ gourde*, cruche*, balourd

domain /dəʊ'meɪn/ N domaine *m* ◆ **in the ~ of science** dans le domaine des sciences ; → **public** COMP **domain name** N nom *m* de domaine

dome /dəʊm/ N *(on building)* dôme *m*, coupole *f* ; *(liter = stately building)* édifice *m* ; *[of hill]* sommet *m* arrondi, dôme *m* ; *[of skull]* calotte *f* ; *[of heaven, branches]* dôme *m*

domed /dəʊmd/ ADJ *[forehead]* bombé ; *[building]* à dôme, à coupole

Domesday Book /'duːmzdeɪˌbʊk/ N Domesday Book *m*

domestic /də'mestɪk/ ADJ 1 *(= household) (gen)* domestique ; *[fuel]* à usage domestique ; *[quarrel] (within family)* de famille ; *(between married couple)* conjugal ◆ ~ **bliss** les joies *fpl* de la vie de famille ◆ **she gets regular ~ help at the weekends** elle a une aide ménagère qui vient tous les week-ends ◆ **the ~ chores** les travaux *mpl* ménagers, les tâches *fpl* ménagères ◆ ~ **harmony** l'harmonie *f* du ménage
2 *(= home-loving)* **she was never a very ~ sort of person** elle n'a jamais vraiment été une femme d'intérieur
3 *(Econ, Pol = internal) [policy, affairs, flight, politics, news, problems, market]* intérieur (-eure *f*) ; *[currency, economy, production]* national ; *[sales]* sur le marché intérieur ◆ **(intended) for ~ consumption** *(lit) [product, commodity]* destiné à la consommation intérieure ; *(fig) [speech, statement]* réservé au public national
4 *(= domesticated)* **the ~ cat/rabbit/chicken** *etc* le chat/lapin/poulet *etc* domestique
N 1 *(= worker)* domestique *mf*
2 *(Brit Police * = fight)* querelle *f* domestique
COMP **domestic appliance** N appareil *m* ménager
domestic heating oil N fioul *m* domestique
domestic rates NPL *(Brit) anciens impôts locaux*
domestic science N arts *mpl* ménagers
domestic science college N école *f* d'arts ménagers
domestic science teaching N enseignement *m* ménager
domestic servants NPL domestiques *mfpl*, employé(e)s *m(f)pl* de maison
domestic service N ◆ **she was in ~ service** elle était employée de maison *or* domestique
domestic spending N *(NonC)* dépenses *fpl* intérieures
domestic staff N *[of hospital, institution]* personnel *m* auxiliaire ; *[of private house]* domestiques *mfpl*
domestic violence N violence *f* domestique *or* familiale

domestically /də'mestɪkəlɪ/ ADV ◆ **only two of the banks are ~ owned** seules deux de ces banques sont détenues par des capitaux nationaux ◆ ~ **produced goods** biens *mpl* produits à l'intérieur du pays ◆ **he's not very ~ inclined** ce n'est pas vraiment un homme d'intérieur

domesticate /də'mestɪkeɪt/ VT 1 *(lit) [+ animal]* domestiquer 2 *(* fig, hum) [+ person]* apprivoiser

domesticated /də'mestɪkeɪtɪd/ ADJ 1 *[animal]* domestiqué 2 * *[person]* **she's very ~** c'est une vraie femme d'intérieur ◆ **he's not very ~** ce n'est pas vraiment un homme d'intérieur

domestication /dəmestɪ'keɪʃən/ N *[of animal]* domestication *f*

domesticity /ˌdəʊmesˈtɪsɪtɪ/ N 1 (= *home life*) vie *f* de famille, vie *f* casanière (*slightly pej*) 2 (= *love of household duties*) goût *m* pour les tâches ménagères

domicile /ˈdɒmɪsaɪl/ (*Admin, Fin, Jur*) N domicile *m* VT domicilier ◆ **~d at** [*person*] domicilié à, demeurant à ◆ **he is currently ~d in Berlin** il est actuellement domicilié à Berlin, il demeure actuellement à Berlin ◆ **to ~ a bill with a bank** domicilier un effet à une banque

domiciliary /ˌdɒmɪˈsɪlɪərɪ/ ADJ domiciliaire

domiciliation /ˌdɒmɪsɪlɪˈeɪʃən/ N [*of bill, cheque*] domiciliation *f*

dominance /ˈdɒmɪnəns/ N (*gen: Ecol, Genetics, Psych*) dominance *f* (*over* sur) ; [*of person, country etc*] prédominance *f*

dominant /ˈdɒmɪnənt/ ADJ 1 (= *predominant, assertive*) dominant ◆ **she is the ~ partner in their marriage** dans leur couple c'est elle qui commande 2 (*Mus*) de dominante ◆ **~ seventh** septième *f* de dominante 3 (*Genetics*) dominant 4 [*animal, individual, species*] dominant ◆ **the ~ male of the group** le mâle dominant du groupe N (*Mus*) dominante *f* ; (*Ecol, Genetics*) dominance *f*

dominate /ˈdɒmɪneɪt/ VTI dominer

dominating /ˈdɒmɪneɪtɪŋ/ ADJ [*character, personality*] dominateur (-trice *f*)

domination /ˌdɒmɪˈneɪʃən/ N domination *f*

dominatrix /ˌdɒmɪˈneɪtrɪks/ N (pl **dominatrices** /ˌdɒmɪnəˈtraɪsiːz/) (= *sexual partner*) dominatrice *f* ; (= *dominant woman*) femme *f* dominatrice, maîtresse femme *f*

domineer /ˌdɒmɪˈnɪəʳ/ VI agir en maître, se montrer autoritaire

domineering /ˌdɒmɪˈnɪərɪŋ/ ADJ dominateur (-trice *f*), impérieux, autoritaire

Dominica /ˌdɒmɪˈniːkə/ N (*Geog*) la Dominique

Dominican¹ /dəˈmɪnɪkən/ ADJ (*Geog*) dominicain N Dominicain(e) *m(f)* COMP **the Dominican Republic** N la République dominicaine

Dominican² /dəˈmɪnɪkən/ ADJ, N (*Rel*) dominicain(e) *m(f)*

dominion /dəˈmɪnɪən/ N 1 (*NonC*) domination *f*, empire *m* (*over* sur) ◆ **to hold ~ over sb** maintenir qn sous sa domination *or* sous sa dépendance 2 (= *territory*) territoire *m*, possessions *fpl* ; (*Brit Pol*) dominion *m* COMP **Dominion Day** N (*Can*) fête *f* de la Confédération

domino /ˈdɒmɪnəʊ/ N (pl **dominoes**) 1 domino *m* ◆ **to play ~es** jouer aux dominos ◆ **banks started collapsing like ~es** les banques se sont écroulées les unes après les autres 2 (= *costume, mask, person*) domino *m*
COMP **domino effect** N effet *m* d'entraînement
domino theory N (*Pol*) théorie *f* des dominos, théorie *f* du proche en proche

Don /dɒn/ N (= *river*) Don *m*

don¹ /dɒn/ N 1 (*Brit Univ* *) professeur *m* d'université (*surtout à Oxford et à Cambridge*) 2 (= *Spanish nobleman*) don *m* 3 (*US*) chef *m* de la Mafia

don² /dɒn/ VT [+ *garment*] revêtir, mettre

donate /dəʊˈneɪt/ VT faire don de, donner ◆ **to ~ blood** donner son sang ◆ **~d by ...** offert par ...

donation /dəʊˈneɪʃən/ N 1 (*NonC* = *act of giving*) donation *f* 2 (= *gift*) don *m* ◆ **to make a ~ to a fund** faire un don à une caisse

done /dʌn/ VB (ptp of **do¹**) ◆ **what's ~ cannot be undone** ce qui est fait est fait ◆ **that's just not ~!** cela ne se fait pas ! ◆ **it's as good as ~** c'est comme si c'était fait ◆ **a woman's work is never ~** (*Prov*) une femme n'est jamais au bout de sa tâche ◆ **~!** (*Comm*) marché conclu !, entendu ! ◆ **consider it ~!** c'est comme si c'était fait ! ADJ → **do¹** 1 ◆ **is it the ~ thing ?** est-ce que cela se fait ? ◆ **it's not the ~ thing** ça ne se fait pas ◆ **it's not yet a ~ deal, since the agreement has to be approved by the owners** ce n'est pas encore chose faite, l'accord doit être approuvé par les propriétaires 2 (* = *tired out*) claqué *, crevé * ◆ **I'm absolutely ~!** ‡ je n'en peux plus !, je suis crevé ! * 3 (= *cooked*) cuit ◆ **is it ~ yet?** est-ce que c'est cuit ? ◆ **well ~** [*steak*] bien cuit

donee /ˌdəʊˈniː/ N (*Jur*) donataire *mf*

doner /ˈdɒnəʳ/ N (also **doner kebab**) donner kebab *m* ≈ sandwich *m* grec

dong /dɒŋ/ N 1 (= *sound of bell*) dong *m* 2 (= *unit of currency*) dông *m* 3 (*‡ = *penis*) zob *‡ *m*

dongle /ˈdɒŋgl/ N (*Comput*) boîtier *m* de sécurité

donjon /ˈdʌndʒən/ N donjon *m*

donkey /ˈdɒŋkɪ/ N 1 âne(sse) *m(f)*, baudet * *m* ◆ **she hasn't been here for ~'s years** * (*Brit*) il y a une éternité *or* ça fait une paye * qu'elle n'est pas venue ici ; → **hind²** 2 (* = *fool*) âne *m*, imbécile *mf*
COMP **donkey derby** N (*Brit*) course *f* à dos d'âne
donkey engine N auxiliaire *m*, petit cheval *m*, cheval *m* alimentaire
donkey jacket N (*Brit*) grosse veste *f*
donkey ride N promenade *f* à dos d'âne
donkey-work N (*Brit*) ◆ **the ~-work** le gros du travail

donnish /ˈdɒnɪʃ/ ADJ [*person*] cérébral ; [*humour, manner*] d'intellectuel

donor /ˈdəʊnəʳ/ N (*to charity etc*) donateur *m*, -trice *f* ; (*Med*) [*of blood, organ for transplant*] donneur *m*, -euse *f* ◆ **sperm/organ/bone marrow/kidney ~** donneur de sperme/d'organe/de moelle osseuse/de rein
COMP **donor card** N carte *f* de donneur d'organes
donor country N pays *m* donateur
donor insemination N insémination *f* artificielle
donor organ N organe *m* de donneur
donor sperm N sperme *m* de donneur

don't /dəʊnt/ VB ⇒ **do not** ; → **do¹** N ◆ **~s** choses *fpl* à ne pas faire ; → **do¹** COMP **don't knows** * NPL (*gen*) sans opinion *mpl* ; (= *voters*) indécis *mpl* ◆ **there were ten in favour, six against, and five "don't knows"** il y avait dix pour, six contre et cinq "sans opinion"

donut /ˈdəʊnʌt/ N (*US*) ⇒ **doughnut**

doodah * /ˈduːdɑː/, **doodad** * (*US*) /ˈduːdæd/ N (= *gadget*) petit bidule * *m*

doodle /ˈduːdl/ VI griffonner (distraitement) N griffonnage *m*

doodlebug * /ˈduːdlbʌg/ N (*Brit*) bombe *f* volante ; (*US*) petit véhicule *m*

doohickey * /ˌduːˈhɪkɪ/ N (*US*) machin * *m*, truc * *m*, bidule * *m*

doolally ‡ /duːˈlælɪ/ ADJ dingo ‡, barjo ‡

doom /duːm/ N (= *ruin*) ruine *f*, perte *f* ; (= *fate*) destin *m*, sort *m* VT condamner (*to* à) destiner (*to* à) ◆ **~ed to failure** voué à l'échec ◆ **the project was ~ed from the start** le projet était voué à l'échec dès le début
COMP **doom-laden** ADJ lugubre, sinistre
doom-monger N ⇒ **doomsayer**

doomsayer /ˈduːmseɪəʳ/ N prophète *m* de malheur

doomsday /ˈduːmzdeɪ/ N jour *m* du Jugement dernier ◆ **till ~** (*fig*) jusqu'à la fin des temps
COMP **doomsday cult** N secte *f* apocalyptique
doomsday scenario N Scénario *m* catastrophe

doomwatch /ˈduːmwɒtʃ/ N attitude *f* pessimiste, catastrophisme *m*

doomwatcher /ˈduːmwɒtʃəʳ/ N prophète *m* de malheur, oiseau *m* de mauvais augure

doomy /ˈduːmɪ/ ADJ lugubre

door /dɔːʳ/ N 1 [*of house, room, cupboard*] porte *f* ; [*of train, plane, car*] portière *f* ◆ **he shut** *or* **closed the ~ in my face** il m'a fermé la porte au nez ◆ **he came through** *or* **in the ~** il est passé par la porte ◆ **"pay at the door"** (*Theat etc*) "billets à l'entrée" ◆ **to get tickets on the ~** prendre les billets à l'entrée ◆ **to go from ~ to ~** (*gen*) aller de porte en porte ; [*salesman*] faire du porte à porte ; see also **comp** ◆ **he lives two ~s down** *or* **up the street** il habite deux portes plus loin ◆ **out of ~s** (au-)dehors ; → **answer, front, next door**
2 (*phrases*) **to lay sth at sb's ~** imputer qch à qn, charger qn de qch ◆ **to open the ~ to further negotiations** ouvrir la voie à des négociations ultérieures ◆ **to leave** *or* **keep the ~ open for further negotiations** laisser la porte ouverte à des négociations ultérieures ◆ **to close** *or* **shut the ~ on** *or* **to sth** barrer la route à qch, rendre qch irréalisable ◆ **there was resistance to the idea at first but now we're pushing at an open ~** (*Brit*) cette idée a rencontré beaucoup de réticences au départ, mais maintenant tout marche comme sur des roulettes ◆ **as one ~ closes, another one opens** il y aura d'autres occasions ◆ **to be on the ~** (*Theat etc*) être à l'entrée ◆ **to open ~s** (*fig*) ouvrir des portes ◆ **a Harvard degree opens ~s** un diplôme de l'université de Harvard ouvre beaucoup de portes ; → **death, show**
COMP **door chain** N chaîne *f* de sûreté
door curtain N portière *f* (*tenture*)
door handle N poignée *f or* bouton *m* de porte ; [*of car*] poignée *f* de portière
door-knocker N marteau *m* (de porte), heurtoir *m*
door-locking mechanism N [*of car, train*] dispositif *m* de verrouillage des portières
door scraper N grattoir *m*
door-to-door ADJ ◆ **~-to-~ delivery** livraison *f* à domicile ◆ **we deliver ~-to-~** nous livrons à domicile ◆ **~-to-~ salesman** ⇒ **doorstep salesman** ; → **doorstep** ◆ **~-to-~ selling** (*Brit*) démarchage *m*, vente *f* à domicile, porte-à-porte *m inv*

doorbell /ˈdɔːbel/ N sonnette *f* ◆ **he heard the ~ ring** il entendit sonner (à la porte) ◆ **there's the ~!** on sonne (à la porte) !

doorframe /ˈdɔːfreɪm/ N chambranle *m*, châssis *m* de porte

doorjamb /ˈdɔːdʒæm/ N montant *m* de porte, jambage *m*

doorkeeper /ˈdɔːkiːpəʳ/ N ⇒ **doorman**

doorknob /ˈdɔːnɒb/ N poignée *f or* bouton *m* de porte

doorman /ˈdɔːmən/ N (pl **-men**) [*of hotel*] portier *m* ; [*of block of flats*] concierge *m* ; [*of nightclub etc*] videur *m*

doormat /ˈdɔːmæt/ N 1 (*lit*) paillasson *m* 2 (* = *downtrodden person*) paillasson *m*, carpette * *f*

doornail /ˈdɔːneɪl/ N clou *m* de porte ; → **dead**

doorpost /ˈdɔːpəʊst/ N montant *m* de porte, jambage *m* ; → **deaf**

doorstep /ˈdɔːstep/ N 1 (*lit*) pas *m* de porte, seuil *m* ◆ **he left it on my ~** il l'a laissé devant ma porte ◆ **the bus stop is just at my ~** l'arrêt du bus est (juste) devant ma porte ◆ **we don't want trouble/a motorway on our ~** nous ne voulons pas d'embêtements dans notre voisinage/d'autoroute dans notre arrière-cour 2 (* = *hunk of bread, sandwich*) grosse tartine *f* VT (*Brit* *) ◆ **to ~ sb** (*Pol*) faire du démarchage électoral chez qn ; (*Press*) aller chez qn pour l'interviewer (*contre son gré*)
COMP **doorstep salesman** N (pl **doorstep salesmen**) (*Brit*) démarcheur *m*, vendeur *m* à domicile
doorstep selling N démarchage *m*

doorstepping * /ˈdɔːstepɪŋ/ N 1 (*Pol*) démarchage *m* électoral 2 (*Press*) *porte-à-porte pratiqué par certains journalistes*

doorstop(per) /ˈdɔːstɒp(əʳ)/ N butoir *m* de porte

doorway /ˈdɔːweɪ/ N (gen) porte *f* ◆ **in the** ~ dans l'embrasure de la porte

doozy * /ˈduːzɪ/ N (US) ◆ **a** ~ **of a moustache** une sacrée moustache

dopamine /ˈdəʊpəmiːn/ N dopamine *f*

dope /dəʊp/ N [1] (‡ = *drugs, esp marijuana*) dope * *f* ; (*for athlete, horse*) (produit *m*) dopant *m* ; (*US* ‡ = *drug addict*) drogué(e) *m(f)*, toxico * *mf* ◆ **to take** ~‡, **to be on** ~‡, **to do** ~‡ (*US*) se droguer

[2] (*NonC:* ‡ = *information*) tuyaux * *mpl* ◆ **to give sb the** ~ tuyauter * *or* affranchir * qn ◆ **what's the** ~ **on ...?** qu'est-ce qu'on a comme tuyaux * sur ... ?

[3] (* = *stupid person*) andouille‡ *f*

[4] (= *varnish*) enduit *m*

[5] (*added to petrol*) dopant *m*

[6] (*for explosives*) absorbant *m*

VT [+ *horse, person*] doper ; [+ *food, drink*] mettre une drogue *or* un dopant dans ◆ **he was ~d (up) to the eyeballs** * il était complètement défoncé‡

COMP **dope fiend** † * N drogué(e) *m(f)*

dope peddler‡, **dope pusher**‡ N revendeur *m*, -euse *f* de drogue, dealer * *m*

dope test * N test *m* antidopage VT faire subir un test antidopage à

▸ **dope out** * VT SEP (*US*) deviner, piger *

dopey * /ˈdəʊpɪ/ ADJ (= *drugged*) drogué, dopé ; (= *very sleepy*) (à moitié) endormi ; (= *stupid*) abruti *

doping /ˈdəʊpɪŋ/ N dopage *m*

Doppler effect /ˈdɒplərɪˌfekt/ N effet *m* Doppler *or* Doppler-Fizeau

dopy /ˈdəʊpɪ/ ADJ ⇒ **dopey**

Dordogne /dɔrˈdɔɲ/ N (= *region, river*) Dordogne *f*

Doric /ˈdɒrɪk/ ADJ (*Archit*) dorique

dork‡ /dɔːk/ N abruti(e) * *m(f)*

dorm * /dɔːm/ N (*Scol*) ⇒ **dormitory**

dormancy /ˈdɔːmənsɪ/ N [*of volcano*] inactivité *f* ; [*of plant*] dormance *f* ; [*of virus*] latence *f*

dormant /ˈdɔːmənt/ ADJ [1] [*animal, plant, passion*] dormant ; [*virus*] latent ; [*volcano*] endormi ; [*law*] inappliqué ; [*title*] tombé en désuétude ; (*Banking*) [*account*] sans mouvement ◆ **the** ~ **season** (*Bot*) la saison de dormance ◆ **to lie** ~ [*plan, organization*] être en sommeil ; [*disease*] être latent ; [*bacterium, virus*] être à l'état latent [2] (*Her*) dormant ◆ **a lion** ~ un lion dormant

dormer (window) /ˈdɔːmə(ˈwɪndəʊ)/ N lucarne *f*

dormice /ˈdɔːmaɪs/ NPL of **dormouse**

dormie /ˈdɔːmɪ/ ADJ (*Golf*) dormie

dormitory /ˈdɔːmɪtrɪ/ N dortoir *m* ; (*US Univ*) résidence *f* universitaire

COMP **dormitory suburb** N (*esp Brit*) banlieue *f* dortoir

dormitory town N (*esp Brit*) ville *f* dortoir

Dormobile ® /ˈdɔːməbiːl/ N (*Brit*) camping-car *m*, autocaravane *f*

dormouse /ˈdɔːmaʊs/ N (pl **dormice**) loir *m*

Dors abbrev of **Dorset**

dorsal /ˈdɔːsl/ ADJ dorsal

dory[1] /ˈdɔːrɪ/ N (= *fish*) dorée *f*, saint-pierre *m inv*

dory[2] /ˈdɔːrɪ/ N (= *boat*) doris *m*

DOS /dɒs/ N (abbrev of **disk operating system**) DOS *m*

dosage /ˈdəʊsɪdʒ/ N (= *dosing*) dosage *m* ; (= *amount*) dose *f* ; (*on medicine bottle*) posologie *f*

dose /dəʊs/ N [1] (*Pharm*) dose *f* ◆ **give him a** ~ **of medicine** donne-lui son médicament ◆ **in small/large ~s** à faible/haute dose ◆ **it went through her like a** ~ **of salts** * (*hum*) ça lui a donné la courante‡ ◆ **she's all right in small ~s** * elle est supportable à petites doses ◆ **to give sb a** ~ **of his own medicine** rendre à qn la monnaie de sa pièce [2] (= *bout of illness*) attaque *f* (*of* de) ◆ **to have a** ~ **of flu** avoir une bonne grippe *

VT [+ *person*] administrer un médicament à ◆ **to** ~ **o.s. (up) with painkillers** se bourrer de médicaments

dosh‡ /dɒʃ/ N (*Brit* = *money*) fric‡ *m*, pognon‡ *m*

doss‡ /dɒs/ (*Brit*) N [1] (= *bed*) pieu‡ *m* ; (= *place*) endroit *m* où pioncer‡ ; (= *sleep*) roupillon * *m* [2] (= *easy task*) ◆ **he thought the course would be a** ~ il croyait que ce stage serait du gâteau * *or* serait fastoche *

VI [1] (= *sleep*) pioncer‡ ; (*in dosshouse*) coucher à l'asile (de nuit) [2] (= *pass time aimlessly:* also **doss around**) glander‡

▸ **doss down**‡ VI pioncer‡ (quelque part)

dosser‡ /ˈdɒsəʳ/ N (*Brit* = *vagrant*) clochard(e) *m(f)*

dosshouse‡ /ˈdɒshaʊs/ N asile *m* (de nuit)

dossier /ˈdɒsɪeɪ/ N dossier *m*

Dosto(y)evsky /ˌdɒstɔrˈefskɪ/ N Dostoïevski *m*

DOT /ˌdiːəʊˈtiː/ N (*US*) (abbrev of **Department of Transportation**) → **transportation**

dot /dɒt/ N (*over i, on horizon, Math, Mus*) point *m* ; (*on material*) pois *m* ◆ **~s and dashes** (*in Morse code*) points *mpl* et traits *mpl* ◆ ~, ~, ~ (*in punctuation*) points de suspension ◆ **they arrived on the** ~ **of 9pm** *or* **at 9pm on the** ~ ils sont arrivés à 9 heures pile *or* tapantes ◆ **in the year** ~ * (*Brit*) il y a belle lurette * ◆ **he's wanted to be a barrister since the year** ~ ça fait belle lurette * qu'il veut devenir avocat ◆ **she's been a socialist since the year** ~ * elle est socialiste depuis toujours, c'est une socialiste de la première heure

VT [+ *paper, wall*] pointiller ◆ **to** ~ **an i** mettre un point sur un i ◆ **to** ~ **one's i's (and cross one's t's)** (*fig*) mettre les points sur les i ◆ **a field ~ted with flowers** un champ parsemé de fleurs ◆ **hotels ~ted around the island** des hôtels éparpillés dans l'île ◆ **there were paintings ~ted around the room** il y avait des tableaux un peu partout sur les murs de la pièce ; see also **dotted**

COMP **dot-matrix printer** N imprimante *f* matricielle

dotage /ˈdəʊtɪdʒ/ N [1] (= *senility*) gâtisme *m* ◆ **to be in one's** ~ être gâteux [2] (= *old age*) vieux jours *mpl* ◆ **he's spending his** ~ **in southern France** il passe ses vieux jours dans le sud de la France [3] (= *blind love*) adoration *f* folle (*on* pour)

dotcom, dot.com /dɒtˈkɒm/ N dotcom *f*, point com *f*

dote /dəʊt/ VI (= *be senile*) être gâteux, être gaga *

▸ **dote on** VT FUS [+ *person*] être fou de ; [+ *thing*] raffoler de

doting /ˈdəʊtɪŋ/ ADJ [1] (= *devoted*) ◆ **her** ~ **father** son père qui l'adore [2] (= *senile*) gâteux ◆ **a** ~ **old fool** un vieux gâteux

dotted /ˈdɒtɪd/ ADJ [1] ◆ ~ **line** ligne *f* pointillée *or* en pointillé ; (*on road*) ligne *f* discontinue ◆ **to tear along the** ~ **line** détacher suivant le pointillé ◆ **to sign on the** ~ **line** (*lit*) signer sur la ligne pointillée *or* sur les pointillés ; (*fig*) (= *agree officially*) donner son consentement (en bonne et due forme) ◆ **a** ~ **bow tie** un nœud papillon à pois [2] (*Mus*) ~ **note/crotchet** note *f*/noire *f* pointée ◆ ~ **rhythm** notes *fpl* pointées

dotterel /ˈdɒtrəl/ N pluvier *m* (guignard)

dotty * /ˈdɒtɪ/ ADJ (*Brit*) toqué * piqué * ◆ **to be** ~ **about sb/sth** être toqué * de qn/qch ◆ **to go** ~ perdre la boule *

double /ˈdʌbl/ ADJ [1] (= *twice as great*) double *gen before n* ◆ **a** ~ **helping of ice cream** une double part de glace ◆ **a** ~ **whisky/brandy** un double whisky/cognac ◆ **three** ~ **brandies** trois doubles cognacs

[2] (= *twofold; in pairs*) double *gen before n* ◆ **the** ~ **six** (*Dice, Dominoes etc*) le double-six ◆ **a box with a** ~ **bottom** une boîte à double fond ◆ **with a** ~ **meaning** à double sens ◆ **to serve a** ~ **purpose** avoir une double fonction

[3] (= *for two people*) pour deux personnes ◆ **a** ~ **ticket** un billet pour deux personnes

[4] (*in numerals, letters*) ◆ ~ **oh four** (= *004*) zéro zéro quatre ◆ ~ **three four seven** (= *3347*) trois mille trois cent quarante-sept ; (*in phone number*) trente-trois quarante-sept ◆ **my name is Bell, B E** ~ **L** mon nom est Bell, B, E, deux L ◆ **spelt with a** ~ **"p"** écrit avec deux "p"

[5] (= *underhand, deceptive*) ◆ **to lead a** ~ **life** mener une double vie ◆ **to play a** ~ **game** jouer un double jeu ; see also **comp**

ADV [1] (= *twice*) deux fois ◆ **to cost/pay** ~ coûter/payer le double *or* deux fois plus ◆ **it costs** ~ **what it did last year** ça coûte deux fois plus que l'année dernière ◆ **she earns** ~ **what I get** elle gagne deux fois plus que moi, elle gagne le double de ce que je gagne ◆ **he's** ~ **your age** il est deux fois plus âgé que toi, il a le double de ton âge ◆ **her salary is** ~ **what it was five years ago** son salaire est le double de ce qu'il était il y a cinq ans

[2] (= *in two, twofold*) ◆ **to fold sth** ~ plier qch en deux ◆ **to bend** ~ se plier en deux ◆ **bent** ~ **with pain** tordu de douleur, plié en deux par la douleur ◆ **to see** ~ voir double

N [1] (= *twice a quantity, number, size etc*) double *m* ◆ **12 is the** ~ **of 6** 12 est le double de 6 ◆ ~ **or quits** quitte ou double ◆ **at** *or* **on the** ~ (*fig* = *quickly*) au pas de course

[2] [*of whisky etc*] double *m*

[3] (= *exactly similar thing*) réplique *f* ; (= *exactly similar person*) double *m*, sosie *m* ; (*Cine* = *stand-in*) doublure *f* ; → **body, stunt**[1] ; (*Theat* = *actor taking two parts*) acteur *m*, -trice *f* qui tient deux rôles (*dans la même pièce*) ; (*Cards*) contre *m* ; (*other games*) double *m* ; (*Betting*) pari *m* doublé (*sur deux chevaux dans deux courses différentes*)

[4] (also **double bedroom**) chambre *f* pour deux personnes

NPL **doubles** (*Tennis*) double *m* ◆ **mixed ~s** double *m* mixte ◆ **ladies'/men's ~s** double *m* dames/messieurs ◆ **a ~s player** un joueur *or* une joueuse de double

VT [1] (= *multiply by two*) [+ *number, salary, price*] doubler

[2] (= *fold in two:* also **double over**) plier en deux, replier, doubler

[3] (*Theat*) **he ~s the parts of courtier and hangman** il joue les rôles *or* il a le double rôle du courtisan et du bourreau ◆ **he's doubling the hero's part for Tony Brennan** il est la doublure de Tony Brennan dans le rôle du héros

[4] (*Cards*) [+ *one's opponent, his call*] contrer ; [+ *one's stake*] doubler ◆ ~**!** (*Bridge*) contre !

VI [1] [*prices, incomes, quantity etc*] doubler

[2] (= *run*) courir, aller au pas de course

[3] (*Cine*) **to** ~ **for sb** doubler qn

[4] (*Bridge*) contrer

[5] (*US fig*) **to** ~ **in brass**‡ avoir une corde supplémentaire à son arc

COMP **double act** N duo *m*

double-acting ADJ à double effet

double agent N agent *m* double

double album N (*Mus*) double album *m*

double bar N (*Mus*) double barre *f*

double-barrelled ADJ [*shotgun*] à deux coups ; (*fig*) [*plan, question*] à deux volets ; (*Brit*) [*surname*] à rallonge *

double bass N contrebasse *f*

double bassoon N contrebasson *m*

double bed N grand lit *m*, lit *m* à deux places

double bedroom N chambre *f* pour deux personnes ; (*in hotel*) chambre *f* double

double bend N *(Brit: on road)* virage *m* en S
double bill N *(Cine etc)* double programme *m*
double bind * N situation *f* insoluble *or* sans issue, impasse *f*
double-blind ADJ *[test, experiment, method]* en double aveugle
double bluff N ◆ **it's actually a ~ bluff** il *(or* elle *etc)* dit la vérité en faisant croire que c'est du bluff
double boiler N ⇒ **double saucepan**
double-book VI *[hotel, airline etc]* faire du surbooking *or* de la surréservation VT *[+ room, seat]* réserver pour deux personnes différentes
double booking N surréservation *f*, surbooking *m*
double bounce N *(Tennis)* double rebond *m* VI *[ball]* doubler
double-breasted ADJ *[jacket]* croisé
double-check VTI revérifier N revérification *f*
double chin N double menton *m*
double-chinned ADJ qui a un double menton
double-click VI *(Comput)* cliquer deux fois *(on* sur) double-cliquer *(on* sur)
double-clutch VI *(US)* ⇒ **double-declutch**
double consonant N consonne *f* redoublée
double cream N *(Brit)* crème *f* fraîche épaisse *or* à fouetter
double-cross * VT trahir, doubler * N traîtrise *f*, duplicité *f*
double-date VI sortir à deux couples
double-dealer N fourbe *m*
double-dealing N double jeu *m*, duplicité *f* ADJ hypocrite, faux jeton *
double-decker N (= *bus*) autobus *m* à impériale ; (= *aircraft*) deux-ponts *m inv* ; (= *sandwich*) sandwich *m* club
double-declutch VI faire un double débrayage
double density N → **density**
double-digit ADJ *(gen)* à deux chiffres
double-dipper N *(US pej)* cumulard(e) * *m(f)*
double-dipping N *(US pej)* cumul *m* d'emplois *or* de salaires
double door N porte *f* à deux battants
double Dutch * N *(Brit)* baragouin * *m*, charabia * *m* ◆ **to talk ~ Dutch** baragouiner ◆ **it was ~ Dutch to me** c'était de l'hébreu pour moi *
double eagle N *(Golf)* albatros *m*
double-edged ADJ *(lit, fig) [blade, remark, praise, benefit]* à double tranchant ◆ **a ~-edged sword** *(lit, fig)* une arme à double tranchant
double entendre N ambiguïté *f*, mot *m (or* expression *f)* à double sens
double-entry book-keeping N comptabilité *f* en partie double
double exposure N *(Phot)* surimpression *f*, double exposition *f*
double-faced ADJ *[material]* réversible ; *(pej) [person]* hypocrite
double fault N *(Tennis)* double faute *f* VI faire une double faute
double feature N *(Cine) programme comportant deux longs métrages*
double-figure ADJ ⇒ **double-digit**
double first N *(Univ)* mention *f* très bien dans deux disciplines
double flat N *(Mus)* double bémol *m*
double-glaze VT *(Brit)* ◆ **to ~-glaze a window** poser un double vitrage
double glazing N *(Brit: gen)* double vitrage *m* ◆ **to put in ~ glazing** (faire) installer un double vitrage
double helix N double hélice *f*
double indemnity N *(US Insurance)* indemnité *f* double
double jeopardy N *(US Jur) mise en cause de l'autorité de la chose jugée*
double-jointed ADJ désarticulé
double-knit(ting) N (= *wool*) laine *f* épaisse ADJ en laine épaisse
double knot N double nœud *m*
double lock N serrure *f* de sécurité
double-lock VT fermer à double tour
double major N *(US Univ)* double *f* dominante
double marking N *(Educ)* double correction *f*
double negative N double négation *f*
double-park VT garer en double file VI stationner *or* se garer en double file
double-parking N stationnement *m* en double file
double pneumonia N pneumonie *f* double
double-quick * ADV en deux temps trois mouvements * ADJ ◆ **in ~-quick time** en deux temps trois mouvements *
double room N chambre *f* double *or* pour deux personnes
double saucepan N casserole *f* pour bain-marie *or* à double fond
double sharp N *(Mus)* double dièse *m*
double-sided ADJ *(Comput) [disk]* double face
double-space VT *(Typ)* taper avec un double interligne ◆ **~-spaced** à double interligne
double spacing N ◆ **in ~ spacing** à double interligne
double standard N ◆ **to have ~ standards** faire deux poids, deux mesures ◆ **there's a ~ standard operating here** il y a deux poids, deux mesures ici ◆ **they were accused of (operating) ~ standards** on les a accusés de partialité *or* discrimination
double star N étoile *f* double
double stopping N *(Mus)* doubles cordes *fpl*
double take * N ◆ **to do a ~ take** devoir y regarder à deux fois
double talk N (= *gibberish*) charabia *m* ; (= *deceptive talk*) paroles *fpl* ambiguës *or* trompeuses
double taxation agreement N convention *f* relative aux doubles impositions
double time N *(at work)* ◆ **to earn ~ time** être payé (au tarif) double ◆ **to get/pay ~ time** gagner/payer le double ◆ **in ~ time** *(US Mil)* au pas redoublé ; see also **time**
double track N *(Cine)* double bande *f* ; (= *tape*) double piste *f*
double track line N *(Rail)* ligne *f* à deux voies
double vision N vision *f* double ◆ **to get** *or* **have ~ vision** voir double
double wedding N double mariage *m*
double whammy * N double coup *m* dur *
double white lines NPL lignes *fpl* blanches continues
double windows NPL doubles fenêtres *fpl*
double yellow lines NPL double bande *f* jaune *(marquant l'interdiction de stationner)*
double yolk N ◆ **egg with a ~ yolk** œuf *m* à deux jaunes

► **double back** VI *[animal, person]* revenir sur ses pas ; *[road]* faire un brusque crochet ◆ **to ~ back on itself** *[line]* former une boucle en épingle à cheveux
VT SEP *[+ blanket]* rabattre, replier ; *[+ page]* replier

► **double over** VI ⇒ **double up 1**
VT SEP ⇒ **double vt 2**

► **double up** VI 1 (= *bend over sharply*) se plier, se courber ◆ **to ~ up with laughter/pain** être plié en deux *or* se tordre de rire/de douleur
2 (= *share room*) partager une chambre *(with* avec)
3 *(Brit Betting)* parier sur deux chevaux

doublespeak /ˈdʌblspiːk/ N *(pej)* double langage *m*

doublet /ˈdʌblɪt/ N 1 *(Dress)* pourpoint *m*, justaucorps *m* 2 *(Ling)* doublet *m*

doublethink * /ˈdʌblθɪŋk/ N ◆ **to do a ~** *tenir un raisonnement ou suivre une démarche où l'on s'accommode de contradictions flagrantes*

doubleton /ˈdʌbltən/ N *(Cards)* deux cartes *fpl* d'une (même) couleur, doubleton *m*

doubling /ˈdʌblɪŋ/ N *[of number, letter]* redoublement *m*, doublement *m*

doubloon /dʌˈbluːn/ N *(Hist)* doublon *m*

doubly /ˈdʌblɪ/ ADV doublement ◆ **divorce is always traumatic, and ~ so when there are children** le divorce est toujours traumatisant, et il l'est doublement quand il y a des enfants ◆ **in order to make ~ sure** pour plus de sûreté ◆ **to work ~ hard** travailler deux fois plus dur

doubt /daʊt/ LANGUAGE IN USE 15.1, 16.1, 26.3
N doute *m*, incertitude *f* ◆ **there is room for ~** il est permis de douter ◆ **there is some ~ about whether he'll come or not** on ne sait pas très bien s'il viendra ou non ◆ **to have one's ~s about sth** avoir des doutes sur *or* au sujet de qch ◆ **I have my ~s (about) whether he will come** je doute qu'il vienne ◆ **to cast** *or* **throw ~(s) on sth** mettre qch en doute, jeter le doute sur qch ◆ **without (a) ~, without the slightest ~** sans aucun doute, sans le moindre doute ◆ **it is beyond all ~** c'est indéniable *or* incontestable ◆ **beyond ~** ADV indubitablement, à n'en pas douter ADJ indubitable ◆ **he'll come without any ~** il viendra sûrement, il n'y a pas de doute qu'il viendra
◆ **in doubt** ◆ **it is not in ~** *[outcome, result etc]* cela ne fait aucun doute ◆ **I am in (some) ~ about his honesty** j'ai des doutes sur son honnêteté ◆ **the outcome is in ~** l'issue est indécise ◆ **I am in no ~ about** *or* **as to what he means** je n'ai aucun doute sur ce qu'il veut dire ◆ **to be in great ~ about sth** avoir de sérieux doutes au sujet de qch, douter fortement de qch ◆ **his honesty is in ~** *(in this instance)* son honnêteté est en doute ; *(in general)* son honnêteté est sujette à caution ◆ **if** *or* **when in ~** en cas de doute
◆ **no doubt(s)** ◆ **I have no ~(s) about it** je n'en doute pas ◆ **no ~ about it!** cela va sans dire ! ◆ **this leaves no ~ that ...** on ne peut plus douter que ... + *subj* ◆ **there is no ~ that ...** il n'y a pas de doute que ... + *indic* ◆ **there's no ~ that he'll come** il viendra sûrement, il n'y a pas de doute qu'il viendra ◆ **no ~ he will come tomorrow** sans doute viendra-t-il demain ◆ **no ~** sans doute ; → **benefit**
VT *[+ person, sb's honesty, truth of statement]* douter de ◆ **I ~ it (very much)** j'en doute (fort) ◆ **I ~ed (the evidence of) my own eyes** je n'en croyais pas mes yeux
◆ **to doubt whether/if/that ...** douter que ... ◆ **I ~ whether he will come** je doute qu'il vienne ◆ **I ~ if that is what she wanted** je doute que ce soit ce qu'elle voulait ◆ **I don't ~ that he will come** je ne doute pas qu'il vienne ◆ **she didn't ~ that he would come** elle ne doutait pas qu'il viendrait
VI douter *(of* de) avoir des doutes *(of* sur) ne pas être sûr *(of* de)
COMP **doubting Thomas** N sceptique *mf* ◆ **to be a ~ing Thomas** être comme saint Thomas

doubter /ˈdaʊtəʳ/ N incrédule *mf*, sceptique *mf*

doubtful /ˈdaʊtfʊl/ LANGUAGE IN USE 16.2 ADJ 1 (= *unconvinced*) *[person]* peu convaincu ◆ **to be ~ of sth** douter de qch ◆ **to be ~ about sb/sth** douter de qn/qch, avoir des doutes sur qn/qch ◆ **I'm a bit ~ (about it)** je n'en suis pas si sûr, j'ai quelques doutes (à ce sujet) ◆ **to be ~ about doing sth** hésiter à faire qch ◆ **he was ~ that** *or* **whether ...** il doutait que ... + *subj* ◆ **he was ~ that** *or* **whether he could ever manage it** il doutait qu'il puisse jamais réussir, il doutait pouvoir jamais réussir
2 (= *questionable, unlikely*) douteux ◆ **it is ~ that** *or* **whether ...** il est douteux que ... + *subj* ◆ **of ~ reliability/quality** d'une fiabilité/qualité douteuse ◆ **in ~ taste** d'un goût douteux ◆ **he's ~ (for the match)** *(Sport* = *unlikely to play)* sa participation (au match) est encore incertaine

doubtfully /ˈdaʊtfəlɪ/ ADV *[frown, shake head etc]* d'un air sceptique ; *[speak]* d'un ton sceptique

doubtfulness /ˈdaʊtfʊlnɪs/ N incertitude *f*

doubtless /ˈdaʊtlɪs/ ADV sans doute, certainement

douceur /duːˈsɜːʳ/ N (= *gift, tip etc*) petit cadeau *m*

douche /duːʃ/ N [1] (= *shower*) douche *f* ◆ **take a ~!**⁑ (*US*) va te faire foutre !⁑ [2] (*Med*) (*vaginal*) douche *f* vaginale ◆ **it was (like) a cold ~** (*fig*) cela a fait l'effet d'une douche froide* VT doucher

dough /dəʊ/ N [1] pâte *f* ◆ **bread ~** pâte *f* à pain [2] (⁑ = *money*) fric⁑ *m*, pognon⁑ *m* COMP **dough-hook** N crochet *m* de pétrissage

doughboy /ˈdəʊbɔɪ/ N [1] (*Culin*) boulette *f* (de pâte) [2] (*US Mil* ⁑) sammy *m* (*soldat américain de la Première Guerre mondiale*)

doughnut /ˈdəʊnʌt/ N beignet *m* ◆ **jam** (*Brit*) or **jelly** (*US*) **~** beignet *m* à la confiture

doughty /ˈdaʊtɪ/ ADJ (*liter*) preux (*liter*), vaillant ◆ **~ deeds** hauts faits *mpl* (*liter*)

doughy /ˈdəʊɪ/ ADJ [*consistency*] pâteux ; [*complexion*] terreux

dour /ˈdʊəʳ/ ADJ (= *austere*) [*person*] sévère, froid ; [*architecture, building, style*] austère, froid ◆ **a ~ Scot** un Écossais à l'air sévère ◆ **he came across on TV as a bit ~** à l'écran il semblait un peu froid

dourly /dʊəlɪ/ ADV [*say*] d'un ton maussade ; [*smile, look at*] d'un air renfrogné ◆ **a ~ conventional man** un homme au conformisme austère

douse /daʊs/ VT [1] (= *drench*) tremper, inonder [2] (= *extinguish*) [+ *flames, light*] éteindre

dove[1] /dʌv/ N colombe *f* (*also Pol*) ; → **turtledove** COMP **dove-grey** ADJ gris perle *inv*

dove[2] /dəʊv/ (*US*) ptp of **dive**

dovecot /ˈdʌvkɒt/, **dovecote** /ˈdʌvkəʊt/ N colombier *m*, pigeonnier *m*

Dover /ˈdəʊvəʳ/ N Douvres ; → **strait** COMP **Dover sole** N sole *f*

dovetail /ˈdʌvteɪl/ N (*Carpentry*) queue *f* d'aronde

VI [1] (= *harmonize*) se rejoindre, concorder ◆ **there may be a place where their interests ~** il y a un peut-être un point sur lequel leurs intérêts se rejoignent *or* concordent

◆ **to dovetail with** concorder avec ◆ **the changes also ~ with plans to modernize the civil service** ces changements concordent également avec le projet de modernisation de la fonction publique

[2] (*Carpentry*) se raccorder (*into* à)

VT [1] (*Carpentry*) assembler à queue d'aronde

[2] (= *harmonize*) [+ *plans etc*] faire concorder, raccorder

COMP **dovetail joint** N (*Carpentry*) assemblage *m* à queue d'aronde

dovish* /ˈdʌvɪʃ/ ADJ (*esp US: Pol fig*) [*person*] partisan(e) *m(f)* de la négociation et du compromis ; [*speech, attitude*] de compromis

Dow* /daʊ/ N ◆ **the ~** l'indice *m* Dow Jones

dowager /ˈdaʊədʒəʳ/ N douairière *f* COMP **dowager duchess** N duchesse *f* douairière

dowdiness /ˈdaʊdɪnɪs/ N manque *m* de chic

dowdy /ˈdaʊdɪ/ ADJ [*person, clothes*] démodé, sans chic

dowel /ˈdaʊəl/ N cheville *f* (en bois), goujon *m* VT assembler avec des goujons, goujonner

dower house /ˈdaʊəhaʊs/ N (*Brit*) petit manoir *m* (de douairière)

Dow Jones /ˌdaʊˈdʒəʊnz/ N ◆ **the ~ average** or **index** l'indice *m* Dow Jones, le Dow Jones

down[1] /daʊn/

> When **down** is an element in a phrasal verb, eg **back down, glance down, play down**, look up the verb.

ADV [1] (*indicating movement to lower level*) en bas, vers le bas ; (= *down to the ground*) à terre, par terre ◆ **~!** (*said to a dog*) couché ! ◆ **~ with traitors!** à bas les traîtres !

◆ **down and down** de plus en plus bas ◆ **to go/fall ~ and ~** descendre/tomber de plus en plus bas

[2] (*indicating position at lower level*) en bas ◆ **~ there** en bas (là-bas) ◆ **I shall stay ~ here** je vais rester ici ◆ **the blinds were ~** les stores étaient baissés ◆ **Douglas isn't ~ yet** Douglas n'est pas encore descendu ◆ **to be ~ for the count** (*Boxing*) être K.-O. ◆ **to kick somebody when they are ~** frapper un homme à terre ◆ **don't hit** or **kick a man when he is ~** on ne frappe pas un homme à terre

◆ **to be down with** (= *ill with*) avoir ◆ **she's ~ with flu** elle a la grippe

◆ **down south** dans le sud ◆ **I was brought up ~ south** j'ai grandi dans le sud ◆ **they're moving ~ south** ils vont s'installer dans le sud ; → **face, head**

[3] (*from larger town, the north, university etc*) **he came ~ from London yesterday** il est arrivé de Londres hier ◆ **we're going ~ to Dover tomorrow** demain nous descendons à Douvres ◆ **he came ~ from Oxford in 1999** (*Univ*) il est sorti d'Oxford en 1999 ◆ **~ East** (*US*) *du* (*or au*) *nord-est de la Nouvelle-Angleterre*

[4] (*indicating diminution in volume, degree, activity*) **the tyres are ~/right ~** les pneus sont dégonflés/à plat ◆ **the pound is ~ against the dollar** la livre est en baisse par rapport au dollar ◆ **we are ~ to our last £5** il ne nous reste plus que 5 livres

◆ **down on** (= *less than*) ◆ **I'm £20 ~ on what I expected** j'ai 20 livres de moins que je ne pensais ◆ **prices are ~ on last year's** les prix sont en baisse par rapport à (ceux de) l'année dernière

◆ **to be down on one's luck** ne pas avoir de chance, être dans une mauvaise passe ◆ **I am ~ on my luck** je n'ai pas de chance, je suis dans une mauvaise passe ◆ **the times when I was ~ on my luck** les moments où les choses allaient mal

[5] (*in writing*) **I've got it (noted) ~ in my diary** je l'ai *or* c'est marqué sur mon agenda ◆ **let's get it ~ on paper** mettons-le par écrit ◆ **did you get ~ what he said?** as-tu noté ce qu'il a dit ? ◆ **to be ~ for the next race** être inscrit dans la prochaine course ; → **note**

[6] (*indicating a series or succession*) **~ to** jusqu'à ◆ **from 1700 ~ to the present** de 1700 à nos jours ◆ **from the biggest ~ to the smallest** du plus grand (jusqu')au plus petit ◆ **from the king ~ to the poorest beggar** depuis le roi jusqu'au plus pauvre des mendiants

[7] (*set phrases*)

◆ **to be down to*** (= *attributable to*) ◆ **any mistakes are entirely ~ to us** s'il y a des erreurs, nous sommes entièrement responsables ◆ **our success is all ~ to him/hard work** c'est à lui seul/à notre travail acharné que nous devons notre succès ◆ **basically, it is ~ to luck** en fait c'est une question de chance ◆ **it's ~ to him to do it** (= *his duty*) c'est à lui de le faire ◆ **it's ~ to him now** c'est à lui de jouer maintenant

[8] ◆ **to be ~ on sb** * avoir une dent contre qn, en vouloir à qn

PREP [1] (*indicating movement to lower level*) du haut en bas de ◆ **he went ~ the hill** (*lit*) il a descendu la colline ; see also **downhill** ◆ **her hair hung ~ her back** ses cheveux lui tombaient dans le dos ◆ **he ran his eye ~ the list** il a parcouru la liste du regard *or* des yeux

[2] (= *at a lower part of*) **he's ~ the hill** il est au pied *or* en bas de la colline ◆ **she lives ~ the street (from us)** elle habite plus bas *or* plus loin (que nous) dans la rue ◆ **it's just ~ the road** c'est tout près, c'est à deux pas ◆ **~ the ages** (*fig*) au cours des siècles

[3] (= *along*) le long de ◆ **he was walking ~ the street** il descendait la rue ◆ **he has gone ~ (to) town** il est allé *or* descendu en ville ◆ **let's go ~ the pub*** allons au pub ◆ **looking ~ this street, you can see ...** si vous regardez le long de cette rue, vous verrez ...

N (*Brit*) ◆ **to have a ~ on sb*** avoir une dent contre qn, en vouloir à qn ; → **up**

ADJ [1] ◆ **to be** or **feel ~** avoir le cafard*, être déprimé

[2] (*Comput*) en panne

[3] (*Brit* †) [*train*] en provenance de la grande ville ◆ **the ~ line** la ligne de la grande ville

[4] ◆ **~ and dirty*** (*esp US*) ◆ **to get ~ and dirty** s'y mettre * ◆ **~ and dirty realism** réalisme *m* cru ◆ **~ and dirty rock** rock *m* primaire

VT * ◆ **to ~ an opponent** terrasser un adversaire ◆ **he ~ed three enemy planes** il a descendu * trois avions ennemis ◆ **to ~ tools** (*Brit*) (= *stop work*) cesser le travail ; (= *strike*) se mettre en grève, débrayer ◆ **he ~ed a glass of beer** il a vidé *or* descendu * un verre de bière

COMP **down-and-out** N SDF *mf* ADJ ◆ **to be ~-and-out** (*Boxing*) aller au tapis pour le compte, être hors de combat ; (= *destitute*) être sur le pavé *or* à la mie

down-at-heel ADJ (*US*) [*person*] miteux ; [*shoe*] éculé

down-bow N (*Mus*) tiré *m*

down-cycle N (*Econ*) cycle *m* de récession

down-in-the-mouth* ADJ abattu, tout triste ◆ **to be ~-in-the-mouth** être abattu *or* tout triste, avoir le moral à zéro* ◆ **to look ~-in-the-mouth** avoir l'air abattu, faire une sale tête

down-market ADJ [*goods, car*] bas de gamme *inv* ; [*newspaper*] populaire ◆ **it's rather ~-market** [*programme etc*] c'est plutôt du genre public de masse ADV ◆ **to go** or **move ~-market** [*company*] se tourner vers le bas de gamme ; [*house purchaser etc*] acheter quelque chose de moins bien

down payment N acompte *m*, premier versement *m* ◆ **to make a ~ payment of £100** payer un acompte de 100 livres, payer 100 livres d'acompte

down-river ADJ, ADV ⇒ **downstream**

down time N (*Comput*) → **downtime**

down-to-earth ADJ réaliste ◆ **he's a very ~-to-earth person** il a les pieds sur terre

down under* ADV (*Brit* = *in Australia/New Zealand*) en Australie/Nouvelle-Zélande, aux antipodes ◆ **from ~ under** d'Australie/de Nouvelle-Zélande

down[2] /daʊn/ N [*of bird, person, plant*] duvet *m* ; [*of fruit*] peau *f* (veloutée) ; → **eiderdown, thistledown**

down[3] /daʊn/ N [1] (= *hill*) colline *f* dénudée ◆ **the Downs** (*Brit*) les Downs *fpl* (*collines herbeuses du sud de l'Angleterre*) [2] (*Brit*) **the Downs** (= *Straits of Dover*) les Dunes *fpl*

downbeat /ˈdaʊnˌbiːt/ N (*Mus*) temps *m* frappé ADJ (= *gloomy*) [*person*] abattu ; [*ending*] pessimiste

downcast /ˈdaʊnˌkɑːst/ ADJ [1] (= *discouraged*) abattu, démoralisé, découragé [2] (= *looking down*) [*eyes*] baissé N (*Min*) aérage *m*

downcry⁑ /ˈdaʊnˌkraɪ/ VT (*US* = *denigrate*) décrier, dénigrer

downdraught, downdraft (*US*) /ˈdaʊn drɑːft/ N (*Weather*) courant *m* descendant

downer /ˈdaʊnəʳ/ N [1] (* = *tranquilliser*) tranquillisant *m*, sédatif *m* [2] ⁑ ◆ **it's a ~** ça fout les boules⁑ ◆ **for divorced people, Christmas can be a ~** Noël peut donner le bourdon* aux divorcés ◆ **to be on a ~** faire de la déprime*

downfall /ˈdaʊnˌfɔːl/ N [*of person, empire*] chute *f*, ruine *f*, effondrement *m* ; [*of hopes*] ruine *f* ; [*of rain*] chute *f* de pluie

downgrade /ˈdaʊnˌɡreɪd/ VT [+ employee] rétrograder (dans la hiérarchie) ; [+ hotel, stock] déclasser ; [+ work, job] dévaloriser, déclasser ◆ **to ~ the importance of sth** minimiser l'importance de qch ◆ **hurricane Isador has been ~d to a tropical storm** l'ouragan Isador est désormais classé comme typhon ◆ **the boy's condition has been ~d from critical to serious** l'état du jeune garçon n'est plus considéré comme très grave mais comme grave N 1 (Rail etc) rampe f, descente f 2 [of stock, bond] déclassement m

downhearted /ˌdaʊnˈhɑːtɪd/ ADJ abattu, découragé ◆ **don't be ~!** ne te laisse pas abattre !

downhill /ˈdaʊnˈhɪl/ ADJ 1 ◆ **during the ~ journey** au cours de la descente ◆ **the course includes a steep ~ slope** le circuit comprend une descente *or* pente abrupte ◆ **it's just a short ~ walk to the station** il n'y a que quelques mètres à descendre pour arriver à la gare, la gare est à deux pas, en bas de la côte ◆ **the accident happened on a ~ stretch of the track** l'accident s'est produit alors que le train descendait une côte

2 (fig) ◆ **it was ~ all the way after that** (= got easier) après cela, tout a été plus facile ; (= got worse) après cela, tout est allé en empirant *or* de mal en pis

3 (Ski) ~ **competition** épreuve f de descente ◆ ~ **course** piste f de descente ◆ ~ **race** (épreuve f de) descente f ◆ ~ **racer** descendeur m, -euse f ◆ ~ **skier** skieur m, -euse f alpin(e) ◆ ~ **ski(ing)** ski m alpin *or* de piste

ADV ◆ **to go ~** [person, vehicle] descendre (la *or* une pente) ; [road] descendre, aller en descendant ; (fig = get worse) [person] être sur une *or* la mauvaise pente ; [company, business etc] péricliter ; [economy] se dégrader ◆ **things just went ~ from there** par la suite les choses n'ont fait qu'empirer

downhome* /ˌdaʊnˈhəʊm/ ADJ (US) (from south) du Sud, sudiste ; (pej) péquenaud *

Downing Street /ˈdaʊnɪŋˌstriːt/ N (Brit) Downing Street (*résidence du Premier ministre britannique*)

DOWNING STREET

Downing Street, dans le quartier de Westminster, est la rue où résident officiellement le Premier ministre (au nº 10) et le chancelier de l'Échiquier (au nº 11). Les médias utilisent souvent les expressions **Downing Street**, « Number Ten » ou « Ten **Downing Street** », pour désigner le Premier ministre ou le gouvernement, à la façon dont on parlerait de "Matignon" en France.

downlighter /ˈdaʊnˌlaɪtəʳ/ N luminaire m (*éclairant vers le bas*)

download /ˈdaʊnˌləʊd/ VT (Comput) télécharger

downloadable /ˈdaʊnˌləʊdəbl/ ADJ téléchargeable

downloading /ˈdaʊnˌləʊdɪŋ/ N (Comput) téléchargement m

downpipe /ˈdaʊnˌpaɪp/ N (Brit) (tuyau m de) descente f

downplay /ˈdaʊnˌpleɪ/ VT (fig) minimiser (l'importance de)

downpour /ˈdaʊnˌpɔːʳ/ N pluie f torrentielle

downright /ˈdaʊnraɪt/ ADJ pur et simple ◆ **a ~ refusal** un refus catégorique ◆ **it's a ~ lie for him to say that ...** il ment carrément *or* effrontément quand il dit que ... ◆ **it's ~ cheek on his part*** il a un sacré culot* *or* toupet* ADV carrément ◆ **it's ~ impossible** c'est carrément impossible, c'est purement et simplement impossible

downshift /ˈdaʊnʃɪft/ (US) VI (in car) rétrograder ; (at work) prendre un poste moins bien payé mais moins stressant N rétrogradation f

downside /ˈdaʊnˌsaɪd/ N 1 (US) ~ **up** sens dessus dessous 2 (= negative aspect) inconvénient m, désavantage m ◆ **on the ~** côté inconvénients, pour ce qui est des inconvénients COMP **downside risk** N [of investment] risque m de baisse *or* de chute du cours

downsize /ˈdaʊnsaɪz/ VT [+ company] réduire les effectifs de, dégraisser* ; (Comput) réduire la taille *or* l'encombrement de VI [company] réduire ses effectifs, dégraisser*

downsizing /ˈdaʊnsaɪzɪŋ/ N [of company] dégraissage m (des effectifs)

downspout /ˈdaʊnspaʊt/ N (US) ⇒ **downpipe**

Down's syndrome /ˈdaʊnzˌsɪndrəʊm/ N trisomie f ◆ **a person with ~** un(e) trisomique ◆ **a ~ baby, a baby with ~** un bébé trisomique

downstage /ˈdaʊnˌsteɪdʒ/ ADV [stand, be] sur l'avant-scène ; [move, point] vers l'avant-scène ◆ **to face ~** faire face au public

downstairs /ˈdaʊnˈsteəz/ ADV (gen) en bas ; (= to or on floor below) à l'étage en-dessous *or* du dessous ; (= to or on ground floor) au rez-de-chaussée ◆ **to go/come ~** descendre (l'escalier) ◆ **to run/crawl** *etc* ~ descendre (l'escalier) en courant/en rampant *etc* ◆ **to rush ~** dévaler l'escalier ◆ **to fall ~** tomber dans les escaliers ◆ **the people ~** (= below) les gens mpl du dessous ; (= on ground floor) les gens mpl d'en bas *or* du rez-de-chaussée

ADJ (= on ground floor) ◆ **they've got a ~ lavatory** ils ont des toilettes en bas ◆ **the ~ phone** le téléphone d'en bas *or* du rez-de-chaussée ◆ **the ~ rooms** les pièces fpl du bas *or* du rez-de-chaussée ◆ **a ~ flat** un appartement au rez-de-chaussée

N ◆ **the ~** * (= ground floor) le rez-de-chaussée ; (= lower floors) les étages mpl inférieurs

downstate /ˈdaʊnˌsteɪt/ (US) N campagne f, sud m de l'État ADJ (= southern) du sud de l'État ◆ ~ **New York** le sud de l'État de New York ADV [be] dans le sud ; [go] vers le sud ◆ **they live ~** ils habitent dans le sud de l'État ◆ **to go ~** aller dans le sud de l'État

downstream /ˈdaʊnˌstriːm/ ADJ, ADV en aval ◆ **to go/move ~** descendre le courant ◆ ~ **industries** (fig) industries fpl d'aval

downstroke /ˈdaʊnˌstrəʊk/ N 1 (in writing) plein m 2 [of piston etc] course f descendante, descente f

downswept /ˈdaʊnˌswept/ ADJ [wings] surbaissé

downswing /ˈdaʊnˌswɪŋ/ N (fig) baisse f, phase f descendante

downtime /ˈdaʊntaɪm/ N [of machine] temps m *or* durée f d'immobilisation ; (Comput) temps m d'arrêt

downtown /ˈdaʊnˈtaʊn/ (US) ADV dans le centre ◆ **to go ~** descendre *or* aller en ville ADJ ◆ ~ **Chicago** le centre de Chicago

downtrend /ˈdaʊntrend/ N tendance f à la baisse

downtrodden /ˈdaʊnˌtrɒdən/ ADJ [person, nation] opprimé

downturn /ˈdaʊntɜːn/ N ⇒ **downswing**

downward /ˈdaʊnwəd/ ADJ [movement, stroke, pull] vers le bas ◆ **there was a ~ slope from the house to the road** la maison était en hauteur par rapport à la route ◆ **they were on a fairly steep ~ slope** ils étaient sur une pente assez raide *or* qui descendait assez fort ◆ **the rain made our ~ path extremely treacherous** la pluie rendait notre descente extrêmement dangereuse ◆ **in a ~ direction** vers le bas ◆ **a ~ trend** une tendance à la baisse ◆ **I'm convinced the economy's on the ~ slope** je suis convaincu que l'économie est sur une mauvaise pente ◆ **the dollar resumed its ~ path today** le dollar a recommencé à baisser aujourd'hui ADV ⇒ **downwards**

downwards /ˈdaʊnwədz/ ADV [go] vers le bas, en bas ◆ **to slope (gently) ~** descendre (en pente douce) ◆ **to look ~** regarder en bas *or* vers le bas ◆ **looking ~** les yeux baissés, la tête baissée ◆ **place the book face ~** posez le livre face en dessous ◆ **from the king ~** (fig) depuis le roi (jusqu'au plus humble), du haut en bas de l'échelle sociale

downwind /ˈdaʊnˌwɪnd/ ADV [be] sous le vent (of, from par rapport à) ; [move] dans la direction du vent ; [sail] sous le vent ◆ **the sparks drifted ~** les étincelles étaient emportées par le vent

downy /ˈdaʊnɪ/ ADJ 1 (= furry) [skin, peach] duveté ; [leaf] duveteux ◆ **covered with fine, ~ hair** couvert de poils fins et soyeux ◆ ~ **softness** douceur f soyeuse 2 (= feathery) [chick] couvert de duvet 3 (= down-filled) garnis de duvet

dowry /ˈdaʊrɪ/ N dot f

dowse /daʊz/ VI pratiquer la rhabdomancie VT ⇒ **douse**

dowser /ˈdaʊzəʳ/ N rhabdomancien(ne) m(f) ; (for water) sourcier m

dowsing /ˈdaʊzɪŋ/ N rhabdomancie f COMP **dowsing rod** N baguette f (de sourcier)

doxology /dɒkˈsɒlədʒɪ/ N doxologie f

doxy †† /ˈdɒksɪ/ N catin † f

doyen /ˈdɔɪən/ N doyen m ◆ **the ~ of ...** le doyen des ...

doyenne /ˈdɔɪen/ N doyenne f

doz. /dʌz/ abbrev of **dozen**

doze /dəʊz/ N somme m ◆ **to have a ~** faire un petit somme VI sommeiller, somnoler

▸ **doze off** VI s'assoupir, s'endormir

dozen /ˈdʌzn/ N douzaine f ◆ **three ~** trois douzaines ◆ **a ~ shirts** une douzaine de chemises ◆ **a round ~** une douzaine tout juste ◆ **half a ~, a half-~** une demi-douzaine ◆ **£1 a ~** une livre la douzaine ◆ **~s of times** des dizaines *or* douzaines de fois ◆ **there are ~s like that** des choses (*or* des gens) comme cela, on en trouve à la douzaine ; → **baker, nineteen, six**

dozy /ˈdəʊzɪ/ ADJ 1 (= sleepy) à moitié endormi, somnolent 2 (Brit * = stupid) empoté*, pas très dégourdi* ◆ **you ~ prat!** imbécile !, espèce d'empoté !

DPhil /diːˈfɪl/ N (abbrev of **Doctor of Philosophy**) ≈ doctorat m (*d'État dans une discipline autre que le droit, la médecine ou la théologie*)

dpi /ˌdiːpiːˈaɪ/ (Comput) (abbrev of **dots per inch**) dpi

DPP /ˌdiːpiːˈpiː/ N (Brit Jur) (abbrev of **Director of Public Prosecutions**) → **director**

Dr /ˈdɒktəʳ/ (abbrev of **Doctor**) ~ **R. Stephenson** (on envelope) Dr R. Stephenson ◆ **Dear ~ Stephenson** (in letters, man) Cher Monsieur ; (woman) Chère Madame ; (if known to writer) Cher Docteur

dr (Comm) abbrev of **debtor, dram, drachma**

drab /dræb/ ADJ [colour] morne ; [clothes] terne ; [surroundings, existence] terne, morne N (NonC = fabric) grosse toile f bise

drabness /ˈdræbnɪs/ N [of place, surroundings, existence] aspect m morne, grisaille f ; [of clothes] aspect m terne

drachm /dræm/ N 1 (Measure, Pharm) drachme f 2 ⇒ **drachma**

drachma /ˈdrækmə/ N (pl **drachmas** *or* **drachmae** /ˈdrækmiː/) (= coin) drachme f

draconian /drəˈkəʊnɪən/ ADJ draconien

Dracula /ˈdrækjʊlə/ N Dracula *m*

draft /drɑːft/ N 1 *(= outline: gen)* avant-projet *m* ; *[of letter]* brouillon *m* ; *[of novel]* premier jet *m*, ébauche *f*
2 *(Comm, Fin: for money)* traite *f*, effet *m* ◆ **to make a ~ on** tirer sur
3 *(Mil = group of men)* détachement *m*
4 *(US Mil = conscript intake)* contingent *m* ◆ **to be ~ age** être en âge de faire son service militaire
5 *(US)* ⇒ **draught**
VT 1 (also **draft out**) *[+ letter]* faire le brouillon de ; *[+ speech] (gen)* écrire, préparer ; *(first draft)* faire le brouillon de ; *(final version)* rédiger ; *(Parl) [+ bill] (Comm, Fin) [+ contract]* rédiger, dresser ; *[+ plan]* esquisser, dresser ; *[+ diagram]* esquisser
2 *(US Mil) [+ conscript]* appeler (sous les drapeaux), incorporer ◆ **to ~ sb to a post/to do sth** *(esp Mil)* détacher *or* désigner qn à un poste/pour faire qch
COMP **draft board** N *(US Mil)* conseil *m* de révision
draft card N *(US Mil)* ordre *m* d'incorporation
draft dodger N *(US Mil)* insoumis *m*
draft letter N brouillon *m* de lettre ; *(more frm)* projet *m* de lettre
draft version N version *f* préliminaire

draftee /dræfˈtiː/ N *(US Mil, fig)* recrue *f*

draftiness /ˈdræftɪnɪs/ N *(US)* ⇒ **draughtiness**

draftsman /ˈdræftsmən/ N (pl **-men**) *(US)* ⇒ **draughtsman 1**

draftsmanship /ˈdræftsmənʃɪp/ N *(US)* ⇒ **draughtsmanship**

draftswoman /ˈdræftswʊmən/ N (pl **-women**) *(US)* ⇒ **draughtswoman**

drafty /ˈdræftɪ/ ADJ *(US)* ⇒ **draughty**

drag /dræg/ N 1 *(for dredging etc)* drague *f* ; *(Naut = cluster of hooks)* araignée *f* ; *(= heavy sledge)* traîneau *m* ; *(= harrow)* herse *f*
2 ⇒ **dragnet**
3 *(= air or water resistance)* résistance *f*, traînée *f*
4 *(= brake shoe)* sabot *m* or patin *m* de frein
5 *(Hunting)* drag *m*
6 *(= hindrance)* frein *m* (on à) ◆ **he's an awful ~ on them** ils le traînent comme un boulet
7 *(* = person)* raseur* *m*, -euse* *f*, casse-pieds* *mf inv* ; *(= tedium)* corvée *f* ◆ **what a ~ to have to go there!** quelle corvée *or* quelle barbe* d'avoir à y aller ! ◆ **this thing is a ~!** quelle barbe ce truc-là !*
8 *(* = pull on cigarette, pipe)* taffe* *f* ◆ **here, have a ~** tiens, tire une taffe*
9 *(* = women's clothing worn by men)* habits *mpl* de femme ◆ **a man in ~** un homme habillé en femme ; *(= transvestite)* un travesti
10 *(US ‡ = influence)* piston *m* ◆ **to use one's ~** travailler dans la coulisse, user de son influence
11 *(US)* **the main ~** la grand-rue
VI 1 *(= trail along) [object]* traîner (à terre) ; *[anchor]* chasser
2 *(= lag behind)* rester en arrière, traîner
3 *[brakes]* frotter, (se) gripper
4 *(fig) [time, work, an entertainment]* traîner ; *[conversation]* (se) traîner, languir ◆ **the minutes ~ged (past** *or* **by)** les minutes s'écoulaient avec lenteur
VT 1 *[+ person, object]* traîner, tirer ; *[+ person]* entraîner ◆ **he ~ged her out of/into the car** il l'a tirée de la voiture/entraînée dans la voiture ◆ **he could barely ~ his injured leg behind him** il se traînait péniblement avec sa jambe blessée ◆ **to ~ one's feet** *(lit = scuff feet)* traîner les pieds ◆ **to ~ one's feet** *or* **one's heels** *(fig)* traîner les pieds ◆ **she accused the government of ~ging its feet** *or* **heels on reforms** elle a accusé le gouvernement de tarder à introduire des réformes ◆ **the government is ~ging its feet** *or* **heels over introducing new legislation** le gouvernement tarde à mettre en place de nouvelles lois ◆ **to ~ anchor** *(Naut)* chasser sur ses ancres ◆ **to ~ the truth from** *or* **out of sb** finir par faire avouer la vérité à qn ◆ **to ~ ass‡** *(US)* glander‡, traînasser
2 *[+ river, lake etc]* draguer (*for* à la recherche de)
3 *(fig = involve) [+ person]* entraîner ; *[+ issue, question etc]* mêler ◆ **don't ~ me into your affairs!** ne me mêle pas à tes histoires ! ◆ **to ~ politics into sth** mêler la politique à qch
COMP **drag and drop** N *(Comput)* glisser-poser *m*
drag artist N travesti *m*
drag coefficient, drag factor N coefficient *m* de pénétration dans l'air, CX *m*
drag lift N *(Ski)* tire-fesses *m inv*
drag queen* N travelo‡ *m*
drag race N course *f* de dragsters
drag shoe N *(= brake shoe)* sabot *m* or patin *m* (de frein)
drag show* N *(Theat)* spectacle *m* de travestis

► **drag about** VI traîner
VT SEP traîner

► **drag along** VT SEP *[+ person]* entraîner (à contrecœur) ; *[+ toy etc]* tirer ◆ **to ~ o.s. along** se traîner, avancer péniblement

► **drag apart** VT SEP séparer de force

► **drag away** VT SEP arracher (*from* à) emmener de force (*from* de) ◆ **she ~ged him away from the television*** elle l'a arraché de devant* la télévision ◆ **she ~ged him away from his work*** elle l'a arraché à son travail ◆ **if you manage to ~ yourself away from the bar*** si tu arrives à t'arracher du bar*

► **drag down** VT SEP entraîner (en bas) ; *(fig)* ◆ **to ~ sb down to one's own level** rabaisser qn à son niveau ◆ **he was ~ged down by the scandal** le scandale l'a discrédité ◆ **his illness is ~ging him down** sa maladie l'affaiblit

► **drag in** VT SEP *(fig) [+ subject, remark]* tenir à placer, amener à tout prix

► **drag on** VI *[meeting, conversation]* traîner en longueur, s'éterniser ; *[conflict]* s'éterniser

► **drag out** VI ⇒ **drag on**
VT SEP *[+ discussion]* faire traîner

► **drag up** VT SEP 1 *(* pej) [+ child]* élever à la diable ◆ **where were you ~ged up?** d'où tu sors ?*
2 *[+ scandal, story]* remettre sur le tapis, déterrer ◆ **the letter ~ged up painful memories for Rose** la lettre a fait res(s)urgir des souvenirs douloureux pour Rose

draggy* /ˈdrægɪ/ ADJ rasoir* *inv*, barbant*

dragnet /ˈdrægnet/ N 1 *(for fish)* seine *f*, drège *f* ; *(for birds)* tirasse *f* 2 *(fig: by police)* coup *m* de filet

dragoman /ˈdrægəʊmən/ N (pl **-mans**) drogman *m*

dragon /ˈdrægən/ N 1 *(= mythical beast, lizard, fierce person)* dragon *m* 2 *(Mil = armoured tractor)* tracteur *m* blindé

dragonfly /ˈdrægənflaɪ/ N libellule *f*, demoiselle *f*

dragoon /drəˈguːn/ N *(Mil)* dragon *m* VT ◆ **to ~ sb into doing sth** contraindre *or* forcer qn à faire qch ◆ **she had been ~ed into the excursion** on l'avait contrainte *or* forcée à prendre part à l'excursion

dragster /ˈdrægstəʳ/ N dragster *m*

dragstrip /ˈdrægstrɪp/ N piste *f* de vitesse *(pour dragsters)*

dragsville‡ /ˈdrægzvɪl/ N *(US)* ◆ **it's utter ~** c'est chiant‡

dragway /ˈdrægweɪ/ N ⇒ **dragstrip**

drain /dreɪn/ N 1 *(in town)* égout *m* ; *(in house)* canalisation *f* sanitaire, tuyau *m* d'écoulement ; *(on washing machine etc)* tuyau *m* d'écoulement ; *(Agr, Med)* drain *m* ; *(= drain cover) (in street)* bouche *f* d'égout ; *(beside house)* puisard *m* ◆ **~s** *(in town)* égouts *mpl* ; *(in house)* canalisations *fpl* sanitaires ; *(Agr)* drains *mpl* ◆ **open ~** égout *m* à ciel ouvert ◆ **to throw one's money down the ~** *(fig)* jeter son argent par les fenêtres ◆ **to go down the ~** *(fig)* tomber à l'eau* ◆ **all his hopes have gone down the ~** tous ses espoirs ont été anéantis
2 *(fig) (on resources, manpower)* ponction *f* (on sur, dans) ; *(on strength)* épuisement *m* (on de) → **brain**
VT *[+ land, marshes]* drainer, assécher ; *[+ vegetables, dishes]* égoutter ; *[+ mine]* vider, drainer ; *[+ reservoir]* vider ; *[+ boiler]* vidanger ; *(Med) [+ wound]* drainer ◆ **to ~ one's glass** *or* **drink** vider son verre ◆ **~ed weight** *[of canned product]* poids *m* net égoutté ◆ **to ~ sb's energy** épuiser qn ◆ **to ~ a country of resources** ponctionner les ressources d'un pays
VI *[liquid]* s'écouler ; *[stream]* s'écouler (into dans) ; *[energy]* s'épuiser
COMP **draining board** N égouttoir *m*, paillasse *f*
draining spoon N écumoire *f*

► **drain away, drain off** VI *[liquid]* s'écouler ; *[strength]* s'épuiser
VT SEP *[+ liquid]* faire couler *(pour vider un récipient)*

drainage /ˈdreɪnɪdʒ/ N *(= act of draining)* drainage *m*, assèchement *m* ; *(= system of drains) (on land)* système *m* de fossés *or* de tuyaux de drainage ; *[of town]* système *m* d'égouts ; *[of house]* système *m* d'écoulement des eaux ; *(= sewage)* eaux *fpl* usées ; *(Geol)* système *m* hydrographique fluvial
COMP **drainage area, drainage basin** N *(Geol)* bassin *m* hydrographique
drainage channel N *(Constr)* barbacane *f*
drainage tube N *(Med)* drain *m*

drainboard /ˈdreɪnbɔːd/ N *(US)* ⇒ **draining board** ; → **drain**

drainer /ˈdreɪnəʳ/ N égouttoir *m*

drainpipe /ˈdreɪnpaɪp/ N tuyau *m* d'écoulement *or* de drainage

drainpipes /ˈdreɪnpaɪps/, **drainpipe trousers** *(Brit)* NPL pantalon-cigarette *m*

drake /dreɪk/ N canard *m* (mâle) ; → **duck¹**

Dralon ® /ˈdreɪlɒn/ N Dralon ® *m*

DRAM, D-RAM /ˈdiːræm/ *(Comput)* (abbrev of **dynamic random access memory**) (mémoire *f*) DRAM *f*

dram /dræm/ N *(Brit)* 1 *(Measure, Pharm)* drachme *f* 2 *(* = small drink)* goutte *f*, petit verre *m*

drama /ˈdrɑːmə/ N 1 *(NonC: gen)* théâtre *m* ◆ **to study ~** étudier l'art *m* dramatique ◆ **English ~** le théâtre anglais 2 *(= play)* drame *m*, pièce *f* de théâtre ; *(fig)* drame *m* 3 *(NonC = quality of being dramatic)* drame *m*
COMP **drama critic** N critique *m* dramatique
drama-doc* N *(TV)* docudrame *m*
drama queen‡ N *(pej)* ◆ **she's such a ~ queen !** quelle comédienne !, elle fait toujours tout un cinéma ◆ **stop being such a ~ queen** arrête ton cinéma*
drama school N école *f* d'art dramatique
drama student N étudiant(e) *m(f)* en art dramatique

dramatic /drəˈmætɪk/ ADJ 1 *(= striking) [change, increase, fall]* spectaculaire ◆ **there has been a ~ decline in birth rates** il y a eu une baisse spectaculaire du taux de natalité ◆ **a fifth year of drought will have ~ effects on the economy** une cinquième année de sécheresse aura des conséquences graves sur l'économie
2 *(= exciting)* **it was a very ~ moment in my life** ç'a été un moment très important de ma

vie ◆ **Elizabeth was there during the afternoon's ~ events** Elizabeth a assisté aux événements dramatiques de cette après-midi

3 *[art, artist, work]* dramatique ◆ **~ irony** ironie *f* dramatique ; → **amateur**

4 *(= theatrical) [effect, entry, gesture]* théâtral ◆ **to make a ~ exit** faire une sortie théâtrale

> ⚠ When it means 'striking' **dramatic** is not translated by **dramatique**.

dramatically /drəˈmætɪkəlɪ/ ADV 1 *(= spectacularly) [change, improve, worsen, increase, affect, alter]* de façon spectaculaire ; *[different, effective, successful]* extraordinairement 2 *(Literat, Theat) [effective, compelling, powerful]* du point de vue théâtral

> ⚠ **dramatiquement** often means 'tragically'. When used as an intensifier it means 'terribly'.

dramatics /drəˈmætɪks/ NPL 1 *(Theat)* art *m* dramatique 2 *(* = fuss)* comédie *f (fig)* → **amateur**

dramatis personae /ˈdræmətɪspɜːˈsəʊnaɪ/ NPL personnages *mpl (d'une pièce etc)*

dramatist /ˈdræmətɪst/ N auteur *m* dramatique, dramaturge *m*

dramatization /ˌdræmətaɪˈzeɪʃən/ N 1 *(Theat, TV) (for theatre)* adaptation *f* pour la scène ; *(for TV)* adaptation *f* pour la télévision ; *(for cinema)* adaptation *f* cinématographique 2 *(= exaggeration)* dramatisation *f*

dramatize /ˈdræmətaɪz/ VT 1 *[+ novel] (for stage)* adapter pour la scène ; *(for film)* adapter pour le cinéma ; *(for TV)* adapter pour la télévision ◆ **they ~d his life story** *(on TV)* l'histoire de sa vie a été portée à l'écran 2 *(esp US) (= make vivid) [+ event]* rendre dramatique *or* émouvant ; *(= exaggerate)* dramatiser

Drambuie ® /dræmˈbjuːɪ/ N Drambuie ® *m*

drank /dræŋk/ VB pt of **drink**

drape /dreɪp/ VT *[+ window, statue, person]* draper *(with* de) ; *[+ room, altar]* tendre *(with* de) ; *[+ curtain, length of cloth]* draper ◆ **she ~d herself over the settee** * elle s'est allongée langoureusement sur le canapé NPL **drapes** *(Brit = hangings)* tentures *fpl* ; *(US = curtains)* rideaux *mpl*

draper /ˈdreɪpəʳ/ N *(Brit)* marchand(e) *m(f)* de nouveautés

drapery /ˈdreɪpərɪ/ N 1 *(= material)* draperie *f*, étoffes *fpl* ; *(= hangings)* tentures *fpl*, draperies *fpl* 2 *(Brit:* also **draper's shop**) magasin *m* de nouveautés

drastic /ˈdræstɪk/ ADJ *[reform, measures, reduction]* drastique, draconien ; *[remedy]* drastique ; *[surgery, change, improvement]* radical ; *[consequences, decline]* dramatique ; *[increase]* considérable, fort ◆ **to make ~ cuts in defence spending** faire *or* opérer des coupes claires dans le budget de la défense

drastically /ˈdræstɪkəlɪ/ ADV *[cut, increase, reduce]* considérablement, drastiquement ; *[change, improve]* radicalement ; *[increase]* considérablement ◆ **defence spending has been ~ cut** on a fait *or* opéré des coupes claires dans le budget de la défense ◆ **~ different** radicalement différent ◆ **it** *or* **things went ~ wrong** les choses ont très mal tourné

drat * /dræt/ EXCL *(euph = damn)* sapristi ! *, diable ! ◆ **~ the child!** au diable cet enfant !, quelle peste * cet enfant !

dratted * /ˈdrætɪd/ ADJ sacré * *before n*, maudit *before n*

draught, draft *(US)* /drɑːft/ N 1 *(= breeze)* courant *m* d'air ; *(for fire)* tirage *m* ◆ **beer on ~** bière *f* à la pression ◆ **to feel the ~** * *(fig: financially)* devoir se serrer la ceinture * ◆ **I felt a ~** * *(esp US: fig = unfriendliness)* j'ai senti un froid *or* qu'il *etc* me traitait avec froideur 2 *(Naut)* tirant *m* d'eau 3 *(= drink)* coup *m* ; *[of medicine]* potion *f*, breuvage *m* ◆ **a ~ of cider** un coup de cidre ◆ **to take a long ~ of sth** avaler une goulée de qch 4 *(Brit)* **(game of) ~s** (jeu *m* de) dames *fpl* 5 *(= rough sketch)* ⇒ **draft noun 1**
COMP *[animal]* de trait ; *[cider, beer]* à la pression
draught excluder N bourrelet *m (de porte, de fenêtre)*

draughtboard /ˈdrɑːftbɔːd/ N *(Brit)* damier *m*

draughtiness, draftiness *(US)* /ˈdrɑːftɪnɪs/ N *(NonC)* courants *mpl* d'air

draughtproof /ˈdrɑːftpruːf/ ADJ calfeutré VT calfeutrer

draughtproofing /ˈdrɑːftpruːfɪŋ/ N calfeutrage *m*

draughtsman /ˈdrɑːftsmən/ N (pl **-men**) 1 *(Art)* dessinateur *m*, -trice *f* ; *(in drawing office)* dessinateur *m*, -trice *f* industriel(le) 2 *(Brit: in game)* pion *m*

draughtsmanship, draftsmanship *(US)* /ˈdrɑːftsmənʃɪp/ N *[of artist]* talent *m* de dessinateur, coup *m* de crayon ; *(in industry)* art *m* du dessin industriel

draughtswoman, draftswoman *(US)* /ˈdræftswʊmən/ N (pl **-women**) *(Art)* dessinatrice *f* ; *(in drawing office)* dessinatrice *f* industrielle

draughty, drafty *(US)* /ˈdrɑːftɪ/ ADJ *[room]* plein de courants d'air ; *[street corner]* exposé à tous les vents *or* aux quatre vents

draw /drɔː/ (pret **drew**, ptp **drawn**) VT 1 *(= pull: gen) [+ object, cord, string, bolt]* tirer ◆ **to ~ a bow** bander un arc ◆ **to ~ the curtains** *(= open)* tirer *or* ouvrir les rideaux ; *(= shut)* tirer *or* fermer les rideaux ◆ **to ~ one's hand over one's eyes** se passer la main sur les yeux ◆ **I drew her arm through mine** j'ai passé *or* glissé son bras sous le mien ◆ **he drew a hand through his hair** il s'est passé la main dans les cheveux ◆ **he drew his chair nearer the fire** il a rapproché sa chaise du feu ◆ **he drew her close to him** il l'a attirée contre lui ◆ **to ~ one's finger along a surface** passer le doigt sur une surface ◆ **to ~ one's belt tighter** serrer sa ceinture ◆ **to ~ smoke into one's lungs** avaler *or* inhaler la fumée *(d'une cigarette)* ◆ **to ~ an abscess** *(Med)* faire mûrir un abcès ◆ **to ~ a bead on sth** *(= aim)* viser qch

2 *(= pull behind) [+ coach, cart, train, trailer etc]* tracter

3 *(= extract, remove) [+ teeth]* extraire, arracher ; *[+ cork]* retirer, enlever ◆ **it was like ~ing teeth** ç'a été la croix et la bannière ◆ **to ~ threads** *(Sewing)* tirer des fils ◆ **to ~ a ticket out of a hat** tirer un billet d'un chapeau ◆ **to ~ one's gun** dégainer son pistolet ◆ **he drew a gun on me** il a sorti un pistolet et l'a braqué sur moi ◆ **to ~ the sword** *(fig)* passer à l'attaque

4 *(= obtain from source) [+ wine]* tirer *(from* de) ; *[+ water] (from tap, pump)* tirer *(from* de) ; *(from well)* puiser *(from* dans) ◆ **to ~ blood from sb** *(Med)* faire une prise de sang à qn ◆ **the stone hit him and drew blood** la pierre l'a frappé et l'a fait saigner ◆ **that remark drew blood** cette remarque blessante a porté ◆ **to ~ a bath** † faire couler un bain ◆ **to ~ (a) breath** aspirer, respirer ; *(fig)* souffler ◆ **to ~ a card from the pack** tirer une carte du jeu ◆ **to ~ trumps** *(Cards)* choisir l'atout ◆ **to ~ the first prize** gagner *or* décrocher le gros lot ◆ **to ~ inspiration from** tirer son inspiration de, puiser son inspiration dans ◆ **to ~ strength from sth** puiser des forces dans qch ◆ **to ~ comfort from sth** trouver un réconfort dans qch ◆ **to ~ a smile from sb** arracher un sourire à qn ◆ **to ~ a laugh from sb** arriver à faire rire qn ◆ **her performance drew tears from the audience** son interprétation a arraché des larmes au public ◆ **her performance drew applause from the audience** son interprétation a été saluée par les applaudissements du public ◆ **I could ~ no reply from him** je n'ai pu tirer de lui aucune réponse ; → **blank**

5 *(Fin)* ◆ **to ~ money from the bank** retirer de l'argent à la banque ◆ **to ~ a cheque on one's account** tirer un chèque sur son compte ◆ **to ~ one's salary** *or* **pay** toucher son salaire ◆ **to ~ one's pension** toucher sa pension

6 *(= attract) [+ attention, customer, crowd]* attirer ◆ **the play has ~n a lot of criticism** la pièce a donné lieu à *or* s'est attiré de nombreuses critiques ◆ **to feel ~n to(wards) sb** se sentir attiré par qn

7 *(= cause to move, do, speak etc)* **her shouts drew me to the scene** ses cris m'ont attiré sur les lieux ◆ **to ~ sb into a plan** entraîner qn dans un projet ◆ **he refuses to be ~n** *(= will not speak)* il refuse de parler ; *(= will not react)* il refuse de se laisser provoquer *or* de réagir ◆ **he would not be ~n on the matter** il a refusé de parler de cette affaire ◆ **to ~ sth to a close** *or* **an end** mettre fin à qch

8 *[+ picture]* dessiner ; *[+ plan, line, circle]* tracer ; *(fig) [+ situation]* faire un tableau de ; *[+ character]* peindre, dépeindre ◆ **to ~ sb's portrait** faire le portrait de qn ◆ **to ~ a map** *(Geog)* dresser une carte ; *(Scol)* faire *or* dessiner une carte ◆ **I ~ the line at scrubbing floors** * je n'irai pas jusqu'à *or* je me refuse à frotter les parquets ◆ **I ~ the line at cheating** * *(myself)* je n'irai pas jusqu'à *or* je me refuse à tricher ; *(in others)* je n'admets pas *or* je ne tolère pas que l'on triche ◆ **we must ~ the line somewhere** il faut se fixer une limite, il y a une limite à tout ◆ **it's hard to know where to ~ the line** il est difficile de savoir où s'arrêter

9 *(= establish, formulate) [+ conclusion]* tirer *(from* de) ; *[+ comparison, parallel, distinction]* établir, faire *(between* entre)

10 *(Naut)* **the boat ~s 4 metres** le bateau a un tirant d'eau de 4 mètres, le bateau cale 4 mètres ◆ **to ~ water** *(= leak)* prendre l'eau

11 *(Sport)* ◆ **to ~ a match** faire match nul ; *(Chess)* faire partie nulle ◆ **they drew one-one** ils ont fait match nul un à un *or* un partout ◆ **Aston Villa have ~n a Czech team in the UEFA Cup** le tirage au sort de la coupe UEFA a désigné une équipe tchèque pour jouer contre Aston Villa

12 *(= infuse) [+ tea]* faire infuser

13 *(Culin) [+ fowl]* vider ; → **hang**

14 *(Hunting)* **to ~ a fox** débusquer *or* lancer un renard

15 *[+ metal]* étirer ; *[+ wire]* tréfiler

VI 1 *(= move, come) [person]* se diriger *(towards* vers) ◆ **to ~ to one side** s'écarter ◆ **to ~ round the table** se rassembler *or* s'assembler autour de la table ◆ **the train drew into the station** le train est entré en gare ◆ **the car drew over towards the centre of the road** la voiture a dévié vers le milieu de la chaussée ◆ **he drew ahead of the other runners** il s'est détaché des autres coureurs ◆ **the two horses drew level** les deux chevaux sont parvenus à la même hauteur ◆ **to ~ near** *[person]* s'approcher *(to* de) ; *[time, event]* approcher ◆ **to ~ nearer (to)** s'approcher un peu plus (de) ◆ **to ~ to an end** *or* **a close** tirer à *or* toucher à sa fin

2 *[chimney, pipe]* tirer ; *[pump, vacuum cleaner]* aspirer

3 *(= be equal) [two teams]* faire match nul ; *(in exams, competitions)* être ex æquo *inv* ◆ **the competitors/the teams drew for second place** les concurrents/les équipes sont arrivé(e)s deuxièmes ex æquo *or* ont remporté la deuxième place ex æquo ◆ **Scotland drew with Ireland** l'Écosse a fait match nul contre l'Irlande

4 *(Cards)* **to ~ for partners** tirer pour les partenaires

5 *(Art)* dessiner ◆ **he ~s well** il dessine bien, il sait bien dessiner ◆ **to ~ from life** dessiner d'après nature

6 *[tea]* infuser

N 1 *(= lottery)* loterie *f*, tombola *f* ; *(= act of drawing a lottery)* tirage *m* ◆ **the ~ is at three o'clock** le tirage est à trois heures ◆ **the ~ for the quarter-finals will take place this morning** *(Sport)* le tirage au sort pour les quarts de finale aura lieu ce matin ; → **luck**

2 *(Sport)* match *m* nul ◆ **the match ended in a ~** le match s'est terminé par un match nul ◆ **five wins and two ~s** cinq victoires et deux (matchs) nuls ◆ **we can get at least a ~ against Holland** nous pouvons au moins faire match nul contre la Hollande

3 *(= attraction)* attraction *f*, succès *m* ; *(Comm)* réclame *f* ◆ **Mel Gibson was the big ~** Mel Gibson était la grande attraction ◆ **the pay was the big ~ of the job** le salaire était l'élément le plus intéressant dans ce travail

4 ◆ **to beat sb to the ~** *(lit)* dégainer plus vite que qn ; *(fig)* devancer qn ◆ **to be quick on the ~** *(lit)* dégainer vite ; *(* fig)* avoir la repartie *or* répartie facile

5 *(Drugs ‡ = hash)* herbe * *f*

COMP **draw poker** N sorte de jeu de poker

draw-sheet N alaise *f*

draw(-top) table N table *f* à rallonge

► **draw along** VT SEP *[+ cart]* tirer, traîner ; *(fig)* *[+ person]* entraîner

► **draw apart** VI s'éloigner *or* s'écarter l'un de l'autre

► **draw aside** VI *[people]* s'écarter

VT SEP *[+ person]* prendre à part ; *[+ object]* écarter

► **draw away** VI 1 *[person]* s'éloigner, s'écarter *(from* de) ; *[car etc]* démarrer ◆ **to ~ away from the kerb** s'éloigner du trottoir

2 *(= move ahead)* *[runner, racehorse etc]* se détacher *(from* de)

VT SEP *[+ person]* éloigner, emmener ; *[+ object]* retirer, ôter

► **draw back** VI *(= move backwards)* (se) reculer, s'écarter *(from* de) faire un mouvement en arrière ; *(fig)* se retirer, reculer *(at, before, from* devant)

VT SEP *[+ person]* faire reculer ; *[+ object, one's hand]* retirer

► **draw down** VT SEP *[+ blind]* baisser ; *(fig)* *[+ blame, ridicule]* attirer *(on* sur)

► **draw in** VI 1 *(in car)* **to ~ in by the kerb** *(= pull over)* se rapprocher du trottoir ; *(= stop)* s'arrêter le long du trottoir

2 *(Brit)* **the days** *or* **nights are ~ing in** *(= get shorter)* les jours raccourcissent

VT SEP 1 *[+ air]* aspirer, respirer

2 *(= attract)* *[+ crowds]* attirer ◆ **the play is ~ing in huge returns** la pièce fait des recettes énormes ◆ **to ~ sb in on a project** *(fig)* recruter qn pour un projet

3 *(= pull in)* rentrer ; *[+ reins]* tirer sur ◆ **to ~ in one's claws** *(gen, also fig)* rentrer ses griffes ; *[cat]* faire patte de velours ; → **horn**

► **draw off** VI *[army, troops]* se retirer

VT SEP 1 *[+ gloves, garment]* retirer, enlever

2 *[+ beer etc]* *(from keg)* tirer ; *(Med)* *[+ blood]* prendre

► **draw on** VI *[time]* avancer

VT SEP 1 *[+ stockings, gloves, garment]* enfiler ; *[+ shoes]* mettre

2 *(fig = encourage)* *[+ person]* entraîner, encourager

VT FUS 1 ⇒ **draw upon**

2 ◆ **he drew on his cigarette** il a tiré sur sa cigarette

► **draw out** VI *(= become longer)* ◆ **the days are ~ing out** les jours rallongent

VT SEP 1 *(= bring out, remove)* *[+ handkerchief, purse]* sortir, tirer *(from* de) ; *[+ money]* *(from bank etc)* retirer *(from* à, de) ; *[+ secret, plan]* soutirer *(from* à) ; *(fig)* *[+ person]* faire parler ◆ **he's shy, try and ~ him out (of his shell)** il est timide, essayez de le faire sortir de sa coquille

2 *(= stretch, extend)* *[+ wire]* étirer ; *(fig)* *[+ speech, meeting]* prolonger ; *[+ meal]* prolonger

► **draw up** VI *(= stop)* *[car etc]* s'arrêter, stopper

VT SEP 1 *[+ chair]* approcher ; *[+ troops]* aligner, ranger ; *[+ boat]* tirer à sec ◆ **to ~ o.s. up (to one's full height)** se dresser de toute sa hauteur

2 *(= formulate, set out)* *[+ inventory]* dresser ; *[+ list, contract, agreement]* dresser, rédiger ; *[+ plan, scheme]* formuler, établir ; *(Fin)* *[+ bill]* établir, dresser

► **draw upon** VT FUS ◆ **to draw upon one's savings** prendre *or* tirer sur ses économies ◆ **to ~ upon one's imagination** faire appel à son imagination

drawback /ˈdrɔːbæk/ N 1 *(= disadvantage)* inconvénient *m*, désavantage *m* *(to* à) 2 *(Tax = refund)* drawback *m*

drawbridge /ˈdrɔːbrɪdʒ/ N pont-levis *m*, pont *m* basculant *or* à bascule

drawee /drɔːˈiː/ N *(Fin)* tiré *m*

drawer¹ /drɔːʳ/ N *[of furniture]* tiroir *m* ; → **bottom, chest¹**

drawer² /ˈdrɔːəʳ/ N 1 *[of cheque etc]* tireur *m* 2 *(Art)* *[of pictures]* dessinateur *m*, -trice *f*

drawers † /drɔːz/ NPL *[of men]* caleçon *m* ; *[of women]* culotte *f*, pantalon(s) † *m(pl)*

drawing /ˈdrɔːɪŋ/ N 1 *(Art)* dessin *m* ◆ **a pencil ~** un dessin au crayon ◆ **a chalk ~** un pastel ◆ **rough ~** esquisse *f* 2 *(NonC = extending, tapering)* *[of metals]* étirage *m*

COMP **drawing account** N *(US)* compte *m* courant

drawing board N planche *f* à dessin ◆ **the scheme is still on the ~ board** le projet est encore à l'étude ◆ **back to the ~ board!** retour à la case départ !

drawing office N *(Brit)* bureau *m* de dessin industriel

drawing paper N *(Art)* papier *m* à dessin

drawing pen N *(Art)* tire-ligne *m*

drawing pin N *(Brit)* punaise *f*

drawing room N salon *m* ; *(larger)* salle *f* *or* salon *m* de réception

drawl /drɔːl/ VI parler d'une voix traînante VT dire *or* prononcer d'une voix traînante N voix *f* traînante ◆ **with a Southern/an aristocratic ~** avec la voix traînante des gens du Sud des États-Unis/des aristocrates ◆ **... he said with a ~** ... dit-il d'une voix traînante

drawn /drɔːn/ VB ptp of **draw** ; see also **long¹**

ADJ 1 *[curtains, blinds]* tiré 2 *(= unsheathed)* *[sword, dagger]* dégainé ◆ **pictures of dragons charging with ~ sword** des images de dragons chargeant sabre au clair ◆ **the police waited with ~ truncheons** *or* **with truncheons ~** les policiers attendaient, matraque en main ; → **dagger** 3 *(= haggard)* *[features]* tiré ; *[person, face]* aux traits tirés ◆ **to look ~** avoir les traits tirés ◆ **face ~ with pain** visage *m* crispé par la douleur 4 *(Sport = equal)* *[match]* nul

COMP **drawn butter** N *(Culin)* beurre *m* fondu

drawn-thread work, drawn work N *(Sewing)* ouvrage *m* à fils tirés *or* à jour(s)

drawstring /ˈdrɔːstrɪŋ/ N cordon *m*

dray /dreɪ/ N *[of brewer]* haquet *m* ; *[of wood, stones]* fardier *m* ; *[of quarry work]* binard *m*

dread /dred/ VT redouter, appréhender ◆ **to ~ doing sth** redouter de faire qch ◆ **to ~ that ...** redouter que ... ne + *subj* ◆ **I ~ to think what goes on in schools these days** je n'ose pas imaginer ce qui se passe dans les écoles de nos jours ◆ **the ~ed Mrs Mitch** la redoutable Mme Mitch ◆ **the ~ed exam/medicine** *(hum)* l'examen/le médicament tant redouté *(hum)* N terreur *f*, effroi *m* ◆ **in ~ of doing sth** dans la crainte de faire qch ◆ **to be** *or* **stand in ~ of sth** redouter qch, vivre dans la crainte de qch ADJ *(liter)* redoutable, terrible

dreadful /ˈdredfʊl/ ADJ 1 *(= horrible, appalling)* *[crime, sight, suffering]* affreux, atroce ; *[disease]* affreux, horrible ; *[weapon]* redoutable ◆ **a ~ mistake** une erreur terrible ◆ **a ~ waste** un gaspillage épouvantable ◆ **he's a ~ coward!** qu'est-ce qu'il peut être lâche ! ◆ **what a ~ thing to happen!** quelle horreur !

2 *(= bad)* *[person, place, moment, situation, weather conditions]* affreux ; *[food]* épouvantable ; *[film, book, play etc]* lamentable ; *[child]* insupportable ◆ **you look ~!** *(= ill, tired)* tu n'as pas l'air bien du tout ! ◆ **you look ~ (in that hat/with that haircut)!** *(= unattractive)* tu es vraiment moche (avec ce chapeau/avec cette coupe de cheveux) ! ◆ **I feel ~!** *(= ill)* je ne me sens pas bien du tout ! ◆ **I feel ~ (about it)!** *(= guilty)* je m'en veux ! ◆ **I feel ~ about John/about what has happened** je m'en veux de ce qui est arrivé à John/de ce qui s'est passé ; → **penny**

dreadfully /ˈdredfəlɪ/ ADV 1 *(= badly)* *[behave, treat sb]* de façon abominable ; *[suffer]* affreusement, atrocement ◆ **I miss him ~** il me manque terriblement ◆ **I had a feeling that something was ~ wrong** j'ai senti que quelque chose de terrible venait de se passer 2 *(* = very)* *[boring, late etc]* affreusement ◆ **I'm ~ sorry** je suis terriblement désolé

dreadlocked /ˈdredlɒkt/ ADJ portant des dreadlocks

dreadlocks /ˈdred,lɒks/ NPL dreadlocks *fpl*

dreadnought /ˈdrednɔːt/ N *(Naut)* cuirassé *m* (d'escadre)

dream /driːm/ LANGUAGE IN USE 8.4 (vb : pret, ptp **dreamed** *or* **dreamt)**

N 1 rêve *m* ◆ **to have a ~ about sb/sth** rêver de qn/qch ◆ **I've had a bad ~** j'ai fait un mauvais rêve *or* un cauchemar ◆ **the whole business was (like) a bad ~** c'était un vrai cauchemar ◆ **sweet ~s!** fais de beaux rêves ! ◆ **to see sth in a ~** voir qch en rêve ◆ **life is but a ~** la vie n'est qu'un songe

2 *(when awake)* ◆ **to be in a ~ *** *(= not paying attention)* être dans les nuages *or* la lune ; *(= daydreaming)* rêvasser

3 *(= fantasy)* rêve *m* ◆ **the man/woman/house of my ~s** l'homme/la femme/la maison de mes rêves ◆ **my ~ is to have a house in the country** mon rêve serait d'avoir une maison à la campagne ◆ **his fondest ~ was to see her again** son vœu le plus cher était de la revoir ◆ **to have ~s of doing sth** rêver de faire qch ◆ **it was like a ~ come true** c'était le rêve ◆ **to make a ~ come true for sb** réaliser le rêve de qn ◆ **in your ~s!** * tu peux toujours rêver ! * ◆ **all his ~s came true** tous ses rêves se sont réalisés ◆ **idle ~s** rêvasseries *fpl* ◆ **rich beyond his wildest ~s** plus riche que dans ses rêves les plus fous ◆ **she achieved success beyond her wildest ~s** son succès a dépassé ses espoirs les plus fous ◆ **never in my wildest ~s would I have thought that ...** jamais, même dans mes rêves les plus fous, je n'aurais imaginé que ... ◆ **everything went like a ~ *** tout est allé comme sur des roulettes *

4 * *(= lovely person)* amour * *m* ; *(= lovely thing)* merveille *f* ◆ **isn't he a ~?** n'est-ce pas qu'il est adorable *or* que c'est un amour ? ◆ **a ~ of a dress** une robe de rêve

ADJ ◆ **a ~ house** une maison de rêve ◆ **his ~ house** la maison de ses rêves

VI 1 *(in sleep)* rêver ◆ **to ~ about** *or* **of sb/sth** rêver de qn/qch ◆ **to ~ about** *or* **of doing sth** rêver qu'on a fait qch ◆ **~ on!** * tu peux toujours rêver ! *

2 *(when awake)* rêvasser, être dans les nuages *or* la lune
3 *(= imagine, envisage)* songer *(of* à) avoir l'idée *(of* de) ◆ **I would never have dreamt of doing such a thing** je n'aurais jamais songé à *or* eu l'idée de faire une chose pareille ◆ **I wouldn't ~ of telling her!** jamais il ne me viendrait à l'idée de lui dire cela ! ◆ **will you come? – I wouldn't ~ of it!** vous allez venir ? – jamais de la vie *or* pas question ! ◆ **I wouldn't ~ of making fun of you** il ne me viendrait jamais à l'idée de me moquer de vous
VT 1 *(in sleep)* rêver, voir en rêve ◆ **to ~ a dream** faire un rêve ◆ **I dreamt that she came** j'ai rêvé qu'elle venait ◆ **you must have dreamt it!** vous avez dû (le) rêver !
2 *(= imagine)* imaginer ◆ **if I had dreamt you would do that ...** si j'avais pu imaginer un instant que tu ferais cela ... ◆ **I didn't ~ he would come!** je n'ai jamais songé *or* imaginé un instant qu'il viendrait !
COMP **dream team** * N équipe *f* de rêve
dream ticket * N *(esp Pol)* équipe *f* de rêve
dream world N *(ideal)* monde *m* utopique ; *(imagination)* monde *m* imaginaire ◆ **he lives in a ~ world** il est complètement détaché des réalités

► **dream away** VT SEP *[+ time]* perdre en rêveries ◆ **to ~ one's life away** passer sa vie à rêvasser

► **dream up** * VT SEP *[+ idea]* imaginer, concevoir ◆ **where did you ~ that up?** où est-ce que vous êtes allé pêcher cela ? *

dreamboat * /ˈdriːmbəʊt/ N ◆ **he's a ~** il est beau comme un dieu

dreamer /ˈdriːməʳ/ N 1 *(lit)* rêveur *m*, -euse *f* 2 *(fig)* rêveur *m*, -euse *f*, songe-creux *m inv* ; *(politically)* utopiste *mf*

dreamily /ˈdriːmɪlɪ/ ADV *[say]* d'un ton rêveur ; *[smile, sigh, look]* d'un air rêveur

dreamland /ˈdriːmlænd/ N pays *m* des rêves *or* des songes ; *(= beautiful place)* pays *m* de rêve

dreamless /ˈdriːmlɪs/ ADJ sans rêves

dreamlike /ˈdriːmlaɪk/ ADJ onirique

dreamt /dremt/ VB pt, ptp of **dream**

dreamtime /ˈdriːmtaɪm/ N *(Austral)* temps *m* du rêve

dreamy /ˈdriːmɪ/ ADJ 1 *(= relaxed, otherworldly) [smile, look, expression]* rêveur ; *[voice, music]* doux (douce *f*), qui fait rêver 2 *(* pej = impractical, idealistic)* rêveur, dans la lune *or* les nuages 3 *(* = wonderful) [house, car, dress]* de rêve ◆ **he's ~!** il est tellement séduisant !

drearily /ˈdrɪərɪlɪ/ ADV *[speak]* d'un ton morne ; *[dress]* de façon terne ◆ **it was a ~ familiar scenario** c'était un scénario trop connu

dreariness /ˈdrɪərɪnɪs/ N *[of surroundings, life]* grisaille *f*, monotonie *f* ; *[of weather]* grisaille *f*

dreary /ˈdrɪərɪ/ ADJ *[place, landscape]* morne ; *[job, work, life]* monotone ; *[day, person]* ennuyeux ; *[weather]* maussade

dredge[1] /dredʒ/ N *(= net, vessel)* drague *f* VT *[+ river, mud]* draguer VI draguer

► **dredge up** VT SEP 1 *(lit)* draguer 2 *(fig) [+ unpleasant facts]* déterrer, ressortir

dredge[2] /dredʒ/ VT *(Culin)* saupoudrer *(with* de ; *on to, over* sur)

dredger[1] /ˈdredʒəʳ/ N *(Naut) (= ship)* dragueur *m* ; *(= machine)* drague *f*

dredger[2] /ˈdredʒəʳ/ N *(Culin)* saupoudreuse *f*, saupoudroir *m*

dredging[1] /ˈdredʒɪŋ/ N *(Naut)* dragage *m*

dredging[2] /ˈdredʒɪŋ/ N *(Culin)* saupoudrage *m*

dregs /dregz/ NPL *(lit, fig)* lie *f* ◆ **the ~ of society** la lie de la société

drench /drentʃ/ VT 1 tremper ◆ **to be ~ed in blood** être baigné de sang ◆ **to be ~ed in sweat** être trempé de sueur, être en nage ◆ **to get ~ed to the skin** se faire tremper jusqu'aux os, se faire saucer * ; → **sun** 2 *(= give medicine to) [+ animal]* administrer *or* faire avaler un médicament à N *(= animal's medicine)* (dose *f* de) médicament *m (pour un animal)*

drenching /ˈdrentʃɪŋ/ N ◆ **to get a ~** se faire tremper *or* saucer * ADJ ◆ **~ rain** pluie *f* battante *or* diluvienne

Dresden /ˈdrezdən/ N 1 *(Geog)* Dresde 2 (also **Dresden china**) porcelaine *f* de Saxe, saxe *m* ◆ **a piece of ~** un saxe

dress /dres/ N 1 robe *f* ◆ **a long/silk/summer ~** une robe longue/de soie/d'été ; → **cocktail, wedding**
2 *(NonC = clothing, way of dressing)* tenue *f* ◆ **articles of ~** vêtements *mpl* ◆ **in eastern/traditional ~** en tenue orientale/traditionnelle ◆ **to be careless in one's ~** avoir une tenue négligée ◆ **he's always very careful in his ~** il s'habille toujours avec beaucoup de recherche, il est toujours élégamment vêtu ; → **evening, full, national**
VT 1 *(= clothe) [+ child, family, recruits, customer]* habiller ◆ **to get ~ed** s'habiller ◆ **he's old enough to ~ himself** *[child]* il est assez grand pour s'habiller tout seul ; see also **dressed**
2 *(Theat) [+ play]* costumer
3 *(= arrange, decorate) [+ gown]* parer, orner ; *(Naut) [+ ship]* pavoiser ◆ **to ~ a shop window** faire la vitrine ◆ **to ~ sb's hair** coiffer qn
4 *(Culin) [+ salad]* assaisonner ; *[+ chicken, crab, game]* préparer
5 *[+ skins]* préparer, apprêter ; *[+ material]* apprêter ; *[+ leather]* corroyer ; *[+ timber]* dégrossir ; *[+ stone]* tailler, dresser
6 *(Agr) [+ field]* façonner
7 *[+ troops]* aligner
8 *[+ wound]* panser ◆ **to ~ sb's wound** panser la blessure de qn
VI 1 s'habiller ◆ **to ~ in black** s'habiller en noir ◆ **to ~ in jeans** porter des jeans ◆ **to ~ as a man** s'habiller en homme ◆ **she ~es very well** elle s'habille avec goût ◆ **to ~ for dinner** se mettre en tenue de soirée ; see also **dressed**
2 *[soldiers]* s'aligner ◆ **right ~!** à droite, alignement !
COMP **dress circle** N *(Theat)* premier balcon *m*, corbeille *f*
dress coat N habit *m*, queue-de-pie *f*
dress code N code *m* vestimentaire
dress designer N couturier *m*
dress length N *(of material)* hauteur *f* (de robe)
dress parade N *(US Mil)* défilé *m* en grande tenue
dress rehearsal N *(Theat)* (répétition *f*) générale *f* ; *(fig)* répétition *f* générale
dress sense N ◆ **he has no ~ sense at all** il ne sait absolument pas s'habiller ◆ **her ~ sense is appalling** elle s'habille d'une façon épouvantable
dress shield N dessous-de-bras *m*
dress shirt N chemise *f* de soirée
dress suit N tenue *f* de soirée
dress uniform N *(Mil)* tenue *f* de cérémonie ; see also **dressed**

► **dress down** VT SEP 1 (* = *scold*) passer un savon à *
2 *[+ horse]* panser
VI *(Brit)* s'habiller décontracté
N ◆ **dressing-down** * → **dressing**
COMP **dress-down day** N *(Comm) jour où le personnel peut s'habiller de manière plus décontractée*

► **dress up** VI 1 *(= put on smart clothes)* se mettre sur son trente et un, s'habiller ◆ **there's no need to ~ up** * il n'y a pas besoin de se mettre sur son trente et un ; see also **dressed**
2 *(= put on fancy dress)* se déguiser ◆ **to ~ up as ...** se déguiser *or* se costumer en ... ◆ **the children love ~ing up** les enfants adorent se déguiser
VT SEP 1 *(= disguise)* déguiser *(as* en)
2 ◆ **it dresses up the skirt** cela rend la jupe plus habillée

dressage /ˈdresɑːʒ/ N dressage *m*

dressed /drest/ ADJ habillé ◆ **casually ~** habillé de façon décontractée ◆ **fully ~** entièrement habillé ◆ **smartly ~** vêtu avec élégance, élégamment vêtu ◆ **well-~** bien habillé ◆ **~ in a suit/in white** vêtu d'un costume/de blanc ◆ **to be ~ for the country/for town/for jogging/for gardening** être habillé pour la campagne/pour la ville/pour faire du jogging/pour jardiner ◆ **~ as a man/a cowboy/an astronaut** *etc* habillé en homme/cow-boy/astronaute *etc* ◆ **to be ~ up to the nines** * *(Brit)*, **to be all ~ up** * être sur son trente et un * ◆ **all ~ up and nowhere to go** * *(hum)* fringué(e) * comme un prince (*or* une princesse) et tout ça pour rien ◆ **she was ~ to kill** * elle était superbement habillée, prête à faire des ravages ; see also **dress**
COMP **dressed crab** N crabe *m* tout préparé

dresser[1] /ˈdresəʳ/ N 1 *(Theat)* habilleur *m*, -euse *f* ; *(Comm:* also **window dresser**) étalagiste *mf* 2 ◆ **she's a stylish ~** elle s'habille avec chic ; → **hairdresser** 3 *(= tool) (for wood)* raboteuse *f* ; *(for stone)* rabotin *m*

dresser[2] /ˈdresəʳ/ N 1 *(= furniture)* buffet *m*, vaisselier *m* 2 *(US)* ⇒ **dressing table** ; → **dressing**

dressing /ˈdresɪŋ/ N 1 *(= providing with clothes)* habillement *m* ◆ **~ always takes me a long time** je mets beaucoup de temps à m'habiller ; → **hairdressing**
2 *(Med)* pansement *m*
3 *(Culin) (= presentation)* présentation *f* ; *(= seasoning)* assaisonnement *m*, sauce *f* ; *(= stuffing)* farce *f* ◆ **oil and vinegar ~** vinaigrette *f* ; → **salad**
4 *(= manure)* engrais *m*, fumages *mpl*
5 *(for material, leather)* apprêt *m*
6 *(Constr)* parement *m*
COMP **dressing case** N nécessaire *m* de toilette, trousse *f* de toilette *or* de voyage
dressing-down * N ◆ **to give sb a ~-down** passer un savon à qn * ◆ **to get a ~-down** recevoir *or* se faire passer un savon *, se faire enguirlander *
dressing gown N *(Brit)* robe *f* de chambre ; *(made of towelling)* peignoir *m* ; *(= negligée)* déshabillé *m*
dressing room N *(in house)* dressing (-room) *m* ; *(Theat)* loge *f* ; *(US: in shop)* cabine *f* d'essayage
dressing station N *(Mil)* poste *m* de secours
dressing table N coiffeuse *f*
dressing table set N accessoires *mpl* pour coiffeuse
dressing-up N déguisement *m*

dressmaker /ˈdresmeɪkəʳ/ N couturière *f*

dressmaking /ˈdresmeɪkɪŋ/ N couture *f*

dressy * /ˈdresɪ/ ADJ chic

drew /druː/ VB pt of **draw**

drey /dreɪ/ N nid *m* (d'écureuil)

dribble /ˈdrɪbl/ VI 1 *[liquid]* tomber goutte à goutte, couler lentement ; *[baby]* baver ◆ **to ~ back/in** *etc [people]* revenir/entrer *etc* par petits groupes *or* un par un 2 *(Sport)* dribbler VT 1 *(Sport) [+ ball]* dribbler 2 ◆ **he ~d his milk all down his chin** son lait lui dégoulinait le long du menton N 1 *[of water]* petite goutte *f* 2 *(Sport)* dribble *m*

dribbler /ˈdrɪbləʳ/ N *(Sport)* dribbleur *m*

driblet /ˈdrɪblɪt/ N *[of liquid]* gouttelette *f* ◆ **in ~s** *(lit)* goutte à goutte ; *(fig)* au compte-gouttes

dribs and drabs /ˈdrɪbzənˈdræbz/ NPL petites quantités *fpl* ◆ **in ~** *(gen)* petit à petit, peu à peu ; *[arrive]* en *or* par petits groupes ; *[pay, give]* au compte-gouttes

dried /draɪd/ VB pt, ptp of **dry** ADJ *[flowers, mushrooms, onions, tomatoes]* séché ; *[beans]* sec (sèche *f*) ; *[eggs, milk, yeast]* en poudre ◆ **~ fruit** fruits *mpl* secs

COMP **dried out** * ADJ *[alcoholic]* désintoxiqué
dried-up ADJ *(= dry) [food]* ratatiné ; *[river-bed, stream, oasis]* desséché ; *[well, spring]* tari ; *(= wizened) [person]* ratatiné ◆ **a little ~-up old man** un petit vieillard ratatiné

drier /ˈdraɪəʳ/ N ⇒ **dryer**

drift /drɪft/ VI 1 *(on sea, river etc)* aller à la dérive, dériver ; *(in wind/current)* être poussé *or* emporté (par le vent/le courant) ; *[plane]* dériver ; *[snow, sand etc]* s'amonceler, s'entasser ; *[sounds]* se faire entendre ◆ **to ~ downstream** descendre la rivière emporté par le courant ◆ **to ~ away/out/back** *etc [person]* partir/sortir/revenir *etc* d'une allure nonchalante ◆ **he was ~ing aimlessly about** il flânait (sans but), il déambulait

2 *(fig) [person]* se laisser aller, aller à la dérive ; *[events]* tendre *(towards* vers) ◆ **to let things ~** laisser les choses aller à la dérive *or* à vau-l'eau ◆ **he ~ed into marriage** il s'est retrouvé marié ◆ **to ~ into crime** sombrer peu à peu dans la délinquance ◆ **to ~ from job to job** aller d'un travail à un autre ◆ **the nation was ~ing towards a crisis** le pays allait vers la crise

3 *(Rad)* se décaler

N 1 *(NonC) (= driving movement or force)* mouvement *m*, force *f* ; *[of air, water current]* poussée *f* ◆ **the ~ of the current** *(= speed)* la vitesse du courant ; *(= direction)* le sens *or* la direction du courant ◆ **carried north by the ~ of the current** emporté vers le nord par le courant ◆ **the ~ towards the cities** le mouvement vers les villes ◆ **the ~ of events** le cours *or* la tournure des événements

2 *(= mass) [of clouds]* traînée *f* ; *[of dust]* nuage *m* ; *[of falling snow]* rafale *f* ; *[of fallen snow]* congère *f*, amoncellement *m* ; *[of sand, leaves]* amoncellement *m* ; *(Geol = deposits)* apports *mpl*

3 *(NonC) (= act of drifting) [of ships, aircraft]* dérive *f*, dérivation *f* ; *[of projectile]* déviation *f*, dérivation *f* ; *(= deviation from course)* dérive *f* ; *(Ling)* évolution *f* (de la langue) ◆ **continental ~** dérive *f* des continents

4 *(* = general meaning)* ◆ **to get** *or* **catch** *or* **follow sb's ~** comprendre où qn veut en venir, comprendre le sens général des paroles de qn ◆ **(you) get my ~?** tu as pigé ? *, tu vois ce que je veux dire ?

5 *(Min)* galerie *f* chassante

COMP **drift anchor** N ancre *f* flottante
drift ice, drifting ice N glaces *fpl* flottantes
drift net N filet *m* dérivant, traîne *f*

► **drift apart** VI *(fig)* s'éloigner l'un de l'autre

► **drift off** VI *(fig = fall asleep)* se laisser gagner par le sommeil

drifter /ˈdrɪftəʳ/ N 1 *(= boat)* chalutier *m*, drifter *m* 2 *(= person)* personne *f* qui se laisse aller *or* qui n'a pas de but dans la vie ◆ **he's a bit of a ~** il manque un peu de stabilité

driftwood /ˈdrɪftwʊd/ N bois *m* flotté

drill¹ /drɪl/ N *(for metal, wood)* foret *m*, mèche *f* ; *(for oil well)* trépan *m* ; *(for DIY)* perceuse *f* ; *(Min)* perforatrice *f*, foreuse *f* ; *(for roads)* marteau-piqueur *m* ; *[of dentist]* roulette *f*, fraise *f* (de dentiste) ◆ **electric (hand) ~** perceuse *f* électrique ; → **pneumatic** VT *[+ wood, metal]* forer, percer ; *[+ tooth]* fraiser ◆ **to ~ an oil well** forer un puits de pétrole VI forer, effectuer des forages *(for* pour trouver)

drill² /drɪl/ N *(NonC) (esp Mil = exercises etc)* exercice(s) *m(pl)*, manœuvre(s) *f(pl)* ; *(in grammar etc)* exercices *m* ◆ **what's the ~?** * *(fig)* quelle est la marche à suivre ? ◆ **he doesn't know the ~** * il ne connaît pas la marche à suivre VT *[+ soldiers]* faire faire l'exercice à ◆ **these troops are well-~ed** ces troupes sont bien entraînées ◆ **to ~ pupils in grammar** faire faire des exercices de grammaire à des élèves ◆ **to ~ good manners into a child** inculquer les bonnes manières à un enfant ◆ **I ~ed it into him that he must not ...** je lui ai bien enfoncé dans la tête qu'il ne doit pas ... VI *(Mil)* faire l'exercice, être à l'exercice

COMP **drill sergeant** N *(Mil)* sergent *m* instructeur

drill³ /drɪl/ *(Agr)* N *(= furrow)* sillon *m* ; *(= machine)* drill *m*, semoir *m* VT *[+ seeds]* semer en sillons ; *[+ field]* tracer des sillons dans

drill⁴ /drɪl/ N *(= fabric)* coutil *m*, treillis *m*

drilling¹ /ˈdrɪlɪŋ/ N *(NonC) [of metal, wood]* forage *m*, perçage *m* ; *(by dentist)* fraisage *m* ◆ **~ for oil** forage *m* (pétrolier)

COMP **drilling platform** N plateforme *f* de forage
drilling rig N derrick *m* ; *(at sea)* plateforme *f*
drilling ship N navire *m* de forage

drilling² /ˈdrɪlɪŋ/ N *(Mil)* exercices *mpl*, manœuvres *fpl*

drillion ‡ /ˈdrɪljən/ N *(US)* ◆ **a ~ dollars** des tonnes de dollars, des milliards et des milliards de dollars

drily /ˈdraɪlɪ/ ADV 1 *(= with dry humour) [say, observe]* d'un air *or* ton pince-sans-rire 2 *(= unemotionally)* flegmatiquement

drink /drɪŋk/ (vb : pret **drank**, ptp **drunk**) N 1 *(= liquid to drink)* boisson *f* ◆ **have you got ~s for the children?** est-ce que tu as des boissons pour les enfants ? ◆ **there's food and ~ in the kitchen** il y a de quoi boire et manger à la cuisine ◆ **may I have a ~?** est-ce que je pourrais boire quelque chose ? ◆ **to give sb a ~** donner à boire à qn ◆ **he's a big ~ of water** * quelle (grande) asperge ! *

2 *(= glass of alcoholic drink)* verre *m* ; *(before meal)* apéritif *m* ; *(after meal)* digestif *m* ◆ **have a ~!** tu prendras bien un verre ? ◆ **let's have a ~** allons prendre *or* boire un verre ◆ **let's have a ~ on it** allons boire un verre pour fêter ça ◆ **I need a ~!** j'ai besoin de boire un verre ! ◆ **he likes a ~** il aime bien boire un verre ◆ **to ask friends in for ~s** inviter des amis à venir prendre un verre ◆ **to stand sb a ~** offrir un verre à qn, offrir à boire à qn ◆ **to stand a round of ~s** payer une tournée ◆ **to stand ~s all round** payer une tournée générale ◆ **he had a ~ in him** * il avait un coup dans le nez * ; → **short, soft, strong**

3 *(NonC = alcoholic liquor)* la boisson, l'alcool *m* ◆ **to be under the influence of ~** être en état d'ébriété ◆ **to be the worse for ~** avoir un coup dans le nez * ◆ **to take to ~** se mettre à boire ◆ **to smell of ~** sentir l'alcool ◆ **his worries drove him to ~** ses soucis l'ont poussé à boire *or* l'ont fait sombrer dans la boisson ◆ **it's enough to drive you to ~!** ça vous donne envie de boire pour oublier ! ; → **demon**

4 *(‡ = sea)* baille ‡ *f* ◆ **to be in the ~** être à la baille ‡

VT *[+ wine, coffee]* boire, prendre ; *[+ soup]* manger ◆ **would you like something to ~?** voulez-vous boire quelque chose ? ◆ **give me something to ~** donnez-moi (quelque chose) à boire ◆ **is the water fit to ~?** est-ce que l'eau est potable ? ◆ **this coffee isn't fit to ~** ce café n'est pas buvable ◆ **to ~ sb's health** boire à la santé de qn ◆ **this wine should be drunk at room temperature** ce vin se boit chambré ◆ **he ~s all his wages** il boit tout ce qu'il gagne ◆ **to ~ sb under the table** faire rouler qn sous la table ◆ **to ~ o.s. senseless** boire jusqu'à ne plus tenir debout ; → **death, toast**

VI boire ◆ **he doesn't ~** il ne boit pas ◆ **his father drank** son père buvait ◆ **to ~ from the bottle** boire à (même) la bouteille ◆ **to ~ out of a glass** boire dans un verre ◆ **"don't drink and drive"** *(on notice)* "boire ou conduire, il faut choisir" ◆ **to ~ like a fish** * boire comme un trou * ◆ **to ~ to sb/to sb's success** boire à *or* porter un toast à qn/au succès de qn

COMP **drink driver** N *(Brit)* conducteur *m*, -trice *f* en état d'ébriété *or* d'ivresse
drink-driving N *(Brit)* conduite *f* en état d'ébriété *or* d'ivresse
drink-driving campaign N *(Brit)* campagne *f* contre l'alcool au volant
drink problem N ◆ **the ~ problem** le problème de l'alcoolisme ◆ **to have a ~ problem** trop boire

► **drink away** VT SEP *[+ fortune]* boire ; *[+ sorrows]* noyer (dans l'alcool)

► **drink down** VT SEP avaler, boire d'un trait

► **drink in** VT SEP *[plants, soil]* absorber, boire ; *(fig) [+ story]* avaler * ◆ **he drank in the fresh air** il a respiré *or* humé l'air frais ◆ **the children were ~ing it all in** les enfants n'en perdaient pas une miette * *or* une goutte *

► **drink up** VI boire, vider son verre ◆ **~ up!** finis *or* bois ton verre !

VT SEP ◆ **to drink sth up** finir son verre (*or* sa tasse) de qch

drinkable /ˈdrɪŋkəbl/ ADJ *(= not poisonous) [water]* potable ; *(= palatable) [wine etc]* buvable

drinker /ˈdrɪŋkəʳ/ N buveur *m*, -euse *f* ◆ **whisky ~** buveur *m*, -euse *f* de whisky ◆ **he's a hard** *or* **heavy ~** il boit beaucoup, il boit sec

drinking /ˈdrɪŋkɪŋ/ N ◆ **eating and ~** manger et boire ◆ **he wasn't used to ~** il n'avait pas l'habitude de boire ◆ **there was a lot of heavy ~** on a beaucoup bu ◆ **his problem was ~** son problème c'était qu'il buvait ◆ **his ~ caused his relationship to break up** son alcoolisme a détruit son couple ◆ **she left him because of his ~** elle l'a quitté parce qu'il buvait ◆ **I don't object to ~ in moderation** je ne vois pas d'inconvénient à boire *or* à ce que l'on boive avec modération ◆ **~ by the under-18s must be stopped** il faut empêcher les jeunes de moins de 18 ans de boire

COMP **drinking bout** N beuverie *f*
drinking chocolate N chocolat *m* (en poudre)
drinking companion N ◆ **one of his ~ companions** un de ses compagnons de beuverie
drinking fountain N *(in street)* fontaine *f* publique ; *(in office, toilets etc)* jet *m* d'eau potable
drinking session N ⇒ **drinking bout**
drinking song N chanson *f* à boire
drinking spree N ⇒ **drinking bout**
drinking straw N paille *f*
drinking trough N abreuvoir *m*, auge *f*
drinking-up time N *(Brit) dernières minutes pour finir son verre avant la fermeture d'un pub*
drinking water N eau *f* potable

drip /drɪp/ VI *[water, sweat, rain]* dégoutter, dégouliner ; *[tap]* couler, goutter ; *[cheese, washing]* s'égoutter ; *[hair, trees etc]* dégoutter, ruisseler *(with* de) ◆ **the rain was ~ping down the wall** la pluie dégouttait *or* dégoulinait le long du mur ◆ **sweat was ~ping from his brow** son front ruisselait de sueur ◆ **to be ~ping with sweat** ruisseler de sueur, être en nage ◆ **his hands were ~ping with blood** ses mains ruisselaient de sang ◆ **the walls were ~ping (with water)** les murs suintaient ◆ **his voice was ~ping with sarcasm** *(liter)* il avait un ton profondément sarcastique ; see also **dripping**

VT *[+ liquid]* faire tomber *or* laisser tomber goutte à goutte ; *[+ washing, cheese]* égoutter ◆ **you're ~ping paint all over the place** tu mets de la peinture partout

N 1 *(= sound) [of water, rain]* bruit *m* de l'eau qui tombe goutte à goutte ; *[of tap]* bruit *m* d'un robinet qui goutte

[2] (= *drop*) goutte *f*
[3] (* fig = spineless person) lavette* *f*
[4] *(Med)* (= *liquid*) perfusion *f* ; (= *device*) goutte-à-goutte *m inv* ◆ **to put up a ~** mettre un goutte-à-goutte ◆ **to be on a ~** être sous perfusion ; → **intravenous**
[5] *(Archit:* also **dripstone**) larmier *m*

COMP **drip-dry** ADJ *[shirt]* qui ne nécessite aucun repassage VT *(Comm: on label)* "ne pas repasser"
drip-feed VT *(Med)* alimenter par perfusion ; (= *gradually release) [money, information]* donner au compte-gouttes ◆ **to ~-feed money into sth** injecter de l'argent au compte-gouttes dans qch
drip mat N dessous-de-verre *m inv*
drip pan N *(Culin)* lèchefrite *f*

dripping /ˈdrɪpɪŋ/ N [1] *(Culin)* graisse *f* (de rôti) ◆ **bread and ~** tartine *f* à la graisse [2] (= *action) [of water etc]* égouttement *m* ADJ [1] (= *leaking) [tap, gutter]* qui goutte *or* coule [2] (= *soaking) [person, hair, clothes, washing]* trempé ; *[tree]* ruisselant, qui dégoutte ◆ **he's ~ wet*** il est trempé jusqu'aux os ◆ **my coat is ~ wet*** mon manteau est trempé ; see also **drip** COMP **dripping pan** N *(Culin)* lèchefrite *f*

drippy* /ˈdrɪpɪ/ ADJ *[person]* gnangnan* *inv* ; *[music, book]* cucul*

drivability /ˌdraɪvəˈbɪlɪtɪ/ N maniabilité *f*, manœuvrabilité *f*

drive /draɪv/ (vb : pret **drove**, ptp **driven**) N [1] (= *car journey*) promenade *f or* trajet *m* en voiture ◆ **to go for a ~** faire une promenade en voiture ◆ **it's about one hour's ~ from London** c'est à environ une heure de voiture de Londres
[2] (= *private road: into house, castle*) allée *f*
[3] *(Golf)* drive *m* ; *(Tennis)* coup *m* droit, drive *m*
[4] (= *energy*) dynamisme *m*, énergie *f* ; *(Psych)* besoin *m*, instinct *m* ◆ **the sex ~** les pulsions *fpl* sexuelles ◆ **to have plenty of ~** avoir du dynamisme *or* de l'énergie ◆ **to lack ~** manquer de dynamisme *or* d'énergie
[5] *(Pol, Comm)* campagne *f* ; *(Mil)* poussée *f* ◆ **a ~ to boost sales** une campagne de promotion des ventes ◆ **an output ~** un effort de production ◆ **a recruitment ~** une campagne de recrutement ◆ **the ~ towards democracy** le mouvement en faveur de la démocratie ; → **export, whist**
[6] *(Tech = power transmission)* commande *f*, transmission *f* ; → **front, left², rear¹**
[7] *(Comput) (for disk)* unité *f* de disques ; *(for tape)* dérouleur *m*
VT [1] *[+ cart, car, train]* conduire ; *[+ racing car]* piloter ; *[+ passenger]* conduire, emmener (en voiture) ◆ **he ~s a lorry/taxi** *(for a living)* il est camionneur/chauffeur de taxi ◆ **he ~s a Peugeot** il a une Peugeot ◆ **he ~s racing cars** il est pilote de course ◆ **to ~ sb back/off** *etc (in car)* ramener/emmener *etc* qn en voiture ◆ **I'll ~ you home** je vais vous ramener (en voiture), je vais vous reconduire chez vous ◆ **she drove me down to the coast** elle m'a conduit *or* emmené (en voiture) jusqu'à la côte ◆ **he drove his car straight at me** il s'est dirigé *or* il a dirigé sa voiture droit sur moi ◆ **measures that would ~ a coach and horses through the reforms** *(esp Brit)* des mesures qui sonneraient le glas des réformes
[2] *[+ people, animals]* chasser *or* pousser (devant soi) ; *(Hunting) [+ game]* rabattre ; *[+ clouds]* charrier, chasser ; *[+ leaves]* chasser ◆ **to ~ sb out of the country** chasser qn du pays ◆ **the dog drove the sheep into the farm** le chien a fait rentrer les moutons à la ferme ◆ **the gale drove the ship off course** la tempête a fait dériver le navire ◆ **the wind drove the rain against the windows** le vent rabattait la pluie contre les vitres ; → **corner**
[3] (= *operate) [+ machine] [person]* actionner, commander ; *[steam etc]* faire fonctionner ◆ **machine driven by electricity** machine fonctionnant à l'électricité
[4] *[+ nail]* enfoncer ; *[+ stake]* enfoncer, ficher ; *[+ rivet]* poser ; *(Golf, Tennis)* driver ; *[+ tunnel]* percer, creuser ; *[+ well]* forer, percer ◆ **to ~ a nail home** enfoncer un clou à fond ◆ **to ~ a point home** réussir à faire comprendre un argument ◆ **to ~ sth into sb's head** enfoncer qch dans la tête de qn ◆ **to ~ sth out of sb's head** faire sortir qch de la tête de qn ◆ **to ~ a bargain** conclure un marché ◆ **to ~ a hard bargain with sb** soutirer le maximum à qn ◆ **he ~s a hard bargain** il ne fait pas de cadeau
[5] *(fig)* **to ~ sb hard** surcharger qn de travail, surmener qn ◆ **to ~ sb mad** rendre qn fou ◆ **to ~ sb potty*** rendre qn dingue* ◆ **to ~ sb to despair** réduire qn au désespoir ◆ **to ~ sb to rebellion** pousser *or* inciter qn à la révolte ◆ **to ~ sb to do** *or* **into doing sth** pousser qn à faire qch ◆ **I was driven to it** j'y ai été poussé malgré moi, j'y ai été contraint ; → **distraction**
VI [1] (= *be the driver*) conduire ; (= *go by car*) aller en voiture ◆ **to ~ away/back** *etc* partir/revenir *etc* (en voiture) ◆ **she drove down to the shops** elle est allée faire des courses (en voiture) ◆ **can you ~?, do you ~?** savez-vous conduire ?, vous conduisez ? ◆ **to ~ at 50km/h** rouler à 50 km/h ◆ **to ~ on the right** rouler à droite ◆ **did you come by train? – no, we drove** êtes-vous venus en train ? – non, (nous sommes venus) en voiture ◆ **we have been driving all day** nous avons roulé toute la journée ◆ **she was about to ~ under the bridge** elle s'apprêtait à s'engager sous le pont
[2] ◆ **the rain was driving in our faces** la pluie nous fouettait le visage

COMP **drive-by shooting** N *coups de feu tirés d'une voiture en marche*
drive-in ADJ, N drive-in *m inv* ◆ **~-in cinema** ciné-parc *m*, drive-in *m inv*
drive-thru, drive-through (Brit) N drive-in *m inv* ADJ *[store, restaurant]* drive-in, où l'on est servi dans sa voiture ◆ **the ~-thru business** le secteur des drive-in
drive-time N *(Rad)* heure *f* de pointe
drive-up window N *(US)* guichet *m* pour automobilistes

► **drive along** VI *[vehicle]* rouler, circuler ; *[person]* rouler
VT SEP *[wind, current]* chasser, pousser

► **drive at** VT FUS *(fig = intend, mean)* en venir à, vouloir dire ◆ **what are you driving at?** où voulez-vous en venir ?, que voulez-vous dire ?

► **drive away** VI *[car]* démarrer ; *[person]* s'en aller *or* partir en voiture
VT SEP *(lit, fig) [+ person, suspicions, cares]* chasser

► **drive back** VI *[car]* revenir ; *[person]* rentrer en voiture
VT SEP [1] (= *cause to retreat: Mil etc)* repousser, refouler ◆ **the storm drove him back** la tempête lui a fait rebrousser chemin
[2] (= *convey back*) ramener *or* reconduire (en voiture)

► **drive down** VT SEP *[+ prices, costs]* faire baisser

► **drive in** VI *[car]* entrer ; *[person]* entrer (en voiture)
VT SEP *[+ nail]* enfoncer ; *[+ screw]* visser

► **drive off** VI [1] ⇒ **drive away vi**
[2] *(Golf)* driver
VT SEP ⇒ **drive away vt sep**
VT FUS *[+ ferry]* débarquer de

► **drive on** VI *[person, car]* poursuivre sa route ; *(after stopping)* reprendre sa route, repartir
VT SEP (= *incite, encourage*) pousser *(to* à ; *to do sth, to doing sth* à faire qch)

► **drive on to** VT FUS *[+ ferry]* embarquer sur

► **drive out** VI *[car]* sortir ; *[person]* sortir (en voiture)
VT SEP *[+ person]* faire sortir, chasser ; *[+ thoughts, desires]* chasser

► **drive over** VI venir *or* aller en voiture ◆ **we drove over in two hours** nous avons fait le trajet en deux heures
VT SEP (= *convey*) conduire en voiture
VT FUS (= *crush*) écraser

► **drive up** VI *[car]* arriver ; *[person]* arriver (en voiture)
VT FUS ◆ **the car drove up the road** la voiture a remonté la rue

driveability /ˌdraɪvəˈbɪlɪtɪ/ N ⇒ **drivability**

drivel* /ˈdrɪvl/ N *(NonC)* bêtises *fpl*, imbécillités *fpl* ◆ **what (utter) ~!** quelles bêtises *or* imbécillités ! VI radoter ◆ **what's he ~ling (on) about?** qu'est-ce qu'il radote ?*

driveline /ˈdraɪvlaɪn/ N *[of vehicle]* transmission *f*

driven /ˈdrɪvn/ VB ptp of **drive**

-driven /ˈdrɪvn/ ADJ *(in compounds)* ◆ **chauffeur-driven** conduit par un chauffeur ◆ **electricity-driven** fonctionnant à l'électricité ◆ **steam-driven** à vapeur

driver /ˈdraɪvəʳ/ N [1] *[of car]* conducteur *m*, -trice *f* ; *[of taxi, truck, bus]* chauffeur *m*, conducteur *m*, -trice *f* ; *[of racing car]* pilote *m* ; *(Brit) [of train]* mécanicien *m*, conducteur *m*, -trice *f* ; *[of cart]* charretier *m* ; *(Sport: in horse race etc)* driver *m* ◆ **car ~s** les automobilistes *mpl* ◆ **to be a good ~** bien conduire ◆ **he's a very careful ~** il conduit très prudemment ; → **lorry, racing** [2] *[of animals]* conducteur *m*, -trice *f* ; → **slave** [3] (= *golf club*) driver *m* [4] *(Comput)* driver *m*, pilote *m* [5] (= *force*) moteur *m*

COMP **driver education** N *(US Scol)* cours *mpl* de conduite automobile *(dans les lycées)*
driver's license N *(US)* ⇒ **driving licence**
driver's seat N ⇒ **driving seat**

driveshaft /ˈdraɪvʃɑːft/ N *[of vehicle, machine]* arbre *m* de transmission

drivetrain /ˈdraɪvtreɪn/ N ⇒ **driveline**

driveway /ˈdraɪvweɪ/ N ⇒ **drive noun 2**

driving /ˈdraɪvɪŋ/ N conduite *f* ◆ **his ~ is awful** il conduit très mal ◆ **bad ~** conduite *f* imprudente *or* maladroite ◆ **~ is his hobby** conduire est sa distraction favorite
ADJ [1] *[necessity]* impérieux, pressant ; *[ambition]* sans bornes, démesurée ◆ **the ~ force behind the reforms** le moteur des réformes
[2] ◆ **~ rain** pluie *f* battante

COMP **driving belt** N courroie *f* de transmission
driving instructor N moniteur *m*, -trice *f* d'auto-école
driving lesson N leçon *f* de conduite
driving licence N *(Brit)* permis *m* de conduire
driving mirror N rétroviseur *m*
driving range N *(Golf)* practice *m*
driving school N auto-école *f*
driving seat N place *f* du conducteur ◆ **to be in the ~ seat** *(lit)* être au volant ; *(fig)* être aux commandes, diriger les opérations
driving test N examen *m* du permis de conduire ◆ **to pass one's ~ test** avoir son permis (de conduire) ◆ **to fail one's ~ test** rater son permis (de conduire)
driving wheel N *(Tech)* roue *f* motrice

DRIVING LICENCE, DRIVER'S LICENSE

En Grande-Bretagne, le permis de conduire (**driving licence**) s'obtient en deux étapes, les apprentis conducteurs n'ayant pendant un certain temps qu'un permis provisoire (« provisional licence »). Il n'est pas obligatoire de l'avoir sur soi mais il faut pouvoir le présenter au commissariat dans les sept jours qui suivent une interpellation.

Aux États-Unis, l'âge d'obtention du permis (**driver's license**) varie suivant les États de quinze à vingt et un ans. Les apprentis conducteurs ou les adolescents peuvent obtenir un permis spécial (« learner's license » ou « junior's license ») qui n'est valable que pour certains trajets précis, celui du lycée par exemple. Le permis de conduire américain sert souvent de carte d'identité et doit être porté par son titulaire. Il doit être renouvelé tous les quatre, cinq ou six ans selon les États.

drizzle /ˈdrɪzl/ **N** bruine *f*, crachin *m* **VI** bruiner, pleuviner **VT** *(Culin)* ◆ **~ the salad with oil, ~ some oil over the salad** verser un filet d'huile sur la salade

drizzly /ˈdrɪzlɪ/ **ADJ** ◆ **~ rain** bruine *f*, crachin *m*

droll /drəʊl/ **ADJ** *(= comic)* drôle

dromedary /ˈdrɒmɪdərɪ/ **N** dromadaire *m*

drone /drəʊn/ **N** [1] *(= bee)* abeille *f* mâle, faux-bourdon *m* ; *(pej = idler)* fainéant(e) *m(f)* [2] *(= sound) [of bees]* bourdonnement *m* ; *[of engine, aircraft]* ronronnement *m* ; *(louder)* vrombissement *m* ; *(fig = monotonous speech)* débit *m* monotone [3] *(Mus)* bourdon *m* [4] *(= robot plane)* avion *m* téléguidé, drone *m* **VI** *[bee]* bourdonner ; *[engine, aircraft]* ronronner ; *(louder)* vrombir ; *(= speak monotonously:* also **drone away, drone on**) faire de longs discours ◆ **he ~d on about politics** il n'a pas arrêté de parler politique ◆ **he ~d on and on for hours** il a parlé pendant des heures et des heures **VT** ◆ **to ~ a speech** débiter un discours d'un ton monotone

drongo /ˈdrɒŋgəʊ/ **N** [1] *(esp Austral * = person)* crétin(e)* *m(f)* [2] *(= bird)* drongo *m*

drool /druːl/ **VI** *(lit)* baver ; *(* fig)* radoter ◆ **to ~ over sth*** fig) baver d'admiration *or* s'extasier devant qch

droop /druːp/ **VI** *[body]* s'affaisser ; *[shoulders]* tomber ; *[head]* pencher ; *[eyelids]* s'abaisser ; *[flowers]* commencer à se faner ; *[feathers, one's hand]* retomber ◆ **his spirits ~ed** ça l'a déprimé ◆ **he was ~ing in the heat** il était accablé par la chaleur **VT** *[+ head]* baisser **N** *[of body]* affaissement *m* ; *[of eyelids]* abaissement *m*

droopy /ˈdruːpɪ/ **ADJ** *[moustache, tail, breasts]* pendant ; *(hum = tired)* mou (molle *f*)

drop /drɒp/ **N** [1] *[of liquid]* goutte *f* ◆ **~s** *(Med)* gouttes *fpl* ◆ **~ by ~** goutte à goutte ◆ **there's only a ~ left** il n'en reste qu'une goutte ◆ **to fall in ~s** tomber en gouttes ◆ **we haven't had a ~ of rain** nous n'avons pas eu une goutte de pluie ◆ **would you like a whisky? – just a ~!** un petit whisky ? – (juste) une goutte *or* une larme ! ◆ **he's had a ~ too much*** il a bu un coup de trop* ; → **nose, teardrop**

[2] *(= pendant) [of chandelier]* pendeloque *f* ; *[of earring]* pendant *m*, pendeloque *f* ; *[of necklace]* pendentif *m*

[3] *(= fall) [of temperature]* baisse *f* (in de) ; *[of prices]* baisse *f*, chute *f* (in de) ◆ **a ~ of 3.1 per cent** *(in sales, applications)* une baisse de 3,1 pour cent ◆ **~ in voltage** *(Elec)* chute *f* de tension ; → **hat**

[4] *(= difference in level)* dénivellation *f*, descente *f* brusque ; *(= abyss)* précipice *m* ; *(= fall)* chute *f* ; *(= distance of fall)* hauteur *f* de chute ; *(Climbing)* vide *m* ; *[of gallows]* trappe *f* ; *(= parachute jump)* saut *m* (en parachute) ◆ **there's a ~ of 10 metres between the roof and the ground** il y a (une hauteur de) 10 mètres entre le toit et le sol ◆ **sheer ~** descente *f* à pic ◆ **to have/get the ~ on sb** *(US fig)* avoir/prendre l'avantage sur qn

[5] *(= delivery)* livraison *f* ; *(from plane)* parachutage *m*, droppage *m* ◆ **to make a ~** *[gangster]* faire une livraison

[6] *(= hiding place: for secret letter etc)* cachette *f*

[7] *(Theat:* also **drop curtain**) rideau *m* d'entracte ; → **backdrop**

[8] *(= sweet)* → **acid, chocolate**

VT [1] *[+ rope, ball, cup etc] (= let fall)* laisser tomber ; *(= release, let go)* lâcher ; *[+ bomb]* lancer, larguer ; *[+ liquid]* verser goutte à goutte ; *[+ one's trousers etc]* baisser ; *[+ price]* baisser ; *(from car) [+ person, thing]* déposer ; *(from boat) [+ cargo, passengers]* débarquer ◆ **I'll ~ you here** *(from car etc)* je vous dépose *or* laisse ici ◆ **to ~ one's eyes/voice** baisser les yeux/la voix ◆ **to ~ a letter in the postbox** poster une lettre, mettre une lettre à la boîte ◆ **to ~ soldiers/supplies by parachute** parachuter des soldats/du ravitaillement ◆ **to be ~ped** *[parachutist]* sauter ◆ **he ~ped the ball over the net** *(Tennis)* il a fait un amorti derrière le filet ◆ **to ~ a goal** *(Rugby)* marquer un drop ◆ **to ~ the ball** *(US fig)* ne pas être à la hauteur ; → **anchor, brick, curtain, curtsy, stitch**

[2] *(* = kill) [+ bird]* abattre ; *[+ person]* descendre*

[3] *(= utter casually) [+ remark, clue]* laisser échapper ◆ **to ~ a word in sb's ear** glisser un mot à l'oreille de qn ◆ **he let ~ that he had seen her** *(accidentally)* il a laissé échapper qu'il l'avait vue ; *(deliberately)* il a fait comprendre qu'il l'avait vue ; → **hint**

[4] *[+ letter, card]* envoyer, écrire (to à) ◆ **to ~ sb a line** écrire un (petit) mot à qn ◆ **~ me a note** écrivez-moi *or* envoyez-moi un petit mot

[5] *(= omit) [+ word, syllable] (spoken)* avaler ; *(written)* omettre ◆ **to ~ one's h's** *or* **aitches** ne pas prononcer les "h"

[6] *(= abandon) [+ habit, idea]* renoncer à ; *[+ work]* abandonner ; *(Scol etc) [+ subject]* abandonner, laisser tomber ; *[+ plan]* renoncer à, ne pas donner suite à ; *[+ discussion, conversation]* abandonner ; *[+ programme, word, scene from play]* supprimer ; *[+ friend, girlfriend, boyfriend]* laisser tomber ◆ **to ~ everything** tout laisser tomber ◆ **to be ~ped from a team** être rayé d'une équipe ◆ **let's ~ the subject** parlons d'autre chose, n'en parlons plus ◆ **~ it!*** laisse tomber !*

[7] *(= lose) [+ money]* perdre, laisser ; *(Cards, Tennis etc) [+ game]* perdre ◆ **to ~ a set/one's serve** perdre un set/son service

[8] *(= give birth to) [animal]* mettre bas ; *(‡ hum) [person]* accoucher ◆ **has she ~ped the sprog yet?** ‡ est-ce qu'elle a déjà eu son gosse ?*

[9] ◆ **to ~ acid** ‡ prendre du LSD

VI [1] *[object]* tomber, retomber ; *[liquids]* tomber goutte à goutte ; *[person]* descendre, se laisser tomber ; *(= sink to ground)* se laisser tomber, tomber ; *(= collapse)* s'effondrer, s'affaisser ◆ **to ~ into sb's arms** tomber dans les bras de qn ◆ **to ~ on one's knees** tomber à genoux ◆ **she ~ped into an armchair** elle s'est effondrée dans un fauteuil ◆ **I'm ready to ~*** je suis claqué* ◆ **~ dead!‡** va te faire voir !*, va te faire foutre !‡ ◆ **to ~ on sb like a ton of bricks*** secouer les puces à qn* ; → **curtain, fly¹, penny, pin**

[2] *(= decrease) [wind]* se calmer, tomber ; *[temperature, voice]* baisser ; *[price]* baisser, diminuer

[3] *(= end) [conversation, correspondence]* en rester là, cesser ◆ **there the matter ~ped** l'affaire en est restée là ◆ **let it ~!*** laisse tomber !*

COMP **drop-add** **N** *(US Univ etc)* remplacement *m* d'un cours par un autre

drop cloth **N** *(US)* bâche *f* de protection

drop-dead‡ **ADV** vachement* ◆ **~-dead gorgeous*** *(Brit)* super* beau (belle *f*)

drop-forge **N** marteau-pilon *m*

drop goal **N** *(Rugby)* drop *m* ◆ **to score a ~ goal** passer un drop

drop hammer **N** ⇒ **drop-forge**

drop handlebars **NPL** guidon *m* de course

drop-in centre **N** *(Brit)* centre *m* d'accueil *(où l'on peut se rendre sans prendre rendez-vous)*

drop kick **N** *(Rugby)* coup *m* de pied tombé, drop *m*

drop-leaf table **N** table *f* à abattants

drop-off **N** *(in sales, interest etc)* diminution *f* (in de)

drop-out **N** *(Rugby)* renvoi *m* aux 22 mètres ; see also **dropout**

dropping out **N** *(Univ etc)* abandon *m*

drop shipment **N** *(Comm)* drop shipment *m*

drop shot **N** *(Tennis)* amorti *m*

drop tag **VT** *(US)* démarquer

drop zone **N** *(Flying)* zone *f* de droppage

► **drop across*** **VI** ⇒ **drop round**

► **drop away** **VI** *[numbers, attendance]* diminuer

► **drop back, drop behind** **VI** rester en arrière, se laisser devancer *or* distancer ; *(in work etc)* prendre du retard

► **drop by** **VI** ◆ **to drop by somewhere/on sb** faire un saut* *or* passer quelque part/chez qn ◆ **we'll ~ by if we're in town** nous passerons si nous sommes en ville

► **drop down** **VI** tomber

► **drop in** **VI** ◆ **to drop in on sb** passer voir qn, faire un saut* chez qn ◆ **to ~ in at the grocer's** passer *or* faire un saut chez l'épicier ◆ **do ~ in if you're in town** passez me voir (*or* nous voir) si vous êtes en ville

► **drop off** **VI** [1] *(= fall asleep)* s'endormir

[2] *[leaves]* tomber ; *[sales, interest]* diminuer

[3] *(* = alight)* descendre

VT SEP *(= set down from car etc) [+ person, parcel]* déposer, laisser

N ◆ **drop-off** → **drop**

► **drop out** **VI** *[contents etc]* tomber ; *(fig)* se retirer, renoncer ; *(from college etc)* abandonner ses études ◆ **to ~ out of a competition** se retirer d'une compétition, abandonner une compétition ◆ **to ~ out of circulation** *or* **out of sight** disparaître de la circulation ◆ **to ~ out (of society)** vivre en marge de la société, se marginaliser

► **drop round*** **VI** passer ◆ **to drop round to see sb** passer *or* aller voir qn ◆ **thanks for ~ping round** merci d'être passé

VT SEP déposer chez moi (*or* toi *etc*)

droplet /ˈdrɒplɪt/ **N** gouttelette *f*

dropout /ˈdrɒpaʊt/ **N** *(from society)* marginal(e) *m(f)* ; *(from college etc)* étudiant(e) *m(f)* qui abandonne ses études **ADJ** ◆ **the ~ rate** le taux d'abandon

dropper /ˈdrɒpəʳ/ **N** *(Pharm)* compte-gouttes *m inv*

droppings /ˈdrɒpɪŋz/ **NPL** *[of bird]* fiente *f* ; *[of animal]* crottes *fpl* ; *[of fly]* chiures *fpl*, crottes *fpl*

dropsical /ˈdrɒpsɪkəl/ **ADJ** hydropique

dropsy /ˈdrɒpsɪ/ **N** hydropisie *f*

drosophila /drɒˈsɒfɪlə/ **N** (pl **drosophilas** *or* **drosophilae** /drɒˈsɒfɪˌliː/) drosophile *f*

dross /drɒs/ **N** *(NonC) (Metal)* scories *fpl*, crasse *f*, laitier *m* ; *(= coal)* menu *m* (de houille *or* de coke), poussier *m* ; *(= refuse)* impuretés *fpl*, déchets *mpl* ◆ **the film was total ~*** *(fig = sth worthless)* ce film était complètement nul

drought /draʊt/ N sécheresse *f*

drove /drəʊv/ VB pt of **drive** N 1 *[of animals]* troupeau *m* en marche ♦ **~s of people** des foules *fpl* de gens ♦ **they came in ~s** ils arrivèrent en foule 2 *(= channel)* canal *m or* rigole *f* d'irrigation

drover /ˈdrəʊvəʳ/ N conducteur *m* de bestiaux

drown /draʊn/ VI se noyer ♦ **he's ~ing in debt** il est criblé de dettes ♦ **he was ~ing in guilt** il était bourrelé de remords ♦ **we were ~ing in data but starved of information** nous étions submergés de données mais privés d'information ♦ **I feel as though I'm ~ing in paperwork** je suis submergé de paperasses, je nage dans la paperasse

VT 1 *[+ person, animal]* noyer ; *[+ land]* inonder, submerger ♦ **because he couldn't swim he was ~ed** il s'est noyé parce qu'il ne savait pas nager ♦ **he's like** *or* **he looks like a ~ed rat** * il est trempé jusqu'aux os *or* comme une soupe ♦ **to ~ one's sorrows** noyer son chagrin ♦ **don't ~ it!** * *(of whisky etc)* n'y mets pas trop d'eau !, ne le noie pas ! ♦ **they were ~ed with offers of help** * ils ont été inondés *or* submergés d'offres d'assistance

2 ⇒ **drown out**

► **drown out** VT SEP *[+ voice, sound, words]* couvrir, étouffer

drowning /ˈdraʊnɪŋ/ ADJ qui se noie ♦ **a ~ man will clutch at a straw** *(Prov)* un homme qui se noie se raccroche à un fétu de paille N 1 *(= death)* noyade *f* ♦ **there were three ~s here last year** trois personnes se sont noyées ici *or* il y a eu trois noyades ici l'année dernière 2 *[of noise, voice]* étouffement *m*

drowse /draʊz/ VI être à moitié endormi *or* assoupi, somnoler ♦ **to ~ off** s'assoupir

drowsily /ˈdraʊzɪlɪ/ ADV *[speak]* d'une voix endormie ♦ **~, she set the alarm clock and went to bed** à moitié endormie, elle mit le réveil et alla se coucher

drowsiness /ˈdraʊzɪnɪs/ N somnolence *f*, engourdissement *m*

drowsy /ˈdraʊzɪ/ ADJ 1 *(= half-asleep) [person, smile, look]* somnolent ; *[voice]* ensommeillé ♦ **he was still very ~** il était encore à moitié endormi ♦ **these tablets will make you ~** ces comprimés vous donneront envie de dormir ♦ **~ with sleep** tout ensommeillé ♦ **to grow ~** s'assoupir ♦ **to feel ~** avoir envie de dormir 2 *(= soporific) [afternoon, atmosphere]* soporifique ; *[countryside, stillness]* assoupi

drub * /drʌb/ VT *(= thrash)* rosser*, rouer de coups ; *(= abuse)* injurier, traiter de tous les noms ; *(= defeat)* battre à plate(s) couture(s) ♦ **to ~ an idea into sb** enfoncer une idée dans la tête de qn ♦ **to ~ an idea out of sb** faire sortir une idée de la tête de qn

drubbing * /ˈdrʌbɪŋ/ N *(= thrashing, defeat)* raclée* *f* ♦ **they suffered a 5-0 ~** ils ont été battus à plate(s) couture(s) 5 à 0 ♦ **to give sb a ~** *(lit, fig)* donner une belle raclée* à qn ♦ **to take a ~** *(fig)* être battu à plate(s) couture(s)

drudge /drʌdʒ/ N bête *f* de somme *(fig)* ♦ **the household ~** la bonne à tout faire VI trimer*, peiner

drudgery /ˈdrʌdʒərɪ/ N *(NonC)* corvée *f*, travail *m* pénible et ingrat ♦ **it's sheer ~!** c'est une vraie corvée !

drug /drʌg/ N *(= medicine)* médicament *m* ; *(illegal)* drogue *f* ; *(Police, Jur)* stupéfiant *m* ♦ **to prescribe a ~** prescrire un médicament ♦ **he's on ~s, he takes ~s** il se drogue ♦ **to use ~s, to do ~s** * se droguer ♦ **~ use** consommation *f* de stupéfiants ♦ **to deal ~s** revendre de la drogue ♦ **police have seized ~s said to have a street value of ten million pounds** la police a saisi des stupéfiants d'une valeur marchande de dix millions de livres ♦ **a ~ on the market** *(fig)* un article *or* une marchandise invendable ♦ **television is a ~** la télévision est une drogue ♦ **~ of choice** *(for particular group)* drogue *f* de prédilection ; → **hard, soft**

VT *[+ person]* droguer; *[+ food, wine etc]* mettre une drogue dans ♦ **his wine had been ~ged with sleeping tablets** on avait mis des somnifères dans son vin ♦ **to be in a ~ged sleep** dormir sous l'effet d'une drogue ♦ **to be ~ged with sleep/from lack of sleep** être abruti de sommeil/par le manque de sommeil

COMP **drug abuse** N usage *m* de stupéfiants
drug abuser N drogué(e) *m(f)*
drug addict N drogué(e) *m(f)*, toxicomane *mf*
drug addiction N toxicomanie *f*
drug check N contrôle *m* antidopage
drug company N compagnie *f* pharmaceutique ♦ **the ~ companies** l'industrie *f* pharmaceutique
drug czar N responsable *mf* de la lutte contre la drogue, Monsieur anti-drogue
drug dealer N revendeur *m*, -euse *f* de drogue
drug dependency N pharmacodépendance *f*
drug habit N ♦ **to have a ~ habit** se droguer
drug peddler, drug pusher N revendeur *m*, -euse *f* de drogue, dealer* *m*
drug raid N *(US)* ⇒ **drugs raid**
drug runner N trafiquant(e) *m(f)* (de drogue)
drug-running N ⇒ **drug traffic**
drugs czar N ⇒ **drug czar**
Drug Squad N *(Police)* brigade *f* des stupéfiants
drugs raid N *(Brit)* opération *f* antidrogue
drugs ring N réseau *m* de trafiquants de drogue
Drugs Squad N ⇒ **Drug Squad**
drugs test N contrôle *m* antidopage
drugs tsar N ⇒ **drug czar**
drug-taker N ⇒ **drug user**
drug-taking N usage *m* de drogue(s) *or* de stupéfiants
drug test N ⇒ **drugs test**
drug traffic(king) N trafic *m* de drogue
drug tsar N ⇒ **drug czar**
drug user N usager *m* de drogue

⚠ When it means 'medicine' **drug** is not normally translated by **drogue**.

drugged /drʌgd/ ADJ *[person, food, drink]* drogué ; *[sleep]* provoqué par une drogue

druggist /ˈdrʌgɪst/ N 1 pharmacien(ne) *m(f)* ♦ **~'s** pharmacie *f* 2 *(US)* gérant(e) *m(f)* de drugstore

druggy * /ˈdrʌgɪ/ N camé(e)* *m(f)*, drogué(e) *m(f)* ADJ *[person]* qui se drogue, qui se came* ; *[music]* de camé*

drugster /ˈdrʌgstəʳ/ N ⇒ **druggy noun**

drugstore /ˈdrʌgstɔːʳ/ N *(US)* drugstore *m* COMP **drugstore cowboy** * N *(US fig)* glandeur* *m*, traîne-savates* *m*

druid /ˈdruːɪd/ N druide *m*

druidic /druːˈɪdɪk/ ADJ druidique

druidism /ˈdruːɪdɪzəm/ N druidisme *m*

drum /drʌm/ N 1 *(Mus = instrument, player)* tambour *m* ♦ **the big ~** la grosse caisse ♦ **the ~s** *(in band, orchestra)* la batterie ♦ **to beat the ~** battre le *or* du tambour ♦ **to beat** *or* **bang the ~ for sb/sth** *(fig)* prendre fait et cause pour qn/qch ♦ **to march to a different ~** choisir une autre voie ; → **kettledrum, tight**

2 *(for oil)* bidon *m* ; *(for tar)* gonne *f* ; *(= cylinder for wire etc)* tambour *m* ; *(= machine part)* tambour *m* ; (also **brake drum**) tambour *m* (de frein) ; *(Comput)* tambour *m* magnétique ; *(= box: of figs, sweets)* caisse *f*

3 *(= sound)* ⇒ **drumming**

4 ⇒ **eardrum**

VI *(Mus)* battre le *or* du tambour ; *[person, fingers]* tambouriner, pianoter *(with* de, avec ; *on* sur) ; *[insect etc]* bourdonner ♦ **the noise was ~ming in my ears** le bruit bourdonnait à mes oreilles ♦ **rain ~med on the roof of the car** la pluie tambourinait sur le toit de la voiture

VT *[+ tune]* tambouriner ♦ **to ~ one's fingers on the table** tambouriner *or* pianoter (des doigts) sur la table ♦ **to ~ one's feet on the floor** taper des pieds ♦ **to ~ sth into sb** *(fig)* seriner qch à qn ♦ **I had tidiness ~med into me** on m'a seriné qu'il fallait être ordonné

COMP **drum and bass** N drum'n'bass *m*
drum brake N frein *m* à tambour
drum kit N batterie *f*
drum machine N boîte *f* à rythme
drum major N *(Brit Mil)* tambour-major *m* ; *(US)* chef *m* des tambours
drum majorette N *(US)* majorette *f*
drum roll N roulement *m* de tambour
drum set N ⇒ **drum kit**

► **drum out** VT SEP *(Mil, fig)* expulser (à grand bruit) *(of* de)

► **drum up** VT SEP *(fig) [+ enthusiasm, support]* susciter ; *[+ supporters]* rassembler, battre le rappel de ; *[+ customers]* racoler, attirer ♦ **to ~ up business** attirer la clientèle

drumbeat /ˈdrʌmbiːt/ N battement *m* de tambour

drumfire /ˈdrʌmfaɪəʳ/ N *(Mil)* tir *m* de barrage, feu *m* roulant

drumhead /ˈdrʌmhed/ N *(Mus)* peau *f* de tambour

COMP **drumhead court-martial** N *(Mil)* conseil *m* de guerre prévôtal
drumhead service N *(Mil)* office *m* religieux en plein air

drumlin /ˈdrʌmlɪn/ N drumlin *m*

drummer /ˈdrʌməʳ/ N 1 (joueur *m* de) tambour *m* ; *(Jazz, Rock)* batteur *m* ♦ **to march to** *or* **hear a different ~** *(fig)* choisir une autre voie 2 *(US Comm* *)* commis *m* voyageur COMP **drummer boy** N petit tambour *m*

drumming /ˈdrʌmɪŋ/ N *[of drum]* bruit *m* du tambour ; *[of insect]* bourdonnement *m* ; *(in the ears)* bourdonnement *m* ; *[of fingers]* tapotement *m*, tambourinage *m*

drumstick /ˈdrʌmstɪk/ N 1 *(Mus)* baguette *f* de tambour 2 *[of chicken, turkey]* pilon *m*

drunk /drʌŋk/ VB ptp of **drink**

ADJ 1 *(lit)* ivre, soûl* ♦ **he was ~ on champagne** il s'était soûlé au champagne ♦ **to get ~ (on champagne)** se soûler* (au champagne) ♦ **to get sb ~ (on champagne)** soûler* qn (au champagne) ♦ **as ~ as a lord** * *(Brit)*, **as ~ as a skunk** * *(US)* soûl comme une grive* *or* un Polonais* ♦ **~ and disorderly** *(Jur)* ≈ en état d'ivresse publique ♦ **to be ~ in charge** *(of vehicle)* conduire en état d'ébriété *or* d'ivresse ; *(at work)* être en état d'ébriété dans l'exercice de ses fonctions ; → **blind, dead**

2 *(fig, liter)* ♦ **~ with** *or* **on success/power** enivré *or* grisé par le succès/pouvoir

N * ivrogne *mf* ; *(on one occasion)* homme *m or* femme *f* soûl(e)*

COMP **drunk driver** N conducteur *m*, -trice *f* en état d'ébriété *or* d'ivresse
drunk driving N *(esp US)* conduite *f* en état d'ébriété *or* d'ivresse

drunkard /ˈdrʌŋkəd/ N ivrogne *mf*

drunken /ˈdrʌŋkən/ ADJ 1 *[person] (= habitually)* ivrogne ; *(= on one occasion)* ivre ♦ **a ~ old man** *(= old drunk)* un vieil ivrogne ♦ **her ~ father** son ivrogne de père 2 *[party]* très arrosé ; *[quarrel, brawl]* d'ivrogne(s) ; *[night, evening]* d'ivresse ; *[voice]* aviné ; *[state]* d'ivresse, d'ébriété ; *[violence]* dû à l'ivresse ♦ **a ~ orgy** une beuverie ♦ **in a ~ rage** *or* **fury** dans un état de fureur dû à l'alcool ♦ **in a ~ stupor** dans une stupeur éthylique 3 *(fig = crooked)* ♦ **at a ~ angle** de travers COMP **drunken driving** N conduite *f* en état d'ébriété *or* d'ivresse

drunkenly /ˈdrʌŋkənlɪ/ ADV 1 (= *while drunk*) [*speak, say, sing*] d'une voix avinée 2 (*fig* = *unsteadily*) [*stumble, stagger*] comme un ivrogne ; [*walk*] en titubant comme un ivrogne ; [*lean*] de travers ◆ **the boat lurched ~** le bateau tanguait dangereusement

drunkenness /ˈdrʌŋkənnɪs/ N (= *state*) ivresse *f*, ébriété *f* ; (= *problem, habit*) ivrognerie *f*

drunkometer /drʌŋˈkɒmɪtəʳ/ N (*US*) alcootest ® *m*

druthers* /ˈdrʌðəz/ N (*US*) ◆ **if I had my ~** s'il ne tenait qu'à moi

dry /draɪ/ ADJ 1 [*object, clothes, ground, air, wind, heat, burn, cough*] sec (sèche *f*) ◆ **when the paint is ~, apply the next coat** une fois la peinture sèche, appliquez la deuxième couche ◆ **her throat/mouth was ~** elle avait la gorge/la bouche sèche ◆ **his mouth was ~ with fear** la peur lui desséchait la bouche ◆ **to be** *or* **feel ~*** (= *thirsty*) avoir le gosier sec* *or* la bouche sèche ◆ **her eyes were ~** (*lit, fig*) elle avait les yeux secs ◆ **there wasn't a ~ eye in the house** tout le monde a eu les larmes aux yeux ◆ **for ~ skin/hair** pour les peaux sèches/cheveux secs ◆ **on ~ land** sur la terre ferme ◆ **to pat sth ~** sécher qch (en tapotant) ◆ **to keep sth ~** tenir qch au sec ◆ **"keep in a dry place"** (*on label*) "tenir au sec" ◆ **as ~ as a bone** complètement sec ; → **high, powder**

2 (= *dried-up*) [*riverbed, lake, well*] à sec ; [*spring, river, valley*] sec (sèche *f*) ; [*oasis*] tari ; [*cow*] qui ne donne plus de lait ◆ **to run ~** [*river, well*] tarir ; [*oil well*] s'assécher ; [*resources*] s'épuiser ◆ **we are going to drink this town ~ by the time we leave** quand nous aurons fini il n'y aura plus une goutte d'alcool dans cette ville

3 (= *not rainy*) [*climate, weather, country, period*] sec (sèche *f*) ; [*day*] sans pluie ◆ **a ~ spell** une période sèche *or* de sécheresse ◆ **the ~ season** la saison sèche ◆ **it was ~ and warm** le temps était sec et chaud ; see also **noun**

4 (= *without butter etc*) ◆ **a piece of ~ toast** une tranche de pain grillé sans beurre

5 [*wine, sherry, vermouth, Madeira*] sec (sèche *f*) ; [*champagne, cider*] brut ◆ **a ~ sherry/white wine** un xérès/vin blanc sec

6 (= *without alcohol*) où l'alcool est prohibé ◆ **a ~ county** (*in US*) une région où l'alcool est prohibé

7 [*humour, wit, person*] pince-sans-rire *inv* ◆ **he has a ~ sense of humour** il est pince-sans-rire, c'est un pince-sans-rire

8 (= *not lively*) [*book, subject, speech, lecture*] aride ◆ **as ~ as dust** ennuyeux comme la pluie

9 (= *cold, unemotional*) [*voice, manner*] froid ◆ **he gave a brief ~ laugh** il rit d'un petit rire sec

10 (*Brit Pol: hum*) pur et dur ◆ **a ~ Tory** un ultraconservateur, une ultraconservatrice

N (*esp Brit*) ◆ **at least you're in the warm and the ~** au moins vous êtes au chaud et au sec

VT [+ *food, skin, hair*] sécher ; (*with cloth*) essuyer, sécher ; [+ *clothes*] (faire) sécher ◆ **"dry away from direct heat"** (*on label*) "ne pas sécher près d'une source de chaleur" ◆ **to ~ one's eyes** *or* **one's tears** sécher ses larmes *or* ses pleurs ◆ **to ~ the dishes** essuyer la vaisselle ◆ **to ~ o.s.** s'essuyer, se sécher

VI sécher ; (*esp Brit* *) [*actor, speaker*] sécher*

COMP **dry-as-dust** ADJ aride, sec (sèche *f*)

dry-bulk cargo ship N vraquier *m*

dry cell N (*Elec*) pile *f* sèche

dry-clean VT nettoyer à sec ◆ **"dry-clean only"** (*on label*) "nettoyage à sec" ◆ **to have a dress ~-cleaned** donner une robe à nettoyer *or* au pressing

dry-cleaner N teinturier *m* ◆ **to take a coat to the ~-cleaner's** porter un manteau à la teinturerie

dry-cleaning N nettoyage *m* à sec, pressing *m*

dry dock N (*Naut*) cale *f* sèche, bassin *m* *or* cale *f* de radoub

dry-eyed ADJ (*lit, fig*) qui a les yeux secs

dry farming N (*Agr*) culture *f* sèche, dry farming *m*

dry fly N (*Fishing*) mouche *f* sèche

dry ginger N ≈ Canada dry ® *m*

dry goods NPL (*Comm*) tissus *mpl* et articles *mpl* de mercerie

dry goods store N (*US*) magasin *m* de tissus et d'articles de mercerie

dry-hump** VI *faire l'amour sans pénétration*

dry ice N neige *f* carbonique

dry measure N mesure *f* de capacité pour matières sèches

dry-roasted ADJ [*peanuts*] grillé à sec

dry rot N pourriture *f* sèche (*du bois*)

dry run (*fig*) N (= *trial, test*) galop *m* d'essai ; (= *rehearsal*) répétition *f* ADJ d'essai

dry shampoo N shampooing *m* sec

dry-shod ADV à pied sec

dry ski slope N piste *f* (de ski) artificielle

dry-stone wall N mur *m* de pierres sèches

► **dry off** VI, VT SEP sécher

► **dry out** VI 1 ⇒ **dry off**

2 * [*alcoholic*] se faire désintoxiquer, suivre une cure de désintoxication

VT SEP * [+ *alcoholic*] désintoxiquer

► **dry up** VI 1 [*stream, well*] se dessécher, (se) tarir ; [*moisture*] s'évaporer ; [*clay*] sécher ; [*cow*] ne plus donner de lait ; [*source of supply, inspiration*] se tarir

2 (= *dry the dishes*) essuyer la vaisselle

3 (* = *fall silent*) se taire ; [*actor, speaker, writer*] sécher* ◆ **~ up!** tais-toi !, boucle-la !**

dryer /ˈdraɪəʳ/ N 1 (= *apparatus*) séchoir *m* ; (*for hands*) sèche-mains *m inv* ; (*for clothes*) sèche-linge *m inv* ; (*for hair*) sèche-cheveux *m inv* ; → **spin, tumble** 2 (*for paint*) siccatif *m*

drying /ˈdraɪɪŋ/ N [*of fruit, crop, wood, clothes*] séchage *m* ; (*with a cloth*) essuyage *m*

COMP **drying cupboard, drying room** N séchoir *m*

drying-up N ◆ **to do the ~-up** essuyer la vaisselle

drying-up cloth N torchon *m*

dryly /ˈdraɪlɪ/ ADV ⇒ **drily**

dryness /ˈdraɪnɪs/ N [*of soil, weather*] sécheresse *f*, aridité *f* ; [*of clothes, skin*] sécheresse *f* ; [*of wit, humour, humorist*] style *m* pince-sans-rire *inv*

drysalter /ˈdraɪˈsɔːltəʳ/ N (*Brit*) marchand *m* de couleurs

drysuit /ˈdraɪsuːt/ N combinaison *f* de plongée

DS /diːˈes/ N (*Brit*) (*Police*) (abbrev of **Detective Sergeant**) → **detective**

DSC /ˌdiːesˈsiː/ N (abbrev of **Distinguished Service Cross**) *médaille militaire*

DSc /ˌdiːesˈsiː/ N (*Univ*) (abbrev of **Doctor of Science**) *doctorat ès sciences*

DSM /ˌdiːesˈem/ N (abbrev of **Distinguished Service Medal**) *médaille militaire*

DSO /ˌdiːesˈəʊ/ N (*Brit*) (abbrev of **Distinguished Service Order**) *médaille militaire*

DSS /ˌdiːesˈes/ N (*Brit: formerly*) (abbrev of **Department of Social Security**) → **department**

DST /ˌdiːesˈtiː/ (*US*) (abbrev of **Daylight Saving Time**) → **daylight**

DT (*Comput*) (abbrev of **data transmission**) → **data**

DTD /ˌdiːtiːˈdiː/ N (abbrev of **Document Type Definition**) DTD *f*

DTI /diːtiːˈaɪ/ N (*Brit Admin*) (abbrev of **Department of Trade and Industry**) → **trade**

DTP /ˌdiːtiːˈpiː/ N (abbrev of **desktop publishing**) PAO *f*

DT's* /diːˈtiːz/ NPL (abbrev of **delirium tremens**) delirium tremens *m*

DU /diːˈjuː/ N (abbrev of **depleted uranium**) UA *m*

dual /ˈdjʊəl/ ADJ [*role, function, strategy, income*] double *before n* N (*Gram*) duel *m*

COMP **dual admissions** NPL (*US Univ etc*) double système *m* d'inscriptions (*avec sélection moins stricte pour étudiants défavorisés*)

dual carriageway N (*Brit*) (route *f* à) quatre voies *f inv* ; → ROADS

dual-control ADJ à double commande

dual controls NPL (*in car, plane*) double commande *f*

dual national N personne *f* ayant la double nationalité, binational(e) *m(f)*

dual nationality N double nationalité *f*

dual ownership N copropriété *f*

dual personality N dédoublement *m* de la personnalité

dual-purpose ADJ à double usage

dualism /ˈdjʊəlɪzəm/ N (*Philos, Pol, Rel*) dualisme *m*

dualist /ˈdjʊəlɪst/ ADJ, N (*Philos*) dualiste *mf*

duality /djʊˈælɪtɪ/ N dualité *f*, dualisme *m*

dub /dʌb/ VT 1 ◆ **to ~ sb a knight** donner l'accolade à qn ; (*Hist*) adouber *or* armer qn chevalier ◆ **to ~ sb "Ginger"** (= *nickname*) surnommer qn "Poil de Carotte" 2 [+ *film*] doubler, postsynchroniser

Dubai /duːˈbaɪ/ N Dubaï *m*

dubbin /ˈdʌbɪn/ N dégras *m*, graisse *f* pour les chaussures

dubbing /ˈdʌbɪŋ/ N [*of film*] doublage *m*, postsynchronisation *f*

dubiety /djuːˈbaɪətɪ/ N doute *m*, incertitude *f*

dubious /ˈdjuːbɪəs/ ADJ 1 (= *suspect*) [*deal, claim, reputation, quality, origin, morality*] douteux ; [*privilege, pleasure*] discutable ◆ **these measures are of ~ benefit** les avantages de ces mesures sont discutables 2 (= *unsure*) ◆ **to be ~ about sth** se montrer dubitatif quant à qch, douter de qch ◆ **I was ~ at first** au début, j'avais des doutes ◆ **I am ~ that** *or* **whether the new law will achieve anything** je doute que cette nouvelle loi serve *subj* à quelque chose ◆ **to look/sound ~** avoir l'air/parler d'un ton dubitatif

dubiously /ˈdjuːbɪəslɪ/ ADV [*look at, smile, frown*] d'un air dubitatif ; [*say*] d'un ton dubitatif ◆ **a piece ~ attributed to Albinoni** un morceau attribué sans doute à tort à Albinoni

Dublin /ˈdʌblɪn/ N Dublin COMP **Dublin Bay prawn** N langoustine *f*

Dubliner /ˈdʌblɪnəʳ/ N habitant(e) *m(f)* *or* natif *m*, -ive *f* de Dublin

ducal /ˈdjuːkəl/ ADJ ducal, de duc

ducat /ˈdʌkɪt/ N ducat *m*

duchess /ˈdʌtʃɪs/ N duchesse *f*

duchy /ˈdʌtʃɪ/ N duché *m*

duck[1] /dʌk/ N 1 canard *m* ; (*female*) cane *f* ◆ **wild ~** canard *m* sauvage ◆ **roast ~** canard *m* rôti ◆ **to play ~s and drakes** (*Brit*) faire des ricochets (sur l'eau) ◆ **to play ~s and drakes with sb** (*Brit* = *treat badly*) traiter qn par-dessus la jambe ◆ **to play at ~s and drakes with one's money** (*Brit*) jeter son argent par les fenêtres, gaspiller son argent ◆ **to get one's ~s in a row*** (*US*) maîtriser la situation ◆ **he took to it like a ~ to water** c'était comme s'il avait fait ça toute sa vie ◆ **yes ~s** * (*Brit*) oui mon chou* ◆ **he's a ~*** c'est un chou* *or* un amour ; → **Bombay, dying, lame**

2 (*Brit Cricket*) **to make a ~, to be out for a ~** faire un score nul

3 (*Stock Exchange*) spéculateur *m*, -trice *f* insolvable

4 (*Mil* = *vehicle*) véhicule *m* amphibie

VI 1 (also **duck down**) se baisser vivement ; (*in fight etc*) esquiver un coup ◆ **to ~ (down) under the water** disparaître sous l'eau

2 ◆ **he ~ed into his office** (= *popped in*) il est passé au bureau ; (*to hide*) il s'est réfugié dans

son bureau ◆ **he ~ed out of the rain** il s'est vite mis à l'abri de la pluie

VT 1 ◆ **to ~ sb** pousser qn sous l'eau

2 *[+ one's head]* baisser vivement ; *[+ blow, question etc]* éviter, esquiver ; *[+ responsibility]* se dérober à ; *[+ decision]* esquiver, éluder

COMP duck-billed platypus N ornithorynque *m*

duck-egg blue ADJ gris-bleu *inv*

duck pond N mare *f* aux canards, canardière *f*

duck shooting N chasse *f* au canard

duck soup‡ **N** *(US)* ◆ **that was ~ soup !** *(= easy)* c'était du gâteau ! *

► **duck out of VT FUS** esquiver ◆ **she ~ed out of going with them** elle s'est esquivée pour ne pas les accompagner ◆ **he ~ed out of the commitment he'd made** il s'est dérobé à ses engagements

duck² /dʌk/ **N** *(= fabric)* coutil *m*, toile *f* fine ◆ **~s** *(Brit = trousers)* pantalon *m* de coutil

duckbill /ˈdʌkbɪl/ **N** ⇒ **duck-billed platypus** ; → **duck**

duckboard /ˈdʌkbɔːd/ **N** caillebotis *m*

duckie * /ˈdʌkɪ/ **N** *(Brit)* ◆ **yes** ~ oui mon chou *

ADJ *(US)* ⇒ **ducky**

ducking /ˈdʌkɪŋ/ **N** plongeon *m*, bain *m* forcé ◆ **to give sb a ~** *(= push under water)* pousser qn sous l'eau ; *(= push into water)* pousser qn dans l'eau ◆ **~ and diving** dérobades *fpl*

duckling /ˈdʌklɪŋ/ **N** *(also Culin)* caneton *m* ; *(female)* canette *f* ; *(older)* canardeau *m*

duckweed /ˈdʌkwiːd/ **N** lentille *f* d'eau, lenticule *f*

ducky * /ˈdʌkɪ/ **ADJ** *(US = cute)* mignon tout plein

duct /dʌkt/ **N** *(for liquid, gas, electricity)* conduite *f*, canalisation *f* ; *(Bot)* trachée *f* ; *(Anat)* canal *m*, conduit *m*

ductile /ˈdʌktaɪl/ **ADJ** *[metal]* ductile ; *[person]* docile

ductless gland /ˌdʌktlɪsˈglænd/ **N** glande *f* endocrine

dud * /dʌd/ **ADJ** *(= defective) [shell, bomb, battery, fuse etc]* qui foire * ; *(= worthless) [cheque]* en bois * ; *[loan]* non remboursé ; *[film, teacher, student]* nul (nulle *f*) ; *(= counterfeit) [note, coin]* faux (fausse *f*) **N** *(= shell)* obus *m* non éclaté ; *(= bomb)* bombe *f* non éclatée ; *(= person)* raté(e) *m(f)* ◆ **this coin is a ~** cette pièce est fausse ◆ **this watch is a ~** c'est de la camelote * cette montre ◆ **Phil was a complete ~ at school** Phil était complètement nul à l'école ◆ **to be a ~ at geography** être nul en géographie ◆ **to be a ~ at tennis** être nul au tennis **NPL duds** †‡ *(= clothes)* nippes † * *fpl*

dude * /d(j)uːd/ *(US)* **N** 1 *(= man)* type * *m*, mec‡ *m* 2 *(= dandy)* dandy *m* ; *(young)* gommeux * *m* 3 *(= Easterner)* habitant(e) *m(f)* de la côte Est **COMP dude ranch N** (hôtel *m*) ranch *m*

DUDE RANCH

Sorte de ranch, authentique ou reconstitué, où les touristes peuvent goûter les joies du Far West. Les amateurs viennent y retrouver la vie du cow-boy : monter à cheval, s'occuper du bétail et dîner autour d'un feu de camp. En argot, un **dude** est un citadin, ou un habitant de la côte Est, trop soigné et trop bien habillé.

dudgeon † /ˈdʌdʒən/ **N** ◆ **in (high) ~** offensé dans sa dignité, furieux

due /djuː/ LANGUAGE IN USE 20.6, 26.3

ADJ 1

◆ **due to** *(= because of)* en raison de ◆ **the match was cancelled ~ to bad weather** le match a été annulé en raison du mauvais temps ◆ **~ to the large number of letters he receives he cannot answer them personally** le nombre de lettres qu'il reçoit étant trop important, il ne peut pas y répondre personnellement ; *(= thanks to)* grâce à ◆ **it was ~ to his efforts that the trip was a success** c'est grâce à ses effort que le voyage a été un succès ◆ **it is largely ~ to them that we are in this strong position** c'est en grande partie grâce à eux que nous sommes en position de force ; *(= caused by)* dû (due *f*) à, attribuable à ◆ **what's it ~ to?** à quoi est-ce dû ? ◆ **accidents ~ to technical failure** les accidents dus à des pannes ◆ **the fall in sales is ~ to high interest rates** la chute des ventes est due au niveau élevé des taux d'intérêt, la chute des ventes s'explique par les taux d'intérêt élevés

◆ **to be due to the fact that ...** *(= because)* être dû au fait que ◆ **this is ~ to the fact that interest rates are lower** cela est dû au fait que les taux d'intérêt sont plus bas

2 *(= expected, scheduled)*

devoir is often used to express this meaning.

◆ **he's ~ in Argentina tomorrow** il devrait arriver *or* il est attendu en Argentine demain ◆ **I am ~ there tomorrow** je dois être là-bas demain ◆ **he's ~ back tomorrow** il doit être de retour demain ◆ **the train is ~ (to arrive) at 2.19** le train doit arriver à 14h19 ◆ **just before the plane was ~ to land** juste avant l'heure d'arrivée prévue de l'avion ◆ **to be ~ in** *[train, ferry, plane]* devoir arriver ◆ **to be ~ out** *[report, figures, book]* devoir être publié ◆ **when is the baby ~?** quand doit naître le bébé ? ◆ **the results are ~ next week** les résultats doivent être rendus la semaine prochaine ◆ **there's an election ~ in March** des élections sont prévues en mars ◆ **with parliamentary elections ~ in less than 3 months' time** les élections législatives étant prévues dans moins de trois mois

3 *(= proper, suitable)* ◆ **to give** *or* **pay ~ attention to sb** prêter à qn l'attention qu'il mérite ◆ **to receive ~ credit (for sth)** être reconnu comme il se doit (pour qch) ◆ **after ~ consideration** après mûre réflexion ◆ **to have ~ regard for sth** respecter pleinement qch ◆ **with/without ~ regard to** *or* **for sth** en tenant pleinement compte/sans tenir pleinement compte de qch ◆ **with (all) ~ respect** sauf votre respect ◆ **with (all) ~ respect to Mrs Harrison** malgré tout le respect que je dois à Mme Harrison ◆ **driving without ~ care and attention** conduite *f* imprudente

◆ **in due course** *or* **time** *(in the future)* en temps utile *or* voulu ◆ **she'll find out about everything in ~ time** elle saura tout en temps utile *or* voulu ◆ **we shall in ~ course be publishing our results** nous publierons nos résultats en temps utile *or* voulu ◆ **in ~ course, she found out that ...** elle finit par découvrir que ...

4 *(= payable) [sum, money]* dû (due *f*) ◆ **I was advised that no further payment was ~** on m'a dit que je ne devais plus rien ◆ **when is the rent ~?** quand faut-il payer le loyer ? ◆ **to fall ~** arriver à échéance ◆ **the sum ~ to me** la somme qui m'est due *or* qui me revient

5 *(= owed, expecting)* **our thanks are ~ to Mr Bertillon** nous tenons à remercier M. Bertillon, notre gratitude va à M. Bertillon ◆ **they must be treated with the respect ~ to their rank/age** ils doivent être traités avec le respect dû à leur rang/âge

◆ **to be due for** ◆ **they are ~ for a shock** *(= going to have)* ils vont avoir un choc ◆ **they were ~ for a break, he thought** *(= should have)* ils devraient prendre des vacances, pensa-t-il ◆ **when you're next ~ for a check-up** lorsqu'il sera temps de passer un contrôle ◆ **to be ~ for completion/demolition/release in 2004** *(= scheduled for)* devoir être terminé/démoli/libéré en 2004 ◆ **he was ~ for retirement in twelve months' time** il devait prendre sa retraite dans un an

PREP

◆ **to be due sth** ◆ **I am ~ £300/six days' holiday** on me doit 300 livres/six jours de congé ◆ **I feel I'm about ~ a holiday!** je pense que je mérite bien des vacances ! ◆ **he had not taken a holiday, but accumulated the leave ~ him** au lieu de prendre des vacances il avait accumulé les jours qu'on lui devait

ADV ◆ **~ north/south** *etc* plein nord/sud *etc* (*of* par rapport à) ◆ **to face ~ north** *[building]* être (en) plein nord ; *[person]* faire face au nord

N ◆ **to give sb his ~** être juste envers qn, faire *or* rendre justice à qn ◆ **(to) give him his ~, he did try hard** il faut (être juste et) reconnaître qu'il a quand même fait tout son possible ; → **devil**

NPL dues *(= fees) [of club etc]* cotisation *f* ; *[of harbour]* droits *mpl* (de port)

COMP due process N *(Jur:* also **due process of law)** *application de la loi selon les procédures prévues*

duel /ˈdjʊəl/ **N** *(lit, fig)* duel *m* ◆ **~ to the death** duel *m* à mort ; → **challenge, fight VI** se battre en duel (*with* contre, avec) **COMP duelling pistol N** pistolet *m* de duel

duellist /ˈdjʊəlɪst/ **N** duelliste *m*

duet /djuːˈet/ **N** duo *m* ◆ **to sing/play a ~** chanter/jouer en duo ◆ **violin ~** duo *m* de violon ◆ **piano ~** morceau *m* à quatre mains

duff¹ /dʌf/ **N** *(Culin)* pudding *m* ◆ **up the ~**‡ en cloque‡ ; → **plum**

duff² /dʌf/ *(Brit)* **ADJ** * 1 *(= non-functional) [machine, watch, gene etc]* détraqué * 2 *(= useless) [suggestion, idea, film, book, record]* nul (nulle *f*) 3 *(= failed) [shot etc]* raté, loupé * **VT** (‡ *= alter, fake*) *[+ stolen goods]* maquiller, truquer

► **duff up**‡ **VT SEP** casser la gueule à‡

duff³‡ /dʌf/ **N** *(US = buttocks)* postérieur *m* ◆ **he just sits on his ~ all day** il ne fiche * rien de la journée ◆ **get off your ~!** magne-toi le train !‡

duffel /ˈdʌfəl/ **N** *gros tissu de laine*

COMP duffel bag N sac *m* de paquetage, sac *m* marin

duffel coat N duffel-coat *m*

duffer * /ˈdʌfəʳ/ **N** nullard(e) * *m(f)* ◆ **he is a ~ at French** il est nul en français

duffle /ˈdʌfəl/ **ADJ** ⇒ **duffel**

dug¹ /dʌg/ **N** mamelle *f*, tétine *f* ; *[of cow]* pis *m*

dug² /dʌg/ **VB** pt, ptp of **dig**

dugong /ˈduːgɒŋ/ **N** dugong *m*

dugout /ˈdʌgaʊt/ **N** *(Mil = trench)* tranchée-abri *f* ; *(= canoe)* pirogue *f*

DUI /ˌdiːjuːˈaɪ/ **N** *(US)* (abbrev of **driving under (the) influence (of alcohol)**) conduite *f* en état d'ébriété

duke /djuːk/ **N** *(= nobleman)* duc *m* **NPL dukes** ‡ *(esp US = fists)* poings *mpl*

dukedom /ˈdjuːkdəm/ **N** *(= territory)* duché *m* ; *(= title)* titre *m* de duc

dulcet /ˈdʌlsɪt/ **ADJ** *(liter)* suave

dulcimer /ˈdʌlsɪməʳ/ **N** tympanon *m*

dull /dʌl/ **ADJ** 1 *(= boring, uneventful) [book, lecture, party, person]* ennuyeux ; *[life, job]* ennuyeux, monotone ; *[place]* morne ; *[food]* quelconque ; *[style]* terne ; *[Stock market]* morose ◆ **there's never a ~ minute** *or* **life is never ~ (with Janet around)** on ne s'ennuie jamais (lorsque Janet est là) ◆ **as ~ as ditchwater** *or* **dishwater** ennuyeux comme la pluie ; → **deadly**

2 *(= not bright or shiny) [light, glow]* faible ; *[colour, eyes, hair, skin, metal]* terne ; *[weather, sky, day]* maussade, gris

3 *(= vague) [pain, sound, feeling]* sourd ◆ **with a ~ thud** *or* **thump** avec un bruit sourd

4 (= *lethargic, withdrawn*) [*person*] abattu
5 (= *slow-witted*) [*person, mind*] borné ◆ **his senses/faculties are growing** ~ ses sens/facultés s'émoussent *or* s'amoindrissent
6 (= *blunt*) [*blade, knife*] émoussé
VT (= *blunt*) [+ *edge, blade*] émousser ; [+ *senses*] émousser, engourdir ; [+ *mind*] engourdir ; [+ *appetite*] calmer ; [+ *pain, grief, impression*] atténuer ; [+ *memories*] estomper ; [+ *pleasure*] émousser ; [+ *sound*] assourdir, amortir ; (*in colour, brightness*) [+ *colour, mirror, metal*] ternir
VI [*eyes*] se voiler ; [*appetite*] diminuer ; [*edge, blade*] s'émousser ; [*light*] baisser
COMP **dull-witted** ADJ dur à la détente *

dullard † * /ˈdʌləd/ N nullard(e) * *m(f)*

dullness /ˈdʌlnɪs/ N 1 (= *slow-wittedness*) lourdeur *f* d'esprit ; [*of senses*] affaiblissement *m* ◆ ~ **of hearing** dureté *f* d'oreille 2 (= *tedium, lack of interest*) [*of book, evening, lecture*] caractère *m* ennuyeux, manque *m* d'intérêt ; [*of person*] personnalité *f* terne ; [*of life*] grisaille *f* ; [*of landscape, room*] tristesse *f* 3 [*of colour, metal, mirror etc*] manque *m or* peu *m* d'éclat, aspect *m* terne ; [*of sound*] caractère *m* sourd *or* étouffé ; [*of weather*] grisaille *f*

dullsville ⁑ /ˈdʌlzvɪl/ N (US) ◆ **it's** ~ **here** on s'emmerde ici ⁑, c'est pas la joie ici *

dully /ˈdʌllɪ/ ADV 1 (= *with a muffled sound*) avec un bruit sourd 2 (= *dimly*) [*glow, gleam*] faiblement 3 (= *without enthusiasm*) [*say, reply*] d'un ton morne ; [*look, nod*] d'un air morne ; [*think*] avec lassitude 4 (= *boringly*) [*talk, write*] d'une manière ennuyeuse

duly /ˈdjuːlɪ/ ADV 1 (= *properly*) [*recorded, completed, authorized, rewarded*] dûment, en bonne et due forme ◆ ~ **elected** dûment élu, élu en bonne et due forme 2 (= *as expected*) comme prévu ◆ **the visitors were** ~ **impressed** comme prévu, les visiteurs ont été impressionnés ◆ **I asked him for his autograph and he** ~ **obliged** je lui ai demandé un autographe et il a accepté

dumb /dʌm/ ADJ 1 (*lit*) muet ◆ ~ **animals** † les bêtes *fpl* ◆ **our** ~ **friends** nos amies les bêtes ; → **deaf, strike** 2 (*fig* = *silent*) muet (*with, from* de) abasourdi (*with, from* de, par) ◆ ~ **insolence** mutisme *m* insolent 3 (*esp US* * = *stupid*) [*person*] bête ; [*action, idea, joke*] stupide ; [*question*] idiot ; [*object, present*] ringard * ◆ **a** ~ **blonde** une blonde évaporée ◆ **to act** ~ faire l'innocent NPL **the dumb** les muets *mpl*
COMP **dumb-ass** ⁑ (US) N con ⁑ *m*, conne ⁑ *f* ADJ à la con ⁑
dumb bomb N (*Mil*) bombe *f* conventionnelle
dumb cluck ⁑ N imbécile *mf*
dumb ox ⁑ N (US) ballot * *m*, andouille * *f*
dumb show N ◆ **in** ~ **show** en mimant, par (des) signes
dumb terminal N (*Comput*) terminal *m* passif
▸ **dumb down** VT SEP [+ *programmes, courses, jobs*] niveler par le bas

dumbbell /ˈdʌmbel/ N (*Sport*) haltère *m*

dumbfound /dʌmˈfaʊnd/ VT abasourdir, ahurir

dumbfounded /dʌmˈfaʊndɪd/ ADJ ahuri, sidéré ◆ **I'm** ~ je suis sidéré, je n'en reviens pas

dumbly /ˈdʌmlɪ/ ADV [*stare, stand, nod*] (= *silently*) en silence ; (*with surprise*) avec stupeur

dumbness /ˈdʌmnɪs/ N mutisme *m* ; (⁑ = *stupidity*) bêtise *f*, niaiserie *f*

dumbo ⁑ /ˈdʌmbəʊ/ N ballot * *m*, andouille * *f*

dumbstruck /ˈdʌmstrʌk/ ADJ frappé de stupeur

dumbwaiter /ˌdʌmˈweɪtəʳ/ N (= *lift*) monte-plat *m* ; (*Brit*) (= *trolley*) table *f* roulante ; (= *revolving stand*) plateau *m* tournant

dum-dum /ˈdʌmdʌm/ N 1 (= *bullet*) balle *f* dum-dum *inv* 2 (⁑ = *stupid person*) crétin(e) *m(f)*, andouille * *f*

dummy /ˈdʌmɪ/ N 1 (*Comm* = *sham object*) objet *m* factice ; (*Comm, Sewing* = *model*) mannequin *m* ; [*of ventriloquist*] marionnette *f* ; (*Theat*) personnage *m* muet, figurant *m* ; (*Fin etc* = *person replacing another*) prête-nom *m*, homme *m* de paille ; [*of book*] maquette *f* ; (*Bridge*) mort *m* ; (*Sport*) feinte *f* ◆ **to sell the** ~ (*Sport*) feinter, faire une feinte de passe ◆ **to sell sb the** ~ feinter qn ◆ **to be** ~ (*Bridge*) faire *or* être le mort ◆ **to play from** ~ (*Bridge*) jouer du mort
2 (*Brit* = *baby's teat*) sucette *f*, tétine *f*
3 (* = *idiot*) andouille * *f*, imbécile *mf* ◆ **"you're a dummy, Mack," she yelled** "Mack, tu es une andouille * *or* un imbécile" hurla-t-elle
ADJ faux (fausse *f*), factice
VI (*Sport*) feinter, faire une feinte de passe
COMP **dummy bridge** N (*Cards*) bridge *m* à trois
dummy element N (*Ling*) postiche *m*
dummy pass N (*Sport*) feinte *f* de passe
dummy run N (*Brit*) (= *air attack*) attaque *f or* bombardement *m* simulé(e) ; (*in manufacturing*) (coup *m* d')essai *m*
dummy symbol N ⇒ **dummy element**

dump /dʌmp/ N 1 (= *pile of rubbish*) tas *m or* amas *m* d'ordures ; (= *place*) décharge *f*, dépotoir *m* ◆ **to be (down) in the ~s** * avoir le cafard *
2 (*Mil*) dépôt *m* ; → **ammunition**
3 (* *pej*) (= *place*) trou *m* perdu * ; (= *house, hotel*) trou *m* à rats *
4 (*Comput*) vidage *m*
5 ◆ **to have a** ~ ⁑ (= *defecate*) couler un bronze ⁑, chier *⁑
VT 1 [+ *rubbish*] déposer, jeter ; [+ *sand, bricks*] décharger, déverser ; (*Comm*) [+ *goods*] vendre *or* écouler à bas prix (*sur les marchés extérieurs*), pratiquer le dumping pour
2 (* = *set down*) [+ *package*] déposer ; [+ *passenger*] poser, larguer * ◆ ~ **your bag on the table** fiche * ton sac sur la table
3 (* = *get rid of*) [+ *thing*] bazarder * ; [+ *boyfriend, girlfriend*] larguer *, plaquer ⁑
4 (*Comput*) [+ *data file etc*] vider ◆ **to** ~ **to the printer** transférer sur l'imprimante
VI (⁑ = *defecate*) couler un bronze ⁑, chier *⁑
COMP **dump bin, dump display** N (*Comm*) présentoir *m* d'articles en vrac
dump truck N ⇒ **dumper**
▸ **dump on** ⁑ VT FUS (= *mistreat*) traiter comme du poisson pourri * ; (= *offload problems on*) se défouler sur

dumper /ˈdʌmpəʳ/ N (*Brit*) (*also* **dumper truck**) tombereau *m*, dumper *m*

dumping /ˈdʌmpɪŋ/ N [*of load, rubbish*] décharge *f* ; (*Ecol: in sea etc*) déversement *m* (de produits nocifs) ; (*Comm*) dumping *m* COMP **dumping ground** N (*lit, fig*) dépotoir *m*

dumpling /ˈdʌmplɪŋ/ N (*Culin: savoury*) boulette *f* (de pâte) ; (* = *person*) boulot *m*, -otte *f*

Dumpster ® /ˈdʌmpstəʳ/ N (US) benne *f* (à ordures)

dumpy * /ˈdʌmpɪ/ ADJ courtaud, boulot

dun¹ /dʌn/ ADJ (= *colour*) brun foncé *inv*, brun grisâtre *inv* N cheval *m* louvet, jument *f* louvette

dun² /dʌn/ N (= *claim*) demande *f* de remboursement VT [+ *debtor*] harceler, relancer ◆ **to** ~ **sb for money owed** harceler *or* relancer qn pour lui faire payer ses dettes

dunce /dʌns/ N âne *m*, cancre * *m* ◆ **to be a** ~ **at maths** être nul en math COMP **dunce's cap** N bonnet *m* d'âne

dunderhead /ˈdʌndəhed/ N imbécile *mf*

Dundonian /dʌnˈdəʊnɪən/ ADJ de Dundee N habitant(e) *m(f) or* natif *m*, -ive *f* de Dundee

dune /djuːn/ N dune *f* COMP **dune buggy** N buggy *m*

dung /dʌŋ/ N (*NonC*) (= *excrement*) excrément(s) *m(pl)*, crotte *f* ; [*of horse*] crottin *m* ; [*of cattle*] bouse *f* ; [*of wild animal*] fumées *fpl* ; (= *manure*) fumier *m* COMP **dung beetle** N bousier *m*

dungarees /ˌdʌŋɡəˈriːz/ NPL salopette *f*

dungeon /ˈdʌndʒən/ N (*underground*) cachot *m* (souterrain) ; (*Hist* = *castle tower*) donjon *m*

dungheap /ˈdʌŋhiːp/, **dunghill** /ˈdʌŋhɪl/ N tas *m* de fumier

dunk /dʌŋk/ VT tremper ◆ **to** ~ **one's bread in one's coffee** tremper son pain dans son café

Dunkirk /dʌnˈkɜːk/ N Dunkerque

dunlin /ˈdʌnlɪn/ N bécasseau *m* variable

dunno ⁑ /dəˈnəʊ/ ⇒ **don't know**

dunnock /ˈdʌnək/ N (*Brit*) accenteur *m* mouchet, fauvette *f* d'hiver *or* des haies

dunny * /ˈdʌnɪ/ N (*Austral*) chiottes ⁑ *fpl*, W.-C. * *mpl*

Duns Scotus /ˈdʌnzˈskɒtəs/ N Duns Scot *m*

duo /ˈdjuːəʊ/ N (pl **duos** *or* **dui** /ˈdjuːiː/) (*Mus, Theat*) duo *m*

duodecimal /ˌdjuːəʊˈdesɪməl/ ADJ duodécimal

duodenal /ˌdjuːəʊˈdiːnl/ ADJ duodénal COMP **duodenal ulcer** N ulcère *m* du duodénum

duodenum /ˌdjuːəʊˈdiːnəm/ N (pl **duodenums** *or* **duodena** /ˈdjuːəʊˈdiːnə/) duodénum *m*

duopoly /djʊˈɒpəlɪ/ N duopole *m*

dupe /djuːp/ VT duper, tromper ◆ **to** ~ **sb into doing sth** amener qn à faire qch en le dupant N dupe *f*

duple /ˈdjuːpl/ ADJ (*gen*) double ; (*Mus*) binaire COMP **duple time** N (*Mus*) rythme *m or* mesure *f* binaire

duplex /ˈdjuːpleks/ ADJ duplex *inv* N (US) (*also* **duplex house**) maison *f* jumelle ; (*also* **duplex apartment**) duplex *m* ; → House COMP **duplex paper** N (*Phot*) bande *f* protectrice

duplicate /ˈdjuːplɪkeɪt/ VT 1 (= *copy*) [+ *document, map, key*] faire un double de ; [+ *film*] faire un contretype de ; (*on machine*) [+ *document*] polycopier ; [+ *action etc*] répéter exactement
2 (= *do again*) refaire ; (= *repeat*) reproduire ◆ **that is merely duplicating work already done** cela revient à refaire le travail qu'on a déjà fait ◆ **he will seek to** ~ **his success overseas at home** il tentera de trouver le même succès dans son pays qu'à l'étranger ◆ **the phenomenon hasn't been ~d elsewhere on anything like the same scale** le phénomène n'a été reproduit nulle part ailleurs dans les mêmes proportions ◆ **to** ~ **results** obtenir deux fois les mêmes résultats
N /ˈdjuːplɪkɪt/ [*of document, map, key, ornament, chair*] double *m* ; (*Jur etc*) duplicata *m inv* ◆ **in** ~ en deux exemplaires
ADJ /ˈdjuːplɪkɪt/ [*copy*] en double ◆ **a** ~ **cheque/receipt** un duplicata du chèque/du reçu ◆ **I've got a** ~ **key** j'ai un double de la clé
COMP **duplicate bridge** N bridge *m* de compétition *or* de tournoi
duplicating machine N duplicateur *m*

duplication /ˌdjuːplɪˈkeɪʃən/ N (*NonC*) [*of document*] copie *f*, duplication *f* ; (*on machine*) polycopie *f* ; [*of work*] répétition *f* inutile ◆ **there is a great deal of** ~ **of effort in research** dans la recherche, les mêmes travaux sont souvent répétés inutilement par plusieurs personnes ◆ **there is some** ~ **between the two departments** il y a un certain chevauchement entre les deux départements

duplicator /ˈdjuːplɪkeɪtəʳ/ N duplicateur *m*

duplicitous /djuːˈplɪsɪtəs/ ADJ fourbe

duplicity /djuːˈplɪsɪtɪ/ N duplicité *f*, fourberie *f*

Dur. abbrev of **Durham**

durability /ˌdjʊərəˈbɪlɪtɪ/ **N** *[of product, material, institution, friendship, solution]* durabilité *f*, caractère *m* durable

durable /ˈdjʊərəbl/ **ADJ** durable ◆ **CDs are more ~ than cassettes** les CD sont plus solides que les cassettes, les CD durent plus longtemps que les cassettes **NPL** **durables** ⇒ **durable goods** **COMP** **durable goods NPL** *(Comm)* biens *mpl* de consommation durables

Duralumin ® /djʊəˈræljʊmɪn/ **N** duralumin *m*

duration /djʊəˈreɪʃən/ **N** durée *f* ◆ **of long ~** de longue durée ◆ **for the ~ of ...** pendant toute la durée de ... ◆ **he stayed for the ~** * *(= for ages)* il est resté une éternité

Durban /ˈdɜːbæn/ **N** Durban

duress /djʊəˈres/ **N** contrainte *f*, coercition *f* ◆ **under ~** sous la contrainte, contraint et forcé *(Jur)*

Durex ® /ˈdjʊəreks/ **N** *(pl inv)* préservatif *m*

durian /ˈdjʊərɪən/ **N** durian *m*

during /ˈdjʊərɪŋ/ **PREP** pendant ; *(= in the course of)* au cours de ◆ **~ working hours** pendant les heures de travail ◆ **~ the night** pendant *or* durant la nuit ◆ **plants need to be protected ~ bad weather** il faut protéger les plantes pendant *or* durant les périodes de mauvais temps ◆ **~ the violence yesterday** au cours des violents incidents d'hier ◆ **~ the past few months** au cours des derniers mois

durst †† /dɜːst/ **VB** pt of **dare**

durum /ˈdjʊərəm/ **N** (also **durum wheat**) blé *m* dur

dusk /dʌsk/ **N** *(= twilight)* crépuscule *m* ; *(= gloom)* (semi-)obscurité *f* ◆ **at ~** au crépuscule, à la tombée de la nuit ◆ **shortly after ~** peu de temps après la tombée de la nuit ◆ **in the ~** entre chien et loup

duskiness /ˈdʌskɪnɪs/ **N** *[of complexion]* teint *m* mat *or* basané

dusky /ˈdʌskɪ/ **ADJ** [1] *(= dark-skinned) [person]* à la peau basanée, au teint basané ; *[complexion]* basané [2] *[colour]* mat ◆ **~ pink** vieux rose *inv*, rose cendré *inv* [3] *(= dim) [room]* sombre

dust /dʌst/ **N** *(NonC)* [1] *(on furniture, ground)* poussière *f* ◆ **there was thick ~, the ~ lay thick** il y avait une épaisse couche de poussière ◆ **I've got a speck of ~ in my eye** j'ai une poussière dans l'œil ◆ **to raise a lot of ~** *(lit)* faire de la poussière ; *(fig)* faire tout un scandale, faire beaucoup de bruit ◆ **to lay the ~** *(lit)* mouiller la poussière ; *(fig)* ramener le calme, dissiper la fumée ◆ **to throw ~ in sb's eyes** *(fig)* jeter de la poudre aux yeux de qn ◆ **to kick up** *or* **raise a ~** * faire un *or* du foin * ◆ **you couldn't see him for ~** * *(Brit)* il s'était volatilisé ; → **ash², bite, shake off**

[2] *[of coal, gold]* poussière *f*, poudre *f*

VT [1] *[+ furniture]* épousseter, essuyer ; *[+ room]* essuyer la poussière dans ◆ **it's done and ~ed** * *(Brit, Austral)* l'affaire est classée

[2] *(with talc, sugar etc)* saupoudrer *(with* de)

VI épousseter

COMP **dust bag N** sac *m* à poussière *(d'aspirateur)*

dust-bath N ◆ **to take a ~-bath** *[bird]* s'ébrouer dans la poussière, prendre un bain de poussière

dust bowl N *(Geog)* désert *m* de poussière, cratère(s) *m(pl)* de poussière

dust cloth N *(US)* chiffon *m* (à poussière)

dust cloud N nuage *m* de poussière

dust cover N *[of book]* jaquette *f* ; *[of furniture]* housse *f* (de protection)

dust devil N tourbillon *m* de poussière

dust jacket N jaquette *f*

dust sheet N housse *f* (de protection)

dust storm N tempête *f* de poussière

dust-up * **N** *(Brit)* accrochage * *m*, bagarre * *f* ◆ **to have a ~-up with sb** *(Brit)* avoir un accrochage * *or* se bagarrer * avec qn

▸ **dust down, dust off VT SEP** épousseter ◆ **to ~ o.s. down** s'épousseter

▸ **dust out VT SEP** *[+ box, cupboard]* épousseter

dustbin /ˈdʌstbɪn/ **N** *(Brit)* poubelle *f*, boîte *f* à ordures **COMP** **dustbin man N** (pl **dustbin men**) *(Brit)* ⇒ **dustman**

dustcart /ˈdʌstkɑːt/ **N** *(Brit)* benne *f* à ordures, camion *m* des éboueurs *or* des boueux *

duster /ˈdʌstəʳ/ **N** [1] *(Brit)* chiffon *m* (à poussière) ; (also **blackboard duster**) chiffon *m* (pour effacer) ; → **feather** [2] *(US)* *(= overgarment)* blouse *f* ; *(= housecoat)* robe *f* d'intérieur [3] *(= device:* also **crop duster**) pulvérisateur *m* d'insecticide *(souvent un avion)*

dustheap /ˈdʌsthiːp/ **N** *(lit)* tas *m* d'ordures ; *(fig)* poubelle *f*, rebut *m*

dusting /ˈdʌstɪŋ/ **N** [1] *[of furniture]* époussetage *m* ◆ **to do the ~** épousseter, essuyer (la poussière) ◆ **to give sth a ~** donner un coup de chiffon à qch [2] *(Culin etc = sprinkling)* saupoudrage *m*

COMP **dusting down N** ◆ **to give sb a ~ down** passer un savon à qn ◆ **to get a ~ down** recevoir un savon

dusting-powder N talc *m*

dustman /ˈdʌstmən/ **N** (pl **-men**) *(Brit)* éboueur *m*, boueux * *m*

dustpan /ˈdʌstpæn/ **N** pelle *f* (à poussière)

dustproof /ˈdʌstpruːf/ **ADJ** antipoussière

dusty /ˈdʌstɪ/ **ADJ** [1] *(= covered in dust)* poussiéreux ◆ **to get ~** se couvrir de poussière [2] *[colour]* cendré ◆ **~ blue** bleu cendré *inv* ◆ **~ pink** vieux rose *inv*, rose cendré *inv* [3] **to give sb a ~ answer** * envoyer paître qn * ◆ **to get** *or* **receive a ~ answer (from sb)** * se faire envoyer paître (par qn) * ◆ **not so ~, not too ~** * pas mal

Dutch /dʌtʃ/ **ADJ** *(gen)* néerlandais, hollandais ; *[ambassador, embassy]* des Pays-Bas ; *[teacher]* de néerlandais ◆ **the ~ School** *(Art)* l'école *f* hollandaise ◆ **~ cheese** fromage *m* de Hollande, hollande *m*

N [1] *(= language)* hollandais *m*, néerlandais *m* ◆ **it's (all) ~ to me** * *(fig)* c'est du chinois *or* de l'hébreu pour moi ; → **double**

[2] *(US fig)* **to be in ~ with sb** * être en disgrâce auprès de qn ◆ **to get one's ~ up** * se mettre en rogne * ◆ **to get into ~** * avoir des ennuis, se mettre dans le pétrin *

NPL **the Dutch** *(loosely)* les Hollandais *mpl* ; *(more correctly)* les Néerlandais *mpl*

ADV ◆ **to go ~** * *(in restaurant)* payer chacun sa part ; *(in cinema, theatre)* payer chacun sa place

COMP **Dutch auction N** enchères *fpl* au rabais

Dutch barn N hangar *m* à récoltes

Dutch cap N diaphragme *m*

Dutch courage N courage *m* puisé dans la bouteille ◆ **the whisky gave him ~ courage** le whisky lui a donné du courage

Dutch door N *(US)* porte *f* à double vantail, porte *f* d'étable

the Dutch East Indies NPL les Indes *fpl* néerlandaises

Dutch elm N orme *m* *(ulmus hollandica)*

Dutch elm disease N champignon *m* parasite de l'orme

Dutch master N maître *m* de l'école hollandaise

Dutch oven N *(= casserole)* grosse cocotte *f* *(en métal)*

Dutch treat N ◆ **to go on a ~ treat** partager les frais

Dutch uncle † * **N** ◆ **to talk to sb like a ~ uncle** dire ses quatre vérités à qn

Dutchman /ˈdʌtʃmən/ **N** (pl **-men**) Hollandais *m* ◆ **if he's a professional footballer, then I'm a ~** je veux bien être pendu si c'est un footballeur professionnel ; → **flying**

Dutchwoman /ˈdʌtʃˌwʊmən/ **N** (pl **-women**) Hollandaise *f*

dutiable /ˈdjuːtɪəbl/ **ADJ** taxable ; *(Customs)* soumis à des droits de douane

dutiful /ˈdjuːtɪfʊl/ **ADJ** *[child]* obéissant ; *[husband, wife]* dévoué ; *[employee]* consciencieux

dutifully /ˈdjuːtɪfəlɪ/ **ADV** consciencieusement ◆ **we laughed/applauded ~** nous avons ri/applaudi consciencieusement

duty /ˈdjuːtɪ/ **LANGUAGE IN USE 10.1**

N [1] *(NonC: moral, legal)* devoir *m*, obligation *f* ◆ **to do one's ~** s'acquitter de *or* faire son devoir *(by sb* envers qn) ◆ **it is my ~ to say that ..., I feel ~ bound to say that ...** il est de mon devoir de dire que ... ◆ **~ calls** le devoir m'appelle ◆ **the** *or* **one's ~ to one's parents** le *or* son devoir envers ses parents ◆ **what about your ~ to yourself?** et ton devoir envers toi-même ? ◆ **to make it one's ~ to do sth** se faire un devoir de faire qch

[2] *(gen pl = responsibility)* fonction *f*, responsabilité *f* ◆ **to take up one's duties** entrer en fonction ◆ **to neglect one's duties** négliger ses fonctions ◆ **my duties consist of ...** mes fonctions consistent à ... ◆ **his duties as presidential adviser** ses fonctions de conseiller du président ◆ **his duties have been taken over by his colleague** ses fonctions ont été reprises par son collègue

[3] *(= work)* **in the course of (one's) ~** dans l'exercice de mes *(or* ses *etc)* fonctions ◆ **to do ~ for sb, to do sb's ~** remplacer qn ◆ **the reading room also does ~ as** *or* **for a library** *(fig)* la salle de lecture fait également fonction *or* office de bibliothèque

◆ **on duty** de service ; *(Med)* de garde ◆ **to be on ~** être de service *or* de garde ◆ **to go on ~** prendre son service

◆ **off duty** ◆ **to be off ~** ne pas être de service *or* de garde ; *(Mil)* avoir quartier libre ◆ **to go off ~** quitter son service

[4] *(Fin = tax)* droit *m*, taxe *f* ; *(at Customs)* frais *mpl* de douane ◆ **to pay ~ on sth** payer un droit *or* une taxe sur qch ; → **death, estate**

COMP **duty call N** visite *f* de politesse

duty-free ADJ hors taxes

duty-free allowance N *quantité autorisée de produits hors taxes (par personne)*

duty-frees * **NPL** *(Brit)* marchandises *fpl* hors taxes

duty-free shop N boutique *f* hors taxes

duty-free shopping N *(NonC)* achat *m* de marchandises hors taxes

duty of care N responsabilité *f* morale *(to* envers)

duty officer N *(Mil)* officier *m* de permanence ; *(Police)* officier *m* de police de service ; *(Admin)* officiel *m* *or* préposé *m* de service

duty paid ADJ dédouané

duty roster, duty rota N liste *f* de service ; *(esp Mil)* tableau *m* de service

duvet /ˈduːveɪ/ **N** couette *f* **COMP** **duvet cover N** housse *f* de couette

DV /diːˈviː/ **ADV** (abbrev of **Deo volente**) Dieu voulant

DVD /ˈdiːviːˌdiː/ **N** (abbrev of **digital versatile disc**) DVD *m* ◆ **~ burner** graveur *m* de DVD ◆ **~ player** lecteur *m* de DVD ◆ **~-Rom** DVD-Rom *m* ◆ **~writer** graveur *m* de DVD

DVD-A /ˌdiːviːdiːˈeɪ/ **N** (abbrev of **digital versatile disc audio**) DVD-A

DVLA /ˌdiːviːelˈeɪ/ **N** *(Brit)* (abbrev of **Driver and Vehicle Licensing Agency**) *service des immatriculations et permis de conduire*

DVM /ˌdiːviːˈem/ **N** *(US Univ)* (abbrev of **Doctor of Veterinary Medicine**) *doctorat vétérinaire*

DVT /ˌdiːviːˈtiː/ **N** *(Med)* (abbrev of **deep vein thrombosis**) TVP *f*

dwarf /dwɔːf/ **N** (pl **dwarfs** *or* **dwarves** /dwɔːvz/) *(= person, animal)* nain(e) *m(f)* ; *(= tree)* arbre *m* nain **ADJ** *[person, tree, star]* nain **VT** [1]

[+ achievement] éclipser ◆ **the US air travel market ~s that of Britain** en comparaison du marché des voyages américains, celui de la Grande-Bretagne semble minuscule ◆ **his figure was ~ed by the huge sign** il semblait minuscule à côté du logo énorme, il était écrasé par le logo énorme 2 *[+ plant]* empêcher de croître

dwarfish /ˈdwɔːfɪʃ/ ADJ *(pej)* nabot(-ote *f*)

dweeb‡ /dwiːb/ N *(esp US)* pauvre mec* *m*

dwell /dwel/ (pret, ptp **dwelt** *or* **dwelled**) VI *(liter)* 1 habiter, demeurer ◆ **to ~ in Glasgow/in France** habiter *or* demeurer à Glasgow/en France 2 *(fig) [interest, difficulty]* résider (*in* dans)

► **dwell on** VT FUS *(= think about)* ne pouvoir s'empêcher de penser à ; *(= talk at length on)* s'étendre sur ; *(Mus) [+ note]* appuyer sur ◆ **don't ~ on it** n'y pense plus ◆ **to ~ on the past** s'appesantir sur le passé, revenir sans cesse sur le passé ◆ **to ~ on the fact that ...** ressasser le fait que ... ◆ **don't let's ~ on it** passons là-dessus, ne nous attardons pas sur ce sujet

► **dwell upon** VT FUS ⇒ **dwell on**

dweller /ˈdweləʳ/ N habitant(e) *m(f)* ; → **country**

dwelling /ˈdwelɪŋ/ N *(Admin or liter:* also **dwelling place)** habitation *f*, résidence *f* ◆ **to take up one's ~** s'installer, élire domicile *(Admin)* COMP **dwelling house** N maison *f* d'habitation

dwelt /dwelt/ VB pt, ptp of **dwell**

DWEM N *(esp US)* (abbrev of **Dead White European Male)** *homme célèbre qui devrait sa réputation à son appartenance au sexe masculin et à la race blanche*

dwindle /ˈdwɪndl/ VI *[strength]* diminuer, décroître ; *[numbers, resources, supplies, interest]* diminuer

► **dwindle away** VI diminuer ; *[person]* dépérir

dwindling /ˈdwɪndlɪŋ/ N diminution *f* (graduelle) ADJ *[number, interest, popularity]* décroissant ; *[resources, supplies, funds]* en baisse ; *[population]* en baisse, décroissant ◆ **~ audiences** un public de moins en moins nombreux

DWP /ˌdiːdʌbljuːˈpiː/ N (abbrev of **Department of Work and Pensions)** → **department**

dye /daɪ/ N *(= substance)* teinture *f*, colorant *m* ; *(= colour)* teinte *f* ◆ **hair ~** teinture *f* pour les cheveux ◆ **fast ~** grand teint *m* ◆ **the ~ will come out in the wash** cela déteindra au lavage ◆ **a villain of the deepest ~** *(fig liter)* une canaille *or* crapule de la pire espèce VT teindre ◆ **to ~ sth red** teindre qch en rouge ◆ **to ~ one's hair** se teindre les cheveux ; → **dyed, tie** VI *[cloth etc]* prendre la teinture, se teindre COMP **dyed-in-the-wool** ADJ *(fig)* bon teint *inv*, invétéré

dyed /daɪd/ ADJ *[hair, fabric]* teint ◆ **~ blond/blue** teint en blond/bleu

dyeing /ˈdaɪɪŋ/ N *(NonC)* teinture *f*

dyer /ˈdaɪəʳ/ N teinturier *m* ◆ **~'s and cleaner's** teinturier *m*

dyestuffs /ˈdaɪstʌfs/ NPL colorants *mpl*

dyeworks /ˈdaɪwɜːks/ NPL teinturerie *f*

dying /ˈdaɪɪŋ/ ADJ 1 *[person, animal, plant, fire]* mourant ◆ **the ~ daylight** les dernières lueurs *fpl* du jour ◆ **the Dying Swan** *(Ballet)* la Mort du Cygne ◆ **the ~ embers** les tisons *mpl* ◆ **to look like a ~ duck (in a thunderstorm)*** *(hum)* avoir l'air pitoyable 2 *(= declining) [custom, industry]* en train de disparaître ◆ **it's a ~ art** c'est un art en voie de disparition ◆ **they are a ~ breed** *(lit, fig)* c'est une espèce en voie de disparition 3 *(= final) [words, wish]* dernier ◆ **with his ~ breath** sur son lit de mort ◆ **till** *or* **until** *or* **to my ~ day** jusqu'à mon dernier jour ◆ **in the ~ minutes of the game** pendant les dernières minutes du match N *(= death)* mort *f* ; *(just before death)* agonie *f* NPL **the dying** les mourants *mpl* ◆ **prayer for the ~** prière *f* des agonisants

dyke /daɪk/ N 1 *(= channel)* fossé *m* ; *(= wall, barrier)* digue *f* ; *(= causeway)* levée *f*, chaussée *f* ; *(Geol)* filon *m* stérile, dyke *m* ; *(Scot dial = wall)* mur *m* 2 (‡ *pej = lesbian)* gouine‡ *f (pej)*

dynamic /daɪˈnæmɪk/ ADJ *(gen, Phys)* dynamique

dynamically /daɪˈnæmɪkəlɪ/ ADV 1 *[develop]* de façon dynamique ; *[work]* avec dynamisme 2 *(Phys)* dynamiquement, du point de vue de la dynamique

dynamics /daɪˈnæmɪks/ N *(NonC)* dynamique *f* *(also Mus)*

dynamism /ˈdaɪnəmɪzəm/ N dynamisme *m*

dynamite /ˈdaɪnəmaɪt/ N 1 *(NonC)* dynamite *f* ; → **stick** 2 *(* fig = dangerous)* **that business is ~** c'est de la dynamite cette affaire ◆ **it's political ~** du point de vue politique, c'est un sujet explosif *or* une affaire explosive ◆ **the book is ~!** ce livre, c'est de la dynamite !* ◆ **asking him to give evidence is potential ~** lui demander de témoigner pourrait amener une situation explosive 3 *(fig)* **she's ~*** *(= terrific)* elle est super* ; *(= full of energy)* elle pète le feu* ; *(= sexy)* elle est supersexy* ◆ **there are some ~ songs on this album*** il y a des chansons à tout casser* dans cet album VT faire sauter à la dynamite, dynamiter

dynamo /ˈdaɪnəməʊ/ N *(esp Brit)* dynamo *f* ◆ **he is a human ~*** il déborde d'énergie

dynastic /daɪˈnæstɪk/ ADJ dynastique

dynasty /ˈdɪnəstɪ/ N dynastie *f*

dyne /daɪn/ N dyne *f*

d'you /djuː/ (abbrev of **do you)** → **do**[1]

dysenteric /ˌdɪsənˈterɪk/ ADJ dysentérique

dysentery /ˈdɪsɪntrɪ/ N dysenterie *f*

dysfunction /dɪsˈfʌŋkʃən/ N dysfonctionnement *m*

dysfunctional /dɪsˈfʌŋkʃənl/ ADJ dysfonctionnel

dyslexia /dɪsˈleksɪə/ N dyslexie *f*

dyslexic /dɪsˈleksɪk/ ADJ, N dyslexique *mf*

dysmenorrhoea, dysmenorrhea *(US)* /ˌdɪsmenəˈrɪə/ N dysménorrhée *f*

dyspepsia /dɪsˈpepsɪə/ N dyspepsie *f*

dyspeptic /dɪsˈpeptɪk/ ADJ, N dyspeptique *mf*, dyspepsique *mf*

dysphasia /dɪsˈfeɪzɪə/ N dysphasie *f*

dyspraxia /dɪspˈræksɪə/ N dyspraxie *f*

dysprosium /dɪsˈprəʊsɪəm/ N dysprosium *m*

dystopia /dɪsˈtəʊpɪə/ N contre-utopie *f*

dystrophy /ˈdɪstrəfɪ/ N dystrophie *f* ; → **muscular**

Ee

E, e /iː/ **N** [1] *(= letter)* E, e *m* ◆ **E for Easy** ≈ E comme Émile [2] *(Mus)* mi *m* ; → **key** [3] (abbrev of **East**) E, est *m* [4] *(Scol)* ≈ faible [5] *(Brit)* (abbrev of **elbow**) **to give sb/get the big E*** *[+ lover]* plaquer‡ *or* laisser tomber qn*/se faire plaquer‡ ; *[+ employee]* virer qn*/se faire virer* [6] *(Drugs = ecstasy)* **E*** ecstasy *m*, ecsta* [7] *(on food packets)* **E numbers** *(Brit)* ≈ additifs *mpl* (alimentaires) ◆ **E25/132** E25/132

e- /iː/ **PREF** *(= electronic)* e-

each /iːtʃ/ **ADJ** chaque ◆ **~ passport** chaque passeport, tout passeport ◆ **~ day** chaque jour, tous les jours ◆ **~ one of us** chacun(e) de *or* d'entre nous ◆ **~ and every one of us** chacun(e) de nous sans exception

PRON [1] *(= thing, person, group)* chacun(e) *m(f)* ◆ **~ of the boys** chacun des garçons ◆ **~ of us** chacun(e) *m(f)* de *or* d'entre nous ◆ **~ of them gave their opinion** chacun a donné son avis, ils ont donné chacun leur avis ◆ **we ~ had our own idea about it** nous avions chacun notre idée là-dessus ◆ **~ more beautiful than the next** *or* **the other** tous plus beaux les uns que les autres ◆ **~ of them was given a present** on leur a offert à chacun un cadeau, chacun d'entre eux a reçu un cadeau ◆ **a little of ~ please** un peu de chaque s'il vous plaît

[2] *(= apiece)* chacun(e) *m(f)* ◆ **we gave them one apple ~** nous leur avons donné une pomme chacun ◆ **two classes of 20 pupils ~** deux classes de 20 élèves (chacune) ◆ **the books are £12 ~** les livres coûtent 12 livres chacun *or* chaque ◆ **roses at one euro ~** des roses à un euro (la) pièce

◆ **each other** l'un(e) l'autre *m(f)*, les uns les autres *mpl*, les unes les autres *fpl* ◆ **they love ~ other** ils s'aiment (l'un l'autre) ◆ **they write to ~ other often** ils s'écrivent souvent ◆ **they were sorry for ~ other** ils avaient pitié l'un de l'autre ◆ **they respected ~ other** ils avaient du respect l'un pour l'autre, ils se respectaient mutuellement ◆ **you must help ~ other** il faut vous entraider ◆ **separated from ~ other** séparés l'un de l'autre ◆ **they used to carry ~ other's books** ils s'aidaient à porter leurs livres

COMP **each way** *(Brit Racing)* **ADJ** *[bet]* sur un cheval placé **ADV** ◆ **to bet on** *or* **back a horse ~ way** jouer un cheval placé

eager /ˈiːgəʳ/ **ADJ** *[person, buyer]* empressé ; *[worker, volunteer]* enthousiaste ; *[lover]* ardent, passionné ; *[search]* avide ; *[pursuit, discussion]* âpre ; *[face]* impatient ◆ **~ anticipation** attente *f* pleine d'impatience ◆ **she is an ~ student of English** elle étudie l'anglais avec enthousiasme *or* ardeur ◆ **~ supporters** *(of cause)* défenseurs *mpl* ardents ; *(Sport)* supporters *mpl* passionnés *or* enthousiastes

◆ **to be eager for** *[+ happiness]* rechercher avidement ; *[+ affection, information]* être avide de ; *[+ vengeance, knowledge]* avoir soif de ; *[+ power, honour]* briguer, convoiter ; *[+ pleasure]* être assoiffé de ; *[+ praise, fame, nomination]* désirer vivement ◆ **to be ~ for change** avoir soif de changement ◆ **to be ~ for sb to do sth** avoir hâte que qn fasse qch ◆ **to be ~ for sth to happen** avoir hâte que qch arrive *subj*

◆ **to be eager to do sth** *(= keen)* désirer vivement faire qch ; *(= impatient)* être impatient *or* avoir hâte de faire qch ◆ **she is ~ to help** elle ne demande qu'à aider ◆ **she is ~ to please** *(= make people happy)* elle ne demande qu'à faire plaisir ; *(= be helpful)* elle ne demande qu'à rendre service

COMP **eager beaver*** **N** *(gen)* personne *f* enthousiaste et consciencieuse ◆ **he's an ~ beaver** *(at work)* il en veut*, il se donne du mal pour réussir

eagerly /ˈiːgəlɪ/ **ADV** *[await, anticipate]* avec impatience ; *[accept]* avec enthousiasme ; *[say]* avec empressement

eagerness /ˈiːgənɪs/ **N** *(NonC) (= excitement)* excitation *f* ; *(= impatience)* impatience *f* ; *(= impetuousness)* ardeur *f* ◆ **~ for sth** soif *f* de qch ◆ **~ to succeed** vif désir *m* de réussir ◆ **~ to learn** soif *f* *or* vif désir *m* d'apprendre ◆ **~ to leave/help/please** empressement *m* à partir/aider/faire plaisir

eagle /ˈiːgl/ **N** [1] *(= bird)* aigle *m* ; *(= lectern)* aigle *m* ; *(= emblem)* aigle *f* ; *(Golf)* eagle *m* ; *(US † = coin) pièce de 10 dollars* ; → **golden**

COMP **eagle eye N** ◆ **to keep an ~ eye on sb/sth** surveiller qn/qch d'un œil attentif ◆ **nothing escapes her ~ eye** rien n'échappe à son œil vigilant
eagle-eyed ADJ aux yeux d'aigle *or* de lynx
eagle owl N grand-duc *m*
eagle ray N aigle *m* de mer
Eagle Scout N *(US) scout du plus haut grade*

eaglet /ˈiːglɪt/ **N** aiglon(ne) *m(f)*

E & OE /ˌiːənd'əʊiː/ (abbrev of **errors and omissions excepted**) se & o

ear[1] /ɪəʳ/ **N** [1] *(= part of body)* oreille *f* ◆ **I'm all ~s!*** je suis tout oreilles *or* tout ouïe ! ◆ **projectiles buzzed around his ~s** des projectiles lui sifflaient aux oreilles ◆ **it all came crashing down around** *or* **about his ~s** tout s'est effondré autour de lui ◆ **your ~s must have been burning!*** vous avez dû entendre vos oreilles siffler ! ◆ **if that should come to his ~s** si cela venait à ses oreilles ◆ **to close** *or* **shut one's ~s to sth** ne pas vouloir entendre qch ◆ **to close** *or* **shut one's ~s to sb** refuser d'écouter qn ◆ **to have** *or* **keep one's ~ to the ground** se tenir au courant ◆ **to have an ~ for music** avoir l'oreille musicale ◆ **to have a good ~** *(for music)* avoir une bonne oreille ◆ **to have an ~** *or* **a good ~ for languages** avoir de l'oreille *or* une bonne oreille pour les langues ◆ **he has the ~ of the President** il a l'oreille du Président ◆ **it goes in one ~ and out (of) the other*** cela lui *(or vous etc)* entre par une oreille et lui *(or vous etc)* sort par l'autre ◆ **to keep one's ~s open** ouvrir l'oreille ◆ **you'll be out on your ~*** **if you're not careful** tu vas te faire vider* si tu ne fais pas attention ◆ **to play by ~** *(Mus)* jouer d'oreille ◆ **I'll play it by ~** *(fig)* je déciderai quoi faire *or* j'improviserai le moment venu ◆ **to set** *or* **put sb on his ~** *(US) (= irritate)* exaspérer qn ; *(= shock)* atterrer qn ◆ **that set them by the ~s!** ça a semé la zizanie (entre eux) ! ◆ **they practically had steam coming out of their ~s*** *(hum)* ils étaient à cran *or* profondément exaspérés ◆ **to find/lend a sympathetic ~** trouver/prêter une oreille attentive ◆ **his proposal found few sympathetic ~s** sa proposition a rencontré peu d'échos ◆ **to be up to the** *or* **one's ~s in work*** avoir du travail pardessus la tête ◆ **to be up to the** *or* **one's ~s in debt** être endetté jusqu'au cou ◆ **he's got money/houses** *etc* **coming out of his ~s*** *(hum)* il a de l'argent/des maisons *etc* à ne plus savoir qu'en faire ◆ **he's got nothing between his ~s*** il n'a rien dans la tête → **bend, box**[2], **clip**[2], **deaf, half**

[2] *[of grain, plant]* épi *m*

COMP *[operation]* à l'oreille
ear, nose and throat department N *(Med)* service *m* d'oto-rhino-laryngologie
ear, nose and throat specialist N oto-rhino-laryngo-logiste *mf*, oto-rhino* *mf*
ear piercing N perçage *m* d'oreilles
ear-piercing ADJ ⇒ **ear-splitting**
ear shell N *(= abalone)* ormeau *m*
ear-splitting ADJ *[sound, scream]* strident, perçant ; *[din]* fracassant
ear stoppers NPL ⇒ **earplugs**
ear trumpet N cornet *m* acoustique

ear[2] /ɪəʳ/ **N** *[of grain, plant]* épi *m*

earache /ˈɪəreɪk/ **N** mal *m* d'oreille(s) ◆ **to have (an) ~** avoir mal à l'oreille *or* aux oreilles

eardrops /ˈɪədrɒps/ **NPL** *(Med)* gouttes *fpl* pour les oreilles

eardrum /ˈɪədrʌm/ **N** *(Anat)* tympan *m*

earful* /ˈɪəfʊl/ **N** ◆ **to give sb an ~** *(= talk a lot)* casser les oreilles* à qn ; *(= scold)* passer un savon* à qn

earhole * /ˈɪəhəʊl/ N (*Brit*) esgourde * *f* ◆ **to give sb a clip** *or* **clout round the** ~ filer une claque à qn *

earl /3:l/ N comte *m* COMP **Earl Grey (tea)** N Earl Grey *m*

earldom /ˈ3:ldəm/ N (*= title*) titre *m* de comte ; (*= land*) comté *m*

earlier /3:lɪəʳ/ (compar of **early**) ADJ 1 (*in past*) [*chapter, edition, meeting, efforts, attempts*] précédent ◆ **at an** ~ **date** (*= formerly*) autrefois, plus tôt ; (*than that specified*) précédemment ◆ **in** ~ **times** autrefois ◆ **his** ~ **symphonies** ses premières symphonies *fpl* ◆ **an** ~ **train** un train plus tôt ◆ **the** ~ **train** le train précédent

2 (*in future*) ◆ **at an** ~ **date** à une date plus rapprochée

ADV 1 (*= nearer beginning of day*) [*get up*] plus tôt

2 (*= previously*) [*leave*] auparavant, plus tôt ◆ **she had left ten minutes** ~ elle était partie dix minutes auparavant *or* plus tôt ◆ ~ **in the evening** plus tôt dans la soirée ◆ ~ **on** (*= formerly*) autrefois ; (*before specified moment*) plus tôt, précédemment ◆ ~ **today** plus tôt dans la journée ◆ **I said** ~ **that ...** tout à l'heure j'ai dit que ... ◆ **not** *or* **no** ~ **than Thursday** pas avant jeudi

earliest /ˈ3:lɪɪst/ (superl of **early**) ADJ 1 (*= first*) [*novel, film*] tout premier ◆ **the** ~ **in a series of murders** le premier en date *or* le tout premier d'une série de meurtres

2 (*= first possible*) ◆ **the** ~ **date he could do it was 31 July** le plus tôt qu'il pouvait le faire était le 31 juillet ◆ **the** ~ **possible date for the election** la première date possible pour la tenue des élections ◆ **at the** ~ **possible moment** le plus tôt possible, au plus tôt ◆ **the** ~ **time you may leave is 4pm** vous ne pouvez pas partir avant 16 heures (au plus tôt) ◆ **at your** ~ **convenience** (*Comm*) dans les meilleurs délais ◆ **the** ~ **delivery time** (*Comm*) le délai de livraison le plus court, le meilleur délai de livraison

ADV ◆ **to arrive/get up** ~ arriver/se lever le tout premier *or* la toute première, être le tout premier *or* la toute première à arriver/se lever ◆ **to flower** ~ être le tout premier *or* la toute première à fleurir

N ◆ **at the** ~ au plus tôt ◆ **the** ~ **he can come is Monday** le plus tôt qu'il puisse venir c'est lundi

earlobe /ˈɪələʊb/ N lobe *m* d'oreille

early /ˈ3:lɪ/ ADJ 1 (*= near beginning of period*) [*years, months, days, settlers, film, book*] premier ; [*childhood*] petit ◆ **it's too** ~ **to say** *or* **tell** il est trop tôt pour le dire ◆ **it is too** ~ **to say** *or* **know what will happen** il est trop tôt pour dire *or* savoir ce qui va se passer ◆ ~ **indications look promising** les premiers signes sont encourageants ◆ ~ **reports suggest that ...** les premières informations semblent indiquer que ... ◆ **the** ~ **(19)60s** le début des années soixante ◆ **in the** ~ **afternoon** en début d'après-midi ◆ **at an** ~ **age** (très) jeune ◆ **from an** ~ **age** dès mon (*or* son *or* leur *etc*) plus jeune âge ◆ **in** ~ **childhood** pendant la petite enfance ◆ **his** ~ **career** les débuts *mpl* de sa carrière ◆ **nausea in** ~ **pregnancy** les nausées du début de la grossesse ◆ **in the** ~ **18th century** au début du 18ᵉ siècle ◆ **in the** ~ **days** au début, au commencement (*of de*) ◆ **the** ~ **days** *or* **stages of the project** les débuts *mpl* du projet ◆ **it's** ~ **days (yet)** * (*esp Brit*) il est (encore) trop tôt pour en juger ◆ **it was** ~ **evening when we finished** nous avons fini tôt dans la soirée ◆ **to be an** ~ **example of sth** être un des premiers exemples de qch ◆ **an** ~ **form of ...** une forme ancienne de ... ◆ **two** ~ **goals** deux buts *mpl* en début de match ◆ ~ **January** début janvier ◆ **by** ~ **January** d'ici début janvier ◆ **in the** ~ **morning** tôt le matin ◆ **an** ~**-morning drive** une promenade matinale en voiture ◆ **in the** ~ **part of the century** au début *or* au commencement du siècle ◆ **in its** ~ **stages** à ses débuts ◆ **this is in a very** ~ **stage of development** c'en est au tout début ◆ **in** ~ **summer** au début de l'été ◆ **in his** ~ **teens** au début de son adolescence, dès treize ou quatorze ans ◆ **to be in one's** ~ **thirties** avoir un peu plus de trente ans ◆ **the** ~ **Tudors** les premiers Tudor *mpl* ◆ **the** ~ **Victorians** les Victoriens *mpl* du début du règne ◆ **an** ~ **Victorian table** une table du début de l'époque victorienne ◆ **in his** ~ **youth** dans sa première *or* prime jeunesse ; see also **earlier, earliest, life**

2 (*in day*) tôt ◆ **don't go, it's still** ~ ne t'en va pas, il est encore tôt *or* il n'est pas tard ◆ **at an** ~ **hour** de bonne heure, très tôt ◆ **at an** ~ **hour of the morning** à une heure matinale ◆ **(in) the** ~ **hours (of the morning)** (dans) les premières heures *fpl* (de la matinée) ◆ **we've got an** ~ **start tomorrow** nous partons tôt *or* de bonne heure demain ◆ **I caught an** ~ **train** j'ai pris un train tôt le matin ◆ **I caught the** ~ **train** j'ai pris le premier train (du matin)

3 (*= before expected time*) [*departure, death, marriage, menopause*] prématuré ; [*spring, flowers, cabbages, crop*] précoce ◆ **to be** ~ [*person*] (*gen*) être en avance ; (*arriving*) arriver en avance ◆ **I'm** ~ (*gen*) je suis en avance ; (*menstrual period*) mes règles ont de l'avance ◆ **I'm a week** ~ (*gen*) je suis une semaine en avance, j'ai une semaine d'avance ; (*menstrual period*) mes règles ont une semaine d'avance ◆ **I was two hours** ~ j'étais deux heures en avance, j'avais deux heures d'avance ◆ **you're** ~ **today** vous arrivez de bonne heure *or* tôt aujourd'hui ◆ **too** ~ trop tôt, trop en avance ◆ **to be** ~ **for an appointment** (*gen*) être en avance à un rendez-vous ; (*arriving*) arriver en avance à un rendez-vous ◆ **to be** ~ **in arriving** arriver avec de l'avance *or* en avance ◆ **to be** ~ **with sth** avoir de l'avance dans qch ◆ **I was** ~ **with the rent** j'ai payé mon loyer en avance ◆ **both my babies were** ~ mes deux bébés sont arrivés avant terme ◆ **Easter is** ~ **this year** Pâques est tôt cette année ◆ **spring was** ~ le printemps était en avance *or* était précoce ◆ **the train is** ~ le train est en avance *or* a de l'avance ◆ **the train is 30 minutes** ~ le train est 30 minutes en avance *or* a 30 minutes d'avance ◆ **we're having an** ~ **holiday this year** nous partons tôt en vacances cette année ◆ **to have an** ~ **lunch** déjeuner tôt ◆ **to have an** ~ **night** (aller) se coucher tôt ◆ **to take an** ~ **bath** * (*Brit fig = withdraw*) prendre une retraite anticipée ◆ **to send sb for an** ~ **bath** (*Brit Ftbl, Rugby*) mettre qn sur la touche ◆ ~ **fruit** (*Comm*) primeurs *mpl* ◆ ~ **vegetables** (*Comm*) primeurs *mpl*

4 (*= occurring in near future*) ◆ **at an** ~ **date** bientôt, prochainement ◆ **to promise** ~ **delivery** (*Comm*) promettre une livraison rapide ◆ **"hoping for an early reply"** (*Comm*) "dans l'espoir d'une prompte réponse" ; see also **earlier, earliest**

ADV 1 (*= near beginning of period*) [*start*] tôt ◆ **as** ~ **as next week** dès la semaine prochaine ◆ ~ **next month/year** tôt le mois prochain/l'année prochaine ◆ ~ **on (in life)** très tôt ◆ ~ **on in his career** au début de sa carrière ◆ ~ **this month/year** tôt dans le mois/l'année ◆ ~ **today** tôt dans la journée ◆ ~ **yesterday** tôt dans la journée d'hier ; see also **earlier**

◆ **early in** ◆ ~ **in 1915** au début de 1915 ◆ ~ **in the year** au début de l'année ◆ ~ **in May** début mai ◆ ~ **in life** tôt dans la vie ◆ ~ **in his life** dans ses jeunes années ◆ ~ **in the book** au début du livre ◆ ~ **in the meeting** au début de la réunion ◆ ~ **in the morning/day** tôt le matin/dans la journée

2 (*= near beginning of day*) [*get up, go to bed, set off*] tôt, de bonne heure ◆ ~ **next day** tôt le lendemain ◆ **too** ~ trop tôt, de trop bonne heure ◆ ~ **to bed,** ~ **to rise (makes a man healthy, wealthy and wise)** (*Prov*) l'avenir appartient à ceux qui se lèvent tôt (*Prov*) see also **bright, earlier, earliest**

3 (*= before usual time*) [*arrive, end*] en avance ; [*flower, harvest*] tôt ◆ **an** ~ **flowering gladiolus** un glaïeul à floraison précoce ◆ **to arrive** ~ **for sth** arriver en avance pour qch ◆ **to arrive five minutes** ~ arriver cinq minutes en avance *or* avec cinq minutes d'avance ◆ **post** ~ expédiez votre courrier à l'avance ◆ **book** ~ **to avoid disappointment** pour éviter toute déception, réservez rapidement *or* le plus tôt possible ◆ **he took his summer holiday** ~ **this year** il a pris ses vacances d'été tôt cette année ◆ **the peaches are ripening** ~ **this year** les pêches seront mûres tôt cette année ◆ **too** ~ trop tôt ; see also **earliest**

4 (*= soon*) ◆ **as** ~ **as possible** le plus tôt possible, dès que possible

COMP **early admission** N (*US Univ*) inscription *f* anticipée

early bird * N lève-tôt * *mf inv* ◆ **it's the** ~ **bird that catches the worm** (*Prov*) l'avenir appartient à ceux qui se lèvent tôt (*Prov*)

Early Christian ADJ, N paléochrétien(ne) *m(f)* ◆ **the** ~ **Christians** les premiers chrétiens *mpl*

the Early Church N l'Église *f* primitive

early closing (day) N (*Brit*) *jour de fermeture l'après-midi* ◆ **it's** ~ **closing (day) today** aujourd'hui les magasins ferment l'après-midi

Early English N (*Archit*) premier gothique *m* anglais

early man N les premiers hommes *mpl* l'homme *m* primitif

early music N la musique ancienne

early retirement N (*gen*) retraite *f* anticipée ; (*Admin*) préretraite *f* ◆ **to take** ~ **retirement** (*gen*) prendre une retraite anticipée ; (*Admin*) partir en préretraite

early riser N lève-tôt * *mf inv*

early warning system N (*Mil, fig*) système *m* d'alerte précoce

earmark /ˈɪəmɑ:k/ N (*fig*) marque *f*, signe *m* distinctif, caractéristique *f* VT [*+ cattle*] marquer ; (*fig*) [*+ object, seat*] réserver (*for* à) ; [*+ funds, person*] assigner, affecter, destiner (*for* à)

earmuff /ˈɪəmʌf/ N cache-oreilles *m inv*

earn /3:n/ VT [*+ money*] gagner ; [*+ salary*] toucher ; (*Fin*) [*+ interest*] rapporter ; [*+ praise, rest*] mériter, gagner ◆ **to** ~ **one's living (doing sth)** gagner sa vie (en faisant qch) ◆ **she** ~**s a** *or* **her living as a freelance TV producer** elle gagne sa vie comme réalisatrice indépendante pour la télévision ◆ **to** ~ **a** *or* **one's crust** (*Brit*) gagner sa croûte * ◆ **to** ~ **an honest crust** (*Brit*) gagner honnêtement sa vie *or* son pain ◆ **he has already** ~**ed his corn** (*Brit*) il nous a déjà rapporté plus qu'il ne nous a coûté ◆ **his success** ~**ed him praise** sa réussite lui a valu des éloges ◆ **his work** ~**ed him the praise of his manager** son travail lui a valu les éloges de son chef ◆ **she** ~**ed a reputation for honesty** elle a acquis une réputation d'honnêteté ◆ **he has** ~**ed his place in history** il a bien mérité de passer à la postérité

VI ◆ **to be** ~**ing** gagner sa vie

COMP **earned income** N revenus *mpl* salariaux, traitement(s) *m(pl)*, salaire(s) *m(pl)*

earning power N (*Econ*) productivité *f* financière ◆ **his** ~**ing power** son salaire *etc* potentiel

earner /ˈ3:nəʳ/ N ◆ **high/low** ~**s** gens *mpl* qui gagnent bien leur vie/qui ont des revenus modestes ◆ **it's a nice little** ~ * (*Brit*) ça rapporte (bien) ◆ **sugar is Fiji's biggest export** ~ le sucre est la plus importante source de revenus à l'exportation des îles Fidji

earnest /ˈ3:nɪst/ ADJ [*person, hope, desire, conversation, discussion*] sérieux ; [*prayer*] fervent

◆ **in earnest** (*= with determination*) sérieusement ; (*= without joking*) sans rire ◆ **this time I am in** ~ cette fois je ne plaisante pas ◆ **it**

started snowing in ~ il a commencé à neiger pour de bon

N 1 (*= guarantee*) garantie *f*, gage *m* ◆ **as an ~ of his good intentions** en gage de ses bonnes intentions

2 (also **earnest money**) arrhes *fpl*

earnestly /ˈɜːnɪstli/ ADV *[say, explain, look at]* avec sérieux ; *[talk, discuss, ask]* sérieusement ; *[hope]* sincèrement ; *[beseech]* instamment ; *[pray]* avec ferveur

earnestness /ˈɜːnɪstnɪs/ N *[of person, tone]* gravité *f*, sérieux *m* ; *[of effort]* ardeur *f* ; *[of demand]* véhémence *f*

earnings /ˈɜːnɪŋz/ NPL *[of person]* salaire *m*, gain(s) *m(pl)* ; *[of business]* profits *mpl*, bénéfices *mpl* COMP **earnings-related** ADJ *[pension, contributions]* proportionnel au salaire

earphone /ˈɪəfəʊn/ N (*Rad, Telec etc*) écouteur *m* ◆ **to listen on ~s** écouter au casque

earpiece /ˈɪəpiːs/ N (*Rad, Telec etc*) écouteur *m*

earplugs /ˈɪəplʌgz/ NPL (*for sleeping*) boules *fpl* Quiès ® ; (*for underwater*) protège-tympans *mpl*

earring /ˈɪərɪŋ/ N boucle *f* d'oreille

earshot /ˈɪəʃɒt/ N ◆ **out of ~** hors de portée de voix ◆ **within ~** à portée de voix

earth /ɜːθ/ N 1 (*NonC = ground, soil*) terre *f* (*Elec*), masse *f* ◆ **to fall to ~** s'écraser au sol ◆ **to plough the ~** labourer la terre ◆ **to come down** *or* **be brought down to ~ (with a bump)** (*fig*) revenir *or* redescendre (brutalement) sur terre (*fig*) ◆ **the ~ moved** (*fig hum*) ça a été le grand frisson ; → **down**¹

2 (*= planet*) ◆ **(the) Earth** la Terre ◆ **on ~** sur terre ◆ **here on ~** ici-bas, en ce bas monde ◆ **it's heaven on ~** c'est le paradis sur terre ◆ **to the ends of the ~** au bout du monde ◆ **where/why/how on ~ ...?** où/pourquoi/comment diable ... ? ◆ **nowhere on ~ will you find ...** nulle part au monde vous ne trouverez ... ◆ **nothing on ~** rien au monde ◆ **she looks like nothing on ~!** à quoi elle ressemble ! ◆ **it tasted like nothing on ~** ça avait un goût vraiment bizarre ◆ **to promise sb the ~** promettre la lune à qn ◆ **it must have cost the ~!*** ça a dû coûter les yeux de la tête ! *

3 *[of fox, badger etc]* terrier *m*, tanière *f* ◆ **to run** *or* **go to ~** *[fox, criminal]* se terrer (*fig*) ◆ **to run sb to ~** dépister qn ◆ **she finally ran him to ~ in the pub** (*hum*) elle a fini par le dénicher au pub ◆ **he ran the quotation to ~ in "Hamlet"** (*hum*) il a déniché la citation dans "Hamlet"

VT (*Brit Elec*) *[+ apparatus]* mettre à la masse *or* à la terre

COMP **earth closet** N fosse *f* d'aisances

earth mother N (*Myth*) déesse *f* de la fertilité ; (*fig*) mère *f* nourricière

earth-moving equipment N engins *mpl* de terrassement

earth sciences NPL sciences *fpl* de la terre

earth-shaking*, **earth-shattering*** ADJ (*fig*) stupéfiant

earth tremor N secousse *f* sismique

► **earth up** VT SEP *[+ plant]* butter

earthborn /ˈɜːθbɔːn/ ADJ (*liter*) humain

earthbound /ˈɜːθbaʊnd/ ADJ (*= moving towards earth*) qui se dirige vers la terre ; *[telescope]* terrestre ; (*= unimaginative*) terre à terre *inv*, terre-à-terre *inv*

earthed /ɜːθt/ ADJ (*Brit Elec*) relié à la terre

earthen /ˈɜːθən/ ADJ de terre, en terre

earthenware /ˈɜːθənwɛəʳ/ N poterie *f*, terre *f* cuite ; (*glazed*) faïence *f* COMP *[jug etc]* en terre cuite (*or* en faïence)

earthiness /ˈɜːθɪnɪs/ N (*fig*) *[of person]* caractère *m* terre à terre *or* terre-à-terre ; (*fig*) *[of humour]* truculence *f*

earthling* /ˈɜːθlɪŋ/ N terrien(ne) *m(f)* (*par opposition à extraterrestre*)

earthly /ˈɜːθli/ ADJ 1 *[being, paradise, possessions]* terrestre 2 (* *fig = possible*) **there is no ~ reason to think that ...** il n'y a pas la moindre raison de croire que ... ◆ **for no ~ reason** sans aucune raison ◆ **he doesn't stand** *or* **hasn't an ~ chance of succeeding** il n'a pas la moindre chance de réussir ◆ **of no ~ use** d'aucune utilité, sans aucun intérêt ◆ **it's no ~ use telling him that** ça ne sert absolument à rien de lui dire ça N (*Brit*) ◆ **not an ~*** pas la moindre chance, pas l'ombre d'une chance

earthman* /ˈɜːθmæn/ N (pl **-men**) terrien *m* (*par opposition à extraterrestre*)

earthmover /ˈɜːθmuːvəʳ/ N bulldozer *m*

earthquake /ˈɜːθkweɪk/ N tremblement *m* de terre, séisme *m* ; → **damage**

earthward(s) /ˈɜːθwəd(z)/ ADV dans la direction de la terre, vers la terre

earthwork /ˈɜːθwɜːk/ N (*Mil, Archeol*) ouvrage *m* de terre ; (*Constr*) terrassement *m*

earthworm /ˈɜːθwɜːm/ N ver *m* de terre

earthy /ˈɜːθi/ ADJ 1 (*= like earth*) *[colour]* ocré ; *[flavour]* légèrement terreux ; *[smell]* terreux, de terre 2 (*= frank*) *[humour, language]* truculent

earwax /ˈɪəwæks/ N cérumen *m*, cire *f*

earwig /ˈɪəwɪg/ N perce-oreille *m* VI * (*= eavesdrop*) écouter aux portes

ease /iːz/ N (*NonC*) 1 (*= well-being, relaxation*) (*mental*) tranquillité *f* ; (*physical*) bien-être *m* ◆ **he lives a life of ~** il a une vie facile ◆ **to take one's ~** prendre ses aises

◆ **at (one's) ease** à l'aise ◆ **she put me at (my) ~** elle m'a mis à l'aise ◆ **not at ~** mal à l'aise ◆ **my mind is at ~ at last** j'ai enfin l'esprit tranquille ◆ **to put** *or* **set sb's mind at ~** tranquilliser qn ◆ **to be at ~ with sb** être à l'aise avec qn ◆ **I like Spain, but I don't feel at ~ with the language** j'aime bien l'Espagne, mais je ne suis pas à l'aise en espagnol ◆ **I'm not really at ~ with the idea of flying** l'idée de prendre l'avion m'angoisse un peu ◆ **to feel ill at ~** se sentir mal à l'aise ◆ **he was ill at ~ with his role as manager** il se sentait mal à l'aise dans son rôle de responsable ◆ **to be** *or* **feel at ~ with oneself** être bien dans sa peau ◆ **(stand) at ~!** (*Mil*) repos !

2 (*= lack of difficulty*) aisance *f*, facilité *f* ◆ **with ~** aisément, facilement ◆ **with the greatest of ~** avec la plus grande facilité, sans la moindre difficulté

◆ **ease of** ◆ **~ of use/reference/access** facilité *f* d'emploi/de consultation/d'accès ◆ **for ~ of reference/access/storage** pour faciliter la consultation/l'accès/le rangement, pour une consultation/un accès/un rangement facile ◆ **we tested them for ~ of use** nous les avons testés pour voir s'ils étaient faciles à utiliser

VT 1 (*= relieve*) *[+ pain]* atténuer, soulager ; *[+ mind]* calmer, tranquilliser ; *[+ pressure, tension]* diminuer, réduire ; *[+ sanctions]* assouplir ; *[+ restrictions]* relâcher ; *[+ shortage, overcrowding]* pallier ; *[+ problem]* atténuer ; *[+ suffering, conscience]* soulager ; *[+ situation]* détendre ; *[+ fears]* apaiser ; *[+ anxiety]* calmer ◆ **ways to ~ the food shortage** des moyens de pallier la pénurie alimentaire ◆ **to ~ traffic congestion in Bangkok/on the motorway** décongestionner Bangkok/l'autoroute ◆ **to ~ the overcrowding in the universities** décongestionner les universités ◆ **to ~ sb's burden** soulager qn d'un poids

2 (*= make easier*) *[+ transition]* faciliter

3 (*= move gently*) ◆ **to ~ a key into a lock** introduire doucement *or* délicatement une clé dans une serrure ◆ **to ~ in the clutch** embrayer en douceur ◆ **she ~d the car into gear** elle a passé la première en douceur ◆ **she ~d out the screw** elle a enlevé doucement *or* délicatement la vis ◆ **he ~d himself into the chair** il s'est laissé glisser dans le fauteuil ◆ **he ~d himself through the gap in the fence** il s'est glissé par le trou de la barrière ◆ **he ~d himself into his jacket** il a passé *or* enfilé doucement sa veste

VI *[pressure, tension, fighting]* diminuer ◆ **the situation has ~d** la situation s'est détendue ◆ **prices have ~d** les prix ont baissé, il y a eu une baisse des prix ◆ **the snow has ~d a bit** il ne neige plus aussi fort ◆ **the wind has ~d a bit** le vent s'est un peu calmé

► **ease back** VI (*US*) ◆ **to ease back on sb/sth** se montrer moins strict envers qn/en ce qui concerne qch

► **ease off** VI *[person]* (*= slow down*) ralentir ; (*= work less hard*) se relâcher ; (*= subside*) *[rain, wind]* se calmer ; *[pressure]* diminuer ; *[work, business]* devenir plus calme ; *[traffic]* diminuer ; *[pain]* se calmer ; *[demand]* baisser

VT SEP *[+ bandage, stamp etc]* enlever délicatement ; *[+ lid]* enlever doucement ◆ **he ~d his foot off the accelerator** il leva le pied (de l'accélérateur)

► **ease up** VI *[person]* (*= relax*) se détendre, se reposer ; (*= make less effort*) relâcher ses efforts ; (*= calm down*) *[situation]* se détendre ◆ **~ up a bit!** vas-y plus doucement ! ◆ **to ~ up on sb/sth** se montrer moins strict envers qn/en ce qui concerne qch

easel /ˈiːzl/ N chevalet *m*

easement /ˈiːzmənt/ N (*US Jur*) droit *m* de passage

easily /ˈiːzɪli/ ADV 1 (*= without difficulty, quickly*) *[accessible, available, recognizable]* facilement ◆ **to tire/break ~** se fatiguer/se casser facilement ◆ **I can ~ fetch him** je peux facilement aller le chercher ◆ **he makes friends ~** il se fait facilement des amis ◆ **just as ~** aussi bien ◆ **as ~ as (if ...)** aussi facilement que (si ...) ◆ **he is ~ led** il est très influençable

2 (*= very possibly*) bien ◆ **he may ~ change his mind** il pourrait bien changer d'avis ◆ **he could ~ be right** il pourrait bien avoir raison

3 (*with superl = unquestionably*) sans aucun doute, de loin ◆ **he was ~ the best candidate** il était de loin le meilleur candidat

4 (*with amounts, measurements etc*) facilement ◆ **that's ~ 50km** ça fait facilement 50 km ◆ **the room is ~ as big as two tennis courts** la pièce fait facilement le double d'un court de tennis

5 (*= in relaxed manner*) *[talk, smile, breathe]* avec décontraction ◆ **"yes", he said ~** "oui", dit-il avec décontraction

easiness /ˈiːzɪnɪs/ N facilité *f*

easing /ˈiːzɪŋ/ N *[of sanctions, laws, restrictions]* assouplissement *m* ; *[of tensions]* relâchement *m*

east /iːst/ N est *m*, orient *m* (*frm*) ◆ **the East** (*gen*) l'Orient *m* ; (*Pol = Iron Curtain*) les pays *mpl* de l'Est ; (*US Geog*) (les États *mpl* de) l'Est *m* ◆ **the mysterious East** l'Orient *m* mystérieux ◆ **to the ~ of ...** à l'est de ... ◆ **in the ~ of Scotland** dans l'est de l'Écosse ◆ **house facing the ~** maison *f* exposée à l'est ◆ **to veer to the ~, to go into the ~** *[wind]* tourner à l'est ◆ **the wind is in the ~** le vent est à l'est ◆ **the wind is (coming** *or* **blowing) from the ~** le vent vient *or* souffle de l'est ◆ **to live in the ~** habiter dans l'Est ; → **far, middle**

ADJ *[coast, wing]* est *inv* ◆ **~ wind** vent *m* d'est ◆ **on the ~ side** du côté est ◆ **East Asia** Asie *f* de l'Est ◆ **in ~ Devon** dans l'est du Devon ◆ **East London** l'est *m* de Londres ◆ **a room with an ~ aspect** une pièce exposée à l'est ◆ **~ transept/door** (*Archit*) transept *m*/portail *m* est *or* oriental ; see also **comp**

ADV *[go, travel, fly]* vers l'est ◆ **go ~ till you get to Manchester** allez vers l'est jusqu'à Manchester ◆ **we drove ~ for 100km** nous avons roulé vers l'est pendant 100 km ◆ **to be (due) ~ of Paris** être (en plein) à l'est de Paris ◆ **to head due ~** *(gen)* se diriger plein est ; *(in plane, ship)* avoir le cap à l'est ◆ **to sail due ~** avoir le cap à l'est ◆ **further ~** plus à l'est ◆ **~ by north/south** est quart nord/sud ◆ **~ by north-~** est quart nord-est

COMP **East Africa** N Afrique *f* orientale, Est *m* de l'Afrique

East African ADJ d'Afrique orientale N Africain(e) *m(f)* de l'Est

East Berlin N Berlin-Est

East Berliner N habitant(e) *m(f)* de Berlin-Est

the East End N (also **the East End of London**) les quartiers *mpl* est de Londres *(quartiers populaires)*

East Ender *(Brit)* N habitant(e) *m(f)* de l'East End (de Londres)

East Europe N *(esp US)* Europe *f* de l'Est

East European ADJ d'Europe de l'Est N Européen(ne) *m(f)* de l'Est

east-facing ADJ exposé à l'est

East German ADJ est-allemand N Allemand(e) *m(f)* de l'Est

East Germany N Allemagne *f* de l'Est

East Indian ADJ des Indes orientales

the East Indies NPL les Indes *fpl* orientales

east-north-east N, ADJ est-nord-est *m*

(the) East Side N *[of New York]* les quartiers *mpl* est de New York

east-south-east N, ADJ est-sud-est *m*

East Timor N Timor *m* oriental

East Timorese ADJ (est-)timorais N Timorais(e) *m(f)* (de l'Est)

East-West relations NPL *(Hist)* relations *fpl* Est-Ouest

eastbound /ˈiːstbaʊnd/ ADJ *[traffic, vehicles]* (se déplaçant) en direction de l'est ; *[carriageway]* est *inv* ◆ **to be ~ on the M8** être sur la M8 en direction de l'est

Easter /ˈiːstəʳ/ N 1 *(Rel)* (also **Easter Day**) Pâques *m* ◆ **~ is celebrated between ...** Pâques est célébré entre ... 2 Pâques *fpl* ◆ **at ~** à Pâques ◆ **Happy ~!** joyeuses Pâques !

COMP *[holidays]* de Pâques

Easter bonnet N chapeau *m* de printemps

the Easter bunny N *(US) personnage censé apporter des friandises aux enfants à Pâques*

Easter communion N ◆ **to make one's ~ communion** faire ses pâques

Easter Day N le jour de Pâques

Easter egg N œuf *m* de Pâques

Easter Island N île *f* de Pâques ◆ **the ~ Island statues** les statues *fpl* de l'île de Pâques

Easter Monday N le lundi de Pâques

Easter parade N défilé *m* pascal

Easter Sunday N le dimanche de Pâques

Easter week N la semaine pascale

easterly /ˈiːstəli/ ADJ *[wind]* d'est ; *[situation]* à l'est, à l'orient *(frm)* ◆ **in an ~ direction** en direction de l'est, vers l'est ◆ **~ aspect** exposition *f* à l'est ADV vers l'est

eastern /ˈiːstən/ ADJ est *inv*, de l'est ◆ **the ~ coast** la côte est *or* orientale ◆ **a house with an ~ outlook** une maison exposée à l'est ◆ **~ wall** mur *m* exposé à l'est ◆ **~ Africa** l'Afrique *f* orientale ◆ **~ France** la France de l'est, l'Est *m* de la France

COMP **the Eastern bloc** N *(Pol)* le bloc de l'Est

the Eastern Church N l'Église *f* d'Orient

Eastern Daylight Time N *(US)* heure *f* d'été de l'Est

Eastern Europe N Europe *f* de l'Est ◆ **Central and Eastern Europe** Europe *f* centrale et orientale

Eastern European Time N heure *f* de l'Europe orientale

Eastern Standard Time N *(US)* heure *f* de l'Est

easterner /ˈiːstənəʳ/ N *(esp US)* homme *m or* femme *f* de l'Est ◆ **he is an ~** il vient de l'Est ◆ **the ~s** les gens *mpl* de l'Est

easternmost /ˈiːstənməʊst/ ADJ le plus à l'est

Eastertide /ˈiːstətaɪd/ N le temps pascal, la saison de Pâques

eastward /ˈiːstwəd/ ADJ *[route]* en direction de l'est ; *[slope]* exposé à l'est ◆ **in an ~ direction** en direction de l'est, vers l'est ADV (also **eastwards**) vers l'est

easy /ˈiːzɪ/ ADJ 1 *(= not difficult) [work, decision, access, victory, option, target]* facile ; *[solution]* facile, de facilité *(pej)* ◆ **there are no ~ answers** il n'y a pas de réponses faciles ◆ **as ~ as pie*** *or* **ABC** *or* **falling off a log*** facile comme tout, simple comme bonjour ◆ **in ~ circumstances** dans l'aisance ◆ **to be far from ~** *or* **none too ~** *or* **no ~ matter** *or* **no ~ task** être loin d'être facile *or* simple ◆ **he came in an ~ first** il est arrivé bon premier ◆ **~ to get on with** facile à vivre ◆ **the flat is within ~ access of the shops** l'appartement est à proximité des commerces ◆ **reducing inflation is a relatively ~ job** réduire l'inflation est chose relativement facile ◆ **~ living, the ~ life** la vie facile ◆ **she's not had an ~ life** elle n'a pas eu la vie facile ◆ **to be ~ prey** *or* **meat* (for sb)** être une cible facile (pour qn) ◆ **it was an ~ mistake to make** c'était une erreur facile à faire ◆ **it's none too ~, it's no ~ task** ce n'est pas simple *or* évident ◆ **~ on the eye*** *(Brit) or* **on the eyes*** *(US) [person]* bien balancé* ; *[thing]* agréable à regarder ◆ **~ on the ear** * agréable à entendre ◆ **to be ~ on the stomach** ne pas être lourd pour l'estomac ◆ **to take the ~ option** *or* **the ~ way out** choisir la solution de facilité ◆ **to take the ~ way out** *(euph = commit suicide)* mettre fin à ses jours ◆ **at an ~ pace** à une allure modérée ◆ **that's the ~ part** c'est ce qu'il y a de plus facile ◆ **burglars hoping for ~ pickings*** cambrioleurs espérant pouvoir faucher* facilement ◆ **there were ~ pickings* to be made in the property market** on pouvait faire de bonnes affaires sur le marché de l'immobilier ◆ **within ~ reach of sth** à distance commode de qch ◆ **to make ~ reading** être facile à lire ◆ **to have an ~ ride** avoir la vie facile ◆ **in** *or* **by ~ stages** par petites étapes ◆ **to be on ~ street*** *(esp US)* se la couler douce* ◆ **to have an ~ time (of it)** avoir la vie belle ◆ **it is ~ for him to do that** il lui est facile de faire cela ◆ **that's ~ for you to say** pour toi, c'est facile à dire ◆ **it is ~ to see that ...** on voit bien que ..., cela se voit que ... ◆ **it's ~ to see why** il est facile de comprendre pourquoi ◆ **it was ~ to get them to be quiet** on a eu vite fait de les faire taire ◆ **he is ~ to work with** il est agréable *or* accommodant dans le travail ; → **mark²**

2 *(= relaxed) [temperament, disposition]* placide ; *[conversation]* tranquille ; *[voice, tone]* paisible ; *[laugh, laughter]* décontracté ; *[style]* facile, aisé ; *[relationship]* facile ; *[manners]* aisé ◆ **on ~ terms with sb** en bons termes avec qn ◆ **I'm ~** * ça m'est égal

3 *(= happy)* ◆ **I don't feel ~ about it** ça me gêne un peu ◆ **I don't feel ~ about leaving the kids with that woman** ça me gêne un peu de laisser les gosses avec cette femme ◆ **to feel ~ in one's mind (about sth)** être tout à fait tranquille *or* ne pas se faire de souci (à propos de qch)

4 *(Fin)* ◆ **on ~ terms** avec facilités de paiement ◆ **~ credit** fonds *mpl* aisément disponibles ◆ **~ market** marché *m* tranquille *or* mou ◆ **prices are ~ today** les prix sont un peu moins hauts aujourd'hui

5 *(* pej = promiscuous) [person]* facile *(pej)* ◆ **she had a reputation for being ~** elle avait la réputation d'être (une femme) facile ◆ **to be an ~ lay** *or (US)* **make** être une Marie-couche-toi-là ◆ **a woman of ~ virtue** † *(euph)* une femme de petite vertu †

ADV 1 *(* = gently)* ◆ **to go ~ on sb/sth** y aller doucement avec qn/qch ◆ **to take it ~, to take things ~** *(= rest)* se la couler douce* ◆ **take it ~!** *(= relax)* t'énerve pas !* ; *(esp US) (when saying goodbye)* à plus !* ◆ **~ does it!, ~ there!** doucement !

2 *(* = without difficulty)* ◆ **to have it ~** se la couler douce* ◆ **that's easier said than done!** c'est plus facile à dire qu'à faire ! ◆ **just get rid of it – easier said than done!** tu n'as qu'à t'en débarrasser – facile à dire ! ◆ **to breathe ~** *(fig = relax)* souffler ◆ **~ come, ~ go!** * ce n'est que de l'argent ! ; see also **comp**

3 *(Mil)* **stand ~!** repos !

COMP **easy-care** ADJ d'entretien facile

easy chair N fauteuil *m* (rembourré)

easy-going ADJ accommodant ; *[person]* facile à vivre, qui ne s'en fait pas ; *[attitude]* complaisant

easy listening N musique *f* légère

easy-listening ADJ *[album, CD]* de musique légère ◆ **~-listening music** musique *f* légère

easy money N *(in prospect)* argent *m* facile à gagner ; *(already made)* argent *m* gagné facilement

easy-peasy* ADJ *(Brit)* fastoche*

eat /iːt/ (pret **ate**, ptp **eaten**) VT 1 *[+ food]* manger ◆ **to ~ (one's) breakfast** déjeuner, prendre son petit déjeuner ◆ **to ~ (one's) lunch** déjeuner ◆ **to ~ (one's) dinner** dîner ◆ **to ~ a meal** prendre un repas ◆ **to have nothing to ~** n'avoir rien à manger *or* à se mettre sous la dent ◆ **to ~ one's fill** manger à sa faim ◆ **fit to ~** mangeable, bon à manger ◆ **she looks good enough to ~** elle est belle à croquer ◆ **to ~ one's words** se rétracter, ravaler ses paroles ◆ **to make sb ~ his words** faire rentrer ses mots dans la gorge à qn ◆ **I'll ~ my hat if ...*** je veux bien être pendu si ... ◆ **I could ~ a horse*** j'ai une faim de loup* ◆ **he won't ~ you*** il ne va pas te manger ◆ **what's ~ing you?**⁑ qu'est ce qui ne va pas ?, qu'est-ce qui te tracasse ? ◆ **he left the other runners ~ing his dust**⁑ il a laissé les autres coureurs loin derrière lui

2 *(⁑ = perform oral sex on)* sucer⁑

VI manger ◆ **to ~ healthily/sensibly** manger des choses saines/de façon équilibrée ◆ **we ~ at eight** nous dînons à 20 heures ◆ **to ~ like a horse** manger comme quatre *or* comme un ogre ◆ **to ~ like a bird** picorer ◆ **to ~ like a pig** manger comme un porc ◆ **he's ~ing us out of house and home*** son appétit va nous mettre à la rue ◆ **to ~ out of sb's hand** *(fig)* faire les quatre volontés de qn ◆ **I've got him ~ing out of my hand** il fait tout ce que je lui dis *or* tout ce que je veux

NPL **eats** ⁑ *(Brit)* bouffe⁑ *f* ; *(on notice)* snacks *mpl* ◆ **let's get some ~s** mangeons quelque chose *or* un morceau

► **eat away** VT SEP *[sea]* saper, éroder ; *[acid, mice]* ronger

► **eat away at** VT FUS *[waves, sea]* éroder ; *[acid, rust, pest]* ronger ; *[rot, damp]* attaquer ◆ **a cancer ~ing away at society** un cancer qui ronge la société ◆ **jealousy was ~ing away at her** elle était rongée de jalousie ◆ **inflation was ~ing away at their capital** l'inflation rongeait leur capital

► **eat in** VI manger chez soi
VT consommer sur place

► **eat into** VT FUS *[acid, insects]* ronger ; *[moths]* manger ; *[expenditure] [+ savings]* entamer, écorner

► **eat out** VI aller au restaurant, déjeuner *or* dîner en ville

VT SEP ◆ **to ~ one's heart out** *(= pine away)* se ronger d'inquiétude ◆ **I've written a novel: Marcel Proust, ~ your heart out!** ⁑ j'ai écrit un roman : Marcel Proust peut aller se rhabiller !*

► **eat up** VI ◆ **eat up !** mangez !

VT SEP (= *finish off*) finir ◆ ~ **up your meat** finis ta viande ◆ ~ **up your meal** finis ton repas, finis de manger ◆ **to be ~en up with envy** être dévoré d'envie *or* rongé par l'envie

VT FUS (*fig* = *consume heavily*) [+ *fuel*] consommer beaucoup de, être gourmand en* ; [+ *resources, profits*] absorber ; [+ *savings*] engloutir ◆ **this car ~s up the miles** cette voiture dévore la route ◆ **this car ~s up petrol** cette voiture est gourmande* (en essence) *or* consomme beaucoup (d'essence) ◆ **it ~s up the electricity/coal** cela consomme beaucoup d'électricité/de charbon

eatable /ˈiːtəbl/ ADJ 1 (= *not poisonous*) [*mushroom, berries etc*] comestible, bon à manger 2 (= *not disgusting*) [*meal etc*] mangeable NPL **eatables** * comestibles *mpl*, victuailles *fpl* (*hum*)

eaten /ˈiːtn/ VB ptp of **eat**

eater /ˈiːtəʳ/ N 1 (= *person*) mangeur *m*, -euse *f* ◆ **to be a big** ~ être un grand *or* gros mangeur ◆ **to be a big meat** ~ être un gros mangeur de viande 2 (* = *eating apple*) pomme *f* à couteau

eatery * /ˈiːtəri/ N restaurant *m*

eating /ˈiːtiŋ/ N ◆ **these apples make good** ~ ces pommes sont bonnes à manger

COMP [*apple*] à couteau, de dessert

eating chocolate N chocolat *m* à croquer

eating disorder N troubles *mpl* du comportement alimentaire

eating hall N (*US*) réfectoire *m*

eating house N (café-)restaurant *m*

eau de Cologne /ˈəʊdəkəˈləʊn/ N eau *f* de Cologne

eaves /iːvz/ NPL avant-toit(s) *m(pl)*

eavesdrop /ˈiːvzdrɒp/ VI écouter aux portes ◆ **to ~ on a conversation** écouter une conversation privée

eavesdropper /ˈiːvzdrɒpəʳ/ N oreille *f* indiscrète

ebb /eb/ N [*of tide*] reflux *m* ; (*Naut*) jusant *m* ◆ ~ **and flow** le flux et le reflux ◆ **the tide is on the** ~ la marée descend ◆ **to be at a low** ~ (*fig*) [*person*] être bien bas ; [*business*] aller mal ◆ **his spirits were at a low** ~ il avait le moral très bas *or* à zéro* ◆ **his funds were at a low** ~ ses fonds étaient bien bas *or* bien dégarnis VI 1 [*tide*] refluer, descendre ◆ **to ~ and flow** monter et baisser 2 (*fig*: also **ebb away**) [*enthusiasm, strength etc*] décliner, baisser ◆ **they watched as her life ~ed away** ils assistaient à ses derniers instants COMP **ebb tide** N marée *f* descendante, reflux *m* ; (*Naut*) jusant *m*

Ebola /iːˈbəʊlə/ N (*Med*) (also **Ebola virus**) virus *m* Ebola

ebonics /eˈbɒniks/ N *argot parlé par des Noirs américains des milieux défavorisés*

ebonite /ˈebənaɪt/ N ébonite *f*

ebony /ˈebəni/ N ébène *f* COMP (= *ebony-coloured*) noir d'ébène ; (= *made of ebony*) en ébène, d'ébène

e-book /ˈiːbʊk/ N livre *m* électronique

EBRD /ˌiːbiːɑːˈdiː/ N (abbrev of **European Bank for Reconstruction and Development**) BERD *f*

ebullience /ɪˈbʌlɪəns/ N exubérance *f*

ebullient /ɪˈbʌlɪənt/ ADJ [*person*] plein de vie, exubérant ; [*spirits, mood*] exubérant

e-business /ˌiːˈbɪznɪs/ N 1 (= *company*) entreprise *f* électronique 2 (= *commerce*) commerce *m* électronique, e-commerce *m*

EC /ˌiːˈsiː/ N (abbrev of **European Community**) CE *f* COMP [*directive, membership, states etc*] de la CE **EC-wide** ADJ, ADV à l'échelle de (toute) la CE

ECB /ˌiːsiːˈbiː/ N (abbrev of **European Central Bank**) BCE *f*

eccentric /ɪkˈsentrɪk/ ADJ (*also Math, Astron*) excentrique N 1 (= *person*) original(e) *m(f)*, excentrique *mf* 2 (*Tech*) excentrique *m*

eccentrically /ɪkˈsentrɪkəlɪ/ ADV [*behave, dress*] de façon excentrique, excentriquement ; [*decorate*] de façon originale

eccentricity /ˌeksənˈtrɪsɪtɪ/ N (*also Math, Astron*) excentricité *f*

Eccles cake /ˈekəlzˌkeɪk/ N *pâtisserie fourrée de fruits secs*

Ecclesiastes /ɪˌkliːzɪˈæstiːz/ N (*Bible*) ◆ **(the Book of)** ~ (le livre de l')Ecclésiaste *m*

ecclesiastic /ɪˌkliːzɪˈæstɪk/ ADJ, N ecclésiastique *m*

ecclesiastical /ɪˌkliːzɪˈæstɪkəl/ ADJ ecclésiastique

ecdysis /ˈekdɪsɪs/ N (pl **ecdyses** /ˈekdɪˌsiːz/) ecdysis *f*

ECG /ˌiːsiːˈdʒiː/, **EKG** (*US*) /ˈiːkeɪˈdʒiː/ N (abbrev of **electrocardiogram, electrocardiograph**) ECG *m*

echelon /ˈeʃəlɒn/ N échelon *m*

echinoderm /ɪˈkiːnədɜːm/ N échinoderme *m*

echo /ˈekəʊ/ N (pl **echoes**) écho *m* ; (*fig*) écho *m*, rappel *m* ◆ **to cheer to the** ~ applaudir à tout rompre

VT (*lit*) répercuter, renvoyer ◆ **he ~ed my words incredulously** (*fig*) il a répété ce que j'avais dit d'un ton incrédule ◆ **"go home?", he ~ed** "rentrer ?", répéta-t-il ◆ **to ~ sb's ideas/remarks** se faire l'écho de la pensée/des remarques de qn ◆ **pinks were chosen to ~ the colours of the ceiling** on a choisi des tons de rose pour rappeler les couleurs du plafond

VI [*sound*] (= *resonate*) retentir, résonner ; (= *bounce back*) se répercuter, faire écho ; [*place*] renvoyer l'écho ◆ **to ~ with music** (*liter*) retentir de musique ◆ **the valley ~ed with their laughter** (*liter*) la vallée résonnait *or* retentissait de leurs rires

COMP **echo chamber** N (*Rad, TV*) chambre *f* sonore

echo-sounder N sondeur *m* (à ultrasons)

echo-sounding N sondage *m* par ultrasons

éclair /eɪˈkleəʳ, ɪˈkleəʳ/ N (*Culin*) éclair *m* (à la crème)

eclampsia /ɪˈklæmpsɪə/ N éclampsie *f*

eclectic /ɪˈklektɪk/ ADJ, N éclectique *mf*

eclecticism /ɪˈklektɪsɪzəm/ N éclectisme *m*

eclipse /ɪˈklɪps/ N (*Astron, fig*) éclipse *f* ◆ **to be in** ~ être éclipsé ◆ **to fall** *or* **go into** ~ être éclipsé ◆ **partial/total** ~ éclipse *f* partielle/totale VT (*Astron, fig*) éclipser COMP **eclipsing binary** N étoile *f* double

ecliptic /ɪˈklɪptɪk/ ADJ écliptique

eclogue /ˈeklɒg/ N églogue *f*

eclosion /ɪˈkləʊʒən/ N éclosion *f*

ecocide /ˈiːkəˌsaɪd/ N écocide *m*

eco-friendly /ˈiːkəʊˌfrendlɪ/ ADJ [*detergent, hairspray etc*] respectueux de l'environnement

E-coli /iːˈkəʊlaɪ/ N (*Med*) E. coli *m*, bactérie *f* Escherischia coli

ecological /ˌiːkəˈlɒdʒɪkəl/ ADJ 1 [*damage, problem, disaster*] écologique 2 (= *ecologically sound*) écologique

ecologically /ˌiːkəˈlɒdʒɪkəlɪ/ ADV [*unacceptable*] écologiquement, d'un point de vue écologique ◆ ~ **aware** sensibilisé aux problèmes écologiques ◆ ~ **harmful** qui nuit à l'environnement ◆ ~ **minded** soucieux de l'environnement ◆ ~ **sound** écologique, respectueux de l'environnement ◆ ~ **speaking** d'un point de vue écologique

ecologist /ɪˈkɒlədʒɪst/ N écologiste *mf*

ecology /ɪˈkɒlədʒɪ/ N écologie *f*

e-commerce /ˈiːˌkɒmɜːs/ N commerce *m* électronique, e-commerce *m*

ecomovement /ˈiːkəʊˌmuːvmənt/ N (*Pol*) mouvement *m* écologique

econometer /ˌɪkəˈnɒmətəʳ/ N économètre *m*

econometric /ɪˌkɒnəˈmetrɪk/ ADJ économétrique

econometrician /ɪˌkɒnəməˈtrɪʃən/ N économétricien(ne) *m(f)*

econometrics /ɪˌkɒnəˈmetrɪks/ N (*NonC*) économétrie *f*

econometrist /ɪˌkɒnəˈmetrɪst/ N ⇒ **econometrician**

economic /ˌiːkəˈnɒmɪk/ ADJ 1 (*Econ*) [*growth, policy, system, crisis, recovery, sanctions, aid*] économique ◆ **the ~ situation** *or* **outlook** la conjoncture (économique) 2 (= *viable, cost-effective*) [*system, factory, mine etc*] rentable (*for sb* pour qn) ◆ **this business is no longer** ~ *or* **an ~ proposition** cette affaire n'est plus rentable ◆ **it is not ~ to do that** ce n'est pas rentable de faire cela ◆ ~ **rate of return** taux *m* de rentabilité économique 3 (= *market-driven*) [*price, rent*] déterminé par le marché

COMP **economic analyst** N spécialiste *mf* de l'analyse économique

economic indicator N indicateur *m* économique

economic management N gestion *f* de l'économie

economic migrant, economic refugee N migrant(e) *m(f)* économique

economical /ˌiːkəˈnɒmɪkəl/ ADJ [*person*] économe ; [*method, vehicle, machine, speed*] économique ; (*fig*) [*style, writing*] sobre, concis ◆ **to be ~ with sth** économiser qch, ménager qch ◆ **to be ~ with the truth** (= *not tell whole truth*) ne pas dire toute la vérité ; (*hum*) (= *lie*) prendre ses aises avec la vérité

economically /ˌiːkəˈnɒmɪkəlɪ/ ADV 1 (*Econ*) [*viable, depressed*] économiquement ; [*feasible, powerful, important*] d'un point de vue économique ; [*develop, suffer*] économiquement, d'un point de vue économique ◆ ~ **speaking** d'un point de vue économique 2 (= *without waste*) [*use, operate, live*] de façon économe 3 (= *concisely*) [*write*] avec sobriété

economics /ˌiːkəˈnɒmɪks/ N (*NonC*) (= *science*) économie *f* politique, science *f* économique ; (= *financial aspect*) côté *m* économique ◆ **the ~ of the situation/the project** le côté économique de la situation/du projet ; → **home**

economist /ɪˈkɒnəmɪst/ N économiste *mf*, spécialiste *mf* d'économie politique

economize /ɪˈkɒnəmaɪz/ VI économiser (*on* sur) faire des économies VT [+ *time, money*] économiser (sur), épargner ◆ **to ~ 20% on the costs** faire *or* réaliser une économie de 20% sur les coûts

economy /ɪˈkɒnəmɪ/ N 1 (= *saving: in time, money etc*) économie *f* (*in* de) ◆ **to make economies in ...** faire des économies de ... ◆ **economies of scale** économies *fpl* d'échelle 2 (*NonC* = *system*) économie *f*, système *m* économique ◆ **the country's ~ depends on ...** l'économie du pays dépend de ... ; → **black, political**

COMP **economy class** N classe *f* économique

economy-class syndrome N syndrome *m* de la classe économique

economy drive N [*of government, firm*] (campagne *f* de) restrictions *fpl* budgétaires ◆ **I'm going on** *or* **having an ~ drive this month** ce mois-ci je m'efforce de faire des économies

economy pack N paquet *m* économique

economy size N taille *f* économique

ecosphere /ˈiːkəʊˌsfɪə/ N écosphère *f*

ecosystem /ˈiːkəʊˌsɪstəm/ N écosystème *m*

eco(-)tax /ˈiːkəʊˌtæks/ N écotaxe *f*

ecoterrorist /ˈiːkəʊˌterərɪst/ N terroriste *mf* écologiste

ecotone /ˈiːkəˌtəʊn/ N écotone *m*

eco-tourism /ˈiːkəʊˌtʊərɪzəm/ N écotourisme *m*

ecotype /ˈiːkəˌtaɪp/ N écotype *m*

eco-village /ˈiːkəʊˌvɪlɪdʒ/ N écovillage *m*

eco-warrior * /ˈiːkəʊˌwɒriə/ N militant(e) *m(f)* écologiste

ecru /ˈekruː/ ADJ, N écru *m*

ECSC /ˌiːsiːesˈsiː/ N *(formerly)* (abbrev of **European Coal and Steel Community**) CECA *f*

ecstasy /ˈekstəsɪ/ N 1 *(= joy)* extase *f (also Rel)*, ravissement *m* ◆ **with ~** avec ravissement, avec extase ◆ **to be in ecstasies over** *[+ object]* s'extasier sur ; *[+ person]* être en extase devant 2 *(Drugs)* ecstasy *m*

ecstatic /eksˈtætɪk/ ADJ *[crowd]* en délire ; *[welcome, reception]* enthousiaste ◆ **to be ~ over** *or* **about sth** être follement heureux de qch

ecstatically /eksˈtætɪkəlɪ/ ADV *[applaud, react]* avec extase ; *[listen, say]* d'un air extasié ◆ **~ happy** follement heureux

ECT /ˌiːsiːˈtiː/ N abbrev of **electroconvulsive therapy**

ectomorph /ˈektəʊˌmɔːf/ N ectomorphe *mf*

ectopic /ekˈtɒpɪk/ ADJ ◆ **~ pregnancy** grossesse *f* extra-utérine

ectoplasm /ˈektəʊplæzəm/ N ectoplasme *m*

ECU /ˈeɪkjuː, ˌiːsiːˈjuː/ N (abbrev of **European Currency Unit**) ECU *m*, écu *m* ◆ **hard ~** écu *m* fort ◆ **weights of currencies in the ~** poids *m* des devises au sein de l'écu

Ecuador /ˈekwədɔːʳ/ N Équateur *m*

Ecuador(i)an /ˌekwəˈdɔːr(ɪ)ən/ ADJ équatorien N Équatorien(ne) *m(f)*

ecumenical /ˌiːkjʊˈmenɪkəl/ ADJ œcuménique

ecumenicism /ˌiːkjʊˈmenɪsɪzəm/, **ecumenism** /iːˈkjuːmənɪzəm/ N œcuménisme *m*

eczema /ˈeksɪmə/ N eczéma *m* ◆ **~ sufferer** personne *f* sujette à l'eczéma

ed. 1 (abbrev of **edition**) éd. ◆ **3rd ~** 3ᵉ éd. 2 (abbrev of **editor**) ◆ **"Chèvrefeuille", ~ J. Lefèvre** "Chèvrefeuille", annoté et commenté par J. Lefèvre ◆ **"Essays in Welsh History", eds. Dodd and Jenkins** "Essays in Welsh History", sous la direction de Dodd et Jenkins

eddy /ˈedɪ/ N *[of water, air]* remous *m*, tourbillon *m* ; *[of snow, dust, smoke]* tourbillon *m* ; *[of leaves]* tournoiement *m*, tourbillon *m* VI *[air, smoke, leaves, snow, dust]* tourbillonner ; *[people]* tournoyer ; *[water]* faire des remous *or* des tourbillons

edelweiss /ˈeɪdlvaɪs/ N edelweiss *m inv*

edema /ɪˈdiːmə/ N (pl **edemata** /ɪˈdiːmətə/) *(esp US)* œdème *m*

Eden /ˈiːdn/ N Éden *m*, paradis *m* terrestre ; → **garden**

edentate /ɪˈdenteɪt/ ADJ, N édenté *m*

edge /edʒ/ N 1 *[of table, plate, cloth, river, cliff, lake]* bord *m* ; *[of road]* bord *m*, côté *m* ; *[of town]* abords *mpl* ; *[of coin]* tranche *f* ; *[of page]* bord *m* ; *(= margin)* marge *f* ; *[of cube, brick]* arête *f* ; *[of forest]* lisière *f*, orée *f* ◆ **at the water's ~** au bord de l'eau ◆ **to stand sth on its ~** poser qch de chant ◆ **the trees at the ~ of the road** les arbres au bord *or* en bordure de la route ◆ **the film had us on the ~ of our seats** *or* *(US)* **chairs** le film nous a tenus en haleine

2 *(= blade) [of knife, razor]* tranchant *m*, fil *m* ◆ **a blade with a sharp ~** une lame bien affilée ◆ **to put an ~ on** *[+ knife, blade]* aiguiser, affiler, affûter

3 *[of ski]* arête *f* ; *(= metal strip)* carre *f*

4 *(fig = brink, verge)* **to be on the ~ of disaster** être au bord du désastre, courir au désastre ◆ **to be on the ~ of tears** être au bord des larmes ◆ **to be on the ~ of extinction** être en voie d'extinction ◆ **that pushed him over the ~** ça a été plus qu'il ne pouvait supporter, ça a été le comble ◆ **to live life on the ~** * être *or* marcher sur le fil du rasoir

5 *(set phrase)*

◆ **on edge** ◆ **he's on ~** il est énervé *or* à cran * ◆ **my nerves are all on ~** j'ai les nerfs en pelote * *or* en boule * ◆ **it sets my teeth on ~** cela me fait grincer les dents

6 *(fig = advantage)* **to have the ~ on** *or* **over** avoir un (léger) avantage sur, l'emporter de justesse sur ◆ **to give sb the ~ on** *or* **over the competition** donner à qn un avantage sur la concurrence ◆ **the company has lost its competitive ~** la société est devenue moins compétitive ◆ **the party has lost its radical ~** le parti n'est plus aussi radical qu'avant

7 *(fig = sharpness)* **to take the ~ off** *[+ sensation]* émousser ; *[+ appetite]* calmer, émousser ◆ **there was an ~ to his voice** on sentait à sa voix qu'il était tendu ◆ **panic gave a sharp ~ to his voice** sous l'effet de la panique, sa voix est devenue tendue ◆ **there was a slightly caustic ~ to his voice** il y avait des intonations caustiques dans sa voix ; → **cutting, rough**

VT 1 *(= put a border on)* border *(with* de) ◆ **~d with lace** bordé de dentelle

2 ◆ **to ~ one's chair nearer the door** rapprocher sa chaise tout doucement de la porte ◆ **to ~ one's way through** *etc* ⇒ **to edge through** VI ◆ **to ~ sb out of his** *(or* **her) job** déloger progressivement qn de son poste ◆ **wage rises have ~d up inflation** la hausse des salaires a entraîné une légère augmentation du taux d'inflation

VI se glisser, se faufiler ◆ **to ~ through/into** *etc* se glisser *or* se faufiler à travers/dans *etc* ◆ **to ~ forward** avancer petit à petit ◆ **to ~ away** s'éloigner tout doucement *or* furtivement ◆ **to ~ up to sb** *(furtively)* s'approcher tout doucement *or* furtivement de qn ; *(shyly)* s'approcher timidement de qn ◆ **share prices ~d up** il y a eu une tendance à la hausse des valeurs boursières ◆ **to ~ out of a room** se glisser hors d'une pièce, sortir furtivement d'une pièce

-edged /edʒd/ ADJ *(in compounds)* 1 *[paper, fabric]* bordé de, avec une bordure de 2 *[knife etc]* **blunt-/sharp-edged** émoussé/bien aiguisé

edgeways /ˈedʒweɪz/, **edgewise** /ˈedʒwaɪz/ ADV de côté ◆ **I couldn't get a word in ~** * je n'ai pas réussi à placer un mot *or* à en placer une *

edginess /ˈedʒɪnɪs/ N *(NonC)* nervosité *f*, énervement *m*, irritation *f*

edging /ˈedʒɪŋ/ N 1 *(gen)* bordure *f* ; *[of ribbon, silk]* liseré *or* liséré *m* 2 *(Ski)* prise *f* de carres COMP **edging shears** NPL cisailles *fpl* à gazon

edgy /ˈedʒɪ/ ADJ *[person, mood]* énervé, à cran *, crispé

edibility /ˌedɪˈbɪlɪtɪ/ N comestibilité *f*

edible /ˈedɪbl/ ADJ 1 *(= not poisonous) [mushroom, berries etc]* comestible, bon à manger 2 *(= not disgusting) [meal etc]* mangeable

COMP **edible crab** N dormeur *m*, tourteau *m*

edible snail N escargot *m* comestible

edict /ˈiːdɪkt/ N *(gen, Jur, Pol)* décret *m* ; *(Hist)* édit *m*

edification /ˌedɪfɪˈkeɪʃən/ N édification *f*, instruction *f*

edifice /ˈedɪfɪs/ N édifice *m*

edify /ˈedɪfaɪ/ VT édifier

edifying /ˈedɪfaɪɪŋ/ ADJ édifiant

Edinburgh /ˈedɪnbərə/ N Édimbourg COMP **the Edinburgh Festival** N le Festival d'Édimbourg

> **EDINBURGH FESTIVAL**
>
> Le Festival d'Édimbourg, qui se tient chaque année durant trois semaines au mois d'août, est l'un des grands festivals européens. Il est réputé pour son programme officiel mais aussi pour son festival « off » (« the Fringe ») qui propose des spectacles aussi bien traditionnels que résolument d'avant-garde. Pendant la durée du Festival se tient par ailleurs, sur l'esplanade du château, un grand spectacle de musique militaire, le « Military Tattoo ».

edit /ˈedɪt/ VT 1 *(= manage) [+ newspaper, magazine]* être rédacteur *(or* rédactrice) en chef de ; *[+ series of texts]* diriger la publication de ; *[+ text, author]* éditer, donner une édition de 2 *(= adapt) [+ article]* mettre au point, préparer ; *[+ dictionary, encyclopedia]* assurer la rédaction de 3 *(Rad, TV) [+ programme]* réaliser ; *[+ film]* monter ; *[+ tape]* mettre au point, couper et recoller 4 *(Comput) [+ file]* éditer N révision *f*

► **edit out** VT SEP supprimer *(of* de) ; *[+ text, film]* couper *(of* de)

editing /ˈedɪtɪŋ/ N *[of magazine]* direction *f* ; *[of newspaper, dictionary]* rédaction *f* ; *[of article, series of texts, tape]* mise *f* au point ; *[of text, author]* édition *f* ; *[of film]* montage *m* ; *(Comput)* édition *f*

edition /ɪˈdɪʃən/ N *[of newspaper, book]* édition *f* ; *[of print, etching]* tirage *m* ◆ **revised ~** édition *f* revue et corrigée ◆ **to bring out an ~ of a text** publier *or* faire paraître l'édition d'un texte ; → **first**

editor /ˈedɪtəʳ/ N 1 *(Press) [of newspaper, magazine]* rédacteur *m*, -trice *f* en chef 2 *(Publishing) [of writer, text, anthology]* éditeur *m*, -trice *f* ; *[of dictionary, encyclopedia]* rédacteur *m*, -trice *f* 3 *(Rad, TV) [of programme]* réalisateur *m*, -trice *f* 4 *(Cine)* monteur *m*, -euse *f* ◆ **political ~** *(Press)* rédacteur *m*, -trice *f* politique ◆ **sports ~** rédacteur *m* sportif, rédactrice *f* sportive ◆ **"letters to the editor"** "courrier des lecteurs", "lettres à la rédaction" ; → **news** 5 *(Comput) (= text editor)* éditeur *m* de texte COMP **editor-in-chief** N rédacteur *m*, -trice *f* en chef

> ⚠ **editor** is only translated by **éditeur** when it means someone who annotates a text, and in the computing sense, (see noun 2,5).

editorial /ˌedɪˈtɔːrɪəl/ ADJ *[budget, board, meeting, comment, control, decision]* de la rédaction ; *[office]* de (la) rédaction ; *[page]* de l'éditorial ; *[policy]* éditorial ◆ **~ assistant** rédacteur *m*, -trice *f* adjoint(e) ◆ **~ staff** *(as team)* rédaction *f* ; *(as individuals)* personnel *m* de la rédaction ◆ **the ~ "we"** le "nous" de modestie *or* d'auteur N *(in newspaper etc)* éditorial *m*, article *m* de tête

editorialist /ˌedɪˈtɔːrɪəlɪst/ N *(US)* éditorialiste *mf*

editorialize /ˌedɪˈtɔːrɪəlaɪz/ VI exprimer une opinion

editorially /ˌedɪˈtɔːrɪəlɪ/ ADV 1 *(= in approach, content) [independent, selective]* du point de vue éditorial 2 *(in opinion piece)* ◆ **the Times commented ~ that ...** le Times a affirmé dans un éditorial que ...

editorship /ˈedɪtəʃɪp/ N 1 *(= position of editor) [of newspaper, magazine]* poste *m* de rédacteur en chef ; *(Rad, TV)* poste *m* de réalisateur 2 *(NonC = act or style of editing) [of newspaper, magazine]* direction *f* ; *[of dictionary, encyclopedia]* rédaction *f* ; *[of text]* édition *f* ◆ **under sb's ~** *or* **the ~ of sb** sous la direction de qn

EDP /ˌiːdiːˈpiː/ N (abbrev of **Electronic Data Processing**) → **electronic**

EDT /ˌiːdiːˈtiː/ N *(US)* (abbrev of **Eastern Daylight Time**) → **eastern**

educable /ˈedjʊkəbl/ ADJ éducable

educate /ˈedjʊkeɪt/ VT (= *teach*) [*teacher, school*] [+ *pupil*] assurer l'instruction de, instruire ; (= *bring up*) [+ *family, children*] élever, éduquer ; [+ *the mind, one's tastes*] former ◆ **the parents' role in educating their children** le rôle des parents dans l'éducation de leurs enfants ◆ **he is being ~d in Paris/at Cambridge** il fait ses études à Paris/Cambridge ◆ **to ~ the public** éduquer le public ◆ **we need to ~ our children about drugs/the environment** il faut que nous sensibilisions nos enfants au problème de la drogue/aux questions d'écologie ◆ **a campaign to ~ people about the dangers of smoking** une campagne de sensibilisation du public aux dangers du tabac *or* du tabagisme ◆ **to ~ sb to believe that ...** (*fig*) enseigner à qn que ...

educated /ˈedjʊkeɪtɪd/ VB ptp of **educate** ADJ [*person*] (= *cultured*) cultivé ; (= *learned, trained*) instruit ; [*work force*] ayant un bon niveau d'éducation *or* d'instruction ; [*voice*] cultivé ; [*palate, ear*] averti ◆ **he's hardly ~ at all** il n'a guère d'instruction ◆ **an ~ mind** un esprit cultivé ; → **guess, well²**

education /ˌedjʊˈkeɪʃən/ N (*gen*) éducation *f* ; (= *teaching*) enseignement *m* ; (= *learning*) instruction *f* ; (= *studies*) études *fpl* ; (= *training*) formation *f* ; (= *knowledge*) culture *f* ; (*as subject studied*) pédagogie *f* ◆ **he had a good ~** il a reçu une bonne éducation ◆ **his ~ was neglected** on a négligé son éducation ◆ **physical/political ~** éducation *f* physique/politique ◆ **he has had very little ~** il n'a pas fait beaucoup d'études ◆ **his ~ was interrupted** ses études ont été interrompues ◆ **she has** *or* **has had a university ~** elle est diplômée d'université, elle a fait des études supérieures ◆ **the ~ he received at school** l'instruction qu'il a reçue à l'école (*or* au lycée *etc*) ◆ **literary/professional ~** formation *f* littéraire/professionnelle ◆ **primary/secondary ~** enseignement *m* primaire/secondaire ◆ **~ is free in Britain** l'instruction est gratuite en Grande-Bretagne, l'enseignement est gratuit en Grande-Bretagne ◆ **the crisis in ~, the ~ crisis** la crise de l'enseignement ◆ **the ~ system** (*gen*) le système éducatif *or* d'éducation ◆ **the French ~ system, the ~ system in France** le système éducatif *or* l'enseignement en France ◆ **people working in ~** les personnes qui travaillent dans l'enseignement ◆ **Secretary for Education** (*US*) ministre *m* de l'Éducation ; → **adult, department, further, minister, secretary**

COMP [*theory, method*] d'enseignement, pédagogique ; [*standards*] d'instruction, scolaire ; [*costs*] de l'enseignement ; (*Pol*) [*budget, minister*] de l'Éducation nationale

the Education Act N (*Brit*) la loi sur l'enseignement

education authority N (*Brit*) ≃ délégation *f* départementale de l'enseignement

Education Committee N (*Brit Scol Admin*) commission *f* du conseil régional chargée des affaires scolaires

education correspondent N (*Press*) correspondant(e) *m(f)* chargé(e) des questions de l'enseignement

education department N (*Brit: of local authority*) ≃ délégation *f* départementale de l'enseignement ; (= *ministry*) ministère *m* de l'Éducation

education page N (*Press*) rubrique *f* de l'enseignement

Education Welfare Officer N (*Brit Scol Admin*) assistant(e) *m(f)* social(e) scolaire

educational /ˌedjʊˈkeɪʃənl/ ADJ [*system, needs, film, book, toy, game*] éducatif ; [*institution, establishment*] d'enseignement ; [*standards*] de l'enseignement ; [*achievement*] (*at school*) scolaire ; (*at university*) universitaire ; [*supplies*] scolaire ; [*theory*] de l'éducation ; [*role, function*] éducateur (-trice *f*) ; [*method, methodology, issue, material*] pédagogique ; [*experience*] instructif ; [*visit, day*] (*for adults*) instructif ; (*for children*) éducatif ◆ **~ opportunities** possibilité *f* de faire des études ◆ **~ qualifications** diplômes *mpl* ◆ **falling ~ standards** la baisse du niveau de l'enseignement

COMP **educational adviser** N (*Scol Admin*) conseiller *m*, -ère *f* pédagogique

educational age N (*US Scol*) niveau *m* scolaire (*d'un élève*)

educational park N (*US*) *complexe scolaire et universitaire*

educational psychologist N psychopédagogue *mf*

educational psychology N psychopédagogie *f*

educational television N (*gen*) télévision *f* éducative ; (*US*) *chaîne de télévision éducative*

educationalist /ˌedjʊˈkeɪʃnəlɪst/ N (*esp Brit*) éducateur *m*, -trice *f*, pédagogue *mf*

educationally /ˌedjʊˈkeɪʃnəlɪ/ ADV [*subnormal, deprived etc*] sur le plan éducatif ◆ **~ sound principles** des principes sains du point de vue pédagogique

educationist /ˌedjʊˈkeɪʃnɪst/ N ⇒ **educationalist**

educative /ˈedjʊkətɪv/ ADJ éducatif, éducateur (-trice *f*)

educator /ˈedjʊkeɪtəʳ/ N (*esp US*) éducateur *m*, -trice *f*

educe /ɪˈdjuːs/ VT (*frm*) dégager, faire sortir

edutainment* /ˌedjʊˈteɪnmənt/ N (*esp US*) (= *games*) jeux *mpl* éducatifs ; (= *TV etc programmes*) émissions *fpl* éducatives pour enfants

Edward /ˈedwəd/ N Édouard *m* ◆ **~ the Confessor** (*Brit Hist*) Édouard le Confesseur

Edwardian /edˈwɔːdɪən/ (*Brit*) ADJ [*England, house, furniture, picture, literature*] édouardien, du début du (20ᵉ) siècle ; [*lady, gentleman*] de l'époque d'Édouard VII ◆ **~ clothes** vêtements *mpl* style 1900 ◆ **in ~ days** à l'époque d'Édouard VII, au début du (20ᵉ) siècle ◆ **the ~ era** ≃ la Belle Époque N *personne qui vivait sous le règne d'Édouard VII ou qui a les caractéristiques de cette époque*

EEC /ˌiːiːˈsiː/ N (abbrev of **European Economic Community**) CEE *f*

EEG /ˌiːiːˈdʒiː/ N (abbrev of **electroencephalogram**) EEG *m*

eek* /iːk/ EXCL aah !

eel /iːl/ N anguille *f* ; → **electric**

eelworm /ˈiːlwɜːm/ N anguillule *f*

e'en /iːn/ ADV (*liter*) ⇒ **even²**

EEOC /ˌiːiːəʊˈsiː/ N (*US*) (abbrev of **Equal Employment Opportunity Commission**) → **equal ;** → **EOC, EEOC**

e'er /ɛəʳ/ ADV (*liter*) ⇒ **ever**

eerie /ˈɪərɪ/ ADJ sinistre, qui donne le frisson

eerily /ˈɪərɪlɪ/ ADV [*deserted, empty*] sinistrement ; [*similar, familiar*] étrangement ◆ **~ quiet/silent** d'un calme/d'un silence inquiétant ◆ **to echo/gleam ~** résonner/luire sinistrement

eery /ˈɪərɪ/ ADJ ⇒ **eerie**

EET /ˌiːiːˈtiː/ N (abbrev of **Eastern European Time**) → **eastern**

eff‡ /ef/ VI ◆ **he was ~ing and blinding** il jurait comme un charretier* ; → **effing**

▸ **eff off**‡ VI aller se faire voir‡

efface /ɪˈfeɪs/ VT (*lit, fig*) effacer, oblitérer (*liter*)

effect /ɪˈfekt/ N 1 (= *result*) effet *m*, conséquence *f* (*on* sur) ; (*Phys*) effet *m* ; [*of wind, chemical, drug*] action *f* (*on* sur) ◆ **this rule will have the ~ of preventing ..., the ~ of this rule will be to prevent ...** cette règle aura pour effet d'empêcher ... ◆ **the ~ of all this is that ...** (*frm*) il résulte de tout ceci que ... ◆ **to feel the ~s of an accident** ressentir les effets d'un accident, se ressentir d'un accident ◆ **the ~s of the new law are already being felt** les effets de la nouvelle loi se font déjà sentir ◆ **to have no ~** ne produire aucun effet ◆ **to be of no ~** (= *have no effect*) être inefficace ; [*law etc*] être inopérant, rester sans effet ◆ **to have an ~ on sth** avoir *or* produire un effet sur qch ◆ **it won't have any ~ on him** ça ne lui fera aucun effet, ça n'aura aucun effet sur lui ◆ **to little ~** sans grand résultat ◆ **to no ~** en vain ◆ **to use to good** *or* **great ~** savoir tirer avantage de ◆ **to such good ~ that ...** si bien que ... ◆ **with ~ from April** (*esp Brit*) à compter du mois d'avril ◆ **with immediate ~** (*frm*) (*esp Brit*) avec effet immédiat

◆ **in effect** (= *in force*) en vigueur ; (= *in reality*) de fait, en réalité

◆ **to put sth into effect** mettre qch à exécution *or* en application

◆ **to come** *or* **go into effect** [*law*] prendre effet, entrer en vigueur ; [*policy*] être appliqué

◆ **to take effect** [*drug*] agir, produire *or* faire son effet ; [*law*] prendre effet, entrer en vigueur

2 (= *impression*) effet *m* ◆ **he said it just for ~** il ne l'a dit que pour faire de l'effet *or* pour impressionner ◆ **to give a good ~** faire (un) bon effet ◆ **to make an ~** faire effet *or* de l'effet

3 (*Cine, Rad, Theat, TV*) (also **sound effect**) effet *m* sonore ; (also **special effect**) effet *m* spécial

4 (= *meaning*) sens *m* ◆ **we got a letter to the same ~** nous avons reçu une lettre dans le même sens

◆ **to that effect** ◆ **he used words to that ~** il s'est exprimé dans ce sens ◆ **... or words to that ~** ... ou quelque chose d'analogue *or* de ce genre

◆ **to the effect that ...** ◆ **his letter is to the ~ that ...** sa lettre nous apprend que ... ◆ **an announcement to the ~ that ...** un communiqué annonçant que ... *or* selon lequel ... ◆ **orders to the ~ that ...** ordres suivant lesquels ...

5 (*frm* = *property*) ◆ **(personal) ~s** effets *mpl* personnels ◆ **"no effects"** (*Banking*) "sans provision" ; → **personal**

VT (*gen*) [+ *reform, reduction, payment*] effectuer ; [+ *cure*] obtenir ; [+ *improvement*] apporter ; [+ *transformation*] opérer, effectuer ; [+ *reconciliation, reunion*] amener ; [+ *sale, purchase*] réaliser, effectuer ◆ **to ~ change** procéder à des changements ◆ **to ~ a saving** faire une économie ◆ **to ~ a settlement** arriver à un accord ◆ **negotiation ~ed the release of the hostages** les négociations ont abouti à *or* ont permis la libération des otages ◆ **to ~ an entry** (*frm*) entrer de force

effective /ɪˈfektɪv/ ADJ 1 (= *successful*) [*action, method, treatment, policy, deterrent, government, politician*] efficace (*against sth* contre qch ; *in doing sth* pour faire qch) ; [*word, remark, argument*] qui porte, qui a de l'effet ◆ **~ life** (*Pharm*) durée *f* effective 2 (= *striking*) [*decoration, pattern, combination*] frappant ◆ **to look ~** faire de l'effet 3 (= *actual*) [*control*] effectif ; [*leader*] véritable 4 (*Econ, Fin*) [*demand, income*] effectif ; [*interest rate*] net, réel 5 (= *operative*) [*law, ceasefire, insurance cover*] en vigueur (*from* à compter de, à partir de) ◆ **to become ~** entrer en vigueur ◆ **to be** *or* **become ~ immediately** prendre effet immédiatement ◆ **~ date** date *f* d'entrée en vigueur 6 (*Mil*) ◆ **~ troops** hommes *mpl* valides NPL **effectives** (*Mil*) effectifs *mpl*

effectively /ɪˈfektɪvlɪ/ ADV 1 (= *successfully*) [*treat, teach, work*] efficacement ◆ **to function ~** bien fonctionner 2 (= *strikingly*) [*contrast*] de manière frappante 3 (= *in effect*) [*prevent, stop*] en réalité

effectiveness /ɪˈfektɪvnɪs/ N (= *efficiency*) efficacité *f* ; (= *striking quality*) effet *m* frappant *or* saisissant

effector /ɪˈfektəʳ/ ADJ effecteur (-trice *f*) N effecteur *m*

effectual /ɪˈfektjʊəl/ ADJ *(frm) [remedy, punishment]* efficace ; *[document, agreement]* valide

effectually /ɪˈfektjʊəlɪ/ ADV *(frm)* efficacement

effectuate /ɪˈfektjʊeɪt/ VT *(frm)* effectuer, opérer, réaliser

effeminacy /ɪˈfemɪnəsɪ/ N caractère *m* efféminé

effeminate /ɪˈfemɪnɪt/ ADJ efféminé

efferent /ˈefərənt/ ADJ efférent

effervesce /ˌefəˈves/ VI 1 *(= fizz) [liquid]* être *or* entrer en effervescence ; *[drinks]* pétiller, mousser ; *[gas]* se dégager (en effervescence) 2 *(fig) [person]* déborder (*with* de) être tout excité

effervescence /ˌefəˈvesns/ N 1 *(= fizziness)* effervescence *f*, pétillement *m* 2 *(fig = liveliness)* excitation *f*

effervescent /ˌefəˈvesnt/ ADJ 1 *(= fizzy) [liquid, tablet]* effervescent ; *[drink]* gazeux 2 *(fig = lively)* plein d'entrain

effete /ɪˈfiːt/ ADJ *(frm) [person]* mou (molle *f*), veule ; *[empire, civilization]* décadent ; *[government]* affaibli ; *[method]* (devenu) inefficace, stérile

effeteness /ɪˈfiːtnɪs/ N *(frm) [of person]* mollesse *f*, veulerie *f (liter)* ; *[of group, civilization]* décadence *f*

efficacious /ˌefɪˈkeɪʃəs/ ADJ *(frm)* efficace (*for sth* pour qch ; *against sth* contre qch)

efficacy /ˈefɪkəsɪ/, **efficaciousness** /ˌefɪˈkeɪʃəsnɪs/ N efficacité *f*

efficiency /ɪˈfɪʃənsɪ/ N *[of person]* capacité *f*, compétence *f* ; *[of method]* efficacité *f* ; *[of organization, system]* efficacité *f*, bon fonctionnement *m* ; *[of machine]* bon rendement *m*, bon fonctionnement *m* COMP **efficiency apartment** N *(US)* studio *m*

efficient /ɪˈfɪʃənt/ ADJ *[person, machine, organization, service, method, use]* efficace ; *[car]* d'un bon rendement ◆ **to be ~ in** *or* **at doing sth** faire qch avec efficacité ◆ **to be ~ in one's use of sth** utiliser qch avec efficacité

efficiently /ɪˈfɪʃəntlɪ/ ADV *[use, manage]* efficacement ; *[deal with]* avec efficacité ◆ **to work ~** *[person]* travailler efficacement ; *[machine]* avoir un bon rendement

effigy /ˈefɪdʒɪ/ N effigie *f* ◆ **in ~** en effigie

effing ‡ /ˈefɪŋ/ *(Brit euph)* ADJ ◆ **this ~ phone !** ce fichu * téléphone ! ◆ **what an ~ waste of time!** merde ! ‡ quelle perte de temps ! ; → **eff** N ◆ **~ and blinding** grossièretés *fpl*

effloresce /ˌeflɒˈres/ VI *(Chem)* effleurir

efflorescence /ˌeflɔːˈresns/ N *(Chem, Med: also liter)* efflorescence *f* ; *(Bot)* floraison *f*

efflorescent /ˌeflɔːˈresnt/ ADJ *(Chem)* efflorescent ; *(Bot)* en fleur(s)

effluence /ˈefluəns/ N émanation *f*, effluence *f (liter)*

effluent /ˈefluənt/ ADJ, N effluent *m*

effluvium /eˈfluːvɪəm/ N (pl **effluviums** *or* **effluvia** /eˈfluːvɪə/) effluve(s) *m(pl)*, émanation *f*, exhalaison *f* ; *(pej)* exhalaison *f or* émanation *f* fétide

efflux /ˈeflʌks/ N ◆ **~ of capital** fuite *f or* exode *m* de capitaux

effort /ˈefət/ N effort *m* ◆ **getting up was an ~** c'était un effort de me (*or se etc*) lever ◆ **it's not bad for a first ~** ça n'est pas (si) mal pour un début ◆ **that's a good ~** * ça n'est pas mal (réussi) ◆ **in an ~ to solve the problem/be polite** *etc* pour essayer de résoudre le problème/d'être poli *etc* ◆ **what do you think of his latest ~?** * qu'est-ce que tu penses de ce qu'il vient de faire ? ◆ **it's a pretty poor ~** * ça n'est pas une réussite *or* un chef-d'œuvre ◆ **the famine relief ~** la lutte contre la famine ◆ **the government's ~ to avoid ...** les efforts *mpl or* les tentatives *fpl* du gouvernement pour éviter ... ◆ **the war ~** l'effort *m* de guerre ◆ **to do sth by ~ of will** faire qch dans un effort de volonté ◆ **with ~** avec difficulté, non sans mal ◆ **without ~** sans peine, sans effort ◆ **it's not worth the ~** cela n'en vaut pas la peine ◆ **it is well worth the ~** cela en vaut vraiment la peine

◆ **to make + effort** ◆ **to make an ~ to do sth** faire un effort pour faire qch, s'efforcer de faire qch ◆ **to make an ~ to concentrate/to adapt** faire un effort de concentration/d'adaptation ◆ **to make every ~ to do sth** *(= try hard)* faire tous ses efforts *or* (tout) son possible pour faire qch, s'évertuer à faire qch ; *(= take great pains)* se donner beaucoup de mal *or* de peine pour faire qch ◆ **to make little ~ to do sth** ne pas faire beaucoup d'effort pour faire qch ◆ **little ~ has been made to investigate this case** on ne s'est pas vraiment donné la peine d'enquêter sur cette affaire ◆ **he made no ~ to be polite** il ne s'est pas donné la peine d'être poli ◆ **he makes no ~** *(Scol)* il ne fait aucun effort, il ne s'applique pas ◆ **do make some ~ to help!** fais un petit effort pour aider !, essaie d'aider un peu ! ◆ **to make the ~ to do sth** faire l'effort de faire qch, se donner le mal de faire qch

effortless /ˈefətlɪs/ ADJ *[movement, style]* fluide ; *[success, victory]* facile ; *[charm, elegance, skill, superiority]* naturel ◆ **with ~ ease** avec une parfaite aisance

effortlessly /ˈefətlɪslɪ/ ADV *[lift, succeed, beat]* sans effort

effrontery /ɪˈfrʌntərɪ/ N effronterie *f* ◆ **to have the ~ to** avoir l'effronterie de

effusion /ɪˈfjuːʒən/ N *[of liquid]* écoulement *m* ; *[of blood, gas]* effusion *f* ; *(fig)* effusion *f*, épanchement *m*

effusive /ɪˈfjuːsɪv/ ADJ *[thanks, greeting, welcome]* chaleureux ; *[praise]* enthousiaste ; *[person]* expansif ◆ **to be ~ in one's thanks/apologies** se confondre en remerciements/excuses

effusively /ɪˈfjuːsɪvlɪ/ ADV *[greet, welcome, praise]* avec effusion ◆ **to thank sb ~** se confondre en remerciements auprès de qn

E-fit /ˈiːfɪt/ N portrait-robot *m* électronique

EFL /ˌiːefˈel/ N (abbrev of **English as a Foreign Language**) → **English** ; → **TEFL, TESL, TESOL, ELT**

EFT /ˌiːefˈtiː/ N (abbrev of **electronic funds transfer**) TEF *m*, transfert *m* électronique de fonds

eft /eft/ N *(= newt)* triton *m* (crêté), salamandre *f* d'eau

EFTA /ˈeftə/ N (abbrev of **European Free Trade Association**) AELE *f*, Association *f* européenne de libre-échange

EFTPOS /ˈeftpɒs/ N (abbrev of **electronic funds transfer at point of sale**) TEF/TPV *m*

EFTS /ˌiːefˈtiːˈes/ N (abbrev of **electronic funds transfer system**) → **electronic**

eg, e.g. /ˌiːˈdʒiː/ ADV (abbrev of **exempli gratia**) *(= for example)* par ex.

egad †† /ɪˈgæd/ EXCL Dieu du ciel ! †

egalitarian /ɪˌgælɪˈteərɪən/ N égalitariste *mf* ADJ *[person]* égalitariste ; *[society, principle, spirit, relationship, policy]* égalitaire

egalitarianism /ɪˌgælɪˈteərɪənɪzəm/ N égalitarisme *m*

egest /ɪˈdʒest/ VT évacuer

egg /eg/ N œuf *m* ◆ **in the ~** dans l'œuf ◆ **~s and bacon** œufs *mpl* au bacon ◆ **a three-minute ~** un œuf à la coque ◆ **to lay an ~** *(lit) [bird etc]* pondre (un œuf) ; (‡ *fig = fail*) faire un fiasco *or* un bide‡ ◆ **to put all one's ~s in one basket** mettre tous ses œufs dans le même panier ◆ **as sure as ~s is ~s**‡ c'est sûr et certain * ◆ **to have ~ on one's face** *(fig)* avoir l'air plutôt ridicule ◆ **he's a good/bad ~** † * c'est un brave/sale type * ; → **boil¹, Scotch**

VT * pousser, inciter (*to do sth* à faire qch)

COMP **egg-and-spoon race** N course *f* (à l'œuf et) à la cuillère

egg custard N = crème *f* renversée

egg flip N lait *m* de poule

egg roll N *(= sandwich)* sandwich *m* à l'œuf ; *(Chinese)* pâté *m* impérial

egg sandwich N sandwich *m* à l'œuf

eggs Benedict N *(NonC: Culin) œufs pochés sur toast et jambon recouverts de sauce hollandaise*

egg-shaped ADJ en forme d'œuf, ovoïde

egg-timer N *(sand)* sablier *m* ; *(automatic)* minuteur *m*

egg whisk N fouet *m*

egg white N blanc *m* d'œuf

egg yolk N jaune *m* d'œuf

► **egg on** VT SEP pousser, inciter (*to do sth* à faire qch)

eggbeater /ˈegbiːtəʳ/ N *(rotary)* batteur *m* (à œufs) ; *(whisk)* fouet *m* ; *(US* ‡ *= helicopter)* hélico * *m*, hélicoptère *m*

eggcup /ˈegkʌp/ N coquetier *m*

egghead * /ˈeghed/ N intello * *mf*

eggnog /ˈegnɒg/ N lait *m* de poule

eggplant /ˈegplɑːnt/ N *(esp US)* aubergine *f*

eggshell /ˈegʃel/ N coquille *f* (d'œuf) ◆ **when I'm with him I feel I'm walking on ~s** quand je suis avec lui, je marche sur des œufs *or* j'ai toujours peur de dire un mot de travers

COMP **eggshell china** N coquille *f* d'œuf *(porcelaine)*

eggshell paint N peinture *f* coquille d'œuf

egis /ˈiːdʒɪs/ N *(US)* ⇒ **aegis**

eglantine /ˈegləntaɪn/ N *(= flower)* églantine *f* ; *(= bush)* églantier *m*

EGM /ˌiːdʒiːˈem/ N (abbrev of **extraordinary general meeting**) AGE *f*

ego /ˈiːgəʊ/ N *(= pride)* amour-propre *m* ◆ **the ~** *(Psych)* l'ego *m*, le moi

COMP **ego-surf** VI *naviguer sur Internet à la recherche de son propre nom ou d'éventuels liens vers sa page personnelle*

ego trip * N ◆ **having his name all over the papers is a great ~ trip for him** avoir son nom dans tous les journaux flatte son amour-propre ◆ **this lecture is just an ~ trip for him** cette conférence ne sert qu'à flatter son amour-propre

egocentric(al) /ˌegəʊˈsentrɪk(əl)/ ADJ égocentrique

egocentricity /ˌegəʊsenˈtrɪsɪtɪ/ N égocentrisme *m*

egoism /ˈegəʊɪzəm/ N égoïsme *m*

egoist /ˈegəʊɪst/ N égoïste *mf*

egoistic(al) /ˌegəʊˈɪstɪk(əl)/ ADJ égoïste

egomania /ˌegəʊˈmeɪnɪə/ N manie *f* égocentrique

egomaniac /ˌegəʊˈmeɪnɪæk/ N égotiste *mf*

egotism /ˈegəʊtɪzəm/ N égotisme *m*

egotist /ˈegəʊtɪst/ N égotiste *mf*

egotistic(al) /ˌegəʊˈtɪstɪk(əl)/ ADJ égotiste

egregious /ɪˈgriːdʒəs/ ADJ *(pej)* énorme *(iro)*, fameux * *before n (iro)* ; *[folly]* extrême ; *[blunder]* monumental

egress /ˈiːgres/ N *(gen: frm)* sortie *f*, issue *f* ; *(Astron)* émersion *f*

egret /ˈiːgrɪt/ N aigrette *f*

Egypt /ˈiːdʒɪpt/ N Égypte *f*

Egyptian /ɪˈdʒɪpʃən/ ADJ égyptien, d'Égypte N Égyptien(ne) *m(f)*

Egyptologist /ˌiːdʒɪpˈtɒlədʒɪst/ N égyptologue *mf*

Egyptology /ˌiːdʒɪpˈtɒlədʒɪ/ **N** égyptologie *f*

eh /eɪ/ **EXCL** hein* ?

Eid /iːd/ **N** (also : **Eid-al-Fitr, Eid-ul-Fitr**) Aïd (el Fitr)

eider /ˈaɪdə^{r}/ **N** (also **eider duck**) eider *m*

eiderdown /ˈaɪdədaʊn/ **N** 1 (= *quilt*) édredon *m* 2 (*NonC: down*) duvet *m* (d'eider)

eidetic /aɪˈdetɪk/ **ADJ** eidétique

Eiffel Tower /ˌaɪfəlˈtaʊə^{r}/ **N** tour *f* Eiffel

Eiger /ˈaɪgə^{r}/ **N** Eiger *m*

eight /eɪt/ **ADJ** huit *inv* ◆ **an ~-hour day** (*Ind etc*) la journée de huit heures ◆ **to do** *or* **work ~-hour shifts** (*Ind etc*) faire des postes *mpl or* des roulements *mpl* de huit heures **N** huit *m inv* (*also Rowing*) ◆ **he's had one over the ~** * il a du vent dans les voiles*, il a un coup dans le nez* ; → **figure** ; *for other phrases see* **six PRON** huit ◆ **there are ~** il y en a huit

eighteen /ˈeɪˈtiːn/ **ADJ** dix-huit *inv* **N** dix-huit *m inv* ; *for phrases see* **six PRON** dix-huit ◆ **there are ~** il y en a dix-huit

eighteenth /ˈeɪˈtiːnθ/ **ADJ** dix-huitième **N** dix-huitième *mf* ; (= *fraction*) dix-huitième *m* ; *for phrases see* **sixth**

eighth /eɪtθ/ **ADJ** huitième ◆ **~ note** (*US Mus*) croche *f* **N** huitième *mf* ; (= *fraction*) huitième *m* ; *for phrases see* **sixth**

eightieth /ˈeɪtɪəθ/ **ADJ** quatre-vingtième **N** quatre-vingtième *mf* ; (= *fraction*) quatre-vingtième *m* ; *for phrases see* **sixth**

eighty /ˈeɪtɪ/ **ADJ** quatre-vingts *inv* ◆ **about ~ books** environ *or* à peu près quatre-vingts livres **N** quatre-vingts *m* ◆ **about ~** environ *or* à peu près quatre-vingts ◆ **~-one** quatre-vingt-un ◆ **~-two** quatre-vingt-deux ◆ **~-first** quatre-vingt-unième ◆ **page ~** la page quatre-vingt ; *for other phrases see* **sixty PRON** quatre-vingts ◆ **there are ~** il y en a quatre-vingts **COMP eighty-six** * **VT** (*US*) (= *refuse to serve*) refuser de servir ; (= *eject*) vider*

Einsteinian /aɪnˈstaɪnɪən/ **ADJ** einsteinien

einsteinium /aɪnˈstaɪnɪəm/ **N** einsteinium *m*

Eire /ˈeərə/ **N** République *f* d'Irlande, Eire *f*

eisteddfod /aɪˈstedfəd/ **N** *concours de musique et de poésie en gallois*

either /ˈaɪðə^{r}, ˈiːðə^{r}/ **ADJ** 1 (= *one or other*) l'un(e) ou l'autre, n'importe lequel (laquelle *f*) (des deux) ◆ **~ day would suit me** l'un ou l'autre jour me conviendrait, l'un de ces deux jours me conviendrait ◆ **I don't like ~ book** je n'aime ni l'un ni l'autre de ces livres ◆ **do it ~ way** faites-le de l'une ou l'autre façon ◆ **~ way*, I can't do anything about it** de toute façon *or* quoi qu'il arrive, je n'y peux rien

2 (= *each*) chaque ◆ **in ~ hand** dans chaque main ◆ **on ~ side of the street** des deux côtés *or* de chaque côté de la rue ◆ **on ~ side lay fields** de part et d'autre s'étendaient des champs

PRON l'un(e) *m(f)* ou l'autre, n'importe lequel (laquelle *f*) (des deux) ◆ **which bus will you take? – ~** quel bus prendrez-vous ? – n'importe lequel ◆ **there are two boxes on the table, take ~** il y a deux boîtes sur la table, prenez celle que vous voulez *or* n'importe laquelle ◆ **I don't believe ~ of them** je ne les crois ni l'un ni l'autre ◆ **give it to ~ of them** donnez-le soit à l'un soit à l'autre ◆ **if ~ is attacked the other helps him** si l'un des deux est attaqué l'autre l'aide

ADV (*after neg statement*) non plus ◆ **he sings badly and he can't act ~** il chante mal et il ne sait pas jouer non plus *or* et il ne joue pas mieux ◆ **I have never heard of him – no, I haven't ~** je n'ai jamais entendu parler de lui – moi non plus

CONJ 1 ◆ **~ ... or** ou (bien) ... ou (bien), soit ... soit ; (*after neg*) ni ... ni ◆ **he must be ~ lazy or stupid** il doit être ou paresseux ou stupide ◆ **he must ~ change his policy or resign** il faut soit qu'il change *subj* de politique soit qu'il démissionne *subj* ◆ **~ be quiet or go out!** tais-toi ou sors d'ici !, ou (bien) tu te tais ou (bien) tu sors d'ici ! ◆ **I have never been ~ to Paris or to Rome** je ne suis jamais allé ni à Paris ni à Rome ◆ **it was ~ him or his sister** c'était soit lui soit sa sœur, c'était ou (bien) lui ou (bien) sa sœur

2 (= *moreover*) **she got a sum of money, and not such a small one ~** elle a reçu une somme d'argent, plutôt rondelette d'ailleurs

ejaculate /ɪˈdʒækjʊleɪt/ **VTI** 1 (= *cry out*) s'exclamer, s'écrier 2 (*Physiol*) éjaculer

ejaculation /ɪˌdʒækjʊˈleɪʃən/ **N** 1 (= *cry*) exclamation *f*, cri *m* 2 (*Physiol*) éjaculation *f*

ejaculatory /ɪˈdʒækjʊlətərɪ/ **ADJ** (*Physiol*) éjaculatoire

eject /ɪˈdʒekt/ **VT** [*pilot, CD, object*] éjecter ; [+ *tenant, troublemaker*] expulser ; [+ *trespasser*] chasser, éconduire ; [+ *customer*] expulser, vider* ◆ **press « ~ »** appuyez sur « éjecter » **VI** [*pilot*] s'éjecter

ejection /ɪˈdʒekʃən/ **N** (*NonC*) [*of person*] expulsion *f* ; [*of pilot, CD, object*] éjection *f* **COMP ejection seat** (*US*) **N** ⇒ **ejector seat**

ejector /ɪˈdʒektə^{r}/ **N** (*Tech*) éjecteur *m* **COMP ejector seat N** siège *m* éjectable

eke /iːk/ **VT** ◆ **to ~ out** (*by adding*) accroître, augmenter ; (*by saving*) économiser, faire durer ◆ **he ~s out his pension by doing odd jobs** il fait des petits travaux pour arrondir sa pension *or* ses fins de mois ◆ **to ~ out a living** *or* **an existence** vivoter

EKG /ˌiːkeɪˈdʒiː/ **N** (*US*) ⇒ **ECG**

el /el/ **N** (*US*) (abbrev of **elevated railroad**) → **elevated**

elaborate /ɪˈlæbərɪt/ **ADJ** [*system, ritual, preparations, drawing, meal, hoax, joke*] élaboré ; [*costume, clothes, style*] recherché ; [*excuse, plan*] compliqué ; [*precautions*] minutieux ◆ **with ~ care** avec un soin minutieux **VT** /ɪˈlæbəreɪt/ élaborer **VI** /ɪˈlæbəreɪt/ donner des détails (*on* sur) entrer dans *or* expliquer les détails (*on* de) **COMP elaborated code N** (*Ling*) code *m* élaboré

elaborately /ɪˈlæbərɪtlɪ/ **ADV** [*decorated, dressed*] avec recherche ; [*carved, planned*] avec minutie

elaboration /ɪˌlæbəˈreɪʃən/ **N** élaboration *f*

élan /eɪˈlɑːn, eɪˈlæn/ **N** allant *m*

elapse /ɪˈlæps/ **VI** s'écouler, (se) passer

elastic /ɪˈlæstɪk/ **ADJ** élastique (*also fig*) **N** 1 (*NonC*) élastique *m* 2 (also **baggage** *or* **luggage elastic**) tendeur *m*, sandow ® *m* **COMP elastic band N** (*esp Brit*) élastique *m* caoutchouc *m*

elastic stockings NPL bas *mpl* à varices

elasticated /ɪˈlæstɪkeɪtɪd/ **ADJ** (*Brit*) élastiqué, à élastique

elasticity /ˌiːlæsˈtɪsɪtɪ/ **N** (*also Econ*) élasticité *f*

Elastoplast ® /ɪˈlæstəˌplɑːst/ **N** (*Brit*) sparadrap *m*

elate /ɪˈleɪt/ **VT** transporter, ravir, enthousiasmer

elated /ɪˈleɪtɪd/ **ADJ** transporté *or* rempli de joie ◆ **to be ~** exulter

elation /ɪˈleɪʃən/ **N** allégresse *f*, exultation *f*

Elba /ˈelbə/ **N** (also **the Island of Elba**) (l'île *f* d')Elbe *f*

Elbe /elb/ **N** (also **the River Elbe**) l'Elbe *f*

elbow /ˈelbəʊ/ **N** [*of person, road, river, pipe, garment*] coude *m* ◆ **to lean one's ~s on** s'accouder à *or* sur, être accoudé à ◆ **to lean on one's ~** s'appuyer sur le coude ◆ **at his ~** à ses côtés ◆ **worn at the ~s** usé aux coudes ◆ **to give sb/get the ~*** (*Brit*) [*lover*] plaquer *or* laisser tomber qn*/se faire plaquer* ; [*employee*] virer qn*/se faire virer* ◆ **he lifts his ~ a bit*** (*euph hum*) il lève le coude*, il picole*

VI ◆ **to ~ through** jouer des coudes

VT ◆ **to ~ sb (in the face)** donner à qn un coup de coude (au visage) ◆ **to ~ sb aside** (*lit*) écarter qn du coude *or* d'un coup de coude ; (*fig*) jouer des coudes pour écarter qn ◆ **to ~ one's way through** *etc* ⇒ **to elbow through vi** ◆ **to ~ one's way to the top** (*fig*) jouer des coudes pour arriver au sommet

COMP elbow grease N ◆ **to use a bit of ~ grease** mettre de l'huile de coude*

elbow joint N articulation *f* du coude

elbow-rest N accoudoir *m*

elbow room N ◆ **to have enough ~ room** (*lit*) avoir de la place pour se retourner ; (*fig*) avoir les coudées franches ◆ **to have no ~ room** (*lit*) être à l'étroit ; (*fig*) ne pas avoir les coudées franches, ne pas avoir de liberté d'action

elder[1] /ˈeldə^{r}/ **ADJ** aîné (*de deux*) ◆ **my ~ sister** ma sœur aînée ◆ **Pliny the ~** Pline l'Ancien ◆ **Alexander Dumas the ~** Alexandre Dumas père ◆ **~ statesman** vétéran *m* de la politique, homme *m* politique chevronné **N** 1 (= *older person*) aîné(e) *m(f)* ◆ **one's ~s and betters** ses aînés 2 (*Rel etc*) [*of Presbyterian Church*] membre *m* du conseil d'une église presbytérienne ◆ **~s** [*of tribe, Church*] anciens *mpl*

elder[2] /ˈeldə^{r}/ **N** (= *plant*) sureau *m*

elderberry /ˈeldəberɪ/ **N** baie *f* de sureau ◆ **~ wine** vin *m* de sureau

elderflower /ˈeldəflaʊə^{r}/ **N** fleur *f* de sureau

elderly /ˈeldəlɪ/ **ADJ** [*person*] âgé ; [*vehicle, machine etc*] plutôt vieux ◆ **he's getting ~** il prend de l'âge, il se fait vieux **NPL the elderly** les personnes *fpl* âgées

eldest /ˈeldɪst/ **ADJ, N** aîné(e) *m(f)* (*de plusieurs*) ◆ **their ~ (child)** leur aîné(e), l'aîné(e) de leurs enfants ◆ **my ~ brother** l'aîné de mes frères

Eleanor /ˈelɪnə^{r}/ **N** Éléonore *f* ◆ **~ of Aquitaine** Aliénor d'Aquitaine

elec abbrev of **electric, electricity**

elect /ɪˈlekt/ **VT** 1 (*by vote*) élire ◆ **he was ~ed chairman/MP** il a été élu président/député ◆ **to ~ sb to the senate** élire qn au sénat 2 (*frm* = *choose*) **to ~ to smoke/stand/stay** *etc* choisir de *or* décider de fumer/rester debout/rester *etc* **ADJ** futur *before n* ◆ **the president ~** le président désigné, le futur président **NPL the elect** (*esp Rel*) les élus *mpl* **COMP elected member N** (*Brit Local Govt*) conseiller *m*, -ère *f* municipal(e) *or* régional(e)

elected official N élu(e) *m(f)*

election /ɪˈlekʃən/ **N** élection *f* ◆ **to hold an ~** tenir une élection ◆ **to stand for ~ (to Parliament)** se présenter aux élections législatives ◆ **her ~ as Tory leader** son élection à la tête du parti conservateur ◆ **his ~ to the presidency** son élection à la présidence ; → **general**

COMP [*speech, agent*] électoral ; [*day, results*] du scrutin ; [*publication*] de propagande électorale

election campaign N campagne *f* électorale

elections judge N (*US Pol*) scrutateur *m*, -trice *f*

electioneer /ɪˌlekʃəˈnɪə^{r}/ **VI** mener une campagne électorale, faire de la propagande électorale

electioneering /ɪˌlekʃəˈnɪərɪŋ/ **N** (= *campaign*) campagne *f* électorale ; (= *propaganda*) propagande *f* électorale **COMP** [*propaganda, publicity*] électoral ; [*speech*] de propagande électorale

elective /ɪˈlektɪv/ **ADJ** 1 (*frm* = *elected*) [*post, official, body, democracy, dictatorship*] électif ◆ **to hold ~ office** (*US*) avoir une fonction élective 2 (*frm* = *with power to elect*) [*body, assembly, power*] électoral 3 (*Med*) [*surgery*] non urgent 4 (*esp US Scol, Univ*) [*course*] facultatif ;

[subject] facultatif, en option **N** *(US Scol, Univ)* *(= course)* cours *m* facultatif

elector /ɪ'lektəʳ/ **N** *(gen, Parl)* électeur *m*, -trice *f* ; *(US Parl)* membre *m* du collège électoral ◆ **Elector** *(Hist)* Électeur *m*, prince *m* électeur

electoral /ɪ'lektərəl/ **ADJ** électoral

COMP electoral boundaries NPL limites *fpl* des circonscriptions (électorales)
electoral college N collège *m* électoral
electoral district, electoral division N *(US)* circonscription *f* (électorale)
the electoral map N *(US)* la carte électorale
electoral register, electoral roll N liste *f* électorale
electoral vote N *(US)* vote *m* des grands électeurs

ELECTORAL COLLEGE

Selon la Constitution des États-Unis, les Américains n'élisent pas directement leur président et leur vice-président, mais élisent des grands électeurs qui forment ensemble le collège électoral et qui s'engagent à voter pour tel ou tel candidat. Chaque grand électeur dispose d'un certain nombre de voix, compris entre 3 et 54 selon l'importance démographique de l'État qu'il représente.

electorally /ɪ'lektərəlɪ/ **ADV** sur le plan électoral

electorate /ɪ'lektərɪt/ **N** électorat *m*, électeurs *mpl*

Electra /ɪ'lektrə/ **N** Électre *f* **COMP Electra complex N** *(Psych)* complexe *m* d'Électre

electric /ɪ'lektrɪk/ **ADJ** électrique ◆ **the atmosphere was ~** l'ambiance était électrique
NPL the electrics * *(Brit)* l'installation *f* électrique

COMP electric arc welding N soudure *f* électrique à l'arc
electric blanket N couverture *f* chauffante
electric blue N bleu *m* électrique
electric-blue ADJ bleu électrique *inv*
electric chair N chaise *f* électrique
electric charge N charge *f* électrique
electric current N courant *m* électrique
electric eel N anguille *f* électrique, gymnote *m*
electric eye N cellule *f* photoélectrique
electric fence N clôture *f* électrifiée
electric field N champ *m* électrique
electric fire N *(Brit)* radiateur *m* électrique
electric furnace N four *m* électrique
electric guitar N guitare *f* électrique
electric heater N ⇒ **electric fire**
electric light N lumière *f* électrique ; *(NonC = lighting)* éclairage *m* électrique
electric mixer N mixeur *m*
electric organ N *(Mus)* orgue *m* électrique ; *(in fish)* organe *m* électrique
electric piano N piano *m* électrique
electric potential N potentiel *m* électrique
electric ray N *(= fish)* raie *f* électrique
electric shock N décharge *f* électrique ◆ **to get an ~ shock** recevoir une décharge électrique ◆ **to give sb an ~ shock** donner une décharge électrique à qn ◆ **~ shock treatment** * *(Med)* (traitement *m* par) électrochocs *mpl*
electric socket N prise *f* électrique *or* de courant
electric storm N orage *m* (électrique)
electric welding N soudure *f* électrique
electric wiring N installation *f* électrique

electrical /ɪ'lektrɪkəl/ **ADJ** électrique

COMP electrical engineer N ingénieur *m* électricien
electrical engineering N électrotechnique *f*
electrical failure N panne *f* dans le circuit électrique
electrical fault N défaut *m* du circuit électrique
electrical fitter N monteur *m* électricien
electrical power N électricité *f*
electrical storm N orage *m* (électrique)

electrically /ɪ'lektrɪkəlɪ/ **ADV** *[heated]* à l'électricité ; *[charged, neutral, self-sufficient]* électriquement ◆ **~ controlled** à commande électrique ◆ **~ operated** *or* **powered** électrique

electrician /ɪlek'trɪʃən/ **N** électricien *m*

electricity /ɪlek'trɪsətɪ/ **N** *(gen)* électricité *f* ◆ **to switch off/on the ~** *(also fig)* couper/rétablir le courant *or* l'électricité ; → **supply**[1]
COMP electricity board N *(Brit)* office *m* régional de l'électricité
electricity strike N grève *f* des employés de l'électricité

electrification /ɪ,lektrɪfɪ'keɪʃən/ **N** électrification *f*

electrify /ɪ'lektrɪfaɪ/ **VT** 1 *(Rail)* électrifier ; *(= charge with electricity)* électriser ◆ **to be electrified** *[village etc]* avoir l'électricité 2 *(fig)* *[+ audience]* électriser, galvaniser **COMP electrified fence N** barrière *f* électrifiée

electrifying /ɪ'lektrɪfaɪɪŋ/ **ADJ** *(fig)* électrisant, galvanisant

electrocardiogram /ɪ,lektrəʊ'kɑːdɪəgræm/ **N** électrocardiogramme *m*

electrocardiograph /ɪ,lektrəʊ'kɑːdɪəgræf/ **N** électrocardiographe *m*

electrochemical /ɪ,lektrəʊ'kemɪkəl/ **ADJ** électrochimique

electrochemistry /ɪ,lektrəʊ'kemɪstrɪ/ **N** électrochimie *f*

electroconvulsive therapy /ɪ'lektrəʊkən,vʌlsɪv'θerəpɪ/ **N** (traitement *m* par) électrochocs *mpl* ◆ **to give sb/have ~** traiter qn/être traité par électrochocs

electrocute /ɪ'lektrəkjuːt/ **VT** électrocuter

electrocution /ɪ,lektrə'kjuːʃən/ **N** électrocution *f*

electrode /ɪ'lektrəʊd/ **N** électrode *f*

electrodialysis /ɪ,lektrəʊdaɪ'ælɪsɪs/ **N** électrodialyse *f*

electrodynamic /ɪ,lektrəʊdaɪ'næmɪk/ **ADJ** électrodynamique

electrodynamics /ɪ,lektrəʊdaɪ'næmɪks/ **N** *(NonC)* électrodynamique *f*

electrodynamometer /ɪ,lektrəʊ,daɪnə'mɒmɪtəʳ/ **N** électrodynamomètre *m*

electroencephalogram /ɪ,lektrəʊen'sefələ,græm/ **N** électro-encéphalogramme *m*

electroencephalograph /ɪ,lektrəʊen'sefələ,græf/ **N** *appareil permettant de faire des électro-encéphalogrammes*

electroencephalography /ɪ'lektrəʊ,ɪnsefə'lɒgrɑːfɪ/ **N** électro-encéphalographie *f*

electroforming /ɪ'lektrəʊ,fɔːmɪŋ/ **N** électroformage *m*

electrolyse /ɪ'lektrəʊ,laɪz/ **VT** électrolyser

electrolyser /ɪ'lektrəʊ,laɪzəʳ/ **N** électrolyseur *m*

electrolysis /ɪlek'trɒlɪsɪs/ **N** électrolyse *f*

electrolyte /ɪ'lektrəʊ,laɪt/ **N** électrolyte *m*

electrolytic /ɪ,lektrəʊ'lɪtɪk/ **ADJ** électrolytique

electrolyze /ɪ'lektrəʊ,laɪz/ **VT** *(US)* ⇒ **electrolyse**

electromagnet /ɪ,lektrəʊ'mægnɪt/ **N** électroaimant *m*

electromagnetic /ɪ,lektrəʊmæg'netɪk/ **ADJ** électromagnétique

electromagnetism /ɪ,lektrəʊ'mægnɪ,tɪzəm/ **N** électromagnétisme *m*

electromechanical /ɪ,lektrəʊmɪ'kænɪkəl/ **ADJ** électromécanique

electromechanics /ɪ,lektrəʊmɪ'kænɪks/ **N** *(NonC)* électromécanique *f*

electrometallurgical /ɪ,lektrəʊ,metə'lɜːdʒɪkəl/ **ADJ** électrométallurgique

electrometallurgist /ɪ,lektrəʊmɪ'tælədʒɪst/ **N** électrométallurgiste *m*

electrometallurgy /ɪ,lektrəʊmɪ'tælədʒɪ/ **N** électrométallurgie *f*

electrometer /ɪlek'trɒmɪtəʳ/ **N** électromètre *m*

electromotive /ɪ,lektrəʊ'məʊtɪv/ **ADJ** électromoteur (-trice *f*)

electron /ɪ'lektrɒn/ **N** électron *m*
COMP *[telescope]* électronique
electron beam N faisceau *m* électronique
electron camera N caméra *f* électronique
electron engineering N génie *m* électronique
electron gun N canon *m* à électrons
electron microscope N microscope *m* électronique

electronegative /ɪ,lektrəʊ'negətɪv/ **ADJ** électronégatif

electronic /ɪlek'trɒnɪk/ **ADJ** électronique

COMP the electronic age N l'ère *f* de l'électronique
electronic banking N opérations *fpl* bancaires électroniques
electronic data processing N traitement *m* électronique de l'information *or* des données
electronic engineer N ingénieur *m* électronicien, électronicien(ne) *m(f)*
electronic engineering N électronique *f*
electronic flash N *(Phot)* flash *m* électronique
electronic funds transfer N transfert *m* électronique de fonds
electronic funds transfer system N système *m* de transfert électronique de fonds
electronic game N jeu *m* électronique
electronic ink N encre *f* électronique
electronic keyboard N clavier *m* électronique
electronic mail N courrier *m* électronique
electronic mailbox N boîte *f* aux lettres électronique
electronic music N musique *f* électronique
electronic news gathering N journalisme *m* électronique
electronic organ N orgue *m* électronique
electronic point of sale N point *m* de vente électronique
electronic publishing N édition *f* électronique
electronic surveillance N surveillance *f* électronique
electronic tag N *(on prisoner)* étiquette *f* électronique
electronic tagging N *(of prisoner)* étiquetage *m* électronique
electronic transfer of funds N transfert *m* électronique de fonds
electronic typewriter N machine *f* à écrire électronique

electronically /ɪlek'trɒnɪkəlɪ/ **ADV** électroniquement

electronics /ɪlek'trɒnɪks/ **N** *(NonC)* électronique *f* ◆ **~ engineer** ingénieur *m* électronicien, électronicien(ne) *m(f)*

electrophysiological /ɪ,lektrəʊ,fɪzɪəʊ'lɒdʒɪkəl/ **ADJ** électrophysiologique

electrophysiologist /ɪ,lektrəʊ,fɪzɪ'ɒlədʒɪst/ **N** électrophysiologiste *mf*

electrophysiology /ɪ,lektrəʊ,fɪzɪ'ɒlədʒɪ/ **N** électrophysiologie *f*

electroplate /ɪ'lektrəʊpleɪt/ **VT** plaquer par galvanoplastie ; *(with gold)* dorer par galvanoplastie ; *(with silver)* argenter par galvanoplastie ◆ **~d nickel silver** ruolz *m* N *(NonC)* articles *mpl* plaqués *etc* par galvanoplastie ; *(= silver)* articles *mpl* de ruolz

electroplating /ɪˈlektrəʊˌpleɪtɪŋ/ N *(= process)* galvanoplastie *f*

electropositive /ɪˌlektrəʊˈpɒzɪtɪv/ ADJ électropositif

electropuncture /ɪˌlektrəʊˈpʌŋktʃəʳ/ N électroponcture *or* électropuncture *f*

electroshock /ɪˈlektrəʊʃɒk/ N électrochoc *m*
COMP **electroshock baton** N matraque *f* électrique
electroshock therapy, electroshock treatment N (traitement *m* par) électrochocs *mpl* ◆ **to give sb ~ therapy** *or* **treatment** traiter qn par électrochocs

electrostatic /ɪˌlektrəʊˈstætɪk/ ADJ électrostatique

electrostatics /ɪˌlektrəʊˈstætɪks/ N *(NonC)* électrostatique *f*

electrosurgery /ɪˌlektrəʊˈsɜːdʒərɪ/ N électrochirurgie *f*

electrotechnological /ɪˌlektrəʊˌteknəˈlɒdʒɪkəl/ ADJ électrotechnique

electrotechnology /ɪˌlektrəʊtekˈnɒlədʒɪ/ N électrotechnique *f*

electrotherapeutics /ɪˌlektrəʊˌθerəˈpjuːtɪks/ N *(NonC)* électrothérapie *f*

electrotherapist /ɪˌlektrəʊˈθerəpɪst/ N électrothérapeute *mf*

electrotherapy /ɪˌlektrəʊˈθerəpɪ/ N électrothérapie *f*

electrotype /ɪˈlektrəʊˌtaɪp/ N galvanotype *m*
VT clicher par galvanotypie

electrovalent bond /ɪˌlektrəʊˈveɪləntbɒnd/ N liaison *f* électrostatique

electrum /ɪˈlektrəm/ N électrum *m*

eleemosynary /ˌeliːɪˈmɒsɪnərɪ/ ADJ *(frm)* de bienfaisance, charitable

elegance /ˈelɪgəns/ N *(NonC)* élégance *f*

elegant /ˈelɪgənt/ ADJ *(lit, fig)* élégant

elegantly /ˈelɪgəntlɪ/ ADV *[dressed]* élégamment, avec élégance ; *[furnished, decorated]* élégamment ; *[written, described]* dans un style élégant ◆ **an ~ simple room** une pièce élégante par sa simplicité ◆ **an ~ simple idea** une idée d'une élégante simplicité

elegiac /ˌelɪˈdʒaɪək/ ADJ élégiaque NPL **elegiacs** poèmes *mpl* élégiaques
COMP **elegiac couplet** N distique *m* élégiaque
elegiac stanza N strophe *f* élégiaque

elegy /ˈelɪdʒɪ/ N élégie *f*

element /ˈelɪmənt/ N 1 *(Chem, Gram, Med, Phys)* élément *m* ; *[of heater, kettle]* résistance *f* ◆ **the ~s** *(= the weather)* les éléments *mpl* ◆ **the four ~s** *(= earth, air, fire, water)* les quatre éléments *mpl* ◆ **to be in/out of one's ~** être/ne pas être dans son élément ◆ **the ~s of mathematics** les éléments *mpl or* les rudiments *mpl* des mathématiques
2 *(= aspect)* dimension *f* ; *(= factor)* élément *m*, facteur *m* ; *(= small part)* part *f* ; *(= group)* élément *m*, composante *f* ◆ **the comic/tragic/sexual ~ in his poetry** la dimension comique/tragique/sexuelle dans sa poésie ◆ **the human ~** l'élément *m* humain ◆ **one of the key ~s of the peace plan** un des éléments clés du plan de paix ◆ **the ~ of chance** le facteur chance ◆ **it's the personal ~ that matters** c'est le rapport personnel qui compte ◆ **an ~ of danger/truth** une part de danger/de vérité ◆ **the communist ~ in the trade unions** la composante communiste dans les syndicats ◆ **the hooligan ~** les éléments *mpl* incontrôlés, les hooligans *mpl* ◆ **the criminal ~** les (éléments *mpl*) criminels *mpl*
3 *(Rel)* ◆ **the Elements** les espèces *fpl*

elemental /ˌelɪˈmentl/ ADJ 1 *(liter = primal) [drive, need]* fondamental ; *[truth]* fondamental, premier *after n* ; *[emotion]* brute ◆ **the ~ violence/fury of the storm** la violence/fureur brute de l'orage 2 *(Chem, Phys, Astron)* élémentaire

elementary /ˌelɪˈmentərɪ/ ADJ élémentaire ◆ **~ geometry course** cours *m* de géométrie élémentaire ◆ **~, my dear Watson!** élémentaire, mon cher Watson !
COMP **elementary education** †† N = enseignement *m* primaire
elementary particle N *(Phys)* particule *f* élémentaire *or* fondamentale
elementary school † N école *f* primaire
elementary schooling † N enseignement *m* primaire
elementary student N *(US)* ≃ élève *mf* du primaire
elementary teacher N *(US Educ)* professeur *m* des écoles

elephant /ˈelɪfənt/ N (pl **elephants** *or* **elephant**) éléphant *m* ◆ **bull/cow ~** éléphant *m* mâle/femelle ◆ **African/Indian ~** éléphant *m* d'Afrique/d'Asie ; → **white** COMP **elephant seal** N éléphant *m* de mer

elephantiasis /ˌelɪfənˈtaɪəsɪs/ N éléphantiasis *f*

elephantine /ˌelɪˈfæntaɪn/ ADJ *(= large)* éléphantesque ; *(= heavy, clumsy)* gauche, lourd ; *[wit]* lourd

elevate /ˈelɪveɪt/ VT hausser, élever *(also Rel)* ; *(fig) [+ voice]* hausser ; *[+ mind]* élever ; *[+ soul]* élever, exalter ◆ **to ~ to the peerage** élever à la pairie, anoblir

elevated /ˈelɪveɪtɪd/ ADJ 1 *(= exalted) [position, status, rank, tone, style, thoughts]* élevé 2 *(= raised) [position, platform, walkway, track]* surélevé
COMP **elevated railroad** N *(US)* métro *m* aérien
elevated train N *(US)* rame *f* de métro aérien

elevating /ˈelɪveɪtɪŋ/ ADJ *[reading]* qui élève l'esprit

elevation /ˌelɪˈveɪʃən/ N 1 *(NonC = raising) [of person, standards, temperature] (also Astron, Rel, Shooting, Surv)* élévation *f* ; *[of blood pressure]* augmentation *f* ◆ **her ~ to the Cabinet/to the rank of Prime Minister** son accession au gouvernement/au rang de Premier ministre ◆ **his ~ to the papacy/to the peerage** son accession à la dignité de pape/au rang de pair ◆ **the ~ of trash to the status of fine art** la camelote élevée au rang des beaux-arts ◆ **angle of ~** *(Shooting)* angle *m* de hausse
2 *(frm = hill, rise)* hauteur *f*, élévation *f*
3 *(= altitude)* altitude *f* ◆ **at an ~ of ...** à une altitude de ...
4 *(Archit) (= drawing)* élévation *f* ; *(= façade) [of building]* façade *f* ◆ **front/north ~** élévation *f* frontale/nord ◆ **sectional ~** coupe *f* (verticale)
5 *(NonC: frm = loftiness) [of mind, spirit]* élévation *f*

elevator /ˈelɪveɪtəʳ/ N 1 *(esp US = lift)* ascenseur *m* ; *(= hoist)* monte-charge *m inv* 2 *(US = grain storehouse)* silo *m* (à élévateur pneumatique) 3 *(Aviat)* gouvernail *m* de profondeur 4 *(US:* also **elevator shoe***)* soulier *m* à talonnette
COMP **elevator car** N *(US)* cabine *f* d'ascenseur
elevator operator N *(US)* liftier *m*, -ière *f*
elevator shaft N *(US)* cage *f* d'ascenseur

eleven /ɪˈlevn/ ADJ onze *inv* N 1 *(= number)* onze *m inv* ◆ **number ~** le numéro onze, le onze ◆ **the ~ plus** *(Brit Scol)* ≃ l'examen *m* d'entrée en sixième 2 *(Sport)* **the French ~** le onze de France ◆ **the first ~** le onze, la première équipe ◆ **the second ~** la deuxième équipe ; *for other phrases see* **six** PRON onze ◆ **there are ~** il y en a onze

elevenses * /ɪˈlevnzɪz/ NPL *(Brit)* ≃ pause-café *f* *(dans la matinée)*

eleventh /ɪˈlevnθ/ ADJ onzième ◆ **at the ~ hour** *(fig)* à la onzième heure, à la dernière minute N onzième *mf* ; *(= fraction)* onzième *m* ; *for phrases see* **sixth**

elf /elf/ N (pl **elves**) *(lit)* elfe *m*, lutin *m*, farfadet *m* ; *(fig)* lutin *m*

elfin /ˈelfɪn/ ADJ 1 *(= delicately attractive) [person]* aux traits délicats ; *[face]* délicat 2 *(Myth) [light, music, dance, creature]* féerique

El Greco /elˈgrekəʊ/ N le Greco

elicit /ɪˈlɪsɪt/ VT *[+ reply, explanation, information]* obtenir *(from* de) ; *[+ reaction, support]* susciter *(from* de la part de) ; *[+ admission, promise]* arracher *(from* à) ◆ **to ~ sympathy from sb** s'attirer la sympathie de qn ◆ **to ~ public sympathy** s'attirer la sympathie du public ◆ **to ~ the facts of a case** tirer une affaire au clair ◆ **to ~ the truth about a case** jeter la lumière sur une affaire

elide /ɪˈlaɪd/ VT 1 *(Ling)* élider ◆ **to be ~d** s'élider 2 *[+ distinctions]* gommer

eligibility /ˌelɪdʒəˈbɪlɪtɪ/ N *(for election)* éligibilité *f* ; *(for employment)* admissibilité *f*

eligible /ˈelɪdʒəbl/ ADJ *(for membership, office)* éligible *(for* à) ; *(for job)* admissible *(for* à) ◆ **to be ~ for a pension** avoir droit à la retraite, pouvoir faire valoir ses droits à la retraite *(frm)* ◆ **to be ~ for promotion** remplir les *or* satisfaire aux conditions requises pour obtenir de l'avancement ◆ **an ~ bachelor** un beau *or* bon parti ◆ **he's very ~** * c'est un très bon parti

Elijah /ɪˈlaɪdʒə/ N Élie *m*

eliminate /ɪˈlɪmɪneɪt/ VT 1 *[+ alternative, suspicion, competitor, candidate]* éliminer, écarter ; *[+ possibility]* écarter, exclure ; *[+ competition, opposition, suspect]* éliminer ; *[+ mark, stain]* enlever, faire disparaître ; *[+ bad language, expenditure, detail]* éliminer, supprimer ; *(Math, Physiol)* éliminer 2 *(* = kill)* supprimer, éliminer

elimination /ɪˌlɪmɪˈneɪʃən/ N élimination *f* ◆ **by (the process of) ~** par élimination

eliminator /ɪˈlɪmɪneɪtəʳ/ N *(Sport)* (épreuve *f*) éliminatoire *f*

Elisha /ɪˈlaɪʃə/ N Élisée *m*

elision /ɪˈlɪʒən/ N élision *f*

elite /ɪˈliːt/ N *(= select group)* élite *f* ADJ 1 *(= select) [group, unit, force, troops]* d'élite ; *[school, university]* prestigieux 2 *(Typ)* élite *inv*

elitism /ɪˈliːtɪzəm/ N élitisme *m*

elitist /ɪˈliːtɪst/ ADJ, N élitiste *mf*

elixir /ɪˈlɪksəʳ/ N élixir *m* ◆ **the ~ of life** l'élixir *m* de (longue) vie ◆ **~ of youth** élixir *m* de jeunesse

Elizabeth /ɪˈlɪzəbəθ/ N Élisabeth *f*

Elizabethan /ɪˌlɪzəˈbiːθən/ ADJ élisabéthain N Élisabéthain(e) *m(f)*

elk /elk/ N (pl **elk** *or* **elks**) élan *m* ◆ **Canadian ~** orignal *m*

ellipse /ɪˈlɪps/ N *(Math)* ellipse *f*

ellipsis /ɪˈlɪpsɪs/ N (pl **ellipses** /ɪˈlɪpsiːz/) *(Gram)* ellipse *f*

ellipsoid /ɪˈlɪpsɔɪd/ ADJ, N ellipsoïde *m*

elliptic(al) /ɪˈlɪptɪk(əl)/ ADJ *(Gram, Math, fig)* elliptique

elliptically /ɪˈlɪptɪk(ə)lɪ/ ADV 1 *(= in elliptical path) [move]* en ellipse 2 *(= not explicitly) [speak, write]* de manière elliptique

elm /elm/ N *(= tree, wood)* orme *m* ◆ **young ~** ormeau *m* ; → **Dutch**

elocution /ˌeləˈkjuːʃən/ N élocution *f*, diction *f*

elocutionist /ˌeləˈkjuːʃənɪst/ N *(= teacher)* professeur *m* d'élocution *or* de diction ; *(= entertainer)* diseur *m*, -euse *f*

elongate /ˈiːlɒŋgeɪt/ VT (gen) allonger, étirer ; [+ line] prolonger VI s'allonger, s'étirer

elongation /ˌiːlɒŋˈgeɪʃən/ N (gen) allongement m ; [of line etc] prolongement m ; (Astron, Med) élongation f

elope /ɪˈləʊp/ VI [man, woman] s'enfuir ◆ **they ~d** ils se sont enfuis ensemble

elopement /ɪˈləʊpmənt/ N fugue f (amoureuse)

eloquence /ˈeləkwəns/ N éloquence f

eloquent /ˈeləkwənt/ ADJ [person, speech, look, gesture, silence, proof] éloquent ; [hands] expressif ◆ **to be ~ about** or **on sth** parler avec éloquence de qch ; → **wax²**

eloquently /ˈeləkwəntlɪ/ ADV [speak, express] éloquemment, avec éloquence ; [write] avec éloquence ; [demonstrate] éloquemment

El Salvador /elˈsælvəˌdɔːʳ/ N Salvador m ◆ **to ~** au Salvador ◆ **in ~** au Salvador

else /els/ ADV ◆ **if all ~ fails** si rien d'autre ne marche ◆ **how ~ can I do it?** comment est-ce que je peux le faire autrement ? ◆ **there is little ~ to be done** il ne reste pas grand-chose d'autre à faire ◆ **they sell books and toys and much ~ (besides)** ils vendent des livres, des jouets et bien d'autres choses (encore) ◆ **not much ~** pas grand-chose d'autre ◆ **what ~?** quoi d'autre ? ◆ **what ~ could I do?** que pouvais-je faire d'autre ? ◆ **where ~?** à quel autre endroit ? ◆ **who ~?** qui d'autre ?

◆ **anybody/anything** etc **else** ◆ **anybody ~ would have done it** n'importe qui d'autre l'aurait fait ◆ **is there anybody ~ there?** y a-t-il quelqu'un d'autre ? ◆ **I'd prefer anything ~** tout mais pas ça ! ◆ **have you anything ~ to say?** avez-vous quelque chose à ajouter ? ◆ **anything ~?** (= have you anything more to tell, me, give me etc) c'est tout ? ; (in shop) ce sera tout ? ◆ **will there be anything ~ sir?** désirez-vous autre chose monsieur ? ◆ **I couldn't do anything ~ but leave** il ne me restait plus qu'à partir ◆ **can you do it anywhere ~?** pouvez-vous le faire ailleurs ? ◆ **you won't find this flower anywhere ~** vous ne trouverez cette fleur nulle part ailleurs

◆ **nobody/nothing** etc **else** ◆ **nobody** or **no one ~** personne d'autre ◆ **nothing ~** rien d'autre ◆ **it was fun if nothing ~** au moins on s'est amusé ◆ **we could do nothing ~** (= nothing more) nous ne pouvions rien faire de plus ; (= no other thing) nous ne pouvions rien faire d'autre ◆ **there's nothing ~ for it** c'est inévitable ◆ **nowhere ~** nulle part ailleurs ◆ **she had nowhere ~ to go** c'est le seul endroit où elle pouvait aller

◆ **someone/something** etc **else** ◆ **someone** or **somebody ~** quelqu'un d'autre ◆ **may I speak to someone ~?** puis-je parler à quelqu'un d'autre ? ◆ **this is someone ~'s umbrella** c'est le parapluie de quelqu'un d'autre ◆ **something ~** autre chose ◆ **she is/it is something ~*** (fig) elle est/c'est vraiment fantastique* ◆ **somewhere ~, someplace ~** (US) ailleurs, autre part

◆ **or else** ou bien, sinon, autrement ◆ **do it or ~ let me** faites-le, ou bien laissez-moi faire ◆ **do it now or ~ you'll be punished** fais-le tout de suite, sinon tu seras puni ◆ **do it or ~!*** vous avez intérêt à le faire !

elsewhere /elsˈweəʳ/ ADV ailleurs, autre part ◆ **from ~** (venu) d'ailleurs ◆ **to go ~** aller ailleurs

ELT /ˌiːelˈtiː/ N (abbrev of **English Language Teaching**) → **English** ; → **TEFL, TESL, TESOL, ELT**

elucidate /ɪˈluːsɪdeɪt/ VT [+ text] élucider ; [+ mystery] élucider, tirer au clair

elucidation /ɪˌluːsɪˈdeɪʃən/ N élucidation f

elude /ɪˈluːd/ VT [+ enemy, pursuit, arrest] échapper à ; [+ question] éluder ; [+ police, justice] se dérober à ◆ **to ~ sb's grasp** échapper aux mains de qn ◆ **the name ~s me** le nom m'échappe ◆ **success ~d him** le succès restait hors de sa portée ◆ **sleep ~d her** elle n'arrivait pas à trouver le sommeil

elusive /ɪˈluːsɪv/ ADJ [person] difficile à joindre ; [animal, truth, happiness] insaisissable ; [quality] indéfinissable ; [goal, target, success, happiness] difficile à atteindre ◆ **the bombers have proved ~ so far** les poseurs de bombe ont jusqu'ici échappé aux recherches

elusively /ɪˈluːsɪvlɪ/ ADV ◆ **to behave ~** se dérober ◆ **... he said ~** ... dit-il pour s'esquiver or pour éluder la question

elusiveness /ɪˈluːsɪvnɪs/ N nature f insaisissable, caractère m évasif

elusory /ɪˈluːsərɪ/ ADJ ⇒ **elusive**

elver /ˈelvəʳ/ N civelle f

elves /elvz/ NPL of **elf**

Elysian /ɪˈlɪzɪən/ ADJ élyséen

elytron /ˈelɪtrɒn/ N (pl **elytra** /ˈelɪtrə/) élytre m

em /em/ N (Typ) cicéro m

'em* /əm/ PERS PRON ⇒ **them**

emaciated /ɪˈmeɪsɪeɪtɪd/ ADJ [person, face] émacié ; [limb] décharné ◆ **to become ~** s'émacier

emaciation /ɪˌmeɪsɪˈeɪʃən/ N émaciation f

email, e-mail /ˈiːmeɪl/ N (Comput) (abbrev of **electronic mail**) e-mail m, courrier m électronique, courriel m (Can) VT ◆ **to ~ sb** envoyer un courrier électronique or un e-mail à qn ◆ **to ~ sth** envoyer qch par courrier électronique

emanate /ˈeməneɪt/ VI [light, odour] émaner (from de) ; [rumour, document, instruction] émaner, provenir (from de)

emanation /ˌeməˈneɪʃən/ N émanation f

emancipate /ɪˈmænsɪpeɪt/ VT [+ women] émanciper ; [+ slaves] affranchir ; émanciper, affranchir, libérer (from de) ◆ **to be ~d from sth** s'affranchir or s'émanciper de qch

emancipated /ɪˈmænsɪpeɪtɪd/ ADJ émancipé, libéré

emancipation /ɪˌmænsɪˈpeɪʃən/ N (NonC) [of mankind, women] émancipation f ; [of slaves] affranchissement m, émancipation f ◆ **black/female ~** émancipation f des Noirs/de la femme

emasculate /ɪˈmæskjʊleɪt/ VT émasculer ADJ /ɪˈmæskjʊlɪt/ émasculé

emasculation /ɪˌmæskjʊˈleɪʃən/ N émasculation f

embalm /ɪmˈbɑːm/ VT (all senses) embaumer

embalmer /ɪmˈbɑːməʳ/ N embaumeur m

embalming /ɪmˈbɑːmɪŋ/ N embaumement m

COMP **embalming fluid** N bain m de natron

embankment /ɪmˈbæŋkmənt/ N [of path, railway line] talus m, remblai m ; [of road] banquette f (de sûreté) ; [of canal, dam] digue f, chaussée f (de retenue) ; [of river] (= mound of earth) berge f ; (= wall of earth) quai m ◆ **the Embankment** (in London) l'un des quais le long de la Tamise

embargo /ɪmˈbɑːgəʊ/ N (pl **embargoes**) (lit) embargo m ◆ **to impose an ~ on** [+ country etc] imposer un embargo contre ; [+ goods] imposer un embargo sur ◆ **arms ~** embargo m sur les armes ◆ **an oil ~** un embargo pétrolier ◆ **to lift an ~** lever l'embargo ◆ **to enforce an ~** appliquer l'embargo ◆ **to put an ~ on sth** (fig) mettre l'embargo sur qch, interdire qch VT mettre l'embargo sur ; (fig = prohibit) interdire

embark /ɪmˈbɑːk/ VT [+ passengers] embarquer, prendre à bord ; [+ goods] embarquer, charger VI (on ship, plane) embarquer (on à bord de, sur) ◆ **to ~ on** (fig) [+ journey] commencer ; [+ business undertaking, deal] s'engager dans, se lancer dans ; [+ doubtful or risky affair, explanation, story] se lancer dans, s'embarquer dans* ; [+ discussion] se lancer dans

embarkation /ˌembɑːˈkeɪʃən/ N [of passengers] embarquement m ; [of cargo] embarquement m, chargement m ◆ **~ card** carte f d'embarquement

embarrass /ɪmˈbærəs/ VT embarrasser, gêner

embarrassed /ɪmˈbærəst/ ADJ 1 [person, silence, laugh] gêné, embarrassé ◆ **there was an ~ silence** il y eut un silence gêné, un ange est passé ◆ **he looked ~** il avait l'air gêné or embarrassé ◆ **I feel ~ about it** cela me gêne or m'embarrasse ◆ **he was ~ about discussing his financial difficulties** cela le gênait or l'embarrassait de parler de ses problèmes financiers ◆ **she was ~ about her spots** ses boutons étaient une source d'embarras pour elle or la rendaient mal à l'aise ◆ **he was ~ at** or **about being the focus of attention** cela le gênait or le mettait dans l'embarras d'être au centre de l'attention ◆ **I was ~ for him** j'étais gêné pour lui ◆ **she was ~ to be seen with him** cela la gênait d'être vue en sa compagnie

2 ◆ **to be financially ~** être dans l'embarras financièrement, avoir des ennuis d'argent

embarrassing /ɪmˈbærəsɪŋ/ ADJ embarrassant, gênant ◆ **to get out of an ~ situation** se tirer d'embarras

embarrassingly /ɪmˈbærəsɪŋlɪ/ ADV ◆ **~ short/few/bad** si court/peu/mauvais que c'en est (or était) embarrassant ◆ **~ for him, he ...** à son grand embarras, il ... ◆ **~, he ...** au grand embarras de tous, il ...

embarrassment /ɪmˈbærəsmənt/ N 1 (= emotion) embarras m, gêne f (at devant) ◆ **to cause sb ~** mettre qn dans l'embarras, embarrasser qn ◆ **financial ~** des ennuis mpl d'argent, des embarras mpl financiers ◆ **it is an ~ of riches: Zola, Flaubert, Balzac, Stendhal** on peut dire qu'on a l'embarras du choix : Zola, Flaubert, Balzac, Stendhal 2 (= source of embarrassment) ◆ **her son is an ~ to her** son fils est une source d'embarras pour elle ◆ **her scar is an ~ to her** sa cicatrice est une source d'embarras pour elle or la rend mal à l'aise

embassy /ˈembəsɪ/ N ambassade f ◆ **the French Embassy** l'ambassade f de France

embattled /ɪmˈbætld/ ADJ 1 (= beleaguered) [city, country, people, army] assiégé 2 (= troubled) [person, government] aux prises avec des difficultés, en difficulté

embed /ɪmˈbed/ VT (in wood) enfoncer ; (in cement) noyer ; (in stone) sceller ; [+ jewel] enchâsser ; (Ling) enchâsser ◆ **~ded in the memory/mind** gravé dans la mémoire/l'esprit

embedding /ɪmˈbedɪŋ/ N action f de sceller, fixation f ; (Ling) enchâssement m

embellish /ɪmˈbelɪʃ/ VT (= adorn) embellir, orner (with de) ; [+ manuscript] relever, enjoliver (with de) ; (fig) [+ tale, account] enjoliver, embellir ; [+ truth] broder sur, orner

embellishment /ɪmˈbelɪʃmənt/ N 1 (= adornment) embellissement m, ornement m ◆ **stripped of ~** dépouillé de tout ornement 2 (= added detail) [of story, truth] embellissement m, enjolivement m 3 (Mus) fioriture f

ember /ˈembəʳ/ N charbon m ardent ◆ **the ~s** la braise ◆ **the dying ~s** les tisons mpl ; → **fan¹**

Ember days /ˈembəˌdeɪz/ NPL (Rel) quatre-temps mpl

embezzle /ɪmˈbezl/ VT détourner VI détourner des fonds

embezzlement /ɪmˈbezlmənt/ N détournement m de fonds

embezzler /ɪmˈbezləʳ/ N escroc m

embitter /ɪmˈbɪtəʳ/ VT [+ person] aigrir, remplir d'amertume ; [+ relations, disputes] envenimer

embittered /ɪmˈbɪtəd/ ADJ *[person, relationship]* aigri, plein d'amertume

embittering /ɪmˈbɪtərɪŋ/ ADJ qui laisse amer

embitterment /ɪmˈbɪtəmənt/ N amertume *f*, aigreur *f*

emblazon /ɪmˈbleɪzən/ VT 1 *(= adorn)* ◆ **to be ~ ed with sth** arborer fièrement qch ◆ **they were wearing t-shirts ~ ed with the company logo** ils portaient des t-shirts arborant fièrement le logo de l'entreprise ◆ **her name was ~ ed across the cover** son nom était imprimé en grosses lettres sur la couverture 2 *(in heraldry)* blasonner

emblem /ˈembləm/ N *(all senses)* emblème *m*

emblematic /ˌembləˈmætɪk/ ADJ *(= characteristic)* typique ◆ **dogs are ~ of faithfulness** *(= symbolic)* les chiens sont un symbole de fidélité

embodiment /ɪmˈbɒdɪmənt/ N 1 incarnation *f*, personnification *f* ◆ **to be the ~ of progress** incarner le progrès ◆ **he is the ~ of kindness** c'est la bonté incarnée *or* personnifiée 2 *(= inclusion)* incorporation *f*

embody /ɪmˈbɒdɪ/ VT 1 *[+ spirit, quality]* incarner ; *[+ one's thoughts, theories] [person]* exprimer, concrétiser, formuler (*in* dans, en) ; *[work]* exprimer, donner forme à, mettre en application (*in* dans) 2 *(= include) [+ ideas] [person]* résumer (*in* dans) ; *[work]* renfermer ; *[+ features] [machine]* réunir

embolden /ɪmˈbəʊldən/ VT 1 enhardir ◆ **to ~ sb to do sth** donner à qn le courage de faire qch, enhardir qn à faire qch 2 *(Typ)* imprimer en gras (*or* mi-gras)

embolism /ˈembəlɪzəm/ N embolie *f*

emboss /ɪmˈbɒs/ VT *[+ metal]* travailler en relief, repousser, estamper ; *[+ leather, cloth]* frapper, gaufrer ; *[+ velvet, paper]* frapper

embossed /ɪmˈbɒst/ ADJ *[lettering, letters, design]* en relief ; *[paper, wallpaper, card]* gaufré ; *[leather] (with stamp)* gaufré ; *(with tool)* repoussé ; *[metal] (with stamp)* estampé ; *(with tool)* repoussé ◆ **~ writing paper** papier *m* à lettres à en-tête en relief ◆ **to be ~ with sth** avoir qch en relief ◆ **leather books ~ in gold** des livres à reliure de cuir estampée d'or

embouchure /ˌɒmbʊˈʃʊəʳ/ N *(Mus)* embouchure *f*

embrace /ɪmˈbreɪs/ VT 1 *(= hug)* étreindre ; *(amorously)* enlacer, étreindre 2 *(fig) [+ religion]* embrasser ; *[+ opportunity]* saisir ; *[+ cause]* épouser, embrasser ; *[+ offer]* profiter de 3 *(= include) [person] [+ theme, experience]* embrasser ; *[+ topics, hypotheses]* inclure ; *[work] [+ theme, period]* embrasser, englober ; *[+ ideas, topics]* renfermer, comprendre ◆ **his charity ~s all mankind** sa charité s'étend à l'humanité tout entière ◆ **an all-embracing review** une revue d'ensemble VI s'étreindre, s'embrasser N *(= hug)* étreinte *f* ◆ **they were standing in a tender ~** ils étaient tendrement enlacés ◆ **he held her in a tender ~** il l'enlaçait tendrement ◆ **to greet sb with a warm ~** accueillir qn en l'étreignant chaleureusement ◆ **locked in an ~** enlacé

embrasure /ɪmˈbreɪʒəʳ/ N embrasure *f*

embrocation /ˌembrəʊˈkeɪʃən/ N embrocation *f*

embroider /ɪmˈbrɔɪdəʳ/ VT broder ; (*fig:* also **embroider on**) *[+ facts, truth]* broder sur ; *[+ story]* enjoliver VI faire de la broderie

embroidery /ɪmˈbrɔɪdərɪ/ N broderie *f*
COMP **embroidery frame** N métier *m or* tambour *m* à broder
embroidery silk N soie *f* à broder
embroidery thread N fil *m* à broder

embroil /ɪmˈbrɔɪl/ VT entraîner (*in* dans) mêler (*in* à) ◆ **to get (o.s.) ~ed in** se laisser entraîner dans, se trouver mêlé à

embroilment /ɪmˈbrɔɪlmənt/ N implication *f* (*in* dans) participation *f* (*in* à)

embryo /ˈembrɪəʊ/ N *(lit, fig)* embryon *m* ◆ **in ~** *(lit)* à l'état *or* au stade embryonnaire ; *(fig)* en germe

embryological /ˌembrɪəˈlɒdʒɪkəl/ ADJ embryologique

embryologist /ˌembrɪˈblədʒɪst/ N embryologiste *mf*

embryology /ˌembrɪˈblədʒɪ/ N embryologie *f*

embryonic /ˌembrɪˈɒnɪk/ ADJ 1 *(lit)* embryonnaire 2 *(fig)* en germe

embus /ɪmˈbʌs/ VT (faire) embarquer dans un car VI s'embarquer dans un car

emcee /ˈemˈsiː/ *(US)* (abbrev of **master of ceremonies**) N *(gen)* maître *m* de cérémonies ; *(in show etc)* animateur *m*, meneur *m* de jeu VT *[+ show etc]* animer

emend /ɪˈmend/ VT *[+ text]* corriger

emendation /ˌiːmenˈdeɪʃən/ N correction *f*

emerald /ˈemərəld/ N *(= stone)* émeraude *f* ; *(= colour)* (vert *m*) émeraude *m*
COMP *(= set with emeralds)* (serti) d'émeraudes ; (also **emerald green**) (vert) émeraude *inv*
the Emerald Isle N *(liter)* l'île *f* d'Émeraude *(Irlande)*
emerald necklace N collier *m* d'émeraudes

emerge /ɪˈmɜːdʒ/ VI *[person, animal]* émerger (*from* de) sortir (*from* de) ; *[truth, facts]* émerger (*from* de) se dégager ; *[difficulties]* surgir, apparaître ; *[new nation]* naître ; *[theory, school of thought]* apparaître, naître ◆ **it ~s (from this) that ...** il (en) ressort que ..., il (en) résulte que ... ◆ **to ~ as ...** *(= turn out to be)* se révéler (être)

emergence /ɪˈmɜːdʒəns/ N *[of truth, facts]* émergence *f* ; *[of new nation, theory, school of thought]* naissance *f*

emergency /ɪˈmɜːdʒənsɪ/ N cas *m* urgent, imprévu *m* NonC ◆ **in case of ~, in an ~** en cas d'urgence ◆ **to be prepared for any ~** être prêt à *or* parer à toute éventualité ◆ **an ~ case** *(Med)* une urgence ◆ **in this ~** dans cette situation critique, dans ces circonstances critiques ◆ **state of ~** état *m* d'urgence ◆ **to declare a state of ~** déclarer l'état d'urgence
COMP *[measures, treatment, operation, repair]* d'urgence ; *[brake, airstrip]* de secours ; *(= improvised) [mast]* de fortune
emergency brake N *(US = handbrake)* frein *m* à main
emergency centre N poste *m* de secours
emergency exit N issue *f or* sortie *f* de secours
emergency force N *(Mil)* force *f* d'urgence *or* d'intervention
emergency landing N atterrissage *m* forcé
emergency powers NPL *(Pol)* pouvoirs *mpl* spéciaux
emergency rations NPL vivres *mpl* de réserve
emergency room N *(US Med)* ⇒ **emergency ward**
emergency service N *(in hospital)* service *m* des urgences ; *(on roads)* service *m* de dépannage
emergency services NPL *(= police etc)* services *mpl* d'urgence, ≃ police-secours *f*
emergency stop N arrêt *m* d'urgence
emergency tax N impôt *m* extraordinaire
emergency telephone N dispositif *m or* borne *f* d'urgence
emergency ward N salle *f* des urgences

emergent /ɪˈmɜːdʒənt/ ADJ *[democracy, movement, group, sexuality]* naissant, émergent ; *(Opt, Philos)* émergent ◆ **emergent nation** pays émergent

emeritus /ɪˈmerɪtəs/ ADJ *(Univ)* ◆ **~ professor, professor ~** professeur *m* honoraire

emery /ˈemərɪ/ N émeri *m*
COMP **emery board** N lime *f* à ongles
emery cloth N toile *f* (d')émeri
emery paper N papier *m* (d')émeri, papier *m* de verre

emetic /ɪˈmetɪk/ ADJ, N émétique *m*

emigrant /ˈemɪgrənt/ N *(just leaving)* émigrant(e) *m(f)* ; *(established)* émigré(e) *m(f)* COMP *[ship, family]* d'émigrants

emigrate /ˈemɪgreɪt/ VI émigrer

emigration /ˌemɪˈgreɪʃən/ N émigration *f*

émigré /ˈemɪgreɪ/ N émigré(e) *m(f)*

Emilia-Romagna /ɪˈmiːlɪərəʊˈmɑːnjə/ N Émilie-Romagne *f*

eminence /ˈemɪnəns/ N 1 *(NonC = distinction)* distinction *f* ◆ **to achieve ~ in one's profession** parvenir à un rang éminent dans sa profession ◆ **to win ~ as a surgeon** acquérir un grand renom comme chirurgien ◆ **the ~ of his position** sa position éminente ◆ **His/Your Eminence** *(Rel)* Son/Votre Éminence 2 *(= high ground)* éminence *f*, élévation *f*

eminent /ˈemɪnənt/ ADJ 1 *(= distinguished) [person]* éminent ◆ **she is ~ in the field of avionics** c'est une sommité dans le domaine de l'avionique 2 *(frm = great)* remarquable ◆ **his ~ good sense** son remarquable bon sens 3 *(Rel)* ◆ **Most Eminent** éminentissime

eminently /ˈemɪnəntlɪ/ ADV *[sensible, reasonable, capable]* parfaitement ; *[respectable, qualified]* éminemment ; *[practical, readable, desirable]* tout à fait ; *[forgettable]* absolument ◆ **to be ~ suitable** convenir parfaitement

emir /eˈmɪəʳ/ N émir *m*

emirate /eˈmɪərɪt/ N émirat *m*

emissary /ˈemɪsərɪ/ N émissaire *m*

emission /ɪˈmɪʃən/ N *(NonC)* dégagement *m*
NPL **emissions** *(= substances)* émissions *fpl*
COMP **emission spectrum** N spectre *m* d'émission
emissions trading N échange *m* (de quotas) d'émissions

emit /ɪˈmɪt/ VT *[+ gas, heat, smoke]* émettre, dégager ; *[+ light, waves]* émettre ; *[+ smell]* dégager, exhaler ; *[+ lava]* répandre ; *[+ sound, chuckle]* émettre

emitter /ɪˈmɪtəʳ/ N *(Elec)* émetteur *m*

Emmy /ˈemɪ/ N (pl **Emmys** *or* **Emmies**) *oscar de la télévision américaine*

emollient /ɪˈmɒlɪənt/ N émollient *m* ADJ *[cream]* émollient ; *(fig) [person]* conciliant

emolument /ɪˈmɒljʊmənt/ N émoluments *mpl*

e-money /ˈiːmʌnɪ/ monnaie *f* électronique, argent *m* virtuel

emote * /ɪˈməʊt/ VI donner dans le sentiment *

emoticon /ɪˈməʊtɪkən/ N *(Comput)* emoticon *m*, smiley *m*

emotion /ɪˈməʊʃən/ N émotion *f*

emotional /ɪˈməʊʃənl/ ADJ 1 *(= psychological) [problem, support, development, detachment, bond, intensity]* affectif ; *[shock, disturbance, impact]* émotif, affectif ◆ **his ~ state** son état émotionnel ◆ **to make an ~ commitment to sb** s'engager vis-à-vis de qn sur le plan affectif ◆ **on an ~ level** sur le plan affectif ◆ **to be on an ~ high/low** * être dans un état d'exaltation *or* sur un petit nuage */déprimé
2 *(= emotive)* ◆ **it is an ~ issue** cette question soulève les passions
3 *(= full of emotion) [person] (by nature)* émotif ; *(on specific occasion)* ému ; *[moment, situation]* de grande émotion ; *[experience, story, appeal, speech, farewell, welcome, outburst, scene, response]* plein d'émotion ; *[decision]* guidé par les sentiments ◆ **he became very ~** il a été très ému ◆ **to be ~ about sth** *(by nature)* s'émouvoir

facilement de qch ◆ **his behaviour was very ~** il a eu un comportement très émotionnel

COMP **emotional baggage** * N *(pej)* expériences *fpl* personnelles ◆ **his ~ baggage** le poids de son vécu personnel

emotional blackmail * N chantage *m* affectif

emotional cripple * N *(pej)* ◆ **to be an ~ cripple** être bloqué sur le plan émotionnel

emotional roller coaster N ◆ **to be on an ~ roller coaster** être pris dans un tourbillon d'émotions

emotional wreck N loque *f* (sur le plan affectif)

emotionalism /ɪˈməʊʃnəlɪzəm/ N émotivité *f*, sensiblerie *f (pej)* ◆ **the article was sheer ~** l'article n'était qu'un étalage de sensiblerie

emotionally /ɪˈməʊʃnəlɪ/ ADV 1 *(= psychologically) [mature, stable, distant, drained]* sur le plan affectif *or* émotionnel ◆ **~ deprived** privé d'affection ◆ **to be ~ disturbed** souffrir de troubles émotifs *or* affectifs ◆ **an ~ disturbed child** un(e) enfant caractériel(le) ◆ **as a doctor, one should never become ~ involved** un médecin ne doit jamais s'impliquer au niveau affectif *or* émotionnel ◆ **to be ~ involved with sb** *(= be in relationship)* avoir une liaison avec qn ◆ **~ I was a wreck** sur le plan émotionnel j'étais une loque 2 *(= with emotion) [speak, describe, react]* avec émotion ◆ **an ~ charged atmosphere** une atmosphère chargée d'émotion ◆ **an ~ worded article** un article qui fait appel aux sentiments

emotionless /ɪˈməʊʃənlɪs/ ADJ *[expression, tone etc]* impassible ; *[person]* imperturbable

emotive /ɪˈməʊtɪv/ ADJ *[issue, question, subject]* qui soulève les passions ; *[language, word]* à connotations émotionnelles

empanel /ɪmˈpænl/ VT *(Jur) [+ jury]* constituer ◆ **to ~ a juror** inscrire quelqu'un sur la liste du jury

empanelment /ɪmˈpænlmənt/ N *[of jury]* constitution *f*

empathetic /ˌempəˈθetɪk/ ADJ compréhensif *(to* envers)

empathetically /ˌempəˈθetɪkəlɪ/ ADV avec compréhension *or* sympathie

empathic /emˈpæθɪk/ ADJ ⇒ **empathetic**

empathize /ˈempəθaɪz/ VI ◆ **to ~ with sb** comprendre ce que ressent qn

empathy /ˈempəθɪ/ N empathie *f* ◆ **to have ~ with sb** comprendre ce que ressent qn ◆ **our ~ with the pain she was suffering** notre compassion *f* pour la douleur qui était la sienne

emperor /ˈempərər/ N empereur *m*

COMP **emperor moth** N paon *m* de nuit

emperor penguin N manchot *m* empereur

emphasis /ˈemfəsɪs/ N (pl **emphases** /ˈemfəsiːz/)

1 *(= accent) (in word, phrase)* accentuation *f*, accent *m* d'intensité ◆ **to speak with ~** parler sur un ton d'insistance ◆ **the ~ is on the first syllable** l'accent d'intensité *or* l'accentuation tombe sur la première syllabe ◆ **to lay** *or* **place ~ on a word** souligner un mot, insister sur *or* appuyer sur un mot

2 *(= importance)* accent *m* ◆ **to lay** *or* **place ~ on one aspect of ...** mettre l'accent sur *or* insister sur un aspect de ... ◆ **the school places special ~ on German** l'école met tout particulièrement l'accent *or* insiste tout particulièrement sur l'allemand ◆ **the government is putting more ~ on domestic issues** le gouvernement met plus l'accent *or* insiste plus sur les affaires nationales ◆ **too much ~ has been placed on ...** on a trop mis l'accent *or* trop insisté sur ... ◆ **special ~ will be given to ...** on accordera une importance toute particulière à ... ◆ **a change** *or* **shift of ~** un changement d'orientation *or* de direction ◆ **the ~ is on sport** on accorde une importance particulière au sport ◆ **this year the ~ is on femininity** *(Fashion)* cette année le mot d'ordre est "féminité"

emphasize /ˈemfəsaɪz/ VT *(= stress) [+ word, fact, point]* insister sur, souligner ; *[+ syllable]* accentuer ; *(= draw attention to) (gen)* accentuer ; *[+ sth pleasant or flattering]* mettre en valeur, faire valoir ◆ **this point cannot be too strongly ~d** on ne saurait trop insister sur ce point ◆ **I must ~ that ...** je dois souligner le fait que ... ◆ **the long coat ~d his height** le long manteau faisait ressortir sa haute taille ◆ **to ~ the eyes with mascara** mettre les yeux en valeur avec du mascara

emphatic /ɪmˈfætɪk/ ADJ 1 *(= forceful) [person]* catégorique ; *[condemnation, denial, rejection, response, statement, declaration]* énergique ◆ **the answer is an ~ yes/no** la réponse est un oui/non catégorique ◆ **to be ~ about sth** insister sur qch ◆ **she's ~ that business is improving** elle affirme catégoriquement que les affaires reprennent ◆ **they were quite ~ that they were not going** ils ont refusé catégoriquement d'y aller ◆ **he was ~ in his defence of the system** il a vigoureusement défendu le système ◆ **they were ~ in denying their involvement** ils ont vigoureusement démenti être impliqués 2 *(= emphasizing) [tone, gesture, nod]* emphatique 3 *(= decisive) [victory, defeat]* écrasant ; *[result, winner]* incontestable

emphatically /ɪmˈfætɪkəlɪ/ ADV 1 *(= forcefully) [say, reply, shake one's head]* énergiquement ; *[deny, reject, refuse]* catégoriquement, énergiquement ◆ **to nod ~** acquiescer énergiquement de la tête 2 *(= definitely) [democratic]* clairement ◆ **politics is most ~ back on the agenda** la politique fait bel et bien un retour en force ◆ **~ not** absolument pas ◆ **yes, ~!** oui, tout à fait ! ◆ **~ no!** non, en aucun cas !, non, absolument pas !

emphysema /emfɪˈsiːmə/ N emphysème *m*

Empire /ˈempaɪər/ ADJ *[costume, furniture]* Empire *inv*

empire /ˈempaɪər/ N *(all senses)* empire *m*

COMP **empire-builder** N *(fig)* bâtisseur *m* d'empires

empire-building N *(fig)* ◆ **he is ~-building, it is ~-building on his part** il joue les bâtisseurs d'empire

the Empire State N *(US)* l'État *m* de New York

the Empire State Building N l'Empire State Building *m*

empiric /emˈpɪrɪk/ ADJ empirique N empiriste *mf* ; *(Med)* empirique *m*

empirical /emˈpɪrɪkəl/ ADJ empirique

empirically /emˈpɪrɪkəlɪ/ ADV *[test]* empiriquement ; *[invalid, testable]* d'un point de vue empirique ◆ **an ~ grounded approach** une approche fondée sur un raisonnement empirique ◆ **~ based knowledge** connaissances *fpl* fondées sur un raisonnement empirique ◆ **~, therefore, four is the answer** empiriquement, donc, la réponse est quatre

empiricism /emˈpɪrɪsɪzəm/ N empirisme *m*

empiricist /emˈpɪrɪsɪst/ ADJ, N empiriste *mf*

emplacement /ɪmˈpleɪsmənt/ N *(Mil)* emplacement *m (d'un canon)*

employ /ɪmˈplɔɪ/ VT *[+ person]* employer *(as* comme) ; *[+ means, method, process]* employer, utiliser ; *[+ time]* employer *(in or by doing sth* à faire qch) ; *[+ force, cunning]* recourir à, employer ; *[+ skill]* faire usage de, employer ◆ **to be ~ed in doing sth** être occupé à faire qch ◆ **he would be better ~ed painting the house** il ferait mieux de repeindre la maison N ◆ **to be in sb's ~** être employé par qn, travailler chez *or* pour qn ; *(of domestic staff)* être au service de qn

employable /ɪmˈplɔɪəbəl/ ADJ *[person]* capable d'entrer sur le marché de l'emploi ◆ **~ skills** compétences *fpl* utilisables

employee /ˌɪmplɔɪˈiː/ N salarié(e) *m(f)* ◆ **to be an ~ of ...** travailler chez ... ◆ **~ benefit** avantage social COMP **employee stock ownership plans** NPL *(US)* actionnariat *m* ouvrier *or* des salariés

employer /ɪmˈplɔɪər/ N employeur *m*, -euse *f* ◆ **~s** *(collectively)* le patronat ◆ **my ~** mon employeur

COMP **employer's contribution** N *(Insurance)* cotisation *f* patronale

employers' federation N syndicat *m* patronal, fédération *f* patronale

employment /ɪmˈplɔɪmənt/ N *(NonC = jobs collectively)* emploi *m NonC* ; *(= a job)* emploi *m*, travail *m* ; *(modest)* place *f* ; *(important)* situation *f* ◆ **full ~** le plein emploi ◆ **in ~** qui travaille, qui a un emploi ◆ **the numbers in ~** les actifs *mpl* ◆ **in sb's ~** employé par qn ; *(domestic staff)* au service de qn ◆ **without ~** sans emploi, au chômage ◆ **conditions/place of ~** conditions *fpl*/lieu *m* de travail ◆ **to seek/find/take up ~ (with)** chercher/trouver/prendre un emploi (chez) ◆ **Secretary for Employment** *(US)* ministre *m* de l'Emploi ; → **department, minister, secretary**

COMP **employment agency** N agence *f* de placement

employment exchange † N *(Brit)* bourse *f* du travail

employment office N *(Brit)* ≃ bureau *m* de l'Agence nationale pour l'emploi

Employment Service N *(US)* ≃ Agence *f* nationale pour l'emploi

employment tribunal N ≃ conseil *m* de prud'hommes

emporium /emˈpɔːrɪəm/ N (pl **emporiums** *or* **emporia** /emˈpɔːrɪə/) *(= shop)* grand magasin *m*, bazar *m* ; *(= market)* centre *m* commercial, marché *m*

empower /ɪmˈpaʊər/ VT 1 *(= authorize)* ◆ **to ~ sb to do sth** autoriser qn à faire qch ; *(Jur)* habiliter qn à faire qch ◆ **to be ~ed to do sth** avoir pleins pouvoirs pour faire qch 2 ◆ **to ~ sb** *(= make stronger)* rendre qn plus fort ; *(= make more independent)* permettre à qn de s'assumer

empowering /ɪmˈpaʊərɪŋ/ ADJ ◆ **such experiences can be ~** ce type d'expérience peut aider les gens à s'assumer

empowerment /ɪmˈpaʊəmənt/ N 1 *(Pol, Sociol)* responsabilisation *f* ◆ **the ~ of minorities** la responsabilisation des minorités 2 *(in workplace)* délégation *f* des responsabilités

empress /ˈemprɪs/ N impératrice *f*

emptiness /ˈemptɪnɪs/ N vide *m* ; *[of pleasures etc]* vanité *f* ◆ **the ~ of life** le vide de l'existence

empty /ˈemptɪ/ ADJ 1 *(= containing nothing) [place, building, container, seat, vehicle, hand, days]* vide *(of sth* de qch) ; *[ship]* vide, lège *(Naut)* ; *[landscape]* désert ; *(Ling)* vide ◆ **she was staring into ~ space** elle regardait fixement dans le vide ◆ **there was an ~ space at the table** il y avait une place vide à la table ◆ **on an ~ stomach** l'estomac vide, à jeun ◆ **his face and eyes were ~ of all expression** son visage et ses yeux étaient dénués de toute expression ◆ **~ of emotion** *or* **feeling** incapable de ressentir la moindre émotion ◆ **to be running on ~** *[car]* avoir le réservoir pratiquement vide ; *(fig) [person]* avoir l'estomac vide ; *[organization]* être à bout de souffle ◆ **~ vessels make most noise** *(Prov)* ce sont les tonneaux vides qui font le plus de bruit ; → **comp**

2 *(= meaningless) [phrase, words, rhetoric]* creux ; *[dream, hope, exercise]* vain ◆ **~ talk** verbiage *m* ◆ **~ promises/threats** promesses *fpl*/menaces *fpl* en l'air ◆ **it's an ~ gesture** c'est un geste

vide de sens *or* un geste qui ne veut rien dire ◆ **my life is ~ without you** ma vie est vide sans toi

3 *(= numb) [person]* vidé ; *[feeling]* de vide ◆ **when I heard the news I felt ~** quand j'ai appris la nouvelle, je me suis senti vidé

NPL **empties** *(= bottles)* bouteilles *fpl* vides ; *(= boxes etc)* boîtes *fpl or* emballages *mpl* vides ; *(= glasses) (in pub etc)* verres *mpl* vides

VT 1 *(= discharge) [+ box, glass, bin, pond, pocket]* vider ; *[+ tank]* vider, vidanger ; *[+ vehicle]* décharger ◆ **the burglars emptied the shop** les voleurs ont dévalisé le magasin ◆ **television has emptied the cinemas** la télévision a vidé les cinémas ◆ **his singing emptied the room** la salle s'est vidée quand il a chanté

2 (also **empty out**) *[+ bricks, books]* sortir ; *[+ rubbish]* vider *(of, from* de ; *into* dans) ; *[+ liquid]* vider *(from* de) verser *(from* de ; *into* dans) transvaser *(into* dans)

VI *[water]* se déverser, s'écouler ; *[river]* se jeter *(into* dans) ; *[building, room, container]* se vider

COMP **empty calories** NPL calories *fpl* inutiles

empty-handed ADJ les mains vides ◆ **to return ~-handed** revenir bredouille *or* les mains vides

empty-headed ADJ sot (sotte *f*), sans cervelle ◆ **an ~-headed girl** une écervelée, une évaporée

empty-nester* N *personne dont les enfants ont quitté la maison*

empyema /ˌempaɪˈiːmə/ N (pl **empyemas** *or* **empyemata** /ˌempaɪˈiːmətə/) empyème *m*

empyrean /ˌempaɪˈriːən/ N *(liter)* ◆ **the ~** l'empyrée *m (liter)*

EMS /ˌiːemˈes/ N (abbrev of **European Monetary System**) SME *m*

EMU /ˌiːemˈjuː/ N (abbrev of **economic and monetary union**) UME *f*

emu /ˈiːmjuː/ N émeu *m*

emulate /ˈemjʊleɪt/ VT imiter ; *(Comput)* émuler

emulation /ˌemjʊˈleɪʃən/ N imitation *f* ; *(Comput)* émulation *f*

emulator /ˈemjʊleɪtəʳ/ N *(Comput)* émulateur *m*

emulsifier /ɪˈmʌlsɪˌfaɪəʳ/ N émulsifiant *m*

emulsify /ɪˈmʌlsɪfaɪ/ VTI émulsionner

emulsion /ɪˈmʌlʃən/ N *(also Phot)* émulsion *f* ◆ **~ (paint)** peinture-émulsion *f* VT peindre *(avec une peinture-émulsion)*

en /en/ N *(Typ)* n *m*, lettre *f* moyenne

enable /ɪˈneɪbl/ VT ◆ **to ~ sb to do sth** *(= give opportunity)* permettre à qn de faire qch, donner à qn la possibilité de faire qch ; *(= give means)* permettre à qn de faire qch, donner à qn le moyen de faire qch ; *(Jur etc = authorize)* habiliter qn à faire qch, donner pouvoir à qn de faire qch COMP **enabling legislation** N loi *f* d'habilitation

-enabled /ɪˈneɪbld/ SUFF ◆ **a WAP-enabled phone** un téléphone WAP ◆ **internet-enabled mobile phones** des téléphones portables pouvant être connectés à Internet

enabler /ɪˈneɪbləʳ/ N ◆ **we are ~s, not service providers** notre vocation n'est pas de fournir des services mais d'aider les gens à trouver des solutions eux-mêmes ◆ **to act as ~s of local artists** encourager les artistes de la région

enact /ɪˈnækt/ VT 1 *(Jur) [+ law, decree]* promulguer, passer ◆ **as by law ~ed** aux termes de la loi, selon la loi 2 *(= perform) [+ play]* représenter, jouer ; *[+ part]* jouer ◆ **the drama which was ~ed yesterday** *(fig)* le drame qui s'est déroulé hier COMP **enacting terms** NPL dispositif *m* d'un jugement

enactment /ɪˈnæktmənt/ N promulgation *f*

enamel /ɪˈnæməl/ N 1 *(NonC: most senses)* émail *m* ◆ **nail ~** vernis *m* à ongles (laqué) ◆ **tooth ~** émail *m* dentaire 2 *(Art)* **an ~** un émail VT émailler

COMP *[ornament, brooch]* en émail

enamel paint N peinture *f* laquée

enamel painting N *(Art)* peinture *f* sur émail

enamel saucepan N casserole *f* en fonte émaillée

enamelled /ɪˈnæməld/ ADJ *[jewellery, bath, saucepan]* en émail ; *[metal]* émaillé

enamelling /ɪˈnæməlɪŋ/ N émaillage *m*

enamelware /ɪˈnæməlweəʳ/ N *(NonC)* articles *mpl* en métal émaillé

enamoured, enamored *(US)* /ɪˈnæməd/ ADJ *(liter or hum)* ◆ **to be ~ of** *[+ person]* être amoureux *or* épris de ; *[+ thing]* être enchanté de, être séduit par ◆ **she was not ~ of the idea** *(hum)* l'idée ne l'enchantait pas

encamp /ɪnˈkæmp/ VI camper VT faire camper

encampment /ɪnˈkæmpmənt/ N campement *m*

encapsulate /ɪnˈkæpsjʊleɪt/ VT incarner (l'essence de) ; *(Pharm, Space)* mettre en capsule

encase /ɪnˈkeɪs/ VT *(= contain)* enfermer, enchâsser *(in* dans) ; *(= cover)* enrober *(in* de)

encash /ɪnˈkæʃ/ VT *(Brit) [+ cheque]* encaisser, toucher

encashment /ɪnˈkæʃmənt/ N *(Brit)* encaissement *m*

encaustic /enˈkɔːstɪk/ ADJ *[painting]* à l'encaustique ; *[tile, brick]* vernissé N *(= painting)* encaustique *f*

encephala /enˈsefələ/ NPL of **encephalon**

encephalic /ˌensɪˈfælɪk/ ADJ encéphalique

encephalitis /ˌensefəˈlaɪtɪs/ N encéphalite *f*

encephalogram /enˈsefələgræm/ N encéphalogramme *m*

encephalon /enˈsefəlɒn/ N (pl **encephala**) encéphale *m*

enchant /ɪnˈtʃɑːnt/ VT 1 *(= put under spell)* enchanter, ensorceler ◆ **the ~ed wood** le bois enchanté 2 *(fig = delight)* enchanter, ravir

enchanter /ɪnˈtʃɑːntəʳ/ N enchanteur *m*

enchanting /ɪnˈtʃɑːntɪŋ/ ADJ ravissant

enchantingly /ɪnˈtʃɑːntɪŋlɪ/ ADV *[dress, dance]* d'une façon ravissante ; *[smile]* d'une façon charmante ◆ **the ~ named "via della Gatta"** la rue au nom charmant de "via della Gatta" ◆ **she is ~ pretty** elle est jolie et pleine de charme ◆ **she is ~ beautiful** elle est belle à ravir

enchantment /ɪnˈtʃɑːntmənt/ N 1 *(= spell)* enchantement *m*, ensorcellement *m* 2 *(fig = appeal)* charme *m* ◆ **the forest had its own peculiar ~** la forêt avait son charme bien particulier ◆ **the many ~s of Venice** les nombreux charmes *mpl or* enchantements *mpl* de Venise

enchantress /ɪnˈtʃɑːntrɪs/ N enchanteresse *f*

enchilada /ˌentʃɪˈlædə/ N 1 *(Culin)* enchilada *f* 2 *(US)* ◆ **big ~** * *(= bigwig)* huile* *f*, grosse légume* *f*

encircle /ɪnˈsɜːkl/ VT *(gen)* entourer ; *[troops, men, police]* encercler, cerner, entourer ; *[walls, belt, bracelet]* entourer, ceindre

encirclement /ɪnˈsɜːklmənt/ N encerclement *m*

encircling /ɪnˈsɜːklɪŋ/ N encerclement *m* ADJ qui encercle ◆ **~ movement** manœuvre *f* d'encerclement

encl. (abbrev of **enclosure(s)**) PJ, pièce(s) *f(pl)* jointe(s)

enclave /ˈenkleɪv/ N enclave *f*

enclitic /ɪnˈklɪtɪk/ N enclitique *m*

enclose /ɪnˈkləʊz/ LANGUAGE IN USE 20.2, 20.3, 20.6

VT 1 *(= fence in)* enclore, clôturer ; *(= surround)* entourer, ceindre *(with* de) ; *(Rel)* cloîtrer ◆ **to ~ within** enfermer dans 2 *(with letter etc)* joindre *(in, with* à) ◆ **to ~ sth in a letter** joindre qch à une lettre, inclure qch dans une lettre ◆ **letter enclosing a receipt** lettre *f* contenant un reçu ◆ **please find ~d** veuillez trouver ci-joint ◆ **the ~d cheque** le chèque ci-joint *or* ci-inclus

enclosed /ɪnˈkləʊzd/ ADJ *[area]* fermé ; *[garden]* clos, clôturé ; *[path]* clôturé ◆ **an ~ space** un espace clos ◆ **an ~ community** *(Rel)* une communauté retirée COMP **enclosed order** N *(Rel)* ordre *m* cloîtré

enclosure /ɪnˈkləʊʒəʳ/ N 1 *(NonC) [of land]* fait *m* de clôturer ; *(Brit Hist)* enclosure *f* 2 *(= ground enclosed)* enclos *m*, enceinte *f* ; *[of monastery]* clôture *f* ; *(= fence etc)* enceinte *f*, clôture *f* ◆ **the ~** *[of racecourse]* le pesage ◆ **the public ~** la pelouse ◆ **the royal ~** l'enceinte *f* réservée à la famille royale 3 *(= document etc enclosed)* pièce *f* jointe, document *m* ci-joint *or* ci-inclus ◆ **"enclosure(s)"** pièce(s) jointe(s) COMP **enclosure wall** N mur *m* d'enceinte

encode /ɪnˈkəʊd/ VTI coder ; *(Comput)* coder, encoder ; *(Ling)* encoder

encoder /ɪnˈkəʊdəʳ/ N *(Comput)* encodeur *m*

encoding /ɪnˈkəʊdɪŋ/ N *[of message]* codage *m* ; *(Comput, Ling)* encodage *m*

encomium /ɪnˈkəʊmɪəm/ N (pl **encomiums** *or* **encomia** /ɪnˈkəʊmɪə/) panégyrique *m*, éloge *m*

encompass /ɪnˈkʌmpəs/ VT *(gen)* couvrir ; *(= include)* englober, comprendre

encore /ɒŋˈkɔːʳ/ EXCL bis ! N /ˈɒŋkɔːʳ/ bis *m*, rappel *m* ◆ **to call for an ~** bisser, crier "bis" ◆ **to play an ~** jouer *or* faire un bis ◆ **the pianist gave several ~s** le pianiste a interprété plusieurs morceaux en rappel *or* a donné plusieurs rappels VT *[+ song, act]* bisser

encounter /ɪnˈkaʊntəʳ/ VT *[+ person]* rencontrer (à l'improviste), tomber sur ; *[+ enemy]* affronter, rencontrer ; *[+ opposition]* se heurter à ; *[+ difficulties]* rencontrer, éprouver ; *[+ danger]* affronter ◆ **to ~ enemy fire** essuyer le feu de l'ennemi N rencontre *f* (inattendue) ; *(Mil)* rencontre *f*, engagement *m*, combat *m* COMP **encounter group** N atelier *m* de psychothérapie de groupe

encourage /ɪnˈkʌrɪdʒ/ VT *[+ person]* encourager ; *[+ arts, industry, projects, development, growth]* encourager, favoriser ; *[+ bad habits]* encourager, flatter ◆ **to ~ sb to do sth** encourager *or* inciter qn à faire qch ◆ **to ~ sb in his belief that ...** confirmer *or* conforter qn dans sa croyance que ... ◆ **to ~ sb in his desire to do sth** encourager le désir de qn de faire qch

encouragement /ɪnˈkʌrɪdʒmənt/ N encouragement *m* ; *(to a deed)* incitation *f* *(to* à) ; *(= support)* encouragement *m*, appui *m*, soutien *m*

encouraging /ɪnˈkʌrɪdʒɪŋ/ ADJ encourageant

encouragingly /ɪnˈkʌrɪdʒɪŋlɪ/ ADV *[say, smile, nod]* de manière encourageante ◆ **the theatre was ~ full** le public était nombreux, ce qui était encourageant ◆ **~, inflation is slowing down** l'inflation est en baisse, ce qui est encourageant

encroach /ɪnˈkrəʊtʃ/ VI *(on sb's land, time, rights)* empiéter *(on* sur) ◆ **the sea is ~ing (on the land)** la mer gagne du terrain (sur la terre ferme) ◆ **to ~ on sb's turf** *(US fig)* marcher sur les plates-bandes de qn ◆ **I followed the road through ~ing trees and bushes** j'ai suivi la route, qui était envahie par les arbres et les buissons

encroachment /ɪnˈkrəʊtʃmənt/ N empiètement *m* *(on* sur) ◆ **a major ~ on the power of the central authorities** un empiètement de taille sur le pouvoir du gouvernement central ◆ **it's a sign of the ~ of commercialism on**

medicine c'est un signe d'envahissement de la médecine par le mercantilisme

encrustation /ɪnkrʌ'steɪʃən/ **N** *[of earth, cement etc]* croûte *f*

encrusted /ɪn'krʌstɪd/ **ADJ** ◆ ~ **with** *[+ jewels, gold]* incrusté de ; *[+ moss, snow]* recouvert (d'une couche) de ◆ **a jewel-~ box** une boîte incrustée de pierres précieuses

encrypt /ɪn'krɪpt/ **VT** *(Comput, Telec, TV)* crypter

encryption /ɪn'krɪpʃən/ **N** *(Comput, Telec, TV)* cryptage *m*

encumber /ɪn'kʌmbə^r/ **VT** *[+ person, room]* encombrer *(with* de) ◆ **~ed with debts** *[person]* criblé de dettes

encumbrance /ɪn'kʌmbrəns/ **N** *(= burden)* fardeau *m* ; *(inhibiting career etc)* handicap *m*, gêne *f* ; *(furniture, skirts etc)* gêne *f* ; *(mortgage)* charge *f* hypothécaire ◆ **to be an ~ to sb** *(fig)* être un fardeau pour qn, être une gêne pour qn

encyclical /ɪn'sɪklɪkəl/ **ADJ, N** encyclique *f*

encyclop(a)edia /ɪn,saɪkləʊ'piːdɪə/ **N** encyclopédie *f* ; → **walking**

encyclop(a)edic /ɪn,saɪkləʊ'piːdɪk/ **ADJ** encyclopédique ◆ **to have an encyclop(a)edic knowledge of sth** avoir une connaissance encyclopédique de qch

encyclop(a)edist /en,saɪkləʊ'piːdɪst/ **N** encyclopédiste *mf*

end /end/

1 NOUN	4 COMPOUNDS
2 TRANSITIVE VERB	5 PHRASAL VERBS
3 INTRANSITIVE VERB	

1 - NOUN

[1] [= farthest part] *[of road, string, table, branch, finger]* bout *m*, extrémité *f* ; *[of procession, line of people]* bout *m*, queue *f* ; *[of garden]* fond *m* ; *[of telephone line]* bout *m* ; *[of spectrum]* extrémité *f* ◆ **the fourth from the ~** le quatrième en partant de la fin ◆ **from ~ to ~** d'un bout à l'autre, de bout en bout ◆ **~ to ~** bout à bout ◆ **the southern ~ of the town** l'extrémité sud de la ville ◆ **the ships collided ~ on** les bateaux se sont heurtés de front ◆ **to the ~s of the earth** jusqu'au bout du monde ◆ **to change ~s** *(Sport)* changer de côté *or* de camp ◆ **you've opened the packet at the wrong ~** vous avez ouvert le paquet par le mauvais bout *or* du mauvais côté ◆ **to be on the wrong ~ of sth** *(fig)* faire les frais de qch ◆ **the ~ of the road** *or* **line** *(fig)* la fin du voyage ◆ **to reach the ~ of the line** *(fig)* être au bout du rouleau ◆ **there was silence at the other ~ of the line** *(Telec)* il y eut un silence à l'autre bout du fil ◆ **at the other ~ of the social scale** à l'autre bout de l'échelle sociale ◆ **he can't see beyond the ~ of his nose** il ne voit pas plus loin que le bout de son nez ◆ **to keep one's ~ up*** se défendre (assez bien) ◆ **to make (both) ~s meet** (faire) joindre les deux bouts ◆ **to play both ~s against the middle*** jouer les uns contre les autres ◆ **how are things at your ~?** comment vont les choses de ton côté ? ◆ **to get one's ~ away** ⁑ s'envoyer en l'air*

[2] [= conclusion] *[of story, chapter, month]* fin *f* ; *[of work]* achèvement *m*, fin *f* ; *[of efforts]* fin *f*, aboutissement *m* ; *[of meeting]* fin *f*, issue *f* ◆ **the ~ of a session** la clôture d'une séance ◆ **the ~ of the world** la fin du monde ◆ **it's not the ~ of the world!*** ce n'est pas la fin du monde ! ◆ **to** *or* **until the ~ of time** jusqu'à la fin des temps ◆ **to read a book to the very ~** lire un livre de A à Z *or* jusqu'à la dernière page ◆ **to get to the ~ of** *[+ supplies, food]* finir ; *[+ work, essay]* venir à bout de ; *[+ troubles]* (se) sortir de ; *[+ holiday]* arriver à la fin de ◆ **we shall never hear the ~ of it** on n'a pas fini d'en entendre parler ◆ **that's the ~ of the matter, that's an ~ to the matter** un point c'est tout, on n'en parle plus ◆ **that was the ~ of that!** on n'en a plus reparlé ! ◆ **to put an ~ to sth, to make an ~ of sth** mettre fin à qch, mettre un terme à qch ◆ **there is no ~ to it all** cela n'en finit plus ◆ **that was the ~ of him** on n'a plus reparlé de lui, on ne l'a plus revu ◆ **to be nearing one's ~** *(euph, liter)* être à (l'article de) la mort, se mourir *(liter)* ◆ **that was the ~ of my watch** ma montre était fichue*

[3] [= remnant] *[of rope, candle]* bout *m* ; *[of loaf, meat]* reste *m*, restant *m*

[4] [= purpose] but *m*, fin *f* ◆ **to this ~, with this ~ in view** dans ce but, à cette fin ◆ **to no ~** en vain ◆ **the ~ justifies the means** *(Prov)* la fin justifie les moyens *(Prov)*

[5] [Sport : of pitch] côté *m*

[6] [Ftbl] ailier *m*

[7] [set structures]

◆ **at the end of** ◆ **at the ~ of the day** à la fin de la journée ; *(fig)* en fin de compte ◆ **at the ~ of three weeks** au bout de trois semaines ◆ **at the ~ of December** à la fin (du mois de) décembre ; *(Comm)* fin décembre ◆ **at the ~ of the winter** à la fin *or* au sortir de l'hiver ◆ **at the ~ of the century** à *or* vers la fin du siècle ◆ **to be at the ~ of one's patience/strength** être à bout de patience/forces

◆ **in the end** ◆ **it succeeded in the ~** cela a réussi finalement *or* en fin de compte ◆ **he got used to it in the ~** il a fini par s'y habituer ◆ **in the ~ they decided to ...** ils ont décidé en définitive de ..., ils ont fini par décider de ...

◆ **no end** * vraiment ◆ **this news depressed me no ~** cette nouvelle m'a vraiment déprimé ◆ **it pleased her no ~** cela lui a fait un plaisir fou *or* énorme

◆ **no end of** * énormément de ◆ **she's had no ~ of problems** elle a eu énormément de problèmes

◆ **on end** *(= upright)* debout ; *(= continuously)* de suite ◆ **to stand a box** *etc* **on ~** mettre une caisse *etc* debout ◆ **his hair stood on ~** ses cheveux se dressèrent sur sa tête ◆ **for two hours on ~** deux heures de suite *or* d'affilée ◆ **for days on ~** jour après jour, pendant des jours et des jours ◆ **for several days on ~** pendant plusieurs jours de suite

◆ **to be at an end** *[action]* être terminé *or* fini ; *[time, period]* être écoulé ; *[material, supplies]* être épuisé ◆ **my patience is at an ~** ma patience est à bout

◆ **to bring sth to an end** ⇒ **end transitive verb**

◆ **to come to an end** ⇒ **end intransitive verb**

2 - TRANSITIVE VERB

[= bring to an end] *[+ work]* finir, terminer ; *[+ period of service]* accomplir ; *[+ speech, writing]* conclure, achever *(with* avec, par) ; *[+ broadcast, series]* terminer *(with* par) ; *[+ speculation, rumour]* mettre fin à, mettre un terme à ; *[+ quarrel, war]* mettre fin à, faire cesser ◆ **to ~ one's days (in Paris/in poverty)** finir ses jours (à Paris/dans la misère) ◆ **to ~ it all** *(= kill oneself)* en finir (avec la vie) ◆ **that was the lie to ~ all lies!** comme mensonge on ne fait pas mieux !* *(iro)* ◆ **the film to ~ all films** le meilleur film qu'on ait jamais fait ◆ **the deal to ~ all deals** l'affaire *f* du siècle*

3 - INTRANSITIVE VERB

[= come to an end] *[speech, programme, holiday, marriage, series]* finir, se terminer ; *[road]* se terminer ; *[insurance cover etc]* expirer, arriver à échéance ◆ **the winter is ~ing** l'hiver tire à sa fin ◆ **where's it all going to ~?** *(fig)* ◆ **where will it all ~?** comment tout cela finira-t-il ? ◆ **word ~ing in an "s"/in "re"** mot se terminant par un "s"/en "re" ◆ **it ~ed in a fight** cela s'est terminé par une bagarre* ◆ **the plan ~ed in failure** le projet s'est soldé par un échec ◆ **the film ~s with the heroine dying** le film se termine par la mort de l'héroïne

4 - COMPOUNDS

end-all N → **be**

end game N *(Cards, Chess)* fin *f* de partie, phase *f* finale du jeu

end house N ◆ **the ~ house in the street** la dernière maison de la rue

end line N *(Basketball)* ligne *f* de fond

end product N *(lit)* produit *m* fini ; *(fig)* résultat *m*

end result N résultat *m* final *or* définitif

end run N *(US fig)* moyen *m* détourné

end table N *(US)* table *f* basse

end user N *(Comput etc)* utilisateur *m* final

end zone N *(US Sport)* zone *f* de but

5 - PHRASAL VERBS

► **end off VT SEP** finir, achever, terminer

► **end up VI** [1] finir, se terminer *(in* en, par) ; *[road]* aboutir *(in* à) ◆ **it ~ed up in a fight** cela s'est terminé par une bagarre*

[2] * *(= finally arrive at)* se retrouver, échouer *(in* à, en) ; *(= finally become)* finir par devenir ◆ **he ~ed up in Paris** il s'est retrouvé à Paris ◆ **you'll ~ up in jail** tu vas finir en prison ◆ **he ~ed up a policeman** il a fini par devenir agent de police ◆ **they ~ed up arresting us** ils ont fini par nous arrêter ◆ **the book she had planned ~ed up (being) just an article** son projet de livre a fini en simple article ◆ **this oil spill could ~ up as the largest in history** cette marée noire pourrait se révéler (être) la plus importante de l'histoire ◆ **he broke his leg and ~ed up being rushed to hospital** il s'est cassé la jambe et a été emmené d'urgence à l'hôpital

endanger /ɪn'deɪndʒə^r/ **VT** *[+ life, interests, reputation]* mettre en danger, exposer ; *[+ future, chances, health]* compromettre **COMP endangered species N** espèce *f* en voie de disparition *or* d'extinction

endear /ɪn'dɪə^r/ **VT** faire aimer *(to* de) ◆ **this ~ed him to the whole country** cela lui a valu l'affection du pays tout entier ◆ **what ~s him to me is ...** ce qui me plaît en lui c'est ... ◆ **to ~ o.s. to everybody** gagner l'affection de tout le monde ◆ **that speech didn't ~ him to the public** ce discours ne l'a pas fait apprécier du public

endearing /ɪn'dɪərɪŋ/ **ADJ** *[person, quality, characteristic]* attachant ; *[habit, manner]* touchant ; *[smile]* engageant

endearingly /ɪn'dɪərɪŋlɪ/ **ADV** *[say, smile]* de façon engageante ; *[admit]* de façon touchante ◆ **~ shy** d'une timidité touchante ◆ **she is ~ unpretentious/childlike** elle est sans prétentions/comme une enfant, ce qui la rend sympathique

endearment /ɪn'dɪəmənt/ **N** ◆ **term of ~** terme *m* d'affection ◆ **words of ~** paroles *fpl* tendres ◆ **~s** *(= words)* paroles *fpl* affectueuses *or* tendres ; *(= acts)* marques *fpl* d'affection

endeavour, endeavor *(US)* /ɪn'devə^r/ **N** *(frm)* [1] *(NonC = effort)* effort *m* ◆ **in all fields or areas of human ~** dans toutes les branches *or* tous les secteurs de l'activité humaine [2] *(= attempt)* tentative *f (to do sth* pour faire qch) ◆ **he made every ~ to go** il a fait tout son possible pour y aller, il a tout fait pour y aller ◆ **in an ~ to please** dans l'intention de plaire, dans un effort pour plaire **VI** s'efforcer, tenter *(to do sth* de faire qch) ; *(stronger)* s'évertuer, s'appliquer *(to do sth* à faire qch)

endemic /en'demɪk/ **ADJ** endémique *(to* à) **N** endémie *f*

endgame /ˈendgeɪm/ N (*Chess, fig*) fin *f* de partie

ending /ˈendɪŋ/ N 1 *[of story, book]* fin *f*, dénouement *m* ; *[of events]* fin *f*, conclusion *f* ; *[of day]* fin *f* ; *(= outcome)* issue *f* ; *[of speech etc]* conclusion *f* ◆ **a story with a happy ~** une histoire qui finit bien ; → **nerve** 2 (*Ling*) terminaison *f*, désinence *f* ◆ **feminine ~** terminaison *f* féminine ◆ **the accusative ~** la flexion de l'accusatif

endive /ˈendaɪv/ N (*curly*) chicorée *f* ; (*smooth, flat*) endive *f*

endless /ˈendlɪs/ ADJ 1 *(= interminable) [day, summer, queue, speech, series, road]* interminable ; *[expanse, stretch, forest, variety, patience]* infini ; *[desert, plain]* infini, sans fin ; *[cycle, list]* sans fin ; *[supply, resources]* inépuisable ; *[discussion, argument]* continuel, incessant ; *[chatter]* intarissable ◆ **an ~ stream of traffic** un flot interminable de voitures ◆ **an ~ round of meetings** une interminable série de réunions ◆ **to go to ~ trouble over sth** se donner un mal fou pour qch ◆ **this job is ~** c'est à n'en plus finir, on n'en voit pas la fin 2 *(= countless) [meetings, questions, problems, hours]* innombrable ; *[possibilities]* innombrable, illimité ; *[times, attempts, arguments]* innombrable, sans nombre COMP **endless belt** N (*Tech*) courroie *f* sans fin

endlessly /ˈendlɪslɪ/ ADV 1 *(= continually) [repeat]* sans cesse ; *[talk, discuss, debate]* sans arrêt ; *[chatter, argue]* continuellement 2 *(= without limit) [stretch]* sans fin, à perte de vue ; *[recycle]* continuellement ◆ **~ long streets** des rues *fpl* qui n'en finissent pas ◆ **~ curious/kind/willing** d'une curiosité/d'une bonté/d'une bonne volonté sans limites ◆ **I find this subject ~ fascinating** ce sujet ne cesse (pas) de me fasciner *or* exerce sur moi une fascination sans fin

endocardia /ˌendəʊˈkɑːdɪə/ NPL of **endocardium**

endocarditis /ˌendəʊkɑːˈdaɪtɪs/ N endocardite *f*

endocardium /ˌendəʊˈkɑːdɪəm/ N (pl **endocardia**) endocarde *m*

endocarp /ˈendəkɑːp/ N endocarpe *m*

endocrine /ˈendəʊkraɪn/ ADJ endocrine ◆ **~ gland** glande *f* endocrine

endocrinologist /ˌendəʊkraɪˈnɒlədʒɪst/ N endocrinologue *mf*, endocrinologiste *mf*

endocrinology /ˌendəʊkrɪˈnɒlədʒɪ/ N endocrinologie *f*

endogamy /enˈdɒgəmɪ/ N endogamie *f*

endogenous /enˈdɒdʒɪnəs/ ADJ *[factor]* endogène

endolymph /ˈendəʊˌlɪmf/ N endolymphe *f*

endometriosis /ˌendəʊˌmiːtrɪˈəʊsɪs/ N endométriose *f*

endometrium /ˌendəʊˈmiːtrɪəm/ N (pl **endometria** /ˌendəʊˈmiːtrɪə/) endomètre *m*

endomorph /ˈendəʊˌmɔːf/ N endomorphe *mf*

endorphin /ˌenˈdɔːfɪn/ N endorphine *f*

endorse /ɪnˈdɔːs/ VT 1 *(= support) [+ claim, candidature, proposal]* appuyer ; *[+ opinion]* souscrire à, adhérer à ; *[+ action, decision]* approuver, sanctionner ; *(= advertise) [+ product, company]* faire de la publicité pour ◆ **to ~ sb as a candidate** appuyer la candidature de qn 2 *(= sign) [+ document, cheque]* endosser ; *(= guarantee) [+ bill]* avaliser ◆ **to ~ an insurance policy** faire un avenant à une police d'assurance ◆ **he has had his licence ~d** (*Brit Jur*) on (lui) a retiré des points sur son permis

endorsee /ˌɪndɔːˈsiː/ N endossataire *mf*, bénéficiaire *mf* d'un endossement

endorsement /ɪnˈdɔːsmənt/ N 1 *(= approval) [of proposal, policy]* adhésion *f* (*of sth* à qch) ; *[of movement, claim, candidate]* appui *m* (*of sb/sth* de qn/qch) ; *[of action, decision, efforts]* approbation *f* (*of sth* de qch) ◆ **a letter of ~** une lettre d'approbation 2 (*NonC = ratification*) *[of treaty]* ratification *f* 3 (*Comm*) *[of product]* recommandation *f* publicitaire ; *[of book]* recommandation *f* ◆ **to receive ~ from sb** être recommandé par qn ◆ **celebrity ~** recommandation *f* publicitaire faite par une personnalité connue 4 (*Brit Jur: on driving licence*) *infraction mentionnée sur le permis de conduire* ◆ **he's already got three ~s** il a déjà perdu des points pour trois infractions au code de la route 5 (*on cheque, document*) endossement *m* 6 *[of insurance policy]* avenant *m* (*to sth* à qch) COMP **endorsement advertising** N *technique publicitaire faisant intervenir des personnalités connues*

endoscope /ˈendəʊˌskəʊp/ N endoscope *m*

endoscopy /ˌenˈdɒskəpɪ/ N endoscopie *f*

endoskeleton /ˌendəʊˈskelɪtən/ N squelette *m* interne, endosquelette *m*

endothermic /ˌendəʊˈθɜːmɪk/ ADJ endothermique

endow /ɪnˈdaʊ/ VT *[+ institution, church]* doter (*with* de) ; *[+ hospital bed, prize, chair]* fonder ◆ **to be ~ed with brains/beauty** *etc* (*fig*) être doté d'intelligence/de beauté *etc* ; → **well**²

endowment /ɪnˈdaʊmənt/ N 1 (*Fin*) (*money for school, college*) dotation *f* ; (*hospital bed, prize, university chair*) fondation *f* 2 *(= portion)* ◆ **to have a generous ~ of sth** être généreusement pourvu *or* doté de qch ◆ **a sense of fair play, the natural ~ of every Briton** un sens du fair-play, la qualité naturelle de tout Britannique COMP **endowment assurance, endowment insurance** N assurance *f* à capital différé **endowment mortgage** N (*Brit*) hypothèque *f* liée à une assurance-vie **endowment policy** N ⇒ **endowment assurance**

endpapers /ˈendpeɪpəz/ NPL (*Typo*) gardes *fpl*, pages *fpl* de garde

endurable /ɪnˈdjʊərəbl/ ADJ supportable, endurable

endurance /ɪnˈdjʊərəns/ N endurance *f* ◆ **to have great powers of ~** avoir beaucoup d'endurance, être très endurant ◆ **a test of human ~** une mise à l'épreuve de l'endurance humaine ◆ **he has come to the end of his ~** il n'en peut plus, il est à bout ◆ **beyond ~, past ~** intolérable, au-delà de ce que l'on peut supporter ◆ **tried beyond ~** excédé COMP **endurance race** N (*Sport*) épreuve *f* de fond **endurance test** N (*Sport, Tech, fig*) épreuve *f* de résistance ; (*for car*) épreuve *f* d'endurance

endure /ɪnˈdjʊəʳ/ VT 1 *(= put up with) [+ pain]* endurer, supporter ; *[+ insults]* supporter, tolérer ; *[+ hardships]* supporter ◆ **she can't ~ being teased** elle ne peut pas supporter *or* souffrir qu'on la taquine *subj* ◆ **I cannot ~ him** je ne peux pas le supporter *or* le voir ◆ **it was more than I could ~** c'était plus que je ne pouvais supporter 2 *(= suffer)* subir ◆ **the company ~d heavy financial losses** la société a subi de grosses pertes financières VI (*frm = last*) *[building, peace, friendship]* durer ; *[book, memory]* rester

enduring /ɪnˈdjʊərɪŋ/ ADJ *[appeal, legacy, quality, peace, friendship, fame, love]* durable ; *[image, grudge]* tenace ; *[illness, hardship]* persistant, qui persiste

endways /ˈendweɪz/, **endwise** /ˈendwaɪz/ ADV (*endways on*) en long, par le petit bout ; *(= end to end)* bout à bout

enema /ˈenɪmə/ N (pl **enemas** *or* **enemata** /ˈenɪmətə/) *(= act)* lavement *m* ; *(= apparatus)* poire *f or* bock *m* à lavement ◆ **to give sb an ~** faire un lavement à qn

enemy /ˈenəmɪ/ N (*Mil*) ennemi *m* ; (*gen*) ennemi(e) *m(f)*, adversaire *mf* ◆ **to make enemies** se faire *or* s'attirer des ennemis ◆ **to make an ~ of sb** (se) faire un ennemi de qn ◆ **he is his own worst ~** il est son pire ennemi, il n'a de pire ennemi que lui-même ◆ **they are deadly enemies** ils sont à couteaux tirés, ils sont ennemis jurés ◆ **corruption is the ~ of the state** (*fig*) la corruption est l'ennemie de l'État ; → **public** COMP *[tanks, forces, tribes]* ennemi ; *[morale, strategy]* de l'ennemi **enemy action** N attaque *f* ennemie ◆ **killed by ~ action** tombé à l'ennemi **enemy alien** N ressortissant(e) *m(f)* d'un pays ennemi **enemy-occupied** ADJ occupé par l'ennemi

energetic /ˌenəˈdʒetɪk/ ADJ *[person, government, action, measure, denial, refusal]* énergique ; *[performance, campaign]* plein d'énergie ; *[activity, sport, game]* énergétique ◆ **he is an ~ campaigner for road safety** il milite énergiquement en faveur de la sécurité sur les routes ◆ **I don't feel very ~** je ne me sens pas d'attaque

energetically /ˌenəˈdʒetɪkəlɪ/ ADV *[deny, campaign]* énergiquement, avec vigueur ; *[nod, wave]* énergiquement

energetics /ˌenəˈdʒetɪks/ N (*NonC*) énergétique *f*

energize /ˈenədʒaɪz/ VT *[+ person]* regonfler ; (*Elec*) alimenter (en courant)

energizing /ˈenədʒaɪzɪŋ/ ADJ énergisant

energy /ˈenədʒɪ/ N 1 (*gen*) énergie *f*, vigueur *f* ◆ **he has a lot of ~** il a beaucoup d'énergie, il est très dynamique ◆ **he seems to have no ~ these days** il semble sans énergie *or* à plat * en ce moment ◆ **I haven't the ~ to start again** (*Brit*) je n'ai pas le courage de (tout) recommencer ◆ **to concentrate one's energies on doing sth** appliquer toute son énergie à faire qch ◆ **with all one's ~** de toutes ses forces ◆ **to put all one's ~** *or* **energies into sth/into doing sth** se consacrer tout entier à qch/à faire qch, appliquer toute son énergie à qch/à faire qch ◆ **to save one's ~ for sth** économiser ses forces pour qch ◆ **he used up all his ~ doing it** il a épuisé ses forces à le faire ◆ **don't waste your ~** * ne te fatigue pas *, ne te donne pas du mal pour rien 2 (*Phys*) énergie *f* ◆ **potential/kinetic ~** énergie *f* potentielle/cinétique ◆ **in order to save ~** pour faire des économies d'énergie ◆ **Department** *or* **Ministry of Energy** ministère *m* de l'Énergie ◆ **Secretary (of State) for** *or* **Minister of Energy** ministre *m* de l'Énergie ; → **atomic** COMP **energy conservation** N conservation *f* de l'énergie **energy conversion** N conversion *f* de l'énergie **energy crisis** N crise *f* énergétique *or* de l'énergie **energy efficiency** N efficacité *f* énergétique **energy-efficient** ADJ économe en énergie **energy-giving** ADJ *[food etc]* énergétique **energy-intensive industry** N industrie *f* grande consommatrice d'énergie **energy level** N (*Phys*) niveau *m* d'énergie **energy-saving** N économies *fpl* d'énergie ADJ d'économie d'énergie **energy-saving campaign** N campagne *f* pour les économies d'énergie

enervated /ˈenɜːveɪtɪd/ ADJ affaibli, mou (molle *f*)

enervating /ˈenɜːveɪtɪŋ/ ADJ débilitant, amollissant

enfeeble /ɪnˈfiːbl/ VT affaiblir

enfeeblement /ɪnˈfiːblmənt/ N affaiblissement *m*

enfilade /ˌenfɪˈleɪd/ (*Mil*) VT soumettre à un tir d'enfilade N tir *m* d'enfilade

enfold /ɪnˈfəʊld/ VT envelopper (*in* de) ◆ **to ~ sb in one's arms** entourer qn de ses bras, étreindre qn

enforce /ɪn'fɔːs/ VT *[+ ruling, the law]* faire obéir *or* respecter ; *[+ agreement, settlement, ceasefire, curfew, sanctions]* faire respecter ; *[+ decision, policy]* mettre en application *or* en vigueur, appliquer ; *[+ discipline, boycott]* imposer ; *[+ argument, rights]* faire valoir ◆ **he ~d the ban on all demonstrations** il a appliqué l'interdiction à toutes les manifestations ◆ **to ~ obedience** se faire obéir ◆ **these laws aren't usually ~d** ces lois ne sont généralement pas appliquées

enforceable /ɪn'fɔːsɪbl/ ADJ *[law]* exécutoire ; *[rules]* applicable

enforced /ɪn'fɔːst/ ADJ *(= imposed)* forcé ◆ **the Frenchman's ~ absence** l'absence forcée du Français ◆ **when she first heard of her ~ retirement ...** lorsqu'elle a appris qu'on la mettait d'autorité à la retraite ...

enforcement /ɪn'fɔːsmənt/ N *[of decision, policy, law]* mise *f* en application *or* en vigueur ; *[of discipline]* imposition *f* ◆ **~ of securities** *(Jur, Fin)* réalisation *f* des sûretés ; → **law** COMP **enforcement action** N *(Jur)* mesure *f* coercitive

enforcer /ɪn'fɔːsəʳ/ N *[of law, rule]* applicateur *m*, -trice *f*

enfranchise /ɪn'fræntʃaɪz/ VT *(= give vote to)* accorder le droit de vote à ; *(= set free)* affranchir

enfranchisement /ɪn'fræntʃaɪzmənt/ N ① *(Pol)* octroi *m* du droit de vote *(of sb* à qn*)* ② *(= emancipation) [of slave]* affranchissement *m*

engage /ɪn'geɪdʒ/ VT ① *(= employ, hire) [+ servant]* engager ; *[+ workers]* embaucher ; *[+ lawyer]* prendre ◆ **to ~ sb's services** s'adjoindre les services de qn ◆ **to ~ o.s. to do sth** *(frm)* s'engager à faire qch

② *(= attract) [+ sb's attention, interest]* éveiller ◆ **to ~ sb in conversation** engager la *or* lier conversation avec qn

③ *(Mil) [+ enemy]* engager le combat avec, attaquer

④ *(Mechanics)* engager ; *[+ gearwheels]* mettre en prise ◆ **to ~ a gear** engager une vitesse ◆ **to ~ gear** mettre en prise ◆ **to ~ the clutch** embrayer ◆ **to ~ the four-wheel drive** passer en quatre roues motrices intégrales *or* en rapport court

VI *[person]* s'engager *(to do sth* à faire qch*)* ; *[wheels]* s'engrener ; *[bolt]* s'enclencher ◆ **to ~ in (a) discussion/conversation** se lancer dans une discussion/conversation *(with* avec*)* ◆ **the clutch didn't ~** l'embrayage n'a pas fonctionné ◆ **to ~ in** *[+ politics, transaction]* se lancer dans ; *[+ controversy]* s'engager dans, s'embarquer dans ◆ **to ~ in competition** entrer en concurrence *(with* avec*)* ◆ **to ~ with sb/sth** s'engager auprès de qn/dans qch ◆ **she found it hard to ~ with office life** elle a eu du mal à se faire à la vie de bureau

engaged /ɪn'geɪdʒd/ LANGUAGE IN USE 24.2, 27.5 ADJ ① *(= betrothed)* ◆ **to be ~ (to be married)** être fiancé *(to* à*)* ◆ **to get ~ (to sb)** se fiancer (à qn) ◆ **the ~ couple** les fiancés *mpl* ② *(Brit Telec) [line, number, telephone]* occupé ◆ **it's ~** ça sonne "occupé" ③ *(= not vacant) [toilet]* occupé ④ *(frm = unavailable) [person]* occupé, pris ◆ **to be otherwise ~** être déjà pris ⑤ *(= involved)* ◆ **~ in sth** *[+ task]* occupé à qch ; *[+ criminal activity]* engagé dans qch ◆ **~ in doing sth** occupé à faire qch ◆ **~ on sth** pris par qch COMP **engaged tone** N *(Brit Telec)* tonalité *f* "occupé" ◆ **I got the** *or* **an ~ tone** ça sonnait "occupé"

engagement /ɪn'geɪdʒmənt/ LANGUAGE IN USE 24.2 N ① *(= appointment)* rendez-vous *m inv* ; *[of actor etc]* engagement *m* ◆ **public ~** obligation *f* officielle ◆ **previous ~** engagement *m* antérieur ◆ **I have an ~** *or* **a previous ~** je suis pris ② *(= betrothal)* fiançailles *fpl* ◆ **a long/short ~** de longues/courtes fiançailles ◆ **to break off one's ~** rompre ses fiançailles ③ *(frm = undertaking)* engagement *m*, obligation *f* ◆ **to give an ~ to do sth** s'engager à faire qch ④ *(Mil)* combat *m*, engagement *m*
COMP **engagement book** N agenda *m*
engagement ring N bague *f* de fiançailles

engaging /ɪn'geɪdʒɪŋ/ ADJ *[person]* charmant ; *[smile, frankness]* engageant ; *[personality]* attachant ; *[manner]* aimable

engender /ɪn'dʒendəʳ/ VT occasionner, créer

engine /'endʒɪn/ N *[of vehicle, boat, non-jet plane]* moteur *m* ; *[of ship]* machine *f* ; *[of jet plane]* réacteur *m* ; *(= locomotive)* locomotive *f* ; *(= device)* machine *f*, moteur *m* ◆ **~s of war** engins de guerre ◆ **to sit facing the ~/with one's back to the ~** *(Rail)* être assis dans le sens de la marche/le sens contraire à la marche ◆ **the private sector is the ~ of economic growth** le secteur privé est le moteur de la croissance économique ; → **jet**[1]
COMP **engine block** N bloc-moteur *m*
engine driver N *(Brit Rail)* mécanicien *m*
engine house N *(US Rail)* ⇒ **engine shed**
engine room N *(Naut)* salle *f or* chambre *f* des machines ; *(fig)* locomotive *f* ◆ **hello, ~ room?** *(over speaking tube)* allô, les machines ?
engine shed N *(Brit Rail)* rotonde *f*
engine unit N bloc-moteur *m*

-engined /'endʒɪnd/ ADJ *(in compounds)* ◆ **twin-engined** à deux moteurs, bimoteur ; → **single**

engineer /ˌendʒɪ'nɪəʳ/ N ① *(professional)* ingénieur *m* ; *(= tradesman)* technicien *m* ; *(= repairer: for domestic appliances etc)* dépanneur *m*, réparateur *m* ◆ **woman ~** (femme *f*) ingénieur *m* ◆ **the Engineers** *(Mil)* le génie ◆ **~ of mines** *(US)* ingénieur *m* des mines ◆ **the TV ~ came** le dépanneur est venu pour la télévision ; → **civil, heating, highway** ② *(Merchant Navy, US Rail)* mécanicien *m* ; *(Navy)* mécanicien *m* de la marine ; → **chief** VT *(lit)* réaliser, concevoir ; *(= bring about)* machiner, manigancer

> ⚠ Be cautious about translating **engineer** by **ingénieur**. An **ingénieur** always has academic qualifications.

engineering /ˌendʒɪ'nɪərɪŋ/ N ① *(NonC) (= subject)* ingénierie *f*, engineering *m* ; *(= work)* technique *f* ◆ **the road is a great feat of ~** la route est une merveille de technique ◆ **the back is a very complicated piece of ~** le dos est une mécanique très complexe ◆ **to study ~** faire des études d'ingénieur ; → **civil, electrical, mechanical** ② *(fig, gen pej)* machination(s) *f(pl)*, manœuvre(s) *f(pl)*
COMP **engineering consultant** N ingénieur-conseil *m*
engineering factory N atelier *m* de construction mécanique
engineering industries NPL industries *fpl* d'équipement
engineering works N *(pl inv)* ⇒ **engineering factory**

England /'ɪŋglənd/ N Angleterre *f*

Englander /'ɪŋgləndə/ N → **little**[1], **new**

English /'ɪŋglɪʃ/ ADJ *(gen)* anglais ; *[monarch]* d'Angleterre ; *[teacher, dictionary]* d'anglais
N anglais *m* ◆ **the King's** *or* **Queen's ~** l'anglais *m* correct ◆ **in plain** *or* **simple ~** en termes très simples
NPL **the English** les Anglais *mpl*
COMP **English as a Foreign Language** N l'anglais *m* langue étrangère ; → TEFL *etc*
English as a Second Language N l'anglais *m* seconde langue
English breakfast N *(in hotel etc)* petit déjeuner *m* anglais
the English Channel N la Manche
English for Special Purposes N l'anglais *m* langue de spécialité
English Heritage N *organisme britannique de protection du patrimoine historique*
English horn N *(US)* cor *m* anglais
English Language Teaching N l'enseignement *m* de l'anglais
English muffin N *(US)* muffin *m*
English-speaker N anglophone *mf*
English-speaking ADJ anglophone

> **ENGLISH**
>
> La prononciation standard de l'anglais parlé en Grande-Bretagne est appelée « Received Pronunciation » ou « RP » et correspond à l'accent du sud-est de l'Angleterre. Cette prononciation est dans l'ensemble celle des milieux cultivés et de la presse audiovisuelle, même si, sur ce plan, les accents régionaux sont aujourd'hui davantage représentés qu'autrefois. L'expression « Standard English » désigne la langue telle qu'elle est enseignée dans les écoles.
>
> L'anglais américain se distingue de l'anglais britannique surtout par sa prononciation mais aussi par des différences orthographiques et sémantiques. Le « Network Standard » désigne l'anglais américain standard, utilisé en particulier dans les médias. En Grande-Bretagne, on associe souvent l'accent à l'origine sociale d'une personne, ce qui est beaucoup moins le cas aux États-Unis.

Englishman /'ɪŋglɪʃmən/ N (pl **-men**) Anglais *m* ◆ **an ~'s home is his castle** *(Prov)* charbonnier est maître chez soi *(Prov)*

Englishwoman /'ɪŋglɪʃwʊmən/ N (pl **-women**) Anglaise *f*

Eng Lit /'ɪŋ'lɪt/ N (abbrev of **English Literature**) littérature *f* anglaise

engorged /ɪn'gɔːdʒd/ ADJ *(frm)* gonflé ◆ **~ with blood** gonflé de sang

engraft /ɪn'grɑːft/ VT *(Agr, Surg, fig)* greffer *(into, on* sur*)*

engram /'engræm/ N engramme *m*

engrave /ɪn'greɪv/ VT *[+ wood, metal, stone]* graver ; *(Typo)* graver au burin ; *(fig)* graver, empreindre ◆ **~d on the heart/the memory** gravé dans le cœur/la mémoire

engraver /ɪn'greɪvəʳ/ N graveur *m*

engraving /ɪn'greɪvɪŋ/ N gravure *f* ; → **wood**
COMP **engraving plate** N *(Typo)* cliché *m* typo

engross /ɪn'grəʊs/ VT ① *[+ attention, person]* absorber, captiver ② *(Jur)* grossoyer

engrossed /ɪn'grəʊst/ ADJ absorbé ◆ **Grace seemed too ~ to notice** Grace semblait trop absorbée pour remarquer quoi que ce soit ◆ **he listened to her with an ~ expression** il l'écoutait, l'air fasciné

◆ **to be engrossed in** *[+ work]* être absorbé par ; *[+ reading, thoughts]* être plongé dans

◆ **to be engrossed in doing sth** être occupé à faire qch ◆ **I was ~ in coping with the demands of a new baby** j'étais occupée à satisfaire aux impératifs posés par l'arrivée du bébé

engrossing /ɪn'grəʊsɪŋ/ ADJ absorbant

engrossment /ɪn'grəʊsmənt/ N *(US Pol)* rédaction *f* définitive d'un projet de loi

engulf /ɪn'gʌlf/ VT engloutir ◆ **to be ~ed in flames** être englouti par les flammes

enhance /ɪn'hɑːns/ VT ① *(= improve, augment) [+ attraction, beauty, status]* mettre en valeur ; *[+ powers]* accroître, étendre ; *[+ value, pleasure]* augmenter ; *[+ position, chances]* améliorer ; *[+ prestige, reputation]* accroître, rehausser ◆ **~d graphics adaptor** adapteur *m* de graphique amélioré ② *(Admin, Fin = increase)* majorer *(by* de*)*

enhancement /ɪn'hɑːnsmənt/ N *[of pension entitlement]* majoration *f* ; *[of conditions]* amélioration *f*

enhancer /ɪnˈhɑːnsəʳ/ **N** (also **flavour enhancer**) agent *m* de sapidité

enharmonic /ˌenhɑːˈmɒnɪk/ **ADJ** enharmonique

enigma /ɪˈnɪgmə/ **N** énigme *f*

enigmatic /ˌenɪgˈmætɪk/ **ADJ** énigmatique

enigmatically /ˌenɪgˈmætɪkəlɪ/ **ADV** *[say]* de façon énigmatique ; *[smile]* d'un air énigmatique

enjambement /ɪnˈdʒæmmənt/ **N** enjambement *m*

enjoin /ɪnˈdʒɔɪn/ **VT** 1 *(= urge) [+ silence, obedience]* imposer *(on* à) ; *[+ discretion, caution]* recommander *(on* à) ◆ **to ~ sb to silence/secrecy** imposer le silence/secret à qn ◆ **to ~ sb to do sth** ordonner *or* prescrire à qn de faire qch 2 *(US)* **to ~ sb from doing sth** *(= forbid)* interdire à qn de faire qch, enjoindre à qn de ne pas faire qch

enjoy /ɪnˈdʒɔɪ/ **VT** 1 *(= take pleasure in)* aimer ◆ **Ross has always ~ed the company of women** Ross a toujours aimé *or* apprécié la compagnie des femmes ◆ **he ~s good food** il aime les bonnes choses ◆ **did you ~ the concert?** le concert vous a-t-il plu ? ◆ **he didn't ~ his years at university** il ne s'est pas plu à la fac ◆ **they greatly** *or* **very much ~ed their holiday** ils se sont beaucoup plu en vacances, ils ont passé de très bonnes vacances ◆ **to ~ a weekend/an evening** passer un bon weekend/une soirée très agréable ◆ **I really ~ed the meal last night** je me suis vraiment régalé hier soir ◆ **the children ~ed their meal** les enfants ont mangé de bon appétit ◆ **to ~ life** jouir de *or* profiter de la vie ◆ **enjoy!** *(US)* bon appétit!

♦ **to enjoy doing sth** aimer faire qch ◆ **I ~ walking and cycling** j'aime faire de la marche et du vélo, j'aime la marche et le vélo ◆ **they ~ed being read to** ils aimaient qu'on leur fasse la lecture ◆ **I ~ed doing it** j'ai pris plaisir à le faire, ◆ **I ~ed playing cricket** ça m'a bien plu de jouer au cricket

♦ **to enjoy oneself** s'amuser ◆ **she was obviously ~ing herself** on voyait qu'elle s'amusait ◆ **did you ~ yourself in Paris?** est-ce que tu t'es bien amusé à Paris ?, est-ce que tu t'es plu à Paris ? ◆ **she always ~s herself in the country** elle se plaît toujours à la campagne, elle est toujours contente d'être à la campagne ◆ **I'm really ~ing myself at the moment** je suis dans une très bonne passe *or* je suis vraiment contente en ce moment ◆ **~ yourself!** amusez-vous bien !

2 *(frm = benefit from) [+ income, rights, health, advantage]* jouir de

enjoyable /ɪnˈdʒɔɪəbl/ **ADJ** agréable ; *[meal]* excellent ◆ **~ sex** rapports *mpl* satisfaisants

enjoyably /ɪnˈdʒɔɪəblɪ/ **ADV** agréablement

enjoyment /ɪnˈdʒɔɪmənt/ **N** *(NonC)* 1 *(= pleasure)* plaisir *m* ◆ **to get ~ from (doing) sth** trouver du plaisir à (faire) qch 2 *(= possession) [of income, rights etc]* jouissance *f*, possession *f* *(of* de)

enlarge /ɪnˈlɑːdʒ/ **VT** *[+ house, territory]* agrandir ; *[+ empire, influence, field of knowledge, circle of friends]* étendre ; *[+ business]* développer, agrandir ; *[+ hole]* élargir, agrandir ; *[+ numbers, majority]* augmenter ; *(Med) [+ organ]* hypertrophier ; *(Phot)* agrandir **VI** 1 *(= grow bigger) [territory]* s'agrandir ; *[empire, influence, field of knowledge, circle of friends]* s'étendre ; *[business]* se développer ; *[hole]* s'élargir ; *(Med) [organ]* s'hypertrophier ; *[pore, pupil]* se dilater 2 *(= explain)* ◆ **to ~ (up)on** *[+ subject, difficulties etc]* s'étendre sur ; *[+ idea]* développer

enlarged /ɪnˈlɑːdʒd/ **ADJ** *[photograph, group, building]* agrandi ; *[force]* plus important ; *[majority]* accru ; *[edition]* augmenté ; *[prostate, gland, organ]* hypertrophié ; *[pore]* dilaté

enlargement /ɪnˈlɑːdʒmənt/ **N** 1 *(NonC = expansion) [of building, city]* agrandissement *m* ; *[of organization]* élargissement *m* ; *[of majority]* élargissement *m*, accroissement *m* 2 *(NonC: Med) [of organ, gland, prostate]* hypertrophie *f* ; *[of pore]* dilatation *f* ; *[of vein]* gonflement *m* ; → **breast** 3 *(Phot = photograph, process)* agrandissement *m*

enlarger /ɪnˈlɑːdʒəʳ/ **N** *(Phot)* agrandisseur *m*

enlighten /ɪnˈlaɪtn/ **VT** éclairer *(sb on sth* qn sur qch)

enlightened /ɪnˈlaɪtnd/ **ADJ** *[person, society, approach, views]* éclairé ◆ **in this ~ age, in these ~ times** *(esp iro)* en ce siècle de lumières ◆ **~ self-interest** individualisme *m* constructif, égoïsme *m* à visage humain

enlightening /ɪnˈlaɪtnɪŋ/ **ADJ** instructif

enlightenment /ɪnˈlaɪtnmənt/ **N** *(NonC) (= explanations)* éclaircissements *mpl* ; *(= knowledge)* instruction *f*, édification *f* ; *(Rel)* illumination *f* ◆ **we need some ~ on this point** nous avons besoin de quelques éclaircissements *or* lumières sur ce point ◆ **the Age of Enlightenment** le Siècle des lumières

enlist /ɪnˈlɪst/ **VI** *(Mil etc)* s'engager, s'enrôler *(in* dans) **VT** *[+ recruits]* enrôler, engager ; *[+ soldiers, supporters]* recruter ◆ **to ~ sb's support/sympathy** s'assurer le concours/la sympathie de qn **COMP enlisted man N** *(US Mil)* simple soldat *m*, militaire *m* du rang ; *(woman)* ≃ caporal *m*

enlistment /ɪnˈlɪstmənt/ **N** 1 *(Mil = enrolment)* enrôlement *m*, engagement *m* *(in sth* dans qch) 2 *(Mil = period)* engagement *m* ◆ **a normal five-year ~** un engagement normal pour cinq ans 3 *(NonC = finding) [of helpers]* recrutement *m*

enliven /ɪnˈlaɪvn/ **VT** *[+ conversation, visit, evening]* animer ; *[+ décor, design]* mettre une note vive dans, égayer

en masse /ɑ̃mæs/ **ADV** en masse

enmesh /ɪnˈmeʃ/ **VT** *(lit, fig)* prendre dans un filet ◆ **to get ~ed in ...** s'empêtrer dans ...

enmity /ˈenmɪtɪ/ **N** inimitié *f*, hostilité *f* *(towards* envers ; *for* pour)

enneathlon /ˌenɪˈæθlɒn/ **N** *(Sport)* ennéathlon *m*

ennoble /ɪˈnəʊbl/ **VT** *(lit)* anoblir ; *(fig) [+ person, mind]* ennoblir, élever

ennui /ˈɒnwiː/ **N** *(NonC)* ennui *m* *(also Literat)*

enologist /iːˈnɒlədʒɪst/ **N** *(US)* ⇒ **oenologist**

enology /iːˈnɒlədʒɪ/ **N** *(US)* ⇒ **oenology**

enormity /ɪˈnɔːmɪtɪ/ **N** 1 *(NonC) [of action, offence]* énormité *f* 2 *(= crime)* crime *m* très grave, outrage *m* ; *(= blunder)* énormité *f*

enormous /ɪˈnɔːməs/ **ADJ** *[person, animal, object, amount, number, power, difference]* énorme ; *[patience]* immense ; *[strength]* prodigieux ; *[stature]* colossal ; *[talent, interest]* formidable

enormously /ɪˈnɔːməslɪ/ **ADV** *[enjoy, vary etc]* énormément ; *[enjoyable, variable etc]* extrêmement ◆ **to be ~ helpful** être d'un immense secours

enosis /ˈenəʊsɪs/ **N** Enôsis *m*

enough /ɪˈnʌf/ **PRON, N** assez, suffisamment

> The partitive **en** is often used with **assez** and **suffisamment**.

◆ **have you got ~?** en avez-vous assez *or* suffisamment ? ◆ **I think you have said ~** je pense que vous en avez assez *or* suffisamment dit ◆ **I've had ~** *(eating)* j'ai assez *or* suffisamment mangé ; *(protesting)* j'en ai assez ◆ **there's more than ~ for all** il y en a largement (assez) *or* plus qu'assez pour tous ◆ **~ said!*** assez parlé !* ◆ **~ is as good as a feast** *(Prov)* il ne faut pas abuser des bonnes choses

♦ **to be enough** suffire, être suffisant ◆ **I think that will be ~** je pense que ça suffira *or* que ce sera suffisant ◆ **that's ~, thanks** ça suffit, merci ◆ **that's ~!, ~ already!*** *(esp US)* ça suffit ! ◆ **~'s ~!** ça suffit comme ça ! ◆ **it is ~ for us to know that ...** il nous suffit de savoir que ...

♦ **enough of** ◆ **I had not seen ~ of his work** je ne connaissais pas assez son travail ◆ **~ of this!** ça suffit comme ça !

♦ **to have had enough of sth** *(= be fed up of)* en avoir assez de qch ◆ **I've had ~ of this novel** j'en ai assez de ce roman ◆ **I've had ~ of listening to her** j'en ai assez de l'écouter

♦ **enough to** ◆ **~ to eat** assez à manger ◆ **he earns ~ to live on** il gagne de quoi vivre ◆ **one song was ~ to show he couldn't sing** une chanson a suffi à prouver qu'il ne savait pas chanter ◆ **this noise is ~ to drive you mad** ce bruit est à (vous) rendre fou ◆ **I've got ~ to worry about (already)** j'ai assez de soucis comme ça

♦ **enough** + *noun* assez de, suffisamment de ◆ **~ books** assez *or* suffisamment de livres ◆ **~ money** assez *or* suffisamment d'argent ◆ **I haven't ~ room** je n'ai pas assez *or* suffisamment de place ◆ **I've had more than ~ wine** j'ai bu bien assez de vin

ADV 1 *(= sufficiently)* assez ◆ **he was close ~ now to see them clearly** il était maintenant assez près pour les voir clairement ◆ **the proposed changes don't go far ~** les changements proposés ne vont pas assez loin ◆ **I was fool ~ to believe him** j'ai été assez bête pour le croire ◆ **that's a good ~ excuse** c'est une assez bonne excuse ◆ **he is good ~ to win** il est assez bon pour gagner ◆ **he is old ~ to go alone** il est assez grand pour y aller tout seul ◆ **are you warm ~?** avez-vous assez chaud ? ◆ **he was well ~ to leave hospital** il allait assez bien pour quitter l'hôpital ◆ **I couldn't get out of there quick ~** je n'avais qu'une envie *or* je n'attendais qu'une chose, c'était de partir ◆ **we have waited long ~** nous avons assez attendu ◆ **it's proof ~ that ...** c'est une preuve suffisante que ... ; → **fair**[1], **sure**

2 *(offhand = tolerably)* assez ◆ **she seemed sincere ~** elle semblait assez sincère ◆ **he writes well ~** il écrit assez bien, il n'écrit pas mal ◆ **it's good ~ in its way** ce n'est pas (si) mal dans son genre*

3 *(intensifying)* **things are difficult ~ as they are** les choses sont bien assez difficiles (comme ça) ◆ **he knows well ~ what I've said** il sait très bien ce que j'ai dit ◆ **oddly** *or* **funnily ~, I saw him too** chose curieuse *or* c'est curieux, je l'ai vu aussi ; → **sure**

enprint /ˈenprɪnt/ **N** *(Phot)* tirage *m* normal

enquire /ɪnˈkwaɪəʳ/ ⇒ **inquire**

enrage /ɪnˈreɪdʒ/ **VT** mettre en rage *or* en fureur, rendre furieux ◆ **he was ~d by this suggestion** cette proposition l'a rendu furieux ◆ **it ~s me to think that ...** j'enrage de penser que ...

enrapture /ɪnˈræptʃəʳ/ **VT** ravir, enchanter ◆ **~d by ...** ravi de ..., enchanté par ...

enrich /ɪnˈrɪtʃ/ **VT** *[+ person, language, collection, mind]* enrichir *(with* en) ; *[+ soil]* fertiliser, amender ; *(Phys)* enrichir ◆ **vitamin-/iron-~ed** enrichi en vitamines/en fer **COMP enriched uranium N** uranium *m* enrichi

enrichment /ɪnˈrɪtʃmənt/ **N** enrichissement *m*

enrol, enroll *(US)* /ɪnˈrəʊl/ **VT** *[+ worker]* embaucher ; *[+ student]* immatriculer, inscrire ; *[+ member]* inscrire ; *[+ soldier]* enrôler **VI** *[worker etc]* se faire embaucher *(as* comme) ; *[student]* se faire immatriculer *or* inscrire, s'inscrire *(in* à ; *for* pour) ; *[soldier]* s'enrôler, s'engager *(in* dans) ◆ **to ~ as a member of a club/party** s'inscrire à un club/un parti **COMP enrolled bill N** *(US Pol)* projet *m* de loi ratifié par les deux Chambres

enrolment, enrollment (US) /ɪnˈrəʊlmənt/ **N** (at school, college, in club, scheme) inscription f (at or in sth à qch) ; (Mil) enrôlement m (in sth dans qch) engagement m (in sth dans qch) ◆ **enrol(l)ment for** or **on** (Brit) or **in** (US) **a course** (Educ) inscription f à un cours ◆ **the school has an ~ of 600 pupils** l'école a un effectif de 600 élèves ◆ **the ideal ~ would be 1,100 members** l'effectif idéal serait de 1 100 membres ◆ **~ has** or **~s have doubled** (at school, college, in club, scheme) les inscriptions ont doublé ; (Mil) les enrôlements or les engagements ont doublé **COMP enrolment fee N** (at school, university) frais mpl de scolarité ; (in club) frais mpl d'adhésion
enrolment figures NPL effectif m

ensconce /ɪnˈskɒns/ **VT** ◆ **to ~ o.s.** bien se caler, bien s'installer ◆ **to be ~d** être bien installé

ensemble /ɑːnsɑːmbl/ **N** (Dress, Mus = collection) ensemble m **ADJ** (Theat) [acting, playing] d'ensemble

enshrine /ɪnˈʃraɪn/ **VT** [+ custom, principle, rights] sauvegarder ; (Rel) enchâsser ◆ **to be ~d in law** être garanti par la loi

enshroud /ɪnˈʃraʊd/ **VT** (liter) ◆ **grey clouds ~ the city** la ville est ensevelie sous des nuages gris ◆ **mist ~ed the land** la terre était noyée sous la brume ◆ **~ed in mystery** enveloppé de mystère

ensign /ˈensaɪn/ **N** 1 /ˈensən/ (= flag) drapeau m ; (Naut) pavillon m ◆ **Red/White Ensign** (Brit) pavillon m de la marine marchande/de la marine de guerre 2 (= emblem) insigne m, emblème m 3 (Mil Hist) (officier m) porte-étendard m inv 4 (US Naut) enseigne m de vaisseau de deuxième classe **COMP ensign-bearer N** porte-étendard m inv

enslave /ɪnˈsleɪv/ **VT** (lit) réduire en esclavage, asservir ; (fig) asservir ◆ **to be ~d by tradition** être l'esclave de la tradition

enslavement /ɪnˈsleɪvmənt/ **N** asservissement m

ensnare /ɪnˈsneəʳ/ **VT** prendre au piège ; [woman, charms] séduire

ensue /ɪnˈsjuː/ **VI** s'ensuivre, résulter (from de)

ensuing /ɪnˈsjuːɪŋ/ **ADJ** [battle, violence, discussion, argument, chaos] qui s'ensuit (or s'ensuivait) ; [months, weeks] suivant, qui suivent (or suivaient etc)

en suite /ɑ̃ˈswiːt/ **ADJ** ◆ **with bathroom ~, with an ~ bathroom** avec salle de bains (attenante)

ensure /ɪnˈʃʊəʳ/ **VT** 1 assurer, garantir ; [+ safety] assurer ◆ **he did everything to ~ that she came** il a tout fait pour qu'elle vienne or pour s'assurer qu'elle viendrait 2 ⇒ **insure 2**

ENT /iːenˈtiː/ (Med) (abbrev of **Ear, Nose and Throat**) ORL f

entail /ɪnˈteɪl/ **VT** 1 (= cause) entraîner ; (= mean) supposer ; [+ expense, work, delay] occasionner ; [+ inconvenience, risk, difficulty] comporter ◆ **vivisection necessarily ~s a great deal of suffering** la vivisection entraîne forcément beaucoup de souffrances ◆ **it ~ed buying a car** cela supposait d'acheter or supposait l'achat d'une voiture ◆ **the job ~s a lot of travel** c'est un poste pour lequel il faut beaucoup voyager 2 (Jur) **to ~ an estate** substituer un héritage ◆ **~ed estate** biens mpl inaliénables

entangle /ɪnˈtæŋgl/ **VT** 1 (= catch up) empêtrer, enchevêtrer ; (= twist together) [+ hair] emmêler ; [+ wool, thread] emmêler, embrouiller ◆ **to become ~d in ropes** s'empêtrer dans des cordages 2 (fig) [+ person] entraîner, impliquer (in dans) mêler (in à) ◆ **to become ~d in an affair** s'empêtrer or se laisser entraîner dans une affaire ◆ **to become ~d in lies/explanations** s'empêtrer dans des mensonges/des explications

entanglement /ɪnˈtæŋglmənt/ **N** 1 (NonC = entwining) enchevêtrement m, emmêlement m 2 (Mil) ◆ **barbed-wire ~s** (réseau m de) barbelés mpl 3 (sexual) liaison f compliquée ◆ **romantic ~** histoire f d'amour compliquée 4 (= difficulty) imbroglio m ◆ **his ~ with the police** son imbroglio avec la police

entente /ɒnˈtɒnt/ **N** entente f ◆ **~ cordiale** entente f cordiale

enter /ˈentəʳ/ **VT** 1 (= come or go into) [+ house etc] entrer dans, pénétrer dans ; [+ vehicle] monter dans, entrer dans ; [+ path, road] s'engager dans ◆ **he ~ed the grocer's** il est entré chez l'épicier or dans l'épicerie ◆ **to ~ harbour** (Naut) entrer au port or dans le port ◆ **the thought never ~ed my head** or **mind** cette pensée ne m'est jamais venue à l'esprit ◆ **he is ~ing his sixtieth year** il entre dans sa soixantième année
2 (= become member of) [+ profession, the army] entrer dans ; [+ university, college] s'inscrire à, se faire inscrire à or dans ◆ **to ~ the Church** se faire prêtre, recevoir la prêtrise ◆ **to ~ society** faire ses débuts dans le monde
3 (= submit, write down) [+ amount, name, fact, order] (on list) inscrire ; (in notebook) noter ; (Comput) [+ data] saisir, entrer ◆ **to ~ an item in the ledger** porter un article sur le livre de comptes ◆ **to ~ a horse for a race** engager or inscrire un cheval dans une course ◆ **to ~ a dog for a show** présenter un chien dans un concours ◆ **to ~ a pupil for an exam/a competition** présenter un élève à un examen/à un concours ◆ **he has ~ed his son for Eton** il a inscrit son fils (à l'avance) à Eton ◆ **to ~ a protest** élever une protestation ◆ **to ~ an appeal** (Jur) interjeter appel ◆ **to ~ an appearance** (Jur) comparaître (en justice)
VI 1 entrer ◆ **~ Macbeth** (Theat) entre Macbeth
2 ◆ **to ~ for a race** s'inscrire pour une course ◆ **to ~ for an exam** s'inscrire à un examen

► **enter into VT FUS** 1 [+ explanation, apology] se lancer dans ; [+ correspondence, conversation] entrer en ; [+ plot] prendre part à ; [+ negotiations] entamer ; [+ contract] passer ; [+ alliance] conclure
2 [+ sb's plans, calculations] entrer dans ◆ **to ~ into the spirit of the game** (lit, fig) entrer dans le jeu ◆ **her money doesn't ~ into it at all** son argent n'y est pour rien or n'a rien à voir là-dedans

► **enter on VT FUS** ⇒ **enter upon**

► **enter up VT SEP** [+ sum of money, amount] inscrire ; [+ diary, ledger] tenir à jour

► **enter upon VT FUS** [+ course of action] s'engager dans ; [+ career] débuter dans, entrer dans ; [+ negotiations] entamer ; [+ alliance] conclure ; (Jur) [+ inheritance] prendre possession de

enteric /enˈterɪk/ **ADJ** entérique **COMP enteric fever N** (fièvre f) typhoïde f

enteritis /ˌentəˈraɪtɪs/ **N** entérite f

enterostomy /ˌentəˈrɒstəmɪ/ **N** entérostomie f

enterotomy /ˌentəˈrɒtəmɪ/ **N** entérotomie f

enterovirus /ˌentərəʊˈvaɪrəs/ **N** entérovirus m

enterprise /ˈentəpraɪz/ **N** 1 (= undertaking, company) entreprise f 2 (NonC = initiative) esprit m d')initiative f, esprit m entreprenant ; → **free COMP Enterprise Allowance Scheme N** (Brit) aide à la création d'entreprise accordée aux chômeurs

enterprising /ˈentəpraɪzɪŋ/ **ADJ** [person, company] plein d'initiative ; [idea] hardi ◆ **that was ~ of you!** vous avez fait preuve d'initiative !

enterprisingly /ˈentəpraɪzɪŋlɪ/ **ADV** (= showing initiative) de sa (or leur etc) propre initiative ; (daringly) hardiment, audacieusement

entertain /ˌentəˈteɪn/ **VT** 1 (= amuse) [+ audience] amuser, divertir ; (= keep occupied) [+ guests, children] distraire ◆ **Liverpool ~ed the crowd with some brilliant football** Liverpool a diverti le public avec un football brillant
2 (= offer hospitality to) [+ guests] recevoir ◆ **to ~ sb to dinner** (frm) (at restaurant) offrir à dîner à qn ; (at home) recevoir qn à dîner
3 (= have in mind) [+ possibility] envisager ; [+ intention, suspicion, doubt, hope] nourrir ; [+ proposal] accueillir ◆ **to ~ the thought of doing sth** envisager de faire qch ◆ **she doesn't really want to ~ the thought** elle ne veut pas vraiment considérer cette éventualité ◆ **I wouldn't ~ it for a moment** je repousserais tout de suite une telle idée ◆ **to ~ a claim** (Insurance, Jur etc) admettre une réclamation, faire droit à une réclamation
VI 1 (= amuse) [+ comic, entertainer, book, film] divertir
2 (= offer hospitality) recevoir ◆ **do you ~ often?** vous recevez beaucoup ?

entertainer /ˌentəˈteɪnəʳ/ **N** artiste mf (de music-hall etc), fantaisiste mf ◆ **a well-known radio ~** un(e) artiste bien connu(e) à la radio ◆ **he's a born ~** c'est un amuseur né

entertaining /ˌentəˈteɪnɪŋ/ **ADJ** divertissant **N** ◆ **she loves ~** elle adore recevoir ; (more formal occasions) elle adore donner des réceptions ◆ **this is a lovely room for ~** c'est la pièce idéale pour recevoir or pour des réceptions ◆ **this dish is ideal for ~** c'est un plat idéal quand on reçoit

entertainingly /ˌentəˈteɪnɪŋlɪ/ **ADV** [say, talk] d'une façon divertissante ◆ **~ cynical** d'un cynisme divertissant

entertainment /ˌentəˈteɪnmənt/ **N** 1 (NonC = amusement) divertissements mpl ◆ **the cinema is their favourite form of ~** le cinéma est leur loisir or divertissement préféré ◆ **this was not his idea of an evening's ~** ce n'était pas comme ça qu'il voyait un divertissement pour une soirée ◆ **family/popular ~** divertissement m familial/populaire ◆ **much to the ~ of ...** au grand divertissement de ... ◆ **for your ~ we have invited ...** (gen) pour vous divertir nous avons invité ... ; (on TV, radio show) pour vous faire plaisir nous avons invité ... ◆ **to make one's own ~** se divertir soi-même ; → **light²**
2 (= show) spectacle m ◆ **the world of ~** le monde du spectacle
3 (Comm) [of clients, guests] réception f
COMP entertainment allowance N ⇒ **entertainment expenses**
entertainment expenses NPL frais mpl de représentation
entertainment tax N taxe f sur les spectacles

enthral(l) /ɪnˈθrɔːl/ **VT** 1 [book, film, talk, performance, spectacle, story] captiver ; [scenery, entertainer, actor] charmer ; [idea, thought] enchanter ; [beauty, charm] séduire, ensorceler 2 (†† = enslave) asservir

enthralled /ɪnˈθrɔːld/ **ADJ** (by book, film, talk, performance, spectacle, story) captivé ; (by scenery, entertainer, actor) charmé ; (by idea) enchanté ◆ **the children listened, enthral(l)ed** les enfants écoutaient, captivés ◆ **to hold sb enthral(l)ed** captiver qn

enthralling /ɪnˈθrɔːlɪŋ/ **ADJ** [story, film, day] passionnant ; [beauty] ensorcelant

enthrone /ɪnˈθrəʊn/ **VT** [+ king] placer sur le trône, introniser ; [+ bishop] introniser ◆ **to sit ~d** (liter) trôner ◆ **~d in the hearts of his countrymen** vénéré par ses compatriotes

enthronement /ɪnˈθrəʊnmənt/ **N** (lit) couronnement m, intronisation f ; (fig) consécration f

enthuse /ɪnˈθuːz/ **VI** ◆ **to ~ over sb/sth** porter qn/qch aux nues, parler avec (beaucoup d')enthousiasme de qn/qch **VT** enthousiasmer

enthusiasm /ɪnˈθuːzɪæzəm/ **N** 1 (NonC) enthousiasme m (for pour) ◆ **without ~** sans enthousiasme ◆ **her visit generated little ~ among local people** sa visite a provoqué peu d'enthousiasme parmi les habitants ◆ **they showed little ~ for the scheme** ils ont manifesté peu d'enthousiasme pour le projet, ils n'ont pas vraiment été enthousiasmés par le projet ◆ **the idea filled her with ~** l'idée l'a enthousiasmée ◆ **she has great ~ for life** elle a une véritable passion pour la vie [2] *(= pet interest)* passion *f* ◆ **photography is one of her many ~s** la photographie est une de ses nombreuses passions

enthusiast /ɪnˈθuːzɪæst/ **N** enthousiaste *mf* ◆ **he is a jazz/bridge/sport** *etc* **~** il se passionne pour le *or* il est passionné de jazz/bridge/sport *etc* ◆ **all these football ~s** tous ces passionnés de football ◆ **a Vivaldi ~** un(e) fervent(e) de Vivaldi

enthusiastic /ɪn,θuːzɪˈæstɪk/ **ADJ** enthousiaste ◆ **~ about** *[+ painting, chess, botany]* passionné de ; *[+ plan, suggestion]* enthousiasmé par ◆ **he was very ~ about the plan** le projet l'a beaucoup enthousiasmé ◆ **~ about doing sth** enthousiaste à l'idée de faire qch ◆ **he was ~ in his praise** il a fait des éloges enthousiastes ◆ **he was less than ~ (about/about doing sth)** il n'était pas du tout enthousiaste (à propos de/pour faire qch) ◆ **to make sb ~ (about sth)** enthousiasmer qn (pour qch) ◆ **to wax ~ (about sth)** s'enthousiasmer (pour qch)

enthusiastically /ɪn,θuːzɪˈæstɪkəlɪ/ **ADV** avec enthousiasme

entice /ɪnˈtaɪs/ **VT** attirer, entraîner ; *(with food, false promises)* allécher ; *(with prospects)* séduire ◆ **to ~ sb to do** entraîner qn (par la ruse) à faire ◆ **to ~ sb away from sb/sth** éloigner qn de qn/qch

enticement /ɪnˈtaɪsmənt/ **N** *(= act)* séduction *f* ; *(= attraction)* attrait *m*

enticing /ɪnˈtaɪsɪŋ/ **ADJ** *[prospect, invitation, offer, idea]* séduisant ◆ **to look ~** *[person]* être séduisant ; *[food]* être appétissant ; *[water]* être tentant

enticingly /ɪnˈtaɪsɪŋlɪ/ **ADV** *[display]* de façon attrayante ◆ **an ~ simple way of life** un style de vie d'une simplicité séduisante

entire /ɪnˈtaɪəʳ/ **ADJ** [1] *(before singular noun)* (tout) entier ; *(before plural noun)* entier ◆ **the ~ town/street** la ville/la rue (tout) entière ◆ **~ families/cities** des familles/des villes entières ◆ **one of the best films in the ~ history of the cinema** l'un des meilleurs films de toute l'histoire du cinéma ◆ **the ~ night** toute la nuit, la nuit (tout) entière ◆ **the ~ time** tout le temps ◆ **the ~ world** le monde entier ◆ **he has my ~ confidence** j'ai entièrement confiance en lui, il a mon entière confiance ◆ **I'd never seen anything like it in my ~ life** de toute ma vie je n'avais rien vu de semblable [2] *(= uncastrated) [animal]* entier

entirely /ɪnˈtaɪəlɪ/ **ADV** *[change]* du tout au tout ; *[depend on, devote to]* entièrement ; *[satisfied, different, clear, possible, happy, convinced]* tout à fait ; *[new]* totalement ; *[free]* absolument ◆ **I ~ agree** je suis entièrement *or* tout à fait d'accord ◆ **made ~ of wood** entièrement fait en bois ◆ **it's ~ up to you** c'est à toi de décider, c'est toi qui décides ◆ **she's ~ the wrong person for the job** ce n'est vraiment pas la personne qui convient pour ce travail ◆ **the accident was ~ the fault of the other driver** l'accident était entièrement de la faute de l'autre conducteur ◆ **to be ~ a matter for sb/sth** relever entièrement de la compétence de qn/qch ◆ **to be another matter ~, to be an ~ different matter** être une tout autre affaire ◆ **was she right? – not ~** avait-elle raison ? – pas entièrement *or* complètement

entirety /ɪnˈtaɪərətɪ/ **N** intégralité *f*, totalité *f* ◆ **in its ~** en (son) entier, intégralement

entitle /ɪnˈtaɪtl/ **VT** [1] *(= bestow right on)* autoriser, habiliter *(Jur) (to do sth* à faire qch) ◆ **to ~ sb to sth** donner droit à qch à qn ◆ **this voucher ~s you to three half-price recordings** ce bon vous donne droit à trois disques à moitié prix ◆ **to be ~d to sth** avoir droit à qch ◆ **you should claim all that you're ~d to** vous devriez réclamer tout ce à quoi vous avez droit ◆ **you're ~d to a bit of fun!** tu as bien le droit de t'amuser un peu ! ◆ **I'm ~d to my own opinion** j'ai bien le droit d'avoir ma propre opinion ◆ **to ~ sb to do sth** donner à qn le droit de faire qch ◆ **to be ~d to do sth** *(by position, qualifications)* avoir qualité pour faire qch, être habilité à faire qch *(Jur)* ; *(by conditions, rules)* avoir le droit *or* être en droit de faire qch ◆ **he is quite ~d to believe that ...** il est tout à fait en droit de croire que ... ◆ **to be ~d to vote** *(Pol = have right of suffrage)* avoir le droit de vote ; *(in union election, for committee etc)* avoir voix délibérative

[2] *[+ book]* intituler ◆ **to be ~d** s'intituler

entitlement /ɪnˈtaɪtəlmənt/ **N** droit *m* (to à)
COMP **entitlement program** **N** *(US Pol)* programme *m* social

entity /ˈentɪtɪ/ **N** entité *f* ; → **legal**

entomb /ɪnˈtuːm/ **VT** mettre au tombeau, ensevelir ; *(fig)* ensevelir

entombment /ɪnˈtuːmmənt/ **N** mise *f* au tombeau, ensevelissement *m*

entomological /,entəməˈlɒdʒɪkəl/ **ADJ** entomologique

entomologist /,entəˈmɒlədʒɪst/ **N** entomologiste *mf*

entomology /,entəˈmɒlədʒɪ/ **N** entomologie *f*

entourage /,ɒntʊˈrɑːʒ/ **N** entourage *m*

entr'acte /ˈɒntrækt/ **N** entracte *m*

entrails /ˈentreɪlz/ **NPL** *(lit, fig)* entrailles *fpl*

entrain /ɪnˈtreɪn/ **VT** *(Rail)* faire monter dans un train ; *(= carry along)* entraîner **VI** monter dans un train

entrance[1] /ˈentrəns/ **N** [1] *(= way in) (gen)* entrée *f* (to de) ; *[of cathedral]* portail *m* ; *(= hall)* entrée *f*, vestibule *m* ; → **tradesman**

[2] *(= act of entering)* entrée *f* ◆ **on his ~** à son entrée ◆ **to make an ~** *(esp Theat)* faire son entrée ◆ **his ~ into politics** son entrée dans la politique

[3] *(= right to enter)* admission *f* ◆ **~ to a school** admission *f* à *or* dans une école ◆ **to gain ~ to a university** être admis à *or* dans une université ◆ **children get free ~ (to the zoo)** l'entrée (du zoo) est gratuite pour les enfants

COMP **entrance examination** **N** examen *m* d'entrée ; *(Admin)* concours *m* de recrutement
entrance fee **N** *(at museum, cinema etc)* prix *m or* droit *m* d'entrée ; *(Brit: for club, association etc)* droit *m* d'inscription
entrance hall **N** hall *m* (d'entrée)
entrance permit **N** visa *m* d'entrée
entrance qualifications **NPL** *(Educ)* diplômes *mpl* exigés à l'entrée
entrance ramp **N** *(US: on highway)* bretelle *f* d'accès
entrance requirements **NPL** *(Educ)* qualifications *fpl* exigées à l'entrée
entrance ticket **N** billet *m* d'entrée

entrance[2] /ɪnˈtrɑːns/ **VT** ravir, enchanter ◆ **she stood there ~d** elle restait là extasiée *or* en extase

entrancing /ɪnˈtrɑːnsɪŋ/ **ADJ** enchanteur (-teresse *f*), ravissant

entrancingly /ɪnˈtrɑːnsɪŋlɪ/ **ADV** *[dance, sing]* à ravir ; *[smile]* d'une façon ravissante *or* séduisante ◆ **she is ~ beautiful** elle est belle à ravir ◆ **it's ~ simple** c'est d'une merveilleuse simplicité

entrant /ˈentrənt/ **N** *(to profession)* nouveau venu *m*, nouvelle venue *f* (to dans, en) ; *(in race)* concurrent(e) *m(f)*, participant(e) *m(f)* ; *(in competition)* candidat(e) *m(f)*, concurrent(e) *m(f)* ; *(in exam)* candidat(e) *m(f)*

entrap /ɪnˈtræp/ **VT** prendre au piège ◆ **to ~ sb into doing sth** amener qn à faire qch par la ruse *or* la feinte

entrapment /ɪnˈtræpmənt/ **N** *(Jur) incitation policière à commettre un délit qui justifiera ensuite l'arrestation de son auteur*

entreat /ɪnˈtriːt/ **VT** supplier, implorer *(sb to do sth* qn de faire qch) ◆ **listen to him, I ~ you** écoutez-le, je vous en supplie *or* je vous en conjure ◆ **to ~ sth of sb** demander instamment qch à qn ◆ **to ~ sb for help** implorer le secours de qn

entreating /ɪnˈtriːtɪŋ/ **ADJ** suppliant, implorant **N** supplications *fpl*

entreatingly /ɪnˈtriːtɪŋlɪ/ **ADV** *[look]* d'un air suppliant ; *[ask]* d'un ton suppliant, d'une voix suppliante

entreaty /ɪnˈtriːtɪ/ **N** prière *f*, supplication *f* ◆ **at his ~** sur ses instances *fpl* ◆ **they ignored my entreaties** ils sont restés sourds à mes prières *or* supplications ◆ **a look/gesture of ~** un regard/un geste suppliant

entrée /ˈɒntreɪ/ **N** [1] *(= first course)* entrée *f* [2] *(US) (= main course)* plat *m* de résistance

entrench /ɪnˈtrentʃ/ **VT** *(Mil)* retrancher

entrenched /ɪnˈtrentʃd/ **ADJ** [1] *(pej = established) [position, idea, attitude]* arrêté ; *[belief, behaviour, practice, racism, suspicion]* enraciné ; *[interests, power, bureaucracy]* bien établi ; *[person]* inflexible ◆ **to become ~** *[position, idea, attitude]* devenir trop arrêté ; *[belief, behaviour, practice, racism, suspicion]* s'enraciner ; *[interests, power, bureaucracy]* s'établir fermement ; *[person]* se retrancher sur ses positions ◆ **the recession is still well ~** la récession s'est installée, la récession dure ◆ **you're too ~ in the past** vous êtes trop replié sur le passé ◆ **he remained ~ in his position** il ne démordait pas de son point de vue ◆ **to be ~ in the belief/view that ...** ne pas démordre de l'idée que .../du point de vue selon lequel ...

[2] *(Mil) [troops, position]* retranché

entrenchment /ɪnˈtrentʃmənt/ **N** [1] *(Mil)* retranchement *m* [2] *(= establishment) [of rights, standards] (gen)* établissement *m* ; *(by constitution, law)* validation *f*

entrepôt /ˈɒntrəpəʊ/ **N** entrepôt *m*

entrepreneur /,ɒntrəprəˈnɜːʳ/ **N** entrepreneur *m (chef d'entreprise)*

entrepreneurial /,ɒntrəprəˈnɜːrɪəl/ **ADJ** *[person, company]* entreprenant ; *[initiative]* audacieux ◆ **to have ~ flair** avoir l'esprit d'entreprise, avoir le sens de l'initiative

entrepreneurship /,ɒntrəprəˈnɜːʃɪp/ **N** esprit *m* d'entreprise

entropy /ˈentrəpɪ/ **N** entropie *f*

entrust /ɪnˈtrʌst/ **VT** *[+ secrets, valuables, letters]* confier (to à) ; *[+ child]* confier *(to sb* à qn, à la garde de qn) ; *[+ prisoner]* confier (to à la garde de) ◆ **to ~ sb/sth to sb's care** confier *or* remettre qn/qch aux soins de qn ◆ **to ~ sb with a task** charger qn d'une tâche, confier à qn une tâche ◆ **to ~ sb with the job of doing sth** charger qn de faire qch, confier à qn le soin de faire qch

entry /ˈentrɪ/ **N** [1] *(= action)* entrée *f* ; *(in competition)* participation *f* ◆ **to make an ~** faire son entrée ◆ **to make one's ~** *(Theat)* entrer en scène ◆ **"no entry"** *(on gate etc)* "défense d'entrer", "entrée interdite" ; *(in one-way street)* "sens interdit"

[2] *(= way in: gen)* entrée *f* ; *[of cathedral]* portail *m*

3 (= item) [of list] inscription f ; [of account book, ledger] écriture f ; [of dictionary, encyclopedia] (= term) article m ; (= headword) adresse f, entrée f ◆ **single/double** ~ (Accounting) comptabilité f en partie simple/double ◆ ~ **in the log** (Naut) entrée f du journal de bord

4 (Sport etc = participant(s)) **there is a large** ~ **for the 200 metres** il y a une longue liste de concurrents pour le 200 mètres ◆ **there are only three entries** (for race, competition) il n'y a que trois concurrents ; (for exam) il n'y a que trois candidats

COMP **entry condition** N (Ling) condition f d'admission (à un système)
entry examination N examen m d'entrée
entry fee N (at museum, cinema etc) prix m or droit m d'entrée ; (Brit: for club, association etc) droit m d'inscription
entry form N feuille f d'inscription
entry-level ADJ (Comput) de base; [model, car, product] d'entrée de gamme
entry permit N visa m d'entrée
entry phone N interphone m
entry qualifications NPL (Educ) diplômes mpl exigés à l'entrée
entry requirements NPL (Educ) qualifications fpl exigées à l'entrée
entry visa N ⇒ **entry permit**
entry word N (US Lexicography) entrée f, adresse f

entryism /ˈentrɪɪzəm/ N entrisme m

entryist /ˈentrɪɪst/ N, ADJ entriste mf

entryway /ˈentrɪweɪ/ N entrée f, hall m d'entrée

entwine /ɪnˈtwaɪn/ VT [+ stems, ribbons] entrelacer ; [+ garland] tresser ; (= twist around) enlacer (with de) ◆ **to ~ itself around** s'enrouler autour de VI s'entrelacer, s'enlacer (around autour de)

enumerate /ɪˈnjuːməreɪt/ VT énumérer, dénombrer

enumeration /ɪˌnjuːməˈreɪʃən/ N énumération f, dénombrement m

enunciate /ɪˈnʌnsɪeɪt/ VT [+ sound, word] prononcer, articuler ; [+ principle, theory] énoncer, exposer ◆ **to ~ clearly** bien articuler

enunciation /ɪˌnʌnsɪˈeɪʃən/ N [of sound, word] articulation f ; [of theory] énonciation f, formulation f ; [of problem] énoncé m ◆ **he has good ~** il articule bien

enuresis /ˌenjʊˈriːsɪs/ N énurésie f

enuretic /ˌenjʊˈretɪk/ ADJ énurétique

envelop /ɪnˈveləp/ VT envelopper (also fig) ◆ **~ed in a blanket** enveloppé dans une couverture ◆ **~ed in clouds/snow** enveloppé de nuages/neige ◆ **~ed in mystery** enveloppé or entouré de mystère

envelope /ˈenvələʊp/ N [of letter, balloon, airship] enveloppe f ; (Bio, Bot) enveloppe f, tunique f ; (Math) enveloppe f ◆ **to put a letter in an ~** mettre une lettre sous enveloppe ◆ **in a sealed ~** sous pli cacheté ◆ **in the same ~** sous le même pli ◆ **it sounds as if it was written on the back of an ~** on dirait que ça a été rédigé à la hâte ◆ **to push (back) the ~** repousser les limites

envelopment /ɪnˈveləpmənt/ N enveloppement m

envenom /ɪnˈvenəm/ VT (lit, fig) envenimer

enviable /ˈenvɪəbl/ ADJ enviable

enviably /ˈenvɪəblɪ/ ADV ◆ ~ **slim** d'une minceur enviable ◆ **a city with ~ little crime** une ville dont on peut envier le faible taux de criminalité ◆ **an ~ high academic standard** un niveau scolaire élevé qui fait envie

envious /ˈenvɪəs/ ADJ [person, glance] envieux ◆ **you're going to Barbados? – I'm very ~** tu vas à la Barbade ? – je t'envie beaucoup ◆ **to be ~ of sb/sth** envier qn/qch ◆ **people were ~ of his success** son succès a fait des envieux ◆ **to be ~ that ...** être envieux du fait que ... + subj ◆ **to cast ~ eyes** or **an ~ eye at sb/sth** jeter un regard envieux sur qn/qch

enviously /ˈenvɪəslɪ/ ADV avec envie

environment /ɪnˈvaɪərənmənt/ N 1 (= surroundings: physical) cadre m, environnement m ; (social, moral) milieu m ◆ **he has a good working ~** il travaille dans un cadre agréable ◆ **to be in a safe ~** [child, vulnerable person] être dans un environnement protégé ◆ **pupils in our schools must be taught in a safe ~** les élèves de notre pays doivent pouvoir étudier en toute sécurité ◆ **the twins were brought up in different ~s** les jumeaux ont été élevés dans des milieux différents ◆ **working-class ~** milieu m ouvrier ◆ **cultural ~** milieu m culturel ◆ **in order to survive in a hostile ~** pour survivre dans un milieu hostile ◆ **are people's characters determined by heredity or ~?** le caractère est-il déterminé par l'hérédité ou par l'environnement ? ◆ **the economic ~ is becoming increasingly global** l'environnement économique se mondialise de plus en plus

2 (natural) environnement m ; (Bio, Bot, Geog) milieu m ◆ **our ~ is awash with other forms of pollution** notre environnement est affecté par une multitude d'autres formes de pollution ◆ **natural ~** milieu m naturel

◆ **the environment** l'environnement ◆ **pollution/protection of the ~** la pollution/la protection de l'environnement ◆ **he expressed grave concern for the ~** il a exprimé de graves inquiétudes quant à l'environnement ◆ **Secretary (of State) for** or **Minister of the Environment** (Brit) ministre mf de l'Environnement ◆ **Department** or **Ministry of the Environment** ministère m de l'Environnement

COMP **Environment Agency** (Brit) N agence f de protection de l'environnement
environment-friendly ADJ qui respecte l'environnement
Environment Protection Agency N (US) agence f de protection de l'environnement

> ⚠ Be cautious about translating **environment** by **environnement**, which is generally used for physical and natural environments.

environmental /ɪnˌvaɪərənˈmentl/ ADJ 1 (= ecological) [issues, matters, problems] écologique, environnemental ; [impact, effects, research] sur l'environnement ; [change] d'écosystème ; [policy] de l'environnement ; [group, movement] écologiste ; [disaster] écologique ◆ ~ **awareness** conscience f écologique ◆ **to take account of ~ concerns** tenir compte des considérations écologiques or environnementales ◆ ~ **damage** dommages mpl causés à l'environnement ◆ ~ **regulations** lois fpl sur (la protection de) l'environnement

2 (= situational) [factors] lié à l'environnement ; [influence] de l'environnement ◆ **the illness is caused by genetic rather than ~ factors** cette maladie est due à des facteurs génétiques plutôt qu'au milieu ambiant

COMP **environmental health** N (Brit) hygiène f publique
Environmental Health Department N (Brit) département m d'hygiène publique
Environmental Health Officer N (Brit) inspecteur m de l'hygiène publique
Environmental Health Service N (Brit) service m d'hygiène publique
Environmental Protection Agency N (US Admin) ≈ ministère m de l'Environnement
environmental studies NPL étude f de l'environnement, études fpl écologiques

environmentalism /ɪnˌvaɪərənˈmentəˌlɪzəm/ N écologie f, science f de l'environnement

environmentalist /ɪnˌvaɪərənˈmentəlɪst/ N écologiste mf, environnementaliste mf

environmentally /ɪnˌvaɪərənˈmentəlɪ/ ADV 1 (= ecologically) [sensitive] écologiquement ◆ **to be ~ conscious** or **aware** être sensibilisé aux problèmes de l'environnement ◆ **to be ~ friendly** or **correct** respecter l'environnement ◆ **to be ~ harmful** nuire à l'environnement ◆ ~ **sound policies** des politiques respectueuses de l'environnement 2 (= from living conditions) ◆ **to suffer from an ~ acquired** or **induced disease** souffrir d'une maladie due aux conditions de vie

environs /ɪnˈvaɪərənz/ NPL abords mpl, alentours mpl

envisage /ɪnˈvɪzɪdʒ/ VT (= foresee) prévoir ; (= imagine) envisager ◆ **it is ~d that ...** on prévoit que ... ◆ **an increase is ~d next year** on prévoit une augmentation pour l'année prochaine ◆ **it is hard to ~ such a situation** il est difficile d'envisager une telle situation ◆ **to ~ sb** or **sb's doing sth** imaginer or penser que qn fera qch

envision /ɪnˈvɪʒən/ VT (esp US) (= conceive of) imaginer ; (= foresee) prévoir

envoy[1] /ˈenvɔɪ/ N (gen) envoyé(e) m(f), émissaire m ; (= diplomat: also **envoy extraordinary**) ministre m plénipotentiaire, ambassadeur m extraordinaire

envoy[2] /ˈenvɔɪ/ N (Poetry) envoi m

envy /ˈenvɪ/ N envie f, jalousie f ◆ **out of ~** par envie, par jalousie ◆ **filled with ~** dévoré de jalousie ◆ **it was the ~ of everyone** cela faisait or excitait l'envie de tout le monde ; → **green** VT [+ person, thing] envier ◆ **to ~ sb sth** envier qch à qn

enzyme /ˈenzaɪm/ N enzyme f

EOC /ˌiːəʊˈsiː/ N (Brit) (abbrev of **Equal Opportunities Commission**)

EOC, EEOC

La Commission pour l'égalité des chances (**Equal Opportunities Commission** ou **EOC**) est un organisme britannique chargé de veiller à ce que les femmes perçoivent à travail égal un salaire égal à celui des hommes et qu'elles ne fassent pas l'objet d'une discrimination sexiste. La Commission pour l'égalité des races (« Commission for Racial Equality ») veille pour sa part à ce qu'il n'y ait pas de discrimination sur la base de la race ou de la religion.

Aux États-Unis, la Commission pour l'égalité des chances (**Equal Employment Opportunity Commission** ou **EEOC**) lutte contre toutes les formes de discrimination raciale, religieuse ou sexuelle sur le lieu de travail. Les entreprises pratiquant une quelconque discrimination peuvent être poursuivies devant la justice fédérale.

Eocene /ˈiːəʊˌsiːn/ ADJ, N éocène m

eolithic /ˌiːəʊˈlɪθɪk/ ADJ éolithique

eon /ˈiːɒn/ N ⇒ **aeon**

eosin(e) /ˈiːəʊsɪn/ N éosine f

EP /ˌiːˈpiː/ N (abbrev of **extended play**) 45 tours m double durée

EPA /ˌiːpiːˈeɪ/ N (US Admin) (abbrev of **Environmental Protection Agency**) → **environmental**

epaulet(te) /ˈepɔːlet/ N épaulette f

épée /ˈepeɪ/ N fleuret m

ephedrine /ˈefɪdrɪn/ N éphédrine f

ephemera /ɪˈfemərə/ N (pl **ephemeras** or **ephemerae** /ɪˈfeməˌriː/) (= insect) éphémère m

NPL (= *transitory items*) choses *fpl* éphémères ; (= *collectables*) babioles *fpl (d'une époque donnée)*

ephemeral /ɪˈfemərəl/ ADJ (*Bot, Zool, fig*) éphémère

ephemerid /ɪˈfemərɪd/ N éphémère *m*

ephemeris /ɪˈfemərɪs/ N (pl **ephemerides** /ˌefɪˈmerɪˌdiːz/) éphéméride *f*

Ephesians /ɪˈfiːʒənz/ N Éphésiens *mpl*

Ephesus /ˈefɪsəs/ N Éphèse

epic /ˈepɪk/ ADJ (*Literat*) épique ; (= *tremendous*) héroïque, épique ◆ **Manchester United's ~ victory** la victoire épique de Manchester United ◆ **an ~ power-struggle** une lutte homérique *or* épique N épopée *f*, poème *m or* récit *m* épique ◆ **an ~ of the screen** (*Cine*) un film à grand spectacle

epicarp /ˈepɪkɑːp/ N épicarpe *m*

epicene /ˈepɪsiːn/ ADJ (*frm*) [*manners, literature*] efféminé ; (*Gram*) épicène

epicentre, epicenter (US) /ˈepɪsentəʳ/ N épicentre *m*

epicure /ˈepɪkjʊəʳ/ N (fin) gourmet *m*, gastronome *mf*

epicurean /ˌepɪkjʊəˈriːən/ ADJ, N épicurien(ne) *m(f)*

epicureanism /ˌepɪkjʊəˈrɪənɪzəm/ N épicurisme *m*

Epicurus /ˌepɪˈkjʊərəs/ N Épicure *m*

epicyclic /epɪˈsaɪklɪk/ ADJ ◆ **~ gear** *or* **train** train *m* épicycloïdal

epidemic /ˌepɪˈdemɪk/ N épidémie *f* ADJ épidémique ◆ **to reach ~ proportions** atteindre des proportions épidémiques

epidemiologist /ˌepɪdemɪˈɒlədʒɪst/ N épidémiologiste *mf*

epidemiology /ˌepɪdemɪˈɒlədʒɪ/ N épidémiologie *f*

epidermis /ˌepɪˈdɜːmɪs/ N épiderme *m*

epidiascope /ˌepɪˈdaɪəˌskəʊp/ N épidiascope *m*

epididymis /ˌepɪˈdɪdɪmɪs/ N (pl **epididymides** /ˌepɪdɪˈdɪmɪˌdiːz/) épididyme *m*

epidural /ˌepɪˈdjʊərəl/ ADJ, N ◆ **~ (anaesthetic)** péridurale *f*

epigenesis /ˌepɪˈdʒenɪsɪs/ N (*Bio*) épigénèse *f* ; (*Geol*) épigénie *f*

epiglottis /ˌepɪˈglɒtɪs/ N (pl **epiglottises** *or* **epiglottides** /ˌepɪˈglɒtɪˌdiːz/) épiglotte *f*

epigram /ˈepɪgræm/ N épigramme *f*

epigrammatic(al) /ˌepɪgrəˈmætɪk(əl)/ ADJ épigrammatique

epigraph /ˈepɪgrɑːf/ N épigraphe *f*

epilator /ˈepɪleɪtəʳ/ N épilateur *m*

epilepsy /ˈepɪlepsɪ/ N épilepsie *f*

epileptic /ˌepɪˈleptɪk/ ADJ épileptique ◆ **~ fit** crise *f* d'épilepsie N épileptique *mf*

epilogue /ˈepɪlɒg/ N épilogue *m*

epinephrine /ˌepəˈnefrɪn/ N (*US*) adrénaline *f*

Epiphany /ɪˈpɪfənɪ/ N (*Rel*) Épiphanie *f*, jour *m* des Rois ; (*fig*) révélation *f*

epiphytic /ˌepɪˈfɪtɪk/ ADJ épiphyte

episcopacy /ɪˈpɪskəpəsɪ/ N épiscopat *m*

Episcopal /ɪˈpɪskəpəl/ ADJ (*Rel: of Church*) épiscopalien

episcopal /ɪˈpɪskəpəl/ ADJ (*of bishop*) épiscopal

Episcopalian /ɪˌpɪskəˈpeɪlɪən/ ADJ épiscopalien N membre *m* de l'Église épiscopalienne ◆ **the ~s** les épiscopaliens *mpl*

episcopate /ɪˈpɪskəpɪt/ N épiscopat *m*

episcope /ˈepɪˌskəʊp/ N (*Brit*) épiscope *m*

episiotomy /əˌpiːzɪˈɒtəmɪ/ N épisiotomie *f*

episode /ˈepɪsəʊd/ N (= *event*) (*TV*) épisode *m* ; (*Med*) crise *f*

episodic /ˌepɪˈsɒdɪk/ ADJ épisodique

epistemic /ˌepɪˈstiːmɪk/ ADJ épistémique

epistemological /ɪˌpɪstɪməˈlɒdʒɪkəl/ ADJ épistémologique

epistemology /ɪˌpɪstəˈmɒlədʒɪ/ N épistémologie *f*

epistle /ɪˈpɪsl/ N épître *f* ; (*Admin* = *letter*) courrier *m* ◆ **Epistle to the Romans/Hebrews** *etc* (*Bible*) Épître *f* aux Romains/Hébreux *etc*

epistolary /ɪˈpɪstələrɪ/ ADJ épistolaire

epitaph /ˈepɪtɑːf/ N épitaphe *f*

epithelium /ˌepɪˈθiːlɪəm/ N (pl **epitheliums** *or* **epithelia** /ˌepɪˈθiːlɪə/) épithélium *m*

epithet /ˈepɪθet/ N épithète *f*

epitome /ɪˈpɪtəmɪ/ N [*of idea, subject*] quintessence *f* ◆ **she's the ~ of virtue** elle est la vertu incarnée *or* personnifiée, elle est l'exemple même de la vertu

epitomize /ɪˈpɪtəmaɪz/ VT [*person*] [*+ quality, virtue*] incarner, personnifier ; [*thing*] illustrer parfaitement ◆ **these dishes ~ current cooking trends** ces plats illustrent parfaitement les tendances de la cuisine contemporaine ◆ **it ~d everything he hated** c'était l'illustration parfaite de tout ce qu'il détestait

EPNS /ˌiːpiːenˈes/ (abbrev of **electroplated nickel silver**) → **electroplate**

EPO /ˌiːpiːˈəʊ/ N (abbrev of **erythropoietin**) EPO *f*

epoch /ˈiːpɒk/ N époque *f*, période *f* ◆ **to mark an ~** (*fig*) faire époque, faire date COMP **epoch-making** ADJ qui fait époque, qui fait date

eponym /ˈepənɪm/ N éponyme *m*

eponymous /ɪˈpɒnɪməs/ ADJ éponyme

EPOS /ˈiːpɒs/ N (abbrev of **electronic point of sale**) TPV *m*, terminal *m* point de vente ◆ **has the shop got ~?** est-ce que le magasin est équipé d'un TPV ?

epoxide /ɪˈpɒksaɪd/ N époxyde *m* ◆ **~ resin** ⇒ **epoxy resin** ; → **epoxy**

epoxy /ɪˈpɒksɪ/ N (also **epoxy resin**) résine *f* époxyde

EPROM /ˈiːprɒm/ N (*Comput*) (abbrev of **erasable programmable read only memory**) EPROM *f*

Epsom salts /ˌepsəmˈsɔːlts/ NPL epsomite *f*, sulfate *m* de magnésium

equable /ekwəbl/ ADJ [*temperament, climate*] égal, constant ◆ **he is very ~** il a un tempérament très égal

equably /ˈekwəblɪ/ ADV [*say*] tranquillement, calmement ; [*respond to*] calmement

equal /ˈiːkwəl/ LANGUAGE IN USE 5.2

ADJ 1 (*gen, Math*) égal ◆ **to be ~ to sth** être égal à qch, égaler qch ; **see also 2** ◆ **~ in number** égal en nombre ◆ **to be ~ in size** être de la même taille ◆ **~ pay** égalité *f* des salaires ◆ **~ pay for ~ work** à travail égal salaire égal ◆ **~ pay for women** salaire égal pour les femmes ◆ **~ rights** égalité *f* des droits ◆ **an ~ sum of money** une même somme d'argent ◆ **with ~ indifference** avec la même indifférence ◆ **with ~ enthusiasm** avec le même enthousiasme ◆ **each party has ~ access to the media** chaque parti a le même accès aux médias ◆ **they are about ~** (*in value etc*) ils se valent à peu près ◆ **to talk to sb on ~ terms** parler à qn d'égal à égal ◆ **other** *or* **all things being ~** toutes choses (étant) égales par ailleurs ◆ **to be on ~ terms** *or* **an ~ footing (with sb)** être sur un pied d'égalité (avec qn) ◆ **to come ~ first/second** *etc* être classé premier/deuxième *etc* ex æquo

2 (= *capable*) ◆ **to be ~ to sth** être à la hauteur de qch ◆ **the guards were ~ to anything** les gardes pouvaient faire face à n'importe quoi ◆ **to be ~ to doing sth** être de force à *or* de taille à faire qch ◆ **she did not feel ~ to going out** elle ne se sentait pas le courage *or* la force de sortir

3 (†† = *equable*) [*temperament*] égal

N égal(e) *m(f)* ◆ **our ~s** nos égaux *mpl* ◆ **to treat sb as an ~** traiter qn d'égal à égal ◆ **she has no ~** elle n'a pas sa pareille, elle est hors pair ◆ **she is his ~** (*in rank, standing*) elle est son égale

VT (*gen, Math*) égaler (in en) ◆ **not to be ~led** sans égal, qui n'a pas son égal ◆ **there is nothing to ~ it** il n'y a rien de tel *or* de comparable ◆ **let x ~ y** (*Math*) si x égale y

COMP **Equal Employment Opportunity Commission** N (*US*) Commission *f* pour l'égalité des chances ; → **EOC, EEOC**

equal opportunities NPL chances *fpl* égales

Equal Opportunities Commission N (*Brit*) Commission *f* pour l'égalité des chances ; → **EOC, EEOC, QUANGO**

equal opportunities employer, equal opportunity employer N employeur *m* qui ne fait pas de discrimination

Equal Rights Amendment N (*US*) *amendement constitutionnel en faveur de l'égalité des droits*

equal(s) sign N signe *m* d'égalité *or* égal

equal time N (*US Rad, TV*) droit *m* de réponse (à l'antenne)

equality /ɪˈkwɒlɪtɪ/ N égalité *f* ◆ **~ in the eyes of the law** égalité *f* devant la loi ◆ **~ of opportunity** l'égalité *f* des chances ◆ **the Equality State** le Wyoming

equalization /ˌiːkwəlaɪˈzeɪʃən/ N (*NonC*) [*of wealth*] répartition *f* ; [*of income, prices*] égalisation *f* ; [*of retirement ages*] nivellement *m* ; [*of account*] régularisation *f* ◆ **to work towards the ~ of opportunities** œuvrer pour l'égalité des chances

equalize /ˈiːkwəlaɪz/ VT [*+ rights, opportunities*] garantir l'égalité de ; [*+ chances*] équilibrer ; [*+ wealth, possessions*] niveler ; [*+ income, prices*] égaliser ; [*+ accounts*] régulariser VI (*Brit Sport*) égaliser

equalizer /ˈiːkwəlaɪzəʳ/ N 1 (*Sport*) but *m* (*or* point *m*) égalisateur 2 (*US* ✻) (= *revolver*) pétard * *m*, revolver *m* ; (= *rifle*) flingue * *m*

equally /ˈiːkwəlɪ/ LANGUAGE IN USE 26.1, 26.2 ADV 1 (= *evenly*) [*divide, share*] en parts égales ◆ **~ spaced** à espaces réguliers

2 (= *in the same way*) [*treat*] de la même manière ◆ **this applies ~ to everyone** ceci s'applique à tout le monde de la même manière ◆ **this applies ~ to men and to women** ceci s'applique aussi bien aux hommes qu'aux femmes

3 (= *just as*) [*important, impressive, true, difficult*] tout aussi ; [*clear*] également ◆ **her mother was ~ disappointed** sa mère a été tout aussi déçue ◆ **~ qualified candidates** des candidats *mpl* ayant les mêmes qualifications ◆ **to be ~ successful** [*person*] réussir aussi bien ; [*artist, exhibition*] avoir autant de succès ◆ **~ gifted brothers** frères *mpl* également *or* pareillement doués ◆ **they were ~ guilty** (*gen*) ils étaient aussi coupables l'un que l'autre, ils étaient coupables au même degré ◆ **she did ~ well in history** (*Jur*) elle a eu de tout aussi bons résultats en histoire ◆ **~ as good/bad** tout aussi bon/mauvais, aussi bon/mauvais l'un que l'autre

4 (= *by the same token*) ◆ **the country must find a solution to unemployment. Equally, it must fight inflation** le pays doit trouver une solution au chômage ; de même, il doit lutter contre l'inflation ◆ **she cannot marry him, but ~ she cannot live alone** elle ne peut pas l'épouser mais elle ne peut pas non plus vivre seule

equanimity /ˌekwəˈnɪmɪtɪ/ N égalité *f* d'humeur, équanimité *f* (*frm*) ◆ **with ~** avec sérénité, d'une âme égale

equate /ɪˈkweɪt/ VT (*= identify*) assimiler (*with* à) ; (*= compare*) mettre sur le même pied (*with* que) ; (*Math*) mettre en équation (*to* avec) ; (*= make equal*) égaler, égaliser ◆ **to ~ Eliot with Shakespeare** mettre Eliot sur le même pied que Shakespeare ◆ **to ~ black with mourning** assimiler le noir au deuil ◆ **to ~ supply and demand** égaler *or* égaliser l'offre à la demande

equation /ɪˈkweɪʒən/ N 1 (*Math, Chem*) équation *f* ◆ **that doesn't even enter the ~** ça n'entre même pas en ligne de compte ; → **quadratic, simple, simultaneous** 2 (*= comparison*) ◆ **the ~ of sth with sth, the ~ between sth and sth** l'assimilation *f* de qch à qch COMP **equation of time** N (*Astron*) équation *f* du temps

equator /ɪˈkweɪtəʳ/ N équateur *m* (terrestre), ligne *f* équinoxiale ◆ **at the ~** sous l'équateur

equatorial /ˌekwəˈtɔːrɪəl/ ADJ équatorial ◆ **Equatorial Guinea** la Guinée équatoriale

equerry /ɪˈkwerɪ/ N écuyer *m* (*au service d'un membre de la famille royale*)

equestrian /ɪˈkwestrɪən/ ADJ équestre N (*gen*) cavalier *m*, -ière *f* ; (*in circus*) écuyer *m*, -ère *f*

equestrianism /ɪˈkwestrɪəˌnɪzəm/ N (*Sport*) hippisme *m*, sports *mpl* équestres

equidistant /ˈiːkwɪˈdɪstənt/ ADJ équidistant, à égale distance ◆ **Orléans is ~ from Tours and Paris** Orléans est à égale distance de Tours et de Paris

equilateral /ˈiːkwɪˈlætərəl/ ADJ équilatéral

equilibrium /ˌiːkwɪˈlɪbrɪəm/ N (pl **equilibriums** *or* **equilibria** /ˌiːkwɪˈlɪbrɪə/) (*physical, mental*) équilibre *m* ◆ **to lose one's ~** (*physically*) perdre l'équilibre ; (*mentally*) devenir déséquilibré ◆ **in ~** en équilibre

equine /ˈekwaɪn/ ADJ [*species, profile*] chevalin

equinoctial /ˌiːkwɪˈnɒkʃəl/ ADJ équinoxial ; [*gales, tides*] d'équinoxe

equinox /ˈiːkwɪnɒks/ N équinoxe *m* ◆ **vernal** *or* **spring ~** équinoxe *m* de printemps, point *m* vernal ◆ **autumnal ~** équinoxe *m* d'automne

equip /ɪˈkwɪp/ VT 1 (*= fit out*) [*+ factory*] équiper, outiller ; [*+ kitchen, laboratory, ship, soldier, worker, astronaut*] équiper ◆ **to ~ a room as a laboratory** aménager une pièce en laboratoire ◆ **to ~ a household** monter un ménage ◆ **to be ~ped to do sth** [*factory etc*] être équipé pour faire qch ◆ **to be ~ped for a job** (*fig*) avoir les compétences nécessaires pour un emploi ; → **ill, well**[2] 2 (*= provide*) **to ~ with** [*+ person*] équiper de, pourvoir de ; [*+ ship, car, factory, army etc*] équiper de, doter de ◆ **to ~ o.s. with** s'équiper de, se munir de ◆ **he is well ~ped with cookery books** il est bien monté *or* pourvu en livres de cuisine ◆ **to ~ a ship with radar** installer le radar sur un bateau

equipage /ˈekwɪpɪdʒ/ N équipage *m* (*chevaux et personnel*)

equipment /ɪˈkwɪpmənt/ N (*gen*) équipement *m* ; (*for office, laboratory, camping etc*) matériel *m* ◆ **factory ~** outillage *m* ◆ **lifesaving ~** matériel *m* de sauvetage ◆ **electrical ~** appareillage *m* électrique ◆ **domestic ~** appareils *mpl* ménagers ◆ **~ grant** prime *f or* subvention *f* d'équipement

equipoise /ˈekwɪpɔɪz/ N (*frm*) équilibre *m*

equisetum /ˌekwɪˈsiːtəm/ N (pl **equisetums** *or* **equiseta** /ˌekwɪˈsiːtə/) equisetum *m*, prèle *f*

equitable /ˈekwɪtəbl/ ADJ équitable

equitably /ˈekwɪtəblɪ/ ADV équitablement

equitation /ˌekwɪˈteɪʃən/ N (*frm*) équitation *f*

equity /ˈekwɪtɪ/ N 1 (*NonC = fairness*) équité *f* 2 (*Econ*) (also **owner's equity, shareholder's equity, equity capital**) fonds *mpl or* capitaux *mpl* propres, capital *m* actions ◆ **equities** (*Brit Stock Exchange*) actions *fpl* cotées en bourse 3 (*Jur = system of law*) équité *f* 4 (*Brit*) **Equity** *syndicat des acteurs*

COMP **Equity card** N (*Brit Theat*) *carte de membre du syndicat des acteurs*

equity issue N (*Econ*) émission *f* de capital

equity-linked policy N (*Econ*) police *f* d'assurance-vie indexée sur le cours des valeurs boursières

equivalence /ɪˈkwɪvələns/ N équivalence *f*

equivalent /ɪˈkwɪvələnt/ LANGUAGE IN USE 5.3 ADJ équivalent ◆ **to be ~ to** être équivalent à, équivaloir à N équivalent *m* (*in* en) ◆ **the French ~ of the English word** l'équivalent en français du mot anglais ◆ **man ~** (*in industry*) unité-travailleur *f*

equivocal /ɪˈkwɪvəkəl/ ADJ [*reply, statement, attitude, behaviour, results, evidence*] équivoque, ambigu (-guë *f*) ; [*person*] (*= ambiguous*) équivoque ; (*= undecided*) indécis (*about sth* quant à qch)

equivocally /ɪˈkwɪvəkəlɪ/ ADV d'une manière équivoque *or* ambiguë

equivocate /ɪˈkwɪvəkeɪt/ VI user de faux-fuyants *or* d'équivoques, parler (*or* répondre *etc*) de façon équivoque

equivocation /ɪˌkwɪvəˈkeɪʃən/ N (*often pl*) paroles *fpl* équivoques ◆ **without ~** sans équivoque *or* ambiguïté

ER 1 (abbrev of **Elizabeth Regina**) la reine Élisabeth 2 (*US Med*) (abbrev of **emergency room**) (salle *f* des) urgences *fpl*

er /ɜːʳ/ INTERJ euh

ERA /ˌiːɑːrˈeɪ/ N 1 (*US*) (abbrev of **Equal Rights Amendment**) → **equal** 2 (*Brit*) (abbrev of **Education Reform Act**) loi *f* sur la réforme de l'enseignement

era /ˈɪərə/ N (*Geol, Hist*) ère *f* ; (*gen*) époque *f*, temps *m* ◆ **the Communist ~** l'ère du communisme ◆ **the Christian ~** l'ère *f* chrétienne ◆ **the ~ of crinolines** le temps des crinolines ◆ **the Gorbachov ~** les années Gorbachev ◆ **a new ~ of economic growth** une nouvelle période de croissance économique ◆ **the end of an ~** la fin d'une époque ◆ **to mark an ~** marquer une époque, faire époque

eradicate /ɪˈrædɪkeɪt/ VT [*+ injustice, discrimination, poverty*] éradiquer, supprimer ; [*+ disease*] éradiquer, éliminer ; [*+ weeds*] éliminer

eradication /ɪˌrædɪˈkeɪʃən/ N (*NonC*) [*of injustice, discrimination*] suppression *f* ; [*of poverty, disease, corruption*] éradication *f* ; [*of weeds*] élimination *f*

erasable /ɪˈreɪzəbl/ ADJ effaçable COMP **erasable programmable read only memory** N (*Comput*) mémoire *f* morte programmable effaçable

erase /ɪˈreɪz/ VT 1 [*+ writing, marks*] effacer, gratter ; (*with rubber*) gommer ; (*Comput, Recording*) effacer ; [*+ memory*] bannir 2 (*US* ‡ *= kill*) liquider‡, tuer COMP **erase head** N tête *f* d'effacement

eraser /ɪˈreɪzəʳ/ N (*esp US = rubber*) gomme *f*

Erasmus /ɪˈræzməs/ N Érasme *m*

erasure /ɪˈreɪʒəʳ/ N grattage *m*, effacement *m*

erbium /ˈɜːbɪəm/ N erbium *m*

ere /ɛəʳ/ (††, *liter*) PREP avant ◆ **~ now** déjà ◆ **~ then** d'ici là ◆ **~ long** sous peu CONJ avant que + *subj*

erect /ɪˈrekt/ ADJ 1 (*= upright*) [*person, head, plant, stem*] droit ; [*tail, ears*] dressé ◆ **her posture is very ~** elle se tient très droite ◆ **to hold o.s.** *or* **stand ~** se tenir droit 2 [*penis, clitoris*] en érection ; [*nipples*] durci ADV [*walk*] (*= on hind legs*) debout ; (*= not slouching*) droit VT [*+ temple, statue*] ériger, élever ; [*+ wall, flats, factory*] bâtir, construire ; [*+ machinery, traffic signs*] installer ; [*+ scaffolding, furniture*] monter ; [*+ altar, tent, mast, barricade*] dresser ; (*fig*) [*+ theory*] bâtir ; [*+ obstacles, barrier*] élever

erectile /ɪˈrektaɪl/ ADJ érectile

erection /ɪˈrekʃən/ N 1 [*of penis*] érection *f* ◆ **to have** *or* **get an ~** avoir une érection ◆ **to maintain an ~** maintenir une érection 2 (*NonC = construction*) [*of statue, monument*] érection *f* ; [*of building, wall, fence*] construction *f* ; [*of scaffolding*] montage *m* ; [*of altar, tent, mast, barricade*] dressage *m* ; (*fig*) [*of theory, obstacle, barrier*] édification *f* 3 (*= structure*) structure *f*

erectly /ɪˈrektlɪ/ ADV droit

erector /ɪˈrektəʳ/ N (*= muscle*) érecteur *m* COMP **erector set** N (*US = toy*) jeu *m* de construction

erg /ɜːg/ N (*Phys, Geol*) erg *m*

ergative /ˈɜːgətɪv/ ADJ (*Ling*) ergatif

ergo /ˈɜːgəʊ/ CONJ (*frm, hum*) par conséquent

ergonomic /ˌɜːgəʊˈnɒmɪk/ ADJ ergonomique

ergonomically /ˌɜːgəʊˈnɒmɪkəlɪ/ ADV [*designed*] conformément à l'ergonomie ; [*sound, sensible*] du point de vue ergonomique

ergonomics /ˌɜːgəʊˈnɒmɪks/ N (*NonC*) ergonomie *f*

ergonomist /ɜːˈgɒnəmɪst/ N ergonome *mf*

ergot /ˈɜːgət/ N (*Agr*) ergot *m* ; (*Pharm*) ergot *m* de seigle

ergotism /ˈɜːgətɪzəm/ N ergotisme *m*

Erie /ˈɪərɪ/ N ◆ **Lake ~** le lac Érié

Erin /ˈɪərɪn/ N (††, *liter*) Irlande *f*

Eritrea /ˌerɪˈtreɪə/ N Érythrée *f*

Eritrean /ˌerɪˈtreɪən/ ADJ érythréen N Érythréen(ne) *m(f)*

erk‡ /ɜːk/ N (*Brit*) (*= airman*) bidasse * *m* ; (*= seaman*) mataf * *m*

ERM /ˌiːɑːrˈem/ N (abbrev of **Exchange Rate Mechanism**) → **exchange**

ermine /ˈɜːmɪn/ N (pl **ermines** *or* **ermine**) (*= animal, fur, robes*) hermine *f*

ERNIE /ˈɜːnɪ/ N (*Brit*) (abbrev of **Electronic Random Number Indicator Equipment**) *ordinateur qui sert au tirage des numéros gagnants des bons à lots*

erode /ɪˈrəʊd/ VT 1 [*water, wind, sea*] éroder ; [*acid, rust*] ronger, corroder 2 (*fig*) [*+ power, authority, support*] éroder ; [*+ confidence*] saper ; [*+ advantages*] grignoter ; [*inflation*] [*+ value*] amoindrir VI [*rock, soil*] s'éroder ; [*value*] s'amoindrir

▸ **erode away** VT désagréger VI se désagréger

erogenous /ɪˈrɒdʒənəs/ ADJ érogène

Eroica /ɪˈrəʊɪkə/ N (*Mus*) ◆ **the ~ Symphony** la symphonie Héroïque

Eros /ˈɪərɒs/ N Éros *m*

erosion /ɪˈrəʊʒən/ N 1 [*of soil, rock, cliff*] érosion *f* ; [*of metal*] corrosion *f* ; (*Med*) érosion *f* ◆ **coastal ~** érosion *f* littorale ◆ **soil ~** érosion *f* du sol ◆ **wind ~** érosion *f* éolienne ◆ **cervical ~** érosion *f* cervicale ◆ **gum ~** érosion *f* gingivale *or* des gencives 2 (*= reduction*) [*of power, authority, support, confidence, belief, freedom, rights*] érosion *f* ; [*of moral standards*] dégradation *f* ◆ **the ~ of the euro through inflation** l'érosion *f or* l'effritement *m* de l'euro du fait de l'inflation

erosive /ɪˈrəʊzɪv/ ADJ [*power*] d'érosion ; [*effect*] de l'érosion

erotic /ɪˈrɒtɪk/ ADJ érotique

erotica /ɪˈrɒtɪkə/ NPL (*Art*) art *m* érotique ; (*Literat*) littérature *f* érotique ; (*Cine*) films *mpl* érotiques

erotically /ɪˈrɒtɪkəlɪ/ ADV érotiquement ◆ **an ~ charged novel** un roman plein d'érotisme

eroticism /ɪˈrɒtɪsɪzəm/ N érotisme *m*

erotomania /ɪˌrɒtəʊˈmeɪnɪə/ N érotomanie *f*

err /ɜːʳ/ VI (= *be mistaken*) se tromper ; (= *sin*) pécher, commettre une faute ◆ **to ~ in one's judgement** faire une erreur de jugement ◆ **to ~ on the side of caution** pécher par excès de prudence ◆ **to ~ is human** l'erreur est humaine

errand /ˈerənd/ N commission *f*, course *f* ◆ **to go on** *or* **run ~s** faire des commissions *or* des courses ◆ **to be on an ~** être en course ◆ **an ~ of mercy** une mission de charité ; → **fool¹** COMP **errand boy** N garçon *m* de courses

errant /ˈerənt/ ADJ (= *sinful*) dévoyé ; (= *wandering*) errant ; → **knight**

errata /eˈrɑːtə/ NPL of **erratum**

erratic /ɪˈrætɪk/ ADJ [*person, behaviour, moods*] fantasque ; [*driving, performance, progress, movements, sales, pulse*] irrégulier ; [*nature*] irrégulier, changeant ◆ **we work ~ hours** nos heures de travail sont très irrégulières

erratically /ɪˈrætɪkəlɪ/ ADV [*behave, act*] de manière fantasque ; [*work, play*] de façon irrégulière ; [*drive*] de manière imprévisible, dangereusement

erratum /eˈrɑːtəm/ N (pl **errata**) erratum *m* (errata *pl*)

erroneous /ɪˈrəʊnɪəs/ ADJ erroné

erroneously /ɪˈrəʊnɪəslɪ/ ADV à tort

error /ˈerəʳ/ N 1 (= *mistake*) erreur *f* (*also Math*), faute *f* ◆ **to make** *or* **commit an ~** faire (une) erreur, commettre une erreur, se tromper ◆ **it would be an ~ to underestimate him** on aurait tort de le sous-estimer ◆ **~ of judgement** erreur *f* de jugement ◆ **~ in calculation** erreur *f* de calcul ◆ **compass ~** (*Naut*) variation *f* du compas ◆ **~s and omissions excepted** (*Comm*) sauf erreur ou omission ◆ **~ message** (*Comput*) message *m* d'erreur ; → **margin, spelling** 2 (*NonC*) erreur *f* ◆ **in ~** par erreur, par méprise ◆ **to be in/fall into ~** (*Rel*) être/tomber dans l'erreur ◆ **to see the ~ of one's ways** revenir de ses erreurs

ersatz /ˈɛəzæts/ ADJ 1 (= *fake*) soi-disant ◆ **an ~ Victorian shopping precinct** un centre commercial soi-disant victorien 2 (= *substitute*) ~ **coffee** ersatz *m* de café

erstwhile /ˈɜːstwaɪl/ (*o.f or liter*) ADJ d'autrefois, d'antan (*liter*) ADV autrefois, jadis

eructate /ɪˈrʌkteɪt/ VI (*frm*) éructer

erudite /ˈerʊdaɪt/ ADJ [*person, work*] érudit, savant ; [*word*] savant

eruditely /ˈerʊdaɪtlɪ/ ADV d'une manière savante, avec érudition

erudition /ˌerʊˈdɪʃən/ N érudition *f*

erupt /ɪˈrʌpt/ VI 1 [*volcano*] (*begin*) entrer en éruption ; (*go on erupting*) faire éruption ◆ **~ing volcano** volcan *m* en éruption

2 [*war, fighting, violence, riots, argument, protests, scandal*] éclater ; [*crisis*] se déclencher ◆ **to ~ in(to) violence** tourner à la violence ◆ **the town ~ed in riots** la ville est devenue (subitement) le théâtre de violentes émeutes ◆ **the car ~ed in flames** la voiture s'est embrasée ◆ **she ~ed (in anger) when she heard the news** sa colère a explosé quand elle a entendu la nouvelle ◆ **the crowd ~ed into applause/laughter** la foule a éclaté en applaudissements/de rire ◆ **the children ~ed into the room** les enfants ont fait irruption dans la pièce

3 (*Med*) [*spots*] sortir, apparaître ; [*tooth*] percer ◆ **his face had ~ed (in spots)** son visage s'était soudain couvert de boutons ◆ **a rash had ~ed across his chest** sa poitrine s'était soudain couverte de boutons

eruption /ɪˈrʌpʃən/ N 1 [*of volcano*] éruption *f* ◆ **a volcano in a state of ~** un volcan en éruption 2 [*of violence, laughter*] explosion *f* ; [*of crisis*] déclenchement *m* ; [*of anger*] explosion *f*, accès *m* ; [*of radicalism, fundamentalism*] vague *f* ◆ **since the ~ of the scandal/the war** depuis que le scandale/la guerre a éclaté ◆ **this could lead to the ~ of civil war** cela pourrait faire éclater une guerre civile 3 (*Med*) [*of spots, rash*] éruption *f*, poussée *f* ; [*of tooth*] percée *f*

erysipelas /ˌerɪˈsɪpɪləs/ N érysipèle *or* érésipèle *m*

erythrocyte /ɪˈrɪθrəʊˌsaɪt/ N érythrocyte *m*

ESA /ˌiːesˈeɪ/ N (abbrev of **European Space Agency**) ASE *f*

Esau /ˈiːsɔː/ N Ésaü *m*

escalate /ˈeskəleɪt/ VI [*fighting, bombing, violence*] s'intensifier ; [*tension, hostilities*] monter ; [*costs*] monter en flèche ◆ **the war is escalating** c'est l'escalade de la guerre ◆ **prices are escalating** c'est l'escalade des prix VT [+ *fighting, violence*] intensifier ; [+ *prices, wage claims*] faire monter en flèche

escalation /ˌeskəˈleɪʃən/ N (= *intensification*) [*of violence*] escalade *f*, intensification *f* ; [*of fighting, conflict, war*] intensification *f* ; [*of tension, hostilities*] montée *f* ; [*of costs, prices*] montée *f* en flèche ◆ **nuclear ~** surenchère *f* dans la course aux armements nucléaires COMP **escalation clause** N (*Comm*) clause *f* d'indexation *or* de révision

escalator /ˈeskəleɪtəʳ/ N escalier *m* roulant *or* mécanique, escalator *m* COMP **escalator clause** N (*Comm*) clause *f* d'indexation *or* de révision

escalope /ˈeskəˌlɒp/ N (*Brit*) escalope *f* ◆ **veal ~** escalope *f* de veau

escapade /ˈeskəˌpeɪd/ N (= *misdeed*) fredaine *f* ; (= *prank*) frasque *f* ; (= *adventure*) équipée *f*

escape /ɪsˈkeɪp/ VI 1 (= *get away*) [*person, animal*] (*from person, incident, accident*) échapper (*from sb* à qn) ; (*from place*) s'échapper (*from* de) ; [*prisoner*] s'évader (*from* de) ◆ **to ~ from sb/from sb's hands** échapper à qn/des mains de qn ◆ **to ~ from captivity** [*person*] s'évader ; [*animal*] s'échapper (*du zoo etc*) ◆ **an ~d prisoner** un évadé ◆ **to ~ from a country** fuir un pays ◆ **to ~ to a neutral country** s'enfuir dans *or* gagner un pays neutre ◆ **to ~ with a warning** s'en tirer avec un (simple) avertissement ◆ **he ~d with a few scratches** il s'en est tiré avec quelques égratignures ◆ **he only just ~d with his life** il a failli y laisser la vie, il a failli y rester* ◆ **to ~ from poverty** échapper à la pauvreté ◆ **to ~ from the world/the crowd** fuir le monde/la foule ◆ **to ~ from reality** s'évader (du réel) ◆ **to ~ from o.s.** se fuir ◆ **she wanted to ~ from her marriage** elle voulait échapper à la vie de couple

2 [*water, steam, gas*] s'échapper, fuir

VT 1 (= *avoid*) [+ *pursuit, death, arrest, capture, prosecution, poverty, criticism*] échapper à ; [+ *consequences*] éviter ; [+ *punishment*] se soustraire à ◆ **he narrowly ~d injury/being run over** il a failli être blessé/écrasé ◆ **he ~d death or serious injury by no more than a few centimetres** quelques centimètres de plus et il était tué ou gravement blessé ◆ **to ~ detection** *or* **notice** ne pas se faire repérer ◆ **to ~ one's pursuers** échapper à ses poursuivants ◆ **this species has so far managed to ~ extinction** cette espèce a jusqu'à présent réussi à échapper à l'extinction

2 (= *elude, be forgotten by*) échapper à ◆ **his name ~s me** son nom m'échappe ◆ **nothing ~s him** rien ne lui échappe ◆ **it had not ~d her** *or* **her notice that ...** elle n'avait pas été sans s'apercevoir que ..., il ne lui avait pas échappé que ...

N [*of person*] fuite *f*, évasion *f* ; [*of animal*] fuite *f* ; [*of water, gas*] fuite *f* ; [*of steam, gas in machine*] échappement *m* ◆ **to plan an ~** combiner un plan d'évasion ◆ **to make an** *or* **one's ~** (*from person, incident, accident*) s'échapper ; (*from place*) s'évader ; [*prisoner*] s'évader ◆ **to have a lucky** *or* **narrow ~** l'échapper belle ◆ **~ from reality** évasion *f* (hors de la réalité) ◆ **~ (key)** (*Comput*) touche *f* d'échappement ◆ **press ~** appuyez sur la touche d'échappement

COMP **escape artist** N ⇒ **escapologist**
escape chute N (*in aircraft*) toboggan *m* de secours
escape clause N (*Jur*) clause *f* dérogatoire *or* de sauvegarde
escape device N dispositif *m* de sortie *or* de secours
escape hatch N sas *m* de secours
escape key N (*Comput*) touche *f* d'échappement
escape mechanism N (*lit*) mécanisme *m* de défense *or* de protection ; (*Psych*) fuite *f* (*devant la réalité*)
escape pipe N tuyau *m* d'échappement *or* de refoulement, tuyère *f*
escape plan N plan *m* d'évasion
escape route N (*on road*) voie *f* de détresse ; (*fig*) échappatoire *f*
escape valve N soupape *f* d'échappement
escape velocity N (*Space*) vitesse *f* de libération

escapee /ɪskeɪˈpiː/ N (*from prison*) évadé(e) *m(f)*

escapement /ɪsˈkeɪpmənt/ N [*of clock, piano*] échappement *m*

escapism /ɪsˈkeɪpɪzəm/ N envie *f* de fuir la réalité ◆ **it's sheer ~!** c'est simplement s'évader du réel !

escapist /ɪsˈkeɪpɪst/ N personne *f* qui fuit la réalité *or* qui se réfugie dans l'imaginaire ADJ [*film, reading etc*] d'évasion

escapologist /ˌeskəˈpɒlədʒɪst/ N (*lit*) virtuose *mf* de l'évasion ; (*fig*) champion(ne) *m(f)* de l'esquive

escarpment /ɪsˈkɑːpmənt/ N escarpement *m*

eschatology /ˌeskəˈtɒlədʒɪ/ N eschatologie *f*

eschew /ɪsˈtʃuː/ VT (*frm*) éviter ; [+ *wine etc*] s'abstenir de ; [+ *temptation*] fuir

escort /ˈeskɔːt/ N 1 (*Mil, Naut*) escorte *f* ; (= *guard of honour*) escorte *f*, cortège *m* ◆ **under the ~ of ...** sous l'escorte de ... ◆ **under ~** sous escorte 2 (*female*) hôtesse *f* ; (*male, at dance*) cavalier *m* ; (= *prostitute*) call-boy *m* VT /ɪsˈkɔːt/ (*Mil, Naut, gen*) escorter ; (= *accompany*) accompagner, escorter ◆ **to ~ sb in** (*Mil, Police*) faire entrer qn sous escorte ; (*gen*) (= *accompany*) faire entrer qn ◆ **to ~ sb out** (*Mil, Police*) faire sortir qn sous escorte ; (*gen*) raccompagner qn jusqu'à la sortie

COMP **escort agency** N agence *f* de rencontres
escort duty N ◆ **to be on ~ duty** [*soldiers*] être assigné au service d'escorte ; [*ship*] être en service d'escorte
escort vessel N (*Naut*) vaisseau *m* *or* bâtiment *m* d'escorte, (vaisseau *m*) escorteur *m*

escrow /ˈeskrəʊ/ N (*Jur*) dépôt *m* fiduciaire *or* conditionnel ◆ **in ~** en dépôt fiduciaire, en main tierce COMP **escrow account** N (*Fin*) compte *m* bloqué

escudo /esˈkuːdəʊ/ N (pl **escudos**) escudo *m*

escutcheon /ɪsˈkʌtʃən/ N (*Her*) écu *m*, écusson *m* ; → **blot**

ESF /ˌiːesˈef/ N (abbrev of **European Social Fund**) FSE *m*

esker /ˈeskəʳ/ N (*Geol*) os *m*

Eskimo /ˈeskɪməʊ/ N 1 Esquimau(de) *m(f)* 2 (= *language*) esquimau *m* ADJ esquimau(de) *f*, eskimo *inv* ◆ **~ dog** chien *m* esquimau

ESL /ˌiːesˈel/ N (*Educ*) (abbrev of **English as a Second Language**) → **English**

esophagus /ɪˈsɒfəgəs/ N (pl **esophaguses** *or* **esophagi** /ɪˈsɒfəˌdʒaɪ/) œsophage *m*

esoteric /ˌesəʊˈterɪk/ ADJ ésotérique

esoterica /ˌesəʊˈterɪkə/ NPL objets *mpl* ésotériques

ESP /ˌiːesˈpiː/ N 1 (abbrev of **extrasensory perception**) → **extrasensory** 2 (abbrev of **English for Special Purposes**) → **English**

esp. abbrev of **especially**

espadrille /ˌespəˈdrɪl/ N espadrille *f*

espalier /ɪˈspæljəʳ/ N (= *trellis*) treillage *m* d'un espalier ; (= *tree*) arbre *m* en espalier ; (= *method*) culture *f* en espalier VT cultiver en espalier

esparto /eˈspɑːtəʊ/ N (also **esparto grass**) alfa *m*

especial /ɪsˈpeʃəl/ ADJ particulier, spécial

especially /ɪsˈpeʃəlɪ/ LANGUAGE IN USE 26.3 ADV 1 (= *particularly*) surtout, en particulier ◆ **the garden is beautiful, ~ in summer** le jardin est beau, surtout en été ◆ **~ as** *or* **since it's so late** d'autant plus qu'il est tard ◆ **skincare becomes vitally important, ~ as we get older** les soins de la peau deviennent d'une importance vitale, surtout *or* en particulier quand on vieillit ◆ **he has mellowed considerably, ~ since he got married** il est beaucoup plus détendu, surtout depuis son mariage ◆ **more ~ as ...** d'autant plus que ... ◆ **you ~ ought to know** tu devrais le savoir mieux que personne ◆ **why me ~?** pourquoi moi en particulier ?
2 (= *expressly*) spécialement ◆ **I came ~ to see you** je suis venu spécialement pour te voir ◆ **to do sth ~ for sb/sth** faire qch spécialement pour qn/qch
3 (= *more than usual*) particulièrement ◆ **is she pretty? – not ~** elle est jolie ? – pas particulièrement *or* spécialement ◆ **read this passage ~ carefully** lisez ce passage avec un soin tout particulier

Esperantist /ˌespəˈræntɪst/ N espérantiste *mf*

Esperanto /ˌespəˈræntəʊ/ N espéranto *m* ADJ en espéranto

espionage /ˌespɪəˈnɑːʒ/ N espionnage *m*

esplanade /ˌespləˈneɪd/ N esplanade *f*

espousal /ɪˈspaʊzəl/ N [*of cause, values, theory*] adhésion *f* (*of* à)

espouse /ɪsˈpaʊz/ VT 1 [+ *cause, values, theory*] épouser, embrasser 2 (†† = *marry*) [+ *person*] épouser

espresso /esˈpresəʊ/ N (café *m*) express *m* COMP **espresso bar** N café *m* (*où l'on sert du café express*)

espy /ɪsˈpaɪ/ VT (*o.f or frm*) apercevoir, aviser (*frm*)

Esq. N (*Brit frm*) (abbrev of **esquire**) ◆ **Brian Smith ~** M. Brian Smith (*sur une enveloppe etc*)

esquire /ɪsˈkwaɪəʳ/ N 1 (*Brit: on envelope etc*) → **Esq.** 2 (*Brit Hist*) écuyer *m*

essay /ˈeseɪ/ N 1 (= *schoolwork*) rédaction *f* ; (*longer*) dissertation *f* ; (= *published work*) essai *m* ; (*US Univ*) mémoire *m* 2 (*liter* = *attempt*) essai *m* VT /eˈseɪ/ (*liter*) (= *try*) essayer, tenter (*to do sth* de faire qch) ; (= *test*) mettre à l'épreuve COMP **essay test** N (*US Educ*) épreuve *f* écrite

> ⚠ When it means a piece written by a student, **essay** is not translated by **essai**.

essayist /ˈeseɪɪst/ N essayiste *mf*

essence /ˈesəns/ N (*gen, Chem, Philos*) essence *f* ; (*Culin*) extrait *m* ◆ **the ~ of what was said** l'essentiel *m* de ce qui a été dit ◆ **the novel captures the ~ of life in the city** le roman rend l'essence de la vie dans la ville ◆ **the ~ of stupidity*** le comble de la stupidité ◆ **he embodies the very ~ of socialism** il incarne l'essence même du socialisme ◆ **the divine ~** l'essence *f* divine ◆ **speed/accuracy is of the ~** la vitesse/la précision est essentielle *or* s'impose ◆ **in ~** essentiellement COMP **essence of violets** N essence *f* de violette

essential /ɪˈsenʃəl/ LANGUAGE IN USE 10.1, 10.3 ADJ [*equipment, action*] essentiel, indispensable (*to* à) ; [*fact*] essentiel ; [*role, point*] capital, essentiel ; [*question*] essentiel, fondamental ; [*commodities*] essentiel, de première nécessité ; (*Chem*) essentiel ◆ **speed/accuracy is ~** la vitesse/la précision est essentielle ◆ **it is ~ to act quickly** il est indispensable *or* essentiel d'agir vite ◆ **it is ~ that ...** il est indispensable que ... + *subj* ◆ **it's not ~** ce n'est pas indispensable ◆ **the ~ thing is to act** l'essentiel est d'agir ◆ **man's ~ goodness** la bonté essentielle de l'homme
N qualité *f* (*or* objet *m etc*) indispensable ◆ **the ~s** l'essentiel *m* ◆ **in (all) ~s** pour l'essentiel, de manière générale ◆ **to see to the ~s** s'occuper de l'essentiel ◆ **accuracy is an ~** *or* **one of the ~s** la précision est une des qualités indispensables *or* est indispensable ◆ **the ~s of German grammar** (= *basics*) des notions *fpl* fondamentales de grammaire allemande
COMP **essential oil** N huile *f* essentielle

essentially /ɪˈsenʃəlɪ/ ADV [*correct, good, different*] essentiellement ◆ **it's ~ a landscape of rolling hills and moors** c'est essentiellement un paysage de collines ondulantes et de landes ◆ **she was ~ a generous person** au fond c'était quelqu'un de généreux ◆ **~, it is a story of ordinary people** c'est avant tout l'histoire de gens ordinaires ◆ **things will remain ~ the same** pour l'essentiel, les choses ne changeront pas

Essex Girl* /ˈesɪksgɜːl/ N (*Brit pej*) minette *f*

Essex Man* (pl **Essex Men** /ˌesɪksˈmæn/) N (*Brit pej*) beauf‡ *m*

EST /ˌiːesˈtiː/ (*US*) (abbrev of **Eastern Standard Time**) → **eastern**

est. 1 (*Comm etc*) (abbrev of **established**) ◆ **~ 1900** ≈ maison *f* fondée en 1900 2 abbrev of **estimate(d)**

establish /ɪsˈtæblɪʃ/ VT 1 (= *set up*) [+ *government*] constituer, mettre en place ; [+ *state, business*] fonder, créer ; [+ *factory*] implanter ; [+ *society, tribunal*] constituer ; [+ *laws, custom*] instaurer ; [+ *relations*] établir, nouer ; [+ *post*] créer ; [+ *power, authority*] asseoir ; [+ *peace, order*] faire régner ; [+ *list*] dresser, établir ; [+ *sb's reputation*] établir ◆ **to ~ one's reputation as a scholar/writer** se faire une réputation de savant/comme écrivain
◆ **to establish o.s.** s'imposer ◆ **he is aiming to ~ himself as the team's No. 1 goalkeeper** il cherche à s'imposer comme meilleur gardien de but de l'équipe ◆ **the company is eager to ~ itself internationally** la société cherche à s'imposer au plan international
2 (= *ascertain*) établir ; (= *show*) montrer, prouver ◆ **they are seeking to ~ the cause of death** ils cherchent à établir la cause du décès ◆ **these studies ~ed that smoking can cause cancer** ces études ont montré que le tabac peut provoquer des cancers
COMP **establishing shot** N (*Cine*) plan *m* de situation

> ⚠ Check the meaning and object of the verb **to establish** before translating it by **établir**.

established /ɪsˈtæblɪʃt/ ADJ [*order, authority, religion, tradition, company, reputation, truth*] établi ; [*clientele*] régulier ◆ **it's an ~ fact that ...** c'est un fait établi que ... ◆ **~ 1850** (*Comm*) ≈ maison fondée en 1850 ; see also **long¹** COMP **the Established Church** N (*Brit*) l'Église *f* anglicane

establishment /ɪsˈtæblɪʃmənt/ N 1 (*NonC* = *creation*) [*of organization, business, system, scheme, post*] création *f* ; [*of regime, custom*] instauration *f* ; [*of relations, reputation, identity, peace, order*] établissement *m* ; [*of tribunal*] constitution *f*
2 (*NonC* = *proving*) [*of innocence, guilt*] établissement *m*, preuve *f*
3 (= *institution, business*) établissement *m* ◆ **commercial/educational ~** établissement *m* commercial/scolaire ◆ **research ~** institut *m* de recherche ◆ **military ~** centre *m* militaire
4 (= *ruling class*) ◆ **the Establishment** l'establishment *m* ◆ **to be against the Establishment** être contre l'establishment ◆ **to join the Establishment** rejoindre l'establishment ◆ **a pillar of the French Establishment** un pilier de l'establishment français ◆ **the medical/political/religious ~** l'establishment *m* médical/politique/religieux
5 (*Mil, Naut* = *personnel*) effectif *m* ◆ **a peacetime ~ of 132,000 men** un effectif en temps de paix de 132 000 hommes ◆ **war ~** effectif *m* en temps de guerre
6 (*frm* = *household*) maisonnée *f* ◆ **to keep up a large ~** avoir un grand train de maison
ADJ ◆ **the ~ view of history** la vue de l'histoire selon l'establishment ◆ **~ figure** personnalité *f* de l'establishment

estate /ɪsˈteɪt/ N 1 (= *land*) propriété *f*, domaine *m* ; (*esp Brit*) (also **housing estate**) lotissement *m*, cité *f* ◆ **country ~** terre(s) *f(pl)* ; → **real**
2 (*Jur* = *possessions*) bien(s) *m(pl)* ; [*of deceased*] succession *f* ◆ **he left a large ~** il a laissé une grosse fortune (en héritage) ◆ **to liquidate the ~** liquider la succession
3 (= *order, rank, condition*) état *m* ◆ **the three ~s** les trois états ◆ **the third ~** le Tiers État, la bourgeoisie ◆ **the fourth ~** la presse, le quatrième pouvoir ◆ **a man of high/low ~** (*liter*) un homme de haut rang/de basse extraction ◆ **to grow to** *or* **reach man's ~** (*liter*) parvenir à l'âge d'homme, atteindre sa maturité
4 (*Brit*) ⇒ **estate car**
COMP **estate agency** N (*esp Brit*) agence *f* immobilière
estate agent N (*esp Brit*) agent *m* immobilier
estate car N (*Brit*) break *m*
estate duty, **estate tax** (*US*) N (*Jur*) droits *mpl* de succession

esteem /ɪsˈtiːm/ VT 1 (= *think highly of*) [+ *person*] avoir de l'estime pour, estimer ; [+ *quality*] apprécier ◆ **our (highly) ~ed colleague** notre (très) estimé collègue *or* confrère 2 (= *consider*) estimer, considérer ◆ **I ~ it an honour (that ...)** je m'estime très honoré (que ... + *subj*) ◆ **I ~ it an honour to do this** je considère comme un honneur de faire cela N estime *f*, considération *f* ◆ **to hold sb in high ~** tenir qn en haute estime, avoir une haute opinion de qn ◆ **to hold sth in high ~** avoir une haute opinion de qch ◆ **he went up/down in my ~** il est monté/a baissé dans mon estime

ester /ˈestə/ (*Chem*) N ester *m*

esthete /ˈiːsθiːt/ N ⇒ **aesthete**

Esthonia /esˈtəʊnɪə/ N ⇒ **Estonia**

estimable /ˈestɪməbl/ ADJ (*frm*) estimable, digne d'estime

estimate /ˈestɪmət/ N 1 estimation *f* ; (*Comm*) devis *m* ◆ **this figure is five times the original ~** ce chiffre est cinq fois supérieur à l'estimation initiale ◆ **at a conservative ~** au bas mot ◆ **the painting is worth $28 million at the lowest ~** le tableau vaut 28 millions de dollars au bas mot ◆ **give me an ~ for (building) a greenhouse** (*Comm*) donnez-moi *or* établissez-moi un devis pour la construction d'une serre ◆ **give me an ~ of what your trip will cost** donnez-moi une idée du coût de votre voyage ◆ **to form an ~ of sb's capabilities** évaluer les capacités de qn ◆ **his ~ of 400 people was very far out** il s'était trompé de beaucoup en évaluant le nombre de gens à 400 ◆ **this price is only a rough ~** ce prix n'est que très approximatif ◆ **at a rough** ~ approximativement ; → **preliminary**

[2] *(Admin, Pol)* **the ~s** le budget ◆ **the Army ~s** le budget de l'armée

VT /ˈestɪmeɪt/ estimer, juger *(that* que) ; *[+ cost, number, price, quantity]* estimer, évaluer ; *[+ distance, speed]* estimer, apprécier ◆ **his fortune is ~d at …** on évalue sa fortune à … ◆ **I ~ that there must be 40 of them** j'estime qu'il doit y en avoir 40, à mon avis il doit y en avoir 40

estimated /ˈestɪmeɪtɪd/ ADJ *[number, cost, figure]* estimé ◆ **an ~ 60,000 refugees have crossed the border** environ 60 000 réfugiés auraient traversé la frontière ◆ **~ time of arrival/departure** horaire *m* prévu d'arrivée/de départ ◆ **~ cost** coût *m* estimé

estimation /ˌestɪˈmeɪʃən/ N [1] jugement *m*, opinion *f* ◆ **in my ~** à mon avis, selon moi [2] *(= esteem)* estime *f*, considération *f* ◆ **he went up/down in my ~** il est monté/a baissé dans mon estime

estimator /ˈestɪmeɪtəʳ/ N expert *m (de compagnie d'assurances)*

Estonia /eˈstəʊnɪə/ N Estonie *f*

Estonian /eˈstəʊnɪən/ ADJ estonien N [1] Estonien(ne) *m(f)* [2] *(= language)* estonien *m*

estrange /ɪsˈtreɪndʒ/ VT brouiller *(from* avec) éloigner *(from* de) ◆ **to become ~d (from)** se brouiller (avec) ◆ **the ~d couple** le couple désuni ◆ **her ~d husband** son mari, dont elle est séparée

estrangement /ɪsˈtreɪndʒmənt/ N *[of people]* séparation *f (from sb* d'avec qn) ; *[of couple]* désunion *f* ; *[of countries]* brouille *f* ◆ **a feeling of ~** un sentiment d'éloignement ◆ **the ~ between the couple** la désunion du couple

estrogen /ˈestrədʒən, ˈiːstrədʒən/ N *(US)* ⇒ **oestrogen**

estrus /ˈiːstrəs/ N *(US)* ⇒ **oestrus**

estuary /ˈestjʊərɪ/ N estuaire *m* COMP **Estuary English** N *(Brit) façon de parler chez certaines personnes de la région de Londres, où les t, l et h ne se prononcent pas*

ET /iːˈtiː/ *(US)* (abbrev of **Eastern Time**) *heure sur la côte est*

ETA /ˌiːtiːˈeɪ/ N (abbrev of **estimated time of arrival**) → **estimated**

e-tail /ˈiːteɪl/ N commerce *m* électronique, e-commerce *m* COMP **e-tail site** N site *m* de commerce électronique *or* d'e-commerce

e-tailer /ˈiːteɪləʳ/ N détaillant *m* électronique

e-tailing /ˈiːteɪlɪŋ/ N commerce *m* de détail électronique ADJ ◆ **an ~ business** une entreprise de commerce électronique

et al /etˈæl/ (abbrev of **and others**) et autres

etc /ɪtˈsetərə/ (abbrev of **et cetera**) etc

et cetera, etcetera /ɪtˈsetərə/ ADV et caetera NPL **the etceteras** les extras *mpl*

etch /etʃ/ VTI *(Art, Typo)* graver à l'eau forte ◆ **~ed on his memory** gravé dans sa mémoire

etching /ˈetʃɪŋ/ N [1] *(NonC)* gravure *f* à l'eau-forte [2] *(= picture)* (gravure *f* à l')eau-forte *f* COMP **etching needle** N pointe *f* (sèche)

ETD /ˌiːtiːˈdiː/ N (abbrev of **estimated time of departure**) → **estimated**

eternal /ɪˈtɜːnl/ ADJ *[beauty, love, life, youth]* éternel ◆ **can't you stop this ~ quarrelling?** allez-vous cesser vos querelles perpétuelles ? ◆ **he was the ~ practical joker** c'était l'éternel farceur N ◆ **the Eternal** l'Éternel *m* COMP **the Eternal City** N la Ville éternelle **the eternal triangle** N l'éternel triangle *m* amoureux

eternally /ɪˈtɜːnəlɪ/ ADV [1] *(= everlastingly) [exist, be damned]* éternellement [2] *(= constantly) [grateful, optimistic, cheerful, young]* éternellement ◆ **he's ~ complaining** il est perpétuellement en train de se plaindre

eternity /ɪˈtɜːnɪtɪ/ N éternité *f* ◆ **it seemed like an ~ that we had to wait** nous avons eu l'impression d'attendre une éternité ◆ **we waited an ~*** nous avons attendu une éternité COMP **eternity ring** N *bague offerte en gage de fidélité*

ethane /ˈiːθeɪn/ N éthane *m*

ethanol /ˈeθənɒl/ N alcool *m* éthylique, éthanol *m*

ether /ˈiːθəʳ/ N *(Chem, Phys)* éther *m* ◆ **the ~** *(liter)* l'éther *m*, les espaces *mpl* célestes ◆ **over the ~** *(Rad)* sur les ondes

ethereal /ɪˈθɪərɪəl/ ADJ *(= delicate)* éthéré, aérien ; *(= spiritual)* éthéré, sublime

ethic /ˈeθɪk/ N morale *f*, éthique *f* ; → **work**

ethical /ˈeθɪkəl/ ADJ *(= moral)* éthique, moral ◆ **not ~** contraire à la morale COMP **ethical code** N *(Med)* code *m* déontologique, déontologie *f* **ethical drug** N médicament *m* sur ordonnance **ethical investment** N investissement *m* éthique

ethically /ˈeθɪklɪ/ ADV *[behave, act]* conformément à l'éthique ; *[sound, unacceptable, wrong]* sur le plan éthique, d'un point de vue éthique ; *[opposed]* d'un point de vue éthique

ethics /ˈeθɪks/ N *(NonC = study)* éthique *f*, morale *f* NPL *(= system, principles)* morale *f* ; *(= morality)* moralité *f* ◆ **medical ~** éthique *f* médicale, code *m* déontologique ; → **code**

Ethiopia /ˌiːθɪˈəʊpɪə/ N Éthiopie *f*

Ethiopian /ˌiːθɪˈəʊpɪən/ ADJ éthiopien N Éthiopien(ne) *m(f)*

ethnic /ˈeθnɪk/ ADJ [1] *(= racial) [origin, community, group, conflict, tension]* ethnique [2] *(= expatriate) [population]* d'ethnie différente ◆ **~ Germans** personnes *fpl* d'ethnie allemande [3] *(= non-Western) [music, food, jewellery]* exotique N *(esp US)* membre *m* d'une minorité ethnique COMP **ethnic cleansing** N *(euph)* purification *f* ethnique **ethnic minority** N minorité *f* ethnique

ethnically /ˈeθnɪklɪ/ ADV *[diverse, distinct, pure, clean, homogeneous, divided]* sur le plan ethnique ◆ **~ based republics** républiques *fpl* fondées sur l'origine ethnique *or* sur des critères ethniques ◆ **an ~ mixed country** un pays comprenant divers groupes ethniques ◆ **~ related violence** violences *fpl* ethniques ◆ **the town had been ~ cleansed** la ville avait subi une purification ethnique

ethnicity /eθˈnɪsɪtɪ/ N [1] *(NonC)* ethnicité *f* [2] *(= ethnic group)* ethnie *f*

ethnocentric /ˈeθnəʊˈsentrɪk/ ADJ ethnocentrique

ethnographer /eθˈnɒgrəfəʳ/ N ethnographe *mf*

ethnographic(al) /ˌeθnəˈgræfɪk(əl)/ ADV ethnographique

ethnography /eθˈnɒgrəfɪ/ N ethnographie *f*

ethnolinguistics /ˌeθnəʊlɪŋˈgwɪstɪks/ N *(NonC)* ethnolinguistique *f*

ethnologic(al) /ˌeθnəˈlɒdʒɪk(əl)/ ADJ ethnologique

ethnologist /eθˈnɒlədʒɪst/ N ethnologue *mf*

ethnology /eθˈnɒlədʒɪ/ N ethnologie *f*

ethologist /ɪˈθɒlədʒɪst/ N éthologue *mf*

ethology /ɪˈθɒlədʒɪ/ N éthologie *f*

ethos /ˈiːθɒs/ N philosophie *f* ◆ **the company/party ~** la philosophie de l'entreprise/du parti

ethyl /ˈiːθaɪl/ N éthyle *m* COMP **ethyl acetate** N acétate *m* d'éthyle

ethylene /ˈeθɪliːn/ N éthylène *m*

e-ticket /ˈiːtɪkɪt/ N billet *m* électronique (titre de transport acheté en ligne)

etiolated /ˈiːtɪəleɪtɪd/ ADJ *(Bot, fig frm)* étiolé

etiology /ˌiːtɪˈɒlədʒɪ/ N ⇒ **aetiology**

etiquette /ˈetɪket/ N étiquette *f*, convenances *fpl* ◆ **~ demands that …** les convenances exigent *or* l'étiquette exige que … + *subj* ◆ **diplomatic ~** protocole *m* ◆ **court ~** cérémonial *m* de cour ◆ **that isn't good ~** c'est contraire aux convenances, c'est un manquement à l'étiquette ◆ **it's against medical ~** c'est contraire à la déontologie médicale ◆ **it's not professional ~** c'est contraire aux usages de la profession

Etna /ˈetnə/ N (also **Mount Etna**) l'Etna *m*

Eton /ˈiːtən/ N *prestigieuse école anglaise* COMP **Eton crop** N coupe *f* à la garçonne

Etonian /iːˈtəʊnɪən/ *(Brit)* N *élève du collège d'Eton* ADJ du collège d'Eton

Etruria /ɪˈtrʊərɪə/ N Étrurie *f*

Etruscan /ɪˈtrʌskən/ ADJ étrusque N [1] *(= person)* Étrusque *mf* [2] *(= language)* étrusque *m*

ETV /ˌiːtiːˈviː/ N *(US)* (abbrev of **Educational Television**) → **educational**

etymological /ˌetɪməˈlɒdʒɪkəl/ ADJ étymologique

etymologically /ˌetɪməˈlɒdʒɪkəlɪ/ ADV étymologiquement

etymology /ˌetɪˈmɒlədʒɪ/ N étymologie *f*

EU /ˈiːˈjuː/ N (abbrev of **European Union**) UE *f*

eucalyptus /ˌjuːkəˈlɪptəs/ N (pl **eucalyptuses** *or* **eucalypti** /ˌjuːkəˈlɪptaɪ/) *(Bot, Pharm)* eucalyptus *m* COMP **eucalyptus oil** N huile *f* essentielle d'eucalyptus

Eucharist /ˈjuːkərɪst/ N Eucharistie *f*

Eucharistic /ˌjuːkəˈrɪstɪk/ ADJ eucharistique

euchre /ˈjuːkəʳ/ *(US)* N euchre *m (jeu de cartes)*

Euclid /ˈjuːklɪd/ N Euclide *m*

Euclidean /juːˈklɪdɪən/ ADJ euclidien

eugenic /juːˈdʒenɪk/ ADJ eugénique

eugenics /juːˈdʒenɪks/ N *(NonC)* eugénique *f*, eugénisme *m*

eulogistic /ˌjuːləˈdʒɪstɪk/ ADJ *(frm)* élogieux

eulogize /ˈjuːlədʒaɪz/ VT faire l'éloge *or* le panégyrique de VI faire l'éloge *or* le panégyrique *(about, over* de)

eulogy /ˈjuːlədʒɪ/ N *(gen)* panégyrique *m* ; *(at funeral service)* oraison *f or* éloge *m* funèbre

eunuch /ˈjuːnək/ N eunuque *m*

euphemism /ˈjuːfəmɪzəm/ N euphémisme *m (for* pour)

euphemistic /ˌjuːfəˈmɪstɪk/ ADJ euphémique

euphemistically /ˌjuːfəˈmɪstɪkəlɪ/ ADV euphémiquement, par euphémisme ◆ **~ described/known as …** décrit/connu par euphémisme comme …

euphonic /juːˈfɒnɪk/ ADJ euphonique

euphonium /juːˈfəʊnɪəm/ N euphonium *m*

euphonius /juːˈfəʊnɪəs/ ADJ ⇒ **euphonic**

euphony /ˈjuːfənɪ/ N euphonie *f*

euphorbia /juːˈfɔːbɪə/ N euphorbe *f*

euphoria /juːˈfɔːrɪə/ N euphorie *f*

euphoric /juːˈfɒrɪk/ ADJ euphorique

Euphrates /juːˈfreɪtiːz/ N Euphrate *m*

euphuism /ˈjuːfjuːɪzəm/ N préciosité *f*, euphuisme *m*

Eurasia /jʊəˈreɪʃə/ N Eurasie *f*

Eurasian /jʊəˈreɪʃn/ ADJ *[population]* eurasien ; *[continent]* eurasiatique N Eurasien(ne) *m(f)*

Euratom /jʊəˈrætəm/ N (abbrev of **European Atomic Energy Community**) Euratom *m*, CEEA *f*

eureka /jʊəˈriːkə/ EXCL eurêka !

eurhythmics /juːˈrɪðmɪks/ N *(NonC)* gymnastique *f* rythmique

Euripides /jʊˈrɪpɪdiːz/ N Euripide *m*

euro /ˈjʊərəʊ/ N *(= currency)* euro *m*

euro... /ˈjʊərəʊ/ PREF euro...

Eurobond /ˈjʊərəʊˌbɒnd/ N euro-obligation *f*

Eurocentric /ˌjʊərəʊˈsentrɪk/ ADJ eurocentrique

Eurocheque /ˈjʊərəʊˌtʃek/ N eurochèque *m* COMP **Eurocheque card** N carte *f* Eurochèque

Eurocommunism /ˈjʊərəʊˌkɒmjʊnɪzəm/ N eurocommunisme *m*

Eurocrat /ˈjʊərəʊˌkræt/ N eurocrate *mf*

Eurocurrency /ˈjʊərəʊˌkʌrənsɪ/ N eurodevise *f*

Eurodollar /ˈjʊərəʊˌdɒləʳ/ N eurodollar *m*

Euroland /ˈjʊərəʊlænd/ N Euroland *m*

Euromarket /ˈjʊərəʊˌmɑːkɪt/ N Communauté *f* économique européenne

Euro MP /ˌjʊərəʊemˈpiː/ N député(e) *m(f)* européen(ne)

Europe /ˈjʊərəp/ N Europe *f* ◆ **to go into ~, to join ~** *(Brit Pol)* entrer dans l'Union européenne

European /ˌjʊərəˈpiːən/ ADJ européen
N Européen(ne) *m(f)*
COMP **European Atomic Energy Community** N Communauté *f* européenne de l'énergie atomique
European Bank for Reconstruction and Development N Banque *f* européenne pour la reconstruction et le développement
European Coal and Steel Community N Communauté *f* européenne du charbon et de l'acier
European Commission N Commission *f* des communautés européennes
European Community N Communauté *f* européenne
European Court of Human Rights N Cour *f* européenne des droits de l'homme
European Court of Justice N Cour *f* de justice européenne *or* des communautés européennes
European Currency Unit N unité *f* de compte européenne, unité *f* monétaire européenne
European Defence Community N Communauté *f* européenne de défense
European Economic Community N Communauté *f* économique européenne
European Free Trade Association N Association *f* européenne de libre-échange
European Monetary System N Système *m* monétaire européen
European monetary union N Union *f* monétaire européenne
European Parliament N Parlement *m* européen
European plan N *(US: in hotel)* chambre *f* sans les repas
European Regional Development Fund N Fonds *m* européen de développement régional
European Social Fund N Fonds *m* social européen
European Space Agency N Agence *f* spatiale européenne
European standard N *(= industrial standard)* norme *f* européenne
European Union N Union *f* européenne

Europeanize /ˌjʊərəˈpɪəˈˌnaɪz/ VT européaniser

Europhile /ˈjʊərəʊfaɪl/ N, ADJ europhile *mf*

europium /jʊˈrəʊpɪəm/ N europium *m*

Europol /ˈjʊərəʊpɒl/ N Europol *m*

Eurosceptic /ˈjʊərəʊˌskeptɪk/ N eurosceptique *mf*

Euro-size /ˈjʊərəʊˌsaɪz/ N *(Comm)* ◆ **~ 1** modèle *m* E 1

Eurostar ® /ˈjʊərəʊˌstɑːʳ/ N Eurostar ® *m*

Eurosterling /ˈjʊərəʊˌstɜːlɪŋ/ N eurosterling *m*

Eurotunnel ® /ˈjʊərəʊˌtʌnl/ N Eurotunnel ® *m*

Eurovision /ˈjʊərəʊˌvɪʒən/ N Eurovision *f* COMP **Eurovision Song Contest** N Concours *m* Eurovision de la chanson

Eurozone /ˈjʊərəʊzəʊn/ N zone *f* euro

Eurydice /jʊˈrɪdɪsɪ/ N Eurydice *f*

Eustachian tube /juːˈsteɪʃəntjuːb/ N trompe *f* d'Eustache

eustatic /juːˈstætɪk/ ADJ eustatique

euthanasia /ˌjuːθəˈneɪzɪə/ N euthanasie *f* ; → **voluntary**

evacuate /ɪˈvækjʊeɪt/ VT *(all senses)* évacuer

evacuation /ɪˌvækjʊˈeɪʃən/ N évacuation *f*

evacuee /ɪˌvækjʊˈiː/ N évacué(e) *m(f)*

evade /ɪˈveɪd/ VT *[+ blow, difficulty]* esquiver, éviter ; *[+ pursuers]* échapper à, tromper ; *[+ obligation]* se soustraire à ; *[+ punishment]* échapper à, se soustraire à ; *[+ sb's gaze]* éviter ; *[+ question]* éluder ; *[+ law]* tourner, contourner ◆ **to ~ military service** se soustraire à ses obligations militaires ◆ **to ~ taxes/customs duty** frauder le fisc/la douane ◆ **happiness still ~d him** le bonheur continuait de lui échapper

> ⚠ In French, **s'évader** means 'to escape'.

evaluate /ɪˈvæljʊeɪt/ VT *[+ damages]* évaluer *(at* à) déterminer le montant de ; *[+ property, worth]* évaluer *(at* à) déterminer la valeur de ; *[+ effectiveness, usefulness]* mesurer ; *[+ evidence, reasons, argument]* peser, évaluer ; *[+ sb's work, performance]* évaluer ◆ **try to ~ the achievements of Victorian architects** *(in essay etc)* essayez d'évaluer l'apport des architectes de l'époque victorienne ◆ **the market situation is difficult to ~** les tendances du marché sont difficiles à apprécier

evaluation /ɪˌvæljʊˈeɪʃən/ N évaluation *f*

evaluative /ɪˈvæljʊətɪv/ ADJ *[criteria, research, report]* d'évaluation ◆ **~ judgement** *or* **assessment** évaluation *f*

evanescent /evəˈnesnt/ ADJ *(liter)* évanescent

evangelical /ˌiːvænˈdʒelɪkəl/ ADJ *(Rel)* évangélique ◆ **with ~ fervour** *(fig)* avec une verve de tribun N évangélique *mf*

evangelicalism /ˌiːvænˈdʒelɪkəlɪzəm/ N évangélisme *m*

evangelism /ɪˈvændʒəlɪzəm/ N évangélisation *f*

evangelist /ɪˈvændʒəlɪst/ N *(Bible)* évangéliste *m* ; *(= preacher)* évangélisateur *m*, -trice *f* ; *(= itinerant)* évangéliste *m*

evangelize /ɪˈvændʒəlaɪz/ VT évangéliser, prêcher l'Évangile à VI prêcher l'Évangile

evaporate /ɪˈvæpəreɪt/ VT *[+ liquid]* faire évaporer VI *[liquid]* s'évaporer ; *[hopes]* s'envoler ; *[dreams, fear, anger]* se dissiper COMP **evaporated milk** N lait *m* condensé non sucré

evaporation /ɪˌvæpəˈreɪʃən/ N évaporation *f*

evasion /ɪˈveɪʒən/ N dérobade *f* ◆ **an ~ of their moral duty to ...** une dérobade devant l'obligation morale de ... ◆ **they were angered by this ~ of responsibility** cette dérobade a provoqué leur colère ◆ **his testimony was full of contradictions and ~s** son témoignage était truffé de contradictions et de faux-fuyants ; → **tax**

> ⚠ The French word **évasion** means 'escape'.

evasive /ɪˈveɪzɪv/ ADJ *[person, answer]* évasif *(about sth* à propos de qch) ; *[eyes]* fuyant ◆ **to take ~ action** *(Mil)* user de manœuvres dilatoires ; *(gen)* esquiver *or* contourner la difficulté

evasively /ɪˈveɪzɪvlɪ/ ADV *[reply]* évasivement ; *[smile]* d'un air évasif

evasiveness /ɪˈveɪzɪvnɪs/ N manières *fpl* évasives

Eve /iːv/ N Ève *f*

eve¹ /iːv/ N veille *f* ; *(Rel)* vigile *f* ◆ **on the ~ of sth/of doing sth** *(lit, fig)* à la veille de qch/de faire qch ; → **Christmas**

eve² /iːv/ N *(liter = evening)* soir *m*

even¹ /ˈiːvən/ N ⇒ **eve²**

even² /ˈiːvən/ ADJ 1 *(= smooth, flat) [surface]* plat, plan ; *[ground]* plat ◆ **to make ~** égaliser ; → **keel**

2 *(= regular) [progress]* régulier ; *[temperature, breathing, step, temper, distribution]* égal ◆ **his work is not ~** son travail est inégal

3 *(= equal) [quantities, distances, values]* égal ◆ **our score is ~** nous sommes à égalité ◆ **they are an ~ match** *(Sport)* la partie est égale ; *(fig)* ils sont (bien) assortis ◆ **the odds** *or* **chances are about ~** *(fig)* les chances sont à peu près égales ◆ **I'll give you ~ money** *(esp Brit) or* **~ odds** *(US)* **that ...** il y a une chance sur deux pour que ... + *subj*

◆ **to get even** prendre sa revanche ◆ **this was my chance to get ~** c'était l'occasion ou jamais de prendre ma revanche ◆ **to get ~ with sb** rendre à qn la monnaie de sa pièce, rendre la pareille à qn ◆ **don't get mad, get ~** * inutile de se mettre en colère, il faut plutôt rendre la pareille ◆ **I'll get ~ with you for that** je te revaudrai ça

4 *(= calm) [voice, tones, temper]* égal

5 ◆ **~ number/date** nombre *m*/jour *m* pair

ADV même ◆ **~ in the holidays** même pendant les vacances ◆ **~ the most optimistic** même les plus optimistes ◆ **~ the guards were asleep** même les gardes dormaient ◆ **without ~ saying goodbye** sans même dire au revoir ◆ **I have ~ forgotten his name** j'ai oublié jusqu'à son nom, j'ai même oublié son nom ◆ **they ~ denied its existence** ils ont été jusqu'à nier *or* ils ont même nié son existence

◆ **even** + *comparative* encore ◆ **~ better** encore mieux ◆ **~ more easily** encore plus facilement ◆ **~ less money** encore moins d'argent

◆ *negative* + **even** même ◆ **he can't ~ swim** il ne sait même pas nager ◆ **not ~ his mother believed him** même sa mère ne le croyait pas

◆ **even if** même si + *indic* ◆ **~ if they lose this match they'll win the championship** même s'ils perdent ce match ils remporteront le championnat

◆ **even so** quand même ◆ **~ so he was disappointed** il a quand même *or* pourtant été déçu ◆ **yes but ~ so ...** oui mais quand même ...

◆ **and even then** et malgré tout ◆ **we made maximum concessions and ~ then nothing materialised** nous avons fait le maximum de concessions et malgré tout il n'y a rien eu de concret ◆ **... and ~ then she wasn't happy ...** mais elle n'était toujours pas contente

◆ **even though** bien que + *subj* ◆ **~ though I am not shy, I felt self-conscious** bien que je ne sois pas timide, je me sentais mal à l'aise ◆ **living standards improved, ~ though they remained far lower than in neighbouring countries** le niveau de vie augmentait, mais il restait pourtant bien plus bas que dans les pays voisins

♦ **even as** *(liter)* *(= exactly when)* alors même que ♦ **~ as he spoke, the door opened** alors même qu'il disait cela, la porte s'ouvrit
VT *[+ surface]* égaliser
NPL **evens** *(esp Brit)* ♦ **the bookmakers are offering ~s** les bookmakers le donnent un contre un
COMP **evens favourite** N *(esp Brit)* favori *m* à un contre un
even-handed ADJ impartial, équitable
even-handedly ADV impartialement, équitablement
even-handedness N impartialité *f*, équité *f*
even-steven * ADV *[divide]* en deux (parts égales) ADJ *(= quits)* quitte *(with* avec) ♦ **it's ~-steven** * **whether we go or stay** peut-être qu'on partira, peut-être qu'on restera
even-tempered ADJ d'humeur égale, placide
► **even out** VT SEP *[+ burden, taxation]* répartir *or* distribuer plus également *(among* entre) ; *[+ prices]* égaliser
► **even up** VT SEP égaliser ♦ **that will ~ things up** cela rétablira l'équilibre ; *(financially)* cela compensera

evening /ˈiːvnɪŋ/ N soir *m* ; *(length of time)* soirée *f* ♦ **all ~** toute la soirée ♦ **every ~** tous les soirs, chaque soir ♦ **every Monday ~** tous les lundis soir(s) ♦ **the previous ~** la veille au soir ♦ **that ~** ce soir-là ♦ **this ~** ce soir ♦ **tomorrow ~** demain soir ♦ **one fine summer ~** (par) une belle soirée d'été ♦ **the warm summer ~s** les chaudes soirées d'été ♦ **a long winter ~** une longue soirée d'hiver ♦ **in the ~(s)** le soir ♦ **to go out in the ~** sortir le soir ♦ **6 o'clock in the ~** 6 heures du soir ♦ **in the ~ of life** *(liter)* au soir de la vie ♦ **on the ~ of his birthday** le soir de son anniversaire ♦ **on the ~ of the next day** le lendemain soir ♦ **on the ~ of the twenty-ninth** le vingt-neuf au soir ♦ **to spend one's ~ reading** passer sa soirée à lire ♦ **let's have an ~ out** *(tonight)* si on sortait ce soir ? ; *(some time)* nous devrions sortir un de ces soirs ♦ **it's her ~ out** c'est le soir où elle sort ; → **good**
COMP **evening class** N cours *m* du soir
evening dress N *[of man]* tenue *f* de soirée, habit *m* ; *[of woman]* robe *f* du soir ♦ **in ~ dress** *(man)* en tenue de soirée ; *(woman)* en robe du soir
evening fixture, evening match N *(Sport)* (match *m* en) nocturne *f*
evening paper N journal *m* du soir
evening performance N (représentation *f* en) soirée *f*
evening prayer(s) N(PL) office *m* du soir
evening primrose oil N huile *f* d'onagre
evening service N *(Rel)* service *m* (religieux) du soir
evening star N étoile *f* du berger

evenly /ˈiːvənlɪ/ ADV 1 *(= equally)* *[distribute]* également ; *[mix]* de façon homogène ; *(= steadily)* *[breathe, beat, flow]* régulièrement ♦ **to divide/split sth ~** diviser/répartir qch en parts égales ♦ **~ matched** de force égale ♦ **~ spaced** à intervalles réguliers ♦ **an ~ grey sky** un ciel uniformément gris ♦ **keep your weight ~ balanced** répartissez bien votre poids ♦ **spread the butter ~** étalez le beurre uniformément ♦ **the cuts were ~ spread throughout the various departments** les réductions budgétaires ont été réparties uniformément entre les divers services 2 *(= calmly)* *[say, ask, reply]* d'une voix égale ; *[watch]* d'un air égal

evenness /ˈiːvənnɪs/ N *[of movements, performance]* régularité *f* ; *[of ground]* caractère *m* plan, planéité *f* ♦ **~ of temper** égalité *f* d'humeur

evensong /ˈiːvənsɒŋ/ N *(Rel)* vêpres *fpl*, office *m* du soir *(de l'Église anglicane)*

event /ɪˈvent/ N 1 *(= happening)* événement *m* ♦ **course of ~s** (déroulement *m* des) événements *mpl* ♦ **in the course of ~s** par la suite ♦ **in the normal** *or* **ordinary course of ~s** normalement ♦ **after the ~** après coup ♦ **it's quite an ~** c'est un (véritable) événement ♦ **a new book by Tyler is always an ~** un nouveau roman de Tyler est toujours un événement ♦ **Easter is a major ~ in the Philippines** Pâques est une fête très importante aux Philippines ♦ **an exam, or even a social ~ makes me nervous** les examens, ou même une sortie, sont sources d'angoisse ; → **happy**
2 *(= public occasion)* manifestation *f* ♦ **an exciting programme of ~s** un calendrier de manifestations très intéressant
3 *(= case)* cas *m* ♦ **in that ~** dans ce cas ♦ **in any ~** en tout cas, de toute façon ♦ **in either ~** dans l'un ou l'autre cas
♦ **in the event** *(Brit)* en fait, en l'occurrence ♦ **the meeting was scheduled to last one hour, in the ~ it lasted four** la réunion devait durer une heure, mais en l'occurrence *or* en fait elle en a duré quatre
♦ **in the event of** en cas de ♦ **in the ~ of death** en cas de décès ♦ **in the ~ of his failing** *(frm)* au cas où il échouerait ♦ **in the ~ of default** *(Jur)* en cas de défaillance *or* de manquement
♦ **in the event that** dans l'hypothèse où, dans le cas où ♦ **in the unlikely ~ that ...** dans l'hypothèse *or* dans le cas improbable où ...
4 *(Sport)* épreuve *f* ; *(Racing)* course *f* ♦ **field ~s** lancers *mpl* et sauts *mpl* ♦ **track ~s** épreuves *fpl* sur piste ♦ **a major sporting ~** une date très importante du calendrier sportif ; → **three**
COMP **event horizon** N *(Astron)* horizon *m* des événements

eventer /ɪˈventəʳ/ N *(Horse-riding)* participant(e) *m(f)* à un concours complet

eventful /ɪˈventfʊl/ ADJ *[life, day, period, journey]* mouvementé, fertile en événements

eventide /ˈiːvəntaɪd/ N *(liter)* tombée *f* du jour, soir *m* COMP **eventide home** N maison *f* de retraite

eventing /ɪˈventɪŋ/ N *(Horse-riding)* concours *m* complet

eventual /ɪˈventʃʊəl/ ADJ *(= ultimate)* *[aim]* ultime ; *[result]* final ♦ **whatever the ~ outcome ...** quel que soit le résultat final ... ♦ **the project is doomed to ~ failure** le projet est voué à l'échec ♦ **the ~ winner of the election** le candidat qui a finalement remporté les élections ♦ **he lost in the semi-final to the ~ winner, McCormack** il a perdu en demi-finale contre McCormack, qui a fini par gagner le tournoi ♦ **it resulted in the ~ disappearance of ...** cela a abouti finalement à la disparition de ...

⚠ Be careful not to translate **eventual** by **éventuel**, which means 'possible'.

eventuality /ɪˌventʃʊˈælɪtɪ/ N éventualité *f*

eventually /ɪˈventʃʊəlɪ/ ADV 1 *(= finally)* finalement ♦ **he'll do it ~** il finira par le faire ♦ **he ~ became Prime Minister** il est finalement devenu *or* il a fini par devenir Premier ministre ♦ **he ~ agreed that she was right** il a fini par admettre qu'elle avait raison 2 *(= ultimately)* un jour ♦ **~ your child will leave home** un jour votre enfant quittera la maison

⚠ Be careful not to translate **eventually** by **éventuellement**, which means 'possibly'.

eventuate /ɪˈventʃʊˌeɪt/ VI *(US)* (finir par) se produire ♦ **to ~ in ...** se terminer par ...

ever /ˈevəʳ/ ADV 1 *(= at any time)* jamais ; *(in questions)* jamais, déjà ♦ **nothing ~ happens** il ne se passe jamais rien ♦ **if you ~ see her** si jamais vous la voyez ♦ **I haven't ~ seen her** je ne l'ai jamais vue ♦ **you won't see him ~ again** tu ne le reverras (plus) jamais ♦ **do you ~ see her? est-ce qu'il vous arrive de la voir ?** ♦ **have you ~ seen her?** l'avez-vous déjà vue ? ♦ **have you ~ seen anything like it?, did you ~ see the like?** avez-vous jamais vu une chose pareille ? ♦ **did you ~!** * a-t-on jamais vu cela ?, (ça) par exemple !
♦ **if ever** ♦ **we seldom if ~ go** nous n'y allons pour ainsi dire jamais ♦ **now if ~ is the moment to do this** c'est le moment ou jamais de faire cela ♦ **he's a liar if ~ there was one** c'est le dernier des menteurs
♦ **never, ever** * ♦ **I can never, ~ forgive myself** jamais au grand jamais je ne me le pardonnerai
♦ *comparative* + **than ever** ♦ **more beautiful than ~** plus beau que jamais ♦ **faster than ~** plus vite que jamais
♦ *superlative* + **ever** ♦ **the best meal I have ~ eaten** le meilleur repas que j'aie jamais fait ♦ **the best grandmother ~** la meilleure grand-mère du monde ♦ **it remains the best album ~ for many fans** pour beaucoup de fans c'est toujours le meilleur album de tous ♦ **the coldest night ~** la nuit la plus froide qu'on ait jamais connue
2 *(= always)* toujours, sans cesse ♦ **he was ~ ready to check his facts** il était toujours disposé à vérifier ses informations ♦ **mother, ~ the optimist, tried to look on the bright side** maman, toujours optimiste, essayait de voir le bon côté des choses ♦ **the danger is ~ present** le danger est toujours là ♦ **her ~ present anxiety** son angoisse constante *or* de tous les instants ♦ **all he ~ does is sleep** il ne fait que dormir, tout ce qu'il sait faire c'est dormir
♦ **ever after** ♦ **~ after, their affection will be tinged with anxiety** dorénavant, leur affection sera toujours mêlée d'inquiétude ♦ **they lived happily ~ after** ils vécurent (toujours) heureux
♦ **ever since** depuis ♦ **~ since I was a boy** depuis mon enfance ♦ **~ since I have lived here** depuis que j'habite ici ♦ **~ since (then) they have been very careful** depuis (lors) *or* depuis ce moment-là ils sont très prudents
♦ **ever and anon** († , *liter*) de temps à autre, parfois
♦ **as ever** comme toujours ♦ **he was, as ~, totally alone** il était tout seul, comme toujours
♦ **yours ever** *(Brit: in letters)* amical souvenir, cordialement (à vous)
3 *(= constantly)* de plus en plus ♦ **they grew ~ further apart** ils s'éloignèrent de plus en plus l'un de l'autre ♦ **~ increasing anxiety** inquiétude *f* croissante ♦ **the government is coming under ~ increasing pressure** le gouvernement est soumis à des pressions de plus en plus importantes
4 *(intensive)* **as quickly as ~ you can** aussi vite que vous le pourrez ♦ **the first ~** le tout premier ♦ **as if I ~ would!** *(esp Brit)* moi, faire ça ! ♦ **why ~ didn't you tell me?** pourquoi donc *or* pourquoi diable ne m'en as-tu pas parlé ? ♦ **why ~ not?** mais enfin, pourquoi pas ?, pourquoi pas, Grand Dieu ? ♦ **where ~ can he have got to?** † où a-t-il bien pu passer ?
♦ **ever so** * *(Brit)* *(= very)* ♦ **~ so slightly drunk** (un) tant soit peu ivre ♦ **~ so pretty** joli comme tout ♦ **he is ~ so nice** il est tout ce qu'il y a de plus gentil ♦ **I'm ~ so sorry** je regrette infiniment, je suis (vraiment) désolé ♦ **thank you ~ so much, thanks ~ so** * merci mille fois, merci bien ♦ **she is ~ so much prettier than her sister** elle est autrement plus jolie que sa sœur
♦ **ever such** *(Brit)* ♦ **it's ~ such a pity** c'est vraiment dommage

Everest /ˈevərɪst/ N ♦ **(Mount) ~** mont *m* Everest, Everest *m*

everglade /ˈevəgleɪd/ N *(US)* terres *fpl* marécageuses

Everglades /ˈevəgleɪdz/ N Everglades *mpl*

evergreen /ˈevəgriːn/ ADJ 1 *[tree, shrub]* vert, à feuilles persistantes 2 *(fig) [song]* qui ne vieillit pas ; *[subject of conversation]* qui revient toujours N 1 *(= tree)* arbre *m* vert *or* à feuilles persistantes ; *(= plant)* plante *f* à feuilles persistantes 2 *(fig = song etc)* chanson *f etc* qui ne vieillit pas 3 *(US)* crédit *m* permanent non confirmé
COMP **evergreen oak** N yeuse *f*, chêne *m* vert
the Evergreen State N *(US)* l'État *m* de Washington

everlasting /ˌevəˈlɑːstɪŋ/ ADJ *(God)* éternel ; *[gratitude, mercy]* infini, éternel ; *[fame, glory]* éternel, immortel ; *[materials]* inusable, qui ne s'use pas COMP **everlasting flower** N immortelle *f*

everlastingly /ˌevəˈlɑːstɪŋlɪ/ ADV éternellement

evermore /ˌevəˈmɔːʳ/ ADV toujours ◆ **for ~** à tout jamais

every /ˈevrɪ/ ADJ 1 *(= each)* tout, chaque, tous *(or* toutes) les ◆ **~ shop in the town** tous les magasins *or* chaque magasin de la ville ◆ **not ~ child has the same advantages** les enfants n'ont pas tous les mêmes avantages ◆ **not ~ child has the advantages you have** tous les enfants n'ont pas les avantages que tu as ◆ **he spends ~ penny he earns** il dépense tout ce qu'il gagne (jusqu'au dernier sou) ◆ **~ child had brought something** chaque enfant avait apporté quelque chose ◆ **~ movement causes him pain** chaque *or* tout mouvement lui fait mal ◆ **from ~ country** de tous (les) pays ◆ **at ~ moment** à tout moment, à chaque instant ◆ **at ~ opportunity** à chaque occasion ◆ **of ~ sort** de toute sorte ◆ **from ~ side** de toute part ◆ **of ~ age** de tout âge ◆ **he became weaker ~ day** il devenait chaque jour plus faible *or* plus faible de jour en jour

2 *(for emphasis)* ◆ **I have ~ confidence in him** j'ai pleine confiance en lui ◆ **there is ~ chance that he will come** il y a toutes les chances qu'il vienne ◆ **you have ~ reason to complain** vous avez tout lieu de vous plaindre ◆ **I have ~ reason to think that ...** j'ai toutes les raisons de penser que ..., j'ai tout lieu de penser que ... ◆ **there was ~ prospect of success** tout laissait augurer d'un succès

3 *(showing recurrence)* tout ◆ **~ fifth day, ~ five days** tous les cinq jours, un jour sur cinq ◆ **one man in ~ ten** un homme sur dix ◆ **~ quarter of an hour** tous les quarts d'heure ◆ **~ few days** tous les deux ou trois jours ◆ **once ~ week** une fois par semaine ◆ **~ 15 metres** tous les 15 mètres

◆ **every other ..., every second ...** ◆ **~ other** *or* **second child** un enfant sur deux ◆ **~ other** *or* **second day** tous les deux jours, un jour sur deux ◆ **~ other Wednesday** un mercredi sur deux ◆ **to write on ~ other line** écrire en sautant une ligne sur deux

4 *(after poss)* tout, chacun, moindre ◆ **his ~ action** chacune de ses actions, tout ce qu'il faisait ◆ **his ~ wish** son moindre désir, tous ses désirs

5 *(in phrases)* **~ little helps** *(Prov)* les petits ruisseaux font les grandes rivières *(Prov)* ◆ **~ man for himself (and the devil take the hindmost)** chacun pour soi ; *(= save yourself)* sauve qui peut ! ◆ **~ man to his trade** à chacun son métier ◆ **in ~ way** *(= from every point of view)* à tous (les) égards, en tous points ; *(= by every means)* par tous les moyens ; → **bit**[1]

◆ **every bit as ...** tout aussi ... ◆ **he is ~ bit as clever as his brother** il est tout aussi intelligent que son frère ◆ **he is ~ bit as much of a liar as his brother** il est tout aussi menteur que son frère

◆ **every last ...** ◆ **~ last biscuit/chocolate** *etc* tous les biscuits/chocolats *etc* jusqu'au dernier ◆ **they drank ~ last drop of wine** ils ont bu tout le vin jusqu'à la dernière goutte

◆ **every now and then, every now and again** de temps en temps, de temps à autre

◆ **every (single) one** ◆ **you must examine ~ one** il faut les examiner tous, sans exception ◆ **~ single one of these peaches is bad** toutes ces pêches sans exception sont pourries ◆ **~ one of us is afraid of something** tous autant que nous sommes nous craignons quelque chose ◆ **~ one of them was there** ils étaient tous là ◆ **~ (single) one of them** chacun d'eux, tous, sans exception ◆ **~ one of them had brought something** chacun d'entre eux avait apporté quelque chose, ils avaient tous apporté quelque chose

◆ **every so often** de temps en temps, de temps à autre

◆ **every + time** chaque fois ◆ **~ time (that) I see him** chaque fois que je le vois ◆ **~ single time** chaque fois sans exception ◆ **her cakes are perfect ~ time** ses gâteaux sont parfaitement réussis à chaque fois ◆ **give me Paris ~ time!** * c'est Paris sans hésiter !

everybody /ˈevrɪbɒdɪ/ PRON tout le monde, chacun ◆ **~ has finished** tout le monde a fini ◆ **~ has his** *or* **their own ideas about it** chacun a ses idées là-dessus ◆ **~ else** tous les autres ◆ **~ knows ~ else here** tout le monde se connaît ici ◆ **~ knows that** tout le monde *or* n'importe qui sait cela ◆ **~ who is anybody** tous les gens qui comptent

everyday /ˈevrɪdeɪ/ ADJ *[thing, clothes, object, world]* de tous les jours ; *[situation, language]* courant ; *[activity, task, life]* de tous les jours, quotidien ; *[occurrence, problem]* quotidien ◆ **fabrics for ~ use** des tissus *mpl* pour tous les jours ◆ **it's too expensive for ~ use** c'est trop cher pour un usage courant ◆ **words in ~ use** mots *mpl* d'usage courant ◆ **~ people** gens *mpl* ordinaires

everyman /ˈevrɪmæn/ N Monsieur *m* tout-le-monde

everyone /ˈevrɪwʌn/ PRON ⇒ **everybody**

everyplace /ˈevrɪpleɪs/ ADV *(US)* ⇒ **everywhere**

everything /ˈevrɪθɪŋ/ PRON tout ◆ **~ is ready** tout est prêt ◆ **~ you have** tout ce que vous avez ◆ **stamina is ~** l'endurance compte plus que tout, l'essentiel c'est l'endurance ◆ **success isn't ~** le succès n'est pas tout ◆ **and ~ (like that)** * et tout et tout *

everywhere /ˈevrɪweəʳ/ ADV partout ◆ **~ in the world** partout dans le monde, dans le monde entier ◆ **~ you go you meet the British** où qu'on aille *or* partout où l'on va, on rencontre des Britanniques

evict /ɪˈvɪkt/ VT *(from house, lodgings, meeting)* expulser

eviction /ɪˈvɪkʃən/ N expulsion *f* COMP **eviction order** N mandat *m* d'expulsion

evidence /ˈevɪdəns/ N *(NonC)* 1 *(= testimony)* témoignage *m* ◆ **the clearest possible ~** la preuve manifeste ◆ **the ~ of the senses** le témoignage des sens ◆ **on the ~ of this document** à en croire ce document ◆ **there is no ~ to support this theory** cette théorie n'est étayée par aucun élément solide ◆ **there is no ~ to suggest a link between the two conditions** rien ne permet d'affirmer qu'il existe un lien entre les deux maladies

2 *(Jur) (= data)* preuve *f* ; *(= testimony)* témoignage *m*, déposition *f* ◆ **to give ~** témoigner, déposer ◆ **to give ~ for/against sb** témoigner *or* déposer en faveur de/contre qn ◆ **to call sb to give ~** convoquer qn pour qu'il témoigne ◆ **to take sb's ~** recueillir la déposition de qn ◆ **there isn't enough ~ to charge her** il n'y a pas assez de preuves pour l'inculper ◆ **to turn King's** *or* **Queen's ~** *(Brit)*, **to turn State's ~** *(US)* témoigner contre ses complices

3 *(= indication)* signe *m*, marque *f* ◆ **there is ~ of widespread fraud** il y a lieu de penser que la fraude est répandue ◆ **to show ~ of** *[+ impatience, worry]* donner des signes de ; *[+ bombing, erosion]* porter les traces de ◆ **his kidneys showed ~ of infection** on a trouvé dans ses reins des signes d'infection ◆ **his features bore ~ of the agony he had endured** ses traits étaient marqués par les épreuves qu'il avait subies ◆ **there was no ~ of the security forces on the streets** il n'y avait aucun signe de la présence dans la rue des forces de sécurité

4 *(set structure)*

◆ **in evidence** *[object]* en évidence ◆ **his father was nowhere in ~** il n'y avait aucune trace de son père ◆ **few soldiers were in ~** on rencontrait *or* voyait peu de soldats ◆ **poverty is still very much in ~** on voit encore beaucoup de gens pauvres ◆ **a man very much in ~ at the moment** un homme très en vue à l'heure actuelle ◆ **whatever you say may be held in ~ against you** tout ce que vous direz pourra être retenu contre vous

VT manifester, témoigner de

> ⚠ **evidence** is rarely translated by the French word **évidence**, which does not mean 'proof'.

evident /ˈevɪdənt/ ADJ évident ◆ **that is very ~** c'est l'évidence même ◆ **we must help her, that's ~** il fait l'aider, c'est évident *or* cela va de soi ◆ **he's guilty, that's ~** il est coupable, c'est évident *or* cela saute aux yeux ◆ **it was ~ from the way he walked** cela se voyait à sa démarche ◆ **it is ~ from his speech that ...** il ressort de son discours que ...

evidently /ˈevɪdəntlɪ/ LANGUAGE IN USE 15.1 ADV 1 *(= apparently)* apparemment ◆ **~ he feared I was going to refuse** il craignait apparemment que je refuse ◆ **was it suicide? – ~ not** était-ce un suicide ? – apparemment non ◆ **are they going too? – ~** ils y vont aussi ? – apparemment oui 2 *(= obviously)* manifestement, de toute évidence ◆ **they ~ knew each other** manifestement *or* de toute évidence, ils se connaissaient ◆ **that is ~ not the case** ce n'est manifestement pas le cas ◆ **~, such men are usually extremely wealthy** évidemment, de tels hommes sont généralement extrêmement riches

evil /ˈiːvl/ ADJ *[person]* méchant, malfaisant ; *[deed, practice, system, consequence, influence]* néfaste ; *[power]* malfaisant ; *[place]* maléfique ; *[spell, reputation]* mauvais ; *[smell]* infect ◆ **to have an ~ tongue** *[person]* être mauvaise langue ◆ **he had his ~ way with her** *(hum)* il est arrivé à ses fins avec elle ◆ **to have an ~ temper** avoir un sale caractère ◆ **(to put off) the ~ day** *or* **hour** (remettre à plus tard) le moment fatidique

N mal *m* ◆ **the powers** *or* **forces of ~** les forces *fpl* du mal ◆ **to wish sb ~** vouloir du mal à qn ◆ **to speak ~ of sb** dire du mal de qn ◆ **of two ~s one must choose the lesser** de deux maux, il faut choisir le moindre ◆ **it's the lesser ~** c'est le moindre mal ◆ **social ~s** maux *mpl* sociaux ◆ **the ~s of drink** les conséquences *fpl* funestes de la boisson ◆ **one of the great ~s of our time** un des grands fléaux de notre temps

COMP **the evil eye** N le mauvais œil ◆ **to give sb the ~ eye** jeter le mauvais œil à qn
evil-minded ADJ malveillant, mal intentionné
the Evil One N le Malin
evil-smelling ADJ nauséabond
evil spirit N esprit *m* malfaisant

evildoer /ˌiːvlˈduːəʳ/ N personnage *m* infâme

evilly /ˈiːvɪlɪ/ ADV avec malveillance

evince /ɪˈvɪns/ VT *(frm) [+ surprise, desire]* manifester ; *[+ qualities, talents]* faire preuve de

eviscerate /ɪˈvɪsəreɪt/ VT *(frm)* éventrer, éviscérer

evocation /ˌevəˈkeɪʃən/ N évocation *f*

evocative /ɪˈvɒkətɪv/ ADJ [1] *(= reminiscent) [name, description, memory, atmosphere, scent]* évocateur (-trice *f*) ◆ **to be ~ of sth** évoquer qch [2] *(Occultism) [incantation, magic]* évocatoire

evocatively /ɪˈvɒkətɪvlɪ/ ADV *[describe]* dans un style évocateur ◆ **~ named cocktails** des cocktails aux noms évocateurs ◆ **the ~ named "Valley of the Moon"** le lieu portant le nom évocateur de « la Vallée de la Lune »

evoke /ɪˈvəʊk/ VT *[+ spirit, memories]* évoquer ; *[+ admiration]* susciter

evolution /ˌiːvəˈluːʃən/ N [1] *(Bio, Zool etc)* évolution *f (from* à partir de) ; *[of language, events]* évolution *f* ; *[of culture, technology, machine]* évolution *f*, développement *m* [2] *[of troops, skaters etc]* évolutions *fpl*

evolutionary /ˌiːvəˈluːʃnərɪ/ ADJ *(Bio, Zool etc)* évolutionniste ; *(gen) [stage, process]* d'évolution

evolutionism /ˌiːvəˈluːʃənɪzəm/ N évolutionnisme *m*

evolutionist /ˌiːvəˈluːʃənɪst/ ADJ, N évolutionniste *mf*

evolve /ɪˈvɒlv/ VT *[+ system, theory, plan]* élaborer, développer VI *(gen, Bio)* évoluer ◆ **to ~ from** se développer à partir de

e-voting /ˈiːvəʊtɪŋ/ N vote *m* électronique

ewe /juː/ N brebis *f* COMP **ewe lamb** N agnelle *f*

ewer /ˈjuːəʳ/ N aiguière *f*

ex /eks/ PREP *(Comm)* ≈ départ, sortie ◆ **price ~ factory, price ~ works** *(Brit)* prix *m* départ *or* sortie usine ◆ **price ~ warehouse** prix *m* départ *or* sortie entrepôt ; → **ex dividend, ex officio** N * *(= ex-wife etc)* ex * *mf*

ex- /eks/ PREF ex-, ancien ◆ **ex-chairman** ancien président *m*, ex-président *m* ◆ **he's my ex-boss** c'est mon ancien patron ; → **ex-husband, ex-service**

exacerbate /ɪgˈzæsəˌbeɪt, ɪkˈsæsəˌbeɪt/ VT *[+ problem, situation]* aggraver ; *[+ pain, disease, hatred]* exacerber

exact /ɪgˈzækt/ ADJ [1] *(= precise) [number, amount, cause, time, translation, details]* exact ; *[copy]* conforme à l'original, exact ◆ **to be ~ about sth** *[person]* préciser qch ◆ **can you be more ~?** pouvez-vous préciser un peu ? ◆ **can you be more ~ about how many came?** pouvez-vous préciser le nombre des gens qui sont venus ? ◆ **he's 44, to be ~** il a 44 ans, pour être précis ◆ **he gave ~ instructions as to what had to be done** il a donné des instructions précises sur ce qu'il fallait faire ◆ **what were his ~ instructions?** quelles étaient ses instructions exactes ? ◆ **to be an ~ likeness of sb/sth** ressembler parfaitement à qn/qch ◆ **until this ~ moment** jusqu'à ce moment précis ◆ **to be the ~ opposite of sb/sth** être aux antipodes *or* tout le contraire de qn/qch ◆ **the ~ same thing*** exactement la même chose ◆ **these were his ~ words** c'est ce qu'il a dit, mot pour mot

[2] *(= meticulous) [person, study, work]* méticuleux ; *[analysis, instrument]* précis

VT *[+ money, obedience etc]* exiger *(from* de) ◆ **to ~ revenge** se venger ◆ **to ~ a high price for sth** faire payer qch cher

COMP **exact science** N science *f* exacte

exacting /ɪgˈzæktɪŋ/ ADJ *[person]* exigeant ; *[task, activity, profession, work]* astreignant, qui exige beaucoup d'attention

exaction /ɪgˈzækʃən/ N *(= act)* exaction *f (pej)* ; *(= money exacted)* impôt *m*, contribution *f* ; *(= excessive demand)* extorsion *f*

exactitude /ɪgˈzæktɪtjuːd/ N exactitude *f*

exactly /ɪgˈzæktlɪ/ LANGUAGE IN USE 11.2, 16.1 ADV *(= precisely) [match, imitate]* exactement ◆ **to look ~ like sb** ressembler trait pour trait à qn, être tout le portrait de qn ◆ **I wanted to get things ~ right** je voulais que tout soit parfait ◆ **at ~ 5 o'clock** à 5 heures pile *or* précises ◆ **it is 3 o'clock ~** il est 3 heures pile *or* précises, il est exactement 3 heures ◆ **~ one hour** une heure exactement ◆ **I had ~ $3** j'avais exactement 3 dollars ◆ **~ in the middle** en plein milieu ◆ **~ 10m high** exactement 10 m de haut ◆ **~ the same thing** exactement la même chose ◆ **that's ~ what I was thinking** c'est exactement ce que je pensais ◆ **I found it somewhere over there – where ~?** je l'ai trouvé quelque part par là – où exactement ? ◆ **~ what are you implying?** qu'est-ce que tu veux dire par là *or* au juste ? ◆ **~ what are you looking for?** qu'est-ce que tu cherches au juste ? ◆ **so I was wrong – ~** alors j'avais tort – exactement ◆ **he didn't ~ say no, but ...** il n'a pas vraiment dit non, mais ... ◆ **we don't ~ know** nous ne savons pas au juste

◆ **not exactly** ◆ **is she sick? – not ~** est-elle malade ? – pas exactement *or* pas vraiment ◆ **it's easy work, but not ~ interesting** c'est facile, mais pas vraiment ce qu'on appelle intéressant ◆ **you refused? – well not ~ ...** tu as refusé ? – euh, pas vraiment ... ◆ **this is not ~ what we need at the moment** *(iro)* il ne manquait plus que ça

exactness /ɪgˈzæktnɪs/ N *(NonC) [of measurement, words, definition]* précision *f* ; *[of translation]* fidélité *f* ; *[of copy, description]* exactitude *f*

exaggerate /ɪgˈzædʒəreɪt/ VT [1] *(= overstate) [+ dangers, fears, size, beauty, story, importance, effect]* exagérer ; *[+ problem]* exagérer l'importance de ◆ **the press ~d the number of victims** les médias ont gonflé le nombre des victimes [2] *(= emphasize)* accentuer ◆ **the dress ~d her paleness** la robe accentuait sa pâleur VI exagérer, forcer la note ◆ **he always ~s a little** il exagère *or* il en rajoute* toujours un peu

exaggerated /ɪgˈzædʒəreɪtɪd/ ADJ *[claim, view, politeness, gesture, report]* exagéré ; *[praise]* outré ◆ **an ~ sense of one's own importance** une trop haute opinion de soi-même

exaggeratedly /ɪgˈzædʒəreɪtɪdlɪ/ ADV *[polite]* exagérément ; *[laugh]* d'une manière exagérée

exaggeration /ɪgˌzædʒəˈreɪʃən/ N exagération *f*

exalt /ɪgˈzɔːlt/ VT *(in rank, power)* élever *(à un rang plus important)* ; *(= extol)* porter aux nues, exalter

exaltation /ˌegzɔːlˈteɪʃən/ N *(NonC)* exaltation *f*

exalted /ɪgˈzɔːltɪd/ ADJ *(= high) [rank, position, style]* élevé ; *[person]* haut placé, de haut rang ; *(= elated) [mood, person]* exalté

exam /ɪgˈzæm/ N (abbrev of **examination noun 2)** examen *m*, exam * *m*

examination /ɪgˌzæmɪˈneɪʃən/ N [1] *(Scol, Univ)* *(= test)* examen *m* ; *(each paper)* épreuve *f* ◆ **class ~** *(Scol)* composition *f* ◆ **the June/September ~s** *(Univ etc)* la session de juin/de septembre

[2] *(= study, inspection)* examen *m* ; *[of machine, premises]* inspection *f*, examen *m* ; *[of question]* étude *f*, considération *f* ; *[of accounts]* vérification *f* ; *[of passports]* contrôle *m* ◆ **Customs' ~** fouille *f* douanière ◆ **expert's ~** expertise *f* ◆ **close ~** examen *m* approfondi *or* détaillé ◆ **on ~** après examen ◆ **on close ~, his papers proved to be false** un examen approfondi *or* détaillé révéla que ses papiers étaient des faux ; → **medical**

[3] *(Jur) [of suspect, accused]* interrogatoire *m* ; *[of witness]* audition *f* ; *[of case, documents]* examen *m* ◆ **legal ~** examen *m* légal ; → **cross**

COMP **examination board** N *(Brit Scol)* *comité chargé de l'organisation des examens scolaires nationaux*

examination candidate N *(Scol etc)* candidat(e) *m(f)*

examination paper N *(= exam)* examen *m*, épreuve *f* ; *(= question paper)* questions *fpl* *or* sujet *m* d'examen ; *(= answer paper)* copie *f*

examination script N *(Brit) (= answer paper)* copie *f* ; *(= question paper)* questions *fpl* *or* sujet *m* d'examen

examine /ɪgˈzæmɪn/ LANGUAGE IN USE 26.1, 26.2 VT [1] *(gen, Med)* examiner ; *[+ machine]* inspecter ; *[+ document, dossier, question, problem, proposition]* examiner ; *[+ accounts]* vérifier ; *[+ passport]* contrôler ; *(Customs) [+ luggage]* inspecter, fouiller ◆ **to ~ a question thoroughly** examiner une question à fond [2] *[+ pupil, candidate]* faire passer un examen à ; *(orally)* interroger *(on* sur) [3] *(Jur) [+ witness]* interroger ; *[+ suspect, accused]* interroger, faire subir un interrogatoire à ; *[+ case, document, evidence]* examiner

COMP **examining board** N *(Brit Scol)* ⇒ **examination board** *(Univ) (for doctorates)* jury *m* de thèse

examining magistrate N *(Jur: in France)* juge *m* d'instruction

examinee /ɪgˌzæmɪˈniː/ N candidat(e) *m(f)*

examiner /ɪgˈzæmɪnəʳ/ N examinateur *m*, -trice *f (in* de) → **board, oral, outside**

example /ɪgˈzɑːmpl/ LANGUAGE IN USE 26.1, 26.2 N exemple *m* ◆ **for ~** par exemple ◆ **to set a good ~** donner l'exemple ◆ **to be an ~** *[person, sb's conduct, deeds]* être un exemple *(to* pour) ◆ **she's an ~ to us all** c'est un exemple pour nous tous ◆ **to take sb as an ~** prendre exemple sur qn ◆ **to follow sb's ~** suivre l'exemple de qn ◆ **following the ~ of ...** à l'instar de ... ◆ **to hold sb/sth up as an ~** ériger qn/qch en exemple ◆ **to make an ~ of sb** punir qn pour l'exemple ◆ **to punish sb as an ~ to others** punir qn pour l'exemple ◆ **to quote the ~ of ...** citer l'exemple de ... ◆ **to quote sth as an ~** citer qch en exemple ◆ **here is an ~ of the work** voici un échantillon du travail

exasperate /ɪgˈzɑːspəreɪt/ VT *[+ person]* exaspérer ; *[+ feeling]* exaspérer, exacerber

exasperated /ɪgˈzɑːspəreɪtɪd/ ADJ exaspéré ◆ **~ at** *or* **by** *or* **with sb/sth** exaspéré par qn/qch

exasperating /ɪgˈzɑːspəreɪtɪŋ/ ADJ exaspérant

exasperatingly /ɪgˈzɑːspəreɪtɪŋlɪ/ ADV de manière exaspérante ◆ **~ slow/stupid** d'une lenteur/d'une stupidité exaspérante

exasperation /ɪgˌzɑːspəˈreɪʃən/ N exaspération *f* ◆ **"hurry!" he cried in ~** "dépêchez-vous !" cria-t-il, exaspéré

ex cathedra /ˌekskəˈθiːdrə/ ADJ, ADV ex cathedra

excavate /ˈekskəveɪt/ VT *[+ ground]* creuser, excaver ; *(Archeol)* fouiller ; *[+ trench]* creuser ; *[+ remains]* déterrer VI *(Archeol)* faire des fouilles

excavation /ˌekskəˈveɪʃən/ N [1] *(NonC) [of tunnel etc]* creusement *m*, percement *m* ◆ **~ work** excavations *fpl* [2] *(Archeol = activity, site)* fouilles *fpl*

excavator /ˈekskəveɪtəʳ/ N [1] *(= machine)* excavateur *m* *or* excavatrice *f* [2] *(Archeol = person)* fouilleur *m*, -euse *f*

exceed /ɪkˈsiːd/ VT *(in value, amount, length of time etc)* dépasser, excéder *(in* en ; *by* de) ; *[+ powers] [person]* outrepasser ; *[decision etc]* excéder ; *[+ expectations, limits, capabilities]* dépasser ; *[+ desires]* aller au-delà de, dépasser ◆ **to ~ one's authority** commettre un abus de pouvoir ◆ **to ~ the speed limit** dépasser la vitesse permise, commettre un excès de vitesse ◆ **a fine not ~ing £50** une amende ne dépassant pas *or* n'excédant pas 50 livres

exceedingly /ɪk'si:dɪŋlɪ/ ADV extrêmement ◆ **his behaviour troubles me** ~ je suis extrêmement troublé par son comportement

excel /ɪk'sel/ VI briller, exceller ◆ **to** ~ **in** *or* **at French/tennis** briller en français/au tennis VT ◆ **to** ~ **o.s.** se surpasser, se distinguer

excellence /'eksələns/ N excellence *f*

Excellency /'eksələnsɪ/ N Excellence *f* ◆ **Your/His** *or* **Her** ~ Votre/Son Excellence

excellent /'eksələnt/ LANGUAGE IN USE 13 ADJ excellent ◆ **what an** ~ **idea!** (quelle) excellente idée ! ◆ ~**!** parfait ! ◆ **that's** ~**!** c'est parfait !

excellently /'eksələntlɪ/ ADV admirablement

excelsior /ek'selsjɔ:ʳ/ N (*US = wood shavings*) copeaux *mpl* d'emballage

except /ɪk'sept/ PREP 1 sauf, excepté, à l'exception de ◆ **all** ~ **the eldest daughter** tous, excepté la fille aînée, tous, la fille aînée exceptée ◆ ~ **(for)** à part, à l'exception de ◆ ~ **(that)** sauf que, excepté que ◆ ~ **if** sauf si ◆ ~ **when** sauf quand, excepté quand 2 (*after neg and certain interrogs*) sinon ◆ **what can they do** ~ **wait?** que peuvent-ils faire sinon attendre ? CONJ († *liter*) à moins que + ne + *subj* ◆ ~ **he be a traitor** à moins qu'il ne soit un traître VT excepter, exclure (*from* de) faire exception de ◆ **not** *or* **without** ~**ing** sans excepter, sans oublier ◆ **always** ~**ing** à l'exception (bien entendu) de, exception faite (bien entendu) de ◆ **present company** ~**ed** exception faite des personnes présentes

excepting /ɪk'septɪŋ/ PREP, CONJ ⇒ **except**

exception /ɪk'sepʃən/ N 1 (*NonC*) exception *f* ◆ **without** ~ sans exception ◆ **with the** ~ **of ...** à l'exception de ..., exception faite de ... ◆ **to take** ~ **to** (*= demur*) trouver à redire à, désapprouver ; (*= be offended*) s'offenser de, s'offusquer de ◆ **I take** ~ **to that remark** je suis indigné par cette remarque

2 (*= singularity*) exception *f* ◆ **to make an** ~ faire une exception (*to sth* à qch ; *for sb/sth* pour qn/qch) ◆ **these strokes of luck are the** ~ ces coups de chance sont l'exception ◆ **this case is an** ~ **to the rule** ce cas est *or* constitue une exception à la règle ◆ **the** ~ **proves the rule** l'exception confirme la règle ◆ **with this** ~ à cette exception près, à ceci près ◆ **apart from a few** ~**s** à part quelques exceptions, à de rares exceptions près

exceptionable /ɪk'sepʃnəbl/ ADJ (*= open to objection*) [*conduct*] répréhensible, blâmable ; [*proposal*] inadmissible, inacceptable

exceptional /ɪk'sepʃənl/ ADJ (*gen*) exceptionnel ; (*Jur*) [*provisions*] dérogatoire ◆ **to apply** ~ **arrangements (to)** (*Jur*) appliquer un régime dérogatoire (à) COMP **exceptional child** N (pl **exceptional children**) (*US Scol*) (*gifted*) enfant *mf* surdoué(e) ; (*handicapped, mentally*) enfant *mf* handicapé(e) mental(e) ; (*physically*) enfant *mf* handicapé(e)

exceptionally /ɪk'sepʃənəlɪ/ ADV exceptionnellement

excerpt /'eksɜ:pt/ N (*Literat, Mus etc*) extrait *m*, passage *m* VT (*Literat, Mus*) extraire

excess /ɪk'ses/ N 1 (*NonC*) [*of precautions, enthusiasm*] excès *m* ; [*of details, adjectives*] luxe *m*, surabondance *f* ◆ **to** ~ (jusqu')à l'excès ◆ **to take** *or* **carry to** ~ pousser à l'excès, pousser trop loin ◆ **carried to** ~ outré ◆ **in** ~ **of** [*number*] supérieur à ◆ **in** ~ **of 50 people have died** plus de 50 personnes sont mortes ◆ **to drink to** ~ boire à l'excès *or* avec excès ◆ **the** ~ **of imports over exports** l'excédent *m* des importations sur les exportations

2 (*Brit Insurance*) franchise *f*

3 ◆ ~**es** (*= debauchery*) excès *mpl* ; (*= cruelty, violence*) excès *mpl*, abus *m* ; (*= overindulgence*) excès *mpl*, écart *m* ◆ **the** ~**es of the regime** les abus *or* excès du régime

COMP [*weight, production*] excédentaire
excess baggage N (*NonC*) excédent *m* de bagages
excess demand N (*Econ*) demande *f* excédentaire
excess employment N suremploi *m*
excess fare N (*Transport*) supplément *m*
excess luggage N ⇒ **excess baggage**
excess postage N (*Brit*) surtaxe *f* (*pour affranchissement insuffisant*)
excess profits tax N impôt *m* sur les bénéfices exceptionnels
excess supply N (*Econ*) excès *m* de l'offre *or* sur offre

excessive /ɪk'sesɪv/ ADJ [*amount, quantity, use, force, speed, demands*] excessif ; [*ambition*] démesuré ; [*praise*] outré ◆ ~ **drinking** abus *m* d'alcool *or* de boissons alcoolisées

excessively /ɪk'sesɪvlɪ/ ADV [*drink, eat*] à l'excès, avec excès ; [*optimistic, proud, ambitious, cautious, centralized*] par trop ; [*boring, pretty*] excessivement ◆ **do you worry** ~ **about work?** avez-vous tendance à vous faire trop de souci pour votre travail ? ◆ **his behaviour was impeccable, sometimes** ~ **so** il se conduisait de manière irréprochable, parfois jusqu'à l'excès

exchange /ɪks'tʃeɪndʒ/ VT [+ *gifts, letters, glances, blows*] échanger ; [+ *houses, cars, jobs*] faire un échange de ◆ **to** ~ **one thing for another** échanger une chose contre une autre ◆ **they** ~**d a few words** ils échangèrent quelques mots ◆ **to** ~ **words with sb** (*euph = quarrel*) avoir des mots avec qn ◆ **to** ~ **contracts** (*Conveyancing*) ≈ signer les contrats

N 1 [*of objects, prisoners, ideas, secrets, notes, greetings*] échange *m* ◆ **to gain/lose on the** ~ gagner/perdre au change ◆ ~ **of contracts** (*Conveyancing*) ≈ signature *f* des contrats

◆ **in exchange** en échange (*for* de) ◆ **to give one thing in** ~ **for another** échanger une chose contre une autre

2 (*Fin*) change *m* ◆ **foreign** ~ **office** bureau *m* de change ◆ **at the current rate of** ~ au cours actuel du change ◆ **the dollar** ~ le change du dollar ◆ **on the (stock)** ~ à la Bourse ; → **bill[1], foreign**

3 (also **telephone exchange**) central *m* ; (also **labour exchange**) bourse *f* du travail

4 ⇒ **exchange visit**

COMP [*student, teacher*] participant(e) *m(f)* à un échange
exchange control N (*Fin*) contrôle *m* des changes ◆ ~ **control regulations** réglementation *f* des changes
exchange law N droit *m* cambial
exchange rate N taux *m* de change
exchange rate mechanism N mécanisme *m* du taux de change
exchange restrictions NPL restrictions *fpl* de change
exchange value N contre-valeur *f*
exchange visit N (*Educ etc*) échange *m* ◆ **to be on an** ~ **visit** faire partie d'un échange

exchangeable /ɪks'tʃeɪndʒəbl/ ADJ échangeable (*for* contre)

exchequer /ɪks'tʃekəʳ/ N 1 (*= state treasury*) ministère *m* des Finances ; → **chancellor** 2 (* *= one's own funds*) fonds *mpl*, finances *fpl* COMP **exchequer bond** N obligation *f* du Trésor

excisable /ek'saɪzəbl/ ADJ imposable, soumis aux droits de régie

excise[1] /'eksaɪz/ N taxe *f* (*on* sur), accise *f* (*Belg, Can*) ◆ **the Excise** (*Brit*) ≈ l'administration *f* des impôts indirects
COMP **excise duties** NPL (*Brit*) impôts *mpl* indirects
excise laws NPL (*US*) *lois sur le commerce des boissons*

excise[2] /ek'saɪz/ VT 1 (*gen*) retrancher, supprimer 2 (*Med*) exciser

exciseman /'eksaɪzmæn/ N (pl **-men**) (*Brit*) agent *m* du fisc (*chargé du recouvrement des impôts indirects*)

excision /ek'sɪʒən/ N (*frm*) 1 (*Med*) excision *f* 2 (*NonC = act of deletion*) [*of words, clause*] suppression *f* 3 (*= deleted passage: in film, play, book*) coupure *f*

excitability /ɪk,saɪtə'bɪlɪtɪ/ N excitabilité *f*, nervosité *f*

excitable /ɪk'saɪtəbl/ ADJ [*person, animal, temperament*] (*also Med*) excitable ◆ **to be in an** ~ **state** être tendu

excitableness /ɪk'saɪtəbəlnɪs/ N excitabilité *f*, nervosité *f*

excite /ɪk'saɪt/ VT 1 [+ *person, animal*] (*gen, also sexually*) exciter ; (*= rouse enthusiasm in*) passionner ◆ **to** ~ **o.s.** s'exciter, s'énerver 2 [+ *sentiments, envy, attention, pity*] exciter ; [+ *imagination, passion*] exciter, enflammer ; [+ *desire, anger*] exciter, aviver ; [+ *admiration*] exciter, susciter ; [+ *curiosity*] exciter, piquer ◆ **to** ~ **enthusiasm/interest in sb** enthousiasmer/intéresser qn ◆ **the issue has** ~**d a great deal of debate** le sujet a suscité de nombreux débats 3 (*Med*) [+ *nerve*] exciter, stimuler

excited /ɪk'saɪtɪd/ ADJ 1 (*= exhilarated*) [*person, voice, shout, laugh, imagination*] excité ; [*chatter*] animé ; (*sexually*) excité ◆ **he was** ~ **to hear of this development** il était tout excité d'apprendre ce fait nouveau ◆ **he is** ~ **at the prospect** il est tout excité à cette idée ◆ **I'm really** ~ **about it** je suis tout excité à cette idée ◆ **he was** ~ **about going on holiday** il était tout excité à l'idée de partir en vacances ◆ **to become** *or* **get** ~ s'exciter ◆ **it's nothing to get** ~ **about** il n'y a pas de quoi s'énerver 2 (*= agitated*) [*person, gesture*] nerveux ; [*state*] de nervosité ◆ **to get** ~ **(about sth)** s'énerver (à propos de qch) ◆ **don't get** ~**!** du calme !, ne t'énerve pas ! 3 (*Phys*) [*atom, molecule*] excité

excitedly /ɪk'saɪtɪdlɪ/ ADV [*say, talk, chatter*] sur un ton animé, avec animation ; [*grin*] d'un air excité ; [*laugh*] avec excitation ; [*behave*] avec agitation ; [*run*] tout excité ◆ **to wave** ~ gesticuler

excitement /ɪk'saɪtmənt/ N [*of people*] excitation *f* ; [*of event*] fièvre *f* ◆ **the** ~ **of the departure** l'excitation *or* la fièvre du départ ◆ **the** ~ **of a trip to the fair** la perspective excitante d'une visite à la fête foraine ◆ **the** ~ **of the elections** la fièvre des élections ◆ **to be in a state of great** ~ être dans un état de très grande excitation ◆ **the** ~ **of victory** l'ivresse *f* de la victoire ◆ **the book caused great** ~ **in literary circles** le livre a fait sensation dans les milieux littéraires ◆ **there was great** ~ **when she announced that ...** elle a suscité un grand émoi lorsqu'elle a annoncé que ... ◆ **he likes** ~ il aime les émotions fortes ◆ **she's looking for a bit of** ~ **in her life** elle cherche à donner un peu de piquant à sa vie ◆ **this sport has plenty of** ~**s** ce sport est excitant à bien des égards ◆ **the** ~ **of getting a book published** l'excitation que l'on ressent à la publication d'un livre ◆ **the** ~ **of being in love** l'ivresse *f* que l'on ressent lorsqu'on est amoureux ◆ **sexual** ~ excitation *f* sexuelle ◆ **with growing** ~ **he turned the key in the lock** de plus en plus excité, il a tourné la clé dans la serrure

exciting /ɪk'saɪtɪŋ/ ADJ (*= exhilarating*) [*activity, experience, opportunity, idea, news, book*] passionnant ; (*sexually*) [*person*] excitant ◆ **he's** ~ **to be with** c'est passionnant d'être avec lui ◆ **very** ~ (absolument *or* tout à fait) passionnant ◆ **not very** ~ pas très *or* bien passionnant ◆ **how** ~**!** comme c'est excitant *or* passionnant ! ◆ **we had an** ~ **time** nous avons passé des moments passionnants ◆ **to be** ~ **to sb** être excitant *or* palpitant pour qn

excitingly /ɪk'saɪtɪŋlɪ/ ADV [*describe*] de façon passionnante ◆ **an** ~ **original writer** un écrivain d'une originalité passionnante

excl. abbrev of **excluding, exclusive (of)**

exclaim /ɪks'kleɪm/ VI (gen) s'exclamer ◆ **he ~ed in surprise when he saw it** il a laissé échapper une exclamation de surprise en le voyant ◆ **to ~ at sth** *(indignantly)* s'exclamer d'indignation devant qch ; *(admiringly)* s'exclamer d'admiration devant qch VT s'écrier *(that* que) ◆ **"at last!" she ~ed** "enfin !" s'écria-t-elle

exclamation /ˌekskləˈmeɪʃən/ N exclamation *f* COMP **exclamation mark, exclamation point** (US) N point *m* d'exclamation

exclamatory /ɪks'klæmətərɪ/ ADJ exclamatif

exclude /ɪks'klu:d/ VT *(from team, society)* exclure *(from* de) ; *(Brit: from school)* exclure temporairement ; *(from list)* écarter *(from* de) ne pas retenir ; *(from meeting, discussions, process)* écarter, exclure ; *[+ possibility]* exclure, écarter ; *[+ sun's rays, germs]* faire écran à ◆ **red meat is ~d from this diet** ce régime interdit la viande rouge ◆ **women were ~d from participation/from competing** les femmes n'avaient pas le droit de participer/de prendre part à la compétition ◆ **to ~ sth from consideration** refuser de prendre qch en considération ◆ **to ~ from the jurisdiction of** soustraire à la compétence de ◆ **the price ~s VAT** le prix est hors taxe ◆ **£200, excluding VAT** 200 livres, hors taxe ◆ **a meal here costs about €15 per head excluding wine** un repas ici coûte environ 15 € par personne, vin non compris

excluding /ɪks'klu:dɪŋ/ PREP à l'exclusion de, à part

exclusion /ɪks'klu:ʒən/ N exclusion *f (from* de) ◆ **to the ~ of ...** à l'exclusion de ...
COMP **exclusion clause** N clause *f* d'exclusion
exclusion order N *(Brit Jur) (from country)* interdiction *f* de territoire *or* de séjour ; *(against spouse)* interdiction *f* de domicile conjugal
exclusion zone N zone *f* d'exclusion

exclusionary /ɪks'klu:ʒənərɪ/ ADJ *[practice]* d'exclusion

exclusive /ɪks'klu:sɪv/ ADJ 1 *(= select) [person, friendship, interest, occupation]* exclusif ; *[club]* fermé ; *[district, resort, hotel, restaurant]* chic *inv* ; *[gathering]* sélect 2 *(= sole) [use, offer, contract, property, story, picture]* exclusif ◆ **~ to readers of ...** exclusivement pour les lecteurs de ... ◆ **this special offer is ~ to (readers of) this magazine** cette offre spéciale est réservée à nos lecteurs ◆ **an interview ~ to ...** une interview exclusive accordée à ... ◆ **to have ~ rights to sth** avoir l'exclusivité de qch 3 *(= not including)* ◆ **to be ~ of sth** exclure qch ◆ **~ of postage and packing** frais d'expédition non compris ◆ **from 15 to 20 June ~** du 15 au 19 juin inclus ◆ **~ of taxes** *(Comm)* hors taxes, taxes non comprises ; → **mutually** N *(Press)* exclusivité *f*

exclusively /ɪks'klu:sɪvlɪ/ ADV exclusivement ◆ **available ~ from ...** en vente exclusivement chez ... ◆ **~ available to readers of ...** réservé exclusivement aux lecteurs de ...

exclusivity /ˌɪksklu:'sɪvətɪ/ N exclusivité *f*

excommunicate /ˌekskə'mju:nɪkeɪt/ VT excommunier

excommunication /'ekskəˌmju:nɪ'keɪʃən/ N excommunication *f*

ex-con ‡ /ˌeks'kɒn/ N ancien taulard ‡ *m*

excoriate /ɪk'skɔ:rɪeɪt/ VT *(frm) [+ person]* chapitrer ; *[+ organization]* condamner ; *[+ idea]* fustiger

excrement /'ekskrɪmənt/ N excrément *m*

excrescence /ɪks'kresns/ N *(lit, fig)* excroissance *f*

excreta /ɪks'kri:tə/ NPL excrétions *fpl* ; *(= excrement)* excréments *mpl*, déjections *fpl*

excrete /ɪks'kri:t/ VT excréter ; *[plant]* sécréter

excretion /ɪks'kri:ʃən/ N excrétion *f*, sécrétion *f*

excretory /ɪk'skri:tərɪ/ ADJ *(Physiol)* excréteur (-trice *f*), excrétoire

excruciating /ɪks'kru:ʃɪeɪtɪŋ/ ADJ *[pain, suffering, sight, sound, boredom]* insoutenable ; *[death]* atroce ; *[joke]* lamentable ◆ **I was in ~ pain** je souffrais comme un damné ◆ **in ~ detail** dans les moindres détails

excruciatingly /ɪks'kru:ʃɪeɪtɪŋlɪ/ ADV *[painful]* atrocement ; *[difficult, humiliating]* affreusement ◆ **~ funny** désopilant

exculpate /'ekskʌlpeɪt/ VT *[+ person]* disculper, innocenter *(from* de) ◆ **to ~ sb of** *or* **from responsibility** juger qn non responsable

excursion /ɪks'kɜ:ʃən/ N excursion *f*, balade * *f* ; *(on foot, cycle)* randonnée *f* ; *(fig = digression)* digression *f*
COMP **excursion ticket** N billet *m* excursion
excursion train N train *m* spécial *(pour excursions)*

excusable /ɪks'kju:zəbl/ ADJ excusable, pardonnable

excuse /ɪks'kju:z/ LANGUAGE IN USE 18.1
VT 1 *(= justify) [+ action, person]* excuser ◆ **such rudeness cannot be ~d** une telle impolitesse est inexcusable ◆ **to ~ o.s.** s'excuser *(for* de) présenter ses excuses
2 *(= pardon)* excuser *(sb for having done* qn d'avoir fait) ◆ **to ~ sb's insolence** excuser l'insolence de qn, pardonner à qn son insolence ◆ **one can be ~d for not understanding what she says** il est excusable de ne pas comprendre ce qu'elle dit ◆ **if you will ~ the expression, ~ my French** *(hum)* passez-moi l'expression ◆ **and now if you will ~ me, I have work to do** et maintenant, si vous voulez bien m'excuser, j'ai du travail à faire ◆ **~ me for wondering if ...** permettez-moi de me demander si ... ◆ **~ me!** excusez-moi !, (je vous demande) pardon ! ◆ **~ me, but I don't think this is true** excusez-moi, mais je ne crois pas que ce soit vrai ◆ **~ me for not seeing you out** excusez-moi si je ne vous raccompagne pas *or* de ne pas vous raccompagner
3 *(= exempt)* exempter *(sb from sth* qn de qch) dispenser *(sb from sth* qn de qch ; *sb from doing sth* qn de faire qch) excuser ◆ **you are ~d** *(to children)* vous pouvez vous en aller ◆ **he ~d himself after ten minutes** au bout de dix minutes, il s'est excusé et est parti ◆ **to ask to be ~d** demander à être excusé ◆ **he was ~d from the afternoon session** on l'a dispensé d'assister à la séance de l'après-midi ◆ **to ~ sb from an obligation** dispenser qn d'une obligation
N /ɪks'kju:s/ 1 *(= reason, justification)* excuse *f* ◆ **there is no ~ for it, it admits of no ~** *(frm)* c'est inexcusable ◆ **his only ~ was that ...** sa seule excuse était que ... ◆ **that is no ~ for his leaving so abruptly** cela ne l'excuse pas d'être parti si brusquement ◆ **in ~ for** pour s'excuser de ◆ **without ~** sans excuse ; → **ignorance**
2 *(= pretext)* excuse *f*, prétexte *m* ◆ **a lame ~** une piètre excuse, une excuse boiteuse ◆ **to find an ~ for sth** trouver une excuse à qch ◆ **I have a good ~ for not going** j'ai une bonne excuse pour ne pas y aller ◆ **to make an ~ for sth/for doing** *(gen)* trouver une *or* des excuse(s) à qch/pour faire ◆ **he's just making ~s** il se cherche des excuses ◆ **he is always making ~s to get away** il trouve *or* invente toujours des excuses pour s'absenter ◆ **what's your ~ this time?** qu'avez-vous comme excuse cette fois-ci ? ◆ **he gave the bad weather as his ~ for not coming** il a prétexté *or* allégué le mauvais temps pour ne pas venir ◆ **it's only an ~** ce n'est qu'un prétexte ◆ **his success was a good ~ for a family party** ce succès a fourni le prétexte à une fête de famille
COMP **excuse-me (dance)** N *(Brit) danse où l'on change de partenaire*, ≃ danse *f* du balai

ex-directory /ˌeksdɪ'rektərɪ/ LANGUAGE IN USE 27.5 ADJ *(Brit Telec)* qui ne figure pas dans l'annuaire ≃ qui est sur la liste rouge ADV ◆ **he's gone ~** il s'est fait mettre sur la liste rouge

ex dividend /'eks'dɪvɪˌdend/ ADJ *(St Ex)* ex-dividende

exec * /ɪg'zek/ N (abbrev of **executive**) cadre *m*

execrable /'eksɪkrəbl/ ADJ exécrable

execrably /'eksɪkrəblɪ/ ADV exécrablement

execrate /'eksɪkreɪt/ VT *(liter)* 1 *(= hate)* exécrer 2 *(= curse)* maudire

execration /ˌeksɪ'kreɪʃən/ N *(liter)* 1 *(NonC)* exécration *f (liter)*, horreur *f* ◆ **to hold in ~** exécrer *(liter)* 2 *(= curse)* malédiction *f*, imprécation *f*

executable /'eksɪkju:təbl/ ADJ exécutable ◆ **~ program** *(Comput)* application *f*

executant /ɪg'zekjʊtənt/ N *(Mus)* interprète *mf*, exécutant(e) *m(f)*

execute /'eksɪkju:t/ VT 1 *(= carry out) [+ order, piece of work, dance, movement]* exécuter ; *[+ work of art]* réaliser ; *[+ project, plan]* exécuter, mettre à exécution ; *[+ purpose, sb's wishes]* accomplir ; *[+ duties]* exercer, remplir ; *[+ task]* accomplir, s'acquitter de ; *(Comput) [+ command, program]* exécuter ; *(Mus)* exécuter, interpréter ; *(Jur) [+ will]* exécuter ; *[+ document]* valider ; *[+ deed]* signer ; *[+ contract]* valider 2 *(= put to death)* exécuter

execution /ˌeksɪ'kju:ʃən/ N 1 *(= carrying out) [of task, order, will, warrant, dance, sculpture]* exécution *f* ; *[of plan]* exécution *f*, réalisation *f* ; *[of wishes]* accomplissement *m* ; *[of song]* interprétation *f* ; *[of treaty]* application *f* ◆ **in the ~ of his duties** dans l'exercice *m* de ses fonctions ◆ **to carry** *or* **put sth into ~** mettre qch à exécution 2 *(= killing)* exécution *f*

executioner /ˌeksɪ'kju:ʃnə^r/ N (also **public executioner**) bourreau *m*, exécuteur *m* des hautes œuvres

executive /ɪg'zekjʊtɪv/ ADJ 1 *[power, decision, function, role]* directorial ; *[position, pay]* de cadre ; *[car]* de fonction ◆ **the ~ arm of the organization** l'organe exécutif de l'organisation ◆ **~ capability** capacité *f* d'exécution
2 *(esp Brit * = up-market) [briefcase, chair]* de luxe ◆ **~ class** classe *f* affaires
N 1 *(= person)* cadre *m* ◆ **senior/junior ~** cadre *m* supérieur/moyen ◆ **a Shell/IBM ~** un cadre (de chez) Shell/IBM ◆ **a sales/production ~** un cadre du service des ventes/du service production ◆ **a woman** *or* **female ~** une femme cadre ; → **chief**
2 *(= managing group: of organization)* bureau *m* ◆ **to be on the ~** faire partie du bureau ◆ **the trade union/party ~** le bureau du syndicat/du parti
3 *(= part of government)* (pouvoir *m*) exécutif *m*
COMP **executive agreement** N *(US Pol) accord conclu entre chefs d'État*
executive board N conseil *m* de direction
executive branch N organe *m* exécutif
executive burnout N épuisement *m* du cadre
executive chairman N (pl **executive chairmen**) directeur *m* exécutif
executive committee N comité *m* exécutif
executive council N conseil *m* exécutif *or* de direction ; *(US Pol)* conseil *m* exécutif
executive director N directeur *m* exécutif
executive lounge N salon *m* classe affaires
the Executive Mansion N *(US) (= White House)* la Maison-Blanche ; *(= Governor's house)* la résidence officielle du gouverneur *(d'un État américain)*
executive member N membre *m* du bureau exécutif
the Executive Office of the President N *(US)* le cabinet du président *(des États-Unis)*, la Présidence *(des États-Unis)*

executive officer N *[of organization]* cadre *m* administratif ; *(US Mil, Naut)* commandant *m* en second
executive order N *(US)* décret-loi *m*
executive president N président *m* exécutif
executive privilege N *(US Pol) privilège du président de ne pas communiquer certaines informations*
executive producer N producteur *m* exécutif
executive relief N *(NonC: euph)* = le cinq à sept du cadre
executive secretary N secrétaire *mf* de direction
executive session N *(US Govt)* séance *f* à huis clos
the executive suite (of offices) N les bureaux *mpl* de la direction
executive toy N *(for play)* gadget *m* de bureau ; *(as status symbol)* gadget *m* de luxe

Executive Privilege

Le « privilège de l'exécutif » est le droit dont bénéficie le président des États-Unis de ne pas divulguer au Congrès ou au pouvoir judiciaire certaines informations jugées confidentielles ou devant rester secrètes pour des raisons de sécurité nationale. Plusieurs présidents ont tenté d'obtenir un droit au secret total, y compris pour des motifs personnels, mais la Cour suprême s'y est opposée. Ainsi, pendant l'affaire du Watergate, elle a rejeté la requête du président Nixon, qui invoquait ce privilège pour refuser de livrer des enregistrements à la commission d'enquête du Sénat.

executor /ɪgˈzekjʊtəʳ/ N *(Jur)* exécuteur *m* testamentaire

executrix /ɪgˈzekjʊtrɪks/ N (pl **executrixes** or **executrices** /ɪgˌzekjʊˈtraɪsiːz/) *(Jur)* exécutrice *f* testamentaire

exegesis /ˌeksɪˈdʒiːsɪs/ N (pl **exegeses** /ˌeksɪˈdʒiːsiːz/) exégèse *f*

exemplar /ɪgˈzemplɑː/ N *(= model)* exemple *m*, modèle *m*

exemplary /ɪgˈzemplərɪ/ ADJ exemplaire ◆ ~ **in one's conduct** d'une conduite exemplaire
COMP **exemplary damages** NPL *(Jur)* dommages-intérêts *mpl* pour préjudice moral

exemplification /ɪgˌzemplɪfɪˈkeɪʃən/ N exemplification *f*

exemplify /ɪgˈzemplɪfaɪ/ VT *(= be example of)* être un exemple de ; *(= illustrate)* illustrer ◆ **exemplified copy** *(Jur)* expédition *f*, copie *f* certifiée

exempt /ɪgˈzempt/ ADJ exempt *(from* de) VT exempter *(from sth* de qch) dispenser *(from doing sth* de faire qch)

exemption /ɪgˈzempʃən/ N exonération *f (from* de) ; *(Educ)* dispense *f (from* de) ; *(Jur)* dérogation *f* ◆ **tax** ~ exonération *f* fiscale

exercise /ˈeksəsaɪz/ N 1 *(NonC = putting into practice) [of right, caution, power]* exercice *m* ; *[of religion]* pratique *f*, exercice *m* ◆ **in the ~ of his duties** dans l'exercice de ses fonctions
2 *(= physical exertion)* exercice *m* ◆ **to take ~** faire de l'exercice ◆ **to do (physical) ~s every morning** faire de la gymnastique tous les matins
3 *(= task)* exercice *m* ◆ **a grammar ~** un exercice de grammaire
4 *(Mil etc: gen pl)* exercice *m*, manœuvre *f* ◆ **to go on (an) ~** *(Mil)* aller à l'exercice ; *(Naut)* partir en manœuvre ◆ **NATO ~s** manœuvres *fpl* de l'OTAN
5 *(= sth carried out)* opération *f* ◆ **an ~ in public relations/in management** *etc* une opération de relations publiques/de gestion des affaires *etc* ◆ **a cost-cutting ~** une opération de réduction des coûts ◆ **an ~ in futility** le type même de l'entreprise inutile
NPL **exercises** *(US = ceremony)* cérémonies *fpl*
VT 1 *(= exert) [+ body, mind]* exercer ; *[+ troops]* faire faire l'exercice à ; *[+ horse]* exercer ◆ **to ~ one's dog** faire courir son chien
2 *(= use, put into practice) [+ one's authority, control, power]* exercer ; *[+ a right]* exercer, user de ; *[+ one's talents]* employer, exercer ; *[+ patience, tact, restraint]* faire preuve de ◆ **to ~ care in doing sth** apporter du soin à faire qch, s'appliquer à bien faire qch
3 *(frm = preoccupy)* préoccuper ◆ **the problem which is exercising my mind** le problème qui me préoccupe
VI faire de l'exercice
COMP **exercise bike** N vélo *m* d'appartement
exercise book N *(for writing in)* cahier *m* (d'exercices *or* de devoirs) ; *(= book of exercises)* livre *m* d'exercices
exercise yard N *[of prison]* cour *f* (de prison)

exerciser /ˈeksəsaɪzəʳ/ N *(= person)* personne *f* qui fait de l'exercice ; *(= machine)* exerciseur *m*

exercycle /ˈeksəsaɪkl/ N vélo *m* d'appartement

exert /ɪgˈzɜːt/ VT 1 *[+ pressure, control, influence, power* 'authority*]* exercer ; *[+ force]* employer 2 ◆ **to ~ o.s.** *(physically)* se dépenser ; *(= take trouble)* se donner du mal, s'appliquer ◆ **to ~ o.s. to do sth** s'efforcer de faire qch ◆ **he didn't ~ himself unduly** il ne s'est pas donné trop de mal, il ne s'est pas trop fatigué ◆ **don't ~ yourself!** *(iro)* ne vous fatiguez pas !

exertion /ɪgˈzɜːʃən/ N 1 effort *m* ◆ **by his own ~s** par ses propres moyens ◆ **after the day's ~s** après les fatigues *fpl* de la journée ◆ **it doesn't require much ~** cela n'exige pas un grand effort 2 *(NonC) [of force, strength]* emploi *m* ; *[of authority, influence]* exercice *m* ◆ **by the ~ of a little pressure** *(lit)* en exerçant une légère pression ; *(fig)* en utilisant la manière douce

exeunt /ˈeksɪʌnt/ VI *(Theat)* ils sortent ◆ **~ Macbeth and Lady Macbeth** Macbeth et Lady Macbeth sortent

exfoliate /eksˈfəʊlɪeɪt/ VT *(Bio, Geol)* exfolier ; *(Cosmetics)* gommer VI *(Bio, Geol)* s'exfolier ; *(Cosmetics)* se faire un gommage (de la peau)
COMP **exfoliating cream** N crème *f* exfoliante

exfoliation /eksˌfəʊlɪˈeɪʃən/ N *(Bio, Geol)* exfoliation *f* ; *(Cosmetics)* gommage *m* ◆ **frequent ~ is good for the skin** un gommage fréquent est bon pour la peau

ex gratia /ˌeksˈgreɪʃə/ ADJ *[payment]* à titre gracieux

exhalation /ˌekshəˈleɪʃən/ N 1 *(= act)* exhalation *f* 2 *(= odour, fumes etc)* exhalaison *f*

exhale /eksˈheɪl/ VT 1 *(= breathe out)* expirer *(Physiol)* 2 *(= give off) [+ smoke, gas, perfume]* exhaler VI expirer ◆ **~ please** expirez s'il vous plaît ◆ **he ~d slowly in relief** il a laissé échapper un long soupir de soulagement

exhaust /ɪgˈzɔːst/ VT 1 *(= use up) [+ supplies, energy, mine, subject]* épuiser ◆ **to ~ sb's patience** pousser qn à bout 2 *(= tire)* épuiser, exténuer ◆ **to ~ o.s. (doing sth)** s'épuiser (à faire qch) N *(= exhaust system)* échappement *m* ; *(= pipe)* tuyau *m* or pot *m* d'échappement ; *(= fumes)* gaz *m* d'échappement

exhausted /ɪgˈzɔːstɪd/ ADJ 1 *(= tired out) [person]* épuisé *(from doing sth* d'avoir fait qch) ◆ **their horses were ~ from** *or* **with the chase** la poursuite avait épuisé leurs chevaux ◆ **I'm ~** je suis épuisé, je n'en peux plus 2 *(= used up) [supplies, savings, mine]* épuisé ◆ **my patience is ~** ma patience est à bout ◆ **until funds are ~** jusqu'à épuisement des fonds

exhaustible /ɪgˈzɔːstɪbl/ ADJ *[resources]* non renouvelable ; *[patience]* limité, qui a des limites

exhausting /ɪgˈzɔːstɪŋ/ ADJ épuisant

exhaustion /ɪgˈzɔːstʃən/ N épuisement *m*

exhaustive /ɪgˈzɔːstɪv/ ADJ *[list, study, report, analysis, research, investigation]* exhaustif ; *[coverage]* exhaustif, complet (-ète *f*) ; *[search]* minutieux ; *[tests]* approfondi, poussé ◆ **to make an ~ study of sth** étudier qch à fond *or* de manière exhaustive

exhaustively /ɪgˈzɔːstɪvlɪ/ ADV *[research, cover, list, describe]* de manière exhaustive ; *[study]* à fond, de manière exhaustive ◆ **they searched the area ~** ils ont minutieusement fouillé la région

exhaustiveness /ɪgˈzɔːstɪvnɪs/ N exhaustivité *f*

exhibit /ɪgˈzɪbɪt/ VT 1 *(= put on display) [+ painting, handicrafts]* exposer ; *[+ merchandise]* exposer, étaler ; *[+ animal]* montrer
2 *[+ courage, skill, ingenuity]* faire preuve de, déployer ; *[+ tendencies]* montrer, afficher ; *[+ behaviour]* afficher ; *[+ symptoms]* présenter ◆ **some people may ~ allergic reactions to this substance** certaines personnes développent *or* présentent des réactions allergiques à cette substance
VI *[artist, sculptor]* exposer ◆ **dog breeders who ~ all over the country** des éleveurs de chiens qui participent à des concours dans tout le pays
N 1 *(= object on display: in exhibition)* pièce *f* exposée *(dans un musée etc)*
2 *(Jur)* pièce *f* à conviction ◆ **~ A** première pièce *f* à conviction
3 *(US = exhibition)* exposition *f* ◆ **a photography ~** une exposition de photographies

exhibition /ˌeksɪˈbɪʃən/ N 1 *(= show) [of paintings, furniture etc]* exposition *f* ; *[of articles for sale]* étalage *m* ◆ **the Van Gogh ~** l'exposition *f* Van Gogh ◆ **to make an ~ of o.s.** se donner en spectacle 2 *(= act of exhibiting) [of technique etc]* démonstration *f* ; *[of film]* présentation *f* ◆ **what an ~ of bad manners!** quel étalage de mauvaises manières ! 3 *(Brit Univ)* bourse *f* (d'études)
COMP **exhibition centre** N centre *m* d'expositions
exhibition match N *(Sport)* match-exhibition *m*

exhibitioner /ˌeksɪˈbɪʃənəʳ/ N *(Brit Univ)* boursier *m*, -ière *f*

exhibitionism /ˌeksɪˈbɪʃənɪzəm/ N exhibitionnisme *m*

exhibitionist /ˌeksɪˈbɪʃənɪst/ ADJ, N exhibitionniste *mf*

exhibitor /ɪgˈzɪbɪtəʳ/ N exposant(e) *m(f) (dans une exposition)*

exhilarate /ɪgˈzɪləreɪt/ VT *[sea air etc]* vivifier ; *[music, wine, good company]* rendre euphorique ◆ **to be** *or* **feel ~d** être en pleine euphorie

exhilarating /ɪgˈzɪləreɪtɪŋ/ ADJ *[experience, time, feeling, ride]* grisant ; *[air, breeze]* vivifiant ; *[activity]* exaltant ◆ **it is ~ to do that** c'est grisant de faire cela

exhilaration /ɪgˌzɪləˈreɪʃən/ N ivresse *f*, euphorie *f*

exhort /ɪgˈzɔːt/ VT exhorter *(sb to sth* qn à qch ; *sb to do sth* qn à faire qch)

exhortation /ˌegzɔːˈteɪʃən/ N exhortation *f (to sth* à qch ; *to do sth* à faire qch) ◆ **despite ~s to investors to buy** bien que l'on ait exhorté les investisseurs à acheter

exhumation /ˌekshjuːˈmeɪʃən/ N exhumation *f*
COMP **exhumation order** N *(Jur)* autorisation *f* d'exhumer

exhume /eksˈhjuːm/ VT exhumer

ex-husband /ˌeksˈhʌzbənd/ N ex-mari *m*

exigence /ˈeksɪdʒəns/, **exigency** /ˈeksɪdʒənsɪ/ N *(frm) (= urgency)* urgence *f* ; *(= emergency)* circonstance *f* or situation *f* critique ; *(gen pl = de-*

mand) exigence *f* ◆ **according to the exigencies of the situation** selon les exigences de la situation

exigent /ˈeksɪdʒənt/ ADJ *(frm)* *(= urgent)* urgent, pressant ; *(= exacting)* exigeant

exiguity /ˌegzɪˈgjuːɪtɪ/ N *(frm)* exiguïté *f*

exiguous /ɪgˈzɪgjʊəs/ ADJ *(frm)* *[space]* exigu (-güe *f*) ; *[savings, income, revenue]* maigre

exile /ˈeksaɪl/ N 1 *(= person)* exilé(e) *m(f)* 2 *(NonC = condition: lit, fig)* exil *m* ◆ **in ~** en exil ◆ **to send into ~** envoyer en exil, exiler ◆ **to go into ~** s'exiler VT exiler, bannir *(from* de)

exiled /ˈeksaɪld/ ADJ exilé, en exil

exist /ɪgˈzɪst/ VI 1 *(= be in existence: gen, Philos)* exister ◆ **everything that ~s** tout ce qui existe ◆ **does God ~?** est-ce que Dieu existe ? ◆ **might life ~ on Mars?** est-ce qu'il peut y avoir de la vie sur Mars ? ◆ **it only ~s in her imagination** cela n'existe que dans son imagination ◆ **the understanding which ~s between the two countries** l'entente qui règne *or* existe entre les deux pays ◆ **the ceasefire now ~s in name only** à présent, le cessez-le-feu n'existe plus que sur le papier ◆ **to continue to ~** *[situation, conditions, doubt]* subsister ; *[institution]* rester en place ; *[person] (after death)* continuer à exister ◆ **to cease to ~** cesser d'exister, disparaître ◆ **there ~s a large number of people who ...** il existe un grand nombre de gens qui ... ◆ **there ~s a possibility** *or* **the possibility ~s that she is still alive** il se peut qu'elle soit toujours vivante

2 *(= live)* vivre, subsister ◆ **we cannot ~ without water** nous ne pouvons pas vivre *or* subsister sans eau ◆ **we ~ on an income of just £90 per week** nous vivons *or* subsistons avec seulement 90 livres par semaine ◆ **she ~s on junk food** elle se nourrit de cochonneries

existence /ɪgˈzɪstəns/ N 1 *(NonC)* *[of God, person, object, institution]* existence *f* ◆ **to be in ~** exister ◆ **to come into ~** voir le jour ◆ **to call into ~** faire naître, créer ◆ **it passed** *or* **went out of ~ ten years ago** cela n'existe plus depuis dix ans ◆ **the only one in ~** le seul *or* la seule qui existe *subj or* qui soit 2 *(= life)* existence *f*, vie *f*

existent /ɪgˈzɪstənt/ ADJ *(frm)* existant

existential /ˌegzɪˈstenʃəl/ ADJ existentiel

existentialism /ˌegzɪˈstenʃəlɪzəm/ N existentialisme *m*

existentialist /ˌegzɪˈstenʃəlɪst/ ADJ, N existentialiste *mf*

existing /ɪgˈzɪstɪŋ/ ADJ *[system, arrangements, customers, facilities, product, border]* actuel ; *[law, order]* existant ◆ **under ~ circumstances** dans les circonstances actuelles

exit /ˈeksɪt/ N 1 *(from stage, competition, motorway)* sortie *f* ◆ **to make one's ~** *(Theat)* quitter la scène, faire sa sortie ; *(gen)* sortir, quitter les lieux 2 *(= way out, door)* sortie *f* ; → **emergency** 3 *(voluntary euthanasia society)* **Exit** ≈ Mourir dans la Dignité VI 1 *(Theat)* **~ the King** le roi sort 2 *(= leave)* sortir, faire sa sortie 3 *(Comput)* sortir VT *(Comput)* *[+ file, program, application]* sortir de, quitter

COMP **exit interview** N entretien *m* de sortie ; *(following redundancy)* entretien *m* de licenciement

exit permit N permis *m* de sortie

exit poll N *(at election)* sondage *m* effectué à la sortie des bureaux de vote

exit ramp N *(US: on highway)* bretelle *f* d'accès

exit strategy N stratégie *f* de repli

exit visa N visa *m* de sortie

ex nihilo /ˌeksˈnɪhɪləʊ/ ADV ex nihilo

exocrine /ˈeksəʊˌkraɪn/ ADJ exocrine

exodus /ˈeksədəs/ N exode *m* ◆ **there was a general ~** il y a eu un exode massif ◆ **Exodus** *(Bible)* l'Exode *m*

ex officio /ˌeksəˈfɪʃɪəʊ/ *(frm)* ADV *[act]* ès qualités ADJ *[member]* de droit

exonerate /ɪgˈzɒnəreɪt/ VT *(= prove innocent)* disculper *(from* de) innocenter ; *(= release from obligation)* dispenser *(from* de)

exoneration /ɪgˌzɒnəˈreɪʃən/ N disculpation *f* *(from sth* de qch)

exorbitance /ɪgˈzɔːbɪtəns/ N *[of demands]* outrance *f* ; *[of price]* énormité *f*

exorbitant /ɪgˈzɔːbɪtənt/ ADJ *[price, cost, charge, demands]* exorbitant ; *[profit]* faramineux

exorbitantly /ɪgˈzɔːbɪtəntlɪ/ ADV *[expensive]* démesurément ◆ **an ~ high salary** un salaire exorbitant ◆ **~ priced** d'un prix exorbitant ◆ **to pay sb/charge sb ~** payer qn/faire payer à qn des sommes exorbitantes

exorcise /ˈeksɔːsaɪz/ VT exorciser *(of* de)

exorcism /ˈeksɔːsɪzəm/ N exorcisme *m*

exorcist /ˈeksɔːsɪst/ N exorciste *mf*

exoskeleton /ˌeksəʊˈskelɪtən/ N exosquelette *m*

exosphere /ˈeksəʊˌsfɪəʳ/ N exosphère *f*

exoteric /ˌeksəʊˈterɪk/ ADJ *[doctrine]* exotérique ; *[opinions]* populaire

exothermic /ˌeksəʊˈθɜːmɪk/ ADJ exothermique

exotic /ɪgˈzɒtɪk/ ADJ exotique ◆ **an ~-sounding name** un nom aux consonances exotiques N *(= plant)* plante *f* exotique

exotica /ɪgˈzɒtɪkə/ NPL objets *mpl* exotiques

exotically /ɪgˈzɒtɪklɪ/ ADV *[dressed]* d'une manière exotique ◆ **~ named** au nom exotique

exoticism /ɪgˈzɒtɪsɪzəm/ N exotisme *m*

expand /ɪkˈspænd/ VT *[+ gas, liquid, metal]* dilater ; *[+ one's business, trade, ideas]* développer ; *[+ production]* accroître, augmenter ; *[+ number]* augmenter ; *[+ study]* élargir ; *[+ influence, empire]* étendre ; *[+ range]* élargir, étendre ; *(Math)* *[+ formula]* développer ◆ **to ~ one's knowledge** élargir ses connaissances ◆ **to ~ one's experience** élargir son expérience ◆ **exercises to ~ one's chest** exercices *mpl* physiques pour développer le torse ◆ **she ~ed the story into a novel** elle a développé l'histoire pour en faire un roman ◆ **they have ~ed their workforce to 300** ils ont porté le nombre de leurs employés à 300 ◆ **this ~ed board membership to 21** cela a porté à 21 le nombre des membres du conseil d'administration

VI 1 *[gas, liquid, metal]* se dilater ; *[business, trade, ideas]* se développer ; *[production]* s'accroître, augmenter ; *[study]* s'élargir ; *[influence, empire]* s'étendre ; *[knowledge]* s'élargir ◆ **the market is ~ing** le marché est en expansion ◆ **the market is ~ing rapidly** le marché connaît une rapide expansion ◆ **the economy ~ed by 3.9% in 1996** l'économie a connu une croissance de 3,9% en 1996 ◆ **they've ~ed into the European market** ils ont étendu leur activités au marché européen ◆ **they've ~ed into new products** ils ont diversifié leurs produits ◆ **a former radio presenter who has ~ed into television** un ancien présentateur de radio qui s'est reconverti dans la télévision ; see also **expanding**

2 ◆ **to ~ (up)on** développer

expanded /ɪkˈspændɪd/ ADJ *(Metal, Tech)* expansé ◆ **~ polystyrene** polystyrène *m* expansé

expander /ɪkˈspændəʳ/ N → **chest²**

expanding /ɪkˈspændɪŋ/ ADJ *[metal etc]* qui se dilate ; *[bracelet]* extensible ; *[market, industry, profession]* en expansion ◆ **the ~ universe** l'univers *m* en expansion ◆ **the ~ universe theory** la théorie de l'expansion de l'univers ◆ **~ file** classeur *m* extensible ◆ **a job with ~ opportunities** un emploi qui offre un nombre croissant de débouchés ◆ **a rapidly ~ industry** une industrie en pleine expansion

expanse /ɪkˈspæns/ N étendue *f*

expansion /ɪkˈspænʃən/ N *[of gas]* expansion *f*, dilatation *f* ; *[of business]* expansion *f*, agrandissement *m* ; *[of trade]* développement *m*, expansion *f* ; *[of production]* accroissement *m*, augmentation *f* ; *(territorial, economic, colonial)* expansion *f* ; *[of subject, idea]* développement *m* ; *(Math)* développement *m* ; *(Gram)* expansion *f*

COMP **expansion bottle** N *[of car]* vase *m* d'expansion

expansion card N *(Comput)* carte *f* d'extension

expansion slot N *(Comput)* emplacement *m or* logement *m* pour carte supplémentaire

expansion tank N ⇒ **expansion bottle**

expansionary /ɪkˈspænʃənərɪ/ ADJ expansionniste

expansionism /ɪkˈspænʃənɪzəm/ N expansionnisme *m*

expansionist /ɪkˈspænʃənɪst/ ADJ, N expansionniste *mf*

expansive /ɪkˈspænsɪv/ ADJ 1 *(= affable)* *[person, mood, gesture]* expansif ; *[smile]* chaleureux 2 *(frm = grand)* *[area, lawn]* étendu ; *[room]* spacieux ; *[view]* étendu, bien dégagé 3 *(= expanding)* *[economy, business]* en expansion ; *[phase]* d'expansion ◆ **to have ~ ambitions** avoir des ambitions conquérantes 4 *(Phys)* *(= causing expansion)* expansif ; *(= capable of expanding)* expansible, dilatable

expansively /ɪkˈspænsɪvlɪ/ ADV 1 *(= affably)* *[say, smile]* chaleureusement, avec chaleur ◆ **to gesture ~** faire de grands gestes 2 *(= in detail)* ◆ **he wrote ~ to his son** il a écrit de longues lettres à son fils ◆ **he talked ~ of his travels** il a longuement raconté ses voyages

expansiveness /ɪkˈspænsɪvnɪs/ N *[of person]* expansivité *f* ; *[of welcome, smile]* chaleur *f*

expat * /eksˈpæt/ N (abbrev of **expatriate**) expatrié(e) *m(f)* ◆ **the ~ community** la communauté des expatriés

expatiate /ɪkˈspeɪʃɪeɪt/ VI discourir, disserter *(upon* sur)

expatriate /eksˈpætrɪət/ N expatrié(e) *m(f)* ◆ **British ~s** ressortissants *mpl* britanniques établis à l'étranger ADJ *[person]* expatrié ; *[family, community]* d'expatriés VT /eksˈpætrɪeɪt/ expatrier

expect /ɪkˈspekt/ VT → **expected** 1 *(= anticipate)* s'attendre à ; *(= predict)* prévoir ; *(with confidence)* escompter ; *(= count on)* compter sur ; *(= hope for)* espérer ◆ **I ~ed that, I ~ed as much** je m'y attendais ◆ **he failed, as we had ~ed** il a échoué, comme nous l'avions prévu ◆ **this suitcase is not as heavy as I ~ed** cette valise n'est pas aussi lourde que je le croyais, je m'attendais à ce que cette valise soit plus lourde ◆ **I did not ~ that from him** je ne m'attendais pas à cela de lui ◆ **we were ~ing rain** nous nous attendions à de la pluie ◆ **he did not have the success he ~ed** il n'a pas eu le succès qu'il escomptait ◆ **to ~ that ...** s'attendre à ce que ... + *subj* ◆ **I ~ that he'll come** je pense qu'il viendra ◆ **to ~ to do sth** penser *or* compter faire qch ◆ **I ~ him to come** je m'attends à ce qu'il vienne ◆ **we were ~ing war** on attendait la guerre ◆ **I know what to ~** je sais à quoi m'attendre *or* m'en tenir ◆ **well what do** *or* **did you ~?** il fallait t'y attendre !, ce n'est pas surprenant ! ◆ **to ~ the worst** s'attendre au pire ◆ **as ~ed** comme on s'y attendait, comme prévu ◆ **as might have been ~ed, as was to be ~ed** comme on pouvait *or* comme il fallait s'y attendre ◆ **that was to be ~ed** c'était à prévoir, il fallait s'y attendre ◆ **it is ~ed that ...** on s'attend à ce que ... + *subj* ◆ **it is hardly to be ~ed that ...** il ne faut pas *or* guère s'attendre à ce que ... + *subj*

◆ **to be expected to do sth** ◆ **she is ~ed to make an announcement this afternoon** elle doit faire une déclaration cet après-midi ◆ **inflation is ~ed to rise this year** on s'attend à ce que l'inflation augmente *subj* cette année ◆ **what am I ~ed to do about it?** qu'est-ce que je suis censé faire ? ◆ **the talks are ~ed to last two or three days** les négociations devraient durer *or* on s'attend à ce que les négociations durent *subj* deux ou trois jours

2 *(= suppose)* ◆ **I ~ so** je crois que oui, je crois* ◆ **we're not going to win – I ~ not** nous n'allons pas gagner – je crois bien que non ◆ **this work is very tiring – yes, I ~ it is** ce travail est très fatigant – oui, je m'en doute *or* je veux bien le croire ◆ **I ~ he'll soon have finished** je pense *or* suppose qu'il aura bientôt fini ◆ **I ~ you're tired** vous devez être fatigué, je suppose que vous êtes fatigué

3 *(= demand)* attendre *(sth from sb* qch de qn) demander *(sth from sb* qch à qn) ; *(stronger)* exiger *(sth from sb* qch de qn) ◆ **you can't ~ too much from him** il ne faut pas trop lui en demander ◆ **the company ~s employees to be punctual** l'entreprise attend de ses employés qu'ils soient ponctuels ◆ **what do you ~ of me?** qu'attendez-vous *or* qu'exigez-vous de moi ? ◆ **to ~ sb to do sth** vouloir que qn fasse qch ; *(stronger)* exiger *or* demander que qn fasse qch ◆ **I ~ you to tidy your own room** tu devras ranger ta chambre toi-même ◆ **what do you ~ me to do about it?** que voulez-vous que j'y fasse ? ◆ **you can't ~ them to take it/him seriously** comment voulez-vous qu'ils prennent cela/qu'ils le prennent au sérieux ? ◆ **are we ~ed to leave now?** est-ce que nous sommes censés *or* est-ce qu'on doit partir tout de suite ?

4 *(= await) [+ person, thing, action, letter, phone call]* attendre ◆ **I am ~ing her tomorrow/this evening/at 7pm** elle doit venir demain/ce soir/à 19 heures ◆ **we are ~ing it this week** *[stock, delivery]* nous devons le recevoir cette semaine ◆ **I am ~ing them for dinner** ils doivent venir dîner ◆ **~ me when you see me!*** vous (me) verrez bien quand je serai là !*, ne m'attendez pas ! ◆ **we'll ~ you when we see you*** on ne t'attend pas à une heure précise

5 ◆ **to be ~ing a baby** attendre un enfant

VI ◆ **she is ~ing*** elle attend un enfant

expectancy /ɪk'spektənsɪ/ **N** attente *f* ; *(= hopefulness)* espoir *m* ◆ **an air of ~** une atmosphère d'impatience contenue ◆ **a look of ~** un regard plein d'espoir ◆ **awaited with eager ~** attendu avec une vive impatience ; → **life**

expectant /ɪks'pektənt/ **ADJ** 1 *(= future) [mother, father]* futur *before n* 2 *(= excited) [person, crowd]* impatient ; *[silence, hush, face, eyes, smile]* plein d'attente ◆ **with an ~ look on one's face** le visage plein d'attente ◆ **an ~ atmosphere** une atmosphère d'impatience contenue

expectantly /ɪk'spektəntlɪ/ **ADV** *[look at, smile]* avec l'air d'attendre quelque chose ◆ **to wait ~** attendre avec impatience

expectation /ˌekspek'teɪʃən/ **N** *(= sth expected)* attente f, espérance *f* ◆ **contrary to all ~(s)** contre toute attente ◆ **to come up to sb's ~s** répondre à l'attente *or* aux espérances de qn ◆ **beyond ~** au-delà de mes *(or de nos etc)* espérances ◆ **his (financial) ~s are good** ses perspectives financières sont bonnes ◆ **his promise has raised ~s that a settlement may be near** sa promesse a laissé espérer qu'une solution était proche ◆ **I shouldn't have raised my ~s so high** je n'aurais pas dû avoir de si grandes espérances ◆ **there is every ~ of/no ~ of a cold winter** il y a toutes les chances/peu de chances que l'hiver soit rude ◆ **there is little ~ that the negotiations will succeed** on ne s'attend guère à ce que les négociations aboutissent

◆ **in + expectation** ◆ **in ~ of ...** en prévision de ... ◆ **to live in ~** vivre dans l'expectative ◆ **I waited in the ~ that she would come** j'ai attendu dans l'espoir qu'elle viendrait ◆ **happiness in ~** du bonheur en perspective

expected /ɪk'spektɪd/ **ADJ** *[phone call, letter, news]* qu'on attendait ; *[change, growth]* attendu ; *[arrival]* prévu ; *[profit, loss]* escompté ◆ **the ~ letter never came** la lettre qu'on attendait n'est jamais arrivée ◆ **their ~ time of arrival is 6 o'clock** on les attend à 6 heures, ils doivent arriver à 6 heures ◆ **what is their ~ time/date of arrival?** à quelle heure/quand doivent-ils arriver ? ◆ **six weeks was the ~ time it would take to resolve such an inquiry** six semaines était le temps qu'il fallait escompter pour répondre à une demande de ce genre ◆ **she had been born before the ~ time** elle était née avant terme ◆ **less than half the ~ number turned out to the demonstration** les manifestants étaient moitié moins nombreux que prévu ◆ **next year's ~ $1.8 billion deficit** le déficit escompté de 1,8 milliard de dollars pour l'année prochaine

expectorant /ɪk'spektərənt/ **N, ADJ** expectorant *m*

expectorate /ɪk'spektəreɪt/ **VTI** expectorer

expedience /ɪk'spiːdɪəns/, **expediency** /ɪk'spiːdɪənsɪ/ **N** *(= convenience)* opportunité *f* ; *(= self-interest)* opportunisme *m* ; *(= advisability) [of project, course of action]* opportunité *f*

expedient /ɪk'spiːdɪənt/ **ADJ** 1 *(= suitable, convenient)* indiqué, opportun 2 *(= politic)* politique, opportun ◆ **this solution is more ~ than just** cette solution est plus politique que juste ◆ **it would be ~ to change the rule** il serait opportun de changer le règlement **N** expédient *m*

expedite /'ekspɪdaɪt/ **VT** *[+ preparations, process]* accélérer ; *[+ work, operations, legal or official matters]* activer, hâter ; *[+ business, task]* expédier ; *[+ deal]* s'efforcer de conclure ; *(o.f or frm = dispatch)* expédier

expedition /ˌekspɪ'dɪʃən/ **N** 1 *(= journey)* expédition *f* ; *(= shorter trip)* tour *m* ; *(= group of people)* (membres *mpl* d'une) expédition *f* ◆ **a fishing ~** une partie de pêche 2 *(NonC: o.f or frm = speed)* promptitude *f*

expeditionary /ˌekspɪ'dɪʃənrɪ/ **ADJ** expéditionnaire ◆ **~ force** *(Mil)* corps *m* expéditionnaire

expeditious /ˌekspɪ'dɪʃəs/ **ADJ** *(frm)* expéditif

expeditiously /ˌekspɪ'dɪʃəslɪ/ **ADV** *(frm)* promptement *(liter)* ◆ **as ~ as possible** aussi rapidement que possible

expel /ɪk'spel/ **VT** *(from country, meeting)* expulser ; *(from society, party)* exclure ; *(from school)* renvoyer ; *[+ the enemy]* chasser ; *[+ gas, liquid]* évacuer, expulser ; *(from the body)* évacuer ; *[+ foetus]* expulser

expend /ɪk'spend/ **VT** 1 *(= spend) [+ time, energy]* consacrer *(on sth* à qch ; *on doing sth* à faire qch) ; *[+ money]* dépenser *(on sth* pour qch ; *on doing sth* pour faire qch) 2 *(= use up) [+ ammunition, resources]* épuiser

expendability /ɪkˌspendə'bɪlɪtɪ/ **N** ◆ **its ~** le peu de valeur qu'on y attache

expendable /ɪk'spendəbl/ **ADJ** *(= not indispensable) [person, luxury, troops, aircraft]* dont on peut se passer ; *(= disposable) [rocket, launcher]* non récupérable ◆ **~ stores** *(Mil)* matériel *m* de consommation **N** consommable *m*

expenditure /ɪk'spendɪtʃər/ **N** *(NonC)* 1 *(= money spent)* dépense(s) *f(pl)* ; *(Accounting = outgoings)* sortie *f* ◆ **public ~** dépenses *fpl* publiques ◆ **to limit one's ~** limiter ses dépenses ◆ **a project which involves heavy ~** un projet qui entraîne de grosses dépenses ◆ **income and ~** recettes *fpl* et dépenses *fpl* 2 *(= spending) [of money, time, energy]* dépense *f* ; *[of resources]* utilisation *f* ◆ **the ~ of public funds on this project** l'utilisation *f* des fonds publics pour ce projet 3 *(= using up) [of ammunition, resources]* épuisement *m*

expense /ɪk'spens/ **N** 1 *(NonC)* dépense *f*, frais *mpl* ; *(Accounting: on account statement)* charge *f*, frais *mpl* ◆ **regardless of ~** même si ça revient cher ◆ **that will involve him in some ~** cela lui occasionnera des frais ◆ **at my ~** à mes frais ◆ **at public ~** aux frais de l'État ◆ **at little ~** à peu de frais ◆ **at great ~** à grands frais ◆ **to go to the ~ of buying a car** aller jusqu'à acheter une voiture ◆ **to put sb to ~** faire faire *or* causer des dépenses à qn ◆ **to put sb to great ~** occasionner de grosses dépenses à qn ◆ **to go to great ~ on sb's account** engager de grosses dépenses pour qn ◆ **to go to great ~ (to repair the house)** faire beaucoup de frais (pour réparer la maison) ◆ **don't go to any ~ over our visit** ne faites pas de frais pour notre visite ◆ **to live at other people's ~** vivre aux frais *or* à la charge des autres ; → **spare**

2 *(fig)* **at the ~ of** *[+ person, one's health, happiness, peace of mind]* au détriment de ◆ **to have a good laugh at sb's ~** bien rire aux dépens de qn ◆ **to get rich at other people's ~** s'enrichir aux dépens d'autrui *or* au détriment des autres

NPL expenses frais *mpl*, dépenses *fpl* ◆ **he gets all his ~s paid** il se fait rembourser tous ses frais *or* toutes ses dépenses ◆ **your ~s will be entirely covered** vous serez défrayé entièrement *or* en totalité ◆ **after all ~s have been paid** tous frais payés

COMP expense account N *(Comm)* frais *mpl* de représentation ◆ **this will go on his ~ account** cela passera aux frais de représentation *or* sur sa note de frais ◆ **~ account lunch** déjeuner *m* qui passe aux frais de représentation *or* sur la note de frais

expenses sheet N note *f* de frais

expensive /ɪk'spensɪv/ **ADJ** *[goods, shop, restaurant, country, city]* cher ; *[journey]* qui coûte cher, onéreux ; *[hobby, holiday, undertaking]* coûteux ; *[mistake]* qui coûte cher ◆ **to be ~** coûter cher, valoir cher ◆ **to come ~*** revenir cher ◆ **to have ~ tastes** avoir des goûts de luxe ◆ **it is very ~ to live in London** c'est très cher *or* ça revient très cher de vivre à Londres ◆ **bringing up children is an ~ business** c'est cher *or* ça revient cher d'élever des enfants

expensively /ɪk'spensɪvlɪ/ **ADV** *[buy, sell]* très cher ; *[equipped, furnished, educated]* à grands frais ; *[dressed]* de façon coûteuse ◆ **to live ~** mener grand train

expensiveness /ɪk'spensɪvnɪs/ **N** cherté *f*

experience /ɪk'spɪərɪəns/ LANGUAGE IN USE 19.2

N 1 *(NonC = knowledge, wisdom)* expérience *f* ◆ **~ of life/of men** expérience *f* du monde/des hommes ◆ **~ shows that ...** l'expérience montre que ... ◆ **in my ~** d'après mon expérience ◆ **I know by ~** je sais par expérience ◆ **from my own** *or* **personal ~** d'après mon expérience personnelle ◆ **I know from bitter ~ that ...** j'ai appris à mes dépens que ... ◆ **he has no ~ of real grief** il n'a jamais éprouvé *or* ressenti un vrai chagrin ◆ **he has no ~ of living in the country** il ne sait pas ce que c'est que de vivre à la campagne

2 *(NonC = practice, skill)* pratique *f*, expérience *f* ◆ **practical ~** pratique *f* ◆ **business ~** expérience *f* des affaires ◆ **he has a lot of teaching ~** il a une longue pratique *or* expérience de l'enseignement ◆ **he has considerable ~ in selecting ...** il possède une expérience considérable dans la sélection de ... ◆ **he has considerable driving ~** c'est un conducteur très expérimenté ◆ **he lacks ~** il manque d'expérience *or* de pratique ◆ **have you any previous ~ (in this kind of work)?** avez-vous déjà fait ce genre de travail ? ◆ **I've (had) no ~ of driving this type of car** je n'ai jamais conduit une voiture de ce type ◆ **~ preferred (but not**

essential) *(in job advert)* expérience souhaitable (mais non indispensable *or* essentielle) [3] *(= event experienced)* expérience *f*, aventure *f* ◆ **I had a pleasant/frightening ~** il m'est arrivé une aventure agréable/effrayante ◆ **she's had** *or* **gone through some terrible ~s** elle a subi de rudes épreuves ◆ **it was a new ~ for me** c'était une nouveauté *or* une expérience nouvelle pour moi ◆ **we had many unforgettable ~s there** nous y avons vécu *or* passé bien des moments inoubliables ◆ **she swam in the nude and it was an agreeable ~** elle a nagé toute nue et a trouvé l'expérience agréable ◆ **it wasn't an ~ I would care to repeat** ça n'est pas une aventure que je tiens à recommencer ◆ **unfortunate ~** mésaventure *f*

VT [1] *(= undergo) [+ misfortune, hardship]* connaître ; *[+ setbacks, losses]* essuyer ; *[+ privations]* souffrir de ; *[+ conditions]* être confronté à ; *[+ ill treatment]* subir ; *[+ difficulties]* rencontrer ◆ **he doesn't know what it is like to be poor for he has never ~d it** il ne sait pas ce que c'est que d'être pauvre car il n'en a jamais fait l'expérience *or* cela ne lui est jamais arrivé ◆ **he ~s some difficulty in speaking** il a du mal *or* il éprouve de la difficulté à parler

[2] *(= feel) [+ sensation, terror, remorse]* éprouver ; *[+ emotion, joy, elation]* ressentir

experienced /ɪkˈspɪərɪənst/ **ADJ** *[person]* expérimenté ◆ **we need someone more ~** il nous faut quelqu'un qui ait plus d'expérience *or* quelqu'un de plus expérimenté ◆ **she is not ~ enough** elle n'a pas assez d'expérience ◆ **"experienced driver required"** "on recherche chauffeur : expérience exigée" ◆ **with an ~ eye** d'un œil exercé ◆ **to the ~ eye/ear** pour un œil exercé/une oreille exercée ◆ **to be sexually ~** être expérimenté (sexuellement) ◆ **to be ~ in sth** être expérimenté en *or* dans qch, être rompu à qch ◆ **to be ~ in the trade** avoir du métier ◆ **to be ~ in doing sth** avoir l'habitude de faire qch

experiential /ɪkˌspɪərɪˈenʃəl/ **ADJ** *(frm, Philos)* qui résulte de l'expérience, dont on a fait l'expérience ◆ **~ learning** apprentissage expérientiel

experiment /ɪkˈsperɪmənt/ **N** *(Chem, Phys)* expérience *f* ; *(fig)* expérience *f*, essai *m* ◆ **to carry out an ~** faire une expérience ◆ **by way of ~, as an ~** à titre d'essai *or* d'expérience **VI** /ɪkˈsperɪˌment/ *(Chem, Phys)* faire une expérience, expérimenter ; *(fig)* faire une *or* des expérience(s) ◆ **to ~ with a new vaccine** expérimenter un nouveau vaccin ◆ **to ~ on guinea pigs** faire des expériences sur des cobayes ◆ **they are ~ing with communal living** ils font l'expérience de la vie communautaire

experimental /ɪkˌsperɪˈmentl/ **ADJ** *[technique, method, evidence, research, novel]* expérimental ◆ **~ scientist/psychologist/physicist** expert *m* en sciences expérimentales/psychologie expérimentale/physique expérimentale ◆ **to be at** *or* **in the ~ stage** en être au stade expérimental ◆ **he gave an ~ tug at the door handle** il a tiré un peu sur la porte pour voir

experimentally /ɪkˌsperɪˈmentəlɪ/ **ADV** [1] *(= scientifically) [study, test]* expérimentalement [2] *(= to see what happens) [try out, introduce]* pour voir, à titre expérimental ◆ **he lifted the cases ~ to see how heavy they were** il a soupesé les valises pour voir si elles étaient lourdes

experimentation /ɪkˌsperɪmenˈteɪʃən/ **N** expérimentation *f*

experimenter /ɪkˈsperɪmentəʳ/ **N** expérimentateur *m*, -trice *f*

expert /ˈekspɜːt/ **N** spécialiste *mf (in, on, at* en) connaisseur *m (in, on* en) ; *(= officially qualified)* expert *m* ◆ **he is an ~ on wines** *or* **a wine ~** c'est un grand *or* fin connaisseur en vins ◆ **he is an ~ on the subject** c'est un expert en la matière ◆ **~ at pigeon shooting** spécialiste *mf* du tir aux pigeons ◆ **19th century ~** spécialiste *mf* du 19ᵉ siècle ◆ **he's an ~ at repairing watches** il est expert à réparer les montres ◆ **he's an ~ at that sort of negotiation** il est spécialiste de ce genre de négociations ◆ **with the eye of an ~** *[examine]* d'un œil *or* regard connaisseur ; *[judge]* en connaisseur, en expert ◆ **~'s report** *or* **valuation** expertise *f*

ADJ *[carpenter, acrobat, hands, approach]* expert *(at or in sth* en qch ; *at or in doing sth* à faire qch) ; *[advice, opinion, help, attention, knowledge, evidence]* d'un expert ; *[treatment]* spécialisé ◆ **to be ~ at** *or* **in sth/in** *or* **at doing sth** être expert en qch/à faire qch ◆ **he ran an ~ eye over the photographs** il a regardé les photographies d'un œil expert ◆ **not noticeable except to the ~ eye** que seul un œil expert peut remarquer ◆ **with an ~ touch** avec une habileté d'expert *or* l'habileté d'un expert ◆ **he is ~ in this field** il est expert en la matière

COMP expert appraisal N expertise *f*
expert system N *(Comput)* système *m* expert
expert valuation N ⇒ **expert appraisal**
expert witness N témoin *m* expert

expertise /ˌekspəˈtiːz/ **N** *(= knowledge)* expertise *f* ; *(= competence)* compétence *f (in* en)

expertly /ˈekspɜːtlɪ/ **ADV** de façon experte

expertness /ˈekspɜːtnɪs/ **N** ⇒ **expertise**

expiate /ˈekspɪeɪt/ **VT** expier

expiation /ˌekspɪˈeɪʃən/ **N** expiation *f* ◆ **in ~ of ...** en expiation de ...

expiatory /ˈekspɪətərɪ/ **ADJ** expiatoire

expiration /ˌekspaɪəˈreɪʃən/ **N** [1] ⇒ **expiry** [2] *(= breathing out)* expiration *f* [3] (†† *= death)* trépas *m (liter)*, décès *m*

expire /ɪkˈspaɪəʳ/ **VI** [1] *[lease, passport, licence, insurance, contract]* expirer ; *[period, time limit]* arriver à terme [2] *(liter = die)* expirer, rendre l'âme *or* le dernier soupir [3] *(= breathe out)* expirer

expiry /ɪkˈspaɪərɪ/ **N** *[of time limit, period, term of office]* expiration *f*, fin *f* ; *[of passport, lease]* expiration *f* ◆ **date of ~, ~ date** *(gen)* date *f* d'expiration ; *(on label)* à utiliser avant ... ◆ **date of ~ of the lease** expiration *f or* terme *m* du bail

explain /ɪkˈspleɪn/ LANGUAGE IN USE 18.4, 26.3 **VT** [1] *(= make clear) [+ how sth works, rule, meaning of a word, situation, motives, thoughts]* expliquer ; *[+ mystery]* élucider, éclaircir ; *[+ reasons, points of view]* exposer ◆ **~ what you want to do** expliquez ce que vous voulez faire ◆ **"it's raining" she ~ed** "il pleut" expliqua-t-elle ◆ **that is easy to ~, that is easily ~ed** cela s'explique facilement ◆ **this may seem confused, I will ~ myself** ceci peut paraître confus, je m'explique donc ◆ **I can ~** je peux (m')expliquer ◆ **let me ~** je m'explique ◆ **to ~ why/how** *etc* expliquer pourquoi/comment *etc* ◆ **he ~ed to us why he had been absent** il nous a expliqué pourquoi il avait été absent ◆ **to ~ to sb how to do sth** expliquer à qn comment (il faut) faire qch

[2] *(= account for) [+ phenomenon]* expliquer ; *[+ behaviour]* expliquer, justifier ◆ **the bad weather ~s why he is absent** le mauvais temps explique son absence *or* qu'il soit absent ◆ **come now, ~ yourself!** allez, expliquez-vous !

▸ **explain away VT SEP** justifier, trouver une explication convaincante à

explainable /ɪkˈspleɪnəbl/ **ADJ** explicable ◆ **that is easily ~** cela s'explique facilement

explanation /ˌekspləˈneɪʃən/ **N** [1] *(= act, statement)* explication *f*, éclaircissement *m* ◆ **a long ~ of what he meant by democracy** une longue explication de ce qu'il entendait par la démocratie ◆ **an ~ of how to do sth** une explication sur la manière de faire qch ◆ **these instructions need some ~** ces instructions demandent quelques éclaircissements [2] *(= cause, motive)* explication *f* ◆ **to find an ~ for sth** trouver l'explication de qch [3] *(NonC = justification)* explication *f*, justification *f* ◆ **has he something to say in ~ of his conduct?** est-ce qu'il peut fournir une explication à sa conduite ? ◆ **what do you have to say in ~?** comment expliquez-vous la chose ?

explanatory /ɪkˈsplænətərɪ/ **ADJ** explicatif

expletive /ɪkˈspliːtɪv/ **N** *(= exclamation)* exclamation *f*, interjection *f* ; *(= oath)* juron *m* ; *(Gram)* explétif *m* **ADJ** *(Gram)* explétif

explicable /ɪkˈsplɪkəbl/ **ADJ** explicable

explicably /ɪkˈsplɪkəblɪ/ **ADV** d'une manière explicable

explicate /ˈekspl̩ɪˌkeɪt/ **VT** *(frm)* expliciter

explicit /ɪkˈsplɪsɪt/ **ADJ** explicite *(about sth* à propos de qch ; *in sth* dans qch) ◆ **to be ~ in doing sth** faire qch de façon explicite ◆ **he was ~ on this point** il a été explicite sur ce point ◆ **in ~ detail** avec des détails explicites ◆ **sexually ~** sexuellement explicite

explicitly /ɪkˈsplɪsɪtlɪ/ **ADV** explicitement

explode /ɪkˈspləʊd/ **VI** *[bomb, boiler, plane]* exploser, éclater ; *[gas]* exploser, détoner ; *[building, ship, ammunition]* exploser, sauter ; *[joy, anger]* éclater ; *[person]* (*: from rage, impatience*)* exploser ◆ **to ~ with laughter** éclater de rire **VT** *[+ bomb]* faire exploser ; *(fig) [+ theory, argument]* faire voler en éclats ; *[+ rumour]* couper court à ◆ **to ~ the myth that ...** démolir le mythe selon lequel ... **COMP exploded drawing, exploded view N** éclaté *m*

exploit /ˈeksplɔɪt/ **N** *(heroic)* exploit *m*, haut fait *m* ; *(= feat)* prouesse *f* ◆ **~s** *(= adventures)* aventures *fpl* **VT** /ɪkˈsplɔɪt/ [1] *(= use unfairly) [+ workers, sb's credulity]* exploiter [2] *(= make use of) [+ minerals, land, talent]* exploiter ; *[+ situation]* profiter de, tirer parti de

exploitable /ɪkˈsplɔɪtəbl/ **ADJ** exploitable

exploitation /ˌeksplɔɪˈteɪʃən/ **N** exploitation *f*

exploitative /ɪkˈsplɔɪtətɪv/ **ADJ** exploiteur (-trice *f*)

exploration /ˌeksplə'reɪʃən/ **N** *(Med, lit, fig)* exploration *f* ◆ **voyage of ~** voyage *m* d'exploration *or* de découverte ◆ **preliminary ~** *[of ground, site]* reconnaissance *f*

exploratory /ɪkˈsplɒrətərɪ/ **ADJ** *(= investigative) [expedition, digging, drilling]* d'exploration ; *(= preliminary) [talks]* exploratoire ; *[meeting, trip, approach, stage]* préliminaire ◆ **the ~ nature of the discussions** la nature préliminaire des discussions ◆ **~ study** *(Jur)* étude *f* prospective ◆ **to have ~ surgery** *or* **an ~ operation** *(Med)* subir une exploration

explore /ɪkˈsplɔːʳ/ **VT** *[+ territory, house, question, matter]* explorer ; *(Med)* sonder ; *(fig) [+ issue, proposal]* étudier sous tous ses aspects ◆ **to go exploring** partir en exploration *or* à la découverte ◆ **to ~ every corner of a house/garden** explorer chaque recoin d'une maison/d'un jardin ◆ **to ~ the ground** *(lit, fig)* tâter *or* sonder le terrain ◆ **to ~ every avenue** examiner toutes les possibilités ◆ **to ~ the possibilities** étudier les possibilités ◆ **to ~ an agreement** examiner les modalités d'un éventuel accord

explorer /ɪkˈsplɔːrəʳ/ **N** [1] *(= person)* explorateur *m*, -trice *f* [2] *(US = dental probe)* sonde *f*

explosion /ɪkˈspləʊʒən/ **N** [1] *[of bomb, boiler, plane]* explosion *f* ◆ **nuclear ~** explosion *f* nucléaire ◆ **to carry out a nuclear ~** effectuer un essai nucléaire [2] *[of anger, laughter, joy]* explosion *f* ; *[of violence]* flambée *f* ◆ **an ~ of colour/light** une soudaine débauche de couleurs/de lumière ◆ **an ~ in demand for sth** une explosion de la demande en qch ◆ **an ~ of interest in sth** une explosion d'intérêt pour qch ◆ **price ~** flambée *f* des prix ; → **population**

explosive /ɪk'spləʊsɪv/ ADJ 1 *(lit, fig) [device, charge, power, applause, growth, situation, issue, person, temper]* explosif ; *[gas, matter]* explosible ; *[mixture] (lit)* détonant, explosif ; *(fig)* détonant 2 *(Phon)* ⇒ **plosive** N *(gen, Chem)* explosif *m* ; → **high**

explosively /ɪk'spləʊsɪvlɪ/ ADV 1 *(= with bang) [react, erupt]* en explosant 2 *(= angrily)* **"are you mad?" he asked** ~ "tu es fou, ou quoi ?" demanda-t-il furieux *or* aboya-t-il

explosiveness /ɪk'spləʊsɪvlɪ/ N explosibilité *f* ◆ **the ~ of this situation** le caractère explosif de la situation

expo /'ekspəʊ/ N (abbrev of **exposition 2**) expo *f*

exponent /ɪk'spəʊnənt/ N *[of cause]* champion(ne) *m(f)* ; *[of theory]* défenseur *m*, partisan *m* ; *(Math, Gram)* exposant *m* ◆ **the principal ~ of this movement/this school of thought** le chef de file *or* le principal représentant de ce mouvement/de cette école de pensée ◆ **he's a great ~ of this new approach** c'est un chaud partisan de cette nouvelle approche ◆ **a leading ~ of the test-tube baby technique** l'un des principaux adeptes de la technique de la fécondation in vitro

exponential /,ekspəʊ'nenʃəl/ ADJ exponentiel ◆ **~ distribution** *(Stat)* distribution *f* exponentielle

exponentially /,ekspəʊ'nenʃəlɪ/ ADV de manière exponentielle

export /ɪk'spɔːt/ VT 1 *[+ product]* exporter *(to* vers) ◆ **countries which ~ coal** pays *mpl* exportateurs de charbon
2 *(Comput) [+ document]* exporter
VI exporter *(to* vers)
N /'ekspɔːt/ 1 *(NonC)* exportation *f* ◆ **for ~ only** réservé à l'exportation
2 *(= object, commodity)* (article *m* d')exportation *f* ◆ **invisible ~s** exportations *fpl* invisibles ◆ **ban on ~s, ~ ban** interdiction *f* des exportations
3 *(= beer)* bière forte
COMP /'ekspɔːt/ *[goods, permit]* d'exportation ; *[director]* du service export, des exportations
export credit N crédit *m* à l'exportation
export drive N campagne *f* pour (encourager) l'exportation
export duty N droit *m* de sortie
export earnings NPL recettes *fpl* d'exportation
export-orientated, export-oriented ADJ à vocation exportatrice
export reject N article *m* impropre à l'exportation
export trade N commerce *m* d'exportation, export *m*

exportable /ɪk'spɔːtəbl/ ADJ exportable

exportation /,ekspɔː'teɪʃən/ N *(NonC)* exportation *f*, sortie *f*

exporter /ɪk'spɔːtə^r^/ N *(= person)* exportateur *m*, -trice *f* ; *(= country)* pays *m* exportateur

expose /ɪk'spəʊz/ VT 1 *(= uncover, leave unprotected)* découvrir, exposer ; *[+ wire, nerve, body part]* mettre à nu, dénuder ◆ **to ~ to radiation/rain/sunlight** exposer à des radiations/à la pluie/au soleil ◆ **to ~ to danger** mettre en danger ◆ **to ~ o.s. to criticism/ridicule** s'exposer à la critique/au ridicule ◆ **a dress which leaves the back ~d** une robe qui découvre *or* dénude le dos ◆ **to be ~d to view** s'offrir à la vue ◆ **apples turn brown when ~d to air** les pommes brunissent au contact de l'air ◆ **digging has ~d the remains of a temple** les fouilles ont mis au jour les restes d'un temple ◆ **~d parts** *[of machinery]* parties *fpl* apparentes ◆ **to ~ a child (to die)** *(Hist)* exposer un enfant ◆ **he ~d himself to the risk of losing his job** il s'est exposé à perdre sa place, il a risqué de perdre sa place ◆ **to ~ o.s.** *(Jur: indecently)* commettre un outrage à la pudeur
2 *(= display) [+ goods]* étaler, exposer ; *[+ pictures]* exposer ; *[+ one's ignorance]* afficher, étaler
3 *(= unmask, reveal) [+ vice]* mettre à nu ; *[+ scandal, plot, lie]* révéler, dévoiler ; *[+ secret]* éventer ; *(= denounce) [+ person]* démasquer, dénoncer *(as* comme étant) ◆ **the affair ~d him as a fraud** cette affaire a montré que c'était un imposteur
4 *(Phot)* exposer

exposé /eks'pəʊzeɪ/ N révélation *f*

exposed /ɪk'spəʊzd/ ADJ 1 *(= unprotected) [troops, flank]* à découvert, exposé ; *[location, hillside, garden]* exposé ; *[ground]* découvert ; *(Climbing) [passage, section]* aérien ; *(= uncovered) [brickwork, plaster, wire, skin, nerve]* à nu ; *[body part]* dénudé ; *[machine part]* apparent ◆ **the house is in a very ~ position** la maison est très exposée ◆ **an ~ position** *(Mil)* un (lieu) découvert ◆ **~ to the wind** exposé au vent 2 *(= vulnerable) [person]* exposé aux regards ◆ **to feel ~** *[person]* se sentir exposé ◆ **his position is very ~** sa position l'expose aux regards 3 *(Phot) [film]* exposé

exposition /,ekspə'zɪʃən/ N 1 *(NonC) [of facts, theory, plan]* exposition *f* ; *[of text]* exposé *m*, commentaire *m*, interprétation *f* ; *(Mus)* exposition *f* 2 *(= exhibition)* exposition *f*

expostulate /ɪk'spɒstjʊleɪt/ *(frm)* VT protester
VI ◆ **to ~ with sb about sth** faire des remontrances à qn au sujet de qch

expostulation /ɪk,spɒstjʊ'leɪʃən/ N *(frm)* protestation *f*

exposure /ɪk'spəʊʒə^r^/ N 1 *(to substance, radiation, sunlight, noise)* exposition *f (to sth* à qch) ◆ **to risk ~ to a virus** risquer d'être mis en contact avec un virus ◆ **to undergo ~ to new ideas** être exposé à de nouvelles idées ◆ **avoid the ~ of children to violent images on television** évitez d'exposer les enfants aux images violentes de la télévision ; → **indecent**
2 *(= hypothermia)* hypothermie *f* ◆ **to die of ~** mourir de froid ◆ **to suffer from ~** souffrir d'hypothermie
3 *(NonC = revelation, unmasking) [of secret, corruption, scandal]* révélation *f* ; *[of person]* dénonciation *f* ◆ **public ~** *[of affair, corruption, scandal]* révélation *f* publique ; *[of person]* dénonciation *f* publique
4 *(NonC = publicity)* ◆ **media ~** couverture *f* médiatique ◆ **to get an enormous amount of ~ on television** faire l'objet d'une abondante couverture télévisée
5 *(Phot = photograph)* pose *f* ◆ **a 36-~ film, a film with 36 ~s** une pellicule 36 poses ◆ **to make an ~** *(= take photograph)* prendre une photo ; *(= develop photograph)* développer un cliché
6 *(NonC: Phot = amount of light)* exposition *f* ; → **double, multiple**
7 *(NonC: Phot)* (also **exposure time**) temps *m* de pose
8 *(NonC = position) [of house]* exposition *f* ◆ **southern/eastern ~** exposition *f* au sud/à l'est ◆ **a house with a northern ~** une maison exposée au nord
COMP **exposure index** N *(Phot)* indice *m* de pose
exposure meter N posemètre *m*, photomètre *m*
exposure value N indice *m* de lumination

expound /ɪk'spaʊnd/ VT *[+ theory]* expliquer ; *[+ one's views]* exposer ; *[+ the Bible]* expliquer, interpréter

ex-president /,eks'prezɪdənt/ N ex-président *m*, ancien président *m*

express /ɪk'spres/ LANGUAGE IN USE 6.3
VT 1 *(= make known) [+ appreciation, feelings, sympathy]* exprimer ; *[+ opinions]* émettre, exprimer ; *[+ surprise, displeasure]* exprimer, manifester ; *[+ thanks]* présenter, exprimer ; *[+ a truth, proposition]* énoncer ; *[+ wish]* formuler ◆ **to ~ o.s.** s'exprimer ◆ **I haven't the words to ~ my thoughts** les mots me manquent pour traduire ma pensée ◆ **they have ~ed (an) interest in ...** ils se sont montrés intéressés par ..., ils ont manifesté de l'intérêt pour ...
2 *(in another language or medium)* rendre, exprimer ; *[face, actions]* exprimer ; *(Math)* exprimer ◆ **this ~es exactly the meaning of the word** ceci rend exactement le sens du mot ◆ **you cannot ~ that so succinctly in French** on ne peut pas l'exprimer aussi succinctement en français
3 *[+ juice]* exprimer, extraire ; *[+ breast milk]* tirer
4 *(= send) [+ letter, parcel]* expédier par exprès
ADJ 1 *(= explicit) [order, instruction]* exprès (-esse *f*) ; *[purpose, intention]* délibéré ◆ **with the ~ purpose of doing sth** dans le seul but *or* dans le but délibéré de faire qch
2 *(= fast) [letter, delivery, mail]* exprès *inv* ; *[service]* express *inv*
ADV *[send]* en exprès *or* par Chronopost ®
N 1 *(= train)* rapide *m*
2 ◆ **to send sth by ~** envoyer qch en exprès
COMP **express coach** N (auto)car *m* express
express company N compagnie *f* de messageries exprès
express delivery, express mail N *(Brit Post = system)* distribution *f* exprès ◆ **to send sth by ~ delivery** *or* **mail** envoyer qch en exprès *or* par Chronopost ®
express rifle N fusil *m* de chasse express
express train N train *m* express

expressage /ɪk'spresɪdʒ/ N *(US) (= service)* service *m* de messagerie exprès ; *(= charge for service)* frais *mpl* de messagerie exprès

expression /ɪk'spreʃən/ N 1 *[of opinions]* expression *f* ; *[of friendship, affection]* témoignage *m* ; *[of joy]* manifestation *f* ◆ **to give ~ to one's fears** formuler ses craintes ◆ **to find ~ (in)** se manifester (dans *or* par) ◆ **from Cairo came ~s of regret at the attack** Le Caire a exprimé ses regrets après cette attaque
2 *(= facial expression)* expression *f* ◆ **a face devoid of ~** un visage sans expression
3 *(NonC = feeling)* expression *f* ◆ **to play with ~** jouer avec expression
4 *(= phrase)* expression *f* ; *(= turn of phrase)* tournure *f* ; *(Math)* expression *f* ◆ **an original/common ~** une tournure originale/expression courante ◆ **it's an ~ he's fond of** c'est une expression *or* une tournure qu'il affectionne ◆ **a figurative ~** une expression figurée ◆ **set** *or* **fixed ~** locution *f*
COMP **expression mark** N *(Mus)* signe *m* d'expression

expressionism /ɪk'spreʃə,nɪzəm/ N expressionnisme *m*

expressionist /ɪk'spreʃə,nɪst/ ADJ, N expressionniste *mf*

expressionless /ɪk'spreʃənlɪs/ ADJ *[person, face, eyes, look]* sans expression ; *[voice]* monotone, monocorde ; *[playing, style]* plat

expressive /ɪk'spresɪv/ ADJ *[face, look, voice, gesture, music, language]* expressif ; *[power, ability, capability, skill]* d'expression ◆ **she's very ~** *(= eloquent)* elle est très éloquente ◆ **to be ~ of sth** *(frm)* exprimer qch

expressively /ɪk'spresɪvlɪ/ ADV d'une manière expressive

expressiveness /ɪk'spresɪvnɪs/ N *[of face]* caractère *m* expressif, expressivité *f* ; *[of words]* force *f* expressive ; *[of music, language]* expressivité *f* ; *[of gesture]* éloquence *f* ◆ **a picture remarkable for its ~** un tableau remarquable par (la force de) l'expression

expressly /ɪk'spreslɪ/ ADV *[forbid, exclude, allow, design, make, write]* expressément ; *[state]* explicitement ◆ ~ **illegal** expressément interdit par la loi

expressman /ɪk'spresmæn/ N (pl **-men**) *(US)* employé *m* de messageries exprès

expresso /ɪk'spresəʊ/ N ⇒ **espresso**

expressway /ɪk'spresweɪ/ N *(esp US)* voie *f* express, autoroute *f* urbaine ; → ROADS

expropriate /eks'prəʊprɪeɪt/ VT *[+ person, land]* exproprier

expropriation /eks,prəʊprɪ'eɪʃən/ N expropriation *f*

expulsion /ɪk'spʌlʃən/ N expulsion *f*, bannissement *m* ; *(Scol etc)* renvoi *m*, exclusion *f* définitive COMP **expulsion order** N arrêté *m* d'expulsion

expunge /ɪk'spʌndʒ/ VT *(frm: from book)* supprimer ◆ **to ~ sth from the record** supprimer *or* effacer qch

expurgate /'ekspɜːgeɪt/ VT *(frm)* expurger ◆ **~d edition** édition *f* expurgée

exquisite /ɪk'skwɪzɪt/ ADJ 1 *(= fine)* exquis ◆ **a woman of ~ beauty** une femme d'une exquise beauté ◆ **in ~ detail** dans les moindres détails 2 *(liter = intense)* *[pleasure, satisfaction]* exquis ; *[pain]* lancinant ; *[care]* minutieux

exquisitely /ɪk'skwɪzɪtlɪ/ ADV *[dress, make, decorate, paint, embroider, describe]* de façon exquise ◆ **~ beautiful/delicate/polite** d'une beauté/délicatesse/politesse exquise ◆ **~ detailed** *[picture, tapestry etc]* plein de détails exquis ◆ **he gave us an ~ detailed account of the accident** il nous a raconté l'accident dans ses moindres détails

ex-service /,eks'sɜːvɪs/ ADJ *(Brit Mil)* ayant servi dans l'armée

ex-serviceman /,eks'sɜːvɪsmæn/ N (pl **ex-servicemen**) ancien militaire *m* ; *(= war veteran)* ancien combattant *m*

ex-servicewoman /,eks'sɜːvɪswʊmən/ N (pl **ex-servicewomen**) femme *f* militaire à la retraite ; *(= war veteran)* ancienne combattante *f*

ext *(Telec)* (abbrev of **extension**) poste *m*

extant /ek'stænt/ ADJ *(frm)* qui existe encore, existant ◆ **the only ~ manuscript** le seul manuscrit conservé ◆ **a few examples are still ~** quelques exemples subsistent (encore)

extemporaneous /ɪk,stempə'reɪnɪəs/, **extemporary** /ɪk'stempərərɪ/ ADJ improvisé, impromptu

extempore /ɪk'stempərɪ/ ADV impromptu, sans préparation ADJ improvisé, impromptu ◆ **to give an ~ speech** improviser un discours, faire un discours au pied levé

extemporize /ɪk'stempəraɪz/ VTI improviser

extend /ɪk'stend/ VT 1 *(= enlarge)* *[+ house, property]* agrandir ; *[+ research]* porter *or* pousser plus loin ; *[+ powers]* étendre, augmenter ; *[+ business]* étendre, accroître ; *[+ knowledge]* élargir, accroître ; *[+ limits]* étendre ; *[+ period, time allowed]* prolonger ; *[+ insurance cover]* augmenter le montant de ◆ **to ~ the field of human knowledge/one's sphere of influence** élargir le champ des connaissances/sa sphère d'influence ◆ **to ~ the frontiers of a country** reculer les frontières d'un pays ◆ **a course that ~s students' understanding of British history** un cours qui permet aux étudiants d'approfondir leur connaissance de l'histoire britannique ◆ **to ~ one's vocabulary** enrichir *or* élargir son vocabulaire ◆ **to ~ a time limit (for sth)** accorder un délai (pour qch)

2 *(= prolong)* *[+ street, line]* prolonger (by de) ; *[+ visit, leave]* prolonger ◆ **to ~ one's stay by two weeks** prolonger son séjour de deux semaines ◆ **to be fully ~ed** *[ladder, telescope]* être entièrement déployé

3 *(= offer, give)* *[+ help]* apporter ; *[+ hospitality, friendship]* offrir ; *[+ thanks, condolences, congratulations]* présenter ; *[+ credit, loan]* consentir ◆ **to ~ a welcome to sb** souhaiter la bienvenue à qn ◆ **to ~ an invitation** faire *or* lancer une invitation

4 *(= stretch out)* *[+ arm]* étendre ◆ **to ~ one's hand (to sb)** tendre la main (à qn)

5 *(= make demands on)* *[+ person, pupil]* pousser à la limite de ses capacités, faire donner son maximum à

VI *[wall, estate]* s'étendre (to, *as far as* jusqu'à) ; *[table]* s'allonger ; *[meeting, visit]* se prolonger, continuer (*over* pendant ; *for* durant) ◆ **the caves ~ for some 10 kilometres** les grottes s'étendent sur quelque 10 kilomètres ◆ **a footballing career that ~ed from 1974 to 1990** une carrière de footballeur qui a duré de 1974 à 1990 ◆ **holidays which ~ into September** des vacances qui durent *or* se prolongent jusqu'en septembre ◆ **the table ~s to 220cm** la table peut s'allonger jusqu'à 220 cm, avec ses rallonges, cette table fait 220 cm ◆ **enthusiasm which ~s even to the children** enthousiasme qui gagne même les enfants

extendable /ɪk'stendəbl/ ADJ *[ladder]* à rallonge ; *[contract, lease]* renouvelable

extended /ɪk'stendɪd/ ADJ prolongé ; *[holiday, leave]* longue durée ◆ **for an ~ period** pendant une période supplémentaire ◆ **an ~ play record** un disque double (durée) ◆ **~ care facilities** *(US Med)* soins *mpl* pour convalescents ◆ **the ~ family** *(Sociol)* la famille étendue COMP **extended memory** N *(Comput)* mémoire *f* étendue

extendible /ɪk'stendəbl/ ADJ ⇒ **extendable**

extensible /ɪk'stensɪbl/ ADJ extensible

extension /ɪk'stenʃən/ LANGUAGE IN USE 27.4, 27.7

N 1 *(to building)* ◆ **to build an ~ (to a building)** agrandir (un bâtiment) ◆ **to have an ~ built onto a house** faire agrandir une maison ◆ **there is an ~ at the back of the house** la maison a été agrandie à l'arrière ◆ **come and see our ~** venez voir, nous avons fait agrandir ◆ **the kitchen/bathroom ~** la nouvelle partie de la maison occupée par la cuisine/la salle de bains ◆ **a new ~ to the library** une nouvelle annexe de la bibliothèque

2 *(= continuation)* prolongement *m* (to *or* of sth de qch) ; *(= extra part)* *(for table, electric flex, pipe)* rallonge *f* ; (also **hair extension**) *(clip-on)* postiche *m* ; *(permanent)* extension *f* ◆ **motorway ~** prolongement *m* d'une autoroute ◆ **the building of an ~ to a golf course** l'agrandissement *m* d'un terrain de golf ◆ **~ to an insurance policy** *(= extra cover)* extension *f* d'une assurance ; *(in duration)* prolongation *f* d'une assurance ◆ **an ~ of o.s./one's personality** un prolongement de soi-même/sa personnalité

3 *(= extra time)* prolongation *f* (to *or* of sth de qch) ◆ **there will be no ~ of the deadline** le délai ne sera pas prolongé ◆ **to grant an ~ of a deadline** accorder un délai supplémentaire ◆ **to get an ~ (of time for payment)** obtenir un délai ◆ **~ of due date** *(Jur, Fin)* report *m* d'échéance délai *m*

4 *(= development)* *[of rights, powers]* extension *f* ; *[of idea, concept]* développement *m* ◆ **the role of women within the family and, by ~, within the community** le rôle des femmes dans la famille et, par extension, au sein de la communauté ◆ **the logical ~ of sth** la suite logique de qch

5 *(Telec)* *(in house)* appareil *m* supplémentaire ; *(in office)* poste *m* ◆ **you can get me on ~ 308** vous pouvez me joindre au poste 308

6 *(= provision)* *[of credit]* allocation *f*

COMP **extension cable, extension cord** *(US)* N rallonge *f*

extension courses NPL *cours dispensés par l'institut d'éducation permanente d'une université*

extension ladder N échelle *f* coulissante

extension lead N ⇒ **extension cable**

extension light N (lampe *f*) baladeuse *f*

extension tube N *(for camera lens)* tube-allonge *m* ; *(for vacuum cleaner)* tube-rallonge *m*

extensive /ɪk'stensɪv/ ADJ *[area, grounds, knowledge, powers, range, collection]* étendu ; *[damage, alterations, experience]* considérable ; *[plans, reforms]* de grande envergure ; *[research, discussions]* approfondi ; *[tests]* nombreux ; *[list]* long (longue *f*) ; *[menu]* varié ; *[tour]* complet (-ète *f*) ◆ **to make ~ use of sth** beaucoup utiliser qch ◆ **her visit got ~ coverage in the press** sa visite a fait l'objet de très nombreux articles dans la presse *or* d'une large couverture médiatique ◆ **to undergo ~ surgery** *(= one operation)* subir une opération longue et complexe ; *(= series of operations)* subir une série d'interventions chirurgicales ◆ **~ farming** agriculture *f* extensive

⚠ **extensive** is only translated by **extensif** in the agricultural sense.

extensively /ɪk'stensɪvlɪ/ ADV *[travel, work, write]* beaucoup ; *[alter, damage]* considérablement ; *[revise, discuss]* en profondeur ; *[grow, quote, report]* abondamment ◆ **to use sth ~** beaucoup utiliser qch ◆ **an ~ used method** une méthode très répandue ◆ **the story was covered ~ in the press** cette histoire a fait l'objet de nombreux articles dans la presse *or* d'une large couverture médiatique ◆ **the subject has been ~ researched** cette question a fait l'objet de recherches approfondies ◆ **the band has toured ~** le groupe a fait des tournées un peu partout ◆ **to advertise ~ in the papers** *[company]* faire énormément de publicité dans les journaux ; *[individual]* faire passer de nombreuses annonces dans les journaux

extensor /ɪk'stensəʳ/ N (muscle *m*) extenseur *m*

extent /ɪk'stent/ N 1 *(= size)* étendue *f*, superficie *f* ; *(= length)* longueur *f* ◆ **an avenue lined with trees along its entire ~** une allée bordée d'arbres sur toute sa longueur ◆ **to open to its fullest ~** ouvrir entièrement *or* tout grand ◆ **over the whole ~ of the ground** sur toute la superficie du terrain ◆ **she could see the full ~ of the park** elle voyait le parc dans toute son étendue

2 *(= range, scope)* *[of damage]* importance *f*, ampleur *f* ; *[of commitments, losses]* importance *f* ; *[of knowledge, activities, power, influence]* étendue *f*

3 *(= degree)* mesure *f*, degré *m* ◆ **to what ~?** dans quelle mesure ? ◆ **to some *or* a certain ~** jusqu'à un certain point *or* degré, dans une certaine mesure ◆ **to a large ~** en grande partie ◆ **to a small *or* slight ~** dans une faible mesure, quelque peu ◆ **to the *or* such an ~ that ...** à tel point que ..., au point que ... ◆ **to the ~ of doing sth** au point de faire qch

extenuate /ɪk'stenjʊeɪt/ VT atténuer ◆ **extenuating circumstances** circonstances *fpl* atténuantes

extenuation /ɪk,stenjʊ'eɪʃən/ N atténuation *f*

exterior /ɪk'stɪərɪəʳ/ ADJ *[wall, door, lighting, paint, decorating, world]* extérieur (-eure *f*) ; *[surface]* extérieur (-eure *f*), externe ◆ **~ to sth** extérieur à qch ◆ **paint for ~ use** peinture *f* pour l'extérieur N *[of house, box]* extérieur *m* ; *(Art, Cine)* extérieur *m* ◆ **on the ~** à l'extérieur ◆ **underneath his rough ~, he ...** sous ses dehors rudes, il ...

COMP **exterior angle** N *(Math)* angle *m* externe

exterior decoration N peintures *fpl* extérieures

exteriorize /ɪk'stɪərɪə,raɪz/ VT *(Med, Psych)* extérioriser

exterminate /ɪk'stɜːmɪ,neɪt/ VT *[+ pests, group of people]* exterminer ; *[+ race]* anéantir ; *[+ disease, beliefs, ideas]* éradiquer

extermination /ɪkˌstɜːmɪˈneɪʃən/ **N** *[of race, animals]* extermination *f* ; *[of disease]* éradication *f* ◆ **mass ~** extermination *f* massive **COMP** **extermination camp N** camp *m* d'extermination

exterminator /ɪkˈstɜːmɪˌneɪtəʳ/ **N** *(US = rat-catcher etc)* employé(e) *m(f)* de la désinfection

extern /ˈekstɜːn/ **N** *(US Med)* externe *mf*

external /ɪkˈstɜːnl/ **ADJ** 1 *(= outer, exterior) [wall]* extérieur (-eure *f*) ; *[surface]* extérieur (-eure *f*), externe ; *[injury]* superficiel ; *[ear, gills]* externe ◆ **~ skeleton** exosquelette *m* ◆ **"for external use only"** *(Pharm)* "à usage externe"
2 *(= outside, from outside) [pressure, factor, reality, world]* extérieur (-eure *f*) ; *(Comm) [mail]* externe ; *[phone call] (outgoing)* vers l'extérieur ; *(incoming)* de l'extérieur
3 *(= foreign) [debt]* extérieur (-eure *f*) ◆ **the European commissioner for ~ affairs** le commissaire européen aux affaires *or* chargé des affaires extérieures
N *(fig)* ◆ **the ~s** l'extérieur *m*, les apparences *fpl* ◆ **the ~s of our faith** les manifestations *fpl* extérieures de notre foi ◆ **to look at the ~s of an issue** ne voir que l'aspect superficiel d'une question
COMP **external auditor N** *(Brit Fin)* vérificateur *m*, -trice *f* de comptes (externe)
external degree N *(Brit Univ) diplôme délivré par une université à des personnes non régulièrement inscrites*
external examiner N *(Brit Univ)* examinateur *m*, -trice *f* extérieur(e)
external student N *(Brit Univ)* étudiant(e) *mf* externe
external trade N *(US)* commerce *m* extérieur

externalize /ɪkˈstɜːnəˌlaɪz/ **VT** extérioriser

externally /ɪkˈstɜːnəlɪ/ **ADV** *[impose]* de l'extérieur ; *[express]* extérieurement ◆ **~ mounted cameras** des caméras *fpl* installées à l'extérieur ◆ **he remained ~ calm** il est resté calme extérieurement ◆ **a cream to be applied ~** une crème à usage externe ◆ **"to be used externally"** "à usage externe"

extinct /ɪkˈstɪŋkt/ **ADJ** 1 *(= no longer existing) [animal, species, tribe, way of life, language]* disparu ; *[custom]* tombé en désuétude ◆ **to be ~** avoir disparu ◆ **to become ~** disparaître ◆ **to be nearly ~** être en voie d'extinction ◆ **are good manners ~?** les bonnes manières n'existent-elles plus ? 2 *(= not active) [volcano]* éteint

extinction /ɪkˈstɪŋkʃən/ **N** *(NonC) [of animal, species, race, family]* extinction *f*, disparition *f* ; *[of hopes]* anéantissement *m* ; *[of debt]* amortissement *m* ; *[of fire]* extinction *f*

extinguish /ɪkˈstɪŋgwɪʃ/ **VT** *[+ fire, light]* éteindre ; *[+ candle]* éteindre, souffler ; *[+ hopes]* anéantir, mettre fin à ; *[+ debt]* amortir

extinguisher /ɪkˈstɪŋgwɪʃəʳ/ **N** extincteur *m* ; → **fire**

extirpate /ˈekstəˌpeɪt/ **VT** extirper

extirpation /ˌekstəˈpeɪʃən/ **N** *(NonC)* extirpation *f*

extirpator /ˈekstəˌpeɪtəʳ/ **N** *(Agr, Tech)* extirpateur *m*

extn *(Telec)* (abbrev of **extension**) poste *m*

extol /ɪkˈstəʊl/ **VT** *[+ person]* porter aux nues, chanter les louanges de ; *[+ act, quality]* prôner, exalter ◆ **to ~ the virtues of ...** chanter les louanges de ...

extort /ɪkˈstɔːt/ **VT** *[+ promise, money]* extorquer, soutirer *(from* à) ; *[+ consent, promise, confession, secret]* arracher *(from* à) ; *[+ signature]* extorquer

extortion /ɪkˈstɔːʃən/ **N** *(also Jur)* extorsion *f* ◆ **this is sheer ~!** *(fig)* c'est du vol (manifeste) !

extortionate /ɪkˈstɔːʃənɪt/ **ADJ** exorbitant

extortioner /ɪkˈstɔːʃənəʳ/, **extortionist** /ɪkˈstɔːʃənɪst/ **N** extorqueur *m*, -euse *f*

extra /ˈekstrə/ **ADJ** 1 *(= additional) [homework, bus, chair, costs, troops, effort]* supplémentaire ◆ **to work ~ hours** faire des heures supplémentaires ◆ **take an ~ pair of shoes** prends une autre paire de chaussures ◆ **I've set an ~ place at table** j'ai ajouté un couvert ◆ **for ~ safety** pour plus de sécurité ◆ **take ~ care!** fais bien attention ! ◆ **to earn an ~ £20 a week** gagner 20 livres de plus par semaine ◆ **there is an ~ charge for wine, the wine is ~** le vin est en supplément ◆ **there's no ~ charge for the wine** il n'y a pas de supplément pour le vin, le vin est compris ◆ **take some ~ money just to be on the safe side** prends un peu plus d'argent, on ne sait jamais *or* au cas où* ◆ **the ~ money will come in handy** l'argent en plus *or* l'argent supplémentaire pourra toujours servir ◆ **the ~ money required to complete the project** le montant supplémentaire *or* l'argent requis pour terminer le projet ◆ **to go to ~ expense** faire des frais ◆ **~ pay** supplément *m* de salaire, sursalaire *m* ; *(Mil)* supplément *m* de solde ◆ **postage and packing ~** frais d'expédition en sus ◆ **95p ~ for postage and packing** 95 pence de plus pour les frais d'expédition
2 *(= spare)* ◆ **these copies are ~** ces exemplaires sont en surplus
ADV 1 *(= more money)* ◆ **to pay/charge ~ (for sth)** payer/faire payer un supplément (pour qch) ◆ **a room with a bath costs ~** les chambres avec salle de bains coûtent plus cher, il y a un supplément pour les chambres avec salle de bains
2 *(= especially) [cautious]* encore plus ◆ **he was ~ polite/nice to her** il a été tout poli/gentil avec elle ◆ **take ~ special care when washing those glasses** faites très attention en lavant ces verres ◆ **he expected to do ~ well in the exam** il s'attendait à réussir brillamment à l'examen ◆ **to work ~ hard** travailler d'arrache-pied ◆ **~ large** *[garment]* très grand ; *[eggs, tomatoes etc]* très gros ◆ **~ virgin** *[oil]* extra vierge
N 1 *(= perk)* à-côté *m* ◆ **~s** *(= expenses)* frais *mpl* supplémentaires ◆ **singing and piano are ~s** *(= options)* les leçons de chant et de piano sont en option ◆ **those little ~s** *(= luxuries)* ces petites gâteries *fpl* ◆ **there are no hidden ~s** il n'y a pas de frais supplémentaires
2 *(in restaurant = extra dish)* supplément *m*
3 *(Cine, Theat = actor)* figurant(e) *m(f)*
4 *(US = gasoline)* super(carburant) *m*
COMP **extra time N** *(esp Brit Sport)* prolongations *fpl* ◆ **the match went to ~ time** on a joué les prolongations ◆ **after ~ time** après prolongation(s)

extra... /ˈekstrə/ **PREF** 1 *(= outside)* extra... ; → **extramarital** 2 *(= specially, ultra)* extra... ◆ **extradry** *[wine etc]* très sec ; *[champagne, vermouth]* extra-dry *inv* ◆ **extrafine** extrafin ◆ **extrasmart** ultrachic *inv* ◆ **extrastrong** *[person]* extrêmement fort ; *[material]* extrasolide ; → **extra-special**

extract /ɪkˈstrækt/ **VT** *[+ juice, minerals, oil, bullet, splinter]* extraire *(from* de) ; *[+ tooth]* arracher *(from* à) ; *[+ cork]* tirer *(from* de) ; *[+ confession, permission, promise]* arracher *(from* à) ; *[+ information]* tirer *(from* de) ; *[+ money]* tirer *(from* de) soutirer *(from* à) ; *[+ meaning]* tirer, dégager *(from* de) ◆ **to ~ pleasure from sth** tirer du plaisir de qch ◆ **to ~ DNA from sth** extraire l'ADN de qch ◆ **to ~ the square root** *(Math)* extraire la racine carrée **N** /ˈekstrækt/ 1 *[of book, film, play etc]* extrait *m* ◆ **~s from Voltaire** morceaux *mpl* choisis de Voltaire 2 *(Pharm)* extrait *m* ; *(Culin)* extrait *m*, concentré *m* ◆ **meat ~** extrait *m* de viande

extraction /ɪkˈstrækʃən/ **N** 1 *(NonC) [of minerals, coal, oil]* extraction *f* ; *[of fluid, bone marrow]* prélèvement *m* ◆ **the ~ of confessions through torture** le fait d'arracher des aveux par la torture 2 *(NonC = descent)* origine *f* ◆ **to be of Scottish ~, to be Scottish by ~** être d'origine écossaise 3 *(Dentistry)* extraction *f*

extractor /ɪkˈstræktəʳ/ **N** extracteur *m* **COMP** **extractor fan N** *(Brit)* ventilateur *m*
extractor hood N *(Brit)* hotte *f* aspirante

extracurricular /ˈekstrəkəˈrɪkjʊləʳ/ **ADJ** *(Scol)* parascolaire, hors programme ; *[sports]* en dehors des heures de classe

extraditable /ˈekstrəˌdaɪtəbl/ **ADJ** *[offence]* qui peut donner lieu à l'extradition ; *[person]* passible *or* susceptible d'extradition

extradite /ˈekstrəˌdaɪt/ **VT** extrader

extradition /ˌekstrəˈdɪʃən/ **N** extradition *f* **COMP** **extradition warrant N** mandat *m* d'extradition

extragalactic /ˌekstrəgəˈlæktɪk/ **ADJ** extragalactique **COMP** **extragalactic nebula N** nébuleuse *f* extragalactique

extralinguistic /ˌekstrəlɪŋˈgwɪstɪk/ **ADJ** extralinguistique

extramarital /ˈekstrəˈmærɪtl/ **ADJ** en dehors du mariage

extramural /ˈekstrəˈmjʊərəl/ **ADJ** 1 *(esp Brit) [course]* hors faculté *(donné par des professeurs accrédités par la faculté et ouvert au public)* ◆ **~ lecture** conférence *f* publique ◆ **Department of Extramural Studies** *(Brit Univ)* ≃ Institut *m* d'éducation permanente ◆ **~ sports** *(US Scol) sports pratiqués entre équipes de différents établissements* 2 *[district]* extra-muros *inv*

extraneous /ɪkˈstreɪnɪəs/ **ADJ** 1 *(= irrelevant) [matter, issue, detail, thought]* sans rapport avec le sujet ◆ **~ to** étranger à 2 *(frm = external) [noise]* extérieur (-eure *f*)

extranet /ˈekstrənet/ **N** extranet *m*

extraordinaire /eksˌtrɔːdɪˈneəʳ/ **ADJ** *(after n: esp hum)* ◆ **George Kuchar, film-maker ~** George Kuchar, cinéaste hors du commun

extraordinarily /ɪkˈstrɔːdnrɪlɪ/ **ADV** extraordinairement ◆ **~, nobody was killed in the explosion** fait extraordinaire, personne n'a été tué par l'explosion

extraordinary /ɪkˈstrɔːdnrɪ/ **ADJ** *[person, behaviour, appearance, success, courage, tale, speech]* extraordinaire ; *[insults]* incroyable ; *[violence]* inouï ◆ **there's nothing ~ about that** cela n'a rien d'extraordinaire, il n'y a rien d'extraordinaire à cela ◆ **I find it ~ that he hasn't replied** je trouve inouï qu'il n'ait pas répondu ◆ **it's ~ to think that ...** il est extraordinaire de penser que ... ◆ **it's ~ how much he resembles his brother** c'est inouï ce qu'il peut ressembler à son frère ◆ **what an ~ thing to say!** quelle idée saugrenue ! ◆ **the ~ thing is that he's right** ce qu'il y a d'extraordinaire c'est qu'il a *or* ait raison ◆ **an ~ meeting of the shareholders** une assemblée extraordinaire des actionnaires ◆ **an Extraordinary General Meeting of the Union** *(Brit)* une assemblée générale extraordinaire du syndicat ; see also **envoy**[1]

extrapolate /ɪkˈstræpəleɪt/ **VT** extrapoler *(from* à partir de)

extrapolation /ɪkˌstræpəˈleɪʃən/ **N** extrapolation *f*

extrasensory /ˈekstrəˈsensərɪ/ **ADJ** extrasensoriel **COMP** **extrasensory perception N** perception *f* extrasensorielle

extra-special /ˌekstrəˈspeʃəl/ **ADJ** exceptionnel ◆ **to take ~ care over sth** apporter un soin tout particulier à qch ◆ **~ occasion** grande occasion *f*

extraterrestrial /ˌekstrətɪˈrestrɪəl/ **ADJ, N** extraterrestre *mf*

extraterritorial /ˈekstrəˌterɪˈtɔːrɪəl/ **ADJ** d'exterritorialité, d'extraterritorialité

extravagance /ɪk'strævəgəns/ N 1 *(= excessive spending)* prodigalité *f* ; *(= thing bought)* dépense *f* excessive, folie *f* ◆ **gross mismanagement and financial** ~ une mauvaise gestion flagrante et des dépenses excessives ◆ **buying a yacht is sheer** ~ acheter un yacht est une pure folie 2 *(= wastefulness)* gaspillage *m* 3 *(= action, notion)* extravagance *f*, fantaisie *f*

extravagant /ɪk'strævəgənt/ ADJ 1 *(financially) [person]* dépensier ; *[tastes]* de luxe ; *[gift]* somptueux ; *[price]* exorbitant, prohibitif ◆ ~ **spending** dépenses *fpl* excessives ◆ **it seems** ~ **to hire a car** ça paraît exagéré de louer une voiture ◆ **it was very** ~ **of him to buy this ring** il a fait une folie en achetant cette bague ◆ **to lead an** ~ **lifestyle** mener un train de vie fastueux ◆ **to be** ~ **with one's money** être dépensier ◆ **to be** ~ **with electricity** gaspiller l'électricité 2 *(= exaggerated) [person, behaviour, dress, talk, claims]* extravagant ; *[praise]* outré ◆ **to be** ~ **in one's praise of sb/sth** faire un éloge outré de qn/qch

extravagantly /ɪk'strævəgəntlɪ/ ADV *[spend]* sans compter ; *[use]* avec prodigalité ; *[entertain]* sans regarder à la dépense ; *[furnish]* avec luxe ; *[behave, dress]* d'une façon extravagante ; *[praise, thank]* à outrance ; *[expensive]* excessivement ; *[eccentric, gifted]* extrêmement ◆ **to live** ~ mener un train de vie fastueux ◆ **an** ~ **large bouquet of flowers** un énorme bouquet de fleurs ◆ ~ **elegant** d'une élégance extravagante

extravaganza /ɪk,strævə'gænzə/ N *(Literat, Mus)* fantaisie *f* ; *(= story)* histoire *f* extravagante *or* invraisemblable ; *(= show)* spectacle *m* somptueux ; *(= whim)* folie *f*, caprice *m*

extravehicular /,ekstrəvɪ'hɪkjʊləʳ/ ADJ *(Space)* extravéhiculaire

extravert /'ekstrə,vɜːt/ N, ADJ ⇒ **extrovert**

extreme /ɪk'striːm/ ADJ *(gen)* extrême ; *[praise, flattery]* outré *after n* ◆ **of** ~ **importance** d'une extrême importance ◆ **of** ~ **urgency** d'une extrême urgence, extrêmement urgent ◆ **in** ~ **danger** en très grand danger ◆ **the** ~ **end** l'extrémité *f* ◆ ~ **old age** l'extrême vieillesse *f* ◆ **he died in** ~ **poverty** il est mort dans une misère extrême ◆ **in the** ~ **distance** au loin ◆ **the** ~ **north** l'extrême nord *m* ◆ **to the** ~ **right** à l'extrême droite ◆ **the** ~ **left/right** *(Pol)* l'extrême gauche *f*/droite *f* ◆ **to be** ~ **in one's opinions** avoir des opinions extrêmes, être extrémiste

N extrême *m* ◆ **in the** ~ *[difficult, irritating, wealthy, helpful, interesting]* à l'extrême ◆ **to go from one** ~ **to the other** passer d'un extrême à l'autre ◆ ~**s of temperature** des écarts *mpl* extrêmes de température ◆ ~**s meet** les extrêmes se touchent ◆ **to go to** ~**s** pousser les choses à l'extrême ◆ **I won't go to that** ~ je ne veux pas aller jusqu'à ces extrémités

COMP **extreme sport** N sport *m* extrême
extreme unction N extrême-onction *f*

extremely /ɪk'striːmlɪ/ ADV *[happy, difficult, important, high, helpful]* extrêmement ◆ **to be** ~ **talented/successful** avoir énormément de talent/succès

extremism /ɪk'striːmɪzəm/ N extrémisme *m*

extremist /ɪk'striːmɪst/ ADJ, N extrémiste *mf*

extremity /ɪk'stremɪtɪ/ N 1 *(= furthest point)* extrémité *f* ◆ **extremities** *(= hands and feet)* extrémités *fpl* 2 *[of despair, happiness]* extrême *or* dernier degré *m* ; *(= extreme act)* extrémité *f* ◆ **to drive sb to extremities** pousser qn à une extrémité 3 *(= danger, distress)* extrémité *f* ◆ **to help sb in his** ~ venir en aide à qn qui est aux abois

extricate /'ekstrɪkeɪt/ VT *[+ object]* dégager *(from* de) ◆ **to** ~ **o.s.** s'extirper *(from* de) ; *(fig)* se tirer *(from* de) ◆ **to** ~ **sb from a nasty situation** tirer qn d'un mauvais pas

extrication /,ekstrɪ'keɪʃən/ N *[of object]* dégagement *m* ◆ **to be in debt without hope of** ~ être endetté sans espoir de s'en sortir

extrinsic /ek'strɪnsɪk/ ADJ extrinsèque

extroversion /,ekstrə'vɜːʃən/ N extraversion *or* extroversion *f*

extrovert /'ekstrəʊ,vɜːt/ *(esp Brit)* ADJ extraverti *or* extroverti N extraverti(e) *or* extroverti(e) *m(f)* ◆ **he's an** ~ il s'extériorise (beaucoup)

extroverted /'ekstrəʊ,vɜːtɪd/ ADJ *(esp US)* ⇒ **extrovert**

extrude /ɪk'struːd/ VT rejeter *(from* hors de) expulser *(from* de) ; *[+ metal, plastics]* extruder

extrusion /ɪk'struːʒən/ N extrusion *f*

extrusive /ɪk'struːsɪv/ ADJ extrusif

exuberance /ɪg'zjuːbərəns/ N *[of person]* exubérance *f* ; *[of vegetation]* exubérance *f*, luxuriance *f* ; *[of words, images]* richesse *f*, exubérance *f*

exuberant /ɪg'zjuːbərənt/ ADJ *[person, personality, mood, style, film, music]* exubérant ; *[growth, vegetation]* exubérant, luxuriant ; *[colour]* vif ; *[painting]* d'un style exubérant

exuberantly /ɪg'zjuːbərəntlɪ/ ADV 1 *(= high-spiritedly) [laugh, embrace]* avec exubérance ◆ **to be** ~ **happy** manifester une joie exubérante 2 *(Bot = vigorously)* ◆ **to grow** ~ être luxuriant

exude /ɪg'zjuːd/ VI suinter, exsuder *(from* de) VT *[+ resin, blood]* exsuder ◆ **to** ~ **water** *or* **moisture** suinter ◆ **he** ~**d charm** le charme lui sortait par tous les pores ◆ **he** ~**s confidence** il respire la confiance en soi

exult /ɪg'zʌlt/ VI *(= rejoice)* se réjouir *(in* de ; *over* à propos de) exulter ; *(= triumph)* jubiler, chanter victoire ◆ **to** ~ **at finding** *or* **to find** se réjouir grandement *or* exulter de trouver

exultant /ɪg'zʌltənt/ ADJ *[person, mood, tone, expression]* jubilant, triomphant ; *[joy]* triomphant ◆ **to be** *or* **feel** ~, **to be in an** ~ **mood** être d'humeur joyeuse

exultantly /ɪg'zʌltəntlɪ/ ADV en exultant, en jubilant

exultation /,egzʌl'teɪʃən/ N exultation *f*, jubilation *f*

exurbia /eks'ɜːbɪə/ N *(US)* la banlieue aisée

ex-wife /,eks'waɪf/ N (pl **ex-wives**) ex-femme *f*

ex-works /,eks'wɜːks/ ADJ *(Brit Comm) [price]* départ usine ; see also **ex** prep

eye /aɪ/

1 NOUN	3 COMPOUNDS
2 TRANSITIVE VERB	4 PHRASAL VERB

1 - NOUN

1 of person, animal œil *m* (yeux *pl*) ◆ **to have brown** ~**s** avoir les yeux marron ◆ **a girl with blue** ~**s** une fille aux yeux bleus ◆ **before my very** ~**s** sous mes yeux ◆ **it's there in front of your very** ~**s** tu l'as sous les yeux, c'est sous ton nez * ◆ **with tears in her** ~**s** les larmes aux yeux ◆ **to have the sun in one's** ~**s** avoir le soleil dans les yeux ◆ **I haven't got** ~**s in the back of my head** je n'ai pas des yeux dans le dos ◆ **he must have** ~**s in the back of his head!** il n'a pas les yeux dans sa poche ! ◆ **to let one's** ~ **rest on sb/sth** poser son regard sur qn/qch ◆ **I've never set** *or* **clapped** * *or* **laid** ~**s on him** je ne l'ai jamais vu de ma vie ◆ **use your** ~**s!** tu es aveugle ? ◆ ~**s front!** *(Mil)* fixe ! ◆ ~**s right!** *(Mil)* tête (à) droite ! ◆ **an** ~ **for an** ~ **and a tooth for a tooth** œil pour œil, dent pour dent ◆ **for your eyes only** *(fig)* ultraconfidentiel ◆ **"eyes only"** *(US: on documents)* "top secret"

2 of object *[of needle]* chas *m*, œil *m* (œils *pl*) ; *[of potato, peacock's tail]* œil *m* (yeux *pl*) ; *[of hurricane]* œil *m* ; *[of camera]* objectif *m* ; *(= photoelectric cell)* œil *m* électrique ◆ **the** ~ **of the storm** *(fig)* l'œil *m* du cyclone

3 set structures

◆ **to close** *or* **shut one's eyes to** ◆ **to close** *or* **shut one's** ~**s to sb's shortcomings** fermer les yeux sur les faiblesses de qn ◆ **to close** *or* **shut one's** ~**s to the evidence** refuser *or* nier l'évidence ◆ **to close** *or* **shut one's** ~**s to the dangers of sth/to the truth** refuser de voir les écueils de qch/la vérité en face ◆ **one can't close** *or* **shut one's** ~**s to the fact that ...** il faut bien reconnaître que ... ◆ **he preferred to close his** ~**s to the possibility of war** il refusait d'envisager la guerre

◆ **to get one's eye in** ajuster son coup d'œil

◆ **to give sb the eye** * faire de l'œil * à qn

◆ **to have an eye for** ◆ **she has an** ~ **for a bargain** elle flaire *or* elle reconnaît tout de suite une bonne affaire ◆ **she has** *or* **she's got an** ~ **for antiques** elle a le coup d'œil pour les antiquités

◆ **to have eyes for** ◆ **he only had** ~**s for her** il n'avait d'yeux que pour elle ◆ **they only have** ~**s for the championship** ils ne pensent qu'au championnat

◆ **to have (got) one's/an eye on** ◆ **he's got his** ~ **on the championship** il lorgne le championnat ◆ **I've already got my** ~ **on a house** j'ai déjà une maison en vue ◆ **to have an** ~ **on sb for a job** avoir qn en vue pour un poste ◆ **he had his** ~ **on a job in the Foreign Office** il visait un poste au ministère des Affaires étrangères

◆ **to keep + eye(s)** ◆ **he couldn't keep his** ~**s open** * il dormait debout ◆ **to keep one's** ~**s wide open** garder les yeux grand(s) ouverts ◆ **to keep one's** ~ **on the ball** *(lit)* fixer la balle ; *(fig)* rester vigilant ◆ **keeping his** ~ **on the bear, he seized his gun** sans quitter l'ours des yeux, il a empoigné son fusil ◆ **keep your** ~ **on the main objective** ne perdez pas de vue le but principal ◆ **to keep an** ~ **on things** *or* **on everything** * garder la boutique * ◆ **will you keep an** ~ **on the baby/shop?** vous pouvez surveiller le bébé/le magasin ? ◆ **to keep an** ~ **on expenditure** surveiller ses dépenses ◆ **to keep one's** ~**s open** *or* **peeled**‡ *or* **skinned**‡ ouvrir l'œil ◆ **keep your** ~**s open for** *or* **keep an** ~ **out for a hotel** * essayez de repérer * un hôtel ◆ **to keep a strict** ~ **on sb** surveiller qn de près, tenir qn à l'œil *

◆ **to make eyes at sb** * faire de l'œil à qn *

◆ **to open sb's eyes to** ◆ **this will open his** ~**s to the truth** ça va lui ouvrir *or* dessiller les yeux

◆ **to take one's eye off** ◆ **he didn't take his** ~**s off her** il ne l'a pas quittée des yeux ◆ **he couldn't take his** ~**s off the cakes** il ne pouvait pas s'empêcher de lorgner les gâteaux, il dévorait les gâteaux des yeux ◆ **to take one's** ~ **off the ball** *(lit)* arrêter de fixer le ballon ; *(fig)* avoir un moment d'inattention

◆ **all eyes** ◆ **all** ~**s are on him** tous les regards sont tournés vers lui ◆ **all** ~**s are on the conference** tous les regards convergent sur la conférence ◆ **to be all** ~**s** * être tout yeux

◆ **eye to eye** ◆ **to see** ~ **to** ~ **with sb** *(on specific issue)* partager le point de vue de qn, être d'accord avec qn ◆ **we rarely see** ~ **to** ~ nous sommes rarement d'accord

◆ **my eye** ◆ **my** ~**!**‡ mon œil !‡ ◆ **it's all my** ~‡ tout ça, c'est des foutaises *

◆ **in + eye(s)** *(fig)* ◆ **it hits you in the** ~ cela saute aux yeux ◆ **that's one in the** ~ **for him** * c'est bien fait pour lui *or* pour sa poire‡ ◆ **in the** ~**s of ...** aux yeux de ... ◆ **in his** ~**s** à ses yeux ◆ **in the** ~**s of the law** au regard de *or* aux yeux de la loi

◆ **through sb's eyes** ◆ **to look at sth through someone else's** ~**s** examiner qch du point de vue de quelqu'un d'autre ◆ **to look at a ques-**

tion through the ~s of an economist envisager une question du point de vue de l'économiste

♦ **under the eye of** sous la surveillance de, sous l'œil de

♦ **up to the/one's eyes** ♦ **to be up to one's ~s in work** être débordé (de travail) ♦ **to be up to one's ~s in paperwork** être dans la paperasserie jusqu'au cou* ♦ **to be up to one's ~s in debt** être endetté jusqu'au cou ♦ **he's in it up to the** *or* **his ~s*** *(in crime, plot, conspiracy)* il est mouillé* jusqu'au cou

♦ **with + eye(s)** ♦ **with one's ~s closed** *or* **shut** les yeux fermés ♦ **with ~s half-closed** *or* **half-shut** les yeux mi-clos ♦ **with my own ~s** de mes propres yeux ♦ **I saw him with my own ~s** je l'ai vu de mes propres yeux ♦ **he went into it with his ~s wide open** *or* **with open ~s** il s'y est lancé en toute connaissance de cause ♦ **I could do it with my ~s shut** *(fig)* je pourrais le faire les yeux fermés ♦ **with an ~ to the future** en prévision de l'avenir ♦ **to look at a house with an ~ to buying** visiter une maison que l'on envisage d'acheter ♦ **he's a man with an ~ for quality** c'est un homme qui sait reconnaître la bonne qualité ♦ **a writer with an ~ for detail** un auteur qui a le sens du détail ♦ **with a critical/a jealous/an uneasy** *etc* **~** d'un œil critique/jaloux/inquiet *etc* ; → **catch, fall, far, half, look, main, mind, open, private, run**

2 - TRANSITIVE VERB

[+ person] regarder, mesurer du regard ; *[+ thing]* regarder, observer ♦ **to ~ sb from head to toe** toiser qn de la tête aux pieds

3 - COMPOUNDS

eye candy* N *(= woman)* belle fille *f* ; *(= man)* beau mec* *m*

eye-catcher N personne *f (or chose f)* qui attire l'œil

eye-catching ADJ *[dress, colour]* qui attire l'œil ; *[publicity, poster]* accrocheur

eye contact N ♦ **to establish/avoid ~ contact with sb** regarder/éviter de regarder qn dans les yeux

eye doctor N *(US)* oculiste *mf* ; *(prescribing)* ophtalmologue *mf*

eye job* N *opération de chirurgie esthétique aux yeux*

eye level N ♦ **at ~ level** au niveau des yeux

eye-level grill N gril *m* surélevé

eye-opener* N *(= surprise)* révélation *f*, surprise *f* ; *(US) (= drink)* petit verre *m* pris au réveil ♦ **that was an ~-opener for him** cela lui a ouvert les yeux ♦ **his speech was an ~-opener** son discours a été très révélateur

eye-patch N cache *m*, bandeau *m*

eye socket N orbite *f*

eye test N examen *m* de la vue

4 - PHRASAL VERB

► **eye up*** VT SEP *(Brit)* reluquer* ♦ **he was ~ing up the girls** il reluquait les filles

eyeball /ˈaɪbɔːl/ 1 N globe *m* oculaire ♦ **to stand ~ to ~ with sb*** se trouver nez à nez avec qn ♦ **to be up to one's ~s in work*** être débordé (de travail) ♦ **to be up to one's ~s in debt/paperwork*** être endetté/être dans la paperasserie jusqu'au cou* 2 VT ⁑ zieuter⁑

eyebank /ˈaɪbæŋk/ N *(Med)* banque *f* des yeux

eyebath /ˈaɪbɑːθ/ N *(esp Brit)* œillère *f*

eyebrow /ˈaɪbraʊ/ 1 N sourcil *m* COMP **eyebrow pencil** N crayon *m* à sourcils **eyebrow tweezers** NPL pince *f* à épiler

eyecup /ˈaɪkʌp/ N *(US)* ⇒ **eyebath**

-eyed /aɪd/ ADJ *(in compounds)* ♦ **big-eyed** aux grands yeux ♦ **brown-eyed** aux yeux marron ♦ **one-eyed** *(lit)* borgne ; *(* fig)* miteux, minable ; → **dry, hollow**

eyedrops /ˈaɪdrɒps/ NPL gouttes *fpl* pour les yeux, collyre *m*

eyeful /ˈaɪfʊl/ N ♦ **he got an ~ of mud** il a reçu de la boue plein les yeux ♦ **she's quite an ~*** cette fille, c'est un régal pour l'œil, elle est vraiment canon* ♦ **get an ~ of this!⁑** vise un peu ça !⁑

eyeglass /ˈaɪglɑːs/ N monocle *m*

eyeglasses /ˈaɪglɑːsɪz/ NPL *(esp US)* lunettes *fpl*

eyelash /ˈaɪlæʃ/ N cil *m*

eyelet /ˈaɪlɪt/ N œillet *m (dans du tissu etc)*

eyelid /ˈaɪlɪd/ N paupière *f*

eyeliner /ˈaɪlaɪnəʳ/ N eye-liner *m*

eyepiece /ˈaɪpiːs/ N oculaire *m*

eyeshade /ˈaɪʃeɪd/ N visière *f*

eyeshadow /ˈaɪʃædəʊ/ N fard *m* à paupières

eyesight /ˈaɪsaɪt/ N vue *f* ♦ **to have good ~** avoir une bonne vue *or* de bons yeux ♦ **to lose one's ~** perdre la vue ♦ **his ~ is failing** sa vue baisse

eyesore /ˈaɪsɔːʳ/ N *objet ou construction qui choque la vue* ♦ **these ruins are an ~** ces ruines sont une horreur *or* sont hideuses

eyestrain /ˈaɪstreɪn/ N ♦ **to have ~** avoir les yeux fatigués

eyetooth /ˈaɪtuːθ/ N (pl **eyeteeth** /ˈaɪtiːθ/) canine *f* supérieure ♦ **I'd give my eyeteeth* for a car like that/to go to China** qu'est-ce que je ne donnerais pas pour avoir une voiture comme ça/pour aller en Chine

eyewash /ˈaɪwɒʃ/ N 1 *(Med)* collyre *m* 2 **that's a lot of ~⁑** *(= nonsense)* ce sont des fadaises, c'est du vent ; *(to impress)* c'est de la frime*, c'est de la poudre aux yeux

eyewear /ˈaɪwɛəʳ/ N *(NonC)* lunettes *fpl*, lunetterie *f*

eyewitness /ˈaɪˌwɪtnɪs/ 1 N témoin *m* oculaire *or* direct COMP **eyewitness account** N *(in media)* récit *m* de témoin oculaire ; *(to police)* déposition *f* de témoin oculaire

eyrie /ˈɪərɪ/ N aire *f (d'aigle)*

Ezekiel /ɪˈziːkɪəl/ N Ézéchiel *m*

e-zine /ˈiːziːn/ N e-zine *m*

Ff

F, f /ef/ **N** 1 (= *letter*) F, f *m* ◆ **F for Freddy, F for fox** *(US)* F comme François ; see also **f-word, f-number, f-stop** 2 *(Mus)* fa *m* 3 *(Scol = mark)* faible 4 abbrev of **Fahrenheit** 5 (abbrev of **fiscal year**) → **fiscal**

FA /ˌefˈeɪ/ *(Brit)* 1 (abbrev of **Football Association**) fédération anglaise de football 2 ⁎ (abbrev of **Fanny Adams**) → **Fanny**

fa /fɑː/ **N** *(Mus)* fa *m*

FAA /ˌefeɪˈeɪ/ **N** *(US)* (abbrev of **Federal Aviation Administration**) → **federal**

fab⁎ /fæb/, **fabby**⁎ /ˈfæbɪ/ **ADJ** *(Brit)* (abbrev of **fabulous**) sensass*

Fabian /ˈfeɪbɪən/ **N** *(Pol)* Fabien(ne) *m(f)* **ADJ** fabien **COMP** **Fabian Society** **N** Association *f* fabienne

fable /ˈfeɪbl/ **N** *(Literat, fig)* fable *f* ; → **fact**

fabled /ˈfeɪbld/ **ADJ** légendaire

fabric /ˈfæbrɪk/ **N** 1 (= *cloth*) tissu *m*, étoffe *f* ◆ **cotton ~s** cotonnades *fpl* ◆ **woollen ~s** lainages *mpl* 2 *[of building, system]* structure *f* ◆ **the social ~ of our country** le tissu social de notre pays **COMP** **fabric conditioner, fabric softener** **N** produit *m* assouplissant

fabricate /ˈfæbrɪkeɪt/ **VT** 1 (= *manufacture*) *[+ goods]* fabriquer 2 (= *invent*) *[+ story, account]* inventer, fabriquer ; *[+ evidence]* fabriquer ; *[+ document]* contrefaire ◆ **to ~ an allegation** avancer une allégation ◆ **to ~ an invoice** établir une fausse facture

fabrication /ˌfæbrɪˈkeɪʃən/ **N** 1 (= *lie*) ◆ **it is (a) pure ~** c'est une invention pure et simple 2 *(NonC = invention) [of story, account]* invention *f* ; *[of document]* fabrication *f* ◆ **~ of evidence** *(Jur)* fabrication *f* de (fausses) preuves 3 (= *manufacturing*) *[of goods]* fabrication *f*

fabulist /ˈfæbjʊlɪst/ **N** *(Literat)* fabuliste *m*

fabulous /ˈfæbjʊləs/ **ADJ** 1 (= *incredible*) fabuleux 2 (* = *wonderful*) *[prize, holiday, opportunity, weather]* fabuleux ◆ **~ prices** des prix astronomiques ◆ **~!** chouette ! * 3 *(liter = mythical) [beast, monster]* fabuleux *(liter)*

fabulously /ˈfæbjʊləslɪ/ **ADV** *[wealthy, rich]* fabuleusement ; *[expensive]* incroyablement ◆ **to be ~ successful** avoir un succès fabuleux

façade /fəˈsɑːd/ **N** *(Archit, fig)* façade *f*

face /feɪs/

1 NOUN
2 TRANSITIVE VERB
3 INTRANSITIVE VERB
4 COMPOUNDS
5 PHRASAL VERBS

1 - NOUN

1 Anat visage *m* ◆ **a pleasant ~** un visage agréable ◆ **he stuck his ~ out of the window** il a passé la tête par la fenêtre ◆ **I know that ~, that ~ is familiar** ce visage me dit quelque chose ◆ **injuries to the ~** blessures à la face *or* au visage ◆ **to have one's ~ lifted** se faire faire un lifting ◆ **to put one's ~ on*** se faire une beauté* ◆ **he won't show his ~ here again** il ne remettra plus les pieds ici ◆ **to go red in the ~** rougir ◆ **I could never look him in the ~ again** je ne pourrais plus le regarder en face ◆ **to be written across** *or* **all over** *or* **on sb's ~** se lire sur le visage de qn ◆ **you're lying, it's written all over your ~!** * tu mens, ça se lit sur ton visage !

◆ **in one's face** ◆ **the rain was blowing in our ~s** la pluie nous fouettait le visage ◆ **it blew up in my ~** *(lit)* ça m'a explosé à la figure ◆ **his plan blew up in his ~** son plan s'est retourné contre lui ; → **in-your-face**

◆ **in the face of** ◆ **courage in the ~ of the enemy** courage *m* face à l'ennemi ◆ **they remained defiant in the ~ of international condemnation** ils persistaient à défier la condamnation internationale ◆ **in the ~ of this threat** devant cette menace, face à cette menace ◆ **to smile in the ~ of adversity** garder le sourire (malgré les problèmes) ◆ **he succeeded in the ~ of great difficulties** il a réussi en dépit de grandes difficultés

◆ **to sb's face** ◆ **he told him so to his ~** il le lui a dit en face *or* sans détour ◆ **he told him the truth to his ~** il lui a dit la vérité sans détour

◆ **face to face** ◆ **to come ~ to ~ with** (= *meet*) se trouver face à face *or* nez à nez avec ; (= *confront*) *[+ problem, difficulty]* devoir affronter ◆ **to bring two people ~ to ~** confronter deux personnes ; see also **compounds**

◆ **to be off one's face**⁎ *(Brit)* être bourré⁎

◆ **out of sb's face**⁎ ◆ **get out of my ~ !** fous-moi la paix !⁎

2 = front ◆ **he was lying ~ down(wards)** *(on ground)* il était face contre terre *or* à plat ventre ; *(on bed, sofa)* il était à plat ventre ◆ **he was lying ~ up(wards)** il était allongé sur le dos ◆ **to fall (flat) on one's ~** *(lit)* tomber à plat ventre, tomber face contre terre ; *(fig)* se planter*

3 = expression mine *f* ◆ **to make** *or* **pull ~s (at)** faire des grimaces (à) ◆ **to make** *or* **pull a (disapproving) ~** faire la moue ◆ **to put a bold** *or* **brave ~ on things** faire bonne contenance ◆ **they're trying to put a good ~ on it** ils font contre mauvaise fortune bon cœur ◆ **to set one's ~ against sth** s'élever contre qch ◆ **to set one's ~ against doing sth** se refuser à faire qch

4 = appearance visage *m* ◆ **to change the ~ of a town** changer le visage d'une ville ◆ **the changing ~ of Malaysian politics** le visage changeant de la politique malaise ◆ **the unacceptable ~ of capitalism** la face inacceptable du capitalisme

◆ **on the face of it** à première vue

5 * = person visage *m* ; (= *celebrity*) nom *m* (connu) ◆ **a familiar ~** un visage familier ◆ **among familiar ~s** parmi des visages familiers *or* connus ◆ **the new committee includes many of the same old ~s** on retrouve les mêmes visages dans le nouveau comité ◆ **we need some new** *or* **fresh ~s on the team** notre équipe a besoin de sang neuf

6 of building façade *f*

7 of clock cadran *m*

8 Climbing *[of mountain]* face *f* ; *[of cliff]* paroi *f* ◆ **the north ~ of the Eiger** la face nord de l'Eiger

9 = surface *[of coin]* côté *m* ; *[of the earth]* surface *f* ; *[of document]* recto *m* ; *[of playing card]* face *f*, dessous *m* ◆ **it fell ~ up/down** *[playing card, photo]* elle est tombée face en dessus/en dessous ; *[coin]* elle est tombée côté face/pile ◆ **to turn sth ~ up** retourner *or* mettre qch à l'endroit ◆ **he vanished off the ~ of the earth** il a complètement disparu

10 Typ œil *m*

11 = prestige **to lose ~** * perdre la face ; → **loss**

12 = impertinence ◆ **to have the ~*** to do sth avoir le toupet* de faire qch

2 - TRANSITIVE VERB

1 = turn one's face towards faire face à ◆ **he turned and ~d the man** il se retourna et fit face à l'homme ◆ **~ this way!** tournez-vous de ce côté !

2 = have one's face towards faire face à, être en face de ◆ **he was facing me** il me faisait face ◆ **facing one another** en face l'un de l'autre, l'un en face de l'autre ◆ **the two boys ~d each other** les deux garçons se faisaient face *or* étaient face à face ◆ **he was facing the wall** il était face au mur ◆ **to ~ both ways** *(fig)* ménager la chèvre et le chou

3 [= have its front towards] *(gen)* faire face à ; *(= look out onto) [building, window]* faire face à, donner sur ◆ **the seats were all facing the platform** les sièges faisaient tous face à l'estrade ◆ **the picture facing page 16** l'illustration en regard de *or* en face de la page 16 ◆ **which way does the house ~?** comment la maison est-elle orientée ? ◆ **the house ~s north** la maison est orientée au nord

4 [= confront] *[problem, task, situation]* se présenter à ◆ **two problems/tasks ~d them** deux problèmes/tâches se présentaient à eux, ils se trouvaient devant deux problèmes/tâches ◆ **the problem facing us** le problème devant lequel nous nous trouvons *or* qui se pose à nous ◆ **the economic difficulties facing the country** les difficultés économiques que rencontre le pays *or* auxquelles le pays doit faire face

◆ **faced with** ◆ **the government, ~d with renewed wage demands ...** le gouvernement, confronté à de nouvelles revendications salariales ... ◆ **he was ~d with a class who refused to cooperate** il se trouvait face à *or* confronté à une classe qui refusait de coopérer ◆ **~d with the task of deciding, he ...** se trouvant dans l'obligation de prendre une décision, il ... ◆ **he was ~d with having to pay £100** *or* **with a bill for £100** il se voyait contraint *or* obligé de payer (une note de) 100 livres ◆ **he was ~d with the possibility that they might refuse** il risquait de les voir refuser ◆ **he was ~d with the prospect of doing it himself** il risquait d'avoir à le faire lui-même ◆ **~d with the prospect of having to refuse, he ...** face à *or* devant la perspective d'avoir à refuser, il ...

◆ **to face sb with sth** ◆ **you must ~ him with this choice/the decision** vous devez le contraindre à faire face à ce choix/cette décision ◆ **you must ~ him with the truth** vous devez le contraindre à regarder la vérité en face

5 [= look at honestly] *[+ problem]* faire face à ; *[+ truth]* regarder en face ◆ **she ~d the problem at last** elle a enfin fait face au problème ◆ **to ~ the music** braver l'orage *or* la tempête ◆ **sooner or later he'll have to ~ the music** tôt ou tard, il va devoir braver l'orage *or* la tempête ◆ **to ~ (the) facts** regarder les choses en face, se rendre à l'évidence ◆ **she won't ~ the fact that he's not going to come back** elle ne veut pas se rendre à l'évidence et admettre qu'il ne reviendra pas ◆ **let's ~ it*** regardons les choses en face

◆ **can't/couldn't face** ◆ **I can't ~ doing it** je n'ai pas le courage de le faire ◆ **I can't ~ breakfast this morning** je ne peux rien avaler ce matin ◆ **I can't ~ him/the washing up** je n'ai pas le courage de le voir/de faire la vaisselle ◆ **I couldn't ~ this alone** je ne pourrais pas y faire face tout seul

6 [= risk incurring] *[+ fine, charges, prison, defeat, death]* risquer ; *[+ unemployment, redundancy]* être menacé de ◆ **he ~s life in prison if convicted** il risque la prison à vie s'il est reconnu coupable ◆ **many people were facing redundancy** beaucoup de gens étaient menacés de licenciement *or* risquaient d'être licenciés

7 [= line] *[+ wall]* revêtir (*with* de) ; *(Sewing)* doubler ◆ **the hood is ~d with silk** la capuche est doublée de soie

3 - INTRANSITIVE VERB

1 [person] *(= turn one's face)* se tourner (*towards* vers) ; *(= be turned)* être tourné (*towards* vers) faire face (*towards* à) ◆ **he was facing towards the audience** il faisait face au public ◆ **right ~!** *(US Mil)* à droite, droite ! ◆ **about ~!** *(US Mil)* demi-tour !

2 [house] être exposé *or* orienté ◆ **a window facing south** une fenêtre orientée au sud ◆ **a room facing towards the sea** une chambre donnant sur la mer

4 - COMPOUNDS

face card N *(US)* figure *f (de jeu de cartes)*
face cloth N ⇒ **face flannel**
face cream N crème *f* pour le visage
face flannel N *(Brit)* ≃ gant *m* de toilette
face guard N *(Baseball)* visière *f* de protection
face-lift N lifting *m* ◆ **to have a ~-lift** se faire faire un lifting ◆ **to give a ~-lift*** **to** *(fig) [+ house] (exterior)* ravaler la façade de ; *(interior)* retaper ; *[+ political party, company]* rajeunir l'image de ◆ **the town/the park/the garden has been given a ~-lift*** la ville/le parc/le jardin a fait peau neuve
face mask N masque *m* ; *(Cosmetics)* masque *m* (de beauté)
face-off N *(Hockey)* remise *f* en jeu ; *(fig)* confrontation *f*
face pack N masque *m* (de beauté)
face powder N poudre *f* de riz
face-saver N → **face-saving**
face-saving ADJ qui sauve la face N ◆ **it was clearly a piece of ~-saving** *or* **a ~-saver on their part** ils ont visiblement fait cela pour sauver la face
face-to-face ADJ face à face, nez à nez ◆ **~-to-~ discussion** *(TV etc)* face à face *m inv*, face-à-face *m inv*
face value N valeur *f* nominale ◆ **to take a statement at (its) ~ value** *(fig)* prendre une déclaration au pied de la lettre ◆ **to take sb at ~ value** juger qn sur les apparences ◆ **you can't take it at (its) ~ value** il ne faut pas vous laisser tromper par les apparences

5 - PHRASAL VERBS

► **face about** VI *(Mil)* faire demi-tour
► **face down** VT SEP *(esp US)* défier du regard
► **face out*** VT SEP *(Brit)* ◆ **to face it out** faire front ◆ **to ~ out a crisis** faire face à *or* affronter une crise
► **face up to** VT FUS *[+ danger, difficulty]* faire face à, affronter ; *[+ responsibilities]* faire face à ◆ **to ~ up to the fact that ...** admettre *or* accepter (le fait) que ...

faceless /ˈfeɪslɪs/ ADJ *[person]* sans visage ; *[place]* anonyme ◆ **he thinks politicians are just ~ wonders** pour lui, les hommes politiques sont tous les mêmes

facer* /ˈfeɪsəʳ/ N *(Brit)* ◆ **it was a real ~** c'était un sacré* problème

facet /ˈfæsɪt/ N *(lit, fig)* facette *f*

faceted /ˈfæsɪtɪd/ ADJ à facettes

facetious /fəˈsiːʃəs/ ADJ *[person]* facétieux

facetiously /fəˈsiːʃəslɪ/ ADV facétieusement

facetiousness /fəˈsiːʃəsnɪs/ N *[of person]* esprit *m* facétieux ; *[of remark]* caractère *m or* côté *m* facétieux ; *(= jokes)* facéties *fpl*

facia /ˈfeɪʃə/ N ⇒ **fascia**

facial /ˈfeɪʃəl/ ADJ *[nerve, muscles, massage]* facial ; *[expression]* du visage ; *[injury]* au visage ◆ **~ features** traits *mpl* (du visage) N * soin *m* (complet) du visage ◆ **to have a ~** se faire faire un soin du visage ◆ **to give o.s. a ~** se faire un nettoyage de peau
COMP **facial hair** N poils *mpl* du visage
facial scrub N exfoliant *m*, produit *m* gommant (pour le visage)
facial wash N lotion *f* (pour le visage)

facially /ˈfeɪʃəlɪ/ ADV ◆ **~ disfigured** défiguré ◆ **to be ~ scarred** avoir une (*or* des) cicatrice(s) au visage ◆ **they are ~ similar** leurs visages se ressemblent

facies /ˈfeɪʃɪiːz/ N *(pl inv)* faciès *m*

facile /ˈfæsaɪl/ ADJ *(pej) [talk, idea, style]* superficiel ; *[optimism, solution, comparison, victory]* facile *(pej)* ; *[question]* simpliste ◆ **it is ~ to suggest that ...** c'est un peu facile de suggérer que ...

facilely /ˈfæsaɪllɪ/ ADV aisément

facilitate /fəˈsɪlɪteɪt/ VT faciliter VI *(= act as mediator)* faire office de facilitateur (*or* de facilitatrice) ; *(= act as group leader)* faire office d'animateur (*or* d'animatrice)

facilitator /fəˈsɪlɪteɪtəʳ/ N *(= mediator)* facilitateur *m*, -trice *f* ; *(= group leader)* animateur *m*, -trice *f*

facility /fəˈsɪlɪtɪ/ N 1 ◆ **facilities** *(= equipment, material)* équipements *mpl* (*for* de) ; *(= place, installation)* installations *fpl* ◆ **military facilities** installations *fpl* militaires ◆ **sports/educational facilities** équipements *mpl* sportifs/scolaires ◆ **storage facilities** *(industrial)* installations *fpl* d'entreposage, entrepôts *mpl* ; *(in house = wardrobes, cupboards etc)* espaces *mpl* de rangement ◆ **a large hotel with all facilities** un grand hôtel doté de tout le confort moderne ◆ **toilet facilities** toilettes *fpl*, sanitaires *mpl* ◆ **health care facilities** services *mpl* de santé, infrastructure *f* médicale ◆ **child care facilities** *(= crèches)* crèches *fpl* ; *(for older children)* garderies *fpl* ◆ **we offer facilities for childminding from 8am to 8pm** nous proposons une crèche *or* garderie pour les enfants de 8 heures à 20 heures ◆ **play facilities for young children** un espace de jeu pour les petits enfants ◆ **there are no facilities for children/the disabled** ce n'est pas aménagé pour les enfants/les handicapés ◆ **the flat has no cooking facilities** l'appartement n'est pas équipé pour faire la cuisine

2 *(= means (of doing sth))* moyens *mpl* (*for* de) possibilité *f* (*for doing sth* de faire qch) ◆ **transport/production facilities** moyens *mpl* de transport/de production ◆ **a ~ for converting part of one's pension into ...** la possibilité de convertir une partie de sa retraite en ... ◆ **the bank offers the ~ to pay over 50 weeks** la banque offre la possibilité d'étaler les paiements sur 50 semaines ◆ **we have no ~** *or* **facilities for disposing of toxic waste** nous ne sommes pas en mesure d'éliminer les déchets toxiques ◆ **you will have all facilities** *or* **every ~ for study** vous aurez toutes facilités *or* tout ce qu'il faut pour étudier ◆ **a computer with the ~ to reproduce speech** un ordinateur capable de reproduire le son de la voix ◆ **the machine does not have the ~ to run this program** l'appareil ne permet pas d'exécuter ce programme ; → **overdraft**

3 *(Tech etc = device)* mécanisme *m* ; *(Comput)* fonction *f* ◆ **the clock has a stopwatch ~** le réveil peut aussi servir de chronomètre ◆ **the oven has an automatic timing ~** le four est doté d'un minuteur automatique ◆ **there's a ~ for storing data** *(Comput)* il y a une fonction de mise en mémoire des données

4 *(= place, building)* ◆ **the museum has a ~ where students can work** le musée met à la disposition des étudiants un endroit où travailler ◆ **student facilities include a library and language laboratory** les étudiants disposent notamment d'une bibliothèque et d'un laboratoire de langues ◆ **a newly-built manufacturing ~** une nouvelle usine ◆ **nuclear ~** *(= arms factory)* usine *f* nucléaire ; *(= power station)* centrale *f* nucléaire

5 *(NonC = ease)* facilité *f* ◆ **to write/speak/express o.s. with ~** écrire/parler/s'exprimer avec facilité *or* aisance

6 *(= person's talent, ability)* **her ~ in** *or* **for learning, her learning ~** sa facilité à apprendre ◆ **he has a great ~ for languages/maths** il est très doué pour les langues/les maths, il a beaucoup de facilité en langues/maths

facing /ˈfeɪsɪŋ/ N *(Constr)* revêtement *m* ; *(Sewing)* revers *m*

-facing /ˈfeɪsɪŋ/ ADJ *(in compounds)* ◆ **south/north~** exposé au sud/au nord ◆ **rear/forward~ seats** *(on train)* sièges *mpl* placés dans le sens contraire de la marche/dans le sens de la marche

facsimile /fækˈsɪmɪlɪ/ N fac-similé *m* ◆ **in ~** en fac-similé

COMP **facsimile machine** N télécopieur *m*
facsimile transmission N télécopie *f*

fact /fækt/ LANGUAGE IN USE 26.1, 26.3

N 1 *(= sth known, accepted as true)* fait *m* ◆ **the ~ that he is here** le fait qu'il est là *or* qu'il soit là ◆ **it is a ~ that ...** il faut bien reconnaître que ..., il est de fait que ... *(frm)* ◆ **in view of the ~ that ...** étant donné que ... ◆ **despite the ~ that ...** bien que ... + *subj* ◆ **is it a ~ that ...?** est-il vrai que ... + *subj or indic* ? ◆ **is that a ~?** *(iro)* vraiment ? ◆ **(and) that's a ~** c'est certain *or* sûr ◆ **I know it for a ~** j'en suis sûr ◆ **to know (it) for a ~ that ...** être certain que ... ◆ **let's stick to the ~s** tenons-nous-en aux faits ◆ **we haven't got all the ~s and figures yet** nous ne disposons pas encore de tous les éléments ◆ **interesting ~s and figures about the different peoples of Africa** des informations intéressantes sur les différents peuples d'Afrique ◆ **it's a ~ of life (that ...)** la vie est ainsi faite (que ...) ◆ **it's time he knew the ~s of life** *(gen)* il est temps de lui apprendre les choses de la vie *or* qu'on le mette devant les réalités de la vie ; *(about sex)* il est temps qu'il sache comment les enfants viennent au monde ; → **face**

2 *(NonC) (= reality)* faits *mpl*, réalité *f* ◆ **story founded on ~** histoire *f* basée sur des faits *or* sur la réalité ◆ **~ and fiction** le réel et l'imaginaire ◆ **he can't tell ~ from fiction** *or* **from fable** il ne sait pas séparer le vrai du faux ◆ **the ~ of the matter is that ...** le fait est que ... ◆ **I accept what he says as ~** je ne mets pas en doute la véracité de ses propos

◆ **in + fact** en fait ; *(reinforcing sth)* effectivement ◆ **he had promised to send the books and in ~ they arrived the next day** il avait promis d'envoyer les livres et ils sont effectivement arrivés le lendemain ◆ **it was a terrible party, in ~ I only stayed for half an hour** la soirée était nulle, en fait, je ne suis resté qu'une demi-heure ◆ **only I knew that Phyllis was, in ~, David's sister** j'étais le seul à savoir que Phyllis était en fait la sœur de David ◆ **it sounds rather simple, but in (actual) ~** *or* **in point of ~ it's very difficult** cela paraît plutôt simple, mais en fait *or* en réalité, c'est très difficile

3 *(Jur)* fait *m*, action *f* ; → **accessary**

COMP **fact-finding** ADJ ◆ **~-finding committee** commission *f* d'enquête ◆ **they were on a ~-finding mission** *or* **trip** *or* **visit to the war front** ils étaient partis en mission d'inspection au front ◆ **~-finding session** séance *f* d'information
fact sheet N fiche *f* d'informations

faction[1] /ˈfækʃən/ N 1 *(= group)* faction *f* 2 *(NonC = strife)* discorde *f*, dissension *f*

faction[2] /ˈfækʃən/ N *(Theat, Cine = mixture of fact and fiction)* docudrame *m*

factional /ˈfækʃənl/ ADJ *[fighting, violence, rivalry]* entre factions ; *[leader]* de faction

factionalism /ˈfækʃənlɪzəm/ N querelles *fpl* intestines

factionalize /ˈfækʃənlaɪz/ VT diviser (en factions)

factious /ˈfækʃəs/ ADJ factieux

factitious /fækˈtɪʃəs/ ADJ artificiel

factitive /ˈfæktɪtɪv/ ADJ *(Gram)* factitif

factoid /ˈfæktɔɪd/ N pseudo-information *f*

factor /ˈfæktəʳ/ N 1 *(gen, Bio, Math)* facteur *m*, élément *m* ◆ **risk ~** facteur *m* de risque ◆ **~ of safety, safety ~** *(Tech)* facteur *m* de sécurité ◆ **the human ~** le facteur humain ◆ **determining** *or* **deciding ~** facteur *m* déterminant *or* décisif ◆ **a (crucial) ~ in determining/deciding sth** un facteur (essentiel) lorsqu'il s'agit de déterminer/décider qch ◆ **price is very much a determining ~ in deciding which car to buy** le prix est un critère important *or* déterminant lors de l'achat d'une voiture ◆ **the scandal was a contributing ~ in his defeat** le scandale a contribué à sa défaite ◆ **output has risen by a ~ of ten** la production a été multipliée par dix ; → **common, prime**

2 *[of sun cream]* **(sun protection) ~ 20** indice *m* (de protection) 20

3 *(= agent)* agent *m* ; *(Scot) (= estate manager)* régisseur *m*, intendant *m*

COMP **factor analysis** N *(Stat)* analyse *f* factorielle
factor VIII, factor 8 N *(Med)* facteur *m* 8

► **factor in** VT SEP *(esp US)* prendre en compte

factorage /ˈfæktərɪdʒ/ N 1 *(Comm)* commission *f* 2 *(Fin)* commission *f* d'affacturage *or* de factoring

factorial /fækˈtɔːrɪəl/ ADJ factoriel N factorielle *f*

factoring /ˈfæktərɪŋ/ N affacturage *m*, factoring *m*

factorize /ˈfæktəˌraɪz/ VT *(Math)* mettre en facteurs

factory /ˈfæktərɪ/ N usine *f* ◆ **shoe/soap** *etc* **~** usine *f or* fabrique *f* de chaussures/de savon *etc* ◆ **car/textile** *etc* **~** usine *f* d'automobiles/de textile *etc* ◆ **arms/china/tobacco ~** manufacture *f* d'armes/de porcelaine/de tabac

COMP **Factory Acts** NPL *(Brit)* législation *f* industrielle
factory chimney N cheminée *f* d'usine
factory farm N ferme *f* industrielle
factory farming N élevage *m* industriel
factory floor N ateliers *mpl* ◆ **workers on the ~ floor** ouvriers *mpl*
factory-fresh ADJ tout droit sorti de l'usine
factory hand N ⇒ **factory worker**
factory inspector N inspecteur *m* du travail
factory outlet N magasin *m* d'usine
factory ship N navire-usine *m*
factory work N *(NonC)* travail *m* en *or* d'usine
factory worker N ouvrier *m*, -ière *f* (d'usine)

factotum /fækˈtəʊtəm/ N factotum *m*, intendant *m* ◆ **general ~** *(hum)* bonne *f* à tout faire *(fig, hum)*

factual /ˈfæktjʊəl/ ADJ *[information, basis, evidence, account]* factuel ; *[error]* sur les faits, de fait ; *[knowledge]* des faits

factually /ˈfæktjʊəlɪ/ ADV *[accurate, correct, wrong]* dans les faits ◆ **~ based** tiré de *or* basé sur des faits réels ◆ **she told her story ~ and without emotion** elle a raconté son histoire factuellement et sans trace d'émotion

faculty /ˈfækəltɪ/ N 1 faculté *f* ◆ **the mental faculties** les facultés *fpl* mentales ◆ **to have all one's faculties** avoir toutes ses facultés ◆ **critical ~** le sens critique 2 *(NonC = aptitude)* aptitude *f*, facilité *f (for doing sth* à faire qch) 3 *(Univ)* faculté *f* ◆ **the Faculty of Arts** la faculté des Lettres ◆ **the medical ~** la faculté de médecine ◆ **the Faculty** *(US)* le corps enseignant ; → **law, science**

COMP **faculty advisor** N *(US Univ) (for student)* directeur *m*, -trice *f* d'études ; *(for club)* animateur *m*, -trice *f*
Faculty board N *(Univ)* Conseil *m* de faculté
Faculty board meeting N réunion *f* du Conseil de faculté
faculty lounge N *(US Scol)* salle *f* des professeurs
Faculty meeting N ⇒ **Faculty board meeting**

fad /fæd/ N *(personal)* marotte *f*, manie *f* ; *(in society in general)* engouement *m*, mode *f* ◆ **she has her ~s** elle a ses (petites) marottes *or* manies ◆ **her latest food ~** sa dernière lubie en matière de nourriture ◆ **a passing ~** un engouement, une lubie

faddish /ˈfædɪʃ/, **faddy** /ˈfædɪ/ ADJ *(Brit) [person]* capricieux, à marottes ; *[distaste, desire]* capricieux

fade /feɪd/ VI 1 *[colour]* passer, perdre son éclat ; *[material]* passer, se décolorer ; *[light]* baisser, diminuer ; *[flower]* se faner, se flétrir ◆ **guaranteed not to ~** *[fabric]* garanti bon teint ◆ **the daylight was fast fading** le jour baissait rapidement

2 (also **fade away**) *[thing remembered, vision]* s'effacer ; *[interest, enthusiasm]* diminuer, décliner ; *[sound]* s'affaiblir ; *[smile]* s'évanouir ; *[one's sight, memory, hearing etc]* baisser ◆ **the castle ~d from sight** le château disparut aux regards ◆ **her voice ~d into silence** sa voix s'est éteinte ◆ **the sound is fading** *(Rad)* il y a du fading ◆ **our hopes had ~d** nos espoirs s'étaient évanouis ◆ **hopes are fading of finding any more survivors** l'espoir de découvrir d'autres survivants s'amenuise ◆ **to ~ into the background** *[person]* se fondre dans le décor ◆ **my fears for Philip ~d into the background** mes craintes pour Philip furent reléguées au second plan ◆ **a singer who ~d into obscurity after just one hit record** un chanteur qui est retombé dans l'anonymat après seulement un tube*

3 *(liter = die) [person]* dépérir

VT 1 *[+ curtains etc]* décolorer ; *[+ colours, flowers]* faner

2 *(Rad) [+ conversation]* couper par un fondu sonore ◆ **to ~ one scene into another** *(Cine, TV)* faire un fondu enchaîné

N ⇒ **fade-out**

COMP **fade-in** N *(Cine)* fondu *m* en ouverture ; *(TV)* apparition *f* graduelle ; *(Rad)* fondu *m* sonore
fade in-fade out N fondu *m* enchaîné
fade-out N *(Cine)* fondu *m* en fermeture ; *(TV)* disparition *f* graduelle ; *(Rad)* fondu *m* sonore

► **fade away** VI ⇒ **fade** VI 2

► **fade in** VI *(Cine, TV)* apparaître en fondu
VT SEP *(Cine, TV)* faire apparaître en fondu ; *(Rad)* monter
N ◆ **fade-in** → **fade**

► **fade out** VI *[sound]* faiblir ; *(Cine, TV) [picture]* disparaître en fondu ; *(Rad) [music, dialogue]* être coupé par un fondu sonore
VT SEP *(Cine, TV)* faire disparaître en fondu ; *(Rad)* couper par un fondu sonore
N ◆ **fade-out** → **fade**

faded /ˈfeɪdɪd/ ADJ *[material]* décoloré, passé ; *[jeans]* délavé ; *[flowers]* fané, flétri ; *[beauty]* défraîchi, fané

faecal, fecal *(US)* /ˈfiːkəl/ ADJ fécal

faeces, feces *(US)* /ˈfiːsiːz/ NPL excréments *mpl*, fèces *fpl (SPÉC)*

faerie, faery /ˈfɛərɪ/ († *or liter*) N féerie *f* ADJ imaginaire, féerique

Faeroes /ˈfɛərəʊz/ NPL ⇒ **Faroes**

faff* /fæf/ VI *(Brit)* ◆ **to ~ about** *or* **around** glandouiller‡

fag /fæg/ N 1 *(Brit ‡ = cigarette)* clope* *f* 2 *(esp US ‡ pej = homosexual)* pédé‡ *m* 3 *(NonC: Brit † *) corvée *f* ◆ **what a ~!** quelle corvée ! 4 *(Brit Scol) petit élève au service d'un grand* VT *(Brit)* 1 (also **fag out**) *[+ person, animal]* éreinter, épuiser ◆ **to be ~ged (out)** ‡ être claqué* *or* crevé* 2 ◆ **I can't be ~ged** ‡ j'ai la flemme* *(to do sth* de faire qch) VI *(Brit Scol)* ◆ **to ~ for sb** faire les menues corvées de qn

COMP **fag end** N
1 ‡ *[of cigarette]* mégot* *m* 2 *(= remainder)* restant *m*, reste *m* ; *[of conversation]* dernières bribes *fpl*
fag hag‡ N fille *f* à pédés‡

faggot¹, fagot *(US)* /ˈfægət/ **N** 1 *(= wood)* fagot *m* 2 *(Brit Culin)* ≃ crépinette *f*

faggot²‡ /ˈfægət/ **N** *(esp US pej)* *(= homosexual)* pédé‡ *m*, tante‡ *f*

fah /fɑː/ **N** *(Mus)* fa *m*

Fahrenheit /ˈfærənhaɪt/ **ADJ** Fahrenheit *inv* ◆ ~ **thermometer/scale** thermomètre *m*/échelle *f* Fahrenheit ◆ **degrees** ~ degrés *mpl* Fahrenheit

fail /feɪl/ LANGUAGE IN USE 11.2

VI 1 *(= be unsuccessful)* *[person] (gen)* échouer ; *(in exam)* échouer, être recalé* *or* collé* ; *[plans, attempts, treatment]* échouer, ne pas réussir ; *[negotiations]* ne pas aboutir, échouer ; *[play, show]* faire *or* être un four ; *[bank, business]* faire faillite ◆ **to** ~ **in an exam/in Latin** échouer *or* être recalé* à un examen/en latin ◆ **to** ~ **by five votes/by ten minutes** échouer à cinq voix près/à dix minutes près ◆ **to** ~ **miserably** *or* **dismally** échouer lamentablement ◆ **he** ~**ed in his attempt to take control of the company** sa tentative de prendre le contrôle de la société a échoué ◆ **to** ~ **in one's duty** faillir à *or* manquer à son devoir

2 *(= grow weak)* *[hearing, eyesight, health]* faiblir, baisser ; *[person, invalid, voice]* s'affaiblir ◆ **his eyes are** ~**ing** sa vue faiblit *or* baisse ◆ **his heart/lungs/liver** ~**ed** il a eu une défaillance cardiaque/pulmonaire/hépatique ◆ **the daylight was beginning to** ~ le jour commençait à baisser

3 *(= run short)* *[power, gas, electricity, water supply]* manquer ◆ **crops** ~**ed because of the drought** la sécheresse a causé la perte des récoltes

4 *(= break down)* *[engine]* tomber en panne ; *[brakes]* lâcher

VT 1 *[+ examination]* échouer à, être recalé* *or* collé* à ◆ **to** ~ **Latin** échouer *or* être recalé* en latin ◆ **to** ~ **one's driving test** échouer à *or* être recalé* à son permis (de conduire)

2 *[+ candidate]* recaler*, coller*

3 *(= let down)* *[+ business partner]* manquer à ses engagements envers ; *[+ friend, colleague, loved one]* *(= disappoint)* décevoir ; *(= neglect)* délaisser ◆ **don't** ~ **me!** je compte sur vous ! ◆ **he felt that he'd** ~**ed his family** il avait le sentiment d'avoir manqué à ses devoirs envers sa famille ◆ **his heart** ~**ed him** le cœur lui a manqué ◆ **words** ~ **me!** les mots me manquent ! ◆ **his memory often** ~**s him** sa mémoire lui fait souvent défaut, sa mémoire le trahit souvent

4 *(= omit)* ◆ **to** ~ **to do sth** manquer de faire qch ◆ **he never** ~**s to write** il ne manque jamais d'écrire ◆ **he** ~**ed to visit her** il a omis de lui rendre visite ◆ **he** ~**ed to meet the deadline** il n'est pas parvenu à respecter les délais ◆ **he** ~**ed to keep his word** il a manqué à sa parole ◆ **he** ~**ed to turn up for dinner** il ne s'est pas montré au dîner ◆ **they** ~**ed to make any progress/to get an agreement** ils n'ont absolument pas progressé/ne sont pas parvenus à un accord ◆ **she never** ~**s to amaze me** elle me surprendra toujours ◆ **I** ~ **to see why** je ne vois pas pourquoi ◆ **I** ~ **to understand** je n'arrive pas à comprendre ; *(Jur)* ◆ **to** ~ **to appear** faire défaut ◆ **he was fined for** ~**ing to stop at a red light** *(Jur)* il a eu une amende *or* contravention pour avoir brûlé un feu rouge

N 1 ◆ **without** ~ *[happen, befall]* immanquablement ; *[come, do]* chaque fois, sans exception ; *(implying obligation)* sans faute ◆ **every morning without** ~**, she takes the dog for a walk** chaque matin sans exception, elle sort son chien ◆ **I'll bring you the money first thing in the morning without** ~ je vous apporterai l'argent sans faute, demain à la première heure ◆ **you must take these tablets every day without** ~ il faut que vous preniez ces cachets tous les jours sans faute *or* sans exception

2 *(Scol, Univ)* échec *m* ◆ **she got a** ~ **in history** elle a échoué *or* elle a été recalée* en histoire

COMP **fail-safe ADJ** *[device, mechanism]* à sûreté intégrée

failed /feɪld/ **ADJ** *[attempt, coup, marriage, businessman, writer]* raté ; *[bank]* en faillite ◆ **it's a** ~ **ideology** c'est une idéologie qui a échoué

failing /ˈfeɪlɪŋ/ **N** défaut *m* **PREP** à défaut de ◆ ~ **this** sinon ◆ ~ **which we ...** sinon *or* faute de quoi nous ... ◆ **drugs can often help. Failing this, surgery may be required** les médicaments sont souvent efficaces, sinon, *or* dans le cas contraire, on peut avoir recours à la chirurgie **ADJ** *[eyesight, health, memory]* défaillant ; *[marriage]* qui va à vau-l'eau ; *[light]* qui baisse ; *[economy]* déprimé, en récession ◆ **"failing"** *(US Scol)* "faible"

failure /ˈfeɪljəʳ/ **N** 1 *(= lack of success)* *[of person, plan]* échec *m* ; *[of bank, business]* faillite *f* ; *[of discussions, negotiations]* échec *m*, fiasco *m* ◆ **academic** ~ l'échec *m* scolaire (*or* universitaire) ◆ **I was surprised by her** ~ **in the exam** j'ai été surpris qu'elle échoue à cet examen ◆ **after two** ~**s he gave up** il a abandonné après deux échecs ◆ **the play was a** ~ la pièce a fait un four *or* a été un fiasco ◆ **this new machine/this plan is a total** ~ cette nouvelle machine/ce projet est un fiasco complet ◆ **his** ~ **to convince them** son incapacité *or* son impuissance à les convaincre ; → **rate¹**

2 *(= unsuccessful person)* raté(e) *m(f)* ◆ **to be a** ~ **at maths** être nul en math ◆ **to be a** ~ **at gardening** ne pas être doué pour le jardinage ◆ **he's a** ~ **as a writer** *(= poor writer)* il ne vaut rien comme écrivain ; *(= unsuccessful writer)* il n'a pas eu de succès en tant qu'écrivain

3 *(= insufficiency)* *[of electricity]* panne *f* ◆ ~ **of oil/water supply** manque *m* de pétrole/d'eau ◆ ~ **of the crops** perte *f* des récoltes

4 *(Med)* **heart/kidney/liver** ~ défaillance *f* cardiaque/rénale/hépatique

5 *(= breakdown)* *[of engine]* panne *f*

6 *(= omission)* ◆ **his** ~ **to answer** le fait qu'il n'a pas répondu ◆ **because of his** ~ **to help us** du fait qu'il ne nous a pas aidés ◆ **the government's** ~ **to comply with EU legal obligations** le non-respect des lois de l'UE de la part du gouvernement ◆ ~ **to appear** *(Jur)* défaut *m* de comparution *or* de comparaître ◆ ~ **to observe a bylaw** inobservation *f* d'un règlement (de police)

fain †† /feɪn/ **ADV** volontiers ◆ **I would** ~ **be dead** puissé-je périr

faint /feɪnt/ **ADJ** 1 *(= slight, not pronounced)* *[sound, smell, trace, breathing]* léger ; *[marking, writing]* à peine visible ; *[colour]* pâle ; *(= vague)* *[recollection, memory, idea]* vague ; *[suspicion]* léger ; *[hope]* faible, léger ; *(= weak)* *[voice, light, breathing, smile]* faible ; *[protest]* sans conviction ◆ **to grow** ~**er** s'affaiblir, diminuer ◆ **a** ~ **feeling of unease** un vague sentiment de gêne ◆ **she made a** ~ **attempt to make him laugh** elle a essayé vaguement de le faire rire ◆ **I haven't the** ~**est idea (about it)** je n'en ai pas la moindre idée ◆ **I never felt the** ~**est desire to cry** je n'ai jamais eu la moindre envie de pleurer ◆ ~ **heart never won fair lady** *(Prov)* qui n'ose rien n'a rien *(Prov)* → **damn**

2 *(= unwell)* *[person]* prêt à s'évanouir *or* à défaillir ◆ **to feel** ~ se sentir mal ◆ **to be/grow** ~ **with hunger** défaillir/commencer à défaillir de faim

N évanouissement *m*, défaillance *f* ◆ **to fall in a** ~ s'évanouir, avoir une défaillance

VI *(= lose consciousness)* s'évanouir ◆ **he** ~**ed from the shock/the pain** le choc/la douleur lui a fait perdre connaissance ◆ **to be** ~**ing** *(= feel weak)* *(from hunger etc)* défaillir *(from* de*)*

COMP **fainting fit, fainting spell** *(US)* **N** évanouissement *m*

faint-ruled paper N papier *m* réglé (en impression légère)

fainthearted /ˌfeɪntˈhɑːtɪd/ **ADJ** timoré ◆ **it's not for the** ~ *[venture, investment]* ça demande un certain courage ; *(= not for the oversensitive)* ce n'est pas pour les personnes sensibles

faintheartedly /ˌfeɪntˈhɑːtɪdlɪ/ **ADV** sans courage, avec pusillanimité

faintheartedness /ˌfeɪntˈhɑːtɪdnɪs/ **N** pusillanimité *f*

faintly /ˈfeɪntlɪ/ **ADV** 1 *(= slightly)* *[glow, smell of]* légèrement ; *[odd, strange, silly]* un peu ; *[ridiculous, absurd, familiar]* vaguement ; *[surprised, embarrassed, annoyed, uncomfortable]* légèrement ◆ ~ **amusing** vaguement amusant ◆ **in a** ~ **disappointed tone** d'un ton un peu déçu, avec une nuance de déception dans la voix ◆ **to be** ~ **reminiscent of sth** rappeler vaguement qch 2 *(= lightly)* *[breathe, write]* légèrement ; *(= weakly)* *[breathe, say, call]* faiblement ◆ **to smile** ~ esquisser un faible *or* un vague sourire ◆ **to sigh** ~ pousser un léger soupir

faintness /ˈfeɪntnɪs/ **N** 1 *[of sound, voice etc]* faiblesse *f* ; *[of breeze etc]* légèreté *f* 2 *(= dizziness)* vertiges *mpl*

fair¹ /feəʳ/ **ADJ** 1 *(= just)* *[person, decision]* juste, équitable ; *[price]* juste ; *[deal]* équitable, honnête ; *[competition, match, fight, player]* loyal, correct ; *[profit]* justifié, mérité ◆ **he is strict but** ~ il est sévère mais juste *or* équitable ◆ **be** ~**: it's not their fault** sois juste : ce n'est pas de leur faute ◆ **it's not** ~ ce n'est pas juste ◆ **as is (only)** ~ et ce n'est que justice, comme de juste ◆ **to be** ~ **(to him)** *or* **let's be** ~ **(to him), he thought he had paid for it** rendons-lui cette justice, il croyait l'avoir payé ◆ **it wouldn't be** ~ **to his brother** ce ne serait pas juste vis-à-vis de son frère ◆ **this isn't** ~ **on anyone/either of us** ce n'est juste pour personne/ni pour toi ni pour moi ◆ **it's** ~ **to say that ...** il est juste de dire que ... ◆ **it's (a)** ~ **comment** la remarque est juste ◆ **to get** *or* **have a** ~ **crack of the whip** avoir la chance de montrer de quoi on est capable ◆ **to give sb a** ~ **deal** agir équitablement envers qn, être fair-play *inv* avec qn ◆ ~ **enough!** d'accord !, très bien ! ◆ **all this is** ~ **enough, but ...** tout cela est très bien mais ..., d'accord mais ... ◆ **it's a** ~ **exchange** c'est équitable, c'est un échange honnête ◆ ~ **exchange is no robbery** *(Prov)* échange n'est pas vol ◆ **he was** ~ **game for the critics** c'était une proie rêvée *or* idéale pour les critiques ◆ ~**'s** ~**!** ce n'est que justice ! ◆ **all's** ~ **in love and war** en amour comme à la guerre, tous les coups sont permis ◆ **by** ~ **means or foul** par tous les moyens, par n'importe quel moyen ◆ **that's a** ~ **point** c'est juste ◆ **to give sb a** ~ **shake** *(US)* agir équitablement envers qn, être fair-play *inv* avec qn ◆ **he got his** ~ **share of the money** il a eu tout l'argent qui lui revenait (de droit) ◆ **he's had his** ~ **share of trouble*** il a eu sa part de soucis ◆ ~ **shares for all** (à) chacun son dû ◆ **it was all** ~ **and square** tout était très correct *or* régulier ◆ **he's** ~ **and square** il est honnête *or* franc ◆ **to get a** ~ **trial** bénéficier d'un procès équitable ◆ **to give sb** ~ **warning of sth** prévenir qn honnêtement de qch ◆ ~ **wear and tear** usure *f* normale

2 *(= considerable)* *[sum]* considérable ; *[number]* respectable ◆ **their garden's a** ~ **size** leur jardin est de taille respectable ◆ **there's a** ~ **amount of money left** il reste pas mal d'argent ◆ **he's travelled a** ~ **amount** il a pas mal voyagé ◆ **to have travelled a** ~ **distance** *or* **way** avoir fait un bon bout de chemin ◆ **to go at a** ~ **pace** aller bon train, aller à (une) bonne allure

3 *(= average)* *[work, achievements]* passable, assez bon ◆ **"fair"** *(Scol: as mark)* "passable" ◆ **it's**

~ **to middling** c'est passable, ce n'est pas mal ◆ **in ~ condition** en assez bon état

4 *(= reasonable) [guess, assessment]* juste ; *[idea]* précis ◆ **he has a ~ chance of success** il a des chances de réussir ◆ **he is in a ~ way to doing it** il y a de bonnes chances pour qu'il le fasse ◆ **~ sample** échantillon *m* représentatif

5 *(= light-coloured) [hair]* blond ; *[complexion, skin]* clair, de blond(e) ◆ **she's ~** elle est blonde, c'est une blonde

6 *(= fine) [weather]* beau (belle *f*) ; *[wind]* propice, favorable ◆ **it will be ~ and warm tomorrow** il fera beau et chaud demain ◆ **it's set ~** le temps est au beau fixe

7 *(† or liter = beautiful) [person, place]* beau (belle *f*) ◆ **~ words** belles phrases *fpl or* paroles *fpl* ◆ **the ~ lady of some brave knight of old** la belle dame de quelque brave chevalier du temps jadis ◆ **this ~ city of ours** cette belle ville qui est la nôtre ◆ **~ promises** belles promesses *fpl* ◆ **with one's own ~ hands** *(hum)* de ses blanches mains

8 *(= clean, neat)* propre, net ◆ **~ copy** *(rewritten)* copie *f* au propre *or* au net ; *(= model answer)* corrigé *m* ◆ **to make a ~ copy of sth** recopier qch au propre *or* au net

ADV 1 ◆ **to play ~** jouer franc jeu ◆ **to act ~ and square** se montrer juste ◆ **the branch struck him ~ and square in the face** la branche l'a frappé au beau milieu du visage *or* en plein (milieu du) visage ◆ **the car ran ~ and square into the tree** la voiture est entrée de plein fouet *or* en plein dans l'arbre

2 *(‡ or dial)* ⇒ **fairly 3**

3 †† *[speak]* courtoisement ◆ **~ spoken** qui parle avec courtoisie

COMP fair-haired ADJ blond, aux cheveux blonds ◆ **~-haired girl** blonde *f* ◆ **the ~-haired boy*** *(US fig)* le chouchou*, le chéri
fair-minded ADJ impartial, équitable
fair play N fair-play *m*
fair-sized ADJ assez grand, d'une bonne taille
fair-skinned ADJ à la peau claire
fair trade N commerce *m* équitable
fair-trade price N *(US)* prix *m* imposé
fair-weather friends NPL les amis *mpl* des beaux jours

fair² /fɛəʳ/ N *(gen)* foire *f* ; *(Comm)* foire *f* ; *(for charity)* fête *f*, kermesse *f* ; *(Brit:* also **funfair***)* fête *f* foraine ◆ **the Book Fair** *(Comm)* le Salon *or* la Foire du livre ; → **world**

fairground /ˈfɛəgraʊnd/ N champ *m* de foire

fairing /ˈfɛərɪŋ/ N *[of vehicle, plane]* carénage *m*

fairly /ˈfɛəlɪ/ ADV 1 *(= moderately)* assez ◆ **he plays ~ well** il joue assez bien ◆ **he's ~ good** il est assez bon, il n'est pas mauvais ◆ **they lead a ~ quiet life** ils mènent une vie plutôt tranquille ◆ **I'm ~ sure that ...** je suis presque sûr que ... ◆ **~ soon** d'ici peu de temps 2 *(= justly) [treat, compare, judge, share, distribute]* équitablement ; *[obtain]* honnêtement, loyalement ; *[call, describe]* honnêtement ; *[claim, argue]* à juste titre 3 *(† = positively)* carrément ◆ **he was ~ beside himself with rage** il était carrément hors de lui ◆ **he ~ flew across the room** il a traversé la pièce en trombe 4 ◆ **~ and squarely** ⇒ **fair and square** ; → **fair¹**

fairness /ˈfɛənɪs/ N 1 *(= lightness) [of hair]* couleur *f* blonde, blondeur *f* ; *[of skin]* blancheur *f*

2 *(= honesty, justice)* équité *f* ; *[of decision, judgment]* équité *f*, impartialité *f* ◆ **in** *or* **out of all ~** en toute justice ◆ **in ~ to him** pour être juste envers lui

COMP Fairness Doctrine N *(US)* principe *m* de l'impartialité

> **FAIRNESS DOCTRINE**
>
> Aux États-Unis, le principe de l'impartialité ou **Fairness Doctrine** impose aux stations de radio et aux chaînes de télévision de faire entendre différents points de vue sur les grandes questions de société et de respecter un certain équilibre dans le temps d'antenne accordé aux principaux candidats lors des élections locales et nationales. Il ne s'agit pas d'une loi, mais d'un principe déontologique qui bénéficie du soutien du Congrès.

fairway /ˈfɛəweɪ/ N *(Naut)* chenal *m*, passe *f* ; *(Golf)* fairway *m*

fairy /ˈfɛərɪ/ N 1 fée *f* ◆ **the wicked ~** la fée Carabosse ◆ **she's his good ~** elle est sa bonne fée ◆ **he's away with the fairies*** *(hum)* il a une araignée au plafond*

2 *(‡ pej = homosexual)* pédé‡ *m*, tapette‡ *f*

ADJ *[gift]* magique ◆ **a ~ helper** une bonne fée

COMP fairy cycle N bicyclette *f* d'enfant
fairy footsteps NPL *(iro)* pas *mpl* (légers) de danseuse *(iro)*
fairy godmother N *(lit)* bonne fée *f* ; *(fig)* marraine *f* gâteau* *inv*
fairy lights NPL guirlande *f* électrique
fairy-like ADJ féerique, de fée
fairy queen N reine *f* des fées
fairy story, fairy tale N conte *m* de fées ; *(= untruth)* histoire *f* à dormir debout*
fairy-tale ADJ *[character, place] (lit)* de conte de fées ; *(fig)* enchanteur (-teresse *f*) ◆ **the hotel is set in ~-tale surroundings** l'hôtel est situé dans un cadre enchanteur ◆ **a ~-tale ending** un dénouement romanesque

fairyland /ˈfɛərɪlænd/ N royaume *m* des fées ; *(fig)* féerie *f*

faith /feɪθ/ N 1 *(NonC) (= trust, belief)* foi *f*, confiance *f* ◆ **Faith, Hope and Charity** la foi, l'espérance et la charité ◆ **~ in God** foi *f* en Dieu ◆ **to have ~ in sb** avoir confiance en qn ◆ **to have ~ in sb's ability/judgement** se fier aux compétences/au jugement de qn ◆ **I've lost ~ in him** je ne lui fais plus confiance ◆ **to put one's ~ in, to pin one's ~ on*** mettre tous ses espoirs en

2 *(= religion)* religion *f* ◆ **the Christian ~** la religion *or* la foi chrétienne ◆ **people of different ~s** des gens de confessions différentes

3 *(NonC)* ◆ **to keep ~ with sb** tenir ses promesses envers qn ◆ **to break ~ with sb** manquer à sa parole envers qn

4 *(NonC)* ◆ **good ~** bonne foi *f* ◆ **to do sth in all good ~** faire qch en toute bonne foi ◆ **bad ~** mauvaise foi *f* ◆ **to act in bad ~** agir de mauvaise foi

COMP faith healer N guérisseur *m*, -euse *f*
faith healing N guérison *f* par la foi

faithful /ˈfeɪθfʊl/ **ADJ** *[person, translation, copy, account]* fidèle (to à) ◆ **to be ~ to sb's wishes** respecter les désirs de qn ◆ **26 years' ~ service** 26 années de bons et loyaux services ◆ **my ~ old car** ma bonne vieille voiture **NPL the faithful** *(Rel) (= Christians)* les fidèles *mpl* ; *(= Muslims)* les croyants *mpl* ◆ **the (party) ~** *(Pol)* les fidèles *mpl* du parti

faithfully /ˈfeɪθfəlɪ/ ADV *[report, translate, reproduce]* fidèlement ; *[serve]* loyalement ◆ **to promise ~** donner sa parole ◆ **Yours ~** *(esp Brit: in letter writing)* Veuillez agréer, Messieurs, mes salutations distinguées, Je vous prie d'agréer, Messieurs, l'expression de mes sentiments distingués

faithfulness /ˈfeɪθfʊlnɪs/ N *[of person]* fidélité *f* (to à) loyauté *f* (to envers) ; *[of account, translation]* fidélité *f*, exactitude *f* ; *[of copy]* conformité *f*

faithless /ˈfeɪθlɪs/ ADJ déloyal, perfide

faithlessness /ˈfeɪθlɪsnɪs/ N *(NonC)* déloyauté *f*, perfidie *f*

fake /feɪk/ N 1 faux *m* ◆ **the passport/document/certificate was a ~** le passeport/le document/le certificat était (un) faux ◆ **the diamond was a ~** c'était un faux diamant ◆ **the pistol was a ~** le pistolet était faux, c'était un faux pistolet ◆ **the bomb was a ~** c'était une fausse bombe ◆ **he's a ~** c'est un imposteur

2 *(US Sport)* feinte *f*

ADJ *[document, passport, painting, beam, banknote, jewel, fur]* faux (fausse *f*) ; *[blood]* factice ; *[elections, trial, photograph, interview]* truqué ◆ **a ~ suntan** un bronzage artificiel ◆ **a ~ Mackintosh chair** une fausse chaise Mackintosh

VT 1 *[+ document] (= counterfeit)* faire un faux de ; *(= alter)* maquiller, falsifier ; *(Art) [+ picture]* faire un faux de, contrefaire ; *[+ beam, furniture, signature]* imiter ; *[+ photograph, sound tape, trial]* truquer ; *[+ accounts]* falsifier ; *(Rad, TV) [+ interview]* truquer, monter d'avance ◆ **to ~ illness/death** faire semblant d'être malade/mort ◆ **to ~ orgasm** simuler l'orgasme ◆ **to ~ a pass** *(US Sport)* feinter

2 *(US = ad-lib) [+ tune]* improviser

VI faire semblant ; *(US Sport)* feinter

fakir /ˈfɑːkɪəʳ/ N fakir *m*

falcon /ˈfɔːlkən/ N faucon *m*

falconer /ˈfɔːlkənəʳ/ N fauconnier *m*

falconry /ˈfɔːlkənrɪ/ N fauconnerie *f*

Falkland /ˈfɔːlklənd/ **NPL the Falklands** ⇒ **the Falkland Islands**

COMP Falkland Islander N habitant(e) *m(f)* des (îles) Malouines *or* Falkland
the Falkland Islands NPL les îles *fpl* Malouines *or* Falkland

fall /fɔːl/ (vb : pret **fell**, ptp **fallen**) N 1 *(lit, fig = tumble)* chute *f* ◆ **to have a ~** tomber, faire une chute ◆ **to be heading** *or* **riding for a ~** courir à l'échec, aller au-devant de la défaite ; → **free**

2 *(= lowering: in price, demand, temperature)* baisse *f* (in de) ; *(more drastic)* chute *f* (in de) ; *(Fin)* dépréciation *f*, baisse *f*

3 *(= shower of objects etc) [of rocks, snow]* chute *f* ◆ **~ of earth** éboulement *m*, éboulis *m*

4 *(Mil) (= defeat)* chute *f*, prise *f* ◆ **the ~ of Saigon** la chute *or* la prise de Saïgon ◆ **the ~ of the Bastille** la prise de la Bastille

5 *(Rel)* ◆ **the Fall (of Man)** la chute (de l'homme)

6 *(= slope) [of ground, roof]* pente *f*, inclinaison *f*

7 *(US = autumn)* automne *m* ◆ **in the ~** en automne

NPL falls *(= waterfall)* chute *f* d'eau, cascade *f* ◆ **the Niagara Falls** les chutes du Niagara

VI

> For set expressions such as **fall ill/pregnant/lame, fall short**, etc, look up the other word

1 *(= tumble) [person, object]* tomber ◆ **he fell into the river** *[person]* il est tombé dans la rivière ◆ **to ~ out of a tree/off a bike** tomber d'un arbre/de vélo ◆ **to ~ over a chair** tomber en butant contre une chaise ◆ **he let the cup ~** il a laissé tomber la tasse ◆ **to ~ on one's feet** *(lit, fig)* retomber sur ses pieds ◆ **to ~ on one's ass**** *(US: lit, fig)* se casser la gueule‡ ; → **wayside**

2 *(= collapse) [building]* s'écrouler, s'effondrer ◆ **he fell into bed exhausted** il s'est effondré sur son lit, épuisé

3 *(= find o.s.)* ◆ **he fell among thieves** il est tombé aux mains de voleurs

4 *(= rain down) [rain, leaves, bombs]* tomber

5 *(= drop) [temperature, price, level]* baisser, tomber ; *[wind]* tomber ; *[voice]* baisser ◆ **his face fell** son visage s'est assombri *or* s'est allongé ◆ **to let ~ a hint that ...** laisser entendre que ..., donner à entendre que ...

6 (= *hang*) ♦ **her hair fell to her shoulders** les cheveux lui tombaient sur les épaules ♦ **the curtains ~ to the floor** les rideaux vont jusqu'au sol ♦ **the dress ~s beautifully** la robe tombe très bien

7 (= *descend*) [*night, darkness*] tomber

8 (also **fall away**) [*ground*] descendre en pente ♦ **the ground fell steeply to the valley floor** le terrain descendait en pente raide vers le fond de la vallée

9 (= *be defeated*) [*country, city, fortress*] tomber ; [*government*] tomber, être renversé

10 (*Rel* = *sin*) tomber, pécher ; → **grace**

11 (*Mil* = *die*) [*soldier etc*] tomber (au champ d'honneur)

12 (= *throw o.s.*) ♦ **they fell into each other's arms** ils sont tombés dans les bras l'un de l'autre ♦ **to ~ to** *or* **on one's knees** tomber à genoux ♦ **he was ~ing over himself to be polite*** il faisait de gros efforts pour être poli ♦ **they were ~ing over each other to get it*** ils se battaient pour l'avoir ; → **neck**

13 (= *occur*) tomber ♦ **Christmas Day ~s on a Sunday** Noël tombe un dimanche ♦ **the accent ~s on the second syllable** l'accent tombe sur la deuxième syllabe ♦ **the students ~ into three categories** les étudiants se divisent en trois catégories

COMP **fall-back position** N solution *f* de secours *or* de réserve

fall guy‡ N (= *scapegoat*) bouc *m* émissaire ; (= *easy victim*) pigeon* *m*, dindon *m* de la farce

fall line N (*Geog*) ligne *f* de séparation entre un plateau et une plaine côtière ; (*Ski*) ligne *f* de plus grande pente

fall-off N ⇒ **falling-off** ; → **falling**

► **fall about*** VI (*Brit fig:* also **fall about laughing**) se tordre de rire

► **fall apart** VI [*house, furniture*] s'effondrer ; [*scheme, plan, deal*] tomber à l'eau ; [*person, one's life*] s'effondrer ; (*in exam etc*) perdre tous ses moyens ♦ **their marriage is ~ing apart** leur couple est en train de se briser

► **fall away** VI [*ground*] descendre en pente ; [*plaster*] s'écailler ; [*numbers, attendances*] diminuer ; [*anxiety, fears*] se dissiper, s'évanouir ♦ **his supporters are ~ing away** ses partisans sont en train de le déserter *or* de l'abandonner

► **fall back** VI (= *retreat, also Mil*) reculer, se retirer ♦ **to ~ back on sth** (*fig*) avoir recours à qch ♦ **some money to ~ back on** un peu d'argent en réserve ♦ **gold shares fell back a point** les mines d'or ont reculé *or* se sont repliées d'un point

► **fall behind** VI rester en arrière, être à la traîne ; [*racehorse, runner*] se laisser distancer ; (*in cycle race*) décrocher ♦ **to ~ behind with one's work** prendre du retard dans son travail ♦ **she fell behind with the rent** elle était en retard pour son loyer

VT FUS ♦ **to fall behind sb** (*in work etc*) prendre du retard sur qn

► **fall down** VI 1 [*person, book*] tomber (par terre) ; [*building*] s'effondrer, s'écrouler ; [*tree*] tomber

2 (= *fail*) [*person*] échouer ; [*plans*] tomber à l'eau ; [*hopes*] s'évanouir ♦ **to ~ down on the job** se montrer incapable de faire le travail, ne pas être à la hauteur ♦ **he fell down badly that time** il s'est vraiment pris les pieds dans le tapis cette fois ♦ **that was where we fell down** c'est là que nous avons achoppé ♦ **she fell down on the last essay** elle a raté la dernière dissertation

► **fall for** VT FUS 1 (= *become very keen on*) ♦ **to fall for sb*** tomber amoureux de qn ♦ **to ~ for an idea*** *etc* s'enthousiasmer pour une idée *etc*

2 (*pej*) (= *be taken in by*) ♦ **to fall for a suggestion** se laisser prendre à une suggestion ♦ **he really fell for it!*** il s'est vraiment laissé prendre !, il s'est vraiment fait avoir !*

► **fall in** VI 1 [*building*] s'effondrer, s'écrouler ♦ **she leaned over the pool and fell in** elle s'est penchée au-dessus de la piscine et elle est tombée dedans

2 (*Mil*) [*troops*] former les rangs ; [*one soldier*] rentrer dans les rangs ♦ **~ in!** à vos rangs !

VT SEP [+ *troops*] (faire) mettre en rangs

► **fall into** VT FUS [+ *trap, ambush*] tomber dans ; [+ *disfavour, disgrace, disuse*] tomber en ; [+ *despair, anarchy*] sombrer dans ; [+ *recession*] s'enfoncer dans ♦ **to ~ into a deep sleep** tomber dans un profond sommeil ♦ **to ~ into conversation with sb** entamer une conversation avec qn, se mettre à parler avec qn ♦ **to ~ into debt** s'endetter ♦ **to ~ into bad habits** prendre *or* contracter de mauvaises habitudes ♦ **to ~ into temptation** (= *be tempted*) être tenté ; (= *give in to temptation*) succomber à la tentation ♦ **she fell into a deep depression** elle a sombré dans la dépression, elle a fait une grave dépression ♦ **to ~ into decline** connaître le déclin ♦ **the city fell into decline at the end of the 16th century** le déclin de la ville remonte à la fin du 16e siècle ♦ **to ~ into ruin** tomber en ruine ♦ **the mansion fell into decay** *or* **ruin 20 years ago** le manoir a commencé à se délabrer *or* à tomber en ruine il y a 20 ans ♦ **ancient civilizations that fell into decay** les civilisations anciennes qui ont connu le déclin ; → **line**[1]

► **fall in with** VT FUS 1 (= *meet*) [+ *person*] rencontrer ; [+ *group*] se mettre à fréquenter ♦ **he fell in with a bad crowd** il s'est mis à avoir de mauvaises fréquentations

2 (= *agree to*) [+ *proposal, suggestion*] accepter ♦ **to ~ in with sb's views** se ranger au point de vue de qn

3 (= *fit in*) ♦ **this decision fell in very well with our plans** cette décision a cadré avec nos projets

► **fall off** VI 1 (*lit*) tomber ; (*Climbing*) dévisser

2 [*supporters*] déserter ; [*sales, numbers, attendances*] diminuer ; [*curve on graph*] décroître ; [*interest*] se relâcher, tomber ; [*enthusiasm*] baisser, tomber

N ♦ **fall-off** ⇒ **falling-off** ; → **falling**

► **fall on** VT FUS 1 (= *alight on, encounter*) ♦ **her eyes fell on a strange object** son regard est tombé sur un objet étrange ♦ **strange sounds fell on our ears** des bruits étranges parvinrent à nos oreilles ♦ **to ~ on bad** *or* **hard times** tomber dans la misère, avoir des revers de fortune

2 ⇒ **fall upon**

► **fall out** VI 1 (= *quarrel*) se brouiller, se fâcher (*with* avec)

2 (*Mil*) rompre les rangs ♦ **~ out!** rompez !

3 (= *come to pass*) advenir, arriver ♦ **everything fell out as we had hoped** tout s'est passé comme nous l'avions espéré

VT SEP [+ *troops*] faire rompre les rangs à

► **fall over** VI tomber (par terre)

► **fall through** VI ♦ **all their plans have fallen through** tous leurs projets ont échoué *or* sont tombés à l'eau

► **fall to** VI 1 (= *begin*) ♦ **he fell to wondering if ...** il s'est mis à se demander si ...

2 (= *start eating*) se mettre à l'œuvre, attaquer (un repas)

VT FUS (= *be one's duty*) ♦ **it falls to me to say** il m'appartient de dire, c'est à moi de dire

► **fall under** VT FUS (= *be subject to*) ♦ **to fall under suspicion** devenir suspect

► **fall upon** VT FUS 1 (= *attack*) se jeter sur, se lancer sur ♦ **to ~ upon the enemy** (*Mil*) fondre *or* s'abattre sur l'ennemi ♦ **the wrath of God fell upon them** (*liter*) la colère de Dieu s'abattit sur eux

2 (= *be incumbent on*) ♦ **the responsibility falls upon you** la responsabilité retombe sur vous

3 (= *find*) trouver, découvrir ♦ **to ~ upon a way of doing sth** trouver *or* découvrir un moyen de faire qch

fallacious /fə'leɪʃəs/ ADJ fallacieux

fallaciousness /fə'leɪʃəsnɪs/ N caractère *m* fallacieux

fallacy /'fæləsɪ/ N (= *false belief*) erreur *f*, illusion *f* ; (= *false reasoning*) faux raisonnement *m*, sophisme *m*

fallback /'fɔːlbæk/ N recul *m*, repli *m* ♦ **as a ~ they will start building their own dealer network** ils vont mettre sur pied un réseau de distribution pour avoir une position de repli

fallen /'fɔːlən/ VB ptp of **fall** ADJ 1 [*object*] tombé ♦ **~ leaf** feuille *f* morte 2 (*morally*) perdu ; [*angel*] déchu ♦ **~ idol** idole *f* déchue NPL **the fallen** (*Mil*) ceux *mpl* qui sont morts à la guerre, ceux *mpl* qui sont tombés au champ d'honneur COMP **fallen arches** NPL (*Med*) affaissement *m* de la voûte plantaire

fallibility /ˌfælɪ'bɪlɪtɪ/ N faillibilité *f*

fallible /'fæləbl/ ADJ faillible ♦ **everyone is ~** tout le monde peut se tromper

falling /'fɔːlɪŋ/ VB prp of **fall** ADJ [*prices, profits, standards, inflation*] en baisse ; [*water, snow, leaf*] qui tombe ♦ **"beware (of) falling rocks"** "attention : chutes de pierres"

COMP **falling evil** †† N ⇒ **falling sickness**

falling market N (*Stock Exchange*) marché *m* à la baisse N

falling-off N réduction *f*, diminution *f*, décroissance *f* (*in* de)

falling-out* N ♦ **to have a ~-out (with sb)** se brouiller (avec qn)

falling sickness †† N (= *epilepsy*) haut mal †† *m*, mal caduc †† *m*

falling star N étoile *f* filante

Fallopian /fə'ləʊpɪən/ ADJ ♦ **~ tube** trompe *f* utérine *or* de Fallope

fallout /'fɔːlaʊt/ N (*NonC*) retombées *fpl* (radioactives) ; (*fig*) retombées *fpl*, répercussions *fpl* COMP **fallout shelter** N abri *m* antiatomique

fallow /'fæləʊ/ N (*Agr*) jachère *f* ADJ 1 (*Agr*) [*land*] en jachère ♦ **the land lay ~** la terre était en jachère 2 (= *inactive*) ♦ **a ~ period** *or* **time** un passage à vide COMP **fallow deer** N daim *m*

false /fɔːls/ ADJ 1 (= *artificial, fake*) [*beard, eyelashes, passport, banknote*] faux (fausse *f*) ♦ **a box with a ~ bottom** une boîte à double fond ♦ **~ ceiling** faux plafond *m* ♦ **~ hem** faux ourlet *m*

2 (= *wrong*) [*information, accusation, impression, hope, rumour*] faux (fausse *f*) ; (= *untrue*) [*promise*] faux (fausse *f*), mensonger ♦ **to give ~ evidence** fournir un faux témoignage ♦ **to make a ~ confession** faire de faux aveux ♦ **he was forced into a ~ confession** on lui a extorqué des aveux ♦ **he gave the police a ~ name** il a donné un faux nom à la police ♦ **he had assumed a ~ identity** il vivait sous une fausse identité ♦ **to bear ~ witness** †† porter un faux témoignage ♦ **under ~ pretences** (*gen*) sous des prétextes fallacieux ; (*Jur*) par des moyens frauduleux ♦ **to put a ~ interpretation on sth** mal interpréter qch ♦ **~ expectations** faux espoirs *mpl* ♦ **a ~ sense of security** une illusion de sécurité ♦ **~ move** *or* **step** faux pas *m* ♦ **to make a ~ move, to take a ~ step** faire un faux pas

3 (*Jur* = *wrongful*) ♦ **~ arrest/imprisonment** arrêt *m*/détention *f* arbitraire

4 (= *insincere*) [*person*] faux (fausse *f*) ♦ **~ laughter** rire *m* forcé ♦ **~ modesty** fausse modestie *f* ♦ **to ring ~** sonner faux ♦ **in a ~ position** en porte-à-faux

5 (= *unfaithful*) ♦ **to be ~ to one's wife** † tromper sa femme

ADV (*liter*) ♦ **to play sb ~** trahir qn

COMP **false alarm** N *(lit, fig)* fausse alerte *f*
false beginner N faux *or* grand débutant *m*
false dawn N lueurs *fpl* annonciatrices de l'aube ; *(fig)* lueur *f* d'espoir trompeuse
false economy N fausse économie *f*
false friend N *(also Ling)* faux ami *m*
false-hearted ADJ fourbe
False Memory Syndrome N syndrome *m* du faux souvenir
false negative *(Med)* N résultat *m* faussement négatif, faux négatif *m* ADJ *[result]* faussement négatif
false positive *(Med)* N résultat *m* faussement positif, faux positif *m* ADJ *[result]* faussement positif
false ribs NPL fausses côtes *fpl*
false start N *(Sport, also fig)* faux départ *m*
false teeth NPL fausses dents *fpl*, dentier *m*

falsehood /'fɔ:lshʊd/ N [1] *(= lie)* mensonge *m* ◆ **to tell a** ~ mentir, dire un mensonge [2] *(NonC)* faux *m* ◆ **truth and** ~ le vrai et le faux [3] *(NonC)* ⇒ **falseness**

falsely /'fɔ:lslɪ/ ADV *[claim, declare, report]* faussement ; *[accuse]* à tort, faussement ; *[convict, imprison, believe]* à tort ◆ ~ **cheerful** d'une gaieté feinte

falseness /'fɔ:lsnɪs/ N fausseté *f* ; († *or liter*) *[of lover]* infidélité *f*

falsetto /fɔ:l'setəʊ/ N *(Mus)* fausset *m* ADJ *[voice, tone]* de fausset, de tête

falsies * /'fɔ:lsɪz/ NPL faux seins *mpl*

falsification /,fɔ:lsɪfɪ'keɪʃən/ N falsification *f*

falsify /'fɔ:lsɪfaɪ/ VT [1] *(= forge) [+ document]* falsifier ; *[+ evidence]* maquiller ; *(= misrepresent) [+ story, facts]* dénaturer ; *[+ accounts, figures, statistics]* truquer [2] *(= disprove) [+ theory]* réfuter

falsity /'fɔ:lsɪtɪ/ N ⇒ **falseness**

falter /'fɔ:ltə^r/ VI *[voice, speaker]* hésiter, s'entrecouper ; *(= waver)* vaciller, chanceler ; *[courage, memory]* faiblir ◆ **her steps ~ed** elle chancela VT (also **falter out**) *[+ words, phrases]* bredouiller

faltering /'fɔ:ltərɪŋ/ ADJ *[voice]* hésitant, entrecoupé ; *[steps]* chancelant

falteringly /'fɔ:ltərɪŋlɪ/ ADV *[speak]* d'une voix hésitante *or* entrecoupée ; *[walk]* d'un pas chancelant *or* mal assuré

fame /feɪm/ N *(gen)* gloire *f*, renommée *f* ; *(= celebrity)* célébrité *f* ◆ **he wanted** ~ il voulait devenir célèbre ◆ **to win** ~ **for o.s.** se rendre célèbre ◆ **this book brought him** ~ ce livre l'a rendu célèbre ◆ ~ **and fortune** la gloire et la fortune ◆ **Margaret Mitchell of "Gone with the Wind"** ~ Margaret Mitchell, le célèbre auteur de "Autant en emporte le vent" ◆ **Bader of 1940** ~ Bader, devenu célèbre en 1940 ; → **ill**

famed /feɪmd/ ADJ célèbre, renommé *(for* pour)

familial /fə'mɪlɪəl/ ADJ *(frm)* familial

familiar /fə'mɪljə^r/ ADJ [1] *(= usual, well-known) [sight, scene, street]* familier ; *[complaint, event, protest]* habituel ◆ **the problems are all too** ~ ces problèmes sont, hélas, bien connus ◆ **his face is** ~ je l'ai déjà vu quelque part, son visage me dit quelque chose * ◆ **his voice seems** ~ **(to me)** il me semble connaître sa voix ◆ **he's a** ~ **figure in the town** c'est un personnage bien connu *or* tout le monde le connaît de vue dans la ville ◆ **it's a** ~ **feeling** c'est une sensation bien connue ; see also **face**
[2] *(= conversant)* ◆ **to be** ~ **with sth** bien connaître qch, être au fait de qch ◆ **to make o.s.** ~ **with** se familiariser avec ◆ **he is** ~ **with our customs** il connaît bien nos coutumes
[3] *(= intimate)* familier, intime ◆ ~ **language** langue *f* familière ◆ **to be on** ~ **terms with sb** bien connaître qn ◆ ~ **spirit** démon *m* familier ◆ **he got much too** ~ *(pej)* il s'est permis des familiarités *(with* avec)

N [1] *(= familiar spirit)* démon *m* familier
[2] *(= friend)* familier *m*

familiarity /fə,mɪlɪ'ærɪtɪ/ N [1] *(NonC) [of sight, event etc]* caractère *m* familier *or* habituel [2] *(NonC: with book, poem, customs etc)* familiarité *f (with* avec) (parfaite) connaissance *f (with* de) ◆ ~ **breeds contempt** *(Prov)* la familiarité engendre le mépris [3] *(= intimacy)* familiarité *f* ◆ **the** ~ **with which she greeted the head waiter** la familiarité avec laquelle elle a salué le maître d'hôtel ; *(pej) (gen pl)* ◆ **familiarities** familiarités *fpl*, privautés *fpl*

familiarize /fə'mɪlɪəraɪz/ VT ◆ **to** ~ **sb with sth** familiariser qn avec qch, habituer qn à qch ◆ **to** ~ **o.s. with** se familiariser avec

familiarly /fə'mɪljəlɪ/ ADV *[say, greet]* avec familiarité ◆ **the "Jade Palace",** ~ **known as "Jo's Place"** le "Jade Palace", "Jo's Place" pour les intimes

family /'fæmɪlɪ/ N *(all senses)* famille *f* ◆ **has he any** ~**?** *(= relatives)* a-t-il de la famille ? ; *(= children)* a-t-il des enfants ? ◆ **he comes from a** ~ **of six children** il vient d'une famille de six enfants ◆ **it runs in the** ~ cela tient de famille ◆ **my** ~ **are all tall** dans ma famille tout le monde est grand ◆ **they'd like to start a** ~ ils aimeraient avoir des enfants ◆ **of good** ~ de bonne famille ◆ **he's one of the** ~ il fait partie *or* il est de la famille

COMP *[dinner, jewels, likeness, name]* de famille ; *[Bible, life]* familial, de famille
family allowance N *(Brit Admin: formerly)* allocations *fpl* familiales
family business N entreprise *f* familiale, affaire *f* de famille
family butcher N boucher *m* de quartier
family circle N *(= family members)* cercle *m* familial ; *(US Theat)* deuxième balcon *m*
family court N *(US Jur)* ≃ tribunal *m* de grande instance *(s'occupant des affaires familiales)*
family credit N *(Brit Admin)* ≃ complément *m* familial
Family Crisis Intervention Unit N *(US Police)* ≃ police-secours *f (intervenant en cas de drames familiaux)*
the Family Division N *(Brit Jur)* tribunal *m* des affaires familiales
family doctor N médecin *m* de famille, généraliste *m*
family friend N ami(e) *m(f)* de la famille
family grouping N *(Scol) regroupement de classes de primaire de sections différentes*
Family Health Services Authority N *(Brit) autorité supervisant les professions de santé*
family hotel N pension *f* de famille
family income supplement N *(Brit Admin: formerly)* ≃ complément *m* familial
family man N (pl **family men**) ◆ **he's a** ~ **man** il aime la vie de famille
family-minded ADJ ◆ **to be ~-minded** avoir le sens de la famille
family name N nom *m* de famille
family planning N planning *m* familial
family planning clinic N centre *m* de planning familial
family practice N *(US Med)* médecine *f* générale
family practitioner N *(US Med)* médecin *m* de famille, (médecin) généraliste *m*
family room N *(esp US: in house)* salle *f* de séjour *(réservée à la famille plutôt qu'aux invités)* ; *(Brit: in pub) salle autorisée aux enfants* ; *(in hotel)* chambre *f* familiale
family-size(d) packet N *(Comm)* paquet *m* familial
family therapy N thérapie *f* familiale
family tree N arbre *m* généalogique
family unit N *(Sociol)* cellule *f* familiale
family values NPL valeurs *fpl* familiales
family viewing N *(TV)* ◆ **it's (suitable for)** ~ **viewing** c'est un spectacle familial *or* pour toute la famille
family way † * N ◆ **she's in the** ~ **way** elle est enceinte, elle attend un enfant

famine /'fæmɪn/ N famine *f*

famished /'fæmɪʃt/ ADJ affamé ◆ **I'm absolutely** ~ * je meurs de faim, j'ai une faim de loup ◆ ~ **looking** d'aspect famélique

famous /'feɪməs/ ADJ [1] *(= well-known)* célèbre *(for* pour) ◆ ~ **last words!** * *(iro)* on verra bien !, c'est ce que tu crois ! ◆ **so when's this** ~ **party going to be?** *(iro)* alors, cette fameuse soirée, quand est-ce qu'elle va avoir lieu ? [2] († * *= excellent)* fameux, formidable *

famously /'feɪməslɪ/ ADV [1] ◆ **a** ~ **rich/arrogant film star** une vedette de cinéma connue pour sa richesse/son arrogance ◆ **Quentin Tarantino, who once** ~ **said ...** Quentin Tarantino, dont tout le monde connaît la fameuse boutade ... ◆ **Marlon Brando** ~ **refused an Oscar in 1972** Marlon Brando, comme chacun le sait, a refusé un oscar en 1972 ◆ **there have been hurricanes in England, most** ~ **in 1987** il y a eu des ouragans en Angleterre, dont le plus connu en 1987 [2] († * *= well)* ◆ **to get on** *or* **along** ~ s'entendre comme larrons en foire * ◆ **to get on** *or* **along** ~ **with sb** s'entendre à merveille avec qn ◆ **to go** ~ marcher rudement * bien

fan¹ /fæn/ N éventail *m* ; *(mechanical)* ventilateur *m* ; *(Agr)* tarare *m* ◆ **electric** ~ ventilateur *m* électrique VT [1] *[+ person, object]* éventer ◆ **to** ~ **the fire** attiser le feu ◆ **to** ~ **the embers** souffler sur la braise ◆ **to** ~ **o.s.** s'éventer [2] *[+ violence, hatred]* attiser ; *[+ fears]* aviver, attiser [3] *(US* ⁑ *= smack)* corriger, flanquer * une fessée à
COMP **fan-assisted oven** N four *m* à chaleur tournante
fan belt N courroie *f* de ventilateur
fan heater N *(Brit)* radiateur *m* soufflant
fan light N imposte *f (semi-circulaire)*
fan oven N four *m* à chaleur pulsée
fan-shaped ADJ en éventail
fan vaulting N *(Archit)* voûte(s) *f(pl)* en éventail
► **fan out** VI *[troops, searchers]* se déployer (en éventail) VT SEP *[+ cards etc]* étaler (en éventail)

fan² /fæn/ N *[of person] (gen)* admirateur *m*, -trice *f* ; *[of personality, pop star, music style]* fan *mf* ; *[of sports team]* supporter *m* ; *[of work of art]* amateur *m* ◆ **I'm definitely not one of his ~s** je suis loin d'être un de ses admirateurs ◆ **he is a jazz/bridge/sports/rugby** *etc* ~ c'est un mordu * *or* un fana * de jazz/bridge/sport/rugby *etc* ◆ **football** ~ amateur *m or* fan *m* de football ◆ **movie** ~ cinéphile *mf*, passionné(e) *m(f)* de cinéma ◆ **a Vivaldi** ~ un grand amateur de Vivaldi
COMP **fan club** N *(Cine etc)* cercle *m or* club *m* de fans ; *(fig)* cercle *m* d'adorateurs *or* de fervents (admirateurs) ◆ **the Colin Smith** ~ **club** le club des fans de Colin Smith
fan letters NPL ⇒ **fan mail**
fan mail N courrier *m* des fans ◆ **she receives lots of** ~ **mail** elle reçoit beaucoup de lettres d'admirateurs
fan site N ⇒ **fansite**

fanatic /fə'nætɪk/ N fanatique *mf* ◆ **a religious** ~ un fanatique religieux ◆ **(s)he's a football** ~ c'est un(e) fana * de football

fanatical /fə'nætɪkl/ ADJ fanatique ◆ **to be** ~ **about sth** être un(e) fanatique de qch

fanatically /fə'nætɪklɪ/ ADV fanatiquement

fanaticism /fə'nætɪsɪzəm/ N fanatisme *m*

fanciable * /'fænsɪəbl/ ADJ *(Brit)* pas mal du tout *

fancied /'fænsɪd/ ADJ imaginaire ; see also **fancy**

fancier /ˈfænsɪəʳ/ **N** ◆ **dog ~** *(= connoisseur)* connaisseur *m*, -euse *f* en chiens ; *(= breeder)* éleveur *m*, -euse *f* de chiens

fanciful /ˈfænsɪfʊl/ **ADJ** *(= whimsical) [person]* capricieux, fantasque ; *[ideas]* fantasque ; *(= imaginative) [design, drawing]* plein d'imagination, imaginatif ; *[story, account]* fantaisiste

fancy /ˈfænsɪ/ **N** 1 *(= whim)* caprice *m*, fantaisie *f* ◆ **a passing ~** une lubie ◆ **as the ~ takes her** comme l'idée la prend ◆ **he only works when the ~ takes him** il ne travaille que quand cela lui plaît *or* lui chante *

2 *(= taste, liking)* goût *m*, envie *f* ◆ **to take a ~ to sb** *(gen)* se prendre d'affection pour qn ; *(= have a crush on)* avoir le béguin * *or* une tocade * pour qn ◆ **to take a ~ to sth** se mettre à aimer qch, prendre goût à qch ◆ **it took** *or* **caught** *or* **tickled his ~** *[story etc]* cela a frappé son imagination ◆ **the hat took** *or* **caught my ~** ce chapeau m'a fait envie *or* m'a tapé dans l'œil * ◆ **the story caught the public's ~** cette histoire a frappé les esprits

3 *(NonC = fantasy)* imagination *f*, fantaisie *f* ◆ **that is in the realm of ~** cela appartient au domaine de l'imaginaire, c'est chimérique

4 *(= delusion)* chimère *f*, fantasme *m* ; *(= whimsical notion)* idée *f* fantasque ◆ **I have a ~ that ...** j'ai idée que ...

5 *(Culin)* gâteau *m* à la crème *(fait de génoise fourrée)*

VT 1 *(esp Brit) (= want)* avoir envie de ; *(= like)* aimer ◆ **do you ~ going for a walk?** as-tu envie *or* ça te dit * d'aller faire une promenade ? ◆ **do you ~ a drink?** ça vous dirait de prendre un verre ? ◆ **I don't ~ the idea** cette idée ne me dit rien ◆ **he fancies himself** * *(Brit)* il ne se prend pas pour rien *(iro)* ◆ **he fancies himself as an actor** * il se prend pour un acteur ◆ **he fancies her** * *(Brit)* il s'est entiché * d'elle ◆ **Omar is strongly fancied for the next race** *(Racing)* Omar est très coté *or* a la cote pour la prochaine course

2 *(= imagine)* se figurer, s'imaginer ; *(= rather think)* croire, penser ◆ **he fancies he can succeed** il se figure pouvoir réussir, il s'imagine qu'il peut réussir ◆ **I rather ~ he's gone out** je crois (bien) qu'il est sorti ◆ **he fancied he heard the car arrive** il a cru entendre arriver la voiture ◆ **I ~ we've met before** j'ai l'impression que nous nous sommes déjà rencontrés ◆ **~ that!** * voyez-vous ça ! ◆ **~ anyone doing that!** les gens font de ces choses ! ◆ **~ seeing you here!** * tiens ! vous ici ! ◆ **~ him winning!** * qui aurait cru qu'il allait gagner !

ADJ 1 *[clothes, shoes, hat, pattern] (= sophisticated)* sophistiqué ; *(= showy)* tape-à-l'œil *inv* ◆ **~ food** des plats compliqués ◆ **good plain food, nothing ~** de la nourriture simple, sans chichis ◆ **~ cakes** pâtisseries *fpl*

2 *(gen pej = expensive) [restaurant, shop, school]* chic *inv* ◆ **with his ~ house and his ~ car how can he know what being poor is like?** avec sa belle maison et sa belle voiture, comment peut-il savoir ce que c'est que d'être pauvre ?

3 *(pej = pretentious) [idea, cure]* fantaisiste ; *[word, language]* recherché

4 *(= high) [price]* exorbitant

5 *(= high-quality) [products, foodstuffs]* de luxe

COMP **fancy dress** **N** *(NonC)* déguisement *m* ◆ **in ~ dress** déguisé, travesti ◆ **to go in ~ dress** se déguiser

fancy-dress ball **N** bal *m* masqué *or* costumé

fancy-free **ADJ** ◆ **he is ~-free** c'est un cœur à prendre ; → **footloose**

fancy goods **NPL** *(Comm)* articles *mpl* de luxe

fancy man * **N** (pl **fancy men**) *(pej)* amant *m*, jules * *m*

fancy woman * **N** (pl **fancy women**) *(pej)* maîtresse *f*, poule * *f* *(pej)*

fancy work **N** *(NonC)* ouvrages *mpl* d'agrément

fandango /fænˈdæŋgəʊ/ **N** (pl **fandangos**) fandango *m*

fanfare /ˈfænfeəʳ/ **N** fanfare *f* *(morceau de musique)* ◆ **the product was launched with** *or* **in a ~ of publicity** il y a eu un grand tapage publicitaire pour le lancement du produit ◆ **the plan was announced amid** *or* **with much ~** le projet a été annoncé en fanfare

fanfold paper /ˈfænfəʊldˈpeɪpəʳ/ **N** *(Comput)* papier *m* accordéon

fang /fæŋ/ **N** *[of dog, vampire]* croc *m*, canine *f* ; *[of snake]* crochet *m*

Fanny /ˈfænɪ/ **N** 1 abbrev of **Frances** 2 *(Brit)* **sweet ~ Adams**⁑ que dalle⁑

fanny /ˈfænɪ/ **N** 1 *(US: *)* *(= buttocks)* cul*⁎ *m*, fesses * *fpl* 2 *(Brit: *⁎= vagina)* chatte*⁎ *f*

fansite /ˈfænsaɪt/ **N** site *m* de fans

fantabulous⁑ /fænˈtæbjʊləs/ **ADJ** super-chouette *

fantail /ˈfænteɪl/ **N** (also **fantail pigeon**) pigeon-paon *m*

fantasia /fænˈteɪzjə/ **N** *(Literat, Mus)* fantaisie *f*

fantasist /ˈfæntəzɪst/ **N** doux rêveur *m*

fantasize /ˈfæntəsaɪz/ **VI** *(gen, Psych)* avoir des fantasmes, fantasmer *(about* sur)

fantastic /fænˈtæstɪk/ **ADJ** 1 *(* = fabulous, terrific) [person, achievement, opportunity, news]* fantastique, formidable ◆ **it's ~ to see you again!** c'est formidable de te revoir ! ◆ **you look ~!** *(= healthy)* tu as une mine superbe ; *(= attractive)* tu es superbe ! 2 *(* = huge) [amount, profit, speed]* phénoménal 3 *(= exotic) [creature, world]* fantastique ; → **trip** 4 *(= improbable) [story, adventure, idea]* invraisemblable

fantastical /fænˈtæstɪkl/ **ADJ** *[story, place, world]* fantastique ; *[account, architecture]* fantasque

fantastically /fænˈtæstɪkəlɪ/ **ADV** 1 *(= extraordinarily) [complicated]* fantastiquement, extraordinairement ; *[expensive, rich]* fabuleusement 2 *(= imaginatively) [wrought, coloured]* fantastiquement

fantasy /ˈfæntəzɪ/ **N** 1 *(= dream)* fantasme *m*, rêve *m* ◆ **sexual ~** fantasme *m* sexuel ◆ **one of my fantasies is to own a boat** l'un des mes rêves c'est d'avoir un bateau ◆ **I had fantasies of revenge** je rêvais de vengeance ◆ **she has fantasies about her teacher** elle fantasme sur son professeur

2 *(NonC) (= imagination)* imagination *f* ◆ **it stimulated her sense of ~** cela stimulait son imagination ◆ **a world of ~, a ~ world** un monde imaginaire ◆ **the realm of ~** le domaine de l'imaginaire ◆ **the tales you've been telling me are all ~** les histoires que tu m'as racontées sont complètement fantaisistes ◆ **she dismissed the allegations as pure ~** elle a décrété que ces accusations étaient complètement fantaisistes

3 *(Literat, Mus)* fantaisie *f*

COMP **fantasy football** **N** *jeu qui consiste à constituer des équipes de football virtuelles avec des joueurs existants*

> ⚠ **fantasy** is only translated by **fantaisie** in literary and musical contexts.

fanzine /ˈfænziːn/ **N** (abbrev of **fan magazine**) fanzine *m*

FAO /ˌefeɪˈəʊ/ **N** (abbrev of **Food and Agriculture Organization**) FAO *f*

FAQ **ABBR** *(Comm)* (abbrev of **free alongside quay**) FLQ **N** *(Comput)* (abbrev of **frequently asked questions**) FAQ *f*

far /fɑːʳ/ (compar **farther** *or* **further**, superl **farthest** *or* **furthest**) **ADV** 1 *(= a long way)* loin ◆ **is it ~?** c'est loin ? ◆ **is it ~ to London?** c'est loin pour aller à Londres ? ◆ **we live quite ~** nous habitons assez loin ◆ **have you come ~?** vous venez de loin ? ◆ **he carried** *or* **took the joke too ~** il a poussé trop loin la plaisanterie ◆ **~ be it from me to try to dissuade you** loin de moi l'idée de vous dissuader ◆ **they came from ~ and wide** *or* **~ and near** ils sont venus de partout

◆ **how far ?** ◆ **how ~ is it to Glasgow?** combien y a-t-il de kilomètres jusqu'à Glasgow ? ◆ **how ~ is it from Glasgow to Edinburgh?** combien y a-t-il (de kilomètres) de Glasgow à Édimbourg ? ◆ **how ~ are you going?** jusqu'où allez-vous ? ◆ **how ~ have you got with your plans?** où en êtes-vous de vos projets ?

◆ **to get + far** ◆ **he won't get ~** il n'ira pas loin ◆ **ten dollars won't get us very ~!** * on n'ira pas loin avec dix dollars !

◆ **to go + far** aller loin ◆ **he'll go ~** *(= do well)* il ira loin ◆ **to make one's money go ~** faire durer son argent ◆ **£10 doesn't go ~ these days** avec 10 livres, on ne va pas bien loin de nos jours ◆ **that will go ~ towards placating him** cela contribuera beaucoup à le calmer ◆ **this scheme does not go ~ enough** ce projet ne va pas assez loin ◆ **I would even go so ~ as to say that ...** j'irais même jusqu'à dire que ..., je dirais même que ... ◆ **that's going too ~** cela dépasse les bornes *or* la mesure ◆ **I wouldn't go that ~** je n'irais pas jusque-là ◆ **now you're going a bit too ~** alors là vous allez un peu trop loin ◆ **he's gone too ~ this time!** il est vraiment allé trop loin cette fois ! ◆ **he has gone too ~ to back out now** il est trop engagé pour reculer maintenant

◆ **as far as, so far as** ◆ **we went as ~ as the town** nous sommes allés jusqu'à la ville ◆ **we didn't go as** *or* **so ~ as the others** nous ne sommes pas allés aussi loin que les autres ◆ **as** *or* **so ~ as I know** (pour) autant que je (le) sache ◆ **as ~ as I can** dans la mesure du possible ◆ **as** *or* **so ~ as I can tell** si je ne m'abuse ◆ **as ~ as the eye can see** à perte de vue ◆ **as** *or* **so ~ as that goes** pour ce qui est de cela ◆ **as** *or* **so ~ as I'm concerned** en ce qui me concerne, pour ma part

◆ **by far** de loin, de beaucoup ◆ **this is by ~ the best** *or* **the best by ~** ceci est de très loin ce qu'il y a de mieux ◆ **he's the oldest by ~, he's by ~ the oldest** il est beaucoup plus âgé que les autres

◆ **far above** loin au-dessus ◆ **~ above the hill** loin au-dessus de la colline ◆ **he is ~ above the rest of the class** il est de loin supérieur au *or* il domine nettement le reste de la classe

◆ **far and away** de loin ◆ **it's ~ and away the most expensive** c'est de loin le plus cher

◆ **far away** loin ◆ **he wasn't ~ away when I saw him** il n'était pas loin quand je l'ai vu ◆ **~ away in the distance** au loin, dans le lointain ◆ **they live not ~ away** ils habitent près d'ici

◆ **far back** ◆ **the bungalow was set ~ back from the road** le bungalow était en retrait de la route ◆ **as ~ back as I can remember** d'aussi loin que je m'en souvienne ◆ **as ~ back as 1945** dès 1945, déjà en 1945 ◆ **how ~ back does all this go?** *(in time)* tout ça remonte à quand ?

◆ **far beyond** bien au-delà ◆ **he ventured into the forest and ~ beyond** il s'est aventuré dans la forêt et même bien au-delà ◆ **~ beyond the forest** très loin au-delà de la forêt ◆ **it's ~ beyond what I can afford** c'est bien au-dessus de mes moyens ◆ **I can't look ~ beyond May** je ne sais pas très bien ce qui se passera après le mois de mai

◆ **far from** loin de ◆ **we live not ~ from here** nous habitons tout près d'ici ◆ **your work is ~ from satisfactory** votre travail est loin d'être satisfaisant ◆ **~ from it!** loin de là !, tant s'en faut ! ◆ **~ from liking him I find him rather objectionable** bien loin de l'aimer, je le trouve (au contraire) tout à fait désagréable ◆ **I am ~ from believing him** je suis très loin de le croire

♦ **far gone** ♦ **he was ~ gone** (= *ill*) il était bien bas ; (* = *drunk*) il était bien parti *
♦ **far into** ♦ **~ into the night** tard dans la nuit ♦ **they went ~ into the forest** ils se sont enfoncés (loin) dans la forêt, ils ont pénétré très avant dans la forêt
♦ **far off** (= *in the distance*) au loin, dans le lointain ♦ **he wasn't ~ off when I caught sight of him** il n'était pas loin quand je l'ai aperçu ♦ **his birthday is not ~ off** c'est bientôt son anniversaire, son anniversaire approche ♦ **she's not ~ off fifty** elle n'est pas loin de la cinquantaine
♦ **far out** (= *distant*) ♦ **~ out at sea** au (grand) large ♦ **~ out on the branch** tout au bout de la branche ; see also **far-**
♦ **so far** ♦ **just so ~, so ~ and no further** jusque-là mais pas plus loin ♦ **so ~ so good** jusqu'ici ça va ♦ **so ~ this year** jusqu'ici cette année ♦ **we have ten volunteers so ~** nous avons dix volontaires pour l'instant *or* jusqu'à présent

2 (*as intensifier*) **~ too expensive/too slow/too dangerous** beaucoup *or* bien trop cher/trop lent/trop dangereux ♦ **this is ~ better** c'est beaucoup *or* bien mieux ♦ **this is ~ and away the best** ceci est de très loin ce qu'il y a de mieux ♦ **it is ~ more serious** c'est (bien) autrement sérieux ♦ **she is ~ prettier than her sister** elle est bien plus jolie que sa sœur ♦ **you're not ~ wrong** tu ne t'es pas trompé de beaucoup, tu n'es pas très loin de la vérité ♦ **it's not ~ wrong** c'est à peu près ça
♦ **to be far out** *or* **far off** (= *wrong*) [*person*] se tromper lourdement, être loin du compte ; [*estimates, guesses*] être loin du compte ; [*opinion polls*] se tromper lourdement ; [*calculations*] être complètement erroné ♦ **you're not ~ out** *or* **off** tu ne t'es pas trompé de beaucoup, tu n'es pas très loin de la vérité ♦ **it's not ~ out** c'est à peu près ça

ADJ 1 (= *distant: liter*) [*country, land*] lointain, éloigné ♦ **it's a ~ cry from what he promised** on est loin de ce qu'il a promis
2 (= *further away*) autre, plus éloigné ♦ **on the ~ side of** de l'autre côté de ♦ **at the ~ end of** à l'autre bout de, à l'extrémité de ♦ **in the ~ north of Scotland** tout au nord de l'Écosse
3 (*Pol*) **the ~ right/left** l'extrême droite *f*/gauche *f*

COMP **the Far East** N l'Extrême-Orient *m*
the Far North N (= *Arctic or polar regions*) le Grand Nord
the Far West N (*US*) le Far West, l'Ouest *m* américain

far- /fɑːʳ/ PREF ♦ **~distant** lointain ♦ **Far-Eastern** d'Extrême-Orient ♦ **~fetched** [*explanation, argument*] tiré par les cheveux ; [*idea, scheme, suggestion*] bizarre ♦ **~flung** (= *remote*) éloigné ♦ **~off** lointain, éloigné ♦ **~out** * (= *modern*) d'avant-garde ; (= *superb*) super *, génial ♦ **~reaching** [*reforms*] d'une grande portée ; [*changes, consequences, effects, implications*] très important ♦ **~seeing** [*person*] prévoyant ; [*decision, measure*] pris avec clairvoyance ♦ **~sighted** (*US* = *long-sighted*) hypermétrope ; (*in old age*) presbyte ; (*fig*) [*person*] prévoyant ; [*policy*] à long terme ; see also **farsightedness**

farad /ˈfærəd/ N farad *m*

faraway /ˈfɑːrəweɪ/ ADJ 1 (*lit*) [*country*] lointain ; [*village, house*] éloigné 2 (*fig*) [*look*] distrait, absent ; [*voice*] lointain

farce /fɑːs/ N 1 **the whole thing's a ~!** tout ça c'est grotesque ♦ **the elections were a ~** les élections furent une mascarade ♦ **the election campaign degenerated into ~** la campagne électorale a tourné à la farce 2 (*Theat*) farce *f*

farcical /ˈfɑːsɪkəl/ ADJ 1 (= *comical*) [*episode, attempt, scene*] burlesque ; (= *ridiculous, grotesque*) risible ; [*situation*] grotesque, risible 2 (*Theat*) ♦ **~ comedy** farce *f*

fare /fɛəʳ/ N 1 (= *charge*) (*on tube, subway, bus etc*) prix *m* du ticket *or* du billet ; (*on train, boat, plane*) prix *m* du billet ; (*in taxi*) prix *m* de la course ♦ **~s, please!** (*in bus*) ≈ les billets, s'il vous plaît ! ♦ **~s are going to go up** les tarifs *mpl* (des transports) vont augmenter ♦ **let me pay your ~** laissez-moi payer pour vous ♦ **I haven't got the ~** je n'ai pas assez d'argent pour le billet ; → **half, return**
2 (= *passenger*) voyageur *m*, -euse *f* ; (*of taxi*) client(e) *m(f)*
3 (*NonC* = *food*) nourriture *f* ♦ **traditional Christmas ~** les plats *mpl* traditionnels de Noël ♦ **vegetarian dishes are now standard ~ in many restaurants** les plats végétariens figurent désormais au menu de nombreux restaurants ♦ **old black-and-white films are standard ~ on late-night TV** les vieux films en noir et blanc figurent régulièrement au programme de fin de soirée à la télévision ; → **bill¹**

VI ♦ **he ~d better at his second attempt** il a mieux réussi à sa deuxième tentative ♦ **she has ~d better in France than in Britain** elle a mieux réussi en France qu'en Grande-Bretagne ♦ **the dollar ~d well on the stock exchange today** le dollar s'est bien comporté à la Bourse aujourd'hui ♦ **how did you ~?** († *or hum*) comment ça s'est passé ?, comment ça a marché ? *

COMP **fare-dodger** N (*Brit*) voyageur *m*, -euse *f* sans billet, resquilleur * *m*, -euse * *f*
fare-dodging N resquillage * *m*
fare stage N [*of bus*] section *f*
fare war N guerre *f* des tarifs
fare zone N (*US*) ⇒ **fare stage**

fare-thee-well /fɛəðiːˈwel/, **fare-you-well** /fɛəjuːˈwel/ N (*US*) ♦ **to a ~** (= *to perfection*) [*imitate etc*] à la perfection ; (= *very much, very hard*) au plus haut point

farewell /fɛəˈwel/ N, EXCL adieu *m* ♦ **to say** *or* **make one's ~s** faire ses adieux ♦ **to take one's ~ of** faire ses adieux à ♦ **to say** *or* **bid** † **~ to** (*lit*) dire adieu à ♦ **you can say ~ to your chances of promotion!** tu peux dire adieu à tes chances de promotion !, ta promotion, tu peux faire une croix dessus ! * COMP [*dinner etc*] d'adieu

farinaceous /ˌfærɪˈneɪʃəs/ ADJ farinacé, farineux

farm /fɑːm/ N ferme *f*, exploitation *f* agricole ♦ **pig/chicken/trout ~** élevage *m* de porcs/poulets/truites ♦ **to work on a ~** travailler dans une ferme ; → **fish, sheep**
VT [+ *land*] cultiver ; [+ *fish, salmon, deer*] faire l'élevage de ; see also **farmed**
VI être agriculteur *m*, -trice *f*
COMP **farm animal** N animal *m* de (la) ferme
farm gate price N (*Econ*) prix *m* à la production *or* au producteur
farm labourer N ⇒ **farm worker**
farm produce N (*NonC*) produits *mpl* agricoles *or* de la ferme
farm worker N ouvrier *m*, -ière *f* agricole

► **farm out** * VT SEP [+ *shop*] mettre en gérance ♦ **to ~ out work** recourir à un sous-traitant ♦ **the firm ~ed out the plumbing to a local tradesman** l'entreprise a confié la plomberie à un sous-traitant local ♦ **she ~ed her children out on her sister-in-law** elle a donné ses enfants à garder à sa belle-sœur

farmed /fɑːmd/ ADJ [*fish etc*] d'élevage

farmer /ˈfɑːməʳ/ N agriculteur *m*, -trice *f*, fermier *m*, -ière *f* ♦ **angry ~s** des agriculteurs en colère COMP **farmers' market** N marché *m* de producteurs

farmhand /ˈfɑːmhænd/ N ⇒ **farm worker**

farmhouse /ˈfɑːmhaʊs/ N ferme *f* ♦ **~ kitchen** cuisine *f* de style fermier
COMP **farmhouse cheese** N fromage *m* fermier
farmhouse loaf N (*Brit*) pain *m* de campagne

farming /ˈfɑːmɪŋ/ N (*gen*) agriculture *f* ♦ **he's always been interested in ~** il s'est toujours intéressé à l'agriculture ♦ **vegetable/fruit ~** culture *f* maraîchère/fruitière ♦ **pig/mink ~** élevage *m* de porcs/de visons ♦ **the ~ of this land** la culture *or* l'exploitation de cette terre ; → **dairy, factory, mixed**
COMP [*methods, techniques*] de culture
farming communities NPL collectivités *fpl* rurales

farmland /ˈfɑːmlænd/ N terres *fpl* cultivées *or* arables

farmstead /ˈfɑːmsted/ N ferme *f*

farmyard /ˈfɑːmjɑːd/ N cour *f* de ferme

Faroes /ˈfɛərəʊz/ NPL ♦ **the ~** (also **the Faroe Islands**) les îles *fpl* Féroé *or* Faeroe

Faroese /ˌfɛərəʊˈiːz/ N 1 (*pl inv* = *person*) Féroïen(ne) *m(f)*, Féringien(ne) *m(f)* 2 (= *language*) féroïen *m* ADJ féroïen, féringien, des îles Féroé

farrago /fəˈrɑːgəʊ/ N (pl **farragos** *or* **farragoes**) méli-mélo * *m*, mélange *m*

farrier /ˈfærɪəʳ/ N (*esp Brit*) maréchal-ferrant *m*

farrow /ˈfærəʊ/ VTI mettre bas N portée *f* (de cochons)

Farsi /ˈfɑːsiː/ N farsi *m*

farsightedness /ˌfɑːˈsaɪtɪdnɪs/ N 1 (*fig*) prévoyance *f* 2 (*lit*) hypermétropie *f* ; (*in old age*) presbytie *f*

fart ‡ /fɑːt/ N pet * *m* ♦ **he's a boring old ~** (*pej* = *person*) c'est un mec rasoir * *or* un vieux schnoque * VI péter ‡
► **fart about** ‡, **fart around** ‡ VI glander ‡ ♦ **stop ~ing about and do some work!** arrête de glander et bosse un peu ! ‡

farther /ˈfɑːðəʳ/ (compar of **far**) ADV plus loin ♦ **how much ~ is it?** c'est encore loin ? ♦ **it is ~ than I thought** c'est plus loin que je ne pensais ♦ **have you got much ~ to go?** est-ce que vous avez encore loin à aller ? ♦ **we will go no ~** (*lit*) nous n'irons pas plus loin ; (*fig*) nous en resterons là ♦ **I can't go any ~** (*lit*) je ne peux pas aller plus loin ; (*fig*) je n'en peux plus ♦ **I got no ~ with him** je ne suis arrivé à rien de plus avec lui ♦ **nothing could be ~ from the truth** rien n'est plus éloigné de la vérité ♦ **nothing is ~ from my thoughts** rien n'est plus éloigné de ma pensée ♦ **I can't see any ~ than the next six months** je n'arrive pas à voir au-delà des six prochains mois ♦ **to get ~ and ~ away** s'éloigner de plus en plus ♦ **~ back** plus (loin) en arrière ♦ **push it ~ back** repousse-le plus loin ♦ **move ~ back** reculez-vous ♦ **~ back than 1940** avant 1940 ♦ **a little ~ up** (*on wall etc*) un peu plus haut ; (*along path*) un peu plus loin ♦ **~ away, ~ off** plus éloigné, plus loin ♦ **he went ~ off than I thought** il est allé plus loin que je ne pensais ♦ **~ on, ~ forward** plus en avant, plus loin ♦ **we're no ~ forward after all that** (*fig*) on n'est pas plus avancé après tout ça
ADJ plus éloigné, plus lointain ♦ **at the ~ end of the room** à l'autre bout de la salle, au fond de la salle ♦ **at the ~ end of the branch** à l'autre bout *or* à l'extrémité de la branche

farthest /ˈfɑːðɪst/ (superl of **far**) ADJ le plus éloigné ♦ **in the ~ depths of the forest** au fin fond de la forêt ♦ **they went by boat to the ~ point of the island** ils se sont rendus en bateau à l'extrémité de l'île ♦ **the ~ way** la route la plus longue ♦ **it's 5km at the ~** il y a 5 km au plus *or* au maximum ADV le plus loin

farthing /ˈfɑːðɪŋ/ N *quart d'un ancien penny* ♦ **I haven't a ~** je n'ai pas le sou ; → **brass**

FAS /ˌefeɪˈes/ (*Comm*) (abbrev of **free alongside ship**) FLB

fascia /ˈfeɪʃə/ N (pl **fasciae** /ˈfeɪʃɪˌiː/) (*Brit*) 1 (*on building*) panneau *m* 2 (*in car*) tableau *m* de bord 3 (*for mobile phone*) façade *f*

fascicle /ˈfæsɪkl/, **fascicule** /ˈfæsɪkjuːl/ N (Bot) rameau *m* fasciculé ; *[of book]* fascicule *m*

fascinate /ˈfæsɪneɪt/ VT [1] *(= interest) [speaker, tale]* fasciner, captiver ; *[sight]* fasciner [2] *[snake]* fasciner

fascinated /ˈfæsɪneɪtɪd/ ADJ *[person]* fasciné, captivé ; *[look, smile]* fasciné

fascinating /ˈfæsɪneɪtɪŋ/ ADJ *[person, place, sight, story]* fascinant ; *[book, film]* captivant ; *[subject]* passionnant ◆ **it'll be ~ to see how she reacts** ce sera très intéressant de voir sa réaction

fascinatingly /ˈfæsɪneɪtɪŋlɪ/ ADV ◆ **~ interesting** d'un intérêt exceptionnel ◆ **~, his thesis is that ...** chose très intéressante, sa thèse est que ...

fascination /ˌfæsɪˈneɪʃən/ N fascination *f* ◆ **his ~ with the cinema** la fascination qu'exerce sur lui le cinéma ◆ **I don't understand the ~ of this book** je ne comprends pas la fascination que ce livre exerce sur les gens ◆ **he listened in ~** il écoutait, fasciné ◆ **she has developed a ~ for Impressionist painting** elle se passionne maintenant pour la peinture impressionniste

fascism /ˈfæʃɪzəm/ N fascisme *m*

fascist /ˈfæʃɪst/ ADJ, N fasciste *mf*

fascistic /fəˈʃɪstɪk/ ADJ fasciste

fashion /ˈfæʃən/ N [1] (NonC = *manner*) façon *f*, manière *f* ◆ **in a strange ~** d'une façon *or* manière bizarre ◆ **in (a) similar ~** d'une façon *or* manière similaire, pareillement ◆ **after a ~** *[manage]* tant bien que mal ◆ **I can cook after a ~** je me débrouille en cuisine, sans plus ◆ **it worked, after a ~** ça a marché plus ou moins bien ◆ **after the ~ of** à la manière de ◆ **in the French ~** à la française ◆ **in his own ~** à sa manière *or* façon ◆ **it's not my ~ to lie** (*frm*) ce n'est pas mon genre de mentir

[2] (*lit, fig = latest clothes, style, ideas*) mode *f* ◆ **it's the latest ~** c'est la dernière mode *or* le dernier cri ◆ **she always wears the latest ~s** elle est toujours habillée à la dernière mode ◆ **the Paris ~s** les collections *fpl* (de mode) parisiennes ◆ **a man of ~** un homme élégant ◆ **~s have changed** la mode a changé ◆ **to set the ~ for** lancer la mode de ◆ **to bring sth into ~** mettre qch à la mode ◆ **to come into ~** devenir à la mode ◆ **it is the ~ to say that** il est de bon ton de dire cela ◆ **it's no longer the ~ to send children away to school** ça ne se fait plus de mettre les enfants en pension

◆ **in fashion** à la mode ◆ **boots are back in ~** les bottes sont revenues à la mode

◆ **out of fashion** démodé, passé de mode ◆ **to go out of ~** se démoder

[3] (*= habit*) coutume *f*, habitude *f* ◆ **as was his ~** selon sa coutume *or* son habitude

VT *[+ carving]* façonner ; *[+ model]* fabriquer ; *[+ dress]* confectionner

COMP **fashion-conscious** ADJ ◆ **to be ~-conscious** suivre la mode

fashion designer N (*gen*) styliste *mf*, modéliste *mf* ◆ **the great ~ designers** (*= Givenchy etc*) les grands couturiers *mpl*

fashion editor N rédacteur *m*, -trice *f* de mode

fashion house N maison *f* de couture

fashion magazine N magazine *m* *or* journal *m* de mode

fashion model N mannequin *m* (*personne*)

fashion parade N défilé *m* de mannequins, présentation *f* de collections

fashion plate N gravure *f* de mode ◆ **she's a real ~ plate*** on dirait une gravure de mode, elle a l'air de sortir d'un magazine de mode

fashion show N présentation *f* de modèles *or* de collections ◆ **to go to the Paris ~ shows** faire les collections parisiennes

fashion victim* N victime *f* de la mode

fashionable /ˈfæʃnəbl/ ADJ *[clothes, shop, restaurant, subject, idea]* à la mode ; *[hotel]* chic *inv* ; *[district]* prisé ; *[person]* (*= stylish*) à la mode ; (*= in the public eye*) en vue ; *[artist, writer]* à la mode ◆ **it is ~ to criticize these theories** il est à la mode de critiquer ces théories

fashionably /ˈfæʃnəblɪ/ ADV *[dress]* à la mode ◆ **~ long hair** des cheveux longs comme c'est la mode ◆ **she was ~ late** elle était en retard, juste ce qu'il faut

fashionista* /ˌfæʃəˈnɪstə/ N victime *f* de la mode

fast¹ /fɑːst/ ADJ [1] (*= speedy*) rapide ◆ **she's a ~ walker/runner/reader** elle marche/court/lit vite ◆ **~ train** rapide *m* ◆ **he's a ~ thinker** il a l'esprit très rapide ◆ **a grass court is ~er** (*Tennis*) le jeu est plus rapide sur gazon ◆ **~ film** (*Phot*) pellicule *f* rapide ◆ **to pull a ~ one on sb*** rouler qn*, avoir qn* ; see also **comp**

[2] **to be ~** *[clock, watch]* avancer ◆ **my watch is five minutes ~** ma montre avance de cinq minutes

[3] († *= dissipated*) *[person]* léger, de mœurs légères ◆ **~ life** *or* **living** vie *f* dissolue (*liter*) ◆ **~ woman** femme *f* légère *or* de mœurs légères ◆ **a ~ set** une bande de noceurs* ◆ **one of the ~ set** un noceur *or* une noceuse

[4] (*= firm*) *[rope, knot, grip]* solide ◆ **to make a boat ~** amarrer un bateau ◆ **they're ~ friends** ils sont très amis

[5] *[colour]* bon teint *inv*, grand teint *inv* ◆ **is the dye ~?** est-ce que ça déteindra ?, est-ce que la teinture s'en ira ?

ADV [1] (*= quickly*) vite, rapidement ◆ **don't speak so ~** ne parlez pas si vite ◆ **how ~ can you type?** à quelle vitesse pouvez-vous taper (à la machine) ? ◆ **the environment is ~ becoming a major political issue** l'environnement est en train de prendre une place importante dans les débats politiques ◆ **he ran off as ~ as his legs could carry him** il s'est sauvé à toutes jambes ◆ **not so ~!** (*interrupting*) doucement !, minute !* ◆ **he'd do it ~ enough if ...** il ne se ferait pas prier si ... ◆ **the holidays can't come ~ enough for me** vivement les vacances ! ◆ **as ~ as I advanced he drew back** à mesure que j'avançais, il reculait ; → **furious**

[2] (*= firmly, securely*) ferme, solidement ◆ **to be ~ asleep** dormir à poings fermés ◆ **to be stuck ~** *[person, door, window, lid]* être coincé ◆ **a door shut ~** une porte bien close ◆ **to stand ~** tenir bon *or* ferme, ne pas lâcher pied ◆ **to play ~ and loose with sb** se jouer de qn, traiter qn à la légère ; → **hard, hold**

[3] ◆ **~ by the church** †† qui jouxte l'église

COMP **fast bowler** N (*Cricket*) lanceur *m*, -euse *f* rapide

fast breeder (reactor) N (*Phys*) (réacteur *m*) surgénérateur *m*, (réacteur *m*) surrégénérateur *m*

fast-flowing ADJ *[river, stream]* au cours rapide

fast food N (*= food*) prêt-à-manger *m* ; (*= place*) (*also* **fast-food restaurant**) fast-food *m*

fast-food chain N chaîne *f* de fast-foods

fast-food industry, fast-food trade N secteur *m* des fast-foods, restauration *f* rapide

fast forward N avance *f* rapide

fast-forward VT faire avancer rapidement VI *[tape]* avancer rapidement

fast-growing ADJ *[economy, market, business]* en plein essor

the fast lane N (*lit*) ≈ la voie de gauche ◆ **to be in the ~ lane** (*fig*) avoir une vie trépidante, vivre à 100 à l'heure* ◆ **life in the ~ lane** la vie trépidante

fast-moving ADJ (*gen*) rapide ; (*fig*) (*= active, rapidly-changing*) *[industry, sector]* en mouvement constant ◆ **~-moving consumer goods** biens *mpl* de consommation à rotation rapide

fast-selling ADJ à écoulement rapide

fast-track N (*in organization*) filière *f* ultrarapide ◆ **her career was on the ~-track** elle progressait rapidement dans sa carrière ◆ **this put the company on a ~-track to privatization** cela a accéléré la privatisation de l'entreprise ADJ *[approach]* expéditif ; (*Univ*) ◆ **~-track degree** diplôme *m* de formation accélérée VT *[+ employee]* accélérer la carrière de

fast-tracking N *[of personnel]* avancement *m* rapide

fast² /fɑːst/ VI jeûner, rester à jeun ; (*Rel*) jeûner, faire maigre N jeûne *m* ◆ **to break one's ~** rompre le jeûne ◆ **~ day** (*Rel*) jour *m* maigre *or* de jeûne

fastback /ˈfɑːstbæk/ N (*Brit = car*) voiture *f* à hayon

fasten /ˈfɑːsn/ VT [1] (*lit*) attacher (*to* à) ; (*with rope, string etc*) lier (*to* à) ; *[+ dress]* fermer, attacher ; *[+ shoelaces]* attacher, nouer ; *[+ box]* fermer (solidement) ◆ **to ~ two things together** attacher deux choses ensemble *or* l'une à l'autre ◆ **to ~ one's seat belt** attacher *or* mettre sa ceinture de sécurité ◆ **it wasn't properly ~ed** (*= attached*) ce n'était pas bien attaché ; (*= closed*) ce n'était pas bien fermé

[2] *[+ responsibility]* attribuer (*on sb* à qn) ; *[+ crime]* imputer (*on sb* à qn) ◆ **to ~ the blame on sb** rejeter la faute sur (le dos de) qn ◆ **you can't ~ it on me!** tu ne peux pas me mettre ça sur le dos ! ◆ **to ~ one's hopes on sb/sth** placer *or* mettre tous ses espoirs dans qn/qch ◆ **to ~ one's eyes on sth** fixer son regard *or* les yeux sur qch

VI *[dress]* s'attacher ; *[box, door, lock, window]* se fermer

► **fasten down** VT SEP fixer en place

► **fasten on** VT SEP fixer (en place)

VT FUS ⇒ **fasten upon**

► **fasten on to** VT FUS [1] ⇒ **fasten upon**

[2] se cramponner à, s'accrocher à ◆ **he ~ed on to my arm** il s'est cramponné *or* accroché à mon bras

► **fasten up** VT SEP *[+ dress, coat]* fermer, attacher

► **fasten upon** VT FUS saisir ◆ **to ~ upon an excuse** saisir un prétexte ◆ **to ~ upon the idea of doing sth** se mettre en tête (l'idée) de faire qch

fastener /ˈfɑːsnəʳ/, **fastening** /ˈfɑːsnɪŋ/ N *[of box, bag, necklace, book]* fermoir *m* ; *[of garment]* fermeture *f* ; (*= button*) bouton *m* ; (*= hook*) agrafe *f* ; (*= press stud*) bouton-pression *m*, pression *f* ; (*= zip*) fermeture *f* éclair ® *inv* ◆ **a zip ~** une fermeture éclair ® ◆ **a Velcro ® ~** une fermeture velcro ® ◆ **a snap ~** un bouton-pression, une pression

fastidious /fæsˈtɪdɪəs/ ADJ *[work, research]* minutieux ; *[person]* (*= meticulous*) méticuleux, minutieux ; (*= demanding about detail*) tatillon, pointilleux ; (*= particular about cleanliness*) tatillon ; (*= easily disgusted*) délicat ◆ **their inspectors are very ~** leurs inspecteurs sont très pointilleux *or* tatillons ◆ **he's ~ about security/hygiene** il est pointilleux en ce qui concerne la sécurité/l'hygiène ◆ **she's too ~ to eat there** elle est trop délicate pour manger là ◆ **this film is not for the ~** ce film n'est pas pour les esprits délicats *or* pour les personnes trop délicates

> ⚠ **fastidieux** does not mean **fastidious**, but 'boring'.

fastidiously /fæsˈtɪdɪəslɪ/ ADV [1] (*= meticulously*) *[check, copy]* méticuleusement ◆ **~ clean** d'une propreté méticuleuse ◆ **his ~ tidy flat** son appartement impeccablement rangé [2] (*pej = with distaste*) *[examine]* en faisant le délicat

fastidiousness /fæsˈtɪdɪəsnɪs/ N (*= meticulousness*) méticulosité *f* (*liter*), minutie *f* ; (*= concern about detail*) caractère *m* tatillon

fastigiate /fæˈstɪdʒɪɪt/ ADJ fastigié

fastness /ˈfɑːstnɪs/ N [1] *[of colours]* solidité *f* ◆ **to test a fabric for colour ~** tester la résistance au lavage d'un tissu [2] (NonC = *speed*) rapidité *f*, vitesse *f* 3 (= *stronghold*) place *f* forte ◆ **mountain** ~ repaire *m* de montagne

fat /fæt/ **N** (*gen, also Anat*) graisse *f* ; (*on raw meat*) graisse *f*, gras *m* ; (*on cooked meat*) gras *m* ; (*for cooking*) matière grasse *f* ◆ **try to cut down the amount of ~ in your diet** essayez de manger moins gras *or* moins de matières grasses ◆ **to fry sth in deep ~** (faire) frire *or* cuire qch dans un bain de friture ◆ **animal/vegetable ~** graisse *f* animale/végétale ◆ **beef/mutton ~** graisse *f* de bœuf/de mouton ◆ **pork ~** saindoux *m* ◆ **body ~** tissu *m* adipeux ◆ **he's got rolls of ~ round his waist** il a des bourrelets de graisse autour de la taille ◆ **the ~'s in the fire** ça va barder* *or* chauffer* ◆ **to live off the ~ of the land** vivre grassement

ADJ 1 [*person, animal, stomach, thighs, cheeks*] gros (grosse *f*) ; [*face*] joufflu ◆ **to get** *or* **grow** *or* **become ~** devenir gros, grossir ◆ **she has got a lot ~ter** elle a beaucoup grossi ◆ **it makes you look ~ter** ça te grossit ◆ **to grow ~ (on sth)** (*fig*) s'engraisser (de qch) ◆ **it's not** *or* **the show's not over until the ~ lady sings*** (*hum*) il ne faut jamais désespérer ◆ **a ~ year** une bonne année ◆ **can't you get that into your ~ head ?*** tu ne peux pas te mettre ça dans la caboche* ? ◆ **get it into your ~ head that you can't come with us*** mets-toi bien dans la tête que tu ne peux pas venir avec nous

2 [*meat, bacon*] gras (grasse *f*)

3 [*book, volume*] gros (grosse *f*), épais (épaisse *f*) ; [*wallet*] bien garni

4 * [*profit, fee, cheque, salary*] gros (grosse *f*)

5 (* *iro*) ◆ **~ chance (of that) !** ça m'étonnerait ! ◆ **he wants to be a racing driver – ~ chance!** il veut être pilote de course – il n'a aucune chance ! ◆ **a ~ chance he's got of winning the lottery!** tu parles qu'il risque de gagner à la loterie !* ◆ **you've got a ~ chance of seeing her!** comme si tu avais la moindre chance de la voir !

◆ **(a) fat lot*** ◆ **a ~ lot he cares!** comme si ça lui faisait quelque chose ! ◆ **a ~ lot of good that did!** nous voilà bien avancés ! ◆ **a ~ lot of good lying did you!** ça t'a avancé à quoi, de mentir ? ◆ **a ~ lot of good such a promise will be!** ça nous fait une belle jambe ! ◆ **it'll be a ~ lot of good to phone now** tu parles si ça sert à quelque chose de téléphoner maintenant ! (*iro*) ◆ **(a) ~ lot of help she was (to me)!** c'est fou ce qu'elle m'a aidé ! (*iro*) ◆ **a ~ lot you did to help!** tu as vraiment été d'un précieux secours ! (*iro*) ◆ **a ~ lot he knows about it!** comme s'il y connaissait quelque chose ! ◆ **that's a ~ lot of use!** pour ce que ça sert ! (*iro*) ◆ **that's a ~ lot of use to me!** c'est fou ce que ça m'aide !* (*iro*) ◆ **a ~ lot that's worth!** c'est fou ce que ça a comme valeur !* (*iro*)

VT †† 1 ⇒ **fatten vt**

2 ◆ **to kill the ~ted calf** tuer le veau gras

COMP fat-ass (*‡, US pej*) **N** (*man*) gros lard* *m* (*pej*) ; (*woman*) grosse vache* *f* (*pej*) **ADJ** obèse (*pej*)

fat cat N gros richard* *m*

fat city * **N** (*US*) ◆ **to be in ~ city** être plein aux as*

fat farm‡ **N** (*esp US*) clinique *f* d'amaigrissement

fat-free ADJ [*diet*] sans matières grasses, sans corps gras

fat-headed * **ADJ** idiot, imbécile

fatal /ˈfeɪtl/ **ADJ** 1 (= *causing death*) [*injury, illness, accident, shot, dose*] mortel ; [*blow*] mortel, fatal ; [*consequences, result, delay*] fatal ◆ **to be ~ to** *or* **for sb** être fatal pour *or* à qn 2 (= *disastrous*) [*mistake, weakness*] fatal ; [*flaw*] malheureux ; [*influence*] néfaste, pernicieux ◆ **~ attraction** attraction *f* irrésistible ◆ **to be ~ to** *or* **for sb/sth** porter un coup fatal *or* le coup de grâce à qn/qch ◆ **it would be ~ to do that** ce serait une erreur fatale de faire cela 3 (= *fateful*) [*day*] fatidique

fatalism /ˈfeɪtəlɪzəm/ **N** fatalisme *m*

fatalist /ˈfeɪtəlɪst/ **N, ADJ** fataliste *mf*

fatalistic /ˌfeɪtəˈlɪstɪk/ **ADJ** fataliste

fatality /fəˈtælɪtɪ/ **N** 1 (= *person killed*) mort *m* ; (= *fatal accident*) accident *m* mortel ◆ **there were no fatalities** il n'y a pas eu de morts ◆ **road fatalities** accidents *mpl* mortels de la route 2 (*NonC*) fatalisme *m* ◆ **a growing sense of pessimism and ~** un sentiment croissant de pessimisme et de fatalisme

fatally /ˈfeɪtəlɪ/ **ADV** 1 [*wounded, injured, shot*] mortellement ◆ **~ ill** condamné 2 [*undermine, damage, weaken*] irrémédiablement ◆ **~ flawed** voué à l'échec 3 (= *disastrously*) **it is ~ easy to forget it** c'est beaucoup trop facile de l'oublier ◆ **to be ~ attracted to sb/sth** être irrésistiblement attiré par qn/qch

⚠ **fatalement** does not mean **fatally**, but 'inevitably'.

fatback /ˈfætˌbæk/ **N** ≈ lard *m* maigre

fate /feɪt/ **N** 1 (= *force*) destin *m*, sort *m* ◆ **the Fates** (*Myth*) les Parques *fpl* ◆ **what ~ has in store for us** ce que le destin *or* le sort nous réserve ; → **tempt** 2 (= *one's lot*) sort *m* ◆ **to leave sb to his ~** abandonner qn à son sort ◆ **to meet one's ~** trouver la mort ◆ **it met with a strange ~** cela a eu une destinée curieuse ◆ **to meet with** *or* **suffer the same ~** connaître *or* subir le même sort ◆ **to face a similar ~** risquer de subir le même sort ◆ **to settle** *or* **seal sb's ~** décider du sort de qn ◆ **it was a ~ worse than death** c'était un sort pire que la mort, la mort eût été mille fois préférable

fated /ˈfeɪtɪd/ **ADJ** [*friendship, person*] voué au malheur ◆ **they were ~ to meet again** il était dit qu'ils se reverraient

fateful /ˈfeɪtfʊl/ **ADJ** [*day, night, moment, words*] fatidique ; [*decision, consequence, journey*] fatal ; [*meeting*] décisif ◆ **to be ~ for sb** être fatal pour qn

fathead * /ˈfæthed/ **N** débile *mf*

father /ˈfɑːðəʳ/ **N** 1 père *m* ◆ **from ~ to son** de père en fils ◆ **like ~ like son** (*Prov*) tel père tel fils (*Prov*) ◆ **to act like a ~** agir en père *or* comme un père ◆ **he was like a ~ to me** il était comme un père pour moi ◆ **there was the ~ and mother of a row!*** il y a eu une dispute épouvantable ! ; see also **comp**

2 (= *founder, leader*) père *m*, créateur *m* ◆ **the ~ of modern jazz/French Impressionism** le père du jazz moderne/de l'impressionnisme français ◆ **the Fathers of the Church** les Pères *mpl* de l'Église ; → **city**

3 (*Rel* = *priest, monk etc*) père *m* ◆ **Father Paul** le (révérend) père Paul, l'abbé *m* Paul ◆ **yes, Father** oui, mon père ◆ **the Capuchin Fathers** les pères *mpl* capucins ; → **holy**

4 (*Rel*) (= *God*) ◆ **Our Father** Notre Père ◆ **the Our Father** (= *prayer*) le Notre Père

NPL fathers ancêtres *mpl*, pères *mpl*

VT [+ *child*] engendrer ◆ **he ~ed three children** il a eu trois enfants ◆ **he was unable to ~ a child** il ne pouvait pas avoir d'enfants

COMP Father Christmas N (*Brit*) le père Noël

father confessor N (*Rel*) directeur *m* de conscience, père *m* spirituel

father figure N figure *f* de père ◆ **he is the ~ figure** il joue le rôle du père

father-in-law N (*pl* **fathers-in-law**) beau-père *m*

Father's Day N la fête des Pères

Father Time N (*also* **Old Father Time**) le Temps

fatherhood /ˈfɑːðəhʊd/ **N** paternité *f*

fatherland /ˈfɑːðəlænd/ **N** patrie *f*

fatherless /ˈfɑːðəlɪs/ **ADJ** orphelin de père, sans père

fatherly /ˈfɑːðəlɪ/ **ADJ** paternel

fathom /ˈfæðəm/ **N** (*Naut*) brasse *f* (= 1,83 *m*) ◆ **a channel with five ~s of water** un chenal de 9 m de fond ◆ **to lie 25 ~s deep** *or* **down** reposer par 45 m de fond **VT** (*Naut*) sonder ; (*fig*) (*also* **fathom out**) [+ *mystery*] pénétrer ; [+ *person*] (finir par) comprendre ◆ **I just can't ~ it (out)** je n'y comprends absolument rien

fathomless /ˈfæðəmlɪs/ **ADJ** (*lit*) insondable ; (*fig*) insondable, impénétrable

fatigue /fəˈtiːg/ **N** 1 fatigue *f*, épuisement *m* 2 (= *jadedness*) **donor ~, charity ~** la lassitude des donateurs ◆ **compassion ~ has set in** la compassion s'est émoussée ◆ **they blamed the low election turn-out on voter ~** ils ont attribué la faible participation électorale à la lassitude des électeurs ; → **battle, combat** 3 (*Mil*) corvée *f* ◆ **to be on ~** être de corvée **NPL fatigues** (*Mil*) ⇒ **fatigue dress VT** fatiguer, lasser ; (*Tech*) [+ *metals etc*] fatiguer

COMP fatigue dress N (*Mil*) tenue *f* de corvée, treillis *m*

fatigue duty N (*Mil*) corvée *f*

fatigue limit N (*Tech*) limite *f* de fatigue

fatigue party N (*Mil*) corvée *f*

fatigued /fəˈtiːgd/ **ADJ** las (lasse *f*), fatigué

fatiguing /fəˈtiːgɪŋ/ **ADJ** fatigant, épuisant

fatness /ˈfætnɪs/ **N** [*of person*] embonpoint *m*, corpulence *f*

fatso‡ /ˈfætsəʊ/ **N** (*pl* **fatsos** *or* **fatsoes**) (*pej*) gros lard‡ *m*

fatstock /ˈfætstɒk/ **N** (*Agr*) animaux *mpl* de boucherie

fatten /ˈfætn/ **VT** (*also* **fatten up**) engraisser ; (*by force-feeding*) gaver **VI** (*also* **fatten out**) engraisser, grossir

fattening /ˈfætnɪŋ/ **ADJ** [*food*] qui fait grossir **N** (*also* **fattening-up**) engraissement *m* ; (*by force-feeding*) gavage *m*

fatty /ˈfætɪ/ **ADJ** 1 (= *greasy*) [*food*] gras (grasse *f*) ◆ **they have a fattier diet than us** ils mangent plus gras que nous 2 (*Anat, Bio*) [*tissue*] adipeux **N** * gros *m* (bonhomme), grosse *f* (bonne femme) ◆ **hey ~!** eh toi le gros (*or* la grosse) !

COMP fatty acid N acide *m* gras

fatty degeneration N (*Med*) dégénérescence *f* graisseuse

fatuity /fəˈtjuːɪtɪ/ **N** stupidité *f*, sottise *f*

fatuous /ˈfætjʊəs/ **ADJ** [*person, remark*] idiot, stupide ; [*smile*] stupide, niais

fatuously /ˈfætjʊəslɪ/ **ADV** sottement, stupidement

fatuousness /ˈfætjʊəsnɪs/ **N** ⇒ **fatuity**

fatwa /ˈfætwə/ **N** (*Rel*) fatwa *f*

faucet /ˈfɔːsɪt/ **N** (*US*) robinet *m*

faugh /fɔː/ **EXCL** pouah !

fault /fɔːlt/ **N** 1 (*in person, scheme*) défaut *m* ; (*in machine*) défaut *m*, anomalie *f* ; (= *mistake*) erreur *f* ◆ **in spite of all her ~s** malgré tous ses défauts ◆ **her big ~ is ...** son gros défaut est ... ◆ **a mechanical ~** un défaut technique ◆ **a ~ has been found in the engine** une anomalie a été constatée dans le moteur ◆ **the ~ lay in the production process** l'anomalie se situait au niveau de la production ◆ **there is a ~ in the gas supply** il y a un défaut dans l'arrivée du gaz ◆ **an electrical ~** un défaut du circuit électrique

◆ **to a fault** ◆ **she is generous to a ~** elle est généreuse à l'excès

◆ **to be at fault** être fautif, être coupable ◆ **you were at ~ in not telling me** vous avez eu tort de ne pas me le dire ◆ **he's at ~ in this matter** il est fautif *or* c'est lui le fautif dans cette affaire ◆ **my memory was at ~** ma mémoire m'a trompé *or* m'a fait défaut

◆ **to find fault** ◆ **to find ~ with sth** trouver à redire à qch, critiquer qch ◆ **to find ~ with sb** critiquer qn ◆ **I have no ~ to find with him** je n'ai rien à lui reprocher ◆ **he is always finding ~** il trouve toujours à redire

2 *(NonC = blame, responsibility)* faute *f* ◆ **whose ~ is it?** c'est la faute à qui ?, qui est fautif ? ◆ **whose ~ is it if we're late?** *(iro)* et à qui la faute si nous sommes en retard ? ◆ **the ~ lies with him** c'est de sa faute, c'est lui le responsable ◆ **it's not my ~** ce n'est pas (de) ma faute ◆ **it's all your ~** c'est entièrement (de) ta faute ◆ **it's your own ~** vous n'avez à vous en prendre qu'à vous-même ◆ **it happened through no ~ of mine** ce n'est absolument pas de ma faute si c'est arrivé ◆ **through no ~ of her own, she ...** sans qu'elle y soit pour quelque chose, elle ...

3 *(Tennis)* faute *f*

4 *(Geol)* faille *f*

VT ◆ **to ~ sth/sb** trouver des défauts à qch/ chez qn ◆ **you can't ~ him** on ne peut pas le prendre en défaut ◆ **you can't ~ her on her handling of the situation** la manière dont elle a géré la situation est irréprochable ◆ **I can't ~ his reasoning** je ne trouve aucune faille dans son raisonnement

COMP **fault-find** VI ◆ **she's always ~-finding** elle trouve toujours à redire, elle est toujours en train de critiquer

fault-finder N mécontent(e) *m(f)*, grincheux *m*, -euse *f*

fault-finding ADJ chicanier, grincheux N critiques *fpl*

fault line N *(Geol)* ligne *f* de faille ; *(fig)* faille *f*

fault plane N *(Geol)* plan *m* de faille

fault-tolerant ADJ *(Comput)* à tolérance de pannes, insensible aux défaillances

faultless /ˈfɔːltlɪs/ ADJ *[person, behaviour]* irréprochable ; *[work, manners, dress]* impeccable, irréprochable ; *[performance]* parfait ◆ **he spoke ~ English** il parlait un anglais impeccable

faultlessly /ˈfɔːltlɪslɪ/ ADV impeccablement

faulty /ˈfɔːltɪ/ ADJ *[work]* défectueux, mal fait ; *[machine]* défectueux ; *[style]* incorrect, mauvais ; *[reasoning]* défectueux, erroné

faun /fɔːn/ N faune *m*

fauna /ˈfɔːnə/ N (pl **faunas** or **faunae** /ˈfɔːniː/) faune *f*

Faust /faʊst/ N Faust *m*

Faustian /ˈfaʊstɪən/ ADJ faustien

faux pas /fəʊˈpɑː/ N *(pl inv)* impair *m*, bévue *f*, gaffe* *f*

fava bean /ˈfɑːvəbiːn/ N *(US)* fève *f*

fave* /feɪv/ ADJ favori N favori(te) *m(f)*

favela /fɑːˈveɪlə/ N favela *f*

favour, favor (US) /ˈfeɪvəʳ/ LANGUAGE IN USE 13

N 1 *(= act of kindness) (small)* service *m* ; *(more major)* faveur *f* ◆ **to do sb a ~, to do a ~ for sb** rendre (un) service à qn, faire *or* accorder une faveur à qn ◆ **to ask sb a ~, to ask a ~ of sb** demander un service à qn, solliciter une faveur de qn *(frm)* ◆ **he did it as a ~ to his brother** il l'a fait pour rendre service à son frère ◆ **I'll return this ~** je vous revaudrai ça ◆ **I would consider it a ~ if you ...** je vous serais très reconnaissant si vous ... ◆ **do me a ~ and ...** sois gentil et ... ◆ **you're not doing yourself any ~s (by refusing to cooperate)** tu ne te facilites pas les choses (en refusant de coopérer) ◆ **do me a ~!*** *(iro)* tu te fous de moi !* ◆ **a woman's ~s** les faveurs *fpl* d'une femme ◆ **your ~ of the 7th inst.** *(Comm)* votre honorée † du 7 courant

2 *(NonC = approval, regard)* faveur *f*, approbation *f* ◆ **to be in ~** *[person]* être en faveur, avoir la cote* ; *[style, fashion]* être à la mode *or* en vogue ◆ **to be out of ~** *[person]* ne pas être en faveur, ne pas avoir la cote* ; *[style, fashion]* être démodé *or* passé de mode ◆ **to be in ~ with sb** être bien vu de qn, jouir des bonnes grâces de qn ◆ **to win sb's ~, to find ~ with sb** *[person]* s'attirer les bonnes grâces de qn ; *[suggestion]* gagner l'approbation de qn ◆ **to get back into sb's ~** rentrer dans les bonnes grâces de qn ◆ **to look with ~ on sth** approuver qch ◆ **to look with ~ on sb** bien considérer qn

3 *(NonC = support, advantage)* faveur *f*, avantage *m* ◆ **the court decided in her ~** le tribunal lui a donné gain de cause ◆ **the decision/ judgement went in his ~** la décision a été prise/le jugement a été rendu en sa faveur ◆ **it's in our ~ to act now** c'est (à) notre avantage d'agir maintenant ◆ **the exchange rate is in our ~** le taux de change joue en notre faveur *or* pour nous ◆ **the traffic lights are in our ~** les feux sont pour nous ◆ **circumstances were all working in her ~** les circonstances lui étaient (entièrement) favorables ◆ **that's a point in his ~** c'est quelque chose à mettre à son actif, c'est un bon point pour lui ◆ **he's got everything in his ~** il a tout pour lui ◆ **will in ~ of sb** testament *m* en faveur de qn ◆ **cheque in ~ of sb** chèque *m* payable à qn ◆ **"balance in your favour"** *(Banking)* "solde en votre faveur"

4 ◆ **to be in ~ of sth** être pour qch, être partisan(e) de qch ◆ **to be in ~ of doing sth** être d'avis de faire qch ◆ **they voted in ~ of accepting the pay offer** ils ont voté en faveur de la proposition de salaire

5 *(NonC = partiality)* faveur *f*, indulgence *f* ◆ **to show ~ to sb** accorder un traitement de faveur à qn, favoriser qn ; → **curry², fear**

6 *(= ribbon, token)* faveur *f*

VT *[+ political party, scheme, suggestion]* être partisan de ; *[+ undertaking]* favoriser, appuyer ; *[+ person]* préférer ; *[+ candidate, pupil]* montrer une préférence pour ; *[+ team, horse]* être pour ; *(† or dial = resemble)* ressembler à ◆ **I don't ~ the idea** je ne suis pas partisan de cette idée ◆ **he ~ed us with a visit** il a eu l'amabilité *or* la bonté de nous rendre visite ◆ **he did not ~ us with a reply** *(iro)* il n'a même pas eu l'amabilité *or* la bonté de nous répondre ◆ **the weather ~ed the journey** le temps a favorisé le voyage ◆ **circumstances that ~ this scheme** circonstances *fpl* favorables à ce projet ◆ **tax cuts which ~ the rich** des réductions d'impôts qui avantagent *or* favorisent les riches

favourable, favorable (US) /ˈfeɪvərəbl/ LANGUAGE IN USE 13 ADJ 1 *(= positive) [reaction, impression, opinion, report]* favorable ; *[comparison]* flatteur ◆ **to be ~ to sb/sth** être favorable à qn/qch ◆ **to show sth in a ~ light** montrer qch sous un jour favorable 2 *(= beneficial) [terms, deal]* avantageux *(for sb/sth* pour qn/ qch) ; *[position]* bon ; *[treatment] (gen)* bon ; *(= preferential)* de faveur 3 *[climate, weather, wind]* favorable *(for, to* à)

favourably, favorably (US) /ˈfeɪvərəblɪ/ ADV 1 *(= approvingly) [respond, react, receive]* favorablement ; *[look upon, consider]* d'un œil favorable ◆ **to impress sb ~** faire une impression favorable à qn ◆ **~ disposed** bien disposé 2 *(= advantageously) [placed]* bien ◆ **to compare ~ with sb/sth** soutenir la comparaison avec qn/ qch ◆ **he was always being compared ~ with his sister** on l'a toujours trouvé mieux que sa sœur ◆ **few would compare themselves ~ with him** peu de personnes se jugeraient meilleures que lui

favoured, favored (US) /ˈfeɪvəd/ ADJ favorisé ◆ **the ~ few** les élus *mpl* ◆ **most ~ nation clause** clause *f* de la nation la plus favorisée

favourite, favorite (US) /ˈfeɪvərɪt/ LANGUAGE IN USE 7.4 N *(gen)* favori(te) *m(f)*, préféré(e) *m(f)* ; *(at court, Racing)* favori(te) *m(f)* ◆ **he's his mother's ~** c'est le préféré de sa mère ◆ **he is a universal ~** tout le monde l'adore ◆ **that song is a great ~ of mine** cette chanson est une de mes préférées ◆ **he sang a lot of old ~s** il a chanté beaucoup de vieux succès ; → **hot** ADJ favori(te) *m(f)*, préféré ◆ **~ son** *(US) (Pol)* candidat à la présidence soutenu officiellement par son parti dans son État ; *(gen)* enfant *m* chéri *(de sa ville natale etc)*

favouritism, favoritism (US) /ˈfeɪvərɪtɪzəm/ N favoritisme *m*

fawn¹ /fɔːn/ N faon *m* ADJ *(= colour)* fauve

fawn² /fɔːn/ VI ◆ **to ~ (up)on sb** *[dog]* faire fête à qn ; *[person]* flatter qn (servilement), lécher les bottes de qn*

fawning /ˈfɔːnɪŋ/ ADJ *[person, manner]* servile, flagorneur ; *[dog]* trop démonstratif, trop affectueux

fax /fæks/ N *(= machine)* fax *m*, télécopieur *m* ; *(= transmission)* fax *m*, télécopie *f* ◆ **~ number** numéro *m* de fax *or* de télécopie ◆ **by ~** par fax *or* télécopie VT *[+ document]* faxer, envoyer par fax *or* par télécopie ; *[+ person]* envoyer un fax à ◆ **~ me your reply** répondez-moi par fax

fay /feɪ/ N *(†† or liter)* fée *f*

faze* /feɪz/ VT décontenancer ◆ **all that jargon didn't seem to ~ her in the least** elle n'a pas du tout eu l'air décontenancée par tout ce jargon

FBI /ˌefbiːˈaɪ/ N *(US)* (abbrev of **Federal Bureau of Investigation**) FBI *m*

FCC /ˌefsiːˈsiː/ N *(US)* (abbrev of **Federal Communications Commission**) → **federal**

FCO /ˌefsiːˈəʊ/ N *(Brit)* (abbrev of **Foreign and Commonwealth Office**) → **foreign**

FD /efˈdiː/ 1 *(US)* (abbrev of **Fire Department**) → **fire** 2 *(Brit)* (abbrev of **Fidei Defensor**) Défenseur *m* de la foi 3 *(Comm)* (abbrev of **free delivered at dock**) livraison *f* franco à quai

FDA /ˌefdiːˈeɪ/ N *(US)* (abbrev of **Food and Drug Administration**) FDA *f*

> **FDA**
>
> La **Food and Drug Administration** ou **FDA** est l'organisme qui a pour mission de tester l'innocuité des aliments, additifs alimentaires, médicaments et cosmétiques aux États-Unis, et de délivrer les autorisations de mise sur le marché.

FE /efˈiː/ N (abbrev of **Further Education**) → **further**

fealty /ˈfiːəltɪ/ N *(Hist)* fidélité *f*, allégeance *f*

fear /fɪəʳ/ LANGUAGE IN USE 6.2, 16.2

N 1 *(= fright)* peur *f* ; *(= worry, apprehension)* crainte *f* ◆ **he obeyed out of ~** il a obéi sous l'effet de la peur ◆ **I couldn't move from** *or* **for ~** j'étais paralysé de peur ◆ **a sudden ~ came over him** la peur s'est soudain emparée de lui ◆ **~ of death/failure/rejection** la peur de la mort/de l'échec/du rejet *or* d'être rejeté ◆ **~ of flying** la peur des voyages en avion *or* de l'avion ◆ **~ of heights** vertige *m* ◆ **grave ~s have arisen for the safety of the hostages** on est dans la plus vive inquiétude en ce qui concerne le sort des otages ◆ **there are ~s that ...** on craint que ... ne + *subj* ◆ **there are ~s that many more refugees will die** on craint que beaucoup d'autres réfugiés ne meurent ◆ **he has ~s for his sister's life** il craint pour la vie de sa sœur ◆ **to have a ~ of** avoir peur de ◆ **have no ~(s)** ne craignez rien, soyez sans crainte ◆ **without ~ or favour** impartialement, sans distinction de personnes ◆ **in ~ and trembling** en tremblant de peur

◆ **for fear of** de peur de ◆ **the authorities had closed the university for ~ of violence** les autorités avaient fermé l'université de peur d'incidents violents ◆ **for ~ of waking him** de peur de le réveiller

◆ **for fear (that ...)** de peur que ... ne + *subj* ◆ **for ~ that he might wake** de peur qu'il ne se réveille

♦ **in fear of** ♦ **to stand in ~ of sb/sth** craindre *or* redouter qn/qch ♦ **he lived in ~ of being discovered** il craignait toujours d'être découvert, il a vécu dans la peur d'être découvert ♦ **to go in ~ of one's life** craindre pour sa vie

2 *(NonC = awe)* crainte *f*, respect *m* ♦ **the ~ of God** la crainte *or* le respect de Dieu ♦ **to put the ~ of God into sb** * *(= frighten)* faire une peur bleue à qn ; *(= scold)* passer à qn une semonce *or* un savon * qu'il n'oubliera pas de si tôt

3 *(= risk, likelihood)* risque *m*, danger *m* ♦ **there's not much ~ of his coming** il est peu probable qu'il vienne, il ne risque guère de venir ♦ **there's not much ~ of us making that kind of money!** nous ne risquons pas de gagner des sommes pareilles ! ♦ **there's no ~ of that!** ça ne risque pas d'arriver ! ♦ **no ~!** * jamais de la vie !, pas de danger ! *

VT craindre, avoir peur de ♦ **to ~ the worst** redouter *or* craindre le pire ♦ **to ~ God** craindre Dieu ♦ **they ~ed being attacked again** ils craignaient d'être à nouveau attaqués ♦ **the man most ~ed by the people living here** l'homme le plus craint par ici ♦ **the loss of sovereignty ~ed by some** la perte de souveraineté que redoutent certains ♦ **the situation is less serious than first** *or* **originally ~ed** la situation est moins grave qu'on ne le craignait ♦ **minorities were ~ed and disliked** les minorités inspiraient crainte et antipathie ♦ **the ~ed secret police** la police secrète tant redoutée ♦ **300 are ~ed dead/drowned** 300 personnes seraient mortes/se seraient noyées ♦ **a policeman is missing, ~ed dead** un policier est porté disparu, probablement mort

♦ **to fear that ...** avoir peur que *or* craindre que ... (ne) + *subj* ♦ **many people ~ that there might be a war** beaucoup craignent *or* ont peur qu'il n'y ait une guerre ♦ **it is ~ed that the death toll may rise** on craint que le bilan ne s'alourdisse ♦ **they ~ed that a strike might destabilize the government** ils craignent qu'une grève ne déstabilise le gouvernement

♦ **to fear to do sth** avoir peur de faire qch ♦ **many women ~ to go out at night** beaucoup de femmes ont peur de sortir le soir

♦ **I fear ...** *(frm)* ♦ **I ~ I am late** *(apologizing)* je crois bien que je suis en retard, je suis désolé d'être en retard ♦ **I ~ he won't come** j'ai bien peur *or* je crains bien qu'il ne vienne pas ♦ **I ~ so** je crains que oui, hélas oui ♦ **I ~ not** je crains que non, hélas non ♦ **it's raining, I ~** il pleut, hélas

♦ **to be feared** *(= worthy of fear)* ♦ **he's a man to be ~ed** c'est un homme redoutable ♦ **such a man was not to be ~ed** il n'y avait rien à craindre de cet homme ♦ **there was nothing to be ~ed** il n'y avait rien à craindre

VI ♦ **to ~ for one's life** craindre pour sa vie ♦ **I ~ for him** j'ai peur *or* je tremble pour lui ♦ **he ~s for the future of the country** l'avenir du pays lui inspire des craintes *or* des inquiétudes ♦ **we ~ for their safety** nous craignons pour leur sécurité ♦ **never ~!** ne craignez rien !, n'ayez crainte ! ♦ **~ not!** (†, *hum*) n'ayez crainte !

fearful /ˈfɪəfʊl/ ADJ 1 *(= frightening) [spectacle, noise]* effrayant, affreux ; *[accident]* épouvantable 2 († *= extreme*) affreux ♦ **it really is a ~ nuisance** c'est vraiment empoisonnant * *or* embêtant * ♦ **she's a ~ bore** Dieu ! qu'elle est *or* peut être ennuyeuse ! 3 *(= timid) [person]* peureux, craintif ♦ **I was ~ of waking her** je craignais de la réveiller

fearfully /ˈfɪəfəlɪ/ ADV 1 *(= timidly) [say, ask]* craintivement 2 († *= extremely*) *[expensive, hot]* affreusement, terriblement ♦ **she's ~ ugly** elle est laide à faire peur

fearfulness /ˈfɪəfʊlnɪs/ N *(= fear)* crainte *f*, appréhension *f* ; *(= shyness)* extrême timidité *f*

fearless /ˈfɪəlɪs/ ADJ intrépide, courageux ♦ **~ of** *(liter)* sans peur *or* appréhension de

fearlessly /ˈfɪəlɪslɪ/ ADV *[fight]* courageusement ♦ **to be ~ outspoken** avoir le courage de ses opinions

fearlessness /ˈfɪəlɪsnɪs/ N intrépidité *f*

fearsome /ˈfɪəsəm/ ADJ *[opponent]* redoutable ; *[apparition]* terrible, effroyable

fearsomely /ˈfɪəsəmlɪ/ ADV effroyablement, affreusement

feasibility /ˌfiːzəˈbɪlɪtɪ/ N 1 *(= practicability) [of plan, suggestion]* faisabilité *f* ♦ **~ of doing sth** possibilité *f* de faire qch ♦ **to doubt the ~ of a scheme** douter qu'un plan soit réalisable 2 *(= plausibility) [of story, report]* vraisemblance *f*, plausibilité *f* COMP **feasibility study** N étude *f* de faisabilité

feasible /ˈfiːzəbl/ ADJ 1 *(= practicable) [plan, suggestion]* faisable, possible ♦ **can we do it? – yes, it's quite ~** pouvons-nous le faire ? – oui, c'est tout à fait possible *or* faisable ♦ **it would be ~ to put all the data on one disk** il serait possible de rassembler toutes les données sur une seule disquette ♦ **it was not economically ~ to keep the school open** il n'était pas économiquement viable de maintenir ouverte cette école 2 *(= likely, probable) [story, theory]* plausible, vraisemblable

feasibly /ˈfiːzəblɪ/ ADV ♦ **he could ~ still be alive** il se pourrait bien qu'il soit encore vivant

feast /fiːst/ N 1 *(lit, fig)* festin *m*, banquet *m* ♦ **to be the spectre** *or* **ghost** *or* **skeleton at the ~** *(Brit)* jeter une ombre sur les réjouissances ♦ **it's ~ or famine** c'est l'abondance ou la famine 2 *(Rel)* fête *f* ♦ **~ day** (jour *m* de) fête *f* ♦ **the ~ of St John** la Saint-Jean ♦ **the ~ of the Assumption** la fête de l'Assomption ; → **movable** VI banqueter, festoyer ♦ **to ~ on sth** *(lit)* se régaler de qch ; *(fig)* se délecter de qch VT († *or liter*) *[+ guest]* fêter, régaler ♦ **to ~ o.s.** se régaler ♦ **to ~ one's eyes on** repaître ses yeux de, se délecter à regarder

feat /fiːt/ N exploit *m*, prouesse *f* ♦ **~ of architecture** *etc* chef-d'œuvre *m or* triomphe *m* de l'architecture *etc* ♦ **~ of arms** fait *m* d'armes ♦ **~ of skill** tour *m* d'adresse ♦ **getting him to speak was quite a ~** cela a été un tour de force *or* un exploit de (réussir à) le faire parler

feather /ˈfeðəʳ/ N plume *f* ; *[of wing, tail]* penne *f* ♦ **the scholarship was a ~ in his cap** il pouvait être fier d'avoir obtenu la bourse ♦ **you could have knocked me down** *or* **over with a ~!** * les bras m'en sont tombés, j'en suis resté baba * *inv* ; → **bird, light², white**

VT 1 *[+ arrow etc]* empenner ♦ **to ~ one's nest** *(fig)* faire sa pelote ♦ **to ~ one's nest at sb's expense** s'engraisser sur le dos de qn

2 *[+ propeller]* mettre en drapeau ♦ **to ~ an oar** *(Rowing)* plumer

COMP *[mattress etc]* de plumes ; *[headdress]* à plumes

feather bed N lit *m* de plume(s) ; (* *= sinecure*) sinécure *f*, bonne planque * *f*

feather-bed VT *(fig) [+ person, project]* surprotéger ; *[+ child]* élever dans du coton ; *[+ workforce]* protéger *(afin de lutter contre les licenciements économiques)*

feather boa N boa *m* (de plumes)

feather cut N *(Hairdressing)* dégradé *m* court

feather duster N plumeau *m*

feather-edged ADJ en biseau

featherbedding /ˈfeðəbedɪŋ/ N *(Ind)* protection *f* excessive de la main-d'œuvre

featherbrain /ˈfeðəbreɪn/ N écervelé(e) *m(f)*

featherbrained /ˈfeðəbreɪnd/ ADJ écervelé

feathered /ˈfeðəd/ ADJ *[bird]* à plumes ♦ **our ~ friends** nos amis à plumes

featheredge /ˈfeðəredʒ/ N *(Carpentry)* biseau *m*

feathering /ˈfeðərɪŋ/ N plumage *m*, plumes *fpl*

featherweight /ˈfeðəweɪt/ *(Boxing)* N poids *m* plume *inv* ADJ *[championship etc]* poids plume *inv*

feathery /ˈfeðərɪ/ ADJ *[texture, feel]* duveteux, doux (douce *f*) comme la plume ; *[mark, design]* plumeté

feature /ˈfiːtʃəʳ/ N 1 *(facial)* trait *m* (du visage) ♦ **the ~s** la physionomie ♦ **to have delicate ~s** avoir les traits fins

2 *[of person] (physical)* trait *m* ; *[of personality]* caractéristique *f* ; *[of machine, countryside, building]* caractéristique *f*, particularité *f* ♦ **her most striking ~ is her hair** le plus remarquable, c'est ses cheveux ♦ **one of his most outstanding ~s is his patience** une de ses caractéristiques les plus remarquables est sa patience ♦ **one of the main ~s in the kidnapping story was ...** un des éléments les plus frappants dans l'affaire du kidnapping a été ... ♦ **scepticism is a ~ of our age** le scepticisme est caractéristique de notre temps ♦ **personal attacks have been a ~ of these elections** ces élections ont été marquées par une série d'attaques personnelles

3 *(Cine)* grand film *m*, long métrage *m* ; *(Press) [of column]* chronique *f* ♦ **this cartoon is a regular ~ in "The Observer"** cette bande dessinée paraît régulièrement dans "The Observer"

4 *(Ling)* (also **distinctive feature**) trait *m* distinctif

VT 1 *(= give prominence to) [+ person, event, story]* mettre en vedette ; *[+ name, news]* faire figurer ♦ **this film ~s an English actress** ce film a pour vedette une actrice anglaise ♦ **a film featuring John Wayne** un film avec John Wayne ♦ **the murder was ~d on the front page** le meurtre était à la une ♦ **a new album featuring their latest hit single** un nouvel album où figure leur dernier tube *

2 *(= depict)* représenter

3 *(= have as one of its features) [machine etc]* être doté *or* équipé de

VI 1 *(Cine)* jouer (*in* dans)

2 *(gen)* figurer ♦ **fish often ~s on the menu** le poisson figure souvent au menu ♦ **the story ~d on all of today's front pages** cette histoire faisait aujourd'hui la une de tous les journaux

COMP **feature article** N *(Press)* article *m* de fond

feature(-length) film N *(Cine)* long métrage *m*

feature story N ⇒ **feature article**

feature writer N *(Press)* journaliste *mf*

-featured /ˈfiːtʃəd/ ADJ *(in compounds)* ♦ **delicate/heavy-featured** aux traits délicats/lourds

featureless /ˈfiːtʃəlɪs/ ADJ *[landscape, building]* monotone

Feb. abbrev of **February**

febrifuge /ˈfebrɪfjuːdʒ/ ADJ, N fébrifuge *m*

febrile /ˈfiːbraɪl/ ADJ fébrile, fiévreux

February /ˈfebrʊərɪ/ N février *m* ; *for phrases see* **September**

fecal /ˈfiːkəl/ ADJ *(US)* ⇒ **faecal**

feces /ˈfiːsiːz/ NPL *(US)* ⇒ **faeces**

feckless /ˈfeklɪs/ ADJ *[person]* inepte, incapable ; *[attempt]* maladroit ♦ **a ~ girl** une tête sans cervelle, une évaporée

fecund /ˈfiːkənd/ ADJ fécond

fecundity /fɪˈkʌndɪtɪ/ N fécondité *f*

Fed /fed/ ABBR *(esp US)* abbrev of **Federal, Federated** *and* **Federation** N 1 *(US* *)* (abbrev of **federal officer**) agent *m or* fonctionnaire *m* fédéral 2 *(US)* (abbrev of **Federal Reserve Bank**) → **federal**

fed /fed/ VB (pret, ptp **feed**) ♦ **well ~** bien nourri COMP **fed up** * ADJ ♦ **to be ~ up** en avoir assez, en avoir marre * ♦ **I'm ~ up waiting for him** j'en ai marre * de l'attendre ♦ **he got ~ up with it** il en a eu assez, il en a eu marre * ♦ **to be ~ up**

to the back teeth* en avoir ras le bol* *(with doing sth de faire qch)*

fedayee /fəˈdɑːjiː/ **N** (pl **fedayeen**) fedayin *m inv*

federal /ˈfedərəl/ **ADJ** fédéral

N *(US Hist)* fédéral *m*, nordiste *m*

COMP Federal Aviation Administration N *(US)* Direction *f* générale de l'aviation civile

Federal Bureau of Investigation N *(US)* FBI *m*

Federal Communications Commission N *(US Admin)* ≈ Conseil *m* supérieur de l'audiovisuel

Federal court N *(US Jur)* cour *f* fédérale

federal crop insurance N *(US) système fédéral d'indemnisation des agriculteurs en cas de catastrophe naturelle*

federal holiday N *(US)* jour *m* férié

Federal Housing Administration N *(US)* commission *f* de contrôle des prêts au logement

Federal Insurance Contributions Act N *(US) (= law) loi sur les cotisations de Sécurité sociale* ; *(= contribution)* ≈ cotisations *fpl* de Sécurité sociale

federal land bank N *(US Fin)* banque *f* fédérale agricole

Federal Maritime Board N *(US)* Conseil *m* supérieur de la Marine marchande

Federal Republic of Germany N Allemagne *f* fédérale, République *f* fédérale d'Allemagne

Federal Reserve Bank N Federal Reserve Bank *f*

federalism /ˈfedərəlɪzəm/ **N** fédéralisme *m*

federalist /ˈfedərəlɪst/ **ADJ, N** fédéraliste *mf*

federate /ˈfedəreɪt/ **VT** fédérer **VI** se fédérer **ADJ** /ˈfedərɪt/ fédéré

federation /ˌfedəˈreɪʃən/ **N** fédération *f*

federative /ˈfedərətɪv/ **ADJ** fédératif ♦ **the Federative Republic of ...** la République fédérative de ...

fedora /fəˈdɔːrə/ **N** chapeau *m* mou, feutre *m* mou

fee /fiː/ **N** *[of doctor, lawyer]* honoraires *mpl* ; *[of artist, speaker, footballer]* cachet *m* ; *[of director, administrator]* jetons *mpl* de présence ; *[of private tutor]* appointements *mpl* ; *(Scol, Univ etc) (for tuition)* frais *mpl* de scolarité ; *(for examination)* droits *mpl* ; *(for board)* prix *m* de la pension ♦ **what's his ~?** combien prend-il ? ♦ **is there a ~?** est-ce qu'il faut payer ? ♦ **you can borrow more books for a small ~** *or* **on payment of a small ~** contre une somme modique vous pouvez emprunter d'autres livres ♦ **~ or other charges** *(Jur)* redevances *fpl* ou autres droits ♦ **~ for appeal** *(Jur)* taxe *f* de recours ; → **entrance¹, licence, membership COMP fee-paying ADJ** *[pupil]* qui paie ses études ; *[school]* privé

fee-splitting N *(US: gen)* partage *m* des honoraires ; *[of doctors]* dichotomie *f*

feeble /ˈfiːbl/ **ADJ** 1 *(= weak) [person, light, voice]* faible 2 *(pej = pathetic) [excuse, response]* piètre ; *[attempt]* vague ; *[joke]* médiocre ♦ **don't be so ~!** quelle mauviette tu fais !

COMP feeble-minded ADJ imbécile

feeble-mindedness N imbécillité *f*

feebleness /ˈfiːblnɪs/ **N** *[of person, pulse, light, voice]* faiblesse *f*

feebly /ˈfiːblɪ/ **ADV** *[smile, shine]* faiblement ; *[say, explain]* sans grande conviction

feed /fiːd/ (vb : pret, ptp **fed**) **N** 1 *(NonC, gen)* nourriture *f* ; *(= pasture)* pâture *f* ; *(= hay etc)* fourrage *m* ♦ **animal/cattle/chicken** *etc* **~** nourriture *f or* aliments *mpl* pour animaux/bétail/volailles *etc* ♦ **he's off his ~*** *[baby]* il n'a pas d'appétit

2 *(= portion of food)* ration *f* ; *[of baby] (breast-fed)* tétée *f* ; *(bottle-fed)* biberon *m* ; *(solid)* repas *m* ♦ **we had a good ~*** on a bien bouffé*

3 *(Theat * = comedian's cue line)* réplique *f* ; *(= straight man)* faire-valoir *m inv*

4 *(= part of machine)* mécanisme *m* d'alimentation ♦ **sheet paper ~** *(Comput)* chargeur *m* feuille à feuille

VT 1 *(= provide food for) (gen)* nourrir ; *[+ army]* nourrir, ravitailler ; *(= give food to) [+ child, invalid, animal]* donner à manger à ; *(Brit) [+ baby]* nourrir ; *[+ baby bird]* donner la becquée à ♦ **there are six people/mouths to ~ in this house** il y a six personnes/bouches à nourrir dans cette maison ♦ **I have three hungry mouths to ~** j'ai trois bouches à nourrir ♦ **what do you ~ your cat on?** que donnez-vous à manger à votre chat ? ♦ **he can ~ himself now** *[child]* il sait manger tout seul maintenant ♦ **to ~ sth to sb** donner qch à manger à qn ♦ **you shouldn't ~ him that** vous ne devriez pas lui donner cela à manger

2 *[+ plant] [ground, sap etc]* nourrir ; *(with fertilizer, plant food)* donner de l'engrais à

3 *(fig)* **to ~ sb information** fournir des informations à qn ♦ **to ~ sb lies** raconter des mensonges à qn ♦ **we've fed him all the facts*** nous lui avons fourni toutes les données ♦ **to ~ sb a line*** essayer de faire avaler une histoire à qn ♦ **to ~ one's habit*/one's heroin habit*** se procurer sa drogue/son héroïne

4 *[+ fire]* entretenir, alimenter ; *[+ furnace, machine]* alimenter ♦ **two rivers ~ this reservoir** deux rivières alimentent ce réservoir ♦ **to ~ the parking meter*** rajouter une pièce dans le parcmètre ♦ **to ~ sth into a machine** mettre *or* introduire qch dans une machine ♦ **to ~ data into a computer** entrer des données dans un ordinateur ♦ **blood vessels that ~ blood to the brain** des vaisseaux sanguins qui irriguent le cerveau ; → **flame**

5 *(Theat *) [+ comedian]* donner la réplique à ; *(= prompt)* souffler à

VI *[animal]* manger, se nourrir ; *(on pasture)* paître, brouter ; *[baby]* manger ; *(at breast)* téter ♦ **to ~ on** *(lit, fig)* se nourrir de ♦ **nationalism ~s on old hatreds** le nationalisme se nourrit de vieilles haines

COMP feed grains NPL céréales *fpl* fourragères

► **feed back VT SEP** *[+ information, results]* donner (en retour)

► **feed in VT SEP** *[+ tape, wire]* introduire *(to dans)* ; *[+ facts, information]* fournir *(to à)*

► **feed up VT SEP** *[+ animal]* engraisser ; *[+ geese]* gaver ; *[+ person]* faire manger plus *or* davantage

ADJ ♦ **fed up *** → **fed**

feedback /ˈfiːdbæk/ **N** 1 *(gen)* réactions *fpl* ; *(Comm) (from questionnaire etc)* information *f* en retour, retour *m* d'information ♦ **I haven't had any ~ from him yet** je n'ai encore eu aucune réaction de sa part ♦ **to give sb ~ on sth** faire part à qn de ses réactions *or* impressions sur qch 2 *(Elec)* réaction *f* ; *(unwanted)* réaction *f* parasite ; *(Cybernetics)* rétroaction *f*, feed-back *m*

feedbag /ˈfiːdbæg/ **N** *[of livestock]* sac *m* de nourriture ; *(US = nosebag)* musette *f*

feeder /ˈfiːdəʳ/ **N** 1 *(= eater: person, animal)* mangeur *m*, -euse *f* ♦ **peonies are quite heavy ~s** *(= need water)* les pivoines ont besoin de beaucoup d'eau ; *(= need fertilizer)* les pivoines ont besoin de beaucoup d'engrais 2 *(= device) (for chickens)* mangeoire *f* automatique ; *(for cattle)* nourrisseur *m* automatique ; *(for machine)* chargeur *m* 3 *(Elec)* ligne *f* d'alimentation 4 *(Brit) (= bib)* bavoir *m* ; *(= bottle)* biberon *m*

COMP *[canal]* d'amenée ; *[railway]* secondaire ; *[road]* d'accès ; *[team, league]* servant de réservoir, jouant le rôle de réservoir

feeder primary (school) N *(Brit Scol) école primaire d'où sont issus les élèves d'un collège donné*

feeder stream N affluent *m*

feeding /ˈfiːdɪŋ/ **N** *(= food)* alimentation *f* ; *(= action of feeding animal)* nourrissage *m*

COMP feeding bottle N *(esp Brit)* biberon *m*

feeding frenzy N *(fig)* ♦ **the press was in a ~ frenzy** les organes de presse se sont déchaînés

feeding grounds NPL *(gen)* aire *f* de nourrissage ; *[of grazing animals]* pâtures *fpl*, pâturages *mpl*

feeding stuffs NPL nourriture *f or* aliments *mpl* (pour animaux)

feeding time N *[of baby] (breast-feeding)* heure *f* de la tétée ; *(bottle-feeding)* heure *f* du biberon ; *[of toddler]* heure *f* du repas ; *[of animal] (in zoo)* heure *f* de nourrir les animaux

feedpipe /ˈfiːdpaɪp/ **N** tuyau *m* d'amenée

feedstuffs /ˈfiːdstʌfs/ **NPL** nourriture *f or* aliments *mpl* (pour animaux)

feel /fiːl/

vb : pret, ptp felt

LANGUAGE IN USE 6.2, 8.4, 11.1

1 NOUN	3 INTRANSITIVE VERB
2 TRANSITIVE VERB	4 PHRASAL VERBS

1 - NOUN

1 [= texture] toucher *m* ♦ **to know sth by the ~ (of it)** reconnaître qch au toucher ♦ **the fabric has a papery ~** le grain de ce tissu ressemble à celui du papier

2 [= sensation] sensation *f* ♦ **she liked the ~ of the sun on her face** elle aimait sentir le soleil sur son visage ♦ **I don't like the ~ of wool against my skin** je n'aime pas le contact de la laine contre ma peau, je n'aime pas porter de la laine à même la peau

3 [= impression] ♦ **he wants to get the ~ of the factory** il veut se faire une impression générale de l'usine ♦ **you have to get the ~ of a new car** il faut se faire à une nouvelle voiture ♦ **the palms bring a Mediterranean ~ to the garden** les palmiers donnent un aspect méditerranéen au jardin ♦ **the room has a cosy ~** on se sent bien dans cette pièce ♦ **there's a nostalgic ~ to his music** il y a quelque chose de nostalgique dans sa musique ♦ **I don't like the ~ of it** ça ne me dit rien de bon *or* rien qui vaille

4 [= intuition] **to have a ~ for languages** être doué pour les langues ♦ **to have a ~ for English** être doué en anglais ♦ **to have a ~ for music** avoir l'oreille musicale ♦ **to have a ~ for doing sth** savoir s'y prendre pour faire qch

2 - TRANSITIVE VERB

1 [= touch] toucher ; *(= explore with one's fingers)* palper ♦ **she felt the jacket to see if it was made of wool** elle a palpé *or* touché la veste pour voir si c'était de la laine ♦ **~ the envelope and see if there's anything in it** palpez l'enveloppe pour voir s'il y a quelque chose dedans ♦ **to ~ sb's pulse** tâter le pouls de qn

♦ **to feel one's way** *(lit)* avancer *or* marcher à tâtons ♦ **he got out of bed and felt his way to the telephone** il s'est levé et a avancé *or* marché à tâtons jusqu'au téléphone ♦ **you'll have to ~ your way** *(fig)* il faut y aller à tâtons ♦ **we are ~ing our way towards an agreement** nous tâtons le terrain pour parvenir à un accord ♦ **I'm still ~ing my way around** *(fig)* j'essaie de m'y retrouver ♦ **she's still ~ing her way in her new job** elle n'est pas encore complètement habituée à son nouveau travail, elle est encore en train de se familiariser avec son nouveau travail

2 [= experience physically] *[+ blow, caress]* sentir ; *[+ pain]* sentir, ressentir ♦ **I felt a few drops of rain** j'ai senti quelques gouttes de pluie ♦ **I'm**

so cold I can't ~ anything j'ai si froid que je ne sens plus rien ◆ **she could ~ the heat from the radiator** elle sentait la chaleur du radiateur ; see also **3** ◆ **I can ~ something pricking me** je sens quelque chose qui me pique ◆ **he felt it move** il l'a senti bouger

3 [= be affected by, suffer from] ◆ **to ~ the heat/cold** être sensible à la chaleur/au froid ◆ **I don't ~ the heat much** la chaleur ne me gêne pas beaucoup ◆ **she really ~s the cold** elle est très frileuse ◆ **she felt the loss of her father greatly** elle a été très affectée par la mort de son père

4 [= experience emotionally] *[+ sympathy, grief]* éprouver, ressentir ◆ **you must ~ the beauty of this music before you can play it** il faut que vous sentiez *subj* la beauté de cette musique avant de pouvoir la jouer vous-même ◆ **the effects will be felt later** les effets se feront sentir plus tard ◆ **he felt a great sense of relief** il a éprouvé *or* ressenti un grand soulagement ◆ **I ~ no interest in this at all** cela ne m'intéresse pas du tout ◆ **they're starting to ~ the importance of this match** ils commencent à prendre conscience de l'importance de ce match ◆ **I felt myself blush** *or* **blushing** je me suis senti rougir

5 [= think, believe] ◆ **I ~ he has spoilt everything** à mon avis, il a tout gâché ◆ **I ~ that he ought to go** j'estime qu'il devrait partir ◆ **he felt it necessary to point out ...** il a jugé *or* estimé nécessaire de faire remarquer ... ◆ **I ~ strongly that ...** je suis convaincu que ... ◆ **if you ~ strongly about it** si cela vous tient à cœur, si cela vous semble important ◆ **what do you ~ about this idea?** que pensez-vous de cette idée ? ◆ **I can't help ~ing that something is wrong** je ne peux m'empêcher de penser que quelque chose ne va pas ◆ **I ~ it in my bones*** *or* **waters**⁑ **that Scotland will score** l'Écosse va marquer, je le sens !, quelque chose me dit que l'Écosse va marquer

3 - INTRANSITIVE VERB

1 [physically] se sentir ◆ **how do you ~ today?** comment vous sentez-vous aujourd'hui ? ◆ **I ~ much better** je me sens beaucoup mieux ◆ **you'll ~ all the better for a rest** vous vous sentirez mieux après vous être reposé ◆ **he doesn't ~ quite himself today** il ne se sent pas tout à fait dans son assiette aujourd'hui ◆ **to ~ old/ill** se sentir vieux/malade ◆ **to ~ cold/hot/hungry/thirsty/sleepy** avoir froid/chaud/faim/soif/sommeil ◆ **he felt like a young man again** il se sentait redevenu jeune homme ◆ **I ~ like a new man/woman** je me sens un autre homme/une autre femme

2 [emotionally, intellectually] **I couldn't help ~ing envious** je ne pouvais pas m'empêcher d'éprouver de la jalousie ◆ **I ~ sure that ...** je suis sûr que ... ◆ **they don't ~ able to recommend him** ils estiment qu'ils ne peuvent pas le recommander ◆ **he ~s confident of success** il s'estime capable de réussir ◆ **we felt very touched by his remarks** nous avons été très touchés par ses remarques ◆ **I don't ~ ready to see her again yet** je ne me sens pas encore prêt à la revoir ◆ **I ~ very bad about leaving you here** cela m'ennuie beaucoup de vous laisser ici ◆ **how do you ~ about him?** que pensez-vous de lui ? ◆ **what does it ~ like** *or* **how does it ~ to know that you are a success?** quel effet cela vous fait-il de savoir que vous avez réussi ?

♦ **to feel for sb** compatir aux malheurs de qn ◆ **we ~ for you in your sorrow** nous partageons votre douleur ◆ **I ~ for you!** comme je vous comprends !

♦ **to feel like sth/doing sth** (= *want*) avoir envie de qch/de faire qch ◆ **I ~ like an ice cream** j'ai envie d'une glace ◆ **do you ~ like a walk?** ça vous dit d'aller vous promener ? ◆ **if you ~ like it** si ça te dit ◆ **I don't ~ like it** je n'en ai pas envie, ça ne me dit rien

3 [= have impression] ◆ **I felt as if I was going to faint** j'avais l'impression que j'allais m'évanouir ◆ **I ~ as if there's nothing we can do** j'ai le sentiment *or* j'ai bien l'impression que nous ne pouvons rien faire

4 [= give impression] **to ~ hard/soft** *[object]* être dur/doux au toucher ◆ **the house ~s damp** la maison donne l'impression d'être humide ◆ **his shirt ~s as if it's made of silk** on dirait que sa chemise est en soie (quand on la touche) ◆ **we were going so fast it felt as if we were flying** on allait si vite qu'on avait l'impression de voler ◆ **it ~s like rain** on dirait qu'il va pleuvoir ◆ **it ~s like thunder** on dirait qu'il va y avoir de l'orage

5 [= grope] (also **feel about, feel around**) tâtonner, fouiller ◆ **she felt (about** *or* **around) in her pocket for some change** elle a fouillé dans sa poche pour trouver de la monnaie ◆ **he was ~ing (about** *or* **around) in the dark for the door** il tâtonnait dans le noir pour trouver la porte

4 - PHRASAL VERBS

► **feel out*** VT SEP *[+ person]* sonder, tâter le terrain auprès de

► **feel up**⁑ VT SEP ◆ **to feel sb up** peloter* qn

feeler /ˈfiːləʳ/ N *[of insect]* antenne *f* ; *[of octopus]* tentacule *m* ◆ **to put out** *or* **throw out ~s (to discover)** tâter le terrain (pour essayer de découvrir) COMP **feeler gauge** N *(Tech)* calibre *m* (d'épaisseur)

feelgood /ˈfiːlgʊd/ ADJ ◆ **the ~ factor** *(Pol)* l'euphorie *f* passagère ◆ **the lack of a ~ factor among customers** l'érosion de la confiance des consommateurs ◆ **a ~ movie** un film qui met de bonne humeur

feeling /ˈfiːlɪŋ/ LANGUAGE IN USE 6.2 N 1 *(NonC: physical)* sensation *f* ◆ **I've lost all ~ in my right arm** j'ai perdu toute sensation dans le bras droit, mon bras droit ne sent plus rien ◆ **a ~ of cold, a cold ~** une sensation de froid

2 *(= awareness, impression)* sentiment *m* ◆ **a ~ of isolation** un sentiment d'isolement ◆ **he had the ~ (that) something terrible was going to happen to him** il avait le sentiment qu'il allait lui arriver quelque chose de terrible ◆ **I've got a funny ~ she will succeed** j'ai comme l'impression qu'elle va réussir ◆ **I know the ~!** je sais ce que c'est *or* ce que ça fait ! ◆ **the ~ of the meeting was that ...** dans l'ensemble, les participants (à la réunion) pensaient que ... ◆ **there was a general ~ that ...** on avait l'impression que ..., le sentiment général a été que ... ; → **strong**

3 *(= emotion)* sentiment *m* ◆ **~s** sentiments *mpl*, sensibilité *f* ◆ **he appealed to their ~s rather than their reason** il faisait appel à leurs sentiments plutôt qu'à leur raison ◆ **you can imagine my ~s** tu t'imagines ce que je ressens (*or* j'ai ressenti *etc*) ◆ **~s ran high about the new motorway** la nouvelle autoroute a déchaîné les passions ◆ **his ~s were hurt** il était blessé ◆ **I didn't mean to hurt your ~s** je ne voulais pas te blesser *or* te vexer ◆ **to have ~s for sb** avoir des sentiments pour qn ; → **hard**

4 *(NonC) (= sensitivity)* émotion *f*, sensibilité *f* ; *(= compassion)* sympathie *f* ◆ **she sang with ~** elle a chanté avec sentiment ◆ **he spoke with great ~** il a parlé avec chaleur *or* avec émotion ◆ **he doesn't show much ~ for his sister** il ne fait pas preuve de beaucoup de sympathie pour sa sœur ◆ **he has no ~ for the suffering of others** les souffrances d'autrui le laissent insensible ◆ **he has no ~ for music** il n'apprécie pas du tout la musique ◆ **he has a certain ~ for music** il est assez sensible à la musique ◆ **ill** *or* **bad ~** animosité *f*, hostilité *f*

feelingly /ˈfiːlɪŋlɪ/ ADV *[speak, write]* avec émotion, avec chaleur

feet /fiːt/ NPL of **foot**

feign /feɪn/ VT *[+ surprise]* feindre ; *[+ madness]* simuler ◆ **to ~ illness/sleep** faire semblant d'être malade/de dormir ◆ **~ed modesty** fausse modestie *f*, modestie *f* feinte

feint /feɪnt/ N *(Boxing, Fencing, Mil)* feinte *f* ◆ **to make a ~** faire une feinte (*at* à) VI feinter COMP **feint-ruled paper** N papier *m* à réglure fine

feist* /faɪst/ N *(US)* roquet *m (chien)*

feisty* /ˈfaɪstɪ/ ADJ 1 *(= lively)* fougueux 2 *(US = quarrelsome)* bagarreur*

feldspar /ˈfeldspɑːʳ/ N ⇒ **felspar**

felicitate /fɪˈlɪsɪteɪt/ VT *(frm)* féliciter, congratuler

felicitous /fɪˈlɪsɪtəs/ ADJ *(frm)* heureux

felicity /fɪˈlɪsɪtɪ/ N *(frm) (= happiness)* félicité *f*, bonheur *m* ; *(= aptness)* bonheur *m*

feline /ˈfiːlaɪn/ ADJ, N félin(e) *m(f)*

fell¹ /fel/ VB pt of **fall**

fell² /fel/ VT *[+ tree, enemy]* abattre ; *[+ ox]* assommer, abattre

fell³ /fel/ N *(Brit) (= mountain)* montagne *f*, mont *m* ◆ **the ~s** *(= moorland)* la lande

fell⁴ /fel/ ADJ *(liter) [blow]* féroce, cruel ; *[disease]* cruel ; → **swoop**

fell⁵ /fel/ N *(= hide, pelt)* fourrure *f*, peau *f* (d'animal)

fella⁑ /ˈfelə/ N *(= chap)* type* *m* ; *(= boyfriend)* petit ami *m*

fellate /fɪˈleɪt/ VT faire une fellation à

fellatio /fɪˈleɪʃɪəʊ/, **fellation** /fɪˈleɪʃən/ N fellation *f* ◆ **to perform fellatio on sb** faire une fellation à qn

fellow /ˈfeləʊ/ N 1 * type* *m*, homme *m* ◆ **a nice ~** un brave type* ◆ **an old ~** un vieux (bonhomme) ◆ **a poor old ~** un pauvre vieux ◆ **poor little ~** pauvre petit *m* (bonhomme *m or* gars *m*) ◆ **a young ~** un jeune homme ◆ **my dear** *or* **good ~** † mon cher ◆ **look here, old ~** † écoute, mon vieux ◆ **this journalist ~** un journaliste

2 *(= comrade)* camarade *m*, compagnon *m* ; *(= equal, peer)* pair *m*, semblable *m* ◆ **~s in misfortune** frères *mpl* dans le malheur, compagnons *mpl* d'infortune ; → **schoolfellow**

3 *[of association, society etc]* membre *m*, associé *m (d'une société savante, d'une académie)*

4 *(US Univ)* boursier *m*, -ière *f* ; *(Brit Univ)* ≈ chargé *m* de cours *(souvent membre du conseil d'administration)* ; → **research**

COMP **fellow being** N semblable *mf*, pareil(le) *m(f)*
fellow citizen N concitoyen(ne) *m(f)*
fellow countryman (pl **fellow countrymen**), **fellow countrywoman** (pl **fellow countrywomen**) N compatriote *mf*
fellow creature N semblable *mf*, pareil(le) *m(f)*
fellow feeling N sympathie *f*
fellow inmate N codétenu(e) *m(f)*
fellow member N confrère *m*, consœur *f*
fellow men NPL semblables *mpl*
fellow passenger N compagnon *m* de voyage, compagne *f* de voyage
fellow student N condisciple *mf*
fellow traveller N *(lit)* compagnon *m* de voyage, compagne *f* de voyage ; *(Pol) (with communists)* communisant(e) *m(f)*, cryptocommuniste *mf* ; *(gen)* sympathisant(e) *m(f)*
fellow worker N *(in office)* collègue *mf* ; *(in factory)* camarade *mf* (de travail)

fellowship /ˈfeləʊʃɪp/ **N** 1 (NonC) (= *comradeship*) camaraderie *f* ; (*Rel etc*) communion *f* 2 (= *society etc*) association *f*, corporation *f* ; (*Rel*) confrérie *f* 3 (= *membership of learned society*) titre *m* de membre *or* d'associé (*d'une société savante*) 4 (*US Univ* = *scholarship*) bourse *f* universitaire ; (*Brit Univ* = *post*) poste *m* d'enseignement et de recherche ; see also **fellow noun 4**

felon /ˈfelən/ **N** (*Jur*) criminel(le) *m(f)*

felonious /fɪˈləʊnɪəs/ **ADJ** (*Jur*) criminel

felony /ˈfelənɪ/ **N** (*Jur*) crime *m*, forfait *m*

felspar /ˈfelspɑːʳ/ **N** feldspath *m*

felt¹ /felt/ **VB** pt, ptp of **feel**

felt² /felt/ **N** feutre *m* ; → **roofing**
COMP de feutre
felt hat **N** feutre *m* (*chapeau*)
felt-tip (pen) **N** feutre *m* (*crayon*)

fem * /fem/ **N** ⇒ **femme 2**

fem. /fem/ 1 abbrev of **female** 2 abbrev of **feminine**

female /ˈfiːmeɪl/ **ADJ** 1 (= *of feminine gender*) [*animal, plant*] femelle ; [*subject, slave*] du sexe féminin ◆ **a ~ child** une fille, un enfant du sexe féminin ◆ **~ students** étudiantes *fpl* ◆ **~ labour** main-d'œuvre *f* féminine ◆ **~ cat/camel** chatte *f*/chamelle *f* 2 (= *relating to women*) [*company, vote*] des femmes ; [*sex, character, quality, organs, health problems*] féminin 3 (*Elec*) femelle **N** (= *person*) femme *f*, fille *f* ; (= *animal, plant*) femelle *f* ◆ **some ~ he works with** * (*pej*) une bonne femme avec qui il bosse * (*pej*)
COMP **female circumcision** **N** excision *f*
female condom **N** préservatif *m* féminin
female impersonator **N** (*Theat*) travesti *m*

Femidom ® /ˈfemɪdɒm/ **N** Femidom ® *m*

feminine /ˈfemɪnɪn/ **ADJ** (*also Gram*) féminin **N** (*Gram*) féminin *m* ◆ **in the ~** au féminin **COMP** **feminine hygiene** **N** hygiène *f* féminine

femininity /ˌfemɪˈnɪnɪtɪ/ **N** féminité *f*

feminism /ˈfemɪnɪzəm/ **N** féminisme *m*

feminist /ˈfemɪnɪst/ **N, ADJ** féministe *mf*

feminize /ˈfemɪnaɪz/ **VT** féminiser

femme /fæm, fem/ **N** 1 ◆ **~ fatale** femme *f* fatale 2 * partenaire *f* passive (*dans un couple de lesbiennes*)

femoral /ˈfemərəl/ **ADJ** fémoral

femur /ˈfiːməʳ/ **N** (pl **femurs** *or* **femora** /ˈfemərə/) fémur *m*

fen /fen/ **N** (*Brit*) (also **fenland**) marais *m*, marécage *m* ◆ **the Fens** les plaines *fpl* marécageuses du Norfolk

fence /fens/ **N** 1 barrière *f*, clôture *f* ; (*Racing*) obstacle *m* ◆ **to sit on the ~** (*fig*) ménager la chèvre et le chou, s'abstenir de prendre position ◆ **to mend one's ~s** * **with sb** se réconcilier avec qn ◆ **they're mending their ~s** * **(with each other)** ils sont en train de se réconcilier ; → **barbed**
2 (= *machine guard*) barrière *f* protectrice
3 * [*of stolen goods*] receleur *m*, fourgue * *m*
VT 1 (also **fence in**) [*+ land*] clôturer, entourer d'une clôture
2 [*+ question*] éluder
3 * [*+ stolen goods*] fourguer *, receler
VI (*Sport*) faire de l'escrime ; (*fig*) éluder la question, se dérober ◆ **to ~ with sword/sabre** *etc* (*Sport*) tirer à l'épée/au sabre *etc*
COMP **fence-mending** **N** (*esp Pol*) rétablissement *m* de bonnes relations, réconciliation *f* ◆ **~-mending mission** mission *f* de conciliation

► **fence in** **VT SEP** 1 (*lit*) ⇒ **fence vt 1**
2 (*fig*) **to feel ~d in by restrictions** se sentir gêné *or* entravé par des restrictions

► **fence off** **VT SEP** [*+ piece of land*] séparer par une clôture

fenced /fenst/ **ADJ** [*of field, garden*] clôturé ◆ **a ~ area** *or* **enclosure** un enclos

fencer /ˈfensəʳ/ **N** escrimeur *m*, -euse *f*

fencing /ˈfensɪŋ/ **N** 1 (*Sport*) escrime *f* 2 (*for making fences*) matériaux *mpl* pour clôture
COMP **fencing master** **N** maître *m* d'armes
fencing match **N** assaut *m* d'escrime ; (*fig*) prise *f* de bec
fencing school **N** salle *f* d'armes

fend /fend/ **VI** ◆ **to ~ for o.s.** se débrouiller (tout seul)

► **fend off** **VT SEP** [*+ blow*] parer ; [*+ attack*] détourner ; [*+ attacker*] repousser ; [*+ question*] écarter, éluder

fender /ˈfendəʳ/ **N** (*in front of fire*) garde-feu *m inv* ; (*US: on car*) aile *f* ; (*US: on train*) chasse-pierres *m inv* ; (*Naut*) défense *f*, pare-battage *m inv* **COMP** **fender-bender** * **N** accrochage *m* ◆ **it was just a ~-bender** ce n'était qu'un accrochage *or* que de la tôle froissée *

fenestration /ˌfenɪsˈtreɪʃən/ **N** (*Archit*) fenêtrage *m* ; (*Med*) fenestration *f* ; (*Bot, Zool*) aspect *m* fenêtré

feng shui /ˌfeŋˈʃuːɪ/ **N** feng-shui *m*

Fenian /ˈfiːnɪən/ (*Brit Hist*) **N** 1 Fenian *m* (*membre d'un groupe révolutionnaire américain fondé en 1858 pour l'indépendance de l'Irlande*) 2 (*pej*, *) sale catho *mf* irlandais(e) (*pej*) **ADJ** 1 Fenian ◆ **the ~ defeat at Gabhra** la défaite des Fenians à Gabhra 2 (*pej*, *) catho *

fennel /ˈfenl/ **N** fenouil *m*

fenugreek /ˈfenjʊˌgriːk/ **N** fenugrec *m*

feral /ˈfɪərəl/ **ADJ** sauvage

ferment /fəˈment/ **VI** (*lit, fig*) fermenter **VT** (*lit, fig*) faire fermenter **N** /ˈfɜːment/ (*lit*) ferment *m* ; (*fig*) agitation *f*, effervescence *f* ◆ **to be in (a state of)** ~ être en ébullition

fermentation /ˌfɜːmenˈteɪʃən/ **N** (*lit, fig*) fermentation *f*

fermium /ˈfɜːmɪəm/ **N** fermium *m*

fern /fɜːn/ **N** fougère *f*

ferocious /fəˈrəʊʃəs/ **ADJ** 1 (= *fierce*) [*animal, person, battle, fighting*] féroce ; [*attack, assault*] violent ; [*knife, teeth*] redoutable 2 (= *intense*) [*competition*] acharné ; [*debate*] houleux ; [*argument*] violent ; [*energy*] farouche 3 (= *severe*) [*heat*] accablant ; [*weather, violent storm*] épouvantable ; [*thirst*] terrible

ferociously /fəˈrəʊʃəslɪ/ **ADV** 1 (= *violently*) [*beat, kick, struggle*] violemment ◆ **to fight ~** [*person*] se battre âprement ; [*animal*] se battre férocement *or* avec férocité 2 (= *extremely*) [*independent*] farouchement ; [*difficult, complicated*] furieusement ; [*clever, intelligent, funny*] terriblement ◆ **to be ~ competitive** avoir un esprit de compétition acharné ◆ **~ determined** d'une détermination farouche ◆ **~ loyal** d'une fidélité à toute épreuve

ferociousness /fəˈrəʊʃəsnɪs/, **ferocity** /fəˈrɒsɪtɪ/ **N** férocité *f*

Ferrara /fəˈrɑːrə/ **N** Ferrare

ferret /ˈferɪt/ **N** furet *m* **VI** 1 (also **ferret about, ferret around**) fouiller, fureter ◆ **she was ~ing (about *or* around) in the cupboard** elle furetait dans le placard 2 ◆ **to go ~ing** chasser au furet

► **ferret out** **VT SEP** [*+ secret, person*] dénicher, découvrir

ferric /ˈferɪk/ **ADJ** ferrique

Ferris wheel /ˈferɪswiːl/ **N** grande roue *f* (*dans une foire*)

ferrite /ˈferaɪt/ **N** ferrite *f*

ferro- /ˈferəʊ/ **PREF** ferro-

ferroconcrete /ˈferəʊˈkɒŋkriːt/ **N** béton *m* armé

ferrous /ˈferəs/ **ADJ** ferreux

ferrule /ˈferuːl/ **N** virole *f*

ferry /ˈferɪ/ **N** (also **ferryboat**) (*large*) ferry-boat *m* ; (*small*) bac *m* ; (*Can*) traversier *m* ; (*between ship and quayside*) va-et-vient *m inv* ; → **air, car**
VT 1 (also **ferry across, ferry over**) [*+ person, car, train*] faire passer *or* traverser (en bac *or* par bateau *or* par avion *etc*) 2 (*fig* = *transport*) [*+ people*] transporter, emmener ; [*+ things*] porter, apporter ◆ **he ferried voters to and from the polls** il a fait la navette avec sa voiture pour emmener les électeurs au bureau de vote ◆ **I can't be expected to ~ you around all the time** je ne peux tout de même pas te servir de taxi en permanence

ferryman /ˈferɪmən/ **N** (pl **-men**) passeur *m*

fertile /ˈfɜːtaɪl/ **ADJ** [*soil, land*] fertile ; [*person*] fertile, fécond ; [*animal, egg, mind*] fécond ◆ **the ~ period** *or* **time** la période de fécondité ◆ **to have a ~ imagination** (*gen pej*) avoir une imagination fertile ◆ **to be (a) ~ ground for sb/sth** (*fig*) être un terrain propice pour qn/qch
COMP **the Fertile Crescent** **N** le Croissant fertile

fertility /fəˈtɪlɪtɪ/ **N** [*of soil, land, man*] fertilité *f* ; [*of woman, animal*] fécondité *f*, fertilité *f* ◆ **~ of invention** (*frm*) fertilité *f* d'imagination
COMP [*cult, symbol*] de fertilité
fertility drug **N** médicament *m* contre la stérilité

fertilization /ˌfɜːtɪlaɪˈzeɪʃən/ **N** [*of land, soil*] fertilisation *f* ; [*of animal, plant, egg*] fécondation *f*

fertilize /ˈfɜːtɪlaɪz/ **VT** [*+ land, soil*] fertiliser, amender ; [*+ animal, plant, egg*] féconder

fertilizer /ˈfɜːtɪlaɪzəʳ/ **N** engrais *m*, fertilisant *m* ◆ **artificial ~** engrais *m* chimique

fervent /ˈfɜːvənt/ **ADJ** [*admirer, advocate, prayer*] fervent ; [*supporter, belief, desire*] ardent ◆ **to be a ~ believer in sth** être un adepte de qch ◆ **my ~ hope is that ...** je souhaite vraiment *or* ardemment que ... ◆ **it is my ~ wish that ...** je souhaite ardemment que ...

fervently /ˈfɜːvəntlɪ/ **ADV** [*hope, believe*] ardemment ; [*say, pray, support*] avec ferveur ; [*religious, anti-Communist*] profondément ◆ **~ opposed to sth** profondément opposé à qch ◆ **~ patriotic** d'un ardent patriotisme

fervid /ˈfɜːvɪd/ **ADJ** ⇒ **fervent**

fervour, fervor (*US*) /ˈfɜːvəʳ/ **N** ferveur *f*

fess up * /fesˈʌp/ **VI** (*esp US*) avouer ; [*criminal*] avouer, passer aux aveux

fest * /fest/ **N** 1 (= *festival*) ◆ **jazz/film ~** festival *m* de jazz/de cinéma 2 (= *extravaganza*) festival *m*, débauche *f* ◆ **gore ~** film *m* d'horreur (*où le sang coule à flots*)

fester /ˈfestəʳ/ **VI** [*cut, wound*] suppurer ; [*anger*] gronder ; [*resentment*] couver ◆ **resentments are starting to ~** le ressentiment couve

festival /ˈfestɪvəl/ **N** 1 (= *cultural event*) festival *m* ◆ **the Edinburgh Festival** le festival d'Édimbourg → EDINBURGH FESTIVAL 2 (= *religious event*) fête *f*

festive /ˈfestɪv/ **ADJ** [*food, decorations*] de fête ◆ **the ~ season** la période des fêtes ◆ **to be in a ~ mood** avoir envie de faire la fête ◆ **your house is looking very ~** (*for party, Christmas*) ta maison a vraiment un air de fête ◆ **there was little sign of festive cheer** ils n'avaient pas le cœur à la fête

festivity /fesˈtɪvɪtɪ/ **N** 1 (also **festivities**) fête *f*, réjouissances *fpl* ◆ **an air of ~** un air de fête 2 (= *festival*) fête *f*

festoon /fesˈtuːn/ **N** feston *m*, guirlande *f* **VT** (*Sewing*) festonner ; (= *bedeck*) orner ◆ **the town was ~ed with flags** il y avait des drapeaux partout dans la ville ◆ **the room was ~ed with**

flowers la pièce était ornée de fleurs ◆ **the pagoda was ~ed with lights** la pagode était décorée *or* ornée de lumières

feta /ˈfetə/ **N** (also **feta cheese**) feta *f*

fetal /ˈfiːtl/ **ADJ** *(US)* ⇒ **foetal**

fetch /fetʃ/ **VT** ① *(= go and get) [+ person, thing]* aller chercher ; *(= bring) [+ person]* amener ; *[+ thing]* apporter ◆ **~ (it)!** *(to dog)* rapporte !, va chercher ! ② *(= sell for) [+ money]* rapporter ◆ **they won't ~ much** ils ne rapporteront pas grand-chose ◆ **it ~ed a good price** ça a atteint un bon prix ③ *[+ blow]* flanquer* **VI** ① *(fig)* **to ~ and carry for sb** faire la bonne pour qn ② *(Naut)* manœuvrer **N** *(Naut)* fetch *m*

▸ **fetch in*** **VT SEP** *[+ person]* faire (r)entrer ; *[+ thing]* rentrer

▸ **fetch out*** **VT SEP** *[+ person]* faire sortir ; *[+ thing]* sortir *(of* de*)*

▸ **fetch up** **VI** * finir par arriver, se retrouver *(at* à ; *in* dans*)* **VT SEP** ① *[+ object]* apporter, monter ; *[+ person]* faire monter ② *(Brit * = vomit)* rendre, vomir

fetching* /ˈfetʃɪŋ/ **ADJ** *[person]* ravissant, charmant ; *[dress, hat]* seyant, ravissant

fetchingly /ˈfetʃɪŋlɪ/ **ADV** d'une façon charmante

fête /feɪt/ **N** *(Brit)* fête *f* ; *(for charity)* fête *f*, kermesse *f* ◆ **village ~** fête *f* de village **VT** *[+ person]* faire la fête à ; *[+ success, arrival]* fêter

fetid /ˈfetɪd/ **ADJ** fétide, puant

fetish /ˈfetɪʃ/ **N** fétiche *m* ; *(Psych)* objet *m* de fétichisation ◆ **she makes a real ~ of** *or* **has a real ~ about cleanliness** elle est obsédée par la propreté, c'est une maniaque de la propreté ◆ **to have a foot ~** être fétichiste du pied

fetishism /ˈfetɪʃɪzəm/ **N** fétichisme *m*

fetishist /ˈfetɪʃɪst/ **N** fétichiste *mf* ◆ **to be a silk/foot ~** être fétichiste de la soie/du pied

fetishistic /ˌfetɪˈʃɪstɪk/ **ADJ** fétichiste

fetishize /ˈfetɪʃaɪz/ **VT** *(frm)* fétichiser

fetlock /ˈfetlɒk/ **N** *(= joint)* boulet *m* ; *(= hair)* fanon *m*

fetoscope /ˈfiːtəʊˌskəʊp/ **N** fœtoscope *m*

fetoscopy /fiːˈtɒskəpɪ/ **N** fœtoscopie *f*

fetter /ˈfetəʳ/ **VT** *[+ person]* enchaîner, lier ; *[+ horse, slave]* entraver ; *(fig)* entraver **NPL** **fetters** *[of prisoner]* fers *mpl*, chaînes *fpl* ; *[of horse, slave] (fig)* entraves *fpl* ◆ **in ~s** dans les fers *or* les chaînes ◆ **to put a prisoner in ~s** mettre un prisonnier aux fers

fettle /ˈfetl/ **N** ◆ **in fine** *or* **good ~** en pleine forme

fettucine /ˌfetəˈtʃiːnɪ/ **N** *(NonC)* fettucine *fpl*

fetus /ˈfiːtəs/ **N** *(US)* ⇒ **foetus**

feu /fjuː/ **N** *(Scot Jur)* bail *m* perpétuel *(à redevance fixe)* **COMP** **feu duty** **N** loyer *m* (de la terre)

feud¹ /fjuːd/ **N** querelle *f (entre deux clans)*, vendetta *f* ◆ **family ~s** querelles *fpl* de famille **VI** se quereller, se disputer ◆ **to ~ with sb** être l'ennemi juré de qn, être à couteaux tirés avec qn

feud² /fjuːd/ **N** *(Hist)* fief *m*

feudal /ˈfjuːdl/ **ADJ** féodal ◆ **the ~ system** le système féodal

feudalism /ˈfjuːdəlɪzəm/ **N** *(Hist)* féodalité *f* ; *(fig) [of society, institution]* féodalisme *m*

fever /ˈfiːvəʳ/ **N** *(Med, fig)* fièvre *f* ◆ **to run a ~** avoir de la fièvre ◆ **he has no ~** il n'a pas de fièvre ◆ **gambling ~** le démon du jeu ◆ **a ~ of impatience** une impatience fébrile ◆ **enthusiasm reached ~ pitch** l'enthousiasme était à son comble ◆ **election ~** fièvre *f* électorale ◆ **the nation is in the grip of World Cup ~** la fièvre de la Coupe du Monde s'est emparée du pays ◆ **the country has succumbed to war ~** le pays a succombé à la fièvre de la guerre ; → **glandular, scarlet** **COMP** **fever blister** **N** bouton *m* de fièvre

fevered /ˈfiːvəd/ **ADJ** ① *(liter) [brow]* brûlant de fièvre ② *(fig) [imagination]* exalté, enfiévré

feverish /ˈfiːvərɪʃ/ **ADJ** ① *(Med) [person]* fiévreux, fébrile ; *[illness]* accompagné de fièvre ② *(fig) [person, excitement, atmosphere, activity]* fiévreux ; *[speculation, pace]* effréné ◆ **~ with excitement** dans un état d'excitation fiévreuse *or* fébrile

feverishly /ˈfiːvərɪʃlɪ/ **ADV** *[work]* fiévreusement, fébrilement ; *[try]* fébrilement

feverishness /ˈfiːvərɪʃnɪs/ **N** ① *(Med)* état *m* fébrile ② *(fig)* fébrilité *f*

few /fjuː/ **ADJ, PRON** ① *(= not many)* peu (de) ◆ **~ books** peu de livres ◆ **very ~ books** très peu de livres ◆ **~ of them came** peu d'entre eux sont venus, quelques-uns d'entre eux seulement sont venus ◆ **~ (people) come to see him** peu de gens viennent le voir ◆ **he is one of the ~ people who is able to do this** c'est l'une des rares personnes qui puisse le faire *or* à pouvoir le faire ◆ **we have worked hard in the past ~ days** nous avons travaillé dur ces jours-ci *or* ces derniers jours ◆ **these past ~ weeks** ces dernières semaines ◆ **the next ~ days** les (quelques) jours qui viennent ◆ **with ~ exceptions** à de rares exceptions près ◆ **the exceptions are ~** les exceptions sont rares *or* peu nombreuses ◆ **she goes to town every ~ days** elle va à la ville tous les deux ou trois jours ◆ **~ and far between** rares ◆ **such occasions are ~ and far between** de telles occasions sont rares ◆ **we are very ~ (in number)** nous sommes peu nombreux ◆ **our days are ~** *(liter)* nos jours sont comptés ◆ **I'll spend the remaining ~ minutes alone** je passerai seul le peu de *or* les quelques minutes qui me restent ◆ **there are always the ~ who think that ...** il y a toujours la minorité qui croit que ... ◆ **the ~ who know him** les rares personnes qui le connaissent ◆ **the Few** *(= Battle of Britain heroes) les héros de la Bataille d'Angleterre* ; → **happy, word**

② *(after adv)* **I have as ~ books as you** j'ai aussi peu de livres que vous ◆ **I have as ~ as you** j'en ai aussi peu que vous ◆ **there were as ~ as six objections** il n'y a eu en tout et pour tout que six objections ◆ **how ~ there are!** il n'y en a (vraiment) pas beaucoup ! ◆ **how ~ they are!** il n'y en a (vraiment) pas beaucoup ! ◆ **however ~ books you (may) buy** même si l'on achète peu de livres ◆ **however ~ there may be** si peu qu'il y en ait ◆ **I've got so ~ already (that ...)** j'en ai déjà si peu (que ...) ◆ **so ~ have been sold** on en a (*or* ils en ont) vendu si peu ◆ **so ~ books** tellement peu *or* si peu de livres ◆ **there were too ~** il y en avait trop peu ◆ **too ~ cakes** trop peu de gâteaux ◆ **there were three too ~** il en manquait trois ◆ **ten would not be too ~** dix suffiraient, il (en) suffirait de dix ◆ **I've got too ~ already** j'en ai déjà (bien) trop peu ◆ **he has too ~ books** il a trop peu de livres ◆ **there are too ~ of you** vous êtes trop peu nombreux, vous n'êtes pas assez nombreux ◆ **too ~ of them realize that ...** trop peu d'entre eux sont conscients que ...

③ *(set structures)*

◆ **a few** quelques(-uns), quelques(-unes) ◆ **a ~ books** quelques livres *mpl* ◆ **I know a ~ of these people** je connais quelques-unes de ces personnes ◆ **a ~** *or (liter)* **some ~ thought otherwise** certains *or (liter)* d'aucuns pensaient autrement ◆ **I'll take just a ~** j'en prendrai quelques-uns (*or* quelques-unes) seulement ◆ **I'd like a ~ more** j'en voudrais quelques-un(e)s de plus ◆ **quite a ~ books** pas mal* de livres ◆ **we'll go in a ~ minutes** nous partirons dans quelques minutes ◆ **a ~ of us** quelques-un(e)s d'entre nous ◆ **there were only a ~ of us** nous n'étions qu'une poignée ◆ **we must wait a ~ more days** il nous faut attendre encore quelques jours *or* attendre quelques jours de plus

◆ **quite a few, a good few** ◆ **quite a ~ did not believe him** pas mal* de gens ne l'ont pas cru ◆ **I saw a good ~** *or* **quite a ~ people there** j'y ai vu pas mal* de gens ◆ **he has had a good ~ (drinks)** il a pas mal* bu ◆ **a good ~ of the books are ...** (un) bon nombre de ces livres sont ...

fewer /ˈfjuːəʳ/ **ADJ, PRON** (compar of **few**) moins (de) ◆ **we have sold ~ this year** nous en avons moins vendu cette année ◆ **he has ~ books than you** il a moins de livres que vous ◆ **we are ~ (in number) than last time** nous sommes moins nombreux que la dernière fois ◆ **~ people than we expected** moins de gens que nous n'en attendions ◆ **there are ~ opportunities for doing it** les occasions de le faire sont plus rares, il y a moins d'occasions de le faire ◆ **no ~ than 37 pupils were ill** il y a eu pas moins de 37 élèves malades ◆ **the ~ the better** moins il y en a mieux c'est *or* mieux ça vaut ◆ **few came and ~ stayed** peu sont venus et encore moins sont restés

fewest /ˈfjuːɪst/ **ADJ, PRON** (superl of **few**) le moins (de) ◆ **he met her on the ~ occasions possible** il l'a rencontrée le moins souvent possible ◆ **we were ~ in number then** c'est à ce moment-là que nous étions le moins nombreux ◆ **we sold ~ last year** c'est l'année dernière que nous en avons le moins vendu ◆ **I've got (the) ~** c'est moi qui en ai le moins ◆ **he has (the) ~ books** c'est lui qui a le moins de livres

fey /feɪ/ **ADJ** *(pej = affected)* mignard, minaudier

fez /fez/ **N** (pl **fezzes**) fez *m*

ff (abbrev of **and the following**) sqq

FFA /ˌefefˈeɪ/ **N** (abbrev of **Future Farmers of America**) *club agricole*

FH **N** (abbrev of **fire hydrant**) → **fire**

FHA /ˌefeɪtʃˈeɪ/ **N** *(US)* (abbrev of **Federal Housing Administration**) → **federal** ◆ **~ loan** *prêt à la construction*

fiancé /fɪˈɑːŋseɪ/ **N** fiancé *m*

fiancée /fɪˈɑːŋseɪ/ **N** fiancée *f*

fiasco /fɪˈæskəʊ/ **N** (pl **fiascos** *or* **fiascoes**) fiasco *m* ◆ **the whole undertaking was a ~** *or* **ended in a ~** l'entreprise a tourné au désastre *or* a été un fiasco total

fiat /ˈfaɪæt/ **N** décret *m*, ordonnance *f*

fib* /fɪb/ **N** bobard* *m* **VI** raconter des bobards* ◆ **you're ~bing!** tu plaisantes ?

fibber /ˈfɪbəʳ/ **N** blagueur* *m*, -euse* *f*, menteur *m*, -euse *f* ◆ **you ~!** espèce de menteur !

fibre, fiber *(US)* /ˈfaɪbəʳ/ **N** ① *[of wood, cotton, muscle]* fibre *f* ◆ **cotton ~** fibre *f* de coton ◆ **synthetic ~s** fibres *fpl* synthétiques, synthétiques *mpl* ◆ **a man of great moral ~** un homme d'une grande force morale ② *(dietary)* fibres *fpl* alimentaires ◆ **a diet high in ~** *(= eating régime)* un régime riche en fibres ; *(= food eaten)* une alimentation riche en fibres

COMP **fibre optics** **NPL** la fibre optique
fibre-tip (pen) **N** *(Brit)* stylo *m* pointe fibre

fibreboard, fiberboard *(US)* /ˈfaɪbəbɔːd/ **N** panneau *m* de fibres

fibrefill, fiberfill *(US)* /ˈfaɪbəfɪl/ **N** rembourrage *m* synthétique

fibreglass, fiberglass *(US)*, **Fiberglas** ® *(US)* /ˈfaɪbəglɑːs/ **N** fibre *f* de verre

fibreoptic, fiberoptic *(US)* /ˌfaɪbərˈɒptɪk/ **ADJ** ◆ **~ cable** câble *m* en fibres optiques ◆ **~ link** liaison *f* par fibre optique

fibrescope, fiberscope *(US)* /ˈfaɪbəskəʊp/ **N** fibroscope *m*

fibril /ˈfaɪbrɪl/, **fibrilla** /faɪˈbrɪlə/ **N** fibrille *f*

fibrillation /ˌfaɪbrɪˈleɪʃən/ **N** fibrillation *f*

fibrin /ˈfɪbrɪn/ N fibrine *f*

fibrinogen /fɪˈbrɪnədʒən/ N fibrinogène *m*

fibroid /ˈfaɪbrɔɪd/ N ⇒ **fibroma**

fibroma /faɪˈbrəʊmə/ N (pl **fibromas** *or* **fibromata** /faɪˈbrəʊmətə/) fibrome *m*

fibrositis /ˌfaɪbrəˈsaɪtɪs/ N aponévrite *f*

fibrous /ˈfaɪbrəs/ ADJ fibreux

fibula /ˈfɪbjʊlə/ N (pl **fibulas** *or* **fibulae** /ˈfɪbjʊˌliː/) péroné *m*

FICA /ˌefaɪsiːˈeɪ/ N (*US*) (abbrev of **Federal Insurance Contributions Act**) → **federal**

fickle /ˈfɪkl/ ADJ *[friend, follower, supporter]* inconstant ; *[lover, husband]* volage, inconstant ; *[fate, weather]* changeant, capricieux

fickleness /ˈfɪklnɪs/ N inconstance *f*

fiction /ˈfɪkʃən/ N [1] (*NonC: Literat*) ◆ **(works of)** ~ œuvres *fpl* de fiction ◆ **a writer of** ~ un romancier ◆ **light** ~ romans *mpl* faciles à lire ; → **science, truth** [2] (*= fabrication*) fiction *f* ◆ **his account was a complete** ~ son récit était une invention du début à la fin ◆ **there is still this** ~ **that you can find a job if you try hard enough** (*= unjustified belief*) il y a encore des gens qui s'imaginent qu'il suffit d'un peu de persévérance pour trouver du travail ◆ **total recycling is a** ~ l'idée de pouvoir tout recycler relève du mythe [3] (*NonC = the unreal*) le faux ; → **fact**

fictional /ˈfɪkʃənl/ ADJ (*Literat*) *[character]* imaginaire, fictif ; *[hero, setting]* imaginaire ; *[film, drama]* de fiction ; *[account, device]* romanesque ; (*= unreal*) *[plans, figures]* fictif

fictionalize /ˈfɪkʃənəlaɪz/ VT romancer ◆ **a ~d account of his journey** un récit romancé de son voyage

fictitious /fɪkˈtɪʃəs/ ADJ (*= false*) *[name, address]* faux (fausse *f*) ; (*Literat*) *[character, story]* imaginaire, fictif ; *[setting]* imaginaire

Fid. Def. (abbrev of **Fidei Defensor**) (*= Defender of the Faith*) Défenseur *m* de la foi

fiddle /ˈfɪdl/ N [1] (*= violin*) violon *m* ; → **fit¹, second¹**
[2] (*esp Brit * = cheating*) truc* *m*, combine* *f* ◆ **it was all a** ~ tout ça c'était une combine* ◆ **tax** ~ fraude *f* fiscale ◆ **he's on the** ~ il traficote*
VI [1] (*Mus*) jouer du violon ◆ **to ~ while Rome burns** se perdre en futilités au lieu d'agir
[2] ◆ **do stop fiddling (about** *or* **around)!** tiens-toi donc tranquille ! ◆ **to ~ (about** *or* **around) with a pencil** tripoter un crayon ◆ **he's fiddling (about** *or* **around) with the car** il bricole la voiture
[3] (*esp Brit * = cheat*) faire de la fraude, traficoter*
VT [1] (*esp Brit **) *[+ accounts, expenses claim]* truquer ◆ **to ~ one's tax return** truquer sa déclaration d'impôts
[2] (*Mus*) jouer du violon
COMP **fiddle-faddle** * EXCL quelle blague ! *

▸ **fiddle about, fiddle around** VI ◆ **he's fiddling about in the garage** il est en train de bricoler dans le garage ◆ **we just ~d about yesterday** on n'a rien fait de spécial hier, on a seulement traînassé hier ; see also **fiddle vi 2**

fiddler /ˈfɪdləʳ/ N [1] joueur *m*, -euse *f* de violon, violoneux* *m* (*gen pej*) [2] (*esp Brit * = cheat*) combinard* *m*

fiddlesticks * /ˈfɪdlstɪks/ EXCL quelle blague ! *

fiddling /ˈfɪdlɪŋ/ ADJ futile, insignifiant ◆ ~ **little jobs** menus travaux *mpl* sans importance N (*NonC: * = dishonesty*) combine(s)* *f(pl)*

fiddly * /ˈfɪdlɪ/ ADJ *[job, task]* minutieux, délicat ; *[machinery]* difficile à manier ◆ ~ **to open** difficile à ouvrir ◆ **this is a rather ~ dish to prepare** c'est un plat qui est délicat à réaliser ◆ **prawns are ~ to eat** les crevettes ne sont pas faciles à manger ◆ ~ **bits*** fioritures *fpl*

fidelity /fɪˈdelɪtɪ/ N fidélité *f* ; → **high**

fidget /ˈfɪdʒɪt/ VI (*= wriggle*: also **fidget about, fidget around**) remuer, gigoter* ; (*= grow impatient*) donner des signes d'impatience ◆ **stop ~ing!** reste donc tranquille !, arrête de bouger ! ◆ **to ~ (about** *or* **around) with sth** tripoter qch ◆ **to be ~ing to do sth** trépigner d'impatience de faire qch N ◆ **to be a** ~ *[child]* être très remuant, ne pas tenir en place ; *[adult]* ne pas tenir en place ◆ **to have the ~s*** avoir la bougeotte*

fidgety /ˈfɪdʒɪtɪ/ ADJ (*= jittery*) agité ; (*physically*) remuant, agité ◆ **to feel** ~ ne pas tenir en place, être agité

fiduciary /fɪˈdjuːʃɪərɪ/ ADJ, N fiduciaire *mf*

fie /faɪ/ EXCL (*archaic or hum*) ◆ ~ **(up)on you!** honni sois-tu ! †† (*also hum*)

fief /fiːf/ N fief *m*

fiefdom /ˈfiːfdəm/ N (*Hist, fig*) fief *m*

field /fiːld/ N [1] (*Agr etc*) champ *m* ; (*Miner*) gisement *m* ◆ **in the ~s** dans les champs, aux champs ; → **coalfield, goldfield, oilfield**
[2] (*= real environment*) terrain *m* ◆ **this machine had a year's trial in the** ~ cette machine a eu un an d'essais sur le terrain ◆ **to be first in the ~ with sth** (*Comm*) être le premier à lancer qch ◆ **work in the** ~ enquête *f* sur place *or* sur le terrain
[3] (*Mil*) champ *m* ◆ ~ **of battle** champ *m* de bataille ◆ **to take the** ~ entrer en campagne ◆ **to hold the** ~ se maintenir sur ses positions ◆ **to die on** *or* **in the** ~ tomber *or* mourir au champ d'honneur
[4] (*Sport*) terrain *m* ◆ **the** ~ (*Racing*) les concurrents *mpl* (*sauf le favori*) ; (*Hunting*) les chasseurs *mpl* ◆ **football** ~ terrain *m* de football ◆ **to take the** ~ entrer en jeu ◆ **to hold off the** ~ (*Sport*) tenir bon face à ses adversaires ; (*fig*) tenir bon face à la concurrence
[5] (*= sphere of activity, knowledge*) domaine *m* ◆ **in the ~ of painting** dans le domaine de la peinture ◆ **it's outside my** ~ ce n'est pas de mon domaine ◆ **his particular ~ is Renaissance painting** la peinture de la Renaissance est sa spécialité, son domaine de spécialité est la peinture de la Renaissance
[6] (*Phys*) (also **field of force**) champ *m* ◆ ~ **of vision** champ *m* visuel *or* de vision ◆ **gravitational** ~ champ *m* de gravitation ; → **magnetic**
[7] (*Comput*) champ *m* ◆ **(semantic)** ~ (*Ling*) champ *m* (sémantique)
[8] (*= expanse*) étendue *f* ; (*Her*) champ *m* ◆ **on a ~ of blue** (*Her*) en champ d'azur
VT (*Sport*) *[+ ball]* attraper ; *[+ team]* faire jouer ◆ **to ~ questions** répondre au pied levé (à des questions)
VI (*Sport*) être joueur de champ
COMP **field day** N (*Mil*) jour *m* de grandes manœuvres ; (*gen*) jour *m* faste, grand jour *m* ◆ **to have a ~ day** s'en donner à cœur joie ◆ **the ice-cream sellers had a ~ day*** les marchands de glaces ont fait des affaires en or *or* d'or ce jour-là ◆ **the press had a ~ day with the story** la presse a fait ses choux gras de cette histoire
field event N (*Athletics*) concours *m*
field glasses NPL jumelles *fpl*
field grown ADJ de plein champ
field gun N canon *m* (de campagne)
field hand N (*US*) ouvrier *m*, -ière *f* agricole
field hockey N (*US*) hockey *m* sur gazon
field of honour N champ *m* d'honneur
field hospital N (*Mil*) antenne *f* chirurgicale ; (*Hist*) hôpital *m* de campagne
field house N (*US*) (*for changing*) vestiaire *m* ; (*= sports hall*) complexe *m* sportif (couvert)
field kitchen N (*Mil*) cuisine *f* roulante
field label N (*Ling*) (indication *f* de) domaine *m*
field marshal N (*Brit Mil*) ≃ maréchal *m*
field mushroom N agaric *m* champêtre
field officer N (*Mil*) officier *m* supérieur
field service N (*US Admin*) antenne *f* (*d'un service administratif*)
field sports NPL activités *fpl* de plein air (*surtout la chasse et la pêche*)
field study N étude *f or* enquête *f* sur le terrain
field term N (*US Univ*) stage *m* pratique
field-test VT soumettre aux essais sur le terrain, tester sur le terrain
field tests NPL essais *mpl* sur le terrain
field trials NPL *[of machine etc]* essais *mpl* sur le terrain ; (*Med*) essais *mpl* cliniques
field trip N (*Educ*) sortie *f* éducative ; (*longer*) voyage *m* d'étude
field work N (*Archeol, Geol*) recherches *fpl or* enquête *f* sur le terrain ; (*Social Work*) travail *m* social (*sur le terrain*)
field worker N (*Archeol, Geol*) archéologue *mf* (*or* géologue *mf etc*) de terrain ; (*Social Work*) ≃ travailleur *m*, -euse *f* social(e) (*allant sur le terrain*)

fielder /ˈfiːldəʳ/ N (*Cricket*) joueur *m* de champ

fieldfare /ˈfiːldfɛəʳ/ N (*= bird*) litorne *f*

fieldmouse /ˈfiːldmaʊs/ N (pl **-mice**) (*Zool*) mulot *m*, rat *m* des champs

fieldsman /ˈfiːldzmən/ N (pl **-men**) (*Cricket*) joueur *m* de champ

fieldstrip /ˈfiːldstrɪp/ VT (*US Mil*) *[+ firearm]* démonter (pour inspection)

fiend /fiːnd/ N [1] (*= demon*) démon *m* ; (*= cruel person*) monstre *m*, démon *m* ◆ **the Fiend** (*= the Devil*) le Malin ◆ **that child's a real** ~* cet enfant est un petit monstre *or* est infernal* [2] (** = fanatic*) enragé(e) *m(f)*, mordu(e)* *m(f)* ◆ **tennis** ~ enragé(e) *m(f) or* mordu(e)* *m(f)* de tennis ◆ **drug** ~ † toxicomane *mf* ; → **sex**

fiendish /ˈfiːndɪʃ/ ADJ [1] (*= cruel*) *[despot]* monstrueux ; *[act, look]* diabolique ; *[cruelty]* extrême ◆ **to take a ~ delight in doing sth** prendre un malin plaisir à faire qch [2] (*= ingenious*) *[plot, device]* diabolique [3] (** = difficult*) *[problem, difficulty]* infernal

fiendishly /ˈfiːndɪʃlɪ/ ADV [1] (*= evilly*) ◆ **to laugh** ~ éclater d'un rire diabolique [2] (** = extremely*) *[difficult, complicated, expensive]* abominablement ; *[simple]* diaboliquement ; *[funny]* terriblement ◆ ~ **clever** *[person]* d'une intelligence redoutable ; *[plot, device]* extrêmement ingénieux

fierce /fɪəs/ ADJ *[animal, person, look, tone, battle]* féroce ; *[attack, argument]* violent ; *[debate]* houleux, acharné ; *[opposition, opponent, resistance, determination]* farouche ; *[loyalty]* à toute épreuve ; *[criticism, critic]* virulent ; *[heat, storm]* terrible ; *[wind]* violent ◆ **to take a ~ pride in sth** être extrêmement fier de qch ◆ **he has a ~ temper** il est d'un tempérament explosif ◆ **competition for the post was** ~ la concurrence pour le poste a été rude

fiercely /ˈfɪəslɪ/ ADV *[resist, fight, defend]* avec acharnement ; *[oppose]* farouchement ; *[criticize]* violemment ; *[say]* d'un ton féroce ◆ **to burn** ~ flamber ◆ ~ **independent** farouchement indépendant ◆ **to be ~ competitive** avoir un esprit de compétition acharné

fierceness /ˈfɪəsnɪs/ N *[of person, animal]* férocité *f* ; *[of passion, sun]* ardeur *f* ; *[of love, fighting, competition, heat, fire]* intensité *f*

fiery /ˈfaɪərɪ/ ADJ *[colour]* rougeoyant ; *[sunset]* embrasé ; *[hair, eyes]* flamboyant ; *[person, character, personality, nature]* fougueux ; *[temper]* explosif ; *[speech, rhetoric]* enflammé ; *[food]* (très) épicé, qui emporte la bouche ; *[drink]* qui emporte la bouche ◆ **the ~ furnace** (*Bible*) la fournaise ardente ◆ **a ~ inferno** un terrible brasier ◆ **the ~ heat of the desert** la chaleur torride du désert ◆ ~ **orange/red** orange/rouge flamboyant *inv* COMP **fiery-tempered** ADJ irascible, coléreux

fiesta /fɪˈestə/ N fiesta *f*

FIFA /ˈfiːfə/ N (abbrev of **Fédération internationale de football-association**) FIFA *f*

fife /faɪf/ N fifre *m (instrument)*

FIFO /ˈfaɪfəʊ/ N (abbrev of **first in, first out**) PEPS *m*

fifteen /fɪfˈtiːn/ ADJ quinze *inv* ◆ **about ~ books** une quinzaine de livres ◆ **her ~ minutes of fame** sa minute de célébrité N 1 quinze *m inv* ◆ **about** ~ une quinzaine 2 *(Rugby)* quinze *m* ◆ **the French** ~ le quinze de France ; *for other phrases see* **six** PRON quinze ◆ **there are** ~ il y en a quinze

fifteenth /fɪfˈtiːnθ/ ADJ quinzième N quinzième *mf* ; *(= fraction)* quinzième *m* ; *for phrases see* **sixth**

fifth /fɪfθ/ ADJ cinquième ◆ **~-rate** de dernier ordre, de dernière catégorie ; *for other phrases see* **sixth**

N 1 *(gen)* cinquième *mf* ; *(= fraction)* cinquième *m* ◆ **to take the Fifth** *(US Jur)* invoquer le cinquième amendement pour refuser de répondre ; *(* fig)* refuser de parler ; → FIFTH AMENDMENT ; *for other phrases see* **sixth**

2 *(Mus)* quinte *f*

3 *(US) (= measurement)* le cinquième d'un gallon *(= 75 cl)* ; *(= bottle)* bouteille *f (d'alcool)*

COMP **Fifth Amendment** N *(US Jur)* cinquième amendement *m* (de la constitution) ◆ **to plead the Fifth Amendment** invoquer le cinquième amendement pour refuser de répondre

fifth column N cinquième colonne *f*

fifth columnist N membre *m* de la cinquième colonne

FIFTH AMENDMENT

Le cinquième amendement de la Constitution des États-Unis protège le citoyen contre certains abus de pouvoir. Ainsi, on ne peut incarcérer une personne ou lui confisquer ses biens sans procès ; on ne peut non plus la juger deux fois pour un même délit. Enfin, tout citoyen peut invoquer cet amendement ("to plead **the Fifth Amendment**" ou "to take **the Fifth**") pour refuser de fournir des éléments de preuve susceptibles de se retourner contre lui. À l'époque du maccarthysme, le cinquième amendement a été invoqué par diverses personnalités présumées coupables d'activités antiaméricaines. → BILL OF RIGHTS

fiftieth /ˈfɪftɪɪθ/ ADJ cinquantième N cinquantième *mf* ; *(= fraction)* cinquantième *m* ; *for phrases see* **sixth**

fifty /ˈfɪftɪ/ ADJ cinquante *inv* ◆ **about ~ books** une cinquantaine de livres N cinquante *m inv* ◆ **about** ~ une cinquantaine ; *for other phrases see* **sixty** PRON cinquante ◆ **there are** ~ il y en a cinquante COMP **fifty-fifty** ADJ, ADV moitié-moitié, fifty-fifty * ◆ **to go ~-~ with sb** partager moitié-moitié *or* fifty-fifty * avec qn ◆ **we have a ~-~ chance of success** nous avons cinquante pour cent de chances *or* une chance sur deux de réussir ◆ **it was a ~-~ deal** ils ont *(or* nous avons *etc)* fait moitié-moitié *or* fifty-fifty *

fig /fɪg/ N 1 *(= fruit)* figue *f* ; (also **fig tree**) figuier *m* 2 *(† *)* **I don't care a** ~ je m'en fiche * ◆ **I don't give a ~ what people think** je me fiche * de ce que les gens pensent ◆ **I don't give a ~ for that** je m'en moque comme de ma première chemise * ◆ **a ~ for all your principles!** vos principes, je m'assois dessus ! * COMP **fig leaf** N (pl **fig leaves**) feuille *f* de figuier ; *(on statue)* feuille *f* de vigne ◆ **the agreement was merely a ~ leaf for the government to hide behind** l'accord n'a fait que servir de couverture au gouvernement

fig. abbrev of **figure noun 2**

fight /faɪt/ (vb : pret, ptp **fought**) N 1 *(between persons)* bagarre * *f* ; *(Mil)* combat *m*, bataille *f* ; *(Boxing)* combat *m* ; *(against disease, poverty etc)* lutte *f* (*against* contre) ; *(= quarrel)* dispute *f* ◆ **to have a ~ with sb** se battre avec qn, se bagarrer * avec qn ; *(= argue)* se disputer avec qn ◆ **he put up a good** ~ *(lit, fig)* il s'est bien défendu ◆ ~ **for life** *(of sick person)* lutte *f* contre la mort ◆ **the ~ for survival** la lutte pour la survie ◆ **the country's ~ for independence** la lutte du pays pour son indépendance ◆ **we're going to make a ~ of it** nous n'allons pas nous laisser faire, nous allons contre-attaquer ◆ **we won't go down without a ~** nous n'abandonnerons pas sans nous être battus ; → **pick**

2 *(NonC = spirit)* **there was no ~ left in him** il n'avait plus envie de lutter, il n'avait plus de ressort ◆ **he certainly shows** ~ il faut reconnaître qu'il sait montrer les dents *or* qu'il ne se laisse pas faire

VI *[person, animal]* se battre (*with* avec ; *against* contre) ; *[troops, countries]* se battre (*against* contre) ; *(fig)* lutter (*for* pour ; *against* contre) ; *(= quarrel)* se disputer (*with* avec) ◆ **the boys were ~ing in the street** les garçons se battaient *or* se bagarraient * dans la rue ◆ **the dogs were ~ing over a bone** les chiens se disputaient un os ◆ **he went down ~ing** il s'est battu jusqu'au bout ◆ **to ~ against sleep** lutter contre le sommeil ◆ **to ~ against disease** lutter contre *or* combattre la maladie ◆ **to ~ for sb** *(lit, fig)* se battre pour qn ◆ **to ~ for one's life** *(lit, fig)* lutter contre la mort ◆ **to be ~ing for breath** respirer à grand-peine ◆ **to ~ shy of sth/sb** fuir devant qch/qn, tout faire pour éviter qch/qn ◆ **to ~ shy of doing sth** éviter à tout prix de *or* répugner à faire qch

VT *[+ person, army]* se battre avec *or* contre ; *[+ fire, disease]* lutter contre, combattre ◆ **to ~ a battle** livrer bataille ◆ **to ~ a losing battle against sth** *(fig)* mener un combat perdu d'avance contre qch ◆ **we're ~ing a losing battle** c'est un combat perdu d'avance ◆ **to ~ a duel** se battre en duel ◆ **to ~ a campaign** *(Pol etc)* mener une campagne, faire campagne ◆ **to ~ a case** *(Jur) [plaintiff]* aller en justice ; *[defendant]* se défendre ; *[defence lawyer]* plaider une cause ◆ **we shall ~ this decision all the way** nous combattrons cette décision jusqu'au bout ◆ **to ~ one's way out through the crowd** sortir en se frayant un passage à travers la foule

► **fight back** VI *(in fight)* rendre les coups, répondre ; *(Mil)* se défendre, résister ; *(in argument)* répondre, se défendre ; *(after illness)* se remettre, réagir ; *(Sport)* se reprendre, effectuer une reprise

VT SEP *[+ tears]* refouler ; *[+ despair]* lutter contre ; *[+ doubts]* vaincre

► **fight down** VT SEP *[+ anxiety, doubts]* vaincre ; *[+ desire]* refouler, réprimer

► **fight off** VT SEP 1 *(lit, Mil) [+ attack]* repousser ◆ **she fought off her attackers** elle a repoussé *or* mis en fuite ses agresseurs

2 *(fig) [+ disease, sleep]* lutter contre, résister à ; *[+ criticisms]* répondre à

► **fight on** VI continuer le combat *or* la lutte

► **fight out** VT SEP ◆ **they fought it out** *(lit)* ils se sont bagarrés * pour régler la question ; *(fig)* ils ont réglé la question en se disputant

fightback /ˈfaɪtbæk/ N *(Brit Sport)* reprise *f*

fighter /ˈfaɪtəʳ/ N 1 *(Boxing)* boxeur *m*, pugiliste *m* ◆ **he's a** ~ *(fig)* c'est un battant ; → **prize**¹ 2 (also **fighter aircraft, fighter plane**) avion *m* de chasse, chasseur *m*

COMP **fighter-bomber** N *(= plane)* chasseur *m* bombardier, avion *m* de combat polyvalent

fighter pilot N pilote *m* de chasse

fighting /ˈfaɪtɪŋ/ N *(Mil)* combat *m* ; *(in classroom, pub etc)* bagarres * *fpl* ◆ **there was some ~ in the town** il y a eu des échauffourées dans la ville ◆ ~ **broke out between police and demonstrators** des incidents ont éclaté entre la police et les manifestants ; → **street** ADJ *[person]* combatif ; *(Mil) [troops]* de combat ◆ ~ **soldier** *or* **man** *(Mil)* combattant *m* ◆ **he's got a lot of ~ spirit** c'est un battant, il en veut * ◆ **there's a ~ chance for her recovery** elle a une assez bonne chance de s'en remettre ◆ ~ **cock/dog** coq *m*/chien *m* de combat ◆ ~ **fit** *(esp Brit)* en pleine forme ◆ ~ **forces** *(Mil)* forces *fpl* armées ◆ ~ **fund** fonds *m* de soutien ◆ ~ **line** front *m* ◆ ~ **strength** effectif *m* mobilisable ◆ ~ **talk** *or* **words** paroles *fpl* de défi

figment /ˈfɪgmənt/ N ◆ **a ~ of the imagination** une invention *or* création de l'imagination ◆ **it's all a ~ of his imagination** il l'a purement et simplement inventé, il a inventé ça de toutes pièces

figurative /ˈfɪgjʊrətɪv/ ADJ 1 *(= metaphorical) [language]* figuré, métaphorique ◆ **in the literal and in the ~ sense** *or* **meaning** au (sens) propre et au (sens) figuré 2 *(Art)* figuratif

figuratively /ˈfɪgjʊrətɪvlɪ/ ADV au sens figuré ◆ **both literally and** ~ au propre comme au figuré ◆ ~ **speaking** métaphoriquement parlant

figure /ˈfɪgəʳ/ N 1 chiffre *m* ◆ **in round ~s** en chiffres ronds ◆ **I can't give you the exact ~s** je ne peux pas vous donner les chiffres exacts ◆ **the crime/unemployment** *etc* **~s** les chiffres de la criminalité/du chômage *etc* ◆ **to put a ~ to sth** chiffrer qch ◆ **can you put a ~ to** *or* **on that?** est-ce que vous pouvez me donner un chiffre ? ◆ **he's good at ~s** il est doué pour le calcul ◆ **there's a mistake in the ~s** il y a une erreur de calcul ◆ **a three-~ number** un nombre *or* un numéro de trois chiffres ◆ **to get into double ~s** atteindre la dizaine ◆ **to reach three ~s** atteindre la centaine ◆ **he earns well into five ~s** il gagne bien plus de dix mille livres ◆ **to bring** *or* **get inflation/unemployment** *etc* **down to single ~s** faire passer l'inflation/le chômage *etc* en dessous (de la barre) des 10% ◆ **to sell sth for a high** ~ vendre qch cher *or* à un prix élevé ◆ **I got it for a low** ~ je l'ai eu pour pas cher *or* pour peu de chose

2 *(= diagram, drawing) [of animal, person etc]* figure *f*, image *f* ; *(Math)* figure *f* ◆ **he drew the ~ of a bird** il a dessiné (la silhouette d')un oiseau

3 *(= human form)* forme *f*, silhouette *f* ◆ **I saw a ~ approach** j'ai vu une forme *or* une silhouette s'approcher ◆ **she's a fine ~ of a woman** c'est une belle femme ◆ **he cut a poor** *or* **sorry** ~ il faisait piètre figure ◆ **she cuts a fine ~ in that dress** elle a grand air *(frm) or* elle a beaucoup d'allure dans cette robe

4 *(= shape: of person)* ligne *f* ◆ **to improve one's** ~ soigner sa ligne ◆ **to keep one's** ~ garder la ligne ◆ **she has a good** ~ elle est bien faite *or* bien tournée ◆ **think of your ~!** pense à ta ligne ! ◆ **she doesn't have the ~ for that dress** elle n'est pas faite pour porter cette robe

5 *(= important person)* figure *f*, personnage *m* ◆ **the great ~s of history** les grandes figures *fpl or* les grands personnages *mpl* de l'histoire ◆ **a ~ of fun** un guignol ; → **public**

6 *(Literat)* figure *f* ◆ ~ **of speech** figure *f* de rhétorique ◆ **it's just a ~ of speech** ce n'est qu'une façon de parler

7 *(Mus)* figure *f* mélodique

8 *(Dancing, Skating)* figure *f*

VT 1 *(esp US = guess)* penser, supposer ◆ **I ~ it like this** je vois la chose comme ceci ◆ **I ~ he'll come** je pense *or* suppose qu'il va venir ◆ **go ~** allez comprendre ! *

2 *(= imagine)* penser, s'imaginer

3 *(= represent)* représenter ; *(= illustrate by diagrams)* illustrer par un *or* des schéma(s), mettre sous forme de schéma

4 (= decorate) orner ; [+ silk etc] brocher, gaufrer ◆ ~d **velvet** velours m façonné
5 (Mus) ~d **bass** basse f chiffrée
VI 1 (= appear) figurer ◆ **he ~d in a play of mine** il a joué or tenu un rôle dans une de mes pièces ◆ **his name doesn't ~ on this list** son nom ne figure pas sur cette liste
2 (esp US * = make sense) **it doesn't ~** ça n'a pas de sens ◆ **that ~s** ça paraît logique
COMP **figure-conscious** * ADJ ◆ **to be ~-conscious** penser à sa ligne
figure-hugging ADJ [dress] moulant
figure of eight, figure eight (US) N huit m ◆ **draw a ~ of eight** dessinez un huit
figure-skate VI (in competition) faire les figures imposées (en patinage) ; (in display etc) faire du patinage artistique
figure skater N patineur m, -euse f artistique
figure skating N (in competition) figures fpl imposées ; (in display etc) patinage m artistique
► **figure in** * VT SEP (US) inclure, compter ◆ **it's ~d in** c'est inclus, c'est compris
► **figure on** VT FUS (esp US) (= take account of) tenir compte de ; (= count on) compter sur ; (= expect) s'attendre (doing sth à faire qch) ◆ **you can ~ on 30** tu peux compter sur 30 ◆ **I was figuring on doing that tomorrow** je pensais faire ça demain ◆ **I hadn't ~d on that** je n'avais pas tenu compte de ça ◆ **I wasn't figuring on having to do that** je ne m'attendais pas à devoir faire ça
► **figure out** VT SEP 1 (= understand) arriver à comprendre ; (= resolve) résoudre ◆ **I can't ~ that guy out at all** je n'arrive pas du tout à comprendre ce type* ◆ **I can't ~ out how much it comes to** je n'arrive pas à (bien) calculer à combien ça s'élève ◆ **I can't ~ it out** ça me dépasse *
2 (= work out, plan) calculer ◆ **they had it all ~d out** ils avaient calculé leur coup

figurehead /ˈfɪgəhed/ N 1 (gen) chef m de file 2 [of ship] figure f de proue

figurine /ˌfɪgəˈriːn/ N figurine f

Fiji /ˈfiːdʒiː/ N Fidji ; (also **the Fiji Islands**) les îles fpl Fidji ◆ **in ~** à or aux Fidji

Fijian /fɪˈdʒiːən/ ADJ fidjien N 1 Fidjien(ne) m(f) 2 (= language) fidjien m

filament /ˈfɪləmənt/ N filament m

filariasis /ˌfɪləˈraɪəsɪs/ N filariose f

filbert /ˈfɪlbɜːt/ N aveline f

filch * /fɪltʃ/ VT voler, chiper *

file¹ /faɪl/ N (for wood, fingernails etc) lime f ; → **nailfile** VT limer ◆ **to ~ one's nails** se limer les ongles ◆ **to ~ through the bars** limer les barreaux
► **file away** VT SEP limer (pour enlever)
► **file down** VT SEP limer (pour raccourcir)

file² /faɪl/ N (= folder) dossier m, chemise f ; (with hinges) classeur m ; (for drawings) carton m ; (for card index) fichier m ; (= cabinet) classeur m ; (= papers) dossier m ; (Comput) fichier m ◆ **to put a document on the ~** joindre une pièce au dossier ◆ **do we have a ~ on her?** est-ce que nous avons un dossier sur elle ? ◆ **there's something in or on the ~ about him** le dossier contient des renseignements sur lui ◆ **to be on ~** [person, fingerprints] être fiché ◆ **to be on police ~s** être fiché par la police ◆ **to keep sb's details on ~** garder les coordonnées de qn ◆ **to keep information about sth on ~** avoir un dossier or des renseignements sur qch ◆ **to keep a ~ on sb/sth** avoir un dossier sur qn/qch ◆ **they closed the ~ concerning his death** ils ont classé le dossier concernant sa mort ◆ **they closed the ~ on that case** ils ont classé cette affaire ◆ **data on ~** (Comput) données fpl fichées ◆ **material on ~, ~ material** archives fpl ; → **student, single**
VT 1 (also **file away**) [+ notes] classer ; [+ letters] ranger, classer ; (into file) joindre au dossier
2 (Comput) classer, stocker
3 (Jur) **to ~ a claim** déposer une requête or demande ◆ **to ~ a claim for damages** intenter un procès en dommages-intérêts ◆ **to ~ an accident claim** (Insurance) faire une déclaration d'accident ◆ **to ~ a petition** déposer une requête or demande ◆ **to ~ a petition (in bankruptcy), to ~ for bankruptcy** déposer son bilan ◆ **to ~ a suit against sb** intenter un procès à qn ; → **submission**
COMP **file cabinet** N (US) classeur m (meuble)
file card N fiche f
file clerk N (US) documentaliste mf
file management N (Comput) gestion f de fichiers
file manager N (Comput) gestionnaire m de fichiers
file-sharing N (Comput) partage m de fichiers ◆ **file-sharing program / software** programme/logiciel de partage de fichiers
file transfer protocol N (Comput) protocole m de transfert de fichiers
► **file for** VT FUS (Jur) ◆ **to file for divorce** demander le divorce ◆ **to ~ for bankruptcy** déposer son bilan ◆ **to ~ for custody (of the children)** demander la garde des enfants

file³ /faɪl/ N file f ◆ **in Indian ~** à la or en file indienne ◆ **in single ~** à la or en file ; → **rank¹**
VI ◆ **to ~ in/out** etc entrer/sortir etc en file ◆ **to ~ past** défiler ◆ **the soldiers ~d past the general** les soldats ont défilé devant le général ◆ **they ~d slowly past the ticket collector** ils sont passés lentement les uns après les autres devant le contrôleur

filename /ˈfaɪlneɪm/ N (Comput) nom m de fichier

filet /fɪˈleɪ/ (US) ⇒ **fillet**

filial /ˈfɪlɪəl/ ADJ filial

filiation /ˌfɪlɪˈeɪʃən/ N filiation f

filibuster /ˈfɪlɪbʌstəʳ/ N 1 (Pol) obstruction f parlementaire 2 (= pirate) flibustier m VI (Pol) faire de l'obstruction parlementaire

filibusterer /ˈfɪlɪˌbʌstərəʳ/ N (Pol) obstructionniste mf

filigree /ˈfɪlɪgriː/ N filigrane m (en métal) COMP en filigrane

filing /ˈfaɪlɪŋ/ N 1 [of documents] classement m ◆ **to do the ~** s'occuper du classement 2 (Jur) [of claim etc] enregistrement m
COMP **filing box** N fichier m (boîte)
filing cabinet N classeur m (meuble)
filing clerk N (esp Brit) documentaliste mf

filings /ˈfaɪlɪŋz/ NPL limaille f ◆ **iron ~** limaille f de fer

Filipino /ˌfɪlɪˈpiːnəʊ/ ADJ philippin N 1 (= person) Philippin(e) m(f) 2 (= language) tagalog m

fill /fɪl/ VT 1 [+ bottle, bucket, hole] remplir (with de) ; [+ cake, pastry] fourrer (with de) ; [+ teeth] plomber ◆ **smoke ~ed the room** la pièce s'est remplie de fumée ◆ **the wind ~ed the sails** le vent a gonflé les voiles ◆ **to ~ o.s. with** [+ chocolate etc] se gaver de ◆ **the thought ~s me with pleasure/horror/hope** cette pensée me réjouit/m'horrifie/me remplit d'espoir ◆ **~ed with admiration** rempli or plein d'admiration ◆ **~ed with emotion/anger** très ému/en colère ◆ **~ed with despair** désespéré, plongé dans le désespoir ◆ **he was trying to ~ his day** il essayait d'occuper sa journée
2 [+ post, job] [employer] pourvoir ◆ **to ~ a vacancy** [employer] pourvoir un emploi ; [employee] prendre un poste vacant ◆ **the position is already ~ed** le poste est déjà pourvu or pris ◆ **he ~s all our requirements** il répond à toutes nos conditions ◆ **to ~ a need** répondre à un besoin ◆ **to ~ a void or a gap** remplir or combler un vide ◆ **to ~ an order** (esp US, Comm) livrer une commande
VI (also **fill up**) [bath] se remplir, s'emplir ; [bus, hall] se remplir ◆ **to ~ with water** [hole] se remplir d'eau ◆ **her eyes ~ed with tears** ses yeux se sont remplis de larmes
N ◆ **to eat one's ~** manger à sa faim, se rassasier ◆ **he had eaten his ~** il était rassasié ◆ **to have/drink one's ~** avoir/boire tout son content ◆ **she's had her ~ of married life** elle en a assez de la vie conjugale ◆ **we've had our ~ of disappointments** nous avons trop souvent été déçus
COMP **fill-in** N (gen = temporary employee) remplaçant(e) m(f) ◆ **I'm only a ~-in** (fig) je fais office de bouche-trou *
► **fill in** VI ◆ **to fill in for sb** remplacer qn (temporairement)
VT SEP 1 [+ form, questionnaire] remplir ; [+ account, report] compléter ◆ **would you ~ in the details for us?** (fig) (on questionnaire) pourriez-vous compléter le questionnaire ? ; (verbally) pourriez-vous nous donner quelques précisions ? ◆ **to ~ sb in (on sth)** * mettre qn au courant (de qch)
2 [+ hole] boucher ◆ **to ~ in gaps in one's knowledge** combler des lacunes dans ses connaissances ◆ **draw the outline in black and ~ it in in red** dessinez le contour en noir et remplissez-le en rouge
3 (* fig = beat up) casser la gueule à *
N ◆ **fill-in** → **fill**
► **fill out** VI 1 [sails etc] gonfler, s'enfler
2 (= become fatter) [person] forcir, se fortifier ◆ **her cheeks or her face had ~ed out** elle avait pris de bonnes joues
VT SEP 1 [+ form, questionnaire] remplir
2 [+ story, account, essay] étoffer
► **fill up** VI 1 ⇒ **fill** VI
2 (with petrol) faire le plein (d'essence)
3 (with tears) avoir les larmes aux yeux
VT SEP 1 [+ tank, cup] remplir ◆ **to ~ o.s. up with** [+ chocolates etc] se gaver de ◆ **~ it or her up!** * (with petrol) (faites) le plein !
2 [+ hole] boucher
3 (Brit) [+ form, questionnaire] remplir

-filled /fɪld/ ADJ (in compounds) ◆ **cream/chocolate-filled** fourré à la crème/au chocolat ◆ **foam-filled** rempli de mousse ◆ **tear-filled** plein de larmes ◆ **hate-filled eyes** des yeux pleins de haine ◆ **he was found dead in his fume-filled car** il a été trouvé mort dans sa voiture remplie de gaz d'échappement

filler /ˈfɪləʳ/ N 1 (= utensil) récipient m (de remplissage) ; [of bottle] remplisseuse f ; (= funnel) entonnoir m 2 (NonC: for cracks in wood, plaster etc) enduit m or produit m de rebouchage 3 (TV, Rad) intermède m (entre deux programmes) ; (Press) article m bouche-trou inv
COMP **filler cap** N (on car) bouchon m de réservoir

-filler /ˈfɪləʳ/ N (in compounds) ◆ **the team is a real stadium-filler** cette équipe fait le plein chaque fois qu'elle joue ◆ **Beethoven's Second Piano Concerto, the standard programme-filler** le Deuxième concerto pour piano de Beethoven, qui figure souvent au programme des concerts ◆ **space-filler** * bouche-trou * m

fillet /ˈfɪlɪt/, **filet** (US) /fɪˈleɪ/ N 1 (Culin) [of beef, pork, fish] filet m ◆ **veal ~** (NonC) longe f de veau ; (one piece) escalope f de veau ◆ **~ of beef/sole** filet m de bœuf/de sole 2 (for the hair) serre-tête m inv VT [+ meat] désosser ; [+ fish] découper en filets ◆ **~ed sole** filets mpl de sole
COMP **fillet steak** N (NonC) filet m de bœuf ; (one slice) bifteck m dans le filet ; (thick) chateaubriand m

filling /ˈfɪlɪŋ/ N 1 (in tooth) plombage m ◆ **my ~'s come out** mon plombage est parti or a sauté 2 (in pie, tart, sandwich) garniture f ;

(= stuffing) farce f ◆ **chocolates with a coffee ~** chocolats mpl fourrés au café ADJ [food] substantiel COMP **filling station** station-service f, poste m d'essence

fillip /ˈfɪlɪp/ N (with finger) chiquenaude f, pichenette f ; (fig) coup m de fouet (fig) ◆ **our advertisements gave a ~ to our business** notre publicité a donné un coup de fouet à nos affaires

filly /ˈfɪlɪ/ N 1 (= horse) pouliche f 2 († * = girl) jeune fille f

film /fɪlm/ N 1 (esp Brit = movie) film m ◆ **to go to a ~** aller voir un film ◆ **the ~ is on at the Odeon just now** le film passe actuellement à l'Odéon ◆ **he wants to be in ~s** il veut travailler dans le cinéma ◆ **he's been in many ~s** il a joué dans beaucoup de films ; → **feature**
2 (Phot) film m, pellicule f ; (Typ) film m ◆ **I need a ~ for my camera** j'ai besoin d'une pellicule or un film pour mon appareil
3 (for wrapping food) film m transparent or étirable ; (in goods packaging etc) film m plastique
4 (= thin layer) [of dust, mud] couche f, pellicule f ; [of mist] voile m ; [of oil, water] film m
VT (gen) [+ news, event, play] filmer ; [+ scene] [director] filmer, tourner ; [camera] tourner
VI (= make a film) faire or tourner un film ◆ **they were ~ing all day** ils ont tourné toute la journée ◆ **they were ~ing in Spain** le tournage avait lieu en Espagne
COMP [archives, history etc] du cinéma
film camera N caméra f
film director N cinéaste mf
film fan N cinéphile mf, amateur mf de cinéma
film festival N festival m du cinéma or du film
film library N cinémathèque f
film-maker N cinéaste mf
film-making N (= filming) tournage m ; (more gen) le cinéma
film noir N film m noir
film première N première f
film rating N (Brit) système de classification des films ; → MOVIE RATING
film rights NPL droits mpl d'adaptation (cinématographique)
film script N scénario m
film sequence N séquence f (de film)
film set N plateau m de tournage ; see also **filmset**
film speed N sensibilité f de la pellicule
film star N vedette f (de cinéma), star f
film studio N studio m (de cinéma)
film test N bout m d'essai ◆ **to give sb a ~ test** faire tourner un bout d'essai à qn
► **film over** VI [windscreen, glass] s'embuer

filming /ˈfɪlmɪŋ/ N (Cine) tournage m

filmography /fɪlˈmɒgrəfɪ/ N filmographie f

filmset /ˈfɪlmset/ VT (Typ) photocomposer

filmsetter /ˈfɪlmsetəʳ/ N (Typ) photocomposeuse f

filmsetting /ˈfɪlmsetɪŋ/ N (Typ) (= machine) photocomposition f ; (= person) photocompos(it)eur m

filmstrip /ˈfɪlmstrɪp/ N film m (pour projection) fixe

filmy /ˈfɪlmɪ/ ADJ [fabric, material] léger, vaporeux ; [clothing] léger et transparent ◆ **~ curtains** voilages mpl

filo /ˈfiːləʊ/ N (also **filo pastry**) pâte f à filo

Filofax ® /ˈfaɪləʊ,fæks/ N Filofax ® m

filter /ˈfɪltəʳ/ N 1 (gen) filtre m ; → **colour, oil**
2 (Brit: in traffic lights) flèche f (permettant à une file de voitures de passer)
VT [+ liquids, phone calls] filtrer ; [+ air] purifier, épurer
VI 1 [light, liquid, sound] filtrer ◆ **the light ~ed through the shutters** la lumière filtrait à travers les volets ◆ **to ~ back/in/out** [people] revenir/entrer/sortir par petits groupes ◆ **horror stories were beginning to ~ out of the prison** des récits effroyables commençaient à filtrer de la prison ; see also **filter out** ◆ **news of the massacre began to ~ in** on a commencé petit à petit à avoir des renseignements sur le massacre ◆ **reports ~ed through that he was dead** des bruits selon lesquels il était mort commençaient à filtrer
2 **to ~ to the left** [car, driver] prendre la voie or la file de gauche pour tourner
COMP **filter bed** N bassin m de filtration
filter cigarette N cigarette f (à bout) filtre
filter coffee N café m filtre
filter lane N file f (matérialisée sur la chaussée)
filter light N (on road) flèche f (de feux de signalisation)
filter paper N papier m filtre
filter tip N (= cigarette, tip) bout m filtre
filter-tipped ADJ à bout filtre
► **filter out** VT SEP [+ impurities] éliminer par filtrage ; (fig) éliminer

filth /fɪlθ/ N 1 (lit) saleté f, crasse f ; (= excrement) ordure f 2 (fig) saleté f, ordure f (liter) ◆ **this book is sheer ~** ce livre est une vraie saleté ◆ **the ~ shown on television** les saletés or les grossièretés fpl que l'on montre à la télévision ◆ **all the ~ he talks** toutes les grossièretés qu'il débite

filthy /ˈfɪlθɪ/ ADJ 1 (= dirty) crasseux ◆ **to live in ~ conditions** vivre dans la crasse ◆ **~ with mud** couvert or maculé de boue ◆ **~ dirty** d'une saleté répugnante or dégoûtante 2 (= disgusting) [creature, insect, habit] dégoûtant ; [substance] infect ◆ **you ~ liar!** espèce de sale menteur ! ◆ **~ rich*** bourré* de fric ; → **lucre** 3 (= obscene) [joke, book] obscène ; [language] ordurier ◆ **to have a ~ mind** avoir l'esprit mal tourné ◆ **~ talk** grossièretés fpl, propos mpl orduriers 4 (= angry) ◆ **to give sb a ~ look** lancer un regard noir à qn ◆ **to have a ~ temper** avoir un tempérament explosif ◆ **to be in a ~ temper** être d'une humeur massacrante 5 * [weather, night] dégueulasse*

filtrate /ˈfɪltreɪt/ N filtrat m

filtration /fɪlˈtreɪʃən/ N filtration f

fin /fɪn/ N 1 [of fish] nageoire f ; [of shark] aileron m ; [of aircraft, spacecraft] empennage m ; [of ship] dérive f ; [of radiator] ailette f ; [of diver] palme f 2 (US ⁑ = five-dollar bill) billet m de cinq dollars

finagle /fɪˈneɪgəl/ (US) VI resquiller VT ◆ **to ~ sb out of sth** carotter* qch à qn

finagler /fɪˈneɪgləʳ/ N (US) resquilleur m, -euse f

final /ˈfaɪnl/ LANGUAGE IN USE 26.1
ADJ 1 (= last) [minute, stage, match, chapter] dernier ◆ **to make a ~ attempt to do sth** faire une dernière tentative pour faire qch ◆ **one ~ point** (in speech, lecture) enfin, un dernier point ◆ **to put the ~ touches to sth** mettre la dernière main à qch ◆ **a ~-year student** un étudiant de dernière année
2 (= conclusive) [decree, result, approval, answer, draft] définitif ◆ **the judges' decision is ~** la décision des arbitres est sans appel ◆ **to have the ~ say** avoir le dernier mot ◆ **and that's ~!** un point c'est tout !, point final ! ; → **analysis, arbiter, say**
3 (= ultimate) [humiliation] suprême ◆ **the ~ irony is that he ...** comble de l'ironie, il ... ◆ **he paid the ~ penalty for his crime** il a payé son crime de sa vie
4 (Philos) [cause] final
N 1 (Sport: US) (also **finals**) finale f
2 (Press) ◆ **late night ~** dernière édition f (du soir)
NPL **finals** (Univ) examens mpl de dernière année
COMP **the final curtain** N (Theat) la chute du rideau
final demand N (for payment) dernier rappel m
final dividend N (Fin) solde m de dividende
final edition N (Press) dernière édition f
final examinations NPL (Univ) examens mpl de dernière année
the Final Four NPL (US Basketball) les demi-finalistes mpl
final instalment N (Fin) versement m libératoire
final notice N (for payment) dernier rappel m
the Final Solution N (Hist) la solution finale
the final whistle N (Ftbl) le coup de sifflet final

finale /fɪˈnɑːlɪ/ N (Mus, fig) finale m ◆ **the grand ~** (fig) l'apothéose f

finalist /ˈfaɪnəlɪst/ N (Sport) finaliste mf ; (Univ) étudiant qui passe ses examens de dernière année

finality /faɪˈnælɪtɪ/ N [of decision etc] caractère m définitif, irrévocabilité f ◆ **to say sth with an air of ~** dire qch sur un ton sans réplique

finalization /,faɪnəlaɪˈzeɪʃən/ N [of deal] finalisation f ; [of text, report] rédaction f définitive ; [of details] mise f au point ; [of arrangements, plans] mise f au point des détails

finalize /ˈfaɪnəlaɪz/ VT [+ text, report] rédiger la version définitive de, finaliser ; [+ arrangements, plans, preparations] mettre au point les derniers détails de, mettre la dernière main à ; [+ details] mettre au point ; [+ decision] confirmer ; [+ date] fixer de façon définitive ◆ **their divorce is now ~d** le divorce est maintenant prononcé

finally /ˈfaɪnəlɪ/ LANGUAGE IN USE 26.1, 26.2 ADV 1 (= eventually) enfin, finalement ◆ **women ~ got the vote in 1918** les femmes ont enfin or finalement obtenu le droit de vote en 1918 2 (= lastly) pour finir, pour terminer ◆ **~ I would like to say ...** pour terminer or pour finir je voudrais dire ... 3 (= definitively) [decide, settle] définitivement

finance /faɪˈnæns/ N (NonC) finance f ◆ **high ~** la haute finance ◆ **Minister/Ministry of Finance** ministre m/ministère m des Finances
NPL **finances** finances fpl ◆ **his ~s aren't sound** ses finances ne sont pas solides ◆ **the country's ~s** la situation financière du pays ◆ **he hasn't the ~s to do that** il n'a pas les finances or les fonds mpl pour cela VT [+ scheme etc] (= supply money for) financer, commanditer ; (= obtain money for) trouver des fonds pour
COMP (Press) [news, page] financier
finance bill N (Parl) projet m de loi de finances
finance company, finance house N compagnie f financière, société f de financement

financial /faɪˈnænʃəl/ ADJ (gen) financier ◆ **to depend on sb for ~ support** dépendre financièrement de qn
COMP **financial accounting** N comptabilité f générale
financial aid office N (in US university) service m des bourses
financial management N gestion f financière
financial plan N plan m de financement
financial services NPL services mpl financiers
Financial Times index, Financial Times Stock Exchange 100 Index N (Brit) indice m FT
financial year N (Brit) exercice m budgétaire

financially /faɪˈnænʃəlɪ/ ADV [secure, independent, viable] financièrement ◆ **to benefit ~** profiter financièrement ◆ **to be struggling ~** avoir des problèmes financiers ◆ **~, things are a bit tight** financièrement, la situation n'est pas facile

financier /faɪˈnænsɪəʳ/ N financier m

finch /fɪntʃ/ N pinson m, fringillidé m (SPEC)

find /faɪnd/ (pret, ptp **found**) VT 1 (gen) trouver ; [+ lost person or object] retrouver ◆ **he was**

trying to ~ his gloves il cherchait ses gants, il essayait de retrouver ses gants ◆ **I never found my keys** je n'ai jamais retrouvé mes clés ◆ **to ~ one's place in a book** retrouver sa page dans un livre ◆ **they soon found him again** ils l'ont vite retrouvé ◆ **we left everything as we found it** nous avons tout laissé tel quel ◆ **he was found dead in bed** on l'a trouvé mort dans son lit ◆ **this flower is found all over England** on trouve cette fleur *or* cette fleur se trouve partout en Angleterre ◆ **to ~ its mark** atteindre son but ◆ **to ~ work** trouver du travail ◆ **who will ~ the money for the trip?** qui va trouver l'argent pour le voyage ? ◆ **I can't ~ the money to do it** je ne peux pas trouver l'argent nécessaire pour le faire ◆ **go and ~ me a needle** va me chercher une aiguille ◆ **can you ~ me a pen?** peux-tu me trouver un stylo ?

♦ **find + way** ◆ **they couldn't ~ the way back** ils n'ont pas pu trouver le chemin du retour ◆ **I'll ~ my way about all right by myself** je trouverai très bien mon chemin tout seul ◆ **can you ~ your own way out?** pouvez-vous trouver la sortie tout seul ? ◆ **to ~ one's way into a building** trouver l'entrée d'un bâtiment ◆ **it found its way into my bag** ça s'est retrouvé *or* ça a atterri* dans mon sac ◆ **it found its way into his essay** ça s'est glissé dans sa dissertation

♦ **(all) found** ◆ **wages £150 all found** salaire de 150 livres logé (et) nourri ◆ **wages 500 dollars and found** *(US)* salaire de 500 dollars logé (et) nourri

♦ **... to be found** ◆ **the castle is to be found near Tours** le château se trouve près de Tours ◆ **there are no more to be found** il n'en reste plus ◆ **when we got back he was nowhere to be found** lorsque nous sommes rentrés, il avait disparu ◆ **your book is not** *or* **nowhere to be found** on ne parvient pas à retrouver votre livre, votre livre reste introuvable

♦ **to find oneself (...)** ◆ **he found himself at last** il a enfin trouvé sa voie ◆ **they found themselves on a boat** ils se sont retrouvés sur un bateau ◆ **I found myself smiling/looking/wondering** je me suis surpris à sourire/regarder/me demander ◆ **I found myself thinking that ...** je me suis surpris à penser que ... ◆ **to my surprise, I found myself having fun** à mon grand étonnement, je me suis amusé ◆ **I found myself quite at sea among all those scientists** je me suis senti complètement perdu au milieu de tous ces scientifiques

2 *(fig)* trouver *(that* que) ◆ **I can never ~ anything to say to him** je ne trouve jamais rien à lui dire ◆ **to ~ the courage to do sth** trouver le courage de faire qch ◆ **I can't ~ time to read** je n'arrive pas à trouver le temps de lire ◆ **to ~ one's voice** *(fig)* trouver son style ◆ **to ~ one's feet** s'adapter, s'acclimater ◆ **to ~ some difficulty in doing sth** éprouver une certaine difficulté à faire qch ◆ **I couldn't ~ it in my heart to refuse** je n'ai pas eu le cœur de refuser ◆ **how did you ~ him?** *(in health)* comment l'avez-vous trouvé ? ◆ **how did you ~ the steak?** comment avez-vous trouvé le bifteck ? ◆ **I ~ her very pleasant** je la trouve très agréable ◆ **we're sure you'll ~ the film exciting!** nous sommes sûrs que vous trouverez ce film captivant ! ◆ **I ~ that I have plenty of time** il se trouve que j'ai tout le temps qu'il faut ; → **expression, fault, favour**

♦ **to find it + adj** ◆ **he found it impossible to leave** il n'arrivait pas à partir ◆ **he ~s it difficult/impossible to walk** il lui est difficile/impossible de marcher ◆ **he ~s it tiring/encouraging** *etc* il trouve que c'est fatigant/encourageant *etc* ◆ **you won't ~ it easy** vous ne trouverez pas cela facile

3 *(= perceive, realize)* constater *(that* que) ; *(= discover)* découvrir, constater *(that* que) ; *[+ cure]* découvrir ; *[+ solution]* trouver, découvrir ; *[+ answer]* trouver ◆ **you will ~ that I am right** vous verrez *or* vous constaterez que j'ai raison ◆ **it has been found that one person in ten does this** on a constaté qu'une personne sur dix fait cela ◆ **I went there yesterday, only to ~ her out** j'y suis allé hier, mais elle était sortie

4 *(Jur)* **to ~ sb guilty** déclarer qn coupable ◆ **how do you ~ the accused?** quel est votre verdict ? ◆ **the court found that ...** le tribunal a conclu que ...

VI *(Jur)* ◆ **to ~ for/against the accused** se prononcer en faveur de/contre l'accusé

N trouvaille *f* ◆ **that was a lucky ~** nous avons *(or* vous avez *etc)* eu de la chance de trouver cela

► **find out** VI 1 *(= make enquiries)* se renseigner *(about* sur)

2 *(= discover)* **we didn't ~ out about it in time** nous ne l'avons pas su *or* appris à temps ◆ **your mother will ~ out if you ...** ta mère le saura si tu ...

VT SEP 1 *(= discover)* découvrir *(that* que) ; *[+ answer]* trouver ; *[+ sb's secret, character]* découvrir ◆ **I found out what he was really like** j'ai découvert son vrai caractère

2 *(= discover the misdeeds etc of) [+ person]* démasquer ◆ **he thought we wouldn't know, but we found him out** il pensait que nous ne saurions rien, mais nous l'avons démasqué *or* nous avons découvert le pot aux roses *

finder /ˈfaɪndər/ N 1 *(of lost object)* personne *f* qui trouve ; *(Jur)* inventeur *m*, -trice *f* ◆ **~s keepers (losers weepers)!** (celui) qui le trouve le garde (et tant pis pour celui qui l'a perdu) ! 2 *[of telescope]* chercheur *m* ; → **viewfinder** COMP **finder's fee** N *(US)* prime *f* d'intermédiaire

findings /ˈfaɪndɪŋz/ NPL 1 *(= conclusions, deductions) [of person, committee]* conclusions *fpl*, constatations *fpl* ; *[of scientist, researcher]* conclusions *fpl*, résultats *mpl* (des recherches) ; *(Jur)* conclusions *fpl*, verdict *m* 2 *(= objects etc unearthed)* découvertes *fpl*

fine[1] /faɪn/ N amende *f*, contravention *f (esp Aut)* ◆ **I got a ~ for going through a red light** j'ai eu une amende *or* j'ai attrapé une contravention pour avoir brûlé un feu rouge VT condamner à une amende, donner une contravention à *(esp Aut)* ◆ **he was ~d £30** il a eu une amende de 30 livres, il a eu 30 livres d'amende ◆ **they ~d him heavily** ils l'ont condamné à une lourde amende ◆ **he was ~d for exceeding the speed limit** il a eu une amende *or* une contravention pour excès de vitesse ◆ **she was ~d for possession of drugs** elle a été condamnée à une amende pour détention de stupéfiants

fine[2] /faɪn/ ADJ 1 *(= excellent) [performer, player, piece of work]* excellent ; *[place, object, example]* beau (belle *f*) ; *[view]* superbe ◆ **the ~st footballer of his generation** le meilleur footballeur de sa génération ◆ **to be in ~ form** être en pleine forme ◆ **you're doing a ~ job** vous faites un excellent travail ◆ **to be in ~ health** être en bonne santé ◆ **it's a ~ thing to help others** c'est beau d'aider autrui ◆ **it was his ~st hour** *or* **moment** ce fut son heure de gloire ; see also **finest** ; → **fettle, figure**

2 *(= acceptable)* bien *inv* ◆ **how was I? – you were ~** comment je me suis débrouillé ? – bien ◆ **the wallpaper looks ~** le papier peint est bien ◆ **you look ~** tu es très bien ◆ **your idea sounds ~** votre idée semble bonne ◆ **the coffee's just ~** le café est parfait ◆ **everything's ~** tout va bien ◆ **everything's going to be just ~** tout va bien se passer ◆ **isn't the basket a bit too small? – it'll be ~** est-ce que le panier n'est pas un peu trop petit ? – ça ira ◆ **any questions? no? ~!** des questions ? non ? parfait ! ◆ **it's ~ to interrupt me** vous pouvez m'interrompre ◆ **it's ~ for men to cry** il n'y a rien de mal à ce que les hommes pleurent ◆ **it's ~ for two** c'est très bien pour deux personnes ◆ **the hotel is ~ for a weekend break** l'hôtel convient pour un séjour d'un week-end ◆ **this bike is ~ for me** ce vélo me convient ◆ **these apples are ~ for cooking** ces pommes sont parfaites comme pommes à cuire ◆ **that's all very ~, but ...** c'est bien beau *or* bien joli mais ...

3 *(= not unwell)* ◆ **to be ~** aller bien ◆ **a glass of water and I'll be ~** un verre d'eau et ça ira ◆ **don't worry, I'm sure he'll be ~** ne t'inquiète pas, je suis sûr qu'il se remettra ◆ **to feel ~** se sentir bien ◆ **he looks ~** il a l'air en forme ◆ **how are you? – ~ thanks** comment allez-vous ? – bien, merci

4 *(= without problems)* ◆ **she'll be ~, the others will look after her** il ne lui arrivera rien, les autres s'occuperont d'elle ◆ **I'll be ~ on my own** je me débrouillerai très bien tout seul

5 *(expressing agreement)* très bien ◆ **I'll be back by lunchtime – ~!** je serai de retour à l'heure du déjeuner – très bien ! ◆ **that's ~ by** *or* **with me** d'accord ◆ **if you want to give me a hand, that's ~ by me** si tu veux me donner un coup de main, je veux bien ◆ **it'll take me a couple of days – that's ~ by** *or* **with me** ça va me prendre quelques jours – d'accord ◆ **anything she wanted was usually ~ with him** il était en général d'accord avec tout ce qu'elle demandait ◆ **shall we have another beer? – ~ by me** *or* **sounds ~ to me!** on prend encore une bière ? – bonne idée !

6 *(iro)* ◆ **that's ~ for you to say** c'est facile à dire ◆ **a ~ friend you are!** c'est beau l'amitié ! ◆ **that's another ~ mess you've got(ten) me into!** tu m'as encore mis dans un beau pétrin ! ◆ **you're a ~ one!** t'es bon, toi ! * ◆ **you're a ~ one to talk!** ça te va bien de dire ça ! ◆ **~ words** belles paroles *fpl*

7 *(= honourable, refined) [person]* bien *inv* ; *[feelings]* raffiné ◆ **he has no ~r feelings** il n'a aucune noblesse de sentiment

8 *(= superior) [food, ingredients]* raffiné ; *[wine]* fin ; *[furniture, china, fabric, clothes]* beau (belle *f*), raffiné ; *[jewellery]* précieux ; *[metal]* pur ; *[workmanship]* délicat ◆ **~ gold** or *m* fin ◆ **meat of the ~st quality** viande *f* de première qualité ◆ **~ ladies and gentlemen** les beaux messieurs *mpl* et les belles dames *fpl* ◆ **she likes to play at being the ~ lady** elle aime jouer les grandes dames

9 *(= delicate) [fabric, powder, rain, hair, features, bones]* fin ; *[net, mesh]* à mailles fines ; *[mist]* léger ; → **print**

10 *(= subtle) [adjustment]* minutieux ; *[detail, distinction]* subtil ◆ **there's a ~ line between genius and madness/fact and fiction** entre le génie et la folie/la réalité et la fiction, la marge est étroite *or* la distinction est subtile ◆ **not to put too ~ a point on it** pour parler franchement ◆ **the ~r points of English grammar** les subtilités de la grammaire anglaise

11 *[weather, day]* beau (belle *f*) ◆ **it's been ~ all week** il a fait beau toute la semaine ◆ **all areas will be ~ tomorrow** il fera beau partout demain ◆ **coastal areas will be ~** il fera beau sur la côte ◆ **I hope it keeps ~ for you!** j'espère que vous continuerez à avoir beau temps ! ◆ **one ~ day** un beau jour ◆ **one of these ~ days** un de ces quatre matins, un de ces jours

ADV 1 *(* = well)* bien ◆ **you're doing ~!** tu te débrouilles bien ! * ◆ **we get on ~** nous nous entendons bien ◆ **that suits me ~** ça me convient très bien

2 *(= not coarsely)* ◆ **to chop sth ~** hacher qch menu ◆ **to cut sth ~** *(lit)* couper qch finement ◆ **to cut it ~** *(fig)* ne pas se laisser de marge ◆ **you're cutting it too ~** vous comptez trop juste

COMP **fine art** N (= *subject*) beaux-arts *mpl* ; (= *works*) objets *mpl* d'art ◆ **the ~ arts** les beaux-arts *mpl* ◆ **a ~ art** un véritable art ◆ **to get sth down** *or* **off to a ~ art** faire qch à la perfection
fine-drawn ADJ *[wire, thread]* finement étiré
fine-grained ADJ *[wood]* au grain fin ; *(Phot)* à grain fin
fine-spun ADJ *[yarn]* très fin, ténu
fine tooth-comb N peigne *m* fin ◆ **he went through the documents with a ~ tooth-comb** il a passé les documents au peigne fin *or* au crible
fine-tune VT *(fig) [+ production, the economy]* régler avec précision
fine-tuning N réglage *m* minutieux

► **fine down** VI (= *get thinner*) s'affiner
VT SEP (= *reduce*) réduire ; (= *simplify*) simplifier ; (= *refine*) raffiner

finely /ˈfaɪnlɪ/ ADV 1 *[crafted, carved]* finement ; *[written, painted]* avec finesse ◆ **~ detailed** aux détails précis 2 *[chop]* menu ; *[cut, slice]* en tranches fines ; *[grate, grind]* fin ◆ **to dice sth ~** couper qch en petits dés 3 (= *delicately*) ◆ **the case was ~ balanced** l'issue du procès était tangente ◆ **the distinction was ~ drawn** la distinction était très subtile ◆ **a ~ judged speech** un discours avec des propos bien choisis ◆ **a ~ tuned car** une voiture réglée avec précision ◆ **a ~ tuned mind** un esprit aiguisé

fineness /ˈfaɪnnɪs/ N 1 *[of hair, powder, features, wine, material, china, clothes]* finesse *f* ; *[of workmanship]* délicatesse *f* ; *[of feelings]* noblesse *f* ; *[of detail, point, distinction]* subtilité *f* 2 *[of metal]* titre *m*

finery /ˈfaɪnərɪ/ N parure † *f* ◆ **she wore all her ~** elle était parée de ses plus beaux atours † ◆ **wedding guests in all their ~** les invités d'un mariage vêtus de leurs plus beaux habits

finesse /fɪˈnes/ N finesse *f* ; *(Cards)* impasse *f* ◆ **with ~** avec finesse, finement VI *(Cards)* ◆ **to ~ against the King** faire l'impasse au roi VT 1 (= *manage skilfully*) *[+ details]* peaufiner ; *[+ problem, questions]* aborder avec finesse ; (= *avoid*) esquiver ◆ **the skier ~d the difficulties of the mountain** le skieur s'est joué des difficultés de la montagne ◆ **no doubt he will try to ~ the problem** *(pej)* il cherchera sans doute à esquiver le problème 2 *(Cards)* **to ~ the Queen** faire l'impasse en jouant la dame

finest /ˈfaɪnɪst/ NPL *(US: iro = police)* ◆ **Chicago's/the city's ~** la police de Chicago/de la ville ◆ **one of New York's ~** un agent de police new-yorkais

finger /ˈfɪŋgəʳ/ N 1 *(Anat)* doigt *m* ◆ **first** *or* **index ~** index *m* ; → **little¹, middle, ring¹** ◆ **between ~ and thumb** entre le pouce et l'index ◆ **to count on one's ~s** compter sur ses doigts ◆ **I can count on the ~s of one hand the number of times he has ...** je peux compter sur les doigts d'une main le nombre de fois où il a ... ◆ **to point one's ~ at sb** montrer qn du doigt ; see also **noun 2**
2 *(fig phrases)* ◆ **he wouldn't lift a ~ to help me** il ne lèverait pas le petit doigt pour m'aider ◆ **to point the ~ at sb** (= *accuse*) montrer qn du doigt ; (= *identify*) identifier qn ◆ **to point the ~ of suspicion at sb** faire peser des soupçons sur qn ◆ **to point the ~ of blame at sb** faire porter le blâme à qn ◆ **to keep one's ~s crossed** croiser les doigts ◆ **(keep your) ~s crossed!** croisons les doigts ! ◆ **keep your ~s crossed for me!** souhaite-moi bonne chance ! ◆ **to put** *or* **stick two ~s up at sb*** *(Brit)*, **to give sb the ~*** ≈ faire un bras d'honneur* à qn ◆ **to put one's ~ on the difficulty** mettre le doigt sur la difficulté ◆ **there's something wrong, but I can't put my ~ on it** il y a quelque chose qui cloche* mais je ne peux pas mettre le doigt dessus ◆ **to put the ~ on sb*** (= *betray*) dénoncer qn ; (= *indicate as victim*) désigner qn comme victime ◆ **to pull** *or* **get one's ~ out**‡ se décarcasser* ◆ **pull your ~ out!**‡ remue-toi !* ; → **green, pie, pulse¹, thumb**
3 *[of cake etc]* petite part *f* ; *[of whisky]* doigt *m* ; *[of land]* langue *f*
VT 1 (= *touch*) toucher *or* manier (des doigts) ; *(pej)* tripoter ; *[+ money]* palper ; *[+ keyboard, keys]* toucher
2 *(Mus = mark fingering on)* doigter, indiquer le doigté sur
3 *(esp US: ‡ = betray)* moucharder*, balancer‡
COMP **finger alphabet** N alphabet *m* des sourds-muets
finger board N *(Mus)* touche *f (de guitare ou de violon etc)*
finger bowl N rince-doigts *m inv*
finger buffet N buffet *m* d'amuse-gueule(s)
finger-dry VT ◆ **to ~-dry one's hair** passer les doigts dans ses cheveux pour les faire sécher
finger exercises NPL *(for piano etc)* exercices *mpl* de doigté
finger food N (= *appetizers*) amuse-gueule(s) *m(pl)* ◆ **these make ideal ~ food for kids** ce sont des choses que les enfants peuvent facilement manger avec les doigts
finger painting N peinture *f* avec les doigts
finger plate N *(on door)* plaque *f* de propreté

fingering /ˈfɪŋgərɪŋ/ N 1 *(Mus)* doigté *m* 2 (= *fine wool*) laine *f* (fine) à tricoter 3 *[of goods in shop etc]* maniement *m*

fingermark /ˈfɪŋgəmɑːk/ N trace *f or* marque *f* de doigts

fingernail /ˈfɪŋgəneɪl/ N ongle *m*

fingerprint /ˈfɪŋgəprɪnt/ N empreinte *f* digitale VT *[+ car, weapon]* relever les empreintes digitales sur ; *[+ room, building]* relever les empreintes digitales dans ; *[+ person]* relever les empreintes digitales de COMP **fingerprint expert** N spécialiste *mf* en empreintes digitales, expert *m* en dactyloscopie

fingerstall /ˈfɪŋgəstɔːl/ N doigtier *m*

fingertip /ˈfɪŋgətɪp/ N bout *m* du doigt ◆ **all the basic controls are at your ~s** toutes les commandes principales sont à portée de votre main ◆ **I had the information at my ~s** (= *near to hand*) j'avais ces informations à portée de main ◆ **he's a politician to his ~s** c'est un homme politique jusqu'au bout des ongles
COMP **fingertip control** N ◆ **a machine with ~ control** une machine d'un maniement (très) léger
fingertip hold N *(Climbing)* gratton *m*
fingertip search N fouille *f* minutieuse

finial /ˈfaɪnɪəl/ N fleuron *m*, épi *m* (de faîtage)

finicky /ˈfɪnɪkɪ/ ADJ *[person]* pointilleux, tatillon ; *[work, job]* minutieux, qui demande de la patience ◆ **don't be so ~!** ne fais pas le (*or* la) difficile ! ◆ **she is ~ about her food** elle est difficile pour *or* sur la nourriture

finish /ˈfɪnɪʃ/ N 1 (= *end*) fin *f* ; *[of race]* arrivée *f* ; *(Climbing)* sortie *f* ; *(Hunting)* mise *f* à mort ◆ **to be in at the ~** *(fig)* assister au dénouement (d'une affaire) ◆ **a fight to the ~** un combat sans merci ◆ **to fight to the ~** se battre jusqu'au bout ◆ **from start to ~** du début à la fin ; → **photo**
2 (= *surface, look*) *[of woodwork, manufactured articles]* finition *f* ◆ **it's a solid car but the ~ is not good** la voiture est solide mais les finitions sont mal faites ◆ **a car with a two-tone ~** une voiture (peinte) en deux tons ◆ **paint with a matt ~** peinture *f* mate ◆ **paint with a gloss ~** laque *f* ◆ **table with an oak ~** *(stained)* table *f* teintée chêne ; *(veneered)* table *f* plaquée *or* à placage chêne ◆ **a table with rather a rough ~** une table à la surface plutôt rugueuse
VT *[+ activity, work, letter, game, meal, supplies, cake]* finir, terminer ◆ **~ your soup** finis *or* mange ta soupe ◆ **to ~ doing sth** finir de faire qch ◆ **I'm in a hurry to get this job ~ed** je suis pressé de finir *or* de terminer ce travail ◆ **to ~ a book** finir *or* terminer un livre ◆ **to put the ~ing touch** *or* **touches to sth** mettre la dernière main *or* la touche finale à qch ◆ **that last mile nearly ~ed me*** ces derniers quinze cents mètres ont failli m'achever *or* m'ont mis à plat* ; see also **finished**
VI 1 *[book, film, game, meeting]* finir, se terminer ; *[holiday, contract]* prendre fin ; *[runner, horse]* arriver, terminer ; *(Stock Exchange)* clôturer, terminer ; *(Climbing)* sortir ◆ **the meeting was ~ing** la réunion tirait à sa fin ◆ **our shares ~ed at $70** nos actions cotaient 70 dollars en clôture *or* en fin de séance ◆ **he ~ed by saying that ...** il a terminé en disant que ... ◆ **to ~ well** *(in race)* arriver en bonne position ◆ **to ~ first** arriver *or* terminer premier
2 ◆ **I've ~ed with the paper** je n'ai plus besoin du journal ◆ **I've ~ed with politics once and for all** j'en ai fini avec la politique, j'ai dit une fois pour toutes adieu à la politique ◆ **she's ~ed with him*** *(in relationship)* elle l'a plaqué* ◆ **you wait till I've ~ed with you!*** attends un peu que je te règle ton compte !*
COMP **finish line** N *(US)* ligne *f* d'arrivée

► **finish off** VI terminer, finir ◆ **let's ~ off now** maintenant finissons-en ◆ **to ~ off with a glass of brandy** terminer par *or* sur un verre de cognac ◆ **the meeting ~ed off with a prayer** la réunion a pris fin sur une prière, à la fin de la réunion on a récité une prière
VT SEP 1 *[+ work]* terminer, mettre la dernière main à
2 *[+ food, meal]* terminer, finir ◆ **~ off your potatoes!** finis *or* mange tes pommes de terre !
3 (* *fig = kill*) *[+ person, wounded animal]* achever ◆ **his illness last year almost ~ed him off** sa maladie de l'année dernière a failli l'achever

► **finish up** VI 1 ⇒ **finish off vi**
2 se retrouver ◆ **he ~ed up in Rome** il s'est retrouvé à Rome, il a fini à Rome
VT SEP ⇒ **finish off vt sep 2**

finished /ˈfɪnɪʃt/ ADJ 1 (= *at end of activity*) ◆ **to be ~** *[person]* avoir fini ◆ **to be ~ doing sth** *(US)* avoir fini de *or* terminé de faire qch ◆ **to be ~ with sth** (= *have completed*) avoir fini qch ◆ **he was ~ with marriage** le mariage, pour lui, c'était fini ◆ **to be ~ with sb** *(after questioning)* en avoir fini avec qn ; (= *have had enough of*) ne plus vouloir entendre parler de qn
2 (= *at its end*) ◆ **to be ~** *[fighting, life]* être fini ; *[performance, trial]* être fini *or* terminé
3 (= *tired*) ◆ **to be ~*** être crevé*
4 (= *without a future*) ◆ **to be ~** *[politician, sportsperson, career]* être fini
5 (= *decorated*) ◆ **the room is ~ in red** la pièce a des finitions rouges ◆ **the bedroom is ~ with cream curtains** les rideaux crème complètent harmonieusement le décor de la chambre ◆ **the jacket is beautifully ~ with hand-sewn lapels** la veste est joliment finie avec des revers cousus main ◆ **beautifully ~ wood** du bois magnifiquement fini
6 (= *final*) *[product, goods, painting, film]* fini ; *[result]* final ◆ **the ~ article** (= *product*) le produit fini ; (= *piece of writing*) la version finale ◆ **he's the ~ article*** il est génial*

finisher /ˈfɪnɪʃəʳ/ N *(Sport)* ◆ **a fast ~** un finisseur *or* une finisseuse rapide ◆ **a strong ~** un bon finisseur, une bonne finisseuse ◆ **a good ~** *(Ftbl)* un bon buteur ; *(Rugby, Hockey etc)* un bon marqueur, une bonne marqueuse

finishing /ˈfɪnɪʃɪŋ/ N *(Ftbl)* dons *mpl* de buteur ; *(Rugby, Hockey etc)* dons *mpl* de marqueur ◆ **his ~ is excellent** c'est un très bon buteur *or* marqueur
COMP **finishing line** N ligne *f* d'arrivée ◆ **to cross the ~ line** *(Sport)* franchir la ligne d'arrivée ; *(fig)* toucher au but ◆ **we'll never make it to the ~ line with this project** nous ne verrons jamais le bout de ce projet

finishing school N institution *f* pour jeunes filles (de bonne famille)

finite /ˈfaɪnaɪt/ ADJ 1 (= *limited*) [*number, set, being, world, universe*] fini ; [*amount, period, life, resources*] limité 2 (Gram) [*verb*] *dont la forme est fixée par le temps et la personne* ; [*clause*] *à forme verbale fixée par le temps et la personne* COMP **finite state grammar** N grammaire *f* à états finis

fink‡ /fɪŋk/ (US *pej*) N (= *strikebreaker*) jaune* *m* ; (= *informer*) mouchard* *m*, indic* *m* ; (= *unpleasant person*) sale type *m* VT moucharder*, dénoncer

► **fink out**‡ VI (US) échouer, laisser tomber

Finland /ˈfɪnlənd/ N Finlande *f*

Finn /fɪn/ N (*gen*) Finlandais(e) *m(f)* ; (also **Finnish speaker**) Finnois(e) *m(f)*

Finnish /ˈfɪnɪʃ/ ADJ [*gen*] finlandais ; [*ambassador, embassy*] de Finlande ; [*teacher*] de finnois ; [*literature, culture, civilization*] finnois N (= *language*) finnois *m*

Finno-Ugric /ˈfɪnəʊˈuːgrɪk/, **Finno-Ugrian** /ˈfɪnəʊˈuːgrɪən/ N, ADJ finno-ougrien *m*

fiord /fjɔːd/ N fjord *or* fiord *m*

fir /fɜːʳ/ N (also **fir tree**) sapin *m* ◆ ~ **cone** pomme *f* de pin

fire /faɪəʳ/ N 1 (*gen*) feu *m* ; (= *blaze*) incendie *m* ◆ ~! au feu ! ◆ **forest** ~ incendie *m* de forêt ◆ **to insure o.s. against** ~ s'assurer contre l'incendie ◆ **to lay/light/make up the** ~ préparer/allumer/faire le feu ◆ **come and sit by the** ~ venez vous installer près du feu *or* au coin du feu ◆ **I was sitting in front of a roaring** ~ j'étais assis devant une belle flambée ◆ ~ **and brimstone** (*fig*) les tourments *mpl* (*liter*) de l'enfer ; see also **comp** ◆ **by** ~ **and sword** par le fer et par le feu ◆ **he would go through** ~ **and water for her** il se jetterait dans le feu pour elle ◆ **to have** ~ **in one's belly** avoir le feu sacré ; → **play**

◆ **on fire** ◆ **the house was on** ~ la maison était en feu *or* en flammes ◆ **the chimney was on** ~ il y avait un feu de cheminée

◆ **to catch fire** (*lit*) prendre feu ; (*fig*) [*play, film, idea*] décoller ◆ **her dress caught** ~ sa robe s'est enflammée *or* a pris feu ◆ **the issue caught** ~ la question est devenue brûlante *or* délicate

◆ **to set fire to sth, to set sth on fire** mettre le feu à qch ◆ **to set the world on** ~ révolutionner le monde ◆ **he'll never set the world** *or* **the Thames** (Brit) *or* **the heather** (*Scot*) **on** ~ il n'impressionnera jamais par ses prouesses

2 (*Brit* = *heater*) radiateur *m* ; → **electric**

3 (*Mil*) feu *m* ◆ **to open** ~ ouvrir le feu, faire feu ◆ ~! feu ! ◆ **between two ~s** (*fig*) entre deux feux ◆ **under** ~ sous le feu de l'ennemi ◆ **to come under** ~, **to draw** ~ (*Mil*) essuyer le feu (de l'ennemi) ; (*fig* = *be criticized*) essuyer des critiques ◆ **to return** ~ riposter par le feu ◆ **to hang** *or* **hold** ~ [*guns*] faire long feu ; (*on plans etc*) traîner (en longueur) ◆ **small-arms/cannon/mortar** ~ tirs *mpl* d'artillerie/de canon/de mortier ◆ **to hold one's** ~ (= *stop firing*) suspendre le tir ; (= *hold back*) ne pas tirer ◆ **to fight** ~ **with** ~ combattre le feu par le feu ; → **ceasefire, line¹**

4 (*NonC* = *passion*) ardeur *f*, feu *m* (*liter*)

VT 1 (= *set fire to*) incendier, mettre le feu à ; (*fig*) [+ *imagination, passions, enthusiasm*] enflammer, exciter ◆ **~d with the desire to do sth** brûlant de faire qch ; → **gas, oil**

2 [+ *gun*] décharger, tirer ; [+ *rocket*] tirer ; (* = *throw*) balancer* ◆ **to** ~ **a gun at sb** tirer (un coup de fusil) sur qn ◆ **to** ~ **a shot** tirer un coup de feu (*at* sur) ◆ **without firing a shot** sans tirer un coup (de feu) ◆ **to** ~ **a salute** *or* **a salvo** lancer *or* tirer une salve ◆ **to** ~ **a salute of 21 guns** saluer de 21 coups de canon ◆ **she ~d an elastic band at me*** elle m'a tiré dessus* avec un élastique ◆ **to** ~ **(off) questions at sb** bombarder qn de questions ◆ **"your name?" he suddenly ~d at me** "votre nom ?" me demanda-t-il à brûle-pourpoint

3 (* = *dismiss*) virer*, renvoyer ◆ **you're ~d!** vous êtes viré* *or* renvoyé !

4 [+ *pottery*] cuire ; [+ *furnace*] chauffer

VI 1 [*person*] (*gen*) tirer ; (*Mil, Police*) tirer, faire feu (*at* sur) ; [*gun*] partir ◆ **the revolver failed to** ~ le coup n'est pas parti ◆ ~ **away** (*fig*) vas-y !, tu peux y aller

2 [*engine*] tourner ◆ **it's only firing on two cylinders** il n'y a que deux cylindres qui marchent ; see also **cylinder** ◆ **the engine is firing badly** le moteur tourne mal

COMP **fire alarm** N alarme *f* d'incendie

fire-and-brimstone ADJ [*sermon, preacher*] apocalyptique

fire appliance N (*Brit*) (= *vehicle*) voiture *f* de pompiers ; (= *fire extinguisher*) extincteur *m*

fire blanket N couverture *f* anti-feu

fire brigade N (*esp Brit*) (brigade *f* des) (sapeurs-)pompiers *mpl*

fire chief N (US) capitaine *m* des pompiers

fire clay N (*Brit*) argile *f* réfractaire

fire curtain N (*Theat*) rideau *m* de fer

fire department N (US) ⇒ **fire brigade**

fire door N porte *f* coupe-feu

fire drill N exercice *m* d'évacuation (*en cas d'incendie*)

fire-eater N (*lit*) cracheur *m* de feu ; (*fig*) belliqueux *m*, -euse *f*

fire engine N (= *vehicle*) voiture *f* de pompiers ; (= *apparatus*) pompe *f* à incendie

fire escape N (= *staircase*) escalier *m* de secours ; (= *ladder*) échelle *f* d'incendie

fire exit N sortie *f* de secours

fire extinguisher N extincteur *m*

fire fighter N (= *fireman*) pompier *m* ; (*volunteer*) pompier *m* volontaire

fire-fighting N lutte *f* contre les incendies *or* anti-incendie, (*fig*) gestion *f* de l'urgence ADJ [*equipment, team*] de lutte contre les incendies *or* anti-incendie

fire hazard N ◆ **it's a** ~ **hazard** cela pourrait provoquer un incendie

fire hydrant N bouche *f* d'incendie

fire insurance N assurance-incendie *f*

fire irons NPL garniture *f* de foyer, accessoires *mpl* de cheminée

fire marshal N (US) ⇒ **fire chief**

fire power N (*Mil*) puissance *f* de feu

fire practice N ⇒ **fire drill**

fire prevention N mesures *fpl* de sécurité *or* de prévention contre l'incendie

fire-raiser N (*Brit*) incendiaire *mf*, pyromane *mf*

fire-raising N (*Brit*) pyromanie *f*

fire regulations NPL consignes *fpl* en cas d'incendie

fire retardant ADJ, N ignifuge *m*

fire risk N ⇒ **fire hazard**

fire sale N (*lit*) *vente de marchandises légèrement endommagées dans un incendie* ; (*fig*) braderie *f* ◆ ~ **sale prices** prix *mpl* massacrés

fire screen N écran *m* de cheminée

fire service N ⇒ **fire brigade**

fire station N caserne *f* de pompiers

fire trap N ◆ **it's a** ~ **trap** c'est une véritable souricière en cas d'incendie

fire truck N (US) ⇒ **fire engine**

fire warden N (US) responsable *mf* de la lutte contre les incendies *or* anti-incendie

fire watcher N guetteur *m* (*dans la prévention contre les incendies*)

fire watching N surveillance *f* contre les incendies

► **fire away** VI → **fire vi 1**

► **fire off** VT SEP → **fire vt 2**

► **fire up** VT SEP (*fig*) [+ *person*] enthousiasmer ; [+ *imagination*] exciter ◆ **to get ~d up about sth** s'enthousiasmer pour qch

firearm /ˈfaɪərˌɑːm/ N arme *f* à feu

fireback /ˈfaɪəbæk/ N [*of chimney*] contrecœur *m*, contre-feu *m*

fireball /ˈfaɪəbɔːl/ N (= *meteor*) bolide *m* ; (= *lightning, nuclear*) boule *f* de feu ; (*Mil*) bombe *f* explosive ◆ **he's a real** ~ il pète le feu*

Firebird /ˈfaɪəbɜːd/ N ◆ **The** ~ (*Mus*) l'Oiseau *m* de feu

firebomb /ˈfaɪəbɒm/ N bombe *f* incendiaire VT lancer une (*or* des) bombe(s) incendiaire(s) sur

firebrand /ˈfaɪəbrænd/ N (*lit*) brandon *m* ◆ **he's a real** ~ (= *energetic person*) il pète le feu* ; (*causing unrest*) c'est un fauteur de troubles

firebreak /ˈfaɪəbreɪk/ N pare-feu *m*, coupe-feu *m*

firebrick /ˈfaɪəbrɪk/ N brique *f* réfractaire

firebug* /ˈfaɪəbʌg/ N incendiaire *mf*, pyromane *mf*

firecracker /ˈfaɪəˌkrækəʳ/ N pétard *m*

firedamp /ˈfaɪədæmp/ N (*Min*) grisou *m*

firedogs /ˈfaɪədɒgz/ NPL chenets *mpl*

firefight /ˈfaɪəfaɪt/ N (*Mil*) échange *m* de coups de feu

firefly /ˈfaɪəflaɪ/ N luciole *f*

fireguard /ˈfaɪəgɑːd/ N (*in hearth*) pare-feu *m*, pare-étincelles *m* ; (*in forest*) pare-feu *m*, coupe-feu *m*

firehouse /ˈfaɪəhaʊs/ N (US) ⇒ **fire station** ; → **fire**

firelight /ˈfaɪəlaɪt/ N lueur *f* du feu ◆ **by** ~ à la lueur du feu

firelighter /ˈfaɪəˌlaɪtəʳ/ N allume-feu *m* ; (= *sticks*) ligot *m*

fireman /ˈfaɪəmən/ N (pl **-men**) (*in fire brigade*) (sapeur-)pompier *m* ; (*Rail*) chauffeur *m* COMP **fireman's lift** N ◆ **to give sb a ~'s lift** (*Brit*) porter qn sur l'épaule

fireplace /ˈfaɪəpleɪs/ N cheminée *f*, foyer *m*

fireplug /ˈfaɪəplʌg/ N (US) ⇒ **fire hydrant** ; → **fire**

fireproof /ˈfaɪəpruːf/ VT ignifuger ADJ [*material*] ignifugé, ininflammable COMP **fireproof dish** N (*Culin*) plat *m* allant au feu

fireproof door N porte *f* ignifugée *or* à revêtement ignifuge

fireside /ˈfaɪəsaɪd/ N foyer *m*, coin *m* du feu ◆ ~ **chair** fauteuil *m* club ; (*without arms*) chauffeuse *f*

firestorm /ˈfaɪəstɔːm/ N (*lit*) incendie *m* dévastateur ◆ **a** ~ **of protest** (US) un tollé (général), une levée de boucliers ◆ **a** ~ **of criticism** une avalanche de critiques ◆ **a** ~ **of controversy** une vive controverse

firewall /ˈfaɪəwɔːl/ N (*Internet*) mur *m* pare-feu

firewater* /ˈfaɪəˌwɔːtəʳ/ N alcool *m*, gnôle* *f*

firewood /ˈfaɪəwʊd/ N bois *m* de chauffage, bois *m* à brûler

firework /ˈfaɪəwɜːk/ N (fusée *f* de) feu *m* d'artifice NPL **fireworks** (also **firework(s) display**) feu *m* d'artifice

firing /ˈfaɪərɪŋ/ N 1 [*of pottery*] cuite *f*, cuisson *f* 2 (*Mil*) tir *m* ; (= *gun battle*) fusillade *f* COMP **firing hammer** N [*of firearm*] percuteur *m*

firing line N ligne *f* de tir ◆ **to be in the** ~ **line** (*lit*) être dans la ligne de tir ; (*fig*) être sous le feu des attaques ◆ **to be in sb's** ~ **line** (*fig*) être la cible de qn ◆ **to be out of the** ~ **line** (*fig*) ne plus être sous le feu des attaques

firing pin N ⇒ **firing hammer**

firing squad N peloton *m* d'exécution

firm¹ /fɜːm/ N (= *company*) entreprise *f* ◆ **there are four doctors in the** ~* (*Brit Med*) quatre médecins partagent le cabinet ◆ **the Firm*** (= *Mafia*) la Mafia

firm² /fɜːm/ ADJ 1 *(= hard) [fruit, ground, muscles, breasts, handshake]* ferme • **the cake should be ~ to the touch** le gâteau doit être ferme au toucher

2 *(= steady, secure) [table, ladder]* stable ; *[voice]* ferme • **a sofa that provides ~ support for the back** un canapé qui maintient bien le dos • **to get** *or* **take a ~ grip** *or* **hold on** *(lit) [object, person]* saisir fermement • **to have** *or* **keep a ~ grip** *or* **hold on** *(lit) [object, person]* tenir fermement ; see also **adj 3**

3 *(= strong, solid) [grasp, understanding]* bon ; *[foundation, base, support]* solide • **to be on a ~ footing** *[finances, relationship]* être sain • **to put sth on a ~ footing** établir qch sur une base solide • **to be in ~ control of sth, to keep sth under ~ control** tenir qch bien en main • **it is my ~ belief that ...** je crois fermement que ... • **to be a ~ believer in sth** croire fermement à qch • **it is my ~ conviction that ...** je suis fermement convaincu que ... • **to have a ~ grasp of sth** *[subject, theory]* avoir une connaissance solide de qch • **they became ~ friends** ils sont devenus de grands amis • **he's a ~ favourite (with the young)** c'est le grand favori *m* (des jeunes) • **to have** *or* **keep a ~ grip on power** tenir (fermement) les rênes du pouvoir • **to have** *or* **keep a ~ grip on spending** surveiller de près les dépenses

4 *(= resolute, determined) [person, leadership]* ferme ; *[action, measure]* sévère • **to be ~ about sth** être ferme à propos de qch • **with a ~ hand** d'une main ferme • **to be ~ with sb, to take a ~ hand with sb** être ferme avec qn • **to take a ~ line** *or* **stand (against sth)** adopter une attitude ferme (contre qch) • **to hold** *or* **stand ~ (against sth)** tenir bon (face à qch)

5 *(= definite, reliable) [agreement, conclusion, decision]* définitif ; *[commitment, intention]* ferme ; *[promise]* formel ; *[information, news]* sûr ; *[evidence]* solide ; *[date]* fixé, arrêté • **~ offer** *(Comm)* offre *f* ferme

6 *(Fin) [price]* ferme, stable ; *[currency]* stable • **the pound was ~ against the dollar** la livre était ferme par rapport au dollar • **to hold ~** rester stable *or* ferme

VT ⇒ **firm up vt sep**

VI ⇒ **firm up vi**

▸ **firm up** VI *[plans, programme]* se préciser ; *[muscles, stomach]* se raffermir ; *(Fin) [currency]* se consolider

VT SEP *[+ plans etc]* préciser ; *[+ muscles, stomach]* raffermir ; *(Fin) [+ currency]* consolider

firmament /ˈfɜːməmənt/ N firmament *m* • **she's a rising star in the political/movie ~** c'est une étoile montante du monde politique/du monde du cinéma

firmly /ˈfɜːmlɪ/ ADV *[fix, base]* solidement ; *[anchor]* profondément, solidement ; *[root]* profondément ; *[shut, establish, stick]* bien ; *[hold, believe, maintain, reject, tell]* fermement ; *[speak, say]* avec fermeté ; *[deny]* formellement • **~ in place** bien en place • **legs ~ planted on the ground** les jambes bien plantées sur le sol • **the jelly is ~ set** la gelée est bien ferme • **to be ~ committed to doing sth** s'être engagé à faire qch • **to be ~ in control of the situation** avoir la situation bien en main • **~ entrenched attitudes** des attitudes très arrêtées • **~ held opinions** des convictions *fpl* • **~ opposed to sth** fermement opposé à qch • **she had her sights ~ set on a career** elle avait bien l'intention de faire carrière

firmness /ˈfɜːmnɪs/ N *[of person, object, handshake, currency]* fermeté *f* ; *[of step, voice, manner]* fermeté *f*, assurance *f* • **~ of purpose** détermination *f*

firmware /ˈfɜːmwɛəʳ/ N *(Comput)* microprogramme *m*

first /fɜːst/ ADJ premier • **the ~ of May** le premier mai • **the twenty-~ time** la vingt et unième fois • **Charles the First** Charles Premier, Charles Ier • **in the ~ place** en premier lieu, d'abord • **~ principles** principes *mpl* premiers • **~ ascent** *(Climbing)* première *f* • **he did it the very ~ time** il l'a fait du premier coup • **it's not the ~ time and it won't be the last** ce n'est pas la première fois et ce ne sera pas la dernière • **they won for the ~ and last time in 1932** ils ont gagné une seule et unique fois en 1932 *or* pour la première et la dernière fois en 1932 • **there's always a ~ time** il y a un début à tout • **I haven't got the ~ idea** * je n'en ai pas la moindre idée • **she doesn't know the ~ thing about it** elle est complètement ignorante là-dessus • **~ things ~!** les choses importantes d'abord ! • **she's past her ~ youth** elle n'est plus de la première *or* prime jeunesse • **of the ~ water** *(fig)* de tout premier ordre ; see also **comp** ; → **first-class, floor, love, offender, sight**

♦ **first thing** • **he goes out ~ thing in the morning** *(= at early hour)* il sort très tôt le matin ; *(= soon after waking)* il sort dès qu'il est levé • **I'll do it ~ thing in the morning** *or* **~ thing tomorrow** je le ferai dès demain matin, je le ferai demain à la première heure • **take the pills ~ thing in the morning** prenez les pilules dès le réveil

ADV 1 *(= at first)* d'abord ; *(= firstly)* d'abord, premièrement ; *(= in the beginning)* au début ; *(= as a preliminary)* d'abord, au préalable • **~ you take off the string, then you ...** d'abord on enlève la ficelle, ensuite ..., premièrement on enlève la ficelle, deuxièmement on ... • **when we ~ lived here** quand nous sommes venus habiter ici • **he accepted but ~ he wanted ...** il a accepté mais au préalable *or* d'abord il voulait ... • **he's a patriot ~ and a socialist second** il est patriote avant d'être socialiste, chez lui, le patriote l'emporte sur le socialiste • **she arrived ~** elle est arrivée la première • **to come ~** *(= arrive)* arriver le premier ; *(in exam, competition)* être reçu premier • **my family comes ~** ma famille passe avant tout *or* compte plus que tout le reste • **one's health comes ~** il faut penser à sa santé d'abord, la santé est primordiale • **she comes ~ with him** pour lui, elle compte plus que tout *or* elle passe avant tout le reste • **it comes ~ with him** pour lui, c'est ça qui compte avant tout *or* c'est ça qui passe en premier • **~ come ~ served** les premiers arrivés seront les premiers servis • **you go ~!** *(gen)* allez-y d'abord ; *(in doorway)* passez devant !, après vous ! • **ladies ~!** les dames d'abord !, place aux dames ! • **women and children ~** les femmes et les enfants d'abord • **he says ~ one thing and then another** il se contredit sans cesse, il dit tantôt ceci, tantôt cela • **she looked at ~ one thing then another** elle regardait tantôt ceci, tantôt cela • **~ you agree, then you change your mind!** d'abord *or* pour commencer tu acceptes, et ensuite tu changes d'avis ! • **I must finish this ~** il faut que je termine *subj* ceci d'abord

♦ **first and foremost** tout d'abord, en tout premier lieu

♦ **first and last** avant tout

♦ **first of all, first off** * tout d'abord

2 *(= for the first time)* pour la première fois • **when did you ~ meet him?** quand est-ce que vous l'avez rencontré pour la première fois ?

3 *(= in preference)* plutôt • **I'd die ~!** plutôt mourir ! • **I'd resign ~!** je préfère démissionner !, plutôt démissionner ! • **I'd give up my job ~, rather than do that** j'aimerais mieux renoncer à mon travail que de faire cela

N 1 premier *m*, -ière *f* • **he was among the very ~ to arrive** il est arrivé parmi les tout premiers • **they were the ~ to come** ils sont arrivés les premiers • **he was among the ~ to meet her** il a été l'un des premiers à la rencontrer • **another ~ for Britain** *(= achievement)* une nouvelle première pour la Grande-Bretagne • **~ in, ~ out** premier entré, premier sorti • **the ~ I heard of it was when ...** je n'étais pas au courant, je l'ai appris quand ... • **that's the ~ I've heard of it!** c'est la première fois que j'entends parler de ça !

♦ **at first** d'abord, au commencement, au début

♦ **from first to last** du début *or* depuis le début (jusqu')à la fin

♦ **from the first** • **they liked him from the ~** ils l'ont aimé dès le début *or* dès le premier jour

2 (also **first gear**) première *f* (vitesse) • **in ~** en première

3 *(Brit Univ)* **he got a ~** ≈ il a eu sa licence avec mention très bien • **to get a double ~** *obtenir sa licence avec mention très bien dans deux disciplines*

COMP **first aid** N → **first aid**

first aider N secouriste *mf*

First Amendment (of the Constitution) N *(in US)* • **the First Amendment** le premier amendement de la constitution des États-Unis *(sur la liberté d'expression et de pensée)*

first base N *(Baseball)* première base *f* • **he didn't even get to ~ base** * *(fig)* il n'a même pas franchi le premier obstacle • **these ideas didn't even get to ~ base** ces idées n'ont jamais rien donné • **to get to ~ base with sb** * *(sexually)* aborder les préliminaires avec qn

first blood N • **to draw ~ blood** remporter le premier round *or* le premier tour

first-born ADJ, N premier-né *m*, première-née *f*

first-class ADJ → **first-class**

the first couple N *(US Pol)* le couple présidentiel

first cousin N cousin(e) *m(f)* germain(e) *or* au premier degré

first-day cover N *(Post)* émission *f* du premier jour

first edition N première édition *f* ; *(valuable)* édition *f* originale *or* princeps

first-ever ADJ tout premier

the first family N *(US Pol)* la famille du président

first floor N • **on the ~ floor** *(Brit)* au premier (étage) ; *(US)* au rez-de-chaussée

first-foot *(Scot)* N *première personne à franchir le seuil d'une maison le premier janvier* VI *rendre visite à ses parents ou amis après minuit à la Saint-Sylvestre*

first-footing N *(Scot) coutume écossaise de rendre visite à ses parents ou amis après minuit à la Saint-Sylvestre* ; → HOGMANAY

first form N *(Brit Scol)* ≈ (classe *f* de) sixième *f*

first fruits NPL *(fig)* premiers résultats *mpl*

first-generation ADJ de la première génération • **he's a ~-generation American** c'est un Américain de première génération

first grade N *(US Scol)* cours *m* préparatoire

first hand N • **I got it at ~ hand** c'est une information de première main

first-hand ADJ *[article, news, information]* de première main

first lady N première dame *f* ; *(US Pol)* première dame *f* des États-Unis *(ou personne servant d'hôtesse à sa place)* • **the ~ lady of jazz** la plus grande dame du jazz

first language N première langue *f*

first lieutenant N *(Brit Navy)* lieutenant *m* de vaisseau ; *(US Airforce)* lieutenant *m*

first mate N *(on ship)* second *m*

First Minister N *(in Scotland) chef du gouvernement régional écossais*

first name N prénom *m*, nom *m* de baptême • **my ~ name is Ellis** mon prénom est Ellis

first-name ADJ • **to be on ~-name terms with sb** appeler qn par son prénom

the first-named N *(frm)* le premier, la première

first night N *(Theat etc)* première *f*

first-nighter N *(Theat etc)* habitué(e) *m(f)* des premières

first officer N *(on ship)* ⇒ **first mate**

first-past-the-post system N *(Pol)* système *m* majoritaire à un tour

first performance N (Cine, Theat) première f ; (Mus) première audition f
first person N (Gram) première personne f
first-rate ADJ → **first-rate**
first school N (Brit) école f primaire
First Secretary N (in Wales) chef du gouvernement régional gallois
first strike capability N (Mil) capacité f de première frappe
first-time buyer N (primo-)accédant m à la propriété
first-timer* N 1 (= novice) débutant(e) m(f) 2 ⇒ **first-time buyer**
first violin N premier violon m
the First World N les pays mpl industrialisés
the First World War N la Première Guerre mondiale
first year infants NPL (Brit Scol) cours m préparatoire

-first /fɜːst/ ADV (in compounds) ◆ **feet-first** les pieds devant ; → **head**

first aid /ˈfɜːstˈeɪd/ N premiers secours mpl or soins mpl, secours mpl d'urgence ; (= subject of study) secourisme m ◆ **to give ~** donner les soins or secours d'urgence
COMP **first-aid box** N ⇒ **first-aid kit**
first-aid classes NPL cours mpl de secourisme
first-aid kit N trousse f de premiers secours or à pharmacie
first-aid post, first-aid station N poste m de secours
first-aid worker N secouriste mf

first-class /ˌfɜːstˈklɑːs/ ADJ 1 (= first-rate) [food, facilities, service, hotel] excellent ; [candidate, administrator] remarquable, exceptionnel ◆ **to have a ~ brain** être d'une intelligence exceptionnelle 2 [travel, flight] en première (classe) ; [ticket, passenger, carriage, compartment] de première (classe) 3 [mail, letter, stamp] en tarif prioritaire ◆ **~ postage** tarif m prioritaire 4 (Univ) ◆ **a ~ (honours) degree** ≈ une licence avec mention très bien ◆ **a ~ honours graduate** ≈ un(e) diplômé(e) qui a obtenu la mention très bien ◆ **to graduate with ~ honours** ≈ obtenir son diplôme avec la mention très bien ADV [travel, fly] en première classe ; (Post) [send, go] en tarif prioritaire

firstly /ˈfɜːstlɪ/ LANGUAGE IN USE 26.1, 26.2 ADV d'abord, premièrement, en premier lieu

first-rate /ˈfɜːstˈreɪt/ ADJ excellent ◆ **to do a ~ job** faire un excellent travail ◆ **he's a ~ translator** c'est un traducteur de premier ordre or un excellent traducteur

firth /fɜːθ/ N (gen Scot) estuaire m, bras m de mer ◆ **the Firth of Clyde** l'estuaire m de la Clyde

fiscal /ˈfɪskəl/ ADJ fiscal ; → **procurator** N (Scot Jur) ≈ procureur m de la République
COMP **fiscal drag** N ralentissement de l'économie dû à une fiscalisation excessive, fiscal drag m (SPEC)
fiscal year N année f fiscale, exercice m fiscal

fiscalist /ˈfɪskəlɪst/ N fiscaliste mf

fish /fɪʃ/ N (pl **fish** or **fishes**) poisson m ◆ **I caught two ~** j'ai pris deux poissons ◆ **to play a ~** fatiguer un poisson ◆ **I've got other ~ to fry** j'ai d'autres chats à fouetter ◆ **there are plenty more ~ in the sea** (gen) les occasions ne manquent pas ; (relationship) un(e) de perdu(e) dix de retrouvé(e)s ◆ **it's neither ~ nor fowl (or nor flesh) nor good red herring** ce n'est ni chair ni poisson ◆ **he's like a ~ out of water** il est comme un poisson hors de l'eau ◆ **he's a queer ~!*** c'est un drôle de numéro* or de lascar* (celui-là) ! ◆ **they consider him a poor ~*** ils le considèrent comme un pauvre type* ◆ **the Fishes** (Astron) les Poissons mpl ; → **big, cold, drink, goldfish, kettle**
VI pêcher ◆ **to go ~ing** aller à la pêche ◆ **to go salmon ~ing** aller à la pêche au saumon ◆ **to ~ for trout** pêcher la truite ◆ **to ~ in troubled waters** pêcher en eau trouble (fig) ◆ **to ~ for compliments** chercher les compliments ◆ **to ~ for information** aller à la pêche (aux informations) ◆ **~ or cut bait*** (US) allez, décide-toi !
VT [+ trout, salmon] pêcher ; [+ river, pool] pêcher dans ; (fig) (= find) pêcher* ◆ **they ~ed the cat out of the well** ils ont repêché le chat du puits ◆ **he ~ed a handkerchief from his pocket** il a extirpé un mouchoir de sa poche ◆ **where on earth did you ~ that (up) from?*** où diable as-tu été pêcher ça ?*
COMP **fish and chips** N (pl inv) poisson m frit et frites
fish-and-chip shop N friterie f
fish cake N croquette f de poisson
fish-eye N (in door) œil m panoramique
fish-eye lens N fish-eye m
fish factory N conserverie f de poisson
fish farm N centre m de pisciculture
fish farmer N pisciculteur m, -trice f
fish farming N pisciculture f
fish fingers NPL (Brit) bâtonnets mpl de poisson
fish fork N fourchette f à poisson ; see also **fish knife**
fish fry N (US) pique-nique m (où l'on fait frire du poisson)
fish glue N colle f de poisson
fish hook N hameçon m
fish kettle N poissonnière f
fish knife N (pl **fish knives**) couteau m à poisson ◆ **~ knife and fork** couvert m à poisson ; see also **fish fork**
fish ladder N échelle f à poissons
fish manure N engrais m de poisson
fish market N (retail) marché m au poisson ; (wholesale) criée f
fish meal N (= fertilizer) guano m de poisson ; (= feed) farine f de poisson
fish paste N (Culin) beurre m de poisson
fish-pole N (US) canne f à pêche
fish shop N poissonnerie f
fish slice N (Brit Culin) pelle f à poisson
fish sticks NPL (US) ⇒ **fish fingers**
fish store N (US) ⇒ **fish shop**
fish story* N (US) histoire f de pêcheur, histoire f marseillaise
fish-tail VI (US) [car] chasser
fish tank N aquarium m

► **fish out** VT SEP (from water) sortir, repêcher ; (from box, drawer etc) sortir, extirper (from de) ◆ **he ~ed out a piece of string from his pocket** il a extirpé un bout de ficelle de sa poche ◆ **to ~ sb out of a river** repêcher qn d'une rivière

► **fish up** VT SEP (from water) pêcher, repêcher ; (from bag etc) sortir ; see also **fish vt**

fishbone /ˈfɪʃbəʊn/ N arête f

fishbowl /ˈfɪʃbəʊl/ N bocal m (à poissons)

fisher /ˈfɪʃəʳ/ N pêcheur m

fisherman /ˈfɪʃəmən/ N (pl **-men**) pêcheur m ◆ **he's a keen ~** il aime beaucoup la pêche ◆ **~'s tale** (Brit fig) histoire f de pêcheur, histoire f marseillaise

fishery /ˈfɪʃərɪ/ N 1 (= area) zone f de pêche 2 (= industry) secteur m de la pêche 3 (= farm) établissement m piscicole

fishing /ˈfɪʃɪŋ/ N pêche f ◆ **"fishing prohibited"** "pêche interdite", "défense de pêcher" ◆ **"private fishing"** "pêche réservée"
COMP **fishing boat** N barque f de pêche ; (bigger) bateau m de pêche
fishing expedition N ◆ **to go on a ~ expedition** (lit) aller à la pêche ; (fig) chercher à en savoir plus long
fishing fleet N flottille f de pêche
fishing grounds NPL pêches fpl, lieux mpl de pêche
fishing harbour N port m de pêche
fishing line N ligne f de pêche
fishing net N (on fishing boat) filet m (de pêche) ; [of angler, child] épuisette f
fishing permit N permis m or licence f de pêche
fishing port N port m de pêche
fishing rod N canne f à pêche
fishing tackle N attirail m de pêche

fishmonger /ˈfɪʃˌmʌŋgəʳ/ N (esp Brit) marchand(e) m(f) de poisson, poissonnier m, -ière f ◆ **~'s (shop)** poissonnerie f

fishnet /ˈfɪʃnet/ N (on fishing boat) filet m (de pêche) ; [of angler] épuisette f COMP [tights, stockings] résille inv

fishplate /ˈfɪʃpleɪt/ N (Rail) éclisse f

fishpond /ˈfɪʃpɒnd/ N bassin m à poissons ; (in fish farming) vivier m

fishwife /ˈfɪʃwaɪf/ N (pl **-wives**) marchande f de poisson, poissonnière f ; (pej) harengère f, poissarde f ◆ **she talks like a ~** (pej) elle a un langage de poissarde, elle parle comme une marchande de poisson

fishy /ˈfɪʃɪ/ ADJ 1 [smell] de poisson ◆ **it smells ~ in here** ça sent le poisson ici ◆ **it tastes ~** ça a un goût de poisson 2 (* = suspicious) louche, douteux ◆ **the whole business seems or smells very ~ to me** toute cette histoire m'a l'air bien louche ◆ **it seems or smells rather ~** ça ne me paraît pas très catholique*

fissile /ˈfɪsaɪl/ ADJ fissile

fission /ˈfɪʃən/ N fission f ; → **nuclear**

fissionable /ˈfɪʃnəbl/ ADJ fissible

fissure /ˈfɪʃəʳ/ N (gen) fissure f, crevasse f ; (in brain) scissure f

fissured /ˈfɪʃəd/ ADJ fissuré

fist /fɪst/ N poing m ◆ **he hit me with his ~** il m'a donné un coup de poing ◆ **he shook his ~ at me** il m'a menacé du poing COMP **fist fight** N pugilat m, bagarre f à coups de poing ◆ **to have a ~ fight (with sb)** se battre à coups de poing (avec qn)

fistful /ˈfɪstfʊl/ N poignée f

fisticuffs /ˈfɪstɪkʌfs/ NPL coups mpl de poing

fistula /ˈfɪstjʊlə/ N (pl **fistulas** or **fistulae** /ˈfɪstjʊliː/) fistule f

fit¹ /fɪt/ ADJ 1 [person] (= suitable, suited) capable (for de) ; (= worthy) digne (for de) ◆ **he isn't ~ to rule the country** (= not capable) il n'est pas capable de gouverner le pays ; (= not worthy) il n'est pas digne de gouverner le pays ◆ **he's not ~ to drive** il n'est pas en mesure de conduire ◆ **I'm not ~ to be seen** je ne suis pas présentable ◆ **that shirt isn't ~ to wear** cette chemise n'est pas mettable ◆ **~ to eat** (= palatable) mangeable ; (= not poisonous) comestible, bon à manger ◆ **~ to drink** (= palatable) buvable ; (= not poisonous) potable ◆ **~ for habitation, ~ to live in** habitable ◆ **~ for (human) consumption** propre à la consommation ◆ **to be ~ for a job** (= qualified) avoir la compétence nécessaire pour faire un travail ◆ **a meal ~ for a king** un repas digne d'un roi ◆ **to be ~ for nothing** être incapable de faire quoi que ce soit, être bon à rien ◆ **to be ~ for the bin** être bon à jeter à la poubelle
2 (= right and proper) convenable, correct ; [time, occasion] propice ◆ **it is not ~ that you should be here** (frm) votre présence est inconvenante (frm) ◆ **it is not a ~ moment to ask that question** ce n'est pas le moment de poser cette question ◆ **he's not ~ company for my son** ce n'est pas une bonne fréquentation pour mon fils ◆ **to see or think ~ to do sth** trouver or juger bon de faire qch ◆ **I'll do as I think or see ~** je ferai comme bon me semblera ◆ **will she come? – if she sees ~** est-ce qu'elle viendra ? – oui, si elle le juge bon
3 (= healthy) en bonne santé ; (= in trim) en forme ; (* Brit = attractive) bien foutu* ◆ **to be**

as ~ as a fiddle être en pleine forme, se porter comme un charme ◆ **she is not yet ~ to travel** elle n'est pas encore en état de voyager ◆ **~ for duty** *(after illness)* en état de reprendre le travail ; *(Mil)* en état de reprendre le service ◆ **will he be ~ for Saturday's match?** *(footballer etc)* sera-t-il en état de jouer samedi ?, sera-t-il suffisamment en forme pour le match de samedi ? ; → **keep**

4 *(* = ready)* **to laugh ~ to burst** se tenir les côtes, rire comme un(e) bossu(e)* *or* une baleine* ◆ **to be ~ to drop** tomber de fatigue ◆ **~ to be tied**‡ *(US = angry)* furibard*

N ◆ **your dress is a very good ~** votre robe est tout à fait à votre taille ◆ **these trousers aren't a very good ~** ce pantalon n'est pas vraiment à ma *(or* sa *etc)* taille ◆ **the crash helmet was a tight ~ on his head** *(= too tight)* le casque était un peu trop juste pour lui ; *(= good fit)* le casque était exactement à sa taille

VT 1 *(= be the right size for) [clothes, shoes]* aller à ◆ **this coat ~s you well** ce manteau vous va bien *or* est bien à votre taille ◆ **the dress ~s her like a glove** cette robe lui va comme un gant ◆ **the washing machine is too big to ~ this space** la machine à laver est trop grande pour entrer dans cet espace ◆ **the key doesn't ~ the lock** cette clé ne correspond pas à la serrure ◆ **you can put these units together to ~ the shape of your kitchen** vous pouvez assembler les éléments en fonction de la forme de votre cuisine ◆ **the cover is tailored to ~ the seat** la housse est faite pour s'adapter au siège ◆ **roll out the pastry to ~ the top of the pie** abaisser la pâte au rouleau pour recouvrir la tourte ◆ **sheets to ~ a double bed** des draps pour un grand lit ◆ **"one size fits all"** "taille unique" ◆ **"to fit ages 5 to 6"** "5-6 ans" ◆ **"to fit waist sizes 70 to 75cm"** "tour de taille 70-75 cm" ; → **cap**

2 *(= find space or time for)* **you can ~ five people into this car** il y a de la place pour cinq dans cette voiture ◆ **to ~ a dental appointment into one's diary** trouver un créneau dans son emploi du temps pour un rendez-vous chez le dentiste, caser* un rendez-vous chez le dentiste dans son emploi du temps ◆ **I can't ~ any more meetings into my schedule** je n'ai pas le temps pour d'autres réunions dans mon emploi du temps, il m'est impossible de caser* d'autres réunions dans mon emploi du temps

3 *(= correspond to, match) [+ mood, definition, stereotype]* correspondre à ; *[+ needs]* répondre à ◆ **the building has been adapted to ~ the needs of disabled people** ce bâtiment a été adapté pour répondre aux besoins des handicapés ◆ **his speech was tailored to ~ the mood of the conference** son discours était adapté à l'ambiance du congrès ◆ **a man ~ting this description** un homme répondant à ce signalement ◆ **to ~ the circumstances** être adapté aux circonstances ◆ **this hypothesis appears to ~ the facts** cette hypothèse semble concorder avec les faits ◆ **the facts ~ the theory** les faits concordent avec la théorie ◆ **she doesn't ~ the profile** *or* **picture of a typical drug smuggler** elle ne correspond pas à l'idée que l'on se fait *or* à l'image que l'on a d'un trafiquant de drogue ◆ **he doesn't ~ my image of a good teacher** il ne correspond pas à l'idée que je me fais d'un bon professeur ◆ **the punishment should ~ the crime** le châtiment doit être proportionné au crime ◆ **the curtains didn't ~ the colour scheme** les rideaux n'allaient pas avec les couleurs de la pièce, la couleur des rideaux jurait avec le reste

4 *[+ garment]* ajuster

5 *(= put in place)* mettre ; *(= fix)* fixer *(on* sur*)* ; *(= install)* poser, mettre ◆ **he ~ted it to the side of the instrument** il l'a mis *or* fixé sur le côté de l'instrument ◆ **to ~ a key in the lock** engager une clé dans la serrure ◆ **to ~ two things together** assembler *or* ajuster deux objets ◆ **~ part A to part B** assemblez la pièce A avec la pièce B ◆ **to ~ sth into place** mettre qch en place ◆ **I had a new window ~ted** on m'a posé *or* installé une nouvelle fenêtre ◆ **to have a new kitchen ~ted** se faire installer une nouvelle cuisine ◆ **car ~ted with a radio** voiture *f* équipée d'une radio ◆ **to ~ lights to a bicycle, to ~ a bicycle with lights** installer des feux sur un vélo ◆ **he has been ~ted with a new hearing aid** on lui a mis *or* posé un nouvel appareil auditif

6 *(frm)* ◆ **to ~ sb for sth/to do sth** préparer qn *or* rendre qn apte à qch/à faire qch ◆ **to ~ o.s. for a job** se préparer à un travail

VI 1 ◆ **the dress doesn't ~ very well** cette robe n'est pas à sa taille *or* ne lui va pas ◆ **it ~s like a glove** *[garment]* cela me *(or* vous *etc)* va comme un gant ; *[suggestion]* cela me *(or* leur *etc)* convient parfaitement

2 *(= be the right size, shape etc)* ◆ **this key/part doesn't ~** ce n'est pas la bonne clé/pièce ◆ **the saucepan lid doesn't ~** le couvercle ne va pas sur la casserole ◆ **it should ~ on this end somewhere** cela doit aller *or* se mettre là au bout (quelque part)

3 *(= have enough room)* entrer, tenir ◆ **it's too big to ~ into the box** c'est trop grand pour entrer *or* tenir dans la boîte ◆ **the clothes won't ~ into the suitcase** les vêtements ne vont pas entrer *or* tenir dans la valise ◆ **a computer small enough to ~ into your pocket** un ordinateur qui tient dans la poche ◆ **my CV ~s onto one page** mon CV tient en une page ◆ **seven people in one car? We'll never ~!** sept personnes dans une voiture ? Il n'y aura jamais assez de place !

4 *(fig = add up, match) [facts]* cadrer ◆ **it doesn't ~ with what he said to me** ça ne correspond pas à *or* ne cadre pas avec ce qu'il m'a dit ◆ **how does this idea ~ into your overall plan?** comment cette idée s'inscrit-elle dans votre plan d'ensemble ? ◆ **people don't always ~ neatly into categories** les gens ne rentrent pas toujours facilement dans des catégories bien définies ◆ **his face doesn't ~ here** il détonne ici ◆ **suddenly everything ~ted into place** soudain, tout est devenu clair ◆ **it all ~s (into place) now!** tout s'explique !

▸ **fit in** **VI** 1 *(= add up, match) [fact]* cadrer ◆ **this doesn't ~ in with what I was taught at school** ceci ne correspond pas à *or* ne cadre pas avec ce que l'on m'a appris à l'école

2 *(= integrate)* **at school she has problems ~ting in** *(with other children)* à l'école elle a du mal à s'intégrer ; *(= getting used to lessons etc)* elle a du mal à s'adapter à l'école ◆ **he has ~ted in well with the other members of our team** il s'est bien entendu avec les autres membres de notre équipe, il s'est bien intégré dans notre équipe

3 *(into room, car etc = have room)* **will we all ~ in?** y aura-t-il assez de place pour nous tous ?, allons-nous tous entrer *or* tenir ? ◆ **will the toys all ~ in?** y aura-t-il assez de place pour tous les jouets ? ◆ **the box is too small for all his toys to ~ in** la boîte est trop petite pour contenir tous ses jouets

VT SEP 1 *(= find room for) [+ object, person]* faire entrer, trouver de la place pour ◆ **can you ~ another book in?** y a-t-il encore de la place pour un livre ?

2 *(= adapt)* adapter, faire concorder ◆ **I'll try to ~ my plans in with yours** je tâcherai de m'adapter en fonction de tes plans

3 *(= find time for) [+ person]* prendre, caser* ◆ **the doctor can ~ you in tomorrow at three** le docteur peut vous prendre demain à 15 heures ◆ **have you got time to ~ in a quick meeting?** avez-vous le temps d'assister à une réunion rapide ?

▸ **fit on** **VI** ◆ **the bottle top won't ~ on** le bouchon de la bouteille n'est pas adapté

VT SEP *[+ object]* mettre

▸ **fit out** **VT SEP** 1 *[+ expedition, person]* équiper

2 *(= furnish) [+ room, office, building]* aménager ◆ **to ~ a room/building out with sth** installer qch dans une pièce/un bâtiment ◆ **they've ~ted one room out as an office** ils ont transformé *or* aménagé une pièce en bureau

3 *[+ ship]* armer

▸ **fit up** **VT SEP** 1 ◆ **they've fitted their house up with a burglar alarm** ils ont installé une alarme dans leur maison ◆ **they've ~ted one room up as an office** ils ont transformé *or* aménagé une pièce en bureau

2 *(* Brit = frame)* ◆ **to fit sb up** faire porter le chapeau à qn

fit² /fɪt/ **N** 1 *(Med)* attaque *f* ; *[of epilepsy]* crise *f* ◆ **~ of coughing** quinte *f* de toux ◆ **to have** *or* **throw* a ~** avoir *or* piquer* une crise ◆ **she'll have a ~ when we tell her*** elle va avoir une attaque *or* elle va piquer une crise quand on lui dira ça* ; → **blue, epileptic, faint**

2 *(= outburst)* mouvement *m*, accès *m* ◆ **in a ~ of anger** dans un mouvement *or* accès de colère ◆ **a ~ of crying** une crise de larmes ◆ **to be in ~s (of laughter)** se tordre de rire ◆ **to get a ~ of the giggles** avoir le fou rire

◆ **in fits and starts** par à-coups

VI *(Med)* faire une attaque

fitful /ˈfɪtfʊl/ **ADJ** *[sleep]* troublé, agité ; *[showers]* intermittent ; *[breeze]* capricieux, changeant ◆ **~ enthusiasm/anger** des accès *mpl* d'enthousiasme/de colère ◆ **to have a ~ night** passer une nuit agitée

fitfully /ˈfɪtfəlɪ/ **ADV** *[sleep, doze]* de façon intermittente ; *[work]* par à-coups ◆ **the sun shone ~** le soleil faisait de brèves apparitions

fitment /ˈfɪtmənt/ **N** 1 *(Brit) (= built-in furniture)* meuble *m* encastré ; *(= cupboard)* placard *m* encastré ; *(in kitchen)* élément *m* (de cuisine) 2 *(= part: for vacuum cleaner, mixer etc)* accessoire *m* ◆ **it's part of the light ~** cela fait partie du luminaire

fitness /ˈfɪtnɪs/ **N** 1 *(= health)* santé *f* ; *(= physical trimness)* forme *f* 2 *(= suitability) [of remark]* à-propos *m*, justesse *f* ; *[of person]* aptitude *f (for* à*)*

COMP **fitness centre** **N** centre *m* de fitness *or* de culture physique

fitness fanatic*, **fitness freak*** **N** *(pej)* fana* *mf* de culture physique

fitness instructor **N** professeur *mf* de fitness *or* de culture physique

fitness programme **N** programme *m* de fitness *or* de culture physique

fitness room **N** salle *f* de fitness *or* de culture physique

fitness test **N** *(Sport)* test *m* de condition physique

fitted /ˈfɪtɪd/ **ADJ** 1 *(Brit) [wardrobe, kitchen units]* encastré ; *[kitchen]* intégré ; *[bedroom]* meublé ; *[bathroom]* aménagé ◆ **a fully-~ kitchen** une cuisine entièrement équipée 2 *(= tailored) [jacket, shirt]* ajusté 3 *(frm = suited)* ◆ **~ to do sth** apte à faire qch ◆ **well/ill ~ to do sth** vraiment/pas vraiment fait pour faire qch ◆ **~ for** *or* **to a task** apte pour une tâche

COMP **fitted carpet** **N** moquette *f* ◆ **the room has a ~ carpet** la pièce est moquettée

fitted sheet **N** drap-housse *m*

fitter /ˈfɪtəʳ/ **N** 1 *[of machine, device]* monteur *m* ; *[of carpet]* poseur *m* 2 *(Dress)* essayeur *m*, -euse *f*

fitting /ˈfɪtɪŋ/ **ADJ** *[remark]* pertinent, juste **N** 1 *(Dress)* essayage *m* 2 *(Brit: gen pl: in house etc)* **~s** installations *fpl* ◆ **bathroom ~s** installations *fpl* sanitaires ◆ **electrical ~s** installations *fpl* électriques, appareillage *m* électrique ◆ **furniture and ~s** mobilier *m* et installations *fpl* ◆ **office ~s** équipement *m* de bureau ; → **light¹**

COMP **fitting room** **N** salon *m* d'essayage

-fitting /ˈfɪtɪŋ/ ADJ *(in compounds)* ◆ **ill-fitting** qui ne va pas ◆ **wide-fitting** large ; → **close¹, loose, tight**

fittingly /ˈfɪtɪŋlɪ/ ADV *[dress]* convenablement (pour l'occasion) ; *[titled, named]* de façon appropriée ◆ **a ~ exciting finish to a magnificent match** une fin passionnante à la hauteur de la qualité du match ◆ **the speech was ~ solemn** le discours avait la solennité qui convenait ◆ **~, he won his first world title before his home crowd** comme il convient, il a remporté son premier titre mondial devant son public

five /faɪv/ ADJ cinq *inv* N cinq *m* ◆ **to take ~** * *(esp US)* faire une pause ; *for other phrases see* **six** NPL **fives** *(Sport) sorte de jeu de pelote (à la main)* PRON cinq ◆ **there are ~** il y en a cinq

COMP **five-and-dime, five-and-ten** N *(US)* bazar *m*
five-a-side (football) N *(Brit)* football *m* à cinq
five-by-five * ADJ *(US fig)* aussi gros que grand
Five Nations Tournament N *(Rugby)* tournoi *m* des cinq nations
five-o'clock shadow N barbe *f* d'un jour
five spot * N *(US)* billet *m* de cinq dollars
five-star hotel N hôtel *m* cinq étoiles
five-star restaurant N ≈ restaurant *m* trois étoiles
five-year ADJ quinquennal
five-year man * N *(US Univ: hum)* éternel redoublant *m*
five-year plan N plan *m* quinquennal

fiver * /ˈfaɪvəʳ/ N *(Brit)* billet *m* de cinq livres ; *(US)* billet *m* de cinq dollars

fix /fɪks/ VT [1] *(= make firm) (with nails etc)* fixer ; *(with ropes etc)* attacher ◆ **to ~ a stake in the ground** enfoncer un pieu en terre ◆ **to ~ bayonets** *(Mil)* mettre (la) baïonnette au canon ; see also **fixed**
[2] *(= direct, aim) [+ gun, camera, radar]* diriger *(on* sur) ; *[+ attention]* fixer *(on* sur) ◆ **to ~ one's eyes on sb/sth** fixer qn/qch du regard ◆ **all eyes were ~ed on her** tous les regards *or* tous les yeux étaient fixés sur elle ◆ **he ~ed him with an angry glare** il l'a fixé d'un regard furieux ◆ **to ~ sth in one's mind** graver *or* imprimer qch dans son esprit ◆ **to ~ one's hopes on sth** mettre tous ses espoirs en qch ◆ **to ~ the blame on sb** attribuer *or* faire endosser la responsabilité à qn
[3] *(= arrange, decide)* décider, arrêter ; *[+ time, price]* fixer, arrêter ; *[+ limit]* fixer, établir ◆ **on the date ~ed** à la date convenue ◆ **nothing has been ~ed yet** rien n'a encore été décidé, il n'y a encore rien d'arrêté *or* de décidé
[4] *(Phot)* fixer
[5] * arranger, préparer ◆ **to ~ one's hair** se passer un coup de peigne ◆ **can I ~ you a drink?** vous prendrez bien un verre ? ◆ **I'll go and ~ us something to eat** je vais vite (nous) préparer un petit quelque chose à manger
[6] *(= deal with)* arranger ; *(= mend)* réparer ◆ **don't worry, I'll ~ it all** ne vous en faites pas, je vais tout arranger ◆ **he ~ed it with the police before he organized the demonstration** il a attendu d'avoir le feu vert* de la police *or* il s'est arrangé avec la police avant d'organiser la manifestation ◆ **I'll soon ~ him** *, **I'll ~ his wagon** * *(US)* je vais lui régler son compte ◆ **to ~ a flat tyre** réparer un pneu
[7] *(* = rig, corrupt) [+ person, witness, jury] (gen)* corrompre ; *(= bribe)* acheter, soudoyer ; *[+ match, fight, election, trial]* truquer ; *[+ prices]* fixer (de manière déloyale)
VI *(US = intend)* ◆ **to be ~ing to do sth** * avoir l'intention de faire qch, compter faire qch
N [1] * ennui *m*, embêtement* *m* ◆ **to be in/get into a ~** être/se mettre dans le pétrin* *or* dans de beaux draps ◆ **what a ~!** nous voilà dans de beaux draps *or* dans le pétrin !*
[2] *(⁑ = dose) [of drugs] (= injection)* piqûre *f*, piquouse⁑ *f* ; *[of coffee, chocolate, caffeine]* dose* *f* ◆ **to get** *or* **give o.s. a ~** *(Drugs)* se shooter⁑, se piquer ◆ **I need my daily ~ of coffee/chocolate** *etc (hum)* il me faut ma dose quotidienne de café/chocolat *etc*
[3] *(= position of plane or ship)* position *f* ◆ **I've got a ~ on him now** j'ai sa position maintenant ◆ **to take a ~ on** *[+ ship]* déterminer la position de ◆ **I can't get a ~ on it** * *(fig)* je n'arrive pas à m'en faire une idée claire
[4] *(= trick)* ◆ **it's a ~** * c'est truqué, c'est une combine*

COMP **fixing bath** N *(Phot) (= liquid)* bain *m* de fixage, fixateur *m* ; *(= container)* bac *m* de fixateur

► **fix on** VT FUS choisir ◆ **they finally ~ed on that house** leur choix s'est finalement arrêté sur cette maison
VT SEP *[+ lid]* fixer, attacher

► **fix up** VI s'arranger *(to do sth* pour faire qch)
VT SEP arranger, combiner ◆ **I'll try to ~ something up** je tâcherai d'arranger quelque chose ◆ **let's ~ it all up now** décidons tout de suite ◆ **to ~ sb up with sth** trouver qch pour qn

fixated /fɪkˈseɪtɪd/ ADJ *(Psych)* qui fait une fixation ; *(fig)* obsédé *(on* par)

fixation /fɪkˈseɪʃən/ N [1] *(Chem, Phot)* fixation *f* [2] ◆ **to have a ~ about** *or* **on** *or* **with sth** faire une fixation sur qch

fixative /ˈfɪksətɪv/ N fixatif *m*

fixed /fɪkst/ ADJ [1] *(= set) [amount, position, time, intervals, stare, price]* fixe ; *[smile, grin]* figé ; *[idea]* arrêté ; *(Ling) [stress, word order]* fixe ◆ **(of) no ~ abode** *or* **address** *(Jur)* sans domicile fixe ◆ **there's no ~ agenda** il n'y a pas d'ordre du jour bien arrêté ◆ **with ~ bayonets** baïonnette au canon
[2] *(= rigged) [election, trial, match, race]* truqué ; *[jury]* soudoyé, acheté
[3] * ◆ **how are we ~ for time ?** on a combien de temps ?, on en est où question temps* ? ◆ **how are you ~ for cigarettes?** il te reste combien de cigarettes ?, tu en es où question cigarettes* ? ◆ **how are you ~ for tonight?** tu es libre ce soir ?, tu as prévu quelque chose ce soir ? ◆ **how are you ~ for transport?** comment fais-tu question transport* ?

COMP **fixed assets** NPL *(Comm)* immobilisations *fpl*
fixed cost contract N marché *m* à prix forfaitaire
fixed costs NPL *(Comm)* frais *mpl* fixes
fixed decimal point N virgule *f* fixe
fixed disk N *(Comput)* disque *m* fixe
fixed exchange rate N *(Econ)* taux *m* de change fixe
fixed menu N (menu *m* à) prix *m* fixe
fixed penalty (fine) N amende *f* forfaitaire
fixed point N ⇒ **fixed decimal point**
fixed-point notation *or* **representation** N *(Comput)* notation *f* en virgule fixe
fixed-rate financing N financement *m* à taux fixe
fixed star N étoile *f* fixe
fixed-term contract N contrat *m* à durée déterminée
fixed-term tenancy N location *f* à durée déterminée
fixed-wing aircraft N aéronef *m* à voilure fixe

fixedly /ˈfɪksɪdlɪ/ ADV *[stare]* fixement ◆ **to smile ~** avoir un sourire figé

fixer /ˈfɪksəʳ/ N [1] *(Phot)* fixateur *m* [2] *(⁑ = person)* combinard(e)⁑ *m(f)*

fixings /ˈfɪksɪŋz/ NPL [1] *(= nuts and bolts)* visserie *f* [2] *(US Culin)* garniture *f*, accompagnement *m*

fixity /ˈfɪksɪtɪ/ N *[of stare]* fixité *f* ◆ **his ~ of purpose** sa détermination inébranlable

fixture /ˈfɪkstʃəʳ/ N [1] *(gen pl: in building)* installation *f* fixe ; *(Jur)* immeuble *m*, bien *m* immeuble ◆ **the house was sold with ~s and fittings** *(Brit)* on a vendu la maison avec les aménagements intérieurs ◆ **€2,000 for ~s and fittings** *(Brit)* 2 000 € de reprise ◆ **lighting ~s** appareillage *m* électrique ◆ **she's a ~** * *(fig)* elle fait partie du mobilier* [2] *(Brit Sport)* match *m* (prévu), rencontre *f* ◆ **~ list** calendrier *m*

fizz /fɪz/ VI *[drink]* pétiller, mousser ; *[steam etc]* siffler N [1] pétillement *m*, sifflement *m* [2] *(fig)* punch* *m* ◆ **they need to put some ~ into their election campaign** leur campagne électorale a besoin d'un peu plus de nerf [3] ⁑ champ⁑ *m*, champagne *m* ; *(US)* eau *f* or boisson *f* gazeuse

► **fizz up** VI monter (en pétillant), mousser

fizzle /ˈfɪzl/ VI pétiller

► **fizzle out** VI *[firework]* rater *(une fois en l'air)* ; *[party, event]* se terminer ; *[book, film, plot]* se terminer en queue de poisson ; *[plans]* tomber à l'eau ; *[enthusiasm, interest]* tomber

fizzy /ˈfɪzɪ/ ADJ *(esp Brit) [soft drink]* pétillant, gazeux ; *[wine]* mousseux, pétillant

fjord /fjɔːd/ N ⇒ **fiord**

FL abbrev of **Florida**

Fla. abbrev of **Florida**

flab * /flæb/ N *(= fat)* graisse *f* superflue, lard* *m*

flabbergast * /ˈflæbəgɑːst/ VT sidérer* ◆ **I was ~ed at this** ça m'a sidéré*

flabbiness /ˈflæbɪnɪs/ N *[of muscle, flesh]* aspect *m* flasque ; *(fig)* mollesse *f*

flabby /ˈflæbɪ/ ADJ [1] *(physically) [thighs, face, stomach, muscles]* mou (molle *f*), flasque ; *[person, skin]* flasque [2] *(= ineffectual) [country, economy]* mou (molle *f*)

flaccid /ˈflæksɪd/ ADJ *[muscle, flesh]* flasque, mou (molle *f*)

flaccidity /flækˈsɪdɪtɪ/ N flaccidité *f*

flack /flæk/ N *(US Cine, Press)* attaché(e) *m(f)* de presse VI être attaché(e) de presse

flag¹ /flæg/ N [1] drapeau *m* ; *(Naut)* pavillon *m* ◆ **~ of truce, white ~** drapeau *m* blanc ◆ **black ~** *[of pirates]* pavillon *m* noir ◆ **~ of convenience, ~ of necessity** *(US)* pavillon *m* de complaisance ◆ **they put the ~s out** * *(Brit fig)* ils ont fêté ça ◆ **with (all) ~s flying** *(fig)* en pavoisant ◆ **to go down with ~s flying** *(Naut)* couler pavillon haut ; *(fig)* mener la lutte jusqu'au bout ◆ **to keep the ~ flying** *(fig)* maintenir les traditions ◆ **to fly the ~ for one's country** défendre les couleurs de son pays ◆ **to wrap** *or* **drape o.s. in the ~** *(esp US)* servir ses intérêts personnels sous couvert de patriotisme ; → **red, show**
[2] *[of taxi]* **the ~ was down** ≈ le taxi était pris
[3] *(for charity)* insigne *m (d'une œuvre charitable)*
[4] *(Comput)* drapeau *m*
VT [1] orner *or* garnir de drapeaux ; *[+ street, building, ship]* pavoiser
[2] *(= mark page)* signaler *(avec une marque)* ; *(Comput)* signaler *(avec un drapeau)*

COMP **flag carrier** N *(= airline)* compagnie *f* nationale
Flag Day N *(US)* le 14 juin *(anniversaire du drapeau américain)*
flag day N *(Brit)* journée *f* de vente d'insignes *(pour une œuvre charitable)* ◆ **~ day in aid of the war-blinded** journée *f* des *or* pour les aveugles de guerre
flag officer N *(Naut)* officier *m* supérieur
flag-waving *(fig)* N déclarations *fpl* cocardières ADJ *[politicians, patriots etc]* cocardier

► **flag down** VT SEP *[+ taxi, bus, car]* héler, faire signe à ; *[police]* faire signe de s'arrêter à

flag² /flæg/ VI *[athlete, walker]* faiblir ; *[worker]* fléchir, se relâcher ; *[conversation]* traîner, languir ; *[interest, spirits]* faiblir ; *[enthusiasm]* tomber ; *[sales]* fléchir ; *[market]* faiblir ; *[economy, economic recovery]* s'essouffler ; *[film, novel, album]* faiblir ◆ **he's ~ging** il ne va pas fort ◆ **the film begins well but starts ~ging towards the middle** le film commence bien mais se met à faiblir vers le milieu

flag[3] / flæg / N (*= iris*) iris *m* (des marais)

flag[4] / flæg / N (also **flagstone**) dalle *f*

flagellant /ˈflædʒələnt/ N 1 (*Rel*) flagellant *m* 2 (*sexual*) adepte *mf* de la flagellation

flagellate /ˈflædʒəleɪt/ ADJ, N (*Bio*) flagellé *m* VT flageller

flagellation /ˌflædʒəˈleɪʃən/ N flagellation *f*

flagellum /fləˈdʒeləm/ N (pl **flagellums** *or* **flagella** /fləˈdʒelə/) flagelle *m*

flageolet /ˌflædʒəʊˈlet/ N 1 (*Mus*) flageolet *m* 2 (also **flageolet bean**) flageolet *m*

flagged / flægd / ADJ *[floor]* dallé

flagon /ˈflægən/ N (*of glass*) (grande) bouteille *f* ; (*larger*) bonbonne *f* ; (*= jug*) (grosse) cruche *f*

flagpole /ˈflægpəʊl/ N mât *m* (*portant le drapeau*) ◆ **to run an idea/proposal up the ~** * lancer une idée/proposition pour tâter le terrain ◆ **let's run this up the ~ (and see who salutes it)** proposons cela (et voyons les réactions)

flagrant /ˈfleɪgrənt/ ADJ flagrant

flagrante delicto /fləˈgræntɪdɪˈlɪktəʊ/ ◆ **in ~** ADV en flagrant délit

flagrantly /ˈfleɪgrəntlɪ/ ADV *[abuse, disregard]* de manière flagrante ; *[silly, untrue, unequal]* manifestement ; *[provocative]* ouvertement ◆ **~ unjust/indiscreet** d'une injustice/d'une indiscrétion flagrante

flagship /ˈflægʃɪp/ N (*Naut*) vaisseau *m* amiral ; (*Comm*) produit *m* phare COMP (*Comm*) *[product, store, company, TV programme]* phare

flagstaff /ˈflægstɑːf/ N mât *m* (*portant le drapeau*) ; (*Naut*) mât *m* de pavillon

flagstone /ˈflægstəʊn/ N ⇒ **flag**[4]

flail / fleɪl / N (*Agr*) fléau *m* VT (*Agr*) *[+ corn]* battre au fléau VI *[arms]* (also **flail about**) battre l'air

flair /flɛəʳ/ N 1 (*= talent*) flair *m* ; (*= perceptiveness*) perspicacité *f* ◆ **to have a ~ for** avoir un don pour ◆ **to have a ~ for getting into trouble** (*iro*) avoir le don pour s'attirer des ennuis 2 (*= style, elegance*) style *m*

flak / flæk / N 1 (*Mil*) (*= firing*) tir *m* antiaérien *or* de DCA ; (*= guns*) canons *mpl* antiaériens *or* de DCA ; (*= flashes*) éclairs *mpl* 2 (** = criticism*) critiques *fpl* ◆ **he got a lot of ~ (for that)** il s'est fait descendre en flammes (pour ça) ◆ **he got a lot of ~ from ...** il s'est fait éreinter par ... COMP **flak-jacket** N gilet *m* pare-balles *inv* **flak ship** N bâtiment *m* de DCA

flake / fleɪk / N 1 *[of snow, cereal]* flocon *m* ; *[of paint]* écaillure *f* ; *[of rust]* écaille *f* ; see also **cornflakes** 2 (** = eccentric*) barjo* *mf* VI (also **flake off**) *[stone, plaster]* s'effriter, s'écailler ; *[paint]* s'écailler ; *[skin]* peler, se desquamer (*Med*) VT (also **flake off**) effriter, écailler ◆ **~d almonds** (*Culin*) amandes *fpl* effilées COMP **flake-white** N blanc *m* de plomb

► **flake off** VI 1 → **flake** vt 2 (*US*) ◆ **flake off !** ** fous le camp ! **, de l'air ! *

► **flake out** ** VI (*Brit*) (*= collapse*) tomber dans les pommes*, tourner de l'œil* ; (*= fall asleep*) s'endormir *or* tomber (tout d'une masse) ◆ **to be ~d out** être crevé* *or* à plat*

flakey ** /ˈfleɪkɪ/ ADJ ⇒ **flaky**

flaky /ˈfleɪkɪ/ ADJ 1 floconneux 2 ** bizarre, excentrique N* ◆ **to chuck** *or* **throw a flaky** piquer une crise* COMP **flaky pastry** N pâte *f* feuilletée

flambé /ˈflɒːmbeɪ/ ADJ flambé VT flamber ◆ **~ed steaks** steaks *mpl* flambés

flamboyance /flæmˈbɔɪəns/ N extravagance *f*

flamboyant /flæmˈbɔɪənt/ ADJ 1 *[colour]* flamboyant, éclatant ; *[person, character]* haut en couleur ; *[rudeness]* ostentatoire ; *[speech]* retentissant ; *[style, dress, manners]* extravagant 2 (*Archit*) flamboyant

flame / fleɪm / N 1 flamme *f* ; (*fig*) *[of passion, enthusiasm]* flamme *f*, ardeur *f* ◆ **to feed** *or* **fan the ~s** (*lit*) attiser le feu ; (*fig*) jeter de l'huile sur le feu

◆ **in flames** en flammes, en feu ◆ **to go up in ~s** (*= catch fire*) s'embraser ; (*= be destroyed by fire*) être détruit par le feu ; (*fig*) partir en fumée

2 ◆ **she's one of his old ~s** * c'est un de ses anciens béguins*

VI *[fire]* flamber ; *[passion]* brûler ◆ **her cheeks ~d** ses joues se sont empourprées

VT (*Internet*) envoyer des messages d'insulte à

COMP **flame-coloured** ADJ (rouge) feu *inv*
flame gun N ⇒ **flamethrower**
flame-proof dish N plat *m* allant au feu
flame red N rouge *m* vif
flame-red ADJ rouge vif
flame retardant ADJ, N ignifuge *m*
flame war N (*Internet*) échange *m* d'insultes

► **flame up** VI *[fire]* flamber

flamenco /fləˈmeŋkəʊ/ ADJ, N flamenco *m*

flamethrower /ˈfleɪmˌθrəʊəʳ/ N lance-flammes *m inv*

flaming /ˈfleɪmɪŋ/ ADJ 1 (*= burning*) *[sun, fire]* ardent ; *[torch]* allumé 2 (*in colour*) *[sunset]* embrasé ◆ **~ red hair** des cheveux d'un roux flamboyant 3 (** = furious*) *[row]* violent 4 (*esp Brit * = damn*) fichu*, satané* ◆ **the ~ car's locked** cette fichue *or* satanée voiture est fermée à clé ◆ **it's a ~ nuisance!** c'est vraiment enquiquinant !* ADV (*esp Brit **) ◆ **he's ~ useless !** il est complètement nul !* ◆ **you get so ~ worked up about everything!** c'est pas possible de s'énerver comme ça pour un rien !*

flamingo /fləˈmɪŋgəʊ/ N (pl **flamingos** *or* **flamingoes**) flamant *m* (rose)

flammable /ˈflæməbl/ ADJ inflammable

flan / flæn / N (*= tart*) tarte *f* ; (*savoury*) ≃ quiche *f* ; (*US*) (*= custard*) flan *m* au caramel

Flanders /ˈflɑːndəz/ N Flandres *fpl*, Flandre *f* COMP **Flanders poppy** N coquelicot *m*

flange / flændʒ / N (*on wheel*) boudin *m* ; (*on pipe*) collerette *f*, bride *f* ; (*on I-beam*) aile *f* ; (*on railway rail*) patin *m* ; (*on tool*) rebord *m*, collet *m*

flanged / flændʒd / ADJ *[wheel]* à boudin, à rebord ; *[tube]* à brides ; *[radiator]* à ailettes

flank / flæŋk / N (*Anat, Geog, Mil*) flanc *m* ; (*Culin*) flanchet *m* VT 1 flanquer ◆ **~ed by two policemen** flanqué de *or* encadré par deux gendarmes 2 (*Mil*) flanquer ; (*= turn the flank of*) contourner le flanc de

flanker /ˈflæŋkəʳ/ N (*Rugby*) ailier *m*

flannel /ˈflænl/ N 1 (*NonC = fabric*) flanelle *f* 2 (*Brit*: also **face flannel**) ≃ gant *m* de toilette 3 (*Brit * fig = waffle*) baratin* *m* NPL **flannels** (*Brit = trousers*) pantalon *m* de flanelle VI (*Brit * = waffle*) baratiner* COMP de flanelle

flannelette /ˌflænəˈlet/ N finette *f*, pilou *m* COMP *[sheet]* de finette, de pilou

flap / flæp / N 1 *[of wings]* battement *m*, coup *m* ; *[of sails]* claquement *m* 2 *[of pocket, envelope, hat, tent, book cover]* rabat *m* ; *[of counter, table]* abattant *m* ; (*= door in floor*) trappe *f* ; (*for cats*) chatière *f* ; (*on aircraft wing*) volet *m* ◆ **a ~ of skin** un morceau de peau 3 (** = panic*) ◆ **to be in a ~** être dans tous ses états ◆ **to get into a ~** se mettre dans tous ses états, paniquer 4 (*Phon*) battement *m* VI 1 *[wings]* battre ; *[shutters]* battre, claquer ; *[sails]* claquer ◆ **his cloak ~ped about his legs** sa cape lui battait les jambes ◆ **his ears must be ~ping** * ses oreilles doivent siffler* 2 (** = be panicky*) paniquer ◆ **stop ~ping!** pas de panique !, t'affole pas !* VT *[bird]* ◆ **to ~ its wings** battre des ailes

flapdoodle * /ˈflæpˌduːdəl/ N blague* *f*, balivernes *fpl*

flapjack /ˈflæpdʒæk/ N (*Culin*) (*= biscuit*) galette *f* (à l'avoine) ; (*US*) (*= pancake*) crêpe *f* épaisse

flapper † * /ˈflæpəʳ/ N *garçonne des années 1920*

flare /flɛəʳ/ N 1 (*= light*) *[of torch, fire, sun]* éclat *m*, flamboiement *m*

2 (*= signal*) feu *m*, signal *m* (lumineux) ; (*Mil*) fusée *f* éclairante, fusée-parachute *f* ; (*for plane's target*) bombe *f* éclairante *or* de jalonnement ; (*for runway*) balise *f*

3 (*Dress*) évasement *m*

NPL **flares** * pantalon *m* à pattes d'éléphant

VI 1 *[match]* s'enflammer ; *[candle]* briller ; *[sunspot]* brûler

2 *[violence, fighting]* éclater ◆ **tempers ~d** les esprits se sont (vite) échauffés

3 *[sleeves, skirt]* s'évaser, s'élargir ; *[nostrils]* se dilater, se gonfler

VT *[+ skirt, trouser legs]* évaser ; *[+ nostrils]* dilater, gonfler ◆ **~d skirt** jupe *f* évasée ◆ **~d trousers** pantalon *m* à pattes d'éléphant

COMP **flare path** N (*for planes*) piste *f* balisée
flare-up N *[of fire]* recrudescence *f* ; *[of fighting]* intensification *f* (soudaine) ; (*= outburst of rage*) accès *m* de colère ; (*= sudden dispute*) altercation *f*, prise *f* de bec*

► **flare out** VI → **flare vi 3**

► **flare up** VI *[fire]* s'embraser, prendre (brusquement) ; *[person]* s'emporter ; *[political situation]* exploser ; *[anger, fighting, revolt]* éclater ; *[disease]* se réveiller, reprendre ; *[epidemic]* éclater, se déclarer (soudain) ◆ **he ~s up at the slightest thing** il est très soupe au lait

N ◆ **flare-up** → **flare**

flash / flæʃ / N 1 (*= sudden light*) (*from torch, car headlights, explosion, firework*) lueur *f* soudaine ; (*of flame, jewels*) éclat *m* ◆ **a ~ of light** un jet de lumière ◆ **a ~ of lightning, a lightning ~** un éclair

2 (*= brief moment*) ◆ **it happened in a ~** c'est arrivé en un clin d'œil ◆ **it came to him in a ~ that ...** l'idée lui est venue tout d'un coup que ... ◆ **~ of genius** *or* **inspiration** (*gen*) éclair *m* de génie ; (*= brainwave*) idée *f* de génie ◆ **(with) a ~ of anger** *or* **temper** (dans) un mouvement de colère ◆ **staring at the photo of him, I had a sudden ~ of recognition** en le regardant sur la photo, je l'ai subitement reconnu ◆ **in a ~ of memory, she saw ...** la mémoire lui revenant soudain, elle a vu ... ◆ **a ~ of humour** un trait d'humour ◆ **a ~ of wit** une boutade ◆ **a ~ in the pan** (*Pol etc: for new movement, idea, party*) un feu de paille (*fig*) (*= person's fad*) lubie *f* ; → **hot**

3 (*= brief glimpse*) coup *m* d'œil ◆ **a ~ of colour/of blue** (*= briefly seen colour*) une note soudaine de couleur/de bleu ; (*= small amount of colour*) une note de couleur/de bleu ◆ **give us a ~!** ** fais voir ! ◆ **despite his illness, there were ~es of the old Henry** malgré sa maladie, il y avait des moments où Henry redevenait lui-même ◆ **she has ~es of the future** elle a des visions fugitives de l'avenir

4 (also **newsflash**) flash *m* (d'information)

5 (*Mil*) écusson *m*

6 (*Phot*) flash *m*

7 (*US*) ⇒ **flashlight**

8 (*US = bright student*) petit(e) doué(e) *m(f)*

VI 1 *[light]* (*on and off*) clignoter ; *[diamond]* étinceler ; *[eyes]* lancer des éclairs ◆ **lightning ~ed** il y a eu des éclairs ◆ **a beam of light ~ed across his face** un trait de lumière éclaira soudain son visage ◆ **the sunlight ~ed on the water** l'eau scintillait (au soleil) ◆ **the blade of the knife ~ed in the sunlight** la lame du couteau brillait au soleil ◆ **to ~ on and off** clignoter ◆ **~ing light** *[of police car, ambulance etc]* gyrophare *m* ; *[of answerphone, warning signal]* lumière *f* clignotante ◆ **her eyes ~ed with anger** ses yeux lançaient des éclairs

2 *(= move quickly)* **to ~ in/out/past** *etc [person, vehicle]* entrer/sortir/passer *etc* comme un éclair ◆ **the day ~ed by** *or* **past** on n'a pas vu la journée passer ◆ **the thought ~ed through** *or* **across his mind that ...** un instant, il a pensé que ... ◆ **his whole life ~ed before him** il a revu le film de sa vie ◆ **a look of terror/anger ~ed across her face** une expression de terreur/de colère passa fugitivement sur son visage ◆ **a message ~ed (up) onto the screen** un message est apparu sur l'écran

3 *(* = expose o.s. indecently)* s'exhiber

VT 1 *[+ light]* projeter ◆ **to ~ a torch on** diriger une lampe torche sur ◆ **to ~ a torch in sb's face** diriger une lampe torche dans les yeux de qn ◆ **to ~ one's headlights, to ~ the high beams** *(US)* faire un appel de phares *(at sb* à qn)

2 *(= show quickly)* **to ~ one's passport/ID card** montrer rapidement son passeport/sa carte d'identité ◆ **the screen was ~ing a message at me** l'écran m'envoyait un message ◆ **these images were ~ed across television screens all around the world** ces images sont apparues sur les écrans de télévision du monde entier ◆ **she ~ed him a look of contempt** elle lui a jeté un regard de mépris ◆ **to ~ a smile at sb** lancer un sourire éclatant à qn

3 *(= flaunt) [+ diamond ring]* étaler (aux yeux de tous), mettre (bien) en vue ◆ **don't ~ all that money around** n'étale pas tout cet argent comme ça

ADJ * ⇒ **flashy**

COMP **flash bulb** N *(Phot)* ampoule *f* de flash
flash burn N *(Med)* brûlure *f (causée par un flux thermique)*
flash card N *(Scol)* fiche *f (support pédagogique)*
flash flood N crue *f* subite
flash-forward N projection *f* dans le futur
flash gun N *(Phot)* flash *m*
flash Harry †* N *(Brit pej)* frimeur* *m*
flash meter N *(Phot)* flashmètre *m*
flash pack N emballage *m* promotionnel
flash photography N *(Phot)* photographie *f* au flash
flash point N *(Chem)* point *m* d'ignition ◆ **the situation had nearly reached ~ point** la situation était explosive
flash powder N *(Phot)* photopoudre *m*

flashback /ˈflæʃbæk/ N 1 *(Cine)* flash-back *m inv*, retour *m* en arrière 2 *(Psych)* flash-back *m inv*

flashcube /ˈflæʃkjuːb/ N *(Phot)* flash *m* (cube)

flasher /ˈflæʃəʳ/ N 1 *(= light, device)* clignotant *m* 2 *(* = person committing indecent exposure)* exhibitionniste *m*

flashily /ˈflæʃɪlɪ/ ADV de façon tape-à-l'œil

flashing /ˈflæʃɪŋ/ N 1 *(on roof)* revêtement *m* de zinc, noue *f* 2 *(* = indecent exposure)* exhibitionnisme *m*

flashlight /ˈflæʃlaɪt/ N *(Phot)* flash *m* ; *(esp US = torch)* torche *f* or lampe *f* électrique ; *(on lighthouse etc)* fanal *m*

flashy /ˈflæʃɪ/ ADJ *(pej) [person]* tapageur ; *[jewellery, car]* tape-à-l'œil *inv*, clinquant ; *[dress]* tape-à-l'œil *inv*, voyant ; *[colour, taste]* criard, tapageur

flask /flɑːsk/ N *(Pharm)* fiole *f* ; *(Chem)* ballon *m* ; *(= bottle)* bouteille *f* ; *(for pocket)* flasque *f* ; (also **vacuum flask**) bouteille *f* isotherme, (bouteille *f*) thermos ® *f*

flat[1] /flæt/ ADJ 1 *[countryside, surface, the earth]* plat ; *[tyre]* dégonflé, à plat ◆ **a ~ dish** un plat creux ◆ **~ roof** toit *m* plat *or* en terrasse ◆ **~ nose** nez *m* épaté *or* camus ◆ **a ~ stomach** un ventre plat ◆ **he was lying ~ on the floor** il était (étendu) à plat par terre ◆ **to fall ~** *[event, joke]* tomber à plat ; *[scheme]* ne rien donner ◆ **lay the book ~ on the table** pose le livre à plat sur la table ◆ **the earthquake laid the whole city ~** le tremblement de terre a rasé la ville entière ◆ **as ~ as a pancake*** *[tyre]* complètement à plat ; *[surface, countryside]* tout plat ◆ **to be in a ~ spin*** *(Brit)* être dans tous ses états ; see also comp

2 *(= dull) [taste, style]* monotone, plat ; *(= unexciting) [event, experience]* morne, sans intérêt ; *[battery]* à plat ; *(= not fizzy) [beer etc]* éventé ◆ **I was feeling rather ~** je n'avais pas la pêche* ◆ **the beer is ~** *(= not fizzy)* la bière est éventée ; *(= insipid)* la bière a un goût fade

3 *(Mus) (= off-key)* trop grave ◆ **B ~** *(= semitone lower)* si *m* bémol

4 *[refusal, denial]* net (nette *f*), catégorique ◆ **and that's ~!*** un point c'est tout !*

5 *(Comm)* **~ rate of pay** salaire *m* fixe ◆ **~ rate** *[of price, charge]* forfait *m*

6 *(= not shiny) [colour]* mat

7 *(= stable) [price]* stationnaire, stable ◆ **house prices have stayed ~** les prix de l'immobilier ont atteint un palier

8 *(US) (= penniless)* **to be ~**‡ être fauché (comme les blés)*, n'avoir plus un rond*

ADV 1 ◆ **he told me ~ that ...** il m'a dit carrément *or* sans ambages que ... ◆ **he turned it down ~** il l'a carrément refusé, il l'a refusé tout net ◆ **to be ~ broke**‡ être fauché (comme les blés)*, n'avoir plus un rond* ◆ **in ten seconds ~** en dix secondes pile

◆ **flat out*** ◆ **to go ~ out** *(esp Brit) [person]* courir à fond de train ; *[car]* rouler à fond de train ◆ **to go ~ out for sth** *(esp Brit)* faire tout son possible pour avoir qch ◆ **to be ~ out** *(= exhausted)* être à plat* *or* vidé* ; *(= asleep)* dormir, ronfler* *(fig) (= drunk)* être complètement rétamé, être KO* ◆ **to be working ~ out** *(esp Brit)* travailler d'arrache-pied ◆ **to be lying ~ out** être étendu *or* couché de tout son long

2 *(Mus) [sing, play]* faux, trop bas

N 1 *[of hand, blade]* plat *m*

2 *(Geog) (= dry land)* plaine *f* ; *(= marsh)* marécage *m* ; → **salt**

3 *(Mus)* bémol *m*

4 *(= flat tyre)* crevaison *f*, pneu *m* crevé

5 *(Racing)* **the ~** ⇒ **flat racing, flat season** ◆ **on the ~** sur le plat

COMP **flat bed** N *[of lorry]* plateau *m*
flat-bed lorry N camion *m* à plateau
flat-bed scanner N scanner *m* à plat
flat-bottomed boat N bateau *m* à fond plat
flat cap N *(Brit)* casquette *f*
flat car N *(US Rail)* wagon *m* plat
flat-chested ADJ ◆ **she is ~-chested** elle est plate, elle n'a pas de poitrine
flat feet NPL ◆ **to have ~ feet** avoir les pieds plats
flat-iron N fer *m* à repasser
flat-out‡ *(US)* ADJ complet, absolu ADV complètement
flat pack N meuble *m* en kit ◆ **it arrives as a ~ pack** c'est livré en kit
flat-pack ADJ en kit
flat race N course *f* de plat
flat racing N course *f* de plat
flat rate amount N *(Fin, Jur)* montant *m* forfaitaire
flat screen N *(TV)* écran *m* plat
flat season N *(Racing)* saison *f* des courses de plat
flat silver N *(US)* couverts *mpl* en argent
flat top N *(= haircut)* coupe *f* en brosse

flat[2] /flæt/ N *(Brit)* appartement *m* COMP **flat-hunting** N ◆ **to go ~-hunting** chercher un appartement

flatfish /ˈflætfɪʃ/ N (pl **flatfish** *or* **flatfishes**) poisson *m* plat

flatfoot‡ /ˈflætfʊt/ N (pl **-foots** *or* **-feet**) *(US = policeman)* flic* *m*

flatfooted /ˌflætˈfʊtɪd/ ADJ *(lit)* aux pieds plats ; *(* fig = tactless) [person, approach]* maladroit ADV *(= wholeheartedly)* tout de go* ◆ **to catch sb ~*** prendre qn par surprise

flatlet /ˈflætlɪt/ N *(Brit)* studio *m*

flatly /ˈflætlɪ/ ADV 1 *(= firmly) [refuse, deny, reject]* catégoriquement ◆ **to be ~ against sth** être catégoriquement contre qch ◆ **to be ~ opposed to sth** être catégoriquement opposé à qch 2 *(= unemotionally) [say, state]* avec impassibilité 3 *(= absolutely)* **to be ~ inconsistent with sth** être absolument incompatible avec qch

flatmate /ˈflætmeɪt/ N ◆ **my ~** la personne avec qui je partage l'appartement ; *(both renting)* mon colocataire, ma colocataire

flatness /ˈflætnɪs/ N 1 *[of countryside, surface]* manque *m* de relief, aspect *m* plat ; *[of curve]* aplatissement *m* 2 *[of refusal]* netteté *f* 3 *(= dullness)* monotonie *f*

flatten /ˈflætn/ VT 1 *(= make less bumpy) [+ path, road]* aplanir ; *[+ metal]* aplatir 2 *(= destroy) [wind, storm] [+ crops]* coucher, écraser ; *[+ tree]* abattre ; *[bombing, earthquake] [+ town, building]* raser ; *(* = knock over) [+ person]* étendre* ◆ **to ~ o.s. against** s'aplatir *or* se plaquer contre 3 *(* = defeat)* écraser* 4 *(Mus) [+ tone, pitch, note]* bémoliser 5 *[+ battery]* mettre à plat

▸ **flatten out** VI *[countryside, road]* s'aplanir ; *[aircraft]* se redresser ; *[curve]* s'aplatir VT SEP *[+ path]* aplanir ; *[+ metal]* aplatir ; *[+ map, newspaper]* ouvrir à plat

flatter /ˈflætəʳ/ VT *(all senses)* flatter ◆ **he ~s himself he's a good musician** il se flatte d'être bon musicien ◆ **I was ~ed to be invited** j'étais flatté d'avoir été invité ◆ **you ~ yourself!** tu te flattes !

flatterer /ˈflætərəʳ/ N flatteur *m*, -euse *f*, flagorneur *m*, -euse *f (pej)*

flattering /ˈflætərɪŋ/ ADJ 1 *[person, remark, behaviour]* flatteur *(to sb* pour qn) ◆ **they listened to him with a ~ interest** ils l'ont écouté avec un intérêt flatteur ◆ **to be ~ about sb** parler de qn en termes flatteurs 2 *[clothes, colour]* flatteur ◆ **it wasn't a very ~ photo (of him)** ce n'était pas une photo qui l'avantageait beaucoup ◆ **lighter shades are more ~ to your complexion** les tons clairs sont plus flatteurs pour votre teint *or* conviennent mieux à votre teint

flatteringly /ˈflætərɪŋlɪ/ ADV flatteusement

flattery /ˈflætərɪ/ N flatterie *f* ◆ **~ will get you nowhere/everywhere** *(hum)* la flatterie ne mène à rien/mène à tout

flatties* /ˈflætɪz/ NPL chaussures *fpl* basses *or* à talon plat

flattop* /ˈflættɒp/ N *(US)* porte-avions *m*

flatulence /ˈflætjʊləns/ N flatulence *f*

flatulent /ˈflætjʊlənt/ ADJ flatulent

flatware /ˈflætweəʳ/ N *(US) (= plates)* plats *mpl* et assiettes *fpl* ; *(= cutlery)* couverts *mpl*

flatworm /ˈflætwɜːm/ N plathelminthe *m*, ver *m* plat

flaunt /flɔːnt/ VT *[+ wealth]* étaler, afficher ; *[+ jewels]* faire étalage de ; *[+ knowledge]* faire étalage *or* parade de ; *[+ boyfriend etc]* afficher ◆ **she ~ed her femininity at him** elle lui jetait sa féminité à la tête ◆ **to ~ o.s.** s'exhiber

flautist /ˈflɔːtɪst/ N *(esp Brit)* flûtiste *mf*

flavour, flavor *(US)* /ˈfleɪvəʳ/ N goût *m*, saveur *f* ; *[of ice cream, sweet, yoghurt, jelly]* parfum *m* ; *(in processed foods)* arôme *m* ◆ **with a rum ~** (parfumé) au rhum ◆ **a slight ~ of irony** une légère pointe d'ironie ◆ **the film gives the ~ of Paris in the twenties** le film rend bien l'atmosphère du Paris des années vingt ◆ **to be (the) ~ of the month*** être la coqueluche du moment VT *(with fruit, spirits)* parfumer *(with* à) ; *(with herbs, spices)* aromatiser, assaisonner ◆ **to ~ a sauce with garlic** relever une sauce avec de l'ail ◆ **pineapple-~ed** (parfumé) à l'ananas COMP **flavour enhancer** N agent *m* de sapidité, exhausteur *m* de goût *or* de saveur

flavourful, flavorful *(US)* /ˈfleɪvəˌfəl/ ADJ goûteux

flavouring, flavoring *(US)* /ˈfleɪvərɪŋ/ N *(in cake, yoghurt, ice cream)* parfum *m* ◆ **vanilla ~** parfum *m* vanille

flavourless, flavorless *(US)* /ˈfleɪvəlɪs/ ADJ insipide, sans saveur

flavoursome /ˈfleɪvəsəm/ ADJ *(US)* goûteux

flaw /flɔː/ N *(in character)* défaut *m*, imperfection *f* ; *(in argument, reasoning)* faille *f* ; *(in wood)* défaut *m*, imperfection *f* ; *(in gemstone, marble)* défaut *m*, crapaud *m* ; *(Jur: in contract, procedure)* vice *m* de forme ; *(= obstacle)* problème *m* ◆ **everything seems to be working out, but there's just one ~** tout semble s'arranger, il n'y a qu'un problème

VT ◆ **the plan was ~ed by its dependence on the actions of others** le plan avait un point faible : il dépendait des actions des autres ◆ **his career was ~ed by this incident** cet incident a nui à sa carrière ◆ **the elections were ~ed by widespread irregularities** les élections ont été entachées de très nombreuses irrégularités ◆ **the team's performance was seriously ~ed by their inexperience** le manque d'expérience de l'équipe a sérieusement nui à ses résultats

flawed /flɔːd/ ADJ *[person, character]* imparfait ; *[object, argument, reasoning, plot]* défectueux

flawless /ˈflɔːlɪs/ ADJ parfait, sans défaut ◆ **he spoke ~ English** il parlait un anglais impeccable, il parlait parfaitement l'anglais

flax /flæks/ N lin *m*

flaxen /ˈflæksən/ ADJ *[hair]* (blond) filasse *inv*, de lin *(liter)* ; *[fabric]* de lin ◆ **~-haired** aux cheveux (blond) filasse, aux cheveux de lin *(liter)*

flay /fleɪ/ VT 1 *(= beat) [+ person, animal]* fouetter, rosser ; *(= criticize)* éreinter 2 *[+ animal] (= skin)* écorcher

flea /fliː/ N puce *f* ◆ **to send sb away** *or* **off with a ~ in his ear*** envoyer promener* qn, envoyer qn sur les roses* ; → **sand**
COMP **flea collar** N *[of dog, cat]* collier *m* antipuces
flea market N marché *m* aux puces
flea-pit⁑ N *(Brit = cinema)* ciné* *m* miteux
flea powder N poudre *f* anti-puces
flea-ridden ADJ *(lit) [person, animal]* couvert de puces ; *[place]* infesté de puces ; *(fig)* miteux

fleabag⁑ /ˈfliːbæg/ N *(Brit = person)* sac *m* à puces* ; *(US = hotel)* hôtel *m* minable

fleabite /ˈfliːbaɪt/ N *(lit)* piqûre *f* de puce ; *(fig)* vétille *f*, broutille *f*

fleabitten /ˈfliːˌbɪtn/ N *(lit)* infesté de puces ; *(fig)* miteux

fleck /flek/ N *[of colour]* moucheture *f* ; *[of foam]* flocon *m* ; *[of blood, light]* petite tache *f* ; *[of dust]* particule *f* VT tacheter, moucheter ◆ **dress ~ed with mud** robe *f* éclaboussée de boue ◆ **blue ~ed with white** bleu moucheté de blanc ◆ **sky ~ed with little clouds** ciel *m* pommelé ◆ **hair ~ed with grey** cheveux *mpl* qui commencent à grisonner

fled /fled/ VB pt, ptp of **flee**

fledged /fledʒd/ ADJ → **fully**

fledg(e)ling /ˈfledʒlɪŋ/ N 1 *(= bird)* oiselet *m*, oisillon *m* 2 *(fig = novice)* novice *mf*, débutant(e) *m(f)* COMP *[industry, democracy]* jeune ; *[dancer, writer, poet]* débutant

flee /fliː/ (pret, ptp **fled**) VI fuir *(before* devant) s'enfuir *(from* de) ◆ **they fled** ils ont fui, ils se sont enfuis ◆ **they fled to Britain/to their parents'** ils se sont enfuis en Grande-Bretagne/chez leurs parents ◆ **I fled when I heard she was expected** je me suis sauvé *or* j'ai pris la fuite lorsque j'ai appris qu'elle devait venir ◆ **to ~ from temptation** fuir la tentation VT *[+ town, country]* s'enfuir de ; *[+ famine, war, temptation, danger]* fuir

fleece /fliːs/ N 1 *[of sheep]* toison *f* ; → **golden** 2 *(= garment)* (laine *f*) polaire *f* VT 1 *(= rob)* voler ; *(= swindle)* escroquer, filouter ; *(= overcharge)* estamper* 2 *[+ sheep]* tondre COMP **fleece-lined** ADJ doublé de mouton

fleecy /ˈfliːsɪ/ ADJ *[blanket, lining]* laineux ; *[jacket]* en laine polaire ; *[cloud]* floconneux

fleet¹ /fliːt/ N *[of ships]* flotte *f* ; *[of cars, buses, lorries]* parc *m* ; → **admiral, fishing**
COMP **fleet admiral** N *(US)* amiral *m*
Fleet Air Arm N *(Brit)* aéronavale *f*
fleet chief petty officer N *(Brit)* major *m*

fleet² /fliːt/ ADJ (also **fleet-footed, fleet of foot**) rapide, au pied léger

fleeting /ˈfliːtɪŋ/ ADJ *[smile, glance, thought]* fugitif ; *[memory]* fugace ◆ **a ~ visit** une visite en coup de vent ◆ **to catch** *or* **get a ~ glimpse of sb/sth** entrapercevoir qn/qch ◆ **to make a ~ appearance** faire une brève apparition ◆ **for a ~ moment** l'espace d'un instant ◆ **the ~ years** *(liter)* les années *fpl* qui fuient

fleetingly /ˈfliːtɪŋlɪ/ ADV *[think, wonder]* un bref *or* court instant ; *[see, appear]* fugitivement ◆ **to smile ~ at sb** adresser un sourire fugitif à qn

Fleet Street /ˈfliːtˌstriːt/ N *(Brit) les milieux de la presse londonienne*

Fleming /ˈflemɪŋ/ N Flamand(e) *m(f)*

Flemish /ˈflemɪʃ/ ADJ flamand N *(= language)* flamand *m* NPL **the Flemish** les Flamands *mpl*

flesh /fleʃ/ N 1 *[of person, animal]* chair *f* ; *[of fruit, vegetable]* chair *f*, pulpe *f* ◆ **to put on ~** *[animal]* engraisser ◆ **to make sb's ~ creep** *or* **crawl** donner la chair de poule à qn ◆ **creatures of ~ and blood** êtres *mpl* de chair et de sang ◆ **I'm only ~ and blood** je ne suis qu'un homme *(or* qu'une femme) comme les autres ◆ **my own ~ and blood** la chair de ma chair ◆ **it is more than ~ and blood can stand** c'est plus que la nature humaine ne peut endurer ◆ **in the ~** en chair et en os, en personne ◆ **to put ~ on the bare bones of a proposal** étoffer une proposition ; → **pound¹**
2 *(Rel liter)* ◆ **he's gone the way of all ~** *(= died)* il a payé son tribut à la nature † ◆ **the sins of the ~** les péchés *mpl* de la chair ◆ **the ~ is weak** la chair est faible
COMP **flesh colour** N couleur *f* chair ; *(Art)* carnation *f*
flesh-coloured ADJ (couleur *f*) chair *inv*
flesh tints NPL *(Art)* carnations *fpl*
flesh wound N blessure *f* superficielle

► **flesh out** VT SEP *(fig) [+ essay, speech]* étoffer ; *[+ idea, proposal, agreement]* développer ◆ **to ~ out the details of an agreement** développer les éléments d'un accord ◆ **the author needs to ~ out his characters more** il faut que l'auteur étoffe davantage ses personnages

fleshly /ˈfleʃlɪ/ ADJ *(liter) [creature, love]* charnel ; *[pleasures]* charnel, de la chair

fleshpots /ˈfleʃpɒts/ NPL lieux *mpl* de plaisir

fleshy /ˈfleʃɪ/ ADJ *[face]* rebondi, joufflu ; *[cheeks]* rebondi ; *[nose, fruit, leaf]* charnu ; *[person]* grassouillet

flew /fluː/ VB pt of **fly³**

flex /fleks/ VT *[+ body, knees]* fléchir, ployer *(pour assouplir)* ◆ **to ~ one's muscles** *(lit)* faire jouer ses muscles, bander *(liter)* ses muscles ; *(fig)* faire étalage de sa force N *(Brit) [of lamp, iron]* fil *m* (souple) ; *[of telephone]* cordon *m* ; *(heavy duty)* câble *m*

flexi* /ˈfleksɪ/ N ⇒ **flexitime**

flexibility /ˌfleksɪˈbɪlɪtɪ/ N *[of material, person, attitude, approach]* souplesse *f*, flexibilité *f* ; *[of body]* souplesse *f* ; *[of working hours, system]* flexibilité *f* ; *[of machine, device]* flexibilité *f*, souplesse *f* d'emploi

flexible /ˈfleksəbl/ ADJ 1 *[object, material]* flexible, souple ; *[person, limbs, joints, body]* souple 2 *(fig) [person, approach, system, plans]* flexible, souple ; *[working hours, budget]* flexible ◆ **I'm ~** *(fig)* je peux toujours m'arranger ◆ **to be ~ in one's approach** faire preuve de souplesse COMP **flexible response** N *(Mil)* riposte *f* graduée

flexibly /ˈfleksəblɪ/ ADV *[respond, adapt, apply]* avec souplesse ; *[work]* avec flexibilité ◆ **to interpret a rule ~** interpréter une règle avec une certaine souplesse

flexion /ˈflekʃən/ N flexion *f*, courbure *f*

flexitime /ˈfleksɪˌtaɪm/ N *(esp Brit)* horaire *m* flexible *or* à la carte ◆ **to work ~** avoir un horaire flexible *or* à la carte ◆ **we work 35 hours' ~ a week** on travaille 35 heures hebdomadaires en horaire flexible

flexor /ˈfleksəʳ/ ADJ, N fléchisseur *m*

flibbertigibbet* /ˈflɪbətɪˈdʒɪbɪt/ N tête *f* de linotte, étourdi(e) *m(f)*

flick /flɪk/ N 1 *[of tail, duster]* petit coup *m* ; *(with finger)* chiquenaude *f*, pichenette *f* ; *(with wrist)* petit mouvement *m* (rapide) ◆ **at the ~ of a switch** rien qu'en appuyant sur un bouton ◆ **let's have a quick ~ through your holiday snaps** jetons un petit coup d'œil à tes photos de vacances
2 *(Brit * = film)* film *m* ◆ **the ~s** le ciné*, le cinoche⁑
VT donner un petit coup à ◆ **he ~ed the horse lightly with the reins** il a donné au cheval un (tout) petit coup avec les rênes ◆ **I'll just ~ a duster round the sitting room** je vais passer un petit coup de chiffon dans le salon ◆ **to ~ a ball of paper at sb** envoyer d'une chiquenaude une boulette de papier à qn ◆ **he ~ed his cigarette ash into the ashtray** il a fait tomber la cendre de sa cigarette dans le cendrier
COMP **flick knife** N (pl **flick knives**) *(Brit)* (couteau *m* à) cran *m* d'arrêt

► **flick off** VT SEP *[+ dust, ash]* enlever d'une chiquenaude

► **flick out** VI, VT SEP ◆ **the snake's tongue flicked out** ◆ **the snake ~ed its tongue out** le serpent a dardé sa langue

► **flick over** VT SEP *[+ pages of book]* feuilleter, tourner rapidement

► **flick through** VT FUS *[+ pages of book, document]* feuilleter, lire en diagonale ◆ **to ~ through the TV channels** zapper

flicker /ˈflɪkəʳ/ VI *[flames, light]* danser ; *(before going out)* trembloter, vaciller ; *[needle on dial]* osciller ; *[eyelids]* ciller ◆ **the snake's tongue ~ed in and out** le serpent a dardé sa langue N *[of flames, light]* danse *f* ; *(before going out)* vacillement *m* ◆ **without a ~** *(fig)* sans sourciller *or* broncher ◆ **a ~ of hope** une lueur d'espoir ◆ **a ~ of doubt** l'ombre *f* d'un doute ◆ **a ~ of annoyance** un geste d'humeur ◆ **without a ~ of a smile** sans l'ombre d'un sourire VT ◆ **to ~ one's eyelids** battre des cils

flickering /ˈflɪkərɪŋ/ ADJ *(gen)* tremblant ; *[flames]* dansant ; *(before going out)* vacillant ; *[needle]* oscillant

flickertail /ˈflɪkəˌteɪl/ N *(US)* spermophile *m* d'Amérique du Nord COMP **the Flickertail State** N le Dakota du Nord

flier /ˈflaɪəʳ/ N 1 *(= aviator)* aviateur *m*, -trice *f* ◆ **to be a good ~** *[passenger]* supporter (bien) l'avion ◆ **to be a bad ~** ne pas supporter *or* mal supporter l'avion ; → **high** 2 *(US) (= fast train)* rapide *m* ; *(= fast coach)* car *m* express 3 ◆ **to take a ~** *(= leap)* sauter avec élan ; *(US * fig = take a risk)* foncer tête baissée 4 *(Stock Ex-*

change) (folle) aventure *f* 5 *(= handbill)* prospectus *m*

flight¹ /flaɪt/ **N** 1 *(NonC = action, course) [of bird, insect, plane]* vol *m* ; *[of ball, bullet]* trajectoire *f* ◆ **the principles of** ~ les rudiments *mpl* du vol *or* de la navigation aérienne ◆ **in** ~ en plein vol ◆ **the Flight of the Bumblebee** *(Mus)* le Vol du bourdon

2 *(= plane trip)* vol *m* ◆ ~ **number 776 from/to Madrid** le vol numéro 776 en provenance/à destination de Madrid ◆ **did you have a good ~?** le vol s'est bien passé ?, vous avez fait (un) bon voyage ?

3 *(fig)* **a ~ of fancy** *(= harebrained idea)* une idée folle ; *(= figment of imagination)* une pure invention ◆ **to indulge** *or* **engage in a ~ of fancy** avoir des idées folles ◆ **in my wildest ~s of fancy** dans mes rêves les plus fous ; → **reconnaissance, test**

4 *(= group) [of birds]* vol *m*, volée *f* ; *[of planes]* escadrille *f* ◆ **in the first** *or* **top ~ of scientists/novelists** parmi les scientifiques/les romanciers les plus marquants ◆ **a firm in the top ~** une entreprise prestigieuse

5 ◆ ~ **of stairs** escalier *m*, volée *f* d'escalier ◆ **we had to climb three ~s to get to his room** nous avons dû monter trois étages pour arriver à sa chambre ◆ **he lives three ~s up** il habite au troisième ◆ ~ **of hurdles** série *f* de haies ◆ ~ **of terraces** escalier *m* de terrasses

COMP flight attendant N steward *m*/hôtesse *f* de l'air, agent *m* de bord

flight bag N (petit) sac *m* de voyage, bagage *m* à main

flight box N enregistreur *m* de vol

flight control N *(on ground)* contrôle *m* aérien ; *(in aircraft)* commande *f* de vol

flight crew N équipage *m*

flight data recorder N enregistreur *m* de données de vol

flight deck N *[of plane]* poste *m or* cabine *f* de pilotage ; *[of aircraft carrier]* pont *m* d'envol

flight engineer N mécanicien *m* de bord

flight lieutenant N *(Brit)* capitaine *m* (de l'armée de l'air)

flight log N suivi *m* de vol

flight path N trajectoire *f* (de vol)

flight plan N plan *m* de vol

flight recorder N enregistreur *m* de vol

flight sergeant N *(Brit)* ≈ sergent-chef *m* (de l'armée de l'air)

flight simulator N simulateur *m* de vol

flight-test VT essayer en vol

flight² /flaɪt/ **N** *(NonC = act of fleeing)* fuite *f* ◆ **to put to ~** mettre en fuite ◆ **to take (to) ~** prendre la fuite, s'enfuir ◆ **the ~ of capital abroad** la fuite *or* l'exode *m* des capitaux à l'étranger

flightless /ˈflaɪtlɪs/ **ADJ** incapable de voler ◆ ~ **bird** ratite *m*, oiseau *m* coureur

flighty /ˈflaɪtɪ/ **ADJ** *(gen)* frivole ; *(in love)* volage, inconstant

flimflam‡ /ˈflɪmˌflæm/ *(US)* **N** *(= nonsense)* balivernes *fpl*, blague* *f* **ADJ** ◆ **a ~ man** *or* **artist** un filou, un escroc **VT** *(= swindle)* rouler*, blouser*

flimsily /ˈflɪmzɪlɪ/ **ADV** ◆ ~ **built** *or* **constructed** (d'une construction) peu solide ◆ **his thesis was ~ argued** sa thèse était assez faiblement étayée

flimsiness /ˈflɪmzɪnɪs/ **N** *[of dress]* finesse *f* ; *[of house]* caractère *m* peu solide ; *[of paper]* minceur *f* ; *[of excuse, reasoning]* faiblesse *f*, futilité *f*

flimsy /ˈflɪmzɪ/ **ADJ** 1 *(= fragile) [object, structure, construction]* peu solide ; *[fabric]* peu résistant 2 *(= thin) [fabric]* léger, mince ; *[garment]* léger, fin ; *[paper]* mince 3 *(= feeble) [evidence]* peu convaincant ; *[excuse]* piètre ; *[grounds]* peu solide **N** *(Brit = type of paper)* papier *m* pelure *inv*

flinch /flɪntʃ/ **VI** broncher, tressaillir ◆ **to ~ from a task** reculer devant une tâche ◆ **he didn't ~ from warning her** il ne s'est pas dérobé au devoir de la prévenir ◆ **without ~ing** sans sourciller *or* broncher

fling /flɪŋ/ (vb : pret, ptp **flung**) **N** * 1 *(= spree)* ◆ **to go on a ~** aller faire la noce *or* la foire* ; *(in shops)* faire des folies ◆ **youth must have its ~** il faut que jeunesse se passe *(Prov)* ◆ **to have a last** *or* **final ~** *(= do sth foolish)* faire une dernière folie ; *[sportsman etc]* faire un dernier exploit ◆ **to have a final ~ at beating one's opponent/winning the championship** tenter une dernière fois de battre son adversaire/de remporter le championnat ; → **highland**

2 *(= affair)* aventure *f* ◆ **he had a brief ~ with my sister** il a eu une brève aventure avec ma sœur

VT *[+ object, stone]* jeter, lancer *(at sb* à qn ; *at sth* sur qch) ; *[+ remark, insult]* lancer *(at sb* à qn) ◆ **he flung his opponent to the ground** il a jeté son adversaire à terre ◆ **to ~ sb into jail** jeter *or* flanquer* qn en prison ◆ **to ~ the window open** ouvrir toute grande la fenêtre ◆ **the door was flung open** la porte s'est ouverte brusquement ◆ **to ~ one's arms round sb** *or* **sb's neck** sauter *or* se jeter au cou de qn ◆ **to ~ a coat over one's shoulders** jeter un manteau sur ses épaules ◆ **to ~ one's coat on/off** enfiler/enlever son manteau d'un geste brusque ◆ **to ~ an accusation at sb** lancer une accusation contre qn ◆ **to ~ o.s. off a bridge/under a train** se jeter d'un pont/sous un train ◆ **to ~ o.s. to the ground/to one's knees** se jeter à terre/à genoux ◆ **to ~ o.s. into a job/a hobby** se jeter *or* se lancer à corps perdu dans un travail/une activité ◆ **she flung herself* at him** elle s'est jetée à sa tête ◆ **she flung herself onto the sofa** elle s'est affalée sur le canapé

► **fling away VT SEP** *[+ unwanted object]* jeter, ficher en l'air* ; *(fig) [+ money]* gaspiller, jeter par les fenêtres

► **fling back VT SEP** *[+ ball etc]* renvoyer ; *[+ one's head]* rejeter en arrière ; *[+ curtains]* ouvrir brusquement

► **fling off VT SEP** *(fig liter)* se débarrasser de

► **fling out VT SEP** *[+ person]* flanquer* *or* mettre à la porte ; *[+ unwanted object]* jeter, ficher en l'air*

► **fling up VT SEP** jeter en l'air ◆ **to ~ one's arms up in exasperation** lever les bras en l'air *or* au ciel en signe d'exaspération

flint /flɪnt/ **N** *(gen)* silex *m* ; *(for cigarette lighter)* pierre *f* (à briquet) ; → **clay COMP** *[axe]* de silex

flint glass N flint(-glass) *m*

flintlock /ˈflɪntlɒk/ **N** fusil *m* à silex

flinty /ˈflɪntɪ/ **ADJ** 1 *(Geol) [soil, ground, rocks]* siliceux 2 *(= cruel) [person]* dur, insensible ; *[heart]* de pierre ; *[eyes, look]* dur

flip /flɪp/ **N** 1 chiquenaude *f*, petit coup *m* ◆ **to decide/win sth on the ~ of a coin** décider/gagner qch en tirant à pile ou face

2 *(Flying *)* petit tour *m* en zinc‡

VT donner un petit coup à, donner une chiquenaude à ; *(US) [+ pancake]* faire sauter ◆ **to ~ a coin** tirer à pile ou face ◆ **to ~ a book open** ouvrir un livre d'une chiquenaude *or* d'une pichenette ◆ **to ~ one's lid‡, to ~ one's wig‡** *or* *(US)* **one's top‡** éclater, exploser *(fig)*

VI (‡ : also **flip out**) *(angrily)* piquer une crise* *(over* à cause de) ; *(ecstatically)* devenir dingue* *(over* de)

ADJ *[remark, repartee]* désinvolte

EXCL * zut !*

COMP flip-flop → **flip-flop**

flip side N *[of record]* autre face *f*, face *f* B ; *(fig)* envers *m*

flip-top bin N poubelle *f* à couvercle pivotant

► **flip out VI** → **flip vi**

► **flip over VT SEP** *[+ stone]* retourner d'un coup léger ; *[+ pages]* feuilleter

► **flip through VT FUS** *[+ book]* feuilleter

flipboard /ˈflɪpbɔːd/, **flipchart** /ˈflɪptʃɑːt/ **N** tableau *m* de conférence

flip-flop /ˈflɪpflɒp/ **N** 1 *(Comput)* bascule *f* (bistable) 2 *(esp US fig = change of opinion)* volte-face *f* **NPL flip-flops** *(= sandals)* tongs *fpl* **VI** *(US fig)* faire volte-face

flippancy /ˈflɪpənsɪ/ **N** *[of attitude]* désinvolture *f* ; *[of speech, remark]* irrévérence *f*, légèreté *f*

flippant /ˈflɪpənt/ **ADJ** *[person, remark]* désinvolte ◆ **to sound ~** sembler désinvolte

flippantly /ˈflɪpəntlɪ/ **ADV** avec désinvolture, irrévérencieusement, cavalièrement

flipper /ˈflɪpəʳ/ **N** *[of seal, whale, penguin]* nageoire *f* ◆ **~s** *[of swimmer]* palmes *fpl*

flipping* /ˈflɪpɪŋ/ **ADJ** *(Brit)* fichu* *before n*, maudit *before n* **ADV** *(Brit) [rude, stupid, cold]* drôlement* ◆ **it's ~ impossible!** c'est vraiment impossible ! ◆ **~ heck!, ~ hell!** zut !

flirt /flɜːt/ **VI** flirter *(with* avec) ◆ **to ~ with danger** flirter avec le danger ◆ **to ~ with an idea** caresser une idée **N** ◆ **he's a ~** c'est un dragueur, il aime flirter

flirtation /flɜːˈteɪʃən/ **N** flirt *m*, amourette *f*

flirtatious /flɜːˈteɪʃəs/ **ADJ** qui aime flirter, flirteur †

flirty* /ˈflɜːtɪ/ **ADJ** *[person, behaviour]* dragueur ; *[clothes]* sexy *inv*

flit /flɪt/ **VI** 1 *[bats, butterflies]* voleter, voltiger ◆ **the idea ~ted through his head** l'idée lui a traversé l'esprit 2 *[person]* **to ~ in/out** *etc (Brit: lightly)* entrer/sortir *etc* avec légèreté ; *(US: affectedly)* entrer/sortir *etc* en minaudant ◆ **to ~ about** *(Brit)* se déplacer avec légèreté ; *(US)* marcher à petits pas maniérés 3 *(Brit = move house stealthily)* déménager à la cloche de bois ; *(N Engl, Scot = move house)* déménager **N** 1 *(N Engl, Scot = house move)* déménagement *m* ◆ **to do a (moonlight) ~** *(Brit)* déménager à la cloche de bois 2 *(US ‡ = homosexual)* pédale‡ *f*, tapette‡ *f*

flitch /flɪtʃ/ **N** flèche *f* (de lard)

flitting /ˈflɪtɪŋ/ **N** *(N Engl, Scot)* déménagement *m*

flivver‡ /ˈflɪvəʳ/ **N** *(US)* tacot* *m*, guimbarde* *f*

float /fləʊt/ **N** 1 *(Fishing, Plumbing)* flotteur *m*, flotte *f* ; *(of cork)* bouchon *m* ; *(of seaplane)* flotteur *m*

2 *(= vehicle in a parade)* char *m* ; → **milk**

3 (also **cash float**) fonds *m* de caisse

4 *(esp US = drink) milk-shake ou soda contenant une boule de glace*

VI *(on water, in air)* flotter ; *[ship]* être à flot ; *[swimmer]* faire la planche ; *(Fin) [currency]* flotter ◆ **the raft ~ed down the river** le radeau a descendu la rivière ◆ **to ~ back up to the surface** remonter à la surface (de l'eau) ◆ **the balloon ~ed up into the sky** le ballon s'est envolé dans le ciel ◆ **music ~ed through the air** une musique flottait dans l'air ◆ **the idea ~ed into his mind** l'idée lui a traversé l'esprit

VT 1 *[+ boat]* faire flotter, mettre à flot *or* sur l'eau ; *(= refloat)* remettre à flot *or* sur l'eau ; *[+ wood etc]* faire flotter ◆ **to ~ logs downstream** faire flotter des rondins au fil de l'eau ◆ **it doesn't ~ my boat*** ça ne me branche pas*

2 *[+ idea, project, plan]* lancer

3 *(Fin) [+ currency]* laisser flotter ; *[+ company]* fonder, créer ◆ **to ~ a share issue** émettre des actions ◆ **to ~ a loan** lancer *or* émettre un emprunt

COMP float plane N *(US)* hydravion *m*

► **float around* VI** *[rumour, news]* circuler, courir ◆ **have you seen my glasses ~ing**

around anywhere? as-tu vu mes lunettes quelque part ?

► **float away** VI dériver, partir à la dérive

► **float off** VI *[wreck]* se renflouer, se déséchouer

VT SEP *[+ wreck]* renflouer, remettre à flot

► **float round** * VI ⇒ **float around**

floatation /fləʊˈteɪʃən/ N ⇒ **flotation**

floating /ˈfləʊtɪŋ/ ADJ *[leaves, debris etc]* flottant ; *[population]* fluctuant N 1 *[of boat]* mise *f* en flottement 2 *(Fin) [of loan]* lancement *m* ; *[of currency]* flottement *m*, flottaison *f*

COMP **floating assets** NPL *(Fin)* capitaux *mpl* circulants

floating currency N *(Fin)* devise *f* flottante

floating currency rate N *(Fin)* taux *m* de change flottant

floating debt N *(Fin)* dette *f* à court terme *or* flottante

floating decimal (point) N *(Math)* virgule *f* flottante

floating dock N *(Naut)* dock *m* flottant

floating exchange N *(Fin)* change *m* flottant

floating point representation N *(Comput)* notation *f* en virgule flottante

floating restaurant N restaurant *m* flottant

floating rib N *(Anat)* côte *f* flottante

floating vote N *(Brit Pol)* vote *m* flottant

floating voter N *(Brit Pol)* électeur *m*, -trice *f* indécis(e)

flocculent /ˈflɒkjʊlənt/ ADJ floconneux

flock¹ /flɒk/ N *[of sheep, geese]* troupeau *m* ; *[of birds]* vol *m*, volée *f* ; *[of people]* foule *f*, troupeau *m (pej)* ; *(Rel)* ouailles *fpl* ◆ **they came in ~s** ils sont venus en masse VI aller *or* venir en masse, affluer ◆ **to ~ in/out** *etc* entrer/sortir *etc* en foule ◆ **to ~ together** s'assembler ◆ **to ~ round sb** s'attrouper *or* s'assembler autour de qn

flock² /flɒk/ N *(NonC) [of wool]* bourre *f* de laine ; *[of cotton]* bourre *f* de coton COMP **flock (wall)paper** N papier *m* velouté *or* tontisse

floe /fləʊ/ N banquise *f*, glaces *fpl* flottantes

flog /flɒg/ VT 1 flageller, fustiger ◆ **to ~ an idea to death** * *or* **into the ground** * rabâcher une idée ; → **dead** 2 *(Brit* ‡ *= sell)* fourguer * ◆ **how much did you ~ it for?** tu en as tiré combien ? *

flogging /ˈflɒgɪŋ/ N flagellation *f*, fustigation *f* ; *(Jur)* fouet *m (sanction)*

flood /flʌd/ N 1 *(gen)* inondation *f* ; (also **flood tide**) marée *f* haute ◆ **"flood"** *(notice on road)* ≈ "attention route inondée" ◆ **the Flood** *(Bible)* le déluge ◆ **river in ~** rivière *f* en crue ◆ **~s of tears** un torrent *or* déluge de larmes ◆ **a ~ of light** un flot de lumière ◆ **a ~ of letters/protests** un déluge de lettres/de protestations ◆ **a ~ of immigrants** un afflux massif d'immigrants

2 ⇒ **floodlight**

VT 1 *[+ fields, town]* inonder, submerger ; *(fig)* inonder ◆ **he was ~ed with letters/with applications** il a été inondé de lettres/de demandes ◆ **room ~ed with light** pièce *f* inondée de lumière

2 *[storm, rain] [+ river, stream]* faire déborder ◆ **to ~ the market** *[suppliers, goods]* inonder le marché *(with* de)

3 *[+ carburettor]* noyer

VI *[river]* déborder, être en crue ◆ **people ~ed into the square** la foule a envahi la place ◆ **refugees ~ed across the border** les réfugiés ont franchi la frontière en masse, des flots de réfugiés ont franchi la frontière

COMP **flood control** N prévention *f* des inondations

flood damage N dégâts *mpl* des eaux

flood plain N zone *f* inondable

flood tide N marée *f* haute

► **flood back** VI *[memories, worries]* (also **come flooding back**) resurgir ◆ **it brought all the memories ~ing back** cela a fait resurgir tous les souvenirs

► **flood in** VI *[sunshine]* entrer à flots ; *[people]* entrer en foule, affluer

► **flood out** VT SEP *[+ house]* inonder ◆ **the villagers were ~ed out** les inondations ont forcé les villageois à évacuer leurs maisons

floodgate /ˈflʌdgeɪt/ N vanne *f*, porte *f* d'écluse ◆ **these changes would open the ~s to ...** ces changements seraient la porte ouverte à ...

flooding /ˈflʌdɪŋ/ N inondation *f*

floodlight /ˈflʌdlaɪt/ (pret, ptp **floodlit**) VT *[+ buildings]* illuminer ; *(Sport) [+ match]* éclairer (aux projecteurs) N *(= device)* projecteur *m* ; *(= light)* lumière *f* (des projecteurs) ◆ **to play a match under ~s** jouer un match en nocturne

floodlighting /ˈflʌdlaɪtɪŋ/ N *[of building]* illumination *f* ; *[of match]* éclairage *m* (aux projecteurs)

floodlit /ˈflʌdlɪt/ VB pt, ptp of **floodlight**

floodwater(s) /ˈflʌd,wɔːtə(z)/ N(PL) eaux *fpl* de crue

flooey ‡ /ˈfluːɪ/ ADJ ◆ **to go ~** se détraquer *

floor /flɔːʳ/ N 1 *(gen)* sol *m* ; *(wooden)* plancher *m*, parquet *m* ; *(for dance)* piste *f* (de danse) ; *[of valley, ocean]* fond *m* ; *(fig) [of prices]* plancher *m* ◆ **stone/tiled ~** sol *m* dallé/carrelé ◆ **put it on the ~** pose-le par terre *or* sur le sol ◆ **she was sitting on the ~** elle était assise par terre *or* sur le sol ◆ **to take to the ~** *(= dance)* aller sur la piste (de danse) ◆ **last year, sales went through the ~** l'année dernière les ventes ont chuté ◆ **property prices have dropped through the ~** les prix sur le marché immobilier se sont effondrés ; → **wipe**

2 *(in public speaking)* ◆ **a question from the ~ of the house** une question de l'auditoire *m or* de l'assemblée *f* ◆ **to hold the ~** garder la parole ◆ **to take the ~** *(= speak)* prendre la parole ◆ **to cross the ~ (of the House)** *(Parl)* ≈ s'inscrire à un parti opposé

3 *(= storey)* étage *m* ◆ **first ~** *(Brit)* premier étage *m* ; *(US)* rez-de-chaussée *m* ◆ **on the first ~** *(Brit)* au premier (étage) ; *(in two-storey building)* à l'étage ; *(US)* au rez-de-chaussée ◆ **he lives on the second ~** *(Brit)* il habite au deuxième étage *or* au second ; *(US)* il habite au premier (étage) ◆ **we live on the same ~** nous habitons au même étage *or* sur le même palier ; → **ground¹**

4 *(Stock Exchange)* enceinte *f* de la Bourse ◆ **on/off the ~** en/hors Bourse

VT 1 faire le sol de ; *(with wooden boards)* planchéier, parqueter

2 *(= knock down) [+ opponent]* terrasser ; *(Boxing)* envoyer au tapis

3 *(* = silence)* réduire au silence ; *(* = baffle, perplex)* désorienter, dérouter ; *(Sport = defeat)* battre à plates coutures ◆ **this argument ~ed him** il n'a rien trouvé à répondre

COMP **floor area** N *[of flat, offices etc]* surface *f* au sol

floor covering N revêtement *m* de sol

floor exercises NPL exercices *mpl* au sol

floor lamp N *(US)* lampadaire *m*

floor leader N *(US Pol)* chef *m* de file

floor manager N *(TV)* régisseur *m* de plateau ; *(in shop)* chef *m* de rayon

floor plan N *(Archit)* plan *m* de niveau

floor polish N encaustique *f*, cire *f*

floor polisher N *(= tool)* cireuse *f*

floor show N attractions *fpl*, spectacle *m* de variétés *(dans un restaurant, cabaret etc)*

floor space N *(gen)* place *f* (par terre) ; *(in store, warehouse, trade fair)* surface *f* au sol

floorboard /ˈflɔːbɔːd/ N planche *f (de plancher)*, latte *f*

floorcloth /ˈflɔːklɒθ/ N serpillière *f*

flooring /ˈflɔːrɪŋ/ N *(= floor)* sol *m* ; *(made of wood)* plancher *m*, parquet *m* ; *(tiled)* carrelage *m* ; *(= material)* revêtement *m* (de sol)

floorwalker /ˈflɔː,wɔːkəʳ/ N *(US Comm)* chef *m* de rayon

floozy ‡ /ˈfluːzɪ/ N poule * *f*, pouffiasse ‡ *f*

flop /flɒp/ VI 1 *(= drop)* s'effondrer, s'affaler ◆ **he ~ped down on the bed/in a chair** il s'est effondré *or* s'est affalé sur le lit/dans un fauteuil ◆ **his hair ~ped over his left eye** ses cheveux lui tombaient sur l'œil gauche 2 *(US* ‡ *= sleep)* roupiller * 3 *(= fail) [play, film, record]* faire un four *or* un flop ; *[scheme etc]* être un fiasco *or* un bide * ◆ **he ~ped as Hamlet** son interprétation d'Hamlet a fait un four N (* *= failure) [of business venture, scheme]* fiasco *m* ◆ **the play was a ~** la pièce a été un four *or* un bide * ◆ **he was a terrible ~** il a lamentablement raté son coup

► **flop over** * *(US)* VI ◆ **to flop over to a new idea** adopter une nouvelle idée

flophouse * /ˈflɒphaʊs/ N *(US)* asile *m* de nuit

flopover * /ˈflɒpəʊvəʳ/ N *(US TV)* cascade *f* d'images

floppy /ˈflɒpɪ/ ADJ *[hat]* à bords flottants ; *[clothes]* lâche, flottant ; *[rabbit, dog ears]* tombant N ⇒ **floppy disk**

COMP **floppy disk** N *(Comput)* disquette *f*

floppy (disk) drive N *(Comput)* lecteur *m* de disquettes

flora /ˈflɔːrə/ N (pl **floras** *or* **florae** /ˈflɔːriː/) flore *f*

floral /ˈflɔːrəl/ ADJ *[fabric, dress, wallpaper, curtains]* fleuri, à fleurs ; *[print]* à fleurs ; *[design]* à fleurs, floral ; *[fragrance, perfume]* de fleurs ; *[arrangement, display]* floral ◆ **material with a ~ pattern** étoffe *f* à motifs floraux COMP **floral tributes** NPL fleurs *fpl* et couronnes *fpl*

Florence /ˈflɒrəns/ N Florence

Florentine /ˈflɒrəntaɪn/ ADJ florentin

floret /ˈflɒrɪt/ N *(Bot)* fleuron *m* ◆ **cauliflower/broccoli ~s** morceaux *mpl* de chou-fleur/brocoli

floribunda /flɔrəˈbʌndə/ N polyanta floribunda *m*

florid /ˈflɒrɪd/ ADJ 1 *(= ornate) [language, literary style, wallpaper, architecture]* très chargé 2 *(= ruddy) [person, face, complexion]* rubicond, rougeaud

Florida /ˈflɒrɪdə/ N Floride *f* ◆ **in ~** en Floride

florin /ˈflɒrɪn/ N florin *m (ancienne pièce de deux shillings)*

florist /ˈflɒrɪst/ N fleuriste *mf* ◆ **~'s shop** magasin *m* de fleurs, fleuriste *m*

floss /flɒs/ N bourre *f* de soie ; (also **dental floss**) fil *m* dentaire ; → **candy** VTI ◆ **to ~ (one's teeth)** utiliser du fil dentaire

flossy * /ˈflɒsɪ/ ADJ *(US)* ultrachic *inv*, d'un brillant superficiel

flotation /fləʊˈteɪʃən/ N 1 *(lit) [of boat]* action *f* de flotter ; *[of log]* flottage *m* 2 *(Fin) [of share, loan]* lancement *m* ; *[of company]* constitution *f*, création *f*

COMP **flotation collar** N *(Space)* flotteur *m (de module lunaire)*

flotation compartment N caisse *f* de flottaison

flotation tank N caisse *f* de flottaison

flotilla /fləˈtɪlə/ N flottille *f*

flotsam /ˈflɒtsəm/ N *(NonC)* épave *f* (flottante) ◆ **~ and jetsam** *(lit)* épaves *fpl* flottantes et rejetées ◆ **the ~ and jetsam of our society** *(fig)* les laissés-pour-compte de notre société

flounce /flaʊns/ VI ◆ **to ~ in/out** *etc* entrer/sortir *etc* dans un mouvement d'humeur *(or* d'indignation *etc)* N 1 *(= gesture)* geste *m* impatient, mouvement *m* vif 2 (*= frill: on clothes, curtain*) volant *m*

flounced /flaʊnst/ **ADJ** *[skirt, dress]* à volants

flounder[1] /ˈflaʊndəʳ/ **N** (pl **flounder** or **flounders**) (*= fish*) flet *m*

flounder[2] /ˈflaʊndəʳ/ **VI** (*= move with difficulty*) patauger (péniblement) ; (*violently*) se débattre ◆ **we ~ed along in the mud** nous avons poursuivi notre chemin en pataugeant dans la boue ◆ **I watched him ~ing about in the water** je le regardais se débattre dans l'eau ◆ **he ~ed through the rest of the speech** il a fini le discours en bredouillant ◆ **he ~ed on in bad French** il continuait de baragouiner en mauvais français ◆ **his career was ~ing** sa carrière traversait une mauvaise passe ◆ **the company/economy was ~ing** la société/l'économie battait de l'aile

flour /ˈflaʊəʳ/ **N** farine *f* **VT** fariner
COMP **flour bin** **N** boîte *f* à farine
flour mill **N** minoterie *f*
flour shaker **N** saupoudreuse *f* (à farine)
flour sifter **N** tamis *m* à farine

flourish /ˈflʌrɪʃ/ **VI** *[plant, animal]* bien venir, se plaire ; *[business, town, market]* prospérer ; *[person]* s'épanouir ; *[literature, the arts, painting]* fleurir, être en plein essor ◆ **the children were all ~ing** les enfants étaient épanouis *or* en pleine forme ◆ **the local fox population was ~ing** les renards prospéraient *or* se multipliaient dans la région ◆ **racism and crime ~ed in poor areas** le racisme et la criminalité se développaient dans les quartiers pauvres ◆ **drug traffickers continued to ~** les trafiquants de drogue ont continué à prospérer *or* à faire des affaires
VT *[+ stick, book, object]* brandir
N (*= curve, decoration*) fioriture *f*, ornement *m* ; (*in handwriting*) fioriture *f* ; (*under signature*) parafe *m or* paraphe *m* ; (*Mus*) fioriture *f* ◆ **he took the lid off with a ~** il a enlevé le couvercle avec un grand geste du bras

flourishing /ˈflʌrɪʃɪŋ/ **ADJ** *[business, economy, career]* prospère, florissant ; *[garden]* florissant ; *[plant, town]* qui prospère ; *[market]* en expansion ; → **flourish**

floury /ˈflaʊərɪ/ **ADJ** *[hands]* enfariné ; *[potatoes]* farineux ; *[loaf, dish]* saupoudré de farine, fariné

flout /flaʊt/ **VT** *[+ orders, advice]* faire fi de, passer outre à ; *[+ conventions, society]* mépriser, se moquer de

flow /fləʊ/ **VI** 1 (*= run*) *[river, blood from wound]* couler ; *[tide]* monter, remonter ◆ **to ~ back** refluer ◆ **to ~ out of** *[liquid]* s'écouler de, sortir de ◆ **to ~ past sth** passer devant qch ◆ **the river ~s into the sea** le fleuve se jette dans la mer ◆ **the water ~ed over the fields** l'eau s'est répandue dans les champs ◆ **tears were ~ing down her cheeks** les larmes coulaient *or* ruisselaient sur ses joues
2 (*= circulate*) *[electric current, blood in veins]* circuler ◆ **traffic ~ed freely** la circulation était fluide
3 (*= move, stream*) ◆ **to ~ in** *[people]* affluer, entrer à flots ◆ **refugees continue to ~ in from the war zone** les réfugiés continuent à affluer de la zone des conflits ◆ **the money keeps ~ing in** l'argent continue à rentrer ◆ **let the music ~ over you** laissez la musique vous envahir, laissez-vous envahir par la musique ◆ **a surge of hatred ~ed through my blood** j'ai soudain ressenti une bouffée de haine ; → **land**
4 (*= abound*) **the wine ~ed all evening** le vin a coulé à flots toute la soirée ◆ **his words ~ed readily** les mots lui venaient facilement
5 *[dress, hair etc]* flotter, ondoyer
6 (*fig*) ◆ **to ~ from** (*= result*) découler de, résulter de
N 1 *[of tide]* flux *m* ; *[of river]* courant *m* ◆ **he stopped the ~ of blood** il a arrêté l'écoulement *m or* l'épanchement *m* du sang ◆ (**menstrual**) **~** flux *m* menstruel
2 (*= circulation*) *[of electric current, blood in veins]* circulation *f* ◆ **it hindered the ~ of traffic** ça a ralenti la circulation
3 (*fig = movement, flood*) *[of donations, orders, replies, words]* flot *m* ◆ **the interruption in the ~ of oil from Iran** l'arrêt de l'approvisionnement en pétrole iranien ◆ **the phone rang, interrupting the ~ of conversation** le téléphone a sonné, interrompant le déroulement de la conversation ◆ **the ~ of information** le flux d'informations ◆ **to be in full ~** *[speaker]* être sur sa lancée ◆ **to go with the ~** suivre le mouvement ; → **ebb**
COMP **flow chart, flow diagram, flow sheet** **N** (*gen*) organigramme *m* ; (*Comput*) ordinogramme *m* ; (*Admin, Ind*) organigramme *m*, graphique *m* d'évolution

flower /ˈflaʊəʳ/ **N** 1 (*lit*) fleur *f* ◆ **in ~** en fleurs ◆ **to say sth with ~s** dire qch avec des fleurs ◆ **"no flowers by request"** "ni fleurs ni couronnes"
2 (*fig*) *[of group, generation]* (fine) fleur *f*, élite *f* ◆ **the ~ of the army** la (fine) fleur *or* l'élite *f* de l'armée ; → **bunch**
VI (*lit, fig*) fleurir
COMP **flower arrangement** **N** (*= art*) art *m* floral ; (*= exhibit*) composition *f* florale, arrangement *m* floral
flower arranging **N** art *m* floral
flower bed **N** platebande *f*, parterre *m*
flower children **NPL** ⇒ **flower people**
flower garden **N** jardin *m* d'agrément
flower head **N** capitule *m*
flower people **NPL** (*fig*) hippies *mpl*, babas cool * *mpl*
flower power **N** flower power *m*
flower seller **N** marchand(e) *m(f)* de fleurs ambulant(e), bouquetière † *f*
flower shop **N** fleuriste *m*, magasin *m* de fleurs ◆ **at the ~ shop** chez le fleuriste
flower show **N** floralies *fpl* ; (*smaller*) exposition *f* de fleurs

flowered /ˈflaʊəd/ **ADJ** *[fabric, garment]* à fleurs

flowering /ˈflaʊərɪŋ/ **N** (*lit*) floraison *f* ; (*fig*) floraison *f*, épanouissement *m* ◆ **the ~ of creative genius** l'épanouissement *m* du génie créateur **ADJ** (*= in flower*) en fleurs ; (*= which flowers*) à fleurs **COMP** **flowering shrub** **N** arbuste *m* à fleurs

flowerpot /ˈflaʊəpɒt/ **N** pot *m* de fleurs

flowery /ˈflaʊərɪ/ **ADJ** 1 *[fragrance, perfume]* fleuri, de fleurs ; *[fabric, dress, wallpaper]* fleuri, à fleurs ; *[meadow, field]* fleuri, couvert de fleurs 2 (*fig = elaborate*) *[speech, language]* fleuri

flowing /ˈfləʊɪŋ/ **ADJ** *[water]* qui coule ; *[tide]* montant ; *[hair, beard, skirt]* flottant ; *[movement]* fluide, plein d'aisance ; *[style]* coulant, fluide ◆ **the car's ~ lines** les lignes douces *or* fluides de la voiture ; → **fast[1]**

flown /fləʊn/ **VB** ptp of **fly[3]** → **high**

fl. oz (abbrev of **fluid ounce**) → **fluid**

flu /fluː/ **N** (abbrev of **influenza**) grippe *f* ; → **Asian**

flub * /flʌb/ (*US*) **VT** louper *, rater * **VI** rater * **N** ratage * *m*, erreur *f*

fluctuate /ˈflʌktjʊeɪt/ **VI** *[prices, rate, temperature]* varier, fluctuer ; *[person, attitude]* varier (*between* entre)

fluctuation /ˌflʌktjʊˈeɪʃən/ **N** fluctuation *f*, variation *f*

flue /fluː/ **N** *[of chimney]* conduit *m* (de cheminée) ; *[of stove]* tuyau *m* (de poêle) **COMP** **flue brush** **N** hérisson *m* (*de ramoneur*)

fluency /ˈfluːənsɪ/ **N** (*in speech*) facilité *f or* aisance *f* (d'élocution) ; (*in writing*) facilité *f*, aisance *f* ◆ **his ~ in English** son aisance (à s'exprimer) en anglais

fluent /ˈfluːənt/ **ADJ** 1 (*in foreign language*) **he is ~ in Italian, he speaks ~ Italian, his Italian is ~** il parle couramment l'italien ◆ **to become ~ in German** acquérir une bonne maîtrise de l'allemand 2 (*= eloquent*) *[style]* coulant ; *[talker, debater]* éloquent ◆ **to be a ~ speaker** parler avec aisance ◆ **to be a ~ reader** lire avec facilité *or* aisance ◆ **to be a ~ writer** avoir la plume facile ◆ **she speaks in ~ sentences** *[baby]* elle fait des phrases 3 (*= graceful*) *[movement]* fluide, plein d'aisance

fluently /ˈfluːəntlɪ/ **ADV** *[speak foreign language]* couramment ; *[speak, read, write, move, play]* avec facilité, avec aisance

fluey * /ˈfluːɪ/ **ADJ** (*Brit*) ◆ **to feel ~** se sentir grippé

fluff /flʌf/ **N** (*NonC: on birds, young animals*) duvet *m* ; (*from material*) peluche *f* ; (*= dust on floors*) mouton(s) *m(pl)* (*de poussière*) ◆ **a bit of ~** *‡ (*fig = girl*) une nénette * **VT** 1 (*also* **fluff out**) *[+ feathers]* ébouriffer ; *[+ pillows, hair]* faire bouffer 2 (* *= do badly*) *[+ audition, lines in play, exam]* rater *, louper *

fluffy /ˈflʌfɪ/ **ADJ** 1 (*= soft*) *[wool]* doux (douce *f*) ; *[slipper]* molletonné ; *[sweater, towel]* pelucheux ; *[hair]* duveteux ; *[kitten, rabbit]* au pelage duveteux ; *[cloud]* floconneux ◆ **~ toy** (*= soft toy*) peluche *f* 2 (*= light*) *[cake, rice, mashed potatoes]* léger ; *[egg, mixture]* mousseux ; *[omelette]* soufflé

fluid /ˈfluːɪd/ **ADJ** *[substance]* liquide ; *[shape]* doux (douce *f*) ; *[style]* fluide, coulant ; *[drawing, outline]* fluide ; *[movement]* fluide, plein d'aisance ; *[situation]* fluide, fluctuant ; *[plan]* flou **N** fluide *m* (*also Chem*), liquide *m* ◆ **he's on ~s only** (*as diet*) il ne prend que des (aliments) liquides
COMP **fluid assets** **NPL** (*US Fin*) liquidités *fpl* disponibilités *fpl*
fluid ounce **N** *mesure de capacité* (*Brit : 0,028 litres, US : 0,030 litres*)

fluidity /fluːˈɪdɪtɪ/ **N** *[of gas, liquid, situation]* fluidité *f* ; *[of style, speech]* aisance *f*, fluidité *f*

fluke[1] /fluːk/ **N** (*= chance event*) coup *m* de chance *or* de veine * extraordinaire, hasard *m* extraordinaire ◆ **by a (sheer) ~** par un hasard extraordinaire **ADJ** *[coincidence, circumstances]* extraordinaire ◆ **he scored a ~ goal** il a marqué un but tout à fait par hasard

fluke[2] /fluːk/ **N** *[of anchor]* patte *f* (*d'ancre*) ; *[of arrow, harpoon]* barbillon *m*

fluke[3] /fluːk/ **N** (*= parasite*) douve *f* (du foie *etc*)

fluky /ˈfluːkɪ/ **ADJ** 1 *[wind]* capricieux 2 ⇒ **fluke[1]**

flume /fluːm/ **N** 1 (*= ravine*) ravin *m* 2 (*= channel*) chenal *m* 3 (*in swimming pool*) toboggan *m*

flummery /ˈflʌmərɪ/ **N** (*Culin*) bouillie *f* ; (*fig*) flagornerie *f*

flummox * /ˈflʌməks/ **VT** *[+ person]* démonter, couper le sifflet à * ◆ **he was ~ed** ça lui avait coupé le sifflet *, il était complètement démonté

flung /flʌŋ/ **VB** pret, ptp of **fling** → **far-**

flunk * /flʌŋk/ (*esp US*) **VI** (*= fail*) être recalé * *or* collé * ; (*= shirk*) se dégonfler * **VT** 1 (*= fail*) **to ~ French/an exam** être recalé * *or* être collé * en français/à un examen ◆ **they ~ed ten candidates** ils ont recalé * *or* collé * dix candidats 2 (*= give up*) laisser tomber

► **flunk out** *‡ (*US*) **VI** se faire virer * (*of* de) **VT SEP** virer *, renvoyer

flunk(e)y /ˈflʌŋkɪ/ **N** (*lit*) laquais *m* ; (*fig*) larbin * *m*

fluorescein /ˌflʊəˈresɪːn/ **N** fluorescéine *f*

fluorescence /flʊəˈresns/ **N** fluorescence *f*

fluorescent /flʊəˈresnt/ ADJ *[lighting, bulb, colour, dye, paint]* fluorescent ; *[clothes]* fluorescent, fluo* *inv* COMP **fluorescent strip** N tube *m* fluorescent *or* au néon

fluoridation /ˌflʊərɪˈdeɪʃən/ N fluoration *f*

fluoride /ˈflʊəraɪd/ N fluorure *m* COMP **fluoride toothpaste** N dentifrice *m* fluoré *or* au fluor

fluorine /ˈflʊəriːn/ N fluor *m*

fluorite /ˈflʊəraɪt/ N *(US)* fluorite *f*, spath *m* fluor

fluorspar /ˈflʊəspɑːʳ/ N spath *m* fluor, fluorite *f*

flurry /ˈflʌrɪ/ N *[of snow]* rafale *f* ; *[of wind]* rafale *f*, risée *f* ; *(fig)* agitation *f*, émoi *m* ◆ **a ~ of activity** un débordement d'activité ◆ **a ~ of protest** une vague de protestations ◆ **in a ~ of excitement** dans un frisson d'agitation VT agiter, effarer ◆ **to get flurried** perdre la tête, s'affoler (*at* pour)

flush[1] /flʌʃ/ N 1 *(in sky)* lueur *f* rouge, rougeoiement *m* ; *[of blood]* afflux *m* ; *(= blush)* rougeur *f* ◆ **(hot) ~es** *(Med)* bouffées *fpl* de chaleur

2 *[of beauty, health, youth]* éclat *m* ; *[of joy]* élan *m* ; *[of excitement]* accès *m* ◆ **in the (first) ~ of victory** dans l'ivresse de la victoire ◆ **she's not in the first ~ of youth** elle n'est pas dans sa première jeunesse

3 *[of lavatory]* chasse *f* (d'eau)

VI 1 *[face, person]* rougir ◆ **to ~ crimson** s'empourprer, rougir jusqu'aux oreilles ◆ **to ~ with shame/anger** rougir de honte/de colère

2 **the toilet won't ~** la chasse d'eau ne marche pas

VT nettoyer à grande eau ; *[+ drain, pipe]* curer à grande eau ◆ **to ~ the toilet** *or* **lavatory** tirer la chasse (d'eau) ◆ **to ~ sth down the toilet** *or* **lavatory** faire passer qch dans les toilettes

► **flush away** VT SEP *(down sink/drain)* faire partir par l'évier/par l'égout ; *(down lavatory)* faire partir (en tirant la chasse d'eau)

► **flush out** VT SEP *(with water)* nettoyer à grande eau

flush[2] /flʌʃ/ ADJ 1 au même niveau (*with* que) au *or* à ras (*with* de) ◆ **~ with the ground** à ras de terre, au ras de terre ◆ **a door ~ with the wall** une porte dans l'alignement du mur ◆ **a cupboard ~ with the wall** un placard encastré dans le mur ◆ **~ against** tout contre 2 ◆ **to be ~ (with money)** * être en fonds, avoir des sous* VT ◆ **to ~ a door** affleurer une porte

flush[3] /flʌʃ/ VT (*also* **flush out**) *[+ game, birds]* lever ; *[+ person]* forcer à se montrer

► **flush out** VT FUS ◆ **they flushed them out of their hiding places** ils les ont forcés à sortir de leur cachette, ils les ont fait sortir de leur cachette ◆ **they tried to ~ out illegal workers operating in the country** ils ont essayé de chasser les travailleurs clandestins du pays

flush[4] /flʌʃ/ N *(Cards)* flush *m* ; → **royal**

flushed /ˈflʌʃt/ ADJ *[person]* tout rouge ; *[face, cheeks]* tout rouge, enflammé ◆ **~ with anger** rouge *or* empourpré de colère ◆ **~ with fever/embarrassment/excitement** rouge de fièvre/d'embarras/d'excitation ◆ **~ with success** grisé par le succès ◆ **white flowers ~ with pink** des fleurs blanches colorées de rose

fluster /ˈflʌstəʳ/ VT énerver, troubler ◆ **to get ~ed** s'énerver, se troubler N agitation *f*, trouble *m* ◆ **in a ~** énervé, troublé ◆ **to be all of a ~** être dans tous ses états

flute /fluːt/ N *(= musical instrument, wine glass)* flûte *f*

fluted /ˈfluːtɪd/ ADJ 1 *[pillar]* cannelé ; *[flan dish]* à cannelures 2 *[tone, note]* flûté

fluting /ˈfluːtɪŋ/ N cannelures *fpl*

flutist /ˈfluːtɪst/ N *(US)* flûtiste *mf*

flutter /ˈflʌtəʳ/ VI 1 *[flag, ribbon]* flotter ; *[bird, moth, butterfly]* voleter, voltiger ; *[wings]* battre ◆ **the bird ~ed about the room** l'oiseau voletait çà et là dans la pièce ◆ **the butterfly ~ed away** le papillon a disparu en voletant *or* voltigeant ◆ **a leaf came ~ing down** une feuille est tombée en tourbillonnant

2 *[person]* papillonner, virevolter

3 *[heart, pulse]* palpiter

VT *[+ fan, paper]* jouer de ◆ **the bird ~ed its wings** l'oiseau a battu des ailes ◆ **to ~ one's eyelashes** battre des cils (*at sb* dans la direction de qn)

N 1 *[of eyelashes, wings]* battement *m* ; *[of heart, pulse]* palpitation *f* ◆ **there was a ~ of fear in her voice** sa voix trahissait la peur ◆ **to feel a ~ of excitement at the prospect of ...** être tout excité à l'idée de ... ◆ **(all) in a ~** tout troublé, dans un grand émoi

2 *(Brit *)* **to have a ~** *(= gamble)* parier (de petites sommes) (*on* sur) ; *(Stock Exchange)* boursicoter

fluvial /ˈfluːvɪəl/ ADJ fluvial

flux /flʌks/ N *(NonC)* 1 changement *m* continuel, fluctuation *f* ◆ **to be in a state of ~** changer sans arrêt, fluctuer continuellement 2 *(Med)* flux *m*, évacuation *f* (*de sang etc*) ; *(Phys)* flux *m* ; *(Metal)* fondant *m*

fly[1] /flaɪ/ N *(= insect, Fishing)* mouche *f* ◆ **they were dropping*** *or* **dying like flies** ils tombaient* *or* mouraient comme des mouches ◆ **small businesses were dropping like flies in the recession*** les petites entreprises faisaient faillite les unes après les autres à cause de la récession ◆ **he wouldn't harm** *or* **hurt a ~** il ne ferait pas de mal à une mouche ◆ **I wish I were a ~ on the wall** j'aimerais être une petite souris ; see also **comp** ◆ **there's a ~ in the ointment** il y a un ennui *or* un hic* ◆ **he's the ~ in the ointment** c'est lui l'empêcheur de tourner en rond ◆ **there are no flies on him*** il n'est pas né d'hier, il n'est pas tombé de la dernière pluie ; → **housefly**

COMP **fly-blown** ADJ *(lit)* couvert *or* plein de chiures de mouches ; *(fig)* très défraîchi

fly fishing N pêche *f* à la mouche

fly killer N insecticide *m*

fly-on-the-wall documentary N documentaire *m* pris sur le vif

fly paper N papier *m* tue-mouches

fly rod N *(Fishing)* canne *f* à mouche

fly spray N bombe *f* insecticide

fly swat(ter) N tapette *f*

fly trap N *(= device)* attrape-mouches *m inv* ; → **Venus**

fly[2] /flaɪ/ ADJ *(esp Brit = astute)* malin (-igne *f*), rusé

fly[3] /flaɪ/ (pret **flew**, ptp **flown**) VI 1 *[bird, insect, plane]* voler ; *[air passenger]* aller *or* voyager en avion ; *[pilot]* piloter un (*or* des) avion(s) ◆ **I don't like ~ing** je n'aime pas (prendre) l'avion ◆ **I always ~** je voyage toujours en avion, je prends toujours l'avion ◆ **how did you get here? – I flew** comment es-tu venu ? – par *or* en avion ◆ **to ~ over London** survoler Londres, voler au-dessus de Londres ◆ **the planes flew past** *or* **over at 3pm** les avions sont passés à 15 heures ◆ **to ~ over the Channel** survoler la Manche ◆ **to ~ across the Channel** *[bird, plane]* traverser la Manche ; *[passenger]* traverser la Manche (en avion) ◆ **to ~ away** *[bird]* s'envoler ◆ **all her worries flew away** tous ses soucis se sont envolés ◆ **we flew in from Rome this morning** nous sommes venus de Rome en *or* par avion ce matin ◆ **to ~ off** *[bird, plane]* s'envoler ; *[passenger]* partir en avion, s'envoler (*to* pour) ◆ **a bee flew in through the window** une abeille est entrée par la fenêtre ◆ **fur was ~ing, feathers were ~ing** ça bardait*, il y avait du grabuge* ◆ **that will make the fur** *or* **feathers ~!** il va y avoir du grabuge !* ◆ **he is ~ing high** *(fig)* il a beaucoup de succès, il réussit très bien ◆ **the company is ~ing high** l'entreprise marche très bien ◆ **to find that the bird has flown** trouver l'oiseau envolé ◆ **~ right, sonny*** *(US)* surtout pas de bêtises, fiston* ; → **fury**

2 *(fig) [time]* passer vite, filer* ; *[sparks]* jaillir, voler ; *[car, people]* filer* ◆ **to ~ in/out/back** *etc* *[person]* entrer/sortir/retourner *etc* à toute vitesse *or* à toute allure ◆ **it's late, I must ~!** il est tard, il faut que je me sauve *subj* ! ◆ **to ~ to sb's assistance** voler au secours de qn ◆ **to ~ in the face of danger/accepted ideas** défier le danger/les idées reçues ◆ **to ~ in the face of authority** battre en brèche l'ordre établi ◆ **to ~ into a rage** *or* **a passion** s'emporter, se mettre dans une violente colère ◆ **to ~ off the handle*** s'emporter, sortir de ses gonds ◆ **to let ~ at sb** *(in angry words)* s'en prendre violemment à qn, prendre qn violemment à partie ; *(by shooting)* tirer sur qn ◆ **to ~ at sb** sauter *or* se ruer sur qn ◆ **to ~ at sb's throat** sauter à la gorge de qn ◆ **the door flew open** la porte s'est ouverte brusquement ◆ **the handle flew off** la poignée s'est détachée brusquement *or* soudain ; → **send, spark**

3 *(= flee)* fuir (*before* devant) s'enfuir (*from* de) ◆ **to ~ from temptation** fuir la tentation ◆ **~ for your life!** fuyez !

4 *[flag]* flotter ◆ **her hair was ~ing in the wind** ses cheveux flottaient au vent ; → **flag**[1]

VT 1 *[+ aircraft]* piloter ; *[+ person]* emmener en avion ; *[+ goods]* transporter par avion ; *[+ standard, admiral's flag]* arborer ◆ **to ~ the French flag** *(Naut)* battre pavillon français ◆ **the building was ~ing the French flag** le drapeau français flottait sur l'immeuble ◆ **to ~ a kite** *(lit)* faire voler un cerf-volant ; *(fig)* lancer un ballon d'essai *(fig)* ◆ **to ~ great distances** faire de longs voyages en avion ◆ **to ~ the Atlantic/the Channel** *etc* traverser l'Atlantique/la Manche, *etc* en avion ◆ **to ~ Air France** voler sur Air France ◆ **we will ~ you to Italy and back for £350** nous vous proposons un vol aller et retour pour l'Italie pour 350 livres

2 ◆ **to ~ the country** s'enfuir du pays ; → **coop, nest**

N 1 *(on trousers: also* **flies***)* braguette *f* ; *(on tent)* auvent *m*

2 *(= vehicle)* fiacre *m*

3 *[of flag]* battant *m*

4 *(set phrase)*

◆ **on the fly** *(= quickly)* sur-le-champ ; *(= while busy)* tout en faisant autre chose ; *(Comput)* à la volée, en direct ◆ **people who can make decisions on the ~** les gens capables de prendre des décisions sur-le-champ

NPL **flies** *(Theat)* cintres *mpl*, dessus *mpl*

COMP **fly-button** N bouton *m* de braguette

fly-by-night N *(= irresponsible person)* tout-fou* *m* ; *(= decamping debtor)* débiteur *m*, -trice *f* qui déménage à la cloche de bois *or* qui décampe en douce* ADJ *[person]* tout-fou* *m only* ; *[firm, operation]* véreux

fly-drive N *(Travel)* formule *f* avion plus voiture

fly-drive holiday N (vacances *fpl* en) formule *f* *or* forfait *m* avion plus voiture

fly hack N *(Rugby)* ⇒ **fly kick**

fly half N *(Rugby)* demi *m* d'ouverture

fly kick N *(Rugby)* coup *m* de pied à suivre

fly-post VT *(Brit)* coller des affiches illégalement

fly-posting N *(Brit)* affichage *m* illégal

fly sheet N *(Brit)* feuille *f* volante

fly-tipping N décharge *f* sauvage

flyaway /ˈflaɪəˌweɪ/ ADJ *[hair]* rebelle, difficile ; *(= frivolous)* frivole, futile

flyboy * /ˈflaɪbɔɪ/ N *(US)* pilote *m* *(de l'armée de l'air)*

flyby /ˈflaɪbaɪ/ N *(US)* (pl **flybys**) ⇒ **flypast**

flycatcher /ˈflaɪˌkætʃəʳ/ N 1 *(= bird)* gobe-mouches *m inv* 2 *(= plant)* plante *f* carnivore 3 *(= trap)* attrape-mouches *m inv*

flyer /ˈflaɪəʳ/ N ⇒ **flier**

flying /ˈflaɪɪŋ/ N *(= action)* vol *m* ; *(= activity)* aviation *f* ◆ **he likes ~** *[passenger]* il aime (prendre) l'avion ; *[pilot]* il aime piloter ◆ **he's afraid of ~** il a peur de prendre l'avion ◆ **to go ~** *(lit)* faire de l'avion ; *(= fall over)* aller valdinguer* ; → **formation, stunt¹**

ADJ *[animal, insect]* volant ; *[debris]* projeté ◆ **~ glass** éclats *mpl* de verre ◆ **~ jump** *or* **leap** saut *m* avec élan ◆ **to take a ~ jump** *or* **leap** sauter avec élan ◆ **with ~ colours** haut la main

COMP **flying ambulance** N *(= plane)* avion *m* sanitaire ; *(= helicopter)* hélicoptère *m* sanitaire
flying boat N hydravion *m*
flying bomb N bombe *f* volante
flying buttress N arc-boutant *m*
flying doctor N médecin *m* volant
the Flying Dutchman N *(Mus)* le Vaisseau fantôme ; *(= legend)* le Hollandais volant
flying fish N poisson *m* volant, exocet *m*
flying fortress N forteresse *f* volante
flying fox N roussette *f*
flying machine N machine *f* volante, appareil *m* volant
flying officer N *(Brit Mil)* lieutenant *m* de l'armée de l'air
flying picket N piquet *m* de grève volant
flying saucer N soucoupe *f* volante
Flying Squad N *(Brit Police)* brigade *f* volante *(de la police judiciaire)*
flying start N *(Sport)* départ *m* lancé ◆ **to get off to a ~ start** *[racing car, runner]* prendre un départ très rapide *or* en flèche ; *[scheme, plan]* prendre un bon *or* un excellent départ
flying suit N combinaison *f* (de vol)
flying time N heures *fpl or* temps *m* de vol
flying trapeze N trapèze *m* volant

flyleaf /ˈflaɪliːf/ N (pl **-leaves**) page *f* de garde

flyover /ˈflaɪˌəʊvəʳ/ N 1 *(Brit : on road)* autopont *m* ; *(temporary)* toboggan *m* 2 *(US= planes)* défilé *m* aérien

flypast /ˈflaɪpɑːst/ N *(Brit)* défilé *m* aérien

flyweight /ˈflaɪweɪt/ N *(Boxing)* poids *m* mouche

flywheel /ˈflaɪwiːl/ N volant *m* *(Tech)*

FM /efˈem/ 1 (abbrev of **Field Marshal**) → **field** 2 (abbrev of **frequency modulation**) FM 3 (abbrev of **Foreign Minister**) → **foreign**

FMB /ˌefemˈbiː/ N *(US)* (abbrev of **Federal Maritime Board**) → **federal**

FMD /ˌefemˈdiː/ N (abbrev of **foot-and-mouth disease**) → **foot**

f-number /ˈefˌnʌmbəʳ/ N *(Phot)* ouverture *f (du diaphragme)*

FO *(Brit)* (abbrev of **Foreign Office**) → **foreign**

foal /fəʊl/ N *(= horse)* poulain *m* ; *(= donkey)* ânon *m* ◆ **the mare is in ~** la jument est pleine
VI mettre bas

foam /fəʊm/ N *[of beer etc]* mousse *f* ; *[of sea]* écume *f* ; *(in fire fighting)* mousse *f (carbonique)* ; *(at mouth)* écume *f* ◆ **the ~** *(liter)* les flots *mpl (liter)* VI *[sea]* écumer, moutonner ; *[soapy water]* mousser, faire de la mousse ◆ **to ~ at the mouth** *[animal]* baver, écumer ; *[person]* *(lit)* avoir de l'écume aux lèvres ; *(fig)* écumer de rage

COMP **foam-backed** ADJ *[carpet]* à sous-couche de mousse
foam bath N bain *m* moussant
foam plastic N mousse *f* de plastique
foam rubber N caoutchouc *m* mousse ®
foam sprayer N extincteur *m* à mousse

► **foam up** VI *[liquid in container]* mousser

foamy /ˈfəʊmɪ/ ADJ *[waves, sea]* écumeux ; *[beer]* mousseux

FOB /efəʊˈbiː/ *(Comm)* (abbrev of **free on board**) FOB

fob /fɒb/ VT ◆ **to ~ sth off on sb, to ~ sb off with sth** refiler* *or* fourguer* qch à qn ◆ **to ~ sb off with promises** se débarrasser de qn par de belles promesses N († = *pocket*) gousset *m* (de pantalon) ; *(= ornament)* breloque *f* COMP **fob watch** N montre *f* de gousset

FOC /efəʊˈsiː/ *(Comm)* (abbrev of **free of charge**) → **free**

focal /ˈfəʊkəl/ ADJ focal
COMP **focal distance** N ⇒ **focal length**
focal infection N *(Med)* infection *f* focale
focal length N distance *f* focale, focale *f*
focal plane N plan *m* focal
focal plane shutter N *(Phot)* obturateur *m* focal *or* à rideau
focal point N *(Opt)* foyer *m* ; *(in building, gardens)* point *m* de convergence ; *(= main point) [of meeting, discussions]* point *m* central *or* focal
focal ratio N diaphragme *m*

foci /ˈfəʊkaɪ/ NPL of **focus**

fo'c'sle /ˈfəʊksl/ N ⇒ **forecastle**

focus /ˈfəʊkəs/ N (pl **focuses** *or* **foci**) 1 *(Math, Phys)* foyer *m*
2 *(Phot)* **the picture is in/out of ~** l'image est nette/floue, l'image est/n'est pas au point ◆ **to bring a picture into ~** mettre une image au point
3 *(= main point) [of illness, unrest]* foyer *m*, siège *m* ◆ **to be the ~ of a controversy** être au centre d'une controverse ◆ **to keep sth in ~** ne pas perdre de vue qch ◆ **to bring sth into ~** centrer l'attention sur qch ◆ **he was the ~ of attention** il était le centre d'attraction
4 *(= purpose, direction) [of person, policy]* objectif *m* ; *[of film, play, plot]* cohérence *f* ◆ **his ~ on foreign policy** la priorité qu'il accorde à la politique étrangère ◆ **the report's ~ is on corruption** le rapport traite essentiellement de la corruption ◆ **to shift one's ~** réorienter ses priorités
VT 1 *[+ instrument, camera]* mettre au point ◆ **to ~ the camera** faire le point
2 *(= direct) [+ light, heat rays]* faire converger ; *[+ beam, ray]* diriger *(on* sur*)* ; *[+ attention]* concentrer *(on* sur*)* ◆ **to ~ one's eyes on sth** fixer ses yeux sur qch ◆ **all eyes were ~ed on him** il était le point de mire de tous
VI 1 *(Phot)* mettre au point *(on* sur*)*
2 ◆ **to ~ on** *[eyes]* se fixer sur, accommoder sur ; *[person]* fixer son regard sur ◆ **my eyes won't ~, I can't ~ properly** je vois trouble, je ne peux pas accommoder
3 *[heat, light, rays]* converger *(on* sur*)*
4 *(= concentrate)* **we must ~ on raising funds** il faut nous concentrer sur la collecte des fonds ◆ **the meeting ~ed on the problems of the unemployed** la réunion a surtout porté sur les problèmes des chômeurs ◆ **the report ~es on new technologies** le rapport est essentiellement axé sur les nouvelles technologies
COMP **focus group** N *(Pol, TV etc)* groupe *m* de discussion

focus(s)ed /ˈfəʊkəst/ ADJ *[person]* déterminé

fodder /ˈfɒdəʳ/ N fourrage *m* ; → **cannon**

FOE, FoE (abbrev of **Friends of the Earth**) → **friend**

foe /fəʊ/ N *(liter, lit, fig)* ennemi(e) *m(f)*, adversaire *mf*

foetal, fetal *(esp US)* /ˈfiːtl/ ADJ fœtal ◆ **in a ~ position** dans la position du fœtus, dans une position fœtale

foetid /ˈfiːtɪd/ ADJ ⇒ **fetid**

foetus /ˈfiːtəs/ N fœtus *m*

fog /fɒg/ N 1 *(on land)* brouillard *m* ; *(at sea)* brume *f*, brouillard *m* (de mer) 2 *(fig)* brouillard *m*, confusion *f* ◆ **to be in a ~** être dans le brouillard, ne plus savoir où l'on en est 3 *(Phot)* voile *m* VT 1 *[+ mirror, glasses]* embuer 2 *(fig) [+ person]* embrouiller, brouiller les idées à ◆ **to ~ the issue** *(accidentally)* embrouiller *or* obscurcir la question ; *(purposely)* brouiller les cartes 3 *[+ photo]* voiler
VI 1 *[mirror, glasses]* (also **fog over** *or* **up**) s'embuer ; *[landscape]* s'embrumer 2 *(Phot) [negative]* se voiler
COMP **fog bank** N banc *m* de brume
fog signal N *(for ships)* signal *m* de brume ; *(for trains)* pétard *m*

fogbound /ˈfɒgbaʊnd/ ADJ pris dans la brume, bloqué par le brouillard

fogey * /ˈfəʊgɪ/ N ◆ **old ~** vieille baderne* *f*, vieux schnock* *m* ◆ **young ~** *jeune BCBG très vieux jeu dans ses goûts et ses opinions*

foggy /ˈfɒgɪ/ ADJ 1 *(= misty) [night]* de brouillard ; *[landscape, weather]* brumeux ; *[street]* enveloppé de brouillard ◆ **it is ~** il y a du brouillard ◆ **on a ~ day** par un jour de brouillard 2 *(fig = confused) [brain]* embrumé ; *[state]* de confusion ◆ **I haven't the foggiest (idea** *or* **notion)!*** je n'en ai pas la moindre idée COMP **Foggy Bottom** * N *(US hum) surnom du ministère américain des Affaires étrangères*

foghorn /ˈfɒghɔːn/ N corne *f or* sirène *f* de brume ◆ **she has a voice like a ~** elle a une voix tonitruante *or* de stentor

foglamp *(Brit)* /ˈfɒglæmp/, **foglight** /ˈfɒglaɪt/ N feu *m* de brouillard

foible /ˈfɔɪbl/ N marotte *f*, petite manie *f*

foie gras /fwɑːˈgrɑː/ N foie *m* gras

foil¹ /fɔɪl/ N 1 *(NonC = metal sheet)* feuille *f or* lame *f* de métal ; (also **cooking** *or* **kitchen foil**) papier *m* d'aluminium, (papier *m*) alu* *m* ◆ **fish cooked in ~** poisson *m* cuit (au four) dans du papier d'aluminium ; → **tinfoil** 2 *(fig)* ◆ **to act as a ~ to sb/sth** servir de faire-valoir à qn/qch, mettre qn/qch en valeur

foil² /fɔɪl/ N *(Fencing)* fleuret *m*

foil³ /fɔɪl/ VT *[+ attempts]* déjouer ; *[+ plans]* contrecarrer

foist /fɔɪst/ VT ◆ **to ~ sth (off) on sb** refiler* *or* repasser* qch à qn ◆ **this job was ~ed (off) on to me** c'est moi qui ai hérité de ce boulot* ◆ **to ~ o.s. on (to) sb** s'imposer à qn ; *(as uninvited guest)* s'imposer *or* s'installer chez qn

fold¹ /fəʊld/ N *(in paper, cloth, skin, earth's surface)* pli *m* ◆ **~s** *(Geol)* plissement *m*
VT 1 *[+ paper, blanket, bed, chair]* plier ; *[+ wings]* replier ◆ **to ~ a page in two** plier une feuille en deux ◆ **to ~ one's arms** (se) croiser les bras ◆ **to ~ one's hands** *(in prayer)* joindre les mains
2 *(= wrap up)* envelopper *(in* dans*)* entourer *(in* de*)* ◆ **to ~ sb/sth in one's arms** serrer qn/qch dans ses bras, étreindre qn/qch ◆ **hills ~ed in mist** *(liter)* des collines enveloppées de brume
3 *(Culin) [+ eggs, flour]* incorporer *(into* à*)*
VI 1 *[chair, table]* se (re)plier
2 *(* = fail) [newspaper]* disparaître, cesser de paraître ; *[business]* fermer (ses portes) ; *[play]* quitter l'affiche, être retiré de l'affiche ◆ **they ~ed last year** *[business etc]* ils ont mis la clé sous la porte l'année dernière
COMP **fold-up** ADJ *[chair, table etc]* pliant, escamotable

► **fold away** VI *[table, bed]* (être capable de) se (re)plier
VT SEP *[+ clothes, newspaper]* plier et ranger

► **fold back** VT SEP *[+ shutters]* ouvrir, rabattre ; *[+ bedclothes, collar]* replier, rabattre

► **fold down** VT SEP *[+ chair]* plier ◆ **to ~ down the corner of a page** corner une page

► **fold in** VT SEP *(Culin) [+ eggs, flour]* incorporer

► **fold over** VT SEP *[+ paper]* plier, replier ; *[+ blanket]* replier, rabattre

► **fold up** VI ⇒ **fold**¹ **VI**
VT SEP *[+ paper etc]* plier, replier

fold² /fəʊld/ **N** *(= enclosure)* parc *m* à moutons ; *(Rel)* sein *m* de l'Église ◆ **to come back to the ~** *(fig)* rentrer au bercail

...fold /fəʊld/ **SUF** ◆ **twentyfold ADJ** par vingt **ADV** vingt fois ; → **twofold**

foldaway /ˈfəʊldə,weɪ/ **ADJ** *[bed]* pliant, escamotable

folder /ˈfəʊldəʳ/ **N** 1 *(= file)* chemise *f* ; *(with hinges)* classeur *m* ; *(for drawings)* carton *m* ; *(papers)* dossier *m* 2 *(Comput)* répertoire *m* 3 *(= leaflet)* dépliant *m*, brochure *f*

folding /ˈfəʊldɪŋ/ **ADJ** *[bed, table, bicycle, screen]* pliant
COMP **folding door N** porte *f* (en) accordéon
folding money * **N** *(US)* billets *mpl* de banque
folding seat (also **folding stool**) **N** pliant *m* ; *(in car, theatre)* strapontin *m*

foldout /ˈfəʊldaʊt/ **N** encart *m*

foliage /ˈfəʊlɪɪdʒ/ **N** feuillage *m*

foliation /,fəʊlɪˈeɪʃən/ **N** *(Bot)* foliation *f*, feuillaison *f* ; *[of book]* foliotage *m* ; *(Geol)* foliation *f* ; *(Archit)* rinceaux *mpl*

folic acid /,fəʊlɪkˈæsɪd/ **N** acide *m* folique

folio /ˈfəʊlɪəʊ/ **N** *(= sheet)* folio *m*, feuillet *m* ; *(= volume)* (volume *m*) in-folio *m*

folk /fəʊk/ **N** 1 *(pl = people:* also **folks**) gens *mpl f adj before n* ◆ **they are good ~(s)** ce sont de braves gens ◆ **a lot of ~(s) believe ...** beaucoup de gens croient ... ◆ **there were a lot of ~ at the concert** il y avait beaucoup de gens *or* de monde au concert ◆ **old ~(s)** les personnes *fpl* âgées, les vieux *mpl (pej)* ◆ **young ~(s)** les jeunes *mpl*, les jeunes gens *mpl* ◆ **my old ~s** *(= parents)* mes vieux * *mpl* ◆ **hello ~s!** * bonjour tout le monde ! * ; → **country, old**
2 *(pl = people in general:* also **folks**) les gens *mpl*, on ◆ **what will ~(s) think?** qu'est-ce que les gens vont penser ?, qu'est-ce qu'on va penser ? ◆ **~ get worried when they see that** les gens s'inquiètent quand ils voient ça
3 *(*: pl = relatives)* **~s** famille *f*, parents *mpl* ◆ **my ~s** ma famille, mes parents *mpl*, les miens *mpl*
4 *(NonC)* ⇒ **folk music**
COMP **folk art N** art *m* populaire
folk dance, folk dancing N danse *f* folklorique
folk etymology N étymologie *f* populaire
folk medicine N médecine *f* traditionnelle
folk memory N mémoire *f* collective
folk music N *(gen)* musique *f* folklorique ; *(contemporary)* musique *f* folk *inv*, folk *m*
folk rock N folk-rock *m*
folk singer N *(gen)* chanteur *m*, -euse *f* de chansons folkloriques ; *(contemporary)* chanteur *m*, -euse *f* folk *inv*
folk tale N conte *m* populaire
folk wisdom N bon sens *m or* sagesse *f* populaire

folklore /ˈfəʊklɔːʳ/ **N** traditions *fpl* populaires

folksong /ˈfəʊksɒŋ/ **N** *(gen)* chanson *f or* chant *m* folklorique ; *(contemporary)* chanson *f* folk *inv*

folksy * /ˈfəʊksɪ/ **ADJ** 1 *(= rustic) [furniture, charm]* rustique ; *[clothes]* de style rustique 2 *(US = affable) [person]* sans façon(s) ; *[manner]* sans prétentions ; *[comment, story, speech, humour]* plein de sagesse populaire

follicle /ˈfɒlɪkl/ **N** follicule *m*

follow /ˈfɒləʊ/ LANGUAGE IN USE 26.3
VT 1 *[+ person, road, vehicle, roadsigns]* suivre ; *(in procession)* aller *or* venir à la suite de, suivre ; *[+ suspect]* filer ◆ **to ~ sb in/out** *etc* suivre qn (qui entre/sort *etc*) ◆ **he ~ed me into the room** il m'a suivi dans la pièce ◆ **we're being ~ed** on nous suit ◆ **~ that car!** suivez cette voiture ! ◆ **~ me** suivez-moi ◆ **they ~ed the guide** ils ont suivi le guide ◆ **he'll be a difficult man to ~** *(fig)* il sera difficile de lui succéder ◆ **to have sb ~ed** faire filer qn ◆ **the detectives ~ed the suspect for a week** les détectives ont filé le suspect pendant une semaine ◆ **a bodyguard ~ed the president everywhere** un garde du corps accompagnait le président partout ◆ **he arrived first, ~ed by the ambassador** il est arrivé le premier, suivi de l'ambassadeur ◆ **this was ~ed by a request for ...** ceci a été suivi d'une demande de ... ◆ **the boat ~ed the coast** le bateau suivait *or* longeait la côte ◆ **~ your nose** * continuez tout droit ◆ **he ~ed his father into the business** il a pris la succession de son père ◆ **the earthquake was ~ed by an epidemic** une épidémie a suivi le tremblement de terre ◆ **the dinner will be ~ed by a concert** le dîner sera suivi d'un concert ◆ **the years ~ed one another** les années se suivaient *or* se succédaient ◆ **night ~s day** la nuit succède au jour
2 *[+ fashion]* suivre, se conformer à ; *[+ instructions, course of study]* suivre ; *[+ sb's orders]* exécuter ; *[+ serial, strip cartoon]* lire (régulièrement) ; *[+ speech, lecture]* suivre, écouter (attentivement) ◆ **to ~ sb's advice/example** suivre les conseils/l'exemple de qn ◆ **do you ~ football?** vous suivez le football ? ◆ **which team do you ~?** tu es supporter de quelle équipe ?
◆ **to follow suit** *(= do likewise)* en faire autant, faire de même ◆ **to ~ suit (in clubs** *etc*) *(Cards)* fournir (à trèfle *etc*)
3 *[+ profession]* exercer, suivre ; *[+ career]* poursuivre ◆ **to ~ the sea** *(liter)* être *or* devenir marin
4 *(= understand)* suivre, comprendre ◆ **do you ~ me?** vous me suivez ? ◆ **I don't quite ~ (you)** je ne vous suis pas bien *or* pas tout à fait
VI 1 *(= come after)* suivre ◆ **to ~ right behind sb, to ~ hard on sb's heels** être sur les talons de qn ◆ **to ~ in sb's footsteps** *or* **tracks** *(fig)* suivre les traces *or* marcher sur les traces de qn ◆ **what is there to ~?** *(at meals)* qu'est-ce qu'il y a après ?, qu'est-ce qui suit ? ◆ **we had ice cream to ~** après *or* ensuite nous avons eu de la glace ◆ **as ~s** *(gen)* comme suit ◆ **his argument was as ~s** son raisonnement était le suivant
2 *(= result)* s'ensuivre, résulter *(from* de) ◆ **it ~s that ...** il s'ensuit que ... + *indic* ◆ **it doesn't ~ that ...** il ne s'ensuit pas nécessairement que ... + *subj or indic*, cela ne veut pas forcément dire que ... + *subj or indic* ◆ **that doesn't ~** pas forcément, les deux choses n'ont rien à voir ◆ **that ~s from what he said** cela découle de ce qu'il a dit
3 *(= understand)* suivre, comprendre
COMP **follow-my-leader N** *(Brit) jeu où les enfants doivent imiter tous les mouvements d'un joueur désigné*
follow-on N *(Cricket) nouveau tour à la défense du guichet*
follow-the-leader N *(US)* ⇒ **follow-my-leader**
follow-through N *(to a project, survey)* suite *f*, continuation *f* ; *(Billiards)* coulé *m* ; *(Golf, Tennis)* accompagnement *m* (du coup)
follow-up N *(on file, case)* suivi *m (on, of* de) ; *[of event, programme] (coming after another)* suite *f (to* de) ; *[of letter, circular]* rappel *m* ; *(by sales representative)* relance *f* ; *(= visit)* → **follow-up visit** ◆ **this course is a ~-up to the beginners' course** ce cours fait suite au cours pour débutants
follow-up call N ◆ **to make a ~-up call** appeler pour donner suite à une lettre (*or* un fax *etc*)
follow-up care N *(Med)* soins *mpl* post-hospitaliers *or* de postcure
follow-up interview N entretien *m* complémentaire, second entretien *m*
follow-up letter N lettre *f* de rappel *or* relance
follow-up study, follow-up survey N étude *f* complémentaire
follow-up telephone call N ⇒ **follow-up call**
follow-up visit N *(Med, Social Work etc)* visite *f* de contrôle

► **follow about, follow around VT SEP** suivre (partout), être toujours sur les talons de

► **follow on VI** 1 *(= come after)* suivre ◆ **you go ahead and I'll ~ on when I can** allez-y, je vous suivrai quand je pourrai
2 *(= result)* résulter *(from* de) ◆ **it ~s on from what I said** cela découle de ce que j'ai dit, c'est la conséquence logique de ce que j'ai dit

► **follow out VT SEP** *[+ idea, plan]* poursuivre jusqu'au bout *or* jusqu'à sa conclusion ; *[+ order]* exécuter ; *[+ instructions]* suivre

► **follow through**
VI *(Billiards)* faire *or* jouer un coulé ; *(Golf, Tennis)* accompagner son coup *or* sa balle
VT SEP *[+ idea, plan]* poursuivre jusqu'au bout *or* jusqu'à sa conclusion
N ◆ **follow-through** → **follow**

► **follow up**
VI 1 *(= pursue an advantage)* exploiter un *or* tirer parti d'un avantage
2 *(Ftbl etc)* suivre l'action
VT SEP 1 *(= benefit from) [+ advantage, success, victory]* exploiter, tirer parti de ; *[+ offer]* donner suite à
2 *(= not lose track of)* suivre ◆ **we must ~ this business up** il faudra suivre cette affaire ◆ **this is a case to ~ up** *(gen, Police, Jur)* c'est une affaire à suivre ; *(Med)* c'est un cas à suivre ◆ **"to be followed up"** *(gen, Police, Jur)* "affaire à suivre" ; *(Med)* "cas à suivre"
3 *(= reinforce) [+ victory]* asseoir ; *[+ remark]* faire suivre *(with* de) compléter *(with* par) ◆ **they ~ed up the programme with another equally good** ils ont donné à cette émission une suite qui a été tout aussi excellente ◆ **they ~ed up their insults with threats** ils ont fait suivre leurs insultes de menaces
N ◆ **follow-up ADJ** → **follow**

follower /ˈfɒləʊəʳ/ **N** 1 *[of political, military leader]* partisan(e) *m(f)* ; *[of religious leader, artist, philosopher]* disciple *m* ; *[of religion, theory, tradition]* adepte *mf* ◆ **~s of fashion** les adeptes *mfpl* de la mode ◆ **as all football ~s know** comme le savent tous les amateurs de football 2 († *= admirer)* amoureux *m*, -euse *f*, admirateur *m*, -trice *f*

following /ˈfɒləʊɪŋ/ **ADJ** suivant ◆ **the ~ day** le jour suivant, le lendemain ◆ **he made the ~ remarks** il a fait les remarques suivantes *or* les remarques que voici
N 1 *[of political, military leader]* partisans *mpl* ; *[of religion, theory, tradition]* adeptes *mpl* ; *[of religious leader, artist, philosopher]* disciples *mpl* ; *(Sport)* supporters *mpl* ◆ **he has a large ~** il a de nombreux partisans *or* disciples
2 ◆ **he said the ~** il a dit ceci ◆ **see the ~ for an explanation** *(in documents)* voir ce qui suit pour toute explication ◆ **his argument was the ~** son raisonnement était le suivant ◆ **the ~ have been chosen** *(= people)* les personnes suivantes ont été retenues ; *(= books)* les livres suivants ont été retenus
PREP 1 *(= after)* après ◆ **~ the concert there will be ...** après le concert il y aura ...
2 *(= as a result of)* (comme) suite à ◆ **~ your letter ...** *(Comm)* (comme) suite à *or* en réponse à votre lettre ... ◆ **~ our meeting** (comme) suite à notre entretien
COMP **following wind N** vent *m* arrière

folly /ˈfɒlɪ/ **N** 1 *(NonC = foolishness)* folie *f*, sottise *f* ◆ **it's sheer ~ to do that** c'est de la pure folie *or* de la démence de faire cela 2 *(= foolish thing, action)* sottise *f*, folie *f* 3 *(Archit)* folie *f*

foment /fəʊˈment/ **VT** *(lit, fig)* fomenter

fomentation /,fəʊmenˈteɪʃən/ **N** *(lit, fig)* fomentation *f*

fond /fɒnd/ ADJ [1] (= *loving*) *[person, smile]* affectueux ; *[look]* tendre ♦ **to bid a ~ farewell to sb/sth** faire de tendres adieux à qn/qch
♦ **fond of** ♦ **to be ~ of sb** bien aimer qn ♦ **to become** *or* **grow ~ of sb** se prendre d'affection pour qn ♦ **to be ~ of sth** aimer beaucoup qch ♦ **to become** *or* **grow ~ of sth** se mettre à aimer qch ♦ **to be very ~ of music** aimer beaucoup la musique, être très mélomane ♦ **to be ~ of sweet things** être friand de sucreries, aimer les sucreries ♦ **to be ~ of doing sth** aimer beaucoup faire qch
[2] (= *pleasant*) *[memory]* très bon, très agréable
[3] (= *foolish*) *[belief]* naïf (naïve *f*) ; *[hope]* fou (folle *f*)
[4] (= *dear*) *[hope]* fervent ; *[dream, wish]* cher

fondant /ˈfɒndənt/ N (bonbon *m*) fondant *m*
COMP **fondant icing** N glaçage *m* fondant

fondle /ˈfɒndl/ VT caresser

fondly /ˈfɒndlɪ/ ADV [1] (= *affectionately*) *[remember, think of]* avec tendresse ; *[say]* affectueusement, tendrement ♦ **to smile ~ at sb** faire un tendre sourire à qn [2] (= *foolishly*) *[imagine, believe, hope]* naïvement

fondness /ˈfɒndnɪs/ N *(for things)* prédilection *f*, penchant *m* (*for* pour) ; *(for people)* affection *f*, tendresse *f* (*for* pour)

fondue /ˈfɒnduː/ N fondue *f*

font /fɒnt/ N [1] *(Rel)* fonts *mpl* baptismaux [2] *(Typo)* ⇒ **fount 2**

fontanel(le) /ˌfɒntəˈnel/ N fontanelle *f*

food /fuːd/ N [1] *(NonC = sth to eat)* nourriture *f* ♦ **there was no ~ in the house** il n'y avait rien à manger *or* il n'y avait pas de nourriture dans la maison ♦ **there's not enough ~** il n'y a pas assez à manger, il n'y a pas assez de nourriture ♦ **most of the ~ had gone bad** la plus grande partie de la nourriture *or* des vivres s'était avariée ♦ **to give sb ~** donner à manger à qn ♦ **to give the horses their ~** faire manger les chevaux, donner à manger aux chevaux ♦ **what's that? – it's ~ for the horse** qu'est-ce que c'est ? – c'est de la nourriture pour *or* c'est de quoi manger pour le cheval ♦ **to buy ~** acheter à manger, faire des provisions ♦ **the cost of ~** le prix des denrées alimentaires *or* de la nourriture ♦ **~ and clothing** la nourriture et les vêtements ♦ **to be off one's ~** * avoir perdu l'appétit, n'avoir plus d'appétit ♦ **the ~ is very good here** la nourriture est très bonne ici, on mange très bien ici ♦ **he likes plain ~** il aime les nourritures simples, il aime se nourrir simplement ♦ **it gave me ~ for thought** cela m'a donné à penser *or* à réfléchir
[2] (= *specific substance*) *(gen)* aliment *m* ; *(soft, moist, for poultry, dogs, cats, pigs etc)* pâtée *f* ♦ **a new ~ for babies/for pigs** un nouvel aliment pour les bébés/pour les cochons ♦ **pet ~** aliments *mpl* pour animaux ♦ **tins of dog/cat ~** des boîtes de pâtée pour chiens/chats ♦ **all these ~s must be kept in a cool place** tous ces aliments doivent être conservés au frais ; → **frozen, health**
[3] *(for plants)* engrais *m*
COMP **food additive** N additif *m* alimentaire
food aid N aide *f* alimentaire
Food and Agriculture Organization N Organisation *f* des Nations Unies pour l'alimentation et l'agriculture
Food and Drug Administration N *(US)* FDA *f* ; → **FDA**
food chain N chaîne *f* alimentaire ♦ **to enter** *or* **get into the ~ chain** entrer dans la chaîne alimentaire
food colouring N colorant *m* alimentaire
food counter N *(in shop)* rayon *m* (d')alimentation
food crop N culture *f* vivrière
food grains NPL céréales *fpl* vivrières
food group N groupe *m* d'aliments
food mixer N mixer *m*, mixeur *m*
food parcel N colis *m* de vivres
food poisoning N intoxication *f* alimentaire
food prices NPL prix *mpl* des denrées alimentaires *or* de la nourriture
food processing N *(industrial)* transformation *f* des aliments ♦ **the ~ processing industry** l'industrie *f* agroalimentaire
food processor N robot *m* ménager *or* de cuisine
food rationing N rationnement *m* alimentaire
food shares NPL *(Stock Exchange)* valeurs *fpl* de l'agroalimentaire
food stamps NPL *(US)* bons *mpl* de nourriture *(pour indigents)*
Food Standards Agency N *(Brit)* services *mpl* de l'hygiène alimentaire
food subsidy N subvention *f* sur les denrées alimentaires
food supplies NPL vivres *mpl*
food technology N technologie *f* des produits alimentaires
food value N valeur *f* nutritive
food wrap N film *m* alimentaire

foodie * /ˈfuːdɪ/ N gourmet *m*, fine bouche *f or* gueule * *f*

foodstuffs /ˈfuːdstʌfs/ NPL denrées *fpl* alimentaires, aliments *mpl*

foofaraw /ˈfuːfəˌrɔː/ N histoires * *fpl*, cirque * *m*, pétard * *m*

fool[1] /fuːl/ N [1] imbécile *mf*, idiot(e) *m(f)* ♦ **stupid ~!** espèce d'imbécile *or* d'idiot ! ♦ **don't be a ~!** ne sois pas stupide ! ♦ **I felt such a ~** je me suis vraiment senti bête ♦ **some ~ of a doctor** *, **some ~ doctor** * un imbécile *or* un abruti * de médecin ♦ **he was a ~ not to accept** il a été bête *or* stupide de ne pas accepter ♦ **what a ~ I was to think ...** ce que j'ai pu être bête de penser ... ♦ **he's more of a ~ than I thought** il est (encore) plus bête que je ne pensais ♦ **he was ~ enough to accept** il a été assez stupide pour accepter, il a eu la bêtise d'accepter ♦ **to play** *or* **act the ~** faire l'imbécile ♦ **he's no ~** il est loin d'être bête ♦ **he's nobody's ~** il n'est pas né d'hier *or* tombé de la dernière pluie ♦ **more ~ you!** * ce que tu es bête ! ♦ **he made himself look a ~** *or* **he made a ~ of himself in front of everybody** il s'est rendu ridicule devant tout le monde ♦ **to make a ~ of sb** (= *ridicule*) ridiculiser qn, se payer la tête de qn * ; (= *trick*) avoir * *or* duper qn ♦ **to play sb for a ~** mener qn en bateau *, rouler * qn ♦ **I went on a ~'s errand** (= *go somewhere*) j'y suis allé pour rien ; (= *do something*) je me suis dépensé en pure perte ♦ **any ~ can do that** n'importe quel imbécile peut faire ça ♦ **to live in a ~'s paradise** se bercer d'illusions *or* d'un bonheur illusoire ♦ **a ~ and his money are soon parted** *(Prov)* aux idiots l'argent file entre les doigts ♦ **there's no ~ like an old ~** *(Prov)* il n'y a pire imbécile qu'un vieil imbécile ♦ **~s rush in (where angels fear to tread)** *(Prov)* c'est de l'inconscience
[2] (= *jester*) bouffon *m*, fou *m*
VI (= *act silly*) ♦ **stop ~ing!** arrête de faire l'idiot *or* l'imbécile ! ♦ **no ~ing** *, **he really said it** sans blague *, il a vraiment dit ça ♦ **I was only ~ing** je ne faisais que plaisanter, c'était pour rire
♦ **to fool with** (= *mess with*) *[+ drugs, drink, electricity]* toucher à * ♦ **she's not someone you should ~ with** avec elle on ne plaisante pas
VT berner, duper ♦ **you won't ~ me so easily!** vous n'arriverez pas à me berner *or* duper si facilement ! ♦ **it ~ed nobody** personne n'a été dupe ♦ **don't ~ yourself** ne te fais pas d'illusions
ADJ *(US *)* ⇒ **foolish**
COMP **fooling about, fooling around** N bêtises *fpl*
fool's gold N *(Geol)* pyrite *f* ♦ **to go after ~'s gold** *(fig) se lancer dans un projet insensé en espérant faire de l'argent*

► **fool about, fool around** VI [1] (= *waste time*) perdre son temps ♦ **stop ~ing about and get on with your work** cesse de perdre ton temps et fais ton travail
[2] (= *play the fool*) faire l'imbécile ♦ **stop ~ing about!** arrête de faire l'imbécile !, cesse tes pitreries ! ♦ **to ~ about with sth** (= *play with*) faire l'imbécile avec qch ; (= *mess with*) *[+ drugs, drink, electricity]* toucher à qch *
[3] (= *have an affair*) avoir une liaison *or* une aventure ; (= *have affairs*) avoir des liaisons *or* des aventures
N ♦ **fooling about** *or* **around** → **fool[1]**

fool[2] /fuːl/ N *(Brit Culin:* also **fruit fool***)* (sorte de) mousse *f* de fruits ♦ **gooseberry ~** ≃ mousse *f* de groseilles à maquereaux

foolery /ˈfuːlərɪ/ N *(NonC)* (= *foolish acts*) sottises *fpl*, bêtises *fpl* ; (= *behaviour*) bouffonnerie *f*, pitrerie(s) *f(pl)*

foolhardiness /ˈfuːlˌhɑːdɪnɪs/ N témérité *f*, imprudence *f*

foolhardy /ˈfuːlˌhɑːdɪ/ ADJ téméraire, imprudent

foolish /ˈfuːlɪʃ/ ADJ [1] (= *foolhardy*) *[person]* idiot, bête ; *[action, decision, statement, mistake]* stupide ♦ **don't be so ~** ne fais pas l'idiot(e), ne sois pas bête ♦ **don't do anything ~** ne faites pas de bêtises ♦ **she had done something very ~** elle avait fait une grosse bêtise ♦ **what a ~ thing to do!** quelle bêtise ! ♦ **it would be ~ to believe her** ce serait stupide de la croire ♦ **I was ~ enough to do it** j'ai été assez bête pour le faire ♦ **it was ~ of him to say such a thing** c'était stupide de sa part de dire une chose pareille [2] (= *ridiculous*) *[person, question]* ridicule ♦ **to make sb look ~** rendre qn ridicule

foolishly /ˈfuːlɪʃlɪ/ ADV [1] (= *unwisely*) *[behave, act, ignore, forget, admit]* bêtement ♦ **~ romantic** d'un romantisme stupide ♦ **~, I allowed myself to be persuaded** bêtement, je me suis laissé persuader [2] (= *ridiculously*) *[say, grin]* bêtement, sottement

foolishness /ˈfuːlɪʃnɪs/ N *(NonC)* bêtise *f*, sottise *f*

foolproof /ˈfuːlpruːf/ ADJ *[method]* infaillible ; *[piece of machinery]* indéréglable

foolscap /ˈfuːlskæp/ N (also **foolscap paper**) ≃ papier *m* ministre
COMP **foolscap envelope** N enveloppe *f* longue
foolscap sheet N feuille *f* de papier ministre
foolscap size N format *m* ministre

foot /fʊt/ N (pl **feet**) [1] *[of person, horse, cow etc]* pied *m* ; *[of dog, cat, bird]* patte *f* ♦ **to be on one's feet** *(lit)* être *or* se tenir debout ; *(fig: after illness)* être sur pied, être rétabli ♦ **I'm on my feet all day long** je suis debout toute la journée ♦ **to fall** *or* **land on one's feet** *(lit, fig)* retomber sur ses pieds ♦ **to think on one's feet** *(lit, fig)* agir sur le moment ♦ **to stand on one's own (two) feet** voler de ses propres ailes, se débrouiller tout seul ♦ **to have a ~ in both camps** *or* **each camp** avoir un pied dans chaque camp ♦ **to go on ~** aller à pied ♦ **to get** *or* **to rise to one's feet** se lever, se mettre debout ♦ **to bring sb to his feet** faire lever qn ♦ **to put** *or* **set sb on his feet again** *(fig) (healthwise)* remettre qn d'aplomb *or* sur pied ; *(financially)* remettre qn en selle ♦ **to keep one's feet** garder l'équilibre ♦ **to keep one's feet on the ground** *(fig)* garder les pieds sur terre ♦ **to get one's feet on the ground** *(US fig)* (= *establish o.s.*) trouver ses marques ; (= *re-establish o.s.*) retrouver ses marques ♦ **feet first** les pieds devant ♦ **it's very wet under ~** c'est très mouillé par terre ♦ **he was trampled under ~ by the horses** les chevaux l'ont piétiné

◆ **to get under sb's feet** venir dans les jambes de qn ◆ **the children have been under my feet the whole day** les enfants ont été dans mes jambes toute la journée ◆ **to put one's ~ down** * *(in car = accelerate)* appuyer sur le champignon * ◆ **you've got to put your ~ down** *(= be firm)* il faut réagir ◆ **he let it go on for several weeks before finally putting his ~ down** il l'a supporté pendant plusieurs semaines avant d'y mettre le holà ◆ **to put one's ~ in it** * mettre les pieds dans le plat ◆ **to put one's best ~ forward** *(= hurry)* se dépêcher, allonger *or* presser le pas ; *(= do one's best)* faire de son mieux ◆ **he didn't put a ~ wrong** il n'a pas commis la moindre erreur *or* maladresse ◆ **to start off** *or* **get off on the right/wrong ~** *[people, relationship]* être bien/mal parti ◆ **I got off on the wrong ~ with him** j'ai mal commencé avec lui ◆ **to get one's** *or* **a ~ in the door** *(fig)* faire le premier pas, établir un premier contact ◆ **to get one's feet under the table** * *(Brit fig)* s'installer ◆ **to put one's feet up** * (s'étendre *or* s'asseoir pour) se reposer un peu ◆ **to take the weight off one's feet** (s'asseoir pour) se reposer un peu ◆ **to have one ~ in the grave** * avoir un pied dans la tombe ◆ **to be dying** *or* **dead on one's feet** * *(= exhausted)* être (complètement) à plat ◆ **the business is dying on its feet** * c'est une affaire qui périclite ◆ **to run sb off his feet** * fatiguer *or* éreinter qn ◆ **she is absolutely run off her feet** * elle est débordée, elle n'en peut plus, elle ne sait plus où donner de la tête ◆ **to set ~ on land** poser le pied sur la terre ferme ◆ **I've never set ~ there** je n'y ai jamais mis le(s) pied(s) ◆ **never set ~ here again!** ne remettez jamais les pieds ici ! ◆ **my ~!** * mon œil ! *, à d'autres ! ◆ **the boot** *(Brit) or* **the shoe** *(US)* **is on the other ~ now** les rôles sont inversés maintenant ; → **cold, drag, find, ground¹**

2 *[of hill, bed, stocking, sock]* pied *m* ; *[of table]* bout *m* ; *[of page, stairs]* bas *m* ◆ **at the ~ of the page** au *or* en bas de la page

3 *(= measure)* pied *m* (anglais) *(= 30,48 cm)*

4 *(NonC: Mil)* infanterie *f* ◆ **ten thousand ~** dix mille fantassins *mpl or* soldats *mpl* d'infanterie ◆ **the 91st of ~** le 91ᵉ (régiment) d'infanterie

5 *(Poetry)* pied *m*

VT ◆ **to ~ the bill** * payer (la note *or* la douloureuse *) ◆ **to ~ it** * *(= walk)* (y) aller à pied *or* à pinces * ; *(= dance)* danser

COMP **foot-and-mouth (disease)** N fièvre *f* aphteuse
foot brake N frein *m* à pied
foot-dragging N lenteurs *fpl*, atermoiements *mpl*
foot fault N *(Tennis)* faute *f* de pied
foot fault judge N juge *m* de ligne de fond
foot passengers NPL *[of ferry]* passagers *mpl* sans véhicule
foot patrol N *(Police, Mil)* patrouille *f* à pied
foot patrolman N (pl **foot patrolmen**) *(US Police)* agent *m* de police
foot rot N piétin *m*
foot soldier N fantassin *m*

footage /ˈfʊtɪdʒ/ N *(gen, also Cine = length)* ≃ métrage *m* ; *(= material on film)* séquences *fpl* *(about, on* sur) ◆ **they showed some ~ of the riots/the concert** ils ont diffusé quelques séquences sur les émeutes/le concert

football /ˈfʊtbɔːl/ **N** 1 *(= sport) (Brit)* football *m*, foot * *m* ; *(US)* football *m* américain ; → **table**

2 *(= ball)* ballon *m* (de football) ; → **political**

COMP *[ground, match, team, coach]* de football
football hooligan N *(Brit)* hooligan *m*, houligan *m*
football hooliganism N *(NonC: Brit)* hooliganisme *m*, houliganisme *m*
football league N championnat *m* de football ◆ **the Football League** *(Brit) la fédération britannique de football*
football player N *(Brit)* joueur *m*, -euse *f* de football, footballeur *m* ; *(US)* joueur *m*, -euse *f* de football américain
football pools NPL *(Brit)* ≃ loto *m* sportif, pronostics *mpl* (sur les matchs de football) ◆ **to do the ~ pools** ≃ jouer au loto sportif ◆ **he won £200 on the ~ pools** ≃ il a gagné 200 livres au loto sportif
football season N saison *f* de football
football special N *(Brit Rail)* train *m* de supporters *(d'une équipe de football)*

footballer /ˈfʊtbɔːləʳ/ N *(Brit)* joueur *m* de football, footballeur *m*

footballing /ˈfʊtbɔːlɪŋ/ ADJ *[skills, career]* de footballeur ; *[hero]* du football ◆ **the great ~ nations** les grandes nations du football ◆ **he's got a ~ injury** il s'est blessé lors d'un match de football

footbath /ˈfʊtbɑːθ/ N bain *m* de pieds

footboard /ˈfʊtbɔːd/ N marchepied *m*

footbridge /ˈfʊtbrɪdʒ/ N passerelle *f*

-footed /ˈfʊtɪd/ ADJ *(in compounds)* ◆ **light-footed** au pied léger ; → **four**

footer /ˈfʊtəʳ/ N *(Typo, Comput)* titre *m* en bas de page

-footer /ˈfʊtəʳ/ N *(in compounds)* ◆ **a 15~** *(= boat)* ≃ un bateau de 5 mètres de long ; → **six**

footfall /ˈfʊtfɔːl/ N (bruit *m* de) pas *mpl*

footgear /ˈfʊtgɪəʳ/ N chaussures *fpl*

foothills /ˈfʊthɪlz/ NPL contreforts *mpl*

foothold /ˈfʊthəʊld/ N prise *f* (de pied) ◆ **to get** *or* **gain a ~** *(lit)* prendre pied ; *(fig) [newcomer]* se faire (progressivement) accepter ; *[idea, opinion, fascism etc]* se répandre, se propager ◆ **to gain a ~ in a market** *(Comm)* prendre pied sur un marché

footie *, **footy** * /ˈfʊtɪ/ N *(Brit)* foot * *m*

footing /ˈfʊtɪŋ/ N 1 *(lit)* prise *f* (de pied) ◆ **to lose** *or* **miss one's ~** perdre son équilibre *or* l'équilibre 2 *(= position, basis)* **to get a ~ in society** se faire une position dans le monde ◆ **to be on a friendly ~ with sb** être en termes amicaux avec qn ◆ **on an equal ~** sur un pied d'égalité ◆ **on a war ~** sur le pied de guerre ◆ **to put sth on an official ~** officialiser qch, rendre qch officiel ◆ **on the ~ that ...** *(Jur)* en supposant que ...

footle * /ˈfuːtl/ VI ◆ **to ~ about** *(= clown around)* faire l'âne ; *(= waste time)* perdre son temps à des futilités

footlights /ˈfʊtlaɪts/ NPL *(Theat)* rampe *f* ◆ **the lure of the ~** l'attrait du théâtre *or* des planches *

footling /ˈfuːtlɪŋ/ ADJ insignifiant, futile

footlocker /ˈfʊtˌlɒkəʳ/ N *(US Mil)* cantine *f*

footloose /ˈfʊtluːs/ ADJ libre (de toute attache) ◆ **~ and fancy-free** libre comme l'air

footman /ˈfʊtmən/ N (pl **-men**) valet *m* de pied

footmark /ˈfʊtmɑːk/ N empreinte *f* (de pied)

footnote /ˈfʊtnəʊt/ N *(lit)* note *f* en bas de (la) page ; *(fig)* post-scriptum *m*

footpath /ˈfʊtpɑːθ/ N *(= path)* sentier *m* ; see also **public** *(Brit) (= pavement)* trottoir *m* ; *(by highway)* chemin *m*

footplate /ˈfʊtpleɪt/ **N** *(esp Brit Rail)* plateforme *f (d'une locomotive)* **COMP** **footplate workers** NPL ⇒ **footplatemen**

footplatemen /ˈfʊtpleɪtmən/ NPL *(esp Brit Rail)* agents *mpl* de conduite

footprint /ˈfʊtprɪnt/ N *(lit)* empreinte *f* (de pied) ; *(fig) (of appliance, machine, computer)* surface *f* d'encombrement ; *(of satellite)* empreinte *f*

footpump /ˈfʊtpʌmp/ N pompe *f* à pied

footrest /ˈfʊtrest/ N *(= part of chair)* repose-pieds *m inv* ; *(= footstool)* tabouret *m (pour les pieds)*

Footsie * /ˈfʊtsɪ/ N (abbrev of **Financial Times Stock Exchange 100 Index**) → **financial** ◆ **(the) ~** l'indice *m* Footsie

footsie * /ˈfʊtsɪ/ N ◆ **to play ~ with sb** faire du pied à qn

footslog * /ˈfʊtslɒg/ VI ◆ **I've been ~ging around town** j'ai fait toute la ville à pied

footslogger * /ˈfʊtslɒgəʳ/ N *(= walker)* marcheur *m*, -euse *f* ; *(= soldier)* pousse-cailloux †* *m inv*

footsore /ˈfʊtsɔːʳ/ ADJ aux pieds endoloris *or* douloureux ◆ **to be ~** avoir mal aux pieds

footstep /ˈfʊtstep/ N pas *m* ; → **follow**

footstool /ˈfʊtstuːl/ N tabouret *m (pour les pieds)*

footway /ˈfʊtweɪ/ N ⇒ **footpath**

footwear /ˈfʊtwɛəʳ/ N chaussures *fpl*

footwork /ˈfʊtwɜːk/ N *(NonC: Sport, Dancing)* jeu *m* de jambes ◆ **legal/financial/political ~** manœuvre *f* juridique/financière/politique

footy * /ˈfʊtɪ/ N ⇒ **footie**

fop /fɒp/ N dandy *m*

foppish /ˈfɒpɪʃ/ ADJ *[manners, behaviour, clothes]* de dandy ◆ **a ~ man** un dandy

FOR /ˌefəʊˈɑːʳ/ *(Comm)* (abbrev of **free on rail**) → **free**

for /fɔːʳ/

1 PREPOSITION 2 CONJUNCTION

When **for** is part of a phrasal verb, eg **look for**, **make for**, **stand for**, look up the verb. When it is part of a set combination, eg **a gift/taste for**, **for sale/pleasure**, **eager/fit/noted for**, look up the other word.

1 - PREPOSITION

1 pour ◆ **a letter ~ you** une lettre pour toi ◆ **is this ~ me?** c'est pour moi ? ◆ **a collection ~ the homeless** une quête pour les *or* en faveur des sans-abri ◆ **he went there ~ a rest** il y est allé pour se reposer ◆ **it is warm ~ January** il fait bon pour (un mois de) janvier ◆ **he's tall ~ his age** il est grand pour son âge ◆ **it's okay ~ a first attempt** ce n'est pas mal pour une première tentative ◆ **there is one French passenger ~ every ten English** il y a un passager français pour dix Anglais ◆ **~ or against** pour ou contre ◆ **I'm ~ helping him** je suis pour l'aider, je suis partisan de l'aider ◆ **I've got some news ~ you** j'ai du nouveau à t'apprendre, j'ai des nouvelles pour toi ◆ **a cloth ~ polishing silver** un chiffon pour astiquer l'argenterie ◆ **it's not ~ cutting wood** ça n'est pas fait pour couper du bois ◆ **what's this knife ~ ?** à quoi sert ce couteau ? ◆ **he had a bag ~ a pillow** il avait un sac en guise d'oreiller ◆ **it's time ~ dinner** c'est l'heure du dîner, il est l'heure de dîner ◆ **I decided that it was the job ~ me** j'ai décidé que ce travail était fait pour moi *or* que c'était le travail qu'il me fallait

2 = going to pour ◆ **is this the train ~ Paris?** c'est bien le train pour Paris ? ◆ **this isn't the bus ~ Lyons** ce n'est pas le bus pour Lyon ◆ **trains ~ Paris go from platform one** les trains pour Paris *or* à destination de Paris partent du quai numéro un ◆ **he swam ~ the shore** il a nagé vers le rivage ◆ **where are you ~ ?** où allez-vous ?

3 [= on behalf of] ◆ ~ **me/you** *etc* à ma/ta *etc* place ◆ **I'll see her ~ you if you like** je peux aller la voir à ta place si tu veux ◆ **will you go ~ me?** est-ce que vous pouvez y aller à ma place ?

4 [= as in] comme ◆ **D ~ Daniel** D comme Daniel

5 [= in exchange for] ◆ **I'll give you this book ~ that one** je vous échange ce livre-ci contre celui-là ◆ **he'll do it ~ £25** il le fera pour 25 livres

> When used with **pay** and **sell**, **for** is not translated.

◆ **to pay €10 ~ a ticket** payer un billet 10 € ◆ **I sold it ~ £20** je l'ai vendu 20 livres

6 [= because of] pour ◆ ~ **this reason** pour cette raison ◆ **to go to prison ~ theft** aller en prison pour vol ◆ **to choose sb ~ his ability** choisir qn pour *or* en raison de sa compétence

7 [= from] de ◆ ~ **fear of being left behind** de peur d'être oublié ◆ **to jump ~ joy** sauter de joie

8 [= up to] à ◆ **that's ~ him to decide** c'est à lui de décider ◆ **it's not ~ you to blame him** ce n'est pas à vous de le critiquer ◆ **it's not ~ me to say** ce n'est pas à moi de le dire

9 [= in spite of] malgré ◆ ~ **all his wealth** malgré toute sa richesse ◆ ~ **all that, you should have warned me** malgré tout, vous auriez dû me prévenir, vous auriez quand même dû me prévenir ◆ ~ **all he promised to come, he didn't** malgré ses promesses, il n'est pas venu, bien qu'il ait promis de venir, il ne l'a pas fait

10 [= for a distance of] sur, pendant ◆ **a road lined with trees ~ 3km** une route bordée d'arbres sur 3 km ◆ **there was nothing to be seen ~ miles** il n'y avait rien à voir pendant des kilomètres ◆ **we walked ~ 2km** nous avons marché (pendant) 2 km ◆ **there were small drab houses ~ mile upon mile** des petites maisons monotones se succédaient pendant *or* sur des kilomètres et des kilomètres

11 [time in the past or future] pendant ◆ **he suffered terribly ~ six months** il a horriblement souffert pendant six mois

> With certain verbs **pendant** may be omitted.

◆ **I worked/stayed there ~ three months** j'y ai travaillé/j'y suis resté (pendant) trois mois ◆ **he went away ~ two weeks** il est parti (pendant) quinze jours ◆ **I'll be away ~ a month** je serai absent (pendant) un mois

> When **for** indicates an intention, the translation is **pour**.

◆ **Christian went ~ a week, but stayed ~ a year** Christian était parti pour une semaine, mais il est resté un an

> When **for** refers to future time, it is translated by **pour** after **aller** and **partir**.

◆ **he's going there ~ six months** il y va pour six mois ◆ **I am going away ~ a few days** je pars (pour) quelques jours ◆ **he won't be back ~ a week** il ne sera pas de retour avant huit jours

12 [uncompleted states and actions] depuis, ça fait ... que (*less frm*)

> French generally uses the present and imperfect where English uses the perfect and past perfect.

◆ **he's been here ~ ten days** il est ici depuis dix jours, ça fait dix jours qu'il est ici ◆ **I have known her ~ five years** je la connais depuis cinq ans, ça fait cinq ans que je la connais ◆ **I have been working here ~ three months** je travaille ici depuis trois mois, ça fait trois mois que je travaille ici ◆ **I had known her ~ years** je la connaissais depuis des années ◆ **I had been working there ~ three months when ...** je travaillais là depuis trois mois quand ... ◆ **he hasn't worked ~ two years** il n'a pas travaillé depuis deux ans, ça fait deux ans qu'il ne travaille pas ◆ **she hadn't seen him ~ three months** elle ne l'avait pas vu depuis trois mois, cela faisait trois mois qu'elle ne l'avait pas vu

13 [phrases with infinitive] ◆ **their one hope is ~ him to return** leur seul espoir est qu'il revienne ◆ **the best would be** *or* **it would be best ~ you to go away** le mieux serait que vous vous en alliez *subj* ◆ ~ **this to be possible** pour que cela soit possible ◆ **I brought it ~ you to see** je l'ai apporté pour que vous le voyiez *subj* ◆ **there is still time ~ him to come** il a encore le temps d'arriver

14 [exclamations]

◆ **for it !*** ◆ **now ~ it !** (bon, alors) on y va ! ◆ **you're ~ it!** qu'est-ce que tu vas prendre !*, ça va être ta fête !* ◆ **I'll be ~ it if he catches me here!** qu'est-ce que je vais prendre * s'il me trouve ici !

◆ **oh for ... !** ◆ **oh ~ a cup of tea!** je donnerais n'importe quoi pour une tasse de thé ! ◆ **oh ~ a chance of revenge!** si seulement je pouvais me venger !

2 – CONJUNCTION

[liter = because] car ◆ **I avoided him, ~ he was rude and uncouth** je l'évitais car il était impoli et grossier

forage /ˈfɒrɪdʒ/ **N** fourrage *m* **VI** fourrager, fouiller (*for* pour trouver) **COMP** **forage cap N** (*Mil*) calot *m*

foray /ˈfɒreɪ/ **N** (*Mil*) incursion *f*, raid *m* (*into* en) ; (*fig: into business, politics, acting etc*) incursion *f* (*into* dans) ◆ **to go on** *or* **make a ~** (*Mil*) faire une incursion *or* un raid ◆ **we made a short ~ into town** on a fait une petite expédition en ville **VI** faire une incursion *or* un raid

forbad(e) /fəˈbæd/ **VB** pret of **forbid**

forbear /fɔːˈbɛəʳ/ (pret **forbore**, ptp **forborne**) **VI** (*frm*) s'abstenir ◆ **to ~ from doing sth, to ~ to do sth** s'abstenir *or* se garder de faire qch ◆ **he forbore to make any comment** il s'abstint de tout commentaire

forbearance /fɔːˈbɛərəns/ **N** patience *f*, tolérance *f*

forbearing /fɔːˈbɛərɪŋ/ **ADJ** patient, tolérant

forbears /ˈfɔːbɛəz/ **NPL** ⇒ **forebears**

forbid /fəˈbɪd/ **LANGUAGE IN USE 9.3, 9.5, 10.4** (pret **forbad(e)**, ptp **forbidden**) **VT** 1 (*= not allow*) défendre, interdire ◆ **to ~ sb to do sth, to ~ sb from doing sth** interdire à qn de faire qch ◆ **to ~ sb alcohol** défendre *or* interdire l'alcool à qn ◆ **I ~ you to!** je vous l'interdis ! ◆ **it is ~den to do that** il est défendu *or* interdit de faire cela ◆ **they are ~den to do that** ils n'ont pas le droit de faire cela, il leur est défendu *or* interdit de faire cela ◆ **that's ~den** c'est défendu *or* interdit ◆ **~den by law** interdit par la loi ◆ **smoking is (strictly) ~den** il est (formellement) interdit de fumer ◆ **"smoking forbidden"** (*on sign*) "défense de fumer" ◆ **preaching was ~den to women** il était défendu *or* interdit aux femmes de prêcher

2 (*= prevent*) empêcher ◆ **his pride ~s him to ask for** *or* **from asking for help, his pride ~s his asking for help** (*more frm*) sa fierté l'empêche de demander de l'aide ◆ **custom ~s any modernization** la coutume empêche toute modernisation ◆ **God** *or* **Heaven ~!** * grands dieux non ! ◆ **God** *or* **Heaven ~ that this might be true!** (*liter*) pourvu que ça ne soit pas vrai ! (*liter*) ◆ **God** *or* **Heaven ~ that he should come here!** pourvu qu'il ne vienne pas ici ◆ **God** *or* **Heaven ~ (that) I should do anything illegal** Dieu me garde de faire quoi que ce soit d'illégal

forbidden /fəˈbɪdn/ **LANGUAGE IN USE 9.5, 10.4** **VB** pt of **forbid** **ADJ** [*food, book, place, love*] interdit ; [*subject, word*] tabou ; [*feelings*] défendu ◆ **that's ~ territory** *or* **ground** (*fig*) c'est un sujet tabou

COMP **the Forbidden City N** la Cité interdite

forbidden fruit N (*Bible or fig*) fruit *m* défendu

forbidding /fəˈbɪdɪŋ/ **ADJ** [*person*] à l'allure sévère ; [*expression*] sévère ; [*place*] inhospitalier ; [*building*] menaçant

forbiddingly /fəˈbɪdɪŋlɪ/ **ADV** [*look at, frown*] de façon rébarbative ◆ **a ~ prison-like building** un bâtiment aux allures rébarbatives de prison

forbore /fɔːˈbɔːʳ/ **VB** pt of **forbear**

forborne /fɔːˈbɔːn/ **VB** ptp of **forbear**

force /fɔːs/ **LANGUAGE IN USE 10.3**

N 1 (*NonC*) (*= strength*) force *f*, violence *f* ; (*Phys*) force *f* ; [*of phrase, word*] force *f*, poids *m* ◆ ~ **of gravity** pesanteur *f* ◆ **centrifugal/centripetal ~** force *f* centrifuge/centripète ◆ **to use ~** employer la force (*to do sth* pour faire qch) ◆ **by sheer ~** par la simple force ◆ **by ~ of** à force de ◆ ~ **of circumstances** force *f* des choses ◆ **from ~ of habit** par la force de l'habitude ◆ **through** *or* **by sheer ~ of will** purement à force de volonté ◆ **by (sheer) ~ of personality** uniquement grâce à sa personnalité ◆ ~ **of a blow** violence *f* d'un coup ◆ **to resort to ~** avoir recours à la force ◆ **to settle a dispute by ~** régler une querelle par la force ◆ **his argument lacked ~** son argument manquait de conviction ◆ **I don't quite see the ~ of his argument** je ne vois pas bien la force de son argument ; → **brute**

◆ **in(to) force** ◆ **the rule is now in ~** le règlement est désormais en vigueur ◆ **the police were there in ~** la police était là en force ◆ **they came in ~ to support him** ils sont venus en force pour lui apporter leur soutien ◆ **to come into ~** [*law, prices*] entrer en vigueur *or* en application

2 (*= power*) force *f* ◆ **the ~s of Nature** les forces *fpl* de la nature ◆ **he is a powerful ~ in the Trade Union movement** il exerce un grand pouvoir au sein du mouvement syndical ◆ **there are several ~s at work** plusieurs influences entrent en jeu ; → **life**

3 (*= body of men*) force *f* ◆ **the ~s** (*Brit Mil*) les forces *fpl* armées ◆ **allied ~s** (*Brit Mil*) armées *fpl* alliées ◆ **the ~*** (*Police*) la police ; see also **police** ; → **join, land, sale**

VT 1 (*= constrain*) forcer, obliger (*sb to do sth* qn à faire qch) ◆ **to be ~d to do sth** être forcé *or* obligé de faire qch ◆ **to ~ o.s. to do sth** se forcer *or* s'obliger à faire qch ◆ **I find myself ~d to say that ...** je me vois contraint de dire que ... ◆ **he was ~d to conclude that ...** il a été forcé de conclure que ...

2 (*= impose*) [*+ conditions, obedience*] imposer (*on sb* à qn) ◆ **the decision was ~d on me by events** cette décision m'a été imposée par les événements, ce sont les événements qui m'ont dicté cette décision ◆ **they ~d action on the enemy** ils ont contraint l'ennemi à se battre ◆ **I don't want to ~ myself on you, but ...** je ne veux pas m'imposer, mais ... ◆ **to ~ the issue** enfoncer le clou

3 (*= push, thrust*) pousser ◆ **to ~ books into a box** fourrer des livres dans une caisse ◆ **he ~d himself through the gap in the hedge** il s'est frayé un passage par un trou dans la haie ◆ **to ~ one's way into** entrer *or* pénétrer de force dans ◆ **to ~ one's way through sth** se frayer un passage à travers qch ◆ **to ~ a bill through Parliament** forcer la Chambre à voter une loi ◆ **the lorry ~d the car off the road** le camion a forcé la voiture à quitter la route

4 (*= break open*) [*+ lock*] forcer ◆ **to ~ (open) a drawer/a door** forcer un tiroir/une porte ◆ **to ~ sb's hand** (*fig*) forcer la main à qn

5 (*= extort*) arracher ; (*stronger*) extorquer (*from* à) ◆ **he ~d a confession from me** il m'a arraché *or* extorqué une confession ◆ **we ~d**

the secret out of him nous lui avons arraché le secret

6 *[+ plants]* forcer, hâter ◆ **to ~ the pace** forcer l'allure *or* le pas

7 ◆ **he ~d a reply/a smile, he ~d himself to reply/smile** il s'est forcé à répondre/à sourire

VI *(Bridge)* faire un forcing

COMP **force-feed** VT *(gen)* nourrir de force ; *[+ animal]* gaver ◆ **he was ~-fed** on l'a nourri de force ◆ **as a child she was ~-fed (on) Shakespeare** quand elle était petite elle a été gavée de Shakespeare

forcing bid N *(Bridge)* annonce *f* forcée *or* de forcing

forcing house N *(Agr)* forcerie *f* ; *(fig)* pépinière *f*

► **force back** VT SEP 1 *[+ enemy]* obliger à reculer, faire reculer ; *[+ crowd]* repousser, faire reculer

2 ◆ **to force back one's desire to laugh** réprimer son envie de rire ◆ **to ~ back one's tears** refouler ses larmes

► **force down** VT SEP 1 *[+ aircraft]* forcer à atterrir

2 *[+ prices, inflation, unemployment]* faire baisser

3 ◆ **to force food down** se forcer à manger ◆ **if you ~ the clothes down you will get more into the suitcase** si tu tasses les vêtements tu en feras entrer plus dans la valise

► **force out** VT SEP 1 faire sortir (de force) ◆ **he ~d the cork out** il a sorti le bouchon en forçant ◆ **they ~d the rebels out into the open** ils ont forcé *or* obligé les insurgés à se montrer ◆ **small farmers will be ~d out of the market** les petits exploitants seront éliminés du marché

2 ◆ **he forced out a reply/an apology** il s'est forcé à répondre/à s'excuser

► **force up** VT SEP *[+ prices, inflation, unemployment]* faire monter

forced /fɔːst/ LANGUAGE IN USE 10.1 ADJ 1 *(= imposed) [marriage, repatriation]* forcé 2 *(= artificial) [smile, laughter]* forcé ; *[conversation]* peu naturel ◆ **to sound ~** *[words]* faire peu naturel ; *[laughter]* sembler forcé 3 *[plant]* forcé

COMP **forced entry** N *(Law)* entrée *f* avec effraction

forced labour N travaux *mpl* forcés

forced landing N atterrissage *m* forcé

forced march N marche *f* forcée

forced savings NPL épargne *f* forcée

forceful /ˈfɔːsfʊl/ ADJ 1 *(= hard) [blow, kick, punch]* violent 2 *(= vigorous) [person, personality, intervention]* énergique ; *[action, reminder]* vigoureux ; *[argument]* convaincant ; *[statement, speech]* énergique ◆ **to be ~ in doing sth** faire qch énergiquement ◆ **he was ~ in condemning the regime** *or* **in his condemnation of the regime** il a condamné énergiquement le régime

forcefully /ˈfɔːsfəlɪ/ ADV 1 *(= using force) [push, knock]* avec force, violemment ; *[remove, administer]* avec fermeté ; *(= forcibly)* de force 2 *[say, express, remind]* avec force ; *[argue]* avec force, avec vigueur ; *[act, intervene]* avec détermination ◆ **it struck him ~ that ...** il lui est apparu avec force *or* avec une évidence frappante que ...

forcefulness /ˈfɔːsfʊlnɪs/ N 1 *(= force) [of blow, kick, punch]* force *f*, violence *f* 2 *(= vigour) [of person]* détermination *f* ; *[of argument, attack]* force *f*

forcemeat /ˈfɔːsmiːt/ N *(Culin)* farce *f*, hachis *m* *(de viande et de fines herbes)*

forceps /ˈfɔːseps/ NPL (also **pair of forceps**) forceps *m* ◆ **~ delivery** accouchement *m* au forceps

forcible /ˈfɔːsəbl/ ADJ 1 *(= forced) [repatriation, feeding]* forcé 2 *(= powerful) [affirmation, speech, reminder]* vigoureux COMP **forcible entry** N *(by thief)* entrée *f* par effraction ◆ **to make a ~ entry** *(by police)* entrer de force

forcibly /ˈfɔːsəblɪ/ ADV 1 *(= by force) [remove, eject, annex]* de force, par la force ; *[repatriate, separate, feed]* de force ; *[restrain]* par la force 2 *(= powerfully) [strike]* avec force ; *[argue, express]* énergiquement ◆ **to bring sth ~ home to sb** forcer qn à prendre conscience de qch

ford /fɔːd/ N gué *m* VT passer à gué

fordable /ˈfɔːdəbl/ ADJ guéable

fore /fɔːʳ/ ADJ 1 *[foot, limb]* antérieur ◆ **near ~** antérieur gauche ◆ **off ~** antérieur droit ; see also **foreleg** 2 *(on ship, plane)* avant *inv* ◆ **the ~ watch** *(on ship)* le quart de proue N 1 ◆ **to come to the ~** *[person]* se mettre en évidence, se faire remarquer ; *[sb's courage]* se manifester ◆ **he was well to the ~ during the discussion** il a été très en évidence pendant la discussion ◆ **to the ~** *(= at hand)* à portée de main 2 *(= front of ship)* avant *m* ADV *(on ship)* à l'avant ◆ **~ and aft** de l'avant à l'arrière EXCL *(Golf)* gare !, attention !

COMP **fore and aft rig** N gréement *m* aurique

fore and aft sail N voile *f* aurique

forearm /ˈfɔːrɑːm/ N avant-bras *m inv*

forebears /ˈfɔːbeəz/ NPL *(liter)* aïeux *mpl (liter)*

forebode /fɔːˈbəʊd/ VT présager, annoncer

foreboding /fɔːˈbəʊdɪŋ/ N pressentiment *m*, prémonition *f* ◆ **to have a ~ that** avoir le pressentiment que, pressentir que ◆ **to have ~s** avoir des pressentiments *or* des prémonitions ◆ **with many ~s he agreed to do it** il a consenti à le faire en dépit de *or* malgré toutes ses appréhensions ADJ qui ne présage rien de bon, menaçant

forecast /ˈfɔːkɑːst/ (pret, ptp **forecast**) VT prévoir N 1 *(gen)* prévisions *fpl* ; *(Betting)* pronostic *m* ◆ **according to all the ~s** selon toutes les prévisions ◆ **sales ~** prévisions *fpl* de vente ◆ **the racing ~** les pronostics *mpl* hippiques *or* des courses 2 (also **weather forecast**) bulletin *m* météorologique, météo* *f* ◆ **the ~ is good** les prévisions sont bonnes, la météo* est bonne

forecaster /ˈfɔːˌkɑːstəʳ/ N *(Weather)* météorologue *mf* ; *(Econ, Pol)* prévisionniste *mf* ; *(Sport)* pronostiqueur *m*, -euse *f*

forecastle /ˈfəʊksl/ N *(Naut)* gaillard *m* d'avant ; *(Merchant Navy)* poste *m* d'équipage

foreclose /fɔːˈkləʊz/ VT *(Jur)* saisir ◆ **to ~ (on) a mortgage** saisir un bien hypothéqué VI saisir le bien hypothéqué

foreclosure /fɔːˈkləʊʒəʳ/ N saisie *f*

forecourt /ˈfɔːkɔːt/ N *(esp Brit)* avant-cour *f*, cour *f* de devant ; *[of petrol station]* devant *m*

foredeck /ˈfɔːdek/ N pont *m* avant

foredoomed /fɔːˈduːmd/ ADJ *(liter)* condamné d'avance, voué à l'échec

forefathers /ˈfɔːˌfɑːðəz/ NPL aïeux *mpl (liter)*, ancêtres *mpl*

forefinger /ˈfɔːˌfɪŋgəʳ/ N index *m*

forefoot /ˈfɔːfʊt/ N (pl **-feet**) *[of horse, cow]* pied *m* antérieur *or* de devant ; *[of cat, dog]* patte *f* antérieure *or* de devant

forefront /ˈfɔːfrʌnt/ N ◆ **in** *or* **at the ~ of** *[+ research, technology, progress]* à la pointe de ◆ **in** *or* **at the ~ of their minds** au premier plan *or* au centre de leurs préoccupations ◆ **to bring sth to the ~** mettre qch en évidence, faire ressortir qch

foregather /fɔːˈgæðəʳ/ VI se réunir, s'assembler

forego /fɔːˈgəʊ/ (pret **forewent**, ptp **foregone**) VT renoncer à, se priver de

foregoing /ˈfɔːgəʊɪŋ/ ADJ précédent ; *(in legal document)* susdit ◆ **according to the ~** d'après ce qui précède

foregone /ˈfɔːgɒn/ ADJ ◆ **it was a ~ conclusion** c'était à prévoir, c'était joué d'avance ◆ **it's a ~ conclusion that ...** il ne fait aucun doute que ...

foreground /ˈfɔːgraʊnd/ N *(Art, Phot)* premier plan *m* ◆ **in the ~** au premier plan VT *(lit)* *[+ object in photo, picture]* mettre en premier plan ; *(fig) [+ issue, problem]* mettre en avant

forehand /ˈfɔːhænd/ *(Tennis)* N coup *m* droit COMP **forehand drive** N coup *m* droit

forehand volley N volée *f* de coup droit

forehead /ˈfɒrɪd/ N front *m* ◆ **on his ~** au front

foreign /ˈfɒrən/ ADJ 1 *[person, country, language, food, car]* étranger ; *[holiday, travel]* à l'étranger ; *[goods, produce]* de l'étranger ; *[politics, trade, debt]* extérieur (-eure *f*) ; *(incoming)* étranger ; *(abroad)* à l'étranger ; *[news]* du monde ◆ **he comes from a ~ country** il vient de l'étranger ◆ **our relations with ~ countries** nos rapports avec l'étranger

2 *(= alien)* ◆ **~ to** étranger à ◆ **lying is quite ~ to him** *or* **to his nature** le mensonge lui est (complètement) étranger

3 *(= extraneous) [matter, object, substance]* étranger

COMP **foreign affairs** NPL affaires *fpl* étrangères ◆ **Minister of Foreign Affairs** ministre *m* des Affaires étrangères ◆ **Ministry of Foreign Affairs** ministère *m* des Affaires étrangères ◆ **Secretary (of State) for Foreign Affairs** *(Brit)* ≃ ministre *m* des Affaires étrangères

foreign agent N *(= spy)* agent *m* étranger ; *(Comm)* représentant *m* à l'étranger

Foreign and Commonwealth Office N *(Brit)* ministère *m* des Affaires étrangères et du Commonwealth

foreign body N *(Med)* corps *m* étranger

foreign-born ADJ né à l'étranger

foreign correspondent N correspondant(e) *m(f)* à l'étranger

foreign currency N devises *fpl* étrangères

foreign exchange N *(= system)* change *m* ; *(= currency)* devises *fpl* ◆ **the ~ exchange market** le marché des changes

Foreign Legion N Légion *f* (étrangère)

Foreign Minister N ministre *m* des Affaires étrangères

Foreign Ministry N ministère *m* des Affaires étrangères

foreign national N ressortissant(e) *m(f)* étranger (-ère *f*)

Foreign Office N *(Brit)* ≃ ministère *m* des Affaires étrangères

foreign-owned ADJ *(Econ, Comm)* sous contrôle étranger

foreign policy N politique *f* étrangère *or* extérieure

foreign relations NPL relations *fpl* extérieures

Foreign Secretary N *(Brit)* ≃ ministre *m* des Affaires étrangères

foreign service N *(esp US)* service *m* diplomatique

foreigner /ˈfɒrənəʳ/ N étranger *m*, -ère *f*

foreknowledge /fɔːˈnɒlɪdʒ/ N fait *m* de savoir à l'avance, connaissance *f* anticipée ◆ **I had no ~ of his intentions** je ne savais pas à l'avance ce qu'il avait l'intention de faire ◆ **it presupposes a certain ~ of ...** ceci présuppose une certaine connaissance anticipée de ...

foreland /ˈfɔːlənd/ N *(= headland)* cap *m*, promontoire *m*

foreleg /ˈfɔːleg/ N *[of horse, cow]* jambe *f* antérieure ; *[of dog, cat]* patte *f* de devant

forelock /ˈfɔːlɒk/ N mèche *f*, toupet *m* ◆ **to touch** *or* **tug one's ~ to sb** *(Brit) (lit)* saluer qn en portant la main à son front ; *(fig)* faire des courbettes à *or* devant qn ◆ **to take Time by the ~** *(liter)* saisir l'occasion aux cheveux

foreman /ˈfɔːmən/ N (pl **-men**) 1 *(in workplace)* contremaître *m*, chef *m* d'équipe 2 *[of jury]* président *m*

foremast /ˈfɔːmɑːst/ N *(Naut)* mât *m* de misaine

foremost /ˈfɔːməʊst/ ADJ 1 *(= chief) [authority, expert, writer, scholar]* plus grand, plus éminent ◆ **~ among contemporary writers is ...** le premier d'entre tous les écrivains contemporains est ... ◆ **to be ~ in sb's mind** être au premier plan des pensées *or* des préoccupations de qn ◆ **they were ~ in calling for an end to the war** ils ont été les plus actifs pour appeler à la fin de la guerre 2 *(Naut)* le *or* la plus en avant ADV 1 *(= above all)* tout d'abord ◆ **first and ~** d'abord et avant tout 2 *(= forwards)* en avant

forename /ˈfɔːneɪm/ N prénom *m*

forenoon /ˈfɔːnuːn/ N matinée *f*

forensic /fəˈrensɪk/ ADJ 1 (also **forensics** : *Med, Jur) [test, laboratory]* médico-légal 2 *(frm = lawyerly) [skill, eloquence]* du barreau N **forensics** *(NonC) (= science)* médecine *f* légale ; *(= police department)* département *m* médicolégal
COMP **forensic evidence** N preuves *fpl* relevées lors d'une expertise médicolégale
forensic expert N expert *m* médicolégal
forensic medicine N médecine *f* légale
forensic science N expertise *f* médicolégale ◆ **~ science laboratory** ≃ laboratoire *m* de police scientifique
forensic scientist N médecin *m* légiste
forensics expert N ⇒ **forensic expert**

forepaw /ˈfɔːpɔː/ N patte *f* antérieure *or* de devant

foreplay /ˈfɔːpleɪ/ N préliminaires *mpl (amoureux)*

forequarters /ˈfɔːˌkwɔːtəz/ NPL quartiers *mpl* de devant

forerunner /ˈfɔːˌrʌnəʳ/ N 1 *(= sign, indication)* signe *m* avant-coureur, présage *m* ; *(= person)* précurseur *m* ; *[of machine, invention]* ancêtre *m* 2 *(Ski)* ouvreur *m*

foresail /ˈfɔːseɪl/ N *(Naut)* (voile *f* de) misaine *f*

foresee /fɔːˈsiː/ (pret **foresaw**, ptp **foreseen**) VT prévoir

foreseeable /fɔːˈsiːəbl/ ADJ prévisible ◆ **in the ~ future** dans un avenir prévisible

foreshadow /fɔːˈʃædəʊ/ VT *[event etc]* présager, annoncer, laisser prévoir

foreshore /ˈfɔːʃɔːʳ/ N *[of beach]* plage *f* ; *(Geog)* estran *m*

foreshorten /fɔːˈʃɔːtn/ VT 1 *(Art) [+ perspective, view, shape, figure]* faire un raccourci de ; *(Phot)* déformer par un effet de téléobjectif ◆ **~ed view** raccourci *m* 2 *(frm: in duration, size)* raccourcir

foreshortening /fɔːˈʃɔːtnɪŋ/ N *(Art, Phot)* raccourci *m*

foresight /ˈfɔːsaɪt/ N prévoyance *f* ◆ **lack of ~** imprévoyance *f* ◆ **to have the ~ to do sth** faire preuve de prévoyance en faisant qch, avoir la bonne idée de faire qch au bon moment

foreskin /ˈfɔːskɪn/ N prépuce *m*

forest /ˈfɒrɪst/ N forêt *f* ◆ **he can't see the ~ for the trees** *(US)* les arbres lui cachent la forêt
COMP **Forest Enterprise** N *(Brit)* Office des Forêts
forest fire N incendie *m* de forêt
forest ranger N garde *m* forestier

forestall /fɔːˈstɔːl/ VT *[+ competitor]* devancer ; *[+ desire, eventuality, objection]* anticiper, prévenir

forested /ˈfɒrɪstɪd/ ADJ boisé

forester /ˈfɒrɪstəʳ/ N forestier *m*

forestry /ˈfɒrɪstrɪ/ N sylviculture *f*, foresterie *f*
COMP **the Forestry Commission** N *ancien nom de l'Office des Forêts en Grande-Bretagne*

foretaste /ˈfɔːteɪst/ N avant-goût *m* ◆ **the riot provided a ~ of the civil war to come** l'émeute donna un avant-goût de ce que serait la guerre civile

foretell /fɔːˈtel/ (pret, ptp **foretold**) VT prédire

forethought /ˈfɔːθɔːt/ N prévoyance *f* ◆ **lack of ~** imprévoyance *f*

forever, for ever /fərˈevəʳ/ ADV 1 *(= eternally) [live, last, remember]* toujours ◆ **I'll love you ~** je t'aimerai toujours ◆ **Manchester United ~!** vive Manchester United ! ◆ **~ and ever** à jamais, éternellement 2 *(= definitively) [go, change, disappear, lose, close]* définitivement, pour toujours ◆ **he left ~** il est parti pour toujours 3 *(* = a long time) [take]* une éternité ; *[wait]* jusqu'à la saint-glinglin* ◆ **the meeting lasted ~** la réunion n'en finissait pas 4 *(= constantly)* ◆ **to be ~ doing sth** être sans arrêt en train de faire qch 5 *(= unfailingly) [cheerful, suspicious]* toujours

forewarn /fɔːˈwɔːn/ VT prévenir, avertir ◆ **~ed is forearmed** *(Prov)* un homme averti en vaut deux *(Prov)*

foreword /ˈfɔːwɜːd/ N avant-propos *m inv*, avertissement *m* (au lecteur)

forex /ˈfɔːreks/ N *(Fin)* ◆ **~ market** marché *m* des changes ◆ **~ dealer** cambiste *mf*

forfeit /ˈfɔːfɪt/ VT 1 *(= lose) [+ property]* perdre (par confiscation) ; *[+ one's rights]* perdre, être déchu de ; *[+ one's life, health]* payer de ; *[+ sb's respect]* perdre 2 *(= abandon)* abandonner N 1 *(gen)* prix *m*, peine *f* 2 *(for non-performance of contract)* dédit *m* ◆ **~s** *(= game)* gages *mpl (jeu de société)* ◆ **to pay a ~** *(in game)* avoir un gage ADJ *(liter) (= liable to be taken)* susceptible d'être confisqué ; *(= actually taken)* confisqué ◆ **his life was ~** *(= he died)* il le paya de sa vie ; *(= he might die)* il pourrait le payer de sa vie

forfeiture /ˈfɔːfɪtʃəʳ/ N *[of property]* perte *f* (par confiscation) ; *[of right etc]* perte *f*, déchéance *f*

forgather /fɔːˈgæðəʳ/ VI ⇒ **foregather**

forgave /fəˈgeɪv/ VB pt of **forgive**

forge /fɔːdʒ/ VT 1 *(= fake) [+ signature, banknote]* contrefaire ; *[+ document]* faire un faux de ; *[+ painting]* faire un faux de, contrefaire ; *[+ evidence]* fabriquer ; *(= alter)* maquiller, falsifier ◆ **a ~d passport/ticket** un faux passeport/billet ◆ **to ~ a certificate** *(= create new one)* faire un faux certificat ; *(= alter existing one)* maquiller *or* falsifier un certificat ◆ **the date on the certificate had been ~d** la date figurant sur le certificat avait été falsifiée ◆ **to ~ a Renoir** faire un faux Renoir ◆ **a ~d painting** un faux *(tableau)* ◆ **a ~d Renoir** un faux Renoir ◆ **it's ~d** c'est un faux 2 *[+ metal]* forger 3 *(= establish) [+ alliance, ties, links]* forger ; *[+ coalition]* former ; *[+ agreement, compromise]* établir ; *[+ solution]* parvenir à ◆ **to ~ one's identity** construire son identité VI ◆ **to ~ ahead** prendre de l'avance ; *(Racing)* foncer N forge *f*

forger /ˈfɔːdʒəʳ/ N faussaire *mf* ; *(Jur)* contrefacteur *m*

forgery /ˈfɔːdʒərɪ/ N 1 *(NonC) [of banknote, signature, document, will] (= counterfeiting)* contrefaçon *f* ; *(= altering)* falsification *f* ; *[of story]* invention *f* ; *(Jur)* contrefaçon *f* (frauduleuse) ◆ **to prosecute sb for ~** poursuivre qn pour faux (et usage de faux) ◆ **art/cheque/banknote ~** contrefaçon d'œuvres d'art/de chèques/de billets de banque 2 *(= thing forged: work of art, document, passport, will)* faux *m* ◆ **the signature was a ~** la signature était fausse

forget /fəˈget/ LANGUAGE IN USE 1.1 (pret **forgot**, ptp **forgotten**)
VT 1 *[+ name, fact, experience]* oublier ◆ **I've forgotten all my Spanish** j'ai oublié tout l'espagnol que je savais *or* tout mon espagnol ◆ **she never ~s a face** elle a la mémoire des visages ◆ **I shall never ~ what he said** je n'oublierai jamais ce qu'il a dit ◆ **I ~ who said ...** je ne sais plus qui a dit ... ◆ **not ~ting ...** sans oublier ... ◆ **we completely forgot the time** nous avons complètement oublié l'heure ◆ **and don't you ~ it!*** et tâche de ne pas oublier !, tu as intérêt à ne pas oublier ! ◆ **she'll never let him ~ it** elle ne manque pas une occasion de le lui rappeler ◆ **let's ~ it!** passons *or* on passe l'éponge ! ; *(= let's drop the subject)* ça n'a aucune importance ◆ **~ it!** *(to sb thanking)* ce n'est rien ! ; *(to sb pestering)* laissez tomber ! ; *(to sb hopeful)* n'y comptez pas ! ◆ **to ~ to do sth** oublier *or* omettre de faire qch ◆ **I've forgotten how to do it** je ne sais plus comment on fait ◆ **it's easy to ~ how to do it** c'est facile d'oublier comment on fait ◆ **I forgot (that) I'd seen her** j'ai oublié que je l'avais vue
2 ◆ **to ~ o.s.** *(= be altruistic)* s'oublier, oublier son propre intérêt ◆ **to ~ o.s.** *or* **one's manners** oublier toutes ses bonnes manières, s'oublier *(liter)* ◆ **he drinks to try to ~ himself** il boit pour oublier ◆ **he forgot himself and ...** *(= be distracted)* dans un moment de distraction, il ...
3 *(= leave behind) [+ umbrella, passport, gloves etc]* oublier, laisser
VI oublier ◆ **I completely forgot, I forgot all about it** j'ai complètement oublié, ça m'est complètement sorti de l'esprit ◆ **I've forgotten all about it (already)** je n'y pense (déjà) plus ◆ **~ about it!*** n'y pensez plus ! ◆ **he seemed willing to ~ about the whole business** il semblait prêt à passer l'éponge sur l'affaire ◆ **you can ~ about your promotion** tu peux dire adieu à ta promotion ◆ **I forgot about having to go to the dentist** j'ai oublié que je devais aller chez le dentiste
COMP **forget-me-not** N *(= plant)* myosotis *m*
forget-me-not blue N (bleu *m*) myosotis *m inv*

forgetful /fəˈgetfʊl/ ADJ *(= absent-minded)* distrait ; *(= careless)* négligent, étourdi ◆ **he is very ~** il a très mauvaise mémoire, il oublie tout ◆ **how ~ of me!** que je suis étourdi ! ◆ **~ of the danger** oublieux du danger

forgetfulness /fəˈgetfʊlnɪs/ N *(= absent-mindedness)* manque *m* de mémoire ; *(= carelessness)* négligence *f*, étourderie *f* ◆ **in a moment of ~** dans un moment d'oubli *or* d'étourderie

forgettable /fəˈgetəbəl/ ADJ peu mémorable

forgivable /fəˈgɪvəbl/ ADJ pardonnable

forgivably /fəˈgɪvəblɪ/ ADV ◆ **to act** *or* **behave ~** avoir un comportement pardonnable *or* excusable ◆ **he was ~ tense/rude** il était tendu/malpoli, ce qu'on pouvait lui pardonner

forgive /fəˈgɪv/ (pret **forgave**, ptp **forgiven**) /fəˈgɪvn/ VT 1 *[+ person, sin, mistake]* pardonner ◆ **to ~ sb (for) sth** pardonner qch à qn ◆ **to ~ sb for doing sth** pardonner à qn de faire qch ◆ **~ me for asking, but ...** excuse-moi de demander, mais ... ◆ **you must ~ him his rudeness** pardonnez-lui son impolitesse ◆ **one could be ~n for thinking ...** on serait excusable *or* pardonnable de penser ... ◆ **~ me, but ...** pardonnez-moi *or* excusez-moi, mais ... ◆ **we must ~ and forget** nous devons pardonner et oublier 2 *(frm)* ◆ **to ~ (sb) a debt** faire grâce (à qn) d'une dette

forgiveness /fəˈgɪvnɪs/ N *(NonC) (= pardon)* pardon *m* ; *(= compassion)* indulgence *f*, clémence *f*

forgiving /fəˈgɪvɪŋ/ ADJ indulgent, clément

forgo /fɔːˈgəʊ/ VT ⇒ **forego**

forgot /fəˈgɒt/ VB pt of **forget**

forgotten /fəˈgɒtn/ VB ptp of **forget**

fork /fɔːk/ N 1 *(at table)* fourchette *f* ; *(for digging)* fourche *f* 2 *[of branches]* fourche *f* ; *[of roads, railways]* embranchement *m* ◆ **take the left** ~ *(giving directions)* prenez à gauche à l'embranchement VT 1 *(also* **fork over***)* *[+ hay, ground]* fourcher 2 ◆ **he ~ed the beans into his mouth** il enfournait* ses haricots (à coups de fourchette) VI *[roads]* bifurquer ◆ **we ~ed right on leaving the village** nous avons pris or bifurqué à droite à la sortie du village ◆ ~ **left for Oxford** prenez or bifurquez à gauche pour Oxford COMP **fork-lift truck** N chariot *m* élévateur (à fourche)

► **fork out*** VI casquer‡ VT SEP *[+ money]* allonger‡, abouler‡

► **fork over** VT SEP ⇒ **fork vt 1**

► **fork up** VT SEP 1 *[+ soil]* fourcher 2 * ⇒ **fork out vt sep**

forked /fɔːkt/ ADJ fourchu ◆ **to speak with (a) ~ tongue** avoir la langue fourchue COMP **forked lightning** N éclair *m* en zigzags

forkful /ˈfɔːkfʊl/ N ◆ **a ~ of mashed potato** une pleine fourchette de purée

forlorn /fəˈlɔːn/ ADJ 1 *(= miserable) [person]* solitaire et malheureux, triste et délaissé ; *[voice]* triste ; *[expression]* de tristesse et de délaissement ◆ **to look** ~ avoir l'air triste et délaissé 2 *(= desolate) [area]* désolé ; *[building]* abandonné ; *[road]* désert 3 *(= despairing) [attempt, effort]* désespéré, vain ◆ **it is a ~ hope** c'est un mince espoir ◆ **in the ~ hope of sth/doing sth** dans le fol espoir de qch/de faire qch

forlornly /fəˈlɔːnlɪ/ ADV 1 *(= miserably) [stand, sit, wait, stare]* d'un air triste et délaissé, tristement 2 *(= despairingly) [hope]* en vain ; *[try]* désespérément

form /fɔːm/ N 1 *(= type, particular kind)* forme *f*, sorte *f* ◆ **the various ~s of energy** les différentes formes d'énergie ◆ **you could say it was a ~ of apology** on pourrait appeler cela une sorte d'excuse ◆ **a new ~ of government** une nouvelle forme de gouvernement ◆ **a different ~ of life** *(= life-form)* une autre forme de vie ; *(= way of life)* un autre mode de vie

2 *(= style, condition)* forme *f* ◆ **in the ~ of** sous forme de ◆ **medicine in the ~ of tablets** or **in tablet** ~ médicament *m* sous forme de comprimés ◆ **the first prize will take the ~ of a trip to Rome** le premier prix sera un voyage à Rome ◆ **what ~ should my application take?** comment dois-je présenter or formuler ma demande ? ◆ **their discontent took various ~s** leur mécontentement s'est manifesté de différentes façons ◆ **the same thing in a new** ~ la même chose sous une forme nouvelle or un aspect nouveau ◆ **her letters are to be published in book** ~ ses lettres doivent être publiées sous forme de livre ◆ **the plural** ~ *(Gram)* la forme du pluriel

3 *(NonC: Art, Literat, Mus etc)* forme *f* ◆ ~ **and content** la forme et le fond

4 *(NonC = shape)* forme *f* ◆ **to take** ~ prendre forme ◆ **his thoughts lack** ~ ses pensées manquent d'ordre

5 *(= figure)* forme *f* ◆ **the human** ~ la forme humaine ◆ **I saw a ~ in the fog** j'ai vu une forme or une silhouette dans le brouillard

6 *(Philos) (= structure, organization)* forme *f* ; *(= essence)* essence *f* ; *(Ling)* forme *f*

7 *(NonC: esp Brit = etiquette)* forme *f*, formalité *f* ◆ **for ~'s sake, as a matter of** ~ pour la forme ◆ **it's good/bad ~ to do that** cela se fait/ne se fait pas

8 *(= formula, established practice)* forme *f*, formule *f* ◆ **he pays attention to the ~s** il respecte les formes ◆ **choose another ~ of words** choisissez une autre expression or tournure ◆ **the correct ~ of address for a bishop** la manière correcte de s'adresser à un évêque ◆ ~ **of worship** liturgie *f*, rites *mpl* ◆ **what's the ~?** † * quelle est la marche à suivre ?

9 *(= document) (gen: for applications etc)* formulaire *m* ; *(for telegram, giro transfer)* formule *f* ; *(for tax returns)* feuille *f* ; *(= card)* fiche *f* ◆ **printed** ~ imprimé *m* ◆ **to fill up** or **in** or **out a** ~ remplir un formulaire ; → **application, tax**

10 *(NonC: esp Brit = fitness)* forme *f* ◆ **on** ~ en forme ◆ **he's not on ~, he's off** ~ or **out of** ~ il n'est pas en forme ◆ **in fine** or **great ~, on top** ~ en pleine forme

11 ◆ **to study (the)** ~ *(Brit Racing)* ≈ préparer son tiercé ; *(fig)* établir un pronostic

12 *(Brit = bench)* banc *m*

13 *(Brit Scol = class)* classe *f* ◆ **he's in the sixth** ~ ≈ il est en première

14 *(NonC: Brit = criminal record)* ◆ **he's got** ~ ‡ il a fait de la taule‡

VT 1 *(= shape)* former, construire ◆ **he ~s his sentences well** il construit bien ses phrases ◆ **he ~ed the clay into a ball** il a roulé or pétri l'argile en boule ◆ **he ~ed it out of a piece of wood** *(liter)* il l'a façonné or fabriqué dans un morceau de bois

2 *(= train, mould) [+ child]* former, éduquer ; *[+ sb's character]* façonner, former

3 *(= develop) [+ habit]* contracter ; *[+ plan]* mettre sur pied ◆ **to ~ an opinion** se faire or se former une opinion ◆ **to ~ an impression** se faire une impression ◆ **you mustn't ~ the idea that** ... il ne faut pas que vous vous mettiez dans la tête que ...

4 *(= organize, create) [+ government]* former ; *[+ coalition, alliance]* constituer ; *(Comm) [+ company]* former, créer ◆ **to ~ a committee** former un comité ◆ **to ~ a new political party** former or créer un nouveau parti politique

5 *(= constitute)* composer, former ◆ **to ~ part of** faire partie de ◆ **the ministers who ~ the government** les ministres qui composent or constituent le gouvernement ◆ **those who ~ the group** les gens qui font partie du groupe ◆ **to ~ a** or **the basis for** former or constituer la base de, servir de base à

6 *(= take the shape or order of) [+ pattern, picture]* former, faire ◆ **to ~ a line** se mettre en ligne, s'aligner ◆ ~ **a circle please** mettez-vous en cercle s'il vous plaît ◆ **to ~ a queue** se mettre en file, former la queue ◆ **to ~ fours** *(Mil)* se mettre par quatre ◆ **the road ~s a series of curves** la route fait or dessine une série de courbes

7 *(Gram)* ◆ **to ~ the plural** former le pluriel

VI *[queue, group, company, crystal, deposits, blood clots]* se former ; *[idea]* prendre forme ◆ **an idea ~ed in his mind** une idée a pris forme dans son esprit

COMP **form feeder** N *(Comput)* dispositif *m* de changement de page
form leader N *(Brit Scol)* ≈ chef *m* de classe
form letter N lettre *f* type
form master, form mistress N ≈ professeur *m* principal
form room N salle *f* de classe *(affectée à une classe particulière)*
form tutor N ⇒ **form master** or **mistress**

► **form up** VI se mettre or se ranger en ligne, s'aligner ◆ ~ **up behind your teacher** mettez-vous or rangez-vous en ligne derrière votre professeur

formal /ˈfɔːməl/ ADJ 1 *(= polite, ceremonial) [person]* cérémonieux, protocolaire ; *[behaviour, handshake, welcome, relationship]* cérémonieux ; *[dinner, occasion, function]* protocolaire, officiel ; *[clothes]* habillé ; *[letter]* respectant les convenances ; *[politeness]* formel ; *[language, style]* soutenu ; *[word]* de style soutenu ◆ **don't be so** ~ ne faites pas tant de cérémonies ◆ **lunch was a ~ affair** le déjeuner était protocolaire ◆ **a ~ dance** un bal habillé

2 *(= official) [talks, statement, request, complaint, acceptance, surrender]* officiel ◆ ~ **contract** contrat *m* en bonne et due forme ◆ ~ **denial** démenti *m* formel or officiel ◆ ~ **instructions** instructions *fpl* formelles

3 *(= in design) [garden]* à la française ; *[room]* solennel

4 *(= professional)* ◆ **he had no ~ training/qualifications** il n'avait pas vraiment de formation/de qualifications ◆ **he had little ~ education** or **schooling** il a quitté l'école assez tôt ◆ **his ~ education stopped after primary school** il n'a pas fait d'études secondaires ◆ **I've had no ~ training as an actor** je n'ai pas suivi de cours de théâtre

5 *(= structural) [perfection]* formel

6 *(= superficial, in form only)* de forme ◆ **a certain ~ resemblance** une certaine ressemblance dans la forme

COMP **formal dress** N tenue *f* de cérémonie ; *(= evening dress)* tenue *f* de soirée
formal grammar N grammaire *f* formelle
formal language N langage *m* formel
formal logic N logique *f* formelle

formaldehyde /fɔːˈmældɪhaɪd/ N formol *m*, formaldéhyde *m*

formalin(e) /ˈfɔːməlɪn/ N formol *m*

formalism /ˈfɔːməlɪzəm/ N formalisme *m*

formalist /ˈfɔːməlɪst/ ADJ, N formaliste *mf*

formalistic /ˌfɔːməˈlɪstɪk/ ADJ formaliste

formality /fɔːˈmælɪtɪ/ N 1 *(NonC) (= convention)* formalité *f* ; *(= stiffness)* raideur *f*, froideur *f* ; *(= ceremoniousness)* cérémonie *f NonC* 2 formalité *f* ◆ **it's a mere** or **just a** ~ ce n'est qu'une simple formalité ◆ **the formalities** les formalités *fpl* ◆ **let's do without the formalities!** dispensons-nous des formalités !, faisons au plus simple !

formalize /ˈfɔːməlaɪz/ VT officialiser

formally /ˈfɔːməlɪ/ ADV 1 *(= politely) [say, shake hands]* cérémonieusement ◆ **his behaviour was ~ correct** son comportement était cérémonieux 2 *(= officially) [announce, approve, agree, open, launch]* officiellement ◆ ~ **charged** mis en examen ◆ **we have been ~ invited** nous avons reçu une invitation officielle 3 **to be ~ dressed** *(= smartly)* être en tenue de cérémonie ; *(= in evening dress)* être en tenue de soirée 4 *(= academically) [teach]* en tant que matière spécifique ◆ **to have been ~ trained** avoir reçu une formation professionnelle 5 *(in design)* ◆ **a ~ laid-out garden** un jardin à la française

format /ˈfɔːmæt/ N 1 *(= type, kind) [of computer data, document, camera film, publication]* format *m* ; *[of video]* système *m* ◆ **newspapers in tabloid or broadsheet** ~ des journaux de format tabloïd ou de grand format ◆ **the film will be shown in wide-screen** ~ *(Cine)* le film sera projeté sur grand écran ; *(TV)* le film sera diffusé en format grand écran ◆ **dictionaries published in both paper and electronic** ~ des dictionnaires publiés à la fois en version papier et en version électronique ◆ **available in cassette or CD** ~ disponible en cassette ou CD

2 *(= structure, presentation) [of book, newspaper, page]* présentation *f* ; *[of TV, radio programme]* forme *f*, présentation *f* ; *[of event, competition]* forme *f* ◆ **dictionaries published in three-column** ~ des dictionnaires publiés dans une présentation sur trois colonnes ◆ **large-~ books** livres *mpl* grand format

VT 1 *(Comput)* formater

2 *(gen)* concevoir le format or la présentation de

formation /fɔːˈmeɪʃən/ N 1 *(NonC) [of child, character]* formation *f* ; *[of plan]* élaboration *f* ; *[of government]* formation *f* ; *[of classes, courses]* organisation *f*, mise *f* en place ; *[of club]* création *f* ; *[of committee]* création *f*, mise *f* en place 2 *(NonC: Mil etc)* formation *f*, disposition *f* ◆ **battle** ~ formation *f* de combat ◆ **in close** ~ en ordre serré 3 *(Geol)* formation *f*

COMP **formation dance, formation dancing** N danse *f* de groupe
formation flying N vol *m* en formation

formative /ˈfɔːmətɪv/ ADJ formateur (-trice *f*) ◆ **he spent his ~ years in London** *(= his childhood)* il a passé son enfance à Londres ◆ **this was a ~ period in his life** c'était une période déterminante dans sa vie N *(Gram)* formant *m*, élément *m* formateur

formatting /ˈfɔːmætɪŋ/ N *(Comput)* formatage *m*

-formed /ˈfɔːmd/ ADJ *(in compounds)* ◆ **fully-formed** *[baby, animal]* complètement formé *or* développé ◆ **half-formed** à moitié formé *or* développé ; → **well[2]**

former[1] /ˈfɔːməʳ/ N *(= tool)* gabarit *m*

former[2] /ˈfɔːməʳ/ LANGUAGE IN USE 26.2

ADJ 1 *(= previous) [president, employee, home]* ancien *before n* ; *[strength, authority]* d'autrefois ◆ **the ~ Soviet Union** l'ex-Union *f* soviétique ◆ **the ~ Yugoslavia** l'ex-Yougoslavie *f* ◆ **my ~ wife/husband** mon ex-femme/ex-mari ◆ **the college is a ~ mansion** le collège est un ancien manoir ◆ **to restore sth to its ~ glory** redonner à qch sa splendeur d'autrefois ◆ **the buildings have now been restored to their ~ glory** les bâtiments rénovés ont retrouvé leur ancienne splendeur *or* leur splendeur d'antan *(liter)* ◆ **he was a (pale) shadow of his ~ self** il n'était plus que l'ombre de lui-même ◆ **he was very unlike his ~ self** il ne se ressemblait plus du tout ◆ **in a ~ life** au cours d'une vie antérieure ◆ **in ~ years** *or* **times** *or* **days** autrefois ◆ **the radicals of ~ days** les radicaux d'autrefois

2 *(as opposed to latter)* ◆ **the ~ option/alternative** la première option/alternative ◆ **your ~ suggestion** votre première suggestion

PRON celui-là, celle-là ◆ **the ~ ... the latter** celui-là ... celui-ci ◆ **of the two ideas I prefer the ~** des deux idées je préfère celle-là *or* la première ◆ **the ~ is the more expensive of the two systems** ce premier système est le plus coûteux des deux, des deux systèmes, c'est le premier le plus coûteux ◆ **of the two possible solutions, I prefer the ~** entre les deux solutions, je préfère la première, entre les deux, je préfère la première solution

COMP **former pupil** N *(Scol)* ancien(ne) élève *m(f)*

-former /ˈfɔːməʳ/ N *(in compounds: Scol)* élève *mf* de ... ◆ **fourth-former** ≈ élève *mf* de troisième

formerly /ˈfɔːməlɪ/ ADV autrefois ◆ **Lake Malawi, ~ Lake Nyasa** le lac Malawi, anciennement *or* autrefois lac Nyassa

formic /ˈfɔːmɪk/ ADJ formique

Formica ®/fɔːˈmaɪkə/ N formica ® *m*, plastique *m* laminé

formidable /ˈfɔːmɪdəbl/ ADJ 1 *(= daunting) [person, opposition]* redoutable, terrible ; *[task, challenge]* redoutable ; *[obstacle]* terrible 2 *(= prodigious) [person, talent, reputation]* phénoménal ; *[combination]* impressionnant

formidably /ˈfɔːmɪdəblɪ/ ADV *(= extremely)* terriblement, redoutablement ◆ **~ armed** redoutablement bien armé, aux armes redoutables

formless /ˈfɔːmlɪs/ ADJ 1 *(= amorphous) [shape, image]* informe ; *[terror, apprehension]* indéfini 2 *(pej = unstructured) [book, play, film, record]* dépourvu de structure

Formosa /fɔːˈməʊsə/ N *(formerly)* Formose *m or f*

Formosan /fɔːˈməʊsən/ ADJ formosan

formula /ˈfɔːmjʊlə/ N 1 (pl **formulas** *or* **formulae** /ˈfɔːmjʊliː/) *(gen, also Chem, Math etc)* formule *f* ◆ **a ~ for averting** *or* **aimed at averting the strike** une formule visant à éviter la grève ◆ **winning ~** formule *f* idéale ◆ **peace ~** forme *f* de paix ◆ **pay/pricing ~** système *m* de fixation des salaires/prix 2 *(= baby milk)* lait *m* maternisé 3 *(in motor racing)* ◆ **Formula One/Two/Three** la formule un/deux/trois ◆ **a ~-one car** une voiture de formule un COMP **formula milk** N lait *m* maternisé

formulaic /ˌfɔːmjʊˈleɪɪk/ ADJ *[language, plot, response, TV programme]* convenu, stéréotypé ◆ **~ phrase** *or* **expression** expression *f* convenue

formulate /ˈfɔːmjʊleɪt/ VT formuler

formulation /ˌfɔːmjʊˈleɪʃən/ N 1 *(NonC = forming, creation) [of idea, theory, proposal]* formulation *f* ; *[of policy, plan, product]* élaboration *f* 2 *(= formula) [of treaty, settlement]* formule *f* ◆ **this ~ was acceptable to both sides** cette formule convenait aux deux parties 3 *(= medicine)* formule *f* 4 *(= saying)* formule *f*

fornicate /ˈfɔːnɪkeɪt/ VI forniquer

fornication /ˌfɔːnɪˈkeɪʃən/ N fornication *f*

forsake /fəˈseɪk/ (pret **forsook**, ptp **forsaken**) VT *(liter) [+ person]* abandonner, délaisser ; *[+ place]* quitter ; *[+ habit]* renoncer à

forsaken /fəˈseɪkən/ VB (pt **forsake**) → **godforsaken** ADJ ◆ **an old ~ farmhouse** une vieille ferme abandonnée

forsook /fəˈsʊk/ VB pt of **forsake**

forsooth /fəˈsuːθ/ ADV (†† *or hum*) en vérité, à vrai dire ◆ **~!** par exemple !

forswear /fɔːˈswɛəʳ/ (pret **forswore** /fɔːˈswɔːʳ/, ptp **forsworn** /fɔːˈswɔːn/) VT *(frm) (= renounce)* renoncer à, abjurer ; *(= deny)* désavouer ◆ **to ~ o.s.** *(= perjure)* se parjurer

forsythia /fɔːˈsaɪθɪə/ N forsythia *m*

fort /fɔːt/ N *(Mil)* fort *m* ; *(small)* fortin *m* ◆ **to hold the ~** *(fig)* monter la garde *(hum)*, assurer la permanence COMP **Fort Knox** N Fort Knox *m (réserve d'or des États-Unis)* ◆ **they have turned their home into (a) Fort Knox** ils ont transformé leur maison en une véritable forteresse

forte[1] /ˈfɔːtɪ, (US) fɔːt/ N fort *m* ◆ **generosity is not his ~** la générosité n'est pas son fort

forte[2] /ˈfɔːtɪ/ ADJ, ADV *(Mus)* forte

forth /fɔːθ/ ADV

> When **forth** is an element in a phrasal verb, eg **pour forth, sally forth, venture forth**, look up the verb.

1 († *or frm = out*) de l'avant ◆ **to go back and ~ between ...** aller et venir entre ..., faire la navette entre ... ◆ **the thunderstorm burst ~** l'orage a éclaté ◆ **to come ~** *(= forward)* s'avancer ; *(= outside)* sortir ◆ **to pour ~ a torrent of invective** vomir un torrent d'injures ◆ **to stretch ~ one's hand** tendre la main ; → **bring forth, hold forth** 2 *(= onward)* ◆ **and so ~** et ainsi de suite ◆ **from this day ~** *(frm)* dorénavant, désormais

forthcoming /fɔːθˈkʌmɪŋ/ ADJ 1 *(= imminent) [event, visit, election, album etc]* prochain ◆ **in a ~ book, he examines ...** dans un prochain livre *or* dans un livre qui va bientôt sortir, il examine ... 2 *(= available)* ◆ **to be ~** *[money, funds, aid, support]* être disponible ◆ **no evidence of this was ~** on n'avait aucune preuve de cela ◆ **no answer was ~** il n'y a pas eu de réponse 3 *(= communicative) [person]* communicatif ◆ **to be ~ on** *or* **about sth** être disposé à parler de qch

forthright /ˈfɔːθraɪt/ ADJ *[person, manner, answer, remark]* franc (franche *f*), direct ; *[language]* direct ; *[statement]* sans détour ◆ **in ~ terms** sans détour ◆ **to be ~ in one's response** donner une réponse franche ◆ **to be ~ in saying sth** dire qch ouvertement ◆ **to be ~ about sth** ne pas mâcher ses mots à propos de qch

forthwith /ˈfɔːθˈwɪθ/ ADV *(frm)* sur-le-champ

fortieth /ˈfɔːtɪɪθ/ ADJ quarantième N quarantième *mf* ; *(= fraction)* quarantième *m* ; *for phrases see* **sixth**

fortification /ˌfɔːtɪfɪˈkeɪʃən/ N fortification *f*

fortify /ˈfɔːtɪfaɪ/ VT 1 *[+ place]* fortifier, armer *(against* contre) ; *[+ person]* réconforter ◆ **fortified place** place *f* forte ◆ **have a drink to ~ you** *(hum)* prenez un verre pour vous remonter 2 *[+ wine]* accroître la teneur en alcool de ; *[+ food]* renforcer en vitamines ◆ **fortified wine** ≈ vin *m* doux, vin *m* de liqueur

fortitude /ˈfɔːtɪtjuːd/ N courage *m*, force *f* d'âme

fortnight /ˈfɔːtnaɪt/ N *(esp Brit)* quinzaine *f*, quinze jours *mpl* ◆ **a ~'s holiday** quinze jours de vacances ◆ **a ~ tomorrow** demain en quinze ◆ **adjourned for a ~** remis à quinzaine ◆ **for a ~** pour une quinzaine, pour quinze jours ◆ **in a ~, in a ~'s time** dans quinze jours ◆ **a ~ ago** il y a quinze jours

fortnightly /ˈfɔːtnaɪtlɪ/ *(esp Brit)* ADJ *[newspaper]* bimensuel ; *[visit]* tous les quinze jours ; *[cycle]* de quinze jours ADV tous les quinze jours

FORTRAN, Fortran /ˈfɔːtræn/ N fortran *m*

fortress /ˈfɔːtrɪs/ N *(= prison)* forteresse *f* ; *(= medieval castle)* château *m* fort ◆ **~ Europe** la forteresse Europe ; → **flying**

fortuitous /fɔːˈtjuːɪtəs/ ADJ fortuit, accidentel

fortuitously /fɔːˈtjuːɪtəslɪ/ ADV fortuitement, par hasard

fortunate /ˈfɔːtʃənɪt/ ADJ *[coincidence, choice]* heureux ; *[circumstances]* favorable ◆ **to be ~** *[person]* avoir de la chance ◆ **we are ~ that ...** nous avons de la chance que ... ◆ **it is ~ that ...** c'est une chance que ... ◆ **it was ~ for him that ...** heureusement pour lui que ... ◆ **they were ~ to escape** ils ont eu de la chance de s'échapper ◆ **I was ~ enough to go to a good school** j'ai eu la chance de fréquenter une bonne école ◆ **to be ~ in one's career** avoir de la chance dans sa carrière ◆ **to be ~ in having a wonderful mother** avoir la chance d'avoir une mère merveilleuse ◆ **she is in the ~ position of having plenty of choice** elle a la chance d'avoir plein d'options ◆ **how ~!** quelle chance !

fortunately /ˈfɔːtʃənɪtlɪ/ LANGUAGE IN USE 26.3
ADV heureusement *(for* pour)

fortune /ˈfɔːtʃən/ N 1 *(= luck)* chance *f*, fortune *f* ◆ **by good ~** par chance, par bonheur ◆ **I had the good ~ to meet him** j'ai eu la chance *or* le bonheur de le rencontrer ◆ **to try one's ~** tenter sa chance ◆ **~ favoured him** la chance *or* la fortune lui a souri ◆ **the ~s of war** la fortune des armes ; → **seek**

2 *(= destiny)* **to tell sb's ~** dire la bonne aventure à qn ◆ **to tell ~s** dire la bonne aventure ◆ **whatever my ~ may be** quel que soit le sort qui m'est réservé

3 *(= riches)* fortune *f* ◆ **to make a ~** faire fortune ◆ **he made a ~ on it** il a gagné une fortune avec ça ◆ **to come into a ~** hériter d'une fortune ◆ **a man of ~** un homme d'une fortune *or* d'une richesse considérable ◆ **to marry a ~** épouser une grosse fortune ◆ **to spend/cost/lose a (small) ~** dépenser/coûter/perdre une (petite) fortune

COMP **fortune cookie** N *(US)* beignet *m* chinois *(renfermant un horoscope ou une devise)*
fortune hunter N *(man)* coureur *m* de dot ; *(woman)* femme *f* intéressée
fortune-teller N diseur *m*, -euse *f* de bonne aventure ; *(with cards)* tireuse *f* de cartes
fortune-telling N (art *m* de la) divination ; *(with cards)* cartomancie *f*

forty /ˈfɔːtɪ/ ADJ quarante *inv* ◆ **about ~ people** une quarantaine de personnes ◆ **to have ~ winks*** faire un petit somme, piquer un roupillon* N quarante *m inv* ◆ **about ~** une quarantaine ◆ **the lower ~-eight** *(US = states)* les quarante-huit États américains *(à l'exclusion de l'Alaska et de Hawaï)* ; *for other phrases see* **sixty** PRON quarante ◆ **there are ~** il y en a quarante

COMP **forty-niner** N (US) prospecteur *m* d'or *(de la ruée vers l'or de 1849)*

forum /ˈfɔːrəm/ N (pl **forums** *or* **fora** /ˈfɔːrə/) [1] *(Hist)* forum *m* [2] *(fig)* tribune *f* ◆ **the newspaper provided a ~ for his ideas** le journal lui a servi de tribune pour ses idées ◆ **the meetings are a ~ for political debate** ces réunions constituent un forum politique

forward /ˈfɔːwəd/

> When **forward** is an element in a phrasal verb, eg **bring forward**, **come forward**, **step forward**, look up the verb.

ADV (also **forwards**) en avant ◆ **to rush ~** se précipiter *or* s'élancer (en avant) ◆ **to go ~** avancer ◆ **to go straight ~** aller droit devant soi ◆ **~!, ~ march!** *(Mil)* en avant, marche ! ◆ **from that moment ~** à partir de ce moment-là ◆ **to push o.s. ~** *(lit, fig)* se mettre en avant ◆ **to come ~** *(fig)* se présenter ◆ **he went backward(s) and ~(s) between the station and the house** il allait et venait entre *or* il faisait la navette entre la gare et la maison ◆ **to put the clocks ~** avancer les pendules ; → **bring forward**

PREP ◆ **~ of** à l'avant de

ADJ [1] *(= in front, ahead) [movement]* en avant, vers l'avant ◆ **the ~ ranks of the army** les premiers rangs de l'armée ◆ **this seat is too far ~** ce siège est trop en avant

[2] *(= well-advanced) [season, plant]* précoce ; *[child]* précoce, en avance ◆ **I'm no further ~ (with this problem)** me voilà bien avancé ! *(iro)*

[3] *(= bold)* effronté ◆ **that was rather ~ of him** c'était assez effronté de sa part

[4] *(Comm) [prices, delivery]* à terme

N *(Sport)* avant *m*

VT [1] *(= advance) [+ career, cause, interests]* favoriser, faire avancer

[2] *(= dispatch) [+ goods]* expédier, envoyer ; *(= send on) [+ letter, parcel]* faire suivre ◆ **please ~** faire suivre SVP, prière de faire suivre

COMP **forward buying** N achat *m* à terme

forward gear N marche *f* avant

forwarding address N *(gen)* adresse *f* de réexpédition ; *(Comm)* adresse *f* pour l'expédition ◆ **he left no ~ing address** il est parti sans laisser d'adresse

forwarding agent N *(Comm)* transitaire *m*

forward line N *(Mil)* première ligne *f* ; *(Sport)* ligne *f* des avants

forward-looking ADJ *[person]* ouvert sur *or* tourné vers l'avenir ; *[plan]* tourné vers l'avenir

forward pass N *(Rugby)* (passe *f*) en-avant *m inv*

forward planning N planification *f*

forward post N *(Mil)* avant-poste *m*, poste *m* avancé

forward sale N vente *f* à terme

forward slash N barre *f* oblique

forwardness /ˈfɔːwədnɪs/ N *[of seasons, plants, children]* précocité *f* ; *(= boldness)* effronterie *f*

forwards /ˈfɔːwədz/ ADV ⇒ **forward adv**

Fosbury flop /ˈfɒzbərɪˌflɒp/ N *(Sport)* rouleau *m* dorsal

fossick* /ˈfɒsɪk/ VI *(Austral)* ◆ **to ~ for sth** fouiller partout pour trouver qch

fossil /ˈfɒsl/ **N** fossile *m* ◆ **he's an old ~ *!** c'est un vieux fossile * *or* une vieille croûte * !

COMP **fossil energy** N énergie *f* fossile

fossil fuel N combustible *m* fossile

fossil hunter N collectionneur *m* de fossiles

fossilization /ˌfɒsɪlaɪˈzeɪʃən/ N fossilisation *f*

fossilized /ˈfɒsɪlaɪzd/ ADJ fossilisé ; *(fig, pej) [person, customs]* fossilisé, figé ; *(Ling) [form, expression]* figé

foster /ˈfɒstəʳ/ **VT** [1] *[+ child] [family]* prendre en placement ; *[authorities]* placer dans une famille nourricière ◆ **the authorities ~ed the child with Mr and Mrs Moore** les autorités ont placé l'enfant chez M. et Mme Moore [2] *(= encourage) [+ friendship, development]* favoriser, encourager [3] *(= entertain) [+ idea, thought]* entretenir, nourrir

COMP *[child]* adoptif, placé dans une famille ; *[father, parents, family]* adoptif, nourricier ; *[brother, sister]* adoptif

foster home N famille *f* nourricière *or* d'accueil

foster mother N mère *f* nourricière *or* adoptive *(d'un enfant placé)*

fostering /ˈfɒstərɪŋ/ N placement *m* familial *or* en famille d'accueil ◆ **the couple has been approved for ~** le couple a obtenu l'autorisation d'accueillir un enfant *(en placement familial)*

fought /fɔːt/ VB pt, ptp of **fight**

foul /faʊl/ **ADJ** [1] *(= disgusting) [place]* immonde, dégoûtant ; *[water]* croupi ; *[air]* vicié ; *[breath]* fétide ; *[person]* infect, ignoble ; *[smell]* infect, nauséabond ; *[taste, food]* infect ◆ **to smell ~** puer

[2] *(esp Brit * = bad) [day]* épouvantable ◆ **~ luck** terrible malchance *f* ◆ **~ weather** *(gen)* sale temps *m*, temps *m* de chien ; *(Naut)* gros temps *m* ◆ **the weather was ~** le temps était infect

[3] *(esp liter = vile) [crime]* ignoble, odieux ; *[behaviour]* odieux ; *[slander, lie]* odieux, vil (vile *f*) ◆ **~ deed** acte *m* crapuleux

[4] *(= offensive) [language, abuse]* grossier ◆ **to have a ~ mouth** être mal embouché ◆ **to have a ~ temper** avoir un sale caractère ◆ **in a ~ mood** *or* **temper** d'une humeur massacrante

[5] *(= unfair: Sport) [shot]* mauvais ; *[tackle]* irrégulier ◆ **by ~ means** par des moyens déloyaux ; → **fair¹** ◆ **a ~ blow** un coup déloyal *or* en traître ; → **cry**

[6] ◆ **to fall** *or* **run ~ of sb** se mettre qn à dos ◆ **to fall** *or* **run ~ of the law/authorities** avoir maille à partir avec la justice/les autorités ◆ **to fall** *or* **run ~ of a ship** *(Naut)* entrer en collision avec un bateau

N *(Sport)* coup *m* défendu *or* irrégulier ; *(Boxing)* coup *m* bas ; *(Ftbl)* faute *f* ◆ **technical/personal ~** *(Basketball)* faute *f* technique/personnelle

VT [1] *(= pollute) [+ air, water]* polluer ; *[+ beaches]* polluer, souiller

[2] *[dog] [+ pavement, garden, grass]* souiller ◆ **to ~ one's own nest** causer sa propre perte

[3] *(= entangle) [+ fishing line, rope]* emmêler ; *[+ mechanism, propeller, anchor]* s'emmêler dans

[4] *(= clog) [+ pipe, chimney, gun barrel]* encrasser, obstruer

[5] *(Sport)* commettre une faute contre

[6] *(= collide with) [+ ship]* entrer en collision avec

VI *(= become entangled or jammed)* ◆ **to ~ on sth** *[rope, line]* s'emmêler dans qch, s'entortiller dans qch ; *[mechanism]* se prendre dans qch

COMP **foul-mouthed** ADJ mal embouché

foul play N *(Sport)* jeu *m* irrégulier ; *(Cards)* tricherie *f* ; *(Jur)* acte *m* criminel ◆ **he suspected ~ play** il soupçonnait qu'il y avait quelque chose de louche ◆ **the police found a body but do not suspect ~ play** la police a découvert un cadavre mais écarte l'hypothèse d'un meurtre

foul-smelling ADJ puant, nauséabond, fétide

foul-tasting ADJ infect

foul-tempered ADJ ◆ **to be ~-tempered** *(habitually)* avoir un caractère de cochon ; *(on one occasion)* être d'une humeur massacrante

foul-up * N confusion *f*

► **foul out** VI *(Basketball)* être exclu *(pour cinq fautes personnelles)*

► **foul up** VT SEP [1] ⇒ **foul vt 1**

[2] * *[+ relationship]* ficher en l'air * ◆ **that has ~ed things up** ça a tout fichu en l'air * *or* gâché

N ◆ **foul-up** * → **foul**

found¹ /faʊnd/ VB pt, ptp of **find**

found² /faʊnd/ VT *[+ town, school]* fonder, créer ; *[+ hospital]* fonder ; *[+ business enterprise]* fonder, constituer ; *[+ colony]* établir, fonder ; *(fig) [+ belief, opinion]* fonder, baser *(on* sur) ; *[+ suspicion]* baser ◆ **our society is ~ed on this** notre société est fondée là-dessus ◆ **the novel is/my suspicions were ~ed on fact** le roman est basé/mes soupçons reposaient sur *or* étaient basés sur des faits réels

found³ /faʊnd/ VT *(Metal)* fondre

foundation /faʊnˈdeɪʃən/ **N** [1] *(NonC = founding) [of town, school, hospital, business]* fondation *f*, création *f*

[2] *(= establishment)* fondation *f* ◆ **Carnegie Foundation** fondation *f* Carnegie ◆ **research ~** fondation *f* consacrée à la recherche ◆ **charitable ~** organisation *f* *or* fondation *f* caritative

[3] *(Constr)* ◆ **~s** fondations *fpl* ◆ **to lay the ~s of** *(lit)* faire *or* jeter les fondations de ; see also **4**

[4] *(fig = basis) [of career, social structure]* base *f* ; *[of idea, religious belief, theory]* base *f*, fondement *m* ◆ **agriculture is the ~ of their economy** l'agriculture est la base *or* le fondement de leur économie ◆ **to lay the ~s of sth** poser les bases *or* les fondements de qch ◆ **his work laid the ~(s) of our legal system** son travail a posé les bases de notre système judiciaire ◆ **without ~** *[rumour, allegation, report, fears etc]* sans fondement ◆ **to rock** *or* **shake sth to its ~s** profondément secouer *or* ébranler qch

[5] (also **foundation cream**) fond *m* de teint

COMP **foundation course** N *(Brit Univ)* cours *m* d'initiation *or* d'introduction

foundation cream N fond *m* de teint

foundation garment N gaine *f*, combiné *m*

foundation stone N *(Brit)* pierre *f* commémorative ◆ **to lay the ~ stone** *(lit, fig)* poser la première pierre

founder¹ /ˈfaʊndəʳ/ **N** fondateur *m*, -trice *f*

COMP **founder member** N *(Brit)* membre *m* fondateur

founder² /ˈfaʊndəʳ/ VI *[ship]* sombrer ; *[horse] (in mud etc)* s'embourber, s'empêtrer ; *(from fatigue)* (se mettre à) boiter ; *[plans]* s'effondrer, s'écrouler ; *[hopes]* s'en aller en fumée

founding /ˈfaʊndɪŋ/ **N** ⇒ **foundation noun 1**

COMP **founding fathers** NPL (US) pères *mpl* fondateurs *(qui élaborèrent la Constitution fédérale des États-Unis)*

foundling /ˈfaʊndlɪŋ/ N enfant *mf* trouvé(e) *f* ◆ **~ hospital** hospice *m* pour enfants trouvés

foundry /ˈfaʊndrɪ/ N fonderie *f*

fount /faʊnt/ N [1] *(liter = spring)* source *f* ◆ **the ~ of knowledge/wisdom** la source du savoir/de la sagesse [2] *(Brit Typ)* fonte *f*

fountain /ˈfaʊntɪn/ **N** [1] *(lit)* fontaine *f* [2] (also **drinking fountain**) fontaine *f* d'eau potable [3] *[of light, sparks]* gerbe *f* ; → **soda** **COMP** **fountain pen** N stylo *m* (à) plume

fountainhead /ˈfaʊntɪnhed/ N source *f*, origine *f* ◆ **to go to the ~** aller (directement) à la source, retourner aux sources

four /fɔːʳ/ **ADJ** quatre *inv* ◆ **it's in ~ figures** c'est dans les milliers ◆ **open to the ~ winds** ouvert à tous les vents *or* aux quatre vents ◆ **to the ~ corners of the earth** aux quatre coins du monde ◆ **the Four Hundred** (US) *l'élite sociale* ; → **stroke**

N quatre *m inv* ◆ **on all ~s** à quatre pattes ◆ **a ~** *(Rowing)* un quatre ◆ **will you make up a ~ for bridge?** voulez-vous faire le quatrième au bridge ? ◆ **to hit a ~** *(Cricket)* marquer quatre courses *or* points ◆ **he hit three ~s** il a marqué trois fois quatre courses *or* points ; → **form** ; *for other phrases see* **six**

PRON quatre ◆ **there are ~** il y en a quatre

COMP **four-ball** ADJ, N *(Golf)* fourball *m*

four-by-four N *(= vehicle)* 4 x 4 *m*

four-colour (printing) process N *(Typ)* quadrichromie *f*

four-door ADJ *[car]* (à) quatre portes

four-engined ADJ *[plane]* quadrimoteur ◆ **~-engined plane** quadrimoteur *m*

four-eyes *‡* N binoclard(e) * *m(f)*

four-flush *‡* VI *(US)* bluffer *

four-flusher *‡* N *(US)* bluffeur * *m*, -euse * *f*

four-footed ADJ quadrupède, à quatre pattes

four-four time N *(Mus)* ◆ **in ~-~ time** à quatre/quatre

four-handed ADJ *[piano music]* à quatre mains

Four-H club N *(US) club éducatif de jeunes ruraux*

four-in-hand N *(= coach)* attelage *m* à quatre

four-leaf clover, four-leaved clover N trèfle *m* à quatre feuilles

four-legged ADJ à quatre pattes, quadrupède *(frm)*

four-legged friend N *(hum)* compagnon *m* à quatre pattes

four-letter word N *(fig)* obscénité *f*, gros mot *m* ◆ **he let out a ~-letter word** il a sorti le mot de cinq lettres *(euph)*

four-minute mile N *(Sport) course d'un mille courue en quatre minutes*

four-part ADJ *[song]* à quatre voix ; *[serial]* en quatre épisodes

four-part harmony N *(Mus)* harmonie *f* à quatre voix

four-poster N lit *m* à baldaquin *or* à colonnes

four-seater N *(= car)* (voiture *f* à) quatre places *f inv*

four-star ADJ *(= high-quality)* de première qualité N ⇒ **four-star petrol**

four-star general N *(US)* général *m* à quatre étoiles

four-star petrol N *(Brit)* super(carburant) *m*

four-stroke ADJ, N (moteur *m*) à quatre temps

four-way stop N *(US = crossroads) carrefour sans priorité autre que l'ordre d'arrivée*

four-wheel drive N *(NonC)* propulsion *f* à quatre roues motrices ; *(= car)* voiture *f* à quatre roues motrices ◆ **with ~-wheel drive** à quatre roues motrices

fourchette /fʊə'ʃet/ N fourchette *f* vulvaire

fourfold /'fɔːfəʊld/ ADJ quadruple ADV au quadruple

fourscore /'fɔːskɔːʳ/ ADJ, N *(liter)* quatre-vingts *m* ◆ **~ and ten** quatre-vingt-dix *m*

foursome /'fɔːsəm/ N *(= game)* partie *f* à quatre ; *(= two women, two men)* deux couples *mpl* ◆ **we went in a ~** nous y sommes allés à quatre

foursquare /'fɔːskweəʳ/ ADJ *(= square)* carré ; *(= firm) [attitude, decision]* ferme, inébranlable ; *(= forthright) [account, assessment]* franc (franche *f*)

fourteen /'fɔː'tiːn/ ADJ, N quatorze *m inv* ; *for phrases see* **six** PRON quatorze ◆ **there are ~** il y en a quatorze

fourteenth /'fɔː'tiːnθ/ ADJ quatorzième ◆ **Louis the Fourteenth** Louis Quatorze *or* XIV N quatorzième *mf* ; *(= fraction)* quatorzième *m* ◆ **the ~ of July** le quatorze juillet, la fête du quatorze juillet ; *for other phrases see* **sixth**

fourth /fɔːθ/ ADJ quatrième ◆ **the ~ dimension** la quatrième dimension ◆ **he lives on the ~ floor** *(Brit)* il habite au quatrième (étage) ; *(US)* il habite au cinquième (étage) ◆ **to change into ~ gear** passer en quatrième ◆ **the ~ estate** le quatrième pouvoir

N quatrième *mf* ; *(US) (= fraction)* quart *m* ; *(Mus)* quarte *f* ◆ **we need a ~ for our game of bridge** il nous faut un quatrième pour notre bridge ◆ **the Fourth of July** *(US)* le 4 juillet *(fête nationale américaine)* ; *for other phrases see* **sixth**

COMP **fourth-class matter** N *(US Post)* paquet-poste *m* ordinaire

fourth finger N annulaire *m*

fourth-rate ADJ *(fig)* de dernier ordre, de dernière catégorie

the Fourth World N *(Pol)* le quart-monde

> **FOURTH OF JULY**
>
> Le 4 juillet, ou jour de l'indépendance ("Independence Day") est la grande fête nationale des États-Unis. Marquant la signature de la déclaration d'indépendance en 1776 (et, par conséquent, la naissance du pays), cette commémoration est l'occasion de manifestations patriotiques diverses : feux d'artifice, défilés, etc.

fourthly /'fɔːθlɪ/ ADV quatrièmement, en quatrième lieu

fowl /faʊl/ N ① *(= hens etc: collective n)* volaille *f*, oiseaux *mpl* de basse-cour ; *(= one bird)* volatile *m*, volaille *f* ◆ **roast ~** volaille *f* rôtie ② †† oiseau *m* ◆ **the ~s of the air** *(liter)* les oiseaux *mpl* ; → **fish, waterfowl, wildfowl** VI ◆ **to go ~ing** chasser le gibier à plumes

COMP **fowling piece** N fusil *m* de chasse léger, carabine *f*

fowl pest N peste *f* aviaire

fox /fɒks/ N ① *(= animal)* renard *m* ◆ **a (sly) ~** *(fig)* un fin renard ② *(US ‡ = girl)* fille *f* sexy *, jolie fille *f* VT *(= puzzle: esp Brit)* rendre perplexe ; *(= deceive)* tromper, berner ◆ **I was completely ~ed** j'étais vraiment perplexe

COMP **fox cub** N renardeau *m*

fox fur N (fourrure *f* de) renard *m*

fox terrier N fox *m*, fox-terrier *m*

foxed /fɒkst/ ADJ *[book, paper]* marqué de rousseurs

foxglove /'fɒksglʌv/ N digitale *f* (pourprée)

foxhole /'fɒkshəʊl/ N terrier *m* de renard, renardière *f* ; *(Mil)* gourbi *m*

foxhound /'fɒkshaʊnd/ N chien *m* courant, foxhound *m*

foxhunt /'fɒkshʌnt/ N chasse *f* au renard

foxhunting /'fɒks,hʌntɪŋ/ N chasse *f* au renard ◆ **to go ~** aller à la chasse au renard

foxtrot /'fɒkstrɒt/ N fox-trot *m*

foxy /'fɒksɪ/ ADJ ① *(= crafty)* finaud, rusé ② *(esp US *)* ◆ **~ lady** fille *f* sexy *, jolie fille *f*

foyer /'fɔɪeɪ/ N *[of theatre]* foyer *m* ; *[of hotel]* foyer *m*, hall *m* ; *(US) [of house]* vestibule *m*, entrée *f*

FP /ef'piː/ *(US)* abbrev of **fireplug**

FPA /,efpiː'eɪ/ N (abbrev of **Family Planning Association**) Mouvement *m* pour le planning familial

fr (abbrev of **franc**) F

Fr. *(Rel)* ① (abbrev of **Father**) ◆ **R. Frost** *(on envelope)* le Révérend Père R. Frost ② abbrev of **friar**

fracas /'frækɑː/ N *(= scuffle)* rixe *f*, échauffourée *f* ; *(= noise)* fracas *m*

fractal /'fræktəl/ N *(Math)* objet *m* fractal, fractale *f*

fraction /'frækʃən/ N *(Math)* fraction *f* ; *(fig)* fraction *f*, partie *f* ◆ **for a ~ of a second** pendant une fraction de seconde ◆ **she only spends a ~ of what she earns** elle ne dépense qu'une infime partie de ce qu'elle gagne ◆ **can you move it a ~ higher/to the left?** peux-tu le déplacer un tout petit peu vers le haut/vers la gauche ? ; → **decimal, vulgar**

fractional /'frækʃənl/ ADJ *(Math)* fractionnaire ; *(fig)* infime, tout petit

COMP **fractional distillation** N distillation *f* fractionnée

fractional note N *(US)* petite coupure *f*

fractional part N fraction *f*

fractionally /'frækʃnəlɪ/ ADV un tout petit peu ◆ **to be ~ ahead** avoir un tout petit peu d'avance ◆ **to be ~ behind** être un tout petit peu en arrière, être très légèrement derrière ◆ **to move sth ~ higher/to the left** déplacer qch un tout petit peu vers le haut/vers la gauche

fractious /'frækʃəs/ ADJ *[child]* grincheux, pleurnicheur ; *[old person]* grincheux, hargneux

fracture /'fræktʃəʳ/ N fracture *f* VT fracturer ◆ **she ~d her hip** elle s'est fracturé la hanche VI se fracturer

frag *‡* /fræg/ *(US Mil)* N grenade *f* offensive VT tuer *or* blesser d'une grenade *(un officier etc)*

fragile /'frædʒaɪl/ ADJ ① *(= delicate) [object, beauty, health, economy]* fragile ; *[person]* fragile ; *(from age, ill health)* frêle ; *[truce, peace, happiness]* précaire, fragile ; *[situation]* délicat ◆ **"fragile: handle with care"** *(notice on boxes)* "fragile" ② *(* gen hum = weak)* patraque *, mal fichu *

fragility /frə'dʒɪlɪtɪ/ N fragilité *f*

fragment /'frægmənt/ N *[of china, bone]* fragment *m* ; *[of paper, metal, glass]* fragment *m*, (petit) morceau *m* ; *(from bomb)* éclat *m* ; *[of information]* élément *m* ◆ **he smashed it to ~s** il l'a réduit en miettes ◆ **the window smashed into ~s** le fenêtre s'est brisée en mille morceaux ◆ **~s of food/DNA, food/DNA ~s** fragments *mpl* de nourriture/d'ADN ◆ **~s of conversation** bribes *fpl* de conversation VT /fræg'ment/ fragmenter ; *[organization, system]* faire éclater VI /fræg'ment/ se fragmenter ; *[organization, system]* éclater

fragmental /fræg'mentl/ ADJ fragmentaire ; *(Geol)* clastique

fragmentary /'frægməntərɪ/ ADJ fragmentaire

fragmentation /,frægmen'teɪʃən/ N fragmentation *f* COMP **fragmentation grenade** N *(Mil)* grenade *f* à fragmentation

fragmented /fræg'mentɪd/ ADJ *[story, version]* morcelé, fragmentaire ; *[organization, system]* éclaté

fragrance /'freɪgrəns/ N *(= smell)* parfum *m*, senteur *f* ; *(= perfume)* parfum *m* ◆ **a new ~ by Chanel** un nouveau parfum de Chanel COMP **fragrance-free** ADJ sans parfum

fragrant /'freɪgrənt/ ADJ *[flowers, herbs, spices, food]* parfumé, odorant ◆ **the air was ~ with the scent of roses** le parfum des roses embaumait l'air

fraidy-cat * /'freɪdɪkæt/ ADJ *(US: baby talk)* trouillard(e) *‡ *m(f)*, poule *f* mouillée

frail /freɪl/ ADJ *[person]* frêle ; *[object]* frêle, fragile ; *[health, happiness, ego]* fragile ; *[hope]* faible

frailty /'freɪltɪ/ N *[of person, health, happiness]* fragilité *f* ; *(morally)* faiblesse *f*

frame /freɪm/ N ① *(= supporting structure) [of building]* charpente *f* ; *[of bicycle]* cadre *m* ; *[of boat]* carcasse *f* ; *[of car]* châssis *m* ; *[of racket]* armature *f*, cadre *m*

② *(= border, surround) [of picture]* cadre *m*, encadrement *m* ; *[of embroidery, tapestry]* cadre *m* ; *[of window, door]* châssis *m*, chambranle *m*

③ ◆ **~s** *[of spectacles]* monture *f*

④ *(Cine)* photogramme *m* ; *(Phot)* image *f*

⑤ *[of human, animal] (= body)* corps *m* ; *(= skeleton)* ossature *f* ◆ **his large ~** son grand corps

⑥ *(fig = structure)* cadre *m* ◆ **this proposal is beyond the ~ of the peace agreement** cette proposition dépasse le cadre du traité de paix ◆ **the new ~ of government** la nouvelle structure du gouvernement ◆ **~ of mind** humeur *f*, disposition *f* d'esprit ◆ **I'm not in the right ~ of mind for this job** *or* **to do this job** je ne suis pas d'humeur à faire ce travail ◆ **to be in a positive/relaxed ~ of mind** être positif/décontracté ◆ **~ of reference** *(Math, fig)* système *m* de référence ◆ **to be in the ~ for sth** *(= in the running)* être dans la course pour qch

⑦ *(in garden)* châssis *m*, cloche *f*

⑧ *(‡ = set-up:* also **frame-up***)* coup *m* monté

⑨ *(for weaving)* métier *m*

VT 1 *[+ picture]* encadrer ◆ **he appeared ~d in the doorway** il apparut dans l'encadrement de la porte ◆ **her face was ~d by a mass of curls** son visage était encadré par une profusion de boucles ◆ **a lake ~d by trees** un lac entouré d'arbres *or* encadré par des arbres

2 *(= construct) [+ house]* bâtir *or* construire la charpente de

3 *(= conceive) [+ idea, plan]* concevoir, formuler ; *[+ plot]* combiner ; *[+ sentence]* construire ; *[+ question, issue]* formuler ◆ **she ~d the issue rather differently** elle a formulé la question assez différemment ◆ **the debate is being ~d in terms of civil rights** on aborde la question du point de vue des droits civils

4 *(Phot)* ◆ **to ~ a subject** cadrer un sujet

5 (⁑ : also **frame up**) **to ~ sb (up), to have sb ~d** monter un coup contre qn *(pour faire porter l'accusation contre lui)* ◆ **he claimed he had been ~d** il a prétendu être victime d'un coup monté ◆ **I've been framed !** c'est un coup monté !

COMP **frame house** N maison *f* à charpente de bois

frame rucksack N sac *m* à dos à armature

frame tent N tente *f* à armature intégrée

frame-up⁑ N coup *m* monté, machination *f*

frameless /ˈfreɪmlɪs/ ADJ *[spectacles]* sans monture

framer /ˈfreɪməʳ/ N (also **picture framer**) encadreur *m*, euse *f*

framework /ˈfreɪmwɜːk/ N 1 *(lit = frame) (gen)* structure *f* ; *(for building, furniture)* charpente *f* 2 *(fig = basis)* cadre *m* ◆ **within the ~ of ...** dans le cadre de ... ◆ **to establish the legal ~ for sth** établir le cadre légal de qch ◆ **the ~ of society** la structure de la société COMP **framework agreement** N accord-cadre *m*

framing /ˈfreɪmɪŋ/ N 1 *(= frame of picture, photo)* encadrement *m* 2 *(= composition of picture)* cadrage *m*

franc /fræŋk/ N franc *m* COMP **franc area** N zone *f* franc

France /frɑːns/ N France *f* ◆ **in ~** en France

franchise /ˈfræntʃaɪz/ N 1 *(Pol)* droit *m* de vote 2 *(Comm)* franchise *f* VT franchiser

franchisee /ˌfræntʃaɪˈziː/ N franchisé(e) *m(f)*

franchiser /ˈfræntʃaɪzəʳ/ N franchiseur *m*

Francis /ˈfrɑːnsɪs/ N François *m*, Francis *m* ◆ **Saint ~ of Assisi** saint François d'Assise

Franciscan /frænˈsɪskən/ ADJ, N franciscain *m*

francium /ˈfrænsiəm/ N francium *m*

Franco* /ˈfræŋkəʊ/ ADJ *(Can)* canadien français

franco /ˈfræŋkəʊ/ ADV *(Comm)* franco ◆ **~ frontier/domicile** franco frontière/domicile

Franco- /ˈfræŋkəʊ/ PREF franco- ◆ **~British** franco-britannique

francophile /ˈfræŋkəʊfaɪl/ ADJ, N francophile *mf*

francophobe /ˈfræŋkəʊfəʊb/ ADJ, N francophobe *mf*

francophone /ˈfræŋkəʊfəʊn/ ADJ, N francophone *mf*

frangipane /ˈfrændʒɪpeɪn/, **frangipani** /ˌfrændʒɪˈpɑːnɪ/ N (pl **frangipanes** *or* **frangipane**) *(= perfume, pastry)* frangipane *f* ; *(= shrub)* frangipanier *m*

Franglais* /ˈfrɑ̃ɡle/ N franglais *m*

Frank /fræŋk/ N *(Hist)* Franc *m*, Franque *f*

frank¹ /fræŋk/ ADJ *[person, comment, admission]* franc (franche *f*) ◆ **to be ~ (with you) ...** pour être franc ... ◆ **I'll be quite ~ with you** je vais être très franc avec vous

frank² /fræŋk/ VT *[+ letter]* affranchir COMP **franking machine** N machine *f* à affranchir

frank³* /fræŋk/ N *(US = sausage)* (saucisse *f* de) Francfort *f*

Frankenstein /ˈfræŋkənstaɪn/ N Frankenstein *m*

frankfurter /ˈfræŋkˌfɜːtəʳ/ N *(= sausage)* saucisse *f* de Francfort

Frankfurt(-on-Main) /ˈfræŋkfɜːtˌɒnˈmeɪn/ N Francfort(-sur-le-Main)

frankincense /ˈfræŋkɪnsens/ N encens *m*

Frankish /ˈfræŋkɪʃ/ ADJ *(Hist)* franc (franque *f*) N *(= language)* francique *m*, langue *f* franque

frankly /ˈfræŋklɪ/ ADV franchement ◆ **(quite) ~, I don't give a damn*** franchement, je m'en fiche complètement ◆ **the book deals ~ with the subject of Alzheimer's** le livre parle sans détours de la maladie d'Alzheimer

frankness /ˈfræŋknɪs/ N franchise *f*

frantic /ˈfræntɪk/ ADJ *[person]* dans tous ses états ; *[shout, phone call]* désespéré ; *[search]* affolé ; *[desire, pace]* effréné ; *[effort, activity, rush]* frénétique ; *[week, day]* fou (folle *f*) ◆ **to become** *or* **get ~** s'affoler ◆ **~ with worry** fou (folle *f*) d'inquiétude ◆ **he/it drives me ~*** il/ça me rend dingue*

frantically /ˈfræntɪkəlɪ/ ADV *[try, search]* désespérément ; *[work, write]* comme un(e) forcené(e) ; *[scramble]* comme un fou *or* une folle ◆ **to be ~ busy** avoir un boulot* fou, être débordé ◆ **to wave ~ to sb** faire des gestes frénétiques de la main à qn

frappé /ˈfræpeɪ/ N *(US)* boisson *f* glacée

frat* /fræt/ N *(US Univ)* ⇒ **fraternity noun 1**

fraternal /frəˈtɜːnl/ ADJ fraternel ◆ **~ twins** faux jumeaux *mpl*

fraternity /frəˈtɜːnɪtɪ/ N 1 *(NonC)* fraternité *f* ; *(US Univ)* association *f* d'étudiants ; → SORORITY, FRATERNITY 2 *(= group)* confrérie *f* ◆ **the hunting ~** la confrérie des chasseurs ◆ **the yachting ~** le monde de la navigation de plaisance ◆ **the criminal ~** la pègre COMP **fraternity pin** N *(US Univ)* insigne *m* de confrérie

fraternization /ˌfrætənaɪˈzeɪʃən/ N fraternisation *f*

fraternize /ˈfrætənaɪz/ VI fraterniser *(with* avec)

fratricidal /ˌfrætrɪˈsaɪdl/ ADJ fratricide

fratricide /ˈfrætrɪsaɪd/ N *(= act)* fratricide *m* ; *(frm, liter = person)* fratricide *mf*

fraud /frɔːd/ N 1 *(= criminal deception)* fraude *f*, imposture *f* ; *(financial)* escroquerie *f* ; *(= misappropriation)* détournement *m* de fonds ; *(Jur)* fraude *f* ◆ **~ and deception** abus *m* de confiance ◆ **tax ~** fraude *f* fiscale ◆ **credit card ~** escroquerie *f* à la carte de crédit 2 *(= person)* imposteur *m*, fraudeur *m*, -euse *f* ; *(= object)* attrape-nigaud *m* ◆ **he turned out to be a ~** il s'est révélé être un imposteur ◆ **you're such a ~! You haven't even got a temperature!** quel simulateur ! Tu n'as même pas de fièvre ! ◆ **the document was a complete ~** le document avait été monté de toutes pièces COMP **Fraud Squad** N *(Police)* service *m* de la répression des fraudes

fraudster /ˈfrɔːdstəʳ/ N fraudeur *m*, -euse *f*

fraudulence /ˈfrɔːdjʊləns/, **fraudulency** /ˈfrɔːdjʊlənsɪ/ N caractère *m* frauduleux

fraudulent /ˈfrɔːdjʊlənt/ ADJ frauduleux COMP **fraudulent conversion** N *(Jur)* malversation *f*, détournement *m* de fonds

fraudulently /ˈfrɔːdjʊləntlɪ/ ADV frauduleusement

fraught /frɔːt/ ADJ 1 *(= filled)* ◆ **to be ~ with difficulty/danger** présenter de multiples difficultés/dangers ◆ **~ with tension** lourd de tension 2 *(= anxious) [person]* tendu, angoissé ; *[situation, meeting, relationship, morning]* tendu

fray¹ /freɪ/ N rixe *f*, échauffourée *f* ; *(Mil)* combat *m* ◆ **ready for the ~** *(lit, fig)* prêt à se battre ◆ **to enter the ~** *(fig)* descendre dans l'arène, entrer en lice

fray² /freɪ/ VT *[+ cloth, garment]* effilocher, effiler ; *[+ cuff]* user le bord de, râper ; *[+ trousers]* user le bas de, râper ; *[+ rope]* user, raguer *(Naut)* ◆ **tempers were getting ~ed** on commençait à perdre patience *or* s'énerver ◆ **my nerves are ~ed** je suis à bout (de nerfs) VI *[cloth, garment]* s'effilocher, s'effiler ; *[rope]* s'user, se raguer *(Naut)* ◆ **his sleeve was ~ing at the cuff** sa manche était usée *or* râpée au poignet ◆ **to ~ at** *or* **around the edges*** *(fig) [marriage, alliance]* battre de l'aile ◆ **he looked rather ~ed around the edges*** il ne semblait pas en grande forme

frazzle* /ˈfræzl/ N 1 ◆ **worn to a ~** claqué*, crevé* ◆ **she's worn to a ~ getting ready for the competition** la préparation de la compétition la crève* ◆ **she had worn herself to a ~** elle s'était crevée à la tâche* 2 ◆ **burnt to a ~** carbonisé, calciné VT 1 *(= exhaust)* crever* ◆ **my brain's ~d!** j'ai la tête farcie !* ◆ **his nerves were ~d** il était à bout (de nerfs) 2 *(= burn)* (faire) carboniser, (faire) cramer*

FRCP /ˌefɑːsiːˈpiː/ N *(Brit)* (abbrev of **Fellow of the Royal College of Physicians**) *membre de l'Académie royale de médecine*

FRCS /ˌefɑːsiːˈes/ N *(Brit)* (abbrev of **Fellow of the Royal College of Surgeons**) *membre de l'Académie royale de chirurgie*

freak /friːk/ N 1 *(= abnormal person or animal)* monstre *m*, phénomène *m* ; *(= eccentric)* phénomène *m* ; *(= absurd idea)* lubie *f*, idée *f* saugrenue *or* farfelue* ◆ **~ of nature** accident *m* de la nature ◆ **his winning was really just a ~** il n'a gagné que grâce à un hasard extraordinaire

2 (⁑ *= fanatic)* ◆ **he's an acid ~** il est accro* à l'acide ◆ **a jazz ~** un(e) dingue* *or* un(e) fana* du jazz ◆ **a health food ~** un(e) fana* de l'alimentation naturelle *or* de la bouffe bio* ◆ **a speed ~** un(e) fana* de la vitesse

ADJ *[storm, weather]* exceptionnel ; *[error]* bizarre ; *[victory]* inattendu

COMP **freak-out**⁑ N défonce⁑ *f*

freak show N exhibition *f* de monstres *(dans une foire)*

VI ⇒ **freak out 1,2 vt sep**

► **freak out**⁑ VI 1 *(= get angry)* piquer une de ces crises*

2 *(= panic)* flipper*

3 *(= get high on drugs)* se défoncer⁑ ◆ **to ~ out on LSD** se défoncer⁑ au LSD

VT SEP ◆ **to freak sb out** *(= surprise)* en boucher un coin à qn* ; *(= make angry)* foutre qn en boule⁑ *or* en pétard⁑ ; *(= panic)* faire flipper qn*

N ◆ **freak-out**⁑ → **freak**

freaking⁑ /ˈfriːkɪŋ/ *(US)* ADV foutrement⁑ ◆ **it's ~ hot in here** il fait vachement* chaud ici ADJ foutu⁑

freakish /ˈfriːkɪʃ/ ADJ *(gen)* bizarre ; *[weather]* anormal ; *[idea]* saugrenu, insolite

freakishly /ˈfriːkɪʃlɪ/ ADV *[hot, cold]* anormalement

freaky* /ˈfriːkɪ/ ADJ bizarre

freckle /ˈfrekl/ N tache *f* de rousseur VI se couvrir de taches de rousseur

freckled /ˈfrekld/ ADJ plein de taches de rousseur, taché de son

Frederick /ˈfredrɪk/ N Frédéric *m*

free /friː/

1 ADJECTIVE	4 NOUN
2 ADVERB	5 COMPOUNDS
3 TRANSITIVE VERB	6 PHRASAL VERB

1 - ADJECTIVE

1 = at liberty, not captive or tied *[person, animal]* libre ♦ **they tied him up but he managed to get ~** ils l'ont attaché mais il a réussi à se libérer ♦ **to go ~** *[prisoner]* être relâché, être mis en liberté ♦ **all these dangerous people still go ~** tous ces gens dangereux sont encore en liberté ♦ **to set a prisoner ~** libérer *or* mettre en liberté un prisonnier ♦ **they had to cut the driver ~ from the wreckage** ils ont dû dégager le conducteur du véhicule accidenté ♦ **he left the end of the rope ~** il a laissé libre le bout de la corde ♦ **she opened the door with her ~ hand** elle a ouvert la porte avec sa main libre ♦ **to have one's hands ~** *(lit, fig)* avoir les mains libres ♦ **to have a ~ hand to do sth** *(fig)* avoir carte blanche pour faire qch ♦ **to give sb a ~ hand** donner carte blanche à qn

2 = unrestricted, unhindered *[person]* libre ; *[choice, access]* libre *before n* ♦ **~ elections** élections *fpl* libres ♦ **~ press** presse *f* libre ♦ **~ translation** traduction *f* libre ♦ **the fishing is ~** la pêche est autorisée ♦ **to be/get ~ of sb** se débarrasser/être débarrassé de qn ♦ **~ and easy** décontracté, désinvolte ♦ **as ~ as a bird** *or* **(the) air** *(Brit)* libre comme l'air ; see also **compounds**

♦ **(to be) free to do sth** ♦ **I'm not ~ to do it** je ne suis pas libre de le faire ♦ **he was ~ to refuse** il était libre de refuser ♦ **you're ~ to choose** vous êtes libre de choisir, libre à vous de choisir ♦ **I am leaving you ~ to do as you please** je vous laisse libre de faire comme bon vous semble, je vous laisse carte blanche ♦ **her aunt's death set her ~ to follow her own career** la mort de sa tante lui a donné toute liberté pour poursuivre sa carrière

♦ **to feel free (to do sth)** ♦ **can I borrow your pen? – feel ~*** est-ce que je peux vous emprunter votre stylo ? – je vous en prie *or* faites ♦ **please feel ~ to ask questions** n'hésitez pas à poser des questions ♦ **a school where children feel ~ to express themselves** une école où les enfants se sentent libres de s'exprimer

♦ **free from** *or* **of** *(= without)* ♦ **to be ~ from** *or* **of care/responsibility** être dégagé de tout souci/de toute responsabilité ♦ **to be ~ from** *or* **of pain** ne pas souffrir ♦ **~ from the usual ruling** non soumis au règlement habituel ♦ **a surface ~ from** *or* **of dust** une surface dépoussiérée ♦ **area ~ of malaria** zone *f* non touchée par la malaria ♦ **a world ~ of nuclear weapons** un monde sans armes nucléaires *or* dénucléarisé ♦ **the elections have been ~ of violence** les élections se sont déroulées sans violence ♦ **the company is now ~ of government control** la société n'est plus contrôlée par le gouvernement ♦ **~ of tax** *or* **duty** exonéré, hors taxe

3 Pol = autonomous, independent *[country, state]* libre ; *[government]* autonome, libre ♦ **the Free French** *(Hist)* les Français *mpl* libres ♦ **the ~ world** le monde libre ♦ **it's a ~ country!** *(fig)* on est en république ! *, on peut faire ce qu'on veut ici !

4 = costing nothing *[object, ticket, sample]* gratuit ♦ **he got a ~ ticket** il a eu un billet gratuit ♦ **"free mug with each towel"** "une chope gratuite pour tout achat d'une serviette" ♦ **admission ~**, **~ admission** entrée *f* gratuite *or* libre ♦ **it's ~ of charge** c'est gratuit ; see also **compounds** ♦ **~ delivery, delivery ~** *(Comm)* livraison *f* gratuite, franco de port ♦ **~ delivered at dock** *(Comm)* livraison *f* franco à quai ♦ **as a ~ gift** *(Comm)* en prime, en cadeau ♦ **~ offer** *(Comm)* offre *f* gratuite ♦ **~ sample** *(Comm)* échantillon *m* gratuit ♦ **there's no such thing as a ~ lunch** tout se paie ♦ **to get a ~ ride*** *(fig)* profiter de la situation

5 = not occupied *[room, seat, hour, person]* libre ♦ **there are only two ~ seats left** il ne reste que deux places de libre ♦ **is this table ~?** cette table est-elle libre ? ♦ **I will be ~ at 2 o'clock** je serai libre à 14 heures

6 = lavish, profuse généreux, prodigue ♦ **to be ~ with one's money** dépenser son argent sans compter ♦ **you're very ~ with your advice** *(iro)* vous êtes particulièrement prodigue de conseils *(iro)* ♦ **he makes ~ with all my things** il ne se gêne pas pour se servir de mes affaires ♦ **to make ~ † with a woman** prendre des libertés *or* se permettre des familiarités avec une femme

7 Ling *[morpheme]* libre

8 Chem *[gas]* libre, non combiné

2 - ADVERB

1 = without payment *[give, get, travel]* gratuitement, gratis* ♦ **we got in ~** *or* **for ~*** nous sommes entrés gratuitement *or* gratis* ♦ **they'll send it ~ on request** ils l'enverront gratuitement sur demande

2 = without restraint *[run about]* en liberté

3 expressing release ♦ **the screw had worked itself ~** la vis s'était desserrée ♦ **to pull ~** se dégager, se libérer ♦ **to wriggle ~** *[person]* se libérer en se tortillant ; *[fish]* se libérer en frétillant

3 - TRANSITIVE VERB

1 = liberate *[+ nation, slave]* affranchir, libérer

2 = untie *[+ person, animal]* détacher ; *[+ knot]* défaire, dénouer ; *[+ tangle]* débrouiller

3 = release *[+ caged animal, prisoner]* libérer ; *[+ person] (from wreckage)* dégager, désincarcérer ; *(from burden)* soulager, débarrasser ; *(from tax)* exempter, exonérer ♦ **to ~ o.s. from** *(lit, fig)* se débarrasser de, se libérer de ♦ **to ~ sb from anxiety** libérer *or* délivrer qn de l'angoisse

4 = unblock *[+ pipe]* débloquer, déboucher

4 - NOUN

♦ **the land of the ~** le pays de la liberté

5 - COMPOUNDS

free agent N ♦ **to be a ~ agent** avoir toute liberté d'action
free alongside quay ADJ *(Comm)* franco à quai
free alongside ship ADJ *(Comm)* franco le long du navire
free association N *(Psych)* libre association *f*
Free Church *(Brit)* N église *f* non-conformiste ADJ non-conformiste
free climbing N escalade *f* libre
free clinic N *(US Med)* dispensaire *m*
free collective bargaining N négociation *f* salariale libre *(sans limite imposée par l'État)*
free(-)diving N plongée *f* libre
free enterprise N libre entreprise *f*
free-enterprise economy N économie *f* de marché
free fall N *(Space, Parachuting, Econ)* chute *f* libre ♦ **in ~ fall** en chute libre ♦ **to go into ~ fall** entamer une chute libre
free fight N mêlée *f* générale
free-fire zone N *(Mil)* secteur *m or* zone *f* de tir libre
free flight N *(in plane)* vol *m* libre
free-floating ADJ *(in water)* qui flotte librement ; *(in outer space)* qui flotte librement dans l'espace ; *(fig) [person]* sans attaches
free-for-all N mêlée *f* générale
free hit N *(Sport)* coup *m* franc
free house N *(Brit)* pub *m (qui n'appartient pas à une chaîne)* ; → PUB
free kick N *(Sport)* coup *m* franc
free labour N *(= non-union)* main-d'œuvre *f* non syndiquée
free love N amour *m* libre
free market, free-market economy N économie *f* de marché
free-marketeer N partisan *m* de l'économie de marché
free of charge ADV *(Comm)* gratuitement
free on board ADJ *(Comm)* franco à bord
free on rail ADJ *(Comm)* franco wagon
free period N *(Educ)* heure *f* de libre *or* sans cours
free port N port *m* franc
free radical N *(Chem)* radical *m* libre
free-range egg N œuf *m* de poule élevée en plein air
free-range poultry N poulets *mpl* élevés en plein air
free shot N lancer *m* franc, coup *m* franc
free speech N liberté *f* de parole
free spirit N esprit *m* libre
free-spirited ADJ *[person]* libre d'esprit ; *[ways]* libre
free-standing ADJ *[furniture]* sur pied
the Free State N *(US)* le Maryland
free-styling N *(Ski)* ski *m* acrobatique
free throw N *(US Sport)* lancer *m* franc
free-to-air ADJ *(TV)* gratuit
free trade N *(Econ)* libre-échange *m*
free-trader N *(Econ)* libre-échangiste *m*
free-trade zone N *(Econ)* zone *f* franche
free verse N *(Literat)* vers *m* libre
free vote N vote *m* en conscience *(sans consigne de vote)*
free will N *(Philos)* libre arbitre *m* ♦ **he did it of his own ~ will** il l'a fait de son propre gré
free-will gift N don *m* volontaire
free-will offering N offrande *f* volontaire

6 - PHRASAL VERB

► **free up** VT SEP *[+ money, resources]* dégager ; *[+ staff]* libérer ♦ **to ~ up some time to do sth** trouver du temps pour faire qch

-free /friː/ ADJ *(in compounds)* ♦ **salt-free** sans sel ♦ **stress-free** sans stress ♦ **trouble-free** sans problèmes

freebase* /ˈfriːbeɪs/ *(Drugs)* N freebase‡ *m (forme de cocaïne purifiée)* VT ♦ **to ~ cocaine** fumer du freebase‡ VI fumer du freebase‡

freebie‡ /ˈfriːbɪ/ N *(= free gift)* (petit) cadeau *m* ; *(= free trip)* voyage *m* gratis* *or* à l'œil* ; *(= free newspaper)* journal *m* gratis* ADJ gratis*

freeboard /ˈfriːbɔːd/ N (hauteur *f* de) franc-bord *m*

freebooter /ˈfriːˌbuːtəʳ/ N *(= buccaneer)* pirate *m* ; *(Hist)* flibustier *m*

freedom /ˈfriːdəm/ N liberté *f* ♦ **~ of action** liberté *f* d'action *or* d'agir ♦ **~ of association/choice/information/speech** liberté *f* d'association/de choix/d'information/de parole ♦ **~ of the press** liberté *f* de la presse ♦ **~ of worship** liberté *f* religieuse *or* du culte ♦ **~ of the seas** franchise *f* des mers ♦ **to give sb ~ to do as he wishes** laisser les mains libres à qn, donner carte blanche à qn ♦ **to speak with ~** parler en toute liberté ♦ **~ from care/responsibility** le fait d'être dégagé de tout souci/de toute responsabilité ♦ **to give sb the ~ of a city** nommer qn citoyen d'honneur d'une ville ♦ **he gave me the ~ of his house** il m'a laissé la libre disposition de sa maison

COMP **freedom fighter** N guérillero *m*, partisan *m*
Freedom of Information Act N *(US Jur)* loi *f* sur la liberté d'information

FREEDOM OF INFORMATION ACT

Aux États-Unis, la loi sur la liberté d'information ou **Freedom of Information Act** oblige les organismes fédéraux à divulguer les informations qu'ils détiennent à quiconque en fait la demande, sauf pour des raisons spécifiques liées au secret-défense, aux secrets de fabrication ou à la protection de la vie privée. Cette loi, particulièrement utile pour les journalistes, a permis la publication de renseignements jusqu'alors gardés secrets sur certaines affaires délicates comme la guerre du Vietnam et les activités d'espionnage illégales du FBI.

Freefone ® /ˈfriːfəʊn/ N *(Brit Telec)* ≈ numéro *m* vert ® VT ◆ **to find out more, freefone 77 88 99** pour plus de renseignements, appelez le 77 88 99 (numéro vert) *or* appelez notre numéro vert 77 88 99

freehand /ˈfriːhænd/ ADJ, ADV à main levée

freehold /ˈfriːhəʊld/ *(Brit)* N propriété *f* foncière libre *(à perpétuité)* ADV en propriété libre

freeholder /ˈfriːhəʊldəʳ/ N *(Brit)* propriétaire *mf* foncier (-ière *f*) *(à perpétuité)*

freelance /ˈfriːlɑːns/ N free-lance *mf*, collaborateur *m*, -trice *f* indépendant(e) ; *(= journalist)* pigiste *mf* ADJ *[journalist, designer, player]* indépendant, free-lance *inv* ; *[work, writing]* en indépendant, en free-lance VI travailler en free-lance *or* en indépendant ADV *[work]* en free-lance, en indépendant ◆ **to go ~** se mettre à travailler en free-lance *or* en indépendant

freelancer /ˈfriːlɑːnsəʳ/ N free-lance *mf*, collaborateur *m*, -trice *f* indépendant(e) ; *(= journalist)* pigiste *mf*

freeload * /ˈfriːləʊd/ VI vivre en parasite

freeloader * /ˈfriːləʊdəʳ/ N parasite *m*, pique-assiette *mf*

freely /ˈfriːlɪ/ ADV 1 *(= unrestrictedly) [travel, elect]* en toute liberté ; *[operate]* librement, en toute liberté ; *[express, translate, adapt]* librement ; *[talk, speak]* franchement, librement ◆ **to move ~** *[person]* se déplacer en toute liberté ; *[machine part]* jouer librement ◆ **traffic is moving** *or* **flowing ~** la circulation est fluide ◆ **to be ~ available** *[drugs, commodity, help, information]* être facile à trouver 2 *(= willingly) [give, share]* généreusement ; *[lend, admit]* volontiers 3 *(= liberally) [spend]* sans compter ; *[use, perspire]* abondamment ◆ **the wine was flowing ~** le vin coulait à flots

freeman /ˈfriːmən/ N (pl **-men**) *(Hist)* homme *m* libre ◆ **~ of a city** citoyen *m* d'honneur d'une ville

freemason /ˈfriːˌmeɪsn/ N franc-maçon *m*

freemasonry /ˈfriːˌmeɪsənrɪ/ N franc-maçonnerie *f*

Freephone ® /ˈfriːfəʊn/ ⇒ **Freefone**

Freepost ® /ˈfriːpəʊst/ N *(Brit)* port *m* payé

freesia /ˈfriːzɪə/ N freesia *m*

freestyle /ˈfriːstaɪl/ N (also **freestyle swimming**) nage *f* libre

freethinker /ˌfriːˈθɪŋkəʳ/ N libre-penseur *m*, -euse *f*

freethinking /ˌfriːˈθɪŋkɪŋ/ ADJ libre penseur N libre pensée *f*

freeware /ˈfriːweəʳ/ N logiciel *m* gratuit

freeway /ˈfriːweɪ/ N *(US)* autoroute *f* *(sans péage)* ; → ROADS

freewheel /ˌfriːˈwiːl/ *(Brit)* VI *[cyclist]* se mettre en roue libre, être en roue libre ; *[motorist]* rouler au point mort N *[of bicycle]* roue *f* libre

freewheeler /ˌfriːˈwiːləʳ/ N *(fig)* insouciant(e) *m(f)*

freewheeling /ˌfriːˈwiːlɪŋ/ ADJ *[person]* insouciant ; *[scheme, lifestyle]* peu orthodoxe ; *[discussion]* libre

freeze /friːz/ (pret **froze**, ptp **frozen**) VI 1 *[liquid] (lit)* geler ; *[food]* se congeler ◆ **it will ~ hard tonight** il gèlera dur cette nuit ◆ **to ~ to death** mourir de froid ◆ **the lake has frozen** le lac est gelé ◆ **the windscreen was frozen** le pare-brise était givré ◆ **this dish ~s well** ce plat se congèle bien ◆ **the fallen apples had frozen to the ground** les pommes tombées étaient collées au sol par le gel

2 *(fig = stop)* se figer ◆ **he froze (in his tracks** *or* **to the spot)** il est resté figé sur place ◆ **the smile froze on his lips** son sourire s'est figé sur ses lèvres ◆ **~!** pas un geste ! ; see also **freezing, frozen**

VT 1 *[+ liquid]* geler ; *[+ food]* congeler ; *(industrially)* surgeler ◆ **she froze him with a look** elle lui a lancé un regard qui l'a glacé sur place

2 *(= stop, block) [+ assets, credit, wages]* geler, bloquer ; *[+ prices, bank account]* bloquer ◆ **can you ~ it?** *(Cine = hold image)* tu peux t'arrêter sur l'image ? ; see also **frozen**

N 1 *(= cold snap)* temps *m* de gelée, gel *m* ◆ **the big ~ of 1948** le grand gel de 1948

2 *[of prices, wages, credit]* blocage *m*, gel *m* ◆ **a wage(s)/price(s) ~, a ~ on wages/prices** un blocage *or* gel des salaires/des prix ◆ **a ~ on new staff appointments** un gel de l'embauche ◆ **a ~ on nuclear weapons testing/programmes** un gel des essais nucléaires/des programmes d'armes nucléaires

COMP **freeze-dry** VT lyophiliser

freeze-frame N *[of film, video]* arrêt *m* sur image

freeze-up N gel *m*

▸ **freeze out** VT SEP ◆ **to freeze sb out (from sth)** tenir qn à l'écart (de qch)

▸ **freeze over** VI *[lake, river]* geler ; *[windscreen]* givrer ◆ **the river has frozen over** la rivière est gelée

▸ **freeze up** VI *[pipes, lake, river]* geler

VT SEP ◆ **the pipes were frozen up last winter** les conduits ont gelé l'hiver dernier

N ◆ **freeze-up** → **freeze**

freezer /ˈfriːzəʳ/ N 1 *(domestic)* congélateur *m* ; *(industrial)* surgélateur *m* 2 *(in fridge:* also **freezer compartment***)* *(one-star)* freezer *m* ; *(two-star)* conservateur *m* ; *(three-star)* congélateur *m* 3 *(US = ice cream maker)* sorbetière *f*

COMP **freezer bag** N sac *m* congélation

freezer centre N magasin *m* de surgelés

freezer container N barquette *f* congélation

freezer film N plastique *m* spécial congélation

freezer foil N aluminium *m* spécial congélation

freezer tray N bac *m* à glace

freezing /ˈfriːzɪŋ/ ADJ 1 *(= icy) [temperatures, weather, wind, rain, night]* glacial 2 (also **freezing cold**) *[person]* gelé ; *[water, room]* glacial ◆ **my hands are ~** j'ai les mains gelées ◆ **it's ~** il fait un froid glacial ◆ **it's ~ in here** on gèle ici ◆ **in the ~ cold** dans le froid glacial N *[of food]* congélation *f*, gel *m*

COMP **freezing fog** N brouillard *m* givrant

freezing point N point *m* de congélation ◆ **below ~ point** au-dessous de zéro (centigrade)

freezing rain N pluie *f* verglaçante

freight /freɪt/ N *(= transporting)* transport *m* ; *(= price, cost)* fret *m* ; *(= goods moved)* fret *m*, cargaison *f* ; *(esp Brit = ship's cargo)* fret *m* ◆ **~ paid** *(Comm)* port *m* payé ◆ **~ and delivery paid** *(US Comm)* franco de port ◆ **to send sth by ~** faire transporter qch ◆ **air ~** transport *m* par avion, fret *m* aérien VT *[+ goods]* transporter

COMP **freight agent** N transitaire *mf*

freight car N *(US Rail)* wagon *m* de marchandises, fourgon *m*

freight charges NPL frais *mpl* de transport, fret *m*

freight forwarder N transporteur *m*

freight note N bordereau *m* d'expédition

freight plane N avion-cargo *m*, avion *m* de fret

freight terminal N terminal *m* de fret

freight train N train *m* de marchandises

freight yard N dépôt *m* des marchandises

freightage /ˈfreɪtɪdʒ/ N *(= charge)* fret *m* ; *(= goods)* fret *m*, cargaison *f*

freighter /ˈfreɪtəʳ/ N *(= ship)* cargo *m*, navire *m* de charge ; *(= plane)* avion-cargo *m*, avion *m* de fret

freightliner /ˈfreɪtˌlaɪnəʳ/ N train *m* de marchandises en conteneurs

French /frentʃ/ ADJ *(gen)* français ; *[ambassador, embassy, monarch]* de France ; *[teacher]* de français ◆ **the ~ way of life** la vie française ◆ **~ cooking** la cuisine française ◆ **the ~ people** les Français *mpl* ; see also **comp**

N *(= language)* français *m* ◆ **excuse** *or* **pardon my ~** * *(apologizing for swearing)* passez-moi l'expression

NPL **the French** les Français *mpl* ; → **free**

COMP **the French Academy** N l'Académie *f* française

French bean N *(Brit)* haricot *m* vert

French bread N pain *m* à la française

French Canadian ADJ canadien français N *(= person)* Canadien(ne) français(e) *m(f)* ; *(= language variety)* français *m* canadien

French chalk N craie *f* de tailleur

French cricket N *forme simplifiée du cricket jouée par les enfants*

French door N *(US)* porte-fenêtre *f*

French dressing N *(Culin) (= vinaigrette)* vinaigrette *f* ; *(US) (= salad cream)* sauce *f* (à) salade

French Equatorial Africa N Afrique *f* équatoriale française

French fried potatoes, French fries NPL (pommes *fpl* de terre) frites *fpl*

French-fry VT *(US)* frire à la friteuse

French Guiana N Guyane *f* française

French horn N *(Mus)* cor *m* d'harmonie

French kiss ‡ N baiser *m* profond *or* avec la langue, patin ‡ *m* VT embrasser avec la langue, rouler un patin ‡ à VI s'embrasser avec la langue, se rouler un patin ‡

French knickers NPL (petite) culotte-caleçon *f*

French leave N ◆ **to take ~ leave** filer à l'anglaise *

French letter * N *(= contraceptive)* capote *f* anglaise *

French loaf N baguette *f* *(de pain)*

French marigold N œillet *m* d'Inde

French pastry N pâtisserie *f*

French pleat N *(Hairdressing)* chignon *m* banane

French polish N *(Brit)* vernis *m* (à l'alcool)

French-polish VT *(Brit)* vernir (à l'alcool)

the French Riviera N la Côte d'Azur

French seam N *(Sewing)* couture *f* anglaise

French-speaking ADJ francophone ; → **Switzerland**

French stick N ⇒ **French loaf**

French toast N *(Brit) (= toast)* pain *m* grillé d'un seul côté ; *(= fried bread in egg)* pain *m* perdu

French West Africa N Afrique *f* occidentale française

French window N porte-fenêtre *f*

Frenchify /ˈfrentʃɪfaɪ/ VT franciser ◆ **his Frenchified ways** *(pej)* ses maniérismes copiés sur les Français

Frenchman /ˈfrentʃmən/ N (pl **-men**) Français *m*

Frenchwoman /ˈfrentʃwʊmən/ N (pl **-women**) Française *f*

frenetic /frɪˈnetɪk/ ADJ *[person]* très agité ; *[activity, pace, applause, shouts]* frénétique ; *[effort]* désespéré ; *[period, time]* trépidant

frenetically /frɪˈnetɪklɪ/ ADV *[work, rush, think, try]* frénétiquement ; *[busy]* extrêmement

frenzied /ˈfrenzɪd/ ADJ *[attack]* sauvage ; *[activity, atmosphere, haste, applause, crowd, fans]* frénétique ; *[efforts, shouts]* désespéré

frenziedly /ˈfrenzɪdlɪ/ ADV *[run, shake, dance]* frénétiquement ; *[work]* comme un fou *or* une folle ◆ **a ~ busy** *or* **hectic time** une période d'activité frénétique

frenzy /ˈfrenzɪ/ N frénésie *f* ◆ **~ of delight** transport *m* de joie ◆ **to be in a ~** être au comble de l'excitation ◆ **a ~ of activity** une activité folle ◆ **a religious/media ~** un délire religieux/médiatique

frequency /ˈfriːkwənsɪ/ N fréquence *f* ; → **high, ultrahigh, very**
COMP **frequency band** N *(Elec)* bande *f* de fréquence
frequency distribution N *(Stat)* distribution *f* des fréquences
frequency modulation N *(Elec)* modulation *f* de fréquence

frequent /ˈfriːkwənt/ ADJ *[rests, breaks, changes, trains]* fréquent, nombreux ; *[absences, headaches, colds, occurrence, use]* fréquent ; *[reports]* nombreux ; *[complaint, criticism]* courant, que l'on entend souvent ◆ **it's quite ~** c'est très courant, cela arrive souvent ◆ **to make ~ visits** *or* **trips to …, to be a ~ visitor to …** aller fréquemment à … ◆ **he is a ~ visitor (to our house)** c'est un habitué (de la maison) VT /frɪˈkwent/ fréquenter, hanter
COMP **frequent flyer** N ◆ **he's a ~ flyer** il prend beaucoup l'avion
frequent-flyer ADJ *[scheme, programme]* de fidélisation
frequent wash shampoo N shampoing *m* (pour) usage fréquent

frequentative /frɪˈkwentətɪv/ ADJ, N *(Gram)* fréquentatif *m*, itératif *m*

frequenter /frɪˈkwentəʳ/ N *[of restaurant, pub]* habitué(e) *m(f)* ◆ **~s of theatres/public libraries** habitués *mpl* des théâtres/des bibliothèques municipales ◆ **he was a great ~ of night clubs** il courait les boîtes de nuit, c'était un habitué des boîtes de nuit

frequently /ˈfriːkwəntlɪ/ ADV fréquemment
COMP **frequently asked questions** NPL *(Comput)* questions *fpl* fréquentes

fresco /ˈfreskəʊ/ N (pl **frescoes** *or* **frescos**) *(= pigment, picture)* fresque *f* ◆ **to paint in ~** peindre à fresque

fresh /freʃ/ ADJ 1 *(= not stale) [food, flavour, smell]* frais (fraîche *f*) ; *[clothes, towel]* propre ◆ **is this milk ~?** ce lait est-il frais ? ◆ **is my breath ~?** ai-je l'haleine fraîche ?
2 *(= recent) [blood, tracks, scent, news]* frais (fraîche *f*) ; *[scar, wound]* récent ; *[memories]* proche ◆ **it's still ~ in my mind** *or* **memory** c'est encore tout frais dans ma mémoire ◆ **a ~ coat of paint** une nouvelle couche de peinture ◆ **"fresh paint"** "peinture fraîche"
3 *(= new, renewed) [evidence, approach, fighting, outbreak, supplies]* nouveau (nouvelle *f*) ◆ **a ~ sheet of paper** une nouvelle feuille de papier ◆ **she applied ~ lipstick** elle a remis du rouge à lèvres ◆ **to make a ~ pot of tea** refaire du thé ◆ **he poured himself a ~ drink** il s'est reversé à boire ◆ **to take a ~ look at sth** regarder qch sous un jour nouveau ◆ **(to make) a ~ start** (prendre) un nouveau départ ◆ **a ~ face** *(= new person)* un nouveau visage ◆ **~ fields (and pastures new)** nouveaux horizons *mpl* ; see also **break, heart**
4 *(= not dried or processed) [pasta, fruit, vegetables, herbs, juice, cream, flowers]* frais (fraîche *f*) ◆ **~ coffee** café *m* (moulu)
5 *(= rested) [person, horse]* frais (fraîche *f*) ◆ **to feel ~** être frais et dispos ◆ **he/she is as ~ as a daisy** il est frais comme un gardon/elle est fraîche comme une rose ◆ **to have a ~ complexion** avoir le teint frais
6 *(= refreshing, original) [approach, style, humour, writing]* original
7 *(= cool, invigorating) [day, wind, breeze]* frais (fraîche *f*)
8 († * = cheeky) culotté * ◆ **that's enough of that ~ talk!** ça suffit avec ces familiarités ! ◆ **to be** *or* **get ~ (with sb)** *(= cheeky)* être impertinent (avec qn) ; *(sexually)* prendre des libertés (avec qn), se permettre des familiarités (avec qn)
ADV 1 *(= straight)* ◆ **milk ~ from the cow** du lait fraîchement trait ◆ **fish ~ from the lake** du poisson qui sort tout juste du lac ◆ **the bread is ~ from the oven** le pain sort à l'instant *or* est frais sorti du four ◆ **~ from** *or* **out of school** frais émoulu du lycée ◆ **~ from the war** tout juste de retour de la guerre ◆ **tourists ~ off the plane** des touristes tout juste débarqués de l'avion ◆ **to come ~ to sth** aborder qch sans idées préconçues
2 ◆ **to be ~ out of sth** * être en panne * de qch
COMP **fresh air** N air *m* frais ◆ **I'm going out for some ~ air** *or* **for a breath of ~ air** je sors prendre l'air *or* le frais ◆ **in the ~ air** au grand air, en plein air ; see also **breath**
fresh-air fiend * N amoureux *m*, -euse *f* du grand air
fresh breeze N *(Naut)* bonne brise *f*
fresh-faced ADJ au visage juvénile
fresh gale N *(Naut)* coup *m* de vent
fresh water N *(= not salt)* eau *f* douce

freshen /ˈfreʃn/ VI *[wind, air]* fraîchir VT *[+ air]* désodoriser ; *[+ breath, complexion]* rafraîchir ◆ **can I ~ your drink for you?** je vous en ressers ?, encore une goutte ?

► **freshen up** VI *(= wash o.s.)* faire un brin de toilette ; *(= touch up make-up)* se refaire une beauté * VT SEP *[+ invalid etc]* faire un brin de toilette à ; *[+ child]* débarbouiller ; *[+ room, paintwork]* rafraîchir ◆ **accessories to ~ up your summer wardrobe** des accessoires pour égayer votre garde-robe estivale ◆ **the new players will ~ up the team** les nouveaux joueurs vont apporter du sang neuf dans *or* à l'équipe ◆ **chewing gum to ~ the breath up** du chewing-gum pour rafraîchir l'haleine ◆ **to ~ o.s. up** ⇒ **to freshen up vi**

freshener /ˈfreʃnəʳ/ N (also **skin freshener**) lotion *f* tonique ; (also **air freshener**) désodorisant *m*

fresher /ˈfreʃəʳ/ N *(Brit Univ)* bizut(h) *m*, étudiant(e) *m(f)* de première année COMP **freshers' week** N *(Brit Univ)* semaine *f* d'accueil des étudiants

freshet /ˈfreʃɪt/ N *(= flood)* crue *f* rapide, inondation *f* brutale ; *(into sea)* (petit) cours *m* d'eau qui se jette dans la mer

freshly /ˈfreʃlɪ/ ADV *[ground, grated, dug]* fraîchement ◆ **~ baked bread** du pain qui sort *or* frais sorti du four ◆ **~ caught fish** du poisson fraîchement pêché ◆ **~-cut flowers** des fleurs fraîchement cueillies *or* qui viennent d'être coupées ◆ **~ made coffee** du café qui vient d'être fait ◆ **~ painted** qui vient d'être peint ◆ **~ squeezed orange juice** du jus d'oranges pressées

freshman /ˈfreʃmən/ N (pl **-men**) *(US Univ)* ≃ bizut(h) *m*

freshness /ˈfreʃnɪs/ N *[of air, food, fruit, milk, wind]* fraîcheur *f* ; *[of manner]* franchise *f*, spontanéité *f* ; *[of outlook, approach]* fraîcheur *f*, jeunesse *f* ; *[of colour]* fraîcheur *f*, gaieté *f*

freshwater /ˈfreʃˌwɔːtəʳ/ ADJ *[fish, plant, lake]* d'eau douce

fret¹ /fret/ VI 1 *(= become anxious)* se tracasser (*about* à propos de) ; *[baby]* pleurer, geindre ◆ **don't ~!** ne t'en fais pas !, ne te tracasse pas ! ◆ **she ~s over the slightest thing** elle se fait du mauvais sang *or* elle se tracasse pour un rien ◆ **the child is ~ting for its mother** le petit réclame sa mère en pleurant 2 ◆ **to ~ (at the bit)** *[horse]* ronger le mors VT ◆ **to ~ o.s.** * se tracasser, se faire de la bile N ◆ **to be in a ~** * se biler *

fret² /fret/ VT *[+ wood]* découper, chantourner ◆ **the stream has ~ted its way through the rock** le ruisseau s'est frayé un passage dans le rocher

fret³ /fret/ N *[of guitar]* touchette *f*

fretful /ˈfretfʊl/ ADJ *[person]* irritable ; *[baby, child]* grognon, pleurnicheur ; *[sleep]* agité ; *[tone]* plaintif

fretfully /ˈfretfəlɪ/ ADV *[say]* *(= anxiously)* d'un ton irrité ; *(= complainingly)* d'un ton plaintif *or* pleurnichard ◆ **to cry ~** *[baby]* pleurnicher, être grognon

fretfulness /ˈfretfʊlnɪs/ N irritabilité *f*

fretsaw /ˈfretsɔː/ N scie *f* à chantourner *or* à découper

fretwork /ˈfretwɜːk/ N *(= piece)* pièce *f* chantournée ; *(= work)* découpage *m*

Freudian /ˈfrɔɪdɪən/ ADJ *(Psych, fig)* freudien ◆ **that's very ~!** c'est révélateur ! N freudienne *m(f)*, disciple *mf* de Freud COMP **Freudian slip** N lapsus *m* (révélateur)

FRG /ˌefɑːˈdʒiː/ N (abbrev of **Federal Republic of Germany**) RFA *f*

Fri. N abbrev of **Friday**

friable /ˈfraɪəbl/ ADJ friable

friar /ˈfraɪəʳ/ N moine *m*, frère *m* ◆ **Friar John** frère Jean

friary /ˈfraɪərɪ/ N confrérie *f*

fricassee /ˈfrɪkəsiː/ N fricassée *f*

fricative /ˈfrɪkətɪv/ *(Ling)* ADJ spirant, fricatif N spirante *f*, fricative *f*

friction /ˈfrɪkʃən/ N 1 *(Phys)* friction *f*, frottement *m* ; *(Ling)* friction *f* ; *(fig)* friction *f* ◆ **there is a certain amount of ~ between them** il y a des frictions entre eux 2 (also **friction climbing**) adhérence *f*
COMP **friction feed** N *(on printer)* entraînement *m* par friction
friction tape N *(US)* chatterton *m*

Friday /ˈfraɪdɪ/ N vendredi *m* ◆ **~ the thirteenth** vendredi treize ; → **good ;** *for other phrases see* **Saturday**

fridge /frɪdʒ/ N *(esp Brit)* (abbrev of **refrigerator**) frigo * *m*, frigidaire ® *m*
COMP **fridge-freezer** N réfrigérateur *m* avec partie congélateur
fridge magnet N magnet *m*

fried /fraɪd/ VB pt, ptp of **fry²**

friend /frend/ N ami(e) *m(f)* ; *(= schoolmate, workmate)* camarade *mf*, copain * *m*, copine * *f* ; *(= helper, supporter)* ami(e) *m(f)* ◆ **a ~ of mine** un de mes amis ◆ **~s of ours** des amis (à nous) ◆ **he's one of my son's ~s** c'est un ami *or* un copain * de mon fils ◆ **her best ~** sa meilleure amie ◆ **a doctor/lawyer ~ of mine** un ami médecin/avocat ◆ **it's a girl's best ~** c'est le rêve de chaque femme ◆ **he's no ~ of mine** je ne le compte pas au nombre de mes amis ◆ **to make ~s with sb** devenir ami avec qn, se lier d'amitié avec qn ◆ **he made a ~ of him** il en a fait son ami ◆ **he makes ~s easily** il se fait facilement des amis, il se lie facilement ◆ **to be ~s with sb** être ami *or* lié avec qn ◆ **let's be ~s again** on fait la paix ? ◆ **close ~s** amis *mpl* intimes ◆ **we're just good ~s** on est simplement amis ◆ **we're all ~s here** nous sommes entre amis ◆ **a ~ of the family** un ami de la famille ◆ **a ~ in need (is a ~ indeed)** *(Prov)* c'est dans le besoin que l'on connaît ses vrais amis

◆ **the best of ~s must part** il n'est si bonne compagnie qui ne se sépare (*Prov*) ◆ **he's been a true ~ to us** il a fait preuve d'une véritable amitié envers nous ◆ **a ~ at court** (*fig*) un ami influent ◆ **to have ~s at court** (*fig*) avoir des amis influents *or* des protections ◆ **my honourable ~** (*Parl*) ◆ **my learned ~** (*Jur*) mon cher *or* distingué confrère, ma distinguée collègue ◆ **~ of the poor** bienfaiteur *m or* ami *m* des pauvres ◆ **Friends of the Earth** les Amis *mpl* de la Terre ◆ **Friends of the National Theatre** (Société *f* des) Amis du Théâtre National ◆ **Society of Friends** (*Rel*) Société *f* des Amis

friendless /ˈfrendlɪs/ ADJ seul, isolé, sans amis

friendliness /ˈfrendlɪnɪs/ N gentillesse *f*

friendly /ˈfrendlɪ/ ADJ [1] (= *amiable*) [*person*] gentil (*to sb* avec qn) ; [*child*] gentil, affectueux ; [*cat, dog*] affectueux ; [*manner, smile, gesture, atmosphere, argument, fight*] amical ; [*face*] avenant ; [*welcome*] chaleureux ; [*service*] sympathique ; [*advice*] d'ami ; [*place*] accueillant ◆ **that wasn't a very ~ thing to do** ce n'était pas très gentil de faire cela ◆ **unions ~ to management** syndicats favorables à la direction ◆ **to feel ~ towards sb** être bien disposé envers qn ◆ **it's nice to see a ~ face!** ça fait plaisir de voir un visage sympathique ! ; → **neighbourhood**

[2] (= *friends*) ◆ **we're quite ~** nous sommes assez amis ◆ **to be ~ with sb** être ami avec qn ◆ **to become** *or* **get ~ with sb** se lier d'amitié avec qn ◆ **to be on ~ terms with sb** avoir des rapports d'amitié avec qn ◆ **to get ~** * (*sexually*) se permettre des familiarités (*pej*)

[3] (*Pol*) [*country, nation, government*] ami ; [*port*] de pays ami

N (also **friendly match**) (*Brit*) → **comp**

COMP **friendly fire** N (*Mil, fig*) tirs *mpl* de son propre camp

the Friendly Islands NPL les îles *fpl* des Amis

friendly match N (*Sport*) match *m* amical

friendly society N (*Brit*) société *f* de prévoyance, mutuelle *f*

-friendly /ˈfrendlɪ/ ADJ (*in compounds*) ◆ **customer-friendly** [*shop*] soucieux de sa clientèle, accueillant ; [*policy, prices*] favorable aux consommateurs ◆ **child-friendly** [*shop*] aménagé pour les enfants ; [*beach, kitchen*] sûr *or* non dangereux pour les enfants ◆ **dolphin-friendly tuna** thon *m* pêché en respectant les dauphins ◆ **reader-friendly** soucieux de ses lecteurs ; → **environment, gay, ozone, user**

friendship /ˈfrendʃɪp/ N amitié *f* ◆ **out of ~** par amitié

frier /fraɪəʳ/ N ⇒ **fryer**

fries * /fraɪz/ NPL (*esp US*) frites *fpl*

Friesian /ˈfriːʒən/ ADJ, N ⇒ **Frisian**

frieze¹ /friːz/ N (*Archit*) frise *f*

frieze² /friːz/ N (= *fabric*) ratine *f*

frig‡ /frɪg/ VI ◆ **to ~ about** *or* **around** déconner‡

frigate /ˈfrɪgɪt/ N frégate *f* (*Naut*)

frigging*‡ /ˈfrɪgɪŋ/ ADV foutrement‡ ADJ foutu‡

fright /fraɪt/ N [1] frayeur *f*, peur *f* ◆ **to shout out in ~** pousser un cri de frayeur ◆ **to be paralysed with ~** être paralysé par la peur ◆ **to take ~** prendre peur, s'effrayer (*at de*) ◆ **to get** *or* **have a ~** avoir peur ◆ **to get the ~ of one's life** avoir la frayeur de sa vie ◆ **to give sb a ~** faire peur à qn ◆ **it gave me such a ~** ça m'a fait une de ces peurs* *or* une belle peur ; → **stage** [2] (* = *person*) **she's** *or* **she looks a ~** elle est à faire peur

frighten /ˈfraɪtn/ VT effrayer, faire peur à ◆ **did he ~ you?** est-ce qu'il vous a fait peur ? ◆ **it nearly ~ed him out of his wits*** *or* **his skin***, **it ~ed the life out of him*** cela lui a fait une peur bleue ◆ **to ~ sb into doing sth** faire peur à qn pour qu'il fasse qch ◆ **he was ~ed into doing it** il l'a fait sous le coup de la peur ◆ **she is easily ~ed** elle prend peur facilement, elle est peureuse

► **frighten away, frighten off** VT SEP [*+ birds*] effaroucher ; [*+ children etc*] chasser (en leur faisant peur) ; (*fig*) [*+ buyers, investors etc*] décourager (en leur faisant peur)

frightened /ˈfraɪtnd/ ADJ effrayé ◆ **to be ~ (of sb/sth)** avoir peur (de qn/qch) ◆ **to be ~ of doing** *or* **to do sth** avoir peur de faire qch ◆ **to be ~ about (doing) sth** avoir peur à l'idée de (faire) qch ◆ **to be ~ that ...** avoir peur que ... ◆ **to be ~ to death*** **(that ...)** être mort de peur (que ...) ◆ **to be ~ to death*** **of sb/sth** avoir une peur bleue de qn/qch ◆ **to be ~ out of one's wits*** avoir une peur bleue ◆ **like a ~ rabbit** comme un animal effarouché

frighteners‡ /ˈfraɪtnəz/ NPL (*Brit*) ◆ **to put the ~ on sb** foutre les jetons‡ à qn

frightening /ˈfraɪtnɪŋ/ ADJ effrayant ◆ **it is ~ to think that ...** ça fait peur de penser que ...

frighteningly /ˈfraɪtnɪŋlɪ/ ADV [*ugly, thin*] à faire peur ; [*expensive*] effroyablement ◆ **we came ~ close to losing all our money** nous avons vraiment failli perdre tout notre argent

frightful /ˈfraɪtfʊl/ ADJ [1] (*liter* = *horrifying*) [*sight, experience*] épouvantable, effroyable [2] († * = *awful*) [*mistake, prospect, possibility, clothes, hat, wallpaper*] affreux ; [*person*] détestable ◆ **he's a ~ bore** il est terriblement ennuyeux ◆ **I know I'm being a ~ nuisance, but ...** je ne voudrais pas vous importuner davantage, mais ...

frightfully /ˈfraɪtfəlɪ/ ADV [1] (*liter* = *horrifyingly*) [*suffer*] effroyablement [2] (*Brit*: † * = *very*) terriblement ◆ **I'm ~ sorry** je suis vraiment désolé ◆ **it's ~ nice of you** c'est vraiment trop gentil à vous

frightfulness /ˈfraɪtfʊlnɪs/ N [*of crime, situation, behaviour*] atrocité *f*, horreur *f*

frigid /ˈfrɪdʒɪd/ ADJ [1] (*sexually*) frigide [2] (= *unfriendly*) [*smile, stare, atmosphere, silence*] glacial [3] (*Geog, Weather*) glacial

frigidity /frɪˈdʒɪdɪtɪ/ N (*sexual*) frigidité *f* ; (*gen*) froideur *f*

frill /frɪl/ N [1] [*of dress*] ruche *f*, volant *m* ; [*of shirt front*] jabot *m* ; [*of cuff*] ruche *f* [2] (*fig*) ◆ **~s** chichis* *mpl* ◆ **without any ~s** simple, sans chichis* ◆ **I want a cheap deal with no ~s** je veux quelque chose de simple et pas cher ◆ **these services are not ~s or luxuries** ces services ne sont pas du tout du superflu ou du luxe ; → **furbelow, no** [3] (*Culin*) papillote *f* [4] (*of bird, lizard*) collerette *f*

frilly /ˈfrɪlɪ/ ADJ [1] [*shirt, dress, cushion*] à fanfreluches ; [*underwear*] à dentelle [2] [*style, speech*] plein de fioritures

fringe /frɪndʒ/ N [1] (*Brit* = *hair*) frange *f*

[2] [*of rug, shawl*] frange *f*

[3] (= *edge*) [*of forest*] bordure *f*, lisière *f* ; [*of crowd*] derniers rangs *mpl* ◆ **on the ~ of the forest** en bordure de forêt, à la lisière de la forêt ◆ **to live on the ~(s) of society** vivre en marge de la société ◆ **a party on the ~(s) of British politics** un parti en marge de la politique britannique ◆ **the outer ~s** [*of town*] la périphérie ; → **lunatic**

VT [1] [*+ rug, shawl*] franger (*with de*)

[2] (*fig*) **a lake ~d with trees** un lac bordé d'arbres

COMP **fringe area** N (*TV*) zone *f* limite (de réception)

fringe benefits NPL avantages *mpl* annexes ; (*company car etc*) avantages *mpl* en nature

fringe festival N festival *m* off ; → EDINBURGH FESTIVAL

fringe group N groupe *m* marginal

fringe meeting N (*Pol*) réunion *f* d'un groupe marginal

fringe theatre N (*Brit*) théâtre *m* d'avant-garde *or* expérimental

fringing reef N (*Geog*) récif *m* frangeant

frippery /ˈfrɪpərɪ/ N (*esp Brit: pej*) (= *cheap ornament*) colifichets *mpl* ; (*on dress*) fanfreluches *fpl* ; (= *ostentation*) préciosité *f*, maniérisme *m*

Frisbee ® /ˈfrɪzbɪ/ N frisbee ® *m*

Frisian /ˈfrɪʒən/ ADJ frison ◆ **the ~ Islands** les îles *fpl* Frisonnes N [1] Frison(ne) *m(f)* [2] (= *language*) frison *m*

frisk /frɪsk/ VI gambader VT [*+ criminal, suspect*] fouiller

friskiness /ˈfrɪskɪnɪs/ N vivacité *f*

frisky /ˈfrɪskɪ/ ADJ (= *lively*) vif, sémillant ◆ **to be feeling ~** (*hum: sexually*) être d'humeur folâtre

frisson /ˈfriːsɒn/ N frisson *m*

fritillary /frɪˈtɪlərɪ/ N fritillaire *f*

fritter¹ /ˈfrɪtəʳ/ VT (also **fritter away**) [*+ money, time, energy*] gaspiller

fritter² /ˈfrɪtəʳ/ N (*Culin*) beignet *m* ◆ **apple ~** beignet *m* aux pommes

fritz‡ /frɪts/ (*US*) N ◆ **on the ~** en panne

► **fritz out**‡ VI tomber en panne

frivolity /frɪˈvɒlɪtɪ/ N frivolité *f*

frivolous /ˈfrɪvələs/ ADJ [*person, object, activity*] (= *lighthearted*) frivole ; (= *futile*) futile ; [*attitude, behaviour, remark*] frivole, léger

frivolously /ˈfrɪvələslɪ/ ADV de façon frivole, frivolement

frizz /frɪz/ VT [*+ hair*] faire friser *or* frisotter VI friser, frisotter

frizzle /ˈfrɪzl/ VI grésiller VT [1] (= *cook*) faire griller ; (= *overcook*) laisser brûler ◆ **~d bacon** bacon *m* grillé [2] ◆ **a man with ~d white hair** un homme aux cheveux blancs frisés

frizzy /ˈfrɪzɪ/ ADJ [*hair*] crépu, crêpelé

fro /frəʊ/ ADV ◆ **to and ~** de long en large ◆ **to go to and ~ between** aller et venir entre, faire la navette entre ◆ **journeys to and ~ between London and Edinburgh** allers *mpl* et retours *mpl* entre Londres et Édimbourg

frock /frɒk/ N [1] † [*of woman, baby*] robe *f* [2] [*of monk*] froc † *m* COMP **frock coat** N redingote *f*

frog¹ /frɒg/ N [1] (= *animal*) grenouille *f* ◆ **to have a ~ in one's throat** avoir un chat dans la gorge [2] (*pej*) **Frog**‡ Français(e) *m(f)*

COMP **frog-march** VT ◆ **to ~-march sb in/out** *etc* (= *hustle*) faire entrer/sortir qn de force

frogs' legs NPL (*Culin*) cuisses *fpl* de grenouilles

frog² /frɒg/ N (*Dress*) brandebourg *m*, soutache *f*

frogging /ˈfrɒgɪŋ/ N (*Dress*) soutaches *fpl*

Froggy‡ /ˈfrɒgɪ/ N (*Brit pej*) Français(e) *m(f)*

frogman /ˈfrɒgmən/ N (pl **-men**) homme-grenouille *m*

frogspawn /ˈfrɒgspɔːn/ N frai *m* de grenouille

frolic /ˈfrɒlɪk/ VI (also **frolic about, frolic around**) [*people*] (*gen, hum*) batifoler* ; [*lambs*] gambader N [*of lambs*] gambades *fpl* ; (= *prank*) espièglerie *f*, gaminerie *f* ; (= *merrymaking*) ébats *mpl* ; (*hum: sexual*) batifolage *m*

frolicsome /ˈfrɒlɪksəm/ ADJ folâtre, badin

from /frɒm/ PREP [1] (*place: starting point*) de ◆ **~ house to house** de maison en maison ◆ **~ town to town** de ville en ville ◆ **to jump ~ a wall** sauter d'un mur ◆ **to travel ~ London to Paris** voyager de Londres à Paris ◆ **train ~ Manchester** train *m* (en provenance) de Manchester ◆ **programme transmitted ~ Lyons** émission *f* retransmise depuis Lyon ◆ **he comes ~ London** il vient de Londres, il est (originaire) de Londres ◆ **he comes ~ there** il en vient ◆ **where are you ~?, where do you come ~?** d'où êtes-vous (originaire) ? ◆ **I see where you're coming ~*** *(= understand)* je comprends maintenant

[2] *(time: starting point)* à partir de, de ◆ **(as) ~ 14 July** à partir du 14 juillet ◆ **~ that day onwards** à partir de ce jour-là ◆ **~ beginning to end** du début (jusqu')à la fin ◆ **~ her childhood onwards ...** dès son enfance ... ◆ **~ time to time** de temps en temps ◆ **~ day to day** de jour en jour ◆ **~ year to year** d'année en année ◆ **counting ~ last Monday** à dater de lundi dernier ◆ **five years ~ now** dans cinq ans

[3] *(distance: lit, fig)* de ◆ **the house is 10km ~ the coast** la maison est à 10 km de la côte ◆ **it is 10km ~ there** c'est à 10 km de là ◆ **to go away ~ home** quitter la maison ◆ **not far ~ here** pas loin d'ici ◆ **far ~ blaming you** loin de vous le reprocher

[4] *(origin = coming from)* de, de la part de ; *(= inspired by)* d'après ◆ **a letter ~ my mother** une lettre de ma mère ◆ **tell him ~ me** dites-lui de ma part ◆ **an invitation ~ the Smiths** une invitation (de la part) des Smith ◆ **memories ~ his childhood** des souvenirs *mpl* de son enfance ◆ **painted ~ life** peint d'après nature ◆ **~ a picture by Picasso** d'après un tableau de Picasso

[5] *(used with prices, numbers)* à partir de, depuis ◆ **wine ~ 2 euros a bottle** vins à partir de 2 € la bouteille ◆ **there were ~ 10 to 15 people there** il y avait là entre 10 et 15 personnes *or* de 10 à 15 personnes ◆ **take 12 ~ 18** *(Math)* soustrayez 12 de 18 ◆ **3 ~ 8 leaves 5** *(Math)* 8 moins 3 égalent 5

[6] *(source)* **to drink ~ a stream/a glass** boire à un ruisseau/dans un verre ◆ **to drink straight ~ the bottle** boire à (même) la bouteille ◆ **he took it ~ the cupboard** il l'a pris dans le placard ◆ **he put the box down and took a book ~ it** il a posé la caisse et en a sorti *or* tiré un livre ◆ **to take sth ~ a shelf** prendre qch sur une étagère ◆ **to pick sb ~ the crowd** choisir qn dans la foule ◆ **a quotation ~ Racine** une citation (tirée) de Racine ◆ **here's an extract ~ it** en voici un extrait ◆ **to speak ~ notes** parler avec des notes ◆ **~ your point of view** à *or* de votre point de vue ◆ **to draw a conclusion ~ the information** tirer une conclusion des renseignements

[7] *(prevention, escape, deprivation etc)* à, de ◆ **take the knife ~ that child!** enlevez *or* prenez le couteau à cet enfant ! ◆ **he took/stole it ~ them** il le leur a pris/volé ◆ **he prevented me ~ coming** il m'a empêché de venir ◆ **the news was kept ~ her** on lui a caché la nouvelle ◆ **to shelter ~ the rain** s'abriter de la pluie

[8] *(change)* de ◆ **~ bad to worse** de mal en pis ◆ **price increase ~ one franc to one franc fifty** augmentation de prix d'un franc à un franc cinquante ◆ **he went ~ office boy to director in five years** de garçon de bureau, il est passé directeur en cinq ans

[9] *(cause, reason)* **to die ~ fatigue** mourir de fatigue ◆ **he died ~ his injuries** il est mort des suites de ses blessures ◆ **~ what I heard ...** d'après ce que j'ai entendu ... ◆ **~ what I can see ...** à ce que je vois ... ◆ **~ the look of things ...** à en juger par les apparences ... ◆ **~ the way he talks you would think that ...** à l'entendre, on penserait que ...

[10] *(difference)* de ◆ **he is quite different ~ the others** il est complètement différent des autres ◆ **to distinguish the good ~ the bad** distinguer le bon du mauvais

[11] *(with other preps and advs)* ◆ **seen ~ above** vu d'en haut ◆ **~ above the clouds** d'au-dessus des nuages ◆ **I saw him ~ afar** je l'ai vu de loin ◆ **she was looking at him ~ over the wall** elle le regardait depuis l'autre côté du mur ◆ **~ under the table** de dessous la table

fromage frais /ˌfrɒmɑːʒˈfreɪ/ N *(Culin)* fromage *m* blanc

frond /frɒnd/ N *[of fern]* fronde *f* ; *[of palm]* feuille *f*

front /frʌnt/ [N] [1] *(= leading section) [of boat, car, train etc]* avant *m* ; *[of class, crowd, audience]* premier rang *m* ; *(= part facing forward) [of cupboard, shirt, dress]* devant *m* ; *[of building]* façade *f*, devant *m* ; *[of book] (= beginning)* début *m* ; *(= cover)* couverture *f* ; *[of postcard, photo]* recto *m* ◆ **she was lying on her ~*** elle était couchée sur le ventre ◆ **it fastens at the ~** cela se ferme devant ◆ **she spilt it down the ~ of her dress** elle l'a renversé sur le devant de sa robe ◆ **he pushed his way to the ~ of the crowd** il s'est frayé un chemin jusqu'au premier rang de la foule ◆ **to come to the ~** *(fig = become known, successful)* se faire connaître *or* remarquer, percer

◆ **in front** *[be, stand, walk, put]* devant ; *[send, move, look]* en avant ◆ **in ~ of the table** devant la table ◆ **to send sb on in ~** envoyer qn en avant ◆ **he was walking in ~** il marchait devant ◆ **to be in ~** *(Sport)* mener

◆ **in (the) front** ◆ **to sit in the ~ (of the car)** ◆ **to sit in ~** être assis à l'avant (de la voiture) ◆ **to sit in the ~ of the train/bus** s'asseoir en tête de *or* du train/à l'avant du bus ◆ **in the ~ of the class** au premier rang de la classe ◆ **in the ~ of the book** au début du livre

◆ **up front** *(= in the front)* ◆ **let's go and sit up ~** allons nous asseoir devant ◆ **he was very up ~ about it** *(= frank)* il a été très franc ◆ **to pay up ~** *(= in advance)* payer d'avance

[2] *(Mil, Pol)* front *m* ◆ **to fall at the ~** mourir au front ◆ **there was fighting on several ~s** on se battait sur plusieurs fronts ◆ **on all ~s** sur tous les fronts, de tous côtés ◆ **we must present a common ~** nous devons offrir un front uni, il faut faire front commun ; → **home**

[3] *(Weather)* front *m* ◆ **cold/warm ~** front *m* froid/chaud

[4] *(Brit:* also **sea front)** *(= beach)* bord *m* de mer, plage *f* ; *(= prom)* front *m* de mer ◆ **along the ~** *(= on the beach)* en bord de mer ; *(= on the prom)* sur le front de mer ◆ **a house on the ~** une maison sur le front de mer

[5] *(liter = forehead)* front *m*

[6] *[of spy, criminal]* couverture *f (fig)* ◆ **it's all just a ~ with him** *(fig)* ◆ **he's just putting on a ~** ce n'est qu'une façade ◆ **he's putting on a brave ~** *(fig)* il fait bonne contenance

[ADJ] [1] de devant, (en) avant ◆ **~ garden** jardin *m* de devant ◆ **on the ~ cover** en couverture ◆ **~ door** *[of house]* porte *f* d'entrée *or* principale ; *[of car]* porte *f* avant ◆ **in the ~ end of the train** en tête de *or* du train, à l'avant du train ◆ **~ line(s)** *(Mil)* front *m* ◆ **to be in the ~ line** *(fig)* être en première ligne, être aux avant-postes ◆ **the ~ page** *(Press)* la première page, la une* ◆ **on the ~ page** *(Press)* en première page, à la une* ; see also **comp** ◆ **the ~ panel** *[of machine]* le panneau de devant, la face avant ◆ **in the ~ rank** *(fig)* parmi les premiers ◆ **~ room** pièce *f* donnant sur la rue, pièce *f* de devant ; *(= lounge)* salon *m* ◆ **in the ~ row** au premier rang ◆ **to have a ~ seat** *(lit)* avoir une place (assise) au premier rang ; *(fig)* être aux premières loges *(fig)* ◆ **~ tooth** dent *f* de devant ◆ **~ wheel** roue *f* avant ; see also **comp** ; → **row**[1]

[2] de face ◆ **~ view** vue *f* de face ◆ **~ elevation** *(Archit)* élévation *f* frontale

[ADV] par devant ◆ **to attack ~ and rear** attaquer par devant et par derrière ◆ **eyes ~!** *(Mil)* fixe !

[VI] [1] ◆ **to ~ on to** donner sur ◆ **the house ~s north** la maison fait face *or* est exposée au nord ◆ **the windows ~ on to the street** les fenêtres donnent sur la rue

[2] ◆ **to ~ for sb** servir de façade à qn

[VT] [1] *[+ building]* donner une façade à ◆ **house ~ed with stone** maison *f* avec façade en pierre

[2] *(Brit = lead, head) [+ company, organization, team]* diriger, être à la tête de ; *[+ rock group]* être le chanteur *or* la chanteuse de

[3] *[+ TV show]* présenter

[COMP] **the front bench** N *(Brit Parl = people) (government)* les ministres *mpl* ; *(opposition)* les membres *mpl* du cabinet fantôme

the front benches NPL *(Brit Parl) (= place) le banc des ministres et celui des membres du cabinet fantôme* ; *(= people)* ≃ les chefs de file des partis politiques

front burner N ◆ **to be on the ~ burner** être une question prioritaire, être au centre des préoccupations ◆ **it's on my ~ burner** j'y pense, je m'en occupe

front crawl N *(Swimming)* crawl *m*

front-end financing N financement *m* initial

front-end payment N versement *m* initial

front-end processor N *(Comput)* (processeur *m*) frontal *m*

front-line ADJ *[troops, news]* du front ; *[countries, areas]* limitrophe *or* voisin *(d'un pays en guerre)*

front-line player N *(US Sport)* avant *m*

front-loader, front-loading washing machine N lave-linge *m* à chargement frontal

front matter N pages *fpl* liminaires

front money N acompte *m*, avance *f*

front office N *(US Comm) (= place)* administration *f* ; *(= managers)* direction *f*

front organization N ◆ **it's merely a ~ organization** cette organisation n'est qu'une façade *or* une couverture

front-page news N gros titres *mpl*, manchettes *fpl* ◆ **it was ~-page news for a month** cela a fait la une* (des journaux) pendant un mois

front-rank ADJ de premier plan

front runner N *(Athletics)* coureur *m* de tête ◆ **he is a ~ runner for the party leadership** *(fig)* c'est l'un des favoris pour la présidence du parti

front-to-back engine N moteur *m* longitudinal

front vowel N *(Ling)* voyelle *f* antérieure

front-wheel drive N *(= car, system)* traction *f* avant

frontage /ˈfrʌntɪdʒ/ N *[of shop]* devanture *f*, façade *f* ; *[of house]* façade *f* ◆ **~ road** *(US)* contre-allée *f*

frontal /ˈfrʌntl/ [ADJ] [1] *[assault, attack]* de front ◆ **to make a ~ assault** *or* **attack on sth** attaquer qch de front ◆ **~ impact** *(in car)* choc *m* frontal [2] *(Anat, Weather)* frontal [3] *[nudity]* de face ; → **full** [N] *(Rel)* parement *m*

frontbencher /ˌfrʌntˈbentʃəʳ/ N *(Brit Parl) (government)* ministre *m* ; *(opposition)* membre *m* du cabinet fantôme ; → BACKBENCHER

frontier /ˈfrʌntɪəʳ/ [N] *(lit, fig)* frontière *f* ◆ **they're pushing back the ~s of science** ils font reculer les frontières de la science ◆ **the ~** *(US Hist) la limite des terres colonisées*, la Frontière

[COMP] *[town, zone, tribe]* frontalier

frontier dispute N incident *m* de frontière

frontier post, frontier station N poste *m* frontière

frontier technology N technologie *f* de pointe

frontiersman /ˈfrʌntɪəzmən/ N (pl **-men**) *(US Hist)* habitant *m* de la Frontière ; see also **frontier noun**

frontispiece /ˈfrʌntɪspiːs/ N frontispice *m*

frontman /ˈfrʌntmən/ N (pl **-men**) *(TV etc)* présentateur *m*

frontwards /ˈfrʌntwədz/ ADV en avant, vers l'avant

frosh* /frɒʃ/ N *(US Univ)* ≃ bizut(h) *m*

frost /frɒst/ [N] gel *m*, gelée *f* ; (also **hoarfrost**) givre *m*, gelée *f* blanche ◆ **late ~s** gelées *fpl* tardives *or* de printemps ◆ **ten degrees of ~**

(Brit) dix degrés au-dessous de zéro ; → **ground¹, jack** VT (= ice) [+ cake] glacer ; see also **frosted** COMP **frost-free** ADJ [fridge] à dégivrage automatique

► **frost over, frost up** VI [window] se givrer, se couvrir de givre

frostbite /ˈfrɒstbaɪt/ N engelures fpl ◆ **to get ~ in one's hands** avoir des engelures aux mains

frostbitten /ˈfrɒst,bɪtn/ ADJ [hands, feet] gelé ; [rosebushes, vegetables] gelé, grillé par la gelée or le gel

frostbound /ˈfrɒstbaʊnd/ ADJ [ground] gelé

frosted /ˈfrɒstɪd/ ADJ 1 (= frost-covered) [grass, plants, windows, windscreen] couvert de givre 2 (Cosmetics) [eyeshadow, nail varnish, lipstick] nacré 3 (Culin) (= iced) recouvert d'un glaçage ; (= sugared) recouvert de sucre COMP **frosted glass** N (for window) verre m dépoli ; (for drink) verre m givré

frostily /ˈfrɒstɪlɪ/ ADV [greet, reply] sur un ton glacial ◆ **she smiled ~ at him** elle lui a adressé un sourire glacial

frosting /ˈfrɒstɪŋ/ N (Culin) (= icing) glace f, glaçage m ; (= icing sugar) sucre m glace

frosty /ˈfrɒstɪ/ ADJ 1 (= cold) [night, morning, weather] de gelée, glacial ; [air, weather] glacial ◆ **it is ~** il gèle 2 (= frost-covered) [ground, grass, window, windscreen] couvert de givre 3 (= unfriendly) [person] glacial, froid ; [atmosphere, reception, response, relations, smile] glacial ; [look] froid

froth /frɒθ/ N 1 [of liquids in general] écume f, mousse f ; [of beer] mousse f ; (around the mouth) écume f ◆ **a ~ of lace** un bouillon de dentelle 2 (= frivolous talk) propos mpl futiles ◆ **his speech was all ~ and no substance** son discours n'avait aucune substance, ce n'était que du vent ◆ **the novel is nothing but silly romantic ~** ce roman est d'un romantisme mièvre et stupide VI écumer, mousser ◆ **the beer ~ed over the edge of the glass** la mousse débordait du verre (de bière) ◆ **waves ~ed over the deck** des vagues passaient par-dessus le pont dans un nuage d'écume ◆ **a cup of ~ing coffee** une tasse de café mousseux ◆ **to ~ at the mouth** [dog] avoir de l'écume à la gueule ; [angry person] écumer de rage

frothy /ˈfrɒθɪ/ ADJ 1 (= bubbly) [beer, milk shake, coffee, mixture] mousseux ; [water] mousseux, écumeux ; [sea] écumeux 2 (= frilly) [dress, underwear, lace] léger, vaporeux 3 (= not serious) [operetta, comedy] léger

frown /fraʊn/ N froncement m (de sourcils) ◆ **to give a ~** froncer les sourcils ◆ **he looked at her with a disapproving ~** il l'a regardée en fronçant les sourcils d'un air désapprobateur ◆ **a puzzled/worried ~ crossed his face** il fronça les sourcils d'un air perplexe/inquiet VI froncer les sourcils ◆ **to ~ at sb** regarder qn en fronçant les sourcils ; (at child) faire les gros yeux à qn ◆ **he ~ed at the news/the interruption** la nouvelle/l'interruption l'a fait tiquer

► **frown (up)on** VT FUS (fig) [+ person, suggestion, idea] désapprouver ◆ **such behaviour is ~ed upon** un tel comportement est mal accepté

frowning /ˈfraʊnɪŋ/ ADJ [person, face, expression] renfrogné ; [look, glance] sombre

frowsty * /ˈfraʊstɪ/ ADJ (Brit) ⇒ **frowsy 1**

frowsy, frowzy /ˈfraʊzɪ/ ADJ 1 [room] qui sent le renfermé 2 [person, clothes] négligé, peu soigné

froze /frəʊz/ VB pt of **freeze**

frozen /ˈfrəʊzn/ VB ptp **freeze**

ADJ 1 [lake, ground, pipe, corpse] gelé ◆ **to be ~ solid** or **hard** être complètement gelé

2 (= preserved) [vegetables, meat, meal] (industrially) surgelé ; (at home) congelé ; [embryo, sperm] congelé

3 (* = very cold) [person, fingers] gelé ◆ **I'm ~ (stiff)** je suis gelé (jusqu'aux os) ◆ **my hands are ~ (stiff)** j'ai les mains (complètement) gelées ◆ **~ to death*** frigorifié* ; → **bone, marrow**

4 (= immobile) figé ◆ **~ in horror/with fear** glacé d'horreur/de peur ◆ **~ to the spot** cloué sur place ◆ **~ in time** figé dans le temps

5 (Econ, Fin) [prices, wages, account, credit] gelé, bloqué

COMP **frozen assets** NPL actifs mpl gelés or bloqués

frozen food N (industrially) aliments mpl surgelés ; (at home) aliments mpl congelés

frozen food compartment N partie f congélateur, freezer m

frozen shoulder N (Med) épaule f ankylosée

frozen wastes NPL déserts mpl de glace

frozen yoghurt N glace f au yaourt

FRS /ˌefɑːrˈes/ (abbrev of **Fellow of the Royal Society**) = membre m de l'Académie des sciences

fructification /ˌfrʌktɪfɪˈkeɪʃən/ N fructification f

fructify /ˈfrʌktɪfaɪ/ VI fructifier

fructose /ˈfrʌktəʊs/ N fructose m

frugal /ˈfruːgəl/ ADJ [person] (gen) économe (with sth de qch) ; (pej) pingre ; [life, meal] frugal ◆ **to be ~ with one's money** faire attention à la dépense ; (pej) être pingre

frugality /fruːˈgælɪtɪ/ N [of meal] frugalité f ; [of person] frugalité f ; (fig) parcimonie f

frugally /ˈfruːgəlɪ/ ADV [live] simplement ; [eat] frugalement ; [use] parcimonieusement

fruit /fruːt/ N 1 (collective n) fruit m ◆ **may I have some ~?** puis-je avoir un fruit ? ◆ **a piece of ~** (= whole fruit) un fruit ; (= segment) un morceau or quartier de fruit ◆ **~ is good for you** les fruits sont bons pour la santé ◆ **several ~s have large stones** plusieurs espèces de fruits ont de gros noyaux ◆ **the ~s of the earth** les fruits de la terre ; → **bear¹, dried, forbidden**

◆ **to be in fruit** [tree, bush] porter des fruits

2 (= benefits) fruit m ◆ **the ~(s) of his labour(s)** les fruits de son travail ◆ **it is the ~ of much hard work** c'est le fruit d'un long travail ◆ **the ~s of victory/one's success** les fruits de la victoire/de sa réussite ◆ **one of the main ~s of the meeting was ...** un des principaux acquis de la réunion a été ... ◆ **the ~ of thy womb** or **loins** (liter) le fruit de tes entrailles ; → **bear¹, first, reap**

3 ◆ **hullo, old ~ !** †* salut, mon pote !*

4 (US ✱ pej = homosexual) pédé✱ m, tapette✱ f

VI [tree] donner

COMP **fruit basket** N corbeille f à fruits

fruit bat N roussette f

fruit bowl N coupe f à fruits

fruit cocktail N macédoine f de fruits (en boîte)

fruit cup N (= drink) boisson f aux fruits (parfois faiblement alcoolisée) ; (US) (coupe f de) fruits mpl rafraîchis

fruit dish N (for dessert, small) petite coupe f or coupelle f à fruits ; (large) coupe f à fruits, compotier m ; (basket) corbeille f à fruits

fruit drop N bonbon m au fruit

fruit farm N exploitation f or entreprise f fruitière

fruit farmer N arboriculteur m (fruitier)

fruit farming N arboriculture f (fruitière), culture f fruitière

fruit fly N mouche f du vinaigre, drosophile f

fruit gum N (Brit) boule f de gomme (bonbon)

fruit juice N jus m de fruit(s)

fruit knife N (pl **fruit knives**) couteau m à fruits

fruit machine N (Brit) machine f à sous

fruit salad N salade f de fruits

fruit salts NPL (Med) sels mpl purgatifs

fruit tree N arbre m fruitier

fruitcake /ˈfruːtkeɪk/ N 1 (Culin) cake m 2 (Brit ✱ = eccentric person) cinglé(e)* m(f) ◆ **he's as nutty as a ~** il est complètement timbré*

fruiterer /ˈfruːtərəʳ/ N (Brit) marchand(e) m(f) de fruits, fruitier m, -ière f ◆ **at the ~'s (shop)** chez le fruitier, à la fruiterie

fruitful /ˈfruːtfʊl/ ADJ 1 (= profitable) [relationship, discussion, career] fructueux ; [meeting] utile, fécond ; [life] productif ◆ **a ~ source of information** une mine de renseignements ◆ **it would be more ~ to do that** il serait plus utile or avantageux de faire cela 2 [land, soil, plant] fécond (liter)

fruitfully /ˈfruːtfəlɪ/ ADV fructueusement

fruitfulness /ˈfruːtfʊlnɪs/ N 1 [of discussion, partnership] caractère m fructueux or profitable 2 [of soil] fertilité f, fécondité f ; [of plant] fécondité f

fruition /fruːˈɪʃən/ N [of aims, plans, ideas] réalisation f ◆ **to bring to ~** réaliser, concrétiser ◆ **to come to ~** se réaliser

fruitless /ˈfruːtlɪs/ ADJ 1 (= vain) [search, quest, effort, attempt, exercise] vain ; [discussion, talks] stérile ◆ **she spent a ~ morning trying to ...** elle a perdu toute une matinée à essayer de ... ◆ **it is ~ to try** il est vain d'essayer 2 (= infertile) [plant] stérile

fruity /ˈfruːtɪ/ ADJ 1 (= like fruit) [flavour, taste, smell] fruité, de fruit ; [wine, oil] fruité 2 (= mellow) [voice] bien timbré ; [laugh] chaleureux 3 (Brit * = lewd) [remark] salé ; [joke] corsé, salé 4 (✱ = crazy) dingue* 5 (US ✱ pej = homosexual) homo*

frump /frʌmp/ N bonne femme f mal fagotée or mal ficelée* ◆ **she's an old ~** c'est une vieille rombière* f

frumpish /ˈfrʌmpɪʃ/, **frumpy** /ˈfrʌmpɪ/ ADJ [person] mal fagoté, mal ficelé* ◆ **frumpy clothes** des vêtements mpl qui font mémé*

frustrate /frʌsˈtreɪt/ VT 1 (= thwart) [+ attempts, plans] contrecarrer, faire échouer ; [+ plot] déjouer, faire échouer ◆ **he was ~d in his efforts to win** malgré tous ses efforts, il n'a pas réussi à gagner ◆ **to ~ sb's hopes** frustrer or tromper les espoirs de qn ◆ **a stumbling block which has ~d the peace process** un obstacle qui a entravé le processus de paix ◆ **rescuers were ~d in their search by bad weather** (= hindered) le mauvais temps a gêné les sauveteurs dans leurs recherches ; (= stopped) le mauvais temps a empêché les sauveteurs de mener leurs recherches à bien 2 (= irritate, annoy) [+ person] contrarier, énerver ◆ **it really ~s me when people interrupt me** ça me contrarie or ça m'énerve que l'on m'interrompe

frustrated /frʌsˈtreɪtɪd/ ADJ 1 (= thwarted, unfulfilled) [person] contrarié ; (stronger) frustré ; [love, desire] frustré ; [ambition] déçu, contrarié ◆ **in a ~ effort to speak to him** dans un vain effort pour lui parler ◆ **he's a ~ poet/intellectual** c'est un poète/un intellectuel frustré or manqué ◆ **to be ~ in one's ambitions** être frustré dans ses ambitions ◆ **he feels very ~ in his present job** il se sent très frustré dans son poste actuel 2 (= irritated) énervé ◆ **I get ~ when people criticize my work** cela m'énerve quand les gens critiquent mon travail 3 (sexually) frustré

frustrating /frʌsˈtreɪtɪŋ/ ADJ contrariant ; (stronger) frustrant ◆ **how ~! I've lost my keys** que c'est contrariant, j'ai perdu mes clés ! ◆ **it's very ~ having** or **to have no money** c'est vraiment frustrant de ne pas avoir d'argent

frustration /frʌsˈtreɪʃən/ N frustration f (also Psych) ◆ **don't take your ~s out on me!** ce n'est pas parce que tu es frustré qu'il faut t'en prendre à moi !

fry[1] /fraɪ/ COLLECTIVE N [of fish] fretin *m* ; [of frogs] têtards *mpl* ; → **small**

fry[2] /fraɪ/ (pret, ptp **fried**) VT (= deep-fry) (faire) frire ; (= shallow-fry) faire revenir ; [+ steak] poêler ◆ **to ~ eggs** faire des œufs sur le plat ◆ **fried eggs** œufs *mpl* sur le plat ◆ **fried fish** poisson *m* frit ◆ **fried food is fattening** les fritures *fpl* font grossir ◆ **fried potatoes** (= chips) pommes *fpl* (de terre) frites ; (= sauté) pommes *fpl* (de terre) sautées ◆ **fried rice** riz *m* cantonais ; → **fish, French** VI frire N friture *f* COMP **fry-pan** N (US) poêle *f* (à frire)
fry-up * N (Brit = dish) *plat composé de saucisses, œufs, bacon etc cuits à la poêle*

fryer /fraɪəʳ/ N sauteuse *f*

frying /fraɪɪŋ/ N ◆ **there was a smell of ~** il y avait une odeur de friture
COMP **frying pan** N poêle *f* (à frire) ◆ **to jump out of the ~ pan into the fire** tomber de mal en pis, tomber de Charybde en Scylla *(liter)*
frying steak N steak *m* (à poêler)

FSA /ˌefes'eɪ/ N (Brit Fin) 1 (abbrev of **Financial Services Authority**) *organisme de régulation du secteur financier* 2 (abbrev of **Food Standards Agency**) *agence britannique de contrôle de la sécurité alimentaire*, ≃ AFSSA *f*

f-stop /'efstɒp/ N (Phot) ouverture *f* (du diaphragme)

FT /ef'tiː/ (abbrev of **Financial Times**) → **financial**

ft. abbrev of **foot** or **feet**

ftp /'eftiːpiː/ (abbrev of **file transfer protocol**) ftp *m*

FTSE (100) index /ˌfʊtsɪ(wʌn"hʌndrəd)'ɪndeks/ N indice *m* FTSE or FT

fuchsia /'fjuːʃə/ N fuchsia *m*

fuck**/fʌk/ N 1 (= act) baise** *f* ◆ **she's a good ~** c'est un bon coup*
2 ◆ **fire me ? like ~ (they will) !** me virer ? mon cul (qu'ils vont le faire) !** ◆ **~ knows!** je n'en sais foutre rien !*
3 (US = person) ◆ **you dumb ~ !** espèce de pauvre débile* !
VT baiser** ◆ **~!, ~ it!** putain de merde !** ◆ **~ me!** putain !*, merde alors !* ◆ **~ you!** va te faire foutre !**
VI baiser**
COMP **fuck-all**** N (Brit) rien *m* de rien ◆ **I know ~-all about it** j'en sais foutrement rien*

► **fuck about****, **fuck around**** VI déconner* ◆ **to ~ about** or **around with sth** tripoter* qch
VT SEP emmerder*

► **fuck off**** VI foutre le camp* ◆ **~ off!** va te faire foutre !**, va te faire enculer !**

► **fuck over**** VT SEP (US) faire une vacherie à *, baiser ** ◆ **they're just ~ing us over!** ils sont en train de nous baiser !**

► **fuck up**** VT SEP [+ plans] foutre la merde dans* ; [+ people] foutre dans la merde*
VI merder*

fucker**/'fʌkəʳ/ N connard* *m*, connasse* *f*

fucking** /'fʌkɪŋ/ ADJ ◆ **~ hell !** putain de bordel !**, putain de merde !** ◆ **~ bastard/bitch** espèce *f* de salaud**/salope** ◆ **this ~ machine** cette putain* de machine ◆ **this ~ phone** ce putain* de téléphone ◆ **where's the ~ phonebook?** où est le foutu* annuaire ? ◆ **I haven't a ~ clue** je n'en sais foutrement* rien
ADV foutrement* ◆ **it's ~ cold** il fait un putain* de froid ◆ **this is a ~ great idea** c'est une putain* de bonne idée ◆ **it's ~ brilliant!, it's ~ A! putain***, c'est génial ! ◆ **don't be ~ stupid!** fais pas le con !* ◆ **a ~ awful film** un film complètement con* ◆ **you ~ well know what I mean!** mais putain*, tu sais très bien ce que je veux dire ! ◆ **I don't ~ know!** j'en sais foutrement* rien ! ◆ **I don't ~ believe this!** putain, c'est pas possible !*

fuckwit**/'fʌkwɪt/ N peigne-cul** *m*

fuddled /'fʌdld/ ADJ [ideas] embrouillé, confus ; [person] (= muddled) désorienté, déconcerté ; (= tipsy) éméché, gris

fuddy-duddy * /'fʌdɪˌdʌdɪ/ ADJ (= old-fashioned) [person, ideas] vieux jeu *inv* ; (= fussy) [person] tatillon, maniaque N vieux machin* *m*, vieux (vieille *f*) schnock* *mf* or schnoque* *mf*

fudge /fʌdʒ/ N 1 (Culin) caramel(s) *m(pl)* (mou(s)) ◆ **a piece of ~** un caramel 2 (Press) (= space for stop press) emplacement *m* de la dernière heure ; (= stop press news) (insertion *f* de) dernière heure, dernières nouvelles *fpl* 3 (* = dodging) faux-fuyants *mpl*, échappatoires *fpl* ◆ **the wording is a total ~** le libellé est très vague or flou EXCL * balivernes ! VT * 1 (= fake up) [+ story, excuse] monter ; (= tamper with) [+ accounts, figures, results] truquer 2 (= dodge) [+ question, issue] esquiver, éluder VI (* = dodge issue) esquiver le problème

fuel /fjʊəl/ N (NonC, for aircraft, rocket, heating) combustible *m* ; (for car engine) carburant *m* ◆ **what kind of ~ do you use in your central heating?** quel combustible utilisez-vous dans votre chauffage central ? ◆ **it's no longer a cheap ~** ce n'est plus une forme or une source d'énergie économique ; (fig) ◆ **to add ~ to the flames** or **fire** jeter de l'huile sur le feu ◆ **the statistics gave him ~ for further attacks on the government** les statistiques lui ont fourni des munitions pour renforcer ses attaques contre le gouvernement
VT 1 [+ stove, furnace] alimenter (en combustible) ; [+ ships, aircraft] ravitailler en combustible or carburant
2 [+ anger, tension, controversy] attiser ; [+ fear, speculation] nourrir, alimenter
VI [ship, engine, aircraft] se ravitailler en combustible or en carburant ◆ **a ~ling stop** une escale technique
COMP [bill, costs] de chauffage
fuel-efficient ADJ économique
fuel gauge N jauge *f* de carburant
fuel injection N injection *f* (de carburant)
fuel injection engine N moteur *m* à injection
fuel injector N injecteur *m* (de carburant)
fuel oil N mazout *m*, fioul *m*
fuel pump N pompe *f* d'alimentation
fuel rod N crayon *m* combustible
fuel saving N économies *fpl* de carburant (or de combustible etc)
fuel-saving ADJ qui réduit la consommation de carburant (or de combustible etc)
fuel-saving device N économiseur *m* de carburant
fuel tank N réservoir *m* à carburant ; [of ship] soute *f* à mazout

fug * /fʌg/ N (esp Brit = smell) (stale) forte odeur *f* de renfermé ; (smoky) forte odeur *f* de fumée ◆ **what a ~!** (ce que) ça pue le renfermé or la fumée !

fuggy * /'fʌgɪ/ ADJ (esp Brit) [room] (= stale) qui sent le renfermé, mal aéré ; (= smoky) enfumé ; [atmosphere] confiné

fugitive /'fjuːdʒɪtɪv/ N fugitif *m*, -ive *f*, fuyard(e) *m(f)* ◆ **he was a ~ from justice** il fuyait la justice ADJ 1 (= running away) [person] fugitif, en fuite 2 (liter = fleeting) [thought, impression] fugitif ; [happiness] fugace, éphémère

fugue /fjuːg/ N (Mus, Psych) fugue *f*

fulcrum /'fʌlkrəm/ N (pl **fulcrums** or **fulcra** /'fʌlkrə/) 1 (lit) pivot *m*, point *m* d'appui 2 (fig) pivot *m* ◆ **she is the ~ of our team** elle est le pivot de notre équipe

fulfil, fulfill (US) /fʊl'fɪl/ VT [+ task, prophecy] accomplir, réaliser ; [+ order] exécuter ; [+ condition, function] remplir ; [+ plan, ambition] réaliser ; [+ desire, hopes] satisfaire, répondre à ; [+ promise] tenir ; [+ one's duties] s'acquitter de, remplir ; [+ contract] remplir, respecter ◆ **all my prayers have been ~led** toutes mes prières ont été exaucées ◆ **to feel** or **be ~led** être épanoui

fulfilling /fʊl'fɪlɪŋ/ ADJ épanouissant

fulfilment, fulfillment (US) /fʊl'fɪlmənt/ N [of duty, desire] accomplissement *m* ; [of prayer, wish] exaucement *m* ; [of conditions, plans] réalisation *f*, exécution *f* ; (= satisfied feeling) épanouissement *m*, (sentiment *m* de) contentement *m* ◆ **to have a sense of ~** se sentir or être épanoui

full /fʊl/

1 ADJECTIVE	3 COMPOUNDS
2 ADVERB	

1 – ADJECTIVE

1 [= filled] [container, stomach] plein, rempli ; [room, hall, theatre] comble, plein ; [hotel, bus, train] complet (-ète *f*) ◆ **we're ~ (up) for July** nous sommes complets pour juillet ◆ **I'm ~ (up)!** * (= not hungry) je n'en peux plus !, j'ai trop mangé ! ◆ **you'll work better on a ~ stomach** tu travailleras mieux le ventre plein or après avoir mangé ◆ **to play to a ~ house** (Theat) jouer à guichets fermés ◆ **"house full"** (Theat) "complet" ◆ **I have a ~ day/morning ahead of me** j'ai une journée/matinée chargée devant moi ◆ **he's had a ~ life** il a eu une vie (bien) remplie ◆ **his heart was ~** (liter) il avait le cœur gros

◆ **full of** plein de ◆ **pockets ~ of money** des poches pleines d'argent ◆ **the house was ~ of people** la maison était pleine de monde ◆ **the papers were ~ of the murder** les journaux ne parlaient que du meurtre ◆ **a look ~ of hate** un regard plein or chargé de haine ◆ **he's ~ of hope** il est plein or rempli d'espoir ◆ **he's ~ of good ideas** il est plein de or il déborde de bonnes idées ◆ **~ of one's own importance** pénétré de son importance, plein de suffisance ◆ **~ of oneself** imbu de soi-même ◆ **to die ~ of years** (liter) mourir chargé d'ans (liter) ; → **life**

2 [= complete] ◆ **I waited two ~ hours** j'ai attendu deux bonnes heures ◆ **a ~ 10 kilometres** 10 bons kilomètres, pas moins de 10 kilomètres ◆ **~ employment** plein emploi *m* ◆ **to pay ~ fare** payer plein tarif ◆ **in ~ flight** en plein vol ◆ **~ and frank discussions** un franc échange de vues ◆ **ask for ~ information** demandez des renseignements complets ◆ **we must have ~er information** il nous faut des informations plus complètes or un complément d'information ◆ **until ~er information is available** en attendant d'en savoir plus ◆ **the ~ particulars** tous les détails ◆ **to pay ~ price for sth** (for goods) acheter qch au prix fort ; (for tickets, fares) payer qch plein tarif ◆ **at ~ speed** à toute vitesse ◆ **~ speed ahead, ~ steam ahead!** (Naut) en avant toute ! ◆ **to go ~ steam ahead** (fig) avancer à plein régime ◆ **battalion at ~ strength** bataillon *m* au (grand) complet ◆ **in ~ uniform** en grande tenue ; see also **compounds**

3 [in titles] ◆ **a ~ colonel** un colonel ◆ **a ~ general** un général d'armée, ≃ un général à cinq étoiles ◆ **~ member** membre *m* à part entière ◆ **~ professor** (Univ: esp US) professeur *m* (titulaire d'une chaire)

4 [= ample] [lips] charnu ; [face] plein, joufflu ; [figure] replet (-ète *f*), rondelet ; [skirt, trousers, blouse] large, ample ; (Naut) [sails] plein, gonflé ◆ **clothes for the ~er figure** des vêtements pour personnes fortes

2 - ADVERB

◆ **to hit sb ~ in the face** frapper qn en plein visage ◆ **to look sb ~ in the face** regarder qn droit dans les yeux ◆ **to turn the volume/sound up ~** mettre le volume/le son à fond

♦ **full on** ◆ **he had his headlights ~ on** il était en pleins phares ◆ **the heater was ~ on** le chauffage était à fond ◆ **she turned the tap ~ on** elle a ouvert le robinet à fond ◆ **the car hit the deer ~ on** la voiture a heurté le cerf de plein fouet ; → **full-on**

♦ **full out*** ◆ **to go ~ out** (= *work*) mettre la gomme* ◆ **we'll be going ~ out to win the championship** on va se défoncer* pour gagner le championnat

♦ **full well** *[know, understand]* fort bien, parfaitement ◆ **to realize ~ well that ...** se rendre parfaitement compte que ...

♦ **in full** ◆ **to write one's name in ~** écrire son nom en entier ◆ **to publish a letter in ~** publier une lettre intégralement ◆ **text in ~** texte *m* intégral ◆ **he paid in ~** il a tout payé

♦ **to the full** pleinement ◆ **to live one's life to the ~** vivre pleinement sa vie

3 - COMPOUNDS

full beam N *(Brit Aut)* ◆ **to drive (with one's headlights) on ~ beam** rouler en pleins phares

full-blooded ADJ (= *vigorous*) *[person]* vigoureux, robuste ; (= *of unmixed race*) de race pure

full-blown ADJ *[flower]* épanoui ; *[crisis, disaster, war, epidemic]* généralisé ◆ **he has ~-blown Aids** il a un sida avéré *or* déclaré ◆ **he's a ~-blown doctor/architect** il est médecin/architecte de plein droit

full-bodied ADJ *[wine]* qui a du corps

full-court press N *(US fig)* ◆ **to give sb the ~-court press** * exercer une forte pression sur qn

full-cream milk N lait *m* entier *or* non écrémé

full dress N *(Mil)* grande tenue *f* ; (= *evening dress*) tenue *f* de soirée

full-dress ADJ *[clothes]* de cérémonie ◆ **~-dress debate** *(Parl)* débat *m* dans les règles ◆ **they had a ~-dress discussion on what should be done** ils ont eu un débat de fond pour décider de la conduite à tenir

full English breakfast N petit-déjeuner *m or* breakfast *m* complet

full-face ADJ *[photograph]* de face ; *[helmet]* intégral

full-fashioned ADJ *(US)* ⇒ **fully-fashioned** ; → **fully**

full-featured ADJ ⇒ **fully-featured**

full-fledged ADJ *(US)* ⇒ **fully-fledged** ; → **fully**

full frontal N nu *m* intégral de face

full-frontal ADJ *[photograph]* d'un nu intégral de face ; *[view]* de face ◆ **~-frontal assault** *or* **attack** attaque *f* de front

full-grown ADJ *[child]* parvenu au terme de sa croissance ; *[animal, man, woman]* adulte

full house N *(Cards)* full *m*

full-length ADJ *[portrait, mirror]* en pied ; *[dress, coat]* long ; *[curtains]* tombant jusqu'au sol ; *[film]* (de) long métrage

full moon N pleine lune *f*

full name N nom *m* et prénom(s) *m(pl)*

full-on* ADJ ◆ **~-on military intervention** intervention *f* militaire massive ◆ **they had a ~-on traditional wedding** c'était un mariage traditionnel, fait dans les règles

full-page ADJ *[advert, article]* (en) pleine page

full pay N ◆ **to be suspended on ~ pay** être suspendu de ses fonctions sans perte de salaire

full-scale → **full-scale**

full score N *(Mus)* grande partition *f* ; *(Brit Sport)* ⇒ **full-time score**

full-size(d) ADJ (= *life-sized*) *[model, drawing]* grandeur nature *inv* ; (= *adult-sized*) *[bicycle, bed]* taille adulte

full stop N *(Brit Gram)* point *m* ◆ **I'm not going, ~ stop!*** je n'y vais pas, un point c'est tout ! ◆ **his career seems to have come to a ~ stop** il semble que sa carrière soit au point mort

full-strength ADJ *[cigarettes]* très fort ; *[solution]* non dilué

full term N ◆ **to come** *or* **go to ~ term** *[baby]* arriver à terme ; *[pregnancy]* arriver à terme, être mené à terme ADV ◆ **to be carried ~ term** *[baby]* arriver à terme ◆ **to go ~ term** *[woman]* accoucher à terme

full-term ADJ *[baby]* né à terme ; *[pregnancy, delivery, birth]* à terme

full-throated ADJ *[laugh, shout]* retentissant

full time ADV *[work]* à temps plein, à plein temps N *(Brit Sport)* fin *f* de match

full-time ADJ *[employment]* à plein temps ◆ **she's a ~-time secretary** elle est secrétaire à plein temps ◆ **it's a ~-time job looking after those children*** s'occuper de ces enfants est un travail à temps plein ◆ **~-time score** *(Sport)* score *m* final

full word N *(Ling)* mot *m* principal

---

fullback /ˈfʊlbæk/ N *(Sport)* arrière *m*

fuller's earth /ˌfʊləzˈɜːθ/ N terre *f* savonneuse

fullness /ˈfʊlnɪs/ N 1 *[of details]* abondance *f* ; *[of description]* *(in novel, story)* richesse *f* ; *[of voice, sound, garment]* ampleur *f* ◆ **the police were impressed by the ~ of her description** la police a été impressionnée par l'exhaustivité de sa description ◆ **~ of flavour** richesse *f* de goût ◆ **this cut gives some ~ to the hairstyle** cette coupe donne du volume *or* du gonflant à la coiffure 2 *(liter)* ◆ **out of the ~ of his sorrow** le cœur débordant de chagrin ◆ **in the ~ of time** (= *eventually*) avec le temps ; (= *at predestined time*) en temps et lieu

full-scale /ˌfʊlˈskeɪl/ ADJ 1 (= *thorough-going*) *[war, conflict]* total, généralisé ; *[riot]* véritable ; *[attack, search, negotiations, debate, investigation]* de grande envergure ; *[review, retreat]* complet (-ète *f*) ; *[industrial production]* à plein rendement 2 (= *life-size*) *[drawing, model, replica]* grandeur nature *inv*

fully /ˈfʊlɪ/ ADV 1 (= *completely*) *[use, load]* au maximum, à plein ; *[justify]* complètement ; *[understand]* très bien ; *[convinced, satisfied]* entièrement, complètement ; → **laden**

2 (= *at least*) au moins, bien ◆ **~ 600** 600 au moins ◆ **~ half the workforce** une bonne moitié des effectifs, la moitié au moins des effectifs ◆ **it is ~ two hours since he went out** il y a au moins *or* bien deux heures qu'il est sorti

COMP **fully-fashioned** ADJ *(Dress)* moulant

fully-featured ADJ *(Comput, Elec)* entièrement équipé

fully-fitted kitchen N cuisine *f* entièrement équipée

fully-fledged ADJ

1 ◆ **~-fledged bird** oiseau *m* qui a toutes ses plumes 2 *(fig)* *[system]* véritable, à part entière ◆ **he's now a ~-fledged doctor/architect** *(Brit)* il est maintenant médecin/architecte de plein droit ◆ **a ~-fledged British citizen** *(Brit)* un citoyen britannique à part entière

fulmar /ˈfʊlməʳ/ N fulmar *m*

fulminate /ˈfʌlmɪneɪt/ VI fulminer, pester *(against* contre) COMP **fulminate of mercury** N fulminate *m* de mercure

fulmination /ˌfʊlmɪˈneɪʃən/ N (also **fulminations**) invective(s) *f(pl)* *(against sb/sth* contre qn/qch)

fulness /ˈfʊlnɪs/ N ⇒ **fullness**

fulsome /ˈfʊlsəm/ ADJ *(gen pej* = *extravagant)* *[praise, tribute, welcome, compliments, thanks]* outré, excessif ; *[tone]* excessivement élogieux ; *[manner]* obséquieux ◆ **to be ~ in one's praise** faire des éloges outrés

fulsomely /ˈfʊlsəmlɪ/ ADV abondamment, excessivement

fumarole /ˈfjuːməˌrəʊl/ N fumerolle *f*

fumble /ˈfʌmbl/ VI (also **fumble about, around**) *(in the dark)* tâtonner ; *(in one's pockets)* fouiller ◆ **to ~ (about) for sth in the dark** chercher qch à tâtons dans l'obscurité ◆ **to ~ (about) for sth in a pocket/a drawer** fouiller dans une poche/un tiroir pour trouver qch ◆ **to ~ with sth** tripoter qch (maladroitement) ◆ **he was fumbling with the zip** il tripotait la fermeture-éclair ◆ **to ~ for words** chercher ses mots

VT *[+ object]* manier gauchement *or* maladroitement ◆ **he ~d the key in the lock** il tentait maladroitement d'engager la clé dans la serrure ◆ **to ~ the ball** *(Sport)* mal attraper la balle ◆ **their fumbling attempts to arrange a settlement** leurs tentatives maladroites pour arriver à un accord ◆ **I ~d the question I was trying to ask** je me suis emmêlé les pinceaux* en essayant de poser ma question

fume /fjuːm/ VI 1 (* = *be furious*) rager ◆ **he's fuming** il est furibard* *or* furax* *inv* 2 *[liquids, gases]* exhaler des vapeurs, fumer N ◆ **~s** *(gen)* exhalaisons *fpl*, émanations *fpl* ◆ **factory ~s** fumées *fpl* d'usine ◆ **petrol ~s** vapeurs *fpl* d'essence ◆ **car exhaust ~s** gaz *mpl* d'échappement

fumigate /ˈfjuːmɪgeɪt/ VT désinfecter par fumigation, fumiger *(frm)*

fumigation /ˌfjuːmɪˈgeɪʃən/ N fumigation *f*

fun /fʌn/ N *(NonC* = *amusement)* amusement *m* ◆ **he had great** *or* **good ~** il s'est bien *or* beaucoup amusé ◆ **have ~!*** amusez-vous bien ! ◆ **he's great** *or* **good ~** il est très drôle, on s'amuse bien avec lui ◆ **the book is great** *or* **good ~** le livre est très amusant ◆ **sailing is good ~** c'est amusant de faire de la voile ◆ **what ~!** ce que c'est drôle *or* amusant ! ◆ **for ~, in ~** pour rire *or* plaisanter ◆ **I don't see the ~ of it** je ne trouve pas cela drôle ◆ **I only did it for the ~ of it** je ne l'ai fait que pour m'amuser ◆ **I'm not doing this for the ~ of it** je ne fais pas cela pour m'amuser *or* pour mon plaisir ◆ **it's not much ~ for us** ce n'est pas très amusant, cela ne nous amuse pas beaucoup ◆ **it's only his ~** il fait cela pour rire, c'est tout ◆ **to spoil the ~, to spoil his** (*or* **our** *etc*) **~** *[person]* jouer les trouble-fête *or* les rabat-joie ; *[event, weather]* gâcher son (*or* notre *etc*) plaisir ◆ **the children had ~ and games at the picnic** les enfants se sont follement amusés pendant le pique-nique ◆ **there'll be ~ and games over this decision*** *(iro)* cette décision va faire du potin* *or* du boucan* ◆ **he's having ~ and games with the au pair girl*** *(euph)* il ne s'ennuie pas avec la jeune fille au pair *(euph)* ◆ **we had a bit of ~ getting the car started*** (= *difficulty*) pour faire partir la voiture ça n'a pas été de la rigolade* *or* ça n'a pas été une partie de plaisir ◆ **did he go? – like ~ he did!*** y est-il allé ? – tu rigoles *or* tu parles !*

♦ **to make fun of** *or* **poke fun at sb/sth** se moquer de qn/qch

ADJ * marrant*, rigolo* ◆ **it's a ~ thing to do** c'est marrant à faire* ◆ **she's a really ~ person** elle est vraiment marrante* *or* rigolote*

COMP **fun fur** N fausse fourrure *f* ADJ en fausse fourrure

fun house N *(US) attraction foraine comprenant des planchers mouvants, des miroirs déformants, etc*

fun-loving ADJ ◆ **she's a ~-loving girl** elle aime s'amuser

fun run N course *f* de fond pour amateurs

function /ˈfʌŋkʃən/ N 1 (= *role*) *[of heart, tool etc]* fonction *f* ; *[of person]* fonction *f*, charge *f* ◆ **in his ~ as judge** en sa qualité de juge ◆ **it is not part of my ~ to do that** cela n'entre pas dans mes fonctions, il ne m'appartient pas de

faire cela ; → **bodily** 2 *(= meeting)* réunion *f* ; *(= reception)* réception *f* ; *(= official ceremony)* cérémonie *f* publique 3 *(Math, Ling, Comput)* fonction *f* 4 *(fig = depend on)* ◆ **to be a ~ of sth** être en fonction de qch VI fonctionner, marcher ◆ **to ~ as** *[person, thing]* faire fonction de, servir de, jouer le rôle de
COMP **function key** N *(Comput)* touche *f* de fonction
function room N salle *f* de réception
function word N *(Ling)* mot-outil *m*

functional /ˈfʌŋkʃnəl/ ADJ 1 *(gen)* fonctionnel 2 *(= in working order)* en état de marche

functionalism /ˈfʌŋkʃnəlɪzəm/ N fonctionnalisme *m*

functionalist /ˈfʌŋkʃnəlɪst/ ADJ, N fonctionnaliste *mf*

functionality /fʌŋkʃəˈnælɪtɪ/ N fonctionnalité *f*

functionally /ˈfʌŋkʃnəlɪ/ ADV fonctionnellement

functionary /ˈfʌŋkʃənərɪ/ N employé(e) *m(f)* *(d'une administration)* ; *(in civil service, local government)* fonctionnaire *mf*

fund /fʌnd/ N 1 *(Fin)* caisse *f*, fonds *m* ◆ **to start a ~** lancer une souscription ◆ **~s** fonds *mpl* ◆ **to be in ~s** être en fonds ◆ **the public ~s** les fonds publics ◆ **no ~s** *(Banking)* défaut *m* de provision ◆ **he hasn't the ~s to buy a house** il n'a pas les fonds nécessaires pour acheter une maison ; → **raise, secret**
2 *(= supply) [of humour, good sense etc]* fond *m* ◆ **a ~ of knowledge** un trésor de connaissances ◆ **he has a ~ of funny stories** il connaît des quantités d'histoires
VT *[+ debt]* consolider ; *[+ project]* financer, assurer le financement de ; *[+ firm]* doter en capital ; *[+ account]* alimenter
COMP **fund manager** N gestionnaire *mf* de fonds *or* de portefeuille
fund-raiser N *(= person)* collecteur *m*, -trice *f* de fonds ; *(= dinner etc)* dîner *m etc* organisé pour collecter des fonds
fund-raising N collecte *f* de fonds ADJ *[dinner, event]* organisé pour collecter des fonds

fundamental /ˌfʌndəˈmentl/ ADJ fondamental, essentiel ◆ **this is ~ to the smooth running of the company** c'est essentiel *or* fondamental pour la bonne marche de l'entreprise ◆ **it is ~ to our understanding of the problem** c'est fondamental *or* essentiel si nous voulons comprendre le problème N 1 principe *m* essentiel *or* de base ◆ **when you get down to (the) ~s** quand on en vient à l'essentiel 2 *(Mus)* fondamental *m*
COMP **fundamental particle** N *(Phys)* particule *f* élémentaire
fundamental research N recherche *f* fondamentale

fundamentalism /ˌfʌndəˈmentəlɪzəm/ N intégrisme *m*, fondamentalisme *m*

fundamentalist /ˌfʌndəˈmentəlɪst/ ADJ, N intégriste *mf*

fundamentally /ˌfʌndəˈmentəlɪ/ ADV *[different, wrong]* fondamentalement, radicalement ; *[agree, affect, alter]* fondamentalement ◆ **~ important** d'une importance fondamentale ◆ **he is ~ good** c'est quelqu'un de fondamentalement bon ◆ **the plan is ~ flawed** le plan est vicié à la base ◆ **to disagree ~ with sb/sth** être en profond désaccord avec qn/qch ◆ **~, it's a love story** au fond, c'est une histoire d'amour

fundholder /ˈfʌndˌhəʊldəʳ/, **fundholding doctor** /ˈfʌndhəʊldɪŋˈdɒktəʳ/, **fundholding GP** /ˌfʌndhəʊldɪŋdʒiːˈpiː/ N *(Brit Admin)* *généraliste ayant obtenu le droit de gérer son propre budget*

funding /ˈfʌndɪŋ/ N financement *m* ◆ **they're hoping to get government ~ for the scheme** ils espèrent obtenir un financement *or* des fonds du gouvernement pour ce programme

fundus /ˈfʌndəs/ N (pl **fundi** /ˈfʌndaɪ/) fond *m* (de l'utérus)

funeral /ˈfjuːnərəl/ N *(gen)* obsèques *fpl (frm)* ; *(grander)* funérailles *fpl* ; *(= burial)* enterrement *m* ; *(= cremation)* incinération *f* ; *(in announcements)* obsèques *fpl* ◆ **that's your ~!** * c'est ton problème ! ; → **state**
COMP **funeral director** N entrepreneur *m* de pompes funèbres
funeral home N *(US)* ⇒ **funeral parlour**
funeral march N marche *f* funèbre
funeral oration N oraison *f* funèbre
funeral parlour N funérarium *m*, salon *m* funéraire *m (Can)*
funeral procession N *(on foot)* cortège *m* funèbre ; *(in car)* convoi *m* mortuaire
funeral pyre N bûcher *m* (funéraire)
funeral service N service *m or* cérémonie *f* funèbre

funerary /ˈfjuːnərərɪ/ ADJ funéraire

funereal /fjuːˈnɪərɪəl/ ADJ *[expression, atmosphere]* funèbre, lugubre ; *[voice]* sépulcral, lugubre

funfair /ˈfʌnfeəʳ/ N *(Brit)* fête *f* (foraine)

fungal /ˈfʌŋgəl/ ADJ *[infection]* fongique

fungi /ˈfʌŋgaɪ/ NPL of **fungus**

fungible /ˈfʌndʒɪbəl/ ADJ fongible

fungicide /ˈfʌndʒɪsaɪd/ N fongicide *m*

fungoid /ˈfʌŋgɔɪd/, **fungous** /ˈfʌŋgəs/ ADJ *(Med)* fongueux ; *(Bot)* cryptogamique

fungus /ˈfʌŋgəs/ N (pl **fungi** *or* **funguses**) *(Bot: generic term) (= mushrooms etc)* champignon *m* ; *(= mould)* moisissure *f* ; *(Med)* mycose *f* ; *(* hum = beard)* barbe *f*

funicular /fjuːˈnɪkjʊləʳ/ ADJ funiculaire N (also **funicular railway**) funiculaire *m*

funk[1] /fʌŋk/ N *(Mus)* ◆ **~ (music)** funk *m*

funk[2] * /fʌŋk/ N *(Brit)* ◆ **to be in a (blue) ~** † *(= frightened)* avoir la trouille * VT ◆ **he ~ed it** il s'est dégonflé *, il a cané *

funker * /ˈfʌŋkəʳ/ N *(= skiver)* planqué(e) * *m(f)*

funky[1] /ˈfʌŋkɪ/ ADJ *[music, rhythm]* funky *inv*

funky[2] * /ˈfʌŋkɪ/ *(US)* ADJ 1 *(= excellent)* super * *inv*, génial * ; *(= fashionable)* à la page, qui a le look * 2 *(= smelly)* qui cocotte *, qui pue

funnel /ˈfʌnl/ N 1 *(for pouring through)* entonnoir *m* 2 *(Brit) [of ship, engine]* cheminée *f* VT (faire) passer dans un entonnoir ; *(fig)* canaliser

funnily * /ˈfʌnɪlɪ/ ADV 1 *(= strangely) [behave, walk]* bizarrement ◆ **~ enough ...** curieusement ... 2 *(= amusingly)* drôlement, comiquement

funny /ˈfʌnɪ/ ADJ 1 *(= amusing) [person, joke, story, book, film, play]* drôle, amusant ; *[accent, voice, walk]* comique ◆ **it's not ~** ça n'a rien de drôle ◆ **what's so ~?** qu'est-ce qu'il y a de drôle ? ◆ **don't (try to) be ~** n'essaie pas d'être drôle ◆ **to make a ~ face** faire une grimace amusante ; see also **adj 2** ◆ **to see the ~ side of sth** voir le côté amusant *or* comique de qch
2 (* = *strange*) bizarre ◆ **~-peculiar (or ~-ha-ha)?** drôle bizarre (ou drôle amusant) ? ◆ **he's ~ that way** il est bizarre pour ça ◆ **the meat tastes ~** la viande a un drôle de goût ◆ **a ~ idea** une drôle d'idée ◆ **to feel ~** *(= ill)* ne pas être dans son assiette ◆ **to go ~** *[machine]* se détraquer ◆ **to make a ~ face** faire une drôle de tête ; see also **adj 1** ◆ **I have a ~ feeling I'm going to regret this** j'ai comme l'impression que je vais le regretter ◆ **(it's) ~ you should say that** c'est bizarre que vous disiez *subj* cela ◆ **the ~ thing (about it) is that ...** ce qu'il y a de drôle c'est que ... ◆ **~! I thought he'd left** bizarre ! je croyais qu'il était parti ◆ **it's a ~ old world** c'est tout de même bizarre *or* curieux
3 (* = *fishy*) louche * ◆ **~ business** magouilles * *fpl* ◆ **don't try anything ~!** * ne fais pas le malin *or* la maligne !
N *(US)* ◆ **the funnies** *(Press *: gen pl)* les bandes *fpl* dessinées
COMP **funny bone** * N petit juif * *m*
funny cigarette * N joint * *m*
funny farm * N maison *f* de fous
funny girl * N *(= comedian)* comique *f*
funny handshake * N poignée *f* de main rituelle
funny man * N (pl **funny men**) *(= comedian)* comique *m*
funny money * N *(= large amount)* sommes *fpl* astronomiques ; *(= counterfeit)* fausse monnaie *f*

fur /fɜːʳ/ N 1 *[of animal]* pelage *m*, fourrure *f* ◆ **the cat has beautiful ~** le chat a un beau pelage *or* une belle fourrure ; → **fly**[3] 2 *(often pl = animal skins)* fourrure(s) *f(pl)* ◆ **she was dressed in ~s** elle portait des fourrures *or* de la fourrure 3 *(= limescale)* (dépôt *m* de) calcaire *m* ◆ **to have ~ on one's tongue** avoir la langue pâteuse *or* chargée VI (also **fur up**) *[kettle, pipe, boiler]* s'entartrer VT ◆ **his tongue is ~red** sa langue est chargée *or* pâteuse
COMP *[jacket etc]* de fourrure
fur coat N manteau *m* de fourrure
fur trade N industrie *f* de la fourrure

furbelow † /ˈfɜːbɪləʊ/ N falbala *m* ◆ **(frills and) ~s** fanfreluches *fpl*, falbalas *mpl*

furbish /ˈfɜːbɪʃ/ VT *(= polish)* fourbir, astiquer, briquer ; *(= smarten)* remettre à neuf, rénover

furious /ˈfjʊərɪəs/ ADJ 1 *(= angry) [person]* furieux *(about or at or over sth* de qch) ◆ **she was ~ at being disturbed** elle était furieuse d'avoir été dérangée ◆ **to be ~ at *or* with sb (for doing sth)** être furieux contre qn (parce qu'il a fait qch) ◆ **to be ~ with o.s. for doing sth** s'en vouloir d'avoir fait qch ◆ **I was ~ that I'd lost** j'étais furieux d'avoir perdu ◆ **I was ~ that he'd come** j'étais furieux qu'il soit venu ◆ **she was ~ to find that ...** elle a été furieuse de découvrir que ... ◆ **to get ~** se mettre en rage *(with sb* contre qn)
2 *(= energetic) [pace]* effréné ; *[speed]* fou (folle *f*) ; *[activity]* débordant, frénétique ; *[effort]* vigoureux, acharné ◆ **the action of the film was fast and ~** le rythme du film était endiablé ◆ **the fun was fast and ~** la fête battait son plein
3 *(= violent) [row, reaction, attack, protest]* violent ; *[debate]* houleux ; *[battle, struggle]* acharné ; *[storm, sea]* déchaîné

furiously /ˈfjʊərɪəslɪ/ ADV 1 *(= angrily) [say]* d'un ton furieux, furieusement ; *[react]* furieusement ; *[argue]* avec emportement ◆ **to be ~ angry** être dans une colère noire, être hors de soi 2 *(= frantically) [work, scribble]* comme un(e) forcené(e) ; *[fight, lobby]* avec acharnement ; *[drive]* à une allure folle ; *[ride]* à bride abattue ◆ **~ busy/jealous** extrêmement occupé/jaloux ◆ **her heart was beating ~** son cœur battait la chamade

furl /fɜːl/ VT *(Naut) [+ sail]* ferler, serrer ; *[+ umbrella, flag]* rouler ◆ **the flags are ~ed** les drapeaux sont en berne

furlong /ˈfɜːlɒŋ/ N furlong *m (201,17 m)*

furlough /ˈfɜːləʊ/ *(US)* N 1 *(Mil)* permission *f*, congé *m* ◆ **on ~** en permission 2 *(at work)* chômage *m* technique VT *[+ worker]* mettre au chômage technique

furnace /ˈfɜːnɪs/ N *(industrial)* fourneau *m*, four *m* ; *(for central heating)* chaudière *f* ◆ **this room is like a ~** cette pièce est une vraie fournaise
COMP **furnace room** N chaufferie *f*

furnish /ˈfɜːnɪʃ/ VT 1 *[+ house]* meubler *(with* de) ◆ **~ed flat** *(Brit)* ◆ **~ed apartment** *(US)* appartement *m* meublé ◆ **in ~ed rooms** en meublé 2 *(= supply) [+ object, information, excuse, reason]* fournir ◆ **to ~ sb with sth** pourvoir *or* munir qn de qch ◆ **to ~ an army with provisions** ravitailler une armée COMP **furnishing fabrics** NPL tissus *mpl* d'ameublement

furnishings /ˈfɜːnɪʃɪŋz/ NPL mobilier *m*, ameublement *m* ◆ **house sold with ~ and fittings** maison *f* vendue avec objets mobiliers divers

furniture /ˈfɜːnɪtʃəʳ/ N (*NonC*) meubles *mpl*, mobilier *m* ◆ **a piece of ~** un meuble ◆ **I must buy some ~** il faut que j'achète des meubles ◆ **the ~ was very old** les meubles étaient très vieux, le mobilier était très vieux ◆ **the ~ was scanty** l'ameublement était insuffisant, c'était à peine meublé ◆ **one settee and three chairs were all the ~** un sofa et trois chaises constituaient tout l'ameublement *or* le mobilier ◆ **he treats her as part of the ~** il la traite comme si elle faisait partie du décor ◆ **he's like part of the ~** (*regular: in pub etc*) il fait partie des meubles ◆ **dining-room ~** des meubles *mpl or* du mobilier *m* de salle à manger

COMP **furniture depot** N garde-meubles *m inv*
furniture mover N (*US*) déménageur *m*
furniture polish N encaustique *f*
furniture remover N déménageur *m*
furniture shop N magasin *m* d'ameublement *or* de meubles
furniture store N ⇒ **furniture depot** *or* **furniture shop**
furniture van N camion *m* de déménagement

furore /fjʊəˈrɔːrɪ/, **furor** (*US*) /fjʊˈrɔːʳ/ N (*= protests*) scandale *m* ; (*= enthusiasm*) débordement *m* d'enthousiasme ◆ **the incident caused a ~** cet incident a fait scandale

furrier /ˈfʌrɪəʳ/ N fourreur *m*

furrow /ˈfʌrəʊ/ N (*Agr*) sillon *m* ; (*in garden etc*) rayon *m* ; (*on brow*) ride *f* ; (*liter: on sea*) sillage *m* ; → **ridge** VT [*+ earth*] sillonner ; [*+ face, brow*] rider

furry /ˈfɜːrɪ/ ADJ 1 [*animal*] à poil ; [*body, tail*] poilu ; [*leaf*] duveteux 2 (*= fleecy*) [*hat, slippers*] en fausse fourrure ; [*material*] qui ressemble à de la fourrure ◆ **~ toy** (*= soft toy*) peluche *f* 3 (*fig*) [*kettle, pipe*] entartré ; (*Brit*) [*tongue*] chargé, pâteux ; [*teeth*] recouvert de tartre, entartré

COMP **furry dice** NPL (*Brit*) dés *mpl* en feutrine (*qu'on accroche au rétroviseur*)
furry friend N (*hum*) ami *m* à fourrure

further /ˈfɜːðəʳ/ LANGUAGE IN USE 19.1, 20.2, 21.1, 26.2 (compar of **far**)

ADV 1 ⇒ **farther adv**

2 (*= more*) davantage, plus ◆ **he questioned us no ~** il ne nous a pas interrogés davantage, il ne nous a pas posé d'autres questions ◆ **without troubling any ~** sans se tracasser davantage, sans plus se tracasser ◆ **I got no ~ with him** je ne suis arrivé à rien de plus avec lui ◆ **unless I hear any ~** à moins qu'on ne me prévienne du contraire, sauf avis contraire ◆ **until you hear ~** jusqu'à nouvel avis ◆ **we heard nothing ~ from him** nous n'avons plus rien reçu de lui, nous n'avons pas eu d'autres nouvelles de lui *or* de sa part ◆ **this mustn't go any ~** (*fig*) il ne faut pas que cela aille plus loin ◆ **I think we should take this matter ~** je pense que nous devrions poursuivre cette affaire *or* que nous ne devrions pas nous en tenir là ◆ **and ~ I believe ...** et de plus je crois ... ◆ **he said that he would do it and ~ that he wanted to** il a dit qu'il le ferait et en outre *or* et en plus qu'il avait envie de le faire ◆ **to study/examine an issue ~** approfondir l'étude/l'examen d'une question ◆ **~ to your letter** (*Comm*) comme suite à votre lettre

ADJ 1 ⇒ **farther adj**

2 (*= additional*) nouveau (nouvelle *f*), supplémentaire ◆ **until ~ notice** jusqu'à nouvel ordre ◆ **to refer** *or* **remand a case for ~ inquiry** (*Jur*) renvoyer une cause pour complément d'information *or* d'instruction ◆ **without ~ delay** sans autre délai, sans plus attendre ◆ **without ~ ado** sans plus de cérémonie ◆ **upon ~ consideration** après plus ample réflexion, à la réflexion ◆ **awaiting ~ details** en attendant de plus amples détails ◆ **one or two ~ details** un ou deux autres points ◆ **please send me ~ details of ...** (*in letter*) veuillez m'envoyer de plus amples renseignements sur *or* concernant ... ◆ **there are one or two ~ things I must say** il y a encore une ou deux remarques que j'aimerais faire, j'ai encore une ou deux remarques à faire

VT [*+ one's interests, a cause, one's career, aims*] servir ◆ **to ~ one's education** pour compléter sa formation ◆ **this has ~ed the peace process** cela a contribué à l'avancement du processus de paix ◆ **this has ~ed our understanding of the disease** cela nous a aidés à mieux comprendre cette maladie

COMP **Further Education, further education** N enseignement *m* postscolaire ; see also **college**
Further Education Funding Council N (*Brit*) *organisme de financement de l'enseignement postscolaire*

furtherance /ˈfɜːðərəns/ N [*of career*] avancement *m* ◆ **this is seen as a ~ of the negotiation process** on considère que cela fait avancer les négociations ◆ **in ~ of sth** pour avancer *or* servir qch ; ◆ **in ~ of one's own interests** pour servir ses propres intérêts ◆ **in ~ of their claim for increased subsidies** pour étayer leur demande de subventions supplémentaires

furthermore /ˌfɜːðəˈmɔːʳ/ ADV en outre, de plus

furthermost /ˈfɜːðəməʊst/ ADJ le plus éloigné, le plus lointain

furthest /ˈfɜːðɪst/ ⇒ **farthest**

furtive /ˈfɜːtɪv/ ADJ [*action, behaviour, look*] furtif ; [*person*] sournois ◆ **she sneaked out for a ~ cigarette** elle s'éclipsa pour fumer furtivement une cigarette *or* pour fumer en douce *

furtively /ˈfɜːtɪvlɪ/ ADV furtivement, à la dérobée

fury /ˈfjʊərɪ/ N [*of person*] fureur *f*, furie *f* ; [*of storm, wind*] fureur *f*, violence *f* ; [*of struggle*] acharnement *m* ◆ **to be in a ~** être en furie, être dans une rage *or* colère folle ◆ **to put sb into a ~** mettre qn dans une colère folle ◆ **to fly into a ~** entrer en fureur *or* en furie, se mettre dans une rage folle ◆ **she's a little ~** c'est une petite furie *or* harpie ◆ **the Furies** (*Myth*) les Furies *fpl*, les Euménides *fpl*

◆ **like fury*** ◆ **to work like ~** travailler d'arrache-pied *or* comme un fou ◆ **to run like ~** courir comme un dératé

furze /fɜːz/ N (*NonC*) ajoncs *mpl*

fuse, fuze (*US*) /fjuːz/ VT 1 (*= unite*) [*+ metal*] fondre, mettre en fusion

2 (*fig*) faire fusionner, réunir

3 (*Brit Elec*) faire sauter ◆ **to ~ the television** (*or* **the iron** *or* **the lights** *etc*) faire sauter les plombs

4 (*= fit with fuse*) [*+ bomb*] amorcer ◆ **to ~ a plug** équiper une prise d'un fusible

VI 1 [*metals*] fondre ; (*fig:* also **fuse together**) fusionner

2 (*Brit Elec*) **the television** (*or* **the lights** *etc*) **~d** les plombs ont sauté

N 1 (*Elec = wire*) fusible *m*, plomb *m* ◆ **to light the ~** (*fig*) mettre la machine en marche, mettre les choses en branle ◆ **this incident lit the ~ which led to the war** cet incident a été le détonateur de la guerre ◆ **to have a short ~ ***, **to be on a short ~ *** (*fig*) se mettre facilement en rogne *, être soupe au lait

2 (*Elec = blow-out*) ◆ **there's been a ~ somewhere** il y a un fusible de sauté quelque part

3 [*of bomb etc*] amorce *f*, détonateur *m* ; (*Min*) cordeau *m*

COMP **fuse box** N (*gen*) boîte *f* à fusibles, coupe-circuit *m inv* ; (*in car*) boîte *f* à fusibles
fuse wire N fusible *m*

fused /fjuːzd/ ADJ (*Elec*) [*electrical equipment, plug*] avec fusible incorporé

fusel /ˈfjuːzl/ N (also **fusel oil**) fusel *m*, huile *f* de fusel

fuselage /ˈfjuːzəlɑːʒ/ N fuselage *m*

fusible /ˈfjuːzɪbl/ ADJ ◆ **~ metal** *or* **alloy** alliage *m* fusible

fusilier /ˌfjuːzɪˈlɪəʳ/ N (*Brit*) fusilier *m*

fusillade /ˌfjuːzɪˈleɪd/ N fusillade *f*

fusion /ˈfjuːʒən/ N (*Metal*) fonte *f*, fusion *f* ; (*Phys, Mus*) fusion *f* ; [*of parties, races*] fusion *f*, fusionnement *m* ◆ **~ cooking** cuisine *f* fusion

fuss /fʌs/ N (*NonC*) (*= commotion stirred up*) tapage *m* ; (*= excitement, agitation in reaction to sth*) agitation *f* ; (*= complaints, objections, difficulties*) histoires *fpl* ◆ **I think all this ~ is only a publicity stunt** je pense que tout ce tapage n'est qu'un truc publicitaire ◆ **the company introduced new working conditions with the minimum of ~** la société a mis en place de nouvelles conditions de travail sans que cela provoque trop d'agitation *or* de remous ◆ **the government's proposals have caused a great deal of ~** les propositions du gouvernement ont provoqué beaucoup d'agitation *or* de remous ◆ **I'm sick of all this ~!** j'en ai assez de toute cette agitation *or* de toutes ces histoires ! ◆ **I don't know what all the ~ is about** je ne sais pas pourquoi on fait tant d'histoires ◆ **a lot of ~ about nothing** beaucoup de bruit pour rien ◆ **what a ~ just to get a passport!** que d'histoires rien que pour obtenir un passeport ! ◆ **we got married very quietly. We didn't want a big ~** nous nous sommes mariés sans cérémonie. Nous voulions quelque chose de simple ◆ **without (any) ~** [*marry, be buried etc*] simplement, en toute simplicité ◆ **he just gets down to work without any ~** il se met au travail sans faire toute une histoire ◆ **to make a ~, to kick up a ~ *** faire un tas d'histoires * ◆ **to make a ~ about** *or* **over sth** (*justifiably*) protester à propos de qch, ne pas laisser passer qch ; (*unjustifiably*) faire des histoires pour qch, faire tout un plat de qch * ◆ **you were quite right to make a ~** vous avez eu tout à fait raison de protester *or* de ne pas laisser passer ça ◆ **don't make such a ~ about accepting** ne faites pas tant de manières pour accepter ◆ **to make a ~ of** (*Brit*) *or* **over** (*US*) **sb** être aux petits soins pour qn

VI (*= become excited*) s'agiter ; (*= rush around busily*) s'affairer, faire la mouche du coche ; (*= worry*) se tracasser, s'en faire * ◆ **to ~ over sb** être aux petits soins pour qn ; (*pej*) embêter * qn (par des attentions excessives) ◆ **don't ~ over him** laisse-le tranquille ◆ **stop ~ing, Mum! I'll be OK** ne te tracasse Maman, ça ira

VT [*+ person*] ennuyer, embêter *

► **fuss about, fuss around** VI s'affairer, faire la mouche du coche

fussbudget* /ˈfʌsˌbʌdʒɪt/ N (*US*) ⇒ **fusspot**

fussed* /fʌst/ ADJ (*Brit*) ◆ **I'm not ~ (about going)** ça m'est égal (d'y aller)

fussily /ˈfʌsɪlɪ/ ADV (*pej*) 1 (*= painstakingly*) [*check, adjust*] de façon tatillonne 2 (*pej = overelaborately*) ◆ **~ ornate** tarabiscoté ◆ **~ dressed** habillé de façon apprêtée

fussiness /ˈfʌsɪnɪs/ N [*of person*] caractère *m* tatillon *or* pointilleux ; [*of style*] caractère *m* tarabiscoté *or* surchargé

fusspot* /ˈfʌspɒt/ N (*= nuisance*) enquiquineur * *m*, -euse * *f* ; (*= finicky person*) coupeur *m*, -euse *f* de cheveux en quatre ◆ **don't be such a ~!** ne fais pas tant d'histoires !, arrête d'enquiquiner le monde ! *

fussy /ˈfʌsɪ/ ADJ 1 (*esp pej = exacting*) [*person, cat*] tatillon (*about sth* sur qch) pointilleux ◆ **to be a ~ eater** être difficile sur la nourriture ◆ **tea or coffee? – I'm not ~ *** thé ou café ? – ça m'est égal 2 *(pej = overelaborate) [design, style, furnishings, details]* trop recherché ; *[food]* (trop) élaboré ◆ **that dress is too ~** cette robe n'est pas assez simple

fustian /ˈfʌstɪən/ **N** futaine *f*

fusty /ˈfʌstɪ/ **ADJ** 1 *(pej = old-fashioned) [person]* vieux jeu *inv* ; *[organization]* poussiéreux, vieillot ; *[image, ideas]* suranné, vieillot 2 *(= musty) [smell]* de renfermé, de moisi ; *[place, clothes, furnishings]* qui sent le renfermé

futile /ˈfjuːtaɪl/ **ADJ** *[attempt, hope, effort, ambition, protest, search]* vain ; *[exercise]* futile ◆ **it would be ~ to try to defend the town** il serait vain d'essayer de défendre la ville ◆ **it was a brave, but ~ gesture** c'était un geste courageux mais vain

> ⚠ **futile** is rarely translated by the French word **futile**, see above.

futility /fjuːˈtɪlɪtɪ/ **N** *[of attempt, hope, ambition]* caractère *m* vain ; *[of life, war, situation]* absurdité *f*

futon /ˈfuːtɒn/ **N** futon *m*

future /ˈfjuːtʃəʳ/ **N** 1 avenir *m* ◆ **what the ~ holds for us** ce que l'avenir nous réserve ◆ **does Britain's ~ lie within the EU?** l'avenir de la Grande-Bretagne est-il dans l'UE ? ◆ **there is a real ~ for bright young people in this firm** cette entreprise offre de réelles possibilités d'avenir pour des jeunes gens doués ◆ **he believed his ~ lay with her** *(in relationship, business)* il pensait que son avenir était lié à elle ◆ **in (the) ~** à l'avenir ◆ **in the near ~, in the not too distant ~** bientôt, dans un proche avenir *(more frm)* ◆ **in ~ I'll be more careful** dorénavant *or* désormais je ferai plus attention ◆ **there's no ~ in this type of research** ce type de recherche n'a aucun avenir ◆ **there's no ~ in it** * *[+ product, method, relationship]* cela n'a aucun avenir ; *[+ measures, way of behaving]* ça n'aboutira à rien, ça ne servira à rien

2 *(Gram)* futur *m* ◆ **in the ~** au futur

NPL futures *(Stock Exchange)* opérations *fpl* à terme ◆ **~s market** marché *m* à terme ◆ **coffee ~s** café *m* (acheté) à terme

ADJ *[prospects, plans, role]* futur ; *[king, queen]* futur *before n* ◆ **her ~ husband** son futur mari ◆ **~ generations** les générations *fpl* futures *or* à venir ◆ **at a** *or* **some ~ date** à une date ultérieure ◆ **in ~ years** dans les années à venir ◆ **for ~ reference** pour référence ultérieure

COMP future perfect (tense) **N** futur *m* antérieur

future tense **N** futur *m* ◆ **in the ~ tense** au futur

futurism /ˈfjuːtʃərɪzəm/ **N** futurisme *m*

futurist /ˈfjuːtʃərɪst/ **N** 1 *(esp US = futurologist)* futurologue *mf* 2 *(Art)* futuriste *mf*

futuristic /ˌfjuːtʃəˈrɪstɪk/ **ADJ** futuriste

futurity /fjuːˈtjʊərɪtɪ/ **N** *(frm = future time)* futur *m*

futurologist /ˌfjuːtʃərˈɒlədʒɪst/ **N** futurologue *mf*

futurology /ˌfjuːtʃərˈɒlədʒɪ/ **N** futurologie *f*, prospective *f*

fuze /fjuːz/ *(US)* ⇒ **fuse**

fuzz /fʌz/ **N** *(NonC = light growth) (on body)* duvet *m*, poils *mpl* fins ; *(on head)* duvet *m*, cheveux *mpl* fins ; *(= frizzy hair)* cheveux *mpl* crépus *or* crêpelés (et bouffants) **NPL the fuzz** ‡ *(= police)* la flicaille ‡, les flics * *mpl*

fuzzily /ˈfʌzɪlɪ/ **ADV** *[worded]* de manière confuse ◆ **you're thinking ~** vous n'avez pas les idées claires

fuzzy /ˈfʌzɪ/ **ADJ** 1 *(= indistinct) [photograph, picture]* flou ; *[sound, voice]* confus, indistinct ; *[writing]* indistinct 2 *(= confused) [idea, brain, details, distinction]* confus ; *[memory]* imprécis, vague ◆ **to be ~ about** *or* **on sth** n'avoir qu'une idée confuse de qch 3 *(= downy)* duveteux ; *(= frizzy) [hair]* crépu 4 *(= furry) [material, sweater]* pelucheux 5 ◆ **to be** *or* **feel ~(-headed)** * *(from drink)* être dans les vapes *

COMP fuzzy dice **NPL** *(US)* ⇒ **furry dice**

fuzzy logic **N** *(Comput)* logique *f* floue

fwd *(esp Comm)* abbrev of **forward**

f-word /ˈefˌwɜːd/ **N** *(euph = fuck)* ◆ **the ~** le mot "fuck" ‡, un gros mot

FX * /ˈefˈeks/ **NPL** *(Cine = special effects)* effets *mpl* spéciaux

FY **N** *(Fin)* (abbrev of **fiscal year**) → **fiscal**

FYI (abbrev of **for your information**) → **information**

Gg

G, g /dʒiː/ **N** 1 (= *letter*) G, g *m* ◆ **G for George** ≃ G comme Georges 2 (*Mus*) sol *m* ; → **key** 3 (*Phys = gravity, acceleration*) g *m* 4 (‡ abbrev of **grand**)(*Brit*) mille livres *fpl* ; (*US*) mille dollars *mpl* 5 (*Scol = mark*) (abbrev of **good**) bon

COMP **G7** **N** G7 *m* ◆ **G7 summit** sommet *m* du G7
G8 **N** G8 *m*
G-force **N** force *f* gravitationnelle
G-man‡ **N** (pl **G-men**) (*US*) agent *m* du FBI
G spot **N** point *m* G
G-string **N** (*Mus*) (corde *f* de) sol *m* ; (= *garment*) cache-sexe *m inv*, string *m*
G-suit **N** (*Space*) combinaison *f* spatiale *or* anti-g

g. 1 (abbrev of **gram(s)**) g *inv* 2 (abbrev of **gravity**) g

GA abbrev of **Georgia**

gab * /gæb/ **N** bagou(t) * *m* ◆ **to have a ~ (about sth)** papoter (à propos de qch) ; → **gift** **VI** (= *chatter*) papoter (*about* à propos de) ; (= *reveal secret*) vendre la mèche

gabardine /ˌgæbəˈdiːn/ **N** gabardine *f*

gabble /ˈgæbl/ **VTI** (= *talk indistinctly*) bafouiller ; (= *talk unintelligibly*) baragouiner * ◆ **he ~d on about the accident** (= *talk quickly*) il nous a fait une description volubile de l'accident ◆ **he ~d (out) an excuse** il a bafouillé une excuse ◆ **"where are they, where are they?", he ~d** "où sont-ils, où sont-ils ?", a-t-il bafouillé ◆ **they were gabbling away in French** ils jacassaient en français **N** baragouin * *m*, charabia * *m*

gabbro /ˈgæbrəʊ/ **N** gabbro *m*

gabby‡ /ˈgæbɪ/ **ADJ** jacasseur, bavard comme une pie

gable /ˈgeɪbl/ **N** pignon *m*
COMP **gable end** **N** pignon *m*
gable roof **N** comble *m* sur pignon(s)

gabled /ˈgeɪbld/ **ADJ** à pignon(s)

Gabon /gəˈbɒn/ **N** Gabon *m* ◆ **in ~** au Gabon

Gabonese /ˌgæbəˈniːz/ **ADJ** gabonais **N** Gabonais(e) *m(f)*

gad[1] /gæd/ **N** (*Agr*) aiguillon *m*

gad[2] /gæd/ **VI** ◆ **to ~ about** vadrouiller * ◆ **she spent the summer ~ding about (in) Italy** elle a passé l'été à vadrouiller * en Italie

gad[3] * /gæd/ **EXCL** (also **by gad**) sapristi ! †, bon sang !

gadabout /ˈgædəˌbaʊt/ **N** vadrouilleur * *m*, -euse * *f*

gadfly /ˈgædflaɪ/ **N** taon *m* ; (*fig = harassing person*) mouche *f* du coche

gadget /ˈgædʒɪt/ **N** 1 (= *device*) (petit) appareil *m* 2 (* = *thingummy*) (petit) truc * *m or* bidule * *m*, gadget *m*

gadgetry /ˈgædʒɪtrɪ/ **N** [*of car etc*] gadgets *mpl*

gadolinium /ˌgædəˈlɪnɪəm/ **N** gadolinium *m*

Gael /geɪl/ **N** Gaël *mf*

Gaelic /ˈgeɪlɪk, ˈgælɪk/ **ADJ** gaélique **N** (= *language*) gaélique *m* **COMP** **Gaelic coffee** **N** irish coffee *m*

gaff[1] /gæf/ **N** (*Fishing*) gaffe *f* ; (*Naut*) corne *f* ◆ **to stand the ~**‡ (*US*) encaisser *, tenir **VT** gaffer, harponner

gaff[2]‡ /gæf/ **N** (*Brit*) (= *home*) piaule * *f* ; (= *music hall etc*) beuglant‡ *m*

gaff[3]‡ /gæf/ **N** (= *nonsense*) foutaises‡ *fpl* ; → **blow**[1]

gaffe /gæf/ **N** gaffe *f*, impair *m*

gaffer /ˈgæfə^r/ **N**‡ 1 ◆ **an old ~** un vieux (bonhomme) 2 (*Brit*) (= *foreman*) contremaître *m* ; (= *boss*) patron *m*, chef *m* 3 (*Cine*) chef *m* électricien **COMP** **gaffer tape** **N** ruban *m* adhésif

gag /gæg/ **N** 1 (*in mouth*) bâillon *m* ; (*Med*) ouvre-bouche *m inv* ◆ **the new law will effectively put a ~ on the free press** la nouvelle loi aura pour effet de bâillonner la presse libre 2 * (= *joke*) blague *f*, plaisanterie *f* ; (= *hoax*) canular *m* ; (*by comedian, unscripted*) improvisation *f* comique ; (*visual*) gag *m* **VT** (*lit*) bâillonner ; (*fig = silence*) bâillonner, museler ◆ **he was bound and ~ged** on l'a attaché et bâillonné **VI** 1 (* = *retch*) avoir des haut-le-cœur ◆ **to be ~ging to do sth**‡ mourir d'envie de faire qch ◆ **to be ~ging for it**‡ (*sex*) être en chaleur‡ 2 (* = *joke*) plaisanter, blaguer ; [*comedian*] faire une *or* des improvisation(s) comique(s) **COMP** **gag law** *, **gag rule** * **N** (*US*) loi *f* limitant la durée des délibérations

gaga‡ /ˈgɑːgɑː/ **ADJ** (= *senile*) gaga * *f inv*, gâteux ; (= *crazy*) cinglé *

gage /geɪdʒ/ **N** 1 (= *challenge*) défi *m* ; (= *glove*) gant *m* 2 (= *pledge*) gage *m*, garantie *f* ; (= *article pledged*) gage *m* 3 (*US Tech*) ⇒ **gauge noun** **VT** (*US Tech*) ⇒ **gauge vt**

gaggle /ˈgægl/ **N** (*lit, hum*) troupeau *m* **VI** [*geese*] cacarder

gaiety /ˈgeɪɪtɪ/ **N** (*NonC*) gaieté *f*

gaily /ˈgeɪlɪ/ **ADV** 1 (= *brightly*) [*painted, dressed*] de couleurs vives ; [*decorated*] de façon gaie ◆ **~ coloured** aux couleurs vives 2 (= *cheerily*) [*chatter*] gaiement 3 (= *thoughtlessly*) tranquillement

gain /geɪn/ **N** (= *profit*) gain *m*, profit *m* ; (= *increase in value of asset*) plus-value *f* ; (*fig*) avantage *m* ; (= *increase*) augmentation *f* ; (*in wealth*) accroissement *m* (*in* de) ; (*in knowledge etc*) acquisition *f* (*in* de) ◆ **to do sth for (financial) ~** faire qch pour le profit ◆ **his loss is our ~** là où il perd nous gagnons ◆ **a ~ in weight** une augmentation de poids ◆ **there have been ~s of up to three points** (*on Stock Exchange*) des hausses allant jusqu'à trois points ont été enregistrées ◆ **Labour made ~s in the South** (*in election*) les travaillistes ont progressé *or* sont en progression dans le sud

NPL **gains** (= *profits*) bénéfices *mpl*, gains *mpl* ; (= *winnings*) gains *mpl*

VT 1 [+ *money, approval, respect*] gagner, obtenir ; [+ *liberty*] obtenir ; [+ *support, supporters*] s'attirer ; [+ *friends*] se faire ◆ **what have you ~ed by doing that?** qu'est-ce que tu as gagné à faire ça ? ◆ **he'll ~ nothing by being rude** il ne gagnera rien à être impoli ◆ **these shares have ~ed three points** ces valeurs ont enregistré une hausse de trois points ◆ **my watch has ~ed five minutes** ma montre a pris cinq minutes d'avance ◆ **we were unable to ~ access to his files** nous n'avons pas pu avoir accès à ses fichiers ◆ **did they ~ access to the property?** ont-ils réussi à entrer dans la propriété ? ◆ **to ~ sb's confidence** gagner la confiance de qn ◆ **to ~ control (of)** prendre le contrôle (de) ◆ **his troops ~ed control after heavy fighting** ses troupes ont pris le contrôle après des combats acharnés ◆ **to ~ back control over sth** reprendre le contrôle de qch ◆ **to ~ entry** (*to building*) réussir à entrer ◆ **she ~ed entry to the system by using a stolen password** elle s'est introduite dans le système à l'aide d'un mot de passe volé ◆ **to ~ sb's goodwill** gagner les bonnes grâces de qn ◆ **to ~ a hearing** (= *make people listen*) se faire écouter ; (*with king etc*) obtenir une audience ◆ **Cyprus ~ed independence from Britain in 1960** Chypre, ancienne colonie britannique, est devenue indépendante en 1960 ◆ **to ~ one's objective** atteindre son objectif ◆ **Labour has ~ed three seats** (*in election*) les travaillistes ont gagné trois nouveaux sièges ◆ **Labour has ~ed three seats from the Conservatives** les travaillistes ont pris trois sièges aux conservateurs

2 (= *acquire more*) **to ~ ground** (*Mil*) gagner du terrain ; (*fig*) gagner du terrain, progresser ◆ **to ~ momentum** (*lit*) prendre de la vitesse ; (*fig*) prendre de l'ampleur, gagner du terrain ◆ **to ~ speed** prendre de la vitesse ◆ **to ~ time** gagner du temps (*by doing sth* en faisant qch)

3 (also **gain in**) **to ~ experience** acquérir de l'expérience ◆ **to ~ popularity** gagner en popularité ◆ **to ~ prestige** gagner en prestige

♦ **to ~ strength** *[person, movement]* devenir plus fort ; *[storm, hurricane]* devenir plus violent ; *[market]* se raffermir ♦ **to ~ weight** prendre du poids ♦ **she's ~ed 3kg (in weight)** elle a pris 3 kg

4 *(= reach) [+ place]* atteindre, parvenir à

VI 1 *(= benefit)* gagner

2 ♦ **to ~ in** *(= acquire more)* → **vt 3**

3 *[watch]* avancer ; *[runners]* prendre de l'avance ♦ **he hasn't ~ed by the exchange** il n'a pas gagné au change

► **gain (up)on** VT FUS 1 *(Sport, fig) (= catch up with)* rattraper ; *(= outstrip)* prendre de l'avance sur

2 *[sea]* gagner sur

gainer /ˈgeɪnəʳ/ N *(= person)* gagnant(e) *m(f)* ; *(Stock Exchange)* valeur *f* en hausse ♦ **there were more losers than ~s** il y avait davantage de perdants que de gagnants ♦ **he is the ~ by it** c'est lui qui y gagne

gainful /ˈgeɪnfʊl/ ADJ *[occupation] (= worthwhile)* utile, profitable ; *(= lucrative)* lucratif, rémunérateur (-trice *f*) ♦ **to be in ~ employment** avoir un emploi rémunéré

gainfully /ˈgeɪnfəlɪ/ ADV ♦ **to be ~ employed** *(= in paid work)* avoir un emploi rémunéré ; *(= doing sth useful)* ne pas perdre son temps ♦ **there was nothing that could ~ be said** il n'y avait pas grand-chose à dire

gainsay /ˌgeɪnˈseɪ/ VT (pret, ptp **gainsaid** /ˌgeɪnˈsed/) *[+ person]* contredire ; *[+ account, statement]* contredire, démentir ; *[+ fact]* nier ♦ **the facts cannot be gainsaid** on ne peut pas nier les faits, ces faits sont indéniables ♦ **the evidence cannot be gainsaid** ces preuves sont irrécusables ♦ **her argument cannot be gainsaid** son argument est irréfutable ♦ **there's no ~ing it** c'est indéniable, on ne peut pas le nier

gait /geɪt/ N démarche *f* ♦ **with an awkward ~** d'une démarche *or* d'un pas gauche ♦ **to have a rolling ~** rouler *or* balancer les hanches ♦ **to have a shuffling ~** marcher en traînant les pieds

gaiter /ˈgeɪtəʳ/ N guêtre *f*

gal † * /gæl/ N ⇒ **girl noun**

gal. (pl **gal.** *or* **gals.**) abbrev of **gallon**

gala /ˈgɑːlə/ N fête *f*, gala *m* ♦ **opening/closing ~** gala *m* d'ouverture/de clôture ♦ **swimming/sports ~** grand concours *m* de natation/d'athlétisme

COMP *[evening, dinner, concert]* de gala

gala day N jour *m* de gala *or* de fête

gala dress N tenue *f* de gala

gala night N soirée *f* de gala

gala occasion N grande occasion *f*

galactic /gəˈlæktɪk/ ADJ galactique

galantine /ˈgælәntiːn/ N galantine *f*

Galapagos /gəˈlæpəgəs/ NPL ♦ **the ~ (Islands)** les (îles *fpl*) Galapagos *fpl*

Galatians /gəˈleɪʃənz/ NPL *(Bible)* Galates *mpl*

galaxy /ˈgæləksɪ/ N *(Astron)* galaxie *f* ; *(fig) [of talent]* constellation *f*, brillante assemblée *f*

gale /geɪl/ N coup *m* de vent, grand vent *m* ♦ **a force 8 ~** un vent de force 8 ♦ **it was blowing a ~** le vent soufflait très fort ♦ **there's a ~ blowing in through that window** c'est une véritable bourrasque qui entre par cette fenêtre ♦ **~s of laughter** grands éclats *mpl* de rire

COMP **gale force winds** NPL vent *m* soufflant en tempête, coups *mpl* de vent

gale warning N *(Met)* avis *m* de coup de vent

galena /gəˈliːnə/ N galène *f*

Galicia /gəˈlɪʃɪə/ N *(in Central Europe)* Galicie *f* ; *(in Spain)* Galice *f*

Galician /gəˈlɪʃɪən/ ADJ galicien N Galicien(ne) *m(f)*

Galilean[1] /ˌgæləˈliːən/ ADJ *(Bible, Geog)* galiléen N Galiléen(ne) *m(f)* ♦ **the ~** *(Bible)* le Christ

Galilean[2] /ˌgælɪˈleɪən/ ADJ *(Phys, Astron)* galiléen

Galilee /ˈgælɪliː/ N Galilée *f* ♦ **the Sea of ~** le lac de Tibériade, la mer de Galilée

Galileo /ˌgælɪˈleɪəʊ/ N Galilée *m*

gall[1] /gɔːl/ N *(= bile) (in humans)* bile *f* ; *(in animals)* bile *f*, fiel *m* ; *(fig = bitterness)* fiel *m*, amertume *f* ♦ **she had the ~ to say that ...** elle a eu l'effronterie de dire que ... COMP **gall-bladder** N vésicule *f* biliaire

gall[2] /gɔːl/ N *(on animal)* écorchure *f*, excoriation *f* ; *(on plant)* galle *f* VT *(= annoy)* irriter, exaspérer ♦ **it ~s me that ...** cela m'irrite *or* m'exaspère que ... ♦ **it ~s me to have to admit it** cela m'irrite *or* m'exaspère d'avoir à le reconnaître

gall. (pl **gall.** *or* **galls.**) abbrev of **gallon**

gallant /ˈgælənt/ ADJ 1 *(† = brave) [soldier]* brave, vaillant *(liter)* ♦ **~ conduct** bravoure *f*, vaillance *f* *(liter)* ♦ **a ~ deed** une action d'éclat 2 *(= plucky) [effort, attempt]* courageux, héroïque ; *[fight]* héroïque 3 *(liter = elegant) [appearance, dress]* élégant 4 /gəˈlænt/ *(= chivalrous) [gentleman, gesture]* galant N /gəˈlænt/ galant *m*

gallantly /ˈgæləntlɪ/ ADV 1 *(= bravely) [fight, battle]* bravement, vaillamment *(liter)* 2 /gəˈlæntlɪ/ *(= chivalrously)* galamment

gallantry † /ˈgæləntrɪ/ N 1 *(= bravery)* bravoure *f* vaillance *f* *(liter)* 2 *(= chivalrousness)* galanterie *f*

galleon /ˈgælɪən/ N galion *m*

gallery /ˈgælərɪ/ N 1 *(Archit) (= passageway, long room, outside balcony)* galerie *f* ; *(= inside balcony)* tribune *f* ; *(in cave, mine)* galerie *f* ; → **minstrel, press, shooting** 2 (also **art gallery**) *(state-owned)* musée *m* (d'art) ; *(private, selling paintings)* galerie *f* (de tableaux *or* d'art) ; *(US) (= auction room)* salle *f* des ventes 3 *(Theat)* dernier balcon *m*, poulailler * *m* ♦ **in the ~** au dernier balcon, au poulailler * ♦ **to play to the ~** *(fig)* poser *or* parler pour la galerie

galley /ˈgælɪ/ N 1 *(= ship)* galère *f* ; *(= ship's kitchen)* coquerie *f* 2 *(Typ)* galée *f* ; (also **galley proof**) (épreuve *f* en) placard *m*

COMP **galley slave** N galérien *m*

galley west ADV *(US)* ♦ **to knock sth ~ west** chambarder * qch, mettre la pagaille dans qch

Gallic /ˈgælɪk/ ADJ *(= of Gaul)* gaulois ; *(= French)* français ♦ **~ charm** charme *m* latin ♦ **the ~ Wars** la guerre des Gaules

gallic /ˈgælɪk/ ADJ *(Chem)* gallique

Gallicism /ˈgælɪsɪzəm/ N gallicisme *m*

gallimaufry /ˌgælɪˈmɔːfrɪ/ N fatras *m*

galling /ˈgɔːlɪŋ/ ADJ *(= irritating)* irritant, exaspérant

gallinule /ˈgælɪnjuːl/ N ♦ **common ~** poule *f* d'eau

gallium /ˈgælɪəm/ N gallium *m*

gallivant /ˌgælɪˈvænt/ VI (also **gallivant about, gallivant around**) *(for pleasure)* se balader ♦ **I have to earn my living while you go ~ing around Europe!** il faut que je gagne ma vie pendant que tu te balades en Europe !

gallon /ˈgælən/ N gallon *m* *(Brit = 4,546 l, US = 3,785 l)*

gallop /ˈgæləp/ N galop *m* ♦ **to go for a ~** aller galoper ♦ **to break into a ~** prendre le galop, se mettre au galop ♦ **at a *or* the ~** au galop ♦ **at full ~** *(horse)* au grand galop, ventre à terre ; *(rider)* au grand galop, à bride abattue ♦ **after a quick ~ through the history of the Roman Empire, the author turns to ...** après avoir évoqué rapidement l'histoire de l'empire romain, l'auteur en vient à ... VI *[horse, rider]* galoper ♦ **to ~ away/back** *etc* partir/revenir *etc* au galop ♦ **to go ~ing down the street** *(fig)* descendre la rue au galop ♦ **to ~ through a book** * lire un livre à toute vitesse VT *[+ horse]* faire galoper

galloping /ˈgæləpɪŋ/ ADJ 1 *[horse]* au galop ; *[hooves, pace]* de cheval au galop 2 *(Med) [pneumonia, pleurisy, consumption]* galopant ; *(Econ) [economy, interest rates, prices]* qui s'emballe ♦ **~ inflation** inflation *f* galopante

gallows /ˈgæləʊz/ N (pl **gallowses** *or* **gallows**) *(NonC)* (also **gallows tree**) gibet *m*, potence *f* ♦ **he'll end up on the ~** il finira à la potence *or* par la corde

COMP **gallows bird** * N gibier *m* de potence

gallows humour N humour *m* macabre

gallstone /ˈgɔːlstəʊn/ N calcul *m* biliaire

Gallup /ˈgæləp/ N Gallup *m* COMP **Gallup poll** ® N sondage *m* Gallup

galoot * /gəˈluːt/ N *(US)* balourd * *m*

galop /ˈgæləp/ N galop *m* *(danse)*

galore /gəˈlɔːʳ/ ADV en abondance, à gogo * ♦ **bargains ~** de bonnes affaires à profusion

galosh /gəˈlɒʃ/ N *(gen pl)* ♦ **~es** caoutchoucs *mpl* *(enfilés par-dessus les chaussures)*

galumph * /gəˈlʌmf/ VI ♦ **to go ~ing in/out** *etc* *(clumsily)* entrer/sortir *etc* en courant maladroitement ; *(happily)* entrer/sortir *etc* en sautillant gaiement ♦ **a ~ing great girl** une grande fille à la démarche gauche

galvanic /gælˈvænɪk/ ADJ *(Elec)* galvanique ; *[jerk]* crispé ; *[effect]* galvanisant, électrisant

galvanism /ˈgælvənɪzəm/ N galvanisme *m*

galvanization /ˌgælvənaɪˈzeɪʃən/ N galvanisation *f*

galvanize /ˈgælvənaɪz/ VT 1 *(Elec, Med)* galvaniser ♦ **~d iron** fer *m* galvanisé 2 *(fig) [+ person, group]* galvaniser ; *[+ discussions, debate]* animer ; *[+ market, economy]* stimuler, donner une impulsion à ♦ **to ~ sb into action** pousser qn à agir ♦ **to ~ sb to do sth, to ~ sb into doing sth** pousser qn à faire qch

galvanometer /ˌgælvəˈnɒmɪtəʳ/ N galvanomètre *m*

galvanoscope /ˈgælvənəˌskəʊp/ N galvanoscope *m*

Gambia /ˈgæmbɪə/ N ♦ **(the) ~** la Gambie

Gambian /ˈgæmbɪən/ N Gambien(ne) *m(f)* ADJ gambien

gambit /ˈgæmbɪt/ N *(Chess)* gambit *m* ; *(fig)* manœuvre *f*, ruse *f* ; → **opening**

gamble /ˈgæmbl/ N entreprise *f* risquée, pari *m* ♦ **a political ~** un pari politique ♦ **life's a ~** la vie est un jeu de hasard ♦ **it's a pure ~** c'est affaire de chance ♦ **it was a bit of a ~ but ...** c'était un peu risqué mais ... ♦ **the ~ came off *or* paid off** ça a payé de prendre ce risque ♦ **to take a ~** prendre un risque ♦ **to take a ~ on it** prendre le risque ♦ **we're really taking a ~ with him** nous prenons vraiment un risque avec lui ♦ **the party is taking a ~ that they will be elected** le parti mise sur le fait qu'il remportera les élections ♦ **to have a ~ on a horse** miser sur un cheval ♦ **to have a ~ on the stock exchange** jouer à la Bourse

VI 1 *(lit)* jouer *(on* sur ; *with* avec*)* ♦ **to ~ on the stock exchange** jouer à la Bourse

2 *(fig)* ♦ **to ~ on** miser sur ♦ **we had been gambling on fine weather** nous avions misé sur le beau temps ♦ **to ~ on doing sth** *(confident of success)* compter faire qch ; *(less sure)* penser faire qch ♦ **Labour was gambling on winning support from the trade unions** les travaillistes comptaient *or* pensaient obtenir le soutien des syndicats ♦ **he was gambling on her being late *or* that she would be late** il comptait sur le fait qu'elle serait en retard ♦ **to ~ with sb's**

life jouer avec la vie de qn ◆ **to ~ with one's future** mettre en jeu son avenir

▸ **gamble away** VT SEP *[+ money etc]* perdre *or* dilapider au jeu

gambler /ˈgæmbləʳ/ **N** *(lit)* joueur *m*, -euse *f* ◆ **he's a bit of a ~** *(fig = risk-taker)* il a le goût du risque, il aime prendre des risques ; → **big** comp **COMP Gamblers Anonymous** N *association venant en aide aux joueurs invétérés*

gambling /ˈgæmblɪŋ/ **N** *(= action)* jeu *m* ; *(= games played)* jeux *mpl* d'argent ◆ **his ~ ruined his family** sa passion du jeu a entraîné la ruine de sa famille ◆ **he believes ~ is wrong** il pense que les jeux d'argent sont un vice
COMP gambling debts NPL dettes *fpl* de jeu
gambling den, gambling hell *, **gambling house, gambling joint** * *(US)* N *(pej)* maison *f* de jeu, tripot *m (pej)*
gambling losses NPL pertes *fpl* au jeu

gamboge /gæmˈbuːʒ/ N gomme-gutte *f*

gambol /ˈgæmbəl/ **N** gambade *f*, cabriole *f* **VI** gambader, cabrioler ◆ **to ~ away/back** *etc* partir/revenir *etc* en gambadant *or* cabriolant

gambrel /ˈgæmbrəl/ N (also **gambrel roof**) toit *m* brisé

game¹ /geɪm/ **N** 1 *(gen)* jeu *m* ; *(= match) [of football, rugby, cricket]* match *m* ; *[of tennis, billiards, chess]* partie *f* ; *[of bridge]* manche *f* ◆ **a ~ of cards** une partie de cartes ◆ **card ~s** jeux *mpl* de cartes ◆ **video ~s** jeux *mpl* vidéo *inv* ◆ **the wonderful ~ of football** le jeu merveilleux qu'est le football ◆ **England's next ~ is against Spain** le prochain match que jouera l'Angleterre sera contre l'Espagne ◆ **a ~ of skill/of chance** un jeu d'adresse/de hasard ◆ **he plays a good ~ of chess** il est bon aux échecs, il joue bien aux échecs ◆ **~, set and match** *(Tennis)* jeu, set et match ◆ **~ (to) Johnston** *(Tennis)* jeu Johnston ◆ **it isn't a ~, you know!** ce n'est pas un jeu tu sais ! ◆ **it's all part of the ~** cela fait partie des règles du jeu ◆ **to have the ~ in one's hands** être sur le point de gagner ◆ **to be the only ~ in town** *(esp US) [person, company, plan]* être le seul valable *or* digne de considération ◆ **to be on the ~** * *[prostitute]* faire le trottoir * ; → **highland, indoor, play**

◆ **to have** *or* **play a game of** *(chess etc)* faire une partie de ; *(football etc)* jouer un match de

◆ **game(s) all** ◆ **they were ~ all** *(Tennis)* ils étaient à un jeu partout ; *(Bridge)* ils étaient à une manche partout ◆ **it was three ~s all** *(Tennis)* on était à trois jeux partout ; *(Bridge)* on était à trois manches partout

2 *(= style of playing)* ◆ **in the second set my ~ picked up** au deuxième set mon jeu s'est amélioré ◆ **he's off his ~** il n'est pas en forme ◆ **to put sb off his** *(or* **her** *etc)* **~** troubler qn

3 *(= strategy)* manège *m*, (petit) jeu *m* ◆ **they are playing a complicated political ~** ils se livrent à un manège politique très complexe ◆ **the ~s people play when they fall in love** le petit jeu *or* le manège auquel se livrent les gens amoureux ◆ **can't you see his little ~?** tu ne vois pas qu'il mijote *or* manigance quelque chose ? ◆ **don't play his ~** n'entre pas dans son jeu ◆ **we soon saw through his ~** nous avons vite vu clair dans son (petit) jeu ◆ **two can play at that ~** à bon chat bon rat *(Prov)* ◆ **I wonder what his ~ is** * je me demande ce qu'il mijote * *or* manigance ◆ **to spoil sb's ~** déjouer les manigances *or* machinations de qn ◆ **what's your (little) ~?** * à quoi tu joues ? * ◆ **what's the ~?** * *(= what's happening?)* qu'est-ce qui se passe ? ; *(= what are you doing?)* à quoi tu joues ? * ; → **fun, give away, play, waiting**

◆ **to beat sb at his** *(or* **her** *etc)* **own game** battre qn sur son propre terrain

◆ **the game is up** tout est fichu * *or* à l'eau ◆ **they saw the ~ was up** ils ont vu que la partie était perdue ◆ **OK, the ~'s up!** ça suffit maintenant, tu es démasqué !

4 *(* = activity)* **I'm new to this ~** c'est nouveau pour moi ◆ **he was new to the ~ and didn't see the pitfalls** il était trop inexpérimenté pour voir qu'il y avait des pièges ◆ **how long have you been in this ~?** * cela fait combien de temps que vous faites ça ? ◆ **it's a profitable ~** c'est une entreprise rentable ◆ **I'm too old for this ~** ce n'est plus de mon âge

5 *(Culin, Hunting)* gibier *m* ◆ **big/small ~** gros/petit *or* menu gibier *m* ; see also **big, fair¹**

NPL games *(Brit Scol)* sport *m*, activités *fpl* physiques et sportives ◆ **to be good at ~s** être sportif ◆ **we have ~s on Thursdays** nous avons EPS le jeudi

VI *(= gamble)* jouer

ADJ 1 *(= ready, prepared)* prêt *(to do sth* à faire qch) ◆ **are you ~?** tu en as envie ? ◆ **I'm ~ if you are** je marche si tu marches ◆ **he's ~ for anything** il est prêt à tout, il ne recule devant rien

2 *(= brave)* courageux

COMP game birds NPL gibier *m NonC* à plume
game fish N poissons *mpl* d'eau douce
game laws NPL réglementation *f* de la chasse
game park N ⇒ **game reserve**
game pie N *(Culin)* pâté *m* de gibier en croûte
game plan N *(lit, fig)* stratégie *f* ◆ **what's the ~ plan?** *(fig)* comment va-t-on s'organiser ?
game reserve N réserve *f* naturelle
games console N *(Comput)* console *f* de jeux (vidéo)
game show N *(TV)* jeu *m* télévisé ; *(Rad)* jeu *m* radiophonique
games master, games mistress N *(Scol)* professeur *m* d'éducation physique
game theory N théorie *f* des jeux
game warden N garde-chasse *m* ; *(on reserve)* gardien *m* chargé de la protection des animaux

game² /geɪm/ ADJ *(= lame) [arm, leg]* estropié

gamebag /ˈgeɪmbæg/ N gibecière *f*, carnassière *f*

gamecock /ˈgeɪmkɒk/ N coq *m* de combat

gamekeeper /ˈgeɪm,kiːpəʳ/ N garde-chasse *m*

gamelan /ˈgæmɪ,læn/ N gamelan *m*

gamely /ˈgeɪmlɪ/ ADV hardiment

gamepad /ˈgeɪmpæd/ N manette *f* de jeux, gamepad *m*

gameplay /ˈgeɪmpleɪ/ N *(Comput)* jouabilité *f*

gamer * /ˈgeɪməʳ/ N *(= computer-game player)* amateur *m*, -trice *f* de jeux vidéo

gamesmanship /ˈgeɪmzmənʃɪp/ N ◆ **a successful piece of ~** un stratagème couronné de succès ◆ **an element of political ~** une part de stratégie politique ◆ **to be good at ~** savoir utiliser les règles (du jeu) à son avantage

gamester /ˈgeɪmstəʳ/ N joueur *m*, -euse *f*

gamete /ˈgæmiːt/ N gamète *m*

gamin /ˈgæmɛ̃/ N gamin *m*

gamine /gæˈmiːn/ **N** *(= cheeky girl)* gamine *f* (espiègle) ; *(= tomboy)* garçon *m* manqué **COMP** *[appearance, hat]* gamin
gamine haircut N ◆ **she had a ~ haircut** elle avait les cheveux coupés à la garçonne

gaming /ˈgeɪmɪŋ/ **N** 1 *(Comput)* jeu *m* 2 ⇒ **gambling** **COMP gaming laws** NPL réglementation *f* des jeux d'argent

gamma /ˈgæmə/ **N** gamma *m*
COMP gamma radiation N rayons *mpl* gamma
gamma rays NPL ⇒ **gamma radiation**

gammon /ˈgæmən/ **N** *(Brit) (= bacon)* quartier *m* de lard fumé ; *(= ham)* jambon *m* fumé **COMP gammon steak** N (épaisse) tranche *f* de jambon fumé *or* salé

gammy * /ˈgæmɪ/ ADJ *(Brit)* ⇒ **game²**

gamp * /gæmp/ N *(Brit hum)* pépin * *m*, pébroc *m*

gamut /ˈgæmət/ N *(Mus, fig)* gamme *f* ◆ **to run the ~ of** *(fig)* passer par toute la gamme de ◆ **his facial expressions ran the ~ from pain to terror** son visage est passé par toute la gamme des expressions de la douleur à la terreur

gamy /ˈgeɪmɪ/ ADJ *[meat etc]* au goût de gibier

gander /ˈgændəʳ/ N 1 *(= bird)* jars *m* ; → **sauce** 2 *(= look)* ◆ **to take a ~** * filer * un coup d'œil *(at* vers)

G&T, G and T /,dʒiːənˈtiː/ N (abbrev of **gin and tonic**) → **gin¹**

ganef * /ˈgɑːnəf/ N *(US)* escroc *m*, filou *m*

gang /gæŋ/ **N** *[of workmen]* équipe *f* ; *[of criminals]* bande *f*, gang *m* ; *[of youths, children, friends etc]* bande *f* ; *[of prisoners]* convoi *m* ; *(Tech) [of tools]* série *f* (d'outils multiples) ◆ **do you want to be in our ~?** veux-tu faire partie de notre bande ? ◆ **they roam the streets in ~s** ils traînent dans les rues en bandes ; → **chain**
COMP the Gang of Four N *(Pol)* la bande des Quatre
gang rape N viol *m* collectif
gang warfare N guerre *f* des gangs

▸ **gang together** * VI se mettre ensemble *or* à plusieurs *(to do sth* pour faire qch)

▸ **gang up** * VI se mettre à plusieurs *(to do sth* pour faire qch) ◆ **to ~ up on** *or* **against sb** * se liguer contre qn, se mettre à plusieurs contre qn

gangbang * /ˈgæŋ,bæŋ/ N *(= rape)* viol *m* collectif

gangbanger * /ˈgæŋ,bæŋəʳ/ N *(US = gang member)* membre *m* d'un gang

gangbusters * /ˈgæŋbʌstəʳz/ NPL *(US)* ◆ **to be going ~** marcher super bien * ◆ **to come on like ~** rouler des mécaniques *

ganger /ˈgæŋəʳ/ N *(Brit)* chef *m* d'équipe *(de travailleurs)*

Ganges /ˈgændʒiːz/ N Gange *m*

gangland * /ˈgæŋ,lænd/ N ◆ **~ boss** chef *m* de gang ◆ **~ killing** règlement *m* de comptes (entre gangs)

ganglia /ˈgæŋglɪə/ NPL of **ganglion**

gangling /ˈgæŋglɪŋ/ ADJ *[person]* dégingandé ◆ **a ~ boy** un échalas, une perche *(hum)*

ganglion /ˈgæŋglɪən/ N (pl **ganglia** *or* **ganglions**) ganglion *m* ; *(fig) [of activity]* centre *m*

gangly /ˈgæŋglɪ/ ADJ ⇒ **gangling**

gangplank /ˈgæŋ,plæŋk/ N passerelle *f* (de débarquement) ; *(Naut)* échelle *f* de coupée

gangrene /ˈgæŋgriːn/ **N** gangrène *f* **VI** se gangréner

gangrenous /ˈgæŋgrɪnəs/ ADJ gangreneux ◆ **to go ~** se gangrener

gangsta rap /ˈgænstə,ræp/ N gangsta rap *m*

gangster /ˈgæŋstəʳ/ **N** gangster *m*, bandit *m* **COMP** *[story, film]* de gangsters

gangsterism /ˈgæŋstərɪzəm/ N gangstérisme *m*

gangway /ˈgæŋ,weɪ/ N passerelle *f* ; *(Brit) (in bus etc)* couloir *m* ; *(in theatre)* allée *f* ◆ **~!** dégagez !

ganja /ˈgændʒə/ N ganja *f*

gannet /ˈgænɪt/ N fou *m* (de Bassan)

gantry /ˈgæntrɪ/ N *(for crane)* portique *m* ; *(Space)* tour *f* de lancement ; *(Rail)* portique *m* (à signaux) ; *(for barrels)* chantier *m*

gaol /dʒeɪl/ *(Brit)* ⇒ **jail**

gaoler /ˈdʒeɪləʳ/ N *(Brit)* ⇒ **jailer**

gap /gæp/ **N** 1 trou *m*, vide *m* ; *(in wall)* trou *m*, brèche *f* ; *(in hedge)* trou *m*, ouverture *f* ; *(in print, text)* espace *m*, blanc *m* ; *(between floorboards)* interstice *m* ; *(in pavement)* brèche *f* ; *(between curtains)* intervalle *m* ; *(in clouds, fog)* trouée *f* ;

(between teeth) écart *m*, interstice *m* ; *(= mountain pass)* trouée *f* ; *(in writing)* blanc *m* ◆ **to stop up** *or* **fill in a ~** boucher un trou, combler un vide

2 *(in time)* intervalle *m* ; *(in timetable)* trou *m* ; *(in conversation, narrative)* interruption *f*, vide *m* ; *(in education)* lacune *f*, manque *m* ◆ **a ~ in his memory** un trou de mémoire ◆ **he left a ~ which will be hard to fill** il a laissé un vide qui sera difficile à combler ◆ **the four-month ~ between the ceasefire and the elections** l'intervalle de quatre mois entre le cessez-le-feu et les élections ◆ **production was resumed after a three-year ~** *or* **a ~ of three years** la production a repris après une interruption de trois ans ◆ **after a ~ of three years** *or* **a three-year ~, Henry was born** trois ans plus tard, Henry est né ◆ **she returned after a ~ of four years** elle est rentrée après une absence de quatre ans ◆ **on the last lap she closed the ~ (between them) to 4.2 seconds** au dernier tour de piste elle est revenue à 4,2 secondes de sa concurrente ◆ **policies designed to close the ~ between the salaries of public and private sector employees** des mesures visant à réduire l'écart entre les salaires du secteur public et ceux du secteur privé ◆ **tax increases to close the ~ between spending and revenue** des augmentations d'impôt afin de réduire l'écart entre les dépenses et les recettes ◆ **to close the ~ in the balance of payments** supprimer le déficit dans la balance des paiements ◆ **the ~ between rich and poor is closing/widening** l'écart entre les riches et les pauvres se réduit/se creuse ◆ **a ~ in the market** un créneau ◆ **the software ~ is the biggest problem** l'insuffisance en matière de logiciel constitue le problème majeur ◆ **the trade ~** le déficit commercial ; → **bridge[1], credibility, generation**

COMP **gap financing** N crédit *m* (de) relais

gap-toothed ADJ *[person]* *(= teeth wide apart)* aux dents écartées ; *(= teeth missing)* brèche-dent † *inv*, à qui il manque une (*or* des) dent(s) ; *[smile, grin]* édenté

gap year N ◆ **he spent his ~ year in India** avant d'entrer à l'université, il a passé un an en Inde

gape /geɪp/ VI 1 *(= open mouth) [person]* bâiller, ouvrir la bouche toute grande ; *[bird]* ouvrir le bec tout grand ; *[seam etc]* bâiller ; *[chasm, abyss]* être béant 2 *(= stare)* rester bouche bée, bayer aux corneilles ◆ **to ~ at sb/sth** regarder qn/qch bouche bée N *(= stare)* regard *m* ébahi

gaping /ˈgeɪpɪŋ/ ADJ *[hole, chasm, wound]* béant ; *[mouth, eyes]* grand ouvert ; *[onlooker, tourist]* bouche bée *inv*

gappy /ˈgæpɪ/ ADJ *[teeth]* écartés ; *[structure, hedge]* avec des vides

garage /ˈgærɑːʒ/ N 1 garage *m* 2 (also **garage music**) garage *m* VT garer, mettre au garage COMP *[door, wall]* de garage

garage band N *(Mus)* groupe *m* de musique garage

garage mechanic N mécanicien *m*

garage proprietor N garagiste *m*

garage sale N vente *f* d'objets usagés *(chez un particulier)*, vide-grenier *m* ; → CAR-BOOT SALE, GARAGE SALE

garage space N *(NonC)* place *f* pour se garer ◆ **there is ~ space for three cars** il y a de la place pour trois voitures

garageman /ˈgærɑːʒmən/ N (pl **-men**) mécanicien *m*

garaging /ˈgærɑːʒɪŋ/ N *(NonC)* place *f* pour se garer ◆ **there is ~ for three cars** il y a de la place pour trois voitures

garb /gɑːb/ N *(NonC: gen hum)* costume *m*, atours *mpl (liter)* ◆ **in medieval ~** en costume médiéval VT *(gen passive)* vêtir *(in* de)

garbage /ˈgɑːbɪdʒ/ N *(NonC: esp US)* ordures *fpl*, détritus *mpl* ; *(= food waste)* déchets *mpl* ; *(fig)* *(= worthless objects)* rebut *m* ; *(= nonsense)* foutaises‡ *fpl* ; *(Comput)* (informations *fpl*) parasites *mpl* ◆ **~ in, ~ out** *(Comput)* qualité d'entrée égale qualité de sortie, garbage in garbage out

COMP **garbage can** N *(US)* boîte *f* à ordures, poubelle *f*

garbage chute N *(US)* vide-ordures *m inv*

garbage collector N *(US)* éboueur *m*

garbage disposal unit N *(US)* broyeur *m* d'ordures

garbage man N (pl **garbage men**) *(US)* ⇒ **garbage collector**

garbage shute N *(US)* ⇒ **garbage chute**

garbage truck N *(US)* camion *m* des éboueurs

garble /ˈgɑːbl/ VT embrouiller

garbled /ˈgɑːbld/ ADJ *[account, version, message]* embrouillé ; *[words, speech]* confus

Garda[1] /ˈgɑːdə/ N ◆ **Lake ~** le lac de Garde

Garda[2] /ˈgɑːdə/ N (pl **Gardaí** /ˈgɑːdiː/) *(Ir)* agent *m* de police ◆ **the ~** *or* **~í** *la police irlandaise*

garden /ˈgɑːdn/ N jardin *m* ◆ **the Garden of Eden** le Paradis terrestre, le jardin d'Éden ◆ **~s** *(public)* parc *m*, jardin *m* public ; *[of manor house etc]* jardin *m* ◆ **herb ~** jardin *m* d'herbes aromatiques ◆ **vegetable ~** (jardin *m*) potager *m* ◆ **in the ~** dans le jardin, au jardin ◆ **everything in the ~'s lovely** *or* **rosy** tout va pour le mieux ; → **back, flower, kitchen**

VI jardiner, faire du jardinage ◆ **I like ~ing** j'aime le jardinage, j'aime jardiner

COMP **garden apartment** N *(US)* ⇒ **garden flat**

garden centre N jardinerie *f*

garden city N *(Brit)* cité-jardin *f*

garden flat N appartement *m* en rez-de-jardin

garden gnome N nain *m* de jardin

garden hose N tuyau *m* d'arrosage

garden of remembrance N jardin *m* du souvenir *(dans un cimetière)*

garden party N garden-party *f*, réception *f* en plein air

garden path N *(fig)* ◆ **to lead sb up the ~ path** * mener qn en bateau *

garden produce N *(NonC)* produits *mpl* maraîchers

garden seat N banc *m* de jardin

garden shears NPL cisaille *f* de jardinier

garden snail N escargot *m*

the Garden State N *(US)* le New Jersey

garden suburb N banlieue *f* résidentielle *(aménagée par un paysagiste)*

garden tools NPL outils *mpl* de jardinage

garden-variety ADJ *(US)* *(= ordinary)* simple, ordinaire ; *(= standard)* d'un modèle standard *or* ordinaire

garden wall N mur *m* de jardin ◆ **he lives just over the ~ wall from us** il habite juste à côté de chez nous

gardener /ˈgɑːdnəʳ/ N jardinier *m*, -ière *f* ◆ **I'm no ~** je ne connais rien au jardinage ◆ **he's a good ~** il est très bon jardinier ; → **landscape**

gardenia /gɑːˈdiːnɪə/ N gardénia *m*

gardening /ˈgɑːdnɪŋ/ N jardinage *m* ; see also **garden, landscape** COMP **gardening tools** NPL outils *mpl* de jardinage

garfish /ˈgɑːfɪʃ/ N (pl **garfish** *or* **garfishes**) orphie *f*

gargantuan /gɑːˈgæntjʊən/ ADJ gargantuesque

gargle /ˈgɑːgl/ VI se gargariser *(with* à) se faire un gargarisme *(with* avec) N gargarisme *m*

gargoyle /ˈgɑːgɔɪl/ N gargouille *f*

garish /ˈgeərɪʃ/ ADJ *[colour]* criard ; *[clothes]* aux couleurs criardes, tapageur ; *[décor]* criard, tapageur ; *[light]* cru

garishly /ˈgeərɪʃlɪ/ ADV *[decorated, painted, dressed]* de couleurs criardes ◆ **~ coloured** aux couleurs criardes ◆ **~ lit** crûment éclairé

garishness /ˈgeərɪʃnɪs/ N *[of clothes, décor, building]* aspect *m* criard *or* tapageur ; *[of colours]* crudité *f*, violence *f*

garland /ˈgɑːlənd/ N guirlande *f* ◆ **a ~ of flowers/holly** une guirlande de fleurs/de houx VT orner de guirlandes, enguirlander

garlic /ˈgɑːlɪk/ N *(NonC)* ail *m* ; → **clove[1]**

COMP **garlic bread** N pain *m* à l'ail

garlic mushrooms NPL champignons *mpl* à l'ail

garlic press N presse-ail *m inv*

garlic salt N sel *m* d'ail

garlic sausage N saucisson *m* à l'ail

garlicky /ˈgɑːlɪkɪ/ ADJ *[flavour, smell]* d'ail ; *[sauce]* à l'ail ; *[food]* aillé ; *[breath]* qui sent l'ail

garment /ˈgɑːmənt/ N vêtement *m*

garner /ˈgɑːnəʳ/ VT (also **garner in, garner up**) *[+ grain etc]* rentrer, engranger ; *(fig)* *[+ information, reviews]* recueillir N *(liter)* *(= granary)* grenier *m* ; *(= anthology)* recueil *m*

garnet /ˈgɑːnɪt/ N *(= gem, colour)* grenat *m* ADJ (also **garnet-coloured**) grenat *inv* COMP *[ring]* de grenat(s)

garnish /ˈgɑːnɪʃ/ VT orner, parer *(with* de) ; *(Culin)* décorer *(with* avec) N décoration *f*

garnishee /ˌgɑːnɪˈʃiː/ N *(Jur)* saisi *m*

garnishing /ˈgɑːnɪʃɪŋ/ N *(Culin)* décoration *f*

garnishment /ˈgɑːnɪʃmənt/ N *(Jur)* saisie-arrêt *f*

garnishor /ˈgɑːnɪʃəʳ/ N *(Jur)* saisissant *m*

garotte /gəˈrɒt/ VT, N ⇒ **garrotte**

garret /ˈgærət/ N *(= room)* mansarde *f* ; *(= attic)* grenier *m*

garrison /ˈgærɪsən/ N garnison *f* VT *[+ fort etc]* placer une garnison dans ; *[+ troops]* mettre en garnison ; *[regiment]* être en garnison dans

COMP **garrison life** N vie *f* de garnison

garrison town N ville *f* de garnison

garrison troops NPL troupes *fpl* de garnison

garrotte /gəˈrɒt/ VT *(= strangle)* étrangler ; *(Spanish Hist)* faire périr par le garrot N *(gen)* cordelette *f (pour étrangler)* ; *(Spanish Hist)* garrot *m*

garrulous /ˈgærʊləs/ ADJ *[person]* loquace, volubile ; *(liter)* *[stream]* babillard *(liter)*

garrulously /ˈgærʊləslɪ/ ADV *[talk]* avec volubilité

garrulousness /ˈgærʊləsnɪs/ N loquacité *f*, volubilité *f*

garter /ˈgɑːtəʳ/ N *(gen)* jarretière *f* ; *(for men's socks)* fixe-chaussette *m* ; *(US: from belt)* jarretelle *f* ◆ **Order of the Garter** *(Brit)* Ordre *m* de la Jarretière ◆ **Knight of the Garter** *(Brit)* chevalier *m* de l'Ordre de la Jarretière

COMP **garter belt** N *(US)* porte-jarretelles *m inv*

garter stitch N *(Knitting)* point *m* mousse

gas /gæs/ N (pl **gas(s)es**) 1 *(Chem, Culin, Phys, Med etc)* gaz *m inv* ; *(Min)* méthane *m*, grisou *m* ; *(Mil)* gaz *m* (asphyxiant *or* vésicant *etc*) ; *(= anaesthetic)* (gaz *m*) anesthésique *m* ◆ **to cook by** *or* **with ~** faire la cuisine au gaz ◆ **to turn on/off the ~** allumer/fermer *or* éteindre le gaz ◆ **the dentist gave me ~** le dentiste m'a fait une anesthésie au gaz ◆ **(combined) ~ and electric cooker** cuisinière *f* mixte ; → **laughing, natural, supply[1]**

2 (US: also **gasoline**) essence *f* ◆ **to step on the ~** * *[driver]* appuyer sur le champignon * ; *(fig)* se magner *, se presser ◆ **to take one's foot off the ~** * ralentir

3 *(= chat)* ◆ **to have a ~** ‡ tailler une bavette * *(about* à propos de)

4 (‡ *= fun)* rigolade * *f* ◆ **it was a real ~!** quelle rigolade ! *, ce qu'on s'est marrés ! ‡

VT *(gen)* asphyxier ; *(Mil)* gazer ◆ **to ~ o.s.** *(gen)* s'asphyxier ; *(= commit suicide)* se suicider au gaz

VI 1 *(Chem)* dégager des gaz
2 (⁑ = *talk, chat*) papoter
COMP *[industry]* du gaz, gazier ; *[engine]* à gaz
gas bracket N applique *f* à gaz
gas burner N ⇒ **gas jet**
gas carrier N (= *ship*) méthanier *m*
gas central heating N ⇒ **gas-fired central heating**
gas chamber N chambre *f* à gaz
gas cooker N cuisinière *f* à gaz, gazinière *f* ; *(portable)* réchaud *m* à gaz
gas-cooled reactor N réacteur *m* graphite-gaz
gas cylinder N bonbonne *f* de gaz
gas explosion N *(gen)* explosion *f* (causée par une fuite) de gaz ; *(in coal mine)* explosion *f or* coup *m* de grisou
gas fire N appareil *m* de chauffage à gaz ◆ **to light the ~ fire** allumer le gaz
gas-fired ADJ chauffé au gaz
gas-fired central heating N chauffage *m* central au gaz
gas fitter N installateur *m*, -trice *f* d'appareils à gaz
gas fittings NPL installation *f* de gaz
gas fixture N ⇒ **gas bracket**
gas guzzler⁑ N (*US* = *car*) voiture *f* qui consomme énormément d'essence *or* qui suce⁑ beaucoup
gas heater N appareil *m* de chauffage à gaz ; *(for heating water)* chauffe-eau *m inv* (à gaz)
gas hog * N *(US)* ⇒ **gas guzzler**
gas jet N brûleur *m* à gaz
gas lamp N lampe *f* à gaz
gas lighter N *(for cooker etc)* allume-gaz *m inv* ; *(for cigarettes)* briquet *m* à gaz
gas lighting N éclairage *m* au gaz
gas main N canalisation *f* de gaz
gas mantle N manchon *m* à incandescence
gas meter N compteur *m* à gaz
gas mileage N *(US)* consommation *f* d'essence
gas oil N gasoil *m*
gas oven N four *m* à gaz ◆ **he put his head in the ~ oven** il s'est suicidé en se mettant la tête dans le four à gaz ◆ **she felt like putting her head in the ~ oven** elle avait envie de se jeter par la fenêtre
gas pedal N *(US)* (pédale *f* d')accélérateur *m*
gas-permeable ADJ *[lens]* perméable à l'oxygène
gas pipe N tuyau *m* à gaz
gas pipeline N gazoduc *m*
gas pump N *(US Aut)* pompe *f* à essence
gas range N fourneau *m* à gaz
gas ring N (= *part of cooker*) brûleur *m* ; (= *small stove*) réchaud *m* à gaz
gas station N *(US)* station-service *f*
gas stove N *(portable)* réchaud *m* à gaz ; *(larger)* cuisinière *f or* fourneau *m* à gaz
gas tank N *(US)* réservoir *m* à essence
gas tap N *(on pipe)* robinet *m* à gaz ; *(on cooker)* bouton *m* (de cuisinière à gaz)
gas turbine N turbine *f* à gaz
gas worker N gazier *m*

► **gas up** * VI (*US* = *get fuel*) faire le plein (de carburant)

gasbag /ˈgæsbæg/ N (enveloppe *f* de) ballon *m* à gaz ; (⁑ *pej*) (= *talkative person*) moulin *m* à paroles * *(pej)* ; (= *boastful person*) baratineur* *m*, -euse* *f*

Gascon /ˈgæskən/ ADJ gascon N Gascon(ne) *m(f)*

Gascony /ˈgæskənɪ/ N Gascogne *f*

gaseous /ˈgæsɪəs/ ADJ gazeux

gash /gæʃ/ N *(in flesh)* entaille *f*, estafilade *f* ; *(on face)* balafre *f* ; *(in cloth, leather)* grande déchirure *f* VT *[+ flesh]* entailler, entamer ; *[+ face]* balafrer ; *[+ cloth, leather]* déchirer ◆ **she ~ed her arm** elle s'est entaillé *or* s'est entamé le bras ADJ (*Brit* ⁑ = *surplus*) de trop, en surplus

gasholder /ˈgæs,həʊldəʳ/ N gazomètre *m*

gasket /ˈgæskɪt/ N 1 *[of piston]* garniture *f* de piston ; *[of joint]* joint *m* d'étanchéité ; *[of cylinder head]* joint *m* de culasse ; → **blow¹** 2 *(Naut)* raban *m* de ferlage

gaslight /ˈgæslaɪt/ N lumière *f* du gaz ◆ **by ~** au gaz, à la lumière du gaz

gaslit /ˈgæslɪt/ N éclairé au gaz

gasman * /ˈgæsmən/ N (pl **-men**) employé *m* du gaz, gazier *m*

gasmask /ˈgæsmæsk/ N masque *m* à gaz

gasohol /ˈgæsəʊhɒl/ N *(US)* carburol *m*

gasoline /ˈgæsəʊliːn/ *(US)* N essence *f*
COMP **gasoline gauge** N jauge *f* d'essence
gasoline-powered ADJ à essence

gasometer /gæˈsɒmɪtəʳ/ N *(Brit)* gazomètre *m*

gasp /gɑːsp/ N halètement *m* ◆ **to give a ~ of surprise/fear** *etc* avoir le souffle coupé par la surprise/la peur *etc* ◆ **to be at one's last ~** * être au bout du rouleau ◆ **to the last ~** jusqu'au dernier souffle ◆ **11,000 years ago, at the last ~ of the ice age** il y a 11 000 ans, juste à la fin de l'ère glaciaire
VI (= *choke*) haleter, suffoquer ; *(from astonishment)* avoir le souffle coupé ◆ **to make sb ~** *(lit, fig)* couper le souffle à qn ◆ **to ~ for breath** *or* **air** haleter, suffoquer ◆ **I'm ~ing * for a cup of tea/a cigarette** (= *want desperately*) je meurs d'envie de boire une tasse de thé/de fumer une cigarette ◆ **I was ~ing!** * (= *thirsty*) je mourrais de soif
VT *(in quiet voice)* souffler ◆ **"no!" she ~ed** "non !" souffla-t-elle ◆ **the young man ~ed his thanks** *(in strangled voice)* le jeune homme remercia d'une voix entrecoupée ◆ **"you're beautiful," he ~ed out** "vous êtes belle" dit-il d'une voix entrecoupée

gasper⁑ /ˈgɑːspəʳ/ N *(Brit)* sèche⁑ *f*, clope⁑ *f or m*

gassed⁑ /gæst/ ADJ (= *drunk*) bourré⁑

gassy /ˈgæsɪ/ ADJ gazeux ; (* *pej*) *[person]* bavard, jacasseur

gastric /ˈgæstrɪk/ ADJ gastrique
COMP **gastric flu** N grippe *f* gastro-intestinale
gastric juices NPL sucs *mpl* gastriques
gastric ulcer N ulcère *m* de l'estomac

gastritis /gæsˈtraɪtɪs/ N gastrite *f*

gastroenteritis /ˌgæstrəʊˌentəˈraɪtɪs/ N gastroentérite *f*

gastroenterologist /ˈgæstrəʊˈentəˌrɒlədʒɪst/ N gastroentérologue *mf*

gastroenterology /ˈgæstrəʊˈentəˌrɒlədʒɪ/ N gastroentérologie *f*

gastrointestinal /ˌgæstrəʊɪnˈtestɪnl/ ADJ *[problems, disorders, system]* gastro-intestinal

gastronome /ˈgæstrənəʊm/ N gastronome *mf*

gastronomic /ˌgæstrəˈnɒmɪk/ ADJ gastronomique

gastronomist /gæsˈtrɒnəmɪst/ N gastronome *mf*

gastronomy /gæsˈtrɒnəmɪ/ N gastronomie *f*

gastropod /ˈgæstrəpɒd/ N gastéropode *m*

gasworks /ˈgæswɜːks/ N (pl *inv*) usine *f* à gaz

gat¹ †† /gæt/ VB pt of **get**

gat² †⁑ /gæt/ N (*US*) (= *gun*) flingue⁑ *m*, pétard⁑ *m*

gate /geɪt/ N 1 *[of castle, town, airport]* porte *f* ; *[of field, level crossing]* barrière *f* ; *[of garden]* porte *f*, portail *m* ; *(large, metallic)* grille *f* (d'entrée) ; *(low)* portillon *m* ; *(tall, into courtyard etc)* porte *f* cochère ; *(in Metro)* portillon *m* ; *[of lock, sluice]* vanne *f*, porte *f* (d'écluse) ; *[of sports ground]* entrée *f* ◆ **the factory/castle** *etc* **~** (= *entrance*) l'entrée *f* de l'usine/du château *etc* ◆ **five-bar ~** ≃ barrière *f* ◆ **to give sb the ~** ⁑ *(US)* *[+ employee]* virer* qn ; *[+ boyfriend etc]* plaquer* qn ◆ **to get the ~** ⁑ *(US)* (= *be dismissed*) être viré*
2 *(Sport)* (= *attendance*) spectateurs *mpl* ; (= *money*) recette *f*, entrées *fpl* ◆ **there was a ~ of 5,000** il y avait 5 000 spectateurs ◆ **the match got a good ~** le match a fait beaucoup d'entrées
3 *(Ski)* porte *f*
4 *(Comput)* porte *f*
VT (*Brit* *: *Scol, Univ*) consigner, coller*
COMP **gated community** N (*esp US*) enclave *f* (résidentielle) protégée
gate-leg(ged) table N table *f* anglaise, table *f* à abattants
gate money N *(Sport)* recette *f*, (montant *m* des) entrées *fpl*

...gate /geɪt/ N *(in compounds)* ◆ **Dianagate** scandale *m* Diana ◆ **Irangate** Irangate *m* ; see also **Watergate**

gâteau /ˈgætəʊ/ N (pl **gâteaux** /ˈgætəʊz/) *(Brit)* grand gâteau *m* fourré

gatecrash /ˈgeɪtkræʃ/ VI *(without invitation)* s'introduire sans invitation ; *(without paying)* resquiller* VT s'introduire (sans invitation) dans ◆ **to ~ a match** assister à un match sans payer

gatecrasher /ˈgeɪt,kræʃəʳ/ N *(without invitation)* intrus(e) *m(f)* ; *(without paying)* resquilleur* *m*, -euse* *f*

gatefold /ˈgeɪtfəʊld/ N *(US Publishing)* dépliant *m* encarté

gatehouse /ˈgeɪthaʊs/ N *[of castle]* corps *m* de garde ; *[of park etc]* maison *f* du gardien

gatekeeper /ˈgeɪt,kiːpəʳ/ N *[of block of flats etc]* portier *m*, -ière *f* ; *[of factory etc]* gardien(ne) *m(f)* ; *(Rail)* garde-barrière *mf*

gatepost /ˈgeɪtpəʊst/ N montant *m* (de porte) ◆ **between you, me and the ~** * soit dit entre nous

gateway /ˈgeɪtweɪ/ N entrée *f* ◆ **New York, the ~ to America** New York, porte de l'Amérique ◆ **it proved the ~ to success/fame/fortune** cela ouvrit toutes grandes les portes du succès/de la gloire/de la fortune

gather /ˈgæðəʳ/ VT 1 (also **gather together**) *[+ people]* rassembler, réunir ; *[+ objects]* rassembler, ramasser ; *[+ troops]* amasser
2 (= *draw, attract*) attirer ; *(Typ)* *[+ pages]* assembler ◆ **the programme ~ed an audience of 20 million viewers** cette émission a été regardée par 20 millions de téléspectateurs ◆ **the accident ~ed quite a crowd** l'accident a attiré pas mal de monde
3 (= *collect*) *[+ flowers]* cueillir ; *[+ wood, sticks, mushrooms]* ramasser ; *[+ taxes]* percevoir ; *[+ information, data, evidence]* réunir ◆ **to ~ dirt** s'encrasser ◆ **to ~ dust** *(lit, fig)* prendre la poussière ◆ **to ~ momentum** *(lit)* prendre de la vitesse ; *(fig)* *[political movement, pressure group]* prendre de l'ampleur ◆ **to ~ one's thoughts** se concentrer ◆ **to ~ speed, to ~ way** *(Naut)* prendre de la vitesse ◆ **to ~ strength** *[person]* reprendre des forces ; *[feeling, movement]* se renforcer ◆ **she is trying to ~ support for her ideas/her candidacy** elle essaie d'obtenir des appuis pour ses idées/sa candidature ◆ **to ~ volume** croître en volume
4 ◆ **she ~ed him in her arms** elle l'a serré dans ses bras ◆ **he ~ed her to him** il l'a serrée contre lui ◆ **he ~ed his cloak around him** il a ramené son manteau contre lui ◆ **she ~ed up her skirts** elle a ramassé ses jupes ◆ **her hair was ~ed into a bun** ses cheveux étaient ramassés en chignon ◆ **he was ~ed to his fathers** *(liter: euph)* il alla rejoindre ses ancêtres *or* aïeux
5 *(Sewing)* froncer ◆ **a ~ed skirt** une jupe froncée

6 (= infer) déduire, conclure ◆ **I ~ from this report (that)** … je conclus or je déduis de ce rapport (que) … ◆ **I ~ from the papers that …** d'après ce que disent les journaux, je déduis or je crois comprendre que … ◆ **I ~ from him that …** je comprends d'après ce qu'il me dit que … ◆ **what are we to ~ from that?** que devons-nous en déduire ? ◆ **as far as I can ~, from what I could ~** à ce que je comprends ◆ **I ~ she won't be coming** d'après ce que j'ai compris, elle ne viendra pas ◆ **as you will have ~ed** comme vous avez dû le deviner ◆ **as will be ~ed from my report** comme il ressort de mon rapport ◆ **so I ~** c'est ce que j'ai cru comprendre ◆ **I ~ed that** j'avais compris

VI 1 (= collect) [people] se rassembler, se réunir ; [troops] s'amasser ; [objects] s'accumuler ; [clouds] se former, s'amonceler ; [dust] s'accumuler, s'amasser ◆ **they ~ed round him** ils se sont groupés or se sont rassemblés autour de lui ◆ **a crowd had ~ed in front of the embassy** une foule s'était formée devant l'ambassade ◆ **a crowd of demonstrators had ~ed** des manifestants s'étaient rassemblés

2 (= increase) (in volume, intensity etc) croître, grandir ; (in size, content etc) grossir ; see also **gathering**

3 [abscess] mûrir ; [pus] se former ◆ **tears ~ed in her eyes** ses yeux se remplirent de larmes

N (Sewing) fronce f

▸ **gather in** VT SEP [+ crops] rentrer, récolter ; [+ money, taxes] faire rentrer, percevoir ; [+ contributions] recueillir ; [+ papers, essays] ramasser ◆ **the dress is ~ed in at the waist** la robe est froncée à la taille

▸ **gather round** VI faire cercle, s'approcher ◆ **~ round!** approchez-vous ! ◆ **~ round, children!** approchez-vous les enfants !

▸ **gather together** VI s'amasser, se rassembler

VT SEP ⇒ **gather vt 1** ◆ **to ~ o.s. together** (= collect one's thoughts) se recueillir, se concentrer ; (for jump etc) se ramasser

▸ **gather up** VT SEP [+ papers, clothes, toys] ramasser ◆ **to ~ up the threads of a discussion** rassembler les principaux arguments d'une discussion ◆ **to ~ up one's courage** rassembler son courage ◆ **to ~ up one's dignity** essayer de paraître digne ◆ **to ~ up one's strength** rassembler ses forces ◆ **to ~ o.s. up** (for jump etc) se ramasser ◆ **he ~ed himself up to his full height** il s'est redressé de toute sa hauteur ; see also **gather vt 3**

gatherer /ˈgæðərəʳ/ N cueilleur m, -euse f ; see also **hunter-gatherer**

gathering /ˈgæðərɪŋ/ N 1 (NonC = act) [of people] rassemblement m ; [of objects] accumulation f, amoncellement m ; [of fruits etc] cueillette f ; [of crops] récolte f ◆ **the ~ of information/evidence may take several weeks** réunir les informations/les preuves pourrait prendre plusieurs semaines

2 (= group of people) assemblée f, réunion f ; (= act of meeting) rassemblement m ◆ **a family ~** une réunion de famille ◆ **a ~ of 12 heads of state** une rencontre de 12 chefs d'État ◆ **~s of more than 20 people were forbidden** les rassemblements de plus de 20 personnes étaient interdits

3 (NonC: Sewing) fronces fpl, froncis m

ADJ [dusk, darkness, gloom] grandissant ; [crowd] en train de se former ◆ **the ~ clouds** les nuages qui s'amoncellent (or s'amoncelaient) ◆ **the ~ storm** l'orage qui se prépare (or se préparait) ◆ **with ~ speed** de plus en plus vite

-gathering /ˈgæðərɪŋ/ N (in compounds) ◆ **information- or intelligence-gathering** collecte f de renseignements

gator * /ˈgeɪtəʳ/ N (US) ⇒ **alligator**

GATT /gæt/ N (abbrev of **General Agreement on Tariffs and Trade**) GATT m

gauche /gəʊʃ/ ADJ gauche, maladroit

gaucheness /ˈgəʊʃnɪs/ N gaucherie f, maladresse f

gaucho /ˈgaʊtʃəʊ/ N gaucho m

gaudily /ˈgɔːdɪlɪ/ ADV [decorated, painted, dressed] de couleurs voyantes ◆ **~ coloured** aux couleurs voyantes or crues ◆ **~ patterned** aux motifs voyants

gaudy /ˈgɔːdɪ/ ADJ [clothes] aux couleurs voyantes ; [bird, fish] aux couleurs éclatantes ; [colour] voyant, cru ; [display etc] tapageur N (Brit Univ) fête f annuelle (de collège)

gauge /geɪdʒ/ N (= standard measure) calibre m ; (of railway) écartement m ; (of fabric) jauge f ; (= instrument) jauge f, indicateur m ◆ **oil ~** indicateur m or jauge f du niveau d'huile ◆ **the survey was seen as a good ~ of employment trends** l'enquête a été considérée comme un bon indicateur des tendances de l'emploi ◆ **opinion polls are not an accurate ~ of popular feeling** les sondages ne permettent pas d'évaluer avec justesse le sentiment populaire

VT 1 (= measure) [+ nut, temperature] mesurer ; [+ oil] jauger ; [+ wind] mesurer la vitesse de ; [+ screw, gun] calibrer ; [+ sb's abilities] évaluer ; [+ course of events] prévoir ◆ **to ~ a distance** (by looking) évaluer une distance à vue d'œil ◆ **"she's out," he said, gauging my reaction** "elle est sortie," dit-il, essayant de deviner ma réaction ◆ **I tried to ~ whether she was pleased or not** j'ai essayé de deviner si elle était contente ou pas ◆ **we must try to ~ how strong public opinion is** nous devons essayer d'évaluer le poids de l'opinion publique ◆ **to ~ the right moment** calculer le bon moment

2 [+ tools] standardiser

-gauge /geɪdʒ/ SUF (in compounds) ◆ **narrow-/standard-/broad-gauge railway** voie f étroite/à écartement normal/à grand écartement

Gaul /gɔːl/ N (= country) Gaule f ; (= person) Gaulois(e) m(f)

Gaullism /ˈgəʊlɪzəm/ N gaullisme m

Gaullist /ˈgəʊlɪst/ ADJ, N gaulliste mf

gaunt /gɔːnt/ ADJ 1 (= thin and pale) [person, face, features] hâve ; [body, figure] émacié ◆ **he looks ~** il a les traits tirés 2 (= grim) [building] austère ; [tree] squelettique

gauntlet /ˈgɔːntlɪt/ N (= glove) gant m (à crispin) ; (= part of glove) crispin m ; [of armour] gantelet m ◆ **to throw down/take up the ~** (Hist, also fig) jeter/relever le gant ◆ **to run the ~** (Mil Hist) passer par les baguettes ; (Naut Hist) courir la bouline ◆ **they ran the ~ of enemy submarines** ils risquaient d'être la cible de sous-marins ennemis ◆ **he had to run the ~ through the crowd** il a dû foncer à travers une foule hostile ◆ **he ran the ~ of public criticism** il essuya le feu des critiques du public

gauss /gaʊs/ N (pl inv) gauss m

gauze /gɔːz/ N (all senses) gaze f

gauzy /ˈgɔːzɪ/ ADJ vaporeux

gave /geɪv/ VB pt of **give**

gavel /ˈgævl/ N marteau m (de président de réunion, de commissaire-priseur)

gavotte /gəˈvɒt/ N gavotte f

Gawd ‡ /gɔːd/ EXCL (Brit = God) mon Dieu !, bon Dieu ! *

gawk /gɔːk/ N godiche * f, grand dadais * m VI rester bouche bée (at devant)

gawker * /ˈgɔːkəʳ/ N badaud m

gawky /ˈgɔːkɪ/ ADJ godiche *, empoté

gawp * /gɔːp/ VI (Brit) ⇒ **gape vi**

gay /geɪ/ ADJ 1 (= homosexual) [person, community, movement] homosexuel, gay inv ; [group, club, bar] gay inv ◆ **~ men and women** homosexuels mpl et lesbiennes fpl ◆ **~ rights** droits mpl des homosexuels ◆ **~ sex** rapports mpl homosexuels 2 († = cheerful) [person, company, occasion] joyeux ; [music, party, appearance, colour] gai ; [laughter] enjoué, gai ; [costume] aux couleurs gaies ◆ **to become ~(er)** s'égayer ◆ **with ~ abandon** avec une belle désinvolture ◆ **to lead a or the ~ life** mener une vie de plaisirs, mener joyeuse vie ◆ **to have a ~ time** prendre du bon temps N homosexuel(le) m(f) ◆ **Gay Liberation (Movement), Gay Lib** * (mouvement m pour) la libération des homosexuels or la libération gay COMP **gay-friendly** ADJ [place, environment] où les homosexuels sont très bien acceptés

gayness /ˈgeɪnɪs/ N [of homosexual] homosexualité f

Gaza strip /ˈgɑːzəˈstrɪp/ N bande f de Gaza

gaze /geɪz/ N regard m (fixe) ◆ **his ~ met mine** son regard a croisé le mien VI regarder ◆ **to ~ into space** regarder dans or fixer le vide ◆ **to ~ at** or (liter) **upon sth** regarder or contempler qch ◆ **they ~d into each other's eyes** ils se regardaient les yeux dans les yeux ◆ **to ~ out of the window** regarder fixement par la fenêtre ◆ **to ~ at o.s. in the mirror** se regarder fixement dans le miroir

▸ **gaze about, gaze around** VI regarder autour de soi

gazebo /gəˈziːbəʊ/ N (pl **gazebos** or **gazeboes**) belvédère m (pavillon)

gazelle /gəˈzel/ N (pl **gazelles** or **gazelle**) gazelle f

gazette /gəˈzet/ N (= official publication) (journal m) officiel m ; (= newspaper) gazette f VT publier à l'Officiel ◆ **to be ~d** (Mil etc) avoir sa nomination publiée à l'Officiel

gazetteer /ˌgæzɪˈtɪəʳ/ N index m (géographique)

gazpacho /gəzˈpætʃəʊ/ N gaspacho m

gazump /gəˈzʌmp/ VT (Brit) ◆ **he was ~ed** le vendeur est revenu sur sa promesse de vente en acceptant une meilleure offre

gazumping /gəˈzʌmpɪŋ/ N (Brit) le fait de revenir sur une promesse de vente d'une maison pour accepter une offre plus élevée

gazunder /gəˈzʌndəʳ/ (Brit) VI revenir sur une promesse d'achat immobilier pour tenter de faire baisser le prix VT (Brit) ◆ **to be ~ed** être obligé de baisser son prix à la dernière minute

GB /dʒiːˈbiː/ (abbrev of **Great Britain**) GB

GBH /dʒiːbiːˈeɪtʃ/ (Brit) (= crime) (abbrev of **grievous bodily harm**) → **grievous**

GC /ˈdʒiːsiː/ N (Brit) (abbrev of **George Cross**) → **George**

GCE /dʒiːsiːˈiː/ N (Brit Educ) (abbrev of **General Certificate of Education**) (formerly) ◆ **~ "O" level** ≈ brevet m ◆ **~ "A" level** ≈ baccalauréat m

GCH N (abbrev of **gas(-fired) central heating**) → **gas**

GCHQ /ˌdʒiːsiːeɪtʃˈkjuː/ N (Brit) (abbrev of **Government Communications Headquarters**) service gouvernemental d'interception des communications

GCSE /ˌdʒiːsiːesˈiː/ N (Brit Educ) (abbrev of **General Certificate of Secondary Education**) ≈ brevet m des collèges

GCSE

En Angleterre, au pays de Galles et en Irlande du Nord, le **General Certificate of Secondary Education** ou **GCSE** est l'équivalent du brevet des collèges français. À l'issue de cet examen, qui se passe généralement à l'âge de seize ans, l'élève peut soit quitter l'école, soit préparer les « A levels », qui correspondent au baccalauréat français. L'équivalent écossais du **GCSE** porte le nom de « Standard Grades ». → A LEVELS

Gdansk /gdænsk/ N Gdansk

Gdns abbrev of **Gardens**

GDP /dʒi:di:'pi:/ N (abbrev of **gross domestic product**) → **gross**

GDR /dʒi:di:'ɑ:r/ N (abbrev of **German Democratic Republic**) → **German**

gear /gɪər/ N 1 (= *mechanism*) *[of vehicle]* embrayage *m* ; (= *speed*) vitesse *f* ◆ **a problem with the ~s** (= *mechanical fault*) un problème d'embrayage ◆ **the car slipped** *or* **jumped out of ~** la vitesse a sauté ◆ **to accelerate** *or* **move (up) through the ~s** accélérer en passant toutes les vitesses les unes après les autres ◆ **to move down through the ~s** ralentir en rétrogradant ◆ **first** *or* **bottom** *or* **low ~** première *f* (vitesse) ◆ **second/third/fourth ~** deuxième *f*/troisième *f*/quatrième *f* (vitesse) ◆ **top ~** *(Brit)* ◆ **high ~** *(US)* (= *fifth*) cinquième *f* (vitesse) ◆ **in second ~** en seconde

♦ **in gear** *[vehicle]* en prise ◆ **the car was in ~** la voiture était en prise ◆ **she put the car into ~** elle a mis la voiture en prise ◆ **not in ~** au point mort

♦ **out of gear** ◆ **it's out of ~** ce n'est pas *or* plus en prise

♦ **to change** *or* **shift + gear** ◆ **to change** *or (US)* **to shift ~** changer de vitesse ◆ **to change** *or (US)* **to shift into third ~** passer en troisième (vitesse) ◆ **to change** *or (US)* **to shift ~s** *(fig)* se réadapter

♦ **to get + in(to) gear** ◆ **to get in(to) ~** * *(fig) [person, process]* démarrer ◆ **the electoral campaign is getting into ~** la campagne électorale démarre ◆ **he helped her get her life back in(to) ~ after the divorce** il l'a aidée à commencer une vie nouvelle après le divorce ◆ **to get one's brain in(to) ~** * faire travailler ses méninges * ◆ **to get one's arse**** *(Brit) or* **ass**** *(US)* **in(to) ~** se remuer le cul**

♦ **to move into + gear** *(fig)* ◆ **after the war life suddenly moved into top ~** après la guerre, la vie a soudain pris un rythme effréné ◆ **military production moved into high ~** la production militaire a atteint sa vitesse maximale ; → **engage, reverse**

2 *(NonC)* (= *equipment*) équipement *m*, matériel *m* ; (= *harness*) harnachement *m* ; *(for camping, skiing, climbing, photography)* matériel *m*, équipement *m* ; *(for sewing, painting)* matériel *m* ; *(for gardening)* matériel *m*, outils *mpl* ◆ **fishing** *etc* **~** matériel *m or* équipement *m* de pêche *etc*

3 *(NonC: * = belongings)* affaires *fpl* ◆ **he leaves his ~ all over the house** il laisse traîner ses affaires dans toute la maison

4 *(NonC: Brit = clothing)* vêtements *mpl* ◆ **I used to wear trendy ~** avant je portais des vêtements branchés ◆ **he's going to wear a top hat and all the ~** il va porter un haut-de-forme et toute la panoplie ◆ **he had his tennis ~ on** il était en tenue de tennis ◆ **put on your tennis ~** mets tes affaires de tennis

5 *(NonC = apparatus)* mécanisme *m*, dispositif *m* ◆ **safety ~** mécanisme *m or* dispositif *m* de sécurité ; → **landing**[1], **steering**

6 *(Tech)* engrenage *m* ◆ **mechanical components such as ~s and bearings** les composants mécaniques tels que les engrenages et les paliers

7 * (= *drugs*) came* *f* ; (= *heroin*) héro* *f*

ADJ *(US * = great)* super *

VT 1 adapter ◆ **they ~ed their output to seasonal demands** ils ont adapté leur production à la demande saisonnière ◆ **classrooms ~ed to the needs of disabled students** des salles de classe adaptées aux besoins des étudiants handicapés ◆ **the factory was not ~ed to cope with an increase of production** l'usine n'était pas à même de faire face à une augmentation de la production ◆ **~ed to the cost of living** indexé ◆ **we both ~ our lives to the children** nous aménageons tous les deux notre vie en fonction des enfants ◆ **movies ~ed primarily to a US audience** des films s'adressant essentiellement à un public américain ◆ **training is ~ed to make staff more efficient** la formation est conçue pour rendre le personnel plus compétent

2 *[+ wheel]* engrener

VI s'engrener

COMP **gear change** N *(Brit)* changement *m* de vitesse

gear lever N *(Brit)* levier *m* de (changement de) vitesse

gear ratio N *[of cycle]* braquet *m*

gear stick N ⇒ **gear lever**

► **gear down** VI *(Tech)* démultiplier

► **gear up** VI 1 *(Tech)* produire une multiplication

2 (= *get ready*) ◆ **they are gearing up for a general election** ils se préparent pour des législatives ◆ **Japan is ~ing up to produce 2 million cars a year** le Japon se prépare à produire 2 millions de voitures par an

3 *(Brit Fin) [company]* s'endetter, augmenter le taux d'endettement

VT SEP (* = *make ready*) ◆ **he is gearing himself up for the presidential elections** il se prépare pour les élections présidentielles ◆ **satellites that are ~ed up to look for missiles** des satellites équipés pour la détection des missiles ◆ **the club is ~ed up for success** le club est fin prêt et compte bien gagner ◆ **they were all ~ed up for the new sales campaign** ils étaient parés *or* fin prêts pour la nouvelle campagne de ventes

gearbox /'gɪəbɒks/ N boîte *f* de vitesses

gearing /'gɪərɪŋ/ N *(Tech)* embrayage *m* ; *(Brit Fin)* taux *m* d'endettement

gearshift /'gɪəʃɪft/ N *(US)* ⇒ **gear change, gear lever**

gearwheel /'gɪəwi:l/ N *[of bicycle]* pignon *m*

gecko /'gekəʊ/ N (pl **geckos** *or* **geckoes**) gecko *m*

GED /,dʒi:i:'di:/ N *(US Educ)* (abbrev of **general equivalency diploma**) *diplôme d'études secondaires obtenu en candidat libre*

geddit* /'gedɪt/ EXCL ◆ **~ ?** tu piges ? *

gee[1] * /dʒi:/ EXCL *(esp US)* eh bien ! ◆ **~ whiz!** mince alors ! * COMP **gee-whiz** ADJ *(US) [product, gadget]* tape-à-l'œil *inv*

gee[2] /dʒi:/ VT ◆ **to ~ sb up** * motiver qn ◆ **~ up!** *(to horse)* hue ! COMP **gee-gee** N *(baby talk)* dada *m*

geek * /gi:k/ N *(esp US)* débile * *mf*

geeky * /'gi:kɪ/ ADJ *(esp US)* débile *

geese /gi:s/ NPL of **goose**

geezer † * /'gi:zər/ N *(esp Brit)* bonhomme * *m*, gus * *m* ◆ **(silly) old ~** vieux schnock * *m*

gefilte /gə'fɪltə/ ADJ *(US)* ◆ **~ fish** ≈ boulettes *fpl* de poisson

Geiger counter /'gaɪgə,kaʊntər/ N compteur *m* Geiger

geisha /'geɪʃə/ N (pl **geisha** *or* **geishas**) geisha *f*

gel[1] /dʒel/ N (= *substance*) *(gen)* gel *m* ; *(Pharm)* gel *m*, colloïde *m* VI 1 *[jelly]* prendre 2 *[plan]* prendre tournure ; *[people] (into team, group)* s'intégrer (with à) ; *[partnership, team]* se souder

gel[2] /gel/ N († *or hum*) ⇒ **girl**

gelatin(e) /'dʒelətɪ:n/ N gélatine *f*

gelatinous /dʒɪ'lætɪnəs/ ADJ gélatineux

geld /geld/ VT *[+ horse]* hongrer ; *[+ pig etc]* châtrer

gelding /'geldɪŋ/ N 1 (= *horse*) (cheval *m*) hongre *m* 2 *(NonC)* castration *f*

gelignite /'dʒelɪgnaɪt/ N plastic *m*

gelt* /gelt/ N *(US)* fric * *m*

gem /dʒem/ N 1 *(lit)* gemme *f*, pierre *f* précieuse 2 *(fig = work of art)* (vrai) bijou *m*, merveille *f* ◆ **this painting is a real ~** ce tableau est une merveille ◆ **the cathedral is a ~ of Gothic architecture** la cathédrale est un joyau de l'architecture gothique ◆ **a perfect ~ of a hotel** un hôtel absolument charmant ◆ **Duval is a ~ of a writer** Duval est un écrivain remarquable ◆ **I must read you this little ~ from the newspaper** il faut que je te lise cette perle dans le journal ◆ **thanks, Pat, you're a ~** merci, Pat, tu es un amour *or* un ange ◆ **Naomi's a ~ of a girl!** Naomi est un amour ! COMP **the Gem State** N *(US)* l'Idaho *m*

Gemini /'dʒemɪnaɪ/ NPL *(Astron)* Gémeaux *mpl* ◆ **I'm (a) ~** *(Astrol)* je suis (des) Gémeaux

Geminian /,dʒemɪ'naɪən/ N ◆ **to be a ~** être (des) Gémeaux ADJ *[person]* du signe des Gémeaux ; *[tendency, characteristic]* propre aux Gémeaux

gem(m)ology /dʒe'mɒlədʒɪ/ N gemmologie *f*

gemstone /'dʒemstəʊn/ N gemme *f*

gen * /dʒen/ *(Brit)* N ◆ **to give sb the ~ on sth** donner à qn tous les tuyaux * sur qch ◆ **what's the ~ on this?** qu'est-ce qu'on sait là-dessus ? ◆ **I want all the ~ on him** je veux tout savoir sur lui ◆ **have you got the ~ on the new house?** avez-vous une documentation sur la nouvelle maison ?

► **gen up*** VI ◆ **to gen up on sth** se rancarder sur qch*

VT SEP ◆ **to be genned up on** être tout à fait au courant de, être bien renseigné sur

Gen. *(Mil)* (abbrev of **general**) ◆ **J. Smith** *(on envelope)* le général Smith

gen. abbrev of **general** *and* **generally**

gendarme /'dʒɒndɑ:m/ N *(Climbing)* gendarme *m*

gender /'dʒendər/ N 1 *(Gram)* genre *m* ◆ **common ~** * genre *m* commun ◆ **to agree in ~** *(Gram)* s'accorder en genre 2 (= *sex*) sexe *m* ◆ **discrimination on grounds of ~** discrimination *f* sexuelle

COMP **gender bender*** N *personne qui s'habille de façon androgyne*

gender bias N parti pris *m* contre les femmes (*or* les hommes)

the gender gap N le décalage entre hommes et femmes

gender politics NPL politique *f* des sexes

gender reassignment N changement *m* de sexe

gender selection N *[of baby]* sélection *f* du sexe

gender studies N *étude sociologique de la différence sexuelle*

gendered /'dʒendəd/ ADJ *(frm)* sexué

gene /dʒi:n/ N gène *m*

COMP **gene mapping** N *(Bio)* cartographie *f* génétique *or* génique

gene pool N bagage *m or* patrimoine *m* héréditaire (de l'espèce)

gene therapy N thérapie *f* génétique

genealogical /,dʒi:nɪə'lɒdʒɪkəl/ ADJ généalogique

genealogist /,dʒi:nɪ'ælədʒɪst/ N généalogiste *mf*

genealogy /ˌdʒiːnɪˈælədʒɪ/ N généalogie *f*

genera /ˈdʒenərə/ NPL of **genus**

general /ˈdʒenərəl/ ADJ 1 *[approval, attitude, interest, decline]* général ◆ **as a ~ rule** en règle générale ◆ **the ~ deterioration of English society** la dégradation générale de la société anglaise ◆ **this type of behaviour is fairly ~** ce genre de comportement est assez répandu ◆ **there was ~ agreement** il y avait un consensus ◆ **there was a ~ agreement that self-regulation was working well** de l'avis général, l'autorégulation fonctionnait bien ◆ **our aim is to raise ~ awareness of the problems** notre but est de sensibiliser les gens *or* le grand public aux problèmes ◆ **the book was a ~ favourite** tout le monde aimait ce livre ◆ **in ~ use** d'usage courant ◆ **a ~ sense of well-being** un sentiment diffus de bien-être ◆ **to give sb a ~ idea of a subject** donner à qn un aperçu d'un sujet ◆ **to give sb a ~ outline of a subject** exposer à qn les grandes lignes de qch

◆ **in general** en général ◆ **we need to improve the education system in ~** il nous faut améliorer le système éducatif en général ◆ **in ~, the changes were beneficial** dans l'ensemble, les changements ont été bénéfiques

◆ **for general use** ◆ **the vaccine could be ready for ~ use by next year** le vaccin pourrait être mis à la disposition du public d'ici l'année prochaine ◆ **the best printer for ~ use** la meilleure imprimante multifonctions

2 *(= overall)* général ◆ **~ maintenance** maintenance *f* générale ◆ **~ costs** frais *mpl* généraux

3 *(= unspecific) [answer, discussion, enquiry]* d'ordre général ◆ **in ~ terms** d'une manière générale

4 *(= rough, approximate)* ◆ **in the ~ direction of the village** dans la direction approximative du village

◆ **the general idea** ◆ **the ~ idea is to turn the place into a theme park** en gros, il s'agit de faire de cet endroit un parc à thème ◆ **I've got the ~ idea** je vois en gros de quoi il s'agit ◆ **I get the ~ idea** * je vois

5 *(= non-specialist) [labourer]* non spécialisé ◆ **the ~ reader** le lecteur moyen ; → **secretary**

6 *(after official title)* général, en chef

N *(Mil)* général *m* ◆ **~ (of the Air Force)** *(US)* général *m* de l'armée de l'air ; → **brigadier**

COMP **general anaesthetic** N *(Med)* anesthésique *m* général

the General Assembly N l'assemblée *f* générale

General Certificate of Education N *(Brit Educ) examen passé à 18 ans,* ≈ baccalauréat *m* ; → **GCE**

General Certificate of Secondary Education N *(Brit Educ) examen passé à 16 ans,* ≈ brevet *m* des collèges ; → **GCSE**

general confession N *(Rel) (Church of England)* confession *f* collective *(lors de la prière en commun)* ; *(Roman Catholic Church)* confession *f* générale

general costs NPL frais *mpl* généraux

general dealer N *(US)* ⇒ **general shop**

general degree N *(Univ) licence non spécialisée*

general delivery N *(US, Can Post)* poste *f* restante

general election N élections *fpl* législatives

general expenses NPL dépenses *fpl* générales

general factotum N *(Brit) (lit)* factotum *m* ; *(fig)* bonne *f* à tout faire

general headquarters NPL *(Mil)* quartier *m* général

general holiday N jour *m* férié

general hospital N centre *m* hospitalier

general insurance N assurances *fpl* IARD *(incendies, accidents, risques divers)*

general knowledge N connaissances *fpl* générales, culture *f* générale

general linguistics N *(NonC)* linguistique *f* générale

General Manager N directeur *m* général

general medicine N médecine *f* générale

general meeting N assemblée *f* générale ; → **annual**

General Officer Commanding N *(Mil)* général *m* commandant en chef

general partnership N *(Jur, Fin)* société *f* en nom collectif

General Post Office N *(Brit Govt: formerly)* Postes *fpl* et Télécommunications *fpl* ; *(= building)* poste *f* centrale

general practice N *(Brit Med) (= work)* médecine *f* générale ; *(= place)* cabinet *m* de médecine générale ◆ **to be in ~ practice** faire de la médecine générale

general practitioner N *(Med)* (médecin *m*) généraliste *m*

the general public N le grand public

general-purpose ADJ *[tool, substance]* universel, multi-usages ; *[dictionary]* général

general science N *(Scol) physique, chimie et biologie* ◆ **~ science teacher** professeur *m* de physique, chimie et biologie

General Secretary N secrétaire *m* général

general servant N domestique *mf (non spécialisé)*

general shop N épicerie *f* générale

general staff N *(Mil)* état-major *m*

general store N *(US)* épicerie *f* générale

general strike N grève *f* générale

General Studies NPL *(Brit Scol) cours de culture générale pour élèves spécialisés*

generalissimo /ˌdʒenərəˈlɪsɪməʊ/ N généralissime *m*

generalist /ˈdʒenərəlɪst/ N généraliste *mf* ADJ généraliste

generality /ˌdʒenəˈrælɪtɪ/ N 1 *(gen pl)* généralité *f*, considération *f* générale ◆ **we talked only of generalities** nous n'avons parlé que de généralités *or* qu'en termes généraux ◆ **to talk in generalities** dire des généralités 2 ◆ **the ~ of** *(= most of)* la plupart de 3 *(NonC)* caractère *m* général ◆ **a rule of great ~** une règle très générale

generalization /ˌdʒenərəlaɪˈzeɪʃən/ N généralisation *f*

generalize /ˈdʒenərəlaɪz/ VTI *(gen, Med)* généraliser

generally /ˈdʒenərəlɪ/ ADV 1 *(= on the whole) [accurate]* en général, généralement ; *[true]* en règle générale ◆ **~, the course is okay** dans l'ensemble, le cours est bien 2 *(= usually)* d'une manière générale, d'habitude ◆ **I ~ get the bus to work** d'habitude je vais au travail en bus 3 *(= widely) [available]* partout ; *[accepted]* généralement, communément 4 *(= in general terms)* ◆ **to talk ~ about sth** dire des généralités sur qch ◆ **~ speaking** en règle générale

generalship /ˈdʒenərəlʃɪp/ N *(Mil)* tactique *f*

generate /ˈdʒenəreɪt/ VT *[+ electricity, heat]* produire ; *[+ income, wealth]* générer ; *[+ interest]* susciter ; *[+ publicity]* faire ; *[+ work, jobs]* créer ◆ **to ~ excitement** susciter l'enthousiasme

COMP **generating set** N groupe *m* électrogène

generating station N centrale *f* électrique

generating unit N groupe *m* électrogène

generation /ˌdʒenəˈreɪʃən/ N 1 génération *f* ◆ **the younger ~** la jeune génération ◆ **the postwar ~** la génération d'après-guerre ◆ **the leading artist of his ~** l'artiste le plus en vue de sa génération ◆ **within a ~** en l'espace d'une génération ◆ **a new ~ of computers** une nouvelle génération d'ordinateurs ◆ **first-/second-~** *(Comput etc)* de la première/de la seconde génération ◆ **he is a first-/second-~ American** c'est un Américain de première/seconde génération ; → **rising** 2 *(NonC) (= generating) [of electricity, heat]* production *f* ; *[of hatred etc]* engendrement *m* ; *(Ling)* génération *f*

COMP **the generation gap** N le conflit des générations

generational /ˌdʒenəˈreɪʃənl/ ADJ *(= within one generation)* de sa *(or* leur *etc)* génération ; *(= between generations)* des générations

generative /ˈdʒenərətɪv/ ADJ *(Ling)* génératif

COMP **generative grammar** N grammaire *f* générative

generator /ˈdʒenəreɪtə^r^/ N *(Elec)* groupe *m* électrogène ; *(in power station)* génératrice *f* ; *(for steam)* générateur *m* ; *(for gas)* gazogène *m*

generatrix /ˈdʒenəˌreɪtrɪks/ N (pl **generatrices** /ˈdʒenəˌreɪtrɪˌsiːz/) *(Math)* génératrice *f*

generic /dʒɪˈnerɪk/ ADJ *(gen, Ling, Med)* générique N *(Med = drug)* (médicament *m*) générique *m*

generically /dʒɪˈnerɪkəlɪ/ ADV génériquement

generosity /ˌdʒenəˈrɒsɪtɪ/ N *(NonC)* générosité *f*

generous /ˈdʒenərəs/ ADJ *[person, amount, gift, offer]* généreux ; *[supply]* ample ◆ **to be in a ~ mood** être d'humeur généreuse ◆ **to be ~ in one's praise of sth** ne pas tarir d'éloges pour qch ◆ **that's very ~ of you** c'est très généreux de ta part ◆ **to be ~ with one's time** ne pas être avare de son temps

generously /ˈdʒenərəslɪ/ ADV *[give, reward, offer, pardon, season]* généreusement ; *[say]* avec générosité ◆ **~ cut** *[garment]* ample

genesis /ˈdʒenɪsɪs/ N (pl **geneses** /ˈdʒenɪsiːz/) genèse *f*, origine *f* ◆ **Genesis** *(Bible)* la Genèse

genetic /dʒɪˈnetɪk/ ADJ *(Bio) (= of the genes)* génétique, génique ; *(= hereditary)* génétique ; *(Philos)* génétique

COMP **genetic code** N *(Bio)* code *m* génétique

genetic counselling N conseil *m* génétique

genetic engineering N génie *m* génétique, manipulations *fpl* génétiques

genetic fingerprint N empreinte *f* génétique

genetic fingerprinting N système *m* d'empreinte génétique

genetic map N carte *f* génétique

genetic pollution N pollution *f* génétique

genetic screening N test *m* de dépistage génétique

genetically /dʒɪˈnetɪkəlɪ/ ADV *[determined, programmed]* génétiquement ◆ **~ engineered** génétiquement manipulé ◆ **~ modified** génétiquement modifié

geneticist /dʒɪˈnetɪsɪst/ N généticien(ne) *m(f)*

genetics /dʒɪˈnetɪks/ N *(NonC)* génétique *f*

Geneva /dʒɪˈniːvə/ N Genève ◆ **Lake ~** le lac Léman *or* de Genève COMP **Geneva Convention** N convention *f* de Genève

genial /ˈdʒiːnɪəl/ ADJ *[person, atmosphere]* cordial ; *[face]* avenant ; *[smile, look, tone]* engageant ; *[climate]* doux (douce *f*), clément ; *[warmth]* réconfortant ◆ **a ~ host** un hôte sympathique

geniality /ˌdʒiːnɪˈælɪtɪ/ N *[of person, smile]* cordialité *f* ; *[of climate]* douceur *f*, clémence *f*

genially /ˈdʒiːnɪəlɪ/ ADV cordialement

genie /ˈdʒiːnɪ/ N (pl **genii**) génie *m*, djinn *m* ◆ **the ~ is out of the bottle** *(fig)* le mal est fait ◆ **to let the ~ out of the bottle** commettre l'irréparable ◆ **to put the ~ back in the bottle** chercher à réparer l'irréparable

genii /ˈdʒiːnɪaɪ/ NPL of **genie, genius 4**

genital /ˈdʒenɪtl/ ADJ génital NPL **genitals** organes *mpl* génitaux

COMP **genital herpes** N herpès *m* génital

genital warts NPL vésicules *fpl* génitales

genitalia /ˌdʒenɪˈteɪlɪə/ NPL organes *mpl* génitaux

genitive /ˈdʒenɪtɪv/ *(Gram)* ADJ *[case]* génitif ◆ **~ ending** flexion *f* du génitif N génitif *m* ◆ **in the ~** au génitif

genius /ˈdʒiːnɪəs/ N [1] *(NonC)* *(= cleverness)* génie *m* ; *(= ability, aptitude)* génie *m* *(for* de) don *m* extraordinaire *(for* pour) ◆ **man of ~** (homme *m* de) génie *m* ◆ **his ~ lay in his ability to assess ...** il était supérieurement doué pour juger ... ◆ **her real ~ as a designer** son véritable génie en design ◆ **he has a ~ for publicity** il a le génie de la publicité ◆ **to have ~** avoir du génie ◆ **to have a ~ for doing sth** avoir le don pour faire qch ◆ **she has a ~ for controversy** elle a le don de la polémique ◆ **he's got a ~ for saying the wrong thing** il a le don de *or* un don pour dire ce qu'il ne faut pas ◆ **a flash** *or* **stroke of ~** un trait de génie

[2] (pl **geniuses**) génie *m* ◆ **he's a ~** c'est un génie, il est génial

[3] *(NonC = distinctive character)* *[of period, country etc]* génie *m* (particulier)

[4] (pl **genii**) *(= spirit)* génie *m* ◆ **evil ~** mauvais génie *m*

Genoa /ˈdʒenəʊə/ N Gênes

genocidal /ˌdʒenəʊˈsaɪdl/ ADJ génocide

genocide /ˈdʒenəʊsaɪd/ N génocide *m*

Genoese /ˌdʒenəʊˈiːz/ ADJ génois N *(pl inv)* Génois(e) *m(f)*

genome /ˈdʒiːnəʊm/ N *(Bio)* génome *m*

genotype /ˈdʒenəʊtaɪp/ N génotype *m*

genre /ˈʒɑːŋrə/ N genre *m* ; (also **genre painting**) tableau *m* de genre

gent /dʒent/ N (abbrev of **gentleman**) [1] *(Comm)* **~s' outfitters** magasin *m* d'habillement *or* de confection pour hommes ◆ **~s' shoes** *etc* *(Comm)* chaussures *fpl etc* (pour) hommes ◆ **the ~s** *(Brit)* les toilettes *fpl* (pour hommes) ◆ **"gents"** *(Brit: sign)* "messieurs" [2] * monsieur *m*, type* *m* ◆ **he's a (real) ~** c'est un monsieur (tout ce qu'il y a de) bien

genteel /dʒenˈtiːl/ ADJ [1] *(= refined)* *[person, behaviour, manners]* distingué ; *[upbringing, resort, district]* comme il faut ; *[atmosphere]* raffiné ; *[institution]* respectable ◆ **to live in ~ poverty** vivre dignement dans la pauvreté [2] *(= affected)* affecté ◆ **she has a very ~ way of holding her glass** elle a une façon très affectée de tenir son verre ; → **shabby**

genteelly /dʒenˈtiːlɪ/ ADV [1] *(= with refinement)* *[sit, eat, drink]* de façon distinguée [2] *(= affectedly)* *[behave]* d'une manière affectée ◆ **she coughed ~ behind her hand** elle toussa d'une manière affectée derrière sa main

gentian /ˈdʒenʃɪən/ N gentiane *f* ◆ **~ blue** bleu *m* gentiane ◆ **~ violet** bleu *m* de méthylène

Gentile /ˈdʒentaɪl/ N Gentil(e) *m(f)* ADJ des Gentils

gentility /dʒenˈtɪlɪtɪ/ N *(iro)* prétention *f* à la distinction *or* au bon ton ; *(† = good birth)* bonne famille *f*, bonne naissance *f*

gentle /ˈdʒentl/ ADJ [1] *(= kind, mild)* *[person, animal, voice, smile]* doux (douce *f*) ◆ **to be ~ with sb** être doux avec qn ◆ **be ~ with me** vas-y doucement ◆ **to have a ~ disposition** être doux de nature ◆ **her ~ manner** sa douceur ◆ **(as) ~ as a lamb** doux comme un agneau ◆ **~ reader** *(† or hum)* aimable lecteur *m*

[2] *(= not violent or strong)* *[movement, touch, sound, breeze]* léger ; *[transition]* sans heurts ; *[exercise]* modéré ; *[slope, curve, colour]* doux (douce *f*) ; *[landscape]* d'une grande douceur ◆ **to cook over a ~ heat** faire cuire à feu doux ◆ **to apply ~ pressure** presser légèrement ◆ **the car came to a ~ stop** la voiture s'est arrêtée doucement ◆ **a ~ stroll** une petite promenade tranquille

[3] *(= not harsh)* *[detergent, cleaning product, beauty product]* doux (douce *f*) ◆ **it is ~ on the skin** ça n'irrite pas la peau

[4] *(= discreet)* *[hint, rebuke, reminder]* discret (-ète *f*) ◆ **to poke ~ fun at sb** se moquer gentiment de qn ◆ **to use a little ~ persuasion** utiliser la manière douce ◆ **a little ~ persuasion will get him to help** si nous le persuadons en douceur il nous aidera

[5] *(† = wellborn:* also **of gentle birth**) bien né *(liter)* ◆ **~ knight** †† noble chevalier *m*

COMP **the gentle** *or* **gentler sex** † N *(liter)* le beau sexe †

> ⚠ **gentil** in French does not mean **gentle**, but 'nice'.

gentlefolk /ˈdʒentlfəʊk/ NPL gens *mpl* de bonne famille

gentleman /ˈdʒentlmən/ (pl **-men**) N [1] *(= man)* monsieur *m* ◆ **there's a ~ to see you** il y a un monsieur qui voudrait vous voir ◆ **the ~ from ...** *(US Pol)* Monsieur le député de ... ◆ **"gentlemen"** *(sign)* "messieurs"

[2] *(= man of breeding)* homme *m* bien élevé, gentleman *m* ◆ **he is a perfect ~** c'est un vrai gentleman ◆ **a ~ never uses such language** un monsieur bien élevé ne se sert jamais de mots pareils ◆ **one of nature's gentlemen** un gentleman né ◆ **to behave like a ~** se comporter en gentleman ◆ **be a ~ and take Emily home** sois galant *or* comporte-toi en gentleman et ramène Emily chez elle ◆ **he's no ~!** ce n'est pas un gentleman ! ◆ **~'s ~** *(hum)* valet *m* de chambre

[3] *(= man of substance)* rentier *m* ◆ **to lead the life of a ~** vivre de ses rentes

[4] *(at court etc)* gentilhomme *m*

COMP **gentleman-at-arms** N (pl **gentlemen-at-arms**) gentilhomme *m* de la garde

gentleman-farmer N (pl **gentlemen-farmers**) gentleman-farmer *m*

gentleman-in-waiting N (pl **gentlemen-in-waiting**) gentilhomme *m* *(attaché à la personne du roi etc)*

gentleman's agreement N gentleman's agreement *m*, accord *m* reposant sur l'honneur

gentlemen's club N *(esp Brit)* club *privé réservé aux hommes*

gentlemanly /ˈdʒentlmənlɪ/ ADJ *[man]* bien élevé ; *[manner, behaviour, conduct]* courtois ; *[voice, appearance, sport]* distingué

gentlemen /ˈdʒentlmən/ NPL of **gentleman**

gentleness /ˈdʒentlnɪs/ N douceur *f*

gentlewoman /ˈdʒentlwʊmən/ N (pl **-women**) *(by birth)* dame *f* *or* demoiselle *f* de bonne famille ; *(at court)* dame *f* d'honneur *or* de compagnie

gently /ˈdʒentlɪ/ ADV [1] *(= kindly)* *[say, rebuke]* avec douceur, gentiment ; *[smile, remind, suggest]* gentiment [2] *(= not violently or strongly)* *[move, shake, caress]* doucement ; *[push, touch]* doucement, avec douceur ; *[exercise]* doucement, sans forcer ◆ **~ does it!** doucement ! ◆ **~ sloping hills** des collines en pente douce ◆ **the road slopes ~ down to the river** la route descend en pente douce vers la rivière ◆ **to simmer ~** faire cuire à feu doux ◆ **to deal ~ with sb** ménager qn, ne pas bousculer qn [3] *(= nobly)* ◆ **~ born** † de bonne naissance †

gentrification /ˌdʒentrɪfɪˈkeɪʃən/ N *[of area]* embourgeoisement *m*

gentrified /ˈdʒentrɪˌfaɪd/ ADJ *[area, houses etc]* embourgeoisé ◆ **to become ~** s'embourgeoiser

gentrify /ˈdʒentrɪfaɪ/ VT *[+ area]* embourgeoiser

gentry /ˈdʒentrɪ/ N *(= aristocracy)* aristocratie *f* ; *(in Britain = lesser nobility)* petite noblesse *f*, gentry *f*

genuflect /ˈdʒenjʊflekt/ VI *(lit)* faire une génuflexion ◆ **to ~ to** *or* **in front of** *(fig)* se prosterner devant

genuflexion, genuflection *(US)* /ˌdʒenjʊˈflekʃən/ N génuflexion *f*

genuine /ˈdʒenjʊɪn/ ADJ [1] *(= authentic)* *[refugee, picture, manuscript, antique, coin]* authentique ; *[democracy, leather, wool, silver]* véritable ; *(Comm)* *[goods]* garanti d'origine ◆ **a ~ Persian rug** un authentique tapis persan ◆ **it's the ~ article** * c'est du vrai [2] *(= real)* *[emotion, belief, enthusiasm, interest, offer]* sincère ; *[laughter, disbelief]* franc (franche *f*) ; *[tears]* vrai, sincère ; *[difficulty]* véritable ◆ **this was a ~ mistake** c'était vraiment une erreur ◆ **a ~ buyer** *(Comm)* un acheteur sérieux [3] *(= sincere)* *[person, relationship]* sincère COMP **genuine assets** NPL *(Accounting)* actif *m* réel

genuinely /ˈdʒenjʊɪnlɪ/ ADV *[interested]* sincèrement, vraiment ; *[concerned, surprised]* réellement ; *[worried, upset, sorry, democratic]* vraiment, réellement ; *[funny, pleased]* vraiment ◆ **she ~ believed that ...** elle croyait vraiment *or* sincèrement que ... ◆ **I ~ want to help** je veux vraiment *or* sincèrement aider ◆ **he is ~ committed to reform** il est profondément partisan de la réforme

genuineness /ˈdʒenjʊɪnnɪs/ N [1] *(= authenticity)* authenticité *f* [2] *(= sincerity)* sincérité *f*

genus /ˈdʒenəs/ N (pl **genera** *or* **genuses**) *(Bio)* genre *m*

geocentric /ˌdʒiːəʊˈsentrɪk/ ADJ géocentrique

geochemical /ˌdʒiːəʊˈkemɪkəl/ ADJ géochimique

geochemist /ˌdʒiːəʊˈkemɪst/ N géochimiste *mf*

geochemistry /ˌdʒiːəʊˈkemɪstrɪ/ N géochimie *f*

geode /ˈdʒiːəʊd/ N géode *f*

geodesic /ˌdʒiːəʊˈdesɪk/ ADJ géodésique ◆ **~ dome** dôme *m* géodésique ◆ **~ line** géodésique *f*

geodesy /dʒiːˈɒdɪsɪ/ N géodésie *f*

geodetic /ˌdʒiːəʊˈdetɪk/ ADJ ⇒ **geodesic**

geographer /dʒɪˈɒɡrəfəʳ/ N géographe *mf*

geographic(al) /dʒɪəˈɡræfɪk(əl)/ ADJ géographique ◆ **~(al) mile** mille *m* marin *or* nautique

geographically /dʒɪəˈɡræfɪkəlɪ/ ADV *[isolated]* géographiquement

geography /dʒɪˈɒɡrəfɪ/ N *(= science)* géographie *f* ◆ **policemen who knew the local ~** des policiers qui connaissaient la topographie du quartier

geological /dʒɪəʊˈlɒdʒɪkəl/ ADJ géologique ◆ **~ survey** *(US)* Bureau *m* de recherches géologiques et minières

geologically /dʒɪəˈlɒdʒɪkəlɪ/ ADV géologiquement

geologist /dʒɪˈɒlədʒɪst/ N géologue *mf*

geology /dʒɪˈɒlədʒɪ/ N géologie *f*

geomagnetic /ˌdʒiːəʊmæɡˈnetɪk/ ADJ géomagnétique ◆ **~ storm** orage *m* géomagnétique

geomagnetism /ˌdʒiːəʊˈmæɡnɪˌtɪzəm/ N géomagnétisme *m*

geometric(al) /dʒɪəʊˈmetrɪk(əl)/ ADJ géométrique ◆ **~(al) mean** *(Math)* moyenne *f* géométrique ◆ **by ~(al) progression** selon une progression géométrique ◆ **~(al) series** série *f* géométrique

geometrically /dʒɪəˈmetrɪkəlɪ/ ADV *[arranged]* géométriquement ◆ **~ patterned** à motifs géométriques

geometrician /ˌdʒɪˌɒmɪˈtrɪʃən/ N géomètre *mf*

geometry /dʒɪˈɒmɪtrɪ/ N géométrie *f*

geomorphic /ˌdʒiːəʊˈmɔːfɪk/ ADJ géomorphique

geomorphologic(al) /ˌdʒiːəʊˌmɔːfəˈlɒdʒɪkəl/ ADJ géomorphologique

geomorphology /ˌdʒiːəʊmɔːˈfɒlədʒɪ/ N géomorphologie *f*

geonomics /ˌdʒiːəʊˈnɒmɪks/ N (NonC) géographie *f* économique

geophysical /ˌdʒiːəʊˈfɪzɪkəl/ ADJ géophysique

geophysicist /ˌdʒiːəʊˈfɪzɪsɪst/ N géophysicien(ne) *m(f)*

geophysics /ˌdʒiːəʊˈfɪzɪks/ N (NonC) géophysique *f*

geopolitical /ˌdʒiːəupəˈlɪtɪkəl/ ADJ géopolitique

geopolitics /ˌdʒiːəʊˈpɒlɪtɪks/ N (NonC) géopolitique *f*

Geordie * /ˈdʒɔːdɪ/ N (Brit) *natif de Tyneside*

George /dʒɔːdʒ/ N Georges *m* ◆ **by ~!** † * mon Dieu ! ◆ **~ Cross** *or* **Medal** (Brit) ≈ médaille *f* du courage

georgette /dʒɔːˈdʒet/ N (also **georgette crêpe**) crêpe *f* georgette

Georgia /ˈdʒɔːdʒɪə/ N (= *country and US state*) Géorgie *f* ◆ **in ~** en Géorgie

Georgian /ˈdʒɔːdʒɪən/ ADJ [1] (Brit Hist) *[period] des rois George I*^er^ *à George IV (1714-1830)* ; (Archit) *[architecture, house, style]* géorgien *(entre 1714 et 1830)* [2] (Geog) *[person, language]* géorgien ; *[town]* de Géorgie ; *[capital]* de la Géorgie

geoscience /ˌdʒiːəʊˈsaɪəns/ N science(s) *f(pl)* de la terre

geoscientist /ˌdʒiːəʊˈsaɪəntɪst/ N spécialiste *mf* des sciences de la terre

geostationary /ˌdʒiːəʊˈsteɪʃənərɪ/ ADJ géostationnaire

geosynchronous /ˌdʒiːəʊˈsɪŋkrənəs/ ADJ géosynchrone

geosyncline /ˌdʒiːəʊˈsɪnklaɪn/ N géosynclinal *m*

geothermal /ˌdʒiːəʊˈθɜːməl/ ADJ géothermique ◆ **~ power** énergie *f* géothermique

geothermally /ˌdʒiːəʊˈθɜːməlɪ/ ADJ géothermiquement

geotropic /ˌdʒiːəʊˈtrɒpɪk/ ADJ géotropique

geotropically /ˌdʒiːəʊˈtrɒpɪkəlɪ/ ADV géotropiquement

geotropism /dʒɪˈɒtrəpɪzəm/ N géotropisme *m*

geranium /dʒɪˈreɪnɪəm/ N géranium *m* ADJ (*colour*) (also **geranium red**) rouge géranium *inv*

gerbil /ˈdʒɜːbɪl/ N gerbille *f*

geriatric /ˌdʒerɪˈætrɪk/ ADJ [1] *[hospital]* gériatrique ; *[ward]* de gériatrie ; *[patient]* de service de gériatrie ; *[nurse]* spécialisé en gériatrie ◆ **~ care** *or* **nursing** soins *mpl* aux vieillards ◆ **~ medicine** gériatrie *f* ◆ **~ social work** aide *f* sociale aux vieillards [2] (* *pej*) *[judge, rock star]* gaga * (*pej*) ; *[government]* de vieux gâteux * (*pej*) ◆ **a ~ car** un vieux tacot * (*pej*) ◆ **a ~ horse** un vieux canasson * (*pej*) N [1] (Med) malade *mf* gériatrique [2] (* *pej*) vieillard(e) *m(f)*

geriatrics /ˌdʒerɪˈætrɪks/ N (NonC) gériatrie *f*

germ /dʒɜːm/ N [1] (Bio, *also fig*) germe *m* ◆ **the ~ of an idea** un embryon d'idée, le germe d'une idée [2] (Med) microbe *m*, germe *m*

COMP **germ carrier** N (Med) porteur *m* de microbes

germ cell N (= *gamete*) cellule *f* germinale *or* reproductrice, gamète *m*

germ-free ADJ stérile, stérilisé

germ-killer N germicide *m*

germ warfare N (NonC) guerre *f* bactériologique

German /ˈdʒɜːmən/ ADJ (*gen*) allemand ; *[ambassador, embassy]* d'Allemagne ; *[teacher]* d'allemand ◆ **East/West ~** d'Allemagne de l'Est/de l'Ouest, est-/ouest-allemand N [1] Allemand(e) *m(f)* [2] (= *language*) allemand *m*

COMP **the German Democratic Republic** N la République démocratique allemande

German measles N rubéole *f*

German sheep dog, German shepherd N chien *m* loup, berger *m* allemand

German speaker N germanophone *mf*

German-speaking ADJ qui parle allemand ; *[nation]* germanophone ; → **Switzerland**

germane /dʒɜːˈmeɪn/ ADJ pertinent (*to* pour, par rapport à)

Germanic /dʒɜːˈmænɪk/ ADJ germanique

germanium /dʒɜːˈmeɪnɪəm/ N germanium *m*

germanophile /dʒɜːˈmænəʊfaɪl/ N germanophile *mf*

germanophobe /dʒɜːˈmænəʊfəʊb/ N germanophobe *mf*

Germany /ˈdʒɜːmənɪ/ N Allemagne *f* ◆ **East/West ~** Allemagne *f* de l'Est/de l'Ouest

germicidal /ˌdʒɜːmɪˈsaɪdl/ ADJ germicide

germicide /ˈdʒɜːmɪsaɪd/ N germicide *m*

germinal /ˈdʒɜːmɪnəl/ ADJ embryonnaire

germinate /ˈdʒɜːmɪneɪt/ VI germer VT faire germer

germination /ˌdʒɜːmɪˈneɪʃən/ N germination *f*

germproof /ˈdʒɜːmpruːf/ ADJ résistant aux microbes

gerontocracy /ˌdʒerɒnˈtɒkrəsɪ/ N gérontocratie *f*

gerontologist /ˌdʒerɒnˈtɒlədʒɪst/ N gérontologue *mf*

gerontology /ˌdʒerɒnˈtɒlədʒɪ/ N gérontologie *f*

gerrymander /ˈdʒerɪmændə^r^/ VI faire du charcutage électoral N ⇒ **gerrymandering**

gerrymandering /ˈdʒerɪmændərɪŋ/ N charcutage *m* électoral

gerund /ˈdʒerənd/ N (*in English*) gérondif *m*, substantif *m* verbal ; (*in Latin*) gérondif *m*

gerundive /dʒɪˈrʌndɪv/ ADJ du gérondif N adjectif *m* verbal

gesso /ˈdʒesəʊ/ N *[of moulding etc]* plâtre *m* (de Paris) ; (Art) gesso *m*

Gestalt /gəˈʃtɑːlt/ N (pl **Gestalts** *or* **Gestalten** /gəˈʃtɑːltən/) gestalt *f* ◆ **~ psychology** gestaltisme *m*

Gestapo /gesˈtɑːpəʊ/ N Gestapo *f*

gestate /dʒesˈteɪt/ VI être en gestation VT (Bio) garder en gestation ; *[+ work of art]* mûrir ; *[+ anger]* couver

gestation /dʒesˈteɪʃən/ N gestation *f*

gesticulate /dʒesˈtɪkjʊleɪt/ VI faire de grands gestes (*at sb* pour attirer l'attention de qn) VT exprimer par gestes

gesticulation /dʒesˌtɪkjʊˈleɪʃən/ N gesticulation *f*

gestural /ˈdʒestʃərəl/ ADJ gestuel

gesture /ˈdʒestʃə^r^/ N (*lit, fig*) geste *m* ◆ **a ~ of good will** un geste de bonne volonté ◆ **friendly ~** geste *m or* témoignage *m* d'amitié ◆ **a ~ of defiance** un signe de méfiance ◆ **they did it as a ~ of support** ils l'ont fait pour manifester leur soutien ◆ **what a nice ~!** quelle délicate attention ! VI ◆ **to ~ to sb to do sth** faire signe à qn de faire qch ◆ **he ~d towards the door** il désigna la porte d'un geste ◆ **he ~d with his head towards the safe** il a indiqué le coffre d'un signe de tête ◆ **he ~d at Derek to remain seated** il a fait signe à Derek de rester assis VT mimer, exprimer par gestes

get /get/

vb : pret, ptp **got**, ptp (US) **gotten**

1 TRANSITIVE VERB	3 COMPOUNDS
2 INTRANSITIVE VERB	4 PHRASAL VERBS

1 - TRANSITIVE VERB

[1] [= have, receive, obtain] avoir

avoir covers a wide range of meanings, and like **get** is unspecific.

◆ **I go whenever I ~ the chance** j'y vais dès que j'en ai l'occasion ◆ **he's got a cut on his finger** il a une coupure au doigt ◆ **he got a fine** il a eu une amende ◆ **she ~s a good salary** elle a un bon salaire ◆ **not everyone ~s a pension** tout le monde n'a pas la retraite ◆ **you need to ~ permission from the owner** il faut avoir la permission du propriétaire ◆ **I got a lot of presents** j'ai eu beaucoup de cadeaux ◆ **he got first prize** il a eu le premier prix ◆ **you may ~ a surprise** tu pourrais avoir une surprise

Some **get** + noun combinations may take a more specific French verb.

◆ **we can ~ sixteen channels** nous pouvons recevoir seize chaînes ◆ **it was impossible to ~ help** il était impossible d'obtenir de l'aide ◆ **he got help from the others** il s'est fait aider par les autres ◆ **first I need to ~ a better idea of the situation** je dois d'abord me faire une meilleure idée de la situation ◆ **I think he got the wrong impression** je pense qu'il s'est fait des idées ◆ **they ~ lunch at school** ils déjeunent *or* ils mangent à l'école ◆ **he got his money by exploiting others** il s'est enrichi en exploitant les autres ◆ **if I'm not working I ~ no pay** si je ne travaille pas je ne suis pas payé ◆ **this area doesn't ~ much rain** il ne pleut pas beaucoup dans cette région ◆ **she got a reputation for infallibility** elle a acquis une réputation d'infaillibilité ◆ **they got interesting results** ils ont obtenu des résultats intéressants ◆ **we'll ~ a sandwich in town** on prendra *or* mangera un sandwich en ville ◆ **this room ~s a lot of sun** cette pièce est très ensoleillée ◆ **I didn't ~ a very good view of it** je ne l'ai pas bien vu ◆ **he got two years** il s'est pris * deux ans de prison

◆ **have/has got** ◆ **I've got toothache** j'ai mal aux dents ◆ **I have got three sisters** j'ai trois sœurs ◆ **how many have you got?** combien en avez-vous ? ◆ **she's got too much to do** elle a trop (de choses) à faire ◆ **I've got it!** (= *have safely*) (ça y est) je l'ai !, je le tiens ! ◆ **you're okay, I've got you!** ne t'en fais pas, je te tiens ! ; see also **have**

[2] [= find] trouver ◆ **they can't ~ jobs** ils n'arrivent pas à trouver de travail ◆ **he got me a job** il m'a trouvé un emploi ◆ **it's difficult to ~ a hotel room in August** c'est difficile de trouver une chambre d'hôtel en août ◆ **you ~ different kinds of ...** on trouve plusieurs sortes de ... ◆ **you'll ~ him at home if you phone this evening** tu le trouveras chez lui si tu appelles ce soir ◆ **I've been trying to ~ you all week** ça fait une semaine que j'essaie de t'avoir ◆ **you can ~ me on this number/the mobile** tu peux m'appeler à ce numéro/sur mon portable

[3] [= buy] acheter ◆ **where do they ~ their raw materials?** où est-ce qu'ils achètent leurs matières premières ? ◆ **to ~ sth cheap** acheter qch bon marché ◆ **I'll ~ some milk** je prendrai *or* j'achèterai du lait

[4] [= fetch] aller chercher ◆ **I must go and ~ some bread** il faut que j'aille chercher *or* acheter du pain ◆ **quick, ~ help!** allez vite chercher de l'aide ! ◆ **can you ~ my coat from the cleaners?** est-ce que tu peux aller chercher mon manteau au pressing ? [BUT] **can I ~ you a drink?** est-ce que je peux vous offrir quelque chose ?

[5] [= take] prendre ◆ **I'll ~ the bus** je vais prendre le bus ◆ **I don't ~ the local paper** je ne prends pas le journal local

[6] [= pick up] aller chercher ◆ **phone me when you arrive and I'll come and ~ you** appelle-moi quand tu arrives et j'irai te chercher

7 [= call in] appeler ◆ **we had to ~ the doctor/a plumber** nous avons dû appeler le médecin/un plombier

8 [= prepare] préparer ◆ **she was ~ting breakfast** elle préparait le petit déjeuner

9 [= catch] *[+ disease, fugitive]* attraper ; *[+ name]* entendre, comprendre ; *[+ details]* comprendre ◆ **you'll ~ a cold** tu vas attraper un rhume ◆ **they've got the thief** ils ont attrapé le voleur ◆ **I didn't ~ your name** je n'ai pas entendu *or* compris votre nom ◆ **to ~ sb alone** *or* **to o.s.** être seul à seul avec qn ◆ **it ~s me here** *[pain]* ça me fait mal ici ◆ **we'll ~ them yet !** on leur revaudra ça ! ◆ **I'll ~ you !** je te revaudrai ça ! ◆ **he'll ~ you for that !** qu'est-ce que tu vas prendre !* ◆ **he's got it bad for her*** il est fou d'elle

10 [= understand] ◆ **~ it ?*** t'as pigé ?*, tu saisis ?* ◆ **I don't ~ it*** je ne comprends pas, je ne saisis pas* ◆ **you've got it in one!*** tu as tout compris ! ◆ **I don't ~ you*** je ne vous suis pas ◆ **I don't ~ the joke** je ne vois pas ce qu'il y a de drôle ◆ **I don't ~ your meaning*** je ne vous suis pas ◆ **he got the point immediately** il a tout de suite tout compris ◆ **let me ~ this right, you're saying that ...** alors, si je comprends bien, tu dis que ... ◆ **don't ~ me wrong** comprenez-moi bien

11 [= answer] ◆ **can you ~ the phone ?** est-ce que tu peux répondre ? ◆ **I'll ~ it!** j'y vais !

12 [* = annoy] agacer ◆ **that's what really ~s me** c'est ce qui m'agace le plus

13 [set structures]

◆ **to get** + *adjective*

This construction is often translated by a verb alone. Look up the relevant adjective.

◆ **don't ~ the carpet dirty !** ne salis pas la moquette ! ◆ **to ~ one's hands dirty** se salir les mains ◆ **to ~ sb drunk** enivrer *or* soûler qn ◆ **you're ~ting me worried** tu m'inquiètes

◆ **to get sth done** *(by someone else)* faire faire qch ◆ **to ~ one's hair cut** se faire couper les cheveux ◆ **I need to ~ my car serviced** je dois faire réviser ma voiture ◆ **he knows how to ~ things done!** il sait faire activer les choses ! ◆ **when do you think you'll ~ it finished?** *(do oneself)* quand penses-tu avoir fini ? ◆ **you can't ~ anything done round here** il est impossible de travailler ici

◆ **to get sb/sth to do sth** ◆ **~ him to clean the car** fais-lui laver la voiture ◆ **I'll ~ her to ring you back** je lui demanderai de te rappeler

réussir or **pouvoir** may be used when speaking of achieving a result.

◆ **we eventually got her to change her mind** nous avons finalement réussi à *or* pu la faire changer d'avis ◆ **I couldn't ~ the washing machine to work** je n'ai pas réussi à *or* pu faire marcher la machine à laver ◆ **I couldn't ~ the sauce to thicken** je n'ai pas réussi à *or* pu épaissir la sauce ◆ **to ~ sth going** *[+ machine]* (réussir à *or* pouvoir) faire marcher qch

◆ **to get sb/sth somewhere** ◆ **to ~ sth downstairs** descendre qch ◆ **they got him home somehow** ils l'ont ramené chez lui tant bien que mal ◆ **how can we ~ it home?** comment faire pour l'apporter à la maison ? ◆ **threatening me will ~ you nowhere** tu n'obtiendras rien en me menaçant ◆ **to ~ sth upstairs** monter qch ◆ **where does that ~ us?** où est-ce que ça nous mène ?

◆ **to get sb/sth** + *preposition* ◆ **to ~ sb by the arm** saisir qn par le bras ◆ **to ~ sb by the throat** prendre qn à la gorge ◆ **I didn't ~ much for it** on ne m'en a pas donné grand-chose ◆ **he ~s a lot of money for his paintings** il gagne beaucoup d'argent avec ses tableaux ◆ **he ~s his red hair from his mother** il a les cheveux roux de sa mère ◆ **I don't ~ much from his lectures** je ne tire pas grand-chose de ses cours ◆ **the bullet got him in the arm** la balle l'a atteint au bras ◆ **try to ~ him into a good mood** essaie de le mettre de bonne humeur ◆ **he managed to ~ the card into the envelope** il a réussi à faire entrer la carte dans l'enveloppe ◆ **to ~ o.s into a difficult position** se mettre dans une situation délicate ◆ **we got him on to the subject of the war** nous l'avons amené à parler de la guerre ◆ **she ~s a lot of pleasure out of gardening** elle prend beaucoup de plaisir à jardiner ◆ **we'll never ~ anything out of him** nous n'en tirerons jamais rien, nous ne tirerons jamais rien de lui ◆ **I couldn't ~ the stain out of the tablecloth** je n'ai pas réussi à enlever la tache sur la nappe ◆ **to ~ sth past the customs** réussir à passer qch à la douane ◆ **I don't know how it got past the inspectors** je ne sais pas comment ça a échappé à la surveillance des inspecteurs ◆ **to ~ sb round the throat** prendre qn à la gorge ◆ **I'll never ~ the car through here** je n'arriverai jamais à faire passer la voiture par ici ◆ **to ~ sth to sb** faire parvenir qch à qn ◆ **to ~ a child to bed** mettre un enfant au lit, coucher un enfant

2 - INTRANSITIVE VERB

1 [= go] aller *(to* à ; *from* de) ; *(= arrive)* arriver ; *(= be)* être ◆ **how do you ~ there?** comment fait-on pour y aller ? ◆ **can you ~ there from London by bus?** est-ce qu'on peut y aller de Londres en bus ? ◆ **what time do you ~ to Sheffield?** à quelle heure arrivez-vous à Sheffield ? ◆ **he should ~ here soon** il devrait bientôt être là ◆ **to ~ to the top** *(lit, fig)* arriver *or* parvenir au sommet ; see also **top**[1]

◆ **to get** + *adverb/preposition* ◆ **to ~ after sb** essayer d'attraper qn ◆ **we won't ~ anywhere with him** nous n'arriverons à rien avec lui ◆ **you won't ~ anywhere if you behave like that** tu n'arriveras à rien en te conduisant comme ça ◆ **I got as far as speaking to him** je lui ai même parlé ◆ **how did that box ~ here?** comment cette boîte est-elle arrivée ici ? ◆ **what's got into him?** qu'est-ce qui lui prend ? ◆ **we're ~ting nowhere** on n'avance pas ◆ **we're ~ting nowhere fast*** on fait du sur place* ◆ **now we're ~ting somewhere!*** enfin du progrès ! ◆ **how's your thesis going? – I'm ~ting there** où en es-tu avec ta thèse ? – ça avance ◆ **your garden is lovely! – yes, we're ~ting there!** votre jardin est très joli ! – oui, ça prend tournure ! ◆ **where did you ~ to?** où étais-tu donc passé ? ◆ **where can he have got to?** où est-il passé ? ◆ **where have you got to?** *(in book, work)* où en êtes-vous ? ◆ **don't let it ~ to you*** ne te fais pas de bile* pour ça ◆ **to ~ with it*** se mettre à la mode *or* dans le vent* ◆ **this is serious business and the government had better ~ with it** *(= become aware)* c'est là un problème grave et le gouvernement ferait bien d'en prendre conscience

2 [= go away] ◆ **~ !**‡ fous le camp !‡

3 [set structures]

◆ **to get** + *adjective*

This construction is often translated by a verb alone.

◆ **I hope you'll ~ better soon** j'espère que tu vas vite te remettre ◆ **things are ~ting complicated** les choses se compliquent ◆ **this is ~ting expensive** ça commence à faire cher ◆ **she's afraid of ~ting fat** elle a peur de grossir ◆ **it's ~ting late** il se fait tard ◆ **how do people ~ like that?** comment peut-on en arriver là ? ◆ **I'm ~ting nervous** je commence à avoir le trac ◆ **he's ~ting old** il vieillit, il se fait vieux ◆ **this is ~ting ridiculous** ça devient ridicule ◆ **how stupid can you ~?** il faut vraiment être stupide ! ◆ **he soon ~s tired** il se fatigue vite ◆ **to ~ used to sth/to doing sth** s'habituer à qch/à faire qch

◆ **to get** + *past participle (passive)* ◆ **she often ~s asked for her autograph** on lui demande souvent son autographe ◆ **he got beaten up** il s'est fait tabasser* ◆ **several windows got broken** plusieurs fenêtres ont été brisées ◆ **to ~ killed** se faire tuer ◆ **to ~ paid** se faire payer

Reflexive verbs are used when the sense is not passive.

◆ **to ~ dressed** s'habiller ◆ **to ~ married** se marier ◆ **to ~ washed** se laver

◆ **to get to** + *infinitive* ◆ **it got to be quite pleasant after a while** c'est devenu assez agréable au bout d'un moment ◆ **he's ~ting to be an old man** il se fait vieux ◆ **it's ~ting to be impossible** ça devient impossible ◆ **she never ~s to drive the car*** on ne la laisse jamais conduire ◆ **to ~ to know sb** apprendre à connaître qn ◆ **we soon got to like them** nous les avons vite appréciés ◆ **we got to like him in the end** nous avons fini par l'apprécier ◆ **students only ~ to use the library between 2pm and 8pm** les étudiants ne peuvent utiliser la bibliothèque qu'entre 14 heures et 20 heures

◆ **have got to** + *infinitive (= must)* ◆ **you've got to come** il faut que vous veniez *subj* ◆ **have you got to go and see her?** est-ce que vous êtes obligé d'aller la voir ? ◆ **I haven't got to leave yet** je ne suis pas obligé de partir tout de suite ◆ **you've got to be joking!** tu plaisantes !

◆ **to get** + *-ing (= begin)* ◆ **to ~ going** se mettre en route, partir ◆ **I got talking to him in the train** j'ai parlé avec lui dans le train, nous avons engagé la conversation dans le train ◆ **I got to thinking that ...*** je me suis dit que ...

3 - COMPOUNDS

get-at-able* ADJ *[place]* accessible, d'accès facile ; *[person]* accessible

get-rich-quick scheme* N *projet pour faire fortune rapidement*

get-together N (petite) réunion *f*

get-up-and-go* N ◆ **he's got lots of ~-up-and-go** il a beaucoup d'allant *or* de dynamisme, il est très dynamique

get-well card N carte *f* de vœux (pour un prompt rétablissement)

4 - PHRASAL VERBS

► **get about** VI 1 *(= move about) [person]* se déplacer ◆ **he ~s about with a stick/on crutches** il marche *or* se déplace avec une canne/des béquilles ◆ **she ~s about quite well despite her handicap** elle arrive assez bien à se déplacer malgré son handicap ◆ **she's old, but she still ~s about quite a bit** elle est âgée mais elle est encore très active ◆ **he's ~ting about again now** *(after illness)* il est de nouveau sur pied 2 *(= travel)* voyager ◆ **she ~s about a lot** elle voyage beaucoup 3 *[news]* circuler ◆ **the story had got about that ...** des rumeurs circulaient selon lesquelles ... ◆ **it has got about that ...** le bruit court que ... ◆ **I don't want it to ~ about** je ne veux pas que ça s'ébruite

► **get above** VT FUS ◆ **to get above o.s.** avoir la grosse tête* ◆ **you're ~ting above yourself!** pour qui te prends-tu ?

► **get across** VI *(lit)* traverser ; *[meaning, message]* passer ◆ **I think the message is ~ting across** je pense que le message commence à passer ◆ **the message is ~ting across that people must ...** les gens commencent à comprendre qu'on doit ... ◆ **that was what got across to me** c'est ce que j'ai compris ◆ **he didn't ~ across to the audience** le courant n'est pas passé entre le public et lui ◆ **he managed to ~ across to her at last** il a enfin réussi à se faire entendre d'elle VT SEP *(lit)* faire traverser, faire passer ; *[+ ideas, intentions, desires]* communiquer (*to sb* à qn) ◆ **to ~ sth across to sb** faire comprendre qch à qn VT FUS (*= annoy*) ◆ **to get across sb** se faire mal voir de qn

► **get ahead** VI (*lit*) prendre de l'avance ; (*in career*) monter en grade

► **get along** VI 1 (*= go*) aller (*to* à) ; (*= leave*) s'en aller ◆ **I must be ~ting along** il faut que je m'en aille ◆ **~ along with you!*** (*= go away*) va-t-en !, file !* ; (*Brit*) (*= stop joking*) à d'autres ! 2 (*= manage*) se débrouiller ◆ **to ~ along without sth/sb** se débrouiller sans qch/qn 3 (*= progress*) [*work*] avancer ; [*student, invalid*] faire des progrès ◆ **he's ~ting along well in French** il fait de gros progrès en français 4 (*= be on good terms*) (bien) s'entendre ◆ **they ~ along very well (together)** ils s'entendent très bien ◆ **I don't ~ along with him at all** je ne m'entends pas du tout avec lui

► **get around** VI ⇒ **get about** VT SEP ⇒ **get round** VT SEP VT FUS ⇒ **get round** VT FUS

► **get at** VT FUS 1 (*= reach*) [*+ object, component, person, place*] atteindre ◆ **sometimes children are used to ~ at their parents** on se sert parfois des enfants pour atteindre les parents ◆ **the dog got at the meat** le chien a touché à la viande ◆ **the goat was trying to ~ at the cabbages** la chèvre essayait de manger les choux ◆ **the rich and powerful are difficult to ~ at** les riches et les puissants sont difficiles à approcher ◆ **let me ~ at him!*** attends un peu que je l'attrape *subj* ! 2 (*= find, ascertain*) [*+ facts, truth*] découvrir 3 (*= suggest*) ◆ **what are you ~ting at ?** où voulez-vous en venir ? 4 (*Brit = attack, jibe at*) s'en prendre à ◆ **she's always ~ting at her brother** elle s'en prend toujours à son frère ◆ **I feel got at** je me sens visé 5 (** = influence*) suborner ◆ **there's a danger witnesses will be got at** les témoins risquent d'être subornés

► **get away** VI 1 (*= leave*) s'en aller, partir ; [*vehicle*] partir ◆ **to ~ away from a place** quitter un endroit ◆ **I usually ~ away from work/the office at six** je quitte généralement (le travail/le bureau) à 6 heures ◆ **I'll try to ~ away from work early** j'essaierai de quitter plus tôt ◆ **I couldn't ~ away any sooner** je n'ai pas pu me libérer plus tôt ◆ **we are not going to be able to ~ away this year** nous n'allons pas pouvoir partir en vacances cette année ◆ **~ away!** allez-vous-en ! ◆ **~ away (with you)!*** à d'autres ! 2 (*= escape*) s'échapper ◆ **to ~ away from** [*+ prison*] s'échapper de ; [*+ people, situation*] échapper à ; [*+ idea*] renoncer à ◆ **he was trying to ~ away when he was shot** il essayait de s'échapper quand on lui a tiré dessus ◆ **she moved here to ~ away from the stress of city life** elle est venue s'installer ici pour échapper au stress de la vie citadine ◆ **it's time we got away from this idea** il est temps que nous renoncions à cette idée ◆ **he went to the Bahamas to ~ away from it all** il est allé aux Bahamas pour laisser tous ses ennuis *or* problèmes derrière lui ◆ **the doctor told her she must ~ away from it all** le médecin lui a ordonné de partir se reposer loin de tout ◆ **the thief got away with the money** le voleur est parti avec l'argent ◆ **you can't ~ away from it!, there's no ~ting away from it!** on ne peut pas y couper !* VT SEP 1 (*= take*) emmener ; (*= move away*) éloigner ; (*= send off*) expédier ◆ **you must ~ her away to the country for a while** il faut que vous l'emmeniez *subj* passer quelque temps à la campagne 2 (*= remove*) ◆ **to get sth away from sb** enlever qch à qn

► **get away with** VT (*= suffer no consequences*) ◆ **she got away with saying outrageous things** elle a tenu impunément des propos choquants ◆ **he broke the law and got away with it** il violait la loi sans être inquiété *or* en toute impunité ◆ **you'll never ~ away with that!** on ne te laissera pas passer ça !* ◆ **he ~s away with murder*** il peut se permettre de faire n'importe quoi ◆ **he got away with a mere apology** (*= escape lightly*) il en a été quitte pour une simple excuse ◆ **we can ~ away with just repainting it** on pourrait se contenter de le repeindre

► **get back** VI 1 (*= return*) revenir ◆ **to ~ back (home)** rentrer chez soi ◆ **to ~ back to bed** se recoucher, retourner au lit ◆ **to ~ back upstairs** remonter, retourner en haut ◆ **life is starting to ~ back to normal** la vie reprend son cours ◆ **to ~ back to work** se remettre au travail, reprendre le travail ◆ **to ~ back to the point** revenir au sujet ◆ **let's ~ back to why you didn't come yesterday** revenons à la question de savoir pourquoi vous n'êtes pas venu hier ◆ **let's ~ back to what we were talking about** revenons à nos moutons ◆ **to ~ back to sb*** recontacter qn ; (*on phone also*) rappeler qn ◆ **can I ~ back to you on that?*** puis-je vous recontacter à ce sujet ? ; (*on phone*) puis-je vous rappeler à ce sujet ? ; see also **get on** VT FUS 2 (*= move backwards*) reculer ◆ **~ back!** reculez ! VT SEP 1 (*= recover*) [*+ sth lent*] récupérer ; [*+ sth lost, stolen*] retrouver, récupérer ; [*+ strength*] reprendre ; [*+ one's husband, partner etc*] faire revenir ◆ **he's trying desperately to ~ her back** il essaie désespérément de la faire revenir ◆ **now that we've got you back** maintenant que tu nous es revenu ◆ **I won't ~ my car back until Thursday** je n'aurai pas ma voiture avant jeudi ◆ **I was afraid I wouldn't ~ my passport back** j'avais peur qu'on ne me rende pas mon passeport ◆ **to ~ one's money back** se faire rembourser, récupérer son argent 2 (*= replace*) remettre en place 3 (*= return*) rendre ◆ **I'll ~ it back to you as soon as I can** je vous le rendrai dès que possible 4 (*= take home*) [*+ person*] raccompagner, reconduire ◆ **he was drunk and I was trying to ~ him back home** il était ivre et j'essayais de le raccompagner chez lui

► **get back at*** VT FUS (*= retaliate against*) prendre sa revanche sur

► **get by** VI 1 (*= pass*) passer ◆ **let me ~ by** laissez-moi passer 2 (*= manage*) arriver à s'en sortir* ◆ **by doing two part-time jobs she just ~s by** elle arrive tout juste à s'en sortir* avec deux emplois à mi-temps ◆ **she ~s by on very little money** elle arrive à s'en sortir* *or* elle se débrouille* avec très peu d'argent ◆ **he'll ~ by!** il s'en sortira !*

► **get down** VI 1 descendre (*from, off* de) ◆ **may I ~ down?** (*at table*) est-ce que je peux sortir de table ? ◆ **to ~ down on one's knees** se mettre à genoux ◆ **~ down!** (*= climb down*) descends ! ; (*= lie down*) couche-toi ! 2 (*esp US* ‡ *= enjoy oneself*) s'éclater‡ VT SEP 1 (*from upstairs, attic*) descendre ; (*from shelf*) prendre 2 (** = swallow*) [*+ food, pill*] avaler 3 (*= make note of*) noter, prendre (en note) 4 (*= depress*) déprimer ◆ **he ~s me down** il me fiche le cafard*, il me déprime ◆ **all the worry has got him down** tous ces soucis l'ont déprimé *or* lui ont mis le moral à zéro* ◆ **don't let it ~ you down!** ne te laisse pas abattre !

► **get down to** VT FUS ◆ **to ~ down to doing sth** se mettre à faire qch ◆ **to ~ down to work** se mettre au travail ◆ **you'll have to ~ down to it** il faut vous y mettre ◆ **when you ~ down to it there's not much difference between them** en y regardant de plus près il n'y a pas grande différence entre eux ◆ **to ~ down to business** passer aux choses sérieuses ◆ **let's ~ down to the details** regardons ça de plus près

► **get in** VI 1 [*person*] (*= enter*) entrer ; (*= be admitted to university, school*) être admis ; (*= reach home*) rentrer ; [*rain, water*] pénétrer, s'introduire ◆ **do you think we'll ~ in?** tu crois qu'on réussira à entrer ? 2 (*= arrive*) [*train, bus, plane*] arriver 3 (*Parl = be elected*) [*member*] être élu ; [*party*] accéder au pouvoir VT SEP 1 (*lit*) faire entrer ; [*+ screw, nail*] enfoncer ; [*+ crops, harvest*] rentrer ◆ **I managed to ~ it in** (*into case*) j'ai réussi à le faire entrer dedans *or* le caser ◆ **did you ~ your essay in on time?** as-tu rendu *or* remis ta dissertation à temps ? 2 (*= plant*) [*+ seeds*] planter, semer ; [*+ bulbs*] planter 3 (*= buy*) [*+ groceries, beer*] acheter ◆ **to ~ in supplies** s'approvisionner, faire des provisions 4 (*= summon*) [*+ doctor, police, tradesman*] faire venir 5 (*= fit in*) glisser ◆ **he got in a reference to his new book** il a glissé une allusion à son dernier livre ◆ **it was hard to ~ a word in** c'était difficile de placer un mot ◆ **he managed to ~ in a game of golf** il a réussi à trouver le temps de faire une partie de golf ; → **eye, hand**

► **get in on*** VT FUS ◆ **he managed to get in on the deal/the trip** il s'est débrouillé pour se joindre à l'affaire/au voyage ; see also **act** noun 3

► **get into** VT FUS 1 (*= enter*) [*+ house, park*] entrer dans, pénétrer dans ; [*+ car, train*] monter dans ◆ **to ~ into a club** devenir membre d'un club ◆ **he got into a good university** il a été admis dans une bonne université ◆ **to ~ into politics** entrer en politique ◆ **how did I ~ into all this?** comment me suis-je fourré* là-dedans ? ◆ **to ~ into the way of doing sth** (*= make a habit of*) prendre l'habitude de faire qch ◆ **I don't know what has got into him** je ne sais pas ce qui lui a pris ; → **company, habit, mischief** 2 [*+ clothes*] mettre ◆ **I can't ~ into these jeans any more** je ne peux plus rentrer dans ce jean

► **get in with** VT FUS 1 (*= gain favour of*) (réussir à) se faire bien voir de ◆ **he tried to ~ in with the headmaster** il a essayé de se faire bien voir du directeur 2 (*= become friendly with*) se mettre à fréquenter ◆ **he got in with local drug dealers** il s'est mis à fréquenter les trafiquants de drogue du quartier

► **get off** VI 1 (*from vehicle*) descendre ◆ **to tell sb where to ~ off*** envoyer promener qn*, envoyer qn sur les roses* 2 (*= depart*) [*person*] partir ; [*car*] démarrer ; [*plane*] décoller ◆ **to ~ off to a good start** (*lit*) prendre un bon départ ; (*fig*) partir du bon pied ◆ **to ~ off (to sleep)** s'endormir 3 (*= escape*) s'en tirer ◆ **to ~ off with a reprimand/a fine** en être quitte pour une réprimande/une amende 4 (*= leave work*) finir, quitter ; (*= take time off*) se libérer ◆ **we ~ off at 5 o'clock** nous finissons *or* nous quittons à 5 heures ◆ **I can't ~ off early today** je ne peux pas m'en aller de bonne heure aujourd'hui ◆ **can you ~ off tomorrow?** est-ce que tu peux te libérer demain ? VT SEP 1 [*+ bus, train*] descendre de 2 (*= remove*) [*+ clothes, shoes*] enlever ; [*+ stains*] faire partir, enlever 3 (*= dispatch*) [*+ mail*] expédier, envoyer ◆ **I'll phone you once I've got the children off to school** je t'appellerai une fois que les enfants seront partis à l'école ◆ **to ~ a child off to sleep** faire dormir un enfant 4 (*= save from punishment*) faire acquitter ◆ **a good lawyer will ~ him off** un bon avocat le tirera d'affaire *or* le fera acquitter 5 (*= learn*) ◆ **to ~ sth off (by heart)** apprendre qch (par cœur) 6 (*from shore*) [*+ boat*] renflouer ; (*from boat*) [*+ crew, passengers*] débarquer VT FUS 1 ◆ **to ~ off a bus/a bike** descendre d'un bus/d'un vélo ◆ **to ~ off a ship** descendre à terre ◆ **he got off his horse** il est descendu de cheval ◆ **to ~ off a chair** se lever d'une chaise ◆ **~ (up) off the floor!** levez-vous ! ◆ **I wish he would ~ off my back!*** si seulement il pouvait me ficher la paix* ! ◆ **let's ~ off this subject of conversation** parlons d'autre chose ◆ **we've rather got off the subject** nous nous sommes plutôt éloignés du sujet 2 (** = be excused*) ◆ **to ~ off gym** se faire dispenser des cours de gym ◆ **to ~ off work** se libérer

► **get off on**‡ VT FUS [*+ pornography, power, violence*] prendre son pied avec‡ ◆ **these guys ~ off on other guys** ces mecs, ce sont les hommes qui les excitent

► **get off with** * VT FUS *(Brit)* draguer *

► **get on** VI 1 *(on to bus, bike)* monter ; *(on to ship)* monter à bord 2 *(= advance, make progress)* avancer, progresser ◆ **how are you ~ting on?** comment ça marche ? * ◆ **how did you ~ on?** ça a bien marché ? *, comment ça s'est passé ? ◆ **she's ~ting on very well with Russian** elle fait de gros progrès en russe ◆ **to be ~ting on** * se faire vieux, prendre de la bouteille * ◆ **he's ~ting on for 40** il approche de la quarantaine ◆ **time is ~ting on** il se fait tard ◆ **it's ~ting on for 3 o'clock** il n'est pas loin de 3 heures ◆ **I must be ~ting on now** il faut que j'y aille ◆ **this will do to be ~ting on with** ça ira pour le moment ◆ **there were ~ting on for 100 people** il y avait pas loin de 100 personnes ◆ **we have ~ting on for 500 copies** nous avons près de *or* pas loin de 500 exemplaires 3 *(esp Brit = succeed)* réussir, arriver ◆ **if you want to ~ on, you must ...** si tu veux réussir, tu dois ... ◆ **to ~ on in life** *or* **in the world** réussir dans la vie *or* faire son chemin 4 *(= agree)* s'entendre *(with* avec) ◆ **we don't ~ on** nous ne nous entendons pas ◆ **I ~ on well with her** je m'entends bien avec elle VT SEP 1 *(= put on)* *[+ clothes, shoes]* mettre, enfiler 2 *(Culin)* ◆ **I've got the potatoes on** j'ai mis les pommes de terre sur le feu ◆ **I've got the dinner on** j'ai mis le repas en route VT FUS ◆ **to ~ on a horse** monter sur un cheval ◆ **to ~ on a bicycle** monter sur *or* enfourcher une bicyclette ◆ **to ~ on a ship** monter à bord (d'un navire) ◆ **to ~ on a bus/train** monter dans un bus/un train ◆ **to ~ back on one's feet** se remettre debout

► **get on to** VT FUS 1 ⇒ **get on** VT FUS 2 *(esp Brit)* *(= get in touch with)* se mettre en rapport avec ; *(= speak to)* parler à ; *(= ring up)* téléphoner à 3 *(= start talking about)* aborder ◆ **we got on to (the subject of) money** nous avons abordé le sujet de l'argent

► **get on with** VT FUS 1 *(= continue)* continuer ◆ **while they talked she got on with her work** pendant qu'ils parlaient, elle continua à travailler ◆ **while he was ~ting on with the job** pendant qu'il continuait à travailler ◆ **~ on with it!, ~ on with the job!** allez, au travail ! 2 *(= start on)* se mettre à ◆ **I'd better ~ on with the job!** il faut que je m'y mette !

► **get out** VI 1 sortir *(of* de) ; *(from vehicle)* descendre *(of* de) ◆ **to ~ out of bed** se lever ◆ **~ out!** sortez ! ◆ **~ out of here!** *(lit)* sors d'ici ! ;*(US * = I don't believe it)* à d'autres ! 2 *(= escape)* s'échapper *(of* de) ◆ **to ~ out of** *(fig)* *[+ task, obligation]* échapper à ; *[+ difficulty]* surmonter ◆ **you'll have to do it, you can't ~ out of it** il faut que tu le fasses, tu ne peux pas y échapper *or* y couper * ◆ **some people will do anything to ~ out of paying taxes** certaines personnes feraient n'importe quoi pour éviter de payer des impôts ◆ **he's trying to ~ out of going to the funeral** il essaie de trouver une excuse pour ne pas aller à l'enterrement 3 *[news]* se répandre, s'ébruiter ; *[secret]* être éventé ◆ **wait till the news ~s out!** attends que la nouvelle soit ébruitée ! ; → **jail** VT SEP 1 *(= bring out)* *[+ object]* sortir *(of* de) ; *[+ words, speech]* prononcer, sortir * ; *[+ book]* *[publisher]* publier, sortir ; *[library-user]* emprunter, sortir ◆ **~ the cards out and we'll have a game** sors les cartes et on va faire une partie ◆ **he got his diary out of his pocket** il sortit son agenda de sa poche 2 *(= remove)* *[+ nail]* arracher ; *[+ tooth]* extraire, arracher ; *[+ stain]* enlever, faire partir ◆ **to ~ the cork out of a bottle** déboucher une bouteille ◆ **I can't ~ it out of my mind** je ne peux pas chasser cela de mon esprit, ça me trotte dans la tête * sans arrêt 3 *(= free)* *[+ person]* faire sortir *(of* de) ◆ **they hope he'll ~ them out of their difficulties** ils espèrent qu'il les sortira de ce mauvais pas ◆ **it ~s me out of the house** ça me fait sortir (de chez moi) 4 *(= prepare)* *[+ list]* établir, dresser

► **get over** VI 1 *(= go)* aller ; *(= come)* venir ; *(= cross)* traverser ; *[message, meaning]* passer * ; *[speaker]* se faire entendre VT FUS 1 *(= cross)* *[+ river, road]* traverser ; *[+ fence]* *[horse]* franchir, sauter par-dessus ; *[person]* escalader, passer par-dessus 2 *(= recover from)* ◆ **to ~ over an illness** guérir *or* se remettre d'une maladie ◆ **to ~ over sb's death** se consoler *or* se remettre de la mort de qn ◆ **I can't ~ over it** je n'en reviens pas ◆ **I can't ~ over the fact that ...** je n'en reviens pas que ... + *subj* ◆ **I can't ~ over how much he's changed** je n'en reviens pas de voir combien il a changé ◆ **you'll ~ over it!** tu n'en mourras pas ! ◆ **she never really got over him** * elle ne l'a jamais vraiment oublié 3 *(= overcome)* *[+ obstacle, difficulty]* surmonter ; *[+ problem]* résoudre VT SEP 1 *(lit)* *[+ person, animal, vehicle]* faire passer ◆ **we couldn't ~ the car over** nous n'avons pas pu faire passer la voiture 2 *(= communicate)* faire comprendre ; *[+ ideas]* communiquer ◆ **I couldn't ~ it over to him that he had to come** je n'ai pas pu lui faire comprendre qu'il devait venir ◆ **he couldn't ~ his ideas over to his readers** il était incapable de communiquer ses idées à ses lecteurs

► **get over with** VT SEP *(= have done with)* en finir ◆ **let's ~ it over with** finissons-en ◆ **I was glad to ~ the injections over with** j'étais content d'en avoir fini avec ces piqûres

► **get round** VI ⇒ **get about** VT SEP ◆ **to ~ sb round to one's way of thinking** rallier qn à son point de vue VT FUS 1 *(= circumvent)* *[+ obstacle, difficulty, law, regulation]* contourner 2 *(= coax, persuade)* *[+ person]* amadouer *

► **get round to** * VT FUS ◆ **to ~ round to doing sth** trouver le temps de faire qch ◆ **I don't think I'll ~ round to it before next week** je ne pense pas trouver le temps de m'en occuper avant la semaine prochaine

► **get through** VI 1 *[news]* parvenir *(to* à) ; *[signal]* être reçu ◆ **I think the message is ~ting through to him** je pense qu'il commence à comprendre 2 *(= be accepted, pass)* *[candidate]* être reçu, réussir ; *[motion, bill]* passer, être voté ◆ **to ~ through to the third round** *[team]* se qualifier pour le troisième tour 3 *(Telec)* obtenir la communication ◆ **I phoned you several times but couldn't ~ through** je t'ai appelé plusieurs fois mais je n'ai pas pu t'avoir ◆ **I got through to him straight away** j'ai réussi à lui parler tout de suite 4 *(= communicate with)* ◆ **to get through to sb** communiquer avec qn ◆ **he can't ~ through to his son at all** il n'arrive pas du tout à communiquer avec son fils 5 *(= finish)* terminer, finir ◆ **I won't ~ through before 6 o'clock** je n'aurai pas terminé *or* fini avant 6 heures ◆ **to ~ through with sb/sth** * en finir avec qn/qch VT FUS 1 *[+ hole, window]* passer par ; *[+ hedge]* traverser, passer à travers ; *[+ crowd]* se frayer un chemin dans *or* à travers ; *(Mil)* *[+ enemy lines]* enfoncer, franchir 2 *(= do)* *[+ work]* faire ; *[+ book]* lire (en entier) ◆ **we've got a lot of work to ~ through** nous avons beaucoup de travail à faire ◆ **he got through a lot of work** il a abattu beaucoup de besogne 3 *(= consume, use, spend)* *[+ supplies]* utiliser, consommer ; *[+ money]* dépenser ; *[+ food]* manger ; *[+ drink]* boire ◆ **we ~ through a lot of nappies** nous utilisons beaucoup de couches ◆ **we ~ through £150 per week** nous dépensons 150 livres par semaine 4 *(= survive)* ◆ **how are they going to ~ through the winter ?** comment vont-ils passer l'hiver ? ◆ **we couldn't ~ through a day without arguing** pas un jour ne se passait sans que nous ne disputions VT SEP 1 *[+ person, object]* faire passer ◆ **we couldn't ~ the sofa through the door** on ne pouvait pas faire passer le sofa par la porte ◆ **to ~ the message through to sb that ...** faire comprendre à qn que ... ◆ **I can't ~ it through to him that ...** je n'arrive pas à lui faire comprendre que ... 2 *(= have approved)* ◆ **to ~ a bill through** faire adopter un projet de loi 3 *(Scol)* ◆ **he got his pupils through** il y est pour beaucoup dans le succès de ses élèves à l'examen ◆ **it was his English that got him through** c'est grâce à son anglais qu'il a été reçu

► **get together** VI se retrouver ◆ **let's ~ together on Thursday and decide what to do** si on se retrouvait jeudi pour décider de ce qu'on va faire ? ◆ **this is the only place where villagers can ~ together** c'est le seul endroit où les gens du village peuvent se retrouver *or* se réunir ◆ **you'd better ~ together with him before you decide** vous feriez bien de le voir avant de prendre une décision VT SEP *[+ people]* rassembler, réunir ; *[+ thoughts, ideas]* rassembler ; *[+ team, group]* former ; *[+ money]* rassembler, collecter ◆ **let me just ~ my things together** je rassemble mes affaires et j'arrive

► **get under** VI *(= pass underneath)* passer par-dessous VT FUS ◆ **to ~ under a fence/a rope** *etc* passer sous une barrière/une corde *etc*

► **get up** VI 1 *(= rise)* *[person]* se lever *(from* de) ; *[wind]* se lever ◆ **the sea is ~ting up** la houle se lève ◆ **what time did you ~ up?** à quelle heure t'es-tu levé ? 2 *(on a chair, on stage)* monter VT FUS *[+ tree, ladder]* monter à ; *[+ hill]* monter, grimper VT SEP 1 *(lit)* *[+ person]* *(up stairs, hill)* faire monter ; *[+ thing]* monter ; *[+ sail]* hisser ◆ **to ~ up speed** prendre de la vitesse 2 *(from bed)* *[+ person]* faire lever ; *(= wake)* réveiller 3 *(= organize)* *[+ play, show]* monter ; *[+ concert]* organiser ; *[+ story]* fabriquer, forger ◆ **to ~ up a petition** organiser une pétition 4 *(= prepare, arrange)* *[+ article for sale]* apprêter, préparer ; *[+ book]* présenter 5 *(= dress)* ◆ **she was very nicely got up** elle était très bien mise ◆ **a tramp got up in a velvet jacket** un clochard affublé d'une veste de velours ◆ **to ~ o.s. up as** se déguiser en 6 *(= study)* *[+ history, literature etc]* travailler, bûcher * ; *[+ speech, lecture]* préparer

► **get up to** VT FUS 1 *(= catch up with)* rattraper 2 *(= reach)* arriver à ◆ **I've got up to page 17** j'en suis à la page 17 ◆ **where did we ~ up to last week?** où en étions-nous *or* où en sommes-nous arrivés la semaine dernière ? 3 *(* = be involved in, do)* ◆ **to ~ up to mischief** faire des bêtises *or* des sottises ◆ **you never know what he'll ~ up to next** on ne sait jamais ce qu'il va inventer *or* fabriquer * ◆ **do you realize what they've been ~ting up to?** est-ce que tu sais ce qu'ils ont trouvé le moyen de faire ? ◆ **what have you been ~ting up to lately?** *(hum)* qu'est-ce que tu deviens ?

getaway /'getəweɪ/ N 1 *(= start)* *(in car)* démarrage *m* ; *(Racing)* départ *m* 2 *(= escape)* *[of criminals]* fuite *f* ◆ **to make a** *or* **one's ~** s'enfuir ◆ **they had a ~ car waiting** ils avaient une voiture pour s'enfuir ◆ **the gangsters' ~ car was later found abandoned** on a retrouvé abandonnée la voiture qui avait permis aux gangsters de s'enfuir 3 *(= short holiday)* escapade *f*

Gethsemane /geθ'semənɪ/ N Gethsémani

getup * /'getʌp/ N *(= clothing)* mise *f*, tenue *f*, accoutrement *m* *(pej)* ; *(= fancy dress)* déguisement *m* ; *(= presentation)* présentation *f*

geum /'dʒiːəm/ N benoîte *f*

gewgaw /'gjuːgɔː/ N bibelot *m*, babiole *f*

geyser /'giːzə^r^, (US) 'gaɪzər/ N *(Geol)* geyser *m* ; *(Brit: in house)* chauffe-eau *m inv*

Ghana /'gɑːnə/ N Ghana *m* ◆ **in ~** au Ghana

Ghanaian /gɑː'neɪən/ ADJ ghanéen N Ghanéen(ne) *m(f)*

ghastly /'gɑːstlɪ/ ADJ 1 *(= awful, horrendous)* *[person]* horrible ; *[war, murder, news, clothes, wallpaper, building]* horrible, affreux ; *[situation, experi-*

ence] épouvantable [2] *(= frightening)* effrayant [3] *(= serious) [mistake, headache, pain]* terrible, épouvantable [4] *(= pale) [appearance]* mortellement pâle ; *[pallor]* mortel ; *[light]* spectral ◆ **to look ~** avoir une mine de déterré

ghee /giː/ N beurre *m* clarifié

Ghent /gent/ N Gand

gherkin /'gɜːkɪn/ N *(Culin)* cornichon *m*

ghetto /'getəʊ/ N (pl **ghettos** or **ghettoes**) *(lit, fig)* ghetto *m* COMP **ghetto-blaster*** N (gros) radiocassette *m*

ghettoization /ˌgetəʊaɪ'zeɪʃən/ N ghettoïsation *f* ; *(fig)* marginalisation *f*

ghettoize /'getəʊˌaɪz/ VT ghettoïser ; *(fig)* marginaliser

Ghibelline /'gɪbɪˌlaɪn/ N Gibelin *m*

ghost /gəʊst/ N *(= apparition)* fantôme *m* ; *(fig)* ombre *f* ; *(TV)* filage *m* ; *(†† = soul)* âme *f* ◆ **I don't believe in ~s** je ne crois pas aux fantômes ◆ **he gave the ~ of a smile** il a eu un vague sourire ◆ **I haven't a ~ of a chance** je n'ai pas la moindre chance *or* pas l'ombre d'une chance ◆ **to give up the ~*** *(liter, hum) (= die)* rendre l'âme ; *(= stop trying)* baisser les bras ◆ **my alarm clock's finally given up the ~** mon réveil a fini par rendre l'âme ◆ **you look like** *or* **as if you've seen a ~!** on dirait que tu as vu un revenant ! ; → **holy**

VT ◆ **his book was ~ed by a journalist** c'est un journaliste qui lui a servi de nègre pour (écrire) son livre

COMP *[film, story]* de revenants, de fantômes ; *[ship]* fantôme

ghost image N *(TV)* filage *m*

ghost town N ville *f* morte

ghost train N *(Brit: at funfair)* train *m* fantôme

ghost-write VT ⇒ **ghost vt**

ghost writer N nègre *m*

ghostly /'gəʊstlɪ/ ADJ [1] spectral, fantomatique [2] *(††: Rel etc)* spirituel

ghoul /guːl/ N goule *f* ; *(= grave robber)* déterreur *m* de cadavres ◆ **he's a ~** *(fig)* il est morbide, il a des goûts dépravés

ghoulish /'guːlɪʃ/ ADJ *(= morbid, ghoul-like)* de goule ; *(pej) [person, curiosity, desire, humour, tastes]* morbide

ghoulishly /'guːlɪʃlɪ/ ADV *(= morbidly)* de façon morbide

GHQ /ˌdʒiːeɪtʃ'kjuː/ N *(Mil etc)* (abbrev of **General Headquarters**) GQG *m*

GI* /dʒiː'aɪ/ *(US)* N (also **GI Joe**) soldat *m* (américain), GI *m* ADJ militaire ◆ **~ bill** *(Univ) loi sur les bourses pour anciens combattants* ◆ **~ bride** *épouse étrangère d'un GI*

giant /'dʒaɪənt/ N géant *m* ◆ **he is a ~ of a man** c'est un géant ◆ **the ~ of opera, Luciano Pavarotti** le monstre sacré de l'opéra, Luciano Pavarotti ◆ **the Giant's Causeway** *(Geog)* la chaussée des Géants ◆ **electronics/chemicals ~** *(fig)* géant *m* de l'électronique/de l'industrie chimique

ADJ *[tree, star etc]* géant ; *[strides]* de géant ; *[helping, amount]* gigantesque ; *[packet, size]* géant

COMP **giant-killer** N *(Sport)* vainqueur *m* surprise *(équipe de second plan qui parvient à battre une grande équipe)*

giant-killing ADJ ◆ **the team's ~-killing act against Manchester United** la victoire surprise de l'équipe contre le géant Manchester United ◆ **Spain's ~-killing French Open champion** l'outsider espagnol qui a tombé les meilleurs joueurs aux Internationaux de France

giant panda N grand panda *m*

giant slalom N *(Ski)* slalom *m* géant

giantess /'dʒaɪəntɪs/ N géante *f*

gibber /'dʒɪbəʳ/ VI *[person, ape etc]* baragouiner* ◆ **to ~ with rage/fear** bégayer *or* bafouiller de colère/de peur ◆ **~ing idiot*** crétin *m* patenté* ◆ **I was a ~ing wreck by this stage** j'étais alors à bout de nerfs

gibberish /'dʒɪbərɪʃ/ N *(NonC)* charabia* *m* ◆ **he's talking ~*** il dit n'importe quoi*

gibbet /'dʒɪbɪt/ N potence *f*, gibet *m*

gibbon /'gɪbən/ N gibbon *m*

gibbous /'gɪbəs/ ADJ *(= hump-backed)* gibbeux *(liter)*, bossu ◆ **~ moon** lune *f* dans le deuxième *or* troisième quartier

gibe /dʒaɪb/ VI [1] ◆ **to ~ at sb** railler qn, se moquer de qn [2] *(Naut) [boat]* virer lof pour lof ; *[sail]* passer d'un bord à l'autre du mât N raillerie *f*, moquerie *f*

giblets /'dʒɪblɪts/ NPL abattis *mpl*, abats *mpl (de volaille)*

Gibraltar /dʒɪ'brɔːltəʳ/ N Gibraltar ◆ **in ~** à Gibraltar ; → **rock², strait**

giddily /'gɪdɪlɪ/ ADV *(= unsteadily)* en titubant ; *(= dizzyingly)* à donner/à en avoir le vertige ◆ **to be ~ high** *[figures etc]* atteindre des sommets vertigineux

giddiness /'gɪdɪnɪs/ N *(NonC) (Med)* vertiges *mpl*, étourdissements *mpl* ; *(= lightheartedness)* légèreté *f* ; *(= heedlessness)* étourderie *f* ◆ **a bout of ~** un vertige, un étourdissement

giddy¹ /'gɪdɪ/ ADJ *[person] (= dizzy)* pris de vertige *or* d'un étourdissement ; *(= heedless)* étourdi, écervelé ; *(= not serious)* léger ; *[height]* vertigineux, qui donne le vertige ◆ **I feel ~** la tête me tourne ◆ **to turn** *or* **go ~** être pris de vertige ◆ **to make sb ~** donner le vertige à qn ◆ **~ spells** vertiges *mpl*, étourdissements *mpl* ◆ **being there gave me a ~ pleasure** être là me procurait un plaisir grisant ◆ **she was ~ with excitement** l'idée *(or* l'émerveillement *etc)* la grisait ◆ **the ~ heights of senior management** *(fig, iro)* les hautes sphères de la direction générale ◆ **that's the ~ limit!‡** ça c'est le bouquet !* ; → **spell²**

giddy² /'gɪdɪ/ EXCL *(to horse)* ◆ **~ up !** hue !

GIFT /gɪft/ N (abbrev of **Gamete Intrafallopian Transfer**) fivète *f*

gift /gɪft/ N [1] *(= present)* cadeau *m*, présent *m* ; *(Comm)* prime *f*, cadeau *m* ◆ **New Year ~** étrennes *fpl* ◆ **it was a ~** *(lit)* c'était un cadeau ; *(* fig = it was easy)* c'était du gâteau* ◆ **I wouldn't have it as a ~** on m'en ferait cadeau que je n'en voudrais pas ◆ **"free gift inside the packet"** *(Comm)* "ce paquet contient un cadeau"

[2] *(Jur etc)* don *m*, donation *f* ◆ **to make sb a ~ of sth** faire don *or* cadeau de qch à qn ◆ **in the ~ of** à la discrétion de ; → **deed**

[3] *(= talent)* don *m (for* de, pour) talent *m (for* pour) ◆ **he has a ~ for maths** il a un don pour les maths *or* le don des maths ◆ **she has a ~ for teaching** elle a un don pour l'enseignement, elle est très douée pour l'enseignement ◆ **he has great artistic ~s** il a de grands dons artistiques ◆ **to have the ~ of the gab*** avoir la langue bien pendue, avoir du bagout*

VT *(esp Jur)* donner ◆ **to be ~ed with patience** *etc (fig)* être doué de patience *etc*

COMP **gift horse** N **don't look a ~ horse in the mouth** *(Prov)* à cheval donné on ne regarde point la bouche *(Prov)*, on ne critique pas le cadeau qu'on reçoit *(Prov)*

gift shop N boutique *f* de cadeaux

gift token, gift voucher N chèque-cadeau *m*

gifted /'gɪftɪd/ ADJ *(fig)* doué *(for* pour) ◆ **the ~ child** l'enfant *m* surdoué

giftwrap /'gɪftræp/ VT ◆ **to ~ a package** faire un paquet-cadeau ◆ **could you ~ it for me?** pouvez-vous me faire un paquet-cadeau ? N ⇒ **giftwrapping**

giftwrapped /'gɪftræpt/ ADJ sous emballage-cadeau

giftwrapping /'gɪftræpɪŋ/ N emballage-cadeau *m*

gig /gɪg/ N [1] *(= vehicle)* cabriolet *m* ; *(= boat)* petit canot *m*, youyou *m* [2] *(Mus* * = jazz, pop concert)* concert *m* ◆ **they had a regular ~ at the Cavern** ils jouaient régulièrement au Cavern ◆ **comedy ~s** *(Theat)* numéros *mpl* de comique [3] *(US fig: *)* job* *m* temporaire VI * *(Mus)* jouer live *or* sur scène ◆ **he spent ten years ~ging in bars** *[stand-up comedian]* il a passé dix ans à jouer dans les bars

gigabyte /'dʒɪgəˌbaɪt/ N gigaoctet *m*

gigaflop /'gaɪgəˌflɒp/ N milliard *m* d'opérations en virgule flottante par seconde

gigahertz /'dʒɪgəˌhɜːts/ N gigahertz *m*

gigantic /dʒaɪ'gæntɪk/ ADJ gigantesque

gigantically /dʒaɪ'gæntɪkəlɪ/ ADV ◆ **~ fat** démesurément gros ◆ **to be ~ successful** avoir un succès énorme

gigantism /dʒaɪ'gæntɪzəm/ N gigantisme *m*

gigawatt /'dʒɪgəˌwɒt/ N gigawatt *m*

giggle /'gɪgl/ VI rire sottement, glousser ◆ **stop giggling!** ne riez pas sottement comme ça ! ◆ **she was giggling helplessly** elle ne pouvait pas se retenir de rire sottement *or* de glousser ◆ **"stop that!" she ~d** "arrête !" dit-elle en gloussant N petit rire *m* sot *or* nerveux, gloussement *m* sot *or* nerveux ◆ **to have/get the ~s** avoir/attraper le fou rire ◆ **she had a fit of the ~s** elle avait le fou rire ◆ **it was a bit of a ~*** *(Brit)* ça nous a bien fait rigoler* ◆ **he did it for a ~*** *(Brit)* il a fait ça pour rigoler*

giggly /'gɪglɪ/ ADJ qui rit bêtement *or* glousse (sans arrêt)

GIGO /'giːgəʊ, ˌdʒiːaɪdʒiː'əʊ/ (abbrev of **garbage in, garbage out**) → **garbage**

gigolo /'ʒɪgələʊ/ N *(sexually)* gigolo *m* ; *(= dancing partner)* danseur *m* mondain

gigot /'ʒiːgəʊ, 'dʒɪgət/ N *(Culin)* gigot *m*

Gila /'hiːla/ N ◆ **~ monster** monstre *m* de Gila, héloderme *m*

Gilbertian /gɪl'bɜːtɪən/ ADJ *(Brit)* ≃ vaudevillesque

gild /gɪld/ VT (pret **gilded**, ptp **gilded** or **gilt**) dorer ◆ **to ~ the lily** renchérir sur la perfection ◆ **to ~ the pill** dorer la pilule ◆ **~ed youth** la jeunesse dorée

gilding /'gɪldɪŋ/ N dorure *f*

Giles /dʒaɪlz/ N Gilles *m*

gill¹ /gɪl/ N *[of mushrooms]* lamelle *f* ◆ **~s** *[of fish]* ouïes *fpl*, branchies *fpl* ◆ **he was looking somewhat green** *or* **pale around the ~s*** il était (devenu) vert

gill² /dʒɪl/ N *(Brit = measure)* quart *m* de pinte *(= 0,142 l)*

gillie /'gɪlɪ/ N *(Scot)* gillie *m*, accompagnateur *m (d'un chasseur, d'un pêcheur etc)*

gillyflower /'dʒɪlɪˌflaʊəʳ/ N giroflée *f*

gilt /gɪlt/ VB ptp of **gild** N *(= gold)* dorure *f* ◆ **to take the ~ off the gingerbread** enlever tout le charme, gâter le plaisir NPL **gilts** *(Brit Fin)* ⇒ **gilt-edged securities** ADJ doré

COMP **gilt-edged** ADJ *[book]* doré sur tranche ; *(fig)* de tout premier ordre

gilt-edged securities NPL *(Brit Fin) (government-issued)* fonds *mpl or* obligations *fpl* d'État ; *(= safe investment)* valeurs *fpl* de tout repos *or* de père de famille

gilt-edged stock N ⇒ **gilt-edged securities**

gilt-head N *(= fish)* daurade *f*, dorade *f*

gimbal(s) /'dʒɪmbəl(z)/ N cardan *m*

gimcrack /'dʒɪmkræk/ ADJ ringard

gimlet /'gɪmlɪt/ N vrille *f* ◆ **to have eyes like ~s, to be ~-eyed** avoir des yeux perçants, avoir un regard perçant

gimme* /'gɪmiː/ ⇒ **give me**

gimmick /'gɪmɪk/ N (gen) truc* m ; (Theat = catch phrase) réplique f à effet ; (= gadget) gadget m ; (US) (= trick) truc* m, combine f ♦ **advertising ~** truc* m or procédé m publicitaire ♦ **election ~** procédé m pour s'attirer des suffrages ♦ **it's just a sales ~** c'est simplement un gadget promotionnel or une astuce promotionnelle

gimmickry /'gɪmɪkrɪ/ N gadgets mpl

gimmicky /'gɪmɪkɪ/ ADJ (pej) qui relève du gadget

gimp* /gɪmp/ (US) N (= person) boiteux m, -euse f ♦ **to walk with a ~** boiter VI boiter

gimpy /'gɪmpɪ/ ADJ (US) boiteux

gin¹ /dʒɪn/ N 1 gin m ♦ **~ and tonic** gin-tonic m ♦ **~ and it** (Brit) gin-vermouth m ; → **pink¹** 2 (Cards: also **gin rummy**) variante du rami

COMP **gin mill*** N (US) bar m, saloon m

gin sling N gin-fizz m

gin² /dʒɪn/ N 1 (Brit: also **gin trap**) piège m 2 (Tech: also **cotton gin**) égreneuse f (de coton)

ginger /'dʒɪndʒəʳ/ N gingembre m ; (fig) énergie f, pêche* f ♦ **Ginger** (= nickname) Poil m de Carotte ADJ 1 [hair] roux (rousse f), rouquin* ♦ **a ~ tom** un chat roux 2 (Culin) [biscuit etc] au gingembre

COMP **ginger ale, ginger beer** (Brit) N boisson f gazeuse au gingembre

ginger group N (Brit: esp Pol) groupe m de pression

ginger nut N gâteau m sec au gingembre

ginger pop* N ⇒ **ginger ale**

ginger snap N ⇒ **ginger nut**

► **ginger up** VT SEP (Brit) [+ person] secouer, secouer les puces à* ; [+ action, event] mettre de la vie or de l'entrain dans ♦ **the banks are desperately trying to ~ up the housing market** les banques essaient désespérément de stimuler or dynamiser le marché de l'immobilier ♦ **he ~ed up his talk with a few jokes** il a relevé or égayé sa causerie de quelques plaisanteries

gingerbread /'dʒɪndʒəbred/ N pain m d'épice ADJ (Culin) en pain d'épice ; (Archit *) [style] tarabiscoté ♦ **~ man** bonhomme m en pain d'épice

gingerly /'dʒɪndʒəlɪ/ ADJ [prod] léger, doux (douce f) ; [touch] délicat ADV avec précaution

gingery /'dʒɪndʒərɪ/ ADJ 1 (= colour) [hair] avec des reflets roux ; [cloth etc] dans les tons roux 2 [taste] de gingembre ♦ **it tastes (very) ~** ça a (fort) goût de gingembre

gingham /'gɪŋəm/ N vichy m

gingivitis /,dʒɪndʒɪ'vaɪtɪs/ N gingivite f

gink* /gɪŋk/ N (US pej) (drôle de) type* m

ginkgo /'gɪŋkgəʊ/ N ginkgo m

ginormous* /dʒaɪ'nɔːməs/ ADJ gigantesque

ginseng /dʒɪn'seŋ/ N ginseng m COMP [tea, tablets] au ginseng

Gioconda /dʒə'kɒndə/ N ♦ **La ~** la Joconde ♦ **~ smile** sourire m énigmatique or sibyllin

gippy* /'dʒɪpɪ/ ADJ (Brit) ♦ **to have a ~ tummy** avoir la courante*

gipsy /'dʒɪpsɪ/ N (gen) bohémien(ne) m(f) ; (Spanish) gitan(e) m(f) ; (Central European) Tsigane or Tzigane mf ; (pej) romanichel(le) m(f) COMP [caravan, custom] de bohémien, de gitan, tsigane, de romanichel (pej) ; [music] des gitans, tsigane

gipsy cab N (US) taxi m clandestin

gipsy driver N (US) chauffeur m de taxi clandestin

gipsy moth N zigzag m

giraffe /dʒɪ'rɑːf/ N girafe f ♦ **baby ~** girafeau m

gird /gɜːd/ (pret, ptp **girded** or **girt**) VT (liter = encircle) ceindre (liter) ; († = clothe) revêtir (with de) ♦ **to ~ o.s. for a fight** (fig = get ready) se préparer au combat ♦ **to ~ (up) one's loins** (liter) se préparer (to do sth à faire qch ; for sth pour qch)

► **gird on** VT SEP [+ sword etc] ceindre (liter)

► **gird up** VT SEP [+ robe] ceindre ; see also **gird**

girder /'gɜːdəʳ/ N poutre f ; (smaller) poutrelle f

girdle¹ /'gɜːdl/ N (= belt: lit, fig) ceinture f ; (= corset) gaine f VT (fig liter) ceindre (with de)

girdle² /'gɜːdl/ N (Culin) ⇒ **griddle noun**

girl /gɜːl/ N 1 (jeune) or (petite) fille f ♦ **the ~ who looks after the children** la jeune fille qui s'occupe des enfants ♦ **a little ~** une petite fille, une fillette ♦ **the little ~s were watching television** les petites filles or les fillettes regardaient la télévision ♦ **she's a nice ~** c'est une fille bien ♦ **that ~ gets on my nerves** cette fille m'énerve ♦ **a ~ of 17** une (jeune) fille de 17 ans ♦ **an English ~** une jeune Anglaise ♦ **a little English ~** une petite Anglaise ♦ **poor little ~** pauvre petite f ♦ **the Smith ~s** les filles des Smith ♦ **I'll really give you something to cry about, my ~** je vais te donner une bonne raison de pleurer, ma fille* ♦ **~s' school** école f (or lycée m etc) de filles

2 (= daughter) fille f ; (= pupil) élève f ; (= servant) bonne f ; (= factory-worker) ouvrière f ; (= shop assistant) vendeuse f, jeune fille f ; (* = sweetheart) petite amie f ♦ **old ~** (Brit Scol) ancienne élève f ♦ **yes, old ~*** oui, ma vieille* ♦ **the old ~*** (= wife) la patronne*, la bourgeoise* ; (= mother) ma mère or vieille* ♦ **the old ~* next door** la vieille dame or la vieille* d'à côté

COMP **girl band** N (Mus) girlband m

girl Friday N (in office) aide f de bureau

girl guide N (Brit) éclaireuse f ; (Roman Catholic) guide f

girl's blouse* N ♦ **he's a big ~'s blouse** c'est une vraie mauviette ♦ **you big ~'s blouse!** quelle mauviette tu fais !

girl scout N (US) ⇒ **girl guide**

girl-watching N (US) ♦ **to go ~-watching** aller reluquer* les filles

girlfriend /'gɜːlfrend/ N [of boy] petite amie f ; [of girl] amie f, copine f

girlhood /'gɜːlhʊd/ N enfance f, jeunesse f

girlie, girly* /'gɜːlɪ/ ADJ de filles ♦ **~ magazine** magazine m de charme (ou fesses*)

girlish /'gɜːlɪʃ/ ADJ [boy] efféminé ; [behaviour, appearance] (woman's) de petite fille, de jeune fille ; (man's, boy's) efféminé

giro /'dʒaɪrəʊ/ N (Brit *: also **giro cheque**) ≃ mandat m postal (servant au paiement des prestations de chômage ou de maladie) ♦ **bank ~ system** système m de virement bancaire ♦ **National Giro** ≃ Comptes mpl Chèques Postaux ♦ **by ~ transfer** (Fin) par virement postal (or bancaire)

girt /gɜːt/ VB pt, ptp **gird** N ⇒ **girth 2**

girth /gɜːθ/ N 1 (= circumference) [of tree] circonférence f ; [of waist/hips etc] tour m (de taille/de hanches etc) ♦ **in ~** de circonférence, de tour ♦ **his (great) ~** sa corpulence 2 [of saddle] sangle f ♦ **to loosen the ~s** dessangler

gist /dʒɪst/ N (NonC) [of report, conversation etc] fond m, essentiel m ; [of question] point m principal ♦ **to get the ~ of sth** comprendre l'essentiel de qch ♦ **give me the ~ of what he said** résumez-moi ce qu'il a dit, en deux mots

git* /gɪt/ N (Brit pej) 1 (= idiot) (man) con* m ; (woman) conne* f ♦ **stupid ~!** espèce de con(ne) !* 2 (= unpleasant person) (man) salaud* m ; (woman) salope* f ♦ **he's a miserable old ~** c'est un vieux con*

give /gɪv/

vb : pret **gave**, ptp **given**

1 TRANSITIVE VERB	4 COMPOUNDS
2 INTRANSITIVE VERB	5 PHRASAL VERBS
3 NOUN	

1 - TRANSITIVE VERB

When **give** is part of a set combination, eg **give evidence, give a party, give a yawn**, look up the other word.

1 donner (to à) ; [+ gift] offrir (to à) ; [+ one's time] consacrer, donner (to à) ♦ **to ~ sb something to eat/drink** donner à manger/à boire à qn ♦ **can you ~ him something to do?** pouvez-vous lui donner quelque chose à faire ? ♦ **what are you going to ~ her?** qu'est-ce que tu vas lui offrir ? ♦ **to ~ one's daughter in marriage** † donner sa fille en mariage † ♦ **she gave herself to him** † elle s'est donnée à lui † ♦ **it was not ~n to him to achieve happiness** il ne lui a pas été donné de trouver le bonheur ♦ **to ~ sb one's trust** donner or accorder sa confiance à qn ♦ **he gave his life or himself to helping the poor** il a consacré sa vie aux pauvres BUT **she gave us a wonderful meal** elle nous a préparé un délicieux repas ♦ **to ~ sb a look** jeter or lancer un regard à qn ♦ **~ me a gas cooker every time!** * pour moi rien ne vaut une gazinière ! ♦ **children ? ~ me dogs any time !** des enfants ? je préfère de loin les chiens !

give + noun may be translated by a verb alone.

♦ **can you ~ me a bed for the night?** pouvez-vous me loger pour la nuit ? ♦ **they gave us a lot of help** ils nous ont beaucoup aidés ♦ **I'll ~ you a call** je vous appellerai, je vous passerai un coup de fil

♦ **to be given** (= receive)

In French the recipient is not made the subject of a passive construction.

♦ **she was ~n a huge bouquet** on lui a donné or offert un énorme bouquet ♦ **we were ~n a warm reception** on nous a accueillis chaleureusement ♦ **the suggestion will be ~n serious consideration** cette suggestion sera soigneusement examinée ♦ **six footballers were ~n honours** six footballeurs ont reçu une distinction honorifique ♦ **he was ~n a knighthood** il a été fait chevalier

♦ **to give and take** ♦ **one must ~ and take** il faut faire des concessions ; see also **compounds**

♦ **give or take** ♦ **~ or take a few minutes** à quelques minutes près ♦ **a hundred people, ~ or take a few** à peu près cent personnes

2 = cause, cause to feel faire ♦ **it gave me a shock** ça m'a fait un choc ♦ **keying ~s me a pain in my wrist** si je tape au clavier, ça me fait mal au poignet ♦ **it gave me a funny feeling** ça m'a fait un drôle d'effet ♦ **to ~ sb to believe sth** donner à croire qch à qn, laisser entendre qch à qn ♦ **I was ~n to understand that ...** on m'avait laissé entendre que ..., on m'avait donné à croire que ... ♦ **her grandchildren ~ her a lot of pleasure** ses petits-enfants lui procurent beaucoup de plaisir ♦ **it ~s me great pleasure to introduce ...** c'est avec grand plaisir que je vous présente ... ♦ **it gave us a good laugh*** on a bien rigolé*

3 = pass on ♦ **OK, I'll ~ him the message** d'accord, je lui ferai la commission, d'accord, je le lui dirai ♦ **you've ~n me your cold** tu m'as passé or refilé* ton rhume ♦ **~ him my love** faites-lui mes amitiés

4 = put through to passer ◆ **could you ~ me Mr Smith/extension 231?** pouvez-vous me passer M. Smith/le poste 231 ?

5 with time expressions ◆ **~ him time to get home** laissez-lui le temps de rentrer ◆ **~ me time and I'll manage it** laissez-moi du temps et j'y arriverai ◆ **~ yourself time to think about it before you decide** prends le temps de réfléchir avant de te décider ◆ **(just) ~ me time!** attends un peu !, ne me bouscule pas ! ◆ **I can't ~ you any longer, you must pay me now** je ne peux plus vous accorder de délai, il faut que vous payiez maintenant ◆ **I can ~ you half an hour tomorrow** je peux vous consacrer une demi-heure demain ◆ **the doctors gave him two years (to live)** les médecins lui ont donné deux ans (à vivre) ◆ **how long do you ~ that marriage?** combien de temps crois-tu que ce mariage tiendra ? ◆ **I can ~ him ten years** * *(in age)* il est de dix ans mon cadet

6 + name, address, description donner *(to* à) ◆ **what name did he ~?** quel nom a-t-il donné ? ◆ **she was unable to ~ the police a description of her attacker** elle a été incapable de donner une description de son agresseur à la police ◆ **to ~ one's decision** rendre *or* faire connaître sa décision ◆ **he gave the cause of death as asphyxia** il a conclu à une mort par asphyxie ◆ **~n under my hand and seal** *(Jur)* signé

7 = utter *[+ answer]* donner ; *[+ sigh, cry]* pousser ◆ **they haven't yet ~n their answer** ils n'ont pas encore donné de réponse, ils n'ont pas encore rendu leur réponse

8 = pay payer ; *(= offer)* offrir, donner ◆ **what did you ~ for it?** combien l'avez-vous payé ? ◆ **I'd ~ a lot/anything to know** je donnerais gros/n'importe quoi pour savoir ◆ **what will you ~ me for it?** combien m'en offrez-vous *or* m'en donnez-vous ? ◆ **I don't ~ much for his chances** je ne donne pas cher de ses chances

9 = punish with *[+ lines, detention]* donner *(to* à) ◆ **the teacher gave him 100 lines** le professeur lui a donné 100 lignes ◆ **the judge gave him five years** le juge l'a condamné à cinq ans de prison

10 = perform, do, deliver *[+ lecture]* faire, donner ; *[+ play]* donner, présenter

11 = produce donner, produire ◆ **cows ~ more milk when ...** les vaches donnent *or* produisent plus de lait lorsque ... ◆ **two surveys gave good results** deux études ont donné *or* produit de bons résultats ◆ **it ~s a total of 100** cela fait 100 en tout ◆ **this lamp doesn't ~ much light** cette lampe éclaire mal

12 frm = toast ◆ **I ~ you the Queen !** je lève mon verre à la santé de la Reine !

13 idiomatic expressions ◆ **he gave as good as he got** il a rendu coup pour coup ◆ **~ it all you've got!** * mets-y le paquet ! * ◆ **I wouldn't have it if you gave it to me** * tu m'en ferais cadeau que je n'en voudrais pas ◆ **I'll ~ him something to cry about!** * je lui apprendrai à pleurer ! ◆ **to ~ sb what for**‡, **to ~ it to sb**‡ passer un savon à qn *, faire sa fête à qn‡ ◆ **he wants £100? I'll ~ him £100!** * *(iro)* il veut 100 livres ? il peut toujours courir ! * ◆ **I'll ~ you that** *(agreeing)* je suis d'accord là-dessus ◆ **don't ~ me that!** * ne me raconte pas d'histoires ! * ◆ **OK, now ~!**‡*(US)* allez accouche !‡

14 set structures

♦ **to give way**[1] *(= collapse) [bridge, beam, ceiling, floor]* s'effondrer *(beneath, under* sous) ; *[ground]* céder, se dérober *(beneath, under* sous) ; *[cable, rope]* céder, (se) casser ; *[legs]* fléchir, mollir ◆ **his strength gave way** les forces lui ont manqué ◆ **after months of stress his health gave way** après des mois de stress, il a eu de graves problèmes de santé *or* sa santé a flanché

♦ **to give way**[2] *(= yield) [person]* céder *(to sth* à qch) ; *(= stand back)* s'écarter, se pousser ; *(= agree)* finir par donner son accord, finir par consentir ; *[troops] (= withdraw)* reculer, se retirer ; *[car, traffic]* céder le passage *(to* à) ◆ **"give way"** *(roadsign)* "cédez le passage", "vous n'avez pas la priorité" ◆ **"give way to traffic from the right"** *(roadsing)* "priorité à droite" ◆ **I gave way to temptation** j'ai cédé à la tentation ◆ **he gave way to their demands** il a cédé à leurs revendications ◆ **don't ~ way to despair** ne cédez pas au désespoir, ne désespérez pas ◆ **to ~ way to an impulse** céder à une impulsion ◆ **she gave way to tears** elle n'a pas pu retenir ses larmes ◆ **his shock gave way to anger** sa surprise a fait place *or* laissé place à la colère

2 - INTRANSITIVE VERB

1 = collapse céder *(beneath, under* sous) ◆ **the axle gave and fell on me** l'essieu a cédé et m'est tombé dessus ◆ **the chair gave under his weight** la chaise a cédé sous son poids

2 = yield *[floor]* fléchir ; *[cloth, elastic]* se détendre, se relâcher ◆ **the floor gave slightly under his feet** le parquet fléchissait légèrement sous son poids

3 esp US ◆ **what ~s ?** * alors, qu'est-ce qui se passe ?

3 - NOUN

* = flexibility ◆ **there is a lot of ~ in this rope** cette corde est très élastique ◆ **there isn't a lot of ~ in these proposals** il n'y a pas beaucoup de souplesse dans ces propositions ◆ **how much ~ has there been on their side?** est-ce qu'ils se sont montrés prêts à faire des concessions ?

4 - COMPOUNDS

give-and-take N *(NonC)* concessions *fpl* mutuelles ◆ **there must be a certain amount of ~-and-take** il faut que chacun fasse des concessions *or* y mette un peu du sien

5 - PHRASAL VERBS

► **give away** VT SEP 1 *(= bestow, distribute) [+ prizes]* distribuer ; *[+ bride]* conduire à l'autel ; *[+ money, goods]* donner ◆ **we've got 200 CDs to ~ away** nous avons 200 CD à donner ◆ **at this price I'm giving it away** à ce prix-là c'est un cadeau *or* c'est donné 2 *(= concede)* faire cadeau de ◆ **we gave away a silly goal** nous leur avons bêtement fait cadeau d'un but 3 *(= tell, betray) [+ names, details]* donner ; *[+ secrets]* révéler ◆ **to ~ sb away** *[+ person, accomplice]* dénoncer *or* donner * qn ; *[reaction, expression]* trahir qn ◆ **to ~ o.s. away** se trahir ◆ **don't ~ anything away** ne dis rien ◆ **his face gave nothing away** son visage ne trahissait aucune émotion ◆ **to ~ the game away** * vendre la mèche *

► **give back** VT SEP *[+ object, freedom]* rendre *(to* à) ; *[+ echo]* renvoyer ; *[+ image]* refléter ◆ **they have been ~n back their property** leurs biens leur ont été restitués *or* rendus

► **give forth** VT SEP *[+ sound]* émettre, faire entendre

► **give in** VI *(= surrender)* capituler ; *(= yield)* céder *(to* à) ◆ **the troops gave in after three weeks** les troupes ont capitulé au bout de trois semaines ◆ **I pestered my parents until they gave in** j'ai harcelé mes parents jusqu'à ce qu'ils cèdent *or* capitulent ◆ **I ~ in!** *(in games)* j'abandonne ! ; *(in guessing)* je donne ma langue au chat ! * VT SEP *[+ essay, exam paper, key]* rendre ; *[+ manuscript, report]* remettre

► **give off** VT SEP *[+ heat]* dégager, émettre ; *[+ gas, smell, aura]* dégager ◆ **the carpets and curtains gave off a smell of mould** la moquette et les rideaux dégageaient une odeur de moisi ◆ **they gave off a sense of assurance** on sentait chez eux une assurance naturelle

► **give on to** VT FUS *[door, window]* donner sur

► **give out** VI *[supplies]* s'épuiser ; *[patience]* être à bout ; *[heart]* lâcher ◆ **after two weeks their food had ~n out** au bout de deux semaines leurs provisions étaient épuisées ◆ **one of his lungs gave out entirely** un de ses poumons a lâché ◆ **all machines ~ out eventually** les machines ne sont pas éternelles ◆ **my strength is giving out** je suis à bout de forces, je n'en peux plus VT SEP 1 *(= distribute) [+ books, food]* distribuer 2 *(= make known) [+ information, details]* donner ◆ **it was ~n out that ...** on a annoncé que ... 3 *[+ radio signal]* émettre 4 *(= utter)* ◆ **he gave out a scream of pain** il poussa un cri de douleur ; see also **give vt 7** 5 ⇒ **give off**

► **give over** * VT FUS *(= stop) [+ studies, activities]* arrêter ◆ **to ~ over doing sth** cesser de faire qch, arrêter de faire qch ◆ **~ over!** arrête !, ça suffit !

► **give over to** VT SEP *(= dedicate, devote)* consacrer ◆ **most of the garden is ~n over to vegetables** la majeure partie du jardin est consacrée au potager ◆ **many cinemas are ~n over to bingo** de nombreux cinémas ont été transformés en salles de bingo ◆ **to ~ o.s. over to** *[+ activity, drink]* s'adonner à ; *[+ children, family]* se consacrer à

► **give up** VI abandonner, laisser tomber * ◆ **they were on the point of giving up when ...** ils étaient sur le point d'abandonner *or* de laisser tomber * lorsque ... ◆ **I ~ up** j'abandonne, je capitule ; *(in guessing)* je donne ma langue au chat * ◆ **don't ~ up!** tenez bon ! VT SEP 1 *(= renounce) [+ interests]* abandonner ; *[+ seat, territory]* céder ; *[+ habit, idea, hope, claim]* renoncer à ; *[+ job]* quitter ; *[+ business]* se retirer de ; *[+ subscription]* résilier ◆ **when she went to university she gave up her old friends** quand elle est entrée à l'université elle a cessé de voir ses vieux amis ◆ **to ~ up the struggle** abandonner la partie ◆ **I gave it up as a bad job** (comme ça ne menait à rien) j'ai laissé tomber * ◆ **she gave him up as a bad job** * comme elle n'arrivait à rien avec lui elle l'a laissé tomber * 2 *(= stop)* arrêter, cesser ◆ **to ~ up smoking** arrêter de fumer, renoncer au tabac ◆ **I've ~n up trying to persuade her** j'ai renoncé à essayer de la convaincre ◆ **eventually he gave up trying** au bout d'un moment il a renoncé 3 *(= deliver, hand over)* ◆ **to give o.s. up** se rendre, se constituer prisonnier ◆ **she gave the baby up for adoption** elle a fait adopter le bébé 4 *(= abandon hope for) [+ expected visitor]* ne plus attendre ◆ **the doctors had ~n him up** les médecins le croyaient condamné ◆ **to ~ sb up for lost** considérer qn comme perdu ◆ **to ~ sb up for dead** croire qn mort 5 * *(US = applaud)* ◆ **give it up for Whitney Houston !** veuillez accueillir Whitney Houston sous vos applaudissements !

► **give up on** VT FUS 1 *(= renounce) [+ idea]* renoncer à ◆ **I finally gave up on it** j'ai fini par y renoncer ◆ **the car/washing machine has ~n up on me** * la voiture/la machine à laver m'a lâché * 2 *(= stop expecting) [+ visitor]* ne plus attendre ; *(= lose faith in)* perdre espoir en

giveaway /ˈgɪvəweɪ/ N *(fig)* révélation *f* involontaire ; *(Comm = free gift)* cadeau *m* (publicitaire) ; *(US Rad, TV)* jeu *m* radiophonique *or* télévisé *(doté de prix)* ADJ *[price]* dérisoire ◆ **it was a real ~ when he said that ...** il s'est vraiment trahi en disant que ... ◆ **the fact that she knew his name was a ~** le simple fait qu'elle sache son nom était révélateur ◆ **what a ~!** là tu t'es trahi (*or* il s'est trahi ! *etc*)

given /ˈgɪvn/ LANGUAGE IN USE 17.1 VB ptp of **give** ADJ 1 donné, déterminé ◆ **at a ~ time** à un moment donné ◆ **of a ~ size** d'une taille donnée *or* bien déterminée ◆ **under the ~ conditions** compte tenu des conditions 2 ◆ **~ the**

triangle ABC soit *or* étant donné le triangle ABC ◆ ~ **that he is capable of learning** à supposer qu'il soit capable d'apprendre 3 *(= having inclination)* ◆ **I am not ~ to lying** je n'ai pas l'habitude de mentir ◆ **he's ~ to laziness** il est enclin à la paresse PREP ◆ ~ **the opportunity** si l'occasion se présentait ◆ ~ **patience** avec de la patience N ◆ **this is a ~** c'est une donnée de base COMP **given name** N nom *m* de baptême

giver /ˈgɪvəʳ/ N donateur *m*, -trice *f* ; *(on Stock Exchange)* preneur *m*, -euse *f* d'option, optionnaire *mf*

giving /ˈgɪvɪŋ/ ADJ généreux

gizmo* /ˈgɪzməʊ/ N machin* *m*, truc* *m*

gizzard /ˈgɪzəd/ N gésier *m* ; → **stick**

GLA /ˌdʒiːelˈeɪ/ N *(Brit)* abbrev of **Greater London Authority**

glacé /ˈglæseɪ/ ADJ *(Culin)* [*fruit*] glacé, confit ◆ ~ **icing** glaçage *m*

glacial /ˈgleɪsɪəl/ ADJ 1 *(Geol)* glaciaire ; [*wind, winter*] glacial ; *(Chem)* cristallisé, en cristaux ◆ **at a ~ pace, with ~ slowness** incroyablement lentement 2 [*person, stare, atmosphere*] glacial

glaciated /ˈgleɪsɪeɪtɪd/ ADJ *(Geol)* ◆ ~ **landscape** relief *m* glaciaire

glaciation /ˌgleɪsɪˈeɪʃən/ N glaciation *f*

glacier /ˈglæsɪəʳ/ N glacier *m*

glaciological /ˌglæsɪəˈlɒdʒɪkəl/ ADJ glaciologique

glaciologist /ˌglæsɪˈɒlədʒɪst/ N glaciologue *mf*

glaciology /ˌglæsɪˈɒlədʒɪ/ N glaciologie *f*

glad /glæd/ ADJ 1 *(= pleased)* ◆ **to be ~ (about sth)** être bien content (de qch) ◆ **I had a great time – I'm ~** je me suis beaucoup amusé – j'en suis ravi *or* bien content ◆ **he was ~ of a chance to change the subject** il était content de pouvoir changer de sujet ◆ **I'd be ~ of some help with this** j'aimerais bien qu'on m'aide (à faire ça) ◆ **I'm ~ that you came** je suis bien content que vous soyez venu ◆ **I'm ~ that I've come** je suis bien content d'être venu ◆ **to be ~ to do sth** *(= happy)* être bien content de faire qch ; *(= willing)* se faire un plaisir de faire qch ◆ **I shall be ~ to come** ça me fera plaisir de venir ◆ ~ **to know you!** très heureux de faire votre connaissance ! ◆ **to be only too ~ to do sth** ne pas demander mieux que de faire qch 2 *(†, liter = happy)* [*news*] heureux ; [*occasion*] joyeux ◆ **to give sb the ~ tidings** annoncer à qn la bonne nouvelle

COMP **glad eye** † N *(Brit)* ◆ **to give sb the ~ eye** * faire de l'œil* à qn
glad hand * N *(esp US)* ◆ **to give sb the ~ hand** accueillir qn les bras ouverts
glad-hand * VT *(US)* accueillir avec effusion
glad rags * NPL belles fringues* *fpl* ◆ **to put on one's ~ rags** mettre ses plus belles fringues

gladden /ˈglædn/ VT [*+ person*] réjouir ◆ **to ~ sb's heart** réjouir qn ◆ **it ~s the heart** ça fait chaud au cœur ◆ **to be ~ed to see** *etc* être heureux de voir *etc*

glade /gleɪd/ N clairière *f*

gladiator /ˈglædɪeɪtəʳ/ N gladiateur *m*

gladiatorial /ˌglædɪəˈtɔːrɪəl/ ADJ *(fig)* conflictuel ◆ ~ **politics** politique *f* de la confrontation

gladiolus /ˌglædɪˈəʊləs/ N (pl **gladiolus** *or* **gladioluses** *or* **gladioli** /ˌglædɪˈəʊlaɪ/) glaïeul *m*

gladly /ˈglædlɪ/ LANGUAGE IN USE 3.1 ADV *(= happily)* avec plaisir ; *(= willingly)* volontiers ◆ **will you help me? – ~** voulez-vous m'aider ? – volontiers *or* avec plaisir

gladness /ˈglædnɪs/ N joie *f*, contentement *m*

glam* /glæm/ ADJ abbrev of **glamorous** COMP **glam rock*** N *(Mus)* glam-rock *m (mouvement musical des années 70)*

glamor /ˈglæməʳ/ N *(US)* ⇒ **glamour**

glamorize /ˈglæməraɪz/ VT [*+ place, event, act etc*] montrer *or* présenter sous un jour séduisant

glamorous /ˈglæmərəs/ ADJ [*person, clothes, photo, atmosphere*] glamour *inv* ; [*lifestyle*] de star ; [*restaurant, café*] chic ; [*occasion*] éclatant ; [*production*] somptueux ; [*job*] prestigieux

glamour /ˈglæməʳ/ N [*of person*] glamour *m* ; [*of occasion*] éclat *m* ; [*of situation etc*] prestige *m* ; [*of distant countries, journeys*] séduction *f* ◆ **the ~ of show biz** le côté glamour du monde du show-biz ◆ **the ~ of life in Hollywood** le côté glamour de la vie d'Hollywood ◆ **the ~ of being on television** le prestige que confère un passage à la télévision

COMP **glamour boy*** N beau mec* *m*
glamour girl* N pin up* *f inv*, beauté *f*
glamour model N pin up *f inv*

glamourpuss* /ˈglæməpʊs/ N *(female)* pin up *f inv* ; *(male)* beau mec* *m*

glance /glɑːns/ N 1 regard *m*, coup *m* d'œil ◆ **Susan and I exchanged a ~** Susan et moi avons échangé un regard ◆ **at a ~** d'un coup d'œil ◆ **at first ~** au premier coup d'œil, à première vue ◆ **without a backward ~** *(lit)* sans se retourner ; *(fig)* sans plus de cérémonie ◆ **to have** *or* **take a ~ at** jeter un coup d'œil sur *or* à ◆ **to steal a ~ at sb/sth** jeter un coup d'œil furtif sur *or* à qn/qch
2 *(= gleam)* [*of light*] lueur *f* ; [*of metal*] reflet *m* ◆ **a ~ of sunlight** un rayon de soleil
VI 1 *(= look)* jeter un coup d'œil (*at* sur, à), lancer un regard (*at* à) ◆ **she ~d in my direction** elle a jeté un coup d'œil vers moi ◆ **he picked up the book and ~d through it** il a pris le livre et l'a feuilleté
2 *(= glint)* étinceler
3 ◆ **to ~ off** [*bullet*] ricocher sur ; [*arrow, sword*] dévier sur

▸ **glance away** VI détourner le regard

▸ **glance down** VI jeter un coup d'œil en bas, regarder en bas

▸ **glance off** VI [*bullet etc*] ricocher, dévier ; [*arrow, sword*] dévier

▸ **glance round** VI *(= behind)* regarder en arrière ; *(= round about)* jeter un coup d'œil autour de soi

▸ **glance up** VI *(= raise eyes)* lever les yeux ; *(= look upwards)* regarder en l'air

glancing /ˈglɑːnsɪŋ/ ADJ [*blow*] oblique

gland /glænd/ N glande *f* ; *(Tech)* presse-étoupe *m inv*

glanders /ˈglændəz/ N *(= horse disease)* morve *f*

glandes /ˈglændiːz/ NPL of **glans**

glandular /ˈglændjʊləʳ/ ADJ glandulaire COMP **glandular fever** N mononucléose *f* infectieuse

glans /glænz/ N (pl **glandes**) ◆ ~ **(penis)** gland *m*

glare /gleəʳ/ VI 1 [*person*] lancer un regard furieux (*at* à) 2 [*sun, lights*] être éblouissant, briller avec éclat N 1 [*of person*] regard *m* furieux ◆ **"no" he said with a ~** "non", dit-il en lançant un regard furieux ◆ **he gave me an angry ~** il m'a lancé un regard furieux 2 [*of light*] éclat *m* aveuglant, lumière *f* éblouissante ; *(while driving)* éblouissement *m* ◆ **the ~ of publicity** le feu des projecteurs *(fig)*

glaring /ˈgleərɪŋ/ ADJ *(= angry)* [*eyes, look*] brillant de colère ; *(= blinding)* [*light, sun*] éblouissant ; *(pej) (= blatant)* [*example, error, contradiction*] flagrant ; [*omission*] manifeste ◆ **the ~ weakness of that argument** la faiblesse manifeste de cet argument

glaringly /ˈgleərɪŋlɪ/ ADV *(pej)* ◆ **it is ~ obvious (that ...)** c'est une évidence aveuglante (que ...) ◆ **a ~ obvious error** une erreur d'une évidence aveuglante

glasnost /ˈglæznɒst/ N glasnost *f*

glass /glɑːs/ N 1 *(NonC)* verre *m* ◆ **pane of ~** carreau *m*, vitre *f* ◆ **window ~** verre *m* à vitre ◆ **I cut myself on the broken ~** je me suis coupé avec l'éclat de verre ◆ **there was some broken ~ in the dustbin** il y avait du verre cassé dans la poubelle ; see also **glassed** ; → **cut, plate**
2 *(= tumbler)* verre *m* ; *(= glassful)* (plein) verre *m* ◆ **a ~ of wine** un verre de vin ◆ **a wine ~** un verre à vin ◆ **she cut her hand on a broken ~** elle s'est coupé la main avec un verre cassé ; → **balloon, beer, champagne**
3 *(NonC: also* **glassware***)* *(gen)* verrerie *f*, objets *mpl* de *or* en verre ; *(= glasses)* gobeleterie *f*
4 *(= mirror)* miroir *m*, glace *f* ; *(Opt)* lentille *f* ; *(also* **magnifying glass***)* verre *m* grossissant, loupe *f* ; *(= telescope)* longue-vue *f* ; *(= barometer)* baromètre *m* ; *(Comm etc)* vitrine *f* ◆ **the ~ is falling** *(= barometer)* le baromètre baisse ◆ **under ~** [*plants*] sous châssis ◆ **object displayed under ~** objet *m* exposé en vitrine
VT *(Brit *)* avec une bouteille *(or un verre)*
COMP [*bottle, ornament*] de verre, en verre
glass case N *(for display)* vitrine *f* ; [*of clock etc*] globe *m* ◆ **to keep sth in a ~ case** garder qch sous verre
glass ceiling* N *niveau professionnel où les femmes ont tendance à plafonner*
glass door N porte *f* vitrée
glass eye N œil *m* de verre
glass factory N ⇒ **glassworks**
glass fibre N fibre *f* de verre COMP en fibre de verre
glass industry N industrie *f* du verre, verrerie *f*
glass slipper N pantoufle *f* de verre
glass wool N laine *f* de verre

glassblower /ˈglɑːsbləʊəʳ/ N souffleur *m* (de verre)

glassblowing /ˈglɑːsbləʊɪŋ/ N soufflage *m* (du verre)

glasscloth /ˈglɑːsklɒθ/ N essuie-verres *m inv*, torchon *m* à verres

glasscutter /ˈglɑːskʌtəʳ/ N *(= tool)* diamant *m*, coupe-verre *m inv* ; *(= person)* vitrier *m*

glassed /glɑːst/, **glassed-in** /ˈglɑːstɪn/ ADJ [*cubicle*] vitré ◆ **~-in shower** cabine *f* de douche *(à parois de verre)* ◆ **~-in porch** véranda *f*

glasses /ˈglɑːsɪz/ NPL *(= spectacles)* lunettes *fpl* ; *(= binoculars)* jumelles *fpl* ; see also **sunglasses**

glassful /ˈglɑːsfʊl/ N (plein) verre *m*

glasshouse /ˈglɑːshaʊs/ N *(Brit: for plants)* serre *f* ; *(US = glassworks)* verrerie *f (fabrique)* ◆ **in the ~*** *(Brit Mil)* au trou* ◆ **people who live in glass houses shouldn't throw stones** *(Prov)* avant de critiquer, tu ferais bien de balayer devant ta porte

glasspaper /ˈglɑːspeɪpəʳ/ N *(Brit)* papier *m* de verre

glassware /ˈglɑːsweəʳ/ N verrerie *f*, objets *mpl* de *or* en verre

glassworks /ˈglɑːswɜːks/ N *(pl inv)* verrerie *f (fabrique)*

glassy /ˈglɑːsɪ/ ADJ [*substance*] vitreux ; [*surface*] uni, lisse ; [*water, sea*] transparent, lisse comme un miroir ◆ ~ **eyes** *or* **look** regard *m* perdu *or* vague ; *(from drink, drugs)* regard *m* vitreux *or* terne ; *(from displeasure)* regard *m* froid
COMP **glassy-eyed** ADJ au regard vide ; *(from drugs, drink)* au regard terne *or* vitreux ; *(from displeasure)* au regard froid

Glaswegian /glæsˈwiːdʒən/ N ◆ **he's a ~** il est de Glasgow ADJ de Glasgow

glaucoma /glɔːˈkəʊmə/ N glaucome *m*

glaucous /ˈglɔːkəs/ ADJ glauque

glaze /gleɪz/ VT 1 [+ door, window] vitrer ; [+ picture] mettre sous verre ; → **double** 2 [+ pottery, tiles] vernisser ; [+ leather] vernir ; [+ cotton etc] satiner, lustrer ; [+ paper, photograph, cake, meat] glacer N 1 (NonC, on pottery, leather, tiles etc) vernis m ; (on cotton etc) lustre m ; (on paper, photograph) glacé m ; (Culin) glaçage m 2 (= substance) (for tiles etc) glaçure f ; (for pottery) vernis m 3 (US = ice) verglas m

► **glaze over** VI [person] prendre un air absent ◆ **his eyes ~d over** (boredom) il prit un air absent ; (dying) ses yeux sont devenus vitreux

glazed /gleɪzd/ ADJ 1 [door, window etc] vitré ; [picture] sous verre 2 [pottery, tiles] vernissé ; [leather] glacé, verni ; [material] lustré, satiné ; [paper, photograph] brillant ; [cake, meat] glacé ; (US ‡ = drunk) bourré‡, ivre ◆ **his eyes** or **he had a ~ look** il avait les yeux ternes or vitreux

glazier /'gleɪzɪəʳ/ N vitrier m

glazing /'gleɪzɪŋ/ N 1 (= act) [of windows] vitrage m, pose f de vitres ; [of pottery] vernissage m 2 (= glass) vitrage m, vitres fpl ; see also **double, triple**

GLC /,dʒiːel'siː/ N (Brit: formerly) (abbrev of **Greater London Council**) ancienne administration centrale à Londres

gleam /gliːm/ N lueur f, rayon m (de lumière) ; [of metal] reflet m ; [of water] miroitement m ◆ **a ~ of hope/interest** une lueur d'espoir/d'intérêt ◆ **with a fanatical ~ in his eye** avec une lueur fanatique dans le regard ◆ **there was a ~ in her eye when she looked at me** il y avait une lueur dans ses yeux quand elle m'a regardé ◆ **the product is still only a ~ in an engineer's eye** ce produit n'est encore qu'une idée en germe dans la tête d'un ingénieur ◆ **almost 20 years before you were even a ~ in your father's eye** (hum) près de 20 ans avant que ton père n'ait même imaginé de te concevoir

VI [lamp, star, eyes etc] luire ; [polished metal, shoes etc] reluire ; [knife, blade etc] luire, briller ; [water] miroiter ◆ **his eyes ~ed with mischief** ses yeux luisaient or brillaient de malice ◆ **his eyes ~ed almost wickedly** il avait une sorte de lueur mauvaise dans les yeux ◆ **his hair ~ed in the sun** ses cheveux brillaient au soleil ◆ **his forehead ~ed with sweat** son front était luisant de sueur ◆ **his skin ~ed with health** sa peau resplendissait de santé

gleaming /'gliːmɪŋ/ ADJ [lamp, star, metal, shoes] brillant ; [kitchen] étincelant

glean /gliːn/ VTI (lit, fig) glaner

gleaner /'gliːnəʳ/ N glaneur m, -euse f

gleanings /'gliːnɪŋz/ NPL glanure(s) f(pl)

glebe /gliːb/ N (Rel) terre f attachée à un bénéfice ecclésiastique ; (liter) terre f, glèbe f (liter)

glee /gliː/ N 1 (NonC) joie f, jubilation f ◆ **his victory was greeted with ~** sa victoire a été accueillie dans l'allégresse ◆ **in great ~** jubilant ◆ **they were rubbing their hands in ~** ils se frottaient les mains en jubilant 2 (Mus) chant m choral à plusieurs voix ◆ **~ club** chorale f

gleeful /'gliːfʊl/ ADJ jubilant ; [smile, look] de jubilation

gleefully /'gliːfəlɪ/ ADV [say, point out] en jubilant ◆ **to laugh ~** rire avec jubilation

glen /glen/ N vallée f, vallon m

glib /glɪb/ ADJ (pej) [answer, style, excuse] désinvolte ; [speech, phrase, lie] facile, désinvolte ; [person] qui a la langue bien pendue or la parole facile ◆ **~ talk** propos mpl or paroles fpl en l'air ◆ **to make ~ promises** faire des promesses en l'air

glibly /'glɪblɪ/ ADV (pej) avec désinvolture

glibness /'glɪbnɪs/ N [of answer, speech, style] désinvolture f ; [of person] facilité f de parole

glide /glaɪd/ VI 1 ◆ **to ~ in/out** etc [person] (silently) entrer/sortir etc sans bruit ; (in stately way, gracefully) entrer/sortir etc avec grâce ; [ghost] entrer/sortir etc en flottant ; [car, ship] entrer/sortir etc en glissant ◆ **time ~d past** le temps s'écoula 2 (Ski) glisser 3 [birds] planer ; [plane] planer, faire du vol plané ◆ **he ~d down to land** il a atterri en vol plané VT faire glisser, faire avancer en douceur N 1 glissement m ; (Dancing) glissé m, glissade f ; (Ski) glisse f 2 (Mus) port m de voix ; (Phon) glissement m 3 (Flying) vol m plané

glider /'glaɪdəʳ/ N 1 (= aircraft) planeur m ◆ **~ pilot** pilote m de planeur 2 (US = swing) balancelle f

gliding /'glaɪdɪŋ/ N (in glider) vol m à voile ; (in other aircraft) vol m plané ; (gen) (= movement) glissement m ADJ (Anat) ◆ **~ joint** arthrodie f

glimmer /'glɪməʳ/ VI [lamp, light, fire] luire ; [water] miroiter N [of light, candle etc] lueur f ; [of water] miroitement m ◆ **a ~ of hope** une lueur d'espoir ◆ **not a ~ of intelligence** pas la moindre lueur d'intelligence

glimmering /'glɪmərɪŋ/ N ⇒ **glimmer noun** ADJ étincelant, scintillant

glimpse /glɪmps/ N [of the truth, the future, sb's meaning] aperçu m ◆ **a ~ into the future** un aperçu de l'avenir ◆ **to catch a ~ of** (person, thing) entrevoir or apercevoir (un bref instant) ; (the truth, the future etc) entrevoir, pressentir VT entrevoir or apercevoir (un bref instant)

glint /glɪnt/ N [of light] trait m de lumière, éclair m ; [of metal] reflet m ◆ **he had a ~ in his eye** il avait une étincelle or une lueur dans le regard ◆ **with the ~ of triumph in his eye** avec une étincelle or une lueur de triomphe dans les yeux VI [metal object, glass, wet road] luire, briller ; [eyes] briller ◆ **the sea ~ed in the sun** la mer miroitait au soleil ◆ **sunlight ~ed on his spectacles** ses lunettes renvoyaient la lumière éblouissante du soleil

glissade /glɪ'seɪd/ (Climbing) N (also **standing glissade**) ramasse f VI descendre en ramasse

glissando /glɪ'sændəʊ/ ADV glissando

glisten /'glɪsn/ VI [water] miroiter, scintiller ; [wet surface] luire ; [light] scintiller ; [metal object] briller, miroiter ◆ **her eyes ~ed (with tears)** ses yeux brillaient (de larmes) ◆ **his face was ~ing with sweat** son visage était luisant de sueur N miroitement m, scintillement m

glister †† /'glɪstəʳ/ ⇒ **glitter**

glitch * /glɪtʃ/ N pépin m

glitter /'glɪtəʳ/ VI [snow, ice, lights] scintiller, briller ; [jewel] scintiller, étinceler ; [water] miroiter, scintiller ◆ **her eyes ~ed** (with hatred) ses yeux brillaient de haine ; (with greed) ses yeux brillaient de convoitise ◆ **all that ~s is not gold** (Prov) tout ce qui brille n'est pas or (Prov) N scintillement m ; (fig) éclat m

glitterati * /,glɪtə'rɑːtiː/ NPL ◆ **the ~** le beau monde, les célébrités fpl

glittering /'glɪtərɪŋ/ ADJ [stars, lights, ice, jewel] étincelant, scintillant ; [eyes] brillant, étincelant ; (fig) [career, future] brillant ; [occasion, social event] somptueux ◆ **~ prizes** prix mpl fabuleux ◆ **a ~ array of celebrities** une brillante assemblée de célébrités

glittery /'glɪtərɪ/ ADJ (lit, fig) étincelant

glitz * /glɪts/ N faste m

glitzy * /'glɪtsɪ/ ADJ fastueux

gloaming /'gləʊmɪŋ/ N (liter) crépuscule m ◆ **in the ~** au crépuscule, entre chien et loup

gloat /gləʊt/ VI (pej) exulter, jubiler * ◆ **to ~ over** (money, possessions) jubiler * à la vue (or à l'idée) de ◆ **he was ~ing over** or **about his success** son succès le faisait jubiler * ◆ **that's nothing to ~ over** or **about!** il n'y a pas de quoi jubiler ! * ◆ **he was ~ing that he was going to win** il affirmait en jubilant * qu'il allait gagner

gloating /'gləʊtɪŋ/ (pej) N exultation f or jubilation f malveillante ADJ jubilatoire

glob /glɒb/ N [of liquid] globule m ; [of clay etc] petite boule f

global /'gləʊbl/ ADJ 1 (= worldwide) [economy, trade, market, recession, climate, system, problem, issue] mondial ; [peace] universel, mondial ◆ **a ~ ban on nuclear testing** une interdiction totale des essais nucléaires ◆ **on a ~ scale** à l'échelle mondiale ◆ **~ capitalism** le capitalisme mondial 2 (= comprehensive) [sum, view] global, entier ◆ **~ search and replace** (Comput) recherche f et remplacement m automatiques

COMP **the global village** N le village planétaire

global warming N réchauffement m de la planète

> ⚠ **global** is only translated by the French word **global** when it means 'comprehensive'.

globalization /,gləʊbəlaɪ'zeɪʃən/ N mondialisation f

globalize /'gləʊbəlaɪz/ VI [company] passer à l'échelle mondiale VT [+ economy, business, culture] mondialiser ◆ **rock music has become ~d** le rock s'est mondialisé

globally /'gləʊbəlɪ/ ADV 1 (= worldwide, in world terms) [sell, compete, think] à l'échelle mondiale ◆ **a ~ familiar trade name** une marque mondialement connue or connue dans le monde entier ◆ **~, the risks are huge** à l'échelle planétaire, les risques sont énormes 2 (= universally) universellement

> ⚠ **globally** is not translated by **globalement**, which means 'as a whole'.

globe /gləʊb/ N (= sphere) globe m, sphère f ; (with map on it) globe m ; (= lampshade etc) globe m ; (= fishbowl) bocal m ; (Anat) globe m ◆ **the ~** (Geog) le globe, la terre ◆ **all over the ~** sur toute la surface du globe ◆ **countries on the far side of the ~** les pays à l'autre bout du monde

COMP **globe artichoke** N artichaut m

globe lightning N éclair m en boule

globe-trotter N globe-trotter mf

globe-trotting N voyages mpl à travers le monde

globefish /'gləʊbfɪʃ/ N (pl **globefish** or **globefishes**) poisson-globe m

globular /'glɒbjʊləʳ/ ADJ globulaire ; (= like globe) en forme de globe

globule /'glɒbjuːl/ N gouttelette f

glockenspiel /'glɒkən,spiːl/ N glockenspiel m

gloom /gluːm/ N (= darkness) obscurité f, ténèbres fpl ; (= melancholy) mélancolie f, tristesse f ◆ **to cast a ~ over sth** assombrir qch ◆ **to cast a ~ over sb** rendre qn sombre, attrister qn ◆ **a ~ descended on us** la tristesse s'est abattue sur nous ◆ **it was all ~ and doom** * tout allait mal ◆ **economic ~** morosité f économique

gloomily /'gluːmɪlɪ/ ADV [say] d'un air sombre

gloomy /'gluːmɪ/ ADJ [person, thoughts, sky, look, mood] sombre ; (stronger) lugubre ; [weather, day, outlook] morose, déprimant ; [voice, place] morne ; (stronger) lugubre ◆ **to feel ~** se sentir morose ◆ **to look ~** [person] avoir l'air sombre or morose ; [future] être sombre ◆ **he took a ~ view of everything** il voyait tout en noir

gloop * /gluːp/ N pâte f visqueuse

glop * /glɒp/ N crasse f

glorification /,glɔːrɪfɪ'keɪʃən/ N glorification f

glorified /'glɔːrɪfaɪd/ ADJ ◆ **the drug is nothing but a ~ painkiller** ce médicament n'est rien de plus qu'un vulgaire calmant ◆ **the referendum was no more than a ~ opinion poll** le référendum n'était qu'un vulgaire sondage ◆ **the "luxury hotel" was nothing but a ~ boarding house** le soi-disant "hôtel de luxe" n'était qu'une pension de famille ◆ **he's a sort of ~ secretary** il ne fait que du secrétariat amélioré

glorify /ˈglɔːrɪfaɪ/ VT 1 *(= glamorize) [+ war, violence]* faire l'apologie de ◆ **the film doesn't ~ violence** le film ne fait pas l'apologie de la violence ; *[+ person, villain]* glorifier, célébrer ◆ **songs ~ing war** des chansons qui célèbrent la guerre ◆ **a video which glorifies soccer hooligans** un clip qui glorifie les hooligans 2 *(= praise) [+ God]* glorifier, rendre gloire à

gloriole /ˈglɔːrɪəʊl/ N nimbe *m*

glorious /ˈglɔːrɪəs/ ADJ 1 *(* = beautiful) [view, scenery]* splendide, magnifique ; *[sunshine, weather, day]* radieux, magnifique ◆ **a ~ mess** *(iro)* un joli *or* beau gâchis 2 *(* = enjoyable) [feeling, holiday]* merveilleux 3 *(= illustrious) [career, future]* brillant ; *[years, days, era]* glorieux ; *[victory]* éclatant ◆ **~ deed** action *f* d'éclat COMP **the Glorious Revolution** N *(Brit Hist)* la Glorieuse Révolution, la Seconde Révolution d'Angleterre *(1688-89)*

gloriously /ˈglɔːrɪəslɪ/ ADV 1 *(* = wonderfully) [happy]* merveilleusement ◆ **a ~ sunny day** une journée radieuse ◆ **~ hot weather** un temps chaud et radieux 2 *(= triumphantly) [succeed, win]* glorieusement ◆ **~ successful** glorieusement réussi

glory /ˈglɔːrɪ/ N 1 *(= celebrity) (NonC)* gloire *f (also Rel)* ◆ **a moment of ~** un moment de gloire ◆ **to have one's moment of ~** avoir son heure de gloire ◆ **to give ~ to God** rendre gloire à Dieu ◆ **to the greater ~ of God** pour la plus grande gloire de Dieu ◆ **Christ in ~** le Christ en majesté *or* en gloire ◆ **the saints in ~** les glorieux *mpl* ◆ **Solomon in all his ~** Salomon dans toute sa gloire ◆ **covered with ~** couvert de gloire ◆ **Rome at the height of its ~** Rome à l'apogée *or* au sommet de sa gloire ◆ **she was in her ~ *** **as president of the club** elle était tout à fait à son affaire en tant que présidente du club ◆ **she led her team to Olympic ~** elle a mené son équipe à la gloire lors des Jeux olympiques ◆ **to go to ~** † * *(= die)* aller ad patres * ◆ **~ be!** † * Seigneur !, grand Dieu ! ◆ **Old Glory** * *(US)* le drapeau américain ; → **former²**
2 *(= beauty)* **the church was the village's greatest ~** l'église était le principal titre de gloire du village ◆ **the roses that are the ~ of the garden** les roses, joyaux du jardin
◆ **in all its** (*or* **his** *or* **her** *etc*) **glory** dans toute sa gloire ◆ **spring arrived in all its ~** le printemps est arrivé dans toute sa gloire *or* splendeur
◆ **glories** *(= masterpieces)* chefs-d'œuvre *mpl* ◆ **this sonnet is one of the glories of English poetry** ce sonnet est un des chefs-d'œuvre *or* fleurons de la poésie anglaise ◆ **the artistic glories of the Italian Renaissance** les chefs-d'œuvre *or* les joyaux de la Renaissance italienne ◆ **past glories** la gloire passée ◆ **for all its past glories, it's just a computer company like any other** malgré sa gloire passée, c'est une société informatique comme les autres ◆ **those happy hours spent reminiscing about past glories** ces bons moments passés à évoquer les exploits passés ◆ **the general's military glories** les exploits militaires du général ; see also **crowning**
VI ◆ **to ~ in sth** *(= be proud of)* être très fier de qch ; *(= revel in)* se glorifier de qch ; *(= enjoy)* savourer qch ◆ **he gloried in his reputation as a troublemaker** il se glorifiait de sa réputation de fauteur de troubles ◆ **the café glories in the name of "The Savoy"** *(iro)* le café porte le nom ronflant de "Savoy"
COMP **glory hole** * N capharnaüm * *m* ; *(Naut)* cambuse *f*

Glos abbrev of **Gloucestershire**

gloss¹ /glɒs/ N 1 *(= shine) [of metal, ceramic, paintwork, polished surface]* lustre *m* ; *[of silk, satin]* lustre *m*, éclat *m* ; *[of person's hair, animal's coat]* brillant *m* ◆ **to take the ~ off** *(metal etc)* dépolir ; *(fig) (event, success)* retirer *or* enlever tout son charme *or* attrait à ; *(victory, compliment)* gâcher ◆ **to lose its ~** *[metal etc]* se dépolir ; *(fig) [event, success]* perdre tout son charme *or* son attrait ; *[victory, compliment]* être gâché ◆ **to put a ~** *or* **an optimistic ~ on sth** *(fig)* présenter qch sous un jour favorable, enjoliver qch 2 *(= paint)* peinture *f* brillante *or* laquée VT *[+ metal etc]* faire briller, polir COMP *[paint]* brillant, laqué ; *[paper]* glacé, brillant **gloss finish** N brillant *m*
► **gloss over** VT FUS *(= play down)* glisser sur, passer sur ; *(= cover up)* dissimuler

gloss² /glɒs/ N *(= insertion)* glose *f* ; *(= note)* commentaire *m* ; *(= interpretation)* paraphrase *f*, interprétation *f* VT commenter, gloser

glossary /ˈglɒsərɪ/ N glossaire *m*, lexique *m*

glossematics /ˌglɒsəˈmætɪks/ N *(NonC)* glossématique *f*

glossily /ˈglɒsɪlɪ/ ADV ◆ **~ packaged** luxueusement conditionné ◆ **a ~ presented** *or* **produced brochure** une brochure luxueusement présentée

glossolalia /ˌglɒsəˈleɪlɪə/ N glossolalie *f*

glossy /ˈglɒsɪ/ ADJ *[fur, material]* luisant, lustré ; *[photograph]* sur papier brillant ; *[paint]* brillant, laqué ; *[hair]* brillant ; *[leaves]* vernissé ; *[metal]* brillant, poli ; *[red, black etc]* brillant ◆ **~ magazine/brochure** magazine *m*/brochure *f* de luxe *(sur papier couché)* ◆ **~ paper** *(Typ)* papier *m* couché ; *(esp Phot)* papier *m* brillant *or* glacé ◆ **~ production** *(film)* superproduction *f* (luxueuse) N *(Brit)* ◆ **the glossies** * les magazines *mpl* de luxe

glottal /ˈglɒtl/ ADJ *(Anat)* glottique ; *(Ling)* glottal COMP **glottal stop** N *(Ling)* coup *m* de glotte

glottis /ˈglɒtɪs/ N (pl **glottises** *or* **glottides** /ˈglɒtɪˌdiːz/) glotte *f*

Gloucs abbrev of **Gloucestershire**

glove /glʌv/ N *(gen, also Baseball, Boxing)* gant *m* ◆ **the ~s are off!** j'y vais (*or* il y va *etc*) sans prendre de gants ! ; → **fit¹, hand, kid, rubber¹**
VT ganter ◆ **his ~d hand** sa main gantée ◆ **white-~d** ganté de blanc
COMP **glove box, glove compartment** N *(in car)* boîte *f* à gants, vide-poches *m*
glove factory N ganterie *f (fabrique)*
glove maker N gantier *m*, -ière *f*
glove puppet N marionnette *f* (à gaine)
glove shop N ganterie *f (magasin)*

glover /ˈglʌvəʳ/ N gantier *m*, -ière *f*

glow /gləʊ/ VI *[coal, fire]* rougeoyer ; *[sky]* rougeoyer, s'embraser ; *[metal]* luire ; *[cigarette end, lamp]* luire ; *[colour, jewel]* rutiler ; *[complexion, face]* rayonner ; *[eyes]* rayonner, flamboyer ◆ **her cheeks ~ed** elle avait les joues toutes rouges ◆ **to ~ red** rougeoyer ◆ **the autumn leaves ~ed red and yellow in the sunlight** le feuillage rouge et jaune de l'automne resplendissait sous la lumière du soleil ◆ **streetlamps ~ing orange in the dusk** les réverbères répandant leur lumière orange au crépuscule ◆ **he was ~ing with health** il était florissant (de santé) ◆ **to ~ with enthusiasm** brûler d'enthousiasme ◆ **she ~ed with pride** elle rayonnait de fierté ◆ **his face ~ed with pleasure** son visage rayonnait de plaisir ◆ **~ing with confidence** respirant la confiance
N *[of coal, fire, metal]* rougeoiement *m* ; *[of sun]* feux *mpl*, embrasement *m* ; *[of complexion, skin]* éclat *m* ; *[of colour, jewel]* éclat *m* ; *[of lamp]* lueur *f* ; *[of passion]* feu *m* ; *[of youth]* ardeur *f* ◆ **a ~ of enthusiasm** un élan d'enthousiasme
COMP **glow-worm** N ver *m* luisant

glower /ˈglaʊəʳ/ VI lancer des regards mauvais *or* noirs ◆ **to ~ at sb/sth** lancer à qn/qch des regards mauvais *or* noirs N regard *m* noir

glowering /ˈglaʊərɪŋ/ ADJ *[look]* mauvais, noir

glowing /ˈgləʊɪŋ/ ADJ *[coals, fire]* rougeoyant ; *[sky]* rougeoyant, embrasé ; *[colour, jewel]* rutilant ; *[lamp, cigarette end]* luisant ; *[eyes]* brillant, de braise ; *[complexion, skin]* rayonnant, éclatant ; *[person]* florissant (de santé) ; *[words, report, tribute, review, praise]* élogieux ◆ **to give a ~ account/description of sth** raconter/décrire qch en termes élogieux ◆ **to speak of sb/sth in ~ terms** parler de qn/qch en termes élogieux ◆ **to paint sth in ~ colours** présenter qch en rose ◆ **to get ~ references** *(from job)* être chaudement recommandé

gloxinia /glɒkˈsɪnɪə/ N gloxinia *m*

glucose /ˈgluːkəʊs/ N glucose *m*

glue /gluː/ N colle *f*
VT coller *(to, on à)* ◆ **she ~d the pieces together** *(from broken object)* elle a recollé les morceaux ; *(from kit etc)* elle a collé les morceaux ensemble ◆ **I ~d the plate back together** j'ai recollé l'assiette ◆ **to ~ sth back on** recoller qch ◆ **to ~ sth down** coller qch ◆ **the fabric is ~d in place** le tissu est fixé avec de la colle ◆ **he stood there ~d to the spot** * il était là comme s'il avait pris racine ◆ **his face was ~d to the window** son visage était collé à la vitre ◆ **to keep one's eyes ~d to sb/sth** * avoir les yeux fixés sur qn/qch, ne pas détacher les yeux de qn/qch ◆ **~d to the television** * cloué devant *or* rivé à la télévision ◆ **we were ~d to our seats** * nous étions cloués à nos sièges
COMP **glue ear** N *(Med)* otite *f* séreuse
glue-sniffer N sniffeur * *m*, -euse * *f* de colle
glue-sniffing N intoxication *f* à la colle *or* aux solvants

gluey /ˈgluːɪ/ ADJ gluant, poisseux

glum /glʌm/ ADJ *[person, face]* sombre ; *(stronger)* lugubre ; *[appearance]* sombre, morne ; *[thoughts]* noir ◆ **to feel ~** avoir des idées noires, avoir le cafard ◆ **a ~ silence** un silence lugubre

glumly /ˈglʌmlɪ/ ADV *[say, look at]* d'un air sombre *or* abattu

glut /glʌt/ VT *(gen)* gaver ; *(Comm) [+ market, economy]* saturer *(with de)* ◆ **~ted with food** repu, gavé ◆ **he ~ted himself on pizza** il s'est gavé de pizza N *[of foodstuffs, goods]* surplus *m*, excès *m* ◆ **there is a ~ of ...** il y a excès de ...

glutamate /ˈgluːtəmeɪt/ N → **monosodium glutamate**

glutamic /gluˈtæmɪk/ ADJ ◆ **~ acid** acide *m* glutamique

gluteal /gluˈtiːəl/ ADJ fessier

gluten /ˈgluːtən/ N gluten *m* COMP **gluten-free** ADJ sans gluten

glutenous /ˈgluːtənəs/ ADJ glutineux

gluteus /ˈgluːtɪəs/ N (pl **glutei** /ˈgluːtɪaɪ/) fessier *m* COMP **gluteus maximus/medius/minimus** N grand/moyen/petit fessier *m*

glutinous /ˈgluːtɪnəs/ ADJ visqueux, gluant

glutton /ˈglʌtn/ N glouton(ne) *m(f)*, gourmand(e) *m(f)* ◆ **to be a ~ for work** être un bourreau de travail ◆ **he's a ~ for punishment** il est masochiste

gluttonous /ˈglʌtənəs/ ADJ glouton, goulu

gluttony /ˈglʌtənɪ/ N gloutonnerie *f*

glycerin(e) /ˌglɪsəˈriːn/ N glycérine *f*

glycerol /ˈglɪsərɒl/ N glycérol *m*

glycin(e) /ˈglaɪsiːn/ N glycine *f*

glycogen /ˈglaɪkəʊdʒen/ N glycogène *m*

glycol /ˈglaɪkɒl/ **N** glycol *m*

GM /ˌdʒiːˈem/ **N** 1 (abbrev of **General Manager**) DG *m* 2 (abbrev of **George Medal**) → **George** **ADJ** (abbrev of **genetically modified**) → **genetically**

gm (abbrev of **gram(me)**) g *inv*

GMAT /ˌdʒiːemˈeɪtiː/ **N** (*US Univ*) (abbrev of **Graduate Management Admission Test**) *test d'admission pour des études de commerce de troisième cycle*

GM-free /ˈdʒiːemfriː/ **ADJ** sans OGM

GMOs /ˌdʒiːemˈəuz/ **NPL** (abbrev of **genetically modified organisms**) OGM *mpl*

GMS /ˌdʒiːemˈes/ **N** (*Telec*) (abbrev of **Global Messaging System**) GMS *m*

GMT /ˌdʒiːemˈtiː/ (abbrev of **Greenwich Mean Time**) GMT

GMWU /ˌdʒiːemdʌbliuːˈjuː/ **N** (*Brit*) (abbrev of **General and Municipal Workers Union**) *syndicat*

gnarled /nɑːld/ **ADJ** *[tree, roots, hands, fingers]* noueux ; *[old man, old woman]* ratatiné

gnash /næʃ/ **VT** ♦ **to ~ one's teeth** *[person]* grincer des dents ; *[animal]* montrer ses dents en grognant **VI** *[person's teeth]* grincer ♦ **its teeth were ~ing** *[animal's teeth]* il (*or* elle) montrait ses dents en grognant

gnashing /ˈnæʃɪŋ/ **N** ♦ **~ of teeth** grincement *m* de dents **ADJ** grinçant

gnat /næt/ **N** moucheron *m* **COMP** **gnat's piss**** **N** pisse *f* d'âne*

gnaw /nɔː/ **VI** (*lit, fig*) ronger ♦ **to ~ at** *or* **on a bone** ronger un os ♦ **the rat had ~ed through the electric cable** le rat avait complètement rongé la câble électrique ♦ **remorse/desire ~ed at him** le remords/le désir le rongeait ♦ **the secret still ~ed at her** le secret la tourmentait toujours **VT** *[+ bone etc]* ronger ♦ **~ed by remorse** rongé par le remords

► **gnaw off** **VT SEP** ronger complètement

gnawing /ˈnɔːɪŋ/ **ADJ** *[fear, doubt, guilt, hunger, pain]* tenaillant ♦ **I had a ~ feeling that...** j'étais tenaillé par le sentiment que...

gneiss /naɪs/ **N** gneiss *m*

gnocchi /ˈnɒkɪ/ **NPL** gnocchis *mpl*

gnome /nəum/ **N** gnome *m*, lutin *m* **COMP** **the Gnomes of Zurich** **NPL** (*Brit fig = bankers*) les gnomes de Zurich

gnomic /ˈnəumɪk/ **ADJ** gnomique

gnostic /ˈnɒstɪk/ **ADJ, N** gnostique *mf*

gnosticism /ˈnɒstɪˌsɪzəm/ **N** gnosticisme *m*

GNP /ˌdʒiːenˈpiː/ **N** (*Econ*) (abbrev of **gross national product**) PNB *m*

gnu /nuː/ **N** (pl **gnus** *or* **gnu**) gnou *m*

GNVQ /ˌdʒiːenviːˈkjuː/ **N** (*Brit Scol*) (abbrev of **General National Vocational Qualification**) *diplôme professionnel national*

go /gəu/

vb : 3rd pers sg pres **goes**, pret **went**, ptp **gone**

1 INTRANSITIVE VERB
2 MODAL VERB
3 TRANSITIVE VERB
4 NOUN
5 ADJECTIVE
6 COMPOUNDS
7 PHRASAL VERBS

When **go** is part of a set combination, eg **go cheap**, **go to the bad**, **go too far**, **go down the tubes**, **go smoothly**, look up the other word.

1 - INTRANSITIVE VERB

1 [= proceed, travel, move] aller ; *[vehicle]* (*referring to speed/manner of moving*) rouler ♦ **where are you going?** où allez-vous ? ♦ **to ~ to do sth** aller faire qch ♦ **he's gone to see his mother** il est allé *or* parti voir sa mère ♦ **who goes there?** qui va là ? ♦ **I wouldn't ~ as far as to say that** je n'irais pas jusque là ♦ **she was going too fast** elle roulait *or* allait trop vite ♦ **there he goes !** le voilà ! ♦ **we can talk as we ~** nous pouvons parler en chemin ♦ **you can ~ next** vous pouvez passer devant ; ♦ (*in game*) **whose turn is it to ~ ?** c'est à qui de jouer ? ♦ **add the sugar, stirring as you ~** ajoutez le sucre, en remuant au fur et à mesure

♦ **to go** + *preposition* ♦ **the train goes at 90km/h** le train roule à *or* fait du 90 km/h ♦ **to ~ down the hill** descendre la colline ♦ **to ~ for a walk** (aller) se promener, (aller) faire une promenade ♦ **the train goes from London to Glasgow** le train va de Londres à Glasgow ♦ **where do we ~ from here?** qu'est-ce qu'on fait maintenant ? ♦ **to ~ on a journey** faire un voyage ♦ **it's going on three** (*US*) il est bientôt trois heures, il va bientôt être trois heures ♦ **to ~ to France/to Canada/to London** aller en France/au Canada/à Londres ♦ **to ~ to the swimming pool/cinema/Champs Élysées** aller à la piscine/au cinéma/aux Champs Élysées ♦ **he went to Paris/to his aunt's** il est allé *or* il s'est rendu à Paris/chez sa tante ♦ **she went to the headmaster** elle est allée voir *or* trouver le principal ♦ **to ~ to the doctor** aller chez le *or* voir le médecin ♦ **to ~ to sb for sth** aller demander qch à qn, aller trouver qn pour qch ♦ **the child went to his mother** l'enfant est allé vers sa mère ♦ **to ~ up the hill** monter la colline ♦ **I went up to $1,000** (*at auction*) je suis monté jusqu'à 1 000 dollars ; see also **phrasal verbs**

♦ **to go** + *-ing* ♦ **to ~ fishing/shooting** aller à la pêche/à la chasse ♦ **to ~ riding** (aller) faire du cheval ♦ **to ~ swimming** (aller) nager ♦ **don't ~ looking for trouble!** ne va pas t'attirer des ennuis ! ♦ **don't ~ getting upset*** ne te mets pas dans ces états

♦ **go and ...** ♦ **I'll ~ and check the train times** je vais vérifier les horaires de trains ♦ **~ and get me it!** va me le chercher ! ♦ **don't ~ and tell her I gave it you*** ne va pas lui dire *or* raconter que je te l'ai donné

go and is often not translated.

♦ **~ and shut the door!** ferme *or* va fermer la porte ! ♦ **don't ~ and do that!*** ne fais pas ça !

Note how indignation, regret etc are expressed in the following:

♦ **now you've gone and broken the zip!*** ça y est*, tu as cassé la fermeture éclair ! ♦ **I wish I hadn't gone and spent all that money!*** si seulement je n'avais pas dépensé tout cet argent ! ♦ **what have they gone and done to him?*** qu'est-ce qu'ils ont bien pu lui faire ?

2 [= depart] partir, s'en aller ; (*= disappear*) disparaître ; *[time]* passer, s'écouler ; (*= be sacked*) être licencié ; (*= be abolished*) être aboli *or* supprimé ; (*= be finished*) *[money]* filer ♦ **when does the train ~?** quand part le train ? ♦ **everybody had gone** tout le monde était parti ♦ **my bag has gone** mon sac a disparu ♦ **we must go** *or* **must be going** il faut qu'on y aille ♦ **go!** (*Sport*) partez ! ♦ **50 workers are to ~ at ...** 50 ouvriers doivent être licenciés à ... ♦ **after I go** *or* **have gone** après mon départ ♦ **after a week all our money had gone** en l'espace d'une semaine, nous avions dépensé tout notre argent ♦ **he'll have to ~** *[employee]* on ne peut pas le garder ; *[official, minister]* il doit démissionner ♦ **the car will have to ~** on va devoir se séparer de la voiture ♦ **there goes my chance of promotion !** je peux faire une croix sur ma promotion ! ; ♦ (*at auction*) **going, going, gone !** une fois, deux fois, trois fois, adjugé, vendu !

♦ **to let sb go** (*= allow to leave*) laisser partir qn ; (*euph = make redundant*) se séparer de qn ; (*= stop gripping*) lâcher qn

♦ **to let go** *or* **leave go** lâcher prise ♦ **let ~!, leave ~!** lâchez !

♦ **to let go** *or* **leave go of sth/sb** lâcher qch/qn ♦ **eventually parents have to let ~ of their children** (*psychologically*) tôt ou tard, les parents doivent laisser leurs enfants voler de leur propres ailes

♦ **to let sth go** ♦ **they have let their garden ~** ils ont laissé leur jardin à l'abandon ♦ **we'll let it ~ at that** n'en parlons plus ♦ **you're wrong, but let it ~** vous avez tort, mais passons

♦ **to let o.s. go** se laisser aller

3 [= operate, start] *[car, machine]* démarrer ; (*= function*) *[machine, watch, car]* marcher ♦ **how do you make this ~?** comment est-ce que ça marche ? ♦ **to be going** *[machine, engine]* être en marche ♦ **the washing machine was going so I didn't hear the phone** la machine à laver était en marche, si bien que je n'ai pas entendu le téléphone ♦ **to make a party ~** mettre de l'ambiance dans une soirée

♦ **to get going** *[person]* (*= leave*) ♦ **let's get going !** allons-y ! ♦ **to get going on** *or* **with sth** (*= start*) s'occuper de qch ♦ **I've got to get going on my tax** il faut que je m'occupe *subj* de mes impôts ♦ **once he gets going ...** une fois lancé ...

♦ **to get sth going** *[+ machine]* mettre en marche ; *[+ car]* faire démarrer ; *[+ work, dinner]* mettre en train ♦ **to get things going** activer les choses

♦ **to keep going** (*= continue*) *[person]* continuer ; *[business]* réussir à se maintenir à flot ♦ **it's okay, keep going!** ne te dérange pas, continue ! ♦ **the police signalled her to stop but she kept going** la police lui a fait signe de s'arrêter mais elle a continué son chemin ♦ **she was under great strain but kept going somehow** elle avait beaucoup de soucis mais réussissait malgré tout à tenir le coup ♦ **will the Prime Minister be able to keep going until the spring ?** est-ce que le Premier ministre pourra se maintenir au pouvoir jusqu'au printemps ? ♦ **it wouldn't keep going** *[machine]* elle s'arrêtait tout le temps ; *[car]* elle n'arrêtait pas de caler

♦ **to keep sb/sth going** ♦ **this medicine/hope kept her going** ce médicament/cet espoir lui a permis de tenir (le coup) ♦ **a cup of coffee is enough to keep her going all morning** elle réussit à tenir toute la matinée avec un café ♦ **I gave them enough money to keep them going for a week or two** je leur ai donné assez d'argent pour tenir une semaine ou deux ♦ **to keep a factory going** maintenir une usine en activité

4 [= begin] ♦ **there he goes again !** le voilà qui recommence ! ♦ **here goes!*** allez, on y va !

5 [= progress] aller, marcher ♦ **the project was going well** le projet marchait bien ♦ **how's it going?, how goes it?** (comment) ça va ? ♦ **the way things are going** au train où vont les choses, si ça continue comme ça ♦ **I hope all will ~ well** j'espère que tout ira bien ♦ **all went well for him until ...** tout a bien marché *or* s'est bien passé pour lui jusqu'au moment où ...

6 [= turn out] *[events]* se passer ♦ **how did your holiday ~?** comment se sont passées tes vacances ? ♦ **the evening went very well** la soirée s'est très bien passée ♦ **let's wait and see how things ~** attendons de voir ce qui va se passer ♦ **I don't know how things will ~** je ne sais pas comment ça va se passer, je ne sais pas comment les choses vont tourner* ♦ **that's the way things ~, I'm afraid** c'est malheu-

reux mais c'est comme ça ; *(esp US)* ◆ **what goes ?** * quoi de neuf ?

7 = extend aller, s'étendre ◆ **the garden goes as far as the river** le jardin va *or* s'étend jusqu'à la rivière ◆ **$50 does not ~ very far** on ne va pas très loin avec 50 dollars

8 = belong aller ◆ **the books ~ in that cupboard** les livres vont dans ce placard-là ◆ **this screw goes here** cette vis va là

9 = become devenir ◆ **the biscuits have gone soft** les biscuits sont devenus mous *or* ont ramolli ◆ **have you gone mad?** tu es (devenu) fou ? ◆ **she went pale** elle est devenue pâle, elle a pâli ◆ **you're not going to ~ all sentimental/shy/religious on me !** * tu ne vas pas me faire le coup * des grands sentiments/de la timidité/de la ferveur religieuse ! ◆ **the lights went red** les feux sont passés au rouge ◆ **the constituency went Labour at the last election** aux dernières élections la circonscription est passée aux travaillistes

10 = break, yield *[rope, cable]* céder ; *[fuse]* sauter ; *[bulb]* griller ; *[material]* être usé ◆ **the lining's going** la doublure est usée ◆ **jeans tend to ~ at the knees** les jeans ont tendance à s'user aux genoux ◆ **this jumper has gone at the elbows** ce pull est troué aux coudes ◆ **there goes another button!** encore un bouton de décousu !

11 = fail *[sight]* baisser ; *[strength]* manquer ◆ **his mind is going** il n'a plus toute sa tête ◆ **his nerve was beginning to ~** il commençait à paniquer *or* à perdre la tête ◆ **my voice has gone** je n'ai plus de voix ◆ **my voice is going** je n'ai presque plus de voix ◆ **his health is going** il commence à avoir des problèmes de santé ◆ **his hearing is going** il devient sourd

12 euph = die partir ◆ **after I go** *or* **have gone** quand je serai parti, quand je ne serai plus là ◆ **he's gone!** il est parti, c'est fini !

13 = be sold ◆ **how much do you think the house will ~ for ?** combien crois-tu que la maison va être vendue ?

14 = be given *[prize, reward, inheritance]* aller, revenir *(to* à)

15 = be current, be accepted *[story, rumour]* circuler ◆ **the story goes that ...** le bruit court *or* circule que ... ◆ **anything goes these days** * tout est permis de nos jours ◆ **that goes without saying** cela va sans dire ◆ **what he says goes** c'est lui qui fait la loi ◆ **what I say goes around here** c'est moi qui commande ici

16 * = say sortir *, faire * ◆ **he goes to me: "what do you want?"** il me sort * *or* il me fait : "qu'est-ce que tu veux ?"

17 = apply ◆ **she mustn't say a word, and that goes for you too** elle ne doit pas dire un mot et c'est valable pour toi aussi ◆ **that goes for me too** *(= I agree with that)* je suis (aussi) de cet avis ◆ **as far as your suggestion goes ...** pour ce qui est de ta suggestion ...

◆ **as far as it goes** ◆ **this explanation is fine, as far as it goes, but ...** cette explication n'est pas mauvaise, mais ...

18 = available

◆ **to be going** ◆ **are there any jobs going?** y a-t-il des postes vacants ? ◆ **there just aren't any jobs going** il n'y a pas de travail ◆ **is there any coffee going?** est-ce qu'il y a du café ? ◆ **I'll have whatever's going** donnez-moi *or* je prendrai de ce qu'il y a

19 = be sung, played ◆ **the tune goes like this** voici l'air ◆ **I don't know how the song goes** je ne connais pas cette chanson ◆ **how does it ~?** c'est comment *or* quoi la chanson ?

20 = make specific sound or movement faire ; *[bell, clock]* sonner ◆ **~ like that with your left foot** faites comme ça avec votre pied gauche

21 = serve ◆ **the money will ~ to compensate the accident victims** cet argent servira à dédommager les victimes de l'accident ◆ **the qualities that ~ to make a great man** les qualités qui font un grand homme

22 Math ◆ **4 into 12 goes 3 times** 12 divisé par 4 égale 3 ◆ **2 won't ~ exactly into 11** 11 divisé par 2, ça ne tombe pas juste

23 * euph aller aux toilettes ◆ **do you need to ~?** tu as envie d'aller aux toilettes ? ◆ **I need to ~** j'ai une envie pressante

24 implying comparison

◆ **as ... go** ◆ **he's not bad, as estate agents ~** il n'est pas mauvais pour un agent immobilier ◆ **it's a fairly good garage as garages go** comme garage cela peut aller *or* ce n'est pas trop mal

25 = be disposed of, elapse ◆ **seven down and three to ~** en voilà sept de faits, il n'en reste plus que trois ◆ **there is a week to ~ before the election** il reste une semaine avant les élections

26 US = take away ◆ **to ~** à emporter ◆ **two hot-dogs to ~** deux hot-dogs à emporter

2 - MODAL VERB

indicating future

◆ **to be going to** + *infinitive* aller ◆ **I'm going to phone him this afternoon** je vais l'appeler cet après-midi ◆ **it's going to rain** il va pleuvoir ◆ **I was just going to do it** j'allais le faire, j'étais sur le point de le faire ◆ **I was going to do it yesterday but I forgot** j'allais le faire *or* j'avais l'intention de le faire hier mais j'ai oublié

3 - TRANSITIVE VERB

1 = travel *[+ distance]* faire ◆ **we had gone only 3km** nous n'avions fait que 3 km ◆ **the car was fairly going it** * la voiture roulait *or* filait à bonne allure

◆ **to go it alone** *(gen)* se débrouiller tout seul ; *(Pol etc)* faire cavalier seul

◆ **to go one better** aller encore plus loin, renchérir

2 Cards, Gambling ◆ **he went three spades** il a annoncé trois piques ◆ **he went £50 on the red** il a misé 50 livres sur le rouge ◆ **I can only ~ £15** je ne peux mettre que 15 livres

3 = make sound faire ◆ **he went "psst"** "psst", fit-il

4 - NOUN

(pl goes)

1 NonC = energy ◆ **to be full of ~** être plein d'énergie, être très dynamique ◆ **there's no ~ about him** il n'a aucun ressort, il est mou

2 NonC : * = activity, motion ◆ **it's all ~ !** ça n'arrête pas ! ◆ **to be always on the ~** être toujours sur la brèche ◆ **to keep sb on the ~** ne pas laisser souffler qn ◆ **he's got two projects on the ~ at the moment** il a deux projets en chantier actuellement

3 * = attempt tentative *f*, coup *m* ◆ **at one** *or* **a ~** d'un seul coup ◆ **it's your ~** *(in games)* c'est ton tour, c'est à toi (de jouer)

◆ **to have a go** *(= try)* essayer, tenter le coup ◆ **to have a ~ at sth** essayer de faire qch ◆ **to have another ~** réessayer, faire une nouvelle tentative ◆ **have another ~!** essaie encore une fois !, réessaie ! ◆ **to have a ~ at sb** *(verbally)* s'en prendre à qn * ; *(physically)* se jeter sur qn ◆ **the public is warned not to have a ~** *(at criminal)* il est demandé au public de ne rien tenter *or* de ne pas s'approcher du criminel

4 * = event, situation ◆ **it's a rum ~** c'est une drôle de situation ◆ **they've had a rough ~ of it** ils ont traversé une mauvaise période

5 = success ◆ **to make a ~ of sth** réussir qch ◆ **they decided to try to make a ~ of their marriage** ils ont décidé de donner une chance à leur couple ◆ **no ~!** * rien à faire ! ◆ **it's all the ~** * ça fait fureur, c'est le dernier cri

5 - ADJECTIVE

esp Space : * paré pour la mise à feu ◆ **all systems (are) ~** *(gen)* tout est OK ◆ **you are ~ for moon-landing** vous avez le feu vert pour l'alunissage

6 - COMPOUNDS

go-ahead ADJ *(esp Brit) [person, government]* dynamique, qui va de l'avant ; *[business, attitude]* dynamique N ◆ **to give sb the ~-ahead (for sth/to do sth)** * donner le feu vert à qn (pour qch/pour faire qch)

go-between N intermédiaire *mf*

go-by * N ◆ **to give sth/sb the ~-by** laisser tomber * qch/qn

go-cart N *(= vehicle)* kart *m* ; *(= toy)* chariot *m (que se construisent les enfants)* ; *(= handcart)* charrette *f* ; *(= pushchair)* poussette *f* ; *(= baby-walker)* trotteur *m*

go-carting N *(Sport)* karting *m*

go-faster stripe * N liseré *m* sport *(sur la carrosserie d'une voiture)*

go-getter * N fonceur * *m*, -euse * *f*

go-getting * ADJ *[person]* fonceur * ; *[approach, attitude]* de battant

go-kart N kart *m*

go-karting N *(Sport)* karting *m*

go-kart track N piste *f* de karting

go-slow (strike) N *(Brit)* grève *f* perlée

7 - PHRASAL VERBS

► **go about** VI 1 circuler, aller ◆ **he goes about in a Rolls** il roule en Rolls ◆ **to ~ about barefoot/in torn jeans** se promener pieds nus/en jean déchiré ◆ **they ~ about in gangs** ils vont *or* circulent en bandes ◆ **he's going about with disreputable people** il fréquente des gens peu recommandables ◆ **he always goes about telling people what to do** il est toujours en train de dire aux gens ce qu'ils doivent faire

2 *[rumour]* courir, circuler

3 *(Naut = change direction)* virer de bord

VT FUS 1 *(= deal with) [+ task, duties]* ◆ **he went about the task methodically** il a procédé *or* il s'y est pris de façon méthodique ◆ **he knows how to ~ about it** il sait s'y prendre ◆ **we must ~ about it carefully** nous devons y aller doucement ◆ **how does one ~ about getting seats?** comment s'y prend-on *or* comment fait-on pour avoir des places ?

2 *(= be occupied with)* ◆ **to go about one's work** vaquer à ses occupations *or* travaux ◆ **to ~ about one's business** vaquer à ses affaires

► **go across** VI *(= cross)* traverser ◆ **she went across to Mrs. Smith's** elle est allée en face chez Mme Smith

VT FUS *[+ river, road]* traverser

► **go after** VT FUS *(= follow)* suivre ; *(= attack)* attaquer ◆ **~ after him!** suivez-le ! ◆ **we're not going after civilian targets** nous n'attaquons pas les cibles civiles ◆ **the press went after him mercilessly** la presse s'est acharnée contre lui ◆ **to ~ after a job** poser sa candidature à un poste, postuler à un emploi ◆ **he saw the job advertised and decided to ~ after it** il a vu une annonce pour ce poste et a décidé de poser sa candidature

► **go against** VT FUS 1 *(= prove hostile to) [vote, judgement, decision]* être défavorable à ◆ **the decision went against him** la décision lui a été défavorable ◆ **everything began to ~ against us** tout se liguait contre nous

2 *(= oppose)* aller à l'encontre de ◆ **conditions which went against national interests** des conditions qui allaient à l'encontre des intérêts nationaux ◆ **to ~ against the tide** aller contre le courant *or* à contre-courant ◆ **to ~ against public opinion** aller à contre-courant de l'opinion (publique) ◆ **to ~ against sb's wishes** s'opposer à la volonté *or* aux volontés

de qn ◆ **it goes against my conscience** ma conscience s'y oppose ◆ **it goes against my principles** cela va à l'encontre de mes principes, c'est contre mes principes

► **go ahead** VI (also **go on ahead**) passer devant *or* en tête ◆ **~ ahead!** allez-y ! ◆ **the exhibition will ~ ahead as planned** l'exposition aura lieu comme prévu ◆ **to ~ ahead with a plan/project** mettre un plan/projet à exécution

► **go along** VI aller ◆ **why don't you ~ along too?** pourquoi n'iriez-vous pas aussi ? ◆ **I'll tell you as we ~ along** je vous le dirai en cours de route *or* en chemin ◆ **I check as I ~ along** je vérifie au fur et à mesure ◆ **to ~ along with sb** *(lit)* aller avec qn, accompagner qn ; *(= agree with)* être d'accord avec qn ◆ **I'd ~ along with you on that** je suis d'accord avec toi sur ce point ◆ **I don't ~ along with you there** là, je ne suis pas d'accord avec vous ◆ **I can't ~ along with that at all** je ne suis pas du tout d'accord là-dessus, je suis tout à fait contre ◆ **the other parties are unlikely to ~ along with the plan** il est peu probable que les autres partis acceptent ce projet

► **go around** VI [1] ⇒ **go about, go round**
[2] ◆ **what goes around comes around** tout finit par se payer

► **go at** VT FUS *(= attack)* *[+ person]* attaquer, se jeter sur ; *(= undertake)* *[+ task]* s'atteler à ◆ **he went at it with a will** il s'y est mis avec acharnement

► **go away** VI partir, s'en aller ; *(on holiday)* partir (en vacances), aller en vacances ; *[pain]* disparaître ◆ **he's gone away with my keys** il est parti avec mes clés ◆ **we're not going away this year** nous n'allons nulle part *or* nous ne partons pas cette année ◆ **don't ~ away with the idea that ...** * n'allez pas penser que ... ◆ **I think we need to ~ away and think about this** je pense que nous devons prendre le temps d'y réfléchir

► **go back** VI [1] *(= return)* retourner ◆ **we went back to the beach after lunch** nous sommes retournés à la plage après le déjeuner ◆ **shall we ~ back now? It's getting dark** il est peut-être temps qu'on rentre *or* qu'on y aille, il commence à faire nuit ◆ **to ~ back to a point** revenir sur un point ◆ **to ~ back to the beginning** revenir au début ◆ **to ~ back to work** reprendre le travail ◆ **to ~ back to bed** aller se recoucher
[2] *(= retreat)* reculer
[3] *(in time)* remonter ◆ **my memories don't ~ back so far** mes souvenirs ne remontent pas aussi loin ◆ **the family goes back to the Norman Conquest** la famille remonte à la conquête normande ◆ **we ~ back a long way** on se connaît depuis longtemps
[4] *(= revert)* revenir *(to à)* ◆ **I don't want to ~ back to the old system** je ne veux pas revenir à l'ancien système ◆ **to ~ back to one's former habits** retomber dans ses anciennes habitudes
[5] *(= extend)* s'étendre ◆ **the garden goes back to the river** le jardin s'étend jusqu'à la rivière ◆ **the cave goes back 300 metres** la grotte a 300 mètres de long

► **go back on** VT FUS *[+ decision, promise]* revenir sur

► **go before** VI *(lit)* aller au devant ◆ **all that has gone before** *(fig = happen earlier)* tout ce qui s'est passé avant ◆ **those who are** *or* **have gone before** *(euph = die)* ceux qui sont partis avant nous ◆ **to ~ before a court/judge** comparaître devant un tribunal/juge

► **go below** VI *(Naut)* descendre dans l'entrepont

► **go by** VI *[person]* passer ; *[period of time]* (se) passer, s'écouler ◆ **we've let the opportunity ~ by** nous avons raté *or* laissé passer l'occasion ◆ **as time goes by** à mesure que le temps passe, avec le temps ◆ **in days** (*or* **years**) **gone by** autrefois, jadis

VT FUS [1] *(= judge by)* ◆ **if first impressions are anything to ~ by** s'il faut se fier à sa première impression ◆ **that's nothing to ~ by** ce n'est pas une référence ◆ **you can't ~ by what he says** on ne peut pas se fier à ce qu'il dit ◆ **to ~ by appearances** juger d'après les apparences ◆ **the only thing the police have got to ~ by ...** le seul indice dont dispose la police ...
[2] *(= be guided by)* suivre ◆ **to ~ by the instructions** suivre les instructions ◆ **if they prove I was wrong I'll ~ by what they say** s'ils prouvent que j'avais tort, je me rallierai à leur point de vue

► **go down** VI [1] *(= descend)* descendre ◆ **to ~ down to the coast** aller *or* descendre sur la côte
[2] *(= fall)* *[person]* tomber ; *[boxer]* aller au tapis ; *[building]* s'écrouler
[3] *(= sink)* *[ship]* couler, sombrer ; *[person]* couler
[4] *(= crash)* *[plane]* s'écraser
[5] *(Brit Univ)* *[student]* *(= go on holiday)* partir en vacances ; *(= finish studies)* terminer (ses études), quitter l'université ◆ **the university goes down on 20 June** les vacances universitaires commencent le 20 juin
[6] *(= set)* *[sun, moon]* se coucher
[7] *(= be swallowed)* ◆ **it went down the wrong way** j'ai (*or* il a *etc*) avalé de travers
[8] *(= be accepted, approved)* ◆ **I wonder how that will ~ down with her parents** je me demande comment ses parents vont prendre ça ◆ **to ~ down well/badly** être bien/mal accueilli ◆ **it went down well** ça a été bien accueilli ◆ **the suggestion didn't ~ down well with the locals** cette proposition a été mal accueillie par la population locale
[9] *(= subside)* *[tide]* descendre ; *[temperature]* baisser ◆ **the floods are going down** les eaux commencent à se retirer
[10] *(= lessen)* *[amount, numbers, rate]* diminuer ; *[value, price, standards]* baisser ◆ **the house has gone down in value** la maison s'est dépréciée ◆ **this neighbourhood has gone down** ce quartier s'est dégradé
[11] *(= be defeated, fail)* être battu *(to par)* ; *(Bridge)* chuter ; *(= fail examination)* échouer, être recalé *(in en)* ◆ **Spain went down to Scotland 2-1** *(Ftbl)* l'Espagne a été battue 2 à 1 par l'Écosse
[12] *(= be relegated)* *[team]* être relégué ◆ **to ~ down a class** *(Scol)* redescendre d'une classe
[13] *(Comput = break down)* tomber en panne
[14] *(Theat)* *[curtain]* tomber ◆ **when the curtain goes down** lorsque le rideau tombe ; *[lights]* s'éteindre
[15] *(= go as far as)* aller ◆ **~ down to the bottom of the page** allez *or* reportez-vous au bas de la page
[16] *[balloon, tyre]* se dégonfler ◆ **my ankle's OK, the swelling has gone down** ma cheville va bien, elle a désenflé
[17] *(= be noted, remembered)* ◆ **to ~ down to posterity** passer à la postérité
[18] *(Mus = lower pitch)* ◆ **can you ~ down a bit ?** vous pouvez chanter (*or* jouer) un peu plus bas ?

► **go down as** VT FUS *(= be regarded as)* être considéré comme ; *(= be remembered as)* passer à la postérité comme ◆ **the victory will ~ down as one of the highlights of the year** cette victoire restera dans les mémoires comme l'un des grands moments de l'année

► **go down on**** VT FUS sucer**

► **go down with** * VT FUS attraper ◆ **to ~ down with flu** attraper la grippe ; see also **go down**

► **go for** VT FUS [1] *(= attack)* attaquer ◆ **he went for me with a knife** il m'a attaqué avec un couteau ◆ **~ for him!** *(to dog)* mors-le !
[2] *(* = like)* ◆ **she went for him in a big way** elle en pinçait* pour lui, elle a craqué* pour lui ◆ **I don't ~ for that sort of talk** je n'aime pas qu'on parle comme ça ◆ **I don't ~ much for poetry** je ne raffole pas de la poésie ◆ **to tend to ~ for** avoir tendance à préférer
[3] *(= strive for)* essayer d'avoir ; *(= choose)* choisir ◆ **~ for it!** * vas-y ! ◆ **I decided to ~ for it** * j'ai décidé de tenter le coup
[4] ◆ **he's got a lot going for him** * il a beaucoup d'atouts ◆ **the theory has a lot going for it** cette théorie a de nombreux mérites

► **go forth** VI *(liter, frm)* [1] *[person]* s'en aller ◆ **they went forth to battle** ils s'en sont allés à la bataille
[2] ◆ **the order went forth that ...** il fut décrété que ... ◆ **the word went forth that ...** il a été annoncé que ...

► **go forward** VI [1] *(= move ahead)* *[person, vehicle]* avancer ; *[economy]* progresser ; *[country]* aller de l'avant
[2] *(= take place)* avoir lieu
[3] *(= continue)* maintenir ◆ **if they ~ forward with these radical proposals** s'ils maintiennent ces propositions radicales

► **go in** VI [1] *(= enter)* entrer ◆ **they went in by the back door** ils sont entrés par la porte de derrière ◆ **I must ~ in now** il faut que je rentre *subj* maintenant ◆ **~ in and win!** allez, bonne chance !
[2] *(= attack)* attaquer ◆ **the troops are going in tomorrow** les troupes attaquent demain ◆ **British troops will not ~ in alone** les troupes britanniques ne seront pas les seules à se battre
[3] *[sun, moon]* se cacher *(behind* derrière)

► **go in for** VT FUS [1] *[+ examination]* se présenter à ; *[+ position, job]* poser sa candidature à, postuler à *or* pour ; *[+ competition, race]* prendre part à
[2] *[+ sport]* pratiquer ; *[+ hobby]* se livrer à ; *[+ style]* être porté sur, affectionner ; *[+ medicine, accounting, politics]* faire ◆ **she goes in for very high heels** elle affectionne les très hauts talons ◆ **I don't ~ in for bright colours** je ne suis pas (très) porté sur les couleurs vives, je ne raffole pas des couleurs vives ◆ **he doesn't ~ in much for reading** il n'aime pas beaucoup lire ◆ **we don't ~ in for eating in expensive restaurants** nous n'avons pas pour habitude de manger dans des restaurants chers ◆ **he's going in for science** il va faire des sciences

► **go into** VT FUS [1] *(= take up)* *[+ profession, field]* ◆ **he doesn't want to ~ into industry** il ne veut pas travailler dans l'industrie
[2] *(= embark on)* *[+ explanation]* se lancer dans ◆ **he went into a long explanation** il s'est lancé *or* embarqué dans une longue explication ◆ **to ~ into details** rentrer dans les détails ◆ **let's not ~ into that now** laissons cela pour le moment ◆ **to ~ into fits of laughter** être pris de fou rire
[3] *(= investigate)* étudier ◆ **this matter is being gone into** on étudie la question ◆ **we haven't got time to ~ into that now** nous n'avons pas le temps de nous pencher sur ce problème ◆ **to ~ into a question in detail** approfondir une question
[4] *(= be devoted to)* *[time, money, effort]* être investi dans ◆ **a lot of money went into the research** on a investi beaucoup d'argent dans la recherche

► **go in with** VT FUS *(= share costs)* se cotiser avec ◆ **she went in with her sister to buy the present** elle s'est cotisée avec sa sœur pour acheter le cadeau

► **go off** VI [1] *(= leave)* partir, s'en aller ; *(Theat)* quitter la scène ◆ **they went off together** ils sont partis ensemble ◆ **she went off at 3 o'clock** *(= go off duty)* elle est partie à 3 heures, elle a quitté (son travail) à 3 heures

2 *[alarm clock]* sonner ; *[alarm]* se déclencher ◆ **the gun didn't ~ off** le coup n'est pas parti ◆ **the pistol went off in his hand** le coup est parti alors qu'il tenait le pistolet dans sa main

3 *(= stop) [light, radio, TV]* s'éteindre ; *[heating]* s'arrêter, s'éteindre

4 *(Brit = deteriorate) [meat]* s'avarier, se gâter ; *[milk]* tourner ; *[butter]* rancir ; *[athlete]* être en méforme

5 *(= lose intensity) [pain]* s'apaiser, passer

6 *(= go to sleep)* s'endormir

7 *[event]* se passer ◆ **the evening went off very well** la soirée s'est très bien passée

VT FUS *(Brit *)* ◆ **I'm starting to ~ off the idea** ça ne me dit plus grand-chose ◆ **I've gone off skiing** le ski ne me tente plus beaucoup ◆ **I used to like him, but I've gone off him lately** je l'aimais bien mais depuis un certain temps il m'agace

► **go off with** VT FUS *[+ thing, person]* partir avec ◆ **she went off with my umbrella** elle est partie avec mon parapluie ◆ **his wife went off with another man** sa femme est partie avec un autre homme

► **go on** VI 1 *(= fit)* ◆ **the lid won't ~ on** le couvercle ne ferme pas bien ◆ **the cover won't ~ on** ça ne rentre pas dans la housse

2 *(= proceed on one's way) (without stopping)* poursuivre son chemin ; *(after stopping)* continuer sa route ; *(by car)* reprendre la route ◆ **after a brief chat she went on to church** après avoir bavardé quelques instants, elle a continué sa route vers l'église ◆ **~ on, it's fun!** * vas-y, tu vas voir, c'est super ! * ; → **go ahead**

3 *(= continue)* continuer *(doing sth* de *or* à faire qch) ◆ **to ~ on speaking** continuer de *or* à parler ; *(after pause)* reprendre (la parole) ◆ **~ on with your work** continuez votre travail ◆ **~ on trying!** essaie encore ! ◆ **~ on!** continuez ! ◆ **~ on (with you)!** * allons donc !, à d'autres ! * ◆ **the war went on until 1945** la guerre a continué *or* s'est prolongée jusqu'en 1945 ◆ **if you ~ on doing that, you'll get into trouble** si tu continues à faire ça, tu vas avoir des ennuis ◆ **that's enough to be going on with** ça suffit pour l'instant

4 *(* = talk)* ◆ **to go on about sth** ne pas arrêter de parler de qch ◆ **don't ~ on about it!** ça va, j'ai compris ! ◆ **she just goes on and on** elle radote ◆ **he goes on and on about it** il n'arrête pas d'en parler

5 *(* = nag)* **to ~ on at sb** s'en prendre à qn ◆ **she went on (and on) at him** elle n'a pas cessé de s'en prendre à lui ◆ **she's always going on at him about doing up the kitchen** elle n'arrête pas de le harceler pour qu'il refasse la cuisine

6 *(= proceed)* passer ◆ **to ~ on to another matter** passer à une autre question ◆ **he went on to say that ...** puis il a dit que ... ◆ **he retired from football and went on to become a journalist** il a abandonné le football et est devenu journaliste ◆ **he goes on to Holland tomorrow** il repart demain pour la Hollande

7 *(= happen)* se dérouler ; *(for a stated time)* durer ◆ **several matches were going on at the same time** plusieurs matchs se déroulaient en même temps ◆ **how long has this been going on?** depuis combien de temps est-ce que ça dure ? ◆ **the rioting went on all night** les émeutes ont duré toute la nuit ◆ **while this was going on** pendant ce temps, au même moment ◆ **what's going on here?** qu'est-ce qui se passe ici ?

8 *(= pass)* ◆ **things got easier as time went on** avec le temps les choses sont devenues plus faciles ◆ **as the day went on he became more and more anxious** au fil des heures, il devenait de plus en plus inquiet

9 *(*: gen pej = behave)* ◆ **that's no way to ~ on** c'est une conduite inacceptable ! ◆ **what a way to ~ on!** en voilà des manières !

10 *(Theat = enter)* entrer en scène

11 *(= progress) [person, patient]* se porter, aller ◆ **how is he going on?** comment va-t-il *or* se porte-t-il ? ◆ **life went on uneventfully** la vie poursuivit son cours paisiblement

12 *(* = approach)* ◆ **she's going on 50** elle va sur la cinquantaine, elle frise* la cinquantaine ◆ **Ann's 25 going on 50** Ann a 25 ans mais elle a les réactions d'une femme de 50 ans

VT FUS 1 *(= be guided by)* ◆ **you've got to ~ on the facts** il faut s'appuyer sur les faits ◆ **what have you got to ~ on?** de quels indices *or* de quelles pistes disposez-vous ? ◆ **we don't have much to ~ on yet** nous n'avons pas beaucoup d'indices pour l'instant ◆ **the police had no clues to ~ on** la police n'avait aucun indice sur lequel s'appuyer

2 *(= appreciate, be impressed by)* ◆ **I don't ~ much on that** ⁑ ça ne me dit pas grand-chose*

► **go on for** VT FUS ◆ **it's going on for 100km** c'est à une centaine de kilomètres ◆ **it's going on for 5 o'clock** il est près de 5 heures ◆ **he's going on for 50** il va sur la cinquantaine

► **go out** VI 1 *(= leave)* sortir ◆ **to ~ out of a room** sortir d'une pièce ◆ **to ~ out shopping** aller faire des courses ◆ **to ~ out for a meal** aller au restaurant ◆ **he goes out a lot** il sort beaucoup ◆ **she doesn't ~ out with him any more** elle ne sort plus avec lui ◆ **to ~ out to work** (aller) travailler ◆ **most mothers have to ~ out to work** la plupart des mères de famille doivent travailler

2 *[style]* passer de mode, se démoder ; *[custom]* disparaître ; *[fire, light]* s'éteindre ◆ **he was so tired he went out like a light*** il était si fatigué qu'il s'est endormi comme une masse* ◆ **all the fun has gone out of it now** ce n'est plus aussi drôle maintenant

3 *(= travel)* aller *(to* à) ◆ **she went out to Bangkok to join her husband** elle est allée rejoindre son mari à Bangkok

4 *[sea]* se retirer ; *[tide]* descendre ◆ **the tide** *or* **the sea goes out 2km** la mer se retire sur 2 km

5 ◆ **my heart went out to him** j'ai été vraiment désolé pour lui ◆ **all our sympathy goes out to you** nous pensons à vous en ces moments douloureux

6 *(Cards etc)* terminer

7 *(= be issued) [pamphlet, circular]* être distribué ; *[invitation]* être envoyé ; *(= be broadcast) [radio programme, TV programme]* être diffusé ◆ **an appeal has gone out for people to give blood** un appel a été lancé pour encourager les dons de sang ◆ **the programme goes out on Friday evenings** l'émission passe *or* est diffusée le vendredi soir

8 *(Sport = be eliminated)* être éliminé, se faire sortir* ◆ **our team went out to a second division side** notre équipe a été éliminée *or* s'est fait sortir* par une équipe de deuxième division

9 *(= end) [year]* finir, se terminer

► **go over** VI 1 *(= cross)* aller ◆ **to ~ over to France** aller en France ◆ **she went over to Mrs Smith's** elle est allée chez Mme Smith ◆ **his speech went over well** son discours a été bien reçu *or* est bien passé ◆ **the ball went over into the field** le ballon est passé par-dessus la haie (*or* le mur *etc*) et il est tombé dans le champ

2 *(= be overturned) [vehicle]* se retourner ; *[boat]* chavirer, se retourner

VT FUS 1 *(= examine) [+ accounts, report]* examiner, vérifier ; *[doctor] [+ patient]* examiner ◆ **to ~ over a house** visiter une maison ◆ **I went over his essay with him** j'ai regardé sa dissertation avec lui

2 *(= rehearse, review) [+ speech]* revoir ; *[+ facts, points]* récapituler ◆ **to ~ over sth in one's mind** repasser qch dans son esprit ◆ **to ~ over the events of the day** repasser les événements de la journée ◆ **let's ~ over the facts again** récapitulons les faits

3 *(= touch up)* retoucher, faire des retouches à ◆ **to ~ over a drawing in ink** repasser un dessin à l'encre

► **go over to** VT FUS passer à ◆ **we're going over to a new system** nous passons à un nouveau système ◆ **I've gone over to a new brand of coffee** j'ai changé de marque de café ◆ **to ~ over to the enemy** passer à l'ennemi

► **go round** VI 1 *(= turn)* tourner ◆ **my head is going round** j'ai la tête qui tourne

2 *(= go the long way)* faire le tour ; *(= make a detour)* faire un détour ◆ **there's no bridge, we'll have to ~ round** il n'y a pas de pont, il faut faire le tour ◆ **we went round by Manchester** nous avons fait un détour par Manchester

3 ◆ **to ~ round to sb's house/to see sb** aller chez qn/voir qn

4 *(= be sufficient)* suffire (pour tout le monde) ◆ **there's enough food to ~ round** il y a assez à manger pour tout le monde ◆ **to make the money ~ round** joindre les deux bouts*

5 *(= circulate) [bottle, document, story]* circuler ; *[rumour]* courir, circuler

6 ⇒ **go about VI**

► **go through** VI *(= be agreed, voted) [proposal]* être accepté ; *[law, bill]* passer, être voté ; *[business deal]* être conclu, se faire ; *(Sport = qualify)* se qualifier ◆ **the deal did not ~ through** l'affaire n'a pas été conclue *or* ne s'est pas faite

VT FUS 1 *(= suffer, endure)* subir, endurer ◆ **after all he's gone through** après tout ce qu'il a subi *or* enduré ◆ **we've all gone through it** nous sommes tous passés par là, nous avons tous connu cela ◆ **he's going through a very difficult time** il traverse une période difficile

2 *(= examine) [+ list]* éplucher ; *[+ book]* parcourir ; *[+ mail]* regarder, dépouiller ; *[+ subject, plan]* étudier ; *[+ one's pockets]* fouiller dans ; *(at customs) [+ suitcases, trunks]* fouiller ◆ **I went through my drawers looking for a pair of socks** j'ai cherché une paire de chaussettes dans mes tiroirs ◆ **I went through his essay with him** j'ai regardé sa dissertation avec lui

3 *(= use up) [+ money]* dépenser ; *(= wear out)* user ◆ **to ~ through a fortune** engloutir une fortune ◆ **he goes through a pair of shoes a month** il use une paire de chaussures par mois ◆ **he has gone through the seat of his trousers** il a troué le fond de son pantalon ◆ **this book has already gone through 13 editions** ce livre en est déjà à sa 13e édition

4 *(= carry out) [+ routine, course of study]* suivre ; *[+ formalities]* remplir, accomplir ; *[+ apprenticeship]* faire

► **go through with** VT FUS *(= persist with) [+ plan, threat]* mettre à exécution ◆ **in the end she couldn't ~ through with it** en fin de compte elle n'a pas pu le faire ◆ **he pleaded with her not to ~ through with the divorce** il l'a suppliée de ne pas continuer la procédure de divorce

► **go to** VI ◆ **~ to !** †† allons donc !

VT FUS ◆ **~ to it !** allez-y !

► **go together** VI *[colours]* aller (bien) ensemble ; *[events, conditions, ideas]* aller de pair ◆ **poor living conditions and TB ~ together** la tuberculose va de pair avec les mauvaises conditions de vie ◆ **they ~ well together** ils vont bien ensemble ◆ **Ann and Peter are going together** Ann et Peter sortent ensemble

► **go under** VI 1 *(= sink) [ship]* sombrer, couler ; *[person]* couler

2 *(= fail) [business person]* faire faillite ; *[business]* couler, faire faillite

► **go up** VI 1 *(= rise)* *[price, value, temperature]* monter, être en hausse ; *(Theat)* *[curtain]* se lever ; *[lights]* s'allumer ; *[cheer]* s'élever ◆ **three teams are hoping to ~ up to the second division** trois équipes espèrent monter *or* passer en deuxième division ◆ **houses are going up near the park** on construit des maisons près du parc ◆ **when the curtain goes up** lorsque le rideau se lève ◆ **to ~ up in price** augmenter ◆ **to ~ up a class** *(Scol)* monter d'une classe

2 *(= climb)* monter, aller en haut ; *(= go upstairs to bed)* monter se coucher

3 *(= travel north)* aller, monter ◆ **I'm going up to Manchester tomorrow** demain je vais *or* je monte à Manchester

4 *(= approach)* ◆ **I wanted to ~ up and talk to him** je voulais m'approcher de lui et lui parler ◆ **a man went up to him and asked him the time** un homme s'est approché et lui a demandé l'heure

5 *(= explode, be destroyed)* *[building]* sauter, exploser

6 *(Brit Univ)* entrer à l'université ◆ **he went up to Oxford** il est entré à Oxford

VT FUS *[+ hill]* monter, gravir ◆ **to ~ up the stairs** monter l'escalier, monter les marches d'un escalier ◆ **to ~ up the street** monter la rue

► **go with** VT FUS 1 *(= accompany)* *[circumstances, event, conditions]* aller (de pair) avec ◆ **ill health goes with poverty** la pauvreté et la mauvaise santé vont de pair ◆ **the house goes with the job** le logement va avec le poste ◆ **to ~ with the times** vivre avec son temps ◆ **to ~ with the crowd** *(lit)* suivre la foule ; *(fig)* faire comme tout le monde

2 *(= harmonize with, suit)* *[colours]* aller bien avec, se marier avec ; *[furnishings]* être assorti à ; *[behaviour, opinions]* cadrer avec, s'accorder avec ◆ **I want a hat to ~ with my new coat** je cherche un chapeau assorti à mon *or* qui aille avec mon nouveau manteau ◆ **his accent doesn't ~ with his appearance** son accent ne correspond pas à son apparence

3 *(= agree with)* *[+ person]* être de l'avis de ; *[+ idea]* souscrire à ◆ **I'll ~ with you there** là, je suis de votre avis ◆ **yes, I'd ~ with that** je suis d'accord sur ce point

4 (* *= choose)* opter pour, choisir ◆ **we decided to ~ with the first option** nous avons décidé d'opter pour la première solution *or* de choisir la première option

5 (* : also **go steady with**) sortir avec

► **go without** VI se priver de tout ◆ **mothers feed their children and ~ without themselves** les mères nourrissent leurs enfants et se privent elles-mêmes de tout

VT FUS se priver de, se passer de

---

goad /gəʊd/ N 1 *(lit)* aiguillon *m* 2 *(fig)* *(= spur, impetus)* aiguillon *m*, stimulation *f* ; *(= irritant)* source *f* d'agacement, cause *f* d'irritation VT 1 *[+ cattle]* aiguillonner, piquer 2 *(fig)* aiguillonner, stimuler ◆ **to ~ sb into doing sth** talonner *or* harceler qn jusqu'à ce qu'il fasse qch ◆ **he was ~ed into replying** il a été piqué au point de répondre ◆ **his insults ~ed her into action** ses insultes l'ont fait passer à l'action

► **goad on** VT SEP aiguillonner, stimuler ◆ **to ~ sb on to doing sth** inciter qn à faire qch

goal /gəʊl/ N 1 *(gen = aim)* but *m*, objectif *m* ◆ **his ~ was to become president** son objectif *or* son but était de devenir président, il avait pour ambition *or* pour but de devenir président ◆ **her ~ was in sight** elle approchait du but ◆ **the ~ is to raise as much money as possible** le but *or* l'objectif est d'obtenir autant d'argent que possible ◆ **to set a ~** fixer un objectif ◆ **to set o.s. a ~** se fixer un but *or* un objectif

2 *(Sport)* but *m* ◆ **to keep ~, to play in ~** être gardien de but ◆ **to win by three ~s to two** gagner par trois buts à deux ◆ **the ball went into the ~** le ballon est entré dans le but

COMP **goal-area** N *(Sport)* surface *f* de but

goal average, goal difference N *(Brit Ftbl)* goal-average *m*

goal difference N *(Sport)* différence *f* de buts, goal-average *m*

goal-kick N *(Ftbl)* coup *m* de pied de renvoi (aux six mètres)

goal-line N ligne *f* de but

goal post N montant *m or* poteau *m* de but ◆ **to move the ~ posts** *(fig)* changer les règles du jeu

goal scorer N buteur *m* ◆ **the main ~ scorer was Jones** c'est Jones qui a marqué le plus de buts

goalie * /'gəʊlɪ/ N (abbrev of **goalkeeper**) goal *m*

goalkeeper /'gəʊlki:pəʳ/ N gardien *m* de but, goal *m*

goalkeeping /'gəʊlki:pɪŋ/ N jeu *m* du gardien de but

goalless /'gəʊllɪs/ ADJ 1 *(Sport)* *[match]* au score vierge, sans but marqué ◆ **a ~ draw** un match nul zéro à zéro 2 *(= aimless)* sans but

goalmouth /'gəʊlmaʊθ/ N ◆ **in the ~** juste devant les poteaux

goat /gəʊt/ N 1 chèvre *f* ; *(= he-goat)* bouc *m* ; *(= young goat)* chevreau *m*, chevrette *f* ; → **sheep** 2 *(Brit)* **to act the ~** * faire l'imbécile *or* l'andouille * 3 *(fig = irritate)* ◆ **to get sb's ~** * taper sur le système * *or* les nerfs * de qn

COMP **goat('s) cheese** N fromage *m* de chèvre

the goat God N *(Myth)* le divin chèvre-pied, le dieu Pan

goatee /gəʊ'ti:/ N barbiche *f*, bouc *m*

goatherd /'gəʊthɜ:d/ N chevrier *m*, -ière *f*

goatskin /'gəʊtskɪn/ N *(= clothing)* peau *f* de chèvre *or* de bouc ; *(= container)* outre *f* en peau de bouc

goatsucker /'gəʊtsʌkəʳ/ N *(US = bird)* engoulevent *m*

gob /gɒb/ N 1 (‡ *= spit)* crachat *m*, mollard‡ *m* 2 *(esp Brit:* ‡ *= mouth)* gueule‡ *f* ◆ **shut your ~!** ferme-la !*, ta gueule !‡ 3 *(US Navy* ‡*)* marin *m*, mataf‡ *m* VI (‡ *= spit)* cracher *(at* sur*)* COMP **gob-stopper** * N *(Brit)* (gros) bonbon *m*

gobbet * /'gɒbɪt/ N petit bout *m*

gobble /'gɒbl/ N *[of turkey]* glouglou *m* VI *[turkey]* glousser, glouglouter VT (also **gobble down, gobble up**) *[+ food]* engloutir, engouffrer ◆ **don't ~!** ne mange pas si vite !

gobbledegook, gobbledygook * /'gɒbldɪgu:k/ N charabia * *m*

gobbler * /'gɒbləʳ/ N *(= turkey)* dindon *m*

Gobi /'gəʊbɪ/ N ◆ **~ Desert** désert *m* de Gobi

goblet /'gɒblɪt/ N *(= stem glass)* verre *m* à pied ; *(= cup)* coupe *f*

goblin /'gɒblɪn/ N lutin *m*, farfadet *m*

gobshite ‡ /'gɒbʃaɪt/ N *(= idiot)* peigne-cul‡ *m*

gobsmacked ‡ /'gɒb,smækd/ ADJ *(Brit)* sidéré *, estomaqué *

goby /'gəʊbɪ/ N (pl **goby** *or* **gobies**) gobie *m*

GOC /,dʒi:əʊ'si:/ N *(Mil)* (abbrev of **General Officer Commanding**) → **general**

god /gɒd/ N 1 dieu *m*, divinité *f* ; *(fig)* dieu *m*, idole *f* ◆ **money is his ~** l'argent est son dieu

2 ◆ **God** Dieu *m* ◆ **God the Father, the Son, the Holy Spirit** Dieu le Père, le Fils et le Saint-Esprit ◆ **he thinks he's God** il se prend pour Dieu ◆ **he thinks he's God's gift** * **to women** il se prend pour Don Juan ◆ **to play God with people's lives** *(pej)* jouer avec la vie des gens ◆ **God's acre** († *= cemetery)* cimetière *m* ◆ **God's own country** * *(US)* les États-Unis *mpl*

3 *(phrases)* ◆ **(my) God!** * mon Dieu ! ◆ **God Almighty!** ‡ Dieu tout puissant ! ◆ **God help him!** * (que) Dieu lui vienne en aide ! ◆ **God help you** * **(if your mother ever finds out about this!)** (si ta mère apprend ça) je te souhaite bien de la chance ! ◆ **God bless you/her/him!** Dieu te/la/le bénisse ! ◆ **God (only) knows** * Dieu seul le sait, allez donc savoir * ◆ **and God (only) knows what else** * et Dieu sait quoi ◆ **God knows I've tried** * Dieu sait si j'ai essayé ◆ **God knows where he's got to** * allez savoir *or* Dieu sait où il est passé ! ◆ **he went God knows where** * il est parti Dieu sait où ◆ **for God's sake!** *, **for the love of God!** * *(crossly)* nom d'un chien ! * ; *(imploringly)* pour l'amour du ciel ! ◆ **by God, I'll get you for this!** * nom d'un chien *or* nom de Dieu je te le ferai payer ! * ◆ **God willing** s'il plaît à Dieu ◆ **I wish to God I hadn't told him!** * si seulement je ne lui avais rien dit ! ◆ **would to God that ...** † plût à Dieu que ... *+ subj* ◆ **ye ~s!** †† grands dieux ! ; → **help, hope, love, man, name, thank, tin**

4 *(Brit Theat)* ◆ **the ~s** * le poulailler *

COMP **god-awful** ‡ ADJ *(gen)* vraiment affreux ; *[weather, place]* pourri ; *[book, film etc]* complètement nul(le) *m(f)*

god-botherer * N *(pej)* bigot(e) * *m(f)* *(pej)*

god-fearing ADJ (très) religieux, (très) croyant ◆ **any ~-fearing man** tout croyant digne de ce nom

god-slot * N *(Brit TV)* créneau *m* horaire des émissions religieuses

godchild /'gɒdtʃaɪld/ N (pl **-children**) filleul(e) *m(f)*

goddammit ‡ /gɒ'dæmɪt/ EXCL *(US)* nom de Dieu !‡, bon sang ! *

goddam(n) ‡ /'gɒdæm/, **goddamned** ‡ /'gɒdæmd/ ADJ sacré *before n*, fichu * *before n*, foutu‡ *before n* ◆ **it's no ~(ned) use!** ça ne sert à rien ! *

goddaughter /'gɒddɔ:təʳ/ N filleule *f*

goddess /'gɒdɪs/ N déesse *f* ; *(fig)* idole *f*

godfather /'gɒdfɑ:ðəʳ/ N *(lit, fig)* parrain *m* ◆ **to stand ~ to a child** être parrain d'un enfant ; *(at ceremony)* tenir un enfant sur les fonts baptismaux

godforsaken /'gɒdfə,seɪkən/ ADJ *[town, place]* perdu, paumé * ; *[person]* malheureux, misérable ◆ **~ existence** chienne *f* de vie * ◆ **~ spot** trou *m* perdu *or* paumé *

godhead /'gɒdhed/ N divinité *f*

godless /'gɒdlɪs/ ADJ *[person, action, life]* impie

godlike /'gɒdlaɪk/ ADJ divin

godliness /'gɒdlɪnɪs/ N dévotion *f* ; see also **cleanliness**

godly /'gɒdlɪ/ ADJ *[person]* dévot(e) *m(f)*, pieux ; *[actions, life]* pieux

godmother /'gɒdmʌðəʳ/ N marraine *f* ◆ **to stand ~ to a child** être marraine d'un enfant ; *(at ceremony)* tenir un enfant sur les fonts baptismaux ; → **fairy**

godparent /'gɒdpɛərənt/ N *(= godfather)* parrain *m* ; *(= godmother)* marraine *f* NPL **godparents** ◆ **his ~s** son parrain et sa marraine

godsend /'gɒdsend/ N aubaine *f*, bénédiction *f* ◆ **to be a** *or* **come as a ~** être une bénédiction *or* aubaine *(to* pour*)*

godson /'gɒdsʌn/ N filleul *m*

godspeed † /'gɒdspi:d/ EXCL bonne chance !, bon voyage !

godsquad * /'gɒdskwɒd/ N *(pej)* bande *f* d'illuminés *(pej)*, ≃ les bigots * *mpl (pej)*,

goer /ˈgəʊəʳ/ N 1 *(= horse, runner)* fonceur *m*, -euse *f* 2 *(* = feasible idea)* bon plan* *m*, bonne idée *f* 3 *(= woman)* ◆ **she's a real ~** ⁑ elle démarre au quart de tour⁑

...goer /ˈgəʊəʳ/ N *(in compounds)* ◆ **cinemagoer** cinéphile *mf* ; → **opera-goer**

goes /gəʊz/ VB → **go**

Goethe /ˈgøːtə/ N Goethe *m*

gofer /ˈgəʊfəʳ/ N coursier *m*, -ière *f*

goggle /ˈgɒgl/ VI * *[person]* rouler de gros yeux ronds ; *[eyes]* être exorbités, sortir de la tête ◆ **to ~ at sb/sth** regarder qn/qch en roulant de gros yeux ronds NPL **goggles** *[of motorcyclist]* lunettes *fpl* protectrices *or* de motocycliste ; *[of skindiver]* lunettes *fpl* de plongée ; *(industrial)* lunettes *fpl* protectrices *or* de protection ; *(* = glasses)* besicles *fpl (hum)*
COMP **goggle-box**⁑ N *(Brit)* télé* *f*
goggle-eyed ADJ *(gen)* aux yeux exorbités ◆ **he sat ~-eyed in front of the TV** * il était assis devant la télé*, les yeux exorbités

go-go /ˈgəʊgəʊ/ ADJ 1 *(US) [market, stocks]* spéculatif ; *(* = dynamic) [team]* plein d'allant ; *[years, days]* prospère, de vaches grasses* ◆ **the ~ 1980s** la décennie prospère des années 1980 2 *(Brit Fin) [investment, fund]* à haut rendement et à haut risque, hautement spéculatif
COMP **go-go dance** N *danse exécutée par des personnes légèrement vêtues (pour les clients d'une boîte de nuit, etc)*
go-go dancer, go-go girl N *jeune fille qui danse légèrement vêtue (pour les clients d'une boîte de nuit, etc)*

going /ˈgəʊɪŋ/ N 1 *(= departure)* départ *m* ; → **coming**
2 *(= progress) (lit, fig)* ◆ **that was good ~** ça a été rapide ◆ **it was slow ~** on n'avançait pas ; *(in work, task)* les progrès étaient lents ◆ **it was hard ~** on a eu du mal, ça a été dur* ◆ **the meeting was hard** *or* **tough ~** la réunion était laborieuse
3 *(= conditions) (gen)* état *m* du sol *or* du terrain *(pour la marche etc)* ; *(Racing)* état *m* du sol *or* du terrain ◆ **it's rough ~** *(walking)* on marche mal ; *(in car)* la route est mauvaise ◆ **he got out while the ~ was good*** il est parti au bon moment ◆ **when the ~ gets tough, the tough get ~** *(Prov)* quand ça se met à être dur, les durs s'y mettent *(Prov)* → **heavy**
ADJ 1 ◆ **the ~ rate/price** le tarif/le prix normal
2 *(after superlative adj: *)* ◆ **it's the best thing ~** il n'y a rien de mieux (à l'heure actuelle) ◆ **the best computer game ~** le meilleur jeu électronique du moment *or* sur le marché ◆ **you must be the biggest fool ~** tu es vraiment le roi des imbéciles
COMP **a going concern** N *(Comm)* une affaire florissante *or* qui marche ◆ **the Empire was still a ~ concern** l'Empire était toujours une réalité
going-over N (pl **goings-over**) *[of accounts]* vérification *f*, révision *f* ; *(medical)* examen *m* ; *(= cleaning) [of rooms, house etc]* nettoyage *m* ; *(fig = beating)* brutalités *fpl*, passage *m* à tabac* ◆ **to give sth a good** *or* **thorough ~-over** *(= check)* inspecter qch soigneusement, soumettre qch à une inspection en règle ; *(= clean)* nettoyer qch à fond
goings-on * NPL *(pej) (= behaviour)* activités *fpl* (louche), manigances *fpl* ; *(= happenings)* événements *mpl* ◆ **fine ~s-on!*** c'est du joli ! ◆ **your letters keep me in touch with ~s-on at home** tes lettres me tiennent au courant de ce qui se passe à la maison

-going /ˈgəʊɪŋ/ ADJ *(in compounds)* ◆ **church-going Christian** chrétien *m* pratiquant ◆ **the theatre-going public** le public amateur de théâtre, les amateurs de théâtre ; → **easy, ocean** N *(in compounds)* ◆ **church-going/theatre-going has declined over the last ten years** depuis dix ans les gens vont de moins en moins à l'église/au théâtre

goitre, goiter *(US)* /ˈgɔɪtəʳ/ N goitre *m*

Golan /ˈgəʊlæn/ N ◆ **the ~ Heights** le plateau du Golan

gold /gəʊld/ N 1 *(NonC)* or *m* ◆ **£500 in ~** 500 livres en or ◆ **a pot** *or* **crock of ~** *(= money)* une mine d'or ; *(= desired object etc)* un oiseau rare ; → **good, heart, rolled**
2 ⇒ **gold medal**
ADJ 1 *(= made of gold) [watch, tooth]* en or ; *[coin, ingot, bullion]* d'or ; *[letters, lettering]* d'or, doré
2 *(= yellow) [paint]* doré ◆ **a green and ~ flag** un drapeau vert et or *inv* ; see also **comp**
COMP **gold braid** N *(Mil)* galon *m* or
Gold Card N *(Comm, Fin)* ≈ Gold Card, Gold MasterCard ®
gold-clause loan N *(Jur, Fin)* emprunt *m* avec garantie-or
Gold Coast N *(Hist: in Africa)* Côte-de-l'Or *f* ; *(US *: fig)* quartiers *mpl* chic *(souvent en bordure d'un lac)*
gold digger N
1 *(lit)* chercheur *m* d'or 2 *(fig pej)* ◆ **she's a ~ digger** c'est une aventurière
gold disc N *(Mus)* disque *m* d'or
gold dust N *(lit)* poudre *f* d'or ◆ **to be like ~ dust** *(esp Brit)* être une denrée rare
gold-exchange standard N *(Econ)* étalon *m* de change-or
gold fever N la fièvre de l'or
gold-filled ADJ *[tooth]* aurifié
gold filling N *(Dentistry)* obturation *f* en or, aurification *f*
gold foil N feuille *f* d'or
gold-headed cane N canne *f* à pommeau d'or
gold lace N *(on uniform)* ⇒ **gold braid**
gold leaf N feuille *f* d'or, or *m* en feuille
gold medal N médaille *f* d'or
gold mine N *(lit, fig)* mine *f* d'or ◆ **he's sitting on a ~ mine** il est assis sur une véritable mine d'or
gold miner N mineur *m (dans une mine d'or)*
gold mining N extraction *f* de l'or
gold plate N *(= coating)* mince couche *f* d'or ; *(= dishes)* vaisselle *f* d'or ◆ **to eat off ~ plates** *(fig)* rouler sur l'or, nager dans l'opulence
gold-plated ADJ *(lit)* plaqué *or inv* ; *(* fig) [deal, contract]* qui doit rapporter gros
the gold pool N *(Fin)* le pool de l'or
gold record N ⇒ **gold disc**
gold reserves NPL *(Econ)* réserves *fpl* d'or
gold-rimmed spectacles NPL lunettes *fpl* à montures en or
gold rush N ruée *f* vers l'or
gold standard N étalon-or *m* ◆ **to come off** *or* **leave the ~ standard** abandonner l'étalon-or
Gold Star Mother N *(US Hist)* mère *f* d'un soldat mort au combat
gold stone N aventurine *f*

goldbrick /ˈgəʊldbrɪk/ N 1 *(lit)* barre *f* d'or 2 *(US fig) (= good deal)* affaire *f* en or ; *(* = shirker)* tire-au-flanc* *m* VI *(US * = shirk)* tirer au flanc*

goldcrest /ˈgəʊldkrest/ N roitelet *m* huppé

golden /ˈgəʊldən/ ADJ 1 *(= yellow) [hair]* doré, d'or ; *[suntan, sand, light, colour]* doré ; *(Culin:* also **golden-brown)** bien doré
2 *(liter = made of gold) [cross, chain, locket]* en or ; *(fig) [voice]* d'or, en or
3 *(= happy, prosperous) [years]* doré ; *[future]* en or ◆ **a ~ era** un âge d'or ◆ **~ hours** heures *fpl* précieuses *or* merveilleuses ; see also **golden age, goose, silence**
COMP **golden age** N âge *m* d'or
golden boy* N *(popular)* enfant *m* chéri ; *(gifted)* jeune prodige *m* ; *(financially successful)* golden boy *m*
golden-brown ADJ *[tan, skin]* brun doré *inv* ; *(Culin)* bien doré
the golden calf N le veau d'or
golden deed N action *f* d'éclat
Golden Delicious (apple) N (pomme *f*) golden *f*
golden eagle N aigle *m* royal *or* doré
the Golden Fleece N la Toison d'or
Golden Gate N *(US Geog)* ◆ **the Golden Gate (Bridge)** le pont de la Golden Gate
golden girl* N *(popular)* enfant *f* chérie ; *(gifted, successful)* jeune prodige *m*
golden goal N *(Sport)* but *m* en or
golden handcuffs* NPL *prime d'encouragement (à rester à un poste)*
golden handshake N grosse prime *f* de départ
golden hello N prime *f* d'embauche
golden jubilee N *(Brit)* cinquantième *m* anniversaire, jubilé *m*
the golden mean N le juste milieu
golden number N nombre *m* d'or
golden oldie* N *(= pop song, performer, sportsperson)* vieille star *f*
golden opportunity N occasion *f* en or
golden oriole N loriot *m* d'Europe
golden parachute* N *prime de licenciement (prévue dans le contrat d'un cadre en cas de rachat de l'entreprise)*
golden pheasant N faisan *m* doré
golden remedy N remède *m* souverain *or* infaillible
golden retriever N golden retriever *m (chien)*
golden rod N *(= plant)* verge *f* d'or
golden rule N règle *f* d'or
golden share N *(Stock Exchange)* action *f* privilégiée
the Golden State N *(US)* la Californie
golden syrup N *(Brit)* sirop *m* de sucre roux
the Golden Triangle N le Triangle d'or
golden wedding (anniversary) N noces *fpl* d'or
golden yellow ADJ jaune d'or

goldfield /ˈgəʊldfiːld/ N région *f or* terrain *m* aurifère

goldfinch /ˈgəʊldfɪntʃ/ N chardonneret *m*

goldfish /ˈgəʊldfɪʃ/ (pl **goldfish** *or* **goldfishes**) N poisson *m* rouge, cyprin *m* (doré) COMP **goldfish bowl** N bocal *m* (à poissons) ◆ **to live in a ~ bowl** *(fig)* vivre comme dans un bocal en verre

Goldilocks /ˈgəʊldɪlɒks/ N Boucles d'Or *f*

goldsmith /ˈgəʊldsmɪθ/ N orfèvre *m* ◆ **~'s shop** magasin *m or* atelier *m* d'orfèvre ◆ **~'s trade** orfèvrerie *f*

golf /gɒlf/ N golf *m* ; → **clock** VI faire du golf, jouer au golf
COMP **golf ball** N balle *f* de golf ; *(on typewriter)* boule *f*, sphère *f* ◆ **~ ball typewriter** machine *f* à écrire à boule *or* à sphère
golf club N *(= stick)* club *m or* crosse *f* (de golf) ; *(= place)* club *m* de golf
golf course N (terrain *m* de) golf *m*
golf links NPL ⇒ **golf course**
golf widow N ◆ **she's a ~ widow** son mari la délaisse pour aller jouer au golf, son mari lui préfère le golf

golfer /ˈgɒlfəʳ/ N joueur *m*, -euse *f* de golf, golfeur *m*, -euse *f*

golfing /ˈgɒlfɪŋ/ ADJ *[equipment, trousers]* de golf ◆ **to go on a ~ holiday** partir en vacances faire du golf N golf *m*

Golgotha /ˈgɒlgəθə/ N Golgotha

Goliath /gəʊˈlaɪəθ/ N *(lit, fig)* Goliath *m*

golliwog /ˈgɒlɪwɒg/ N *(Brit)* poupée *f* nègre de chiffon *(aux cheveux hérissés)*

golly * /ˈgɒlɪ/ EXCL ◆ **(by) ~ !** mince (alors) !*, bon sang !* ◆ **and by ~ he did it!** et il l'a fait nom de Dieu ! N *(Brit)* ⇒ **golliwog**

golosh /gəˈlɒʃ/ N ⇒ **galosh**

Gomorrah /gəˈmɒrə/ N Gomorrhe

gonad /ˈgəʊnæd/ N gonade *f*

gonadotrophin /ˌɡɒnədəʊˈtrəʊfɪn/, **gonadotropin** /ˌɡɒnədəʊˈtrəʊpɪn/, N gonadotrophine *f*

gonadotropic /ˌɡɒnədəʊˈtrəʊpɪk/ ADJ gonadotrope

gondola /ˈɡɒndələ/ N 1 (= *boat*) gondole *f* 2 *[of balloon, airship]* nacelle *f* 3 (*in supermarket*) gondole *f* ; (*US Rail:* also **gondola car**) wagon-tombereau *m*

gondolier /ˌɡɒndəˈlɪəʳ/ N gondolier *m*

Gondwana /ɡɒndˈwɑːnə/ N (also **Gondwanaland**) Gondwana *m*

gone /ɡɒn/ VB ptp of **go** ADJ 1 ◆ **to be ~** *[object, enthusiasm etc]* avoir disparu ◆ **the coffee is all ~** il n'y a plus de café ◆ **the trees have been ~ for years** cela fait des années qu'il n'y a plus d'arbres ◆ **~ are the days when ...** le temps n'est plus où ... ◆ **he is ~** il est parti ; (*euph = dead*) il n'est plus ◆ **to be long ~** ne plus exister depuis longtemps ◆ **to be far ~** (= *ill*) être très bas *or* mal ; (* = *drunk, on drugs*) être cassé‡ ◆ **she was six months ~** * (= *pregnant*) elle était enceinte de six mois ◆ **to be ~ on sb** * en pincer pour qn * ◆ **be ~!** († *or hum*) allez-vous-en ! 2 (*Brit* = *after*) **it's just ~ three** il est 3 heures et quelques ◆ **it was ~ four before he came** il était plus de 4 heures *or* 4 heures passées quand il est arrivé

goner * /ˈɡɒnəʳ/ N ◆ **to be a ~** être fichu * *or* foutu‡

gong /ɡɒŋ/ N 1 (*Mus*) gong *m* 2 (*Brit hum = medal*) médaille *f*

gonna * /ˈɡənə/ (*esp US*) ⇒ **going to**

gonorrhoea /ˌɡɒnəˈrɪə/ N blennorragie *f*

gonzo‡ /ˈɡɒnzəʊ/ ADJ (*US*) (= *crazy*) déjanté ; *[journalist] qui s'implique dans les événements qu'il relate (et se comporte souvent de façon excentrique)*

goo * /ɡuː/ N matière *f* visqueuse *or* gluante ; (= *sentimentality*) sentimentalité *f* à l'eau de rose COMP **goo-goo eyes** * N (*US*) ◆ **to make goo-goo eyes at sb** (*hum*) faire les yeux doux à qn

good /ɡʊd/

compar **better**, superl **best**

1 ADJECTIVE
2 ADVERB
3 NOUN
4 NPL
5 COMPOUNDS

1 – ADJECTIVE

When **good** is part of a set combination, eg **a good thrashing**, **in a good temper**, **a good deal of**, **good heavens**, look up the noun.

1 = pleasant *[trip, holiday, news, mood]* bon ; *[weather, life]* beau (belle *f*) ◆ **his ~ nature** son bon caractère ◆ **I've got some ~ news for you** j'ai de bonnes nouvelles pour toi ◆ **have you had a ~ day?** est-ce que tu as passé une bonne journée ? ◆ **I've had a ~ life** j'ai eu une belle vie ◆ **we had a ~ time** nous nous sommes bien amusés ◆ **there are ~ times ahead** l'avenir est prometteur ◆ **he's a ~ chap** * c'est un brave *or* chic type * ◆ **it's too much** *or* **you can have too much of a ~ thing** c'est presque trop

♦ **it's good to** ◆ **it's ~ to be here** cela fait plaisir d'être ici ◆ **it's ~ to see you looking so well** ça fait plaisir de te voir en si bonne forme ◆ **it's ~ to see you** je suis content de te voir ◆ **it's ~ to talk** ça fait du bien de parler ◆ **it's ~ to be alive** il fait bon vivre ◆ **it's too ~ to be true** c'est trop beau pour être vrai

2 = kind gentil ◆ **be ~ to him** soyez gentil avec lui ◆ **that's very ~ of you** c'est très gentil de votre part, vous êtes bien gentil ◆ **I tried to find something ~ to say about him** j'ai essayé de trouver quelque chose de bien à dire sur lui ◆ **would you be ~ enough to tell me** auriez-vous l'obligeance de me dire ◆ **perhaps you'd be ~ enough to check your facts before accusing me** vous feriez peut-être mieux de vérifier les faits avant de m'accuser

3 = efficient, competent bon ◆ **she was a ~ wife and mother** elle a été une bonne épouse et une bonne mère ◆ **I've got a ~ teacher/doctor/lawyer** j'ai un bon professeur/médecin/avocat ◆ **I think I'm as ~ as him** je pense que je suis aussi bon que lui ◆ **40% of candidates are not ~ enough to pass** 40% des candidats ne sont pas assez bons pour être reçus ◆ **he's as ~ a player as his brother** il joue aussi bien que son frère

♦ **good at** (*academic subject*) bon en ◆ **~ at French** bon en français ◆ **he's ~ at everything** il est bon en tout ◆ **she's ~ at singing** elle chante bien ◆ **she's ~ at putting people at their ease** elle sait mettre les gens à l'aise

♦ **good with** ◆ **she's ~ with children/dogs** elle sait s'y prendre avec les enfants/les chiens ◆ **she's ~ with her hands** elle est habile de ses mains

4 = upright, virtuous ◆ **he's a ~ man** c'est un homme bon ◆ **a ~ and holy man** un saint homme ◆ **to live** *or* **lead a ~ life** mener une vie vertueuse ◆ **he sounds too ~ to be true!** mais c'est une vraie perle ! ◆ **to do ~ works** faire de bonnes œuvres ◆ **the 12 ~ men and true** les 12 jurés

5 = respected ◆ **send us a photo of your ~ self** envoyez-nous une photo de vous ◆ **your ~ lady (wife)** (*hum*) Madame votre épouse ◆ **yes, my ~ man** (*hum*) oui, mon brave

6 = well-behaved *[child, animal]* sage ◆ **be ~!** sois sage ! ◆ **be a ~ girl!** sois sage ! ◆ **Andrew was as ~ as gold** Andrew a été sage comme une image

7 = at ease ◆ **I feel ~** je me sens bien ◆ **I don't feel too ~ about that** * (= *ashamed*) j'ai un peu honte de moi ◆ **I started to feel ~ about myself** j'ai commencé à me sentir bien dans ma peau *

8 = close *[friend]* bon ◆ **he's a ~ friend of mine** c'est un bon ami à moi ◆ **my ~ friend Laura** ma bonne amie Laura

9 = high quality de qualité ◆ **always use ~ ingredients** utilisez toujours des ingrédients de qualité ◆ **it's made of ~ leather** c'est en cuir de bonne qualité ◆ **it's important to have ~ equipment** il est important d'avoir du matériel de qualité *or* du bon matériel BUT **nothing was too ~ for his wife** rien n'était trop beau pour sa femme ◆ **this is my only ~ dress** c'est la seule robe habillée que j'aie

10 = creditable *[result, mark]* bon ◆ **200 was a ~ score in those conditions** 200 était un bon résultat dans ces conditions ◆ **he came in a ~ third** il s'est honorablement classé troisième

11 = satisfactory *[reason, excuse]* bon, valable ◆ **unless you have a ~ excuse** à moins que vous n'ayez une bonne excuse *or* une excuse valable ◆ **it's as ~ a way as any other** c'est une façon comme une autre

♦ **good enough** ◆ **that's ~ enough for me** cela me suffit ◆ **that's not ~ enough** ça ne suffit pas ◆ **a refreshment voucher! that's not ~ enough!** un bon pour une boisson ! mais vous vous moquez de moi ! ◆ **it's just not ~ enough!** (*indignantly*) c'est lamentable !, c'est inadmissible ! ◆ **it is not ~ enough to say parents control what children watch** cela ne suffit pas de dire que les parents doivent surveiller ce que regardent leurs enfants

12 = beneficial bon (*for* pour) ◆ **milk is ~ for children** le lait est bon pour les enfants ◆ **it's ~ for you** c'est bon pour la santé ◆ **this climate is not ~ for one's health** ce climat est mauvais pour la santé *or* est insalubre BUT **the shock was ~ for him** le choc lui a été salutaire ◆ **all this excitement isn't ~ for me !** (*hum*) toutes ces émotions, ça ne me vaut rien ! ◆ **it's ~ for the soul !** (*hum*) ça forme le caractère !

♦ **what's good for** ◆ **if you know what's ~ for you you'll say yes** si tu as le moindre bon sens tu accepteras ◆ **what's ~ for the consumer isn't necessarily ~ for the economy** ce qui est bon pour le consommateur ne l'est pas forcément pour l'économie

♦ **more than is good for** ◆ **they tend to eat and drink more than is ~ for them** ils ont tendance à boire et à manger plus que de raison ◆ **some children know more than is ~ for them** certains enfants en savent plus qu'ils ne le devraient

13 = wholesome, in sound condition bon ◆ **the water of the well is still ~** l'eau du puits est encore bonne *or* saine ◆ **their stock of food is still ~** leurs stocks de nourriture sont encore bons ◆ **how ~ is her eyesight?** est-ce qu'elle a une bonne vue ? ◆ **his hearing is ~** il entend bien ◆ **to stay ~** *[food]* (bien) se conserver

14 = attractive joli, beau (belle *f*) ◆ **she's got a ~ figure** elle a un joli corps, elle est bien faite ◆ **you've got ~ hair** tu as de beaux cheveux ◆ **she's got ~ legs** elle a de jolies jambes ◆ **you have to be of ~ appearance** vous devez bien présenter ◆ **you look ~ in that** ◆ **that looks ~ on you** ça vous va bien ◆ **you look ~ !** (= *healthy*) tu as bonne mine ! ; (= *well-dressed*) tu es très bien comme ça !

15 Naut ◆ **the ~ ship Domino** le Domino

16 = advantageous, favourable *[terms, deal, offer]* intéressant ; *[omen, opportunity]* bon ◆ **it would be a ~ thing to ask him** il serait bon de lui demander ◆ **it's a ~ chance to sort things out** c'est l'occasion ou jamais de régler le problème ; (*Gambling*) ◆ **I've had a ~ day** la chance était avec moi aujourd'hui ◆ **he's on to a ~ thing** * il a trouvé le filon * *or* un bon filon * ◆ **this is as ~ a time as any to do it** autant le faire maintenant ◆ **you've never had it so ~ !** * la vie n'a jamais été aussi facile

17 = lucky ◆ **it's a ~ thing** *or* **job I was there** heureusement que j'étais là, c'est une chance que j'aie été là ◆ **that's a ~ thing!** tant mieux !, très bien !

18 = upper-class ◆ **to live at a ~ address** habiter dans un beau quartier ◆ **he's got no money but he's of ~ family** il n'a pas d'argent mais il est de bonne famille

19 = reliable, valid *[car, tools, machinery]* bon ◆ **it's a ~ little car** c'est une bonne petite voiture ◆ **he is a ~ risk** (*financially*) c'est un client sûr ◆ **is his credit ~ ?** peut-on lui faire crédit ?

♦ **good for** ◆ **this ticket is ~ for three months** ce billet est valable trois mois ◆ **he's ~ for another 20 years yet** * il en a encore bien pour 20 ans ◆ **my car is ~ for another few years** ma voiture fera *or* tiendra bien encore quelques années ◆ **I'm ~ for another mile or two** je me sens de force à faire quelques kilomètres de plus ◆ **he is** *or* **his credit is ~ for £9,000** on peut lui faire crédit jusqu'à 9 000 livres ◆ **what** *or* **how much is he ~ for?** de combien (d'argent) dispose-t-il ? ◆ **he's ~ for £500** (= *will lend*) il nous (*or* vous *etc*) prêtera bien 500 livres ◆ **are you ~ for another beer?** * tu reprendras bien une autre bière ? ; see also **compounds**

20 = thorough ◆ **to have a ~ cry** pleurer un bon coup *or* tout son soûl

Verb + adverb may be used in French, instead of adjective + noun. For combinations other than the following, look up the noun.

◆ **give it a ~ rinse** rincez-le bien *or* à grande eau ◆ **give it a ~ stir** mélangez-le bien

21 = considerable, not less than bon, grand ◆ **a ~ distance** une bonne distance ◆ **it will take you a ~ hour** il vous faudra une bonne heure ◆ **we waited a ~ fifteen minutes** nous avons

attendu un bon quart d'heure ◆ **a ~ 8 kilometres** 8 bons kilomètres, 8 kilomètres au moins

22 in greetings ◆ ~ **afternoon** *(early)* bonjour ; *(later)* bonsoir ; *(on leaving)* bonsoir ◆ ~ **day** † (= *goodbye*) au revoir ; (= *good morning*) bonjour ◆ ~ **evening** bonsoir ◆ ~ **morning** bonjour ◆ **Robert sends (his) ~ wishes** Robert envoie ses amitiés ◆ **with every ~ wish, with all ~ wishes** *(in letter)* cordialement

23 in exclamations ◆ **oh ~, Tom's just arrived** tiens justement, Tom vient d'arriver ◆ **very ~, sir!** (très) bien monsieur ! ◆ **~ for YOU!, ~ on you!** bravo ! ◆ **(that's) ~!** bien !, excellent ! ◆ **that's a ~ one!** *[joke, story]* elle est (bien) bonne celle-là ! * *(iro)*, à d'autres ! * ◆ **~ one!** * (= *well done, well said*) bravo ! *(also iro)*

24 emphatic use ◆ **we had a ~ long talk** nous avons bien *or* longuement discuté ◆ **a ~ long walk** une bonne *or* une grande promenade ◆ **they're expecting it to take a ~ long time** ils pensent que ça va prendre un bon bout de temps ◆ **~ old Charles!** * ce (bon) vieux Charles ! ◆ **~ strong shoes** de bonnes chaussures

◆ **good and ...** * ◆ **the soup was served ~ and hot** la soupe a été servie bien chaude ◆ **I'll go when I'm ~ and ready** je partirai quand ça me chante * ◆ **I told him off ~ and proper** * je lui ai passé un bon savon *, je l'ai bien engueulé ‡

25 set structures

◆ **as good as** (= *practically*) pratiquement, pour ainsi dire ◆ **his career is as ~ as over** sa carrière est pratiquement terminée ◆ **the matter is as ~ as settled** c'est comme si l'affaire était réglée, l'affaire est pour ainsi dire *or* pratiquement réglée ◆ **she as ~ as told me that ...** elle m'a dit à peu de chose près que ..., elle m'a pour ainsi dire déclaré que ... ◆ **it was as ~ as a holiday** c'étaient presque des vacances ◆ **he as ~ as called me a liar** il n'a pas dit que je mentais mais c'était tout comme *, il m'a pratiquement traité de menteur ◆ **it's as ~ as saying that ...** autant dire que ... ◆ **he was as ~ as his word** il a tenu promesse

◆ **as good as new** *[thing]* comme neuf (neuve *f*) ◆ **in a day or so he'll be as ~ as new** *[person]* dans un jour ou deux il sera complètement rétabli

◆ **to make good** (= *succeed*) faire son chemin, réussir ; *[ex-criminal]* s'acheter une conduite * ; (= *compensate for*) *[+ deficit]* combler ; *[+ deficiency, losses]* compenser ; *[+ expenses]* rembourser ; (= *put right*) *[+ injustice, damage]* réparer ◆ **to make ~ an assertion** justifier une affirmation ◆ **to make ~ one's escape** réussir son évasion ◆ **to make ~ a loss to sb** dédommager qn d'une perte ◆ **to make ~ a promise** tenir une promesse ◆ **they were sure he would make ~ his threat** ils étaient sûrs qu'il mettrait sa menace à exécution

2 - ADVERB

* = well bien ◆ **you did ~** tu as bien fait ◆ **how are you? – ~!** *(esp US)* comment vas-tu ? – bien ! ◆ **to be in ~ with sb** être dans les petits papiers * de qn

3 - NOUN

1 = virtue, righteousness bien *m* ◆ **~ and evil may co-exist within one family** le bien et le mal peuvent se côtoyer au sein d'une même famille ◆ **for ~ or ill** pour le meilleur et *or* ou pour le pire ◆ **he is a power for ~** il exerce une bonne influence ◆ **there's some ~ in him** il a de bons côtés

2 = good deeds ◆ **to do ~** faire le bien ◆ **she's up to no ~** * elle prépare un mauvais coup *

3 = advantage, profit bien *m* ◆ **it's for his own ~** c'est pour son bien ◆ **I did it for your ~** je l'ai fait pour ton bien ◆ **for the ~ of the country** pour le bien du pays ◆ **the common ~** l'intérêt *m* commun ◆ **a lot of ~ that's done!** nous voilà bien avancés ! ◆ **a lot of ~ that's done you!** te voilà bien avancé ! ◆ **he'll come to no ~** il finira mal

◆ **to do sb good** faire du bien à qn ◆ **that will do you ~** cela vous fera du bien ◆ **what ~ will that do you?** ça t'avancera à quoi ? ◆ **a (fat) lot of ~ that will do (you)!** * tu seras bien avancé !, ça te fera une belle jambe ! * ◆ **much ~ may it do you!** grand bien te fasse ! ◆ **a lot of ~ that's done him!** le voilà bien avancé ! ◆ **it does my heart ~ to see him** ça me réjouit de le voir

4 = use ◆ **what's the ~?** à quoi bon ? ◆ **what's the ~ of hurrying?** à quoi bon se presser ? ◆ **it's not much ~ to me** *[advice, suggestion]* ça ne m'avance pas à grand-chose ; *[object, money]* ça ne me sert pas à grand-chose ◆ **if that is any ~ to you** si ça peut t'être utile *or* te rendre service ◆ **is he any ~?** *[worker/singer etc]* est-ce qu'il est bon ? ◆ **that won't be much ~** cela ne servira pas à grand-chose

◆ **no good** (= *useless*) ◆ **it's no ~** ça ne sert à rien ◆ **it's no ~ saying that** ça ne sert à rien de dire cela, inutile de dire cela ◆ **it's no ~ worrying** ça ne sert à rien de se faire du souci ◆ **it's no ~, I'll never get it finished in time** il n'y a rien à faire, je n'arriverai jamais à le finir à temps ◆ **that's no ~** ça ne va pas ◆ **that's no ~, it's too thick** ça ne va pas, c'est trop épais ◆ **I'm no ~ at maths** je suis mauvais en maths

5 → **goods**

6 set structures

◆ **for good** pour de bon ◆ **he's gone for ~** il est parti pour de bon ◆ **for ~ and all** une (bonne) fois pour toutes ◆ **to settle down for ~** se fixer définitivement

◆ **to the good** ◆ **we were £50 to the ~** nous avions fait 50 livres de bénéfice ◆ **that's all to the ~!** tant mieux !, c'est autant de gagné !

4 - NPL

the good (= *people*) les bons *mpl* ◆ **the ~ and the bad** les bons *mpl* et les méchants *mpl* BUT **the ~ die young** ce sont toujours les meilleurs qui partent les premiers

5 - COMPOUNDS

the Good Book N la Bible
good-for-nothing ADJ bon *or* propre à rien N bon *m*, bonne *f* à rien, propre *mf* à rien
Good Friday N Vendredi *m* saint
good-hearted ADJ qui a bon cœur, bon
good-heartedness N bonté *f*
good-humoured ADJ *[person]* de bonne humeur, jovial ; *[appearance, smile etc]* jovial ; *[joke]* sans malice
good-humouredly ADV avec bonne humeur, avec bonhomie
good-looker * N (= *man*) beau gosse * *m* ; (= *woman*) belle *or* jolie fille *f* ; (= *horse*) beau cheval *m*
good-looking ADJ beau (belle *f*), bien *inv*
good looks NPL beauté *f*
good-natured ADJ *[person]* accommodant, facile à vivre ; *[smile, laughter]* bon enfant *inv*
good-naturedly ADV gentiment
Good Neighbor Policy N *(US Pol)* politique *f* de bon voisinage
good-oh * EXCL *(Brit, Austral)* youpi
good-sized ADJ assez grand ; *[portion]* bon (*f* bonne) ◆ **a ~-sized steak** un bon (gros) steak
good-tempered ADJ *[person]* qui a bon caractère ; *[smile, look]* aimable, gentil
good-time girl * N *(pej)* fille *f* qui ne pense qu'à s'amuser *or* qu'à prendre du bon temps

---

goodbye /ˌgʊdˈbaɪ/ EXCL au revoir ◆ **to say** *or* **bid** † **~ to sb** dire au revoir à qn, faire ses adieux à qn *(frm)* ◆ **~ to all that!** fini tout cela ! ◆ **you can say ~ to all your hopes** tu peux dire adieu à toutes tes espérances ◆ **you can say ~ to peace and quiet!** tu peux dire adieu à ta tranquillité ! ◆ **you can kiss it ~!** * tu peux faire une croix dessus ! *

goodie * /ˈgʊdɪ/ ⇒ **goody**

goodish /ˈgʊdɪʃ/ ADJ assez bon *or* bien

goodly /ˈgʊdlɪ/ ADJ 1 (= *reasonable*) *[number, supply]* considérable ; *[portion, amount]* gros (grosse *f*) ; *[size]* grand ◆ **to have a ~ share of sth** avoir plus que sa part de qch 2 († *or liter* = *attractive*) *[appearance]* beau (belle *f*), gracieux

goodness /ˈgʊdnɪs/ N 1 *[of person]* bonté *f* ◆ **out of the ~ of his heart** par pure gentillesse ◆ **(my) ~!** *, **~ gracious!** * juste ciel !, bonté divine ! ◆ **~ (only) knows** * Dieu (seul) sait ◆ **for ~' sake** * pour l'amour de Dieu ◆ **I wish to ~ I had gone there!** * si seulement j'y étais allé ! ◆ **I wish to ~ I had never met him!** * si seulement j'avais pu ne jamais le rencontrer !, si seulement je ne l'avais jamais rencontré ! ; → **surely, thank** 2 *(in food)* qualités *fpl* nutritives ◆ **to be full of natural ~** être plein de bonnes choses

goodnight /gʊdˈnaɪt/ EXCL bonsoir, bonne nuit ◆ **to bid sb ~** souhaiter le *or* dire bonsoir à qn ◆ **to give sb a ~ kiss** embrasser qn *(en lui disant bonne nuit)*

goods /gʊdz/ NPL 1 *(Comm)* marchandises *fpl*, articles *mpl* ◆ **leather ~** articles *mpl* de cuir, maroquinerie *f* ◆ **knitted ~** articles *mpl* en tricot ◆ **to have the ~ on sb** * *(US)* en savoir long sur qn ; → **consumer, deliver** 2 *(Jur)* biens *mpl*, meubles *mpl* ◆ **all his ~ and chattels** tous ses biens et effets

COMP **goods service** N *(Brit Rail)* ◆ **to send by fast/slow ~ service** envoyer en grande/petite vitesse
goods siding N *(Brit Rail)* voie *f* de garage pour wagons de marchandises
goods station N *(Brit Rail)* gare *f* de marchandises
goods train N *(Brit Rail)* train *m* de marchandises
goods wagon N *(Brit Rail)* wagon *m* de marchandises
goods yard N *(Brit Rail)* dépôt *m or* cour *f* des marchandises

goodwill /ˌgʊdˈwɪl/ N 1 bonne volonté *f* ◆ **to gain sb's ~** se faire bien voir de qn ◆ **~ mission** *or* **tour** *(Pol)* visite *f* d'amitié 2 (= *willingness*) zèle *m* ◆ **to work with ~** travailler de bon cœur *or* avec zèle 3 *(Comm* = *customer connections)* (biens *mpl*) incorporels *mpl*, clientèle *f* ; *(Accounting* = *intangible assets)* survaloir *m*, goodwill *m* ◆ **the ~ goes with the business** les incorporels sont vendus *or* la clientèle est vendue avec le fonds de commerce COMP **goodwill ambassador** N ambassadeur *m*, -drice *f* de bonne volonté

goody * /ˈgʊdɪ/ EXCL (also **goody goody**) chic ! *, chouette ! * N 1 (= *person*) ◆ **the goodies and the baddies** * les bons *mpl* et les méchants *mpl* 2 ◆ **goodies** * (= *treats*) friandises *fpl* ; (= *gifts*) petits cadeaux *mpl*

COMP **goody bag** * N sachet *m* de cadeaux, pochette *f* de cadeaux promotionnels
goody-goody * ADJ *(pej)* ◆ **to be goody-goody** *[child]* être l'image du petit garçon (*or* de la petite fille) modèle ; *[adult]* être un vrai petit saint N modèle *m* de vertu *(iro)*, petit(e) saint(e) * *m(f)*
goody two-shoes * N *(pej)* modèle *m* de vertu *(iro)*, petit(e) saint(e) * *m(f)*

gooey * /ˈguːɪ/ ADJ (= *sticky*) *[substance, mess]* gluant ; *[cake, dessert]* fondant ; *(pej)* (= *sentimental*) *[film, story]* à l'eau de rose *(pej)* ◆ **to go (all) ~** devenir bêtement sentimental ◆ **women went ~ over him** il faisait fondre toutes les femmes

goof * /guːf/ N (= *idiot*) toqué(e) ‡ *m(f)* VI faire une gaffe, gaffer *

► **goof around** * VI *(US)* faire l'imbécile
► **goof off** * VI *(US)* tirer au flanc

► **goof up** * VI (US) faire une gaffe, gaffer* VT SEP gâcher

goofball * /ˈguːfbɔːl/ N 1 *(= drug)* barbiturique *m* 2 *(US = eccentric person)* fantaisiste *mf*, numéro* *m*

goofy * /ˈguːfɪ/ ADJ *(= mad)* maboul*, toqué* ; *(esp US) (= silly)* niais

Google ® /ˈguːgl/ N Google ® *m* VI faire *or* lancer une recherche Google VT *(= do search on)* *[+ person]* googler, *chercher des renseignements sur (qn) au moyen d'Internet*

googly /ˈguːglɪ/ N *(Cricket) balle lancée de manière à tromper le batteur sur la direction qu'elle va prendre*

gook * /guːk/ N (US) 1 *(= slime)* substance *f* visqueuse ; *(= dirt)* crasse *f* ◆ **what's this ~?** qu'est-ce que c'est que cette saloperie* ? 2 *(pej = Asian etc)* Asiate *mf (pej)*

goolies ** /ˈguːlɪz/ NPL couilles** *fpl*

goon * /guːn/ N *(= fool)* idiot(e) *m(f)*, imbécile *mf* ; (US) *(= hired thug)* homme *m* de main ; *(= prison camp guard)* garde-chiourme *m*

gooney bird * /ˈguːnɪˌbɜːd/ N (US) albatros *m*

goop * /guːp/ N *(esp US)* substance *f* visqueuse

goosander /guːˈsændəʳ/ N harle *m* bièvre

goose /guːs/ (pl **geese**) N oie *f* ◆ **all his geese are swans** il exagère tout le temps, il en rajoute toujours ◆ **to kill the ~ that lays the golden eggs** tuer la poule aux œufs d'or ◆ **don't be such a ~!** † * ne sois pas si bébête ! * ◆ **silly little ~!** * petite dinde ! * ; → **boo, cook, mother** VT *(esp US * = prod) donner un petit coup sur les fesses de*

COMP **goose bumps** NPL ⇒ **goose pimples**
goose chase N → **wild**
goose flesh N ⇒ **goose pimples**
goose pimples NPL ◆ **to come out in ~ pimples** avoir la chair de poule ◆ **that gives me ~ pimples** cela me donne la chair de poule
goose-step N pas *m* de l'oie VI faire le pas de l'oie ◆ **to ~-step along/in** *etc* avancer/entrer *etc* au pas de l'oie

gooseberry /ˈgʊzbərɪ/ N *(= fruit)* groseille *f* à maquereau ; (also **gooseberry bush**) groseillier *m* ◆ **to play ~** *(Brit)* tenir la chandelle

goosegog * /ˈgʊzgɒg/ N *(Brit)* ⇒ **gooseberry**

GOP /ˌdʒiːəʊˈpiː/ N (US) (abbrev of **Grand Old Party**) → **grand**

gopher /ˈgəʊfəʳ/ N 1 *(= squirrel)* spermophile *m* ; *(= rodent)* gauphre *m*, gaufre *m* 2 ⇒ **gofer** 3 *(Comput)* gopher *m* COMP **the Gopher State** N (US) le Minnesota

gorblimey * /ˌgɔːˈblaɪmɪ/ ADJ *[accent]* populaire EXCL *(Brit)* nom d'un chien ! *

Gordian /ˈgɔːdɪən/ N ◆ **to cut** *or* **untie the ~ knot** trancher le nœud gordien

gore¹ /gɔːʳ/ N *(= blood)* sang *m*

gore² /gɔːʳ/ VT *(= injure)* encorner, blesser d'un coup de corne ◆ **~d to death** tué d'un coup de corne

gore³ /gɔːʳ/ N *(Sewing)* godet *m* ; *[of sail]* pointe *f* VT *[+ sail]* mettre une pointe à ◆ **~d skirt** jupe *f* à godets

gorge /gɔːdʒ/ N 1 *(Geog)* gorge *f*, défilé *m* 2 *(Anat)* gorge *f*, gosier *m* ◆ **it makes my ~ rise** cela me soulève le cœur VT ◆ **to ~ o.s.** se gaver *(with* de) VI se gaver *(on* de)

gorgeous /ˈgɔːdʒəs/ ADJ 1 *(= beautiful) [scenery, sunset, colour, house]* superbe, splendide ; *[weather, day]* formidable, superbe ; *[food, wine]* sensationnel ◆ **to look ~** avoir l'air superbe ◆ **to smell ~** sentir délicieusement bon 2 *(* = attractive) [person]* superbe ; *[eyes, hair]* splendide ◆ **a ~ blonde** une superbe blonde ◆ **a ~ hunk** un mec* superbe ◆ **hi, ~!** *(to female)* salut, beauté ! * ; *(to male)* salut, playboy ! * 3 *(liter = sumptuous) [clothes, fabric, jewellery, building]* somptueux

gorgeously /ˈgɔːdʒəslɪ/ ADV *[embroidered, dressed]* superbement, splendidement ◆ **~ coloured** aux couleurs superbes *or* splendides

Gorgons /ˈgɔːgənz/ NPL *(Myth)* Gorgones *fpl*

gorilla /gəˈrɪlə/ N 1 *(= animal)* gorille *m* 2 *(* pej) (= bodyguard)* gorille* *m*

Gorki, Gorky /ˈgɔːkɪ/ N Gorki *m*

gormandize /ˈgɔːməndaɪz/ VI *(pej)* se goinfrer*, s'empiffrer*

gormless * /ˈgɔːmlɪs/ ADJ *(Brit)* empoté

gorse /gɔːs/ N *(NonC)* ajoncs *mpl* ◆ **~ bush** ajonc *m*

gory /ˈgɔːrɪ/ ADJ sanglant ◆ **tell me all the ~ details!** * *(hum)* raconte-moi tous les détails sordides ! *(hum)*

gosh * /gɒʃ/ EXCL dites donc !, mince alors ! *

goshawk /ˈgɒshɔːk/ N autour *m*

gosling /ˈgɒzlɪŋ/ N oison *m*

gospel /ˈgɒspəl/ N 1 évangile *m* ◆ **the Gospel according to St John** l'Évangile selon saint Jean ◆ **that's ~** * *(fig)* c'est parole d'évangile ◆ **to take** *or* **accept sth as ~** * accepter qch comme *or* prendre qch pour parole d'évangile 2 *(= music)* gospel *m*

COMP **gospel music** N gospel *m*
Gospel oath N serment *m* prêté sur l'Évangile
gospel song N gospel *m*, negro-spiritual *m*
gospel truth N *(fig)* ◆ **it's the ~ truth** * c'est parole d'évangile, c'est la vérité pure

gossamer /ˈgɒsəməʳ/ N 1 *(NonC) (= cobweb)* fils *mpl* de la Vierge ; *(= gauze)* gaze *f* ; *(= light fabric)* tulle *m*, gaze *f* 2 *(US = waterproof)* imperméable *m* léger ADJ *[thread, garment, wings] (= light)* arachnéen *(liter)*, léger ◆ **~ thin** très fin, fin comme de la gaze

gossip /ˈgɒsɪp/ N 1 *(NonC: pej = rumours)* commérages *mpl (pej)*, cancans *mpl (pej)* ; *(in newspaper)* échos *mpl*, potins *mpl (pej)* ◆ **I never listen to ~** je n'écoute jamais les commérages *or* les cancans ◆ **what's the latest ~?** quels sont les derniers potins ? ◆ **a piece of ~** un cancan, un ragot 2 *(= chat)* **we had a good old ~** on a bien papoté* 3 *(= person)* bavard(e) *m(f)*, commère *f (pej)* ◆ **he's a real ~** c'est une vraie commère VI 1 *(= chat)* bavarder, papoter 2 *(pej: maliciously)* cancaner, faire des commérages *(about* sur)

COMP **gossip column** N *(Press)* échos *mpl*
gossip columnist, gossip writer N échotier *m*, -ière *f*

gossiping /ˈgɒsɪpɪŋ/ ADJ *(= chatting)* bavard ; *(pej)* cancanier N *(idle)* bavardage *m*, papotage *m* ; *(pej: malicious)* commérage *m*

gossipy * /ˈgɒsɪpɪ/ ADJ *[style, book, letter]* plein de bavardages ; *(pej) [person]* cancanier *(pej)*

got /gɒt/ VB (pt, ptp of **get**) see also **have**

gotcha * /ˈgɒtʃə/ EXCL *(= I've got you)* 1 *(= I see)* pigé ! * 2 *(when catching sb, catching sb out)* je te tiens ! * ; *(when hitting, killing sb)* je t'ai eu ! *

Goth¹ /gɒθ/ N Goth *m*

Goth², goth /gɒθ/ *(esp Brit)* N 1 *(= person)* fan *mf* de goth 2 *(Mus)* goth *m (mouvement musical des années 80)* 3 *(= fashion)* mode *f* goth ADJ goth

Gothic /ˈgɒθɪk/ ADJ 1 *(Archit, Literat, Cine) (genuine)* gothique ; *(in Gothic style)* de style gothique 2 *(Hist)* des Goths N *(Archit, Ling etc)* gothique *m*

COMP **Gothic Revival** N *(Archit)* néogothique *m*
Gothic script N *(Printing)* écriture *f* gothique

gotta * /ˈgɒtə/ MODAL AUX VB *(esp US = have got to)* ◆ **I/he's/they ~ go** je dois/il doit/ils doivent partir

gotten /ˈgɒtn/ VB (US) ptp of **get**

gouache /gʊˈɑːʃ/ N gouache *f*

gouge /gaʊdʒ/ N gouge *f* VT 1 *[+ wood etc]* gouger ◆ **to ~ a hole in sth** creuser un trou dans qch 2 *(US * fig = overcharge etc)* estamper*, arnaquer

► **gouge out** VT SEP *(with gouge)* gouger ; *(with thumb, pencil etc)* évider ◆ **to ~ sb's eyes out** arracher les yeux à qn

goujons /ˈguːʒɒn/ NPL *(Culin) croquettes de poisson ou de poulet*

goulash /ˈguːlæʃ/ N goulache *m*, goulasch *m*

gourd /gʊəd/ N *(= fruit)* gourde *f* ; *(= container)* gourde *f*, calebasse *f*

gourmand /ˈgʊəmənd/ N gourmand(e) *m(f)*, glouton(ne) *m(f)*

gourmet /ˈgʊəmeɪ/ N gourmet *m*, gastronome *mf* ADJ *[food, restaurant]* gastronomique

gout /gaʊt/ N *(Med)* goutte *f*

gouty /ˈgaʊtɪ/ ADJ *[person, joint, condition]* goutteux

gov * /gʌv/ N abbrev of **governor 2**

Gov. N abbrev of **governor 1**

govern /ˈgʌvən/ VT 1 *(= rule) [person, government] [+ country]* gouverner, diriger ; *[+ province, city]* administrer ; *(= direct) [+ household, business, company]* diriger, gérer ; *[+ affairs]* administrer, gérer ◆ **she ~ed Britain from 1979 to 1990** elle a gouverné la Grande-Bretagne de 1979 à 1990

2 *(= control) [law, rule, principle] [+ conduct, behaviour, treatment]* régir ◆ **~ed by the laws of England** *(Jur)* régi par le droit anglais ◆ **international guidelines ~ing the export of arms** les directives internationales régissant l'exportation des armes ◆ **there are strict rules ~ing how much lawyers can charge** il existe des règles strictes fixant le montant des honoraires des avocats

3 *(= influence) [+ events]* déterminer, régir ; *[+ opinions]* guider ; *[+ speed]* déterminer

4 *(fig frm) [+ passions, emotions]* maîtriser, dominer ◆ **to ~ one's temper** se maîtriser

5 *(Gram)* régir

VI *(Pol)* gouverner

governance /ˈgʌvənəns/ N *(frm) (= governing)* gouvernement *m* ; *(= authority)* autorité *f*

governess /ˈgʌvənɪs/ N gouvernante *f*, institutrice *f (à domicile)*

governing /ˈgʌvənɪŋ/ ADJ *[party, coalition]* au pouvoir ; *[council, board]* d'administration ; *[committee]* directeur (-trice *f*) ; see also **self-governing;** → **self**

COMP **governing body** N *[of sport]* comité *m* directeur ; *[of professional association]* conseil *m* d'administration ; *[of school]* conseil *m* d'établissement ; *[of university]* conseil *m* d'université
governing class N classe *f* gouvernante
governing principle N principe *m* directeur

government /ˈgʌvənmənt/ N *[of country]* gouvernement *m* ; *[of province, city]* administration *f* ; *(= Cabinet of ministers)* gouvernement *m* ; *(= the State:* also **central government**) État *m*, pouvoirs *mpl* publics ; *(= local, municipal, regional)* administration *f* territoriale ; *(= political régime)* régime *m* politique ◆ **a project financed by the ~** un projet financé par l'État ◆ **a presidential/democratic system of ~** un régime présidentiel/démocratique ◆ **we've had five years of socialist ~** on a eu cinq années de gouvernement *or* gestion socialiste ; see also **local**

COMP *[policy, decision, intervention, spending]* gouvernemental, du gouvernement ; *[backing]* du gouvernement ; *[grant]* gouvernemental, d'État ; *[responsibility, loan]* de l'État, public (-ique *f*)
Government Accounting Office N (US) ≃ Cour *f* des comptes
government action N *(gen)* action *f* gouvernementale ; *(Insurance)* fait *m* du prince
government bond N *(Fin)* obligation *f* d'État

government corporation N (US) régie *f* d'État
government department N département *m or* service *m* gouvernemental
government expenditure N dépenses *fpl* publiques
Government House N (Brit) palais *m or* résidence *f* du gouverneur
government issue ADJ *[equipment]* fourni par le gouvernement ; *[bonds etc]* émis par le gouvernement
government monopoly N monopole *m* d'État
government-owned corporation N établissement *m* public autonome
Government Printing Office N (US) ≃ Imprimerie *f* nationale
government securities NPL (Fin) fonds *mpl or* titres *mpl* d'État
government stock N (Fin) fonds *mpl* publics *or* d'État

governmental /ˌgʌvənˈmentl/ ADJ gouvernemental, du gouvernement

governor /ˈgʌvənəʳ/ N 1 *[of state, bank]* gouverneur *m* ; *(esp Brit) [of prison]* directeur *m*, -trice *f* ; *[of institution]* administrateur *m*, -trice *f* ; *(Brit Scol)* ≃ membre *m* d'un conseil d'établissement *(de lycée ou d'IUT)* ◆ ~ **general** *(Brit)* gouverneur *m* général 2 *(Brit ⁑) (= employer)* patron *m* ; *(= father)* paternel* *m* ◆ **thanks ~!** merci chef *or* patron ! 3 *(in mechanism)* régulateur *m* ; *(= speed control device)* limiteur *m* de vitesse

governorship /ˈgʌvənəʃɪp/ N fonctions *fpl* de gouverneur ◆ **during my** ~ pendant la durée de mes fonctions (de gouverneur)

govt. abbrev of **government**

gown /gaʊn/ N robe *f* ; *(Jur, Univ)* toge *f* ; → **town** VT *(liter)* revêtir *(in* de*)* habiller *(in* de*)*

goy /gɔɪ/ N (pl **goys** *or* **goyim** /ˈgɔɪɪm/) goy *mf*

GP /dʒiːˈpiː/ N (abbrev of **General Practitioner**) (médecin *m*) généraliste *m* ◆ **he's/she's a** ~ il/elle est (médecin) généraliste ◆ **to go to one's** ~ aller voir son médecin généraliste *or* traitant

GPA /ˌdʒiːpiːˈeɪ/ N (US) (abbrev of **grade point average**) → **grade**

GPMU /ˌdʒiːpiːemˈjuː/ N (Brit) (abbrev of **Graphical, Paper and Media Union**) *syndicat*

GPO /dʒiːpiːˈəʊ/ N 1 *(Brit Govt: formerly)* (abbrev of **General Post Office**) → **general** 2 *(US)* (abbrev of **Government Printing Office**) → **government**

GPS /dʒiːpiːˈes/ N (abbrev of **global positioning system**) GPS *m*

gr. abbrev of **gross adj 5**

grab /græb/ N 1 ◆ **to make a ~ for** *or* **at sth** faire un geste *or* un mouvement vif pour saisir qch ◆ **to be up for ~s*** *(= available)* être disponible ◆ **there are big money prizes up for ~s** il y a de grosses sommes d'argent à gagner
2 *(esp Brit) [of excavator]* benne *f* preneuse
VT 1 *(lit = take hold of) [+ object, one's belongings]* saisir ◆ **to ~ sth away from sb** arracher qch à qn, enlever qch à qn d'un geste brusque ◆ **he ~bed the pen from me** il m'a arraché le stylo ◆ **~ hold of this for a minute** tiens ça une minute ◆ **he ~bed (hold of) me** il m'a empoigné ◆ **she ~bed (hold of) him by the arm** elle l'a saisi *or* empoigné par le bras ◆ **I managed to ~ him before he left** *(fig)* j'ai réussi à lui mettre la main dessus avant qu'il s'en aille
2 *(= seize unlawfully) [+ land, power]* s'emparer de
3 *(* = snatch) [+ quick snack, sandwich]* avaler ; *[+ cigarette]* fumer rapidement ; *[+ seat]* prendre ◆ **I'll ~ a quick shower** je vais prendre une douche vite fait* ◆ **to ~ a quick nap** piquer un roupillon*
4 *(fig = attract, win) [+ sb's attention]* attirer, accaparer ; *(= take) [+ opportunity]* saisir ◆ **to ~ the headlines** *[person, story]* faire la une ◆ **they're trying to ~ a share of the market** ils essaient de prendre une part de marché ◆ **he ~bed* the audience at once** il a tout de suite captivé l'auditoire ◆ **that really ~bed* me** ça m'a vraiment emballé* ◆ **how does that ~ you?*** qu'est-ce que tu en dis ?*
VI ◆ **to ~ at a rope** essayer d'agripper une corde ◆ **don't ~!** *(to child)* doucement !, ne te jette pas dessus !
COMP **grab bag*** N (US) *(lit)* sac *m* (pour jouer à la pêche miraculeuse) ; *(fig)* mélange *m* hétéroclite

grabby* /ˈgræbɪ/ ADJ *(= greedy) [person]* gourmand *(fig)*, accapareur

grace /greɪs/ N 1 *(NonC) [of person, animal, movement]* grâce *f*
2 *(Rel)* grâce *f* ◆ **by the ~ of God** par la grâce de Dieu ◆ **there but for the ~ of God go I** cela aurait tout aussi bien pu être moi ◆ **in a state of ~** en état de grâce ◆ **to fall from ~** *(Rel)* perdre la grâce ; *(fig hum)* tomber en disgrâce, ne plus avoir la cote* ◆ **to say ~** *(before meals)* dire le bénédicité ; *(after meals)* dire les grâces ; → **year**
3 *(phrases)* ◆ **to be in sb's good/bad ~s** être bien/mal vu de qn, être en faveur/défaveur auprès de qn ◆ **to get into sb's good/bad ~s** se faire bien/mal voir de qn ◆ **to do sth with good/bad ~** faire qch de bonne/mauvaise grâce ◆ **he had the (good) ~ to apologize** il a eu la bonne grâce de s'excuser ◆ **his saving ~** ce qui le rachète *(or* rachetait *etc)* ; → **air**
4 *(NonC = respite)* grâce *f*, répit *m* ◆ **a day's ~** un jour de grâce *or* de répit ◆ **days of ~** *(Comm)* jours *mpl* de grâce ◆ **as an act of ~, he ...** *(Jur)* en exerçant son droit de grâce, il ...
5 *(= title)* ◆ **His Grace (the Archbishop)** Monseigneur l'Archevêque, Son Excellence l'Archevêque ◆ **His Grace (the Duke)** Monsieur le duc ◆ **Her Grace (the Duchess)** Madame la duchesse ◆ **yes, your Grace** oui, Monseigneur *(or* Monsieur le duc *or* Madame la duchesse)
6 *(Myth)* ◆ **the (three) Graces** les trois Grâces *fpl*
VT 1 *(= adorn)* orner, embellir *(with* de*)*
2 honorer *(with* de*)* ◆ **the queen ~d the performance with her presence** la reine honora la représentation de sa présence
COMP **grace-and-favour** N (Brit) ◆ **~-and-favour residence** *résidence attribuée à une personne pour la durée de sa vie par un roi ou un noble* ◆ **he has the use of the room on a ~-and-favour basis** *(fig)* il a l'usage de cette pièce (à titre gratuit)
grace note N *(Mus)* (note *f* d')ornement *m*
grace period N *(Jur, Fin)* délai *m* de grâce *or* de carence

graceful /ˈgreɪsfʊl/ ADJ *[movement, animal, person]* gracieux ; *[building, apology, retraction, refusal]* élégant

gracefully /ˈgreɪsfəlɪ/ ADV *[move]* avec grâce, gracieusement ; *[dance, accept, withdraw]* avec grâce ; *[retire]* avec dignité ; *[apologize]* élégamment, avec grâce ◆ **to admit defeat ~** s'avouer vaincu de bonne grâce ◆ **to grow old ~** vieillir avec grâce

gracefulness /ˈgreɪsfʊlnɪs/ N ⇒ **grace noun 1**

graceless /ˈgreɪslɪs/ ADJ *[dance, movement, building]* sans grâce ; *[person, refusal]* inélégant, peu courtois

gracious /ˈgreɪʃəs/ ADJ 1 *(frm = kindly) [person]* bienveillant ; *[smile, gesture]* gracieux, bienveillant ; *(= courteous) [person, smile, gesture]* courtois, affable ; *[action]* courtois, plein de bonne grâce ◆ **our ~ Queen** notre gracieuse souveraine ◆ **by the ~ consent of** par la grâce de ◆ **to be ~ to sb** se montrer bienveillant à l'égard de qn 2 *(= elegant) [house, room, gardens]* d'une élégance raffinée ; *[era]* fastueux ◆ **~ living** la vie de luxe 3 *(† = merciful) [God]* miséricordieux ◆ **Lord be ~ unto him** Seigneur, accordez-lui votre miséricorde EXCL * ◆ **(good** *or* **goodness) ~!** juste ciel !, bonté divine ! ◆ **(good** *or* **goodness) ~ yes!** bien sûr que oui ! ◆ **(good** *or* **goodness) ~ no!** jamais de la vie ! ◆ **(good** *or* **goodness) ~ me!** oh, mon Dieu !

graciously /ˈgreɪʃəslɪ/ ADV 1 *(frm = courteously) [wave, smile]* gracieusement, avec grâce ; *[accept, agree]* de bonne grâce ; *[consent, allow]* gracieusement ◆ **the king was ~ pleased to accept** *(frm)* le roi eut la bonté d'accepter, le roi accepta gracieusement 2 *(= elegantly) [live]* avec raffinement 3 *(= mercifully)* miséricordieusement

graciousness /ˈgreɪʃəsnɪs/ N *(NonC) [of person]* bienveillance *f (towards* envers*)* ; *[of house]* élégance *f* raffinée ; *[of God]* miséricorde *f*

grad* /græd/ N (US) abbrev of **graduate**

gradate /grəˈdeɪt/ VT graduer VI être gradué

gradation /grəˈdeɪʃən/ N gradation *f*

grade /greɪd/ N 1 *[of goods] (= quality)* qualité *f* ; *(= size)* calibre *m* ◆ **high-~ meat/fruit** viande *f*/fruits *mpl* de premier choix *or* de première qualité ◆ **high-~ steel/coal** acier *m*/charbon *m* de haute qualité ◆ **small-/large-~ eggs** œufs *mpl* de petit/gros calibre
2 *(= category, type)* catégorie *f* ◆ **prices vary according to the ~ of the hostel** le prix varie en fonction de la catégorie de l'établissement ◆ **a union that represents every ~ of staff** un syndicat qui représente toutes les catégories de personnel ◆ **the lowest ~ of skilled worker** la catégorie la plus basse des ouvriers qualifiés ◆ **the highest ~ of clerical post** la catégorie supérieure *or* la plus élevée des employés de bureau ◆ **make sure you install the right ~ of glass for the job** veillez à installer le type de verre qui convient ◆ **using a coarse ~ of steel wool** en utilisant une laine de verre épaisse
3 *(in hierarchy: in company etc)* échelon *m* ; *(in public sector)* grade *m* ; *(Mil = rank)* rang *m* ◆ **to go up a ~** monter d'un échelon ◆ **salary ~** échelon *m* (salarial) ◆ **she's on salary ~ three** elle est à l'indice trois ◆ **every ~ of competence** tous les niveaux de compétence
◆ **to make the grade** y arriver ◆ **he'll never make the ~** il n'y arrivera jamais, il ne sera jamais à la hauteur ◆ **she wanted to be a dancer, but failed to make the ~** elle voulait être danseuse, mais elle n'y est pas arrivée
4 *(= mark)* note *f* ◆ **~s for effort** *etc* note *f* d'application *etc* ◆ **to get good/poor ~s** avoir de bonnes/mauvaises notes
5 *(US Scol = class)* année *f* ; → GRADE
6 *(= gradation on scale)* degré *m*
7 *(Climbing)* degré *m* (de difficulté)
8 *(US = slope)* rampe *f*, pente *f*
9 *(US = ground level)* ◆ **at ~** au niveau du sol
VT 1 *(= sort out) [+ produce, accommodation, colours, questions]* classer ; *(by size) [+ apples, eggs etc]* calibrer ◆ **the exercises are ~d according to difficulty** les exercices sont classés selon leur degré de difficulté ◆ **to ~ sb according to performance/seniority** *(Comm)* classer qn en fonction de son rendement/ancienneté
2 *(= make progressively easier, more difficult, darker, lighter etc) [+ work, exercises, colours etc]* graduer ; see also **graded**
3 *(Scol = mark) [+ pupil, work]* noter
4 *(Agr:* also **grade up***)* améliorer par sélection
5 *(US = level) [+ ground]* niveler
COMP **grade book** N *(US Scol)* registre *m or* cahier *m* de notes
grade crossing N *(US Rail)* passage *m* à niveau
grade inflation N *(US Educ)* surnotation *f*

grade point (average) N *(US Educ)* (note *f*) moyenne *f*
grade school N *(US)* école *f* primaire
grade separation N *(US : on road)* séparation *f* des niveaux de circulation
grade sheet N *(US Educ)* relevé *m* de notes
► **grade down** VT SEP mettre *or* placer dans une catégorie inférieure
► **grade up** VT SEP mettre *or* placer dans une catégorie supérieure ; see also **grade vt 4**

GRADE

Aux États-Unis et au Canada, on désigne sous le nom de **grade** chacune des douze années de la scolarité obligatoire, depuis le cours préparatoire (first **grade**) jusqu'à la terminale (twelfth **grade**). On notera les surnoms donnés aux élèves des quatre dernières années : « freshman » (petit nouveau) en 9e année (la première année du deuxième cycle du secondaire), « sophomore » en 10e année, « junior » en 11e et « senior » en terminale.

graded /'greɪdɪd/ ADJ *[charges, rates, tax] (= increasing)* progressif ; *(= decreasing)* dégressif ; *[tests, exercises]* classé par degré de difficulté ◆ **a ~ series of transformations** une série progressive de transformations ◆ **~ reader** méthode *f* de lecture progressive

grader /'greɪdəʳ/ N *(US Scol)* correcteur *m* ; *(Constr)* niveleuse *f*

gradient /'greɪdiənt/ N *(esp Brit)* pente *f*, inclinaison *f* ; *(Math, Phys)* gradient *m* ◆ **a ~ of one in ten** *or* **10%** une inclinaison *or* une déclivité de 10%

grading /'greɪdɪŋ/ N *(gen)* classification *f* ; *(by size)* calibrage *m* ; *(Scol etc)* notation *f*

gradual /'grædjʊəl/ ADJ *[process, progress]* graduel ; *[change, improvement, withdrawal, reduction]* graduel, progressif ; *[decline, recovery, reform]* progressif ; *[slope]* doux (douce *f*) N *(Rel)* graduel *m*

gradualism /'grædjʊəlɪzm/ N *(Pol, Geol etc)* gradualisme *m*

gradually /'grædjʊəlɪ/ ADV peu à peu, petit à petit, progressivement

graduate /'grædjʊeɪt/ VT 1 *(= mark out) [+ thermometer, container]* graduer (in en)
2 *(= make progressively easier, more difficult, darker etc) [+ work, exercises, colours etc]* graduer ◆ **to ~ payments** *[buyer]* payer par fractionnements progressifs *(or dégressifs)*
3 *(US Scol, Univ)* conférer un diplôme à
VI 1 *(Univ)* ≈ obtenir sa licence *(or* son diplôme *etc)* ; *(US Scol)* ≃ obtenir son baccalauréat ◆ **he ~d as an architect/a teacher** *etc* il a eu son diplôme d'architecte/de professeur *etc*
2 *[colours etc]* se changer graduellement ◆ **to ~ to ...** virer progressivement à ...
N /'grædjʊɪt/ 1 *(Univ)* ≈ licencié(e) *m(f)*, diplômé(e) *m(f)*
2 *(Pharm)* verre *m* (or bocal *m etc*) gradué
ADJ /'grædjʊɪt/ *(Univ) [teacher, staff]* ≃ diplômé, licencié ◆ **~ assistant** étudiant(e) *m(f)* chargé(e) de travaux dirigés, moniteur *m*, -trice *f* ◆ **~ course** études *fpl* de troisième cycle ◆ **Graduate Record Examination** *(US Univ) examen d'entrée dans le second cycle* ◆ **~ school** *(US)* troisième cycle *m* d'université ◆ **~ student** *(US)* étudiant(e) *m(f)* de troisième cycle ◆ **~ studies** *(US)* études *fpl* de troisième cycle

graduated /'grædjʊeɪtɪd/ ADJ *[tube, flask]* gradué ; *[tax]* progressif ◆ **in ~ stages** par paliers, progressivement COMP **graduated pension scheme** N *(Brit)* ≃ régime *m* de retraite complémentaire

graduation /ˌgrædjʊ'eɪʃən/ N 1 *(Univ, also US Scol) (= ceremony)* cérémonie *f* de remise des diplômes ; *(by student)* obtention *f* du diplôme ◆ **I'm hoping to get a good job after ~** j'espère trouver un bon emploi une fois que j'aurai (obtenu) mon diplôme
2 *(on container, instrument)* graduation *f*
COMP **graduation ceremony** N cérémonie *f* de remise des diplômes
graduation day N jour *m* de la remise des diplômes

GRADUATION

La **graduation** est la cérémonie de remise des diplômes universitaires. C'est un événement important, où les étudiants, revêtus de leur toge et de leur toque noires, reçoivent officiellement leurs diplômes des mains du recteur. Les familles assistent à la cérémonie et les photos prises à cette occasion occupent généralement une place d'honneur dans les intérieurs anglo-saxons. Aux États-Unis, le terme désigne aussi la cérémonie qui marque la fin des études secondaires.

Graeco- *(Brit)*, **Greco-** *(esp US)* /'griːkəʊ/ PREF gréco-
COMP **Graeco-Roman** ADJ *[art, sculpture]* gréco-romain
Graeco-Roman wrestling N lutte *f* gréco-romaine

graffiti /grə'fiːtɪ/ N *(NonC)* graffiti *m* ◆ **~ artist** graffiteur *m*, -euse *f (artiste)*

graft /grɑːft/ N 1 *(Agr)* greffe *f*, greffon *m*, ente *f* ; *(Med)* greffe *f* ◆ **they did a skin ~** ils ont fait une greffe de la peau ◆ **they did a kidney ~ on him** on lui a greffé un rein 2 *(esp US = corruption)* corruption *f* 3 *(Brit *)* **(hard) ~** *(= work)* boulot* *m* acharné VT 1 *(Agr, Med)* greffer *(on sur)* 2 *(= get by bribery)* obtenir par la corruption ; *(= get by swindling)* obtenir par (l')escroquerie VI *(= engage in bribery)* donner *(or* recevoir) des pots-de-vin *or* enveloppes* ; *(= swindle)* faire de l'escroquerie

grafter /'grɑːftəʳ/ N 1 *(= swindler etc)* escroc *m*, chevalier *m* d'industrie *(liter)* 2 *(Brit * = hard worker)* bourreau *m* de travail

graham cracker /'greɪəmkrækəʳ/ N *(US)* biscuit *m* à la farine complète

graham flour /'greɪəmflaʊəʳ/ N farine *f* complète

grail /greɪl/ N ◆ **the Holy Grail** le Saint Graal

grain /greɪn/ N 1 *(NonC)* céréale(s) *f(pl)* ; *(US)* blé *m*
2 *(= single grain) [of cereal, salt, sand etc]* grain *m* ; *(fig) [of sense, malice]* grain *m*, brin *m* ; *[of truth]* ombre *f*, miette *f* ◆ **a few ~s of rice** quelques grains de riz ◆ **that's a ~ of comfort** c'est une petite consolation ; → **salt**
3 *(in leather, also Phot)* grain *m* ; *(in wood, meat)* fibre *f* ; *(in cloth)* fil *m* ; *(in stone, marble)* veine *f* ◆ **with the ~** dans le sens de la fibre *(or* de la veine *etc)* ◆ **against the ~** en travers de la fibre *(or* de la veine *etc)* ◆ **it goes against the ~ for him to apologize** cela va à l'encontre de sa nature de s'excuser ◆ **I'll do it, but it goes against the ~** je le ferai, mais pas de bon cœur *or* mais cela va à l'encontre de mes idées
4 *(= weight) mesure de poids (= 0,065 gramme)*
VT 1 *[+ salt etc]* grener, grainer ; *[+ powder]* granuler ◆ **finely ~ed** à grain fin ◆ **coarse ~ed** à gros grain
2 *[+ leather, paper]* greneler ; *(= paint in imitation of wood)* veiner
COMP **grain alcohol** N alcool *m* de grain
grain elevator N *(US)* silo *m* à céréales

graininess /'greɪnɪnɪs/ N *(Phot)* grain *m*

grainy /'greɪnɪ/ ADJ *(Phot)* qui a du grain ; *[substance]* granuleux

gram /græm/ N gramme *m*

gram flour /'græmflaʊəʳ/ N farine *f* de pois chiches

grammar /'græməʳ/ N 1 *(NonC)* grammaire *f* ◆ **that is bad ~** cela n'est pas grammatical ; → **generative** 2 (also **grammar book**) (livre *m* de) grammaire *f*
COMP **grammar checker** N correcteur *m* grammatical
grammar school N *(in Britain)* ≃ lycée *m (avec examen d'entrée)* ; *(in US)* ≃ école *f* primaire ; → COMPREHENSIVE SCHOOL

grammarian /grə'meərɪən/ N grammairien(ne) *m(f)*

grammatical /grə'mætɪkəl/ ADJ 1 *[structure, sentence]* grammatical ; *[rule, error]* de grammaire, grammatical 2 *(= correct)* grammaticalement correct ◆ **he speaks perfectly ~ English** il parle un anglais parfaitement correct du point de vue grammatical

grammaticality /grəmætɪ'kælɪtɪ/ N grammaticalité *f*

grammatically /grə'mætɪkəlɪ/ ADV *[correct]* du point de vue grammatical ◆ **to write ~** écrire des phrases grammaticalement correctes ◆ **to speak ~** s'exprimer correctement d'un point de vue grammatical

grammaticalness /grə'mætɪkəlnɪs/ N grammaticalité *f*

grammatologist /ˌgræmə'tɒlədʒɪst/ N grammatologue *mf*

grammatology /ˌgræmə'tɒlədʒɪ/ N grammatologie *f*

gramme /græm/ N *(Brit)* ⇒ **gram**

Grammy /'græmɪ/ N (pl **Grammys** *or* **Grammies**) *(US) prix récompensant les meilleurs disques*

gramophone /'græməfəʊn/ N *(esp Brit)* phonographe *m*
COMP **gramophone needle** N aiguille *f* de phonographe
gramophone record N disque *m*

Grampian /'græmpɪən/ N ◆ **the ~ Mountains, the ~s** les (monts *mpl*) Grampians *mpl*

gramps* /græmps/ N *(US)* pépé* *m*, papy* *m*

grampus /'græmpəs/ N (pl **grampuses**) dauphin *m* de Risso

gran* /græn/ N *(Brit)* mémé* *f*, mamie* *f*

Granada /grə'nɑːdə/ N Grenade

granary /'grænərɪ/ N grenier *m (à blé etc)* COMP **Granary** ® ADJ *[bread, loaf, roll]* aux céréales

grand /grænd/ ADJ 1 *(= impressive) [architecture]* grandiose ; *[building, staircase]* majestueux ; *[person]* éminent ; *[job]* prestigieux ; *[occasion, chorus, concert]* grand ◆ **to make a ~ entrance** faire une entrée majestueuse ◆ **in the ~ manner** en souverain(e) *m(f)* ◆ **on a ~ scale** à très grande échelle ◆ **to do things on a ~ scale** faire les choses en grand ◆ **to live in ~ style** mener la grande vie ◆ **to make a ~ gesture** *(fig)* faire un geste grandiose
2 *(= ambitious) [scheme, strategy, design]* ambitieux
3 *(† * = excellent) [person]* super* *inv* ◆ **we had a ~ time** c'était formidable ◆ **it was a ~ game** le match a été magnifique
4 *(in names)* ◆ **the Grand Hotel** le Grand Hôtel
N 1 *(pl inv: *) (Brit)* mille livres *fpl* ; *(US)* mille dollars *mpl*
2 (also **grand piano**) piano *m* à queue *or* de concert ; → **baby**
COMP **the Grand Canyon** N le Grand Canyon ◆ **the Grand Canyon State** l'Arizona *m*
grand duchy N grand-duché *m* ◆ **the Grand Duchy of Luxembourg** le grand-duché de Luxembourg
grand duke N grand-duc *m*
grand finale N grande finale *f*
grand jury N *(in US)* jury *m* d'accusation
grand larceny N *(US Jur)* vol *m* qualifié

grand mal N (= *illness*) épilepsie *f* (essentielle) ; (= *seizure*) crise *f* (d'épilepsie) convulsive
grand master N (*Chess*) grand maître *m*
the Grand National N (*Brit Racing*) le Grand National
grand old man N (pl **grand old men**) ◆ **the ~ old man of English politics** le grand monsieur de la politique anglaise
the Grand Old Party N (*US*) le parti républicain
grand opening N grande inauguration *f*
grand opera N grand opéra *m*
grand piano N piano *m* à queue *or* de concert
Grand Prix N (*Motor Racing*) Grand Prix *m* ◆ **the French/Monaco** *etc* **Grand Prix** le Grand Prix de France/de Monaco *etc*
grand slam N (*Bridge, Sport*) grand chelem *m*
grand staircase N escalier *m* d'honneur
grand total N (*gen*) somme *f* globale ; (*Math*) résultat *m* final ◆ **we get to the ~ total of ...** (*fig*) nous arrivons au chiffre impressionnant de ...
the Grand Tour N (*Hist*) le tour d'Europe ◆ **we did a** *or* **the ~ tour of the Louvre** nous avons fait le tour complet *or* une visite complète du Louvre
Grand Unified Theory N (*Phys*) théorie *f* de la grande unification
grand vizier N grand vizir *m*

GRAND JURY

Dans le système judiciaire américain, le **grand jury** est le jury d'accusation, qui décide si une personne devra comparaître devant le jury de jugement (« trial jury » ou « petit jury »), qui statuera sur son éventuelle culpabilité.
Composé de 12 à 23 personnes, le **grand jury** se réunit à huis clos ; il a le droit de citer des témoins à comparaître.

grandchild /'grænt∫aɪld/ N petit(e)-enfant *m(f)*, petit-fils *m*, petite-fille *f* NPL **grandchildren** petits-enfants *mpl*

grand(d)ad * /'grændæd/, **grand(d)addy** * (*US*) /'grændædɪ/ N grand-papa * *m*, pépé * *m*, papi * *m*, bon-papa * *m*

granddaughter /'grændɔːtəʳ/ N petite-fille *f*

grandee /græn'diː/ N (*in Spain*) grand *m* d'Espagne ; (*fig*) grand personnage *m*

grandeur /'grændjəʳ/ N [*of person*] grandeur *f* ; [*of scenery, house*] splendeur *f*, magnificence *f* ; [*of character, style*] noblesse *f* ; [*of position*] éminence *f* ◆ **an air of ~** une allure grandiose

grandfather /'grændfɑːðəʳ/ N grand-père *m*
COMP **grandfather clause** N (*US fig: in law*) clause *f* d'antériorité
grandfather clock N (horloge *f*) comtoise *f*, horloge *f* de parquet

grandiloquence /græn'dɪləkwəns/ N grandiloquence *f*

grandiloquent /græn'dɪləkwənt/ ADJ (*frm*) grandiloquent

grandiloquently /græn'dɪləkwəntlɪ/ ADV (*frm*) avec grandiloquence

grandiose /'grændɪəʊz/ ADJ grandiose ; [*style*] grandiloquent, pompeux

grandly /'grændlɪ/ ADV [1] (= *impressively*) [*stand*] majestueusement ◆ **to live ~** mener grand train ◆ **~ decorated** au décor majestueux [2] (= *pompously*) [*announce*] solennellement ; [*speak, say, call*] pompeusement ; [*behave*] avec majesté

grandma * /'grændmɑː/ N grand-maman * *f*, mémé * *f*, mamie * *f*, bonne-maman * *f*

grandmother /'grænmʌðəʳ/ N grand-mère *f*

grandpa * /'grænpɑː/ N ⇒ **grand(d)ad**

grandparent /'grændpɛərənt/ N (= *grandfather*) grand-père *m* ; (= *grandmother*) grand-mère *f* NPL **grandparents** grands-parents *mpl*

grandson /'grænsʌn/ N petit-fils *m*

grandstand /'grændstænd/ N (*Sport*) tribune *f* ◆ **to have a ~ view** (*fig*) être aux premières loges (*fig*) VI (*US* * *fig*) jouer pour la galerie ◆ **~ play** * (*US fig*) amusement *m* pour la galerie

grandstanding /'grændstændɪŋ/ N (*political*) démagogie *f*

grange /greɪndʒ/ N [1] (*esp Brit* = *country house*) château *m*, manoir *m* [2] (*US* = *farm*) ferme *f* ◆ **the Grange** (*US Hist*) la Fédération agricole [3] ⇒ **granary noun**

granger /'greɪndʒəʳ/ N (*US*) fermier *m*

granite /'grænɪt/ N granit *m*
COMP de granit **the Granite City** N (*Brit*) Aberdeen
the Granite State N (*US*) le New Hampshire

grannie, granny /'grænɪ/ N * mamie *f*, grand-maman *f*
COMP **granny bond** * N ≈ bon *m* du Trésor indexé
granny flat * N petit appartement *m* indépendant (*en annexe*)
granny glasses * NPL petites lunettes *fpl* cerclées de métal
granny knot N nœud *m* de vache
Granny Smith (apple) N granny smith *f inv*
granny specs * NPL ⇒ **granny glasses**

granola /græ'nəʊlə/ N (*US*) muesli *m* (*aux pépites de céréales*)

grant /grɑːnt/ VT [1] (= *accord*) [+ *favour, permission*] accorder ; [+ *wish, prayer*] exaucer ; [+ *request*] accéder à ; [+ *money*] accorder, octroyer ; [+ *pension*] accorder, allouer ◆ **to ~ sb permission to do sth** accorder à qn l'autorisation de faire qch ◆ **to ~ sb his request** accéder à la requête de qn ◆ **to be ~ed one's wish** voir son souhait exaucé ◆ **they were ~ed an extension of three weeks** on leur a accordé un délai de trois semaines ◆ **to ~ sb political asylum** accorder l'asile politique à qn ◆ **I beg your pardon! – ~ed!** je vous demande pardon ! – je vous en prie ! ◆ **God ~ that ...** plaise à Dieu que ... (+ *subj*)
[2] (= *admit*) admettre, concéder ◆ **to ~ a proposition** admettre la vérité d'une proposition ◆ **it must be ~ed that ...** il faut admettre *or* reconnaître que ... ◆ **I ~ you that** je vous l'accorde ◆ **I ~ that he is honest** je vous accorde qu'il est honnête
[3] (*set phrases*)
◆ **to take sb for granted** ◆ **one does tend to take one's parents for ~ed** c'est vrai que nous avons tendance à ne pas apprécier *or* à faire peu de cas de tout ce que nos parents font pour nous ◆ **he takes her for ~ed** il ne fait aucun cas de tout ce qu'elle fait pour lui ◆ **stop taking me for ~ed!** arrête de faire comme si je n'existais pas !
◆ **to take sth for granted** (= *regard as normal*) ◆ **we take our democracy for ~ed** pour nous la démocratie est quelque chose qui va de soi *or* est une évidence ◆ **people who took this luxury for ~ed** les gens pour qui ce luxe était quelque chose de normal ◆ **I take Net access so much for ~ed that ...** pour moi, avoir accès à l'Internet est quelque chose de tellement normal que ... ◆ **to take sb's agreement for ~ed** considérer l'accord de qn comme allant de soi *or* comme acquis ◆ **researchers should avoid taking too much for ~ed** les chercheurs doivent veiller à ne pas avoir trop de certitudes ◆ **he seemed to take it for ~ed that he should speak first** il semblait trouver tout naturel qu'on lui donne la parole en premier ◆ **you take too much for ~ed** (= *take too many liberties*) vous vous croyez tout permis, vous prenez trop de libertés ; (= *assume things are further forward than they are*) si vous croyez que c'est facile ...
◆ **to take (it) for granted that ...** (= *assume*) supposer que ... ◆ **I just took for ~ed that she was going straight home** j'ai supposé qu'elle rentrait directement ◆ **we may take it for ~ed that he will come** nous pouvons tenir pour certain *or* nous pouvons compter qu'il viendra
N [1] (*NonC*) [*of favour, permission*] octroi *m* ; [*of land*] concession *f* ; (*Jur*) [*of property*] cession *f* ; [*of money, pension*] allocation *f* ◆ **~ of a patent** (*Jur*) délivrance *f* d'un brevet
[2] (= *sum given*) subvention *f*, allocation *f* ; (*Brit*) (= *scholarship*) bourse *f* ◆ **they have a government ~ to aid research** ils ont une subvention gouvernementale d'aide à la recherche ◆ **to be on a ~** [*student*] avoir une bourse ◆ **he's on a ~ of £900** il a une bourse de 900 livres ; → **improvement**
COMP **grant-aided** ADJ subventionné par l'État
grant-in-aid N (pl **grants-in-aid**) subvention *f* de l'État
grant-maintained school N (*Brit*) *établissement scolaire financé par l'État plutôt que par une collectivité locale*

granted /'grɑːntɪd/ CONJ ◆ **~ that this is true** en admettant que ce soit vrai ADV ◆ **~, he doesn't look too bad for his age** c'est vrai, il n'est pas mal pour son âge EXCL soit !, d'accord !

grantee /,grɑː n'tiː/ N (*Jur: gen*) bénéficiaire *mf* ; [*of patent*] impétrant *m*

granular /'grænjʊləʳ/ ADJ granuleux

granulate /'grænjʊleɪt/ VT [+ *metal, powder*] granuler ; [+ *salt, sugar, soil*] grener, grainer ; [+ *surface*] rendre grenu
COMP **granulated paper** N papier *m* grenelé
granulated sugar N sucre *m* semoule
granulated surface N surface *f* grenue

granule /'grænjuːl/ N granule *m*

grape /greɪp/ N (grain *m* de) raisin *m* ◆ **~s** raisin *m NonC*, raisins *mpl* ◆ **to harvest the ~s** vendanger, faire la (*or* les) vendange(s) ; → **bunch, sour**
COMP **grape harvest** N vendange *f*
grape hyacinth N muscari *m*
grape juice N jus *m* de raisin

grapefruit /'greɪpfruːt/ N (pl **grapefruit** *or* **grapefruits**) pamplemousse *m*

grapeshot /'greɪp∫ɒt/ N mitraille *f*

grapevine /'greɪpvaɪn/ N [1] (*lit*) vigne *f* [2] (*fig*) **I hear on** *or* **through the ~ that ...** j'ai appris par le téléphone arabe *or* par mes services de renseignement que ...

graph /grɑːf/ N (*gen*) graphique *m* ; (*Ling*) graphe *m* VT tracer le graphique *or* la courbe de
COMP **graph paper** N papier *m* quadrillé ; (*in millimetres*) papier *m* millimétré
graph plotter N table *f* traçante

grapheme /'græfiːm/ N graphème *m*

graphic /'græfɪk/ ADJ [1] (= *horrifying*) [*account, description*] cru ; (= *explicit*) [*sex, violence*] explicite ◆ **to describe sth in ~ detail** faire une description très crue de qch [2] (= *vivid*) [*description*] imagé [3] (*Art, Math*) graphique
COMP **graphic artist** N graphiste *mf*
the graphic arts NPL les arts *mpl* graphiques
graphic design N graphisme *m*
graphic designer N maquettiste *mf*, graphiste *mf*
graphic display N (*Comput*) visualisation *f* graphique
graphic equalizer N égaliseur *m* graphique
graphic novel N bande *f* dessinée, BD *f*

graphical /'græfɪkəl/ ADJ (*gen, also Math*) graphique
COMP **graphical display unit** N (*Comput*) visuel *m* graphique
graphical user interface N (*Comput*) interface *f* graphique, interface *f* GUI

graphically /'græfɪkəlɪ/ ADV *[describe, explain]* de manière très réaliste ; *[illustrate, demonstrate, display]* très clairement ◆ **to be ~ clear** être tout à fait évident

graphics /'græfɪks/ N 1 *(NonC) (= art of drawing)* art *m* graphique ; *(Math etc = use of graphs)* (utilisation *f* des) graphiques *mpl* ; *(Comput)* traitement *m* graphique, graphiques *mpl* 2 *(pl = sketches)* représentations *fpl* graphiques, graphisme *m* ◆ **~ by ...** (TV *etc*) art *m* graphique (de) ... ; → **computer**
COMP **graphics card** N *(Comput)* carte *f* graphique
graphics tablet N tablette *f* graphique

graphite /'græfaɪt/ N graphite *m*, mine *f* de plomb

graphologist /græ'fɒlədʒɪst/ N graphologue *mf*

graphology /græ'fɒlədʒɪ/ N graphologie *f*

grapnel /'græpnəl/ N grappin *m*

grapple /'græpl/ N (also **grappling hook** *or* **iron**) grappin *m* VT (= *pick up with a grapple*) saisir avec un grappin *or* au grappin VI ◆ **to ~ with** *[+ person]* lutter avec ; *[+ problem, task, book, subject]* se colleter avec, se débattre avec

grasp /grɑːsp/ VT 1 (= *seize*) *[+ object]* saisir, empoigner ◆ **to ~ sb's hand** saisir *or* empoigner la main de qn ; → **nettle**
2 *(fig) [+ power]* s'emparer de ; *[+ opportunity]* saisir
3 (= *understand*) saisir, comprendre ◆ **she soon ~ed what was going on** elle a vite compris ce qui se passait
N 1 (= *hold*) prise *f* ; *(stronger)* poigne *f* ◆ **a strong ~** une forte poigne ◆ **to lose one's ~** *(lit)* lâcher prise ◆ **to lose one's ~ on** *or* **of sth** *(lit)* lâcher qch ; *(fig)* ne plus être au fait de qch ◆ **to let sth/sb slip out of** *or* **from one's ~** *(fig)* laisser échapper qch/qn ◆ **to have sb/sth in one's ~** (= *have power over*) avoir *or* tenir qn/qch sous son emprise ◆ **to have sth within one's ~** *(lit, fig)* avoir qch à portée de la main ◆ **peace is now within our ~** la paix est à présent à notre portée
2 (= *understanding*) compréhension *f* ◆ **he has a good ~ of basic mathematics** il a de bonnes bases en mathématiques ◆ **he has no ~ of our difficulties** il ne se rend pas compte de nos difficultés, il ne saisit pas la nature de nos difficultés ◆ **it is beyond my ~** je n'y comprends rien, cela me dépasse ◆ **this subject is within everyone's ~** ce sujet est à la portée de tout le monde

► **grasp at** VT FUS 1 *(lit)* essayer d'agripper
2 *(fig) [+ hope]* chercher à se raccrocher à ; *[+ opportunity]* chercher à saisir ; see also **straw**

grasping /'grɑːspɪŋ/ ADJ *[arm, hand]* crochu ; *(fig)* cupide, avide

grass /grɑːs/ N 1 *(NonC)* herbe *f* ; (= *lawn*) gazon *m*, pelouse *f* ; (= *grazing*) herbage *m*, pâturage *m* ◆ **"keep off the grass"** "défense de marcher sur la pelouse" ◆ **at ~** au vert ◆ **to put under ~** *(Agr)* enherber, mettre en pré ◆ **to put out to ~** *[+ horse]* mettre au vert ; *(fig) [+ person]* mettre sur la touche ◆ **to play on ~** *(Tennis)* jouer sur herbe *or* sur gazon ◆ **to let the ~ grow under one's feet** laisser traîner les choses, laisser passer son temps ◆ **to kick** *or* **put sth into the long ~** reléguer qch aux oubliettes ◆ **he can hear the ~ growing*** rien ne lui échappe ◆ **the ~ is (always) greener on the other side of the fence** ailleurs, l'herbe est toujours plus verte ; → **blade, green**
2 *(Bot)* ◆ **~es** graminées *fpl*
3 (‡ = *marijuana*) herbe* *f*
4 ‡ (= *telltale*) balance‡ *f*, mouchard* *m* ; (= *informer*) indic* *m*
VT (also **grass over**) *[+ garden, square]* gazonner ; *[+ field, land]* couvrir d'herbe, enherber
VI ‡ moucharder* ◆ **to ~ on sb** donner* *or* vendre* qn
COMP **grass court** N *(Tennis)* court *m* (en gazon) ◆ **to play on a ~ court** jouer sur herbe *or* sur gazon
grass cutter N (grosse) tondeuse *f* à gazon
grass green N vert *m* pré
the grass roots NPL *[of movement, party]* la base ◆ **~-roots candidate/movement** *etc* *(Pol)* candidat *m*/mouvement *m* *etc* populaire
grass skirt N pagne *m* végétal *(des Hawaïennes)*
grass snake N couleuvre *f*
grass widow N *(esp US) (divorced)* divorcée *f* ; *(separated)* femme *f* séparée (de son mari) ◆ **I'm a ~ widow this week*** *(Brit fig)* cette semaine je suis célibataire *f* *(hum)* *or* sans mari
grass widower N *(esp US) (divorced)* divorcé *m* ; *(separated)* homme *m* séparé (de sa femme)

grasshopper /'grɑːshɒpəʳ/ N sauterelle *f*

grassland /'grɑːslænd/ N *(NonC)* prairie *f*, herbages *mpl*

grassy /'grɑːsɪ/ ADJ 1 *[land]* herbeux, herbu 2 *[wine, flavour]* herbacé

grate[1] /greɪt/ N (= *metal framework*) grille *f* de foyer ; (= *fireplace*) âtre *m*, foyer *m* ◆ **a fire in the ~** un feu dans l'âtre

grate[2] /greɪt/ VT 1 *(Culin) [+ cheese, carrot etc]* râper 2 (= *make noise with*) *[+ metallic object]* faire grincer ; *[+ chalk]* faire grincer *or* crisser
VI *[metal]* grincer ; *[chalk]* grincer, crisser (on sur) ◆ **to ~ on the ears** écorcher les oreilles ◆ **it ~d on his nerves** cela lui tapait sur les nerfs* *or* le système* ◆ **his constant chatter ~d on me** son bavardage incessant me tapait sur les nerfs* *or* m'agaçait

grateful /'greɪtfʊl/ LANGUAGE IN USE 2.1, 4, 19.1, 19.4, 20.1, 20.3, 20.6, 21, 22 ADJ *[person]* reconnaissant (*to* à ; *for* de) ; *[smile]* de reconnaissance ◆ **I am ~ for your support** je vous suis reconnaissant de votre soutien ◆ **I should be ~ if you would come** je serais très heureux si vous pouviez venir ◆ **he sent me a very ~ letter** il m'a envoyé une lettre exprimant sa vive reconnaissance ◆ **with ~ thanks** avec mes (*or* nos *etc*) plus sincères remerciements ◆ **I would be ~ if you could send me ...** *(in letter)* je vous saurais gré *or* je vous serais reconnaissant de bien vouloir m'envoyer ... ◆ **he was ~ that she had told him the truth** il était heureux qu'elle lui ait dit la vérité

gratefully /'greɪtfəlɪ/ ADV avec gratitude ◆ **all donations ~ received** tous les dons seront les bienvenus

grater /'greɪtəʳ/ N râpe *f* ◆ **cheese ~** râpe *f* à fromage

gratification /ˌgrætɪfɪ'keɪʃən/ N (= *pleasure*) satisfaction *f*, plaisir *m* ; (= *fulfilment*) *[of desires etc]* assouvissement *m* ◆ **to his ~ he learnt that ...** à sa grande satisfaction il apprit que ... ◆ **sensual ~** le plaisir sensuel ◆ **sexual ~** la satisfaction sexuelle, le plaisir sexuel

gratify /'grætɪfaɪ/ VT (= *please*) *[+ person]* faire plaisir à, être agréable à ; (= *fulfil*) *[+ desire etc]* satisfaire, assouvir ; *[+ whim]* satisfaire ◆ **I was gratified to hear that ...** j'ai appris avec grand plaisir que ..., cela m'a fait plaisir d'apprendre que ...

gratifying /'grætɪfaɪɪŋ/ ADJ (= *pleasing*) agréable, plaisant ; (= *flattering*) *[attentions]* flatteur ◆ **it is ~ to learn that ...** il est très agréable d'apprendre que ..., j'ai (*or* nous avons) appris avec plaisir que ... ◆ **it is ~ that everyone reacted in a professional way** cela fait plaisir de voir que tout le monde a réagi avec professionnalisme

gratin /'grætɛ̃/ N gratin *m*

grating[1] /'greɪtɪŋ/ N grille *f*

grating[2] /'greɪtɪŋ/ ADJ *[voice, sound]* grinçant N *(NonC = sound)* grincement *m*

gratis /'grætɪs/ ADV gratuitement ADJ gratuit

gratitude /'grætɪtjuːd/ LANGUAGE IN USE 22 N reconnaissance *f*, gratitude *f* (*towards* envers ; *for* de)

gratuitous /grə'tjuːɪtəs/ ADJ gratuit

gratuitously /grə'tjuːɪtəslɪ/ ADV ◆ **~ violent/nasty/cruel** d'une violence/méchanceté/cruauté gratuite ◆ **~ offensive** qui cherche à choquer sans justification

gratuity /grə'tjuːɪtɪ/ N 1 *(Brit Mil)* prime *f* de démobilisation 2 (= *tip*) pourboire *m*, gratification *f* 3 (*to a retiring employee*) prime *f* de départ

gravamen /grə'veɪmen/ N (pl **gravamina** /grə'væmɪnə/) *(Jur)* ≈ principal chef *m* d'accusation

grave[1] /greɪv/ N tombe *f* ; *(more elaborate)* tombeau *m* ◆ **from beyond the ~** d'outre-tombe ◆ **he went to his ~ a bitter man** il est mort aigri ◆ **he'll go to an early ~** il aura une fin prématurée ◆ **he sent her to an early ~** il est responsable de sa mort prématurée ◆ **you'll send me to an early ~!** *(hum)* tu veux ma mort ? ◆ **someone is walking over my ~*** j'ai eu un frisson ◆ **Mozart must be turning in his ~*** Mozart doit se retourner dans sa tombe* ; → **dig, foot, silent**

grave[2] /greɪv/ ADJ (= *serious, solemn*) grave ◆ **to have ~ doubts about sth** douter sérieusement de qch

grave[3] /grɑːv/ ADJ *(Typ) [accent]* grave

gravedigger /'greɪvdɪgəʳ/ N fossoyeur *m*

gravel /'grævəl/ N 1 *(NonC)* gravier *m* ; *(finer)* gravillon *m* 2 *(Med)* lithiase *f* VT couvrir de gravier
COMP **gravel path** N allée *f* de gravier
gravel pit N carrière *f* de cailloux

gravelly /'grævəlɪ/ ADJ 1 (= *stony*) *[road, soil, riverbed]* graveleux 2 *(fig = rough) [voice]* râpeux

gravely /'greɪvlɪ/ ADV 1 (= *solemnly*) *[say, ask, nod]* gravement 2 (= *badly, extremely*) ◆ **~ ill** gravement malade ◆ **~ wounded** grièvement *or* gravement blessé ◆ **~ displeased** extrêmement mécontent ◆ **~ concerned** extrêmement *or* profondément inquiet

graven †† /'greɪvən/ ADJ taillé, sculpté ◆ **~ image** *(Rel etc)* image *f* (gravée) ◆ **~ on his memory** gravé dans sa mémoire

graveness /'greɪvnɪs/ N *(NonC: all senses)* gravité *f*

graverobber /'greɪvrɒbəʳ/ N déterreur *m* de cadavres

graveside /'greɪvsaɪd/ N ◆ **at the ~** (= *beside the grave*) près de la tombe ; (= *at the burial ceremony*) à l'enterrement

gravestone /'greɪvstəʊn/ N pierre *f* tombale

graveyard /'greɪvjɑːd/ N cimetière *m* ◆ **the ~ of so many political careers** la ruine de tant de carrières politiques ◆ **a ~ cough** une toux caverneuse *or* qui sent le sapin* ◆ **~ shift*** *(US fig hum)* le poste *or* l'équipe *f* de nuit COMP **graveyard slot** N plage *f*, horaire d'écoute minimale

gravid /'grævɪd/ ADJ *(frm)* gravide

graving dock /'greɪvɪŋdɒk/ N *(Naut)* bassin *m* de radoub

gravitas /'grævɪtæs/ N *[of person]* gravité *f*

gravitate /'grævɪteɪt/ VI 1 *(fig)* graviter (*round* autour de) être attiré (*towards* par) ◆ **these students ~ towards medicine, law and engineering** ces étudiants sont plutôt attirés par la médecine, le droit et les études d'ingénieur 2 *(Phys)* graviter (*round* autour de) ◆ **to ~ to the bottom** se déposer *or* descendre au fond (*par gravitation*)

gravitation /ˌgrævɪ'teɪʃən/ N *(Phys, fig)* gravitation *f* (*round* autour de ; *towards* vers)

gravitational /ˌɡrævɪˈteɪʃənl/ ADJ gravitationnel ◆ ~ **constant/field/force** constante *f*/champ *m*/force *f* de gravitation COMP **gravitational pull** N gravitation *f*

gravity /ˈɡrævɪtɪ/ N *(NonC)* [1] *(Phys)* pesanteur *f* ◆ ~ **feed** alimentation *f* par gravité ; → **centre, law, specific** [2] *(= seriousness)* gravité *f*, sérieux *m* ◆ **to lose one's** ~ perdre son sérieux

gravy /ˈɡreɪvɪ/ N [1] *(Culin)* sauce *f* au jus *m* de viande [2] *(US* ‡*) (= easy money)* profit *m* facile, bénef‡ *m* ; *(= dishonest money)* argent *m* mal acquis

COMP **gravy boat** N saucière *f*

gravy train‡ N *(fig)* ◆ **to be on** *or* **ride the** ~ **train** avoir trouvé le bon filon‡ ◆ **to get on the** ~ **train** trouver une bonne planque‡

gray /ɡreɪ/ *(esp US)* ⇒ **grey**

grayish /ˈɡreɪɪʃ/ ADJ *(esp US)* ⇒ **greyish**

grayling /ˈɡreɪlɪŋ/ N (pl **grayling** *or* **graylings**) *(= fish)* ombre *m* (de rivière)

graze[1] /ɡreɪz/ VI *[animal]* brouter, paître ; *[person]* grignoter VT [1] *[cattle] [+ grass]* brouter, paître ; *[+ field]* pâturer (dans) [2] *[farmer] [+ cattle]* paître, faire paître

graze[2] /ɡreɪz/ VT [1] *(= touch lightly)* frôler, effleurer ◆ **it only ~d him** cela n'a fait que l'effleurer ◆ **to ~ bottom** *(Naut)* labourer le fond [2] *(= scrape) [+ skin, hand etc]* érafler, écorcher ◆ **to ~ one's knees** s'écorcher les genoux ◆ **the bullet ~d his arm** la balle lui a éraflé le bras N écorchure *f*, éraflure *f*

grazing /ˈɡreɪzɪŋ/ N *(NonC:* also **grazing land)** pâturage *m* ; *(= act)* pâture *f*

GRE /dʒiːɑːrˈiː/ N *(US Univ)* (abbrev of **Graduate Record Examination**) → **graduate**

grease /ɡriːs/ N *(gen, also Culin)* graisse *f* ; *(= lubricant)* lubrifiant *m*, graisse *f* ; *(= dirt)* crasse *f*, saleté *f* ◆ **to remove the ~ from sth** dégraisser qch ◆ **his hair is thick with** ~ il a les cheveux très gras ; → **axle, elbow** VT graisser ; *(= lubricate)* lubrifier, graisser ◆ **like ~d lightning*** en quatrième vitesse*, à toute pompe* ◆ **to move like a ~d pig*** *(US)* filer comme un zèbre* ; → **palm**[1]**, wheel**

COMP **grease gun** N (pistolet *m*) graisseur *m*

grease monkey‡ N mécano* *m*

grease nipple N graisseur *m*

grease remover N dégraisseur *m*

grease-stained ADJ graisseux

greasepaint /ˈɡriːspeɪnt/ N fard *m* gras ◆ **stick of** ~ crayon *m* gras

greaseproof paper /ˈɡriːspruːfˈpeɪpəʳ/ N papier *m* sulfurisé

greaser‡ /ˈɡriːsəʳ/ N [1] *(= mechanic)* mécano* *m* [2] *(= motorcyclist)* motard* *m* [3] *(pej = ingratiating person)* lèche-bottes* *m* [4] *(US pej = Latin American)* Latino-Américain *m*, ≈ métèque* *m*

greasiness /ˈɡriːsɪnɪs/ N aspect *m* or état *m* graisseux ; *(= slipperiness) [of road]* surface *f* grasse *or* glissante

greasy /ˈɡriːsɪ/ ADJ [1] *[hair, skin, ointment, food, surface]* gras (grasse *f*) ; *[overalls, tools]* graisseux ◆ ~ **hands** mains *fpl* pleines de graisse, mains *fpl* graisseuses ◆ **the road (surface) was** ~ la chaussée était grasse [2] *(pej = smarmy)* obséquieux

COMP **greasy pole** N *(lit)* mât *m* de cocagne ◆ **to climb (up) the ~ pole** *(Brit fig)* progresser au prix de grands efforts

greasy spoon* N *(pej)* gargote* *f (pej)*

great /ɡreɪt/ ADJ [1] *(= large) [building, tree, cloud]* grand ◆ **A or B, whichever is the ~er** choisir entre A et B le chiffre ayant la valeur la plus élevée

[2] *(= considerable) [effort, success]* grand ◆ **a player of ~ ability** un joueur très doué ◆ **to live to a ~ age** parvenir à un âge avancé ◆ **he did not live to a ~ age** il n'a pas vécu très vieux ◆ **despite his ~ age, he ...** malgré son grand âge, il ... ◆ **with ~ care** avec grand soin, avec beaucoup de soin ◆ **a ~ deal** beaucoup ◆ **a ~ deal of sth** beaucoup *or* énormément de qch ◆ **to study sth in ~ depth** étudier qch à fond ◆ **with ~ difficulty** avec de grandes difficultés ◆ **to a ~ extent** dans une large mesure ◆ **she has a ~ eye for detail** elle a vraiment le coup d'œil pour les détails ◆ **I have a ~ hatred of ...** j'éprouve une violente haine pour ... ◆ **to be a ~ help** être d'une grande aide ◆ **to take a ~ interest in sb/sth** s'intéresser énormément à qn/qch ◆ **a ~ many** un grand nombre ◆ **a ~ many people** un grand nombre de gens ◆ **a ~ many of us** beaucoup d'entre nous ◆ **there is a ~ need for improvement** des améliorations s'imposent ◆ **I have no ~ opinion of ...** je n'ai pas une haute opinion de ... ◆ **at a ~ pace** à vive allure ◆ **are you in ~ pain?** avez-vous très mal ? ◆ **a ~ sense of team spirit** un esprit d'équipe remarquable ◆ **it was all a ~ shock** tout cela fut un choc terrible ◆ **a ~ variety of opinions** des avis très variés ◆ **she has ~ willpower** elle a une forte volonté

[3] *(= important) [achievement, event, issue, city, country]* grand ◆ **America can be ~ again** l'Amérique peut retrouver sa grandeur

[4] *(= eminent) [scientist, footballer etc]* éminent ◆ **a ~ man** un grand homme ◆ **he has a ~ future** il a un bel *or* grand avenir (devant lui) ◆ **the ~ masters** les grands maîtres ◆ **the ~est names in football/poetry** *etc* les plus grands noms du football/de la poésie, *etc*

[5] *(* = excellent) [person, place]* super* *inv* ; *[holiday, idea]* sensationnel*, génial* ◆ **you were ~!** tu as été sensationnel !* ◆ **he's the ~est!** il est formidable ! ◆ **that's ~!** *(lit, iro)* c'est super !* ◆ **I feel ~** je me sens en pleine forme ◆ **my wife isn't feeling so ~** ma femme ne se sent pas trop bien ◆ **this cook book is ~ for desserts** ce livre de cuisine est excellent pour les desserts ◆ **you look ~** *(= healthy)* tu as vraiment bonne mine ; *(= attractive)* tu es superbe ◆ **we had a ~ time** c'était merveilleux ◆ **it was ~ fun** c'était très amusant ◆ **wouldn't it be ~ to live here?** ça ne serait pas merveilleux de vivre ici ? ; see also **gun, shake**

[6] *(= enthusiastic)* ◆ **he's a ~ angler** il est passionné de pêche ◆ **he's a ~ arguer** il est toujours prêt à discuter ◆ **he was a ~ friend of Huxley** c'était un grand ami de Huxley ◆ **they are ~ friends** ce sont de grands amis ◆ **he's a ~ one for cathedrals*** il adore visiter les cathédrales ◆ **he's a ~ one for criticizing others*** il ne rate pas une occasion de critiquer les autres ◆ **he was a ~ womaniser** c'était un grand coureur de jupons ◆ **he's ~ on jazz*** *(US)* il est mordu* de jazz

[7] *(* = expert)* ◆ **he's a ~ teacher** c'est un excellent professeur ◆ **he's ~ at football/maths** il est doué pour le football/les maths ◆ **he's ~ on baroque music** il est incollable* en musique baroque

[8] *(in exclamations)* ◆ **Great Scott** *or* **Heavens !** † grands dieux !

[9] *(in titles)* ◆ **Alexander the Great** Alexandre le Grand ◆ **Catherine the Great** Catherine II la Grande

[10] *(= pregnant)* ◆ **to be ~ with child** †† être enceinte

ADV * [1] *(= excellently)* super bien* ◆ **she's doing ~** elle s'en tire super bien* ◆ **we get on ~** nous nous entendons super bien* ◆ **everything's going ~** *[life]* tout va super bien* ; *[activity, business]* tout marche comme sur des roulettes*

[2] ◆ ~ **big** *[object, animal, kiss]* énorme ◆ **a ~ big Italian wedding** un mariage italien en grand

EXCL * *(= brilliant)* super*, génial* ◆ **oh ~, just what I need!** super*, j'avais vraiment besoin de ça !

N *(Oxford Univ)* ◆ **Greats** ≈ licence *f* de lettres classiques

NPL **the great** les grands *mpl*

COMP **great ape** N grand singe *m*, anthropoïde *m*

great auk N grand pingouin *m*

great-aunt N grand-tante *f*

the Great Australian Bight N la Grande Baie Australienne

the Great Barrier Reef N la Grande Barrière de corail

the Great Bear N *(Astron)* la Grande Ourse

Great Britain N Grande-Bretagne *f* ; → GREAT BRITAIN

Great Dane N *(= dog)* danois *m*

the Great Dividing Range N la cordillère australienne

Greater London N le grand Londres *m*

Greater London Authority conseil municipal de Londres

Greater Manchester N l'agglomération *f* de Manchester

greatest common divisor, greatest common factor N *(Math)* plus grand commun diviseur *m*

great-grandchild N (pl **great-grandchildren**) arrière-petit-fils *m*, arrière-petite-fille *f* ◆ **my ~-grandchildren** mes arrière-petits-enfants *mpl*

great-granddaughter N arrière-petite-fille *f*

great-grandfather N arrière-grand-père *m*, bisaïeul *m (liter)*

great-grandmother N arrière-grand-mère *f*, bisaïeule *f (liter)*

great-grandparent N *(= great-grandfather)* arrière-grand-père *m* ; *(= great-grandmother)* arrière-grand-mère *f* ◆ **~-grandparents** arrière-grands-parents *mpl*

great-grandson N arrière-petit-fils *m*

great-great-grandfather N arrière-arrière-grand-père *m*, trisaïeul *m (liter)*

great-great-grandson N arrière-arrière-petit-fils *m*

great-hearted ADJ au grand cœur, magnanime

the Great Lakes NPL les Grands Lacs *mpl*

Great Leap Forward N *(in China)* le Grand Bond en avant

great-nephew N petit-neveu *m*

great-niece N petite-nièce *f*

the Great Plains NPL les Grandes Plaines *fpl*

the Great Powers NPL *(Pol)* les grandes puissances *fpl*

great tit N *(= bird)* mésange *f* charbonnière

great-uncle N grand-oncle *m*

the Great Wall of China N la Grande Muraille de Chine

the Great War N la Grande Guerre, la guerre de 14-18

the Great White Way* N *(esp US)* Broadway *m*

GREAT BRITAIN, UNITED KINGDOM

Dans l'usage courant, il est fréquent d'employer les mots **Britain** ou **England** pour désigner l'ensemble du Royaume-Uni, mais cet usage est impropre.

La Grande-Bretagne, **Great Britain** ou **Britain** en anglais, est, strictement parlant, un terme géographique. Il désigne la plus grande des îles Britanniques et englobe donc l'Écosse et le pays de Galles. Avec l'Irlande, l'île de Man et les îles Anglo-Normandes, la Grande-Bretagne constitue les îles Britanniques ou **British Isles**, qui sont également une notion géographique puisqu'elles comprennent deux pays : le Royaume-Uni (capitale : Londres) et la République d'Irlande (capitale : Dublin).

Le Royaume-Uni (de Grande-Bretagne et d'Irlande du Nord), en anglais **United Kingdom (of Great Britain and Northern Ireland)** ou **UK**, est la désignation officielle d'une entité politique. Ses citoyens sont des Britanniques.

greatcoat /ˈgreɪtkəʊt/ N pardessus *m* ; *(Mil)* manteau *m*, capote *f*

greater /ˈgreɪtəʳ/, **greatest** /ˈgreɪtɪst/ ADJ compar, superl of **great**

greatly /ˈgreɪtlɪ/ ADV *[regret]* vivement ; *[surprise]* beaucoup ; *[prefer]* de beaucoup ; *[admire, influence, increase]* énormément ; *[improve]* considérablement ; *[exaggerate]* largement ; *[diminish]* fortement, considérablement ♦ **to be ~ superior to sb/sth** être nettement supérieur à qn/qch ♦ **this is ~ to be feared/regretted** *(frm)* il y a tout lieu de le craindre/de le regretter

greatness /ˈgreɪtnɪs/ N *[of person, achievement, country, city]* grandeur *f* ; *[of work of art]* grandeur *f*, splendeur *f*

grebe /griːb/ N grèbe *m*

Grecian /ˈgriːʃən/ *(liter)* ADJ grec (grecque *f*) ♦ **hair in a ~ knot** coiffure *f* à la grecque N *(= Greek)* Grec(que) *m(f)*

Greco- /ˈgriːkəʊ/ *(esp US)* ⇒ **Graeco-**

Greece /griːs/ N Grèce *f*

greed /griːd/ N *(NonC, for food)* gourmandise *f* ; *(for money, power etc)* avidité *f*, cupidité *f*

greedily /ˈgriːdɪlɪ/ ADV *[eat, drink]* goulûment ♦ **he eyed the food** ~ il a regardé la nourriture d'un air vorace *or* goulu ♦ **he licked his lips** ~ il s'est léché les babines

greediness /ˈgriːdɪnɪs/ N ⇒ **greed**

greedy /ˈgriːdɪ/ ADJ *(for food)* gourmand ; *(for money, power etc)* avide (*for* de) rapace, cupide ♦ **~ for gain** âpre au gain ♦ **don't be ~!** *(at table)* ne sois pas si gourmand ! ; *(gen)* n'en demande pas tant ! ♦ **~ guts**‡ *(pej)* goinfre *m*, bâfreur* *m* ; → **hog**

Greek /griːk/ ADJ *(gen)* grec (grecque *f*) ; *[ambassador, embassy, monarch]* de Grèce ; *[teacher]* de grec ♦ **~ scholar** *or* **expert** helléniste *mf* N 1 Grec(que) *m(f)* 2 *(= language)* grec *m* ♦ **ancient/modern** ~ grec *m* classique/moderne ♦ **that's (all) ~ to me*** tout ça c'est de l'hébreu *or* du chinois pour moi*

COMP **Greek Cypriot** N Chypriote *mf* grec (grecque *f*) ADJ chypriote grec

Greek god N *(Myth)* dieu *m* grec ♦ **to be a ~ god** *(= handsome man)* être beau comme un dieu

Greek-letter society N *(US Univ) association d'étudiants désignée par une combinaison de lettres grecques* ; → PHI BETA KAPPA

Greek Orthodox Church N Église *f* orthodoxe grecque

Greek tragedy N *(Theat)* tragédie *f* grecque

green /griːn/ ADJ 1 *(in colour)* vert ♦ **dark** ~ vert *inv* foncé *inv* ♦ **light** ~ vert *inv* clair *inv* ♦ **pale** ~ vert *inv* pâle *inv* ♦ **the ~ shoots of recovery** les premiers signes *mpl* de reprise ♦ **he looked quite** ~ *(fig)* il était vert ♦ **to turn** *or* **go** ~ *[person]* verdir ♦ **she went** ~ elle *or* son visage a verdi ♦ **to be/turn ~ with envy** *(fig)* être/devenir vert de jalousie ♦ **to make sb ~ with envy** rendre qn vert de jalousie ; see also **comp**

2 *(= unripe) [fruit]* vert, pas mûr ; *[banana, tomato, wood]* vert ; *[bacon]* non fumé ♦ **~ corn** blé *m* en herbe ♦ **~ meat** viande *f* crue

3 * *(= inexperienced)* jeune, inexpérimenté ; *(= naïve)* naïf (naïve *f*) ♦ **I'm not as ~ as I look!** je ne suis pas si naïf que j'en ai l'air ! ♦ **he's as ~ as grass** c'est un blanc-bec*

4 *(* = ecological) [issues, movement, company, policy, product]* écologique ; *[vote, voters]* vert ; *[party]* écologique, vert ; *[person]* écolo* *inv* ♦ **~ awareness** prise *f* de conscience des problèmes écologiques

5 *(liter = flourishing)* vert, vigoureux ♦ **to keep sb's memory** ~ chérir la mémoire de qn ♦ **memories still** ~ souvenirs *mpl* encore vivaces *or* vivants

N 1 *(= colour)* vert *m* ♦ **dressed in** ~ habillé de *or* en vert

2 *(= lawn)* pelouse *f*, gazon *m* ; (also **village green**) ≈ place *f* (du village) *(gazonnée)* ; *(Golf)* vert *m* ; (also **bowling green**) *terrain gazonné pour le jeu de boules*

NPL **greens** 1 *(Brit = vegetables)* légumes *mpl* verts

2 *(Pol)* ♦ **the Greens** les Verts *mpl*

ADV *(Pol)* ♦ **to vote** ~ voter vert ♦ **to think** ~ penser écologie

COMP **green bean** N haricot *m* vert

green belt N *(Brit Town Planning)* ceinture *f* verte

the Green Berets NPL *(Mil)* les bérets *mpl* verts

green card N *(in Brit = driving insurance)* carte *f* verte ; *(in US) (= work permit)* permis *m* de travail

Green Cross Code N *(Brit) code de prévention routière destiné aux enfants*

green currency N monnaie *f* verte

green-eyed ADJ aux yeux verts ; *(fig)* jaloux, envieux ♦ **the ~-eyed monster** *(fig)* la jalousie

green fingers NPL *(Brit)* ♦ **he's got ~ fingers** il a la main verte *or* le pouce vert

green goddess* N *(Brit)* voiture *f* de pompiers *(de l'armée)*

green light N *(= traffic light)* feu *m* vert ♦ **to give sb/sth the ~ light** *(fig)* donner le feu vert à qn/qch ♦ **to get the ~ light from sb** obtenir *or* recevoir le feu vert de qn

the Green Mountain State N *(US)* le Vermont

green onion N *(US)* ciboule *f*

Green Paper N *(Brit Pol)* ≃ livre *m* blanc

the Green Party N *(Brit Pol)* les Verts *mpl*

green peas NPL petits pois *mpl*

green pepper N poivron *m* vert

the green pound N *(Econ)* la livre verte

green power N *(US) [of money]* puissance *f* de l'argent

green revolution N *(Econ, Agr)* révolution *f* verte

green room N *(Theat)* foyer *m* des acteurs *or* des artistes

green salad N salade *f* (verte)

green tea N thé *m* vert

green thumb N *(US)* ⇒ **green fingers**

green vegetables NPL légumes *mpl* verts

green-welly* ADJ *(pej)* ♦ **the ~-welly brigade** les gens huppés qui vivent à la campagne

green woodpecker N pivert *m*, pic-vert *m*

GREEN-WELLY BRIGADE

En Grande-Bretagne, les personnes qui pratiquent l'équitation, la chasse et la pêche portent souvent des bottes en caoutchouc vertes. Ces passe-temps étant traditionnellement ceux d'une certaine élite sociale, les bottes vertes sont devenues un signe social distinctif. L'expression **green-welly brigade** est parfois utilisée pour évoquer certains aspects déplaisants du comportement de la haute société.

greenback* /ˈgriːnbæk/ N *(US = dollar)* dollar *m*

greenery /ˈgriːnərɪ/ N verdure *f*

greenfield site /ˈgriːnfiːldsaɪt/ N terrain *m* en dehors de la ville

greenfinch /ˈgriːnfɪntʃ/ N verdier *m*

greenfly /ˈgriːnflaɪ/ N (pl **greenfly** *or* **greenflies**) puceron *m* (des plantes)

greengage /ˈgriːn,geɪdʒ/ N *(Brit)* reine-claude *f*

greengrocer /ˈgriːngrəʊsəʳ/ N *(Brit)* marchand(e) *m(f)* de fruits et légumes ♦ **~'s (shop)** magasin *m* de fruits et légumes

greenhorn /ˈgriːnhɔːn/ N blanc-bec *m*

greenhouse /ˈgriːnhaʊs/ N serre *f* ♦ **the ~ effect** *(Ecol)* l'effet *m* de serre ♦ **~ gas** *(Ecol)* gaz *m* contribuant à l'effet de serre

greening /ˈgriːnɪŋ/ N *(NonC)* sensibilisation *f* à l'environnement

greenish /ˈgriːnɪʃ/ ADJ tirant sur le vert, verdâtre *(pej)* ♦ **~-blue/-yellow/-brown** bleu/jaune/brun tirant sur le vert

Greenland /ˈgriːnlənd/ N Groenland *m* ♦ **in** ~ au Groenland ADJ groenlandais

Greenlander /ˈgriːnləndəʳ/ N Groenlandais(e) *m(f)*

Greenlandic /griːnˈlændɪk/ ADJ groenlandais N *(= language)* groenlandais *m*

greenmail /ˈgriːnmeɪl/ N *(US Stock Exchange)* chantage *m* financier *(pour revendre au prix fort à une société les actions qui ont été achetées lors d'un raid)*

greenness /ˈgriːnnɪs/ N couleur *f* verte, vert *m* ; *[of countryside etc]* verdure *f* ; *[of wood, fruit etc]* verdeur *f*

Greenpeace /ˈgriːn,piːs/ N Greenpeace *m*

greenshank /ˈgriːnʃæŋk/ N *(= bird)* chevalier *m* aboyeur

greenstick fracture /ˈgriːnstɪkfræktʃəʳ/ N *(Med)* fracture *f* incomplète *or* en bois vert

greenstuff /ˈgriːnstʌf/ N verdure *f* ; *(Culin)* légumes *mpl* verts, verdure *f*

greensward †† /ˈgriːnswɔːd/ N pelouse *f*, gazon *m*, tapis *m* de verdure

Greenwich /ˈgrenɪtʃ, ˈgrenɪdʒ/ N ♦ **~ (mean) time** heure *f* de Greenwich

greenwood /ˈgriːnwʊd/ N *(liter)* ♦ **the ~** la forêt verdoyante

greeny* /ˈgriːnɪ/ ADJ ⇒ **greenish**

greet[1] /griːt/ VT *[+ person]* *(= say or wave hello to)* saluer ; *(= invite, welcome)* accueillir ♦ **they ~ed him with cries of delight** ils l'ont accueilli avec des cris de joie ♦ **he ~ed me with the news that ...** il m'a accueilli en m'apprenant que ... ♦ **the statement was ~ed with laughter** la déclaration fut accueillie *or* saluée par des rires ♦ **this was ~ed with relief by everyone** ceci a été accueilli avec soulagement par tous ♦ **to ~ the ear** parvenir à l'oreille ♦ **an awful sight ~ed me** *or* **my eyes** un spectacle affreux s'offrit à mes regards

greet[2] /griːt/ VI *(Scot = weep)* pleurer

greeting /ˈgriːtɪŋ/ N salut *m*, salutation *f* ; *(= welcome)* accueil *m* ♦ **~s** compliments *mpl*, salutations *fpl* ♦ **Xmas ~s** vœux *mpl* de Noël ♦ **~(s) card** carte *f* de vœux ♦ **he sent ~s to my brother** il s'est rappelé au bon souvenir de mon frère ♦ **my mother sends you her ~s** ma mère vous envoie son bon souvenir

gregarious /grɪˈgeərɪəs/ ADJ *[animal, instinct, tendency]* grégaire ; *[person]* sociable ♦ **man is ~** l'homme est un animal grégaire

Gregorian /grɪˈgɔːrɪən/ ADJ grégorien

COMP **Gregorian calendar** N calendrier *m* grégorien

Gregorian chant N chant *m* grégorien

Gregory /ˈgregərɪ/ N Grégoire *m*

gremlin* /ˈgremlɪn/ N diablotin *m* (malfaisant)

Grenada /greˈneɪdə/ N Grenade *f* ♦ **in** ~ à la Grenade

grenade /grɪˈneɪd/ N grenade *f* ; → **hand, stun**

Grenadian /greˈneɪdɪən/ ADJ grenadin N Grenadin(e) *m(f)*

grenadier /,grenəˈdɪəʳ/ N grenadier *m (soldat)*

grenadine /ˈgrenədiːn/ N grenadine *f*

grew /gruː/ VB pt of **grow**

grey, gray *(US)* /greɪ/ ADJ 1 *(in colour)* gris ♦ **dark** ~ gris *inv* foncé *inv* ♦ **light** ~ gris *inv* clair *inv* ♦ **pale** ~ gris *inv* pâle *inv* ♦ **he is totally** ~ *(hair)* il a les cheveux complètement gris ♦ **he** *or* **his hair is going** *or* **turning** ~ il grisonne, ses cheveux grisonnent ♦ **he nearly went ~ over it** il s'en est fait des cheveux blancs ♦ **~ skies** ciel *m* gris ♦ **it was a ~ day** *(lit)* c'était un jour gris ; *(fig)* c'était un jour triste ◆ **the men in ~ suits** *(Pol hum) les membres influents du parti conservateur*

2 *(= ashen) [person, face, complexion]* blême ◆ **to turn ~** blêmir

3 *(= bleak) [time, world]* morne ; *[outlook, prospect]* sombre, morne ; *(= boring) [person, image]* terne ; *[city, town]* morne, triste

4 *(= older people's) [vote, market]* des plus de 55 ans, des seniors

N 1 *(= colour)* gris *m* ◆ **dressed in ~** habillé de *or* en gris ◆ **hair touched with ~** cheveux *mpl* grisonnants

2 *(= horse)* cheval *m* gris

VI *[hair]* grisonner ◆ **~ing hair** cheveux *mpl* grisonnants ◆ **a ~ing man** un homme aux cheveux grisonnants ◆ **he was ~ing at the temples** il avait les tempes grisonnantes

COMP **grey area** N zone *f* d'ombre ◆ **a ~ area between truth and lies** une zone d'ombre entre la vérité et le mensonge ◆ **the law on compensation is a ~ area** la loi sur l'indemnisation comporte des zones d'ombre
Grey Friar N franciscain *m*
grey-haired ADJ aux cheveux gris, grisonnant
grey market N marché *m* gris
grey matter N *(Anat)* substance *f* grise ; *(* = intelligence)* matière *f* grise
grey mullet N mulet *m*, muge *m*
grey seal N phoque *m* gris
grey squirrel N écureuil *m* gris, petit-gris *m*
grey wagtail N bergeronnette *f* des ruisseaux
grey wolf N loup *m* (gris)

greybeard /ˈgreɪbɪəd/ N *(liter)* vieil homme *m*

Greyhound /ˈgreɪhaʊnd/ N ◆ **~ (bus)** Greyhound *mpl*

GREYHOUND

Les cars de tourisme de la compagnie **Greyhound** sillonnent tout le territoire des États-Unis. Ce moyen de transport très répandu et bon marché perpétue symboliquement la tradition des grandes migrations américaines. La compagnie propose un abonnement forfaitaire appelé "Ameripass" qui permet de voyager sans restriction dans l'ensemble du pays.

greyhound /ˈgreɪhaʊnd/ N *(= dog)* lévrier *m* ; *(= bitch)* levrette *f* COMP **greyhound racing** N courses *fpl* de lévriers

greying /ˈgreɪɪŋ/ ADJ → **grey vi**

greyish /ˈgreɪɪʃ/ ADJ tirant sur le gris, grisâtre *(pej)* ; *[hair, beard]* grisonnant

greylag goose /ˈgreɪlæggu:s/ N oie *f* cendrée

greyness /ˈgreɪnɪs/ N *(= colour)* couleur *f* grise ; *(= semi-dark)* pénombre *f* ; *[of atmosphere, weather, day]* morosité *f* ; *[of person]* fadeur *f*

grid /grɪd/ N 1 *(= grating)* grille *f*, grillage *m* ; *(= network of lines on chart, map etc, also Rad)* grille *f* ; *(Theat)* gril *m (pour manœuvrer les décors)* ; *(= electrode)* grille *f* ; *(Brit Elec = system)* réseau *m* ; *(Surv)* treillis *m* ◆ **the (national) ~** *(Brit Elec)* le réseau électrique (national) 2 ⇒ **gridiron**
COMP **grid map** N carte *f or* plan *m* quadrillé(e) *or* à grille
grid reference N référence *f* de grille

gridded /ˈgrɪdɪd/ ADJ quadrillé

griddle /ˈgrɪdl/ N *(Culin)* plaque *f* en fonte *(pour cuire)* ; *(= part of stove)* plaque *f* chauffante VT *(Culin)* cuire sur une plaque COMP **griddle cake** N (sorte *f* de) crêpe *f* épaisse

gridiron /ˈgrɪdaɪən/ N 1 *(= utensil)* gril *m* 2 *(American Ftbl)* terrain *m* de football américain

gridlock /ˈgrɪdlɒk/ N *(US)* bouchon *m* ; *(fig) (in talks etc)* impasse *f*

gridlocked /ˈgrɪdlɒkt/ ADJ *(esp US)* 1 *(lit) [road]* embouteillé ; *[traffic]* bloqué 2 *(fig) [government, negotiations]* dans une impasse

grief /gri:f/ N 1 *(NonC)* chagrin *m*, peine *f* ◆ **to come to ~** *[vehicle, rider, driver]* avoir un accident ; *[plan, marriage etc]* échouer ◆ **a bungee jumper came to ~ during recording for a TV programme** un sauteur à l'élastique a eu un accident lors de l'enregistrement d'une émission télévisée ◆ **good ~!*** ciel !, grands dieux ! 2 *(= cause of grief)* (cause *f* de) chagrin *m* 3 *(* = trouble)* embêtements* *mpl*, ennuis *mpl* ◆ **to give sb ~** embêter* qn, en faire voir de toutes les couleurs à qn ◆ **the bank's been giving me ~ about my overdraft** la banque m'a fait des histoires à cause de mon découvert
COMP **grief counselling** N thérapie *f* du deuil
grief-stricken ADJ accablé de douleur, affligé

grievance /ˈgri:vəns/ N *(= ground for complaint)* grief *m*, sujet *m* de plainte ; *(= complaint)* doléance *f* ; *(in industrial relations)* différend *m*, conflit *m* ◆ **to have a ~ against sb** avoir un grief *or* un sujet de plainte contre qn, en vouloir à qn ◆ **he had a sense of ~** il avait le sentiment profond d'être victime d'une injustice ; → **redress**

grieve /gri:v/ VT peiner, chagriner ◆ **it ~s us to see** nous sommes peinés de voir ◆ **it ~s us to learn that …** nous avons la douleur d'apprendre que …, c'est avec beaucoup de peine que nous apprenons que … ◆ **in a ~d tone** d'un ton peiné *or* chagriné VI avoir de la peine *or* du chagrin *(at, about, over* à cause de) ◆ **to ~ for sb/sth** pleurer qn/qch ◆ **I didn't have any time to ~** je n'avais pas le temps de pleurer

grieving /ˈgri:vɪŋ/ ADJ *[family, relatives]* éploré ◆ **the ~ process** le travail de deuil

grievous /ˈgri:vəs/ *(frm)* ADJ *[injury, damage, error, injustice]* grave ; *[wound]* grave, sérieux ; *[setback]* sérieux ; *[loss]* cruel ; *[blow]* sévère ; *[news]* pénible, affreux ; *[crime, offence]* odieux COMP **grievous bodily harm** N *(Jur)* ≈ coups *mpl* et blessures *fpl*

grievously /ˈgri:vəslɪ/ ADV *(frm) [hurt, offend]* terriblement ◆ **~ injured** *or* **wounded** grièvement blessé ◆ **to wrong sb ~** gravement léser qn ◆ **to be ~ mistaken** se tromper lourdement

griffin /ˈgrɪfɪn/ N *(Myth)* griffon *m*

griffon /ˈgrɪfən/ N *(= mythical beast, dog)* griffon *m*

grift‡ /grɪft/ *(US)* N filouterie* *f*, escroquerie *f* VI filouter*, vivre d'escroquerie

grifter‡ /ˈgrɪftəʳ/ N *(US)* escroc *m*, filou *m*

grill /grɪl/ N 1 *(= cooking utensil)* gril *m* ; *(= food)* grillade *f* ; *(= restaurant)* (also **grillroom**) rôtisserie *f*, grill *m* ◆ **brown it under the ~** faites-le dorer au gril ; → **mixed** 2 ⇒ **grille** VT 1 *(Culin)* (faire) griller ◆ **~ed fish** poisson *m* grillé 2 *(fig = interrogate)* cuisiner*, mettre sur la sellette VI *(Culin)* griller COMP **grill pan** N *(Brit)* plateau *m* à grillades *(avec poignée)*

grille /grɪl/ N *(= grating)* grille *f* ; *[of convent etc]* grille *f* ; *[of door]* judas *m* ; (also **radiator grille**) *[of car]* calandre *f*

grilling /ˈgrɪlɪŋ/ N *(fig = interrogation)* interrogatoire *m* serré ◆ **to give sb a ~** cuisiner* qn, mettre qn sur la sellette

grim /grɪm/ ADJ 1 *(= dire, gloomy) [place, situation, warning, outlook, news]* sinistre ◆ **to hold** *or* **hang** *or* **cling on to sth like** *or* **for ~ death** se cramponner à qch de toutes ses forces ◆ **things are looking pretty ~** les perspectives ne sont guère réjouissantes ◆ **~ necessity** la dure *or* cruelle nécessité ◆ **the ~ reality of hospital work** la dure réalité du travail à l'hôpital ◆ **the ~ truth** la vérité brutale

2 *[person, face, expression] (= stern, angry)* sévère ; *(= worried)* sombre ; *[smile]* sans joie ; *[humour]* macabre ; *[voice]* sombre ◆ **to look ~** *(= angry)* avoir une mine sévère ; *(= worried)* avoir une mine sombre ◆ **with ~ determination** avec une volonté inflexible

3 *(* = bad)* nul* ◆ **his singing's pretty ~** il chante comme une casserole ◆ **to feel ~** *(= unwell)* ne pas être dans son assiette

COMP **the Grim Reaper** N ≈ la Faucheuse *(liter)*

grimace /grɪˈmeɪs/ N grimace *f* VI *(from disgust, pain etc)* grimacer, faire la grimace ; *(for fun)* faire des grimaces ◆ **he ~d at the taste/the sight of …** il a fait une grimace en goûtant/voyant …

grime /graɪm/ N *(NonC)* crasse *f*, saleté *f*

grimly /ˈgrɪmlɪ/ ADV *[frown, look at]* d'un air sévère ; *[continue, hold on]* avec détermination ; *[fight, struggle]* farouchement ◆ **~ determined** farouchement déterminé ◆ **to smile ~** avoir un sourire amer ◆ **he nodded ~** l'air sombre, il acquiesça d'un signe de tête ◆ **"no surrender", they said ~** "nous ne nous rendrons pas", dirent-ils, farouchement déterminés ◆ **"this is not good enough" he said ~** "ça ne va pas" dit-il d'un air sévère

grimness /ˈgrɪmnɪs/ N *[of situation]* caractère *m* sinistre ; *[of sight, face, person]* aspect *m* lugubre *or* sinistre

grimy /ˈgraɪmɪ/ ADJ crasseux

grin /grɪn/ VI 1 *(= smile)* sourire ; *(broadly)* avoir un large *or* grand sourire ◆ **his ~ning face confronts us on the television** son visage souriant est là, devant nous, sur l'écran de télévision ◆ **to ~ broadly at sb** adresser un large sourire à qn ◆ **to ~ from ear to ear, to ~ like a Cheshire cat** avoir un sourire fendu jusqu'aux oreilles ◆ **we must just ~ and bear it** il faut le prendre avec le sourire, il faut faire contre mauvaise fortune bon cœur 2 *(in pain)* avoir un rictus, grimacer ; *[snarling dog]* montrer les dents VT ◆ **he ~ned his approval** il a manifesté son approbation d'un large sourire N *(= smile)* (large) sourire *m* ; *(in pain)* rictus *m*, grimace *f* de douleur

grind /graɪnd/ (pret, ptp **ground**) N 1 *(= sound)* grincement *m*, crissement *m*

2 *(* = dull hard work)* boulot* *m* pénible ; *(particular task)* corvée *f* ◆ **the daily ~** le boulot* quotidien ◆ **she found housework a ~** le ménage était une corvée pour elle ◆ **the tiresome ~ of preparing for exams** la vraie corvée que sont les révisions pour les examens

3 *(US * = swot)* bûcheur *m*, -euse *f*

VT 1 *[+ corn, coffee, pepper etc]* moudre ; *(= crush)* écraser, broyer ; *(US) [+ meat]* hacher ; *(in mortar)* piler, concasser ◆ **to ~ sth to a powder** pulvériser qch, réduire qch en poudre ◆ **the metal will have to be ground into tiny pieces** il faudra réduire le métal en petits morceaux ◆ **to ~ one's teeth** grincer des dents ◆ **dirt ground into the carpet** saleté *f* incrustée dans le tapis ◆ **he ground his heel into the soil** il a enfoncé son talon dans la terre ◆ **to ~ the faces of the poor** opprimer les pauvres ; see also **ground²**

2 *(= polish) [+ gems]* égriser, polir ; *[+ knife, blade]* aiguiser *or* affûter (à la meule), meuler ; *[+ lens]* polir ; → **axe**

3 *(= turn) [+ handle]* tourner ; *[+ barrel organ]* faire jouer, jouer de ◆ **to ~ a pepper mill** tourner un moulin à poivre

VI 1 grincer ◆ **the ship was ~ing against the rocks** le navire heurtait les rochers en grinçant ◆ **tanks were ~ing south** des chars progressaient péniblement en direction du sud ◆ **to ~ to a halt** *or* **a standstill** *[vehicle]* s'arrêter *or* s'immobiliser dans un grincement de freins ; *[process, production, negotiations etc]* s'enliser ◆ **the traffic had ground to a halt** *or* **a standstill** il y avait un bouchon

2 (* = work hard) bosser * dur or ferme

► **grind away** * VI bosser * dur or ferme ♦ **to ~ away at grammar** bûcher* or potasser* la grammaire

► **grind down** VT SEP 1 (l t) pulvériser

2 (fig) (= oppress) opprimer, écraser ; (= wear down) [+ one's opponents etc] avoir à l'usure ♦ **ground down by poverty** accablé par la misère ♦ **he gradually ground down all opposition to his plans** il a écrasé petit à petit toute tentative d'opposition à ses plans ; see also **grind vi 1**

► **grind on** VI [person] continuer péniblement or laborieusement ; [year, week, day etc] s'écouler péniblement ; [war] s'éterniser implacablement

► **grind out** VT SEP ♦ **to grind out a tune on a barrel organ** jouer un air sur un orgue de Barbarie ♦ **he ground out an oath** il a proféré un juron entre ses dents ♦ **he managed to ~ out two pages of his essay** il est laborieusement arrivé à pondre * or à écrire deux pages de sa dissertation

► **grind up** VT SEP pulvériser

grinder /ˈgraɪndəʳ/ N 1 (= apparatus) broyeur m, moulin m ; (= tool) meuleuse f ; (for sharpening) affûteuse f, meule f à aiguiser 2 (= person) broyeur m, -euse f ; (for knives) rémouleur m, -euse f ; → **organ** 3 (= tooth) molaire f 4 (US Culin *) grand sandwich m mixte

grinding /ˈgraɪndɪŋ/ N (NonC = sound) grincement m ADJ 1 (= oppressive) ♦ **poverty** misère f noire ♦ **~ hard work** travail m très pénible ♦ **~ tedium** ennui m mortel 2 (= grating) [noise] grinçant ♦ **to make a ~ noise** grincer ♦ **to come to a ~ halt** [process, production, negotiations] s'enrayer brusquement ; [vehicle] s'arrêter brusquement ♦ **to bring sth to a ~ halt** [+ process, production, negotiations] mettre brusquement un terme à qch ; [+ vehicle] arrêter qch dans un grincement ♦ **the traffic came to** or **was brought to a ~ halt** la circulation a fini par se bloquer

grindingly /ˈgraɪndɪŋlɪ/ ADV ♦ **to be ~ hard work** être terriblement dur ♦ **to be a ~ slow process** être horriblement long ♦ **the routine became ~ familiar** la routine est devenue terriblement pesante

grindstone /ˈgraɪndstəʊn/ N meule f (à aiguiser) ♦ **to keep sb's nose to the ~** faire travailler qn sans répit or relâche ♦ **to keep one's nose to the ~** travailler sans répit or relâche

gringo /ˈgrɪŋgəʊ/ N (US pej) gringo m, Ricain(e) m(f)

grip /grɪp/ N 1 (= handclasp) poigne f ; (= hold) prise f ; (= control) mainmise f ♦ **he held my arm in a vice-like ~** il me tenait le bras d'une poigne d'acier, il me serrait le bras comme un étau ♦ **she tightened her ~ on my arm** elle a serré mon bras plus fort ♦ **he has a strong ~** il a de la poigne or une bonne poigne ♦ **cold weather had a firm ~ on the capital** un froid intense régnait dans la capitale ♦ **environmentalism has taken a firm ~ on Europe** l'écologisme est solidement implanté en Europe ♦ **they're struggling to maintain their ~ on power** ils s'efforcent de maintenir leur mainmise sur le pouvoir ♦ **rebel forces are tightening their ~ on the capital** les rebelles resserrent l'étau sur la capitale

♦ **to get a grip** * (= control oneself) se ressaisir ♦ **he told himself to get a ~** il s'est dit "ressaisis-toi !"

♦ **to get a grip on** or **of o.s.** * se ressaisir ♦ **get a ~ on yourself!** ressaisis-toi ! ♦ **I had to get a ~ of myself not to panic** j'ai dû me faire violence pour ne pas paniquer

♦ **to keep a grip on o.s.** * se maîtriser, se contrôler

♦ **to get a grip on** or **of sth** (= get hold of) empoigner qch

♦ **to get a grip on** (= control) [+ inflation] contrôler ; [+ party, power] prendre le contrôle de ; [+ situation] prendre en main

♦ **to lose one's grip** (on object) lâcher prise ; (= lose control) perdre le contrôle de la situation ♦ **Brown is showing signs of losing his ~** il semble que Brown soit en train de perdre le contrôle de la situation ♦ **he's losing his ~** * [old person] il perd un peu les pédales * ♦ **I must be losing my ~!** * (hum) je baisse ! *

♦ **to lose one's grip on sth** [+ object] lâcher ♦ **he lost his ~ on the rope** il a lâché la corde ♦ **the President was losing his ~ on power** le président perdait le contrôle du pouvoir ♦ **to lose one's ~ on reality** perdre le sens de la réalité

♦ **in the grip of** en proie à ♦ **a region in the ~ of severe drought** une région en proie à une grave sécheresse ♦ **the country was in the ~ of an epidemic of minor crime** le pays était en proie à une véritable épidémie de délinquance ♦ **in the ~ of winter** paralysé par l'hiver ♦ **country in the ~ of a general strike** pays paralysé par une grève générale

♦ **to fall into the grip of sb** or **sth** ♦ **he fell into the ~ of the dictator** il est tombé sous l'emprise du dictateur ♦ **she fell into the ~ of anorexia** elle est devenue anorexique

2 [of tyre] adhérence f

3 (= handle) poignée f ; (on racket) prise f de raquette ; (on golf club, bat) prise f

4 (= suitcase) valise f ; (US) (= bag) (also **gripsack**) sac m de voyage

5 (TV, Cine: also **key grip**: US) machiniste mf caméra

NPL **grips** ♦ **to come** or **get to ~s with a problem** s'attaquer à un problème, s'efforcer de résoudre un problème ♦ **we have never had to come to ~s with such a situation** nous n'avons jamais été confrontés à pareille situation

VT 1 (= grasp) [+ rope, handrail, sb's arm] saisir ; [+ pistol, sword etc] saisir, empoigner ; (= hold) serrer, tenir serré ♦ **to ~ sb's hand** (= grasp) saisir la main de qn ; (= hold) tenir la main de qn serrée ♦ **to ~ the road** [tyres] adhérer à la chaussée ♦ **the car ~s the road well** la voiture tient bien la route

2 [fear etc] saisir, étreindre ♦ **~ped by terror** saisi de terreur

3 (= interest strongly) [film, story etc] captiver ♦ **a film that really ~s you** un film vraiment palpitant, un film qui vous prend vraiment

VI [wheels] adhérer, mordre ; [screw, vice, brakes] mordre ; [anchor] crocher (sur le fond)

COMP **grip strip** N (for carpet) bande f adhésive (pour tapis)

gripe /graɪp/ VT (= anger) ♦ **this ~d him** * cela lui a mis l'estomac en boule * VI (* = grumble) ronchonner, rouspéter * (at contre) N 1 (Med: also **gripes**) coliques fpl 2 (NonC) ♦ **his main ~ was that …** * son principal sujet de plainte or de rogne * était que … COMP **gripe water** N (Brit) calmant m (pour coliques infantiles)

griping /ˈgraɪpɪŋ/ ADJ ♦ **~ pain(s)** coliques fpl N (NonC: * = grumbling) rouspétance * f, ronchonnements * mpl

grippe /grɪp/ N (US) grippe f

gripping /ˈgrɪpɪŋ/ ADJ (= exciting) palpitant

grisly /ˈgrɪzlɪ/ ADJ (= gruesome) macabre, sinistre ; (= terrifying) horrible, effroyable

grist /grɪst/ N blé m (à moudre) ♦ **it's all ~ for** or **to his mill** cela apporte de l'eau à son moulin ♦ **any media coverage is useful - it's all ~ to the mill** toute couverture médiatique est utile : c'est toujours bon à prendre

gristle /ˈgrɪsl/ N (NonC) nerfs mpl (surtout dans la viande cuite)

gristly /ˈgrɪslɪ/ ADJ [meat] tendineux

grit /grɪt/ N (NonC) 1 (= sand) sable m ; (= gravel) gravillon m ; (= rock: also **gritstone**) grès m ; (for fowl) gravier m ♦ **I've got (a piece of) ~ in my eye** j'ai une poussière dans l'œil 2 (* fig = courage) cran * m ♦ **he's got ~** il a du cran * NPL **grits** (US) gruau m de maïs VI craquer, crisser VT 1 ♦ **to ~ one's teeth** serrer les dents 2 ♦ **to ~ a road** sabler une route, répandre du sable sur une route

gritter /ˈgrɪtəʳ/ N camion m de sablage

gritty /ˈgrɪtɪ/ ADJ 1 (= stony, grainy) [soil, ash] graveleux ; [road] sablé ; [floor] plein de grains de sable ; [texture] grumeleux ; [fruit] graveleux, grumeleux ♦ **these leeks/mussels are ~** il y a du sable dans ces poireaux/dans ces moules 2 (* = courageous) [person, determination] solide ♦ **the team's ~ display** la performance courageuse de l'équipe 3 (= unsentimental) [realism] cru ; [film, drama, account] réaliste

grizzle /ˈgrɪzl/ VI (Brit) (= whine) pleurnicher, geindre ; (= complain) ronchonner *

grizzled /ˈgrɪzld/ ADJ [hair, beard, man] grisonnant

grizzly /ˈgrɪzlɪ/ ADJ 1 (= grey) grisâtre ; [hair, person] grisonnant 2 (= whining) pleurnicheur, geignard N (also **grizzly bear**) grizzly m

groan /grəʊn/ N [of pain] gémissement m, plainte f ; [of disapproval, dismay] grognement m ♦ **this news was greeted with ~s** cette nouvelle a été accueillie par des murmures (désapprobateurs) VI 1 (in pain) gémir, pousser un or des gémissement(s) (with de) ; (in disapproval, dismay) grogner ♦ **he ~ed inwardly at the thought** il étouffa un grognement à cette idée 2 (= creak) [planks] gémir ; [door] crier ♦ **the table ~ed under the weight of the food** la table ployait sous le poids de la nourriture ♦ **the ~ing board** (o.f or hum) la table ployant sous l'amoncellement de victuailles VT (in pain) dire en gémissant ; (in disapproval, dismay) dire en grommelant

groat /grəʊt/ N (Brit) ancienne petite pièce de monnaie

groats /grəʊts/ NPL gruau m d'avoine or de froment

grocer /ˈgrəʊsəʳ/ N épicier m, -ière f ♦ **at the ~'s (shop)** à l'épicerie, chez l'épicier

grocery /ˈgrəʊsərɪ/ N 1 (= shop) épicerie f ♦ **he's in the ~ business** il est dans l'épicerie 2 (= provisions) ♦ **I spent $25 on groceries** j'ai dépensé 25 dollars en épicerie or en provisions ♦ **all the groceries are in this basket** toute l'épicerie est dans ce panier

grog /grɒg/ N grog m

groggy * /ˈgrɒgɪ/ ADJ [person] (= weak) faible ; (= unsteady) groggy * ; (from blow etc) groggy *, sonné * ; [voice] faible ♦ **I still feel a bit ~** je me sens toujours un peu sonné * or groggy *

grogram /ˈgrɒgrəm/ N gros-grain m

groin /grɔɪn/ N 1 (Anat) aine f 2 (Archit) arête f 3 ⇒ **groyne**

grommet /ˈgrɒmɪt/ N 1 (= metal eyelet) œillet m 2 (Med) drain m transtympanique

groom /gruːm/ N 1 (for horses) valet m d'écurie, palefrenier m 2 (also **bridegroom**) (just married) (jeune) marié m ; (about to be married) (futur) marié m 3 (in royal household) chambellan m VT [+ horse] panser ♦ **the cat was ~ing itself** le chat faisait sa toilette ♦ **to ~ each other** [primates] s'épouiller ♦ **to ~ o.s.** [person] se pomponner, s'arranger ♦ **well-~ed** [person] très soigné ; [hair] bien coiffé ♦ **to ~ sb for a post** préparer or former qn pour un poste ♦ **she is being ~ed for stardom** on la prépare à devenir une star ♦ **he is ~ing him as his successor** il en a fait son poulain

grooming /ˈɡruːmɪŋ/ N 1 *(= care)* soins *mpl* de toilette *or* de beauté ; *(= appearance)* apparence *f* (impeccable) ◆ ~ **products** produits *mpl* de toilette *or* de beauté 2 *[of horse]* pansage *m* ; *[of dog]* toilettage *m*

groove /ɡruːv/ N 1 *(in wood, plank, head of screw, for sliding door)* rainure *f* ; *(for pulley)* gorge *f* ; *(in column)* cannelure *f* ; *(in record)* sillon *m* ; *(in penknife blade)* onglet *m* 2 *(Mus * = rhythm)* groove *m* ◆ **to get into the** ~ trouver son rythme 3 * ◆ **to be in the** ~ *(= up-to-date) [person, place]* être dans le vent * *or* coup * ◆ **he's in the** *or* **a** ~ il a le vent en poupe * ◆ **he's (stuck) in a** ~ il s'est encroûté 4 *(US = great)* ◆ **it's a** ~ * c'est sensationnel *, c'est le pied * VT 1 *(= put groove in)* rainurer, rainer (SPEC) 2 *(US = like)* ◆ **I ~ it** * ça me botte * VI 1 (US *) prendre son pied * 2 *(* = dance)* danser ◆ **to ~ to the music** danser au rythme de la musique

groovy * /ˈɡruːvɪ/ ADJ *(= marvellous)* sensass * *inv*, vachement bien * ; *(= up-to-date)* dans le vent *

grope /ɡrəʊp/ VI tâtonner, aller à l'aveuglette ◆ **to ~ (around) for sth** *(in a room etc)* chercher qch à tâtons *or* à l'aveuglette ◆ **I ~d (around) in my bag for the keys** j'ai fouillé dans mon sac pour trouver les clés ◆ **to ~ for words** chercher ses mots ◆ **scientists are groping towards a cure** les chercheurs s'efforcent de trouver un remède ◆ **to be groping in the dark** *(fig)* être dans le brouillard VT 1 ◆ **to ~ one's way towards** avancer à tâtons *or* à l'aveuglette vers ◆ **to ~ one's way in/out** *etc* entrer/sortir *etc* à tâtons *or* à l'aveuglette 2 *(*, pej = touch sexually)* peloter *, tripoter * N *(pej: sexual)* ◆ **to have a** ~ * *[couple]* se peloter *

groping /ˈɡrəʊpɪŋ/ ADJ 1 *(= tentative) [attempt]* tâtonnant, timide ◆ **we have a ~ awareness of how it works** nous commençons plus ou moins à comprendre comment cela fonctionne 2 *(pej)* ◆ ~ **hands** * mains *fpl* baladeuses N 1 (also **gropings**) *(= tentative attempts)* tâtonnements *mpl* 2 *(*, pej)* pelotage * *m*

gropingly /ˈɡrəʊpɪŋlɪ/ ADV en tâtonnant, à tâtons

grosgrain /ˈɡrəʊɡreɪn/ N gros-grain *m*

gross /ɡrəʊs/ ADJ 1 *(= massive) [injustice]* flagrant ; *[inequalities, abuse, violation, mismanagement, incompetence]* grave ; *[exaggeration, simplification, error]* grossier ◆ ~ **ignorance** ignorance *f* crasse ◆ **that is a ~ understatement** c'est le moins que l'on puisse dire ◆ **it is a ~ exaggeration to say that ...** c'est une grossière exagération que d'affirmer que ...

2 *(* = disgusting) [person, behaviour, food]* dégoûtant, répugnant ; *[clothes]* moche *

3 *(= crude) [remarks, jokes]* grossier

4 *(pej = fat)* énorme

5 *[income, profit, weight etc]* brut

ADV *[pay, weigh]* brut ◆ **she earns £30,000 ~ per annum** elle gagne 30 000 livres brut par an

N 1 ◆ **in (the)** ~ *(= wholesale)* en gros, en bloc ; *(fig)* en général, à tout prendre

2 *(pl inv = twelve dozen)* grosse *f*, douze douzaines *fpl*

VT (+ *amount*) réaliser *or* dégager un bénéfice brut de

COMP **gross domestic income** N revenu *m* intérieur brut

gross domestic product N produit *m* intérieur brut

gross indecency N atteinte *(f)* sexuelle

gross misconduct N faute *(f)* grave

gross national product N produit *m* national brut

gross negligence N *(gen)* extrême négligence *f* ; *(Jur)* ≃ faute *f* grave

gross output N production *f* brute

► **gross out** * VT (US) débecter *

► **gross up** VT FUS *[+ interest, dividend, amount]* calculer le montant brut *or* la valeur brute de

grossly /ˈɡrəʊslɪ/ ADV 1 *(= very much) [exaggerate, overestimate, underestimate]* grossièrement ; *[overpaid, underpaid]* nettement ; *[inadequate]* nettement, largement ; *[inaccurate]* totalement ; *[misleading, inefficient, irresponsible]* terriblement ◆ ~ **unfair** d'une injustice flagrante ◆ **to be ~ negligent** *(gen)* commettre une négligence grave ; *(Jur)* ≃ commettre une faute grave ◆ **the health service is ~ underfunded** les services de santé manquent cruellement de fonds 2 *(= disgustingly) [behave, talk]* de façon grossière, grossièrement 3 *(gen, Med)* ◆ ~ **overweight** obèse

grossness /ˈɡrəʊsnɪs/ N 1 *(= coarseness)* grossièreté *f* 2 *(= fatness)* obésité *f*

grot * /ɡrɒt/ N (NonC) *(= dirt)* crasse *f* ; *(fig)* inepties *fpl*

grotesque /ɡrəʊˈtesk/ ADJ 1 *(= hideous) [appearance]* monstrueux ; *[idea, proposal]* grotesque ; *[sight, spectacle]* choquant 2 *(Art)* grotesque N grotesque *m*

grotesquely /ɡrəʊˈteskli/ ADV *(= hideously) [distorted, deformed, swollen]* monstrueusement ; *[simplistic]* ridiculement

grotto /ˈɡrɒtəʊ/ N (pl **grottos** *or* **grottoes**) grotte *f*

grotty * /ˈɡrɒtɪ/ ADJ (Brit) *(= dirty) [clothes]* cradingue * ; *(= horrible) [place, food]* minable * ◆ **to feel** ~ *(= unwell)* être mal fichu *

grouch * /ɡraʊtʃ/ VI râler * N *(= person)* râleur * *m*, -euse * *f* ◆ **his main ~ is that ...** *(= complaint)* il râle * surtout parce que ...

grouchiness * /ˈɡraʊtʃɪnɪs/ N caractère *m* ronchon * *or* grincheux

grouchy * /ˈɡraʊtʃɪ/ ADJ ronchon *, grincheux

ground[1] /ɡraʊnd/ N 1 (NonC) ◆ **the** ~ *(= surface for walking on)* la terre, le sol ◆ **above** ~ en surface ◆ **below (the)** ~ sous terre ◆ **to fall to the** ~ tomber par terre ◆ **to knock sb to the** ~ faire tomber qn (par terre) ◆ **burnt to the** ~ réduit en cendres ◆ **to lie/sit (down) on the** ~ se coucher/s'asseoir par terre *or* sur le sol ◆ **to have one's feet (firmly) on the** ~ *(fig)* avoir les pieds sur terre ◆ **to get off the** ~ *[plane etc]* décoller ; *[scheme etc]* démarrer ◆ **to get sth off the** ~ *(fig)* (faire) démarrer qch ◆ **to go to** ~ *(lit, fig)* se terrer ◆ **to run a fox to** ~ poursuivre un renard jusqu'à son terrier ◆ **to run sb to** ~ *(fig)* mettre la main sur qn ◆ **that suits me down to the** ~ * ça me va tout à fait ◆ **to run** *or* **drive a car into the** ~ user une voiture jusqu'à ce qu'elle soit bonne pour la casse ◆ **to run a business into the** ~ laisser péricliter une entreprise ◆ **to run sb into the** ~ user *or* épuiser qn ◆ **to run o.s. into the ~ (with work)** s'épuiser (au travail) ◆ **to cut the ~ from under sb's feet** couper l'herbe sous le pied de qn ; → **ear[1]**, **high, thick, thin**

2 (NonC) *(= piece of land)* terrain *m* ; *(larger)* domaine *m*, terres *fpl* ; *(= soil)* sol *m*, terre *f*, terrain *m* ; *(fig)* terrain *m* ◆ **to till the** ~ labourer la terre ◆ **stony** ~ sol *m* *or* terrain *m* caillouteux ; see also **stony** ◆ **all this ~ is owned by Lord Carrick** toutes ces terres appartiennent à Lord Carrick ◆ **neutral** ~ *(lit, fig)* terrain *m* neutre ◆ **to meet sb on his own** ~ *(fig)* affronter qn sur son propre terrain ◆ **to be sure of one's** ~ *(fig)* être sûr de son fait ◆ **to be on dangerous** ~ être sur un terrain glissant ◆ **on familiar** ~ en terrain familier *or* connu ◆ **we're on fairly firm** *or* **solid** ~ nous sommes sur un terrain assez solide ◆ **to change one's** ~ *(fig)* changer son fusil d'épaule ◆ **to give** ~ *(Mil, also fig)* céder du terrain ◆ **to go over the same ~ again** *(fig: in discussion etc)* ressasser les mêmes questions ◆ **to hold one's** ~ tenir bon, ne pas lâcher prise ◆ **to lose** ~ *(Mil, also gen)* perdre du terrain ; *[party, politician]* être en perte de vitesse ◆ **sterling lost ~ against the other European currencies** la livre a perdu du terrain face aux autres monnaies européennes ◆ **to clear the** ~ *(fig)* déblayer le terrain ◆ **to shift one's** ~ changer son fusil d'épaule ◆ **to stand one's** ~ tenir bon ; → **break, common, cover, gain**

3 *(= area for special purpose)* terrain *m* ◆ **football** ~ terrain *m* de football ; → **landing[1]**, **parade, recreation**

4 ◆ **~s** *(= gardens etc)* → **grounds**

5 *(US Elec)* terre *f* ; *(in car etc)* masse *f*

6 *(gen pl = reason)* motif *m*, raison *f* ◆ **~s for divorce/dismissal** motifs *mpl* de divorce/licenciement ◆ **~s for prosecution** chefs *mpl* d'accusation ◆ **~(s) for complaint** grief *m* ◆ **there are ~s for believing that ...** il y a lieu de penser que ... ◆ **the situation gives ~s for anxiety** la situation est préoccupante ◆ **the latest figures give (us) ~s for optimism** les derniers chiffres (nous) permettent d'être optimistes ◆ **on personal/medical ~s** pour (des) raisons personnelles/médicales ◆ **on what ~s?** à quel titre ? ◆ **on the ~(s) of** pour raison de ◆ **on the ~(s) that ...** en raison du fait que ... ◆ **on the ~ that ...** *(Jur)* au motif que ...

7 *(= background)* fond *m* ◆ **on a blue** ~ sur fond bleu

VT 1 *[+ plane, pilot]* empêcher de voler, interdire de voler à ; *(= keep on ground)* retenir au sol

2 *(*: as punishment) [+ teenager]* priver de sortie

3 *[+ ship]* faire s'échouer ◆ **the tanker was ~ed (on the rocks)** le pétrolier s'était échoué (sur les rochers)

4 *(US Elec)* mettre à la terre ; *(in car etc)* mettre à la masse

5 *(= base)* fonder *(on, in* sur) ◆ **her argument was ~ed in** *or* **on fact** son argument était fondé sur des faits ◆ **the story isn't ~ed in reality** cette histoire n'est pas fondée sur la réalité ; → **well[2]**

VI *[ship]* s'échouer

COMP **ground angle shot** N *(Phot, Cine)* contre-plongée *f*

ground attack N *(Mil)* offensive *f* terrestre

ground bait N *(Fishing)* amorce *f* de fond

ground bass N *(Mus)* basse *f* contrainte *or* obstinée

ground cloth N (US) tapis *m* de sol

ground colour N *(= background colour)* fond *m*

ground control N *(at airport)* contrôle *m* au sol

ground crew N *(at airport)* équipe *f* au sol

ground floor N *(esp Brit)* rez-de-chaussée *m* ◆ **he got in on the ~ floor** *(fig)* il est là depuis le début

ground-floor ADJ *(esp Brit) [flat, room]* au rez-de-chaussée ; *[window]* du rez-de-chaussée

ground forces NPL *(Mil)* forces *fpl* terrestres

ground frost N gelée *f* blanche

ground ice N glaces *fpl* de fond

ground ivy N lierre *m* terrestre

ground level N ◆ **at ~ level** au niveau du sol

ground plan N *(= scale drawing)* plan *m* (au sol) ; *(= basic sketch)* esquisse *f*

ground rent N *(esp Brit)* redevance *f* foncière

ground rules NPL *(gen)* procédure *f* ◆ **we can't change the ~ rules at this stage** *(fig)* on ne peut pas changer les règles du jeu maintenant

ground staff N *(at airport)* personnel *m* au sol

ground-to-air missile N *(Mil)* missile *m* sol-air

ground-to-ground missile N *(Mil)* missile *m* sol-sol

ground troops NPL *(Mil)* armée *f* de terre

ground water N *(Geol)* nappe *f* phréatique

ground wire N *(US Elec)* fil *m* de terre ; *(in car etc)* fil *m* de masse

ground zero N *(Mil: of nuclear explosion)* point *m* de radiation maximum au sol

Ground Zero N *(in US)* Ground Zero *m*

ground[2] /ɡraʊnd/ VB pt, ptp of **grind** ADJ *[coffee, spices etc]* moulu ◆ ~ **beef** *(US Culin)* bœuf *m* haché ◆ ~ **glass** *(rough surface)* verre *m* dépoli ; *(powdered)* verre *m* pilé ◆ ~ **rice** farine *f* de riz

groundbreaking /ˈgraʊndbreɪkɪŋ/ ADJ révolutionnaire

groundhog /ˈgraʊndhɒg/ N (US) marmotte *f* d'Amérique COMP **Groundhog Day** N (US) jour *m* de la marmotte d'Amérique

GROUNDHOG DAY

Groundhog Day est une tradition américaine selon laquelle on peut prédire l'arrivée du printemps en observant le comportement de la marmotte d'Amérique, censée sortir de son hibernation le 2 février. Si le soleil brille ce jour-là, la marmotte est tellement effrayée par son ombre qu'elle prolonge son hibernation de six semaines, ce qui signifie que l'hiver se prolongera d'autant. La sortie de la marmotte est filmée chaque année à Punxsutawney, en Pennsylvanie, et l'événement est diffusé à l'échelle nationale.

grounding /ˈgraʊndɪŋ/ N 1 (*in education*) bases *fpl* (*in* en) ♦ **she had a good ~ in French** elle avait de bonnes bases en français 2 [*of ship*] échouage *m* 3 [*of plane*] interdiction *f* de vol

groundless /ˈgraʊndlɪs/ ADJ sans fondement, infondé

groundnut /ˈgraʊndnʌt/ N (*esp Brit*) arachide *f* COMP **groundnut oil** N huile *f* d'arachide

grounds /graʊndz/ NPL 1 (*also* **coffee grounds**) marc *m* (de café) 2 (= *gardens etc*) parc *m*

groundsel /ˈgraʊnsl/ N séneçon *m*

groundsheet /ˈgraʊndʃiːt/ N tapis *m* de sol

ground(s)keeper /ˈgraʊndzkiːpəʳ/ N (US) ⇒ **groundsman**

groundsman /ˈgraʊndzmən/ (pl **-men**) N [*of playing field*] gardien *m* (de stade) ; [*of park*] garde *m* (de parc) ; [*of cemetery*] gardien *m* (de cimetière)

groundspeed /ˈgraʊndspiːd/ N [*of aircraft*] vitesse *f* au sol

groundswell /ˈgraʊndswel/ N (*lit, fig*) lame *f* de fond

groundwork /ˈgraʊndwɜːk/ N (*gen*) travail *m* préparatoire, préparation *f* ; [*of novel, play etc*] plan *m*, canevas *m*

group /gruːp/ N (*gen, also Gram, Comm, Mus*) groupe *m* ♦ **in ~s of four** par groupes de quatre ♦ **to stand in ~s** former des petits groupes ♦ **to form a ~ round sth/sb** se grouper *or* se rassembler autour de qch/qn ♦ **literary ~** cercle *m* littéraire ; → **blood, in, pressure**

VI (*also* **group together**) [*people*] se grouper, se regrouper ♦ **to ~ round sth/sb** se grouper *or* se rassembler autour de qch/qn

VT (*also* **group together**) [*+ objects, people*] rassembler, réunir ; [*+ ideas, theories, numbers*] grouper ♦ **the children ~ed themselves around the teacher** les enfants se sont groupés *or* rassemblés autour du professeur ♦ **pupils are ~ed according to age and ability** les élèves sont répartis en groupes en fonction de leur âge et de leurs aptitudes

COMP **group booking** N réservation *f* de groupe
group captain N (*Brit Aviat*) colonel *m* de l'armée de l'air
group dynamics NPL dynamique *f* de(s) groupe(s)
group insurance N (*NonC*) assurance *f* groupe
the Group of Eight N (*Pol*) le groupe des Huit
the Group of Seven N (*Pol*) le groupe des Sept
group practice N (*Med*) cabinet *m* (de groupe *or* d'association)
group sex N ♦ **to take part in ~ sex** faire l'amour à plusieurs
group theory N (*Math*) théorie *f* des ensembles
group therapist N (*Psych*) (psycho)thérapeute *mf* (de groupe)
group therapy N (*Psych*) (psycho)thérapie *f* de groupe
group work N (*Social Work*) travail *m* en groupe *or* en équipe

grouper /ˈgruːpəʳ/ N mérou *m*

groupie * /ˈgruːpɪ/ N groupie * *f*

grouping /ˈgruːpɪŋ/ N groupement *m* ♦ **~s of companies** (*Fin, Jur*) regroupements *mpl* d'entreprises

groupware /ˈgruːpweəʳ/ N (*NonC: Comput*) groupware *m* COMP **groupware package** N logiciel *m* de productivité de groupe

grouse¹ /graʊs/ (= *bird*) N (pl **grouse** *or* **grouses**) grouse *f* ; → **black, red**

COMP **grouse-beating** N ♦ **to go ~-beating** faire le rabatteur (*à la chasse à la grouse*)
grouse moor N chasse *f* réservée (*où l'on chasse la grouse*)
grouse-shooting N ♦ **to go ~-shooting** chasser la grouse, aller à la chasse à la grouse

grouse² * /graʊs/ VI (= *grumble*) rouspéter *, râler * (*at, about* contre) ♦ **stop grousing!** arrête de rouspéter ! * N ♦ **to have a ~ (about sth)** (= *complain*) rouspéter * *or* râler * (contre qch) ♦ **I have a big ~ about the firm's attitude** j'ai de bonnes raisons de rouspéter * *or* râler * contre l'attitude de l'entreprise

grout /graʊt/ N enduit *m* de jointoiement ; (*on floor*) coulis *m*, enduit *m* de ragréage VT jointoyer

grouting /ˈgraʊtɪŋ/ N (*between tiles*) joints *mpl* ; (= *sealant*) mastic *m*

grove /grəʊv/ N bosquet *m* ♦ **olive ~** oliveraie *f* ♦ **pine ~** pinède *f*

grovel /ˈgrɒvl/ VI (*lit*) être à plat ventre ; (*searching for something*) ramper ; (*fig*) (= *humble oneself*) se mettre à plat ventre, ramper (*to, before* devant)

grovelling /ˈgrɒvlɪŋ/ ADJ (*lit*) rampant ; (*fig*) servile

grow /grəʊ/ (pret **grew**, ptp **grown**) VI 1 (= *get taller, bigger, longer etc physically*) [*plant, hair*] pousser ; [*person*] grandir ; [*animal*] grandir, grossir ; [*tumour*] grossir ; [*crystal*] se former ♦ **she's letting her hair ~** elle se laisse pousser les cheveux ♦ **that plant does not ~ in England** cette plante ne pousse pas en Angleterre ♦ **the plant ~s from a bulb/from seed** c'est une plante à bulbe/que l'on sème ♦ **to ~ to a height of 60cm** atteindre 60 cm (de haut) ♦ **he has ~n (by) 5cm** il a grandi de 5 cm ♦ **haven't you ~n!** comme tu as grandi *or* poussé ! * ; see also **grow into**

2 (= *increase, develop*) [*numbers, amount*] augmenter, grandir ; [*club, group*] s'agrandir ; [*population, rage, fear, love, influence, knowledge*] augmenter, s'accroître ; [*economy, market*] être en expansion ♦ **their friendship grew as time went on** leur amitié a grandi avec le temps ♦ **our friendship grew from a common interest in gardening** notre amitié s'est développée à partir d'un goût commun pour le jardinage ♦ **fears are ~ing for the safety of the hostages** on craint de plus en plus pour la sécurité des otages ♦ **pressure is ~ing on him to resign** on fait de plus en plus pression sur lui pour qu'il démissionne ♦ **their policies kept the economy ~ing** grâce à leur politique, la croissance de l'économie s'est maintenue ♦ **the economy/market is ~ing at** *or* **by 3% a year** l'économie/le marché connaît une croissance de 3% par an ♦ **the population is ~ing at** *or* **by 2% a year** la population augmente de 2% par an ♦ **we have ~n away from each other** avec le temps, nous nous sommes éloignés l'un de l'autre

♦ **to grow** + *adj* ♦ **he grew bitter** il est devenu amer ♦ **to ~ big(ger)** grandir ♦ **to ~ old(er)** vieillir ♦ **to ~ red(der)** rougir ♦ **to ~ angry** se fâcher, se mettre en colère ♦ **to ~ rare(r)** se faire (plus) rare ♦ **to ~ used to sth** s'habituer *or* s'accoutumer à qch

♦ **to grow in** + *noun* ♦ **to ~ in popularity** devenir plus populaire ♦ **to ~ in confidence** prendre de l'assurance ♦ **to ~ in strength** se renforcer ♦ **to ~ in wisdom/beauty** (*liter*) croître en sagesse/beauté

♦ **to grow to do sth** commencer à faire qch ♦ **to ~ to like/dislike/fear sth** commencer à aimer/détester/redouter qch ♦ **I'm ~ing to like him a bit more** je commence à l'apprécier un peu plus ♦ **I had ~n to like him** j'avais fini par l'apprécier

VT [*+ plants, crops*] cultiver, faire pousser ; [*+ one's hair, beard, nails*] laisser pousser ; [*+ crystal*] fabriquer ♦ **organically-~n vegetables** légumes *mpl* biologiques ♦ **she has ~n her hair (long)** elle s'est laissé pousser les cheveux ♦ **it's ~n a new leaf** une nouvelle feuille vient de pousser *or* d'apparaître ♦ **to ~ horns** commencer à avoir des cornes

COMP **grow bag** N sac *m* de culture

► **grow apart** VI s'éloigner peu à peu (l'un de l'autre *or* les uns des autres)

► **grow in** VI [*nail*] s'incarner ; [*hair*] repousser

► **grow into** VT FUS 1 (= *become*) devenir ♦ **to ~ into a man** devenir un homme ♦ **he's ~n into quite a handsome boy** il est devenu très beau garçon (en grandissant)

2 [*+ clothes*] devenir assez grand pour mettre ♦ **he grew into the job** peu à peu, il a appris les ficelles du métier ♦ **to ~ into the habit of doing sth** prendre (avec le temps) l'habitude de faire qch

► **grow on** VT FUS [*habit etc*] s'imposer peu à peu à ; [*book, music etc*] plaire de plus en plus à ♦ **his paintings ~ on you** plus on regarde ses tableaux, plus on les apprécie

► **grow out** VI ♦ **to let one's dyed hair grow out** laisser repousser ses cheveux (*pour éliminer la teinture*), attendre que ses cheveux retrouvent leur couleur naturelle

VT SEP ♦ **if you don't like the perm, you'll just have to grow it out** si la permanente ne vous plaît pas, vous n'avez qu'à vous laisser repousser les cheveux

► **grow out of** VT FUS [*+ clothes*] devenir trop grand pour ♦ **he's ~n out of this jacket** cette veste est (devenue) trop petite pour lui ♦ **he grew out of his asthma/acne** son asthme/acné lui a passé avec le temps ♦ **to ~ out of the habit of doing sth** perdre l'habitude de faire qch

► **grow up** VI 1 [*person, animal*] devenir adulte ♦ **when I ~ up I'm going to be a doctor** quand je serai grand je serai médecin ♦ **~ up!** * arrête tes enfantillages !

2 [*friendship, hatred etc*] se développer ; [*custom*] se répandre

grower /ˈgrəʊəʳ/ N 1 (= *person*) producteur *m*, -trice *f*, cultivateur *m*, -trice *f* ♦ **vegetable ~** maraîcher *m*, -ère *f* ; → **rose²** 2 ♦ **this plant is a slow ~** c'est une plante à croissance lente

growing /ˈgrəʊɪŋ/ ADJ 1 [*plant*] qui pousse ♦ **~ crops** récoltes *fpl* sur pied ♦ **fast-/slow-~** à croissance rapide/lente 2 [*child*] en cours de croissance, qui grandit ♦ **he's a ~ boy** il est en pleine croissance 3 (= *increasing*) [*number, amount*] grandissant, qui augmente ; [*friendship, hatred*] grandissant, croissant ♦ **a ~ opinion** une opinion de plus en plus répandue ♦ **a ~ feeling of frustration** un sentiment croissant *or* grandissant de frustration ♦ **to have a ~ desire to do sth** avoir de plus en plus envie de faire qch N (= *getting bigger*) croissance *f* ; (*Agr*) culture *f*

COMP **growing pains** * NPL (*Med*) douleurs *fpl*

de croissance ; *[of business, project]* difficultés *fpl* de croissance
growing season N *(Agr)* période *f* de croissance

growl /graʊl/ VI *[animal]* grogner, gronder *(at* contre) ; *[person]* grogner, ronchonner* ; *[thunder]* gronder VT *[+ reply etc]* grogner, grommeler N grognement *m*, grondement *m* ◆ **to give a ~** grogner

grown /grəʊn/ VB (ptp **grow** ;) see also **home comp** ADJ *[person]* adulte ◆ **he's a ~ man** il est adulte

grown-up /ˌgrəʊnˈʌp/ ADJ 1 *(= adult) [children]* adulte ◆ **when he is ~** quand il sera grand 2 *(= mature) [child, adolescent]* mûr ; *[behaviour]* de grande personne ◆ **your brother's very ~ for his age** ton frère est très mûr pour son âge ◆ **you think you're so ~!** tu te prends pour une grande personne ! ◆ **she looks very ~** elle fait très grande personne *or* très adulte ◆ **try to be more ~ about it** ne sois pas aussi puéril 3 * *[talk, subject]* d'adultes N grande personne *f*, adulte *mf* ◆ **the ~s** les grandes personnes *fpl*

growth /grəʊθ/ N 1 *(NonC = development) [of plant]* croissance *f*, développement *m* ; *[of person]* croissance *f* ◆ **to reach full ~** *[person]* avoir fini de grandir
2 *(NonC = increase) [of numbers, amount]* augmentation *f* ; *[of business, trade]* expansion *f*, croissance *f (in de)* ; *[of club, group]* croissance *f* ; *[of influence, economy]* croissance *f*, développement *m* ; *[of knowledge, love, friendship]* développement *m* ◆ **these measures encourage ~** *(Econ)* ces mesures favorisent la croissance ◆ **the ~ of public interest in ...** l'intérêt croissant du public pour ...
3 *(= what has grown)* pousse *f*, poussée *f* ◆ **a thick ~ of weeds** des mauvaises herbes qui ont poussé dru ◆ **a five days' ~ of beard** une barbe de cinq jours ◆ **she had a new ~ of hair** ses cheveux se sont mis à repousser
4 *(Med = tumour)* tumeur *f* ◆ **benign/malignant ~** tumeur *f* bénigne/maligne
COMP *[potential, prospects, forecast]* de croissance, d'expansion
growth area N *(= sector of economy)* secteur *m* en (pleine) expansion ; *(= region)* région *f* en (pleine) expansion
growth factor N *(Med)* facteur *m* de croissance
growth hormone N hormone *f* de croissance
growth industry N secteur *m* en (pleine) expansion *or* en plein essor
growth market N marché *m* en (pleine) expansion *or* en plein essor
growth rate N taux *m* de croissance
growth shares NPL *(Brit)* valeurs *fpl* de croissance
growth stock N *(US)* ⇒ **growth shares**

groyne /grɔɪn/ N *(esp Brit)* brise-lames *m inv*

Grozny /ˈgrɒznɪ/ N Grozny

grub /grʌb/ N 1 *(= larva)* larve *f* ; *(in apple etc)* ver *m*, asticot *m* 2 *(NonC: * = food)* boustifaille* *f*, bouffe* *f* ◆ **~'s up!** à la soupe !* VT *[animal] [+ ground, soil]* fouir VI (also **grub about, grub around**) fouiller, fouiner *(in, among* dans) COMP **Grub Street*** N *(Brit)* le monde des écrivaillons
► **grub up** VT SEP *[+ soil]* fouir ; *[+ object]* déterrer

grubbiness /ˈgrʌbɪnɪs/ N saleté *f*

grubby /ˈgrʌbɪ/ ADJ *(= dirty) [person, object]* malpropre, sale ; *(pej) (= sordid)* sale, sordide ◆ **I don't want him to get his ~ hands on it** je ne veux pas qu'il y touche (avec ses pattes sales) ◆ **the ~ business of selling arms** le sordide commerce des armes

grubstake* /ˈgrʌbsteɪk/ N *(US) (Hist)* avance *f* faite à un prospecteur ◆ **to put up a ~ for sb*** *(Fin)* fournir les fonds nécessaires à qn *(pour le lancement d'une entreprise ou d'un projet)* VT accorder une avance à ; *(Fin)* financer *(pendant la phase de lancement)*

grudge /grʌdʒ/ VT ◆ **to ~ doing sth** faire qch à contrecœur, rechigner à faire qch ◆ **she ~s paying £20 a ticket** cela lui fait mal au cœur de payer 20 livres le billet ◆ **he ~s her even the food she eats** il lui mesure jusqu'à sa nourriture, il lésine même sur sa nourriture ◆ **do you ~ me these pleasures?** me reprochez-vous ces (petits) plaisirs ? ◆ **they ~d him his success** ils lui en voulaient de sa réussite ◆ **I won't ~ you $5** je ne vais pas te refuser 5 dollars N rancune *f* ◆ **to bear** *or* **have a ~ against sb** en vouloir à qn, garder rancune à qn COMP **grudge match*** N (pl **grudge matches**) *(Sport, fig)* règlement *m* de comptes

grudging /ˈgrʌdʒɪŋ/ ADJ *[consent, approval, support]* réticent ; *[apology, praise]* fait à contrecœur ◆ **he won their ~ admiration/respect** à contrecœur, ils ont fini par l'admirer/le respecter ◆ **to be ~ in one's support for sth** apporter un soutien réticent à qch

grudgingly /ˈgrʌdʒɪŋlɪ/ ADV à contrecœur

gruel /grʊəl/ N gruau *m*

gruelling, grueling (US) /ˈgrʊəlɪŋ/ ADJ éreintant

gruesome /ˈgruːsəm/ ADJ horrible, épouvantable ◆ **in ~ detail** jusque dans les plus horribles détails

gruesomely /ˈgruːsəmlɪ/ ADV *(with vb)* d'une manière horrible ; *(with adj)* horriblement

gruff /grʌf/ ADJ bourru

gruffly /ˈgrʌflɪ/ ADV *[say]* d'un ton bourru

gruffness /ˈgrʌfnɪs/ N *[of person, manner]* brusquerie *f* ; *[of voice]* ton *m* bourru

grumble /ˈgrʌmbl/ VI *[person]* maugréer *(at, about* contre) ; *[thunder]* gronder N 1 grognement *m*, ronchonnement* *m* ◆ **to do sth without a ~** faire qch sans ronchonner* ◆ **after a long ~ about ...** après avoir longtemps maugréé contre ... 2 ◆ **~s** récriminations *fpl*

grumbling /ˈgrʌmblɪŋ/ N *(NonC)* récriminations *fpl* ADJ *[person]* grognon, grincheux ◆ **a ~ sound** un grondement COMP **grumbling appendix** N appendicite *f* chronique

grummet /ˈgrʌmɪt/ N ⇒ **grommet**

grump /grʌmp/ N *(= person)* grognon *m*, ronchon *m* NPL **grumps** ◆ **to have the ~s** être de mauvais poil*

grumpily /ˈgrʌmpɪlɪ/ ADV *[say]* d'un ton maussade

grumpiness /ˈgrʌmpɪnɪs/ N *(permanent)* mauvais caractère *m* ◆ **sorry for my ~ yesterday** désolé d'avoir été de mauvais poil* hier

grumpy /ˈgrʌmpɪ/ ADJ grognon, bougon

grunge /grʌndʒ/ N grunge *m*

grungy* /ˈgrʌndʒɪ/ ADJ crado* *inv*, cradingue*

grunt /grʌnt/ VTI grogner ◆ **to ~ a reply** grommeler *or* grogner une réponse ◆ **"no", he ~ed** "non", grommela-t-il N 1 grognement *m* ◆ **to give a ~** pousser *or* faire entendre un grognement ; *(in reply)* répondre par un grognement 2 *(US * = soldier)* fantassin *m*, biffin* *m*

gruppetto /gruːˈpetəʊ/ N (pl **gruppetti** /gruːˈpetiː/) *(Mus)* gruppetto *m*

gryphon /ˈgrɪfən/ N ⇒ **griffin**

GSM /ˌdʒiːesˈem/ N *(Telec)* (abbrev of **Global System for Mobile Communications**) GSM *m*

GSOH* N (abbrev of **good sense of humour**) sens *m* de l'humour

GT /ˈdʒiːˈtiː/ N (abbrev of **gran turismo**) GT *f*

Gt (abbrev of **Great**) gd (gde *f*), grand ◆ **~ Britain** la Grande-Bretagne ◆ **~ Yarmouth** Great Yarmouth

GTi /ˌdʒiːtiːˈaɪ/ N (abbrev of **gran turismo injection**) GTi *f*

GU *(US Post)* abbrev of **Guam**

guacamole /ˌgwɑːkəˈməʊlɪ/ N *(Culin)* guacamole *m*

Guadeloupe /ˌgwɑːdəˈluːp/ N Guadeloupe *f*

Guam /gwɑːm/ N Guam

guano /ˈgwɑːnəʊ/ N *(NonC)* guano *m*

guarantee /ˌgærənˈtiː/ N 1 *(gen, Comm = promise, assurance)* garantie *f* ◆ **to be under ~** être sous garantie ◆ **there is a year's ~ on this watch** cette montre est garantie un an, cette montre a une garantie d'un an ◆ **a ~ against defective workmanship** une garantie contre les malfaçons ◆ **"money-back guarantee with all items"** "remboursement garanti sur tous les articles" ◆ **you have** *or* **I give you my ~ that ...** je vous garantis que ... ◆ **there's no ~ that it will happen** il n'est pas garanti *or* dit que cela arrivera ◆ **there's no ~ that it actually happened** il n'est pas certain que cela soit arrivé ◆ **health is not a ~ of happiness** la santé n'est pas une garantie de bonheur
2 *(Jur etc = pledge, security)* garantie *f*, caution *f* ◆ **~ for a bill** *(Fin)* aval *m* d'une traite ◆ **to give sth as (a) ~** donner qch en garantie ◆ **he left his watch as a ~ of payment** il a laissé sa montre en gage ◆ **what ~ can you offer?** quelle caution pouvez-vous donner ?
3 ⇒ **guarantor**
VT 1 *(Comm) [+ goods etc]* garantir *(against* contre) ◆ **to ~ sth for two years** garantir qch (pour) deux ans ◆ **~d not to rust** garanti inoxydable ◆ **~d price** prix *m* garanti
2 *(= assure) [+ sb's safety, freedom, rights]* garantir ◆ **I will ~ his good behaviour** je me porte garant de sa bonne conduite ◆ **I ~ that it won't happen again** je vous garantis que cela ne se reproduira pas ◆ **I can't ~ that he will come** je ne peux pas garantir qu'il viendra ◆ **we can't ~ good weather** nous ne pouvons pas garantir le beau temps *or* qu'il fera beau
3 *(Fin)* ◆ **to ~ a loan** se porter garant *or* caution d'un emprunt ◆ **I will ~ him for a £500 loan** je lui servirai de garant *or* de caution pour un emprunt de 500 livres ◆ **~d student loan** *(US Univ)* prêt *m* d'honneur *(à un étudiant)*
COMP **guarantee form** N garantie *f (fiche)*

guarantor /ˌgærənˈtɔːʳ/ N garant(e) *m(f)*, caution *f* ◆ **to stand ~ for sb** se porter garant *or* caution de qn ◆ **will you be my ~ for the loan?** me servirez-vous de garant *or* de caution pour cet emprunt ?

guaranty /ˈgærəntɪ/ N *(Fin)* garantie *f*, caution *f* ; *(= agreement)* garantie *f* ; *(= person)* garant(e) *m(f)*

guard /gɑːd/ N 1 *(NonC)* garde *f*, surveillance *f* ; *(Mil)* garde *f* ◆ **to put a ~ on sb/sth** faire surveiller qn/qch ◆ **to come off ~** finir son tour de garde ◆ **to be on ~** être de garde *or* de faction ◆ **to go on ~** prendre son tour de garde ◆ **to keep** *or* **stand ~** être de garde, monter la garde ◆ **to keep** *or* **stand ~ on** *(against attack)* garder ; *(against theft, escape)* surveiller ◆ **to stand ~ over sb/sth** monter la garde auprès de qn/qch ◆ **to be under ~** être sous surveillance *or* sous bonne garde ◆ **to keep sb under ~** garder qn sous surveillance ◆ **he was taken under ~ to ...** il a été emmené sous escorte à ... ; → **mount**
2 *(NonC) (Boxing, Fencing)* garde *f* ◆ **on ~!** *(Sport)* en garde !
3 *(= as protection)* ◆ **he wears goggles as a ~ against accidents** il porte des lunettes protectrices
4 *(= wariness)* ◆ **to be on one's ~** se méfier *(against* de) être *or* se tenir sur ses gardes *(against* contre) ◆ **to put sb on his ~** mettre qn en garde *(against* contre) ◆ **to be off (one's) ~** ne pas être *or* ne pas se tenir sur ses gardes ◆ **to**

catch sb off (his) ~ prendre qn au dépourvu ◆ **to put sb off (his)** ~ tromper la vigilance de qn ◆ **to drop one's** ~ relâcher sa vigilance, baisser sa garde (*fig*)

5 (*Mil etc*) (*= squad of men*) garde *f* ; (*= one man*) garde *m* ◆ **to change (the)** ~ (*Mil*) faire la relève de la garde ◆ **one of the old** ~ un vieux de la vieille* ◆ **the Guards** (*Brit Mil*) les régiments *mpl* de la garde royale ; → **lifeguard, security**

6 (*Brit Rail*) chef *m* de train

7 (*on machine*) dispositif *m* de sûreté ; (*on sword*) garde *f* ; → **fireguard**

8 (*Basketball*) ◆ **left/right** ~ arrière *m* gauche/droit

VT (*against attack*) garder (*from, against* contre) ; (*against theft, escape*) surveiller ; (*Cards, Chess*) garder ; (*fig*) [*+ one's tongue, passions etc*] surveiller ◆ **the frontier is heavily ~ed** la frontière est solidement gardée ◆ **the dog ~ed the house** le chien gardait la maison ◆ ~ **it with your life!** veillez bien dessus ! ◆ **to ~ o.s. against sth** (*fig*) se prémunir contre qch

COMP guard dog N chien *m* de garde

guard duty N (*Mil*) ◆ **to be on ~ duty** être de garde *or* de faction

guard of honour N (*lit, fig*) garde *f* d'honneur ; (*on either side*) haie *f* d'honneur

guard's van N (*Brit Rail*) fourgon *m*

► **guard against** VT FUS se protéger contre, se prémunir contre ◆ **to ~ against doing sth** (bien) se garder de faire qch ◆ **in order to ~ against this** pour éviter cela ◆ **we must try to ~ against this happening again** nous devons essayer d'empêcher que cela ne se reproduise

guarded /ˈgɑːdɪd/ ADJ [*person*] sur ses gardes ; [*response, remark*] circonspect, prudent ; [*support, smile*] réservé ; [*optimism*] prudent ◆ **he is ~ about his intentions** il se garde de trop révéler ses intentions ◆ **a closely** *or* **carefully ~ secret** un secret bien gardé ◆ **to give a ~ welcome to sth** accueillir qch avec réserve

guardedly /ˈgɑːdɪdlɪ/ ADV [*say*] avec circonspection, prudemment ◆ ~ **optimistic** d'un optimisme prudent

guardedness /ˈgɑːdɪdnɪs/ N circonspection *f*

guardhouse /ˈgɑːdhaʊs/ N (*Mil*) (*for guards*) corps *m* de garde ; (*for prisoners*) salle *f* de police

guardian /ˈgɑːdɪən/ N **1** gardien(ne) *m(f)*, protecteur *m*, -trice *f* **2** [*of minor*] tuteur *m*, -trice *f* ADJ gardien

COMP guardian angel N ange *m* gardien

Guardian reader N (*Brit*) lecteur *m*, -trice *f* du Guardian

GUARDIAN READER

« Dis-moi quel quotidien tu lis, et je te dirai qui tu es » : cet adage est particulièrement valable en Grande-Bretagne, où les gens ont une image stéréotypée des lecteurs des différents quotidiens. Les lecteurs du **Guardian**, quotidien de centre gauche, se comptent surtout parmi la gauche bourgeoise et intellectuelle, les enseignants, les travailleurs sociaux etc. Le « Sun » se situerait à l'autre extrême.

guardianship /ˈgɑːdɪənʃɪp/ N (*Jur*) tutelle *f*

guardrail /ˈgɑːdreɪl/ N [*of staircase*] rampe *f* ; [*of balcony*] balustrade *f*, rambarde *f* ; [*of road*] glissière *f* de sécurité

guardroom /ˈgɑːdrʊm/ N (*Mil*) corps *m* de garde

guardsman /ˈgɑːdzmən/ N (pl **-men**) (*Brit Mil*) soldat *m* de la garde royale, garde *m* ; (*US*) soldat *m* de la garde nationale

Guatemala /ˌgwɑːtɪˈmɑːlə/ N Guatemala *m* ◆ **in** ~ au Guatemala

Guatemalan /ˌgwɑːtɪˈmɑːlən/ ADJ guatémaltèque N Guatémaltèque *mf*

guava /ˈgwɑːvə/ N (*= fruit*) goyave *f* ; (*= tree*) goyavier *m*

gubbins* /ˈgʌbɪnz/ N (*Brit*) **1** (*= thing*) machin* *m*, truc* *m* **2** (*= silly person*) crétin* *m*, imbécile *m*

gubernatorial /ˌguːbənəˈtɔːrɪəl/ ADJ (*esp US*) de *or* du gouverneur

gudgeon¹ /ˈgʌdʒən/ N (*= fish*) goujon *m*

gudgeon² /ˈgʌdʒən/ N [*of hinge*] tourillon *m* ; (*in boat*) goujon *m* COMP **gudgeon pin** N (*Brit*) (*in car*) axe *m* de piston

guelder rose /ˌgeldəˈrəʊz/ N boule-de-neige *f*

Guelf, Guelph /gwelf/ N guelfe *m*

Guernsey /ˈgɜːnzɪ/ N **1** (*Geog*) Guernesey *f* ◆ **in** ~ à Guernesey **2** (also **Guernsey cow**) vache *f* de Guernesey

guernsey /ˈgɜːnzɪ/ N (*= garment*) ≈ pull *m* marin

guerrilla /gəˈrɪlə/ N guérillero *m*

COMP [*tactics etc*] de guérilla

guerrilla band N troupe *f* de partisans *or* de guérilleros

guerrilla financing N (*US*) financement *m* indépendant

guerrilla group N ⇒ **guerrilla band**

guerrilla strike N [*of workers*] grève *f* sauvage

guerrilla war(fare) N guérilla *f*

guess /ges/ N supposition *f*, conjecture *f* ◆ **to have** *or* **make a ~ (at sth)** essayer de deviner (qch) ◆ **he made a wild** ~ il a lancé une réponse au hasard ◆ **(I'll give you) three ~es!** essaie de deviner ! ◆ **that was a good ~!** tu as deviné juste ! ◆ **that was a good ~ but ...** c'est une bonne idée, mais ... ◆ **how did you know? – it was just a lucky** ~ comment as-tu deviné ? – j'ai dit ça au hasard ◆ **my ~ is that he refused** d'après moi, il aura *or* a refusé ◆ **it's anyone's ~ who will win*** impossible de prévoir qui va gagner ◆ **will he come tomorrow? – it's anyone's ~*** viendra-t-il demain ? – qui sait ? *or* Dieu seul le sait ◆ **at a ~ I would say there were 200** à vue de nez, il y en a 200 ◆ **at a rough** ~ à vue de nez ◆ **an educated** ~ une supposition éclairée ◆ **your ~ is as good as mine!*** je n'en sais pas plus que toi !

VT **1** (also **guess at**) [*+ answer, name etc*] deviner ; (*= estimate*) [*+ height, numbers etc*] estimer, évaluer ; (*= surmise*) supposer, conjecturer (*that* que) ◆ **to ~ sb's age** deviner l'âge de qn ◆ **you've ~ed (it)!** tu as deviné !, c'est ça ! ◆ **I ~ed as much** je m'en doutais ◆ **I don't weigh the ingredients, I just ~ the quantities** je ne pèse pas les ingrédients, je le fais au pif* ◆ **I ~ed him to be about 20, I ~ed (that) he was about 20** je lui donnais à peu près 20 ans ◆ ~ **how heavy he is** devine combien il pèse ◆ **can you ~ what it means?** devine ce que ça veut dire ◆ ~ **what!*** tu sais quoi ? ◆ ~ **who!*** devine qui c'est ! ◆ **you'll never ~ who's coming to see us!** tu ne devineras jamais qui va venir nous voir !

2 (*= believe, think*) supposer, penser ◆ **he'll be about 40 I ~** je lui donnerais la quarantaine ◆ **I ~ she's decided not to come** je suppose qu'elle a décidé de ne pas venir ◆ **I ~ so** sans doute, oui ◆ **I ~ not** non

VI deviner ◆ **(try to) ~!** essaie de deviner !, devine un peu ! ◆ **you'll never ~!** tu ne devineras jamais ! ◆ **to ~ right** deviner juste ◆ **to ~ wrong** tomber à côté ◆ **to keep sb ~ing** laisser qn dans le doute ◆ **to ~ at the height of a building/the number of people present** évaluer *or* estimer (au jugé) la hauteur d'un bâtiment/le nombre de personnes présentes

COMP guessing game N ◆ **to play a ~ing game** jouer aux devinettes

guesstimate* /ˈgestɪmɪt/ N (*NonC*) estimation *f* approximative VT calculer au pifomètre*

guesswork /ˈgeswɜːk/ N conjecture *f*, hypothèse *f* ◆ **it was sheer** ~ ce n'étaient que des conjectures ◆ **by** ~ en devinant, au jugé ◆ **it's far too important a decision to be left to** ~ c'est une décision bien trop importante pour être prise au hasard *or* au jugé ◆ **to take the ~ out of sth** rendre qch plus précis

guest /gest/ N (*at home*) invité(e) *m(f)*, hôte *mf* ; (*at table*) convive *mf* ; (*in hotel*) client(e) *m(f)* ; (*in boarding house*) pensionnaire *mf* ; (*TV, Rad*) invité(e) *m(f)* ◆ ~ **of honour** invité(e) *m(f)* d'honneur ◆ **we were their ~s last summer** nous avons été invités chez eux l'été dernier ◆ **be my ~!*** je vous en prie ! ; → **houseguest, paying**

VI (*TV, Rad*) ◆ **to ~ on sb's show** être invité sur le plateau de qn ◆ **and ~ing on tonight's show we have Linda Roberts** et pour l'émission de ce soir, notre invitée est Linda Roberts

COMP guest appearance N ◆ **to make a ~ appearance on sb's show** être invité sur le plateau de qn

guest artist N invité(e) *m(f)* spécial(e)

guest book N livre *m* d'or

guest list N liste *f* des invités

guest night N *soirée où les membres d'un club peuvent inviter des non-membres*

guest room N chambre *f* d'amis

guest speaker N conférencier *m*, -ière *f* (*invité(e) par un club, une organisation*)

guesthouse /ˈgesthaʊs/ N (*Brit: gen*) pension *f* de famille ; (*in monastery etc*) hôtellerie *f*

guestworker /ˈgestwɜːkəʳ/ N travailleur *m*, -euse *f* immigré(e)

guff* /gʌf/ N (*NonC*) idioties *fpl*, conneries*⁑ *fpl*

guffaw /gʌˈfɔː/ VI s'esclaffer N gros (éclat *m* de) rire *m*

GUI /ˈguːɪ/ N (*Comput*) (abbrev of **graphical user interface**) interface *f* graphique, interface *f* GUI

Guiana /gaɪˈænə/ N Guyanes *fpl* ◆ **in** ~ aux Guyanes

guidance /ˈgaɪdəns/ N **1** conseils *mpl* ; (*= counselling*) guidance *f* ◆ **he needs some ~ about how** *or* **as to how to go about it** il a besoin de conseils quant à la façon de procéder ◆ **your ~ was very helpful** vos conseils ont été très utiles ◆ **for your** ~ pour votre gouverne, à titre d'indication *or* d'information ; see also **child, vocational** **2** [*of rocket etc*] guidage *m*

COMP guidance counselor N (*US Scol*) conseiller *m*, -ère *f* d'orientation

guidance system N (*for missile*) système *m* de guidage ; (*for ship*) système *m* de navigation

guide /gaɪd/ N **1** (*= person*) guide *m* ◆ **you must let reason be your** ~ il faut vous laisser guider par la raison

2 (*= indication*) guide *m*, indication *f* ◆ **this figure is only a** ~ ce chiffre n'est donné qu'à titre indicatif ◆ **last year's figures will be a good** ~ les statistiques de l'année dernière serviront d'indication générale ◆ **these results are not a very good ~ as to his ability** ces résultats ne reflètent pas vraiment ses compétences ◆ **as a rough ~, count four apples to the pound** comptez en gros quatre pommes par livre

3 (*= guidebook*) guide *m* (touristique) ◆ ~ **to Italy** guide *m* d'Italie

4 (*= book of instructions*) guide *m*, manuel *m* ◆ **beginner's ~ to sailing** manuel *m* d'initiation à la voile

5 (*for curtains etc*) glissière *f* ; (*on sewing machine*) pied-de-biche *m*

6 (*Brit:* also **girl guide**) éclaireuse *f* ; (*Roman Catholic*) guide *f*

VT 1 [*+ stranger, visitor*] guider, piloter ; [*+ blind person*] conduire, guider ◆ **he ~d us through the town** il nous a pilotés *or* guidés à travers la ville ◆ **he ~d us to the main door** il nous a montré le chemin jusqu'à la porte d'entrée ◆ **they had only a compass to ~ them** ils n'avaient qu'une boussole pour s'orienter

◆ **guided by** ◆ **be ~d by your instinct** laisse-toi guider par ton instinct ◆ **his method of working was ~d by four principles** sa méthode de travail obéissait à quatre principes ◆ **governments should be ~d by a simple rule ...** les gouvernements devraient respecter une règle simple ...

2 [*+ rocket, missile*] guider

COMP **guide dog** N chien *m* d'aveugle
guide line N (*for writing*) ligne *f* (*permettant une écriture horizontale régulière*) ; (*= rope*) main *f* courante ; see also **guideline**
guide price N prix *m* indicatif

guidebook /ˈgaɪdbʊk/ N guide *m* (touristique)

guided /ˈgaɪdɪd/ ADJ [*rocket etc*] téléguidé
COMP **guided missile** N missile *m* téléguidé
guided tour N visite *f* guidée

guideline /ˈgaɪdlaɪn/ N 1 (*= rough guide*) indication *f* ; (*= advice*) conseil *m* ◆ **an IQ test is merely a ~** un test de QI ne donne qu'une indication (générale) ◆ **I gave her a few ~s on how to look after a kitten** je lui ai donné quelques conseils sur la manière de s'occuper d'un chaton ◆ **follow these simple ~s for a healthy diet** pour vous alimenter sainement, il suffit de suivre ces conseils 2 (*= official directive*) directive *f* (*on* sur) ◆ **judges are expected to follow clear ~s when awarding damages** les juges sont censés suivre des directives claires dans les affaires de dommages-intérêts ◆ **safety/health ~s** directives *fpl* concernant la santé/sécurité, directives *fpl* de santé/sécurité

guidepost /ˈgaɪdpəʊst/ N poteau *m* indicateur

guider /ˈgaɪdəʳ/ N cheftaine *f*

guiding /ˈgaɪdɪŋ/ ADJ [*ideology*] dominant ; [*policy, rule*] de base ◆ **he assumed a ~ role in his nephew's life** il a servi de mentor à son neveu ◆ **~ light, ~ star** (*fig*) guide *m* ◆ **our ~ principle is that the interests of children are paramount** le principe qui nous guide est que les intérêts des enfants passent avant tout ◆ **the ~ principle behind conservation** le principe de base de la défense de l'environnement ◆ **~ force** moteur *m* ◆ **he is the ~ force behind these reforms** il est le moteur de ces réformes ◆ **he needs a ~ hand from time to time** de temps en temps, il faut le remettre sur la bonne voie

guild /gɪld/ N 1 (*Hist*) guilde *f*, corporation *f* ◆ **goldsmiths' ~** guilde *f* des orfèvres 2 association *f*, confrérie *f* ◆ **the church ~** le conseil paroissial ◆ **women's ~** association *f* féminine

guilder /ˈgɪldəʳ/ N (pl **guilders** *or* **guilder**) florin *m*

guildhall /ˈgɪldhɔːl/ N (*Hist*) maison *f* des corporations ; (*= town hall*) hôtel *m* de ville

guile /gaɪl/ N (*NonC*) (*= deceit*) fourberie *f*, duplicité *f* ; (*= cunning*) ruse *f*

guileful /ˈgaɪlfʊl/ ADJ (*= deceitful*) fourbe, trompeur ; (*= cunning*) rusé

guileless /ˈgaɪllɪs/ ADJ candide, sans malice

guillemot /ˈgɪlɪmɒt/ N guillemot *m*

guillotine /ˌgɪləˈtiːn/ N (*for beheading*) guillotine *f* ; (*for paper-cutting*) massicot *m* ◆ **a ~ was imposed on the bill** (*Parl*) la durée des débats sur le projet de loi a été limitée VT [*+ person*] guillotiner ; [*+ paper*] massicoter ◆ **to ~ a bill** (*Parl*) limiter la durée des débats sur un projet de loi

guilt /gɪlt/ N (*NonC*) culpabilité *f* ◆ **he was tormented by ~** il était torturé par un sentiment de culpabilité ◆ **to have ~ feelings about sth/sb** avoir un sentiment de culpabilité à cause de qch/envers qn COMP **guilt complex** N (*Psych*) complexe *m* de culpabilité

guiltily /ˈgɪltɪlɪ/ ADV [*say*] d'un ton coupable ; [*look away*] d'un air coupable ; [*think*] avec un sentiment de culpabilité

guiltless /ˈgɪltlɪs/ ADJ innocent (*of* de)

guilty /ˈgɪltɪ/ ADJ 1 (*also Jur*) [*person*] coupable (*of* de) ◆ **I've been ~ of that myself** j'ai moi-même commis la même erreur ◆ **he was ~ of taking the book without permission** il s'est rendu coupable d'avoir pris le livre sans permission ◆ **to be found ~/not ~ (of sth)** être déclaré coupable/non coupable (de qch) ◆ **to plead ~/not ~ (to sth)** plaider coupable/non coupable (de qch) ◆ **how do you plead? ~ or not ~?** plaidez-vous coupable ou non coupable ? ◆ **a ~ verdict, a verdict of ~** un verdict de culpabilité ◆ **a not ~ verdict, a verdict of not ~** un verdict d'acquittement ◆ **the judge took into account his ~ plea** *or* **his plea of ~** le juge a tenu compte du fait qu'il avait plaidé coupable ◆ **the court accepted a not ~ plea** *or* **a plea of not ~** la cour l'a acquitté

2 (*= ashamed*) [*smile, thought*] coupable ; [*silence*] chargé de culpabilité ◆ **to look ~** avoir l'air coupable ◆ **he had a ~ look on his face** il avait une expression coupable ◆ **to feel ~** culpabiliser, avoir mauvaise conscience ◆ **to make sb feel ~** culpabiliser qn, donner mauvaise conscience à qn ◆ **to feel ~ about sth** se sentir coupable de qch ◆ **I felt ~ that I had not thanked her** je culpabilisais *or* j'avais mauvaise conscience de ne pas l'avoir remerciée

3 (*= shameful*) [*secret*] honteux ; [*pleasure*] inavouable, coupable

COMP **guilty conscience** N mauvaise conscience *f* ◆ **I have a ~ conscience about not writing** j'ai mauvaise conscience de ne pas avoir écrit
the guilty party N le coupable

Guinea /ˈgɪnɪ/ N (*Geog*) ◆ **(the Republic of) ~** la (République *f* de) Guinée *f* ; see also **equatorial**
COMP **Guinea-Bissau** N Guinée-Bissau *f*
guinea-fowl N (*pl inv*) pintade *f*
guinea-pig N (*= animal*) cochon *m* d'Inde, cobaye *m* ; (*fig*) cobaye *m* ◆ **to be a guinea-pig** (*fig*) servir de cobaye

guinea /ˈgɪnɪ/ N (*Brit: formerly = money*) guinée *f* (*= 21 shillings*)

Guinean /ˈgɪnɪən/ ADJ guinéen N Guinéen(ne) *m(f)*

guise /gaɪz/ N ◆ **in a new ~** sous une autre forme ◆ **in** *or* **under the ~ of scientific research** sous l'apparence de *or* sous couvert de recherche scientifique ◆ **under the ~ of doing sth** sous prétexte de faire qch ◆ **a portrait of the king in the ~ of a Roman emperor** un portrait du roi en empereur romain

guitar /gɪˈtɑːʳ/ N guitare *f*

guitarist /gɪˈtɑːrɪst/ N guitariste *mf*

Gujarat, Gujerat /ˌgʊdʒəˈrɑːt/ N Gujarat *m*, Gujerat *m* ◆ **in ~** au Gujarat

Gujarati, Gujerati /ˌgʊdʒəˈrɑːtɪ/ ADJ du Gujarat N 1 (*= person*) Gujarati *mf* 2 (*Ling*) gujarati *m*

gulag /ˈguːlæg/ N goulag *m*

gulch /gʌlʃ/ N (*US*) ravin *m*

gulf /gʌlf/ N 1 (*in ocean*) golfe *m* ◆ **the (Persian) Gulf** le golfe Persique, le Golfe 2 (*= difference*) fossé *m* COMP **the Gulf of Aden** N le golfe d'Aden
the Gulf of Alaska N le golfe d'Alaska
the Gulf of Mexico N le golfe du Mexique
the Gulf States NPL (*Middle East*) les États *mpl* du Golfe ; (*in US*) les États *mpl* du golfe du Mexique
the Gulf Stream N le Gulf Stream
the Gulf War N la guerre du Golfe
Gulf War syndrome N (*NonC: Med*) syndrome *m* de la guerre du Golfe

gull¹ /gʌl/ N (*= bird*) goéland *m*, mouette *f* ◆ **common ~** goéland *m* cendré COMP **gull-wing door** N porte *f* papillon

gull² /gʌl/ VT duper, rouler * N (*= dupe*) gogo * *m*

gullet /ˈgʌlɪt/ N (*Anat*) œsophage *m* ; (*= throat*) gosier *m* ◆ **it really stuck in my ~** (*fig*) ça m'est resté en travers de la gorge *

gulley /ˈgʌlɪ/ N ⇒ **gully**

gullibility /ˌgʌlɪˈbɪlɪtɪ/ N crédulité *f*

gullible /ˈgʌlɪbl/ ADJ crédule

gully /ˈgʌlɪ/ N 1 (*= ravine*) ravine *f*, couloir *m* ; (*Climbing*) couloir *m* 2 (*= drain*) caniveau *m*, rigole *f*

gulp /gʌlp/ N 1 (*= action*) coup *m* de gosier ; (*from emotion*) serrement *m* de gorge ◆ **to swallow sth in one ~** avaler qch d'un seul coup ◆ **he emptied the glass in one ~** il a vidé le verre d'un (seul) trait ◆ **"yes" he replied with a ~** "oui" répondit-il la gorge serrée *or* avec une boule dans la gorge

2 (*= mouthful*) [*of food*] bouchée *f* ; [*of drink*] gorgée *f* ◆ **he took a ~ of milk** il a avalé une gorgée de lait

VT 1 (*also* **gulp down**) [*+ food*] engloutir, avaler tout rond ; [*+ drink*] avaler d'un trait ◆ **don't ~ your food** mâche ce que tu manges

2 ◆ **"I'm sorry," he ~ed** "désolé", répondit-il la gorge serrée *or* avec une boule dans la gorge

VI essayer d'avaler ; (*from emotion*) avoir un serrement à la gorge ◆ **he ~ed** sa gorge s'est serrée *or* s'est contractée

► **gulp back** VT SEP ◆ **to gulp back one's tears/sobs** ravaler *or* refouler ses larmes/sanglots

gum¹ /gʌm/ N (*Anat*) gencive *f*
COMP **gum disease** N gingivite *f*
gum shield N protège-dents *m*

gum² /gʌm/ N 1 (*NonC*) (*Bot*) gomme *f* ; (*esp Brit = glue*) gomme *f*, colle *f* ; (*= rubber*) caoutchouc *m* 2 (*NonC*) chewing-gum *m* 3 (*= sweet*) (*also* **gumdrop**) boule *f* de gomme VT (*= put gum on*) gommer ; (*= stick*) coller (*to* à) ◆ **~med envelope/label** enveloppe *f*/étiquette *f* collante *or* gommée ◆ **to ~ sth back on** recoller qch ◆ **to ~ down an envelope** coller *or* cacheter une enveloppe
COMP **gum arabic** N gomme *f* arabique
gum tree N gommier *m* ◆ **to be up a ~ tree** * (*Brit*) être dans le pétrin *

► **gum up** * VT SEP [*+ machinery, plans*] bousiller * ◆ **it's ~med up the works** ça a tout bousillé *

gum³ * /gʌm/ N (*euph*) ◆ **by ~!** * nom d'un chien ! *, mince alors ! *

gumball * /ˈgʌmbɔːl/ N (*US*) (*= chewing gum*) boule *f* de chewing-gum ; (*pej = person*) andouille * *f* ; (*hum*) (*on police car*) gyrophare *m*, bulle ‡ *f*

gumbo /ˈgʌmbəʊ/ N (*US, Can*) (*= vegetable*) gombo *m* ; (*= soup*) soupe *f* au(x) gombo(s)

gumboil /ˈgʌmbɔɪl/ N fluxion *f* dentaire, abcès *m* à la gencive

gumboots /ˈgʌmbuːts/ NPL (*esp Brit*) bottes *fpl* de caoutchouc

gumdrop /ˈgʌmdrɒp/ N boule *f* de gomme

gummy /ˈgʌmɪ/ ADJ [*substance, surface*] collant

gumption * /ˈgʌmpʃən/ N (*NonC*) jugeote * *f*, bon sens *m* ◆ **use your ~!** un peu de jugeote ! * ◆ **he's got a lot of ~** il sait se débrouiller

gumshoe ‡ /ˈgʌmʃuː/ N (*US = detective*) privé * *m*

gumshoes /ˈgʌmʃuːz/ NPL (US) (= *overshoes*) caoutchoucs *mpl* ; (= *sneakers*) (chaussures *fpl* de) tennis *mpl*

gun /gʌn/ N 1 (= *handgun*) revolver *m*, pistolet *m* ; (= *rifle*) fusil *m* ; (= *cannon*) canon *m* ◆ **he's got a ~!** il est armé ! ◆ **the thief was carrying a ~** le voleur avait une arme (à feu), le voleur était armé ◆ **to draw a ~ on sb** braquer une arme sur qn ◆ **to hold** *or* **put a ~ to sb's head** (*fig*) mettre le couteau *or* le pistolet sous la gorge de qn ◆ **a 21-~ salute** une salve de 21 coups de canon ◆ **the ~s** (*Mil*) les canons *mpl*, l'artillerie *f* ◆ **the big ~s** (*Mil*) les gros canons *mpl*, l'artillerie *f* lourde ; * (*fig* = *people*) les grosses légumes* *fpl*, les huiles* *fpl* ◆ **to bring out the big ~s** (*fig*) brandir un argument massue ◆ **to be going great ~s*** (*fig*) [*business*] marcher très fort* ; [*person*] être en pleine forme ; see also **blow**[1] ◆ **he's the fastest ~ in the West** c'est la meilleure gâchette de l'Ouest ◆ **with (all) ~s blazing** tout feu tout flamme *inv* ◆ **to be under the ~** (*esp US*) être dans une situation critique ; → **jump, son, stick**
2 (*Brit* = *member of shooting party*) fusil *m*
3 (*US* ‡: also **gunman**) bandit *m* armé
4 (*Tech*) pistolet *m* ◆ **paint ~** pistolet *m* à peinture ; see also **grease**
VT (*esp US Aut*) ◆ **to ~ the engine** faire ronfler le moteur ◆ **to ~ it*** appuyer sur le champignon*
VI * ◆ **to be ~ning for sb** chercher qn*, essayer d'avoir qn ◆ **watch out, he's ~ning for you!** fais gaffe*, il te cherche !
COMP **gun barrel** N canon *m* de fusil *or* de revolver
gun carriage N affût *m* de canon ; (*at funeral*) prolonge *f* d'artillerie
gun control N (*US*) réglementation *f* du port d'armes
gun cotton N fulmicoton *m*, coton-poudre *m*
gun crew N (*Mil*) peloton *m* *or* servants *mpl* de pièce
gun dog N chien *m* de chasse
the gun laws NPL (*US*) les lois *fpl* sur le port d'armes
gun licence, gun license (*US*) N permis *m* de port d'armes
gun room N (*in house*) armurerie *f* ; (*Brit Naut*) poste *m* des aspirants
gun-shy ADJ qui a peur des coups de feu *or* des détonations ; (*fig*) qui n'a pas le courage de ses opinions
gun turret N (*Mil etc*) tourelle *f*
▸ **gun down** VT SEP abattre

Gun Control

Aux États-Unis, la réglementation du port d'armes est un sujet très controversé. Le droit pour tous les citoyens de détenir des armes à feu est inscrit dans la Constitution et certains lobbies encouragent fortement la pratique de l'autodéfense. Cependant, la montée de la violence préoccupe de nombreux Américains et a conduit à mettre en place une législation plus restrictive ; en particulier, beaucoup d'armes semi-automatiques ont été interdites.

gunboat /ˈgʌnbəʊt/ N (*Naut*) canonnière *f* COMP **gunboat diplomacy** N politique *f* de la canonnière, politique *f* de force

gunfight /ˈgʌnfaɪt/ N échange *m* de coups de feu, fusillade *f*

gunfighter /ˈgʌnfaɪtəʳ/ N (*esp US*) professionnel *m* de la gâchette, tireur *m*

gunfire /ˈgʌnfaɪəʳ/ N [*of rifles etc*] coups *mpl* de feu, fusillade *f* ; [*of cannons*] feu *m* *or* tir *m* d'artillerie

gunge* /gʌndʒ/ N (*NonC*: *Brit*) magma *m* infâme*

gung ho* /ˈgʌŋˈhəʊ/ ADJ fonceur

gungy* /ˈgʌndʒɪ/ ADJ visqueux, poisseux

gunk* /gʌŋk/ N (*NonC*) ⇒ **gunge**

gunmaker /ˈgʌnmeɪkəʳ/ N armurier *m*

gunman /ˈgʌnmən/ N (pl **-men**) bandit *m* armé ; (*Pol*) terroriste *m*

gunmetal /ˈgʌnmetl/ N bronze *m* à canon ADJ (= *colour*) vert-de-gris *inv*

gunnel /ˈgʌnl/ N ⇒ **gunwale**

gunner /ˈgʌnəʳ/ N (*Mil, Naut*) artilleur *m* ; (*Brit Mil*) canonnier *m*

gunnery /ˈgʌnərɪ/ N 1 (= *science, art, skill*) tir *m* au canon 2 (*Mil* = *guns*) artillerie *f* COMP **gunnery officer** N (*Mil*) officier *m* d'artillerie

gunny /ˈgʌnɪ/ N (*NonC*) toile *f* de jute grossière ; (also **gunny bag, gunny sack**) sac *m* de jute

gunplay /ˈgʌnpleɪ/ N (*US*) échange *m* de coups de feu

gunpoint /ˈgʌnpɔɪnt/ N ◆ **to have** *or* **hold sb at ~** tenir qn sous la menace d'un revolver *or* d'un fusil ◆ **he did it at ~** il l'a fait sous la menace d'un revolver *or* d'un fusil

gunpowder /ˈgʌnpaʊdəʳ/ N poudre *f* à canon ◆ **the Gunpowder Plot** (*Brit Hist*) la conspiration des Poudres

gunrunner /ˈgʌnrʌnəʳ/ N trafiquant *m* d'armes

gunrunning /ˈgʌnrʌnɪŋ/ N contrebande *f* *or* trafic *m* d'armes

gunsel* /ˈgʌnsl/ N (*US* = *gunman*) flingueur* *m*

gunship /ˈgʌnʃɪp/ N (also **helicopter gunship**) hélicoptère *m* de combat

gunshot /ˈgʌnʃɒt/ N (= *sound*) coup *m* de feu ◆ **within ~** à portée de fusil ◆ **out of ~** hors de portée de fusil COMP **gunshot wound** N blessure *f* par balle ◆ **to get a ~ wound** être blessé par balle, recevoir un coup de feu

gunslinger‡ /ˈgʌnslɪŋəʳ/ N (*US* = *gunman*) flingueur* *m*

gunsmith /ˈgʌnsmɪθ/ N armurier *m*

gunwale /ˈgʌnl/ N (*Naut*) plat-bord *m*

guppy /ˈgʌpɪ/ N guppy *m*

gurdwara /gɜːdˈwɑːrəʳ/ N gurdwara *m*

gurgle /ˈgɜːgl/ N [*of water, rain*] gargouillis *m*, glouglou *m* ; [*of stream*] murmure *m* ; [*of laughter*] gloussement *m* ; [*of baby*] gazouillis *m* ◆ **to give a ~ of delight** gazouiller de joie VI [*water*] glouglouter, gargouiller ; [*stream*] murmurer ; [*person*] (*with delight*) gazouiller ; (*with laughter*) glousser

Gurkha /ˈgɜːkə/ N Gurkha *m*

gurnard /ˈgɜːnəd/ N (pl **gurnard** *or* **gurnards**) grondin *m*

gurney /ˈgɜːnɪ/ (*US*) N lit *m* à roulettes

guru /ˈgʊruː/ N (*lit, fig*) gourou *m*

gush /gʌʃ/ N [*of oil, water, blood*] jaillissement *m*, bouillonnement *m* ; [*of tears, words*] flot *m* ; (* *pej*) effusion(s) *f(pl)*, épanchement(s) *m(pl)* VI 1 (*lit, fig*) jaillir ◆ **to ~ in/out/through** *etc* [*water etc*] entrer/sortir/traverser *etc* en bouillonnant 2 (* *pej*) [*person*] se répandre en compliments (*over/about* sur/au sujet de) en rajouter*

gusher* /ˈgʌʃəʳ/ N 1 (= *oil well*) puits *m* jaillissant (de pétrole) 2 (= *effusive person*) ◆ **to be a ~** être trop exubérant

gushing /ˈgʌʃɪŋ/ ADJ [*water etc*] jaillissant ; (*pej*) [*person, enthusiasm, welcome*] trop exubérant

gushy* /ˈgʌʃɪ/ ADJ [*person*] trop exubérant ; [*language*] dithyrambique

gusset /ˈgʌsɪt/ N (*Sewing*) soufflet *m*

gussy* /ˈgʌsɪ/ VT (*US*) ◆ **to ~ sth up** retaper* qch

gust /gʌst/ N 1 [*of wind*] rafale *f*, bourrasque *f* ; [*of smoke*] bouffée *f* ; [*of flame*] jet *m* ◆ **a ~ of rain** une averse ◆ **the wind was blowing in ~s** le vent soufflait en rafales ◆ **~s of 100km/h** des rafales de 100 km/h 2 (*fig*) [*of rage etc*] accès *m*, bouffée *f* ◆ **a ~ of laughter** un grand éclat de rire VI [*wind*] souffler en rafales ◆ **wind ~ing to force 7** vent *m* (en rafales) atteignant force 7

gustatory /ˈgʌstətərɪ/ ADJ gustatif

gusto /ˈgʌstəʊ/ N (*NonC*) enthousiasme *m*, plaisir *m* ◆ **with ~** avec brio *or* verve ◆ **he ate his meal with great ~** il a dévoré son repas

gusty /ˈgʌstɪ/ ADJ [*weather*] venteux ◆ **a ~ day** un jour de grand vent ◆ **~ wind** du vent en rafales

gut /gʌt/ N (*Anat*) boyau *m*, intestin *m* ; (*Med*: *for stitching*) catgut *m* ; (*Mus etc*) (corde *f* de) boyau *m* ◆ **~s** (*Anat*) boyaux *mpl* ◆ **my ~s ache!**‡ j'ai mal au bide‡ ◆ **to work** *or* **sweat one's ~s out**‡ se crever* au travail ◆ **I hate his ~s**‡ je ne peux pas le blairer‡ ◆ **the ~s* of his speech/of the problem** l'essentiel de son discours/du problème ; → **bust**[2]
NPL **guts** * (= *courage*) cran* *m* ◆ **he's got ~s** il a du cran* ◆ **he's got no ~s** il n'a rien dans le ventre*, il manque de cran* ◆ **it takes a lot of ~s to do that** il faut beaucoup de cran* pour faire ça
ADJ (*fig*) [*reaction*] instinctif ; (*negative*) viscéral ◆ **I've got a ~ feeling about it** je le sens au fond de moi-même ◆ **my ~ feeling** *or* **instinct is that ...** instinctivement, je sens que ... ◆ **~ reaction** première réaction *f*, réaction *f* instinctive
VT (*Culin*) [+ *animal*] vider, étriper ; [+ *fish*] vider ; * [+ *book etc*] piller* ◆ **fire ~ted the house** le feu n'a laissé que les quatre murs de la maison ◆ **the vandals ~ted the hall** les vandales n'ont laissé de la salle que les murs ; see also **gutted**
COMP **gut-churning** ADJ abominable, effroyable
gut course* N (*US Univ*) enseignement *m* de base
gut-wrenching ADJ abominable, effroyable

gutless* /ˈgʌtlɪs/ ADJ (= *cowardly*) dégonflé*

gutsy* /ˈgʌtsɪ/ ADJ 1 (= *plucky*) courageux 2 (= *substantial*) [*food, wine*] corsé ; [*music, song*] musclé*

gutta-percha /ˌgʌtəˈpɜːtʃə/ N (*NonC*) gutta-percha *f*

gutted‡ /ˈgʌtɪd/ ADJ (*Brit* = *disappointed*) écœuré

gutter /ˈgʌtəʳ/ N [*of roof*] gouttière *f* ; [*of road*] caniveau *m* ◆ **the language of the ~** le langage de la rue ◆ **to rise from the ~** sortir du ruisseau VI [*candle*] couler ; [*flame*] vaciller, crachoter COMP **gutter-press** N presse *f* de bas étage *or* à scandales

guttering /ˈgʌtərɪŋ/ N (*NonC*) gouttières *fpl*

guttersnipe /ˈgʌtəsnaɪp/ N gamin(e) *m(f)* des rues

guttural /ˈgʌtərəl/ ADJ guttural N (*Phon* †) gutturale *f*

guv‡ /gʌv/ N ⇒ **gov** ; → **governor 2**

guvnor‡ /ˈgʌvnəʳ/ N ⇒ **governor 2**

Guy /gaɪ/ N Guy *m* COMP **Guy Fawkes Night** N (*Brit*) *fête célébrée le 5 novembre*

GUY FAWKES NIGHT

En Grande-Bretagne, **Guy Fawkes Night** se fête le 5 novembre en mémoire de l'exécution du principal conjuré de la Conspiration des poudres (1605). Cette fête est prétexte à feux d'artifices et à feux de joie sur lesquels on brûle traditionnellement une effigie de **Guy Fawkes** (the guy) sous la forme d'une poupée de chiffon. Dans les jours qui précèdent, les enfants promènent cette effigie dans les rues et abordent les passants pour leur demander "a penny for the guy".

guy¹ /gaɪ/ N 1 *(esp US *)* type* *m*, mec* *m* ◆ **the good/bad ~s** les bons *mpl*/les méchants *mpl* ◆ **nice ~** chic type* *m*, type *m* bien* ◆ **hi, ~s!** salut les mecs !* ◆ **what are you ~s doing tonight?** qu'est-ce que vous faites ce soir, les mecs ?* ◆ **the ~s** *(US = friends)* les copains *mpl* ; → **fall** 2 *(Brit) effigie de Guy Fawkes* ; → GUY FAWKES NIGHT VT *(= make fun of)* tourner en ridicule

guy² /gaɪ/ N (also **guy rope**) corde *f* de tente

Guyana /gaɪ'ænə/ N Guyana *f*

Guyanese /ˌgaɪə'niːz/ ADJ guyanais N Guyanais(e) *m(f)*

guzzle /'gʌzl/ VT 1 *[person] [+ food]* bâfrer*, bouffer* ; *[+ drink]* siffler* 2 *(* fig) [car] [+ fuel, petrol]* bouffer*

guzzler /'gʌzlə^r/ N goinfre *mf* ; → **gas**

gybe /dʒaɪb/ VI ⇒ **gibe vi 2**

gym /dʒɪm/ N 1 (abbrev of **gymnastics**) gymnastique *f*, gym* *f* 2 (abbrev of **gymnasium**) gymnase *m* ; *(Scol)* gymnase *m*, salle *f* de gym*
COMP **gym shoes** NPL chaussures *fpl* de gym*
gym slip *(Brit)*, **gym suit** *(US)* N tunique *f (d'écolière)*

gymkhana /dʒɪm'kɑːnə/ N *(esp Brit)* gymkhana *m*

gymnasium /dʒɪm'neɪzɪəm/ N (pl **gymnasiums** or **gymnasia** /dʒɪm'neɪzɪə/) gymnase *m* ; *(Scol)* gymnase *m*, salle *f* de gymnastique

gymnast /'dʒɪmnæst/ N gymnaste *mf*

gymnastic /dʒɪm'næstɪk/ ADJ *[ability]* en gymnastique ; *[exercise, routine, championship]* de gymnastique ; *[leap]* acrobatique

gymnastics /dʒɪm'næstɪks/ N 1 *(pl = exercises)* gymnastique *f* ◆ **to do ~** faire de la gymnastique ◆ **mental ~** gymnastique *f* intellectuelle 2 *(NonC = art, skill)* gymnastique *f*

gynae* /'gaɪnɪ/ abbrev of **gynaecological, gynaecology**

gynaecological, gynecological *(US)* /ˌgaɪnɪkə'lɒdʒɪkəl/ ADJ gynécologique

gynaecologist, gynecologist *(US)* /ˌgaɪnɪ'kɒlədʒɪst/ N gynécologue *mf*

gynaecology, gynecology *(US)* /ˌgaɪnɪ'kɒlədʒɪ/ N gynécologie *f*

gyp* /dʒɪp/ N 1 *(US) (= swindler)* arnaqueur* *m* ; *(= swindle)* escroquerie *f* 2 *(Brit)* ◆ **my leg is giving me ~** j'ai atrocement *or* sacrément* mal à la jambe 3 *(Brit Univ)* domestique *m* VT *(US)* ◆ **to ~ sb out of sth** escroquer qch à qn

gyppo* /'dʒɪpəʊ/ N *(Brit)* manouche* *mf*

gypsophila /dʒɪp'sɒfɪlə/ N gypsophile *f*

gypsum /'dʒɪpsəm/ N *(NonC)* gypse *m*

gypsy /'dʒɪpsɪ/ N ⇒ **gipsy**

gyrate /ˌdʒaɪə'reɪt/ VI 1 *(= dance)* tournoyer ; *(suggestively)* onduler de façon suggestive 2 *(= spin)* tournoyer 3 *(= fluctuate)* fluctuer

gyration /ˌdʒaɪə'reɪʃən/ N *[of dancer, gymnast]* acrobatie *f* ; *(suggestive)* mouvement *m* suggestif ; *[of currency, stockmarket]* fluctuation *f*

gyratory /ˌdʒaɪə'reɪtərɪ/ ADJ giratoire

gyro /'dʒaɪərəʊ/ N abbrev of **gyrocompass, gyroscope**

gyrocompass /'dʒaɪərəʊ'kʌmpəs/ N gyrocompas *m*

gyrofrequency /ˌdʒaɪərəʊ'friːkwənsɪ/ N gyrofréquence *f*

gyromagnetic /ˌdʒaɪrəʊmæg'netɪk/ ADJ gyromagnétique

gyroscope /'dʒaɪərəˌskəʊp/ N gyroscope *m*

gyroscopic /ˌdʒaɪərə'skɒpɪk/ ADJ gyroscopique

gyrostabilizer /ˌdʒaɪərəʊ'steɪbɪlaɪzə^r/ N gyrostabilisateur *m*

gyrostat /'dʒaɪrəʊˌstæt/ N gyrostat *m*

Hh

H, h /eɪtʃ/ N 1 (= letter) H, h *m* ◆ **H for Harry, H for How** (US) ≃ H comme Hector ; → **drop** 2 (Drugs) H * poudre* *f* (Drugs), héroïne *f*
COMP **H-bomb** N bombe *f* H
H grade N (Scot Scol) ⇒ **Higher Grade** ; → **higher**

ha[1] /hɑː/ EXCL ha !, ah ! ◆ ~, ~! (surprise, irony) ha ! ha ! ; (laughter) hi ! hi ! hi !

ha[2] N (abbrev of **hectare**) ha

habeas corpus /ˈheɪbɪəsˈkɔːpəs/ N (Jur) habeas corpus *m* ; → **writ**[1]

haberdasher /ˈhæbədæʃəʳ/ N (= person) (Brit) mercier *m*, -ière *f* ; (US) chemisier *m*, -ière *f* ◆ **~'s** (Brit) mercerie *f* ; (US) confection *f* pour hommes

haberdashery /ˌhæbəˈdæʃərɪ/ N (Brit) mercerie *f* ; (US) confection *f* pour hommes

habit /ˈhæbɪt/ N 1 habitude *f* ◆ **good ~s** bonnes habitudes *fpl* ◆ **eating ~s** habitudes *fpl* alimentaires ◆ **a survey of British reading ~s** une étude sur ce que lisent les Britanniques ◆ **I'm worried about his drinking ~s** je m'inquiète de son penchant pour la boisson ◆ **to be in the ~ of doing sth** avoir pour habitude *or* avoir l'habitude de faire qch ◆ **he was talking very loudly, as he was in the ~ of doing when nervous** il parlait très fort comme il avait l'habitude de le faire quand il était tendu ◆ **I don't make a ~ of it** je ne le fais pas souvent ◆ **you can do it this time, but don't make a ~ of it** d'accord pour cette fois, mais il ne faut pas que cela devienne une habitude ◆ **let's hope he doesn't make a ~ of it** espérons qu'il n'en prendra pas l'habitude ◆ **to get** *or* **fall into bad ~s** prendre de mauvaises habitudes ◆ **to get into/out of the ~ of doing sth** prendre/perdre l'habitude de faire qch ◆ **to get sb into the ~ of doing sth** faire prendre à qn l'habitude de faire qch, habituer qn à faire qch ◆ **to get out of a ~** (= lose the habit) perdre une habitude ; (= get rid of a habit) se débarrasser *or* se défaire d'une habitude ◆ **I've got out of the ~ of going to the cinema** j'ai perdu l'habitude d'aller au cinéma, je ne vais pratiquement plus au cinéma ◆ **to have a ~ of doing sth** avoir l'habitude de faire qch ◆ **his ~ of staring at people unnerved her** cette habitude qu'il avait de fixer les gens la troublait ◆ **he had a bad ~ of listening in to other people's conversations** il avait la mauvaise habitude d'écouter les conversations des autres ◆ **history has a ~ of repeating itself** l'histoire a tendance à se répéter ◆ **to do sth out of** *or* **from ~** faire qch par habitude ◆ **~ of mind** tournure *f* d'esprit ◆ **old ~s die hard** (Prov) les mauvaises habitudes ont la vie dure (Prov) → **creature, force**
2 ◆ **to have a ~** (= drug-taking) être toxicomane ; (= smoking) avoir une dépendance à la nicotine ◆ **they couldn't cure him of the ~** ils n'ont pas réussi à le désaccoutumer *or* le faire décrocher* ; → **kick**
3 (= costume) [of monk, nun] habit *m* ; (also **riding habit**) tenue *f* d'équitation
COMP **habit-forming** ADJ qui crée une accoutumance

habitability /ˌhæbɪtəˈbɪlɪtɪ/ N habitabilité *f*

habitable /ˈhæbɪtəbl/ ADJ habitable

habitat /ˈhæbɪtæt/ N habitat *m*

habitation /ˌhæbɪˈteɪʃən/ N 1 (NonC) habitation *f* ◆ **the house showed signs of ~** la maison avait l'air habitée ◆ **unfit for human ~** inhabitable 2 (= dwelling-place) habitation *f*, domicile *m* ; (= settlement) établissement *m*, colonie *f*

habitual /həˈbɪtjʊəl/ ADJ 1 (= customary) [action, smile, expression, practice, courtesy] habituel ◆ **to become ~** devenir une habitude 2 (= regular) [drug user, drinker, liar] invétéré ◆ **~ criminal** *or* **offender** multirécidiviste *mf*

habitually /həˈbɪtjʊəlɪ/ ADV habituellement

habituate /həˈbɪtjʊeɪt/ VT habituer, accoutumer (sb to sth qn à qch)

hacienda /ˌhæsɪˈendə/ N (US) hacienda *f*

hack[1] /hæk/ N 1 (= cut) entaille *f* ; (= blow) (grand) coup *m* ; (= kick) coup *m* de pied
2 (= cough) toux *f* sèche
3 (Comput) ⇒ **hacker**
VT 1 (= cut) hacher, tailler ◆ **to ~ sth to pieces** tailler qch en pièces ◆ **the victims had been ~ed to death** les victimes avaient été massacrées à coups de hache ◆ **we ~ed our way through the jungle** nous nous sommes frayé un chemin dans la jungle à coups de machette
2 (Brit Sport = kick) ◆ **to ~ the ball away** renvoyer le ballon
3 ‡ ◆ **he just can't ~ it** (= can't manage it) il est complètement largué‡ ; (= can't stand it) il déteste ça, ça lui donne des boutons* ◆ **can he ~ it as a police chief?** est-ce qu'il tiendra le choc* en tant que chef de la police ?
4 (Brit ‡) ◆ **I'm ~ed off** (= fed up) j'en ai ras le bol‡ (with sb/sth de qn/qch) ; (= annoyed) je l'ai mauvaise* ◆ **I'm really ~ed off with her!** (= annoyed) je suis en rogne* contre elle !
5 (Comput) [+ system, file] s'introduire dans
VI 1 (= cut) ◆ **to ~ at sth** (essayer de) couper qch (au couteau *or* à la hache *etc*)
2 (= cough) tousser (d'une toux sèche)
3 (= be computer enthusiast) être un(e) mordu(e)* d'informatique ◆ **she had managed to ~ into the system** (= break into system) elle avait réussi à s'introduire dans le système
COMP **hacking cough** N toux *f* sèche
► **hack around** VI (US) traîner
► **hack down** VT SEP [+ person] massacrer à coups de couteau (*or* de hache *or* d'épée *etc*) ; [+ tree] abattre
► **hack out** VT SEP enlever grossièrement à coups de couteau (*or* de hache *or* d'épée *etc*)
► **hack up** VT SEP hacher, tailler en pièces

hack[2] /hæk/ N 1 (Brit) (= horse) cheval *m* de selle ; (hired) cheval *m* de louage ; (worn-out) haridelle *f*, rosse *f* ; (= ride) promenade *f* à cheval ◆ **to go for a ~** (aller) se promener à cheval
2 (pej) (= journalist) journaleux *m*, -euse *f* (pej) ; (= politician) politicard(e) *m(f)* (pej) ◆ **the party ~s** (Pol) les politicards *mpl* (pej) du parti ◆ **a ~ writer, a literary ~** un écrivaillon, un plumitif
3 (US ‡) (= vehicle) taxi *m* ; (= driver) chauffeur *m* de taxi
VI 1 (Brit = ride) monter (à cheval) ◆ **to go ~ing** (aller) se promener à cheval
2 (US = operate cab) faire le taxi*
COMP **hacking jacket** N (Brit) veste *f* de cheval *or* d'équitation
hack reporter N ◆ **to be a ~ reporter** tenir la rubrique des chiens écrasés, faire les chiens écrasés
hack work N ⇒ **hack writing**
hack writer N (pej) → **noun 2**
hack writing N (NonC) écrits *mpl* alimentaires ; (pej) travail *m* d'écrivaillon (pej)
► **hack up** VI [horse] (= win easily) l'emporter facilement ◆ **the favourite ~ed up by 12 lengths** le favori l'a emporté facilement avec 12 longueurs d'avance

hacker /ˈhækəʳ/ N (Comput) (= enthusiast) mordu(e)* *m(f)* d'informatique ; (= pirate) pirate *m* informatique

hacking /ˈhækɪŋ/ N (Comput) (= enthusiasm) engouement *m* pour l'informatique ; (= piracy) piratage *m* informatique

hackle /ˈhækl/ N plume *f* du cou NPL **hackles** poils *mpl* du cou ◆ **his ~s rose at the very idea** (fig) ça le hérissait d'y penser ◆ **to get sb's ~s up, to raise sb's ~s** hérisser qn

hackman /ˈhækmən/ N (pl **-men**) (US = cabdriver) chauffeur *m* de taxi

hackney cab /ˈhæknɪkæb/, **hackney carriage** /ˈhæknɪkærɪdʒ/ N voiture *f* de place *or* de louage

hackneyed /ˈhæknɪd/ ADJ *[word, image]* banal ; *[theme, subject]* rebattu ; *[metaphor]* usé ◆ **~ expression** *or* **phrase** cliché *m*, lieu *m* commun

hacksaw /ˈhæksɔː/ N scie *f* à métaux

had /hæd/ VB pt, ptp of **have**

haddock /ˈhædək/ N (pl **haddock** *or* **haddocks**) églefin *m or* aiglefin *m* ◆ **smoked ~** haddock *m*

Hades /ˈheɪdiːz/ N *(Myth) (= the underworld)* les enfers *mpl* ; *(= god)* Hadès *m*

hadj /hædʒ/ N (pl **hadjes**) ⇒ **hajj**

hadn't /ˈhædnt/ ⇒ **had not** ; → **have**

Hadrian /ˈheɪdrɪən/ N Hadrien *m* COMP **Hadrian's Wall** N le mur d'Hadrien

haematemesis, hematemesis *(US)* /ˌhiːməˈtemɪsɪs/ N hématémèse *f*

haematic, hematic *(US)* /hiːˈmætɪk/ ADJ hématique

haematite, hematite *(US)* /ˈhiːməˌtaɪt/ N hématite *f*

haematological, hematological *(US)* /ˌhiːmətəˈlɒdʒɪkəl/ ADJ hématologique

haematologist, hematologist *(US)* /ˌhiːməˈtɒlədʒɪst/ N hématologue *mf*, hématologiste *mf*

haematology, hematology *(US)* /ˌhiːməˈtɒlədʒɪ/ N hématologie *f*

haematolysis, hematolysis *(US)* /ˌhiːməˈtɒlɪsɪs/ N (pl **haematolyses** /ˌhiːməˈtɒlɪsiːz/) ⇒ **haemolysis**

haematoma, hematoma *(US)* /ˌhiːməˈtəʊmə/ N (pl **haematomas** *or* **haematomata** /ˌhiməˈtəʊmətə/) hématome *m*

haemodialyser, hemodialyzer *(US)* /ˌhiːməʊˈdaɪəˌlaɪzəʳ/ N rein *m* artificiel

haemodialysis, hemodialysis *(US)* /ˌhiːməʊdaɪˈælɪsɪs/ N hémodialyse *f*

haemoglobin, hemoglobin *(US)* /ˌhiːməʊˈgləʊbɪn/ N hémoglobine *f*

haemolysis, hemolysis *(US)* /hɪˈmɒlɪsɪs/ N (pl **haemolyses** /hɪˈmɒlɪˌsiːz/) hémolyse *f*

haemophilia, hemophilia *(US)* /ˌhiːməʊˈfɪlɪə/ N hémophilie *f*

haemophiliac, hemophiliac *(US)* /ˌhiːməʊˈfɪlɪæk/ ADJ, N hémophile *mf*

haemoptysis, hemoptysis *(US)* /hɪˈmɒptɪsɪs/ N (pl **haemoptyses** /hɪˈmɒptɪˌsiːz/) hémoptysie *f*

haemorrhage, hemorrhage *(US)* /ˈhemərɪdʒ/ N hémorragie *f* VI faire une hémorragie

haemorrhoids, hemorrhoids *(US)* /ˈhemərɔɪdz/ NPL hémorroïdes *fpl*

haemostasis, hemostasis *(US)* /ˌhiːməʊˈsteɪsɪs/ N hémostase *f*

hafnium /ˈhæfnɪəm/ N hafnium *m*

haft /hɑːft/ N *[of knife]* manche *m* ; *[of sword]* poignée *f* VT emmancher, mettre un manche à

hag /hæg/ N *(= ugly old woman)* vieille sorcière *f* ; *(= witch)* sorcière *f* ; *(* = unpleasant woman)* mégère *f* COMP **hag-ridden** ADJ *(gen)* tourmenté ◆ **he's ~-ridden** *(henpecked husband)* sa femme n'arrête pas de le houspiller

haggard /ˈhægəd/ ADJ *(= careworn)* défait ; *(= wild in appearance)* hagard ◆ **to look ~** avoir la mine défaite

haggis /ˈhægɪs/ N haggis *m (plat écossais à base d'abats de mouton, traditionnellement cuit dans une panse de mouton)*

haggle /ˈhægl/ VI *(= bargain)* marchander ; *(= quibble)* chicaner ◆ **to ~ about** *or* **over the price** *(= bargain)* débattre le prix ; *(= quibble)* chicaner sur le prix ◆ **they ~d over the terms of the agreement** ils ont chicané sur les termes de l'accord

haggling /ˈhæglɪŋ/ N *(= bargaining)* marchandage *m* ; *(= quibbling)* ergotage *m*

hagiographer /ˌhægɪˈɒgrəfəʳ/ N hagiographe *mf*

hagiography /ˌhægɪˈɒgrəfɪ/ N hagiographie *f*

Hague /heɪg/ N ◆ **The ~** La Haye

hah /hɑː/ EXCL ha !, ah !

ha-ha /ˈhɑːˈhɑː/ N *(Brit) (= fence)* clôture *f* en contrebas ; *(= ditch)* saut-de-loup *m*

haiku /ˈhaɪkuː/ N *(pl inv)* haïku *m*

hail[1] /heɪl/ N 1 *(NonC: Met)* grêle *f* 2 *(fig) [of stones, bullets, blows]* grêle *f*, pluie *f* ◆ **a ~ of gunfire** une pluie *or* grêle de balles VI grêler ◆ **it is ~ing** il grêle

hail[2] /heɪl/ VT 1 *(= acclaim)* saluer *(as* comme) ◆ **she has been ~ed as the greatest novelist of her generation** elle a été saluée comme la plus grande romancière de sa génération ◆ **the agreement was ~ed as a breakthrough** l'accord a été salué comme un événement capital

2 *(† = acknowledge)* acclamer *(as* comme) ◆ **he was ~ed as emperor** on l'acclama *or* il fut acclamé comme empereur

3 ◆ **(all) ~ !** † salut à vous !, je vous salue !

4 *(= call loudly) [+ ship, taxi, person]* héler ◆ **within ~ing distance** à portée de (la) voix

VI *(frm)* ◆ **to ~ from** *[ship]* être en provenance de ; *[person]* être originaire de ◆ **a ship ~ing from London** un navire en provenance de Londres ◆ **they ~ from Leeds** ils sont originaires de Leeds ◆ **where do you ~ from?** d'où êtes-vous ?

N appel *m*

COMP **hail-fellow-well-met** ADJ ◆ **to be ~-fellow-well-met** se montrer d'une familiarité excessive

Hail Mary N *(Rel)* Je vous salue Marie *m inv*, Ave *m inv*

► **hail down** VT SEP *[+ taxi]* héler

hailstone /ˈheɪlstəʊn/ N grêlon *m*

hailstorm /ˈheɪlstɔːm/ N averse *f* de grêle

hair /heəʳ/ N 1 *(NonC) [of human] (on head)* cheveux *mpl* ; *(on body)* poils *mpl* ◆ **he has black ~** il a les cheveux noirs ◆ **a man with long ~** un homme aux cheveux longs ◆ **a fine head of ~** une belle chevelure ◆ **to wash one's ~** se laver les cheveux ◆ **to do one's ~** se coiffer ◆ **her ~ always looks nice** elle est toujours bien coiffée ◆ **to have one's ~ done** se faire coiffer ◆ **she always does my ~ very well** elle me coiffe toujours très bien ◆ **to get one's ~ cut** se faire couper les cheveux ◆ **to put one's ~ up** relever ses cheveux ◆ **to let one's ~ down** * *(fig)* se laisser aller ◆ **keep your ~ on!*** *(Brit)* du calme ! ◆ **he gets in my ~** * *(= is annoying)* il me tape sur les nerfs * *or* sur le système * ◆ **I wish you'd get out of my ~ * while I'm working** j'aimerais bien que tu ne sois pas tout le temps dans mes jambes quand je travaille ◆ **to get sb out of one's ~** *(= get rid of them)* se débarrasser de qn ◆ **it made my ~ stand on end** cela m'a fait dresser les cheveux sur la tête

2 *[of human] (= single hair) (on head)* cheveu *m* ; *(on body)* poil *m* ◆ **I'm starting to get some grey ~s** je commence à avoir des cheveux gris *or* à grisonner ◆ **(with) not a ~ out of place** tiré à quatre épingles ◆ **not a ~ of his head was harmed** on n'a pas touché à un seul de ses cheveux ◆ **this will put ~s on your chest** * *(hum: spicy food, strong drink etc)* ça te rendra plus viril ◆ **it was hanging by a ~** cela ne tenait qu'à un cheveu ◆ **he won the race by a ~** il a gagné la course de justesse *or* d'un cheveu ; → **hair's breadth, split, turn**

3 *[of animal] (= single hair)* poil *m* ; *(NonC)* pelage *m* ; *[of horse]* pelage *m*, robe *f* ; *(= bristles)* soies *fpl* ◆ **I'm allergic to cat ~** je suis allergique aux poils de chat ◆ **try a ~ of the dog (that bit you)*** reprends un petit verre pour faire passer ta gueule de bois *

COMP *[sofa, mattress]* de crin

hair appointment N rendez-vous *m* chez le coiffeur

hair bulb N bulbe *m* pileux

hair care N soins *mpl* capillaires *or* du cheveu

hair clippers NPL tondeuse *f (de coiffeur)*

hair conditioner N après-shampooing *m*, baume *m* démêlant

hair cream N crème *f* capillaire

hair-curler N bigoudi *m*

hair-dryer N *(hand-held)* sèche-cheveux *m inv*, séchoir *m* (à cheveux) ; *(freestanding)* casque *m*

hair extension N *(clip-on)* postiche *m* ; *(permanent)* extension *f*

hair follicle N follicule *m* pileux

hair gel N gel *m* (coiffant *or* pour les cheveux)

hair grip N *(Brit)* pince *f* à cheveux

hair implant N implants *mpl* capillaires

hair lacquer N laque *f (pour cheveux)*

hair oil N huile *f* capillaire

hair-raising * ADJ *[experience, story]* terrifiant, à (vous) faire dresser les cheveux sur la tête ◆ **driving in Paris is a ~-raising business** c'est terrifiant de conduire dans Paris

hair remover N crème *f* dépilatoire

hair restorer N antichute *m*

hair roller N rouleau *m (bigoudi)*

hair's breadth N ◆ **the bullet missed him by a ~'s breadth** la balle l'a manqué de justesse *or* d'un cheveu ◆ **the car missed the taxi by a ~'s breadth** la voiture a évité le taxi de justesse ◆ **the country is within a ~'s breadth of civil war** le pays est à deux doigts de la guerre civile ◆ **she was within a ~'s breadth of selling the business** elle était à deux doigts de vendre l'affaire ADJ ◆ **they won the election with a ~'s breadth majority** ils ont remporté les élections d'un cheveu *or* de justesse ◆ **this performance earned him a ~'s breadth victory** grâce à cette performance, il l'a emporté *or* il a gagné de justesse ◆ **they had a ~'s breadth escape from their pursuers** ils ont échappé à leurs poursuivants de justesse

hair shirt N *(Rel)* haire *f*, cilice *m*

hair slide N *(Brit)* barrette *f*

hair specialist N capilliculteur *m*, -trice *f*

hair-splitter N coupeur *m*, -euse *f* de cheveux en quatre

hair-splitting N ergotage *m*, pinaillage * *m*

hair spray N laque *f (pour cheveux)*

hair style N coiffure *f*

hair stylist N coiffeur *m*, -euse *f*

hair transplant N implants *mpl* capillaires

hair-trigger ADJ *[temper]* explosif

hairball /ˈheəbɔːl/ N *[of cat]* boule *f* de poils

hairband /ˈheəbænd/ N bandeau *m*

hairbrained /ˈheəbreɪnd/ ADJ ⇒ **harebrained**

hairbrush /ˈheəbrʌʃ/ N brosse *f* à cheveux

haircloth /ˈheəklɒθ/ N étoffe *f* de crin

haircut /ˈheəkʌt/ N ◆ **to have** *or* **get a ~** se faire couper les cheveux ◆ **I'd like a ~** je voudrais une coupe ◆ **I like your ~** j'aime bien ta coupe de cheveux

hairdo * /ˈheəduː/ N coiffure *f* ◆ **do you like my ~?** tu aimes ma coiffure ?, tu aimes mes cheveux comme ça ? *

hairdresser /ˈheədresəʳ/ N coiffeur *m*, -euse *f* ◆ **I'm going to the ~'s** je vais chez le coiffeur COMP **hairdresser's (salon** *or* **shop)** N salon *m* de coiffure

hairdressing /ˈheədresɪŋ/ N *(NonC = skill, job)* coiffure *f (métier)*

COMP **hairdressing appointment** N rendez-vous *m* chez le coiffeur

hairdressing salon N salon *m* de coiffure

-haired /heəd/ ADJ *(in compounds)* ◆ **long-haired** *[person]* aux cheveux longs ; *[animal]* à longs poils ◆ **short-haired** *[person]* aux cheveux courts ; *[animal]* à poils ras ; → **curly, fair**[1]

hairless /ˈhɛəlɪs/ ADJ *[head]* chauve ; *[face, chin]* imberbe ; *[body, legs]* glabre ; *[animal]* sans poils

hairline /ˈhɛəlaɪn/ N *(on head)* naissance *f* des cheveux ; *(in handwriting)* délié *m* ; → **recede** COMP **hairline crack** N *(gen)* fine fissure *f* ; *(Med)* mince *or* légère fêlure *f*
hairline fracture N *(Med)* fêlure *f*

hairnet /ˈhɛənet/ N résille *f*, filet *m* à cheveux

hairpiece /ˈhɛəpiːs/ N postiche *m*

hairpin /ˈhɛəpɪn/ N épingle *f* à cheveux COMP **hairpin bend, hairpin curve** *(US)* N virage *m* en épingle à cheveux

hairspring /ˈhɛəsprɪŋ/ N (ressort *m*) spiral *m* *(de montre)*

hairy /ˈhɛərɪ/ ADJ 1 *(= covered with hair) [person, body]* poilu ; *[animal]* très poilu ; *[chest, legs, spider, leaf]* velu ◆ **a mammal's ~ coat** le pelage épais d'un mammifère 2 * *(= scary)* ◆ **his driving is a bit ~** sa façon de conduire file la pétoche* ◆ **there were some ~ moments on the mountain bends** on a eu des sueurs froides dans les virages de montagne

Haiti /ˈheɪtɪ/ N Haïti *f or m* ◆ **in ~** en Haïti

Haitian /ˈheɪʃɪən/ ADJ haïtien N Haïtien(ne) *m(f)*

hajj /hædʒ/ N (pl **hajjes**) hadj *m*

hake /heɪk/ N (pl **hake** *or* **hakes**) *(Brit)* colin *m*, merlu *m*

halal /hæˈlæl/ ADJ *[meat, butcher]* halal *inv or* hallal *inv*

halberd /ˈhælbəd/ N hallebarde *f*

halcyon /ˈhælsɪən/ N *(Myth, Orn)* alcyon *m* ADJ *[years, period]* de bonheur ◆ **~ days** jours *mpl* de bonheur, jours *mpl* heureux

hale /heɪl/ ADJ *[person]* vigoureux, robuste ◆ **to be ~ and hearty** *(gen)* être en pleine santé ; *[old person]* avoir bon pied bon œil

half /hɑːf/ (pl **halves**) N 1 *(of one whole)* moitié *f* ◆ **to take ~ of sth** prendre la moitié de qch ◆ **two halves make a whole** deux demis font un entier ◆ **the two halves of the brain** les deux hémisphères du cerveau ◆ **inflation rose in the first ~ of this year** l'inflation a augmenté au cours du premier semestre de l'année ◆ **I spent ~ the night thinking about it** j'ai passé la moitié de la nuit à y penser ◆ **she was working with ~ her usual energy** elle travaillait avec beaucoup moins d'énergie que de coutume ◆ **in ~ a second*** en moins de rien ◆ **to listen with ~ an ear** n'écouter que d'une oreille ◆ **you can see that with ~ an eye** ça saute aux yeux, ça crève les yeux ◆ **and that's not the ~ of it!*, I haven't told you the ~ of it yet!*** et c'est pas tout !* ◆ **my better** *or* **other ~*** *(hum)* ma douce moitié ◆ **to see how the other ~ lives*** voir comment vivent les autres
◆ **and a half** ◆ **two and a ~** deux et demi ◆ **two and a ~ hours/weeks, two hours/weeks and a ~** deux heures/semaines et demie ◆ **two and a ~ kilos, two kilos and a ~** deux kilos et demi ◆ **that was a day/an exam and a ~!*** ça a été une sacrée journée/un sacré examen !*, je te raconte pas ma journée/mon examen !*
◆ **by half** ◆ **to cut by ~** *[+ costs, prices, budget, workforce]* réduire de moitié ◆ **he's too clever/cheeky by ~*** c'est un petit malin/impertinent ◆ **the film was too sentimental by ~*** ce film était bien trop sentimental
◆ **by halves** ◆ **he doesn't do things by halves** il ne fait pas les choses à moitié *or* à demi
◆ **to go halves** ◆ **will you go halves with me in buying the book?** veux-tu qu'on achète ce livre ensemble, en payant chacun la moitié ?, est-ce que tu partagerais avec moi le prix de ce livre ? ◆ **we always go halves on the phone bill** nous partageons toujours la note de téléphone en deux ◆ **we went halves on a taxi** nous avons partagé un taxi
◆ **in half** ◆ **to cut sth in ~** *[+ object]* couper qch en deux ◆ **to cut in ~** *[+ costs, prices, budget, workforce]* réduire de moitié ◆ **the plate broke in ~** l'assiette s'est cassée en deux
2 *(of a number of things or people)* moitié *f* ◆ **~ of the books are in French** la moitié des livres sont en français ◆ **nearly ~ of all marriages end in divorce** près de la moitié des couples divorcent ◆ **100 employees, ~ of whom are part-time** 100 employés, dont la moitié sont à temps partiel ◆ **they don't know how to drive, ~ of them** la plupart d'entre eux ne savent pas conduire
3 *[of rail ticket]* **outward ~** billet *m* aller ◆ **return ~** billet *m* de retour
4 *(Sport = part of match)* mi-temps *f* ◆ **the first/second ~** la première/seconde mi-temps
5 *(Sport = player)* demi *m* ◆ **left/right ~** *(Ftbl)* demi *m* gauche/droite
6 *(Scol = term)* semestre *m*
7 *(Brit:* also **half-pint)** demi *m* ◆ **a ~ of Guinness please** un demi de Guinness, s'il vous plaît
ADJ demi ◆ **a ~ cup, ~ a cup** une demi-tasse ◆ **three ~ cups** trois demi-tasses ◆ **a ~ bottle of wine** une demi-bouteille de vin ◆ **a ~-point cut in interest rates** une réduction d'un demi pour cent des taux d'intérêt ◆ **~ man ~ beast** mi-homme mi-bête ◆ **there are no ~ measures** il n'y a pas de demi-mesures ◆ **this plan smacks of ~ measures** ce plan ne propose que des demi-mesures ◆ **he never does anything by ~ measures, there are no ~ measures with him** il ne fait jamais les choses à moitié ; see also **comp, tick¹**
ADV 1 *(= 50%)* ◆ **a mixture of ~ milk, ~ cream** un mélange moitié lait moitié crème, un mélange de lait et de crème, moitié-moitié ◆ **a ~-million dollars/people** un demi-million de dollars/personnes ◆ **the book was ~ in French, ~ in English** le livre était à moitié en français, à moitié en anglais ◆ **he's ~ French ~ English** il est de père français et de mère anglaise (*or* de père anglais et de mère française) ◆ **he is ~ as big as his sister** il est deux fois plus petit que sa sœur ◆ **he earns ~ as much as you** il gagne deux fois moins que vous ◆ **she earns ~ as much again as him** elle gagne une fois et demi(e) son salaire ◆ **a PC costs ~ as much again in Europe as in America** les PC coûtent une fois et demi(e) plus cher en Europe qu'en Amérique ◆ **his company's sales fell ~ as much again as last year** les ventes de son entreprise ont connu une baisse de 50% de plus que l'année dernière ; see also **comp**
2 *(= partially, partly)* à moitié ◆ **~ asleep** à moitié endormi ◆ **~-buried** à moitié *or* à demi enterré ◆ **the work is only ~ done** le travail n'est qu'à moitié fait ◆ **she has only ~ recovered from her illness** elle n'est qu'à moitié remise de sa maladie ◆ **he only ~ understands** il ne comprend qu'à moitié ◆ **I've only ~ read it** *(= didn't read carefully)* je ne l'ai lu qu'à moitié ; *(= haven't finished reading)* je n'en ai lu que la moitié ◆ **she was ~ laughing ~ crying** elle était partagée entre le rire et les larmes, elle était entre rire et larmes ◆ **~ angry, ~ amused** mi-fâché, mi-amusé
3 *(= rather, almost)* un peu ◆ **I'm ~ afraid that ...** j'ai un peu peur que ... + ne + *subj* ◆ **he was ~ ashamed to admit it** il avait un peu honte de l'admettre ◆ **I ~ think (that) ...** je serais tenté de penser que ... ◆ **I'm ~ inclined to do it** je suis tenté de le faire ◆ **I ~ suspect that ...** je soupçonne que ... ; see also **comp**
4 *(Brit *: emphatic)* ◆ **he wasn't ~ bad to look at !** il était rudement* *or* drôlement* beau ! ◆ **she didn't ~ swear!** elle a juré comme un charretier ! ◆ **she didn't ~ cry!** elle a pleuré comme une Madeleine ! ◆ **not ~!** tu parles !*, et comment !
5 *(in telling the time)* ◆ **it is ~ past three** il est trois heures et demie ◆ **what time is it? – ~ past** quelle heure est-il ? – la demie ; see also **comp**
COMP **half-a-crown** N *(Brit: formerly = value)* une demi-couronne ; → **half-crown**
half-a-dollar N *(US = value)* un demi-dollar ; *(Brit* ⁑*: formerly)* une demi-couronne ; → **half-dollar**
half-a-dozen N une demi-douzaine ; → **half-dozen**
half-and-half ADV moitié-moitié N *(US = milk and cream)* mélange mi-crème mi-lait
half-an-hour N une demi-heure ; → **half-hour**
half-assed⁑ ADJ *(US)* foireux⁑, nul
half-baked ADJ *(Culin)* à moitié cuit ; *(fig, pej) [plan, idea]* qui ne tient pas debout, à la noix* ; *[attempt]* maladroit ◆ **a ~-baked philosopher/politician** un philosophe/politicien à la manque*
half-binding N *[of book]* demi-reliure *f*
half-blind ADJ à moitié aveugle
half-blood N *(US)* ⇒ **half-breed**
half-board N *(Brit: in hotel)* demi-pension *f*
half-breed N *(= person)* métis(se) *m(f)* ADJ (also **half-bred)** *[person]* métis(se) ; *[animal]* hybride
half-brother N demi-frère *m*
half-caste ADJ, N métis(se) *m(f)*
half-century N demi-siècle *m*
half-circle N demi-cercle *m*
half-clad ADJ à demi vêtu
half-closed ADJ à demi fermé, à moitié fermé
half-cock N ◆ **to go off at ~-cock** *(fig) [plan etc]* rater
half-cocked ADJ *[gun]* à moitié armé, au cran de sûreté ; *(fig) [plan, scheme]* mal préparé, bâclé ◆ **to go off ~-cocked** *(fig)* rater
half-conscious ADJ à demi conscient
half-convinced ADJ à demi convaincu, à moitié convaincu
half-cooked ADJ à moitié cuit
half-crazy ADJ à moitié fou (folle *f*)
half-crown N *(Brit: formerly = coin)* demi-couronne *f* ; → **half-a-crown**
half-cup bra N soutien-gorge *m* à balconnet
half-cut †⁑ ADJ *(Brit)* bourré⁑
half-day N demi-journée *f* ◆ **to have a ~-day (holiday)** avoir une demi-journée (de congé)
half-dazed ADJ à demi hébété
half-dead ADJ *(lit, fig)* à moitié mort, à demi mort *(with* de)
half-deaf ADJ à moitié sourd
half-deck N *(Naut)* demi-pont *m*
half-digested ADJ *(lit, fig)* mal digéré
half-dollar N *(US = coin)* demi-dollar *m* ; → **half-a-dollar**
half-dozen N demi-douzaine *f* ; → **half-a-dozen**
half-dressed ADJ à demi vêtu
half-drowned ADJ à moitié noyé
half-educated ADJ ◆ **he is ~-educated** il n'est pas très instruit
half-empty ADJ à moitié vide VT vider à moitié
half-fare N demi-tarif *m* ADV *[pay]* demi-tarif
half-fill VT remplir à moitié
half-forgotten ADJ à moitié oublié
half-frozen ADJ à moitié gelé
half-full ADJ à moitié plein
half-grown ADJ à mi-croissance
half-hearted ADJ *[person, welcome]* peu enthousiaste ; *[manner]* tiède ; *[attempt]* timide
half-heartedly ADV *[welcome]* sans enthousiasme ; *[try]* sans conviction
half-heartedness N tiédeur *f* ; *[of person, welcome]* manque *m* d'enthousiasme ; *[of attempt]* manque *m* de conviction
half-hitch N demi-clef *f*
half holiday N *(Brit)* demi-journée *f* de congé
half-hour N demi-heure *f* ◆ **the clock struck the ~-hour** l'horloge a sonné la demie (de l'heure) ◆ **on the ~-hour** à la demie ADJ *[wait, delay]* d'une demi-heure ; → **half-an-hour**
half-hourly ADV toutes les demi-heures ADJ d'une demi-heure

half-jokingly ADV en plaisantant à moitié
half-landing N palier *m* de repos
half-length N *(Swimming)* demi-longueur *f* ADJ *[portrait]* en buste
half-lie N demi-mensonge *m*
half-life N *(Phys)* demi-vie *f*
half-light N demi-jour *m*
half-mad ADJ à moitié fou (folle *f*)
half-marathon N semi-marathon *m*
half-mast N ◆ **at ~-mast** *[flag]* en berne ; *[trousers]* qui tombe
half-moon N demi-lune *f* ; *(on fingernail)* lunule *f*
half-naked ADJ à demi nu, à moitié nu
half-nelson N *(Wrestling)* étranglement *m*
half-note N *(US Mus)* blanche *f*
half open VT entrouvrir, entrebâiller
half-open ADJ *[eye, mouth]* entrouvert ; *[window, door]* entrouvert, entrebâillé
half pay N ◆ **to be on ~ pay** *(gen)* toucher un demi-salaire ; *(Mil)* toucher une demi-solde
half-pint N ≈ quart *m* de litre ; (* = *small person)* demi-portion * *f* ◆ **a ~-pint (of beer)** ≈ un demi
half price N ◆ **at ~ price** à moitié prix ◆ **the goods were reduced to ~ price** le prix des articles était réduit de moitié ◆ **children are admitted (at) ~ price** les enfants paient demi-tarif ◆ **a ~-price hat** un chapeau à moitié prix
half-raw ADJ à moitié cru
half rest N *(US Mus)* demi-pause *f*
half seas over †‡ ADJ parti *, dans les vignes du Seigneur
half-serious ADJ à moitié sérieux
half-shut ADJ à moitié fermé
half-sister N demi-sœur *f*
half-size N *[of shoes]* demi-pointure *f* ADJ ◆ **~-size(d) model** modèle *m* réduit de moitié
half-sleeve N manche *f* mi-longue
half-staff N *(US)* ◆ **at ~-staff** en berne
half-starved ADJ à demi mort de faim, affamé
half term N *(Brit Educ) congé en milieu de trimestre*, petites vacances *fpl*
half-timbered ADJ à colombage
half time N 1 *(Sport)* mi-temps *f* ◆ **at ~ time** à la mi-temps 2 *(= work)* mi-temps *m* ◆ **on ~ time** à mi-temps ◆ **they are working ~ time** ils travaillent à mi-temps
half-time ADJ ◆ **~-time score** score *m* à la mi-temps
half-tone N *(US Mus)* demi-ton *m* ; *(Art)* demi-teinte *f* ; *(Phot)* similigravure *f*
half-track N *(= tread)* chenille *f* ; *(= vehicle)* half-track *m*
half-truth N demi-vérité *f*
half-understood ADJ compris à moitié, mal compris
half volley N *(Tennis)* demi-volée *f*
half-yearly *(esp Brit)* ADJ semestriel(le) *m(f)* ADV tous les six mois, chaque semestre

halfback /ˈhɑːfbæk/ N *(Sport)* demi *m*

halfpenny /ˈheɪpnɪ/ N (pl **halfpennies** *or* **halfpence** /ˈheɪpəns/) demi-penny *m* ◆ **he hasn't got a ~** il n'a pas le *or* un sou ADJ d'un demi-penny

halfway /ˈhɑːfˈweɪ/ ADV *(in distance)* à mi-chemin ◆ **to be ~ along the road** être à mi-chemin ◆ **~ along (the line of cars** *etc***)** vers le milieu (de la file de voitures *etc*) ◆ **~ between ...** *(lit, fig)* à mi-chemin entre ... ◆ **~ down (the hill)** à mi-pente, à mi-côte ◆ **~ up (the pipe/tree** *etc***)** à mi-hauteur (du tuyau/de l'arbre *etc*) ◆ **he was ~ down/up the stairs** il avait descendu/monté la moitié de l'escalier ◆ **her hair reaches ~ down her back** ses cheveux lui arrivent au milieu du dos ◆ **to stretch ~ around the world** faire la moitié de la terre ◆ **they've travelled ~ around the world** *(lit)* ils ont fait la moitié du tour de la terre ; *(fig)* ils ont beaucoup voyagé ◆ **(to be) ~ there** (être) à mi-chemin ◆ **~ through the book/film** au milieu du livre/du film ◆ **turn the fish over ~ through** retournez le poisson en milieu de cuisson ◆ **~ to Paris** à mi-chemin de Paris ◆ **anything ~ decent will be incredibly expensive** pour avoir quelque chose d'à peu près correct, il faut compter une fortune ◆ **to go ~** *(lit)* faire la moitié du chemin ◆ **the decision goes ~ to giving the strikers what they want** cette décision va dans le sens des revendications des grévistes ◆ **I'll meet you ~** *(lit)* j'irai à votre rencontre, je ferai la moitié du chemin ; *(fig)* coupons la poire en deux, faisons un compromis ◆ **to meet trouble ~** se créer des ennuis

COMP **halfway hostel** N ⇒ **halfway house 1**
halfway house N 1 *(for rehabilitation)* centre *m* de réadaptation 2 *(= compromise)* compromis *m* ◆ **it's a ~ house between dance and drama** c'est à mi-chemin entre la danse et le théâtre 3 *(Hist = inn)* hôtellerie *f* relais
halfway line N *(Ftbl)* ligne *f* médiane

halfwit /ˈhɑːfwɪt/ N idiot(e) *m(f)*, imbécile *mf*

halfwitted /hɑːfˈwɪtɪd/ ADJ idiot, imbécile

halibut /ˈhælɪbət/ N (pl **halibut** *or* **halibuts**) flétan *m*

halitosis /ˌhælɪˈtəʊsɪs/ N mauvaise haleine *f*

hall /hɔːl/ N 1 *(= large public room)* salle *f* ; *[of castle, public building]* (grande) salle *f* ; (also **village hall, church hall**) salle *f* paroissiale ; *(Brit Univ) (= refectory)* réfectoire *m* ; → **concert, music, town** 2 *(= mansion)* château *m*, manoir *m* 3 *(Theat)* ◆ **to play the ~s** faire du music-hall 4 *(= entrance way) [of house]* entrée *f* ; *[of hotel]* hall *m* 5 *(US = corridor)* couloir *m* 6 *(Univ:* also **hall of residence** *(Brit)*, **residence hall** *(US))* résidence *f* universitaire ◆ **to live** *or* **be in ~** habiter en résidence universitaire *or* en cité universitaire

COMP **Hall of Fame** N panthéon *m* ◆ **his records have earned him a place in the jazz Hall of Fame** ses disques lui ont valu une place au panthéon du jazz
hall porter N *(Brit) (in blocks of flats)* concierge *mf* ; *(in hotel)* portier *m*
hall tree N *(US)* ⇒ **hallstand**

hallelujah /ˌhælɪˈluːjə/ EXCL, N alléluia *m* ◆ **the Hallelujah Chorus** l'Alléluia

hallmark /ˈhɔːlmɑːk/ N 1 *[of gold, silver]* poinçon *m* 2 *(fig)* marque *f* ◆ **the ~ of genius** la marque du génie ◆ **this attack bears the ~ of a terrorist incident** cet attentat porte la marque d'une organisation terroriste, cet attentat a tout d'un acte terroriste ◆ **excellent service is the ~ of a good restaurant** un bon restaurant se distingue par l'excellence de son service ◆ **the dry wit that has always been his ~** l'humour pince-sans-rire qui l'a toujours caractérisé VT poinçonner

hallo /həˈləʊ/ EXCL *(Brit)* ⇒ **hello**

halloo /həˈluː/ EXCL *(Hunting)* taïaut ! ; *(gen)* ohé ! N appel *m* VI *(Hunting)* crier taïaut ; *(gen)* appeler (à grands cris)

hallow /ˈhæləʊ/ VT sanctifier, consacrer ◆ **~ed be Thy name** que Ton nom soit sanctifié

hallowed /ˈhæləʊd/ ADJ 1 *(= holy)* saint, béni ◆ **on ~ ground** en terre sacrée 2 *(= venerable) [right, tradition, institution]* sacré ◆ **the ~ halls of the White House** *(hum)* la vénérable enceinte de la Maison Blanche ◆ **the ~ portals of the headmaster's office** *(hum)* l'entrée de ce lieu sacré qu'est le bureau du directeur

Halloween, Hallowe'en /ˌhæləʊˈiːn/ N Halloween *m*

HALLOWEEN

La fête d'**Halloween**, célébrée le 31 octobre (jour où, pensait-on, les morts venaient rendre visite aux vivants), est une très ancienne tradition dans les pays anglo-saxons. À cette occasion, les enfants déguisés en sorcières et en fantômes frappent aux portes de leurs voisins pour leur demander des bonbons et de l'argent ; aux États-Unis, cette coutume est connue sous le nom de « trick or treat », car les enfants menacent de vous jouer un mauvais tour (« trick ») si vous ne leur donnez pas un petit cadeau (« treat »), en général des bonbons.

hallstand /ˈhɔːlstænd/ N portemanteau *m*

hallucinant /həˈluːsɪnənt/ N hallucinogène *m*

hallucinate /həˈluːsɪˌneɪt/ VI avoir des hallucinations

hallucination /həˌluːsɪˈneɪʃən/ N hallucination *f*

hallucinatory /həˈluːsɪnətərɪ/ ADJ *[drug]* hallucinogène ; *[state, effect, vision]* hallucinatoire

hallucinogen /ˌhæluːˈsɪnədʒən/ N hallucinogène *m*

hallucinogenic /həˌluːsɪnəʊˈdʒenɪk/ ADJ hallucinogène

hallway /ˈhɔːlweɪ/ N ⇒ **hall noun 4**

halo /ˈheɪləʊ/ N (pl **halo(e)s**) *[of saint]* auréole *f*, nimbe *m* ; *(Astron)* halo *m*

halogen /ˈhæləˌdʒen/ N halogène *m* COMP **halogen lamp** N lampe *f* (à) halogène

halt[1] /hɔːlt/ N 1 halte *f*, arrêt *m* ◆ **five minutes' ~** cinq minutes d'arrêt ◆ **to come to a ~** *[person]* faire halte, s'arrêter ; *[vehicle]* s'arrêter ; *[process]* être interrompu ◆ **the commander called a ~** le commandant a ordonné que l'on s'arrête ◆ **the referee called a ~** *(Ftbl etc)* l'arbitre a sifflé un arrêt de jeu ◆ **to call a ~ to sth** mettre fin à qch ◆ **to call for a ~ to sth** demander l'arrêt de qch ◆ **her government called for an immediate ~ to the fighting** son gouvernement a demandé l'arrêt immédiat des combats 2 *(Brit Rail)* halte *f* VI faire halte, s'arrêter ◆ **~!** halte ! VT *[+ vehicle]* faire arrêter ; *[+ process]* interrompre COMP **halt sign** N *(on road)* (panneau *m*) stop *m*

halt[2] †† /hɔːlt/ ADJ *(= lame)* boiteux NPL **the halt** les estropiés *mpl*

halter /ˈhɔːltəʳ/ N 1 *[of horse]* licou *m*, collier *m* ; *(= hangman's noose)* corde *f (de pendaison)* 2 *(Dress:* also **halterneck**) ◆ **a dress with a ~ top** une robe dos nu ADJ *(Dress:* also **halterneck**) *[top, dress]* dos nu *inv*

halterneck /ˈhɔːltəˈnek/ N dos-nu *m inv* ADJ dos nu *inv*

halting /ˈhɔːltɪŋ/ ADJ *[speech, efforts, progress]* hésitant ; *[voice]* haché, hésitant ; *[verse]* boiteux ; *[style]* heurté ◆ **in ~ French/German** dans un français/allemand hésitant

haltingly /ˈhɔːltɪŋlɪ/ ADV *[speak]* de façon hésitante

halve /hɑːv/ VT 1 *(= divide in two) [+ object]* couper en deux 2 *(= reduce by half) [+ expense, time]* réduire *or* diminuer de moitié ◆ **the quantities if cooking for one** pour une personne, réduisez les quantités de moitié VI *[sales, figures]* être réduit de moitié

halves /hɑːvz/ NPL of **half**

halyard /ˈhæljəd/ N *(Naut)* drisse *f*

ham /hæm/ N 1 *(= meat)* jambon *m* ◆ **~ and eggs** œufs *mpl* au jambon 2 *(Anat) [of animal]* cuisse *f* 3 *(Theat *: pej)* cabotin(e) * *m(f) (pej)* 4 *(Rad *)* radioamateur *m* COMP *[sandwich]* au jambon
ham acting N cabotinage * *m*

ham-fisted, ham-handed ADJ maladroit, gauche

► **ham up*** VT SEP *(Theat)* *[+ part, speech]* forcer ◆ **to ~ it up** forcer son rôle

Hamburg /ˈhæmbɜːg/ N Hambourg

hamburger /ˈhæm,bɜːgəʳ/ N *(gen)* hamburger *m* ; *(US:* also **hamburger meat***)* viande *f* hachée

Hamitic /hæˈmɪtɪk/ ADJ chamitique

Hamlet /ˈhæmlət/ N Hamlet *m*

hamlet /ˈhæmlɪt/ N *(village)* hameau *m*

hammer /ˈhæməʳ/ N *(= tool: also Sport, of piano)* marteau *m* ; *(of gun)* chien *m* ◆ **the ~ and sickle** la faucille et le marteau ◆ **to come under the ~** *(at auction)* être mis aux enchères

◆ **to go at it hammer and tongs** s'en donner à cœur joie ◆ **they were going at it ~ and tongs** *(= having sex)* ils s'en donnaient à cœur joie ; *(= fighting)* ils se battaient comme des chiffonniers ; *(= working)* ils y mettaient tout leur cœur ; *(= arguing, debating)* ils discutaient âprement

VT 1 *[+ metal]* battre au marteau, marteler ◆ **to ~ a nail into a plank** enfoncer un clou dans une planche (à coups de marteau) ◆ **to ~ the table with one's fists** frapper du poing sur la table ◆ **to ~ sb/sth into the ground** *(fig)* venir à bout de qn/qch ◆ **to ~ a point home** insister sur un point ◆ **to ~ into shape** *[+ metal]* façonner (au marteau) ; *(fig)* *[+ plan, agreement]* mettre au point ◆ **I tried to ~ some sense into him** j'ai essayé de lui faire entendre raison ◆ **I'd had it ~ed into me that ...** on m'avait enfoncé dans la tête que ...

2 *(Brit* = defeat)* battre à plate(s) couture(s) ; *(= criticize severely)* descendre en flammes, éreinter ; *(= damage severely)* frapper de plein fouet ◆ **the firm had been ~ed by the recession** l'entreprise avait été frappée de plein fouet par la récession ◆ **the report ~s motorists who drink and drive** le rapport incrimine les automobilistes qui conduisent en état d'ivresse

3 *[+ stockbroker]* déclarer failli *or* en faillite

VI *(lit)* donner des coups de marteau ◆ **he was ~ing at the door** il frappait à la porte à coups redoublés ◆ **he was ~ing away on the piano** il tapait sur le piano (comme un sourd) ◆ **to ~ away at a problem** s'acharner à résoudre un problème ◆ **my heart was ~ing** mon cœur battait très fort

COMP **hammer blow** N *(lit)* coup *m* de marteau ; *(fig)* coup *m* terrible *(for pour)* ◆ **to deal a ~ blow to sth** porter un rude coup *or* un coup terrible à qch

hammer drill N perceuse *f* à percussion

► **hammer down** VT SEP *[+ nail]* enfoncer ; *[+ metal]* aplatir au marteau ; *[+ loose plank]* fixer

► **hammer in** VT SEP enfoncer (au marteau) ◆ **he ~ed the nail in with his shoe** il a enfoncé le clou avec sa chaussure

► **hammer out** VT SEP *[+ metal]* étirer (au marteau) ; *(fig)* *[+ plan, agreement]* élaborer (avec difficulté) ; *[+ difficulties]* démêler ; *[+ verse, music]* marteler ◆ **to ~ out a solution** finir par trouver une solution

► **hammer together** VT SEP *[+ pieces of wood etc]* assembler au marteau

hammerhead /ˈhæməhed/ N *(= shark)* requin *m* marteau

hammering /ˈhæmərɪŋ/ N 1 *(lit)* *(= action)* martelage *m* ; *(= sound)* martèlement *m* 2 * : *(fig)* *(= defeat)* raclée* *f*, dérouillée* *f* ; *(= criticism)* éreintement *m*, descente *f* en flammes ◆ **to take a ~*** *[team, boxer, player]* prendre une raclée* *or* une dérouillée* ; *[book, play, film]* se faire esquinter* *or* éreinter

hammertoe /ˈhæmətəʊ/ N orteil *m* en marteau

hammock /ˈhæmək/ N hamac *m*

hammy* /ˈhæmɪ/ ADJ *[actor]* qui force son rôle ; *[performance]* trop théâtral

hamper¹ /ˈhæmpəʳ/ N panier *m* d'osier, manne *f* ; *(for oysters, fish, game)* bourriche *f* ◆ **a ~ of food** un panier garni *(de nourriture)* ; → **picnic**

hamper² /ˈhæmpəʳ/ VT *[+ person]* gêner, handicaper ; *[+ movement efforts]* gêner, entraver

hamster /ˈhæmstəʳ/ N hamster *m*

hamstring /ˈhæmstrɪŋ/ N tendon *m* du jarret VT couper les jarrets à ; *(fig)* *[+ person]* couper ses moyens à, paralyser ; *[+ plan]* entraver ; *[+ activity]* paralyser COMP **hamstring injury** N claquage *m* (au jarret)

hand /hænd/

LANGUAGE IN USE 26.2

1 NOUN	3 COMPOUNDS
2 TRANSITIVE VERB	4 PHRASAL VERBS

1 - NOUN

1 = part of body main *f* ◆ **he took her by the ~** il l'a prise par la main ◆ **to take sth with both ~s** prendre qch à deux mains ◆ **he's very good with his ~s** il est très adroit de ses mains ◆ **give me your ~** donne-moi la main ◆ **my ~s are tied** j'ai les mains liées ◆ **I could do it with one ~ tied behind my back** je pourrais le faire les yeux fermés ◆ **we're forced to do it with one ~** *or* **both ~s** *or* **our ~s tied behind our back** nous sommes pieds et poings liés

2 in marriage main *f* ◆ **he asked for her ~** † il a demandé sa main ◆ **to give sb one's ~** † accorder sa main à qn †

3 = help coup *m* de main ◆ **could you give** *or* **lend me a ~?** tu peux me donner un coup de main ? ◆ **would you like a ~ with moving that?** tu veux un coup de main pour déplacer ça ? ◆ **to lend a ~** donner un coup de main

4 = influence influence *f* ◆ **you could see his ~ in everything the committee did** on reconnaissait son influence dans tout ce que faisait le comité

5 person *(= worker)* ouvrier *m*, -ière *f* ; *(= member of crew)* membre *m* d'équipage ◆ **I sailed round Java, with a couple of ~s** j'ai fait le tour de Java en voilier avec un équipage de deux personnes ◆ **the ship was 26 ~s short of her complement** il manquait 26 hommes à l'équipage du bateau ◆ **the ship was lost with all ~s** le navire a disparu corps et biens ◆ **all ~s on deck** tout le monde sur le pont ; *(fig)* ◆ **the wedding's next week, so it's all ~s on deck** le mariage a lieu la semaine prochaine, alors on a besoin de tout le monde

6 of clock, watch aiguille *f* ◆ **the ~s of the clock were pointing to midday** les aiguilles de l'horloge indiquaient midi ◆ **the big/little ~** la grande/petite aiguille

7 Cards *(= cards one has)* main *f*, jeu *m* ; *(= game)* partie *f* ◆ **I've got a good ~** j'ai une belle main *or* un beau jeu ◆ **we played a ~ of bridge** nous avons fait une partie de bridge

8 = handwriting écriture *f* ◆ **she recognized his neat ~** elle a reconnu son écriture bien nette ◆ **the letter was written in his own ~** la lettre était écrite de sa propre main

9 Measure paume *f* ◆ **a horse 13 ~s high** un cheval de 13 paumes

10 Culin ◆ **~ of bananas** régime *m* de bananes ◆ **~ of pork** jambonneau *m*

11 set structures

◆ *preposition/article/possessive +* **hand(s)** ◆ **many suffered at the ~s of the secret police** beaucoup de gens ont souffert aux mains de la police secrète ◆ **their defeat at the ~s of Manchester** *(Sport)* leur défaite face à Manchester ◆ **to lead sb by the ~** conduire qn par la main ◆ **for four ~s** *(Mus)* à quatre mains ◆ **she had a book in her ~** elle avait un livre à la main ◆ **she was holding the earrings in her ~** elle tenait les boucles d'oreilles dans sa main ◆ **he wanted £100 in his ~** il a demandé 100 livres de la main à la main ◆ **my life is in your ~s** ma vie est entre vos mains ◆ **in one's own ~s** entre ses mains ◆ **our destiny is in our own ~s** notre destinée est entre nos mains ◆ **to put o.s. in sb's ~s** s'en remettre à qn ◆ **to put sth into sb's ~s** confier qch à qn ◆ **she put the firm into her daughter's ~s** elle a confié l'entreprise à sa fille ◆ **to fall into the ~s of** tomber aux mains *or* entre les mains de ◆ **the children are now off our ~s** maintenant nous n'avons plus besoin de nous occuper des enfants ◆ **to get sth off one's ~s** se débarrasser *or* se décharger de qch ◆ **I'll take it off your ~s** je vous en débarrasse ? ◆ **we've got a difficult job on our ~s** une tâche difficile nous attend ◆ **he'll have a real battle on his ~s** un véritable combat l'attend ◆ **he had time on his ~s** il avait du temps de reste ◆ **to sit on one's ~s** rester sans rien faire ◆ **goods left on our** (*or* **their** *etc*) **~s** marchandises *fpl* invendues ◆ **the hedgehog ate out of his ~** le hérisson lui mangeait dans la main ◆ **she's got the boss eating out of her ~** elle fait marcher le patron au doigt et à l'œil ◆ **it is out of his ~s** ce n'est plus lui qui s'en occupe

◆ **hand(s)** *+ preposition/adverb* ◆ **she won ~s down** elle a gagné haut la main ◆ **to get one's ~ in** se faire la main ◆ **to have a ~ in** *[+ task, achievement]* jouer un rôle dans ; *[+ crime]* être mêlé à, être impliqué dans ◆ **Lee scored a goal and had a ~ in two others** Lee a marqué un but et a contribué à en marquer deux autres ◆ **the president himself had a ~ in the massacre** le président lui-même était impliqué dans le massacre ◆ **I had no ~ in it** je n'y suis pour rien ◆ **to take a ~ in sth/in doing sth** contribuer à qch/à faire qch ◆ **everybody took a ~ in the preparations for the party** tout le monde a participé aux préparatifs de la fête ◆ **the government took a ~ in drawing up the plan** le gouvernement a contribué à l'élaboration du projet ◆ **to keep one's ~ in** garder la main ◆ **he can't keep his ~s off the money** il ne peut pas s'empêcher de toucher à l'argent ◆ **keep your ~s off my sweets!*** touche pas à mes bonbons !* ◆ **~s off!*** bas les pattes !* ◆ **~s off our village!*** laissez notre village tranquille ! ◆ **to get one's ~s on sth** mettre la main sur qch ◆ **just wait till I get my ~s on him!*** attends un peu que je lui mette la main dessus ! ◆ **I wish I could lay my ~s on a good dictionary** si seulement je pouvais mettre la main sur *or* dénicher un bon dictionnaire ◆ **she read everything she could get** *or* **lay her ~s on** elle a lu tout ce qui lui tombait sous la main ◆ **to put** *or* **set one's ~ to sth** entreprendre qch ◆ **he can set his ~ to most things** il y a peu de choses qu'il ne sache (pas) faire ◆ **~s up!** *(at gun point)* haut les mains ! ; *(in school)* levez la main ! ◆ **~s up who'd like some chocolate!** levez la main si vous voulez du chocolat !

◆ *adjective +* **hand(s)** ◆ **she's no bad ~ at acting** ce n'est pas une mauvaise actrice ◆ **they gave him a big ~** ils l'ont applaudi bien fort ◆ **a big ~, please, for Mr John Turner** applaudissez bien fort M. John Turner ◆ **he grabbed the opportunity with both ~s** il a sauté sur l'occasion ◆ **I am leaving you in Penny's very capable ~s** je te laisse entre les mains de Penny ◆ **on every ~** partout ◆ **to rule with a firm ~** gouverner d'une main ferme ◆ **at first ~** de première main ◆ **I've got my ~s full at the moment** je suis débordé en ce moment ◆ **to have one's ~s full with** avoir fort à faire avec ◆ **to be in good ~s** être en (de) bonnes mains ◆ **King Henry ruled with a heavy ~** le roi Henri a dirigé le pays d'une main de fer ◆ **on the left ~** du côté gauche, à gauche ◆ **he's an old ~ (at this game)!** il connaît la musique ! ◆ **he's an old ~ at blackmail** le chantage, ça le connaît ◆ **the director was an old ~ at Racine** il (*or* elle) n'en était pas à sa première mise en scène de Racine ◆ **to give with one ~ and take away with the other** donner d'un côté *or* d'une main et reprendre de l'autre ◆ **on the one ~ ..., on the other ~** d'une part ..., d'autre part ◆ **yes, but on the other ~ he is very rich** oui, mais (par ailleurs) il est très riche ◆ **on the right ~** du côté droit, à droite ◆ **to gain** *or* **get the upper ~** prendre l'avantage *or* le dessus ◆ **to get into the wrong ~s** tomber dans *or* entre de mauvaises mains ; → **left², right**

◆ **hand(s)** + *noun* ◆ **he's making money ~ over fist** il fait des affaires en or ◆ **we're losing money ~ over fist** nous perdons de l'argent à une vitesse phénoménale ◆ **he was bound ~ and foot** il était pieds et poings liés ◆ **I refuse to wait on my husband ~ and foot** je refuse d'être l'esclave de mon mari ◆ **she expected to be waited on ~ and foot** elle voulait être servie comme une princesse ◆ **they are ~ in glove** ils sont de mèche ◆ **he's ~ in glove with them** il est de mèche avec eux ◆ **the authorities often worked ~ in glove with criminals** les autorités ont souvent travaillé en étroite collaboration avec des criminels ◆ **they were walking along ~ in ~** ils marchaient (la) main dans la main ◆ **research and teaching go ~ in ~** la recherche et l'enseignement vont de pair *or* sont indissociables ◆ **she hauled herself up the rope ~ over ~** elle a grimpé à la corde en s'aidant des deux mains ◆ **from ~ to ~** de main en main ◆ **on (one's) ~s and knees** à quatre pattes ◆ **to live from ~ to mouth** vivre au jour le jour ◆ **he doesn't like putting his ~ in his pocket** il n'aime pas mettre la main à la poche ◆ **he never does a ~'s turn*** (*Brit*) il ne fiche* jamais rien

◆ *verb* + **hand(s)** ◆ **to force sb's ~** forcer la main à qn ◆ **to put** *or* **hold one's ~s up to sth** se déclarer coupable de qch ◆ **to show one's ~** dévoiler son jeu ◆ **to stay one's ~** (*liter*) se retenir ◆ **he turned his ~ to writing** il s'est mis à écrire ◆ **he can turn his ~ to anything** il sait tout faire

◆ **at hand** (= *close by*) à portée de (la) main ◆ **having the equipment at ~ will be very helpful** ce sera très pratique d'avoir l'équipement à portée de (la) main ◆ **summer is (close) at ~** † l'été *m* est (tout) proche

◆ **by hand** à la main ◆ **made by ~** fait (à la) main ◆ **the letter was written by ~** la lettre était manuscrite *or* écrite à la main ◆ **the letter was delivered by ~** quelqu'un a apporté la lettre

◆ **in hand** ◆ **Guy was at the door, briefcase in ~** Guy était à la porte, son attaché-case à la main ◆ **he opened the door, gun in ~** il a ouvert la porte, pistolet au poing ◆ **he had the situation well in ~** il avait la situation bien en main ◆ **to take sb/sth in ~** prendre qn/qch en main ◆ **to take o.s. in ~** se prendre en main ◆ **Scotland are behind, but have a game in ~** l'Écosse est derrière, mais il lui reste un match à jouer ◆ **he had £6,000 in ~** il avait 6 000 livres de disponibles ◆ **let's concentrate on the job in ~** revenons à nos moutons

◆ **off hand** ◆ **I don't know off ~** je ne pourrais pas le dire de tête

◆ **on hand** sur place ◆ **there are experts on ~ to give you advice** il y a des experts sur place pour vous conseiller

◆ **out of hand** (= *instantly*) d'emblée ◆ **to dismiss sth out of ~** rejeter qch d'emblée ◆ **to get out of ~** [*situation, spending, crowd*] échapper à tout contrôle

◆ **to hand** sous la main ◆ **I haven't got the letter to ~** je n'ai pas la lettre sous la main ◆ **the information to ~** les renseignements *mpl* disponibles ◆ **she seized the first weapon to ~** elle s'est emparée de la première arme venue

2 - TRANSITIVE VERB

[= give] donner (*to* à) ; (= *hold out*) tendre (*to* à) ◆ **to ~ sb sth, to ~ sth to sb** donner qch à qn ◆ **you've got to ~ it to him* - he did it very well** il faut reconnaître qu'il l'a très bien fait, il n'y a pas à dire, il l'a très bien fait ◆ **it was ~ed to him on a plate*** on le lui a apporté sur un plateau (d'argent)

3 - COMPOUNDS

hand-baggage N ⇒ **hand-luggage**
hand controls NPL commandes *fpl* manuelles
hand cream N crème *f* pour les mains
hand-drier, hand-dryer N sèche-mains *m inv*
hand grenade N (*Mil*) grenade *f*
hand-held ADJ portable
hand-knitted ADJ tricoté à la main
hand lotion N lotion *f* pour les mains
hand-luggage N (*NonC*) bagages *mpl* à main
hand-me-down* N vêtement *m* déjà porté ◆ **it's a ~-me-down from my sister** c'est un vêtement qui me vient de ma sœur
hand-out N (= *leaflet*) prospectus *m* ; (*at lecture, meeting*) polycopié *m* ; (= *press release*) communiqué *m* ; (= *money: from government, official body*) aide *f*, subvention *f* ; (= *alms*) aumône *f*
hand-painted ADJ peint à la main
hand-pick VT [+ *fruit, vegetables etc*] cueillir à la main ; (*fig*) trier sur le volet
hand-picked ADJ [*fruit, vegetables etc*] cueilli à la main ; (*fig*) trié sur le volet
hand print N empreinte *f* de main
hand-printed ADJ imprimé à la main
hand puppet N marionnette *f* à gaine
hand-reared ADJ [*animal*] élevé *or* nourri au biberon
hands-free ADJ [*telephone*] mains libres ◆ **~s-free kit** *or* **set** kit *m* mains libres
hand signal N [1] (*gen*) geste *m*, signe *m* [2] [*of driver*] signe *m* de la main
hands-off ADJ (*fig*) [*policy etc*] de non-intervention
hands-on ADJ [*experience*] pratique ; [*exhibition*] interactif (*où l'on peut toucher les objets*)
hand-spray N (= *shower attachment*) douchette *f* (amovible) ; (= *plant spray*) spray *m*
hand-stitched ADJ cousu (à la) main
hand-to-hand ADJ, ADV ◆ **to fight ~-to-~** combattre corps à corps ◆ **a ~-to-~ fight** un corps à corps ◆ **~-to-~ fighting** du corps à corps
hand-to-mouth ADJ ◆ **to lead a ~-to-mouth existence** vivre au jour le jour
hand towel N essuie-mains *m inv*
hand wash VT laver à la main ◆ **"hand wash only"** "lavage à la main"
hand-woven ADJ tissé à la main

4 - PHRASAL VERBS

► **hand around** VT SEP ⇒ **hand round**

► **hand back** VT SEP rendre (*to* à)

► **hand down** VT SEP [1] (*lit*) ◆ **hand me down the vase** descends-moi le vase ◆ **he ~ed me down the dictionary from the top shelf** il a pris le dictionnaire qui était en haut de l'étagère et me l'a passé [2] (*fig*) transmettre ◆ **the farm's been ~ed down from generation to generation** cette ferme s'est transmise de génération en génération ◆ **these tales are ~ed down from mother to daughter** ces histoires se transmettent de mère en fille [3] (*Jur*) [+ *decision*] rendre

► **hand in** VT SEP remettre (*to* à) ◆ **~ this in at the office** remettez cela à quelqu'un au bureau ◆ **your wallet's been ~ed in at reception** [+ *lost item*] on a rapporté votre portefeuille à la réception

► **hand on** VT SEP [1] (= *pass to sb else*) donner (*to* à) passer (*to* à) [2] ⇒ **hand down 2**

► **hand out** VT SEP distribuer ◆ **to ~ out advice** donner des conseils

► **hand over** VI (*fig*) ◆ **to hand over to sb** (*gen*) passer le relais à qn ; (*at meeting*) passer le micro à qn ; (*Rad, TV*) passer l'antenne à qn VT SEP [+ *book, object*] remettre (*to* à) ; [+ *criminal, prisoner*] livrer (*to* à) ; [+ *authority, powers*] (= *transfer*) transmettre (*to* à) ; (= *surrender*) céder (*to* à) ; [+ *property, business*] céder (*to* à)

► **hand round** VT SEP [+ *bottle, papers*] faire circuler ; [+ *cakes*] (faire) passer (à la ronde) ; [*hostess*] offrir

► **hand up** VT SEP passer (*de bas en haut*)

---

handbag /ˈhændbæg/ N sac *m* à main

handball /ˈhændbɔːl/ N [1] (= *sport*) handball *m* [2] (*Ftbl* = *offence*) faute *f* de main

handbasin /ˈhænd,beɪsn/ N lavabo *m*

handbasket /ˈhændbɑːskɪt/ N → **hell**

handbell /ˈhændbel/ N sonnette *f*

handbill /ˈhændbɪl/ N prospectus *m*

handbook /ˈhænd,bʊk/ N [1] (= *manual*) manuel *m* ; see also **teacher** [2] (= *guidebook*) (*for tourist*) guide *m* ; (*to museum*) catalogue *m*

handbrake /ˈhænd,breɪk/ N (*Brit*) frein *m* à main ◆ **to take the ~ off, to release the ~** enlever le frein à main ◆ **you've left the ~ on** tu as laissé le frein à main COMP **handbrake turn** N virage *m* au frein à main

h. & c. (abbrev of **hot and cold (water)**) → **hot**

handcar /ˈhændkɑːʳ/ N (*Rail*) draisine *f*

handcart /ˈhændkɑːt/ N charrette *f* à bras ; → **hell**

handclap /ˈhændklæp/ N (*Brit*) ◆ **a thunderous ~** un tonnerre d'applaudissements ◆ **to get the slow ~** se faire siffler

handclasp /ˈhændklɑːsp/ N poignée *f* de main

handcraft /ˈhændkrɑːft/ N ⇒ **handicraft**

handcuff /ˈhændkʌf/ N menotte *f* VT mettre *or* passer les menottes à ◆ **to be ~ed** avoir les menottes aux poignets

-handed /ˈhændɪd/ ADJ (*in compounds*) ◆ **one-handed** d'une main, avec une main ; → **empty, left², short**

Handel /ˈhændəl/ N Händel *or* Haendel *m*

handful /ˈhændfʊl/ N [1] (= *fistful*) [*of coins, objects etc*] poignée *f* ◆ **his hair started falling out by the ~** *or* **in ~s** il a commencé à perdre ses cheveux par poignées ◆ **she was swallowing sleeping pills by the ~** elle se bourrait de somnifères [2] (= *small number*) poignée *f* ◆ **there was only a ~ of people at the concert** il n'y avait qu'une poignée de gens au concert ◆ **only a tiny ~ of companies did well in the recession** très peu d'entreprises ont prospéré pendant la récession [3] (= *nuisance*) ◆ **the children can be a ~*** les enfants me donnent parfois du fil à retordre

handgrip /ˈhændgrɪp/ N (*on cycle, machine*) poignée *f*

handgun /ˈhændgʌn/ N pistolet *m*

handhold /ˈhændhəʊld/ N prise *f*

handicap /ˈhændɪkæp/ N [1] (= *disability*) handicap *m* ; (= *disadvantage*) désavantage *m* ◆ **his appearance is a great ~** son aspect physique le handicape beaucoup ◆ **to be under a great ~** avoir un désavantage *or* un handicap énorme ; → **physical** [2] (*Sport*) handicap *m* ◆ **weight ~** [*of racehorse*] surcharge *f* ◆ **time ~** handicap *m* (de temps) VT (*also Sport, fig*) handicaper ◆ **the industry was ~ped by antiquated machinery** la vétusté des machines constituait un handicap pour ce secteur

handicapped /ˈhændɪkæpt/ ADJ handicapé ◆ **a physically ~ child** un enfant handicapé physique NPL **the handicapped** les handicapés *mpl* ◆ **the mentally/physically ~** les handicapés *mpl* mentaux/physiques

handicraft /'hændɪkrɑːft/ N (= work) artisanat *m*, travail *m* artisanal ; (= skill) habileté *f* manuelle NPL **handicrafts** (= products) objets *mpl* artisanaux

handily /'hændɪlɪ/ ADV [1] (= conveniently) [placed] commodément [2] (US = easily) [win] haut la main

handiness /'hændɪnɪs/ N [1] (= usefulness) [of object, method, approach] côté *m* pratique, commodité *f* ; (= ease of control) [of car, boat] maniabilité *f* [2] (= nearness) **because of the ~ of the library** parce que la bibliothèque est (*or* était) si proche [3] (= skill) [of person] adresse *f*, dextérité *f*

handiwork /'hændɪwɜːk/ N œuvre *f* ◆ **the architect stepped back to admire his ~** l'architecte a fait un pas en arrière pour admirer son œuvre ◆ **the fire was the ~ of an arsonist** l'incendie était l'œuvre d'un pyromane

handjob** /'hænddʒɒb/ N ◆ **to give sb a ~** branler qn** ◆ **to give o.s. a ~** se branler**

handkerchief /'hæŋkətʃɪf/ N mouchoir *m* ; (fancy) pochette *f*

handle /'hændl/ N [1] [of basket, bucket] anse *f* ; [of broom, spade, knife] manche *m* ; [of door, drawer, suitcase] poignée *f* ; [of handcart] brancard *m* ; [of saucepan] queue *f* ; [of pump, stretcher, wheelbarrow] bras *m* ◆ **(starting) ~** [of car] manivelle *f*

[2] (= understanding) **models give us a ~ on some aspects of the natural world** les modèles nous aident à comprendre certains aspects de la nature ◆ **to have a ~ on** [+ problem, state of affairs] comprendre ; (= control) [+ situation, spending] maîtriser ◆ **my subject is something not many people have a ~ on** peu de gens ont une idée de mon sujet

[3] ◆ **to have a ~ to one's name** †* avoir un nom à rallonge* ; → **fly**[3]

VT [1] (= cope with) [+ difficult person] s'y prendre avec ; [+ stress] supporter ◆ **he knows how to ~ his son** il sait s'y prendre avec son fils ◆ **this child is very hard to ~** cet enfant est très difficile ◆ **she cannot ~ pressure** elle ne supporte pas la pression ◆ **it was more than I could ~** c'était plus que je ne pouvais supporter ◆ **I don't know if I can ~ the job** je ne sais pas si je serai à la hauteur ◆ **I could have ~d it better than I did** j'aurais pu mieux m'y prendre ◆ **you didn't ~ that very well!** vous ne vous y êtes pas très bien pris !

[2] (= deal with) [+ customers, clients, case] s'occuper de ; [+ business] traiter ◆ **I'll ~ this** je m'en charge, je vais m'en occuper ◆ **do you ~ tax matters?** est-ce que vous vous occupez de fiscalité ? ◆ **three lawyers had already refused to ~ the case** trois avocats avaient déjà refusé de s'occuper de l'affaire ◆ **which judge is handling the case?** quel juge est chargé de l'affaire ? ◆ **we don't ~ that type of business** nous ne traitons pas ce type d'affaires ◆ **we have to be careful when handling these issues** nous devons traiter ces questions avec prudence ◆ **the hospital doesn't ~ emergencies** l'hôpital n'a pas de service d'urgences ◆ **Orly ~s 5 million passengers a year** 5 millions de voyageurs passent par Orly chaque année ◆ **we ~ 200 passengers a day** 200 voyageurs par jour passent par nos services ◆ **can the port ~ big ships?** le port peut-il accueillir les gros bateaux ? ◆ **she ~s large sums of money in her job** elle manie de grosses sommes d'argent dans son travail

[3] (= manage) gérer ◆ **they doubt the government's ability to ~ the economy** ils doutent de la capacité du gouvernement à gérer l'économie ◆ **he ~d the situation very well** il a très bien géré la situation

[4] (= touch) [+ fruit, food] toucher à ◆ **please do not ~ the goods** prière de ne pas toucher aux marchandises ◆ **to ~ the ball** (Ftbl) toucher le ballon de la main, faire une faute de main

[5] (= move by hand) manipuler, manier ◆ **they had to ~ radioactive materials** ils ont dû manipuler des substances radioactives ◆ **his hands were sore from handling bales of straw** il avait mal aux mains d'avoir manié des bottes de paille ◆ **"handle with care"** (label) "fragile" ◆ **the crowd ~d him roughly** (lit) la foule l'a malmené ; (fig) la foule l'a hué

[6] (= control) [+ ship] manœuvrer, gouverner ; [+ car] conduire, manœuvrer ; [+ weapon] manier, se servir de ◆ **the boat was very easy to ~** le bateau était très facile à manœuvrer *or* gouverner ◆ **he knows how to ~ a gun** il sait se servir d'un revolver *or* manier un revolver ◆ **these dogs can be difficult to ~** ces chiens sont parfois difficiles à contrôler

[7] (= stock, deal in) avoir, faire ◆ **we don't ~ that type of product** nous ne faisons pas ce genre de produit ◆ **to ~ stolen goods** receler des objets volés ◆ **she was convicted of handling explosives** elle a été condamnée pour détention d'explosifs

VI ◆ **to ~ well/badly** [ship] être facile/difficile à manœuvrer ; [car, gun] être facile/difficile à manier ; [horse] répondre bien/mal aux aides

handlebar /'hændlbɑːʳ/ N (also **handlebars**) guidon *m* COMP **handlebar moustache** N (hum) moustache *f* en guidon de vélo*

-handled /'hændld/ ADJ (in compounds) ◆ **a wooden-handled spade** une pelle au manche de bois *or* avec un manche de bois

handler /'hændləʳ/ N [1] (also **dog handler**) maître-chien *m* [2] [of stock] manutentionnaire *mf*

handling /'hændlɪŋ/ N [of ship] manœuvre *f* ; [of car] maniement *m* ; [of goods in warehouse] manutention *f* ; (= fingering) maniement *m*, manipulation *f* ; [of stolen goods] recel *m* ◆ **~ of drugs** trafic *m* de drogue ◆ **his ~ of the matter** la façon dont il a géré l'affaire ◆ **the judge's ~ of witnesses was criticized** on a critiqué la manière dont le juge a traité les témoins ◆ **a new system to speed up the ~ of complaints** un nouveau système pour accélérer le traitement des réclamations ◆ **the government's ~ of the economy** la manière dont le gouvernement gère l'économie ◆ **toxic waste requires very careful ~** les déchets toxiques doivent être manipulés avec beaucoup de précaution ◆ **to get some rough ~** [person, object] se faire malmener

COMP **handling charges** NPL frais *mpl* de manutention

handmade /,hænd'meɪd/ ADJ fait (à la) main

handmaid(en) /'hændmeɪd(ə)n/ N († *or* liter: lit, fig) servante *f*

handover /'hændəʊvəʳ/ N [of company, colony] cession *f* ◆ **the ~ of power** la passation des pouvoirs ◆ **during the prisoner's ~ to the police ...** lorsque le prisonnier a été remis à la police ...

handrail /'hændreɪl/ N [of stairs] rampe *f*, main *f* courante ; [of bridge, quay] garde-fou *m*

handsaw /'hændsɔː/ N scie *f* à main, scie *f* égoïne

handset /'hændset/ N (Telec) combiné *m*

handshake /'hændʃeɪk/ N [1] poignée *f* de main ; → **golden** [2] (Comput) prise *f* de contact

handsome /'hænsəm/ ADJ [1] (= attractive) [man, face, features, building, object] beau (belle *f*) ◆ **a ~ woman** une belle femme ◆ **~ is as ~ does** (Prov) l'air ne fait pas la chanson, l'habit ne fait pas le moine [2] (= large) [sum] coquet ◆ **a ~ price/salary** un bon prix/salaire ◆ **to win a ~ victory** remporter une belle victoire ◆ **to win by a ~ margin** gagner haut la main [3] (= generous) [conduct, compliment, gift] généreux ◆ **to make a ~ apology for sth** se confondre en excuses pour qch

handsomely /'hænsəmlɪ/ ADV [1] (= attractively) [illustrated] joliment ; [dressed] avec élégance [2] (= generously) [pay, reward, behave] généreusement ; [contribute] généreusement, avec générosité ◆ **to apologize ~** se confondre en excuses [3] (= convincingly) [win] haut la main ◆ **this strategy paid off ~** cette stratégie s'est révélée payante

handspring /'hændsprɪŋ/ N saut *m* de mains

handstand /'hændstænd/ N appui *m* renversé, équilibre *m* sur les mains ◆ **to do a ~** faire un appui renversé *or* un équilibre sur les mains

handwork /'hændwɜːk/ N ⇒ **handiwork**

handwringing /'hændrɪŋɪŋ/ N paroles *fpl* affligées, manifestation *f* de compassion

handwrite /'hændraɪt/ VT écrire à la main

handwriting /'hændraɪtɪŋ/ N écriture *f* ◆ **he has seen the ~ on the wall** (US) il mesure la gravité de la situation ◆ **the ~ is on the wall** la catastrophe est imminente

handwritten /'hændrɪtən/ ADJ manuscrit, écrit à la main

handy /'hændɪ/ ADJ [1] (= useful) [tool, hint, method] pratique ◆ **a ~ little car** une petite voiture bien pratique ◆ **I brought a torch just in case – that's ~!** j'ai apporté une lampe de poche à tout hasard – bonne idée ! ◆ **he's coming to see us tomorrow – that's ~!** il vient nous voir demain – ça tombe bien ! ◆ **to come in ~** être bien utile

[2] * (= conveniently close) proche ◆ **in a ~ place** à portée de (la) main ◆ **the shops are very ~** les magasins sont tout près ◆ **to be ~ for the shops** être à proximité des magasins ◆ **to keep** *or* **have sth ~** avoir qch à portée de (la) main

[3] (= skilful) adroit (de ses mains) ◆ **he's ~ around the home** il est bricoleur ◆ **he's ~ in the kitchen** il se débrouille bien en cuisine ◆ **to be ~ with sth** savoir bien se servir de qch

[4] [ship] maniable

COMP **handy-pack** N emballage *m* à poignée

handyman /'hændɪmæn/ N (pl **-men**) (do-it-yourself) bricoleur *m* ; (= servant) factotum *m*, homme *m* à tout faire

hang /hæŋ/ (pret, ptp **hung**) VT [1] (= suspend) [+ lamp] suspendre, accrocher (on à) ; [+ curtains, hat, decorations] accrocher ; [+ painting] (gen) accrocher ; (in gallery) (= exhibit) exposer ; [+ door] monter ; [+ wallpaper] poser, tendre ; [+ dangling object] laisser pendre ◆ **to ~ clothes on the line** étendre du linge ◆ **he hung the rope over the side of the boat** il a laissé pendre le cordage par-dessus bord ◆ **to ~ one's head** baisser la tête

[2] (Culin) [+ game] faire faisander

[3] (= decorate) décorer (with de) ◆ **trees hung with lights** des arbres décorés de lumières ◆ **walls hung with modern paintings** des murs décorés de tableaux modernes ◆ **a study hung with hessian** un bureau tapissé *or* tendu de jute ◆ **balconies hung with flags** des balcons pavoisés

[4] (pret, ptp **hanged**) [+ criminal] pendre ◆ **he was ~ed for murder** il fut pendu pour meurtre ◆ **he was ~ed, drawn and quartered** il a été pendu, éviscéré et écartelé ◆ **he ~ed himself** il s'est pendu ◆ **(may) as well be ~ed for a sheep as a lamb** quitte à être punis, autant l'être pour un crime qui en vaille la peine

[5] († *: in phrases) ◆ **~ him !** qu'il aille se faire voir !* ◆ **(I'll be) ~ed if I know!** je veux bien être pendu si je le sais !* ◆ **I'm ~ed if I'm waiting until he decides to come back** je serais fou d'attendre *or* je ne vois pas pourquoi j'attendrais qu'il se décide à revenir ◆ **~ it (all)!** zut !*

VI 1 *[rope, dangling object]* pendre, être accroché *or* suspendu (*on, from* à) ; *[drapery]* tomber ◆ **a suit that ~s well** un costume qui tombe bien ◆ **her hair hung down her back** *(not put up)* elle avait les cheveux dénoués ; *(long)* ses cheveux lui tombaient dans le dos ◆ **her hair hung loose about her shoulders** ses cheveux flottaient sur ses épaules ◆ **a picture ~ing on the wall** un tableau accroché au mur ◆ **to ~ out of the window** *[person]* se pencher par la fenêtre ; *[thing]* pendre à la fenêtre ◆ **I was left ~ing by my fingertips** *(lit)* je me suis retrouvé agrippé au rocher (*or* au bord de la fenêtre *etc*) ; *(fig)* je n'avais plus qu'un mince espoir de m'en tirer ◆ **just ~ loose!**‡ *(esp US)* essaie d'être relax !* ◆ **to ~ tough*** *(esp US)* tenir bon, s'accrocher* ; → **balance**

2 *(= hover)* planer, peser ◆ **a damp fog hung over the valley** un brouillard chargé d'humidité planait sur la vallée ◆ **a haze of expensive perfume ~s around her** les effluves d'un parfum de luxe flottent autour d'elle ◆ **the hawk hung motionless in the sky** le faucon était comme suspendu dans le ciel ◆ **a constant threat of unemployment ~s over us** *or* **our heads** la menace constante du chômage pèse sur nous ◆ **the question was left ~ing in the air** la question est restée en suspens ◆ **time hung heavy (on his hands)** il trouvait le temps long

3 *[criminal]* être pendu ◆ **he ought to ~** il devrait être pendu ◆ **he'll ~ for it** cela lui vaudra la corde *or* d'être pendu ◆ **to be sentenced to ~** être condamné à la corde (*for sth* pour qch) ◆ **he was sentenced to ~ for killing a woman** il a été condamné à être pendu pour avoir tué une femme

4 (*US* ‡) ⇒ **hang about**

N * 1 ◆ **to get the ~ of** *(= learn to use) [+ machine, tool, device]* comprendre *or* piger* comment utiliser ; *(= grasp meaning of) [+ letter, book]* (arriver à) comprendre ◆ **to get the ~ of doing sth** attraper le coup pour faire qch ◆ **you'll soon get the ~ of it** *(of device, process etc)* tu auras vite fait de t'y mettre ◆ **she's getting the ~ of her new job** elle commence à s'habituer à son nouveau travail ◆ **I am getting the ~ of it!** ça y est, je saisis !

2 ◆ **I don't give a ~** † je m'en fiche*

COMP **hang-glider** **N** *(= aircraft)* deltaplane ® *m*, aile *f* delta ; *(= person)* libériste *mf*

hang-gliding **N** deltaplane ® *m*, vol *m* libre ◆ **to go ~-gliding** faire du deltaplane ®, pratiquer le vol libre

hang-out* **N** *(= place)* lieu *m* de prédilection

hang-up* **N** *(= complex)* complexe *m* (*about* à cause de) ◆ **to have a ~-up about one's body** être mal dans son corps, être complexé ◆ **to have a ~-up about spiders** avoir la phobie des araignées, avoir une peur maladive des araignées ◆ **to have sexual ~-ups** avoir des blocages (sexuels)

► **hang about, hang around** **VI** *(= loiter, pass time)* traîner ; *(= wait)* attendre ◆ **he's always ~ing about here** il est toujours à traîner par ici ◆ **he got sick of ~ing around waiting for me** il en a eu marre* de m'attendre ◆ **they always ~ around together** ils sont toujours ensemble ◆ **Ann used to ~ around with the boys** Ann traînait avec les garçons ◆ **to keep sb ~ing about** faire attendre *or* poireauter* qn ◆ **this is where they usually ~ about** c'est là qu'ils se trouvent habituellement ◆ **~ about!*** attends ! ◆ **~ about*, I know that guy!** attends, je le connais, ce type* !

VT FUS ◆ **the crowd who hung around the cafe** les habitués du café

► **hang back** **VI** *(in walking etc)* rester en arrière, hésiter à aller de l'avant ◆ **she hung back from suggesting this** elle hésitait à le proposer ◆ **they hung back on closing the deal** ils tardaient à conclure l'affaire ◆ **he should not ~ back (on this decision) any longer** il est temps qu'il prenne une décision *or* qu'il se décide

► **hang down** **VI** pendre

► **hang in*** **VI** (also **hang in there**) s'accrocher ◆ **~ in there, Bill, you're going to make it** accroche-toi, Bill, tu vas t'en sortir

► **hang on** **VI** 1 *(* = wait)* attendre ◆ **~ on!** attendez ! ; *(on phone)* ne quittez pas ! ◆ **~ on a sec, I'll come with you** attends une seconde, je viens avec toi ◆ **I had to ~ on for ages** *(on phone)* j'ai dû attendre des siècles

2 *(= hold out)* tenir bon ◆ **he managed to ~ on till help came** il réussit à tenir bon jusqu'à l'arrivée des secours ◆ **Manchester United hung on to take the Cup** Manchester United a tenu bon et a remporté le championnat ◆ **to ~ on by one's fingernails** *or* **fingertips** *(lit)* être agrippé *or* cramponné au rocher (*or* au bord de la fenêtre *etc*) ; *(fig)* n'avoir plus qu'un mince espoir de s'en tirer ◆ **~ on in there*** ⇒ **hang in there** ; → **hang in**

3 ◆ **to hang on to sth** * *(= cling on to)* s'accrocher à qch, rester cramponné à qch ; *(= keep, look after)* garder qch ◆ **~ on to the branch** cramponne-toi à la branche, ne lâche pas la branche ◆ **to ~ on to one's lead** conserver son avance ◆ **to ~ on to power** s'accrocher au pouvoir

VT FUS 1 *(lit, fig)* se cramponner à, s'accrocher à ◆ **to ~ on sb's arm** se cramponner *or* s'accrocher au bras de qn ◆ **to ~ on sb's words** *or* **every word** boire les paroles de qn, être suspendu aux lèvres de qn

2 *(= depend on)* dépendre de ◆ **everything ~s on his decision** tout dépend de sa décision ◆ **everything ~s on whether he saw her or not** le tout est de savoir s'il l'a vue ou non

VT SEP *(esp US)* ◆ **to ~ one on** * se cuiter‡, se biturer‡

► **hang out** **VI** 1 *[tongue]* pendre ; *[shirt tails etc]* pendre (dehors), pendouiller* ◆ **let it all ~ out!**‡ défoulez-vous !

2 * *(= live)* percher*, crécher‡ ; *(= loiter aimlessly)* traîner ◆ **to ~ out with sb** frayer avec qn

3 *(= resist)* **they are ~ing out for a 5% rise*** ils insistent pour obtenir une augmentation de 5%

VT SEP *[+ streamer]* suspendre (dehors) ; *[+ washing]* étendre (dehors) ; *[+ flag]* arborer ◆ **to ~ sb out to dry*** *(= abandon them)* abandonner qn à son sort

N ◆ **hang-out** * → **hang**

► **hang together** **VI** 1 *(= unite) [people]* se serrer les coudes

2 *(= be consistent) [argument]* se tenir ; *[story]* tenir debout ; *[statements]* s'accorder, concorder ◆ **her ideas don't always ~ together very well as a plot** ses intrigues sont souvent décousues

► **hang up** **VI** *(Telec)* raccrocher ◆ **to ~ up on sb** raccrocher au nez de qn ; see also **hung**

VT SEP *[+ hat, picture]* accrocher, pendre (*on* à, sur) ◆ **to ~ up the receiver** *(Telec)* raccrocher ◆ **to ~ up one's hat** *(= retire)* raccrocher* ◆ **the goalkeeper announced he was ~ing up his boots for good** le gardien de but a annoncé qu'il raccrochait pour de bon ; → **hung**

N ◆ **hang-up** * → **hang**

► **hang with*** **VT FUS** *(esp US)* frayer avec*

hangar /ˈhæŋəʳ/ **N** hangar *m*

hangdog /ˈhæŋdɒg/ **N** ◆ **to have a ~ look** *or* **expression** avoir un air de chien battu

hanger /ˈhæŋəʳ/ **N** (also **coat hanger**) cintre *m* ; *(= hook)* patère *f* **COMP** **hanger-on** **N** (pl **hangers-on**) parasite *m* ◆ **he's just one of the ~s-on** *(= person)* c'est juste l'un de ces parasites ◆ **there was a crowd of ~s-on** il y avait toute une foule de parasites

hanging /ˈhæŋɪŋ/ **N** 1 *(= execution)* pendaison *f* ◆ **they want to bring back ~** ils veulent réintroduire la pendaison 2 *(NonC)* accrochage *m*, suspension *f* ; *[of bells, wallpaper]* pose *f* ; *[of door]* montage *m* ; *[of picture]* accrochage *m* 3 *(= curtains etc)* **~s** tentures *fpl*, draperies *fpl* ◆ **bed ~s** rideaux *mpl* de lit **ADJ** *[bridge, staircase]* suspendu ; *[door]* battant ; *[lamp, light]* pendant ; *[sleeve]* tombant

COMP **hanging basket** **N** panier *m* suspendu

hanging committee **N** *(Art)* jury *m* d'exposition

the Hanging Gardens of Babylon **NPL** les jardins *mpl* suspendus de Babylone

hanging judge **N** *(Hist) juge qui envoyait régulièrement à la potence* ; *(fig)* juge *m* impitoyable

hanging offence **N** *(lit)* crime *m* punissable de pendaison ◆ **it's not a ~ offence** *(fig)* ce n'est pas un crime

hanging wardrobe **N** penderie *f*

hangman /ˈhæŋmən/ **N** (pl **-men**) 1 *(= executioner)* bourreau *m* 2 *(= game)* pendu *m* ◆ **to play ~** jouer au pendu

hangnail /ˈhæŋneɪl/ **N** petite peau *f*, envie *f*

hangover /ˈhæŋəʊvəʳ/ **N** 1 *(after drinking)* ◆ **to have a ~** avoir la gueule de bois* 2 *(= relic)* ◆ **this problem is a ~ from the previous administration** c'est un problème que nous avons hérité de l'administration précédente

Hang Seng Index /ˌhæŋseŋˈɪndeks/ **N** indice *m* Hang Seng

hank /hæŋk/ **N** *[of wool]* écheveau *m*

hanker /ˈhæŋkəʳ/ **VI** ◆ **to ~ for** *or* **after** rêver de

hankering /ˈhæŋkərɪŋ/ **N** ◆ **to have a ~ for sth/to do sth** rêver de qch/de faire qch

hankie*, **hanky*** /ˈhæŋkɪ/ **N** abbrev of **handkerchief**

hanky-panky* /ˈhæŋkɪˈpæŋkɪ/ **N** *(suspicious)* entourloupes* *fpl* ; *(= fooling around)* bêtises *fpl* ; *(sexual)* batifolage *m* ◆ **there's some ~ going on** *(suspicious)* il se passe quelque chose de louche, il y a là quelque chose de pas très catholique* ◆ **there were reports of political ~** le bruit courait qu'il se passait des choses louches en politique

Hannibal /ˈhænɪbəl/ **N** Hannibal *m*

Hanoi /hæˈnɔɪ/ **N** Hanoi

Hanover /ˈhænəʊvəʳ/ **N** Hanovre ◆ **the house of ~** *(Brit Hist)* la maison *or* la dynastie de Hanovre

Hanoverian /ˌhænəʊˈvɪərɪən/ **ADJ** hanovrien

Hansard /ˈhænsɑːd/ **N** Hansard *m* *(procès verbal des débats du parlement britannique)*

Hanseatic /ˌhænzɪˈætɪk/ **ADJ** ◆ **the ~ League** la Hanse, la Ligue hanséatique

hansom /ˈhænsəm/ **N** (also **hansom cab**) cab *m*

Hants /hænts/ abbrev of **Hampshire**

Hanukkah /ˈhɑːnəkə/ **N** *(Rel)* Hanoukka *f*

ha'pence † /ˈheɪpəns/ **NPL** of **ha'penny**

ha'penny † /ˈheɪpnɪ/ **N** ⇒ **halfpenny**

haphazard /ˌhæpˈhæzəd/ **ADJ** désordonné ◆ **in a somewhat ~ fashion** de manière un peu désordonnée ◆ **the whole thing was very ~** tout était fait au petit bonheur ◆ **they have a ~ approach to film-making** leur façon de réaliser des films laisse une grande place au hasard

haphazardly /ˌhæpˈhæzədlɪ/ **ADV** *[arrange, select]* au hasard

hapless /ˈhæplɪs/ **ADJ** infortuné *before n*, malheureux *before n*

happen /ˈhæpən/ **VI** 1 arriver, se passer ◆ **something ~ed** il est arrivé *or* il s'est passé quelque chose ◆ **what's ~ed?** qu'est-ce qui s'est passé ?, qu'est-il arrivé ? ◆ **just as if nothing had ~ed** comme si de rien n'était

◆ **whatever ~s** quoi qu'il arrive *subj or* advienne ◆ **don't let it ~ again!** et que cela ne se reproduise pas ! ◆ **these things ~** ce sont des choses qui arrivent ◆ **what has ~ed to him?** *(= befallen)* qu'est-ce qui lui est arrivé ? ; *(= become of)* qu'est-ce qu'il est devenu ? ◆ **if anything ~ed to me my wife would have enough money** s'il m'arrivait quelque chose ma femme aurait assez d'argent ◆ **something has ~ed to him** il lui est arrivé quelque chose ◆ **a funny thing ~ed to me this morning** il m'est arrivé quelque chose de bizarre ce matin ◆ **let's pretend it never ~ed** faisons comme si rien ne s'était passé ◆ **she switched on the ignition. Nothing ~ed** elle a mis le contact. Il ne s'est rien passé ◆ **it's al ~ing!** * il s'en passe des choses !

2 *(= come about, chance)* **how does it ~ that ...?** comment se fait-il que ... + *subj* ? ◆ **it might ~ that ...** il se pourrait que ... + *subj* ◆ **it so ~ed that ...** il s'est trouvé que ... + *indic* ◆ **it so ~s that I'm going there today, as it ~s I'm going there today** il se trouve que j'y vais aujourd'hui

◆ **to happen to do sth** ◆ **he ~ed to tell me that ...** il me disait justement que ... ◆ **do you ~ to have a pen?** aurais-tu par hasard un stylo ? ◆ **how did you ~ to go?** comment se fait-il que tu y sois allé ? ◆ **we ~ed to discover we had a friend in common** nous avons découvert par hasard que nous avions un ami commun ◆ **I looked in the nearest paper, which ~ed to be the Daily Mail** j'ai regardé dans le premier journal qui m'est tombé sous la main. Il s'est trouvé que c'était le Daily Mail ◆ **I ~ to know he is not rich** je sais qu'en fait, il n'est pas riche ◆ **if he does ~ to see her** s'il lui arrive de la voir

► **happen (up)on** † VT FUS [+ *object*] trouver par hasard ; [+ *person*] rencontrer par hasard

happening /ˈhæpnɪŋ/ N événement *m* ; *(Theat)* happening *m* ADJ * branché *

happenstance * /ˈhæpənstæns/ N ◆ **by ~** par hasard

happily /ˈhæpɪlɪ/ ADV 1 *[say, talk, play] (= contentedly)* d'un air heureux ; *(= merrily)* gaiement ◆ **to smile ~** avoir un sourire épanoui *or* de bonheur ◆ **it all ended ~** tout s'est bien terminé ◆ **I'm a ~ married man** je suis heureux en ménage ◆ **they lived ~ ever after** ils vécurent heureux 2 *(= without difficulty) [live together, work together etc]* sans problème 3 *(= willingly) [offer, lend]* volontiers 4 *(= fortunately)* heureusement ◆ **~, no one was hurt** heureusement, personne n'a été blessé ◆ **~ for him, he can afford it** heureusement pour lui, il peut se le permettre 5 *(= felicitously) [express, word]* avec bonheur ◆ **a ~ chosen word** un mot choisi avec bonheur

happiness /ˈhæpɪnɪs/ LANGUAGE IN USE 24.3 N bonheur *m*

happy /ˈhæpɪ/ LANGUAGE IN USE 3.2, 11.2, 23.2, 23.3, 23.6, 24, 25

ADJ 1 *(= joyful, glad) [person, smile, time]* heureux ◆ **a ~ feeling** un sentiment de bonheur ◆ **to have a ~ ending** bien se terminer ◆ **to have ~ memories of sb/sth** garder un bon souvenir *or* de bons souvenirs de qn/qch ◆ **to be ~ about sth** être heureux de qch ◆ **as ~ as Larry** *or* **a sandboy** *or* **a clam** *or* **a lark, ~ as the day is long** *(US)* heureux comme un poisson dans l'eau, heureux comme un roi ◆ **we're just one big ~ family** *(firm, school etc)* nous formons une grande famille, nous sommes comme une grande famille ◆ **to be ~ for sb** se réjouir pour qn ◆ **can't you just be ~ for me?** tu ne peux pas te réjouir pour moi ? ◆ **I'm ~ that I came** je suis content d'être venu ◆ **I'm ~ that you came** je suis content que vous soyez venu ◆ **I'm ~ to say that ...** j'ai le plaisir de vous dire que ... ◆ **I'm just ~ to have a job** je m'estime heureux d'avoir un emploi

2 *(= contented, at ease) [person]* content, heureux ; *[childhood, life, marriage, retirement, family]* heureux ◆ **I'm ~ here reading** je suis très bien ici à lire ◆ **we like to keep the customers/sponsors ~** nous voulons que nos clients/sponsors soient satisfaits ◆ **you're not just saying that to keep me ~?** tu ne dis pas ça juste pour me faire plaisir ? ◆ **to be ~ with** *or* **about sth** être satisfait de qch ◆ **I'm not ~ with this new car** je ne suis pas satisfait de cette nouvelle voiture ◆ **I'm not ~ about leaving him alone** ça ne me plaît pas trop de le *or* je n'aime pas trop le laisser seul ◆ **are you ~ now?** *(said in reproach)* t'es content maintenant ? *

3 *(= willing, glad)* ◆ **to be ~ to do sth** bien vouloir faire qch ◆ **she was quite ~ to stay there alone** cela ne l'ennuyait *or* la dérangeait pas (du tout) de rester là toute seule ◆ **I'm always ~ to oblige** à votre service ◆ **I would be ~ to have your comments** n'hésitez pas à me faire part de vos commentaires ◆ **I'd be more than** *or* **only too ~ to do that** je le ferais volontiers ; → **slap, trigger**

4 *(in greetings)* ◆ **~ birthday!** bon anniversaire ! ◆ **"happy birthday to you!"** *(in song)* "joyeux anniversaire !" ◆ **"happy 40th birthday"** *(on card)* "40 ans : joyeux anniversaire !" ◆ **~ Christmas!** joyeux Noël ! ◆ **~ Easter!** joyeuses Pâques ! ◆ **~ New Year!** bonne année ! ◆ **~ holidays!** *(US)* joyeuses fêtes ! ◆ **~ days!** * *(as toast)* tchin-tchin ! * ; see also **return**

5 *(*, euph = tipsy)* éméché *, gris *

6 *(= fortunate) [chance, coincidence]* heureux ◆ **the ~ few** les rares privilégiés *mpl*

7 *(= felicitous) [phrase, words, outcome]* heureux ◆ **it's not a ~ thought** ce n'est pas une perspective réjouissante

COMP **happy-clappy** ADJ *(pej) [service] qui se déroule dans une allégresse collective*

the happy couple N les jeunes mariés *mpl*

the happy event N *(= birth)* l'heureux événement *m*

happy families N *(= card game)* jeu *m* des sept familles

happy-go-lucky ADJ *[person, attitude]* insouciant ◆ **the arrangements were very ~-go-lucky** c'était organisé au petit bonheur (la chance) ◆ **to do sth in a ~-go-lucky way** faire qch au petit bonheur (la chance) *or* à la va comme je te pousse *

happy hour N *(US)* heure *f* du cocktail *or* de l'apéritif ; *(Brit) heure, généralement en début de soirée, pendant laquelle les consommations sont à prix réduit*

happy hunting ground N *[of Native Americans]* paradis *m* des Indiens d'Amérique ◆ **a ~ hunting ground for collectors** le paradis des collectionneurs

happy medium N juste milieu *m* ◆ **to strike a ~ medium** trouver le juste milieu

Hapsburg /ˈhæpsbɜːg/ N Habsbourg ◆ **the ~s** les Habsbourg *mpl*

hara-kiri /ˈhærəˈkɪrɪ/ N hara-kiri *m* ◆ **to commit ~** faire hara-kiri

harangue /həˈræŋ/ VT [+ *crowd*] haranguer (*about* à propos de) ; [+ *individual*] sermonner (*about* à propos de) ◆ **he tried to ~ the crowd into action** il a essayé de haranguer la foule pour qu'elle agisse N *(to crowd)* harangue *f* ; *(to individual)* sermon *m*

harass /ˈhærəs/ VT 1 *(= harry) [+ troops, the enemy, crowd]* harceler ◆ **don't ~ me!** arrête de me harceler ! ◆ **they complained of being routinely ~ed by the police** ils se sont plaints de harcèlements répétés de la part de la police ◆ **he sexually ~ed her** il la harcelait sexuellement 2 *(= worry)* tracasser ; *(stronger)* harceler, tourmenter ◆ **~ed by doubts** harcelé de doutes

> ⚠ **harasser** in French means 'to exhaust'.

harassed /ˈhærəst/ ADJ *(= hassled)* harcelé ; *(= overburdened)* stressé ◆ **I'm feeling a bit ~** je suis un peu stressé

harassment /ˈhærəsmənt/ N harcèlement *m* ◆ **police ~** harcèlement *m* de la part de la police ; → **sexual**

harbinger /ˈhɑːbɪndʒəʳ/ N *(liter)* signe *m* avant-coureur *(liter)*, présage *m* ◆ **a ~ of doom** un funeste présage

harbour, harbor (US) /ˈhɑːbəʳ/ N *(for boats)* port *m* ; *(fig)* havre *m (liter)*, refuge *m* ◆ **Dover Harbour** *(in names)* port *m* de Douvres ◆ **the ship was lying in the ~** le navire était au port *or* avait mouillé dans le port ; → **outer**

VT 1 *(= give shelter to)* héberger, abriter ◆ **to ~ a criminal** receler un criminel *(Jur)* ◆ **they accused the government of ~ing terrorists** ils ont accusé le gouvernement d'avoir fermé les yeux sur la présence de terroristes

2 *[+ suspicions]* entretenir, nourrir ; *[+ fear, hope]* entretenir ◆ **to ~ a grudge against sb** garder rancune à qn ◆ **she ~s no regrets** elle ne nourrit aucun regret

3 *[+ dirt, dust]* retenir, garder ◆ **the river still ~s crocodiles** des crocodiles habitent encore le fleuve ◆ **the cat's fur ~s various parasites** divers parasites trouvent refuge dans la fourrure du chat

COMP **harbour dues, harbour fees** NPL *(Jur, Comm)* droits *mpl* de port

harbour master N capitaine *m* de port

harbour station N gare *f* maritime

hard /hɑːd/ ADJ 1 *(= firm) [object, substance, ground, bed, fruit]* dur ; *[mud, snow]* durci ; *[muscle]* ferme ; ◆ **to become** *or* **get** *or* **go** *or* **grow ~** durcir ◆ **the ground was baked/frozen ~** le sol était durci par la chaleur/par le gel ◆ **the lake was frozen ~** le lac était complètement gelé ◆ **to set ~** *[plaster, concrete, clay etc]* bien prendre

2 *(= difficult) [problem, question, exam, choice, decision, work]* difficile ; *[task]* pénible, dur ; *[battle, fight]* rude ; *[match]* âprement disputé ◆ **it is ~ to do that** il est difficile de faire cela ◆ **to find it ~ to do sth** avoir du mal à faire qch, trouver difficile de faire qch ◆ **I find it ~ to believe that ...** j'ai du mal à croire que ... ◆ **their prices are ~ to beat** leurs prix sont imbattables ◆ **to be ~ to open/close/translate** *etc* être difficile *or* dur à ouvrir/fermer/traduire *etc* ◆ **good managers are ~ to find these days** il est difficile de trouver de bons cadres de nos jours ◆ **that's a ~ question to answer** c'est une question à laquelle il est difficile de répondre ◆ **it was a ~ decision to make** c'était une décision difficile à prendre ◆ **I've had a ~ day** ma journée a été dure ◆ **a ~ day's work** une rude journée de travail ◆ **it's ~ work!** c'est dur ! ◆ **a ~ day's sunbathing on the beach** *(hum)* une rude journée *or* une journée fatigante passée à bronzer sur la plage *(hum)* ◆ **she's had a very ~ life** elle a eu une vie très dure ◆ **it's a ~ life** *(also iro)* la vie est dure ◆ **it's a ~ life being a man** *(also iro)* c'est dur d'être un homme ◆ **she's having a ~ time at the moment** elle traverse une période difficile ◆ **she had a ~ time of it after her husband's death** elle a traversé une période difficile après la mort de son mari ◆ **to have a ~ time doing sth** avoir du mal *or* des difficultés à faire qch ◆ **you'll have a ~ time trying to get him to help you** vous allez avoir du mal à le persuader de vous aider ◆ **to give sb a ~ time** * en faire voir de toutes les couleurs à qn ◆ **the kids are giving me a ~ time at the moment** * les enfants sont vraiment pénibles en ce moment ◆ **times are ~** les temps sont durs ◆ **those were ~ times** c'était une époque difficile ◆ **he**

always has to do it *or* **things the ~ way** il faut toujours qu'il cherche *subj* la difficulté ◆ **to learn the ~ way** l'apprendre à ses dépens ◆ **to play ~ to get*** se faire désirer ; see also **drive**

3 *(= committed)* ◆ **he's a ~ worker** il est travailleur ◆ **he's a ~ drinker** il boit beaucoup, il boit sec

4 *(= forceful) [blow, kick, punch]* violent ◆ **give it a ~ push** pousse fort ◆ **she gave the rope a ~ tug** elle a tiré la corde d'un coup sec ◆ **he had a ~ fall** il a fait une mauvaise chute ◆ **a ~ blow** *(fig)* un coup dur *(for, to sb/sth* pour qn/qch) → **knock**

5 *(= unsympathetic) [person, face, look, smile, voice]* dur ◆ **to have a ~ heart** avoir le cœur dur ◆ **no ~ feelings!** sans rancune ! ◆ **to show there are no ~ feelings** pour montrer qu'il n'y a pas de rancune entre nous *(or eux etc)* ◆ **to grow ~** s'endurcir

6 *(= harsh, severe) [winter, climate]* rude, rigoureux ; *[frost]* fort ; *[light, colour]* cru ; *[treatment]* dur ; *[rule, decision]* sévère ◆ **to take a ~ line with sb/on sth** se montrer dur *or* intransigeant avec qn/lorsqu'il s'agit de qch ; see also **comp** ◆ **to be ~ on sb** *[person]* être dur avec qn ◆ **aren't you being a bit ~ on yourself?** n'es-tu pas un peu trop dur avec toi-même ? ◆ **to be ~ on sb/sth** *(= damaging) [situation, circumstances]* être difficile *or* éprouvant pour qn/qch ◆ **the light was ~ on the eyes** la lumière fatiguait les yeux ◆ **children are ~ on their shoes** les enfants usent leurs chaussures en un rien de temps ◆ **~ cheese*** *or* **lines*!** *(Brit)* tant pis pour toi ! ◆ **~ luck!** pas de chance *or* de veine* ! ◆ **it was ~ luck that he didn't win** il n'a vraiment pas eu de chance de ne pas gagner ◆ **it's ~ luck on him** il n'a vraiment pas de chance ◆ **he told me another ~ luck story** il m'a encore raconté ses malheurs ◆ **his ~ luck story failed to move me** il n'a pas réussi à m'émouvoir avec ses malheurs

7 *(= tough)* **she thinks she's really ~*** *[person]* elle se considère comme une dure

8 *(= indisputable) [information]* sûr ; *[evidence]* tangible ◆ **there are ~ facts to support our arguments** il y a des faits concrets pour soutenir nos arguments ◆ **the ~ facts of the matter are that ...** ce qu'il y a de sûr et certain, c'est que ... ◆ **what we want is ~ news** ce qu'il nous faut, c'est une information sérieuse

9 *(= strong) [drink]* fortement alcoolisé, fort ; *[drug]* dur ◆ **~ porn*** porno *m* hard* ◆ **the ~ stuff*** *(= whisky)* le whisky ; *(= drugs)* les drogues dures ◆ **a drop of the ~ stuff*** un petit coup* de whisky

10 *[water]* dur

11 *(Med) [tissue]* sclérosé, scléreux

12 *(esp Brit)* ◆ **the ~ left/right** *(Pol)* la gauche/droite dure

13 *(Phon, Ling) [sound]* dur ; *[consonant] (= not palatalized)* dur ; *(= velar)* fort, dur †

14 *(Stock Exchange) [market, stock, rate]* soutenu, ferme

ADV 1 *(= energetically, assiduously) [push, pull, rain, snow]* fort ; *[work]* dur ; *[study]* assidûment ; *[laugh]* aux éclats ; *[cry]* à chaudes larmes ; *[listen]* de toutes ses oreilles ; *[think]* bien ◆ **tug the rope ~** tire sur la corde d'un coup sec ◆ **she slammed the door ~** elle a claqué violemment la porte ◆ **to fall down ~** tomber lourdement ◆ **to run ~** courir de toutes ses forces ◆ **to hold on ~** tenir bon ◆ **to hit ~** frapper fort, cogner dur ; see also **hit** ◆ **to beg ~** supplier ◆ **to look ~ at** *[+ person]* dévisager ; *[+ thing]* bien regarder ◆ **he tried really ~** il a vraiment essayé ◆ **you must try ~er** il faut faire plus d'efforts ◆ **no matter how ~ I try, I ...** j'ai beau essayer, je ... ◆ **as ~ as one can** de toutes ses forces ◆ **to be ~ at work** *or* **at it*** travailler *or* bosser* dur ◆ **she works ~ at keeping herself fit** elle fait de gros efforts pour rester en forme ◆ **he likes to work ~ and play ~** il met autant d'énergie à travailler qu'à s'amuser ◆ **to clamp down ~ on sb** prendre des sanctions très sévères contre qn

◆ **to be hard pushed** *or* **put (to it) to do sth** avoir beaucoup de mal à faire qch

2 *(= as far as possible) [turn]* ◆ **~ left** à fond à gauche ◆ **~ right** à fond à droite ◆ **~ a-port** *(Naut)* bâbord toute ◆ **~ a-starboard** *(Naut)* tribord toute ◆ **~ astern** *(Naut)* arrière toute ◆ **~ about** *(Naut)* demi-tour toute

3 *(= badly)* ◆ **to take sth ~** être très affecté par qch ◆ **it'll go ~ for him if ...** ça ira mal pour lui si ... ◆ **she feels ~ done by** *(by person)* elle se sent brimée ; *(by life)* elle trouve qu'elle n'a pas eu de chance dans la vie

4 *(= closely)* ◆ **to follow** *or* **come ~ behind** *or* **upon sth** suivre qch de très près ◆ **~ by sth** † tout près de qch ◆ **it was ~ on 10 o'clock** † il était bientôt 10 heures ; → **heel**[1]

COMP **hard-and-fast** ADJ *[timetable]* strict ; *[position]* inflexible ; *[conclusion]* définitif ; *[evidence]* concluant ; *[rule]* absolu

hard-ass** N *(US)* dur(e) *m(f)* à cuire*

hard-bitten ADJ *(fig)* dur à cuire*

hard-boiled ADJ *[egg]* dur ; *(fig) [person]* dur à cuire*

hard cash N *(Fin)* espèces *fpl*, argent *m* liquide

hard cheese N *(= type of cheese)* fromage *m* à pâte pressée ; see also **f**

hard cider N *(US)* cidre *m*

hard copy N *(Comput)* tirage *m*, sortie *f* papier

hard core N

1 *(= group) [of supporters, objectors, offenders]* noyau *m* dur 2 *(for roads)* matériaux *mpl* pour assise, couche *f* de fondation ; see also **hardcore**

hard-core ADJ *(= extreme) [criminal, hooligan]* irrécupérable ; *(= uncompromising)* pur et dur ; *[support, opposition]* inconditionnel ◆ **~-core pornography** pornographie *f* hard

hard court N *(Tennis)* court *m* en dur

hard currency N *(Fin)* devise *f* forte

hard disk N *(Comput)* disque *m* dur

hard disk drive N *(Comput)* unité *f* de disque dur

hard-drinking ADJ qui boit beaucoup *or* sec

hard-earned ADJ *[money, salary]* durement gagné ; *[holiday]* bien mérité

hard-edged ADJ *[shadow, shape]* aux contours nets ; *[style]* intransigeant

hard-faced, hard-featured ADJ au visage sévère, aux traits durs

hard-fought ADJ *[battle]* acharné ; *[election, competition]* âprement disputé

hard hat N *[of motorcyclist, construction worker]* casque *m* ; *(= riding hat)* bombe *f* ; *(esp US fig = construction worker)* ouvrier *m* du bâtiment

hard-hat ADJ *(esp US fig)* réactionnaire

hard-headed ADJ réaliste, qui a la tête sur les épaules ◆ **~-headed businessman** homme *m* d'affaires réaliste ; see also **hardhead**

hard-hearted ADJ insensible, au cœur dur ◆ **he was very ~-hearted towards them** il était très dur avec eux

hard-hitting ADJ *(fig) [report, news programme]* sans complaisance

hard labour, hard labor *(US)* N *(Jur)* travaux *mpl* forcés

hard-line ADJ *[person]* (pur et) dur ; *[stance, policy]* dur, intransigeant

hard-liner N *(gen)* pur(e) *m(f)* et dur(e) *m(f)* ◆ **the ~-liners** *(in political party)* la ligne dure (du parti)

hard loan N *(Fin)* prêt *m* aux conditions commerciales *or* du marché

hard mint candy N *(US)* bonbon *m* à la menthe

hard-nosed ADJ dur, intraitable

hard of hearing ADJ dur d'oreille

the hard-of-hearing NPL les malentendants *mpl*

hard-on** N ◆ **to have a ~-on** bander**

hard-packed snow N neige *f* tassée ; *(by wind)* congère *f*

hard palate N voûte *f* du palais, palais *m* dur

hard pressed ADJ *[staff]* sous pression ; *[consumers, homeowners]* en difficulté financière ; *[economy]* en difficulté ◆ **to be ~ pressed to do sth** avoir beaucoup de mal à faire qch ◆ **to be ~ pressed for money** être vraiment à court d'argent

hard rock N *(Mus)* hard rock *m*

hard sauce N *(US) crème au beurre*

hard-sell N *(Comm)* vente *f* agressive ◆ **~-sell tactics** stratégie *f* de vente agressive ◆ **~-sell approach** *(gen)* approche *f* agressive

hard shoulder N *(esp Brit: on road)* bande *f* d'arrêt d'urgence

hard-up* ADJ *(= penniless)* fauché*, sans le sou ◆ **I'm ~-up** je suis fauché* *or* à sec* ◆ **they must be ~-up if ...** *(fig)* les choses doivent aller mal (pour eux) si ... ◆ **to be ~-up for sth** *(gen)* être à court de qch, manquer de qch

hard-wearing ADJ *[shoes, clothes, material]* solide, résistant

hard-wired ADJ *(Comput)* câblé

hard-won ADJ *[victory, battle, freedom, independence]* durement gagné, remporté de haute lutte ; *[promotion]* bien mérité

hard-working ADJ *(gen)* travailleur ; *[student, pupil]* travailleur, bûcheur*

hardback /ˈhɑːdbæk/ ADJ *[book]* relié, cartonné N livre *m* relié *or* cartonné

hardball /ˈhɑːdbɔːl/ N *(US)* base-ball *m* ◆ **to play ~*** *(fig)* employer la manière forte, ne pas prendre de gants

hardboard /ˈhɑːdbɔːd/ N *(NonC)* isorel ® *m*, panneau *m* dur (de fibres de bois)

hardcore /ˌhɑːdˈkɔːʳ/ N *(Mus)* hardcore *m* ; see also **hard**

hardcover /ˈhɑːdˌkʌvəʳ/ ADJ, N *(US)* ⇒ **hardback**

harden /ˈhɑːdn/ VT 1 *[+ substance]* durcir ; *[+ steel]* tremper ; *[+ muscle]* affermir, durcir ◆ **his years in the Arctic ~ed him considerably** les années qu'il a passées dans l'Arctique l'ont considérablement endurci ◆ **to ~ o.s. to sth** s'endurcir *or* s'aguerrir à qch ◆ **to ~ one's heart** s'endurcir ◆ **this ~ed his heart** cela lui a endurci le cœur ◆ **my heart ~ed against her** je lui ai fermé mon cœur 2 *(Fin)* ◆ **to ~ credit** restreindre le crédit ; see also **hardened** 3 *(Med) [+ arteries]* scléroser VI 1 *[substances]* durcir ; *[steel]* se tremper ◆ **his voice ~ed** sa voix se fit dure ◆ **the look on his face ~ed** son regard s'est durci 2 *(Fin) [shares, prices]* se raffermir ◆ **the market ~ed** le marché s'affermit 3 *(Med) [arteries]* se scléroser

hardened /ˈhɑːdnd/ ADJ *[substance]* durci ; *[steel]* trempé ; *[criminal, sinner]* endurci ; *[drinker]* invétéré ◆ **~ drug addicts** des toxicomanes endurcis ◆ **I'm ~ to it** j'ai l'habitude, ça ne me fait plus rien ◆ **a world ~ to political injustice** un monde qui est devenu insensible à l'injustice politique

hardening /ˈhɑːdnɪŋ/ N 1 *[of substance]* durcissement *m* ; *[of steel]* trempe *f* ; *(fig)* durcissement *m*, endurcissement *m* ◆ **I noticed a ~ of his attitude** j'ai remarqué que son attitude se durcissait 2 *(Fin) [of currency, prices]* raffermissement *m* 3 *(Med)* induration *f*, sclérose *f* COMP **hardening of the arteries** N *(Med)* artériosclérose *f*

hardhead /ˈhɑːdhed/ N *(= person)* réaliste *mf* ; see also **hard**

hardihood /ˈhɑːdɪhʊd/ N hardiesse *f*

hardiness /ˈhɑːdɪnɪs/ N robustesse *f*

hardly /ˈhɑːdlɪ/ ADV 1

> When it means 'barely', **hardly** can generally be translated using the expression **à peine**.

◆ **he can ~ write** il sait à peine écrire, c'est à peine s'il sait écrire ◆ **I can ~ hear you** je vous entends à peine ◆ **he was given ~ 24 hours to pack his bags** c'est à peine si on lui a donné 24 heures pour faire ses bagages ◆ ~ **had he got home than the phone started ringing** à peine était-il rentré chez lui que le téléphone se mit à sonner ◆ ~ **a day goes by without someone visiting** il est rare qu'une journée se passe sans qu'il y ait une visite ◆ **you'll ~ believe it** vous aurez de la peine *or* du mal à le croire

Note the use of **presque** in the following examples.

◆ ~ **anyone knew** presque personne n'était au courant ◆ **these animals are found ~ anywhere else** ces animaux ne se trouvent presque nulle part ailleurs ◆ **you have ~ eaten anything** tu n'as presque rien mangé ◆ ~ **ever** presque jamais ◆ **I ~ know you** je vous connais à peine, je ne vous connais presque pas ◆ **Nicki had ~ slept** Nicki avait à peine dormi, Nicki n'avait presque pas dormi

2 *(expressing doubt, scepticism, irony)* ~! *(= not at all)* certainement pas ! ; *(= not exactly)* pas précisément ! ◆ **he would ~ have said that** il n'aurait tout de même pas dit cela ◆ **it's ~ surprising his ideas didn't catch on** il n'est guère surprenant que ses idées ne soient pas devenues populaires ◆ **it's ~ his business if ...** ce n'est guère son affaire si ... ◆ **I need ~ point out that ...** je n'ai pas besoin de faire remarquer que ...

hardness /ˈhɑːdnɪs/ N dureté *f* ◆ ~ **of hearing** surdité *f* (partielle) ◆ **his ~ of heart** sa dureté de cœur ◆ **the ~ of the market** *(Fin)* le raffermissement du marché

hardscrabble /ˈhɑːdˌskræbəl/ ADJ *(US)* *[farmer, farm]* misérable

hardship /ˈhɑːdʃɪp/ N ☐ *(NonC)* *(= circumstances)* épreuves *fpl* ; *(= suffering)* souffrance *f* ; *(= poverty)* pauvreté *f* ; *(= deprivation)* privation *f* ◆ **he has suffered great ~** il a connu de dures épreuves ◆ **periods of economic ~** des périodes de difficultés économiques ◆ **many students are experiencing severe financial ~** beaucoup d'étudiants ont de gros problèmes d'argent ◆ **there's a certain amount of ~ involved but it's worth it** ça sera dur mais ça en vaut la peine ◆ **a life of ~** une vie pleine d'épreuves ◆ **being posted to Cairo was no ~ at all** être posté au Caire n'avait rien de désagréable ◆ **it's no great ~ to go and see her once a month** ce n'est pas la mer à boire d'aller la voir une fois par mois

2 ◆ **~s** épreuves *fpl*, privations *fpl* ◆ **the ~s of war** les privations *fpl or* les rigueurs *fpl* de la guerre ◆ **many families are suffering economic ~s** de nombreuses familles ont des problèmes financiers

COMP **hardship clause** N *(Jur)* clause *f* de sauvegarde

hardtack /ˈhɑːdtæk/ N *(Mil)* biscuit *m* ; *(Naut)* galette *f*

hardtop /ˈhɑːdtɒp/ N *(= car roof)* hard-top *m* ; *(= car)* voiture *f* à hard-top

hardware /ˈhɑːdwɛəʳ/ N *(NonC)* *(Comm)* quincaillerie *f* *(marchandises)* ; *(Mil etc)* matériel *m* ; *(Comput, Space)* matériel *m* hardware *m*

COMP **hardware dealer** N quincaillier *m*, -ière *f*

hardware shop *(Brit)*, **hardware store** *(US)* N quincaillerie *f*

hardwood /ˈhɑːdwʊd/ N *(= tree)* feuillu *m* ; *(= wood)* bois *m* dur, bois *m* de feuillu COMP de feuillu, de bois dur

hardy /ˈhɑːdɪ/ ADJ 1 *(= tough)* *[person, animal]* robuste ; *[plant]* rustique 2 *(= brave)* *[person]* hardi, intrépide

COMP **hardy annual** N *(= plant)* annuelle *f* rustique ; *(fig)* *(= topic)* sujet *m* rebattu, sujet *m* bateau

hardy perennial N *(= plant)* vivace *f* rustique ; *(fig)* sujet *m* rebattu, sujet *m* bateau

hare /hɛəʳ/ N lièvre *m* ◆ ~ **and hounds** *(= game)* (sorte de) jeu *m* de piste ◆ **to run with the ~ and hunt with the hounds** ménager la chèvre et le chou ; → **jug, mad** VI *(Brit)* ◆ **to ~ away** *or* **off** * partir en trombe *or* à fond de train COMP **hare coursing** N chasse *f* au lièvre

harebell /ˈhɛəbel/ N campanule *f*

harebrained /ˈhɛəbreɪnd/ ADJ *[person]* écervelé ; *[plan, scheme]* insensé ◆ **to be ~** *[person]* être une tête de linotte, être écervelé

harelip /ˌhɛəˈlɪp/ N *(Med)* bec-de-lièvre *m*

harem /hɑːˈriːm/ N harem *m*

haricot /ˈhærɪkəʊ/ N *(Brit)* (also **haricot bean**) haricot *m* blanc

hark /hɑːk/ VI *(liter)* ◆ **to ~ to** écouter, prêter une oreille attentive à ◆ ~! († *or liter*) écoutez ! ◆ ~ **at him!** * *(Brit)* mais écoutez-le (donc) ! *

▸ **hark back** VI revenir *(to* à*)* ◆ **to ~ back to sth** revenir sur qch, ressasser qch

harken /ˈhɑːkən/ VI ⇒ **hearken**

Harlequin /ˈhɑːlɪkwɪn/ N *(Theat)* Arlequin *m* ◆ ~ **costume** costume *m* bigarré *or* d'Arlequin

Harley Street /ˈhɑːlɪˌstriːt/ N *(Brit)* Harley Street *(haut lieu de la médecine privée à Londres)*

harlot †† /ˈhɑːlət/ N catin *f* † *(pej)*

harm /hɑːm/ N mal *m* ◆ **to do sb ~** faire du mal à qn ◆ **he never did any ~ to anyone** il n'a jamais fait de mal à personne ◆ **a bit of exercise never did anyone any ~** un peu d'exercice physique n'a jamais fait de mal à personne ◆ **the ~'s done now** le mal est fait maintenant ◆ **no ~ done!** il n'y a pas de mal ! ◆ **it can't do you any ~** ça ne peut pas te faire de mal ◆ **it will do more ~ than good** cela fera plus de mal que de bien ◆ **to cut taxes would do the economy more ~ than good** une réduction des impôts ferait plus de mal que de bien à l'économie ◆ **he means no ~** il n'a pas de mauvaises intentions ◆ **he doesn't mean us any ~** il ne nous veut pas de mal ◆ **you will come to no ~** il ne t'arrivera rien ◆ **make sure that no ~ comes to him** fais en sorte qu'il ne lui arrive rien de mal ◆ **I don't see any ~ in it, I see no ~ in it** je n'y vois aucun mal ◆ **there's no ~ in an occasional drink** un petit verre de temps en temps ne peut pas faire de mal ◆ **there's no ~ in asking** on peut toujours demander

◆ **in harm's way** en danger ◆ **they'd been put in ~'s way** on les avait mis en danger

◆ **out of harm's way** ◆ **keep** *or* **stay out of ~'s way** *(= out of danger)* mettez-vous en sûreté ; *(= out of the way)* ne restez pas ici, c'est dangereux ◆ **to keep a child out of ~'s way** mettre un enfant à l'abri du danger ◆ **put the vase out of ~'s way** mets ce vase en lieu sûr

VT *[+ person]* *(= damage)* faire du tort à, nuire à ; *(= hurt)* faire du mal à ; *[+ crops, harvest, building]* endommager ; *[+ object]* abîmer ; *[+ reputation, interests, cause]* nuire à ◆ **this will ~ his case considerably** cela desservira ses intérêts ◆ **products which ~ the environment** des produits nocifs pour l'environnement ; → **fly¹**

harmful /ˈhɑːmfʊl/ ADJ *[substance, rays, effects]* nocif ◆ **to be ~ to** *(physically)* être nuisible à *or* mauvais pour ; *(morally)* porter préjudice à

harmless /ˈhɑːmlɪs/ ADJ *[animal, substance, device, joke]* inoffensif *(to* pour*)* ; *[hobby, pleasure, entertainment, diversion]* innocent ; *[rash, cyst, growth]* bénin (-igne *f*) ◆ **it's just a bit of ~ fun** ce n'est pas bien méchant ◆ **he's ~** * il n'est pas bien méchant ◆ **to hold ~** *(Jur)* tenir à couvert

harmlessly /ˈhɑːmlɪslɪ/ ADV 1 *(= without causing damage)* *[explode]* sans dommages 2 *(= inoffensively)* *[gossip]* de façon inoffensive ◆ **it all started ~ enough** au début ce n'était qu'un jeu

harmonic /hɑːˈmɒnɪk/ ADJ *(Math, Mus, Phys)* harmonique NPL **harmonics** 1 *(= science)* harmonie *f* ; *(= overtones)* harmoniques *mpl* 2 *(Phys)* harmoniques *mpl or fpl*

harmonica /hɑːˈmɒnɪkə/ N harmonica *m*

harmonious /hɑːˈməʊnɪəs/ ADJ *(gen, Mus)* harmonieux

harmoniously /hɑːˈməʊnɪəslɪ/ ADV 1 *[live together, work together]* en harmonie ; *[blend, combine]* harmonieusement, avec harmonie 2 *[sing]* harmonieusement

harmonium /hɑːˈməʊnɪəm/ N harmonium *m*

harmonize /ˈhɑːmənaɪz/ VI *(Mus)* chanter en harmonie ; *[colours etc]* s'harmoniser *(with* avec*)* VT *(gen, Mus)* harmoniser

harmony /ˈhɑːmənɪ/ N *(Mus)* harmonie *f* ; *(fig)* harmonie *f*, accord *m* ◆ **in perfect ~** en parfaite harmonie, en parfait accord ◆ **they work together in ~** ils travaillent ensemble en harmonie ◆ **in ~ with** en harmonie *or* en accord avec ◆ **to live in ~ with nature** vivre en harmonie avec la nature ; → **close¹**

harness /ˈhɑːnɪs/ N *[of horse]* harnais *m*, harnachement *m* ; *[of loom, parachute]* harnais *m* ; *(Climbing)* baudrier *m* ◆ **to get back in(to) ~** * *(fig = back to work)* reprendre le collier ◆ **to die in ~** * *(fig)* mourir debout *or* à la tâche ◆ **to work in ~ (with sb)** *(fig)* travailler en tandem (avec qn) VT 1 *[+ horse]* harnacher ◆ **to ~ a horse to a carriage** atteler un cheval à une voiture 2 *[+ river, resources, energy, power, anger, talents]* exploiter

Harold /ˈhærəld/ N Harold *m*

harp /hɑːp/ N harpe *f* VI * ◆ **to ~ on (about) sth** rabâcher qch ◆ **stop ~ing on about it!** cesse de nous rebattre les oreilles avec ça ! ◆ **she's always ~ing on about her problems** elle nous rebat les oreilles de ses problèmes ◆ **I don't want to ~ on about it** je ne veux pas revenir toujours là-dessus ◆ **to ~ back to sth** revenir sur qch, ressasser qch

harpist /ˈhɑːpɪst/ N harpiste *mf*

harpoon /hɑːˈpuːn/ N harpon *m* VT harponner

harpsichord /ˈhɑːpsɪkɔːd/ N clavecin *m*

harpsichordist /ˈhɑːpsɪkɔːdɪst/ N claveciniste *mf*

harpy /ˈhɑːpɪ/ N *(Myth)* harpie *f* ◆ **old ~** *(pej)* vieille harpie *f or* sorcière *f*

harridan /ˈhærɪdən/ N *(frm)* harpie *f*, sorcière *f*

harried /ˈhærɪd/ ADJ *[look, expression]* soucieux

harrier /ˈhærɪəʳ/ N 1 *(= dog)* harrier *m* ◆ **~s** meute *f* 2 ◆ **~s** *(= cross-country runners)* coureurs *mpl* de cross 3 *(= bird)* busard *m*

Harris Tweed ® /ˌhærɪsˈtwiːd/ N (gros) tweed *m* *(des Hébrides)*

harrow /ˈhærəʊ/ N herse *f* VT 1 *(Agr)* herser 2 *(fig)* *[+ person]* tourmenter, torturer

harrowing /ˈhærəʊɪŋ/ ADJ *[story, account, film]* poignant ; *[experience]* extrêmement pénible ; *[photo, picture]* difficile à supporter N *(Agr)* hersage *m*

Harry /ˈhærɪ/ N (dim of **Henry**) Harry ; → **flash**

harry /ˈhærɪ/ VT *[+ country]* dévaster, ravager ; *[+ person]* harceler ; *(Mil)* harceler

harsh /hɑːʃ/ ADJ 1 *(= severe)* *[words, criticism, reality, truth, measures]* dur ; *[person, verdict, sentence, punishment]* sévère, dur ◆ **the ~ facts of ...** la dure réalité de ... ◆ **he said many ~ things about his opponents** il n'a pas été tendre avec ses adversaires ◆ **to be ~ on sb** être dur avec qn 2 *(= inhospitable)* *[conditions, environment]* dur ; *[climate, winter, weather]* rude, rigoureux 3 *(= rough, hard)* *[colour, voice, cry]* criard ; *[sound]* discordant ; *[light]* cru ; *[whisper, breathing]* rauque ; *[contrast]* fort ; *[wool, fabric]* rêche ; *[wine, whisky, tobacco]* âpre, râpeux ;

[cleaner, detergent] corrosif ◆ **the ~ glare of the sun** l'éclat éblouissant du soleil

harshly /ˈhɑːʃlɪ/ ADV *[treat, criticize, judge]* sévèrement ; *[say]* rudement, durement ; *[laugh]* d'un rire jaune *or* amer

harshness /ˈhɑːʃnɪs/ N 1 *(= severity) [of manner]* rudesse *f* ; *[of words, conditions]* dureté *f* ; *[of fate, climate]* rigueur *f* ; *[of punishment, laws]* sévérité *f* 2 *(= roughness) (to the touch)* rudesse *f*, dureté *f* ; *(to the taste)* âpreté *f* ; *(to the ear)* discordance *f*

hart /hɑːt/ N (pl **harts** *or* **hart**) cerf *m*

harumph /həˈrʌmf/ VTI bougonner

harum-scarum * /ˈhɛərəmˈskɛərəm/ ADJ tête de linotte *inv* N tête *f* de linotte

harvest /ˈhɑːvɪst/ N *[of corn]* moisson *f* ; *[of fruit]* récolte *f*, cueillette *f* ; *[of grapes]* vendange *f* ; *(fig)* moisson *f* ◆ **to get in the ~** faire la moisson, moissonner ◆ **a bumper potato ~** une récolte de pommes de terre exceptionnelle ◆ **poor ~s** mauvaises récoltes *fpl* ; see also **reap** VT *[+ corn]* moissonner ; *[+ fruit]* récolter, cueillir ; *[+ grapes]* vendanger, récolter ; *[+ organ, egg]* prélever ; *[+ reward, information]* récolter ◆ **to ~ the fields** faire les moissons, moissonner (les champs) VI faire la moisson, moissonner

COMP **harvest festival** N fête *f* de la moisson

harvest home N *(= festival)* fête *f* de la moisson ; *(= season)* fin *f* de la moisson

harvest moon N pleine lune *f* (de l'équinoxe d'automne)

harvest time N ◆ **at ~ time** pendant *or* à la moisson

harvester /ˈhɑːvɪstəʳ/ N *(= machine)* moissonneuse *f* ; *(= person)* moissonneur *m*, -euse *f* ; → **combine**

harvestman /ˈhɑːvɪstmən/ N (pl **-men**) *(= insect)* faucheur *m*

has /hæz/ → **have** COMP **has-been** * N *(= person)* has been * *m inv* ; *(= hat, carpet etc)* vieillerie *f*, vieux truc * *m* ◆ **he's/she's a ~-been** * il/elle a fait son temps

hash[1] /hæʃ/ N 1 *(* = mess)* gâchis *m* ◆ **he made a ~ of it** il a raté son affaire ◆ **I'll settle his ~** * je vais lui régler son compte *

2 *(Culin) plat en sauce à base de viande hachée et de légumes*

3 *(Drugs *: also* **hashish**) hasch * *m*

VT *(Culin)* hacher

COMP **hash brownies** NPL petits gâteaux *mpl* au haschisch

hash browns NPL *(Culin)* pommes *fpl* de terre sautées *(servies au petit déjeuner)*

hash cookies NPL ⇒ **hash brownies**

hash house * N *(US)* gargote *f*

hash house slinger * N *(US)* serveur *m*, -euse *f* dans une gargote

► **hash out** * VT SEP 1 ⇒ **hash over**

2 *(= solve)* finir par résoudre

► **hash over** * VT SEP *[+ problem, plan, difficulty]* discuter ferme de ◆ **this subject has been ~ed over a great deal** on a discuté en long et en large de ce sujet

► **hash up** VT SEP 1 *(Culin)* hacher menu

2 *(= spoil)* ◆ **he really hashed it up** * il a raté son affaire

N ◆ **hash-up** * ⇒ **hash noun 1**

hash[2] /hæʃ/ (pl **hashes**) N *(Typ)* dièse *m* COMP **hash key** N *(on keyboard, phone)* touche *f* dièse

hashish /ˈhæʃɪʃ/ N haschisch *or* haschich *m*

hasn't /ˈhæznt/ ⇒ **has not** ; → **have**

hasp /hɑːsp/ N *[of door, lid, window]* moraillon *m* ; *[of book cover, necklace]* fermoir *m*

Hassidic /hæˈsɪdɪk/ ADJ hassidique

hassle * /ˈhæsl/ N 1 *(= fuss)* histoire *f* ; *(= worries)* tracas *mpl* ◆ **what a ~!** quelle histoire ! ◆ **legal ~s** tracas *mpl* juridiques ◆ **it's a ~!** c'est toute une histoire *or* affaire ! ◆ **it's no ~!** ce n'est pas un problème ! ◆ **it isn't worth the ~** ça ne vaut pas la peine * ◆ **preparing for a wedding is such a ~** la préparation d'un mariage, c'est toute une affaire ◆ **commuting's a bit of a ~** les trajets quotidiens sont un peu embêtants ◆ **charcoal's a real ~ to light** ce n'est pas une mince affaire d'allumer du charbon de bois

2 *(US) (= squabble)* chamaillerie * *f*, bagarre * *f* ; *(= bustle, confusion)* pagaille *f*

VT *(= harass)* embêter, enquiquiner * ◆ **stop hassling me, will you?** arrête donc de m'embêter *or* de m'enquiquiner * ◆ **he was continually being ~d for money** on l'embêtait sans arrêt pour lui demander de l'argent

VI *(US = quarrel)* se battre *(with sb* avec qn ; *over sth* à propos de qch)

hassock /ˈhæsək/ N coussin *m* (d'agenouilloir)

hast †† /hæst/ *(liter)* ◆ **thou ~** ⇒ **you have** ; → **have**

haste /heɪst/ N hâte *f* ; *(excessive)* précipitation *f* ◆ **why all this ~?** pourquoi tant de précipitation ? ◆ **to do sth in ~** faire qch à la hâte *or* en hâte ◆ **in their ~ to explain what had happened, they ...** dans leur précipitation à expliquer ce qui s'était passé, ils ... ◆ **in great ~** en toute hâte ◆ **to make ~** † se hâter *(to do sth* de faire qch) ◆ **more ~ less speed** *(Prov)* hâtez-vous lentement ◆ **marry in ~, repent at leisure** *(Prov)* qui se marie sans réfléchir aura tout le loisir de s'en repentir

hasten /ˈheɪsn/ VI se hâter, s'empresser *(to do sth* de faire qch) ◆ **... I ~ to add ...** je m'empresse d'ajouter, ... j'ajoute tout de suite ◆ **to ~ down/away** *etc* se hâter de descendre/partir *etc*, descendre/partir *etc* à la hâte VT *(gen)* hâter, accélérer ; *[+ reaction]* activer ◆ **to ~ one's step** presser le pas, accélérer l'allure *or* le pas ◆ **to ~ sb's departure** hâter le départ de qn ◆ **to ~ sb's/sth's demise** précipiter la fin de qn/qch ◆ **the strikes that ~ed the collapse of the Soviet Union** les grèves qui ont précipité l'effondrement de l'Union soviétique

hastily /ˈheɪstɪlɪ/ ADV hâtivement ; *(= excessively quickly)* précipitamment ◆ **a ~ arranged press conference** une conférence de presse organisée à la hâte ◆ **he ~ suggested that ...** il s'est empressé de suggérer que ..., il a suggéré précipitamment que ... ◆ **to act ~ in doing sth** agir avec précipitation *or* à la hâte en faisant qch

Hastings /ˈheɪstɪŋz/ N ◆ **the Battle of ~** la bataille de Hastings

hasty /ˈheɪstɪ/ ADJ 1 *(= hurried) [departure, escape, retreat]* précipité ; *[glance, examination, visit, sketch, kiss]* rapide ◆ **to eat a ~ breakfast** prendre son petit déjeuner en hâte ◆ **to bid a ~ goodbye to sb** dire précipitamment au revoir à qn 2 *(= rash) [action, decision, words]* hâtif ; *[marriage]* précipité ◆ **don't be ~** pas de précipitation ◆ **perhaps I was a bit ~** *(in actions)* j'ai sans doute agi avec précipitation ; *(in speaking)* j'ai sans doute parlé trop vite ◆ **to have a ~ temper** s'emporter facilement

hat /hæt/ N chapeau *m* ◆ **to put on one's ~** mettre son chapeau ◆ **~ in hand** *(lit)* chapeau bas ; *(fig)* obséquieusement ◆ **~s off!** chapeau bas ! ◆ **to take one's ~ off to sb** tirer son chapeau à qn ◆ **~s off to them for helping the homeless!** leur action en faveur des SDF mérite un (grand) coup de chapeau ◆ **to keep sth under one's ~** * garder qch pour soi ◆ **keep it under your ~!** * motus ! ◆ **to pass round the ~** *or (US)* **to pass the ~ for sb** faire la quête pour qn ◆ **she wears two ~s** *(fig)* elle a deux casquettes ◆ **speaking with my accountant's ~ on** (si je te parlais) en tant que comptable ◆ **putting on my nationalistic ~ ...** en tant que nationaliste ... ◆ **at the drop of a hat** *[act, make speech]* au pied levé ; *[leave, shoot, get angry]* pour un oui pour un non

COMP **hat shop** N magasin *m* de chapeaux

hat tree N *(US)* ⇒ **hatstand**

hat trick N 1 ◆ **to score a ~ trick** *(gen Sport)* réussir trois coups *(or* gagner trois matchs *etc)* consécutifs ; *(Ftbl)* marquer trois buts dans un match ; *(Cricket)* éliminer trois batteurs en trois balles 2 *(Conjuring)* tour *m* du chapeau

hatband /ˈhætbænd/ N ruban *m* de chapeau

hatbox /ˈhætbɒks/ N carton *m* à chapeaux

hatch[1] /hætʃ/ VT 1 *[+ chick, egg]* faire éclore ; → **chicken** 2 *[+ plot]* ourdir *(liter)*, tramer ; *[+ plan]* couver VI *(also* **hatch out**) *[chick, egg]* éclore N *(= brood)* couvée *f*

hatch[2] /hætʃ/ N 1 *(Naut: also* **hatchway**) écoutille *f* ; *(= floodgates)* vanne *f* d'écluse ◆ **under ~es** dans la cale ◆ **down the ~!** * *(drinking)* cul sec ! * 2 *(Brit: also* **service** *or* **serving hatch**) passe-plats *m inv*, guichet *m* 3 *(= car)* ⇒ **hatchback**

hatch[3] /hætʃ/ VT *(Art)* hachurer

hatchback /ˈhætʃbæk/ N *(= car)* voiture *f* à hayon

hatcheck /ˈhættʃek/ N *(also* **hatcheck girl, hatcheck man**) préposé(e) *m(f)* au vestiaire

hatchery /ˈhætʃərɪ/ N couvoir *m (local pour l'incubation des œufs, notamment de poisson)*

hatchet /ˈhætʃɪt/ N hachette *f* ; → **bury**

COMP **hatchet-faced** ADJ au visage en lame de couteau

hatchet job N *(fig)* démolissage *m* ◆ **to do a ~ job on sb** démolir qn

hatchet man * N (pl **hatchet men**) *(US = hired killer)* tueur *m* (à gages) ; *(fig) (in industry etc)* homme *m* de main ◆ **he was the company's ~ man when they sacked 200 workers** c'est lui que l'entreprise a chargé de faire tomber les têtes quand elle a licencié 200 ouvriers

hatching[1] /ˈhætʃɪŋ/ N *[of chicks, eggs] (= act)* éclosion *f* ; *(= brood)* couvée *f*

hatching[2] /ˈhætʃɪŋ/ N *(Art)* hachures *fpl*

hatchway /ˈhætʃweɪ/ N passe-plats *m inv*

hate /heɪt/ LANGUAGE IN USE 7.3

VT haïr ; *(weaker)* détester, avoir horreur de ◆ **she ~s him like poison** elle le hait à mort ; *(weaker)* elle ne peut pas le voir en peinture * ◆ **what he ~s most of all is ...** ce qu'il déteste le plus au monde c'est ... ◆ **I ~ it when people accuse me of lying** je déteste *or* j'ai horreur que les gens m'accusent de mentir ◆ **to ~ o.s.** s'en vouloir *(for doing sth* de faire qch) ◆ **I ~d myself for writing that letter** je m'en voulais d'avoir écrit cette lettre ◆ **to ~ doing sth, to ~ to do sth** détester faire qch, avoir horreur de faire qch ◆ **he ~s being** *or* **to be ordered about** il a horreur *or* il ne peut pas souffrir qu'on lui donne *subj* des ordres ◆ **I ~ being late** je déteste être en retard, j'ai horreur d'être en retard ◆ **she ~s me having any fun** elle ne supporte pas que je m'amuse ◆ **I ~ to tell you this, but ...** *[+ bad news]* ça m'embête beaucoup de te dire ça, mais ... ◆ **I ~ to tell you this, but we're out of mayonnaise** j'ai bien peur qu'il n'y ait plus de mayonnaise ◆ **I ~ to admit it, but you were right** je suis obligé d'admettre que vous aviez raison ◆ **I ~ seeing her in pain** je ne peux pas supporter de la voir souffrir ◆ **I would ~ to keep him waiting** je ne voudrais surtout pas le faire attendre ◆ **I ~ to rush you but I have another appointment later on** je ne voudrais pas vous bousculer mais j'ai un autre rendez-vous plus tard ◆ **I would ~ him to think that ...** je ne voudrais surtout pas qu'il pense que ...

N *(NonC)* haine *f* ; → **pet**[1]

COMP **hate campaign** N campagne *f* de dénigrement
hate mail N lettres *fpl* d'injures

hated /ˈheɪtɪd/ ADJ haï, détesté

hateful /ˈheɪtfʊl/ ADJ 1 (= *horrible*) odieux 2 (= *full of hate*) haineux

hath †† /hæθ/ ⇒ **has** ; → **have**

hatless /ˈhætlɪs/ ADJ sans chapeau

hatpin /ˈhætpɪn/ N épingle *f* à chapeau

hatrack /ˈhætræk/ N porte-chapeaux *m inv*

hatred /ˈheɪtrɪd/ N (NonC) haine *f* ◆ **racial ~** la haine raciale ◆ **he developed a bitter ~ of the police** il s'est mis à vouer une haine féroce à la police ◆ **the brothers killed their father out of ~** la haine a poussé les frères à tuer leur père ◆ **to feel ~ for sb/sth** haïr qn/qch

hatstand /ˈhætstænd/ N portemanteau *m*

hatter /ˈhætəʳ/ N chapelier *m* ; → **mad**

haughtily /ˈhɔːtɪlɪ/ ADV [*say, reply, dismiss, ignore*] avec arrogance, avec morgue (*liter*)

haughtiness /ˈhɔːtɪnɪs/ N arrogance f, morgue *f* (*liter*)

haughty /ˈhɔːtɪ/ ADJ (*pej*) [*person, manner, tone, look*] hautain

haul /hɔːl/ N 1 (= *journey*) **the long ~ between Paris and Aurillac** le long voyage entre Paris et Aurillac ◆ **it's a long ~** (*lit, fig*) la route est longue ◆ **revitalizing the economy will be a long ~** relancer l'économie prendra beaucoup de temps ◆ **over the long ~** (*esp US fig*) sur le long terme
2 (= *catch*) [*of fish*] prise *f* ◆ **a good ~** une belle prise, un beau coup de filet
3 (= *booty*) butin *m* ◆ **the thieves made a good ~** les voleurs ont eu un beau butin ◆ **a drugs ~** une saisie de drogue ◆ **police have recovered a ~ of machine guns** la police a récupéré tout un stock de mitraillettes ◆ **what a ~!** * (*fig*) quelle récolte !
VT 1 (= *pull*) traîner, tirer ◆ **to ~ o.s. on to sth** se hisser sur qch ◆ **he ~ed himself to his feet** il s'est levé à grand-peine ◆ **to ~ sb over the coals** passer un savon* à qn, réprimander sévèrement qn ◆ **she was ~ed before magistrates for refusing to pay the fine** * elle a été traînée devant les tribunaux parce qu'elle avait refusé de payer l'amende ◆ **to ~ ass**‡ (*US*) se barrer‡, mettre les bouts‡
2 (= *transport by truck*) camionner
3 (*Naut*) haler ◆ **to ~ a boat into the wind** faire lofer un bateau
VI (*Naut*) [*boat*] lofer ; [*wind*] refuser

► **haul down** VT SEP (*gen*) [+ *object*] descendre (*en tirant*) ; [+ *flag, sail*] affaler, amener

► **haul in** VT SEP [+ *line, catch*] amener ; [+ *drowning man*] tirer (de l'eau)

► **haul up** VT SEP (*gen*) [+ *object*] monter (*en tirant*) ; [+ *flag, sail*] hisser ◆ **to ~ o.s. up** se hisser ◆ **to ~ up a boat** (*Naut*) (*aboard ship*) rentrer une embarcation (à bord) ; (*on to beach*) tirer un bateau au sec ◆ **to be ~ed up in court** * être traîné devant les tribunaux ◆ **he was ~ed up for speeding** * il a été interpellé parce qu'il roulait trop vite

haulage /ˈhɔːlɪdʒ/ N (= *business*) transport *m* routier ; (= *charge*) frais *mpl* de transport
COMP **haulage company** N (*Brit*) entreprise *f* de transports (routiers)
haulage contractor N ⇒ **haulier**

hauler /ˈhɔːləʳ/ N (*US*) 1 ⇒ **haulier** 2 (= *vehicle*) camion *m*, poids *m* lourd

haulier /ˈhɔːlɪəʳ/ N (*Brit*) (= *company*) entreprise *f* de transports (routiers) ; (= *person in charge*) entrepreneur *m* de transports (routiers), transporteur *m* ; (= *driver*) camionneur *m*, routier *m*

haunch /hɔːntʃ/ N hanche *f* ◆ **~es** [*of animal*] derrière *m*, arrière-train *m* ◆ **(squatting) on his ~es** (*person*) accroupi ; (*dog etc*) assis (sur son derrière) ◆ **~ of venison** cuissot *m* de chevreuil

haunt /hɔːnt/ VT (*lit, fig*) hanter ◆ **he used to ~ the café in the hope of seeing her** il hantait le café dans l'espoir de la voir ◆ **to be ~ed by memories** être hanté par des souvenirs ◆ **he is ~ed by the fear of losing all his money** il est hanté par la peur de *or* il a la hantise de perdre tout son argent ◆ **the decision to leave her children now ~s her** elle est hantée par le remords parce qu'elle a décidé d'abandonner ses enfants ◆ **lack of money ~ed successive projects** le manque d'argent a été la plaie de *or* a nui à tous les projets ; see also **haunted**
N [*of criminals*] repaire *m* ◆ **one of the favourite ~s of this animal is ...** un des lieux où l'on trouve souvent cet animal est ... ◆ **it is a favourite ~ of artists** c'est un lieu fréquenté par les artistes ◆ **that café is one of his favourite ~s** ce café est un de ses lieux favoris *or* de prédilection ◆ **familiar childhood ~s** des lieux de prédilection de son (*or* mon *etc*) enfance

haunted /ˈhɔːntɪd/ ADJ [*house*] hanté ; [*look, expression*] égaré ; [*face, eyes*] hagard ◆ **he looks ~** il a un air égaré *or* hagard

haunting /ˈhɔːntɪŋ/ ADJ [*tune*] obsédant, qui vous hante ; [*image, beauty, memory, doubt, cry*] N ◆ **there have been several ~s here** il y a eu plusieurs apparitions ici

hauntingly /ˈhɔːntɪŋlɪ/ ADV ◆ **~ beautiful** d'une beauté envoûtante

haute couture /ˌəʊt kuːˈtʊəʳ/ N haute couture *f*

haute cuisine /ˌəʊtˌkwɪˈziːn/ N haute cuisine *f*

hauteur /əʊˈtɜː/ N hauteur *f* (*pej*), morgue *f* (*liter*)

Havana /həˈvænə/ N 1 La Havane 2 ◆ **a ~ (cigar)** un havane

have /hæv/

vb : 3rd pers sg pres **has**, pret, ptp **had**

LANGUAGE IN USE 10

1 AUXILIARY VERB
2 MODAL VERB
3 TRANSITIVE VERB
4 NOUN
5 PHRASAL VERBS

When **have** is part of a set combination, eg **have a look/walk, have a good time, have breakfast/lunch**, look up the noun.

1 - AUXILIARY VERB

1 avoir

avoir is the auxiliary used with most verbs to form past tenses. For important exceptions see **2**.

◆ **I ~ eaten** j'ai mangé ◆ **I ~ been** j'ai été ◆ **I had been** j'avais été ◆ **I had eaten** j'avais mangé ◆ **haven't you grown!** comme tu as grandi ! ◆ **once he'd explained the situation I felt better** une fois qu'il m'eut expliqué la situation, je me suis senti mieux

Note the agreement of the past participle with the preceding direct object.

◆ **I haven't seen him** je ne l'ai pas vu ◆ **I haven't seen her** je ne l'ai pas vue ◆ **I hadn't seen him** je ne l'avais pas vu ◆ **had I seen her** *or* **if I had seen her I would have spoken to her** si je l'avais vue, je lui aurais parlé ◆ **having seen them** les ayant vus ◆ **I left immediately after I had seen her** je suis parti tout de suite après l'avoir vue

When describing uncompleted states or actions, French generally uses the present and imperfect where English uses the perfect and past perfect.

◆ **I ~ lived** *or* **~ been living here for ten years/since January** j'habite ici depuis dix ans/depuis janvier ◆ **I had lived** *or* **had been living there for ten years** j'habitais là depuis dix ans

◆ **to have just ...** venir de ... ◆ **I ~ just seen him** je viens de le voir ◆ **I had just spoken to him** je venais de lui parler ◆ **I've just come from London** j'arrive à l'instant de Londres

2 être

être is the auxiliary used with all reflexives, and the following verbs when used intransitively: **aller, arriver, descendre, devenir, entrer, monter, mourir, naître, partir, passer, rentrer, rester, retourner, revenir, sortir, tomber, venir**.

◆ **I ~ gone** je suis allé ◆ **I've made a mistake** je me suis trompé ◆ **I had gone** j'étais allé ◆ **I had made a mistake** je m'étais trompé

3 in tag questions : seeking confirmation n'est-ce pas ◆ **you've seen her, haven't you?** vous l'avez vue, n'est-ce pas ? ◆ **he hasn't told anyone, has he?** il n'en a parlé à personne, n'est-ce pas ? ◆ **you haven't lost it, ~ you?** tu ne l'as pas perdu, n'est-ce pas ?

4 in tag responses ◆ **he's got a new job – oh has he ?** il a un nouveau travail – ah bon ? ◆ **you've dropped your book – so I ~!** vous avez laissé tomber votre livre – en effet *or* ah oui, c'est vrai !

(mais) si or **(mais) non** are used to contradict.

◆ **you haven't seen her – yes I ~!** vous ne l'avez pas vue – (mais) si ! ◆ **you've made a mistake – no I haven't!** vous vous êtes trompé – (mais) non !

oui or **non** are often sufficient when answering questions.

◆ **have you met him? – yes I ~** est-ce que tu l'as rencontré ? – oui ◆ **has he arrived? – no he hasn't** est-ce qu'il est arrivé ? – non

5 avoiding repetition of verb ◆ **~ you ever been there ? if you ~ ...** y êtes-vous déjà allé ? si oui, ... ◆ **~ you tried it? if you haven't ...** est-ce que vous avez goûté ça ? si vous ne l'avez pas fait, ... ; → **so, neither, nor**

2 - MODAL VERB

◆ **to have to** + *infinitive* devoir, falloir

falloir is always used in the third person singular, in an impersonal construction.

◆ **they ~ to work hard** ils doivent travailler dur, il faut qu'ils travaillent *subj* dur ◆ **they had to work hard** ils ont dû travailler dur, il a fallu qu'ils travaillent *subj* dur ◆ **you're going to ~ to work hard!** tu vas devoir travailler dur !, il va falloir que tu travailles *subj* dur ! ◆ **I ~ (got) to speak to you at once** je dois vous parler *or* il faut que je vous parle *subj* immédiatement ◆ **I'll ~ to leave now or I'll miss the train** il faut que je parte, sinon je vais rater mon train ◆ **he had to pay all the money back** il a dû tout rembourser ◆ **don't you ~ to get permission?** est-ce qu'on ne doit pas demander la permission ? ◆ **do you ~ to go now?, ~ you got to go now?** est-ce que vous devez partir tout de suite ? ◆ **she was having to get up at six each morning** elle devait se lever à 6 heures tous les matins ◆ **we've had to work late twice this week** nous avons dû rester travailler tard deux fois cette semaine ◆ **we shall ~ to find an alternative** nous allons devoir *or* il nous faudra trouver une autre solution ◆ **the locks will ~ to be changed** il va falloir changer les serrures ◆ **what kind of equipment would you ~ to have?** quel type de matériel vous faudrait-il ? ◆ **it's got to be** *or* **it has to be the biggest scandal this year** c'est sans aucun doute le plus gros scandale de l'année ◆ **it still has to be proved** ça reste à prouver ◆ **do you ~ to make such a noise ?** tu es vraiment forcé de faire tout ce bruit ?, tu ne pourrais pas faire un peu moins de bruit ?

♦ **don't/doesn't have to** + *infinitive*

Note that **falloir** and **devoir** are not used.

◆ **he doesn't ~ to work** il n'a pas besoin de travailler ◆ **you didn't ~ to tell her!** tu n'avais pas besoin de le lui dire ! ◆ **if you're a member you don't ~ to pay** si vous êtes membre vous n'avez pas besoin de payer ◆ **it's nice not to ~ to work on Saturdays** c'est agréable de ne pas avoir à travailler le samedi ◆ **I don't ~ to do it** je ne suis pas obligé *or* forcé de le faire

3 - TRANSITIVE VERB

1 [= possess] avoir ◆ **I ~** *or* **I've got three books** j'ai trois livres ◆ **~ you got** *or* **do you ~ a suitcase?** avez-vous une valise ? ◆ **she has blue eyes** elle a les yeux bleus ◆ **he's got big feet** il a de grands pieds ◆ **I've got an idea** j'ai une idée ◆ **~ you got this jumper in black?** est-ce que vous avez ce pull en noir ? ◆ **sorry, that's all I ~** désolé, c'est tout ce que j'ai ◆ **I haven't (got) any more** je n'en ai plus ◆ **she has** *or* **she's got a shop** elle tient *or* a une boutique ◆ **~ you got the time (on you)?** est-ce que vous avez *or* avez-vous l'heure ? ◆ **I ~ (got) nothing to do** je n'ai rien à faire ◆ **I ~ (got) letters to write** j'ai des lettres à écrire ◆ **I didn't ~ any spades** *(Cards)* je n'avais pas de piques ◆ **he has flu** il a la grippe ◆ **I've (got) a headache** j'ai mal à la tête ◆ **I had my camera ready** j'avais mon appareil tout prêt ◆ **I'll ~ everything ready** je veillerai à ce que tout soit prêt ◆ **I ~ (got) no German** je ne parle pas un mot d'allemand

2 [= eat, drink, take] ◆ **he had an egg for breakfast** il a mangé un œuf au petit déjeuner ◆ **I'll just ~ a sandwich** je vais juste prendre *or* manger un sandwich ◆ **I've had some more** j'en ai repris ◆ **shall we ~ a coffee?** est-ce qu'on prend un café ? ◆ **to ~ tea with sb** prendre le thé avec qn ◆ **I've had a couple of aspirins** j'ai pris deux aspirines

♦ **will you have ... ?** *(in offers)* ◆ **will you ~ tea or coffee ?** voulez-vous *or* prendrez-vous du thé ou du café ? ◆ **will you ~ some more?** voulez-vous en reprendre ?

3 [= spend] passer ◆ **what sort of day have you had?** est-ce que tu as passé une bonne journée ? ◆ **to ~ a pleasant evening** passer une bonne soirée

4 [= smoke] fumer ◆ **he had a cigarette** il a fumé une cigarette

5 [= receive, obtain, get] avoir, recevoir ◆ **to ~ news from sb** avoir *or* recevoir des nouvelles de qn ◆ **we had a lot of visitors** nous avons eu *or* reçu beaucoup de visites ◆ **I had a birthday card from him** il m'a envoyé une carte d'anniversaire ◆ **there are no newspapers to be had** on ne trouve pas de journaux

Note the use of **falloir** to translate **must have/have to have**.

◆ **I must ~ £50 at once** il me faut 50 livres immédiatement ◆ **I must** *or* **~ to have them by this afternoon** il me les faut pour cet après-midi ◆ **I must ~ more time** il me faut davantage de temps

6 [= hold, catch] tenir ◆ **he had me by the throat/the hair** il me tenait à la gorge/par les cheveux ◆ **the dog had (got) him by the ankle** le chien le tenait par la cheville ◆ **I ~** *or* **I've got him where I want him!*** je le tiens ! ◆ **there you ~ me !** là tu me poses une colle !

7 [= give birth to] **to ~ a child** avoir un enfant ◆ **she is having a baby in April** elle va avoir un bébé en avril ◆ **our cat has had kittens** notre chatte a eu des petits

8 [‡ = have sex with] coucher* avec

9 [set structures]

♦ **to let sb have** *(= give)* donner à qn ◆ **let me ~ your address** donnez-moi votre adresse ◆ **I'll let you ~ the books tomorrow** je vous donnerai les livres demain ◆ **I'll let you ~ it for 20 euros** je vous le cède pour 20 euros

♦ **to have it that** ◆ **he will ~ it that Paul is guilty** il soutient que Paul est coupable ◆ **he won't ~ it that Paul is guilty** il n'admet pas que Paul soit coupable ◆ **rumour has it that ...** le bruit court que ...

♦ **won't have** *or* **am not having** *(= refuse to accept)* ◆ **I won't ~** *or* **am not having this nonsense !** je ne tolérerai pas ces enfantillages ! ◆ **I won't ~** *or* **am not having this sort of behaviour!** je ne tolérerai pas une conduite pareille ! ◆ **I won't ~ it!** je ne tolérerai pas ça ! ◆ **I won't ~ him risking his neck on that motorbike** je ne tolérerai pas qu'il risque sa vie sur cette moto ◆ **I'm not having any!‡** ça ne prend pas !*

♦ **would + have** *(= wish)* ◆ **as fate would ~ it, he did not get the letter** la fatalité a voulu qu'il ne reçoive pas la lettre ◆ **what would you ~ me do?** que voulez-vous que je fasse ? ◆ **I would ~ you know that ...** sachez que ...

♦ **to have sth done** faire faire qch ◆ **to ~ sth mended** faire réparer qch ◆ **~ it mended!** fais-le réparer ! ◆ **to ~ one's hair cut** se faire couper les cheveux ◆ **they killed him, or had him killed** ils l'ont tué ou ils l'ont fait tuer ◆ **I've had the brakes checked** j'ai fait vérifier les freins

♦ **to have sb do sth** faire faire qch à qn ◆ **I had him clean the car** je lui ai fait nettoyer la voiture

♦ **to have sb doing sth** ◆ **he had us all helping with the dinner** il nous avait tous mis à contribution pour préparer le dîner ◆ **she soon had them all reading and writing** elle réussit très rapidement à leur apprendre à lire et à écrire

♦ **to have sth stolen/broken** *etc* ◆ **he had his car stolen** il s'est fait voler sa voiture, on lui a volé sa voiture ◆ **he had his worst fears confirmed** ses pires craintes se sont réalisées ◆ **I've had three windows broken this week** j'ai eu trois fenêtres cassées cette semaine

♦ **had better** *(= should)* ◆ **I had better go now** il vaut mieux que j'y aille ◆ **you'd better not tell him that!** tu ferais mieux de ne pas lui dire ça !

♦ **to be had*** se faire avoir ◆ **you've been had** tu t'es fait avoir*, on t'a eu*

♦ **to have had it*** ◆ **I've had it** *(= am done for)* je suis fichu* *or* foutu‡ ; *(= fed up:* also **I've had it up to here** *or* **I've had that)** j'en ai par-dessus la tête !*, j'en ai marre !*, j'en ai ras-le-bol !*

♦ **to have to do with** ◆ **I ~ (got) nothing to do with it** je n'y suis pour rien ◆ **that has nothing to do with it** ça n'a rien à voir

4 - NOUN

◆ **the ~s and the ~-nots** les riches *mpl* et les pauvres *mpl* ◆ **the ~-nots** les démunis *mpl*, les déshérités *mpl*

5 - PHRASAL VERBS

▸ **have at** VT FUS *(in swordfight etc)* ◆ **have at thee !** †† défends-toi !

▸ **have down** VT SEP ◆ **we are having the Smiths down for a few days** nous avons invité les Smith à venir passer quelques jours chez nous

▸ **have in** VT SEP 1 *[+ doctor]* faire venir ◆ **we'll ~ them in and discuss it** nous allons les faire venir pour en discuter 2 ◆ **to have it in for sb*** garder *or* avoir une dent contre qn 3 ◆ **to have it in one** en être capable ◆ **she has got it in her** elle en est capable

▸ **have it away‡, have it off‡** VI *(Brit)* ◆ **to have it away** *or* **off with sb** ‡ s'envoyer‡ qn, se taper‡ qn ◆ **they were having it off** ‡ ils s'envoyaient en l'air‡

▸ **have on** VT SEP 1 *[+ clothes]* porter ◆ **he had nothing on** il était tout nu 2 *(Brit = have planned)* ◆ **I've got so much on this week that ...** j'ai tant à faire cette semaine que ... ◆ **I've (got) nothing on this evening** je suis libre ce soir 3 *(Brit * = tease) [+ person]* faire marcher* 4 * ◆ **Richard has nothing on him !** Richard ne lui arrive pas à la cheville ! ◆ **the police ~ nothing on me** la police n'a pas de preuve contre moi

▸ **have out** VT SEP 1 ◆ **to have a tooth out** se faire arracher une dent 2 ◆ **to have it out with sb** s'expliquer avec qn

▸ **have round** VT SEP *[+ friends, neighbours]* inviter

▸ **have up** VT SEP ◆ **to be had up** passer en jugement *(for sth* pour qch ; *for doing sth* pour avoir fait qch)

have-a-go /'hævəgəʊ/ * ADJ ◆ **~ hero** *intrépide qui n'hésite pas à intervenir lorsqu'il est témoin d'un délit*

haven /'heɪvn/ N 1 ◆ **a ~ of** *[+ peace, tranquillity etc]* un havre de ◆ **a ~ for** *[+ animals, refugees]* un refuge pour ; *[+ artists, writers]* un refuge de 2 *(liter = harbour)* port *m* ; → **safe, tax**

haven't /'hævnt/ ⇒ **have not** ; → **have**

haver /'heɪvəʳ/ VI *(N Engl, Scot)* dire des âneries

haversack /'hævəsæk/ N *(over shoulder)* musette *f* ; *(on back)* sac *m* à dos ; *(Mil)* havresac *m*, musette *f*

havoc /'hævək/ N *(NonC)* ravages *mpl* ; *(less serious)* dégâts *mpl* ◆ **to cause** *or* **create ~** faire des dégâts ◆ **to wreak ~** causer des ravages ◆ **violent storms wreaked ~ on the French Riviera** de violents orages ont ravagé la Côte d'Azur *or* ont causé des ravages sur la Côte d'Azur ◆ **stress can wreak ~ on the immune system** le stress peut perturber sérieusement *or* dérégler le système immunitaire ◆ **this wreaked ~ with their plans** cela a bouleversé tous leurs projets ◆ **to wreak ~ on sb's life** complètement bouleverser la vie de qn ◆ **to play ~ with** *(schedule, routine, plans)* bouleverser ; *(health, skin)* être très mauvais pour ◆ **spicy food can play ~ with your stomach** les aliments épicés peuvent vous déranger l'estomac ◆ **his drug habit played ~ with his career** sa toxicomanie a gravement perturbé sa carrière

haw¹ /hɔː/ N *(Bot)* cenelle *f*

haw² /hɔː/ VI ◆ **to hem and ~, to hum and ~** balancer

Hawaii /hə'waɪiː/ N Hawaï *or* Hawaii ◆ **in ~** à Hawaï *or* Hawaii

Hawaiian /hə'waɪjən/ ADJ hawaïen ◆ **the ~ Islands** les îles *fpl* Hawaï *or* Hawaii N 1 Hawaïen(ne) *m(f)* 2 *(= language)* hawaïen *m*
COMP **Hawaiian guitar** N guitare *f* hawaïenne
Hawaiian shirt N chemise *f* hawaïenne
Hawaiian Standard Time N *(US)* heure *f* de Hawaï

hawfinch /'hɔːfɪntʃ/ N gros-bec *m*

hawk¹ /hɔːk/ N 1 *(= bird)* faucon *m* ◆ **to have eyes like a ~** avoir un regard d'aigle *or* des yeux de lynx ◆ **to watch sb like a ~** surveiller qn de près, avoir qn à l'œil* 2 *(Pol fig)* faucon *m* ◆ **~s and doves** faucons *mpl* et colombes *fpl* VI chasser au faucon COMP **hawk-eyed** ADJ au regard d'aigle, aux yeux de lynx

hawk² /hɔːk/ **VI** (also **hawk up**) *(= clear one's throat)* se racler la gorge **VT** ◆ **to ~ sth up** cracher qch

hawk³ /hɔːk/ **VT** *(= peddle)* colporter ; *(in street)* crier *(des marchandises)*

hawker /ˈhɔːkəʳ/ **N** *(street)* colporteur *m* ; *(door-to-door)* démarcheur *m*, -euse *f*

Hawkeye /ˈhɔːkaɪ/ **N** *(US)* habitant(e) *m(f)* de l'Iowa **COMP** **the Hawkeye State** **N** l'Iowa *m*

hawkish /ˈhɔːkɪʃ/ **ADJ** belliciste

hawser /ˈhɔːzəʳ/ **N** haussière or aussière *f*

hawthorn /ˈhɔːθɔːn/ **N** aubépine *f*

hay /heɪ/ **N** foin *m* ◆ **to make ~** *(Agr)* faner, faire les foins ◆ **to make ~ while the sun shines** *(Prov)* ≈ battre le fer pendant qu'il est chaud ◆ **to make ~ of** * *(argument)* démolir * ; *(enemy, team)* battre à plate(s) couture(s) ◆ **that ain't ~** ⁑ *(US fig)* c'est pas rien * ; → **hit, roll**
COMP **hay fever** **N** rhume *m* des foins
hay fork **N** fourche *f* à foin

haycock /ˈheɪkɒk/ **N** meulon *m* (de foin)

hayloft /ˈheɪlɒft/ **N** grenier *m* à foin, fenil *m*

haymaker /ˈheɪmeɪkəʳ/ **N** *(= worker)* faneur *m*, -euse *f* ; *(Boxing) (= blow)* uppercut *m* magistral

haymaking /ˈheɪmeɪkɪŋ/ **N** fenaison *f*, foins *mpl*

hayrick /ˈheɪrɪk/ **N** ⇒ **haystack**

hayride /ˈheɪraɪd/ **N** *(esp US) promenade dans une charrette de foin*

hayseed ⁑ /ˈheɪsiːd/ **N** *(US pej)* péquenaud ⁑ *m*

haystack /ˈheɪstæk/ **N** meule *f* de foin

haywire * /ˈheɪwaɪəʳ/ **ADJ** ◆ **to go ~** *[person]* perdre la tête or la boule * ; *[plans]* être perturbé ; *[equipment etc]* se détraquer

hazard /ˈhæzəd/ **N** 1 *(= risk)* risque *m* ; *(stronger)* danger *m*, péril *m* ◆ **natural ~s** risques *mpl* naturels ◆ **to be a safety ~** constituer un danger, être dangereux ◆ **to pose a ~ (to sb/sth)** présenter un risque (pour qn/qch) ◆ **this waste is an environmental ~** ces déchets présentent un risque pour l'environnement ◆ **pesticides posed the greatest ~ to health** les pesticides présentaient le plus gros risque pour la santé ; → **fire, health, occupational**
2 *(= chance)* hasard *m*
3 *(Golf etc)* obstacle *m* naturel, hazard *m*
VT 1 *(= venture to make) [+ remark, forecast]* hasarder ◆ **to ~ a suggestion** hasarder une proposition ◆ **to ~ an attempt** risquer une tentative ◆ **to ~ a guess** hasarder une hypothèse ◆ **she ~ed a guess that ...** elle a hasardé l'hypothèse que ... ◆ **"I could do it," she ~ed** "je pourrais le faire," se risqua-t-elle à dire
2 *(= risk) [+ life, reputation, one's fortune]* risquer ; *(= endanger)* mettre en danger
COMP **hazard (warning) lights** **NPL** feux *mpl* de détresse, warning *mpl*

> ⚠ When it means 'danger' **hazard** is not translated by **hasard**.

hazardous /ˈhæzədəs/ **ADJ** dangereux *(to or for sb/sth* pour qn/qch) **COMP** **hazardous waste** **N** déchets *mpl* dangereux

haze¹ /heɪz/ **N** brume *f* (légère) ◆ **a ~ of cigarette smoke filled the room** de la fumée de cigarette emplissait la pièce ◆ **a ~ of dust** un nuage de poussière ◆ **to be in a ~** *(fig)* être dans le brouillard ◆ **in a ~ of alcohol** dans les brumes de l'alcool ; → **heat**

haze² /heɪz/ **VT** *(US Univ)* bizuter

hazel /ˈheɪzl/ **N** *(= tree)* noisetier *m*, coudrier *m* **ADJ** *(colour)* (couleur) noisette *inv* ◆ **~ eyes** yeux *mpl* (couleur) noisette
COMP **hazel grouse** **N** gélinotte *f* (des bois)
hazel grove **N** coudraie *f*

hazelnut /ˈheɪzlnʌt/ **N** noisette *f*

hazelwood /ˈheɪzlwʊd/ **N** (bois *m* de) noisetier *m*

haziness /ˈheɪzɪnɪs/ **N** 1 *(= mist)* brume *f* 2 *(= lack of clarity) [of ideas, memory]* flou *m*, manque *m* de précision

hazing /ˈheɪzɪŋ/ **N** *(US Univ)* bizutage *m*

hazy /ˈheɪzɪ/ **ADJ** 1 *(= misty) [sunshine, sun]* voilé ; *[day, sky]* brumeux ; *[view] (with mist)* brumeux ; *(with heat, vapour, dust)* flou ◆ **it's very ~ today** *(with mist)* il y a beaucoup de brume aujourd'hui ; *(with vapour, heat, dust)* l'air est vaporeux aujourd'hui ◆ **~ blue** bleu pastel *inv* 2 *(= indistinct) [outline, vision, details]* flou ; *[notion, idea, memory]* vague ◆ **to be ~ about sth** *[person]* n'avoir qu'une vague idée de qch

HDD **N** *(Comput)* (abbrev of **hard disk drive**) → **hard**

HDTV **N** (abbrev of **high definition television**) TVHD *f*

HE /ˌeɪtʃˈiː/ 1 (abbrev of **His** or **Her Excellency**) SE 2 (abbrev of **high explosive**) → **high**

he /hiː/ **PERS PRON** 1 *(unstressed)* il ; *(Rel)* **He** Il ◆ **~ has come** il est venu ◆ **here ~ is** le voici ◆ **~ is a doctor** il est médecin, c'est un médecin ◆ **~ is a small man** c'est un homme petit 2 *(stressed)* lui ; *(Rel)* Lui ◆ **it is ~** *(frm)* c'est lui ◆ **if I were ~** *(frm)* si j'étais lui, si j'étais à sa place ◆ **younger than ~** *(frm)* plus jeune que lui ◆ **HE didn't do it** ce n'est pas lui qui l'a fait 3 *(+ rel pron)* celui ◆ **~ who or that can** celui qui peut **N** 1 * mâle *m* ◆ **it's a ~** *(animal)* c'est un mâle ; *(baby)* c'est un garçon 2 *(Scol)* ◆ **you're ~ !** * (c'est toi le) chat !
COMP mâle **he-bear** **N** ours *m* mâle
he-goat **N** bouc *m*
he-man * **N** (pl **he-men**) (vrai) mâle *m*, macho * *m*

head /hed/

1 NOUN	4 COMPOUNDS
2 TRANSITIVE VERB	5 PHRASAL VERB
3 INTRANSITIVE VERB	

1 - NOUN

1 Anat tête *f* ◆ **to hit sb on the ~** frapper qn à la tête ◆ **~ down** *(= upside down)* la tête en bas ; *(= looking down)* la tête baissée ◆ **to keep one's ~ down** * *(= avoid trouble)* garder un profil bas ; *(= work hard)* travailler dur ◆ **~ hanging** la tête baissée ◆ **~ downwards** la tête en bas ◆ **~ first, ~ foremost** la tête la première ◆ **my ~ aches, I've got a bad ~** * j'ai mal à la tête or au crâne * ◆ **I've got a bit of a ~** * j'ai un peu mal au crâne * ◆ **~ of hair** chevelure *f* ◆ **to stand on one's ~** faire le poirier ◆ **I could do it standing on my ~** c'est simple comme bonjour ◆ **to stand or turn sth on its ~** prendre le contre-pied de qch ◆ **she is a ~ taller than her sister, she is taller than her sister by a ~** elle dépasse sa sœur d'une tête ◆ **to win by a (short) ~** *[horse]* gagner d'une (courte) tête ◆ **to give a horse its ~** lâcher la bride à un cheval ◆ **to give sb his ~** lâcher la bride à qn ◆ **to give (sb) ~** *⁑ *(esp US)* tailler une pipe *⁑ (à qn) ◆ **to keep one's ~ above water** *(lit)* garder la tête au-dessus de l'eau ; *(fig)* se maintenir à flot ◆ **to have a big or swollen ~** *(fig)* avoir la grosse tête * ◆ **to put or lay one's ~ on the block** *(fig)* risquer gros ◆ **it's completely above my ~** *(fig)* cela me dépasse complètement ◆ **to get in or be in over one's ~** * être complètement dépassé ◆ **he gave orders over my ~** il a donné des ordres sans me consulter ◆ **he went over my ~ to the director** il m'a court-circuité et est allé voir le directeur ◆ **his ideas went right over my ~** ses idées me dépassaient complètement ◆ **he's got his ~ in the sand** il pratique la politique de l'autruche ◆ **to have one's ~ up one's arse** *⁑ *(Brit = be confused)* dérailler * ◆ **to have one's ~ up one's ass** *⁑ *(US = be heedless)* marcher à côté de ses pompes ⁑ ◆ **he was talking his ~ off** * il n'arrêtait pas de parler ◆ **to sing/shout one's ~ off** * chanter/crier à tue-tête ◆ **to laugh one's ~ off** rire aux éclats or à gorge déployée ◆ **on your own ~ be it!** à vos risques et périls ! ◆ **~ to wind** *(Naut)* vent debout ◆ **~ on** ⇒ **head-on**

◆ **a head, per head** par tête ◆ **they paid €5 a ~ or per ~** ils ont payé 5 € par tête

◆ **from head to foot** or **toe** de la tête aux pieds ◆ **covered from ~ to foot or toe in mud** couvert de boue de la tête aux pieds ◆ **he was dressed in black from ~ to foot or toe** il était habillé en noir de la tête aux pieds ◆ **he was trembling from ~ to foot** il tremblait de tout son corps

◆ **head and shoulders** ◆ **he stands ~ and shoulders above everybody else** *(lit)* il dépasse tout le monde d'une tête ; *(fig)* il surpasse tout le monde ◆ **she is ~ and shoulders above her sister in maths** elle est cent fois meilleure que sa sœur en maths

◆ **head over heels** ◆ **to turn or go ~ over heels** *(accidentally)* faire la culbute ; *(on purpose)* faire une galipette ◆ **to be/fall ~ over heels in love with sb** être/tomber follement or éperdument amoureux de qn

2 = mind, intellect tête *f* ◆ **weak or soft** * **in the ~** un peu demeuré * ◆ **to count in one's ~** calculer mentalement or de tête ◆ **I can't do it in my ~** je ne peux pas faire or calculer ça de tête ◆ **to get sth into one's ~** * s'enfoncer or se mettre qch dans la tête ◆ **I wish he would get it into his ~** * **that ...** j'aimerais qu'il se mette dans la tête que ... ◆ **I can't get that into his ~** * je ne peux pas lui mettre ça dans la tête ◆ **he has taken it into his ~ that ...** il s'est mis dans la tête que ... ◆ **to take it into one's ~ to do sth** se mettre en tête de or s'aviser de faire qch ◆ **it didn't enter his ~ to do it** il ne lui est pas venu à l'idée or à l'esprit de le faire ◆ **you never know what's going on in his ~** on ne sait jamais ce qui lui passe par la tête ◆ **what put that (idea) into his ~?** qu'est-ce qui lui a mis cette idée-là dans la tête ? ◆ **that tune has been running through my ~ all day** j'ai eu cet air dans la tête or cet air m'a trotté dans la tête toute la journée ◆ **she's got her ~ screwed on (right)** * elle a la tête sur les épaules ◆ **two ~s are better than one** deux avis valent mieux qu'un ◆ **we put our ~s together** * nous y avons réfléchi ensemble ◆ **don't bother or worry your ~ about it** * ne vous en faites pas pour cela ◆ **to keep one's ~** garder son sang-froid ◆ **to lose one's ~** perdre la tête ◆ **he has no ~ for heights** il a le vertige ◆ **the wine/his success went to his ~** le vin/son succès lui est monté à la tête ◆ **he has gone or he is off his ~** * il a perdu la boule * ◆ **to get one's ~ together or straight** * reprendre le dessus ◆ **to get one's ~ round sth** * *(= understand)* piger * qch ; *(= come to accept)* accepter qch ◆ **it does my ~ in** * ça me prend la tête *

◆ **a (good) head (for)** ◆ **she has a good ~ for figures** elle a des dispositions pour or elle est douée pour le calcul ◆ **she has a good ~ for heights** elle n'a jamais le vertige ◆ **she has a good business ~** elle a le sens des affaires ◆ **she has a good ~ on her shoulders** elle a de la tête

◆ **out of one's head** ◆ **I can't get it out of my ~** je ne peux pas me sortir ça de la tête, ça me trotte dans la tête ◆ **he couldn't get her out of his ~** il ne pouvait pas s'empêcher de penser à elle ◆ **his name has gone out of my ~** son nom m'est sorti de la tête or de la mémoire ◆ **it's gone right out of my ~** ça m'est tout à fait sorti de la tête ◆ **to be out of one's ~** * *(= mad)* être cinglé * or dingue * ; *(= drunk)* être bituré * or pété * ; *(= high on drugs)* être défoncé * or pété *

3 of cattle (*pl inv*) ◆ **20 ~ of cattle** 20 têtes *fpl or* pièces *fpl* de bétail ◆ **20 ~ of oxen** 20 bœufs *mpl*

4 specific part [*of flower, nail, pin, hammer, mast*] tête *f* ; [*of arrow*] pointe *f* ; [*of spear*] fer *m* ; [*of cane*] pommeau *m* ; [*of bed*] chevet *m*, tête *f* ; [*of violin*] crosse *f* ; (*on beer*) mousse *f*, faux col * *m* ; (*on tape recorder*) tête *f* (*de lecture, d'enregistrement*)

5 = top end [*of page, staircase*] haut *m* ; [*of pillar*] chapiteau *m* ; [*of jetty, pier*] extrémité *f* ◆ **at the ~ of** (*lake, valley*) à l'extrémité de ; (*table*) au (haut †) bout de ; (*procession*) en tête de ; (*fig = in charge of: army, organization, company*) à la tête de ◆ **at the ~ of the list/the queue** en tête de liste/de file ◆ **to be at the ~ of the field** *or* **pack** (*Sport*) mener la course

6 of vegetable [*of lettuce, cabbage*] pomme *f* ; [*of celery*] pied *m*

7 of abscess, pimple tête *f* ◆ **it's coming to a ~** [*abscess, pimple*] ça mûrit ; (*fig, gen*) ça devient critique ◆ **it all came to a ~ when he met her yesterday** les choses sont arrivées au point critique quand il l'a rencontrée hier ◆ **to bring things to a ~** précipiter les choses

8 = leader chef *m* ◆ **~ of department** [*of company*] chef *m* de service ; [*of shop*] chef *m* de rayon ; see also **9** ◆ **~ of state** chef *m* d'État ◆ **the ~ of the government** le chef du gouvernement ◆ **the ~ of the family** le chef de famille

9 Brit Scol ⇒ **headmaster** *or* **headmistress** ◆ **~ of French/Maths** *etc* (*Scol*) ≈ professeur *m* coordinateur de français/de maths *etc* ◆ **~ of department** [*of school, college*] professeur *mf* responsable de département

10 = title titre *m* ; (= *subject heading*) rubrique *f* ◆ **under this ~** sous ce titre *or* cette rubrique

11 of coin face *f* ◆ **to toss ~s or tails** jouer à pile ou face ◆ **~s or tails?** pile ou face ? ◆ **~s I win!** face je gagne ! ◆ **he called ~s** il a annoncé "face" ◆ **I can't make ~ (n)or tail of what he's saying** je ne comprends rien à ce qu'il dit ◆ **I can't make ~ (n)or tail of it** je n'y comprends rien

12 Drugs * → **acid**

13 Comput tête *f* ◆ **reading/writing ~** tête *f* de lecture/d'écriture

2 - TRANSITIVE VERB

1 + group of people être à la tête de ; [*+ procession, list, poll*] venir *or* être en tête de ◆ **Dr Grey ~s our research team** le docteur Grey est à la tête de notre équipe de chercheurs ◆ **a coalition government ~ed by the former opposition leader** un gouvernement de coalition dirigé par l'ancien leader de l'opposition

2 = direct **he got in the car and ~ed it towards town** il est monté dans la voiture et a pris la direction de *or* il s'est dirigé vers la ville ◆ **to ~ a ship for port** mettre le cap sur le port

3 = put at head of [*+ chapter*] intituler ◆ **to ~ a chapter/a letter** *etc* **with sth** mettre qch en tête d'un chapitre/d'une lettre *etc*

4 Ftbl **to ~ the ball** faire une tête

3 - INTRANSITIVE VERB

1 = go, move **to ~ for** *or* **towards, to be ~ed for** *or* **towards** [*person, vehicle*] se diriger vers ; [*ship*] mettre le cap sur ◆ **he ~ed up the hill** il s'est mis à monter la colline ◆ **he was ~ing home(wards)** il était sur le chemin du retour ◆ **they were ~ing back to town** ils rentraient *or* retournaient à la ville ◆ **he's ~ing for a disappointment** il va vers une déception ◆ **he's ~ing for trouble** il va avoir des ennuis ◆ **they're ~ing for victory** ils sont bien partis pour gagner ◆ **they're ~ing straight for disaster** ils vont droit au désastre

2 * = head off, leave mettre les voiles *

4 - COMPOUNDS

[*buyer, assistant etc*] principal

head-banger * **N** (= *heavy metal fan*) enragé(e) * *m(f)* de heavy metal ; (= *mad person*) cinglé(e) * *m(f)*

head boy N (*Brit Scol*) *élève de terminale chargé d'un certain nombre de responsabilités*

head clerk N (*Comm*) premier commis *m*, chef *m* de bureau ; (*Jur*) principal *m*

head cold N rhume *m* de cerveau

head gardener N jardinier *m* en chef

head girl N (*Brit Scol*) *élève de terminale chargée d'un certain nombre de responsabilités*

head-guard N (*Sport*) casque *m* de protection

head height N ◆ **at ~ height** à hauteur d'homme

head lad N (*Racing*) premier garçon *m*

head nurse N (*US*) infirmier *m*, -ière *f* en chef

head office N siège *m* social, agence *f* centrale

head of steam N pression *f* ◆ **to build up** *or* **work up a ~ of steam** (*fig*) (= *get worked up*) se mettre dans tous ses états ; (= *build momentum*) [*movement*] prendre de l'ampleur ◆ **to get** *or* **build up a ~ of steam for sth** (*fig*) obtenir un ferme soutien pour qch

head of water N colonne *f* d'eau, hauteur *f* de chute

head-on ADV [*confront, tackle, meet*] de front ◆ **to collide** *or* **crash ~-on** se heurter de plein fouet ◆ **to collide ~-on with sth, to crash ~-on into sth** heurter qch de plein fouet **ADJ** [*smash, collision*] frontal ; [*conflict, clash, confrontation*] direct

head post office N bureau *m* central des postes, poste *f* principale

head restraint N ⇒ **headrest**

head shop N (*US*) boutique *f* hippie

head start N (*fig*) ◆ **to have a ~ start** être avantagé dès le départ (*over or on sb* par rapport à qn)

head teacher N (*Brit Scol*) ⇒ **headmaster** *or* **headmistress**

head to head ADV ◆ **to compete ~ to ~ with sb** affronter directement qn ; (*Comm*) être en concurrence directe avec qn

head-to-head ADJ [*contest, competition*] direct **N** affrontement *m* direct

head waiter N maître *m* d'hôtel

5 - PHRASAL VERB

► **head off VI** partir (*for* pour ; *towards* vers) ◆ **he ~ed off onto the subject of …** il est passé à la question de … **VT SEP** [*+ enemy*] forcer à se rabattre ; [*+ person*] (*lit*) détourner de son chemin ; (*fig*) détourner (*from* de) ; [*+ questions*] parer, faire dévier

► **head up VT FUS** [*+ organization, team*] diriger

headache /ˈhedeɪk/ **N** 1 (*lit*) mal *m* de tête ◆ **to have a ~** avoir mal à la tête ◆ **he suffers from terrible ~s** il souffre de terribles maux de tête 2 (*fig*) problème *m* ◆ **at least that's not my ~** au moins ce n'est pas mon problème ◆ **it was a real ~** ça n'a pas été une mince affaire ◆ **the decision created a major ~ for the Government** cette décision a sérieusement compliqué la tâche du gouvernement ◆ **his teenage daughter is a real ~** sa fille est une adolescente impossible

headband /ˈhedbænd/ **N** bandeau *m*

headboard /ˈhedbɔːd/ **N** [*of bed*] tête *f* de lit

headbutt /ˈhedbʌt/ **N** coup *m* de tête **VT** donner un coup de tête à

headcase * /ˈhedkeɪs/ **N** cinglé(e) * *m(f)*

headcheese /ˈhedtʃiːz/ **N** (*US*) fromage *m* de tête

headcount /ˈhedkaʊnt/ **N** 1 (= *count*) comptage *m*, vérification *f* du nombre de personnes présentes ◆ **let's do a ~** comptons-les, comptons combien ils sont 2 (= *number of employees*) nombre *m* d'employés

headdress /ˈheddres/ **N** (*of lace*) coiffe *f* ; (*of feathers*) coiffure *f*

headed /ˈhedɪd/ **ADJ** (*Brit*) ◆ **~ writing paper** *or* **notepaper** papier *m* à lettres à en-tête

-headed /ˈhedɪd/ **ADJ** (*in compounds*) ◆ **bare-headed** nu-tête *inv* ◆ **curly-headed** frisé, aux cheveux frisés ; → **hard**

header /ˈhedəʳ/ **N** 1 * (= *dive*) plongeon *m* ; (= *fall*) chute *f or* plongeon *m* (la tête la première) ◆ **to take a ~** (= *fall*) tomber par terre la tête la première ◆ **to take** *or* **do a ~ into the water** piquer une tête dans l'eau ◆ **the dollar took a ~ in share trading today** le dollar a chuté en Bourse aujourd'hui 2 (*Ftbl*) tête *f* 3 (*Constr*) boutisse *f* 4 (*Comput*) en-tête *m*

headfirst /ˌhedˈfɜːst/ **ADV** (*lit*) la tête la première ◆ **she rushed ~ into marriage** (*fig*) elle s'est précipitée dans le mariage

headgear /ˈhedgɪəʳ/ **N** (*NonC*) 1 (= *hat*) chapeau *m* ; (= *cap*) casquette *f* ◆ **she was wearing the most outrageous ~** elle portait un chapeau des plus extravagants ◆ **protective ~** (*for policeman*) casque *m* ; (= *riding hat*) bombe *f* 2 (= *part of costume*) coiffure *f* ◆ **the men of the tribe wear brightly-coloured ~** les hommes de la tribu portent des coiffures très colorées ◆ **she was wearing elaborate Egyptian-style ~** elle portait une coiffure très élaborée, de style égyptien

headhunt /ˈhedhʌnt/ **VI** (*fig*) recruter des cadres pour une entreprise **VT** recruter ◆ **she has been ~ed by several firms** plusieurs entreprises ont essayé de la recruter

headhunter /ˈhedhʌntəʳ/ **N** (*lit*) chasseur *m* de têtes ; (*fig*) (*in recruiting personnel*) chasseur *m* de têtes, recruteur *m* de cadres

headhunting /ˈhedhʌntɪŋ/ **N** chasse *f* de têtes

headiness /ˈhedɪnɪs/ **N** 1 (= *strength*) [*of wine*] goût *m* capiteux ◆ **the ~ of her perfume was almost intoxicating** son parfum capiteux était presque enivrant 2 (= *exhilaration*) exaltation *f* ◆ **the ~ of the unknown** l'exaltation de l'inconnu

heading /ˈhedɪŋ/ **N** (= *title: at top of page, chapter, article, column of figures*) titre *m* ; (= *subject title*) rubrique *f* ; (*printed: on letter, document*) en-tête *m* ◆ **chapter ~** (*gen*) tête *f* de chapitre ; (= *title*) titre *m* ◆ **under this ~** sous ce titre *or* cette rubrique ◆ **this comes under the ~ of …** c'est sous la rubrique … ◆ **under the ~ of "Science" may be found …** sous la rubrique "Sciences" on peut trouver … ◆ **the essay was divided into several ~s** la dissertation était divisée en plusieurs chapitres ; → **tariff**

headlamp /ˈhedlæmp/ **N** ⇒ **headlight**

headland /ˈhedlənd/ **N** promontoire *m*, cap *m*

headless /ˈhedlɪs/ **ADJ** [*body, nail*] sans tête ; [*organism*] acéphale ; → **chicken**

headlight /ˈhedlaɪt/ **N** (*Brit*) [*of car*] phare *m* ; [*of train*] fanal *m*, feu *m* avant

headline /ˈhedlaɪn/ **N** [*of newspaper*] gros titre *m* ; (*Rad, TV*) grand titre *m* ◆ **it's in the ~s in the papers** c'est en gros titre *or* en manchette dans les journaux ◆ **the ~s were full of the story** cette histoire faisait les gros titres *or* la une de tous les journaux ◆ **to hit the ~s** * [*story, person*] faire les gros titres *or* la une ; [*scandal, crime etc*] défrayer la chronique ◆ **the story never made the ~s** cette histoire n'a jamais fait les gros titres *or* la une ◆ **have you seen the ~s?** as-tu vu les (gros) titres ? ◆ **here are the news ~s** (*Rad, TV*) voici les titres de l'actualité *or* de notre journal ◆ **here are the ~s again** et maintenant le rappel des titres ◆ **I only heard the ~s** je n'ai entendu que les (grands) titres

VT 1 [*+ story*] mettre en manchette ◆ **a story ~d "Fraud in high places"** un article intitulé "Fraude en haut lieu"

2 [+ festival, event] être en tête de l'affiche de ◆ **his ambition was to ~ the Albert Hall before he was 30** son ambition était d'être en tête d'affiche à l'Albert Hall avant ses 30 ans
VI être en tête d'affiche
COMP **headline news** N ◆ **to be** *or* **make ~ news** faire les gros titres
headline rate of inflation N (Econ) *l'indice des prix prenant notamment en compte les taux d'intérêt des emprunts logement*

headliner* /ˈhedlaɪnəʳ/ N (US Mus, Theat) vedette *f*

headlock /ˈhedlɒk/ N ◆ **to get/have sb in a ~** cravater qn/avoir cravaté qn

headlong /ˈhedlɒŋ/ ADV (lit, fig) [run, rush, plunge] tête baissée ◆ **she fell ~ down the stairs** elle est tombée la tête la première dans les escaliers ◆ **avoid rushing ~ into another relationship** évitez de vous précipiter tête baissée dans une nouvelle liaison ADJ (lit, fig) [fall] vertigineux ◆ ~ **dash** *or* **rush** ruée *f* ◆ **they made a ~ dash for the door** ils se sont rués vers la porte ◆ **the army was in ~ flight** l'armée était en pleine débandade

headman /ˈhedmən/ N (pl **-men**) chef *m* (d'une tribu etc)

headmaster /ˈhedmɑːstəʳ/ N (Brit gen) directeur *m* ; [of French lycée] proviseur *m* ; [of college] principal *m* ; (US Scol) directeur *m* d'école privée

headmistress /ˈhedmɪstrɪs/ N (Brit gen) directrice *f* ; [of French lycée] proviseur *m* ; [of college] principale *f* ; (US Scol) directrice *f* d'école privée

head-on /ˈhedˈɒn/ ADV ◆ **to confront** *or* **meet** *or* **tackle ~** [+ problem, issue] attaquer *or* aborder de front ; [+ enemies] attaquer de front ; [+ criticism, threat] faire face à ◆ **to collide** *or* **crash** *or* **meet ~** se heurter de plein fouet ◆ **to collide ~ with sth, to crash ~ into sth** heurter qch de plein fouet ADJ [smash, collision] frontal ; [conflict, clash, confrontation] direct

headphones /ˈhedfəʊnz/ NPL casque *m* (à écouteurs)

headquarter /ˈhedkwɔːtəʳ/ VT ◆ **the company is ~ed in Chicago** la société a son siège à Chicago

headquarters /ˈhedkwɔːtəz/ NPL [of bank, company, political party] siège *m* ; (Mil) quartier *m* général COMP **headquarters staff** N (Mil) état-major *m*

headrest /ˈhedrest/ N appui-tête *m*, repose-tête *m*

headroom /ˈhedrʊm/ N (in vehicle) hauteur *f* de l'habitacle ◆ **there is not enough ~** (gen) le plafond est trop bas *or* n'est pas assez haut ◆ **have you got enough ~?** vous avez assez d'espace (en hauteur) ? ◆ **"5 metres headroom"** (on roadsign) "hauteur limite : 5 mètres" ◆ **there is standing ~ throughout** (on boat) on peut se tenir debout partout ◆ **there is sitting ~ only** (on boat) on ne tient qu'assis

headscarf /ˈhedskɑːf/ N foulard *m*

headset /ˈhedset/ N ⇒ **headphones**

headship /ˈhedʃɪp/ N (= post) poste *m* de directeur ◆ **under the ~ of Mr Winfield** sous la direction de M. Winfield

headshrinker* /ˈhedʃrɪŋkəʳ/ N psy* *mf*

headsman † /ˈhedzmən/ N (pl **-men**) bourreau *m*

headsquare /ˈhedskweəʳ/ N foulard *m*

headstand /ˈhedstænd/ N ◆ **to do a ~** faire le poirier

headstone /ˈhedstəʊn/ N 1 [of grave] pierre *f* tombale 2 (Archit) clef *f* de voûte, pierre *f* angulaire

headstrong /ˈhedstrɒŋ/ ADJ (= obstinate) têtu ; (= rash) impétueux

headwaters /ˈhedwɔːtəz/ NPL sources *fpl*

headway /ˈhedweɪ/ N progrès *m* ◆ **to make ~** (in journey, studies etc) avancer, faire des progrès ; [ship] faire route ◆ **I didn't make much ~ with him** je n'ai pas fait beaucoup de progrès avec lui

headwind /ˈhedwɪnd/ N vent *m* contraire ; (Naut) vent *m* debout

headword /ˈhedwɜːd/ N entrée *f*, adresse *f*

heady /ˈhedɪ/ ADJ [scent, wine] capiteux ; [days, experience, atmosphere, brew, mixture] grisant ◆ **the ~ delights of ...** les plaisirs grisants de ... ◆ **the ~ heights of ...** les sommets vertigineux de ... ◆ **it's ~ stuff*** **(for sb)** c'est grisant (pour qn) ◆ **to be ~ with success** être grisé par le succès ◆ **the air was ~ with spices** les épices rendaient l'air enivrant

heal /hiːl/ VI (also **heal over, heal up**) [wound] se cicatriser VT [+ person] guérir (of de) ; [+ wound] cicatriser ; (fig) [+ differences] régler ; [+ troubles] apaiser ◆ **time will ~ the pain** votre chagrin s'estompera avec le temps ◆ **to ~ the breach** (fig) combler le fossé, effectuer une réconciliation

healer /ˈhiːləʳ/ N guérisseur *m*, -euse *f* ; → **faith**

healing /ˈhiːlɪŋ/ N [of person] guérison *f* ; [of wound] cicatrisation *f* ADJ [ointment] cicatrisant ; [properties] médicinal, curatif ; [powers] de guérison ; [words] apaisant ◆ **the ~ process** le processus de guérison ◆ **to have ~ hands** avoir des talents de guérisseur

health /helθ/ N santé *f* ◆ **in good/poor ~** en bonne/mauvaise santé ◆ **poverty can cause poor ~** la pauvreté peut être la cause de problèmes de santé ◆ **he suffers from poor ~** il est en mauvaise santé ◆ **to have ~ problems** avoir des problèmes de santé ◆ **the ~ benefits of a vegetarian diet** les effets bénéfiques pour la santé d'un régime végétarien ; see also **comp** ◆ **to regain one's ~** recouvrer la santé, guérir ◆ **the ~ of the economy** la santé de l'économie ◆ **to drink (to) sb's ~** boire à la santé de qn ◆ **your ~!, good ~!** à votre santé ! ◆ **Department of/Secretary of State for Health and Social Security** (Brit: formerly) ◆ **Department/Secretary of Health and Human Services** (US) ministère *m*/ministre *m* de la Santé et des Affaires sociales ◆ **Department of Health** (Brit) ≈ ministère *m* de la Santé ; → **national, restore**
COMP **the Health and Safety Executive** N (Brit) ≈ l'inspection *f* du travail
Health Authority N (Brit) administration *f* régionale de la santé publique
health benefits NPL (Admin) prestations *fpl* maladie
health care N (= services) services *mpl* de santé ; (= treatment) soins *mpl* médicaux ◆ **the ~ care system** le système de santé publique ◆ **the ~ care industry** le secteur médical ◆ **~ care benefits** prestations *fpl* de santé
health care worker N membre *m* du personnel soignant
health centre N ≈ centre *m* médicosocial
health check N visite *f* médicale ; (more thorough) bilan *m* de santé
health club N club *m* de (re)mise en forme
health education N (Scol) hygiène *f*
health farm N établissement *m* de remise en forme
health foods NPL aliments *mpl* diététiques
health food shop, health food store (US) N magasin *m* or boutique *f* de produits diététiques
health-giving ADJ → **healthful**
health hazard N risque *m* pour la santé
health insurance N assurance *f* maladie
health maintenance organization N (US) *organisme médical privé*
health officer N inspecteur *m*, -trice *f* de la santé (publique)
health resort N (= spa town) station *f* thermale, ville *f* d'eaux ; (in mountains) station *f* climatique
health risk N ⇒ **health hazard**
Health Service N (Brit) → NHS ◆ **I got my glasses on the Health Service** ≈ la Sécurité sociale m'a remboursé mes lunettes
health service N (US Univ) infirmerie *f*
Health Service doctor N (Brit) ≈ médecin *m* conventionné
health spa N centre *m* de cure, station *f* thermale
health visitor N (Brit) ≈ infirmière *f* visiteuse
health warning N (on cigarette packet) *mise en garde du ministère de la Santé*

HEALTH MAINTENANCE ORGANIZATION

Aux États-Unis, les **health maintenance organizations** sont des organismes privés qui dispensent des soins médicaux (y compris hospitaliers) à leurs adhérents. Dans une volonté de maîtrise des coûts, ces organismes insistent sur la médecine préventive et obligent à consulter des médecins agréés. En ce sens, ils diffèrent des assurances médicales privées avec lesquelles on les assimile parfois.

healthful /ˈhelθfʊl/ ADJ sain

healthily /ˈhelθɪlɪ/ ADV [live, eat, grow] sainement ◆ **a recipe which is ~ low in fat** une recette saine du fait de sa faible teneur en graisses ◆ **~ cynical/irreverent** d'un cynisme/d'une irrévérence salutaire ◆ **to be ~ contemptuous of sth** montrer un mépris sain de qch ◆ **to be ~ sceptical of sth** faire preuve d'un scepticisme salutaire à l'égard de qch

healthy /ˈhelθɪ/ ADJ 1 (= in good health) [person, animal, plant] en bonne santé ; [body, skin, hair, cell, sexuality] sain ; [appetite] solide ◆ **he is very ~** il est en très bonne santé ◆ **to stay ~** rester en bonne santé ◆ **her skin/she had a ~ glow** sa peau/elle éclatait de santé ◆ **a ~ mind in a ~ body** un esprit sain dans un corps sain
2 (fig = thriving) [economy, bank, relationship] sain ; [bank account] bien approvisionné ◆ **to make** *or* **earn a ~ living** gagner confortablement sa vie
3 (= health-giving) [food, lifestyle, attitude] sain ; [climate, air] salubre ; [exercise] bon pour la santé, salutaire ◆ **to have a ~ diet** manger sainement ◆ **~ eating** une alimentation saine ◆ **advice on ~ living** conseils *mpl* pour vivre sainement
4 (= wholesome, desirable) [profit] substantiel ; [scepticism] salutaire, de bon aloi ; [doubts] légitime ◆ **to have a ~ respect for sb/sth** apprécier qn/qch à sa juste valeur ◆ **the economy is showing ~ growth** l'économie connaît une croissance équilibrée ◆ **a ~ dose of caution/scepticism** une bonne dose de prudence/scepticisme ◆ **his interest in this is not very ~** l'intérêt qu'il y porte n'est pas très sain

heap /hiːp/ N 1 tas *m* ◆ **in a ~** en tas ◆ **to collapse/fall in a ~** [person] s'effondrer/tomber comme une masse ◆ **to be at the top/the bottom of the ~** (fig) être en haut/en bas de l'échelle
2 (* fig) tas* *m*, masse* *f* ◆ **~s of** (money, people, ideas) des tas* de ◆ **she has ~s of enthusiasm** elle déborde d'enthousiasme ◆ **they got ~s of criticism for this decision** ils ont été très critiqués pour cette décision ◆ **we've got ~s of time** nous avons largement le temps, nous avons tout notre temps ◆ **~s of times** des tas* de fois, mille fois ◆ **to have ~s of** *or* **a whole ~ of things to do** avoir un tas* *or* des masses* de choses à faire ◆ **~s better** drôlement* mieux

◆ **(to be in) a whole ~ of trouble** (avoir) tout un tas * d'ennuis ◆ **the news struck him all of a ~** ⁑ la nouvelle lui a coupé bras et jambes *or* l'a éberlué * ◆ **he was struck all of a ~** ⁑ il en est resté baba *

3 (⁑ = *car*) tas *m* de ferraille *

VT 1 ⇒ **heap up**

2 *(fig)* ◆ **to ~ gifts on sb** couvrir qn de cadeaux ◆ **to ~ favours on sb** combler qn de faveurs ◆ **to ~ praise on sb** couvrir qn d'éloges ◆ **to ~ abuse/scorn on sb** accabler *or* couvrir qn d'injures/de mépris ◆ **to ~ work on sb** accabler qn de travail ◆ **to ~ coals of fire on sb's head** rendre le bien pour le mal à qn

► **heap up** **VT SEP** empiler ◆ **to ~ sth up on top of sth** empiler *or* entasser qch sur qch ◆ **she ~ed her plate up with cakes** elle a empilé des gâteaux sur son assiette, elle a chargé son assiette de gâteaux

heaped /hiːpt/ **ADJ** 1 *[basket]* très chargé ◆ **shelves ~ with piles of old books** des étagères croulant sous des piles de vieux livres ◆ **a sofa ~ with cushions** un canapé où s'entassent des coussins *or* disparaissant sous les coussins 2 *(Culin)* **a ~ spoonful** une grosse cuillerée ◆ **a ~ teaspoonful** une cuiller à café bien pleine

heaping /hiːpɪŋ/ **ADJ** *(US)* ⇒ **heaped 2**

hear /hɪəʳ/ **LANGUAGE IN USE 21.1** (pret, ptp **heard**)

VT 1 entendre ◆ **did you ~ what he said?** avez-vous entendu ce qu'il a dit ? ◆ **can you ~ him?** vous l'entendez (bien) ? ◆ **I can't ~ you!** je ne vous entends pas ! ◆ **I ~ you speaking** je vous entends parler ◆ **you're not going, do you ~ (me)?** tu n'iras pas, tu m'entends ? ◆ **I ~ you** (= *understand*) je comprends ◆ **I heard him say that ...** je l'ai entendu dire que ... ◆ **I heard someone come in** j'ai entendu entrer quelqu'un *or* quelqu'un entrer ◆ **a noise was heard** un bruit se fit entendre ◆ **he was heard to say that ...** on l'a entendu dire que ... ◆ **to make o.s. heard** se faire entendre ◆ **I couldn't ~ myself think** * je ne m'entendais plus penser ◆ **to ~ him (talk) you'd think he was an expert** à l'entendre, on dirait que c'est un expert ◆ **I have heard it said that ..., I've heard tell that ...** j'ai entendu dire que ... ◆ **I've heard tell of ...** j'ai entendu parler de ... ◆ **to ~ voices** *(lit, fig)* entendre des voix ◆ **let's ~ it for ...** * *(call for applause)* un grand bravo pour ..., on applaudit bien fort ...

2 (= *learn*) *[+ piece of news, facts]* apprendre ◆ **have you heard the news?** connaissez-vous la nouvelle ? ◆ **have you heard the rumour that they're going to leave?** avez-vous entendu la rumeur selon laquelle ils partiraient ? ◆ **we've been ~ing reports of roads blocked by snow** nous avons entendu à la radio que les routes étaient bloquées par la neige ◆ **have you heard the story about her trip to Paris?** tu as entendu ce qui s'est passé quand elle est allée à Paris ? ◆ **have you heard the one about the Scotsman who ...** tu connais l'histoire de l'Écossais qui ... ◆ **we've heard it all before** ce n'est pas la première fois qu'on entend cette histoire ◆ **I've been ~ing bad things about him** on m'a dit du mal de lui ◆ **I've never heard such rubbish!** jamais je n'ai entendu pareilles âneries ! ◆ **he had heard that they had left** on lui avait dit qu'ils étaient partis ◆ **I ~ you've been ill** il paraît que vous avez été malade, on m'a dit que vous avez été malade ◆ **did you ~ whether or not she's accepted the job?** savez-vous si elle a accepté (ou non) le poste ?

3 (= *listen to*) *[+ lecture etc]* assister à, écouter ◆ **to ~ a case** *(Jur)* entendre une cause ◆ **the court has been ~ing evidence that he was ...** le tribunal a entendu des témoignages selon lesquels il aurait été ... ◆ **to ~ mass** *(Rel)* assister à *or* entendre la messe ◆ **Lord, ~ our prayers** Seigneur, écoutez nos prières ◆ **to ~ a child's lessons** faire répéter *or* réciter ses leçons à un enfant

VI 1 entendre ◆ **he does not *or* cannot ~ very well** il n'entend pas très bien

2 (= *get news*) recevoir *or* avoir des nouvelles *(from de)* ◆ **I ~ from my daughter every week** je reçois *or* j'ai des nouvelles de ma fille chaque semaine ◆ **you will ~ from me soon** vous aurez bientôt de mes nouvelles ◆ **hoping to ~ from you** *(in informal letter)* en espérant avoir bientôt de tes nouvelles ; *(in formal letter)* dans l'attente de vous lire ◆ **you'll be ~ing from me!** *(threatening)* tu vas avoir de mes nouvelles !, tu vas entendre parler de moi ! ◆ **to ~ about** *or* **of sb/sth** *(gen)* entendre parler de qn/qch ; (= *have news of*) avoir des nouvelles de qn/qch ◆ **I ~ about** *or* **of him from his mother** j'ai de ses nouvelles par sa mère, sa mère me donne de ses nouvelles ◆ **he wasn't heard of for a long time** on n'entendit plus parler de lui pendant longtemps ◆ **he was never heard of again** on n'a plus jamais entendu parler de lui ◆ **the ship was never heard of again** on n'a jamais retrouvé trace du navire ◆ **I've never heard of him!** je ne le connais pas !, connais pas ! * ◆ **everyone has heard of him** tout le monde a entendu parler de lui ◆ **I've never heard of such a thing!** je n'ai jamais entendu parler d'une chose pareille ! ◆ **I ~ about nothing else!** j'en ai les oreilles rebattues ! ◆ **I won't ~ of you going there** je ne veux absolument pas que tu y ailles ◆ **no! I won't ~ of it!** non, je ne veux pas en entendre parler ! ◆ **can I help you with the washing-up? – I wouldn't ~ of it!** je peux vous aider à faire la vaisselle ? – (il n'en est) pas question !

EXCL ◆ **hear, hear !** bravo !

► **hear out** **VT SEP** *[+ person, story]* écouter jusqu'au bout

heard /hɜːd/ **VB** pt, ptp of **hear**

hearer /ˈhɪərəʳ/ **N** auditeur *m*, -trice *f* ◆ **~s** auditoire *m*, auditeurs *mpl*

hearing /ˈhɪərɪŋ/ **N** 1 *(NonC = sense)* ouïe *f* ◆ **to have good ~** avoir l'ouïe fine ◆ **his ~'s not very good** il n'entend pas très bien ◆ **within ~ (distance)** à portée de voix ◆ **in my ~** en ma présence, devant moi ; → **hard**

2 (= *chance to be heard*) ◆ **to give sb a fair ~** *(gen)* écouter ce que qn a à dire ◆ **he was refused a ~** on refusa de l'entendre, on refusa d'écouter ce qu'il avait à dire ◆ **to condemn sb without a ~** condamner qn sans l'entendre ◆ **he got a sympathetic ~** on l'a écouté avec bienveillance

3 (= *meeting*) *[of commission, committee etc]* séance *f* ◆ **court ~** *(Jur)* audience *f* ◆ **to give sb a fair ~** accorder à qn un procès équitable ◆ **they demanded a proper ~ of their complaint** ils ont exigé que leur plainte soit correctement entendue ◆ **disciplinary ~** conseil *m* de discipline ◆ **full ~** *(Jur)* audience *f* contradictoire

ADJ *[person]* qui entend (bien)

COMP **hearing aid** **N** appareil *m* acoustique, audiophone *m*, sonotone ® *m*

Hearing Dog **N** chien *m* de malentendant

hearing-impaired **ADJ** (= *deaf*) sourd ; (= *hard of hearing*) malentendant **N** ◆ **the ~-impaired** (= *deaf*) les sourds *mpl* ; (= *hard of hearing*) les malentendants *mpl*

hearken /ˈhɑːkən/ **VI** († *or liter*) prêter l'oreille *(to à)*

hearsay /ˈhɪəseɪ/ **N** ◆ **from** *or* **by ~** par ouï-dire ◆ **it's only ~** ce ne sont que des rumeurs *or* des on-dit **COMP** *[report, account]* fondé sur des ouï-dire **hearsay evidence** **N** *(Jur)* preuve *f* par commune renommée *or* par ouï-dire

hearse /hɜːs/ **N** corbillard *m*, fourgon *m* mortuaire

heart /hɑːt/

LANGUAGE IN USE 22, 26.1

1 NOUN 2 PLURAL NOUN 3 COMPOUNDS

1 - NOUN

1 Anat cœur *m* ◆ **to have a weak ~** avoir le cœur malade, être cardiaque ◆ **to clasp sb to one's ~** *(liter)* serrer qn sur son cœur

2 seat of feelings, emotions cœur *m* ◆ **a battle for the ~s and minds of ...** une bataille pour séduire ... ◆ **it did my ~ good to see them** cela m'a réchauffé le cœur de les voir ◆ **I didn't have the ~ to tell him, I couldn't find it in my ~ to tell him** je n'ai pas eu le cœur de le lui dire ◆ **he knew in his ~ that it was a waste of time** au fond de lui-même, il savait bien que c'était une perte de temps ◆ **in his ~ of ~s he thought ...** dans son for intérieur *or* au fond de lui-même, il pensait ... ◆ **his ~ isn't in it** le cœur n'y est pas ◆ **his ~ isn't in his work** il n'a pas le cœur à l'ouvrage ◆ **his ~ is in the right place** il a bon cœur ◆ **this is an issue which is close to** *or* **dear to his ~** c'est un sujet qui lui tient à cœur ◆ **that part of the country was very dear to her ~** cette région du pays était très chère à son cœur ◆ **to be in good ~** avoir le moral ◆ **a man after my own ~** un homme selon mon cœur ◆ **with all my ~** de tout mon cœur ◆ **have a ~!** * pitié ! * ◆ **to lose one's ~ to sb** tomber amoureux de qn ◆ **to take sth to ~** prendre qch à cœur ◆ **don't take it to ~** ne prenez pas cela trop à cœur ◆ **it cut me to the ~** cela m'a profondément blessé ◆ **he left with a heavy ~** il est parti le cœur gros ◆ **he has set his ~ on a new car, his ~ is set on a new car** il veut à tout prix une nouvelle voiture ◆ **he has set his ~ on going to Paris** il veut à tout prix aller à Paris, il rêve d'aller à Paris ◆ **my ~ was in my mouth, I had my ~ in my mouth** mon cœur battait la chamade ◆ **to eat/drink to one's ~'s content** manger/boire tout son soûl ◆ **it was his ~'s desire** c'était son plus cher désir *or* ce qu'il désirait le plus au monde ◆ **to have a ~ of gold/stone** avoir un cœur en or/de pierre ◆ **~ and soul** corps et âme ◆ **he put his ~ and soul into his work** il s'est donné à son travail corps et âme

♦ **from + heart** du cœur ◆ **a cry from the ~** un cri du cœur ◆ **a plea from the ~** un appel du fond du cœur ◆ **to speak from the ~** parler du fond du cœur ◆ **from the bottom of one's ~** du fond du cœur

♦ **at heart** au fond ◆ **I'm an optimist at ~** au fond je suis optimiste ◆ **she's still a child at ~** elle est restée très enfant ◆ **we have your (best) interests at ~** vos intérêts nous tiennent à cœur

♦ **by heart** par cœur ◆ **to know by ~** *or* **off by ~** * *[+ text, song, poem]* savoir par cœur ; *[+ subject, plan, route]* connaître par cœur ◆ **to learn sth by ~** *or* **off by ~** * apprendre qch par cœur

3 = courage courage *m* ◆ **to put new** *or* **fresh ~ into sb** redonner (du) courage à qn ◆ **to lose/take ~** perdre/prendre courage ◆ **we may take ~ from the fact that ...** le fait que ... devrait nous encourager

4 = centre *[of town]* cœur *m*, centre *m* ◆ **in the ~ of the forest** au cœur *or* au (beau) milieu de la forêt, en pleine forêt ◆ **in the ~ of the desert** au cœur *or* au (fin) fond du désert ◆ **in the ~ of the country** en pleine campagne ◆ **the ~ of the matter** le fond du problème, le vif du sujet

5 = middle part *[of cabbage, lettuce, celery]* cœur *m* ; *[of artichoke]* fond *m*, cœur *m*

2 - PLURAL NOUN

hearts *(Cards)* cœur *m* ◆ **queen/six of ~s** dame *f*/six *m* de cœur ; *for other phrases see* **club**

3 - COMPOUNDS

heart attack N crise *f* cardiaque
heart case N cardiaque *mf*
heart complaint, heart condition N maladie *f* de cœur ◆ **to have a ~ complaint** *or* **condition** être cardiaque
heart disease N maladie *f* de cœur
heart failure N *(gen)* insuffisance *f* cardiaque ; *(= cardiac arrest)* arrêt *m* du cœur
heart-lung machine N cœur-poumon *m* (artificiel)
heart-rate N rythme *m* cardiaque
heart-rate monitor N moniteur *m* cardiaque
heart-searching N ◆ **after much ~-searching he ...** après s'être longuement interrogé, il ...
heart-shaped ADJ en (forme de) cœur
heart surgeon N chirurgien *m* cardiologue
heart surgery N chirurgie *f* du cœur
heart-throb* N *(= person)* idole *f*, coqueluche *f* ; *(US)* ⇒ **heartbeat**
heart-to-heart ADJ intime, à cœur ouvert ADV à cœur ouvert N ◆ **to have a ~-to-~ (with sb)** * parler à cœur ouvert (avec qn)
heart transplant N greffe *f* du cœur
heart trouble N ◆ **to have ~ trouble** souffrir du cœur, être cardiaque ◆ **~ trouble in the over-50s** les troubles cardiaques dont on souffre après la cinquantaine

heartache /ˈhɑːteɪk/ N chagrin *m*, peine *f*

heartbeat /ˈhɑːtbiːt/ N 1 *(= single beat)* battement *m* de *or* du cœur, pulsation *f* 2 *(= rhythm of heart, pulse)* battements *mpl* de *or* du cœur, pouls *m* ◆ **her ~ is very weak** son pouls est très faible

heartbreak /ˈhɑːtbreɪk/ N immense chagrin *m* *or* douleur *f* ◆ **the relationship ended in ~** la relation s'est terminée dans la douleur ◆ **the group split up, causing ~ to millions of fans** le groupe s'est séparé, au grand désespoir de millions de fans

heartbreaker /ˈhɑːtbreɪkəʳ/ N *(man)* bourreau *m* des cœurs ; *(woman)* femme *f* fatale

heartbreaking /ˈhɑːtbreɪkɪŋ/ ADJ *[story, sight]* qui fend le cœur ; *[appeal, cry, sound]* déchirant, qui fend le cœur ◆ **it was ~ to see him like that** c'était à fendre le cœur de le voir comme ça

heartbroken /ˈhɑːtbrəʊkn/ ADJ ◆ **to be ~** avoir un immense chagrin ; *(stronger)* avoir le cœur brisé ; *[child]* avoir un gros chagrin ◆ **she was ~ about it** elle en a eu un immense chagrin ; *(stronger)* elle en a eu le cœur brisé ◆ **her ~ parents** ses parents, complètement désespérés

heartburn /ˈhɑːtbɜːn/ N brûlures *fpl* d'estomac

-hearted /ˈhɑːtɪd/ ADJ *(in compounds)* ◆ **open-hearted** sincère ◆ **warm-hearted** chaleureux ; → **broken, hard**

hearten /ˈhɑːtn/ VT encourager, donner du courage à

heartening /ˈhɑːtnɪŋ/ ADJ encourageant, réconfortant ◆ **it's very ~ to see so many young writers emerging** c'est très encourageant *or* réconfortant de voir apparaître tant de jeunes écrivains ◆ **it's ~ that the crime figures have dropped so significantly** il est encourageant *or* réconfortant de voir que la criminalité a connu une telle baisse

heartfelt /ˈhɑːtfelt/ ADJ qui vient du fond du cœur ◆ **to make a ~ appeal** lancer un appel du fond du cœur ◆ **~ sympathy** condoléances *fpl* sincères

hearth /hɑːθ/ N foyer *m*, âtre † *m* COMP **hearth rug** N devant *m* de foyer

heartily /ˈhɑːtɪlɪ/ ADV 1 *(= enthusiastically)* *[laugh]* de bon cœur ; *[say, welcome]* chaleureusement ; *[applaud]* avec enthousiasme ; *[eat]* de bon appétit ; *[drink, sing]* avec entrain ; *[recommend]* vivement ; *[agree]* pleinement ; *[congratulate, endorse]* de tout cœur 2 *(= thoroughly)* *[glad, relieved, sorry]* profondément ◆ **to be ~ sick of*** *or* **fed up with*** **sb/sth** en avoir vraiment par-dessus la tête* de qn/qch ◆ **to dislike sb ~** détester cordialement qn ◆ **to dislike sth ~** avoir une profonde aversion pour qch

heartland /ˈhɑːtlænd/ N (also **heartlands**) *[of country, continent]* cœur *m*, centre *m* ◆ **the Tory ~** le bastion traditionnel des conservateurs

heartless /ˈhɑːtlɪs/ ADJ *[person]* sans cœur ; *[treatment]* cruel

heartlessly /ˈhɑːtlɪslɪ/ ADV *[say, deceive]* sans pitié ◆ **~ cruel** d'une cruauté impitoyable

heartlessness /ˈhɑːtlɪsnɪs/ N *[of person]* manque *m* de cœur

heartrending /ˈhɑːtrendɪŋ/ ADJ *[cry, appeal]* déchirant, qui fend le cœur ; *[sight]* qui fend le cœur ◆ **it was ~ to see him** c'était à fendre le cœur de le voir

heartsick /ˈhɑːtsɪk/ ADJ ◆ **to be ~** avoir la mort dans l'âme

heartstrings /ˈhɑːtstrɪŋz/ NPL ◆ **to pull at** *or* **tug (at)** *or* **touch sb's ~** jouer sur la corde sensible de qn

heartwarming /ˈhɑːtwɔːmɪŋ/ ADJ réconfortant, qui réchauffe le cœur

hearty /ˈhɑːtɪ/ ADJ 1 *(= enthusiastic)* *[welcome, thanks]* chaleureux ; *[applause]* enthousiaste ; *[slap, pat, thump]* bon *before n* ; *[appetite]* solide ◆ **he gave a ~ laugh** il eut un bon rire franc ◆ **to bid sb a ~ welcome** accueillir chaleureusement qn ◆ **he's a ~ eater** c'est un gros mangeur ; → **hale**
2 *(= substantial)* *[food, soup]* consistant ; *[meal]* copieux ; *[helping]* généreux
3 *(pej = bluff)* *[person, greeting]* trop exubérant ; *[voice]* retentissant
4 *(= wholehearted)* *[endorsement, condemnation]* sans réserves ◆ **to be in ~ agreement with sb/sth** être absolument d'accord avec qn/qch ◆ **please accept my ~** *or* **heartiest congratulations** *(in letter)* je vous adresse mes plus vives félicitations ◆ **to have a ~ dislike of sb** détester cordialement qn ◆ **to have a ~ dislike of sth** avoir une profonde aversion pour qch
N * 1 *(= person)* gai luron † *m*
2 *(Naut)* ◆ **heave ho, my hearties !** oh ! hisse ! les gars ! *

heat /hiːt/ N 1 *(NonC: gen, Phys)* chaleur *f* ◆ **extremes of ~ and cold** extrêmes *mpl* de chaleur et de froid ◆ **I can't stand ~** je ne supporte pas la chaleur ◆ **how can you work in this ~?** *(indoor temperature)* comment pouvez-vous travailler dans cette fournaise ? ; *(in hot weather)* comment pouvez-vous travailler par cette chaleur ? ◆ **if you can't stand the ~ get out of the kitchen** *(fig)* que ceux qui trouvent la situation intenable s'en aillent ◆ **in the ~ of the day** au (moment le) plus chaud de la journée ◆ **in the summer ~** dans la chaleur de l'été ◆ **we were trying to stay cool in the 35-degree ~** nous essayions de nous rafraîchir alors qu'il faisait 35 degrés ◆ **at a low ~** *(Culin)* à feu doux ◆ **cook over a low/medium ~** cuire à feu doux/moyen ◆ **lower the ~ and allow to simmer** *(Culin)* réduire le feu et laisser mijoter ◆ **in the ~ of the moment/the battle/the argument** dans le feu de l'action/du combat/de la discussion ◆ **in the ~ of his departure they forgot ...** dans l'agitation qui a entouré son départ, ils ont oublié ... ◆ **"certainly not!" she responded with some ~** "certainement pas !" répondit-elle avec feu ◆ **the issue was debated with some ~** cette question a fait l'objet d'un débat houleux ◆ **we had no ~ all day at the office** nous avons été sans chauffage toute la journée au bureau ◆ **to turn on the ~** *(in house, office)* mettre le chauffage ◆ **to put** *or* **turn the ~ on sb*** faire pression sur qn ◆ **to turn up the ~ on sb*** accentuer la pression sur qn ◆ **the ~ is on *** on est sous pression ◆ **it'll take the ~ off us*** ça nous permettra de souffler *or* de respirer un peu ; → **red, specific, white**
2 *(Sport)* (épreuve *f*) éliminatoire *f* ; → **dead**
3 *(NonC)* *(= sexual readiness of animal)* chaleur *f*, rut *m* ◆ **in** *or* *(Brit)* **on ~** en chaleur, en rut
4 *(US)* ◆ **the ~** ‡ *(= the police)* les flics ‡ *mpl*
VT *(gen)* chauffer ; *(Med)* *[+ blood]* échauffer ; *(fig)* enflammer
VI *[liquid etc]* chauffer ; *[room]* se réchauffer
COMP **heat constant** N *(Phys)* constante *f* calorifique
heat efficiency N rendement *m* thermique *or* calorifique
heat exchanger N échangeur *m* de chaleur
heat exhaustion N épuisement *m* dû à la chaleur
heat haze N brume *f* de chaleur
heat lightning N éclair(s) *m(pl)* de chaleur
heat loss N perte *f* calorifique
heat rash N irritation *f* *or* inflammation *f* (due à la chaleur)
heat-resistant, heat-resisting ADJ ⇒ **heatproof**
heat-seeking ADJ *[missile]* thermoguidé, guidé par infrarouge
heat-sensitive ADJ sensible à la chaleur
heat shield N *(Space)* bouclier *m* thermique
heat treatment N *(Med)* traitement *m* par la chaleur, thermothérapie *f*
► **heat up** VI *[liquid etc]* chauffer ; *[room]* se réchauffer
VT SEP réchauffer

heated /ˈhiːtɪd/ ADJ 1 *[swimming pool, greenhouse, towel rail]* chauffé 2 *(= impassioned)* *[debate, discussion]* passionné ; *[argument, exchange, words]* vif ◆ **to become** *or* **get** *or* **grow ~** *[person, debate, argument etc]* s'échauffer COMP **heated rollers** NPL bigoudis *mpl* *or* rouleaux *mpl* chauffants

heatedly /ˈhiːtɪdlɪ/ ADV *[say]* avec emportement ; *[argue]* avec feu, fougueusement ; *[debate]* avec feu, avec passion ; *[deny]* farouchement

heater /ˈhiːtəʳ/ N *(gen: for room)* appareil *m* de chauffage, radiateur *m* ; *(for water)* chauffe-eau *m inv* ; *[of car]* chauffage *m* ; → **electric, immersion**

heath /hiːθ/ N 1 *(esp Brit = moorland)* lande *f* 2 *(= plant)* bruyère *f*

heathen /ˈhiːðən/ *(pej)* ADJ *(= unbelieving)* païen ; *(= barbarous)* barbare, sauvage N (pl **heathens** *or* **heathen**) païen(ne) *m(f)*, les païens *mpl* ; *(= savages)* les barbares *mpl*, les sauvages *mpl*

heathenish /ˈhiːðənɪʃ/ ADJ *(pej)* *(= unbelieving)* de païen ; *(= barbarous)* barbare

heathenism /ˈhiːðənɪzəm/ N *(pej)* paganisme *m*

heather /ˈheðəʳ/ N bruyère *f*

Heath Robinson* /hiːθˈrɒbɪnsən/ ADJ *(Brit)* bricolé

heating /ˈhiːtɪŋ/ N chauffage *m* ; → **central**
COMP **heating apparatus** N *(= heater)* appareil *m* de chauffage ; *(= equipment)* appareils *mpl* de chauffage
heating engineer N chauffagiste *m*
heating plant N système *m* *or* installation *f* de chauffage
heating power N pouvoir *m* calorifique
heating system N système *m* de chauffage

heatproof /ˈhiːtpruːf/ ADJ *[material]* résistant *inv* à la chaleur ; *[dish]* allant *inv* au four

heatpump /ˈhiːtpʌmp/ N pompe *f* à chaleur, thermopompe *f*

heatstroke /ˈhiːtstrəʊk/ **N** (NonC) coup *m* de chaleur

heatwave /ˈhiːtweɪv/ **N** vague *f* de chaleur

heave /hiːv/ (vb : pret, ptp **heaved**) **N** *[of sea]* houle *f* ; *[of bosom]* soulèvement *m* ◆ **to give a ~** (= *lift, throw, tug etc*) faire un effort pour soulever (*or* lancer *or* tirer *etc*) ◆ **to give sb the ~(-ho)** *‡ *[employer]* sacquer * *or* virer * qn ; *[boyfriend, girlfriend]* plaquer * qn

VT (= *lift*) lever *or* soulever (avec effort) ; (= *pull*) tirer (avec effort) ; (= *drag*) traîner (avec effort) ; (= *throw*) lancer ◆ **he ~d Barney to his feet** il a soulevé Barney (avec effort) pour le mettre debout ◆ **he ~d himself up off his stool** il s'est levé de son tabouret avec effort ◆ **to ~ a sigh of relief** pousser un gros soupir de soulagement

VI 1 *[sea, chest]* se soulever ; *[person]* (= *pant*) haleter ; (= *retch*) avoir des haut-le-cœur *or* des nausées ; (= *vomit*) vomir ◆ **his stomach was heaving** son estomac se soulevait

2 (*Naut*) (pret, ptp **hove**) **to ~ into sight** *or* **view** apparaître

COMP heave-ho EXCL (*Naut*) oh ! hisse !

► **heave to** (pret, ptp **hove to**) (*Naut*) **VI** se mettre en panne

VT SEP mettre en panne

► **heave up VT SEP** (= *vomit*) vomir

heaven /ˈhevn/ **N** 1 (= *paradise*) ciel *m*, paradis *m* ◆ **to go to ~** aller au ciel, aller au paradis ◆ **in ~** au ciel, au *or* en paradis ◆ **our Father which art in ~** notre Père qui êtes aux cieux ◆ **he was in ~** *or* **in seventh ~** il était au septième ciel *or* aux anges ◆ **I thought I'd died and gone to ~!** * j'étais au septième ciel *or* aux anges ◆ **it was ~** * c'était divin *or* merveilleux ◆ **he found a ~ on earth** il a trouvé son paradis sur terre ◆ **the shop was a chocolate-lover's ~!** ce magasin était un paradis pour les amateurs de chocolat ! ◆ **an injustice that cries out to ~** une injustice criante *or* flagrante ◆ **~ help you** * **(if your mother ever finds out about this)** (si ta mère apprend ça) je te souhaite bien de la chance ◆ **what in ~'s name does that mean?** * mais qu'est-ce que ça veut bien dire ? ◆ **~ (only) knows what/when** *etc* Dieu sait quoi/quand *etc* ◆ **when will you come back? – ~ (only) knows!** quand reviendras-tu ? – Dieu seul le sait ! ◆ **~ knows I've tried** Dieu sait *or* m'est témoin que j'ai essayé ◆ **(good) ~s!** * mon Dieu !, Seigneur !, ciel ! (*hum*) ◆ **for ~'s sake** * pour l'amour de Dieu * *or* du ciel * ◆ **I wish to ~** * **he were still here!** si seulement il était encore là ! ◆ **I wish to ~** * **I'd never met you!** si seulement je ne t'avais jamais rencontré ! ; → **forbid, move, stink, thank**

2 (*gen liter*) **the ~s** (= *sky*) le ciel, le firmament (*liter*) ◆ **the ~s opened** le ciel se mit à déverser des trombes d'eau

COMP heaven-sent ADJ providentiel

heavenly /ˈhevnlɪ/ **ADJ** (*lit*) céleste, du ciel ; (*fig*) (= *delightful*) divin, merveilleux

COMP heavenly body N corps *m* céleste

Heavenly Father N (*Rel*) Père *m* céleste

heavenward(s) /ˈhevnwəd(z)/ **ADV** *[go]* vers le ciel ◆ **to look ~(s)** lever les yeux au ciel

heavily /ˈhevɪlɪ/ **ADV** 1 (= *much*) *[rely on, influence, censor, subsidize]* fortement ; *[rain]* à verse, très fort ; *[snow]* à gros flocons, très fort ; *[bleed, sweat]* abondamment ; *[smoke, drink]* beaucoup ; *[gamble]* gros ; *[criticize]* vivement ; *[tax]* lourdement ; *[fortified]* solidement ; *[populated]* densément ; *[wooded]* très ◆ **he spoke in ~ accented English** il parlait anglais avec un fort accent ◆ **~ armed** fortement armé ◆ **~ bandaged** entouré d'un épais pansement ◆ **to be ~ booked in advance** être en grande partie réservé à l'avance ◆ **his face was ~ bruised** il avait la figure toute meurtrie ◆ **~ in debt** fortement endetté ◆ **to be ~ defeated** subir une défaite écrasante ◆ **to be ~ disguised** avoir un déguisement très élaboré ◆ **~ edited** plein de corrections ◆ **~ fined** condamné à une lourde amende ◆ **~ guarded** fortement gardé ◆ **~ involved in** *or* **with** (*politics, interest group*) fortement engagé dans ; (*drugs, illegal business*) fortement impliqué dans ◆ **~ laden** lourdement chargé ◆ **his ~ lined face** son visage tout parcheminé *or* ridé ◆ **~ made-up eyes** yeux *mpl* très maquillés *or* fardés ◆ **~ outnumbered** très inférieur en nombre ◆ **~ pregnant** près d'accoucher, dans un état de grossesse avancée ◆ **a ~ pregnant mare** une jument près de mettre bas ◆ **~ scented flowers** des fleurs au parfum lourd *or* capiteux ◆ **~ sedated** sous l'influence de fortes doses de calmants ◆ **~ spiced** fortement épicé ◆ **~ underlined** souligné d'un gros trait ◆ **~ weighted in sb's favour/against sb** fortement favorable/défavorable à qn ◆ **the rain/snow was falling ~** il pleuvait/neigeait très fort ◆ **to borrow ~** emprunter de fortes sommes ◆ **to invest ~** beaucoup investir ◆ **to lose ~** (*Gambling*) perdre gros ; (*Sport, Pol*) subir une défaite écrasante

2 ◆ **to be ~ into** * *[+ sports, music, computers etc]* être un(e) mordu(e) de * ◆ **he's ~ into drugs/heroin/health foods** son truc *, c'est la drogue/l'héroïne/l'alimentation bio

3 (= *deeply*) *[breathe, pant]* bruyamment ; *[sleep, sigh]* profondément

4 (= *clumsily*) *[sit down, fall, land, lean, move]* lourdement ; *[walk]* d'un pas lourd

5 (= *solidly*) ◆ **~ built** costaud, solidement bâti ◆ **her attacker is described as aged 30-40 and ~ built** son agresseur aurait entre 30 et 40 ans et serait de forte carrure

6 (= *slowly*) *[say]* d'une voix accablée

7 (= *richly*) *[encrusted, embroidered, gilded]* richement

heaviness /ˈhevɪnɪs/ **N** *[of person, animal, load]* poids *m* ◆ **the ~ of his movements** la lourdeur dans ses mouvements ◆ **a sensation of ~ in the limbs** une sensation de lourdeur dans les membres ◆ **the ~ of the blood loss** l'importance *f* de l'hémorragie ◆ **hormones to reduce the ~ of your period** des hormones qui rendraient vos règles moins abondantes ◆ **~ of heart** tristesse *f*

heavy /ˈhevɪ/ **ADJ** 1 (*gen*) lourd ◆ **to make sth heavier** alourdir qch ◆ **how ~ are you?** combien pesez-vous ? ◆ **heavier than air** plus lourd que l'air ◆ **barley bread is ~ on the stomach** le pain d'orge est peu digeste ◆ **to fall into a ~ sleep** s'endormir comme une masse ◆ **a ~ sigh** un gros soupir ◆ **his voice was ~ with sarcasm** son ton était très sarcastique

2 (= *violent*) **a ~ blow** (*lit*) un coup violent ; (*fig*) un rude coup ◆ **they suffered a ~ defeat** ils ont subi une lourde défaite ◆ **the plane made a ~ landing** l'avion a fait un atterrissage brutal ◆ **he got really ~ with me** * (= *threatening*) il est devenu menaçant

3 (= *severe*) **a ~ cold** (*Med*) un gros rhume ◆ **~ periods** (*Med*) des règles *fpl* abondantes

4 (*describing features*) **~ eyes** yeux cernés *mpl* ◆ **eyes ~ with sleep** yeux *mpl* lourds de sommeil ◆ **a man of ~ build** un homme solidement bâti *or* de forte constitution ◆ **~ features** gros traits *mpl*, traits *mpl* épais

5 (*in quantity, number*) *[population]* dense ; *[crop]* abondant ; *[loss, fine]* gros (grosse *f*) *before n*, lourd ; *[payments]* important ◆ **there were ~ casualties** il y a eu de nombreuses victimes ◆ **a ~ concentration of ...** une forte concentration de ... ◆ **the traffic was ~** la circulation était dense ◆ **I was caught up in ~ traffic** j'ai été pris dans un ralentissement ◆ **my car is ~ on petrol** ma voiture consomme beaucoup (d'essence) ◆ **salads ~ on carrots** des salades avec beaucoup de carottes

6 (= *difficult, demanding*) *[task, work]* lourd, pénible ◆ **we've got a very ~ schedule** nous avons un planning très lourd ◆ **I've had a ~ day** j'ai eu une journée chargée ◆ **the going was ~ because of the rain** le terrain était lourd à cause de la pluie ◆ **he did all the ~ work** c'est lui qui a fait le gros travail ◆ **it's ~ stuff** * (= *not superficial*) c'est du solide * ; (= *difficult, tedious*) c'est indigeste

◆ **heavy going** (= *difficult*) difficile ◆ **he found things ~ going without Jim's experience and contacts** c'était difficile pour lui sans l'expérience et les contacts de Jim ◆ **this book is very ~ going** ce livre est très indigeste

7 (*describing habits*) **to be a ~ drinker/smoker** boire/fumer beaucoup, être un grand buveur/fumeur ◆ **to be a ~ sleeper** avoir le sommeil profond *or* lourd ◆ **~ drug use** consommation *f* excessive de drogues ◆ **~ viewer** (TV) téléspectateur *m*, -trice *f* assidu(e)

8 (= *not subtle*) *[humour, irony]* lourd ◆ **to play the ~ father** jouer les pères autoritaires

9 *[rain, shower]* fort *before n*, gros (grosse *f*) *before n* ; *[fog]* épais (-aisse *f*) ; *[sky]* couvert, lourd ◆ **~ dew** forte rosée *f* ◆ **~ sea** grosse mer *f* ◆ **a ~ sea was running** la mer était grosse

◆ **heavy weather** (*Naut*) gros temps *m* ◆ **he made ~ weather of it** il s'est compliqué la tâche *or* l'existence * ◆ **he made ~ weather of cleaning the car** il s'est compliqué la vie pour laver la voiture

10 (= *pregnant*) **~ with young** (*animal*) gravide ◆ **to be ~ with child** † (*liter*) être grosse

11 (*Mil*) **~ artillery, ~ guns** artillerie *f* lourde, grosse artillerie *f* ◆ **~ (gun)fire** feu *m* nourri ◆ **~ fighting** combats *mpl* acharnés ◆ **~ shelling** bombardements *mpl* intensifs

ADV lourd, lourdement ◆ **to weigh** *or* **lie ~ on** peser lourd sur ◆ **he's ~ into** * **health foods** (*US fig*) il est à fond dans l'alimentation bio *, son truc, c'est l'alimentation bio * ; see also **lie**[1]

N 1 (*Boxing*) poids *m* lourd

2 (* = *bouncer etc*) costaud * *m*

3 (*Brit* * = *newspaper*) grand journal *m*

COMP heavy bodies NPL (*Phys*) corps *mpl* graves

heavy breather N (*on phone*) *personne qui fait des appels téléphoniques anonymes obscènes*

heavy cream N (*US*) crème *f* fraîche épaisse *or* à fouetter

heavy crude (oil) N brut *m* lourd

heavy cruiser N (*Naut*) croiseur *m* lourd

heavy-duty ADJ *[carpet]* résistant ; *[equipment]* à usage industriel

heavy goods vehicle N poids *m* lourd

heavy-handed ADJ *[person]* (= *severe*) dur ; (= *tactless, clumsy*) maladroit ; *[tactics]* dur, répressif ; *[style]* lourd

heavy-handedly ADV (*with severity*) durement ; (= *tactlessly*) maladroitement

heavy-hearted ADJ ◆ **to be ~-hearted** avoir le cœur gros

heavy industry N industrie *f* lourde

heavy-laden ADJ lourdement chargé

heavy metal N (*Chem*) métal *m* lourd ; (*Mus*) heavy metal *m*

heavy-set ADJ costaud

heavy type N (*Typ*) caractères *mpl* gras

heavy water N eau *f* lourde

heavyweight /ˈhevɪweɪt/ **N** (*Boxing*) poids *m* lourd ; (* *fig* = *influential person*) (grosse) pointure *f* **ADJ** 1 (*Boxing*) *[bout, champion, class]* poids lourds *inv* ◆ **a ~ boxer** un poids lourd 2 (= *serious*) *[issue, subject, newspaper, interviewer, political commentator]* sérieux 3 (= *thick*) *[cloth, plastic]* épais (-aisse *f*) ; *[wallpaper]* fort

Hebe *‡ /hiːbɪ/ **N** (*US pej*) youpin(e) *‡ *m(f)*

Hebraic /hɪˈbreɪɪk/ **ADJ** hébraïque

Hebrew /ˈhiːbruː/ **ADJ** hébreu *m only*, hébraïque **N** 1 (*Hist*) Hébreu *m*, Israélite *mf* ◆ **~s** (*Bible*) Hébreux *mpl* 2 (= *language*) hébreu *m*

Hebrides /ˈhebrɪdiːz/ NPL ◆ **the ~** les Hébrides fpl

heck * /hek/ EXCL zut ! *, flûte ! * N ◆ **a ~ of a lot** une sacrée quantité * ◆ **I'm in one ~ of a mess** je suis dans un sacré pétrin * ◆ **what the ~ is he doing?** que diable * peut il bien faire ? ◆ **what the ~ did he say?** qu'est-ce qu'il a bien pu dire ? ◆ **what the ~!** et puis flûte * *or* zut * !

heckle /ˈhekl/ VTI chahuter

heckler /ˈheklər/ N *(Pol etc)* (élément *m*) perturbateur *m*

heckling /ˈheklɪŋ/ N chahut *m*

hectare /ˈhektɑːr/ N hectare *m*

hectic /ˈhektɪk/ ADJ 1 *[life, lifestyle] (= busy)* trépidant ; *(= eventful)* mouvementé ; *[journey, day]* mouvementé ; *[schedule]* très chargé ; *[activity]* fiévreux ; *[pace]* trépidant ; *[traffic]* intense ◆ **we've had three ~ days** on n'a pas arrêté pendant trois jours 2 *(Med) [person, colour]* fiévreux COMP **hectic fever** N fièvre *f* hectique

hectogramme, hectogram *(US)* /ˈhektəʊɡræm/ N hectogramme *m*

hectolitre, hectoliter *(US)* /ˈhektəʊˌliːtər/ N hectolitre *m*

Hector /ˈhektər/ N Hector *m*

hector /ˈhektər/ VT harceler VI ◆ **stop ~ing!** arrête de harceler les gens !

hectoring /ˈhektərɪŋ/ ADJ ◆ **in a ~ voice** d'un ton autoritaire *or* impérieux

Hecuba /ˈhekjʊbə/ N Hécube *f*

he'd /hiːd/ ⇒ **he had, he would** ; → **have, would**

hedge /hedʒ/ N 1 haie *f* ◆ **beech ~** haie *f* de hêtres

2 *(fig)* ◆ **a ~ against inflation** une protection contre l'inflation

VI 1 *(= not be direct) (in answering)* se dérober ; *(in explaining, recounting etc)* expliquer *or* raconter *etc* avec des détours ◆ **don't ~** dis-le franchement ◆ **to ~ on a question/promise** éviter de répondre à une question/de s'engager

2 *(= protect o.s.)* **to ~ against sth** se prémunir contre qch

VT 1 (also **hedge about, hedge in**) entourer d'une haie, enclore ◆ **~d (about *or* in) with difficulties** *(fig)* plein de difficultés ◆ **the offer was ~d around with conditions** l'offre était assortie d'une série de conditions

2 *[+ bet, risk]* couvrir ◆ **to ~ one's bets** *(fig)* se couvrir *(fig)* ◆ **"I can't give you an answer now", he ~d** "je ne peux pas vous répondre maintenant", dit-il en se dérobant

3 **to ~ the issue** esquiver la question

COMP **hedge clippers** NPL cisailles *fpl* à haie

hedge fund N *(Fin)* hedge fund *m*, fonds *m* spéculatif

hedge trimmer N taille-haie *m*

► **hedge off** VT SEP *[+ garden]* entourer d'une haie ; *[+ part of garden]* séparer par une haie *(from* de)

hedgehog /ˈhedʒhɒɡ/ N hérisson *m*

hedgehop /ˈhedʒhɒp/ VI *(in plane)* faire du rase-mottes

hedger /ˈhedʒər/ N *(Fin)* arbitragiste *m (en couverture de risques)*

hedgerow /ˈhedʒrəʊ/ N haie *f*

hedgesparrow /ˈhedʒspærəʊ/ N fauvette *f* des haies *or* d'hiver

hedonism /ˈhiːdənɪzəm/ N hédonisme *m*

hedonist /ˈhiːdənɪst/ ADJ, N hédoniste *mf*

hedonistic /ˌhiːdəˈnɪstɪk/ ADJ hédoniste

heebie-jeebies ‡ /ˈhiːbɪˈdʒiːbɪz/ NPL ◆ **to give sb the ~** *(revulsion)* donner la chair de poule à qn ; *(fright, apprehension)* flanquer la frousse * *or* la trouille ‡ à qn

heed /hiːd/ VT tenir compte de N ◆ **to take ~ of sth, to pay *or* give ~ to sth** tenir compte de qch ◆ **take no ~ of what they say** ne faites pas attention à ce qu'ils disent ◆ **to pay no ~ to sb** ne pas écouter qn ◆ **pay no ~ to these rumours** ne faites pas attention à ces rumeurs ◆ **he paid no ~ to the warning** il n'a tenu aucun compte de cet avertissement ◆ **to take ~ to do sth** prendre soin de faire qch

heedless /ˈhiːdlɪs/ ADJ *(= not thinking)* étourdi ; *(= not caring)* insouciant ◆ **~ of what was going on** inattentif à ce qui se passait ◆ **~ of danger, she ...** sans se soucier du danger, elle ... ◆ **~ of complaints** sans tenir compte des réclamations

heedlessly /ˈhiːdlɪslɪ/ ADV sans faire attention

heehaw /ˈhiːhɔː/ N hi-han *m* VI faire hi-han, braire

heel[1] /hiːl/ N 1 *[of foot, sock, shoe, tool, golf club, bow]* talon *m* ; *[of hand]* hypothénar *m (Anat)* ◆ **high ~s** talons *mpl* hauts ◆ **shoes with high ~s** chaussures *fpl* à talons hauts ◆ **at sb's ~s** sur les talons de qn ◆ **to be (hot) on sb's ~s** marcher sur les talons de qn ◆ **they followed close *or* hard on his ~s** ils étaient sur ses talons ◆ **this meeting follows hot on the ~s of last month's talks** cette réunion arrive juste après les négociations du mois dernier ◆ **to be snapping at sb's ~s** * *(fig)* essayer de prendre la place de qn ◆ **to take to one's ~s, to show a clean pair of ~s** prendre ses jambes à son cou ◆ **he turned on his ~ and left** il a tourné les talons et est parti ◆ **under the ~ of** *(fig)* sous le joug *or* la botte de ◆ **~!** *(to dog)* au pied ! ◆ **he brought the dog to ~** il a fait venir le chien à ses pieds ◆ **to bring sb to ~** *(fig)* rappeler qn à l'ordre, faire rentrer qn dans le rang ; → **click, cool down, kick**

2 *(† * = unpleasant man)* salaud ‡ *m*

VT 1 *[+ shoes]* remettre *or* refaire un talon à

2 *(Rugby) [+ ball]* talonner ; see also **back**

COMP **heel-bar** N talon-minute *m*

heel-piece N *[of sock etc]* talon *m* (renforcé)

heel[2] /hiːl/ VI (also **heel over**) *[ship]* gîter, donner de la bande ; *[truck, structure]* s'incliner *or* pencher (dangereusement)

heeled /hiːld/ ADJ 1 → **well**[2] 2 *(US* ‡ *= armed)* armé

heeling /ˈhiːlɪŋ/ N *(Rugby)* talonnage *m*

heft * /heft/ VT *(= lift)* soulever ; *(= feel weight of)* soupeser

hefty * /ˈheftɪ/ ADJ 1 *(= big) [person]* costaud *, maous * (-ousse * *f*) ; *[object, fine, increase, meal]* de taille * ; *[profit]* gros (grosse *f*) ; *[bill]* salé * ; *[fees]* très élevé ◆ **a ~ sum** une jolie somme, une coquette somme 2 *(= powerful) [kick, slap, punch]* formidable

Hegelian /hɪˈɡeɪlɪən/ ADJ hégélien

hegemony /hɪˈɡemənɪ/ N hégémonie *f*

Hegira /ˈhedʒɪrə/ N hégire *f*

heifer /ˈhefər/ N génisse *f*

heigh /heɪ/ EXCL hé !, eh ! ◆ **~-ho!** eh bien !

height /haɪt/ N 1 *[of object, building]* hauteur *f* ; *[of person]* taille *f* ; *[of mountain]* altitude *f* ; *[of star, sun]* élévation *f* ◆ **what ~ are you?** combien mesurez-vous ? ◆ **he is 5 foot 9 inches in ~, his ~ is 5 foot 9 inches** il fait 1 mètre 75 ◆ **of average ~** de taille moyenne ◆ **her weight is about normal for her ~** son poids est à peu près normal par rapport à sa taille ◆ **he drew himself up to his full ~** il s'est dressé de toute sa hauteur ◆ **a building 40 metres in ~** un bâtiment qui a *or* un bâtiment de 40 mètres de haut ◆ **at shoulder ~** à hauteur des épaules ◆ **~ above sea level** altitude *f* au-dessus du niveau de la mer

2 *(= high place)* éminence *f*, hauteur *f* ◆ **the ~s** les sommets *mpl* ◆ **fear of ~s** *(gen)* vertige *m* ◆ **to be afraid of ~s** avoir le vertige ◆ **his performance never reached the ~s** *(fig)* il n'a jamais brillé ; → **giddy**[1], **head**

3 *(= altitude) [of plane]* altitude *f* ◆ **to gain/lose ~** gagner *or* prendre/perdre de l'altitude

4 *(fig) (= best point) [of fortune]* apogée *m* ; *[of success]* point *m* culminant ; *[of glory]* sommet *m* ; *[of grandeur]* sommet *m*, faîte *m* ; *[of absurdity, folly]* comble *m* ◆ **at the ~ of his power** au summum de sa puissance ◆ **at the ~ of his career** à l'apogée *or* au sommet de sa carrière ◆ **at the ~ of his fame** au sommet de sa gloire ◆ **he is at the ~ of his powers** il est en pleine possession de ses moyens ◆ **at the ~ of summer/the storm/the battle** au cœur de l'été/l'orage/la bataille ◆ **at the ~ of the season** au plus fort de la saison ◆ **the season is at its ~** la saison bat son plein ◆ **the ~ of fashion** la toute dernière mode, le dernier cri ◆ **the ~ of luxury** le comble du luxe ◆ **the ~ of bad manners/arrogance/bad taste** le comble de l'impolitesse/de l'arrogance/du mauvais goût ◆ **during the war emigration was at its ~** pendant la guerre l'émigration a atteint son niveau le plus haut ◆ **at its ~ the company employed 12,000 people** à son apogée la société employait 12 000 personnes ◆ **the crisis was at its ~** la crise avait atteint son paroxysme

COMP **height gauge** N *(= altimeter)* altimètre *m*

heighten /ˈhaɪtn/ VT *[+ effect, absurdity, interest, tension, fear]* augmenter, intensifier ; *[+ flavour]* relever ◆ **it will ~ people's awareness of the problem** cela rendra les gens plus conscients du problème ◆ **this has ~ed concern that the elections may not go ahead** cela fait craindre encore plus que les élections n'aient pas lieu VI *[tension]* augmenter, monter ; *[fear]* s'intensifier, devenir plus vif

heightened /ˈhaɪtnd/ ADJ *[competition]* accru ; *[sense]* très aigu ◆ **the attack comes amid ~ tension in the region** cette attaque est survenue alors que la tension s'accroît dans la région ◆ **this has brought ~ concern about food shortages** cela a augmenté les craintes de pénurie de nourriture ◆ **~ emotions** des sentiments *mpl* exacerbés ◆ **her ~ sense of injustice** son sens très aigu de l'injustice ◆ **she looked at him with ~ interest** elle l'a regardé avec un intérêt accru ◆ **this gave her a ~ awareness of ...** cela lui a permis de mieux se rendre compte de ... ◆ **with ~ colour** *[person]* le teint animé

heinous /ˈheɪnəs/ ADJ odieux, atroce

heir /ɛər/ N héritier *m*, légataire *mf* *(to* de) ◆ **he is ~ to a fortune** il héritera d'une fortune ◆ **~ to the throne** héritier *m* du trône *or* de la couronne ◆ **rightful ~** héritier *m* légitime *or* naturel ◆ **to fall ~ to sth** hériter de qch

COMP **heir apparent** N (pl **heirs apparent**) héritier *m* présomptif

heir-at-law N (pl **heirs-at-law**) *(Jur)* héritier *m* légitime *or* naturel

heir presumptive N (pl **heirs presumptive**) héritier *m* présomptif *(sauf naissance d'un héritier en ligne directe)*

heiress /ˈɛəres/ N héritière *f* ◆ **he married an ~** il a épousé une riche héritière

heirloom /ˈɛəluːm/ N héritage *m* ◆ **this silver is a family ~** c'est de l'argenterie de famille ◆ **you can't sell that, it's an ~!** tu ne peux pas vendre ça, c'est un bien de famille !

heist * /haɪst/ *(esp US)* N *(= robbery)* hold-up *m* inv ; *(= burglary)* casse ‡ *m* VT voler

held /held/ VB pt, ptp of **hold**

Helen /ˈhelɪn/ N Hélène *f* ◆ **~ of Troy** Hélène *f* de Troie

helical /ˈhelɪkəl/ ADJ hélicoïdal ◆ **~ spring** ressort *m* hélicoïdal

helices /ˈhelɪˌsiːz/ **NPL** of **helix**

helicopter /ˈhelɪkɒptəʳ/ [N] hélicoptère *m* ◆ **transfer** *or* **transport by ~** héliportage *m* ◆ **transferred** *or* **transported by ~** héliporté

[VT] *(esp US) [+ person, goods]* transporter en hélicoptère ◆ **to ~ in/out** *etc* amener/évacuer *etc* par hélicoptère

[COMP] *[patrol, rescue]* en hélicoptère ; *[pilot]* d'hélicoptère

helicopter gunship N hélicoptère *m* de combat

helicopter station N héligare *f*

heliograph /ˈhiːlɪəʊɡrɑːf/ N héliographe *m*

heliostat /ˈhiːlɪəʊstæt/ N héliostat *m*

heliotrope /ˈhiːlɪətrəʊp/ [N] [1] *(= plant)* héliotrope *m* [2] *(= colour)* ≈ violet *m* [ADJ] ≈ violet

helipad /ˈhelɪˌpæd/ N hélistation *f*

heliport /ˈhelɪpɔːt/ N héliport *m*

helium /ˈhiːlɪəm/ N hélium *m*

helix /ˈhiːlɪks/ N (pl **helixes** *or* **helices** /ˈhelɪˌsiːz/) *(Anat)* hélix *m*

he'll /hiːl/ ⇒ **he will** ; → **will**

hell /hel/ [N] [1] *(Rel)* enfer *m* ; *(Myth)* les enfers *mpl* ◆ **in ~** *(gen, Rel)* en enfer ; *(Myth)* aux enfers ◆ **the ~ of the labour camps** l'enfer des camps de travail ◆ **to make sb's life ~** rendre la vie de qn infernale ◆ **when ~ freezes over** quand les poules auront des dents, à la Saint-Glinglin* ◆ **all ~ broke** *or* **was let loose*** ça a été une pagaille* monstre ◆ **when he heard about it all ~ broke** *or* **was let loose*** quand il l'a appris il a fait une scène épouvantable ◆ **life became ~** la vie est devenue infernale ◆ **it's ~ on earth*** c'est l'enfer ◆ **a living ~** un véritable enfer ◆ **we've been to ~ and back*** ça a été l'enfer *or* l'horreur (mais on s'en est sortis) ◆ **we're going to ~ in a handbasket** *or* **handcart**‡ la situation est catastrophique* pour nous ◆ **~ hath no fury like a woman scorned** *(Prov)* rien n'est plus à craindre qu'une femme blessée ◆ **come ~ or high water** quoi qu'il arrive ◆ **the boyfriend from ~*** le pire des petits amis ◆ **the holiday from ~*** des vacances de cauchemar ◆ **to ride ~ for leather** aller à un train d'enfer ◆ **he went off home ~ for leather** il est rentré chez lui au triple galop

[2] ‡ *(emphatic phrases)* **there'll be ~ to pay** ça va barder* ◆ **he did it for the ~ of it** *(gen)* il l'a fait parce que ça lui chantait ; *(= to annoy people)* il l'a fait pour embêter le monde ◆ **to play (merry) ~ with** *[+ plans, routine, schedule]* bouleverser ; *[+ health, skin]* être très mauvais pour ◆ **they beat the ~ out of me** ils m'ont roué de coups ◆ **I hope to ~ you're right** j'espère sacrément* que tu as raison ◆ **to give sb ~** *(= make their life a misery)* faire mener une vie infernale à qn ; *(= scold)* faire sa fête à qn*, passer une engueulade‡ à qn ◆ **my back's giving me ~** mon dos me fait horriblement mal* ◆ **the children give her ~** les enfants lui en font voir de toutes les couleurs ◆ **to go through ~** vivre un enfer *or* l'enfer ◆ **I put Brian through ~** j'en ai fait voir de toutes les couleurs à Brian ◆ **oh ~!** flûte !*, merde !‡ ◆ **~ and damnation!**‡, **~'s bells** *or* **teeth!** † *(Brit)* sacrebleu !* ◆ **to ~ with him!** qu'il aille se faire voir !* ◆ **to ~ with it!** la barbe !* ◆ **get the ~ out of here!** fous le camp !‡ ◆ **let's get the ~ out of here** barrons-nous‡ ◆ **he got the ~ out** il a foutu le camp‡ ◆ **to scare the ~ out of sb** faire une peur bleue à qn*, ficher la frousse à qn* ◆ **go to ~!** va te faire voir* *or* foutre‡ ! ◆ **will you do it? – the ~ I will!** tu le feras ? – tu parles* *or* tu rigoles‡ !

♦ **as hell** ◆ **I was angry as ~** j'étais vachement en boule* ◆ **it's (as) hot/cold as ~** on crève* de chaud/froid ◆ **they sure as ~ haven't been trained properly** une chose est sûre, ils n'ont pas été correctement formés

♦ **hell of a**‡ ◆ **to make a ~ of a noise** faire un boucan *or* un raffut du diable* ◆ **a ~ of a lot of cars** tout un tas de bagnoles* ◆ **a ~ of a lot of people** des masses* de gens ◆ **he's a ~ of a nice guy** c'est un type vachement bien* ◆ **we had a ~ of a time** *(= bad)* ça n'a pas été marrant‡, on en a bavé‡ ; *(= good)* on s'est vachement marrés‡, ça a été terrible‡ *or* du tonnerre‡ ◆ **they had one ~ of a fight** ils se sont étripés ◆ **there'll be a ~ of a row** ça va barder*

♦ **like hell** ◆ **to work like ~** travailler comme un forçat ◆ **to run like ~** courir comme un dératé* *or* un fou ◆ **it hurts like ~** ça fait vachement* mal ◆ **I missed her like ~** elle me manquait vachement* ◆ **will you do it? – like ~ (I will)!** tu le feras ? – tu parles* *or* tu rigoles‡ !

♦ **what/where** *etc* **the hell ...** ◆ **what the ~!** *(in surprise)* merde alors !‡ ; *(dismissive)* qu'est-ce que ça peut bien faire ! ◆ **what the ~ does he want now?** qu'est-ce qu'il peut bien vouloir maintenant ? ◆ **what the ~ is he doing?** qu'est-ce qu'il peut bien fabriquer* *or* foutre‡ ? ◆ **what the ~ did he say?** qu'est-ce qu'il a bien pu raconter ? ◆ **what the ~'s going on?** mais enfin qu'est-ce qui se passe ?, mais bon sang* qu'est-ce qui se passe ? ◆ **where the ~ have I put it?** où est-ce que j'ai bien pu le foutre ?‡ ◆ **where the ~ have you been?** mais où t'étais passé, bon sang ?* ◆ **how the ~ did you get in?** mais comment t'as fait pour entrer ?* ◆ **why the ~ did you do it?** qu'est-ce qui t'a pris de faire ça ?

[COMP] **hell-raiser**‡ N ◆ **to be a ~-raiser** mener une vie de patachon* *or* de bâton de chaise*

hell-raising‡ N vie *f* de patachon* *or* de bâton de chaise*

hell's angel N *(= person)* Hell's Angel *m*

hellacious‡ /heˈleɪʃəs/ ADJ *(US)* [1] *(= terrible) [fighting]* infernal ; *[car crash]* effroyable [2] *(= wild) [party]* dingue* [3] *(= excellent) [vacation]* d'enfer*

hellbent* /ˌhelˈbent/ ADJ ◆ **to be ~ on doing sth** *or (US)* **to do sth** vouloir à tout prix faire qch

hellcat /ˈhelkæt/ N *(pej)* harpie *f*, mégère *f*

hellebore /ˈhelɪˌbɔːʳ/ N (h)ellébore *m*

Hellene /ˈheliːn/ N Hellène *mf*

Hellenic /heˈliːnɪk/ ADJ hellénique

Hellenistic /ˌhelɪˈnɪstɪk/ ADJ hellénistique

heller‡ /ˈheləʳ/ N *(US)* vrai démon* *m*

hellfire /helˈfaɪəʳ/ N flammes *fpl* de l'enfer

hellhole* /ˈhelhəʊl/ N bouge *m*

hellion* /ˈheljən/ N *(US)* chahuteur *m*, trublion *m*

hellish /ˈhelɪʃ/ [ADJ] *(lit) [vision]* cauchemardesque ; *[intentions, actions]* diabolique ; *(*fig = very unpleasant) [time, place, job]* infernal ; *[problems]* épouvantable [ADV] †* *[expensive, difficult]* sacrément

hellishly* /ˈhelɪʃlɪ/ ADV horriblement

hello /həˈləʊ/ **LANGUAGE IN USE 21.2** EXCL *(in greeting)* bonjour ! ; *(on phone)* allô ! ; *(to attract attention)* hé !, ohé ! ; *(in surprise)* tiens ! ◆ **~ there!** bonjour !

helluva‡ /ˈheləvə/ ⇒ **hell of a** ; → **hell**

helm /helm/ [N] *(Naut)* barre *f* ◆ **to be at the ~** *(Naut, fig)* être à *or* tenir la barre ◆ **to take (over) the ~** *(fig)* prendre la barre [VT] tenir la barre de [VI] être à *or* tenir la barre, barrer

helmet /ˈhelmɪt/ N casque *m* ; → **crash¹**

helmeted /ˈhelmɪtɪd/ ADJ casqué

helminth /ˈhelmɪnθ/ N helminthe *m*

helmsman /ˈhelmzmən/ N (pl **-men**) *(Naut)* timonier *m*, homme *m* de barre

help /help/ **LANGUAGE IN USE 4**

[N] [1] *(gen)* aide *f* ; *(in emergency)* secours *m* ◆ **~!** *(in danger etc)* au secours !, à l'aide ! ; *(in dismay)* mince ! ◆ **thank you for your ~** merci de votre aide ◆ **with his brother's ~** avec l'aide de son frère ◆ **~ was at hand in the form of my sister** ma sœur est venue à mon secours ◆ **with the ~ of a knife/a computer** à l'aide d'un couteau/d'un ordinateur ◆ **he did it without ~** il l'a fait tout seul ◆ **to shout for ~** appeler *or* crier au secours, appeler à l'aide ◆ **to ask sb for ~** demander de l'aide à qn ◆ **ask the pharmacist for ~** demandez conseil au pharmacien ◆ **to go to sb's ~** aller au secours de qn, prêter secours *or* assistance à qn ◆ **to come to sb's ~** venir à l'aide de qn *or* en aide à qn ◆ **to be of ~ to sb** *[person, machine, training]* rendre service à qn ◆ **can I be of ~?** je peux vous aider ? ◆ **I was glad to be of ~** j'ai été content d'avoir pu rendre service ◆ **it was of no ~ (at all)** cela n'a servi à rien (du tout) ◆ **you've been a great ~** vous m'avez vraiment rendu service ◆ **you're a great ~!** *(iro)* tu es d'un précieux secours ! *(iro)* ◆ **you can't get decent (domestic) ~ nowadays** on ne trouve plus de bons employés de maison de nos jours ◆ **she has no ~ in the house** elle n'a personne pour l'aider à la maison ◆ **we need more ~ in the shop** il nous faut davantage de personnel au magasin ◆ **he's beyond ~** *(fig)* on ne peut plus rien pour lui ◆ **there's no ~ for it** il n'y a rien à faire, on n'y peut rien ; → **voluntary**

[2] *(= cleaner)* femme *f* de ménage ; → **daily, home, mother**

[VT] [1] *(gen)* aider *(sb to do sth* qn à faire qch) ; *(in emergency)* secourir ◆ **let me ~ you with that suitcase** je vais vous aider avec votre valise ◆ **she ~s her son with his homework** elle aide son fils à faire ses devoirs ◆ **he got his brother to ~ him** il s'est fait aider par son frère ◆ **that doesn't ~ much** cela ne sert pas à *or* n'arrange pas grand-chose ◆ **that won't ~ you** cela ne vous servira à rien ◆ **God ~s those who ~ themselves** *(Prov)* aide-toi et le ciel t'aidera *(Prov)* ◆ **so ~ me God!** je le jure devant Dieu ! ◆ **so ~ me*** **I'll kill him!** je le tuerai, je le jure ! ◆ **this money will ~ to save the church** cet argent contribuera à sauver l'église ◆ **every little ~s** les petits ruisseaux font les grandes rivières *(Prov)* ◆ **can I ~ you?** *(in shop, to customer at counter)* vous désirez ? ; *(to customer browsing)* je peux vous aider ? ◆ **to ~ each other** *or* **one another** s'entraider ◆ **he is ~ing the police with their inquiries** *(euph)* il est en train de répondre aux questions de la police ◆ **it ~s industry/exports** cela favorise l'industrie/les exportations ◆ **to ~ sb across/down/in** *etc* aider qn à traverser/à descendre/à entrer *etc* ◆ **to ~ sb up/down/out with a suitcase** aider qn à monter/à descendre/à sortir une valise ◆ **to ~ sb (up) to his feet** aider qn à se lever ◆ **to ~ sb on/off with his coat** aider qn à mettre/à enlever son manteau

[2] *(= serve)* ◆ **to ~ o.s.** se servir ◆ **he ~ed himself to vegetables** il s'est servi de légumes ◆ **~ yourself to wine/bread** prenez du vin/du pain, servez-vous de vin/de pain ◆ **just ~ yourself to leaflets** voilà des prospectus, servez-vous ◆ **~ yourself!** servez-vous ! ◆ **he's ~ed himself to my pencil*** *(euph)* il m'a piqué mon crayon*

[3] *(with can, cannot, etc)* **I couldn't ~ laughing** je ne pouvais pas m'empêcher de rire ◆ **one cannot ~ wondering whether ...** on ne peut s'empêcher de se demander si ... ◆ **one can't ~ but wonder/be impressed** on ne peut s'empêcher de se demander/d'être impressionné ◆ **it can't be ~ed** tant pis !, on n'y peut rien ! ◆ **I can't ~ it if he always comes late** je n'y peux rien *or* ce n'est pas de ma faute s'il arrive toujours en retard ◆ **he can't ~ it** ce n'est pas de sa faute, il n'y peut rien ◆ **why are you laughing? – I can't ~ it** pourquoi riez-vous ? – c'est plus fort que moi ◆ **we just can't ~ ourselves** c'est plus fort que nous ◆ **not if I can ~ it!** sûrement pas !, il faudra d'abord me passer sur le corps ! *(hum)* ◆ **he won't come if I can ~ it** je vais faire tout mon possible pour l'empêcher de venir ◆ **can I ~ it if it rains?** est-ce que c'est de ma

faute s'il pleut ? ◆ **it's rather late now – I can't ~ that, you should have come earlier** il est un peu tard maintenant – je n'y peux rien, tu aurais dû venir plus tôt ◆ **he can't ~ his temperamental nature** il n'arrive pas à se corriger de son humeur instable ◆ **he can't ~ his deafness** ce n'est pas de sa faute s'il est sourd ◆ **he can't ~ being stupid** ce n'est pas de sa faute s'il est idiot ◆ **don't say more than you can ~** n'en dites pas plus qu'il ne faut

COMP **help desk** N service *m* d'assistance

help menu N *(Comput)* menu *m* d'assistance

► **help along** VT SEP *[+ person]* aider à marcher ; *[+ scheme]* (faire) avancer, faire progresser

► **help out**

VI aider, donner un coup de main ; *(financially)* dépanner* ◆ **I ~ out with the secretarial work** j'aide à faire le secrétariat

VT SEP *(gen)* aider, donner un coup de main à ; *(financially)* dépanner*, tirer d'embarras ◆ **to ~ each other out** s'entraider

► **help up** VT SEP ◆ **to help sb up** aider qn à se lever

helper /ˈhelpəʳ/ N aide *mf*

helpful /ˈhelpfʊl/ ADJ 1 *(= cooperative) [person, staff]* obligeant *(to sb* avec qn) ◆ **you have been most ~** c'était très aimable à vous ◆ **you're not being very ~** tu ne m'aides pas beaucoup 2 *(= useful) [suggestion, book, tool]* utile ; *[medicine]* efficace ◆ **to be ~ in doing sth** contribuer à faire qch

helpfully /ˈhelpfəlɪ/ ADV *[say]* avec obligeance ; *[provide, suggest, explain]* obligeamment

helpfulness /ˈhelpfʊlnɪs/ N obligeance *f*

helping /ˈhelpɪŋ/ N *(at table)* portion *f* ◆ **to take a second ~ of sth** reprendre de qch ◆ **I've had three ~s** j'en ai repris deux fois ◆ **the public appetite for huge ~s of nostalgia** le goût du public pour de grosses bouffées de nostalgie

ADJ secourable ◆ **to give** *or* **lend a ~ hand (to)** aider, donner un coup de main (à)

helpless /ˈhelplɪs/ ADJ *[victim, baby, old person]* sans défense *(against sth* contre qch) ; *[invalid]* impotent, sans défense ; *[situation]* désespéré ; *[feeling, gesture]* d'impuissance ◆ **he is quite ~ (in this matter)** il n'y peut rien, il ne peut rien y faire ◆ **she looked at him with a ~ expression** elle lui jeta un regard d'impuissance ◆ **to feel ~ (against sth)** se sentir désarmé (devant qch) ◆ **he was ~ to resist** il a été incapable de résister ◆ **to be ~ with laughter** être mort de rire

helplessly /ˈhelplɪslɪ/ ADV 1 *(= impotently) [struggle, try, say]* désespérément ; *[stand, look on]* sans pouvoir rien faire ; *[agree]* en désespoir de cause ◆ **he was lying ~ on the ground** il était allongé par terre, sans pouvoir bouger 2 *(= uncontrollably) [sob, cry, sneeze]* sans pouvoir se retenir ; *[drift]* inexorablement ◆ **to laugh ~** être mort de rire ◆ **to get ~ drunk** se soûler jusqu'à ne plus pouvoir tenir debout ◆ **to feel ~ angry** être en proie à une colère impuissante

helplessness /ˈhelplɪsnɪs/ N *[of victim, baby, old person]* impuissance *f* *(against sth* face à qch ; *before sth* devant qch) ; *[of invalid]* impotence *f* ◆ **feelings of ~** un sentiment d'impuissance ◆ **the ~ of the situation** le fait que la situation soit désespérée

helpline /ˈhelplaɪn/ N *(esp Brit)* service *m* d'assistance téléphonique ; *(Comm)* ≈ numéro *m* vert *(pour renseignements sur un produit)*

helpmate /ˈhelpmeɪt/, **helpmeet** † /ˈhelpmiːt/ N *(= spouse)* époux *m*, épouse *f* ; *(= female companion)* dame *f* de compagnie

Helsinki /helˈsɪŋkɪ/ N Helsinki

helter-skelter /ˈheltəˈskeltəʳ/ ADV *[run]* pêle-mêle ADJ *[rush]* désordonné N 1 *(= rush)* débandade *f*, bousculade *f* 2 *(Brit: in fairground)* toboggan *m*

hem¹ /hem/ N ourlet *m* ; *(= edge)* bord *m* ◆ **I've let the ~ down on my skirt** j'ai défait l'ourlet de ma jupe pour la rallonger, j'ai rallongé ma jupe VT *(= sew)* ourler

► **hem in** VT SEP *[+ houses, objects, people]* cerner ; *[rules etc]* entraver ◆ **I feel ~med in** je me sens oppressé ◆ **they are ~med in by rigid contracts** ils sont pris dans le carcan de contrats rigides

hem² /hem/ VI → **haw²**

hema(t)... /ˈhiːmə(t)/ PREF *(US)* ⇒ **haema(t)...**

hemato... /ˈhiːmətəʊ/ PREF *(US)* ⇒ **haemato...**

hemicycle /ˈhemɪsaɪkl/ N hémicycle *m*

hemiplegia /ˌhemɪˈpliːdʒɪə/ N hémiplégie *f*

hemiplegic /ˌhemɪˈpliːdʒɪk/ ADJ, N hémiplégique *mf*

hemisphere /ˈhemɪsfɪəʳ/ N hémisphère *m* ◆ **the northern ~** l'hémisphère *m* nord *or* boréal ◆ **the southern ~** l'hémisphère *m* sud *or* austral

hemispheric /ˈhemɪsferɪk/ ADJ 1 *(Geog)* ◆ **Northern ~ summers** les étés *mpl* de l'hémisphère nord *or* boréal 2 *(US Pol) [relations, solidarity]* entre pays du nord et du sud de l'Amérique ; *[policy]* concernant les relations entre pays du nord et du sud de l'Amérique ◆ **a sense of ~ identity** un sentiment d'identité américaine 3 *(Med, Psych) [asymmetry]* hémisphérique ; *[specialization, activity]* de l'un des hémisphères (du cerveau)

hemistich /ˈhemɪstɪk/ N hémistiche *m*

hemline /ˈhemlaɪn/ N (bas *m* de l')ourlet *m* ◆ **~s are lower this year** les robes rallongent cette année

hemlock /ˈhemlɒk/ N 1 *(= plant, poison)* ciguë *f* 2 *(= tree)* (also **hemlock spruce**) sapin *m* du Canada, sapin-ciguë *m*

hem(o)... /ˈhiːm(əʊ)/ PREF *(US)* ⇒ **haem(o)...**

hemp /hemp/ N *(= plant, fibre)* chanvre *m* ; *(= drug)* chanvre *m* indien

hemstitch /ˈhemstɪtʃ/ VT ourler à jour N point *m* d'ourlet

hen /hen/ N 1 poule *f* ; *(= female bird)* femelle *f* ◆ **~ bird** oiseau *m* femelle 2 *(Scot)* **here you are, ~*** voilà, ma petite dame*

COMP **hen harrier** N busard *m* Saint-Martin

hen night*, **hen party*** N *(esp Brit)* soirée *f* entre femmes *(or filles)*

henbane /ˈhenbeɪn/ N *(= plant)* jusquiame *f* (noire), herbe *f* aux poules

hence /hens/ LANGUAGE IN USE 26.3 ADV 1 *(frm = therefore)* d'où ◆ **~ the name** d'où son nom ◆ **inflation is rising: ~, new economic policies are needed** l'inflation est en hausse ; d'où la nécessité de prendre de nouvelles mesures économiques ◆ **it will drive up the price of oil, and ~ the price of petrol** ça fera monter le prix du pétrole, et par conséquent celui de l'essence ◆ **the lack of blood, and ~ oxygen, in the brain** le manque de sang, et par conséquent *or* et donc d'oxygène, dans le cerveau 2 *(frm = from now)* d'ici ◆ **two years ~** d'ici deux ans 3 († † *= from here)* d'ici ◆ **(get thee) ~!** hors d'ici !

henceforth /hensˈfɔːθ/, **henceforward** /hensˈfɔːwəd/ ADV *(frm)* dorénavant, désormais

henchman /ˈhentʃmən/ N (pl **-men**) *(pej)* homme *m* de main ; *(Hist)* écuyer *m*

hencoop /ˈhenkuːp/ N cage *f* à poules

henhouse /ˈhenhaʊs/ N poulailler *m*

henna /ˈhenə/ N henné *m* VT *[+ hair]* teindre au henné ◆ **to ~ one's hair** se faire un henné

henpecked /ˈhenpekt/ ADJ ◆ **he's a ~ husband** sa femme le mène par le bout du nez

Henry /ˈhenrɪ/ N Henri *m* ; → **hooray**

hep* /hep/ N (abbrev of **hepatitis**) hépatite *f* ◆ **~ A/B** hépatite A/B ADJ † *(= with-it)* dans le vent* ◆ **to be ~ to sth** *(US)* être au courant de qch

heparin /ˈhepərɪn/ N héparine *f*

hepatitis /ˌhepəˈtaɪtɪs/ N hépatite *f* ◆ **~ A/B/C** hépatite *f* A/B/C

heptagon /ˈheptəgən/ N *(Geom)* heptagone *m*

heptagonal /hepˈtægənəl/ ADJ *(Geom)* heptagonal

heptathlon /hepˈtæθlən/ N heptathlon *m*

her /hɜːʳ/ PERS PRON 1 *(direct, unstressed)* la ; *(before vowel)* l' ; *(stressed)* elle ◆ **I see ~** je la vois ◆ **I have seen ~** je l'ai vue ◆ **I know HIM but I have never seen HER** lui je le connais, mais elle je ne l'ai jamais vue

2 *(indirect)* lui ◆ **I gave ~ the book** je lui ai donné le livre ◆ **I'm speaking to ~** je lui parle

3 *(after prep etc)* elle ◆ **I am thinking of ~** je pense à elle ◆ **without ~** sans elle ◆ **she took her books with ~** elle a emporté ses livres ◆ **if I were ~** si j'étais elle ◆ **it's ~** c'est elle ◆ **younger than ~** plus jeune qu'elle

4 celle ◆ **to ~ who might complain, I should point out that ...** à celle qui se plaindrait, je ferais remarquer que ... ◆ **the articles are of no value except to ~ who had once owned them** ces articles n'ont aucune valeur sauf pour celle à qui ils appartenaient autrefois

POSS ADJ son, sa, ses ◆ **~ book** son livre ◆ **~ table** sa table ◆ **~ friend** son ami(e) *m(f)* ◆ **~ clothes** ses vêtements

Hera /ˈhɪərə/ N Héra *f*

Heracles /ˈherəˌkliːz/ N Héraclès *m*

Heraclitus /ˌherəˈklaɪtəs/ N Héraclite *m*

herald /ˈherəld/ N héraut *m* ◆ **the ~ of spring** *(fig, liter)* le messager du printemps *(liter)* VT annoncer ◆ **to ~ (in)** annoncer l'arrivée de ◆ **tonight's game is being ~ed as the match of the season** *(Ftbl)* on présente le match de ce soir comme le plus important de la saison

heraldic /heˈrældɪk/ ADJ héraldique ◆ **~ bearing** armoiries *fpl*, blason *m*

heraldry /ˈherəldrɪ/ N *(NonC) (= science)* héraldique *f* ; *(= coat of arms)* blason *m* ; *(ceremonial)* pompe *f* héraldique ◆ **book of ~** armorial *m*

herb /hɜːb, (US) ɜːb/ N herbe *f* ◆ **~s** *(Culin)* fines herbes *fpl* ◆ **pot ~s** herbes *fpl* potagères ◆ **medicinal ~s** herbes *fpl* médicinales, simples *mpl*

COMP **herb garden** N jardin *m* d'herbes aromatiques

herb tea N infusion *f*, tisane *f*

herbaceous /hɜːˈbeɪʃəs/ ADJ herbacé ◆ **~ border** bordure *f* de plantes herbacées

herbage /ˈhɜːbɪdʒ/ N *(Agr)* herbages *mpl* ; *(Jur)* droit *m* de pacage

herbal /ˈhɜːbəl/ ADJ d'herbes N herbier *m (livre)*

COMP **herbal medicine** N phytothérapie *f*

herbal remedy N remède *m* à base de plantes

herbal tea N infusion *f*, tisane *f*

herbalism /ˈhɜːbəlɪzəm/ N phytothérapie *f*

herbalist /ˈhɜːbəlɪst/ N herboriste *mf*

herbarium /hɜːˈbɛərɪəm/ N (pl **herbariums** *or* **herbaria** /hɜːˈbɛərɪə/) herbier *m (collection)*

herbicide /ˈhɜːbɪsaɪd/ N herbicide *m*

herbivore /ˈhɜːbɪvɔːʳ/ N herbivore *m*

herbivorous /hɜːˈbɪvərəs/ ADJ herbivore

Herculean /ˌhɜːkjʊˈliːən/ ADJ herculéen

Hercules /ˈhɜːkjuliːz/ N *(Myth)* Hercule *m* ; *(fig) (= strong man)* hercule *m*

herd /hɜːd/ N 1 *[of cattle, goats, elephants]* troupeau *m* ; *[of stags]* harde *f* ; *[of horses]* troupe *f*, bande *f* ◆ **to ride ~ on sb** *(US)* avoir l'œil sur qn 2 * *[of people]* troupeau *m*, foule *f* ◆ **to follow the ~** *(fig)* être comme un mouton de

Panurge ; → **common** 3 (†† = *person)* pâtre *m (liter)* ; → **cowherd, goatherd** VT *[+ animals]* mener en troupeau ◆ **to ~ into/onto** *etc [+ people]* faire entrer/monter *etc* en troupeau dans

COMP **herd instinct** N instinct *m* grégaire

► **herd together** VI *[animals, people]* s'attrouper, s'assembler en troupeau VT SEP *[+ animals, people]* rassembler

herdsman /hɜːdzmən/ N (pl **-men**) gardien *m* de troupeau ; *(= shepherd)* berger *m* ; *(= cowman)* vacher *m*, bouvier *m*

here /hɪəʳ/ ADV 1 *(place)* ici ◆ **I live ~** j'habite ici ◆ **come ~** venez ici ◆ **~!** *(at roll call)* présent ! ◆ **he's ~ at last** le voici enfin, il est enfin là *or* arrivé ◆ **spring is ~** c'est le printemps, le printemps est là ◆ **my sister ~ says …** ma sœur que voici dit … ◆ **this man ~ saw it** cet homme-ci l'a vu ◆ **Mr Moore is not ~ just now** M. Moore n'est pas là *or* ici en ce moment ◆ **are you there? – yes I'm ~** vous êtes là ? – oui je suis là ◆ **I shan't be ~ this afternoon** je ne serai pas là cet après-midi ◆ **I'm ~ to help** je suis là pour vous aider ◆ **I'm ~ to tell you (that) …** je suis venu vous dire (que) … ◆ **~ below** ici-bas

◆ **here and there** çà et là, par-ci par-là

◆ **here, there and everywhere** un peu partout

◆ **neither here nor there** ◆ **it's neither ~ nor there** tout cela n'a aucun rapport

◆ **here and now** sur-le-champ ◆ **I must warn you ~ and now that …** il faut que je vous prévienne tout de suite que …

◆ *preposition* + **here** ◆ **about** *or* **around ~** par ici ◆ **far from ~** loin d'ici ◆ **put it in ~** mettez-le ici ◆ **come in ~** venez (par) ici ◆ **in ~ please** par ici s'il vous plaît ◆ **near ~** près d'ici ◆ **over ~** ici ◆ **it's cold up ~** il fait froid ici (en haut) ◆ **up to** *or* **down to ~** jusqu'ici ◆ **from ~ to London** d'ici (jusqu')à Londres ◆ **it's 10km from ~ to Paris** il y a 10 km d'ici à Paris

◆ **here** + *verb structure (showing, announcing etc)* ◆ **~ I am** me voici ◆ **~ is my brother** voici mon frère ◆ **~ are the others** voici les autres ◆ **~ we are at last** nous voici enfin arrivés ◆ **~ we are!** *(bringing sth)* voici ! ◆ **~ you are!** *(giving sth)* tenez ! ◆ **~ come my friends** voici mes amis qui arrivent ◆ **~ goes!*** allons-y !, c'est parti !* ◆ **~ we go again!** c'est reparti !*, (et) voilà que ça recommence ! ◆ **~ lies …** ci-gît …

◆ **here's to …** ◆ **~'s to you!** à la tienne !, à la vôtre ! ◆ **~'s to your success!** à votre succès !

2 *(time)* alors, à ce moment-là ◆ **it's ~ that the real test will come** ce sera l'épreuve de vérité ◆ **~ I think it is appropriate to draw your attention to …** je pense qu'il convient maintenant d'attirer votre attention sur …

EXCL ◆ **~, I didn't promise that at all!** dites donc, je n'ai jamais promis cela ! ◆ **~, you try to open it** * tiens, essaie de l'ouvrir, alors ◆ **~, hold this a minute** * tiens-moi ça une minute

COMP **the here and now** N le présent, l'instant *m* présent

hereabouts /hɪərəbaʊts/ ADV par ici

hereafter /hɪərˈɑːftəʳ/ ADV *(= in the future)* après, plus tard ; *(in document = following this)* ci-après ; *(= after death)* dans l'autre monde *or* vie N ◆ **the ~** l'au-delà *m*

hereby /hɪəˈbaɪ/ ADV *(Comm, Jur) (in letter)* par la présente ; *(in document)* par le présent document ; *(in act)* par le présent acte ; *(in will)* par le présent testament ; *(in declaration)* par la présente (déclaration)

hereditaments /ˌherɪˈdɪtəmənts/ NPL *(Jur) biens meubles ou immeubles transmissibles par héritage*

hereditary /hɪˈredɪtərɪ/ ADJ héréditaire ◆ **a ~ peer** un lord héréditaire

heredity /hɪˈredɪtɪ/ N hérédité *f*

herein /hɪəˈrɪn/ ADV *(frm) (= in this matter)* en ceci, en cela ; *(= in this writing)* ci-inclus

hereinafter /ˌhɪərɪnˈɑːftəʳ/ ADV *(Jur)* ci-après, dans la suite des présentes

hereof /hɪərˈɒv/ ADV *(frm)* de ceci, de cela ◆ **the provisions ~** *(Jur)* les dispositions *fpl* des présentes

heresy /ˈherəsɪ/ N hérésie *f* ◆ **an act of ~** une hérésie

heretic /ˈherətɪk/ N hérétique *mf*

heretical /hɪˈretɪkəl/ ADJ hérétique

hereto /hɪəˈtuː/ ADV *(Jur)* à ceci, à cela ◆ **the parties ~** *(Jur)* les parties *fpl* aux présentes

heretofore /ˌhɪətʊˈfɔːʳ/ ADV *(frm) (= up to specified point)* jusque-là ; *(= up to now)* jusqu'ici ; *(= previously)* ci-devant

hereupon /ˌhɪərəˈpɒn/ ADV *(frm)* là-dessus, sur ce

herewith /ˌhɪəˈwɪð/ ADV *(frm)* avec ceci ◆ **I am sending you ~** je vous envoie ci-joint *or* sous ce pli ◆ **I enclose ~ a copy of …** veuillez trouver ci-joint une copie de …

heritable /ˈherɪtəbl/ ADJ *[objects, property]* transmissible ; *[intelligence]* héréditaire

heritage /ˈherɪtɪdʒ/ N 1 *(= legacy)* héritage *m* ◆ **the country's communist ~** l'héritage communiste du pays ◆ **the law is a ~ of the Thatcher era** cette loi est un héritage des années Thatcher 2 *(= historical wealth)* patrimoine *m* ◆ **our cultural/national ~** notre patrimoine culturel/national ◆ **steel mills are becoming part of the ~ industry** les anciennes aciéries font maintenant partie des circuits du tourisme industriel et historique

COMP **heritage centre** N *(Brit)* petit musée *m* local

hermaphrodite /hɜːˈmæfrədaɪt/ ADJ, N hermaphrodite *m*

hermaphroditic /hɜːmæfrəˈdɪtɪk/ ADJ hermaphrodite

Hermes /ˈhɜːmiːz/ N Hermès *m*

hermetic /hɜːˈmetɪk/ ADJ *(gen, also Literat)* hermétique

hermetically /hɜːˈmetɪkəlɪ/ ADV hermétiquement ◆ **~ sealed** hermétiquement fermé

hermit /ˈhɜːmɪt/ N *(lit, fig)* ermite *m* COMP **hermit crab** N bernard-l'(h)ermite *m inv*

hermitage /ˈhɜːmɪtɪdʒ/ N ermitage *m*

hernia /ˈhɜːnɪə/ N (pl **hernias** *or* **herniae** /ˈhɜːnɪˌiː/) hernie *f*

hero /ˈhɪərəʊ/ (pl **heroes**) N 1 héros *m* ◆ **his boyhood ~** le héros de son enfance ◆ **the ~ of the hour** le héros du jour ; → **land** 2 ⇒ **hero sandwich**

COMP **hero sandwich** N *(US)* grand sandwich *m* mixte

hero's welcome N ◆ **to give sb a ~'s welcome** accueillir qn comme un héros

hero-worship N culte *m* (du héros) VT aduler, idolâtrer

Herod /ˈherəd/ N Hérode *m* ; → **out-Herod**

heroic /hɪˈrəʊɪk/ ADJ héroïque ◆ **to put up ~ resistance** résister héroïquement

COMP **heroic couplet** N *(Poetry)* distique *m* héroïque

heroic verse N *(NonC: Poetry)* vers *mpl* héroïques ◆ **in ~ verse** en décasyllabes

heroically /hɪˈrəʊɪkəlɪ/ ADV héroïquement ◆ **she managed, ~, to keep a straight face** *(hum)* elle réussit, à grand-peine, à garder son sérieux

heroics /hɪˈrəʊɪks/ NPL actes *mpl* de bravoure ◆ **no ~!** ne joue pas les héros !

heroin /ˈherəʊɪn/ N héroïne *f (drogue)*

COMP **heroin addict** N héroïnomane *mf*

heroin addiction N héroïnomanie *f*

heroin user N héroïnomane *mf*

heroine /ˈherəʊɪn/ N héroïne *f (femme)*

heroism /ˈherəʊɪzəm/ N héroïsme *m*

heron /ˈherən/ N héron *m*

herpes /ˈhɜːpiːz/ N herpès *m* ; → **genital**

herring /ˈherɪŋ/ N (pl **herrings** *or* **herring**) hareng *m* ; → **fish, red**

COMP **herring boat** N harenguier *m*

herring gull N goéland *m* argenté

the herring-pond * N *(= the Atlantic)* la mare aux harengs *(hum)*, l'Atlantique Nord

herringbone /ˈherɪŋbəʊn/ N *(lit)* arête *f* de hareng ; *(Archit)* appareil *m* en épi ; *(Ski)* (also **herringbone climb**) montée *f* en canard

COMP **herringbone pattern** N (dessin *m* à) chevrons *mpl*

herringbone stitch N point *m* d'épine (en chevron)

hers /hɜːz/ POSS PRON le sien, la sienne, les siens, les siennes ◆ **my hands are clean, ~ are dirty** mes mains sont propres, les siennes sont sales ◆ **~ is a specialized department** sa section est une section spécialisée ◆ **this book is ~** ce livre est à elle, ce livre est le sien ◆ **the house became ~** la maison est devenue la sienne ◆ **it is not ~ to decide** ce n'est pas à elle de décider, il ne lui appartient pas de décider ◆ **is this poem ~?** ce poème est-il d'elle ?

◆ **… of hers** ◆ **a friend of ~** un de ses amis (à elle) ◆ **it's no fault of ~** ce n'est pas de sa faute (à elle) ◆ **no advice of ~ could prevent him** aucun conseil de sa part ne pouvait l'empêcher ◆ **that car of ~** *(pej)* sa fichue* voiture ◆ **that stupid son of ~** *(pej)* son idiot de fils ◆ **that temper of ~** *(pej)* son sale caractère

herself /hɜːˈself/ PERS PRON *(reflexive, direct and indirect)* se ; *(emphatic)* elle-même ; *(after prep)* elle ◆ **she has hurt ~** elle s'est blessée ◆ **she poured ~ a whisky** elle s'est servie un whisky ◆ **"why not?" she said to ~** "pourquoi pas ?" se dit-elle ◆ **she told me ~** elle me l'a dit elle-même ◆ **I saw the girl ~** j'ai vu la jeune fille elle-même *or* en personne ◆ **she kept three for ~** elle s'en est réservé trois ◆ **he asked her for a photo of ~** il lui a demandé une photo d'elle ◆ **she hasn't been ~ lately** *(= not behaving normally)* elle n'est pas dans son état normal ces temps-ci ; *(= not feeling well)* elle n'est pas dans son assiette ces temps-ci

◆ **(all) by herself** toute seule

Herts /hɑːts/ abbrev of **Hertfordshire**

hertz /hɜːts/ N *(pl inv)* hertz *m*

he's /hiːz/ ⇒ **he is, he has** ; → **be, have**

hesitancy /ˈhezɪtənsɪ/ N hésitation *f*

hesitant /ˈhezɪtənt/ ADJ hésitant ◆ **to be ~ to do** *or* **about doing sth** hésiter à faire qch

hesitantly /ˈhezɪtəntlɪ/ ADV *[say]* avec hésitation ; *[enter]* en hésitant ◆ **she stood ~ in the doorway** elle se tenait indécise sur le pas de la porte

hesitate /ˈhezɪteɪt/ LANGUAGE IN USE 3.1, 20.2, 21.2

VI hésiter *(over, about, at* sur, devant ; *to do sth* à faire qch) ◆ **he didn't ~ at the idea of leaving her** il l'a quittée sans hésiter ◆ **he never once ~d over publishing the article** il n'a pas hésité une seconde avant de publier cet article ◆ **the President has been hesitating over whether to attend the conference** le président hésite à assister à la conférence ◆ **I will not ~ to take unpopular decisions** je n'hésiterai pas à prendre des décisions impopulaires ◆ **she ~d about going in for politics** elle hésitait à entrer dans la politique ◆ **don't ~ to ask me** n'hésitez pas à me demander ◆ **please do not ~ to contact our Customer Service Department** n'hésitez pas à contacter notre service clientèle ◆ **he ~s at nothing** il ne recule devant rien, rien ne l'arrête ◆ **he who ~s is lost** *(Prov)* une minute d'hésitation peut coûter cher

hesitation /ˌhezɪˈteɪʃən/ N hésitation *f* ◆ **without the slightest ~** sans la moindre hésitation ◆ **I have no ~ in saying that ...** je n'hésite pas à dire que ... ◆ **... he said after some ~ ...** dit-il après un moment d'hésitation ◆ **I had no ~ about taking the job** j'ai accepté le travail sans la moindre hésitation

Hesperides /heˈsperɪˌdiːz/ NPL ◆ **the ~** les Hespérides *fpl*

hessian /ˈhesɪən/ (*esp Brit*) N (toile *f* de) jute *m* COMP (= *made of hessian*) en (toile de) jute

het /het/ ADJ * N hétéro* *mf* COMP **het up*** ADJ excité, énervé ◆ **he gets ~ up about the slightest thing** il se met dans tous ses états à propos d'un rien

hetero* /ˈhetərəʊ/ N, ADJ hétéro* *mf*

heterodox /ˈhetərədɒks/ ADJ hétérodoxe

heterodoxy /ˈhetərədɒksɪ/ N hétérodoxie *f*

heterogeneity /ˌhetərəʊdʒəˈniːətɪ/ N hétérogénéité *f*

heterogeneous /ˈhetərəʊˈdʒiːnɪəs/ ADJ hétérogène

heterosexism /ˈhetərəʊˈseksɪzm/ N discrimination *f* à l'égard des homosexuels

heterosexual /ˈhetərəʊˈseksjʊəl/ ADJ, N hétérosexuel(le) *m(f)*

heterosexuality /ˌhetərəʊˌseksjʊˈælɪtɪ/ N hétérosexualité *f*

heuristic /hjʊəˈrɪstɪk/ ADJ heuristique

heuristics /hjʊəˈrɪstɪks/ N (*NonC*) heuristique *f*

hew /hjuː/ VT (pret **hewed** /hjuːd/, ptp **hewn** *or* **hewed** /hjuːn/) [*+ stone*] tailler, équarrir ; [*+ wood*] couper ; [*+ coal*] abattre ◆ **to ~ sth out of wood/stone** tailler qch dans du bois/la pierre VI (pret, ptp **hewed**) (*US*) ◆ **to ~ to sth** se conformer à qch, suivre qch

hewer /ˈhjuːəʳ/ N [*of stone, wood*] équarrisseur *m* ; [*of coal*] haveur *m*, piqueur *m*

hex¹ /heks/ (*esp US*) N (= *spell*) sort *m* ; (= *witch*) sorcière *f* VT jeter un sort à

hex² /heks/ N (*Comput*) ◆ **~ code** code *m* hexadécimal

hexadecimal /ˌheksəˈdesɪməl/ ADJ, N hexadécimal *m*

hexagon /ˈheksəgən/ N hexagone *m*

hexagonal /hekˈsægənəl/ ADJ hexagonal

hexagram /ˈheksəˌgræm/ N hexagramme *m*

hexameter /hekˈsæmɪtəʳ/ N hexamètre *m*

hexathlon /hekˈsæθlən/ N hexathlon *m*

hey /heɪ/ EXCL hé !, ohé ! ◆ **~ presto!** (*said by magician*) passez muscade ! ; (*fig*) ô miracle ! ◆ **what the ~!** (*US*) et puis zut !*

heyday /ˈheɪdeɪ/ N [*of the music hall, the railways etc*] âge *m* d'or, beaux jours *mpl* ◆ **in his ~** (= *in his prime*) quand il était dans la force de l'âge ; (= *at his most famous*) à l'apogée de sa gloire ◆ **in the ~ of punk/of the theatre** à l'âge d'or du punk/du théâtre ◆ **in the ~ of flares** à la grande époque des pantalons à pattes d'éléphant

Hezbollah /ˈhezbəˈlɑː/ N Hezbollah *m* ADJ [*guerrillas, leader, stronghold*] du Hezbollah

HGH /ˌeɪtʃdʒiːˈeɪtʃ/ N (*Med*) (abbrev of **human growth hormone**) HCH *f*

HGV /ˌeɪtʃdʒiːˈviː/ N (abbrev of **heavy goods vehicle**) poids *m* lourd ◆ **~ driver** chauffeur *m*, -euse *f* de poids lourd ◆ **~ licence** permis *m* poids lourd

HHS /eɪtʃeɪtʃˈes/ N (*US*) (abbrev of **Health and Human Services**) *ministère de la Santé et des Affaires sociales*

HI abbrev of **Hawaii**

hi* /haɪ/ EXCL 1 (= *greeting*) salut !* 2 (= *hey*) hé !, ohé !

hiatus /haɪˈeɪtəs/ N (pl **hiatuses** *or* **hiatus**) (*in series, manuscript etc*) lacune *f* ; (*Ling, Phon, Poetry*) hiatus *m* ; (*fig*) (= *interruption*) interruption *f*, pause *f* ; (= *difference*) hiatus *m*, décalage *m* ◆ **after a two-week ~** après une interruption de deux semaines ◆ **there was an ~ in his acting life** il y a eu une coupure dans sa carrière d'acteur COMP **hiatus hernia** N (*Med*) hernie *f* hiatale

hibernate /ˈhaɪbəneɪt/ VI hiberner

hibernation /ˌhaɪbəˈneɪʃən/ N hibernation *f* ◆ **in ~** en hibernation

Hibernian /haɪˈbɜːnɪən/ ADJ irlandais N Irlandais(e) *m(f)*

hibiscus /hɪˈbɪskəs/ N (pl **hibiscuses**) hibiscus *m*

hic /hɪk/ EXCL hic !

hiccup, hiccough † /ˈhɪkʌp/ N 1 hoquet *m* ◆ **to have ~s** avoir le hoquet 2 (= *minor setback*) contretemps *m*, ratés *mpl* ◆ **the recent sales ~** la baisse momentanée des ventes que nous avons connue récemment VI hoqueter VT dire en hoquetant

hick⁑ /hɪk/ (*US*) N péquenaud(e)⁑ *m(f)* (*pej*) ADJ [*ideas*] de péquenaud⁑ (*pej*) COMP **hick town** N bled⁑ *m* (*pej*)

hickey* /ˈhɪkɪ/ N (*US*) (= *pimple*) petit bouton *m* ; (= *lovebite*) suçon *m*

hickory /ˈhɪkərɪ/ N hickory *m*, noyer *m* blanc d'Amérique

hidden /ˈhɪdn/ VB ptp of **hide¹** ADJ caché ◆ **to remain ~** rester caché ◆ **~ meaning** sens *m* caché ◆ **"no hidden extras"** "garanti sans suppléments" ◆ **~ tax** impôt *m* déguisé COMP **hidden agenda** N intentions *fpl* cachées

hide¹ /haɪd/ (pret **hid** /hɪd/, ptp **hidden** /ˈhɪdn/ *or* **hid**) †† VT cacher (*from sb* à qn) ; [*+ feelings*] dissimuler (*from sb* à qn) ◆ **to ~ o.s.** se cacher ◆ **I've got nothing to ~** je n'ai rien à cacher *or* à dissimuler ◆ **he's hiding something** il nous cache quelque chose ◆ **to ~ one's face** se cacher le visage ◆ **to ~ sth from sight** dérober qch aux regards ◆ **hidden from sight** dérobé aux regards ◆ **to ~ one's light under a bushel** cacher ses talents ◆ **he doesn't ~ his light under a bushel** ce n'est pas la modestie qui l'étouffe ◆ **clouds hid the sun** des nuages cachaient *or* voilaient le soleil ◆ **the building was hidden by trees and shrubs** le bâtiment était caché par des arbres et des arbustes ◆ **he tried to ~ his disappointment** il a essayé de dissimuler sa déception

VI se cacher (*from sb* de qn) ◆ **he's hiding behind his boss** (*fig*) il se réfugie derrière son patron (*fig*)

N (*Brit*) cachette *f*

COMP **hide-and-(go-)seek** N cache-cache *m*

► **hide away** VI se cacher (*from* de)

VT SEP cacher

► **hide out, hide up** VI se cacher (*from* de)

hide² /haɪd/ N (= *skin*) peau *f* ; (= *leather*) cuir *m* ◆ **they found neither ~ nor hair of him** ils n'ont pas trouvé la moindre trace de son passage ◆ **I haven't seen ~ nor hair of him*** je ne l'ai vu nulle part, il a complètement disparu de la circulation ◆ **when I went to Australia I didn't see ~ nor hair of a kangaroo** quand je suis allé en Australie, je n'ai pas vu l'ombre d'un kangourou ; → **tan** COMP [*chair etc*] de *or* en cuir

hideaway /ˈhaɪdəweɪ/ N cachette *f*, planque* *f*

hidebound /ˈhaɪdbaʊnd/ ADJ [*person*] borné, obtus ; [*view*] étroit, borné

hideous /ˈhɪdɪəs/ ADJ [*appearance, sight, person*] hideux, affreux ; [*crime, attack*] abominable, horrible ; (*fig*) terrible* ◆ **it's been a truly ~ day** ça a été une journée absolument épouvantable

hideously /ˈhɪdɪəslɪ/ ADV [*deformed, ugly*] hideusement ; [*embarrassed*] affreusement ; [*expensive*] horriblement

hideout /ˈhaɪdaʊt/ N ⇒ **hideaway**

hidey-hole* /ˈhaɪdɪhəʊl/ N planque* *f*

hiding¹ /ˈhaɪdɪŋ/ N [*of object*] fait *m* de cacher ; [*of feelings*] dissimulation *f* ; [*of criminals*] recel *m* ◆ **to be in ~** se tenir caché ◆ **to go into ~** se cacher ◆ **to come out of ~** sortir de sa cachette COMP **hiding place** N cachette *f*

hiding² /ˈhaɪdɪŋ/ N (*gen*) raclée* *f* ; (= *punishment*) correction *f* ◆ **to give sb a good ~** donner une bonne raclée* *or* correction à qn ◆ **to take** *or* **get a ~*** (*fig*) prendre une raclée* ◆ **to be on a ~ to nothing*** (*Brit*) être sûr de se ramasser *or* prendre une gamelle*

hie †† /haɪ/ VI se hâter ◆ **~ thee hence!** hors d'ici !

hierarchic(al) /ˌhaɪəˈrɑːkɪk(əl)/ ADJ hiérarchique

hierarchically /haɪəˈrɑːkɪkəlɪ/ ADV hiérarchiquement

hierarchy /ˈhaɪərɑːkɪ/ N hiérarchie *f*

hieratic /haɪəˈrætɪk/ ADJ (*frm*) hiératique

hieroglyph /ˈhaɪərəglɪf/ N hiéroglyphe *m*

hieroglyphic /ˌhaɪərəˈglɪfɪk/ ADJ hiéroglyphique N hiéroglyphe *m*

hieroglyphics /ˌhaɪərəˈglɪfɪks/ NPL (*lit*) écriture *f* hiéroglyphique ; (*fig*) hiéroglyphes *mpl*, écriture *f* hiéroglyphique

hifalutin* /ˌhaɪfəˈluːtɪn/ ADJ ⇒ **highfalutin(g)**

hi-fi /ˈhaɪˈfaɪ/ (abbrev of **high fidelity**) N 1 (also **hi-fi system**) chaîne *f* (hi-fi *inv*) 2 (*NonC*) hi-fi *f inv*, haute fidélité *inv*

COMP [*reproduction, record*] hi-fi *inv*, haute fidélité *inv*

hi-fi equipment N matériel *m* hi-fi *inv*

hi-fi set, hi-fi system N chaîne *f* (hi-fi *inv*)

higgledy-piggledy* /ˈhɪgldɪˈpɪgldɪ/ ADJ, ADV pêle-mêle *inv*

high /haɪ/ ADJ 1 (*in height*) [*building, mountain, wall, shelf, ceiling*] haut ◆ **a ~ fence/hill** une haute clôture/colline ◆ **a building 40 metres ~, a 40-metre ~ building** un bâtiment de 40 mètres de haut, un bâtiment haut de 40 mètres ◆ **the wall is 2 metres ~** le mur fait 2 mètres de haut ◆ **the door is 3 metres ~** la porte fait 3 mètres de haut ◆ **how ~ is that tower?** quelle est la hauteur de cette tour ? ◆ **how ~ is the mountain?** quelle est l'altitude de la montagne ? ◆ **the shelf was too ~ for him to reach** l'étagère était trop haute, il n'arrivait pas à l'atteindre ◆ **the sun was ~ in the sky** le soleil était haut dans le ciel ◆ **at ~ altitude** à haute altitude ◆ **when he was only so ~*** alors qu'il était haut comme trois pommes ◆ **~ cheekbones** pommettes *fpl* saillantes ◆ **on ~ ground** (= *on hill*) en hauteur ; (= *on mountain*) en altitude ◆ **to have** *or* **hold** *or* **occupy the (moral) ~ ground** (= *moral superiority*) être au-dessus de la mêlée ◆ **to take** *or* **claim the (moral) ~ ground** se mettre dans une position moralement plus élevée, prétendre être au-dessus de la mêlée ; see also **comp**

2 (*in degree, number, strength etc*) [*frequency, latitude, tension*] haut *before n* ; [*speed, value*] grand *before n* ; [*fever*] gros (grosse *f*) *before n*, fort *before n* ; [*pressure*] élevé, haut *before n* ; [*salary*] haut *before n*, gros (grosse *f*) *before n* ; [*rent, price*] élevé ; [*number*] grand *before n*, élevé ; [*sound, voice*] aigu (-guë *f*) ; [*note*] haut ; [*complexion*] rougeaud ; [*colour*] vif ; [*polish*] brillant ; [*respect*] grand *before n*, profond ; [*calling, character*] noble ; [*ideal*] noble, grand *before n* ; (*Phon*) [*vowel*] fermé ◆ **this food is ~ in protein** cet aliment contient beaucoup de protéine ◆ **to have ~ blood pressure** avoir de la tension ◆ **his team were of the ~est calibre** son équipe était de très haut niveau ◆ **of ~ caste** de caste supérieure ◆ **official reports say casual-**

ties have been ~ selon les rapports officiels, il y a beaucoup de morts et de blessés ◆ **the new model has been refined to the ~est degree** le nouveau modèle est hautement perfectionné ◆ **to have ~ expectations of sth** placer de grands espoirs en qch ◆ **to have ~ expectations of sb** beaucoup attendre de qn ◆ **~ official** haut fonctionnaire *m* ◆ **to have a ~ opinion of sb/sth** avoir une haute opinion de qn/qch ◆ **she has friends in ~ places** elle a des amis en haut lieu ◆ **allegations of corruption in ~ places** des allégations de corruption en haut lieu ◆ **to buy sth at a ~ price** acheter qch cher ◆ **to pay a ~ price for sth** (*lit, fig*) payer qch cher ◆ **he has a ~ temperature** il a une forte température ◆ **it boils at a ~ temperature** cela bout à une température élevée ◆ **the temperature was in the ~ 30s** la température approchait les quarante degrés ◆ **it's ~ time you went home** il est grand temps que tu rentres *subj* ◆ **to set a ~ value on sth** attacher une grande valeur à qch ◆ **a ~ wind was blowing** il soufflait un vent violent, il faisait grand vent ◆ **in ~ gear** en quatrième (*or* cinquième) vitesse ◆ **the ~est common factor** le plus grand commun diviseur ; see also **comp** ; → **lord, priority, profile, very**

◆ **to be high on** [*+ quality*] ◆ **he's low on looks but ~ on personality** il n'est pas très beau mais il a beaucoup de personnalité ◆ **the film is ~ on humour but low on suspense** le film est plein d'humour mais il n'y a pas beaucoup de suspense

3 (*Culin*) [*game, meat*] avancé, faisandé ; [*butter*] fort, rance

4 * (*= drunk*) parti* ◆ **he was ~** (*= on drugs*) il planait* ◆ **to get ~ on alcohol** s'enivrer ◆ **he was ~ on speed** il planait* après avoir pris du speed ◆ **to be (as) ~ as a kite** planer complètement* ◆ **she was ~ on her latest success** elle était enivrée par son dernier succès

5 († * *fig*) ◆ **to have a ~ old time** s'amuser follement ◆ **there was a ~ old row about it** cela a provoqué une sacrée bagarre* *or* un sacré chambard*

ADV 1 (*in height*) [*climb, jump, throw*] haut ; [*fly*] à haute altitude, à une altitude élevée ◆ **she threw the ball ~ in the air** elle a lancé le ballon très haut ◆ **the balloon rose ~ in the air** le ballon s'est élevé *or* est monté haut dans le ciel ◆ **~ above our heads** bien au-dessus de nos têtes ◆ **how ~ can you jump?** à quelle hauteur pouvez-vous sauter ? ◆ **a plate piled ~ with sandwiches** une assiette avec une grosse pile de sandwiches ◆ **the house was built ~ on the hillside** la maison était construite en haut de la colline ◆ **a house ~ up in the hills** une maison perchée dans les collines ◆ **grapes grown ~ up on the slope** du raisin que l'on fait pousser en haut de la pente ◆ **we saw a bird circling very ~ up** nous avons vu un oiseau décrire des cercles très haut dans le ciel ◆ **~er up** plus haut ◆ **~er up the hill was a small farm** plus haut sur la colline il y avait une petite ferme ◆ **~er and ~er** de plus en plus haut ◆ **unemployment is climbing ~er and ~er** le chômage augmente de plus en plus ◆ **she was quite ~ up in the organization** elle était assez haut placée dans l'organisation ◆ **economic reform is ~ (up) on the agenda** *or* **on the list of priorities** la réforme économique est l'une des (premières) priorités ◆ **to aim ~, to set one's sights ~** (*fig*) viser haut ◆ **to live ~ on the hog** *(*esp US fig*) vivre comme un nabab

2 (*in degree, number, strength etc*) **the numbers go as ~ as 200** les nombres montent jusqu'à 200 ◆ **I had to go as ~ as 60 euros for it** j'ai dû aller *or* monter jusqu'à 60 € pour l'avoir ◆ **to hunt** *or* **look ~ and low for sb** chercher qn partout ◆ **to hunt** *or* **look ~ and low for sth** chercher qch partout *or* dans tous les coins ◆ **to hold one's head (up) ~** avoir la tête haute ◆ **to play ~** [*gambler*] jouer gros (jeu) ◆ **to live ~** mener grand train, mener la grande vie ◆ **the sea is running ~** la mer est grosse *or* houleuse ◆ **the river is running ~** la rivière est en crue ◆ **feelings ran ~** les esprits étaient échauffés ; → **fly¹**

N 1 (*= high point*) ◆ **the cost of living reached a new ~** le coût de la vie a atteint un nouveau record *or* plafond ◆ **the pound closed at a new ~ against the dollar today** la livre a atteint un nouveau plafond par rapport au dollar en clôture aujourd'hui ◆ **his football career reached a new ~ with eight goals in ten matches** sa carrière de footballeur a atteint un nouveau sommet avec huit buts en dix matchs ◆ **car sales reached an all-time ~ of 2.3 million** les ventes de voitures ont atteint un niveau record : 2,3 millions ◆ **~s and lows** (*fig*) les hauts *mpl* et les bas *mpl*

◆ **on high** en haut ◆ **from on ~** d'en haut ◆ **the directive had come down from on ~** la directive était venue d'en haut ◆ **orders from on ~** des ordres venus d'en haut ◆ **God on ~** Dieu qui est au ciel

2 * (*= good feeling*) euphorie *f*

◆ **to be on a high** être euphorique

3 (*= area of high pressure*) ◆ **a ~ over the North Sea** une zone de haute pression sur la mer du Nord

4 (*Rel*) **the Most High** le Très-Haut

COMP **high-ability** ADJ très doué

high altar N maître-autel *m*

high and dry ADJ [*boat*] échoué ◆ **to leave sb ~ and dry** (*fig*) laisser qn en plan*

high and mighty * ADJ ◆ **to be ~ and mighty** se donner de grands airs, faire le grand seigneur (*or* la grande dame)

high-angle shot N (*Cine*) plongée *f*

high beam N (*US*) pleins phares *mpl*

high camp N → **camp²**

High Church N (*Brit*) Haute Église *f* (*anglicane*)

high-class ADJ [*hotel, food, service*] de premier ordre ; [*house*] très bourgeois ; [*neighbourhood, flat*] (de) grand standing ; [*person*] du grand monde ; [*prostitute*] de luxe

high comedy N (*Theat*) comédie *f* sophistiquée ◆ **it was ~ comedy** (*fig*) c'était du plus haut comique

high command N (*Mil*) haut commandement *m*

High Commission N (*Admin*) haut commissariat *m*

High Commissioner N (*Admin*) haut commissaire *m*

High Court N (*Jur*) ≈ Haute Cour *f*

High Court judge N (*Brit*) juge *m* de la Haute Cour

high definition ADJ, N haute définition *f*

high definition television N télévision *f* haute définition

high-density ADJ [*printing, disk*] haute densité *inv*

high-density housing N grands ensembles *mpl*

high dependency ADJ (*Med*) [*bed, unit*] de soins semi-intensifs

high diving N (*NonC: Sport*) plongeon(s) *m(pl)* de haut vol ; see also **diving**

high-end ADJ (*= top-of-the-range*) haut de gamme *inv*

high-energy ADJ [*particle*] de haute énergie

high explosive N explosif *m* (puissant)

high-explosive shell N obus *m* explosif

high fibre diet N (*= eating régime*) régime *m* riche en fibres ; (*= food eaten*) alimentation *f* riche en fibres

high-fidelity N, ADJ haute fidélité *f inv*

high-five * N *geste de salut ou de félicitation où les deux personnes se tapent dans la main*

high-flier, high-flyer N (*in profession*) ambitieux *m*, -euse *f*, jeune loup *m* (*pej*) ; (*at school*) crack* *m*

high-flown ADJ [*style, discourse*] ampoulé

high-flyer N ⇒ **high-flier**

high-flying ADJ [*aircraft*] volant à haute altitude ; [*aim, ambition*] extravagant ; [*person*] ambitieux

high-frequency ADJ de *or* à haute fréquence ; see also **ultrahigh, very**

High German N haut allemand *m*

high-grade ADJ [*goods*] de qualité supérieure, de premier choix

high-grade mineral N minerai *m* à haute teneur

high hand N ◆ **to rule sb with a ~ hand** imposer sa loi à qn

high-handed ADJ autoritaire

high-handedly ADV de manière autoritaire

high-handedness N autoritarisme *m*

high hat N (*= hat*) (chapeau *m*) haut-de-forme *m*

high-hat * ADJ snob, poseur VT snober, traiter de haut VI faire le snob *or* la snobinette

high-heeled shoes N chaussures *fpl* à hauts talons

high heels NPL (*= shoes*) hauts talons *mpl*

high horse N (*fig*) ◆ **to get up/be on one's ~ horse** monter/être sur ses grands chevaux

high-impact ADJ [*aerobics, exercise*] high-impact *inv* ; [*plastic*] résistant *inv* aux chocs

high-income ADJ [*group, country*] à hauts revenus, à revenus élevés

high-interest ADJ (*Fin*) à intérêt élevé

high jinks † * NPL ◆ **to get up to** *or* **have ~ jinks** se payer du bon temps ◆ **there were ~ jinks last night** on s'est amusé comme des fous hier soir

high jump N (*Sport*) saut *m* en hauteur ◆ **he's for the ~ jump!** * (*Brit fig*) (*= going to be scolded, punished*) il est bon pour une engueulade*, qu'est-ce qu'il va prendre !* ; (*= going to be sacked*) il va se faire virer !*

high jumper N (*Sport*) sauteur *m*, -euse *f* en hauteur

high-level ADJ de haut niveau ◆ **~-level committee** (*with great authority*) haute instance *f* ; (*composed of high officials*) comité *m* formé de hauts responsables ◆ **~-level language** langage *m* évolué ◆ **~-level nuclear waste** déchets *mpl* nucléaires à haute activité

high life N ◆ **to live the ~ life** mener la grande vie

high living N la grande vie

High Mass N grand-messe *f*

high-minded ADJ [*person*] à l'âme noble, de caractère élevé ; [*ambition, wish*] noble, élevé

high-necked ADJ à col haut

high noon N plein midi *m* ◆ **it's ~ noon for ...** (*= crisis point*) c'est l'heure de vérité pour ...

high-octane ADJ [*petrol*] à indice d'octane élevé ; (*fig = powerful, exciting*) puissant

high-performance ADJ très performant, à haute performance

high-pitched ADJ (*Mus*) [*voice, sound, note*] aigu (-guë *f*) ; [*song*] (chanté) dans les aigus ; (*Archit*) [*roof*] à forte pente ; [*ambitions*] noble, haut *before n*

high point N [*of visit, holiday*] grand moment *m* ◆ **the ~ point of the show/evening** le clou du spectacle/de la soirée

high-powered ADJ [*car*] très puissant ; (*fig*) [*person*] de haut vol ◆ **~-powered businessman** homme *m* d'affaires de haut vol

high-pressure ADJ (*Tech*) à haute pression ◆ **~-pressure area** (*Weather*) zone *f* de haute pression ◆ **a ~-pressure salesman** un vendeur de choc* ◆ **~-pressure salesmanship** technique *f* de vente agressive

high-priced ADJ coûteux, cher

high priest N grand prêtre *m*

high priestess N grande prêtresse *f*

high-principled ADJ qui a des principes élevés

high-profile ADJ [*position, politician*] très en vue ; [*role*] très influent ; [*issue*] très discuté

high-protein ADJ riche en protéines

high-ranking ADJ haut placé, de haut rang ◆ **~-ranking official** haut fonctionnaire *m*

high resolution N haute résolution *f*

high-resolution ADJ haute résolution *inv*

high-rise N (also **high-rise block, high-rise flats**) tour *f* (d'habitation)

high-risk ADJ à haut risque

high roller* N *(US) (gen)* casse-cou* *m inv* ; *(Gambling)* flambeur‡ *m*

high school N *(US)* ≃ lycée *m* ; *(Brit)* collège *m* or établissement *m* d'enseignement secondaire ◆ **~ school diploma** *(US)* diplôme *m* de fin d'études secondaires, ≃ baccalauréat *m* ; → HIGH SCHOOL

high-scoring ADJ à score élevé

high seas NPL ◆ **on the ~ seas** en haute mer

high season N *(Brit)* haute saison *f*

high-sided vehicle N véhicule *m* haut *(donnant prise au vent)*

high sign* N *(US)* signe *m* convenu *or* d'intelligence ◆ **to give sb a ~ sign** faire un signe d'intelligence à qn

high society N haute société *f*

high-sounding ADJ sonore, grandiloquent *(pej)*

high-speed ADJ *(gen)* ultrarapide ◆ **a ~-speed chase** une course poursuite ◆ **~-speed lens** objectif *m* à obturation (ultra)rapide ◆ **~-speed train** train *m* à grande vitesse, TGV *m*

high-spirited ADJ *[person]* plein d'entrain *or* de vivacité ; *[horse]* fougueux, fringant

high spirits NPL entrain *m*, vivacité *f* ◆ **in ~ spirits** *(= lively, energetic)* plein d'entrain *or* de vivacité ; *(= happy)* tout joyeux

high spot N *(fig) (= climax) [of visit, holiday]* grand moment *m* ◆ **the ~ spot of the show/evening** le clou du spectacle/de la soirée ◆ **to hit the ~ spots*** faire la foire‡ *or* la noce* *(dans un night-club, restaurant etc)*

high stakes NPL *(lit, fig)* ◆ **to play for ~ stakes** jouer gros (jeu)

high street N *(Brit) [of village]* grand-rue *f* ; *[of town]* rue *f* principale

high-street ADJ *(Brit) [shop, store]* qui appartient à une grande chaîne ◆ **the ~-street banks** les grandes banques *fpl*

high-strung ADJ *(US)* ⇒ **highly strung** ; → **highly**

high summer N le cœur de l'été ◆ **in ~ summer** en plein été, au cœur de l'été, au plus chaud de l'été

high table N *(gen)* table *f* d'honneur ; *(Scol, Univ)* table *f* des professeurs *(au réfectoire)*

high tea N *(Brit) repas pris en début de soirée*

high tech N high-tech *m inv*

high-tech ADJ *[equipment, product]* de pointe, de haute technologie ; *[computer]* sophistiqué ; *[company]* high-tech *inv*, de pointe, de haute technologie ; *[industry, medicine]* de pointe, high-tech *inv* ; *[weapon]* de haute technologie ; *[job]* dans un secteur de haute technologie ; *[technique]* de pointe ◆ **the ~-tech age** l'ère *f* des techniques de pointe

high technology N technologie *f* avancée *or* de pointe

high-technology ADJ *[device]* d'une haute technicité ; *[sector]* de pointe

high-tensile steel N acier *m* à résistance élevée

high-tensile wire N fil *m* à résistance élevée

high tension N *(Elec)* haute tension *f*

high-tension ADJ *(Elec)* à haute tension

high tide N marée *f* haute ◆ **at ~ tide** à marée haute

high treason N haute trahison *f*

high-up ADJ *[person, post]* de haut rang, très haut placé N * grosse légume* *f*, huile* *f*

high-velocity ADJ *[rifle, bullet, jet of air]* à grande vitesse

high voltage N haute tension *f*

high-voltage ADJ haute tension *inv*

high water N ⇒ **high tide** ; see also **hell**

high-water mark N niveau *m* des hautes eaux

high wire N *(lit = tightrope)* corde *f* raide ◆ **to be walking the ~ wire** *(fig)* être sur la corde raide

high wire act N *(lit, fig)* numéro *m* de corde raide

high yellow‡* N *(US pej)* mulâtre *m* au teint clair, mulâtresse *f* au teint clair

> **HIGH SCHOOL**
>
> Aux États-Unis, les **high schools** réunissent les quatre années du deuxième cycle du secondaire (15 à 18 ans). Les élèves reçus à leur examen final se voient remettre leur diplôme au cours d'une importante cérémonie appelée « graduation ».
>
> La vie des **high schools** a inspiré de nombreux films et téléfilms américains ; on y voit le rôle qu'y jouent les sports (en particulier le football et le basket-ball) et certaines manifestations mondaines comme le bal de fin d'année des élèves de terminale, le « senior prom ». → GRADE, GRADUATION, PROM

-high /haɪ/ ADJ *(in compounds)* ◆ **to be knee/shoulder-high** arriver aux genoux/épaules

high-achieving /ˌhaɪəˈtʃiːvɪŋ/ ADJ *[manager]* performant

highball /ˈhaɪbɔːl/ N 1 *(esp US = drink)* whisky *m* à l'eau (avec de la glace) 2 (also **highball glass** *or* **tumbler**) grand verre *m* VI *(US‡) (= drive fast)* foncer*

highborn /ˈhaɪbɔːn/ ADJ de haute naissance, bien né

highboy /ˈhaɪbɔɪ/ N *(US)* commode *f (haute)*

highbrow /ˈhaɪbraʊ/ *(slightly pej)* N intellectuel(le) *m(f)* ADJ *[tastes, interests]* d'intellectuel ; *[music]* pour intellectuels

highchair /ˈhaɪtʃɛəʳ/ N chaise *f* haute *(pour enfants)*

higher /ˈhaɪəʳ/ (compar of **high**) ADJ *[animal, primate, species, plant]* supérieur ; *[degree, diploma]* d'études supérieures ◆ **any number ~ than six** tout nombre supérieur à six ◆ **the ~ forms** *or* **classes** *(Scol)* les grandes classes *fpl* ◆ **the ~ income brackets** les tranches *fpl* de revenu(s) supérieur(s) ADV plus haut ; → **high** N *(Scot Scol:* also **Higher)** ⇒ **Higher Grade**

COMP **higher education** N enseignement *m* supérieur

Higher Grade N *(Scot Scol)* diplôme *m* de fin d'études secondaires, ≃ baccalauréat *m* ; → A LEVELS

Higher National Certificate N *(Brit Educ)* ≃ BTS *m*

Higher National Diploma N *(Brit Educ)* ≃ DUT *m*

higher-up* N *(= senior person)* supérieur(e) *m(f)* (hiérarchique)

highfalutin(g)* /ˌhaɪfəˈluːtɪn/ ADJ *[behaviour, language]* affecté, prétentieux ; *[style]* ampoulé

highjack /ˈhaɪdʒæk/ VT ⇒ **hijack**

highjacker /ˈhaɪdʒækəʳ/ N ⇒ **hijacker**

highjacking /ˈhaɪdʒækɪŋ/ N ⇒ **hijacking**

highland /ˈhaɪlənd/ ADJ *(Brit)* ◆ **Highland** *[scenery, air]* des Highlands ; *[holiday]* dans les Highlands NPL **highlands** région *f* montagneuse, montagnes *fpl* ◆ **the Highlands** *(Brit Geog)* les Highlands *mpl*

COMP **Highland fling** N *danse écossaise*

Highland games NPL jeux *mpl* écossais

highlander /ˈhaɪləndəʳ/ N montagnard *m* ◆ **Highlander** *(Brit)* natif *m*, -ive *f* des Highlands

highlight /ˈhaɪlaɪt/ N 1 *(= high point)* ◆ **the ~s of the match/the festival** les temps *mpl* forts du match/du festival ◆ **the ~ of the show/evening** le clou du spectacle/de la soirée 2 *(Art, lit)* rehaut *m* ◆ **to have ~s put in one's hair** se faire faire un balayage *or* des mèches *fpl*

VT 1 *(= emphasize)* souligner, mettre l'accent sur ◆ **his report ~ed the plight of the homeless** son rapport a attiré l'attention sur la situation des SDF ◆ **the incident ~s growing concern about racism** cet incident montre que le racisme inquiète de plus en plus les gens 2 *(with highlighter pen)* surligner ; *(= underline)* souligner ; *(on computer)* sélectionner

highlighter /ˈhaɪˌlaɪtəʳ/ N 1 *(= pen)* surligneur *m* 2 *(for hair)* produit *m* éclaircissant

highly /ˈhaɪlɪ/ ADV 1 *(= very) (gen)* extrêmement ; *[skilled, qualified, unlikely, professional]* hautement ; *[prized]* très ; *[interesting, unusual]* tout à fait ◆ **~ respected** éminemment respecté ◆ **~ acclaimed by the critics** salué par la critique ◆ **~ recommended** *[book, film, play]* hautement recommandé ◆ **she comes ~ recommended** elle est chaudement recommandée ◆ **~ polished** *(= shiny) [furniture, wood]* (bien) astiqué, briqué ; *[gemstone]* (bien) poli ◆ **~ charged** *[atmosphere]* très tendu ; *[occasion, debate]* à l'atmosphère très tendue ◆ **~ seasoned** fortement assaisonné ◆ **to be ~ sexed** avoir de forts appétits sexuels

2 *(= at or to a high level)* ◆ **~-paid** *[person, job]* très bien payé *or* rémunéré ◆ **~-trained** *[professional, scientist, staff]* de haut niveau ; *[sportsman, soldier]* parfaitement entraîné ◆ **~-placed** haut *inv* placé ◆ **~-regarded, ~-rated** très estimé ◆ **~ coloured** *(lit) [picture etc]* haut en couleur ; *(fig) [description]* pittoresque

3 *(with vb)* ◆ **to speak/think ~ of sb/sth** dire/penser beaucoup de bien de qn/qch ◆ **to praise sb ~** chanter les louanges de qn ◆ **I don't rate him very ~ at all** je n'ai pas une très haute opinion de lui ◆ **travelling by car rates very ~ in terms of convenience** la voiture est perçue comme un moyen de transport très pratique

COMP **highly strung** ADJ *(esp Brit)* très nerveux

highness /ˈhaɪnɪs/ N ◆ **His** *or* **Her/Your Highness** Son/Votre Altesse *f* ; → **royal**

highroad /ˈhaɪrəʊd/ N *(esp Brit) (lit)* grand-route *f* ◆ **the ~ to success** la voie de la réussite

hightail* /ˈhaɪteɪl/ VT *(esp US)* ◆ **they ~ed it back to town** ils sont revenus en ville à toute vitesse *or* à tout(e) berzingue‡

highway /ˈhaɪweɪ/ N 1 *(US = main road)* grande route *f*, route *f* nationale 2 (also **public highway**) voie *f* publique ◆ **the king's** *or* **queen's ~** la voie publique ◆ **through the ~s and byways of Sussex** par tous les chemins du Sussex

COMP **highway code** N *(Brit)* code *m* de la route

highway patrol N *(US)* (also **state highway patrol**) police *f* de la route

highway robbery N *(lit)* banditisme *m* de grand chemin ◆ **it's ~ robbery** *(fig)* c'est du vol manifeste *or* caractérisé

Highways Department N *(Admin)* administration *f* des Ponts et Chaussées

highways engineer N ingénieur *m* des Ponts et Chaussées

highwayman /ˈhaɪweɪmən/ N (pl **-men**) *(Hist)* bandit *m* de grand chemin

hijack /ˈhaɪdʒæk/ VT *(lit)* détourner ; *(fig)* récupérer ◆ **they were accused of ~ing the revolution** on les a accusés d'avoir récupéré la révolution N *(lit)* détournement *m* ; *(fig)* récupération *f*

hijacker /ˈhaɪdʒækəʳ/ N pirate *m* (de l'air/de la route/du rail *etc*), auteur *m* d'un détournement

hijacking /ˈhaɪdʒækɪŋ/ N *(lit, fig)* détournement *m*

hike /haɪk/ N 1 randonnée *f* (pédestre) ; *(Mil, Sport)* marche *f* à pied ◆ **to go on** *or* **for a ~** faire une randonnée (pédestre) 2 *(= increase) [of prices etc]* hausse *f*, augmentation *f* VI 1 faire des randonnées (pédestres) ◆ **we spent our holidays hiking in France** nous avons passé nos vacances à faire des randonnées pédestres à travers la France [2] (US = increase) [price etc] augmenter VT ⇒ hike up

▸**hike up** VT SEP [1] (= hitch up) [+ skirt] remonter [2] (= increase) [+ prices, amounts] augmenter

hiker /ˈhaɪkəʳ/ N randonneur m, -euse f

hiking /ˈhaɪkɪŋ/ N randonnées fpl (à pied) COMP
hiking boots NPL chaussures fpl de randonnée or de marche

hilarious /hɪˈlɛərɪəs/ ADJ hilarant

hilariously /hɪˈlɛərɪəslɪ/ ADV comiquement ◆ ~ **funny** hilarant ◆ **Mary Williams plays the ~ incompetent Betty** Mary Williams joue Betty, dont l'incompétence est d'un comique irrésistible

hilarity /hɪˈlærɪtɪ/ N hilarité f ◆ **it caused great** or **much** ~ cela a déchaîné l'hilarité

hill /hɪl/ N colline f ; (= slope) côte f, pente f ; (up) montée f ; (down) descente f ◆ **their house is on a** ~ (in countryside) leur maison est sur une colline ; (in town) leur maison est dans une rue en pente ◆ **he was going up the** ~ (in countryside) il grimpait la colline ; (in town) il remontait la rue ◆ **up** ~ **and down dale, over** ~ **and dale** (liter) par monts et par vaux ◆ **as old as the ~s** vieux comme Hérode ◆ **he's over the** ~* (= old) il se fait vieux ◆ **it doesn't amount to a ~ of beans*** (US) ça n'a aucune importance ; → **ant, molehill, uphill**

COMP **hill climb** N (Sport) course f de côtes
hill climber N ⇒ **hill walker**
hill climbing N ⇒ **hill walking**
hill farmer N (esp Brit) agriculteur pratiquant l'élevage sur hauts pâturages
hill start N (in vehicle) démarrage m en côte
hill walker N randonneur m, -euse f
hill walking N randonnées fpl (en montagne)

hillbilly* /ˈhɪlbɪlɪ/ N (US: gen pej) péquenaud* m (pej), rustaud m (pej) (montagnard du sud des USA) COMP **hillbilly music** N musique f folk inv (originaire des montagnes du sud des USA)

hilliness /ˈhɪlɪnɪs/ N caractère m accidenté

hillock /ˈhɪlək/ N monticule m

hillside /ˈhɪlsaɪd/ N (flanc m de) coteau m ◆ **on the** ~ à flanc de coteau

hilltop /ˈhɪltɒp/ N ◆ **on the** ~ en haut de or au sommet de la colline ADJ [village, site, fortress] perché en haut d'une colline

hilly /ˈhɪlɪ/ ADJ [country] vallonné, accidenté ; [road] qui monte et qui descend

hilt /hɪlt/ N [of sword] poignée f ; [of dagger] manche m ; [of pistol] crosse f ◆ **she's in debt up to the** ~ elle est endettée jusqu'au cou ◆ **we're mortgaged to the** ~ nous nous sommes endettés jusqu'au cou avec l'achat de notre maison (or appartement) ◆ **to back** or **support sb to the** ~ être derrière qn quoi qu'il arrive, soutenir qn à fond ◆ **he played his role to the** ~ il a joué son rôle avec conviction

him, Him (Rel) /hɪm/ PERS PRON [1] (direct, unstressed) le ; (before vowel) l' ; (stressed) lui ◆ **I see** ~ je le vois ◆ **I have seen** ~ je l'ai vu ◆ **I know HER but I've never seen HIM** je la connais, elle, mais lui je ne l'ai jamais vu [2] (indirect) lui ◆ **I give** ~ **the book** je lui donne le livre ◆ **I'm speaking to** ~ je lui parle, c'est à lui que je parle [3] (after prep etc) lui ◆ **I am thinking of** ~ je pense à lui ◆ **I'm proud of** ~ je suis fier de lui ◆ **without** ~ sans lui ◆ **if I were** ~ si j'étais lui, si j'étais à sa place ◆ **it's** ~ c'est lui ◆ **younger than** ~ plus jeune que lui [4] celui ◆ **to** ~ **who might complain, I should point out that ...** à ceux qui se plaindraient, je ferais remarquer que ...

Himalayan /ˌhɪməˈleɪən/ ADJ (gen) himalayen ; [expedition] dans l'Himalaya

Himalayas /ˌhɪməˈleɪəz/ NPL (chaîne f de l') Himalaya m

himself /hɪmˈself/ PERS PRON (reflexive, direct and indirect) se ; (emphatic) lui-même ; (after prep) lui ◆ **he has hurt** ~ il s'est blessé ◆ **he poured** ~ **a whisky** il s'est servi un whisky ◆ **"why not?" he said to** ~ "pourquoi pas ?" se dit-il ◆ **he told me** ~ il me l'a dit lui-même ◆ **I saw the teacher** ~ j'ai vu le professeur lui-même or en personne ◆ **he kept three for** ~ il s'en est réservé trois ◆ **she asked him for a photo of** ~ elle lui a demandé une photo de lui ◆ **there's no work and no future for students like** ~ il n'y a pas de travail et pas d'avenir pour les étudiants comme lui ◆ **he hasn't been** ~ **lately** (= not behaving normally) il n'est pas dans son état normal ces temps-ci ; (= not feeling well) il n'est pas dans son assiette ces temps-ci
◆ **(all) by himself** tout seul

hind¹ /haɪnd/ N (pl **hinds** or **hind**) (= deer) biche f

hind² /haɪnd/ ADJ [legs, feet, paws] de derrière ◆ **to get up on one's** ~ **legs*** (hum) se lever pour parler ◆ **she could** or **would talk the** ~ **leg(s) off a donkey*** c'est un vrai moulin à paroles

hinder¹ /ˈhaɪndəʳ/ ADJ compar of **hind²**

hinder² /ˈhɪndəʳ/ VT (= obstruct, impede) entraver, gêner ; (= delay) retarder ; (= prevent) empêcher, arrêter ◆ **the rescue team's efforts were ~ed by the bad weather** le travail des sauveteurs a été ralenti par le mauvais temps ◆ **we want to help, not** ~, **the progress of the scheme** nous voulons faire avancer le projet, pas l'entraver ◆ **being disabled has done nothing to** ~ **her career** son handicap n'a pas du tout entravé sa carrière ◆ **the heavy jacket ~ed him as he tried to swim** sa lourde veste le gênait pour nager ◆ **poor productivity ~s economic growth** lorsque la productivité est faible, cela entrave la croissance économique ◆ **he does not let racism** ~ **him** il ne se laisse pas arrêter par le racisme ◆ **the rocky terrain ~ed their progress** le terrain rocheux les a ralentis ◆ **poor diet is ~ing her recovery** sa mauvaise alimentation l'empêche de guérir plus vite ◆ **high interest rates are ~ing recovery** les taux d'intérêt élevés font obstacle à la reprise or freinent la reprise ◆ **to** ~ **sb from doing sth** (= prevent) empêcher qn de faire qch ◆ **restrictions that** ~ **them from doing their job** (= impede) des restrictions qui les gênent dans leur travail

Hindi /ˈhɪndɪ/ N (Ling) hindi m

hindmost /ˈhaɪndməʊst/ ADV dernier ; → **devil, every**

hindquarters /ˈhaɪndˌkwɔːtəz/ NPL arrière-train m, train m de derrière

hindrance /ˈhɪndrəns/ N obstacle m ◆ **to be a** ~ **to sb/sth** gêner qn/qch ◆ **he is more of a** ~ **than a help** il gêne plus qu'il n'aide ◆ **these attacks are a** ~ **to reconciliation** ces attaques font obstacle à la réconciliation ◆ **the issue has been a constant** ~ **to normal relations between the two countries** ce problème n'a cessé de faire obstacle à la normalisation des relations entre les deux pays ◆ **they crossed the border without** ~ ils ont traversé la frontière sans problème or difficulté

hindsight /ˈhaɪndsaɪt/ N ◆ **with** or **in** ~, **with the benefit of** ~ avec du recul, rétrospectivement ◆ **it was, in** ~, **a mistaken judgement** rétrospectivement or avec du recul, je pense que c'était une erreur de jugement

Hindu /ˈhɪnduː/ ADJ hindou N hindou(e) m(f)

Hinduism /ˈhɪndʊˌɪzəm/ N hindouisme m

Hindustan /ˌhɪndʊˈstɑːn/ N Hindoustan m

Hindustani /ˌhɪndʊˈstɑːnɪ/ ADJ hindou N [1] Hindoustani(e) m(f) [2] (= language) hindoustani m

hinge /hɪndʒ/ N [of door] gond m, charnière f ; [of box] charnière f ; (fig) pivot m, charnière f ; (= stamp hinge) charnière f ◆ **the door came off its ~s** la porte est sortie de ses gonds VT [+ door] mettre dans ses gonds ; [+ box] mettre des charnières à ◆ **a ~d lid** un couvercle à charnière(s) ◆ **a ~d flap** [of counter] (in shop, bar) abattant m ◆ **the mirror was ~d to a wooden frame** le miroir était fixé à un cadre en bois par des charnières VI [1] (Tech) pivoter (on sur) [2] (fig) ◆ **to** ~ **on** or **upon sth** dépendre de qch ◆ **everything ~s on his decision** tout dépend de sa décision

COMP **hinged girder** N (Tech) poutre f articulée
hinge joint N (Anat) diarthrose f

hint /hɪnt/ N [1] allusion f ◆ **to drop a** ~, **to throw out a** ~ faire une allusion ◆ **to drop a** ~ **that ...** faire une allusion au fait que ... ◆ **he dropped me a** ~ **that he would like an invitation** il m'a fait comprendre or il m'a laissé entendre qu'il aimerait être invité ◆ **he dropped a gentle** ~ **about it** il y a fait une allusion discrète ◆ **a broad** or **strong** or **heavy** ~ une allusion transparente or à peine voilée ◆ **there are strong ~s from the government that ...** le gouvernement a clairement laissé entendre que ... ◆ **I dropped heavy ~s that I'd love a new coat for my birthday** j'ai insisté lourdement sur le fait que je voulais un nouveau manteau pour mon anniversaire ◆ **she gave me a subtle** ~ **not to expect promotion** elle m'a fait comprendre discrètement qu'il ne fallait pas compter sur une promotion ◆ **he knows how to take a** ~ il comprend à demi-mot, il comprend les allusions ◆ **he took the** ~ **and left at once** il a compris sans qu'on ait besoin de lui expliquer et est parti sur-le-champ ◆ **I can take a** ~ (ça va,) j'ai compris ◆ **he can't take a** ~ il ne comprend pas vite ◆ **I'll give you a** ~ **- the answer has two words** je vais vous donner un indice or vous mettre sur la piste : la réponse est en deux mots ◆ **he gave no** ~ **of his feelings** il n'a rien laissé transparaître de ses sentiments ◆ **~s and tips for travellers** conseils mpl aux voyageurs ◆ **~s on maintenance** conseils mpl d'entretien

[2] (= trace) [of colour] touche f ; [of taste, flavour] soupçon m ◆ **she was wearing a** ~ **of eye-shadow** elle avait mis un peu or une touche de fard à paupières ◆ **there was a** ~ **of sadness in his smile** il y avait un je ne sais quoi de triste dans son sourire ◆ **there was a** ~ **of desperation in his voice** il y avait une pointe de désespoir dans sa voix ◆ **there was no** ~ **of apology in his voice** il n'y avait pas la moindre trace de remords dans sa voix ◆ **"why are you here?" she said, with no** ~ **of irony** "que faites-vous ici ?" dit-elle, sans la moindre ironie ◆ **at the first** ~ **of trouble** à la moindre alerte, au moindre problème ◆ **there's a** ~ **of spring in the air** il y a un petit air printanier

VT (= insinuate) insinuer (that que) ◆ **he ~ed strongly that ...** il a lourdement insinué que ... ◆ **he ~ed to me that he was unhappy** il m'a laissé entendre or fait comprendre qu'il était malheureux

VI ◆ **to** ~ **at sth** faire allusion à qch ◆ **what are you ~ing at?** qu'est-ce que vous voulez dire par là ? ◆ **are you ~ing at something?** c'est une allusion ? ◆ **the newspapers ~ed darkly at conspiracies** les journaux ont fait des allusions inquiétantes à des complots ◆ **the president ~ed at the possibility of tax cuts** le président a laissé entendre qu'il pourrait y avoir une baisse des impôts

hinterland /ˈhɪntəlænd/ N arrière-pays m inv

hip¹ /hɪp/ N [1] (Anat) hanche f ◆ **with (one's) hands on (one's) ~s** les mains sur les hanches ◆ **to break one's** ~ se casser le col du fémur ; → **shoot** [2] (Archit) arête f (d'un toit)

COMP **hip bath** N baignoire-sabot f
hip flask N flasque f

hip joint N articulation *f* coxofémorale *or* de la hanche
hip measurement N ⇒ **hip size**
hipped roof N *(Archit)* toit *m* en croupe
hip pocket N poche *f* revolver *inv*
hip replacement (operation) N pose *f* d'une prothèse de la hanche ◆ **she's waiting for/ she's had a ~ replacement** elle attend/on lui a posé une prothèse de la hanche
hip size N tour *m* de hanches ◆ **what is her ~ size?** quel est son tour de hanches ?, combien fait-elle de tour de hanches ?

hip² /hɪp/ N *(= berry)* cynorrhodon *m*

hip³ /hɪp/ EXCL ◆ **~ ~ hurrah !** hip hip hip hourra !

hip⁴ ⁑ /hɪp/ ADJ *(= up-to-date)* branché* VT *(US)* mettre au parfum*

hipbone /ˈhɪpbəʊn/ N os *m* iliaque *or* de la hanche

hip-hop /ˈhɪphɒp/ N hip-hop *m*

hiphuggers /ˈhɪphʌgəz/ NPL pantalon *m* taille basse

hipped /hɪpt/ ADJ *(US)* ◆ **to be ~ on sth** ⁑ être dingue* de qch

-hipped /hɪpt/ ADJ *(in compounds)* ◆ **broad-hipped** large de hanches, aux hanches larges ◆ **narrow-hipped** aux hanches étroites

hippie * /ˈhɪpɪ/ ADJ, N *(in the sixties)* hippie *mf* ; *(modern-day)* baba *mf* cool ◆ **an ageing ~** un hippie sur le retour

hippo * /ˈhɪpəʊ/ N abbrev of **hippopotamus**

Hippocrates /hɪˈpɒkrəˌtiːz/ N Hippocrate *m*

Hippocratic oath /hɪpəʊˈkrætɪk/ N ◆ **the ~** le serment d'Hippocrate

hippodrome /ˈhɪpədrəʊm/ N hippodrome *m*

Hippolytus /hɪˈpɒlɪtəs/ N Hippolyte *m*

hippopotamus /ˌhɪpəˈpɒtəməs/ N (pl **hippopotamuses** *or* **hippopotami** /ˌhɪpəˈpɒtəmaɪ/) hippopotame *m*

hippy¹ * /ˈhɪpɪ/ ⇒ **hippie**

hippy² * /ˈhɪpɪ/ ADJ aux hanches larges, large de hanches

hipster /ˈhɪpstəʳ/ N 1 *(Brit)* ◆ **~ skirt** jupe *f* taille basse ; see also **npl** 2 *(US* *)* jeune homme *m* dans le vent (1940-50) NPL **hipsters** *(Brit)* pantalon *m* taille basse

hire /ˈhaɪəʳ/ N *(NonC: Brit = act of hiring) [of car, boat, clothes, hall]* location *f* ◆ **for ~** *[car, boat, building]* à louer ; *[taxi]* libre ◆ **on ~** en location ◆ **to let out sth on ~** louer qch ◆ **car/cycle/ski ~** location *f* de voitures/de vélos/de skis

VT 1 *(Brit = rent) [+ car, boat, clothes, hall]* louer ◆ **a ~d car** une voiture louée *or* de location

2 *(= employ) [+ person]* engager, embaucher ◆ **~d man** *(for season)* ouvrier *m* saisonnier ; *(on daily basis)* ouvrier *m* à la journée ◆ **a ~d killer** un tueur à gages

VI embaucher, recruter ◆ **she's in charge of all hiring and firing at the company** c'est elle qui est responsable du recrutement et des licenciements au sein de l'entreprise

COMP **hire car** N *(Brit)* voiture *f* de location
hire charges NPL *(Brit)* frais *mpl* de location, prix *m* de (la) location
hire purchase N *(Brit)* achat *m or* vente *f* à crédit, achat *m or* vente *f* à tempérament ◆ **on ~ purchase** à crédit
hire purchase agreement N *(Brit)* contrat *m* de crédit

► **hire out** VT SEP 1 *(Brit = rent out) [+ car, tools]* louer
2 *(US)* ◆ **he hires himself out as a gardener** il loue ses services comme jardinier

hireling /ˈhaɪəlɪŋ/ N *(pej)* mercenaire *m*

Hiroshima /ˌhɪrɒˈʃiːmə/ N Hiroshima

hirsute /ˈhɜːsjuːt/ ADJ velu, poilu

his /hɪz/ POSS ADJ son, sa, ses ◆ **~ book** son livre ◆ **~ table** sa table ◆ **~ friend** son ami(e) ◆ **~ clothes** ses vêtements ◆ **HIS book** son livre à lui ◆ **he has broken ~ leg** il s'est cassé la jambe
POSS PRON le sien, la sienne, les siens, les siennes ◆ **my hands are clean, ~ are dirty** mes mains sont propres, les siennes sont sales ◆ **~ is a specialized department** sa section est une section spécialisée ◆ **this book is ~** ce livre est à lui, ce livre est le sien ◆ **this poem is ~** ce poème est de lui ◆ **the house became ~** la maison est devenue la sienne ◆ **it is not ~ to decide** ce n'est pas à lui de décider, il ne lui appartient pas de décider
◆ **... of his** ◆ **a friend of ~** un de ses amis (à lui) ◆ **it's no fault of ~** ce n'est pas de sa faute (à lui) ◆ **no advice of ~ could prevent her doing it** aucun conseil de sa part ne pouvait l'empêcher de le faire ◆ **that car of ~** *(pej)* sa fichue* voiture ◆ **that stupid son of ~** *(pej)* son idiot de fils ◆ **that temper of ~** *(pej)* son sale caractère ◆ **that awful laugh of ~** *(pej)* ce rire abominable qu'il a

Hispanic /hɪˈspænɪk/ ADJ *(gen)* hispanique ; *(in America)* hispano-américain N Hispano-Américain(e) *m(f)*

Hispano... /hɪˈspænəʊ/ PREF hispano-

hiss /hɪs/ VI *[person, snake]* siffler ; *[cat]* cracher ; *[gas, steam]* chuinter, siffler VT *[+ actor, speaker]* siffler ◆ **"come here", he ~ed** "viens ici", siffla-t-il N sifflement *m* ◆ **~es** *(Theat)* sifflet(s) *m(pl)*

histogram /ˈhɪstəgræm/ N histogramme *m*

histologist /hɪˈstɒlədʒɪst/ N histologiste *mf*

histology /hɪˈstɒlədʒɪ/ N histologie *f*

historian /hɪˈstɔːrɪən/ N historien(ne) *m(f)*

historic /hɪˈstɒrɪk/ ADJ *(gen)* historique ◆ **site of ~ interest** site *m* historique ◆ **a ~ occasion** un événement historique COMP **historic present** N *(Gram)* présent *m* historique *or* de narration

historical /hɪˈstɒrɪkəl/ ADJ *(gen)* historique ◆ **the ~ background to the case** le rappel historique *or* l'historique *m* de l'affaire ◆ **place of ~ interest** monument *m or* site *m* historique ◆ **of ~ importance** d'une importance historique ◆ **a ~ landmark** un événement historique marquant, un jalon dans l'histoire ◆ **a famous ~ figure** un personnage historique célèbre ◆ **from a ~ perspective** d'un point de vue historique ◆ **~ research** recherche *f* historique ◆ **a ~ record** une source historique ◆ **there is no ~ precedent for this** sur le plan historique, il n'y a aucun précédent
COMP **historical linguistics** N *(NonC)* linguistique *f* diachronique
historical novel N roman *m* historique
historical present N *(Gram)* present *m* historique *or* de narration

historically /hɪˈstɒrɪkəlɪ/ ADV *(= traditionally)* traditionnellement ; *(= in historical terms) [important, accurate]* historiquement ; *[consider]* sur le plan historique ◆ **~, there is no precedent for this** sur le plan historique, ceci n'a aucun précédent ◆ **~ speaking** historiquement parlant

historiography /ˌhɪstɒrɪˈɒgrəfɪ/ N historiographie *f*

history /ˈhɪstərɪ/ N histoire *f* ◆ **to make ~** être historique ◆ **she will go down in ~ for what she did** elle entrera dans l'histoire pour ce qu'elle a fait ◆ **it will go down in ~ (as ...)** *[event, day, decision]* cela entrera dans l'histoire (comme étant ...) ◆ **one of the most dramatic moments in Polish ~** un des moments les plus marquants de l'histoire polonaise ◆ **the highest salary in television ~** le salaire le plus élevé de l'histoire de la télévision ◆ **religious ~** l'histoire *f* des religions ◆ **military ~** l'histoire *f* militaire ◆ **that's all ancient ~** c'est de l'histoire ancienne tout cela ◆ **the recent ceasefire agreement is already ~** le récent cessez-le-feu n'est déjà plus qu'un souvenir ◆ **... and the rest is ~** ... le reste appartient à l'histoire ◆ **one mistake and you're ~** * une erreur et tu es fini* ◆ **I don't know the ~ of this necklace** je ne connais pas l'histoire de ce collier ◆ **what is his medical ~?** quel est son passé médical ? ◆ **my family has a ~ of asthma** j'ai des antécédents familiaux d'asthme ◆ **he has a ~ of psychiatric disorders** il a des antécédents de troubles psychiatriques ◆ **the accused had a ~ of violent behaviour** l'accusé était déjà connu pour avoir commis des actes de violence ; → **case¹, natural**

histrionic /ˌhɪstrɪˈɒnɪk/ ADJ théâtral ; *(pej)* histrionique, de cabotin *(pej)* ◆ **~ ability** talent *m* dramatique

histrionically /ˌhɪstrɪˈɒnɪkəlɪ/ ADV d'un air théâtral *or* mélodramatique

histrionics /ˌhɪstrɪˈɒnɪks/ NPL art *m* dramatique ◆ **I'm tired of his ~** *(pej)* j'en ai assez de ses airs dramatiques *or* de son cinéma*

hit /hɪt/ (vb : pret, ptp **hit**) N 1 *(= stroke, blow)* coup *m* ; *(in baseball, cricket)* coup *m* de batte ; *(in tennis)* coup *m* de raquette ; *(fig)* attaque *f* ◆ **the film was a ~ at current government policy** le film était une attaque contre la politique actuelle du gouvernement ; → **free**

2 *(= successful stroke)* coup *m* réussi, beau coup *m* ; *(Fencing)* touche *f* ; *(Mil: with bomb, bullet, shell)* tir *m* réussi ◆ **three ~s and three misses** *(gen)* trois succès et trois échecs ; → **direct, score**

3 *(Comput) (= response from Internet)* réponse *f*, occurrence *f* ; *(= visit to website)* connexion *f*, hit *m*

4 *(gen)* (gros) succès *m* ; *(= song)* tube* *m* ◆ **the play/song was a big ~** la pièce/chanson a eu un énorme succès ◆ **to make a ~ of sth*** réussir (pleinement) qch ◆ **she was** *or* **made a big ~ with my sister** elle a beaucoup plu à ma sœur

5 *(* = dose) [of crack, speed, caffeine etc]* dose* *f* ; → **score**

6 *(* = assassination)* meurtre *m*

VT 1 *(= strike) (once)* frapper ; *(repeatedly)* taper sur ; *(= knock against)* heurter, cogner ; *(= reach)* atteindre ; *(Billiards, Fencing)* toucher ; *(Typ, Comput) [+ key]* appuyer sur ; *(fig = hurt, annoy)* blesser ◆ **he ~ his brother** il a frappé son frère ◆ **he ~ me!** *(once)* il m'a frappé ! ; *(repeatedly)* il m'a tapé dessus ! ◆ **his father used to ~ him** son père le battait ◆ **to ~ sb where it hurts** *(lit: in fight)* frapper qn là où ça fait mal ; *(fig)* toucher qn à son point faible ◆ **she ~ him a blow across the face** *(with hand)* elle l'a frappé au visage ; *(with truncheon etc)* elle lui a donné un coup de matraque *etc* sur le visage ◆ **to ~ one's knee/elbow on** *or* **against sth** se cogner *or* se heurter le genou/coude contre qch ◆ **his head ~ the corner of the table, he ~ his head on the corner of the table** sa tête a cogné contre *or* heurté le coin de la table, il s'est cogné la tête sur le coin de la table ◆ **the stone ~ the window** la pierre a cogné contre la fenêtre ◆ **he ~ the nail with a hammer** il a tapé sur le clou avec un marteau ◆ **to ~ the nail on the head** *(fig)* mettre dans le mille, faire mouche ◆ **that ~ home!** *(fig)* le coup a porté ! ◆ **to ~ the buffers** *(Brit fig) [plan, project]* s'en aller en eau de boudin ◆ **to ~ the wall** *(fig) [athlete etc]* connaître un passage à vide ◆ **to ~ the ground running*** se mettre immédiatement au travail ◆ **he was ~ by flying glass** il a reçu des éclats de verre ◆ **the president was ~ by three bullets** le président a reçu trois balles ◆ **the bullet ~ him in the chest** il a reçu la balle dans la poitrine ◆ **the house was ~ by a bomb** la maison a été atteinte par *or* a reçu une bombe ◆ **the tree was ~ by lightning** l'arbre a été frappé par la foudre ◆ **the hurricane ~ San Francisco yesterday evening** l'ouragan a frappé San Francisco hier soir ◆ **my plane had been ~** mon avion avait été touché ◆ **you won't know what's ~ you when the baby arrives!** * ta vie va être bouleversée par l'arrivée du bébé ; → **down², mark²**

2 *(fig = affect adversely)* toucher ◆ **California was the area hardest ~ by the storms** la Californie a été la région la plus touchée par les tempêtes ◆ **production was ~ by the strike** la production a été touchée par la grève ◆ **the rise in prices will ~ the poorest families first** la hausse des prix affectera *or* touchera d'abord les familles les plus pauvres ◆ **he was hard ~ by his losses** ses pertes l'ont durement touché *or* atteint ◆ **industry has been hard ~ by the recession** l'industrie a été gravement touchée par la récession ◆ **the public was hardest ~ by the strike** c'est le public qui a été touché le plus durement par la grève

3 *(fig)* ◆ **to ~ the papers** *[news, story]* être à la une* des journaux, faire les gros titres des journaux ◆ **what will happen when the story ~s the front page?** que se passera-t-il quand on lira cette histoire en première page des journaux ? ◆ **the car ~* 100mph just before it crashed** la voiture a atteint les 160 km/h juste avant l'accident ◆ **oil prices ~ record levels yesterday** le prix du pétrole a atteint un niveau record hier ◆ **then it ~ me*** *(= realization)* alors ça a fait tilt* ◆ **it suddenly ~ me* that ...** je me suis soudain rendu compte que ..., j'ai soudain réalisé que ... ◆ **you've ~ it!*** ça y est*, tu as trouvé ! ◆ **he ~ me with a six of spades*** *(US Cards)* il m'a flanqué un six de pique ◆ **to ~ sb for 10 dollars**⁑ *(US)* taper* qn de 10 dollars ◆ **to ~ the bottle*** se mettre à picoler* ◆ **to ~ the ceiling*** *or* **the roof*** sortir de ses gonds ◆ **to ~ the deck*** *(= get down)* s'aplatir au sol ; *(= get knocked down) (gen)* tomber par terre ; *[boxer]* aller au tapis ◆ **to ~ the dirt**⁑ s'aplatir au sol ◆ **to ~ the hay**⁑ *or* **the sack**⁑ se pieuter⁑ ◆ **to ~ the road*** *or* **the trail*** se mettre en route ◆ **in May the candidates will ~ the campaign trail** en mai les candidats se lanceront dans la campagne électorale ◆ **to ~ the dance floor*** aller sur la piste (de danse) ◆ **when will Jim ~ town?*** quand est-ce que Jim va débarquer* en ville ? ◆ **we should ~ Las Vegas in a couple of hours** nous devrions arriver à Las Vegas dans une ou deux heures ◆ **to ~ the shops*** *[article]* arriver dans les magasins ; *[person]* faire les magasins ◆ **to ~ the bookshops** *or (US)* **bookstores** *[new publication]* sortir en librairie ◆ **it ~s the spot*** *[food, drink]* ça fait du bien ! ; *(= succeeds)* ça tombe à pic !* ◆ **to ~ sb for six*** *[cold, flu]* lessiver* qn ; *[news]* faire un choc à qn ; → **headline, high, jackpot, skid**

4 *(= collide with)* heurter, rentrer dans* ◆ **the car ~ a pedestrian** la voiture a renversé un piéton

5 *(= find)* trouver, tomber sur ; *[+ problems, difficulties]* rencontrer ◆ **at last we ~ the right road** nous sommes enfin tombés sur la bonne route ◆ **we've ~ a snag** on est tombés sur un os*

VI *(= collide)* se heurter, se cogner *(against* à, contre)

COMP **hit-and-miss** ADV au petit bonheur (la chance), un peu n'importe comment ADJ *[work]* fait au petit bonheur (la chance) ; *[attitude]* désinvolte ; *[technique]* empirique ◆ **it's a ~-and-miss affair** c'est une question de chance ◆ **the way she painted the room was rather ~-and-miss** elle a peint la pièce un peu n'importe comment ◆ **it was all rather ~-and-miss** tout se passait plutôt au petit bonheur (la chance), tout était à la va-comme-je-te-pousse

hit-and-run accident N accident *m* avec délit de fuite

hit-and-run driver N chauffard *m* coupable du délit de fuite

hit-and-run raid N *(Mil)* raid *m* éclair *inv*

hit-and-run strike N grève *f* éclair

hit list N liste *f* noire ◆ **he's on her ~ list** *(fig)* elle l'a dans le collimateur*

hit-or-miss ADV, ADJ ⇒ **hit-and-miss**

hit parade N hit-parade *m*

hit show N *(Theat)* revue *f* à succès ; *(TV)* émission *f* à succès

hit single N *(Mus)* tube* *m*

hit squad * N commando *m* (de tueurs)

► **hit back** VI *(lit)* frapper en retour ; *(fig)* riposter ◆ **to ~ back at sb** *(fig)* se venger de qn ◆ **to ~ back at sb's criticism/suggestions/accusations** riposter à la critique/aux suggestions/aux accusations de qn

VT SEP ◆ **to hit sb back** frapper qn en retour

► **hit off** * VT SEP ◆ **to hit it off with sb** bien s'entendre avec qn ◆ **they ~ it off straight away** ils se sont immédiatement bien entendus ◆ **he has never ~ it off with Douglas** il ne s'est jamais entendu avec Douglas

► **hit on** VT FUS 1 ⇒ **hit upon**

2 *(US *)* *(= try to pick up)* draguer* ; *(= beat)* frapper

► **hit out** VI 1 *(lit)* ◆ **the police hit out with batons and iron bars** la police a distribué des coups de matraque et de barres de fer ◆ **to ~ out at sb** donner un coup à qn

2 *(fig)* riposter ◆ **he ~ out angrily when I suggested it had been his fault** il a riposté avec colère quand j'ai suggéré que c'était de sa faute ◆ **to ~ out at sb** s'en prendre à qn ◆ **to ~ out at sb's criticism/suggestions/accusations** riposter à la critique/aux suggestions/aux accusations de qn

► **hit upon** VT FUS tomber sur, trouver

hitch /hɪtʃ/ N 1 *(= obstacle)* (petit) problème *m* ◆ **there's been a ~** il y a eu un (petit) problème ◆ **there's been a ~ in their plans** leur projet s'est heurté à un obstacle ◆ **after some technical ~es the show finally got under way** après quelques problèmes techniques le spectacle a finalement commencé ◆ **the only ~ is that ...** le seul ennui c'est que ... ◆ **without a ~** sans accroc

2 *(US *: in army or in jail) période passée dans l'armée ou en prison*

3 *(= knot: gen)* nœud *m* ; (also **hitch knot**) deux demi-clés *fpl*

4 ◆ **to give sth a ~ (up)** remonter qch

VT 1 (also **hitch up**) *[+ trousers, skirt]* remonter

2 *(= fasten)* accrocher, attacher, fixer ; *(Naut)* amarrer ◆ **to get ~ed**⁑ se marier ◆ **to ~ one's wagon to a star** *(US)* aspirer à de hautes destinées ◆ **to ~ one's wagon to sb** *(US)* chercher à profiter de la destinée de qn

3 * ◆ **to ~ a lift** *(= be hitch-hiking)* faire du stop* ; *(= get a lift)* être pris en stop* ◆ **to ~ a lift** *or* **a ride to Paris** faire du stop* jusqu'à Paris, être pris en stop* jusqu'à Paris ◆ **she ~ed a lift into town** elle a fait du stop* pour aller en ville, quelqu'un l'a déposée en ville ◆ **I ~ed a ride with a truck driver** j'ai été pris en stop* par un camion *or* un routier

VI * ⇒ **hitch-hike**

COMP **hitch-hike** VI faire du stop* *or* de l'autostop ◆ **they ~-hiked to Paris** ils sont allés à Paris en stop, ils ont fait du stop* *or* de l'autostop jusqu'à Paris

hitch-hiker N auto-stoppeur *m*, -euse *f*

hitch-hiking N auto-stop *m*, stop* *m*

► **hitch up** VT SEP 1 *[+ horses, oxen]* atteler *(to* à)

2 ⇒ **hitch vt 1**

hi-tec(h) /ˈhaɪˈtek/ ADJ ⇒ **high-tech** ; → **high**

hither /ˈhɪðəʳ/ ADV 1 *(†† = to here) [bring]* ici ◆ **come ~!** viens çà ! †† ; see also **come** ◆ **his journey ~** son voyage en ce lieu 2 ◆ **~ and thither** *(Brit)*, **~ and yon** *(US)* *(= to and fro)* çà et là ADJ †† de ce côté-ci

hitherto /ˌhɪðəˈtuː/ ADV jusqu'ici

Hitler /ˈhɪtləʳ/ N Hitler *m* COMP **the Hitler Youth (Movement)** N les jeunesses *fpl* hitlériennes

Hitlerian /hɪtˈlɪərɪən/ ADJ hitlérien

Hitlerism /ˈhɪtlərɪzəm/ N hitlérisme *m*

hitman * /ˈhɪtmæn/ N (pl **-men**) tueur *m* à gages

Hittite /ˈhɪtaɪt/ N 1 Hittite *mf* 2 *(= language)* hittite *m* ADJ hittite

HIV /ˌeɪtʃaɪˈviː/ N *(Med)* (abbrev of **human immunodeficiency virus**) HIV *m*, VIH *m*

COMP **HIV-negative** ADJ séronégatif

HIV-positive ADJ séropositif

HIV-related ADJ associé au sida

HIV virus N virus *m* HIV

hive /haɪv/ N *(= place, also fig)* ruche *f* ; *(with bees in it)* essaim *m* ◆ **a ~ of activity** *or* **industry** *(fig)* une vraie ruche VT mettre dans une ruche VI entrer à la ruche

► **hive off** *(Brit)* VI 1 *(= separate)* se séparer *(from* de) essaimer 2 *(⁑ = rush off)* filer*, se tirer⁑ VT SEP séparer *(from* de) ◆ **they ~d off the infant school to a different building** ils ont déplacé la maternelle pour l'installer dans un autre bâtiment ◆ **the branch might be ~d off into a separate company** il se peut que cette succursale devienne une société indépendante

hives /haɪvz/ NPL *(Med)* urticaire *f*

hiya⁑ /ˈhaɪjə/ EXCL salut !*

Hizbollah, Hizbullah /ˈhɪzbəˈlɑː/ N ⇒ **Hezbollah**

hl (abbrev of **hectolitre(s)**) hl

HM /ˌeɪtʃˈem/ N (abbrev of **His** *or* **Her Majesty**) S.M., Sa Majesté

HMG /ˌeɪtʃemˈdʒiː/ N *(Brit)* (abbrev of **His** *or* **Her Majesty's Government**) → **majesty**

HMI /ˌeɪtʃemˈaɪ/ N *(Brit Educ)* (abbrev of **His** *or* **Her Majesty's Inspector**) ≈ inspecteur *m*, -trice *f* général(e) de l'enseignement secondaire

HMS /ˌeɪtʃemˈes/ N *(Brit)* (abbrev of **His** *or* **Her Majesty's Ship**) → **ship**

HMSO /ˌeɪtʃemesˈəʊ/ N *(Brit)* (abbrev of **His** *or* **Her Majesty's Stationery Office**) → **stationery**

HNC /ˌeɪtʃenˈsiː/ N *(Brit Educ)* (abbrev of **Higher National Certificate**) ≈ BTS *m*

HND /ˌeɪtʃenˈdiː/ N *(Brit Educ)* (abbrev of **Higher National Diploma**) ≈ DUT *m*

ho /həʊ/ EXCL ◆ **~ ~!** ah ah (ah) !

hoagie, hoagy /ˈhəʊgɪ/ N *(US)* grand sandwich *m* mixte

hoard /hɔːd/ N réserves *fpl*, provisions *fpl* ; *(pej)* stock *m* *(pej)* ; *(= treasure)* trésor *m* ◆ **a ~ of food** des provisions *fpl*, des réserves *fpl* ◆ **a ~ of silver and jewels** un trésor composé d'argenterie et de bijoux ; *(pej)* tout un stock d'argenterie et de bijoux ◆ **a squirrel's ~ of nuts** les réserves *or* provisions de noisettes d'un écureuil VT (also **hoard up**) *[+ food etc]* amasser, mettre en réserve ; *(pej)* stocker *(pej)* ; *[+ money]* accumuler, amasser

hoarder /ˈhɔːdəʳ/ N ◆ **to be a ~** ne rien jeter

hoarding¹ /ˈhɔːdɪŋ/ N *(= act of saving)* entassement *m*, accumulation *f* ; *[of capital]* thésaurisation *f*

hoarding² /ˈhɔːdɪŋ/ N 1 *(Brit: for advertisements)* panneau *m* d'affichage *or* publicitaire 2 *(= fence)* palissade *f*

hoarfrost /ˈhɔːˌfrɒst/ N gelée *f* blanche, givre *m*

hoarse /hɔːs/ ADJ *[person]* enroué ; *[voice]* rauque, enroué ◆ **to be ~** avoir la voix rauque, être enroué ◆ **he shouted himself ~** il s'est enroué à force de crier

hoarsely /ˈhɔːslɪ/ ADV d'une voix rauque

hoarseness /ˈhɔːsnɪs/ N enrouement *m*

hoary /ˈhɔːrɪ/ ADJ [1] *[hair]* blanchi, blanc neigeux *inv* ; *[person] (lit, liter:* also **hoary-headed**) chenu *(liter)* ; *(fig)* vénérable ◆ **a ~ old joke** une blague éculée ◆ **a ~ old tradition** une vieille tradition surannée [2] *(Bot)* couvert de duvet blanc

hoax /həʊks/ N canular *m* ◆ **to play a ~ on sb** monter *or* faire un canular à qn ◆ **the phone call was a ~** le coup de téléphone était le fait d'un mauvais plaisant VT faire *or* monter un canular à ◆ **we were completely ~ed** on nous a eus* ◆ **to ~ sb into believing sth** faire croire qch à qn

hob /hɒb/ N *(on cooker)* plan *m* de cuisson ; *(Brit: on old-fashioned cooker)* rond *m* ; *(by fireplace)* plaque *f* (de foyer) *(où la bouilloire etc est tenue au chaud)*

hobble /ˈhɒbl/ VI clopiner, boitiller ◆ **to ~ along** aller clopin-clopant ◆ **to ~ in/out** *etc* entrer/sortir *etc* en clopinant VT *(lit, fig)* entraver N *(for horses)* entrave *f* COMP **hobble skirt** N jupe *f* entravée

hobbledehoy /ˌhɒbldɪˈhɔɪ/ N grand dadais *m*

hobby /ˈhɒbɪ/ N passe-temps *m inv*, hobby *m* ◆ **my hobbies include painting and sailing** la peinture et la voile sont deux de mes hobbies ◆ **he began to paint as a ~** il a commencé la peinture comme passe-temps COMP **hobby-horse** N *(= toy)* tête *f* de cheval *(sur un manche)* ; *(= rocking horse)* cheval *m* à bascule ; *(fig)* sujet *m* favori, dada* *m* ◆ **he's off on his ~-horse** *(fig)* le voilà reparti (sur son dada)

hobbyist /ˈhɒbɪɪst/ N amateur *m* ◆ **a photo ~** un photographe amateur

hobgoblin /ˈhɒbˌɡɒblɪn/ N *(= elf)* lutin *m* ; *(fig) (= bugbear)* croquemitaine *m*

hobnail /ˈhɒbneɪl/ N caboche *f*, clou *m* COMP **hobnail(ed) boots** NPL souliers *mpl* cloutés *or* ferrés

hobnob /ˈhɒbnɒb/ VI ◆ **to ~ with** frayer avec

hobo /ˈhəʊbəʊ/ N (pl **hobo(e)s**) *(US)* [1] *(= tramp)* clochard *m* [2] *(= migratory worker)* saisonnier *m*

Hobson's choice /ˈhɒbsənzˈtʃɔɪs/ N ◆ **it's ~** c'est un choix qui n'en est pas un, ce n'est un choix qu'en apparence

Ho Chi Minh City /ˈhəʊˈtʃiːˈmɪnˈsɪtɪ/ N Hô Chi Minh-Ville

hock¹ /hɒk/ N *[of animal]* jarret *m* ; *[of human]* creux *m* du genou ; *(Culin)* jarret *m* (de bœuf)

hock² /hɒk/ N *(Brit = wine)* vin *m* du Rhin

hock³* /hɒk/ VT *(= pawn)* mettre au clou* N ◆ **in ~** *[object]* au clou*, au mont-de-piété ; *[person]* endetté

hockey /ˈhɒkɪ/ N [1] (also **field hockey**) hockey *m* [2] (also **ice hockey**) hockey *m* sur glace COMP *[match, pitch]* de hockey
hockey player N hockeyeur *m*, -euse *f*, joueur *m*, -euse *f* de hockey
hockey stick N crosse *f* de hockey

hocus-pocus /ˈhəʊkəsˈpəʊkəs/ N *(NonC)* [1] *(= trickery)* ◆ **a bit of ~** des tours de passe-passe [2] *(= mumbo-jumbo)* galimatias *m*

hod /hɒd/ N *(for coal)* seau *m* à charbon ; *(for bricks, mortar)* oiseau *m*, hotte *f*

hodgepodge /ˈhɒdʒpɒdʒ/ N *(esp US)* ⇒ **hotchpotch**

hoe /həʊ/ N houe *f*, binette *f* VT *[+ ground]* biner ; *[+ vegetables, weeds]* sarcler

hoedown /ˈhəʊdaʊn/ N *(US) (= dance)* danse *f* (villageoise) ; *(= party)* bal *m* populaire

hog /hɒg/ N [1] cochon *m*, porc *m* ; *(Brit: castrated)* cochon *m* ◆ **he's a greedy ~** c'est un vrai goinfre ◆ **to go ~ wild*** *(US)* dépasser les bornes ; → **high, road, whole** [2] *(US * = motorbike)* moto* *f* VT * [1] *(= monopolize) [+ best chair etc]* accaparer, monopoliser ; *[+ conversation]* monopoliser ◆ **don't ~ all the sweets** ne garde pas tous les bonbons pour toi ◆ **to ~ the credit** s'attribuer tout le mérite ◆ **to ~ the limelight** monopoliser l'attention [2] *[+ food]* se goinfrer* de

Hogarthian /həʊˈɡɑːθɪən/ ADJ *grotesque à la manière de Hogarth*

Hogmanay /ˌhɒɡməˈneɪ/ N *(Scot)* la Saint-Sylvestre, le réveillon du jour de l'an

> **HOGMANAY**
>
> **Hogmanay** est le nom donné au réveillon du jour de l'An en Écosse. La coutume veut que le 31 décembre on se rende chez ses voisins après minuit en apportant symboliquement un petit cadeau, de la boisson et, parfois, un morceau de charbon en gage de prospérité pour l'année à venir ; cette coutume porte le nom de « first-footing ».

hogshead /ˈhɒɡzhed/ N barrique *f*

hogtie /ˈhɒɡtaɪ/ VT *(US) (lit)* lier les pieds et les poings de ; *(fig)* entraver ◆ **to be ~d** *(lit, fig)* être pieds et poings liés

hogwash /ˈhɒɡwɒʃ/ N *(= pigswill)* eaux *fpl* grasses *(pour nourrir les porcs)* ; *(* = nonsense)* inepties *fpl*

ho hum* /ˈhəʊˈhʌm/ EXCL ◆ **~ ! that's life** eh oui ! c'est la vie ADJ (also **ho-hum**) moyen

hoick* /hɔɪk/ VT *(Brit = lift)* ◆ **to ~ one's trousers up** remonter son pantalon ◆ **to ~ sb out of bed** tirer qn de son lit

hoi polloi /ˌhɔɪpəˈlɔɪ/ NPL *(pej)* ◆ **the ~** la populace

hoist /hɔɪst/ VT hisser, remonter ; *[+ sails, flag]* hisser ◆ **to be ~ with one's own petard** être pris à son propre piège N [1] *(= equipment)* appareil *m* de levage, palan *m* ; *(= winch)* treuil *m* ; *(= crane)* grue *f* ; *(for goods)* monte-charge *m inv* ; *(made of rope)* corde *f*, palan *m* [2] ◆ **to give sth a ~ (up)** hisser *or* remonter qch

hoity-toity /ˈhɔɪtɪˈtɔɪtɪ/ ADJ *(pej = arrogant)* prétentieux, bêcheur*

hoke‡ /həʊk/ VT *(US)* ◆ **to ~ up a movie** forcer les effets d'un film

hokey* /ˈhəʊkɪ/ ADJ *(US)* [1] *(= phoney)* bidon* *inv* ◆ **it's ~** c'est du bidon* [2] *(= corny) [story, song]* cucul la praline* *inv* ; *[excuse]* tiré par les cheveux COMP **hokey-cokey** N *sorte de ronde*

hokum* /ˈhəʊkəm/ N *(US) (= nonsense)* foutaises‡ *fpl* ; *(= sentimentality)* blablabla* *m* sentimental, niaiseries *fpl* ; *(US Cine, Theat)* gros effets *mpl*

hold /həʊld/

vb : pret, ptp held

LANGUAGE IN USE 27

1 NOUN
2 TRANSITIVE VERB
3 INTRANSITIVE VERB
4 PHRASAL VERBS

1 - NOUN

[1] [= grip, clutch] prise *f* ◆ **he loosened his ~** il a desserré sa prise *or* son étreinte *f* ◆ **he loosened his ~ around my arms/my throat** il a desserré son étreinte autour de mes bras/ma gorge ◆ **I tried to break free from his ~** j'ai essayé de me dégager ◆ **to seize ~ of** saisir ◆ **to have ~ of** tenir ◆ **I've got a good** *or* **firm ~ on the rope** je tiens bien *or* bon la corde

[2] [= control, influence] emprise *f* ◆ **the Prime Minister's uneasy ~ over her government** la fragile emprise du Premier ministre sur son gouvernement ◆ **the president has consolidated his ~ on the media** le président a renforcé son emprise sur les médias ◆ **she still has a ~ on him** elle a toujours de l'emprise sur lui

[3] [gen, *also* Climbing] prise *f* ◆ **the rock offered him few ~s** le rocher lui offrait peu de prises

[4] [Wrestling] prise *f* ◆ **no ~s barred** * *(fig)* tous les coups sont (*or* étaient *etc*) permis ◆ **a talk show with no ~s barred** * un débat télévisé où tous les coups sont permis

[5] [of hairspray, hair gel] fixation *f* ◆ **finish with hairspray for extra ~** pour finir, vaporisez de la laque pour obtenir une fixation parfaite

[6] [in ship] cale *f*

[7] [in plane] soute *f*

[8] [set structures]

◆ **to catch hold (of sth)** attraper (qch) ◆ **catch ~!** attrape ! ◆ **he caught ~ of her arm** il l'a attrapée par le bras

◆ **to get/take a hold of** *(= catch)* prendre ◆ **to get a ~ of o.s.** se maîtriser, se contrôler ◆ **get a ~ of yourself!** ressaisis-toi !

◆ **to get hold of** *(= find, trace) [+ object]* dénicher*, (réussir à) se procurer ; *[+ details, information]* réussir à obtenir ; *(= contact) [+ person]* contacter, joindre ◆ **can you get ~ of £500 by tomorrow?** est-ce que tu peux te procurer 500 livres d'ici demain ?* ◆ **where did you get ~ of that hat?** où as-tu déniché* *or* été trouver ce chapeau ? ◆ **children can all too easily get ~ of drugs** les enfants peuvent trop facilement se procurer de la drogue ◆ **where did you get ~ of that idea?** où as-tu été pêcher* *or* trouver cette idée ? ◆ **the press got ~ of the story** la presse s'empara de cette histoire ◆ **we've been trying to get ~ of him all day** nous avons essayé de le contacter *or* le joindre toute la journée

◆ **to take hold** *[fire]* prendre ; *[custom, practice]* se répandre ; *[idea]* faire son chemin ; *[recession, economic recovery, disease]* s'installer ; *[truce, ceasefire]* tenir ◆ **the reforms taking ~ in former Communist states** les réformes engagées dans les anciens États communistes ◆ **take ~!** tiens !

◆ **to keep hold of** tenir fermement, ne pas lâcher ◆ **keep ~ of the idea that ...** dites-vous bien que ...

◆ **on hold** *[phone call, order]* en attente ◆ **to put sb on ~** *(during phone call)* mettre qn en attente ◆ **nuclear testing was put on ~** les essais nucléaires ont été suspendus ◆ **he put his career on ~ to spend more time with his family** il a mis sa carrière entre parenthèses pour consacrer plus de temps à sa famille

2 - TRANSITIVE VERB

[1] [= grasp] tenir ◆ **~ this for a moment** tiens *or* prends ça un moment ◆ **he held my arm** il me tenait le bras ◆ **the dog held the stick in his mouth** le chien tenait le bâton dans sa gueule ◆ **she was ~ing her sister's hand** *(lit, fig)* elle tenait la main de sa sœur ◆ **they were ~ing hands** *(gen)* ils se tenaient par la main ; *[lovers]* ils étaient la main dans la main ◆ **she held him tight** elle l'a serré très fort ◆ **~ him tight or he'll fall** tenez-le bien pour qu'il ne tombe *subj* pas

[2] [= keep in place] ◆ **to ~ sth in place** maintenir qch en place ◆ **the nails ~ the carpet in place** les clous maintiennent la moquette en place ◆ **hair held in place with a clip** des cheveux attachés avec une barrette ◆ **she held the door open** elle a tenu la porte (ouverte) ◆ **a hat held by a ribbon tied under the chin** un chapeau maintenu au moyen d'un ruban noué sous le menton

[3] [= support] supporter ◆ **the ladder won't ~ you** *or* **your weight** l'échelle ne supportera pas ton poids

[4] [= maintain, keep] **to ~ o.s. upright** se tenir droit ◆ **to ~ a note** *(Mus)* tenir une note ◆ **to ~**

sth in mind garder qch à l'esprit ◆ **to ~ an opinion** avoir une opinion ◆ **to ~ sb's attention/interest** retenir l'attention/l'intérêt de qn ◆ **can he ~ an audience?** est-ce qu'il sait tenir son public (en haleine) ? ◆ **this car ~s the road well** cette voiture tient bien la route ◆ **to ~ one's breath** *(lit, fig)* retenir son souffle ◆ **don't ~ your breath!** *(fig)* n'y compte pas trop ! ◆ **it's scheduled to finish in August, but don't ~ your breath** il est prévu que ce soit fini en août mais je n'y compterais pas trop ◆ **~ the line!** *(Telec)* ne quittez pas ! ◆ **I've been ~ing the line for several minutes** *(Telec)* cela fait plusieurs minutes que je suis en ligne *or* que j'attends

5 [= have, possess] *[+ ticket, permit, driving licence]* avoir ; *[+ shares, record]* détenir ◆ **Spain held vast territories in South America** l'Espagne possédait de vastes territoires en Amérique du Sud

6 [= defend successfully] *(gen, Mil)* tenir ◆ **the army held the bridge against the enemy** l'armée a tenu le pont malgré les attaques de l'ennemi ◆ **to ~ one's serve** *(Tennis)* gagner son service

♦ **to hold one's own** *(gen)* (bien) se débrouiller ; *[ill person]* se maintenir ◆ **he can ~ his own in German** il se débrouille très bien en allemand ◆ **he can ~ his own with anybody** il ne s'en laisse pas remontrer

7 [= occupy] *[+ post, position]* avoir, occuper ; *(Rel) [+ living]* jouir de ◆ **he ~s the post of headmaster** il occupe le poste de directeur

8 [= cause to take place] *[+ meeting, election, debate]* tenir ; *[+ conversation]* avoir, tenir ; *(Scol) [+ examination]* organiser ◆ **the exhibition is always held here** l'exposition se tient toujours *or* a toujours lieu ici ◆ **to ~ a service** *(Rel) [priest etc]* célébrer un office ◆ **they are ~ing a service to mark the day when ...** ils ont prévu une cérémonie pour commémorer le jour où ... ◆ **to ~ interviews** *[employer etc]* recevoir des candidats ◆ **the interviews are being held in London** les entretiens ont lieu à Londres

9 [= contain] contenir ◆ **this box will ~ all my books** cette caisse est assez grande pour (contenir) tous mes livres ◆ **this bottle ~s one litre** cette bouteille a une contenance d'un litre *or* peut contenir un litre ◆ **this room ~s 20 people** il y a de la place pour 20 personnes dans cette salle ◆ **what does the future ~ for us?** qu'est-ce que l'avenir nous réserve ? ◆ **I wonder what the future ~s** je me demande ce que l'avenir nous réserve ◆ **she can ~ her drink** *or* **liquor!** * c'est fou ce qu'elle supporte bien l'alcool !

10 [= keep, have charge of] garder ◆ **I will ~ the money until ...** je garderai l'argent jusqu'à ce que ... ◆ **my lawyer ~s these documents** ces documents sont chez mon avocat ◆ **the bank ~s these bills** la banque conserve ces effets ◆ **we don't ~ that information on our files** nous n'avons pas ces informations dans nos fichiers ◆ **the data is held on computer** ces données sont informatisées

11 [= keep back, restrain] *[+ person]* tenir, retenir ◆ **to ~ a train** empêcher un train de partir ◆ **~ the letter until ...** n'envoyez pas la lettre avant que ... + *subj* ◆ **"hold for arrival"** *(US on letters)* "ne pas faire suivre" ◆ **the police held him for two days** la police l'a gardé (à vue) pendant deux jours ◆ **there's no ~ing him** il n'y a pas moyen de l'arrêter ◆ **~ it!** * stop !

12 [= believe, assert] ◆ **to ~ that ...** maintenir que ... ◆ **he ~s that matter does not exist** il maintient que la matière n'existe pas ◆ **to ~ sth to be true** considérer qch comme vrai ◆ **this is held to be true** cela passe pour vrai ◆ **the court held that ...** *(Jur)* la cour a statué que ... ◆ **it was held by the judge that ...** le juge a statué que ... ◆ **the law ~s that ...** la loi prévoit *or* stipule que ... ◆ **he was held guilty of the offence** on pensait que c'était lui qui avait commis le délit ◆ **to ~ sb responsible for sth** tenir qn pour responsable de qch ◆ **to ~ in high esteem** tenir en haute estime

♦ **to hold sth against sb** en vouloir à qn de qch ◆ **I don't ~ it against him** je ne lui en veux pas

3 - INTRANSITIVE VERB

1 [= remain in place] *[rope, nail]* tenir, être solide ◆ **to ~ firm** *or* **tight** *or* **fast** *(= stay in place)* tenir ; see also **tight** ◆ **~ hard!** arrêtez !, minute ! *

2 *[weather]* se maintenir

3 [Telec] **can you ~, please?** ne quittez pas ! ◆ **I've been ~ing for several minutes** cela fait plusieurs minutes que je suis en ligne *or* que j'attends

4 [also **hold good**] *[statement, argument]* être valable ◆ **your argument doesn't ~ (good)** votre argument n'est pas valable ◆ **the theory could still ~** la théorie pourrait tout de même être valable

4 - PHRASAL VERBS

► **hold back**

VI *(lit)* rester en arrière ; *(fig)* se retenir *(from sth* de qch ; *from doing sth* de faire qch) ◆ **I held back from telling him what I really thought** je me suis retenu de lui dire ce que je pensais vraiment

VT SEP 1 *[+ fears, emotions]* maîtriser ; *[+ tears]* retenir ◆ **the police held back the crowd** la police a contenu la foule ◆ **to ~ sb back from doing sth** empêcher qn de faire qch ◆ **they held back the names of the victims** ils n'ont pas divulgué le nom des victimes ◆ **he was ~ing something back from me** il me cachait quelque chose ◆ **his policies have held our country back economically** sa politique a bloqué l'essor économique *or* a freiné le développement (économique) de notre pays

2 *(US Scol) [+ pupil]* faire redoubler ◆ **to be held back** redoubler

► **hold down** VT SEP 1 *(= keep in place)* maintenir en place ; *[+ person]* maintenir ◆ **to ~ one's head down** garder la tête baissée ◆ **we couldn't ~ him down** nous ne sommes pas arrivés à le maintenir au sol

2 *(= keep low) [+ costs, prices, inflation, taxes]* empêcher d'augmenter ◆ **strict government regulation will ~ down costs** le gouvernement empêchera les coûts d'augmenter grâce à une réglementation stricte

3 *[+ job] (= have)* avoir, occuper ; *(= keep)* garder ◆ **she's managed to ~ down a job as well as looking after the children** elle a réussi à continuer de travailler tout en s'occupant des enfants ◆ **he's ~ing down a good job** il a une belle situation ◆ **he can't ~ down a job** il ne garde jamais longtemps le même travail

► **hold forth**

VI faire des discours, disserter ◆ **he was ~ing forth on the subject of religion** il faisait des discours *or* dissertait sur la religion

VT SEP *(frm = hold out)* tendre

► **hold in** VT SEP retenir ◆ **~ your stomach in!** rentre ton ventre ! ◆ **to ~ in one's temper** se contenir, se retenir ◆ **he managed to ~ in his horse** il réussit à maîtriser son cheval ◆ **depression can sometimes be traced to ~ing in anger** le fait de réprimer sa colère peut entraîner la dépression ◆ **go ahead and cry, don't ~ it in** laisse-toi aller et pleure, n'essaie pas de te retenir

► **hold off**

VI ◆ **the rain has held off so far** jusqu'ici il n'a pas plu

VT SEP 1 *(= prevent from approaching)* tenir éloigné *or* à distance ◆ **they held off the enemy** ils tenaient l'ennemi à distance ◆ **try to ~ him off a little longer** *(fig)* essayez de le faire patienter encore un peu ◆ **I can't ~ him off any longer: you'll have to see him** je ne peux pas le faire attendre plus longtemps : il faut que vous le voyiez

2 *(= resist)* ◆ **she held off all challengers to win the race** elle a gagné la course malgré les autres challengers

3 *(= delay)* ◆ **to hold off doing sth** attendre pour faire qch ◆ **they held off eating until she had arrived** ils ont attendu qu'elle soit arrivée pour manger

► **hold on**

VI 1 *(= endure)* tenir bon, tenir le coup * ◆ **despite her aching shoulders, Nancy held on** malgré ses épaules qui lui faisaient mal, Nancy a tenu bon *or* a tenu le coup

2 *(= wait)* attendre ◆ **~ on!** attendez ! ; *(on telephone)* ne quittez pas !

VT SEP maintenir (en place), tenir en place ◆ **this hinge ~s the lid on** cette charnière maintient le couvercle (en place) ◆ **to ~ one's hat on** tenir son chapeau sur sa tête

► **hold on to** VT FUS 1 *(= cling to) [+ rope, raft, branch]* se cramponner à, s'accrocher à ; *(fig) [+ hope, idea]* se raccrocher à

2 *(= keep)* garder ◆ **~ on to this for me** *(= hold it)* tiens-moi ça ; *(= keep it)* garde-moi ça

► **hold out**

VI 1 *(= last) [supplies]* durer ◆ **how long will the food ~ out?** combien de temps est-ce que les provisions vont durer ? ◆ **if his luck ~s out** s'il continue à avoir de la chance

2 *(= endure, resist)* tenir bon, tenir le coup ◆ **to ~ out against** *[+ enemy, attacks]* tenir bon devant ; *[+ change, improvements, progress, threats, fatigue]* résister à ◆ **one prisoner was still ~ing out on the roof of the jail** un prisonnier continuait à résister sur le toit de la prison ◆ **they are ~ing out for more pay** ils continuent de demander une augmentation

VT SEP *[+ object]* tendre *(sth to sb* qch à qn) ◆ **"I'm Nancy" she said, ~ing out her hand** "je m'appelle Nancy" dit-elle en tendant la main ◆ **to ~ out one's arms** ouvrir les bras

VT FUS ◆ **the doctors hold out little hope for him** les médecins ne lui donnent pas beaucoup de chances de s'en tirer ◆ **she's still ~ing out hope that ...** elle conserve toujours l'espoir que ... ◆ **the negotiations held out little hope of a settlement** il y avait peu d'espoir que les négociations aboutissent à un accord ◆ **the scheme ~s out the promise of great financial reward** ce projet promet de rapporter beaucoup d'un point de vue financier

► **hold out on** * VT FUS *[+ price etc]* s'en tenir à ◆ **you've been ~ing out on me!** tu m'as caché quelque chose !

► **hold over** VT SEP remettre ◆ **the meeting was held over until Friday** la réunion a été remise à vendredi

► **hold to**

VT FUS s'en tenir à ◆ **I ~ to what I said** je m'en tiens à ce que j'ai dit ◆ **he held to his religious beliefs** il restait attaché à ses convictions religieuses

VT SEP ◆ **to hold sb to a promise** faire tenir parole à qn ◆ **I'll ~ you to that!** je te prends au mot !

► **hold together**

VI *[objects]* tenir (ensemble) ; *[groups, people]* rester uni ◆ **the coalition will never ~ together for six months** la coalition ne tiendra jamais six mois ◆ **we must ~ together** il faut se serrer les coudes *or* rester unis

VT SEP *[+ objects]* maintenir (ensemble) ; *(fig) [+ political party]* maintenir l'union de ◆ **he held the family together** c'est grâce à lui que la famille est restée unie ◆ **she sought to ~ together the various factions in her party** elle a cherché à réconcilier les différentes factions de son parti

► **hold up**
VI 1 *(lit)* ◆ **that building won't hold up much longer** ce bâtiment ne tiendra plus longtemps debout
2 *[argument]* tenir la route ; *[economy]* tenir le coup ◆ **the evidence doesn't ~ up** ces preuves ne tiennent pas la route
VT SEP 1 *(= raise)* lever, élever ◆ **~ it up higher** tiens-le plus haut ◆ **~ up your hand** levez la main ◆ **~ it up so that we can see it** soulevez-le pour que nous puissions le voir ◆ **to ~ sth up to the light** élever qch vers la lumière ◆ **I'll never be able to ~ my head up again** je ne pourrai plus jamais regarder personne en face ◆ **to ~ sb up to ridicule** tourner qn en ridicule ◆ **he had always been held up as an example to the younger ones** il avait toujours été cité en exemple aux plus jeunes
2 *(= support)* soutenir ◆ **the roof is held up by pillars** le toit est soutenu par des piliers
3 *(= stop)* arrêter ; *(= suspend)* différer, suspendre ; *(= cause delay to)* retarder ◆ **the traffic was held up by the accident** l'accident a ralenti la circulation ◆ **I'm sorry, I was held up** excusez-moi, j'ai été retenu ◆ **violence on the streets could ~ up progress towards reform** la violence dans les rues pourrait retarder les réformes
4 *[robber]* *[+ bank, shop]* faire un hold-up dans, braquer* ; *[+ coach, person]* attaquer (à main armée), braquer*

► **hold with*** **VT FUS** ◆ **I don't hold with that** je désapprouve *or* réprouve cela ◆ **she doesn't ~ with people smoking** elle n'aime pas que l'on fume *subj*

holdall /ˈhəʊldɔːl/ **N** *(Brit)* (sac *m*) fourre-tout *m inv*

holder /ˈhəʊldəʳ/ **N** 1 *[of ticket, card]* détenteur *m*, -trice *f* ; *[of passport, office, post, title of nobility, diploma]* titulaire *mf* ; *[of stocks]* porteur *m*, -euse *f*, détenteur *m*, -trice *f* ; *[of farm]* exploitant *m* ; *(Sport etc)* *[of record]* détenteur *m*, -trice *f* ; *[of title]* détenteur *m*, -trice *f*, tenant(e) *m(f)* ◆ **the ~s of the European Football Championship** les détenteurs *or* les tenants du titre de champion d'Europe de football ◆ **account ~** *(Banking)* titulaire *mf* d'un compte 2 *(= object)* support *m* ◆ **penholder** porte-plume *m inv* ; → **cigarette**

holding /ˈhəʊldɪŋ/ **N** 1 *(= act)* tenue *f* ; 2 *(= possession)* *[of lands]* possession *f*, jouissance *f* ; *[of stocks]* possession *f* 3 *(= farm)* propriété *f*, ferme *f* **NPL holdings** *(Fin)* *(= lands)* avoirs *mpl* fonciers ; *(= stocks)* intérêts *mpl*, participations *fpl* **COMP holding company N** *(Fin)* holding *m*, société *f* de portefeuille

holdout /ˈhəʊldaʊt/ **N** *(US)* *personne qui fait obstacle*, obstacle *m* ◆ **Britain was the only ~ on this agreement** la Grande-Bretagne était le seul pays à faire obstacle à cet accord

holdover* /ˈhəʊldəʊvəʳ/ **N** *(US: esp Pol)* rescapé(e) *m(f)* *(fig)*

holdup /ˈhəʊldʌp/ **N** 1 *(= robbery)* hold-up *m inv*, braquage* *m* 2 *(= delay)* retard *m* ; *(in traffic)* embouteillage *m*, bouchon *m* ◆ **there's been a ~ in the delivery** il y a eu un retard dans la livraison ◆ **a big ~ owing to roadworks** un gros embouteillage *or* bouchon dû aux travaux

hole /həʊl/ **N** 1 trou *m* ; *(in defences, dam)* brèche *f* ; *(in clouds)* trouée *f* ◆ **he spied on them through a ~ in the wall** il les a espionnés en regardant par un trou dans le mur ◆ **these socks are in ~s** *or* **full of ~s** ces chaussettes sont toutes trouées *or* pleines de trous ◆ **to wear a ~ in sth** trouer qch ◆ **to wear into ~s** se trouer ◆ **I need it like I need a ~ in the head!**‡ je n'ai vraiment pas besoin de ça !
2 *[of mouse]* trou *m* ; *[of rabbit, fox]* terrier *m*
3 *(Golf)* trou *m* ◆ **we played nine ~s** nous avons fait neuf trous ; → **comp**
4 *(fig = gap)* ◆ **it made** *or* **blew a ~ in his savings** cela a fait un trou dans ses économies ◆ **to blow a ~ in sb's plans** saborder les plans de qn ◆ **there were some ~s in his theory/his argument** il y avait des failles *fpl* *or* des faiblesses *fpl* dans sa théorie/son argumentation ◆ **the plot is full of ~s** l'intrigue est mal ficelée ◆ **his story's full of ~s** sa version des faits ne tient pas debout ; → **burn¹, knock, pick**
5 *(* = trouble)* **they were in a nasty ~** ils étaient dans un sale pétrin ◆ **he got me out of a ~** il m'a tiré d'embarras *or* d'un mauvais pas
6 *(* pej)* *(= town)* trou *m* (paumé)* ; *(= room, house)* bouge *m*
VT 1 faire un trou dans, trouer ◆ **the ship was ~d by a missile** un missile a fait un trou dans le bateau
2 *(Golf)* *[+ putt]* enquiller ◆ **to ~ a ball in three** faire un *or* le trou en trois ◆ **he ~d the 5th in three** il a fait le (trou numéro) cinq en trois coups, il a fait trois sur le cinq
VI 1 *[socks, pullover]* se trouer
2 *(Golf:* also **hole out)** terminer le trou ◆ **to ~ in one** faire le *or* un trou en un ; see also **comp** ◆ **he ~d from nine feet at the 18th** il a fait le 18ᵉ trou à trois mètres
3 *(Billiards)* bloquer
COMP hole-and-corner ADJ *(pej)* *(= secret)* clandestin, secret (-ète *f*) ; *(= furtive)* furtif ; *(= underhand)* fait en douce*
hole in one N *(Golf)* trou *m* en un
hole in the heart N maladie *f* bleue ◆ **she was born with a ~ in the heart** elle est née avec une malformation cardiaque *or* du cœur
hole-in-the-heart ADJ ◆ **~-in-the-heart baby** enfant *mf* bleu(e) ◆ **~-in-the-heart operation** opération *f* pour communication interventriculaire
hole-in-the-wall* N *(Brit = cash dispenser)* distributeur *m* de billets

► **hole up VI** *[animal, criminal]* se terrer ◆ **she's been ~d up in her study all day** elle a passé toute la journée cloîtrée dans son bureau

holey /ˈhəʊlɪ/ **ADJ** plein de trous, (tout) troué

holiday /ˈhɒlɪdeɪ/ **N** *(esp Brit)* *(= vacation)* vacances *fpl* ; *(= day off)* (jour *m* de) congé *m* ; *(= public holiday)* jour *m* férié ◆ **to take a ~** prendre des vacances *or* un congé ◆ **to take a month's ~** prendre un mois de vacances ◆ **~s with pay, paid ~s** congés *mpl* payés ◆ **tomorrow is a ~** demain est un jour férié ◆ **the school ~(s)** les vacances *fpl* scolaires ◆ **the Christmas ~(s)** les vacances *fpl* de Noël ◆ **we were in ~ mood** on se sentait en vacances ; → **bank²**
◆ **on holiday** en vacances, en congé ◆ **to go on ~** partir en vacances
VI *(esp Brit)* passer les vacances ◆ **they were ~ing at home** ils prenaient leurs vacances à la maison
COMP holiday camp N *(Brit)* *(gen)* camp *m* de vacances ; *(for children only)* colonie *f* *or* camp *m* de vacances
holiday clothes NPL tenue *f* de vacances
holiday feeling N atmosphère *f* *or* ambiance *f* de vacances
holiday home N *(esp Brit)* maison *f* *or* résidence *f* secondaire
holiday job N *(Brit)* emploi *m* temporaire *(pendant les vacances)*
holiday-maker N *(Brit)* vacancier *m*, -ière *f* ; *(in summer)* estivant(e) *m(f)*
holiday pay N *(esp Brit)* congés *mpl* payés ◆ **they don't get ~ pay** ils n'ont pas droit aux congés payés
holiday resort N *(esp Brit)* villégiature *f*, lieu *m* de vacances
holiday season N période *f* des vacances
holiday spirit N air *m* *or* ambiance *f* de vacances ◆ **he's already lost his ~ spirit** il ne se sent déjà plus en vacances
holiday traffic N départs *mpl* en (*or* retours *mpl* de) vacances

holier-than-thou* /ˈhəʊlɪəðənˈðaʊ/ **ADJ** *[person]* imbu de soi-même, supérieur ; *(in religious matters)* pharisien ; *[attitude]* suffisant

holiness /ˈhəʊlɪnɪs/ **N** sainteté *f* ◆ **His Holiness** Sa Sainteté

holism /ˈhəʊlɪzəm/ **N** holisme *m*

holistic /həʊˈlɪstɪk/ **ADJ** holistique

Holland /ˈhɒlənd/ **N** 1 Hollande *f*, Pays-Bas *mpl* ◆ **in ~** en Hollande, aux Pays-Bas 2 **holland** *(= fabric)* toile *f* de Hollande

holler* /ˈhɒləʳ/ *(esp US)* **N** braillement *m* **VTI** (also **holler out**) brailler, beugler* ◆ **to ~ at sb** *(= tell off)* crier après qn

hollow /ˈhɒləʊ/ **ADJ** 1 *(= empty inside)* *[tree, tooth, log, stem]* creux ◆ **to sound ~** *[object]* sonner creux ◆ **to have a ~ feeling in one's stomach** *(from hunger)* avoir le ventre creux ; *(from emotion)* avoir l'estomac noué
2 *(= sunken)* *[cheeks]* creux ; *[eyes]* creux, cave
3 *(= hollow-sounding)* *[laugh]* creux ; *[voice]* caverneux ; *[sound]* *(from box)* creux ; *(from hall, cave)* caverneux ; → **beat**
4 *(= false, empty)* *[person, victory]* faux (fausse *f*) ; *[promise, threat, gesture]* vain ◆ **~ words** des paroles *fpl* creuses ◆ **to have a ~ ring, to ring ~** sonner faux ◆ **a ~ sham** une dérisoire comédie
N *(in ground, gen)* creux *m* ; *(= valley)* cuvette *f* ; *[of back, hand, tree]* creux *m* ; *[of tooth]* cavité *f* ◆ **to have** *or* **hold sb in the ~ of one's hand** mener qn par le bout du nez
VT (also **hollow out**) creuser ; *(= scoop out)* *[+ apple etc]* évider
COMP hollow-cheeked ADJ aux joues creuses *or* creusées
hollow-eyed ADJ aux yeux caves *or* creux

hollowly /ˈhɒləʊlɪ/ **ADV** *[echo]* avec un bruit creux ; *[say]* platement ◆ **to ring ~** sonner creux ◆ **to laugh ~** rire jaune

hollowness /ˈhɒləʊnɪs/ **N** *[of promise, guarantee]* manque *m* de sincérité, vacuité *f*

holly /ˈhɒlɪ/ **N** houx *m* **COMP holly berry N** baie *f* de houx

hollyhock /ˈhɒlɪˌhɒk/ **N** rose *f* trémière

Hollywood /ˈhɒlɪˌwʊd/ **N** Hollywood

holmium /ˈhɒlmɪəm/ **N** holmium *m*

holm oak /ˈhəʊmˈəʊk/ **N** chêne *m* vert, yeuse *f*

holocaust /ˈhɒləkɔːst/ **N** holocauste *m* ◆ **the Holocaust** *(Hist)* l'Holocauste *m*

hologram /ˈhɒləˌgræm/ **N** hologramme *m*

holograph /ˈhɒləgrɑːf/ **N** document *m* (h)olographe **ADJ** (h)olographe

holographic /ˌhɒləˈgræfɪk/ **ADJ** holographique

holography /hɒˈlɒgrəfɪ/ **N** holographie *f*

holophrastic /ˌhɒləˈfræstɪk/ **ADJ** holophrastique

hols* /hɒlz/ **N** *(Brit)* (abbrev of **holidays**) vacances *fpl*

holster /ˈhəʊlstəʳ/ **N** étui *m* de revolver ; *(on saddle)* fonte *f*

holy /ˈhəʊlɪ/ **ADJ** *[object, place, day, book]* saint ◆ **~ war** guerre *f* sainte ◆ **on ~ ground** dans un lieu saint ◆ **the ~ month of Ramadan** le mois sacré du ramadan ◆ **that child is a ~ terror*** cet enfant est un vrai démon ◆ **~ cow** *or* **smoke** *or* **Moses** *or* **Moley** *or* **mackerel!**‡ sacrebleu !* ◆ **~ shit!***‡ nom de Dieu !‡ ◆ **Holy (Mary) Mother of God!**‡ nom de Dieu !‡ ; → **innocent**
N ◆ **the ~ of holies** le saint des saints

COMP **the Holy Alliance** N la Sainte-Alliance
the Holy Bible N la sainte bible
the Holy City N la Ville sainte
Holy Communion N sainte communion *f*
Holy Eucharist N saint sacrement *m*
the Holy Family N la Sainte famille
the Holy Father N le Saint-Père
the Holy Ghost N ⇒ **Holy Spirit**
the Holy Grail N le Saint-Graal ; *(fig)* le graal
Holy Joe * N *(= clergyman)* curé *m* ; *(= sanctimonious person)* bondieusard(e) *m(f)* *(pej)*
the Holy Land N la Terre sainte ◆ **in the Holy Land** en Terre sainte
holy man N (pl **holy men**) saint homme *m*
holy matrimony N les liens *mpl* sacrés du mariage ◆ **they were joined in ~ matrimony** ils ont été unis par les liens sacrés du mariage
the Holy Office N le Saint-Office
holy oil N huile *f* bénite
holy orders NPL ordres *mpl* ◆ **in ~ orders** dans les ordres ◆ **to take ~ orders** entrer dans les ordres
holy picture N image *f* pieuse
the Holy Roman Empire N le Saint Empire romain germanique
the Holy Rood N la sainte Croix
Holy Saturday N samedi *m* saint
Holy Scripture N Écriture *f* sainte
the Holy See N le Saint-Siège
the Holy Sepulchre N le Saint-Sépulcre
the Holy Spirit N le Saint-Esprit, l'Esprit *m* saint
the Holy Trinity N la sainte Trinité
holy water N eau *f* bénite
Holy Week N semaine sainte *f*
Holy Writ † N *(= scripture)* Écriture *f* sainte ◆ **he treats everything she says as if it were Holy Writ** pour lui, tout ce qu'elle dit est parole d'évangile
Holy Year N année *f* sainte

holystone /ˈhəʊlɪstəʊn/ *(Naut)* N brique *f* à pont VT briquer

homage /ˈhɒmɪdʒ/ N *(NonC)* hommage *m* ◆ **to pay ~ to sb/sth** rendre hommage à qn/qch ◆ **in ~ to sb/sth** en hommage à qn/qch

homburg /ˈhɒmbɜːg/ N chapeau *m* mou, feutre *m* (souple)

home /həʊm/ N 1 maison *f*, chez-soi *m* ◆ **to have a ~ of one's own** avoir sa propre maison (*or* son propre appartement) ◆ **he was glad to see his ~ again** il était content de rentrer chez lui ◆ **it is quite near my ~** c'est tout près de chez moi ◆ **his ~ is in Paris** il habite Paris ◆ **I live in Paris but my ~ is in London** je suis de Londres, mais j'habite à Paris en ce moment ◆ **~ for me is Edinburgh** c'est à Édimbourg que je me sens chez moi ◆ **for some years he made his ~ in France** pendant quelques années il a habité en France ◆ **refugees who made their ~ in Britain** les réfugiés qui se sont installés en Grande-Bretagne ◆ **~ for them is England now, they now call England ~** maintenant l'Angleterre c'est leur pays ◆ **Warwick is ~ to some 550 international students** il y a quelque 550 étudiants étrangers à Warwick ◆ **the building is ~ to over 1,000 students** plus de 1 000 étudiants logent dans ce bâtiment ◆ **he is far from ~** il est loin de chez lui ◆ **he has been away from ~ for some months** il est loin de chez lui depuis quelques mois ◆ **there's no place like ~** *(Prov)* ◆ **~ is where the heart is** *(Prov)* on n'est vraiment bien que chez soi ◆ **he has no ~** il n'a pas de foyer ◆ **to give sb/an animal a ~** recueillir qn/un animal chez soi *or* sous son toit ◆ **he made a ~ for his sisters** il a accueilli ses sœurs sous son toit ◆ **it's a ~ from ~** *(Brit) or* **away from ~** *(US)* c'est mon second chez-moi *(or son second chez-soi etc)* ◆ **she has a lovely ~** c'est joli chez elle ◆ **he comes from a broken ~** il vient d'un foyer désuni ◆ **"good home wanted for kitten"** "cherche foyer accueillant pour chaton" ◆ **accidents in the ~** accidents *mpl* domestiques ; → **leave, set up, spiritual**

◆ **at home** chez soi, à la maison ◆ **I'll be at ~ this afternoon** je serai chez moi cet après-midi ◆ **is Paul at ~?** est-ce que Paul est à la maison ? ◆ **Celtic are at ~ to Rangers, Celtic are playing Rangers at ~** *(Ftbl)* le Celtic joue à domicile contre les Rangers, le Celtic reçoit les Rangers ◆ **Mrs Gough is not at ~** *(frm = not receiving visitors)* Mme Gough ne reçoit pas ◆ **Mrs Gough is not at ~ to anyone** *(frm)* Mme Gough ne reçoit personne ◆ **to be** *or* **feel at ~ with sb** se sentir à l'aise avec qn ◆ **he doesn't feel at ~ in English** il n'est pas à l'aise en anglais ◆ **to make o.s. at ~** se mettre à l'aise, faire comme chez soi ◆ **make yourself at ~!** *(fig, also iro)* faites comme chez vous ! ◆ **who's he when he's at ~?** * qui c'est celui-là ?* ◆ **what's that when it's at ~?** * qu'est-ce que c'est que ça ?

2 *(= country of origin)* pays *m* natal, patrie *f* ◆ **at ~ and abroad** ici et *or* chez nous et à l'étranger ◆ **the Russians, at ~ and abroad** les Russes, chez eux et à l'étranger ◆ **to bring sth closer** *or* **nearer (to) ~ for sb** permettre à qn de mieux se rendre compte de qch ◆ **let's concentrate on problems closer** *or* **nearer to ~** occupons-nous de problèmes qui nous concernent plus directement ◆ **her jokes about bald people were a bit too close to ~ for him** ses plaisanteries sur les chauves le touchaient au vif ◆ **Scotland is the ~ of the haggis** l'Écosse est le pays du haggis ◆ **Bordeaux is the ~ of some of the world's finest wines** Bordeaux produit certains des meilleurs vins du monde

3 *(= institution)* maison *f*, institution *f* ; *(shorter-term)* foyer *m* ◆ **children's ~** maison *f* pour enfants ; → **maternity, mental, nursing**

4 *(= habitat of plant/animal)* habitat *m*

5 *(Racing)* arrivée *f*

6 *(Baseball)* base *f* de départ

ADV 1 chez soi, à la maison ◆ **to go ~** rentrer (chez soi *or* à la maison) ◆ **to get ~** rentrer ◆ **I got ~ at 5 o'clock** je suis rentré (chez moi *or* à la maison) à 5 heures ◆ **I'll be ~ at 5 o'clock** je serai à la maison à 5 heures, je rentrerai à 5 heures ◆ **I met him on the journey ~** je l'ai rencontré sur le chemin du retour ◆ **I must write ~** il faut que j'écrive à ma famille ◆ **it's nothing to write ~ about** * ça ne casse pas des briques *, ça ne casse rien * ◆ **to be ~ and dry** *or (US)* **~ free** *(fig)* être arrivé au bout de ses peines

2 *(from abroad)* dans son pays, chez soi ◆ **he came ~ from abroad** il est rentré de l'étranger ◆ **to go** *or* **return ~** rentrer dans son pays

3 *(= right in etc)* à fond ◆ **to drive a nail ~** enfoncer un clou à fond ◆ **to bring sth ~ to sb** faire comprendre *or* faire voir qch à qn ◆ **the horror of the situation was brought ~ to him when ...** l'horreur de la situation lui est apparue pleinement quand ... ◆ **to drive** *or* **hammer sth ~** *(fig)* bien faire comprendre qch ◆ **he nodded the ball ~** *(Ftbl)* il a marqué un but de la tête ◆ **he drove the ball ~ from 15 metres** *(Ftbl)* il a marqué un but grâce à un tir de 15 mètres ◆ **to push ~ an attack** pousser à fond une attaque ; → **hit**

VI revenir *or* rentrer chez soi ; *[pigeons]* revenir au colombier

COMP *[atmosphere]* de famille, familial ; *[troubles]* de famille, domestique ; *(Econ, Pol)* du pays, national ; *[policy, market]* intérieur (-eure *f*)
home address N *(on forms etc)* domicile *m* (permanent) ; *(as opposed to business address)* adresse *f* personnelle
home assembly N ◆ **for ~ assembly** en kit
home-baked ADJ (fait) maison *inv* ◆ **~-baked bread** pain *m* fait maison
home baking N *(= cakes etc)* pâtisseries *fpl* maison
home banking N banque *f* à domicile
home base N *(Baseball)* base *f* de départ
home birth N accouchement *m* à domicile
home brew N *(= beer)* bière *f* faite à la maison ; *(= wine)* vin *m* fait à la maison
home-buying N achats *mpl* de logements ; *(first-time)* accession *f* à la propriété
home comforts NPL confort *m* du foyer
home computer N ordinateur *m* personnel
home cooking N cuisine *f* familiale
the Home Counties NPL *(Brit) les comtés qui entourent Londres*
home country N pays *m* natal *or* d'origine
home delivery N *(Comm) [of meals, shopping]* livraison *f* à domicile ; *(Med) [of baby]* accouchement *m* à domicile
home economics N *(NonC)* économie *f* domestique
home entertainment system N équipement *m* hi-fi, TV et vidéo
home field N *(US)* ⇒ **home ground**
home front N ◆ **on the ~ front** *(Pol, Mil)* à l'intérieur ; *(* hum = at home)* à la maison
home ground N *(Sport)* ◆ **to play at one's ~ ground** jouer sur son terrain *or* à domicile ◆ **to be on ~ ground** *(fig)* être sur son terrain
home-grown ADJ *(= not foreign)* du pays ; *(= from own garden)* du jardin
Home Guard N *(Brit) volontaires pour la défense du territoire (1940-45)*
home heating oil N fuel *m* domestique
home help N *(Brit Social Work) (= person)* aide *f* ménagère ◆ **do you have any ~ help?** *(= assistance)* est-ce que vous avez quelqu'un pour vous aider à la maison ?
home improvement grant N prime *f* à l'amélioration de l'habitat
home improvement loan N prêt *m* pour l'amélioration de l'habitat
home improvements NPL réfection *f* de logements ; *(= DIY)* bricolage *m*
home leave N *(gen)* congé *m* au foyer ; *(Mil)* permission *f*
home life N vie *f* de famille
home loan N prêt *m* immobilier
home-lover N casanier *m*, -ière *f* ; *(woman)* femme *f* d'intérieur
home-loving ADJ casanier
home-made ADJ (fait) maison *inv*
home-maker N femme *f* d'intérieur
home match N *(Sport)* match *m* à domicile
home movie N vidéo *f* amateur
home nations NPL *(Brit)* ◆ **the ~ nations** les quatre nations britanniques
home news N *(gen)* nouvelles *fpl* de chez soi ; *(Pol)* nouvelles *fpl* nationales
the Home Office N *(Brit)* ≃ le ministère de l'Intérieur
home owner N propriétaire *mf*
home ownership N ◆ **~ ownership is on the increase** de plus en plus de gens sont propriétaires de leur logement
home page N *(Comput)* page *f* d'accueil
home port N *(Naut)* port *m* d'attache
home posting N *(Brit: of diplomat, soldier)* affectation *f* au pays
home rule N autonomie *f*
home run N *[of ship, truck]* voyage *m* de retour ; *(Baseball)* coup *m* de circuit ◆ **to hit a ~ run** *(Baseball)* faire *or* réussir un coup de circuit ; *(US fig)* réussir un beau coup
home sales NPL ventes *fpl* intérieures *or* domestiques
Home Secretary N *(Brit)* ≃ ministre *m* de l'Intérieur
home shopping N *(by post, telephone) achat par correspondance ou par téléphone* ; *(by computer, television)* téléachat *m*
home side N *(Sport)* ⇒ **home team**
home State N *(US)* État *m* d'origine
home straight, home stretch N ◆ **to be in the ~ straight** *(Sport)* être dans la (dernière) ligne droite ; *(fig)* toucher au but
home team N *(Ftbl etc)* équipe *f* qui reçoit
home territory N *(fig)* ◆ **to be on one's ~ territory** être sur son terrain

home time N ◆ **it's ~ time** c'est l'heure de rentrer à la maison
home town N ◆ **my ~ town** *(= place of birth)* ma ville natale ; *(= where I grew up)* la ville où j'ai grandi
home truth N ◆ **I'll tell him a few ~ truths** je vais lui dire ses quatre vérités
home video N vidéo *f* amateur
home visit N *(by doctor etc)* visite *f* à domicile
home waters NPL *(Naut)* *(= territorial waters)* eaux *fpl* territoriales ; *(near home port)* eaux *fpl* voisines du port d'attache
▸ **home in on, home on to** VT FUS *[missile]* *(= move towards)* se diriger vers *or* sur ; *(= reach)* atteindre

homebody * /ˈhəʊmbɒdɪ/ N *(esp US)* casanier *m*, -ière *f*, pantouflard(e) * *m(f)* *(pej)*

homebound /ˈhəʊmˈbaʊnd/ ADJ *(= on the way home)* *[traveller]* qui rentre chez soi

homeboy * /ˈhəʊmbɔɪ/ N *(US)* pote * *m*

homecoming /ˈhəʊmkʌmɪŋ/ N 1 *(gen)* retour *m* à la maison ; *(to one's country)* retour *m* au pays ; *(of soldier etc)* retour *m* au foyer 2 *(US Scol, Univ)* fête *f* annuelle *(marquant le début de l'année universitaire)*

homegirl * /ˈhəʊmɡɜːl/ N *(US)* copine * *f*

homeland /ˈhəʊmlænd/ N *(gen)* patrie *f* ; *(in South Africa)* homeland *m*

homeless /ˈhəʊmlɪs/ ADJ sans foyer, sans abri NPL **the homeless** les SDF *mpl* ; → **single**

homelessness /ˈhəʊmlɪsnɪs/ N ◆ **~ is on the increase** il y a de plus en plus de SDF ◆ **what's the government doing about ~?** que fait le gouvernement pour les SDF ?

homelike /ˈhəʊmlaɪk/ ADJ accueillant, confortable

homely /ˈhəʊmlɪ/ ADJ 1 *(esp Brit)* *[person]* aux goûts simples ; *[atmosphere, room, place]* accueillant ; *[dish, food]* simple, familial 2 *(US = plain)* *[person]* sans charme ; *[appearance]* peu attrayant

homeopath /ˈhəʊmɪəʊpæθ/ N homéopathe *mf*

homeopathic /ˌhəʊmɪəʊˈpæθɪk/ ADJ *[medicine, methods]* homéopathique ; *[doctor]* homéopathe

homeopathy /ˌhəʊmɪˈɒpəθɪ/ N homéopathie *f*

Homer /ˈhəʊməʳ/ N Homère *m*

homer /ˈhəʊməʳ/ N 1 *(US Baseball *)* coup *m* de circuit 2 *(Brit = homing pigeon)* pigeon *m* voyageur

Homeric /həʊˈmerɪk/ ADJ homérique

homeroom /ˈhəʊmrʊm/ N *(US Scol)* salle *f* de classe *(affectée à une classe particulière)* COMP **homeroom teacher** N ≈ professeur *m* principal

homesick /ˈhəʊmsɪk/ ADJ nostalgique ◆ **to be ~** *(for place)* avoir le mal du pays ; *(for one's family)* s'ennuyer de sa famille ◆ **to be ~ for sth** avoir la nostalgie de qch

homesickness /ˈhəʊmsɪknɪs/ N mal *m* du pays

homespun /ˈhəʊmspʌn/ ADJ *[cloth]* filé à domicile ; *(fig)* simple, sans recherche N homespun *m*

homestead /ˈhəʊmsted/ *(esp US)* N *(= house etc)* propriété *f* ; *(= farm)* ferme *f* COMP **the Homestead Act** N *(US) la loi agraire de 1862*

homesteader /ˈhəʊmstedəʳ/ N *(US)* colon *m* *(pionnier)*

homeward /ˈhəʊmwəd/ ADJ de retour ◆ **~ journey** (voyage *m* de) retour *m* ADV *(Brit)* (also **homewards**) ◆ **to head ~** partir en direction de chez soi ◆ **to hurry ~** se dépêcher de rentrer chez soi COMP **homeward bound** ADV ◆ **to be ~ bound** être sur le chemin de retour ◆ **~-bound commuters** banlieusards *mpl* rentrant chez eux

homework /ˈhəʊmwɜːk/ N *(Scol)* devoirs *mpl* COMP **homework diary** N cahier *m* de textes
homework exercise N devoir *m*
homework notebook N → **homework diary**

homeworker /ˈhəʊmwɜːkəʳ/ N travailleur *m*, -euse *f* à domicile

homeworking /ˈhəʊmwɜːkɪŋ/ N travail *m* à domicile

homey /ˈhəʊmɪ/ ADJ *(US)* ⇒ **homely 2**

homicidal /ˌhɒmɪˈsaɪdl/ ADJ *[tendencies]* homicide ; *[rage]* meurtrier ◆ **~ maniac** fou *m* dangereux, folle *f* dangereuse

homicide /ˈhɒmɪsaɪd/ N *(= act)* homicide *m* ; *(= person)* homicide *mf*

homie ‡ /ˈhəʊmɪ/ N *(US)* ⇒ **homeboy, homegirl**

homily /ˈhɒmɪlɪ/ N *(Rel)* homélie *f* ; *(fig)* sermon *m*, homélie *f*

homing /ˈhəʊmɪŋ/ ADJ *[missile]* à tête chercheuse COMP **homing device** N tête *f* chercheuse
homing instinct N *[of animal]* instinct *m* de retour (à l'habitat d'origine)
homing pigeon N pigeon *m* voyageur

hominy /ˈhɒmɪnɪ/ N *(US)* maïs *m* concassé COMP **hominy grits** NPL *(US)* bouillie *f* de maïs concassé

homo †‡ /ˈhəʊməʊ/ ADJ, N (abbrev of **homosexual**) *(pej)* pédé‡ *m* *(pej)*, homo * *mf*

homoeopath /ˈhəʊmɪəʊpæθ/ N ⇒ **homeopath**

homoeopathic /ˌhəʊmɪəʊˈpæθɪk/ ADJ ⇒ **homeopathic**

homoeopathy /ˌhəʊmɪˈɒpəθɪ/ N ⇒ **homeopathy**

homoeostasis /ˌhəʊmɪəʊˈsteɪsɪs/ N ⇒ **homeostasis**

homoerotic /ˌhəʊməʊɪˈrɒtɪk/ ADJ homoérotique

homoeroticism /ˌhəʊməʊɪˈrɒtɪsɪzm/ N homoérotisme *m*

homogeneity /ˌhəʊməʊdʒɪˈniːɪtɪ/ N homogénéité *f*

homogeneous /ˌhəʊməˈdʒiːnɪəs/ ADJ homogène

homogenize /həˈmɒdʒənaɪz/ VT homogénéiser

homogenous /həˈmɒdʒɪnəs/ ADJ ⇒ **homogeneous**

homograph /ˈhɒməʊɡrɑːf/ N homographe *m*

homographic /ˌhɒməˈɡræfɪk/ ADJ homographique

homography /hɒˈmɒɡrəfɪ/ N homographie *f*

homonym /ˈhɒmənɪm/ N homonyme *m*

homonymic /ˌhɒməˈnɪmɪk/ ADJ homonymique

homonymy /hɒˈmɒnɪmɪ/ N homonymie *f*

homophobe /ˌhəʊməʊˈfəʊb/ N homophobe *mf*

homophobia /ˌhɒməʊˈfəʊbɪə/ N homophobie *f*

homophobic /ˌhɒməʊˈfəʊbɪk/ ADJ homophobe

homophone /ˈhɒməfəʊn/ N homophone *m*

homophonic /ˌhɒməˈfɒnɪk/ ADJ homophone

homophony /hɒˈmɒfənɪ/ N homophonie *f*

homo sapiens /ˈhəʊməʊˈsæpɪˌenz/ N homo sapiens *m*

homosexual /ˌhɒməʊˈseksjʊəl/ ADJ, N homosexuel(le) *m(f)*

homosexuality /ˌhɒməʊseksjʊˈælɪtɪ/ N homosexualité *f*

homunculus /hɒˈmʌŋkjʊləs/ N (pl **homunculi** /hɒˈmʌŋkjʊlaɪ/) homoncule *m* *or* homuncule *m*

hon * /hʌn/ N *(US)* (abbrev of **honey**) ◆ **hi, ~!** bonjour, chéri(e) !

Hon. *(in titles)* abbrev of **Honorary** *or* **Honourable**

honcho * /ˈhɒntʃəʊ/ N *(US)* patron *m*, grand chef *m*

Honduran /hɒnˈdjʊərən/ ADJ hondurien N Hondurien(ne) *m(f)*

Honduras /hɒnˈdjʊərəs/ N Honduras *m* ◆ **in ~** au Honduras

hone /həʊn/ N pierre *f* à aiguiser VT 1 *[+ craft, abilities, wit, skill]* affiner ◆ **~d to perfection**, **finely ~d** parfaitement affiné ◆ **a finely ~d body** un corps d'athlète 2 *[+ blade]* affûter, affiler ◆ **finely ~d** parfaitement affûté *or* affilé

honest /ˈɒnɪst/ ADJ *[person, action]* honnête *(with sb* avec qn ; *about sth* en ce qui concerne qch) ; *[face]* franc (franche *f*) ; *[answer]* franc (franche *f*), sincère ; *[money, profit]* honnêtement acquis *or* gagné ; *(Jur)* *[goods]* de qualité loyale et marchande ◆ **he's (as) ~ as the day is long** il est on ne peut plus honnête, il est foncièrement honnête ◆ **now, be ~!** *(= say what you think)* allons, dis ce que tu penses ! ; *(= tell the truth, be objective)* allons, sois honnête ! ◆ **to be ~ (with you) ...** à vrai dire ... ◆ **~ (injun)!** * parole d'honneur ! ◆ **~ to goodness** *or* **God!** * *(expressing sincerity)* parole d'honneur ! ; *(expressing impatience)* vingt dieux ! * ◆ **by ~ means** par des moyens honnêtes ◆ **an ~ mistake** une erreur commise en toute bonne foi ◆ **I'd like your ~ opinion of it** j'aimerais que vous me donniez honnêtement votre avis (là-dessus) ◆ **an ~ day's work** une honnête journée de travail ◆ **to earn an ~ penny** *or* **crust** *(hum)* gagner honnêtement sa vie *or* son pain ◆ **I'm trying to turn an ~ penny** j'essaie de me faire de l'argent honnêtement ◆ **the ~ truth** la pure vérité ◆ **(the) God's ~ truth** * la vérité pure ◆ **he made an ~ woman of her** († *or hum*) il a fini par l'épouser ◆ **good, ~ home cooking** de la bonne cuisine bourgeoise
COMP **honest broker** N *(Brit esp Pol)* médiateur *m*, -trice *f*
honest-to-God *, **honest-to-goodness** * ADJ très simple, sans chichi *

honestly /ˈɒnɪstlɪ/ ADV *[act, behave, say, answer]* honnêtement ; *[think, expect]* vraiment ◆ **~?** c'est vrai ? ◆ **I can ~ say that ...** franchement *or* en toute honnêteté, je peux dire que ... ◆ **I ~ believe that ...** je suis convaincu que ... ◆ **no, ~, I'm fine** non, vraiment, je me sens bien ◆ **~, I don't care** honnêtement *or* franchement, ça m'est égal ◆ **I didn't do it, ~** ce n'est pas moi, je le jure *or* parole d'honneur ◆ **quite ~ ...** en toute honnêteté ... ◆ **~, that woman!** * celle-là, alors ! * ◆ **~, this is getting ridiculous!** * enfin, ça devient ridicule !

honesty /ˈɒnɪstɪ/ N 1 *(= integrity, truthfulness)* *[of person]* honnêteté *f* ; *[of words, writing]* franchise *f*, sincérité *f* ; *(= sincerity)* sincérité *f* ◆ **in all ~** en toute honnêteté ◆ **~ is the best policy** *(Prov)* l'honnêteté paie 2 *(Bot)* lunaire *f*, monnaie-du-pape *f* COMP **honesty box** N *boîte où l'on est invité à déposer le montant d'un journal en distribution hors kiosque, d'un trajet impayé, etc*

honey /ˈhʌnɪ/ N 1 miel *m* ◆ **clear/thick ~** miel *m* liquide/solide 2 *(= person)* ◆ **yes, ~** * oui, chéri(e) ◆ **she's a ~** * elle est adorable, c'est un chou *

honeybee /ˈhʌnɪbiː/ N abeille *f*

honeybunch * /ˈhʌnɪbʌntʃ/, **honeybun** * /ˈhʌnɪbʌn/ N *(esp US)* ◆ **hi, ~!** salut, chéri(e) !

honeycomb /ˈhʌnɪkəʊm/ N 1 *(of bees)* rayon *m* de miel 2 *(= fabric)* nid *m* d'abeille VT *(fig)* cribler *(with* de) ◆ **the palace was ~ed with corridors** le palais était un dédale de couloirs COMP *[textile, pattern]* en nid d'abeille

honeydew /ˈhʌnɪdjuː/ N *[of insects]* miellat *m* ; *[of plants]* miellée *f* COMP **honeydew melon** N melon *m* d'hiver *or* d'Espagne

honeyed /ˈhʌnɪd/ ADJ [1] *[scent, taste]* de miel [2] *[words, voice]* mielleux, doucereux

honeymoon /ˈhʌnɪˌmuːn/ [N] *(= trip)* voyage *m* de noces ; *(= period)* lune *f* de miel ◆ **their ~ was spent in Paris** ils sont allés à Paris en voyage de noces ◆ **they spent their ~ at home** ils ont passé leur lune de miel à la maison ◆ **we were on our ~** nous étions en voyage de noces ◆ **while on ~ in Majorca they ...** pendant leur voyage de noces à Majorque, ils ... [VI] passer son voyage de noces ◆ **while ~ing in Majorca we ...** pendant notre voyage de noces à Majorque, nous ...
COMP **honeymoon couple** N jeunes mariés *mpl* (en voyage de noces)
honeymoon period N *(fig)* état *m* de grâce
honeymon suite N suite *f* nuptiale

honeymooner /ˈhʌnɪˌmuːnəʳ/ N jeune marié(e) *m(f)* (en voyage de noces)

honeypot /ˈhʌnɪpɒt/ N *(lit)* pot *m* à miel ◆ **a tourist ~, a ~ for tourists** un lieu qui attire les touristes ; → **bee**

honeysuckle /ˈhʌnɪsʌkəl/ N chèvrefeuille *m*

honeytrap /ˈhʌnɪtræp/ N piège *m* *(dans lequel un criminel est attiré par une femme)*

Hong Kong /ˈhɒŋˈkɒŋ/ N Hong-Kong ◆ **in ~** à Hong-Kong

honk /hɒŋk/ [VI] [1] *[car]* klaxonner ; *[goose]* cacarder [2] *(⁑ = stink)* chlinguer⁑, cocotter * ◆ **it's ~ing in here!** ça chlingue⁑ *or* cocotte * ici ! [VT] ◆ **to ~ the** *or* **one's horn** klaxonner, corner [N] *[of car]* coup *m* de klaxon ® ; *[of goose]* cri *m* ◆ **~, ~!** *[of car]* tut-tut ! ; *[of goose]* coin-coin !

honkie⁑, **honky**⁑ /ˈhɒŋkɪ/ [N] *(US pej)* sale Blanc *m*, sale Blanche *f* COMP **honky-tonk** * N [1] *(US = club)* bastringue * *m* [2] *(Mus)* musique *f* de bastringue *

Honolulu /ˌhɒnəˈluːluː/ N Honolulu

honor /ˈɒnəʳ/ N (US) ⇒ **honour**

honorable /ˈɒnərəbl/ ADJ (US) ⇒ **honourable**

honorably /ˈɒnərəblɪ/ ADV (US) ⇒ **honourably**

honorarium /ˌɒnəˈrɛərɪəm/ N (pl **honorariums** *or* **honoraria** /ˌɒnəˈrɛərɪə/) honoraires *mpl no sg*

honorary /ˈɒnərərɪ/ [ADJ] *[official, member]* honoraire ; *[duties, titles]* honorifique ; *[degree]* accordé à titre honorifique ◆ **to be awarded an ~ doctorate** *(Univ)* être nommé docteur honoris causa COMP **Honorary Secretary** N secrétaire *mf* honoraire

honorific /ˌɒnəˈrɪfɪk/ [ADJ] honorifique [N] titre *m* honorifique

honour, honor (US) /ˈɒnəʳ/ [N] [1] honneur *m* ◆ **it is a great ~ for me** c'est un grand honneur pour moi ◆ **it is an ~ for me to be here** c'est un honneur pour moi que d'être ici ◆ **he is the soul of ~** c'est la probité même ◆ **he is an ~ to his father/his regiment** il fait honneur à son père/son régiment ◆ **to what do we owe this ~?** qu'est-ce qui nous vaut cet honneur ? ◆ **I have the ~ to inform you** *or* **of informing you that ...** *(frm)* j'ai l'honneur de vous informer que ... ◆ **may I have the ~ of accompanying you?** *(frm)* puis-je avoir l'honneur de vous accompagner ? ◆ **to lose one's ~** † *(woman)* être déshonoré † ◆ **(there is) ~ among thieves** *(Prov)* les loups ne se mangent pas entre eux ; → **debt, word**
◆ **do + honour(s)** ◆ **they did me the ~ of inviting me** *(frm)* ils m'ont fait l'honneur de m'inviter ◆ **perhaps you will do me the ~ of dancing with me?** *(frm)* me ferez-vous l'honneur de m'accorder une danse ? ◆ **he does no ~ to the profession** il ne fait pas honneur à sa profession ◆ **to do the ~s** *(= introductions)* faire les présentations *(entre invités)* ; *(of one's house)* faire les honneurs de sa maison
◆ **in honour of ...** en l'honneur de ... ◆ **in his ~** en son honneur
◆ **on + honour** ◆ **to be on one's ~ to do sth** s'être engagé à faire qch ◆ **she put me on my ~ to own up** je lui ai donné ma parole d'honneur que j'avouerais ◆ **on** *or* **upon my ~!** †* parole d'honneur !
[2] *(Mil etc)* **the last ~s** les derniers honneurs *mpl*, le dernier hommage ◆ **with full military ~s** avec les honneurs militaires ; → **guard**
[3] *(frm = title)* **Your/His Honour** Votre/Son Honneur
[4] *(Brit Univ)* **to take ~s in English** ≈ faire une licence d'anglais ◆ **he got first-/second-class ~s in English** ≈ il a eu sa licence d'anglais avec mention très bien/mention bien
[5] *(Bridge)* honneur *m*
[6] *(Brit = award)* distinction *f* honorifique
[VT] [1] *[+ person]* honorer, faire honneur à ◆ **to feel ~ed (to do sth)** être honoré (de faire qch) ◆ **I'm ~ed** je suis très honoré, quel honneur ! ◆ **I'd be ~ed** je serais très honoré ◆ **she ~ed them with her presence** *(gen, iro)* elle les honora de sa présence ◆ **they ~ed us by coming to the ceremony** ils nous firent l'honneur de venir à la cérémonie ◆ **since you have ~ed me with your confidence** puisque vous m'avez fait l'honneur de m'accorder votre confiance ◆ **to ~ one's partner** *(in dancing)* saluer son cavalier *(or* sa cavalière) ◆ **~ed guest** invité(e) *m(f)* d'honneur
[2] *[+ cheque, contract]* honorer ; *[+ ceasefire, agreement]* respecter
COMP **honour-bound** ADJ ◆ **to be ~-bound to do sth** être tenu par l'honneur de faire qch
honors course N (US) *cours réservé aux meilleurs étudiants*
honours course N *(Brit Univ)* ≈ licence *f*
honors degree N (US) licence *f* avec mention
honours degree N *(Brit Univ)* ≈ licence *f*
honor guard N (US) ⇒ **guard of honour** ; → **guard**
Honours List N *(Brit) liste de distinctions honorifiques conférées par le monarque*
honor roll N (US) *(gen)* liste *f* honorifique ; *(Mil)* liste *f* d'anciens combattants ; *(Scol)* liste *f* des meilleurs élèves
honor society N *(US Scol)* club *m* des meilleurs élèves
honor system N (US) système *m* de l'autosurveillance *(dans les écoles et les prisons)*

> **HONOURS LIST**
>
> La **Honours List** est la liste des personnes proposées pour recevoir une distinction honorifique telle qu'un MBE (titre de « Member of the Order of the British Empire ») ou un OBE (titre de « Officer of the Order of the British Empire »). Cette liste, établie par le Premier ministre et approuvée par le monarque, est publiée deux fois par an au moment de la nouvelle année (**New Year's Honours List**) et de l'anniversaire de la reine en juin (**Queen's Birthday Honours List**).

honourable, honorable (US) /ˈɒnərəbl/ ADJ *[person, action, intentions]* honorable ; *[contract, debt]* d'honneur ◆ **an ~ mention** une mention honorable ◆ **the Honourable ...** *(title)* l'honorable ... ◆ **my (right) Honourable friend** *(Brit Parl)* mon (très) honorable collègue ◆ **the (right) Honourable member for Weston** *(Brit Parl)* ≈ Monsieur *(or* Madame) le député de Weston ; → **right**

honourably, honorably (US) /ˈɒnərəblɪ/ ADV honorablement

Hons. *(Univ)* (abbrev of **honours degree**) avec mention

Hon. Sec. N (abbrev of **Honorary Secretary**) → **honorary**

hooch⁑ /huːtʃ/ N *(= alcoholic drink)* gnôle * *f*

hood /hʊd/ [N] [1] *(gen)* capuchon *m* ; *[of executioner etc]* cagoule *f* ; *(Univ)* épitoge *f* ; *[of falcon]* chaperon *m* ◆ **rain ~** capuche *f (en plastique)* [2] *[of car]* *(Brit)* capote *f* ; *(US)* capot *m* [3] *[of pram]* capote *f* ; *(over fire, cooker)* hotte *f* [4] *[of cobra]* capuchon *m* [5] *[of clitoris]* capuchon *m* [6] *(US ⁑ = neighbourhood)* quartier *m* [7] *(⁑ = hoodlum)* truand *m* [VT] *[+ falcon]* chaperonner, enchaperonner

'hood⁑ /hʊd/ N (US) ⇒ **neighborhood**

hooded /ˈhʊdɪd/ [ADJ] *(gen)* *[monk, figure, gunman]* encapuchonné ; *[prisoner]* au visage couvert ; *[coat, jacket]* à capuchon ◆ **he has ~ eyes** il a les paupières tombantes
COMP **hooded crow** N corneille *f* mantelée
hooded falcon N faucon *m* chaperonné *or* enchaperonné

hoodlum /ˈhuːdləm/ N truand *m*

hoodoo * /ˈhuːduː/ [N] *(= bad luck)* guigne * *f*, poisse * *f* ; *(= object, person)* porte-guigne * *m* [VT] porter la guigne * *or* la poisse * à

hoodwink /ˈhʊdˌwɪŋk/ VT tromper, duper ◆ **they ~ed me into accepting** j'ai accepté sur la foi d'informations erronées

hooey * /ˈhuːɪ/ N (US) sornettes *fpl*, conneries⁑ *fpl* ◆ **to talk a lot of ~** dire des bêtises, déconner⁑

hoof /huːf/ [N] (pl **hoofs** *or* **hooves**) sabot *m* *(d'animal)* ◆ **on the ~** sur pied ; → **cloven** [VT] ◆ **to ~ it** ⁑ *(= walk)* aller à pinces * ; (US) *(= dance)* danser, se trémousser COMP **hoof and mouth disease** N (US) fièvre *f* aphteuse

hoofed /huːft/ ADJ à sabots

hoofer⁑ /ˈhuːfəʳ/ N *(esp US = dancer)* danseur *m*, -euse *f* professionnel(le)

hoo-ha * /ˈhuːˌhaː/ N *(= noise)* brouhaha *m*, boucan * *m* ; *(= confusion)* pagaille * *f or* pagaïe * *f* ; *(= bustle)* tohu-bohu *m* ; *(= excitement)* animation *f* ; *(pej) (= fuss)* ◆ **there was a great ~ about it** on en a fait tout un foin * *or* tout un plat *

hook /hʊk/ [N] [1] crochet *m* ; *(for hanging coats)* patère *f* ; *(on dress)* agrafe *f* ; *(Fishing)* hameçon *m* ◆ **~s and eyes** *(Sewing)* agrafes *fpl* ◆ **he swallowed the story ~, line and sinker** * il a gobé * tout ce qu'on lui a raconté, il a tout avalé *(fig)* ◆ **by ~ or by crook** coûte que coûte, par tous les moyens ◆ **to get sb off the ~** * tirer qn d'affaire *or* d'un mauvais pas ◆ **to let sb off the ~** * *[+ wrongdoer]* ficher la paix à qn * ; *[+ sb with problem]* tirer une épine du pied à qn ◆ **he's off the ~** * il est tiré d'affaire ◆ **to get one's ~s into sb/sth** * *(pej)* mettre le grappin sur qn/qch
[2] *(Telec)* ◆ **to take the phone off the ~** décrocher le téléphone ◆ **the phone's off the ~** on a décroché le téléphone ◆ **the phone was ringing off the ~** * (US) le téléphone n'arrêtait pas de sonner
[3] *(Boxing)* crochet *m* ◆ **right ~** crochet *m* (du) droit
[4] *(Golf)* coup *m* hooké
[5] *(Agr)* faucille *f*
[VT] accrocher *(to* à) ; *[+ dress]* agrafer ; *(Naut)* gaffer ; *(Boxing)* donner un crochet à ; *(Fishing)* prendre ; *(Golf)* hooker ◆ **to ~ the ball** *(Rugby)* talonner le ballon ◆ **to ~ a husband** * se trouver un mari ; see also **hooked**
[VI] [1] *(Golf)* hooker
[2] *(US ⁑)* *[prostitute]* faire le tapin⁑ *or* le trottoir *
COMP **hook-nosed** ADJ au nez recourbé *or* crochu
the Hook of Holland N Hoek van Holland
► **hook on** [VI] s'accrocher *(to* à)
[VT SEP] accrocher *(to* à)
► **hook up** [VI] *[dress, skirt]* s'agrafer
[VT SEP] [1] *[+ dress, skirt]* agrafer
[2] *(Rad, TV* *)* faire un duplex entre
[N] ◆ **hookup** * → **hookup**

hookah /'hʊkɑː/ N narguilé *m*

hooked /hʊkt/ ADJ 1 (= *hook-shaped*) [*nose*] recourbé, crochu ◆ **the end of the wire was ~** le bout du fil (de fer) était recourbé 2 (= *having hooks*) muni de crochets *or* d'agrafes *or* d'hameçons ; → **hook** 3 (* *fig*) (= *fascinated*) fasciné (*on* par) accroché* ; (= *dependent*) dépendant (*on* de) ◆ **he's ~ on it** il ne peut plus s'en passer ◆ **to get ~ on** [+ *drugs*] devenir accro* à ; [+ *jazz, television*] devenir enragé* de ◆ **he's really ~ on that girl** il est complètement dingue* de cette fille ◆ **he's become ~ on power** il aime trop le pouvoir : il ne peut plus s'en passer ◆ **once I'd seen the first episode I was ~** après avoir vu le premier épisode j'étais accro* 4 (‡ = *married*) casé*, marié

hooker /'hʊkəʳ/ N 1 (*Rugby*) talonneur *m* 2 (‡ = *prostitute*) putain‡ *f*

hookey * /'hʊkɪ/ N ◆ **to play ~** sécher les cours, faire l'école buissonnière

hookup * /'hʊkʌp/ N (*Rad, TV*) relais *m* temporaire

hookworm /'hʊkwɜːm/ N ankylostome *m*

hooky * /'hʊkɪ/ N ⇒ **hookey**

hooligan /'huːlɪɡən/ N vandale *m*, hooligan *m*

hooliganism /'huːlɪɡənɪzəm/ N vandalisme *m*, hooliganisme *m*

hoop /huːp/ N [*of barrel*] cercle *m* ; (= *toy: in circus, for skirt*) cerceau *m* ; (*Basketball*) (cercle *m* du) panier *m* ; (*Croquet*) arceau *m* ◆ **they put him through the ~(s)** (= *interrogated*) ils l'ont mis sur la sellette ◆ **they put him through** *or* **made him jump through ~s** (= *put to test*) ils l'ont mis à l'épreuve

hoopla /'huːplɑː/ N 1 (*Brit*) jeu *m* d'anneaux (*dans les foires*) 2 (*US* *) ⇒ **hoo-ha**

hoopoe /'huːpuː/ N huppe *f*

hooray /huː'reɪ/ EXCL hourra COMP **Hooray Henry** N (pl **Hooray Henries**) (*Brit pej*) *jeune homme des classes supérieures jovial et bruyant*

hoosegow ‡ /'huːsɡaʊ/ N (*US*) taule‡ *f or* tôle‡ *f*, trou* *m*

Hoosier /'huːʒəʳ/ N (*US*) habitant(e) *m(f)* de l'Indiana ◆ **the ~ State** l'Indiana *m*

hoot /huːt/ N 1 [*of owl*] hululement *m* ; (*esp Brit*) [*of car horn*] coup *m* de klaxon ® ; [*of siren*] mugissement *m* ; [*of train*] sifflement *m* ; (= *jeer*) huée *f* ◆ **she gave a ~ of laughter** elle s'est esclaffée ◆ **I don't give** *or* **care a ~** *or* **two ~s** * je m'en fiche* 2 (* = *amusing thing, person*) ◆ **it was a ~** c'était tordant* *or* marrant* ◆ **she's a ~** elle est impayable* VI [*owl*] hululer ; (*esp Brit*) [*car horn*] klaxonner, corner ; [*siren*] mugir ; [*train*] siffler ; (= *jeer*) huer, pousser des huées ◆ **to ~ with laughter** s'esclaffer, rire aux éclats ◆ **to ~ with derision/delight** pousser des cris moqueurs/de joie VT 1 (also **hoot down**) [+ *actor, speaker*] huer, conspuer 2 ◆ **to ~ the** *or* **one's horn** klaxonner

hooter /'huːtəʳ/ N 1 [*of factory*] sirène *f* ; (*Brit*) [*of car*] klaxon ® *m* ; [*of train*] sifflet *m* 2 (*Brit* ‡ = *nose*) pif* *m*, blair‡ *m* 3 (*US*) ‡ (= *breasts*) **~s** roberts‡ *mpl*

Hoover ® /'huːvəʳ/ (*Brit*) N aspirateur *m* VT ◆ **to hoover a carpet/a room** passer l'aspirateur sur un tapis/dans une pièce ◆ **to hoover sth up** (*lit*) aspirer qch ; (*fig: = consume*) engloutir qch

hooves /huːvz/ NPL of **hoof**

hop¹ /hɒp/ N 1 [*of person, animal*] saut *m* ; [*of bird*] sautillement *m* ◆ **~ skip and jump, ~ step and jump** (*Sport*) triple saut *m* ◆ **it's a ~, skip** *or* **step and jump from here** c'est à deux pas d'ici ◆ **with a ~, skip** *or* **step and jump he was gone** une pirouette et il avait disparu ◆ **to catch sb on the ~** (*Brit*) prendre qn au dépourvu ◆ **to keep sb/be on the ~** * ne pas laisser à qn/ne pas avoir le temps de respirer* 2 († * = *dance*) sauterie † *f* 3 (*in plane*) étape *f* ◆ **from London to Athens in two ~s** de Londres à Athènes en deux étapes ◆ **it's a short ~ from Paris to Brussels** ce n'est qu'un saut de Paris à Bruxelles VI [*person*] (*on one foot*) sauter à cloche-pied ; (= *jump*) sauter ; [*animal*] sauter ; [*bird*] sautiller ◆ **he hopped over to the window** il est allé à cloche-pied jusqu'à la fenêtre ◆ **~ in!** (*in car*) montez ! ◆ **he hopped out of bed** il a sauté du lit ◆ **he hopped onto a plane for London** il a attrapé un avion pour Londres ; → **mad** VT ◆ **to ~ it** * (*Brit*) décamper*, mettre les bouts* *or* les voiles* ◆ **~ it!** * (*Brit*) fiche le camp !* ◆ **he hopped a flight to New York** (*US*) il a attrapé un avion pour New York COMP **hop-o'-my-thumb** N le Petit Poucet

► **hop off** * VI (= *leave*) décamper*, ficher le camp*

hop² /hɒp/ N (= *plant*) (also **hops**) houblon *m* COMP **hop picker** N cueilleur *m*, -euse *f* de houblon **hop-picking** N cueillette *f* du houblon **hop pole** N perche *f* à houblon

hope /həʊp/ LANGUAGE IN USE 8.4, 23, 25.2

N espoir *m* (*of doing sth* de faire qch) espérance *f* (*liter*) (*also Rel*) ◆ **we must live in ~** nous devons vivre d'espoir ◆ **she lives in (the) ~ of seeing her son again** elle continue d'espérer revoir un jour son fils ◆ **in the ~ that ...** dans l'espoir que ... ◆ **in the ~ of sth/of doing sth** dans l'espoir de qch/de faire qch ◆ **to have ~s of doing sth** avoir l'espoir de faire qch ◆ **I haven't much ~ of succeeding** je n'ai pas beaucoup d'espoir de réussir ◆ **to give up ~** cesser d'espérer, perdre espoir ◆ **you should never give up ~** il ne faut jamais perdre espoir ◆ **to give up ~ of doing sth** abandonner l'espoir de faire qch ◆ **past** *or* **beyond (all) ~** sans espoir, désespéré ◆ **the car was smashed beyond any ~ of repair** la voiture était bonne pour la casse ◆ **she hasn't (got) a ~ in hell‡ of being promoted** elle n'a pas la moindre chance d'être promue ◆ **there is no ~ of that** c'est hors de question ◆ **he set out with high ~s** il s'est lancé avec l'espoir de faire de grandes choses ◆ **she had high ~s of winning** elle avait bon espoir de gagner ◆ **her family has great** *or* **high ~s of her** sa famille a de grands espoirs pour elle ◆ **to raise sb's ~s** faire naître l'espoir chez qn ◆ **don't raise her ~s too much** ne lui laisse *or* donne pas trop d'espoir ◆ **don't get your ~s up** *or* **raise your ~s too much** n'y compte pas trop ◆ **to lose (all) ~ of sth/of doing sth** perdre l'espoir *or* tout espoir de qch/de faire qch ◆ **my ~ is that ...** ce que j'espère *or* mon espoir c'est que ... ◆ **you're my last ~** tu es mon dernier espoir ◆ **she's now our best ~** elle représente maintenant notre plus grand espoir ◆ **some ~(s)!** * tu parles !*, tu crois au père Noël !* ; → **dash, faith, hold out**

VI espérer ◆ **to ~ for money/for success** espérer gagner de l'argent/avoir du succès ◆ **they were still hoping for a peaceful solution to the crisis** ils espéraient toujours trouver une solution pacifique à la crise ◆ **we're hoping for fine weather** nous espérons avoir du beau temps *or* qu'il fera beau ◆ **if I were you I shouldn't ~ for too much from the meeting** à votre place je n'attendrais pas trop de la réunion ◆ **don't ~ for too much** n'en attendez pas trop ◆ **it was too much to ~ for (that ...)** ça aurait été trop beau (que ... + *subj*) ◆ **a pay rise would be too much to ~ for** une augmentation ? il ne faut pas rêver ! ◆ **to ~ for better days** espérer (connaître) des jours meilleurs ◆ **we must ~ for better things** il faut espérer que de meilleurs jours viendront *or* que ça ira mieux ◆ **to ~ for the best** espérer que tout se passe au mieux ◆ **to ~ against ~** espérer en dépit de tout

VT espérer ◆ **I ~ (that) he comes** j'espère qu'il viendra ◆ **I ~ to see you, I ~ I'll see you** j'espère te voir ◆ **I ~ to God** *or* **hell‡ she remembers/he doesn't turn up** j'espère vraiment qu'elle s'en souvient/qu'il ne viendra pas ◆ **what do you ~ to gain by that?** qu'espères-tu obtenir par là ? ◆ **the party cannot ~ to win more than a few seats** le parti ne peut pas espérer obtenir plus que quelques sièges ◆ **hoping to hear from you** (*in letter*) dans l'espoir d'avoir de vos nouvelles ◆ **I ~ so** (*answer to question*) j'espère que oui ; (*agreeing with sb's statement*) je l'espère, j'espère bien ◆ **I ~ not** (*answer to question*) j'espère que non ; (*agreeing*) (also **I should hope not**) j'espère bien que non !

COMP **hope chest** N (*US*) (armoire *f or* malle *f* à) trousseau *m*
hoped-for ADJ espéré

hopeful /'həʊpfʊl/ ADJ 1 (= *optimistic*) [*person, face*] plein d'espoir ◆ **to be** *or* **feel ~ (that ...)** avoir bon espoir (que ...) ◆ **I'll ask her but I'm not too ~** je lui demanderai mais je n'y crois pas trop ◆ **to be ~ of doing sth** avoir bon espoir de faire qch 2 (= *promising*) [*sign, future*] prometteur ; [*situation, news*] encourageant N ◆ **the young ~s** (*showing promise*) les jeunes espoirs *mpl* ; (*ambitious*) les jeunes ambitieux *mpl* ; (*hoping for sth*) les jeunes optimistes *mpl* ◆ **the British Olympic ~s** (*hoping to make team*) les candidats *mpl* à la sélection pour l'équipe olympique britannique ; (*hoping to win medal*) les prétendants *mpl* britanniques à une médaille olympique ◆ **presidential ~ Gavin Killip** le candidat à la présidence Gavin Killip

hopefully /'həʊpfəlɪ/ ADV 1 (= *optimistically*) [*say, look at*] avec espoir ◆ **... she asked ~ ...** demanda-t-elle pleine d'espoir 2 (* = *one hopes*) avec un peu de chance ◆ **~ we'll be able to find a solution** avec un peu de chance, nous trouverons une solution ◆ **~ it won't rain** j'espère qu'il ne va pas pleuvoir ◆ **(yes) ~!** je l'espère !, j'espère bien ! ◆ **~ not!** j'espère que non !

hopeless /'həʊplɪs/ ADJ 1 (= *doomed*) [*person, cause, situation, position, attempt*] désespéré ; [*love, task*] impossible ◆ **it's ~!** c'est désespérant ! ◆ **a ~ muddle** *or* **mess** une effroyable pagaille ◆ **in the face of** *or* **against ~ odds** face à une situation désespérée ◆ **to feel ~** (= *in despair*) être désespéré 2 (= *incurable*) [*romantic*] incorrigible ; [*drunk*] invétéré ◆ **he's ~ *, he's a ~ case** * c'est un cas désespéré 3 (* = *useless*) [*person, work*] nul ◆ **he's a ~ teacher** il est nul comme professeur ◆ **to be ~ at maths/sport** être nul en maths/sport ◆ **to be ~ at doing sth** être nul quand il s'agit de faire qch

hopelessly /'həʊplɪslɪ/ ADV 1 (= *despairingly*) avec désespoir 2 (= *impossibly*) [*confused*] totalement ; [*lost*] complètement ◆ **~ naïve** d'une naïveté désespérante ◆ **supplies were ~ inadequate** les provisions manquaient cruellement ◆ **to be ~ in love** *or* **besotted (with sb)** être éperdument amoureux (de qn)

hopelessness /'həʊplɪsnɪs/ N [*of situation*] caractère *m* désespéré ; (= *powerlessness*) sentiment *m* d'impuissance ; (= *despair*) désespoir *m*

hopfield /'hɒpfiːld/ N houblonnière *f*

hophead ‡ /'hɒphed/ N (*US pej*) junkie‡ *mf*

hopper /'hɒpəʳ/ N 1 (= *bin*) trémie *f* 2 (*Austral* *) kangourou *m* COMP **hopper car** N (*Rail*) wagon-trémie *m*

hopscotch /'hɒpskɒtʃ/ N marelle *f*

Horace /'hɒrɪs/ N Horace *m*

Horae /'hɔːriː/ NPL (*Myth*) Heures *fpl*

horde /hɔːd/ N horde *f* (*also pej*), foule *f* ◆ **~s of people** des foules de gens

horizon /hə'raɪzn/ N (*lit*) horizon *m* ; (*fig*) vue *f*, horizon *m* ◆ **on the ~** (*lit, fig*) à l'horizon ◆ **the mountains on the distant ~** les montagnes loin à l'horizon ◆ **a man of limited ~s** un homme aux vues étroites ◆ **to broaden** *or* **expand one's ~s** élargir son horizon *or* ses horizons ◆ **to open new ~s for sb** ouvrir des horizons à qn

horizontal /ˌhɒrɪˈzɒntl/ ADJ horizontal N horizontale *f* COMP **horizontal bar** N barre *f* fixe

horizontally /ˌhɒrɪˈzɒntəlɪ/ ADV horizontalement

hormonal /hɔːˈməʊnəl/ ADJ hormonal

hormone /ˈhɔːməʊn/ N hormone *f*
COMP **hormone replacement therapy** N traitement *m* hormonal substitutif
hormone treatment N traitement *m* hormonal

horn /hɔːn/ N 1 corne *f* ◆ **to draw in** *or* **pull in one's ~s** (= *back down*) diminuer d'ardeur ; (= *spend less*) restreindre son train de vie ; → **dilemma** 2 (*Mus*) cor *m* ; (* = *trumpet*) trompette *f* ; → **French** 3 [*of car*] klaxon ® *m*, avertisseur *m* ; [*of boat*] sirène *f* ◆ **to blow** *or* **sound the** *or* **one's** ~ klaxonner, corner ; → **foghorn** 4 (*US* ‡ = *telephone*) bigophone * *m* ◆ **to get on the ~ to sb** passer un coup de bigophone * à qn 5 [*of saddle*] corne *f*, pommeau *m*
COMP [*handle, ornament*] en corne
horn of plenty N corne *f* d'abondance
horn-rimmed spectacles NPL lunettes *fpl* à monture d'écaille
► **horn in** ‡ VI (*esp US*) mettre son grain de sel

hornbeam /ˈhɔːnbiːm/ N (= *tree*) charme *m*

hornbill /ˈhɔːnbɪl/ N calao *m*

horned /hɔːnd/ ADJ (*gen*) cornu
COMP **horned owl** N duc *m* (= *hibou*)
horned toad N crapaud *m* cornu

hornet /ˈhɔːnɪt/ N frelon *m* ◆ **his inquiries stirred up a ~'s nest** ses investigations ont mis le feu aux poudres ◆ **the case has opened up a ~'s nest of moral and legal concerns** cette affaire soulève une série de questions épineuses, tant morales que juridiques

hornless /ˈhɔːnlɪs/ ADJ sans cornes

hornpipe /ˈhɔːnpaɪp/ N (*Naut*) matelote *f* (*danse*)

horny /ˈhɔːnɪ/ ADJ 1 (‡ = *sexually aroused*) excité * (*sexuellement*) 2 (‡ = *sexually arousing*) sexy * 3 (= *like horn*) corné ; [*hands*] calleux

horology /hɒˈrɒlədʒɪ/ N horlogerie *f*

horoscope /ˈhɒrəskəʊp/ N horoscope *m*

horrendous /hɒˈrendəs/ ADJ épouvantable

horrible /ˈhɒrɪbl/ ADJ 1 (= *horrific*) horrible ; [*moment*] terrible ◆ **the ~ truth** la terrible vérité 2 (= *unpleasant, awful*) épouvantable ; [*clothes*] affreux ; [*mistake*] terrible 3 (* = *unkind*) [*person*] méchant (*to sb* avec qn) ◆ **that's a ~ thing to say!** c'est vraiment méchant *or* terrible de dire des choses pareilles ! ◆ **all the ~ things I said to you** toutes les horreurs que je t'ai dites

horribly /ˈhɒrɪblɪ/ ADV 1 (= *horrifically*) [*die, scream*] d'une manière horrible ; [*mutilated, disfigured, injured*] horriblement ; [*cruel*] très, particulièrement ; [*violent*] terriblement 2 (= *unpleasantly, awfully*) [*expensive, guilty, embarrassed, uncomfortable*] terriblement ◆ **it's all gone ~ wrong** les choses ont très mal tourné ◆ **I'm going to be ~ late** * je vais être affreusement en retard

horrid /ˈhɒrɪd/ ADJ (= *nasty*) [*person*] ignoble ; [*weather, place*] épouvantable ; (= *ugly*) hideux ◆ **a ~ child** une (petite) horreur *

horrific /hɒˈrɪfɪk/ ADJ atroce, horrible

horrifically /hɒˈrɪfɪkəlɪ/ ADV [*injured, burned, beaten*] horriblement ; [*expensive, dangerous*] terriblement

horrified /ˈhɒrɪfaɪd/ ADJ horrifié

horrify /ˈhɒrɪfaɪ/ VT horrifier

horrifying /ˈhɒrɪfaɪɪŋ/ ADJ effrayant

horrifyingly /ˈhɒrɪfaɪɪŋlɪ/ ADV effroyablement

horror /ˈhɒrəʳ/ N (= *feeling, object*) horreur *f* ◆ **to have a ~ of sth/of doing sth** avoir horreur de qch/de faire qch ◆ **the ~s of war** les horreurs *fpl* de la guerre ◆ **to my ~ I realized that ...** je me suis rendu compte avec horreur que ... ◆ **to my ~ he returned with a knife** à ma grande horreur il est revenu un couteau à la main ◆ **they watched in ~ as the train left the tracks** le train a déraillé sous leurs yeux horrifiés ◆ **and then, ~ of ~s *, he said ...** et alors, pour comble de l'horreur, il a dit ... ◆ **you little ~!** * petit monstre ! * ◆ **nine die in motorway ~** (*as headline*) scènes d'horreur sur l'autoroute : neuf morts ; → **chamber**
COMP [*book, film, comic*] d'épouvante
horror story N (*lit*) histoire *f* d'épouvante ; (*fig*) horreur *f*
horror-stricken, horror-struck ADJ glacé d'horreur

horse /hɔːs/ N 1 cheval *m* ◆ **to work like a ~** travailler comme un forcené ◆ **(straight) from the ~'s mouth** de source sûre ◆ **to back the wrong ~** (*lit, fig*) miser sur le mauvais cheval ◆ **that's a ~ of a different colour** cela n'a rien à voir ◆ **hold your ~s!** * arrêtez !, minute ! * ◆ **it's (a case of) ~s for courses** (*Brit*) chacun selon ses compétences ◆ **to change** *or* **switch ~s in midstream** changer de cheval au milieu du gué ◆ **you can take** *or* **lead a ~ to water but you cannot make it drink** (*Prov*) on ne peut pas forcer les gens ; → **dark, eat, gift, white, willing**
2 (*Gym*) cheval *m* d'arçons ; → **clothes**
3 (*NonC: Mil*) cavalerie *f* ◆ **light ~** cavalerie *f* légère
4 (*Drugs* * = *heroin*) blanche * *f*, héroïne *f*
COMP **horse-and-buggy** ADJ (*US*) [*approach, system*] dépassé
horse artillery N troupes *fpl* montées
horse brass N médaillon *m* de cuivre (*fixé à une martingale*)
horse-breaker N dresseur *m*, -euse *f* de chevaux
horse breeder N éleveur *m*, -euse *f* de chevaux
horse chestnut N (= *nut*) marron *m* (d'Inde) ; (*also* **horse chestnut tree**) marronnier *m* (d'Inde)
horse-collar N collier *m* (*de harnais*)
horse-dealer N maquignon *m*
horse-doctor * N vétérinaire *mf*
horse-drawn ADJ tiré par des chevaux, à chevaux
the Horse Guards NPL (*Brit Mil*) (le régiment de) la Garde à cheval
horse latitudes NPL latitudes *fpl* subtropicales
horse-laugh N gros rire *m*
horse manure N crottin *m* de cheval
horse opera * N (*US Cine, TV*) western *m*
horse-race N course *f* de chevaux
horse-racing N courses *fpl* de chevaux, hippisme *m*
horse-riding N (*Brit*) équitation *f*
horse-sense * N (gros) bon sens *m*
horse show N concours *m* hippique
horse-trade VI (*lit*) maquignonner ; (*fig*) négocier âprement
horse-trader N (*lit*) maquignon *m* ; (*fig*) négociateur *m*, -trice *f* redoutable
horse-trading N (*lit*) maquignonnage *m* ; (*fig*) âpres négociations *fpl*
horse trailer N (*US*) ⇒ **horsebox**
horse trials NPL concours *m* hippique
horse vaulting N (*Sport*) saut *m* de cheval
► **horse about** *, **horse around** * VI chahuter, jouer bruyamment ◆ **stop horsing about!** arrêtez de chahuter !

horseback /ˈhɔːsbæk/ N ◆ **on ~** à cheval COMP **horseback riding** N (*esp US*) équitation *f*

horsebox /ˈhɔːsbɒks/ N (*Brit*) fourgon *m* à chevaux, van *m* ; (*in stable*) box *m*

horsecar /ˈhɔːskɑːʳ/ N (*US*) fourgon *m* à chevaux, van *m*

horseflesh /ˈhɔːsfleʃ/ N 1 (= *horses generally*) chevaux *mpl* 2 (= *horsemeat*) viande *f* de cheval

horsefly /ˈhɔːsflaɪ/ N taon *m*

horsehair /ˈhɔːsheəʳ/ N crin *m* (de cheval) ADJ de *or* en crin

horsehide /ˈhɔːshaɪd/ N cuir *m* de cheval

horseless /ˈhɔːslɪs/ ADJ sans cheval COMP **horseless carriage** † N voiture *f* sans chevaux

horseman /ˈhɔːsmən/ N (pl **-men**) cavalier *m* ◆ **he's a good ~** c'est un bon cavalier, il monte bien (à cheval)

horsemanship /ˈhɔːsmənʃɪp/ N (= *skill*) talent *m* de cavalier, monte *f*

horsemeat /ˈhɔːsmiːt/ N viande *f* de cheval

horseplay /ˈhɔːspleɪ/ N chahut *m*

horsepower /ˈhɔːspaʊəʳ/ N puissance *f* (en chevaux) ; (= *unit*) cheval-vapeur *m* ◆ **a ten-~ car** une dix-chevaux

horseradish /ˈhɔːsrædɪʃ/ N (= *plant*) raifort *m* COMP **horseradish sauce** N sauce *f* au raifort

horseshit *‡ /ˈhɔːsʃɪt/ N (*lit*) crottin *m* (de cheval) ; (*fig*) (= *nonsense*) conneries ‡ *fpl*

horseshoe /ˈhɔːsʃuː/ N fer *m* à cheval ADJ en fer à cheval

horsetail /ˈhɔːsteɪl/ N (= *plant*) prêle *f*

horsewhip /ˈhɔːswɪp/ N cravache *f* VT cravacher

horsewoman /ˈhɔːswʊmən/ N (pl **-women**) cavalière *f*, écuyère *f* ◆ **she's a good ~** c'est une bonne cavalière, elle monte bien (à cheval)

hors(e)y * /ˈhɔːsɪ/ ADJ 1 (= *fond of horses*) passionné de chevaux ; (= *fond of riding*) passionné d'équitation 2 (*in appearance*) [*person, face*] chevalin

horticultural /ˌhɔːtɪˈkʌltʃərəl/ ADJ horticole ◆ **~ show** exposition *f* horticole *or* d'horticulture

horticulturalist /ˌhɔːtɪˈkʌltʃərəlɪst/ N ⇒ **horticulturist**

horticulture /ˈhɔːtɪkʌltʃəʳ/ N horticulture *f*

horticulturist /ˌhɔːtɪˈkʌltʃərɪst/ N horticulteur *m*, -trice *f*

hosanna, hosannah /həʊˈzænə/ EXCL hosanna ! N hosanna *m*

hose¹ /həʊz/ N (*gen*) tuyau *m* ; (*also* **garden hose**) tuyau *m* d'arrosage ; (*also* **fire hose**) tuyau *m* d'incendie ; (*Tech*) (*for water*) manche *f* à eau ; (*for air*) manche *f* à air ; (*in car engine*) durite *f* VT (*in garden*) arroser au jet ; [*firemen*] arroser à la lance
► **hose down, hose out** VT SEP laver au jet

hose² /həʊz/ N (pl inv) (*Comm* = *stockings etc*) bas *mpl* ; (*US:* = *tights*) collants *mpl* ; (*Hist*) (= *tights*) chausses *fpl* ; (= *knee breeches*) culotte *f* courte

Hosea /həʊˈzɪə/ N Osée *m*

hosepipe /ˈhəʊzpaɪp/ N (*in garden*) tuyau *m* d'arrosage ; (*of fireman*) tuyau *m* d'incendie COMP **hosepipe ban** N (*Brit*) *interdiction d'arroser pour cause de pénurie d'eau*

hosier /ˈhəʊzɪəʳ/ N bonnetier *m*, -ière *f*

hosiery /ˈhəʊzɪərɪ/ N (*business*) bonneterie *f* ; (*Comm*) (= *stocking department*) (rayon *m* des) bas *mpl* ; (= *stockings*) bas *mpl*

hosp N abbrev of **hospital**

hospice /ˈhɒspɪs/ N (*gen*) hospice *m* ; (*for terminally ill*) établissement *m* de soins palliatifs

hospitable /hɒsˈpɪtəbl/ ADJ [*person, place, welcome*] hospitalier (*to sb* envers qn) accueillant ; [*climate, environment*] favorable (*to sth* à qch) hospitalier

hospitably /hɒsˈpɪtəblɪ/ ADV *[welcome]* de façon accueillante

hospital /ˈhɒspɪtl/ N hôpital *m* ◆ **in ~** à l'hôpital ◆ **people** *or* **patients in ~** (malades *mpl*) hospitalisés *mpl* ◆ **to go into ~** aller à l'hôpital, être hospitalisé ; → **maternity, mental**
COMP *[treatment, staff]* hospitalier ; *[bed etc]* d'hôpital ; *[dispute, strike]* des hôpitaux
hospital administrator N *(Brit)* administrateur *m*, -trice *f* d'hôpital ; *(US)* directeur *m*, -trice *f* d'hôpital
hospital board N conseil *m* d'administration de l'hôpital
hospital case N ◆ **90% of ~ cases are released within three weeks** 90% des patients hospitalisés sortent dans les trois semaines ◆ **this is a ~ case** le patient doit être hospitalisé
hospital doctor N médecin *m* hospitalier ◆ **junior ~ doctor** interne *m* des hôpitaux
hospital facilities NPL structures *fpl* hospitalières
hospital nurse N infirmier *m*, -ière *f* hospitalier (-ière)
hospital service N service *m* hospitalier
hospital ship N navire-hôpital *m*
hospital train N train *m* sanitaire

hospitality /ˌhɒspɪˈtælɪtɪ/ N hospitalité *f* COMP
hospitality suite N salon *m (où sont offerts les rafraîchissements)*

hospitalization /ˌhɒspɪtəlaɪˈzeɪʃən/ N hospitalisation *f*

hospitalize /ˈhɒspɪtəlaɪz/ VT hospitaliser

host[1] /həʊst/ N 1 *(= person receiving guests)* hôte *m* ; (†† = *innkeeper)* patron *m* ; *[of TV, radio show]* animateur *m*, -trice *f*, présentateur *m*, -trice *f* ◆ **mine ~** *(hum)* notre hôte *(hum)* 2 *(Bio, Comput)* hôte *m* VT *[+ radio or TV show]* animer ; *[+ festival, games]* accueillir
COMP *[plant, animal]* hôte ; *[town etc]* qui reçoit
host computer N hôte *m*
host country N *[of conference, games]* pays *m* d'accueil

host[2] /həʊst/ N 1 *(= crowd)* foule *f* ◆ **a ~ of friends** une foule d'amis ◆ **a whole ~ of reasons** toute une série *or* tout un tas* de raisons 2 †† armée *f*

host[3] /həʊst/ N *(Rel)* hostie *f*

hostage /ˈhɒstɪdʒ/ N otage *m* ◆ **to take/hold sb ~** prendre/retenir qn en otage ◆ **to be a ~ to fortune** être le jouet du destin

hostel /ˈhɒstəl/ N 1 *(for students, workers)* foyer *m* ◆ **(youth) ~** auberge *f* de jeunesse 2 († = *inn)* auberge *f* VI ◆ **to go (youth) ~ling** aller passer ses vacances en auberges de jeunesse

hosteller /ˈhɒstələʳ/ N ≈ ajiste *mf*

hostelry /ˈhɒstəlrɪ/ N *(esp Brit* ††*)* hostellerie *f* ; *(hum) (= pub)* auberge *f*

hostess /ˈhəʊstɪs/ N *(gen)* hôtesse *f* ; *(in night club)* entraîneuse *f* ; *[of TV, radio show]* animatrice *f*, présentatrice *f* ; → **air** COMP **hostess trolley** N *(Brit)* table *f* roulante *(avec chauffe-plats)*

hostile /ˈhɒstaɪl, (US) ˈhɒstəl/ ADJ hostile *(to* à*)* ; *(Mil) [fire, force, aircraft]* ennemi COMP **hostile takeover bid** N OPA *f* hostile

hostility /hɒˈstɪlɪtɪ/ N hostilité *f*

hostler †† /ˈɒsləʳ/ N *(US)* ⇒ **ostler**

hot /hɒt/ ADJ 1 *(lit)* chaud ◆ **to be ~** *[person]* avoir (très *or* trop) chaud ; *[thing]* être (très) chaud ; *(Met)* faire (très) chaud ◆ **it's too ~ in here** il fait trop chaud ici ◆ **to get ~** *[person]* commencer à avoir (trop) chaud ; *[thing]* devenir chaud, chauffer ; *(Weather)* commencer à faire chaud ◆ **it was a very ~ day** c'était un jour de grande *or* de forte chaleur ◆ **the ~ sun** le soleil brûlant ◆ **in the ~ weather** pendant les grandes chaleurs ◆ **bread ~ from the oven** pain tout chaud sorti du four ◆ **~ dishes** *(on menu)* plats *mpl* chauds ◆ **I can't drink ~ things** je ne peux pas boire chaud ◆ **the food must be served ~** la nourriture doit être servie bien chaude ◆ **he's had more trips to Paris than I've had ~ dinners*** c'est un grand habitué des voyages à Paris ◆ **~ and cold (running water)** (eau *f* courante) chaude et froide ◆ **to be in ~ water** *(fig)* être dans le pétrin ◆ **to get into ~ water** *(fig)* s'attirer des ennuis ◆ **this subject's too ~ to handle*** ce sujet est trop épineux ◆ **she's too ~ to handle*** il vaut mieux ne pas s'y frotter ◆ **that's a ~ button** *(US)* c'est un sujet épineux ◆ **to be (all) ~ and bothered** *(= perspiring)* être en nage ; *(= flustered)* être dans tous ses états *(about sth* au sujet de qch*)* ◆ **to be/get ~ under the collar*** être/se mettre dans tous ses états *(about sth* au sujet de qch*)* see also **comp** ; → **cake, coal, iron**
2 *(fig) [food, curry]* fort, épicé ; *[spices]* fort ; *[news]* tout(e) frais (fraîche *f*) ; *[contest, dispute, competition]* acharné ; *[topic]* brûlant ; *[temperament]* passionné, violent ◆ **he's got a ~ temper** il a un caractère violent, il est très coléreux ◆ **a ~ war*** *(Pol)* une guerre ouverte ◆ **~ favourite** *(Sport)* grand favori *m* ◆ **~ tip** tuyau *m* sûr* ◆ **to be ~ on the trail** être sur la bonne piste ◆ **to be ~ on sb's trail** être sur les talons de qn ◆ **you're getting ~!** *(in guessing games)* tu brûles ! ◆ **news ~ from the press** informations *fpl* de dernière minute ◆ **the latest designs ~ from Milan** les derniers modèles qui arrivent tout droit de Milan ◆ **to make it** *or* **things ~ for sb*** mettre qn dans une situation délicate ; see also **pursuit**
3 (* = *very good) (gen)* terrible*, sensationnel* ◆ **that's ~** *(esp US)* c'est fantastique ◆ **not so ~** pas formidable*, pas fameux* ◆ **how are things? – not so ~** comment ça va ? – pas terrible* ◆ **he's pretty ~ at maths** c'est un crack* en maths ◆ **he's pretty ~ at football** il joue super bien au foot* ◆ **she is so ~*** *(sexually)* elle est tellement sexy
4 *(= successful) [article for sale]* très recherché, qui a beaucoup de succès ◆ **the hottest show in town*** un spectacle à voir absolument ◆ **Bardot soon became the hottest property*** **in show business** bientôt, on s'est arraché Bardot dans le milieu du show-business
5 *(= stolen)* ◆ **it's ~*** c'est de la fauche*
6 *(= radioactive)* radioactif (-ive *f*)
ADV → **blow**[1]
NPL **hots*** ◆ **to have the ~s for sb** craquer* complètement pour qn
COMP **hot air*** N *(fig) (= nonsense)* blablabla* *m*, foutaises* *fpl* ; *(= empty talk)* du vent ◆ **to blow ~ air** brasser du vent ◆ **he's all ~ air** c'est une grande gueule*
hot-air balloon N ballon *m*, montgolfière *f*
hot-blooded ADJ *(fig)* ardent, passionné
hot-button ADJ *(US)* ◆ **~-button issue** point *m* chaud, question *f* controversée
hot cross bun N brioche *f* du Vendredi saint
hot-desking N partage *m* de bureaux
hot dog N *(Culin)* hot-dog *m*
hot-dogging N *(Ski)* ski *m* acrobatique
hot flash N *(US)* ⇒ **hot flush**
hot flush N *(Med)* bouffée *f* de chaleur
hot gospeller* N prêcheur *m* évangéliste, exalté(e) *m(f)*
hot issue N *(Fin)* émission *f* des valeurs vedettes
hot jazz N hot *m*
hot key N *(Comput)* touche *f* directe
hot line N *(Telec) (gen)* ligne *f* ouverte vingt-quatre heures sur vingt-quatre *(to* avec*)* ; *(Pol)* téléphone *m* rouge *(to* avec*)*
hot money N *(Fin)* capitaux *mpl* spéculatifs *or* fébriles ; *(stolen)* argent *m* volé
hot pants* NPL mini-short *m*
hot pepper N piment *m* rouge
hot potato* N *(fig)* sujet *m* brûlant ◆ **he dropped the idea like a ~ potato** il a (soudain) laissé tomber cette idée
hot press N *(Ir = airing cupboard)* placard-séchoir *m*
hot seat* N *(US = electric chair)* chaise *f* électrique ◆ **to be in the ~ seat** *(fig) (in decision-making)* être en première ligne
hot-selling ADJ qui se vend comme des petits pains
hot shit*** N *(esp US fig)* ◆ **he really thinks he's ~ shit** il ne se prend pas pour de la merde**
hot-shoe N *(Phot)* sabot(-contact) *m*, porte-flash *m*
hot spot* N *(= trouble area)* point *m* névralgique *or* chaud ; *(= night club)* boîte *f* (de nuit) ; *(for wireless access)* borne *f*
hot spring N source *f* chaude
hot stuff* N ◆ **to be ~ stuff** *(= terrific)* être terrible* ; *(= daring) [film etc]* être osé ◆ **he's ~ stuff** *(= clever)* il est génial* ; *(= sexy)* il est sexy*
hot-tempered ADJ emporté, colérique
hot tub N *(esp US)* jacuzzi ® *m*
hot-water bottle N bouillotte *f*
hot-wire* VT *[+ car]* démarrer en faisant se toucher les fils de contact
► **hot up*** *(fig)* VI *(esp Brit)* chauffer* ◆ **things are ~ting up in the Middle East** cela commence à chauffer* au Moyen-Orient ◆ **things are ~ting up** *(at a party)* l'atmosphère commence à chauffer* ◆ **the bars rarely ~ up before 1am** il y a rarement de l'ambiance dans les bars avant une heure du matin
VT SEP *(= to step up)* ◆ **police are ~ting up their surveillance** la police renforce sa surveillance

hotbed /ˈhɒtbed/ N ◆ **a ~ of vice** une sentine de vices ◆ **a ~ of social unrest** un foyer d'agitation sociale

hotcake /ˈhɒtkeɪk/ N *(US)* ⇒ **pancake**

hotchpotch /ˈhɒtʃpɒtʃ/ N salmigondis *m*, fatras *m*

hotel /həʊˈtel/ N hôtel *m* ; *(Austral = pub)* pub *m* ◆ **to stay at a ~** être à l'hôtel
COMP *[furniture, prices, porter]* d'hôtel
hotel industry N industrie *f* hôtelière, hôtellerie *f*
hotel manager N gérant(e) *m(f) or* directeur *m*, -trice *f* d'hôtel
hotel receptionist N réceptionniste *mf* d'hôtel
hotel room N chambre *f* d'hôtel
hotel ship N navire-hôtel *m*
hotel staff N personnel *m* hôtelier *or* de l'hôtel
hotel work N ◆ **he's looking for ~ work** il cherche un travail dans l'hôtellerie
hotel workers NPL personnel *m* hôtelier

hotelier /həʊˈtelɪəʳ/, **hotelkeeper** /həʊˈtel,kiːpəʳ/ N hôtelier *m*, -ière *f*

hotfoot /hɒtˈfʊt/ ADV à toute vitesse, à toute allure VT ◆ **to ~ it*** galoper

hothead /ˈhɒthed/ N *(fig)* tête *f* brûlée ADJ (also **hotheaded**) *[person]* impétueux ; *[attitude]* exalté

hothouse /ˈhɒthaʊs/ N *(lit)* serre *f* (chaude) ; *(fig)* foyer *m* ADJ *(lit)* de serre (chaude) ◆ **a ~ atmosphere** une ambiance très compétitive

hothousing /ˈhɒthaʊzɪŋ/ N *enseignement intensif à l'intention des enfants surdoués*

hotly /ˈhɒtlɪ/ ADV 1 *(= keenly) [debated, disputed]* avec passion ◆ **~ pursued (by sb)** poursuivi de très près (par qn) ◆ **the man ~ tipped to become the next president** l'homme donné comme grand favori de la course à la présidence ◆ **he was ~ tipped to take a gold** il était grand favori pour la médaille d'or ◆ **to be ~ contested** être l'objet d'une lutte acharnée 2 *(= angrily) [deny]* avec virulence ; *[say]* avec feu

hotplate /ˈhɒtpleɪt/ N plaque *f* chauffante

hotpot /ˈhɒtpɒt/ N *(esp Brit Culin) ragoût de viande aux pommes de terre*

hotrod /ˈhɒtrɒd/ N *(US)* (also **hotrod car**) hotrod *m*, voiture *f* gonflée*

hotshot* /ˈhɒtʃɒt/ ADJ *[person]* génial ; *[performance]* de virtuose ◆ **a ~ lawyer** un ténor du barreau N *(= expert)* as *m*, crack* *m* ; *(= important person)* gros bonnet *m*

Hottentot /ˈhɒtəntɒt/ ADJ hottentot N 1 Hottentot *mf* 2 *(= language)* hottentot *m*

houm(o)us /ˈhuːməs/ N ⇒ **hummus**

hound /haʊnd/ N 1 chien *m* courant, chien *m* de meute ; *(hum = any dog)* chien *m* ◆ **the ~s** *(Brit)* la meute ◆ **to ride to ~s** chasser à courre ; → **foxhound, master** 2 *(† pej = person)* canaille *f*, crapule *f* VT *[+ person]* s'acharner sur *or* contre, harceler ◆ **he is constantly ~ing them for advice** il les harcèle constamment pour leur demander conseil ◆ **to be ~ed by the press** être harcelé par la presse ◆ **he was ~ed out of his job** il a été chassé de son travail ◆ **he was ~ed out of town** il a été forcé à quitter la ville ◆ **they ~ed him for the money** ils n'ont pas arrêté de le harceler pour qu'il leur donne l'argent

► **hound down** VT SEP (traquer et) capturer

► **hound out** VT SEP chasser

hour /ˈaʊəʳ/ N 1 *(= period)* heure *f* ◆ **a quarter of an ~** un quart d'heure ◆ **three quarters of an ~** trois quarts d'heure ◆ **half an ~, a half-~** une demi-heure ◆ **an ~ and a half** une heure et demie ◆ **two and a half ~s** deux heures et demie ◆ **~ by ~** heure par heure ◆ **80km an ~** 80 km à l'heure ◆ **four ~s' walk from here** (à) quatre heures de marche d'ici ◆ **London is an ~ away from here** Londres est à une heure d'ici ◆ **to do sth (for) ~ after ~** faire qch heure après heure *or* des heures d'affilée ◆ **to pay sb by the ~** payer qn à l'heure ◆ **she is paid £8 an ~** elle est payée 8 livres (de) l'heure ◆ **getting there would take ~s** il faudrait des heures pour s'y rendre ◆ **she's been waiting for ~s** elle attend depuis des heures ◆ **to be ~s late** *(lit)* être en retard de plusieurs heures ; *(fig)* être terriblement en retard

2 *(= time of day, point in time)* heure *f* ; *(fig)* heure *f*, moment *m* ◆ **on the ~** à l'heure juste (toutes les heures) ◆ **the ~ has come** l'heure est venue, c'est l'heure ◆ **his ~ has come** son heure est venue ◆ **his last ~ neared** sa dernière heure approchait ◆ **the ~ of his execution** l'heure de son exécution ◆ **the darkest ~ of my professional life** le passage le plus noir de ma vie professionnelle ◆ **in the early** *or* **(wee) small ~s (of the morning)** au petit matin *or* jour, aux premières heures (du jour) ◆ **at all ~s (of the day and night)** à toute heure (du jour et de la nuit) ◆ **till all ~s** * jusqu'à une heure avancée de la nuit, jusqu'à très tard ◆ **not at this ~ surely!** tout de même pas à cette heure-ci *or* à l'heure qu'il est ! ◆ **at this late ~** *(fig)* à ce stade avancé ◆ **in his ~ of danger** lorsqu'il était en danger ◆ **the problems of the ~** les problèmes *mpl* du jour *or* de l'heure ◆ **Book of Hours** livre *m* d'Heures ; → **eleventh, half**

3 ◆ **to keep regular ~s** avoir une vie réglée ◆ **to work long ~s** avoir une journée très longue ◆ **after ~s** *(Brit) (of shops, pubs)* après l'heure de fermeture ; *(of offices)* après les heures de bureau ◆ **out of ~s** en dehors des heures d'ouverture ◆ **out of school ~s** en dehors des heures de cours *or* de classe ; → **early, late, office, school**[1]

COMP **hour hand** N *[of watch, clock]* petite aiguille *f*

hourglass /ˈaʊəglɑːs/ N sablier *m* COMP **hourglass figure** N *(fig)* silhouette *f* de rêve

hourly /ˈaʊəlɪ/ ADJ 1 *(= every hour)* ◆ **the ~ news broadcast** les nouvelles diffusées toutes les heures ◆ **the village has an ~ bus service** le village est desservi par un car qui passe toutes les heures ◆ **at ~ intervals** toutes les heures ◆ **at two-~ intervals** toutes les deux heures 2 *(= per hour) [earnings, wage, rate]* horaire ; *[worker, job]* payé à l'heure ◆ **paid on an ~ basis** payé à l'heure 3 *(= constant)* constant ADV 1 *(= every hour) [fly, patrol, update]* toutes les heures 2 *(= per hour) [pay]* à l'heure 3 *(= constantly)* constamment 4 *(= at any moment) [expect]* à tout moment, d'un moment à l'autre

house /haʊs/ N (pl **houses** /ˈhaʊzɪz/) 1 maison *f* ◆ **at my ~** chez moi ◆ **to my ~** chez moi ◆ **she needs more help in the ~** il faudrait qu'elle soit plus aidée à la maison ◆ **she looks after the ~ herself** elle tient son ménage, c'est elle qui s'occupe du ménage ◆ **to keep ~ (for sb)** tenir la maison *or* le ménage (de qn) ◆ **to set up ~** s'installer, monter son ménage ◆ **they've set up ~ together** *(gen)* ils habitent ensemble ; *[couple]* ils se sont mis en ménage ◆ **to put** *or* **set one's ~ in order** *(fig)* mettre de l'ordre dans ses affaires ◆ **to play at ~s, to play ~** *(esp US)* jouer au papa et à la maman ◆ **they got on like a ~ on fire** ils s'entendaient à merveille *or* comme larrons en foire ◆ **to be (as) safe as ~s** être tout à fait sûr, ne présenter aucun risque ◆ **he'll be safe as ~s** il ne courra absolument aucun risque ◆ **their jobs are safe as ~s** ils ne risquent pas du tout de perdre leur emploi, ils ont un emploi tout à fait sûr ◆ **to go round the ~s*** *(Brit = waffle)* parler pour ne rien dire ; → **doll, eat, move, open, public**

2 *(Parl)* **the House** la Chambre ; → **floor**

3 *(Theat etc) (= place)* salle *f* ; *(= audience)* spectateurs *mpl* ◆ **is there a doctor in the ~?** y a-t-il un médecin dans la salle ? ◆ **a full** *or* **good ~** une salle pleine ◆ **to play to full** *or* **packed ~s** faire salle pleine, jouer à guichets fermés ◆ **"house full"** "complet" ◆ **the second ~** la deuxième séance ◆ **to bring the ~ down** faire un tabac*, casser la baraque* ; → **pack**

4 *(Comm)* (also **business house**) maison *f* (de commerce), compagnie *f* ; → **banking**[2], **fashion, publishing** *etc*

◆ **in house** → **in**

◆ **on the house*** aux frais de la maison ◆ **drinks are on the ~!** c'est la tournée du patron !

◆ **out of house** en externe ◆ **the work was done out of ~** le travail a été fait en externe

5 *(of noble family)* maison *f* ; *(Rel)* maison *f* religieuse ; *(Brit Scol)* groupe *m* d'internes ◆ **the House of Windsor** la maison des Windsor

6 *(Mus)* **House (music)** house *f*

VT /haʊz/ *[+ person]* loger, héberger ◆ **she was housing refugees** elle logeait *or* hébergeait des réfugiés ◆ **the town offered to ~ six refugee families** la ville a proposé de loger six familles de réfugiés ◆ **this building ~s five families/a motorcycle museum** ce bâtiment abrite cinq familles/un musée de la moto ◆ **the jail ~s more than a thousand inmates** il y a plus de mille détenus dans cette prison ◆ **the freezer is ~d in the basement** le congélateur est au sous-sol ◆ **the generator is ~d in a large wooden box** le générateur se trouve dans un grand châssis de bois ◆ **the sauna is ~d in their garage** le sauna est (situé) dans leur garage

COMP **house agent** N *(Brit)* agent *m* immobilier

house arrest N assignation *f* à domicile *or* à résidence ◆ **to put sb under ~ arrest** assigner qn à domicile *or* à résidence ◆ **to be under ~ arrest** être assigné à domicile, être en résidence surveillée

house-clean VI *(US)* faire le ménage

house-cleaning N *(US)* ménage *m*, nettoyage *m*

house-hunt VI *(Brit)* chercher une maison (*or* un appartement), être à la recherche d'une maison (*or* d'un appartement)

house-hunting N *(Brit)* recherche *f* d'une maison (*or* d'un appartement)

house-husband N homme *m* au foyer

house journal, house magazine N *[of company, organization]* bulletin *m*, journal *m* interne

house manager N *(Theat)* directeur *m*, -trice *f* de théâtre

house of cards N château *m* de cartes

House of Commons N *(Brit)* Chambre *f* des communes

house of correction N *(US)* maison *f* d'arrêt

House of God N maison *f* de Dieu

House of Lords N *(Brit)* Chambre *f* des lords

House of Representatives N *(US)* Chambre *f* des députés

house organ N ⇒ **house journal**

house-owner N propriétaire *mf* d'une maison

house painter N peintre *m* en bâtiments

house party N *(in country house)* partie *f* de campagne ◆ **I'm having a ~ party next week** *(gen)* j'organise une soirée *or* une fête chez moi la semaine prochaine

house physician N *(Brit) (in hospital)* ≃ interne *mf* en médecine ; *(in hotel etc)* médecin *m (attaché à un hôtel etc)*

house plant N plante *f* d'intérieur

house prices NPL prix *mpl* de l'immobilier

house-proud ADJ *(esp Brit)* ◆ **she's very ~-proud** tout est toujours impeccable chez elle

house red N vin *m* rouge cuvée du patron

house rosé N vin *m* rosé cuvée du patron

house rule N *(gen, Comm)* règle *f* de la maison ◆ **~ rules** *(Comm)* règlement *m* interne

house sale N vente *f* immobilière

house-sit VI ◆ **to ~-sit for sb** garder la maison de qn

house-sitter N *personne qui loge chez qn en son absence*

the Houses of Parliament N *(in Brit) (= building)* le Palais de Westminster ; *(= members)* le Parlement, les Chambres *fpl*

house sparrow N moineau *m* domestique

house style N *(Publishing)* style *m* maison

house surgeon N *(Brit)* ≃ interne *mf* en chirurgie

house-to-house ADJ porte à porte *inv* ◆ **~-to-~ search** perquisition *f* systématique dans le quartier ◆ **to make a ~-to-~ search for sb** aller de porte en porte à la recherche de qn

house-train VT *(Brit) [+ animal]* apprendre à être propre à

house-trained ADJ *(Brit) [animal]* propre ; *(fig) [person]* docile, obéissant

House Un-American Activities Committee N *(US Hist)* Commission *f* des activités antiaméricaines

house-warming (party) N pendaison *f* de crémaillère ◆ **to give a ~-warming (party)** pendre la crémaillère

house white N vin *m* blanc cuvée du patron

house wine N cuvée *f* du patron

HOUSE

Les types de logements portent souvent des noms différents en anglais britannique et en anglais américain ; ainsi, un appartement se dit respectivement « flat » (Brit) et « apartment » (US). Un « condominium » (US) est un immeuble d'habitation dont les appartements appartiennent à des propriétaires individuels alors que les parties communes sont en copropriété.

Les rangées de maisons identiques et contiguës sont appelées « terraced houses » (Brit) ou « row houses » (US). Les « semidetached houses » (Brit) ou « duplex houses » (US) sont des maisons jumelles, tandis que la « detached house » (Brit) est un pavillon.

Deux autres types de maisons répandues aux États-Unis sont les « ranch houses » - de longues bâtisses généralement de plain-pied, et les « colonials », maisons de style 18e siècle en bardeaux ou en briques, comportant souvent un portique.

houseboat /ˈhaʊsbəʊt/ N house-boat *m*

housebound /ˈhaʊsbaʊnd/ ADJ confiné chez soi NPL **the housebound** les personnes *fpl* confinées chez elles

houseboy † /ˈhaʊsbɔɪ/ N (*= servant*) domestique *m* ; (*in former colonies*) boy *m*

housebreaker /ˈhaʊsbreɪkəʳ/ N (*= burglar*) cambrioleur *m*

housebreaking /ˈhaʊsbreɪkɪŋ/ N (*= burglary*) cambriolage *m*

housebroken /ˈhaʊsbrəʊkən/ ADJ (*US*) ⇒ **house-trained** ; → **house**

housecoat /ˈhaʊskəʊt/ N 1 (*= dress*) robe *f* d'intérieur 2 (*= dressing gown*) peignoir *m*

housedress /ˈhaʊsdres/ N ⇒ **housecoat 1**

housefather /ˈhaʊsfɑːðəʳ/ N responsable *m* (de groupe) (*dans une institution*)

housefly /ˈhaʊsflaɪ/ N mouche *f* (commune *or* domestique)

houseful /ˈhaʊsfʊl/ N ◆ **a ~ of people** une pleine maisonnée de gens ◆ **a ~ of dogs** une maison pleine de chiens

houseguest /ˈhaʊsgest/ N invité(e) *m(f)* ◆ **I've got ~s** j'ai des amis à la maison

household /ˈhaʊs,həʊld/ N (*= persons*) (gens *mpl* de la) maison *f*, ménage *m* (*also Admin, Econ*) ◆ **there were seven people in his ~** sa maison était composée de sept personnes ◆ **the whole ~ was there to greet him** tous les gens de la maison étaient là pour l'accueillir ◆ **give below details of your ~** indiquez ci-dessous les personnes qui résident chez vous ◆ **~s with more than three wage-earners** des ménages *or* des familles de plus de trois salariés ◆ **poor ~s** les ménages *mpl* pauvres ◆ **a male-only ~** un appartement (*or* une maison) où il n'y a que des hommes ◆ **Household** (*Brit*) maison *f* royale

COMP [*accounts, expenses, equipment*] de *or* du ménage

household ammonia N ammoniaque *f*

household arts NPL arts *mpl* ménagers

Household Cavalry N (*Brit*) Cavalerie *f* de la Garde Royale

household chores NPL travaux *mpl* ménagers

household gods NPL dieux *mpl* du foyer, pénates *mpl*

household goods NPL (*gen*) (*Comm*) appareils *mpl* ménagers ; (*Econ*) biens *mpl* d'équipement ménager ◆ **all her ~ goods** (*more generally*) ses meubles *mpl* et ses ustensiles *mpl* de ménage

household insurance N assurance *f* sur le contenu de l'habitation

household linen N linge *m* de maison

household name N ◆ **she is a ~ name** elle est connue partout ◆ **Kleeno is a ~ name** Kleeno est une marque très connue

household soap N savon *m* de Marseille

Household troops NPL (*Brit*) Garde *f* royale

household word N ◆ **it's a ~ word** c'est un mot que tout le monde connaît

householder /ˈhaʊs,həʊldəʳ/ N occupant(e) *m(f)* ; (*= owner*) propriétaire *mf* ; (*= lessee*) locataire *mf* ; (*= head of house*) chef *m* de famille

housekeeper /ˈhaʊskiːpəʳ/ N (*in sb else's house*) gouvernante *f* ; (*in institution*) économe *f*, intendante *f* ◆ **his wife is a good ~** sa femme est bonne ménagère *or* maîtresse de maison

housekeeping /ˈhaʊskiːpɪŋ/ N 1 (*= skill*) économie *f* domestique *or* ménagère ; (*= work*) ménage *m* ; (*= management*) gestion *f* ◆ **it's a question of good ~** (*at home*) il s'agit de tenir sa maison en ordre ; (*at work*) il s'agit d'être bon gestionnaire ◆ **they said the job cuts were just good ~** ils ont dit que les licenciements ne relevaient que de la bonne gestion des effectifs 2 (*esp Brit*) (*also* **housekeeping money**) argent *m* du ménage 3 (*Comput*) gestion *f* des disques

houselights /ˈhaʊslaɪts/ NPL (*Theat*) lumières *fpl or* éclairage *m* de la salle

housemaid /ˈhaʊsmeɪd/ N bonne *f* COMP **housemaid's knee** N inflammation *f* du genou

houseman /ˈhaʊsmən/ N (pl **-men**) (*Brit: in hospital*) ≃ interne *mf*

housemartin /ˈhaʊsmɑːtɪn/ N hirondelle *f* de fenêtre

housemaster /ˈhaʊsmɑːstəʳ/ N (*Brit Scol*) *professeur responsable d'un groupe d'internes*

housemate /ˈhaʊsmeɪt/ N ◆ **my ~** la personne avec qui je partage la maison ; (*both renting*) mon *or* ma colocataire

housemistress /ˈhaʊsmɪstrɪs/ N (*Brit Scol*) *professeur responsable d'un groupe d'internes*

housemother /ˈhaʊsmʌðəʳ/ N responsable *f* (de groupe) (*dans une institution*)

houseroom /ˈhaʊsrʊm/ N ◆ **I wouldn't give it ~** je n'en voudrais pas chez moi ◆ **I wouldn't give him ~** (*Brit fig*) je ne veux pas de lui

housetop /ˈhaʊstɒp/ N toit *m* ◆ **to shout** *or* **proclaim sth from the ~s** crier qch sur les toits

housewares /ˈhaʊswɛəz/ NPL (*esp US*) articles *mpl* ménagers

housewife /ˈhaʊs,waɪf/ N (pl **-wives** /waɪvz/) 1 ménagère *f* ; (*as opposed to career woman*) femme *f* au foyer ◆ **a born ~** une ménagère née, une femme au foyer type ◆ **a bored ~** une femme au foyer qui s'ennuie, une ménagère esseulée ◆ **housewives refuse to pay these prices** les ménagères refusent de payer ces prix ◆ **I'd rather be a ~** j'aimerais mieux être femme au foyer 2 /ˈhʌzɪf/ (*= sewing box*) trousse *f* de couture

housewifely /ˈhaʊs,waɪflɪ/ ADJ de ménagère

housewifery /ˈhaʊs,wɪfərɪ/ N tenue *f* du ménage

housewives /ˈhaʊs,waɪvz/ NPL of **housewife**

housework /ˈhaʊswɜːk/ N (*NonC*) ménage *m*, tâches *fpl* ménagères ◆ **to do the ~** faire le ménage

housing /ˈhaʊzɪŋ/ N 1 (*NonC*) logement *m* ◆ **affordable ~ is difficult to find** les logements à des prix abordables sont difficiles à trouver ◆ **there's a lot of new ~** il y a beaucoup de résidences *or* de constructions nouvelles ◆ **the ~ of workers proved difficult** le logement des ouvriers a posé un problème ◆ **Minister/Ministry of Housing** (*Brit*) ◆ **Secretary/Department of Housing and Urban Development** (*US*) ministre *m*/ministère *m* de l'Urbanisme et du Logement ; → **low**[1]

2 (*Tech: for mechanism etc*) boîtier *m* ; (*Archit, Constr*) encastrement *m*

COMP [*matters, problem, crisis*] de *or* du logement

housing association N (*Brit*) (*for providing housing*) *association à but non lucratif qui construit et rénove des logements pour les louer à des prix très raisonnables* ; (*for co-ownership*) association *f* de copropriétaires (*pour faciliter l'accession à la propriété privée*)

housing benefit N (*Admin*) allocation *f* logement

housing conditions NPL conditions *fpl* de logement

housing development N (*US*) ensemble *m* immobilier privé

housing estate N (*Brit*) (*= council-owned flats*) cité *f* ; (*= privately-owned houses*) lotissement *m*

housing list N (*Brit*) *liste d'attente pour obtenir un logement social*

housing project N (*US = place*) ≃ cité *f*

housing scheme N (*Scot*) ⇒ **housing estate**

housing shortage N pénurie *f or* manque *m* de logements ◆ **the current acute ~ shortage** la crise du logement actuelle

housing stock N parc *m* de logements

hove /həʊv/ VB pt, ptp of **heave**

hovel /ˈhɒvəl/ N taudis *m*, masure *f*

hover /ˈhɒvəʳ/ VI 1 [*bird, butterfly*] voltiger (*about* autour de ; *over* au-dessus de) ; [*bird of prey, helicopter, danger, threat*] planer (*above, over* au-dessus de) ; [*person*] (*also* **hover about, hover around**) rôder ; [*smile*] errer ; [*mist, fog*] flotter ◆ **a waiter ~ed over** *or* **round us** un garçon (de café) rôdait *or* tournait autour de nous ◆ **she was ~ing in the doorway** elle hésitait sur le pas de la porte ◆ **he was ~ing between life and death** il restait suspendu entre la vie et la mort ◆ **the exchange rate is ~ing around 140 yen to the dollar** le taux de change tourne autour de *or* avoisine les 140 yens pour un dollar 2 (*= waver*) hésiter (*between* entre)

hovercraft /ˈhɒvəkrɑːft/ N aéroglisseur *m*

hoverport /ˈhɒvəpɔːt/ N hoverport *m*

how /haʊ/ ADV 1 (*= in what way*) comment ◆ **~ did you come?** comment êtes-vous venu ? ◆ **tell me ~ you came** dites-moi comment vous êtes venu ◆ **to learn ~ to do sth** apprendre à faire qch ◆ **I know ~ to do it** je sais le faire ◆ **~ do you like your steak?** comment aimez-vous votre bifteck ? ◆ **~ did you like the steak?** comment avez-vous trouvé le bifteck ? ◆ **~ was the play?** comment avez-vous trouvé la pièce ? ◆ **~ is it that ...?** comment se fait-il que ... + *subj* ? ◆ **~ could you (do such a thing)?** comment as-tu pu faire une chose pareille ? ◆ **~ could you do/say that?** comment as-tu pu faire/dire une chose pareille ? ◆ **~ so?, ~ can that be?** comment cela (se fait-il) ? ◆ **~ come?*** comment ça se fait ?*, pourquoi ? ◆ **~ come you aren't going out?*** pourquoi tu ne sors pas ?* ◆ **and ~!*** et comment !*

◆ **how about ...** * ◆ **~** *or* **~'s*** **about going for a walk?** et si on allait se promener ? ◆ **~ about you?** et toi ? ◆ **~ about that?*** (*US*) ça alors !

◆ **how's that ?*** (*= how possible, in what way*) comment ça ? ; (*= what is your opinion*) qu'est-ce que tu en penses ? ; (*= agreed*) d'accord ?, ça va ? ◆ **~'s that (again)?** (*= please repeat*) vous pouvez répéter ? ◆ **~'s that for size/height?** ça va du point de vue de la taille/de la hauteur ? ◆ **~'s that for clean!** (*admiringly*) c'est ce que j'appelle propre ! ◆ **~'s that for luck?** quelle veine !* ◆ **~'s that for size/height?** ça va pour la taille/la hauteur ?

2 (*health etc*) ◆ **~ are you ?** comment allez-vous ? ◆ **tell me ~ she is** dites-moi comment elle va ◆ **~ do you do?** (*on being introduced*) enchanté ◆ **~ are things?** * comment ça va ? ◆ **~'s business?** comment vont les affaires ? ◆ **~'s life?** * comment ça va ?

3 (*with adj, adv: degree, quantity*) que, comme ◆ **~ glad I am to see you!** que *or* comme je suis content de vous voir ! ◆ **I can't tell you ~ glad I was to leave that place** vous ne pouvez pas savoir à quel point j'étais heureux de quitter cet endroit ◆ **~ splendid!** c'est merveilleux ! ◆ **~ nice!** comme c'est gentil ! ◆ **~ kind of you!** c'est très aimable à vous ! ◆ **~ very astute of you** (*or* **him** *etc*)! quelle finesse ! (*also iro*) ◆ **~ very clever of you!** ce que vous pouvez être intelligent ! ◆ **~ he has grown!** comme il a grandi !, ce qu'il a grandi !* ◆ **~ long is the tunnel?** quelle est la longueur du tunnel ? ◆ **~ long is this film?** combien de temps dure ce film ? ◆ **~ long will you be staying?** combien de temps resterez-vous ? ◆ **~ tall is he?** quelle est sa taille ?, combien mesure-t-il ? ◆ **~ old is he?** quel âge a-t-il ? ◆ **~ soon can you come?** quand pouvez-vous venir ? ◆ **~ much does this book cost?** combien coûte ce livre ?

4 (= that) que ◆ **she told me ~ she had seen the child lying on the ground** elle m'a raconté qu'elle avait vu l'enfant couché par terre

N ◆ **the ~ and the why of it** le comment et le pourquoi de cela

COMP **how-d'ye-do** †* N ◆ **here's a (fine) ~-d'ye-do !** en voilà une affaire !, en voilà une histoire ! * ◆ **it was a real ~-d'ye-do** c'était un joli gâchis ! *

how's-your-father * N (= sex) partie f de jambes en l'air *

how-to ADJ ◆ **a ~-to book on carpentry** un manuel de menuiserie ◆ **a ~-to video on carpentry** une vidéo d'initiation à la menuiserie

howdah /ˈhaʊdə/ N *siège sanglé sur le dos d'un éléphant*

howdy * /ˈhaʊdɪ/ EXCL (US) salut !

however /haʊˈevəʳ/ LANGUAGE IN USE 26.2, 26.3

ADV 1 (= nevertheless) cependant, toutefois ◆ **that is one reason. It is not, ~, the only one** c'est une raison. Ce n'est cependant pas la seule ◆ **losing doesn't seem to matter to women. Most men, ~, can't stand it** cela ne semble pas gêner les femmes de perdre. Par contre *or* en revanche, les hommes détestent cela, cela ne semble pas gêner les femmes de perdre alors que la plupart des hommes détestent cela ◆ **~, he remained unimpressed by my enthusiasm** pourtant, mon enthousiasme ne lui a fait ni chaud ni froid

2 (= no matter how) ◆ **~ tall he may be** *or* **is, ...** il a beau être grand, ..., malgré sa taille, ... ◆ **~ much money he has ...** il a beau être riche ..., même s'il a beaucoup d'argent ... ◆ **~ hard she tried, she couldn't remember my name** malgré tous ses efforts, elle n'arrivait pas à se souvenir de mon nom ◆ **~ great the temptation, don't do it** même si tu es très tenté, ne le fais pas ◆ **~ few people come, we'll do the play** même s'il n'y a pas beaucoup de monde, nous jouerons la pièce ◆ **~ many people there are** quel que soit le nombre de personnes (présentes) ◆ **six or seven people, or ~ many are present** six ou sept personnes, ou selon le nombre de présents

3 (= how on earth: in questions) comment donc ◆ **~ did you manage to do that?** comment donc as-tu réussi à le faire ?

CONJ de quelque manière que + *subj* ◆ **~ we tell her about this, she won't be pleased** de quelque manière que nous le lui disions, elle ne sera pas contente ◆ **~ you may do it, it will never be right** quoi que vous fassiez or de toute façon, ce ne sera jamais bien ◆ **~ that may be** quoi qu'il en soit

howitzer /ˈhaʊɪtsəʳ/ N obusier *m*

howl /haʊl/ N [*of person, animal*] hurlement *m* ; [*of baby*] braillement *m*, hurlement *m* ; [*of wind*] mugissement *m* ◆ **there were ~s of laughter at her remark** sa remarque a provoqué d'énormes éclats de rire VI 1 [*person, animal, wind*] hurler ◆ **to ~ with laughter** rire aux éclats *or* à gorge déployée ◆ **to ~ with delight** pousser des cris de joie ◆ **to ~ with pain/rage** hurler de douleur/de rage ◆ **to ~ with derision** lancer des huées 2 (* = cry) pleurer ; [*baby*] brailler * VT (also **howl out**) hurler, crier ◆ **they ~ed their disapproval** ils hurlaient leur désapprobation

► **howl down** VT SEP huer ◆ **the president was ~ed down by the crowd** le président a été hué par la foule

howler * /ˈhaʊləʳ/ N gaffe * *f*, bourde *f* ◆ **to make a ~** faire une gaffe * *or* une bourde ◆ **schoolboy ~** perle *f* (d'écolier)

howling /ˈhaʊlɪŋ/ N [*of person, animal*] hurlements *mpl* ; [*of wind*] mugissement *m* ADJ 1 [*person, animal, wind*] hurlant 2 (* = terrific) [*success*] monstre

howsoever /haʊsəʊˈevəʳ/ ADV 1 (frm = no matter how) ◆ **~ bad the situation may seem** quelque (*liter*) mauvaise que la situation puisse paraître 2 (†† *or dial* = nevertheless) néanmoins CONJ (frm) ◆ **~ that may be** quoi qu'il en soit

hoy /hɔɪ/ EXCL ohé !

hoyden † /ˈhɔɪdn/ N garçon *m* manqué

hoydenish † /ˈhɔɪdənɪʃ/ ADJ garçonnier, de garçon manqué

HP * /eɪtʃˈpiː/ N (Brit) (abbrev of **hire purchase**) → **hire**

hp /eɪtʃˈpiː/ N (abbrev of **horsepower**) CV

HQ /eɪtʃˈkjuː/ N (abbrev of **headquarters**) QG *m*

HR /eɪtʃˈɑːʳ/ N (abbrev of **human resources**) ressources *fpl* humaines

hr (abbrev of **hour**) h ◆ **28 ~s** 28 h

HRH /ˌeɪtʃɑːrˈeɪtʃ/ N (abbrev of **His** *or* **Her Royal Highness**) SAR

HRT /ˌeɪtʃɑːˈtiː/ N (abbrev of **hormone replacement therapy**) → **hormone**

HS N (US Scol) (abbrev of **high school**) → **high**

HST /ˌeɪtʃesˈtiː/ N 1 (Brit) (abbrev of **high speed train**) ≈ TGV *m* 2 (US) (abbrev of **Hawaiian Standard Time**) → **Hawaiian**

HT (abbrev of **high tension**) → **high**

ht N abbrev of **height**

HTML /ˌeɪtʃtiːemˈel/ (abbrev of **hypertext markup language**) HTML *m*

http /ˌeɪtʃtiːtiːˈpiː/ (Comput) (abbrev of **hypertext transfer protocol**) http

HUAC N (US Hist) (abbrev of **House Un-American Activities Committee**) → **house**

hub /hʌb/ N 1 [*of wheel*] moyeu *m* ; (*fig*) (= centre) centre *m* ; (= cornerstone) pierre *f* angulaire ◆ **a ~ of finance/activity/operations** un centre financier/d'activité/d'opérations *or* opérationnel ◆ **the island's social ~** le centre de la vie sociale de l'île 2 ◆ **~ (airport)** hub *m*, plate-forme *f* de correspondances COMP **hub airport** N (US) plaque *f* tournante du transport aérien

hubba-hubba * /ˈhʌbəˈhʌbə/ EXCL (US) vise un peu ! *

hubbub /ˈhʌbʌb/ N tohu-bohu *m*

hubby ‡ /ˈhʌbɪ/ N (abbrev of **husband**) mari *m*

hubcap /ˈhʌbkæp/ N enjoliveur *m*

hubris /ˈhjuːbrɪs/ N orgueil *m* (démesuré)

huckleberry /ˈhʌklbərɪ/ N (US) myrtille *f*

huckster /ˈhʌkstəʳ/ N (US) (= hawker) colporteur *m* ; (*fig pej*) mercanti *m* ; (* = salesman) vendeur *m* de choc * ; (*in fairground*) bonimenteur *m*

HUD /hʌd/ N (US) (abbrev of **Department of Housing and Urban Development**) → **housing**

huddle /ˈhʌdl/ N [*of people*] petit groupe *m* (compact) ◆ **a ~ of houses in the valley** quelques maisons blotties dans la vallée ◆ **to go into a ~** * se réunir en petit comité (*fig*)

VI 1 (*lit*) se blottir (les uns contre les autres) ◆ **we ~d round the fire** nous nous sommes blottis autour du feu ◆ **the baby birds ~d in the nest** les oisillons se blottissaient les uns contre les autres dans le nid ◆ **spectators huddling under umbrellas** des spectateurs s'abritant tant bien que mal sous leurs parapluies ; see also **huddled**

2 (US fig = meet and discuss) se réunir en petit comité (*fig*)

► **huddle down** VI (= crouch) se recroqueviller, se faire tout petit ; (= snuggle) se blottir, se pelotonner

► **huddle together** VI se serrer *or* se blottir les uns contre les autres ◆ **they were huddling together for warmth** ils se serraient *or* se blottissaient les uns contre les autres pour se tenir chaud ◆ **they ~d together to discuss the proposal** ils ont formé un petit groupe pour discuter de la proposition ; see also **huddled**

► **huddle up** VI se blottir, se pelotonner

huddled /ˈhʌdld/ ADJ ◆ **the chairs were ~ in a corner** les chaises étaient rassemblées *or* groupées dans un coin ◆ **small wooden sheds, ~ under tall pine trees** des petites cabanes groupées sous de hauts sapins ◆ **he lay ~ under the blankets** il était blotti *or* pelotonné sous les couvertures ◆ **the children lay ~ (together) under the blankets** les enfants étaient blottis *or* pelotonnés (les uns contre les autres) sous les couvertures ◆ **she sat ~ in the corner** elle était (assise,) blottie dans le coin ◆ **he was ~ over his books** il était penché sur ses livres

Hudson Bay /ˈhʌdsənˈbeɪ/ N la baie d'Hudson

hue[1] /hjuː/ N ◆ **~ and cry** clameur *f* ◆ **to raise a ~ and cry** crier haro (*against* sur)

hue[2] /hjuː/ N (= colour) teinte *f*, nuance *f*

-hued /hjuːd/ ADJ (*in compounds*) ◆ **many-hued** multicolore

huff[1] * /hʌf/ N ◆ **to be in a ~** être vexé ◆ **to go into a ~** prendre la mouche, se vexer ◆ **he went off** *or* **left in a ~** il s'est vexé et il est parti

huff[2] /hʌf/ VI (*lit*) ◆ **to ~ and puff** souffler comme un bœuf * ; (* = show annoyance) râler *

huffily * /ˈhʌfɪlɪ/ ADV avec (mauvaise) humeur

huffiness * /ˈhʌfɪnɪs/ N mauvaise humeur *f*

huffy * /ˈhʌfɪ/ ADJ (= annoyed) vexé ; (= sulky) boudeur, qui boude ; (= touchy) susceptible

hug /hʌg/ VT 1 (= hold close) serrer dans ses bras, étreindre ; [*bear, gorilla*] écraser entre ses bras ◆ **to ~ one another** s'étreindre ◆ **she stood ~ging herself as if she were cold** elle avait les bras serrés contre sa poitrine comme si elle avait froid ◆ **she ~ged her legs tight to her chest** elle a serré ses jambes contre sa poitrine ◆ **to ~ o.s. over sth** (*fig*) jubiler à l'idée de qch 2 (= keep close to) serrer ◆ **to ~ the shore/wind** [*boat*] serrer la côte/le vent ◆ **to ~ the kerb** [*car*] serrer le trottoir VI s'étreindre ◆ **we ~ged and kissed** nous nous sommes embrassés N étreinte *f* ◆ **to give sb a ~** serrer qn dans ses bras, étreindre qn ◆ **he gave the child a big ~** il a serré l'enfant bien fort dans ses bras ; → **bear**[2]

huge /hjuːdʒ/ ADJ [*person, object, profit, difference, amount, effort*] énorme ; [*success*] énorme, fou (folle *f*) ; [*eyes*] immense ; [*number, increase*] très fort ◆ **on a ~ scale** sur une très grande échelle

hugely /ˈhjuːdʒlɪ/ ADV [*popular, expensive, important, entertaining, enjoyable*] extrêmement ; [*enjoy o.s., vary, increase*] énormément ◆ **a ~ successful film** un film qui a eu un énorme succès *or* un succès fou ◆ **~ influential** très influent ◆ **~ talented** extrêmement doué

hugeness /ˈhjuːdʒnɪs/ N immensité *f*

hugger-mugger †* /ˈhʌgəˌmʌgəʳ/ ADV (= confusedly) pêle-mêle

Hugh /hjuː/ N Hugues *m*

Huguenot /ˈhjuːgənəʊ/ ADJ huguenot N huguenot(e) *m(f)*

huh /hʌ/ EXCL (dismay) oh ! ; (surprise, disbelief) hein ? ; (disgust) berk ! *, beuh !

Hula Hoop ® /ˈhuːləˌhuːp/ N hula-hoop *m*

hulk /hʌlk/ N 1 ◆ **(big) ~ of a man** mastodonte *m* ◆ **I followed his big ~ * into the kitchen** j'ai suivi ce géant dans la cuisine 2 (= prison ship) ponton *m* ; (= wrecked ship) épave *f* ; (= ramshackle ship) vieux rafiot * *m* ; (= wrecked vehicle, building) carcasse *f*

hulking /ˈhʌlkɪŋ/ ADJ massif, imposant ◆ **he was a ~ great brute** * c'était un gros malabar *

hull /hʌl/ N 1 *[of ship]* coque *f* ; *[of plane]* carlingue *f* ; *[of tank]* caisse *f* 2 *[of nuts]* coque *f* ; *[of peas, beans]* cosse *f*, gousse *f* VT 1 *[+ peas]* écosser ; *[+ barley]* monder ; *[+ oats, rice]* décortiquer ; *[+ nuts]* écaler ; *[+ berries]* équeuter 2 *[+ ship, plane]* percer la coque de

hullabaloo * /ˌhʌləbəˈluː/ N *(= noise)* raffut* *m* ◆ **they made** *or* **there was quite a ~ about the missing money** *(= fuss)* on a fait toute une histoire* *or* tout un foin* à propos de l'argent disparu ◆ **I don't know what all the ~ is about** *(= noise)* je ne sais pas d'où vient ce raffut* ; *(= fuss)* je ne comprends pas pourquoi on en fait toute une histoire

hullo /hʌˈləʊ/ EXCL *(esp Brit)* ⇒ **hello**

hum /hʌm/ VI 1 *[insect]* bourdonner ; *[person]* fredonner, chantonner ; *[aeroplane, engine, machine]* vrombir ; *[spinning top, radio]* ronfler ; *[wire]* bourdonner ◆ **then things began to ~** * *(fig)* alors les choses ont commencé à chauffer* *or* à s'animer ; → **haw²** 2 *(Brit* ⁑ *= stink)* chlinguer⁑ VT *[+ tune]* fredonner, chantonner N 1 *[of insect, conversation]* bourdonnement *m* ; *[of aeroplane, engine, machine]* vrombissement *m* ; *[of spinning top, radio]* ronflement *m* 2 *(Brit* ⁑ *= stink)* puanteur *f* EXCL hem !, hum !

human /ˈhjuːmən/ ADJ humain ◆ **he's only ~ after all** après tout, ce n'est qu'un homme ◆ **to lack the ~ touch** manquer de chaleur humaine ◆ **not fit for ~ consumption** impropre à la consommation ; → **decency**
N humain *m*
COMP **human being** N être *m* humain
human cloning N clonage *m* humain
human ecology N écologie *f* humaine
human engineering N ergonomie *f*
human genome N génome *m* humain
human growth hormone N *(Med)* hormone *f* de croissance humaine
human interest N dimension *f* humaine
human interest story N *(Press)* histoire *f* à dimension humaine
human nature N nature *f* humaine ◆ **it's only ~ nature to want revenge** c'est dans la nature humaine de chercher à se venger
human race N race *f* humaine, genre *m* humain
human resource management N gestion *f* des ressources humaines
human resources NPL ressources *fpl* humaines
human rights NPL droits *mpl* de l'homme
human rights campaigner N défenseur *m* des droits de l'homme
human shield N bouclier *m* humain

humane /hjuːˈmeɪn/ ADJ 1 *(= compassionate) [person]* plein d'humanité ; *[attitude]* humain, plein d'humanité ; *[treatment, decision, system]* humain ; *[society]* bienveillant 2 *(= painless)* ◆ **the ~ killing of cattle** l'abattage *m* sans cruauté du bétail
COMP **the Humane Society** N *(in US) société protectrice des animaux,* ≈ SPA *f*
humane studies NPL *études de lettres*

humanely /hjuːˈmeɪnlɪ/ ADV *(= compassionately) [treat]* avec humanité, humainement ; *(= painlessly) [kill, slaughter, rear]* sans cruauté

humaneness /hjuːˈmeɪnnɪs/ N humanité *f*

humanism /ˈhjuːmənɪzəm/ N humanisme *m*

humanist /ˈhjuːmənɪst/ N, ADJ humaniste *mf*

humanistic /ˌhjuːməˈnɪstɪk/ ADJ humaniste

humanitarian /hjuːˌmænɪˈteərɪən/ ADJ, N humanitaire *mf*

humanitarianism /hjuːˌmænɪˈteərɪənɪzəm/ N humanitarisme *m*

humanity /hjuːˈmænɪtɪ/ N humanité *f* NPL **the humanities** les humanités *fpl*, les lettres *fpl*

humanization /ˌhjuːmənaɪˈzeɪʃən/ N humanisation *f*

humanize /ˈhjuːmənaɪz/ VT humaniser

humankind /ˌhjuːmənˈkaɪnd/ N l'humanité *f*, le genre humain

humanly /ˈhjuːmənlɪ/ ADV ◆ **if it is ~ possible** si c'est humainement possible ◆ **we will do all that is ~ possible** nous ferons tout ce qui est humainement possible ◆ **in as quick a time as is ~ possible** aussi vite qu'il est humainement possible de le faire

humanoid /ˈhjuːmənɔɪd/ ADJ, N humanoïde *mf*

humble /ˈhʌmbl/ ADJ 1 *(= lowly) [person, beginnings, home, job]* humble ◆ **of ~ origins** *or* **birth** *(liter)* d'humble naissance ◆ **the ~ potato/earthworm** l'humble pomme de terre/ver de terre ◆ **in my ~ opinion** à mon humble avis ◆ **my ~ abode** *(hum)* mon humble demeure *(hum)* ◆ **I am** *or* **remain, Sir, your ~ servant** † *(in letters)* je suis, Monsieur, votre humble serviteur † ◆ **your ~ servant** *(= oneself)* votre serviteur *(hum)* ◆ **to eat ~ pie** faire amende honorable
2 *(= unassuming) [person]* modeste *(about sth* à propos de qch) ; *[restaurant]* sans prétention
3 ◆ **it makes me (feel) very ~** ça me donne un sentiment de grande humilité
VT *(= humiliate)* rabaisser ; *(Sport)* humilier ◆ **Ted's words ~d me** les paroles de Ted ont été une leçon d'humilité pour moi ◆ **to ~ o.s.** se rabaisser ◆ **I felt ~d** j'ai eu honte de moi ◆ **millions of viewers were ~d by their story** ça a été une leçon d'humilité pour des millions de téléspectateurs ◆ **United were ~d 3-0 at Liverpool** United a été honteusement battu 3 à 0 par Liverpool

humblebee /ˈhʌmblbiː/ N bourdon *m*

humbleness /ˈhʌmblnɪs/ N humilité *f*

humbly /ˈhʌmblɪ/ ADV *[say, beseech, thank, beg sb's pardon]* humblement ; *[suggest]* en toute humilité

humbug /ˈhʌmbʌg/ N 1 *(= person)* charlatan *m* ; *(= talk)* sornettes *fpl* 2 *(Brit = sweet)* bonbon *m* à la menthe EXCL n'importe quoi !

humdinger †⁑ /ˈhʌmdɪŋəʳ/ N ◆ **he's/she's a real ~ !** il/elle est vraiment super !* ◆ **it's a ~!** c'est super* ! ◆ **it's going to be a ~ of a match** ça va être un super* match ◆ **a ~ of a hangover** une épouvantable gueule de bois*

humdrum /ˈhʌmˌdrʌm/ ADJ monotone, banal N monotonie *f*, banalité *f*

humerus /ˈhjuːmərəs/ N (pl **humeri** /ˈhjuːməˌraɪ/) humérus *m*

humid /ˈhjuːmɪd/ ADJ *[climate]* humide et chaud ◆ **it's ~ today** il fait lourd aujourd'hui

humidifier /hjuːˈmɪdɪfaɪəʳ/ N humidificateur *m*

humidify /hjuːˈmɪdɪfaɪ/ VT *[+ room, air]* humidifier

humidity /hjuːˈmɪdɪtɪ/ N humidité *f*

humidor /ˈhjuːmɪdɔːʳ/ N boîte *f* à cigares

humiliate /hjuːˈmɪlɪeɪt/ VT humilier

humiliating /hjuːˈmɪlɪeɪtɪŋ/ ADJ humiliant

humiliatingly /hjuːˈmɪlɪeɪtɪŋlɪ/ ADV d'une manière humiliante, honteusement ◆ **~, he broke down in tears** à sa grande honte, il éclata en sanglots

humiliation /hjuːˌmɪlɪˈeɪʃən/ N humiliation *f*

humility /hjuːˈmɪlɪtɪ/ N humilité *f*

humming /ˈhʌmɪŋ/ N *[of insect, voices]* bourdonnement *m* ; *[of aeroplane, engine, machine]* vrombissement *m* ; *[of person]* fredonnement *m*
COMP **humming-top** N toupie *f* ronflante

hummingbird /ˈhʌmɪŋbɜːd/ N oiseau-mouche *m*, colibri *m*

hummock /ˈhʌmək/ N *(= hillock)* tertre *m*, monticule *m* ; *(in ice field)* hummock *m*

hummus /ˈhʊməs/ N houm(m)ous *m*

humongous ⁑ /hjuˈmɒŋgəs/ ADJ énorme, monstre* ◆ **a ~ row** une mégadispute*, une dispute monstre* ◆ **a ~ box office hit** un mégasuccès* *or* un succès monstre* au box-office ◆ **Streisand is such a ~ star** Streisand est vraiment une superstar

humor /ˈhjuːməʳ/ N, VT *(US)* ⇒ **humour**

-humored /ˈhjuːməd/ ADJ *(US) (in compounds)* ⇒ **-humoured**

humorist /ˈhjuːmərɪst/ N humoriste *mf*

humorless(ly) /ˈhjuːməlɪs(lɪ)/ ADJ, ADV *(US)* → **humourless(ly)**

humorous /ˈhjuːmərəs/ ADJ 1 *(= amusing) [book, comment, writer]* humoristique 2 *(= amused) [expression]* amusé

humorously /ˈhjuːmərəslɪ/ ADV avec humour

humour, humor *(US)* /ˈhjuːməʳ/ N 1 *(= sense of fun)* humour *m* ◆ **I see no ~ in it** je ne vois pas où est l'humour ◆ **this is no time for ~** ce n'est pas le moment de faire de l'humour ◆ **the ~ of the situation** le comique de la situation ◆ **their own inimitable brand of ~** leur humour inimitable 2 *(= temper)* humeur *f* ◆ **to be in (a) good/bad ~** être de bonne/mauvaise humeur ◆ **to be out of ~** être de mauvaise humeur 3 *(Med Hist)* humeur *f* VT *[+ person]* faire plaisir à ; *[+ sb's wishes, whims]* se prêter à, se plier à ◆ **just ~ him!** fais-lui plaisir !

-humoured, -humored *(US)* /ˈhjuːməd/ ADJ *(in compounds)* ◆ **bad-humoured** de mauvaise humeur ; → **good**

humourless, humorless *(US)* /ˈhjuːməlɪs/ ADJ *[person]* qui manque d'humour, qui n'a pas le sens de l'humour ; *[laugh, style]* sans humour

humourlessly, humorlessly *(US)* /ˈhjuːməlɪslɪ/ ADV sans humour

hump /hʌmp/ N 1 *[of person, camel]* bosse *f* 2 *(= hillock)* bosse *f*, mamelon *m* ◆ **we're over the ~ now** * *(fig)* le plus difficile est passé *or* fait maintenant 3 *(Brit)* ◆ **to have** *or* **get the ~** * faire la gueule* VT 1 *(Brit* * *= carry)* porter, trimballer* 2 *(*⁑ *= have sex with)* baiser⁑, sauter⁑ VI *(*⁑ *= have sex)* baiser⁑

humpback /ˈhʌmpbæk/ N 1 *(= person)* bossu(e) *m(f)* ◆ **to have a ~** être bossu 2 (also **humpback whale**) baleine *f* à bosse

humpbacked /ˈhʌmpbækt/ ADJ 1 *[person]* bossu 2 *(Brit) [bridge]* en dos d'âne

humph /hʌmf/ EXCL hum !

humpy /ˈhʌmpɪ/ ADJ *[ground]* inégal, accidenté

humungous ⁑ /hjuˈmʌŋgəs/ ADJ ⇒ **humongous**

humus /ˈhjuːməs/ N humus *m*

Hun /hʌn/ N 1 *(Hist)* Hun *m* 2 *(*⁑ *pej)* Boche⁑ *m (pej)*

hunch /hʌntʃ/ VT ◆ **to ~ one's back** arrondir le dos ◆ **to ~ one's shoulders** se voûter ◆ **~ed shoulders** épaules *fpl* voûtées ◆ **with ~ed shoulders** la tête rentrée dans les épaules ; → **hunched** N 1 *(* = premonition)* pressentiment *m*, intuition *f* ◆ **to have a ~ that ...** avoir (comme une petite) idée que* ... ◆ **it's only a ~** ce n'est qu'une impression ◆ **your ~ paid off** vous avez bien fait de vous fier à votre intuition ◆ **his ~ proved right** son intuition était juste ◆ **to act on a ~, to play a ~** *(esp US)* suivre son intuition 2 *(= hump)* bosse *f* 3 ⇒ **hunk**

hunchback /ˈhʌntʃbæk/ N bossu(e) *m(f)*

hunchbacked /ˈhʌntʃbækt/ ADJ bossu

hunched /ˈhʌntʃt/ ADJ recroquevillé ◆ **she sat ~ over her typewriter** elle était penchée sur sa machine à écrire ◆ **he sat ~ (up) over his books** il était assis courbé *or* penché sur ses livres ◆ **he was ~ forward in his chair** il était penché en avant sur sa chaise ; → **hunch**

hundred /ˈhʌndrəd/ ADJ cent ◆ **a ~ books/chairs** cent livres/chaises ◆ **two ~ chairs** deux cents chaises ◆ **about a ~ books** une centaine de livres

N 1 cent *m* ◆ **about a ~, a ~-odd*** une centaine ◆ **I've got a ~** j'en ai cent ◆ **a** *or* **one ~ and one** cent un ◆ **two ~** deux cents ◆ **two ~ and one** deux cent un ◆ **the ~ and first** le *or* la cent unième ◆ **a ~ per cent** cent pour cent ◆ **it was a ~ per cent successful** cela a réussi à cent pour cent ◆ **in seventeen ~** en dix-sept cents ◆ **in seventeen ~ and ninety-six** en dix-sept cent quatre-vingt-seize ◆ **sold by the ~** *(Comm)* vendus par (lots de) cent ◆ **to live to be a ~** devenir centenaire ◆ **they came in (their) ~s** ils sont venus par centaines ; *for other phrases see* **sixty**

2 *(* fig)* **~s of** des centaines de, des tas* de ◆ **I've told you ~s of times!** je te l'ai dit mille fois !

COMP **the Hundred Days** NPL *(Hist)* les Cent Jours *mpl*

hundreds and thousands NPL *(Brit)* vermicelles *mpl* en sucre

hundred-year-old ADJ centenaire, séculaire *(liter)*

the Hundred Years' War N *(Hist)* la guerre de Cent Ans

hundredfold /ˈhʌndrədfəʊld/ ADJ centuple ADV au centuple

hundredth /ˈhʌndrɪdθ/ ADJ centième N *(= person, thing)* centième *mf* ; *(= fraction)* centième *m*

hundredweight /ˈhʌndrədweɪt/ N *(Brit, Can)* (poids *m* de) cent douze livres *fpl (50,7 kg)* ; *(US)* (poids *m* de) cent livres *fpl (45,3 kg)*

hung /hʌŋ/ VB pret, ptp of **hang** ADJ ◆ **to be ~ like a horse** *or* **a donkey** ‡ être bien monté‡

COMP **hung jury** N jury *m* sans majorité, jury *m* qui ne parvient pas à une décision

hung over* ADJ ◆ **to be ~ over** avoir la gueule de bois*

hung parliament N parlement *m* sans majorité, parlement *m* où aucun parti n'a la majorité

hung up* ADJ *(= tense)* complexé, inhibé ◆ **he's ~ up about it** il en fait tout un complexe* ◆ **to be ~ up on sb/sth** *(= obsessed)* être fou (folle *f*) de qn/qch

Hungarian /hʌŋˈgeərɪən/ ADJ *(gen)* hongrois ; *[ambassador, embassy]* de Hongrie ; *[teacher]* de hongrois N 1 Hongrois(e) *m(f)* 2 *(= language)* hongrois *m*

Hungary /ˈhʌŋgəri/ N Hongrie *f*

hunger /ˈhʌŋgəʳ/ N faim *f* ; *(fig)* faim *f*, soif *f* *(for* de) ◆ **~ to do sth** désir *m* ardent de faire qch VI *(liter)* avoir faim ◆ **to ~ for** *or* **after sth** *(fig)* avoir faim *or* soif de qch *(fig)* ◆ **to ~ to do sth** *(fig)* désirer ardemment faire qch

COMP **the hunger marches** NPL *(Brit Hist)* les marches *fpl* de la faim

hunger strike N grève *f* de la faim ◆ **to go on (a) ~ strike** faire la grève de la faim

hunger striker N gréviste *mf* de la faim

hungrily /ˈhʌŋgrɪli/ ADV *[eat, kiss, smoke]* goulûment ; *[look, listen, wait]* avidement

hungry /ˈhʌŋgri/ ADJ 1 *(for food) [person, animal]* affamé ◆ **to be** *or* **feel ~** avoir faim ◆ **I'm so ~** j'ai tellement faim ◆ **to be very ~** avoir très faim, être affamé ◆ **you look ~** tu as l'air d'avoir faim ◆ **to make sb ~** donner faim à qn ◆ **to go ~** *(= starve)* être affamé, manquer de nourriture ; *(= miss a meal)* sauter un repas ◆ **when he was a child he often went ~** quand il était enfant, il ne mangeait pas toujours à sa faim ◆ **digging the garden is ~ work** ça donne faim de bêcher 2 *(= eager)* ◆ **they were ~ for news** ils attendaient avidement des nouvelles ◆ **the child is ~ for love** cet enfant a besoin d'amour ◆ **~ for success** *[executive]* avide de réussir ; *[artist, writer]* avide de succès

hunk /hʌŋk/ N 1 *[of bread, cheese]* (gros) morceau *m* 2 *(* = attractive man)* beau mec* *m*

hunker /ˈhʌŋkəʳ/ VI ◆ **to ~ down** s'accroupir

hunkers /ˈhʌŋkəz/ NPL fesses *fpl* ◆ **on one's ~** accroupi

hunky* /ˈhʌŋki/ ADJ *[man]* bien foutu* COMP **hunky-dory*** ADJ au poil* ◆ **everything's ~-dory** tout marche comme sur des roulettes*

hunt /hʌnt/ N 1 *(gen)* recherche *f*

2 *(Sport) (= event)* chasse *f* ◆ **elephant/tiger ~** chasse *f* à l'éléphant/au tigre ◆ **the ~ was held on the Duke's land** la partie de chasse a eu lieu sur les terres du duc ◆ **the ~ rode by** *(= hunters)* les chasseurs sont passés à cheval ◆ **the Beaufort ~** l'équipage *m* Beaufort ◆ **the ~ for the missing child** la battue pour retrouver l'enfant disparu ◆ **the ~ for the murderer** la chasse au meurtrier ◆ **her ~ for a husband** sa chasse au mari ◆ **I've had a ~ for my gloves** j'ai cherché mes gants partout ◆ **to be on the ~ for a cheap house** chercher une *or* être à la recherche d'une maison bon marché ◆ **the ~ is on for ...** *(fig)* on cherche ...

VT 1 *(= seek)* chercher ; *(= pursue)* poursuivre, pourchasser

2 *(Sport) [+ fox etc]* chasser, faire la chasse à ◆ **to ~ a horse** monter un cheval à la chasse ◆ **astronomers ~ the sky for black holes** les astronomes cherchent des trous noirs dans le ciel ◆ **I've ~ed my desk for it** j'ai retourné tout mon bureau pour le trouver

VI *(Sport)* chasser ◆ **to go ~ing** aller à la chasse ◆ **to ~ for** *(Sport)* faire la chasse à, chasser ; *(gen) [+ object, details, facts, missing person]* chercher (partout), être à la recherche de ◆ **he is ~ing for a job** il est à la recherche d'un travail ◆ **he ~ed in his pocket for his pen** il a fouillé dans sa poche pour trouver son stylo ◆ **we ~ed around for cardboard and glue** nous avons cherché partout du carton et de la colle ◆ **~ around until you find what you need** fouillez jusqu'à ce que vous trouviez ce dont vous avez besoin

COMP **hunt sabbing*** N *(Brit)* sabotage *m* des chasses à courre

hunt saboteur, hunt sab* N *(Brit) militant qui participe à des actions directes contre les chasses à courre*

► **hunt down** VT SEP *[+ animal]* pourchasser ; *[+ person]* traquer, pourchasser ; *[+ object, facts, details, quotation]* dénicher

► **hunt out** VT SEP dénicher, découvrir

hunter /ˈhʌntəʳ/ N 1 *(= person) (Sport)* chasseur *m* ; *(gen)* poursuivant *m* ; → **lion** 2 *(= horse)* cheval *m* de chasse 3 *(= watch)* (montre *f* à) savonnette *f*

COMP **hunter-gatherer** N chasseur-cueilleur *m* ◆ **they were ~-gatherers** ils vivaient de chasse et de cueillette

hunter-killer submarine N sous-marin *m* nucléaire d'attaque

hunting /ˈhʌntɪŋ/ N 1 *(Sport)* chasse *f* ; *(with dogs)* chasse *f* à courre ; *(also* **fox hunting***)* chasse *f* au renard 2 *(gen = search)* chasse *f (for* à) recherche *f (for* de) → **bargain, house**

COMP **hunting ground** N *(lit, fig)* (terrain *m* de) chasse *f* ; → **happy**

hunting horn N cor *m* or trompe *f* de chasse

hunting lodge N pavillon *m* de chasse

hunting pink N rouge *m* chasseur *inv*

hunting season N saison *f* de chasse

Huntington's chorea /ˌhʌntɪŋtənzkɒˈrɪə/ N chorée *f* de Huntington

huntress /ˈhʌntrɪs/ N *(liter)* chasseresse *f*

huntsman /ˈhʌntsmən/ N (pl **-men**) chasseur *m*

hurdle /ˈhɜːdl/ N *(for fences)* claie *f* ; *(Sport)* haie *f* ; *(fig)* obstacle *m* ◆ **the 100-metre ~s** *(Sport)* le 100 mètres haies ◆ **to take a ~** *(Sport)* franchir une haie ; *(fig)* franchir un obstacle ◆ **to fall at the first ~** *(fig)* échouer au premier obstacle VI *(Sport)* faire de la course de haies

COMP **hurdle champion** N champion(ne) *m(f)* de course de haies

hurdle race N course *f* de haies

hurdles champion N ⇒ **hurdle champion**

hurdles race N ⇒ **hurdle race**

hurdler /ˈhɜːdləʳ/ N *(Sport)* coureur *m*, -euse *f* de haies

hurdling /ˈhɜːdəlɪŋ/ N *(NonC)* course *f* de haies

hurdy-gurdy /ˈhɜːdɪˈgɜːdɪ/ N orgue *m* de Barbarie

hurl /hɜːl/ VT *[+ object, stone]* jeter *or* lancer (avec violence) *(at* contre) ◆ **they were ~ed to the ground by the blast** ils ont été précipités à terre par le souffle de l'explosion ◆ **to ~ o.s. at sb/sth** se ruer sur qn/qch ◆ **they ~ed themselves into the fray** ils se sont jetés dans la mêlée ◆ **he ~ed himself from a 10th floor window** il s'est jeté *or* précipité d'une fenêtre au 10e étage ◆ **they ~ed themselves into the debate** ils se sont jetés à corps perdu dans le débat ◆ **her question ~ed us headlong into a moral quandary** sa question nous a plongés dans un dilemme moral ◆ **to ~ abuse at sb** lancer des injures à qn, accabler *or* agonir qn d'injures

hurley /ˈhɜːlɪ/, **hurling** /ˈhɜːlɪŋ/ N *sport irlandais ressemblant au hockey sur gazon*

hurly-burly /ˈhɜːlɪˈbɜːlɪ/ N *(= commotion)* tohu-bohu *m* ; *(= uproar)* tumulte *m* ◆ **the ~ of politics** le tourbillon de la politique ◆ **the ~ of election campaigning** le tourbillon de la campagne électorale

Huron /ˈhjʊərən/ N ◆ **Lake ~** le lac Huron

hurrah /hʊˈrɑː/, **hurray** /hʊˈreɪ/ N hourra *m* ◆ **~ for Robert!** vive Robert ! ◆ **last ~** *(US) (= last appearance)* dernier tour *m* de piste ; *(= last attempt)* dernière tentative *f* ; *(Pol)* dernière campagne *f* ; → **hip³**

hurricane /ˈhʌrɪkən/ N ouragan *m*

COMP **hurricane-force** ADJ *[wind]* de force 12

hurricane lamp N lampe-tempête *f*

hurried /ˈhʌrɪd/ ADJ *[steps]* précipité, pressé ; *[remark]* dit à la hâte ; *[departure]* précipité ; *[decision]* pris à la hâte ; *[reading, visit, meeting]* très rapide ; *[work]* fait à la hâte, fait à la va-vite* *(pej)* ◆ **a ~ breakfast** un petit déjeuner pris à la hâte ◆ **a ~ goodbye** des adieux précipités ◆ **to pay sb a ~ visit** passer voir qn en coup de vent

hurriedly /ˈhʌrɪdlɪ/ ADV *(= quickly)* en hâte ; *(faster than one would wish)* à la hâte

hurry /ˈhʌrɪ/ N *(= haste)* hâte *f*, précipitation *f* ; *(= eagerness)* empressement *m* ◆ **what's the** *or* **your ~?*** qu'est-ce qui (vous) presse ? ◆ **there's no (great) ~** rien ne presse, il n'y a pas le feu* ◆ **there's no ~ for it** ça ne presse pas

◆ **in a hurry** ◆ **to be in a ~** être pressé ◆ **to be in a ~ to do sth** avoir hâte de faire qch ◆ **it was done in a ~** cela a été fait à la hâte ◆ **he left in a ~** il est parti précipitamment ◆ **I won't do that again in a ~!*** je ne suis pas près de recommencer ! ◆ **he won't come back here in a ~!*** il ne reviendra pas de sitôt !, il n'est pas près de revenir ! ◆ **are you in a ~ for this?** vous en avez un besoin urgent ?, vous en avez besoin tout de suite ?

◆ **in no hurry** ◆ **I'm in no particular ~** je ne suis pas particulièrement pressé ◆ **I'm in no ~ to do that again!*** je ne recommencerai pas de sitôt !, je ne suis pas près de recommencer !

VI 1 se dépêcher, se presser *(to do sth* de faire qch) ◆ **do ~!** dépêchez-vous ! ◆ **don't ~** ne vous pressez *or* dépêchez pas ◆ **I must ~** il faut que je me dépêche *subj or* presse *subj*

2 ◆ **to ~ in/out/through** entrer/sortir/traverser en hâte ◆ **she hurried (over) to her sister's** elle s'est précipitée chez sa sœur ◆ **he hurried after her** il a couru pour la rattraper ◆ **they hurried up the stairs** ils ont monté

l'escalier quatre à quatre ◆ **she hurried home** elle s'est dépêchée de rentrer, elle est rentrée en hâte

VT 1 *[+ person]* bousculer, faire se dépêcher ; *[+ piece of work]* presser ◆ **don't ~ your meal** *(= don't feel you have to rush)* ne vous pressez pas (de manger) ; *(= don't eat too quickly)* ne mangez pas trop vite ◆ **I don't want to ~ you** je ne veux pas vous bousculer ◆ **you can't ~ him, he won't be hurried** vous ne le ferez pas se dépêcher ◆ **this job can't be hurried** ce travail prend du temps ◆ **I won't be hurried into a decision** je refuse de prendre une décision précipitée ; see also **hurried**

2 ◆ **to ~ sb in/out/through** faire entrer/sortir/traverser qn à la hâte *or* en (toute) hâte ◆ **they hurried him to a doctor** ils l'ont emmené d'urgence chez un médecin ◆ **the legislation was hurried through parliament** ils ont fait adopter la loi à toute vitesse par le parlement

COMP **hurry-scurry** VI courir dans tous les sens N bousculade *f*, débandade *f* ADV à la débandade

► **hurry along** VI marcher d'un pas pressé ◆ **~ along please!** pressons un peu, s'il vous plaît !
VT SEP ⇒ **hurry on vt sep**

► **hurry back** VI se presser de revenir (*or* de retourner) ◆ **~ back!** *(to guest)* revenez-nous bientôt ! ◆ **don't ~ back: I'll be here till 6 o'clock** ne te presse pas de revenir, je serai ici jusqu'à 6 heures

► **hurry on** VI ◆ **she hurried on to the next stop** elle s'est pressée de gagner l'arrêt suivant ◆ **they hurried on to the next question** ils sont vite passés à la question suivante ◆ **she hurried on ahead** elle est partie devant, elle est partie en éclaireur
VT SEP *[+ person]* faire se dépêcher ; *[+ work]* activer, accélérer ◆ **we're trying to ~ things on a little** nous essayons d'accélérer *or* d'activer un peu les choses

► **hurry up** VI se dépêcher, se presser ◆ **~ up!** dépêchez-vous ! ◆ **~ up and take your bath** dépêche-toi de prendre ton bain ◆ **~ up with that coffee** *(bringing it)* dépêche-toi d'apporter ce café ; *(drinking it)* dépêche-toi de boire ton café
VT SEP *[+ person]* faire se dépêcher ; *[+ work]* activer, pousser

hurt /hɜːt/ (pret, ptp **hurt**) VT 1 *(= do physical damage to) [+ person]* faire du mal à ◆ **to ~ o.s.** se blesser, se faire mal ◆ **to ~ one's arm** se faire mal au bras ◆ **I hope I haven't ~ you?** j'espère que je ne vous ai pas fait de mal *or* pas blessé ? ◆ **to get ~** se blesser, se faire mal ◆ **someone is bound to get ~** il va y avoir quelqu'un de blessé, quelqu'un va se faire du mal ◆ **a little rest won't ~ him** un peu de repos ne lui fera pas de mal ◆ **a glass of wine never ~ anyone** un verre de vin n'a jamais fait de mal à personne ◆ **it wouldn't ~ you to be a bit more serious** ça ne te ferait pas de mal d'être un peu plus sérieux ; → **fly¹**

2 *(= cause physical pain to) [+ person]* faire mal à ◆ **to ~ o.s., to get ~** se faire mal

3 *(emotionally)* faire de la peine à ◆ **someone is bound to get ~** il y a toujours quelqu'un qui pâtit *or* qui écope* ◆ **what ~ most was ...** ce qui faisait le plus mal c'était ... ◆ **to ~ sb's feelings** blesser qn

4 *(= damage) [+ thing]* abîmer, endommager ; *[+ sb's reputation, career]* nuire à ◆ **an embargo would ~ the economy** un embargo serait mauvais pour *or* aurait un effet néfaste sur l'économie

VI 1 faire mal ◆ **that ~s** ça fait mal ◆ **my arm ~s** mon bras me fait mal ◆ **it doesn't ~ much** ça ne fait pas très mal ◆ **where does it ~?** où avez-vous mal ? ◆ **nothing ~s like the truth** il n'y a que la vérité qui blesse ◆ **it won't ~ for being left for a while** * il n'y aura pas de mal à laisser cela de côté un instant

2 *(= suffer emotionally)* souffrir

N douleur *f* ◆ **to cause (great) ~ to sb** blesser qn (profondément) ◆ **the real ~ lay in his attitude to her** ce qui la blessait vraiment *or* lui faisait vraiment mal c'était l'attitude qu'il avait envers elle ◆ **feelings of ~ and anger** la peine et la colère

ADJ *(lit, fig)* blessé ◆ **she's feeling ~ about it** ça l'a blessée, elle est blessée

hurtful /ˈhɜːtfʊl/ ADJ nocif, nuisible *(to* à) ; *[remark]* blessant ◆ **what a ~ thing (for you) to say!** c'est vraiment blessant ce que tu as dit !

hurtfully /ˈhɜːtfəlɪ/ ADV d'une manière blessante

hurtle /ˈhɜːtl/ VI ◆ **to ~ along** *[car, person]* avancer à toute vitesse *or* allure ◆ **to ~ past sb** passer en trombe devant qn ◆ **the stone ~d through the air** la pierre a fendu l'air ◆ **she went hurtling down the hill** elle a dévalé la pente VT lancer (de toutes ses forces *or* violemment)

husband /ˈhʌzbənd/ N mari *m* ; *(Admin, Jur)* époux *m* ◆ **now they're ~ and wife** ils sont maintenant mari et femme ◆ **the ~ and wife** les conjoints *mpl*, les époux *mpl* ◆ **they were living together as ~ and wife** *(gen)* ils vivaient maritalement ; *(Jur, Admin)* ils vivaient en concubinage VT *(frm) [+ strength]* ménager, économiser ; *[+ supplies, resources]* bien gérer

husbandry /ˈhʌzbəndrɪ/ N *(Agr)* agriculture *f* ; *(fig)* économie *f*, gestion *f* ◆ **good ~** bonne gestion *f* ; → **animal**

hush /hʌʃ/ N silence *m* ◆ **there was a sudden ~, a ~ fell** il y a eu un silence, tout à coup tout le monde s'est tu ◆ **an expectant ~ fell over the crowd** les spectateurs ont retenu leur souffle ◆ **in the ~ of the night** *(liter)* dans le silence de la nuit ◆ **a deathly ~** un silence de mort ; see also **hushed** EXCL chut ! VT *(= silence)* faire taire ; *(= soothe)* apaiser, calmer ◆ **~ your chatter/complaining!** * arrêtez un peu de bavarder/de vous plaindre ! VI se taire

COMP **hush-hush** * ADJ (ultra-)secret (-ète *f*)
hush money * N pot-de-vin *m (pour acheter le silence)*, prix *m* du silence ◆ **to pay sb ~ money** acheter le silence de qn
hush puppy N *(US Culin)* espèce de beignet

► **hush up** VT SEP *[+ scandal, news]* étouffer ; *[+ fact]* cacher ; *[+ person]* faire taire, empêcher de parler

hushed /hʌʃt/ ADJ *[voice, conversation]* étouffé ◆ **there was a ~ silence** *(of embarrassment)* un ange est passé ; *(of expectation)* tout le monde a retenu son souffle ◆ **in ~ amazement they ...** frappés de stupeur, ils ... ◆ **we discussed the situation in ~ whispers** nous avons discuté de la situation à voix basse

husk /hʌsk/ N *[of wheat]* balle *f* ; *[of maize, rice]* enveloppe *f* ; *[of chestnut]* bogue *f* ; *[of nut]* écale *f* ; *[of peas]* cosse *f*, gousse *f* ◆ **rice in the ~** riz *m* non décortiqué VT *[+ maize, rice]* décortiquer ; *[+ nut]* écaler ; *[+ grain]* vanner ; *[+ peas]* écosser ; *[+ barley, oats]* monder

huskily /ˈhʌskɪlɪ/ ADV d'une voix rauque *or* voilée

huskiness /ˈhʌskɪnɪs/ N enrouement *m*

husky¹ /ˈhʌskɪ/ ADJ 1 *(= hoarse) [person]* enroué ; *[voice]* rauque, voilé 2 *(= burly)* costaud*

husky² /ˈhʌskɪ/ N *(= dog)* husky *m*

hussar /hʊˈzɑːʳ/ N hussard *m*

hussy /ˈhʌsɪ/ N *(pej)* dévergondée *f*

hustings /ˈhʌstɪŋz/ NPL *(esp Brit)* plateforme *f* électorale ◆ **he said it on the ~** il l'a dit pendant *or* au cours de sa campagne électorale ◆ **candidates are battling it out at the ~** les élections mettent aux prises les candidats

hustle /ˈhʌsl/ VT 1 *[+ person]* pousser, bousculer ◆ **to ~ sb in/out/away** faire entrer/sortir/partir qn ◆ **they ~d him into a car** ils l'ont poussé dans une voiture ◆ **I won't be ~d into anything** je ne ferai rien si on me bouscule ◆ **I won't be ~d into making a decision** je refuse de prendre une décision précipitée

2 *(= cause to proceed)* **to ~ legislation through** faire voter des lois à la hâte ◆ **to ~ things (on** *or* **along)** faire activer les choses

3 *(US* ✻ *= sell, pass off)* fourguer*, refiler*

VI 1 *(* = hurry)* se manier*, se grouiller*

2 *(esp US *)* *(= make efforts)* se démener ; *(= work hard)* trimer*, turbiner*

3 *(esp US* ✻*) [prostitute]* faire le trottoir* ; *[trader]* fricoter*

N 1 *(= jostling)* bousculade *f* ; *(= activity)* grande activité *f* ◆ **~ and bustle** tourbillon *m* d'activité ◆ **the ~ and bustle of city life** le tourbillon de la vie en ville

2 *(US* ✻*)* racket *m*, activité *f* illégale

hustler * /ˈhʌsləʳ/ N 1 *(= swindler)* arnaqueur *m*, -euse *f* 2 *(= prostitute)* prostitué(e) *m(f)* 3 *(= go-getter)* battant(e) *m(f)*

hut /hʌt/ N *(= primitive dwelling)* hutte *f*, case *f* ; *(= shed)* cabane *f* ; *(Mil)* baraquement *m* ; *(for climbers)* refuge *m* ; *[of shepherd]* cabane *f*, abri *m* ; → **mud**

hutch /hʌtʃ/ N 1 *[of rabbit]* clapier *m* 2 *(US = dresser)* vaisselier *m*

Hutu /ˈhuːtuː/ N Hutu *mf* ADJ hutu *f inv*

HV, h.v. (abbrev of **high voltage**) → **high**

hyacinth /ˈhaɪəsɪnθ/ N 1 *(= plant)* jacinthe *f* ◆ **wild ~** jacinthe *f* des bois *or* sauvage, endymion *m* 2 *(= gemstone)* hyacinthe *f*

hyaena /haɪˈiːnə/ N ⇒ **hyena**

hybrid /ˈhaɪbrɪd/ N 1 *(gen)* hybride *m (between* entre) 2 *(= bicycle)* vélo *m* hybride ADJ hybride
COMP **hybrid system** N système *m* hybride

hybridism /ˈhaɪbrɪdɪzəm/ N hybridisme *m*

hybridization /ˌhaɪbrɪdaɪˈzeɪʃən/ N hybridation *f*

hybridize /ˈhaɪbrɪdaɪz/ VT hybrider, croiser

hydra /ˈhaɪdrə/ N (pl **hydras** *or* **hydrae** /ˈhaɪdriː/) hydre *f*

hydrangea /haɪˈdreɪndʒə/ N hortensia *m*

hydrant /ˈhaɪdrənt/ N prise *f* d'eau ; (also **fire hydrant**) bouche *f* d'incendie

hydrate /ˈhaɪdreɪt/ N hydrate *m* VT hydrater

hydraulic /haɪˈdrɒlɪk/ ADJ hydraulique
COMP **hydraulic brake** N frein *m* hydraulique
hydraulic circuit N circuit *m* hydraulique
hydraulic ramp N pont *m* élévateur
hydraulic suspension N suspension *f* hydraulique

hydraulics /haɪˈdrɒlɪks/ N *(NonC)* hydraulique *f*

hydro /ˈhaɪdrəʊ/ N 1 *(Brit* † *= hotel)* établissement *m* thermal *(hôtel)* 2 *(Can) (= electricity)* énergie *f* hydroélectrique ; *(= power station)* centrale *f* hydroélectrique ADJ *(Can)* hydroélectrique

hydrocarbon /ˌhaɪdrəʊˈkɑːbən/ N hydrocarbure *m*

hydrochloric /ˌhaɪdrəʊˈklɒrɪk/ ADJ chlorhydrique

hydrocyanic /ˌhaɪdrəʊsaɪˈænɪk/ ADJ cyanhydrique

hydrodynamics /ˌhaɪdrəʊdaɪˈnæmɪks/ N *(NonC)* hydrodynamique *f*

hydroelectric /ˌhaɪdrəʊɪˈlektrɪk/ ADJ hydroélectrique COMP **hydroelectric power** N énergie *f* hydroélectrique

hydroelectricity /ˌhaɪdrəʊɪlekˈtrɪsɪtɪ/ N hydroélectricité *f*

hydrofoil /ˈhaɪdrəʊˌfɔɪl/ N hydroptère *m*, hydrofoil *m*

hydrogen /ˈhaɪdrɪdʒən/ N hydrogène *m*
COMP **hydrogen bomb** N bombe *f* à hydrogène
hydrogen peroxide N eau *f* oxygénée

hydrography /haɪˈdrɒɡrəfɪ/ N hydrographie *f*

hydrolysis /haɪˈdrɒlɪsɪs/ N hydrolyse *f*

hydrometer /haɪˈdrɒmɪtəʳ/ N hydromètre *m*

hydropathic /ˌhaɪdrəʊˈpæθɪk/ ADJ hydrothérapique

hydrophilic /ˌhaɪdrəʊˈfɪlɪk/ ADJ hydrophile

hydrophobia /ˌhaɪdrəʊˈfəʊbɪə/ N hydrophobie *f*

hydrophobic /ˌhaɪdrəʊˈfəʊbɪk/ ADJ hydrophobe

hydroplane /ˈhaɪdrəʊˌpleɪn/ N hydroglisseur *m*

hydroponic /ˌhaɪdrəʊˈpɒnɪk/ ADJ hydroponique

hydroponics /ˌhaɪdrəʊˈpɒnɪks/ N *(NonC)* culture *f* hydroponique

hydropower /ˌhaɪdrəʊˈpaʊəʳ/ N énergie *f* hydroélectrique, hydroélectricité *f*

hydrotherapy /ˌhaɪdrəʊˈθerəpɪ/ N hydrothérapie *f*

hydroxide /haɪˈdrɒksaɪd/ N hydroxyde *m*

hyena /haɪˈiːnə/ N hyène *f*

hygiene /ˈhaɪdʒiːn/ N hygiène *f*

hygienic /haɪˈdʒiːnɪk/ ADJ hygiénique

hygienist /ˈhaɪdʒiːnɪst/ N hygiéniste *mf*

hymen /ˈhaɪmen/ N *(Anat)* hymen *m*

hymn /hɪm/ N hymne *m*, cantique *m* ♦ **a ~ to sth** *(fig = celebration)* un hymne à qch VT *(liter)* chanter un hymne à la gloire de
COMP **hymn book** N livre *m* de cantiques
hymn sheet N ♦ **to be singing from the same ~ sheet** parler d'une même voix

hymnal /ˈhɪmnəl/ N livre *m* de cantiques

hype /haɪp/ N 1 *(NonC: * = publicity)* battage *m* publicitaire ; *(in media)* battage *m* médiatique ♦ **it has been the subject of intense media ~** ça a fait l'objet d'un énorme battage médiatique ♦ **he's always been contemptuous of marketing ~** il a toujours méprisé le battage publicitaire des campagnes de marketing
2 *(* = book, product)* livre *m* or produit *m* lancé à grand renfort de publicité
3 *(Drugs ‡) (= syringe)* shooteuse‡ *f* ; *(= injection)* shoot‡ *m* ; *(= addict)* toxico* *mf*, camé(e)* *m(f)*
VT 1 *(* : also* **hype up**) *(= publicize) [+ book, product, film]* faire un énorme battage autour de ♦ **he felt the film was ~d up too much** il a trouvé que l'on avait fait trop de battage autour de ce film
2 *(‡ = increase) [+ numbers, attendance]* augmenter ♦ **to ~ the economy** stimuler l'économie
3 *(‡ = excite)* exciter ; see also **hyped-up**
4 *(US ‡ = cheat) [+ person]* tromper, rouler*
VI *(Drugs ‡: also* **hype up**) se shooter*
COMP **hyped-up‡** ADJ *(= excited)* surexcité ; *(= anxious)* stressé

► **hype up** VI, VT SEP → **hype vi, hyped-up**

hyper* /ˈhaɪpəʳ/ ADJ surexcité

hyperacidity /ˈhaɪpərəˈsɪdɪtɪ/ N hyperacidité *f*

hyperactive /ˌhaɪpərˈæktɪv/ ADJ *[child]* hyperactif

hyperactivity /ˌhaɪpərækˈtɪvɪtɪ/ N suractivité *f* ; *[of child]* hyperactivité *f*, syndrome *m* hyperkinétique *(SPEC)*

hyperbola /haɪˈpɜːbələ/ N (pl **hyperbolas** or **hyperbole** /haɪˈpɜːbəˌliː/) *(Math)* hyperbole *f*

hyperbole /haɪˈpɜːbəlɪ/ N *(Literat)* hyperbole *f*

hyperbolic(al) /ˌhaɪpəˈbɒlɪk(əl)/ ADJ hyperbolique

hypercorrection /ˌhaɪpəkəˈrekʃən/ N hypercorrection *f*

hypercritical /ˌhaɪpəˈkrɪtɪkəl/ ADJ hypercritique

hyperglycaemia, hyperglycemia *(US)* /ˌhaɪpəglaɪˈsiːmɪə/ N hyperglycémie *f*

hyperglycaemic, hyperglycemic *(US)* /ˌhaɪpəglaɪˈsiːmɪk/ ADJ hyperglycémique

hyperinflation /ˌhaɪpərɪnˈfleɪʃən/ N hyperinflation *f*

hyperkinetic /ˌhaɪpəkɪˈnetɪk/ ADJ suractif ; *[child]* hyperactif

hyperlink /ˈhaɪpəlɪŋk/ N lien *m* hypertexte VT créer un lien hypertexte avec

hypermarket /ˈhaɪpəmɑːkɪt/ N *(Brit)* hypermarché *m*

hypermeter /haɪˈpɜːmɪtəʳ/ N vers *m* hypermètre

hypermetropia /ˌhaɪpəmɪˈtrəʊpɪə/, **hypermetropy** /ˌhaɪpəˈmetrəpɪ/ N hypermétropie *f*

hypernym /ˈhaɪpənɪm/ N hyperonyme *m*

hyperrealism /ˌhaɪpəˈrɪəlɪzəm/ N hyperréalisme *m*

hypersensitive /ˌhaɪpəˈsensɪtɪv/ ADJ hypersensible

hypersonic /ˌhaɪpəˈsɒnɪk/ ADJ hypersonique

hypertension /ˌhaɪpəˈtenʃən/ N hypertension *f*

hypertext /ˈhaɪpəˌtekst/ N *(Comput)* hypertexte *m*

hypertrophy /haɪˈpɜːtrəfɪ/ N hypertrophie *f* VT hypertrophier VI s'hypertrophier

hyperventilate /ˌhaɪpɜːˈventɪleɪt/ VI hyperventiler

hyperventilation /ˌhaɪpɜːventɪˈleɪʃən/ N hyperventilation *f*

hyphen /ˈhaɪfən/ N trait *m* d'union

hyphenate /ˈhaɪfəneɪt/ VT mettre un trait d'union à ♦ **~d word** mot *m* à trait d'union

hypnagogic, hypnogogic /ˌhɪpnəˈgɒdʒɪk/ ADJ hypnagogique

hypnosis /hɪpˈnəʊsɪs/ N (pl **hypnoses** /hɪpˈnəʊsiːz/) hypnose *f* ♦ **under ~** sous hypnose

hypnotherapist /ˌhɪpnəʊˈθerəpɪst/ N hypnothérapeute *mf*

hypnotherapy /ˌhɪpnəʊˈθerəpɪ/ N hypnothérapie *f*

hypnotic /hɪpˈnɒtɪk/ ADJ *[state]* hypnotique, d'hypnose ; *[trance, regression, power]* hypnotique ; *[rhythm, effect, eyes, voice]* envoûtant N *(= drug)* hypnotique *m* ; *(= person)* sujet *m* hypnotique

hypnotism /ˈhɪpnətɪzəm/ N hypnotisme *m*

hypnotist /ˈhɪpnətɪst/ N hypnotiseur *m*, -euse *f*

hypnotize /ˈhɪpnətaɪz/ VT *(lit, fig)* hypnotiser ♦ **to ~ sb into doing sth** faire faire qch à qn sous hypnose ♦ **to ~ o.s.** s'hypnotiser

hypoallergenic /ˌhaɪpəʊæləˈdʒenɪk/ ADJ hypoallergénique

hypocentre /ˈhaɪpəʊˌsentəʳ/ N *[of earthquake]* hypocentre *m* ; *[of nuclear blast]* point *m* zéro

hypochondria /ˌhaɪpəʊˈkɒndrɪə/ N *(Med)* hypocondrie *f*

hypochondriac /ˌhaɪpəʊˈkɒndrɪæk/ ADJ *(Med)* hypocondriaque ♦ **my ~ brother** *(gen)* mon frère, ce malade imaginaire N *(Med)* hypocondriaque *mf* ; *(gen)* malade *mf* imaginaire

hypocrisy /hɪˈpɒkrɪsɪ/ N hypocrisie *f*

hypocrite /ˈhɪpəkrɪt/ N hypocrite *mf*

hypocritical /ˌhɪpəˈkrɪtɪkəl/ ADJ hypocrite

hypocritically /ˌhɪpəˈkrɪtɪkəlɪ/ ADV hypocritement

hypodermic /ˌhaɪpəˈdɜːmɪk/ ADJ hypodermique N *(= syringe)* seringue *f* hypodermique ; *(= needle)* aiguille *f* hypodermique ; *(= injection)* injection *f* hypodermique

hypoglossal /ˌhaɪpəˈglɒsəl/ ADJ hypoglosse

hypoglycaemia, hypoglycemia *(US)* /ˌhaɪpəʊglaɪˈsiːmɪə/ N *(Med)* hypoglycémie *f*

hypoglycaemic, hypoglycemic *(US)* /ˌhaɪpəʊglaɪˈsiːmɪk/ ADJ hypoglycémique

hyponym /ˈhaɪpənɪm/ N hyponyme *m*

hyponymy /haɪˈpɒnɪmɪ/ N hyponymie *f*

hypostasis /haɪˈpɒstəsɪs/ N (pl **hypostases** /haɪˈpɒstəsiːz/) *(Rel)* hypostase *f*

hypostatic /ˌhaɪpəʊˈstætɪk/ ADJ *(Rel)* hypostatique

hypotenuse /haɪˈpɒtɪnjuːz/ N hypoténuse *f*

hypothalamus /ˌhaɪpəˈθæləməs/ N (pl **hypothalami** /ˌhaɪpəˈθæləmaɪ/) hypothalamus *m*

hypothermia /ˌhaɪpəʊˈθɜːmɪə/ N hypothermie *f*

hypothesis /haɪˈpɒθɪsɪs/ N (pl **hypotheses** /haɪˈpɒθɪsiːz/) hypothèse *f* ; → **working**

hypothesize /haɪˈpɒθɪˌsaɪz/ VT conjecturer ♦ **it was ~d that …** on est parti de l'hypothèse que … VI se livrer à des conjectures

hypothetic(al) /ˌhaɪpəʊˈθetɪk(əl)/ ADJ hypothétique

hypothetically /ˌhaɪpəʊˈθetɪkəlɪ/ ADV en théorie

hyssop /ˈhɪsəp/ N hysope *f*

hysterectomy /ˌhɪstəˈrektəmɪ/ N hystérectomie *f*

hysteria /hɪsˈtɪərɪə/ N *(Psych)* hystérie *f* ♦ **she felt a wave of mounting ~** *(= panic)* elle se sentait or elle était au bord de la crise de nerfs ♦ **there were signs of ~ among the crowd** la foule semblait être au bord de l'hystérie ♦ **he was completely overcome with ~** il était complètement hystérique ; → **mass**[1]

hysterical /hɪsˈterɪkəl/ ADJ *(Psych)* hystérique ; *(gen) [person]* très nerveux, surexcité ; *(with laughter)* en proie au fou rire ; *[laugh, sobs, weeping]* convulsif ; *(* = hilarious) [joke, scene, comedian]* tordant* ♦ **~ laughter** fou rire *m* ♦ **~ crying** une violente crise de larmes

hysterically /hɪsˈterɪkəlɪ/ ADV *(Med, Psych)* hystériquement ♦ **to weep ~** avoir une violente crise de larmes ♦ **to laugh ~** rire convulsivement, être saisi d'un rire convulsif ♦ **"come here", she shouted ~** "viens ici" hurla-t-elle comme une hystérique ♦ **it was ~ funny*** c'était à se tordre de rire

hysterics /hɪsˈterɪks/ NPL 1 *(= tears, shouts)* (violente) crise *f* de nerfs ♦ **to have ~, to go into ~** avoir une (violente) crise de nerfs ♦ **she was nearly in ~** elle était au bord de la crise de nerfs 2 *(* = laughter)* crise *f* de fou rire ♦ **to have ~, to go into ~** attraper le fou rire ♦ **we were in ~ about it** on a ri aux larmes ♦ **he had us all in ~** il nous a fait rire aux larmes

Hz *(Rad etc)* (abbrev of **hertz**) hz

Ii

I¹, i /aɪ/ N [1] *(= letter)* I, i *m* ◆ **I for Isaac** *(Brit)* ◆ **I for item** *(US)* ≈ I comme Irène ; → **dot** [2] *(Geog)* (abbrev of **Island** *and* **Isle**) I

I² /aɪ/ PERS PRON *(unstressed)* je ; *(before vowel)* j' ; *(stressed)* moi ◆ **he and I are going to sing** lui et moi (nous) allons chanter ◆ **no, I'll do it** non, c'est moi qui vais le faire ◆ **it is I** *(frm)* c'est moi

IA abbrev of **Iowa**

Ia. abbrev of **Iowa**

IAAF /ˌaɪeɪeɪˈef/ N (abbrev of **International Amateur Athletic Federation**) FIAA *f*

IAEA /ˌaɪeiːˈeɪ/ N (abbrev of **International Atomic Energy Agency**) AIEA *f*

iambic /aɪˈæmbɪk/ ADJ iambique N iambe *m*, vers *m* iambique COMP **iambic pentameter** N pentamètre *m* iambique

IBA /ˌaɪbiːˈeɪ/ N *(Brit)* (abbrev of **Independent Broadcasting Authority**) *haute autorité contrôlant les sociétés indépendantes de radiotélévision*

Iberia /aɪˈbɪərɪə/ N Ibérie *f*

Iberian /aɪˈbɪərɪən/ ADJ ibérique N [1] Ibère *mf* [2] *(= language)* ibère *m* COMP **Iberian Peninsula** N péninsule *f* Ibérique

ibex /ˈaɪbeks/ N (pl **ibexes** *or* **ibex** *or* **ibices** /ˈɪbɪˌsiːz/) bouquetin *m*, ibex *m*

ibid /ˈɪbɪd/ (abbrev of **ibidem**) ibid

ibis /ˈaɪbɪs/ N (pl **ibises** *or* **ibis**) ibis *m*

Ibiza /ɪˈbiːθə/ N Ibiza *f* ◆ **in** ~ à Ibiza

IBRD /ˌaɪbiːɑːˈdiː/ N (abbrev of **International Bank for Reconstruction and Development**) BIRD *f*

IBS /ˌaɪbiːˈes/ N (abbrev of **irritable bowel syndrome**) → **irritable**

i/c (abbrev of **in charge**) → **charge**

ICA /ˌaɪsiːˈeɪ/ N [1] *(Brit)* abbrev of **Institute of Contemporary Arts** [2] *(Brit)* abbrev of **Institute of Chartered Accountants** [3] abbrev of **International Cooperation Administration**

ICAO /ˌaɪsiːeɪˈəʊ/ N (abbrev of **International Civil Aviation Organization**) OACI *f*

Icarus /ˈɪkərəs/ N Icare *m*

ICBM /ˌaɪsiːbiːˈem/ N (abbrev of **intercontinental ballistic missile**) ICBM *m*

ice /aɪs/ N [1] *(NonC)* glace *f* ; *(on road)* verglas *m* ; *(for drink)* glaçons *mpl* ◆ **my hands are like** ~ j'ai les mains glacées ◆ **to put sth on** ~ *(lit)* *[+ melon, wine]* mettre qch à rafraîchir avec de la glace ; *[+ champagne]* mettre qch à frapper ; *(fig)* mettre qch en attente *or* au frigidaire* ◆ **to keep sth on** ~ *(lit)* garder qch sur *or* dans de la glace ; *(fig)* garder qch en attente ◆ **"Cinderella on ice"** *(Theat)* "Cendrillon, spectacle sur glace" ◆ **to break the** ~ *(lit) (also in conversation etc)* briser *or* rompre la glace ; *(= broach tricky matter)* entamer le sujet délicat ◆ **that cuts no** ~ *or* **that doesn't cut much** ~ **with me** ça ne me fait aucun effet, ça ne m'impressionne guère ; → **black, cold**

[2] *(Brit:* also **ice cream**) glace *f* ◆ **raspberry** ~ glace *f* à la framboise ; → **water**

[3] (* = *diamonds)* diam(s)* *m(pl)*, diamant(s) *m(pl)*

[4] (* = *drug) drogue à base de méthamphétamine*

VT [1] *[+ cake]* glacer

[2] *(fig)* ◆ **his words ~d her heart** ses paroles l'ont glacée ; → **iced**

COMP **ice age** N période *f* glaciaire

ice-age ADJ (qui date) de la période glaciaire

ice axe N piolet *m*

ice beer N ice beer *m*, bière *f* de glace

ice blue N, ADJ bleu *m* métallique *inv*

ice bucket N seau *m* à glace *or* à champagne

ice climber N glaciériste *mf*

ice-cold ADJ *[drink, hands]* glacé ; *[room, manners, person]* glacial

ice-cool ADJ *[person]* d'un sang-froid à toute épreuve

ice cream N glace *f* ◆ **strawberry ~ cream** glace *f* à la fraise

ice-cream cone, ice-cream cornet *(Brit)* N cornet *m* de glace

ice-cream soda N *(US)* soda *m* avec de la crème glacée

ice-cream van N camionnette *f* de vendeur de glaces

ice cube N glaçon *m*

ice dance N ⇒ **ice dancing**

ice dancer N danseur *m*, -euse *f* sur glace

ice dancing N danse *f* sur glace

ice field N champ *m* de glace

ice floe N banquise *f* (flottante)

ice hammer N marteau-piolet *m*

ice hockey N hockey *m* sur glace

ice lolly N *(Brit)* sucette *f* glacée

ice maiden * N glaçon * *m (fig)*

ice pack N *(Med)* poche *f* de glace ; *(Geog)* banquise *f*

ice pick N pic *m* à glace

ice piton N broche *f* (à glace)

ice rink N patinoire *f*

ice sheet N *(Geol)* couche *f* de glace

ice-shelf N *(Geog)* ice-shelf *m*

ice show N *(Theat)* spectacle *m* sur glace

ice skate N patin *m* (à glace)

ice-skate VI faire du patin (à glace) *or* du patinage (sur glace)

ice skater N patineur *m*, -euse *f* (sur glace)

ice-skating N patinage *m* (sur glace)

ice storm N *(US)* tempête *f* de pluie verglaçante

ice tray N bac *m* à glaçons

ice water N *(US)* eau *f* glacée

ice yacht N char *m* à voile (sur patins)

► **ice over** VI *[windscreen, aircraft wings]* givrer ; *[river]* geler ◆ **the lake has ~d over** le lac a gelé *or* est pris (de glace)

VT SEP ◆ **to be iced over** *[windscreen, aircraft wings]* être givré ; *[river, lake]* être gelé, être pris (de glace)

► **ice up** VI *[windscreen, aircraft, mechanism, lock]* se givrer

VT SEP ◆ **to be iced up** *[windscreen, aircraft wings]* être givré ; *[river, lake]* être gelé, être pris (de glace)

iceberg /ˈaɪsbɜːg/ N iceberg *m* ; (* *fig = person)* glaçon * *m* ; see also **tip¹** COMP **iceberg lettuce** N laitue *f* iceberg *(sorte de laitue croquante)*

iceboat /ˈaɪsbəʊt/ N *(Sport)* char *m* à voile (sur patins) ; *(Naut)* brise-glace(s) *m*

icebound /ˈaɪsbaʊnd/ ADJ *[harbour]* fermé par les glaces ; *[ship]* pris dans les glaces

icebox /ˈaɪsbɒks/ N *(US* † *= refrigerator)* frigidaire ® *m*, réfrigérateur *m* ; *(Brit = freezer compartment)* compartiment *m* à glace, freezer *m* ; *(= insulated box)* glacière *f* ◆ **this room is like an** ~ cette pièce est une vraie glacière, on gèle dans cette pièce

icebreaker /ˈaɪsˌbreɪkəʳ/ N *(Naut)* brise-glace(s) *m* ◆ **as an** ~ *(fig)* pour briser la glace *or* faire connaissance

icecap /ˈaɪskæp/ N calotte *f* glaciaire

iced /aɪst/ ADJ *[coffee, tea]* glacé ; *[melon]* rafraîchi ◆ ~ **water/martini** de l'eau/un martini avec des glaçons ◆ ~ **champagne** champagne *m* frappé

icehouse /ˈaɪshaʊs/ N glacière *f*

Iceland /ˈaɪslənd/ N Islande *f*

Icelander /ˈaɪsləndəʳ/ N Islandais(e) *m(f)*

Icelandic /aɪsˈlændɪk/ ADJ islandais N *(= language)* islandais *m*

iceman /ˈaɪsmæn/ N (pl **-men**) [1] *(US)* marchand *m or* livreur *m* de glace [2] *(Archeol)* homme *m* trouvé dans la glace

I Ching /ˈiːˈtʃɪŋ/ N Yijing *or* Yi-king *m*

ichthyologist /ˌɪkθɪˈɒlədʒɪst/ N ichtyologiste *mf*

ichthyology /ˌɪkθɪˈɒlədʒɪ/ N ichtyologie *f*

ichthyosaurus /ˌɪkθɪəˈsɔːrəs/ N (pl **ichthyosauruses** *or* **ichthyosauri** /ˌɪkθɪəˈsɔːraɪ/) ichtyosaure *m*

icicle /ˈaɪsɪkl/ N glaçon *m (naturel)*

icily /ˈaɪsɪlɪ/ ADV *[say]* sur un ton glacial ; *[smile, stare]* d'un air glacial ◆ ~ **polite** d'une politesse glaciale ◆ ~ **calm** d'un calme glacial

iciness /ˈaɪsɪnɪs/ N 1 *(lit) [of road surface]* état *m* verglacé 2 *(fig) [of manner, tone, stare etc]* froideur *f* extrême

icing /ˈaɪsɪŋ/ N 1 *(NonC: Culin)* glace *f*, glaçage *m* ◆ **chocolate/coffee** *etc* ~ glaçage *m* au chocolat/au café *etc* ; → **butter** 2 *(fig)* **the ~ on the cake** la cerise sur le gâteau COMP **icing sugar** N *(Brit)* sucre *m* glace

icky‡ /ˈɪkɪ/ ADJ *(= messy)* poisseux ; *(fig) (= horrible)* dégueulasse‡

icon /ˈaɪkɒn/ N 1 *(Rel, Comput)* icône *f* 2 *(fig = symbol)* emblème *m* ; *(= idol)* idole *f* ◆ **a feminist/youth/gay** ~ une idole pour les féministes/les jeunes/les homosexuels ◆ **fashion** ~ figure *f* emblématique de la mode

iconic /aɪˈkɒnɪk/ ADJ 1 *(Ling, Comput, Psych)* iconique 2 *(Art) [portrait]* ressemblant à une icône 3 *(culturally) [figure]* emblématique ◆ **to achieve ~ status** devenir une idole

iconoclast /aɪˈkɒnəklæst/ N iconoclaste *mf*

iconoclastic /aɪˌkɒnəˈklæstɪk/ ADJ iconoclaste

iconographer /ˌaɪkɒˈnɒgrəfəʳ/ N iconographe *mf*

iconography /ˌaɪkɒˈnɒgrəfɪ/ N iconographie *f*

ICRC /ˌaɪsiːɑːˈsiː/ N (abbrev of **International Committee of the Red Cross**) CICR *m*

ICT /ˌaɪsiːˈtiː/ N *(Brit Scol)* (abbrev of **Information and Communications Technology**) TIC *fpl*

ICU /ˌaɪsiːˈjuː/ N (abbrev of **intensive care unit**) USI *f*

icy /ˈaɪsɪ/ ADJ 1 *(= frozen) [road, pavement]* verglacé ; *[lake, river, sea]* gelé ◆ ~ **rain** pluie *f* mêlée de grêle ◆ ~ **conditions** *(on roads)* verglas *m* ◆ **it's ~ this morning** il gèle ce matin 2 (also **icy cold**) *[wind, water]* glacial, glacé ; *[hands, feet]* glacé ◆ **it was ~ (cold) yesterday** il faisait un froid glacial hier ◆ **her hands were ~ (cold)** elle avait les mains glacées ◆ **the ~ blast** *(liter or hum)* le vent glacial 3 *(= unfriendly) [stare, silence, tone, reception]* glacial COMP **icy blue** ADJ, N bleu *m* métallique *inv*

ID /aɪˈdiː/ ABBR abbrev of **Idaho** N (abbrev of **identification**) pièce *f* d'identité ◆ **she asked me for some** ~ elle m'a demandé une pièce d'identité ◆ **I had no ~ on me** je n'avais pas de pièce d'identité sur moi
COMP (abbrev of **identification, identity**) *[bracelet, tag, number]* d'identification
ID card N *(gen)* carte *f* d'identité ; *(magnetic)* carte *f* d'identification
ID parade N *(Brit)* séance *f* d'identification (d'un suspect)

id /ɪd/ N *(Psych)* ça *m*

I'd /aɪd/ ⇒ **I had, I should, I would** ; → **have, should, would**

Ida. abbrev of **Idaho**

Idaho /ˈaɪdəˌhəʊ/ N Idaho *m* ◆ **in** ~ dans l'Idaho

IDD /ˌaɪdiːˈdiː/ N *(Brit Telec)* (abbrev of **international direct dialling**) *automatique international*

idea /aɪˈdɪə/ LANGUAGE IN USE 1, 2.2, 11.2 N 1 *(= thought, purpose)* idée *f* ◆ **brilliant** *or* **bright** ~ idée *f* géniale *or* de génie ◆ **good ~!** bonne idée ! ◆ **what an ~!, the very ~ (of it)!** quelle idée !, en voilà une idée ! ◆ **I've got an ~ for a play** j'ai une idée pour une pièce de théâtre ◆ **I haven't the least** *or* **slightest** *or* **foggiest*** ~ je n'en ai pas la moindre idée ◆ **it wasn't my ~!** ce n'est pas moi qui en ai eu l'idée ! ◆ **man/woman of ~s** homme *m*/femme *f* à idées ◆ **he's the ~s man*** *or* **the one with the ~s** c'est lui qui trouve les idées ◆ **the ~ never entered my head** l'idée ne m'en est jamais venue *or* ne m'a jamais effleuré ◆ **to put ~s into sb's head, to give sb ~s** mettre *or* fourrer* des idées dans la tête de qn ◆ **that's the ~!*** c'est ça ! ◆ **what's the big ~?*** ça ne va pas, non ?‡

◆ **the idea of + -ing** ◆ **I can't bear the ~ of selling it** je ne supporte pas l'idée de le vendre ◆ **that gave me the ~ of inviting her** cela m'a donné l'idée de l'inviter ◆ **I suddenly had the ~ of going to see her** d'un seul coup l'idée m'est venue d'aller la voir ◆ **he sent for the books, with the ~ of re-reading them** il s'est fait envoyer ces livres dans l'intention de les relire ◆ **I like the ~ of helping people** l'idée d'aider les gens me plaît ◆ **I like/hate the ~ of living abroad** j'aimerais assez/je détesterais vivre à l'étranger

◆ **idea of +** *noun or noun clause (= conception)* ◆ **if that's your ~ of fun** si c'est ça que tu appelles t'amuser ◆ **that's not my ~ of a holiday** ce n'est pas ce que j'appelle des vacances ◆ **I've got some ~ of what this is all about** j'ai une vague idée de quoi il s'agit ◆ **he gave me a general ~ of what they would do** il m'a donné une idée générale de ce qu'ils allaient faire ◆ **have you any ~ of what he meant to do?** avez-vous idée de ce qu'il voulait faire ? ◆ **this will give you an ~ of how much it will cost** cela permettra de vous faire une idée de ce que ça va coûter ◆ **can you give me a rough ~ of how many you want?** pouvez-vous m'indiquer en gros *or* approximativement combien vous en voulez ?

◆ **the/an idea that** ◆ **what gave you the ~ that I couldn't come?** qu'est-ce qui t'a fait penser que je ne pourrais pas venir ? ◆ **I had an ~ that he'd joined the army** j'avais dans l'idée qu'il s'était engagé dans l'armée ◆ **I hate the ~ that summer's over** je n'arrive pas à me faire à l'idée que l'été est fini

◆ **idea + to** ◆ **it's an ~** *or* **a good ~ to book well in advance** c'est une (bonne) idée de réserver assez longtemps à l'avance ◆ **it was a good/wonderful ~ to come here** c'était une bonne/excellente idée de venir ici ◆ **it might not be a bad ~ to wait a few days** ce ne serait peut-être pas une mauvaise idée d'attendre quelques jours ◆ **the ~ is to reduce expenditure** l'idée est de réduire les dépenses ◆ **whose ~ was it to take this route?** qui a eu l'idée de prendre cet itinéraire ?

◆ **to get + idea** ◆ **where did you get the ~ that I wasn't well?** où as-tu été chercher que je n'allais pas bien ? ◆ **where did you get that ~?** où est-ce que tu as pris cette idée ? ◆ **don't get any ~s!*** ce n'est pas la peine d'y penser ! ◆ **you're getting the ~!*** tu commences à comprendre *or* à piger* ! ◆ **I've got the general ~*** je vois à peu près *or* en gros (ce dont il s'agit) ◆ **to get an ~ into one's head** se mettre une idée dans la tête ◆ **once he gets an ~ into his head** une fois qu'il s'est mis une idée dans la tête ◆ **he got the ~ into his head that she wouldn't help him** il s'est mis dans la tête qu'elle ne l'aiderait pas

◆ **to have no idea** ◆ **I have no ~** je n'en sais rien ◆ **I had no ~ they knew each other** je n'avais aucune idée *or* j'ignorais absolument qu'ils se connaissaient ◆ **he has no ~ what he's doing!** il fait n'importe quoi !* ◆ **it was awful, you've no ~!** c'était terrible, tu ne peux pas t'imaginer !

2 *(= opinion)* idée *f*, opinion *f* ; *(= way of thinking)* façon *f* de penser ◆ **she has some odd ~s about how to bring up children** elle a de drôles d'idées sur l'éducation des enfants ◆ **he is convinced that his ~s are correct** il est convaincu que sa façon de penser est la bonne ◆ **Lord Syme outlined his ~s at a London conference** Lord Syme a exposé sa théorie lors d'une conférence à Londres ◆ **according to his ~** selon sa façon de penser ◆ **his ~s about democracy** ses idées sur la démocratie, sa façon de voir *or* sa conception de la démocratie

ideal /aɪˈdɪəl/ ADJ idéal *(for sb/sth* pour qn/qch ; *for doing sth* pour faire qch) N idéal *m*

idealism /aɪˈdɪəlɪzəm/ N idéalisme *m*

idealist /aɪˈdɪəlɪst/ ADJ, N idéaliste *mf*

idealistic /aɪˌdɪəˈlɪstɪk/ ADJ idéaliste

idealization /aɪˌdɪəlaɪˈzeɪʃən/ N idéalisation *f*

idealize /aɪˈdɪəlaɪz/ VT idéaliser

ideally /aɪˈdɪəlɪ/ ADV 1 *(= preferably)* ◆ ~, **you should brush your teeth after every meal** l'idéal serait de se brosser les dents après chaque repas, pour bien faire il faudrait se brosser les dents après chaque repas ◆ ~, **every child should get individual attention** l'idéal serait que chaque enfant soit suivi individuellement ◆ ~ **I'd like to leave about five** dans l'idéal *or* pour bien faire, j'aimerais partir vers cinq heures 2 *(= perfectly)* ◆ **he is ~ suited to the job** il est parfait pour ce poste ◆ **I'm not ~ placed to give you advice** je ne suis pas le mieux placé pour vous conseiller ◆ **the village is ~ situated** la situation du village est idéale

ident* /ˈaɪdent/ N *(TV)* (also **station ident**) *clip vidéo servant à identifier une chaîne de télévision*

identical /aɪˈdentɪkəl/ ADJ identique *(to* à) ◆ ~ **twins** vrais jumeaux *mpl*, vraies jumelles *fpl*

identically /aɪˈdentɪkəlɪ/ ADV de façon identique ◆ ~ **dressed** vêtus de manière identique, habillés pareil*

identifiable /aɪˈdentɪˌfaɪəbl/ ADJ identifiable ; *[goal, group]* distinct ; *[person]* repérable, reconnaissable ◆ ~ **as a Frenchman** reconnaissable en tant que Français ◆ **it is ~ as a Rembrandt** on voit tout de suite que c'est un Rembrandt ◆ **he's easily ~** il est facilement repérable *or* reconnaissable *(as* comme ; *by* à) ◆ **Chinese rugs are ~ by their design** les tapis chinois se reconnaissent à leur motifs

identification /aɪˌdentɪfɪˈkeɪʃən/ N 1 identification *f (with* avec) ◆ **early ~ of a disease** l'identification précoce d'une maladie ◆ **he's made a formal ~ of the body** il a formellement identifié le corps
2 *(= association)* association *f* ◆ **the ~ of Spain with Catholicism** l'association de l'Espagne au catholicisme
3 *(= empathy)* ◆ **his ~ with the problem** sa compréhension profonde du problème ◆ **an actor's ~ with his character** l'identification *f* d'un acteur avec son personnage
4 *(= proof of identity)* pièce *f* d'identité
COMP **identification mark** N signe *m* particulier *(permettant d'identifier qn ou qch)*
identification papers NPL pièces *fpl or* papiers *mpl* d'identité
identification parade N *(Brit Police)* séance *f* d'identification (d'un suspect)
identification tag N plaque *f* d'identité

identifier /aɪˈdentɪfaɪəʳ/ N *(Comput)* identificateur *m*

identify /aɪˈdentɪfaɪ/ VT 1 *(= recognize)* **the characteristics by which you can ~ an epic** les caractéristiques qui permettent de définir l'épopée ◆ **try to ~ sources of stress in your life** essayez de déterminer les causes de stress dans votre vie quotidienne ◆ **I tried to ~ her perfume** j'ai essayé d'identifier son parfum
2 *(= name)* **many players ~ him as their most troublesome opponent** de nombreux joueurs le considèrent comme leur opposant le plus coriace ◆ **the police have so far identified 10 suspects** la police a jusqu'ici révélé l'identité de 10 suspects ◆ **so far we have just identified the problems** jusqu'ici nous n'avons fait qu'énumérer les problèmes
3 *(= establish identity of)* identifier ◆ **she identified him as the man who had attacked her** elle l'a identifié comme étant son agresseur ◆ **the police have identified the man they want to question** la police a identifié *or* établi l'identité de l'homme qu'elle veut interroger ◆ **to ~ a body** identifier un cadavre

4 (= *discover*) découvrir ◆ **scientists have identified valuable chemicals produced by plants** des chercheurs ont découvert d'importants produits chimiques présents dans les plantes
5 (= *mark out*) **his accent identified him as a local boy** son accent indiquait qu'il était de la région ◆ **she wore a nurse's hat to ~ herself** elle portait un chapeau d'infirmière pour qu'on la reconnaisse ◆ **the badge identified him as Emil Gregory** le badge disait "Emil Gregory", il portait un badge au nom d'Emil Gregory
6 (= *consider as the same*) identifier ◆ **she hates to play the passive women audiences ~ her with** elle déteste les rôles de femmes passives auxquels l'identifie le public ◆ **to ~ o.s. with** s'identifier à *or* avec, s'assimiler à ◆ **he refused to ~ himself with the rebels** il a refusé de s'identifier avec les rebelles ◆ **he refused to be identified with the rebels** il a refusé d'être identifié *or* assimilé aux rebelles
VI s'identifier (*with* avec, à) ◆ **a character the audience can ~ with** un personnage auquel le public peut s'identifier ◆ **I can easily ~ with their problems** je comprends parfaitement leurs problèmes

> ⚠ Check which meaning of **to identify** you are translating before opting for **identifier**.

Identikit ® /aɪˈdentɪkɪt/ N (also **Identikit picture**) portrait-robot *m*, photo-robot *f*

identity /aɪˈdentɪtɪ/ N identité *f* ◆ **proof of ~** pièce *f* d'identité ◆ **a case of mistaken ~** une erreur d'identité ◆ **cultural ~** identité culturelle
COMP **identity card** N (*gen*) carte *f* d'identité ; (*magnetic*) carte *f* d'identification
identity crisis N (*Psych*) crise *f* d'identité
identity disc N plaque *f* d'identité
identity papers NPL pièces *fpl* or papiers *mpl* d'identité
identity parade N (*Brit*) séance *f* d'identification (d'un suspect)

ideogram /ˈɪdɪəgræm/, **ideograph** /ˈɪdɪəgrɑːf/ N idéogramme *m*

ideographic /ˌɪdɪəˈgræfɪk/ ADJ idéographique

ideological /ˌaɪdɪəˈlɒdʒɪkəl/ ADJ idéologique

ideologically /ˌaɪdɪəˈlɒdʒɪkəlɪ/ ADV [*motivated*] idéologiquement ◆ **~ sound/unsound** idéologiquement correct/incorrect, correct/incorrect sur le plan idéologique ◆ **to be ~ opposed to sth** être hostile à qch pour des raisons idéologiques ◆ **~, they are poles apart** du point de vue idéologique, ils sont très éloignés l'un de l'autre

ideologist /ˌaɪdɪˈɒlədʒɪst/ N idéologue *mf*

ideologue /ˈaɪdɪəlɒg/ N idéologue *mf*

ideology /ˌaɪdɪˈɒlədʒɪ/ N idéologie *f*

ides /aɪdz/ NPL ides *fpl*

idiocy /ˈɪdɪəsɪ/ N 1 (*NonC*) stupidité *f*, idiotie *f* (*of doing sth* de faire qch) ◆ **a piece of ~** une stupidité, une idiotie 2 (*Med* ††) idiotie *f*

idiolect /ˈɪdɪəʊlekt/ N idiolecte *m*

idiom /ˈɪdɪəm/ N 1 (= *phrase, expression*) expression *f* or tournure *f* idiomatique, idiotisme *m* 2 (= *language*) [*of country*] idiome *m*, langue *f* ; [*of region*] idiome *m* ; [*of person*] idiome *m*, parler *m* 3 (= *style*) style *m* ◆ **in a minimalist ~** dans un style minimaliste

idiomatic /ˌɪdɪəˈmætɪk/ ADJ idiomatique ◆ **~ expression** expression *f* or tournure *f* idiomatique

idiomatically /ˌɪdɪəˈmætɪkəlɪ/ ADV de façon idiomatique

idiosyncrasy /ˌɪdɪəˈsɪŋkrəsɪ/ N idiosyncrasie *f*, particularité *f* ◆ **it's just one of his little idiosyncrasies** ça fait partie de son côté original

idiosyncratic /ˌɪdɪəsɪŋˈkrætɪk/ ADJ particulier, singulier

idiot /ˈɪdɪət/ N 1 idiot(e) *m(f)*, imbécile *mf* ◆ **to act** or **behave like an ~** se conduire en idiot or en imbécile ◆ **to grin like an ~** sourire bêtement ◆ **to feel like an ~** se sentir bête ◆ **what an ~ I am!** que je suis idiot !, quel imbécile je fais ! 2 (*Med* ††) idiot(e) *m(f)* (de naissance) ; → **village**
COMP **idiot board** N (*TV*) téléprompteur *m*, télésouffleur *m*
idiot box * N (*US TV*) téloche * *f*
idiot-proof * ADJ [*method*] infaillible ; [*machine*] indétraquable, indéréglable

idiotic /ˌɪdɪˈɒtɪk/ ADJ idiot, stupide ◆ **that was ~ of you!** ce que tu as été idiot ! ◆ **what an ~ thing to say!** c'est idiot or stupide de dire une chose pareille !

idiotically /ˌɪdɪˈɒtɪkəlɪ/ ADV stupidement, de façon idiote

idle /ˈaɪdl/ ADJ 1 (= *inactive*) [*person*] inactif ; [*employee*] désœuvré ; [*machinery*] à l'arrêt ; [*factory*] arrêté ; [*land*] inexploité ◆ **this machine is never ~** cette machine n'est jamais à l'arrêt or ne s'arrête jamais ◆ **he has not been ~ during his absence** il n'a pas chômé pendant son absence ◆ **to stand ~** [*machinery, vehicle, factory*] être à l'arrêt ◆ **to lie** or **sit ~** [*money*] dormir ; [*land*] rester inexploité ◆ **~ money** argent *m* qui dort ; → **lie¹**
2 (= *unoccupied, at leisure*) [*person, hours, days*] oisif ◆ **~ time** [*of workers*] temps *m* chômé ; [*of machine*] temps *m* mort, arrêt *m* machine ◆ **to spend one's ~ hours doing sth** passer son temps libre à faire qch ◆ **in an ~ moment** pendant un moment d'oisiveté
3 (*pej* = *lazy*) [*person*] fainéant ◆ **the ~ rich** (*pej*) les riches oisifs *mpl* ; → **bone, devil**
4 († = *unemployed*) sans emploi ◆ **to make sb ~** réduire qn au chômage
5 (= *futile, vain*) [*threat, promise, hope*] vain *before n* ; [*speculation, talk, chatter*] oiseux, vain *before n* ; [*conversation, remark, question*] oiseux, futile ; [*rumour, fear*] sans fondement ◆ **out of ~ curiosity** par pure or simple curiosité ◆ **~ gossip** ragots *mpl* ◆ **that is no ~ boast** ce n'est pas une vaine fanfaronnade ◆ **an ~ dream** un vain rêve ◆ **it would be ~ to do such a thing** il serait vain or futile de faire une telle chose
VI 1 (also **idle about** or **around**) [*person*] paresser, fainéanter ◆ **to ~ about the streets** traîner dans les rues
2 [*engine, machine*] tourner au ralenti
VT (*US*) [*+ person*] mettre au chômage ; [*+ factory*] mettre à l'arrêt

► **idle away** VT SEP ◆ **to idle away one's time** passer le temps (en occupations futiles), s'occuper pour passer le temps ◆ **he ~d the time away in dreamy thought** il passait le temps à rêvasser

idleness /ˈaɪdlnɪs/ N 1 (= *leisure*) oisiveté *f* ; (*pej*) (= *laziness*) paresse *f*, fainéantise *f* ◆ **to live in ~** vivre dans l'oisiveté 2 (= *state of not working*) inaction *f*, inactivité *f* ; (= *unemployment*) chômage *m* 3 [*of threat, wish, question, speculation*] futilité *f*, inutilité *f* ; [*of promises, pleasures*] futilité *f* ; [*of fears*] manque *m* de justification ; [*of words*] manque *m* de sérieux ; [*of effort*] inutilité *f*

idler /ˈaɪdləʳ/ N 1 (= *lazy person*) paresseux *m*, -euse *f*, fainéant(e) *m(f)* 2 (*Tech*) (= *wheel*) roue *f* folle ; (= *pinion*) pignon *m* libre ; (= *pulley*) poulie *f* folle

idling /ˈaɪdlɪŋ/ ADJ ◆ **at ~ speed** au ralenti

idly /ˈaɪdlɪ/ ADV 1 (= *lazily*) [*sit, spend time*] sans rien faire ◆ **to stand** or **sit ~ by (while ...)** rester sans rien faire (pendant que ...) 2 (= *abstractedly*) [*wonder, speculate, think, look at*] vaguement ; [*say, play with*] négligemment ; [*talk*] pour passer le temps ◆ **~ curious** vaguement curieux

idol /ˈaɪdl/ N (*lit, fig*) idole *f* ◆ **a teen ~** une idole des jeunes ◆ **a fallen ~** une idole déchue

idolater /aɪˈdɒlətəʳ/ N idolâtre *mf*

idolatrous /aɪˈdɒlətrəs/ ADJ idolâtre

idolatry /aɪˈdɒlətrɪ/ N (*lit, fig*) idolâtrie *f*

idolize /ˈaɪdəlaɪz/ VT idolâtrer

idyll /ˈɪdɪl/ N (*Literat, also fig*) idylle *f*

idyllic /ɪˈdɪlɪk/ ADJ idyllique

i.e., ie /ˌaɪˈiː/ (abbrev of **id est**) (= *that is*) c.-à-d., c'est-à-dire

if /ɪf/ CONJ 1 (*condition* = *supposing that*) si ◆ **I'll go ~ you come with me** j'irai si tu m'accompagnes ◆ **~ the weather's nice I'll be pleased** s'il fait beau je serai content ◆ **~ the weather were nice I would be pleased** s'il faisait beau je serais content ◆ **~ the weather's nice and (~ it is) not too cold I'll go with you** s'il fait beau et (s'il ne fait or qu'il ne fasse) pas trop froid je vous accompagnerai ◆ **~ I had known, I would have visited them** si j'avais su, je leur aurais rendu visite ◆ **~ you wait a minute, I'll come with you** si vous attendez or voulez attendre une minute, je vais vous accompagner ◆ **~ I were a millionaire, I could ...** si j'étais (un) millionnaire, je pourrais ... ◆ **~ I were you** si j'étais vous, (si j'étais) à votre place ◆ **(even) ~ I knew I wouldn't tell you** même si je le savais, je ne te le dirais pas ◆ **~ they are to be believed** à les en croire ◆ **~ it is true that ...** s'il est vrai que ... + *indic*, si tant est que ... + *subj*
2 (= *whenever*) si ◆ **~ I asked him he helped me** si je le lui demandais il m'aidait ◆ **~ she wants any help she asks me** si elle a besoin d'aide elle s'adresse à moi
3 (= *although*) si ◆ **(even) ~ it takes me all day I'll do it** (même) si cela doit me prendre toute la journée je le ferai ◆ **(even) ~ they are poor at least they are happy** s'ils sont pauvres du moins ils sont heureux ◆ **even ~ it is a good film it's rather long** c'est un bon film bien qu'(il soit) un peu long ◆ **nice weather, ~ rather cold** temps agréable, bien qu'un peu froid ◆ **even ~ he tells me himself I won't believe it** même s'il me le dit lui-même je ne le croirai pas
4 (= *granted that, admitting that*) si ◆ **~ I am wrong, you are wrong too** si je me trompe or en admettant que je me trompe *subj*, vous vous trompez aussi ◆ **(even) ~ he did say that, he didn't mean to hurt you** quand (bien) même il l'aurait dit, il n'avait aucune intention de vous faire de la peine
5 (= *whether*) si ◆ **do you know ~ they have gone?** savez-vous s'ils sont partis ? ◆ **I wonder ~ it's true** je me demande si c'est vrai
6 (= *unless*) **~ ... not** si ... ne ◆ **that's the house, ~ I'm not mistaken** voilà la maison, si je ne me trompe ◆ **they're coming at Christmas ~ they don't change their minds** ils viennent à Noël à moins qu'ils ne changent *subj* d'avis
7 (*phrases*) **underpaid, ~ they are paid at all** mal payés, si tant est qu'on les paie ◆ **~ it weren't for him, I wouldn't go** sans lui, je n'irais pas ◆ **~ it weren't for him, I wouldn't be in this mess** sans lui, je ne serais pas dans ce pétrin ◆ **~ it hadn't been for you, I would have despaired** sans toi, j'aurais désespéré ◆ **well ~ he didn't try to steal my bag!** * (ne) voilà-t-il pas qu'il essaie de me voler mon sac ! * ◆ **~ it isn't our old friend Smith!** tiens ! mais c'est notre bon vieux Smith ! ◆ **~ I know her, she'll refuse** telle que je la connais, elle refusera
◆ **as if** comme, comme si ◆ **he acts as ~ he were rich** il se conduit comme s'il était riche ◆ **as ~**

by chance comme par hasard ◆ **he stood there as ~ he were dumb** il restait là comme (s'il était) muet ◆ **it isn't as ~ we were rich** ce n'est pas comme si nous étions riches, nous ne sommes pourtant pas riches

♦ **if not** sinon ◆ **in practice ~ not in law** dans la pratique sinon d'un point de vue légal ◆ **the old programme was very similar, ~ not the same** l'ancienne émission était très semblable, voire identique ◆ **difficult ~ not impossible** difficile, voire impossible ◆ **they're nothing ~ not efficient** le moins qu'on puisse dire, c'est qu'ils sont efficaces

♦ **if only** *(wishing)* si seulement ◆ **~ only I had known!** si seulement j'avais su ! ◆ **~ only it were that simple!** si seulement c'était aussi simple ! ◆ **I'd better write to her, ~ only to let her know that ...** *(emphatic use)* il faudrait que je lui écrive, ne serait-ce que pour lui faire savoir que ... ◆ **~ only for a moment** ne serait-ce que pour un instant

♦ **if so** si oui, dans ce cas ◆ **are they to be released and ~ so when?** vont-ils être remis en liberté et, si oui *or* dans ce cas, quand ?

N ◆ **~s and buts** les si *mpl* et les mais *mpl* ◆ **it's a big ~** c'est un grand point d'interrogation

iffy* /ˈɪfɪ/ **ADJ** *(= uncertain) [outcome, future]* aléatoire, incertain ; *(= dodgy) [method]* qui craint* ◆ **an ~ neighbourhood** un quartier douteux ◆ **it all seems a bit ~ to me** ça me paraît un peu suspect, ça ne me paraît pas très catholique ◆ **I was feeling a bit ~** je n'étais pas vraiment dans mon assiette

igloo /ˈɪgluː/ **N** igloo *m or* iglou *m*

Ignatius /ɪgˈneɪʃəs/ **N** Ignace *m* ◆ **(St) ~ Loyola** saint Ignace de Loyola

igneous /ˈɪgnɪəs/ **ADJ** igné

ignite /ɪgˈnaɪt/ **VT** 1 *(lit)* mettre le feu à, enflammer 2 *(fig) [passions, interest]* susciter, déclencher ; *[conflict, controversy]* déclencher, être le détonateur de **VI** 1 *(lit)* prendre feu, s'enflammer 2 *(fig) [conflict, controversy]* se déclencher

ignition /ɪgˈnɪʃən/ **N** 1 ignition *f* 2 *[of vehicle] (= system)* allumage *m* ; *(= starting mechanism)* contact *m* ◆ **to switch on/turn off the ~** mettre/couper le contact

COMP **ignition coil N** bobine *f* d'allumage
ignition key N clé *f* de contact
ignition switch N contact *m*

ignoble /ɪgˈnəʊbl/ **ADJ** ignoble, indigne

ignominious /ˌɪgnəˈmɪnɪəs/ **ADJ** *(frm)* ignominieux *(liter)*

ignominiously /ˌɪgnəˈmɪnɪəslɪ/ **ADV** *(frm)* ignominieusement *(liter)*

ignominy /ˈɪgnəmɪnɪ/ **N** ignominie *f*

ignoramus /ˌɪgnəˈreɪməs/ **N** ignare *mf*, ignorant(e) *m(f)*

ignorance /ˈɪgnərəns/ **N** 1 ignorance *f (of* de) ◆ **to be in ~ of sth** ignorer qch ◆ **they lived in blissful ~ of his true identity** ils vivaient dans l'heureuse ignorance de sa véritable identité ◆ **to keep sb in ~ of sth** tenir qn dans l'ignorance de qch, laisser ignorer qch à qn ◆ **in my ~** dans mon ignorance ◆ **~ of the law is no excuse** nul n'est censé ignorer la loi ◆ **his ~ of chemistry** son ignorance en (matière de) chimie ◆ **there is so much public ~ about this problem** c'est un problème totalement méconnu du grand public ◆ **~ is bliss** il vaut mieux ne pas savoir 2 *(= lack of education)* ignorance *f* ◆ **don't show your ~!** ce n'est pas la peine d'étaler ton ignorance !

ignorant /ˈɪgnərənt/ **ADJ** 1 *(= unaware)* **~ of** ignorant de ◆ **to be ~ of the facts** ignorer les faits, être ignorant des faits 2 *(= lacking education) [person]* ignorant ; *[words, behaviour]* d'(un) ignorant ◆ **for fear of appearing ~** par peur de paraître ignorant ; → **pig**

ignorantly /ˈɪgnərəntlɪ/ **ADV** par ignorance

ignore /ɪgˈnɔːʳ/ **VT** 1 *(= take no notice of) [+ interruption, remark, objection, advice, warning]* ne tenir aucun compte de, ignorer ; *[+ sb's behaviour]* ne pas prêter attention à ; *[+ person]* faire semblant de ne pas voir *or* entendre ; *[+ invitation, letter]* ne pas répondre à ; *[+ facts]* méconnaître ; *[+ question]* ne pas répondre à ; *[+ rule, prohibition]* ne pas respecter ; *[+ awkward fact]* faire semblant de ne pas connaître, ne tenir aucun compte de ◆ **I shall ~ your impertinence** je ne relèverai pas votre impertinence ◆ **we cannot ~ this behaviour any longer** nous ne pouvons plus fermer les yeux sur ce genre de comportement 2 *(Jur)* **to ~ a bill** prononcer un verdict d'acquittement

iguana /ɪˈgwɑːnə/ **N** iguane *m*

ikon /ˈaɪkɒn/ **N** ⇒ **icon**

IL abbrev of **Illinois**

ILEA /ˌaɪˌeliːˈeɪ/ **N** *(Brit Educ: formerly)* (abbrev of **Inner London Education Authority**) *services londoniens de l'enseignement*

ileum /ˈɪlɪəm/ **N** *(Anat)* iléon *m*

ilex /ˈaɪleks/ **N** 1 *(= holm oak)* yeuse *f*, chêne *m* vert 2 *(genus = holly)* houx *m*

Iliad /ˈɪlɪəd/ **N** ◆ **the ~** l'Iliade *f*

Ilion /ˈɪlɪən/, **Ilium** /ˈɪlɪəm/ **N** Ilion

ilium /ˈɪlɪəm/ **N** (pl **ilia** /ˈɪlɪə/) *(Anat)* ilion *m*

ilk /ɪlk/ **N** ◆ **of that ~** de cette espèce *or* cet acabit ◆ **people of his ~** des gens de son espèce

I'll /aɪl/ ⇒ **I shall, I will** ; → **shall, will**

ill /ɪl/ **ADJ** (compar **worse**, superl **worst**) 1 *(= unwell)* malade ; *(less serious)* souffrant ◆ **to be ~** être malade *or* souffrant ◆ **to fall** *or* **take** *or* **be taken ~** tomber malade ◆ **to feel ~** ne pas se sentir bien ◆ **to look ~** avoir l'air malade *or* souffrant ◆ **to make sb ~** rendre qn malade ◆ **to be ~ with a fever/pneumonia** avoir de la fièvre/une pneumonie ◆ **~ with anxiety/jealousy** *etc* malade d'inquiétude/de jalousie *etc* ◆ **he's seriously ~ in hospital** il est à l'hôpital dans un état grave ; see also **mentally, terminally**

2 *(= bad)* mauvais, méchant ◆ **~ deed** *(liter)* mauvaise action *f*, méfait *m* ◆ **~ effects** conséquences *fpl* négatives ◆ **of ~ fame** *or* **repute** *(liter) [place]* mal famé ; *[person]* de mauvaise réputation ◆ **house of ~ repute** maison *f* mal famée ◆ **~ health** mauvaise santé *f* ◆ **~ luck** malchance *f* ◆ **by ~ luck** par malheur, par malchance ◆ **as ~ luck would have it, he ...** le malheur a voulu qu'il ... + *subj* ◆ **~ humour** *or* **temper** mauvaise humeur *f* ◆ **~ nature** méchanceté *f* ◆ **~ omen** mauvais augure *m* ◆ **~ feeling** ressentiment *m*, rancune *f* ◆ **no ~ feeling!** sans rancune ! ◆ **~ will** *(gen)* malveillance *f* ; *(= grudge, resentment)* rancune *f* ◆ **I bear him no ~ will** je ne lui en veux pas ◆ **just to show there's no ~ will, I'll do it** je vais le faire, pour bien montrer que je ne suis pas rancunier ◆ **it's an ~ wind that blows nobody any good** *(Prov)* à quelque chose malheur est bon *(Prov)*

N *(NonC = evil, injury)* mal *m* ◆ **to think/speak ~ of sb** penser/dire du mal de qn ◆ **they mean you no ~** ils ne vous veulent aucun mal ; → **good**

NPL **ills** *(= misfortunes)* maux *mpl*, malheurs *mpl*

ADV mal ◆ **he can ~ afford the expense** il peut difficilement se permettre la dépense ◆ **we can ~ afford another scandal** nous ne pouvons guère nous permettre un autre scandale ◆ **to take sth ~** *(liter)* prendre mal qch, prendre qch en mauvaise part ◆ **to go ~ with sb/sth** *(liter)* tourner mal pour qn/qch, aller mal pour qn/qch ◆ **the suggestion was ~-received** la suggestion a été mal accueillie ◆ **to sit ~ with sth** *(liter)* aller mal avec qch ◆ **to bode** *or* **augur ~ for sb** être de mauvais augure pour qn ◆ **it ~ becomes you to do that** *(frm, liter)* il vous sied mal *(frm)* de faire cela

COMP **ill-advised ADJ** *[decision, remark, action]* peu judicieux ◆ **you would be ~-advised to do that** vous auriez tort de faire cela, vous seriez malavisé de faire cela
ill-assorted ADJ mal assorti
ill-at-ease ADJ mal à l'aise
ill-bred ADJ mal élevé
ill-concealed ADJ *[amusement, disdain, disgust]* mal dissimulé
ill-conceived ADJ *[plan, policy]* mal conçu *or* pensé
ill-considered ADJ *[action, words]* irréfléchi ; *[measures]* hâtif
ill-defined ADJ *[goals, powers, task]* mal défini
ill-disposed ADJ mal disposé *(towards* envers)
ill-equipped ADJ mal équipé *(with* en) ◆ **to be ~-equipped to do sth** *(lit)* être mal équipé pour faire qch, ne pas avoir le matériel nécessaire pour faire qch ; *(fig) [person]* être mal armé pour faire qch ◆ **he's ~-equipped for the role of Macbeth** il n'a pas les qualités requises pour jouer Macbeth
ill-fated ADJ *[person]* infortuné, malheureux ; *[day]* fatal, néfaste ; *[action, effort]* malheureux
ill-favoured, ill-favored (US) **ADJ** *(= ugly)* laid, pas aidé par la nature ; *(= objectionable)* déplaisant, désagréable ; *(stronger)* répugnant
ill-fitting ADJ *[shoe, garment]* qui ne va pas (bien) ; *[lid, stopper]* qui ferme mal
ill-formed ADJ *(Ling)* mal formé
ill-founded ADJ *[belief, argument]* mal fondé ; *[rumour]* sans fondement
ill-gotten gains NPL biens *mpl* mal acquis
ill-humoured ADJ de mauvaise humeur, maussade
ill-informed ADJ *[person]* mal renseigné, mal informé ; *[comment, criticism]* mal fondé ; *[essay, speech]* plein d'inexactitudes
ill-judged ADJ peu judicieux, peu sage
ill-mannered ADJ *[person, behaviour]* grossier, impoli
ill-natured ADJ *[person, reply]* désagréable ; *[child]* méchant, désagréable
ill-nourished ADJ mal nourri
ill-omened ADJ de mauvais augure
ill-prepared ADJ mal préparé
ill-starred ADJ *(liter) [person]* né sous une mauvaise étoile, infortuné ; *[day, undertaking]* malheureux, néfaste
ill-suited ADJ ◆ **they are ~-suited (to each other)** ils sont mal assortis ◆ **~-suited to** *[tool, computer]* mal adapté à ◆ **he is ~-suited to this type of work** il ne convient guère à ce genre de travail, il n'est pas vraiment fait pour ce genre de travail
ill-tempered ADJ *(habitually)* désagréable, qui a mauvais caractère ; *(on one occasion)* de mauvaise humeur, maussade
ill-timed ADJ inopportun
ill-treat VT maltraiter
ill-treatment N mauvais traitements *mpl*
ill-use VT maltraiter

Ill. abbrev of **Illinois**

illegal /ɪˈliːgəl/ **ADJ** 1 *(= against the law)* illégal ◆ **it is ~ to do that** il est illégal de faire cela ◆ **it is ~ to sell alcohol to children** la loi interdit la vente d'alcool aux enfants ◆ **to make it ~ to do sth** rendre illégal de faire qch ◆ **~ parking** stationnement *m* illicite *or* interdit ◆ **~ alien** étranger *m*, -ère *f* en situation irrégulière ◆ **~ immigrant** immigré(e) *m(f)* clandestin(e) 2 *(Sport)* irrégulier ◆ **~ tackle** tacle *m* irrégulier 3 *(Comput)* ◆ **~ character** caractère *m* invalide ◆ **~ operation** opération *f* interdite

illegality /ˌɪliːˈgælɪtɪ/ **N** illégalité *f*

illegally /ɪˈliːgəlɪ/ **ADV** illégalement ◆ **to be ~ parked** être en stationnement interdit

illegible /ɪˈledʒəbl/ **ADJ** illisible

illegibly /ɪˈledʒəblɪ/ **ADV** de façon illisible

illegitimacy /ˌɪlɪˈdʒɪtɪməsɪ/ **N** illégitimité *f*

illegitimate /ˌɪlɪˈdʒɪtɪmɪt/ ADJ ① *[child]* illégitime, naturel ② *[action]* illégitime ; *(fig) [argument]* illogique ; *[conclusion]* injustifié

illegitimately /ˌɪlɪˈdʒɪtɪmɪtlɪ/ ADV illégitimement

illiberal /ɪˈlɪbərəl/ ADJ *[law]* restrictif ; *[system, regime]* intolérant ; *[person]* intolérant, étroit d'esprit ; *[view]* étroit

illicit /ɪˈlɪsɪt/ ADJ illicite

illicitly /ɪˈlɪsɪtlɪ/ ADV illicitement

illimitable /ɪˈlɪmɪtəbl/ ADJ illimité, sans limites

Illinois /ˌɪlɪˈnɔɪ/ N Illinois *m* ♦ **in ~** dans l'Illinois

illiteracy /ɪˈlɪtərəsɪ/ N analphabétisme *m*

illiterate /ɪˈlɪtərɪt/ ADJ *[person]* illettré, analphabète ♦ **he is computer ~** il ne connaît rien à l'informatique, il ne s'y connaît pas en informatique N illettré(e) *m(f)*, analphabète *mf*

illness /ˈɪlnɪs/ N maladie *f* ♦ **she died after a long ~** elle est morte à la suite d'une longue maladie

illocutionary /ˌɪləˈkjuːʃənərɪ/ ADJ illocutionnaire

illogical /ɪˈlɒdʒɪkəl/ ADJ illogique

illogicality /ɪˌlɒdʒɪˈkælɪtɪ/ N illogisme *m*

illogically /ɪˈlɒdʒɪkəlɪ/ ADV de façon illogique

illuminate /ɪˈluːmɪneɪt/ VT ① *(gen)* éclairer ; *(for special occasion or effect)* illuminer ♦ **~d sign** enseigne *f* lumineuse ② *(fig) [+ question, subject]* éclairer, faire la lumière sur ③ *(Art) [+ manuscript]* enluminer

illuminating /ɪˈluːmɪneɪtɪŋ/ ADJ *(lit, fig)* éclairant ♦ **his comments proved very ~** ses commentaires se sont révélés très éclairants *or* ont beaucoup éclairci la question ♦ **it would be ~ to compare their stories** on apprendrait beaucoup en comparant leurs histoires

illumination /ɪˌluːmɪˈneɪʃən/ N ① *(NonC, gen)* éclairage *m* ; *(for special effect) [of building]* illumination *f* ② *(fig)* lumière *f*, inspiration *f* ③ *(Brit)* ♦ **~s** *(= decorative lights)* illuminations *fpl* ④ *[of manuscript]* enluminure *f*

illuminator /ɪˈluːmɪneɪtəʳ/ N ① *(= lighting device)* dispositif *m* d'éclairage ② *[of manuscript]* enlumineur *m*

illumine /ɪˈluːmɪn/ VT *(liter)* éclairer

illusion /ɪˈluːʒən/ N illusion *f* ♦ **to be under an ~** avoir *or* se faire une illusion ♦ **to be under the ~ that ...** avoir *or* se faire l'illusion que ... *+ indic* ♦ **to have** *or* **to be under no ~(s)** ne se faire aucune illusion ♦ **I have no ~s about what will happen to him** je ne me fais aucune illusion sur le sort qui l'attend ♦ **no one has any ~s about winning the war** personne ne se fait d'illusions sur l'issue de la guerre ♦ **he cherishes the ~ that ...** il caresse l'illusion que ... ♦ **large wall mirrors give an ~ of space** des grands miroirs au mur créent une impression d'espace ♦ **a tan can give us the ~ of being slimmer** le bronzage peut donner l'impression d'être plus mince ; → **optical**

illusionist /ɪˈluːʒənɪst/ N illusionniste *mf*

illusive /ɪˈluːsɪv/, **illusory** /ɪˈluːsərɪ/ ADJ *(= unreal)* illusoire, irréel ; *(= deceptive)* illusoire, trompeur

illustrate /ˈɪləstreɪt/ LANGUAGE IN USE 26.1 VT ① *[+ book, story]* illustrer ♦ **~d paper** (journal *m or* magazine *m etc*) illustré *m* ② *(fig = exemplify) [+ idea, problem]* illustrer ; *[+ rule]* donner un exemple de ♦ **this can best be ~d as follows** la meilleure illustration qu'on puisse en donner est la suivante ♦ **to ~ that ...** illustrer le fait que ...

illustration /ˌɪləsˈtreɪʃən/ LANGUAGE IN USE 26.2 N illustration *f* ♦ **by way of ~** à titre d'exemple

illustrative /ˈɪləstrətɪv/ ADJ *[example]* explicatif, servant d'explication ♦ **for ~ purposes** à titre d'illustration ♦ **~ of this problem** qui sert à illustrer ce problème

illustrator /ˈɪləstreɪtəʳ/ N illustrateur *m*, -trice *f*

illustrious /ɪˈlʌstrɪəs/ ADJ illustre, célèbre

illustriously /ɪˈlʌstrɪəslɪ/ ADV glorieusement

ILO /ˌaɪelˈəʊ/ N (abbrev of **International Labour Organisation**) OIT *f*

I'm /aɪm/ ⇒ **I am** ; → **be**

image /ˈɪmɪdʒ/ N ① *(= likeness)* image *f* ♦ **God created man in his own ~** Dieu créa l'homme à son image ♦ **real/virtual ~** image *f* réelle/virtuelle ♦ **~ in the glass/mirror** réflexion *f* dans la vitre/le miroir ♦ **he is the (living** *or* **very** *or* **spitting*) ~ of his father** c'est le portrait (vivant) de son père, c'est son père tout craché* ♦ **he's the very ~ of the English aristocrat** c'est l'aristocrate anglais type, c'est l'image même de l'aristocrate anglais ♦ **I had a sudden (mental) ~ of her, alone and afraid** soudain je l'ai vue en imagination, seule et effrayée ♦ **they had quite the wrong ~ of him** ils se faisaient une idée tout à fait fausse de lui ; → **graven, mirror**

② (also **public image**) image *f* (de marque) *(fig)* ♦ **he has to think of his ~** il faut qu'il pense à son image (de marque) ♦ **the tobacco industry is trying to improve its ~** l'industrie du tabac essaie d'améliorer son image (de marque) ♦ **he's got the wrong ~ for that part** *(Cine, Theat etc)* le public ne le voit pas dans ce genre de rôle ; → **brand**

COMP **image-building** N ♦ **it's just ~-building** ça ne vise qu'à promouvoir son (*or* leur *etc*) image de marque

image-conscious ADJ ♦ **he is very ~-conscious** il se soucie beaucoup de son image

image enhancement N *(in computer graphics)* enrichissement *m* d'images

imager /ˈɪmɪdʒəʳ/ N → **magnetic, thermal**

imagery /ˈɪmɪdʒərɪ/ N imagerie *f* ♦ **language full of ~** langage *m* imagé

imaginable /ɪˈmædʒnəbl/ ADJ imaginable ♦ **every activity ~** toutes les activités imaginables ♦ **the most horrible circumstances ~** les circonstances les plus horribles que l'on puisse imaginer ♦ **a place of no ~ strategic value** un endroit qui ne présente pas le moindre intérêt stratégique

imaginary /ɪˈmædʒɪnərɪ/ ADJ *[danger]* imaginaire ; *[character, place]* imaginaire, fictif

imagination /ɪˌmædʒɪˈneɪʃən/ N *(NonC)* imagination *f* ♦ **to have a lively** *or* **vivid ~** avoir une imagination fertile ♦ **he's got ~** il a de l'imagination ♦ **he has little ~** il a peu d'imagination ♦ **a lack of ~** un manque d'imagination ♦ **she lets her ~ run away with her** elle se laisse emporter *or* entraîner par son imagination ♦ **it existed only in his ~** cela n'existait que dans son imagination ♦ **to capture** *or* **catch sb's ~** frapper l'imagination de qn ♦ **it is only** *or* **all (your) ~!** vous vous faites des idées !, vous rêvez ! ♦ **haven't you got any ~?** tu n'as donc aucune imagination ? ♦ **use your ~!** tu n'as pas beaucoup d'imagination ! ; → **appeal** ; see also **stretch**

imaginative /ɪˈmædʒɪnətɪv/ ADJ *[person]* imaginatif, plein d'imagination ; *[book, film, approach]* plein d'imagination ; *[solution, system, device]* inventif

imaginatively /ɪˈmædʒɪnətɪvlɪ/ ADV avec imagination

imaginativeness /ɪˈmædʒɪnətɪvnɪs/ N *[of person]* esprit *m* imaginatif *or* inventif ; *[of thing]* caractère *m* imaginatif *or* inventif

imagine /ɪˈmædʒɪn/ LANGUAGE IN USE 6.2 VT ① *(= picture to o.s.)* (s')imaginer ♦ **~ life 100 years ago** imaginez(-vous) *or* représentez-vous la vie il y a 100 ans ♦ **try to ~ a huge house far from anywhere** essayez d'imaginer *or* de vous imaginer une immense maison loin de tout ♦ **~ (that) you're lying on a beach** imaginez que vous êtes étendu sur une plage ♦ **I can't ~ myself at 60** je ne m'imagine *or* ne me vois pas du tout à 60 ans ♦ **~ a situation in which ...** imaginez (vous) une situation où ... ♦ **(just) ~!** tu (t')imagines ! ♦ **(you can) ~ how I felt!** imaginez *or* vous imaginez ce que j'ai pu ressentir ! ♦ **I can ~ how he must feel** j'imagine ce qu'il doit ressentir ♦ **I can ~!** je m'en doute ! ♦ **~ my surprise when I won!** imaginez ma surprise quand j'ai gagné ! ♦ **(you can) ~ how pleased I was!** vous pensez si j'étais content ! ♦ **it's hard to ~ how bad things were** on a du mal à s'imaginer à quel point les choses allaient mal ♦ **did you ever ~ you'd meet her one day?** est-ce que tu t'étais jamais imaginé *or* douté que tu la rencontrerais un jour ? ♦ **I can just ~ his reaction when he sees her** je vois d'ici sa réaction quand il la verra ♦ **I can't ~ you being nasty to anyone** je ne peux pas imaginer que vous puissiez être désagréable avec qui que ce soit ♦ **I can't ~ living there** je ne me vois pas vivre là ♦ **he's (always) imagining things** il se fait des idées

② *(= suppose, believe)* supposer, imaginer *(that* que) ♦ **you won't want to stay long, I ~** vous ne resterez pas longtemps, je suppose *or* j'imagine ♦ **I didn't ~ he would come** je ne pensais pas qu'il viendrait ♦ **was he meeting someone? – I ~ so** il avait un rendez-vous ? – j'imagine *or* je suppose

③ *(= believe wrongly)* croire, s'imaginer ♦ **don't ~ that I can help you** n'allez pas croire que *or* ne vous imaginez pas que je puisse vous aider ♦ **he fondly ~d she was still willing to obey him** il s'imaginait naïvement qu'elle était encore prête à lui obéir ♦ **I ~d I heard someone speak** j'ai cru entendre parler ♦ **I ~d you to be dark-haired** je vous imaginais avec les cheveux bruns

imaging /ˈɪmɪdʒɪŋ/ N *(Comput)* imagerie *f* ; → **document, thermal**

imaginings /ɪˈmædʒɪnɪŋz/ NPL ♦ **it was beyond our wildest ~** nous n'en espérions pas tant, même dans nos rêves les plus fous

imam /ɪˈmɑːm/ N imam *m*

IMAX ®/ˈaɪmaks/ N IMAX ® *m*

imbalance /ɪmˈbæləns/ N *(lit, fig)* déséquilibre *m* ♦ **the ~ in trade between the two countries** le déséquilibre des échanges commerciaux entre les deux pays

imbalanced /ɪmˈbælənst/ ADJ déséquilibré

imbecile /ˈɪmbəsiːl/ N ① imbécile *mf*, idiot(e) *m(f)* ♦ **to act/speak like an ~** faire/dire des imbécillités *or* des bêtises ♦ **you ~!** espèce d'imbécile *or* d'idiot ! ② *(Med* ††*)* imbécile *mf* ADJ ① *[action, words]* imbécile ; *[person]* imbécile, idiot ② *(Med* ††*)* imbécile

imbecility /ˌɪmbɪˈsɪlɪtɪ/ N ① *(NonC)* imbécillité *f*, stupidité *f* ② *(= act etc)* imbécillité *f*, stupidité *f* ③ *(Med* ††*)* imbécillité *f*

imbed /ɪmˈbed/ VT ⇒ **embed**

imbibe /ɪmˈbaɪb/ VT ① *(= drink)* boire, absorber ; *(fig) [+ ideas, information]* absorber ② *(= absorb) [+ water, light, heat]* absorber VI *(* hum = drink to excess)* s'imbiber d'alcool

imbroglio /ɪmˈbrəʊlɪəʊ/ N imbroglio *m*

imbue /ɪmˈbjuː/ VT *(fig)* imprégner *(with* de) ♦ **~d with** imprégné de

IMF /ˌaɪemˈef/ N *(Econ)* (abbrev of **International Monetary Fund**) FMI *m*

imitable /ˈɪmɪtəbl/ ADJ imitable

imitate /ˈɪmɪteɪt/ VT imiter

imitation /ˌɪmɪˈteɪʃən/ N imitation *f* ♦ **in ~ of** en imitant ♦ **they learnt grammar by ~ of their elders** ils ont appris la grammaire en imitant leurs aînés ♦ **"beware of imitations"**

(Comm) "se méfier des contrefaçons" ◆ **it's only ~** c'est de l'imitation ◆ **I do a pretty good ~ of him** j'arrive assez bien à l'imiter ◆ **~ is the sincerest form of flattery** *(Prov)* il n'est pas de louange plus sincère que l'imitation
COMP *[silk, ivory, gun, fruit]* faux (fausse *f*) *before n*
imitation fur coat N manteau *m* en fourrure synthétique *or* en fausse fourrure
imitation gold N similor *m*
imitation jewellery N faux bijoux *mpl*
imitation leather N imitation *f* cuir, similicuir *m*
imitation marble N faux marbre *m*, similimarbre *m*
imitation mink coat N manteau *m* (en) imitation vison
imitation pearl N perle *f* synthétique, fausse perle *f*
imitation stone N pierre *f* artificielle, fausse pierre *f*

imitative /ˈɪmɪtətɪv/ ADJ *[word, art]* imitatif ; *[person]* imitateur (-trice *f*)

imitator /ˈɪmɪteɪtəʳ/ N imitateur *m*, -trice *f*

immaculate /ɪˈmækjʊlɪt/ ADJ *(= clean) [fabric, garment, colour]* immaculé ; *(= spick and span) [garment, house, hair, figure]* impeccable ◆ **an ~ white shirt** une chemise blanche immaculée
COMP **the Immaculate Conception** N *(Rel)* l'Immaculée Conception *f*

immaculately /ɪˈmækjʊlɪtlɪ/ ADV *[dressed, groomed, behaved]* de façon impeccable ◆ **~ clean** d'une propreté impeccable ◆ **an ~ kept house/car** une maison/voiture impeccablement tenue

immanent /ˈɪmənənt/ ADJ immanent

Immanuel /ɪˈmænjʊəl/ N Emmanuel *m*

immaterial /ˌɪməˈtɪərɪəl/ ADJ [1] *(= unimportant)* négligeable, sans importance ◆ **it is ~ whether he did or not** il importe peu qu'il l'ait fait ou non ◆ **that's (quite) ~** *(= not important)* ça n'a pas d'importance ; *(= not relevant)* ça n'est pas pertinent ◆ **that's ~ to us** peu nous importe ◆ **my presence was ~ to him** il n'avait que faire de ma présence [2] *(Philos etc)* immatériel

immature /ˌɪməˈtjʊəʳ/ ADJ [1] *(= not full-grown) [fruit]* (qui n'est) pas mûr, vert ; *[animal, tree]* jeune [2] *(= childish)* immature ◆ **he's very ~** il est très immature, il manque vraiment de maturité ◆ **he is emotionally ~** il est affectivement immature ◆ **she's just being childish and ~** elle se comporte d'une manière puérile et immature

immaturity /ˌɪməˈtjʊərɪtɪ/ N manque *m* de maturité, immaturité *f*

immeasurable /ɪˈmeʒərəbl/ ADJ *[amount, height, space]* incommensurable ; *[joy, suffering]* incommensurable, infini ; *[precautions, care]* infini ; *[wealth, riches, value]* inestimable

immeasurably /ɪˈmeʒərəblɪ/ ADV *(frm) [better, worse]* infiniment ; *[improve]* infiniment ; *[increase, rise, advance]* dans des proportions illimitées ◆ **to help sb ~** apporter une aide inestimable à qn ◆ **to add ~ to sth** ajouter infiniment à qch

immediacy /ɪˈmiːdɪəsɪ/ N immédiateté *f* ◆ **the ~ of live television** l'immédiateté du direct ◆ **a sense of ~** un sentiment d'immédiateté *or* d'urgence

immediate /ɪˈmiːdɪət/ ADJ [1] *(= instant) [effect, impact, response, results, ceasefire, closure, danger]* immédiat ◆ **with ~ effect** avec effet immédiat ◆ **to come into ~ effect** entrer immédiatement en vigueur ◆ **to take ~ action** agir immédiatement ◆ **for ~ delivery** à livrer immédiatement ◆ **the matter deserves your ~ attention** cette affaire exige une attention immédiate de votre part ◆ **a savings account that allows ~ access to your money** un compte d'épargne qui vous permet d'effectuer des retraits à tout moment ◆ **he has no ~ plans to retire** il n'envisage pas de prendre sa retraite dans l'immédiat
[2] *(= most urgent) [future, needs, priority, threat, problem, issue]* immédiat ◆ **my ~ concern was for the children** mon premier souci a été les enfants ◆ **of more ~ concern is the state of the economy** l'état de l'économie est une préoccupation plus urgente *or* plus immédiate ◆ **his (most) ~ task** sa tâche la plus urgente
[3] *(= direct, nearest)* immédiat ◆ **in sb's ~ vicinity** dans le voisinage immédiat de qn ◆ **to the ~ south** immédiatement au sud ◆ **her ~ predecessor** son prédécesseur immédiat ◆ **in the ~ aftermath of the war** sitôt après la guerre, dans l'immédiat après-guerre ◆ **my ~ family** ma famille immédiate
COMP **immediate constituent** N *(Gram)* constituant *m* immédiat

immediately /ɪˈmiːdɪətlɪ/ ADV [1] *(= at once)* immédiatement, tout de suite ◆ **~ available/obvious/apparent** immédiatement *or* tout de suite disponible/évident/apparent ◆ **~ before/after/afterwards** immédiatement *or* sitôt avant/après/après ◆ **the years ~ following the Second World War** les années qui ont immédiatement suivi la Seconde Guerre mondiale ◆ **~ upon arrival** *or* **arriving** dès l'arrivée [2] *(= directly)* directement ◆ **~ behind/above** directement derrière/au-dessus
CONJ *(esp Brit)* dès que ◆ **~ I returned, I ...** dès mon retour, je ...

immemorial /ˌɪmɪˈmɔːrɪəl/ ADJ immémorial ◆ **from** *or* **since time ~** de toute éternité, de temps immémorial

immense /ɪˈmens/ ADJ *[space]* immense, vaste ; *[size]* immense ; *[possibilities, achievements, fortune, difficulty]* immense, énorme ; *(* esp US = very impressive)* géant*

immensely /ɪˈmenslɪ/ ADV *[rich, successful, popular]* immensément, extrêmement ; *[enjoy, help, vary]* énormément ◆ **~ helpful** *[book, object etc]* extrêmement utile ; *[person]* extrêmement serviable ◆ **to improve ~** s'améliorer énormément

immensity /ɪˈmensɪtɪ/ N immensité *f*

immerse /ɪˈmɜːs/ VT immerger, plonger ; *(Rel)* baptiser par immersion ◆ **to ~ one's head in water** plonger la tête dans l'eau ◆ **to ~ o.s. in sth** *(work, hobby)* se plonger dans qch ◆ **to be ~d in one's work** être absorbé *or* plongé dans son travail

immersion /ɪˈmɜːʃən/ N immersion *f* ; *(fig)* absorption *f* ; *(Rel)* baptême *m* par immersion
COMP **immersion course** N *(Educ)* stage *m or* cours *m* intensif (in de)
immersion heater N *(Brit) (= boiler)* chauffe-eau *m inv* électrique ; *(= device)* thermoplongeur *m*

immigrancy /ˈɪmɪɡrənsɪ/ N *(US)* condition *f* d'immigrant

immigrant /ˈɪmɪɡrənt/ ADJ, N *(newly arrived)* immigrant(e) *m(f)* ; *(well-established)* immigré(e) *m(f)*
COMP **immigrant labour** N ⇒ **immigrant workers**
immigrant workers NPL main-d'œuvre *f* immigrée

immigrate /ˈɪmɪɡreɪt/ VI immigrer

immigration /ˌɪmɪˈɡreɪʃən/ N immigration *f* ◆ **to go through customs and ~** passer la douane et l'immigration
COMP *[policy]* d'immigration ; *[law]* sur l'immigration
immigration authorities NPL services *mpl* de l'immigration
immigration border patrol N *(US Police)* services *mpl* de l'immigration
immigration control N *(= department)* (services *mpl* de) l'immigration *f* ; *(= system)* contrôle *m* de l'immigration
Immigration Department N services *mpl* de l'immigration *f*

imminence /ˈɪmɪnəns/ N imminence *f*

imminent /ˈɪmɪnənt/ ADJ imminent

immobile /ɪˈməʊbaɪl/ ADJ immobile

immobility /ˌɪməʊˈbɪlɪtɪ/ N immobilité *f*

immobilize /ɪˈməʊbɪlaɪz/ VT *(also Fin)* immobiliser

immobilizer *(Brit)* /ɪˈməʊbɪlaɪzəʳ/ N *(in car)* dispositif *m* antidémarrage

immoderate /ɪˈmɒdərɪt/ ADJ *(frm) [desire, appetite]* immodéré, démesuré ; *[conduct]* déréglé

immoderately /ɪˈmɒdərɪtlɪ/ ADV *(frm)* immodérément

immodest /ɪˈmɒdɪst/ ADJ [1] *(= indecent)* impudique, indécent [2] *(= presumptuous)* impudent, présomptueux

immodestly /ɪˈmɒdɪstlɪ/ ADV [1] *(= indecently) [dress]* de façon inconvenante ◆ **to behave ~** avoir une conduite inconvenante [2] *(= presumptuously) [claim]* de façon présomptueuse

immodesty /ɪˈmɒdɪstɪ/ N [1] *(= indecency)* impudeur *f*, indécence *f* [2] *(= presumption)* impudence *f*, présomption *f*

immolate /ˈɪməʊleɪt/ VT *(frm)* immoler

immoral /ɪˈmɒrəl/ ADJ immoral, contraire aux bonnes mœurs ◆ **it is ~ to do that** il est immoral de faire ça ◆ **it would be ~ for him to take the money** il serait immoral qu'il accepte *subj* l'argent ◆ **it is ~ that ...** il est immoral que ... + *subj* ◆ **~ behaviour** un comportement contraire aux bonnes mœurs COMP **immoral earnings** NPL *(Jur)* gains *mpl* résultant d'activités contraires à la morale

immorality /ˌɪməˈrælɪtɪ/ N immoralité *f*

immortal /ɪˈmɔːtl/ ADJ *[person, god]* immortel ; *[fame]* immortel, impérissable ◆ **in the ~ words of La Pasionaria, they shall not pass** selon le mot impérissable de la Pasionaria, ils ne passeront pas N immortel(le) *m(f)*

immortality /ˌɪmɔːˈtælɪtɪ/ N immortalité *f*

immortalize /ɪˈmɔːtəlaɪz/ VT immortaliser

immovable /ɪˈmuːvəbl/ ADJ [1] *[object]* fixe ; *(Jur) [belongings]* immeuble, immobilier [2] *(fig) [courage, decision]* inflexible, inébranlable ◆ **John was ~ in his decision** John était inflexible *or* inébranlable dans sa décision NPL **immovables** *(Jur)* immeubles *mpl*, biens *mpl* immobiliers

immovably /ɪˈmuːvəblɪ/ ADV [1] *[fix, nail down]* de façon inamovible [2] *[determined]* de façon inébranlable ; *[opposed]* irrévocablement

immune /ɪˈmjuːn/ ADJ [1] *(Med) [person]* immunisé *(from, to* contre*)* → **acquired** [2] *(fig = secure from)* **~ from** *or* **to** *(temptation, wish etc)* immunisé *or* blindé* contre ◆ **~ to criticism** immunisé *or* blindé* contre la critique ◆ **he never became ~ to the sight of death** il n'a jamais pu s'habituer à la vue de la mort [3] *(fig = exempt from)* **~ from taxation** exonéré d'impôt ◆ **to be ~ from prosecution** bénéficier de l'immunité
COMP **immune body** N anticorps *m*
immune deficiency N déficience *f* immunitaire
immune response N réaction *f* immunitaire
immune serum N immun-sérum *m*
immune system N système *m* immunitaire

immunity /ɪˈmjuːnɪtɪ/ N *(Med, gen)* immunité *f* *(from, to* contre*)* ◆ **diplomatic/parliamentary ~** immunité *f* diplomatique/parlementaire

immunization /ˌɪmjʊnaɪˈzeɪʃən/ N immunisation *f (against* contre*)*

immunize /ˈɪmjʊnaɪz/ VT immuniser *(against* contre*)*

immunocompromised /ˌɪmjʊnəʊˈkɒmprəmaɪzd/ ADJ immunodéprimé

immunodeficiency /ˌɪmjʊnəʊdɪˈfɪʃənsɪ/ N déficience *f* immunologique

immunodeficient /ˌɪmjʊnəʊdɪˈfɪʃənt/ ADJ immunodéficitaire

immunodepressant /ˌɪmjʊnəʊdɪˈpresnt/ N, ADJ immunodépresseur *m*

immunogenic /ˌɪmjʊnəʊˈdʒenɪk/ ADJ immunogène

immunoglobulin /ˌɪmjʊnəʊˈglɒbjʊlɪn/ N immunoglobuline *f*

immunological /ˌɪmjʊnəʊˈlɒdʒɪkəl/ ADJ immunologique

immunologist /ˌɪmjʊˈnɒlədʒɪst/ N immunologiste *mf*

immunology /ˌɪmjʊˈnɒlədʒɪ/ N immunologie *f*

immunosuppressant /ˌɪmjʊnəʊsʌˈpresnt/ N immunosuppresseur *m* ADJ immunosuppressif

immunosuppression /ˌɪmjʊnəʊsʌˈpreʃən/ N immunosuppression *f*

immunosuppressive /ˌɪmjʊnəʊdɪˈpresɪv/ ADJ immunosuppressif

immunotherapy /ˌɪmjʊnəʊˈθerəpɪ/ N immunothérapie *f*

immure /ɪˈmjʊəʳ/ VT *(frm) (lit)* emmurer ; *(fig)* enfermer

immutability /ɪˌmjuːtəˈbɪlɪtɪ/ N immutabilité *f*, immuabilité *f (frm)*

immutable /ɪˈmjuːtəbl/ ADJ immuable, inaltérable

immutably /ɪˈmuːtəblɪ/ ADV immuablement

imp /ɪmp/ N diablotin *m*, lutin *m* ; *(* = child)* petit(e) espiègle *m(f)*, petit diable *m*

impact /ˈɪmpækt/ N 1 *(= effect)* impact *m*, effets *mpl* ; *(= consequences)* incidences *fpl*, conséquences *fpl* ◆ **the major ~ of this epidemic is yet to come** les effets les plus dramatiques de cette épidémie ne se sont pas encore fait sentir ◆ **the ~ on the environment has not been positive** cela n'a pas eu d'effets positifs sur l'environnement

◆ **to have an impact on sth** avoir des conséquences *or* un impact sur qch ◆ **the bad weather had an ~ on sales** le mauvais temps a eu des conséquences *or* un impact sur les ventes ◆ **such gestures of charity can have little ~ on a problem of this scale** de tels actes de charité n'ont souvent que peu d'impact sur un problème de cette taille

◆ **to make an impact on sb** *(= affect)* produire un impact sur qn ; *(= impress)* faire une forte impression sur qn

2 *[of moving object]* choc *m* ; *[of bullet]* impact *m*, choc *m* ◆ **at the moment of ~** au moment du choc *or* de l'impact

◆ **on impact** au moment du choc *or* de l'impact

VT /ɪmˈpækt/ 1 *(= affect) [+ person]* toucher ◆ **the potential for women to ~ the political process** la possibilité pour les femmes d'exercer une influence sur le système politique ◆ **factors ~ing their mental health** des facteurs qui ont une incidence sur leur santé mentale

2 *(= cause to become impacted)* enfoncer, presser *(into* dans*)*

3 *(= collide with)* percuter, entrer en collision avec

VI /ɪmˈpækt/ 1 *(= influence)* influer *(on* sur*)* ; ◆ **the strategy ~ed on the culture of the company** la stratégie a influé sur la culture d'entreprise ◆ **we're confident that we're not ~ing on the environment** nous sommes persuadés que nous n'avons aucun effet négatif sur l'environnement ◆ **the Gulf crisis also ~ed on this period** les effets de la crise du Golfe se sont également fait sentir sur cette période

◆ **to impact on sb** produire un impact sur qn ◆ **such schemes mean little unless they ~ on people** de tels programmes ne signifient pas grand-chose s'ils n'ont pas d'effet sur les gens

2 *(= hit)* percuter ◆ **the missile ~ed with the ground** le missile a percuté le sol

3 *(= become stuck)* se coincer

COMP **impact printer** N *(Comput)* imprimante *f* à impact

impacted /ɪmˈpæktɪd/ ADJ *(gen = stuck)* coincé ; *[tooth]* inclus, enclavé ; *[fracture]* engrené COMP **impacted area** N *(US)* quartier *m* surpeuplé

impair /ɪmˈpɛəʳ/ VT *[+ abilities, faculties]* détériorer, diminuer ; *[+ relations]* porter atteinte à ; *[+ negotiations]* entraver ; *[+ health]* abîmer, détériorer ; *[+ sight, hearing]* abîmer, affaiblir ; *[+ mind, strength]* diminuer ; *[+ quality]* diminuer, réduire ◆ **extreme heat can ~ judgment** les températures extrêmement élevées peuvent diminuer le sens critique ◆ **anxiety does not necessarily ~ performance** l'anxiété ne nuit pas forcément aux performances

impaired /ɪmˈpɛəd/ ADJ *[sight, hearing]* abîmé, affaibli ; *[faculties, health]* détérioré ; *[strength]* diminué ◆ **if she did survive, she would be in a very ~ state** si elle s'en tirait, elle serait très diminuée N ◆ **the visually ~** les malvoyants *mpl* ◆ **the hearing ~** les malentendants *mpl*

impairment /ɪmˈpɛəmənt/ N 1 *(NonC = weakening) [of judgment, mental functions]* affaiblissement *m*, diminution *f* 2 *(= defect)* déficience *f* ◆ **hearing/visual ~** déficience *f* auditive/visuelle ◆ **speech** *or* **language ~s** *(serious)* troubles *mpl* du langage ; *(= lisp etc)* défauts *mpl* de prononciation

impala /ɪmˈpɑːlə/ N (pl **impalas** *or* **impala**) impala *m*

impale /ɪmˈpeɪl/ VT empaler *(on* sur*)*

impalpable /ɪmˈpælpəbl/ ADJ impalpable

impanel /ɪmˈpænl/ VT ⇒ **empanel**

imparity /ɪmˈpærɪtɪ/ N inégalité *f*

impart /ɪmˈpɑːt/ VT 1 *(= make known) [+ news]* communiquer, faire part de ; *[+ knowledge]* communiquer, transmettre 2 *(= bestow)* donner, transmettre

impartial /ɪmˈpɑːʃəl/ ADJ *[person, attitude, verdict, decision, speech]* impartial, objectif

impartiality /ɪmˌpɑːʃɪˈælɪtɪ/ N impartialité *f*, objectivité *f*

impartially /ɪmˈpɑːʃəlɪ/ ADV impartialement, objectivement

impassable /ɪmˈpɑːsəbl/ ADJ *[barrier, river]* infranchissable ; *[road]* impraticable

impasse /æmˈpɑːs/ N *(lit, fig)* impasse *f* ◆ **to reach an ~** se retrouver dans une impasse

impassioned /ɪmˈpæʃnd/ ADJ *[feeling]* exalté ; *[plea, speech]* passionné

impassive /ɪmˈpæsɪv/ ADJ *[person, attitude, face]* impassible, imperturbable

impassively /ɪmˈpæsɪvlɪ/ ADV impassiblement, imperturbablement

impatience /ɪmˈpeɪʃəns/ N 1 *(= eagerness)* impatience *f (to do sth* de faire qch*)* 2 *(= intolerance)* intolérance *f (of sth* à l'égard de qch ; *with sb* vis-à-vis de qn, à l'égard de qn*)*

impatiens /ɪmˈpeɪʃɪˌenz/ N *(pl inv: = plant)* impatiente *f*

impatient /ɪmˈpeɪʃənt/ ADJ 1 *(= eager) [person, answer]* impatient ◆ **an ~ gesture** un geste d'impatience ◆ **~ to leave** impatient de partir ◆ **to become** *or* **get** *or* **grow ~** s'impatienter ◆ **they are ~ for jobs** ils ont hâte d'obtenir un emploi 2 *(= intolerant)* intolérant *(of sth* à l'égard de qch ; *with sb* vis-à-vis de qn, à l'égard de qn ; *at* par rapport à*)*

impatiently /ɪmˈpeɪʃəntlɪ/ ADV *[wait, say]* impatiemment ; *[nod]* avec impatience ◆ **to look forward ~ to sth** attendre qch avec beaucoup d'impatience

impeach /ɪmˈpiːtʃ/ VT 1 *(Jur = accuse) [+ public official]* mettre en accusation *(en vue de destituer)* ; *(US)* entamer la procédure d'impeachment contre ; *[+ person]* accuser *(for or of sth* de qch ; *for doing sth* de faire qch*)* 2 *(= question, challenge) [+ sb's character]* attaquer ; *[+ sb's motives, honesty]* mettre en doute ◆ **to ~ a witness** *(Jur)* récuser un témoin

impeachable /ɪmˈpiːtʃəbl/ ADJ passible des tribunaux

impeachment /ɪmˈpiːtʃmənt/ N 1 *(Jur) [of public official]* mise *f* en accusation *(en vue d'une destitution)* ; *(US)* procédure *f* d'impeachment ; *[of person]* accusation *f (for sth* de qch ; *for doing sth* de faire qch*)* 2 *[of sb's character]* dénigrement *m* ; *[of sb's honesty]* mise *f* en doute

impeccable /ɪmˈpekəbl/ ADJ *[manners, behaviour, taste]* irréprochable ; *[credentials, timing, English, service, clothes]* impeccable

impeccably /ɪmˈpekəblɪ/ ADV *[dress]* impeccablement ; *[behave]* de façon irréprochable

impecunious /ˌɪmpɪˈkjuːnɪəs/ ADJ *(frm)* impécunieux, nécessiteux

impedance /ɪmˈpiːdəns/ N *(Elec)* impédance *f*

impede /ɪmˈpiːd/ VT *[+ person, progress]* entraver ; *[+ action, success, movement, traffic]* gêner, entraver ◆ **to ~ sb from doing sth** empêcher qn de faire qch

impediment /ɪmˈpedɪmənt/ N 1 obstacle *m*, empêchement *m* ◆ **there was no legal ~ to the marriage** il n'y avait aucun empêchement légal à ce mariage 2 (also **speech impediment**) défaut *m* d'élocution 3 ◆ **~s** ⇒ **impedimenta**

impedimenta /ɪmˌpedɪˈmentə/ NPL *(also Mil)* impedimenta *mpl*

impel /ɪmˈpel/ VT 1 *(= drive forward)* pousser, faire avancer 2 *(= compel)* obliger, forcer *(to do sth* à faire qch*)* ; *(= urge)* inciter, pousser *(to do sth* à faire qch*)* ◆ **to ~ sb to crime** pousser qn au crime ◆ **to ~ sb to action** pousser qn à agir

impend /ɪmˈpend/ VI *(= be about to happen)* être imminent ; *(= menace, hang over) [danger, storm]* menacer ; *[threat]* planer

impending /ɪmˈpendɪŋ/ ADJ imminent

impenetrability /ɪmˌpenɪtrəˈbɪlɪtɪ/ N *[of forest]* impénétrabilité *f* ; *[of book, theory]* caractère *m* hermétique

impenetrable /ɪmˈpenɪtrəbl/ ADJ *[barrier]* infranchissable ; *[forest]* impénétrable ; *[darkness, mystery]* insondable ; *[book, theory]* inaccessible ; *[accent]* incompréhensible

impenetrably /ɪmˈpenɪtrəblɪ/ ADV ◆ **~ thick** d'une épaisseur impénétrable ◆ **~ obscure** d'une obscurité insondable

impenitence /ɪmˈpenɪtəns/ N impénitence *f*

impenitent /ɪmˈpenɪtənt/ ADJ impénitent ◆ **he was quite ~ about it** il ne s'en repentait nullement

impenitently /ɪmˈpenɪtəntlɪ/ ADV sans repentir

imperative /ɪmˈperətɪv/ ADJ 1 *[action, need]* impératif ; *[desire]* pressant, impérieux ◆ **immediate action is ~** il est impératif d'agir immédiatement ◆ **silence is ~** le silence s'impose ◆ **it is ~ to do this** il est impératif de le faire ◆ **it is ~ for him to do this, it is ~ that he (should) do this** il est impératif qu'il le fasse 2 *(Gram)* **~ form/mood** forme *f* impérative/mode *m* impératif ◆ **~ verb** verbe *m* à l'impératif N *(Gram)* impératif *m* ◆ **in the ~ (mood)** à l'impératif, au mode impératif

imperatively /ɪmˈperətɪvlɪ/ ADV 1 *[need]* impérieusement ; *[order]* impérativement 2 *(Gram) [use verb]* à l'impératif

imperceptible /ˌɪmpəˈseptəbl/ ADJ *[sight, movement, sound]* imperceptible (*to* à) ; *[difference]* imperceptible, insensible

imperceptibly /ˌɪmpəˈseptəblɪ/ ADV imperceptiblement

imperceptive /ˌɪmpəˈseptɪv/ ADJ peu perspicace

imperfect /ɪmˈpɜːfɪkt/ ADJ 1 *(= flawed) [world, human being, system, knowledge]* imparfait ; *[goods, copy]* défectueux 2 *(Gram) [tense, ending]* de l'imparfait ; *[verb]* à l'imparfait N *(Gram)* imparfait *m* ◆ **in the ~ (tense)** à l'imparfait
COMP **imperfect competition** N *(Econ)* concurrence *f* imparfaite
imperfect market N *(Econ)* marché *m* imparfait

imperfection /ˌɪmpəˈfekʃən/ N *(in person, moral)* défaut *m* ; *(physical)* imperfection *f* ; *(in skin, paper, policy, system, design)* imperfection *f* (*in sth* de qch) ; *(in china, glass, jewel, cloth)* défaut *m* (*in sth* de qch)

imperfectly /ɪmˈpɜːfɪktlɪ/ ADV imparfaitement

imperial /ɪmˈpɪərɪəl/ ADJ 1 *(Pol)* impérial ◆ **His Imperial Highness/Majesty** Son Altesse/Sa Majesté Impériale
2 *(in Brit = non-metric)* ◆ **~ weights and measures** *système anglo-saxon de poids et mesures* ◆ **~ gallon** ≈ 4,55 litres
N *(= beard)* (barbe *f* à l')impériale *f*
COMP **imperial preference** N *(Brit Hist)* tarif *m* préférentiel *(à l'intérieur de l'Empire britannique)*
imperial system N *système anglo-saxon de poids et mesures*

> **IMPERIAL SYSTEM**
>
> Le système dit « impérial » des poids et mesures reste utilisé en Grande-Bretagne, parallèlement au système métrique, officiellement adopté en 1971 et enseigné dans les écoles. Beaucoup de gens connaissent leur poids en « stones and pounds » et leur taille en « feet and inches ». Les distances sont, elles, données en « miles ».
>
> Aux États-Unis, le système « impérial » est encore officiellement en usage pour toutes les unités de poids et mesures. Cependant, en ce qui concerne les liquides, beaucoup de noms sont les mêmes que dans le système britannique, mais la contenance diffère. D'autre part, les gens se pèsent en « pounds » plutôt qu'en « stones and pounds ».

imperialism /ɪmˈpɪərɪəlɪzəm/ N impérialisme *m*

imperialist /ɪmˈpɪərɪəlɪst/ ADJ, N impérialiste *mf*

imperialistic /ɪmˌpɪərɪəˈlɪstɪk/ ADJ impérialiste

imperially /ɪmˈpɪərɪəlɪ/ ADV majestueusement ; *[say, gesture]* impérieusement

imperil /ɪmˈperɪl/ VT *(liter) [+ sb's life]* mettre en péril *or* danger ; *[+ fortune, one's life]* exposer, risquer ; *[+ health, reputation]* compromettre

imperious /ɪmˈpɪərɪəs/ ADJ *[gesture, look, command]* impérieux ; *[need, desire]* pressant, impérieux

imperiously /ɪmˈpɪərɪəslɪ/ ADV impérieusement

imperishable /ɪmˈperɪʃəbl/ ADJ impérissable

impermanence /ɪmˈpɜːmənəns/ N caractère *m* éphémère

impermanent /ɪmˈpɜːmənənt/ ADJ éphémère, transitoire

impermeable /ɪmˈpɜːmɪəbl/ ADJ *[rock]* imperméable ; *[wall, roof]* étanche

impersonal /ɪmˈpɜːsnl/ ADJ *(also Gram)* impersonnel

impersonality /ɪmˌpɜːsəˈnælɪtɪ/ N côté *m* impersonnel

impersonalize /ˌɪmˈpɜːsənəˌlaɪz/ VT déshumaniser

impersonally /ɪmˈpɜːsnəlɪ/ ADV de façon impersonnelle

impersonate /ɪmˈpɜːsəneɪt/ VT *(gen)* se faire passer pour ; *(Jur)* usurper l'identité de ; *(Theat)* imiter

impersonation /ɪmˌpɜːsəˈneɪʃən/ N *(Theat)* imitation *f* ; *(Jur)* usurpation *f* d'identité ◆ **his Elvis ~** son imitation d'Elvis ◆ **he gave a fair ~ of somebody trying to be friendly** il jouait assez bien le rôle de quelqu'un qui se veut aimable

impersonator /ɪmˈpɜːsəneɪtəʳ/ N *(Theat)* imitateur *m*, -trice *f* ; *(Jur)* usurpateur *m*, -trice *f* d'identité ; → **female**

impertinence /ɪmˈpɜːtɪnəns/ N impertinence *f* ◆ **a piece of ~** une impertinence ◆ **to ask would be an ~** il serait impertinent de demander

impertinent /ɪmˈpɜːtɪnənt/ ADJ *(= impudent)* impertinent (*to sb* envers qn) ◆ **don't be ~!** ne soyez pas impertinent ! ◆ **would it be ~ to ask where exactly you were?** serait-il inconvenant de vous demander où vous étiez exactement ?

impertinently /ɪmˈpɜːtɪnəntlɪ/ ADV 1 *(= impudently)* avec impertinence 2 *(= irrelevantly)* sans pertinence, hors de propos ; *[reply]* à côté de la question

imperturbable /ˌɪmpəˈtɜːbəbl/ ADJ imperturbable

imperturbably /ˌɪmpəˈtɜːbəblɪ/ ADV imperturbablement

impervious /ɪmˈpɜːvɪəs/ ADJ 1 *(= impermeable) [substance, rock]* imperméable (*to* à) ; *[wall, roof]* étanche (*to* à) 2 *(fig)* ◆ **~ to the sufferings of others** insensible aux souffrances d'autrui ◆ **~ to reason** inaccessible *or* sourd à la raison ◆ **~ to threats** indifférent aux menaces ◆ **he is ~ to criticism** la critique le laisse indifférent *or* ne le touche pas ; *(pej)* il est fermé *or* sourd à la critique

impetigo /ˌɪmpɪˈtaɪgəʊ/ N impétigo *m* ; *(in children)* gourme *f*

impetuosity /ɪmˌpetjʊˈɒsɪtɪ/ N impétuosité *f*, fougue *f*

impetuous /ɪmˈpetjʊəs/ ADJ impétueux, fougueux

impetuously /ɪmˈpetjʊəslɪ/ ADV impétueusement, fougueusement

impetuousness /ɪmˈpetjʊəsnɪs/ N ⇒ **impetuosity**

impetus /ˈɪmpɪtəs/ N 1 *(Phys) [of object]* force *f* d'impulsion ; *[of runner]* élan *m* 2 *(fig)* impulsion *f*, élan *m* ◆ **to give (an) ~ to** donner une impulsion *or* un élan à ◆ **she needs a new ~ for her talent** elle a besoin d'une nouvelle impulsion *or* d'un nouvel élan pour exprimer son talent

impiety /ɪmˈpaɪətɪ/ N impiété *f*

impinge /ɪmˈpɪndʒ/ VI 1 *(= make impression)* ◆ **to ~ on sb/sth** affecter *or* toucher qn/qch ◆ **it didn't ~ on his daily life** cela n'affectait pas sa vie quotidienne, cela n'avait pas de répercussion sur sa vie quotidienne 2 ◆ **to ~ on sb's rights** empiéter sur les droits de qn, porter atteinte aux droits de qn ◆ **this legislation could ~ on privacy** cette législation pourrait porter atteinte à la vie privée 3 ◆ **cosmic rays that ~ on the upper atmosphere** les rayons cosmiques qui affectent la couche supérieure de l'atmosphère

impingement /ɪmˈpɪndʒmənt/ N empiètement *m* (*of, on* sur)

impious /ˈɪmpɪəs/ ADJ impie

impiously /ˈɪmpɪəslɪ/ ADV avec impiété

impish /ˈɪmpɪʃ/ ADJ espiègle, malicieux

implacable /ɪmˈplækəbl/ ADJ implacable (*towards sb/sth* envers qn/qch) ◆ **he was ~ in his opposition to the proposal** il a été implacable dans son opposition à la proposition

implacably /ɪmˈplækəblɪ/ ADV implacablement

implant /ɪmˈplɑːnt/ VT 1 *[+ idea]* implanter (*in sb* dans la tête de qn) ; *[+ principle]* inculquer (*in sb* à qn) ; *[+ desire, wish]* inspirer (*in sb* à qn) 2 *(Med)* implanter (*in* dans) VI s'implanter (*in* dans) N /ˈɪmplɑːnt/ *(under skin)* implant *m* ; *(= graft)* greffe *f*

implantation /ˌɪmplɑːnˈteɪʃən/ N *[of ideology, culture]* introduction *f* ; *(Med) [of embryo]* implantation *f*

implausible /ɪmˈplɔːzəbl/ ADJ peu plausible, peu vraisemblable

implausibly /ɪmˈplɔːzəblɪ/ ADV *[big, fat, high]* incroyablement ◆ **his characters are ~ nice** ses personnages sont d'une bonté peu vraisemblable ◆ **they are, rather ~, good friends** chose incroyable, ils sont bons amis

implement /ˈɪmplɪmənt/ N outil *m*, instrument *m* ◆ **~s** équipement *m* NonC, matériel *m* NonC ; *(for gardening, painting, carpentry)* matériel *m*, outils *mpl* ; *(for cooking)* ustensiles *mpl* ◆ **~s of war** matériel *m* de guerre ◆ **farm ~s** matériel *m* *or* outillage *m* agricole VT /ˈɪmplɪment/ *[+ decision, plan, recommendation]* mettre en œuvre, exécuter ; *[+ promise]* accomplir ; *[+ contract]* exécuter ; *[+ law]* mettre en œuvre, appliquer ; *[+ system]* mettre en place ; *[+ idea]* mettre en pratique, réaliser

implementation /ˌɪmplɪmenˈteɪʃən/ N *[of plan]* exécution *f*, réalisation *f* ; *[of law, reform, peace agreement, policy]* mise *f* en œuvre ; *(Comput)* implémentation *f*

implicate /ˈɪmplɪkeɪt/ VT impliquer, compromettre (*in* dans)

implication /ˌɪmplɪˈkeɪʃən/ N 1 *(= possible consequence)* implication *f* ◆ **what are the political ~s?** quelles sont les implications politiques ? ◆ **we shall have to study all the ~s** il nous faudra étudier toutes les conséquences *or* implications possibles ◆ **what are the ~s of the new tax for the poor?** qu'implique ce nouvel impôt pour les pauvres ?
◆ **to have implications** avoir des répercussions ◆ **the low level of investment has ~s for economic growth** la faiblesse des investissements a des répercussions sur la croissance économique
2 *(= suggestion)* **she complained that the ~ was that she was guilty** elle s'est élevée contre le fait que sa culpabilité était sous-entendue ◆ **the ~ was obvious: vote for us and you'll pay less tax** le sous-entendu était clair : votez pour nous, vous paierez moins d'impôts ◆ **his ~ was that the war boosted newspaper circulation** ce qu'il voulait dire c'est que la guerre faisait vendre les journaux ◆ **he didn't realize the full ~ of his words** il n'a pas mesuré toute la portée de ses paroles
◆ **by implication** par voie de conséquence ◆ **his authority, and by ~, that of the whole team, is under threat** son autorité et, par voie de conséquence, celle de l'équipe tout entière, est menacée ◆ **if a product remains unlabelled then, by ~, it doesn't contain GM elements** si un produit ne porte pas d'étiquette, cela implique *or* suppose qu'il ne contient pas d'OGM ◆ **everyone else, by ~, is an extremist** sous-entendu : tous les autres sont des extrémistes

3 *(NonC = involvement)* implication *f (in* dans*)*

> ⚠ Be cautious about translating **implication** by the French word **implication**, which does not mean 'suggestion'.

implicit /ɪmˈplɪsɪt/ ADJ 1 *(= implied) [warning, message, criticism, threat, admission]* implicite *(in* dans*)* ; *[recognition]* tacite 2 *(= unquestioning) [belief, faith, confidence, obedience]* absolu

implicitly /ɪmˈplɪsɪtlɪ/ ADV 1 *(= indirectly) [accept, recognize, criticize]* implicitement 2 *(= unquestioningly) [trust]* totalement ; *[believe]* tout à fait

implied /ɪmˈplaɪd/ ADJ *[criticism, question]* implicite, sous-entendu ; *[threat]* implicite, voilé ; *[message]* implicite
COMP **implied reader** N *(Literat)* lecteur *m (à qui s'adresse implicitement le texte)*
implied term N *(Jur)* clause *f* implicite *or* tacite
implied warranty N *(US Jur)* garantie *f* légale

implode /ɪmˈpləʊd/ VI imploser VT causer l'implosion de COMP **imploded consonant** N *(Phon)* consonne *f* implosive

implore /ɪmˈplɔːʳ/ VT implorer *(sb to do sth* qn de faire qch*)* ◆ **to ~ sb's help** implorer le secours de qn ◆ **I ~ you!** je vous en supplie *or* conjure !

imploring /ɪmˈplɔːrɪŋ/ ADJ *[look, voice]* implorant, suppliant ; *[person]* suppliant

imploringly /ɪmˈplɔːrɪŋlɪ/ ADV *[say]* d'un ton implorant ◆ **to look ~ at sb** supplier qn du regard, regarder qn d'un air implorant

implosion /ɪmˈpləʊʒən/ N implosion *f*

implosive /ɪmˈpləʊzɪv/ ADJ implosif N *(Phon)* implosive *f*

imply /ɪmˈplaɪ/ VT 1 *[person]* suggérer, laisser entendre ; *(= insinuate)* insinuer *(pej)* ◆ **he implied that he would come** il a laissé entendre qu'il viendrait ◆ **he implied that I was lying** il a laissé entendre *or* insinué que je mentais ◆ **are you ~ing that ...?** voulez-vous suggérer *or* insinuer que ... ? ◆ **it is implied that ...** il faut sous-entendre que ..., cela sous-entend que ... ; see also **implied** 2 *(= indicate)* impliquer ◆ **that implies some intelligence** cela implique *or* suppose une certaine intelligence ◆ **the meeting did not ~ the resumption of sales** la rencontre ne signifiait pas que les ventes allaient reprendre ◆ **figures ~ that the economy is getting stronger** les chiffres laissent penser *or* suggèrent que l'économie connaît une embellie ; see also **implied**

impolite /ˌɪmpəˈlaɪt/ ADJ impoli *(to or towards sb* avec *or* envers qn*)* ◆ **it is ~ to do that** il est impoli de faire cela ◆ **it was very ~ of you to do/say that** c'était très impoli de votre part de faire/dire cela

impolitely /ˌɪmpəˈlaɪtlɪ/ ADV impoliment

impoliteness /ˌɪmpəˈlaɪtnɪs/ N impolitesse *f (to, towards* envers*)*

impolitic /ɪmˈpɒlɪtɪk/ ADJ *(frm)* peu politique, impolitique

imponderable /ɪmˈpɒndərəbl/ ADJ, N impondérable *m*

import /ˈɪmpɔːt/ N 1 *(Comm = process, goods)* importation *f (into* en*)* ◆ **~ of goods** importation *f* de marchandises ◆ **~s from England** importations *fpl* en provenance d'Angleterre
2 *(= significance)* importance *f* ◆ **of great/little ~** *[question, issue]* de grande/peu d'importance ; *[argument]* de poids/de peu de poids
3 *(frm = meaning) [of action, decision, speech, words]* sens *m*, signification *f* ; *[of document]* teneur *f*
VT /ɪmˈpɔːt/ 1 *(Comm)* importer ◆ **~ed goods** marchandises *fpl* d'importation *or* importées
2 *(frm = mean, imply)* signifier, vouloir dire
COMP **import duty** N droits *mpl* d'importation, taxe *f* à l'importation
import-export (trade) N import-export *m*
import licence N licence *f* d'importation
import quota N quota *m* à l'importation, contingent *m* d'importation
import surcharge N surtaxe *f* à l'importation
import trade N (commerce *m* d')importation *f*

importance /ɪmˈpɔːtəns/ N importance *f* ◆ **to be of ~** avoir de l'importance ◆ **of some ~** assez important, d'une certaine importance ◆ **of great ~** très important, de grande importance ◆ **it is a matter of great ~ for the future** c'est quelque chose de très important pour l'avenir ◆ **it is of the highest ~ that ...** il est de la plus haute importance que ... + *subj*, il importe au premier chef que ... + *subj* ◆ **it is of ~ to do** il est important de faire, il importe de faire *(frm)* ◆ **it is of no (great) ~** c'est sans (grande) importance ◆ **to give ~ to sth** *[person]* attacher de l'importance *or* du prix à qch ; *[event, development]* accorder *or* donner de l'importance à qch ◆ **we give *or* attach the greatest ~ to establishing the facts** nous accordons *or* attachons la plus haute importance à l'établissement des faits ◆ **man of ~** homme *m* important, personnage *m* (important) ◆ **person of no ~** personne *f* sans importance ◆ **his position gives him considerable ~** sa position lui donne une importance *or* un poids considérable ◆ **he is full of his own ~** il est imbu de lui-même, il est pénétré de son importance ◆ **the ~ of being/doing** l'importance d'être/de faire

important /ɪmˈpɔːtənt/ LANGUAGE IN USE 26.3 ADJ important *(to or for sb/sth* pour qn/qch*)* ; ◆ **that's an ~ consideration** c'est un facteur important ◆ **his family was more ~ to him than politics** sa famille comptait plus pour lui que la politique ◆ **that's not ~** ça n'a pas d'importance, ce n'est pas important ◆ **to make sb feel ~** donner à qn un sentiment d'importance ◆ **he's trying to look ~** il fait l'important, il se donne des airs importants ◆ **it is ~ to do sth** il est important de faire qch ◆ **it is ~ for sb to do sth *or* that sb (should) do sth** il est important que qn fasse qch
◆ **the important thing** l'important *m* ◆ **the ~ thing is not to win but to take part** l'important n'est pas de gagner mais de participer
◆ **the most important thing** le plus important ◆ **the most ~ thing is that you should be happy** l'important *or* le plus important, c'est que tu sois heureux ◆ **her children are the most ~ thing in her life** ses enfants sont ce qu'il y a de plus important dans sa vie ◆ **the most ~ thing to remember is ...** *(factual information)* ce qu'il faut surtout retenir, c'est ... ◆ **the most ~ thing to remember is to do ...** *(advice on interview technique etc)* surtout n'oubliez pas de faire ...

importantly /ɪmˈpɔːtəntlɪ/ ADV 1 *(= significantly)* ◆ **to figure ~ in sth** occuper une place importante dans qch ◆ **to differ ~ from sth** présenter d'importantes différences avec qch ◆ **I was hungry, and, more ~, my children were hungry** j'avais faim et, surtout *or* plus important encore, mes enfants avaient faim 2 *(also* **self-importantly***) [say, strut]* d'un air important

importation /ˌɪmpɔːˈteɪʃən/ N *(Comm)* importation *f*

importer /ɪmˈpɔːtəʳ/ N *(= person)* importateur *m*, -trice *f* ; *(= country)* (pays *m*) importateur *m*

importunate /ɪmˈpɔːtjʊnɪt/ ADJ *(frm) [visitor, demand]* importun, gênant ; *[creditor]* harcelant

importune /ˌɪmpɔːˈtjuːn/ VT *(frm) [questioner, beggar]* importuner, ennuyer ; *[creditor]* harceler, presser ; *(Jur) [prostitute]* racoler VI *(Jur)* racoler ◆ **she was arrested for importuning** elle a été arrêtée pour racolage

importunity /ˌɪmpɔːˈtjuːnɪtɪ/ N *(frm)* importunité *f*

impose /ɪmˈpəʊz/ VT 1 *[+ task, conditions, constraint, rule, obedience, one's opinion]* imposer *(on* à*)* ; *[+ sanctions]* prendre *(on* à l'encontre de*)* ; ◆ **to ~ a fine on sb** condamner qn à une amende ◆ **to ~ a tax on sth** imposer qch, taxer qch ◆ **beware of imposing your tastes on your children** gardez-vous d'imposer vos goûts à vos enfants ◆ **the pressures ~d upon teachers** les pressions que subissent les professeurs ◆ **to ~ itself** s'imposer ◆ **to ~ o.s. (on sb)** s'imposer (à qn) ◆ **to ~ one's presence on sb** imposer sa présence à qn 2 *(Typ)* imposer
VI s'imposer ◆ **I don't want to ~** je ne veux pas m'imposer ◆ **to ~ on sb** abuser de la gentillesse de qn ◆ **to ~ on sb's hospitality** abuser de l'hospitalité de qn

imposing /ɪmˈpəʊzɪŋ/ ADJ imposant, impressionnant

imposition /ˌɪmpəˈzɪʃən/ N 1 *(NonC) [of regulations, ban]* mise *f* en place ◆ **despite the ~ of a curfew** malgré la mise en place d'un couvre-feu ◆ **the ~ of sanctions on Iraq** le fait de prendre des sanctions à l'encontre de l'Irak ◆ **the ~ of a tax on ...** la taxation *or* l'imposition de ... 2 *(= tax imposed)* impôt *m*, taxe *f* 3 *(= burden)* **I know this is an ~, but please hear me out** je sais que j'abuse, mais écoutez-moi, je vous en prie ◆ **she seems to find the presence of guests more of an ~** la présence d'invités semble plutôt la déranger ◆ **it's rather an ~ on her** c'est abuser de sa gentillesse 4 *(Typ)* imposition *f* 5 *(Scol)* punition *f*

> ⚠ The commonest meanings of **imposition** are not translated by the French word **imposition**.

impossibility /ɪmˌpɒsəˈbɪlɪtɪ/ N impossibilité *f (of sth* de qch ; *of doing sth* de faire qch*)* ◆ **it's an ~** c'est une chose impossible, c'est quelque chose d'impossible ; → **physical**

impossible /ɪmˈpɒsəbl/ LANGUAGE IN USE 12, 15.3, 16.3, 16.4, 18.2, 26.3
ADJ impossible ◆ **this cooker is ~ to clean!** cette cuisinière est impossible à nettoyer ! ◆ **it is ~ for him to leave** il lui est impossible *or* il est dans l'impossibilité de partir ◆ **I find it ~ to understand why ...** je n'arrive pas à comprendre pourquoi ... ◆ **to put sb/to be in an ~ position *or* situation** mettre qn/être dans une position *or* situation impossible ◆ **it is/is not ~ that ...** il est/n'est pas impossible que ... + *subj* ◆ **that boy is ~!** * ce garçon est impossible ! *
◆ **to make it impossible** ◆ **the idea was to make it ~ to cheat** le but était de rendre toute tricherie impossible
◆ **to make it impossible for sb to do sth** empêcher qn de faire qch ◆ **a knee injury made it ~ for him to play again** une blessure au genou l'a empêché de rejouer
N impossible *m* ◆ **to do/ask for the ~** faire/demander l'impossible

impossibly /ɪmˈpɒsəblɪ/ ADV *[small, large, late]* incroyablement ; *[expensive]* ridiculement ◆ **~ rude/arrogant** d'une impolitesse/arrogance insupportable ◆ **~ difficult** d'une difficulté insurmontable ◆ **her standards were ~ high** ses exigences étaient impossibles à satisfaire ◆ **he's behaving ~** il se conduit d'une façon impossible ◆ **if, ~, he were to succeed** si, par impossible, il réussissait

impost /ˈɪmpəʊst/ N *(Admin, Fin, Jur)* impôt *m* ; *(Customs)* taxe *f* douanière, droit *m* de douane

imposter, impostor /ɪmˈpɒstəʳ/ N imposteur *m*

imposture /ɪmˈpɒstʃəʳ/ N imposture *f*

impotence /ˈɪmpətəns/ N *(gen, sexual, fig)* impuissance *f* ; † *[of invalid, patient]* impotence *f*

impotent /ˈɪmpətənt/ ADJ 1 *(sexually)* impuissant 2 *(= powerless) [person, organization]* impuissant ; † *[invalid, patient]* impotent ◆ **in ~ rage** *or* **fury** † dans une rage impuissante ◆ **to be ~ in the face of sth** être impuissant face à qch

impound /ɪmˈpaʊnd/ VT 1 *(Jur) [+ property]* confisquer, saisir ; *[+ car]* mettre en fourrière 2 *[+ water]* retenir, endiguer

impoundment /ɪmˈpaʊndmənt/ N 1 *(Jur) [of property]* saisie *f* ; *[of car]* mise *f* en fourrière 2 *[of water]* retenue *f* d'eau 3 *(US Fin) mise en réserve de fonds votés (par le Congrès)*

impoverish /ɪmˈpɒvərɪʃ/ VT appauvrir

impoverished /ɪmˈpɒvərɪʃt/ ADJ pauvre

impoverishment /ɪmˈpɒvərɪʃmənt/ N appauvrissement *m*

impracticability /ɪm,præktɪkəˈbɪlɪtɪ/ N impraticabilité *f*

impracticable /ɪmˈpræktɪkəbl/ ADJ *[idea, plan, scheme, suggestion]* impraticable, irréalisable

impractical /ɪmˈpræktɪkəl/ ADJ *[person]* qui manque d'esprit pratique ; *[plan, idea]* difficilement applicable ; *[clothes]* pas pratique

impracticality /ɪm,præktɪˈkælɪtɪ/ N *[of person]* manque *m* d'esprit pratique ; *[of plan, idea]* côté *m* peu pratique

imprecation /,ɪmprɪˈkeɪʃən/ N *(frm)* imprécation *f*, malédiction *f*

imprecise /,ɪmprɪˈsaɪs/ ADJ imprécis

imprecision /,ɪmprɪˈsɪʒən/ N imprécision *f*, manque *m* de précision

impregnable /ɪmˈpregnəbl/ ADJ *(Mil) [fortress, defences]* imprenable, inexpugnable ; *(fig) [person, position]* inattaquable ; *[argument]* irréfutable

impregnate /ˈɪmpregneɪt/ VT 1 *(= fertilize)* féconder 2 *(= saturate)* imprégner, imbiber *(with* de) ; *(fig)* imprégner, pénétrer *(with* de)

impregnation /,ɪmpregˈneɪʃən/ N 1 *(= fertilization)* fécondation *f* 2 *(= permeation)* imprégnation *f* ◆ **the ~ of paper with chemicals** l'imprégnation du papier par des produits chimiques

impresario /,ɪmpreˈsɑːrɪəʊ/ N imprésario *m*

impress /ɪmˈpres/ VT 1 *[+ person]* impressionner ◆ **to be ~ed by sth** être impressionné par qch ◆ **they were most ~ed by his having everything ready on time** ils ont été très impressionnés par le fait qu'il ait tout préparé à temps ◆ **he is not easily ~ed** il ne se laisse pas facilement impressionner ◆ **I am not ~ed** *(negative opinion, by object, work of art, performance)* ça me laisse froid ; *(by sb's behaviour)* ça ne m'impressionne pas ◆ **I am NOT ~ed!** *(annoyance)* je ne suis pas du tout content ! ◆ **he ~ed me favourably/unfavourably** il m'a fait une bonne/mauvaise impression ◆ **his novel greatly ~ed me** son roman m'a beaucoup impressionné, son roman m'a fait une forte *or* grosse impression ◆ **he does it just to ~ people** il ne le fait que pour épater la galerie
2 imprimer, marquer *(on* sur) ◆ **to ~ a seal on wax** imprimer un sceau sur de la cire ◆ **to ~ sth on sb** *(fig)* faire (bien) comprendre qch à qn ◆ **that day has remained ~ed in my memory** ce jour est resté gravé dans ma mémoire
VI *[object, work of art, performance]* être impressionnant ; *[person]* faire bonne impression
N /ˈɪmpres/ marque *f*, empreinte *f*

impression /ɪmˈpreʃən/ N 1 *(= effect)* impression *f* ◆ **to make an ~ on sb** faire impression *or* de l'effet à qn ◆ **to make an ~ on sth** avoir un effet sur qch ◆ **to make a good/bad ~ on sb** faire bonne/mauvaise impression à qn ◆ **his novel made a lasting ~ on me** son roman m'a laissé une impression durable ◆ **what was your ~ of him?** quelle impression vous a-t-il fait ? ◆ **you have a false ~ of him** vous vous trompez sur son compte ◆ **first ~s count** c'est la première impression qui compte ◆ **she got the wrong ~** elle s'est méprise ◆ **he gave the ~ of being bored** il donnait l'impression de s'ennuyer ◆ **to create an ~ of space** créer une impression d'espace
2 *(= vague idea)* impression *f* ◆ **I was under the ~ that ..., my ~ was that ...** j'avais l'impression que ..., je croyais que ... ◆ **that wasn't my ~!** ce n'est pas l'impression que j'ai eue ! ◆ **his ~s of Paris** les impressions qu'il a gardées de Paris
3 *[of seal, stamp, footprint]* empreinte *f*, trace *f* ; *(on wax)* impression *f* ; *(Dentistry)* empreinte *f*
4 *[of engraving]* impression *f* ; *(esp Brit) [of book]* tirage *m*, édition *f*
5 ◆ **to do ~s (of sb)** faire des imitations (de qn)

impressionable /ɪmˈpreʃnəbl/ ADJ impressionnable ◆ **at an ~ age** à un âge où l'on est impressionnable

impressionism /ɪmˈpreʃənɪzəm/ N *(Art)* impressionnisme *m*

impressionist /ɪmˈpreʃənɪst/ N *(Art)* impressionniste *mf* ; *(Theat = impersonator)* imitateur *m*, -trice *f* ADJ *(Art)* impressionniste

impressionistic /ɪm,preʃəˈnɪstɪk/ ADJ *[story, account, painting]* impressionniste

impressive /ɪmˈpresɪv/ ADJ *[appearance, building, ceremony, person, sight, sum]* impressionnant, imposant ; *[amount, account, achievement, result, speech]* impressionnant

impressively /ɪmˈpresɪvlɪ/ ADV *[big, high, brave etc]* remarquablement ; *[win, perform]* d'une manière impressionnante ◆ **~ large** remarquablement grand, d'une grandeur impressionnante

impressment /ɪmˈpresmənt/ N *[of person]* enrôlement *m* forcé ; *[of property, goods]* réquisition *f*

imprimatur /,ɪmprɪˈmɑːtəʳ/ N *(frm)* imprimatur *m*

imprint /ɪmˈprɪnt/ VT imprimer, marquer *(on* sur) ; *(fig)* imprimer, graver *(on* dans) N /ˈɪmprɪnt/ 1 *(= impression) (lit, fig)* empreinte *f* ; *(Psych)* empreinte *f* perceptive 2 *(Publishing)* ◆ **published under the Collins ~** édité chez Collins

imprinting /ɪmˈprɪntɪŋ/ N *(NonC: Psych)* empreinte *f*

imprison /ɪmˈprɪzn/ VT emprisonner, écrouer ; *(fig)* emprisonner ◆ **they ~ed him for his part in the burglary** ils l'ont emprisonné *or* écroué pour avoir participé au cambriolage ◆ **the judge ~ed him for ten years** le juge l'a condamné à dix ans de prison

imprisonment /ɪmˈprɪznmənt/ N emprisonnement *m*, incarcération *f* ◆ **to sentence sb to seven years' ~/to life ~** condamner qn à sept ans de prison/à la prison à vie *or* à perpétuité ◆ **sentence of life ~** condamnation *f* à la prison à vie *or* à perpétuité ◆ **the prospect of ~** la perspective de la prison

improbability /ɪm,prɒbəˈbɪlɪtɪ/ N 1 *(= unlikelihood) [of outcome]* improbabilité *f* 2 *(= implausibility) [of film, story, plot, excuse]* invraisemblance *f*

improbable /ɪmˈprɒbəbl/ ADJ 1 *(= unlikely) [situation, victory]* improbable ◆ **it is ~ that ...** il est improbable *or* il est peu probable que ... + *subj* 2 *(= implausible) [explanation, story, name]* invraisemblable ◆ **~ as it sounds ...** aussi invraisemblable que cela paraisse ...

improbably /ɪmˈprɒbəblɪ/ ADV invraisemblablement ◆ **she works, ~, in a bank** bizarrement, elle travaille dans une banque

impromptu /ɪmˈprɒmptjuː/ ADV impromptu ADJ impromptu ◆ **to make an ~ speech** faire un discours impromptu *or* au pied levé ◆ **to make an ~ appearance** faire une apparition N *(Mus)* impromptu *m*

improper /ɪmˈprɒpəʳ/ ADJ 1 *(= unsuitable)* déplacé, malséant 2 *(= indecent)* indécent, inconvenant ; *[conduct, suggestion]* indécent ; *[story]* indécent, scabreux 3 *(= dishonest)* malhonnête 4 *(= wrong) [diagnosis]* incorrect, erroné ; *[term]* inexact, impropre ; *[use, interpretation]* abusif, incorrect ; *(Sport) [play etc]* incorrect

improperly /ɪmˈprɒpəlɪ/ ADV 1 *(= indecently)* ◆ **he was ~ dressed** il était habillé de façon inconvenante 2 *(= dishonestly) [act]* de façon irrégulière 3 *(= incorrectly) [test, diagnose, treat]* mal ◆ **a word used ~** un mot employé improprement

impropriety /,ɪmprəˈpraɪətɪ/ N 1 *[of behaviour etc]* inconvenance *f* ◆ **to commit an ~** commettre une inconvenance ◆ **to behave with ~** se conduire avec inconvenance ◆ **financial ~** irrégularités *fpl* financières 2 *(Ling) [of expression, phrase]* impropriété *f*

improv * /ˈɪmprɒv/ N sketch *m* improvisé

improve /ɪmˈpruːv/ VT 1 *(= make better) [+ situation, position, work, health, wording]* améliorer ; *[+ physique]* développer ; *[+ knowledge, machine, invention]* améliorer, perfectionner ; *[+ building, property]* réaménager, rénover ; *[+ site]* aménager, embellir ; *[+ soil, land]* amender, bonifier ◆ **to ~ sb's looks** *or* **appearance** embellir *or* avantager qn ◆ **to ~ one's looks** s'embellir ◆ **to ~ one's chances of doing sth** améliorer *or* augmenter ses chances de faire qch ◆ **how can I ~ my chances at interview?** comment est-ce que je peux améliorer *or* augmenter mes chances de réussite à un entretien ? ◆ **that should ~ his chances of success** cela devrait améliorer ses chances de succès ◆ **$60,000 worth of repairs failed to ~ matters** 60 000 dollars de réparations n'ont pas réussi à améliorer les choses ◆ **she's trying to ~ her mind** elle essaie de se cultiver (l'esprit) ◆ **a book which ~s the mind** un livre qui élève l'esprit ◆ **he wants to ~ his French** il veut se perfectionner en français
2 *(= make good use of)* tirer parti de, profiter de ◆ **to ~ the occasion, to ~ the shining hour** *(hum)* tirer parti de l'occasion, mettre l'occasion à profit
VI 1 *(= get better) [situation, position, health, prospects, chances, weather]* s'améliorer ; *[physique]* se développer ; *[soil]* s'amender, se bonifier ; *[student, patient]* faire des progrès ◆ **the service has ~d** la qualité du service s'est améliorée ◆ **his work is improving** (la qualité de) son travail s'améliore ◆ **his French is improving** il fait des progrès en français ◆ **as medical knowledge ~s** avec l'amélioration des connaissances médicales ◆ **mobile phones have ~d greatly** les téléphones portables se sont beaucoup améliorés ◆ **safety/efficiency/productivity has definitely ~d** il y a eu une nette amélioration au niveau de la sécurité/de l'efficacité/du rendement ◆ **business is improving** les affaires reprennent ◆ **things are improving** les choses vont mieux ◆ **matters haven't ~d much** la situation ne s'est pas beaucoup améliorée ◆ **his chances of success are improving** ses chances de réussir s'améliorent ◆ **to ~ with use** s'améliorer à l'usage ◆ **this wine ~s with age** ce vin se bonifie *or* s'améliore en vieillissant ◆ **he's ~d with age** *(hum)* il s'est amélioré *or* bonifié avec l'âge ◆ **this book ~s on re-reading** ce livre gagne à être relu

2 ◆ **to ~ on sth** faire mieux que qch, apporter des améliorations à qch ◆ **it can't be ~d on** on peut difficilement faire mieux ◆ **she had ~d on her previous performance** elle s'est améliorée depuis sa dernière prestation ◆ **to ~ on sb's offer** *(Comm, Fin)* enchérir sur qn

improved /ɪm'pruːvd/ ADJ meilleur ◆ **much/slightly ~** nettement/légèrement meilleur ◆ **this room looks much ~ after painting** la pièce est beaucoup mieux après avoir été repeinte ◆ **"new improved formula"** *(Comm)* "nouvelle formule"

improvement /ɪm'pruːvmənt/ N 1 *(NonC)* *[of situation, position, health, soil, land]* amélioration *f* ; *[of mind, physique]* développement *m* ; *[of site]* aménagement *m*, embellissement *m* ; *[of building, property]* réaménagement *m*, rénovation *f* ; *[of machine]* perfectionnement *m* ◆ **there's been quite an ~** *(gen)* on constate une nette amélioration ◆ **there has been some ~ in the patient's condition** l'état du malade s'est un peu amélioré ◆ **it is open to ~** ça peut être amélioré ◆ **he has shown some ~ in French** il a fait quelques progrès en français ◆ **this model is an ~ on the previous one** ce modèle est mieux que le précédent ◆ **the new teacher is an ~ on his predecessor** le nouveau professeur est meilleur que son prédécesseur ◆ **they made an ~ on their previous offer** ils ont fait une nouvelle offre plus intéressante ◆ **there is room for ~** *(in situation)* cela pourrait être mieux ; *(in work)* on pourrait faire mieux

2 *(gen pl)* ◆ **~s** améliorations *fpl* aménagements *mpl* ◆ **to carry out ~s to a house** apporter des améliorations à *or* faire des travaux d'aménagement dans une maison

COMP **improvement grant** N subvention *f* pour l'amélioration d'un logement, ≃ prime *f* à l'amélioration de l'habitat

improvidence /ɪm'prɒvɪdəns/ N imprévoyance *f*, manque *m* de prévoyance

improvident /ɪm'prɒvɪdənt/ ADJ *(= not providing for future)* imprévoyant ; *(= extravagant)* prodigue, dépensier

improvidently /ɪm'prɒvɪdəntlɪ/ ADV avec imprévoyance

improving /ɪm'pruːvɪŋ/ ADJ *(= edifying)* édifiant

improvisation /ˌɪmprəvaɪ'zeɪʃən/ N *(gen, Mus)* improvisation *f*

improvise /'ɪmprəvaɪz/ VTI *(gen, Mus)* improviser

imprudence /ɪm'pruːdəns/ N imprudence *f*

imprudent /ɪm'pruːdənt/ ADJ imprudent

imprudently /ɪm'pruːdəntlɪ/ ADV imprudemment

impudence /'ɪmpjʊdəns/ N impudence *f*, effronterie *f*

impudent /'ɪmpjʊdənt/ ADJ impudent, effronté

impudently /'ɪmpjʊdəntlɪ/ ADV impudemment, avec effronterie

impugn /ɪm'pjuːn/ VT *(frm)* *[+ motives, sincerity, judgment]* contester ; *[+ honour, reputation]* porter gravement atteinte à, attaquer

impulse /'ɪmpʌls/ N 1 *(= sudden desire)* impulsion *f* ◆ **rash ~** coup *m* de tête ◆ **on a sudden ~ he ...** pris d'une impulsion soudaine il ... ◆ **a man of ~** un impulsif ◆ **to act on (an) ~** agir par impulsion ◆ **my first ~ was to refuse** ma première impulsion *or* réaction a été de refuser ◆ **he couldn't resist the ~** il n'arrivait pas à résister à l'envie ◆ **she resisted an ~ to smile** elle a réprimé son envie de sourire 2 *(= stimulus)* impulsion *f*, élan *m* ◆ **this gave new ~ to the reform process** ça a donné une nouvelle impulsion *or* un nouvel élan au processus de réforme 3 *(Phys, Elec, Physiol)* impulsion *f*

COMP **impulse buy** N achat *m* d'impulsion

impulse buying N achats *mpl* d'impulsion

impulse purchase N ⇒ **impulse buy**

impulsion /ɪm'pʌlʃən/ N impulsion *f*

impulsive /ɪm'pʌlsɪv/ ADJ 1 *(= spontaneous, acting on impulse)* *[movement]* impulsif, spontané ; *[temperament]* primesautier ; *[temper, passion]* fougueux ; *[act]* impulsif, spontané ; *[remark]* irréfléchi ◆ **she's very ~** elle est très impulsive 2 *(= impelling)* *[force]* irrésistible

impulsively /ɪm'pʌlsɪvlɪ/ ADV de manière impulsive

impulsiveness /ɪm'pʌlsɪvnɪs/ N *(NonC)* caractère *m* impulsif, impulsivité *f*

impunity /ɪm'pjuːnɪtɪ/ N impunité *f* ◆ **with ~** impunément, avec impunité

impure /ɪm'pjʊər/ ADJ *[air, water, milk, motive]* impur ; *[thought, action]* impur, impudique ; *[drug]* frelaté ; *(Archit etc)* *[style]* bâtard

impurity /ɪm'pjʊərɪtɪ/ N impureté *f*

imputation /ˌɪmpjʊ'teɪʃən/ N 1 *(= accusation)* imputation *f* 2 *(NonC)* attribution *f*, imputation *f* *(of sth to sb/sth* de qch à qn/qch)

impute /ɪm'pjuːt/ VT imputer, attribuer *(sth to sb/sth* qch à qn/qch) ◆ **~d rent/value** *(Comm)* loyer *m*/valeur *f* imputé(e) *or* implicite ◆ **~d cost** *(Comm)* coût *m* supplétif, charge *f* supplétive

IN abbrev of **Indiana**

in /ɪn/

1 PREPOSITION	4 PLURAL NOUN
2 ADVERB	5 COMPOUNDS
3 ADJECTIVE	

1 - PREPOSITION

When **in** is the second element in a phrasal verb, eg **ask in**, **fill in**, **look in**, look up the verb. When it is part of a set combination, eg **in the country**, **in ink**, **in danger**, **weak in**, **wrapped in**, look up the other word.

1 place dans ◆ **~ the box** dans la boîte ◆ **~ the street** dans la rue ◆ **~ the shop window** en vitrine ◆ **~ sb's house** chez qn

◆ **in it/them** *(= inside it, inside them)* dedans ◆ **put that ~ it** mets-le dedans ◆ **there's something ~ it** il y a quelque chose dedans ◆ **our bags were stolen, and our passports were ~ them** on nous a volé nos sacs et nos passeports étaient dedans

2 people chez ◆ **a condition rare ~ a child of that age** une maladie rare chez un enfant de cet âge ◆ **it's something I admire ~ her** c'est quelque chose que j'admire chez elle ◆ **we find this theme ~ Dickens** on trouve ce thème chez Dickens ◆ **the party will have a great leader ~ him** le parti trouvera en lui un excellent leader

3 plant, animal chez ◆ **you find this instinct ~ animals** on trouve cet instinct chez les animaux ◆ **a condition common ~ plants, shellfish, and some lizards** une maladie courante chez les plantes, les crustacés et certains lézards

4 with geographical names

◆ **in** + *fem countries, regions, islands* en

Feminine countries usually end in -e.

◆ **~ England/France** en Angleterre/France ◆ **~ Brittany/Provence** en Bretagne/Provence ◆ **~ Sicily/Crete** en Sicile/Crète ◆ **~ Louisiana/Virginia** en Louisiane/Virginie ◆ **~ Cornwall/Bavaria** en Cornouailles/Bavière

en is also used with masculine countries beginning with a vowel.

◆ **~ Iran/Israel** en Iran/Israël

◆ **in** + *masc country* au ◆ **~ Japan/Kuwait** au Japon/Koweït

Note also the following:

◆ **~ the Sahara/Kashmir** au Sahara/Cachemire

◆ **in** + *plural country/group of islands* aux ◆ **~ the United States/West Indies** aux États-Unis/Antilles

◆ **in** + *town/island without article* à ◆ **~ London/Paris** à Londres/Paris ◆ **~ Cuba/Malta** à Cuba/Malte

◆ **in** + *masculine state/French region/county* dans ◆ **~ Poitou/Berry** dans le Poitou/le Berry ◆ **~ Sussex/Yorkshire** dans le Sussex/le Yorkshire

dans is also used with islands with **île** in their name, and many departments.

◆ **~ the Drôme/the Var** dans la Drôme/le Var ◆ **~ the Isle of Man/the Ile de Ré** dans l'île de Man / l'île de Ré BUT **~ Seine-et-Marne/the Vendée** en Seine-et-Marne/Vendée

5 with time expressions *(= in the space of)* en ; *(= after)* dans ◆ **I can't do it ~ two hours** je ne peux pas le faire en deux heures ◆ **he has written twice ~ three years** il a écrit deux fois en trois ans ◆ **it'll be ready ~ three hours** ce sera prêt dans trois heures ◆ **I'll be back ~ a week** je reviendrai dans une semaine ◆ **once ~ a hundred years** une fois tous les cent ans

6 month, year, season en ◆ **~ May** en mai ◆ **~ 2002/September 2002** en 2002/septembre 2002 ◆ **~ summer/autumn/winter** en été/automne/hiver ◆ **~ spring** au printemps

Look up the noun when translating such phrases as **in the morning**, **in the sixties**, **in a minute**, **in a week's time**, **in the end**.

7 = wearing en ◆ **they were all ~ shorts** ils étaient tous en short ◆ **~ his slippers** en pantoufles, dans ses pantoufles ◆ **you look nice ~ that dress** cette robe te va bien, tu es jolie dans cette robe

8 language, medium, material en ◆ **~ French** en français ◆ **~ marble/velvet** en marbre/velours

9 ratio sur ◆ **one man ~ ten** un homme sur dix ◆ **what happened was a chance ~ a million** il y avait une chance sur un million que ce genre de choses arrive ◆ **a one ~ fifty chance of survival** une chance sur cinquante de survie ◆ **they pay 20 pence ~ the pound income tax** ils payent 20 pour cent d'impôts sur le revenu

10 = in respect of ◆ **rough ~ appearance** d'aspect rugueux ◆ **~ that, he resembles his father** en cela, il ressemble à son père

11 following superlative de ◆ **the best pupil ~ the class** le meilleur élève de la classe ◆ **the highest mountain ~ Europe** la plus haute montagne d'Europe, la montagne la plus haute d'Europe

12 = while en ◆ **~ saying this, ~ so saying** en disant cela ◆ **~ trying to save her he fell into the water himself** en essayant de la sauver, il est tombé à l'eau

2 - ADVERB

1 = inside à l'intérieur ◆ **she opened the door and they all rushed ~** elle a ouvert la porte et ils se sont tous précipités à l'intérieur

When **in** means **in it** or **in them**, it is translated by **y**.

◆ **she opened her bag and put the ticket ~** elle a ouvert son sac et y a mis le billet

2 at home, work

♦ **to be in** *[person]* être là ♦ **the boss isn't ~ yet** le patron n'est pas encore là

When **in** means **at home, chez** + pronoun can also be used.

♦ **he's usually ~ on Saturday morning** il est généralement là le samedi matin, il est généralement chez lui le samedi matin ♦ **you're never ~!** tu n'es jamais là !, tu n'es jamais chez toi ! ♦ **is Paul ~?** est-ce que Paul est là ? BUT **there's nobody ~** il n'y a personne

to be in may require a more specific translation.

♦ **the train is ~** le train est en gare ♦ **he's ~ for tests** il est venu faire des analyses ♦ **the essays have to be ~ by Friday** les dissertations doivent être rendues d'ici vendredi ♦ **the harvest is ~** la moisson est rentrée ♦ **the socialists are ~!** les socialistes sont au pouvoir ! ♦ **the fire is still ~** il y a encore du feu ♦ **the screw was not ~ properly** la vis n'était pas bien enfoncée

3 set structures

♦ **in between** ♦ **the pages ~ between are completely blank** les pages du milieu sont vierges ♦ **~ between he will give three concerts** entre-temps *or* dans l'intervalle, il donnera trois concerts

♦ **in between** + *noun/pronoun* entre ♦ **he positioned himself ~ between the two weakest players** il s'est placé entre les deux joueurs les plus faibles ♦ **~ between adventures, he finds time for ...** entre deux aventures, il trouve le temps de ... ; see also **compounds**

♦ **to be in for sth** *(= be threatened with)* ♦ **we are ~ for trouble** * nous allons avoir des ennuis ♦ **you don't know what you're ~ for!** * tu ne sais pas ce qui t'attend ! ♦ **he's ~ for it!** * il va en prendre pour son grade !* ♦ **to be ~ for a competition/exam** *(= to be entered for)* être inscrit à un concours/examen

♦ **to be in on sth** * *(= know about)* ♦ **to be ~ on a plan/secret** être au courant d'un plan/d'un secret ♦ **are you ~ on it?** tu es au courant ?

♦ **in that** *(= seeing that)* ♦ **the new treatment is preferable ~ that ...** le nouveau traitement est préférable car ...

♦ **to be well in with sb** * être dans les petits papiers de qn* ♦ **she's well ~ with the management** elle est bien avec la direction

3 - ADJECTIVE

* = fashionable in *inv*, à la mode ♦ **straw hats are ~** les chapeaux de paille sont à la mode ♦ **it's the ~ place to eat** c'est le restaurant branché* *or* à la mode en ce moment ♦ **it's the ~ thing to ...** c'est très in* *or* à la mode de ... + *infin*

4 - PLURAL NOUN

the ins

1 = details

♦ **the ins and outs** ♦ **to know the ins and outs of a matter** connaître les tenants et aboutissants d'une affaire, connaître une affaire dans ses moindres détails ♦ **she knows the ins and outs of the system** le système n'a plus de secret pour elle, elle connaît le système dans ses moindres détails

2 US Pol * le parti au pouvoir

5 - COMPOUNDS

in-between N ♦ **the in-betweens** ceux qui sont entre les deux ADJ ♦ **it's in-between** c'est entre les deux ♦ **in-between times** dans les intervalles ♦ **it was in-between* weather** c'était un temps mitigé ♦ **a coat for in-between* weather** un manteau de demi-saison

in-built ADJ *(esp Brit) [feeling, tendency]* inné ; *[feature, device]* intégré ♦ **in-built limitation** limite *f* inhérente au système

in-car ADJ *[system, CD player]* embarqué

the in-crowd * N les branchés* *mpl*, les gens *mpl* in ♦ **to be in with the in-crowd** faire partie des branchés* *or* des gens in

in-depth ADJ en profondeur ♦ **in-depth interview** interview *f* en profondeur

in-flight ADJ *[refuelling]* en vol ; *[film, entertainment]* proposé pendant le vol ♦ **in-flight meal** repas *m* servi pendant le vol ♦ **in-flight magazine** magazine *m* de voyage *(destiné aux passagers aériens)*

in-goal area N *(Rugby)* en-but *m inv*

in-group N cercle *m* fermé

in-house ADJ *(= designed for staff) [publication]* interne ; *[training]* en entreprise *or* en interne ; *(= made within company) [video etc]* réalisé en interne ADV *[train, produce etc]* en interne

in-joke N plaisanterie *f* pour initiés

in-laws * NPL *(= parents-in-law)* beaux-parents *mpl* ; *(others)* belle-famille *f*

in-off * N *(Ftbl)* ♦ **the goal was an in-off** le but a été marqué après un cafouillage dans la surface de réparation

in-patient N ⇒ **inpatient**

in-service education N *(US)* formation *f* continue

in-service training N formation *f* continue ♦ **to have in-service training** *[new employee]* faire un stage d'initiation ; *[present employee]* faire un stage de perfectionnement ; *(new subject)* faire un stage de recyclage ♦ **to have in-service training in the use of computers** suivre un stage d'informatique dans son entreprise

in-store ADJ *[detective]* employé par le magasin ; *[theft]* commis par un membre du personnel

in-tray N corbeille *f* "arrivée"

in-your-face*, **in-yer-face*** ADJ cru

-in /ɪn/ N *(in compounds) particule qui désigne une réunion ou un rassemblement* ♦ **a talk-in** une réunion où l'on discute ; → **sit-in, teach**

in. abbrev of **inch**

inability /ˌɪnəˈbɪlɪtɪ/ N incapacité *f (to do sth* de faire qch) inaptitude *f (to do sth* à faire qch)

in absentia /ˌɪnæbˈsentɪə/ ADV *(frm)* en votre *(or leur etc)* absence

inaccessibility /ˈɪnækˌsesəˈbɪlɪtɪ/ N inaccessibilité *f*

inaccessible /ˌɪnækˈsesəbl/ ADJ *(lit, fig)* inaccessible *(to sb/sth* à qn/qch) ♦ **to be ~ by road/by land/by boat/by sea** être inaccessible par la route/par voie terrestre/par bateau/par voie maritime

inaccuracy /ɪnˈækjʊrəsɪ/ N 1 (NonC) *[of calculation, information, translation, quotation, statement]* inexactitude *f* ; *[of person]* imprécision *f*, manque *m* de précision ; *[of expression, term, word]* inexactitude *f*, impropriété *f* 2 *(= error)* inexactitude *f* ♦ **there are several inaccuracies in his account** son rapport contient plusieurs inexactitudes

inaccurate /ɪnˈækjʊrɪt/ ADJ *[information, statement, picture, forecast]* inexact ; *[method, instrument, missile, shot]* imprécis ♦ **he is ~** il fait des erreurs ♦ **the clock is ~** l'horloge n'est pas à l'heure ♦ **it is ~ to say that ...** il est inexact de dire que ...

inaccurately /ɪnˈækjʊrɪtlɪ/ ADV *[answer, quote, report]* avec inexactitude, inexactement ; *[multiply]* incorrectement

inaction /ɪnˈækʃən/ N inaction *f*, inertie *f* ♦ **policy of ~** politique *f* de l'inaction *or* de non-intervention

inactive /ɪnˈæktɪv/ ADJ 1 *[person, animal, lifestyle, bank account]* inactif ; *[member]* non participant 2 *(Chem) [substance]* non actif, inerte 3 *[volcano] (= extinct)* inactif, éteint ; *(= dormant)* assoupi

inactivity /ˌɪnækˈtɪvɪtɪ/ N inactivité *f*

inadequacy /ɪnˈædɪkwəsɪ/ N *[of system, punishment, resources, piece of work]* insuffisance *f* ; *(Psych)* inadaptation *f or* insuffisance *f* socio-affective ♦ **the inadequacies of the current system** les insuffisances du système actuel

inadequate /ɪnˈædɪkwɪt/ ADJ *(= insufficient) [resources, funding, protection, information, preparation, amount]* insuffisant ; *(= unsatisfactory) [facilities, housing, training, response, diet]* inadéquat, inadapté ; *(= incompetent)* incompétent ; *(Psych)* mal adapté *or* inadapté (sur le plan socio-affectif) ♦ **he's ~** il ne fait pas le poids, il n'est pas à la hauteur ♦ **he felt totally ~** il ne se sentait absolument pas à la hauteur ♦ **~ staffing levels** manque *m* de personnel ♦ **the proposed legislation is quite ~ for this purpose** la législation en projet est tout à fait insuffisante *or* inadéquate pour atteindre ce but ♦ **the amount offered is ~ to cover the expenses** la somme proposée ne suffit pas à couvrir les frais N (also **social inadequate**) inadapté(e) *m(f)*

inadequately /ɪnˈædɪkwɪtlɪ/ ADV insuffisamment

inadmissible /ˌɪnədˈmɪsəbl/ ADJ *[attitude, opinion, behaviour]* inadmissible ; *[suggestion, offer]* inacceptable ♦ **~ evidence** *(Jur)* témoignage *m* irrecevable

inadvertence /ˌɪnədˈvɜːtəns/ N manque *m* d'attention, étourderie *f* ♦ **by** *or* **through ~** par inadvertance, par mégarde

inadvertent /ˌɪnədˈvɜːtənt/ ADJ 1 *(= heedless) [person]* insouciant *(to* de) ; *[action]* commis par inadvertance *or* par mégarde ♦ **an ~ insult** une insulte lâchée par étourderie 2 *(= inattentive) [person]* inattentif, étourdi

inadvertently /ˌɪnədˈvɜːtəntlɪ/ ADV par inadvertance *or* mégarde

inadvisability /ˈɪnədˌvaɪzəˈbɪlɪtɪ/ N inopportunité *f (of doing sth* de faire qch)

inadvisable /ˌɪnədˈvaɪzəbl/ LANGUAGE IN USE 2.2 ADJ *[action, scheme]* inopportun, à déconseiller ♦ **it is ~ to do ...** il est déconseillé de faire ...

inalienable /ɪnˈeɪlɪənəbl/ ADJ *(Jur, fig) [rights, affection]* inaliénable

inamorata /ɪnˌæməˈrɑːtə/ N *(liter)* amoureuse *f*

inane /ɪˈneɪn/ ADJ *[person, action]* inepte, bête ; *[question, smile, grin]* bête ♦ **~ remark** observation *f* inepte, ineptie *f* ♦ **what an ~ thing to do!** faut-il être bête pour faire une chose pareille !

inanely /ɪˈneɪnlɪ/ ADV *[grin, laugh]* bêtement ; *[talk]* sottement

inanimate /ɪnˈænɪmɪt/ ADJ inanimé

inanition /ˌɪnəˈnɪʃən/ N inanition *f*

inanity /ɪˈnænɪtɪ/ N ineptie *f*

inapplicable /ɪnˈæplɪkəbl/ ADJ inapplicable *(to* à)

inappropriate /ˌɪnəˈprəʊprɪɪt/ ADJ *[action, behaviour, remark]* inopportun, déplacé ; *[word, expression]* impropre ; *[name]* mal choisi, impropre ; *[moment]* inopportun, mauvais ♦ **it would be ~ for me to comment** il ne m'appartient pas de commenter ♦ **many parents feel it is ~ to discuss finances with their children** beaucoup de parents trouvent inopportun *or* déplacé de parler de questions financières avec leurs enfants

♦ **inappropriate to** + *noun* ♦ **the factory is ~ to the town's needs** l'usine ne répond pas *or* n'est pas adaptée aux besoins de la ville ♦ **clothing ~ to their status** des vêtements qui ne correspondent pas *or* ne sont pas appropriés à leur statut

inappropriately /ˌɪnəˈprəʊprɪɪtlɪ/ ADV *[remark, reply]* mal à propos, inopportunément ◆ **to behave ~** ne pas se comporter comme il faut (*or* fallait *etc*) ; (*= harrass*) se conduire de façon déplacée ◆ **if a colleague is behaving ~, ask him to stop** si l'un de vos collègues se conduit de façon déplacée, demandez-lui d'arrêter ◆ **he was asking questions quite ~** il posait des questions de façon tout à fait inopportune ◆ **he was dressed ~ for ...** il n'était pas habillé comme il fallait pour ...

inappropriateness /ɪnəˈprəʊprɪɪtnəs/ N *[of action, behaviour, remark]* caractère *m* inopportun *or* déplacé ; *[of word]* impropriété *f*

inapt /ɪnˈæpt/ ADJ 1 *[remark, behaviour]* peu approprié 2 *[person]* inapte, incapable

inaptitude /ɪnˈæptɪtjuːd/ N 1 *[of remark, behaviour]* caractère *m* peu approprié 2 *[of person]* inaptitude *f*, incapacité *f*

inarticulacy /ˌɪnɑːˈtɪkjʊləsɪ/ N difficulté *f* à s'exprimer ◆ **he was suddenly reduced to ~** il était soudain incapable de s'exprimer

inarticulate /ˌɪnɑːˈtɪkjʊlɪt/ ADJ 1 (*= incoherent*) *[speech]* mal articulé ; *[sound, noise]* inarticulé ; *[emotion]* inexprimable ◆ **he is ~** (*= unable to express himself*) il s'exprime mal, il n'arrive pas à s'exprimer ; (*in pronunciation*) il articule mal, il avale ses mots ◆ **~ with anger** bafouillant *or* bégayant de colère 2 (*Anat, Bot*) *[body, structure]* inarticulé

inarticulately /ˌɪnɑːˈtɪkjʊlɪtlɪ/ ADV *[mumble]* de manière confuse

inartistic /ˌɪnɑːˈtɪstɪk/ ADJ *[work]* peu artistique, sans valeur artistique ; *[person]* dépourvu de sens artistique, peu artiste

inartistically /ˌɪnɑːˈtɪstɪkəlɪ/ ADV sans talent (artistique), de façon peu artistique

inasmuch /ɪnəzˈmʌtʃ/ ADV ◆ **~ as** (*= seeing that*) attendu que, vu que ; (*= insofar as*) en ce sens que, dans la mesure où

inattention /ˌɪnəˈtenʃən/ N manque *m* d'attention, inattention *f* ◆ **~ to details** manque *m* d'attention pour les détails ◆ **a moment's ~** un moment d'inattention

inattentive /ˌɪnəˈtentɪv/ ADJ (*= not paying attention*) inattentif, distrait ; (*= neglectful*) peu attentionné, négligent (*towards sb* envers qn) ◆ **he was ~ to details** il accordait peu d'attention aux détails ◆ **he was ~ to her requests** il était peu attentif à ses demandes

inattentively /ˌɪnəˈtentɪvlɪ/ ADV distraitement, sans prêter attention

inaudible /ɪnˈɔːdəbl/ ADJ *[sound, whisper, voice]* inaudible ◆ **he was almost ~** il était presque inaudible, on l'entendait à peine ◆ **sounds that are ~ to humans** des sons qui ne sont pas perceptibles à l'oreille humaine

inaudibly /ɪnˈɔːdəblɪ/ ADV *[speak, mumble]* de manière inaudible

inaugural /ɪˈnɔːgjʊrəl/ ADJ inaugural ◆ **~ lecture** (*Univ*) cours *m* inaugural ◆ **~ ceremony** cérémonie *f* d'inauguration *or* d'ouverture

inaugurate /ɪˈnɔːgjʊreɪt/ VT 1 *[+ policy]* inaugurer, mettre en application ; *[+ new rail service etc]* inaugurer ; *[+ era]* inaugurer, commencer 2 *[+ president, official]* investir dans ses fonctions ; *[+ bishop, king, pope]* introniser

inauguration /ɪˌnɔːgjʊˈreɪʃən/ N *[of president, governor, government]* investiture *f* ; *[of bishop, king, pope]* intronisation *f* ; *[of building, institution, service]* inauguration *f* COMP **Inauguration Day** N (*US Pol*) jour *m* de l'investiture du président

INAUGURATION DAY

Les élections présidentielles américaines ont lieu au mois de novembre, mais le nouveau président ne prête serment que deux mois plus tard, le 20 janvier, **Inauguration Day**, à l'occasion d'une cérémonie d'investiture qui se tient dans la ville de Washington.

inauspicious /ˌɪnɔːsˈpɪʃəs/ ADJ *[beginning, event]* peu propice, de mauvais augure ; *[circumstances]* malencontreux, fâcheux

inauspiciously /ˌɪnɔːsˈpɪʃəslɪ/ ADV sous de mauvais auspices

inboard /ˈɪnˌbɔːd/ (*Naut*) ADV à l'intérieur, à bord PREP à bord de ADJ intérieur (-eure *f*) COMP **inboard motor** N (moteur *m*) in-bord *m*

inborn /ˈɪnˌbɔːn/ ADJ *[talent, ability, instinct, desire, fear]* inné ; *[weakness, fault]* congénital

inbound /ˈɪnˌbaʊnd/ ADJ ◆ **an ~ flight from Honduras** un vol en provenance du Honduras ◆ **a plane/flight ~ for Heathrow Airport** un avion/vol arrivant à l'aéroport de Heathrow

inbred /ˈɪnˌbred/ ADJ 1 (*= innate*) inné (*in sb* chez qn) 2 (*Sociol, Bio*) *[family, tribe]* qui possède un fort degré de consanguinité ; *[person]* de parents ayant un fort degré de consanguinité ; *[animal]* issu de la même souche

inbreeding /ˈɪnˌbriːdɪŋ/ N *[of animals]* croisement *m* d'animaux de même souche ◆ **there is a lot of ~ in the tribe** il y a beaucoup d'unions consanguines au sein de la tribu

inc abbrev of **including, inclusive**

Inc. (abbrev of **Incorporated**) SA ◆ **Gough and Gautier ~** Gough et Gautier SA

Inca /ˈɪŋkə/ N (pl **Inca** *or* **Incas**) 1 Inca *mf* 2 (*= language*) quichua *m* ADJ inca *inv*

incalculable /ɪnˈkælkjʊləbl/ ADJ 1 (*= immeasurable*) *[effect, consequences, damage, risk, cost, loss]* incalculable ; *[value, importance, benefit]* inestimable 2 (*= unpredictable*) *[mood]* imprévisible

incandescence /ˌɪnkænˈdesns/ N incandescence *f*

incandescent /ˌɪnkænˈdesnt/ ADJ 1 (*lit = glowing*) incandescent 2 (*fig, liter = radiant*) rayonnant 3 (*= furious*) ◆ **he was ~ (with rage** *or* **fury)** il était blême de rage COMP *[bulb, lamp, light]* à incandescence

incantation /ˌɪnkænˈteɪʃən/ N incantation *f*

incapability /ɪnˌkeɪpəˈbɪlɪtɪ/ N (*Jur, fig*) incapacité *f* (*of doing sth* de faire qch)

incapable /ɪnˈkeɪpəbl/ LANGUAGE IN USE 16.4 ADJ *[person]* incapable (*of doing sth* de faire qch) ; (*Jur*) incapable, inapte ◆ **I'm not ~, I can manage** je ne suis pas invalide, je peux me débrouiller ◆ **~ of violence/tenderness/love/murder** incapable de violence/de tendresse/d'aimer/de commettre un meurtre ◆ **he was ~ of movement** il était incapable de bouger ◆ **~ of proof/analysis** (*frm*) impossible à prouver/analyser ◆ **to be ~ of solution** (*frm*) être insoluble *or* sans solution, ne pouvoir être résolu

incapacitate /ˌɪnkəˈpæsɪteɪt/ VT 1 handicaper ◆ **she was ~d by diabetes** elle était handicapée par ses problèmes de diabète ◆ **to be ~d for work** *or* **from working** être dans l'incapacité de travailler, être en invalidité ◆ **heart problems ~d him** ses problèmes cardiaques l'empêchaient de mener une vie normale 2 (*Jur*) frapper d'incapacité

incapacitated /ˌɪnkəˈpæsɪteɪtɪd/ ADJ handicapé ◆ **he was ~ with severe back pain** il était immobilisé souffrant d'un sérieux mal de dos

incapacitating /ˌɪnkəˈpæsɪteɪtɪŋ/ ADJ ◆ **~ headaches** des maux *mpl* de tête qui empêchent toute activité ◆ **he had an ~ heart condition** ses problèmes cardiaques l'empêchaient de poursuivre des activités normales ◆ **she suffered an ~ stroke** elle a eu une attaque qui l'a laissée handicapée

incapacity /ˌɪnkəˈpæsɪtɪ/ N 1 incapacité *f* (*to do* de faire) incompétence *f* (*to do sth* pour faire qch) impuissance *f* (*to do sth* à faire qch ; *for sth* en matière de qch) 2 (*Jur*) incapacité *f* (légale) COMP **incapacity benefit** N (*Brit*) allocation *f* d'invalidité

incarcerate /ɪnˈkɑːsəreɪt/ VT incarcérer

incarceration /ɪnˌkɑːsəˈreɪʃən/ N incarcération *f*

incarnate /ɪnˈkɑːnɪt/ (*Rel, fig*) ADJ incarné ◆ **the Incarnate Word** (*Rel*) le Verbe incarné ◆ **he's evil/the devil ~** c'est le mal/le diable incarné ◆ **he is cynicism ~** il est le cynisme incarné VT /ˈɪnkɑːneɪt/ incarner

incarnation /ˌɪnkɑːˈneɪʃən/ N (*Rel, fig*) incarnation *f* ◆ **she is the ~ of virtue** c'est la vertu incarnée ◆ **in a previous ~** dans une vie antérieure

incautious /ɪnˈkɔːʃəs/ ADJ *[person]* imprudent ; *[remark, promise, action]* irréfléchi ; *[behaviour]* inconsidéré

incautiously /ɪnˈkɔːʃəslɪ/ ADV imprudemment, sans réfléchir

incendiary /ɪnˈsendɪərɪ/ ADJ (*lit, fig*) incendiaire N (*= bomb*) engin *m or* bombe *f* incendiaire ; (*= arsonist*) incendiaire *mf* ; (*fig*) (*= agitator*) brandon *m* de discorde COMP **incendiary device** N dispositif *m* incendiaire

incense¹ /ɪnˈsens/ VT (*= anger*) mettre en fureur ; (*stronger*) mettre dans une rage folle

incense² /ˈɪnsens/ N encens *m* COMP **incense bearer** N thuriféraire *m*
incense burner N encensoir *m*

incensed /ɪnˈsenst/ ADJ outré (*at, by* de, par) révolté (*at, by* par)

incentive /ɪnˈsentɪv/ N 1 (*= motivation*) motivation *f* ◆ **he has got no ~** il n'a aucune motivation, il n'est absolument pas motivé ◆ **this gave me an ~** cela m'a motivé *or* m'a donné une motivation ◆ **there is no ~ to work hard** rien ne vous incite *or* ne vous pousse à travailler dur ◆ **what ~ is there to work faster?** pour quelle (bonne) raison se mettrait-on à travailler plus vite ? ◆ **they have little ~ to keep going** peu de choses les motivent *or* incitent à continuer ◆ **to provide ~(s) for sth** encourager qch à l'aide de mesures incitatives

2 (*= promised reward*) incitation *f* ◆ **financial/economic ~s** incitations *fpl* financières/économiques ◆ **they offered him an ~** ils lui ont promis qu'il serait récompensé ; see also **tax** COMP **incentive bonus** N prime *f* d'encouragement
incentive discount N remise *f* promotionnelle
incentive payment N ⇒ **incentive bonus**

inception /ɪnˈsepʃən/ N commencement *m*, début *m* ◆ **since its ~** depuis ses débuts

incertitude /ɪnˈsɜːtɪtjuːd/ N incertitude *f*

incessant /ɪnˈsesnt/ ADJ *[complaints]* incessant, perpétuel ; *[rain, efforts]* incessant

incessantly /ɪnˈsesntlɪ/ ADV sans arrêt

incest /ˈɪnsest/ N inceste *m*

incestuous /ɪnˈsestjʊəs/ ADJ (*lit*) incestueux ◆ **they're an ~ lot** (*fig*) ils sont très repliés sur eux-mêmes, ils vivent entre eux

inch /ɪntʃ/ N pouce *m* (*= 2,54 cm*) ◆ **he has grown a few ~es since last year** ≈ il a grandi de quelques centimètres depuis l'année dernière ◆ **not an ~ from my face** *or* **nose** en plein *or* juste devant mon nez ◆ **he couldn't see an ~ in front of him** il n'y voyait pas à deux pas ◆ **not an ~ of the cloth is wasted** on ne perd pas un centimètre de tissu ◆ **not an ~ of French territory will be conceded** on ne cédera pas un pouce de territoire français ◆ **he knows every ~ of the district** il connaît la région comme sa poche *or* (jusque) dans ses moindres recoins ◆ **we searched every ~ of the room** nous avons cherché partout dans la pièce, nous avons passé la pièce au peigne fin ◆ **the police were searching the area ~ by ~** la police passait le quartier au peigne fin ◆ **an ~-by-~ search** une fouille minutieuse ◆ **he wouldn't budge an ~** *(lit)* il n'a pas voulu bouger d'un pouce ; *(fig)* il n'a pas voulu faire la plus petite concession *or* céder d'un pouce ◆ **he's every ~ a soldier** il a tout d'un soldat, il est soldat jusqu'à la moelle ◆ **she's every ~ a lady** c'est une femme du monde jusqu'au bout des ongles, elle a tout d'une femme du monde ◆ **within an ~ of succeeding/of death** *etc* à deux doigts *or* à un doigt de réussir/de la mort *etc* ◆ **they beat him to within an ~ of his life** ils l'ont roué de coups et laissé à deux doigts de la mort ◆ **he missed being run over by ~es** il a été à deux doigts de se faire écraser ◆ **give him an ~ and he'll take a yard** *or* **a mile** vous lui donnez le doigt, il vous prend le bras

VI ◆ **to ~ (one's way) forward/out/in** *etc* avancer/sortir/entrer *etc* peu à peu *or* petit à petit ◆ **to ~ (one's way) through** se frayer peu à peu un passage ◆ **prices are ~ing up** les prix augmentent petit à petit

VT ◆ **to ~ sth forward/in/out** *etc* faire avancer/entrer/sortir *etc* qch peu à peu *or* petit à petit

inchoate /ˈɪnkəʊeɪt/ **ADJ** *(frm)* *(= just begun)* naissant, débutant ; *(= half-formed)* vague, mal défini ; *(= unfinished)* incomplet (-ète *f*), inachevé

inchoative /ɪnˈkəʊətɪv/ **ADJ** *(Ling)* *[aspect, verb]* inchoatif

inchtape /ˈɪntʃteɪp/ **N** centimètre *m* (de couturière)

incidence /ˈɪnsɪdəns/ **N** 1 *[of disease]* fréquence *f*, incidence *f* ; *[of crime]* taux *m* ◆ **the ~ of breast cancer increases with age** la fréquence *or* l'incidence des cancers du sein augmente avec l'âge ◆ **the high ~ of heart disease in men over 40** le taux élevé des maladies cardiaques chez les hommes de plus de 40 ans ◆ **record ~s of pneumonia and bronchitis** un nombre record de cas de pneumonie et de bronchite 2 *(Opt, Phys etc)* incidence *f* ; → **angle**[1]

incident /ˈɪnsɪdənt/ **N** 1 incident *m* ; *(in book, play etc)* épisode *m*, péripétie *f* ◆ **there were several ~s on the border last month** il y a eu plusieurs incidents frontaliers le mois dernier ◆ **two students were killed in separate ~s** deux étudiants ont été tués dans deux incidents différents ◆ **a diplomatic ~** un incident diplomatique ◆ **the Birmingham ~** l'incident de Birmingham *or* qui a eu lieu à Birmingham ◆ **~s of violence** actes *mpl* de violence

2 *(NonC)* **the elections went ahead without ~** les élections se sont poursuivies sans incident ◆ **a novel full of ~** un roman plein de péripéties ◆ **a life full of ~** une vie mouvementée

ADJ 1 *(frm)* **~ to** lié à ◆ **costs ~ to the development of the new model** les coûts liés au développement du nouveau modèle

2 *(Opt)* incident

COMP incident room N *(Police)* bureau *m* de police *(provisoirement installé sur les lieux d'une enquête)*

incidental /ˌɪnsɪˈdentl/ **ADJ** *(= accompanying)* annexe ; *(= secondary)* d'importance secondaire, annexe ; *(= unplanned)* accidentel, fortuit ; *(= relating to a particular incident)* *[detail]* accessoire, secondaire ◆ **I don't know much about the ~ background** je connais mal les circonstances annexes ◆ **teaching is ~ to my main occupation of translating** l'enseignement n'est pour moi qu'une activité annexe par rapport à la traduction ◆ **these minor characters are ~ to the story** ces personnages secondaires ne sont pas essentiels à l'histoire ◆ **the dangers ~ to such exploration** les dangers que comporte une telle exploration

N *[event etc]* chose *f* fortuite ◆ **that's just an ~** ça n'a pas de rapport avec la question ◆ **~s** *(= expenses)* faux frais *mpl* ; *(= objects)* accessoires *mpl*

COMP incidental damages NPL *(Jur)* dommages-intérêts *mpl* accessoires
incidental expenses NPL faux frais *mpl*
incidental music N *(TV)* musique *f* de fond ; *(Theat)* musique *f* de scène ; *(Cine)* musique *f* de film ◆ **the ~ music to the play** la musique qui accompagne la pièce

incidentally /ˌɪnsɪˈdentəlɪ/ **ADV** 1 *(= by the way)* *(at start of sentence)* au fait, à propos ; *(in middle, at end of sentence)* soit dit en passant, entre parenthèses ◆ **~, why have you come?** au fait *or* à propos, pourquoi es-tu venu ? ◆ **the tower, ~, dates from the 12th century** la tour, entre parenthèses, date du 12e siècle 2 *(= casually)* *[mention, happen]* incidemment ◆ **it was only ~ interesting** cela n'avait qu'un intérêt accessoire

incinerate /ɪnˈsɪnəreɪt/ **VT** incinérer

incineration /ɪnsɪnəˈreɪʃən/ **N** incinération *f*

incinerator /ɪnˈsɪnəreɪtəʳ/ **N** *(domestic, industrial)* incinérateur *m* ; *[of crematorium]* four *m* crématoire

incipient /ɪnˈsɪpɪənt/ **ADJ** *[quarrel, disease, revolt]* naissant, qui commence ◆ **the ~ uprising was suppressed** la révolte naissante a été étouffée, la révolte a été écrasée dans l'œuf

incise /ɪnˈsaɪz/ **VT** 1 inciser, faire une incision dans 2 *(Art)* graver

incision /ɪnˈsɪʒən/ **N** incision *f*, entaille *f* ; *(Surg)* incision *f*

incisive /ɪnˈsaɪsɪv/ **ADJ** *[tone, analysis, comment, criticism]* incisif ; *[mind]* pénétrant ◆ **she's very ~** elle a l'esprit très vif

incisively /ɪnˈsaɪsɪvlɪ/ **ADV** *[say]* sur un ton incisif ; *[analyse, criticize]* de façon pénétrante

incisiveness /ɪnˈsaɪsɪvnɪs/ **N** *[of person, comment, criticism, analysis]* perspicacité *f* ◆ **the ~ of his mind** son acuité d'esprit ◆ **the ~ of his tone was almost aggressive** son ton était incisif au point d'en être presque agressif

incisor /ɪnˈsaɪzəʳ/ **N** *(= tooth)* incisive *f*

incite /ɪnˈsaɪt/ **VT** inciter, pousser *(to* à*)* ◆ **to ~ sb to violence/revolt** *etc* inciter *or* pousser qn à la violence/la révolte *etc* ◆ **to ~ sb to do sth** inciter *or* pousser qn à faire qch ◆ **they were ~d to break the law** on les a incités *or* poussés à enfreindre la loi

incitement /ɪnˈsaɪtmənt/ **N** *(NonC)* incitation *f* *(to* à*)*

incivility /ˌɪnsɪˈvɪlɪtɪ/ **N** *(NonC)* impolitesse *f*, incivilité † *f* *(also liter)* ◆ **there was an exchange of incivilities** ils ont échangé des amabilités *(iro)*

incl. abbrev of **including, inclusive**

inclemency /ɪnˈklemənsɪ/ **N** inclémence *f*

inclement /ɪnˈklemənt/ **ADJ** inclément

inclination /ˌɪnklɪˈneɪʃən/ **N** 1 *(= liking, wish)* inclination *f*, penchant *m* ; *(= tendency)* tendance *f* ; *(= desire)* envie *f* ◆ **children with little ~ for schooling** des enfants qui montrent peu d'inclination *or* de penchant pour les études ◆ **she was by ~ generous** elle était généreuse par inclination ◆ **I had no ~ to sleep** je n'avais aucune envie de dormir ◆ **I have neither the time nor the ~ (to do)** je n'ai ni le temps ni l'envie (de faire) ◆ **she's a playwright by ~** elle est auteur dramatique par goût ◆ **to follow one's own ~s** suivre son inclination *or* ses penchants (naturels) ◆ **he has an ~ towards meanness** il a tendance à être mesquin ◆ **her natural ~ was to help him** son inclination naturelle la portait à lui venir en aide

2 *(= slope, leaning)* *[of hill]* inclinaison *f*, pente *f* ; *[of head, body]* inclination *f*

incline /ɪnˈklaɪn/ **VT** 1 *(= bend, bow)* incliner, pencher ◆ **Jack ~d his head very slightly** Jack a très légèrement incliné *or* penché la tête ◆ **~d at an angle of ...** incliné à un angle de ...

2 *(fig: gen pass)* **to ~ sb to do sth** porter qn à faire qch ◆ **to be ~d to do sth** *(= have a tendency to)* avoir tendance à faire qch ; *(= feel desire to)* être enclin à faire qch ◆ **he's ~d to be lazy** il a tendance à être paresseux ◆ **the drawer is ~d to stick** le tiroir a tendance à se coincer ◆ **I'm ~d to think that ...** j'ai tendance à penser que ... ◆ **I'm ~d to believe you** je suis tenté de te croire ◆ **I'm more ~d to believe her than her sister** j'aurais tendance à la croire elle, plutôt que sa sœur ◆ **he's that way ~d** il est comme ça ◆ **to be criminally ~d** avoir des tendances criminelles ◆ **to be artistically ~d** avoir des dispositions pour l'art ◆ **if you feel (so) ~d** si le cœur vous en dit ◆ **to be well** *or* **favourably ~d towards sb** être bien disposé envers qn

VI 1 *(= slope)* s'incliner ; *(= bend, bow)* s'incliner, se pencher

2 *(= tend towards)* **she ~s to the opinion that ...** elle est plutôt d'avis que ..., elle aurait tendance à croire que ... ◆ **he ~s to laziness** il incline à la paresse, il a tendance à être paresseux ◆ **his politics ~ towards socialism** ses idées politiques tendent vers le socialisme

N /ˈɪnklaɪn/ pente *f*, inclinaison *f* ; *(Rail)* plan *m* incliné ◆ **a steep ~** une pente raide

COMP inclined plane N plan *m* incliné

inclose /ɪnˈkləʊz/ **VT** ⇒ **enclose**

inclosure /ɪnˈkləʊʒəʳ/ **N** ⇒ **enclosure**

include /ɪnˈkluːd/ **VT** inclure, comprendre ◆ **the trip will ~ Brazil, Argentina and Chile** le Brésil, l'Argentine et le Chili seront inclus dans le trajet ◆ **the President will ~ this idea in his plan** le Président inclura cette idée dans son plan ◆ **the hostages ~ three Britons** il y a trois Britanniques parmi les otages ◆ **does that remark ~ me?** est-ce que cette remarque s'adresse aussi à moi ? ◆ **he ~d my mother in the invitation** ma mère était comprise dans son invitation ◆ **the invitation ~s everybody** l'invitation s'adresse à tout le monde ◆ **everyone, children ~d** tout le monde, les enfants y compris ◆ **all of us, myself ~d** nous tous, moi y compris ◆ **the district ~s ...** la région comprend ...

◆ **to be included** *(in price)* être compris *or* inclus ◆ **wine was ~d in the price** le vin était compris *or* inclus dans le prix ◆ **"service included/not included"** "service compris/non compris" ◆ **your name is not ~d on the list** votre nom ne figure pas sur la liste ◆ **they were all ~d in the accusation** ils étaient tous visés par l'accusation ◆ **I had worked hard to be ~d in a project like this** j'avais travaillé dur pour participer à un projet comme celui-ci

▸ **include out** * **VT SEP** ◆ **include me out!** ne comptez pas sur moi !

including /ɪnˈkluːdɪŋ/ **PREP** y compris ◆ **that comes to €40 ~ packing** cela fait 40 € y compris l'emballage ◆ **there were six rooms ~ the kitchen** il y avait six pièces y compris la cuisine ◆ **(not) ~ service charge** service (non) compris ◆ **not ~ tax** taxe non comprise ◆ **up to and ~ chapter five** jusqu'au chapitre cinq inclus ◆ **up to and ~ 4 May** jusqu'au 4 mai inclus ◆ **several projects, ~ ...** plusieurs projets, dont ... *or* parmi lesquels ... ◆ **many conditions, ~ allergies, can be treated with homeopathic remedies** beaucoup de maladies, dont *or* et notamment les allergies, peuvent être traitées par l'homéopathie ◆ **several people, ~ my father, had been invited** plusieurs personnes, dont mon père, avaient été invitées

inclusion /ɪn'kluːʒən/ N inclusion *f*

inclusive /ɪn'kluːsɪv/ ADJ 1 *(= comprehensive) [price, package]* tout compris *inv* ; *[amount, sum]* forfaitaire, global ◆ **~ terms** *(Comm)* (prix *m*) tout compris *m* ◆ **~ of postage and packing** port et emballage compris ◆ **all prices are ~ of VAT** tous les prix incluent la TVA ◆ **cost ~ of travel** prix voyage compris ◆ **the course costs £700, ~ of all food, drink and accommodation** le cours coûte 700 livres, nourriture, boissons et logement compris *or* y compris la nourriture, les boissons et le logement ◆ **the course is fully ~ of all costs** le cours inclut *or* comprend tous les frais ; → **all compounds**
2 *(= included)* ◆ **Tuesday to Saturday ~** de mardi à samedi inclus *or* compris ◆ **rows A to M ~** de la rangée A à M incluse *or* comprise ◆ **from 1 to 6 May ~** du 1er au 6 mai inclus ◆ **up to page five ~** jusqu'à la page cinq incluse *or* comprise
3 *(= undiscriminating)* ◆ **a very ~ agenda** un programme très riche ◆ **the conservatoire is far more ~ than before** le conservatoire accueille une clientèle beaucoup plus diversifiée qu'autrefois ◆ **~ language** *(= non-sexist)* langage *m* non sexiste

inclusively /ɪn'kluːsɪvlɪ/ ADV inclusivement

inclusiveness /ɪn'kluːsɪvnɪs/, **inclusivity** /ˌɪnkluː'sɪvɪtɪ/ N inclusivité *f*

incognito /ˌɪnkɒg'niːtəʊ/ ADV *[travel]* incognito ADJ ◆ **to remain ~** garder l'incognito ◆ **to be an ~ traveller** voyager incognito N incognito *m*

incoherence /ˌɪnkəʊ'hɪərəns/ N incohérence *f*

incoherent /ˌɪnkəʊ'hɪərənt/ ADJ *[person, speech, letter]* incohérent ; *[style]* décousu ◆ **an ~ set of objectives** un ensemble incohérent d'objectifs ◆ **he was ~ with rage** la fureur le rendait incohérent ◆ **~ ramblings** des divagations *fpl*, des propos *mpl* incohérents

incoherently /ˌɪnkəʊ'hɪərəntlɪ/ ADV de façon incohérente

incohesive /ˌɪnkəʊ'hiːsɪv/ ADJ sans cohésion

incombustible /ˌɪnkəm'bʌstəbl/ ADJ incombustible

income /'ɪnkʌm/ N revenu(s) *m(pl)* ◆ **families on low ~s, low-~ families** les familles *fpl* à faible revenu ◆ **an ~ of $30,000 a year** un revenu de 30 000 dollars par an ◆ **most of their ~ comes from ...** l'essentiel de leur revenu provient de ... ◆ **private ~** rente(s) *f(pl)* ; → **price, upper**

COMP **income group** N *(Econ)* tranche *f* de revenus ◆ **the lowest ~ group** les économiquement faibles *mpl* ◆ **the middle ~ group** les revenus *mpl* moyens ◆ **the upper** *or* **highest ~ group** les gros revenus *mpl*, les revenus *mpl* élevés
incomes policy N politique *f* des revenus
Income Support N *(Brit Admin)* ≈ revenu *m* minimum d'insertion, RMI *m*
income tax N *(gen)* impôt *m* sur le revenu ; *[of corporations]* impôt *m* sur les bénéfices
income tax inspector N inspecteur *m* des impôts
income tax return N déclaration *f* de revenus, feuille *f* d'impôts

incomer /'ɪnˌkʌmə^r/ N *(Brit = new arrival) (into town, area)* nouveau venu *m*, nouvelle venue *f*, nouvel(le) arrivant(e) *m(f)* ; *(into country)* immigrant(e) *m(f)*

incoming /'ɪnˌkʌmɪŋ/ ADJ 1 *(Mil) [missile]* en approche ; *(Phys) [light, radiation]* reçu ◆ **they would not let him receive ~ calls** ils ne le laissaient pas recevoir d'appels ◆ **this telephone only takes ~ calls** ce téléphone ne prend que les appels de l'extérieur ◆ **~ mail** le courrier à l'arrivée 2 *(= arriving: Travel) [plane, flight]* à l'arrivée 3 *[tide]* montant ; *[waves]* qui arrive 4 *(= new) [president, government]* nouveau (nouvelle *f*) NPL **incomings** *(Accounting)* rentrées *fpl*, recettes *fpl*

incommensurable /ˌɪnkə'menʃərəbl/ ADJ incommensurable (*with* avec)

incommensurate /ˌɪnkə'menʃərɪt/ ADJ 1 *(= out of proportion)* sans rapport (*to* avec) disproportionné (*to* à) ; *(= inadequate)* insuffisant (*to* pour) 2 ⇒ **incommensurable**

incommode † /ˌɪnkə'məʊd/ VT *(frm)* incommoder, gêner

incommodious /ˌɪnkə'məʊdɪəs/ ADJ *(frm) (= inconvenient)* incommode ; *(= not spacious) [house, room]* où l'on est à l'étroit

incommunicable /ˌɪnkə'mjuːnɪkəbl/ ADJ incommunicable

incommunicado /ˌɪnkəmjʊnɪ'kɑːdəʊ/ ADJ ◆ **to be ~** être injoignable ADV ◆ **to be kept** *or* **held ~** être tenu au secret

incomparable /ɪn'kɒmpərəbl/ ADJ incomparable (*to, with* à) ; *[talent, beauty]* incomparable, sans pareil

incomparably /ɪn'kɒmpərəblɪ/ ADV *[better, superior]* incomparablement ◆ **~ beautiful** d'une beauté incomparable

incompatibility /'ɪnkəmˌpætə'bɪlɪtɪ/ N *(gen, Med, Comput)* incompatibilité *f* ◆ **divorce on the grounds of ~** divorce *m* pour incompatibilité d'humeur

incompatible /ˌɪnkəm'pætəbl/ ADJ *(gen, Med, Comput)* incompatible (*with sb/sth* avec qn/qch) ◆ **we were totally ~** il y avait incompatibilité totale entre nous, nous n'étions pas faits pour nous entendre

incompetence /ɪn'kɒmpɪtəns/, **incompetency** /ɪn'kɒmpɪtənsɪ/ N *(gen, Jur)* incompétence *f*

incompetent /ɪn'kɒmpɪtənt/ ADJ *(gen, Jur)* incompétent ◆ **~ teachers** professeurs *mpl* incompétents ◆ **to be ~ in business** être incompétent *or* inapte en affaires ◆ **to be ~ at driving/drawing** être mauvais conducteur/mauvais en dessin ◆ **the court declared him ~ to manage his financial affairs** le tribunal l'a déclaré inapte à s'occuper de ses propres finances N incompétent(e) *m(f)*, incapable *mf*

incomplete /ˌɪnkəm'pliːt/ ADJ *(= unfinished)* incomplet (-ète *f*), inachevé ; *(= with some parts missing) [collection, series, kit, machine]* incomplet (-ète *f*)

incompletely /ˌɪnkəm'pliːtlɪ/ ADV incomplètement

incompleteness /ˌɪnkəm'pliːtnɪs/ N inachèvement *m*

incomprehensible /ɪnˌkɒmprɪ'hensəbl/ ADJ incompréhensible (*to sb* à qn)

incomprehensibly /ɪnˌkɒmprɪ'hensəblɪ/ ADV *[act, react]* de manière incompréhensible ◆ **~ worded** formulé de façon inintelligible *or* incompréhensible ◆ **~, he refused** inexplicablement, il a refusé

incomprehension /ɪnˌkɒmprɪ'henʃən/ N incompréhension *f*

inconceivable /ˌɪnkən'siːvəbl/ ADJ inconcevable

inconceivably /ˌɪnkən'siːvəblɪ/ ADV ◆ **~ stupid** d'une stupidité inconcevable ◆ **almost ~, she survived the accident** il est incroyable qu'elle ait survécu à l'accident

inconclusive /ˌɪnkən'kluːsɪv/ ADJ *[outcome, results, evidence, debate]* peu concluant, peu probant ; *[war, fighting]* non décisif ; *[election]* sans résultats nets ◆ **the last two elections were ~** les deux dernières élections n'ont pas donné de résultats nets

inconclusively /ˌɪnkən'kluːsɪvlɪ/ ADV *[discuss]* d'une manière peu concluante ◆ **to end ~** ne pas produire de résultats tangibles, ne déboucher sur rien

incongruity /ˌɪnkɒŋ'gruːɪtɪ/ N *[of behaviour, dress, remark]* incongruité *f*, inconvenance *f* ; *[of situation]* absurdité *f* ; *[of age, condition]* disproportion *f*, incompatibilité *f*

incongruous /ɪn'kɒŋgrʊəs/ ADJ *(= out of place) [remark, act, name]* incongru, déplacé ; *(= absurd) [situation]* absurde, grotesque ◆ **he was an ~ figure among the tourists** il ne semblait pas à sa place au milieu des touristes ◆ **it was an ~ setting for a wedding** c'était un cadre qui ne semblait pas convenir à un mariage ◆ **it seemed ~ that they should take such a silly idea so seriously** il semblait absurde qu'ils prennent tellement au sérieux une idée aussi stupide ◆ **~ with** peu approprié à

incongruously /ɪn'kɒŋgrʊəslɪ/ ADV *[say, remark, remind, dress]* de façon incongrue ◆ **he wore old jeans, with ~ smart shoes** il portait un vieux jean avec des chaussures d'une élégance incongrue ◆ **the ~ named Million Dollar Hotel** le Million Dollar Hotel, le mal nommé

inconsequent /ɪn'kɒnsɪkwənt/ ADJ *(frm) [person, remark, behaviour, reasoning]* inconséquent

inconsequential /ɪnˌkɒnsɪ'kwenʃəl/ ADJ 1 ⇒ **inconsequent** 2 *(= unimportant)* sans importance, sans conséquence

inconsequentially /ɪnˌkɒnsɪ'kwenʃəlɪ/ ADV *[talk, remark]* de façon inconséquente

inconsiderable /ˌɪnkən'sɪdərəbl/ ADJ insignifiant ◆ **a not ~ sum of money** une somme d'argent non négligeable

inconsiderate /ˌɪnkən'sɪdərɪt/ ADJ *[person]* qui manque d'égards *or* de considération ; *[action, reply]* inconsidéré, irréfléchi ◆ **to be ~ towards sb** manquer d'égards *or* de considération envers qn ◆ **you were very ~, that was very ~ of you** tu as agi sans aucun égard *or* sans aucune considération ◆ **it would be ~ to wake him up** ce serait manquer d'égards *or* de considération que de le réveiller

inconsistency /ˌɪnkən'sɪstənsɪ/ N *[of person]* inconstance *f* ; *[of facts, accusation, behaviour, reasoning]* incohérence *f* ◆ **the ~ of the two statements** les contradictions entre les deux déclarations ◆ **the ~ of his work** le manque de constance de son travail

inconsistent /ˌɪnkən'sɪstənt/ ADJ 1 *(pej = capricious) [person]* inconstant ; *[behaviour]* incohérent 2 *(= variable) [work, quality]* inégal ◆ **the team's been ~ this season** les résultats de l'équipe ont été inégaux cette saison 3 *(= contradictory) [statements, evidence, accounts]* contradictoire ◆ **it is ~ to do that** c'est incohérent *or* inconséquent de faire cela ◆ **to be ~ with sth** *(= contradict)* ne pas concorder avec qch, contredire qch ; *(= be out of keeping with)* ne pas être conforme à qch, ne pas correspondre à qch

⚠ The French word **inconsistant** means 'flimsy'.

inconsolable /ˌɪnkən'səʊləbl/ ADJ inconsolable

inconsolably /ˌɪnkən'səʊləblɪ/ ADV de façon inconsolable

inconspicuous /ˌɪnkən'spɪkjʊəs/ ADJ *[person, action]* qui passe inaperçu ; *[dress]* discret (-ète *f*) ◆ **he tried to make himself ~** il a essayé de passer inaperçu, il s'est efforcé de ne pas se faire remarquer

inconspicuously /ˌɪnkən'spɪkjʊəslɪ/ ADV *[behave, move, sit, wait]* discrètement ; *[dress]* de façon discrète

inconstancy /ɪnˈkɒnstənsɪ/ **N** *(frm) (= fickleness) [of person]* inconstance *f* ; *(= instability)* instabilité *f*

inconstant /ɪnˈkɒnstənt/ **ADJ** 1 *[person] (in friendship)* changeant, instable ; *(in love)* inconstant, volage 2 *(= variable) [weather]* instable, changeant ; *[quality]* variable

incontestable /ˌɪnkənˈtestəbl/ **ADJ** incontestable, indiscutable

incontinence /ɪnˈkɒntɪnəns/ **N** *(Med, also fig frm)* incontinence *f* **COMP incontinence pad N** couche *f* pour incontinent

incontinent /ɪnˈkɒntɪnənt/ **ADJ** 1 *(Med)* incontinent 2 *(fig frm)* intempérant

incontrovertible /ɪnˌkɒntrəˈvɜːtəbl/ **ADJ** *[proof, evidence]* irréfutable, irrécusable ; *[argument]* irréfutable ; *[fact]* indéniable ◆ **it is ~ that ...** il est indéniable que ...

incontrovertibly /ɪnˌkɒntrəˈvɜːtəblɪ/ **ADV** *[true, right]* indéniablement, irréfutablement ; *[prove, demonstrate]* de façon irréfutable, irréfutablement

inconvenience /ˌɪnkənˈviːnɪəns/ **N** 1 *(= disadvantage)* inconvénient *m*, désagrément *m* ◆ **there are ~s in** *or* **to living in the country** il y a des inconvénients à habiter la campagne, habiter la campagne présente des inconvénients *or* des désagréments ◆ **it's one of the ~s of getting old** c'est l'un des inconvénients quand on vieillit

2 *(NonC)* dérangement *m* ◆ **the ~ of a delayed flight** le dérangement occasionné par le retard d'un vol ◆ **to put sb to great ~** causer beaucoup de dérangement à qn ◆ **I don't want to put you to any ~** je ne veux surtout pas vous déranger ◆ **he went to a great deal of ~ to help me** il s'est donné beaucoup de mal pour m'aider ◆ **the management apologizes for any ~ caused by this work** la direction vous prie de bien vouloir excuser la gêne occasionnée par les travaux

VT *(= presume on, impose on)* déranger ; *(= disturb) [noise, smoke etc]* incommoder ; *(stronger)* gêner

inconvenient /ˌɪnkənˈviːnɪənt/ **ADJ** *[time, moment]* inopportun ; *[visitor]* gênant, importun ; *[fact, information, truth]* gênant ; *[arrangement, location]* peu pratique ; *[house, room]* peu pratique, malcommode ◆ **I'm sorry if I've come at an ~ time** excusez-moi si j'arrive à un moment inopportun *or* au mauvais moment ◆ **I can come back later if it is ~** je peux revenir plus tard si je vous dérange ◆ **it is ~ for us to do that** ce n'est pas pratique pour nous de faire cela, cela ne nous arrange pas de faire ça

inconveniently /ˌɪnkənˈviːnɪəntlɪ/ **ADV** *[happen]* malencontreusement ◆ **an ~ designed room/car** une pièce/voiture conçue de façon peu pratique ◆ **the hotel is ~ situated** la situation de l'hôtel est peu pratique

inconvertibility /ˈɪnkənˌvɜːtɪˈbɪlɪtɪ/ **N** non-convertibilité *f*

inconvertible /ˌɪnkənˈvɜːtəbl/ **ADJ** *(Fin etc)* inconvertible

incorporate[1] /ɪnˈkɔːpəreɪt/ **VT** 1 *(= introduce as part) [+ territory, suggestions, revisions]* incorporer, intégrer ◆ **they ~d him into their group** ils l'ont incorporé *or* intégré dans leur groupe ◆ **her proposals were ~d into the project plan** ses propositions ont été incorporées dans l'ébauche du projet ◆ **they refused to ~ environmental considerations into their policies** ils ont refusé d'intégrer *or* de prendre en compte des considérations écologiques dans leur politique

2 *(= include, contain) [+ articles, essays]* contenir, comprendre ; *[+ ideas, thoughts]* rassembler, réunir ◆ **the new cars will ~ a number of major improvements** les nouvelles voitures seront dotées de plusieurs perfectionnements importants

3 *(Comm, Jur) [+ company]* absorber ◆ **~d company** *(esp US)* société *f* à responsabilité limitée ◆ **Smith Robinson Incorporated** *(in name of firm)* Smith Robinson SA

4 *(= mix, add)* incorporer *(into* à*)* ◆ **to ~ eggs into a sauce** incorporer des œufs à une sauce

VI *(Comm)* fusionner *(with* avec*)*

incorporate[2] /ɪnˈkɔːpərɪt/ **ADJ** *(Philos)* incorporel

incorporation /ɪnˌkɔːpəˈreɪʃən/ **N** *(gen)* incorporation *f (in(to) sth* dans qch*)* ; *(Comm, Jur) [of single company]* incorporation *f* ; *(= take-over)* absorption *f (of, by* de, par*)*

incorporator /ɪnˈkɔːpəˌreɪtə[r]/ **N** *(Jur, Fin)* fondateur *m* (d'une société)

incorporeal /ˌɪnkɔːˈpɔːrɪəl/ **ADJ** *(frm)* incorporel

incorrect /ˌɪnkəˈrekt/ **ADJ** *[information, answer, spelling, assessment, behaviour, posture]* incorrect ; *[assumption, belief]* erroné ; *[diet, dress]* inadapté ; *[breathing]* mauvais ◆ **he is ~ (in his assertion/belief that ...)** il se trompe (en affirmant/croyant que ...) ◆ **it is ~ to say that ...** il est incorrect de dire que ... ; → **politically**

incorrectly /ˌɪnkəˈrektlɪ/ **ADV** *[behave, act]* incorrectement ◆ **he sits ~** il se tient mal, il ne se tient pas correctement ◆ **we assumed ~ that ...** nous avons supposé à tort que ...

incorrigible /ɪnˈkɒrɪdʒəbl/ **ADJ** incorrigible

incorrigibly /ɪnˈkɒrɪdʒəblɪ/ **ADV** incorrigiblement

incorruptible /ˌɪnkəˈrʌptəbl/ **ADJ** incorruptible

increase /ɪnˈkriːs/ **VI** *[price, sales, taxes, crime, sorrow, surprise, rage, pain]* augmenter ; *[amount, numbers]* augmenter, croître ; *[demand, strength, population, supply, speed, possessions, riches]* augmenter, s'accroître ; *[trade]* se développer ; *[darkness]* grandir ; *[noise, effort]* s'intensifier ; *[pride]* grandir ; *[business, firm, institution, town]* s'agrandir, se développer ; *[rain, wind]* devenir plus violent, redoubler ; *[friendship]* se renforcer, se consolider ◆ **industrial output ~d by 2% last year** la production industrielle a augmenté de 2% l'année dernière ◆ **to ~ in volume** augmenter de volume, prendre du volume ◆ **to ~ in weight** prendre du poids, s'alourdir ◆ **to ~ in width** s'élargir ◆ **to ~ in height** *[person]* grandir ; *[tree]* pousser ; *[building]* gagner de la hauteur

VT *[+ numbers, strength, taxes, pain]* augmenter *(by* de*)* ; *[+ price, sales]* augmenter, faire monter *(by* de*)* ; *[+ demand, supply, population, possessions, riches]* augmenter, accroître *(by* de*)* ; *[+ delight, pride, rage, sorrow, surprise]* augmenter, ajouter à ; *[+ trade]* développer ; *[+ noise]* intensifier ; *[+ business]* agrandir, développer ; *[+ friendship]* renforcer, consolider ◆ **how can I ~ my chances of winning?** comment puis-je augmenter mes chances de gagner ? ◆ **a poor diet ~s the risk of cancer** une mauvaise alimentation augmente le risque de cancer ◆ **a greatly ~d risk of (getting) heart disease** un risque considérablement accru de contracter une maladie du cœur ◆ **they've ~d her salary by $2,000 a year** ils l'ont augmentée *or* ils ont augmenté son salaire de 2 000 dollars par an ◆ **they've ~d her salary to $50,000 a year** son salaire a été porté à 50 000 dollars par an ◆ **his hours were ~d to 25 per week** ses heures ont été portées à 25 par semaine ◆ **to ~ speed** accélérer ◆ **he ~d his speed to 90km/h** il a accéléré jusqu'à 90 km/h, il a atteint le 90* ◆ **she ~d her efforts** elle redoubla ses efforts *or* redoubla d'efforts

N /ˈɪnkriːs/ *[of price, sales, numbers, pain, workload]* augmentation *f* ; *[of demand, supply, population, speed]* augmentation *f*, accroissement *m* ; *[of trade]* développement *m* ; *[of noise]* intensification *f* ; *[of business]* agrandissement *m*, développement *m* ; *[of crime]* augmentation *f* ; *[of rain, wind]* redoublement *m* ; *[of friendship]* renforcement *m*, consolidation *f* ; *[of effort]* redoublement *m*, intensification *f* ◆ **our sales figures showed no significant ~** nos chiffres de vente n'ont pas connu d'augmentation notable ◆ **an ~ in public spending** une augmentation des dépenses publiques ◆ **there has been an ~ in police activity** la police a intensifié ses activités ◆ **a pay ~, an ~ in pay** une hausse de salaire, une augmentation (de salaire) ◆ **~ in value** *(Fin)* plus-value *f*

◆ **on the increase** ◆ **violent crime is/racial attacks are on the ~** les crimes violents/les agressions raciales sont en augmentation ◆ **the problem of crime is on the ~** le problème de la criminalité s'accentue ◆ **inflation is on the ~** l'inflation est de plus en plus forte ◆ **asthma is on the ~** les cas d'asthme sont de plus en plus nombreux

increasing /ɪnˈkriːsɪŋ/ **ADJ** *[number, amount]* croissant ◆ **there is ~ concern about the effect of these drugs** on se préoccupe de plus en plus de l'effet de ces drogues ◆ **there is ~ evidence to suggest that ...** nous disposons de plus en plus d'éléments qui tendent à prouver que ... ◆ **there are ~ signs that ...** il semble de plus en plus que ... ◆ **there is ~ pressure on her to resign** elle subit des pressions de plus en plus fortes qui la poussent à démissionner

increasingly /ɪnˈkriːsɪŋlɪ/ **ADV** *(= more and more)* de plus en plus ; *(= more and more often)* de plus en plus souvent ◆ **~ well** de mieux en mieux ◆ **~ unreliable** de moins en moins fiable

incredible /ɪnˈkredəbl/ **ADJ** incroyable ◆ **it is ~ that ...** il est incroyable que ... + *subj* ◆ **~ though it may seem ...** aussi incroyable que cela puisse paraître ...

incredibly /ɪnˈkredəblɪ/ **ADV** 1 *(= unbelievably)* incroyablement ◆ **~, he refused** chose incroyable, il a refusé 2 *(= extremely) [big, small, fast, silly etc]* drôlement* ◆ **it was ~ difficult** c'était drôlement* *or* extrêmement difficile

incredulity /ˌɪnkrɪˈdjuːlɪtɪ/ **N** incrédulité *f*

incredulous /ɪnˈkredjʊləs/ **ADJ** *[person]* incrédule ; *[look]* incrédule, d'incrédulité

incredulously /ɪnˈkredjʊləslɪ/ **ADV** *[say]* d'un ton incrédule ; *[watch]* d'un air incrédule

increment /ˈɪnkrɪmənt/ **N** *(in salary)* échelon *m* ; *(Math)* différentielle *f* ; *(Comput)* incrément *m* ; → **unearned VT** *(gen)* augmenter ; *(Comput)* incrémenter

incremental /ˌɪnkrɪˈmentl/ **ADJ** *[benefits]* supplémentaire ; *[cost]* marginal, différentiel ; *[rise, increase]* progressif ; *(Comput)* incrémentiel

COMP incremental plotter N *(Comput)* traceur *m* incrémentiel

incremental value N *(Comm: on index, scale)* valeur *f* indiciaire *or* de l'augmentation

incriminate /ɪnˈkrɪmɪneɪt/ **VT** incriminer, compromettre ◆ **the drugs had been planted to ~ him** les drogues avaient été placées là dans le but de le compromettre *or* de pouvoir l'incriminer ◆ **he was afraid of incriminating himself** il avait peur de se compromettre

incriminating /ɪnˈkrɪmɪneɪtɪŋ/ **ADJ** compromettant ◆ **~ document** pièce *f* à conviction ◆ **~ evidence** *(Jur)* pièces *fpl* à conviction, preuves *fpl* à charge ; *(fig)* pièces *fpl* à conviction

incrimination /ɪnˌkrɪmɪˈneɪʃən/ **N** incrimination *f*

incriminatory /ɪnˈkrɪmɪnətərɪ/ **ADJ** ⇒ **incriminating**

incrustation /ˌɪnkrʌsˈteɪʃən/ **N** incrustation *f*

incubate /ˈɪnkjʊbeɪt/ **VT** 1 *[+ eggs]* couver, incuber 2 *(= grow) [+ bacteria cultures, disease]* incuber 3 *(fig) [+ plan, scheme]* mûrir **VI** *[eggs, bacteria, virus]* être en incubation ; *(fig)* couver

incubation /ˌɪnkjʊˈbeɪʃən/ N 1 *[of eggs, disease]* incubation *f* 2 *(fig) [of plan, scheme]* gestation *f*
COMP **incubation period** N période *f* d'incubation

incubator /ˈɪnkjʊbeɪtəʳ/ N *(for chicks, eggs, babies)* couveuse *f*, incubateur *m* ; *(for bacteria cultures)* incubateur *m* ◆ **to put a baby in an ~** mettre un nouveau-né en couveuse

incubus /ˈɪŋkjʊbəs/ N (pl **incubuses** *or* **incubi** /ˈɪŋkjʊˌbaɪ/) *(= demon)* incube *m* ; *(fig)* cauchemar *m*

incudes /ɪnˈkjuːdiːz/ NPL of **incus**

inculcate /ˈɪnkʌlkeɪt/ VT inculquer *(sth in sb, sb with sth* qch à qn)

inculcation /ˌɪnkʌlˈkeɪʃən/ N inculcation *f*

incumbency /ɪnˈkʌmbənsɪ/ N *[of president, official]* mandat *m* ; *(Rel)* charge *f* ◆ **during his ~** *(gen)* pendant son mandat ; *(Rel)* pendant la durée de sa charge

incumbent /ɪnˈkʌmbənt/ ADJ 1 *(frm)* ◆ **to be ~ (up)on sb to do sth** incomber *or* appartenir à qn de faire qch 2 *(in office)* en exercice ◆ **the ~ President** *(US Pol)* le président en exercice ; *(before elections)* le président sortant N *(Rel, Admin)* titulaire *m* ◆ **the present ~ of the White House** *(US Pol)* l'occupant actuel de la Maison-Blanche

incunabula /ˌɪnkjʊˈnæbjʊlə/ NPL incunables *mpl*

incunabular /ˌɪnkjʊˈnæbjʊləʳ/ ADJ incunable

incur /ɪnˈkɜːʳ/ VT *[+ anger, blame]* s'attirer, encourir ; *[+ risk]* courir ; *[+ obligation, debts]* contracter ; *[+ loss]* subir ; *[+ expenses, costs]* encourir ◆ **a company ~s huge costs if it decides to modernize** une société encourt des dépenses énormes si elle décide de se moderniser ◆ **this would ~ huge costs to the company** ceci coûterait extrêmement cher à la société ◆ **settle the bill in full each month and you won't ~ interest charges** si vous réglez la facture en entier chaque mois, vous ne serez pas soumis au paiement des intérêts

incurable /ɪnˈkjʊərəbl/ ADJ 1 *(Med)* incurable 2 *(fig)* incurable, incorrigible ◆ **he's an ~ romantic** c'est un romantique incorrigible N incurable *mf*

incurably /ɪnˈkjʊərəblɪ/ ADV *(Med, fig)* incurablement ◆ **the ~ ill** les incurables *mpl*

incurious /ɪnˈkjʊərɪəs/ ADJ sans curiosité *(about* en ce qui concerne) incurieux *(liter) (about* de)

incuriously /ɪnˈkjʊərɪəslɪ/ ADV sans curiosité

incursion /ɪnˈkɜːʃən/ N *(Mil)* incursion *f* ; *(fig)* ingérence *f*

incus /ˈɪŋkəs/ N (pl **incudes**) *(Anat)* enclume *f*

Ind. abbrev of **Indiana**

indebted /ɪnˈdetɪd/ ADJ 1 *(Fin)* endetté ◆ **to be ~ to sb for sth** *(lit, fig)* être redevable à qn de qch ◆ **I was ~ to the tune of £13,000** mes dettes s'élevaient à 13 000 livres ◆ **heavily ~ companies** des sociétés *fpl* fortement endettées ◆ **he was ~ to his brother for a large sum** il était redevable d'une grosse somme à son frère 2 *(= grateful)* ◆ **I am ~ to him for pointing out that ...** je lui suis redevable d'avoir fait remarquer que ... ◆ **I am greatly ~ to him for his generosity** je lui dois beaucoup pour sa générosité

indebtedness /ɪnˈdetɪdnɪs/ N 1 *(Fin, Comm)* dette(s) *f(pl)*, endettement *m* ◆ **the company has reduced its ~ to £15 million** la société a réduit son endettement à 15 millions de livres ◆ **the amount of our ~ to the bank is $15,000** notre dette envers la banque s'élève à 15 000 dollars 2 *(fig)* dette(s) *f(pl)* ◆ **my ~ to my friend** ma dette envers mon ami, ce dont je suis redevable à mon ami ◆ **De Palma's ~ to Hitchcock** ce que De Palma doit à Hitchcock

indecency /ɪnˈdiːsnsɪ/ N *(gen)* indécence *f* ; *(Jur:* also **act of indecency)** attentat *m* à la pudeur
COMP **indecency charge** N accusation *f* d'attentat à la pudeur
indecency law N loi *f* sur l'attentat à la pudeur

indecent /ɪnˈdiːsnt/ ADJ indécent ◆ **~ material** documents *mpl* contraires aux bonnes mœurs
COMP **indecent assault** N attentat *m* à la pudeur *(on sb* contre qn)
indecent behaviour N outrage *m* aux bonnes mœurs
indecent exposure N outrage *m* public à la pudeur

indecently /ɪnˈdiːsntlɪ/ ADV 1 *[behave]* indécemment, de façon indécente ◆ **they got married ~ soon after his first wife's funeral** ils se sont mariés si tôt après les obsèques de sa première femme que c'en était indécent 2 *(Jur) [touch]* de façon indécente ◆ **to ~ assault sb** attenter à la pudeur de qn ◆ **to ~ expose oneself** *or* **one's person** commettre un outrage public à la pudeur

indecipherable /ˌɪndɪˈsaɪfərəbl/ ADJ indéchiffrable

indecision /ˌɪndɪˈsɪʒən/ N indécision *f*, irrésolution *f*

indecisive /ˌɪndɪˈsaɪsɪv/ ADJ 1 *(= uncertain) [person, government, manner]* indécis *(about or over sth* à propos de qch) 2 *(= inconclusive) [discussion, argument, result, vote]* peu concluant, peu probant

indecisively /ˌɪndɪˈsaɪsɪvlɪ/ ADV de façon indécise

indecisiveness /ˌɪndɪˈsaɪsɪvnɪs/ N ⇒ **indecision**

indeclinable /ˌɪndɪˈklaɪnəbl/ ADJ indéclinable

indecorous /ɪnˈdekərəs/ ADJ *(frm)* peu convenable, inconvenant

indecorously /ɪnˈdekərəslɪ/ ADV d'une manière inconvenante *or* peu convenable

indecorum /ˌɪndɪˈkɔːrəm/ N *(frm)* manquement *m* aux usages

indeed /ɪnˈdiːd/ LANGUAGE IN USE 26.3 ADV 1 *(indicating confirmation, agreement)* en effet, effectivement ◆ **he promised to help and ~ he helped us a lot** il a promis de nous aider et effectivement il nous a beaucoup aidés ◆ **I am ~ quite tired** je suis en effet assez fatigué ◆ **did you know him? – I did ~** vous le connaissiez ? – oui, tout à fait ◆ **are you coming? – ~ I am** *or* **yes ~!** vous venez ? – mais certainement *or* (mais) bien sûr !

2 *(introducing further information)* d'ailleurs, en fait ◆ **I don't know what she said, ~ I don't want to know** je ne sais pas ce qu'elle a dit, d'ailleurs *or* en fait je ne veux pas le savoir ◆ **he was happy, ~ delighted, to hear the news** il était content, même ravi d'entendre la nouvelle ◆ **I feel, ~ I know he is right** je sens, en fait je sais qu'il a raison

3 *(as intensifier)* vraiment ◆ **that's praise ~ coming from him** venant de lui, c'est vraiment un compliment ◆ **I am very grateful/pleased ~** je suis vraiment reconnaissant/très content ◆ **thank you very much ~** je vous remercie infiniment ◆ **if ~ he were wrong** s'il est vrai qu'il a tort, si tant est qu'il ait tort

4 *(showing interest, irony, surprise etc)* ◆ **(oh) ~?** vraiment ?, c'est vrai ? ◆ **is it ~!, did you** *(or* **he** *etc)* **~!** vraiment ? ◆ **who is that man? – who is he ~?** qui est cet homme ? – ah, là est la question ! ◆ **what was to be done? – what ~?** que faire ? – on peut effectivement se poser la question ! ◆ **I heard it on the wireless – wireless, ~! they're called radios now** je l'ai entendu à la TSF – TSF, vraiment ! ça s'appelle une radio, maintenant

indefatigable /ˌɪndɪˈfætɪgəbl/ ADJ infatigable, inlassable

indefatigably /ˌɪndɪˈfætɪgəblɪ/ ADV inlassablement

indefensible /ˌɪndɪˈfensəbl/ ADJ indéfendable

indefensibly /ˌɪndɪˈfensəblɪ/ ADV d'une manière inexcusable ◆ **he was ~ rude** il a été d'une grossièreté impardonnable *or* inexcusable

indefinable /ˌɪndɪˈfaɪnəbl/ ADJ indéfinissable, vague

indefinably /ˌɪndɪˈfaɪnəblɪ/ ADV vaguement

indefinite /ɪnˈdefɪnɪt/ ADJ 1 *(= unspecified) [period, postponement, size, number, duration]* indéterminé ; *[strike, curfew, ban]* illimité ◆ **for the ~ future** pour un avenir indéterminé ◆ **to be granted ~ leave (of absence)** obtenir un congé à durée indéterminée ◆ **at some ~ time** à un moment quelconque *or* indéterminé 2 *(= vague) [feelings]* indéfini ; *[word]* imprécis ; *[plans]* imprécis, mal défini
COMP **indefinite article** N *(Gram)* article *m* indéfini
indefinite pronoun N *(Gram)* pronom *m* indéfini

indefinitely /ɪnˈdefɪnɪtlɪ/ ADV *[last, continue, stay, detain]* indéfiniment ; *[adjourn, cancel]* pour une durée indéterminée ◆ **the meeting has been postponed ~** la réunion a été reportée à une date indéterminée

indelible /ɪnˈdeləbl/ ADJ *(lit, fig)* indélébile

indelibly /ɪnˈdeləblɪ/ ADV *(lit, fig)* de façon indélébile

indelicacy /ɪnˈdelɪkəsɪ/ N *(frm)* 1 *(NonC) [of person, behaviour] (= tactlessness)* indélicatesse *f*, manque *m* de délicatesse ; *(= indiscreetness)* manque *m* de discrétion 2 *[of action, remark] (= impropriety)* inconvenance *f* ; *(= coarseness)* grossièreté *f* ; *(= tactlessness)* indiscrétion *f*

indelicate /ɪnˈdelɪkɪt/ ADJ *[person] (= indiscreet)* indélicat, peu délicat ; *(= tactless)* manquant de tact, indiscret (-ète *f*) ; *[act, remark] (= out of place)* indélicat, déplacé ; *(= tactless)* indiscret (-ète *f*), manquant de tact ; *(= coarse)* grossier

indemnification /ɪnˌdemnɪfɪˈkeɪʃən/ N 1 *(NonC)* indemnisation *f (for, against* de) 2 *(= sum paid)* indemnité *f*, dédommagement *m*

indemnify /ɪnˈdemnɪfaɪ/ VT 1 *(= compensate)* indemniser, dédommager *(sb for sth* qn de qch) 2 *(= safeguard)* garantir, assurer *(sb against or for sth* qn contre qch)

indemnity /ɪnˈdemnɪtɪ/ N 1 *(= compensation)* indemnité *f*, dédommagement *m* 2 *(= insurance)* assurance *f*, garantie *f*

indent /ɪnˈdent/ VT 1 *(Typ) [+ word, line]* mettre en alinéa *or* en retrait ; *[+ whole paragraph]* mettre en retrait ; *[+ first line of paragraph]* faire un retrait de première ligne de ◆ **~ed line** ligne *f* en alinéa *or* en retrait ◆ **~ two spaces** renfoncez de deux espaces, mettez en alinéa *or* en retrait de deux espaces 2 *[+ border]* denteler, découper *(en dentelant)* ◆ **~ed edge** bord *m* dentelé ◆ **~ed coastline** littoral *m* découpé VI *(Brit Comm)* ◆ **to ~ on sb for sth** passer une commande de qch à qn, commander qch à qn N /ˈɪndent/ 1 *(Brit Comm)* commande *f* 2 ⇒ **indentation**

indentation /ˌɪndenˈteɪʃən/ N 1 *(Typ)* alinéa *m* 2 *(= act)* découpage *m* ; *(= notched edge)* dentelure *f*, découpure *f* ; *[of coastline]* échancrures *fpl*, indentations *fpl* 3 *(= hollow mark)* empreinte *f* ; *(= footprint)* trace *f* de pas ; *(in metal, car)* bosse *f* ◆ **the ~ of tyres on the soft ground** l'empreinte des pneus sur le sol mou

indenture /ɪnˈdentʃəʳ/ N *(Jur)* contrat *m* synallagmatique ; *[of apprentice]* contrat *m* d'apprentissage VT *(Jur)* lier par contrat (synallagmatique) ; *[+ apprentice]* mettre en apprentissage *(to* chez)

independence /ˌɪndɪˈpendəns/ **N** 1 *(gen)* indépendance *f* *(from* par rapport à) ◆ **to show ~** faire preuve d'indépendance, manifester son indépendance 2 *(Pol)* ◆ **the country's first elections since ~** les premières élections du pays depuis l'indépendance ◆ **the country got its ~ in 1970** le pays est devenu indépendant *or* a obtenu son indépendance en 1970 ◆ **Rhodesia gained ~ from Britain in 1978** la Rhodésie s'est affranchie de la tutelle britannique en 1978 **COMP** **Independence Day** **N** *(US)* fête *f* *or* anniversaire *m* de l'Indépendance américaine *(le 4 juillet)*

independent /ˌɪndɪˈpendənt/ **ADJ** 1 *(gen) [person, attitude, artist]* indépendant ; *[radio]* libre ◆ **she was fiercely ~** elle était farouchement indépendante ◆ **he is an ~ thinker** c'est un penseur original ◆ **an Independent member** *(Pol)* un député non inscrit *or* non affilié ◆ **~ means** rentes *fpl*, revenus *mpl* indépendants ◆ **he has ~ means** il a une fortune personnelle 2 *[country, nation]* indépendant *(of* de), autonome ◆ **to become ~** devenir indépendant *or* autonome, s'affranchir 3 *(= unrelated) [proof, research]* indépendant ; *[reports]* émanant de sources indépendantes ◆ **to ask for an ~ opinion** demander un avis indépendant ◆ **there has been no ~ confirmation of this report** aucune source indépendante n'a confirmé cette information 4 *(Gram)* indépendant

N *(Pol)* ◆ **Independent** non-inscrit(e) *m(f)*, non-affilié(e) *m(f)*

COMP **independent school** **N** *(Brit)* établissement *m* d'enseignement privé
independent suspension **N** *[of vehicle]* suspension *f* indépendante
Independent Television Commission **N** *(Brit)* ≃ Conseil *m* supérieur de l'audiovisuel

independently /ˌɪndɪˈpendəntlɪ/ **ADV** *[act, live, think]* de façon indépendante, de façon autonome ; *[research, negotiate, investigate]* séparément ◆ **~ of sb/sth** indépendamment de qn/qch ◆ **to be ~ wealthy** avoir une fortune personnelle ◆ **the two scientists had discovered the virus quite ~** les deux savants avaient découvert le virus chacun de leur côté ◆ **quite ~, he had offered to help** il avait proposé son aide sans même qu'on le lui demande, il avait spontanément proposé son aide

indescribable /ˌɪndɪsˈkraɪbəbl/ **ADJ** indescriptible

indescribably /ˌɪndɪsˈkraɪbəblɪ/ **ADV** ◆ **~ filthy** d'une saleté indescriptible ◆ **it was ~ awful** c'était affreux au-delà de toute expression ◆ **~ beautiful** d'une beauté indescriptible

indestructibility /ˌɪndɪstrʌktəˈbɪlɪtɪ/ **N** indestructibilité *f*

indestructible /ˌɪndɪsˈtrʌktəbl/ **ADJ** indestructible

indeterminable /ˌɪndɪˈtɜːmɪnəbl/ **ADJ** indéterminable

indeterminacy /ˌɪndɪˈtɜːmɪnəsɪ/ **N** indétermination *f*

indeterminate /ˌɪndɪˈtɜːmɪnɪt/ **ADJ** *[age, sex, number, period]* indéterminé ; *[meaning, shape]* imprécis, vague ; *[colour]* imprécis, indéterminé ; *(Math)* indéterminé **COMP** **indeterminate sentence** **N** *(US Jur)* peine *f* de prison de durée indéterminée

indeterminately /ˌɪndɪˈtɜːmɪnɪtlɪ/ **ADV** de façon indéterminée, vaguement

index /ˈɪndeks/ **N** 1 (pl **indexes**) *(= list) (in book, map etc)* index *m*, table *f* alphabétique ; *(on cards, in files: in library etc)* catalogue *m* *or* répertoire *m* (alphabétique) ◆ **to put a book on the Index** *(Rel)* mettre un livre à l'Index
2 (pl **indexes**) *(= pointer) [of instrument]* aiguille *f*, index *m*
3 (pl **indices**) *(= number expressing ratio)* indice *m* ◆ **cost-of-living ~** indice *m* du coût de la vie ◆ **~ of growth/of industrial activity** indice *m* de croissance/de l'activité industrielle ◆ **~ of refraction** *(Opt)* indice *m* de réfraction
4 (also **share index**) indice *m* boursier
5 (pl **indices**) *(fig)* signe *m* (révélateur), indication *f* ◆ **it is an ~ of how much poorer people were then** c'est un signe révélateur de la plus grande pauvreté qui régnait à l'époque ◆ **weeds are an ~ to the character of the soil** les mauvaises herbes sont un indicateur de la nature du sol
6 (pl **indexes**) ◆ **~ (finger)** index *m*
7 (pl **indexes**) *(Typ)* index *m*
8 (pl **indices**) *(Math)* exposant *m*

VT 1 *(= put an index in) [+ book]* ajouter un index *or* une table alphabétique à ◆ **the book is badly ~ed** l'index *or* la table alphabétique du livre est mal fait(e)
2 *(= put into an index) [+ word]* faire figurer dans l'index *or* la table alphabétique ; *(on cards, in files etc) [+ information]* répertorier *or* cataloguer (alphabétiquement) ; *[+ books, diskettes, articles]* classer *(under* sous, à) ◆ **it is ~ed under "Europe"** c'est classé *or* indexé sous "Europe"
3 *[+ wages, prices]* indexer

COMP **index card** **N** fiche *f*
index figure **N** *(Stat)* indice *m*
index finger **N** index *m*
index-linked **ADJ** *(Brit)* indexé
index number **N** ⇒ **index figure**
index-tied **ADJ** ⇒ **index-linked**
index-tracking fund, index-tracker (fund) **N** fonds *m* indiciel

indexation /ˌɪndekˈseɪʃən/ **N** indexation *f*

India /ˈɪndɪə/ **N** Inde *f* ; *(Hist)* les Indes *fpl* **COMP** **India ink** **N** encre *f* de Chine
India paper **N** papier *m* bible
India rubber **N** *(NonC)* *(= substance)* caoutchouc *m* ; *(= eraser)* gomme *f*

Indiaman /ˈɪndɪəmən/ **N** (pl **-men**) *(Naut Hist)* *navire faisant le voyage des Indes*

Indian /ˈɪndɪən/ **ADJ** 1 *(in India)* indien, de l'Inde ; *[ambassador, embassy]* de l'Inde ; *(Hist)* des Indes
2 (also **American Indian**) indien, des Indiens (d'Amérique)

N 1 *(in India)* Indien(ne) *m(f)*
2 (also **American Indian**) Indien(ne) *m(f)* (d'Amérique)
3 *(= language)* amérindien *m*

COMP **Indian clubs** **NPL** massues *fpl (de gymnastique)*
Indian corn **N** maïs *m*
Indian elephant **N** éléphant *m* d'Asie
Indian Empire **N** Empire *m* des Indes
Indian file **N** ◆ **in ~ file** en file indienne
Indian giver * **N** *(US pej)* personne *f* qui reprend ses cadeaux
Indian ink **N** encre *f* de Chine
Indian Mutiny **N** *(Hist)* révolte *f* des Cipayes
Indian National Congress **N** Congrès *m* national indien
Indian Ocean **N** océan *m* Indien
Indian rope trick **N** *tour d'illusionniste consistant à grimper à une corde que l'on a dressée en jouant d'un instrument de musique*
Indian sign † **N** *(US)* sort *m* ◆ **to put an ~ sign on sb** jeter un sort à qn
Indian summer **N** *(= warm weather)* été *m* indien *or* de la Saint-Martin ; *(esp Brit: fig = success late in life)* réussite *f* tardive, succès *m* tardif
Indian tea **N** thé *m* indien *or* de l'Inde
Indian tonic (water) **N** Schweppes ® *m*
Indian wrestling **N** *(US Sport)* bras *m* de fer ; see also **rope**

Indiana /ˌɪndɪˈænə/ **N** Indiana *m* ◆ **in ~** dans l'Indiana

indicate /ˈɪndɪkeɪt/ **VT** 1 *(= point to)* indiquer, montrer ◆ **he ~d a chair and asked me to sit down** il a indiqué *or* montré une chaise et m'a invité à m'asseoir
2 *(= be a sign of)* indiquer ◆ **a change in colour ~s the presence of acid** un changement de couleur indique la présence d'acide ◆ **opinion polls ~ (that) they are losing popularity** les sondages indiquent que leur cote de popularité est en baisse
3 *(= make known) [+ intentions, opinion]* faire connaître, faire part de ; *[+ feelings]* laisser voir, manifester ◆ **he ~d that I was to leave** il m'a fait comprendre que je devais partir ◆ **he ~d that he might resign** il a laissé entendre qu'il pourrait démissionner
4 *(= call for)* indiquer ◆ **the use of penicillin is clearly ~d** le recours à la pénicilline est nettement indiqué ◆ **a new approach to the wages problem is ~d** il convient d'aborder le problème des salaires sous un nouvel angle

VI *(esp Brit: while driving)* mettre son clignotant ◆ **he was indicating (left)** il avait mis son clignotant (à gauche)

indication /ˌɪndɪˈkeɪʃən/ **N** signe *m*, indication *f* ◆ **it was an ~ of his guilt** c'était un signe *or* une indication de sa culpabilité ◆ **we had no ~ that it was going to take place** rien ne laissait prévoir *or* présager que cela allait arriver ◆ **there is every ~ that she's right** tout porte à croire *or* laisse à penser qu'elle a raison ◆ **there are few ~s that they are ready to come to an agreement** rien ne laisse présager qu'ils approchent d'un accord ◆ **all the ~s lead one to believe that …** tout porte à croire que …, il y a toute raison de croire que … ◆ **it is some ~ of how popular she is** cela montre à quel point elle est populaire ◆ **if this result is any ~, he …** à en juger par ce résultat, il … ◆ **to give sb an ~ of one's feelings/intentions** manifester ses sentiments/faire part de ses intentions à qn ◆ **he gave us some ~ of what he meant** il nous a donné une idée de ce qu'il voulait dire ◆ **he gave no ~ that he was ready to compromise** il n'a aucunement laissé entendre qu'il était prêt à transiger

indicative /ɪnˈdɪkətɪv/ **ADJ** 1 ◆ **to be ~ of sth** être révélateur de qch ◆ **to be ~ of the fact that …** montrer que … 2 *(Gram)* indicatif **N** *(Gram:* also **indicative mood***)* (mode *m*) indicatif *m* ◆ **in the ~** à l'indicatif

indicator /ˈɪndɪkeɪtəʳ/ **N** *(= device)* indicateur *m* ; *(= needle on scale etc)* aiguille *f*, index *m* ; *(= indication)* indicateur *m* ; *(Brit:* also **indicator light***)* *(flashing)* clignotant *m* ; *(projecting)* flèche *f* ; *(Ling)* indicateur *m* ◆ **higher output is an ~ that the economy is recovering** *or* **of economic recovery** une augmentation de la production est un indicateur de reprise économique ◆ **economic ~s** indicateurs *mpl* économiques ◆ **altitude/pressure ~** indicateur *m* d'altitude/de pression

indices /ˈɪndɪsiːz/ **NPL** of **index**

indict /ɪnˈdaɪt/ **VT** 1 *(esp US Jur)* mettre en examen ◆ **to ~ sb for sth** *or* **on a charge of sth** inculper qn de qch, mettre qn en examen pour qch 2 *(fig)* accuser, porter une accusation contre

indictable /ɪnˈdaɪtəbl/ **ADJ** *(Jur) [person, action]* attaquable en justice, passible de poursuites ◆ **an ~ offence** un délit grave, une infraction majeure

indictment /ɪnˈdaɪtmənt/ **N** 1 *(Jur)* *(= bill)* acte *m* d'accusation *(for* de) ; *(= process)* mise *f* en examen *(for* pour) ; *(US)* accusation *f (par le jury d'accusation)* ; → GRAND JURY ◆ **bill of ~** *(Brit Hist)* résumé *m* d'instruction *(présenté au jury d'accusation)* ◆ **to bring an ~ against sb (for sth)** inculper qn (de qch) 2 *(fig)* ◆ **such poverty is an ~ of the political system** une telle pauvreté est une véritable mise en cause du système politique ◆ **his speech constituted a damning ~ of government policy** son discours a été un réquisitoire accablant contre la politique du gouvernement ◆ **it is a sad ~ of our times that many old people are afraid to go out alone** c'est un triste signe des temps que beaucoup de personnes âgées n'osent plus sortir seules

indie * /ˈɪndɪ/ N *(Mus)* musique *f or* rock *m* indé

Indies /ˈɪndɪz/ NPL Indes *fpl* ; → **east, west**

indifference /ɪnˈdɪfrəns/ N [1] *(= lack of interest, of feeling)* indifférence *f* *(to* à ; *towards* envers) manque *m* d'intérêt *(to, towards* pour, à l'égard de) ◆ **he greeted the suggestion with ~** il a accueilli la suggestion avec indifférence *or* sans manifester d'intérêt ◆ **it is a matter of supreme ~ to me** cela m'est parfaitement indifférent *or* égal [2] *(= poor quality)* médiocrité *f*

indifferent /ɪnˈdɪfrənt/ ADJ [1] *(= lacking feeling, interest)* indifférent *(to* à) ◆ **the government's ~ attitude to the massacres** l'indifférence manifestée par le gouvernement vis-à-vis des massacres [2] *(pej = mediocre) [talent, performance, player]* médiocre, quelconque ◆ **good, bad or ~** bon, mauvais ou quelconque [3] *(† = impartial)* impartial, neutre

indifferently /ɪnˈdɪfrəntlɪ/ ADV [1] *(= uninterestedly) [say, shrug, look at]* avec indifférence [2] *(pej = badly) [perform, write]* médiocrement [3] *(† = impartially)* ◆ **she went ~ to one shop or the other** elle allait indifféremment dans une boutique ou dans l'autre

indigence /ˈɪndɪdʒəns/ N indigence *f*

indigenous /ɪnˈdɪdʒɪnəs/ ADJ *[people, species, plant, culture, language]* indigène ; *[population]* indigène, autochtone ◆ **the elephant is ~ to India** l'éléphant est un animal indigène en Inde

indigent /ˈɪndɪdʒənt/ ADJ *(frm)* indigent, nécessiteux

indigestible /ˌɪndɪˈdʒestəbl/ ADJ [1] *[food, fibre]* inassimilable (par l'organisme) [2] *(fig) [book, information]* indigeste

indigestion /ˌɪndɪˈdʒestʃən/ N *(NonC: Med)* indigestion *f* ◆ **to have an attack of ~** avoir une indigestion ◆ **he gets a lot of ~** il fait souvent des indigestions

indignant /ɪnˈdɪɡnənt/ ADJ indigné *(at or about sth* de qch ; *with sb* contre qn) ◆ **they were ~ that they were not consulted/that he had not consulted them** ils étaient indignés de ne pas avoir été consultés/qu'il ne les eût pas consultés ◆ **to become** *or* **get ~** s'indigner ◆ **to make sb ~** indigner qn

indignantly /ɪnˈdɪɡnəntlɪ/ ADV avec indignation ; *[say]* d'un air *or* d'un ton indigné

indignation /ˌɪndɪɡˈneɪʃən/ N indignation *f* *(at* devant ; *with* contre) ◆ **she was filled with ~ at their working conditions** leurs conditions de travail la remplissaient d'indignation

indignity /ɪnˈdɪɡnɪtɪ/ N [1] *(= act)* outrage *m*, indignité *f* ◆ **it was the final ~** c'était le comble de l'outrage ◆ **he suffered the ~ of having to ...** il subit l'outrage d'avoir à ... [2] *(NonC)* indignité *f*

indigo /ˈɪndɪɡəʊ/ N (pl **indigos** *or* **indigoes**) indigo *m* ADJ (also **indigo blue**) (bleu) indigo *inv*

indirect /ˌɪndɪˈrekt/ ADJ indirect

COMP **indirect demand** N *(Comm)* demande *f* indirecte

indirect discourse N *(US)* ⇒ **indirect speech**

indirect discrimination N discrimination *f* indirecte

indirect lighting N éclairage *m* indirect

indirect object N *(Gram)* complément *m* d'objet indirect

indirect question N *(gen, Gram)* question *f* indirecte

indirect speech N *(Gram)* discours *m* indirect

indirect tax N impôt *m* indirect

indirect taxation N contributions *fpl* indirectes, impôts *mpl* indirects

indirectly /ˌɪndɪˈrektlɪ/ ADV indirectement

indirectness /ˌɪndɪˈrektnɪs/ N caractère *m* indirect

indiscernible /ˌɪndɪˈsɜːnəbl/ ADJ indiscernable

indiscipline /ɪnˈdɪsɪplɪn/ N indiscipline *f*

indiscreet /ˌɪndɪsˈkriːt/ ADJ *(= tactless)* indiscret (-ète *f*) ; *(= rash)* imprudent *(about sth* à propos de qch)

indiscreetly /ˌɪndɪsˈkriːtlɪ/ ADV *(= tactlessly)* indiscrètement ; *(= rashly)* imprudemment, avec imprudence

indiscretion /ˌɪndɪsˈkreʃən/ N [1] *(NonC) (= tactlessness)* manque *m* de discrétion, indiscrétion *f* ; *(= rashness)* imprudence *f* ; *(= carelessness)* indiscrétion *f* [2] *(= tactless remark, action)* indiscrétion *f* ◆ **an act of ~** une indiscrétion ◆ **a youthful ~** une bêtise *or* une erreur de jeunesse

indiscriminate /ˌɪndɪsˈkrɪmɪnɪt/ ADJ *[killing, violence]* systématique ; *[punishment]* distribué à tort et à travers ◆ **~ use of pesticides** emploi *m* inconsidéré de pesticides ◆ **to be ~ in one's attacks** lancer ses attaques au hasard ◆ **to be ~ in one's viewing habits** ne pas être sélectif dans ses choix de programmes de télévision

indiscriminately /ˌɪndɪsˈkrɪmɪnɪtlɪ/ ADV *[use]* sans discernement ; *[kill, punish]* sans distinction ; *[fire]* au hasard ; *[read, watch TV]* de façon non sélective ◆ **this disease strikes ~** cette maladie frappe tout le monde sans distinction

indispensable /ˌɪndɪsˈpensəbl/ ADJ indispensable *(to* à) ◆ **nobody's ~!** personne n'est indispensable ! ◆ **you're not ~!** on peut se passer de toi !, tu n'es pas indispensable !

indisposed /ˌɪndɪsˈpəʊzd/ ADJ [1] *(= unwell)* indisposé, souffrant [2] *(= disinclined)* peu disposé, peu enclin *(to do sth* à faire qch)

indisposition /ˌɪndɪspəˈzɪʃən/ N [1] *(= illness)* indisposition *f*, malaise *m* [2] *(= disinclination)* manque *m* d'inclination *(to do sth* à faire qch)

indisputable /ˌɪndɪsˈpjuːtəbl/ ADJ incontestable, indiscutable

indisputably /ˌɪndɪsˈpjuːtəblɪ/ LANGUAGE IN USE 26.3 ADV incontestablement, indiscutablement

indissoluble /ˌɪndɪˈsɒljʊbl/ ADJ [1] *[friendship]* indissoluble [2] *(Chem)* insoluble

indissolubly /ˌɪndɪˈsɒljʊblɪ/ ADV *(gen, Jur)* indissolublement

indistinct /ˌɪndɪsˈtɪŋkt/ ADJ *[voice, sound, words, figure, shape]* indistinct ; *[memory]* vague, flou ; *[photograph]* flou

indistinctly /ˌɪndɪsˈtɪŋktlɪ/ ADV *[see, hear, speak]* indistinctement ; *[remember]* vaguement

indistinguishable /ˌɪndɪsˈtɪŋɡwɪʃəbl/ ADJ [1] indifférenciable *(from* de) [2] *(= very slight) [noise, difference, change]* imperceptible, indiscernable

indistinguishably /ˌɪndɪsˈtɪŋɡwɪʃəblɪ/ ADV au point de ne pouvoir être différencié

indium /ˈɪndɪəm/ N indium *m*

individual /ˌɪndɪˈvɪdjʊəl/ ADJ [1] *(= separate) [opinion, attention, portion]* individuel ◆ **served in ~ dishes** servi dans des plats individuels ◆ **Japan has changed ~ aspects of its nuclear policy** le Japon a modifié certains aspects de sa politique nucléaire ◆ **the rights of ~ countries to impose their own laws** le droit de chaque pays à imposer ses propres lois ◆ **divide the salmon among six ~ plates** répartissez le saumon sur six assiettes individuelles

[2] *(= distinctive, characteristic)* personnel, particulier ◆ **he has an ~ style** il a un style personnel *or* bien à lui ◆ **the language she uses is highly ~** elle utilise un langage très personnel *or* particulier

[3] *(Sport)* ◆ **~ pursuit** poursuite *f* individuelle ◆ **~ sports** sports *mpl* individuels

N individu *m* ◆ **each ~ is entitled to ...** tout individu *or* toute personne *or* chacun a droit à ... ◆ **two or more unrelated ~s living together** deux ou plusieurs personnes qui vivent ensemble ◆ **donations from wealthy ~s** des dons de riches particuliers ◆ **enterprising ~s who ...** des audacieux qui ... ◆ **at what age does a child become aware it is an ~?** à quel âge l'enfant se rend-il compte de son individualité ?

individualism /ˌɪndɪˈvɪdjʊəlɪzəm/ N individualisme *m*

individualist /ˌɪndɪˈvɪdjʊəlɪst/ N individualiste *mf*

individualistic /ˌɪndɪˌvɪdjʊəˈlɪstɪk/ ADJ individualiste

individuality /ˌɪndɪˌvɪdjʊˈælɪtɪ/ N individualité *f*

individualize /ˌɪndɪˈvɪdjʊəlaɪz/ VT individualiser, personnaliser ◆ **~d instruction** *(US Scol)* enseignement *m* individualisé

individually /ˌɪndɪˈvɪdjʊəlɪ/ ADV [1] *(= separately) [wrapped, numbered]* individuellement, séparément ◆ **~ responsible for sth** individuellement *or* personnellement responsable de qch ◆ **he spoke to them ~** il leur a parlé à chacun individuellement *or* personnellement ◆ **they're all right ~** pris séparément ils sont très bien [2] *(= uniquely) [decorated]* de façon individualisée *or* personnalisée ◆ **~ designed flats** appartements *mpl* individualisés *or* personnalisés

indivisibility /ˌɪndɪˌvɪzəˈbɪlɪtɪ/ N indivisibilité *f*

indivisible /ˌɪndɪˈvɪzəbl/ ADJ indivisible ; *(Math, Philos)* insécable

indivisibly /ˌɪndɪˈvɪzəblɪ/ ADV indivisiblement, indissolublement

Indo- /ˈɪndəʊ/ PREF indo- ; → **Indo-China**

Indo-China /ˈɪndəʊˈtʃaɪnə/ N Indochine *f*

Indo-Chinese /ˈɪndəʊtʃaɪˈniːz/ ADJ indochinois N Indochinois(e) *m(f)*

indoctrinate /ɪnˈdɒktrɪneɪt/ VT endoctriner ◆ **they've all been ~d** ils sont tous endoctrinés ◆ **to ~ sb with ideas** inculquer des idées à qn ◆ **to ~ sb to do sth** conditionner qn à faire qch ◆ **we have all been strongly ~d to value material things** nous avons tous été fortement conditionnés à valoriser les choses matérielles, on nous a fortement inculqué à tous le sens des choses matérielles ◆ **to ~ sb with political ideas/with hatred of the enemy** inculquer des doctrines politiques/la haine de l'ennemi à qn

indoctrination /ɪnˌdɒktrɪˈneɪʃən/ N endoctrinement *m*

Indo-European /ˈɪndəʊˌjʊərəˈpiːən/ ADJ indo-européen N *(= language)* indo-européen *m*

indolence /ˈɪndələns/ N indolence *f*

indolent /ˈɪndələnt/ ADJ indolent

indolently /ˈɪndələntlɪ/ ADV indolemment

indomitable /ɪnˈdɒmɪtəbl/ ADJ indomptable ◆ **her ~ spirit** sa ténacité à toute épreuve

indomitably /ɪnˈdɒmɪtəblɪ/ ADV *[struggle, continue]* sans jamais se laisser abattre

Indonesia /ˌɪndəʊˈniːzɪə/ N Indonésie *f*

Indonesian /ˌɪndəʊˈniːzɪən/ ADJ indonésien N [1] Indonésien(ne) *m(f)* [2] *(= language)* indonésien *m*

indoor /ˈɪndɔːʳ/ ADJ *[activity, plant, shoes]* d'intérieur ; *[market, swimming pool, tennis court, cycle track]* couvert ; *[sports, athletics, championship]* en salle ; *[job] (in office)* dans un bureau ; *(at home)* à la maison ; *(Cine, Theat) [scene]* d'intérieur ◆ **~ aerial** *(TV)* antenne *f* intérieure ◆ **~ games**

(squash etc) sports *mpl* pratiqués en salle ; *(table games)* jeux *mpl* de société ◆ ~ **photography** photographie *f* d'intérieur

indoors /ɪnˈdɔːz/ ADV *[stay]* *(in building)* à l'intérieur ; *(at home)* chez soi ; *[go, keep, spend time]* à l'intérieur ◆ **to go** ~ rentrer ◆ **to take sb** ~ faire entrer qn ◆ **I can't stay** ~ **forever** je ne peux pas rester enfermé tout le temps ◆ **bring plants** ~ **in October** en octobre, rentrer les plantes

indorse /ɪnˈdɔːs/ VT ⇒ **endorse**

indrawn /ˈɪndrɔːn/ ADJ *(lit)* ◆ **a long** ~ **breath** une longue inspiration ◆ **he received the news with** ~ **breath** *(fig)* l'annonce de la nouvelle lui a coupé le souffle ◆ **the crowd gave a gasp of** ~ **breath** la foule a retenu son souffle

indubitable /ɪnˈdjuːbɪtəbl/ ADJ indubitable

indubitably /ɪnˈdjuːbɪtəblɪ/ ADV indubitablement

induce /ɪnˈdjuːs/ VT ① *(= persuade)* persuader *(sb to do sth* qn de faire qch) inciter *(sb to do sth* qn à faire qch) ◆ **nothing would ever** ~ **me to go back there** rien ne pourrait me décider à retourner là-bas ② *(= bring about)* *[+ reaction]* produire, provoquer ; *[+ sleep, illness, hypnosis]* provoquer ◆ **to** ~ **labour** *(Med)* déclencher l'accouchement *(artificiellement)* ◆ ~**d labour** accouchement *m* déclenché ◆ **she was** ~**d** son accouchement a été déclenché ③ *(Philos = infer)* induire, conclure ④ *(Elec)* produire par induction

-induced /ɪnˈdjuːst/ ADJ *(in compounds)* causé *or* provoqué par ◆ **drug-induced** *[sleep, fit]* causé *or* provoqué par les médicaments *(or* par la drogue *etc)* ◆ **self-induced** intentionnel, volontaire ; *[hypnosis]* autosuggéré

inducement /ɪnˈdjuːsmənt/ N ① *(= reward)* récompense *f* ; *(euph)* *(= bribe)* pot-de-vin *m* *(pej)* ◆ **and as an added** ~ **we are offering ...** et comme avantage supplémentaire nous offrons ... ◆ **he received £100 as an** ~ il a reçu 100 livres à titre de gratification, il a reçu un pot-de-vin *(pej)* de 100 livres ◆ **financial/cash** ~**s** avantages *mpl* financiers/en espèces ② *(NonC = reason for doing sth)* motivation *f* *(to do sth, for doing sth* pour faire qch) encouragement *m* *(to do sth, for doing sth* à faire qch)

induct /ɪnˈdʌkt/ VT *[+ president]* établir dans ses fonctions, installer ; *[+ clergyman]* instituer, installer ; *[+ student]* accueillir *(au début de leur première année d'études)* ; *(US Mil)* incorporer ◆ **to** ~ **sb into the mysteries of ...** initier qn aux mystères de ...

induction /ɪnˈdʌkʃən/ N ① *(NonC)* *(Elec, Philos)* induction *f* ; *[of sleep, hypnosis etc]* provocation *f* ; *(Med)* *[of labour]* déclenchement *m* (provoqué) ② *[of clergyman, president]* installation *f* ; *[of new staff members]* insertion *f*, intégration *f* ; *(US Mil)* incorporation *f*

COMP **induction coil** N *(Elec)* bobine *f* d'induction

induction course, induction training N *(Ind)* stage *m* préparatoire (d'intégration), stage *m* d'accueil et d'orientation

induction year N *(Scol)* *[of teacher]* ≈ année *f* de stage

inductive /ɪnˈdʌktɪv/ ADJ ① *(Logic, Math)* *[reasoning, logic, process]* inductif ② *(Elec)* *[load]* inductif ; *[current]* inducteur (-trice *f*)

indulge /ɪnˈdʌldʒ/ VT ① *(= spoil)* *[+ person]* gâter ; *(= give way to, gratify)* *[+ person, desires, wishes, laziness]* céder à ◆ **he** ~**s her every whim** il lui passe tous ses caprices, il cède à tous ses caprices ◆ **on Saturdays he** ~**s his passion for football** le samedi il s'adonne à sa passion pour le football ◆ ~ **yourself with a glass of chilled white wine** faites-vous plaisir avec un verre de vin blanc bien frais ◆ **go on,** ~ **yourself!** allez, laissez-vous tenter !

② *(Comm = extend time for payment)* *[+ person, firm]* accorder des délais de paiement à

VI ◆ **to** ~ **in sth** se permettre qch ◆ **she** ~**d in a little harmless flirtation** elle s'est permis un petit flirt inoffensif ◆ **we can't afford to** ~ **in cheap speculation** nous ne pouvons pas nous complaire dans des suppositions gratuites ◆ **we don't** ~ **in such underhand tactics** nous ne nous abaissons pas à pratiquer ces tactiques sournoises

indulgence /ɪnˈdʌldʒəns/ N ① *(NonC = tolerance)* indulgence *f*, complaisance *f* ② *(= luxury)* luxe *m* ; *(= treat, food)* gâterie *f* ◆ **he allowed himself the** ~ **of a day off work** il s'est offert le luxe de prendre un jour de congé ◆ **smoking was his one** ~ la cigarette était son seul petit plaisir *or* son seul péché mignon ③ *(Rel)* indulgence *f*

indulgent /ɪnˈdʌldʒənt/ ADJ *(= not severe)* indulgent *(to* envers, pour) ; *(= permissive)* indulgent *(to* envers, pour) complaisant *(to* à l'égard de, pour)

indulgently /ɪnˈdʌldʒəntlɪ/ ADV avec indulgence

Indus /ˈɪndəs/ N Indus *m*

industrial /ɪnˈdʌstrɪəl/ ADJ *[application, experience, psychology, research, training]* industriel ; *[expansion]* industriel, de l'industrie ; *[worker]* de l'industrie ; *[accident, injury, medicine]* du travail ; *[fabric, equipment]* pour l'industrie, industriel

COMP **industrial action** N *(Brit)* action *f* revendicative ; *(= strike)* (mouvement *m* de) grève *f* ◆ **to take** ~ **action** lancer une action revendicative ; *(= go on strike)* se mettre en grève

industrial arts NPL *(US)* enseignement *m* technique

industrial correspondent N *(Brit Press, Rad, TV)* correspondant *m* industriel

industrial design N design *m* (industriel), esthétique *f* industrielle

industrial designer N concepteur-dessinateur *m* industriel, designer *m*

industrial diamond N diamant *m* naturel *or* industriel

industrial disease N maladie *f* professionnelle

industrial dispute N *(Brit)* conflit *m* social

industrial engineering N génie *m* industriel

industrial espionage N espionnage *m* industriel

industrial estate N *(Brit)* zone *f* industrielle

industrial hygiene N hygiène *f* du travail

industrial injury benefit N indemnité *f* d'accident du travail

industrial insurance N assurance *f* contre les accidents du travail, assurance *f* des salariés de l'industrie

industrial park N zone *f* industrielle

industrial psychologist N psychologue *mf* d'entreprise

industrial rehabilitation N réadaptation *f* fonctionnelle

industrial relations NPL relations *fpl* patronat-syndicats ; *(= field of study)* relations *fpl* sociales

Industrial Revolution N *(Hist)* révolution *f* industrielle

industrial school N *(US)* école *f* technique

industrial-strength ADJ ① *(lit)* à usage industriel ② *(* fig = strong)* *[elastic]* bien costaud ; *[face cream]* énergique ◆ **~-strength red wine** du gros rouge costaud *or* qui tache

industrial tribunal N ≈ conseil *m* de prud'hommes

industrial unrest N troubles *mpl* sociaux, agitation *f* ouvrière

industrial vehicle N véhicule *m* industriel

industrial waste N *(Brit)* déchets *mpl* industriels

industrial wastes NPL *(US)* ⇒ **industrial waste**

industrialism /ɪnˈdʌstrɪəlɪzəm/ N industrialisme *m*

industrialist /ɪnˈdʌstrɪəlɪst/ N industriel *m*

industrialization /ɪnˌdʌstrɪəlaɪˈzeɪʃən/ N industrialisation *f*

industrialize /ɪnˈdʌstrɪəlaɪz/ VT industrialiser

industrious /ɪnˈdʌstrɪəs/ ADJ assidu

industriously /ɪnˈdʌstrɪəslɪ/ ADV assidûment, avec assiduité

industriousness /ɪnˈdʌstrɪəsnɪs/ N ⇒ **industry noun 2**

industry /ˈɪndəstrɪ/ N ① industrie *f* ◆ **basic** *or* **heavy** ~ industrie *f* lourde ◆ **the hotel** ~ l'hôtellerie *f*, l'industrie *f* hôtelière ◆ **the tourist** ~ le tourisme, l'industrie *f* touristique ◆ **psychoanalysis has become a real** ~ *(fig)* la psychanalyse est devenue une véritable industrie ; → **coal, textile, trade** ② *(NonC = industriousness)* assiduité *f*, application *f* ◆ **with great** ~ avec beaucoup d'assiduité

COMP **industry standard** N norme *f* industrielle

industry-standard ADJ aux normes industrielles

inebriate /ɪˈniːbrɪɪt/ N *(frm)* alcoolique *mf* ADJ *(frm)* en état d'ébriété VT /ɪˈniːbrɪeɪt/ *(lit, fig)* enivrer, griser

inebriated /ɪˈniːbrɪˌeɪtɪd/ ADJ *(= drunk)* *(lit)* ivre ; *(fig)* enivré, grisé *(by* de)

inebriation /ɪˌniːbrɪˈeɪʃən/, **inebriety** /ˌɪniːˈbraɪətɪ/ N état *m* d'ébriété

inedible /ɪnˈedɪbl/ ADJ *(= not meant to be eaten)* non comestible ; *(= not fit to be eaten)* immangeable

ineducable /ɪnˈedjʊkəbl/ ADJ inéducable

ineffable /ɪnˈefəbl/ ADJ *(liter)* indicible *(liter)*, ineffable

ineffably /ɪnˈefəblɪ/ ADV *(liter)* ineffablement *(liter)*

ineffaceable /ˌɪnɪˈfeɪsəbl/ ADJ ineffaçable, indélébile

ineffective /ˌɪnɪˈfektɪv/ ADJ inefficace *(against sth* contre qch ; *in doing sth* pour faire qch)

ineffectively /ˌɪnɪˈfektɪvlɪ/ ADV *[use]* inefficacement ; *[try]* vainement, en vain

ineffectiveness /ˌɪnɪˈfektɪvnɪs/ N inefficacité *f*

ineffectual /ˌɪnɪˈfektjʊəl/ ADJ ⇒ **ineffective**

ineffectually /ˌɪnɪˈfektjʊəlɪ/ ADV inefficacement

inefficacious /ˌɪnefɪˈkeɪʃəs/ ADJ inefficace

inefficacy /ɪnˈefɪkəsɪ/ N inefficacité *f*

inefficiency /ˌɪnɪˈfɪʃənsɪ/ N *[of action, machine, measures]* inefficacité *f*, insuffisance *f* ; *[of person]* incompétence *f*, manque *m* d'efficacité

inefficient /ˌɪnɪˈfɪʃənt/ ADJ *[person, measures, drug]* inefficace ; *[machine, factory]* peu performant

inefficiently /ˌɪnɪˈfɪʃəntlɪ/ ADV inefficacement ◆ **work done** ~ travail exécuté de façon inefficace

inelastic /ˌɪnɪˈlæstɪk/ ADJ ① *[material]* non élastique ② *(fig)* *[system, regulations]* rigide ; *(Econ)* *[demand, supply]* non élastique ③ *(Phys)* inélastique

inelegant /ɪnˈelɪgənt/ ADJ inélégant, peu élégant

inelegantly /ɪnˈelɪgəntlɪ/ ADV inélégamment

ineligibility /ɪnˌelɪdʒəˈbɪlɪtɪ/ N *(gen)* inéligibilité *f* ; *(Fin)* irrecevabilité *f*

ineligible /ɪnˈelɪdʒəbl/ ADJ *[candidate]* inéligible ◆ **he's** ~ **for social security benefits** il n'a pas droit aux prestations de la Sécurité sociale ◆ **he's** ~ **to vote** il n'a pas le droit de vote ◆ ~ **for military service** inapte au service militaire

ineluctable /ˌɪnɪˈlʌktəbl/ ADJ *(frm)* inéluctable, inévitable

inept /ɪ'nept/ ADJ *(= incompetent)* incompétent ; *(= inappropriate) [remark]* déplacé ◆ **the team's ~ performance** la médiocre performance de l'équipe

ineptitude /ɪ'neptɪtjuːd/ N *(= incompetence)* incompétence *f* ; *(= inappropriateness) [of remark]* caractère *m* déplacé

ineptly /ɪ'neptlɪ/ ADV de façon inepte

ineptness /ɪ'neptnɪs/ N ⇒ **ineptitude**

inequality /ˌɪnɪ'kwɒlɪtɪ/ N inégalité *f*

inequitable /ɪn'ekwɪtəbl/ ADJ inéquitable, injuste

inequity /ɪn'ekwɪtɪ/ N injustice *f*, iniquité *f*

ineradicable /ˌɪnɪ'rædɪkəbl/ ADJ indéracinable, tenace

inert /ɪ'nɜːt/ ADJ *(gen, also Chem, Phys)* inerte ; *(= dull)* morne COMP **inert gas** N gaz *m* inerte

inertia /ɪ'nɜːʃə/ N [1] *[of person]* inertie *f*, apathie *f* [2] *(Chem, Phys)* inertie *f*
COMP **inertia-reel seat belts** NPL ceintures *fpl* (de sécurité) à enrouleurs
inertia selling N *(Brit)* vente *f* forcée par correspondance

inescapable /ˌɪnɪs'keɪpəbl/ ADJ inéluctable, inévitable

inessential /ˌɪnɪ'senʃəl/ ADJ superflu, nonessentiel

inestimable /ɪn'estɪməbl/ ADJ *[gift, friendship]* inestimable, inappréciable ; *[fortune, work]* incalculable

inevitability /ɪnˌevɪtə'bɪlɪtɪ/ N caractère *m* inévitable

inevitable /ɪn'evɪtəbl/ ADJ *[result]* inévitable, inéluctable ; *[day, event]* fatal ◆ **it seems that civil war has become ~** il semble que la guerre civile soit devenue inévitable *or* inéluctable ◆ **it's ~ that new recruits will make errors at first** les nouvelles recrues feront inévitablement *or* fatalement des erreurs au début ◆ **I'm afraid it's ~** j'ai bien peur que ce soit inévitable *or* inéluctable ◆ **the tourist had the ~ camera** le touriste avait l'inévitable *or* l'incontournable appareil-photo N ◆ **the ~** l'inévitable *m*

inevitably /ɪn'evɪtəblɪ/ ADV inévitablement

inexact /ˌɪnɪg'zækt/ ADJ inexact

inexactitude /ˌɪnɪg'zæktɪtjuːd/ N inexactitude *f*

inexactly /ˌɪnɪg'zæktlɪ/ ADV inexactement

inexcusable /ˌɪnɪks'kjuːzəbl/ ADJ inexcusable, impardonnable ◆ **it is ~ that ...** il est inexcusable que ... + *subj* ◆ **it would be ~ to make such a mistake** il serait inexcusable de faire une telle erreur ◆ **that was ~ of you** c'était inexcusable *or* impardonnable de votre part

inexcusably /ˌɪnɪks'kjuːzəblɪ/ ADV *[say, overlook, neglect]* de façon inexcusable *or* impardonnable ◆ **~ lazy/careless** d'une paresse/d'une négligence inexcusable

inexhaustible /ˌɪnɪg'zɔːstəbl/ ADJ inépuisable

inexorable /ɪn'eksərəbl/ ADJ inexorable

inexorably /ɪn'eksərəblɪ/ ADV inexorablement

inexpedient /ˌɪnɪks'piːdɪənt/ ADJ *[action, decision, policy]* inopportun, malavisé

inexpensive /ˌɪnɪks'pensɪv/ ADJ bon marché *inv*, pas cher

inexpensively /ˌɪnɪks'pensɪvlɪ/ ADV *[buy]* à bon marché, à bon compte ; *[live]* à peu de frais

inexperience /ˌɪnɪks'pɪərɪəns/ N inexpérience *f*, manque *m* d'expérience

inexperienced /ˌɪnɪks'pɪərɪənst/ ADJ *[driver, pilot, teacher, doctor]* inexpérimenté ◆ **I am very ~ in matters of this kind** j'ai très peu d'expérience dans ce genre de choses ◆ **doctors are ~ in dealing with this disease** les médecins ont peu d'expérience dans le traitement de cette maladie ◆ **he's too ~ to be president** il manque trop d'expérience pour être président ◆ **to be sexually ~** manquer d'expérience sexuelle

inexpert /ɪn'ekspɜːt/ ADJ inexpert, maladroit (in en)

inexpertly /ɪn'ekspɜːtlɪ/ ADV maladroitement

inexplicable /ˌɪnɪks'plɪkəbl/ ADJ inexplicable

inexplicably /ˌɪnɪks'plɪkəblɪ/ ADV inexplicablement

inexpressible /ˌɪnɪks'presəbl/ ADJ inexprimable

inexpressive /ˌɪnɪks'presɪv/ ADJ inexpressif

inextinguishable /ˌɪnɪks'tɪŋgwɪʃəbl/ ADJ *[fire]* impossible à éteindre *or* à maîtriser ; *[passion, enthusiasm]* indéfectible ; *[thirst, laughter]* inextinguible

in extremis /ɪnɪk'striːmɪs/ ADV *(frm)* in extremis

inextricable /ˌɪnɪks'trɪkəbl/ ADJ inextricable

inextricably /ˌɪnɪks'trɪkəblɪ/ ADV inextricablement

infallibility /ɪnˌfælə'bɪlɪtɪ/ N *(also Rel)* infaillibilité *f*

infallible /ɪn'fæləbl/ ADJ infaillible

infallibly /ɪn'fæləblɪ/ ADV [1] *(= without error) [pronounce, correct]* infailliblement [2] *(= always)* infailliblement, immanquablement

infamous /'ɪnfəməs/ ADJ *[person, place]* tristement célèbre *(for sth* pour qch) ; *[incident]* notoire ; *[case, trial, conduct]* infâme ◆ **his ~ temper** son mauvais caractère notoire

infamy /'ɪnfəmɪ/ N infamie *f*

infancy /'ɪnfənsɪ/ N [1] *(lit)* petite enfance *f*, bas âge *m* ; *(Jur)* minorité *f* ◆ **early ~** toute petite enfance *f* ◆ **child still in ~** enfant *mf* encore en bas âge ◆ **a quarter of these children die in ~** un quart de ces enfants meurent en bas âge [2] *(fig)* enfance *f*, débuts *mpl* ◆ **when radio was still in its ~** quand la radio en était encore à ses débuts *or* à ses premiers balbutiements

infant /'ɪnfənt/ N *(= newborn)* nouveau-né *m* ; *(= baby)* bébé *m*, nourrisson *m* ; *(= young child)* petit(e) enfant *m(f)*, enfant *mf* en bas âge ; *(Jur)* mineur(e) *m(f)* ; *(Brit Scol)* enfant *mf*, petit(e) *m(f) (de quatre à sept ans)*
COMP *[disease]* infantile ; *(fig) [industry, movement, organization]* naissant **infant class** N *(Brit)* ≃ cours *m* préparatoire ◆ **the ~ classes** les classes *fpl* enfantines, les petites classes *fpl*
infant education N enseignement *m* des petits *(entre quatre et sept ans)*
infant mortality N mortalité *f* infantile
infant school N *(Brit)* ≃ cours *m* préparatoire et première année de cours élémentaire *(entre quatre et sept ans)*
infant welfare clinic N centre *m* médicosocial pédiatrique

infanta /ɪn'fæntə/ N infante *f*

infante /ɪn'fæntɪ/ N infant *m*

infanticide /ɪn'fæntɪsaɪd/ N *(= crime)* infanticide *m* ; *(frm) (= killer)* infanticide *mf*

infantile /'ɪnfəntaɪl/ ADJ infantile COMP **infantile paralysis** † N *(= polio)* paralysie *f* infantile †

infantilism /ɪn'fæntɪlɪzəm/ N *(Psych)* infantilisme *m*

infantilize /ɪn'fæntɪlaɪz/ VT infantiliser

infantry /'ɪnfəntrɪ/ N *(NonC: Mil)* infanterie *f NonC*, fantassins *mpl*

infantryman /'ɪnfəntrɪmən/ N fantassin *m* ; → **light²**

infarct /'ɪnfɑːkt/ N *(Med)* infarctus *m*

infarction /ɪn'fɑːkʃən/ N *(Med)* [1] *(= dead tissue)* ⇒ **infarct** [2] *(= forming of dead tissue)* infarcissement *m*

infatuate /ɪn'fætjʊeɪt/ VT *(gen pass)* tourner la tête à ◆ **to be ~d with** *[+ person]* être fou d'amour pour ; *[+ idea]* avoir la tête pleine de, être engoué de ◆ **to become ~d with** *[+ person]* s'enticher de ; *[+ idea]* s'engouer pour ◆ **as soon as he met her he was ~d** il s'est entiché d'elle dès leur première rencontre

infatuation /ɪnˌfætjʊ'eɪʃən/ N *(with person)* amour *m* obsessionnel ; *(with idea, activity)* engouement *m (with sth* pour qch)

infect /ɪn'fekt/ VT [1] *(lit) [+ person, wound]* infecter ; *[+ air, well, blood]* contaminer ◆ **his wound became ~ed** sa blessure s'infecta ◆ **a virus spread by ~ed blood** un virus qui se transmet par du sang contaminé ◆ **to ~ sb with a disease** transmettre *or* communiquer une maladie à qn ◆ **to be ~ed with malaria/hepatitis** être atteint du paludisme/de l'hépatite ◆ **~ed with HIV** séropositif [2] *(fig)* **for a moment I was ~ed by her fear** pendant un moment elle m'a communiqué sa peur ◆ **you can't help being ~ed with his passion for the music** sa passion pour la musique est véritablement contagieuse

infection /ɪn'fekʃən/ N [1] *(lit) [of person, wound]* infection *f* ; *[of air, well, blood]* contamination *f* ◆ **there's some ~ in the wound** la blessure est légèrement infectée ◆ **she has a slight ~** elle a une légère infection ◆ **a throat ~** une angine ◆ **an ear ~** une otite [2] *(fig)* contagion *f*

infectious /ɪn'fekʃəs/ ADJ [1] *(Med) [disease] (= transmissible)* contagieux ; *(= caused by germs)* infectieux [2] *(fig) [person, laugh, enthusiasm, rhythm]* contagieux COMP **infectious hepatitis** N hépatite *f* infectieuse

infectiousness /ɪn'fekʃəsnɪs/ N [1] *(Med)* nature *f* infectieuse [2] *(fig)* contagion *f*

infective /ɪn'fektɪv/ ADJ *[disease] (= transmissible)* contagieux ; *(= caused by germs)* infectieux ; *[agent]* infectieux

infectivity /ˌɪnfek'tɪvɪtɪ/ N infectiosité *f*

infelicitous /ˌɪnfɪ'lɪsɪtəs/ ADJ *(frm)* malheureux, fâcheux

infelicity /ˌɪnfɪ'lɪsɪtɪ/ N *(frm)* [1] *(NonC = misfortune)* malheur *m* [2] *(= tactless act, remark)* maladresse *f*

infer /ɪn'fɜːʳ/ VT [1] *(= conclude)* déduire, conclure *(that* que) ◆ **can we ~ from this that you disagree?** pouvons-nous en déduire *or* en conclure que vous n'êtes pas d'accord ? [2] *(* = imply)* laisser entendre, insinuer ◆ **what are you ~ring?** qu'est-ce que vous insinuez ?

inference /'ɪnfərəns/ N [1] *(= conclusion)* déduction *f*, conclusion *f* ◆ **by ~** par déduction ◆ **the ~ is that he is unwilling to help us** on doit en conclure qu'il n'est pas disposé à nous aider ◆ **to draw an ~ from sth** tirer une conclusion de qch [2] *(* = implication)* insinuation *f*

inferential /ˌɪnfə'renʃəl/ ADJ *[method]* déductif ; *[proof]* obtenu par déduction

inferentially /ˌɪnfə'renʃəlɪ/ ADV par déduction

inferior /ɪn'fɪərɪəʳ/ LANGUAGE IN USE 26.3 ADJ [1] *[person, status, quality]* inférieur (-eure *f*) *(to sb* à qn ; *in sth* en qch) ; *[product]* de qualité inférieure ; *[service, work]* de second ordre ◆ **he makes me feel ~** il me donne un sentiment d'infériorité [2] *(Jur) [court]* ≃ de première instance [3] *(Bot)* infère [4] *(Typ)* **~ letter** indice *m* N *(in quality, social standing)* inférieur *m*, -eure *f* ; *(in authority, rank: also Mil)* subalterne *mf*, subordonné(e) *m(f)*

inferiority /ɪnˌfɪərɪ'ɒrɪtɪ/ N infériorité *f (to* par rapport à) COMP **inferiority complex** N complexe *m* d'infériorité

infernal /ɪn'fɜːnl/ ADJ [1] *(* = terrible) [noise]* infernal ; *[heat, weather]* abominable ; *[car, computer]* satané ◆ **it's an ~ nuisance** c'est vraiment empoisonnant [2] *(Myth, Rel, liter) [regions]* infernal ; *[flames]* de l'enfer

infernally* /ɪnˈfɜːnəlɪ/ ADV *[difficult]* abominablement, épouvantablement ◆ **it is ~ hot** il fait une chaleur infernale *or* abominable

inferno /ɪnˈfɜːnəʊ/ N 1 ◆ **an ~, a blazing ~** un brasier 2 *(liter = hell)* enfer *m*

infertile /ɪnˈfɜːtaɪl/ ADJ *[person, animal, land, soil]* stérile

infertility /ˌɪnfɜːˈtɪlɪtɪ/ N *[of person, animal, land, soil]* stérilité *f*
COMP **infertility clinic** N *service de consultation pour problèmes de stérilité*
infertility treatment N *(Med)* traitement *m* de la stérilité

infest /ɪnˈfest/ VT 1 *(lit) [pest, vermin]* infester ◆ **~ed with** infesté de 2 *(fig) [drugs, bandits]* envahir

infestation /ˌɪnfesˈteɪʃən/ N infestation *f*

infidel /ˈɪnfɪdəl/ N *(liter) (Hist, Rel)* infidèle † *mf* ; *(Rel)* incroyant(e) *m(f)* ADJ infidèle †, incroyant

infidelity /ˌɪnfɪˈdelɪtɪ/ N infidélité *f* ◆ **divorce on the grounds of ~** *(Jur)* divorce *m* pour cause d'adultère

infighting /ˈɪnˌfaɪtɪŋ/ N 1 *(within group)* conflits *mpl or* querelles *fpl* internes, luttes *fpl* intestines *(within* au sein de) 2 *(Mil) (hand-to-hand)* corps à corps *m* ; *(close-range)* combat *m* rapproché ; *(Boxing)* corps à corps *m*

infill /ˈɪnfɪl/ N *(Constr, Geol)* remplissage *m*

infiltrate /ˈɪnfɪlˌtreɪt/ VI *[troops, person, light, liquid, ideas]* s'infiltrer *(into* dans) VT *[+ liquid]* infiltrer *(into* dans ; *through* à travers) ; *(Pol) [+ group, organization]* infiltrer, noyauter ; *(Mil) [troops] [+ territory, city, enemy lines]* s'infiltrer dans ◆ **to ~ troops into a territory, to ~ a territory with troops** envoyer des troupes s'infiltrer dans un territoire

infiltration /ˌɪnfɪlˈtreɪʃən/ N *(Pol, Mil, Med)* infiltration *f (into sth* dans qch)

infiltrator /ˈɪnfɪlˌtreɪtəʳ/ N *(inside organization, country)* agent *m* infiltré ◆ **Western ~s** agents *mpl* de l'Occident

infinite /ˈɪnfɪnɪt/ ADJ *(gen) [number, patience, care]* infini, illimité ; *[possibilities]* illimité ; *(Math, Philos, Rel)* infini ◆ **the choice is ~** le choix est illimité ◆ **an ~ variety of landscapes** une variété infinie de paysages ◆ **God in his ~ mercy** Dieu dans son infinie miséricorde ◆ **it gave her ~ pleasure** cela lui a fait infiniment plaisir ◆ **the organizers, in their ~ wisdom, planned the two events for the same day** *(iro)* les organisateurs, dans leur infinie sagesse, ont programmé les deux manifestations le même jour ◆ **he seemed to have an ~ capacity for cruelty** *(iro)* sa cruauté semblait illimitée N infini *m*

infinitely /ˈɪnfɪnɪtlɪ/ ADV infiniment

infiniteness /ˈɪnfɪnɪtnɪs/ N ⇒ **infinity 3**

infinitesimal /ˌɪnfɪnɪˈtesɪməl/ ADJ *(gen) [amount, majority etc]* infinitésimal, infime ; *(Math)* infinitésimal

infinitesimally /ˌɪnfɪnɪˈtesɪmlɪ/ ADV infiniment

infinitive /ɪnˈfɪnɪtɪv/ *(Gram)* N infinitif *m* ◆ **in the ~** à l'infinitif ADJ infinitif

infinitude /ɪnˈfɪnɪtjuːd/ N ◆ **an ~ of** une infinité de

infinity /ɪnˈfɪnɪtɪ/ N 1 *(= that which is infinite)* infinité *f*, infini *m* ◆ **in time and space or in ~** dans le temps et dans l'espace ou dans l'infinité *or* l'infini 2 *(= infinite quantity, number etc)* infinité *f* ◆ **an ~ of reasons/details/possibilities** une infinité de raisons/détails/possibilités 3 *(= infiniteness)* infinitude *f* ◆ **the ~ of God** l'infinitude *f* de Dieu 4 *(Math)* infini *m* ◆ **to ~** à l'infini

infirm /ɪnˈfɜːm/ ADJ 1 *(= sick)* infirme 2 *(liter)* ◆ **~ of purpose** irrésolu, indécis NPL **the infirm** les infirmes *mpl* ◆ **the old and the ~** les personnes *fpl* âgées et les infirmes *mpl*

infirmary /ɪnˈfɜːmərɪ/ N *(= hospital)* hôpital *m* ; *(in school etc)* infirmerie *f*

infirmity /ɪnˈfɜːmɪtɪ/ N infirmité *f* ◆ **her grandmother's increasing ~** l'infirmité croissante de sa grand-mère ◆ **she bears these infirmities with fortitude** elle supporte ces infirmités avec courage

infix /ɪnˈfɪks/ VT *[+ habit, idea]* inculquer *(in* à) implanter *(in* dans) ; *(Ling)* insérer *(in* dans) N /ˈɪnˌfɪks/ *(Ling)* infixe *m*

inflame /ɪnˈfleɪm/ VT 1 *(fig) [+ courage]* enflammer ; *[+ anger, desire, hatred, discord]* attiser 2 *(Med)* enflammer 3 *(= set alight)* enflammer, mettre le feu à

inflammable /ɪnˈflæməbl/ ADJ 1 *[liquid, substance]* inflammable 2 *(fig) [situation]* explosif

inflammation /ˌɪnfləˈmeɪʃən/ N *(Med, fig)* inflammation *f*

inflammatory /ɪnˈflæmətərɪ/ ADJ 1 *[speech, remark, language]* incendiaire 2 *(Med)* inflammatoire

inflatable /ɪnˈfleɪtɪbl/ ADJ *[dinghy, mattress]* pneumatique, gonflable ; *[toy, rubber ring]* gonflable N *(gen)* objet *m (or* jouet *m etc)* gonflable ; *(= dinghy)* canot *m* pneumatique

inflate /ɪnˈfleɪt/ VT 1 *(lit) [+ tyre, balloon]* gonfler *(with* de) ; *(Med) [+ lung]* dilater 2 *(fig) [+ prices]* gonfler, faire monter ; *[+ bill, account]* gonfler, charger VI *[tyre, balloon, air bag]* se gonfler

inflated /ɪnˈfleɪtɪd/ ADJ 1 *(lit) [tyre, balloon]* gonflé ; *[lung]* dilaté 2 *(fig) [price, cost, salary, insurance claim]* excessif ◆ **~ with pride** bouffi d'orgueil ◆ **he has an ~ ego** il a une très haute opinion de lui-même ◆ **he has an ~ sense of his own importance** il se fait une idée exagérée de sa propre importance

inflation /ɪnˈfleɪʃən/ N 1 *(Econ)* inflation *f* ; *[of prices]* hausse *f* 2 *[of tyre etc]* gonflement *m*
COMP **inflation-proof** ADJ protégé contre l'inflation
inflation rate N taux *m* d'inflation

inflationary /ɪnˈfleɪʃnərɪ/ ADJ inflationniste

inflationist /ɪnˈfleɪʃənɪst/ N partisan(e) *m(f)* d'une politique inflationniste

inflect /ɪnˈflekt/ VT 1 *(Ling) [+ word]* mettre une désinence à ; *(= conjugate)* conjuguer ; *(= decline)* décliner ◆ **~ed form** forme *f* fléchie ◆ **~ed vowel** voyelle *f* infléchie 2 *(= modulate) [+ voice]* moduler ; *(Mus) [+ note]* altérer 3 *(Geom, Opt = bend)* infléchir, dévier VI *(Ling)* ◆ **a verb which ~s** un verbe flexionnel *or* qui prend des désinences ◆ **does this noun ~ in the plural?** ce nom prend-il la marque du pluriel ? ◆ **an ~ing language** une langue désinentielle *or* flexionnelle

inflection /ɪnˈflekʃən/ N 1 *(= modulation) [of voice, tone]* inflexion *f* ; *[of note]* altération *f* 2 *(NonC: Ling) [of word]* flexion *f* ◆ **the ~ of nouns/verbs** la flexion nominale/verbale ◆ **vowel ~** inflexion *f* vocalique 3 *(Ling = affix)* désinence *f* 4 *(= curving) [of body]* inflexion *f*, inclination *f* ; *(Geom, Opt)* inflexion *f*, déviation *f*

inflectional /ɪnˈflekʃənəl/ ADJ *(Ling)* flexionnel ◆ **an ~ ending** une désinence

inflexibility /ɪnˌfleksɪˈbɪlɪtɪ/ N 1 *(lit)* rigidité *f* 2 *(fig)* inflexibilité *f*, rigidité *f*

inflexible /ɪnˈfleksəbl/ ADJ 1 *(lit) [person]* inflexible ; *[object]* rigide 2 *(fig) [system, policy]* rigide ; *[person, rule, position]* inflexible ; *[attitude]* rigide, inflexible

inflexion /ɪnˈflekʃən/ N ⇒ **inflection**

inflict /ɪnˈflɪkt/ VT *[+ punishment, torture, fine, defeat]* infliger *(on* à) ; *[+ pain, suffering]* faire subir, infliger *(on* à) ◆ **to ~ damage** causer des dégâts ◆ **to ~ a wound on sb** infliger une blessure à qn ◆ **the enemy ~ed heavy casualties on us** l'ennemi nous a infligé de lourdes pertes ◆ **to ~ one's company/one's beliefs on sb** imposer sa compagnie/ses croyances à qn

infliction /ɪnˈflɪkʃən/ N 1 *(NonC)* ◆ **another operation would mean further ~ of pain on him** une autre opération reviendrait à lui infliger de nouvelles douleurs 2 *(= misfortune)* affliction *f*

in-flight /ˈɪnˌflaɪt/ ADJ *[refuelling]* en vol ; *[film, entertainment]* proposé pendant le vol ◆ **~ meal** repas *m* servi pendant le vol ◆ **~ magazine** magazine *m* de voyage *(destiné aux passagers aériens)*

inflow /ˈɪnfləʊ/ N 1 *[of water]* afflux *m*, arrivée *f* 2 ⇒ **influx 1** 3 *[of capital]* entrée *f* COMP **inflow pipe** N tuyau *m* d'arrivée ◆ **water-~ pipe** arrivée *f or* adduction *f* d'eau

influence /ˈɪnflʊəns/ N *(gen)* influence *f (on* sur) ◆ **her book had *or* was a great ~ on him** son livre a eu une grande influence sur lui *or* l'a beaucoup influencé ◆ **he has got ~** il a de l'influence ◆ **I've got a lot of ~ with her** j'ai beaucoup d'influence *or* d'ascendant sur elle ◆ **to use one's ~ with sb to get sth** user de son influence auprès de qn pour obtenir qch ◆ **she used her ~ to persuade them to accept the deal** elle a usé de son influence pour les persuader d'accepter le marché ◆ **to exert ~ over sb** exercer une influence sur qn ◆ **he denies having exerted any political ~ over them** il a nié avoir exercé la moindre influence politique sur eux ◆ **I shall bring all my ~ *or* every ~ to bear on him** j'essaierai d'user de toute mon influence pour le persuader ◆ **a man of ~** un homme influent ◆ **she is a good ~ in the school/on the pupils** elle a *or* exerce une bonne influence dans l'établissement/sur les élèves ◆ **she is a disruptive ~** c'est un élément perturbateur

◆ **under + influence** ◆ **under his ~** sous son influence ◆ **under the ~ of his advisers, he ...** influencé par ses conseillers, il ... ◆ **under the ~ of drink/drugs** sous l'effet *or* l'empire de la boisson/des drogues ◆ **convicted of driving under the ~ of drink** *(Jur)* condamné pour conduite en état d'ébriété *or* d'ivresse ◆ **he was a bit under the ~*** il était pompette*

VT *[+ attitude, behaviour, decision, person]* influencer ◆ **don't be ~d by him** ne vous laissez pas influencer par lui ◆ **a friend who ~d me deeply** un ami qui m'a beaucoup influencé *or* marqué ◆ **my dad ~d me to do electronics** mon père m'a encouragé *or* poussé à faire des études d'électronique ◆ **he's easily ~d** il est très influençable, il se laisse facilement influencer ◆ **her music is strongly ~d by jazz** sa musique est fortement influencée par le jazz ◆ **the artist has been ~d by Leonardo da Vinci** cet artiste a été influencé par Léonard de Vinci ◆ **your diet may ~ your risk of getting cancer** votre alimentation peut influer sur les risques que vous avez de développer un cancer
COMP **influence peddling** N trafic *m* d'influence

influential /ˌɪnflʊˈenʃəl/ ADJ influent ◆ **to be ~** avoir de l'influence ◆ **she has ~ friends** elle a des amis influents *or* haut placés

influenza /ˌɪnflʊˈenzə/ N *(NonC)* grippe *f* ◆ **he's got ~** il a la grippe

influx /ˈɪnflʌks/ N 1 *[of people]* afflux *m*, flot *m* ; *[of new ideas, attitudes]* flot *m*, flux *m* ◆ **a great ~ of people into the neighbourhood** un gros afflux d'arrivants dans le voisinage ◆ **the ~ of tourists/foreign workers** l'afflux *or* le flot de touristes/de travailleurs étrangers 2 ⇒ **inflow noun 1** 3 *(= meeting place of rivers)* confluent *m*

info * /ˈɪnfəʊ/ N (NonC) (abbrev of **information**) (gen) renseignements mpl ; (= tips) tuyaux* mpl (about sur)

infobahn /ˈɪnfəʊbɑːn/ N autoroute f de l'information

infomercial /ˈɪnfəʊmɜːʃəl/ N (US) (for product) publireportage m ; (Pol) émission où un candidat présente son programme électoral

inform /ɪnˈfɔːm/ LANGUAGE IN USE 24.5
VT 1 (gen) informer (of de) ; (= warn) avertir (of de) ◆ **to ~ sb of sth** informer qn de qch, faire savoir qch à qn ◆ **"he'd like a word with you", she ~ed me** "il aimerait vous dire un mot" m'a-t-elle dit ◆ **we were ~ed that the factory was to close** nous avons été informés que l'usine allait fermer ◆ **I should like to be ~ed as soon as he arrives** j'aimerais être informé or averti dès qu'il sera là, prévenez-moi dès qu'il arrivera ◆ **keep me ~ed** tenez-moi au courant ◆ **I'd like to be kept ~ed of progress** j'aimerais que l'on me tienne au courant de l'avancement des choses ◆ **they tried to keep us fully ~ed** ils ont essayé de nous tenir pleinement informés ◆ **why was I not ~ed?** pourquoi ne m'a-t-on rien dit ?, pourquoi n'ai-je pas été informé ? ◆ **we must ~ the police** il faut avertir la police ◆ **the public should be ~ed about the dangers of these drugs** il faudrait informer le public or le public devrait être informé des dangers de ces drogues ◆ **she's better ~ed than most of her colleagues** elle est mieux informée que la plupart de ses collègues ◆ **he was not well ~ed about what had been happening** il était mal informé or il n'était pas bien au courant de ce qui s'était passé ; see also **informed**
2 (= contribute to) contribuer à ; (= influence) influencer ◆ **his writing is ~ed by a sound knowledge of philosophy** ses écrits portent la marque d'une solide connaissance de la philosophie
VI ◆ **to ~ against** or **on sb** dénoncer qn

informal /ɪnˈfɔːməl/ ADJ 1 (= relaxed, natural) [person] décontracté, sans façons ; [manner, tone, style, atmosphere] décontracté
2 (Ling) [language, expression] familier
3 (= unceremonious) [party, meal, visit] tout simple, sans cérémonie ; [clothes] décontracté ◆ **it was a very ~ occasion** c'était une occasion dénuée de toute formalité or de tout protocole ◆ **it's just an ~ get-together between friends** ce sera à la bonne franquette ◆ **it will be quite ~** ce sera sans cérémonie or en toute simplicité ◆ **"dress informal"** "tenue de ville"
4 (= unofficial) [talks, meeting] non officiel, informel ; [agreement, acceptance, announcement, communication, visit] non officiel, officieux ; [invitation] non officiel, dénué de caractère officiel ; [group] à caractère non officiel ◆ **there was an ~ arrangement that ...** il y avait une entente officieuse selon laquelle ... ◆ **play is often an important part of ~ education** le jeu joue souvent un rôle important dans l'apprentissage non scolaire

informality /ˌɪnfɔːˈmælɪtɪ/ N [of visit, welcome etc] simplicité f, absence f de formalité ; [of style, language] simplicité f ; [of arrangement, agreement, occasion] caractère m informel or officieux ◆ **the ~ of his manners** (gen) son naturel ; (pej) les familiarités qu'il se permet

informally /ɪnˈfɔːməlɪ/ ADV 1 (= in relaxed manner) [dress] simplement ◆ **she chatted ~ to the children** elle parla aux enfants avec naturel 2 (= unceremoniously, unofficially) [invite] sans cérémonie ; [meet, discuss, agree, arrange] à titre officieux or non officiel ◆ **the policy has been ~ adopted** la politique a été adoptée à titre officieux or non officiel 3 (Ling) [call] familièrement

informant /ɪnˈfɔːmənt/ N 1 (gen, Press) informateur m, -trice f ◆ **my ~ tells me ...** mon informateur me dit que ... ◆ **who is your ~?** de qui tenez-vous cette information ?, quelles sont vos sources ? 2 (= informer) (also **police informant**) indicateur m informateur m (de la police) ◆ **a mafia boss turned police ~** un parrain de la mafia devenu indicateur or informateur 3 (Ling: also **native informant**) informateur m, -trice f

informatics /ˌɪnfəˈmætɪks/ N (NonC) informatique f

information /ˌɪnfəˈmeɪʃən/ LANGUAGE IN USE 19.1, 19.3
N 1 (NonC) (= facts) renseignements mpl, information(s) f(pl) ◆ **a piece of ~** un renseignement, une information ◆ **we will be looking at every piece of ~ we received** nous examinerons chacune des informations que nous avons reçues or chacun des renseignements que nous avons reçus ◆ **to give sb ~ about** or **on sth/sb** renseigner qn sur qch/qn ◆ **to get ~ about** or **on sth/sb** se renseigner sur qch/qn, obtenir des informations sur qch/qn ◆ **to ask for ~ about** or **on sth/sb** demander des renseignements or des informations sur qch/qn ◆ **I need more ~ about it** il me faut des renseignements plus complets or des informations plus complètes ◆ **we are collecting as much ~ as we can on that organization** nous sommes en train de réunir le plus d'informations or de renseignements possible(s) sur cette organisation ◆ **we have no ~ on that point** nous n'avons aucune information or aucun renseignement là-dessus ◆ **until more ~ is available** jusqu'à ce qu'il y ait de plus amples renseignements ◆ **have you any ~ about the accident?** avez-vous des renseignements or des détails sur l'accident ? ◆ **the police are seeking ~ about ...** la police recherche des renseignements sur ..., la police enquête sur ... ◆ **I have ~ that they are being held captive near the border** j'ai des informations selon lesquelles ils seraient retenus en captivité près de la frontière ◆ **our ~ is that he has refused to talk to the press** selon nos renseignements il aurait refusé de parler à la presse ◆ **my ~ is that the President will be making a statement this afternoon** selon mes renseignements le président fera une déclaration cet après-midi ◆ **the police had acted on inadequate ~** la police avait agi à partir d'informations insuffisantes ◆ **I enclose for your ~ a copy of ...** à titre d'information je joins une copie de ... ◆ **for further ~ contact ...** pour plus de or pour de plus amples renseignements, veuillez contacter ... ◆ **"for your information"** (on document) "à titre d'information", "à titre indicatif" ◆ **for your ~, he ...** (gen) nous vous signalons or informons qu'il ... ; (iro) au cas où vous ne le sauriez pas (encore), il ... ; → **tourist**
2 (US Telec) (service m des) renseignements mpl
3 (pl **informations**) (Jur) (= denunciation) dénonciation f ; (= charge) plainte f ◆ **to lay an ~ against sb** (= bring charge against) déposer plainte contre qn ; (= denounce) dénoncer qn à la police
COMP **information bureau** N bureau m d'informations or de renseignements
information content N contenu m informationnel
information desk N accueil m
information exchange N centre m d'échange d'informations
information highway N ⇒ **information superhighway**
information office N ⇒ **information bureau**
information officer N responsable mf de l'information
information overload N surinformation f
information pack N (Brit) documentation f, ensemble m documentaire
information processing N informatique f, traitement m de l'information
information retrieval N recherche f documentaire
information retrieval system N système m de recherche documentaire
information science N informatique f
information scientist N informaticien(ne) m(f)
information service N bureau m d'informations or de renseignements
information superhighway N autoroute f de l'information
information technology N informatique f, technologie f de l'information
information theory N théorie f de l'information

informational /ˌɪnfəˈmeɪʃənl/ ADJ [needs, meeting, documentary, programme] d'information

informative /ɪnˈfɔːmətɪv/ ADJ [book, meeting, article, talk] instructif ◆ **the talk was very ~ about ...** l'exposé était très instructif quant à or au sujet de ...

informatory /ɪnˈfɔːmətərɪ/ ADJ (Bridge) d'information ◆ **~ double** contre m d'appel

informed /ɪnˈfɔːmd/ ADJ [person] informé ; [debate, discussion] approfondi ; [opinion, criticism, point of view] fondé ◆ **an ~ decision** une décision prise en connaissance de cause ◆ **to make an ~ choice** choisir en connaissance de cause ◆ **~ sources** sources fpl bien informées ◆ **~ observers** observateurs mpl bien informés ◆ **there is a body of ~ opinion which claims that there is ...** certains milieux bien informés prétendent qu'il y a ..., selon certains milieux bien informés, il y aurait ... ◆ **an ~ guess** une hypothèse fondée sur la connaissance des faits ; see also **inform**

informer /ɪnˈfɔːməʳ/ N dénonciateur m, -trice f, délateur m, -trice f ◆ **police ~** indicateur m, informateur m (de la police) ◆ **to turn ~** (on specific occasion) dénoncer or vendre ses complices ; (long-term) devenir indicateur or informateur

infotainment /ˌɪnfəʊˈteɪnmənt/ N info-spectacle m, info-divertissement m

infraction /ɪnˈfrækʃən/ N [of law, rule] infraction f (of à)

infra dig * /ˈɪnfrəˈdɪg/ ADJ au-dessous de sa (or ma etc) dignité, indigne or au-dessous de soi (or moi etc), déshonorant

infrared /ˈɪnfrəˈred/ ADJ infrarouge

infrasonic /ˌɪnfrəˈsɒnɪk/ ADJ infrasonore

infrastructure /ˈɪnfrəˌstrʌktʃəʳ/ N infrastructure f

infrequency /ɪnˈfriːkwənsɪ/ N rareté f

infrequent /ɪnˈfriːkwənt/ ADJ peu fréquent

infrequently /ɪnˈfriːkwəntlɪ/ ADV peu souvent, peu fréquemment ◆ **not ~** assez fréquemment

infringe /ɪnˈfrɪndʒ/ VT [+ law, rule] enfreindre, transgresser ◆ **to ~ copyright** ne pas respecter les droits d'auteur ◆ **to ~ a patent** commettre une contrefaçon en matière de brevet ◆ **to ~ sb's rights** empiéter sur or léser les droits de qn ◆ **this law would ~ freedom of speech** cette loi serait contraire au principe de la liberté d'expression ◆ **he ~d his amateur status by accepting money for the race** il a enfreint son statut d'amateur en acceptant d'être payé pour cette course
VI ◆ **to ~ (up)on sb's rights** empiéter sur or léser les droits de qn ◆ **to ~ on sb's privacy** porter atteinte à la vie privée de qn ◆ **measures that ~ on Iraq's sovereignty** des mesures qui portent atteinte à la souveraineté de l'Irak ◆ **laws that ~ upon press freedom** des lois qui portent atteinte à la liberté de la presse

infringement /ɪnˈfrɪndʒmənt/ N [of law] transgression f (of sth de qch) violation f (of sth de qch) ; *[of rule]* infraction *f (of sth* à qch) ; *[of rights, liberties]* atteinte *f (of or on sth* à qch) ◆ **to be in ~ of a law** enfreindre une loi ◆ **~ of copyright** non-respect *m* des droits d'auteur ◆ **~ of patent** contrefaçon *f* de brevet

infuriate /ɪnˈfjʊərɪeɪt/ VT rendre furieux, mettre en fureur ◆ **it ~s me (that ...)** cela me rend fou (que.. + *subj*), cela m'exaspère (que ... + *subj*) ◆ **to be ~d** être furieux ◆ **she was ~d to hear that ...** elle était furieuse d'apprendre que ... ◆ **to be ~d by sth/sb** être exaspéré par qch/qn

infuriating /ɪnˈfjʊərɪeɪtɪŋ/ ADJ exaspérant, rageant

infuriatingly /ɪnˈfjʊərɪeɪtɪŋlɪ/ ADV *[say, reply, laugh]* de façon exaspérante ◆ **~ slow/cheerful** d'une lenteur/gaieté exaspérante ◆ **~ reasonable** raisonnable à un point exaspérant

infuse /ɪnˈfjuːz/ VT infuser *(into* dans) ; *(Culin) [+ tea, herbs]* (faire) infuser ; *(fig) [+ ideas etc]* infuser, insuffler *(into* à) ◆ **to ~ a project with enthusiasm** insuffler de l'enthousiasme dans un projet VI *(Culin) [tea, herbs]* infuser

infusion /ɪnˈfjuːʒən/ N infusion *f*

ingenious /ɪnˈdʒiːnɪəs/ ADJ ingénieux, astucieux

ingeniously /ɪnˈdʒiːnɪəslɪ/ ADV ingénieusement, astucieusement ◆ **~ inventive excuses** des excuses ingénieuses

ingénue /ˌænʒeɪˈnjuː/ N ingénue *f*

ingenuity /ˌɪndʒɪˈnjuːɪtɪ/ N ingéniosité *f*

ingenuous /ɪnˈdʒenjʊəs/ ADJ *(= naïve)* ingénu, naïf (naïve *f*) ; *(= candid)* sincère, franc (franche *f*)

ingenuously /ɪnˈdʒenjʊəslɪ/ ADV ingénument

ingenuousness /ɪnˈdʒenjʊəsnɪs/ N ingénuité *f*

ingest /ɪnˈdʒest/ VT *(Med)* ingérer

ingestion /ɪnˈdʒestʃən/ N *(Med)* ingestion *f*

inglenook /ˈɪŋglnʊk/ N coin *m* du feu COMP **inglenook fireplace** N grande cheminée *f* à l'ancienne

inglorious /ɪnˈglɔːrɪəs/ ADJ peu glorieux ; *(stronger)* déshonorant, honteux

ingloriously /ɪnˈglɔːrɪəslɪ/ ADV *[fall, slip]* piteusement ; *[fail]* lamentablement

ingoing /ˈɪn,gəʊɪŋ/ ADJ *[people, crowd]* qui entre ; *[tenant]* nouveau (nouvelle *f*)

ingot /ˈɪŋgət/ N lingot *m*

ingrained /ˈɪnˈgreɪnd/ ADJ 1 *(= deep-seated) [attitude, prejudice, hostility, distrust]* enraciné *(in sb* chez qn ; *in sth* dans qch) ; *[habit]* invétéré 2 *[dirt, grime]* incrusté ◆ **~ with dirt** encrassé, incrusté de saleté

ingrate /ˈɪngreɪt/ N ingrat(e) *m(f)*

ingratiate /ɪnˈgreɪʃɪeɪt/ VT ◆ **to ~ o.s. with sb** se faire bien voir de qn, s'insinuer dans les bonnes grâces de qn

ingratiating /ɪnˈgreɪʃɪeɪtɪŋ/ ADJ patelin, doucereux

ingratitude /ɪnˈgrætɪtjuːd/ N ingratitude *f*

ingredient /ɪnˈgriːdɪənt/ N *(Culin)* ingrédient *m* ; *[of character etc]* élément *m* ◆ **~s** *(on food packaging)* ingrédients *mpl*, composition *f*

ingress /ˈɪngres/ N *(Jur)* entrée *f* ◆ **to have free ~** avoir le droit d'entrée

ingrowing /ˈɪn,grəʊɪŋ/, **ingrown** *(US)* /ˈɪn,grəʊn/ ADJ ◆ **~ nail** ongle *m* incarné

inguinal /ˈɪŋgwɪnl/ ADJ inguinal

inhabit /ɪnˈhæbɪt/ VT *[+ town, country]* habiter ; *[+ house]* habiter (dans) ◆ **~ed** habité

inhabitable /ɪnˈhæbɪtəbl/ ADJ habitable

inhabitant /ɪnˈhæbɪtənt/ N habitant(e) *m(f)*

inhalant /ɪnˈheɪlənt/ N 1 *(= medicine)* médicament *m* à inhaler 2 *(= solvent)* solvant *m* ; ◆ **~ abuse** prise de solvants

inhalation /ˌɪnhəˈleɪʃən/ N *(gen, Med)* inhalation *f*

inhalator /ˈɪnhəleɪtəʳ/ N ⇒ **inhaler**

inhale /ɪnˈheɪl/ VT *[+ vapour, gas]* inhaler ; *[+ perfume]* respirer, humer ; *[smoker]* avaler VI *[smoker]* avaler la fumée

inhaler /ɪnˈheɪləʳ/ N inhalateur *m*

inharmonious /ˌɪnhɑːˈməʊnɪəs/ ADJ inharmonieux, peu harmonieux

inhere /ɪnˈhɪəʳ/ VI *(frm)* être inhérent *(in* à)

inherent /ɪnˈhɪərənt/ ADJ *[right, power]* inhérent, intrinsèque ; *[dangers, problems, contradictions, risks, weaknesses]* inhérent, propre ; *[value]* intrinsèque ; *(Jur)* propre *(in, to* à) ; ◆ **to be ~ to sb/sth** être inhérent à qn/qch ◆ **the dangers ~ in war** les dangers inhérents *or* propres à la guerre ◆ **with all the ~ difficulties** avec toutes les difficultés qui en découlent ◆ **stress is an ~ part of modern life** le stress fait partie intégrante de la vie moderne ◆ **self-defence is an ~ right of all countries** l'autodéfense est un droit inhérent à tous les pays *or* intrinsèque de chaque pays

inherently /ɪnˈhɪərəntlɪ/ ADV *[involved, dangerous, difficult]* par nature ; *(Philos)* par inhérence ; *(Jur) [entail]* en propre ◆ **there is nothing ~ wrong with the system** le système n'a rien de mauvais en soi ◆ **war is ~ a dirty business** la guerre est par nature une sale affaire

inherit /ɪnˈherɪt/ VT hériter de, hériter *(liter)* ◆ **she ~ed $10,000** elle a hérité de 10 000 dollars ◆ **to ~ a house/fortune** hériter d'une maison/d'une fortune, hériter *(liter)* une maison/une fortune ◆ **to ~ a house/fortune from sb** hériter *(liter)* une maison/une fortune de qn ◆ **he ~ed the estate from his father** il a succédé à son père à la tête du domaine, il a hérité du domaine de son père ◆ **to ~ a title** succéder à un titre, hériter d'un titre ◆ **the new government has ~ed a weak economy** le nouveau gouvernement a hérité d'une économie en mauvaise santé ◆ **she ~ed her mother's beauty** elle a hérité de la beauté de sa mère ◆ **he ~s his patience/his red hair from his father** il tient sa patience/ses cheveux roux de son père ◆ **I've ~ed my brother's coat** *(hum)* j'ai hérité du manteau de mon frère ; see also **inherited**

VI hériter ◆ **she is due to ~ on the death of her aunt** elle doit hériter à la mort de sa tante

inheritance /ɪnˈherɪtəns/ N 1 *(NonC)* succession *f* ◆ **law of ~** *(Jur)* droit *m* de succession 2 *[of individual, family]* héritage *m* ; *[of nation]* patrimoine *m* ◆ **to come into an ~** faire un héritage ◆ **an ~ of $10,000** un héritage de 10 000 dollars ◆ **it's part of our cultural ~** cela fait partie de notre patrimoine culturel ◆ **our genetic ~** notre patrimoine génétique COMP **inheritance tax** N droits *mpl* de succession

inherited /ɪnˈherɪtɪd/ ADJ *[disease, defect]* héréditaire ; *[gene]* hérité ◆ **~ wealth/property** richesse *f*/propriété *f* dont on a hérité

inheritor /ɪnˈherɪtəʳ/ N *(lit, fig)* héritier *m*, -ière *f*

inhibit /ɪnˈhɪbɪt/ VT 1 *[+ growth, development] (= slow down)* freiner ; *(= hinder)* entraver ; *(= prevent)* empêcher ; *[situation, sb's presence] [+ person]* gêner ; *(Psych)* inhiber ◆ **tablets which ~ the desire to eat** des pilules qui coupent la faim, des coupe-faim *mpl* ◆ **orthodox drugs can ~ the action of natural treatments** les médicaments traditionnels peuvent gêner l'action des traitements naturels ◆ **a drug that ~s the formation of blood clots** un médicament qui empêche la formation de caillots de sang ◆ **alcohol can ~ our ability to think logically** l'alcool peut diminuer nos facultés de raisonnement ◆ **stress can ~ a man's sexual performance** le stress peut diminuer *or* amoindrir les capacités sexuelles d'un homme ◆ **to ~ freedom of speech** entraver la liberté d'expression ◆ **to ~ sb from doing sth** *(= restrain)* retenir qn de faire qch ; *(= prevent)* empêcher qn de faire qch ◆ **his presence ~ed the discussion** *(= limited it)* sa présence gênait la discussion ; *(= prevented it)* sa présence empêchait toute discussion ◆ **he was greatly ~ed by his lack of education** *(= held back)* il était handicapé par son manque d'instruction ; *(= embarrassed)* il était très gêné par son manque d'instruction

2 *(Jur = prohibit)* interdire, défendre *(sb from doing sth* à qn de faire qch)

inhibited /ɪnˈhɪbɪtɪd/ ADJ refoulé, inhibé ◆ **he is very ~** il a beaucoup d'inhibitions ◆ **to be sexually ~** être refoulé sexuellement

inhibiting /ɪnˈhɪbɪtɪŋ/ ADJ inhibiteur (-trice *f*)

inhibition /ˌɪnhɪˈbɪʃən/ N 1 *(gen)* complexe *m* ; *(Physiol, Psych)* inhibition *f* 2 *(Jur = prohibition)* interdiction *f*

inhibitory /ɪnˈhɪbɪtərɪ/ ADJ 1 *(Physiol, Psych)* inhibiteur (-trice *f*) 2 *(Jur)* prohibitif

inhospitable /ˌɪnhɒsˈpɪtəbl/ ADJ *[person, behaviour, reception]* inhospitalier, peu accueillant ; *[country, climate]* inhospitalier ; *[weather]* désagréable, inclément *(liter)*

inhospitably /ˌɪnhɒsˈpɪtəblɪ/ ADV *[behave]* de façon *or* manière inhospitalière ◆ **to treat sb ~** se montrer inhospitalier envers qn ◆ **~ cold** *[region, climate]* d'un froid inhospitalier ; *(fig) [person]* d'une froideur glaciale

inhospitality /ˈɪn,hɒspɪˈtælɪtɪ/ N *[of person, country, climate]* inhospitalité *f* ; *[of weather]* inclémence *f (liter)*

inhuman /ɪnˈhjuːmən/ ADJ *(lit, fig)* inhumain

inhumane /ˌɪnhju(ː)ˈmeɪn/ ADJ inhumain

inhumanity /ˌɪnhjuːˈmænɪtɪ/ N inhumanité *f*

inhumation /ˌɪnhjuːˈmeɪʃən/ N *(frm)* inhumation *f*

inimical /ɪˈnɪmɪkəl/ ADJ *(= hostile)* hostile ◆ **~ to** défavorable à, (l')ennemi de

inimitable /ɪˈnɪmɪtəbl/ ADJ inimitable

inimitably /ɪˈnɪmɪtəblɪ/ ADV d'une façon inimitable

iniquitous /ɪˈnɪkwɪtəs/ ADJ inique, profondément injuste

iniquitously /ɪˈnɪkwɪtəslɪ/ ADV de façon inique

iniquity /ɪˈnɪkwɪtɪ/ N iniquité *f*

initial /ɪˈnɪʃəl/ ADJ 1 *[investment, cost, results, period, enthusiasm]* initial ◆ **after the ~ shock, I ...** après le choc initial, je ... ◆ **my ~ reaction was to refuse** ma première réaction *or* ma réaction initiale a été de refuser ◆ **~ reports suggest that hundreds of people have been wounded** selon les premiers rapports il y aurait des centaines de blessés ◆ **in the ~ stages** au début, dans un premier temps ◆ **~ expenses** *[of shop, firm etc]* frais *mpl* d'établissement 2 *(Phon)* initial 3 *(Typ)* **~ letter** initiale *f* N (lettre *f*) initiale *f* ◆ **~s** initiales *fpl* ; *(as signature)* parafe *or* paraphe *m* VT *[+ letter, document]* parafer *or* parapher ; *(= approve)* viser COMP **Initial Teaching Alphabet** N *(Brit Scol) alphabet phonétique d'apprentissage de la lecture*

initialize /ɪˈnɪʃə,laɪz/ VT *(Comput)* initialiser

initially /ɪˈnɪʃəlɪ/ ADV d'abord, au départ ◆ **~, they were wary of him** au départ, ils se méfiaient de lui

initiate /ɪˈnɪʃɪeɪt/ VT 1 *[+ negotiations, discussion, action, reform]* engager, lancer ; *[+ enterprise, fashion]* lancer ; *[+ scheme, programme]* mettre en place ◆ **to ~ sex** prendre l'initiative de l'acte sexuel ◆ **to ~ proceedings against sb** *(Jur)* intenter un procès à qn ◆ **the trip was ~d by the manager** c'est le directeur qui a eu l'initiative du voyage 2 *(Rel etc) [+ person]* initier ◆ **to ~ sb into a science/a secret** initier qn à une science/un secret ◆ **to ~ sb into a society** admettre qn au sein d'une société (secrète) ADJ /ɪˈnɪʃɪɪt/ N initié(e) *m(f)*

initiation /ɪˌnɪʃɪˈeɪʃən/ N 1 *[of negotiations, discussion, action, reform, enterprise, fashion]* lancement *m* ; *[of scheme, programme]* mise *f* en place 2 *(into society)* admission *f (into* dans) initiation *f* ; *(into knowledge, secret)* initiation *f (into* à) COMP **initiation rite** N rite *m* d'initiation

initiative /ɪˈnɪʃətɪv/ N initiative *f* ◆ **to take the ~** prendre l'initiative *(in doing sth* de faire qch) ◆ **the government still has the ~** le gouvernement a gardé l'initiative ◆ **to use one's (own) ~** faire preuve d'initiative ◆ **on one's own ~** de sa propre initiative, par soi-même ◆ **he's got ~** il a de l'initiative ◆ **to have/lose the ~** avoir/perdre l'initiative ◆ **a new peace ~** une nouvelle initiative de paix COMP **initiative test** N test *m* d'initiative

initiator /ɪˈnɪʃɪˌeɪtəʳ/ N auteur *m*, instigateur *m*, -trice *f*

inject /ɪnˈdʒekt/ VT 1 *[+ liquid, gas]* injecter *(into* dans) ◆ **to ~ sb with sth** *(Med)* injecter qch à qn, faire une piqûre *or* une injection de qch à qn ◆ **to ~ sb's arm with penicillin, to ~ penicillin into sb's arm** faire une piqûre *or* injection de pénicilline dans le bras de qn ◆ **he ~s himself** *[diabetic etc]* il se fait ses piqûres ◆ **to ~ drugs** *[addict]* se piquer* ◆ **to ~ heroin** se piquer* à l'héroïne
2 *(fig)* ◆ **to ~ sb with enthusiasm** communiquer *or* insuffler de l'enthousiasme à qn ◆ **I wanted to ~ some humour into my speech** je voulais introduire un peu d'humour dans mon discours ◆ **they need to ~ some new life into their relationship** il faut qu'ils introduisent un peu de nouveauté dans leur relation ◆ **the government are trying to ~ some life into the economy** le gouvernement essaie de relancer l'économie ◆ **she ~ed some money/£5 million into the company** elle a injecté de l'argent/5 millions de livres dans la société
VI *[drug addict]* se piquer*

injection /ɪnˈdʒekʃən/ N *(lit, fig, also Fin = process)* injection *f* ; *(Med, Brit Dentistry = shot)* injection *f*, piqûre *f* ◆ **to give medicine by ~** administrer un remède par injection ◆ **an ~ of new capital** une injection *or* un apport de capital frais ◆ **a $250 million cash ~** un apport de 250 millions de dollars

injector /ɪnˈdʒektəʳ/ N injecteur *m* ; → **fuel**

injudicious /ˌɪndʒuˈdɪʃəs/ ADJ peu judicieux, malavisé

injudiciously /ˌɪndʒuˈdɪʃəslɪ/ ADV peu judicieusement

injunction /ɪnˈdʒʌŋkʃən/ N *(gen)* ordre *m*, recommandation *f* formelle ; *(Jur)* injonction *f* ; *(= court order)* ordonnance *f (to do sth* de faire qch ; *against doing sth* de ne pas faire qch) ◆ **she plans to seek a court ~ to stop publication of the photographs** elle a l'intention de demander une ordonnance pour empêcher la publication des photos ◆ **an ~ banning the sale of the book** une ordonnance interdisant la vente du livre ◆ **to give sb strict ~s to do sth** enjoindre formellement *or* strictement à qn de faire qch

injure /ˈɪndʒəʳ/ VT 1 *(= hurt physically) [+ person, limb]* blesser ◆ **to ~ o.s.** se blesser ◆ **to ~ one's leg** se blesser à la jambe ◆ **no one was ~d** il n'y a pas eu de blessés, personne n'a été blessé ; see also **injured** 2 *(fig) [+ person] (= wrong)* faire du tort à, nuire à ; *(Jur)* porter préjudice à, léser ; *(= offend)* blesser, offenser ; *(= damage) [+ reputation, sb's interests, chances, trade]* compromettre ; *(Comm) [+ cargo, goods]* avarier ◆ **to ~ sb's feelings** offenser qn ◆ **to ~ one's health** compromettre sa santé, se détériorer la santé ; see also **injured**

injured /ˈɪndʒəd/ ADJ 1 *(physically)* blessé ; *(in road accident)* accidenté ; *[limb]* blessé 2 *(fig) [person]* offensé ; *[look, voice]* blessé, offensé ; *[wife, husband]* outragé, trompé ◆ **the ~ party** *(Jur)* la partie lésée NPL **the injured** *(gen)* les blessés *mpl* ; *(in road accident etc)* les accidentés *mpl*, les blessés *mpl*

injurious /ɪnˈdʒʊərɪəs/ ADJ nuisible, préjudiciable *(to* à)

injury /ˈɪndʒərɪ/ N 1 *(physical)* blessure *f* ◆ **to do sb an ~** blesser qn ◆ **you'll do yourself an ~!** tu vas te faire mal ! ◆ **three players have injuries** *(Sport)* il y a trois joueurs (de) blessés 2 *(fig = wrong) (to person)* tort *m*, préjudice *m* ; *(to reputation)* atteinte *f* ; *(Jur)* lésion *f*, préjudice *m* ◆ **to the ~ of sb** au détriment *or* au préjudice de qn ◆ **they awarded him £28,000 to cover ~ to his feelings** il a reçu 28 000 livres en réparation du préjudice moral 3 *(Comm, Naut)* avarie *f* COMP **injury time** N *(Brit Ftbl)* arrêts *mpl* de jeu ◆ **to play ~ time** jouer les arrêts de jeu

injustice /ɪnˈdʒʌstɪs/ N injustice *f* ◆ **to do sb an ~** être *or* se montrer injuste envers qn

ink /ɪŋk/ N 1 encre *f* ◆ **written in ~** écrit à l'encre ; → **Indian, invisible** 2 *[of octopus, cuttlefish]* encre *f*, sépia *f* VT 1 *(Typ) [+ roller]* encrer 2 *(US * fig = sign)* signer
COMP **ink bag** N *[of marine animal]* sac *m or* poche *f* d'encre
ink blot N tache *f* d'encre, pâté *m*
ink blot test N *(Psych)* test *m* de la tache d'encre, test *m* de Rorschach
ink bottle N bouteille *f* d'encre
ink eraser N gomme *f* à encre
ink-jet printer N *(Comput)* imprimante *f* à jet d'encre
ink rubber N ⇒ **ink eraser**

► **ink in** VT SEP repasser à l'encre

► **ink out** VT SEP raturer *or* barrer à l'encre

► **ink over** VT SEP ⇒ **ink in**

inkling /ˈɪŋklɪŋ/ N soupçon *m*, vague *or* petite idée *f* ◆ **I had no ~ that ...** je n'avais pas la moindre idée que ..., je ne me doutais pas du tout que ... ◆ **he had no ~ of what was going on** il n'avait pas la moindre idée de ce qui se passait, il ne se doutait pas du tout de ce qui se passait ◆ **we had some ~ of their plan** nous avions une petite idée de leur plan ◆ **there was no ~ of the disaster to come** rien ne laissait présager le désastre qui allait se produire

inkpad /ˈɪŋkpæd/ N tampon *m* (encreur)

inkpot /ˈɪŋkpɒt/ N encrier *m*

inkstain /ˈɪŋksteɪn/ N tache *f* d'encre

inkstand /ˈɪŋkstænd/ N (grand) encrier *m* (de bureau)

inkwell /ˈɪŋkwel/ N encrier *m* (de pupitre *etc*)

inky /ˈɪŋkɪ/ ADJ 1 *(liter = dark) [colour]* très foncé ; *[sky]* noir *inv* d'encre *or* comme de l'encre ◆ **~ black** noir *inv* d'encre ◆ **~ blue** (d'un) bleu outremer foncé *inv* 2 *(= covered with ink) [finger, paper]* plein d'encre ; *[pad, rubber stamp]* encré

inlaid /ˈɪnˈleɪd/ ADJ *[brooch, sword]* incrusté *(with* de) ; *[box, table]* marqueté ; *[metal]* damasquiné ◆ **ivory ~ with gold** ivoire *m* incrusté d'or ◆ **an ~ floor** un parquet ◆ **~ work** *(= jewels)* incrustation *f* ; *(= wood)* marqueterie *f*

inland /ˈɪnlænd/ ADJ 1 *(= not coastal) [sea, town]* intérieur (-eure *f*) ◆ **~ navigation** navigation *f* fluviale ◆ **~ waterways** canaux *mpl* et rivières *fpl* 2 *(Brit = domestic) [mail, trade]* intérieur (-eure *f*) ADV /ɪnˈlænd/ à l'intérieur ◆ **to go ~** aller dans l'arrière-pays

COMP **the Inland Revenue (Service)** N *(Brit) (= organization, system)* le fisc
Inland Revenue stamp N timbre *m* fiscal

inlay /ˈɪnleɪ/ (vb : pret, ptp **inlaid**) N *[of brooch, sword]* incrustation *f* ; *[of table, box]* marqueterie *f* ; *[of floor]* parquet *m* ; *[of metal]* damasquinage *m* VT /ˌɪnˈleɪ/ *[+ brooch, sword]* incruster *(with* de) ; *[+ table, box]* marqueter ; *[+ floor]* parqueter ; *[+ metal]* damasquiner ; see also **inlaid**

inlet /ˈɪnlet/ N 1 *[of sea]* crique *f*, anse *f* ; *[of river]* bras *m* de rivière 2 *[of engine]* arrivée *f*, admission *f* ; *[of ventilator]* prise *f* (d'air) COMP **inlet pipe** N tuyau *m* d'arrivée ; → **valve**

in loco parentis /ɪnˈləʊkəʊpəˈrentɪs/ ADV en tant que substitut *or* à la place des parents

inmate /ˈɪnmeɪt/ N *[of prison]* détenu(e) *m(f)* ; *[of asylum]* interné(e) *m(f)* ; *[of hospital]* malade *mf*, hospitalisé(e) *m(f)*, pensionnaire* *mf*

inmost /ˈɪnməʊst/ ADJ *[thoughts]* le plus secret, le plus intime ; *[feelings]* le plus intime ◆ **in the ~ part of the temple** au plus profond *or* au cœur du temple ◆ **in one's ~ being** au plus profond de soi-même ◆ **in one's ~ heart** au fond de son cœur

inn /ɪn/ N *(small, wayside)* auberge *f* ; *(larger, wayside)* hostellerie *f* ; *(in town)* hôtel *m* ; († *= tavern)* cabaret † *m*
COMP **inn sign** N enseigne *f* d'auberge
the Inns of Court NPL *(Brit Jur)* les (quatre) écoles *fpl* de droit *(londoniennes)*

innards* /ˈɪnədz/ NPL entrailles *fpl*, intérieurs* *mpl*

innate /ɪˈneɪt/ ADJ *[ability, talent, wisdom, intelligence, conservatism]* inné ; *[dignity]* foncier ; *[distrust]* naturel ◆ **an ~ sense of sth** un sens inné de qch

innately /ɪˈneɪtlɪ/ ADV ◆ **~ aggressive/generous** d'une agressivité/générosité innée, naturellement agressif/généreux

inner /ˈɪnəʳ/ ADJ 1 *[room, court]* intérieur (-eure *f*) ◆ **on the ~ side** à l'intérieur ◆ **they formed an ~ circle within the society** ils formaient un petit noyau *or* un petit cercle (fermé) à l'intérieur de la société
2 *[emotions, thoughts]* intime ; *[life]* intérieur (-eure *f*) ◆ **the ~ child** l'enfant *m* intérieur ◆ **the ~ meaning** le sens intime *or* profond ◆ **the ~ man** *(= spiritual self)* l'homme *m* intérieur ; *(hum) (= stomach)* l'estomac *m* ◆ **the discovery of the ~ self** la découverte de soi ◆ **trust your ~ self** suivez votre instinct
COMP **inner city** N quartiers *mpl* déshérités *(à l'intérieur de la ville)*
inner-city ADJ *[buildings, problems, crime, renewal]* des quartiers déshérités
inner-city areas NPL ⇒ **inner city**
inner-directed ADJ *(esp US)* individualiste
inner dock N *(Naut)* arrière-bassin *m*
inner ear N *(Anat)* oreille *f* interne
inner harbour N arrière-port *m*
inner sole N *[of shoe]* semelle *f* (intérieure)
inner spring mattress N *(US)* matelas *m* à ressorts
inner tube N *[of tyre]* chambre *f* à air

INNER CITY

L'expression **inner city** désigne initialement le centre des villes. Dans l'évolution des villes anglo-saxonnes, les quartiers du centre, délaissés par les classes aisées, se caractérisent souvent par une grande pauvreté, un taux de chômage élevé, de très mauvaises conditions de logement et des tensions entre les groupes ethniques. En ce sens, la notion de **inner city** correspondrait en français aux banlieues à problèmes.

innermost /ˈɪnəməʊst/ ADJ ⇒ **inmost**

inning /ˈɪnɪŋ/ N *(Baseball)* tour *m* de batte

innings /ˈɪnɪŋz/ N *(pl inv)* 1 *(Cricket)* tour *m* de batte 2 *(fig)* tour *m* ◆ **I've had a good ~** j'ai bien profité de l'existence

innit* /ˈɪnɪt/ EXCL (Brit) ◆ ~ ? pas vrai ?*

innkeeper /ˈɪnkiːpəʳ/ N (wayside) aubergiste mf ; (in town) hôtelier m, -ière f

innocence /ˈɪnəsns/ N (gen, Jur) innocence f ; (= simplicity) innocence f, naïveté f ◆ **in all ~** en toute innocence ◆ **in his ~ he believed it all** naïf comme il est (or était etc) il a tout cru, dans son innocence il a tout cru ◆ **to protest one's ~** (Jur) protester de son innocence

Innocent /ˈɪnəsnt/ N (= Papal name) Innocent m

innocent /ˈɪnəsnt/ ADJ 1 (= not guilty, not involved, naive) [person, victim, bystander] innocent (of sth de qch) ◆ **to be found ~ of sth** être déclaré innocent de qch ◆ **as ~ as a newborn babe** innocent comme l'enfant qui vient de naître
2 (= harmless, not malicious) [question, remark, pastime] innocent ◆ **it was the source of much ~ amusement** on s'en est beaucoup amusé mais il n'y avait aucune méchanceté là-dedans ◆ **an ~ mistake** une erreur commise en toute innocence ◆ **~ infringement** (Jur: of patent) contrefaçon f involontaire
3 (frm) ◆ **~ of** (= free from) vierge de (liter), dépourvu de ◆ **a room ~ of all ornament** une pièce vierge de (liter) or dépourvue de tout ornement
N ◆ **he's one of Nature's ~s*, he's a bit of an ~*** c'est un grand innocent ◆ **he tried to come the ~ with me*** il a essayé de jouer aux innocents avec moi ◆ **Massacre of the Holy Innocents** (Rel) massacre m des (saints) Innocents ◆ **Holy Innocents' Day** jour m des saints Innocents

innocently /ˈɪnəsntlɪ/ ADV innocemment, en toute innocence

innocuous /ɪˈnɒkjʊəs/ ADJ inoffensif

innovate /ˈɪnəʊveɪt/ VTI innover

innovation /ˌɪnəʊˈveɪʃən/ N innovation f (in sth en (matière de) qch) changement m (in sth en (matière de) qch) ◆ **to make ~s in sth** apporter des innovations or des changements à qch ◆ **scientific/technical ~s** innovations fpl scientifiques/techniques

innovative /ˈɪnəʊˌveɪtɪv/ ADJ [person, organization, idea, design, approach] novateur (-trice f) ; [product] innovant ◆ **we aim to be ~** nous cherchons à innover

innovator /ˈɪnəʊveɪtəʳ/ N innovateur m, -trice f, novateur m, -trice f

innovatory /ˈɪnəʊˌveɪtərɪ/ ADJ (Brit) ⇒ **innovative**

innuendo /ˌɪnjʊˈendəʊ/ N (pl **innuendo(e)s**) insinuation f, allusion f (malveillante) ◆ **to make ~(e)s about sb** faire des insinuations (malveillantes) à l'égard de qn ◆ **to spread ~(e)s about sb** faire courir des bruits sur qn ◆ **sexual ~** allusions fpl grivoises

Innuit /ˈɪnjuːɪt/ N, ADJ ⇒ **Inuit**

innumerable /ɪˈnjuːmərəbl/ ADJ innombrable, sans nombre ◆ **there are ~ reasons** il y a une infinité de raisons ◆ **I've told you ~ times** je te l'ai dit cent fois ◆ **goals can be pursued in ~ ways** on peut poursuivre un but de cent manières différentes ◆ **she drank ~ cups of coffee** elle a bu un nombre incalculable de tasses de café

innumerate /ɪˈnjuːmərɪt/ ADJ qui n'a pas le sens de l'arithmétique ◆ **he's totally ~** il ne sait pas du tout compter

inoculate /ɪˈnɒkjʊleɪt/ VT vacciner (against sth contre qch) ◆ **to ~ sb with sth** inoculer qch à qn

inoculation /ɪˌnɒkjʊˈleɪʃən/ N inoculation f

inoffensive /ˌɪnəˈfensɪv/ ADJ inoffensif

inoperable /ɪnˈɒpərəbl/ ADJ inopérable

inoperative /ɪnˈɒpərətɪv/ ADJ inopérant

inopportune /ɪnˈɒpətjuːn/ ADJ inopportun

inopportunely /ɪnˈɒpətjuːnlɪ/ ADV inopportunément

inordinate /ɪˈnɔːdɪnɪt/ ADJ [size, number, quantity] démesuré ; [demands] immodéré, extravagant ; [pride, pleasure] extrême ◆ **an ~ amount of luggage/time/money** énormément de bagages/de temps/d'argent ◆ **an ~ sum (of money)** une somme exorbitante or astronomique

inordinately /ɪˈnɔːdɪnɪtlɪ/ ADV [hot, cold, difficult] excessivement ; [proud] infiniment ◆ **to be ~ fond of sth** aimer particulièrement qch

inorganic /ˌɪnɔːˈgænɪk/ ADJ 1 (= artificial) [fibre, material, fertilizer] inorganique 2 (Sci) minéral ◆ **~ chemistry** chimie f inorganique or minérale

inpatient /ˈɪnˌpeɪʃənt/ N malade mf hospitalisé(e)

input /ˈɪnpʊt/ N 1 (= contribution) contribution f, participation f ; [of funds, labour] apport m ; (= ideas) idées fpl ◆ **we need a regular ~ of new ideas** nous avons besoin d'un flux or d'un apport constant de nouvelles idées ◆ **artistic/creative ~** apport m artistique/créatif 2 (Econ) ◆ **~s** input m, intrants mpl ; 3 (in industry) (= materials, parts) consommations fpl intermédiaires 4 (Elec) énergie f, puissance f ; (Tech) [of machine] consommation f 5 (Comput) (= data) données fpl ; (= act of inputting) saisie f, entrée f (de données) VT (Comput) saisir (into sur) entrer (into sth dans qch)
COMP **input data** N (Comput) données fpl en entrée
input/output N (Comput) entrée-sortie f
input/output device N (Comput) périphérique m entrée-sortie
input/output table N (Econ) tableau m d'entrées-sorties

inquest /ˈɪnkwest/ N (Jur) enquête f (criminelle) ; → **coroner**

inquietude /ɪnˈkwaɪətjuːd/ N (liter) inquiétude f

inquire /ɪnˈkwaɪəʳ/ VI se renseigner (about sth sur qch) s'informer (about, after de) ; (= ask) demander ◆ **to ~ after sb/sth** demander des nouvelles de qn/qch, s'informer or s'enquérir (liter) de qn/qch ◆ **I'll go and ~** je vais demander ◆ **~ at the office** demandez au bureau, renseignez-vous au bureau ◆ **"inquire within"** "renseignements ici", "s'adresser ici" ◆ **"inquire at the information desk"** "s'adresser aux renseignements", "s'adresser au bureau de renseignements" ◆ **to ~ into** (subject) faire des recherches or des investigations sur ; (possibilities) se renseigner sur ; (Admin, Jur) (event, situation) enquêter sur, faire une enquête sur
VT demander ◆ **"is something wrong?" he ~d** "il y a quelque chose qui ne va pas ?" a-t-il demandé ◆ **he rang up to ~ how she was** il a téléphoné pour demander or savoir comment elle allait ◆ **he ~d what she wanted** il a demandé ce qu'elle voulait ◆ **I ~d whether my letter had arrived** j'ai demandé si ma lettre était arrivée ◆ **he ~d his way to the cemetery, he ~d how to get to the cemetery** il a demandé le chemin du cimetière

inquiring /ɪnˈkwaɪərɪŋ/ ADJ [attitude, frame of mind] curieux ; [look] interrogateur (-trice f)

inquiringly /ɪnˈkwaɪərɪŋlɪ/ ADV [look] d'un air interrogateur ; [say] d'un ton interrogateur

inquiry /ɪnˈkwaɪərɪ/ N 1 (from individual) demande f de renseignements ◆ **to make inquiries (about sb/sth)** se renseigner (sur qn/qch), demander des renseignements (sur qn/qch) ; see also **noun 2** ◆ **on ~ he found that ...** renseignements pris il a découvert que ... ◆ **a look of ~** un regard interrogateur ◆ **he gave me a look of ~** il m'a interrogé du regard ◆ **"all inquiries to ..."** "pour tous renseignements s'adresser à ..."
2 (Admin, Jur) enquête f, investigation f ◆ **to set up** or **open an ~ (into sth)** ouvrir une enquête (sur qch) ◆ **committee of ~** commission f d'enquête ◆ **to hold an ~ (into sth)** enquêter or faire une enquête (sur qch) ◆ **to call for an ~ into sth** demander une enquête sur qch ◆ **a murder ~** une enquête sur un meurtre ◆ **they are pursuing a new line of ~** ils suivent une nouvelle piste ◆ **the police are making inquiries** la police enquête ; → **help, officer**
3 (Telec, Rail etc) **the Inquiries** les renseignements mpl
COMP **inquiry agent** N détective m privé
inquiry desk, inquiry office N (bureau m de) renseignements mpl

inquisition /ˌɪnkwɪˈzɪʃən/ N investigation f, recherches fpl ; (Jur) enquête f (judiciaire) ◆ **the Inquisition** (Rel) l'Inquisition f

inquisitive /ɪnˈkwɪzɪtɪv/ ADJ curieux, inquisiteur (-trice f) (pej)

inquisitively /ɪnˈkwɪzɪtɪvlɪ/ ADV avec curiosité ; (pej) d'un air inquisiteur

inquisitiveness /ɪnˈkwɪzɪtɪvnɪs/ N curiosité f ; (pej) curiosité f indiscrète, indiscrétion f

inquisitor /ɪnˈkwɪzɪtəʳ/ N (Jur) enquêteur m, -euse f ; (Rel) inquisiteur m

inquisitorial /ɪnˌkwɪzɪˈtɔːrɪəl/ ADJ inquisitorial

inquorate /ɪnˈkwɔːreɪt/ ADJ (Admin) qui n'a pas le quorum, où le quorum n'est pas atteint

inroad /ˈɪnrəʊd/ N (Mil) incursion f (into en, dans) ◆ **to make ~s on** or **into** (fig) (majority, numbers, supplies) entamer ; (sb's rights) empiéter sur ◆ **they have made significant ~s into the commercial aircraft market** ils ont fait une percée importante sur le marché de l'aéronautique commerciale

inrush /ˈɪnˌrʌʃ/ N [of air, water, people] irruption f

ins. (abbrev of **inches**) → **inch**

insalubrious /ˌɪnsəˈluːbrɪəs/ ADJ (gen) insalubre, malsain ; [district] peu recommandable

insane /ɪnˈseɪn/ ADJ (Med) aliéné, dément ; (gen) [person, desire] fou (folle f), insensé ; [project] démentiel ◆ **to become ~** perdre la raison ◆ **to go ~** perdre la raison, devenir fou ◆ **to drive sb ~** rendre qn fou ◆ **he must be ~ to think of going** il faut qu'il soit fou pour envisager d'y aller ◆ **you must be ~!** tu es fou ! ◆ **temporarily ~** pris d'une crise de folie ◆ **~ asylum** (US) asile m d'aliénés ; → **certify** NPL **the insane** (Med) les aliénés mpl

insanely /ɪnˈseɪnlɪ/ ADV [behave] de façon insensée ◆ **to laugh ~** (= hysterically) rire de façon hystérique ◆ **~ possessive/expensive/fast** follement possessif/cher/rapide ◆ **~ jealous** (on one occasion) fou de jalousie ; (by nature) d'une jalousie maladive

insanitary /ɪnˈsænɪtərɪ/ ADJ insalubre, malsain

insanity /ɪnˈsænɪtɪ/ N (Med) aliénation f mentale, démence f ; (gen) folie f, démence f

insatiable /ɪnˈseɪʃəbl/ ADJ (lit, fig) insatiable (for sth de qch)

insatiably /ɪnˈseɪʃəblɪ/ ADV ◆ **to be ~ hungry** avoir une faim insatiable ◆ **to be ~ curious** être d'une curiosité insatiable

inscribe /ɪnˈskraɪb/ VT 1 (in book etc) inscrire ; (on monument etc) inscrire, graver ; [+ surface] marquer, graver ; (fig) [+ ideas] graver, inscrire, fixer ◆ **to ~ a tomb with a name** or **a name on a tomb** graver un nom sur une tombe ◆ **a watch ~d with his name** une montre gravée à son nom ◆ **a watch, ~d "to Laura"** une montre portant l'inscription "à Laura" ◆ **~d stock** (Fin) titres mpl nominatifs or inscrits 2 (= dedicate) [+ book] dédicacer

inscription /ɪnˈskrɪpʃən/ N *(on coin, monument etc)* inscription *f* ; *(on cartoon)* légende *f* ; *(= dedication)* dédicace *f*

inscrutability /ɪnˌskruːtəˈbɪlɪtɪ/ N impénétrabilité *f*

inscrutable /ɪnˈskruːtəbl/ ADJ impénétrable *(to sb/sth* à qn/qch*)*

insect /ˈɪnsekt/ N insecte *m*
COMP **insect bite** N piqûre *f* d'insecte
insect eater N insectivore *m*
insect powder N poudre *f* insecticide
insect repellent ADJ antimoustiques *inv*, insectifuge *(frm)* N *(= cream, ointment etc)* crème *f* (or lotion *f* etc) antimoustiques *inv*, insectifuge *m (frm)*
insect spray N aérosol *m* or bombe *f* insecticide

insecticide /ɪnˈsektɪsaɪd/ ADJ, N insecticide *m*

insectivorous /ˌɪnsekˈtɪvərəs/ ADJ insectivore

insecure /ˌɪnsɪˈkjʊəʳ/ ADJ 1 *(= unsure of oneself)* ◆ **to be ~** manquer d'assurance ; *(Psych)* être anxieux or angoissé ◆ **to feel ~** *(gen)* se sentir mal dans sa peau ; *(= afraid)* ne pas se sentir en sécurité 2 *(= uncertain) [future]* incertain ; *[job, rights]* précaire 3 *(= unsafe, unprotected) [building, lock, door, window, district]* peu sûr 4 *(= not firm, badly fixed) [structure, ladder]* qui n'est pas sûr ; *[rope, rope ladder, load]* mal attaché

insecurity /ˌɪnsɪˈkjʊərɪtɪ/ N *(also Psych)* insécurité *f*

inseminate /ɪnˈsemɪneɪt/ VT inséminer

insemination /ɪnˌsemɪˈneɪʃən/ N insémination *f* ; → **artificial**

insensate /ɪnˈsenseɪt/ ADJ *(frm) (= senseless)* insensé ; *(= inanimate)* inanimé, insensible ; *(= unfeeling)* insensible

insensibility /ɪnˌsensəˈbɪlɪtɪ/ N 1 *(frm Med = unconsciousness)* insensibilité *f*, inconscience *f* 2 *(fig = unfeelingness)* insensibilité *f (to sb/sth* à qn/qch*)* indifférence *f (to sb/sth* pour qn/qch*)*

insensible /ɪnˈsensəbl/ ADJ 1 *(frm = unconscious)* inconscient, sans connaissance ◆ **the blow knocked him ~** le coup lui fit perdre connaissance 2 *(= unaware, impervious)* insensible *(to sth* à qch*)* ◆ **~ to the cold/to shame/to ridicule** insensible au froid/à la honte/au ridicule

insensibly /ɪnˈsensɪblɪ/ ADV *[change, grow]* insensiblement, imperceptiblement

insensitive /ɪnˈsensɪtɪv/ ADJ *(lit, fig: physically or emotionally) [person]* insensible *(to sth* à qch ; *to sb* envers qn*)* ; *[remark, act]* indélicat ; *[policy]* pas assez réfléchi ◆ **policies which are ~ to the needs of ...** des mesures qui ne tiennent pas compte des besoins de ...

insensitivity /ɪnˌsensɪˈtɪvɪtɪ/ N insensibilité *f*

inseparable /ɪnˈsepərəbl/ ADJ inséparable *(from* de*)*

inseparably /ɪnˈsepərəblɪ/ ADV inséparablement ◆ **~ bound up with** or **linked with** inséparablement lié à

insert /ɪnˈsɜːt/ VT insérer *(in, into* dans ; *between* entre*)* ; *[+ paragraph, word]* insérer, introduire *(in* dans*)* ajouter *(in* à*)* ; *[+ knife, finger]* introduire, enfoncer *(in* dans*)* ; *[+ key]* introduire, mettre *(in* dans*)* ; *(Typ) [+ page, leaflet]* encarter, insérer ; *[+ advertisement]* insérer *(in* dans*)* N /ˈɪnsɜːt/ 1 *(= extra pages)* encart *m* ; *(in print) (= advertisement, note, word)* insertion *f* 2 *(Tech)* pièce *f* insérée, ajout *m* ; *(Sewing)* entre-deux *m inv*, incrustation *f*

insertion /ɪnˈsɜːʃən/ N 1 *(NonC)* insertion *f*, introduction *f* 2 ⇒ **insert noun 1** COMP **insertion mark** N *(Typ)* signe *m* d'insertion

INSET /ˈɪnset/ N *(Brit)* (abbrev of **In-Service Education and Training**) formation *f* continue

inset /ˈɪnset/ (pret, ptp **inset**) VT *[+ jewel]* insérer *(into* dans*)* incruster *(into* sur*)* ; *[+ leaflet]* encarter, insérer *(into* dans*)* ; *(in typing, printing) [+ word, line]* rentrer ◆ **to ~ a panel into a skirt** *(Sewing)* rapporter un panneau sur une jupe ◆ **to ~ a map into the corner of a larger one** insérer une carte en cartouche sur une plus grande N *(= diagram)* schéma *m* en cartouche ; *(= map)* carte *f* en cartouche ; *(= portrait)* portrait *m* en cartouche ; *(Typ = leaflet, pages)* encart *m* ; *(Sewing)* entre-deux *m inv*, incrustation *f* ADJ *[gem, pearl]* enchâssé, serti ◆ **~ with** incrusté de

inshore /ˈɪnˈʃɔːʳ/ ADJ *[area, fisherman, navigation, waters]* côtier ; *[fishing boat]* côtier, caboteur ; *[reefs]* près de la côte ◆ **~ fishing** pêche *f* côtière ◆ **~ lifeboat** canot *m* de sauvetage côtier ◆ **~ wind** vent *m* de mer ADV *[be, fish]* près de la côte ; *[blow, flow, go]* vers la côte

inside /ˈɪnˈsaɪd/

> When **inside** is an element in a phrasal verb, eg **step inside**, look up the verb.

ADV 1 dedans, à l'intérieur ◆ **~ and outside** au-dedans et au-dehors ◆ **come** or **step ~!** entrez (donc) ! ◆ **it is warmer ~** il fait plus chaud à l'intérieur ◆ **wait for me ~** attendez-moi à l'intérieur ◆ **let's go ~** rentrons

2 *(* = in jail)* à l'ombre*, au frais*

PREP 1 *(of place)* à l'intérieur de, dans ◆ **he was waiting ~ the house** il attendait à l'intérieur (de la maison) or dans la maison ◆ **she was standing just ~ the gate** *(seen from inside)* elle était juste de ce côté-ci de la barrière ; *(seen from outside)* elle était juste de l'autre côté de la barrière

2 *(of time)* en moins de ◆ **he came back ~ three minutes** or *(US)* **~ of three minutes** il est revenu en moins de trois minutes ◆ **he was well ~ the record time** *(Sport)* il avait largement battu le record

N 1 dedans *m*, intérieur *m* ; *[of house, box, company]* intérieur *m* ◆ **on the ~** à l'intérieur ◆ **walk on the ~ of the pavement** or *(US)* **sidewalk** marchez sur le trottoir du côté maisons ◆ **the door is bolted on** or **from the ~** la porte est fermée au verrou de l'intérieur ◆ **I heard music coming from ~** j'ai entendu de la musique qui venait de l'intérieur

♦ **inside out** ◆ **your coat is ~ out** ton manteau est à l'envers ◆ **her umbrella blew ~ out** son parapluie s'est retourné sous l'effet du vent ◆ **I turned the bag ~ out** j'ai retourné le sac (entièrement) ◆ **he knows his subject ~ out** il connaît son sujet à fond ◆ **he knows the district ~ out** il connaît le quartier comme sa poche ◆ **we know each other ~ out** nous nous connaissons parfaitement ◆ **war turns morality ~ out** la guerre met les valeurs morales sens dessus dessous

2 *(* = stomach:* also **insides***)* ventre *m* ◆ **he felt the fear grip his ~s** il a senti la peur le prendre au ventre

ADJ 1 intérieur (-eure *f*), d'intérieur ◆ **~ pocket** poche *f* intérieure ◆ **~ seat** *[of plane]* place *f* côté fenêtre ◆ **to get ~ information** *(fig)* obtenir des renseignements grâce à des complicités dans la place ◆ **the ~ story** *(Press)* les dessous *mpl* de l'histoire ◆ **it must have been an ~ job*** *(theft etc)* c'est un coup qui a dû être monté de l'intérieur or par quelqu'un de la maison

2 *[wheel, headlight etc] (in Brit)* gauche ; *(in US, Europe etc)* droit ◆ **the ~ lane** *(in Brit)* ≃ la voie de gauche ; *(in US, Europe etc)* ≃ la voie de droite ◆ **to be on** or **hold the ~ track** *(Sport)* être à la corde, tenir la corde ; *(fig)* être le mieux placé

COMP **inside-forward** N *(Sport)* intérieur *m*, inter* *m*
inside-left N *(Sport)* intérieur *m* gauche
inside leg N entrejambe *m*
inside leg measurement N mesure *f* or hauteur *f* de l'entrejambe
inside-right N *(Sport)* intérieur *m* droit

insider /ɪnˈsaɪdəʳ/ N *(gen)* quelqu'un qui connaît les choses de l'intérieur ; *(in firm, organization)* quelqu'un qui est dans la place ; *(esp sb with influence, knowledge, also Stock Exchange)* initié(e) *m(f)* COMP **insider dealing, insider trading** N *(Jur, Fin)* délit *m* d'initiés

insidious /ɪnˈsɪdɪəs/ ADJ insidieux

insidiously /ɪnˈsɪdɪəslɪ/ ADV insidieusement

insight /ˈɪnsaɪt/ N 1 *(= revealing glimpse)* aperçu *m*, idée *f (into* de ; *about* sur*)* ◆ **to give sb an ~ into sth** donner à qn un aperçu de qch ◆ **this gave us new ~s into what's been happening** cela nous a ouvert de nouvelles perspectives sur ce qui s'est passé ◆ **that will give you an ~ into his reasons for doing it** cela vous éclairera sur les raisons qui l'ont poussé à le faire ◆ **to gain ~ into sth** se familiariser avec qch 2 *(= discernment)* perspicacité *f* ◆ **to have great ~** être doué d'une grande perspicacité

insightful /ˈɪnsaɪtfʊl/ ADJ pénétrant, perspicace

insignia /ɪnˈsɪgnɪə/ N (pl **insignias** or **insignia**) insigne *m*

insignificance /ˌɪnsɪgˈnɪfɪkəns/ N insignifiance *f* ; → **pale¹**

insignificant /ˌɪnsɪgˈnɪfɪkənt/ ADJ insignifiant ◆ **not ~** non négligeable ◆ **statistically ~** statistiquement non significatif

insincere /ˌɪnsɪnˈsɪəʳ/ ADJ *[person]* pas sincère, hypocrite ; *[book, smile, remark]* faux (fausse *f*), hypocrite

insincerely /ˌɪnsɪnˈsɪəlɪ/ ADV *[speak, smile, promise]* sans sincérité, de façon hypocrite

insincerity /ˌɪnsɪnˈserɪtɪ/ N manque *m* de sincérité, hypocrisie *f*

insinuate /ɪnˈsɪnjʊeɪt/ VT 1 *(= hint, suggest)* insinuer ◆ **to ~ that ...** insinuer que ... ◆ **to ~ to sb that ...** insinuer à qn que ... ◆ **what are you insinuating?** qu'est-ce que tu veux dire or insinuer par là ? 2 ◆ **to ~ o.s. into sb's favour** s'insinuer dans les bonnes grâces de qn

insinuating /ɪnˈsɪnjʊeɪtɪŋ/ ADJ insinuant

insinuation /ɪnˌsɪnjʊˈeɪʃən/ N 1 *(= suggestion)* insinuation *f*, allusion *f* 2 *(NonC)* insinuation *f*

insipid /ɪnˈsɪpɪd/ ADJ *[food, taste, entertainment, person]* insipide ; *[colour]* fade

insipidity /ˌɪnsɪˈpɪdɪtɪ/ N *[of food, taste, entertainment, person]* insipidité *f* ; *[of colour]* fadeur *f*

insist /ɪnˈsɪst/ LANGUAGE IN USE 4

VI insister ◆ **if you ~** si vous insistez, si vous y tenez ◆ **I won't ~** je n'insisterai pas ◆ **please don't ~** inutile d'insister ◆ **if he refuses, I will ~** s'il refuse, j'insisterai ◆ **to ~ on doing sth** insister pour faire qch, vouloir absolument faire qch ◆ **I ~ on your coming** j'insiste pour que tu viennes, je tiens absolument à ce que tu viennes ◆ **he ~ed on my waiting for him** il a insisté pour que je l'attende, il voulait absolument que je l'attende ◆ **they ~ed on silence** ils ont exigé le silence ◆ **he ~ed on his innocence** il a clamé son innocence, il protestait de son innocence ◆ **they ~ on the right to defend themselves** ils revendiquent leur droit de se défendre eux-mêmes ◆ **he ~ed on the need for dialogue** il a insisté sur le besoin de dialogue ◆ **to ~ on a point in a discussion** insister sur un point dans une discussion

VT 1 *(= demand)* insister ◆ **I must ~ that you let me help** laissez-moi vous aider, j'insiste ◆ **she ~ed that I should come** elle a insisté pour que je vienne ◆ **I ~ that you should come** j'insiste pour que tu viennes, je tiens absolument à ce que tu viennes

2 *(= affirm)* affirmer, soutenir ◆ **he ~s that he has seen her before** il affirme or soutient

l'avoir déjà vue ◆ **"it's not that difficult", she ~ed** "ce n'est pas si difficile" a-t-elle affirmé *or* soutenu

insistence /ɪn'sɪstəns/ **N** insistance *f* ◆ **his ~ on coming with me** l'insistance qu'il met (*or* a mis *etc*) à vouloir venir avec moi ◆ **their ~ on being involved** *or* **that they should be involved** leur insistance à vouloir être associé ◆ **his ~ on his innocence** ses protestations d'innocence ◆ **his ~ on secrecy made her uneasy** son insistance à exiger le secret la mettait mal à l'aise ◆ **with ~** avec insistance ◆ **I did it on** *or* **at his ~** je l'ai fait parce qu'il a insisté

insistent /ɪn'sɪstənt/ **ADJ** *[person, tone, question, attitude, demands]* insistant ◆ **she was (most) ~ (about it)** elle a (beaucoup) insisté (là-dessus)

insistently /ɪn'sɪstəntlɪ/ **ADV** avec insistance

in situ /ɪn,sɪtjuː/ **ADV** *(frm)* in situ, sur place

insofar /,ɪnsəʊ'fɑː/ **ADV** ◆ **~ as** en ce sens que, dans la mesure où

insole /'ɪn,səʊl/ **N** *(removable)* semelle *f* intérieure ; *(part of shoe)* première *f*

insolence /'ɪnsələns/ **N** *(NonC)* insolence *f* *(to* envers)

insolent /'ɪnsələnt/ **ADJ** insolent *(to or with sb* avec qn)

insolently /'ɪnsələntlɪ/ **ADV** insolemment

insolubility /ɪn,sɒljʊ'bɪlɪtɪ/ **N** insolubilité *f*

insoluble /ɪn'sɒljubl/ **ADJ** insoluble

insolvable /ɪn'sɒlvəbl/ **ADJ** insoluble

insolvency /ɪn'sɒlvənsɪ/ **N** *(gen)* insolvabilité *f* ; *(= bankruptcy)* faillite *f*

insolvent /ɪn'sɒlvənt/ **ADJ** *(gen)* insolvable ; *(= bankrupt)* en faillite, en état de cessation de paiement *(Jur)* ◆ **to become ~** *[trader]* tomber en *or* faire faillite ; *[individual]* tomber en déconfiture ◆ **to declare oneself ~** *[trader]* déposer son bilan ; *[individual]* se déclarer insolvable

insomnia /ɪn'sɒmnɪə/ **N** insomnie *f*

insomniac /ɪn'sɒmnɪæk/ **ADJ, N** insomniaque *mf*

insomuch /,ɪnsəʊ'mʌtʃ/ **ADV** ◆ **~ that** à tel point *or* au point que ◆ **~ as** d'autant que

insouciance /ɪn'suːsɪəns/ **N** *(frm)* insouciance *f*

insouciant /ɪn'suːsɪənt/ **ADJ** *(frm)* insouciant *(about sth* de qch)

insp. abbrev of **inspector**

inspect /ɪn'spekt/ **VT** 1 *(= examine) [+ document, object]* examiner (avec attention *or* de près), inspecter ; *(Brit) [+ ticket]* contrôler ; *(Customs) [+ luggage]* visiter ; *[+ machinery]* inspecter, vérifier ; *(Mil, Pol) [+ weapon sites]* inspecter ; *[+ school, teacher]* inspecter ◆ **right to ~ (sth)** *(Jur)* droit *m* de regard (sur qch) 2 *(Mil) [+ troops] (= check)* inspecter ; *(= review)* passer en revue

inspection /ɪn'spekʃən/ **N** 1 *[of document, object]* examen *m* (attentif) ; *(Brit) [of ticket]* contrôle *m* ; *[of machinery]* inspection *f*, vérification *f* ; *[of school]* (visite *f* d')inspection *f* ◆ **close ~** *(gen)* examen *m* minutieux ; *(for checking purposes)* inspection *f* ◆ **customs ~** visite *f* de douane ◆ **factory ~** inspection *f* d'usine ◆ **to make an ~ of sth** effectuer une inspection *or* un contrôle de qch ◆ **on ~ everything proved normal** une vérification a permis de s'assurer que tout était normal ◆ **on closer ~** en regardant de plus près 2 *(Mil) [of troops] (= check)* inspection *f* ; *(= review)* revue *f*

COMP **inspection pit N** *(for car repairs)* fosse *f* (de réparation)

inspector /ɪn'spektəʳ/ **N** 1 *(gen)* inspecteur *m*, -trice *f* ; *(Brit: on bus, train)* contrôleur *m*, -euse *f* ◆ **tax ~, ~ of taxes** *(Brit)* contrôleur *m* or inspecteur *m* des impôts 2 *(Brit)* (also **police inspector**) inspecteur *m* (de police) ; → **chief** 3 *(Brit Scol:* also **schools inspector, inspector of schools**) *(secondary)* inspecteur *m*, -trice *f* d'académie ; *(primary)* inspecteur *m*, -trice *f* primaire

COMP **inspector general N** (pl **inspectors general**) inspecteur *m* général

inspectorate /ɪn'spektərɪt/ **N** *(esp Brit) (= body of inspectors)* corps *m* des inspecteurs, inspection *f* ; *(= office)* inspection *f*

inspiration /,ɪnspə'reɪʃən/ **N** 1 *(NonC)* inspiration *f* ◆ **to draw one's ~ from sth** s'inspirer de qch 2 ◆ **to be an ~ to sb** *[person, thing]* être une source d'inspiration pour qn ◆ **you've been an ~ to us all** vous avez été notre source d'inspiration à tous ◆ **to be the ~ for sth** servir d'inspiration pour qch ◆ **the ~ behind the reforms was a paper written in 1985** les réformes s'inspiraient d'un article écrit en 1985 3 *(= good idea)* inspiration *f* ◆ **to have a sudden ~** avoir une inspiration subite

inspirational /,ɪnspə'reɪʃənl/ **ADJ** *[teacher, leader]* enthousiasmant, stimulant ; *[book, film]* stimulant, inspirant ; *(Rel)* édifiant

inspire /ɪn'spaɪəʳ/ **VT** *[+ person, work of art, action, decision]* inspirer ◆ **the book was ~d by a real person** le livre s'inspirait d'un personnage réel ◆ **to ~ confidence in sb, to ~ sb with confidence** inspirer confiance à qn ◆ **to ~ courage in sb** insuffler du courage à qn ◆ **to ~ sb with an idea** inspirer une idée à qn ◆ **her beauty ~d him to write the song** inspiré par sa beauté, il a écrit cette chanson ◆ **what ~d you to offer to help?** qu'est-ce qui vous a donné l'idée de proposer votre aide ? ◆ **these herbs will ~ you to try out all sorts of exotic-flavoured dishes!** ces herbes vous donneront envie d'essayer toutes sortes de plats aux saveurs exotiques ! ◆ **what ~d you to change your name?** qu'est-ce qui vous a donné l'idée de changer de nom ? ◆ **a political murder ~d by nationalist conflicts** un assassinat politique motivé par les conflits nationalistes

inspired /ɪn'spaɪəd/ **ADJ** 1 *[person, performance, idea, choice]* inspiré ◆ **that was an ~ guess** *or* **a piece of ~ guesswork!** bien deviné ! 2 *(= motivated)* **politically/divinely/classically ~** d'inspiration politique/divine/classique

inspiring /ɪn'spaɪərɪŋ/ **ADJ** 1 *(= edifying, impressive) [story, film, example]* édifiant, inspirant ◆ **the ~ tale of her fight against cancer** l'histoire édifiante de sa lutte contre le cancer ◆ **it wasn't particularly ~** ce n'était pas terrible* 2 *(= stimulating) [teacher, leader]* enthousiasmant, stimulant ; *[book, film]* stimulant, inspirant

inst. **ADV** *(Comm)* (abbrev of **instant**) courant ◆ **the 16th ~** le 16 courant

instability /,ɪnstə'bɪlɪtɪ/ **N** instabilité *f*

instal(l) /ɪn'stɔːl/ **VT** *(gen, Rel)* installer ◆ **to ~(l) o.s. in** s'installer dans

installation /,ɪnstə'leɪʃən/ **N** *(all senses)* installation *f*

instalment, installment (US) /ɪn'stɔːlmənt/ **N** 1 *(= payment)* versement *m* (partiel *or* échelonné) ; *(= down payment)* acompte *m* ; *[of loan, investment, credit]* tranche *f*, versement *m* ◆ **to pay an ~** faire un versement (partiel) ◆ **to pay in** *or* **by ~s** payer en plusieurs versements *or* par traites échelonnées ◆ **~ on account** acompte *m* provisionnel ◆ **annual ~** versement *m* annuel, annuité *f* ◆ **monthly ~** versement *m* mensuel, mensualité *f*

2 *[of story, serial]* épisode *m* ; *[of book]* fascicule *m*, livraison *f* ◆ **this is the first ~ of a six-part serial** *(TV etc)* voici le premier épisode d'un feuilleton qui en comportera six ◆ **this story will appear in ~s over the next eight weeks** ce récit paraîtra par épisodes pendant les huit semaines à venir ◆ **to publish a work in ~s** publier un ouvrage par fascicules

COMP **installment plan N** *(US)* contrat *m* de vente à crédit *or* à tempérament ◆ **to buy on the installment plan** acheter à crédit

instance /'ɪnstəns/ LANGUAGE IN USE 26.2 **N** 1 *(= example)* exemple *m*, cas *m* ; *(= occasion)* circonstance *f*, occasion *f* ◆ **for ~** par exemple ◆ **in the present ~** dans le cas présent, dans cette circonstance ◆ **in many ~s** dans bien des cas ◆ **in the first ~** en premier lieu ◆ **as an ~ of** comme exemple de ◆ **let's take an actual ~** prenons un exemple *or* un cas concret ◆ **this is an ~ of what I was talking about** c'est un exemple de ce dont je parlais ◆ **a serious ~ of corruption** un cas sérieux de corruption 2 *(Jur)* **at the ~ of** sur *or* à la demande de, sur l'instance de **VT** donner en exemple, citer en exemple, faire état de *(more frm)*

instant /'ɪnstənt/ **ADJ** 1 *[obedience, relief, response, effect]* immédiat, instantané ; *[need]* urgent, pressant ◆ **this calls for ~ action** ceci nécessite des mesures immédiates ◆ **~ camera/photography** appareil *m* (photo)/photographie *f* à développement instantané

2 *(Culin) [coffee]* soluble ; *[potatoes]* déshydraté ; *[food]* à préparation rapide ◆ **~ soup** potage *m* (instantané) en poudre

3 *(Comm)* courant ◆ **your letter of the 10th ~** votre lettre du 10 courant

N 1 *(= moment)* instant *m*, moment *m* ◆ **come here this ~** viens ici tout de suite *or* à l'instant ◆ **for an ~** pendant un instant, l'espace d'un instant ◆ **on the ~** tout de suite, à l'instant ◆ **the next ~** l'instant d'après ◆ **I did it in an ~** je l'ai fait en un instant ◆ **I'll be ready in an ~** je serai prêt dans un instant ◆ **in** *or* **at the same ~** au même moment ◆ **he left the ~ he heard the news** il est parti dès qu'il *or* aussitôt qu'il a appris la nouvelle

2 *(lottery = scratchcard) jeu instantané de grattage,* ≃ Tac o Tac ® *m*

COMP **instant messaging N** messagerie *f* instantanée ◆ **instant messaging service/system** service/système de messagerie instantanée

instant replay N *(TV) répétition immédiate d'une séquence ; (= slow-motion)* ralenti *m*

instantaneous /,ɪnstən'teɪnɪəs/ **ADJ** *[event, response]* instantané ◆ **I took an ~ dislike to him** je l'ai tout de suite *or* immédiatement détesté

instantaneously /,ɪnstən'teɪnɪəslɪ/ **ADV** instantanément

instantly /'ɪnstəntlɪ/ **ADV** *[die, be killed]* sur le coup, instantanément ; *[know, recognize]* immédiatement ; *[identifiable, available]* immédiatement ◆ **~ likeable** *[person]* sympathique au premier abord ◆ **the giant panda is ~ recognizable** *or* **identifiable by its black and white coat** le panda géant est immédiatement reconnaissable à son pelage noir et blanc ◆ **~ forgettable** *(= mediocre)* sans aucun intérêt

instead /ɪn'sted/ **ADV** plutôt, au contraire ◆ **if you don't like orange juice, have some mineral water ~** si vous n'aimez pas le jus d'orange, prenez plutôt de l'eau minérale ◆ **forget about dieting and eat normally ~** oubliez votre régime et mangez normalement ◆ **his brother came ~ (of him)** son frère est venu à sa place ◆ **I didn't go to the office, I went to the cinema ~** je ne suis pas allé au bureau, au lieu de cela je suis allé au cinéma

◆ **instead of** ◆ **~ of going to school** au lieu d'aller à l'école, plutôt que d'aller à l'école ◆ **we decided to have dinner at 8 o'clock ~ of 7** nous avons décidé de dîner à 20 heures au lieu de 19 heures ◆ **~ of Louise** à la place de Louise ◆ **this is ~ of a birthday present** c'est à la place d'un cadeau d'anniversaire

instep /'ɪnstep/ **N** 1 *(Anat)* cou-de-pied *m* ◆ **to have a high ~** avoir le pied cambré 2 *[of shoe]* cambrure *f*

instigate /'ɪnstɪgeɪt/ **VT** être l'instigateur de

instigation /ˌɪnstɪˈgeɪʃən/ N instigation *f* ◆ **at sb's ~** à l'instigation de qn

instigator /ˈɪnstɪgeɪtəʳ/ N instigateur *m*, -trice *f* ; *[of riot, plot]* auteur *m*

instil, instill (US) /ɪnˈstɪl/ VT *[+ courage, optimism]* insuffler (*into sb* à qn) ; *[+ knowledge, principles]* inculquer (*into sb* à qn) ; *[+ idea, fact]* faire comprendre (*into sb* à qn) ; *[+ fear]* faire naître (*into sb* chez qn) ◆ **to ~ into sb that ...** faire pénétrer dans l'esprit de qn que ...

instinct /ˈɪnstɪŋkt/ N instinct *m* ◆ **by** *or* **from ~** d'instinct ◆ **to have an ~ for business** *or* **a good business ~** avoir le sens des affaires ADJ /ɪnˈstɪŋkt/ (*liter*) ◆ **~ with** qui exhale *or* respire (*liter*), plein de

instinctive /ɪnˈstɪŋktɪv/ ADJ instinctif

instinctively /ɪnˈstɪŋktɪvlɪ/ ADV instinctivement

instinctual /ɪnˈstɪŋktʃʊəl/ ADJ ⇒ **instinctive**

institute /ˈɪnstɪtjuːt/ VT 1 (= *establish*) *[+ system, rules]* instituer, établir ; (= *found*) *[+ society]* fonder, constituer ◆ **newly ~d** *[post]* récemment créé, de création récente ; *[organization]* de fondation récente 2 (= *set in motion*) *[+ inquiry]* ouvrir ; *[+ action]* entreprendre (*against sb* contre qn) ◆ **to ~ proceedings against sb** intenter un procès contre qn 3 (*Rel*) investir N 1 (*gen*) institut *m* ◆ **Institute of Education** Institut *m* de formation des maîtres ◆ **Institute of Linguistics** *etc* Institut *m* de linguistique *etc* 2 (*US* = *course*) stage *m* (d'études)

institution /ˌɪnstɪˈtjuːʃən/ N 1 (= *organization*) institution *f* ◆ **a religious/political ~** une institution religieuse/politique ◆ **financial/credit/educational ~** établissement *m* financier/de crédit/d'enseignement ◆ **an academic ~** un établissement d'enseignement supérieur

2 (= *feature, custom*) institution *f* ◆ **democratic ~s, the ~s of democracy** les institutions *fpl* démocratiques ◆ **the ~ of marriage** l'institution *f* du mariage ◆ **tea is a great British ~** le thé est une grande institution britannique ◆ **he's been with the firm so long that he's now an ~** (*hum*) il fait partie de l'entreprise depuis si longtemps qu'il en est devenu une véritable institution

3 (= *hospital, mental home etc*) institution *f* ◆ **he has been in ~s all his life** il a passé toute sa vie en institution

4 (*NonC*) *[of system, practice]* institution *f* ; *[of proceedings, inquiry]* ouverture *mf*

5 (*Rel*) *[of priest]* investiture *f*

institutional /ˌɪnstɪˈtjuːʃənl/ ADJ 1 (= *of institutions*) *[reform, structure]* institutionnel ◆ **~ care** soins *mpl* en institution 2 (*Fin, Comm* = *of companies*) *[investors, funds, buying]* institutionnel 3 (*pej* = *reminiscent of institutions*) *[food]* d'internat ; *[atmosphere]* réglementé

institutionalization /ˈɪnstɪˌtjuːʃnəlaɪˈzeɪʃən/ N *[of person]* placement *m* dans une institution ; *[of custom, procedure]* institutionnalisation *f*

institutionalize /ˌɪnstɪˈtjuːʃnəlaɪz/ VT 1 *[+ person]* placer dans une institution 2 *[+ procedure, custom, event etc]* institutionnaliser, donner un caractère officiel à

institutionalized /ˌɪnstɪˈtjuːʃnəlaɪzd/ ADJ 1 (= *living in an institution*) ◆ **~ people** personnes *fpl* vivant en institution 2 (= *dependent*) dépendant ◆ **after all those years in prison, he's become totally ~** après toutes ces années en prison, il est désormais totalement dépendant *or* il a désappris à être autonome 3 (= *ingrained*) *[racism etc]* institutionnalisé ◆ **to become ~** s'institutionnaliser, devenir une institution ◆ **~ religion** (*NonC*) la religion institutionnalisée

instruct /ɪnˈstrʌkt/ VT 1 (= *teach*) *[+ person]* instruire ◆ **to ~ sb in sth** instruire qn en qch, enseigner *or* apprendre qch à qn ◆ **to ~ sb in how to do sth** enseigner *or* apprendre à qn comment (il faut) faire qch 2 (= *order, direct*) *[+ person]* donner des instructions *or* des ordres à ◆ **to ~ sb to do** charger qn de faire, donner pour instructions à qn de faire ◆ **I am ~ed to inform you that ...** (*frm*) je suis chargé de *or* j'ai mission de vous informer que ... 3 (*Brit Jur*) ◆ **to ~ a solicitor** donner ses instructions à un notaire ◆ **to ~ counsel** constituer avocat ◆ **to ~ the jury** *[judge]* donner des instructions au jury (*to do sth* pour qu'il fasse qch)

instruction /ɪnˈstrʌkʃən/ N 1 (*NonC* = *teaching*) instruction *f*, enseignement *m* ◆ **to give ~ to sb (in sth)** instruire qn (en qch) ◆ **driving ~** leçons *fpl* de conduite

2 (*gen pl*) ◆ **~s** instructions *fpl* ; (*Mil*) consigne *f* ; (*Pharm, Tech*) indications *fpl* ◆ **he gave me precise ~s on what to do if ...** il m'a donné des consignes précises *or* des instructions précises sur la conduite à tenir au cas où ... ◆ **I gave ~s for him to be brought to me** j'ai donné des instructions pour qu'on *or* j'ai donné ordre qu'on me l'amène *subj* ◆ **he gave me ~s not to leave until ...** il m'a donné ordre de ne pas partir avant ... ◆ **he was given strict ~s to avoid alcohol** on lui a rigoureusement interdit de boire de l'alcool ◆ **to act according to ~s** (*gen*) se conformer aux instructions ; (*Mil*) se conformer à la consigne ◆ **"instructions for use"** "mode d'emploi" ◆ **the ~s are on the back of the box** le mode d'emploi est (indiqué) au dos de la boîte

COMP **instruction book** N mode *m* d'emploi, notice *f* d'utilisation

instruction manual N manuel *m* d'utilisation

instructive /ɪnˈstrʌktɪv/ ADJ instructif

instructor /ɪnˈstrʌktəʳ/ N 1 (*Sport*) moniteur *m*, -trice *f*, professeur *m* ; (*Mil*) instructeur *m* ; → **driving** 2 (*US Univ*) ≃ assistant *m*

instructress /ɪnˈstrʌktrɪs/ N (*Sport*) monitrice *f*, professeur *m*

instrument /ˈɪnstrʊmənt/ N (*gen*) instrument *m* ; (*Jur*) instrument *m*, acte *m* juridique ; (*Fin*) titre *m*, effet *m* ◆ **to fly by** *or* **on ~s** naviguer aux instruments ◆ **~ of government** instrument *m* du gouvernement ; → **blunt, wind¹** VT /ˌɪnstrʊˈment/ (*Mus*) orchestrer ; (*Jur*) instrumenter

COMP *[flying, landing]* aux instruments (de bord)

instrument board, instrument panel N (*in vehicle plane*) tableau *m* de bord

instrumental /ˌɪnstrʊˈmentl/ ADJ 1 *[role]* déterminant ◆ **to be ~ in sth** jouer un rôle-clé dans qch ◆ **he was ~ in setting up/launching the scheme** il a joué un rôle-clé dans la mise en place/le lancement du projet 2 *[music, composition, arrangement, tuition, ensemble]* instrumental ; *[recording, album]* de musique instrumentale ; *[composer]* d'œuvres instrumentales ◆ **~ performer** instrumentiste *mf*

instrumentalist /ˌɪnstrʊˈmentəlɪst/ N (*Mus*) instrumentiste *mf*

instrumentation /ˌɪnstrʊmenˈteɪʃən/ N (*Mus, Tech*) instrumentation *f*

insubordinate /ˌɪnsəˈbɔːdənɪt/ ADJ insubordonné, indiscipliné

insubordination /ˈɪnsəˌbɔːdɪˈneɪʃən/ N insubordination *f*, indiscipline *f*, désobéissance *f*

insubstantial /ˌɪnsəbˈstænʃəl/ ADJ 1 (= *small*) *[sum, amount]* peu important ; *[meal, work]* peu substantiel ; (= *weak*) *[argument]* sans substance ; *[evidence]* sans fondement ; *[structure]* peu solide 2 (*liter* = *unreal*) *[vision, illusion]* chimérique

insufferable /ɪnˈsʌfərəbl/ ADJ (*frm*) insupportable

insufferably /ɪnˈsʌfərəblɪ/ ADV (*frm*) insupportablement ◆ **it was ~ hot** il faisait une chaleur insupportable

insufficiency /ˌɪnsəˈfɪʃənsɪ/ N insuffisance *f*

insufficient /ˌɪnsəˈfɪʃənt/ ADJ insuffisant

insufficiently /ˌɪnsəˈfɪʃəntlɪ/ ADV insuffisamment

insular /ˈɪnsjələʳ/ ADJ 1 (*pej* = *parochial*) *[person, attitude, views, outlook]* borné (*pej*) ; *[community, existence]* coupé du monde extérieur 2 (*SPEC* = *relating to an island*) insulaire

insularity /ˌɪnsjʊˈlærɪtɪ/ N insularité *f* ; (*fig pej*) *[of person]* étroitesse *f* d'esprit ; *[of community, existence]* fermeture *f* au monde extérieur ; *[of outlook, views]* étroitesse *f*

insulate /ˈɪnsjʊleɪt/ VT 1 (*Elec*) isoler ; (*against cold, heat*) *[+ room, roof]* isoler ; *[+ water tank]* calorifuger ; (*against sound*) *[+ room, wall]* insonoriser ◆ **~d handle** manche *m* isolant ◆ **~d pliers** pince *f* isolante ◆ **insulating material** isolant *m* 2 (*fig*) *[+ person]* (= *separate*) séparer (*from de*) ; (= *protect*) protéger (*against de*) COMP **insulating tape** N (ruban *m*) isolant *m* ; (= *adhesive*) chatterton *m*

insulation /ˌɪnsjʊˈleɪʃən/ N 1 (*NonC*) (*Elec*) isolation *f* ; *[of house, room]* (*against cold*) isolation *f* (calorifuge) ; (*against sound*) insonorisation *f* 2 (*fig*) **they lived in happy ~ from brutal facts** ils vivaient heureux à l'abri de la réalité brutale 3 (*NonC* = *material*) isolant *m*

insulator /ˈɪnsjʊleɪtəʳ/ N (*Elec*) (= *device*) isolateur *m* ; (= *material*) isolant *m*

insulin /ˈɪnsjʊlɪn/ N insuline *f*

COMP *[injection]* d'insuline

insulin shock N (*Med*) choc *m* insulinique

insulin treatment N insulinothérapie *f*, traitement *m* insulinique *or* à l'insuline

insult /ɪnˈsʌlt/ VT (*with words, gestures*) insulter, injurier ; (= *offend*) faire (un) affront à, insulter ◆ **she felt ~ed by his indifference** elle s'est sentie insultée par son indifférence N /ˈɪnsʌlt/ (= *remark*) insulte *f*, injure *f* ; (= *action, affront*) affront *m*, insulte *f* ◆ **to hurl ~s at sb** injurier qn, lancer des insultes à qn ◆ **the book is an ~ to the reader's intelligence** le livre est une insulte à *or* fait affront à l'intelligence du lecteur ◆ **these demands are an ~ to the profession** ces revendications sont un affront à la profession ◆ **an ~ to sb's memory** une insulte à la mémoire de qn ◆ **it was seen as an ~ to Islam** cela a été perçu comme un affront à l'islam ; → **add**

insulting /ɪnˈsʌltɪŋ/ ADJ insultant, injurieux ◆ **to be ~ to sb** *[remarks, comments etc]* être un affront à qn

insultingly /ɪnˈsʌltɪŋlɪ/ ADV *[behave, talk]* de façon insultante ◆ **~ dismissive** dédaigneux au point d'être insultant ◆ **~ sexist** d'un sexisme insultant

insuperable /ɪnˈsuːpərəbl/ ADJ insurmontable

insuperably /ɪnˈsuːpərəblɪ/ ADV ◆ **~ difficult** d'une difficulté insurmontable

insupportable † /ˌɪnsəˈpɔːtəbl/ ADJ insupportable

insurable /ɪnˈʃʊərəbl/ ADJ assurable

insurance /ɪnˈʃʊərəns/ N (*gen*) assurance *f* (*on or for sth* pour qch ; *against* contre) ; (= *policy*) police *f or* contrat *m* d'assurances (*on or for sth* pour qch ; *against sth* contre qch) ; (*fig*) garantie *f* ◆ **he pays £300 a year in ~** il paie 300 livres (de primes) d'assurance par an ◆ **~ on a building** assurance *f* sur le capital immobilier ◆ **to take out ~** contracter une assurance ◆ **to take out ~ against** s'assurer contre, se faire assurer contre ◆ **what does your ~ cover?** que couvre votre police *or* contrat d'assurance ? ◆ **we must extend our ~** nous devons augmenter le montant pour lequel nous sommes assurés

◆ **the ~ runs out on 5 July** l'assurance arrive à échéance le 5 juillet ◆ **to do sth as an ~ against** *(fig)* faire qch comme garantie contre, faire qch pour se prémunir contre ; → **fire, life**

COMP **insurance adjuster** N *(US)* expert *m* en sinistres
insurance agent N agent *m* d'assurances
insurance broker N courtier *m* d'assurances
insurance certificate N attestation *f* d'assurance
insurance claim N (déclaration *f* de) sinistre *m*
insurance company N compagnie *f or* société *f* d'assurances
insurance policy N police *f* d'assurance, assurances * *fpl*
insurance premium N prime *f* (d'assurance)
insurance scheme N régime *m* d'assurances
insurance stamp N *(Brit Admin)* vignette *f or* timbre *m* de contribution à la sécurité sociale
insurance underwriter N *(gen)* assureur *m* ; *(= underwriting company)* réassureur *m*

insurant /ɪnˈʃʊərənt/ N *(SPEC)* assuré(e) *m(f)*, souscripteur *m*, -trice *f*

insure /ɪnˈʃʊəʳ/ VT 1 *[+ car, house]* (faire) assurer ◆ **he ~d his guitar for $1000** il a assuré sa guitare pour 1 000 dollars ◆ **to ~ o.s.** *or* **one's life** s'assurer *or* se faire assurer sur la vie ◆ **I am ~d against fire** je suis assuré contre l'incendie ◆ **we ~d (ourselves) against possible disappointment** *(fig)* nous avons paré aux déceptions possibles ◆ **in order to ~ against any delay ...** pour nous *(or* les *etc)* garantir contre tout retard ...
2 *[+ power, success]* assurer, garantir ◆ **this will ~ that you will be notified when ...** grâce à ceci vous êtes assuré d'être avisé quand ... ◆ **in order to ~ that terrorists do not enter the country** afin de s'assurer que les terroristes n'entrent pas dans le pays ◆ **they want to ~ that their children will be educated properly** ils veulent s'assurer *or* être sûrs que leurs enfants recevront une éducation correcte

insured /ɪnˈʃʊəd/ ADJ, N assuré(e) *m(f)*

insurer /ɪnˈʃʊərəʳ/ N assureur *m*

insurgence /ɪnˈsɜːdʒəns/, **insurgency** /ɪnˈsɜːdʒənsɪ/ N insurrection *f*

insurgent /ɪnˈsɜːdʒənt/ ADJ, N insurgé(e) *m(f)*

insurmountable /ˌɪnsəˈmaʊntəbl/ ADJ insurmontable

insurrection /ˌɪnsəˈrekʃən/ N 1 *(NonC)* insurrection *f* ◆ **to rise in ~** se soulever, s'insurger 2 *(= uprising)* insurrection *f*, soulèvement *m*

insurrectionary /ˌɪnsəˈrekʃnərɪ/ ADJ insurrectionnel

insurrectionist /ˌɪnsəˈrekʃənɪst/ N insurgé(e) *m(f)*

int. ADJ, N (abbrev of **international**) international

intact /ɪnˈtækt/ ADJ intact ◆ **to remain** *or* **survive ~** rester intact

intake /ˈɪnteɪk/ N 1 *(NonC: Tech) [of water]* prise *f*, adduction *f* ; *[of gas, steam]* adduction *f*, admission *f* ; → **air** 2 *(Scol, Univ)* admission(s) *f(pl)*, (nombre *m* des) inscriptions *fpl* ; *(Mil)* contingent *m*, recrues *fpl* ◆ **the latest ~ of young graduates into our company** le dernier contingent de jeunes diplômés recrutés dans notre société ◆ **the US's annual ~ of immigrants** le contingent annuel d'immigrants arrivant aux États-Unis 3 *[of protein, liquid, alcohol etc]* consommation *f* ◆ **food ~** ration *f* alimentaire 4 ◆ **she heard his ~ of breath** elle l'a entendu retenir sa respiration

COMP **intake valve** N soupape *f* d'admission

intangible /ɪnˈtændʒəbl/ ADJ *[quality, presence]* intangible, impalpable N impondérable *m*

COMP **intangible assets** NPL *(Jur)* immobilisations *fpl* incorporelles
intangible property N *(Jur)* biens *mpl* incorporels

integer /ˈɪntɪdʒəʳ/ N (nombre *m*) entier *m*

integral /ˈɪntɪgrəl/ ADJ 1 *[part]* intégrant, constituant ◆ **to be an ~ part of sth, to be ~ to sth** faire partie intégrante de qch 2 *(= whole)* intégral, complet (-ète *f*), entier ◆ **~ payment** paiement *m* intégral 3 *(Math)* intégral ◆ **~ calculus** calcul *m* intégral N *(Math, fig)* intégrale *f*

integrate /ˈɪntɪgreɪt/ VT 1 *(= combine into a whole) [+ people, objects, ideas]* intégrer, incorporer *(in, into* dans) ◆ **talks will now begin about integrating the activities of both companies** l'intégration des activités des deux sociétés va maintenant faire l'objet de négociations ◆ **Ann wanted the conservatory to ~ with the kitchen** Ann voulait qu'il y ait une continuité entre le jardin d'hiver et la cuisine
2 *(= complete by adding parts)* compléter ◆ **an ~d personality** *(Psych)* une personnalité bien intégrée
3 *(= desegregate) [+ races, religions, ethnic groups etc]* intégrer ◆ **to ~ Catholic and non-Catholic schools** intégrer les écoles catholiques et non catholiques ◆ **to ~ a school** *etc* imposer la déségrégation dans un établissement scolaire *etc* ◆ **~d school** établissement *m* scolaire où se pratique l'intégration
4 *(Math)* intégrer
VI 1 *[school, neighbourhood etc]* pratiquer l'intégration raciale
2 *[person, religious or ethnic group etc]* s'intégrer *(into* dans)

integrated /ˈɪntɪgreɪtɪd/ ADJ intégré

COMP **integrated accounting package** N logiciel *m* intégré de comptabilité
integrated circuit N *(Elec)* circuit *m* intégré
integrated course N *(Brit Educ)* cours *m* de formation professionnelle *(pour apprentis)*
integrated day N *(Brit Scol)* journée *f* sans emploi du temps structuré
Integrated Services Digital Network N Réseau *m* numérique à intégration de services
integrated studies NPL *(Brit Scol)* études *fpl* générales *(où les matières ne sont pas différenciées)*

integration /ˌɪntɪˈgreɪʃən/ N *(also Math, Psych)* intégration *f (into* dans) ◆ **racial/social/European ~** intégration *f* raciale/sociale/européenne

integrity /ɪnˈtegrɪtɪ/ N 1 *(= honesty)* intégrité *f*, probité *f* ◆ **a man of ~** un homme intègre 2 *(= totality)* intégrité *f*, totalité *f* ◆ **in its ~** dans son intégrité, dans sa totalité ◆ **territorial ~** l'intégrité *f* du territoire ◆ **the ~ of the nation** l'intégrité *f* de la nation

integument /ɪnˈtegjʊmənt/ N tégument *m*

intellect /ˈɪntɪlekt/ N 1 *(NonC) (= reasoning power)* intellect *m*, intelligence *f* ; *(= cleverness)* intelligence *f*, esprit *m* ◆ **a man of (great) ~** un homme d'une grande intelligence 2 *[of person]* intelligence *f*, esprit *m*

intellectual /ˌɪntɪˈlektjʊəl/ ADJ *(gen)* intellectuel ; *[group, family]* d'intellectuels ◆ **~ property** propriété *f* intellectuelle N intellectuel(le) *m(f)*

intellectualize /ˌɪntɪˈlektjʊəlaɪz/ VT intellectualiser VI ◆ **you always have to ~** il faut toujours que tu intellectualises tout

intellectually /ˌɪntɪˈlektjʊəlɪ/ ADV intellectuellement, sur le plan intellectuel ◆ **~ satisfying/honest** *etc* intellectuellement satisfaisant/honnête *etc*

intelligence /ɪnˈtelɪdʒəns/ N 1 *(NonC)* intelligence *f* ◆ **a man of little ~** un homme peu intelligent *or* de peu d'intelligence ◆ **his book shows ~** son livre est intelligent
2 *(= information)* renseignement(s) *m(pl)*, information(s) *f(pl)* ◆ **latest ~** *(Press)* informations *fpl* de dernière minute
3 ◆ **Military/Naval Intelligence** service *m* de renseignements de l'armée de Terre/de la Marine ◆ **he was in Intelligence during the war** il était dans les services de renseignements pendant la guerre

COMP **intelligence agent** N agent *m* de renseignements, agent *m* secret
Intelligence Corps N *(Brit Mil) service de renseignements et de sécurité militaires*
Intelligence officer N *(Brit Pol)* officier *m* de renseignements
intelligence quotient N quotient *m* intellectuel
Intelligence Service N *(Brit Pol)* services *mpl* secrets *or* de renseignements
intelligence test N test *m* d'intelligence
intelligence work N ◆ **to do ~ work** être dans *or* travailler dans les services de renseignements

intelligent /ɪnˈtelɪdʒənt/ ADJ *(gen)* intelligent ◆ **~ terminal** *(Comput)* terminal *m* intelligent ◆ **the search for ~ life on other planets** la recherche de formes de vie intelligente sur d'autres planètes

intelligently /ɪnˈtelɪdʒəntlɪ/ ADV intelligemment

intelligentsia /ɪnˌtelɪˈdʒentsɪə/ N *(collective sg)* ◆ **the ~** l'intelligentsia *f*, l'élite *f* intellectuelle

intelligibility /ɪnˌtelɪdʒəˈbɪlɪtɪ/ N intelligibilité *f*

intelligible /ɪnˈtelɪdʒəbl/ ADJ intelligible

intelligibly /ɪnˈtelɪdʒəblɪ/ ADV intelligiblement

intemperance /ɪnˈtempərəns/ N *(= lack of self-restraint)* intempérance *f* ; *(= lack of moderation)* manque *m* de modération

intemperate /ɪnˈtempərɪt/ ADJ *(frm) [attitude, comment]* immodéré ; *[language]* sans retenue ; *[person]* intempérant † ; *[haste, zeal]* excessif

intend /ɪnˈtend/ LANGUAGE IN USE 8 VT avoir l'intention ; *[+ gift etc]* destiner *(for* à) ◆ **to ~ to do sth, to ~ doing sth** avoir l'intention de faire qch ◆ **I ~ to go and see him** j'ai l'intention d'aller le voir ◆ **I don't ~ to tell him about it** je n'ai pas l'intention de lui en parler ◆ **I didn't ~ coming to Germany to work ...** je n'avais pas l'intention *or* je n'avais pas prévu de venir en Allemagne pour travailler ... ◆ **I'm sure he didn't ~ that we should hear him** je suis sûr qu'il ne pensait pas que nous allions l'entendre ◆ **his response seemed patronizing, though he hadn't ~ed it that way** le ton de sa réponse semblait condescendant, même si ça n'était pas son intention ◆ **I fully ~ to punish him** j'ai la ferme intention de le punir ◆ **he ~s to be a doctor** il a l'intention de devenir médecin, il se destine à la médecine ◆ **it was ~ed that he should become an accountant** il était prévu qu'il devienne comptable ◆ **this scheme is ~ed to help the poor** ce projet est destiné à venir en aide aux indigents ◆ **~ed for** destiné à ◆ **the money was ~ed for British families** l'argent était destiné aux familles britanniques ◆ **hospital facilities which were ~ed for AIDS patients** des infrastructures hospitalières qui étaient destinées aux malades du sida ◆ **the building was originally ~ed as a sports complex** le bâtiment devait initialement être un complexe sportif ◆ **I ~ed it as a compliment** (dans mon esprit) cela voulait être un compliment ◆ **he ~ed no harm** il l'a fait sans mauvaise intention ◆ **to ~ marriage** avoir des intentions de mariage ◆ **did you ~ that?** est-ce que vous avez fait cela exprès ? ; see also **intended**

intended /ɪnˈtendɪd/ ADJ 1 *(= desired, planned) [target]* visé ; *[effect]* voulu ◆ **the ~ victim (of the attack)** la victime visée (par l'attentat) ◆ **he stayed only ten days of his ~ six-month**

visit il n'est resté que dix jours sur les six mois de visite qu'il avait prévus ② *(= deliberate) [insult etc]* intentionnel, fait intentionnellement **N** † ◆ **his ~** sa promise †, sa future *(hum)* ◆ **her ~** son promis †, son futur *(hum)*

intense /ɪn'tens/ **ADJ** ① *[heat, cold, pain, light, colour, activity, fighting, speculation]* intense ; *[fear, anger, hatred]* violent ; *[interest, enthusiasm, competition]* très vif ② *(= passionate) [person]* sérieux ; *[relationship]* passionné ; *[gaze, expression]* d'une grande intensité

intensely /ɪn'tenslɪ/ **ADV** ① *(= very) [hot, cold, unpleasant, moving]* extrêmement ; *[moved, irritated]* vivement ② *[concentrate, look at]* intensément ; *[hate]* de tout son être ◆ **I dislike her ~** elle me déplaît profondément

intensification /ɪn,tensɪfɪ'keɪʃən/ **N** *[of heat, light, pain, activity, fighting]* intensification *f* ; *[of production]* accélération *f*, intensification *f*

intensifier /ɪn'tensɪfaɪəʳ/ **N** *(Gram)* intensif *m*

intensify /ɪn'tensɪfaɪ/ **VT** intensifier ◆ **to ~ (one's) efforts to do sth** intensifier ses efforts pour faire qch **VI** *[fighting, competition, speculation]* s'intensifier ; *[heat, cold, pain, fear, anger, hatred, light, colour]* augmenter

intensity /ɪn'tensɪtɪ/ **N** *[of anger, hatred, love]* intensité *f*, force *f* ; *[of cold, heat]* intensité *f* ; *[of current, light, sound]* intensité *f*, puissance *f* ; *[of tone]* véhémence *f* ◆ **her ~ disturbs me** son côté sérieux me met mal à l'aise ◆ **capital ~** intensité *f* capitalistique

intensive /ɪn'tensɪv/ **ADJ** *(gen, Ling, Agr)* intensif ◆ **an ~ course in French** un cours accéléré *or* intensif de français

COMP **intensive care** **N** ◆ **to be in ~ care** être en réanimation ◆ **to need ~ care** demander des soins intensifs

intensive care unit **N** *(Med)* service *m* de réanimation, unité *f* de soins intensifs

intensive farming **N** agriculture *f* intensive

-intensive /ɪn'tensɪv/ **ADJ** *(in compounds)* à forte intensité de ◆ **capital-intensive** à forte intensité de capital ; → **energy, labour**

intensively /ɪn'tensɪvlɪ/ **ADV** *[work, campaign, study, farm]* intensivement ◆ **~ reared** *[meat]* provenant d'un élevage intensif

intent /ɪn'tent/ **N** intention *f* ◆ **it was not my ~ to do business with him** il n'était pas dans mes intentions de traiter avec lui, je n'avais pas l'intention de traiter avec lui ◆ **to all ~s and purposes** pratiquement ◆ **with good ~** dans une bonne intention ◆ **to do sth with ~** faire qch de propos délibéré ◆ **with criminal ~** *(Jur)* dans un but délictueux ◆ **with ~ to do sth** dans l'intention *or* le but de faire qch ◆ **he denied possessing a firearm with ~ to endanger life** *(Jur)* il a nié avoir détenu une arme à feu dans le but d'intenter à la vie de quelqu'un ◆ **he signed a letter of ~ to sell his assets** il a signé une lettre d'intention concernant la vente de ses biens ; → **loiter**

ADJ ① *(= absorbed) [face, look, expression]* attentif ◆ **~ on his work/on a jigsaw puzzle** absorbé par son travail/par un puzzle ◆ **he was ~ on what she was saying** il écoutait attentivement ce qu'elle disait

② *(= determined)* ◆ **to be ~ on doing sth** être résolu à faire qch ◆ **~ on revenge** résolu à se venger ◆ **they were ~ on his downfall** ils étaient résolus à provoquer sa perte ◆ **he was so ~ on seeing her that ...** il voulait tellement la voir que ...

intention /ɪn'tenʃən/ LANGUAGE IN USE 8 **N** intention *f* ◆ **it is my ~ to retire** j'ai l'intention de prendre ma retraite ◆ **to have no ~ of doing sth** n'avoir aucune intention de faire qch ◆ **he has every ~ of doing this** il a bien l'intention de le faire ◆ **I haven't the least** *or* **slightest ~ of staying** je n'ai pas la moindre intention de rester ici, il n'est nullement dans mes intentions de rester ici ◆ **with the ~ of doing sth** dans l'intention de *or* dans le but de faire qch ◆ **with this ~** à cette intention, à cette fin ◆ **with good ~s** avec de bonnes intentions ◆ **with the best of ~s** avec les meilleures intentions (du monde) ◆ **what are your ~s?** quelles sont vos intentions ?, que comptez-vous faire ? ◆ **I don't know what his ~s were when he did it** je ne sais pas quelles étaient ses intentions quand il l'a fait ◆ **his ~s are honourable** il a des intentions honorables

intentional /ɪn'tenʃənl/ **ADJ** intentionnel ◆ **how can I blame him? it wasn't ~** comment pourrais-je lui en vouloir ? il ne l'a pas fait exprès *or* ce n'était pas intentionnel

intentionally /ɪn'tenʃnəlɪ/ **ADV** *[mislead, violate, discriminate etc]* intentionnellement ◆ **the authorities consider him ~ homeless** l'administration considère qu'il a délibérément quitté son domicile ◆ **~ vague/misleading** délibérément vague/trompeur ◆ **I didn't hurt you ~** je ne voulais pas te faire du mal

intently /ɪn'tentlɪ/ **ADV** *[listen, look, watch, stare]* intensément ◆ **they were talking ~ about work** ils parlaient travail, l'air absorbé

intentness /ɪn'tentnɪs/ **N** intensité *f* ◆ **~ of purpose** résolution *f*

inter /ɪn'tɜːʳ/ **VT** enterrer, ensevelir

inter- /,ɪntəʳ/ **PREF** *(+ nsg)* entre *+ npl*, inter ... *+ adj* ◆ **~company** entre compagnies ◆ **~regional** interrégional ; see also **inter-city**

interact /,ɪntər'ækt/ **VI** ① *[substances]* (ré)agir l'un sur l'autre, interagir ② *(Comput)* dialoguer (*with* avec) ◆ **we don't ~ very well** *(fig)* le courant passe mal (entre nous)

interaction /,ɪntər'ækʃən/ **N** relation *f* ◆ **the ~ between life and theatre** la relation entre la vie et le théâtre ◆ **~ between individuals** les relations entre individus ◆ **the ~ of politics and the financial markets** l'interaction *or* les relations entre la politique et les marchés financiers ◆ **the ~ between alpha particles** l'interaction entre les particules alpha

> ⚠ Be cautious about translating **interaction** by the French word **interaction**, which is mainly used in technical contexts.

interactive /,ɪntər'æktɪv/ **ADJ** *(gen, Comput)* interactif ◆ **~ computing** traitement *m* interactif, informatique *f* conversationnelle ◆ **~ mode** mode *m* conversationnel *or* interactif

COMP **interactive television** **N** télévision *f* interactive

interactive video **N** vidéo *f* interactive

interactively /,ɪntər'æktɪvlɪ/ **ADV** *(Comput) [work]* en mode conversationnel *or* interactif

inter alia /,ɪntər'ælɪə/ **ADV** *(frm)* notamment, entre autres

interbreed /'ɪntə'briːd/ (pret, ptp **interbred** /'ɪntə'bred/) **VT** *[+ animals]* croiser **VI** se croiser (*with* avec)

intercalate /ɪn'tɜːkəleɪt/ **VT** intercaler

intercalation /ɪn,tɜːkə'leɪʃən/ **N** intercalation *f*

intercampus /,ɪntə'kæmpəs/ **ADJ** *(US Univ)* inter-universitaire

intercede /,ɪntə'siːd/ **VI** intercéder (*with* auprès de ; *for* pour, en faveur de)

intercensal /,ɪntə'sensl/ **ADJ** intercensitaire

intercept /,ɪntə'sept/ **VT** *[+ message, light]* intercepter, capter ; *[+ plane, suspect]* intercepter ; *[+ person]* arrêter au passage **N** interception *f*

interception /,ɪntə'sepʃən/ **N** interception *f*

interceptor /,ɪntə'septəʳ/ **N** *(= aircraft, missile)* intercepteur *m*

intercession /,ɪntə'seʃən/ **N** intercession *f*

interchange /'ɪntə,tʃeɪndʒ/ **N** ① *(NonC) (= exchange)* échange *m* ; *(= alternation)* alternance *f* ② *(on motorway)* échangeur *m* **VT** /,ɪntə'tʃeɪndʒ/ *(= alternate)* faire alterner (*with* avec) ; *(= change positions of)* changer de place, mettre à la place l'un de l'autre ; *(= exchange) [+ gifts, letters, ideas]* échanger (*with sb* avec qn) **VI** *(= change position)* changer de place (*with* avec) ; *(= alternate)* alterner (*with* avec)

interchangeable /,ɪntə'tʃeɪndʒəbl/ **ADJ** interchangeable

interchangeably /,ɪntə'tʃeɪndʒəblɪ/ **ADV** de façon interchangeable

Intercity /,ɪntə'sɪtɪ/ ® **N** *(= train)* rapide *m*

inter-city /,ɪntə'sɪtɪ/ **ADJ** *[travel]* d'une grande ville à une autre ; *[communications, route, service]* interurbain

intercollegiate /'ɪntəkə'liːdʒɪɪt/ **ADJ** entre collèges

intercom /'ɪntəkɒm/ **N** interphone *m* ◆ **over** *or* **on the ~** à l'interphone

intercommunicate /,ɪntəkə'mjuːnɪkeɪt/ **VI** communiquer (réciproquement)

intercommunication /'ɪntəkə,mjuːnɪ'keɪʃən/ **N** intercommunication *f*, communication *f* réciproque

intercommunion /,ɪntəkə'mjuːnɪən/ **N** *(Rel)* intercommunion *f* ; *(gen)* intercommunication *f*

interconnect /,ɪntəkə'nekt/ **VT** *(gen)* connecter (entre eux *or* elles) ; *(Comput) [+ systems]* interconnecter ◆ **~ed facts** faits *mpl* intimement *or* étroitement liés ◆ **~ed rooms** pièces *fpl* communicantes **VI** *[rooms, tunnels]* communiquer (entre eux *or* elles) ; *[parts of a structure]* être relié(e)s (les un(e)s aux autres) ◆ **~ing wall** mur *m* mitoyen

interconnection /'ɪntəkə'nekʃən/ **N** *(Elec)* interconnexion *f* ; *(fig)* lien *m*

intercontinental /'ɪntə,kɒntɪ'nentl/ **ADJ** intercontinental ◆ **~ ballistic missile** missile *m* balistique intercontinental

intercostal /,ɪntə'kɒstl/ **ADJ** intercostal

intercourse /'ɪntəkɔːs/ **N** ① *(NonC)* relations *fpl*, rapports *mpl* ◆ **business/human/social ~** relations *fpl* commerciales/humaines/sociales ② ◆ **sexual ~** rapports *mpl* (sexuels) ◆ **anal ~** sodomie *f* ◆ **to have ~** avoir des rapports (*with* avec)

intercut /,ɪntə'kʌt/ **VT** *(Cine)* ◆ **to ~ sth with sth** entrecouper qch de qch

interdenominational /'ɪntədɪ,nɒmɪ'neɪʃənl/ **ADJ** entre confessions, interconfessionnel

interdental /,ɪntə'dentl/ **ADJ** interdentaire

interdepartmental /'ɪntə,diːpɑːt'mentl/ **ADJ** *(within firm)* entre services ; *(Univ)* entre départements ; *(Pol)* interministériel

interdependence /,ɪntədɪ'pendəns/ **N** interdépendance *f*

interdependent /,ɪntədɪ'pendənt/ **ADJ** interdépendant

interdict /'ɪntədɪkt/ **VT** ① *(Jur, frm)* interdire, prohiber ② *(Rel) [+ priest, person]* jeter l'interdit sur **N** ① *(Jur)* prohibition *f*, interdiction *f* ② *(Rel)* interdit *m*

interdiction /,ɪntə'dɪkʃən/ **N** *(Jur, Rel)* interdiction *f*

interdisciplinarity /,ɪntə,dɪsɪplɪ'nærɪtɪ/ **N** interdisciplinarité *f*

interdisciplinary /,ɪntə'dɪsɪplɪnərɪ/ **ADJ** interdisciplinaire

interest /'ɪntrɪst/ LANGUAGE IN USE 19.2

N ① *(NonC: in sb/sth)* intérêt *m* ◆ **to take** *or* **have an ~ in sb** s'intéresser à qn ◆ **to take** *or* **have an ~ in sth** s'intéresser à qch, prendre de l'intérêt à qch ◆ **he took no further ~ in it** il ne s'y est plus intéressé ◆ **to show an ~ in sb/sth** manifester *or* montrer de l'intérêt pour qn/qch ◆ **to take a great ~ in sb/sth** s'intéresser vivement à qn/qch ◆ **to arouse sb's ~** éveiller l'intérêt de qn ◆ **that's of no ~ to me** ça ne m'intéresse pas, ça a peu d'intérêt pour moi ◆ **a subject of little ~** un sujet présentant peu d'intérêt ◆ **questions of public ~** questions *fpl* d'intérêt public *or* qui intéressent le public ; see also **noun 3** ◆ **she doesn't really need to work - she's doing it just for ~** elle n'a pas vraiment besoin de travailler : elle le fait parce que ça l'intéresse ◆ **it adds ~ to the story** ça ajoute un certain intérêt à l'histoire ◆ **matters of vital ~** questions *fpl* d'un intérêt *or* d'une importance capital(e)

② *(= hobby etc)* ◆ **what are your ~s ?** quelles sont les choses qui vous intéressent ?, à quoi vous intéressez-vous ? ◆ **my main ~ is baroque architecture** mon principal centre d'intérêt est l'architecture baroque ◆ **special ~ holidays** vacances *fpl* à thème

③ *(= advantage, well-being)* intérêt *m*, avantage *m* ◆ **in one's (own) ~(s)** dans son (propre) intérêt ◆ **it is in your own ~ to do so** il est de votre intérêt d'agir ainsi, vous avez tout intérêt à agir ainsi ◆ **to act in sb's ~(s)** agir dans l'intérêt de qn ◆ **in the ~(s) of hygiene/safety** par souci d'hygiène/de sécurité ◆ **in the ~(s) of peace/national security** dans l'intérêt de la paix/la sécurité nationale ◆ **in the public ~** dans l'intérêt public, pour le bien public ◆ **Washington has an ~ in helping Russia with its economy** c'est dans l'intérêt de Washington d'aider économiquement la Russie

④ *(Comm, Jur etc = share stake)* intérêts *mpl*, participation *f* ◆ **I have an ~ in a hairdressing business** j'ai des intérêts dans un salon de coiffure ◆ **he has business ~s abroad** il a des intérêts commerciaux à l'étranger ◆ **Switzerland is looking after British ~s** la Suisse défend les intérêts britanniques ◆ **he has sold his ~ in the firm** il a vendu la participation *or* les intérêts qu'il avait dans l'entreprise ; → **vest²**

⑤ *(= interested parties)* **the coal/oil ~(s)** les (gros) intérêts *mpl* houillers/pétroliers ◆ **shipping ~s** les intérêts *mpl* maritimes ◆ **the landed ~s** les propriétaires *mpl* terriens

⑥ *(NonC: Fin)* intérêt(s) *m(pl)* ◆ **simple/compound ~** intérêts *mpl* simples/composés ◆ **~ on an investment** intérêts *mpl* d'un placement ◆ **loan with ~** prêt *m* à intérêt ◆ **to lend out money at ~** faire un prêt (*or* des prêts) à intérêt ◆ **to bear ~** rapporter un intérêt ◆ **to bear ~ at 8%** donner un intérêt de 8%, porter intérêt à 8% ◆ **to carry ~** rapporter *or* produire des intérêts

VT ① intéresser ◆ **to be ~ed in sth/sb** s'intéresser à qch/qn ◆ **I'm not ~ed in football** le football ne m'intéresse pas, je ne m'intéresse pas au football ◆ **the company is ~ed in buying land** l'entreprise est intéressée par l'achat de terrains ◆ **I'm ~ed in going** ça m'intéresse d'y aller ◆ **I'm not ~ed!** ça ne m'intéresse pas ! ◆ **I'm not ~ed in your excuses!** tes excuses ne m'intéressent pas ! ◆ **I'd be ~ed to see what this man has to offer** je serais curieux de savoir ce que cet homme a à proposer ◆ **they spent time trying to ~ customers in their product** ils ont passé du temps à essayer d'intéresser les clients à leurs produits ◆ **can I ~ you in contributing to ...?** est-ce que cela vous intéresserait de contribuer à ... ? ◆ **can I ~ you in a new computer?** seriez-vous intéressé par un nouvel ordinateur ?

② *(= concern)* intéresser, concerner ◆ **the struggle against inflation ~s us all** la lutte contre l'inflation touche chacun d'entre nous *or* nous concerne tous

COMP **interest-bearing** ADJ *(Fin) [loan]* productif d'intérêt

interest-free ADJ *(Fin)* sans intérêt

interest group N groupe *m* d'intérêt

interest payment N *(Fin)* versement *m* d'intérêts

interest rate N *(Fin)* taux *m* d'intérêt ◆ **at an ~ rate of 10%** à un taux d'intérêt de 10%

interested /ˈɪntrɪstɪd/ ADJ ① *(= attentive) [expression]* d'intérêt ② *(= involved, partial) [person, motive]* intéressé ◆ **to be an ~ party** être une des parties intéressées ◆ **the ~ parties** les intéressés *mpl*, les parties *fpl* intéressées *(Jur)* ; see also **interest**

interesting /ˈɪntrɪstɪŋ/ ADJ *[book, story, idea, person]* intéressant ◆ **the meeting was very ~ for me** cette réunion m'a beaucoup intéressé ◆ **the ~ thing (about it) is that ...** ce qu'il y a d'intéressant (à ce propos), c'est que ...

interestingly /ˈɪntrɪstɪŋlɪ/ ADV de façon intéressante ◆ **~ (enough), he ...** chose intéressante, il ...

interface /ˈɪntəfeɪs/ N ① *(Comput, Phys, Chem)* interface *f* ◆ **user ~** *(Comput)* interface *f* utilisateur ② *(fig)* interface *f*, point *m* de liaison *or* de contact VI ① *(Comput, Tech)* faire interface ② *(fig) [person, organization] (= liaise)* être en liaison *or* en contact *(with* avec) VT *(Tech)* connecter *(with* avec)

interfacing /ˈɪntəfeɪsɪŋ/ N ① *(Sewing)* entoilage *m* ② *(Comput)* interfaçage *m*, interface *f*

interfaith /ˈɪntəfeɪθ/ ADJ *[relations, dialogue]* interreligieux

interfere /ˌɪntəˈfɪəʳ/ VI ① *(= intrude)* **stop interfering!** ne vous mêlez pas de ce qui ne vous regarde pas ! ◆ **he's always interfering** il se mêle toujours de ce qui ne le regarde pas ◆ **he tried to ~ in running the business** il a voulu se mêler de la gestion de l'entreprise ◆ **to ~ in another country's affairs** s'ingérer dans les affaires d'un autre pays

◆ **to interfere with** *(= adversely affect)* affecter ; *[+ plans]* contrarier, contrecarrer ◆ **to ~ with sb's plans** *[weather, accident, circumstances etc]* contrarier *or* contrecarrer les projets de qn ◆ **tiredness ~s with your ability to study** la fatigue affecte l'aptitude à étudier ◆ **alcohol can ~ with your sexual performance** l'alcool peut affecter votre puissance sexuelle ◆ **computer games can ~ with school work** les jeux électroniques peuvent perturber le travail scolaire

② *(sexually)* ◆ **to ~ with sb** abuser de qn ◆ **the child had been ~d with** on avait abusé de l'enfant

③ *(= handle)* ◆ **don't ~ with my camera*** ne touche pas à *or* ne tripote pas mon appareil, laisse mon appareil tranquille*

④ *(Phys)* interférer

interference /ˌɪntəˈfɪərəns/ N *(NonC)* ① *(gen)* ingérence *f* (*in* dans ; *from* de) ◆ **bureaucracy and government ~** l'ingérence des bureaucrates et du gouvernement ◆ **his constant ~ in the lives of his children** la façon dont il se mêle constamment des affaires de ses enfants ◆ **with less ~, we can manage our own affairs** si on nous laisse faire, nous pouvons gérer nos affaires nous-mêmes ◆ **state ~** *(Econ)* ingérence *f* de l'État ◆ **unwarrantable ~** *(Jur)* immixtion *f* ② *(Phys)* interférence *f* ; *(Rad)* parasites *mpl*, interférence *f*

interfering /ˌɪntəˈfɪərɪŋ/ ADJ *[person]* importun ; *[neighbour]* envahissant ◆ **he's an ~ busybody** il se mêle toujours de ce qui ne le regarde pas

interferon /ˌɪntəˈfɪərɒn/ N interféron *m*

intergalactic /ˌɪntəgəˈlæktɪk/ ADJ intergalactique

intergovernmental /ˌɪntəgʌvnˈmentl/ ADJ intergouvernemental

interim /ˈɪntərɪm/ N intérim *m* ◆ **in the ~** dans l'intérim, entre-temps ADJ *[arrangement, report, payment, loan]* provisoire ; *[post, postholder]* par intérim, intérimaire ; *[government]* intérimaire, provisoire ◆ **the ~ period** l'intérim *m* COMP **interim dividend** N dividende *m* intérimaire

interim financing N préfinancement *m*

interior /ɪnˈtɪərɪəʳ/ ADJ intérieur (-eure *f*) N ① *[of building, country]* intérieur *m* ◆ **Minister/Ministry of the Interior** ministre *m*/ministère *m* de l'Intérieur ◆ **Secretary/Department of the Interior** *(US) ministre/ministère de l'Environnement chargé des Parcs nationaux* ② *(Art)* (tableau *m* d')intérieur *m*

COMP **interior angle** N *(Math)* angle *m* interne

interior decoration N décoration *f* d'intérieur

interior decorator N décorateur *m*, -trice *f* d'intérieur

interior design N architecture *f* d'intérieur

interior designer N architecte *mf* d'intérieur

interior sprung mattress N matelas *m* à ressorts

interject /ˌɪntəˈdʒekt/ VT *[+ remark, question]* placer ◆ **"yes" he ~ed** "oui" dit-il soudain

interjection /ˌɪntəˈdʒekʃən/ N interjection *f*

interlace /ˌɪntəˈleɪs/ VT entrelacer, entrecroiser VI s'entrelacer, s'entrecroiser

interlard /ˌɪntəˈlɑːd/ VT entrelarder, entremêler *(with* de)

interleave /ˌɪntəˈliːv/ VT interfolier

interlibrary loan /ˌɪntəˌlaɪbrərɪˈləʊn/ N prêt *m* interbibliothèque

interline /ˌɪntəˈlaɪn/ VT ① *(Typ)* interligner ② *(Sewing)* mettre une triplure à

interlinear /ˌɪntəˈlɪnɪəʳ/ ADJ interlinéaire

interlining /ˌɪntəˈlaɪnɪŋ/ N *(Sewing)* triplure *f*

interlink /ˌɪntəˈlɪŋk/ VI *[parts of a structure]* se rejoindre ; *[factors, problems, aspects]* se lier ; *[bus, train services]* interconnecter ◆ **a transport network with bus and rail services ~ing** un réseau de transport avec interconnexion des services de bus et de train VT ◆ **to be ~ed** *[factors, problems, aspects]* être lié *(with* à)

interlock /ˌɪntəˈlɒk/ VT *[+ part, component]* enclencher VI *(lit) (= click into place)* s'enclencher ; *(= join together)* s'emboîter ; *(fig) [problems, ideas, projects]* être étroitement lié ; *[groups]* avoir des intérêts en commun

interlocutor /ˌɪntəˈlɒkjʊtəʳ/ N interlocuteur *m*, -trice *f*

interloper /ˈɪntələʊpəʳ/ N intrus(e) *m(f)* ; *(Comm)* commerçant *m* marron

interlude /ˈɪntəluːd/ N intervalle *m* ; *(Theat)* intermède *m* ◆ **in the ~** *(gen)* dans l'intervalle, entre-temps ; *(Theat)* pendant l'intermède ◆ **musical ~** interlude *m*, intermède *m* musical

intermarriage /ˌɪntəˈmærɪdʒ/ N *(NonC, within family, tribe etc)* endogamie *f* ; *(between families, tribes etc)* mariage *m*

intermarry /ˈɪntəˈmærɪ/ VI *(within one's own family, tribe etc)* pratiquer l'endogamie ; *(with other family, tribe etc)* se marier entre eux ◆ **to ~ with** se marier avec

intermediary /ˌɪntəˈmiːdɪərɪ/ ADJ, N intermédiaire *mf*

intermediate /ˌɪntəˈmiːdɪət/ ADJ ① intermédiaire ◆ **~ goods** *(Econ)* biens *mpl* intermédiaires ◆ **~ stop** *[of ship, plane]* escale *f* ◆ **the ~ stages of the project** les phases *fpl* *or* étapes *fpl* intermédiaires du projet ② *(Scol etc)* moyen ◆ **~ course/exam** cours *m*/examen *m* (de niveau) moyen N ① *(Sport, Educ etc)* niveau *m* intermédiaire ◆ **language courses for ~s** des cours *mpl* de langue pour les étudiants de niveau intermédiaire ② *(US) (= intermediary)* intermédiaire *mf* ③ *(US = car)* automobile *f* de taille moyenne ④ *(= substance)* substance *f* *or* produit *m* intermédiaire COMP **intermediate-range ballistic missile, intermediate-**

range weapon N *(Mil)* missile *m* à moyenne portée

interment /ɪnˈtɜːmənt/ N enterrement *m*, inhumation *f*

intermezzo /ˌɪntəˈmetsəʊ/ N (pl **intermezzos** *or* **intermezzi** /ˌɪntəˈmetsiː/) *(Mus)* intermezzo *m*

interminable /ɪnˈtɜːmɪnəbl/ ADJ interminable, sans fin

interminably /ɪnˈtɜːmɪnəblɪ/ ADV *[talk, argue, continue]* interminablement ◆ **~ long** interminable

intermingle /ˌɪntəˈmɪŋgl/ VT entremêler (*with* de) mélanger VI se mêler, se mélanger (*with* avec)

intermission /ˌɪntəˈmɪʃən/ N 1 *(gen)* interruption *f*, pause *f* ; *(in hostilities, quarrel, work, session)* trêve *f* ◆ **without ~** *(frm)* sans arrêt, sans relâche 2 *(Cine, Theat)* entracte *m* 3 *(Med)* intermission *f*

intermittent /ˌɪntəˈmɪtənt/ ADJ intermittent ◆ **~ wipe** *[of car]* essuie-glace *m* à balayage intermittent

intermittently /ˌɪntəˈmɪtəntlɪ/ ADV par intermittence

intermodal /ˌɪntəˈməʊdəl/ ADJ *[transport]* intermodal

intern /ɪnˈtɜːn/ VT *(Pol, Mil)* interner *(pour raisons de sécurité)* N /ˈɪntɜːn/ *(US Med)* interne *mf*

internal /ɪnˈtɜːnl/ ADJ 1 *(Med)* interne ◆ **~ bleeding** hémorragie *f* interne ◆ **~ examination** toucher *m* vaginal ◆ **~ injuries** lésions *fpl* internes

2 *(Math, Tech)* interne

3 *[dispute, trouble, reorganization, security]* intérieur (-eure *f*), interne ◆ **~ wars** guerres *fpl* civiles *or* intestines *(liter)* ◆ **~ quarrels** querelles *fpl* intestines ◆ **~ (phone) call** appel *m* *or* communication *f* interne ◆ **~ candidate** candidat *m* interne ◆ **~ mail** courrier *m* interne

4 (= *intrinsic*) *[proof, evidence]* intrinsèque

5 *[hope]* secret (-ète *f*) ◆ **~ conviction** conviction *f* intime

COMP **internal auditor** N contrôleur *m* financier

internal combustion engine N moteur *m* à explosion *or* à combustion interne

internal examiner N *(Univ)* examinateur *m*, -trice *f* interne

internal market N *(in country)* marché *m* intérieur *or* domestique ; *(in European Union)* marché *m* intérieur ; *(in organization)* marché *m* interne

internal medicine N *(US)* médecine *f* interne

internal revenue N *(US)* contributions *fpl* directes

Internal Revenue Service N *(US)* ≃ fisc *m*

internalization /ɪnˌtɜːnəlaɪˈzeɪʃən/ N intériorisation *f*

internalize /ɪnˈtɜːnəˌlaɪz/ VT *[+ skill, fact]* intégrer ; *[+ problem]* intérioriser ; *(Ling)* intérioriser

internally /ɪnˈtɜːnəlɪ/ ADV 1 *(gen, Med)* intérieurement ◆ **to bleed ~** avoir des hémorragies internes ◆ **~ coherent** qui a une cohérence interne ◆ **"to be taken internally"** *(Pharm)* "à usage interne" ◆ **"not to be taken internally"** *(Pharm)* "pour usage externe" 2 (= *within company*) ◆ **software developed ~ at IBM** un logiciel créé au sein d'IBM

international /ˌɪntəˈnæʃnəl/ ADJ international ◆ **~ law** droit *m* international ◆ **~ relations** relations *fpl* internationales ; → **road**

N 1 *(Brit Sport)* (= *match*) match *m* international ; (= *player*) international(e) *m(f)*

2 *(Pol)* **International** Internationale *f* (association)

COMP **International Atomic Energy Agency** N Agence *f* internationale de l'énergie atomique

International Bank for Reconstruction and Development N Banque *f* internationale pour la reconstruction et le développement

International Court of Justice N Cour *f* internationale de Justice

International Date Line N ligne *f* de changement de date *or* de changement de jour

International Labour Organization N Organisation *f* internationale du travail

International Modernism N ⇒ **International Style**

International Monetary Fund N Fonds *m* monétaire international

International Olympic Committee N Comité *m* international olympique

International Phonetic Alphabet N alphabet *m* phonétique international

international reply coupon N coupon-réponse *m* international

International Standards Organization N Organisation *f* internationale de normalisation

International Style N *(Archit)* style *m* international

Internationale /ˌɪntəˌnæʃəˈnɑːl/ N Internationale *f*

internationalism /ˌɪntəˈnæʃnəlɪzəm/ N internationalisme *m*

internationalist /ˌɪntəˈnæʃnəlɪst/ N internationaliste *mf*

internationalize /ˌɪntəˈnæʃnəlaɪz/ VT internationaliser

internationally /ˌɪntəˈnæʃnəlɪ/ ADV *[recognized]* internationalement ; *[discussed, accepted, competitive]* au niveau international ◆ **~ renowned** de réputation internationale, réputé internationalement ◆ **~ respected** respecté dans le monde entier ◆ **to compete ~** *[athlete etc]* participer à des compétitions internationales ; *[company]* être présent sur le marché international ◆ **~, the situation is even worse** sur le plan international, la situation est encore pire

internecine /ˌɪntəˈniːsaɪn/ ADJ *(frm)* *[strife, warfare, feud]* interne ◆ **~ quarrels/battles** querelles *fpl*/luttes *fpl* internes *or* intestines *(liter)*

internee /ˌɪntɜːˈniː/ N *(Mil, Pol)* interné(e) *m(f)*

Internet /ˈɪntəˌnet/ N ◆ **the ~** l'Internet *m*

COMP **Internet café** N cybercafé *m*

Internet connection N connexion *f* Internet

Internet service provider N fournisseur *m* d'accès à Internet

Internet site N site *m* Internet

Internet user N utilisateur *m*, -trice *f* Internet, internaute *mf*

internist /ɪnˈtɜːnɪst/ N *(US Med)* ≃ spécialiste *mf* de médecine interne, interniste *mf*

internment /ɪnˈtɜːnmənt/ N *(Mil, Pol)* internement *m* COMP **internment camp** N camp *m* d'internement

internship /ˈɪntɜːnˌʃɪp/ N *(US Med)* internat *m* ; *(Univ etc)* stage *m* en entreprise

interoperability /ˈɪntəˌrɒpərəˈbɪlɪtɪ/ N *(Comput)* interopérabilité *f*, interfonctionnement *m*

interpenetrate /ˈɪntəˈpenɪtreɪt/ VT imprégner VI s'interpénétrer

interpersonal /ˌɪntəˈpɜːsnl/ ADJ ◆ **~ skills/relationships** compétences *fpl*/relations *fpl* interpersonnelles

interplanetary /ˌɪntəˈplænɪtərɪ/ ADJ *[journey]* interplanétaire ◆ **~ vessel** vaisseau *m* spatial

interplay /ˈɪntəpleɪ/ N *(NonC)* effet *m* réciproque, interaction *f*

Interpol /ˈɪntəˌpɒl/ N Interpol *m*

interpolate /ɪnˈtɜːpəleɪt/ VT *(gen)* interpoler (*into* dans) ; *[+ text, manuscript]* altérer par interpolation

interpolation /ɪnˌtɜːpəˈleɪʃən/ N interpolation *f*

interpose /ˌɪntəˈpəʊz/ VT *[+ remark]* placer ; *[+ objection, veto]* opposer ; *[+ obstacle]* interposer ◆ **to ~ o.s. between** s'interposer entre ◆ **"he rang me just now", she ~d** "il vient de me téléphoner" dit-elle soudain VI intervenir, s'interposer

interpret /ɪnˈtɜːprɪt/ LANGUAGE IN USE 26.1 VT *(all senses)* interpréter VI interpréter, servir d'interprète, faire l'interprète

interpretation /ɪnˌtɜːprɪˈteɪʃən/ N *(all senses)* interprétation *f* ◆ **she put quite a different ~ on the figures** elle a donné à ces chiffres une tout autre interprétation

interpretative /ɪnˈtɜːprɪtətɪv/ ADJ *[article, account]* explicatif ; *[skills, grasp, problems]* d'interprétation ◆ **~ centre** centre *m* d'information

interpreter /ɪnˈtɜːprɪtəʳ/ N (= *person: lit, fig*) interprète *mf* ; *(Comput)* interpréteur *m*

interpreting /ɪnˈtɜːprɪtɪŋ/ N (= *profession*) interprétariat *m*, interprétation *f*

interpretive /ɪnˈtɜːprɪtɪv/ ADJ ⇒ **interpretative**

interracial /ˌɪntəˈreɪʃəl/ ADJ *[marriage]* mixte ; *[problems, violence]* interracial

interregnum /ˌɪntəˈregnəm/ N (pl **interregnums** *or* **interregna** /ˌɪntəˈregnə/) interrègne *m*

interrelate /ˌɪntərɪˈleɪt/ VT mettre en corrélation VI *[concepts]* être en corrélation (*with* avec) ◆ **the way in which we ~ with others** la manière dont nous communiquons avec les autres ◆ **the body and the mind ~** le corps et l'esprit sont étroitement liés

interrelated /ˌɪntərɪˈleɪtɪd/ ADJ étroitement lié

interrelation /ˌɪntərɪˈleɪʃən/, **interrelationship** /ˌɪntərɪˈleɪʃənʃɪp/ N corrélation *f*, lien *m* étroit

interrogate /ɪnˈterəgeɪt/ VT interroger, soumettre à une interrogation ; *(Police)* soumettre à un interrogatoire ; *(Comput)* interroger

interrogation /ɪnˌterəˈgeɪʃən/ N interrogation *f* ; *(Police)* interrogatoire *m* COMP **interrogation mark, interrogation point** N point *m* d'interrogation

interrogative /ˌɪntəˈrɒgətɪv/ ADJ *[look, tone]* interrogateur (-trice *f*) ; *(Ling)* interrogatif N *(Ling)* interrogatif *m* ◆ **in the ~** à l'interrogatif

interrogatively /ˌɪntəˈrɒgətɪvlɪ/ ADV d'un air *or* d'un ton interrogateur ; *(Ling)* interrogativement

interrogator /ɪnˈterəgeɪtəʳ/ N interrogateur *m*, -trice *f*

interrogatory /ˌɪntəˈrɒgətərɪ/ ADJ interrogateur (-trice *f*)

interrupt /ˌɪntəˈrʌpt/ VT *[+ speech, traffic, circuit, holiday]* interrompre ; *[+ communication]* interrompre, couper ; *[+ person] (when talking)* interrompre, couper la parole à ; *(when busy etc)* interrompre ; *[+ view]* gêner, boucher ◆ **to ~ a private conversation** interrompre un tête-à-tête ◆ **the match was ~ed by rain** the match a été interrompu par la pluie ◆ **don't ~!** pas d'interruptions ! ◆ **I don't want to ~, but ...** je ne voudrais pas vous interrompre, mais ...

interruption /ˌɪntəˈrʌpʃən/ N interruption *f* ◆ **without ~** sans interruption, sans arrêt ◆ **an ~ to her career** une interruption dans sa carrière

intersect /ˌɪntəˈsekt/ VT couper, croiser ; *(Math)* intersecter ◆ **the city is ~ed by three waterways** la ville est traversée par trois cours d'eau VI *[lines, wires, roads etc]* se couper, se croiser ; *(Math)* s'intersecter ◆ **~ing arcs/lines** *(Math)* arcs *mpl*/lignes *fpl* intersecté(e)s ◆ **their histories** ~ leurs histoires se croisent ◆ **historical events ~ with our lives** nos vies sont traversées par des événements historiques

intersection /ˌɪntəˈsekʃən/ **N** *(US = crossroads)* croisement *m*, carrefour *m* ; *(Math)* intersection *f*

interservice /ˌɪntəˈsɜːvɪs/ **ADJ** *(Mil)* interarmes *inv*

intersperse /ˌɪntəˈspɜːs/ **VT** semer, parsemer *(among, between* dans, parmi) ◆ **a book ~d with quotations** un livre parsemé *or* émaillé de citations ◆ **a speech ~d with jokes** un discours émaillé de plaisanteries ◆ **a rocky landscape ~d with lakes** un paysage de rochers et de lacs ◆ **periods of tremendous heat ~d with sudden showers** des périodes de très forte chaleur entrecoupées de brusques averses

interstate /ˌɪntəˈsteɪt/ *(US)* **ADJ** *[commerce etc]* entre états **N** (also **interstate highway**) autoroute *f (qui relie plusieurs États)* ; → ROADS

interstellar /ˌɪntəˈsteləʳ/ **ADJ** interstellaire, intersidéral

interstice /ɪnˈtɜːstɪs/ **N** interstice *m*

intertextuality /ˈɪntəˈtekstjuːˈælɪtɪ/ **N** *(Literat)* intertextualité *f*

intertwine /ˌɪntəˈtwaɪn/ **VT** entrelacer ◆ **their destinies are ~d** leurs destins sont inextricablement liés **VI** s'entrelacer ◆ **intertwining branches** branches *fpl* entrelacées ◆ **her fate ~d with his** son destin était inextricablement lié au sien

interurban /ˌɪntəˈɜːbən/ **ADJ** interurbain

interval /ˈɪntəvəl/ **N** 1 *(in time)* intervalle *m* ◆ **at ~s** par intervalles ◆ **at frequent/regular ~s** à intervalles rapprochés/réguliers ◆ **at rare ~s** à intervalles espacés, de loin en loin ◆ **at fortnightly ~s** tous les quinze jours ◆ **there was an ~ for discussion** il y eut une pause pour la discussion ◆ **he has lucid ~s** *(Med)* il a des moments de lucidité ◆ **showery ~s** averses *fpl* ; → **sunny**

2 *(Theat)* entracte *m* ; *(Sport)* mi-temps *f*, pause *f* ; *(Scol)* récréation *f*

3 *(= space between objects)* intervalle *m*, distance *f* ◆ **at ~s of 2 metres** à 2 mètres d'intervalle, à 2 mètres de distance ◆ **rest areas spaced at regular ~s along major roads** des aires de repos aménagées à intervalles réguliers sur les routes principales

4 *(Mus)* intervalle *m* ◆ **second/third ~** intervalle *m* de seconde/de tierce

intervene /ˌɪntəˈviːn/ **VI** 1 *[person]* intervenir *(in* dans) ◆ **the government ~d to resolve the crisis** le gouvernement est intervenu pour résoudre la crise ◆ **Europe would ~ with military force** l'Europe interviendrait militairement 2 *[event, circumstances etc]* survenir, arriver ; *[time]* s'écouler, s'étendre *(between* entre) ◆ **war ~d** survint la guerre ◆ **if nothing ~s** s'il n'arrive *or* ne se passe rien entre-temps ◆ **you never know what might ~ between now and election day** on ne sait jamais ce qui pourrait se passer d'ici les élections **VT** *(= interrupt)* ◆ **"I've told you he's not here", Irene ~d** "je vous ai dit qu'il n'était pas là" coupa Irene

intervening /ˌɪntəˈviːnɪŋ/ **ADJ** *[event]* survenu ; *[period of time]* intermédiaire ◆ **the ~ years were happy** les années qui s'écoulèrent entre-temps furent heureuses, la période intermédiaire a été heureuse ◆ **I had spent the ~ time in London** entre-temps j'étais resté à Londres ◆ **they scoured the ~ miles of moorland** ils ont parcouru les kilomètres de lande qui séparaient les deux endroits

intervention /ˌɪntəˈvenʃən/ **N** intervention *f (in* dans) ◆ **~ price** *(Econ)* prix *m* d'intervention

interventionist /ˌɪntəˈvenʃənɪst/ **N, ADJ** interventionniste *mf*

interview /ˈɪntəvjuː/ LANGUAGE IN USE 19.3, 19.5

N 1 *(for job, place on course etc)* entretien *m* ; *(to discuss working conditions, pay rise etc)* entrevue *f* ◆ **to call** *or* **invite sb to (an) ~** convoquer qn à *or* pour un entretien ◆ **to come to (an) ~** venir pour *or* se présenter à un entretien ◆ **I had an ~ with the manager** j'ai eu un entretien *or* une entrevue avec le directeur ◆ **the ~s will be held next week** les entretiens auront lieu la semaine prochaine

2 *(Press, Rad, TV)* interview *f* ◆ **to give an ~** accorder une interview

VT 1 *(for job, place on course etc)* faire passer un entretien à ◆ **he is being ~ed on Monday** on le convoque (pour) lundi ◆ **she was ~ed for the job** elle a passé un entretien pour le poste

2 *(Press, Rad, TV)* interviewer

3 *(Police)* interroger ◆ **he was ~ed by the police** il a été interrogé par les policiers ◆ **the police want to ~ him** la police le recherche

VI ◆ **we shall be ~ing throughout next week** nous faisons passer des entretiens toute la semaine prochaine

interviewee /ˌɪntəvjʊˈiː/ **N** *(for job, place on course etc)* candidat(e) *m(f) (qui passe un entretien)* ; *(Press, Rad, TV)* interviewé(e) *m(f)*

interviewer /ˈɪntəvjʊəʳ/ **N** *(Press, Rad, TV)* interviewer *m* ; *(in market research, opinion poll)* enquêteur *m*, -trice *f* ◆ **the ~ asked me ...** *(for job etc)* la personne qui m'a fait passer l'entretien m'a demandé ...

inter vivos /ˈɪntəˈviːvɒs/ **ADJ** *(Jur)* ◆ **~ gift** donation *f* entre vifs

intervocalic /ˌɪntəvəʊˈkælɪk/ **ADJ** *(Phon)* intervocalique

interwar /ˈɪntəˈwɔːʳ/ **ADJ** ◆ **the ~ period** *or* **years** l'entre-deux-guerres *m*

interweave /ˌɪntəˈwiːv/ **VT** *[+ threads]* tisser ensemble ; *[+ lines etc]* entrelacer ; *(fig) [+ stories, subplots]* entremêler **VI** s'entrelacer, s'emmêler

intestate /ɪnˈtestɪt/ **ADJ** *(Jur)* intestat *f inv* ◆ **to die ~** mourir ab intestat **COMP** **intestate estate N** succession *f* ab intestat

intestinal /ɪnˈtestɪnl/ **ADJ** intestinal ◆ **~ blockage** occlusion *f* intestinale ◆ **to have ~ fortitude*** *(US fig)* avoir quelque chose dans le ventre*

intestine /ɪnˈtestɪn/ **N** *(Anat)* intestin *m* ◆ **small ~** intestin *m* grêle ◆ **large ~** gros intestin *m*

inti /ˈɪntɪ/ **N** inti *m*

intifada /ˌɪntɪˈfɑːdə/ **N** intifada *f*

intimacy /ˈɪntɪməsɪ/ **N** 1 *(NonC)* intimité *f* 2 *(NonC: sexual)* rapports *mpl* (intimes *or* sexuels) 3 ◆ **intimacies** familiarités *fpl*

intimate /ˈɪntɪmɪt/ **ADJ** 1 *(= close) [friend, friendship, contact]* intime ; *[link, bond]* étroit ; *(sexually)* intime ◆ **to be on ~ terms (with sb)** *(gen)* être intime (avec qn), être très proche (de qn) ; *(sexually)* avoir des relations intimes (avec qn) ◆ **to be ~ with sb** *(euph = have sex with)* avoir des rapports intimes avec qn *(euph)*

2 *(= private, cosy) [conversation, moment, details, restaurant, photo etc]* intime ◆ **an ~ atmosphere** une atmosphère intime *or* d'intimité ◆ **an ~ candlelit dinner for two** un dîner aux chandelles en tête-à-tête

3 *(= detailed)* ◆ **to have an ~ knowledge of sth** avoir une connaissance intime *or* approfondie de qch

N intime *mf*, familier *m*, -ière *f*

VT /ˈɪntɪmeɪt/ *(frm)* 1 *(= hint)* laisser entendre, donner à entendre

2 *(= make known officially)* annoncer *(that* que) ◆ **he ~d his approval, he ~d that he approved** il a annoncé qu'il était d'accord

intimately /ˈɪntɪmɪtlɪ/ **ADV** *[know]* intimement ; *[talk]* en toute intimité ◆ **~ concerned** intimement concerné ◆ **to be ~ involved in** *or* **with a project** être très engagé dans un projet ◆ **to be ~ involved with sb** *(sexually)* avoir des relations intimes avec qn ◆ **~ linked** *or* **connected** étroitement lié ◆ **to be ~ acquainted with sb/sth** connaître intimement qn/qch

intimation /ˌɪntɪˈmeɪʃən/ **N** *(= announcement) (gen)* annonce *f* ; *[of death]* avis *m* ; *[of birth, wedding]* annonce *f* ; *(= notice)* signification *f*, notification *f* ; *(= hint)* suggestion *f* ; *(= sign)* indice *m*, indication *f* ◆ **this was the first ~ we had of their refusal** c'était la première fois qu'on nous notifiait leur refus ◆ **this was the first ~ we had that the company was in financial difficulty** c'était la première fois que nous entendions parler des difficultés financières de l'entreprise ◆ **he gave no ~ that he was going to resign** rien dans son comportement ne permettait de deviner qu'il allait démissionner

intimidate /ɪnˈtɪmɪdeɪt/ **VT** intimider

intimidating /ɪnˈtɪmɪdeɪtɪŋ/ **ADJ** *[person, manner, presence, atmosphere]* intimidant ; *[sight, figure]* impressionnant, intimidant ; *[tactics]* d'intimidation

intimidation /ɪnˌtɪmɪˈdeɪʃən/ **N** *(NonC)* intimidation *f* ; *(Jur)* menaces *fpl*

intimidatory /ɪnˌtɪmɪˈdeɪtərɪ/ **ADJ** *[tactics, telephone call]* d'intimidation ; *[behaviour]* intimidant

into /ˈɪntʊ/

> When **into** is an element in a phrasal verb, eg **break into, enter into, look into, walk into,** look up the verb.

PREP *(gen)* dans ◆ **to come** *or* **go ~ a room** entrer dans une pièce ◆ **to go ~ town** aller en ville ◆ **to get ~ a car** monter dans une voiture *or* en voiture ◆ **he helped his mother ~ the car** il a aidé sa mère à monter dans la *or* en voiture ◆ **she fell ~ the lake** elle est tombée dans le lac ◆ **he went off ~ the desert** il est parti dans le désert ◆ **to put sth ~ a box** mettre qch dans une boîte ◆ **put the book ~ it** mets le livre dedans ◆ **it broke ~ a thousand pieces** ça s'est cassé en mille morceaux ◆ **to change traveller's cheques ~ francs/francs ~ pounds** changer des chèques de voyage contre des francs/des francs contre des livres sterling ◆ **to translate** *or* **put sth ~ French** traduire qch en français ◆ **he went further ~ the forest** il s'est enfoncé dans la forêt ◆ **far ~ the night** tard dans la nuit ◆ **it was ~ 1996** c'était déjà 1996, on était déjà en 1996 ◆ **it continued well ~** *or* **far ~ 1996** cela a continué pendant une bonne partie de 1996 ◆ **he's well ~ his fifties/sixties** il a une bonne cinquantaine/soixantaine d'années ◆ **he's well ~ his seventies/eighties** il a soixante-dix/quatre-vingts ans bien tassés* ◆ **let's not go ~ that again!** ne revenons pas là-dessus ! ◆ **we must go ~ this very carefully** nous devons étudier la question de très près ◆ **4 ~ 12 goes 3** 12 divisé par 4 donne 3 ◆ **the children are ~ everything*** les enfants touchent à tout ◆ **she's ~* health foods/jazz/buying antiques** les aliments naturels/le jazz/acheter des antiquités, c'est son truc* ◆ **to be ~ drugs*** toucher à la drogue* ; → **burst, get into, grow into**

intolerable /ɪnˈtɒlərəbl/ **ADJ** *(= unacceptable)* intolérable ; *(= unbearable)* insupportable, intolérable ◆ **an ~ intrusion into his private life** une intrusion intolérable dans sa vie privée ◆ **the heat was ~** la chaleur était insupportable *or* intolérable ◆ **it is ~ that ...** il est intolérable *or* il n'est pas tolérable que ... + *subj*

intolerably /ɪnˈtɒlərəblɪ/ **ADV** *(frm)* 1 *[high, low, expensive, rude, arrogant etc]* horriblement ◆ **it was ~ hot** il faisait une chaleur intolérable *or* insupportable, il faisait horriblement chaud [2] *(with vb) [annoy, disturb, behave]* de façon intolérable

intolerance /ɪnˈtɒlərəns/ N *(NonC: also Med)* intolérance *f*

intolerant /ɪnˈtɒlərənt/ ADJ intolérant ◆ **to be ~ of** *(gen)* ne pas supporter ; *(Med) [foodstuff, drug etc]* présenter une intolérance à

intolerantly /ɪnˈtɒlərəntlɪ/ ADV avec intolérance

intonation /ˌɪntəʊˈneɪʃən/ N *(Ling, Mus)* intonation *f*

intone /ɪnˈtəʊn/ VT entonner ; *(Rel)* psalmodier

intoxicant /ɪnˈtɒksɪkənt/ ADJ enivrant N *(= alcohol)* alcool *m*, boisson *f* alcoolisée ; *(= narcotic)* stupéfiant *m*

intoxicate /ɪnˈtɒksɪkeɪt/ VT *(lit, fig)* enivrer

intoxicated /ɪnˈtɒksɪkeɪtɪd/ ADJ *(frm = drunk)* en état d'ivresse ◆ **~ by** *or* **with success/victory** *etc* enivré par le succès/la victoire *etc*

intoxicating /ɪnˈtɒksɪkeɪtɪŋ/ ADJ *[drink]* alcoolisé ; *[effect, perfume]* enivrant

intoxication /ɪnˌtɒksɪˈkeɪʃən/ N ivresse *f* ; *(Med)* intoxication *f* (par l'alcool) ; *(fig)* ivresse *f* ◆ **in a state of ~** *(Jur)* en état d'ivresse *or* d'ébriété

intractability /ɪnˌtræktəˈbɪlɪtɪ/ N [1] *(= difficulty) [of problem, dispute]* insolubilité *f (frm)*, caractère *m* insoluble [2] *(= stubbornness) [of person, government]* intransigeance *f*

intractable /ɪnˈtræktəbl/ ADJ *[problem]* insoluble ; *[illness, pain]* réfractaire (à tout traitement) ; *[child, temper]* intraitable, indocile

intramural /ˌɪntrəˈmjʊərəl/ ADJ *[studies, sports, competitions]* à l'intérieur d'un même établissement NPL **intramurals** *(US Scol, Univ)* matchs *mpl* entre élèves (*or* étudiants) d'un même établissement

intramuscular /ˌɪntrəˈmʌskjʊləʳ/ ADJ intramusculaire

intramuscularly /ˌɪntrəˈmʌskjʊləlɪ/ ADV par voie intramusculaire

intranet /ˈɪntrənet/ N intranet *m*

intransigence /ɪnˈtrænsɪdʒəns/ N intransigeance *f*

intransigent /ɪnˈtrænsɪdʒənt/ ADJ, N intransigeant(e) *m(f)*

intransitive /ɪnˈtrænsɪtɪv/ ADJ, N *(Gram)* intransitif *m*

intrauterine /ˌɪntrəˈjuːtəraɪn/ ADJ *[procedure, surgery, insemination, pregnancy]* intra-utérin COMP **intrauterine device** N stérilet *m*, dispositif *m* anticonceptionnel intra-utérin

intravenous /ˌɪntrəˈviːnəs/ ADJ *[injection, fluids, solution]* intraveineux ; *[feeding]* par voie intraveineuse ; *[line, tube, needle]* pour voie intraveineuse ; *[drugs]* administré par voie intraveineuse ◆ **~ drug users/drug use** utilisateurs *mpl*/utilisation *f* de drogue par voie intraveineuse

COMP **intravenous drip** N perfusion *f* intraveineuse, goutte-à-goutte *m*
intravenous injection N (injection *f or* piqûre *f*) intraveineuse *f*

intravenously /ˌɪntrəˈviːnəslɪ/ ADV par voie intraveineuse

intrepid /ɪnˈtrepɪd/ ADJ intrépide

intrepidity /ˌɪntrɪˈpɪdɪtɪ/ N intrépidité *f*

intrepidly /ɪnˈtrepɪdlɪ/ ADV intrépidement

intricacy /ˈɪntrɪkəsɪ/ N *[of problem, plot, pattern, mechanism]* complexité *f* ◆ **the intricacies of English law** les subtilités *fpl* du droit anglais

intricate /ˈɪntrɪkɪt/ ADJ *[mechanism]* complexe ; *[pattern, style]* complexe, très élaboré ; *[plot, problem, situation]* complexe ◆ **all the ~ details** les détails dans toute leur complexité

intricately /ˈɪntrɪkɪtlɪ/ ADV ◆ **~ carved** finement sculpté ◆ **~ designed** *(in conception)* de conception très élaborée ; *(elaborately drawn)* au dessin *or* motif très élaboré ◆ **~ patterned tiles** des carreaux aux motifs complexes *or* élaborés

intrigue /ɪnˈtriːg/ VI intriguer, comploter *(with sb* avec qn ; *to do sth* pour faire qch) VT intriguer ◆ **she ~s me** elle m'intrigue ◆ **go on, I'm ~d** continue, ça m'intrigue ◆ **I'm ~d to hear what she's been saying** je suis curieux de savoir ce qu'elle a dit ◆ **I was ~d with** *or* **by what you said about the case** ce que vous avez dit sur l'affaire m'a intrigué N *(= plot)* intrigue *f* ; *(= love affair)* intrigue *f*, liaison *f* ◆ **political ~** intrigue *f* politique

intriguer /ɪnˈtriːgəʳ/ N intrigant(e) *m(f)*

intriguing /ɪnˈtriːgɪŋ/ ADJ fascinant N *(NonC)* intrigues *fpl*

intriguingly /ɪnˈtriːgɪŋlɪ/ ADV ◆ **~ different** étrangement différent ◆ **~ original** d'une originalité fascinante ◆ **~-titled** au titre fascinant ◆ **~, this was never confirmed** très curieusement, ça n'a jamais été confirmé

intrinsic /ɪnˈtrɪnsɪk/ ADJ intrinsèque ◆ **the sculpture has no ~ value** cette sculpture n'a pas de valeur intrinsèque ◆ **financial insecurity is ~ to capitalism** l'insécurité financière est une caractéristique intrinsèque du capitalisme

intrinsically /ɪnˈtrɪnsɪklɪ/ ADV intrinsèquement ◆ **~ linked** intrinsèquement lié

intro * /ˈɪntrəʊ/ N (abbrev of **introduction**) intro * *f*

introduce /ˌɪntrəˈdjuːs/ VT [1] *(= make acquainted)* présenter ◆ **he ~d me to his friend** il m'a présenté à son ami ◆ **let me ~ myself** permettez-moi de me présenter ◆ **I ~d myself to my new neighbour** je me suis présenté à mon nouveau voisin ◆ **who ~d them?** qui les a présentés ? ◆ **we haven't been ~d** nous n'avons pas été présentés ◆ **may I ~ Mr Smith?** *(frm)* puis-je (me permettre de) vous présenter M. Smith ?

◆ **to introduce sb to sth** faire découvrir qch à qn ◆ **who ~d him to drugs?** qui est-ce qui lui a fait découvrir la drogue ? ◆ **I was ~d to Shakespeare at the age of 11** on m'a fait découvrir Shakespeare quand j'avais 11 ans

[2] *(= announce etc) [+ speaker, programme]* présenter

[3] *(= adopt, bring in) [+ reform, new method, innovation]* mettre en place, introduire ; *[+ practice]* faire adopter, introduire ; *[+ word, species]* introduire ◆ **potatoes were ~d here from America** la pomme de terre nous est venue d'Amérique ◆ **when video cameras were first ~d into the courtroom** le jour où les caméras ont été autorisées pour la première fois dans les salles d'audience ◆ **this ~d a note of irony into the conversation** cela a introduit une note d'ironie dans la conversation

[4] *(= tackle) [+ subject, question]* aborder ◆ **to ~ a bill** *(Parl)* présenter un projet de loi ◆ **he soon ~d the subject of sex** il a rapidement abordé le sujet de la sexualité

[5] *(= put in place)* introduire ; *[+ key etc]* introduire, insérer *(into* dans) ◆ **I ~d him into the firm** je l'ai introduit *or* fait entrer dans l'entreprise ◆ **privatization ~d competition into the telecommunications industry** la privatisation a introduit la concurrence dans l'industrie des télécommunications ◆ **the genes ~d into plants to make them grow faster** les gènes introduits dans les plantes pour accélérer leur croissance

> ⚠ When it means 'make acquainted', **introduce** is not translated by **introduire**.

introduction /ˌɪntrəˈdʌkʃən/ N [1] *(= introducing, putting in place: gen)* introduction *f (into* dans) ; *[of system, legislation]* mise *f* en place ◆ **the company's ~ of new technology** l'introduction par l'entreprise de nouvelles technologies ◆ **his ~ to professional football** ses débuts dans le monde du football professionnel

[2] *(= new phenomenon)* apparition *f* ◆ **the massive changes wrought by the ~ of cheap Internet access** les changements radicaux dûs à l'apparition des abonnements Internet à bas prix

[3] présentation *f (of sb to sb* de qn à qn) ◆ **to give sb an ~** *or* **a letter of ~ to sb** donner à qn une lettre de recommandation auprès de qn ◆ **someone who needs no ~** une personne qu'il est inutile de présenter ◆ **will you make** *or* **do* the ~s?** voulez-vous faire les présentations ?

[4] *(to book etc)* avant-propos *m*, introduction *f*

[5] *(= elementary course)* introduction *f (to* à) manuel *m* élémentaire ◆ **"an introduction to German"** "initiation à l'allemand"

COMP **introduction agency** N club *m* de rencontres

introductory /ˌɪntrəˈdʌktərɪ/ ADJ préliminaire, d'introduction ◆ **a few ~ words** quelques mots d'introduction ◆ **~ remarks** remarques *fpl* (pré)liminaires, préambule *m* ◆ **~ offer** *(Comm)* offre *f* de lancement ◆ **an ~ price of £2.99** un prix de lancement de 2,99 livres

introit /ˈɪntrɔɪt/ N introït *m*

introspection /ˌɪntrəʊˈspekʃən/ N *(NonC)* introspection *f*

introspective /ˌɪntrəʊˈspektɪv/ ADJ introspectif, replié sur soi-même

introspectiveness /ˌɪntrəʊˈspektɪvnɪs/ N tendance *f* à l'introspection

introversion /ˌɪntrəʊˈvɜːʃən/ N introversion *f*

introvert /ˈɪntrəʊvɜːt/ N *(Psych)* introverti(e) *m(f)* ◆ **he's something of an ~** c'est un caractère plutôt fermé ADJ introverti VI *(Psych)* ◆ **to become ~ed** se replier sur soi-même

introverted /ˈɪntrəʊvɜːtɪd/ ADJ *(Psych)* introverti ; *(fig) (= inward-looking) [system, society]* replié sur soi-même

intrude /ɪnˈtruːd/ VI *[person]* être importun, s'imposer ◆ **to ~ on sb's privacy** s'ingérer dans la vie privée de qn ◆ **to ~ on sb's grief** ne pas respecter le chagrin de qn ◆ **to ~ into sb's affairs** s'immiscer *or* s'ingérer dans les affaires de qn ◆ **my family has been ~d upon by the press** la presse s'est immiscée dans la vie privée de ma famille ◆ **I don't want to ~ on your meeting** je ne veux pas interrompre votre réunion ◆ **don't let personal feelings ~** ne vous laissez pas influencer par vos sentiments ◆ **don't let negative thoughts ~** écartez toute pensée négative ◆ **am I intruding?** est-ce que je (vous) dérange ? ; *(stronger)* est-ce que je (vous) gêne ? VT introduire de force *(into* dans) imposer *(into* à) ◆ **to ~ one's views (on sb)** imposer ses idées (à qn)

intruder /ɪnˈtruːdəʳ/ N *(= person, animal)* intrus(e) *m(f)* ; *(= aircraft) avion pénétrant sans autorisation dans un espace aérien* ◆ **the ~ fled when he heard the car** l'intrus s'est enfui en entendant la voiture ◆ **I felt like an ~** je me sentais étranger *or* de trop COMP **intruder alarm** N alarme *f* anti-effraction

intrusion /ɪnˈtruːʒən/ N intrusion *f (into* dans) ◆ **excuse this ~** excusez-moi de vous déranger

intrusive /ɪnˈtruːsɪv/ ADJ *[person, presence]* indiscret (-ète *f*), importun ◆ **~ consonant** *(Ling)* consonne *f* d'appui ◆ **the ~ "r"** *(Ling) le "r" ajouté en anglais en liaison abusive*

intuit /ɪnˈtjuːɪt/ VT ◆ **to ~ that ...** savoir intuitivement *or* par intuition que ..., avoir l'intuition que ... ◆ **he ~s your every thought** il connaît intuitivement toutes vos pensées

intuition /ˌɪntjuːˈɪʃən/ N intuition *f* ◆ **female** *or* **woman's** ~ l'intuition féminine

intuitive /ɪnˈtjuːɪtɪv/ ADJ intuitif

intuitively /ɪnˈtjuːɪtɪvlɪ/ ADV intuitivement ◆ **the plan seemed ~ attractive** intuitivement, ce projet nous (*or* leur *etc*) a plu ◆ **~, the idea seems reasonable to me** intuitivement, je trouve cette idée raisonnable

Inuit /ˈɪnjuːɪt/ N Inuit *mf* ◆ **the ~(s)** les Inuit *mfpl* ADJ inuit *inv*

inundate /ˈɪnʌndeɪt/ VT (*lit, fig*) inonder (*with* de) ◆ **to be ~d with work** être débordé (de travail), être submergé de travail ◆ **to be ~d with visits** être inondé de visiteurs, être débordé de visites ◆ **to be ~d with letters** être submergé de lettres

inundation /ˌɪnʌnˈdeɪʃən/ N inondation *f*

inure /ɪnˈjʊəʳ/ VT ◆ **to be ~d to** [*+ criticism, cold*] être endurci contre ; [*+ sb's charms*] être insensible à ; [*+ pressures*] être habitué à

invade /ɪnˈveɪd/ VT 1 (*gen, Mil, fig*) envahir ◆ **city ~d by tourists** ville *f* envahie par les touristes ◆ **he was suddenly ~d by doubts** il fut soudain envahi de doutes ◆ **cells that have been ~d by a virus** des cellules qui ont été envahies par un virus 2 [*+ privacy*] violer, s'ingérer dans ◆ **to ~ sb's rights** empiéter sur les droits de qn

invader /ɪnˈveɪdəʳ/ N envahisseur *m*, -euse *f* ◆ **the immune system produces antibodies to neutralize the ~** le système immunitaire fabrique des anticorps afin de neutraliser l'envahisseur

invading /ɪnˈveɪdɪŋ/ ADJ [*army, troops*] d'invasion ◆ **the ~ Romans** l'envahisseur romain

invalid¹ /ˈɪnvəlɪd/ N (*= sick person*) malade *mf* ; (*with disability*) invalide *mf*, infirme *mf* ◆ **chronic ~** malade *mf* chronique ◆ **to treat sb like an ~** traiter qn comme un handicapé ADJ (*= ill*) malade ; (*with disability*) invalide, infirme VT /ˈɪnvəliːd/ (*esp Brit Mil*) ◆ **he was ~ed home from the front** il fut rapatrié du front pour blessures (*or* pour raisons de santé) COMP **invalid car, invalid carriage** N (*Brit*) voiture *f* d'infirme *or* pour handicapé

▸ **invalid out** VT SEP (*Mil*) ◆ **to invalid sb out of the army** réformer qn (pour blessures *or* pour raisons de santé)

invalid² /ɪnˈvælɪd/ ADJ (*esp Jur*) non valide, non valable ; [*argument*] nul (nulle *f*) ◆ **to become ~** [*ticket*] ne plus être valable, être périmé ◆ **to declare sth ~** déclarer qch nul

invalidate /ɪnˈvælɪdeɪt/ VT invalider, annuler ; (*Jur*) [*+ judgment*] casser, infirmer ; [*+ will*] rendre nul et sans effet ; [*+ contract*] vicier ; [*+ statute*] abroger

invalidity /ˌɪnvəˈlɪdɪtɪ/ N 1 (*= disability*) invalidité *f* ◆ **~ benefit** (*Brit Admin*) allocation *f* d'invalidité 2 [*of argument*] nullité *f* ; [*of law, election*] invalidité *f*

invaluable /ɪnˈvæljʊəbl/ ADJ inestimable, (très) précieux ◆ **her help has been ~ to me** elle m'a été d'une aide inestimable *or* (très) précieuse ◆ **their advice was ~ (to me)** leurs conseils m'ont été précieux

invariable /ɪnˈvɛərɪəbl/ ADJ invariable

invariably /ɪnˈvɛərɪəblɪ/ ADV invariablement

invariant /ɪnˈvɛərɪənt/ ADJ, N invariant *m*

invasion /ɪnˈveɪʒən/ N 1 (*Mil, fig*) invasion *f* ◆ **a tourist ~** une invasion de touristes 2 [*of rights*] empiètement *m* (*of* sur) ◆ **~ of privacy** (*by journalist, police etc*) intrusion *f* dans la vie privée ◆ **reading her diary was a gross ~ of privacy** lire son journal intime était une intrusion choquante dans sa vie privée

invasive /ɪnˈveɪsɪv/ ADJ (*Med*) [*disease*] (*gen*) qui gagne du terrain ; [*cancer, carcinoma*] invasif ; [*surgery, treatment*] agressif ◆ **the legislation has been criticized as being too ~** cette législation a été critiquée parce qu'elle porterait atteinte à la vie privée

invective /ɪnˈvektɪv/ N (*NonC*) invective *f* ◆ **torrent** *or* **stream of ~** flot *m* d'invectives *or* d'injures ◆ **racist ~** injures *fpl* racistes

inveigh /ɪnˈveɪ/ VI ◆ **to ~ against sb/sth** invectiver qn/qch ; (*more violently*) fulminer *or* tonner contre qn/qch

inveigle /ɪnˈviːgl/ VT ◆ **to ~ sb into sth** entraîner *or* attirer qn dans qch (par la ruse) ◆ **to ~ sb into doing sth** entraîner *or* amener qn à faire qch (par la ruse)

invent /ɪnˈvent/ VT (*lit, fig*) inventer

invention /ɪnˈvenʃən/ N 1 invention *f* ◆ **the ~ of the telephone** l'invention *f* du téléphone ◆ **one of his most practical ~s** une de ses inventions les plus pratiques 2 (*= falsehood*) invention *f*, mensonge *m* ◆ **it was pure ~ on her part** c'était pure invention de sa part ◆ **it was (an) ~ from start to finish** c'était (une) pure invention du début à la fin

inventive /ɪnˈventɪv/ ADJ inventif

inventiveness /ɪnˈventɪvnɪs/ N (*NonC*) esprit *m* inventif *or* d'invention

inventor /ɪnˈventəʳ/ N inventeur *m*, -trice *f*

inventory /ˈɪnvəntrɪ/ N inventaire *m* ; (*US Comm*) stock *m* ◆ **to draw up** *or* **make an ~ of sth** inventorier qch, faire *or* dresser un inventaire de qch ◆ **~ of fixtures** état *m* des lieux VT inventorier COMP **inventory control** N (*US Comm*) gestion *f* des stocks

inverse /ˈɪnvɜːs/ ADJ inverse ◆ **in ~ order** en sens inverse ◆ **in ~ proportion to** inversement proportionnel à ◆ **in ~ ratio (to)** en raison inverse (de) ◆ **an ~ relationship between ...** une relation inverse entre ... N inverse *m*, contraire *m*

inversely /ɪnˈvɜːslɪ/ ADV inversement

inversion /ɪnˈvɜːʃən/ N (*gen*) inversion *f* ; [*of values, roles etc*] (*also Mus*) renversement *m*

invert /ɪnˈvɜːt/ VT 1 [*+ elements, order, words*] inverser, intervertir ; [*+ roles*] renverser, intervertir ◆ **to ~ a process** renverser une opération 2 [*+ cup, object*] retourner N /ˈɪnvɜːt/ (*Psych*) inverti(e) *m(f)* COMP **inverted chord** N (*Mus*) accord *m* renversé **inverted commas** NPL (*Brit*) guillemets *mpl* ◆ **in ~ed commas** entre guillemets **inverted nipples** NPL mamelons *mpl* ombiliqués **inverted snobbery** N snobisme *m* à rebours **invert sugar** N sucre *m* inverti

invertebrate /ɪnˈvɜːtɪbrɪt/ ADJ, N invertébré *m*

invest /ɪnˈvest/ VT 1 (*Fin*) [*+ money, capital, funds*] investir, placer (*in* dans, en) ◆ **to ~ money** faire un *or* des placement(s), placer de l'argent ◆ **I have ~ed a lot of time in this project** j'ai consacré beaucoup de temps à ce projet ◆ **she ~ed a lot of effort in it** elle s'est beaucoup investie 2 (*= endow*) revêtir, investir (*sb with sth* qn de qch) ◆ **to ~ sb as** [*+ monarch, president etc*] élever qn à la dignité de ◆ **the buildings are ~ed with a nation's history** ces bâtiments sont empreints de l'histoire d'une nation 3 (*Mil = surround*) investir, cerner VI investir ◆ **to ~ in shares/property** placer son argent *or* investir dans des actions/dans l'immobilier ◆ **I've ~ed in a new car** je me suis offert une nouvelle voiture

investigate /ɪnˈvestɪgeɪt/ VT [*+ question, possibilities*] examiner, étudier ; [*+ motive, reason*] scruter, sonder ; [*+ crime*] enquêter sur, faire une enquête sur

investigation /ɪnˌvestɪˈgeɪʃən/ N 1 (*NonC*) [*of facts, question*] examen *m* ; [*of crime*] enquête *f* (*of* sur) ◆ **to be under ~ for sth** faire l'objet d'une enquête pour qch ◆ **the matter under ~** la question à l'étude 2 [*of researcher*] investigation *f*, enquête *f* ; [*of policeman*] enquête *f* ◆ **his ~s led him to believe that ...** ses investigations l'ont amené à penser que ... ◆ **criminal ~** enquête *f* criminelle ◆ **to launch an ~** ouvrir une enquête ◆ **preliminary ~** enquête *f* préparatoire *or* préliminaire ◆ **it calls for an immediate ~** cela demande une étude immédiate *or* à être étudié immédiatement ◆ **to call for an immediate ~ into sth** demander que l'on ouvre *subj* immédiatement une enquête sur qch ◆ **to order an ~ into** *or* **of sth** ordonner une enquête sur qch ◆ **we have made ~s** nous avons fait une enquête *or* des recherches

investigative /ɪnˈvestɪˌgeɪtɪv/ ADJ [*journalism, reporter, team, method*] d'investigation

investigator /ɪnˈvestɪgeɪtəʳ/ N investigateur *m*, -trice *f* ; → **private**

investigatory /ɪnˈvestɪˌgeɪtərɪ/ ADJ ◆ **~ group/panel** groupe *m*/commission *f* d'enquête

investiture /ɪnˈvestɪtʃəʳ/ N investiture *f*

investment /ɪnˈvestmənt/ N 1 (*Fin*) investissement *m*, placement *m* ; (*fig, esp Psych*) investissement *m* ◆ **by careful ~ of his capital** en investissant *or* plaçant soigneusement son capital ◆ **he regretted his ~ in the company** il regrettait d'avoir investi dans la firme ◆ **~ in shares** placement *m* en valeurs ◆ **~ in property** placement *m or* investissement *m* immobilier ◆ **we need a major ~ in new technology** il nous faut investir massivement dans les nouvelles technologies ◆ **foreign ~ in the region** les investissements *mpl* étrangers dans la région ◆ **~s** (*= money invested*) placements *mpl*, investissements *mpl* ◆ **return on one's ~s** retour *m* sur investissement ◆ **a portable TV is always a good ~** une télévision portable est toujours un bon investissement 2 (*Mil*) investissement *m* 3 ⇒ **investiture** COMP **investment analyst** N analyste *mf* en placements **investment bank** N (*US*) banque *f* d'affaires *or* d'investissement **investment company** N société *f* d'investissement **investment income** N revenu *m* des placements *or* des investissements **investment management** N gestion *f* de portefeuille **investment manager** N gérant(e) *m(f)* de portefeuille **investment opportunities** NPL investissements *mpl or* placements *mpl* intéressants **investment trust** N société *f* d'investissement

investor /ɪnˈvestəʳ/ N (*gen*) investisseur *m* ; (*= shareholder*) actionnaire *mf* ◆ **(the) big ~s** les gros actionnaires *mpl* ◆ **(the) small ~s** les petits actionnaires *mpl*, la petite épargne *NonC*

inveterate /ɪnˈvetərɪt/ ADJ [*gambler, smoker, liar*] invétéré ; [*traveller*] insatiable ; [*collector*] impénitent ; [*laziness, extravagance*] incurable

invidious /ɪnˈvɪdɪəs/ ADJ [*decision, distinction, choice*] injuste, propre à susciter la jalousie ; [*comparison*] blessant, désobligeant ; [*task*] ingrat, déplaisant

invigilate /ɪnˈvɪdʒɪleɪt/ (*Brit*) VI être de surveillance (à un examen) VT [*+ examination*] surveiller

invigilator /ɪnˈvɪdʒɪleɪtəʳ/ N (*Brit*) surveillant(e) *m(f)* (*à un examen*)

invigorate /ɪnˈvɪgəreɪt/ VT [*+ person*] [*drink, food, thought, fresh air*] redonner des forces à, revigorer ; [*climate, air*] vivifier, tonifier ; [*exercise*] tonifier ; [*+ campaign*] animer ◆ **to feel ~d** se sentir revigoré *or* vivifié

invigorating /ɪn'vɪgəreɪtɪŋ/ ADJ *[climate, air, walk]* vivifiant, tonifiant ; *[speech]* stimulant

invincibility /ɪn,vɪnsɪ'bɪlɪtɪ/ N invincibilité *f*

invincible /ɪn'vɪnsəbl/ ADJ 1 *(= unbeatable)* invincible 2 *(= unshakeable) [faith, belief, spirit]* inébranlable

inviolability /ɪn,vaɪələ'bɪlɪtɪ/ N inviolabilité *f*

inviolable /ɪn'vaɪələbl/ ADJ inviolable

inviolably /ɪn'vaɪələblɪ/ ADV inviolablement

inviolate /ɪn'vaɪəlɪt/ ADJ inviolé

invisibility /ɪn,vɪzə'bɪlɪtɪ/ N invisibilité *f*

invisible /ɪn'vɪzəbl/ ADJ 1 *(lit)* invisible 2 *(fig = ignored)* ignoré ◆ **to feel ~** se sentir ignoré NPL **invisibles** invisibles *mpl*

COMP **invisible earnings** NPL revenus *mpl* invisibles

invisible exports NPL exportations *fpl* invisibles

invisible ink N encre *f* sympathique

invisible mending N stoppage *m*

invisibly /ɪn'vɪzəblɪ/ ADV invisiblement

invitation /,ɪnvɪ'teɪʃən/ LANGUAGE IN USE 25

N invitation *f* ◆ **~ to dinner** invitation *f* à dîner ◆ **the unions have not yet accepted the ~ to attend** les syndicats n'ont pas encore accepté de venir ◆ **their ~ to attend a July conference** leur invitation à participer à une conférence en juillet ◆ **he has refused an ~ to attend the inauguration ceremony** il a refusé d'assister à la cérémonie d'ouverture ◆ **at sb's ~** à *or* sur l'invitation de qn ◆ **by ~ (only)** sur invitation (seulement) ◆ **to send out ~s** envoyer des invitations ◆ **~ to bid** *(Fin)* avis *m* d'appel d'offres ◆ **this lock is an open ~ to burglars!** *(iro)* cette serrure est une véritable invite au cambriolage !

COMP **invitation card** N (carte *f or* carton *m* d')invitation *f*

invitational /,ɪnvɪ'teɪʃənl/ ADJ *(Sport)* ◆ **~ tournament** tournoi *m* sur invitation

invite /ɪn'vaɪt/ LANGUAGE IN USE 25.1

VT 1 *(= ask) [+ person]* inviter *(to do sth* à faire qch) ◆ **to ~ sb to dinner** inviter qn à dîner ◆ **he ~d him for a drink** il l'a invité à prendre un verre ◆ **I've never been ~d to their house** je n'ai jamais été invité chez eux ◆ **he was ~d to the ceremony** il a été invité (à assister) à la cérémonie ◆ **to ~ sb in/up** *etc* inviter qn à entrer/monter *etc* ◆ **that store ~s thieves** *(iro)* ce magasin est une invite au vol

2 *(= ask for) [+ sb's attention, subscriptions etc]* demander, solliciter ◆ **when he had finished he ~d questions from the audience** quand il eut fini il invita le public à poser des questions ◆ **he was ~d to give his opinion** on l'a invité à donner son avis

3 *(= lead to) [+ confidences, questions, doubts, ridicule]* appeler ; *[+ discussion, step]* inviter à ; *[+ failure, defeat]* chercher ◆ **I wouldn't walk home alone, it only ~s trouble** je ne rentrerais pas à pied tout seul, c'est vraiment chercher les ennuis

N /'ɪnvaɪt/ * invitation *f*

▸ **invite out** VT SEP inviter (à sortir) ◆ **he has ~d her out several times** il l'a invitée plusieurs fois à sortir ◆ **I've been ~d out to dinner this evening** j'ai été invité à dîner ce soir

▸ **invite over** VT SEP 1 inviter (à venir) ◆ **they often ~ us over for a drink** ils nous invitent souvent à venir prendre un verre chez eux ◆ **let's ~ them over some time** invitons-les un de ces jours (à venir nous voir)

2 ◆ **he invited me over to his table** il (m'appela et) m'invita à venir m'asseoir à sa table

inviting /ɪn'vaɪtɪŋ/ ADJ *[place, room, atmosphere]* accueillant ; *[dish, smell]* alléchant, appétissant ; *[prospect]* engageant, tentant ◆ **the water looked very ~** *(for swimming)* l'eau était très tentante ◆ **it's not an ~ prospect** ce n'est pas une perspective engageante *or* tentante

invitingly /ɪn'vaɪtɪŋlɪ/ ADV ◆ **to smile ~** sourire d'un air engageant ◆ **the soup steamed ~** la soupe fumait de façon appétissante ◆ **the chocolate sat ~ on his desk** * le chocolat était sur son bureau, telle une invitation à la gourmandise ◆ **the waters of the tropics are ~ clear** les eaux tropicales sont d'une limpidité engageante

in vitro /ɪn'viːtrəʊ/ ADJ, ADV in vitro COMP **in vitro fertilization** N fécondation *f* in vitro

invocation /,ɪnvəʊ'keɪʃən/ N invocation *f*

invoice /'ɪnvɔɪs/ LANGUAGE IN USE 20.6 N facture *f* VT *[+ customer, goods]* facturer ◆ **they will ~ us for the maintenance** ils vont nous facturer l'entretien COMP **invoice clerk** N facturier *m*, -ière *f*

invoicing /'ɪnvɔɪsɪŋ/ N *(NonC)* facturation *f*

invoke /ɪn'vəʊk/ VT 1 *(= call on) [+ God, Muse, mercy, precedent, law]* invoquer ; *[+ memories, atmosphere]* évoquer ◆ **to ~ sb's help** invoquer *or* demander l'aide de qn 2 *(= evoke) [+ spirits, the devil]* évoquer

involuntarily /ɪn'vɒləntərɪlɪ/ ADV involontairement

involuntary /ɪn'vɒləntərɪ/ ADJ involontaire COMP **involuntary manslaughter** N *(Jur)* homicide *m* involontaire

involuted /,ɪnvə'luːtɪd/ ADJ compliqué

involve /ɪn'vɒlv/ VT 1 *(= entail)* impliquer ; *(= cause)* occasionner ; *(= demand)* exiger ◆ **such an attack would inevitably ~ considerable loss of life** une telle attaque ferait inévitablement de très nombreuses victimes ◆ **such a project ~s considerable planning** un tel projet exige une organisation considérable ◆ **will the post ~ much foreign travel?** ce poste impliquera-t-il de nombreux déplacements à l'étranger ? ◆ **make sure you know what the job ~s** il faut que tu saches exactement en quoi consiste ce travail ◆ **my job ~s repetitive hand movements** dans le cadre de mon travail, je fais toujours le même mouvement avec mes mains ◆ **the job would ~ my moving to London** ce travail impliquerait que je m'installe *subj* à Londres ◆ **there will be a good deal of work ~d** cela demandera *or* entraînera beaucoup de travail ◆ **the charges against him ~ allegations of corruption** parmi les accusations portées contre lui, il y a des allégations de corruption

2 *(= implicate, associate)* impliquer *(in* dans) mêler *(in* à) ◆ **we would prefer not to ~ Robert** nous préférerions ne pas mêler Robert à l'affaire *or* ne pas impliquer Robert dans l'affaire ◆ **don't try to ~ me in this scheme** n'essaie pas de me mêler à ce projet ◆ **to ~ sb in a quarrel** mêler qn à une querelle ◆ **the cover-up ~d senior officers** des officiers supérieurs étaient impliqués dans le *or* mêlés au complot ◆ **to get ~d in sth, to ~ o.s. in sth** *(= get dragged into)* se laisser entraîner dans qch ; *(from choice)* s'engager dans qch ◆ **she didn't want to ~ herself in this debate** elle ne voulait pas se laisser entraîner dans ce débat ◆ **she ~d herself** *or* **got ~d in the freedom movement** elle s'est engagée dans le mouvement pour la liberté ◆ **a riot involving a hundred prison inmates** une émeute à laquelle ont pris part cent détenus ◆ **this is going to ~ us in a lot of expense** cela va nous entraîner dans de grosses dépenses ◆ **how did you come to be ~d?** comment vous êtes-vous trouvé impliqué ?

◆ **to involve sb in sth** *(= cause to participate)* faire participer qn à qch ◆ **he ~s me in all aspects of the job** il me fait participer à tous les aspects du travail ◆ **the school likes to ~ parents in their children's education** l'école aime associer les parents à l'éducation de leurs enfants

involved /ɪn'vɒlvd/ ADJ 1 *(= concerned)* concerné ◆ **we are all ~** nous sommes tous concernés ◆ **to feel personally ~** se sentir concerné ◆ **she wasn't directly ~** *(= affected)* elle n'était pas directement concernée ; *(= taking part)* elle n'était pas directement impliquée ◆ **the police became ~** la police est intervenue ◆ **a question of principle is ~** il s'agit d'une question de principe ◆ **the factors/forces/principles ~** les facteurs *mpl*/forces *fpl*/principes *mpl* en jeu ◆ **the vehicles ~** les véhicules *mpl* en cause ◆ **the person ~** l'intéressé(e) *m(f)*

◆ **to be involved in sth** *(= take part in)* participer à ; *[+ sth negative]* être mêlé à ◆ **they were not ~ in the discussions** ils ne participaient pas aux négociations ◆ **an organization for people ~ in agriculture** un organisme pour ceux qui travaillent dans l'agriculture ◆ **he wasn't ~ in the plot** il n'était pas mêlé au complot ◆ **to be ~ in a quarrel** être mêlé à une querelle

◆ **to get involved with sb** *(socially)* se mettre à fréquenter qn ; *(= fall in love with)* avoir une liaison avec qn ◆ **he got ~ with a married woman** il a eu une liaison avec une femme mariée ◆ **she likes him but she doesn't want to get (too) ~** elle l'aime bien, mais elle ne veut pas (trop) s'engager

2 *(= very interested)*

◆ **to be involved in sth** être absorbé par qch ◆ **he was so ~ in politics that he had no time to ...** il était tellement absorbé par la politique qu'il n'avait pas le temps de ...

3 *(= complicated) [situation, relationship, question]* compliqué, complexe ; *[style]* contourné, compliqué ; see also **involve**

involvement /ɪn'vɒlvmənt/ N *(NonC) (= rôle)* rôle *m (in* dans) ; *(= participation)* participation *f (in* à) ◆ **his ~ in the affair/plot** *etc* son rôle dans l'affaire/le complot *etc* ◆ **the increasing ~ of employees in decision-making processes** la participation de plus en plus importante des employés dans la prise de décisions ◆ **his ~ in politics** son engagement *m* dans la politique ◆ **his ~ in social work** son action *f* en matière sociale ◆ **we don't know the extent of her ~** nous ne savons pas dans quelle mesure elle est impliquée ◆ **we have no hard proof of his ~** nous n'avons aucune preuve concrète qu'il ait été impliqué ◆ **she denied any ~ in** *or* **with drugs** elle a nié toute implication dans des histoires de drogues ◆ **they were good friends but there was no romantic ~** ils étaient bons amis mais leur relation n'allait pas plus loin

invulnerability /ɪn,vʌlnərə'bɪlɪtɪ/ N invulnérabilité *f*

invulnerable /ɪn'vʌlnərəbl/ ADJ invulnérable

inward /'ɪnwəd/ ADJ *[movement]* vers l'intérieur ; *[happiness, peace]* intérieur (-eure *f*) ; *[thoughts, desire, conviction]* intime, profond ADV ⇒ **inwards**

COMP **inward investment** N *(NonC: Comm)* investissements *mpl* étrangers

inward-looking ADJ replié sur soi (-même)

inwardly /'ɪnwədlɪ/ ADV *[groan, smile]* intérieurement ◆ **she was ~ furious** en son for intérieur elle était furieuse

inwards /'ɪnwədz/ ADV *[move]* vers l'intérieur ◆ **his thoughts turned ~** il devint songeur

I/O /aɪəʊ/ N (abbrev of **input/output**) E/S *f*

IOC /,aɪəʊ'siː/ N (abbrev of **International Olympic Committee**) CIO *m*

iodide /'aɪədaɪd/ N iodure *m*

iodine /'aɪədiːn/ N iode *m*

iodize /'aɪədaɪz/ VT ioder

iodoform /aɪ'ɒdəfɔːm/ N iodoforme *m*

IOM (abbrev of **Isle of Man**) → **isle**

ion /ˈaɪən/ N ion *m*

Iona /aɪˈəʊnə/ N (île *f* d')Iona *f*

Ionian /aɪˈəʊnɪən/ ADJ ionien ◆ **the ~ Islands** les îles *fpl* Ioniennes ◆ **the ~ (Sea)** la mer Ionienne

Ionic /aɪˈɒnɪk/ ADJ *(Archit)* ionique

ionic /aɪˈɒnɪk/ ADJ *(Chem, Phys)* ionique

ionize /ˈaɪənaɪz/ VT ioniser

ionizer /ˈaɪənaɪzəʳ/ N ioniseur *m*

ionosphere /aɪˈɒnəsfɪəʳ/ N ionosphère *f*

iota /aɪˈəʊtə/ N *(= letter)* iota *m* ; *(fig = tiny amount)* brin *m*, grain *m* ; *(in written matter)* iota *m* ◆ **he won't change an ~ (of what he has written)** il refuse de changer un iota (à ce qu'il a écrit) ◆ **if he had an ~ of sense** s'il avait un grain de bon sens ◆ **not an ~ of truth** pas un brin de vérité, pas un mot de vrai ◆ **it won't make an ~ of difference** cela ne changera absolument rien ◆ **it won't affect us one ~** cela ne nous touchera absolument pas

IOU /ˌaɪəʊˈjuː/ N (abbrev of **I owe you**) reconnaissance *f* de dette ◆ **he gave me an ~ for £20** il m'a signé un reçu de 20 livres

IOW *(Brit)* (abbrev of **Isle of Wight**) → **isle**

Iowa /ˈaɪəʊə/ N Iowa *m* ◆ **in ~** dans l'Iowa

IPA /ˌaɪpiːˈeɪ/ N (abbrev of **International Phonetic Alphabet**) API *m*

IP address /aɪˈpiːədres/ N *(Comput)* (abbrev of **Internet Protocol address**) adresse *f* IP

ipecac(uanha) /ˌɪpɪkæk(jʊˈænə)/ N ipéca(cuana) *m*

IPO /ˌaɪpiːˈəʊ/ N (abbrev of **initial public offering**) IPO *m*

ipso facto /ˈɪpsəʊˈfæktəʊ/ ADJ, ADV ipso facto

IQ /ˌaɪˈkjuː/ N (abbrev of **intelligence quotient**) QI *m*

IR /ˌaɪˈɑːʳ/ N *(Brit)* (abbrev of **Inland Revenue**) ≈ fisc *m*

IRA /ˌaɪɑːrˈeɪ/ N (abbrev of **Irish Republican Army**) IRA *f*

Irak /ɪˈrɑːk/ N ⇒ **Iraq**

Iraki /ɪˈrɑːkɪ/ ADJ, N ⇒ **Iraqi**

Iran /ɪˈrɑːn/ N Iran *m* ◆ **in ~** en Iran

Irangate /ɪˈrɑːngeɪt/ N, ADJ Irangate *m*

Iranian /ɪˈreɪnɪən/ ADJ iranien N 1 Iranien(ne) *m(f)* 2 *(Ling)* iranien *m*

Iraq /ɪˈrɑːk/ N Irak *or* Iraq *m* ◆ **in ~** en Irak

Iraqi /ɪˈrɑːkɪ/ ADJ irakien *or* iraquien N Irakien(ne) *or* Iraquien(ne) *m(f)*

irascibility /ɪˌræsɪˈbɪlɪtɪ/ N irascibilité *f*

irascible /ɪˈræsɪbl/ ADJ irascible, coléreux

irascibly /ɪˈræsɪblɪ/ ADV *[say]* d'un ton irrité

irate /aɪˈreɪt/ ADJ furieux, courroucé *(liter)*

IRBM /ˌaɪɑːbiːˈem/ N (abbrev of **intermediate range ballistic missile**) → **intermediate**

IRC /ˌaɪɑːˈsiː/ N *(Comput)* (abbrev of **Internet Relay Chat**) IRC *m*

ire /aɪəʳ/ N *(liter)* courroux *m (liter)* ◆ **to rouse sb's ~** provoquer le courroux de qn

Ireland /ˈaɪələnd/ N Irlande *f* ◆ **the Republic of ~** la République d'Irlande ; → **northern**

irides /ˈɪrɪdiːz/ NPL of **iris 1**

iridescence /ˌɪrɪˈdesns/ N *[of prism, crystal]* irisation *f* ; *[of plumage etc]* chatoiement *m*

iridescent /ˌɪrɪˈdesnt/ ADJ *[prism, crystal]* irisé ; *[plumage]* chatoyant

iridium /aɪˈrɪdɪəm/ N iridium *m*

iridology /ˌɪrɪˈdɒlədʒɪ/ N iridologie *f*

iris /ˈaɪərɪs/ N 1 (pl **irides**) *[of eye]* iris *m* 2 (pl **irises**) *(= plant)* iris *m*

Irish /ˈaɪərɪʃ/ ADJ *(gen)* irlandais ; *[ambassador, embassy]* d'Irlande ; *[teacher]* d'irlandais N *(= language)* irlandais *m* NPL **the Irish** les Irlandais *mpl*

COMP **Irish coffee** N café *m* irlandais, irish coffee *m*

Irish Free State N *(Hist)* État *m* libre d'Irlande

Irish Republic N République *f* d'Irlande

Irish Sea N mer *f* d'Irlande

Irish stew N ragoût *m* de mouton (à l'irlandaise)

Irish terrier N irish-terrier *m*

Irish wolfhound N lévrier *m* irlandais

Irishman /ˈaɪərɪʃmən/ N (pl **-men**) Irlandais *m*

Irishwoman /ˈaɪərɪʃˈwʊmən/ N (pl **-women**) Irlandaise *f*

irk /ɜːk/ VT contrarier, ennuyer

irksome /ˈɜːksəm/ ADJ *[restriction, person]* ennuyeux ; *[task]* ingrat

iron /ˈaɪən/ N 1 *(NonC = metal)* fer *m* ◆ **old** *or* **scrap ~** ferraille *f NonC* ◆ **a man of ~** *(fig) (unyielding)* un homme de fer ; *(cruel)* un homme au cœur de pierre ◆ **to strike while the ~ is hot** battre le fer pendant qu'il est chaud ◆ **the ~ had entered his soul** *(fig liter)* il avait la mort dans l'âme, il était comme une âme en peine ; → **cast, pump¹, rod, wrought**

2 *(= tool)* fer *m* ; *(for laundry:* also **flat iron***)* fer *m* (à repasser) ◆ **electric ~** fer *m* électrique ◆ **to give a dress an ~*, to run the ~ over a dress** donner un coup de fer à une robe ◆ **to have too many ~s in the fire** mener trop de choses *or* d'affaires de front ◆ **she's got other ~s in the fire** elle a d'autres affaires en train ; → **fire, grapple, solder**

3 *(Golf)* fer *m* ◆ **a number three ~** un fer trois

4 *(NonC: Med)* (sels *mpl* de) fer *m*

5 *(= surgical appliance)* appareil *m* orthopédique ; → **leg**

NPL **irons** *(= fetters)* fers *mpl*, chaînes *fpl* ◆ **to put sb in ~s** mettre qn aux fers ◆ **to be in ~s** *(Naut)* faire chapelle

VT *[+ clothes etc]* repasser ; *(more sketchily)* donner un coup de fer à ◆ **"iron under a damp cloth"** "repasser à la pattemouille" ; → **minimum, non-**

VI *[person]* repasser ; *[clothes etc]* se repasser

COMP *(lit) [tool, bridge]* de *or* en fer ; *(fig) [determination]* de fer, d'acier

the Iron Age N l'âge *m* de fer

the iron and steel industry N l'industrie *f* sidérurgique

the Iron Chancellor N *(Hist)* le Chancelier de fer *(Bismarck)*

iron constitution N ◆ **to have an ~ constitution** avoir une santé de fer

Iron Curtain N *(Pol Hist)* rideau *m* de fer ◆ **the Iron Curtain countries** les pays *mpl* de l'Est, le bloc de l'Est

the Iron Duke N *(Brit Hist)* le Duc de fer *(Wellington)*

iron fist N ◆ **an ~ fist in a velvet glove** une main de fer dans un gant de velours

iron foundry N fonderie *f* de fonte

iron grey ADJ gris *inv* de fer, gris fer *inv* ; *[hair]* gris argenté

iron hand N ◆ **to rule with an ~ hand** gouverner d'une main *or* poigne de fer ; see also **iron fist**

the Iron Lady N *(Brit Pol)* la Dame de fer *(Margaret Thatcher)*

iron lung N *(Med)* poumon *m* d'acier

iron mask N ◆ **the man in the ~ mask** l'homme *m* au masque de fer

iron ore N minerai *m* de fer

iron oxide N oxyde *m* de fer

iron pyrite N pyrite *f*

iron rations NPL vivres *mpl or* rations *fpl* de réserve

iron will N volonté *f* de fer

► **iron out** VT SEP *[+ creases]* faire disparaître au fer ; *(fig) [+ difficulties]* aplanir ; *[+ problems]* régler ◆ **the two sides were unable to ~ out their differences** les deux camps n'ont pas réussi à régler leurs différends

ironclad /ˈaɪənklæd/ N *(= ship)* cuirassé *m* ADJ *(lit) [warship]* cuirassé ; *(fig) [argument, case, guarantee, promise, defence]* en béton ; *[rule]* strict

ironic(al) /aɪˈrɒnɪk(əl)/ ADJ ironique

ironically /aɪˈrɒnɪkəlɪ/ ADV ironiquement ◆ **~, she never turned up** l'ironie de la chose, c'est qu'elle n'est pas venue du tout

ironing /ˈaɪənɪŋ/ N repassage *m* ◆ **to do the ~** repasser, faire le repassage ◆ **it doesn't need ~** cela n'a pas besoin d'être repassé COMP **ironing board** N planche *f* à repasser

ironist /ˈaɪərənɪst/ N adepte *mf* de l'ironie ◆ **the master ~** le maître de l'ironie

ironize /ˈaɪərənaɪz/ VI ironiser VT ◆ **to ~ sb/sth** traiter qn/qch avec ironie

ironmonger /ˈaɪən,mʌŋgəʳ/ N *(Brit)* quincaillier *m*, -ière *f* ◆ **~'s (shop)** quincaillerie *f*

ironmongery /ˈaɪən,mʌŋgərɪ/ N *(Brit)* quincaillerie *f*

ironstone /ˈaɪənstəʊn/ N (also **ironstone china**) terre *f* de fer

ironwork /ˈaɪənwɜːk/ N *(NonC) [of gates, railings etc]* ferronnerie *f*, serrurerie *f* ; *[of parts of construction]* ferronnerie *f*, ferrures *fpl* ◆ **heavy ~** grosse ferronnerie *f or* serrurerie *f*

ironworks /ˈaɪənwɜːks/ N *(pl inv)* usine *f* sidérurgique

irony /ˈaɪərənɪ/ N ironie *f* ◆ **the ~ of the situation was not lost on her** l'ironie de la situation ne lui a pas échappé ◆ **by some ~ of fate, she ...** l'ironie du sort a voulu qu'elle ... ◆ **the ~ of it is that ...** l'ironie de la chose c'est que ... ◆ **one of the great ironies of this story is that ...** le comble de l'ironie (dans cette histoire), c'est que ... ; → **dramatic**

Iroquois /ˈɪrəkwɔɪ/ ADJ iroquois N *(pl inv)* 1 (also **Iroquois Indian**) Iroquois(e) *m(f)* 2 *(= language)* iroquois *m*

irradiate /ɪˈreɪdɪeɪt/ VT 1 *(Med, Nucl = expose to radiation) [+ food, population, tumour, patient]* irradier ◆ **~d foods** aliments *mpl* irradiés 2 *(= illuminate: lit, fig)* illuminer

irradiation /ɪˌreɪdɪˈeɪʃən/ N *(with radiation) [of person, food]* irradiation *f* ; *(with light)* illumination *f*

irrational /ɪˈræʃənl/ ADJ *[person]* qui n'est pas rationnel ; *[conduct]* irrationnel, déraisonnable ; *[fear]* irraisonné, irrationnel ; *[hatred, idea, reaction]* irrationnel ; *[thoughts]* fou (folle *f*) ; *(Math)* irrationnel ◆ **he had become quite ~ about it** c'était un sujet qu'il n'était plus capable d'aborder rationnellement

irrationality /ɪ,ræʃəˈnælɪtɪ/ N irrationalité *f*

irrationally /ɪˈræʃnəlɪ/ ADV *[act, behave]* irrationnellement ; *[think, believe]* en dépit du bon sens, irrationnellement ; *[angry]* sans véritable raison ◆ **~ jealous** d'une jalousie irraisonnée

irreconcilable /ɪˌrekənˈsaɪləbl/ ADJ *[differences, positions]* inconciliable ; *[beliefs, opinions]* inconciliable, incompatible *(with sth* avec qch) ; *[objectives]* incompatible *(with sth* avec qch) ; *[enemy, opponent]* irréconciliable ; *[conflict]* insoluble ; *[hatred]* implacable

irrecoverable /ˌɪrɪˈkʌvərəbl/ ADJ *[object]* irrécupérable ; *[loss]* irréparable, irrémédiable ; *(Fin)* irrécouvrable

irredeemable /ˌɪrɪˈdiːməbl/ ADJ 1 *[error]* irréparable ; *[liar, thief]* invétéré ; *[optimist]* impénitent, incorrigible 2 *(Fin) [loan, bond]* non remboursable ;

irredeemably /ˌɪrɪˈdiːməblɪ/ ADV *[lost, ruined, damaged]* irrémédiablement ◆ **~ evil/incom-**

petent d'une méchanceté/incompétence irrémédiable

irredentism /ˌɪrɪ'dentɪzəm/ N *(fig)* irrédentisme *m*

irredentist /ˌɪrɪ'dentɪst/ ADJ, N *(fig)* irrédentiste *mf*

irreducible /ˌɪrɪ'dju:səbl/ ADJ irréductible

irrefutable /ˌɪrɪ'fju:təbl/ ADJ *[argument, evidence]* irréfutable ; *[testimony]* irrécusable

irregular /ɪ'regjʊlə^r/ ADJ 1 *(gen, Math, Gram) [features, pulse, meals, hours]* irrégulier ◆ **at ~ intervals** à intervalles irréguliers ◆ **he leads a very ~ life** il mène une vie très déréglée ◆ **all this is most ~** *(= against regulations)* tout cela n'est pas du tout régulier ; *(= unorthodox)* cela ne se fait pas ◆ **he is ~ in his attendance at classes** il n'assiste pas régulièrement aux cours ◆ **~ periods** *(Med)* règles *fpl* irrégulières 2 *(= uneven) [surface]* inégal 3 *(Mil) [soldier]* irrégulier NPL *(Mil)* ◆ **the ~s** les irréguliers *mpl*

irregularity /ɪˌregjʊ'lærɪtɪ/ N irrégularité *f* ; *(NonC)* irrégularités *fpl* ; *(Jur, Admin) (in procedure)* vice *m* de forme

irregularly /ɪ'regjʊləlɪ/ ADV irrégulièrement ◆ **~-shaped** aux formes irrégulières

irrelevance /ɪ'reləvəns/, **irrelevancy** /ɪ'reləvənsɪ/ N 1 *(NonC)* manque *m* de pertinence (to par rapport à) ◆ **the ~ of nuclear weapons in this day and age** le fait que les armements nucléaires n'ont plus de raison d'être à l'heure actuelle 2 *(= person, thing)* ◆ **a report full of ~s** or **irrelevancies** un compte rendu qui s'écarte sans cesse du sujet ◆ **the party is rapidly becoming a political ~** ce parti est de plus en plus coupé de la réalité politique ◆ **she dismissed this idea as an ~** elle a écarté cette idée comme étant non pertinente

irrelevant /ɪ'reləvənt/ ADJ 1 *(= unconnected) [facts, details]* non pertinent ; *[question, remark]* hors de propos ◆ **~ to** sans rapport avec ◆ **that's ~ (to the subject)** ça n'a rien à voir, ça n'a aucun rapport ◆ **written in the 1960s, his novels are largely ~ to the concerns of today** écrits dans les années 60, ses romans n'ont guère de rapport avec les préoccupations d'aujourd'hui 2 *(= unimportant)* sans importance ◆ **the cost is ~** le coût n'a pas d'importance ◆ **age should be totally ~ when a player has ability** l'âge ne devrait pas entrer en ligne de compte lorsque le joueur est doué ◆ **many of these issues seem ~ to the younger generation** les jeunes ne se sentent pas concernés par beaucoup de ces questions

irrelevantly /ɪ'reləvəntlɪ/ ADV *[say, add, ask]* hors de propos

irreligion /ˌɪrɪ'lɪdʒən/ N irréligion *f*

irreligious /ˌɪrɪ'lɪdʒəs/ ADJ irréligieux

irremediable /ˌɪrɪ'mi:dɪəbl/ ADJ irrémédiable, sans remède

irremediably /ˌɪrɪ'mi:dɪəblɪ/ ADV irrémédiablement

irremovable /ˌɪrɪ'mu:vəbl/ ADJ *[thing]* immuable ; *[difficulty]* invincible ; *[judge etc]* inamovible

irreparable /ɪ'repərəbl/ ADJ *[harm, wrong]* irréparable ; *[loss]* irréparable, irrémédiable

irreparably /ɪ'repərəblɪ/ ADV irréparablement, irrémédiablement

irreplaceable /ˌɪrɪ'pleɪsəbl/ ADJ irremplaçable

irrepressible /ˌɪrɪ'presəbl/ ADJ *[laughter]* irrépressible ; *[person]* débordant d'activité, exubérant

irrepressibly /ˌɪrɪ'presəblɪ/ ADV *[laugh]* de façon irrépressible ◆ **~ cheerful/optimistic** d'une gaieté/d'un optimisme à toute épreuve

irreproachable /ˌɪrɪ'prəʊtʃəbl/ ADJ irréprochable

irresistible /ˌɪrɪ'zɪstəbl/ ADJ irrésistible (to sb pour qn) ◆ **he is ~ to women** les femmes le trouvent irrésistible

irresistibly /ˌɪrɪ'zɪstəblɪ/ ADV *[attract, remind, impel, spread]* irrésistiblement ◆ **she found him ~ attractive** elle lui trouvait un charme irrésistible

irresolute /ɪ'rezəlu:t/ ADJ irrésolu, indécis, hésitant

irresolutely /ɪ'rezəˌlu:tlɪ/ ADV *[hesitate, pause etc]* d'un air irrésolu or indécis

irresoluteness /ɪ'rezəlu:tnɪs/ N irrésolution *f*, indécision *f*

irrespective /ˌɪrɪ'spektɪv/ ADJ ◆ **~ of** ◆ **they were all the same price, ~ of their quality** ils étaient tous au même prix, indépendamment de leur qualité or quelle que soit la qualité ◆ **~ of race, creed or colour** sans distinction de race, de religion ou de couleur, indépendamment de la race, de la religion ou de la couleur ◆ **~ of whether they are needed** que l'on en ait besoin ou non

irresponsibility /'ɪrɪsˌpɒnsə'bɪlɪtɪ/ N *[of person]* irresponsabilité *f (also Jur)*, légèreté *f* ; *[of act]* légèreté *f*

irresponsible /ˌɪrɪs'pɒnsəbl/ ADJ *[person, behaviour, attitude, action] (also Jur)* irresponsable ; *[remark]* irréfléchi ◆ **it was ~ of her to say that, she was ~ to say that** c'était irresponsable de sa part de dire cela ◆ **it would be ~ of me to encourage you** ce serait irresponsable de ma part si je t'encourageais ◆ **it is ~ to drink and drive** c'est faire preuve d'irresponsabilité de conduire lorsqu'on a bu

irresponsibly /ˌɪrɪs'pɒnsɪblɪ/ ADV *[act, behave]* de façon irresponsable ◆ **~ extravagant** d'une extravagance irresponsable

irretrievable /ˌɪrɪ'tri:vəbl/ ADJ *[harm, damage, loss]* irréparable ; *[object]* irrécupérable ; *(Fin) [debt]* irrécouvrable ◆ **the ~ breakdown of a relationship** la rupture irrémédiable d'une relation ◆ **to divorce on grounds of ~ breakdown** *(Jur)* divorcer pour rupture de la vie commune

irretrievably /ˌɪrɪ'tri:vəblɪ/ ADV irréparablement, irrémédiablement

irreverence /ɪ'revərəns/ N irrévérence *f*

irreverent /ɪ'revərənt/ ADJ irrévérencieux

irreverently /ɪ'revərəntlɪ/ ADV irrévérencieusement

irreversible /ˌɪrɪ'vɜ:səbl/ ADJ *[damage, process, change, decline, disease, brain damage, operation]* irréversible ; *[decision, judgment]* irrévocable

irreversibly /ˌɪrɪ'vɜ:səblɪ/ ADV *[change]* irréversiblement ; *[damage]* de façon irréversible

irrevocable /ɪ'revəkəbl/ ADJ irrévocable

irrevocably /ɪ'revəkəblɪ/ ADV irrévocablement

irrigable /'ɪrɪgəbl/ ADJ irrigable

irrigate /'ɪrɪgeɪt/ VT *(Agr, Med)* irriguer

irrigation /ˌɪrɪ'geɪʃən/ N *(Agr, Med)* irrigation *f*

irritability /ˌɪrɪtə'bɪlɪtɪ/ N irritabilité *f*

irritable /'ɪrɪtəbl/ ADJ *[person] (= cross)* irritable ; *(= irascible)* irascible, coléreux ; *[look, mood]* irritable ; *[temperament, nature]* irascible ◆ **to get** or **grow ~** devenir irritable COMP **irritable bowel syndrome** N syndrome *m* du côlon irritable, colopathie *f* spasmodique

irritably /'ɪrɪtəblɪ/ ADV avec irritation

irritant /'ɪrɪtənt/ N 1 *(= annoying noise, interference etc)* source *f* d'irritation ; *(= contentious issue)* point *m* épineux ◆ **the issue has become a major ~ to the government** cette question donne du fil à retordre au gouvernement 2 *(= substance)* irritant *m* ADJ *[substance, effect]* irritant

irritate /'ɪrɪteɪt/ VT 1 *(= annoy)* irriter, agacer ◆ **to get** or **become ~d** s'irriter 2 *(Med)* irriter

irritating /'ɪrɪteɪtɪŋ/ ADJ 1 *(= annoying)* irritant, agaçant 2 *(Med)* irritant

irritatingly /'ɪrɪteɪtɪŋlɪ/ ADV ◆ **~ slow/smug** d'une lenteur/d'une autosuffisance irritante or agaçante

irritation /ˌɪrɪ'teɪʃən/ N 1 *(NonC = annoyance)* irritation *f*, agacement *m* 2 *(= irritant)* source *f* d'irritation

irruption /ɪ'rʌpʃən/ N irruption *f*

IRS /ˌaɪɑ:'res/ N *(US)* (abbrev of **Internal Revenue Service**) ◆ **the ~** ≈ le fisc

is /ɪz/ → **be**

ISA /ˌaɪes'eɪ/ N *(Brit)* (abbrev of **Individual Savings Account**) plan *m* d'épargne défiscalisé

Isaac /'aɪzək/ N Isaac *m*

Isaiah /aɪ'zaɪə/ N Isaïe *m*

ISBN /ˌaɪesbi:'en/ N (abbrev of **International Standard Book Number**) ISBN *m*

ischium /'ɪskɪəm/ N (pl **ischia** /'ɪskɪə/) ischion *m*

ISDN /ˌaɪesdi:'en/ N (abbrev of **Integrated Services Digital Network**) RNIS *m*

ish* /ɪʃ/ ADV *(Brit)* ◆ **hungry ?** – **~** tu as faim ? – un (petit) peu ◆ **is it good?** – **~** est-ce que c'est bien ? – pas mal *

...ish /ɪʃ/ SUF 1 ...âtre ◆ **blackish** plutôt noir, noirâtre *(pej)* 2 ◆ **she came at threeish** elle est venue vers 3 heures or sur les 3 heures ◆ **it's coldish** il fait un peu froid or frisquet * ◆ **she's fortyish** elle a dans les quarante ans *

isinglass /'aɪzɪŋglɑ:s/ N ichtyocolle *f*

Isis /'aɪsɪs/ N *(Myth)* Isis *f*

Islam /'ɪzlɑ:m/ N Islam *m*

Islamic /ɪz'læmɪk/ ADJ islamique ◆ **the ~ Republic of ...** la République islamique de ...

Islamicist /ɪz'læmɪsɪst/ N islamiste *mf*

Islamism /'ɪzləmɪzəm/ N islamisme *m*

Islamist /'ɪzləmɪst/ N ⇒ **Islamicist**

islamophobia /ɪzˌlæmə'fəʊbɪə/ N islamophobie *f*

island /'aɪlənd/ N *(lit, fig)* île *f* ; *(smaller)* îlot *m* COMP *[people, community]* insulaire
island-hopping* N ◆ **to go ~-hopping** aller d'île en île ADJ ◆ **~-hopping holiday** *vacances passées à aller d'île en île*

islander /'aɪləndə^r/ N insulaire *mf*, habitant(e) *m(f)* d'une île or de l'île

isle /aɪl/ N *(liter)* île *f* ; → **British**
COMP **the Isle of Man** N l'île *f* de Man
the Isle of Wight N l'île *f* de Wight

islet /'aɪlɪt/ N îlot *m*

ism /'ɪzəm/ N doctrine *f*, idéologie *f* ◆ **Marxism or any other ~** le marxisme ou tout autre doctrine or idéologie

isn't /'ɪznt/ ⇒ **is not** ; → **be**

ISO /ˌaɪes'əʊ/ N (abbrev of **International Standards Organization**) ISO *f*

isobar /'aɪsəʊbɑ:^r/ N isobare *f*

Isobel /'ɪzəʊbel/ N Isabelle *f*

isogloss /'aɪsəʊˌglɒs/ N isoglosse *f*

isolate /'aɪsəʊleɪt/ VT *(all senses)* isoler (from de)

isolated /'aɪsəʊleɪtɪd/ ADJ *(gen, Chem, Med etc)* isolé (from sb/sth de qn/qch) ; ◆ **to keep sb/sth ~ (from sb/sth)** tenir qn/qch à l'écart (de qn/qch)

isolation /ˌaɪsəʊ'leɪʃən/ N 1 *(gen, Med)* isolement *m* ◆ **international ~** isolement *m* international ◆ **to be (kept) in ~** *[prisoner]* être maintenu en isolement ◆ **he was in ~ for**

three months il a passé trois mois en isolement

[2] ◆ **in** ~ isolément ◆ **my remarks should not be considered in** ~ mes remarques ne devraient pas être considérées isolément *or* hors contexte ◆ **taken in** ~ **these statements can be dangerously misleading** hors contexte ces déclarations risquent d'être mal interprétées ◆ **no social class can exist in** ~ aucune classe sociale ne peut exister isolément ◆ **to act in** ~ agir seul ◆ **to deal with sth in** ~ traiter de qch à part

[3] *(Chem etc) (= action)* isolation *f* ; *(= state)* isolement *m*

COMP **isolation hospital** N hôpital *m* de quarantaine

isolation ward N salle *f* de quarantaine

isolationism /ˌaɪsəʊˈleɪʃənɪzəm/ N isolationnisme *m*

isolationist /ˌaɪsəʊˈleɪʃənɪst/ ADJ, N isolationniste *mf*

Isolde /ɪˈzɔldə/ N Iseult *or* Iseut *f*

isomer /ˈaɪsəməʳ/ N isomère *m*

isometric /ˌaɪsəʊˈmetrɪk/ ADJ isométrique NPL **isometrics** exercices *mpl* musculaires isométriques

isomorphic /ˌaɪsəʊˈmɔːfɪk/ ADJ isomorphe

isopluvial /ˌaɪsəʊˈpluːvɪəl/ ADJ ◆ ~ **map** carte *f* pluviométrique

isosceles /aɪˈsɒsɪliːz/ ADJ isocèle

isotherm /ˈaɪsəʊθɜːm/ N isotherme *f*

isotonic /ˌaɪsəʊˈtɒnɪk/ ADJ *[contraction, solution]* isotonique

isotope /ˈaɪsəʊtəʊp/ ADJ, N isotope *m*

ISP /ˌaɪesˈpiː/ N (abbrev of **Internet service provider**) fournisseur *m* d'accès à Internet

I-spy /ˈaɪspaɪ/ N *(Brit) jeu où l'on essaie de faire deviner le nom d'un objet à partir de sa première lettre*

Israel /ˈɪzreəl/ N Israël *m* ◆ **in** ~ en Israël

Israeli /ɪzˈreɪlɪ/ ADJ *(gen)* israélien ; *[ambassador, embassy]* d'Israël N (pl **Israelis** *or* **Israeli**) Israélien(ne) *m(f)*

Israelite /ˈɪzrɪəlaɪt/ N israélite *mf*

issue /ˈɪʃuː/ N [1] *(= matter, question)* question *f* ; *(= point)* point *m* ; *(= problem)* problème *m* ◆ **it is a very difficult** ~ c'est une question *or* un problème très complexe ◆ **the** ~ **is whether ...** la question est de savoir si ... ◆ **the main** *or* **key** ~ **is to discover if ...** la question centrale est de découvrir si ... ◆ **that's the main** *or* **key** ~ c'est la question principale *or* le problème principal ◆ **it's not a political** ~ ce n'est pas une question politique ◆ **this needn't become an** ~ **between us** il ne faut pas que ça devienne un problème entre nous ◆ **the real** ~ **was never addressed** le vrai problème *or* la vraie question n'a jamais été posé(e) ◆ **to face the** ~ regarder le problème en face ◆ **to evade** *or* **avoid the** ~ éluder le problème, prendre la tangente

◆ **at issue** ◆ **the point at** ~ le point controversé ◆ **the question at** ~ la question en jeu *or* qui fait problème ◆ **the matter at** ~ l'affaire *f* en jeu ◆ **his integrity is not at** ~ son intégrité n'est pas (mise) en doute *or* en cause ◆ **his political future is at** ~ son avenir politique est (mis) en question *or* en cause ◆ **what is at** ~ **is whether/how ...** la question est de savoir si/comment ...

◆ **to have issues with** *or* **about sth** ◆ **I have always had** ~**s with my weight** mon poids m'a toujours posé problème ◆ **they have** ~**s about the safety of their children** ils sont préoccupés par la sécurité de leurs enfants

◆ **to make an issue of sth** ◆ **he's not expected to make an** ~ **of sanctions** il ne devrait pas insister sur la question des sanctions ◆ **he makes an** ~ **of every tiny detail** il fait une montagne du moindre détail ◆ **I don't want to make an** ~ **of it but ...** je ne veux pas trop insister là-dessus mais ...

◆ **to raise + issue** ◆ **she will raise the** ~ **at next month's conference** elle soulèvera ce problème le mois prochain, à la conférence ◆ **she raised several new** ~**s** elle a soulevé plusieurs points nouveaux ◆ **the priest raised the** ~ **of human rights** le prêtre a soulevé la question des droits de l'homme ◆ **she raised the** ~ **of who was to control the budget** elle a posé la question de savoir qui contrôlerait le budget

◆ **to take issue with** ◆ **to take issue with sb** ne pas être d'accord avec qn, être en désaccord avec qn ◆ **some of you might take** ~ **with me on this matter** certains d'entre vous ne seront peut-être pas d'accord avec moi sur ce point ◆ **I will not take** ~ **with the fact that we have a problem** je ne nierai pas le fait que nous avons un problème ◆ **I feel I must take** ~ **with you on this** je me permets de ne pas partager votre avis là-dessus

[2] *(= release) [of book]* publication *f*, parution *f*, sortie *f* ; *[of goods, tickets]* distribution *f* ; *[of passport, document]* délivrance *f* ; *[of banknote, cheque, stamp]* émission *f*, mise *f* en circulation ; *[of shares]* émission *f* ; *[of proclamation]* parution *f* ; *(Jur) [of warrant, writ, summons]* lancement *m* ◆ **there has been a new** ~ **of banknotes/stamps/shares** il y a eu une nouvelle émission de billets/de timbres/d'actions ◆ **these coins are a new** ~ ces pièces viennent d'être émises

[3] *(= copy, number) [of newspaper, magazine]* numéro *m*, livraison *f* ◆ **in this** ~ dans ce numéro

[4] *(Med)* écoulement *m*

[5] *(NonC: Jur or liter = offspring)* descendance *f*, progéniture *f (liter)* ◆ **without** ~ sans descendance, sans progéniture *(liter)* ◆ **the king and his** ~ le roi et sa descendance *or* ses descendants

[6] *(frm = outcome)* résultat *m*

VT *[+ book]* publier, faire paraître ; *[+ order]* donner ; *[+ goods, tickets]* distribuer ; *[+ passport, document]* délivrer ; *[+ banknote, cheque, shares, stamps]* émettre, mettre en circulation ; *[+ proclamation]* faire ; *[+ threat, ultimatum, warning, warrant, writ]* lancer ; *[+ verdict]* rendre ◆ **to** ~ **a statement** faire une déclaration ◆ **to** ~ **a summons** *(Jur)* lancer une assignation ◆ ~**d to bearer** *(Fin)* émis au porteur ◆ **to** ~ **sth to sb, to** ~ **sb with sth** fournir *or* donner qch à qn ◆ **to be** ~**d with** recevoir ◆ **the children were** ~**d with pencils** on a distribué des crayons aux enfants, les enfants ont reçu des crayons

VI *(liter)* ◆ **to** ~ **forth** *[steam, liquid, people]* jaillir ◆ **to** ~ **from** sortir de ◆ **blood issuing from his mouth, he ...** alors que du sang sortait de sa bouche, il ...

COMP *(esp Mil) [clothing etc]* réglementaire, d'ordonnance

issue price N *(on Stock Exchange)* prix *m* or cours *m* d'émission

issuer /ˈɪʃʊəʳ/ N *(Fin)* émetteur *m*, société *f* émettrice

Istanbul /ˌɪstænˈbuːl/ N Istanbul

isthmus /ˈɪsməs/ N (pl **isthmuses** *or* **isthmi** /ˈɪsmaɪ/) isthme *m*

Istria /ˈɪstrɪə/ N Istrie *f*

IT /ˈaɪˈtiː/ N (abbrev of **information technology**) → **information**

it[1] /ɪt/ PRON [1] *(specific, nominative)* il, elle ; *(accusative)* le, la ; *(before vowel)* l' ; *(dative)* lui ◆ **where is the book? – ~'s on the table** où est le livre ? – il est sur la table ◆ **my machine is old but** ~ **works** ma machine est vieille mais elle marche ◆ **here's the pencil – give** ~ **to me** voici le crayon – donne-le-moi ◆ **if you find the watch give** ~ **to him** si tu trouves la montre, donne-la-lui ◆ **he found the book and brought** ~ **to me** il a trouvé le livre et me l'a apporté ◆ **let the dog in and give** ~ **a drink** fais entrer le chien et donne-lui à boire

[2] ◆ **of** *or* **from** *or* **about** *or* **for** ~ *etc* en ◆ **he's afraid of** ~ il en a peur ◆ **I took the letter out of** ~ j'en ai sorti la lettre ◆ **I feel the better for** ~ ça m'a fait du bien ◆ **I don't care about** ~ ça m'est égal, je m'en fiche* ◆ **speak to him about** ~ parlez-lui-en ◆ **he didn't speak to me about** ~ il ne m'en a pas parlé ◆ **I doubt** ~ *(following French verbs with "de")* j'en doute

[3] ◆ **in** *or* **to** *or* **at** ~ *etc* y ◆ **he fell in** ~ il y est tombé ◆ **he'll be at** ~ *(meeting etc)* il y sera ◆ **he agreed to** ~ il y a consenti ◆ **taste** ~**!** *(following French verbs with "à")* goûtez-y ! ◆ **don't touch** ~ n'y touche pas

[4] ◆ **above** *or* **over** ~ (au-)dessus ◆ **below** *or* **beneath** *or* **under** ~ (au-)dessous, (en-)dessous ◆ **there's the table and your book is on** ~ voilà la table et votre livre est dessus ◆ **a table with a cloth over** ~ une table avec une nappe dessus ◆ **he drew a house with a cloud above** ~ il a dessiné une maison avec un nuage au-dessus ◆ **there is a fence but you can get under** ~ il y a une barrière mais vous pouvez passer (en-)dessous

[5] *(weather, time)* il ◆ ~ **is raining** il pleut ◆ ~**'s hot today** il fait chaud aujourd'hui ◆ ~ **was a warm evening** il faisait doux ce soir-là ◆ ~**'s 3 o'clock** il est 3 heures ◆ ~**'s Wednesday 16 October** nous sommes (le) mercredi 16 octobre

[6] *(impers: non-specific)* ◆ ~ **all frightens me** tout cela m'effraie ◆ ~**'s very pleasant here** c'est agréable *or* bien ici ◆ **who is** ~**?** qui est-ce ? ◆ ~**'s me** c'est moi ◆ **what is** ~**?** qu'est-ce que c'est ? ◆ **what's** ~ **all about?** qu'est-ce qui se passe ?, de quoi s'agit-il ? ◆ **where is** ~**?** où est-ce ?, où est-ce que c'est ? ◆ **that's** ~**!** *(approval)* c'est ça ! ; *(agreement)* exactement !, tout à fait ! ; *(achievement)* ça y est !, c'est fait ! ; *(anger)* ça suffit ! ; *(dismay)* ça y est ! ◆ **how was** ~**?** comment ça s'est passé ?, comment c'était ?* ◆ **what was that noise? –** ~ **was the cat** qu'est-ce que c'était que ce bruit ? – c'était le chat ◆ ~**'s no use trying to see him** ce n'est pas la peine de *or* ça ne sert à rien d'essayer de le voir ◆ ~**'s difficult to understand** c'est difficile à comprendre ◆ ~**'s difficult to understand why** il est difficile de comprendre pourquoi ◆ ~**'s a pity** c'est dommage ◆ **I considered** ~ **pointless to protest** j'ai jugé (qu'il était) inutile de protester ◆ ~**'s fun to go for a swim** c'est amusant d'aller nager ◆ ~ **was your father who phoned** c'est ton père qui a téléphoné ◆ ~ **was Anne I gave** ~ **to** c'est à Anne que je l'ai donné ◆ ~ **can't be helped** on n'y peut rien, on ne peut rien y faire ◆ **the best of** ~ **is that ...** ce qu'il y a de mieux (là-dedans) c'est que ... ◆ **he's not got** ~ **in him to do this job properly** il est incapable de faire ce travail comme il faut ◆ **keep at** ~**!** continuez ! ◆ **let's face** ~ regardons les choses en face ◆ **he's had** ~* il est fichu* ◆ **to be with** ~* être dans le vent* *or* à la page ◆ **to get with** ~*‡ se mettre à la page* ◆ **she's got** ~ **in for me** elle m'en veut, elle a une dent contre moi*

[7] *(in games)* ◆ **you're** ~ **!** c'est toi le chat !

[8] *(* = something special)* ◆ **she really thinks she's** ~ elle se prend vraiment pour le nombril du monde* ◆ **she's got** ~ elle est sexy*

COMP **It-Girl** N * *(Brit)* jeune fille *f* branchée

it[2] /ɪt/ N (abbrev of **Italian**) ◆ **gin and** ~ vermouth-gin *m*

ITA /ˌaɪtiːˈeɪ/ N (abbrev of **Initial Teaching Alphabet**) → **initial**

Italian /ɪˈtæljən/ ADJ *(gen)* italien ; *[ambassador, embassy]* d'Italie ; *[teacher]* d'italien N [1] Italien(ne) *m(f)* [2] *(= language)* italien *m* ; → **Switzerland**

Italianate /ɪˈtæljənɪt/ ADJ *[garden, landscape]* à l'italienne ; *[building, architecture, singing]* de style italien, italianisant

italic /ɪ'tælɪk/ ADJ (Typ) italique ◆ ~ **script** or **writing** écriture f italique NPL **italics** italique m ◆ **to put a word/to write in ~s** mettre un mot/écrire en italique ◆ **"my italics"** "c'est moi qui souligne"

italicize /ɪ'tælɪsaɪz/ VT (Typ) mettre or imprimer en italique

Italo- /ɪ'tæləʊ/ PREF italo-

Italy /'ɪtəlɪ/ N Italie f

ITC /,aɪtiː'siː/ N (Brit) (abbrev of **Independent Television Commission**) ≈ CSA m, *organisme de contrôle de l'audiovisuel*

itch /ɪtʃ/ N (lit) démangeaison f ◆ **I've got an ~ in my leg/back** ma jambe/mon dos me démange, j'ai des démangeaisons à la jambe/dans le dos ◆ **the ~** (= *scabies*) la gale ◆ **I've got an ~** * **for** or **to travel** l'envie de voyager me démange ◆ **the seven-year ~** *le cap des sept ans de mariage*

VI 1 [*person*] éprouver des démangeaisons ◆ **his legs ~** ses jambes le or lui démangent ◆ **my leg/back ~es** ma jambe/mon dos me démange, j'ai des démangeaisons à la jambe/dans le dos ◆ **my eyes are ~ing** j'ai les yeux qui me piquent ◆ **my skin ~es** j'ai la peau qui me gratte or démange

2 * **I was ~ing to get started** cela me démangeait de commencer ◆ **I'm ~ing to tell him the news** la langue me démange de lui annoncer la nouvelle ◆ **he's ~ing for a fight** ça le démange de se battre ◆ **she was ~ing for her contract to end** elle avait hâte que son contrat se termine *subj* ◆ **the people are ~ing for change** les gens attendent un changement avec impatience

VT démanger

itchiness /'ɪtʃɪnɪs/ N démangeaisons fpl

itching /'ɪtʃɪŋ/ N démangeaison f COMP **itching powder** N poil m à gratter

itchy /'ɪtʃɪ/ ADJ ◆ **my eyes are ~** j'ai les yeux qui me piquent ◆ **my skin is** or **feels ~** j'ai la peau qui me gratte or me démange ◆ **my scalp is** or **feels ~, I have an ~ scalp** j'ai le cuir chevelu qui me démange or qui me gratte ◆ **a dry, ~ scalp** un cuir chevelu sec et irrité ◆ **I have an ~ leg** j'ai la jambe qui me démange, j'ai des démangeaisons à la jambe ◆ **I'm** or **I feel all ~** ça me démange de partout, ça me gratte partout ◆ **the baby has an ~ rash** le bébé a des rougeurs qui le démangent ◆ **this sweater is ~** ce pull me gratte ◆ **to have ~ feet** * (*esp Brit fig*) avoir la bougeotte * ◆ **to have ~ fingers** * (*fig*) (= *be impatient to act*) ne pas tenir en place ; (= *be likely to steal*) être kleptomane sur les bords * ◆ **to have an ~ palm** * (*fig, pej*) avoir les doigts crochus * ◆ **to have an ~ trigger finger** * avoir la gâchette facile

it'd /'ɪtd/ ⇒ **it had, it would** ; → **have, would**

item /'aɪtəm/ N (Comm, Comput) article m ; (*in discussion: at meeting*) question f, point m ; (*in variety show*) numéro m ; (*in catalogue, newspaper*) article m ; (*Jur: in contract*) article m ; (*Accounting*) poste m ◆ **an ~ of clothing** un vêtement ◆ **an ~ of food, a food ~** un aliment ◆ **an ~ of jewellery, a jewellery ~** un bijou ◆ **~s on the agenda** questions fpl à l'ordre du jour ◆ **the first ~ on the programme** le premier numéro du programme ◆ **the first ~ on the list** (*gen*) la première chose sur la liste ; (*on shopping list*) le premier article sur la liste ; (*in discussion*) la première question or le premier point sur la liste ◆ **the main ~ in the news, the main news ~** (*Rad, TV*) l'information f principale ◆ **we have several ~s for discussion** nous avons plusieurs points à discuter ◆ **they're an ~** * ils sont ensemble

ADV item, en outre

COMP **item veto** N (US Pol) veto m partiel (*sur un projet de loi*)

itemize /'aɪtəmaɪz/ VT donner le détail de ◆ **an ~d bill** une facture f détaillée

iterate /'ɪtəreɪt/ VT (*frm*) réitérer

itinerant /ɪ'tɪnərənt/ ADJ [*preacher*] itinérant ; [*actor, musician*] ambulant ◆ **~ (lace-)seller** colporteur m, -euse f (de dentelle) ◆ **an ~ lifestyle/childhood** un mode de vie/une enfance nomade ◆ **~ teacher** (*US Scol*) *professeur qui enseigne dans plusieurs établissements*

itinerary /aɪ'tɪnərərɪ/ N itinéraire m

it'll /'ɪtl/ ⇒ **it will** ; → **will**

ITN /,aɪtiː'en/ N (Brit) (abbrev of **Independent Television News**) *chaîne indépendante d'actualités télévisées*

its /ɪts/ POSS ADJ son m *also f before vowel*, sa f, ses pl POSS PRON le sien, la sienne, les siens, les siennes

it's /ɪts/ ⇒ **it is, it has** ; → **be, have**

itself /ɪt'self/ PRON 1 (*emphatic*) lui-même m, elle-même f ◆ **the book ~ is not valuable** le livre (en) lui-même n'est pas de grande valeur ◆ **the chair ~ was covered with ink** la chaise elle-même était couverte d'encre ◆ **you've been kindness ~** vous avez été la gentillesse même ◆ **she fainted in the theatre ~** elle s'est évanouie en plein théâtre or dans le théâtre même ◆ **the involvement of the foreign ministers was ~ a sign of progress** l'engagement des ministres des Affaires étrangères était en soi un signe encourageant ◆ **in the town ~, the atmosphere remained calm** dans la ville même, le calme régnait ◆ **no matter who's elected, the system ~ is not going to change** peu importe qui sera élu, le système en lui-même ne va pas changer

◆ **by itself** ◆ **the door closes by ~** la porte se ferme d'elle-même or toute seule ◆ **this by ~ is not bad** ceci n'est pas un mal en soi ◆ **the mere will to cooperate is by ~ not sufficient** la simple volonté de coopérer n'est pas suffisante en soi

◆ **in itself, in and of itself** en soi ◆ **just reaching the semifinals has been an achievement in ~** arriver en demi-finale a déjà été un exploit en soi ◆ **this in ~ is not bad** ceci n'est pas un mal en soi ◆ **an end in ~** une fin en soi

2 (*reflexive*) se ◆ **the dog hurt ~** le chien s'est fait mal ◆ **the computer can reprogram ~** l'ordinateur peut se reprogrammer tout seul ◆ **a group which calls ~ the freedom movement** un groupe qui se donne le nom de mouvement pour la liberté

ITV /,aɪtiː'viː/ N (Brit) (abbrev of **Independent Television**) *chaîne indépendante de télévision*

IU(C)D /,aɪjuːsiː'diː/ N (abbrev of **intrauterine (contraceptive) device**) DIU m

IV, i.v. /'aɪ'viː/ (abbrev of **intravenous(ly)**) IV, iv

Ivan /'aɪvən/ N Ivan m ◆ **~ the Terrible** Ivan le Terrible

I've /aɪv/ ⇒ **I have** ; → **have**

IVF /,aɪviː'ef/ N (abbrev of **in vitro fertilization**) FIV f

ivory /'aɪvərɪ/ N 1 (NonC) ivoire m 2 (= *object*) ivoire m 3 ◆ **ivories** * (= *piano keys*) touches fpl ; (= *dice*) dés mpl ; (= *teeth*) dents fpl

COMP [*statue, figure*] en ivoire, d'ivoire ; (also **ivory-coloured**) ivoire *inv*

Ivory Coast N Côte-d'Ivoire f

ivory tower N tour f d'ivoire

ivory trade N (= *selling*) commerce m de l'ivoire ; (= *industry*) industrie f de l'ivoire

ivy /'aɪvɪ/ N lierre m COMP **Ivy League** N (US) *les huit grandes universités privées du nord-est* ADJ ≈ BCBG *

> **IVY LEAGUE**
>
> Les universités dites de l'**Ivy League** sont huit universités du nord-est des États-Unis réputées pour la qualité de leur enseignement et qui ont créé une association visant à encourager les compétitions sportives interuniversitaires. Il s'agit des universités de Harvard, Yale, Pennsylvania, Princeton, Columbia, Brown, Dartmouth et Cornell. Le nom de cette « ligue du lierre » vient du fait que la plupart des bâtiments de ces prestigieuses institutions sont recouverts de lierre.
>
> Un **Ivy Leaguer** est un étudiant appartenant à l'une de ces universités, ou toute personne qui en adopte les modes et les comportements.

ivyleaf geranium /'aɪvɪliːfdʒə'reɪnɪəm/ N géranium-lierre m

Jj

J, j /dʒeɪ/ N (= letter) J, j m ◆ **J for Jack, J for John, J for Jig** (US) ≃ J comme Jean

jab /dʒæb/ VT [+ knife, stick] enfoncer, planter (into dans) ◆ **he ~bed his elbow into my side** il m'a donné un coup de coude dans les côtes ◆ **he ~bed the fabric with his needle** il a planté son aiguille dans l'étoffe ◆ **he ~bed a finger at the map** il a montré la carte du doigt VI (Boxing) lancer un coup droit, envoyer un direct (at à) N 1 coup m (donné avec un objet pointu) 2 (Brit * = injection) piqûre f ◆ **I've had my ~** on m'a fait ma piqûre ◆ **tetanus/measles/flu ~** vaccin m contre le tétanos/la rougeole/la grippe 3 (Boxing) direct m ◆ **left/right ~** direct du gauche/du droit

jabber /'dʒæbəʳ/ (pej) VT (also **jabber out**) [+ excuse, explanation] bafouiller, bredouiller ; [+ foreign language] baragouiner ; [+ prayers] marmotter VI 1 (= speak unintelligibly) (also **jabber away**) baragouiner ◆ **they were ~ing (away) in Chinese** ils baragouinaient en chinois 2 (= chatter) (also **jabber on**) jacasser, caqueter ◆ **he was ~ing (on) about his holidays** il parlait à n'en plus finir de ses vacances

jabbering /'dʒæbərɪŋ/ N jacassement m, caquetage m

jacaranda /ˌdʒækə'rændə/ N jacaranda m

jack /dʒæk/ N 1 (for car) cric m

2 (Bowls) cochonnet m, bouchon* m

3 (Cards) valet m

4 (= flag) → **union**

5 **before you could say Jack Robinson*** en moins de temps qu'il n'en faut pour le dire ◆ **I'm all right Jack*** moi, je suis peinard*

6 ◆ **every man ~** chacun ◆ **every man ~ of them** tous tant qu'ils sont (or étaient etc)

NPL **jacks** (= game) osselets mpl

COMP **"Jack and the Beanstalk"** N "Jack et le Haricot magique"

Jack Frost N (le) Bonhomme Hiver

jack-in-office* N (pej) rond-de-cuir qui joue les petits chefs

jack-in-the-box N diable m (à ressort)

jack-knife N (pl **jack-knives**) couteau m de poche VI ◆ **the lorry ~-knifed** la remorque (du camion) s'est mise en travers ◆ **~-knife dive** saut m carpé or de carpe

jack of all trades N (pl **jacks of all trades**) ◆ **he's a ~ of all trades (and master of none)** c'est un touche-à-tout

jack-o'-lantern N feu follet m

jack plug N fiche f mâle, jack m

jack rabbit N gros lièvre m (de l'Ouest américain)

jack shit*°* N (US) que dalle*

Jack Tar*, **jack tar*** N (Naut) marin m, matelot m

Jack-the-lad* N (Brit) petit frimeur* m (pej)

► **jack in*** VT SEP (Brit) plaquer*

► **jack up** VT SEP 1 [+ car] soulever avec un cric ◆ **the car was ~ed up** la voiture était sur le cric 2 (* = raise) [+ prices, wages] faire grimper

jackal /'dʒækɔːl/ N chacal m

jackanapes † /'dʒækəneɪps/ N polisson(ne) m(f)

jackass /'dʒækæs/ N âne m, baudet* m ; (* fig) crétin* m ; → **laughing**

jackboot /'dʒækbuːt/ N 1 botte f cavalière 2 (fig = military dictatorship) régime m totalitaire ◆ **to live under the ~ of** vivre or être sous la botte de ADJ [discipline, method] autoritaire, dictatorial

jackdaw /'dʒækdɔː/ N choucas m

jacket /'dʒækɪt/ N 1 (straight, fitted style, man's) veste f, veston m ; (woman's) veste f ; (padded or blouson style) blouson m ; → **life** 2 [of water boiler] enveloppe f calorifugée ; [of book] jaquette f ; [of record] pochette f ◆ **~ potatoes, potatoes baked in their ~s** (Brit) pommes fpl de terre cuites au four dans leur peau or en robe des champs

jackfruit /'dʒækfruːt/ N (= tree) jaquier m ; (= fruit) jaque m

jackhammer /'dʒækˌhæməʳ/ N (US) marteau-piqueur m

jackleg /'dʒækleg/ ADJ (US) (= not qualified) amateur ; (= dishonest) [work] louche ; (= makeshift) [structure] de fortune

jackpot /'dʒækpɒt/ N gros lot m, jackpot m ◆ **to hit the ~** (lit, fig) (= win prize) gagner le gros lot or le jackpot ; (= be successful) faire un malheur* or un tabac*

jackstraw /'dʒækstrɔː/ N (fig) nullité f COMP **jackstraws** NPL (= game) (jeu m de) jonchets mpl

Jacob /'dʒeɪkəb/ N Jacob m COMP **Jacob's ladder** N l'échelle f de Jacob

Jacobean /ˌdʒækə'biːən/ ADJ jacobéen (-éenne f) (de l'époque de Jacques Iᵉʳ d'Angleterre (1603-1625))

Jacobite /'dʒækəbaɪt/ N Jacobite mf ADJ jacobite

Jacuzzi ® /dʒə'kuːzɪ/ N jacuzzi ® m

jade¹ /dʒeɪd/ N jade m ADJ (colour) (couleur de) jade inv COMP **jade-green** ADJ vert jade inv

jade² /dʒeɪd/ N (= horse) haridelle f, rossinante f ; († pej = prostitute) traînée* f ; († = pert girl) coquine f

jaded /'dʒeɪdɪd/ ADJ [person] las (lasse f) (with or about de) blasé ; [palate] blasé ◆ **his appetite was ~** il avait l'estomac fatigué

Jag* /dʒæg/ N (= car) jag* f, jague* f

jag /dʒæg/ N 1 saillie f, aspérité f 2 (* fig) ◆ **a drinking ~** une cuite* ◆ **they were on a drinking ~ last night** ils se sont bien cuités* or ils ont pris une fameuse cuite* hier soir ◆ **a crying ~** une crise de larmes 3 (Scot) injection f, piqûre f VT (= catch, tear) déchirer

jagged /'dʒægɪd/ ADJ [rocks, edge, glass, metal] déchiqueté ; [tear] irrégulier, en dents de scie ; [hole] aux bords déchiquetés or irréguliers

jaguar /'dʒægjʊəʳ/ N jaguar m

jai alai /'haɪəˌlaɪ/ N (US Sport) ≃ pelote f basque

jail /dʒeɪl/ N prison f ◆ **he is in ~** il est en prison ◆ **he was in ~ for five years** il a fait cinq ans de prison ◆ **to put sb in ~** mettre qn en prison ◆ **to send sb to ~** condamner qn à la prison ◆ **to send sb to ~ for five years** condamner qn à cinq ans de prison ◆ **to break ~** s'évader (de prison) ◆ **to get out of ~** (lit) sortir de prison; (Sport) se ressaisir, reprendre le dessus VT mettre en prison ◆ **to ~ sb for life** condamner qn (à la réclusion) à perpétuité ◆ **to ~ sb for theft/murder** condamner qn à la prison pour vol/meurtre COMP **jail sentence** N peine f de prison ◆ **she got a three-year ~ sentence** elle a été condamnée à (une peine de) trois ans de prison

jailbait* /'dʒeɪlbeɪt/ N (US) mineure f ◆ **she's ~** (NonC) si tu touches à cette fille, tu te retrouves en taule*

jailbird /'dʒeɪlbɜːd/ N récidiviste mf

jailbreak /'dʒeɪlbreɪk/ N évasion f (de prison)

jailbreaker /'dʒeɪlbreɪkəʳ/ N évadé(e) m(f)

jailer /'dʒeɪləʳ/ N geôlier m, -ière f

jailhouse /'dʒeɪlhaʊs/ N prison f

Jain /'dʒaɪn/ ADJ, N (Rel) jaïn (mf) inv

Jainism /'dʒaɪnɪzəm/ N (Rel) jaïnisme m

Jakarta /dʒə'kɑːtə/ N Djakarta or Jakarta

jakes* /dʒeɪks/ N ◆ **the ~** les cabinets mpl

jalapeño /ˌdʒælə'piːnəʊ, hælə'penjəʊ/ N (piment m) jalapenos m

jalop(p)y* /dʒə'lɒpɪ/ N vieux tacot* m, guimbarde f

jalousie /'ʒæluːziː/ N jalousie f (store)

jam¹ /dʒæm/ N 1 (= crush) [of vehicles] embouteillage m ; [of people] foule f, masse f ; → **log¹, traffic**

2 (* = mess) pétrin m ◆ **to be in a ~** être dans le pétrin ◆ **to get into/out of a ~** se mettre dans

le/se tirer du pétrin ◆ **to get sb into/out of a ~** mettre qn dans le/tirer qn du pétrin

3 *(Climbing)* coincement *m*, verrou *m*

VT 1 *(= stuff)* entasser ; *(= thrust)* fourrer, enfoncer ◆ **to ~ clothes into a suitcase** entasser des vêtements dans une valise ◆ **the prisoners were ~med into a small cell** les prisonniers ont été entassés dans une petite cellule ◆ **he ~med his hat on** il a enfoncé son chapeau sur sa tête ◆ **she ~med her hands into her pockets** elle a enfoncé *or* fourré ses mains dans ses poches ◆ **he ~med a handkerchief up his sleeve** il a fourré un mouchoir dans sa manche ◆ **to ~ one's foot on the brake** écraser le frein, enfoncer la pédale de frein

2 *(= wedge) [+ door, window]* coincer ◆ **to be ~med between the wall and the door** être coincé entre le mur et la porte ◆ **he got his finger ~med in the door, he ~med his finger in the door** il s'est coincé le doigt dans la porte ◆ **the coins got ~med in the machine** les pièces se sont coincées dans la machine ◆ **to ~ a door open/shut** coincer *or* bloquer une porte en position ouverte/fermée

3 *(= make unworkable)* (also **jam up**) *[+ lock]* bloquer ; *[+ mechanism]* enrayer, coincer ; *[+ gun, machine]* enrayer ; *[+ hinge]* coincer ; *[+ brake]* bloquer, coincer

4 *(= block) [crowd, cars] [+ street, corridor]* encombrer, embouteiller ◆ **a street ~med with cars** une rue embouteillée ◆ **the street was ~med with people** la rue était noire de monde ◆ **the entrance was ~med with people** des gens bouchaient l'entrée ◆ **spectators ~med the stadium for the match** les spectateurs se sont entassés dans le stade pour le match ◆ **the drain was ~med with rubbish** l'égout était bouché par des ordures

5 *[+ station, broadcast, transmission, radar signal]* brouiller ; *(Telec) [+ line]* encombrer ; *[+ switchboard]* encombrer, saturer

VI 1 *(= become stuck) [door, switch, lever, hinge]* se coincer ; *[mechanism]* s'enrayer, se coincer ; *[gun]* s'enrayer ; *[brake]* se bloquer ◆ **the key ~med in the lock** la clé s'est coincée dans la serrure

2 *(= press tightly)* ◆ **the crowd ~med into the courtroom** la foule s'est entassée dans la salle de tribunal

COMP **jam-full, jam-packed** ADJ *[room]* comble, plein à craquer* ; *[bus]* bondé, plein à craquer* ; *[street, pavements]* noir de monde ; *[container, suitcase]* plein à ras bord

►**jam in** VT SEP *[+ people] (= pack in)* entasser ; *(= trap, wedge)* coincer ◆ **to get ~med in** se retrouver coincé

►**jam on** VT SEP 1 ◆ **to jam on the brakes** écraser le frein, enfoncer la pédale de frein

2 ◆ **to jam on one's hat** enfoncer son chapeau sur sa tête

jam² /dʒæm/ **N** *(esp Brit)* confiture *f* ◆ **cherry ~** confiture *f* de cerises ◆ **you want ~ on it!*** *(Brit)* et quoi encore ? ◆ **to promise ~ tomorrow** promettre des jours meilleurs ◆ **(it's a case of) ~ tomorrow** ça ira mieux demain ; → **money**

COMP *[tart]* à la confiture

jam jar, jam pot N pot *m* à confiture

jam puff N *(Brit)* feuilleté *m* à la confiture

jam roll N *(Brit)* roulé *m* à la confiture

jam³ /dʒæm/ *(Mus)* **N** (also **jam session**) bœuf* *m* jam-session *f* **VI** faire un bœuf*

Jamaica /dʒə'meɪkə/ N Jamaïque *f* ◆ **in ~** à la Jamaïque

Jamaican /dʒə'meɪkən/ **ADJ** jamaïquain ; *[ambassador, embassy]* de la Jamaïque **N** Jamaïquain(e) *m(f)*

jamb /dʒæm/ N *[of door, window]* jambage *m*, montant *m*

jambalaya /,dʒʌmbə'laɪə/ N *plat de la Louisiane à base de riz et de fruits de mer*

jamboree /,dʒæmbə'riː/ N *(= gathering)* grand rassemblement *m* ; *(= merrymaking)* festivités *fpl* ; *(scouts)* jamboree *m* ; *(fig)* réjouissances *fpl*

James /dʒeɪmz/ N Jacques *m*

jamming /'dʒæmɪŋ/ N *(Rad)* brouillage *m* ; *(Telec)* encombrement *m*

jammy /'dʒæmɪ/ ADJ 1 *(lit) [fingers, hands]* poisseux *(de confiture)* 2 *(Brit* ⁑ *= lucky)* verni* ◆ **that was pretty ~!** c'était un coup de veine* *or* de pot* ! ◆ **~ devil** *or* **so-and-so** veinard(e)* *m(f)*

JAN /,dʒeɪeɪ'en/ N *(US)* (abbrev of **Joint Army-Navy**) *organisation commune armée-marine*

Jan. abbrev of **January**

Jane /dʒeɪn/ **N** Jeanne *f* ; → **plain** **COMP** **Jane Doe** N *(US Jur) femme dont on ignore le nom*

jangle /'dʒæŋgl/ **VI** *[bracelets, chains]* cliqueter ; *[saucepans]* retentir avec un bruit de ferraille *or* de casserole ; *[bells]* retentir ◆ **his nerves were jangling** il avait les nerfs à vif **VT** faire cliqueter ◆ **~d nerves** nerfs *mpl* à vif **N** cliquetis *m*

jangling /'dʒæŋglɪŋ/ **ADJ** *[keys, bracelets]* cliquetant ; *[phone, music]* strident **N** *[of keys]* cliquetis *m* ; *[of phone]* sonnerie *f* stridente

janitor /'dʒænɪtə^r/ N *(= doorkeeper)* portier *m* ; *(US, Scot = caretaker)* concierge *m*, gardien *m*

Jansenism /'dʒænsə,nɪzəm/ N jansénisme *m*

Jansenist /'dʒænsənɪst/ ADJ, N janséniste *mf*

January /'dʒænjʊərɪ/ N janvier *m* ; *for phrases see* **September**

Janus /'dʒeɪnəs/ N Janus *m*

Jap /dʒæp/ N *(pej)* (abbrev of **Japanese**) Japonais(e) *m(f)*

Japan /dʒə'pæn/ N Japon *m* ◆ **in ~** au Japon

japan /dʒə'pæn/ **N** laque *f* **VT** laquer

Japanese /,dʒæpə'niːz/ **ADJ** *(gen)* japonais ; *[ambassador, embassy]* du Japon ; *[teacher]* de japonais **N** 1 Japonais(e) *m(f)* 2 *(= language)* japonais *m* **NPL** **the Japanese** les Japonais *mpl*

jape † /dʒeɪp/ N *(= trick)* farce *f*, tour *m* ; *(= joke)* blague* *f*

japonica /dʒə'pɒnɪkə/ N cognassier *m* du Japon

jar¹ /dʒɑː^r/ **N** *(= harsh sound)* son *m* discordant ; *(= jolt: lit, fig)* secousse *f*, choc *m* ◆ **that gave him a nasty ~** *(lit, fig)* cela l'a sérieusement ébranlé *or* secoué

VI 1 *(= sound discordant)* rendre un son discordant ; *(= rattle, vibrate)* vibrer, trembler ◆ **to ~ against sth** cogner sur qch *or* heurter qch (avec un bruit discordant)

2 *(= clash, be out of harmony) [note]* détonner ; *[colours]* jurer (with avec) ; *(fig) [ideas, opinions]* se heurter ◆ **what he says ~s a little** ce qu'il dit sonne faux

VT *[+ structure]* ébranler ; *[+ person]* ébranler, secouer ; *(fig)* commotionner, choquer ◆ **the explosion ~red the whole building** l'explosion a ébranlé tout le bâtiment ◆ **he was badly ~red by the blow** il a été sérieusement commotionné par le choc ◆ **you ~red my elbow** tu m'as cogné le coude

►**jar (up)on** VT FUS irriter, agacer ◆ **this noise ~s (up)on my nerves** ce bruit me met les nerfs en boule* *or* me tape sur les nerfs ◆ **her screams ~ (up)on my ears** ses cris m'écorchent *or* me percent les oreilles

jar² /dʒɑː^r/ N 1 *(of glass)* bocal *m* ; *(of stone, earthenware)* pot *m*, jarre *f* ; → **jam²** 2 *(Brit* * *= drink)* pot* *m*, verre *m* ◆ **we had a few ~s** on a pris quelques verres

jargon /'dʒɑːgən/ N *(= technical language)* jargon *m* ; *(= pompous nonsense)* jargon *m*, charabia* *m*

jarring /'dʒɑːrɪŋ/ ADJ 1 *(= discordant) [noise, voice, colours]* discordant ◆ **to strike a ~ note** *(fig)* détonner 2 *(= jolting)* ◆ **~ shock** secousse *f* 3 *(= upsetting) [experience]* bouleversant

jasmine /'dʒæzmɪn/ N jasmin *m* ◆ **~ tea** thé *m* au jasmin

Jason /'dʒeɪsən/ N Jason *m*

jasper /'dʒæspə^r/ N jaspe *m*

jaundice /'dʒɔːndɪs/ N *(Med)* jaunisse *f*

jaundiced /'dʒɔːndɪst/ ADJ *(fig = bitter)* amer, aigri ◆ **to look on sth with a ~ eye, to take a ~ view of sth** voir qch d'un mauvais œil ◆ **he has a fairly ~ view of things** il voit les choses en noir ◆ **to give sb a ~ look** regarder qn d'un œil torve

jaunt /dʒɔːnt/ N ◆ **to go for a ~** aller faire un tour *or* une virée*

jauntily /'dʒɔːntɪlɪ/ ADV *(= cheerily) [say]* d'une voix enjouée ; *[walk]* d'un pas leste

jauntiness /'dʒɔːntɪnɪs/ N désinvolture *f*

jaunty /'dʒɔːntɪ/ ADJ *(= cheery) [air, tone]* enjoué ; *[step]* leste, vif ; *[hat, clothes]* coquet ◆ **a hat worn at a ~ angle** un chapeau incliné sur le côté de façon guillerette

Java¹ /'dʒɑːvə/ N *(Geog)* Java *f* ◆ **in ~** à Java

Java² ® /'dʒɑːvə/ N *(Comput)* Java *m*

java * /'dʒɑːvə/ N *(US = coffee)* café *m*, kawa* *m*

Javanese /,dʒɑːvə'niːz/ **ADJ** javanais **N** 1 *(pl inv)* Javanais(e) *m(f)* 2 *(= language)* javanais *m*

javelin /'dʒævlɪn/ **N** *(Sport)* javelot *m* ; *(Mil)* javelot *m*, javeline *f* ◆ **the ~** *(= competition)* le (lancer du) javelot

COMP **javelin thrower** N *(Sport)* lanceur *m*, -euse *f* de javelot

javelin throwing N *(NonC)* le lancement *or* le lancer du javelot

jaw /dʒɔː/ **N** 1 *(Anat)* mâchoire *f* ; *[of pincer, vice]* mâchoire *f* ◆ **his ~ dropped (in astonishment)** il en est resté bouche bée ◆ **his ~ was set in concentration** la concentration lui faisait serrer les mâchoires ◆ **his ~ was set in an angry line** sa mâchoire serrée lui donnait un air furieux ◆ **the ~s of death** les bras *mpl* de la mort ◆ **the ~s of hell** *(liter)* les portes *fpl* de l'enfer ; → **lockjaw, lower¹** 2 *(= chat)* ◆ **we had a good old ~** * on a bien papoté* **VI** * *(= chat)* papoter*, tailler une bavette* ; *(= moralize)* faire un sermon* ◆ **he was ~ing (on) about ...** il discourait sur ... *(pej)* **COMP** **jaw-dropping** ADJ stupéfiant

jawbone /'dʒɔːbəʊn/ **N** (os *m*) maxillaire *m* **VT** *(US fig)* chercher à convaincre, exercer des pressions sur

jawboning ⁑ /'dʒɔːbəʊnɪŋ/ N *(US Pol)* pressions *fpl* gouvernementales

jawbreaker /'dʒɔː,breɪkə^r/ N *(US)* *(= word)* mot *m* très difficile à prononcer ; *(= sweet)* bonbon *m* à sucer

-jawed /dʒɔːd/ ADJ *(in compounds)* au menton ... ◆ **square-jawed** au menton carré

jawline /'dʒɔːlaɪn/ N menton *m*

jay /dʒeɪ/ N *(= bird)* geai *m*

Jayhawker /'dʒeɪ,hɔːkə^r/ N *(US)* habitant(e) *m(f)* du Kansas ◆ **the ~ State** le Kansas

jaywalk /'dʒeɪ,wɔːk/ VI traverser la chaussée en dehors des clous

jaywalker /'dʒeɪ,wɔːkə^r/ N piéton(ne) *m(f)* indiscipliné(e)

jaywalking /'dʒeɪ,wɔːkɪŋ/ N *(gen)* indiscipline *f* des piétons ◆ **to be accused of ~** être accusé d'avoir traversé la chaussée en dehors des clous

jazz /dʒæz/ **N** *(Mus)* jazz *m* ◆ **and all that ~** * et tout le bataclan*, et tout ça ; → **hot** **VI** *(US* * *= exaggerate)* exagérer

COMP *[band, club, record]* de jazz

jazz ballet N ballet *m* sur musique de jazz

jazz rock N jazz-rock *m*

►**jazz up** VT SEP 1 *(Mus)* ◆ **to jazz up the classics** mettre les classiques au goût du jour ◆ **a ~ed-up version of the national anthem** une version de l'hymne national mise au goût du jour 2 * [+ occasion] animer ◆ **to ~ up a party** mettre de l'animation dans une soirée ◆ **to ~ up an old dress** égayer *or* rajeunir une vieille robe ◆ **she ~ed her outfit up with a scarf** elle a égayé sa tenue avec un foulard

jazzed * /dʒæzd/ ADJ (US) ◆ **to be ~ for sth** être plein d'entrain à la pensée de qch

jazzman /ˈdʒæzmən/ N (pl **-men**) jazzman *m*

jazzy /ˈdʒæzɪ/ ADJ 1 (* = *showy*) *[clothes, product, car]* voyant, qui en jette* 2 (= *upbeat*) *[music]* vivant, gai ; (= *jazz-like*) *[rhythm, beat]* de jazz

JC (abbrev of **Jesus Christ**) → **Jesus**

JCB ® /ˌdʒeɪsiːˈbiː/ N ABBR pelle *f* hydraulique automotrice

JCR /ˌdʒeɪsiːˈɑːʳ/ N (*Brit Univ*) (abbrev of **Junior Common Room**) → **junior**

JCS /ˌdʒeɪsiːˈes/ N (*US Mil*) (abbrev of **Joint Chiefs of Staff**) → **joint**

jct., jctn abbrev of **junction**

JD /ˌdʒeɪˈdiː/ N (*US* = *Doctor of Laws*) ≃ doctorat *m* en droit

jealous /ˈdʒeləs/ ADJ (= *envious*) *[person, nature, look]* jaloux (of de) ◆ **a ~ rage** une crise de jalousie ◆ **~ feelings** jalousie *f* ◆ **to keep a ~ watch over** *or* **a ~ eye on sb/sth** surveiller qn/qch d'un œil jaloux

jealously /ˈdʒeləslɪ/ ADV *[watch]* d'un œil jaloux ; *[guard, protect]* jalousement ◆ **~ guarded** *[secret, privilege]* jalousement gardé

jealousy /ˈdʒeləsɪ/ N jalousie *f*

Jean /dʒiːn/ N Jeanne *f*

jeans /dʒiːnz/ NPL (also **pair of jeans**) jean *m* ; → **blue**

Jeep ® /dʒiːp/ N jeep ® *f*

jeer /dʒɪəʳ/ N (= *mocking remark*) raillerie *f* ; (*from a crowd*) quolibet *m*, huée *f* VI *[individual]* railler ; *[crowd]* huer, conspuer (*frm*) ◆ **to ~ at sb** se moquer de qn, railler qn VT huer, conspuer

jeering /ˈdʒɪərɪŋ/ ADJ railleur, moqueur N (= *mocking remarks*) railleries *fpl* ; *[of crowd]* huées *fpl*

jeeringly /ˈdʒɪərɪŋlɪ/ ADV *[say]* d'un ton moqueur

Jeez * /dʒiːz/ EXCL bon Dieu ! *, putain ! *

jehad /dʒɪˈhæd/ N ⇒ **jihad**

Jehovah /dʒɪˈhəʊvə/ N Jéhovah *m* COMP **Jehovah's Witness** N Témoin *m* de Jéhovah

jejune /dʒɪˈdʒuːn/ ADJ (*liter*) (= *naive*) naïf (naïve *f*) ; (= *dull*) ennuyeux, plat

jejunum /dʒɪˈdʒuːnəm/ N jéjunum *m*

Jekyll and Hyde /ˈdʒekələnˈhaɪd/ N ◆ **a ~ (character)** une sorte de Docteur Jekyll et Mister Hyde

jell /dʒel/ VI ⇒ **gel**[1]

jellied /ˈdʒelɪd/ ADJ *[eels, meat]* en gelée

Jell-O ®**, jello** /ˈdʒeləʊ/ N (*US Culin*) gelée *f*

jelly /ˈdʒelɪ/ N 1 (*Brit: gen*) gelée *f* ; (*US*) (= *jam*) confiture *f* ◆ **blackcurrant ~** gelée *f* de cassis ◆ **my legs turned to ~** mes jambes se sont dérobées sous moi ; → **petroleum** 2 * ⇒ **gelignite**

COMP **jelly baby** N bonbon *m* à la gélatine (*en forme de bébé*)
jelly bean N bonbon *m* à la gelée
jelly bear N nounours *m* (*bonbon*)
jelly roll N (*US Culin*) gâteau *m* roulé

jellyfish /ˈdʒelɪfɪʃ/ N (pl **jellyfish** *or* **jellyfishes**) méduse *f*

jemmy /ˈdʒemɪ/ (*Brit*) N pince-monseigneur *f* VT ◆ **to ~ sth open** ouvrir qch à l'aide d'une pince-monseigneur

jeopardize /ˈdʒepədaɪz/ VT mettre en péril, compromettre ◆ **the publicity could ~ the entire operation** le fait que les médias en ont parlé pourrait compromettre *or* mettre en péril l'opération tout entière

jeopardy /ˈdʒepədɪ/ N

◆ **to be in jeopardy** *[person, life]* être en péril ◆ **his life is in ~** sa vie est *or* ses jours sont en péril ◆ **his happiness is in ~** son bonheur est menacé ◆ **their marriage is in ~** leur mariage est en jeu ◆ **my business is in ~** mon affaire risque de couler

◆ **to put sth in jeopardy** (= *endanger*) compromettre qch ◆ **these setbacks have put the whole project in ~** ces revers ont compromis le projet tout entier

◆ **to put sb in jeopardy** mettre la vie de qn en péril ◆ **its 325 passengers were put in ~** la vie de ses 325 passagers a été mise en péril

jerbil /ˈdʒɜːbɪl/ N ⇒ **gerbil**

jerboa /dʒɜːˈbəʊə/ N gerboise *f*

jeremiad /ˌdʒerɪˈmaɪəd/ N jérémiade *f*

Jeremiah /ˌdʒerɪˈmaɪə/ N Jérémie *m*

Jericho /ˈdʒerɪˌkəʊ/ N Jéricho

jerk /dʒɜːk/ N 1 (= *push, pull, twist*) secousse *f*, saccade *f* ; (*Med*) réflexe *m* tendineux, crispation *f* nerveuse ◆ **the car moved along in a series of ~s** la voiture a avancé par saccades *or* par à-coups ◆ **the train started with a series of ~s** le train s'est ébranlé avec une série de secousses *or* de saccades

2 (*esp US* * *pej* = *person*) pauvre type* *m* ; → **physical, soda**

VT (= *pull*) tirer brusquement ; (= *shake*) secouer (par saccades), donner une secousse à ◆ **she ~ed her head up** elle a brusquement redressé la tête ◆ **he ~ed the book out of my hand** il m'a brusquement arraché le livre que je tenais à la main ◆ **he ~ed himself free** il s'est libéré d'une secousse ◆ **to ~ out an apology** bafouiller une excuse

VI 1 ◆ **the car ~ed along** la voiture roulait en cahotant ◆ **he ~ed away (from me)** il s'est brusquement écarté de moi

2 *[person, muscle]* se contracter, se crisper

► **jerk off** ** VI se branler **

jerkily /ˈdʒɜːkɪlɪ/ ADV *[move, walk]* d'une démarche saccadée ; *[speak, say]* d'une voix entrecoupée

jerkin /ˈdʒɜːkɪn/ N gilet *m* ; (*Hist*) justaucorps *m*, pourpoint *m*

jerkiness /ˈdʒɜːkɪnɪs/ N *[of walk]* rythme *m* saccadé ; *[of journey]* cahots *mpl* ; *[of style, delivery]* caractère *m* haché

jerkwater town * /ˈdʒɜːkwɔːtəˈtaʊn/ N (*US pej*) trou *m* perdu, bled* *m*

jerky /ˈdʒɜːkɪ/ ADJ *[motion, movement, rhythm]* saccadé ; *[song]* au rythme saccadé

jeroboam /ˌdʒerəˈbəʊəm/ N jéroboam *m*

Jerry † * /ˈdʒerɪ/ N (*Brit*) (= *German*) Boche* *m*

jerry * /ˈdʒerɪ/ N (*Brit* = *chamberpot*) pot *m* (de chambre), Jules* *m*

COMP **jerry-building** N (*NonC*) construction *f* bon marché
jerry-built ADJ *[house]* (construit) en carton-pâte ; (*fig*) *[agreement, plan]* cousu de fil blanc
jerry can N jerrycan *m*

Jersey /ˈdʒɜːzɪ/ N 1 (*Geog*) (île *f* de) Jersey *f* ◆ **in ~** à Jersey 2 (= *breed of cow*) race *f* Jersey ◆ **a ~ (cow)** une vache jersiaise *or* de Jersey

jersey /ˈdʒɜːzɪ/ N (= *pullover*) chandail *m* ; (= *material*) jersey *m* ; → **yellow**

Jerusalem /dʒəˈruːsələm/ N Jérusalem ◆ **the New/Heavenly ~** la Jérusalem nouvelle/céleste COMP **Jerusalem artichoke** N topinambour *m*

jest /dʒest/ N plaisanterie *f* ◆ **in ~** pour rire, en plaisantant ◆ **many a true word is spoken in ~** beaucoup de vérités se disent en plaisantant VI plaisanter, se moquer

jester /ˈdʒestəʳ/ N (*Hist*) bouffon *m* ; (= *joker*) plaisantin *m*, farceur *m*, -euse *f* ◆ **the King's ~** le fou du Roi

jesting /ˈdʒestɪŋ/ ADJ *[remark]* (fait) en plaisantant *or* pour plaisanter N plaisanteries *fpl*

Jesuit /ˈdʒezjʊɪt/ N, ADJ (*Rel, fig*) jésuite *m*

jesuitic(al) /ˌdʒezjʊˈɪtɪk(əl)/ ADJ (*Rel, fig*) jésuitique

Jesus /ˈdʒiːzəs/ N Jésus *m* ◆ **~ Christ** Jésus-Christ *m* ◆ **~ (wept)!** * nom de Dieu ! * ; → **society**

COMP **Jesus freak** * N chrétien(ne) *m(f)* militant(e) branché(e)*
Jesus Movement N Jesus Movement *m*
Jesus sandals NPL nu-pieds *mpl*

jet[1] /dʒet/ N 1 *[of liquid]* jet *m*, giclée *f* ; *[of gas]* jet *m*

2 (also **jet plane**) avion *m* à réaction, jet *m*

3 (= *nozzle*) brûleur *m* ; (*in car engine*) gicleur *m*

VI * voyager en avion *or* en jet ◆ **she's ~ting off to Spain next week** elle prend l'avion pour l'Espagne la semaine prochaine

COMP *[travel]* en jet
jet engine N moteur *m* à réaction, réacteur *m*
jet fighter N chasseur *m* à réaction
jet-foil N hydroglisseur *m*
jet fuel N kérosène *m*
jet lag N fatigue *f* due au décalage horaire
jet-lagged ADJ ◆ **to be ~-lagged** souffrir du décalage horaire
jet-powered, jet-propelled ADJ à réaction
jet propulsion N propulsion *f* par réaction
jet set N jet-set *m or f*
jet-set ADJ *[travellers]* du *or* de la jet-set
jet setter N membre *m* du *or* de la jet-set
jet-setting ADJ *[lifestyle]* du *or* de la jet-set ; *[person]* qui fait partie du *or* de la jet-set
jet ski N scooter *m* des mers, jet-ski *m*
jet-ski VI faire du scooter des mers *or* du jet-ski
jet skiing N (*NonC*) jet-ski *m*
jet stream N jet-stream *m*, courant-jet *m*

jet[2] /dʒet/ N jais *m* COMP **jet-black** ADJ de jais, noir comme jais

jetliner /ˈdʒetˌlaɪnəʳ/ N avion *m* de ligne

jetsam /ˈdʒetsəm/ N 1 (*NonC*) jets *mpl* à la mer ; → **flotsam** 2 (*fig* = *down-and-outs*) épaves *fpl* (*fig*)

jettison /ˈdʒetɪsn/ VT 1 (*from ship*) jeter par-dessus bord, se délester de 2 (*from plane*) *[+ bombs, fuel, cargo]* larguer 3 (*fig*) *[+ idea, system, plans]* abandonner ; *[+ assets, product]* se défaire de

jetty /ˈdʒetɪ/ N (= *breakwater*) jetée *f*, digue *f* ; (= *landing pier*) embarcadère *m*, débarcadère *m* ; (*of wood*) appontement *m*

jetway /ˈdʒetweɪ/ N passerelle *f* télescopique

Jew /dʒuː/ N juif *or* Juif *m*, juive *or* Juive *f* COMP **Jew-baiting** N persécution *f* des juifs
jew's harp N guimbarde *f*

jewel /ˈdʒuːəl/ N 1 bijou *m*, joyau *m* ; (= *gem*) pierre *f* précieuse ; (*in watch*) rubis *m* 2 (*fig*) (= *object, work of art*) bijou *m*, joyau *m* ; (= *person*) perle *f*, trésor *m* ◆ **the ~ in the crown of ...** le joyau de ..., le plus beau fleuron de ... ◆ **his latest book is the ~ in his crown** son dernier livre est le couronnement de sa carrière COMP **jewel case** N (also **jewel box** : *for jewels*) coffret *m* à bijoux ; (*for CD*) boîtier *m* de disque compact

jewelled, jeweled (US) /ˈdʒuːəld/ ADJ orné de bijoux *or* de pierreries ; *[watch]* monté sur rubis

jeweller, jeweler (US) /ˈdʒuːələʳ/ N bijoutier *m* ◆ **~'s (shop)** bijouterie *f*

jewellery, jewelry (US) /ˈdʒuːəlrɪ/ N (*NonC*) bijoux *mpl* ◆ **a piece of ~** un bijou ◆ **jewelry store** (US) bijouterie *f*

Jewess † /ˈdʒuːɪs/ N (*gen pej*) Juive *f*

Jewish /ˈdʒuːɪʃ/ ADJ juif

Jewishness /ˈdʒuːɪʃnɪs/ N judaïté *f*, judéité *f*

Jewry /ˈdʒʊərɪ/ N la communauté juive, les Juifs *mpl*

Jezebel /ˈdʒezəˌbel/ N Jézabel *f*

jib /dʒɪb/ N 1 *(Naut)* foc *m* ♦ **the cut of his ~** †* *(fig)* son allure 2 *[of crane]* flèche *f* VI *[person]* rechigner *(at sth* à qch ; *at doing sth* à faire qch) ; *[horse]* refuser d'avancer ♦ **the horse ~bed at the fence** le cheval a refusé l'obstacle *or* a renâclé devant l'obstacle

jibe¹ /dʒaɪb/ ⇒ **gibe**

jibe² * /dʒaɪb/ VI *(US = agree)* concorder

jiffy * /ˈdʒɪfɪ/ N ♦ **wait a ~** attends une minute *or* une seconde ♦ **in a ~** en moins de deux* COMP **Jiffy bag** ® N enveloppe *f* matelassée

jig /dʒɪg/ N 1 (= *dance)* gigue *f* ♦ **the ~'s up** * *(US fig)* c'est cuit* 2 (= *device for guiding drill)* calibre *m* VI (also **jig about, jig around**) se trémousser, gigoter* ♦ **to ~ up and down** sautiller

jigger¹ /ˈdʒɪgəʳ/ N 1 (= *whisky measure)* mesure *f* d'une once et demie (= *42 ml)* 2 *(esp US* * = *thingummy)* truc* *m*, machin* *m*

jigger² /ˈdʒɪgəʳ/ N (= *flea)* chique *f*

jiggered * † /ˈdʒɪgəd/ ADJ *(Brit)* 1 (= *astonished)* étonné, baba* *f inv* ♦ **well, I'll be ~!** nom d'un chien !* 2 (= *exhausted)* crevé*

jiggery-pokery ✱ /ˈdʒɪgərɪˈpəʊkərɪ/ N *(NonC: Brit)* magouilles* *fpl*, manigances *fpl*

jiggle /ˈdʒɪgl/ VT secouer légèrement

jigsaw /ˈdʒɪgˌsɔː/ N 1 (also **jigsaw puzzle**) puzzle *m* 2 (= *saw)* scie *f* sauteuse

jihad /dʒɪˈhæd/ N *(Rel)* djihad *m*

jilt /dʒɪlt/ VT *[+ lover, girlfriend, boyfriend]* plaquer*, laisser tomber* ♦ **~ed** abandonné, plaqué* ♦ **he was ~ed at the altar** il a été plaqué* par sa fiancée le jour de son mariage

Jim /dʒɪm/ N (dim **James**) Jim *m* COMP **Jim Crow** N *(US = policy)* politique *f* raciste *(envers les Noirs)*

jimjams¹ ✱ /ˈdʒɪmdʒæmz/ N ♦ **to have the ~** *(from revulsion)* avoir des frissons *or* la chair de poule ; *(from fear)* avoir les chocottes* ; *(from drink)* avoir une (*or* des) crise(s) de delirium tremens

jimjams² * /ˈdʒɪmdʒæmz/ NPL *(baby talk)* pyjama *m*

Jimmy /ˈdʒɪmɪ/ N (dim of **James**) Jimmy *m*

jimmy /ˈdʒɪmɪ/ N *(US)* pince-monseigneur *f*

jimson weed /ˈdʒɪmsənˌwiːd/ N *(US Bot)* stramoine *f*, datura *m*

jingle /ˈdʒɪŋgl/ N 1 *[of jewellery etc]* *(musical)* tintement *m* ; *(clinking)* cliquetis *m* 2 (= *tune)* ♦ **(advertising) ~** jingle *m or* sonal *m* publicitaire VI *(musically)* tinter ; (= *clink)* cliqueter VT *(musically)* faire tinter ; (= *clink)* faire cliqueter

jingo /ˈdʒɪŋgəʊ/ N (pl **jingoes**) chauvin *m* ♦ **by ~!** * ça alors !, nom d'une pipe !*

jingoism /ˈdʒɪŋgəʊɪzəm/ N chauvinisme *m*

jingoistic /ˌdʒɪŋgəʊˈɪstɪk/ ADJ chauvin

jink * /dʒɪŋk/ VI *(Brit = zigzag)* zigzaguer ♦ **he ~ed out of the way** il a fait un bond de côté

jinks /dʒɪŋks/ NPL → **high**

jinx * /dʒɪŋks/ N ♦ **to put a ~ on sb** porter la poisse à qn ♦ **to put a ~ on sth** jeter un sort à qch ♦ **there's a ~ on this watch** on a jeté un sort à cette montre VT *[+ person]* porter la guigne* *or* la poisse* à ♦ **to be ~ed** *[person]* avoir la guigne* *or* la poisse* ♦ **this project must be ~ed** un mauvais sort semble peser sur ce projet

jitney ✱ /ˈdʒɪtniː/ N *(US)* 1 pièce *f* de cinq cents 2 *véhicule à itinéraire fixe et à prix modique*

jitterbug /ˈdʒɪtəbʌg/ N 1 (= *dance) danse acrobatique sur rythme de swing ou de boogie-woogie* 2 (* = *panicky person)* froussard(e)* *m(f)*, trouillard(e)✱ *m(f)* VI (= *dance)* danser le jitterbug

jitters * /ˈdʒɪtəz/ NPL frousse* *f* ♦ **to have the ~** *(gen)* être nerveux *or* agité ; *(before performance)* avoir le trac, avoir la frousse* ♦ **to give sb the ~** rendre qn nerveux *or* agité, ficher la frousse à qn*

jittery * /ˈdʒɪtərɪ/ ADJ nerveux, agité ♦ **to be ~** avoir la frousse*

jiujitsu /dʒuːˈdʒɪtsuː/ N ⇒ **jujitsu**

jive /dʒaɪv/ N 1 (= *music, dancing)* swing *m* 2 *(esp US* ✱*)* (= *big talk)* baratin* *m* ; (= *nonsense)* foutaises✱ *fpl* ♦ **stop that ~** arrête de dire tes conneries✱ 3 *(US = type of speech)* argot *m (des Noirs surtout)* VI (= *dance)* danser le swing

Jly abbrev of **July**

Jnr *(Brit)* abbrev of **junior**

Joan /dʒəʊn/ N Jeanne *f* ♦ **~ of Arc** Jeanne *f* d'Arc

Job /dʒəʊb/ N *(Bible)* Job *m* COMP **Job's comforter** N piètre consolateur *m*, -trice *f*
Job's tears N (= *plant)* larme-de-Job *f*

job /dʒɒb/ N 1 (= *employment)* travail *m*, emploi *m* ♦ **to have a ~** avoir un travail *or* un emploi ♦ **to lose one's ~** perdre son travail *or* son emploi ♦ **to look for a ~** chercher du travail *or* un emploi ♦ **he's looking for a ~ as a teacher/manager** il cherche un poste *or* un emploi de professeur/directeur ♦ **her new ~** son nouveau travail ♦ **teaching/manufacturing ~s** emplois *mpl* dans l'enseignement/l'industrie ♦ **nursing ~s** postes *mpl* d'infirmiers ♦ **he has a ~ for the vacation** il a un travail pour les vacances ♦ **7,000 ~s lost** 7 000 suppressions d'emplois ♦ **it's more than my ~'s worth** *(hum)* ça risque de me coûter mon travail ♦ **we've found the right person for the ~** nous avons trouvé la personne qu'il nous faut ♦ **off-the-~ training** formation *f* à l'extérieur ♦ **~s for the boys** * *(Brit)* des boulots pour les (petits) copains* ; → **cushy, loss**

♦ **to get + job** trouver du travail *or* un emploi ♦ **once I'm in America I can get a ~** une fois que je serai en Amérique je pourrai trouver du travail *or* un emploi ♦ **of course she didn't get the ~** évidemment elle n'a pas obtenu le poste

♦ **on the job** ♦ **after 3 years on the ~** au bout de 3 années à ce poste ♦ **everyone learns on the ~** tout le monde apprend sur le tas ♦ **the heavy boots he wore on the ~** les gros bottillons qu'il portait pour travailler ♦ **to stay** *or* **remain on the ~** conserver son emploi *or* poste ♦ **he fell asleep on the ~** ✱ (= *during sex)* il s'est endormi en pleine action* *(hum) or* en faisant l'amour ♦ **on-the-training** *(formal)* formation *f* dans l'entreprise ; *(informal)* formation *f* sur le tas

♦ **to be out of a job** être au chômage

2 (= *piece of work, task)* travail *m*, boulot* *m* ♦ **I have a little ~ for you** j'ai un petit travail *or* un petit boulot* pour vous ♦ **the decorators made a terrible ~ of the kitchen** les peintres ont fait du sale boulot* dans la cuisine ♦ **he's got a ~ to do, he's only doing his ~** il ne fait que son travail ♦ **drinking a lot of water helps the kidneys do their ~** boire beaucoup d'eau facilite le travail des reins ♦ **she's done a fine ~ with her children** elle a bien élevé ses enfants ; → **chin, odd, nose**

♦ **to do the job** * (= *be okay)* faire l'affaire ♦ **it's not ideal but it'll do the ~** ce n'est pas l'idéal mais ça fera l'affaire

♦ **to do a good job** (= *do well)* faire du bon travail ♦ **most thought the United Nations was doing a good ~** la plupart des gens pensaient que les Nations unies faisaient du bon travail ♦ **are our schools doing a good ~?** nos écoles sont-elles efficaces ?

♦ **to make a good job of sth** (= *do sth well)* ♦ **you've made a good ~ of the lawn** tu as bien tondu la pelouse ♦ **they haven't made a good ~ of protecting our countryside** ils n'ont pas protégé nos campagnes comme ils auraient dû ♦ **he has made a good ~ of it** il a fait du bon travail

♦ **to make a better job of sth** ♦ **we could have done a far better ~ of running the project than they have** on aurait pu gérer ce projet beaucoup mieux qu'eux

♦ **to do** *or* **make a poor job of sth** ♦ **he has made a poor ~ of it** il n'a pas réussi ♦ **he tried to keep calm, but did a poor ~ of it** il a essayé de rester calme mais n'y a pas réussi ♦ **Bob did a poor ~ of hiding his disappointment** Bob n'a pas réussi à cacher sa déception

3 (= *duty, responsibility)* travail *m* ♦ **it's not my ~ to supervise him** ce n'est pas à moi *or* ce n'est pas mon travail de contrôler ce qu'il fait ♦ **he knows his ~** il connaît son affaire ♦ **that's not his ~** ce n'est pas de son ressort, ce n'est pas son travail ♦ **I had the ~ of telling them** c'est moi qui ai dû le leur dire

4 (= *state of affairs)* ♦ **it's a good ~ (that) he managed to meet you** c'est heureux *or* c'est une chance qu'il ait pu vous rencontrer ♦ **and a good ~ too!** à la bonne heure ! ♦ **it's a bad ~** c'est une sale affaire ♦ **to give sth/sb up as a bad ~** renoncer à qch/qn en désespoir de cause ♦ **this is just the ~** * *(Brit)* c'est juste *or* exactement ce qu'il faut

5 (= *difficult time)* ♦ **to have a ~ to do sth** *or* **doing sth** avoir du mal à faire qch ♦ **I had a ~ to finish this letter** j'ai eu du mal à finir cette lettre ♦ **it was a ~** *or* **an awful ~ to organize this party** ça a été un sacré* travail *or* tout un travail que d'organiser cette soirée ♦ **it was a (terrible) ~ convincing him** ça a été toute une affaire *or* ça n'a pas été une mince affaire pour le convaincre ♦ **you'll have a ~ finding** *or* **to find a hotel room** vous aurez du mal à trouver une chambre d'hôtel ♦ **I'll show it to him now – you'll have a ~, he's already left!** je le lui montre tout de suite – tu auras du mal, il est déjà parti ! ♦ **you've got a real ~ there!** tu n'es pas au bout de tes peines !

6 (* = *dishonest business)* ♦ **to do a ~** faire un coup ♦ **to pull a ~** monter un coup ♦ **a put-up ~** un coup monté ♦ **remember that bank ~?** tu te rappelles le coup de la banque ?

7 (✱ = *thing)* truc* *m* ♦ **that red ~ over there** ce truc rouge là-bas

VI (= *do casual work)* faire des petits travaux ; *(on Stock Exchange)* négocier, faire des transactions ; (= *profit from public position)* magouiller*

VT (also **job out**) *[+ work]* sous-traiter

COMP **job action** N *(US = strike)* action *f* revendicative, (mouvement *m* de) grève *f*

job analysis N analyse *f* des tâches, analyse *f* statique *or* par poste de travail

Jobcentre N *(Brit)* ≃ ANPE *f*, Agence *f* nationale pour l'emploi

job club N *(Brit)* club *m* d'entraide pour chômeurs

job control language N *(Comput)* langage *m* de contrôle de travaux

job creation N création *f* d'emplois

job creation scheme N plan *m* de création d'emplois

job description N description *f* de poste, profil *m* de l'emploi

job evaluation N évaluation *f* des tâches

job-hop * VI changer fréquemment d'emploi

job hopper * N personne *f* qui change fréquemment d'emploi

job hunting N chasse *f* à l'emploi

job lot N lot *m* d'articles divers ♦ **to sell/buy sth as a ~ lot** vendre/acheter qch en vrac

job offer N offre *f* d'emploi

job queue N *(Comput)* file *f* d'attente des travaux

job rotation N rotation *f* des tâches

job satisfaction N satisfaction *f* au travail ♦ **I get a lot of ~ satisfaction** je trouve beaucoup de satisfaction dans mon travail

job security N sécurité *f* de l'emploi
job seeker N *(Brit Admin)* demandeur *f* d'emploi
job seeker's allowance N *(Brit)* allocation *f* de demandeur d'emploi
job-share *(Brit)* N partage *m* de poste VI partager un poste
job sharing N partage *m* de poste
job title N intitulé *m* de poste

jobber /ˈdʒɒbəʳ/ N *(Brit: on Stock Exchange)* négociant *m* en valeurs (boursières) ; (also **stock jobber**) contrepartiste *mf* ; *(= pieceworker)* ouvrier *m*, -ière *f* à la tâche ; *(= dishonest person)* magouilleur* *m*, -euse* *f*

jobbery /ˈdʒɒbərɪ/ N *(NonC: Brit)* malversation *f*, magouillage *m*

jobbing /ˈdʒɒbɪŋ/ ADJ *(Brit) (paid by the day)* payé à la journée ; *(paid by the task)* à la tâche, à façon N *(NonC: on Stock Exchange)* transactions *fpl* boursières

jobholder /ˈdʒɒb,həʊldəʳ/ N *(= employed person)* personne *f* qui travaille ; *(in specific post)* employé(e) *m(f)*

jobless /ˈdʒɒblɪs/ ADJ sans emploi, au chômage NPL **the jobless** les chômeurs *mpl*, les sans-emploi *mpl* ♦ **the ~ figures** le nombre de chômeurs *or* sans-emploi, les chiffres *mpl* du chômage

joblessness /ˈdʒɒblɪsnɪs/ N chômage *m*

jobsworth* /ˈdʒɒbz,wɜːθ/ N *(Brit) employé qui applique le règlement à la lettre*

Jock* /dʒɒk/ N *(pej)* Écossais *m*

jock /dʒɒk/ N 1 ⇒ **jockstrap** 2 *(US)* sportif *m*

jockey /ˈdʒɒkɪ/ N jockey *m* VI ♦ **to ~ about** se bousculer ♦ **to ~ for position** *(lit, fig)* manœuvrer pour se placer avantageusement ♦ **they were ~ing for office in the new government** ils manœuvraient pour obtenir des postes dans le nouveau gouvernement VT ♦ **to ~ sb into doing sth** manœuvrer qn (habilement) pour qu'il fasse qch, amener adroitement qn à faire qch
COMP **Jockey club** N Jockey-Club *m*
Jockey Shorts ® NPL caleçon *m*

jockstrap /ˈdʒɒkstræp/ N *(Sport)* slip *m* de sport ; *(Med)* suspensoir *m*

jocose /dʒəˈkəʊs/ ADJ *(liter) (= merry)* enjoué, jovial ; *(= jesting)* facétieux

jocosely /dʒəˈkəʊslɪ/ ADV *(liter) [say] (= merrily)* d'un ton enjoué ; *(= jestingly)* facétieusement

jocular /ˈdʒɒkjʊləʳ/ ADJ *(= merry)* enjoué, jovial ; *(= humorous)* plaisant

jocularity /,dʒɒkjʊˈlærɪtɪ/ N jovialité *f*

jocularly /ˈdʒɒkjʊləlɪ/ ADV *[say, ask, speak, discuss]* en plaisantant

jocund /ˈdʒɒkənd/ ADJ jovial, joyeux

jodhpurs /ˈdʒɒdpəz/ NPL jodhpurs *mpl*, culotte *f* de cheval

Joe /dʒəʊ/ N (dim **Joseph**) Jo *m*
COMP **Joe Bloggs*** *(Brit)*, **Joe Blow*** *(US)* N Monsieur tout-le-monde *m*, l'homme *m* de la rue
Joe College* N *(US Univ)* étudiant *m* type américain
Joe Public* N *(Brit)* le public
Joe Six-Pack* *(US)*, **Joe Soap*** *(Brit)* N ⇒ **Joe Bloggs**

jog /dʒɒg/ N 1 *(Sport = run)* jogging *m*, footing *m* ♦ **to go for a ~** aller faire un jogging *or* un footing ♦ **she begins the day with a ~ around the park** elle commence la journée en faisant son jogging *or* footing dans le parc
2 (also **jog-trot**) petit trot *m* ♦ **he set off at a ~ down the path** il s'est mis à descendre le sentier au petit trot ♦ **to go along at a ~(-trot)** aller au petit trot
3 *(= nudge, knock)* légère poussée *f* ; *(with elbow)* coup *m* de coude
VT *(= shake)* secouer, bringuebaler ; *(= nudge)* pousser ♦ **to ~ sb's elbow** pousser le coude de qn ♦ **to ~ sb's memory** rafraîchir la mémoire de qn
VI 1 *(Sport)* faire du jogging, faire du footing
2 cahoter, bringuebaler ♦ **the cart ~s along the path** la charrette cahote *or* bringuebale sur le chemin

► **jog about** VI sautiller
VT SEP remuer

► **jog along** VI *(lit) [person, vehicle]* aller son petit bonhomme de chemin, cheminer ; *(fig) [person]* aller cahin-caha* ; *[piece of work, course of action]* aller tant bien que mal

► **jog around** VTI ⇒ **jog about**

► **jog on** VI ⇒ **jog along**

jogger /ˈdʒɒgəʳ/ N jogger *m*, joggeur *m*, -euse *f*
COMP **jogger's nipple*** N mamelon *m* du jogger

jogging /ˈdʒɒgɪŋ/ N *(Sport)* jogging *m*, footing *m*
COMP **jogging shoes** NPL chaussures *fpl* de jogging
jogging suit N jogging *m*

joggle /ˈdʒɒgl/ VT secouer VI bringuebaler, ballotter N légère secousse *f*

Johannesburg /dʒəʊˈhænɪs,bɜːg/ N Johannesburg

John /dʒɒn/ N 1 Jean *m* 2 *(esp US = lavatory)* ♦ **the john** ‡ les chiottes ‡ *fpl* 3 *(US = prostitute's customer)* ♦ **john** ‡ micheton ‡ *m*
COMP **John Bull** N John Bull *m (Anglais de caricature)*
John Doe N *(US Jur) homme dont on ignore le nom*
John Dory N saint-pierre *m inv*, dorée *f*
John Hancock*, **John Henry*** N *(US fig = signature)* signature *f*, paraphe *m*
John of the Cross N (also **Saint John of the Cross**) saint Jean *m* de la Croix
John Q. Public* N *(US)* le public, le quidam *(hum)*
John the Baptist N (also **Saint John the Baptist**) saint Jean *m* Baptiste

Johnny /ˈdʒɒnɪ/ N 1 dim of **John** 2 ♦ **johnny*** type* *m* 3 *(Brit* † * = *condom:* also **johnny, rubber johnny**) capote *f* (anglaise)*
COMP **Johnny-come-lately** N nouveau venu *m* ; *(= upstart)* parvenu *m*
Johnny Foreigner ‡ N *(Brit pej)* étrangers *mpl*

join /dʒɔɪn/ LANGUAGE IN USE 25.2
VT 1 *(= attach)* attacher, relier ; *(= assemble, put together) [+ parts]* assembler ; *[+ broken pieces]* raccorder ; *(with glue)* recoller ; *(Elec) [+ batteries]* accoupler, connecter ♦ **to ~ (together) two ends of a chain** attacher *or* relier les deux bouts d'une chaîne ♦ **~ part A to part B** *(in instructions)* assemblez l'élément A avec l'élément B ♦ **~ the panels (together) with screws** assemblez les panneaux à l'aide de vis ♦ **they are ~ed at the hip*** *(fig, pej)* ils sont comme cul et chemise*, ils sont inséparables ; → **issue**
2 *(= link)* relier *(to* à*)* ♦ **~ the dots (together) with a line** reliez les points par un trait ♦ **the island was ~ed to the mainland by a bridge** l'île était reliée à la terre par un pont ♦ **to ~ hands** se donner la main ♦ **~ed in marriage** *or* **matrimony** unis par les liens du mariage
3 *(= merge with) [river] [+ another river, the sea]* rejoindre, se jeter dans ; *[road] [+ another road]* rejoindre ♦ **this is where the river ~s the sea** c'est là que le fleuve se jette dans la mer
4 *(Mil, fig)* ♦ **to ~ battle (with)** engager le combat (avec) ♦ **they ~ed forces** ils ont uni leurs forces ♦ **to ~ forces (with sb) to do sth** s'unir (à qn) pour faire qch
5 *(= become member of) [+ club, association, political party]* devenir membre de, adhérer à, s'affilier à ; *[+ university]* entrer à, s'inscrire à ; *[+ circus, religious order]* entrer dans ; *[+ procession]* se joindre à ♦ **to ~ NATO/the European Union** devenir membre de l'OTAN/l'Union européenne ♦ **he ~ed Liverpool** *(Ftbl)* il a rejoint l'équipe de Liverpool ♦ **to ~ the army** s'engager *or* s'enrôler dans l'armée ♦ **to ~ a trade union** s'affilier à un syndicat, se syndiquer ♦ **~ the club!*** *(fig)* tu es en bonne compagnie !
6 *[+ person]* rejoindre, retrouver ♦ **I'll ~ you in five minutes** je vous rejoins *or* retrouve dans cinq minutes ♦ **Paul ~s me in wishing you ...** Paul se joint à moi pour vous souhaiter ... ♦ **Moscow has ~ed Washington in condemning these actions** Moscou, comme Washington, a condamné ces actions ♦ **she ~ed me in support of the idea** elle s'est jointe à moi pour défendre cette idée ♦ **will you ~ us?** *(= come with us)* voulez-vous venir avec nous ? ; *(= be one of our number)* voulez-vous être des nôtres ? ; *(in restaurant)* voulez-vous vous asseoir à notre table ?, je peux *or* puis-je m'asseoir avec vous ? ♦ **will you ~ me in a drink?** *(in restaurant)* voulez-vous prendre un verre avec moi ? ♦ **to ~ one's regiment** rejoindre son régiment ♦ **to ~ one's ship** rallier *or* rejoindre son bâtiment ♦ **to ~ the queue** se mettre à la queue
VI 1 *(= connect) [pieces, parts, edges]* se raccorder *(with* à*)* ; *[ends]* s'attacher
2 *(= link up) [lines]* se rejoindre, se rencontrer
3 *(= merge) [roads, rivers]* se rejoindre ; *(= become a member) [of political party, sports club, leisure club, class, group]* devenir membre ♦ **to ~ in doing sth** *[people]* s'associer pour faire qch ♦ **Moscow and Washington have ~ed in condemning these actions** Moscou et Washington ont toutes deux condamné ces actions
N *(in mended object)* ligne *f* de raccord ; *(Sewing)* couture *f*
COMP **joined case** N *(Jur)* affaire *f* jointe
joined-up ADJ *[writing]* attaché ; *[language, thinking]* cohérent
join-the-dots puzzle N *(Brit) jeu qui consiste à relier des points pour découvrir une figure*

► **join in**
VI participer, se mettre de la partie ♦ **~ in!** *(in singing)* chantez avec nous !
VT FUS *[+ game, activity]* participer à ; *[+ conversation]* prendre part à ; *[+ protests, shouts]* joindre sa voix à ; *[+ thanks, wishes]* se joindre à ; → **chorus**

► **join on**
VI *[links, parts of structure]* se joindre *(to* à*)*
VT SEP fixer ; *(by tying)* attacher

► **join together**
VI ⇒ **join vi 1**
VT SEP ⇒ **join vt 1, 2**

► **join up**
VI *(Mil)* s'engager (dans l'armée)
VT SEP joindre, assembler ; *[+ pieces of wood or metal]* abouter, rabouter ; *(Elec) [+ wires]* connecter, raccorder

joinder /ˈdʒɔɪndəʳ/ N *(Jur)* jonction *f*

joiner /ˈdʒɔɪnəʳ/ N *(Brit = carpenter)* menuisier *m*

joinery /ˈdʒɔɪnərɪ/ N *(Brit)* menuiserie *f*

joint /dʒɔɪnt/ N 1 *(Anat)* articulation *f* ♦ **ankle/knee/elbow ~** articulation *f* de la cheville/du genou/du coude ♦ **out of ~** *[knee, ankle, hip]* démis ; *(fig)* de travers ♦ **to put one's shoulder/wrist** *etc* **out of ~** se démettre l'épaule/le poignet *etc* ♦ **his nose is out of ~** *(fig)* il est dépité ♦ **that put his nose out of ~** ça l'a défrisé* ; → **ball**[1]
2 *(in wood, metal)* articulation *f*, jointure *f* ; *(Geol) (in rock)* diaclase *f* ; → **mitre, universal**
3 *(Brit) [of meat]* rôti *m* ♦ **a cut off the ~** une tranche de rôti
4 * *(= night club)* boîte* *f* ; *(= disreputable pub)* bistro(t)* *m* mal famé ; *(= gambling den)* tripot *m*
5 *(Drugs *)* joint* *m*
ADJ *[statement, action, project, approach, meeting, control]* commun ; *[research]* en commun ; *[effort]* conjugué ♦ **to come ~ first/second** *(in*

race, competition) être classé premier/deuxième ex æquo ◆ **it has to be a ~ decision between you and your husband** votre mari et vous devez prendre cette décision ensemble ◆ **the two bodies are expected to take a ~ decision today** les deux organismes devraient parvenir aujourd'hui à une décision commune ◆ **to make** *or* **take a ~ decision to do sth** décider d'un commun accord de faire qch ◆ **~ consultations** consultations *fpl* bilatérales ◆ **~ obligation** coobligation *f* ◆ **~ responsibility** coresponsabilité *f* ◆ **in ~ names** *[sign]* conjointement

VT 1 *(Brit Culin)* découper (aux jointures)
2 *[+ pipes]* joindre, raccorder

COMP **joint account** N *(Fin)* compte *m* joint
joint agreement N *(for employees)* convention *f* collective
joint and several guarantee N caution *f* solidaire
joint and several liability N responsabilité *f* conjointe et solidaire
joint author N coauteur *m*
Joint Chiefs of Staff NPL *(US)* chefs *mpl* d'état-major (des armées)
joint committee N *(gen)* commission *f* mixte ; *(US Pol)* commission *f* interparlementaire
joint estate N *(Jur)* biens *mpl* communs
joint favourite N ◆ **the horses are ~ favourites** ces chevaux sont les deux favoris
joint financing N cofinancement *m*
joint heir N cohéritier *m*, -ière *f*
joint honours N *(Brit Univ = degree)* ≈ licence *f* préparée dans deux matières *(ayant le même coefficient)*
joint manager N codirecteur *m*, -trice *f*, cogérant(e) *m(f)*
joint mortgage N emprunt *m* logement souscrit conjointement
joint ownership N copropriété *f*
joint partner N coassocié(e) *m(f)*
joint passport N passeport *m* conjoint *(pour mari et femme)*
joint-stock company N *(Fin)* société *f* par actions
joint venture N *(gen)* entreprise *f* commune ; *(Jur, Fin) (= company, operation)* joint-venture *f*

JOINT CHIEFS OF STAFF

Collectivement, les **Joint Chiefs of Staff** (c'est-à-dire les chefs d'état-major des trois corps d'armée) constituent un organe du ministère américain de la Défense ayant pour rôle de conseiller le Président, le Conseil national de sécurité et le ministère de la Défense en matière de défense nationale.

jointed /ˈdʒɔɪntɪd/ ADJ *[doll]* articulé ; *[fishing rod, tent pole]* démontable

jointly /ˈdʒɔɪntlɪ/ ADV conjointement (*with* avec) ◆ **to be ~ responsible** *or* **liable for sth** être conjointement responsable de qch ◆ **~ and severally** *(Jur)* conjointement et solidairement

jointure /ˈdʒɔɪntʃəʳ/ N douaire *m*

joist /dʒɔɪst/ N *(wooden)* solive *f* ; *(metal)* poutrelle *f*

jojoba /həʊˈhəʊbə/ N jojoba *m*

joke /dʒəʊk/ N 1 *(= funny anecdote)* plaisanterie *f*, blague * *f* ◆ **for a ~** pour rire, pour blaguer * ◆ **to make a ~ about sb/sth** plaisanter sur qn/qch ◆ **to make a ~ of sth** tourner qch à la plaisanterie ◆ **he can't take a ~** il ne comprend pas *or* il prend mal la plaisanterie ◆ **it's no ~!** *(= it's not easy)* ce n'est pas une petite affaire ! *(doing sth* que de faire qch) ; *(= it's not enjoyable)* ce n'est pas drôle *or* marrant * *(doing sth* (que) de faire qch) ◆ **what a ~!** *(gen, iro)* ce que c'est drôle ! ◆ **it's a ~!** * *(pej = useless)* c'est de la blague ! ◆ **his behaviour is (getting) beyond a ~** * *(Brit)* il a dépassé les bornes ◆ **the situation is (getting) beyond a ~** * la situation devient alarmante ◆ **the ~ is that ...** le plus drôle c'est que ..., ce qu'il y a de drôle *or* de marrant * c'est que ... ; → **see¹, standing**

2 *(= trick)* tour *m*, farce *f* ◆ **to play a ~ on sb** faire une farce à qn, jouer un tour à qn ; → **practical**

3 *(= object of amusement)* risée *f* ◆ **he is the ~ of the village** il est la risée du village

VI plaisanter, blaguer * ◆ **you're joking!** vous voulez rire !, sans blague ! * ◆ **£100 for that? – you must be joking!** 100 livres pour ça ? – vous n'êtes pas sérieux *or* vous voulez rire ! ◆ **I'm not joking** je ne plaisante pas ◆ **I was only joking** ce n'était qu'une plaisanterie ◆ **you mustn't ~ about his accent** il ne faut pas se moquer de son accent

VT ◆ **you're joking me!** tu plaisantes !, tu me mets en boîte !

joker /ˈdʒəʊkəʳ/ N 1 (* = *idiot*) rigolo * *m* ◆ **some ~ will always start singing** il y aura toujours un rigolo * pour se mettre à chanter 2 *(Cards)* joker *m* ◆ **the ~ in the pack** *(fig)* l'outsider *m*, le joker 3 ⇒ **jokester** 4 *(Jur)* clause *f* ambiguë

jokester /ˈdʒəʊkstəʳ/ N blagueur *m*, -euse *f*, plaisantin *m*

jokey * /ˈdʒəʊkɪ/ ADJ *(= amusing)* rigolo * (-ote * *f*) ; *(= jocular)* blagueur, jovial ◆ **in a ~ way** en plaisantant

joking /ˈdʒəʊkɪŋ/ ADJ *[tone]* de plaisanterie N *(NonC)* plaisanterie *f*, blague * *f* ◆ **~ apart** *or* **aside** plaisanterie *or* blague * à part

jokingly /ˈdʒəʊkɪŋlɪ/ ADV en plaisantant, pour plaisanter ◆ **she ~ referred to her son as "my little monster"** elle appelait son fils "mon petit monstre" pour plaisanter

jollification * /ˌdʒɒlɪfɪˈkeɪʃən/ N *(NonC)* réjouissances *fpl*

jollity /ˈdʒɒlɪtɪ/ N *[of person, atmosphere]* gaieté *f*, joyeuse humeur *f*

jolly /ˈdʒɒlɪ/ ADJ *(esp Brit)* 1 *(= cheerful) [person, atmosphere, smile, mood]* jovial 2 († * = *enjoyable*) amusant ◆ **to have a ~ (old) time** bien s'amuser ADV *(Brit* † * = *very) [good, decent]* drôlement *, rudement * ◆ **you are ~ lucky** tu as une drôle de veine * ◆ **~ good!** *(expressing approval)* très bien ! ◆ **I'm ~ well going** un peu que je vais y aller ! * ◆ **you ~ well will go!** pas question que tu n'y ailles pas ! ◆ **I (should) ~ well hope** *or* **think so!** j'espère bien ! VT ◆ **to ~ sb along** enjôler qn ◆ **they jollied him into joining them** ils l'ont convaincu (en douceur) de se joindre à eux N *(US)* ◆ **to get one's jollies** ‡ prendre son pied ‡ *(from doing sth* en faisant qch)

COMP **jolly boat** N *(Naut)* canot *m*
the Jolly Roger N le pavillon noir

jolt /dʒəʊlt/ VI *[vehicle]* cahoter, tressauter ◆ **to ~ along** avancer en cahotant ◆ **to ~ to a stop** s'arrêter brutalement VT *(lit, fig)* secouer, cahoter ◆ **she was ~ed awake** elle s'est réveillée en sursaut ◆ **to ~ sb into action/into doing sth** *(fig)* pousser qn à agir/à faire qch ◆ **she was ~ed back to reality** elle fut brutalement rappelée à la réalité ◆ **it ~ed her out of her self-pity/depression** ça l'a tellement secouée qu'elle a arrêté de s'apitoyer sur son sort/qu'elle a arrêté de déprimer N 1 *(= jerk) [of vehicle]* secousse *f*, à-coup *m* 2 *(fig)* choc *m* ◆ **it gave me a ~** ça m'a fait un choc

jolting /ˈdʒəʊltɪŋ/ ADJ cahotant N *(NonC)* cahots *mpl*

Jonah /ˈdʒəʊnə/ N Jonas *m* ; *(fig)* porte-malheur *m inv*, oiseau *m* de malheur

Jonas /ˈdʒəʊnəs/ N Jonas *m*

Jonathan /ˈdʒɒnəθən/ N Jonathan *m*

Joneses /ˈdʒəʊnzɪz/ NPL ◆ **to try to keep up with the ~** * ne pas vouloir faire moins bien que le voisin

jonquil /ˈdʒɒŋkwɪl/ N jonquille *f*, narcisse *m* ADJ jonquille *inv*

Jordan /ˈdʒɔːdn/ N *(= country)* Jordanie *f* ◆ **the river ~** le Jourdain

Jordanian /dʒɔːˈdeɪnɪən/ N Jordanien(ne) *m(f)* ADJ jordanien ; *[ambassador, embassy, monarch]* de Jordanie

Joseph /ˈdʒəʊzɪf/ N Joseph *m*

Josephine /ˈdʒəʊzɪfiːn/ N Joséphine *f*

josh ‡ /dʒɒʃ/ *(esp US)* VT charrier *, mettre en boîte * VI blaguer * N mise *f* en boîte *

Joshua /ˈdʒɒʃʊə/ N Josué *m*

joss stick /ˈdʒɒsstɪk/ N bâton *m* d'encens

jostle /ˈdʒɒsl/ VI ◆ **he ~d against me** il m'a bousculé ◆ **to ~ through the crowd** se frayer un chemin (à coups de coudes) à travers la foule ◆ **to ~ for sth** *(lit, fig)* jouer des coudes pour obtenir qch VT bousculer N bousculade *f*

jot /dʒɒt/ N brin *m*, iota *m* ◆ **there is not a ~ of truth in this** il n'y a pas une once de vérité là-dedans ◆ **not one ~ or tittle** pas un iota, pas un brin VT noter, prendre note de

► **jot down** VT SEP noter, prendre note de ◆ **to ~ down notes** prendre *or* griffonner des notes ◆ **to ~ down a few points** prendre note de *or* noter quelques points

jotter /ˈdʒɒtəʳ/ N *(Brit) (= exercise book)* cahier *m* (de brouillon) ; *(= pad)* bloc-notes *m*

jottings /ˈdʒɒtɪŋz/ NPL notes *fpl*

joual /ʒwaːl/ N *(Can)* joual *m*

joule /dʒuːl/ N joule *m*

journal /ˈdʒɜːnl/ N 1 *(= periodical)* revue *f* ; *(= newspaper)* journal *m* ◆ **all our results are published in scientific ~s** tous nos résultats sont publiés dans des revues scientifiques 2 *(= diary)* journal *m* 3 *(Naut)* livre *m* de bord ; *(Comm)* livre *m* de comptes ; *(Jur)* compte rendu *m* COMP **journal bearing** N *(Tech)* palier *m*

journalese /ˌdʒɜːnəˈliːz/ N *(NonC: pej)* jargon *m* journalistique

journalism /ˈdʒɜːnəlɪzəm/ N journalisme *m*

journalist /ˈdʒɜːnəlɪst/ N journaliste *mf*

journalistic /ˌdʒɜːnəˈlɪstɪk/ ADJ *[profession, community, experience, talent, cliché]* de journaliste ; *[style, career]* journalistique

journey /ˈdʒɜːnɪ/ N *(gen)* voyage *m* ; *(short or regular trip)* trajet *m* ; *(distance covered)* trajet *m*, parcours *m* ◆ **to go on a ~** partir en voyage ◆ **to set out on one's ~** se mettre en route ◆ **a two days' ~** un voyage de deux jours ◆ **it's a 50-minute train ~ from Glasgow to Edinburgh** le trajet Glasgow-Édimbourg en train est de *or* prend 50 minutes ◆ **to reach one's ~'s end** arriver à destination ◆ **the ~ from home to office** le trajet de la maison au bureau ◆ **the return ~, the ~ home** le (voyage *or* trajet de) retour ◆ **a car ~** un voyage *or* trajet en voiture ◆ **a long bus ~** un long trajet en autobus ; → **outward** VI voyager ◆ **to ~ on** continuer son voyage COMP **journey time** N durée *f* du trajet

⚠ **journée** means 'day', not **journey**.

journeyman /ˈdʒɜːnɪmən/ N (pl **-men**) artisan *m*
COMP **journeyman baker** N ouvrier *m* boulanger
journeyman joiner N compagnon *m* charpentier

journo * /ˈdʒɜːnəʊ/ N (abbrev of **journalist**) journaliste *mf*, journaleux * *m (pej)*

joust /dʒaʊst/ N joute *f* VI *(lit, fig)* jouter

Jove /dʒəʊv/ N Jupiter *m* ◆ **by ~!** † * sapristi ! *

jovial /ˈdʒəʊvɪəl/ ADJ jovial

joviality /ˌdʒəʊvɪˈælɪtɪ/ N jovialité *f*

jovially /ˈdʒəʊvɪəlɪ/ ADV *[say]* jovialement ; *[laugh]* gaiement

jowl /dʒaʊl/ **N** (= *jaw*) mâchoire *f* ; (= *cheek*) bajoue *f* ; → **cheek**

-jowled /dʒaʊld/ **ADJ** (*in compounds*) ♦ **square-jowled** à la mâchoire carrée

jowly /ˈdʒaʊlɪ/ **ADJ** aux joues flasques

joy /dʒɔɪ/ **N** 1 (*NonC*) joie *f* ♦ **the ~ of my life** mon rayon de soleil ♦ **to my great ~** à ma grande joie
2 (= *enjoyable thing*) plaisir *m* ♦ **the ~s of the seaside** les plaisirs *or* les charmes du bord de la mer ♦ **the ~s of motherhood** les joies *fpl or* satisfactions *fpl* de la maternité ♦ **it was a ~ to see him again** c'était un (vrai) plaisir de le revoir ♦ **this car is a ~ to drive** c'est un (vrai) plaisir de conduire cette voiture ♦ **his dancing was a ~ to watch, it was a ~ to watch him dancing** c'était un (vrai) plaisir *or* délice de le regarder danser ♦ **to be full of the ~s of spring** avoir le cœur joyeux ♦ **I wish you ~ of it!** (*iro*) je vous souhaite bien du plaisir !
3 (*Brit* * = *success*) ♦ **any ~?** alors, ça a marché ? * ♦ **I got no ~ out of it** ça n'a pas marché, ça n'a rien donné ♦ **I got no ~ out of him** avec lui ça n'a rien donné, je n'en ai rien tiré

joyful /ˈdʒɔɪfʊl/ **ADJ** joyeux

joyfully /ˈdʒɔɪfəlɪ/ **ADV** [*greet, sing*] joyeusement

joyfulness /ˈdʒɔɪfʊlnɪs/ **N** (*gen*) joie *f* ♦ **the ~ of the occasion** le caractère joyeux de l'événement

joyless /ˈdʒɔɪlɪs/ **ADJ** [*world*] sans joie ; [*person, experience*] triste

joyous /ˈdʒɔɪəs/ **ADJ** (*liter*) joyeux

joyously /ˈdʒɔɪəslɪ/ **ADV** (*liter*) (*with vb*) avec joie ; (*with adj*) joyeusement

joypad /ˈdʒɔɪpæd/ **N** manette *f* de jeu, joypad *m*

joyride /ˈdʒɔɪˌraɪd/ **N** ♦ **to go for a ~** faire une virée * dans une voiture volée **VI** (also **go joyriding**) faire une virée * dans une voiture volée

joyrider /ˈdʒɔɪˌraɪdəʳ/ **N** jeune chauffard *m* au volant d'une voiture volée

joyriding /ˈdʒɔɪˌraɪdɪŋ/ **N** ♦ **~ is on the increase** il y a de plus en plus de jeunes qui volent une voiture juste pour aller faire une virée

joystick /ˈdʒɔɪstɪk/ **N** (*in plane*) manche *m* à balai ; (*Comput*) manche *m* à balai, manette *f* (de jeu)

JP /ˌdʒeɪˈpiː/ **N** (*Brit Jur*) (abbrev of **Justice of the Peace**) → **justice**

Jr (*US*) (abbrev of **Junior**) Jr

JSA /ˌdʒeɪesˈeɪ/ **N** (*Brit Admin*) (abbrev of **job seeker's allowance**) → **job**

jubilant /ˈdʒuːbɪlənt/ **ADJ** [*person, voice*] débordant de joie ; [*face*] épanoui, radieux ♦ **he was ~** il jubilait

jubilation /ˌdʒuːbɪˈleɪʃən/ **N** (= *emotion*) allégresse *f*, jubilation *f* **NPL** **jubilations** (= *celebrations*) fête *f*, réjouissance(s) *f(pl)*

jubilee /ˈdʒuːbɪliː/ **N** jubilé *m* ; → **diamond**

Judaea /dʒuːˈdiːə/ **N** Judée *f*

Judaeo-Christian, Judeo-Christian (*US*) /dʒuːˌdeɪəʊˈkrɪstɪən/ **ADJ** judéo-chrétien

Judah /ˈdʒuːdə/ **N** Juda *m*

Judaic /dʒuːˈdeɪɪk/ **ADJ** judaïque

Judaism /ˈdʒuːdeɪɪzəm/ **N** judaïsme *m*

Judas /ˈdʒuːdəs/ **N** 1 (= *name*) Judas *m* ♦ **~ Iscariot** Judas *m* Iscariote 2 (= *traitor*) judas *m* 3 (= *peephole*) **judas** judas *m* **COMP** **Judas tree** **N** arbre *m* de Judée, gainier *m*

judder /ˈdʒʌdəʳ/ (*Brit*) **VI** vibrer ; (*stronger*) trépider ♦ **to ~ to a halt** s'arrêter en trépidant **N** vibration *f*, trépidation *f*

Jude /dʒuːd/ **N** Jude *m*

judge /dʒʌdʒ/ **N** 1 (*gen, Jur, Sport*) juge *m* ; (= *member of judging panel*) membre *m* du jury ♦ **(the book of) Judges** (*Bible*) (le livre des) Juges *mpl* ♦ **the ~s' rules** (*Brit Police*) *la procédure criminelle avant un procès* ; see also **comp**
2 (*fig*) connaisseur *m*, juge *m* ♦ **to be a good ~ of character** être bon psychologue, savoir juger les gens ♦ **to be a good ~ of wine** être bon juge en vins, s'y connaître en vins ♦ **I'll be the ~** *or* **let me be the ~ of that** c'est à moi de juger
VT 1 (= *assess*) [+ *person, conduct, competition*] juger ; [+ *qualities*] apprécier
2 (= *consider*) juger, estimer (*that* que) ♦ **to ~ it necessary to do sth** juger *or* estimer nécessaire de faire qch ♦ **you can't ~ a book by its cover** (*Prov*) il ne faut pas se fier aux apparences
VI juger, rendre un jugement ♦ **to ~ for oneself** juger par soi-même ♦ **as far as one can ~, as far as can be ~d** autant qu'on puisse en juger ♦ **judging by** *or* **from** à en juger par *or* d'après
COMP **judge advocate** **N** (pl **judge advocates**) (*Mil, Jur*) assesseur *m* (*auprès d'un tribunal militaire*)
judge of appeal **N** (*Jur*) conseiller *m* à la cour d'appel

judg(e)ment /ˈdʒʌdʒmənt/ **N** 1 (= *opinion*) avis *m* ♦ **to give one's judg(e)ment (on)** donner son avis (sur) ♦ **in my judg(e)ment** selon moi
♦ **to make a judg(e)ment** se faire une opinion ♦ **they had to make a ~ about what they had seen** ils ont dû se faire une opinion sur ce qu'ils venaient de voir ♦ **my job is to make a ~ as to whether a good job has been done** mon rôle est de décider si le travail a été bien fait
♦ **to pass judg(e)ment** (= *criticize*) juger ♦ **it's not for me to pass ~** il ne m'appartient pas de juger
♦ **against one's better judg(e)ment** ♦ **against my better ~ I agreed** j'ai accepté tout en sachant que c'était une erreur
♦ **to sit in judg(e)ment** porter un jugement ; → **reserve**
2 (*Jur, Rel*) jugement *m* ♦ **in a historic ~, the court rejected this argument** le tribunal a rejeté cet argument dans un jugement qui fera date ♦ **to give** *or* **pass ~ (on)** prononcer *or* rendre un jugement (sur) ; → **last¹**
3 (*NonC* = *good sense*) jugement *m* ♦ **to have (sound) judg(e)ment** avoir du jugement ♦ **I respect his ~** j'ai confiance en son jugement ♦ **an error of ~** une erreur de jugement
COMP **judg(e)ment call** **N** (*esp US*) ♦ **to make a judg(e)ment call** prendre une décision en s'en remettant à son jugement personnel
Judg(e)ment Day **N** (*Rel*) le jour du Jugement (dernier)

> ⚠ **judg(e)ment** is not usually translated by **jugement** when it means 'opinion'.

judg(e)mental /dʒʌdʒˈmentəl/ **ADJ** ♦ **he is very judg(e)mental** il porte toujours des jugements catégoriques, il s'érige toujours en juge

judicature /ˈdʒuːdɪkətʃəʳ/ **N** 1 (= *process of justice*) justice *f* 2 (= *body of judges*) magistrature *f* 3 (= *judicial system*) système *m* judiciaire

judicial /dʒuːˈdɪʃəl/ **ADJ** 1 (*Jur*) [*power, function*] judiciaire ; [*decision*] de justice ♦ **~ and extrajudicial documents** actes *mpl* judiciaires et extrajudiciaires ♦ **the ~ process** la procédure judiciaire ♦ **~ appointments** nominations *fpl* judiciaires 2 (= *wise*) [*mind*] sage ♦ **~ faculty** sens *m* critique
COMP **judicial inquiry** **N** enquête *f* judiciaire
judicial murder **N** exécution *f*
judicial proceedings **NPL** poursuites *fpl* judiciaires
judicial review **N** (*Jur*) (*Brit*) réexamen *m* d'une décision de justice (*par une juridiction supérieure*) ; (*US*) examen *m* de la constitutionnalité d'une loi
judicial sale **N** vente *f* forcée *or* judiciaire

judicially /dʒuːˈdɪʃəlɪ/ **ADV** judiciairement

judiciary /dʒuːˈdɪʃɪərɪ/ **ADJ** judiciaire **N** 1 (= *system*) système *m* judiciaire 2 (= *body of judges*) magistrature *f* 3 (= *branch of government*) pouvoir *m* judiciaire

judicious /dʒuːˈdɪʃəs/ **ADJ** (*frm*) judicieux

judiciously /dʒuːˈdɪʃəslɪ/ **ADV** (*frm*) [*use, say*] judicieusement

Judith /ˈdʒuːdɪθ/ **N** Judith *f*

judo /ˈdʒuːdəʊ/ **N** judo *m*

judoka /ˈdʒuːdəʊˌkɑː/ **N** judoka *m*

Judy /ˈdʒuːdɪ/ **N** (dim of **Judith**) → **Punch**

jug /dʒʌg/ **N** 1 (*for water*) carafe *f* ; (*for wine*) pichet *m* ; (*round, heavy, jar-shaped*) cruche *f* ; (*for milk*) pot *m* ; (*for washing water*) broc *m* 2 (‡ = *prison*) taule * *f or* tôle * *f*, bloc * *m* ♦ **in ~** en taule *, au bloc * **VT** 1 (*Culin*) cuire en civet ♦ **~ged hare** civet *m* de lièvre 2 (‡ = *imprison*) coffrer * **COMP** **jug band** **N** (*US*) orchestre *m* (de folk *or* de jazz) improvisé (*utilisant des ustensiles ménagers*)

juggernaut /ˈdʒʌgənɔːt/ **N** 1 (*Brit* = *truck*) gros poids lourd *m*, mastodonte *m* 2 (*fig* = *irresistible force*) **the media/military ~** le pouvoir écrasant des médias/de l'armée ♦ **the ~ of tradition/religion** l'influence écrasante de la tradition/religion 3 (*Rel*) **Juggernaut** Jagannâth *m*

juggins‡ /ˈdʒʌgɪnz/ **N** jobard(e) *m(f)*, cruche * *f*

juggle /ˈdʒʌgl/ **VI** (*lit, fig*) jongler (*with* avec) **VT** [+ *balls, plates, facts, figures*] jongler avec ; [+ *one's time*] essayer de partager ♦ **to ~ a career and a family** jongler pour concilier sa carrière et sa vie de famille

juggler /ˈdʒʌgləʳ/ **N** jongleur *m*, -euse *f*

juggling /ˈdʒʌglɪŋ/ **N** (*NonC*) 1 (*lit: with balls, plates*) jonglerie *f* 2 (*fig* = *clever organization*) **combining career and family requires a lot of ~** il faut beaucoup jongler pour concilier sa carrière et sa famille ♦ **with a bit of ~ I managed to pack everything into one suitcase** avec un peu d'astuce j'ai réussi à tout mettre dans une seule valise 3 (= *trickery*) tours *mpl* de passe-passe **COMP** **juggling act** **N** (*fig*) ♦ **to do a ~ act** tout mener de front ♦ **to do a ~ act with sth** jongler avec qch (*fig*)

jughead‡ /ˈdʒʌghed/ **N** (*US pej*) andouille * *f*

Jugoslav /ˈjuːgəʊˌslɑːv/ **ADJ** yougoslave **N** Yougoslave *mf*

Jugoslavia /ˌjuːgəʊˈslɑːvɪə/ **N** Yougoslavie *f*

jugular /ˈdʒʌgjʊləʳ/ **ADJ** jugulaire **N** (veine *f*) jugulaire *f* ♦ **to go for the ~** frapper au point le plus faible

juice /dʒuːs/ **N** 1 [*of fruit, meat*] jus *m* ♦ **orange ~** jus *m* d'orange 2 (*Physiol*) suc *m* ♦ **digestive ~s** sucs *mpl* digestifs 3 (*US* ‡ = *alcohol*) alcool *m* 4 (* = *electricity, gas*) jus * *m* ; (*Brit* = *petrol*) essence *f* **VT** [+ *fruit, vegetable*] faire du jus (avec)
COMP **juice extractor** **N** (*Brit*) centrifugeuse *f* électrique
juicing orange **N** orange *f* à jus
► **juice up** * **VT SEP** 1 (*US*) [+ *car*] gonfler le moteur de 2 (= *spice up*) [+ *occasion*] mettre de l'ambiance dans ; [+ *image, brand*] donner du punch à *

juicehead‡ /ˈdʒuːshed/ **N** (*US*) poivrot(e) * *m(f)*, alcoolique *mf*

juicer /ˈdʒuːsəʳ/ **N** centrifugeuse *f* électrique

juiciness /ˈdʒuːsɪnɪs/ **N** juteux *m*

juicy /ˈdʒuːsɪ/ **ADJ** 1 (= *succulent*) [*fruit, steak*] juteux 2 * (= *desirable*) [*role, part*] savoureux ; [*deal*] juteux ; (= *interesting*) [*story, scandal, details*] croustillant ♦ **I heard some ~ gossip about him** j'ai entendu des histoires bien croustillantes à son sujet

jujitsu /dʒuːˈdʒɪtsuː/ **N** jiu-jitsu *m*

juju /ˈdʒuːdʒuː/ N *culte africain proche du vaudou*

jujube /ˈdʒuːdʒuːb/ N jujube *m*

jukebox /ˈdʒuːkbɒks/ N juke-box *m*

Jul. abbrev of **July**

julep /ˈdʒuːlep/ N boisson *f* sucrée, sirop *m*, julep *m* ; → **mint²**

Julian /ˈdʒuːlɪən/ N Julien *m* ADJ julien

Juliet /ˈdʒuːlɪet/ N Juliette *f*

Julius /ˈdʒuːlɪəs/ N Jules *m* ◆ ~ **Caesar** Jules *m* César

July /dʒuːˈlaɪ/ N juillet *m* ; *for phrases see* **September**

jumble /ˈdʒʌmbl/ VT (also **jumble up**) [1] *(lit)* *[+ objects, clothes, figures]* mélanger ◆ **to ~ everything (up)** tout mélanger ◆ **his clothes are all ~d up on his bed** ses vêtements sont pêle-mêle *or* en vrac sur son lit ◆ **a ~d mass of wires** un amas de fils entortillés ◆ **can you work out whose famous face has been ~d up in the picture?** *(in magazine)* pouvez-vous recomposer le visage du personnage célèbre qui figure sur cette image ?

[2] *(fig)* *[+ facts, details]* brouiller, embrouiller ◆ **~d thoughts/memories** pensées *fpl*/souvenirs *mpl* confus(es)

N [1] *(lit)* *[of objects]* fouillis *m*, méli-mélo* *m* ◆ **a ~ of toys/papers** un tas de jouets/papiers en vrac ◆ **in a ~** *[objects, papers, toys]* en vrac

[2] **a ~ of words** une suite de mots sans queue ni tête ◆ **a ~ of ideas/thoughts/memories** des idées *fpl*/pensées *fpl*/souvenirs *mpl* confus(es) ◆ **in a ~** *[ideas, thoughts]* confus

[3] *(NonC: Brit = junk, goods at jumble sale)* bric-à-brac *m*

COMP **jumble sale** N *(Brit)* vente *f* de charité *(d'objets d'occasion)*

jumbo /ˈdʒʌmbəʊ/ N * [1] éléphant *m* [2] ⇒ **jumbo jet**

COMP *[order, load, box, bottle, vegetable, prawn, egg]* géant

jumbo jet N jumbo-jet *m*, avion *m* gros porteur

jumbo loan N prêt *m* géant *or* jumbo

jumbo pack N *(gen)* paquet *m* géant ; *[of bottles, cans]* emballage *m* géant

jump /dʒʌmp/ N [1] *(gen)* saut *m* ; *(of fear, nervousness)* sursaut *m* ◆ **to give a ~** faire un saut, sauter ; *(nervously)* sursauter ◆ **at one ~** d'un (seul) bond ◆ **to be one ~ ahead** *(fig)* avoir une longueur d'avance *(of* sur*)* ; ◆ **to get a** *or* **the ~ on sb/sth** *(US)* prendre une longueur d'avance sur qn/qch ◆ **it's a big ~ from medical student to doctor** il y a une grande différence entre être étudiant en médecine et devenir médecin ; → **bungee jumping, high, parachute, running**

[2] *(= increase)* bond *m* ◆ **a ~ in profits/sales/inflation** un bond des profits/des ventes/de l'inflation ◆ **the ~ in prices** la hausse brutale des prix ◆ **a 5% ~ in the unemployment figures** un bond de 5% des chiffres du chômage

[3] *(Comput)* saut *m*

[4] *(Horse-riding)* obstacle *m*

VI [1] *(= leap)* sauter, bondir ◆ **to ~ in/out/across** entrer/sortir/traverser d'un bond ◆ **to ~ across a stream** franchir un ruisseau d'un bond ◆ **to ~ into the river** sauter dans la rivière ◆ **to ~ off a bus/train** sauter d'un autobus/d'un train ◆ **to ~ off a wall** sauter (du haut) d'un mur ◆ **to ~ over a wall/fence/ditch** sauter un mur/une barrière/un fossé ◆ **he managed to ~ clear as the car went over the cliff** il a réussi à sauter hors de la voiture au moment où celle-ci passait par-dessus la falaise ◆ **to ~ up and down** sauter ◆ **to ~ up and down with excitement** bondir d'excitation ◆ **to ~ up and down with anger** trépigner de colère ◆ **to ~ for joy** *(fig)* sauter de joie

[2] *(from nervousness)* sursauter, tressauter ◆ **to make sb ~** *[loud noise]* faire sursauter *or* tressauter qn ◆ **it almost made him ~ out of his skin** * ça l'a fait sauter au plafond* ◆ **his heart ~ed** *(with fear)* il a eu un coup au cœur ; *(with happiness)* son cœur a bondi

[3] *(fig)* *[person]* sauter ◆ **to ~ from one subject to another** sauter (sans transition) d'un sujet à un autre, passer du coq à l'âne ◆ **she ~ed from kitchen assistant to chef** elle est passée directement de simple aide-cuisinière à chef de cuisine ◆ **she ~ed from seventh place to second** elle est passée directement de la septième à la seconde place ◆ **to ~ at** *[+ chance, suggestion, offer]* sauter sur ; *[+ idea]* accueillir avec enthousiasme ◆ **to ~ down sb's throat** * rembarrer qn ◆ **to ~ to conclusions** tirer des conclusions hâtives ◆ **he ~ed to the conclusion that ...** il en a conclu hâtivement que ... ◆ **to ~ to sb's defence** s'empresser de prendre la défense de qn ◆ **~ to it!** * et plus vite que ça ! *, et que ça saute ! *

[4] *[prices, shares, profits, costs]* monter en flèche, faire un bond ◆ **her salary ~ed from $25,000 to $50,000** son salaire est passé d'un seul coup de 25 000 à 50 000 dollars ◆ **losses ~ed to $4.1 million** les pertes ont subitement atteint les 4,1 millions de dollars

VT [1] *[person, horse]* *[+ obstacle, ditch, fence]* sauter, franchir (d'un bond) ◆ **the horse ~ed a clear round** le cheval a fait un parcours d'obstacles sans faute ◆ **the electric current ~s the gap between the two wires** sans que les fils se touchent, le courant électrique passe de l'un à l'autre ◆ **to ~ 2 metres** sauter 2 mètres, faire un saut de 2 mètres

[2] *[rider]* *[+ horse]* faire sauter ◆ **the jockey ~ed his horse over the fence** le jockey a fait sauter l'obstacle à son cheval ◆ **she's ~ing three horses in this competition** *[jockey]* elle monte trois chevaux dans cette épreuve d'obstacles ; *[owner]* elle engage trois chevaux dans cette épreuve d'obstacles

[3] *(= skip)* sauter ◆ **the stylus ~ed a groove** la pointe de lecture a sauté un sillon ◆ **the disease has ~ed a generation** cette maladie a sauté une génération ◆ **the film then ~s ten years to 1996** le film fait alors un bond de dix ans pour arriver en 1996 ◆ **the company's shares ~ed £1.25/3%** les actions de la société ont fait un bond de 1,25 livres/de 3% ◆ **to ~ bail** *(Jur)* ne pas comparaître au tribunal ◆ **to ~ a claim** *(Jur)* s'emparer illégalement d'une concession minière ◆ **to ~ the gun** *(Sport)* partir avant le départ ; (* *fig*) agir prématurément ◆ **to ~ the gun on sb** couper l'herbe sous le pied de qn ◆ **to ~ the lights** *or* **a red light** * *[motorist]* brûler le feu rouge ◆ **to ~ the queue** * *(Brit)* passer avant son tour, resquiller* ◆ **to ~ the points** *[train]* dérailler à l'aiguillage ◆ **to ~ the rails** *(lit)* *[train]* dérailler ; *(esp Brit fig = go wrong)* déraper ◆ **to ~ a train** *(= get on)* sauter dans un train en marche ; *(= get off)* sauter d'un train en marche ◆ **to ~ ship** *(lit)* déserter le navire ; *(fig = join rival organization)* passer dans un autre camp ◆ **to ~ town** * *(US)* quitter la ville

[4] *(= attack)* ◆ **to ~ sb** * sauter sur qn

[5] ** *(esp US = have sex with)* sauter*

COMP **jumped-up** * ADJ *(Brit pej)* *(= pushy)* parvenu ; *(= cheeky)* effronté ; *(= conceited)* prétentieux ◆ **he is a ~ed-up clerk** ce n'est qu'un petit employé qui a monté en grade

jump-jet N avion *m* à décollage vertical

jump jockey N *(Brit Racing)* jockey *m* de steeple-chase

jump leads NPL *(Brit Aut)* câbles *mpl* de démarrage *(pour batterie)*

jump-off N *(Horse-riding)* (épreuve *f*) finale *f* *(d'un concours hippique)*

jump rope N *(US)* corde *f* à sauter

jump seat N strapontin *m*

jump-start → **jump-start**

jump suit N *(gen)* combinaison (-pantalon) *f*, combinaison *f* de saut

► **jump about, jump around** VI sautiller

► **jump down** VI *(gen)* descendre d'un bond *(from* de*)* ◆ **~ down!** *(from wall, bicycle)* sautez !

► **jump in** VI sauter dedans ◆ **he came to the river and ~ed in** arrivé à la rivière il a sauté dedans ◆ **~ in!** *(into vehicle)* montez ! ; *(into swimming pool)* sautez !

► **jump off** VI sauter ◆ **he ~ed off** il a sauté

ADJ ◆ **jumping-off** → **jumping**

N ◆ **jump-off** → **jump**

► **jump on** VI *(onto truck, bus)* ◆ **jump on!** montez ! ◆ **to ~ on(to) one's bicycle** sauter sur son vélo

VT FUS [1] ◆ **to jump on(to) a bus** sauter dans un autobus

[2] (* = *reprimand*) tomber sur

► **jump out** VI sauter *(of* de*)* ◆ **to ~ out of bed** sauter (à bas) du lit ◆ **to ~ out of the window** sauter par la fenêtre ◆ **to ~ out of a car/train** sauter d'une voiture/d'un train ◆ **~ out!** *(from vehicle)* sortez !, descendez ! ◆ **the mistake ~ed out of the page at him** l'erreur dans la page lui a sauté aux yeux

► **jump up** VI se (re)lever d'un bond

ADJ ◆ **jumped-up** * → **jump**

jumper /ˈdʒʌmpəʳ/ N [1] *(Brit = sweater)* pull (-over) *m* [2] *(US = dress)* robe-chasuble *f* [3] *(= one who jumps: person, animal)* sauteur *m*, -euse *f* [4] *(Comput)* cavalier *m* COMP **jumper cables** NPL câbles *mpl* de démarrage *(pour batterie)*

jumping /ˈdʒʌmpɪŋ/ N *(gen)* saut *m* ; *(= equitation)* jumping *m*, concours *m* hippique ADJ *(US* * *= lively)* plein d'animation

COMP **jumping bean** N haricot *m* sauteur

jumping-off place, jumping-off point N *(fig)* tremplin *m* ◆ **they used the agreement as a ~-off place** *or* **point for further negotiations** ils se sont servis de l'accord comme d'un tremplin pour de plus amples négociations

jumping rope N *(US)* corde *f* à sauter

jump-start /ˈdʒʌmpstɑːt/ VT [1] **to ~ a car** *(by pushing)* faire démarrer une voiture en la poussant ; *(with jump leads)* faire démarrer une voiture en branchant sa batterie sur une autre [2] *[+ negotiations, process, economy]* relancer N [1] **to give sb a ~** *(by pushing)* faire démarrer la voiture de qn en la poussant ; *(with jump leads)* faire démarrer la voiture de qn en branchant sa batterie sur une autre [2] *[of negotiations, process, economy]* relance *f*

jumpy * /ˈdʒʌmpɪ/ ADJ *[person]* nerveux ; *[stock market]* instable

Jun. [1] abbrev of **June** [2] (abbrev of **Junior**) Jr

junction /ˈdʒʌŋkʃən/ N [1] *(NonC)* jonction *f* [2] *(Brit)* *(= meeting place)* *[of roads]* bifurcation *f* ; *(= crossroads)* carrefour *m* ; *[of rivers]* confluent *m* ; *[of railway lines]* embranchement *m* ; *[of pipes]* raccordement *m* ; *(= station)* gare *f* de jonction ◆ **leave the motorway at ~ 13** prenez la sortie numéro 13 COMP **junction box** N *(Elec)* boîte *f* de dérivation

juncture /ˈdʒʌŋktʃəʳ/ N [1] *(= joining place)* jointure *f*, point *m* de jonction ; *(Ling)* joncture *f* [2] *(fig = state of affairs)* conjoncture *f* ◆ **at this ~** *(fig = point)* à ce moment

June /dʒuːn/ N juin *m* ; *for phrases see* **September**

COMP **June bug** N hanneton *m*

Jungian /ˈjʊŋɪən/ N *(= follower of Jung)* jungien(ne) *m(f)* ADJ jungien

jungle /ˈdʒʌŋgl/ N [1] jungle *f* [2] *(Mus)* jungle *f*

COMP *[animal, bird]* de la jungle

jungle bunny ** N *(esp US pej)* nègre *m*, négresse *f*, Noir(e) *m(f)*

jungle gym N *(in playground)* cage *f* à poules *or* aux écureuils

jungle juice * N gnôle* *f*

jungle warfare N *(NonC)* combats *mpl* de jungle

junior /ˈdʒuːnɪəʳ/ ADJ 1 *(in age)* (plus) jeune, cadet ◆ **John Smith, Junior** John Smith fils *or* junior ; see also **comp**

2 *(in position) [employee, job]* subalterne ◆ ~ **members of staff** les employés subalternes ◆ **he is ~ to me in the business** il est au-dessous de moi dans l'entreprise ◆ **people at the most ~ level in the company** les petits employés de l'entreprise ; see also **comp**

3 *(Sport) [competition, team, title] (gen)* junior ; *(= under 11)* ≃ de poussins ; *(= 12 to 13)* ≃ de benjamins ; *(= 14 to 15)* ≃ de minimes ; *(= 16 to 17)* ≃ de cadets ; *(= 18 to 19)* ≃ de juniors ◆ **to compete at ~ level** faire partie de l'équipe des poussins *(or* des benjamins *etc)*

N 1 cadet(te) *m(f)* ◆ **he is two years my ~, he is my ~ by two years** il est mon cadet de deux ans

2 *(Brit Scol)* petit(e) élève *m(f) (de 7 à 11 ans)* ; *(US Scol)* élève *mf* de classe de première ; *(US Univ)* étudiant(e) *m(f)* de troisième année

3 *(Sport) (gen)* junior *mf* ; *(= under 11)* ≃ poussin *mf* ; *(= 12 to 13)* ≃ benjamin(e) *m(f)* ; *(= 14 to 15)* ≃ minime *mf* ; *(= 16 to 17)* ≃ cadet(te) *m(f)* ; *(= 18 to 19)* ≃ junior *mf*

COMP **junior class** N ◆ **the ~ classes** les petites classes *fpl (de 7 à 11 ans)*

junior clerk N petit commis *m*

junior college N *(US)* institut *m* universitaire (du premier cycle)

Junior Common Room N *(Brit Univ) (= room)* salle *f* des étudiants ; *(= students)* étudiants *mpl*

junior doctor N interne *m* des hôpitaux

junior executive N jeune cadre *m*

junior high school N *(US)* ≃ collège *m*

Junior League N 1 *(US: for voluntary work) association locale féminine d'aide à la communauté* 2 *(Brit Sport)* championnat *m* junior

junior minister N *(Parl)* sous-secrétaire *m* d'État

junior miss † N *(Comm)* fillette *f (de 11 à 14 ans)*

junior officer N officier *m* subalterne

junior partner N associé(-adjoint) *m*

junior rating N *(Brit Navy)* matelot *m*

junior school N *(Brit)* école *f* primaire *(de 7 à 11 ans)*

junior's license N *(US) permis spécial pour adolescents et autres apprentis conducteurs* ; → DRIVING LICENCE, DRIVER'S LICENSE

junior technician N *(Brit = airman)* soldat *m* de première classe

junior training centre N *(Brit)* centre *m* médico-éducatif

junior varsity sports NPL *(US Univ) sports pratiqués entre les équipes de deuxième division des établissements scolaires et universitaires*

juniper /ˈdʒuːnɪpəʳ/ N genévrier *m* ◆ ~ **berry** baie *f* de genièvre ◆ ~ **berries** genièvre *m*

junk¹ /dʒʌŋk/ N *(NonC) (= discarded objects)* bric-à-brac *m inv*, vieilleries *fpl* ; *(= metal)* ferraille *f* ; *(* = bad quality goods)* camelote * *f* ; *(* = worthless objects)* pacotille *f* ; *(‡ = nonsense)* âneries *fpl* ; *(Drugs *)* came * *f* VT * bazarder *, balancer *

COMP **junk art** N junk art *m (sculptures réalisées à l'aide de déchets)*

junk bond N junk bond *m*, obligation *f* à risque

junk dealer N brocanteur *m*, -euse *f*

junk food * N *(NonC)* ◆ **to eat ~ food** manger des cochonneries *

junk heap N dépotoir *m*

junk mail N *(NonC)* imprimés *mpl* publicitaires *(envoyés par la poste)*

junk market N marché *m* aux puces

junk shop N (boutique *f* de) brocante *f*

junk² /dʒʌŋk/ N *(= boat)* jonque *f*

junket /ˈdʒʌŋkɪt/ N 1 *(Culin)* (lait *m*) caillé *m* 2 *(US = trip at public expense)* voyage *m* aux frais de la princesse * VI faire bombance

junketing /ˈdʒʌŋkɪtɪŋ/ N *(NonC) (= merrymaking)* bombance *f*, bringue ‡ *f* ; *(US * = trip, banquet at public expense)* voyage *m or* banquet *m* aux frais de la princesse *

junkie, junky * /ˈdʒʌŋkɪ/ N drogué(e) *m(f)*, camé(e) * *m(f)* ◆ **a television ~** un accro * de la télé

junkyard /ˈdʒʌŋkjɑːd/ N entrepôt *m* de chiffonnier-ferrailleur

Juno /ˈdʒuːnəʊ/ N Junon *f*

Junr (abbrev of **Junior**) Jr

junta /ˈdʒʌntə/ N junte *f*

Jupiter /ˈdʒuːpɪtəʳ/ N *(Myth)* Jupiter *m* ; *(Astron)* Jupiter *f*

Jura /ˈdʒʊərə/ N (also **Jura Mountains**) Jura *m*

Jurassic /dʒʊˈræsɪk/ ADJ *[period]* jurassique

juridical /dʒʊəˈrɪdɪkəl/ ADJ juridique

jurisdiction /ˌdʒʊərɪsˈdɪkʃən/ N *(Jur)* juridiction *f* ; *(Admin)* compétence *f* ◆ **it comes within our ~** *(Jur)* cela relève de notre juridiction ; *(Admin)* cela relève de notre compétence *or* de nos attributions, c'est de notre ressort ◆ **to be outside sb's ~** *(Jur)* ne pas relever de la juridiction de qn ; *(Admin)* ne pas relever des compétences de qn, sortir des attributions de qn ; → **court**

jurisdictional /ˌdʒʊərɪsˈdɪkʃənl/ ADJ *(US)* ◆ ~ **dispute** conflit *m* d'attributions

jurisprudence /ˌdʒʊərɪsˈpruːdəns/ N droit *m* ; → **medical**

jurist /ˈdʒʊərɪst/ N juriste *m*

juror /ˈdʒʊərəʳ/ N juré *m*

jury¹ /ˈdʒʊərɪ/ N *[of trial]* jury *m*, jurés *mpl* ; *[of examination, exhibition, competition]* jury *m* ◆ **to be on the ~** faire partie du jury ◆ **Ladies and Gentlemen of the ~** Mesdames et Messieurs les jurés ◆ **the ~ is out** *(lit)* le jury s'est retiré pour délibérer ; *(fig)* cela reste à voir ◆ **the ~ is out on whether this is true** reste à voir si c'est vrai ; → **coroner, grand**

COMP **jury box** N banc *m* des jurés

jury duty N *(US, Scot)* ⇒ **jury service**

juryrigging N *constitution d'un jury partisan*

jury service N ◆ **to do ~ service** faire partie d'un jury, être juré ◆ **to be called for ~ service** être appelé à faire partie d'un jury

jury shopping N *(US Jur) recherche du jury idéal (par récusation de jurés)*

the jury system N le système de jugement par jury

jury² /ˈdʒʊərɪ/ ADJ *(Naut)* de fortune, improvisé

juryman /ˈdʒʊərɪmən/ N (pl **-men**) juré *m*

jurywoman /ˈdʒʊərɪwʊmən/ N (pl **-women**) femme *f* juré

just¹ /dʒʌst/

ADVERB

1 = exactly juste, exactement ◆ **it's ~ 9 o'clock** il est 9 heures juste, il est exactement 9 heures ◆ **you're ~ in time** vous arrivez juste à temps ◆ **it took me ~ two hours** il m'a fallu exactement *or* juste deux heures ◆ **it's ~ what I wanted** c'est exactement *or* juste ce que je voulais ◆ **that's ~ what I thought** c'est exactement ce que je pensais ◆ **that's ~ what I was going to say** c'est juste *or* exactement ce que j'allais dire ◆ ~ **how many came we don't know** nous ne savons pas exactement *or* au juste combien de personnes sont venues ◆ ~ **then** *or* **at that moment** à ce moment-là, juste à ce moment ◆ **he has to have everything ~ so** * il faut que tout soit exactement comme il veut

Note the translations of the following examples, where **just** is used for emphasis:

◆ ~ **what are you implying?** qu'est-ce que tu veux dire au juste ? ◆ ~ **what did they hope to achieve!** on se demande bien ce qu'ils s'imaginaient obtenir ! ◆ **I'm sure that's ~ what it was** c'était sûrement ça ◆ ~ **when everything was going so well!** dire que tout allait si bien !

◆ **just on** tout juste ◆ **it cost ~ on 10 euros** ça a coûté tout juste 10 € ◆ **it's ~ on 2 kilos** ça fait tout juste 2 kilos ◆ **it's ~ on nine** il est tout juste 9 heures

2 indicating position juste ◆ ~ **by the church** juste à côté de *or* tout près de l'église ◆ **my house is ~ here** ma maison est juste ici ◆ **it's ~ on the left as you go in** c'est tout de suite à gauche en entrant ◆ ~ **over there** là(, tout près) ◆ ~ **past the station** juste après la gare ◆ **it's ~ to the left of the bookcase** c'est juste à gauche de la bibliothèque

3 = at this or that moment ◆ **we're ~ off** nous partons à l'instant ◆ **I'm ~ coming!** j'arrive ! ◆ **it's okay, I was ~ leaving** ce n'est pas grave, je partais ◆ **are you leaving? – not ~ yet** tu pars ? – pas encore *or* pas tout de suite ◆ **are you ready? – not ~ yet** tu es prêt ? – pas tout à fait

4 referring to recent time ◆ ~ **last week** pas plus tard que la semaine dernière ◆ **I saw him ~ last week** je l'ai vu pas plus tard que la semaine dernière ◆ **this book is ~ out** ce livre vient de paraître

◆ **to have just done sth** venir de faire qch ◆ **he had ~ left** il venait de partir ◆ **I have only ~ heard about it** je viens juste de l'apprendre ◆ **I've ~ this minute finished it** je viens de le finir à l'instant, je viens tout juste de le finir

5 = barely ◆ **we (only) ~ caught the train** nous avons juste eu le temps de sauter dans le train ◆ **I'll ~ catch the train if I hurry** j'aurai tout juste le temps d'attraper le train si je me dépêche ◆ **his voice was ~ audible** sa voix était tout juste audible

◆ **only just** tout juste ◆ **I will only ~ get there on time** j'arriverai tout juste à l'heure ◆ **I have only ~ enough money** j'ai tout juste assez d'argent ◆ **we only ~ missed the train** nous avons raté le train de justesse ◆ **he passed the exam but only ~** il a été reçu à l'examen mais de justesse *or* mais ça a été juste

6 = slightly juste ◆ **he got home ~ after 9 o'clock** il est rentré peu après *or* juste après 9 heures ◆ ~ **after he came** juste après son arrivée ◆ ~ **after this** juste après, tout de suite après ◆ ~ **before Christmas** juste avant Noël ◆ ~ **before it started to rain** juste avant qu'il ne commence à pleuvoir ◆ **that's ~ over the kilo** cela fait juste un peu plus du kilo ◆ ~ **over $10** un peu plus de 10 dollars ◆ ~ **under $10** un peu moins de 10 dollars ◆ **it's ~ after 9 o'clock** il est un peu plus de 9 heures

7 = conceivably ◆ **it may ~ be possible** ce n'est pas totalement exclu ◆ **it's an old trick, but it could ~ work** c'est une vieille astuce mais avec un peu de chance ça pourrait marcher

8 = merely juste, ne … que ◆ **it's ~ a suggestion** c'est juste une suggestion, ce n'est qu'une suggestion ◆ **there will be ~ the two of us** il n'y aura que nous deux, il y aura juste nous deux ◆ ~ **a few** juste quelques-uns ◆ **would you like some? – ~ a little bit** tu en veux ? – juste un petit peu ◆ ~ **a quick note to let you know that …** juste un petit mot pour vous dire que … ◆ **he did it ~ for a laugh** * il l'a fait juste pour rigoler * ◆ **that's ~ your opinion** ça c'est ce que tu penses, ça c'est ton opinion

9 = simply juste, simplement ◆ **I ~ told him to go away** je lui ai juste *or* simplement dit de s'en aller ◆ **I would ~ like to say this** je voudrais juste *or* simplement dire ceci ◆ **don't take any notice of her, she's ~ jealous** ne fais pas attention à elle, elle est tout simplement jalouse

When **just** is used in mitigation, or for emphasis, this is expressed in French in various ways.

◆ **I was ~ wondering if you knew ...** je me demandais si vous saviez ... ◆ **I'm ~ phoning to remind you that ...** je te téléphone juste pour te rappeler que ... ◆ **it's ~ one of those things*** c'est comme ça* ◆ **I ~ can't imagine what's happened to him** je n'arrive tout simplement pas à comprendre *or* j'ai du mal à imaginer ce qui a (bien) pu lui arriver ◆ **you should ~ send it back** vous n'avez qu'à le renvoyer ◆ **~ because YOU think so doesn't mean ...** ce n'est pas parce que tu le crois que ...

10 [= specially] spécialement ◆ **I did it ~ for you** je l'ai fait spécialement pour toi

11 [= absolutely] absolument, tout simplement ◆ **it was ~ marvellous!** c'était absolument *or* tout simplement merveilleux ! ◆ **she's ~ amazing!** elle est tout simplement *or* absolument stupéfiante ! ◆ **that's ~ stupid !** c'est complètement *or* vraiment stupide ◆ **we're managing ~ fine** on s'en sort (sans problème)

12 [in imagination] ◆ **I can ~ see her face if I told her** j'imagine déjà la tête qu'elle ferait si je (le) lui disais ◆ **I can ~ hear the roars of laughter** j'entends déjà les rires (que ça provoquerait)

13 [in commands, requests, threats] ◆ **~ wait here a minute** attends une minute ici ◆ **~ be reasonable** sois donc (un peu) raisonnable ◆ **~ don't ask me to help** ne me demande surtout pas de t'aider ◆ **~ a moment please** un instant s'il vous plaît ◆ **~ imagine!*** rends-toi compte !, tu t'imagines un peu !* ◆ **~ look at that!** regarde-moi ça !* ◆ **~ you do!***, **~ you try it!***, **~ you dare!*** essaie un peu pour voir ! ◆ **~ shut up!*** veux-tu te taire !, tu vas te taire ! ◆ **~ let me get my hands on him!*** celui-là, si je l'attrape !

14 [in rejoinders] ◆ **that's ~ it !, that's ~ the point !** justement ! ◆ **~ so!** exactement ! ◆ **yes, but ~ the same ...** oui, mais tout de même ... ◆ **that's ridiculous! – isn't it ~!** *(Brit)* c'est ridicule ! – ça tu peux le dire ! ◆ **she made a real mess of it – didn't she ~!** *(Brit)* elle a tout gâché – ça tu peux le dire !

15 [set structures]

♦ **just about** *(= approximately)* à peu près ◆ **it's ~ about 3 o'clock** il est à peu près 3 heures ◆ **it's ~ about 5 kilos** ça pèse à peu près 5 kilos ◆ **I think that it was ~ about here that I saw him** je pense que c'est par ici que je l'ai vu ◆ **have you finished? – ~ about** avez-vous fini ? – presque *or* pratiquement ◆ **the incident ~ about ruined him** l'incident l'a pratiquement *or* quasiment ruiné ◆ **I've had ~ about enough** *or* **about as much as I can stand!** j'en ai par-dessus la tête !*, j'en ai vraiment assez !

♦ **to be just about to do sth** être sur le point de faire qch ◆ **we were ~ about to leave** on était sur le point de partir, on allait partir

♦ **just as** ◆ **leave everything ~ as you find it** laissez tout exactement en l'état ◆ **~ as we arrived it began to rain** juste au moment où nous arrivions, il s'est mis à pleuvoir ◆ **come ~ as you are** venez comme vous êtes ◆ **~ as you like** (c'est) comme vous voulez *or* voudrez ◆ **~ as I thought!** c'est bien ce que je pensais ! ◆ **this one is ~ as good as the more expensive model** celui-ci est tout aussi bon que le modèle plus cher

♦ **just as well** ◆ **I wasn't expecting much, which was ~ as well** je ne m'attendais pas à grand-chose, heureusement *or* et c'est tant mieux ◆ **I was driving slowly, and ~ as well** heureusement que je roulais lentement ◆ **we might ~ as well have stayed on a few days longer** on aurait très bien pu rester quelques jours de plus

♦ **just in case** ◆ **~ in case it rains** juste au cas où il pleuvrait ◆ **I'm taking a sleeping bag, ~ in case** j'emmène un sac de couchage, au cas où *or* pour le cas où

♦ **just like** ◆ **he's ~ like his father** *(physically)* c'est le portrait de son père, c'est son père tout craché ; *(in behaviour)* il est comme son père ◆ **they have their problems ~ like the rest of us** eux aussi, ils ont leurs problèmes comme tout le monde ◆ **that's ~ like Robert, always late** c'est bien Robert ça, toujours en retard ◆ **I can't find £1,000 ~ like that** je ne peux pas trouver 1 000 livres comme ça

♦ **just now** *(= a short time ago)* à l'instant, tout à l'heure ◆ **I saw him ~ now** je l'ai vu à l'instant *or* tout à l'heure ◆ **I'm busy ~ now** *(= at the moment)* je suis occupé (pour l'instant) ◆ **he's on the phone ~ now** il est au téléphone

---

just² /dʒʌst/ **ADJ** *(= fair)* juste *(to or towards sb* avec qn) ◆ **it is only ~ to point out that ...** il n'est que juste de faire remarquer que ... ; → **deserts**

justice /ˈdʒʌstɪs/ **N** 1 *(NonC: Jur)* justice *f* ◆ **to bring sb to ~** traduire qn en justice ◆ **~ has been done** justice a été faite ; → **poetic**
2 *(NonC = fairness)* justice *f* ◆ **I must, in (all) ~, say (that) ...** pour être juste, je dois dire (que) ... ◆ **in ~ to him he ..., to do him ~ he ...** pour être juste envers lui, il ..., il faut lui rendre cette justice qu'il ... ◆ **this photograph doesn't do him ~** cette photo ne le flatte pas *or* ne l'avantage pas ◆ **she never does herself ~** elle ne se montre jamais à sa juste valeur ◆ **to do ~ to a meal** faire honneur à un repas
3 *(= judge) (Brit)* juge *m* ; *(US)* juge *m* de la Cour Suprême ; → **lord**
4 *(= justness) [of cause]* bien-fondé *m* ◆ **to dispute the ~ of a claim** contester le bien-fondé d'une réclamation
COMP **Justice Department** **N** *(US)* département *m* de la Justice
Justice of the Peace **N** juge *m* de paix

justifiable /ˌdʒʌstɪˈfaɪəbl/ **ADJ** *[action]* justifié ; *[desire, emotion]* légitime ; *[choice]* défendable ◆ **~ homicide** *(Jur)* homicide *m* justifiable *(commis par qn dans l'exercice de ses fonctions)*

justifiably /ˌdʒʌstɪˈfaɪəblɪ/ **ADV** à juste titre ◆ **he was angry, and ~ so** il était en colère, à juste titre *or* et il y avait de quoi

justification /ˌdʒʌstɪfɪˈkeɪʃən/ **N** 1 *(gen, also Rel)* justification *f (of, for* de, à, pour) ◆ **as a ~ for his action** comme justification de *or* à son acte ◆ **in ~ of** pour justifier ◆ **to have some ~ for doing sth** avoir des raisons de faire qch ◆ **there is no ~ for the recent rise in prices** la hausse récente des prix n'est absolument pas justifiée ◆ **there can be no ~ for these barbaric acts** rien ne saurait justifier ces actes de barbarie ◆ **I knew there was no ~ for what I was doing** je savais que je n'avais aucune raison valable de faire ce que je faisais ◆ **the only ~ for a zoo is education** la seule raison d'être des zoos est leur fonction éducative ◆ **with ~** à juste titre
2 *(Typ, Comput) [of text, page]* justification *f*

justify /ˈdʒʌstɪfaɪ/ **VT** 1 *[+ behaviour, action]* justifier ; *[+ decision]* prouver le bien-fondé de ◆ **to ~ o.s.** se justifier ◆ **this does not ~ his being late** cela ne justifie pas son retard ◆ **the decision was fully justified by economic conditions** la décision était entièrement justifiée par les conditions économiques ◆ **to be justified in doing sth** avoir de bonnes raisons de faire qch ◆ **you're not justified in talking to her like that** rien ne vous autorise à lui parler de cette façon ◆ **am I justified in thinking ...?** est-ce que j'ai raison de penser ... ? 2 *(Typ, Comput) [+ paragraph, text]* justifier ◆ **justified left/right, left/right justified** justifié à gauche/à droite

justly /ˈdʒʌstlɪ/ **ADV** 1 *(= justifiably, deservedly) [proud, famous, claim, accuse]* à juste titre 2 *(= fairly, equitably) [treat, rule, govern, reward]* justement

justness /ˈdʒʌstnɪs/ **N** *[of cause]* justesse *f*

jut /dʒʌt/ **VI** (also **jut out**) faire saillie, dépasser ◆ **he saw a gun ~ting (out) from behind a wall** il a vu le canon d'un fusil dépasser de derrière un mur ◆ **the cliff ~s (out) into the sea** la falaise avance dans la mer ◆ **to ~ (out) over the street/the sea** surplomber la rue/la mer

Jute /dʒuːt/ **N** Jute *m*

jute /dʒuːt/ **N** jute *m*

Juvenal /ˈdʒuːvɪnəl/ **N** Juvénal *m*

juvenile /ˈdʒuːvənaɪl/ **N** *(= human)* adolescent(e) *m(f)*, jeune *mf* ; *(= bird, animal)* jeune *mf*
ADJ 1 *(= young) [animal]* jeune 2 *[violence, employment]* des jeunes ; *[diabetes, arthritis]* juvénile ◆ **~ crime** délinquance *f* juvénile ◆ **~ books** livres *mpl* pour enfants ; see also **comp** ; → **lead¹** 3 *(pej) [behaviour, attitude]* puéril(e) *m(f)*, juvénile
COMP **juvenile court** **N** *(Jur)* tribunal *m* pour enfants
juvenile delinquency **N** délinquance *f* juvénile
juvenile delinquent **N** délinquant(e) *m(f)* juvénile, jeune délinquant(e) *m(f)* ◆ **~ delinquents** l'enfance *f* *or* la jeunesse délinquante
juvenile offender **N** *(Jur)* jeune délinquant(e) *m(f)*

juvenilia /ˌdʒuːvɪˈnɪlɪə/ **NPL** *(frm)* œuvres *fpl* de jeunesse

juxtapose /ˈdʒʌkstəpəʊz/ **VT** juxtaposer

juxtaposition /ˌdʒʌkstəpəˈzɪʃən/ **N** juxtaposition *f* ◆ **to be in ~** se juxtaposer

K, k /keɪ/ **N** [1] (= letter) K, k *m* ◆ **K for King** ≈ K comme Kléber [2] (= thousand) mille *m* ◆ **he earns 30K*** il gagne 30 000 livres (*or* dollars) [3] (Comput) K K *m*

kabala /kæˈbɑːlə/ **N** cabale *f*

kabob /kəˈbɒb/ **N** ⇒ **kebab**

kabuki /kəˈbuːkɪ/ **N** kabuki *m*

Kabul /kəˈbʊl/ **N** Kaboul

kaffeeklatsch /ˈkæfɪklætʃ/ **N** (US) *réunion de femmes qui se retrouvent régulièrement pour bavarder autour d'une tasse de café*

Kaffir /ˈkæfəʳ/ (pej) **N** (pl **Kaffirs** or **Kaffir**) Cafre *mf* **ADJ** cafre

Kafkaesque /ˌkæfkəˈesk/ **ADJ** kafkaïen

kaftan /ˈkæftæn/ **N** caf(e)tan *m*

kagoul(e) /kəˈguːl/ **N** ⇒ **cagoule**

kail /keɪl/ **N** ⇒ **kale**

Kaiser /ˈkaɪzəʳ/ **N** Kaiser *m*

Kalahari /ˌkæləˈhɑːrɪ/ **N** ◆ **the ~ (Desert)** le (désert du) Kalahari

Kalashnikov /kəˈlæʃnɪˌkɒf/ **N** kalachnikov *f*

kale /keɪl/ **N** chou *m* frisé

kaleidoscope /kəˈlaɪdəskəʊp/ **N** (lit, fig) kaléidoscope *m*

kaleidoscopic /kəˌlaɪdəˈskɒpɪk/ **ADJ** kaléidoscopique

Kama Sutra /ˌkɑːməˈsuːtrə/ **N** Kamasutra *m*

kamikaze /ˌkæmɪˈkɑːzɪ/ **N** kamikaze *m* **ADJ** kamikaze

Kampala /ˌkæmˈpɑːlə/ **N** Kampala

Kampuchea /ˌkæmpʊˈtʃɪə/ **N** ◆ **(Democratic) ~** le Kampuchéa (démocratique)

Kampuchean /ˌkæmpʊˈtʃɪən/ **N** Kampuchéen(ne) *m(f)* **ADJ** kampuchéen

Kan. abbrev of **Kansas**

Kanak /kəˈnæk/ **N** canaque *mf*, kanak(e) *m(f)*

kangaroo /ˌkæŋgəˈruː/ **N** kangourou *m* ◆ **to have ~s in one's top paddock*** (Austral) débloquer* **COMP** **kangaroo court N** (pej) tribunal *m* irrégulier

Kans. abbrev of **Kansas**

Kansas /ˈkænzəs/ **N** Kansas *m* ◆ **in ~** dans le Kansas

Kantian /ˈkæntɪən/ **N** kantien(ne) *m(f)* **ADJ** kantien

kaolin /ˈkeɪəlɪn/ **N** kaolin *m*

kapok /ˈkeɪpɒk/ **N** (= material) kapok *m* ; (= tree) fromager *m* **COMP** [cushion] rembourré de kapok

Kaposi's sarcoma /kæˈpəʊsɪzsɑːˈkəʊmə/ **N** (Med) sarcome *m* de Kaposi

kaput* /kəˈpʊt/ **ADJ** [watch, car] fichu*, kaput* *inv* ; [plan] fichu*, foutu*

karabiner /ˌkærəˈbiːnəʳ/ **N** (Climbing) mousqueton *m*

karaoke /ˌkɑːrɪˈəʊkɪ/ **N** karaoké *m*
COMP [competition, singer] de karaoké
karaoke bar N bar *m* karaoké
karaoke machine N karaoké *m*

karat /ˈkærət/ **N** ⇒ **carat**

karate /kəˈrɑːtɪ/ **N** (NonC) karaté *m* **COMP** **karate chop N** coup *m* de karaté (*donné avec le tranchant de la main*)

Kariba /kəˈriːbə/ **N** ◆ **Lake ~** le lac Kariba

karma /ˈkɑːmə/ **N** (Rel) karma *m* ◆ **good/bad ~** (fig) bonnes/mauvaises vibrations *fpl*

kart /kɑːt/ **N** kart *m* **VI** ◆ **to go ~ing** faire du karting

karting /ˈkɑːtɪŋ/ **N** karting *m*

Kashmir /kæʃˈmɪəʳ/ **N** Cachemire *m*

Kashmiri /kæʃˈmɪərɪ/ **N** [1] (= person) Cachemirien(ne) *m(f)* [2] (= language) kashmiri *m*, cachemirien *m* **ADJ** cachemirien

kat /kæt/ **N** ⇒ **khat**

Kate /keɪt/ **N** dim of **Katharine**

Katharine, Katherine /ˈkæθərɪn/, **Kathleen** /ˈkæθliːn/ **N** Catherine *f*

katydid /ˈkeɪtɪdɪd/ **N** sauterelle *f* d'Amérique

katzenjammer* /ˈkætsənˌdʒæməʳ/ **N** (US) [1] (= noise) tapage *m* [2] (= hangover) gueule *f* de bois*

kayak /ˈkaɪæk/ **N** kayak *m*

Kazak(h) /kəˈzɑːk/ **ADJ** kazakh **N** [1] (= person) Kazakh(e) *m(f)* [2] (= language) kazakh *m*

Kazakhstan /ˌkɑːzɑːkˈstæn/ **N** Kazakhstan *m*

kazoo /kəˈzuː/ **N** mirliton *m*

KB (abbrev of **kilobyte**) Ko *m*

KBE /ˌkeɪbiːˈiː/ **N** (Brit) (abbrev of **Knight of the British Empire**) *titre honorifique*

KC /keɪˈsiː/ **N** [1] (Brit Jur) (abbrev of **King's Counsel**) → **counsel** [2] abbrev of **Kansas City**

kcal /ˈkeɪkæl/ **N** (abbrev of **kilocalorie**) kcal

KCB /ˌkeɪsiːˈbiː/ **N** (Brit) (abbrev of **Knight Commander of the Bath**) *titre honorifique*

KD /keɪˈdiː/ **ADJ** (US Comm) (abbrev of **knocked down**) (livré) non monté

kebab /kəˈbæb/ **N** (also **shish kebab**) brochette *f* (de viande) ; (also **doner kebab**) doner kebab *m*

kedge /kedʒ/ (Naut) **N** ancre *f* à jet **VT** haler (sur une ancre à jet)

kedgeree /ˌkedʒəˈriː/ **N** (Brit) kedgeree *m* (*pilaf de poisson avec des œufs durs*)

keel /kiːl/ **N** (Naut) quille *f* ◆ **on an even ~** (Naut) dans ses lignes, à égal tirant d'eau ; (fig) stable ◆ **to keep sth on an even ~** (fig) maintenir qch en équilibre ◆ **to get back on an even ~** retrouver l'équilibre

► **keel over VI** [1] (Naut) chavirer
[2] (* fig) [person] tourner de l'œil*
VT (Naut) (faire) chavirer

keelhaul /ˈkiːlhɔːl/ **VT** (Naut) faire passer sous la quille (*en guise de châtiment*) ; (* fig) passer un savon à*

keen¹ /kiːn/ **LANGUAGE IN USE 19.2** **ADJ** [1] (= eager) ◆ **to be ~ to do sth** or **on doing sth** tenir à faire qch ◆ **to be ~ for** [+ solution, referendum etc] avoir hâte de voir ◆ **she's ~ for a family** elle a envie d'avoir des enfants ◆ **he's not ~ on her coming** il ne tient pas tellement à ce qu'elle vienne ◆ **to be ~ for sb to do sth** or **that sb should do sth** tenir à ce que qn fasse qch ◆ **to await sth with ~ anticipation** attendre qch avec beaucoup d'impatience

[2] (= enthusiastic) [student, amateur] enthousiaste ◆ **a ~ gardener/photographer** un passionné de jardinage/de photo ◆ **a ~ advocate of sth** un fervent partisan de qch ◆ **he tried not to seem too ~** il a essayé de ne pas se montrer trop enthousiaste *or* de ne pas montrer trop d'enthousiasme ◆ **to be ~ on music/cycling** aimer beaucoup la musique/le vélo ◆ **to be ~ on an idea** être emballé* par une idée ◆ **to become** *or* **get ~ on sth** se passionner pour qch ◆ **I got quite ~ on the idea** l'idée m'a séduit ◆ **to be (as) ~ as mustard*** ◆ **to be mustard ~*** (Brit) déborder d'enthousiasme ◆ **to be mad ~ on sth*** être fou de qch

[3] (esp Brit *) ◆ **to be ~ on sb** être inspiré *or* branché* par qn, être attiré par qn ; (= sexually attracted) en pincer* pour qn ◆ **I'm not too ~ on him** il ne me plaît pas beaucoup

[4] (= acute) [desire, interest, disappointment, sense of humour, intellect, intelligence] vif ; [look, gaze, sight] perçant ; [hearing, sense of smell] fin ◆ **to have a ~ sense of** *or* **instinct for sth** avoir un sens aigu de qch ◆ **to have a ~ appetite for sth** (fig) avoir un vif intérêt pour qch ◆ **to have a ~ awareness of sth** être profondément conscient de qch, avoir une conscience vive de qch ◆ **to have a ~ eye** (= good eyesight) avoir la vue perçante ◆ **to have a ~ eye for detail** être minutieux ◆ **to have a ~ ear** (= good hearing) avoir l'oreille *or* ouïe fine ◆ **to have a ~ nose**

for sth *(= sense of smell)* avoir le nez fin *or* du nez pour qch ; *(fig)* savoir flairer qch
5 *(= fierce) [competition]* serré ; *[fight]* acharné
6 *(= sharp) [blade, edge]* tranchant ; *[wind]* pénétrant ; *[frost]* mordant ; *[air]* vif
7 *(esp Brit - competitive) [price]* compétitif
8 *(US * = good)* chouette* ◆ **he plays a ~ game of squash** il se défend bien au squash

keen² /kiːn/ **N** *(= lament)* mélopée *f* funèbre *(irlandaise)* **VI** chanter une mélopée funèbre

keenly /ˈkiːnlɪ/ **ADV** 1 *(= intensely) [interested]* vivement ; *[aware]* profondément ◆ **to feel sth ~** ressentir qch profondément 2 *(= alertly) [listen, watch]* très attentivement 3 *(= eagerly) [awaited, anticipated]* impatiemment, avec impatience 4 *(= fiercely) [fight, debate]* âprement ◆ **~ contested** vivement contesté 5 *(= competitively)* ◆ **~ priced** vendu à un prix compétitif

keenness /ˈkiːnnɪs/ **N** 1 *(= eagerness)* volonté *f* ; *(= haste)* empressement *m* ◆ **the Government's ~ for economic reform** la volonté du gouvernement de mettre en place des réformes économiques ◆ **his ~ to leave** son empressement à partir 2 *(= enthusiasm) [of student, supporter]* enthousiasme *m* 3 *(= acuteness) [of interest, pleasure, grief]* intensité *f* ; *[of pain]* violence *f*, acuité *f* ; *[of cold, wind]* âpreté *f* ; *[of hearing]* finesse *f* ; *[of intelligence, mind]* finesse *f*, pénétration *f* ◆ **~ of sight** acuité *f* visuelle 4 *(= sharpness) [of blade]* tranchant *m*

keep /kiːp/

vb : pret, ptp **kept**

1 TRANSITIVE VERB
2 INTRANSITIVE VERB
3 NOUN
4 COMPOUNDS
5 PHRASAL VERBS

1 - TRANSITIVE VERB

When **keep** is part of a set combination, eg **keep control/a promise/an appointment**, look up the noun.

1 = retain garder, conserver *(more frm)* ◆ **you can ~ this book** tu peux garder ce livre ◆ **if that's what it costs, you can ~ it!*** à ce prix-là, vous pouvez le garder ! ◆ **you must ~ the receipt** il faut garder *or* conserver le reçu ◆ **~ the change!** gardez la monnaie ! ◆ **to ~ one's job** garder *or* conserver son emploi ◆ **this material will ~ its colour/softness** ce tissu garde ses couleurs/sa souplesse ◆ **to ~ sth for o.s.** garder qch (pour soi) ◆ **I bought it for my niece but decided to ~ it for myself** je l'ai acheté pour ma nièce mais j'ai décidé de le garder (pour moi) ◆ **~ it to yourself*** garde-ça pour toi, ne le répète à personne ◆ **I can't ~ telephone numbers in my head** je n'arrive pas à retenir les numéros de téléphone

2 = preserve, put aside garder, mettre de côté ◆ **we're ~ing the best ones for Christmas** nous gardons *or* mettons de côté les meilleurs pour Noël ◆ **you must ~ it in a cold place** il faut le garder *or* le conserver au froid ◆ **I'm ~ing this champagne in case we have visitors** je garde cette bouteille de champagne (en réserve) au cas où nous aurions de la visite

3 = have ready avoir ◆ **I always ~ a blanket and a shovel in the car** j'ai toujours une couverture et une pelle dans la voiture

4 Comm = stock faire, avoir ◆ **we don't ~ that model any more** nous ne faisons plus *or* n'avons plus ce modèle

5 = store, put ranger, mettre ◆ **where does he ~ his passport?** où est-ce qu'il range *or* met son passeport ? ◆ **where do you ~ the sugar?** où est-ce que vous mettez *or* rangez le sucre ? ◆ **~ it somewhere safe** mettez-le en lieu sûr ◆ **she ~s her money under the mattress** elle cache son argent sous son matelas

6 = detain retenir ◆ **they kept him prisoner for two years** ils l'ont retenu *or* gardé prisonnier pendant deux ans ◆ **what kept you?** qu'est-ce qui vous a retenu ? ◆ **I mustn't ~ you** je ne veux pas vous retenir *or* vous retarder ◆ **he was kept in hospital overnight** il a dû passer une nuit à l'hôpital ◆ **he was kept in prison for 20 years** il a passé 20 ans en prison ◆ **they kept the prisoners in a dark room** les prisonniers étaient enfermés dans une salle sombre ◆ **a nasty cold kept her in bed** un mauvais rhume l'a forcée à rester au lit *or* à garder le lit

7 = have *[+ shop]* tenir, avoir ; *[+ house, servant, dog]* avoir ; *[+ pigs, bees, chickens]* élever ◆ **he ~s a good cellar** il a une bonne cave

8 = support subvenir aux besoins de ; *[+ mistress]* entretenir ◆ **you can't ~ a family on that** ça ne suffit pas pour subvenir aux besoins d'une famille *or* pour faire vivre une famille ◆ **I have three children to ~** j'ai trois enfants à ma charge *or* à nourrir ◆ **such a sum would ~ me for a year** une somme pareille me permettrait de vivre pendant un an ◆ **the money ~s me in beer and cigarettes** cet argent me permet d'acheter de la bière et des cigarettes ◆ **our garden ~s us in vegetables all summer** notre jardin nous fournit tout l'été les légumes dont nous avons besoin

9 = observe *[+ law]* observer, respecter ; *[+ vow]* respecter ; *[+ feast day]* célébrer ◆ **to ~ Christmas** célébrer Noël

10 + accounts, diary tenir ◆ **~ a note of this number, in case there's some problem** prends *or* note ce numéro, au cas où il y aurait un problème ; → **count¹, track**

11 † = guard, protect protéger ◆ **God ~ you!** que Dieu vous garde *or* protège !

12 set structures

◆ **to keep sb at sth** ◆ **they kept him at it all day** ils l'ont fait travailler toute la journée ; see also **keep at**

◆ **to keep sth from sb** *(= conceal)* cacher qch à qn ◆ **to ~ a piece of news from sb** cacher une nouvelle à qn ◆ **I know he's ~ing something from me** je sais qu'il me cache quelque chose

◆ **to keep sb from sth** ◆ **the thought kept him from despair** cette pensée l'a empêché de sombrer dans le désespoir

◆ **to keep sb/sth from doing sth** *(= prevent)* empêcher qn/qch de faire qch ◆ **shyness kept him from making new friends** sa timidité l'empêchait de se faire de nouveaux amis ◆ **a spot of oil will ~ it from going rusty** une goutte d'huile l'empêchera de rouiller ◆ **to ~ o.s. from doing sth** se retenir *or* s'abstenir de faire qch ◆ **what can we do to ~ it from happening again?** que pouvons-nous faire pour que ça ne se reproduise pas ?

◆ **to keep sb to sth** ◆ **she kept him to his promise** elle l'a forcé à tenir sa promesse

◆ **to keep o.s. to o.s.** se tenir à l'écart ◆ **she ~s herself to herself** elle n'est pas très sociable, elle ne se mêle pas aux autres ◆ **they ~ themselves to themselves** *[group]* ils font bande à part, ils restent entre eux

◆ **to keep sb/sth** + *-ing* ◆ **to ~ sb waiting** faire attendre qn ◆ **he kept them working all night** il les a fait travailler toute la nuit ◆ **~ him talking while I ...** fais-lui la conversation pendant que je ... ◆ **we want to ~ customers coming back** nous voulons fidéliser notre clientèle ◆ **she managed to ~ the conversation going** elle a réussi à entretenir la conversation ◆ **he kept the engine running** il a laissé le moteur en marche

◆ **to keep** *... + adjective* ◆ **to ~ sth clean** tenir *or* garder qch propre ◆ **cats ~ themselves clean** les chats sont toujours propres ◆ **exercise will ~ you fit** l'exercice physique vous maintiendra en forme ◆ **to ~ inflation as low as possible** maintenir l'inflation au plus bas niveau possible ◆ **you must ~ your bedroom tidy** ta chambre doit toujours être bien rangée *or* en ordre ◆ **to ~ sb informed (of sth)** tenir qn au courant (de qch) ◆ **she kept the plants watered for me** elle a arrosé mes plantes régulièrement

2 - INTRANSITIVE VERB

1 = continue continuer ◆ **to ~ straight on** continuer *or* aller tout droit ◆ **~ north till you get to ...** continuez vers le nord jusqu'à ce que vous arriviez *subj* à ...

2 = remain rester ◆ **she kept inside for three days** elle est restée enfermée chez elle *or* elle n'est pas sortie pendant trois jours ◆ **~ there for a minute** restez là une minute ◆ **to ~ in the middle of the road** rester au milieu de la route

3 in health aller, se porter ◆ **how are you ~ing?** comment allez-vous ?, comment vous portez-vous ? ◆ **to ~ well** aller bien, se porter bien ◆ **she's not ~ing very well** elle ne va pas très bien *or* elle ne se porte pas très bien

4 food se garder, se conserver ◆ **apples that ~ all winter** des pommes qui se gardent *or* se conservent tout l'hiver

5 = wait ◆ **that letter can** *or* **will ~ until tomorrow** cette lettre peut attendre jusqu'à demain

6 set structures

◆ **to keep** + *-ing* ◆ **to ~ doing sth** *(= continue)* continuer à *or* de faire qch ; *(= do repeatedly)* ne pas arrêter de faire qch, ne pas cesser de faire qch ◆ **he kept walking** il a continué à *or* de marcher ◆ **if you ~ complaining** si vous continuez à vous plaindre ◆ **she ~s saying it was my fault** elle ne cesse de dire *or* n'arrête pas de dire que c'était de ma faute ◆ **he kept interrupting us** il n'a pas arrêté *or* cessé de nous couper la parole ◆ **~ smiling!** gardez le sourire !

An adverb is often added to verbs such as **oublier** and **espérer**.

◆ **I ~ leaving things on the bus** j'oublie constamment des choses dans le bus ◆ **I ~ forgetting to pay the gas bill** j'oublie tout le temps de payer la facture de gaz ◆ **I ~ hoping she'll come back** j'espère toujours qu'elle reviendra

◆ **to keep** + *preposition* ◆ **she bit her lip to ~ from crying** elle s'est mordu la lèvre pour s'empêcher de pleurer ◆ **he leaned against the wall to ~ from falling** il s'est appuyé contre le mur pour ne pas tomber ◆ **he's promised to ~ off alcohol** il a promis de ne plus boire ◆ **you'll save money if you ~ off the motorways** vous économiserez de l'argent si vous évitez d'utiliser les autoroutes ◆ **"keep off the grass"** "défense de marcher sur les pelouses" ◆ **~ on this road until you come to ...** suivez cette route jusqu'à ce que vous arriviez *subj* à ... ◆ **~ to the left!** gardez votre gauche ! ◆ **to ~ to one's bed/one's room** garder le lit/la chambre ◆ **she ~s to herself** elle n'est pas très sociable ◆ **they ~ to themselves** *[group]* ils font bande à part, ils restent entre eux ; see also **phrasal verbs**

◆ **to keep** + *adjective* ◆ **~ calm!** reste calme ! ◆ **to ~ fit** se maintenir en forme ; see also **compounds** ◆ **to ~ silent** se taire, rester silencieux ◆ **to ~ still** rester *or* se tenir tranquille

3 - NOUN

1 = livelihood, food ◆ **I got £30 a week and my ~** je gagnais 30 livres par semaine logé et nourri, je gagnais 30 livres par semaine plus le gîte et le couvert ◆ **I need to give my parents money for my ~** je dois donner de l'argent à mes

parents pour participer aux frais de la maison ◆ **in a poem every word must earn its ~** dans un poème chaque mot doit avoir sa raison d'être

2 of castle donjon *m*

3 set structure ◆ **for ~s** * pour toujours

4 - COMPOUNDS

keep-fit N *(Brit)* ◆ **she does ~-fit once a week** elle fait de la gymnastique une fois par semaine ◆ **~-fit (classes)** cours *mpl* de gymnastique ◆ **~-fit exercises** gymnastique *f*

5 - PHRASAL VERBS

► **keep at** VT FUS 1 *(= persevere with)* poursuivre, continuer ◆ **despite his problems he kept at his studies** malgré ses problèmes, il a poursuivi *or* continué ses études ◆ **~ at it!** persévère !, ne baisse pas les bras ! 2 *(= nag at)* harceler ◆ **I kept at them until they paid me** je les ai harcelés jusqu'à ce qu'ils me paient

► **keep away** VI *(lit)* ne pas s'approcher *(from* de) ◆ **~ away from the fire** ne t'approche pas du feu ◆ **he promised to ~ away from drink** il a promis de ne plus toucher une goutte d'alcool ◆ **~ away!** n'approchez pas ! VT SEP empêcher de s'approcher *(from* de) ◆ **the police kept the crowds away** la police a empêché la foule de s'approcher ◆ **~ him away!** ne le laisse pas approcher !

► **keep back** VI ne pas approcher ◆ **~ back!** n'approchez pas !, restez où vous êtes ! VT SEP 1 *(= restrain)* retenir ◆ **he struggled to ~ back his tears** il retenait ses larmes à grand-peine 2 *(= save)* mettre de côté ◆ **~ back some of the parsley to garnish** mettez de côté *or* réservez une partie du persil pour la garniture 3 *(= conceal)* cacher ; *[+ secrets]* ne pas révéler, taire ◆ **I'm sure he's ~ing something back** je suis sûr qu'il me *(or* nous *etc)* cache quelque chose 4 *[+ crowd]* empêcher de s'approcher *(from* de)

► **keep down** VI rester à couvert ◆ **~ down!** baissez-vous !, restez à couvert ! VT SEP 1 *(= control) [+ one's anger]* réprimer, contenir ; *[+ dog]* retenir, maîtriser ◆ **it's just a way to ~ women down** c'est une manière de cantonner les femmes à un statut inférieur ◆ **you can't ~ her down** elle ne se laisse jamais abattre ◆ **he's living proof that you can't ~ a good man down** il est la preuve vivante que quelqu'un qui en veut arrive toujours à s'en sortir ! 2 *(= limit) [+ inflation, costs]* maîtriser ; *[+ number]* limiter ◆ **to ~ prices down** empêcher les prix de monter ◆ **could you ~ the noise down?** est-ce que vous pourriez faire un peu moins de bruit ? 3 *(Scol)* **to ~ a pupil down** faire redoubler une classe à un élève ◆ **to be kept down** redoubler 4 *(= avoid vomiting)* ◆ **she drank some water but couldn't keep it down** elle a bu de l'eau mais elle a tout vomi *or* rendu ◆ **I can't ~ anything down** je ne peux rien garder

► **keep in** VI ◆ **to keep in with sb** rester en bons termes avec qn VT SEP 1 *[+ anger]* contenir BUT **~ your stomach in !** rentre le ventre ! 2 *(Scol)* ◆ **to keep a child in** garder un enfant en retenue, consigner un enfant ◆ **I'm going to ~ her in till she is better** je vais la garder à la maison jusqu'à ce qu'elle soit rétablie

► **keep off** VI *[person]* rester à l'écart *or* à distance ◆ **if the rain ~s off** s'il ne se met pas à pleuvoir VT SEP ◆ **cover it with clingfilm to keep the flies off** recouvrez-le de film alimentaire pour le protéger des mouches ◆ **they want to ~ young people off the streets** ils veulent qu'il n'y ait plus de jeunes qui traînent dans les rues ◆ **~ your hands off!*** pas touche !* ◆ **he kept his hat off** il s'était découvert ; see also **keep intransitive verb 6**

► **keep on** VI 1 *(= continue)* continuer ◆ **if you ~ on like this you'll fail the exam** si tu continues comme ça, tu seras recalé à l'examen ◆ **he kept on reading** il a continué à *or* de lire ◆ **~ on past the church till you get to the school** continuez après l'église jusqu'à (ce que vous arriviez *subj* à) l'école ◆ **I'll ~ on trying** *(on phone)* je rappellerai 2 *(Brit = nag)* ◆ **don't keep on !** * arrête donc un peu !, laisse-moi tranquille ! VT SEP 1 *[+ servant, employee]* garder 2 ◆ **to keep one's hat on** garder son chapeau ; *[man]* rester couvert ; see also **keep intransitive verb 6**

► **keep on about*** VT FUS *(Brit)* ne pas arrêter de parler de ◆ **she ~s on about her important friends** elle n'arrête pas de parler de ses amis haut placés ◆ **he kept on about me being selfish** il n'arrêtait pas de dire que j'étais égoïste

► **keep on at*** VT FUS *(Brit)* harceler ◆ **she kept on at him to look for a job** elle le harcelait pour qu'il cherche du travail

► **keep out** VI rester en dehors ◆ **"keep out"** "défense d'entrer", "accès interdit" ◆ **to ~ out of danger** rester *or* se tenir à l'abri du danger ◆ **to ~ out of a quarrel** ne pas se mêler à une dispute ◆ **~ out of this!, you ~ out of it!** ne te mêle pas de ça ! VT SEP 1 *(= exclude) [+ person, dog]* empêcher d'entrer ◆ **that coat looks as if it will ~ out the cold** ce manteau doit bien protéger du froid ◆ **I'll ~ the kids out of your** *or* **the way so that you two can have a nice evening together** je me débrouillerai pour que les enfants ne vous embêtent pas et que vous puissiez passer la soirée entre vous 2 *(= not involve)* ◆ **let's keep my mother out of this, shall we ?** pas la peine de mêler ma mère à ça, d'accord ? ◆ **racist attitudes are blamed for ~ing black people out of the police** on considère que le racisme décourage les Noirs d'entrer dans la police

► **keep to** VT FUS *[+ promise]* tenir, être fidèle à ; *[+ agreement, rules, schedule]* respecter ; *[+ plan]* s'en tenir à ; *[+ subject]* ne pas s'écarter de, rester dans ◆ **his production/translation ~s close to the original text** sa mise en scène/traduction reste fidèle au texte original ◆ **to ~ to one's bed** garder le lit ◆ **to ~ to a/one's diet** suivre scrupuleusement un/son régime, ne pas faire d'écart à un/son régime ◆ **to ~ to one's ideal weight** rester *or* se maintenir à son poids idéal ; see also **keep verb**

► **keep together** VI *[people]* ne pas se séparer, rester ensemble ◆ **~ together!** ne vous séparez pas, restez ensemble ! VT SEP *[+ objects]* garder ensemble ; *(= keep fixed together)* maintenir ensemble ; *[+ team, group]* maintenir la cohésion de, souder ◆ **it's been hard to ~ the team together** ça n'a pas été facile de souder l'équipe

► **keep under** VT SEP *[+ people, race]* assujettir ; *[+ subordinates]* dominer ; *[+ unruly pupils etc]* se faire obéir de, mater

► **keep up** VI 1 *[prices]* se maintenir ◆ **their spirits are ~ing up** ils ne se découragent pas, ils ne se laissent pas abattre ◆ **I hope the good weather will ~ up** j'espère que le beau temps va continuer *or* se maintenir 2 *(in walk, race, work, achievement)* suivre (le rythme) ; *(in comprehension)* suivre ◆ **to ~ up with sb** *(in walk, race, work, achievement)* suivre qn ; *(in comprehension)* suivre qn ◆ **they went so fast I couldn't ~ up (with them)** ils allaient si vite que je n'arrivais pas à (les) suivre ◆ **I couldn't ~ up with what he was saying** je n'ai pas pu suivre ce qu'il disait ◆ **wage increases have not kept up with inflation** les hausses de salaires n'ont pas suivi le taux d'inflation ◆ **the company has failed to ~ up with the times** la société n'a pas réussi à évoluer ◆ **to ~ up with demand** parvenir à satisfaire la demande ; → **Joneses** 3 *(= stay friends with)* ◆ **to keep up with sb** rester en relations avec qn, garder le contact avec qn VT SEP 1 *[+ pressure, standards, subscription]* maintenir ; *[+ correspondence]* entretenir ; *[+ study]* continuer ◆ **I try to ~ up my German** j'essaie d'entretenir mon allemand ◆ **I couldn't ~ the diet up for more than a week** je n'ai pas réussi à suivre ce régime pendant plus d'une semaine ◆ **they can no longer ~ the payments up** ils n'arrivent plus à payer les traites ◆ **they kept up a constant barrage of criticism** ils ont opposé un flot ininterrompu de critiques ◆ **to ~ up a custom** maintenir *or* perpétuer une tradition ◆ **~ it up!** continuez ! 2 *(= maintain) [+ house, paintwork]* entretenir, maintenir en bon état

---

keeper /'kiːpəʳ/ N *(in museum)* conservateur *m*, -trice *f* ; *(in park, zoo)* gardien(ne) *m(f)* ; (also **gamekeeper**) garde-chasse *m* ; (also **goalkeeper**) gardien(ne) *m(f)* (de but) ◆ **am I my brother's ~?** *(Bible)* suis-je le gardien de mon frère ? ◆ **I'm not his ~** *(fig)* je ne suis pas responsable de lui ; → **beekeeper, goalkeeper, shopkeeper**

keeping /'kiːpɪŋ/ N *(NonC)* 1 *(= care)* garde *f* ◆ **to put sb in sb's ~** confier qn à (la garde de) qn ◆ **to put sth in sb's ~** confier qch à qn ; → **safekeeping**

2 *(= observing) [of rule]* observation *f* ; *[of festival etc]* célébration *f*

3 *(set structures)*

◆ **to be in keeping with** *[+ regulation, law, image]* être conforme à, correspondre à ; *[+ status, tradition]* être conforme à ; *[+ character]* correspondre à ; *[+ surroundings, area]* être en harmonie avec

◆ **to be out of keeping with** *[+ image, character]* ne pas correspondre à ; *[+ status, tradition]* ne pas être conforme à ; *[+ surroundings, area]* détonner dans

keepsake /'kiːpseɪk/ N souvenir *m (objet)*

keester‡ /'kiːstəʳ/ N ⇒ **keister**

keg /keg/ N 1 *(= barrel) [of beer, brandy etc]* tonnelet *m*, baril *m* ; *[of fish]* caque *f* 2 (also **keg beer**) bière *f* en tonnelet

keister‡ /'kiːstəʳ/ N *(US) (= buttocks)* derrière *m*, postérieur* *m* ; *(= case)* mallette *f*

kelly-green /'kelɪ'griːn/ ADJ, N *(US)* vert pomme *m inv*

kelp /kelp/ N *(NonC)* varech *m*

ken /ken/ N ◆ **that is beyond** *or* **outside my ~** ça dépasse mes capacités d'entendement VT *(Scot)* ⇒ **know**

Ken. abbrev of **Kentucky**

kendo /'kendəʊ/ N kendo *m*

kennel /'kenl/ N 1 *[of dog]* niche *f* ; *(pej)* tanière *f* ◆ **~s** *(for breeding)* élevage *m* (de chiens), chenil *m* ; *(for boarding)* chenil *m* ◆ **to put a dog in ~s** mettre un chien dans un chenil 2 *[of fox]* repaire *m*, tanière *f*

Kentucky /ken'tʌkɪ/ N Kentucky *m* ◆ **in ~** dans le Kentucky

Kenya /'kenjə/ N Kenya *m* ◆ **in ~** au Kenya ◆ **Mount ~** le mont Kenya

Kenyan /'kenjən/ N Kényan(e) *m(f)* ADJ kényan

kepi /'keɪpɪ/ N képi *m*

kept /kept/ VB (pret, ptp of **keep**) ◆ **a ~ man/woman** † un homme/une femme entretenu(e)

keratin /'kerətɪn/ N kératine *f*

kerb /kɜːb/ *(Brit)* N 1 *[of pavement]* (bordure *f or* bord *m* du) trottoir *m* ◆ **along the ~** le long du trottoir ◆ **to pull into the ~** s'arrêter (le long du trottoir) ◆ **to hit the ~** *[car]* heurter le trottoir 2 *(Stock Exchange)* **on the ~** en coulisse, après la clôture *(de la Bourse)*

COMP **kerbbroker** N (Stock Exchange) courtier m en valeurs mobilières
kerb crawler N dragueur* m motorisé, conducteur m qui accoste les femmes sur le trottoir
kerb crawling N (NonC) drague* f en voiture
kerb drill N ◆ **to learn one's ~ drill** apprendre à traverser la rue (en toute sécurité)
kerb market N (Stock Exchange) marché m hors-cote, coulisse † f

kerbstone /ˈkɜːbstəʊn/ N bordure f de trottoir

kerchief † /ˈkɜːtʃɪf/ N fichu m, fanchon f

kerfuffle * /kəˈfʌfl/ N (Brit) histoire * f ◆ **what a ~!** quelle histoire ! *, que d'histoires ! *

kernel /ˈkɜːnl/ N 1 [of nut, fruit stone] amande f ; (= seed) grain m ◆ **there's a ~ of truth in what he says** il y a un grain de vérité dans ce qu'il dit 2 (Ling, Comput) noyau m ◆ **~ sentence** (Ling) phrase-noyau f

kerosene /ˈkerəsiːn/ N 1 (= aircraft fuel) kérosène m 2 (US: for stoves, lamps) pétrole m (lampant) COMP **kerosene lamp** N lampe f à pétrole

kestrel /ˈkestrəl/ N crécerelle f

ketch /ketʃ/ N ketch m

ketchup /ˈketʃəp/ N ketchup m

kettle /ˈketl/ N 1 (for water: US) (also **teakettle**) bouilloire f ◆ **the ~'s boiling** l'eau bout (dans la bouilloire) ◆ **I'll just put the ~ on (for some tea)** je vais mettre l'eau à chauffer (pour le thé) 2 (also **fish kettle**) poissonnière f ◆ **that's a fine** or **a pretty ~ of fish** quel micmac ! * ◆ **that's another** or **a different ~ of fish** c'est une autre paire de manches *

kettledrum /ˈketldrʌm/ N (Mus) timbale f

key /kiː/ N 1 (for lock) clé or clef f ◆ **to turn the ~ (in the door)** donner un tour de clé (dans la serrure) ◆ **to leave the ~ in the door** laisser la clé sur la porte ; → **latchkey, lock¹, master**
2 [of clock] clé f or clef f, remontoir m ; [of clockwork toy etc] remontoir m ; (= spanner) clé f de serrage or à écrous
3 (to problem etc) clé f or clef f ◆ **he holds the ~ to the mystery** il détient la clé du mystère ◆ **the ~ to understanding his behaviour is ...** la clé pour comprendre son comportement, c'est ..., l'explication de son comportement, c'est ... ◆ **the ~ to ending this recession** la solution pour mettre fin à la récession
4 (= answers) solutions fpl ; (Scol) corrigé m ; (= explanation) (for map, diagram etc) légende f ; (to symbols, abbreviations) liste f
5 [of piano, computer, typewriter etc] touche f ; [of wind instrument] clé f or clef f ; → **function**
6 (Mus) ton m ◆ **to be in/off ~** être/ne pas être dans le ton ◆ **to go off ~** sortir du ton ◆ **to sing in/off ~** chanter juste/faux ◆ **to play in/off ~** jouer juste/faux ◆ **that note was off ~** cette note était fausse ◆ **in the ~ of C/D** etc en do/ré etc ◆ **in the major ~** en mode majeur ◆ **change of ~** changement m de ton ; → **low¹, minor**
ADJ (= crucial) [role, factor, area, concept] clé inv ◆ **to be a ~ player (in sth)** jouer un rôle-clé (dans qch) ◆ **we will provide additional resources in ~ areas** nous injecterons des fonds supplémentaires dans certains domaines-clés ◆ **a ~ issue** une question fondamentale ◆ **a ~ figure in American politics** l'une des principales personnalités de la scène politique américaine ◆ **a ~ component of ...** une composante essentielle or l'une des principales composantes de ... ◆ **a ~ witness** un témoin essentiel
VT 1 (Comput, Typo: also **key in** or **up**) [+ text, data] saisir
2 ◆ **to ~ one's speech to** or **for one's audience** adapter son discours à son auditoire ◆ **the colour scheme was ~ed to brown** les coloris s'harmonisaient autour du brun
COMP **key card** N (at hotel etc) carte f magnétique
key money N pas m de porte (fig)
key punch N (Comput) perforatrice f à clavier
key ring N porte-clés m inv
key signature N (Mus) armature f
► **key in** VT SEP (Comput, Typ) saisir
► **key up** VT SEP 1 (Comput, Typ) saisir
2 (fig) (= excite) surexciter ; (= make tense) tendre ◆ **she was (all) ~ed up about the interview** elle était excitée or tendue à la perspective de l'entrevue

keyboard /ˈkiːbɔːd/ N [of piano, computer, typewriter etc] clavier m VT (Comput, Typ) saisir NPL **keyboards** (Mus) (instrument m à) clavier m électronique, synthétiseur m ◆ **he's on ~s** il est aux claviers or au synthétiseur
COMP **keyboard instruments** NPL (Mus) instruments mpl à clavier
keyboard operator N (Comput) ⇒ **keyboarder**
keyboard player N (Mus) ◆ **he's a ~ player** il joue du piano (or clavecin etc)
keyboard skills NPL (Comput) compétences fpl de claviste

keyboarder /ˈkiːbɔːdəʳ/ N (Comput) opérateur m, -trice f de saisie, claviste mf

keyboardist /ˈkiːˌbɔːdɪst/ N (Mus) joueur m, -euse f de synthétiseur

keyhole /ˈkiːhəʊl/ N trou m de serrure ◆ **through the ~** par le trou de la serrure
COMP **keyhole saw** N scie f à guichet
keyhole surgery N (Med) chirurgie f endoscopique

keying /ˈkiːɪŋ/ N saisie f (de données)

keynote /ˈkiːnəʊt/ N (Mus) tonique f ; (fig) (= main theme) [of speech, policy] idée-force f
COMP **keynote speaker** N (Pol etc) orateur m principal
keynote speech N discours-programme m

keynoter * /ˈkiːnəʊtəʳ/ N (US) ⇒ **keynote speaker** ; → **keynote**

keypad /ˈkiːpæd/ N (on computer keyboard) pavé m numérique ; (on telephone, calculator etc) clavier m

keystone /ˈkiːstəʊn/ N (Archit, fig) clé or clef f de voûte COMP **the Keystone State** N (US) la Pennsylvanie

keystroke /ˈkiːstrəʊk/ N (Typ, Comput) frappe f

keyword /ˈkiːwɜːd/ N mot-clé m

keyworker /ˈkiːwɜːkəʳ/ N (Med, Social Work) coordonnateur m, -trice f

Kg (abbrev of **kilogram(s)**) kg

KGB /keɪdʒiːˈbiː/ N (in former USSR) KGB m

khaki /ˈkɑːkɪ/ ADJ kaki inv N kaki m

Khartoum /kɑːˈtuːm/ N Khartoum

khat /kæt/ N qat or khat m

Khmer /kmeəʳ/ ADJ khmer (khmère f) N 1 Khmer m, Khmère f 2 (= language) khmer m, cambodgien m
COMP **Khmer Republic** N République f khmère
Khmer Rouge N Khmer m rouge

Khyber Pass /ˌkaɪbəˈpɑːs/ N passe f de Khyber or Khaybar

kHz abbrev of **kilohertz**

kibbutz /kɪˈbʊts/ N (pl **kibbutzim** /kɪˈbʊtsɪm/) kibboutz m

kibitz * /ˈkɪbɪts/ VI (US) (Cards) regarder le jeu de quelqu'un par-dessus son épaule ; (fig) mettre son grain de sel *

kibitzer * /ˈkɪbɪtsəʳ/ N (US) (Cards) spectateur m, -trice f (qui regarde le jeu de quelqu'un par-dessus son épaule) ; (= busybody) mouche f du coche ; (pej) (= disruptive wisecracker) petit malin m, petite maligne f

kibosh ‡ /ˈkaɪbɒʃ/ N ◆ **to put the ~ on sth** mettre le holà à qch

kick /kɪk/ N 1 (= action) coup m de pied ◆ **to give the door a ~** donner un coup de pied dans la porte ◆ **to get a ~ on the leg** recevoir un coup de pied à la jambe ◆ **to aim** or **take a ~ at sb/sth** lancer un coup de pied à qn/qch or dans la direction de qn/qch ◆ **he needs a ~ up the backside** ‡ il a besoin d'un bon coup de pied au cul ‡ ◆ **to give sb a ~ in the pants** * botter * le derrière à or de qn ◆ **this refusal was a ~ in the teeth for her** * ce refus lui a fait l'effet d'une gifle ; → **free**
2 (* = thrill, excitement) ◆ **I get a ~ out of it** j'adore ça ◆ **she got quite a ~ out of seeing Paris** elle était super contente de voir Paris * ◆ **he gets a ~ out of making his sister cry** il prend un malin plaisir à faire pleurer sa sœur ◆ **he did it for ~s** ‡ il l'a fait pour se marrer * or pour rigoler *
3 (* = zest, punch) ◆ **a drink with plenty of ~ in it** une boisson qui vous donne un coup de fouet ◆ **an old man with plenty of ~ left in him** un vieil homme encore plein de punch *
4 (= recoil) [of gun] recul m ◆ **a ~ of the starting handle** un retour de manivelle
5 (fig) ◆ **he's on a fishing ~ now** * son truc * en ce moment c'est la pêche
6 (Ftbl etc) ◆ **he's a good ~** * il a un bon dégagement
VI 1 [person] donner or lancer un coup de pied ; [footballer] shooter ; [baby] (in womb) donner des coups de pied ; (after birth) gigoter * ; [horse] ruer ◆ **to ~ at sb/sth** [person] lancer un coup de pied à qn/qch or en direction de qn/qch ; [horse] lancer une ruade à qn/qch or en direction de qn/qch ◆ **~ing and screaming** à son (or leur etc) corps défendant ◆ **they need to be dragged ~ing and screaming into the 21st century** il faut les forcer à entrer à leur corps défendant dans le XXIe siècle ◆ **to ~ for touch** (Rugby) chercher la touche ◆ **to ~ against the pricks** regimber en pure perte ◆ **to ~ over the traces** (fig) ruer dans les brancards (fig)
2 (* = object to sth) ruer dans les brancards, se rebiffer * ◆ **to ~ (out) at** or **against sth** se rebiffer contre qch *
3 [gun] reculer
VT 1 [person] (gen) donner un coup de pied à ; [+ ball] donner un coup de pied à, botter ; [horse] lancer une ruade à ◆ **she ~ed him in the face/head/shin/stomach** elle lui a donné un coup de pied au visage/à la tête/dans le tibia/dans le ventre ◆ **to ~ one's legs in the air** [baby] gigoter ◆ **to ~ sb's bottom** botter * le derrière or les fesses à qn ◆ **to ~ a goal** (Ftbl etc) marquer un but ◆ **to ~ the ball into touch** (Rugby) botter en touche ◆ **I could have ~ed myself** * je me serais giflé ◆ **to ~ sb in the teeth** * (fig) faire un coup vache * à qn ◆ **to ~ sb when he's (or she's) down** * (fig) frapper qn à terre ◆ **to ~ sb downstairs** (lit) faire descendre qn à coups de pied dans le derrière ; (fig) rétrograder qn ◆ **to ~ sb upstairs** (lit) faire monter qn à coups de pied dans le derrière ; (* fig) catapulter or bombarder * qn à un poste supérieur (pour s'en débarrasser) ; (Brit Pol *) catapulter qn à la Chambre des lords (un député dont on ne veut plus aux Communes) ◆ **I'm going to ~ (some) ass** ‡ (esp US) il y a des coups de pied au cul qui se perdent ‡ ◆ **it ~s ass!** *‡ (esp US) c'est à en tomber sur le cul ! *‡ ◆ **to ~** (Brit) or **~ up** (US) **one's heels** * (= wait around) faire le pied de grue, poireauter * ◆ **to ~ the bucket** ‡ (= die) casser sa pipe ‡
2 (= stop) **to ~ the habit** (gen) arrêter ; [smoker] arrêter de fumer ; [drug addict] décrocher *
COMP **kick boxing** N boxe f française
kick-off N (Ftbl etc) coup m d'envoi ; (* fig = start) [of meeting, ceremony etc] démarrage * m ◆ **the ~-off is at 3pm** (Ftbl) le coup d'envoi est à 15 h ◆ **when's the ~-off?** * (fig) à quelle heure

ça démarre ?* ◆ **for a ~-off*** *(fig)* d'abord, pour commencer
kick pleat N *(Sewing)* pli *m* d'aisance
kick-stand N *[of motorcycle, bicycle]* béquille *f*
kick-start VT *[+ motorcycle]* démarrer au kick ; *(fig) [+ economy]* donner un coup de fouet à ; *[+ negotiations, process]* relancer
kick starter N *[of motorcycle]* kick *m*
kick turn N *(Ski)* conversion *f*
► **kick about, kick around** VI ⁑ *[books, clothes etc]* traîner ; *[person]* traîner, traînasser *(pej)*
VT SEP ◆ **to kick a ball about** *or* **around** donner des coups de pied dans un ballon, taper dans un ballon* ◆ **to ~ sb around** *(= mistreat)* traiter qn sans ménagement, malmener qn ◆ **to ~ an idea around*** *(reflecting)* tourner et retourner une idée ; *(discussing)* débattre une idée
► **kick away** VT SEP 1 *[+ object on ground]* repousser du pied
2 ◆ **he kicked away the last part of the fence** il a démoli à coups de pied ce qui restait de la clôture
► **kick back** VI 1 *[engine]* avoir un retour de manivelle
2 * *(esp US = relax)* se la couler douce*
VT SEP 1 *[+ ball etc]* renvoyer (du pied)
2 *(US ⁑) [+ money]* ristourner
► **kick down** VT SEP *[+ door]* enfoncer à coups de pied ; *[+ hedge, barrier]* démolir à coups de pied
► **kick in** VT SEP 1 *[+ door]* enfoncer à coups de pied ◆ **to ~ sb's teeth in*** casser la figure* *or* la gueule⁑ à qn
2 *(US ⁑ = contribute)* cracher*, abouler⁑
VI (* *= begin, take effect) [drug]* commencer à agir ; *[mechanism, generator]* entrer en action
► **kick off** VI *(Ftbl)* donner le coup d'envoi ; (* fig) démarrer* ◆ **the party ~ed off in great style** la soirée a démarré* en beauté ◆ **it all ~ed off when ...** ce qui a tout déclenché, c'est que ...
VT SEP enlever d'un coup de pied, envoyer valser*
N ◆ **~-off** → **kick**
► **kick out** VI *[horse]* ruer ◆ **the man ~ed out at his assailants** l'homme envoyait de grands coups de pied à ses assaillants ◆ **to ~ out against one's lot/society** *etc* se révolter contre son sort/la société *etc* ; see also **kick vi 2**
VT SEP *(lit)* chasser à coups de pied, flanquer* dehors ; (* fig) flanquer* dehors *or* à la porte
► **kick up** VT SEP *[+ dust]* faire voler ◆ **to ~ up a row*** *or* **a din*** *or* **a racket*** faire du chahut *or* du boucan* ◆ **to ~ up a fuss*** faire des histoires *or* toute une histoire ◆ **he ~ed up a stink⁑ about it** il en a fait tout un plat* ; see also **kick vt 1**

kickback* /ˈkɪkbæk/ N *(= reaction)* réaction *f*, contrecoup *m* ; *(= bribe)* pot-de-vin *m* ; *(= rebate on sale)* ristourne *f*, rabais *m*
kicker /ˈkɪkəʳ/ N *(Rugby)* botteur *m*
kicking⁑ /ˈkɪkɪn/ ADJ ◆ **a really ~ club** une boîte qui bouge* ◆ **a ~ beat** un rythme d'enfer*
kicky⁑ /ˈkɪkɪ/ ADJ excitant, palpitant
kid /kɪd/ N 1 *(= goat)* chevreau *m*, chevrette *f*
2 *(NonC = leather)* chevreau *m* NonC
3 * *(= child)* gosse* *mf*, gamin(e)* *m(f)* ; *(= teenager)* (petit(e)) jeune *m(f)* ◆ **when I was a ~** quand j'étais gosse* ◆ **that's ~'s stuff** *(= easy to do)* un gamin* *or* un gosse* saurait faire ça ; *(= suitable for children)* c'est bon pour des gosses* ◆ **hi, ~!** salut mon vieux (*or* ma vieille) ! ◆ **to be like a ~ in a candy store** *(US)* être aux anges
VT * ◆ **to ~ sb** faire marcher qn* ◆ **no ~ding!, you're ~ding!** sans blague !* ◆ **you can't ~ me** tu ne me la feras pas⁑ ◆ **I ~ you not** je te jure ◆ **who are you trying to ~?** à qui tu veux faire croire ça ? ◆ **to ~ o.s.** se faire des illusions, se fourrer le doigt dans l'œil ◆ **to ~ o.s. that ...** s'imaginer que ...
VI (* : also **kid on**) raconter des blagues* ◆ **he's just ~ding (on)** il te (*or* nous *etc*) fait marcher* ◆ **I was only ~ding (on)** j'ai dit ça pour plaisanter *or* pour rigoler*
COMP **kid brother*** N petit frère *m*
kid gloves NPL gants *mpl* de chevreau ◆ **to handle with ~ gloves** *(fig) [+ person]* ménager, prendre des gants avec* ; *[+ subject]* traiter avec précaution
kid sister* N petite sœur *f*
► **kid on** VI ⇒ **kid vi**
VT SEP * 1 ◆ **to kid sb on** faire marcher qn*, raconter des blagues à qn*
2 *(= pretend)* ◆ **he was kidding on that he was hurt** il faisait semblant d'être blessé

kiddo* /ˈkɪdəʊ/ N mon petit *m*, ma petite *f*
kiddy* /ˈkɪdɪ/ N gosse* *mf*, gamin(e)* *m(f)*
kidnap /ˈkɪdnæp/ VT kidnapper, enlever
kidnapper, kidnaper *(US)* /ˈkɪdnæpəʳ/ N kidnappeur *m*, -euse *f*, ravisseur *m*, -euse *f*
kidnapping, kidnaping *(US)* /ˈkɪdnæpɪŋ/ N enlèvement *m*, kidnapping *m*, rapt *m*
kidney /ˈkɪdnɪ/ N *(Anat)* rein *m* ; *(Culin)* rognon *m*
COMP *[disease etc]* rénal, de(s) reins
kidney bean N haricot *m* rouge *or* de Soissons
kidney dish N haricot *m*
kidney donor N donneur *m*, -euse *f* de rein(s)
kidney machine N *(Med)* rein *m* artificiel ◆ **to be on a ~ machine** être sous rein artificiel *or* en (hémo)dialyse
kidney-shaped ADJ en forme de haricot
kidney specialist N néphrologue *mf*
kidney stone N calcul *m* rénal
kidney transplant N greffe *f* du rein, transplantation *f* rénale
kidology* /kɪˈdɒlədʒɪ/ N *(Brit)* bluff *m*
Kiel /kiːl/ N ◆ **~ Canal** canal *m* de Kiel
kike⁑⁑ /kaɪk/ N *(esp US pej)* youpin(e)⁑⁑ *m(f) (pej)*
Kilimanjaro /ˌkɪlɪmənˈdʒɑːrəʊ/ N ◆ **Mount ~** le Kilimandjaro
kill /kɪl/ N 1 *(at bullfight, hunt)* mise *f* à mort ◆ **the wolves gathered round for the ~** les loups se sont rassemblés pour tuer leur proie ◆ **the tiger had made a ~** le tigre avait tué ◆ **to move in for the ~** *(lit)* s'approcher pour la curée ; *(fig)* guetter le dénouement ◆ **to be in at the ~** *(fig)* assister au dénouement ; *(for unpleasant event)* assister au coup de grâce
2 *(NonC: Hunting = animals killed)* pièces *fpl* tuées, tableau *m* de chasse ◆ **the lion dragged his ~ over to the trees** le lion a traîné (le cadavre de) sa proie sous les arbres
VT 1 tuer ; *(= murder)* assassiner ; *(= gun down)* abattre ; *[+ animal]* tuer ; *(Hunting, Shooting: also in slaughterhouse)* abattre ◆ **the earthquake ~ed five people** le tremblement de terre a fait cinq morts ◆ **the shock ~ed her** c'est le choc qui l'a tuée ◆ **the frost has ~ed my trees** le gel a tué *or* a fait mourir mes arbres ◆ **to be ~ed in action/battle** tomber au champ d'honneur/au combat ◆ **thou shalt not ~** tu ne tueras point ◆ **to ~ two birds with one stone** *(Prov)* faire d'une pierre deux coups *(Prov)* ◆ **it was ~ or cure** *(hum)* c'était un remède de cheval* *(fig)*
2 *(fig) [+ parliamentary bill]* couler ; *[+ proposal, attempt]* faire échouer ; *(Press etc) [+ paragraph, line]* (faire) supprimer ; *[+ story]* interdire la publication de ; *[+ rumour]* étouffer, mettre fin à ; *[+ pain]* supprimer ; *[+ feeling, hope]* détruire ; *[+ flavour, smell]* tuer ; *[+ sound]* étouffer ; *[+ engine, motor]* arrêter ◆ **to ~ time** tuer le temps ◆ **we're just ~ing time** on tue le temps ◆ **to ~ a bottle of whisky** liquider* une bouteille de whisky
3 * ◆ **to ~ o.s. with work** se tuer au travail ◆ **to ~ sb with kindness** accabler qn de prévenances ◆ **he certainly wasn't ~ing himself** le moins qu'on puisse dire c'est qu'il ne se surmenait pas ◆ **don't ~ yourself!** *(iro)* surtout ne te surmène pas ! *(iro)* ◆ **I'll do it (even) if it ~s me** je le ferai même si je dois y laisser ma peau ◆ **this heat is ~ing me** cette chaleur me tue *or* me crève* ◆ **my feet are ~ing me** j'ai un de ces* mal aux pieds ◆ **she was ~ing herself (laughing)** elle était morte de rire, elle était pliée en deux de rire ◆ **this will ~ you!** tu vas (mourir de) rire ! ; → **dressed**
VI *[cancer, drugs, drink etc]* tuer
► **kill off** VT SEP *[+ people]* tuer ; *[+ weeds, disease, bacteria, infection]* éliminer ; *[+ parliamentary bill]* couler

killer /ˈkɪləʳ/ N 1 *(= assassin)* tueur *m*, -euse *f* ; *(= murderer)* assassin *m*, meurtrier *m*, -ière *f* ; → **hire, ladykiller** 2 *(= deadly thing)* **diphtheria was once a ~** autrefois la diphtérie tuait ◆ **it's a ~*** *(fig) (= hard work)* c'est tuant ; *(= very funny)* c'est tordant* ; *(= very impressive)* c'est terrible* *or* formidable COMP *[disease, virus, drug]* mortel
killer bee N abeille *f* tueuse
killer blow N coup *m* décisif, coup *m* de grâce
killer instinct N *(lit)* instinct *m* de meurtre ◆ **he's got the ~ instinct** *(fig)* il est prêt à tout pour réussir ◆ **he lacks the ~ instinct** *(fig)* il manque d'agressivité
killer whale N épaulard *m*, orque *f*
killing /ˈkɪlɪŋ/ N *[of person]* meurtre *m* ; *[of people, group]* tuerie *f*, massacre *m* ; *[of animal] (at abattoir)* abattage *m* ◆ **the ~ of stags is forbidden** il est interdit de tuer les cerfs ◆ **all the ~ sickened him of war** toute cette tuerie lui fit prendre la guerre en horreur ◆ **to make a ~*** *(fig: in buying and selling)* réussir un beau coup
ADJ 1 *[blow, disease, shot]* meurtrier 2 (* *= exhausting) [work]* tuant, crevant* 3 * † *(= hilarious)* tordant*, crevant* †
COMP **killing fields** NPL, **killing ground(s)** N(PL) charniers *mpl*
killing spree N massacre *m* ◆ **to go on a ~ spree** se livrer à un massacre
killingly /ˈkɪlɪŋlɪ/ ADV ◆ **it was ~ funny** c'était crevant* *or* tordant*, c'était à mourir de rire
killjoy /ˈkɪldʒɔɪ/ N rabat-joie *mf inv*
kiln /kɪln/ N four *m* ◆ **pottery ~** four *m* céramique ; → **lime¹**
Kilner jar ® /ˈkɪlnəˌdʒɑːʳ/ N *(Brit)* bocal *m* à conserves
kilo /ˈkiːləʊ/ N (abbrev of **kilogram(me)**) kilo *m*
kiloampère /ˈkɪləʊˌæmpɛəʳ/ N kiloampère *m*
kilobar /ˈkɪləʊˌbɑːʳ/ N kilobar *m*
kilobyte /ˈkɪləʊˌbaɪt/ N *(Comput)* kilo-octet *m*
kilocalorie /ˈkɪləʊˌkælərɪ/ N kilocalorie *f*
kilocycle /ˈkɪləʊˌsaɪkl/ N kilocycle *m*
kilogram(me) /ˈkɪləʊgræm/ N kilogramme *m*
kilohertz /ˈkɪləʊˌhɜːts/ N *(pl inv)* kilohertz *m*
kilolitre, kiloliter *(US)* /ˈkɪləʊˌliːtəʳ/ N kilolitre *m*
kilometre, kilometer *(US)* /ˈkɪləʊˌmiːtəʳ, kɪˈlɒmətəʳ/ N kilomètre *m* ◆ **it is 5 ~s to the nearest town** la ville la plus proche est à 5 kilomètres
kilometric /ˌkɪləʊˈmetrɪk/ ADJ kilométrique
kiloton /ˈkɪləʊˌtʌn/ N kilotonne *f*
kilovolt /ˈkɪləʊˌvəʊlt/ N kilovolt *m*
kilowatt /ˈkɪləʊwɒt/ N kilowatt *m* COMP **kilowatt-hour** N kilowattheure *m*
kilt /kɪlt/ N kilt *m*
kilted /ˈkɪltɪd/ ADJ *[man]* en kilt ◆ **~ skirt** kilt *m*
kilter /ˈkɪltəʳ/ N ◆ **out of ~** détraqué, déglingué* ◆ **out of ~ with** déphasé par rapport à
kimono /kɪˈməʊnəʊ/ N kimono *m*

kin /kɪn/ N (NonC) parents *mpl*, famille *f* ; → **kith, next**

kind /kaɪnd/ LANGUAGE IN USE 4, 22, 25.1

N 1 (= *class, variety, sort, type*) genre *m*, type *m*, sorte *f* ; (= *make*) [*of car, coffee etc*] marque *f* ◆ **this ~ of book** ce genre de livre ◆ **books of all ~s** des livres de tous genres *or* de toutes sortes ◆ **this ~ of thing** ce genre *or* ce type de chose ◆ **what ~ of flour do you want? – the ~ you gave me last time** quelle sorte *or* quel type de farine voulez-vous ? – celle que vous m'avez donnée la dernière fois ◆ **what ~ do you want?** vous en voulez de quelle sorte ? ◆ **what ~ of car is it?** quelle marque de voiture est-ce ? ◆ **what ~ of dog is he?** qu'est-ce que c'est comme (race de) chien ? ◆ **what ~ of man is he?** quel genre *or* quel type d'homme est-ce ? ◆ **he is not the ~ of man to refuse** ce n'est pas le genre d'homme à refuser, il n'est pas homme à refuser ◆ **he's not that ~ of person** ce n'est pas son genre ◆ **I'm not that ~ of girl!** * (*gen*) ce n'est pas mon genre ! ; (*refusing sb's advances*) pour qui me prenez-vous ? ◆ **that's the ~ of person I am** c'est comme ça que je suis (fait) ◆ **what ~ of people does he think we are?** (mais enfin,) pour qui nous prend-il ? ◆ **what ~ of a fool does he take me for?** (non mais *,) il me prend pour un imbécile ! ◆ **what ~ of behaviour is this?** qu'est-ce que c'est que cette façon de se conduire ? ◆ **what ~ of an answer do you call that?** vous appelez ça une réponse ? ◆ **classical music is the ~ she likes most** c'est la musique classique qu'elle préfère ◆ **and all that ~ of thing** et tout ça * ◆ **you know the ~ of thing I mean** vous voyez (à peu près) ce que je veux dire ◆ **I don't like that ~ of talk** je n'aime pas ce genre de propos ◆ **he's the ~ that will cheat** il est du genre à tricher ◆ **I know his ~!** * je connais ce genre de type ◆ **your ~ never do any good** * il n'y a rien de bon à tirer de gens de votre espèce ◆ **he's not my ~** * (*gen*) je n'aime pas les gens de son genre *or* de son espèce ; (*sexually*) ce n'est pas mon genre d'homme ◆ **it's my ~** * **of film** c'est le genre de film que j'aime *or* qui me plaît

◆ **a kind of ...** une sorte *or* une espèce de ..., un genre de ... ◆ **there was a ~ of box in the middle of the room** il y avait une sorte *or* une espèce de boîte au milieu de la pièce ◆ **there was a ~ of tinkling sound** on entendait quelque chose qui ressemblait à un bruit de grelot ◆ **in a ~ of way I'm sorry** * d'une certaine façon je le regrette

◆ **kind of** * ◆ **I was ~ of frightened that ...** j'avais comme peur que ... + ne + *subj* ◆ **I ~ of like that** j'aime assez ça ◆ **I ~ of thought that he would come** j'avais dans l'idée qu'il viendrait ◆ **he was ~ of worried-looking** il avait l'air un peu inquiet, il avait l'air comme qui dirait * inquiet ◆ **it's ~ of blue** c'est plutôt bleu ◆ **aren't you pleased? – ~ of!** tu n'es pas content ? – si, assez !

◆ **of a kind** (*pej*) ◆ **it was beef of a ~** c'était quelque chose qui pouvait passer pour du bœuf ◆ **it was an apology of a ~** ça pouvait ressembler à une excuse ◆ **the cease-fire brought peace of a ~** le cessez-le-feu a introduit une certaine paix

◆ **of the kind** ◆ **something of the ~** quelque chose de ce genre *or* d'approchant ◆ **this is wrong – nothing of the ~!** c'est faux – pas le moins du monde *or* absolument pas ! ◆ **I shall do nothing of the ~!** je n'en ferai rien !, certainement pas ! ◆ **I will have nothing of the ~!** je ne tolérerai pas cela !

2 (= *race, species*) genre *m*, espèce *f* ◆ **they differ in ~** ils sont de genres différents *or* de natures différentes ◆ **they're two of a ~** ils sont du même genre ; (*pej*) ils sont du même acabit ◆ **this painting is perfect of/the only one of its ~** ce tableau est parfait dans/unique en son genre ; → **humankind, mankind**

3 (NonC = *goods as opposed to money*) nature *f* ◆ **to pay/payment in ~** payer/paiement *m* en nature ◆ **I shall repay you in ~** (*fig*) (*after good deed*) je vous revaudrai ça ; (*after bad deed*) je vous rendrai la monnaie de votre pièce

ADJ 1 (= *caring, helpful*) [*person, remark, smile*] gentil ; [*gesture*] aimable ; [*face, voice*] doux (douce *f*), affable ◆ **to be ~ to sb** [*person*] être gentil avec qn ◆ **to be ~ to sb/sth** [*photograph, lighting*] montrer qn/qch à son avantage ; [*clothes*] avantager qn/qch ◆ **to be ~ to animals** être bon avec les animaux ◆ **that's very ~ of you** c'est très gentil *or* (*more frm*) aimable (de votre part) ◆ **life has been ~ to me** j'ai eu de la chance dans la vie, j'ai eu la vie belle ◆ **life has not been ~ to her** la vie ne l'a pas gâtée ◆ **to have a ~ heart** avoir bon cœur ; → **soul**

2 (= *charitable*) [*person*] gentil ; [*comments*] aimable ; [*thought*] délicat, attentionné ◆ **he was very ~ about me** il a dit des choses très gentilles *or* aimables sur moi ◆ **the critics were not ~ to the film** les critiques n'ont pas été tendres avec le film ◆ **the ~est thing that can be said about him is that ...** ce qu'on peut en dire de plus aimable, c'est que ...

3 (*in polite formulae*) ◆ **he was ~ enough to write to me** il a eu la gentillesse de m'écrire ◆ **please be ~ enough to ..., please be so ~ as to ...** veuillez avoir la gentillesse de ... (*frm*) ◆ **would you be ~ enough to ...?, would you be so ~ as to ...?** voudriez-vous avoir la gentillesse *or* l'amabilité de ... ? (*frm*)

4 (= *not harmful*) doux (douce *f*) ◆ **a washing-up liquid that is ~ to your hands** un produit à vaisselle qui n'abîme pas vos mains *or* qui est doux pour vos mains

COMP **kind-hearted** ADJ bon, qui a bon cœur
kind-heartedness N bonté *f*, grand cœur *m*

kinda ‡ /ˈkaɪndə/ ⇒ **kind of** ; → **kind**

kindergarten /ˈkɪndəˌgɑːtn/ N (*gen*) jardin *m* d'enfants ; (*state-run*) (école *f*) maternelle *f* ◆ **she's in ~ now** elle est en maternelle maintenant

kindle /ˈkɪndl/ VT [+ *fire*] allumer ; [+ *wood*] enflammer ; (*fig*) [+ *passion, desire*] allumer, enflammer ; [+ *enthusiasm, interest*] susciter ; [+ *heart*] enflammer VI s'allumer, s'enflammer

kindliness /ˈkaɪndlɪnɪs/ N bienveillance *f*, bonté *f*

kindling /ˈkɪndlɪŋ/ N (NonC = *wood*) petit bois *m*, bois *m* d'allumage

kindly /ˈkaɪndlɪ/ ADV 1 (= *in a caring way*) [*say, speak, treat*] avec bienveillance 2 (= *generously*) [*offer, give, invite*] gentiment, aimablement ◆ **Mr Lea has ~ offered to help us** M. Lea nous a gentiment proposé son aide 3 (= *please*) ◆ **~ be seated** veuillez vous asseoir ◆ **would you ~ pass the salt?** auriez-vous la gentillesse de me passer le sel ? ◆ **will you ~ be quiet!** (*annoyed*) veux-tu te taire ? 4 (= *favourably*) ◆ **to think ~ of sb** apprécier qn ◆ **to look ~ (up)on sb/sth** considérer qn/qch avec bienveillance ◆ **not to take ~ to sb/sth/to doing sth** ne pas apprécier qn/qch/de faire qch ◆ **she didn't take it ~ when I said that** elle n'a pas apprécié quand j'ai dit cela ; → **disposed** ADJ [*person, smile, words*] bienveillant ; [*face, eyes*] doux (douce *f*) ; → **soul**

kindness /ˈkaɪndnɪs/ N 1 (NonC) gentillesse *f*, bonté *f* (*towards* pour, envers) ◆ **to treat sb with ~, to show ~ to sb** être gentil avec *or* envers qn, faire preuve de bonté envers qn ◆ **out of the ~ of his heart** par (pure) bonté d'âme ; → **kill** 2 (= *act of kindness*) gentillesse *f*, attention *f* ◆ **to do sb a ~** rendre service à qn ◆ **he thanked the teachers for all their ~es** il a remercié les professeurs pour toutes leurs petites attentions ◆ **it would be a ~ to let him know** ce serait lui rendre service que de le lui dire

kindred /ˈkɪndrɪd/ N (NonC) (= *relatives*) parents *mpl*, famille *f* ; (= *relationship*) parenté *f* ADJ 1 (= *related*) [*languages, tribes*] apparenté, de la même famille 2 (= *similar*) similaire, semblable, analogue ◆ **to have a ~ feeling for sb** sympathiser avec qn COMP **kindred spirit** N âme *f* sœur

kinesics /kɪˈniːsɪks/ N kinésique *f*

kinesiology /kɪˌniːsɪˈɒlədʒɪ/ N cinésiologie *f*, kinésiologie *f*

kinetic /kɪˈnetɪk/ ADJ (*Phys, Art*) cinétique

kinetics /kɪˈnetɪks/ N (NonC) cinétique *f*

kinfolk /ˈkɪnfəʊk/ NPL ⇒ **kinsfolk**

king /kɪŋ/ N 1 (*lit, fig*) roi *m* ◆ **King Arthur/David** le roi Arthur/David ◆ **(the Book of) Kings** (*Bible*) le livre des Rois ◆ **the ~ of beasts** le roi des animaux ◆ **it cost a ~'s ransom** ça a coûté des sommes fabuleuses ◆ **an oil ~** un roi *or* un magnat du pétrole

2 (*Cards, Chess*) roi *m* ; (*Draughts*) dame *f*

COMP **king cobra** N cobra *m* royal
king penguin N manchot *m* royal
king prawn N (grosse) crevette
King's Bench N (*Brit Jur*) cour *f* supérieure de justice
King's Counsel N (*Jur*) avocat *m* de la Couronne
King's evidence N (*Jur*) ◆ **to turn King's evidence** témoigner contre ses complices
the King's highway N (*Jur*) la voie publique
king-size(d) ADJ (*Comm*) [*cigarette*] long (longue *f*) ; [*packet*] géant ◆ **I've got a ~-size(d) headache** * j'ai un mal de crâne carabiné *
king-size bed N grand lit *m* (*de 1,95 m de large*)
King's Messenger N courrier *m* diplomatique
King's speech N (*Brit*) discours *m* du roi ; → QUEEN'S SPEECH, KING'S SPEECH

kingbolt /ˈkɪŋbəʊlt/ N pivot *m* central, cheville *f* ouvrière

kingcup /ˈkɪŋkʌp/ N (= *buttercup*) bouton *m* d'or ; (= *marsh marigold*) souci *m* d'eau *or* des marais, populage *m*

kingdom /ˈkɪŋdəm/ N royaume *m* ; ◆ **the animal/plant ~** le règne animal/végétal ◆ **the Kingdom of God** le royaume de Dieu ◆ **the Kingdom of Heaven** le royaume des cieux, le royaume céleste ◆ **he's gone to ~ come** * il est parti dans l'autre monde *or* dans un monde meilleur ◆ **to send sb to ~ come** * envoyer qn dans l'autre monde *or* ad patres * ◆ **till ~ come** * jusqu'à la fin des siècles ◆ **in the ~ of the blind (the one-eyed man is king)** (*Prov*) au royaume des aveugles, les borgnes sont rois (*Prov*) → **animal, united**

kingfish * /ˈkɪŋfɪʃ/ N (*US* = *leader*) caïd * *m*

kingfisher /ˈkɪŋfɪʃəʳ/ N martin-pêcheur *m*

kingly /ˈkɪŋlɪ/ ADJ (*lit, fig*) royal, de roi

kingmaker /ˈkɪŋmeɪkəʳ/ N personne *f* qui fait et défait les rois ◆ **the ~s** (*Pol fig*) les gens *mpl* qui font et défont les hommes politiques

kingpin /ˈkɪŋpɪn/ N (*Tech*) pivot *m* central, cheville *f* ouvrière ; (*fig*) pilier *m* ; (*US*) (*in tenpin bowling, skittles*) première quille *f*

kingship /ˈkɪŋʃɪp/ N royauté *f*

kink /kɪŋk/ N (*in rope, tube, wire*) nœud *m* ; (*in paper*) défaut *m* ◆ **to work out** *or* **iron out the ~s** (*fig*) résoudre les problèmes ◆ **her hair has a ~ in it** ses cheveux frisent légèrement VI [*rope, tube, wire*] s'entortiller

kinky /ˈkɪŋkɪ/ ADJ 1 (*: *sexually*) [*person*] aux mœurs spéciales, pervers sur les bords * ; [*activity*] spécial (*euph*) ; [*underwear*] d'un goût spécial ◆ **~ sex** des pratiques sexuelles un peu spéciales ◆ **~ black leather gear** un attirail en cuir noir d'un goût spécial 2 (* = *eccentric*) [*person*] farfelu 3 (= *curly*) [*hair*] frisé COMP **kinky boots** NPL bottes *fpl* de cuir (*ajustées au-dessous du genou*)

kinsfolk /ˈkɪnzfəʊk/ NPL (NonC) parents *mpl*, famille *f*

kinship /ˈkɪnʃɪp/ N (NonC) 1 *(= blood relationship)* parenté *f* 2 *(fig = bond)* affinité *f* ◆ **to feel a deep ~ with sb** avoir de nombreuses affinités avec qn

kinsman /ˈkɪnzmən/ N (pl **-men**) parent *m*

kinswoman /ˈkɪnzˌwʊmən/ N (pl **-women**) parente *f*

kiosk /ˈkiːɒsk/ *(Brit)* N *(for selling: also* **bandstand***)* kiosque *m* ; *(Telec)* cabine *f* téléphonique

kip⁑ /kɪp/ *(Brit)* N *(= bed)* plumard⁑ *m*, pieu⁑ *m* ; *(= nap)* roupillon* *m* ◆ **to get some ~** piquer un roupillon*, pioncer⁑ VI *(also* **kip down***)* se pieuter⁑

kipper /ˈkɪpəʳ/ *(Brit)* N hareng *m* fumé et salé, kipper *m* VT *[+ herring]* fumer et saler COMP **kipper tie** N large cravate *f* *(des années 60)*

kir /kɪəʳ/ N kir *m*

Kirbigrip ®, **kirbygrip** /ˈkɜːbɪˌgrɪp/ N pince *f* à cheveux

Kirg(h)iz /ˈkɜːgɪz/ ADJ kirghiz *inv* N 1 *(= person)* Kirghiz(e) *m(f)* 2 *(= language)* kirghiz *m*

Kirg(h)izia /kɜːˈgɪzɪə/ N Kirghizstan *m*

Kirg(h)izstan /ˌkɜːgɪsˈtɑːn/ N Kirghizstan *m*

Kiribati /ˈkɪrɪbæs/ N Kiribati

kirk /kɜːk/ N *(Scot)* église *f* ◆ **the Kirk** l'Église *f* presbytérienne (d'Écosse)

Kirsch /ˈkɪəʃ/, **Kirschwasser** /ˈkɪəʃˌvɑːsəʳ/ N kirsch *m*

kiss /kɪs/ N baiser *m* ◆ **to give sb a ~** donner un baiser à qn, embrasser qn ◆ **give me a ~** embrasse-moi ; *(to child)* fais-moi une bise* *or* un bisou* ◆ **~ of life** *(esp Brit Med)* bouche-à-bouche *m* ◆ **"love and kisses"** *(in letter)* "bons baisers", "grosses bises"* ◆ **to give the ~ of death to ...** *(fig)* porter le coup fatal à ... ; → **blow¹**

VT 1 embrasser, donner un baiser à ◆ **to ~ sb's cheek** embrasser qn sur la joue ◆ **to ~ sb's hand** baiser la main de qn ◆ **to ~ hands** *(Diplomacy etc)* être admis au baisemain (du roi *or* de la reine) ◆ **they ~ed each other** ils se sont embrassés ◆ **to ~ sb good night/goodbye** embrasser qn en lui souhaitant bonne nuit/en lui disant au revoir, souhaiter bonne nuit/dire au revoir à qn en l'embrassant ◆ **I'll ~ it better** *(to hurt child)* un petit bisou* et ça ira mieux ◆ **to ~ ass**⁑* *(esp US)* faire de la lèche⁑ ◆ **to ~ sb's ass**⁑* *(esp US)* lécher le cul à qn⁑* ◆ **~ my ass!**⁑* *(esp US)* va chier !⁑* ; see also **goodbye**

2 *(= touch lightly: also liter)* frôler ◆ **the ball ~ed the top of the crossbar** le ballon a frôlé la barre transversale

VI s'embrasser ◆ **to ~ and make up** faire la paix ◆ **to ~ and tell** raconter ses secrets d'alcôve

COMP **kiss-and-tell*** ADJ *[story, memoirs]* divulguant des secrets d'alcôve *(avec une personnalité en vue)*

kiss curl N *(Brit)* accroche-cœur *m*

kiss-off⁑ N *(US)* ◆ **to give sb the ~-off** *[+ employee]* virer* qn ; *[+ girlfriend etc]* plaquer⁑ qn

► **kiss away** VT SEP ◆ **she kissed away the child's tears** elle a séché les larmes de l'enfant en l'embrassant

► **kiss back** VT SEP *[+ person]* rendre un baiser à

kissagram /ˈkɪsəˌgræm/ N *baiser télégraphié*

KISSAGRAM

Un **kissagram** est un « baiser télégraphié » adressé à une personne pour lui faire une surprise, par exemple à l'occasion de son anniversaire. Le message est remis par un porteur costumé, qui lit un petit texte et embrasse le destinataire devant tout le monde.

kisser⁑ /ˈkɪsəʳ/ N gueule⁑ *f*

kit /kɪt/ N 1 (NonC) *(= equipment, gear) (for camping, skiing, climbing, photography etc)* matériel *m*, équipement *m* ; *(Mil)* fourniment *m*, fourbi* *m* ; *(= tools)* outils *mpl* ◆ **fishing** *etc* **~** matériel *m or* attirail *m* de pêche *etc* ◆ **the whole ~ and caboodle*** *(US)* tout le bataclan*, tout le fourbi*

2 (NonC: *) *(= belongings)* affaires *fpl* ; *(= clothes)* fringues* *fpl* ; *(for sports)* affaires *fpl* ; *(= luggage)* bagages *mpl* ◆ **get your ~ off!**⁑ à poil !* ◆ **have you got your gym/football ~?** tu as tes affaires de gym/de football ?

3 *(= set of items)* trousse *f* ◆ **puncture-repair ~** trousse *f* de réparations ◆ **first-aid ~** trousse *f* d'urgence *or* de premiers secours ; → **survival**

4 *(= parts for assembly)* kit *m* ◆ **sold in ~ form** vendu en kit ◆ **he built it from a ~** il l'a assemblé à partir d'un kit ◆ **model aeroplane ~** maquette *f* d'avion (à assembler)

COMP **kit car** N voiture *f* en kit

kit inspection N *(Mil)* revue *f* de détail

► **kit out, kit up** VT SEP *(Brit)* 1 *(Mil)* équiper *(with* de*)*

2 ◆ **to kit sb out with sth** équiper qn de qch ◆ **he arrived ~ted out in oilskins** il est arrivé équipé d'un ciré ◆ **he had ~ted himself out in a bright blue suit** il avait mis un costume bleu vif

kitbag /ˈkɪtbæg/ N *(esp Brit)* sac *m* *(de voyage, de sportif, de soldat, de marin etc)*

kitchen /ˈkɪtʃɪn/ N cuisine *f* ; → **thief**

COMP *[table, cutlery, scissors etc]* de cuisine

kitchen cabinet N buffet *m* de cuisine ; *(Pol fig)* proches conseillers *mpl* du Premier ministre ; *(in US)* proches conseillers *mpl* du Président ; → **CABINET**

kitchen-diner, kitchen-dinette N cuisine *f* avec coin-repas

kitchen foil N papier *m* d'aluminium *or* d'alu*

kitchen garden N (jardin *m*) potager *m*

kitchen paper N essuie-tout *m inv*

kitchen police N *(US Mil)* *(= work)* corvée *f* de cuisine ; *(= soldiers)* soldats *mpl* chargés de la corvée de cuisine

kitchen range N fourneau *m* (de cuisine), cuisinière *f*

kitchen roll N ⇒ **kitchen paper**

kitchen salt N sel *m* de cuisine, gros sel *m*

kitchen scales NPL balance *f* (de cuisine)

kitchen sink N évier *m* ◆ **I've packed everything but the ~ sink*** j'ai tout emporté sauf les murs

kitchen-sink drama* N *(Theat)* *théâtre misérabiliste des années 50 et 60*

kitchen soap N savon *m* de Marseille

kitchen unit N élément *m* de cuisine

kitchen utensil N ustensile *m* de cuisine

kitchen waste N déchets *mpl* domestiques

kitchen wastes NPL *(US)* ⇒ **kitchen waste**

kitchenette /ˌkɪtʃɪˈnet/ N kitchenette *f*

kitchenmaid /ˈkɪtʃɪnmeɪd/ N fille *f* de cuisine

kitchenware /ˈkɪtʃɪnwɛəʳ/ N (NonC) *(= dishes)* vaisselle *f or* faïence *f* (de cuisine) ; *(= equipment)* ustensiles *mpl* de cuisine

kite /kaɪt/ N 1 *(= bird)* milan *m* ; *(= toy)* cerf-volant *m* ; → **fly³**, **high** 2 *(Fin *) (= cheque)* chèque *m* en bois* ; *(= bill)* traite *f* en l'air*

COMP **kite balloon** N *(Mil)* ballon *m* d'observation, saucisse *f*

Kite mark N *(Brit Comm)* label *m* de qualité *(délivré par l'Association britannique de normalisation)*

kith /kɪθ/ N ◆ **~ and kin** amis *mpl* et parents *mpl*

kitsch /kɪtʃ/ N (NonC) kitsch *m*, art *m* kitsch *or* pompier ADJ kitsch *inv*, pompier

kitten /ˈkɪtn/ N chaton *m*, petit chat *m* ◆ **to have ~s**⁑ *(Brit fig)* piquer une crise*

kittenish /ˈkɪtənɪʃ/ ADJ *(lit)* de chaton ; *(fig)* de chaton, mutin

kittiwake /ˈkɪtɪweɪk/ N mouette *f* tridactyle

kitty /ˈkɪtɪ/ N 1 *(Cards etc)* cagnotte *f* ; *(* fig)* caisse *f*, cagnotte *f* ◆ **there's nothing left in the ~** il n'y a plus un sou dans la caisse *or* dans la cagnotte 2 *(* = cat)* minet* *m*, minou* *m*

COMP **Kitty Litter** ® N *(US)* litière *f* pour chats

kiwi /ˈkiːwiː/ N 1 *(= bird)* kiwi *m*, aptéryx *m* 2 *(also* **kiwi fruit***)* kiwi *m* 3 *(* = New Zealander)* Néo-Zélandais(e) *m(f)*

KKK /ˌkeɪkeɪˈkeɪ/ abbrev of **Ku Klux Klan**

Klansman /ˈklænzmən/ N membre *m* du Ku Klux Klan

klatch /klætʃ/ N (also **coffee klatch**) *(US)* ⇒ **kaffeeklatsch**

klaxon /ˈklæksn/ N klaxon ® *m*

Kleenex ® /ˈkliːneks/ N (pl **Kleenex** *or* **Kleenexes**) kleenex ® *m*

kleptomania /ˌkleptəʊˈmeɪnɪə/ N kleptomanie *f*

kleptomaniac /ˌkleptəʊˈmeɪnɪæk/ ADJ, N kleptomane *mf*

klieg light /ˈkliːglaɪt/ N *(esp US)* lampe *f* à arc

kludge* /klʌdʒ/ N *(Comput)* bidouille* *f*, kludge *m*

klutz⁑ /klʌts/ N *(US)* empoté(e) *m(f)*, manche* *m*

klystron /ˈklɪstrɒn/ N klystron *m*

km N (abbrev of **kilometre(s)**) km

kmh N (abbrev of **kilometres per hour**) km/h

knack /næk/ N 1 *(= physical dexterity)* tour *m* de main ◆ **to learn** *or* **get the ~ of doing sth** prendre le tour de main pour faire qch ◆ **there's a ~ to it** il y a un tour de main à prendre ◆ **I've lost the ~** j'ai perdu la main 2 *(= talent)* ◆ **to have the ~ of doing sth** avoir le don pour faire qch ; *(iro)* avoir le chic pour faire qch ◆ **she's got a ~ of saying the wrong thing** elle a le chic pour dire ce qu'il ne faut pas ◆ **I never really got the ~ of it** je n'ai jamais compris le truc*

knacker /ˈnækəʳ/ *(Brit)* N 1 *[of horses]* équarrisseur *m* ◆ **to send a horse to the ~'s yard** envoyer un cheval à l'équarrissage 2 *[of boats, houses]* entrepreneur *m* de démolition, démolisseur *m* NPL **knackers** *⁑† *(Brit: = testicles)* couilles*⁑ *fpl* VT ⁑ 1 *(= tire)* crever* 2 *(= break)* bousiller*

knackered⁑ /ˈnækəd/ ADJ *(Brit)* 1 *(= tired out)* crevé*, éreinté* 2 *(= broken, worn out)* nase*, foutu⁑

knapsack /ˈnæpsæk/ N sac *m* à dos, havresac *m*

knave /neɪv/ N († *pej*) filou *m*, fripon † *m* ; *(Cards)* valet *m*

knavery /ˈneɪvərɪ/ N (NonC: *pej*) filouterie *f*, friponnerie † *f*

knavish /ˈneɪvɪʃ/ ADJ *(pej)* de filou, de fripon †

knead /niːd/ VT *[+ dough]* pétrir, travailler ; *[+ muscles]* malaxer

knee /niː/ N genou *m* ◆ **he sank in up to the ~s** il s'est enfoncé jusqu'aux genoux ◆ **these trousers have gone at the ~(s)** ce pantalon est usé aux genoux ◆ **to sit on sb's ~** s'asseoir sur les genoux de qn ◆ **to put a child over one's** ~ donner une fessée à un enfant ◆ **to learn sth at one's mother's** ~ apprendre qch dès son jeune âge ◆ **to go (down) on one's ~s** s'agenouiller, tomber *or* se mettre à genoux ◆ **to go down on one's ~s to sb** *(lit)* tomber *or* se mettre à genoux devant qn ; *(fig)* se mettre à genoux devant qn *(fig)*, supplier qn à genoux ◆ **on bended ~(s)** à genoux ◆ **to bring sb to his ~s** *(fig)* forcer qn à capituler *or* à se soumettre ◆ **it will bring the country/the steel industry to its ~s** ça va mettre le pays/l'industrie sidérurgique à genoux

VT ◆ **to ~ sb in the groin** donner un coup de genou dans le bas-ventre de qn

COMP knee-bend N *(gen, Ski)* flexion *f* (du genou)

knee breeches NPL culotte *f* courte

knee-deep ADJ ◆ **he was ~-deep in mud** la boue lui arrivait aux genoux, il était dans la boue jusqu'aux genoux ◆ **the water was ~-deep** l'eau arrivait aux genoux ◆ **to be ~-deep in paperwork** * être dans la paperasse jusqu'au cou

knee-high ADJ à hauteur de genou ◆ **~-high to a grasshopper** * haut comme trois pommes

knee jerk N réflexe *m* rotulien

knee-jerk ADJ *[reaction, response]* réflexe ◆ **he's a ~-jerk conservative** * c'est un conservateur primaire

knee joint N articulation *f* du genou

knee level N ◆ **at ~ level** à (la) hauteur du genou

knee pants NPL *(US)* bermuda *m*

knee reflex N réflexe *m* rotulien

knees-up‡ N (pl **knees-ups**) *(Brit)* pince-fesses‡ *m*, bringue * *f*

kneecap /ˈniːkæp/ **N** *(Anat)* rotule *f* **VT** tirer dans le genou de

kneecapping /ˈniːˌkæpɪŋ/ N mutilation *f* en tirant dans le genou

kneel /niːl/ (pret, ptp **knelt** *or* **kneeled**) VI (also **kneel down**) s'agenouiller, se mettre à genoux ; *(= be kneeling)* être agenouillé ◆ **he had to ~ on his case to shut it** il a dû se mettre à genoux sur sa valise pour la fermer ◆ **to ~ (down) to** *or* **before sb** *(lit, fig)* se mettre à genoux devant qn

kneepad /ˈniːpæd/ N genouillère *f*

kneeroom /ˈniːrʊm/ N espace *m* pour les jambes

knell /nel/ N glas *m* ◆ **to sound** *or* **toll the (death)** ~ sonner le glas

knelt /nelt/ VB pt, ptp of **kneel**

Knesset /ˈknesɪt/ N ◆ **the** ~ la Knesset

knew /njuː/ VB pt of **know**

knickerbocker /ˈnɪkəˌbɒkəʳ/ **NPL knickerbockers** *(knee-length)* knickers *mpl* ; *(longer)* culotte *f* de golf **COMP knickerbocker glory** N *(Brit)* *coupe glacée faite de glace, de gelée, de crème et de fruits*

knickers /ˈnɪkəz/ NPL 1 *(Brit: woman's)* culotte *f*, slip *m* *(de femme)* ◆ ~!‡ *(annoyed)* mince ! * ; *(disbelieving)* mon œil ! * ◆ **to get one's ~ in a twist**‡ se mettre dans tous ses états ◆ **don't get your ~ in a twist!**‡ ne te mets pas dans cet état ! 2 † ⇒ **knickerbockers** ; → **knickerbocker**

knick-knack /ˈnɪknæk/ N bibelot *m*, babiole *f* ; *(on dress)* colifichet *m*

knife /naɪf/ **N** (pl **knives**) couteau *m* ; (also **pocket knife**) canif *m* ◆ ~, **fork and spoon** couvert *m* ◆ **to turn** *or* **twist the ~ in the wound** *(fig)* retourner le couteau dans la plaie *(fig)* ◆ **he's got his ~ into me** * *(fig)* il s'acharne contre moi ◆ **the knives are out** * *(esp Brit fig)* c'est la guerre ouverte ◆ **the knives are out for him** * *(esp Brit fig)* on en a après lui ◆ **to put** *or* **stick the ~ into sb** *(fig)* blesser qn ◆ **the critics are trying to put the ~ in (him)** les critiques l'attendent au tournant ◆ **it's war to the ~ between them** ils sont à couteaux tirés *(fig)* ◆ **(to go) under the ~** * *(Med)* (passer) sur le billard * ◆ **before you could say ~** * en moins de temps qu'il n'en faut pour le dire ◆ **like a (hot) ~ through butter** *(US = easily)* facilement

VT *[+ person]* donner un coup de couteau à ◆ **she had been ~d** elle avait reçu un coup (*or* des coups) de couteau ; *(to death)* elle avait été tuée à coups de couteau

COMP knife edge N fil *m* d'un couteau ; *[of balance]* couteau *m* ◆ **on a ~ edge** *(fig = tense, anxious)* sur des charbons ardents ◆ **the success of the scheme/the result was balanced on a ~ edge** la réussite du projet/le résultat ne tenait qu'à un fil

knife-edge(d) ADJ *[blade]* tranchant, aiguisé ; *[crease]* bien marqué

knife-grinder N rémouleur *m*

knife pleat N pli *m* couché

knife point N ◆ **to hold sb at ~ point** menacer qn d'un couteau

knife rest N porte-couteau *m*

knife-sharpener N *(on wall, on wheel etc)* affiloir *m*, aiguisoir *m* ; *(long, gen with handle)* fusil *m* (à repasser les couteaux)

knifeman /ˈnaɪfmən/ N *(Brit)* agresseur *m* armé d'un couteau

knifing /ˈnaɪfɪŋ/ N attaque *f* au couteau

knight /naɪt/ **N** chevalier *m* ; *(Chess)* cavalier *m* ◆ **a ~ in shining armour** *(= romantic figure)* un prince charmant ; *(= saviour)* un sauveur, un redresseur de torts **VT** 1 *(Hist)* *[+ squire etc]* adouber, faire chevalier 2 *(Brit)* *[sovereign]* donner l'accolade (de chevalier) à, faire chevalier ◆ **he was ~ed for services to industry** il a été fait chevalier pour services rendus dans l'industrie

COMP knight errant N (pl **knights errant**) *(Hist)* chevalier *m* errant

knight-errantry N *(NonC)* chevalerie *f* errante

Knight of the Garter N chevalier *m* de (l'ordre de) la Jarretière

Knight Templar N (pl **Knights Templars** *or* **Knights Templar**) chevalier *m* de l'ordre du Temple, Templier *m*

knighthood /ˈnaɪthʊd/ N 1 *(= knights collectively)* chevalerie *f* 2 *(Brit = rank)* titre *m* de chevalier ◆ **to get** *or* **receive a ~** être fait chevalier, recevoir le titre de chevalier

knightly /ˈnaɪtlɪ/ ADJ *[courtesy]* chevaleresque ; *[armour]* de chevalier

knit /nɪt/ (pret, ptp **knitted** *or* **knit**) **VT** 1 *[+ garment, blanket etc]* tricoter ◆ **"knit three, purl one"** "trois mailles à l'endroit, une maille à l'envers" ◆ **to ~ sth for sb, to ~ sb sth** tricoter qch pour qn ◆ **~ted jacket** veste *f* tricotée *or* en tricot ◆ **~ted goods** tricots *mpl*, articles *mpl* en maille ; → **close¹, thick** 2 ◆ **to ~ one's brows** froncer les sourcils **VI** 1 tricoter 2 (also **knit together, knit up**) *[bone]* se souder **COMP knit stitch** N maille *f* à l'endroit

► **knit together** **VI** se souder **VT SEP** 1 ◆ **"knit two together"** "tricoter deux mailles ensemble" 2 *(fig)* *[+ family, community]* lier, unir ; *[+ team]* souder

► **knit up** **VI** 1 *[bone]* se souder 2 ◆ **this wool knits up very quickly** cette laine monte très vite **VT SEP** *[+ jersey]* tricoter

knitter /ˈnɪtəʳ/ N tricoteur *m*, -euse *f*

knitting /ˈnɪtɪŋ/ **N** *(NonC)* 1 *(gen)* tricot *m* ; *(industrial)* tricotage *m* ◆ **where's my ~?** où est mon tricot ? ; → **double** 2 *[of bone]* consolidation *f*, soudure *f*

COMP knitting bag N sac *m* à tricot

knitting machine N machine *f* à tricoter, tricoteuse *f*

knitting needle, knitting pin N aiguille *f* à tricoter

knitting wool N laine *f* à tricoter

knitwear /ˈnɪtwɛəʳ/ N *(NonC: Comm)* tricots *mpl*

knives /naɪvz/ NPL of **knife**

knob /nɒb/ N 1 *[of door, instrument]* bouton *m* ; *[of cane, walking stick]* pommeau *m* ; *(= small bump)* bosse *f*, protubérance *f* ; *(on tree)* nœud *m* ◆ **with ~s on** * *(fig)* et encore plus 2 *(= small piece)* *[of cheese etc]* petit morceau *m* ◆ **~ of butter** *(Brit)* noix *f* de beurre 3 (*‡ = *penis)* zob*‡*m*, bitte*‡*f*

knobbly /ˈnɒblɪ/, **knobby** /ˈnɒbɪ/ ADJ noueux

knobkerrie /ˈnɒbˌkerɪ/ N massue *f*

knock /nɒk/ **N** 1 *(= blow)* coup *m* ; *(= collision)* heurt *m*, choc *m* ; *(in engine etc)* cognement *m* ◆ **he got a ~ (on the head etc)** il a reçu *or* pris * un coup (sur la tête *etc*) ◆ **he gave himself a nasty ~ (on the head** *etc***)** il s'est cogné très fort (la tête *etc*)

2 *(at door)* ◆ **there was a ~ at the door** on a frappé (à la porte) ◆ **I heard a ~ (at the door)** j'ai entendu (quelqu'un) frapper (à la porte) ◆ **~, ~!** toc, toc, toc ! ◆ **I'll give you a ~ at 7 o'clock** je viendrai frapper à ta porte à 7 heures

3 *(fig)* *(= setback)* revers *m* ◆ **~s** * *(= criticism)* critiques *fpl* ◆ **to take a ~** *[person]* recevoir un coup *(fig)* ◆ **his pride/credibility has taken a ~** son orgueil/sa crédibilité en a pris un coup ◆ **his confidence has taken a ~** sa confiance a été sérieusement ébranlée ◆ **her professional reputation took a very hard ~** sa réputation professionnelle en a pris un sacré * coup

VT 1 *(= hit, strike)* *[+ object]* frapper ◆ **to ~ a nail into a plank** planter *or* enfoncer un clou dans une planche ◆ **to ~ a nail in (with a hammer/shoe** *etc***)** enfoncer un clou (d'un coup *or* à coups de marteau/de chaussure *etc*) ◆ **he ~ed the ball into the hedge** il a envoyé la balle dans la haie ◆ **she ~ed the knife out of his hand** elle lui a fait tomber le couteau des mains ◆ **to ~ a glass off a table** faire tomber un verre d'une table ◆ **she ~ed the cup to the floor** elle a fait tomber la tasse (par terre) ◆ **to ~ the bottom out of a box** défoncer (le fond d')une boîte ◆ **to ~ the bottom out of an argument** démolir un argument ◆ **this ~ed the bottom out of the market** *(St Ex)* cela a provoqué l'effondrement des cours ◆ **to ~ holes in sth** faire des trous dans qch ◆ **to ~ holes in an argument** battre un argument en brèche ◆ **to ~ sb's confidence** ébranler la confiance de qn ◆ **that ~ed his plans on the head** * *(Brit)* ça a flanqué * par terre *or* démoli ses projets ◆ **it's time to ~ this idea on the head** * il est temps de faire un sort à cette idée ◆ **to ~ some sense into sb** * ramener qn à la raison (par la manière forte) ◆ **to ~ spots off sb** * battre qn à plate(s) couture(s) ◆ **to ~ spots off sth** * être beaucoup mieux que qch ; → **stuffing**

2 *(= hit, strike)* **to ~ sb to the ground** *[person, explosion]* jeter qn à terre, faire tomber qn ; *(= stun)* assommer qn ◆ **to ~ sb unconscious** *or* **cold** *or* **senseless** *or* **silly** * assommer qn ◆ **to ~ sb off balance** faire perdre l'équilibre à qn ◆ **he ~ed the child out of the way** il a brusquement écarté l'enfant ◆ **to ~ sb dead** * épater qn *, en mettre plein la vue à qn * ◆ **go out there and ~ 'em dead!** ‡ montre-leur de quoi tu es capable ! ◆ **to ~ sb on the head** frapper qn à la tête ; *(= stun)* assommer qn ◆ **to ~ sb into the middle of next week**‡ faire voir trente-six chandelles à qn * ◆ **to ~ sth on the head** * *[+ project, idea]* laisser tomber qch ; *[+ relationship]* mettre fin à qch ◆ **his wife's death really ~ed him sideways** * *(Brit = shook him)* la mort de sa femme l'a profondément ébranlé ◆ **confidence in the legal system has been ~ed sideways** * *(Brit)* la confiance dans le système légal a été sérieusement ébranlée ◆ **to ~**

sb for six* (Brit) [cold, flu] lessiver* qn ; [news] faire un choc à qn

3 (= collide with, strike) [person] se cogner dans, heurter ; [vehicle] heurter ◆ **to ~ one's head on** or **against** se cogner la tête contre ◆ **he ~ed his foot against the leg of the table** il a buté contre le pied de la table

4 (Constr) ◆ **to ~ two rooms into one** abattre la cloison entre deux pièces

5 (* = denigrate) [+ person, sb's work] débiner* ; [+ plan, project, idea] dénigrer ◆ **don't ~ it!** arrête de dénigrer ! ◆ **don't ~ it if you haven't tried it!** c'est pas la peine* de critiquer si tu n'as pas essayé !

6 (Scot * = steal) piquer*

VI 1 (= strike, hit) frapper ; (more forcefully) cogner ◆ **to ~ at the door/window** frapper à la porte/la fenêtre ◆ **he ~ed on the table** il a frappé la table, il a cogné sur la table ◆ **his knees were ~ing** il tremblait de peur, il avait les chocottes*

2 (= bump, collide) **to ~ against** or **into sb/sth** se cogner contre qn/qch, heurter qn/qch ◆ **his hand ~ed against the shelf** sa main a heurté l'étagère, il s'est cogné la main contre l'étagère ◆ **he ~ed into the table** il s'est cogné dans or contre la table, il a heurté la table ◆ **the car ~ed into the lamppost** la voiture a heurté le réverbère

3 [car engine] cogner

COMP **knocked down** ADJ (US Comm) [table, shed etc] (livré) non monté

knock-for-knock agreement N (Insurance) convention f d'indemnisation directe de l'assuré

knock-kneed ADJ ◆ **to be ~-kneed** avoir les genoux cagneux

knock-knees NPL ◆ **to have ~-knees** avoir les genoux cagneux

knock-on N (Rugby) en-avant m inv

knock-on effect N répercussions fpl

knock-out agreement N (Jur, Fin) entente f entre enchérisseurs

knock-out drops* NPL soporifique m

knock-up N (Tennis) ◆ **to have a ~-up** faire des balles

► **knock about***, **knock around*** VI (= travel) vadrouiller*, bourlinguer* (fig) (= hang around) traîner, glander* ◆ **he spent many years ~ing about in the provinces** il a passé de nombreuses années à vadrouiller* or bourlinguer* en province ◆ **he has ~ed about a bit** il a beaucoup bourlingué* ◆ **what are all these boxes ~ing about in the garage?** que font tous ces cartons dans le garage ? ◆ **who's he ~ing around with these days?** qui est-ce qu'il fréquente en ce moment ?

VT FUS ◆ **to knock about the world** vadrouiller* de par le monde ◆ **he's ~ing about France somewhere*** il vadrouille* or il se balade* quelque part en France

VT SEP 1 (* = beat) taper sur, frapper ◆ **he ~s her about** il lui tape dessus*

2 [storm, waves] [+ boat] ballotter

3 ◆ **to knock a ball about** or **around** donner des coups de pied dans un ballon, taper dans un ballon*

► **knock back** VI (lit) ◆ **he knocked on the wall and she knocked back** il a frappé au mur et elle a répondu de la même façon

VT SEP * 1 (= drink) s'enfiler*, s'envoyer* ; (= eat) avaler, engloutir

2 (= cost) coûter ◆ **how much did it ~ you back?** ça vous a coûté combien ? ◆ **this watch ~ed me back £120** cette montre m'a coûté 120 livres

3 (fig = shock) sonner* ◆ **the news ~ed her back a bit** la nouvelle l'a un peu sonnée*

4 (*= reject) [+ offer, suggestion] refuser ; [+ person] envoyer balader*

► **knock down** VT SEP 1 [+ object] (= topple) renverser ; (= knock off shelf, table etc) faire tomber ; [+ building, wall etc] abattre, démolir ; [+ door] (= remove) démolir ; (= kick in) défoncer, enfoncer ◆ **he ~ed me down with one blow** il m'a jeté à terre d'un seul coup ; → **feather**

2 (= run over) [vehicle] [+ person] renverser ; [+ lamppost] emboutir ; [+ fence, wall] défoncer ◆ **he got ~ed down by a bus** il a été renversé par un autobus

3 [+ price] baisser ◆ **he ~ed the price down by 10%** il a baissé le prix de 10%, il a fait une remise de 10% sur le prix

4 (at auction) ◆ **to knock down sth to sb** adjuger qch à qn ◆ **it was ~ed down for £10** ça a été adjugé 10 livres

ADJ ◆ **knocked down** → **knock**

► **knock off** VI * (= stop work) s'arrêter (de travailler) ; (= leave work) se casser*, se tirer* ; (= strike) débrayer

VT SEP 1 (lit) [+ object on shelf etc] faire tomber ◆ **I got ~ed off my bike** j'ai été renversé en vélo ◆ **to ~ sb's block off*** casser la figure* à qn

2 (= reduce price by) [+ percentage, amount] faire une remise de ◆ **I'll ~ off £10/10%** je vous fais une remise de 10 livres/de 10% ◆ **she ~ed 15 seconds off the world record** elle a battu le record du monde de 15 secondes

3 * [+ homework, correspondence, piece of work] expédier

4 (Brit * = steal) piquer*

5 (= stop) ◆ **knock it off !** * ça suffit !

6 (* = kill) liquider*

ADJ ◆ **knocking-off** → **knocking**

► **knock on** VT SEP (Rugby) ◆ **to knock the ball on** faire un en-avant

VT FUS ◆ **he's knocking on for fifty*** il frise la cinquantaine

N ◆ **knock-on** ADJ → **knock**

► **knock out** VT SEP 1 [+ nail etc] faire sortir (of de) ◆ **to ~ out one's pipe** débourrer or éteindre sa pipe ◆ **to ~ a window out** [builder] enlever une fenêtre ; [explosion, earthquake] souffler une fenêtre

2 (* = put out of action) [storm, earthquake, bomb] [+ power supply, electricity] couper ; [missile] [+ target] détruire, bousiller*

3 (= stun) [person] assommer ; (Boxing) mettre knock-out or k.-o. ; [drug] sonner*, assommer ◆ **to ~ o.s. out** s'assommer

4 * (= shock, overwhelm) sidérer* ; (= exhaust) mettre à plat*

5 (from competition, contest) éliminer (of de)

► **knock over** VT SEP 1 [+ object] renverser

2 [vehicle] [+ pedestrian] renverser ; [+ lamppost] emboutir ; [+ fence] défoncer ◆ **he was ~ed over by a taxi** il a été renversé par un taxi

► **knock together** VI [glasses, knees] s'entrechoquer

VT SEP 1 (lit) [+ two objects] cogner l'un contre l'autre ◆ **I'd like to ~ their heads together!*** ce sont deux têtes à claques

2 * ⇒ **knock up vt sep 3**

► **knock up** VI (Tennis) faire des balles

VT SEP 1 (lit) [+ handle, lever etc] faire lever d'un coup

2 (Brit = waken) réveiller (en frappant à la porte)

3 (* = make hurriedly) [+ meal] improviser ; [+ shed, furniture] bricoler (en vitesse)

4 (Brit * = exhaust) [+ person] crever*

5 (* = make pregnant) engrosser*

N ◆ **knock-up** → **knock**

knockabout /ˈnɒkəˌbaʊt/ N (esp US Naut) dériveur m, petit voilier m ADJ (esp Brit = boisterous) [fun, humour, style] exubérant ◆ **~ comedy** (Theat) (grosse) farce f

knockback* /ˈnɒkbæk/ N (= setback) contretemps m ◆ **he got** or **received** or **suffered a ~** on l'a envoyé balader*

knockdown /ˈnɒkdaʊn/ ADJ 1 ◆ **a ~ blow** (lit) un coup à assommer un bœuf ; (fig) un coup de boutoir 2 (Brit Comm) ◆ **~ price** prix m très avantageux or intéressant ◆ **"knockdown prices"** (in posters, announcements) "prix sacrifiés" ◆ **to sell at ~ prices** vendre pour une bouchée de pain N (Boxing) knock-down m inv

knocker /ˈnɒkəʳ/ N (also **door-knocker**) marteau m (de porte), heurtoir m NPL **knockers** * (= breasts) nichons* mpl, roberts* mpl

knocking /ˈnɒkɪŋ/ N (NonC) 1 coups mpl ◆ **I can hear ~ at the door** j'entends frapper à la porte 2 (in engine) cognement m

COMP **knocking copy** N (Advertising) publicité f comparative

knocking-off time* N (Ind etc) heure f de la sortie

knocking shop* N (Brit) bordel* m

knockout /ˈnɒkaʊt/ N 1 (Boxing) knock-out m inv 2 (= overwhelming success) ◆ **to be a ~** * [person, record, achievement] être sensationnel* 3 (= competition) compétition f (avec épreuves éliminatoires) ◆ **"It's a Knockout"** (TV: formerly) ≈ "Jeux sans frontières" ADJ 1 (Boxing etc) ◆ **he delivered** or **landed a ~ blow** or **punch** il a mis son adversaire K.-O. ◆ **the ~ blow came in round six** il a été mis K.-O. au sixième round ◆ **~ blow** (fig) coup m terrible 2 (Brit Sport) [competition, tournament] par élimination

knoll /nəʊl/ N (= hillock) tertre m, monticule m

Knossos /ˈnɒsəs/ N Cnossos

knot /nɒt/ N 1 nœud m ◆ **to tie/untie a ~** faire/défaire un nœud ◆ **the marriage ~** le lien du mariage ◆ **to have a ~ in one's stomach** (= feel tense) avoir l'estomac noué, avoir un nœud à l'estomac ; → **granny, reef²**, **slipknot, tie** 2 (Naut = unit of speed) nœud m ◆ **to make 20 ~s** filer 20 nœuds ; → **rate¹** 3 (in wood) nœud m ◆ **a ~ of people** un petit groupe de gens VT [+ rope, scarf, tie, handkerchief] faire un nœud à, nouer ◆ **he ~ted the piece of string to the rope** il a noué la ficelle à la corde ◆ **get ~ted!*** va te faire voir* or foutre* !

► **knot together** VT SEP attacher, nouer

knothole /ˈnɒthəʊl/ N (in wood) trou m (laissé par un nœud)

knotty /ˈnɒtɪ/ ADJ 1 (lit) [wood, muscle, hand] noueux ; [rope, hair] plein de nœuds 2 (fig = thorny) [problem, issue, question] épineux

knout /naʊt/ N knout m

know /nəʊ/

vb : pret **knew**, ptp **known**

LANGUAGE IN USE 16.1

1 TRANSITIVE VERB
2 INTRANSITIVE VERB
3 SET STRUCTURES
4 NOUN
5 COMPOUNDS

1 - TRANSITIVE VERB

Look up set combinations such as **know the ropes, know the score** at the noun.

1 = have knowledge of connaître ◆ **to ~ the details/the results/the truth** connaître les détails/les résultats/la vérité ◆ **I ~ the problem!** je connais le problème ! ◆ **to ~ one's business*** connaître son affaire, s'y connaître

savoir can often also be used.

◆ **to ~ the difference between** connaître or savoir la différence entre ◆ **to ~ French** savoir *or* connaître le français ◆ **that's worth ~ing** c'est bon à savoir ◆ **it was sure to cause trouble, as well he knew** ça allait sûrement faire des histoires et il le savait très bien ◆ **I ~ the problems that arise when ...** je connais les problèmes qui surviennent lorsque ...

When **know** is followed by a clause, **savoir** must be used. Unlike **that**, **que** can never be omitted.

◆ **I ~ (that) you're wrong** je sais que vous avez tort ◆ **I ~ him to be a liar** je sais que c'est un menteur ◆ **I will** *or* **would have you ~ that ...** sachez que ... ◆ **to ~ how to do sth** savoir faire qch ◆ **I ~ how you feel** je sais ce que tu ressens, je connais ça ◆ **you don't ~ how glad/relieved I am to see you** vous ne pouvez pas savoir comme je suis content/soulagé de vous voir ◆ **she ~s what it means to suffer** *or* **what suffering means** elle sait ce qu'est la souffrance ◆ **he ~s what he's talking about** il sait de quoi il parle ◆ **I don't ~ where to begin** je ne sais pas par où commencer ◆ **do you ~ whether she's coming?** est-ce que tu sais si elle vient ? ◆ **I don't ~ why he reacted like that** je ne sais pas pourquoi il a réagi comme ça

2 = be acquainted with *[+ person, place, book, author]* connaître ◆ **I ~ him well** je le connais bien ◆ **do you ~ Paris?** connaissez-vous Paris ? ◆ **to ~ sb by sight/by name/by reputation** connaître qn de vue/de nom/de réputation ◆ **he ~s all his customers by name** il connaît tous ses clients par leur(s) nom(s) ◆ **I don't ~ her to speak to** je ne la connais que de vue ◆ **everyone ~s him as Dizzy** on le connaît sous le nom de Dizzy ◆ **most of us ~ him only as a comedian** la plupart d'entre nous ne le connaissons qu'en tant que comique ◆ **he is ~n as a man of great charm** c'est un homme connu pour son charme, il passe pour un homme plein de charme ◆ **civilisation as we ~ it** la civilisation telle que nous la connaissons

3 = understand ◆ **I don't ~ how you can say that !** comment peux-tu dire une chose pareille ! ◆ **you ~ what I mean** tu vois ce que je veux dire

4 = recognize reconnaître ◆ **to ~ sb by his voice/his walk** reconnaître qn à sa voix/à sa démarche ◆ **I knew him at once** je l'ai reconnu tout de suite ◆ **I ~ real expertise when I see it!** je sais reconnaître un spécialiste quand j'en vois un ! ◆ **she ~s a good thing when she sees it** * elle ne laisse pas passer les bonnes occasions ◆ **he knew he was to blame** il se savait coupable

5 = be certain ◆ **I don't ~ that it's made things any easier** je ne suis pas sûr que ça ait simplifié les choses ◆ **I don't ~ if** *or* **that that is a very good idea** je ne suis pas sûr que ce soit une bonne idée ◆ **I don't ~ if I can do it** je ne suis pas sûr de pouvoir le faire

6 exclamations ◆ **well, what do you ~ !** *(US)* * tiens, tiens ! ◆ **I ~ (what)** *, **let's leave it till tomorrow!** et si on remettait ça à demain ? ◆ **(do) you ~ what** *, **I think she did it!** tu sais quoi, je pense que c'est elle qui a fait ça ! ◆ **she's furious! – don't I ~ it!** * elle est furieuse ! – à qui le dis-tu *or* je suis bien placé pour le savoir ! ◆ **not if I ~ it!** * ça m'étonnerait ! ◆ **that's all you ~ (about it)!** * c'est ce que tu crois ! ◆ **you ~ what you can do with it** *or* **where you can stick it!** ‡ tu peux te le mettre où je pense ! ‡

2 - INTRANSITIVE VERB

savoir ◆ **who ~s?** qui sait ? ◆ **is she nice? – I don't ~** *or* **I wouldn't ~** * est-ce qu'elle est gentille ? – je ne sais pas *or* je n'en sais rien ◆ **how should I ~?** est-ce que je sais (moi) ! *, comment veux-tu que je sache ? ◆ **it'll be expensive, you ~** ça va coûter cher, tu sais ◆ **you ~, that's not a bad idea** tu sais, ce n'est pas une mauvaise idée ◆ **as far as I ~** autant que je sache, à ma connaissance ◆ **not as far as I ~** pas que je sache, pas à ma connaissance ◆ **for all I ~** pour ce que j'en sais ◆ **one never ~s, you never ~** on ne sait jamais ◆ **and afterwards they just don't want to ~** * et après ça ils ne veulent plus en entendre parler

3 - SET STRUCTURES

◆ **to know sth about sth/sb** ◆ **to ~ a lot about sth/sb** en savoir long sur qch/qn ◆ **I don't ~ much about it/him** je ne sais pas grand-chose à ce sujet/je ne le connais pas beaucoup ◆ **I'd like to ~ more (about it)** je voudrais en savoir plus (à ce sujet) ◆ **it's no good lying, I ~ all about it** ce n'est pas la peine de mentir, je sais tout ◆ **she ~s (all) about computers** elle s'y connaît en informatique ◆ **I ~ nothing about music** je n'y connais rien en musique, je ne m'y connais pas du tout en musique ◆ **I ~ nothing about it** je ne sais rien à ce sujet

◆ **to know about sth/sb** ◆ **I didn't ~ about their quarrel** je ne savais pas qu'ils s'étaient disputés, je n'étais pas au courant de leur dispute ◆ **I didn't ~ about the accident** je n'étais pas au courant pour l'accident ◆ **I didn't ~ about that** je n'étais pas au courant ◆ **he ~s about antiques** il s'y connaît en antiquités ◆ **do you ~ about Paul?** tu es au courant pour Paul ? ◆ **I don't ~ about you, but I think it's terrible** je ne sais pas ce que tu en penses mais personnellement je trouve ça affreux ◆ **I don't ~ about you, but I'm hungry!** vous n'avez peut-être pas faim, mais moi si ! ◆ **so you're satisfied? – I don't ~ about that** alors tu es satisfait ? – satisfait c'est beaucoup dire ◆ **I'm not going to school tomorrow – I don't ~ about that!** * je ne vais pas à l'école demain – c'est à voir *or* c'est ce qu'on va voir !

◆ **to know of** *(= be acquainted with)* connaître ; *(= be aware of)* savoir ; *(= learn about)* apprendre ; *(= have heard of)* entendre parler de ◆ **do you ~ of a good hairdresser?** connaissez-vous un bon coiffeur ? ◆ **I ~ of a nice little café** je connais un petit café sympathique ◆ **I'd ~n of his death for some time** je savais depuis quelque temps qu'il était mort ◆ **is he married? – not that I ~ of** il est marié ? – pas que je sache *or* pas à ma connaissance ◆ **I knew of his death through a friend** j'ai appris sa mort par un ami ◆ **I ~ of you through your sister** j'ai entendu parler de vous par votre sœur ◆ **I don't ~ him but I ~ of him** je ne le connais pas mais j'ai entendu parler de lui ◆ **I ~ of no reason why he should have committed suicide** je ne lui connais aucune raison de se suicider ◆ **I ~ of no evidence for this claim** rien à ma connaissance ne permet de l'affirmer

◆ **to know sb/sth from sb/sth** *(= distinguish)* savoir distinguer qn/qch de qn/qch, savoir faire la différence entre qn/qch et qn/qch ◆ **students nowadays don't ~ a pronoun from an adverb** les étudiants ne savent plus distinguer un pronom d'un adverbe ◆ **he doesn't ~ good wine from cheap plonk** * il ne sait pas faire la différence entre un bon vin et une piquette, il est incapable de distinguer un bon vin d'une piquette BUT **he doesn't ~ one end of a horse/hammer from the other** c'est à peine s'il sait ce que c'est qu'un cheval/marteau

◆ **to know sb/sth** *+ infinitive* ◆ **I've never ~n him to smile** je ne l'ai jamais vu sourire ◆ **I've never ~n her to be wrong** je dois dire qu'elle ne se trompe jamais ◆ **I've ~n such things to happen before** ça s'est déjà produit auparavant ◆ **well, it has been ~n (to happen)** enfin, ça c'est déjà vu ◆ **I've never ~n it to rain like this in June** je n'ai jamais vu autant de pluie en juin

◆ **to know better** ◆ **I ~ better than to offer advice** je me garde bien de donner des conseils ◆ **he ~s better than to touch his capital** il est trop prudent pour entamer son capital ◆ **you ought to ~ better than to listen to him** tu sais bien qu'il ne faut pas l'écouter ◆ **you ought to have ~n better** tu aurais dû réfléchir ◆ **he should ~ better at his age** à son âge il devrait avoir un peu plus de bon sens ◆ **they did that because they didn't ~ any better** ils faisaient ça par ignorance ◆ **he says he didn't do it but I ~ better** il dit qu'il n'est pas responsable mais je sais que ce n'est pas vrai *or* que ce n'est pas le cas ◆ **she told him not to go but he thought he knew better** elle lui a dit de ne pas y aller mais il pensait qu'il était plus apte à juger qu'elle ◆ **a lot of people think he's rich but I ~ better** beaucoup de gens pensent qu'il est riche, mais je sais que ce n'est pas vrai *or* que ce n'est pas le cas

◆ **to know best** ◆ **mother ~s best!** maman a toujours raison ! ◆ **you ~ best, I suppose!** bon, puisque tu le dis !

◆ **to get to know** *[+ fact]* apprendre ; *[+ person]* faire plus ample connaissance avec, apprendre à connaître ◆ **I'd like to see you again and get to ~ you better** j'aimerais vous revoir et faire plus ample connaissance avec vous *or* apprendre à mieux vous connaître ◆ **he seems arrogant, but when you get to ~ him you can see he's just shy** il a l'air arrogant, mais quand on le connaît mieux on s'aperçoit que c'est simplement de la timidité

◆ **to let sb know** ◆ **I'll let you ~** je vous le ferai savoir ◆ **I'll let you ~ on Monday** je te dirai *or* te ferai savoir ça lundi ◆ **if you can't come, please let me ~** *(in advance)* préviens-moi si tu ne peux pas venir, s'il te plaît

◆ **to let sb know sth** dire qch à qn ◆ **I'll let you ~ the price as soon as possible** je te dirai combien ça coûte dès que possible ◆ **let me ~ if I can help** si je peux me rendre utile, dites-le-moi ◆ **he soon let me ~ what he thought of it** il n'a pas tardé à me faire savoir ce qu'il en pensait

4 - NOUN

◆ **to be in the know** * être au courant *or* au parfum ‡ ◆ **those in the ~ choose Collins** ceux qui s'y connaissent choisissent Collins

5 - COMPOUNDS

know-all * **N** *(Brit)* (Monsieur) je-sais-tout * *m*, (Madame *or* Mademoiselle) je-sais-tout * *f*

know-how * **N** savoir-faire *m* ◆ **they have the materials to make the missile but they haven't got the ~-how** ils ont le matériel nécessaire à la fabrication du missile mais ils n'ont pas le savoir-faire ◆ **after years in the job he has acquired a lot of ~-how** après des années dans cet emploi il a acquis beaucoup de savoir-faire *or* de métier ◆ **you need quite a bit of ~-how to operate this machine** il faut pas mal s'y connaître pour faire marcher cette machine

know-it-all * **N** *(US)* ⇒ **know-all**

knowable /ˈnəʊəbəl/ **ADJ** connaissable

knowing /ˈnəʊɪŋ/ **ADJ** 1 *(= shrewd)* fin, malin (-igne *f*) ; *(= wise)* sage 2 *(= arch) [look, smile]* entendu **N** ◆ **there's no ~ what she might do** on ne peut pas savoir ce qu'elle va faire ◆ **will he help us? – there's no ~** est-ce qu'il va nous aider ? – on ne peut pas savoir

knowingly /ˈnəʊɪŋlɪ/ **ADV** 1 *(= consciously)* sciemment, intentionnellement 2 *(= archly) [look, smile, nod]* d'un air entendu

knowledge /ˈnɒlɪdʒ/ LANGUAGE IN USE 19.2

N *(NonC)* 1 *(= understanding, awareness)* connaissance *f* ◆ **to have ~ of** avoir connaissance de ◆ **to have no ~ of** ne pas savoir,

ignorer ◆ **to (the best of) my ~** à ma connaissance, pour autant que je sache ◆ **not to my ~** pas à ma connaissance, pas que je sache ◆ **they had never to her ~ complained before** à sa connaissance ils ne s'étaient jamais plaints auparavant ◆ **without his ~** à son insu, sans qu'il le sache ◆ **without the ~ of her mother** à l'insu de sa mère, sans que sa mère le sache ◆ **to bring sth to sb's ~** porter qch à la connaissance de qn ◆ **to bring to sb's ~ that ...** porter à la connaissance de qn le fait que ... ◆ **it has come to my ~ that ...** j'ai appris que ... ◆ **~ of the facts** la connaissance des faits ◆ **it's common** *or* **public ~ that ...** il est de notoriété publique que ...
2 *(= body of knowledge)* savoir *m* ; *(= learning, facts learnt)* connaissances *fpl* ◆ **his ~ will die with him** son savoir mourra avec lui ◆ **my ~ of English is elementary** mes connaissances d'anglais sont élémentaires ◆ **he has a thorough ~ of geography** il a de grandes connaissances en géographie, il possède la géographie à fond ◆ **he has a working ~ of Japanese** il possède les éléments de base du japonais
COMP **knowledge-based system** N *(Comput)* système *m* expert
knowledge engineering N *(Comput)* génie *m* cognitif

knowledgeable /ˈnɒlɪdʒəbl/ ADJ *[person] (in general)* cultivé ; *(in a given subject)* qui s'y connaît ◆ **she's very ~ about cars** elle s'y connaît en voitures

knowledgeably /ˈnɒlɪdʒəblɪ/ ADV de manière compétente

known /nəʊn/ N ptp of **know**
ADJ connu *(to sb* de qn) ◆ **to be ~ for sth/for doing sth** être connu pour qch/pour faire qch ◆ **she wishes to be ~ as Jane Beattie** elle veut se faire appeler Jane Beattie ◆ **he is ~ to be unreliable** il est bien connu qu'on ne peut pas compter sur lui ◆ **he is ~ to have been there/to be dishonest** on sait qu'il y a été/qu'il est malhonnête ◆ **it soon became ~ that ...** on a bientôt su que ... ◆ **to make sth ~ to sb** faire savoir qch à qn ◆ **to make o.s. ~ to sb** se présenter à qn ◆ **to make one's presence ~ to sb** manifester sa présence à qn ◆ **~ to the Ancient Greeks** connu des Grecs de l'antiquité ◆ **to let it be ~ that** faire savoir que ◆ **it is a ~ fact that ...** c'est un fait établi que ... ◆ **an internationally-~ expert** un expert reconnu au plan international ◆ **he is a ~ quantity** on sait ce qu'il vaut ◆ **the most dangerous snake ~ to science** le serpent le plus dangereux que l'on connaisse

knuckle /ˈnʌkl/ N articulation *f or* jointure *f* du doigt ◆ **to graze one's ~s** s'écorcher les articulations des doigts ◆ **to be near the ~** * être limite * ; → **rap** COMP **knuckle-bone** N *(Anat)* articulation *f* du doigt ; *(Culin)* os *m* de jarret
▸ **knuckle down** * VI s'y mettre ◆ **to ~ down to work** s'atteler au travail
▸ **knuckle under** * VI céder

knuckleduster /ˈnʌkl,dʌstəʳ/ N coup-de-poing *m* américain

knucklehead‡ /ˈnʌklhed/ N crétin(e) * *m(f)*, nouille * *f*

knurl /nɜːl/ N *(in wood)* nœud *m* ; *(on screw, nut)* moletage *m* VT *[+ screw, nut]* moleter

KO * /ˈkeɪˈəʊ/ (abbrev of **knockout**) N (pl **KO's**) *(= blow)* K.-O. *m* VT (vb : pret, ptp **KO'd**) /ˈkeɪˈəʊd/ *(gen, Boxing)* mettre K.-O.

koala /kəʊˈɑːlə/ N (also **koala bear**) koala *m*

kohl /kəʊl/ N khôl *m* COMP **kohl pencil** N crayon *m* khôl

kohlrabi /kəʊlˈrɑːbɪ/ N (pl **kohlrabies**) chou-rave *m*

Kolkata /kɒlˈkɑːtə/ N Kolkata *(nouveau nom de Calcutta)*

kook‡ /kuːk/ N (US) dingue * *mf*

kookaburra /ˈkʊkə,bʌrə/ N kookaburra *m* *(oiseau d'Australie)*

kookie‡, **kooky**‡ /ˈkuːkɪ/ ADJ (US) dingue *, cinglé *

kopeck /ˈkəʊpek/ N kopeck *m*

Koran /kɒˈrɑːn/ N Coran *m*

Koranic /kɒˈrænɪk/ ADJ coranique

Korea /kəˈrɪə/ N Corée *f* ◆ **North/South ~** Corée *f* du Nord/du Sud

Korean /kəˈrɪən/ ADJ coréen ◆ **North/South ~** nord-/sud-coréen N 1 Coréen(ne) *m(f)* ◆ **North/South ~** Nord-/Sud-Coréen(ne) 2 *(= language)* coréen *m*

korma /ˈkɔːmə/ N *type de curry souvent préparé à la crème et à la noix de coco*

Kosevo /ˈkɒsə,vəʊ/ N, ADJ ⇒ **Kosovo**

kosher /ˈkəʊʃəʳ/ ADJ 1 *(Rel)* casher *inv*, kasher *inv* 2 (* fig) ◆ **it's ~** c'est OK * ◆ **there's something not quite ~ about him/it** il y a quelque chose de pas très catholique * en lui/là-dedans

Kosova /ˈkɒsəʊvɑː/ N, ADJ ⇒ **Kosovo**

Kosovan /ˈkɒsəvən/, **Kosovar** /ˈkɒsəvɑːʳ/ ADJ kosovar N Kosovar(e) *m(f)*

Kosovo /ˈkɒsə,vəʊ/ N Kosovo *m* ◆ **in ~** au Kosovo ADJ kosovar

Kowloon Peninsula /ˈkaʊluːnpɪˈnɪnsjʊlə/ N péninsule *f* de Kowloon

kowtow /ˈkaʊˈtaʊ/ VI se prosterner ◆ **to ~ to sb** courber l'échine devant qn, faire des courbettes devant qn

KP /keɪˈpiː/ N 1 *(US Mil)* (abbrev of **kitchen police**) → **kitchen** 2 *(Med)* abbrev of **Kaposi's sarcoma**

kph /,keɪpiːˈeɪtʃ/ N (abbrev of **kilometres per hour**) km/h

kraal /krɑːl/ N kraal *m*

Kraut‡ /kraʊt/ N *(pej)* Boche‡ *mf*

Kremlin /ˈkremlɪn/ N Kremlin *m*

kremlinologist /ˈkremlɪˈnɒlədʒɪst/ N kremlinologue *mf*

kremlinology /ˈkremlɪˈnɒlədʒɪ/ N kremlinologie *f*

krill /krɪl/ N *(pl inv)* krill *m*

Krishna /ˈkrɪʃnə/ N *(= deity)* Krisna *or* Krishna ; *(= river)* Krishna *m*, Kistna *m*

Krishnaism /ˈkrɪʃnə,ɪzəm/ N kris(h)naïsme *m*

krona /ˈkrəʊnə/ N couronne *f* (suédoise)

krone /ˈkrəʊnə/ N *(Danish)* couronne *f* (danoise) ; *(Norwegian)* couronne *f* (norvégienne)

Krugerrand /ˈkruːgə,rænd/ N krugerrand *m*

Krum(m)horn /ˈkrʌm,hɔːn/ N *(Mus)* cromorne *m*

krypton /ˈkrɪptɒn/ N krypton *m*

KS abbrev of **Kansas**

Kt *(Brit)* abbrev of **knight**

kudos * /ˈkjuːdɒs/ N *(NonC)* gloire *f* ◆ **to have ~** avoir du prestige ◆ **he got all the ~** c'est lui qui a récolté toute la gloire *or* tous les lauriers

Ku Klux Klan /ˈkuːˈklʌksˈklæn/ N Ku Klux Klan *m*

kummel /ˈkɪməl/ N kummel *m*

kumquat /ˈkʌmkwɒt/ N kumquat *m*

kung fu /ˈkʌŋˈfuː/ N kung-fu *m*

Kuomintang /ˈkwəʊˈmɪnˈtæŋ/ N Kuo-min-tang *m*

Kurd /kɜːd/ N Kurde *mf*

Kurdish /ˈkɜːdɪʃ/ ADJ kurde N *(= language)* kurde *m*

Kurdistan /,kɜːdɪˈstɑːn/ N Kurdistan *m* ◆ **in ~** au Kurdistan

Kuwait /kʊˈweɪt/ N Koweït *m* ◆ **in Koweit** au Koweït

Kuwaiti /kʊˈweɪtɪ/ N Koweïtien(ne) *m(f)* ADJ koweïtien

kvas(s) /kvɑːs/ N kwas *or* kvas *m*

kvetch * /kvetʃ/ VI (US) se plaindre *(about* de) râler *

kW (abbrev of **kilowatt**) kW

kwashiorkor /,kwɑːʃɪˈɔːkɔːʳ/ N kwashiorkor *m*

kWh (abbrev of **kilowatt-hour(s)**) kWh

KY abbrev of **Kentucky**

Kyrgyzstan /,kɜːgɪsˈtɑːn/ N ⇒ **Kirg(h)izstan**

Ll

L, l /el/ N [1] (= *letter*) L, l *m* ◆ **L for London, L for Love** (*US*) ≃ L comme Louis [2] (abbrev of **litre(s)**) l [3] (*US*) **the L*** le métro aérien [4] (*Geog*) (abbrev of **Lake**) L [5] (abbrev of **left**) gauche [6] (abbrev of **large**) L (*pour indiquer la taille sur l'étiquette*) [7] (*Ling*) (abbrev of **Latin**) lat.
COMP **L-driver** N (*Brit*) conducteur *m*, -trice *f* débutant(e)
L-plate N (*Brit*) *plaque signalant la conduite accompagnée ;* [*of driving school*] plaque *f* d'auto-école
L-shaped ADJ en (forme de) L

LA¹ /el'eɪ/ abbrev of **Los Angeles**

LA² abbrev of **Louisiana**

La abbrev of **Lane**

La. abbrev of **Louisiana**

Lab (*Brit Pol*) (abbrev of **Labour**) ADJ travailliste N (*NonC*) le parti travailliste, les travaillistes *mpl*

lab* /læb/ N (abbrev of **laboratory**) labo* *m*
COMP [*work, test*] en laboratoire
lab book N (*Scol etc*) cahier *m* de travaux pratiques
lab coat N blouse *f* blanche
lab technician N technicien(ne) *m(f)* de laboratoire

label /'leɪbl/ N (*lit, fig, Ling*) étiquette *f* ; (= *brand guarantee*) label *m* ◆ **an album on the Technix ~** un album sorti chez Technix *or* sous le label Technix ◆ **he was stuck with the ~ of "political activist"** il avait du mal à se défaire de l'étiquette d'"activiste politique" ; → **luggage**
VT [1] [+ *parcel, bottle*] coller une *or* des étiquette(s) sur ; [+ *goods for sale*] étiqueter ◆ **all packets must be clearly ~led** tous les paquets doivent être clairement étiquetés ◆ **the bottle was not ~led** il n'y avait pas d'étiquette sur la bouteille ◆ **the bottle was ~led "poison"** sur la bouteille il y avait marqué "poison" [2] [+ *person, group*] étiqueter, cataloguer (*pej*) (*as* comme) ◆ **he was ~led a dissident** on l'a étiqueté *or* catalogué comme dissident [3] (*Ling*) marquer

labia /'leɪbɪə/ N (pl of **labium**) lèvres *fpl* (*de la vulve*) ◆ **~ minora/majora** petites/grandes lèvres *fpl*

labial /'leɪbɪəl/ ADJ (*Anat, Phon*) labial N (*Phon*) labiale *f*

labiodental /,leɪbɪəʊ'dentəl/ ADJ labiodental N labiodentale *f*

labiovelar /,leɪbɪəʊ'viːlər/ ADJ, N labiovélaire *f*

labium /,leɪbɪʊm/ N → **labia**

labor /'leɪbər/ (*US*) ⇒ **labour**

laboratory /lə'bɒrətərɪ, (US) 'læbrətɔːrɪ/ N laboratoire *m* ; → **language**
COMP [*experiment, instrument, product*] de laboratoire
laboratory assistant N assistant(e) *m(f)* de laboratoire, laborantin(e) *m(f)*
laboratory equipment N équipement *m* de laboratoire
laboratory school N (*US*) école *f* d'application
laboratory technician N technicien(ne) *m(f)* de laboratoire

laborious /lə'bɔːrɪəs/ ADJ laborieux

laboriously /lə'bɔːrɪəslɪ/ ADV laborieusement

labour, labor (*US*) /'leɪbər/ N [1] (= *work, task*) travail *m* ; (= *hard work*) dur travail *m*, labeur *m* ◆ **a ~ of love** une tâche accomplie pour le plaisir ◆ **the (twelve) ~s of Hercules** les (douze) travaux *mpl* d'Hercule ; → **hard, manual, organized, slave**
[2] (*NonC* = *workers*) main-d'œuvre *f* ◆ **Minister/Ministry of Labour, Secretary/Department of Labour** (*US*) ministre *m*/ministère *m* du Travail ◆ **to withdraw one's ~** faire grève ; → **management, skilled**
[3] (*Pol*) (also **the Labour Party**) ◆ **Labour** le parti travailliste, les travaillistes *mpl* ◆ **he votes Labour** il vote travailliste ◆ **New Labour** le New Labour, le nouveau parti travailliste
[4] (*Med*) travail *m* ◆ **in ~** en travail, en train d'accoucher ◆ **to go into ~** commencer à avoir des contractions ◆ **a 15-hour ~** un accouchement qui a duré 15 heures
ADJ (*Pol*) ◆ **Labour** travailliste
VI [1] (= *work with effort*) travailler dur (*at* à) ; (= *work with difficulty*) peiner (*at* sur) ◆ **to ~ to do sth** peiner pour faire qch ◆ **to ~ up a slope** [*person, car*] gravir péniblement une pente
[2] [*engine, motor*] peiner ; [*ship, boat*] fatiguer
[3] ◆ **to ~ under a delusion** *or* **an illusion** *or* **a misapprehension** être victime d'une illusion ◆ **to ~ under the delusion** *or* **illusion** *or* **misapprehension that ...** s'imaginer que ...
VT insister sur, s'étendre sur ◆ **I won't ~ the point** je n'insisterai pas (lourdement) sur ce point, je ne m'étendrai pas là-dessus
COMP [*dispute, trouble*] ouvrier
labo(u)r agreement N convention *f* collective
labo(u)r camp N camp *m* de travail
Labo(u)r Day N fête *f* du Travail (*Brit : premier lundi de mai ; US, Can : premier lundi de septembre*)
Labour Exchange N (*Brit: formerly*) ≃ Bourse *f* de l'emploi †, Agence *f* pour l'emploi
labo(u)r force N main-d'œuvre *f*, travailleurs *mpl*
labo(u)r-intensive ADJ ◆ **a labo(u)r-intensive industry** une industrie à forte main-d'œuvre ◆ **to be labo(u)r-intensive** nécessiter une main-d'œuvre importante
labo(u)r laws NPL législation *f or* droit *m* du travail
labo(u)r market N marché *m* du travail
labo(u)r movement N (*Pol*) mouvement *m* ouvrier ◆ **the Labo(u)r movement** le mouvement travailliste
labo(u)r pains NPL (*Med*) douleurs *fpl* de l'accouchement
labour relations NPL relations *fpl* du travail
labo(u)r-saving ADJ qui facilite le travail
labo(u)r-saving device N (*in household*) appareil *m* ménager
labo(u)r shortage N pénurie *f* de main-d'œuvre
labo(u)r supply N main-d'œuvre *f* (disponible)
labor union N (*US*) syndicat *m*
labo(u)r ward N (*Med*) salle *f* d'accouchement *or* de travail

> **LABOR DAY**
>
> La fête du Travail aux États-Unis et au Canada est fixée au premier lundi de septembre. Instituée par le Congrès en 1894 après avoir été réclamée par les mouvements ouvriers pendant douze ans, elle a perdu une grande partie de son caractère politique pour devenir un jour férié assez ordinaire et l'occasion de partir pour un long week-end avant la rentrée des classes.

laboured, labored (*US*) /'leɪbəd/ ADJ [1] (= *involving effort*) [*movement*] pénible ; [*debate, negotiations, process, task*] laborieux ◆ **~ breathing** respiration *f* pénible *or* difficile [2] (= *clumsy*) [*joke, pun, rhyme, style*] lourd, laborieux

labourer, laborer (*US*) /'leɪbərər/ N ouvrier *m*, travailleur *m* ; (*on farm*) ouvrier *m* agricole ; (*on roads, building sites etc*) manœuvre *m* ◆ **the ~ is worthy of his hire** (*Prov*) l'ouvrier mérite son salaire ; → **dock¹**

labouring, laboring (*US*) /'leɪbərɪŋ/ ADJ [*work, job*] d'ouvrier ◆ **a ~ man** un ouvrier ◆ **the interests of the ~ man** les intérêts des ouvriers *or* de la population ouvrière ◆ **the ~ class(es)** la classe ouvrière

labourite, laborite (*US*) /'leɪbəraɪt/ N (*Pol*) travailliste *mf*

Labrador /'læbrədɔːr/ N [1] (*Geog*) Labrador *m* ◆ **in ~** au Labrador [2] (= *dog:* also **labrador**) labrador *m*

laburnum /lə'bɜːnəm/ N cytise *m*

labyrinth /'læbɪrɪnθ/ N (*lit, fig*) labyrinthe *m* ◆ **a ~ of streets** un dédale *or* un labyrinthe de rues

labyrinthine /,læbɪ'rɪnθaɪn/ ADJ labyrinthique

lace /leɪs/ N 1 *(NonC = fabric)* dentelle *f* ◆ **dress trimmed with ~** robe *f* bordée de dentelle(s) ◆ **a piece of ~** de la dentelle 2 *[of shoe, corset]* lacet *m* VT 1 (also **lace up**) *[+ shoe, corset]* lacer ◆ **to ~ one's fingers together** joindre les mains 2 ◆ **to ~ with** *[+ alcohol]* arroser de ◆ **tea ~d with whisky** du thé arrosé de whisky ◆ **coffee ~d with cyanide** du café additionné de cyanure ◆ **her comments were ~d with sarcasm/humour** ses propos étaient empreints de sarcasme/d'humour VI (also **lace up**) se lacer
COMP *[collar, curtains]* de *or* en dentelle
lace-ups * NPL ⇒ **lace-up shoes**
lace-up shoes NPL *(Brit)* chaussures *fpl* à lacets

lacemaker /ˈleɪsˌmeɪkəʳ/ N dentellier *m*, -ière *f*

lacemaking /ˈleɪsˌmeɪkɪŋ/ N fabrication *f* de la dentelle, dentellerie *f*

lacerate /ˈlæsəreɪt/ VT *(lit)* *[+ face, skin, clothes]* lacérer ; *(fig)* *[+ person]* déchirer, fendre le cœur de

laceration /ˌlæsəˈreɪʃən/ N *(= act)* lacération *f* ; *(= tear: also Med)* déchirure *f*

lacey /ˈleɪsɪ/ ADJ ⇒ **lacy**

lachrymal /ˈlækrɪməl/ ADJ lacrymal

lachrymose /ˈlækrɪməʊs/ ADJ *(liter)* larmoyant

lack /læk/ LANGUAGE IN USE 17.1
N manque *m* ◆ **through** *or* **for ~ of** faute de, par manque de ◆ **such was their ~ of confidence that ...** ils manquaient tellement de confiance que ... ◆ **there was a complete ~ of interest in my proposals** mes suggestions se sont heurtées à une indifférence totale ◆ **there was no ~ of applicants/customers** ce n'étaient pas les candidats/les clients qui manquaient ; → **try**
VT *[+ confidence, friends, strength, interest]* manquer de ◆ **we ~ the resources** nous manquons de ressources, nous n'avons pas les ressources nécessaires ◆ **he doesn't ~ talent** il ne manque pas de talent, ce n'est pas le talent qui lui manque
VI 1 ◆ **to be ~ing** *[food, money etc]* manquer, faire défaut ◆ **innovation has been sadly ~ing throughout this project** l'innovation a fait cruellement défaut tout au long de ce projet
2 ◆ **to be ~ing in** ◆ **to ~ for** *[person]* manquer de

lackadaisical /ˌlækəˈdeɪzɪkəl/ ADJ *(= listless)* nonchalant, apathique ; *(= lazy)* indolent ; *[work]* fait à la va-comme-je-te-pousse *

lackey /ˈlækɪ/ N laquais *m (also pej)*, larbin * *m (pej)*

lacking * /ˈlækɪŋ/ ADJ *(= stupid)* simplet, demeuré *

lacklustre, lackluster *(US)* /ˈlækˌlʌstəʳ/ ADJ terne, peu brillant

laconic /ləˈkɒnɪk/ ADJ laconique

laconically /ləˈkɒnɪkəlɪ/ ADV laconiquement

lacquer /ˈlækəʳ/ N *(= substance: for wood, hair etc)* laque *f* ; *(= object)* laque *m* ◆ **~ ware** laques *mpl* VT *[+ wood]* laquer ; *(Brit)* *[+ hair]* mettre de la laque sur

lacrosse /ləˈkrɒs/ N lacrosse *m* COMP **lacrosse stick** N crosse *f*

lactase /ˈlækteɪs/ N lactase *f*

lactate /ˈlækteɪt/ N *(Chem)* lactate *m* VI produire du lait

lactation /lækˈteɪʃən/ N lactation *f*

lacteal /ˈlæktɪəl/ ADJ lacté NPL **lacteals** veines *fpl* lactées

lactic /ˈlæktɪk/ ADJ lacté COMP **lactic acid** N acide *m* lactique

lactiferous /lækˈtɪfərəs/ ADJ lactifère

lactogenic /ˌlæktəˈdʒenɪk/ ADJ lactogène

lacto-ovo-vegetarian /ˌlæktəʊˌəʊvəʊˌvedʒɪˈteərɪən/ N lacto-ovo-végétarien(ne) *m(f)*

lactose /ˈlæktəʊs/ N lactose *m*

lacto-vegetarian /ˌlæktəʊˌvedʒɪˈteərɪən/ N lactovégétarien(ne) *m(f)*

lacuna /ləˈkjuːnə/ N (pl **lacunas** *or* **lacunae** /ləˈkjuːniː/) lacune *f*

lacustrine /ləˈkʌstraɪn/ ADJ lacustre

lacy /ˈleɪsɪ/ ADJ *[underwear, shirt, cushion]* *(= made of lace)* en dentelle ; *(= containing lace)* avec des dentelles ◆ **her tights had a ~ pattern** *(= resembling lace)* ses collants avaient un motif de dentelle ◆ **the frost made a ~ pattern** il y avait une dentelle de givre

lad /læd/ N *(esp Brit)* *(= boy)* garçon *m*, gars * *m* ; *(* = son)* fiston * *m* ◆ **when I was a ~** quand j'étais jeune, dans mon jeune temps ◆ **he's only a ~** ce n'est qu'un gosse * *or* un gamin * ◆ **I'm going for a drink with the ~s** * *(Brit)* je vais boire un pot * avec les copains ◆ **come on ~s!** *(Brit)* allez les gars ! * ◆ **he's one of the ~s** * *(Brit)* il fait partie de la bande ◆ **he's a bit of a ~** * *(Brit)* c'est un vrai mec * ; → **stable²** COMP
lad mag N magazine *m* pour homme

ladder /ˈlædəʳ/ N 1 *(lit, fig)* échelle *f* ◆ **to be at the top/bottom of the ~** *(fig)* être en haut/en bas de l'échelle ◆ **the social ~** l'échelle *f* sociale ◆ **to move up the social ~** monter dans l'échelle sociale ◆ **to move up the career ~** monter dans la hiérarchie ◆ **she has reached the top of the career ~** elle est au sommet de sa carrière ◆ **to get on the housing ~** accéder à la propriété ◆ **an evolutionary ~ from monkey to ape to man** l'échelle de l'évolution du singe au grand singe puis à l'homme ; → **rope, stepladder** 2 *(Brit: in tights)* échelle *f*, maille *f* filée ◆ **to have a ~ in one's tights** avoir une échelle à son collant, avoir un collant filé VT *(Brit)* *[+ tights, stocking]* filer, faire une échelle à VI *(Brit)* *[tights, stocking]* filer

ladderproof /ˈlædəpruːf/ ADJ *(Brit)* *[tights, stockings]* indémaillable

laddie * /ˈlædɪ/ N *(esp Scot and dial)* garçon *m*, (petit) gars * *m* ◆ **look here, ~!** dis donc, mon petit * *or* fiston * !

laddish * /ˈlædɪʃ/ ADJ *(Brit)* macho * *inv*

lade /leɪd/ (pret **laded**, ptp **laden**) VT charger

laden /ˈleɪdn/ VB ptp of **lade** ADJ chargé *(with* de) ◆ **fully ~ truck/ship** camion *m*/navire *m* avec un plein chargement

la-di-da * /ˈlɑːdɪˈdɑː/ *(pej)* ADJ *[person]* chochotte * ; *[voice]* maniéré, apprêté ; *[manner]* affecté ADV *[talk, speak]* de façon maniérée *or* affectée

lading /ˈleɪdɪŋ/ N cargaison *f*, chargement *m* ; → **bill¹**

ladle /ˈleɪdl/ N louche *f* VT *[+ soup]* servir (à la louche)
► **ladle out** VT SEP *[+ soup]* servir (à la louche) ; *(* fig)* *[+ money, advice]* prodiguer (à foison)

lady /ˈleɪdɪ/ N 1 *(= woman)* dame *f* ◆ **she's a real ~** c'est une vraie dame ◆ **she's no ~** elle n'a aucune classe ◆ **a little old ~** une petite vieille * ◆ **young ~** *(married)* jeune femme *f* ; *(unmarried)* jeune fille *f* ◆ **look here, young ~!** dites donc, jeune fille ! ◆ **this is the young ~ who served me** *(in shop, restaurant etc)* voilà la demoiselle qui m'a servi ◆ **Ladies and Gentlemen!** Mesdames, Mesdemoiselles, Messieurs ! ◆ **good morning, ladies and gentlemen** bonjour mesdames, bonjour mesdemoiselles, bonjour messieurs ◆ **listen here, ~** * écoutez, ma petite dame * ◆ **the ~ of the house** *(Brit)* la maîtresse de maison ◆ **"The Lady with the Camelias"** *(Literat)* "La Dame aux camélias" ◆ **ladies who lunch** * dames *fpl* de la bonne société ; → **first, leading¹**
2 *(† = wife)* dame *f* ◆ **the headmaster and his ~** le directeur et sa dame † ◆ **your good ~** *(hum)* votre dame * *(also hum)* ◆ **his young ~** * *(= girlfriend)* sa petite amie ; *(= fiancée)* sa fiancée
3 *(in titles)* ◆ **Lady Davenport** lady Davenport ◆ **Sir John and Lady Smith** sir John Smith et lady Smith
4 *(for ladies)* ◆ **ladies' hairdresser** coiffeur *m*, -euse *f* pour dames ◆ **~'s umbrella** parapluie *m* de femme ◆ **he's a ladies' man** *or* **a ~'s man** c'est un homme à femmes
5 ◆ **ladies** (also **ladies' room**) *(= public lavatory)* toilettes *fpl* (pour dames) ◆ **where is the ladies' room?, where is the ladies?** où sont les toilettes (pour dames) ? ◆ **"Ladies"** *(on sign)* "Dames"
6 *(Rel)* ◆ **Our Lady** Notre-Dame *f*
COMP *[engineer etc]* femme *before n*
ladies' auxiliary N *(US Med)* *association de bénévoles s'occupant d'œuvres de bienfaisance dans un hôpital*
Lady Bountiful N généreuse bienfaitrice *f*
Lady Chapel N *(Rel)* chapelle *f* de la (Sainte) Vierge
Lady Day N *(Brit)* la fête de l'Annonciation
lady doctor N femme *f* médecin
lady friend * N amie *f*
lady-in-waiting N (pl **ladies-in-waiting**) dame *f* d'honneur
lady-love N *(† or hum)* ◆ **his ~-love** sa bien-aimée †, la dame de ses pensées *(hum)*
Lady Mayoress N *(Brit)* femme *f* du lord-maire
Lady Muck N ◆ **she thinks she's Lady Muck** * ce qu'elle peut se croire ! *
lady's finger N *(= biscuit)* boudoir *m* ; *(= vegetable)* gombo *m*
lady's maid N femme *f* de chambre *(attachée au service particulier d'une dame)*
lady teacher N femme *f* professeur

ladybird /ˈleɪdɪbɜːd/ N *(Brit)* coccinelle *f*

ladyboy * /ˈleɪdɪbɔɪ/ N *jeune transsexuel ou travesti dans certains pays du Sud-Est asiatique*

ladybug /ˈleɪdɪbʌg/ N *(US)* ⇒ **ladybird**

ladyfinger /ˈleɪdɪˌfɪŋgəʳ/ N *(US Culin)* boudoir *m (biscuit)*

ladykiller /ˈleɪdɪkɪləʳ/ N don Juan *m*, bourreau *m* des cœurs *(hum)*

ladylike /ˈleɪdɪlaɪk/ ADJ *[person]* bien élevé, distingué ; *[manners]* raffiné ◆ **it's not ~ to yawn** une jeune fille bien élevée *or* comme il faut ne bâille pas

ladyship /ˈleɪdɪʃɪp/ N ◆ **Her/Your Ladyship** Madame *f* (la comtesse *or* la baronne *etc*)

lag¹ /læg/ VI rester en arrière, traîner ◆ **he was ~ging behind the others** il était à la traîne ; *(physically)* il traînait derrière les autres ◆ **their country ~s behind ours in car exports** leur pays a du retard *or* est en retard sur le nôtre dans l'exportation automobile ◆ **he now ~s ten points behind the leader** il a maintenant un retard de dix points sur le leader N *(= delay)* retard *m* ; *(between two events)* décalage *m* ; → **jet¹, time**
► **lag behind** VI rester en arrière, traîner ◆ **the government is ~ging behind in the opinion polls** le gouvernement est à la traîne dans les sondages

lag² /læg/ VT *[+ pipes]* calorifuger

lag³ * /læg/ N *(esp Brit)* ◆ **old ~** récidiviste *mf*, cheval *m* de retour

lager /ˈlɑːgəʳ/ N lager *f*, ≃ bière *f* blonde ◆ **~ lout** *(Brit)* voyou *m* imbibé de bière

laggard /ˈlægəd/ N traînard(e) *m(f)*

lagging /ˈlægɪŋ/ N *(NonC)* *(= material)* calorifuge *m* ; *(= act)* calorifugeage *m*

lagniappe /lænˈjæp/ N *(US)* prime *f*

lagoon /ləˈguːn/ N *(gen)* lagune *f* ; *(coral)* lagon *m*

Lagos /ˈleɪgɒs/ N Lagos *m*

lah /lɑː/ N *(Mus)* la *m*

lah-di-dah * /ˌlɑːdɪˈdɑː/ ⇒ **la-di-da**

laicize /ˈleɪɪsaɪz/ VT laïciser

laid /leɪd/ VB pt, ptp of **lay¹**; → **new** COMP **laid-back** * ADJ relax*, décontracté

lain /leɪn/ VB ptp of **lie¹**

lair /lɛəʳ/ N *(lit, fig)* tanière *f*, repaire *m*

laird /lɛəd/ N *(Scot)* laird *m*, propriétaire *m* foncier

laity /ˈleɪɪtɪ/ NPL ◆ **the** ~ les laïcs *or* les laïques *mpl*

lake¹ /leɪk/ N lac *m* ◆ **Lake Michigan** le lac Michigan ◆ **Lake Constance** le lac de Constance ◆ **Lake Geneva** le lac Léman *or* de Genève COMP **the Lake District** N *(Brit Geog)* la région des lacs
lake dwellers NPL *(Hist)* habitants *mpl* d'un village (*or* d'une cité) lacustre
lake dwelling N *(Hist)* habitation *f* lacustre
the Lake poets NPL *(Literat)* les lakistes *mpl*
the Lakes NPL *(Brit Geog)* ⇒ **the Lake District**

lake² /leɪk/ N *(Art)* laque *f*

Lakeland /ˈleɪklænd/ N *(Brit Geog)* la région des lacs

lakeside /ˈleɪksaɪd/ N bord *m* de lac ADJ au bord du (*or* d'un) lac ◆ **along the** ~ le long du lac ◆ **by** *or* **at the** ~ au bord du lac

La-La Land * /ˈlɑːlɑːˌlænd/ N *(esp US) Los Angeles, et plus particulièrement Hollywood*

Lallans /ˈlælənz/ N lallans *m (forme littéraire du dialecte parlé dans les Basses Terres d'Écosse)* ADJ en lallans

lallygag ‡ /ˈlælɪˌgæg/ VI *(US)* ⇒ **lollygag**

lam¹ * /læm/ VT tabasser* VI ◆ **to** ~ **into sb** (= *thrash*) rentrer dans qn* ; (= *scold*) engueuler qn‡

lam² * /læm/ N *(US)* ◆ **on the** ~ en fuite, en cavale‡ ◆ **to take it on the** ~ filer, partir en cavale‡

lama /ˈlɑːmə/ N lama *m (Rel)*

Lamaism /ˈlɑːməˌɪzəm/ N *(Rel)* lamaïsme *m*

Lamaist /ˈlɑːməˌɪst/ ADJ, N *(Rel)* lamaïste *mf*

lamb /læm/ N agneau *m* ◆ **Lamb of God** Agneau de Dieu ◆ **my little** ~! * mon trésor !, mon ange ! ◆ **poor** ~! * pauvre petit(e) ! ◆ **he followed her like a** ~ il l'a suivie sans broncher *or* sans protester ◆ **like a** ~ **to the slaughter** comme un agneau que l'on mène à l'abattoir VI agneler, mettre bas
COMP **lamb chop, lamb cutlet** N côtelette *f* d'agneau
lamb's lettuce N mâche *f*, doucette *f*
lamb's wool N *(NonC)* lambswool *m*, laine *f* d'agneau

lambada /ˌlæmˈbɑːdə/ N lambada *f*

lambast /læmˈbæst/, **lambaste** /læmˈbeɪst/ VT (= *scold*) réprimander ; (= *criticize severely*) éreinter, démolir ; (= *beat*) rosser*

lambent /ˈlæmbənt/ ADJ chatoyant

lambing /ˈlæmɪŋ/ N agnelage *m* ◆ ~ **time**, ~ **season** (période *f* d')agnelage *m*

lambkin /ˈlæmkɪn/ N jeune agneau *m*, agnelet *m* ◆ **my little** ~! * mon trésor *or* ange !

lambrequin /ˈlæmbrɪkɪn/ N lambrequin *m*

lambskin /ˈlæmskɪn/ N (= *skin itself*) peau *f* d'agneau ; (= *material*) agneau *m* NonC ADJ en agneau, d'agneau

lame /leɪm/ ADJ 1 (= *disabled*) *[person]* éclopé ; *[horse]* boiteux ; *[leg]* estropié ◆ **to be** ~ boiter ◆ **to be slightly** ~ boitiller ◆ **to go** *or* **fall** ~ se mettre à boiter ◆ **this horse is** ~ **in one leg** ce cheval boite d'une jambe 2 (= *feeble*) *[excuse]* mauvais ; *[performance]* piètre *before n* ; *[joke]* vaseux ; *[argument]* boiteux 3 *(Poetry) [metre]* boiteux, faux (fausse *f*) VT *[+ person, animal]* estropier N *(US* ‡*)* personne *f* qui n'est pas dans le coup COMP **lame duck** N (= *failure*) canard *m* boiteux ; *(US Pol) homme politique non réélu qui assure l'intérim en attendant l'entrée en fonction de son successeur*

lamé /ˈlɑːmeɪ/ N lamé *m* COMP en lamé ◆ **gold** ~ **jacket** veste *f* lamée or

lamebrain * /ˈleɪmbreɪn/ N crétin(e) *m(f)*

lamebrained * /ˈleɪmbreɪnd/ ADJ crétin

lamely /ˈleɪmlɪ/ ADV *[say, ask]* sans conviction ◆ **to argue** ~ **(that ...)** avancer des arguments boiteux (selon lesquels ...)

lameness /ˈleɪmnɪs/ N *(lit)* claudication *f (frm)*, boiterie *f* ; *(of excuse)* faiblesse *f*

lament /ləˈment/ N 1 lamentation *f* 2 (= *poem*) élégie *f* ; (= *song*) complainte *f* ; *(at funerals)* chant *m* funèbre ; *(for bagpipes etc)* lamentation *f* VT *[+ loss, lack]* regretter ◆ **to** ~ **sb's death** pleurer la mort de qn ◆ **to** ~ **the fact that ...** regretter que ... + *subj* ◆ **"she doesn't believe me!", he ~ed** "elle ne me croit pas !", gémit-il *or* se lamenta-t-il ◆ **our (late)** ~**ed sister** notre regrettée sœur ◆ **the late ~ed James Rose** le regretté James Rose VI se lamenter *(for sur)* ◆ **to** ~ **over one's lost youth** pleurer sa jeunesse perdue

lamentable /ˈlæməntəbl/ ADJ *[state, situation, performance]* lamentable, déplorable ; *[incident]* fâcheux, regrettable

lamentably /ˈlæməntəblɪ/ ADV lamentablement ◆ **there are still** ~ **few women surgeons** il est déplorable qu'il y ait toujours aussi peu de femmes chirurgiens ◆ **there are, ~, no set rules** il n'y a pas, on peut le déplorer, de règles établies

lamentation /ˌlæmənˈteɪʃən/ N lamentation *f* ◆ **(the Book of) Lamentations** *(Bible)* le livre des Lamentations

laminate /ˈlæmɪneɪt/ VT *[+ metal]* laminer ; *[+ book jacket]* plastifier N stratifié *m*

laminated /ˈlæmɪneɪtɪd/ ADJ *[metal]* laminé ; *[glass]* feuilleté ; *[windscreen]* (en verre) feuilleté ; *[book, jacket]* plastifié ◆ ~ **wood** contreplaqué *m*

lamp /læmp/ N 1 (= *light*) lampe *f* ; *[of vehicle]* feu *m* ; → **blowlamp, safety, streetlamp** 2 (= *bulb*) ampoule *f* ◆ **100-watt** ~ ampoule *f* de 100 watts
COMP **lamp bracket** N applique *f*
lamp standard N réverbère *m*

lampblack /ˈlæmpblæk/ N noir *m* de fumée *or* de carbone

lampern /ˈlæmpən/ N lamproie *f* de rivière

lamplight /ˈlæmplaɪt/ N ◆ **by** ~ à la lumière de la (*or* d'une) lampe

lamplighter /ˈlæmplaɪtəʳ/ N allumeur *m* de réverbères

lamplit /ˈlæmplɪt/ ADJ éclairé (par une lampe)

lampoon /læmˈpuːn/ N *(gen)* virulente satire *f* ; *(written)* pamphlet *m*, libelle *m* ; *(spoken)* diatribe *f* VT *[+ person, action, quality]* tourner en dérision ; *(in song)* chansonner

lampoonist /læmˈpuːnɪst/ N *(gen)* satiriste *m* ; (= *writer*) pamphlétaire *m* ; (= *singer*) chansonnier *m*

lamppost /ˈlæmpˌpəʊst/ N réverbère *m*

lamprey /ˈlæmprɪ/ N lamproie *f*

lampshade /ˈlæmpʃeɪd/ N abat-jour *m inv*

lampstand /ˈlæmpstænd/ N pied *m* de lampe

LAN /læn/ N *(Comput)* (abbrev of **local area network)** → **local**

lanai /ləˈnaɪ/ N *(US)* véranda *f*

Lancaster /ˈlæŋkəstəʳ/ N *(Geog)* Lancaster ; *(Hist)* Lancastre

Lancastrian /læŋˈkæstrɪən/ ADJ *(Geog)* lancastrien, de Lancaster ; *(Hist)* de Lancastre N Lancastrien(ne) *m(f)*, natif *m*, -ive *f or* habitant(e) *m(f)* de Lancaster ; *(Hist)* Lancastrien(ne) *m(f)*, natif *m*, -ive *f or* habitant(e) *m(f)* de Lancastre

lance /lɑːns/ N 1 (= *weapon*) lance *f* ; (= *soldier*) lancier *m* 2 *(Med)* lancette *f*, bistouri *m* VT *[+ abscess]* percer ; *[+ finger]* ouvrir COMP **lance corporal** N *(Brit Mil)* caporal *m*

lancer /ˈlɑːnsəʳ/ N (= *soldier*) lancier *m*

lancet /ˈlɑːnsɪt/ N *(Med)* lancette *f*, bistouri *m* COMP **lancet window** N *(Archit)* fenêtre *f* en ogive

Lancs. /læŋks/ N abbrev of **Lancashire**

land /lænd/ N 1 *(NonC: as opposed to sea)* terre *f* ◆ **on** ~ à terre ◆ **over** ~ **and sea** sur terre et sur mer ◆ **dry** ~ terre *f* ferme ◆ **on dry** ~ sur la terre ferme ◆ **to sight** ~ apercevoir la terre ◆ **to go by** ~ voyager par voie de terre ◆ **to make** ~ toucher terre ◆ **to see how the** ~ **lies, to find out the lie** *(Brit) or* **the lay** *(US)* **of the** ~ tâter le terrain, prendre le vent* ◆ **(for)** ~**'s sake!** * *(US)* juste ciel ! *(liter)*
2 *(NonC: Agr)* terre *f* ; (= *countryside*) campagne *f* ◆ **many people have left the** ~ beaucoup d'agriculteurs ont cessé leur activité et quitté la campagne ◆ **to work (on) the** ~ travailler la terre ◆ **to live off the** ~ vivre de la terre ◆ **agricultural** ~ *(suitable for agriculture)* terres *fpl* cultivables ; *(used for agriculture)* terres *fpl* agricoles ◆ **fertile** ~ terre *f* fertile ◆ **grazing** ~ pâturage *m*
3 (= *property*) *(large)* terre(s) *f(pl)* ; *(smaller)* terrain *m* ◆ **she's bought a piece of** ~ elle a acheté un terrain ◆ **get off my** ~! sortez de mon terrain *or* de mes terres !
4 (= *country, nation*) pays *m* ◆ **people of many** ~**s** des gens de nationalités diverses ◆ **throughout the** ~ dans tout le pays ◆ **a** ~ **of contrasts** une terre de contrastes ◆ **a** ~ **of opportunity** un pays où tout le monde a ses chances ◆ **a** ~ **fit for heroes** un pays digne de ses héros ◆ **to be in the** ~ **of the living** être encore de ce monde ◆ ~ **of milk and honey** *or* **flowing with milk and honey** pays *m* de cocagne ◆ **in the Land of Nod** au pays des rêves ; → **law, native, promised**
VT 1 *[+ cargo]* décharger, débarquer ; *[+ passengers]* débarquer ; *[+ aircraft]* poser ; *[+ fish]* prendre ◆ **to** ~ **a blow on sb's cheek/mouth, to** ~ **sb a blow on the cheek/mouth** frapper qn sur la joue/bouche
2 (* = *obtain*) *[+ job, contract, prize]* décrocher*
3 *(Brit* * = *cause to be)* ◆ **to** ~ **sb in it** mettre qn dans de beaux draps *or* dans le pétrin* ◆ **that will** ~ **you in trouble** ça va vous attirer des ennuis ◆ **to** ~ **sb in debt** endetter qn ◆ **buying the house ~ed him in debt** en achetant la maison, il s'est endetté ◆ **that's what ~ed him in jail** c'est comme ça qu'il s'est retrouvé en prison ◆ **his outspoken comments ~ed him in court for slander** son franc-parler lui a valu un procès en diffamation
4 *(Brit* *) ◆ **to be ~ed with sth** (= *left with*) avoir qch *or* rester avec qch sur les bras ; (= *forced to take on*) récolter qch*, devoir se coltiner qch* ◆ **now we're ~ed with all this extra work** maintenant il faut qu'on se coltine* *subj* tout ce boulot* en plus ◆ **I've got ~ed with this job** on m'a collé* ce travail ◆ **being overdrawn could** ~ **you with big bank charges** avec un découvert, vous pourriez vous retrouver à payer d'importants frais bancaires
VI 1 *[aircraft]* atterrir, se poser ; *(on sea)* amerrir ; *(on ship's deck)* apponter ◆ **to** ~ **on the moon** *[rocket, spacecraft]* alunir, se poser sur la lune ; *[person]* atterrir sur la lune ◆ **we ~ed at Orly** nous avons atterri à Orly ◆ **as the plane was coming in to** ~ comme l'avion s'apprêtait à atterrir
2 *[person, object] (gen)* retomber ; (= *fall*) tomber ; *[ski jumper, gymnast]* retomber, se recevoir ◆ **he slipped and ~ed heavily on his arm** il a glissé et est tombé lourdement sur le bras ◆ **to**

~ **awkwardly** mal retomber ◆ **to ~ on sth** *[falling object]* tomber sur qch ; *[person or animal jumping]* retomber *or* atterrir* sur qch ; *[bird, insect]* se poser sur qch ◆ **to ~ on one's feet** *(lit, fig)* retomber sur ses pieds
3 *(from boat)* débarquer
COMP *[breeze]* de terre ; *[prices]* des terrains ; *[defences]* terrestre ; *[law, policy, reform]* agraire ; *[tax]* foncier
land agent N (= *steward*) régisseur *m* ; (= *estate agent*) agent *m* immobilier
land army N ⇒ **land forces**
the (Women's) Land Army N *(Brit) pendant les deux guerres mondiales, corps composé de femmes, chargé des travaux agricoles en l'absence des hommes*
land forces NPL armée *f* de terre, forces *fpl* terrestres
land girl N *(Brit)* membre *m* de la Land Army
land grant college N *(US)* établissement *m* d'enseignement supérieur *(créé grâce à une donation foncière du gouvernement fédéral)*
land line N *(Telec)* ligne *f* terrestre
land mass N bloc *m* continental
land-office N *(US fig)* ◆ **to do a ~-office business** * faire d'excellentes affaires
land ownership N propriété *f* foncière
land patent N *(US)* titre *m* (constitutif) de propriété foncière
land-poor farmer N *(US)* fermier *m* riche en terre mais pauvre en disponibilités
land reform N réforme *f* agraire
land registry N *(Brit)* ≃ bureau *m* du cadastre
Land Rover ® N Land Rover *f*, landrover *f*
Land's End N *(Geog)* Land's End *(pointe sud-ouest de l'Angleterre)*
land worker N ouvrier *m*, -ière *f* agricole
land yacht N char *m* à voile
► **land up** * VI atterrir*, (finir par) se retrouver ◆ **to ~ up in Paris/in jail** atterrir* *or* finir par se retrouver à Paris/en prison ◆ **the report ~ed up on my desk** le rapport a atterri* *or* a fini par arriver sur mon bureau ◆ **we finally ~ed up in a small café** nous avons fini par échouer *or* nous retrouver dans un petit café

landau /ˈlændɔː/ N landau *m (véhicule)*

landed /ˈlændɪd/ ADJ *[proprietor]* foncier, terrien ; *[property]* foncier
COMP **landed gentry** N aristocratie *f* terrienne
landed price N *(Comm)* prix *m* débarqué *or* au débarquement

landfall /ˈlændfɔːl/ N terre *f (aperçue d'un navire)* ◆ **to make ~** (= *see land*) apercevoir la terre ; (= *make land*) accoster

landfill /ˈlændfɪl/ N enfouissement *m* des déchets ◆ **~ site** site *m* d'enfouissement (des déchets)

landing¹ /ˈlændɪŋ/ N 1 *[of aircraft, spacecraft etc]* atterrissage *m* ; *(on sea)* amerrissage *m* ; *(on moon)* alunissage *m* ; *(on deck)* appontage *m* ; → **crash¹, pancake, soft**
2 *(from ship)* débarquement *m* ◆ **the Normandy ~s** *(Mil Hist)* le débarquement (du 6 juin 1944)
3 *[of jumper, gymnast]* réception *f*
COMP **landing card** N carte *f* de débarquement
landing craft N *(Mil)* chaland *m or* navire *m* de débarquement
landing field N terrain *m* d'aviation
landing force N *(Mil)* troupes *fpl* de débarquement
landing gear N *[of plane]* train *m* d'atterrissage
landing ground N terrain *m* d'atterrissage
landing lights NPL *(on aircraft)* phares *mpl* d'atterrissage ; *(on ground)* balises *fpl* (d'atterrissage)
landing net N *(Fishing)* épuisette *f*
landing party N *(from ship)* détachement *m* de débarquement
landing stage N *(Brit)* débarcadère *m*, appontement *m*
landing strip N piste *f* d'atterrissage
landing wheels NPL roues *fpl* du train d'atterrissage

landing² /ˈlændɪŋ/ N *(between stairs)* palier *m* ; (= *storey*) étage *m*

landlady /ˈlændˌleɪdɪ/ N *[of flat, house] (gen)* propriétaire *f* ; (= *live-in owner*) logeuse *f* ; *(Brit) [of pub, guest house]* patronne *f*

landless /ˈlændlɪs/ ADJ sans terre

landlocked /ˈlændlɒkt/ ADJ (= *totally enclosed*) *[country]* enclavé, sans accès à la mer ; *[lake]* qui ne communique pas avec la mer ; (= *almost totally enclosed*) entouré par les terres

landlord /ˈlændˌlɔːd/ N *[of flat, house] (gen)* propriétaire *m* ; (= *live-in owner*) logeur *m* ; *(Brit) [of pub, guest house]* patron *m*

landlubber* /ˈlændˌlʌbəʳ/ N *(hum)* marin *m* d'eau douce *(pej)*

landmark /ˈlændmɑːk/ N 1 *(for navigating)* point *m* de repère ◆ **we used the castle as a ~** le château nous a servi de point de repère 2 (= *famous sight*) *(monument)* grand monument *m* ; *(natural phenomenon)* grand site *m* ◆ **one of the ~s of historic Prague** l'un des grands monuments du vieux Prague 3 (= *momentous event, achievement etc*) jalon *m* ◆ **a ~ in the history of cinema** un jalon dans l'histoire du cinéma ADJ *[decision, ruling, victory]* historique ◆ **this was hailed as a ~ decision** cette décision a été jugée historique ◆ **this is a ~ event** il s'agit d'un événement historique *or* qui fera date

landmine /ˈlændmaɪn/ N mine *f* terrestre

landowner /ˈlændəʊnəʳ/ N propriétaire *m* terrien

landowning /ˈlændəʊnɪŋ/ ADJ *[family]* de propriétaires terriens ◆ **the ~ class** les propriétaires *mpl* terriens

landscape /ˈlændˌskeɪp/ N (= *land, view, picture*) paysage *m* VT *[+ garden]* dessiner ; *[+ bomb site, dirty place etc]* aménager ADJ, ADV *(Comput)* en format paysage
COMP **landscape architect** N architecte *mf* paysagiste
landscape gardener N jardinier *m*, -ière *f* paysagiste
landscape gardening N jardinage *m* paysagiste, paysagisme *m*
landscape mode N *(Comput)* ◆ **to print sth in ~ mode** imprimer qch en format paysage
landscape painter N (peintre *m*) paysagiste *mf*

landscaping /ˈlændˌskeɪpɪŋ/ N *(NonC)* aménagements *mpl* paysagers

landslide /ˈlændˌslaɪd/ N glissement *m* de terrain ; *(loose rocks etc)* éboulement *m* ; *fig Pol:* also **landslide victory**) victoire *f* écrasante ◆ **to win by a ~, to win a ~ victory** remporter une victoire écrasante ◆ **~ majority** majorité *f* écrasante VI *(US Pol)* remporter une victoire électorale écrasante

landslip /ˈlændslɪp/ N *(esp Brit)* glissement *m* de terrain ; *[of loose rocks etc]* éboulement *m*

landward /ˈlændwəd/ ADJ (situé *or* dirigé) du côté de la terre ◆ **~ breeze** brise *f* de mer ◆ **~ side** côté *m* terre ADV (also **landwards**) vers *or* en direction de la terre, vers l'intérieur

lane /leɪn/ N 1 *(in country)* chemin *m*, petite route *f* ; *(in town)* ruelle *f*
2 (= *part of road*) voie *f* ; (= *line of traffic*) file *f* ◆ **"keep in lane"** *ne changez pas de file* ◆ **"get in lane"** *mettez-vous dans or sur la bonne file* ◆ **(to be in) the left-hand ~** (être *or* rouler sur) la voie de gauche ◆ **three-~ road** route *f* à trois voies ◆ **I'm in the wrong ~** je suis dans *or* sur la mauvaise file ◆ **traffic was reduced to a single ~** on ne roulait plus que sur une seule file
3 *(for aircraft, ships, runners, swimmers)* couloir *m* ◆ **air/shipping ~** couloir *m* aérien/de navigation
COMP **lane closure** N fermeture *f* de voie(s) de circulation ◆ **there'll be ~ closures on the M1** certaines voies seront fermées à la circulation sur la M1
lane markings NPL signalisation *f* au sol des voies, signalisation *f* horizontale

langlauf /ˈlɑːŋˌlaʊf/ N *(Ski)* ski *m* de fond ◆ **~ specialist** fondeur *m*, -euse *f* ◆ **~ skier** skieur *m*, -euse *f* de fond

language /ˈlæŋgwɪdʒ/ N 1 (= *particular tongue*) langue *f* ◆ **the French ~** la langue française ◆ **English has become the international ~ of business** l'anglais est devenu la langue internationale des affaires ◆ **he's studying ~s** il fait des études de langues ; → **dead, source**
2 *(NonC = ability to talk)* langage *m* ◆ **the faculty of ~** le langage ◆ **animal ~** le langage des animaux ◆ **the origin of ~** l'origine du langage ◆ **how do children acquire ~?** comment se fait l'acquisition du langage chez les enfants ? ◆ **speaking is one aspect of ~** la parole est l'un des aspects du langage ◆ **he's studying ~** il étudie les sciences du langage
3 (= *specialized terminology: also Comput*) langage *m* ◆ **the formal ~ of official documents** le langage conventionnel des documents officiels ◆ **scientific/legal ~** langage *m* scientifique/juridique ◆ **the ~ of art/science/flowers** le langage de l'art/de la science/des fleurs ◆ **we're not speaking the same ~ here** *(fig)* nous ne parlons pas le même langage ◆ **to speak the ~ of diplomacy/violence** parler le langage de la diplomatie/violence ; → **machine, sign**
4 *(NonC = individual's manner of expression)* langage *m* ◆ **(watch your) ~!** * surveille ton langage ! ◆ **strong** *or* **bad** *or* **foul ~** gros mots *mpl*, grossièretés *fpl*
COMP *[studies, teacher, textbooks, department, school]* de langues ; *[students, degree]* en langues ; *[development]* langagier, linguistique ; *[ability]* à s'exprimer
language barrier N barrière *f* linguistique *or* de la langue
language laboratory, language lab* N laboratoire *m* de langues ◆ **~ lab training** *or* **practice** entraînement *m* en cabines
language school N école *f* de langues

languid /ˈlæŋgwɪd/ ADJ languissant

languidly /ˈlæŋgwɪdlɪ/ ADV avec langueur ◆ **~ graceful/elegant** d'une grâce/élégance langoureuse

languidness /ˈlæŋgwɪdnɪs/ N langueur *f*

languish /ˈlæŋgwɪʃ/ VI *(gen)* (se) languir ; *(in prison)* se morfondre, dépérir

languishing /ˈlæŋgwɪʃɪŋ/ ADJ languissant, langoureux

languor /ˈlæŋgəʳ/ N langueur *f*

languorous /ˈlæŋgərəs/ ADJ langoureux, alangui

lank /læŋk/ ADJ *[hair]* raide et terne ; *[grass, plant]* long (longue *f*) et grêle

lanky /ˈlæŋkɪ/ ADJ grand et maigre, dégingandé

lanolin /ˈlænəʊlɪn/ N lanoline *f*

lantern /ˈlæntən/ N *(all senses)* lanterne *f* ; *(in paper)* lanterne *f* vénitienne, lampion *m* ; → **Chinese, magic**
COMP **lantern-jawed** ADJ aux joues creuses
lantern slide N plaque *f* de lanterne magique

lanthanum /ˈlænθənəm/ N lanthane *m*

lanyard /ˈlænjəd/ N *(gen, Mil)* cordon *m* ; *(Naut)* ride *f* (de hauban)

Lao /laʊ/ N *(pl inv)* Lao *mpl*

Laos /laʊs/ N Laos *m* ◆ **in ~** au Laos

Laotian /'laʊʃɪən/ ADJ laotien N 1 (= *person*) Laotien(ne) *m(f)* 2 (= *language*) laotien *m*

Laotze /'laʊ'tzeɪ/, **Lao-tzu** /'laʊ'tsuː/ N Laozi *m*, Lao-tseu *m*

lap¹ /læp/ N (= *knees*) genoux *mpl*, giron *m* (*gen hum*) ◆ **sitting on his mother's** ~ assis sur les genoux de sa mère ◆ **with her hands in her** ~ les mains sur les genoux ◆ **it fell right into his** ~ * (*fig*) ça lui est tombé tout cuit dans le bec* ◆ **they dropped the problem in his** ~ ils lui ont laissé *or* collé* le problème (à résoudre) ◆ **it's in the** ~ **of the gods** on ne peut que s'en remettre au destin ◆ **(to live) in the** ~ **of luxury** (vivre) dans le plus grand luxe

COMP **lap and shoulder belt** N ceinture *f* (de sécurité) trois points

lap dancer N strip-teaseuse *f* (*qui s'assoit sur les genoux des clients*)

lap dancing N (*esp US*) *numéro de strip-tease où une danseuse s'assoit sur les genoux d'un client*

lap robe N (US) plaid *m* (*pour les genoux*)

lap² /læp/ N (*Sport*) tour *m* de piste ◆ **to run a** ~ faire un tour de piste ◆ **ten-~ race** course *f* en *or* sur dix tours ◆ **on the 10th** ~ au 10e tour ◆ ~ **of honour** (*esp Brit*) tour *m* d'honneur ◆ **we're on the last** ~ (*fig*) on a fait le plus gros *or* le plus difficile, on tient le bon bout* VT (*Sport*) [+ *runner, car*] prendre un tour d'avance sur VI (*Racing*) ◆ **the car was ~ping at 200km/h** la voiture faisait le circuit à 200 km/h de moyenne

lap³ /læp/ VT [+ *milk*] laper VI [*waves*] clapoter (*against* contre)

► **lap up** VT SEP 1 [+ *milk etc*] laper 2 (* *fig*) [+ *information, congratulations, compliments*] avaler, gober ; [+ *attention*] se délecter de ◆ **he ~s up everything you say** il gobe* tout ce qu'on lui dit ◆ **he fairly ~ped it up** il buvait du petit-lait* ◆ **the media are ~ping up this latest scandal** les médias se délectent de *or* font leurs choux gras* de ce dernier scandale

lap⁴ /læp/ VT (= *wrap*) enrouler (*round* autour de) envelopper (*in* de)

► **lap over** VI [*tiles etc*] se chevaucher

laparoscopy /ˌlæpə'rɒskəpɪ/ N laparoscopie *f*, cœlioscopie *f*

laparotomy /ˌlæpə'rɒtəmɪ/ N laparotomie *f*

La Paz /læ'pæz/ N La Paz

lapdog /'læpdɒg/ N petit chien *m* d'appartement, chien *m* de manchon †

lapel /lə'pel/ N revers *m* (*de veston etc*) ◆ ~ **microphone,** ~ **mike*** micro *m* cravate

lapidary /'læpɪdərɪ/ N (= *craftsman*) lapidaire *m* ; (= *craft*) art *m or* métier *m* du lapidaire

lapin /'læpɪn/ N (US) (fourrure *f or* peau *f* de) lapin *m*

lapis lazuli /'læpɪs'læzjʊlaɪ/ N (= *stone*) lapis (-lazuli) *m* ; (= *colour*) bleu *m* lapis(-lazuli)

Lapland /'læpˌlænd/ N Laponie *f*

Laplander /'læpˌlændəʳ/ N Lapon(e) *m(f)*

Lapp /læp/ ADJ lapon(-one *f*) N 1 Lapon(e) *m(f)* 2 (= *language*) lapon *m*

lapping /'læpɪŋ/ N [*of waves*] clapotis *m*

Lappish /'læpɪʃ/ ADJ, N ⇒ **Lapp**

lapse /læps/ N 1 (= *fault*) faute *f* (légère), défaillance *f* ; (= *in behaviour*) écart *m* (de conduite) ◆ **a** ~ **into bad habits** un retour à de mauvaises habitudes ◆ **~s of (good) taste** des fautes *fpl* de goût ◆ **a serious security** ~ une grave défaillance des services de sécurité ◆ **~s of judgement** des erreurs *fpl* de jugement ◆ ~ **of memory, memory** ~ trou *m* de mémoire ◆ ~ **from a diet** entorse *f* à un régime ◆ **a momentary** ~ **of concentration** *or* **attention** un moment d'inattention

2 (= *passage of time*) intervalle *m* ◆ **a** ~ **of time, a time** ~ un laps de temps ◆ **after a** ~ **of ten weeks** au bout de dix semaines, après un intervalle de dix semaines

3 (= *falling into disuse*) [*of custom etc*] disparition *f*, oubli *m* ; [*of right, privilege*] déchéance *f*

VI 1 (= *err*) faire un or des écart(s)

2 (*Rel*) cesser de pratiquer ◆ **to** ~ **from grace** perdre l'état de grâce

3 ◆ **to** ~ **into bad habits** prendre de mauvaises habitudes *or* un mauvais pli ◆ **to** ~ **into silence** se taire ◆ **to** ~ **into unconsciousness** (re)perdre connaissance ◆ **to** ~ **into a coma** tomber dans le coma ◆ **he ~d into reverie** il s'est laissé aller à la rêverie ◆ **he ~d into French** il est repassé au français, il s'est remis à parler français ◆ **she ~d into legal jargon** elle s'est remise à parler le jargon juridique

4 [*act, law*] devenir caduc, tomber en désuétude ; [*contract*] expirer, venir à expiration ; [*ticket, passport*] se périmer ; [*membership, subscription*] prendre fin, venir à expiration ◆ **her insurance policy has ~d** sa police d'assurance est périmée *or* n'est plus valable

lapsed /læpst/ ADJ [*contract, law*] caduc (-uque *f*) ; [*ticket, passport*] périmé ◆ **a** ~ **Catholic** un(e) catholique qui ne pratique plus

laptop (computer) /'læptɒpkəm'pjuːtəʳ/ N (ordinateur *m*) portable *m*

lapwing /'læpwɪŋ/ N vanneau *m*

larboard †† /'lɑːbəd/ (*Naut*) N bâbord *m* ADJ de bâbord

larceny /'lɑːsənɪ/ N (*Jur*) vol *m* simple ◆ **to commit** ~ **by servant** (*US Jur*) commanditer un vol ; → **grand, petty**

larch /lɑːtʃ/ N mélèze *m*

lard /lɑːd/ N saindoux *m* VT (*Culin*) larder (*with* de) ◆ **a speech ~ed with quotations/references to ...** un discours bourré *or* truffé de citations/références à ...

> ⚠ **lard** in French means 'bacon'.

larder /'lɑːdəʳ/ N (= *cupboard*) garde-manger *m inv* ; (= *small room*) cellier *m*

large /lɑːdʒ/ ADJ [*area, town, house, garden, company, object, amount, problem*] grand ; [*person, animal, hand, slice, piece*] gros (grosse *f*) ; [*dose*] fort ; [*sum, share, proportion, group*] important ; [*population*] nombreux, important ; [*family, crowd*] nombreux ; [*losses*] lourd, important ; [*meal*] copieux, grand ◆ **to get** *or* **grow ~(r)** [*stomach*] grossir ; [*population, overdraft*] augmenter ◆ **to make ~r** agrandir ◆ **"large"** (*on clothing label*) L ◆ **the** ~ **size** (*of packet, tube*) le grand modèle ◆ **the ~st size of this dress** la plus grande taille dans ce modèle de robe ◆ **a** ~ **number of them refused** beaucoup d'entre eux ont refusé ◆ ~ **numbers of people came** les gens sont venus nombreux *or* en grand nombre ◆ **a** ~ **slice of his savings** une bonne partie de ses économies ◆ **a** ~ **proportion of the business** une part importante des affaires ◆ **to do sth on a** ~ **scale** faire qch sur une grande échelle *or* en grand ; see also **large-scale** ◆ **to a** ~ **extent** dans une grande mesure ◆ **in (a)** ~ **measure** en grande partie, dans une large mesure ◆ **in** ~ **part** en grande partie ◆ **there he was (as)** ~ **as life** c'était bien lui ◆ **~r than life** [*character*] plus vrai que nature

◆ **at large** (= *at liberty*) en liberté ; (*US Pol*) [*candidate, congressman*] non rattaché à une circonscription électorale ◆ **the prisoner is still at** ~ le prisonnier court toujours *or* est toujours en liberté ◆ **the country/population at** ~ (= *as a whole*) le pays/la population dans son ensemble ; → **ambassador**

◆ **by and large** d'une façon générale, en gros ◆ **taking it by and** ~ à tout prendre

VT ◆ **to** ~ **it*** (*Brit*) faire la fête

COMP **large-hearted** ADJ au grand cœur

large intestine N gros intestin *m*

large-minded ADJ large d'esprit

large-mouth bass N achigan *m* à grande bouche

large-print book N livre *m* imprimé en gros caractères

large-scale ADJ

1 (= *extensive*) [*operation, reforms, research*] de grande envergure ; [*production, fraud*] à grande échelle ; [*immigration, aid, redundancies*] massif ; [*attack*] vaste ; [*unrest*] général 2 [*drawing, map*] à grande échelle 3 (*Comput*) ◆ **very ~-scale integration** intégration *f* à (très) grande échelle

large-size(d) ADJ grand

> ⚠ **large** is rarely translated by the French word **large**, which means 'wide'.

largely /'lɑːdʒlɪ/ ADV [*ignore, forget*] pratiquement ; [*correct, responsible, irrelevant, unchanged*] en grande partie ◆ ~ **forgotten/unnoticed** pratiquement oublié/inaperçu ◆ **the traffic consisted** ~ **of bicycles** le trafic se composait en grande partie de vélos ◆ **these estimates are based** ~ **on conjecture** ces estimations s'appuient en grande partie sur des conjectures ◆ **the town was** ~ **untouched by the hurricane** la ville a été presque complètement épargnée par l'ouragan ◆ **the phenomenon appears to be** ~ **confined to coastal areas** ce phénomène semble presque exclusivement circonscrit aux régions côtières ◆ ~ **because** principalement parce que, surtout parce que ◆ **thanks** ~ **to** notamment grâce à, en raison notamment de

> ⚠ **largely** is not translated by **largement**, which does not mean 'mainly'.

largeness /'lɑːdʒnɪs/ N (= *size*) [*of person, body, object*] grande taille *f* ; [*of number, amount*] importance *f* ; (*fig*) (= *breadth*) largesse *f*

largesse /lɑː'ʒes/ N (*NonC*) (= *generosity*) largesse *f* ; (= *gifts*) largesses *fpl*

largish* /'lɑːdʒɪʃ/ ADJ assez grand ; [*person, body, object*] assez gros (grosse *f*) ; [*amount, proportion*] assez important

largo /'lɑːgəʊ/ ADV, N largo *m inv*

lariat /'lærɪət/ N (= *lasso*) lasso *m* ; (= *tether*) longe *f*

lark¹ /lɑːk/ N (= *bird*) alouette *f* ◆ **to be up** *or* **rise with the** ~ se lever au chant du coq ; → **happy, sing**

lark² †* /lɑːk/ N blague *f* ◆ **we only did it for a** ~ on l'a seulement fait pour rigoler*, on l'a seulement fait histoire de rigoler* ◆ **what a ~!** quelle rigolade !*, la bonne blague ! ◆ **I don't believe in all this horoscope** ~ je ne crois pas à ces histoires d'horoscope

► **lark about*, lark around*** VI faire le fou* ◆ **they were ~ing about with a ball/on their bikes** ils s'amusaient avec une balle/leurs vélos

larkspur /'lɑːkspɜːʳ/ N (= *plant*) pied-d'alouette *m*

larky /'lɑːkɪ/ ADJ espiègle

Larry /'lærɪ/ N (dim of **Laurence, Lawrence**) ; see also **happy**

larva /'lɑːvə/ N (pl **larvae** /'lɑːviː/) larve *f* (*Zool*)

larval /'lɑːvəl/ ADJ larvaire (*Zool*)

laryngitis /ˌlærɪn'dʒaɪtɪs/ N laryngite *f*

larynx /'lærɪŋks/ N (pl **larynxes** *or* **larynges** /lə'rɪndʒiːz/) larynx *m*

lasagna, lasagne /lə'zænjə/ N lasagnes *fpl*

lascivious /lə'sɪvɪəs/ ADJ lascif, luxurieux

lasciviously /lə'sɪvɪəslɪ/ ADV lascivement

lasciviousness /lə'sɪvɪəsnɪs/ N luxure *f*, lascivité *f*

laser /'leɪzəʳ/ N laser *m*

COMP **laser beam** N rayon *m* laser

laser disk N disque *m* laser

laser-guided ADJ *(Mil)* guidé par laser
laser printer N imprimante *f* laser
laser proof N épreuve *f* laser
laser show N spectacle *m* laser
laser surgery N chirurgie *f* au laser
laser weapon N arme *f* laser

lash /læʃ/ N 1 *(= blow from whip)* coup *m* de fouet ◆ **sentenced to ten ~es** condamné à dix coups de fouet ◆ **to feel the ~ of sb's tongue** essuyer les propos cinglants de qn ; → **whiplash**
2 *(also* **eyelash***)* cil *m*
3 *(= thong)* mèche *f*, lanière *f*
VT 1 *[person] (= beat)* frapper (d'un grand coup de fouet), fouetter violemment ; *(= flog)* flageller
2 *[storm]* s'abattre sur ; *[wind]* cingler, fouetter ; *[waves]* fouetter ◆ **the wind ~ed the sea into a fury** le vent a déchaîné la mer ◆ **the storm has been ~ing the Bahamas with high winds and heavy rain** de violentes bourrasques de vent et de pluie se sont abattues sur les Bahamas ◆ **the hailstones ~ed my face** la grêle me cinglait le visage ◆ **to ~ sb with one's tongue** faire des remarques cinglantes à qn
3 ◆ **the lion ~ed its tail** le lion a fouetté l'air de sa queue
4 *(= fasten)* attacher *or* fixer fermement ; *[+ cargo]* arrimer ; *[+ load]* attacher, amarrer ◆ **to ~ sth to a post** attacher solidement qch à un piquet ◆ **he ~ed himself to the life raft** il s'est attaché *or* amarré solidement au radeau de sauvetage
VI ◆ **the rain was ~ing against the window** la pluie fouettait *or* cinglait les carreaux

► **lash about** VI *(in bonds, in pain etc)* se débattre violemment

► **lash down** VI *[rain]* tomber avec violence
VT SEP *[+ cargo]* arrimer

► **lash out** VI 1 ◆ **to lash out at sb (with one's fists/a knife)** envoyer des coups (de poing/de couteau) à qn ◆ **she ~ed out with her fists** elle s'est débattue à coups de poing ◆ **to ~ out at sb** *(verbally)* s'en prendre violemment à qn
2 *(* = spend a lot of money)* faire une folie* ◆ **he ~ed out on a car** il a fait une folie* et s'est payé une voiture
VT SEP * *[+ money]* lâcher*, allonger*

► **lash up** VT SEP *[+ person, dog]* attacher ; *[+ boat]* attacher, amarrer

lashing /ˈlæʃɪŋ/ N 1 *(= flogging)* flagellation *f* ◆ **to give sb a ~** *(lit)* donner le fouet à qn ; *(fig: verbally)* réprimander sévèrement qn, tancer † vertement qn 2 *(= rope)* corde *f* ; *(Naut)* amarre *f* 3 *(esp Brit *)* **with ~s of cream/butter** avec une montagne *or* des tonnes de crème/beurre ◆ **~s of mascara** des tonnes de mascara

lass /læs/ N *(esp Scot and dial) (= girl)* jeune fille *f* ; *(† = sweetheart)* bonne amie † *f*

Lassa fever /ˈlæsəˈfiːvəʳ/ N fièvre *f* de Lassa

lassie /ˈlæsɪ/ N *(esp Scot and dial)* gamine* *f*, gosse* *f*

lassitude /ˈlæsɪtjuːd/ N lassitude *f*

lasso /læˈsuː/ N (pl **lassos** *or* **lassoes**) 1 *(= rope)* lasso *m* 2 *(Climbing)* ⇒ **lassoing** VT prendre au lasso

lassoing /læˈsuːɪŋ/ N *(Climbing)* lancer *m* de corde

last[1] /lɑːst/ ADJ 1 *(= final in series)* dernier *before n* ◆ **the ~ Saturday of the month** le dernier samedi du mois ◆ **the ~ ten pages** les dix dernières pages ◆ **~ but one, second ~** avant-dernier ◆ **the ~ time but one** l'avant-dernière fois ◆ **it's the ~ round but three** il ne reste plus que trois rounds (après celui-ci) ◆ **his office is the second ~** son bureau est l'avant-dernier ◆ **the third and ~ point is that ...** le troisième et dernier point est que ... ◆ **to fight to the ~ man** se battre jusqu'au dernier ◆ **to make it through to the ~ four** *(in tournament)* atteindre les demi-finales ; *(in race)* arriver dans les quatre premiers ; → **every**
2 *(= past, most recent)* dernier *gen after n* ◆ **~ night** *(= evening)* hier soir ; *(= night)* cette nuit, la nuit dernière ◆ **~ week/year** la semaine/l'année *f* dernière ◆ **~ month/summer** le mois/l'été *m* dernier ◆ **~ Monday, on Monday ~** lundi dernier ◆ **for the ~ few days** ces derniers jours, ces jours-ci ◆ **for the ~ few weeks** ces dernières semaines, depuis quelques semaines ◆ **he hasn't been seen these ~ two years** on ne l'a pas vu ces deux dernières années *or* depuis deux ans ◆ **for the ~ two years he has been ...** depuis deux ans il est ... ◆ **the day before ~** avant-hier ◆ **the night/morning before ~** avant-hier soir/matin ◆ **the week before ~** l'avant-dernière semaine ◆ **what did you do ~ time?** qu'avez-vous fait la dernière fois ? ◆ **he was ill (the) ~ time I saw him** il était malade la dernière fois que je l'ai vu ◆ **this time ~ year** l'an dernier à la même époque
3 *(= final) [chance, hope]* dernier ◆ **this is my ~ pound** c'est ma dernière livre ◆ **I'm down to my ~ pound** je n'ai plus *or* il ne me reste plus qu'une seule livre ◆ **he took the ~ sandwich** il a pris le dernier sandwich ◆ **at the ~ minute** à la dernière minute ; see also **comp** ◆ **that was the ~ time I saw him** c'est la dernière fois que je l'ai vu ◆ **that's the ~ time I lend you anything!** c'est la dernière fois que je te prête quelque chose ! ◆ **for the ~ time, shut up!** pour la dernière fois, tais-toi ! ◆ **~ thing (at night)** juste avant de se coucher ◆ **I'll get it, if it's the ~ thing I do** je l'aurai coûte que coûte *or* même si ça doit me coûter la vie ◆ **to fight to the ~ ditch** *(lit, fig)* se battre jusqu'au bout ; see also **comp** ◆ **at one's ~ gasp** *(= dying)* sur le point de mourir, à l'agonie ; *(* = exhausted)* à bout de force ; see also **comp** ◆ **he was on his ~ legs*** il était à bout ◆ **the company is on its ~ legs*** l'entreprise est au bord de la faillite ◆ **the washing machine is on its ~ legs*** la machine à laver va bientôt nous lâcher, la machine à laver va bientôt rendre l'âme ◆ **she always wants to have the ~ word** elle veut toujours avoir le dernier mot ◆ **it's the ~ word in comfort** c'est ce que l'on fait de mieux *or* c'est le dernier cri en matière de confort ; → **first, laugh, stand, straw**
4 *(= least likely or desirable)* dernier ◆ **he's the ~ person to ask** c'est la dernière personne à qui demander ◆ **that's the ~ thing to worry about** c'est le dernier *or* le cadet de mes *(or* tes *etc)* soucis
5 *(Rel)* ◆ **at the Last Judgement** au Jugement dernier ◆ **the ~ rites** les derniers sacrements *mpl* ◆ **the ~ trump** *or* **trumpet** la trompette du Jugement dernier
ADV 1 *(= at the end)* en dernier ◆ **she arrived ~** elle est arrivée en dernier *or* la dernière ◆ **he arrived ~ of all** il est arrivé le tout dernier ◆ **his horse came in ~** son cheval est arrivé (bon) dernier ◆ **~ but not least** enfin et surtout ◆ **~ in, first out** dernier entré, premier sorti ◆ **to leave sth/sb till ~** placer qch/qn en dernier *or* à la fin
2 *(= most recently)* la dernière fois ◆ **when I ~ saw him** quand je l'ai vu la dernière fois, la dernière fois que je l'ai vu ◆ **who dealt ~?** *(Cards)* qui a donné en dernier ?
3 *(= finally)* finalement, pour terminer ◆ **~, I would like to say ...** pour terminer *or* enfin, je voudrais dire ...
N dernier *m*, -ière *f* ◆ **he was the ~ of the Tudors** ce fut le dernier des Tudor ◆ **this is the ~ of the pears** *(one)* c'est la dernière poire ; *(several)* ce sont les dernières poires, voici le reste des poires ◆ **this is the ~ of the cider** c'est tout ce qui reste de *or* comme cidre ◆ **the ~ but one** l'avant-dernier *m*, -ière *f* ◆ **I'd be the ~ to criticize, but ...** ce n'est pas mon genre de critiquer, mais ..., j'ai horreur de critiquer, mais ... ◆ **each one better than the ~** tous meilleurs les uns que les autres ◆ **to stick to one's ~** *(fig)* s'en tenir à ce que l'on sait faire ◆ **to look one's ~ on sth** *(liter)* jeter un ultime regard sur qch ; → **breathe**
◆ **at (long) last** enfin, à la fin ◆ **at (long) ~** enfin ◆ **at long ~ he came** il a enfin fini par arriver ◆ **here he is! – at ~!** le voici ! – enfin *or* ce n'est pas trop tôt !
◆ **the last ...** *(= the end)* ◆ **we shall never hear the ~ of this** on n'a pas fini d'en entendre parler ◆ **you haven't heard the ~ of this!** vous n'avez pas fini d'en entendre parler ! ; *(threatening)* vous aurez de mes nouvelles ! ◆ **the ~ I heard (of her), she was abroad** aux dernières nouvelles, elle était à l'étranger ◆ **I shall be glad to see the ~ of this** je serai content de voir tout ceci terminé *or* de voir la fin de tout ceci ◆ **we were glad to see the ~ of him** nous avons été contents de le voir partir *or* d'être débarrassés de lui ◆ **that was the ~ I saw of him** c'est la dernière fois que je l'ai vu, je ne l'ai pas revu depuis
◆ **to the last** jusqu'au bout, jusqu'à la fin
COMP **last-chance saloon** N *(Brit)* ◆ **it's the ~-chance saloon for them** ◆ **they are drinking in the ~-chance saloon** c'est leur dernière chance
last-ditch, last-gasp ADJ ultime, de dernière minute
last-minute ADJ de dernière minute
last post N *(Brit) (= bugle call)* (sonnerie *f* de l')extinction *f* des feux ; *(at funerals)* sonnerie *f* aux morts
the Last Supper N *(Rel)* la Cène

last[2] /lɑːst/ VI 1 *(= continue) [pain, film, supplies etc]* durer ◆ **it ~ed two hours** cela a duré deux heures ◆ **it's too good to ~** c'est trop beau pour durer *or* pour que ça dure *subj* ◆ **will this good weather ~ till Saturday?** est-ce que le beau temps va durer *or* tenir jusqu'à samedi ?
2 *(= hold out)* tenir ◆ **no one ~s long in this job** personne ne reste longtemps dans ce poste ◆ **after he got pneumonia he didn't ~ long** après sa pneumonie il n'en a pas eu pour longtemps* ◆ **that whisky didn't ~ long** ce whisky n'a pas fait long feu *or* n'a pas duré longtemps
3 *(= remain usable)* durer ◆ **made to ~** fait pour durer ◆ **this table will ~ a lifetime** cette table vous fera toute une vie ◆ **will this material ~?** ce tissu fera-t-il de l'usage ?
VT durer ◆ **this amount should ~ you (for) a week** cela devrait vous durer *or* vous faire une semaine ◆ **I have enough money to ~ me a lifetime** j'ai assez d'argent pour tenir jusqu'à la fin de mes jours ◆ **she must have got enough chocolates to ~ her a lifetime** elle a dû recevoir assez de chocolats pour tenir jusqu'à la fin de ses jours

► **last out** VI *[person]* tenir (le coup) ; *[money]* suffire
VT SEP faire ◆ **he won't ~ the winter out** il ne passera pas *or* ne fera pas l'hiver*, il ne verra pas la fin de l'hiver ◆ **my money doesn't ~ out the month** mon argent ne me fait pas le mois

last[3] /lɑːst/ N *[of cobbler]* forme *f*

Lastex ® /ˈlasteks/ N *(US)* Lastex ® *m*

lasting /ˈlɑːstɪŋ/ ADJ *[friendship, situation, benefit, impression, effect]* durable ◆ **to cause ~ damage to sb/sth** affecter qn/qch de façon durable ◆ **to his ~ shame** à sa plus grande honte

lastly /ˈlɑːstlɪ/ ADV *(= as final point, item)* enfin, en dernier lieu ; *(= as final action)* enfin

latch /lætʃ/ N clenche *f*, loquet *m* ◆ **the door is on** *or* **off the ~** la porte n'est pas fermée à clé ◆ **to leave the door on** *or* **off the ~** fermer la porte sans la verrouiller VT fermer au loquet

► **latch on*** VI 1 *(= grab)* s'accrocher *(to* à) 2 *(= understand)* saisir, piger*

► **latch on to** * VT FUS 1 *(= get possession of)* prendre possession de ; *(= catch hold of)* saisir ; *(US)* *(= obtain)* se procurer ◆ **he ~ed on to me as soon as I arrived** il n'a pas arrêté de me coller* depuis que je suis arrivé ◆ **he ~es on to the slightest mistake** il ne laisse pas passer la moindre erreur 2 *(= understand)* saisir, piger* ; *(= realize)* se rendre compte de, réaliser* ◆ **when children ~ on to the idea that reading is fun** quand les enfants se rendent compte que la lecture est un plaisir

latchkey /'lætʃki:/ N clé *f* (de la porte d'entrée) COMP **latchkey child, latchkey kid** * N *enfant qui rentre à la maison avant ses parents*

late /leɪt/ (compar **later**, superl **latest**) ADJ 1 *(= delayed, after scheduled time)* ◆ **to be ~** *[person]* *(gen)* être en retard ; *(arriving)* arriver en retard ◆ **I'm ~** *(gen)* je suis en retard ; *(menstrual period)* j'ai du retard* *(euph)*, mes règles ont du retard ◆ **to be ~ (in) arriving** arriver avec du retard *or* en retard ◆ **she was ~ (in) returning from work** elle est rentrée du travail en retard ◆ **to be ~ for an appointment** être *or* arriver en retard à un rendez-vous ◆ **I was ~ for work** je suis arrivé au travail en retard ◆ **hurry up, I'm ~ for work** dépêche-toi, je vais arriver en retard au travail ◆ **to be ~ with sth** avoir du retard dans qch ◆ **I was ~ with the rent** *(now paid)* j'avais payé mon loyer en retard ◆ **the train is ~** le train est en retard *or* a du retard ◆ **your essay is ~** vous rendez votre dissertation en retard ◆ **too ~** trop tard ◆ **to make sb ~** mettre qn en retard ◆ **I apologized for my ~ arrival** je me suis excusé d'être arrivé en retard ◆ **we apologize for the ~ arrival of flight XY 709** nous vous prions d'excuser le retard du vol XY 709 ◆ **~ arrivals will not be admitted** les retardataires ne seront pas admis ◆ **his campaign got off to a ~ start** sa campagne a démarré tard ◆ **both my babies were ~** mes deux bébés sont nés *or* arrivés après terme

2 *(with time expressions)* ◆ **to be 20 minutes ~** avoir 20 minutes de retard ◆ **it made me an hour ~** j'ai eu une heure de retard à cause de ça ◆ **the train is 30 minutes ~** le train a 30 minutes de retard ◆ **I'm/I was two hours ~ for work** je vais arriver/je suis arrivé au travail avec deux heures de retard ◆ **a technical problem on the plane made us two hours ~** un problème technique dans l'avion nous a fait arriver avec deux heures de retard ◆ **I'm a week ~** *(gen)* j'ai une semaine de retard ; *(menstrual period)* j'ai une semaine de retard*, mes règles ont une semaine de retard

3 *(= after usual time) [crop, flowers]* tardif ; *[booking]* de dernière minute ◆ **Easter is ~ this year** Pâques est *or* tombe tard cette année ◆ **spring was ~** le printemps était en retard *or* était tardif

4 *(= at advanced time of day)* tard ◆ **it was very ~** il était très tard ◆ **it's getting ~** il se fait tard ◆ **owing to the ~ hour** en raison de l'heure tardive ◆ **at this ~ hour** à cette heure tardive ◆ **to work ~ hours** finir son travail tard le soir, travailler tard le soir ◆ **to keep ~ hours** être un(e) couche-tard* *inv* ◆ **to have a ~ meal/lunch** manger/déjeuner tard ◆ **there's a ~ (-night) film on Saturdays** *(Cine)* le samedi, il y a une séance supplémentaire le soir ◆ **the ~ film tonight is …** *(TV)* le film diffusé en fin de soirée est … ◆ **there's a ~(-night) show on Saturdays** *(Theat)* il y a une seconde représentation en soirée le samedi ◆ **~(-night) opening** *[of shop]* nocturne *f* ◆ **there's ~(-night) opening on Thursdays** les magasins ouvrent en nocturne *or* font nocturne* le jeudi ◆ **~(-night) opening Fridays until 7pm** nocturne jusqu'à 19 heures le vendredi

5 *(= near end of period or series)* **the ~st edition of the catalogue** la toute dernière édition du catalogue ◆ **the subject of her ~r books is …** le sujet de ses derniers livres est … ◆ **two ~ goals** deux buts en fin de match ◆ **at this ~ stage** à ce stade avancé ◆ **he was in his ~ thirties** il approchait de la quarantaine ◆ **in the ~ afternoon** en fin d'après midi ◆ **she was enjoying the cool ~ evening** elle appréciait la fraîcheur de cette fin de soirée ◆ **by ~ morning** à la fin de la matinée ◆ **in ~ June/September** fin juin/septembre, à la fin (du mois de) juin/septembre ◆ **in ~ spring** à la fin du printemps ◆ **it was not until ~ 1989 that …** ce n'est qu'à la fin de l'année 1989 que … ◆ **in the ~ 1980s** à la fin des années 80 ◆ **in the ~ 18th century** à la fin du 18e (siècle) ◆ **in the ~ Middle Ages** à la fin du Moyen Âge ◆ **a ~ Victorian house** une maison de la fin de l'époque victorienne ; see also **later, latest**

6 *(= dead)* feu *(liter)* ◆ **the ~ queen** feu la reine ◆ **the ~ Harry Thomas** feu Harry Thomas ◆ **my ~ wife** ma pauvre *or* défunte *(frm)* femme ◆ **our ~ colleague** notre regretté *(frm)* *or* défunt *(frm)* collègue

ADV 1 *(= after scheduled time) [arrive]* en retard ; *[start, finish, deliver]* avec du retard ◆ **to arrive ~ for sth** *(meeting, dinner, film)* arriver en retard à qch ◆ **we're running ~ this morning** nous sommes en retard ce matin ◆ **the baby was born ~** le bébé est né *or* arrivé après terme ◆ **the baby was born two weeks ~** le bébé est né avec deux semaines de retard ◆ **he turned up two hours ~** il est arrivé avec deux heures de retard ◆ **we're running about 40 minutes ~** nous avons environ 40 minutes de retard ◆ **work on the new motorway started two years ~** la construction de la nouvelle autoroute a commencé avec deux ans de retard ◆ **too ~** trop tard ; see also **later** ; → **better**[1]

2 *(= after usual time)* ◆ **to flower ~** fleurir tard ◆ **her periods started very ~** elle a eu ses premières règles très tard ◆ **they married ~ in life** ils se sont mariés sur le tard ◆ **she had started learning German quite ~ in life** elle avait commencé à apprendre l'allemand assez tard ◆ **she came ~ to acting** elle est devenue comédienne sur le tard ◆ **he had come quite ~ to painting** il s'était mis à la peinture sur le tard

3 *(= at advanced time of day) [work, get up, sleep, start, finish]* tard ◆ **they stayed up talking until very ~** ils sont restés à parler jusque tard dans la nuit ◆ **the chemist is open ~ on Thursdays** la pharmacie est ouverte tard *or* en nocturne le jeudi ◆ **to stay up ~** veiller tard, se coucher tard ◆ **to work ~ at the office** rester tard au bureau pour travailler ◆ **~ at night** tard dans la nuit *or* la soirée ◆ **~ that night** tard dans la nuit *or* la soirée ◆ **~ last night** tard hier soir ◆ **~ in the afternoon** en fin d'après-midi ◆ **~ the previous evening** la veille, en fin de soirée ◆ **it was ~ in the evening before I returned to Baker Street** je ne suis retourné à Baker Street qu'en fin de soirée ◆ **~ into the night** tard dans la nuit ◆ **it is rather ~ in the day to change your mind** *(fig)* c'est un peu tard pour changer d'avis ◆ **it was her intervention, ~ in the day, that saved the scheme** *(fig)* ce fut son intervention, assez tardive, qui sauva le projet

4 *(= near end of period)* **~ in 2001** à la fin de l'année 2001, fin 2001 ◆ **~ in the year** en fin d'année ◆ **~ last year** à la fin de l'année dernière ◆ **~ in May** fin mai ◆ **they scored ~ in the second half** ils ont marqué à la fin de la deuxième mi-temps ◆ **symptoms appear only ~ in the disease** les symptômes n'apparaissent qu'à un stade avancé de la maladie ◆ **very ~ in the proceedings** * tout à la fin, très tard ◆ **it wasn't until relatively ~ in his career that …** ce n'est que vers la fin de sa carrière que …

5 *(= recently)* ◆ **as ~ as last week** pas plus tard que la semaine dernière, la semaine dernière encore ◆ **as ~ as 1950** en 1950 encore ◆ **as ~ as the 1980s** jusque dans les années 1980

◆ **of late** *(= lately)* dernièrement, ces derniers temps ◆ **we haven't seen much of him of ~** on ne l'a pas beaucoup vu ces derniers temps

6 *(frm = formerly)* **Jane Burdon, ~ of Bristol** Jane Burdon, autrefois domiciliée à Bristol ◆ **Carrington, ~ of the Diplomatic Service** Carrington, ancien membre du corps diplomatique

COMP **late developer** N ◆ **he's a ~ developer** il n'est pas précoce, il a mis du temps à sortir de l'enfance
late-night ADJ ◆ **~-night television** émissions *fpl* de fin de soirée ◆ **there's ~-night shopping on Thursdays** le magasin ouvre en nocturne *or* fait nocturne* le jeudi

latecomer /'leɪtkʌmə^r/ N 1 *(lit)* retardataire *mf* ◆ **~s will not be admitted** *(frm)* les retardataires ne seront pas admis 2 *(fig)* ◆ **he is a ~ to politics** il est venu à la politique sur le tard

lateen /lə'ti:n/ N (also **lateen sail**) voile *f* latine

lately /'leɪtlɪ/ ADV ces derniers temps, dernièrement ◆ **till ~** jusqu'à ces derniers temps ; see also **Johnny**

latency /'leɪtənsɪ/ N *(Med)* latence *f*

lateness /'leɪtnɪs/ N 1 *(= not being on time) [of person, train, flight]* retard *m* ◆ **he apologized for his ~** il s'est excusé de son retard ◆ **his boss became exasperated by his constant ~** ses retards perpétuels ont fini par exaspérer son patron 2 ◆ **a crowd had gathered despite the ~ of the hour** une foule s'était formée malgré l'heure tardive

latent /'leɪtənt/ ADJ *[tendency, talent, antagonism, racism, threat]* latent ; *[meaning]* caché
COMP **latent defect** N *(Jur)* vice *m* caché
latent heat N *(Phys)* chaleur *f* latente
latent period N *(Med)* période *f* de latence

later /'leɪtə^r/ (compar of **late**) ADV plus tard ◆ **~ that night** plus tard (dans la soirée) ◆ **even ~** encore plus tard ◆ **two years ~** deux ans plus tard ◆ **~ on** *(in period of time, film)* plus tard ; *(in book)* plus loin ◆ **not** *or* **no ~ than …** pas plus tard que … ◆ **essays must be handed in not ~ than Monday morning** les dissertations devront être remises lundi matin dernier délai *or* au plus tard ◆ **~!** *(when interrupted etc)* tout à l'heure ! ; *(US* * *= goodbye)* à plus !* ◆ **see you ~!*** *(= in a few minutes)* à tout à l'heure ! ; *(longer)* à plus tard ! ; see also **soon**

ADJ 1 *(= subsequent, more recent) [chapter, date]* ultérieur (-eure *f*) ◆ **we'll discuss it at a ~ meeting** nous en discuterons au cours d'une réunion ultérieure *or* d'une autre réunion ◆ **at a ~ meeting they decided …** au cours d'une réunion ultérieure, ils ont décidé … ◆ **I decided to take a ~ train** j'ai décidé de prendre un autre train *or* de partir plus tard ◆ **the ~ train** *(of two)* le train suivant ◆ **a ~ edition** une édition postérieure ◆ **this version is ~ than that one** *(= subsequent)* cette version est postérieure à celle-là

2 *(in period or series)* ◆ **at a ~ stage** plus tard ◆ **at a ~ stage in the negotiations** lors d'une phase ultérieure des négociations ◆ **the ~ 18th century** la fin du 18e (siècle) ◆ **Beethoven's ~ symphonies** les dernières symphonies de Beethoven ◆ **in ~ life** plus tard ◆ **in his ~ years** vers la fin de sa vie

lateral /'lætərəl/ ADJ latéral *(also Phon)* COMP **lateral thinking** N *(esp Brit)* la pensée latérale *(manière non conventionnelle d'aborder les problèmes)*

laterally /'lætərəlɪ/ ADV *(= sideways)* latéralement ; *(= originally)* ◆ **to think ~** pratiquer la pensée latérale, avoir une manière originale d'aborder les problèmes

latest /'leɪtɪst/ (superl of **late**) ADJ 1 *(= most recent)* dernier ◆ **his ~ film** son dernier film ◆ **the ~ in a series of murders** le dernier en date d'une série de meurtres ◆ **the ~ news** les dernières nouvelles *fpl* ◆ **the ~ news (bulletin)** *(Rad, TV)* les dernières informations *fpl* ◆ **his ~ statement** sa dernière déclaration (en date) ◆ **he is the ~ minister to resign** c'est le dernier ministre en date à démissionner ◆ **the very ~ technology** la toute dernière technologie

2 *(= last possible)* limite ◆ **what is the ~ date for applications?** quelle est la date limite de dépôt des candidatures ? ◆ **the ~ date he could do it was 31 July** la dernière date à laquelle il pouvait le faire était le 31 juillet ◆ **the ~ time you may come is 4 o'clock** l'heure limite à laquelle vous pouvez arriver est 4 heures ◆ **the ~ time for doing it is April** il faut le faire en avril au plus tard ◆ **at the ~ possible moment** au tout dernier moment

ADV *(= last)* ◆ **to arrive/get up (the) ~** être le dernier *or* la dernière à arriver/se lever ◆ **to work ~** travailler plus tard que les autres ◆ **to flower (the) ~** fleurir en dernier

N 1 * *(= latest version)* ◆ **it's the ~ in computer games** c'est le dernier cri* en matière de jeux électroniques ◆ **the very ~ in technology** le dernier cri* de la technologie ◆ **have you heard the ~?** *(= news)* tu connais la dernière ?* ◆ **what's the ~ on this affair?** qu'y a-t-il de nouveau sur cette affaire ? ◆ **for the ~ on the riots, over to Ian** *(Rad, TV)* pour les dernières informations sur les émeutes, à vous, Ian ◆ **have you seen his ~?** *(= girlfriend)* tu as vu sa nouvelle ?* ◆ **have you heard his ~?** *(= joke)* tu connais sa dernière ?* ◆ **did you hear about his ~?** *(= exploit)* on t'a raconté son dernier exploit *or* sa dernière prouesse ?

2 *(= latest time)* ◆ **when** *or* **what is the ~ you can come ?** quand pouvez-vous venir, au plus tard ? ◆ **I'll be there by noon at the ~** j'y serai à midi au plus tard ◆ **give me your essay by Monday at the ~** rendez-moi votre dissertation lundi dernier délai *or* au plus tard

latex /ˈleɪteks/ N (pl **latexes** *or* **latices** /ˈlætɪˌsiːz/) latex *m*

lath /lɑːθ/ N (pl **laths** /lɑːðz/) latte *f* ◆ **a ~-and-plaster wall** *un mur fait en lattes et enduit de plâtre*

lathe /leɪð/ N *(= machine)* tour *m* ; → **capstan, power**

lather /ˈlɑːðəʳ/ N 1 *[of soap]* mousse *f* (de savon) 2 *(= sweat) [of horse]* écume *f* ◆ **in a ~** *[horse]* couvert d'écume ; (* *fig* = nervous, anxious) *[person]* agité, dans tous ses états ◆ **to work o.s. up into a ~** * se mettre dans tous ses états ◆ **what's he getting into such a ~ about?** * pourquoi se met-il dans un état pareil ? VT ◆ **to ~ one's face/hands** *etc* se savonner le visage/les mains *etc* VI *[soap]* mousser

latices /ˈlætɪˌsiːz/ NPL of **latex**

latifundia /ˌlætɪˈfʊndɪə/ NPL latifundia *mpl*

Latin /ˈlætɪn/ ADJ 1 *[text, grammar, poet]* latin ; *[lesson]* de latin 2 *[people, temperament, culture]* *(European)* latin ; *(in US)* latino-américain N 1 *(= language)* latin *m* ◆ **late ~** bas latin *m* ◆ **low ~** bas latin *m* ◆ **vulgar ~** latin *m* vulgaire 2 Latin(e) *m(f)* ; *(in US)* Latino-Américain(e) *m(f)*
COMP **Latin America** N Amérique *f* latine
Latin-American ADJ latino-américain, d'Amérique latine N Latino-Américain(e) *m(f)*
latin lover N latin lover *m*
Latin quarter N quartier *m* latin
Latin school N *(US)* ≃ lycée *m* classique

Latinist /ˈlætɪnɪst/ N latiniste *mf*

Latinization /ˌlætɪnaɪˈzeɪʃən/ N latinisation *f*

Latinize /ˈlætɪnaɪz/ VT latiniser

Latino /læˈtiːnəʊ/ N (pl **Latinos**) *(in US)* Latino *mf* COMP **Latino-American** ADJ latino-américain N *(US)* Latino-Américain(e) *m(f)*

latish * /ˈleɪtɪʃ/ ADJ *[hour]* assez avancé, assez tardif ◆ **it's getting ~** il commence à se faire tard ◆ **we had a ~ breakfast** nous avons pris notre petit déjeuner assez *or* plutôt tard ADV assez tard, plutôt tard

latitude /ˈlætɪtjuːd/ N 1 *(Geog)* latitude *f* ◆ **at a ~ of 48° north** à *or* par 48° de latitude Nord ◆ **in these ~s** sous ces latitudes 2 *(NonC = freedom)* latitude *f* ◆ **to give** *or* **allow sb a certain amount of ~** laisser *or* accorder une certaine latitude à qn

latitudinal /ˌlætɪˈtjuːdɪnl/ ADJ latitudinal

latrine /ləˈtriːn/ N latrine(s) *f(pl) gen pl*

latte /ˈlɑːteɪ/ N *(= coffee)* café *m* au lait

latter /ˈlætəʳ/ LANGUAGE IN USE 26.2 *(frm)*
ADJ 1 *(= second of two)* dernier, second ◆ **the ~ proposition was accepted** cette dernière *or* la seconde proposition fut acceptée ◆ **of the two, we prefer the ~ solution** nous préférons la seconde solution ◆ **the ~ half** la seconde moitié ◆ **the ~ half of the month** la seconde quinzaine du mois

2 *(= later)* **the ~ stages of the match produced some fine football** vers la fin du match, il y a eu du très bon football ◆ **the college was destroyed in the ~ stages of the war/the century** le collège a été détruit vers la fin de la guerre/du siècle ◆ **in the ~ years of his life, in his ~ years** les dernières années de sa vie, tard dans sa vie

N ◆ **the ~ is the more expensive of the two systems** ce dernier *or* second système est le plus coûteux des deux ◆ **of these two books the former is expensive but the ~ is not** le premier de ces deux livres est cher mais le second ne l'est pas ◆ **he visited his cousin and uncle - the ~ was ill** il a rendu visite à son cousin et à son oncle : ce dernier était souffrant ◆ **of the two possible solutions, I prefer the ~** je préfère la seconde solution
COMP **latter-day** ADJ moderne, d'aujourd'hui
Latter-Day Saints NPL *(Rel)* Saints *mpl* des derniers jours

latterly /ˈlætəlɪ/ ADV *(frm)* *(= recently)* récemment, dernièrement ; *(= towards end of life)* vers la fin de sa *(or leur etc)* vie ; *(= towards end of period)* vers la fin ◆ **he has lived abroad for many years, ~ in Rome** il a longtemps vécu à l'étranger, maintenant il est à Rome

lattice /ˈlætɪs/ N treillis *m* ; *(= fence)* treillage *m*, claire-voie *f* ; (also **lattice structure**) structure *f* réticulaire
COMP **lattice girder** N poutre *f* en treillis
lattice window N fenêtre *f* treillissée

latticed /ˈlætɪst/ ADJ *[window]* treillissé ; *[fence, wall]* treillagé

latticework /ˈlætɪswɜːk/ N treillis *m*

Latvia /ˈlætvɪə/ N Lettonie *f*

Latvian /ˈlætvɪən/ ADJ lette, letton (-on(n)e *f*) N 1 Lette *mf*, Letton((n)e) *m(f)*, Latvien(ne) *m(f)* 2 *(= language)* lette *m*, letton *m*

laud /lɔːd/ VT *(liter)* louanger *(liter)* ; *(Rel)* louer, glorifier, chanter les louanges de

laudable /ˈlɔːdəbl/ ADJ louable, digne de louanges

laudably /ˈlɔːdəblɪ/ ADV *[behave]* de façon louable ◆ **he was ~ calm** son calme était remarquable ◆ **a ~ objective article** un article d'une louable objectivité

laudanum /ˈlɔːdnəm/ N laudanum *m*

laudatory /ˈlɔːdətərɪ/ ADJ *(frm)* élogieux

laugh /lɑːf/ N 1 rire *m* ◆ **he has a very distinctive ~** il a un rire très caractéristique ◆ **with a ~** *(brief)* dans un éclat de rire ; *(longer)* en riant ◆ **with a scornful ~** avec un rire méprisant *or* dédaigneux ◆ **to give a ~** rire ◆ **to have a good ~ at sb/sth** bien rire de qn/qch ◆ **his act didn't get a single ~** son numéro n'a fait rire personne ◆ **that joke always gets a ~** cette plaisanterie fait toujours rire ◆ **he had the last ~** finalement c'est lui qui a bien ri ◆ **we'll see who has the last ~** on verra bien qui rira le dernier ◆ **the ~ is on you** * c'est toi qui fais les frais de la plaisanterie ◆ **it was a ~ a minute!** *(also iro)* c'était d'un drôle ! *(also iro)* ; → **play, raise**

2 (* = *amusement, amusing time)* ◆ **it was** *or* **we had a good ~** on s'est bien amusés, on a bien rigolé* ◆ **if you want a ~ go to her German class!** si tu veux t'amuser *or* rigoler* va assister à son cours d'allemand ! ◆ **what a ~!** ça, c'est *(or* c'était *etc)* marrant !* ◆ **just for a ~** *or* **for ~s** rien que pour rire, histoire de rire* ◆ **he's always good for a ~** il nous fera toujours bien rire ◆ **his films are always good for a ~** ses films sont toujours drôles ◆ **he's a good ~** on rigole* bien avec lui

VI rire ◆ **you may ~!, it's easy for you to ~!** tu peux toujours rire ! ◆ **you've got to ~** * ◆ **you have to ~** * *(philosophical)* il vaut mieux en rire ◆ **I didn't know whether to ~ or cry** je ne savais plus si je devais rire ou pleurer ◆ **he ~ed until he cried** il pleurait de rire, il riait aux larmes ◆ **to ~ about** *or* **over sth** rire de qch ◆ **there's nothing to ~ about** il n'y a pas de quoi rire ◆ **he never ~s at my jokes** mes plaisanteries ne le font jamais rire ; see also **laugh at** ◆ **she ~ed to herself** elle a ri dans sa barbe, elle a ri sous cape ◆ **to ~ up one's sleeve** rire dans sa barbe, rire sous cape ◆ **he makes me ~** il me fait rire ◆ **don't make me ~** * *(iro = don't be silly)* laisse-moi rire, ne me fais pas rire ◆ **he who ~s last ~s longest** *(Prov)* rira bien qui rira le dernier *(Prov)* ◆ **to ~ in sb's face** rire au nez de qn ◆ **he'll soon be ~ing on the other side of his face** il n'aura bientôt plus envie de rire, il va bientôt rire jaune ◆ **you'll be ~ing on the other side of your face in a minute!** * tu vas le regretter ! ◆ **it's all right for him, he's ~ing** * lui il s'en fiche, il est peinard* ◆ **once we get this contract signed we're ~ing** * une fois ce contrat signé, ce sera dans la poche* ◆ **he's ~ing all the way to the bank** * il n'a pas de problèmes de compte en banque ! ; → **burst out**

VT ◆ **he ~ed a jolly laugh** il eut un rire jovial ◆ **"don't be silly," he ~ed** "ne sois pas idiot", dit-il en riant ◆ **to be ~ed out of court** *[person, idea]* être tourné en ridicule ◆ **they ~ed him to scorn** ils l'ont tourné en dérision ◆ **he ~ed himself silly** * il a ri comme un bossu* *or* une baleine*
COMP **laugh track** N *(US Rad, TV)* (bande *f* sonore de) rires *mpl* préenregistrés

► **laugh at** VT FUS *(lit) [+ person, sb's behaviour]* rire de ; *(unpleasantly)* se moquer de ; *(fig) [+ difficulty, danger]* se rire de

► **laugh down** VT SEP ◆ **they laughed the speaker down** leurs moqueries ont réduit l'orateur au silence

► **laugh off** VT SEP 1 ◆ **to laugh one's head off** * rire comme un bossu* *or* une baleine*

2 *[+ accusation]* écarter d'une plaisanterie *or* d'une boutade ◆ **she managed to ~ it off** elle a réussi à tourner la chose en plaisanterie ◆ **you can't ~ this one off** cette fois tu ne t'en tireras pas par la plaisanterie

laughable /ˈlɑːfəbl/ ADJ *[person, behaviour, idea, suggestion]* ridicule ; *[offer, amount]* dérisoire ◆ **it's ~ to compare him with Gandhi** il est ridicule de le comparer à Gandhi

laughably /ˈlɑːfəblɪ/ ADV ridiculement

laughing /ˈlɑːfɪŋ/ ADJ 1 *[person, face, eyes]* riant, rieur 2 *(= light-hearted)* **this is no ~ matter** il n'y a pas de quoi rire ◆ **I'm in no ~ mood** *(= angry)* je ne suis pas d'humeur à rire ; *(= sad)* je n'ai pas le cœur à rire
COMP **laughing gas** N gaz *m* hilarant
laughing hyena N hyène *f* (tachetée)
laughing jackass N *(= bird)* martin-pêcheur *m* géant

laughing stock N ◆ **he was the ~ stock of the class** il était la risée de la classe ◆ **he made himself a ~ stock** il s'est couvert de ridicule

laughingly /ˈlɑːfɪŋlɪ/ ADV 1 *(= amusedly) [say]* en riant 2 *(= ironically)* ◆ **this patch of lawn that I ~ call my garden** ce carré de gazon que j'appelle pour rire mon jardin ◆ **what the government ~ calls its economic policy** *(= risibly)* ce que le gouvernement appelle sans rire sa politique économique

laughline /ˈlɑːflaɪn/ N *(US: on face)* ride *f* d'expression

laughter /ˈlɑːftə^{r}/ N *(NonC)* rire(s) *m(pl)* ◆ **there was a little nervous ~** on entendit quelques rires nerveux ◆ **there was loud ~ at this remark** cette remarque a provoqué des éclats de rire ◆ **he said amid ~ that ...** il dit au milieu des rires que ... ◆ **~ is good for you** cela fait du bien de rire ◆ **their ~ could be heard in the next room** on les entendait rire dans la pièce à côté ; → **can[2], roar** COMP **laughter line** N *(Brit: on face)* ride *f* d'expression

launch /lɔːntʃ/ N 1 *(= motorboat) (for patrol etc)* vedette *f* ; *(for pleasure)* bateau *m* de plaisance ◆ **police ~** vedette *f* de la police
2 *(= boat carried by warship)* chaloupe *f*
3 *(= launching) [of ship, spacecraft, product]* lancement *m* ; → **window**
VT 1 *[+ ship, satellite, missile]* lancer ; *[+ shore lifeboat etc]* faire sortir ; *[+ ship's boat]* mettre à la mer
2 *[+ company, product, career, scheme, plan]* lancer ; *[+ attack, offensive]* lancer, déclencher ; *[+ inquiry, investigation]* ouvrir ◆ **to ~ a share issue** *(Fin)* émettre des actions, faire une émission d'actions ◆ **it was this novel that really ~ed her as a writer** c'est ce roman qui l'a vraiment lancée en tant qu'écrivain ◆ **the film ~ed her as Hollywood's latest star** le film a fait d'elle la nouvelle star d'Hollywood
VI *(fig: also* **launch forth***)* se lancer ◆ **to ~ into** *[+ speech, explanation, attack]* se lancer dans
COMP **launch pad** N *(Space)* ⇒ **launching pad**
launch party N *(Publishing etc)* réception *f* de lancement
launch vehicle N *(Space)* fusée *f* de lancement

► **launch forth** VI ⇒ **launch vi**

► **launch out** VI *[business, company] (= diversify)* se diversifier ◆ **to ~ out into sth** *[speaker, business]* se lancer dans qch

launcher /ˈlɔːntʃə^{r}/ N *(Mil, Space)* lanceur *m* ; → **missile, rocket**

launching /ˈlɔːntʃɪŋ/ N 1 *[of new ship, missile, satellite]* lancement *m* ; *[of shore lifeboat]* sortie *f* ; *[of ship's boat]* mise *f* à la mer 2 *[of company, product, career]* lancement *m*
COMP **launching ceremony** N cérémonie *f* de lancement
launching pad N *(Space)* rampe *f* de lancement
launching site N *(Mil, Space)* aire *f* de lancement

launder /ˈlɔːndə^{r}/ VT 1 *[+ clothes]* laver ◆ **to send sth to be ~ed** envoyer qch à la blanchisserie *or* au blanchissage 2 *[+ money]* blanchir

Launderette ® /ˌlɔːndəˈret/ N *(Brit)* laverie *f* automatique

laundering /ˈlɔːndərɪŋ/ N 1 *[of clothes]* blanchissage *m* 2 *[of money]* blanchiment *m*

laundress /ˈlɔːndrɪs/ N blanchisseuse *f*

laund(e)rette /ˌlɔːndəˈret/ N laverie *f* automatique

Laundromat ® /ˈlɔːndrəmæt/ N *(US)* → **laund(e)rette**

laundry /ˈlɔːndrɪ/ N 1 *(NonC) (= clean clothes)* linge *m* ; *(= dirty clothes)* linge *m* (sale) ◆ **to do the ~** faire la lessive, laver le linge 2 *(= place)* blanchisserie *f*
COMP **laundry basket** N panier *m* à linge
laundry list N *(lit)* liste *f* de blanchissage ; *(fig pej)* liste *f* interminable
laundry mark N marque *f* de la blanchisserie *or* du blanchissage
laundry van N camionnette *f* de la blanchisserie
laundry worker N blanchisseur *m*, -euse *f* *(employé)*

laureate /ˈlɔːrɪɪt/ ADJ, N lauréat(e) *m(f)* ◆ **(poet) ~** *(in Brit)* poète *m* lauréat

laurel /ˈlɒrəl/ N laurier *m* ◆ **to rest on one's ~s** se reposer sur ses lauriers ◆ **to win one's ~s** se couvrir de lauriers ◆ **you must look to your ~s** ne t'endors pas sur tes lauriers COMP **laurel wreath** N couronne *f* de lauriers

lav* /læv/ N (abbrev of **lavatory**) cabinets *mpl*, W.-C. *mpl*

lava /ˈlɑːvə/ N lave *f*
COMP **lava bed** N champ *m* de lave
lava flow N coulée *f* de lave
lava lamp N lampe *f* à bulles d'huile

lavalier(e) /ˌlævəˈlɪə^{r}/ N *(US)* pendentif *m*

lavatorial /ˌlævəˈtɔːrɪəl/ ADJ scatologique

lavatory /ˈlævətrɪ/ N 1 *(= room)* toilettes *fpl*, W.-C. *mpl* 2 *(Brit = fitting)* (cuvette *f* et siège *m* de) W.-C. *mpl* ◆ **to put sth down the ~** jeter qch dans les W.-C. *or* cabinets ; → **public**
COMP **lavatory bowl** N cuvette *f* de W.-C.
lavatory humour N *(pej)* humour *m* scatologique
lavatory pan N ⇒ **lavatory bowl**
lavatory paper N papier *m* hygiénique
lavatory seat N siège *m* de W.-C.

lavender /ˈlævɪndə^{r}/ N lavande *f*
COMP *[colour]* lavande *inv*
lavender bag N sachet *m* de lavande
lavender-blue ADJ bleu lavande *inv*
lavender water N eau *f* de lavande

laver bread /ˈlɑːvəbred/ N gâteau *m* d'algues

lavish /ˈlævɪʃ/ ADJ 1 *[person]* prodigue *(of, with* de) ◆ **to be ~ with one's money** dépenser sans compter, se montrer prodigue 2 *(= generous) [expenditure]* très considérable ; *[amount]* gigantesque ; *[meal]* plantureux, copieux ; *[helping, hospitality]* généreux ◆ **to bestow ~ praise on sb** se répandre en éloges sur qn VT prodiguer *(sth on sb* qch à qn)

lavishly /ˈlævɪʃlɪ/ ADV *[illustrated, decorated]* somptueusement ; *[equipped, furnished]* somptueusement, luxueusement ◆ **to entertain ~** recevoir somptueusement ◆ **to spend ~** dépenser sans compter ◆ **to tip sb ~** donner un pourboire très généreux à qn

lavishness /ˈlævɪʃnɪs/ N *[of spending]* extravagance *f* ; *[of hospitality, helping]* générosité *f* ; *[of meal]* luxe *m*

law /lɔː/ N 1 *(NonC = set of laws, legislation)* loi *f*, législation *f* ◆ **the ~** la loi ◆ **it's the ~** c'est la loi ◆ **the ~ as it stands** les lois en vigueur, la législation en vigueur ◆ **they're campaigning for a change in the ~** ils font campagne pour une réforme législative ◆ **according to French/European ~** selon la loi *or* la législation française/européenne ◆ **by** *or* **under French/international ~** selon la loi *or* la législation française/internationale ◆ **when a bill becomes ~** *(Parl)* quand un projet de loi est voté ◆ **to be above the ~** être au-dessus des lois ◆ **to keep within the ~** rester dans (les limites de) la légalité ◆ **to take the ~ into one's own hands** (se) faire justice soi-même ◆ **the ~ of the land** la législation *or* les lois du pays ◆ **the ~ of the jungle** la loi de la jungle ◆ **the Law of Moses** la loi de Moïse ◆ **~ and order** l'ordre *m* public ; see also **comp** ◆ **forces of ~ and order** forces *fpl* de l'ordre ◆ **to have the ~ on one's side** avoir la loi pour soi ◆ **he's a ~ unto himself** il ne connaît d'autre loi que la sienne, il fait ce qu'il veut ; → **break, lay down, rule, word**
◆ **against the law** contraire à la loi, illégal
◆ **by law** ◆ **protected/prohibited/permitted by ~** protégé/interdit/autorisé par la loi ◆ **bound** *or* **obliged by ~** légalement obligé ◆ **you must by ~ provide access for the handicapped** vous êtes légalement obligé d'aménager un accès pour les handicapés ◆ **parents who must by ~ remain anonymous** les parents que la loi oblige à rester dans l'anonymat
2 *(NonC = operation of the law)* justice *f* ◆ **the report looks at how women are treated by the ~** ce rapport étudie la façon dont la justice traite les femmes ◆ **court of ~** cour *f* de justice, tribunal *m* ◆ **to go to ~** recourir à la justice ◆ **to take a case to ~** porter une affaire devant les tribunaux, saisir la justice ◆ **to take sb to ~** faire un procès à qn ◆ **I'll have the ~ on you!*** je vous traînerai devant les tribunaux ! ◆ **here's the ~ arriving!*** *(= the police)* voilà les flics !* ; → **arm[1], brush, officer**
3 *(NonC = system, science, profession)* droit *m* ◆ **civil/criminal** *etc* **~** le droit civil/criminel *etc* ◆ **to study** *or* **read ~** faire son *or* du droit ◆ **to practise ~** *[solicitor]* être notaire *m* ; *[barrister]* être avocat(e) ◆ **Faculty of Law** *(Univ)* faculté *f* de droit ; → **common, martial, point**
4 *(= regulation)* loi *f* ◆ **to pass a ~** voter une loi ◆ **several ~s have been passed against pollution** plusieurs lois ont été votées pour combattre la pollution ◆ **is there a ~ against it?** est-ce que c'est interdit par la loi ? ◆ **there should be a ~ against it!** ça devrait être interdit ! ◆ **there's no ~ against it!** * ce n'est pas défendu ! ◆ **framework ~** loi-cadre *f*
5 *(= principle, rule) (also Phys)* loi *f* ; *(Sport)* règle *f* ◆ **the ~ of averages** la loi des probabilités ◆ **the ~ of diminishing returns** la loi des rendements décroissants ◆ **the ~(s) of gravity** la loi de la chute des corps *or* de la pesanteur ◆ **the ~s of nature** les lois *fpl* de la nature ◆ **the ~(s) of supply and demand** la loi de l'offre et de la demande ; → **Murphy, Parkinson's law, sod[2]**
COMP **law-abiding** ADJ respectueux des lois
law-and-order issues NPL questions *fpl* d'ordre public
law-breaking N *(NonC)* violation *f* de la loi ADJ violant *or* enfreignant la loi
law centre, law center (US) N *service de consultations juridiques gratuites*
law clerk N *(US Jur) jeune juriste qui prépare le travail du juge*
law court N cour *f* de justice, tribunal *m*
Law Courts NPL ≈ Palais *m* de justice
law enforcement agency N *(US) service chargé de faire respecter la loi*
law enforcement officer N *(US) personne ayant des pouvoirs de police*
Law Faculty N *(Univ)* faculté *f* de droit
Law Lords NPL *(Brit) juges siégeant à la Chambre des lords*
law school N *(Univ)* faculté *f* de droit ◆ **he's at ~ school** il fait son droit *or* du droit
law student N étudiant(e) *m(f)* en droit

lawbreaker /ˈlɔːˌbreɪkə^{r}/ N personne *f* qui enfreint la loi

lawful /ˈlɔːfʊl/ ADJ *[action]* légal ; *[marriage, child]* légitime ; *[contract]* valide ◆ **it is not ~ to do that** il n'est pas légal de *or* il est illégal de faire cela ◆ **to go about one's ~ business** vaquer à ses occupations

lawfully /ˈlɔːfəlɪ/ ADV légalement

lawgiver /ˈlɔːˌgɪvə^{r}/ N *(Brit)* législateur *m*, -trice *f*

lawless /ˈlɔːlɪs/ ADJ *[country]* sans loi ; *[period]* d'anarchie ; *[person]* sans foi ni loi ◆ **~ behaviour** manque *m* de respect des lois ◆ **we live in an increasingly ~ society** nous vivons dans une société où l'on respecte de moins en moins la loi

lawlessness /ˈlɔːlɪsnɪs/ **N** *[of person]* non-respect *m* des lois ; *[of country, period]* anarchie *f*

lawmaker /ˈlɔːˌmeɪkəʳ/ **N** *(US)* législateur *m*, -trice *f*

lawman /ˈlɔːmæn/ **N** (pl **-men**) *(US)* policier *m*

lawn¹ /lɔːn/ **N** pelouse *f* **COMP** **lawn tennis N** *(on grass)* tennis *m* sur gazon ; *(on hard surface)* tennis *m*

lawn² /lɔːn/ **N** *(= fabric)* batiste *f*, linon *m*

lawnmower /ˈlɔːnmaʊəʳ/ **N** tondeuse *f* (à gazon)

lawrencium /lɔˈrensɪəm/ **N** lawrencium *m*

lawsuit /ˈlɔːsuːt/ **N** *(esp US)* procès *m* ◆ **to bring a ~ against sb** intenter un procès à qn, poursuivre qn en justice

lawyer /ˈlɔːjəʳ/ **N** ① *(= barrister)* avocat *m* ; *(= solicitor) (for sales, wills etc)* notaire *m* ; *(in court for litigation)* avocat *m* ; *(in firm etc)* conseiller *m* juridique
② *(= person trained in law)* juriste *mf*

LAWYER

Il existe deux catégories d'avocats en Grande-Bretagne : les "solicitors" et les "barristers" (appelés "advocates" en Écosse). Les premiers sont à la fois des notaires, qui traitent donc les transactions immobilières, les affaires de succession, etc, et des avocats habilités à plaider au civil dans les instances inférieures. Les seconds sont des avocats plus spécialisés, qui interviennent au pénal ou au civil dans les instances supérieures, y compris pour défendre des affaires dont ils sont saisis par des "solicitors".

Aux États-Unis, les avocats sont appelés "attorneys". Ils travaillent souvent selon le système dit "no win no fee" (c'est-à-dire que le client ne paie les honoraires que s'il a gain de cause), ce qui leur permet de défendre des clients pauvres dans des affaires importantes, avec la perspective d'obtenir des gains importants en cas de succès. Ainsi, les dommages et intérêts demandés dans les affaires civiles sont souvent beaucoup plus élevés qu'en Europe, et les Américains ont volontiers recours aux voies judiciaires pour régler leurs différends.

lax /læks/ **ADJ** ① *[behaviour, discipline, morals]* relâché ; *[person]* négligent ; *[government]* laxiste ; *[pronunciation]* relâché ◆ **to be ~ in doing sth** faire qch avec négligence *or* sans soin ◆ **to be ~ about security/one's work/duties** négliger la sécurité/son travail/ses devoirs ◆ **he's become very ~ recently** il s'est beaucoup relâché récemment ② *(Med) [bowels]* relâché ③ *(Ling) [vowel]* lâche

laxative /ˈlæksətɪv/ **ADJ, N** laxatif *m*

laxity /ˈlæksɪtɪ/, **laxness** /ˈlæksnɪs/ **N** *[of behaviour, discipline, morals]* relâchement *m* ; *[of person]* négligence *f* ; *[of government]* laxisme *m*

lay¹ /leɪ/ (vb : pret, ptp **laid**) **N** ① *[of countryside, district etc]* disposition *f*, configuration *f* ; → **land**
② *(⁑ = sex)* partie *f* de jambes en l'air ◆ **it was a good ~** on a bien baisé⁑ ◆ **she's an easy ~** elle couche* avec n'importe qui, c'est une fille facile ◆ **he's/she's a good ~** il/elle baise bien⁑, c'est un bon coup⁑

VT ① *(= put, place, set) [+ cards, objects]* mettre, poser ; *(= stretch out) [+ cloth etc]* étendre ◆ **he laid his briefcase on the table** il a posé *or* mis sa serviette à plat sur la table ◆ **she laid her hand on my shoulder** elle a posé *or* mis la main sur mon épaule ◆ **he laid his head on the table/the pillow** il a posé sa tête sur la table/l'oreiller ◆ **I didn't ~ a finger on him** je ne l'ai pas touché ◆ **if you so much as ~ a finger on me ...** si tu oses (seulement) lever la main sur moi ... ◆ **I wish I could ~ my hands on a good dictionary** si seulement je pouvais mettre la main sur *or* dénicher un bon dictionnaire ◆ **to ~ hands on a territory** *etc (= seize)* s'emparer d'un territoire *etc* ◆ **to ~ a hand** *or* **hands on sb** *(= strike)* porter *or* lever la main sur qn ◆ **to ~ hands on sb** *(Rel)* faire l'imposition des mains à qn ◆ **to ~ it on the line*** y aller carrément, ne pas y aller par quatre chemins ◆ **he laid it on me*** *(US = explained)* il m'a tout expliqué ◆ **to ~ one on sb⁑** *(Brit) (= hit)* coller un pain⁑ à qn, flanquer une châtaigne* à qn ; *(= trick)* jouer un sale tour à qn ; → **curse, eye, hand, rest, siege**
② *(= put down, install)* poser, mettre ; *[+ bricks, carpet, cable, pipe]* poser ; *[+ mine]* poser, mouiller ◆ **to ~ a road** faire une route ◆ **to ~ a floor with carpet** poser une moquette sur un sol ; → **foundation**
③ *[+ eggs]* pondre ◆ **this bird ~s its eggs in the sand** cet oiseau pond (ses œufs) dans le sable ; see also **egg, new**
④ *(= prepare) [+ fire]* préparer ; *[+ snare, trap]* tendre, dresser *(for* à) ; *[+ plans]* élaborer ◆ **to ~ the table (for lunch)** *(Brit)* mettre la table *or* le couvert (pour le déjeuner) ◆ **all our carefully-laid plans went wrong** tous nos projets si bien élaborés ont échoué ◆ **even the best-laid plans can go wrong** même les projets les mieux élaborés peuvent échouer ; see also **best**
⑤ *(with adjective)* ◆ **to ~ bare one's innermost thoughts/feelings** mettre à nu *or* dévoiler ses pensées les plus profondes/ses sentiments les plus secrets ◆ **to ~ bare one's soul** *(liter)* mettre son âme à nu ◆ **the blow laid him flat** le coup l'étendit par terre *or* l'envoya au tapis ◆ **the storm laid the town flat** la tempête a rasé la ville ◆ **to be laid low** être immobilisé ◆ **he was laid low with flu** il était immobilisé par la grippe, la grippe l'obligeait à garder le lit ◆ **to ~ sb/to ~ o.s. open to criticism** *etc* exposer qn/s'exposer à la critique *etc* ◆ **to ~ waste a town, to ~ a town to waste** ravager *or* dévaster une ville
⑥ *(= impose, place) [+ tax]* faire payer *(on sth* sur qch) ; *[+ burden]* imposer *(on sb* à qn) → **blame, emphasis, responsibility**
⑦ *(= wager) [+ money]* parier, miser *(on* sur) ◆ **I'll ~ you (a fiver*) that ...** je te parie (5 livres) que ... ◆ **to ~ a bet (on sth)** parier (sur qch)
⑧ *(= register, bring to sb's attention) [+ accusation, charge]* porter ◆ **we shall ~ the facts before him** nous lui exposerons les faits ◆ **they laid their plan before him** ils lui ont soumis leur projet ◆ **to ~ a matter before the court** *(Jur)* saisir le tribunal d'une affaire ◆ **he laid his case before the commission** il a porté son cas devant *or* soumis son cas à la commission ◆ **to ~ a complaint** *(Jur)* porter plainte *(against* contre ; *with* auprès de) ◆ **to ~ information** *(Police = inform authorities)* donner des informations, servir d'indicateur ; → **claim**
⑨ *(= suppress) [+ ghost]* exorciser, conjurer ; *[+ doubt, fear]* dissiper ◆ **to ~ the dust** faire tomber la poussière
⑩ *(⁑ = have sex with)* baiser⁑ ◆ **to get laid** baiser⁑, se faire sauter⁑

VI *[bird, fish, insect]* pondre

COMP **lay-by N** *(Brit Aut)* (petite) aire *f* de stationnement *(sur le bas-côté)*
lay days NPL *(Naut)* jours *mpl* de planche, estarie *f*
lay-off N *(= redundancy)* licenciement *m*

► **lay about VT FUS** ◆ **to lay about sb (with a stick)** rouer qn de coups (de bâton)

► **lay alongside** *(Naut)* **VI, VT SEP** accoster

► **lay aside VT SEP** ① *(= save) [+ money, supplies]* mettre de côté
② *(= put away) [+ object]* mettre de côté ◆ **he laid aside his book to greet me** il a posé son livre pour me dire bonjour
③ *(= relinquish) [+ prejudice, scruples]* faire abstraction de ; *[+ differences, disagreements, doubts]* faire taire ; *[+ principles]* se départir de ; *[+ fears, anxieties, doubts]* écarter ; *[+ plans, projects]* abandonner

► **lay away VT SEP** *(US)* ⇒ **lay aside 1**

► **lay back VT SEP** remettre *(on* sur)

► **lay by VT SEP** ⇒ **lay aside 1**
N ◆ **lay-by** → **lay¹**

► **lay down VI** *(Cards)* étaler son jeu *or* ses cartes
VT SEP ① *(= deposit) [+ object, parcel, burden]* poser, déposer ◆ **to ~ down one's cards** poser son jeu *or* ses cartes
② *[+ wine]* mettre en cave
③ *(= give up)* **to ~ down one's arms** déposer ses *or* les armes ◆ **to ~ down one's life for sb** sacrifier sa vie pour qn
④ *(= establish, decide) [+ rule]* établir, poser ; *[+ condition, price]* imposer, fixer ◆ **he laid it down that ...** il décréta *or* stipula que ... ◆ **it is laid down in the rules that ...** il est stipulé dans le règlement que ... ◆ **to ~ down a policy** dicter une politique ◆ **to ~ down the law (to sb) (about sth)** *(fig)* (essayer de) faire la loi (à qn) (sur qch) ◆ **in our house it's my mother who ~s down the law** c'est ma mère qui fait la loi à la maison ◆ **stop ~ing down the law!** arrête de commander !

► **lay in VT SEP** *[+ goods, reserves]* faire provision de ; *(in shop)* emmagasiner ◆ **to ~ in provisions** faire des provisions ◆ **I must ~ in some fruit** il faut que je m'approvisionne *subj* en fruits *or* que je fasse provision de fruits

► **lay into*** **VT FUS** *(= attack verbally)* prendre à partie ; *(= scold)* passer un savon à* ; *(= attack physically)* rentrer dans le chou *or* le lard de*, tomber à bras raccourcis sur ◆ **we really laid into the beer last night** *(fig = devour)* on a descendu pas mal de bière hier soir*

► **lay off VT SEP** *[+ workers]* licencier, débaucher
VT FUS *(* = leave alone)* ◆ **you'd better ~ off the beer/running for a while** tu ferais mieux de t'abstenir de boire/courir pour le moment ◆ **~ off (it)!** *(= stop)* arrête !, ça suffit ! ; *(= don't touch)* pas touche !*, bas les pattes !* ◆ **~ off him!** fiche-lui la paix !* ◆ **I told him to ~ off (it)** je lui ai dit d'arrêter
N ◆ **lay-off** → **lay¹**

► **lay on VT SEP** ① *[+ tax]* mettre ◆ **they ~ on an extra charge for tea** ils ajoutent à la note le prix du thé
② *(Brit) (= install) [+ water, gas]* installer, mettre ; *(= provide) [+ facilities, entertainment]* fournir ◆ **a house with water/gas/electricity laid on** une maison qui a l'eau courante/le gaz/l'électricité ◆ **I'll have a car laid on for you** je mettrai une voiture à votre disposition, je ferai en sorte que vous ayez une voiture à votre disposition ◆ **everything will be laid on** il y aura tout ce qu'il faut ◆ **it was all laid on (for us) so that we didn't have to buy anything** tout (nous) était fourni si bien qu'on n'a rien eu à acheter
③ *[+ varnish, paint]* étaler ◆ **he laid it on thick** *or* **with a trowel*** *(fig)* il en a rajouté* ; → **lay¹**

► **lay out VT SEP** ① *(= plan, design) [+ garden]* dessiner ; *[+ house]* concevoir (le plan de) ; *[+ essay]* faire le plan de ◆ **a well laid-out flat** un appartement bien conçu ◆ **to ~ out page 4** *(Typ)* faire la mise en page de la (page) 4, monter la (page) 4
② *(= get ready, display) [+ clothes]* sortir, préparer ; *[+ goods for sale]* disposer, étaler ◆ **the meal that was laid out for them** le repas qui leur avait été préparé ◆ **to ~ out a body** faire la toilette d'un mort

3 (= present systematically) [+ reasons, events etc] exposer systématiquement
4 (= spend) [+ money] débourser, dépenser (on pour)
5 (= knock out) mettre knock-out or KO
6 (= make an effort) ◆ **to lay o.s. out to do sth** faire tout son possible pour faire qch, se mettre en quatre pour faire qch
N ◆ **layout** → **layout**

► **lay over** (US) VI s'arrêter, faire une halte
N ◆ **layover** → **layover**

► **lay to** (Naut) VI être en panne
VT SEP mettre en panne

► **lay up** VT SEP 1 [+ store, provisions] amasser, entasser ; (in shop) emmagasiner ◆ **to ~ up trouble for o.s.** se préparer des ennuis
2 [+ car] remiser ; [+ boat] désarmer ◆ **he is laid up (in bed) with flu** il est au lit avec la grippe

lay² /leɪ/ VB pt of **lie¹**

lay³ /leɪ/ N (Mus, Poetry) lai m

lay⁴ /leɪ/ ADJ 1 [missionary, school, education] laïque 2 (fig) **to the ~ mind** aux yeux du profane, pour le profane ◆ **~ opinion on this** l'opinion des profanes sur la question
COMP **lay analyst** N psychanalyste non titulaire d'un doctorat
lay brother N frère m convers or lai
lay person N 1 (Rel) laïc m 2 (fig) profane mf, non-initié(e) m(f)
lay reader N prédicateur m laïque
lay sister N sœur f converse

lay⁵ /leɪ/ ADJ (Art) ◆ **~ figure** mannequin m

layabout * /ˈleɪəbaʊt/ N (Brit) fainéant(e) m(f), feignant(e) * m(f)

layaway (plan) /ˈleɪəweɪˌplæn/ N (US Comm) vente f à livraison différée

layback /ˈleɪbæk/ N (Climbing) dülfer f

layer /ˈleɪəʳ/ N 1 [of atmosphere, paint, dust, sand] couche f ; (Geol) couche f, strate f ◆ **several ~s of clothing** plusieurs épaisseurs fpl de vêtements 2 (= hen) ◆ **a good ~** une bonne pondeuse 3 (= plant runner) marcotte f
VT 1 [+ hair] couper en dégradé 2 [+ plant] marcotter
COMP **layer cake** N gâteau m fourré

layette /leɪˈet/ N layette f

laying /ˈleɪɪŋ/ N [of carpet] pose f ◆ **the ~ of wreaths** (ceremony) le dépôt de gerbes ◆ **the ~ on of hands** (Rel) l'imposition f des mains
ADJ ◆ **~ hen** poule f pondeuse

layman /ˈleɪmən/ N (pl **-men**) 1 (Rel) laïc m 2 (fig) profane m, non-initié m ◆ **in ~'s terms** en termes simples

layout /ˈleɪaʊt/ N [of house, school] disposition f, agencement m ; [of garden] plan m, dessin m, disposition f ; [of district] disposition f ; [of essay] plan m ; [of advertisement, newspaper article etc] agencement m, mise f en page ◆ **the ~ of page 4** (Press etc) la mise en page de la (page) 4 ◆ **I don't like the ~ of my hand** (Cards) je n'aime pas mon jeu

layover /ˈleɪˌəʊvəʳ/ N (US) halte f

Lazarus /ˈlæzərəs/ N Lazare m

laze /leɪz/ VI (also **laze about, laze around**) (= be idle) paresser, ne rien faire, traînasser (pej) ◆ **we ~d (about or around) in the sun for a week** nous avons passé une semaine au soleil à ne rien faire, nous avons eu une semaine de farniente au soleil ◆ **stop lazing about or around and do some work!** cesse de perdre ton temps (à ne rien faire) et mets-toi au travail !

► **laze away** VT SEP ◆ **to laze the time away** passer son temps à ne rien faire

lazily /ˈleɪzɪlɪ/ ADV (= idly, languidly) [stretch, get up, yawn, watch] paresseusement ; [smile] avec indolence ◆ **to drift ~** [smoke, cloud] flotter mollement ; [snowflakes] voleter légèrement

laziness /ˈleɪzɪnɪs/ N paresse f, indolence f, fainéantise f

lazy /ˈleɪzɪ/ ADJ 1 (pej = idle) [person] paresseux ◆ **I'm ~ about washing my vegetables** je suis trop paresseux pour laver mes légumes, je ne prends pas la peine de laver mes légumes ◆ **to feel ~** être pris de paresse 2 (pej = sloppy) [attitude] nonchalant, paresseux ; [writing, work] peu soigné ; [style] relâché 3 (= relaxed, languid) [gesture, smile] nonchalant, indolent ; [river] paresseux, lent ; [hour, day, afternoon] de détente ; [lunch, dinner] décontracté ◆ **a ~ drawl** une voix traînante et nonchalante ◆ **we had a ~ holiday on the beach** nous avons passé des vacances reposantes à la plage
COMP **lazy eye** N (Med) amblyopie f
lazy Susan N (= dish) plateau m tournant

lazybones * /ˈleɪzɪbəʊnz/ N feignant(e) * m(f)

lb (abbrev of **libra**) ⇒ **pound¹**

LBO /ˌelbiːˈəʊ/ N (abbrev of **leveraged buyout**) → **leverage**

lbw /ˌelbiːˈdʌbljuː/ N (Cricket) (abbrev of **leg before wicket**) faute du batteur qui met la jambe devant le guichet au moment où la balle arrive

LC N (in US) (abbrev of **Library of Congress**) → **library**

lc (Typ) (abbrev of **lower case**) → **lower¹**

L/C (abbrev of **letter of credit**) → **letter**

LCD /ˌelsiːˈdiː/ N 1 (abbrev of **liquid crystal display**) LCD m 2 (abbrev of **lowest common denominator**) PPDC m

lcd /ˌelsiːˈdiː/ N PPDC m

LCM, lcm /ˌelsiːˈem/ N (abbrev of **lowest common multiple**) PPCM m

Ld (Brit) abbrev of **Lord**

L-dopa /elˈdəʊpə/ N L-dopa f

LDS /ˌeldiːˈes/ N (abbrev of **Licentiate in Dental Surgery**) diplôme m de chirurgien dentiste

LEA /ˌeliːˈeɪ/ N (Brit) (abbrev of **local education authority**) → **local**

lea /liː/ N (liter) pré m

leach /liːtʃ/ VT [+ liquid] filtrer ; [+ particles] lessiver VI [liquid] filtrer (from de ; into dans ; through à travers)

lead¹ /liːd/

vb : pret, ptp **led**

LANGUAGE IN USE 26.3

1 NOUN	4 INTRANSITIVE VERB
2 ADJECTIVE	5 COMPOUNDS
3 TRANSITIVE VERB	6 PHRASAL VERBS

1 - NOUN

1 esp Sport (= front position) tête f ; (= distance or time ahead) avance f ◆ **to be in the ~** (in match) mener ; (in race, league) être en tête ◆ **to go into or take the ~** (in race) prendre la tête ; (in match, league) mener ◆ **to have a three-point ~** avoir trois points d'avance ◆ **to have a two-minute/ten-metre ~ over sb** avoir deux minutes/dix mètres d'avance sur qn
2 = initiative initiative f, exemple m ◆ **to follow sb's ~** suivre l'exemple de qn ◆ **to give the ~** montrer l'exemple ◆ **to give sb a ~** montrer l'exemple à qn ◆ **to take the ~ in doing sth** être le premier à faire qch ◆ **thanks to his ~ the rest were able to** ... grâce à son initiative les autres ont pu ...
3 = clue piste f ◆ **the police have a ~** la police tient une piste ◆ **the footprints gave them a ~** les traces de pas les ont mis sur la piste
4 Theat rôle m principal ◆ **to play the ~** jouer or avoir le rôle principal ◆ **to sing the ~** chanter le rôle principal ◆ **male/female ~** premier rôle m masculin/féminin ◆ **juvenile ~** jeune premier m
5 = leash laisse f ◆ **dogs must be kept on a ~** les chiens doivent être tenus en laisse
6 Elec = flex fil m
7 Press article m à la une ; (= editorial) éditorial m ◆ **the financial crisis is the ~ (story) in this morning's papers** (= headlines) la crise financière fait les gros titres des journaux or est à la une des journaux ce matin
8 Cards **whose ~ is it?** à qui est-ce de jouer ?
9 Comm ◆ **~s and lags** termaillage m, jeu m de termes de paiement

2 - ADJECTIVE

= leading ◆ **~ guitarist** première guitare f ◆ **~ vocalist** (chanteur m) leader m, (chanteuse f) leader f

3 - TRANSITIVE VERB

1 = conduct, show the way to [+ person, horse] conduire, mener (to à) ; [+ procession, parade] être à la tête de ◆ **to ~ sb in/out/across** etc faire entrer/sortir/traverser etc qn ◆ **they led him into the king's presence** on le conduisit devant le roi ◆ **to ~ sb into a room** faire entrer qn dans une pièce ◆ **the guide led them through the courtyard** le guide leur a fait traverser la cour or les a fait passer par la cour ◆ **the first street on the left will ~ you to the church** la première rue à gauche vous mènera à l'église ◆ **what led you to Venice?** qu'est-ce qui vous a amené à Venise ? ◆ **each clue led him to another** chaque indice le menait au suivant ◆ **this ~s me to an important point** cela m'amène à un point important ◆ **to ~ a team onto the field** conduire une équipe sur le terrain

◆ **to lead the way** (= go ahead) aller devant ; (= show the way) (lit, fig) montrer le chemin ◆ **he led the way to the garage** il nous (or les etc) a menés jusqu'au garage ◆ **will you ~ the way?** passez devant, nous vous suivons

2 = be leader of [+ government, movement, party, team] être à la tête de, diriger ; [+ expedition] être à la tête de, mener ; [+ regiment] être à la tête de, commander ; (Ftbl etc) [+ league] être en tête de ; [+ orchestra] (Brit) être le premier violon de ; (US) diriger ◆ **we are looking for someone to ~ our new department** nous cherchons quelqu'un pour assurer la direction de notre nouveau service
3 Sport, fig = be ahead of ◆ **they were ~ing us by 10 metres** ils avaient une avance de 10 mètres sur nous ◆ **to ~ the field** (Sport, fig) venir or être en tête ◆ **our country ~s the world in textiles** notre pays est le leader mondial dans le domaine du textile
4 + life, existence mener ◆ **they ~ a simple life** ils mènent une vie simple
5 = induce, bring porter, amener ◆ **I am led to the conclusion that ...** je suis amené à conclure que ...

◆ **to lead sb to do sth** ◆ **he led me to believe that he would help me** il m'a amené à croire qu'il m'aiderait ◆ **what led you to think that?** qu'est-ce qui vous a amené à penser ça ? ◆ **his financial problems led him to change his attitude** ses problèmes financiers l'ont amené à changer d'attitude

6 Cards jouer ; (Bridge etc: at first trick) attaquer de, entamer ◆ **what is led?** qu'est-ce qui est joué or demandé ?

4 - INTRANSITIVE VERB

1 = be ahead : esp Sport (in match) mener ; (in race) être en tête ◆ **which horse is ~ing?** quel

est le cheval de tête ? ◆ **to ~ by half a length/three points** avoir une demi-longueur/trois points d'avance ◆ **to ~ (by) four goals to three** mener (par) quatre (buts) à trois

2 [= go ahead] aller devant ; *(= show the way)* montrer le chemin ◆ **you ~, I'll follow** passez devant, je vous suis

3 [Jur] ◆ **to ~ for the defence** être l'avocat principal de la défense

4 [Dancing] mener, conduire

5 [= go] *[road, corridor]* mener, conduire ; *[door]* mener (to à) s'ouvrir (to sur) ; *(fig)* mener (to à) ◆ **where is all this ~ing?** *(trend, events)* où cela va-t-il nous mener ? ; *(questions, reasoning)* où veut-il (or voulez-vous etc) en venir ? ◆ **the streets that ~ into/from the square** les rues qui débouchent sur/partent de la place ; see also **lead off**

◆ **to lead to** ◆ **it led to war** cela a conduit à la guerre ◆ **it led to his arrest** cela a abouti à son arrestation ◆ **that will ~ to his undoing** cela causera or sera sa perte ◆ **it led to nothing** ça n'a mené à rien ◆ **this led to their asking to see the president** cela les a amenés à demander à voir le président ◆ **it could ~ to some confusion** cela pourrait créer or occasionner une certaine confusion ◆ **it led to a change in his attitude** cela a provoqué un changement dans son attitude ◆ **one story led to another** une histoire en a amené une autre ◆ **one thing led to another and we ...** une chose en amenant une autre, nous ...

6 [Cards] ◆ **who is it to ~ ?** c'est à qui de commencer ? ◆ **south to ~** *(Bridge)* sud joue

5 - COMPOUNDS

lead-in N introduction *f*, entrée *f* en matière
lead story N *(Press)* → **noun 7**
lead time N *[of project, process]* délais *mpl* (d'exécution or de réalisation) ; *[of stock]* délais *mpl* (de réapprovisionnement) ; *[of new product]* délais *mpl* (de démarrage or de mise en production)
lead-up N préparation *f* (to sth de qch)

6 - PHRASAL VERBS

► **lead away** VT SEP emmener ◆ **he was led away by the soldiers** il a été emmené par les soldats ◆ **they led him away to the cells** ils l'ont conduit en cellule

► **lead back** VT SEP ramener, reconduire ◆ **they led us back to the office** ils nous ont ramenés or reconduits au bureau ◆ **this street ~s you back to the town hall** cette rue vous ramène à l'hôtel de ville

► **lead off** VI *(= begin)* commencer VT FUS *[corridor, path]* partir de ◆ **a passage ~ing off the foyer** un couloir qui part du foyer ◆ **the rooms which ~ off the corridor** les pièces qui donnent sur le couloir VT SEP ⇒ **lead away**

► **lead on** VI *(= lead the way)* marcher devant ◆ **~ on(, Macduff)!** *(hum)* allez-y, je vous suis ! VT SEP 1 *(= tease)* taquiner, faire marcher* ; *(= fool)* duper, avoir* ; *(= raise hopes in)* donner de faux espoirs à ; *(sexually)* allumer* 2 *(= induce)* amener ◆ **they led him on to talk about his experiences** ils l'ont amené à parler de son expérience ◆ **this led him on to say that ...** cela l'amena à dire que ...

► **lead up** VI 1 *[path etc]* conduire ◆ **this road ~s up to the castle** cette route conduit or mène au château ◆ **this staircase ~s up to the roof** cet escalier conduit au or donne accès au toit 2 *(= precede)* précéder ◆ **the years that led up to the war** les années qui ont précédé la guerre ◆ **the events that led up to the revolution** les événements qui ont conduit à la révolution 3 *(= lead on)* ◆ **he led up carefully to his proposal** il a soigneusement amené sa proposition ◆ **what are you ~ing up to?** où voulez-vous en venir ? ◆ **what's all this ~ing up to?** *(= what's he trying to say?)* où veut-il en venir ?

lead² /led/ N 1 *(NonC = metal)* plomb *m* ◆ **they filled** or **pumped him full of ~** * *(hum)* ils l'ont criblé de balles, ils l'ont transformé en écumoire* ; → **red**

2 *(NonC: also* **black lead***)* mine *f* de plomb

3 *[of pencil]* mine *f* ; *[of fishing line]* plomb *m* ; *(for sounding)* plomb *m* (de sonde) ; *(for wheel balancing)* masselotte *f* ◆ **that'll put ~ in your pencil** †‡ *(Brit hum)* ça va te donner de la vigueur (virile) ; → **swing**

4 *(Brit)* **~s** *[of roof]* couverture *f* de plomb ◆ **(window) ~s** plombures *fpl*

COMP *[object, weight etc]* de or en plomb
lead acetate N acétate *m* de plomb
lead balloon* N ◆ **it went down like a ~ balloon** c'est tombé à plat, ça a foiré‡
lead crystal N cristal *m* au plomb
lead-crystal ADJ *[decanter, bowl]* en cristal (au plomb)
lead-free ADJ sans plomb
lead oxide N oxyde *m* de plomb
lead paint N peinture *f* à base de carbonate de plomb
lead pencil N crayon *m* à papier
lead pipe N tuyau *m* de plomb
lead piping N tuyauterie *f* de plomb
lead poisoning N saturnisme *m*
lead replacement petrol N ≈ super *m*
lead shot N *(NonC)* grenaille *f* de plomb

leaded /ˈledɪd/ ADJ 1 ◆ **~ window** fenêtre *f* à petits carreaux ◆ **~ lights** petits carreaux *mpl* 2 *[petrol]* au plomb, qui contient du plomb

leaden /ˈledn/ ADJ 1 († = *made of lead*) de or en plomb 2 *(liter: in colour)* *[sky, clouds]* de plomb, plombé 3 *(= heavy)* *[footsteps, atmosphere]* lourd, pesant ; *[silence]* de mort ; *[translation, dialogue]* lourd 4 *(pej = stodgy)* *[food]* bourratif*
COMP **leaden-eyed** ADJ aux yeux ternes
leaden-limbed ADJ ◆ **to feel ~-limbed** se sentir des membres de plomb

leader /ˈliːdəʳ/ N 1 *[of expedition, gang, tribe]* chef *m* ; *[of club]* dirigeant(e) *m(f)* ; *(= guide)* guide *m* ; *(Climbing)* premier *m* (de cordée) ; *[of riot, strike]* meneur *m*, -euse *f* ; *(Mil)* commandant *m* ; *(Pol)* dirigeant(e) *m(f)*, leader *m* ◆ **they're (the) world ~s in the cosmetics industry** ce sont les leaders mondiaux de l'industrie cosmétique ◆ **he's a born ~** il est né pour commander ◆ **one of the ~s in the scientific field** une des sommités du monde scientifique ◆ **one of the ~s of the trade union movement** l'un des chefs de file or leaders du mouvement syndical ◆ **the ~ of the Labour Party, the Labour ~** le leader or le chef (du parti) travailliste ◆ **opposition ~** leader *m* or chef *m* de l'opposition ◆ **the Iraqi ~** le chef du gouvernement irakien ◆ **political ~s** leaders *mpl* or chefs *mpl* politiques ◆ **religious ~s** chefs *mpl* religieux ◆ **community ~s** notables *mpl* ◆ **the ~ of the orchestra** *(Brit)* le premier violon ; *(US)* le chef d'orchestre ◆ **the ~ for the defence** *(Jur)* l'avocat *m* principal de la défense ; → **follow, world, youth**

2 *(Sport)* *(in race)* *(= runner)* coureur *m* de tête ; *(= horse)* cheval *m* de tête ; *(in league)* leader *m* ◆ **he managed to stay up with the ~s** il a réussi à rester dans les premiers or dans le peloton de tête

3 *(Press)* article *m* principal ; *(= editorial)* éditorial *m* ◆ **~ writer** *(Brit)* éditorialiste *mf*

4 *(Mus)* *(= principal violinist)* premier violon *m* ; *(US)* *(= director)* chef *m* d'orchestre

5 *(Recording)* *(also* **leader tape***)* amorce *f*

6 *(Fishing)* bas *m* de ligne

7 *(Comm: also* **loss leader***)* produit *m* d'appel

8 *(Stock Exchange)* **~s** valeurs *fpl* vedettes

COMP **Leader of the House** N *(Brit Parl)* président *m* de la Chambre *(des communes ou des lords)*

LEADER OF THE HOUSE

Leader of the House désigne le président de la Chambre des communes ou celui de la Chambre des lords. L'un et l'autre ont pour fonction de préparer les débats parlementaires et d'en assurer le bon déroulement. Ils occupent une place importante au sein de l'équipe gouvernementale.

leaderboard /ˈliːdəbɔːd/ N *(Golf)* leaderboard *m*, têtes *fpl* de liste

leadership /ˈliːdəʃɪp/ N 1 *(NonC)* *(= position)* direction *f*, leadership *m* ; *(= action)* direction *f* ◆ **during** or **under his ~** sous sa direction ◆ **they were rivals for the party ~** ils étaient candidats rivaux à la direction du parti ◆ **to take over the ~ of the country** prendre la succession à la tête du pays ◆ **to resign the party ~** démissionner de la tête du parti ◆ **he has ~ potential** il a l'étoffe d'un chef ◆ **what we want to see is firm ~** ce que nous voulons c'est un dirigeant à poigne ◆ **he praised her ~ during the crisis** il a loué la manière dont elle a géré la crise ◆ **the company is suffering from poor ~** la société est mal gérée ◆ **~ skills** qualités *fpl* de leader ◆ **to play** or **take a ~ role (in sth)** jouer un rôle de meneur (dans qch)

2 *(= leaders collectively)* dirigeants *mpl* ◆ **the union ~ has** or **have agreed to arbitration** les dirigeants du syndicat ont accepté de recourir à l'arbitrage

leading¹ /ˈliːdɪŋ/ ADJ 1 *(= important)* important ◆ **a ~ industrialist** un industriel de premier plan ◆ **a ~ industrial nation** une des principales nations industrialisées ◆ **a ~ advocate of economic sanctions** un des principaux partisans des sanctions économiques

2 *(= most important)* principal ◆ **Britain's ~ car manufacturer** le premier or le principal constructeur automobile britannique ◆ **one of the ~ figures of the twenties** un personnage marquant des années vingt ◆ **one of our ~ industries** l'une de nos principales industries ◆ **one of the country's ~ writers** un des écrivains les plus importants or les plus en vue du pays

3 *(Theat, Cine)* *[role, part]* principal ◆ **to play the ~ part** or **role (in a film/play)** être la vedette (d'un film/d'une pièce) ◆ **to play** or **take a ~ part** or **role in sth** *(fig)* jouer un rôle majeur or prépondérant dans qch

4 *(= in foremost position)* *[car, aircraft, battalion]* de tête

5 *(= winning)* *(in race)* *[runner, driver, car]* en tête de course ; *(in league)* *[competitor, club, team]* en tête de classement

COMP **leading aircraft(s)man** (pl **leading aircraft(s)men**), **leading aircraft(s)woman** (pl **leading aircraft(s)women**) N *(Brit)* ≃ soldat *m* (de l'armée de l'air)
leading article N *(Press)* *(Brit)* éditorial *m* ; *(US)* article *m* de tête
leading case N *(Jur)* précédent *m*
leading counsel N *(Brit Jur)* *avocat commis sur une affaire*
leading edge N
1 *[of wing]* ◆ **the ~ edge** le bord d'attaque 2 *(fig)* ◆ **to be at** or **on the ~ edge of technology** être à la pointe de la technologie ◆ **to invest in the ~ edge of technology** investir dans les technologies de pointe
leading lady N *(Cine)* actrice *f* principale ◆ **his ~ lady in that film was Gill Page** sa partenaire principale dans ce film était Gill Page ◆ **the ~ lady was Mary Dodd** *(Theat)* c'est Mary Dodd qui tenait le premier rôle féminin
leading light N ◆ **he is one of the ~ lights in the campaign** c'est un des personnages les plus en vue de la campagne ◆ **she was one of**

the ~ lights in the local drama society c'était une des étoiles du groupe d'art dramatique local ◆ **one of the ~ lights in the economic field** une des sommités *or* lumières en matière d'économie
leading man N (pl **leading men**) *(Cine)* acteur *m* principal ◆ **her ~ man in that film was Will Preston** son partenaire principal dans ce film était Will Preston ◆ **the ~ man was David Penn** *(Theat)* c'est David Penn qui tenait le premier rôle masculin
leading note N *(Mus)* note *f* sensible
leading question N *(Jur, fig: pej)* question *f* tendancieuse
leading rating N *(Brit Navy)* quartier-maître *m* de 1re classe
leading rein N *(Horse-riding)* longe *f*

leading² /ˈledɪŋ/ N *(NonC: Typ)* interligne *f*, blanc *m*

leadworks /ˈledwɜːks/ N fonderie *f* de plomb

leaf /liːf/ (pl **leaves**) N 1 *[of tree, plant]* feuille *f* ◆ **the leaves** les feuilles *fpl*, le feuillage ◆ **in ~** en feuilles ◆ **to come into ~** se couvrir de feuilles ◆ **to shake like a ~** trembler comme une feuille ; → **fig** 2 *[of book]* feuillet *m*, page *f* ◆ **you should take a ~ out of his book** vous devriez prendre exemple sur lui ◆ **to turn over a new ~** s'acheter une conduite ; → **flyleaf** 3 *[of table]* *(on hinges)* rabat *m*, abattant *m* ; *(in groove, removable)* rallonge *f* 4 *(NonC)* *[of metal]* feuille *f* ; → **gold**
COMP **leaf bud** N bourgeon *m* à feuilles
leaf mould, leaf mold *(US)* N *(NonC)* terreau *m* de feuilles
leaf tobacco N tabac *m* en feuilles
► **leaf through** VT FUS *[+ book]* feuilleter, parcourir

leafless /ˈliːflɪs/ ADJ sans feuilles, dénudé

leaflet /ˈliːflɪt/ N 1 (= *publication*) prospectus *m* ; *(Pol, Rel)* tract *m* ; *(for publicity)* dépliant *m*, prospectus *m* ; (= *instruction sheet*) notice *f* explicative, mode *m* d'emploi 2 *(Bot)* foliole *f* VI distribuer des prospectus *or* des tracts *etc* VT *[+ area, street]* distribuer des prospectus *or* des tracts *etc* dans

leafy /ˈliːfɪ/ ADJ *[branch]* couvert de feuilles ; *[tree, plant]* touffu ; *[garden]* luxuriant ; *[lane]* bordé d'arbres (feuillus) ; *[suburb]* vert ◆ **green ~ vegetables** les légumes *mpl* verts à feuilles

league¹ /liːg/ N 1 (= *association*) ligue *f* ◆ **to form a ~ against** se liguer contre ◆ **to be in ~ (with sb)** être de connivence (avec qn)
2 *(Ftbl)* championnat *m* ; *(Baseball)* division *f* ◆ **major/minor ~** *(Baseball)* première/deuxième division *f* ; → **rugby**
3 *(fig = class)* classe *f*, catégorie *f* ◆ **they're in a different** *or* **not in the same ~** ils ne sont pas du même calibre ◆ **in the big ~** dans le peloton de tête, parmi les premiers ◆ **this is way out of your ~!** tu ne fais pas le poids !, tu n'es pas de taille !
COMP **league champions** NPL *(Brit Ftbl)* vainqueurs *mpl* du championnat ◆ **they were the ~ champions last year** ils ont remporté le championnat l'année dernière
league championship N championnat *m*
league leaders NPL ◆ **they are the ~ leaders now** pour le moment ils sont en tête du championnat
league match N *(Brit Ftbl)* match *m* de championnat
League of Nations N Société *f* des Nations
league table N *(Ftbl)* classement *m* du championnat ; *(esp Brit)* *[of schools, companies etc]* palmarès *m*

league² /liːg/ N lieue *f* ◆ **seven-~ boots** bottes *fpl* de sept lieues

leak /liːk/ N 1 *(in bucket, pipe, roof, bottle, pen)* fuite *f* ; *(in boat)* voie *f* d'eau ; *(in shoe)* trou *m* ◆ **to spring a ~** *[bucket, pipe]* se mettre à fuir ; *[boat]* commencer à faire eau ◆ **the ship sprang a ~ in the bow** une voie d'eau s'est déclarée à l'avant du navire ◆ **a gas ~** une fuite de gaz
2 *[of information]* fuite *f* ◆ **a Cabinet ~** une fuite ministérielle ◆ **budget/security ~** fuite *f* concernant le budget/la sécurité
3 (*‡* = *urinate*) ◆ **to take a ~** pisser‡ ◆ **to go for a ~** aller pisser‡
VI 1 *[bucket, pen, pipe, bottle]* fuir ; *[ship]* faire eau ; *[shoe]* prendre l'eau ◆ **the roof ~s** le toit fuit, il y a des fuites dans le toit
2 *[gas, liquid]* fuir, s'échapper ◆ **the acid ~ed (through) onto the carpet** l'acide a filtré jusque dans le tapis
3 *[cabinet, ministry etc]* ◆ **the Cabinet has been ~ing** il y a eu des fuites au sein du cabinet
VT 1 *[+ liquid]* répandre, faire couler ◆ **the tanker had ~ed its contents into the river/all over the road** le contenu du camion-citerne s'était répandu dans la rivière/sur la route
2 *[+ information]* divulguer ; *[+ story, document]* divulguer *(à la presse)*
► **leak in** VI *[spilt liquid]* filtrer ; *[water]* s'infiltrer ◆ **the water is ~ing in through the roof** l'eau entre *or* s'infiltre par le toit
► **leak out** VI *[gas, liquid]* fuir, s'échapper ; *[secret, news]* filtrer, être divulgué ◆ **it finally ~ed out that ...** on a fini par apprendre que ...

leakage /ˈliːkɪdʒ/ N (= *leak*) *[of gas, liquid, information]* fuite *f* ; (= *amount lost*) perte *f*

leakproof /ˈliːkpruːf/ ADJ étanche

leaky /ˈliːkɪ/ ADJ *[roof, pipe, bucket]* qui fuit ; *[boat]* qui fait eau ; *[shoe]* qui prend l'eau

lean¹ /liːn/ (pret, ptp **leaned** *or* **leant**) VI 1 (= *slope*) *[wall, construction etc]* pencher ◆ **I ~ towards the belief that ...** *(fig)* je tends à *or* j'incline à croire que ... ◆ **to ~ towards sb's opinion** tendre à partager l'opinion de qn ◆ **to ~ towards the left** *(Pol)* avoir des sympathies pour la gauche *or* à gauche
2 (= *support o.s., rest*) *[person]* s'appuyer (*(up) against* contre, à ; *on* sur) prendre appui (*(up) against* contre ; *on* sur) ; *(with one's back)* s'adosser (*(up) against* à) s'appuyer (*(up) against* contre, à) ; *(with elbows)* s'accouder (*on* à) ◆ **to be ~ing** être appuyé *or* adossé *or* accoudé ◆ **to be ~ing (up) against the wall** *[ladder, cycle etc]* être appuyé contre le mur ; *[person]* être appuyé contre le mur, être adossé au mur ◆ **to ~ on one's elbows** s'appuyer *or* prendre appui sur les coudes ◆ **to ~ on sb for help** *or* **support** s'appuyer sur qn ◆ **to ~ (heavily) on sb for advice** compter (beaucoup) sur qn pour ses conseils
3 (*** = *apply pressure*) faire pression (*on* sur) forcer la main (*on* à) ◆ **they ~ed on him for payment** ils ont fait pression sur lui pour qu'il paie *subj* ◆ **the editor was ~ing on him for the article** le rédacteur en chef le pressait pour qu'il remette son article
VT *[+ ladder, cycle etc]* appuyer (*(up) against* contre) ◆ **to ~ one's elbows on the table/one's head on sb's shoulder** poser ses coudes sur la table/sa tête sur l'épaule de qn ◆ **she ~ed her weight on the door** elle s'appuya de tout son poids contre la porte
N inclinaison *f*
COMP **lean-to** N (pl **lean-tos**) appentis *m* ◆ **~-to garage/shed** *etc* garage *m*/cabane *f etc* en appentis
► **lean back** VI se pencher en arrière ◆ **to ~ back in an armchair** se laisser aller en arrière dans un fauteuil ◆ **to ~ back against sth** s'adosser contre *or* à qch
VT SEP *[+ chair]* pencher en arrière ◆ **to ~ one's head back** pencher la tête en arrière, renverser la tête (en arrière)
► **lean forward** VI se pencher en avant
VT SEP pencher en avant
► **lean out** VI se pencher au dehors ◆ **to ~ out of the window** se pencher par la fenêtre ◆ **"do not lean out"** "ne pas se pencher au dehors"
VT SEP pencher au dehors ◆ **he leant his head out of the window** il a passé la tête par la fenêtre
► **lean over** VI *[person]* (= *forward*) se pencher en avant ; (= *sideways*) se pencher sur le côté ; *[object, tree]* pencher, être penché ◆ **to ~ over backwards** se pencher en arrière
► **lean up** VI, VT SEP → **lean¹**

lean² /liːn/ ADJ 1 (= *slim*) *[person, body]* mince ; *[animal]* svelte ◆ **to have a ~ build** être mince 2 (= *fatless*) *[meat, beef]* maigre 3 (= *poor*) *[harvest]* maigre, pauvre ◆ **~ diet** régime *m* maigre ◆ **~ years** années *fpl* de vaches maigres ◆ **there are ~ times ahead in the property market** le marché de l'immobilier connaîtra une période difficile ◆ **we had a ~ time of it** on a mangé de la vache enragée ◆ **to go through a ~ patch** traverser une période difficile 4 *[company]* *(through downsizing)* dégraissé ◆ **a ~er, more efficient team** une équipe plus légère et plus efficace N *[of meat]* maigre *m* COMP **lean-burn engine** N moteur *m* à carburant maigre

leaning /ˈliːnɪŋ/ N (= *liking*) penchant *m* (*towards* pour) ; (= *tendency*) tendance *f* (*towards* à) ◆ **I always had a ~ towards sport** j'ai toujours été attiré par le sport ◆ **he has artistic ~s** il a une prédisposition pour les arts, il a des tendances artistiques ◆ **what are his political ~s?** quelles sont ses tendances politiques ? ADJ *[wall, building]* penché COMP **the Leaning Tower of Pisa** N la tour (penchée) de Pise

leanness /ˈliːnnɪs/ N maigreur *f*

leant /lent/ VB pt, ptp of **lean¹**

leap /liːp/ (vb : pret, ptp **leaped** *or* **leapt**) N 1 *(lit)* saut *m*, bond *m* ◆ **to take a ~** bondir, sauter ◆ **at one ~** d'un bond
2 *(fig)* bond *m* ◆ **a ~ in profits/inflation** un bond dans les profits/l'inflation ◆ **there has been a ~ of 13% in profits/sales** les profits/les ventes ont fait un bond de 13% ◆ **Russia's ~ into the market economy** le passage de la Russie à l'économie de marché ◆ **the film takes a ~ into fantasy** le film plonge dans le fantastique ◆ **to make the ~ from singer to actor** réussir à passer de la chanson au cinéma (*or* au théâtre) ◆ **in** *or* **by ~s and bounds** à pas de géant ◆ **a ~ in the dark** un saut dans l'inconnu ◆ **a big** *or* **great ~ forward** un grand bond en avant ◆ **a giant ~ for mankind** un pas de géant pour l'humanité ◆ **(to take** *or* **make) a ~ of faith** *(Rel, fig)* (faire) un acte de foi ◆ **to make a ~ of the imagination** *or* **an imaginative ~** faire preuve de beaucoup d'imagination ◆ **you're making a ~ of logic here that I can't follow** je n'arrive pas à suivre votre logique
VI 1 *[person, animal, fish]* sauter, bondir ; *[flames]* jaillir ◆ **to ~ in/out** *etc* entrer/sortir *etc* d'un bond ◆ **to ~ to one's feet** se lever d'un bond ◆ **he leapt into/out of the car** il sauta dans/de la voiture ◆ **he leapt out of bed** il sauta du lit ◆ **he leapt over to the window** il se précipita à la fenêtre ◆ **to ~ off a bus/train** sauter d'un bus/train ◆ **to ~ over a ditch** franchir un fossé d'un bond, sauter (par-dessus) un fossé ◆ **he leapt into the air** il fit un bond (en l'air) ◆ **the flames leapt into the air** les flammes ont jailli *or* se sont élevées dans les airs ◆ **to ~ to attention** se mettre vivement au garde-à-vous ◆ **he leapt for joy** il a sauté *or* bondi de joie ◆ **the word leapt out at him** *or* **leapt off the page (at him)** le mot lui a sauté aux yeux
2 *(fig)* *[profits, sales, prices, unemployment]* faire un bond ◆ **the shares leapt from 125p to 190p** les actions ont fait un bond de 125 à 190 pence

♦ **the shares leapt (by) 21p to 370p** les actions ont fait un bond de 21 pence pour atteindre la cote de 370 pence ♦ **her heart leapt** son cœur a bondi dans sa poitrine ♦ **my heart leapt at the sight of her** j'ai eu un coup au cœur en la voyant ♦ **to ~ at sth** *[+ chance, suggestion, offer]* sauter sur qch ; *[+ idea]* accueillir qch avec enthousiasme ♦ **to ~ to the conclusion that …** conclure hâtivement que … ♦ **you mustn't ~ to conclusions** il ne faut pas tirer de conclusions hâtives ♦ **to ~ to sb's defence** s'empresser de prendre la défense de qn ; → **look**

VT 1 *[+ stream, hedge etc]* sauter (par-dessus), franchir d'un bond

2 *[+ horse]* faire sauter

3 *(fig)* **to ~ a generation** *[disease, illness, trait]* sauter une génération

COMP **leap year** **N** année *f* bissextile

▸ **leap about** **VI** gambader ♦ **to ~ about with excitement** sauter de joie

▸ **leap up** **VI** 1 *(lit) (off ground)* sauter en l'air ; *(to one's feet)* se lever d'un bond ; *[flame]* jaillir ♦ **the dog leapt up at him** le chien lui a sauté dessus ♦ **he leapt up indignantly** il a bondi d'indignation

2 *(fig) [profits, sales, prices, unemployment]* faire un bond

leapfrog /ˈliːp,frɒg/ **N** saute-mouton *m* **VI** ♦ **to ~ over** *(lit) [+ person]* sauter à saute-mouton par-dessus ; *[+ stool, object]* franchir à saute-mouton ; *(fig)* dépasser **VT** *(fig)* dépasser

leapt /lept/ **VB** (pt, ptp of **leap**)

learn /lɜːn/ (pret, ptp **learned** *or* **learnt**) **VT** 1 *(by study) [+ language, lesson, musical instrument]* apprendre ♦ **to ~ (how) to do sth** apprendre à faire qch ♦ **he's learnt his lesson** *(fig)* il a compris la leçon ♦ **I've learnt a lot since then** *(fig)* je sais à quoi m'en tenir maintenant, maintenant j'ai compris

2 *(= find out) [+ facts, news, results etc]* apprendre ♦ **I was sorry to ~ (that) you had been ill** j'ai appris avec regret que vous aviez été malade ♦ **we haven't yet ~ed whether he recovered** nous ne savons toujours pas s'il est guéri

3 *(Psych = acquire) [behaviour, reaction]* acquérir ♦ **a ~ed reaction** une réaction acquise ♦ **~ed behaviour** comportement *m* acquis

4 *(‡ = teach)* apprendre ♦ **I'll ~ you!** je vais t'apprendre, moi ! * ♦ **that'll ~ you!** ça t'apprendra ! *

VI 1 apprendre ♦ **it's never too late to ~** il n'est jamais trop tard pour apprendre, on apprend à tout âge ♦ **he'll ~!** *(fig iro)* un jour il comprendra ! ♦ **we are ~ing about the Revolution at school** on étudie la Révolution en classe ♦ **to ~ from experience** apprendre par l'expérience ♦ **to ~ from one's mistakes** tirer la leçon de ses erreurs ; → **live**^{1}

2 *(= hear)* ♦ **I was sorry to ~ of** *or* **about your illness** j'ai appris avec regret votre maladie

▸ **learn off** **VT SEP** apprendre par cœur

▸ **learn up** **VT SEP** *(= revise) [+ maths etc]* travailler, bûcher * ; *[+ new facts]* apprendre ♦ **she ~t up all she could about the district** elle a appris tout ce qu'elle a pu sur la région

learned /ˈlɜːnɪd/ **ADJ** *(= erudite) [person, journal, society, essay]* savant ; *[profession]* intellectuel ♦ **my ~ friend** *(Brit Jur)* mon éminent confrère

learnedly /ˈlɜːnɪdlɪ/ **ADV** avec érudition, savamment

learner /ˈlɜːnəʳ/ **N** apprenant(e) *m(f)* ♦ **~ (driver)** *(Brit)* apprenti(e) conducteur *m*, -trice *f* ♦ **you are a quick ~** vous apprenez vite ♦ **a ~s' dictionary** un dictionnaire pour apprenants ♦ **language ~** étudiant(e) *m(f)* en langues ♦ **a ~ of English** un apprenant d'anglais

COMP **learner-centred, learner-centered** *(US)* **ADJ** centré sur l'apprenant

learner's license **N** *(US) permis spécial pour apprentis conducteurs* ; → Driving Licence, Driver's License

learning /ˈlɜːnɪŋ/ **N** *(NonC)* 1 *(= fund of knowledge)* érudition *f*, savoir *m* ♦ **a man of ~** *(in humanities)* un érudit ; *(in sciences)* un savant ♦ **a little ~ is a dangerous thing** *(Prov)* mieux vaut être ignorant qu'à demi-savant ; → **seat**

2 *(= act)* apprentissage *m*, étude *f (of* de*)* ♦ **language** *etc* **~** apprentissage *m or* étude *f* des langues *etc* ♦ **children who are behind in their ~** des enfants qui ont du retard à l'école ♦ **~ develops the memory** apprendre développe la mémoire ♦ **a place of ~** un lieu d'étude ; → **distance, rote**

COMP **learning curve** **N** courbe *f* d'apprentissage *(SPEC)* ♦ **to be on a (steep) ~ curve** devoir apprendre (très) vite, avoir beaucoup à apprendre

learning difficulties, learning disabilities **NPL** difficultés *fpl* d'apprentissage

learning-disabled **ADJ** *(US)* ayant des difficultés d'apprentissage

learning resources centre **N** centre *m* de documentation et d'information

learnt /lɜːnt/ **VB** *(esp Brit)* (pt, ptp of **learn**)

lease /liːs/ **N** 1 *(Jur = contract, duration)* bail *m* ♦ **long ~** bail *m* à long terme ♦ **99-year ~** bail *m* de 99 ans ♦ **to take a house on ~** prendre une maison à bail, louer une maison

2 *(fig)* ♦ **to get** *or* **find** *or* **be given a new ~ of** *(Brit) or* **on** *(US)* **life** *[person]* retrouver un second souffle ♦ **after a career as a comedian, he found a new ~ of life as an actor** après une carrière de comique, il a retrouvé un second souffle en devenant acteur ♦ **it's like getting a new ~ of life!** je retrouve un second souffle ! ; *(stronger)* je me sens revivre ! ♦ **after months of pain and immobility I have found a new ~ of life** après des mois de douleur et d'immobilité j'ai retrouvé une nouvelle jeunesse ♦ **the heart transplant has given him a new ~ of** *or* **on life** sa greffe du cœur lui a donné un regain de vitalité ♦ **printing can give old T-shirts a new ~ of** *or* **on life** l'impression d'un motif peut donner une nouvelle jeunesse à de vieux tee-shirts

VT *[+ house, car etc]* louer à bail

COMP **lease-lend** **N** *(Econ)* prêt-bail *m*

leaseback /ˈliːsbæk/ **N** cession-bail *f* ♦ **~ scheme** *or* **contract** contrat *m* de cession-bail

leasehold /ˈliːshəʊld/ **N** *(= contract)* ≃ bail *m* emphytéotique ; *(= property)* propriété *f* louée à bail **ADJ** *[property, building, land]* loué à bail **ADV** *[buy]* à bail **COMP** **leasehold reform** **N** révision *f* du bail

leaseholder /ˈliːshəʊldəʳ/ **N** ≃ locataire *mf* emphytéotique

leash /liːʃ/ **N** *(for dog)* laisse *f* ♦ **to keep a dog on a ~** tenir un chien en laisse ♦ **to hold** *or* **keep sb on a short** *or* **tight ~** tenir la bride haute à qn ♦ **to give sb a longer ~** *(esp US)* laisser la bride sur le cou à qn

leasing /ˈliːsɪŋ/ **N** crédit-bail *m*

least /liːst/ LANGUAGE IN USE 26.3 (superl of **little**^{2})

ADJ *(= smallest amount of)* le moins de ; *(= smallest)* le moindre, la moindre, le plus petit, la plus petite ♦ **he has (the) ~ money** c'est lui qui a le moins d'argent ♦ **the ~ thing upsets her** la moindre chose *or* la plus petite chose la contrarie ♦ **the principle of ~ effort** le principe du moindre effort ♦ **the ~ common denominator** *(Math)* le plus petit dénominateur commun ♦ **with the ~ possible expenditure** avec le moins de dépenses possible(s) ♦ **that's the ~ of our worries** c'est le moindre *or* le cadet de nos soucis ; → **resistance**

PRON le moins ♦ **you've given me the ~** c'est à moi que tu en as donné le moins ♦ **it's the ~ I can do** c'est le moins que je puisse faire, c'est la moindre des choses ♦ **it's the ~ one can expect** c'est la moindre des choses ♦ **what's the ~ you are willing to accept?** quel prix minimum êtes-vous prêt à accepter ? ♦ **I wasn't the ~ bit surprised** cela ne m'a pas surpris le moins du monde ♦ **~ said soonest mended** *(Prov)* moins on en dit mieux on se porte, moins on en dit et mieux ça vaut ♦ **that's the ~ of it!** s'il n'y avait que ça !, ça, ce n'est rien !

♦ **at least** *(with quantity, comparison)* au moins ; *(parenthetically)* du moins, tout au moins ♦ **it costs $5 at ~** cela coûte au moins 5 dollars ♦ **there were at ~ eight books** il y avait au moins huit livres ♦ **he's at ~ as old as you** il a au moins votre âge ♦ **he eats at ~ as much as I do** il mange au moins autant que moi ♦ **at ~ it's not raining** au moins il ne pleut pas ♦ **you could at ~ have told me!** tu aurais pu au moins me le dire ! ♦ **I can at ~ try** je peux toujours essayer ♦ **he's ill, at ~ that's what he says** il est malade, du moins c'est ce qu'il dit

♦ **at the very least** au moins, au minimum ♦ **it will cost $100 at the very ~** cela coûtera 100 dollars au minimum *or* au bas mot

♦ **in the least** ♦ **not in the ~!** pas du tout ! ♦ **he was not in the ~ tired** *or* **not the ~ bit tired** *or* **not tired in the ~** il n'était pas le moins du monde fatigué ♦ **it didn't surprise me in the ~** cela ne m'a pas surpris le moins du monde ♦ **it doesn't matter in the ~** cela n'a pas la moindre importance

♦ **to say the least** ♦ **I was annoyed, to say the ~ (of it)** j'étais mécontent, c'était le moins qu'on puisse dire ♦ **she was not very wise, to say the ~** elle était pour le moins imprudente ♦ **it wasn't a very good meal, to say the ~ of it** c'était un repas assez médiocre pour ne pas dire plus

ADV le moins ♦ **the ~ expensive** le moins cher ♦ **the ~ expensive car** la voiture la moins chère ♦ **he did it ~ easily of all** *(= least easily of all he did)* c'est ce qu'il a eu le plus de mal à faire ; *(= least easily of all people involved)* c'est lui qui l'a fait le moins facilement de tous ♦ **she is ~ able to afford it** elle est la dernière à pouvoir se l'offrir ♦ **when you are ~ expecting it** quand vous vous y attendez le moins

♦ **least of all** ♦ **he deserves it ~ of all** c'est lui qui le mérite le moins de tous ♦ **nobody seemed amused, ~ of all John** cela ne semblait amuser personne et surtout pas John ♦ **~ of all would I wish to offend him** je ne voudrais surtout pas le froisser

♦ **not least** ♦ **all countries, not ~ the USA** tous les pays, et en particulier les USA ♦ **not ~ because …** notamment *or* entre autres parce que …

COMP **least-worst** * **ADJ** moins pire‡, moins mauvais

leastways * /ˈliːstweɪz/, **leastwise** * /ˈliːstwaɪz/ **ADV** du moins, ou plutôt

leather /ˈleðəʳ/ **N** 1 *(NonC)* cuir *m* ; → **hell, patent** 2 (also **wash leather**) peau *f* de chamois ; → **chamois** 3 *(US ‡ = wallet)* portefeuille *m* **NPL** **leathers** *(= suit)* cuir * *m* ; *(= trousers)* pantalon *m* en cuir **VT** *(* = beat)* tanner le cuir à‡

COMP *[boots, jacket, seat]* de *or* en cuir

leather bar * **N** bar *m* cuir *

leather goods **NPL** *(gen)* articles *mpl* en cuir ; *(fancy goods)* maroquinerie *f*

leatherbound /ˈleðəbaʊnd/ **ADJ** *[book]* relié (en) cuir

Leatherette ® /,leðəˈret/ **N** similicuir *m*, skaï ® *m*

leathering * /ˈleðərɪŋ/ **N** ♦ **to give sb a ~** tanner le cuir à qn‡

leatherjacket /ˈleðə,dʒækɪt/ **N** *(= larva)* larve *f* de tipule

leathern /ˈleðən/ **ADJ** *(= of leather)* de *or* en cuir ; *(= like leather)* tanné

leatherneck* /'leðənek/ N (US) marine *m*, fusilier *m* marin américain

leathery /'leðərɪ/ ADJ *[meat, substance]* coriace ; *[skin]* parcheminé, tanné

leave /liːv/ (vb : pret, ptp **left**) N 1 *(NonC = consent)* permission *f* ◆ **to ask ~ (from sb) to do sth** demander (à qn) la permission de faire qch ◆ **by** *or* **with your ~** avec votre permission ; → **by**

2 *(= holiday) (gen)* congé *m* ; *(Mil)* permission *f* ◆ **how much ~ do you get?** vous avez droit à combien de jours de congé (*or* de jours de permission) ? ◆ **six weeks' ~** permission *f or* congé *m* de six semaines ◆ **to be on ~** être en congé *or* en permission ◆ **on ~ of absence** en congé exceptionnel ; *(Mil)* en permission spéciale ; → **absent, French, sick**

3 *(= departure)* congé *m* ◆ **to take (one's) ~ (of sb)** prendre congé (de qn) ◆ **I must take my ~** il faut que je prenne congé ◆ **have you taken ~ of your senses?** avez-vous perdu la tête *or* la raison ?

VT 1 *(= go away from) [+ town]* quitter, partir de ; *(permanently)* quitter ; *[+ room, building]* sortir de, quitter ; *[+ person, job, one's husband, wife]* quitter ; *[+ one's children]* abandonner ◆ **he left Paris in 2001** il a quitté Paris en 2001 ◆ **we left Paris at 6 o'clock** nous sommes partis de Paris *or* nous avons quitté Paris à 6 heures ◆ **I must ~ you** il faut que je vous quitte *subj* ◆ **you may ~ us** *(frm)* vous pouvez vous retirer *(frm)* ◆ **they were left to die/to starve** on les a laissés mourir/mourir de faim ◆ **he has left this address** il n'habite plus à cette adresse ◆ **he left home in 1989** il a quitté la maison en 1989 ◆ **I left home at 6 o'clock** je suis sorti de chez moi *or* j'ai quitté la maison à 6 heures ◆ **to ~ hospital** sortir de *or* quitter l'hôpital ◆ **the ship left port** le navire a quitté le port ◆ **to ~ prison** sortir de prison ◆ **the car left the road** la voiture a quitté la route ◆ **to ~ the room** *(= go out)* sortir de la pièce ; *(euph = go to toilet)* sortir *(euph)* ◆ **he left school in 2001** *(Brit)* il a quitté l'école en 2001 ; *(US)* il a terminé ses études en 2001 ; *(US = gave up studies)* il a arrêté ses études en 2001 ◆ **he left school at 4pm** il est sorti de l'école *or* il a quitté l'école à 16 heures ◆ **the train left the station** le train est sorti de *or* a quitté la gare ◆ **to ~ the table** se lever de table, quitter la table ◆ **to ~ the track** *or* **rails** *(Rail)* dérailler ; → **love, lurch²**

2 *(= forget) [+ object, keys, umbrella]* laisser, oublier ◆ **he left his umbrella on the train** il a laissé *or* oublié son parapluie dans le train

3 *(= deposit, put)* laisser ◆ **I'll ~ the book for you with my neighbour** je laisserai le livre pour vous chez mon voisin ◆ **has the postman left anything?** est-ce que le facteur a apporté *or* laissé quelque chose ? ◆ **can I ~ my camera with you?, can I ~ you my camera?** puis-je vous confier mon appareil-photo ? ◆ **he left the children with a neighbour** il a laissé *or* confié les enfants à un voisin ◆ **he ~s a widow and one son** il laisse une veuve et un orphelin ◆ **to ~ a message for sb** laisser un message à qn ◆ **to ~ the waiter a tip** laisser un pourboire au garçon ◆ **to ~ word** laisser un mot *or* un message *(with sb for sb* à qn pour qn ; *that* que) ◆ **he left word for Paul to go and see him** il a fait dire à Paul d'aller le voir ◆ **he left word with me for Paul to go and see him** il m'a chargé de dire à Paul d'aller le voir

4 *(= allow to remain)* laisser ◆ **~ it where it is** laisse-le là où il est ◆ **he left half his meal** il a laissé la moitié de son repas ◆ **to ~ a space** *(Typ etc)* laisser un blanc *or* un espace ◆ **to ~ the door open/the phone off the hook** laisser la porte ouverte/le téléphone décroché ◆ **to ~ two pages blank** laisser deux pages blanches ◆ **it left me free for the afternoon** cela m'a laissé l'après-midi de libre, cela m'a libéré pour l'après-midi ◆ **this deal has left me in debt** cette affaire m'a laissé des dettes ◆ **he was left a widower** il est devenu veuf ◆ **he left it lying on the floor** il l'a laissé traîner par terre ◆ **don't ~ that letter lying around** ne laissez pas traîner cette lettre ◆ **to ~ sb on his own** *or* **to himself** laisser qn tout seul ◆ **to ~ sb in peace** *or* **to himself** laisser qn tranquille ◆ **left to himself, he'd never have finished** (tout) seul, il n'aurait jamais fini ◆ **I'll ~ it to you to decide** je te laisse le soin de décider ◆ **I('ll) ~ you to judge** je vous laisse juger ◆ **I'll ~ the matter in your hands** je vous laisse vous occuper de l'affaire, je vous laisse le soin d'arranger cela ◆ **shall we go via Paris? – I'll ~ it to you** et si on passait par Paris ? – je m'en remets à vous *or* je vous laisse décider ◆ **~ it to me!** laissez-moi faire !, je m'en charge ! ◆ **I'll ~ you to it** * je vous laisse (à vos occupations) ◆ **I wanted to ~ myself (with) at least £80 a week** je voulais garder *or* qu'il me reste *subj* au moins 80 livres par semaine ◆ **let's ~ it at that** tenons-nous-en là ◆ **let's ~ it at that for today** restons-en là pour aujourd'hui ◆ **it left a good impression on me** cela m'a fait bonne impression ◆ **to ~ sb in charge of a house/shop** *etc* laisser à qn la garde d'une maison/d'une boutique *etc* ◆ **the boss is out and he's left me in charge** le patron est sorti et m'a laissé la charge de tout ◆ **take it or ~ it** c'est à prendre ou à laisser ◆ **I can take it or ~ it** cela ne me fait ni chaud ni froid ; → **alone, baby, chance, cold, desire, device, go, shelf, stand, stone, unsaid**

5 *(Math)* **three from six ~s three** six moins trois égalent trois ◆ **if you take four from seven, what are you left with?** si tu enlèves quatre de sept, qu'est-ce qui te reste ?

6 *(in will) [+ money]* laisser *(to* à) ; *[+ object, property]* laisser, léguer *(to* à)

7 ◆ **to be left** rester ◆ **what's left?** qu'est-ce qui reste ? ◆ **who's left?** qui est-ce qui reste ? ◆ **there'll be none left** il n'en restera pas ◆ **how many are (there) left?** combien en reste-t-il ? ◆ **there are three cakes left** il reste trois gâteaux ◆ **are there any left?** est-ce qu'il en reste ? ◆ **nothing was left for me but to sell the house** il ne me restait plus qu'à vendre la maison ◆ **I was left with a lot of stock I couldn't sell** je me suis retrouvé avec un gros stock que je ne pouvais pas écouler ◆ **I've got $6 left** il me reste 6 dollars ◆ **I've got a half left** il m'en reste la moitié ◆ **I'll have nothing left** il ne me restera plus rien ◆ **I've no money left** je n'ai plus d'argent ◆ **have you got any left?** est-ce qu'il vous en reste ?

VI *(= go away) [person, train, ship etc]* partir, s'en aller ; *(= resign)* partir, démissionner ◆ **to ~ for Paris** *[person, train]* partir pour Paris ; *[ship]* partir *or* appareiller pour Paris ◆ **it's time we left, it's time for us to ~** il est l'heure de partir *or* que nous partions *subj* ◆ **the train ~s at 4 o'clock** le train part à 4 heures ◆ **he's just left** il vient de partir ◆ **his wife has left** *(permanently)* sa femme est partie

► **leave about, leave around** VT SEP *[+ clothes, possessions etc]* laisser traîner

► **leave aside** VT SEP laisser de côté

► **leave behind** VT SEP 1 *(= not take) [+ person]* laisser, ne pas emmener ; *[+ object]* laisser, ne pas emporter ◆ **he left the children behind in Paris** il a laissé les enfants à Paris ◆ **you'll get left behind if you don't hurry up** on va te laisser là si tu ne te dépêches pas

2 *(= outdistance) [+ opponent in race]* distancer ; *[+ fellow students etc]* dépasser

3 *(= forget) [+ gloves, umbrella etc]* laisser, oublier

► **leave in** VT SEP *[+ paragraph, words etc]* garder, laisser ; *[+ plug]* laisser, ne pas enlever ◆ **~ the cake in for 50 minutes** *(in oven)* laisser cuire le gâteau pendant 50 minutes

► **leave off** VI (* = *stop*) s'arrêter ◆ **where did we ~ off?** *(in work, reading)* où nous sommes-nous arrêtés ? ◆ **~ off!** arrête !, ça suffit ! *

VT SEP 1 (* = *stop*) arrêter *(doing sth* de faire qch)

2 *[+ lid]* ne pas remettre ; *[+ clothes] (= not put back on)* ne pas remettre ; *(= stop wearing)* cesser de porter, abandonner ; *(= not put on)* ne pas mettre

3 *[+ gas, heating, tap]* laisser fermé ; *[+ light]* laisser éteint

4 *(= not add to list) (deliberately)* exclure ; *(accidentally)* oublier, omettre

► **leave on** VT SEP 1 *[+ one's hat, coat etc]* garder, ne pas enlever ; *[+ lid]* ne pas enlever, laisser

2 *[+ gas, heating, tap]* laisser ouvert ; *[+ light]* laisser allumé

► **leave out** VT SEP 1 *(= omit) (accidentally)* oublier, omettre ; *(deliberately)* exclure ; *[+ line in text] (also Mus) [+ note]* sauter ◆ **they left him out** ils l'ont tenu *or* laissé à l'écart ◆ **I'm feeling left out** j'ai l'impression d'être tenu à l'écart ◆ **~ it out!** ‡ arrête ! *

2 *(= not put back)* laisser sorti, ne pas ranger ; *(= leave visible) [+ food, note, etc]* laisser ◆ **I left the box out on the table** j'ai laissé la boîte sortie sur la table ◆ **to ~ sth out in the rain** laisser qch dehors sous la pluie ◆ **to ~ sb out in the cold** *(in cold place)* laisser qn dans le froid ; *(on the sidelines)* laisser qn à l'écart *or* sur la touche ; *(in the lurch)* laisser qn en plan

► **leave over** VT SEP 1 ◆ **this is all the meat that was left over** c'est toute la viande qui reste ◆ **there's nothing left (over)** il ne reste plus rien ◆ **there's never anything left over** il n'y a jamais de restes ◆ **after each child has three there are two left over** quand chaque enfant en a pris trois, il en reste deux ◆ **if there's any money left over** s'il reste de l'argent

2 *(= postpone)* remettre (à plus tard) ◆ **let's ~ this over till tomorrow** remettons cela à demain

-leaved /liːvd/ ADJ *(in compounds)* ◆ **small-leaved** à petites feuilles ◆ **round-leaved** à feuilles rondes ◆ **five-leaved stem** tige *f* à cinq feuilles

leaven /'levn/ N levain *m* VT *(lit)* faire lever ◆ **his speech was ~ed by a few witty stories** son discours était agrémenté de quelques anecdotes spirituelles COMP **leavened bread** N pain *m* au levain

leavening /'levnɪŋ/ N *(lit, fig)* levain *m*

leaves /liːvz/ NPL of **leaf**

leavetaking /'liːvˌteɪkɪŋ/ N adieux *mpl*

leaving /'liːvɪŋ/ N départ *m* COMP **leaving present** N cadeau *m* de départ

leavings /'liːvɪŋz/ NPL restes *mpl*

Lebanese /ˌlebə'niːz/ ADJ libanais N *(pl inv)* Libanais(e) *m(f)* NPL **the Lebanese** les Libanais *mpl*

Lebanon /'lebənən/ N Liban *m* ◆ **in ~** au Liban ; → **cedar**

leccy‡ /'lekɪ/ *(Brit)* N *(= electricity)* courant *m*

lech * /letʃ/ VI ◆ **to ~ after sb** *(= desire)* désirer qn ; *(= behave lecherously)* courir après qn N ⇒ **lecher**

lecher /'letʃəʳ/ N coureur *m* de jupons

lecherous /'letʃərəs/ ADJ lubrique, libidineux *(hum)* ; *[look]* lascif

lecherously /'letʃərəslɪ/ ADV lubriquement, lascivement

lechery /'letʃərɪ/ N *(NonC)* luxure *f*, lubricité *f*

lectern /'lektən/ N lutrin *m*

lector /'lektɔːʳ/ N *(Univ)* lecteur *m*, -trice *f*

lecture /'lektʃəʳ/ N 1 *(gen single occurrence)* conférence *f* ; *(Univ etc: gen one of a series)* cours *m* (magistral) ◆ **to give a ~** faire *or* donner une conférence, faire un cours (*on* sur) ◆ **I went to the ~s on French poetry** j'ai suivi les cours de poésie française ; → **inaugural**

2 (*fig* = *reproof*) réprimande *f*, sermon *m* (*pej*) ◆ **to give** *or* **read sb a ~** sermonner qn (*about* au sujet de)

VI faire *or* donner une conférence (*to* à ; *on* sur) faire un cours (*to* à ; *on* sur) ◆ **he ~s at 10 o'clock** il fait son cours à 10 heures ◆ **he ~s at Bristol** il enseigne dans le supérieur à Bristol ◆ **he ~s in law** il est professeur de droit à l'université ◆ **she ~s on Keats** elle fait cours sur Keats

VT (= *reprove*) réprimander (*for having done* pour avoir fait) sermonner (*pej*) ◆ **he ~d me about my clumsiness** il m'a réprimandé pour ma maladresse

COMP **lecture course** N (*Univ*) cours *m* magistral

lecture hall N amphithéâtre *m*

lecture notes NPL notes *fpl* de cours

lecture room, lecture theatre N (*gen*) salle *f* de conférences ; (*Univ*) amphithéâtre *m*

> ⚠ In French, **lecture** means 'reading'.

lecturer /ˈlektʃərər/ N 1 (= *speaker*) conférencier *m*, -ière *f* 2 (*Brit Univ*) ≃ enseignant(e) *m(f)* du supérieur ◆ **senior ~** ≃ maître *m* de conférences

lectureship /ˈlektʃəʃɪp/ N (*Brit Univ*) ≃ poste *m* d'enseignant(e) du supérieur ◆ **senior ~** ≃ poste *m* de maître de conférences ◆ **he's got a ~ in English at Birmingham University** il enseigne l'anglais à l'université de Birmingham

LED /ˌeliːˈdiː/ N (abbrev of **light-emitting diode**) (diode *f*) LED *f* **COMP** **LED display** N affichage *m* LED

led /led/ VB pt, ptp of **lead[1]**

ledge /ledʒ/ N (*on wall*) rebord *m*, saillie *f* ; (*also* **window ledge**) rebord *m* (de la fenêtre) ; (*on mountain*) saillie *f* ; (*Climbing*) vire *f* ; (*under sea*) (= *ridge*) haut-fond *m* ; (= *reef*) récif *m*

ledger /ˈledʒər/ N (*Accounting*) grand livre *m* **COMP** **ledger line** N (*Mus*) ligne *f* supplémentaire

lee /liː/ N côté *m* sous le vent ◆ **in** *or* **under the ~ of ...** à l'abri de ... ADJ [*side of ship, shore*] sous le vent

leech /liːtʃ/ N (*lit, also fig pej*) sangsue *f* ◆ **he clung like a ~ to me all evening** il est resté pendu à mes basques * toute la soirée

leek /liːk/ N poireau *m*

leer /lɪər/ VI lorgner ◆ **to ~ at sb** lorgner qn N (*evil*) regard *m* mauvais ; (*lustful*) regard *m* concupiscent

leery * /ˈlɪərɪ/ ADJ 1 (*esp US, Can*) ◆ **to be ~ about sth** se méfier de qch 2 [*smile, grin*] lubrique, concupiscent 3 (= *flashy, showy*) [*clothes, car etc*] tape-à-l'œil *inv*

lees /liːz/ NPL [*of wine*] lie *f NonC*

leeward /ˈliːwəd/ (*esp Naut*) ADJ, ADV sous le vent N côté *m* sous le vent ◆ **to ~** sous le vent **COMP** **the Leeward Islands** NPL les îles *fpl* Sous-le-Vent

leeway /ˈliːweɪ/ N 1 (*Naut*) dérive *f*

2 (*fig* = *freedom*) liberté *f* ; (= *margin for action*) latitude *f* ◆ **he gives his children/his staff too much ~** il laisse trop de liberté à ses enfants/à son personnel ◆ **that allows** *or* **gives him a certain (amount of) ~** cela lui donne une certaine liberté d'action *or* marge de manœuvre ◆ **we had ten minutes' ~ to catch the train** nous avions une marge (de sécurité) de dix minutes pour attraper le train ◆ **they want more ~ to make decisions** ils veulent davantage de latitude *or* de liberté pour prendre des décisions ◆ **we had little ~ in our choice of hotel** *or* **in choosing a hotel** nous n'étions pas vraiment libres de choisir notre hôtel ◆ **he has some ~ in deciding how much money to spend** il dispose d'une certaine liberté *or* marge de manœuvre pour les dépenses

left[1] /left/ VB (pt, ptp **leave**)

COMP **left luggage** N (*Brit*) bagages *mpl* en consigne

left-luggage locker N (casier *m* à) consigne *f* automatique

left-luggage office N consigne *f*

left[2] /left/ ADJ gauche ◆ **my ~ arm/foot** mon bras/pied gauche ◆ **~ hand down!** (*to driver*) braquez à gauche ! ◆ **to have two ~ feet** * être maladroit de ses pieds ◆ **to be (way) out in ~ field** * (*esp US*) être (tout à fait) saugrenu ◆ **to come out of ~ field** * (*esp US*) être totalement inattendu ; see also **comp**

ADV [*turn, look*] à gauche ◆ **go** *or* **bear** *or* **turn ~ at the church** tournez *or* prenez à gauche à l'église ◆ **eyes ~!** (*Mil*) tête gauche ! ; → **right**

N 1 gauche *f* ◆ **on your ~** à *or* sur votre gauche ◆ **on the ~** sur la gauche, à gauche ◆ **the door on the ~** la porte de gauche ◆ **to drive on the ~** conduire à gauche ◆ **to the ~** à gauche ◆ **to keep to the ~** [*driver*] tenir sa gauche ◆ **turn it to the ~** tournez-le vers la gauche *or* à gauche

2 (*Pol*) **the Left** la gauche ◆ **he's further to the Left than I am** il est plus à gauche que moi ◆ **the parties of the Left** les partis *mpl* de gauche

3 (*Boxing*) gauche *m* ◆ **he threw a ~ to the jaw** il a porté un direct du gauche à la mâchoire ◆ **he hit him with his ~** il l'a frappé du gauche

COMP **left back** N (*Sport*) arrière *m* gauche

left-click (*Comput*) VI cliquer à gauche VT cliquer à gauche sur

left-footed ADJ [*shot*] du pied gauche ; [*player*] gaucher

left half N (*Sport*) demi *m* gauche

left-hand ADJ à *or* de gauche ◆ **the ~-hand door/page** *etc* la porte/page *etc* de gauche ◆ **~-hand drive car** conduite *f* à gauche (*véhicule*) ◆ **this car is ~-hand drive** cette voiture a la conduite à gauche ◆ **on the ~-hand side** à gauche ◆ **a ~-hand turn** un virage à gauche

left-handed ADJ [*person*] gaucher ; [*screw*] fileté à gauche, avec pas à gauche ; [*scissors etc*] pour gaucher ◆ **~-handed compliment** (= *insincere*) compliment *m* hypocrite ; (= *ambiguous*) compliment *m* ambigu

left-hander N (= *person*) gaucher *m*, -ère *f* ; (* = *blow*) gifle *f or* claque * *f* (*donnée de la main gauche*)

left-of-centre ADJ (*Pol*) de centre gauche

left wing N (*Mil, Sport*) aile *f* gauche ; (*Pol*) gauche *f*

left-wing ADJ [*newspaper, view*] de gauche ◆ **he's very ~-wing** il est très à gauche

left-winger N (*Pol*) homme *m* or femme *f* de gauche ; (*Sport*) ailier *m* gauche

leftie * /ˈleftɪ/ N 1 (*esp Brit: Pol, pej*) gaucho * *mf* (*pej*), gauchiste *mf* 2 (*US* = *left-handed person*) gaucher *m*, -ère *f*

leftish /ˈleftɪʃ/ ADJ ⇒ **leftist adj**

leftism /ˈleftɪzəm/ N (*NonC*) gauchisme *m*

leftist /ˈleftɪst/ (*Pol*) N gauchiste *mf* ADJ de gauche

leftover /ˈleftˌəʊvər/ N (= *throwback*) vestige *m* (*from* de) ◆ **a ~ from the days when ...** un vestige des jours *or* de l'époque où ... NPL **leftovers** (*after meal*) restes *mpl* ADJ restant, qui reste ◆ **a bottle with some ~ wine in it** une bouteille avec un restant de vin ◆ **a ~ bottle of wine** une bouteille de vin qui reste (*or* restait, *etc*)

leftward(s) /ˈleftwəd(z)/ (*Pol, lit*) ADJ orienté vers la gauche ADV vers la gauche

lefty * /ˈleftɪ/ N ⇒ **leftie**

leg /leg/ N 1 [*of person, horse*] jambe *f* ; [*of other animal, bird, insect*] patte *f* ◆ **my ~s won't carry me any further!** je ne tiens plus sur mes jambes ! ◆ **to stand on one ~** se tenir sur un pied *or* une jambe ◆ **to give sb a ~ up** (*lit*) faire la courte échelle à qn ; (* *fig*) donner un coup de pouce à qn ◆ **he hasn't got a ~ to stand on** il ne peut s'appuyer sur rien, il n'a aucun argument valable ◆ **it's got ~s** * (*esp US*) [*idea, plan, story*] ça tient debout ◆ **to pull sb's ~** (= *hoax*) faire marcher qn ; (= *tease*) taquiner qn ◆ **to get one's ~ over**‡ (*Brit*) s'envoyer en l'air‡ ; → **fast[1]**, **hind[2]**, **last[1]**

2 (*Culin*) [*of lamb*] gigot *m* ; [*of beef*] gîte *m* ; [*of veal*] sous-noix *f* ; [*of pork, chicken, frog*] cuisse *f* ; [*of venison*] cuissot *m*

3 [*of table etc*] pied *m* ; [*of trousers, tights etc*] jambe *f* ; → **inside**

4 (= *stage*) [*of journey*] étape *f* ◆ **first ~** (*Ftbl etc*) match *m* aller ◆ **second** *or* **return ~** match *m* retour ◆ **to run/swim the first ~** (*Sport: in relay*) courir/nager la première distance *or* le premier relais

VT ◆ **to ~ it** * (= *run*) cavaler‡ ; (= *flee*) se barrer‡ ; (= *walk*) aller à pied, faire le chemin à pied

COMP **leg bone** N tibia *m*

leg iron N (*Med*) appareil *m* (orthopédique)

leg muscle N muscle *m* de la jambe, muscle *m* jambier (*frm*)

leg-of-mutton sleeve N manche *f* gigot *inv*

leg-pull * N canular *m*

leg-pulling * N mise *f* en boîte *

leg shield N protège-jambe *m*

leg-warmers NPL jambières *fpl*

legacy /ˈlegəsɪ/ N (*Jur*) legs *m* (*de biens mobiliers*) ; (*fig*) legs *m*, héritage *m* ◆ **to leave a ~ to sb** (*Jur*) faire un legs *or* un héritage à qn ; (*fig*) laisser un héritage à qn ◆ **they have left us a ~ of bureaucracy and red tape** ils nous ont légué leur bureaucratie et leur paperasserie ◆ **we are left with the ~ of 40 years of environmental disaster** nous héritons de 40 ans de désastre écologique ◆ **the ~ of the past** l'héritage *m or* le legs du passé ◆ **the tragedy left a ~ of bitterness** cette tragédie a laissé un profond sentiment d'amertume ◆ **this law is a ~ from medieval times** cette loi est un héritage de l'époque médiévale ◆ **the economic ~ of Thatcherism/Communism** l'héritage *m* économique du thatchérisme/du communisme ◆ **this vase is a ~ from the previous tenants** on a hérité ce vase des précédents locataires

COMP **legacy duty, legacy tax** (*US*) N droits *mpl* de succession

legal /ˈliːgəl/ ADJ 1 (= *concerning the law*) [*error, protection*] judiciaire ; [*question, battle, services, framework*] juridique ; [*status*] légal, judiciaire ◆ **to take ~ action against sb** intenter un procès à qn, poursuivre qn en justice ◆ **I am considering taking ~ action** j'envisage d'intenter une action ◆ **to take ~ advice (on** *or* **about** *or* **over sth)** consulter un juriste *or* un avocat (à propos de qch) ◆ **~ loophole** vide *m* juridique ◆ **it's a ~ matter** c'est une question juridique *or* de droit ◆ **in ~ matters** en matière de droit ◆ **to have a fine ~ mind** être un excellent juriste ◆ **to the ~ mind the issue is quite clear** pour un juriste ce problème est tout à fait clair ◆ **for ~ reasons** pour des raisons légales ◆ **he's below the ~ age for driving a car** il n'a pas l'âge légal pour conduire une voiture

2 (= *lawful*) [*act, decision, right, obligation, requirement*] légal

COMP **legal adviser** N conseiller *m*, -ère *f* juridique

legal aid N aide *f* juridictionnelle

legal costs NPL frais *mpl* de justice

legal currency N monnaie *f* légale ◆ **this note is no longer ~ currency** ce billet n'a plus cours

legal department N [*of bank, firm*] service *m* du contentieux

legal document N *(concerning the law)* document *m* juridique ; *(legally valid)* document *m* légal
legal eagle * N as * *m* du barreau
legal entity N personne *f* morale
legal fees NPL frais *mpl* de justice
legal fiction N fiction *f* juridique
legal holiday N *(US)* jour *m* férié
the legal limit N la limite légale
legal offence N infraction *f* à la loi
legal opinion N avis *m* juridique
legal proceedings NPL procès *m*, poursuites *fpl* ◆ **to begin** *or* **start ~ proceedings against sb** engager des poursuites contre qn, intenter un procès à qn
the legal process N la procédure (judiciaire)
the legal profession N *(= lawyers)* les gens *mpl* de loi ; *(= occupation)* ◆ **to go into the ~ profession** faire une carrière juridique
legal redress N réparation *f* en justice
legal representation N représentation *f* en justice
legal successor N ayant cause *m*
legal system N système *m* juridique
legal tender N monnaie *f* légale ◆ **is this ~ tender?** *[banknote]* ce billet a-t-il cours ? ; *[coin]* cette pièce a-t-elle cours ?

legalese * /ˌliːɡəˈliːz/ N *(pej)* jargon *m* des juristes

legalism /ˈliːɡəˌlɪzəm/ N *(pej)* 1 *(word, point, rule etc)* argutie *f* juridique 2 *(turn of mind)* juridisme *m*, légalisme *m*

legalistic /ˌliːɡəˈlɪstɪk/ ADJ *(pej)* légaliste

legalistically /ˌliːɡəˈlɪstɪkəlɪ/ ADV *(frm)* d'un point de vue purement juridique

legality /lɪˈɡælɪtɪ/ N légalité *f*

legalization /ˌliːɡəlaɪˈzeɪʃən/ N légalisation *f*

legalize /ˈliːɡəlaɪz/ VT légaliser

legally /ˈliːɡəlɪ/ ADV *(gen)* légalement ◆ **to acquire sth ~** acquérir qch légalement *or* par des moyens légaux ◆ **~, the whole issue is a nightmare** du point de vue juridique, toute cette question est un cauchemar ◆ **it could be a bit problematic, ~ speaking** du point de vue juridique, ça pourrait poser un problème ◆ **the school is ~ responsible for your child's safety** du point de vue juridique *or* selon la loi, l'école est responsable de la sécurité de vos enfants ◆ **a lorry driver can ~ work eighty-two hours a week** selon la loi, les chauffeurs de poids lourds peuvent travailler jusqu'à 82 heures par semaine

legate /ˈleɡɪt/ N légat *m*

legatee /ˌleɡəˈtiː/ N légataire *mf*

legation /lɪˈɡeɪʃən/ N légation *f*

legator /ˌleɡəˈtɔːʳ/ N testateur *m*, -trice *f*

legend /ˈledʒənd/ N *(all senses)* légende *f* ◆ **a ~ in his own lifetime** une légende de son vivant ◆ **a living ~** une légende vivante

legendary /ˈledʒəndərɪ/ ADJ légendaire ◆ **to achieve ~ status** devenir légendaire

-legged /ˈleɡɪd/ ADJ *(in compounds)* ◆ **four-legged** à quatre pattes, quadrupède *(frm)* ◆ **bare-legged** aux jambes nues ; → **three**

leggings /ˈleɡɪŋz/ NPL *(for woman)* caleçon *m*, leggings *mpl* ; *(= legwarmers)* jambières *fpl* ; *(for baby)* petit pantalon *m* ; *(protective: for walker, farmer)* cuissardes *fpl*

leggo ‡ /leˈɡəʊ/ EXCL ⇒ **let go** ; → **go**

leggy * /ˈleɡɪ/ ADJ *[person]* aux longues jambes ; *(slightly pej) [youth etc]* tout en jambes ; *[animal]* aux longues pattes, haut sur pattes ◆ **a gorgeous ~ blonde** une magnifique blonde aux longues jambes

Leghorn /ˈleɡˌhɔːn/ N *(Geog)* Livourne

legibility /ˌledʒɪˈbɪlɪtɪ/ N lisibilité *f*

legible /ˈledʒəbl/ ADJ lisible

legibly /ˈledʒəblɪ/ ADV de façon lisible

legion /ˈliːdʒən/ N *(lit, fig)* légion *f* ; → **foreign** ADJ légion *inv* ◆ **books on the subject are ~** les ouvrages sur ce sujet sont légion

> **LEGION**
>
> La **British Legion** est un organisme d'aide aux anciens combattants et à leurs familles. Comptant de nombreux clubs locaux, elle organise des collectes au profit des associations caritatives de l'armée le jour anniversaire de l'armistice de la Première Guerre mondiale. C'est le "Poppy Day Appeal".
>
> L'**American Legion** remplit des fonctions similaires et aide à la réinsertion des anciens combattants. D'autre part, elle fait pression auprès du Congrès pour défendre leurs intérêts et milite en faveur d'une forte défense nationale. Elle compte également de nombreux clubs locaux où ses membres peuvent se retrouver.

legionary /ˈliːdʒənərɪ/ N légionnaire *m* ADJ de la légion

legionella /ˌliːdʒəˈnelə/ N légionellose *f*

legionnaire /ˌliːdʒəˈnɛəʳ/ N légionnaire *m* COMP
legionnaire's disease N *(Med)* maladie *f* du légionnaire

legislate /ˈledʒɪsleɪt/ VI légiférer, faire des lois ◆ **to ~ against** faire des lois contre ◆ **the government's decision to ~ for immigration control** la décision du gouvernement de légiférer sur le contrôle de l'immigration ◆ **we can't ~ for people doing that** ça ne servirait à rien d'interdire aux gens de le faire VT ◆ **attempts to ~ a national energy strategy** des tentatives pour mettre en place, par la voie législative, une stratégie nationale de l'énergie ◆ **a clause which allows the EU to ~ a fuller anti-discrimination law** une clause qui permet à l'UE d'adopter une loi plus complète contre la discrimination

legislation /ˌledʒɪsˈleɪʃən/ N 1 *(= body of laws)* législation *f* ; *(= single law)* loi *f* ◆ **a piece of ~** une loi ◆ **to bring in** *or* **introduce ~** mettre en place des dispositions législatives ◆ **the government is considering ~ against ...** le gouvernement envisage de légiférer contre ... ◆ **we are in favour of ~ to abolish ...** nous sommes partisans d'une législation qui abolirait ... ◆ **under the present ~** sous la législation actuelle 2 *(NonC) (= making laws)* élaboration *f* des lois ; *(= enacting)* promulgation *f* des lois

legislative /ˈledʒɪslətɪv/ ADJ *(frm) [reform, assembly, powers, process]* législatif ; *[session]* parlementaire ; *[programme]* de lois ; *[proposals]* de loi ◆ **the ~ body** le (corps) législatif ◆ **a ~ agenda** *(US)* un programme de lois ◆ **~ drafting** *(US)* rédaction *f* des projets de loi

legislator /ˈledʒɪsleɪtəʳ/ N législateur *m*, -trice *f*

legislature /ˈledʒɪslətʃəʳ/ N (corps *m*) législatif *m*

legist /ˈliːdʒɪst/ N légiste *mf*

legit ‡ /ləˈdʒɪt/ ADJ *[business, deal, person]* réglo * ◆ **to go ~** faire les choses dans les règles

legitimacy /lɪˈdʒɪtɪməsɪ/ N légitimité *f*

legitimate /lɪˈdʒɪtɪmɪt/ ADJ 1 *(= lawful) [action, government, business, child]* légitime ◆ **he has a ~ claim to the property** il a légitimement droit à cette propriété ◆ **it's ~ for the international community to intervene** il est légitime que la communauté internationale intervienne 2 *(= valid) [reason, excuse, argument, conclusion]* valable ; *[fear]* légitime ; *[complaint]* fondé ; *[target]* admissible ◆ **for ~ purposes** dans un but légitime, pour des motifs valables ◆ **it's perfectly ~ to raise objections** il est parfaitement légitime de soulever des objections 3 *(Theat)* ◆ **the ~ stage** *or* **theatre** *(gen)* le théâtre sérieux ; *(as opposed to cinema)* le théâtre VT /lɪˈdʒɪtɪmeɪt/ légitimer

legitimately /lɪˈdʒɪtɪmɪtlɪ/ ADV *[act, claim, argue, expect]* légitimement ◆ **a ~ elected government** un gouvernement élu légitimement ◆ **one might ~ believe/ask ...** on est en droit de croire/de demander ...

legitim(iz)ation /lɪˌdʒɪtɪm(aɪˈz)eɪʃən/ N légitimation *f*

legitimize /lɪˈdʒɪtɪmaɪz/ VT légitimer

legless /ˈleɡlɪs/ ADJ 1 *(lit)* sans jambes, cul-de-jatte 2 *(Brit * fig = drunk)* bourré *, rond *

legman * /ˈleɡmæn/ N (pl **-men**) *(Press)* reporter *m* débutant (qui enquête sur le terrain) ; *(gen)* garçon *m* de courses

Lego ® /ˈleɡəʊ/ N Lego ® *m* COMP **Lego brick** N bloc *m* de Lego ®

legroom /ˈleɡrʊm/ N place *f* pour les jambes

legume /ˈleɡjuːm/ N *(gen) (= plant)* légumineuse *f* ; *(= pod)* gousse *f*

leguminous /leˈɡjuːmɪnəs/ ADJ légumineux ◆ **~ plants** fabacées

legwork * /ˈleɡwɜːk/ N *[of reporter, investigator etc]* travail *m* sur le terrain ◆ **I had to do all the ~** *(gen)* c'est moi qui ai dû me déplacer

Leibnitzian /laɪbˈnɪtsɪən/ ADJ leibnizien

Leics. abbrev of **Leicestershire**

Leipzig /ˈlaɪpsɪɡ/ N Leipzig

leisure /ˈleʒəʳ, (US) ˈliːʒəʳ/ N *(NonC)* loisir *m*, temps *m* libre ◆ **she's a lady of ~** *(hum)* elle est rentière *(fig hum)* ◆ **a life of ~** une vie pleine de loisirs, une vie oisive *(pej)* ◆ **in my moments** *or* **hours of ~** à mes moments perdus, pendant mes loisirs ◆ **do it at your ~** prenez tout votre temps ◆ **think about it at (your) ~** réfléchissez-y à tête reposée ◆ **a park where the public can stroll at ~** un parc où l'on peut flâner à sa guise ◆ **he is not often at ~** il n'a pas souvent de temps libre
COMP *[pursuits, activities]* de loisirs ; *[sector]* des loisirs
leisure centre N *(Brit)* centre *m* de loisirs
leisure complex N complexe *m* de loisirs
the leisure industry N l'industrie *f* des loisirs
leisure occupations NPL loisirs *mpl*
leisure suit N costume *m* sport, tenue *f* décontractée
leisure time N loisirs *mpl*, temps *m* libre
leisure wear N *(NonC)* sportswear *m*

leisured /ˈleʒəd/ ADJ *[person, life, existence]* oisif ; *[meal]* tranquille ◆ **the ~ classes** les classes *fpl* oisives

leisurely /ˈleʒəlɪ/ ADJ *[pace, stroll, meal, occupation]* tranquille ◆ **to adopt a ~ approach to sth** aborder qch avec décontraction ◆ **to have a ~ bath** prendre tranquillement un bain ADV tranquillement, sans se presser

leitmotif, leitmotiv /ˈlaɪtməʊˌtiːf/ N *(Mus, fig)* leitmotiv *m*

lem /lem/ N *(Space)* lem *m*, module *m* lunaire

lemma /ˈlemə/ N (pl **lemmas** *or* **lemmata** /ˈlemətə/) *(Ling: gen)* vocable *m* ; *(in computational liguistics)* lemme *m*

lemmatization /ˌleməˌtaɪˈzeɪʃən/ N lemmatisation *f*

lemmatize /ˈlemətaɪz/ VT lemmatiser

lemming /ˈlemɪŋ/ N lemming *m*

lemon /ˈlemən/ N 1 *(= fruit, drink)* citron *m* ; *(= tree)* citronnier *m* ; *(= colour)* citron *m* ; → **bitter** 2 *(* = idiot)* cruche * *f*, imbécile *mf* ; *(= defective object)* cochonnerie * *f* ◆ **I stood there like a ~** j'étais là comme un imbécile *or* une cruche * ADJ *(in colour)* citron *inv*
COMP **lemon balm** N citronnelle *f*, eau *f* de mélisse

lemon cheese, lemon curd N *(Brit)* crème *f* au citron
lemon drink N citronnade *f*
lemon drop N bonbon *m* (acidulé) au citron
lemon grass N citronnelle *f*
lemon grove N plantation *f* de citronniers
lemon juice N jus *m* de citron ; *(= drink)* citron *m* pressé
lemon soda N *(esp US)* limonade *f*
lemon sole N *(Brit)* limande-sole *f*
lemon squash N ≈ citronnade *f*
lemon squeezer N presse-citron *m*, presse-agrumes *m inv*
lemon tea N thé *m* au citron
lemon tree N citronnier *m*
lemon yellow ADJ, N jaune citron *m inv*

lemonade /ˌleməˈneɪd/ N *(still)* citronnade *f* ; *(fizzy)* limonade *f*

lemur /ˈliːməʳ/ N lémurien *m*

lend /lend/ (pret, ptp **lent**) VT 1 *[+ money, possessions]* prêter ◆ **to ~ sb sth, to ~ sth to sb** prêter qch à qn ◆ **to ~ money at 10%** prêter de l'argent à 10% ; → **lease**
2 *(fig)* *[+ importance]* prêter, accorder *(to* à) ; *[+ dignity, mystery]* donner, conférer *(to* à) ◆ **to ~ credibility to sth** donner *or* conférer une certaine crédibilité à qch ◆ **to ~ authority to sth** conférer une certaine autorité à qch ◆ **to ~ an ear (to sb)** prêter l'oreille (à qn), écouter (qn) ; see also **ear**[1] ◆ **to ~ one's name to …** prêter son nom à …, accorder son patronage à …
3 *(reflexive)* ◆ **to ~ itself** *(or* **o.s.) to …** se prêter à … ◆ **the novel doesn't ~ itself to being filmed** ce roman ne se prête pas à une adaptation cinématographique ◆ **the programme doesn't really ~ itself to radio** cette émission ne se prête pas vraiment à la radio ◆ **these problems don't ~ themselves to quick solutions** ces problèmes ne se prêtent pas à des solutions rapides ◆ **he refused to ~ himself to such a dishonest scheme** il a refusé de cautionner un plan aussi malhonnête, il a refusé de se laisser impliquer dans une affaire aussi malhonnête ; → **hand, support, weight**
COMP **lend-lease** N *(US)* ⇒ **lease-lend** ; → **lease**

► **lend out** VT SEP *[+ object, book]* prêter

lender /ˈlendəʳ/ N prêteur *m*, -euse *f* ; → **moneylender**

lending /ˈlendɪŋ/ N prêt *m* ◆ **bank ~** le prêt bancaire
COMP **lending library** N bibliothèque *f* de prêt
lending limit N *(Fin)* plafond *m* de crédit
lending policy N *(Fin)* politique *f* de prêt
lending rate N *(Fin)* taux *m* de prêt, taux *m* d'intérêt débiteur

length /leŋ(k)θ/ N 1 *(NonC: in space)* longueur *f* ◆ **its ~ was 6 metres, it was 6 metres in ~** il faisait 6 mètres de long, sa longueur était de 6 mètres ◆ **what is the ~ of the field?, what ~ is the field?** quelle est la longueur du champ ? ◆ **along the whole ~ of the river** tout le long *or* sur toute la longueur de la rivière ◆ **what ~ do you want?** quelle longueur vous faut-il ?, il vous en faut combien (de long) ? ◆ **what ~ (of cloth) did you buy?** quel métrage (de tissu) as-tu acheté ? ◆ **the ship turns in its own ~** le navire vire sur place ◆ **over the ~ and breadth of England** dans toute l'Angleterre ◆ **to fall full ~, to go** *or* **measure one's ~** tomber *or* s'étaler* de tout son long ; see also **full** ; → **arm**[1]
2 *(NonC: in time)* durée *f* ; *[of book, essay, letter, film, speech]* longueur *f* ◆ **what ~ is the film?, what's the ~ of the film?** quelle est la durée du film ? ◆ **~ of life** durée *f* de vie ◆ **for the whole ~ of his life** pendant toute la durée de sa vie ◆ **for what ~ of time?** pour combien de temps ?, pour quelle durée ? ◆ **for some ~ of time** pendant un certain temps, pendant quelque temps ◆ **the ~ of time he took to do it** le temps qu'il a mis à le faire ◆ **~ of service** ancienneté *f* ◆ **4,000 words in ~** *(essay, book)* de 4 000 mots
◆ **at + length** *(= at last)* enfin, à la fin ◆ **at (great) ~** *(= for a long time)* fort longuement ; *(= in detail)* dans le détail, en long et en large
◆ **to go to the length/to … lengths** ◆ **he went to the ~ of asking my advice** il est allé jusqu'à me demander conseil ◆ **I've gone to great ~s to get it finished** je me suis donné beaucoup de mal pour le terminer ◆ **he would go to any ~(s) to succeed** il ne reculerait devant rien pour réussir ◆ **I didn't think he would go to such ~s to get the job** je n'aurais pas cru qu'il serait allé jusque-là pour avoir le poste
3 *(Sport)* longueur *f* ◆ **to win by a ~** gagner d'une longueur ◆ **he was two ~s behind** il avait deux longueurs de retard ◆ **the race will be swum over six ~s** la course se nagera sur six longueurs ◆ **four ~s of the pool** quatre longueurs de piscine ◆ **he was about three car ~s behind me** il était à trois longueurs de voiture derrière moi
4 *(Phon)* *[of vowel]* quantité *f* ; *[of syllable]* longueur *f*
5 *(= section)* *[of rope, wire]* morceau *m*, bout *m* ; *[of wallpaper]* lé *m*, laize *f* ; *[of cloth]* métrage *m*, pièce *f* ; *[of tubing]* morceau *m*, bout *m* ; *[of track]* tronçon *m* ◆ **cut into metre ~s** coupé en morceaux d'un mètre ◆ **I bought several ~s of dress material** j'ai acheté plusieurs métrages de tissu de confection ◆ **dress/skirt ~** *(Sewing)* hauteur *f* de robe/de jupe
COMP **length mark** N *(Ling)* signe *m* diacritique de longueur

-length /leŋ(k)θ/ ADJ *(in compounds)* ◆ **ankle-length skirt** jupe *f* qui descend jusqu'aux chevilles ◆ **elbow-length sleeve** manche *f* mi-longue ; → **shoulder**

lengthen /ˈleŋ(k)θən/ VT *[+ object]* allonger, rallonger ; *[+ visit, life]* prolonger ; *(Phon)* *[+ vowel]* allonger ◆ **to ~ one's stride** allonger le pas VI *[object, process, cycle, shadows, queue]* s'allonger ; *[visit, silence]* se prolonger ; *[skirts]* rallonger ◆ **the days/nights are ~ing** les jours/nuits rallongent ◆ **the intervals between his visits were ~ing** ses visites s'espaçaient

lengthily /ˈleŋ(k)θɪlɪ/ ADV longuement

lengthways /ˈleŋ(k)θ,weɪz/, **lengthwise** /ˈleŋ(k)θ,waɪz/ ADV dans le sens de la longueur ADJ longitudinal

lengthy /ˈleŋ(k)θɪ/ ADJ très long (longue *f*) ◆ **a ~ process** un processus très long ◆ **~ delays on the M8** de très forts ralentissements sur la M8 ◆ **for a ~ period of time** pendant très longtemps ◆ **patients who have a ~ wait for treatment** les patients qui doivent attendre très longtemps pour être soignés

lenience /ˈliːnɪəns/, **leniency** /ˈliːnɪənsɪ/ N *[of parent, teacher, treatment, view]* indulgence *f* ; *[of government, judge, sentence]* clémence *f*

lenient /ˈliːnɪənt/ ADJ *[parent, teacher, treatment, view]* indulgent *(with sb* avec qn) ; *[government, judge, sentence]* clément

leniently /ˈliːnɪəntlɪ/ ADV *[treat]* avec indulgence

Lenin /ˈlenɪn/ N Lénine *m*

Leningrad /ˈlenɪngræd/ N Leningrad

Leninism /ˈlenɪˌnɪzəm/ N léninisme *m*

Leninist /ˈlenɪnɪst/ ADJ, N léniniste *mf*

lens /lenz/ N *(for magnifying)* lentille *f* ; *[of camera]* objectif *m* ; *[of spectacles]* verre *m* ; (also **contact lens**) lentille *f*, verre *m* de contact ; *[of eye]* cristallin *m* ; → **contact, telephoto lens, wide**
COMP **lens cap** N bouchon *m* d'objectif
lens field N angle *m* de couverture
lens holder N porte-objectif *m inv*
lens hood N pare-soleil *m inv*

Lent /lent/ N *(Rel)* le carême ◆ **in** *or* **during ~** pendant le carême ◆ **to keep ~** observer le carême, faire carême ◆ **I gave it up for ~** j'y ai renoncé pour le carême

lent /lent/ VB (pt, ptp of **lend**)

Lenten /ˈlentən/ ADJ de carême

lentil /ˈlentl/ N lentille *f* ◆ **~ soup** soupe *f* aux lentilles

Leo /ˈliːəʊ/ N *(Astron)* Lion *m* ◆ **I'm (a) ~** *(Astrol)* je suis (du) Lion

Leonardo (da Vinci) /ˌliːəˈnɑːdəʊ(dəˈvɪntʃɪ)/ N Léonard de Vinci *m*

Leonian /liːˈəʊnɪən/ N ◆ **to be a ~** être (du) Lion

leonine /ˈliːənaɪn/ ADJ léonin

leopard /ˈlepəd/ N léopard *m* ◆ **the ~ cannot change its spots** *(Prov)* on ne peut pas changer sa nature, chassez le naturel, il revient au galop

leopardess /ˈlepədes/ N léopard *m* femelle

leopardskin /ˈlepədskɪn/ N peau *f* de léopard

leotard /ˈliːətɑːd/ N justaucorps *m*

leper /ˈlepəʳ/ N *(Med)* lépreux *m*, -euse *f* ; *(fig)* pestiféré *m* ◆ **~ colony** léproserie *f*

lepidoptera /ˌlepɪˈdɒptərə/ NPL lépidoptères *mpl*

lepidopterist /ˌlepɪˈdɒptərɪst/ N lépidoptériste *mf*

leprechaun /ˈleprəkɔːn/ N lutin *m*, farfadet *m* *(dans la mythologie irlandaise)*

leprosy /ˈleprəsɪ/ N lèpre *f*

leprous /ˈleprəs/ ADJ lépreux

lesbian /ˈlezbɪən/ ADJ *[woman, activist, feminist, group, film]* lesbien ; *[couple]* de lesbiennes ; *[relationship, affair]* homosexuel *(entre femmes)* ◆ **~ sex** rapports *mpl* homosexuels entre femmes ◆ **~ and gay community** communauté *f* lesbienne et gay ◆ **~ and gay issues** questions *fpl* concernant les lesbiennes et les gays ◆ **~ and gay movement/rights** mouvement *m*/droits *mpl* des lesbiennes et des gays ◆ **~ and gay people** les lesbiennes *fpl* et les gays *mpl* N lesbienne *f*

lesbianism /ˈlezbɪənɪzəm/ N lesbianisme *m*, homosexualité *f* féminine

lesion /ˈliːʒən/ N lésion *f*

Lesotho /lɪˈsuːtuː/ N Lesotho *m* ◆ **in ~** au Lesotho

less /les/ (compar of **little**[2]) ADJ, PRON *(in amount, size, degree)* moins (de) ◆ **~ butter** moins de beurre ◆ **even ~** encore moins ◆ **even** *or* **still ~ butter** encore moins de beurre ◆ **much ~ milk** beaucoup moins de lait ◆ **a little ~ cream** un peu moins de crème ◆ **~ and ~** de moins en moins ◆ **~ and ~ money** de moins en moins d'argent ◆ **he couldn't have done ~ if he'd tried** il aurait pu difficilement (en) faire moins ◆ **of ~ importance** de moindre importance, de moins d'importance ◆ **I have ~ time for reading** j'ai moins le temps de lire, j'ai moins de temps pour lire ◆ **can't you let me have it for ~?** vous ne pouvez pas me faire un prix ? ◆ **~ of your cheek!*** ça suffit ! ◆ **~ noise please!** moins de bruit s'il vous plaît ! ◆ **~ of that** *or* **it!** assez !, ça suffit ! ◆ **with ~ trouble** avec moins de mal ◆ **he knows little German and ~ Russian** il ne connaît pas bien l'allemand et encore moins le russe ◆ **he has little but I have ~** il n'a pas grand-chose mais j'en ai encore moins ◆ **we must see ~ of her** il faut que nous la voyions *subj* moins souvent
◆ **less … than** moins … que ; *(before a number)* moins de … ◆ **I have ~ than you** j'en ai moins que vous ◆ **I need ~ than that** il m'en faut moins que cela ◆ **I have ~ money than you** j'ai moins d'argent que vous ◆ **it costs ~ than the export model** il coûte moins cher que le modèle d'exportation ◆ **it was ~ money than I expected** c'était moins (d'argent) que je n'es-

comptais ◆ ~ **than half the audience** moins de la moitié de l'assistance ◆ **I got ~ out of it than you did** j'en ai tiré moins de profit que toi ◆ **it took ~ time than I expected** cela a pris moins de temps que je ne pensais ◆ **we eat ~ bread than we used to** nous mangeons moins de pain qu'avant ◆ **he did ~ to help them than his brother did** il a moins fait *or* fait moins pour les aider que son frère ◆ **it is ~ than perfect** on ne peut pas dire que ce soit parfait ◆ **in ~ than a month** en moins d'un mois ◆ **in ~ than no time*** en un rien de temps, en moins de deux* ◆ **not ~ than one kilo** pas moins d'un kilo ◆ **a sum ~ than 10 euros** une somme de moins de 10 € ◆ **it's ~ than you think** c'est moins que vous ne croyez ◆ **I won't sell it for ~ than $10** je ne le vendrai pas à *or* pour moins de 10 dollars

◆ **no less** ◆ **with no ~ skill than enthusiasm** avec non moins d'habileté que d'enthousiasme ◆ **no ~ a person than the Prime Minister** rien moins que le Premier ministre ◆ **he's bought a car, no ~*** il s'est payé une voiture, rien que ça* ◆ **I was told the news by the bishop, no ~*** c'est l'évêque en personne, s'il vous plaît*, qui m'a appris la nouvelle ◆ **he has no ~ than four months' holiday a year** il a au moins quatre mois de vacances par an ◆ **it costs no ~ than £100** ça ne coûte pas moins de 100 livres ◆ **I think no ~ of him for that** il n'est pas descendu dans mon estime pour autant

◆ **the less ...** ◆ **there will be so much the ~ to pay** cela fera autant de moins à payer ◆ **the ~ said about it the better** mieux vaut ne pas en parler ◆ **the ~ you buy the ~ you spend** moins vous achetez, moins vous dépensez ◆ **I think none the ~ of him** *or* **I don't think any the ~ of him for that** il n'est pas descendu dans mon estime pour autant

◆ **nothing less than** rien moins que, tout simplement ◆ **he's nothing ~ than a thief** c'est tout simplement un voleur, ce n'est qu'un voleur ◆ **nothing ~ than a bomb would move them** il faudrait au moins une bombe pour les faire bouger ◆ **nothing ~ than a public apology will satisfy him** il ne lui faudra rien moins que des excuses publiques pour le satisfaire ◆ **it's nothing ~ than disgraceful** le moins qu'on puisse dire c'est que c'est une honte

ADV moins ◆ **you must eat ~** vous devez moins manger, il faut que vous mangiez *subj* moins ◆ **I must see you ~** il faut que je vous voie moins souvent ◆ **to grow ~** diminuer ◆ **that's ~ important** c'est moins important, ça n'est pas si important ◆ **~ and ~** de moins en moins ◆ **still ~, much ~, even ~** encore moins ◆ **~ regularly/often** moins régulièrement/souvent ◆ **whichever is (the) ~ expensive** le moins cher des deux ◆ **he is ~ well known** il est moins (bien) connu ◆ **he was (all) the ~ pleased as he'd refused to give his permission** il était d'autant moins content qu'il avait refusé son autorisation ◆ **he wasn't expecting me but he was none the ~ pleased to see me** il ne m'attendait pas mais il n'en était pas moins content de me voir

◆ **less ... than** moins ... que ◆ **it's ~ expensive than you think** c'est moins cher que vous ne croyez ◆ **he was ~ hurt than frightened** il a eu plus de peur que de mal ◆ **the problem is ~ one of capital than of personnel** ce n'est pas tant *or* c'est moins un problème de capital qu'un problème de personnel ◆ **he was ~ annoyed than amused** il était moins fâché qu'amusé ◆ **it is ~ a short story than a novel** c'est moins une nouvelle qu'un roman

◆ **no less ... than** ◆ **she is no ~ intelligent than you** elle n'est pas moins intelligente que vous ◆ **he criticized the director no ~ than the caretaker** il a critiqué le directeur tout autant que le concierge

◆ **the less ...** + *comparative* ◆ **the ~ he works the ~ he earns** moins il travaille, moins il gagne ◆ **the ~ you worry about it the better** moins vous vous ferez du souci à ce sujet, mieux ça vaudra ; → **more**

PREP moins ◆ **~ 10% discount** moins 10% de remise ◆ **in a year ~ four days** dans un an moins quatre jours

...less /lɪs/ SUF ◆ **hatless** sans chapeau ◆ **childless** sans enfants

lessee /leˈsiː/ N preneur *m*, -euse *f* (à bail)

lessen /ˈlesn/ VT *(gen)* diminuer ; *[+ cost]* réduire ; *[+ anxiety, pain]* atténuer ; *[+ effect, shock]* amortir ; *(Pol) [+ tension]* relâcher VI diminuer, s'amoindrir ; *[pain]* s'atténuer ; *[tension]* se relâcher

lessening /ˈlesnɪŋ/ N *(NonC)* diminution *f*, amoindrissement *m* ◆ **~ of tension** *(Pol)* détente *f*

lesser /ˈlesəʳ/ ADJ [1] moindre ◆ **to a ~ degree** *or* **extent** à un moindre degré, à un degré moindre ◆ **the ~ of two evils** le moindre de deux maux ◆ **we ~ mortals*** *or* **beings*** *(hum)* nous (autres) simples mortels *(hum)* [2] *(in names of animals, plants, places)* petit

COMP **the Lesser Antilles** NPL les Petites Antilles *fpl*

lesser celandine N ficaire *f*

lesser panda N petit panda *m*

lesson /ˈlesn/ N [1] *(gen)* leçon *f* ; *(in school, college etc)* leçon *f*, cours *m* ◆ **a French/geography** *etc* **~** une leçon *or* un cours de français/de géographie *etc* ◆ **swimming/driving ~** leçon *f* de natation/de conduite ◆ **to have** *or* **take ~s in** prendre des leçons de ◆ **to give ~s in** donner des leçons de ◆ **we have ~s from nine to midday** nous avons classe *or* cours de 9 heures à midi ◆ **~s start at 9 o'clock** la classe commence *or* les cours commencent à 9 heures ◆ **let that be a ~ to you!** que cela te serve de leçon ! ; → **private, teach** [2] *(Rel)* leçon *f* ; → **read** COMP **lesson plans** NPL *(Scol)* dossier *m* pédagogique

lessor /leˈsɔːʳ/ N bailleur *m*, -eresse *f*

lest /lest/ CONJ *(liter)* de peur *or* de crainte de + *infin*, de peur *or* de crainte que (+ ne) + *subj* ◆ **he took the map ~ he should get lost** il a pris la carte de peur *or* crainte de se perdre, il a pris la carte au cas où il se perdrait ◆ **I gave him the map ~ he should get lost** je lui ai donné la carte de peur *or* de crainte qu'il (ne) se perde, je lui ai donné la carte au cas où il se perdrait ◆ **~ anyone had forgotten, may I remind you that ...** au cas où certains auraient oublié, permettez-moi de vous rappeler que ... ◆ **I was afraid ~ he should** *or* **might fall** je craignais qu'il ne tombe *subj* *or* ne tombât *subj* *(frm)* ◆ **"lest we forget"** *(on war memorial etc)* "in memoriam"

let[1] /let/ LANGUAGE IN USE 3.1, 9, 26.1 (pret, ptp **let**)

VT [1] *(= allow)* laisser ◆ **to ~ sb do sth** laisser qn faire qch ◆ **he wouldn't ~ us** il n'a pas voulu ◆ **she wanted to help but her mother wouldn't ~ her** elle voulait aider mais sa mère ne l'a pas laissée faire ◆ **I won't ~ you be treated like that** je ne permettrai pas qu'on vous traite *subj* de cette façon ◆ **I won't ~ it be said that ...** je ne permettrai pas que l'on dise que ... ◆ **to ~ sb into a secret** révéler un secret à qn ◆ **don't ~ it get you down*** ne te laisse pas démoraliser pour autant* ◆ **don't ~ me forget** rappelle-le-moi, tu m'y feras penser ◆ **don't ~ the fire go out** ne laisse pas s'éteindre le feu ◆ **~ me have a look** faites voir ◆ **~ me help you** laissez-moi vous aider ◆ **~ me give you some advice** permettez-moi de vous donnez un conseil ◆ **~ me take your coat** laissez-moi vous débarrasser de votre manteau ◆ **~ me tell you ...** que je vous dise ... *or* raconte *subj* ... ◆ **when can you ~ me have it?** quand est-ce que je pourrai l'avoir *or* le prendre ? ◆ **~ him have it!** *(= give)* donnez-le-lui ! ; *(‡ = shoot, strike etc)* règle-lui son compte !* ◆ **~ him be!** laisse-le (tranquille) ! ◆ **(just you) ~ me catch you stealing again!*** que je t'attrape *subj* *or* t'y prenne encore à voler ! ◆ **the hunted man ~ himself be seen** l'homme traqué s'est laissé repérer ◆ **I ~ myself be persuaded** je me suis laissé convaincre ; → **alone, drop, fall, fly**[3]**, go, know, lie**[1]

[2] *(used to form imperative of 1st person)* **~ us** *or* **~'s go for a walk** allons nous promener ◆ **~'s go!** allons-y ! ◆ **~'s get out of here!** filons !, fichons le camp (d'ici) !* ◆ **don't ~'s*** *or* **~'s not start yet** ne commençons pas tout de suite ◆ **don't ~ me keep you** que je ne vous retienne pas ◆ **don't ~ me see you doing that again** que je ne t'y reprenne pas, que je ne te revoie pas faire ça ◆ **~ us pray** prions ◆ **~ me see (now) ..., ~'s see (now) ...** voyons ... ◆ **~ me think** laissez-moi réfléchir ; → **say**

[3] *(used to form imperative of 3rd person)* **if he wants the book, ~ him come and get it himself** s'il veut le livre, qu'il vienne le chercher lui-même *or* il n'a qu'à venir le chercher lui-même ◆ **~ him say what he likes, I don't care** qu'il dise ce qu'il veut, ça m'est égal ◆ **~ no one believe that I will change my mind** que personne ne s'imagine *subj* que je vais changer d'avis ◆ **~ that be a warning to you** que cela vous serve d'avertissement ◆ **~ there be light** que la lumière soit ◆ **just ~ them try!** qu'ils essaient *subj* un peu ! ◆ **~ it be done at once** *(frm)* qu'on le fasse tout de suite ◆ **~ x equal two** *(Math)* soit x égal à deux

[4] *(Med)* **to ~ blood** tirer du sang, faire une saignée

[5] ◆ **to ~ a window/door into a wall** percer *or* ouvrir une fenêtre/porte dans un mur

[6] *(esp Brit = hire out) [+ house etc]* louer, mettre en location ◆ **"flat to let"** "appartement à louer" ◆ **"to let", "to be let"** "à louer"

N *[of house etc]* location *f* ◆ **I'm looking for a long/short ~ for my villa** je cherche à louer ma villa pour une longue/brève période

COMP **let alone** CONJ → **alone**

let-down* N déception *f* ◆ **what a ~-down!** quelle déception ! ◆ **the film was a ~-down after the book** le film était décevant par rapport au livre

let-out N *(Brit)* échappatoire *f*, issue *f*

let-up* N *(= decrease)* diminution *f* ; *(= stop)* arrêt *m* ; *(= respite)* relâchement *m*, répit *m* ◆ **if there is a ~-up in the rain** si la pluie s'arrête un peu ◆ **he worked five hours without (a) ~-up** il a travaillé cinq heures d'affilée *or* sans s'arrêter ◆ **there will be no ~-up in my efforts** je ne relâcherai pas mes efforts

► **let away** VT SEP *(= allow to leave)* laisser partir ◆ **the headmaster ~ the children away early today** le directeur a laissé partir *or* a renvoyé les enfants tôt aujourd'hui ◆ **you can't ~ him away with that!** tu ne peux pas le laisser s'en tirer comme ça !

► **let down**

VT SEP [1] *[+ window]* baisser ; *[+ one's hair]* dénouer, défaire ; *[+ dress]* rallonger ; *[+ tyre]* dégonfler ; *(on rope etc) [+ person, object]* descendre ◆ **to ~ down a hem** défaire un ourlet *(pour rallonger un vêtement)* ◆ **he ~ me down gently** *(fig) (in giving bad news)* il me l'a dit *or* il m'a traité avec ménagement ; *(in punishing etc)* il n'a pas été trop sévère avec moi ; see also **hair**

[2] *(= disappoint, fail)* faire faux bond à, décevoir ◆ **we're expecting you on Sunday, don't ~ us down** nous vous attendons dimanche, nous comptons sur vous *or* ne nous faites pas faux bond ◆ **he's ~ me down several times** il m'a déçu plusieurs fois *or* à plusieurs reprises ◆ **to feel ~ down** être déçu ◆ **that shop has ~ me down before** j'ai déjà été déçu par cette boutique ◆ **the car ~ me down** la voiture m'a joué des tours ◆ **my watch never ~s me down** ma montre est toujours à l'heure ◆ **you've ~ the**

team down ta façon de jouer a beaucoup déçu *or* desservi l'équipe ◆ **you've ~ the side down** *(fig)* tu ne nous *(or* leur) as pas fait honneur ◆ **the weather ~ us down** le beau temps n'a pas été de la partie

N ◆ **let-down** * → **let¹**

► **let in** VT SEP *[+ person, cat]* faire entrer, laisser entrer, ouvrir (la porte) à ◆ **can you ~ him in?** pouvez-vous lui ouvrir (la porte) ? ◆ **the maid ~ him in** la bonne lui a ouvert la porte *or* l'a fait entrer ◆ **he pleaded with us to ~ him in** il nous a suppliés de le laisser entrer *or* de lui ouvrir (la porte) ◆ **they wouldn't ~ me in** ils ne voulaient pas me laisser entrer ◆ **he ~ himself in with a key** il a ouvert (la porte) *or* il est entré avec une clé ◆ **to ~ in water** *[shoes, tent]* prendre l'eau ; *[roof]* laisser entrer *or* passer la pluie ◆ **the curtains ~ the light in** les rideaux laissent entrer la lumière ◆ **this camera ~s the light in** cet appareil-photo laisse passer la lumière ◆ **to ~ the clutch in** *(Driving)* embrayer

◆ **to let sb in for sth** * ◆ **see what you've ~ me in for now!** tu vois dans quelle situation tu me mets maintenant ! ◆ **if I'd known what you were ~ting me in for I'd never have come** si j'avais su dans quoi tu allais m'entraîner je ne serais jamais venu ◆ **you're ~ting yourself in for trouble** tu te prépares des ennuis ◆ **you don't know what you're ~ting yourself in for** tu ne sais pas à quoi tu t'engages ◆ **I ~ myself in for doing the washing-up** je me suis laissé coincer pour la corvée de vaisselle ◆ **I got ~ in for a £5 donation** j'ai dû donner cinq livres

◆ **to let sb in on sth** mettre qn au courant de qch ◆ **can't we ~ him in on it?** ne peut-on pas le mettre au courant ?

► **let off** VT SEP 1 *(= cause to explode, fire etc) [+ bomb]* faire éclater ; *[+ firework]* tirer, faire partir ; *[+ firearm]* faire partir

2 *(= release)* dégager, lâcher ◆ **to ~ off steam** *[boiler, engine]* lâcher *or* dégager de la vapeur ; * *(fig) [person] [+ anger]* décharger sa bile ; *[+ excitement]* se défouler *

3 *(= allow to leave)* laisser partir ◆ **they ~ the children off early today** aujourd'hui ils ont laissé partir *or* renvoyé les enfants de bonne heure ◆ **will you please ~ me off at 3 o'clock?** pourriez-vous s'il vous plaît me laisser partir à 3 heures ?

4 *(= excuse)* dispenser ◆ **to ~ sb off (doing) sth** dispenser qn de (faire) qch ◆ **if you don't want to do it, I'll ~ you off** si tu ne veux pas le faire, je t'en dispense

5 *(= not punish)* ne pas punir, faire grâce à ◆ **he ~ me off** il ne m'a pas puni ◆ **I'll ~ you off this time** je vous fais grâce *or* je ferme les yeux pour cette fois ◆ **the headmaster ~ him off with a warning** le directeur lui a seulement donné un avertissement ◆ **he was ~ off with a fine** il s'en est tiré avec une amende, il en a été quitte pour une amende ◆ **to ~ sb off lightly** laisser qn s'en tirer à bon compte

6 *[+ rooms etc]* louer ◆ **the house has been ~ off in flats** la maison a été louée en plusieurs appartements

► **let on** *

VI *(= tell)* ◆ **I won't ~ on** je ne dirai rien, je garderai ça pour moi ◆ **they knew the answer but they didn't ~ on** ils connaissaient la réponse mais ils n'ont pas pipé ◆ **don't ~ on!** motus ! ◆ **don't ~ on about what they did** ne va pas raconter *or* dire ce qu'ils ont fait ◆ **she didn't ~ on that she'd seen me** elle n'a pas dit qu'elle m'avait vu

VT SEP 1 *(= admit, acknowledge)* dire, aller raconter *(that* que)

2 *(= pretend)* prétendre, raconter *(that* que)

► **let out**

VI ◆ **to let out at sb** *(with fists, stick etc)* envoyer des coups à qn ; *(= abuse)* injurier qn ; *(= speak angrily to)* attaquer qn ; *(= scold)* réprimander qn sévèrement

VT SEP 1 *(= allow to leave) [+ person, cat]* faire *or* laisser sortir ; *(= release) [+ prisoner]* relâcher ; *[+ sheep, cattle]* faire sortir *(of* de) ; *[+ caged bird]* lâcher ◆ **~ me out!** laissez-moi sortir ! ◆ **I'll ~ you out** je vais vous ouvrir la porte *or* vous reconduire ◆ **the watchman ~ me out** le veilleur m'a fait sortir ◆ **he ~ himself out quietly** il est sorti sans faire de bruit, il a ouvert la porte sans faire de bruit ◆ **I'll ~ myself out** pas besoin de me reconduire ◆ **they are ~ out of school at 4** on les libère à 16 heures ◆ **to ~ the air out of a tyre** dégonfler un pneu ◆ **to ~ the water out of the bath** vider l'eau de la baignoire ; → **cat**

2 *[+ fire, candle]* laisser s'éteindre

3 *(= reveal) [+ secret, news]* laisser échapper, révéler ◆ **don't ~ it out that ...** ne va pas raconter que ...

4 *[+ shout, cry]* laisser échapper ◆ **to ~ out a laugh** faire entendre un rire

5 *[+ dress]* élargir ◆ **to ~ one's belt out by two holes** desserrer sa ceinture de deux crans ◆ **to ~ out a seam** défaire une couture *(pour agrandir un vêtement)*

6 *(= remove suspicion from)* disculper, mettre hors de cause ; *(= exclude)* exclure, éliminer ◆ **his alibi ~s him out** son alibi le met hors de cause ◆ **if it's a bachelor you need that ~s me out** si c'est un célibataire qu'il vous faut je ne peux pas faire votre affaire

7 *(esp Brit) [+ house etc]* louer

N ◆ **let-out** → **let¹**

► **let past** VT SEP *[+ person, vehicle, animal, mistake]* laisser passer

► **let through** VT SEP *[+ vehicle, person, light]* laisser passer

► **let up**

VI *[rain]* diminuer ; *[cold weather]* s'adoucir ◆ **he didn't ~ up until he'd finished** il ne s'est accordé aucun répit avant d'avoir fini ◆ **she worked all night without ~ting up** elle a travaillé toute la nuit sans relâche ◆ **what a talker she is, she never ~s up!** quelle bavarde, elle n'arrête pas ! ◆ **to ~ up on sb** * lâcher la bride à qn

VT SEP *(= allow to rise)* ◆ **to ~ sb up** permettre à qn de se lever

N ◆ **let-up** * → **let¹**

let² /let/ N 1 *(Tennis)* let *m*, balle *f* à remettre ◆ **to play a ~** jouer un let, remettre le service ◆ **~ ball** balle *f* de let ◆ **~!** net !, let ! 2 *(Jur)* **without ~ or hindrance** librement, sans empêchement aucun

letch * /letʃ/ VI ⇒ **lech**

lethal /'liːθəl/ ADJ *(= causing death) [poison, chemical, gas, effect, injection, dose]* mortel ; *[attack, blow]* fatal ; *[weapon, explosion]* meurtrier ◆ **(by) ~ injection** (par) injection *f* (d'une dose) mortelle ◆ **a ~ combination** *or* **cocktail (of ...)** *[of drink, drugs etc]* un mélange fatal (de ...) ; *(fig) [of ignorance, fear, poverty etc]* un mélange explosif *or* détonant (de ...) ; *(Pol, Mil)* ◆ **~/non-~ aid** aide *f* militaire/humanitaire ◆ **that stuff is ~!** * *(hum: coffee, beer etc)* c'est infect !

lethargic /lɪ'θɑːdʒɪk/ ADJ 1 *(= tired) [person]* léthargique ; *[movement]* indolent ◆ **to feel ~** se sentir tout mou 2 *[market]* léthargique ◆ **trading was ~** les affaires étaient moroses

lethargy /'leθədʒɪ/ N léthargie *f*

LETS /lets/ N (abbrev of **Local Exchange Trading Scheme** *or* **System**) SEL *m*

let's /lets/ ⇒ **let us** ; → **let¹**

Lett /let/ ADJ, N ⇒ **Latvian**

letter /'letər/ N 1 *[of alphabet]* lettre *f* ◆ **the ~ L** la lettre L ◆ **it was printed in ~s 15cm high** c'était écrit en lettres de 15 cm de haut ◆ **the ~ of the law** la lettre de la loi ◆ **he followed the instructions to the ~** il a suivi les instructions à la lettre *or* au pied de la lettre ◆ **to have a lot of ~s after** *(Brit)* **or behind** *(US)* **one's name** être bardé de diplômes ; → **block, capital, red**

2 *(= written communication)* lettre *f* ◆ **I wrote her a ~** je lui ai écrit une lettre ◆ **thank you for your ~ of 1 June 1996** je vous remercie pour votre lettre du 1er juin 1996 ◆ **were there any ~s for me?** y avait-il du courrier *or* des lettres pour moi ? ◆ **to write a ~ of complaint/support/apology/protest** écrire une lettre de réclamation/de soutien/d'excuse/de protestation ◆ **she apologized/complained by ~** elle a envoyé une lettre d'excuse/de réclamation ◆ **he was invited by ~** il a reçu une invitation écrite ◆ **his appointment to the post was confirmed by ~** il a reçu une lettre confirmant sa nomination ◆ **the news came in a ~ from her brother** une lettre de son frère annonçait la nouvelle ◆ **"The Letters of Virginia Woolf"** "La correspondance de Virginia Woolf", "Les lettres de Virginia Woolf" ; → **covering, love, open**

3 *(= literature)* ◆ **~s** (belles-)lettres *fpl* ◆ **man of ~s** homme *m* de lettres

4 *(US Scol)* distinctions *fpl (pour succès sportifs)*

VT 1 *(= put letter on)* **I've ~ed the packets according to the order they arrived in** j'ai inscrit des lettres sur les paquets selon leur ordre d'arrivée ◆ **she ~ed the envelopes from A to M** elle a marqué les enveloppes de A à M

2 *(= add lettering to)* ◆ **the book cover was ~ed in gold** la couverture du livre portait une inscription en lettres d'or ◆ **the case is ~ed with my initials** l'étui est gravé à mes initiales, mes initiales sont gravées sur l'étui

COMP **letter bomb** N lettre *f* piégée

letter-card N *(Brit)* carte-lettre *f*

letter of acknowledgement N *(Comm)* lettre *f* accusant réception

letter of attorney N *(Jur)* procuration *f*

letter of credence N ⇒ **letters of credence**

letter of credit N *(Fin)* lettre *f* de crédit

letter of intent N lettre *f* d'intention

letter of introduction N lettre *f* de recommandation

letter of request N *(Jur)* commission *f* rogatoire

letter opener N coupe-papier *m inv*

letter paper N papier *m* à lettres

letter-perfect ADJ *(US)* ◆ **to be ~-perfect in sth** connaître qch sur le bout des doigts

letter quality N *(Comput)* qualité *f* "courrier"

letter rogatory N ⇒ **letter of request**

letters of credence NPL *(Diplomacy)* lettres *fpl* de créance

letters patent NPL lettres *fpl* patentes

letter-writer N ◆ **he's a good/bad ~-writer** c'est un bon/mauvais correspondant *or* épistolier *(hum)*

letterbox /'letəbɒks/ N *(esp Brit)* boîte *f* aux *or* à lettres

lettered /'letəd/ ADJ *[person]* lettré ; see also **letter**

letterhead /'letəhed/ N en-tête *m* (de lettre)

lettering /'letərɪŋ/ N (NonC) *(= engraving)* gravure *f* ; *(= letters)* caractères *mpl*

letterpress /'letəpres/ N *(Typ) (= method)* typographie *f* ; *(= text)* texte *m* imprimé

letting /'letɪŋ/ N 1 *[of flat etc]* location *f* 2 → **bloodletting**

lettuce /'letɪs/ N *(as plant, whole)* laitue *f* ; *(leaves, as salad)* salade *f*

leucocyte, leukocyte *(esp US)* /'luːkəˌsaɪt/ N leucocyte *m*

leucotomy, leukotomy *(esp US)* /luːˈkɒtəmɪ/ N leucotomie *f*, lobotomie *f* cérébrale

leukaemia, leukemia *(esp US)* /luːˈkiːmɪə/ N leucémie *f*

leukocyte /ˈluːkəˌsaɪt/ N *(esp US)* ⇒ **leucocyte**

leukotomy /luːˈkɒtəmɪ/ N *(esp US)* ⇒ **leucotomy**

Levant /lɪˈvænt/ N Levant *m*

Levantine /ˈlevəntaɪn/ ADJ levantin N *(Hist)* Levantin(e) *m(f)*

levee¹ /ˈlevɪ/ N *(= raised riverside of silt)* levée *f* naturelle ; *(= man-made embankment)* levée *f*, digue *f* ; *(= ridge surrounding field)* digue *f* ; *(= landing place)* quai *m*

levee² /leˈveɪ/ N *(Hist)* réception *f* royale *(pour hommes)* ; *(at royal bedside)* lever *m* (du roi) ◆ **a presidential ~** *(US)* une réception présidentielle

level /ˈlevl/ N 1 *(lit = height)* niveau *m*, hauteur *f* ◆ **the water reached a ~ of 10 metres** l'eau a atteint un niveau *or* une hauteur de 10 mètres ◆ **water finds its own ~** l'eau trouve son niveau ◆ **at roof ~** au niveau du toit ◆ **the top of the tree was on a ~ with the roof** la cime de l'arbre arrivait au niveau *or* à la hauteur du toit ◆ **she bent down until her eyes were on a ~ with mine** elle s'est baissée pour que ses yeux soient au même niveau que les miens ; → **eye, knee, sea**

2 *(fig: in intellect, achievement)* niveau *m* ◆ **the child will find his own ~** l'enfant trouvera son niveau ◆ **intellectual ~** niveau *m* intellectuel ◆ **he's far above my ~** il est d'un niveau bien supérieur au mien ◆ **the teacher came down to their ~** le professeur s'est mis à leur niveau ◆ **I'm not on his ~ at all** je ne suis pas du tout à son niveau ◆ **his reading/writing is on a ~ with that of his brother** il a le même niveau que son frère en lecture/écriture ◆ **that dirty trick is on a ~ with the other one he played** ce mauvais coup est (bien) à la hauteur du *or* vaut le précédent

3 *(fig: in hierarchy)* niveau *m*, échelon *m* ◆ **social ~** niveau *m* social ◆ **at a higher/lower ~** *(in company)* à un échelon supérieur/inférieur ; *[talks, negotiations]* à un niveau *or* échelon supérieur/inférieur ◆ **at local/national/international ~** au niveau local/national/international ◆ **at departmental ~** à l'échelon départemental ◆ **there were redundancies at all ~s of the organization** il y a eu des licenciements à tous les niveaux *or* échelons de l'organisation ◆ **we need to address the gun problem at grassroots ~** nous devons affronter le problème du port d'armes à la source

4 *(= rate, degree) [of inflation, unemployment, radiation]* niveau *m*, taux *m* ; *[of income, noise, difficulty, violence]* niveau *m* ◆ **the ~ of hormones/insulin in the blood** le taux d'hormones/d'insuline dans le sang ◆ **the ~ of alcohol in the blood** le taux d'alcoolémie ◆ **cholesterol ~(s), ~(s) of cholesterol** taux *m* de cholestérol ◆ **fluoride ~(s)** quantité *f* de fluor dans l'eau ◆ **~ of consciousness** *(Med)* état *m* de conscience ◆ **a higher ~ of consciousness** un niveau de conscience supérieur ◆ **the idea attracted a high ~ of interest** cette idée a suscité beaucoup d'intérêt ◆ **the ~ of support for the government is high/low** beaucoup/peu de gens soutiennent le gouvernement ◆ **the ~ of violence in those societies is very high** il y a énormément de violence dans ces sociétés ◆ **the strike received a fairly low ~ of support** la grève n'a pas vraiment été suivie ◆ **the ~ of public interest in the scheme remains low** le public continue à manifester peu d'intérêt pour ce projet ◆ **these polls do not reflect the true ~ of support for Green policies** ces sondages ne reflètent pas la popularité réelle des mesures écologiques ◆ **the rising ~ of violence** la montée de la violence ◆ **the rising ~ of inflation/unemployment** l'augmentation *f* de l'inflation/du chômage ◆ **there has been a falling/rising ~ of support for their policies** de moins en moins/de plus en plus de gens soutiennent leur politique

5 *(= floor)* niveau *m* ◆ **the house is on four ~s** la maison est sur *or* la maison a quatre niveaux

6 *(Nuclear Industry)* ◆ **high-/intermediate-/low-~ waste** déchets *mpl* de haute/moyenne/faible activité

7 (also **spirit level**) niveau *m* à bulle

8 *(= flat place)* terrain *m* plat

9 *(set phrase)*

◆ **on the level** ◆ **speed on the ~** *[of car, train]* vitesse *f* en palier ◆ **I'm telling you on the ~** * je te le dis franchement ◆ **is this on the ~?** * est-ce que c'est réglo ?* ◆ **is he on the ~?** * est-ce qu'il joue franc-jeu ?, est-ce qu'il est fair-play ?

ADJ 1 *(= flat, not bumpy, not sloping) [surface]* plat, plan, uni ◆ **~ ground** terrain *m* plat *or* plan ◆ **it's dead ~** c'est parfaitement plat ◆ **the tray must be absolutely ~** il faut que le plateau soit parfaitement horizontal ◆ **hold the stick ~** tiens le bâton horizontal *or* à l'horizontale ◆ **a ~ spoonful** une cuillerée rase ◆ **a ~ playing field** *(fig)* une situation équitable pour tout le monde ◆ **a ~ playing field for all companies** une situation équitable pour toutes les entreprises ◆ **to compete on a ~ playing field** être sur un pied d'égalité ◆ **to do one's ~ best (to do sth)** * faire tout son possible *or* faire de son mieux (pour faire qch)

2 *(= equal) (at same standard)* à égalité ; *(at same height)* à la même hauteur ◆ **the two contestants are dead ~** les deux participants sont exactement à égalité ◆ **hold the two sticks absolutely ~ (with each other)** tiens les deux bâtons exactement à la même hauteur ◆ **keep your shoulders ~ throughout the exercise** gardez vos épaules à la même hauteur tout au long de l'exercice ◆ **he knelt down so that their eyes were ~** il s'est agenouillé afin que leurs yeux soient au même niveau ◆ **the dining room is ~ with the garden** la salle à manger est de plain-pied avec le jardin ◆ **~ with the ground** au niveau du sol, à ras du sol ◆ **to be ~ with sb** *(in race)* être à la hauteur de qn ; *(in league)* être à égalité avec qn, avoir le même nombre de points que qn ; *(in one's studies, achievements etc)* être au niveau de *or* au même niveau que qn ; *(in salary, rank)* être à l'échelon de *or* au même échelon que qn, être au même niveau que qn ◆ **to be ~ in seniority with** avoir la même ancienneté que, être au même niveau d'ancienneté que ◆ **to draw ~ with sb** *(esp Brit) (in race)* arriver à la hauteur de *or* à la même hauteur que qn ; *(in league)* arriver dans la même position que qn, arriver au même score que qn ; *(in one's studies, achievements etc)* arriver au niveau de *or* au même niveau que qn ; *(in salary, rank)* arriver au niveau de *or* au même niveau que qn, arriver au même échelon que qn ◆ **she slowed down a little to let the car draw ~ (with her)** elle a ralenti un peu afin de permettre à la voiture d'arriver à sa hauteur

3 *(= steady) [voice, tones]* calme ◆ **she gave him a ~ stare** elle l'a dévisagé calmement ◆ **to keep a ~ head** garder tout son sang-froid ; see also **comp**

4 *(US * = honest) [person, deal]* honnête, régulier

VT 1 *(= make level) [+ site, ground]* niveler, aplanir ; *[+ quantities]* répartir également ◆ **to ~ the score** *(in competition, league etc)* égaliser ◆ **Graf ~led the score to one set all** *(Tennis)* Graf a égalisé à un set partout

2 *(= demolish) [+ building, town]* raser ◆ **to ~ sth to the ground** raser qch

3 *(= aim)* ◆ **to ~ a blow at sb** allonger un coup de poing à qn ◆ **to ~ a gun at sb** braquer *or* pointer un pistolet sur qn ◆ **to ~ an accusation at sb** lancer *or* porter une accusation contre qn ◆ **to ~ criticism at** *or* **against sb** formuler des critiques à l'encontre de qn ◆ **to ~ charges at** *or* **against sb** *(Jur)* porter des accusations contre qn

VI ◆ **I'll ~ with you** je vais être franc avec vous ◆ **you're not ~ling with me about how much it cost** tu ne me dis pas combien ça a coûté

COMP **level crossing** N *(Brit Rail)* passage *m* à niveau

level-headed ADJ équilibré, pondéré

level-pegging ADJ *(Brit)* ◆ **they were ~-pegging** ils étaient à égalité

► **level down** VT SEP *(lit) [+ surface]* aplanir, raboter ; *(fig) [+ standards]* niveler par le bas

N ◆ **levelling down** → **levelling**

► **level off** VI *[statistics, results, prices etc]* se stabiliser ; *[curve on graph]* s'aplatir ; *[aircraft]* amorcer le vol en palier ◆ **output has ~led off over recent months** la production s'est stabilisée ces derniers mois

VT SEP *(= make flat) [+ heap of sand etc]* égaliser, niveler

N ◆ **levelling off** → **levelling**

► **level out** VI *[statistics, results, prices etc]* se stabiliser ; *[curve on graph]* s'aplatir ; *[road etc]* s'aplanir

VT SEP niveler, égaliser

► **level up** VT SEP *[+ ground]* niveler ; *[+ standards]* niveler par le haut

leveling /ˈlevlɪŋ/ *(US)* ⇒ **levelling**

leveller, leveler *(US)* /ˈlevləʳ/ N ◆ **poverty is a great ~** tous les hommes sont égaux dans la misère ◆ **death is the great ~** *(Prov)* nous sommes tous égaux devant la mort

levelling, leveling *(US)* /ˈlevlɪŋ/ N *(NonC: lit, fig)* nivellement *m* ADJ *(fig) [process, effect]* de nivellement

COMP **levelling down** N nivellement *m* par le bas

levelling off N *(gen)* égalisation *f*, nivellement *m* ; *(Econ, Fin)* stabilisation *f*, tassement *m*

levelling rod, levelling staff N mire *f*, jalonmire *m*

levelling up N nivellement *m* par le haut

levelly /ˈlevlɪ/ ADV *(= evenly) [look at, say]* posément

lever /ˈliːvəʳ/ N *(gen, also fig)* levier *m* ; *(small: on machine etc)* manette *f* ◆ **he used it as a ~ to get what he wanted** *(fig)* cela lui a servi de marchepied pour arriver à ses fins ; → **gear** VT ◆ **to ~ sth into position** mettre qch en place (à l'aide d'un levier) ◆ **to ~ sth out/open** extraire/ouvrir qch (au moyen d'un levier) ◆ **they had ~ed open the door with a crowbar** ils avaient ouvert la porte à l'aide d'un levier ◆ **he ~ed himself out of the chair** *(hum)* il s'est extirpé* du fauteuil ◆ **to ~ sb into a post** pistonner qn pour un poste ◆ **to ~ sb out** déloger qn

► **lever up** VT SEP soulever au moyen d'un levier ◆ **he ~ed himself up on one elbow** il s'est soulevé sur un coude ◆ **to ~ up the bank rate** relever le taux d'escompte officiel

leverage /ˈliːvərɪdʒ/ N *(lit)* force *f* (de levier) ; *(fig = influence)* influence *f*, prise *f* *(on or with sb* sur qn) ; *(US Fin)* effet *m* de levier VT *(Fin) [+ company]* augmenter le ratio d'endettement de ◆ **~d buyout** rachat *m* d'entreprise financé par l'endettement

leveret /ˈlevərɪt/ N levraut *m*

leviathan /lɪˈvaɪəθən/ N *(Bible)* Léviathan *m* ; *(fig = ship/organization etc)* navire *m*/organisme *m etc* géant

Levi's ® /ˈliːvaɪz/ NPL Levi's ® *m*

levitate /ˈlevɪteɪt/ VI se soulever *or* être soulevé par lévitation VT soulever *or* élever par lévitation

levitation /ˌlevɪˈteɪʃən/ N lévitation *f*

Leviticus /lɪˈvɪtɪkəs/ N Lévitique *m*

levity /ˈlevɪtɪ/ N *(= frivolity)* manque *m* de sérieux, légèreté *f*

levy /ˈlevɪ/ N [1] *(gen)* prélèvement *m (on sur)* ; *(= tax)* impôt *m*, taxe *f (on sur)* ; *(= amount, act of taxing)* taxation *f* ◆ **import** ~ prélèvement *m* à l'importation ◆ **the political** ~ *(in Brit) cotisation des membres d'un syndicat au parti travailliste* ◆ **training** ~ ≈ taxe *f* d'apprentissage ; → **capital** [2] *(Mil) (= act)* levée *f*, enrôlement *m* ; *(= troops)* troupes *fpl* enrôlées, levée *f* VT [1] *(= impose) [+ tax]* prélever *(on sth* sur qch) ; *[+ fine]* infliger, imposer *(on sb* à qn) [2] *(= collect) [+ taxes, contributions]* lever, percevoir [3] *(Mil)* **to** ~ **troops/an army** lever des troupes/une armée

▸ **levy on** VT FUS *(Jur)* ◆ **to levy on sb's property** saisir (les biens de) qn

lewd /luːd/ ADJ *[comment, picture, gesture, joke]* obscène ◆ **to have a** ~ **expression on one's face** avoir un air lubrique

lewdly /ˈluːdlɪ/ ADV de façon obscène

lewdness /ˈluːdnɪs/ N *[of person]* lubricité *f* ; *[of object, drawing]* obscénité *f*

lexeme /ˈleksiːm/ N lexème *m*

lexical /ˈleksɪkəl/ ADJ lexical ◆ ~ **item** unité *f* lexicale, item *m* lexical

lexicalize /ˈleksɪkəˌlaɪz/ VT lexicaliser

lexicographer /ˌleksɪˈkɒɡrəfəʳ/ N lexicographe *mf*

lexicographical /ˌleksɪkəʊˈɡræfɪkəl/ ADJ lexicographique

lexicography /ˌleksɪˈkɒɡrəfɪ/ N lexicographie *f*

lexicologist /ˌleksɪˈkɒlədʒɪst/ N lexicologue *mf*

lexicology /ˌleksɪˈkɒlədʒɪ/ N lexicologie *f*

lexicon /ˈleksɪkən/ N [1] *(Ling = wordlist, lexis)* lexique *m* [2] *(fig = terminology, language)* vocabulaire *m* ◆ **the word "perestroika" has entered the political** ~ le mot "perestroïka" fait désormais partie du vocabulaire politique

lexis /ˈleksɪs/ N *(Ling)* lexique *m*

Leyland cypress /ˈleɪlənd/ N (pl **Leyland cypresses**) *(Bot)* cyprès *m* hybride de Leyland

LI abbrev of **Long Island**

liability /ˌlaɪəˈbɪlɪtɪ/ N [1] *(NonC)* responsabilité *f* ◆ **don't admit** ~ **for the accident** n'acceptez pas la responsabilité de l'accident ◆ **his** ~ **for the company's debts was limited to $50,000** il n'était responsable qu'à hauteur de 50 000 dollars des dettes de la société

[2] *(NonC)* ◆ ~ **for tax/for paying tax** assujettissement *m* à l'impôt/au paiement de l'impôt ◆ ~ **for military service** obligations *fpl* militaires

[3] *(Fin)* **liabilities** *(= debts)* dettes *fpl*, passif *m* ◆ **assets and liabilities** actif *m* et passif *m* ◆ **to meet one's liabilities** rembourser ses dettes ◆ **current** ~ dettes *fpl* à court terme ◆ **non-current** ~ dettes *fpl* à moyen et long terme

[4] *(= handicap)* ◆ **this car is a** ~ **(for us)** on n'arrête pas d'avoir des problèmes avec cette voiture ◆ **he's a real** ~ ce type est un boulet* ◆ **this issue has become a political** ~ cette question constitue maintenant un handicap politique

COMP **liability insurance** N assurance *f* responsabilité civile ; → **joint, limited, strict**

liable /ˈlaɪəbl/ ADJ [1] ◆ **to be** ~ **to do sth** *(= be likely to)* avoir des chances de faire qch ; *(= risk)* risquer de faire qch ◆ **he's** ~ **to refuse to do it** il risque de refuser de le faire ◆ **he is** ~ **not to come** il y a des chances (pour) qu'il ne vienne pas, il y a peu de chances qu'il vienne ◆ **we are** ~ **to get shot at** on risque de se faire tirer dessus ◆ **we are** ~ **to be in London next week** nous pourrions bien être *or* nous serons probablement à Londres la semaine prochaine ◆ **it's** ~ **to be hot there** il peut faire très chaud là-bas

[2] *(= subject)* ◆ **to be** ~ **to sth** être sujet à qch ◆ **the programme is** ~ **to alteration without notice** la direction se réserve le droit d'apporter sans préavis des modifications à ce programme ◆ **to be** ~ **to imprisonment/a fine** être passible d'emprisonnement/d'une amende ◆ **to be** ~ **to** *or* **for prosecution** s'exposer à des poursuites ◆ **to be** ~ **to** *or* **for duty** *[goods]* être assujetti à des droits ; *[person]* avoir à payer des droits ◆ **to be** ~ **to** *or* **for tax** *[person]* être imposable ; *[thing]* être assujetti à la taxation ◆ **every man of 20 is** ~ **for military service** tout homme de 20 ans est astreint au service militaire ◆ **he is not** ~ **for military service** il a été exempté du service militaire

[3] *(Jur = responsible)* (civilement) responsable *(for sb/sth* de qn/qch) ◆ **jointly and severally** ~ responsable conjointement et solidairement ◆ **to be** ~ **for sb's debts** répondre des dettes de qn ◆ **he is still** ~ **for interest on the loan** il est toujours redevable d'intérêts sur cet emprunt ◆ ~ **for damages** tenu de verser des dommages et intérêts ◆ **you could be** ~ **for hefty damages** on serait en droit de vous demander des dommages et intérêts importants ◆ **to be held** ~ **(for sth)** être tenu (pour) responsable (de qch) ◆ **to be** ~ **in law** *or* **under the law** être responsable devant la loi ◆ **to be** ~ **in law** *or* **under the law to do sth** être tenu, de par la loi, de faire qch, être tenu par la loi de faire qch

liaise /liːˈeɪz/ VI *(Brit)* collaborer ◆ **to** ~ **with** *(= cooperate with)* se concerter avec ; *(= act as go-between)* assurer la liaison avec ◆ **to** ~ **between** assurer la liaison entre ◆ **to** ~ **closely** travailler en étroite collaboration

liaison /liːˈeɪzɒn/ N *(gen, Mil, Phon)* liaison *f*

COMP **liaison committee** N comité *m* de liaison

liaison officer N *(Mil, gen)* officier *m* de liaison

liana /liˈɑːnə/ N liane *f*

liar /ˈlaɪəʳ/ N menteur *m*, -euse *f*

Lib /lɪb/ ADJ, N *(Brit Pol)* (abbrev of **Liberal**) libéral(e) *m(f)* COMP **Lib-Lab*** ADJ *(Brit Pol Hist)* (abbrev of **Liberal-Labour**) ◆ **~-Lab pact** pacte *m* libéral-travailliste

lib* /lɪb/ N abbrev of **liberation**

libation /laɪˈbeɪʃən/ N libation *f*

libber* /ˈlɪbəʳ/ N ⇒ **liberationist**

libel /ˈlaɪbəl/ N *(Jur) (= act)* diffamation *f* (par écrit) ; *(= document)* écrit *m* diffamatoire ◆ **to sue sb for** ~**, to bring an action for** ~ **against sb** intenter un procès en diffamation à qn ◆ **that's (a)** ~! *(fig)* c'est une calomnie ! VT *(Jur)* diffamer (par écrit) ; *(gen)* calomnier, médire de

COMP **libel laws** NPL *(Jur)* lois *fpl* sur la diffamation

libel proceedings NPL, **libel suit** N procès *m* en diffamation

libellous, libelous *(US)* /ˈlaɪbələs/ ADJ diffamatoire

liberal /ˈlɪbərəl/ ADJ [1] *(= broad-minded) [education, régime, society]* libéral ; *[ideas, views]* progressiste ; *[person]* large d'esprit

[2] *(= broad) [interpretation]* libre

[3] *(= generous) [amount, helping, contribution, offer]* généreux ; *[person]* prodigue *(with* de) généreux ; *[supply]* ample, abondant ◆ **a** ~ **amount of** beaucoup de ◆ **she made** ~ **use of the hairspray** elle a utilisé beaucoup de laque ◆ **she made** ~ **use of her sister's make-up and clothes** elle se servait abondamment du maquillage et des vêtements de sa sœur ◆ **because of the** ~ **use of weedkillers and pesticides these days** parce que les herbicides et les pesticides sont utilisés abondamment de nos jours ◆ **the artist's** ~ **use of black** la dominante noire dans l'œuvre de ce peintre

[4] *(Brit Pol)* **Liberal** libéral

N *(Pol)* ◆ **Liberal** libéral(e) *m(f)*

COMP **liberal arts** NPL arts *mpl* libéraux

liberal democracy N démocratie *f* libérale

Liberal Democrat N *(Pol)* libéral(e)-démocrate *m(f)*

the Liberal Democrat Party N *(Brit)* le parti démocrate-libéral

liberal-minded ADJ ⇒ **adj 1**

liberal studies NPL *(Scol etc)* ≈ programme *m* de culture générale

liberalism /ˈlɪbərəlɪzəm/ N *(gen, Pol)* libéralisme *m*

liberality /ˌlɪbəˈrælɪtɪ/ N *(= broad-mindedness)* libéralisme *m* ; *(= generosity)* libéralité *f*, générosité *f*

liberalization /ˌlɪbərəlaɪˈzeɪʃən/ N libéralisation *f*

liberalize /ˈlɪbərəlaɪz/ VT libéraliser

liberally /ˈlɪbərəlɪ/ ADV [1] *(= generously)* généreusement [2] *(= indulgently) [treat]* libéralement

liberate /ˈlɪbəreɪt/ VT *[+ prisoner, slave]* libérer ; *[+ women etc]* libérer, émanciper ; *(Chem) [+ gas]* libérer, dégager ; *(Fin) [+ capital]* dégager

liberated /ˈlɪbəreɪtɪd/ ADJ libéré

liberation /ˌlɪbəˈreɪʃən/ N libération *f* ; *(Fin)* dégagement *m* COMP **liberation theology** N théologie *f* de la libération

liberationist /ˌlɪbəˈreɪʃənɪst/ N *(active)* membre *m* d'un (*or* du) mouvement de libération ; *(sympathiser)* partisan *m* de la libération *(des femmes etc)*

liberator /ˈlɪbəreɪtəʳ/ N libérateur *m*, -trice *f*

Liberia /laɪˈbɪərɪə/ N Libéria *or* Liberia *m* ◆ **in** ~ au Libéria

Liberian /laɪˈbɪərɪən/ ADJ *(gen)* libérien ; *[ambassador, embassy]* du Libéria N Libérien(ne) *m(f)*

libertarian /ˌlɪbəˈteərɪən/ ADJ *[person, attitude, view, policy, politics]* libertaire N libertaire *mf*

libertarianism /ˌlɪbəˈteərɪənɪzəm/ N *(= philosophy)* doctrine *f* libertaire ; *(= sb's characteristic)* idées *fpl* libertaires

libertinage /ˈlɪbətɪnɪdʒ/ N libertinage *m*

libertine /ˈlɪbətiːn/ ADJ, N libertin(e) *m(f)*

Liberty /ˈlɪbətɪ/ N *(= civil rights group) association britannique de défense des libertés civiques*

liberty /ˈlɪbətɪ/ N [1] *(= freedom)* liberté *f* ◆ **individual/political** ~ liberté *f* individuelle/politique

◆ **at liberty** ◆ **the escaped prisoner remains at** ~ le prisonnier évadé est toujours en liberté ◆ **to set sb at** ~ mettre qn en liberté ◆ **to set** *or* **leave sb at** ~ **to do sth** permettre qn à faire qch ◆ **you are at** ~ **to choose** vous êtes libre de choisir, libre à vous de choisir ◆ **I am not at** ~ **to reveal that information** je n'ai pas le droit de révéler ces informations

[2] *(= presumption)* liberté *f* ◆ **to take liberties (with sb)** prendre *or* se permettre des libertés (avec qn) ◆ **to take the** ~ **of doing sth** prendre la liberté *or* se permettre de faire qch ◆ **that was rather a** ~ **on his part** il ne s'est pas gêné ◆ **what a** ~!* quel toupet !*

COMP **liberty bodice** † N ≈ chemise *f* américaine

liberty cap N *(Hist)* bonnet *m* phrygien

liberty hall N *(fig hum)* ◆ **it's** ~ **hall here** * ici tout est permis

libidinal /lɪˈbɪdɪnl/ ADJ libidinal

libidinous /lɪˈbɪdɪnəs/ ADJ *(frm)* libidineux *(liter or hum)*

libido /lɪˈbiːdəʊ/ N libido *f*

Libra /ˈliːbrə/ N *(Astron)* Balance *f* ◆ **I'm (a)** ~ *(Astrol)* je suis (de la) Balance

Libran /ˈliːbrən/ **N** ◆ **to be a** ~ être (de la) Balance

librarian /laɪˈbreərɪən/ **N** bibliothécaire *mf*

librarianship /laɪˈbreərɪənʃɪp/ **N** *(= job)* poste *m* de bibliothécaire ; *(esp Brit) (= science)* bibliothéconomie *f* ; *(= knowledge)* connaissances *fpl* de bibliothécaire ◆ **to do** *or* **study** ~ faire des études de bibliothécaire *or* de bibliothéconomie

library /ˈlaɪbrərɪ/ **N** 1 *(= building, room)* bibliothèque *f* ; → **mobile, public, reference**

2 *(= collection, also Comput)* bibliothèque *f* ; *(= published series)* collection *f*, série *f*

COMP **library book N** livre *m* de bibliothèque

library card N ⇒ **library ticket**

library edition N édition *f* de luxe

Library of Congress N *(US)* Bibliothèque *f* du Congrès

library pictures NPL *(TV)* images *fpl* d'archives

library science N bibliothéconomie *f*

library software N *(Comput)* répertoire *m* de macro-instructions

library ticket N carte *f* de lecteur *or* de bibliothèque

> ⚠ **librairie** in French means 'bookshop', not **library**.

LIBRARY OF CONGRESS

La Bibliothèque du Congrès a été fondée à Washington en 1800, initialement pour servir les besoins des membres du Congrès. Devenue par la suite la Bibliothèque nationale des États-Unis, elle reçoit, au titre du dépôt légal, deux exemplaires de chaque ouvrage publié dans le pays et possède un fonds très riche de manuscrits, partitions de musique, cartes, films et autres enregistrements. D'autre part, c'est elle qui gère la bibliothèque internationale en attribuant les numéros d'ISBN.

librettist /lɪˈbretɪst/ **N** librettiste *mf*

libretto /lɪˈbretəʊ/ **N** (pl **librettos** *or* **libretti** /lɪˈbretiː/) libretto *m*, livret *m*

Librium ® /ˈlɪbrɪəm/ **N** Librium ® *m*

Libya /ˈlɪbɪə/ **N** Libye *f*

Libyan /ˈlɪbɪən/ **N** Libyen(ne) *m(f)* **ADJ** *(gen)* libyen ; *[ambassador, embassy]* de Libye ◆ ~ **Arab Jamahiriya** Jamahiriya *f* arabe libyenne ◆ **the** ~ **Desert** le désert de Libye

lice /laɪs/ **NPL** of **louse**

licence, license *(US)* /ˈlaɪsəns/ **N** 1 *(= permit) (gen)* autorisation *f*, permis *m* ; *(for manufacturing, trading etc)* licence *f* ; *(for driver)* permis *m* ; *(for car)* vignette *f* ; *(for radio, TV)* redevance *f* ; *(= document itself)* fiche *f* de redevance ◆ **driving** ~ *(Brit)* permis *m* de conduire ◆ **export/import** ~ permis *m* d'exporter/d'importer ◆ **pilot's** ~ brevet *m* de pilote ◆ **have you got a** ~ **for this television?** est-ce que vous avez payé votre redevance pour cette télévision ? ◆ **they were married by special** ~ ils se sont mariés avec dispense (de bans) ◆ **to manufacture sth under** ~ fabriquer qch sous licence ; → **marriage, off**

2 *(NonC) (= freedom)* licence *f*, liberté *f* ; *(= excess)* licence *f* ◆ **you can allow some** ~ **in translation** on peut tolérer une certaine licence *or* liberté dans la traduction ; → **poetic**

COMP **licence fee N** *(Brit TV)* redevance *f*

licence number N *[of driving licence]* numéro *m* de permis de conduire ; *[of car]* numéro *m* minéralogique *or* d'immatriculation

licence plate N plaque *f* minéralogique *or* d'immatriculation

> ⚠ Check what kind it is before translating **licence** by the French word **licence**.

license /ˈlaɪsəns/ **N** *(US)* ⇒ **licence**

VT 1 *(= give licence to)* donner une licence à ; *[+ car] [licensing authority]* délivrer la vignette pour ; *[owner]* acheter la vignette de *or* pour ◆ **is that gun** ~**d?** avez-vous un permis pour ce revolver ? ◆ **the shop is** ~**d to sell tobacco** le magasin détient une licence de bureau de tabac ◆ **the shop is** ~**d for the sale of alcoholic liquor** le magasin détient une licence de débit de boissons ◆ ~**d victualler** *(Brit)* patron *m or* gérant *m* d'un pub ◆ **(on)** ~**d premises** *(Brit)* (dans un) établissement ayant une licence de débit de boissons ◆ ~**d product** produit *m* sous licence ◆ ~**d practical nurse** *(US)* infirmier *m*, -ière *f* auxiliaire

2 *(frm = permit)* autoriser *(sb to do sth* qn à faire qch) permettre *(sb to do sth* à qn de faire qch)

COMP **license plate N** *(US)* ⇒ **licence plate**

licensee /ˌlaɪsənˈsiː/ **N** concessionnaire *mf* d'une licence ; *[of pub]* patron(ne) *m(f)*

licenser /ˈlaɪsənsəʳ/ **N** ⇒ **licensor**

licensing /ˈlaɪsənsɪŋ/ **ADJ** ◆ **the** ~ **authority** l'organisme *m or* le service délivrant les permis *(or* les licences *etc)*

COMP **licensing agreement N** *(Comm)* accord *m* de licence

licensing hours NPL *(Brit)* heures *fpl* d'ouverture légales *(des débits de boisson)*

licensing laws NPL *(Brit)* lois *fpl* réglementant la vente d'alcool

LICENSING LAWS

En Grande-Bretagne, les lois réglementant la vente et la consommation d'alcool sont connues sous le nom de **licensing laws**. L'âge minimum pour boire de l'alcool dans les lieux publics est de 18 ans.

Aux États-Unis, chaque État a sa propre législation en la matière. L'âge minimum varie de 18 à 21 ans et, dans certains comtés, il reste rigoureusement interdit de vendre ou de consommer de l'alcool. Dans d'autres, on ne peut acheter les boissons alcoolisées que dans des magasins spécialisés appelés "liquor stores" ou "package stores". La plupart des restaurants et discothèques ont une licence (liquor license) qui les autorise à vendre de l'alcool.

licensor /ˈlaɪsənsəʳ/ **N** *(Jur)* bailleur *m or* bailleresse *f* de licence

licentiate /laɪˈsenʃɪɪt/ **N** diplômé(e) *m(f) (pour pratiquer une profession libérale)*

licentious /laɪˈsenʃəs/ **ADJ** *(frm)* licencieux

licentiousness /laɪˈsenʃəsnɪs/ **N** *(frm)* licence *f*

lichee /ˌlaɪˈtʃiː/ **N** ⇒ **lychee**

lichen /ˈlaɪkən/ **N** lichen *m*

lichgate /ˈlɪtʃgeɪt/ **N** porche *m* de cimetière

licit /ˈlɪsɪt/ **ADJ** licite

lick /lɪk/ **N** 1 coup *m* de langue ◆ **the cat gave me a** ~ le chat m'a donné un coup de langue ◆ **the cat gave my hand a** ~ le chat m'a léché la main ◆ **give me** *or* **let me have a** ~ je peux goûter ? ◆ **to give o.s. a** ~ **and a promise*** faire un (petit) brin de toilette ◆ **a** ~ **of paint** un (petit) coup de peinture ◆ **he didn't do a** ~ **of work*** il n'a rien fichu*

2 (* *= speed)* vitesse *f* ◆ **at a fair** *or* **a good** *or* **one hell of a** ~ en quatrième vitesse*, à toute blinde*

3 *(Mus *)* riff *m*

VT 1 *[person, animal, flames]* lécher ◆ **she** ~**ed the cream off her fingers** elle a léché la crème qu'elle avait sur les doigts ◆ **the cat** ~**ed (at) her hand** le chat lui a léché la main ◆ **the cat** ~**ed its paws** le chat s'est léché les pattes ◆ **to** ~ **sth clean** nettoyer qch à coups de langue ◆ **to** ~ **the bowl out** *or* **clean** lécher le saladier ◆ **to** ~ **one's lips** *(lit)* se lécher les lèvres ; *(fig)* se frotter les mains ◆ **to** ~ **one's chops*** se lécher les babines* ; *(fig)* se frotter les mains, s'en lécher les babines* ◆ **to** ~ **sb's boots** lécher les bottes à qn*, jouer les lèche-bottes* avec qn ◆ **to** ~ **sb's arse**** lécher le cul à qn** ◆ **to** ~ **one's wounds** *(fig)* panser ses blessures *(fig)*

2 * *(= defeat)* écraser*, battre à plate(s) couture(s) ; *(= outdo, surpass)* battre ; *(= thrash)* flanquer une correction à, tabasser* ◆ **I've got it** ~**ed** *[+ problem, puzzle etc]* j'ai trouvé la solution ; *[+ bad habit]* j'ai réussi à m'arrêter ◆ **it's got me** ~**ed** *[problem etc]* cela me dépasse ; → **shape**

► **lick at VT FUS** *[dog, flames]* lécher

► **lick off VT SEP** enlever à coups de langue, lécher ◆ ~ **it off!** lèche-le !

► **lick up VT SEP** lécher ; *[cat]* laper

lickety-split* /ˈlɪkɪtɪˈsplɪt/ **ADV** *(US)* à fond de train

licking* /ˈlɪkɪŋ/ **N** *(= whipping)* rossée* *f*, raclée* *f* ; *(= defeat)* déculottée** *f*

lickspittle /ˈlɪkˌspɪtl/ **N** *(pej)* lèche-botte* *mf*

licorice /ˈlɪkərɪs/ **N** *(US)* ⇒ **liquorice**

lid /lɪd/ **N** 1 *[of pan, box, jar, piano]* couvercle *m* ◆ **the newspaper articles took** *or* **blew the** ~ **off his illegal activities** les articles de presse ont étalé au grand jour ses activités illégales ◆ **that puts the (tin)** ~ **on it!** † * *(= that's the end)* ça c'est un comble *or* le pompon !* ◆ **to keep the** ~ **on sth** *[+ scandal, affair]* étouffer qch ; *[+ crime]* contenir qch ◆ **to keep a** ~ **on prices** enrayer la hausse des prix 2 (also **eyelid**) paupière *f*

lidded /ˈlɪdɪd/ **ADJ** *[container, jar]* à couvercle ◆ **heavily** ~ **eyes** yeux *mpl* aux paupières lourdes

lido /ˈliːdəʊ/ **N** *(= resort)* complexe *m* balnéaire ; *(Brit) (= swimming pool)* piscine *f (en plein air)*

lie¹ /laɪ/ (pret **lay**, ptp **lain**) **VI** 1 *[person etc] (= lie down)* s'allonger, s'étendre ; *(state = be lying)* être allongé *or* étendu ; *(in grave etc)* être enterré ◆ **go and** ~ **on the bed** allez vous allonger *or* vous étendre sur le lit ◆ **don't** ~ **on the grass** ne t'allonge pas sur l'herbe ◆ **he was lying on the floor** *(resting etc)* il était allongé *or* étendu par terre ; *(unable to move)* il était étendu *or* il gisait par terre ◆ **she lay in bed until 10 o'clock** elle est restée *or* a traîné *(pej)* au lit jusqu'à 10 heures ◆ **she was lying in bed** elle était au lit ◆ **she was lying on her bed** elle était allongée *or* étendue sur son lit ◆ **she was lying in bed reading** elle lisait au lit ◆ ~ **on your side** couche-toi *or* allonge-toi sur le côté ◆ **she was lying face downwards** elle était (allongée *or* étendue) à plat ventre ◆ **he was lying asleep** il était allongé et il dormait, il était allongé endormi ◆ **he lay asleep on the bed** il dormait allongé *or* étendu sur le lit ◆ **he lay dead** il était étendu mort ◆ **he lay dead at her feet** il était étendu mort à ses pieds, il gisait à ses pieds ◆ **he lay helpless on the floor** il était étendu *or* il gisait par terre sans pouvoir rien faire ◆ **he was lying still** il était étendu immobile ◆ ~ **still!** ne bouge pas !, reste tranquille ! ◆ **his body was lying on the ground** son corps gisait sur le sol ◆ **he** ~**s in the churchyard** il repose dans le *or* est enterré au cimetière ◆ **the corpse lay in the coffin/the tomb** le corps reposait *or* était dans le cercueil/la tombe ◆ **to** ~ **in state** être exposé solennellement ◆ **here** ~**s** *or* **lieth ...** † *(on tombstone)* ci-gît ... ◆ **to** ~ **low** *(fig) (= hide)* se cacher, rester caché ; *(= stay out of limelight)* ne pas se faire remarquer, se tenir à carreau* ; → **ambush, sleeping, wait**

[2] *[object]* être ; *[place, road]* se trouver, être ; *[land, sea etc]* s'étendre ; *(= remain)* rester, être ◆ **the book lay on the table** le livre était sur la table ◆ **the book lay unopened all day** le livre est resté fermé toute la journée ◆ **the book lay open on the table** le livre était ouvert sur la table ◆ **his food lay untouched while he told us the story** il n'a pas touché à son assiette pendant qu'il nous racontait l'histoire ◆ **his clothes were lying on the floor** ses vêtements étaient par terre ◆ **the contents of the box lay scattered on the carpet** le contenu de la boîte était éparpillé sur le tapis ◆ **our road lay along the river** notre route longeait la rivière ◆ **the road ~s over the hills** la route traverse les collines ◆ **the British team is lying third** l'équipe britannique est troisième *or* en troisième position ◆ **to ~ at anchor** *[ship]* être à l'ancre, avoir mouillé ◆ **obstacles ~ in the way** la route est semée d'embûches ◆ **the money is lying (idle) in the bank** l'argent dort à la banque ◆ **the factory lay idle** personne ne travaillait dans l'usine ◆ **the machines lay idle** les machines étaient arrêtées ◆ **the snow lay two metres deep** il y avait deux mètres de neige ◆ **the snow lay thick** *or* **deep on the ground** il y avait une épaisse couche de neige sur le sol ◆ **this snow will not ~** la neige ne tiendra pas ◆ **the town lay in ruins** la ville était en ruines ◆ **the meal lay heavy on his stomach** le repas lui pesait sur l'estomac ◆ **the crime lay heavy on his conscience** ce crime lui pesait sur la conscience ◆ **the valley/lake/sea lay before us** la vallée/le lac/la mer s'étendait devant nous ◆ **Stroud ~s to the west of Oxford** Stroud est situé à l'ouest d'Oxford ◆ **the years that ~ before us** les années à venir ◆ **a brilliant future ~s before you** vous avez devant vous un brillant avenir ◆ **what ~s before him** *(fig: in future)* ce que lui réserve l'avenir ◆ **what ~s ahead** *(fig)* ce qui reste à venir, ce que réserve l'avenir ◆ **the (whole) world lay at her feet** toutes les portes lui étaient ouvertes ◆ **to let it** *or* **things ~** *(fig)* laisser les choses comme elles sont ; → **land**

[3] *(with abstract subject)* être, résider ◆ **he knows where his interests ~** il sait où sont *or* résident ses intérêts ◆ **what ~s behind his refusal?** quelle est la véritable raison de son refus ? ◆ **the real cause that lay behind the rise in divorce** la vraie cause de la hausse du nombre des divorces ◆ **the trouble ~s in the engine** le problème vient du moteur ◆ **the trouble ~s in his inability to be strict** le problème vient de *or* réside dans son incapacité à être sévère ◆ **the difference ~s in the fact that ...** la différence vient de ce que ... ◆ **the real solution ~s in education** la véritable solution réside dans l'éducation ◆ **the blame ~s with you** c'est vous qui êtes à blâmer, c'est à vous que la faute est imputable ◆ **a curse lay on the family** une malédiction pesait sur la famille ◆ **it does not ~ within my power to decide** il n'est pas en mon pouvoir de décider ◆ **it ~s with you to decide** il vous appartient de décider, c'est à vous (qu'il incombe) de décider ◆ **as far as in me ~s** *(liter, frm)* au mieux de mes possibilités, du mieux que je peux

[4] *(Jur)* *[evidence, appeal]* être recevable

N [1] *(Golf)* *[of ball]* position *f*

[2] *[of land]* configuration *f* ; → **land**

COMP **lie-abed** † N flemmard(e)* *m(f)* (qui traîne au lit)

lie-down N *(Brit)* ◆ **to have a ~-down** s'allonger, se reposer

lie-in N *(Brit)* ◆ **to have a ~-in** faire la grasse matinée

► **lie about, lie around** VI [1] *[objects, clothes, books]* traîner ◆ **don't leave that money lying about** ne laissez pas traîner cet argent

[2] *[person]* traîner, traînasser* *(pej)* ◆ **don't just ~ about all day!** tâche de ne pas traîner *or* traînasser* *(pej)* toute la journée !

► **lie back** VI *(in chair, on bed)* se renverser (en arrière) ◆ **just ~ back and enjoy yourself!** *(fig)* laisse-toi (donc) vivre !

► **lie down** VI *[person, animal]* s'allonger, s'étendre ◆ **she lay down for a while** elle s'est allongée quelques instants ◆ **when I arrived she was lying down** quand je suis arrivé elle était allongée ◆ **~ down!** *(to dog)* couché ! ◆ **to ~ down on the job*** tirer au flanc*, flemmarder* ◆ **to take sth lying down*** *(fig)* encaisser qch* sans broncher, accepter qch sans protester ◆ **he won't take that lying down*** il va se rebiffer*, il ne va pas se laisser faire ◆ **I won't take it lying down*** ça ne va pas se passer comme ça, je ne vais pas me laisser faire ◆ **he's not one to take things lying down*** il n'est pas du genre à tout encaisser sans rien dire

N ◆ **lie-down*** → **lie**[1]

► **lie in** VI [1] *(= stay in bed)* rester au lit, faire la grasse matinée

[2] *(†: in childbirth)* être en couches

N ◆ **lie-in*** → **lie**[1]

► **lie off** VI *(Naut)* rester au large

► **lie over** VI *(= be postponed)* être ajourné, être remis (à plus tard)

► **lie to** VI *(Naut)* être *or* se tenir à la cape

► **lie up** VI [1] *(= stay in bed)* garder le lit *or* la chambre

[2] *(= hide)* se cacher, rester caché

lie[2] /laɪ/ (vb : pret, ptp **lied**) N mensonge *m* ◆ **to tell ~s** mentir, dire des mensonges ◆ **I tell a ~*** je mens, je dis une bêtise ◆ **that's a ~!** vous mentez !, c'est un mensonge ! ◆ **to give the ~ to** *[+ person]* accuser de mentir ; *[+ claim, account]* démentir, contredire ; → **pack, white** VI mentir ◆ **he's lying through** *or* **in his teeth*** il ment effrontément *or* comme un arracheur de dents VT ◆ **he tried to ~ his way out of it** il a essayé de s'en sortir par des mensonges ◆ **he managed to ~ his way into the director's office** il a réussi à s'introduire dans le bureau du directeur sous un prétexte mensonger ◆ **he ~d his way into the job** il a obtenu le poste grâce à des mensonges COMP **lie detector** N détecteur *m* de mensonges

Liechtenstein /ˈlɪktənˌstaɪn/ N Liechtenstein *m* ◆ **in ~** au Liechtenstein ◆ **native** *or* **inhabitant of ~** Liechtensteinois(e) *m(f)* ADJ liechtensteinois

lied /liːd/ N (pl **lieder** /ˈliːdəʳ/) lied *m*

lief †† /liːf/ ADV ◆ **I would as ~ die as tell a lie** j'aimerais mieux mourir que mentir

liege /liːdʒ/ N *(Hist)* [1] (also **liege lord**) seigneur *m*, suzerain *m* ◆ **yes, my ~!** oui, Sire ! [2] (also **liege man**) vassal *m* (lige)

lien /lɪən/ N *(Jur)* privilège *m*, droit *m* de gage ◆ **to have a ~ on the estate of a debtor** avoir un privilège sur les biens d'un débiteur

lienee /lɪəˈniː/ N débiteur-gagiste *m*

lienor /ˈlɪənəʳ/ N créancier-gagiste *m*

lieu /luː/ N ◆ **in ~ of** au lieu de, à la place de ◆ **one month's notice or £2,400 in ~** un mois de préavis ou bien 2 400 livres

Lieut. (abbrev of **Lieutenant**) ~ **J Smith** *(on envelope)* le lieutenant J. Smith

lieutenant /lefˈtenənt, (US) luːˈtenənt/ N [1] *(Brit Army)* lieutenant *m* ; *(Brit, US Navy)* lieutenant *m* de vaisseau ; *(fig = chief assistant)* second *m* ◆ **first ~** *(US Army)* lieutenant *m* ; → **lord** [2] *(US Police)* *(uniformed)* officier *m* de paix ; *(plain clothes)* inspecteur *m* de police

COMP **lieutenant colonel** N *(Brit, US Army, also US Air Force)* lieutenant-colonel *m*

lieutenant commander N *(Navy)* capitaine *m* de corvette

lieutenant general N *(Brit, US Army)* général *m* de corps d'armée ; *(US Air Force)* général *m* de corps aérien

lieutenant-governor N *(Can)* lieutenant-gouverneur *m*

life /laɪf/ N (pl **lives**) [1] *(in general)* vie *f* ◆ **is there (a) ~ after death?** y a-t-il une vie après la mort ? ◆ **I don't believe in ~ after death** je ne crois pas à la vie après la mort ◆ **a matter of ~ and death** une question de vie ou de mort ◆ **to be tired of ~** être las de vivre ◆ **to lay down one's ~ (for sb)** *(liter)* sacrifier sa vie (pour qn), donner sa vie (pour qn) ◆ **to be on trial for one's ~** risquer la peine capitale ◆ **he ran for his ~** il a pris ses jambes à son cou, il s'est sauvé à toutes jambes ◆ **run for your lives!** sauve qui peut ! ◆ **I couldn't for the ~ of me tell you his name*** je ne pourrais absolument pas vous dire son nom ◆ **I couldn't for the ~ of me understand ...*** je n'arrivais absolument pas à comprendre ... ; → **large, loss, still**[2]

◆ **to bring (back) to life** ◆ **to bring sb back to ~** *(= resuscitate)* ranimer qn ◆ **he brought me back to ~** *(fig)* il m'a redonné goût à la vie ◆ **his interpretation brings the character to ~** son interprétation donne vie au personnage ◆ **she brought the party to ~** elle a vraiment animé la soirée ◆ **Victorian England is vividly brought to ~ in this film** ce film est une évocation très vivante de l'Angleterre victorienne

◆ **to come to life** ◆ **he came to ~ again** *(= regained consciousness)* il a repris conscience ◆ **the creature came to ~** la créature s'est animée ◆ **the town came to ~ when the sailors arrived** la ville s'éveillait à l'arrivée des marins

◆ **lose + life** ◆ **to lose one's ~** perdre la vie ◆ **how many lives were lost?** combien de vies cela a-t-il coûté ? ◆ **many lives were lost** beaucoup ont trouvé la mort ◆ **no lives were lost** il n'y a eu aucun mort *or* aucune victime

◆ **take + life** ◆ **to take one's (own) ~** se donner la mort ◆ **to take sb's ~** donner la mort à qn ◆ **when is it acceptable to take a ~?** quand devient-il acceptable de tuer quelqu'un ? ◆ **to take one's ~ in one's hands** jouer sa vie

[2] *(= existence)* vie *f* ◆ **~ went on uneventfully** la vie poursuivit son cours paisible ◆ **~ goes on, ~ must go on** la vie continue ◆ **he lived in France all his ~** il a vécu toute sa vie en France ◆ **~ begins at forty** la vie commence à quarante ans ◆ **she began ~ as a teacher** elle a débuté comme professeur ◆ **how's ~?** comment (ça) va ? ◆ **departed this ~, 27 February 1997** *(on tombstone etc)* enlevé(e) *(liter)* aux siens le 27 février 1997 ◆ **~ isn't worth living** la vie ne vaut pas la peine d'être vécue ◆ **for the rest of his ~** pour le restant de ses jours, pour le reste de sa vie ◆ **at my time of ~** à mon âge ◆ **cats have nine lives** le chat a neuf vies ; → **afterlife, claim, danger, fight, risk, rose**[2]**, save**[1]**, working**

◆ **in + life** ◆ **in early ~, early in ~** de bonne heure, tôt dans la vie ◆ **in her early ~** dans sa jeunesse ◆ **in later ~** plus tard (dans la vie) ◆ **in his later ~** plus tard dans sa vie ◆ **late in ~** sur le tard, à un âge avancé ◆ **they married late in ~** ils se sont mariés sur le tard ◆ **in the next ~** dans l'autre vie ◆ **for the first time in my ~** pour la première fois de ma vie ◆ **never in (all) my ~ have I seen such stupidity** jamais de ma vie je n'ai vu une telle stupidité ◆ **she's in the ~*** *(US)* *(of prostitute)* elle fait le trottoir

◆ **for life** ◆ **to be banned/scarred for ~** être exclu/marqué à vie ◆ **to be jailed for ~** être condamné à perpétuité *or* à la prison à vie ◆ **it will last you for ~** cela vous durera toute votre vie ◆ **friends for ~** amis pour toujours ◆ **a job for ~** un emploi pour la vie ◆ **president for ~** président(e) *m(f)* à vie

[3] *(= living things)* vie *f* ◆ **is there ~ on Mars?** la vie existe-t-elle sur Mars ? ◆ **bird ~** les oiseaux *mpl* ◆ **insect ~** les insectes *mpl* ◆ **animal and plant ~** vie *f* animale et végétale

[4] *(= way of living)* vie *f* ◆ **which do you prefer, town or country ~?** que préférez-vous, la vie à la ville ou (la vie) à la campagne ? ◆ **his ~ was very unexciting** sa vie n'avait rien de passionnant ◆ **to lead a busy ~** avoir une vie bien remplie ◆ **to lead a charmed ~** avoir la chance avec soi ◆ **the good ~** *(= pleasant)* la belle vie ; *(Rel)* la vie d'un saint, une vie sainte ◆ **it's a good ~** c'est la belle vie ◆ **to live one's own ~** vivre sa vie ◆ **to make a new ~ for o.s., to start a new ~** commencer une nouvelle vie ◆ **to lead a quiet ~** mener une vie tranquille ◆ **to have another ~** *or* **a ~ of one's own** avoir sa propre vie ◆ **that washing machine seems to have a ~ of its own** cette machine à laver n'en fait qu'à sa tête ◆ **I do have a ~ outside of work, you know!** il n'y a pas que le travail dans ma vie, vous savez ! ; → **live¹, married, nightlife, private, see¹**

[5] *(= liveliness)* ◆ **there isn't much ~ in our village** notre village n'est pas très vivant *or* est plutôt mort ◆ **there's ~ in the old dog yet** * le bonhomme a encore du ressort ◆ **to be full of ~** être plein de vie ◆ **you need to put a bit of ~ into it** il faut y mettre plus d'ardeur, il faut y aller avec plus d'entrain ◆ **it put new ~ into me** ça m'a fait revivre, ça m'a ragaillardi ◆ **he's the ~ and soul of the party** c'est un boute-en-train, c'est lui qui met l'ambiance

[6] *(in exclamations)* **that's ~!, such is ~!** c'est la vie ! ◆ **get a ~!** * bouge-toi un peu ! * ◆ **not on your ~!** * jamais de la vie ! ◆ **this is the ~!** * voilà comment je comprends la vie ! ◆ **upon my ~!** † seigneur !, diantre ! † ◆ **what a ~!** quelle vie !

[7] *[of car, ship, government, battery etc]* durée *f* de vie ; *[of licence]* validité *f* ◆ **my car's nearing the end of its ~** ma voiture a fait son temps

[8] *(Art)* ◆ **a portrait taken from ~** un portrait d'après nature ◆ **it was Paul to the ~** c'était Paul tout craché *

[9] *(= biography)* vie *f*, biographie *f* ◆ **a ~ of Henry VIII** une biographie d'Henri VIII, la vie d'Henri VIII ◆ **the lives of the Saints** la vie des saints

[10] *(* = life imprisonment)* ◆ **he got ~** il a été condamné à perpétuité *or* à perpète * ◆ **he's doing ~ (for murder)** il a été condamné à perpétuité *or* à perpète * (pour meurtre)

COMP *[subscription etc]* à vie

life-affirming ADJ (humainement) positif

life-and-death struggle N combat *m* à mort, lutte *f* désespérée

life annuity N rente *f* viagère

life assurance N *(esp Brit)* assurance *f* vie, assurance-vie *f*

life class N *(Art)* cours *m* de dessin d'après modèle

life coach N coach *m/f* (personnel)

life cycle N cycle *m* de (la) vie

life-enhancing ADJ revigorant

life expectancy N espérance *f* de vie ◆ **~ expectancy table** table *f* de survie

the life force N la force vitale

life form N forme *f* de vie

life-giving ADJ vivifiant

Life Guards NPL *(Brit Mil)* régiment *m* de cavalerie de la garde royale

life history N ◆ **her ~ history** l'histoire *f* de sa vie ◆ **the ~ history of the salmon** *(Bio)* la vie du saumon

life imprisonment N prison *f* à vie, réclusion *f* à perpétuité

life insurance N ⇒ **life assurance**

life interest N *(Jur)* usufruit *m*

life jacket N gilet *m* de sauvetage ; *(Navy)* brassière *f* (de sauvetage)

life member N membre *m* à vie

life membership N carte *f* de membre à vie ◆ **to be given ~ membership** être nommé *or* fait membre à vie

life-or-death struggle N ⇒ **life-and-death struggle**

life peer N *(Brit)* pair *m* à vie

life peerage N *(Brit)* pairie *f* à vie

life preserver N *(US)* ⇒ **life jacket** ; *(Brit* ‡ *= bludgeon)* matraque *f*

life president N président(e) *m(f)* à vie

life raft N radeau *m* de sauvetage

life-saver N *(= person)* maître *m* nageur *(surveillant un lieu de baignade)* ◆ **that money was a ~-saver** cet argent m'a (or lui a *etc*) sauvé la vie

life-saving N *(= rescuing)* sauvetage *m* ; *(= first aid)* secourisme *m* ADJ de sauvetage

the life sciences NPL les sciences *fpl* de la vie

life sentence N *(Jur)* condamnation *f* à perpétuité

life-size(d) ADJ grandeur nature *inv*

life span N durée *f or* espérance *f* de vie

life story N biographie *f* ◆ **his ~ story** sa biographie, l'histoire *f* de sa vie ◆ **he started telling me his ~ story** * il a commencé à me raconter sa vie

life support machine N *(Space)* équipements *mpl* de vie ; *(Med)* respirateur *m* artificiel ◆ **he's on a ~ support machine** *(Med)* il est sous assistance respiratoire ◆ **to switch off the ~ support machine** *(Med)* débrancher le respirateur artificiel

life's work N œuvre *f* de toute une (or ma *or* sa *etc)* vie

life tenancy N ◆ **to hold a ~ tenancy of a house** être locataire d'une maison à vie

life-threatening ADJ *[disease, emergency]* extrêmement grave

life-vest N *(US)* ⇒ **life jacket**

lifebelt /ˈlaɪfbelt/ N bouée *f* de sauvetage

lifeblood /ˈlaɪfblʌd/ N *(fig)* élément *m* vital *or* moteur, âme *f*

lifeboat /ˈlaɪfbəʊt/ N *(from shore)* bateau *m or* canot *m* de sauvetage ; *(from ship)* chaloupe *f* de sauvetage ◆ **~ station** centre *m or* poste *m* de secours en mer

lifeboatman /ˈlaɪfbəʊtmən/ N (pl **-men**) sauveteur *m* (en mer)

lifebuoy /ˈlaɪfbɔɪ/ N bouée *f* de sauvetage

lifeguard /ˈlaɪfɡɑːd/ N *(on beach)* maître nageur *m* ; *(Mil) (= bodyguard)* garde *m* du corps

lifeless /ˈlaɪflɪs/ ADJ [1] *(= dead) [person, eyes]* sans vie ; *[animal]* mort ; *[body]* sans vie, inanimé [2] *(= inanimate) [object]* inanimé [3] *(= not supporting life) [lake]* stérile ; *[planet]* sans aucune forme de vie [4] *(pej = dull, feeble) [style, novel, description]* plat ; *[voice]* terne ; *[team, player, performer]* sans énergie

lifelessness /ˈlaɪflɪsnɪs/ N *(lit)* absence *f* de vie ; *(fig)* manque *m* de vigueur *or* d'entrain

lifelike /ˈlaɪflaɪk/ ADJ qui semble vivant *or* vrai

lifeline /ˈlaɪflaɪn/ N [1] *(on ship)* main *f* courante ; *(for diver)* corde *f* de sécurité ◆ **it was his ~** *(fig)* c'était vital pour lui [2] *(in palmistry)* ligne *f* de vie

lifelong /ˈlaɪflɒŋ/ ADJ *[ambition]* de toute ma (or sa *etc)* vie ; *[friend, friendship]* de toujours ◆ **it is a ~ task** c'est le travail de toute une vie COMP

lifelong learning N formation *f* tout au long de la vie

lifer‡ /ˈlaɪfəʳ/ N condamné(e) *m(f)* à perpète *

lifestyle /ˈlaɪfstaɪl/ N style *m or* mode *m* de vie ◆ **a ~ change** un changement de mode de vie

lifetime /ˈlaɪftaɪm/ N [1] *(of person)* vie *f* ◆ **it won't happen in** *or* **during my ~** je ne verrai pas cela de mon vivant ◆ **it was the chance/holiday of a ~** c'était la chance/c'étaient les plus belles vacances de ma (or sa *etc)* vie ◆ **the experience of a ~** une expérience inoubliable ◆ **once in a ~** une fois dans la *or* une vie ◆ **the work of a ~** l'œuvre de toute une vie ◆ **a ~'s experience/work** l'expérience/le travail de toute une vie ; → **last²** [2] *(fig = eternity)* éternité *f* ◆ **an hour that seemed (like) a ~** une heure qui semblait une éternité [3] *[of battery, machine etc]* (durée *f* de) vie *f* ; *[of nuclear reactor]* durée *f* de vie

LIFO /ˈlaɪfəʊ/ (abbrev of **last in, first out**) DEPS

lift /lɪft/ N [1] *(Brit) (= elevator)* ascenseur *m* ; *(for goods)* monte-charge *m inv* ; → **service**

[2] *(Ski)* téléski *m*, tire-fesses * *m*, remontée *f* mécanique

[3] ◆ **give the box a ~** soulève la boîte ◆ **can you give me a ~ up, I can't reach the shelf** soulève-moi, s'il te plaît, je n'arrive pas à atteindre l'étagère ; → **airlift, face**

[4] *(= transport)* **can I give you a ~?** est-ce que je peux vous déposer quelque part ? ◆ **I gave him a ~ to Paris** je l'ai pris en voiture *or* je l'ai emmené jusqu'à Paris ◆ **we didn't get any ~s** personne ne s'est arrêté pour nous prendre ◆ **he stood there hoping for a ~** il était là (debout) dans l'espoir d'être pris en stop ; → **hitch**

[5] *(NonC: of wing)* portance *f*

[6] *(fig = boost)* **it gave us a ~** cela nous a remonté le moral *or* nous a encouragés

VT [1] *(= raise)* lever, soulever ; *(Agr) [+ potatoes etc]* arracher ◆ **to ~ sth into the air** lever qch en l'air ◆ **to ~ sb/sth onto a table** soulever qn/qch et le poser *or* pour le poser sur une table ◆ **to ~ sb/sth off a table** descendre qn/qch d'une table ◆ **to ~ sb over a wall** faire passer qn par-dessus un mur ◆ **this suitcase is too heavy for me to ~** cette valise est trop lourde pour que je la soulève *subj* ◆ **to ~ weights** *(Sport)* faire de l'haltérophilie *or* des haltères ◆ **he ~ed his fork to his mouth** il a porté la fourchette à sa bouche ◆ **"lift here"** "soulever ici" ; → **face, finger**

[2] *(= repeal) [+ restrictions]* supprimer, abolir ; *[+ ban, blockade, siege]* lever ◆ **to ~ the prohibition on sth** lever l'interdiction de qch

[3] *(* = steal)* piquer *, chiper * ; → **shoplift**

[4] *(= copy) [+ quotation, passage]* prendre, voler ◆ **he ~ed that idea from Sartre** il a volé *or* pris cette idée à Sartre, il a plagié Sartre

VI *[lid etc]* se soulever ; *[fog]* se lever

COMP **lift attendant** N *(Brit)* liftier *m*, -ière *f*

lift cage N *(Brit)* cabine *f* d'ascenseur

lift-off N *(Space)* décollage *m* ◆ **we have ~-off!** décollage !

lift operator N ⇒ **lift attendant**

lift shaft N *(Brit)* cage *f* d'ascenseur

► **lift down** VT SEP *[+ box, person]* descendre ◆ **to ~ sth down from a shelf** descendre qch d'une étagère

► **lift off** VI *(Space)* décoller

VT SEP *[+ lid]* enlever ; *[+ person]* descendre

N ◆ **lift-off** → **lift**

► **lift out** VT SEP *[+ object]* sortir ; *(Mil) [+ troops] (by plane)* évacuer par avion, aéroporter ; *(by helicopter)* héliporter, évacuer par hélicoptère ◆ **he ~ed the child out of his playpen** il a sorti l'enfant de son parc

► **lift up** VI *[drawbridge etc]* se soulever, basculer

VT SEP *[+ object, carpet, skirt, person]* soulever ◆ **to ~ up one's eyes** lever les yeux ◆ **to ~ up one's head** lever *or* redresser la tête ◆ **he ~ed up his voice** *(liter)* il a élevé la voix

liftboy /ˈlɪftbɔɪ/ N *(Brit)* liftier *m*, garçon *m* d'ascenseur

liftgate /ˈlɪftɡeɪt/ N *(esp US) [of car]* hayon *m*

liftman /ˈlɪftmæn/ N (pl **-men**) *(Brit)* ⇒ **liftboy**

lig‡ /lɪɡ/ VI *(Brit) (at party)* s'inviter ; *(at concert etc)* resquiller *

ligament /ˈlɪɡəmənt/ N ligament *m*

ligature /ˈlɪɡətʃəʳ/ N *(Surg, Typ = act, object)* ligature *f* ; *(Mus)* liaison *f*

ligger‡ /ˈlɪɡəʳ/ N *(Brit) (at party)* personne qui s'invite ; *(at concert etc)* resquilleur * *m*, -euse * *f*

ligging‡ /ˈlɪɡɪŋ/ N *(Brit) (at party)* fait *m* de s'inviter ; *(at concert etc)* resquille * *f*

light[1] /laɪt/ LANGUAGE IN USE 26.3 (vb : pret, ptp **lit** *or* **lighted**)

N 1 *(gen)* lumière *f* ; *(from lamp)* lumière *f*, éclairage *m* ; *(from sun)* lumière *f* ; (also **daylight**) lumière *f*, jour *m* ◆ **we saw several ~s on the horizon** nous avons vu plusieurs lumières à l'horizon ◆ **by the ~ of a candle/the fire/a torch** à la lumière *or* lueur d'une bougie/du feu/d'une lampe de poche ◆ **there were ~s on in several of the rooms** il y avait de la lumière dans plusieurs pièces ◆ **the ~s are on but nobody's (at) home** * *(fig hum)* il (*or* elle *etc*) est complètement dans les nuages ◆ **at first ~** au point du jour ◆ **the ~ was beginning to fail** le jour commençait à baisser ◆ **the ~ isn't good enough to take photographs** il ne fait pas assez clair *or* il n'y a pas assez de lumière pour prendre des photos ◆ **~ and shade** *(Art, Phot)* ombre *f* et lumière *f* ◆ **there's no ~ and shade in their life** leur vie est très monotone ◆ **you're holding it against the ~** vous le tenez à contre-jour ◆ **to stand sth in the ~** mettre qch à la lumière ◆ **to be** *or* **stand in one's own ~** se faire de l'ombre ◆ **you're in my** *or* **the ~** *(daylight)* vous me cachez le jour ; *(electric)* vous me cachez la lumière ◆ **she was sitting with her back to the ~** elle tournait le dos à la lumière ; → **firelight, go out, hide**[1], **electric, moonlight**

2 *(fig)* ◆ **in a good/bad ~** sous un jour favorable/défavorable ◆ **to see things in a new ~** voir les choses sous un nouveau jour ◆ **the incident revealed him in a new ~** l'incident l'a montré sous un jour nouveau ◆ **to see sb/sth in a different ~** voir qn/qch sous un autre jour *or* un jour différent ◆ **to shed** *or* **cast a new ~ on a subject** jeter un jour nouveau sur un sujet ◆ **can you throw any ~ on this question?** pouvez-vous éclaircir cette question ? ◆ **to bring to ~** mettre en lumière, révéler ◆ **the case will be reconsidered in the ~ of new evidence** l'affaire sera revue à la lumière des nouvelles preuves ◆ **in the ~ of recent events, I think we should ...** étant donné les *or* compte tenu des récents événements, je pense que nous devrions ... ◆ **to come to ~** être dévoilé *or* découvert ◆ **new facts have come to ~** on a découvert des faits nouveaux ◆ **in (the) ~ of what you say** à la lumière de ce que vous dites ◆ **I don't see things in that ~** je ne vois pas les choses sous cet angle-là *or* sous ce jour-là ◆ **in the cold ~ of day** à tête reposée ◆ **to see the ~** *(= understand)* comprendre ; *(= see error of one's ways: also Rel)* trouver son chemin de Damas ◆ **to see the ~ (of day)** *(= be born)* venir au monde ; *(= be published etc)* paraître ◆ **there is (a)** *or* **one can see the ~ at the end of the tunnel** on entrevoit la lumière au bout du tunnel

3 *(in eyes)* lueur *f* ◆ **with the ~ of battle in his eyes** (avec) une lueur belliqueuse dans le regard

4 *(= lamp etc)* lampe *f* ◆ **desk ~** lampe *f* de bureau

5 *[of motor vehicle] (gen)* feu *m* ; *(= headlight)* phare *m* ; *[of cycle]* feu *m* ◆ **have you got your ~s on?** as-tu mis tes phares (*or* tes feux) ? ; → **parking, sidelight**

6 **the ~s** *(= traffic lights)* les feux *mpl* (de circulation) ◆ **the ~s aren't working** les feux sont en panne ◆ **the ~s were (at) red** le feu était (au) rouge ◆ **he stopped at the ~s** il s'est arrêté au feu (rouge) ; see also **red**

7 *(for cigarette etc)* feu *m* ◆ **have you got a ~?** avez-vous du feu ? ◆ **to set ~ to sth** *(Brit)* mettre le feu à qch ; → **pilot, strike**

8 *(Archit = window)* fenêtre *f*, ouverture *f* ; → **fan**[1], **leaded, skylight**

ADJ 1 *(in brightness) [evening, room]* clair ◆ **it was growing** *or* **getting ~** il commençait à faire jour ◆ **while it's still ~** pendant qu'il fait encore jour

2 *(in colour) [hair]* clair, blond ; *[colour, complexion, skin]* clair ◆ **~ green** vert clair *inv* ◆ **~ blue** bleu clair *inv*

VT 1 *(= set fire to) [+ candle, cigarette, gas]* allumer ◆ **to ~ a match** frotter *or* gratter une allumette ◆ **a ~ed match** une allumette enflammée ◆ **he lit the fire** il a allumé le feu ◆ **he lit a fire** il a fait du feu ◆ **to ~ a fire under sb** *(esp US)* mettre la pression sur qn

2 *(= illuminate)* éclairer ◆ **lit by electricity** éclairé à l'électricité ◆ **this torch will ~ your way** *or* **the way for you** cette lampe de poche vous éclairera le chemin

VI 1 *[match]* s'allumer ; *[coal, wood]* prendre (feu)

2 ◆ **to ~ into sb** * tomber sur qn (à bras raccourcis)

COMP **light bulb** N *(Elec)* ampoule *f*

light-coloured ADJ clair, de couleur claire

light effects NPL effets *mpl* *or* jeux *mpl* de lumière

light-emitting diode N diode *f* électroluminescente

light fitting N appareil *m* d'éclairage

light-haired ADJ blond

light meter N *(Phot)* posemètre *m*

light pen, light pencil N *(Comput)* photostyle *m*, crayon *m* optique

light pollution N pollution *f* lumineuse

light-sensitive ADJ photosensible

light show N éclairages *mpl*

lights out N l'extinction *f* des feux ◆ **~s out at 9 o'clock** extinction des feux à 21 heures ◆ **~s out!** extinction des feux !, on éteint !

light switch N interrupteur *m*

light wave N onde *f* lumineuse

light-year N année-lumière *f* ◆ **3,000 ~-years away** à 3 000 années-lumière ◆ **that's ~-years away** *(fig)* c'est à des années-lumière

► **light out** † * VI partir à toute vitesse (*for* pour) se barrer *

► **light up**

VI 1 *[lamp]* s'allumer ; *(fig)* s'allumer, s'éclairer ◆ **her eyes/face lit up** son regard/visage s'est éclairé

2 (* *= start to smoke)* allumer une cigarette *or* une pipe *etc*

VT SEP *(= illuminate)* éclairer ◆ **a smile lit up her face** un sourire a éclairé *or* illuminé son visage

ADJ ◆ **lit up** → **lit**

N ◆ **lighting-up** → **lighting**

light[2] /laɪt/ ADJ 1 *(= not heavy) [parcel, weapon, clothes, sleep, meal, wine, soil]* léger ◆ **~er than air** plus léger que l'air ◆ **as ~ as a feather** léger comme une plume ◆ **to be ~ on one's feet** *(gen)* avoir le pas léger *or* la démarche légère ; *(of boxer)* avoir un très bon jeu de jambes ; *(of dancer)* être aérien ◆ **to be a ~ sleeper** avoir le sommeil léger

2 *(fig) (= not serious) [play, music, breeze, punishment, shower]* léger ; *[rain]* petit, fin ; *[work, task] (= easy)* facile ; *(= not strenuous)* peu fatigant ◆ **it is no ~ matter** c'est sérieux, ça n'est pas une plaisanterie ◆ **a ~ fall of snow** une légère chute de neige ◆ **with a ~ heart** le cœur léger ◆ **"woman wanted for light work"** "on demande employée de maison pour travaux légers" ◆ **to make ~ work of sth** faire qch aisément *or* sans difficulté ◆ **to make ~ of sth** prendre *or* traiter qch à la légère

ADV ◆ **to sleep ~** avoir le sommeil léger ◆ **to travel ~** voyager avec peu de bagages

NPL **lights** *(= meat)* mou *m (abats)*

COMP **light aircraft** N petit avion *m*

light ale N *(Brit) sorte de bière blonde légère*

light beer N *(US)* bière *f* basses calories

light comedy N comédie *f* légère

light cream N *(US)* crème *f* liquide

light entertainment N *(NonC: Rad, TV)* variétés *fpl*

light-fingered ADJ ◆ **to be ~-fingered** être chapardeur

light-footed ADJ *(gen)* au pas léger, à la démarche légère ; *[dancer]* aérien

light-headed ADJ *(= dizzy)* étourdi, pris de vertige ; *(= unable to think clearly)* étourdi, hébété ; *(= excited)* exalté, grisé ; *(= thoughtless)* étourdi, écervelé

light-hearted ADJ *[person]* gai, aimable, enjoué ; *[laugh]* joyeux, gai ; *[atmosphere]* joyeux, gai, plaisant ; *[discussion]* enjoué ; *[question, remark]* plaisant, peu sérieux

light-heartedly ADV *(= happily)* joyeusement, allégrement ; *(= jokingly)* en plaisantant ; *(= cheerfully)* de bon cœur, avec bonne humeur

light heavyweight ADJ, N *(Boxing)* (poids *m*) mi-lourd *m*

light industry N industrie *f* légère

light infantry N *(Mil)* infanterie *f* légère

light middleweight ADJ, N *(Boxing)* (poids *m*) superwelter *m* *or* super-mi-moyen *m*

light opera N opérette *f*

light railway N transport *m* urbain sur rail

light reading N lecture *f* distrayante

light vehicles NPL véhicules *mpl* légers

light verse N poésie *f* légère

light welterweight ADJ, N *(Boxing)* (poids *m*) super-léger *m*

light[3] /laɪt/ (pret, ptp **lighted** *or* **lit**) VI ◆ **to ~ (up)on sth** trouver qch par hasard, tomber par chance sur qch ◆ **his eyes lit upon the jewels** son regard est tombé sur les bijoux

lighten[1] /ˈlaɪtn/ VT 1 *(= light up) [+ darkness, face]* éclairer, illuminer 2 *(= make lighter) [+ colour, hair]* éclaircir VI 1 *[sky]* s'éclaircir 2 **it is ~ing** *(of lightning)* il fait *or* il y a des éclairs

lighten[2] /ˈlaɪtn/ VT 1 *(= make less heavy) [+ cargo, burden]* alléger ; *[+ tax]* alléger, réduire 2 *(fig) [+ atmosphere]* détendre ; *[+ discussion]* rendre plus léger ◆ **to ~ sb's mood** dérider qn ◆ **the sunshine did nothing to ~ his mood** malgré le soleil, il ne s'est pas déridé VI *[load]* se réduire ◆ **her heart ~ed at the news** la nouvelle lui a enlevé le poids qu'elle avait sur le cœur *or* lui a ôté un grand poids

► **lighten up** * VI se relaxer, se détendre

lighter[1] /ˈlaɪtəʳ/ N *(for gas cooker)* allume-gaz *m inv* ; (also **cigarette lighter**) briquet *m* ; *(on car dashboard)* allume-cigare *m inv*, allume-cigarette *m inv* ; → **cigar, firelighter, lamplighter**

COMP **lighter flint** N pierre *f* à briquet

lighter fuel N gaz *m* (*or* essence *f*) à briquet

lighter[2] /ˈlaɪtəʳ/ N *(= barge)* péniche *f*, chaland *m* ; *(= for unloading ships)* allège *f*

lighterage /ˈlaɪtərɪdʒ/ N (transport *m* par) ac(c)onage *m* ; *(= fee)* droit *m* d'ac(c)onage

lighthouse /ˈlaɪthaʊs/ N phare *m* COMP **lighthouse keeper** N gardien(ne) *m(f)* de phare

lighting /ˈlaɪtɪŋ/ N *(NonC)* 1 *(Elec)* éclairage *m* ; *(Theat)* éclairages *mpl* 2 *(= act) [of lamp, candle etc]* allumage *m*

COMP **lighting effects** NPL effets *mpl* *or* jeux *mpl* d'éclairage, éclairages *mpl*

lighting engineer N éclairagiste *mf*

lighting fixture N appareil *m* d'éclairage

lighting-up time N *(Brit: for drivers) heure à laquelle les automobilistes sont tenus d'allumer leurs phares*

lightly /ˈlaɪtlɪ/ ADV 1 *(= gently) [walk]* légèrement ; *[stroke]* doucement, délicatement ; *[brush]* délicatement ◆ **she touched his brow ~ with her hand** elle lui a effleuré le front de la main ◆ **bring to the boil and season ~ with pepper** faire bouillir et assaisonner légèrement de poivre ◆ **~ boiled egg** ≈ œuf *m* mollet ◆ **~ cooked** pas trop cuit ◆ **to kiss sb ~** donner un petit baiser à qn ◆ **he kissed me ~ on the lips** il a déposé un petit baiser sur mes lèvres 2 *(= light-heartedly) [speak]* légèrement, à la légère ; *[laugh]* légèrement ; *[remark, say]* d'un ton dégagé ◆ **if this deadline is not met,**

they will not take it ~ si ce délai n'est pas respecté, ils ne le prendront pas à la légère ◆ **to get off** ~ s'en tirer à bon compte

lightness¹ /ˈlaɪtnɪs/ **N** (= *brightness*) clarté *f*

lightness² /ˈlaɪtnɪs/ **N** (*in weight, Culin*) légèreté *f*

lightning /ˈlaɪtnɪŋ/ **N** (= *flash*) éclair *m* ; (= *phenomenon*) foudre *f* ◆ **we saw** ~ nous avons vu un éclair *or* des éclairs ◆ **there was a lot of** ~ il y avait beaucoup d'éclairs ◆ **a flash of** ~ un éclair ◆ **struck by** ~ frappé par la foudre, foudroyé ◆ ~ **never strikes twice in the same place** (*Prov*) la foudre ne frappe *or* ne tombe jamais deux fois au même endroit ◆ **like** ~* avec la rapidité de l'éclair *or* à la vitesse de l'éclair ; → **forked, grease, sheet**

COMP [*attack*] foudroyant ; (*Ind*) [*strike*] surprise *inv* ; [*visit*] éclair *inv*

lightning bug **N** (*US*) luciole *f*

lightning conductor, lightning rod (*US*) **N** paratonnerre *m*

lightship /ˈlaɪtʃɪp/ **N** bateau-phare *m*, bateau-feu *m*

lightweight /ˈlaɪtweɪt/ **ADJ** [*jacket, shoes*] léger ; (*Boxing*) poids léger *inv* **N** (*Boxing*) poids *m* léger ◆ **European** ~ **champion/championship** champion *m*/championnat *m* d'Europe des poids légers

ligneous /ˈlɪgnɪəs/ **ADJ** ligneux

lignite /ˈlɪgnaɪt/ **N** lignite *m*

lignum vitae /ˈlɪgnəmˈvɪtaɪ/ **N** 1 (= *tree*) gaïac *m* 2 (= *wood*) bois *m* de gaïac

Liguria /lɪˈgjʊərɪə/ **N** Ligurie *f*

Ligurian /lɪˈgjʊərɪən/ **ADJ** ligurien

likable /ˈlaɪkəbl/ **ADJ** ⇒ **likeable**

like /laɪk/

LANGUAGE IN USE 3.3, 4, 7, 8, 11.2, 13, 25.2

1 ADJECTIVE	5 NOUN
2 PREPOSITION	6 PLURAL NOUN
3 ADVERB	7 TRANSITIVE VERB
4 CONJUNCTION	8 COMPOUNDS

1 - ADJECTIVE

= similar de ce type *or* genre, analogue ◆ **this technique detects sugar and other** ~ **substances** cette technique permet de détecter le sucre et d'autres substances de ce type *or* analogues ◆ **in** ~ **manner** de la même manière ◆ **they are as** ~ **as two peas (in a pod)** ils se ressemblent comme deux gouttes d'eau

2 - PREPOSITION

1 = in the manner of comme ◆ **he spoke** ~ **an aristocrat** il parlait comme un aristocrate ◆ **he spoke** ~ **the aristocrat he was** il parlait comme l'aristocrate qu'il était ◆ **he behaved** ~ **a fool** il s'est conduit comme un imbécile ◆ ~ **the fool he is, he ...** imbécile comme il l'est, il ... ◆ ~ **an animal in a trap he ...** comme *or* telle une bête prise au piège, il ... ◆ **an idiot** ~ **you** un imbécile comme toi ◆ **she was** ~ **a sister to me** elle était comme une sœur pour moi ◆ **the news spread** ~ **wildfire** la nouvelle s'est répandue comme une traînée de poudre ◆ **to tell it** ~ **it is*** dire les choses comme elles sont

◆ **like that** comme ça ◆ **don't do it** ~ **that** ne fais pas comme ça ◆ **some people are** ~ **that** il y a des gens comme ça ◆ **his father is** ~ **that** son père est comme ça ◆ **it wasn't** ~ **that at all** ce n'est pas comme ça que ça s'est passé ◆ **people** ~ **that can't be trusted** on ne peut pas se fier à des gens pareils *or* à des gens comme ça

◆ **like this** comme ceci, comme ça ◆ **you do it** ~ **this** tu fais comme ceci *or* ça ◆ **it happened** ~ **this ...** voici comment ça s'est passé ..., ça s'est passé comme ça ... ◆ **it was** ~ **this, I'd just got home ...** voilà, je venais juste de rentrer chez moi ... ◆ **I'm sorry I didn't come but it was** ~ **this ...** je m'excuse de ne pas être venu mais c'est que ...

2 in comparisons comme ◆ **to be** ~ **sb/sth** ressembler à qn/qch ◆ **they are very (much)** ~ **one another** ils se ressemblent beaucoup ◆ **he is** ~ **his father** il ressemble à son père, il est comme son père ◆ **he's just** ~ **anybody else** il est comme tout le monde ◆ **the portrait is not** ~ **him** le portrait ne lui ressemble pas *or* n'est pas ressemblant ◆ **his work is rather** ~ **Van Gogh's** son œuvre est un peu dans le style de Van Gogh ◆ **your writing is rather** ~ **mine** vous avez un peu la même écriture que moi, votre écriture ressemble un peu à la mienne ◆ **a house** ~ **mine** une maison comme la mienne ◆ **a hat rather** *or* **something** ~ **yours** un chapeau un peu comme le vôtre *or* dans le genre du vôtre ◆ **I found one** ~ **it** j'en ai trouvé un pareil, j'ai trouvé le même ◆ **I never saw anything** ~ **it!** je n'ai jamais rien vu de pareil ! ◆ **we heard a noise** ~ **a car backfiring** on a entendu comme une pétarade de voiture

3 in descriptions ◆ **what's he** ~ **?** comment est-il ? ◆ **you know what she's** ~* vous savez comment elle est ◆ **what's he** ~ **as a teacher?** comment est-il *or* que vaut-il comme professeur ? ◆ **what was the film** ~**?** comment as-tu trouvé le film ? ◆ **what's the weather** ~ **in Paris?** quel temps fait-il à Paris ? ◆ **that's more** ~ **it!** * voilà qui est mieux !, il y a du progrès !

◆ **something/nothing like** ◆ **it cost something** ~ **$100** cela a coûté dans les 100 dollars, cela a coûté quelque chose comme 100 dollars ◆ **he's called Middlewick or something** ~ **that** il s'appelle Middlewick ou quelque chose comme ça *or* quelque chose d'approchant ◆ **I was thinking of giving her something** ~ **a necklace** je pensais lui offrir un collier ou quelque chose dans ce genre-là *or* quelque chose comme ça ◆ **that's something** ~ **a steak!*** voilà ce que j'appelle *or* ce qui s'appelle un bifteck ! ◆ **there's nothing** ~ **real silk** rien de tel que la soie véritable, rien ne vaut la soie véritable ◆ **that's nothing** ~ **it!** ça n'est pas du tout ça !

4 = typical of ◆ **that's just** ~ **him !** c'est bien de lui ! ◆ **it's not** ~ **him to be late** ça ne lui ressemble pas *or* ça n'est pas son genre d'être en retard ◆ **that's just** ~ **a woman!** voilà bien les femmes !

5 = in the same way as comme, de même que ◆ ~ **me, he is fond of Brahms** comme moi, il aime Brahms ◆ **he,** ~ **me, thinks that ...** comme moi, il pense que ... ◆ **he thinks** ~ **us*** il pense comme nous ◆ **do it** ~ **me*** fais comme moi ◆ **can't you just accept it** ~ **everyone else?** tu ne peux pas simplement l'accepter comme tout le monde ? ◆ ~ **father,** ~ **son** (*Prov*) tel père, tel fils (*Prov*)

6 = such as comme, tel que ◆ **the things she prefers,** ~ **reading and music** les activités qu'elle préfère, telles que la lecture et la musique *or* comme la lecture et la musique

3 - ADVERB

1 = likely ◆ **(as)** ~ **as not** ◆ ~ **enough*** probablement

2 = near **that record's nothing** ~ **as good as this one** ce disque-là est loin d'être aussi bon que celui-ci ◆ **she's more** ~ **30 than 25** elle est plus près de 30 ans que de 25 ◆ **he asked her to do it – ordered her, more** ~**!*** il lui a demandé de le faire – il le lui a ordonné, plutôt !

3 ✱ : conversational filler **he felt tired** ~**, he felt** ~ **tired**(*US*) il se sentait comme qui dirait* fatigué ◆ **I had a fortnight's holiday,** ~**, so I did a bit of gardening** j'avais quinze jours de vacances, alors comme ça* j'ai fait un peu de jardinage

4 - CONJUNCTION

1 * = as comme ◆ **he did it** ~ **I did** il l'a fait comme moi ◆ **he can't play poker** ~ **his brother can** il ne sait pas jouer au poker comme *or* aussi bien que son frère ◆ ~ **we used to** comme nous en avions l'habitude ◆ **it's just** ~ **I say** c'est comme je vous le dis

2 * = as if comme si ◆ **he behaved** ~ **he was afraid** il se conduisait comme s'il avait peur ◆ **it's not** ~ **she's poor, or anything** ce n'est pas comme si elle était pauvre

5 - NOUN

= similar thing ◆ **oranges, lemons and the** ~ les oranges, les citrons et autres fruits de ce genre ◆ **the** ~ **of which we'll never see again** comme on n'en reverra plus jamais ◆ **did you ever see the** ~ **(of it)?*** a-t-on jamais vu une chose pareille ? ◆ **I've never known his** ~ **for ...** il n'a pas son pareil pour ... ◆ **we'll never see his** ~ **again** nous ne verrons plus jamais quelqu'un comme lui *or* son pareil ◆ **the ~s of him*** les gens comme lui *or* de son acabit (*pej*)

6 - PLURAL NOUN

likes goûts *mpl*, préférences *fpl* ◆ **he knows all my ~s and dislikes** il sait tout ce que j'aime et (tout) ce que je n'aime pas

7 - TRANSITIVE VERB

1 + person aimer bien ◆ **I** ~ **him** je l'aime bien ◆ **I don't** ~ **him** je ne l'aime pas beaucoup, il me déplaît ◆ **I've come to** ~ **him** il m'est devenu sympathique, maintenant je l'aime bien ◆ **he is well ~d here** on l'aime bien ici, on le trouve sympathique ici ◆ **how do you** ~ **him?** comment le trouvez-vous ? ◆ **I don't** ~ **the look of him** son allure ne me dit rien qui vaille

2 + object, food, activity aimer (bien) ◆ **I** ~ **that hat** j'aime bien ce chapeau, ce chapeau me plaît ◆ **which do you** ~ **best?** lequel préférez-tu ? ◆ **this plant doesn't** ~ **sunlight** cette plante ne se plaît pas à la lumière du soleil ◆ **I** ~ **oysters but they don't** ~ **me*** j'aime bien les huîtres mais elles ne me réussissent pas ◆ **I** ~ **music/Beethoven/football** j'aime bien la musique/Beethoven/le football ◆ **I** ~ **to have a rest after lunch** j'aime (bien) me reposer après déjeuner ◆ **he ~s to be obeyed** il aime être obéi *or* qu'on lui obéisse ◆ **I** ~ **people to be punctual** j'aime que les gens soient à l'heure, j'aime qu'on soit ponctuel ◆ **I don't** ~ **it when he's unhappy** je n'aime pas ça quand il est malheureux ◆ **well, I** ~ **that!*** (*iro*) ah ça, par exemple ! ◆ **I** ~ **your cheek!*** (*iro*) tu as quand même du toupet !* ◆ **how do you** ~ **Paris?** que pensez-vous de Paris ?, est-ce que Paris vous plaît ? ◆ **how do you** ~ **it here?** (est-ce que) vous vous plaisez ici ? ◆ **your father won't** ~ **it** cela ne plaira pas à ton père, ton père ne sera pas content ◆ **whether he ~s it or not** que cela lui plaise ou non

3 = want, wish aimer (bien), vouloir ◆ **I'd** ~ **to go home** j'aimerais (bien) *or* je voudrais (bien) rentrer chez moi ◆ **I'd have ~d to be there** j'aurais (bien) aimé être là ◆ **I didn't** ~ **to disturb you** je ne voulais pas vous déranger ◆ **I thought of asking him but I didn't** ~ **to** j'ai bien pensé (à) le lui demander mais j'étais gêné ◆ **would you** ~ **a drink?** voulez-vous boire quelque chose ? ◆ **I would** ~ **more time** je voudrais plus de temps ◆ **which one would you** ~**?** lequel voudriez-vous *or* aimeriez-vous ? ◆ **I would** ~ **you to speak to him** je voudrais que tu lui parles *subj* ◆ **would you** ~ **me to go and get it?** veux-tu que j'aille le

chercher ? ◆ **would you ~ to go to Paris?** aimerais-tu aller à Paris ? ◆ **how would you ~ to go to Paris?** est-ce que cela te plairait *or* te dirait* d'aller à Paris ? ◆ **how do you ~ your steak: rare, medium or well done?** vous le voulez comment, votre bifteck : saignant, à point ou bien cuit ? ◆ **how would you ~ a steak?** est-ce que ça te dirait* de manger un bifteck ? ◆ **I can do it when/where/as much as/how I ~** je peux le faire quand/où/autant que/comme je veux ◆ **when would you ~ breakfast?** à quelle heure voulez-vous votre petit déjeuner ? ◆ **whenever you ~** quand vous voudrez ◆ **"As You Like It"** "Comme il vous plaira" ◆ **don't think you can do as you ~** ne croyez pas que vous puissiez faire comme vous voulez *or* comme bon vous semble ◆ **I'll go out as much as I ~** je sortirai autant qu'il me plaira ◆ **come on Sunday if you ~** venez dimanche si vous voulez ◆ **if you ~** si tu veux, si vous voulez ◆ **she can do what(ever) she ~s with him** elle fait tout ce qu'elle veut de lui ◆ **(you can) shout as much as you ~, I won't open the door** crie tant que tu veux *or* voudras, je n'ouvrirai pas la porte ◆ **he can say** *or* **let him say what he ~s, I won't change my mind** il peut dire ce qu'il veut, je ne changerai pas d'avis

8 – COMPOUNDS

like-minded ADJ de même sensibilité ◆ **it was nice to be with ~-minded individuals** c'était agréable d'être en compagnie de gens de même sensibilité

likeable /ˈlaɪkəbl/ ADJ sympathique, agréable

likeableness /ˈlaɪkəblnɪs/ N caractère *m* sympathique *or* agréable

likelihood /ˈlaɪklɪhʊd/ N probabilité *f*, chance *f* ◆ **there is little ~ of his coming** *or* **that he will come** il y a peu de chances *or* il est peu probable qu'il vienne ◆ **there is a strong ~ of his coming** *or* **that he will come** il y a de fortes chances (pour) qu'il vienne, il est très probable qu'il viendra ◆ **there is no ~ of that** cela ne risque pas d'arriver ◆ **in all ~ she ...** selon toute probabilité elle ..., il est fort probable qu'elle ...

likely /ˈlaɪklɪ/ LANGUAGE IN USE 16.2, 26.3

ADJ [1] (= *probable*) [*outcome, result, consequences*] probable ◆ **~ developments in the region** les développements que la région va probablement connaître ◆ **what is the likeliest time to find him at home?** à quelle heure a-t-on le plus de chances de le trouver chez lui ? ◆ **it is ~ that ...** il est probable que ... + *subj*, il y a des chances (pour) que ... + *subj* ◆ **it is not ~ that ...** il est peu probable que ... + *subj*, il y a peu de chances que ... + *subj* ◆ **it is very ~ that ...** il est tout à fait possible que ... + *subj*, il y a de grandes chances (pour) que ... + *subj* ◆ **it's hardly ~ that ...** il n'est guère probable que ... + *subj* ◆ **is it ~ that he would forget?** se peut-il qu'il oublie *subj* ? ◆ **is it ~ that I'd forget?** comment aurais-je pu oublier ?

[2] ◆ **he/it is ~ to ...** il est bien possible qu'il/que cela ... + *subj* ◆ **to be ~ to win/succeed** (*with pleasant outcome*) [*person*] avoir de fortes chances de gagner/réussir ◆ **to be ~ to fail/refuse** (*with unpleasant outcome*) [*person*] risquer d'échouer/de refuser ◆ **it is ~ to sell well/to improve** (*pleasant*) [*thing*] il y a de fortes chances (pour) que cela se vende bien/que cela s'améliore *subj* ◆ **it is ~ to break/make a loss** (*unpleasant*) [*thing*] cela risque de se casser/de ne pas être rentable ◆ **she is ~ to arrive at any time** (*gen*) elle va probablement arriver d'une minute à l'autre ; (*unwelcome*) elle risque d'arriver d'une minute à l'autre ◆ **she is not ~ to come** il est peu probable *or* il y a peu de chances qu'elle vienne ◆ **this trend is ~ to continue** (*gen*) cette tendance va probablement se poursuivre ; (*unpleasant*) cette tendance risque de se poursuivre ◆ **he is not ~ to succeed** il a peu de chances de réussir ◆ **the man most ~ to succeed** l'homme qui a le plus de chances de réussir ◆ **this incident is ~ to cause trouble** cet incident pourrait bien créer *or* risque de créer des problèmes ◆ **that is not ~ to happen** cela a peu de chances de se produire ◆ **they were not ~ to forget it** ils n'étaient pas près de l'oublier

[3] (= *plausible*) [*explanation*] plausible, vraisemblable ◆ **a ~ story** *or* **tale !** (*iro*) elle est bonne, celle-là ! (*iro*) ◆ **a ~ excuse!** (*iro*) belle excuse ! (*iro*)

[4] (= *promising*) ◆ **he's a ~ candidate/recruit** c'est un candidat/une nouvelle recrue qui promet ◆ **a ~ candidate to become** *or* **for Prime Minister** quelqu'un qui a de fortes chances de devenir Premier ministre ◆ **I asked six ~ people** j'ai demandé à six personnes susceptibles de convenir *or* qui me semblaient pouvoir convenir ◆ **he's a ~ young man** c'est un jeune homme qui promet ◆ **it's not a very ~ place for a film festival** (= *surprising choice*) ce n'est pas vraiment l'endroit auquel on penserait pour un festival du cinéma ◆ **he glanced round for a ~-looking person to help him** il chercha des yeux une personne susceptible de l'aider ◆ **a ~ place for him to be hiding** un endroit où il pouvait être caché

ADV [1] ◆ **very** *or* **most ~** très probablement ◆ **it will very** *or* **most ~ rain** il va très probablement pleuvoir ◆ **as ~ as not** sans doute

[2] (*US*) probablement ◆ **some prisoners will ~ be released soon** certains prisonniers seront probablement bientôt libérés

[3] (*esp Brit:* *) ◆ **not ~ !** sûrement pas !* ◆ **are you going? – not ~!** tu y vas ? – sûrement pas *or* ça risque pas !

liken /ˈlaɪkən/ VT comparer (*to* à) ◆ **to ~ sb to a fox/bird/hamster** comparer qn à un renard/un oiseau/un hamster ◆ **he ~ed the situation to a time bomb** il a comparé la situation à une bombe à retardement ◆ **he ~ed himself to the former president** il se comparait à l'ancien président ◆ **X can be ~ed to Y** on peut comparer X et Y

likeness /ˈlaɪknɪs/ N [1] (= *resemblance*) ressemblance *f* (*to* avec) ◆ **I can't see much ~ between them** je ne vois guère de ressemblance entre eux, je ne trouve pas qu'ils se ressemblent *subj* beaucoup ◆ **a strong family ~** un air de famille très marqué ◆ **to bear a ~ to sb/sth** ressembler à qn/qch [2] ◆ **in the ~ of ...** sous la forme *or* l'aspect de ... [3] (= *portrait*) **to draw sb's ~** faire le portrait de qn ◆ **to have one's ~ taken** se faire faire son portrait ◆ **it is a good ~** c'est très ressemblant ◆ **to catch a ~** (*Art, Phot*) saisir une ressemblance

likewise /ˈlaɪkwaɪz/ ADV [1] (= *similarly*) de même ; (= *also*) également, aussi ; (= *moreover*) de plus, en outre ◆ **in Italy football is the national sport, ~ in Britain** en Italie, le football est le sport national ; il en est de même en Grande-Bretagne ◆ **I can talk to him about anything. Likewise with my brother** je peux lui parler de tout ; c'est la même chose avec mon frère *or* il en est de même avec mon frère ◆ **overtures from the Right have ~ been rejected** des ouvertures de la part de la droite ont de même *or* ont également été rejetées ◆ **my wife is well, the children ~** ma femme va bien, les enfants aussi *or* également ◆ **and ~, it cannot be denied that ...** et on ne peut pas nier non plus que ...

[2] (*with vb*) ◆ **to do ~** faire de même

[3] (*in replies*) ◆ **nice to talk to you – ~** * ça m'a fait plaisir de parler avec vous – moi de même

liking /ˈlaɪkɪŋ/ N (*for person*) sympathie *f*, affection *f* (*for* pour) ; (*for thing*) goût *m* (*for* pour) penchant *m* (*for* pour) ◆ **to take a ~ to sb** se prendre d'amitié pour qn ◆ **to take a ~ to (doing) sth** se mettre à aimer (faire) qch ◆ **to have a ~ for sb** avoir de la sympathie pour qn ◆ **to have a ~ for sth** avoir un penchant *or* du goût pour qch, aimer qch ◆ **a ~ for work** le goût du travail ◆ **to your ~, for your ~** à votre goût

lilac /ˈlaɪlək/ N (= *bush, colour, flower*) lilas *m* ◆ **a bunch of white ~** un bouquet de lilas blanc ADJ (*in colour*) lilas *inv*

Lilliputian /ˌlɪlɪˈpjuːʃɪən/ ADJ lilliputien N Lilliputien(ne) *m(f)*

Lilo ® /ˈlaɪˌləʊ/ N matelas *m* pneumatique

lilt /lɪlt/ N [*of speech, song*] rythme *m*, cadence *f* ◆ **a song with a ~ to it** une chanson bien rythmée ◆ **her voice had a pleasant ~ (to it)** sa voix avait des inflexions mélodieuses

lilting /ˈlɪltɪŋ/ ADJ [*song*] cadencé ; [*voice*] aux intonations mélodieuses ; [*movement*] cadencé

lily /ˈlɪlɪ/ N lis *m* ◆ **~ of the valley** muguet *m* ; → **water**

COMP **lily-livered** ADJ poltron
lily pad N feuille *f* de nénuphar
lily-white ADJ (*lit*) d'une blancheur de lis ; (*fig* = *innocent*) blanc (blanche *f*) comme neige ; (*US: for Whites only*) excluant totalement les Noirs

Lima /ˈliːmə/ N Lima COMP **Lima bean** N haricot *m* de Lima

limb /lɪm/ N [1] [*of body*] membre *m* ; [*of tree*] grosse branche *f* ; [*of cross*] bras *m* (*fig*) [*of organisation, company, government*] branche *f* ◆ **to tear ~ from ~** [+ *person*] mettre en pièces ; [+ *animal*] démembrer ◆ **to be out on a ~** (= *isolated*) être isolé ; (= *vulnerable*) être dans une situation délicate ◆ **to go out on a ~** prendre des risques ◆ **~ of Satan** suppôt *m* de Satan ; → **risk** [2] (*Astron*) limbe *m*

-limbed /lɪmd/ ADJ (*in compounds*) ◆ **long-limbed** aux membres longs ◆ **strong-limbed** aux membres forts

limber[1] /ˈlɪmbəʳ/ ADJ [*person*] leste ; [*thing*] souple, flexible

► **limber up** VI (*Sport etc*) se dégourdir, faire des exercices d'assouplissement ; (*fig*) se préparer, se mettre en train ◆ **~ing-up exercises** exercices *mpl* d'assouplissement

limber[2] /ˈlɪmbəʳ/ N [*of gun carriage*] avant-train *m*

limbic /ˈlɪmbɪk/ ADJ limbique

limbless /ˈlɪmlɪs/ ADJ ◆ **~ man** (= *no limbs*) homme *m* sans membres, homme *m* tronc ; (= *limb missing*) homme *m* estropié, homme *m* à qui il manque un bras *or* une jambe ; (*after amputation*) amputé *m* (d'un membre) ◆ **~ ex-servicemen** ≈ (grands) mutilés *mpl* de guerre

limbo[1] /ˈlɪmbəʊ/ N ◆ **in ~** (= *forgotten*) tombé dans l'oubli ; (= *still undecided*) encore dans les limbes *mpl* (*liter*) ; (*Rel*) dans les limbes ◆ **in legal/social ~** dans un vide juridique/social ◆ **negotiations have been in ~ since December** les négociations sont dans une impasse depuis décembre ◆ **refugee children live on in a ~ of hunger and fear** les enfants réfugiés mènent une existence incertaine dominée par la faim et la peur

limbo[2] /ˈlɪmbəʊ/ N (= *dance*) limbo *m* ◆ **~ dancer** danseur *m*, -euse *f* de limbo

lime[1] /laɪm/ N [1] (*Chem*) chaux *f* ; → **quicklime** [2] (also **birdlime**) glu *f* VT [1] [+ *ground*] chauler [2] [+ *twig*] engluer ; [+ *bird*] prendre à la glu, engluer COMP **lime kiln** N four *m* à chaux

lime[2] /laɪm/ N [1] (= *fruit*) citron *m* vert, lime *f* [2] (= *tree*) lime *f* [3] (= *drink*) jus *m* de citron vert ◆ **vodka/lager and ~** vodka *f*/bière *f* citron vert COMP **lime cordial** N sirop *m* de citron vert
lime green N vert *m* jaune *inv*
lime juice N jus *m* de citron vert

lime[3] /laɪm/ N (= *linden:* also **lime tree**) tilleul *m*

limelight /ˈlaɪmlaɪt/ **N** *(Theat)* feux *mpl* de la rampe ◆ **to be in the ~** *(fig)* être sous les projecteurs (de l'actualité) ◆ **to keep out of the ~** ne pas se faire remarquer

limerick /ˈlɪmərɪk/ **N** limerick *m*

> **LIMERICK**
>
> Un **limerick** est un poème humoristique ou burlesque en cinq vers, dont les rimes se succèdent dans l'ordre aabba. Le sujet de ces épigrammes (qui commencent souvent par "There was a ...") est généralement une personne décrite dans des termes crus ou sur un mode surréaliste.

limescale /ˈlaɪmskeɪl/ **N** tartre *m*

limestone /ˈlaɪmstəʊn/ **N** calcaire *m*

Limey * /ˈlaɪmɪ/ **N** *(US, Austral)* Anglais(e) *m(f)*, Angliche* *mf*

limit /ˈlɪmɪt/ **N** (= *furthest point*) *[of territory, experience, vision etc]* limite *f* ; *(fig)* limite *f*, borne *f* ; (= *restriction on amount, number etc*) limitation *f*, restriction *f* ; (= *permitted maximum*) limite *f* ◆ **the city ~s (of Baghdad)** les limites de la ville (de Bagdad) ◆ **we must set a ~ to the expense** il faut limiter *or* restreindre les dépenses ◆ **his anger knows no ~s** sa colère ne connaît pas de limites, sa colère est sans borne(s) ◆ **to go to the ~ to help sb** faire tout son possible pour aider qn ◆ **the 60km/h ~** (= *speed limit*) la limitation de vitesse de 60 km/h ◆ **there is a 60km/h ~ on this road** la vitesse est limitée à 60 km/h sur cette route ; see also **speed** ◆ **that's the ~!*** c'est le comble !, ça dépasse les bornes ! ◆ **he's the ~!*** (= *goes too far*) il dépasse les bornes ! ; (= *amusing*) il est impayable !* ◆ **there are ~s!*** quand même il y a des limites !, il y a des limites à tout ! ◆ **he is at the ~ of his patience/endurance** il est à bout de patience/de forces ◆ **off ~s** *[area, district]* d'accès interdit ; *(on sign)* "accès interdit" ◆ **there is no ~ on the amount you can import** la quantité que l'on peut importer n'est pas limitée ◆ **outside the ~s of ...** en dehors des limites de ... ◆ **over the ~** *(of lorry in weight)* en surcharge, surchargé ; *(of driver on Breathalyser)* qui excède le taux maximal légal d'alcoolémie ◆ **he was three times over the ~** *[driver]* son taux d'alcoolémie était trois fois plus élevé que le maximum légal ◆ **there is a ~ to my patience** ma patience a des limites ◆ **there is a ~ to what one can do** il y a une limite à ce que l'on peut faire, on ne peut (quand même) pas faire l'impossible ◆ **within the ~s of** dans les limites de ◆ **within a 5-mile ~** dans un rayon de 8 kilomètres ◆ **it is true within ~s** c'est vrai dans une certaine limite *or* mesure ◆ **without ~** sans limitation, sans limite ; see also **stretch**

VT [1] (= *restrict*) *[+ speed, time]* limiter (*to* à) ; *[+ expense, power]* limiter, restreindre (*to* à) ; *[+ person]* limiter ◆ **he ~ed questions to 25 minutes** il a limité les questions à 25 minutes ◆ **he ~ed questions to those dealing with education** il a accepté seulement les questions portant sur l'éducation ◆ **to ~ o.s. to a few remarks** se borner à (faire) quelques remarques ◆ **to ~ o.s. to ten cigarettes a day** se limiter à dix cigarettes par jour ◆ **we are ~ed in what we can do** nous sommes limités dans ce que nous pouvons faire

[2] (= *confine*) limiter ◆ **Neo-Fascism is not ~ed to Europe** le néofascisme ne se limite pas à l'Europe ◆ **our reorganization plans are ~ed to Africa** nos projets de réorganisation se limitent à *or* ne concernent que l'Afrique ◆ **the government's attempts to ~ unemployment to 2.5 million** les efforts du gouvernement pour empêcher le chômage de dépasser la barre des 2,5 millions

limitation /ˌlɪmɪˈteɪʃən/ **N** [1] (= *restriction*) limitation *f*, restriction *f* ◆ **the ~ on imports** la limitation *or* la restriction des importations ◆ **there is no ~ on the amount of currency you may take out** il n'y a aucune restriction sur les devises que vous pouvez emporter ◆ **he has/knows his ~s** il a/connaît ses limites ◆ **the ~ of nuclear weapons** la limitation des armements nucléaires ◆ **an exercise in damage ~, a damage-~ exercise** une tentative pour limiter les dégâts ◆ **this drug has one important ~** ce médicament a un inconvénient de taille ◆ **parents tend to blame schools for the educational ~s of their children** les parents ont tendance à tenir l'école pour responsable des insuffisances scolaires de leurs enfants ◆ **~ of movement** restriction *f* des mouvements

[2] *(Jur)* prescription *f*

limited /ˈlɪmɪtɪd/ **ADJ** [1] (= *restricted*) *[number, resources, choice, means, amount, range]* limité ; *[intelligence, person]* borné, limité ◆ **for a ~ period only** pour une durée limitée ◆ **to a ~ extent** jusqu'à un certain point, dans une certaine mesure seulement

[2] *(esp Brit: in company name)* ◆ **Smith and Sons Limited** ≈ Smith et fils, SA

COMP **limited bus** **N** *(US)* ⇒ **limited-stop bus**
limited company **N** *(esp Brit)* (also **private limited company**) ≈ société *f* à responsabilité limitée ; (also **public limited company**) ≈ société *f* anonyme
limited edition **N** *[of book]* édition *f* à tirage limité ; *[of poster, print]* tirage *m* limité ; *[of record]* pressage *m* limité ; *[of car]* série *f* limitée
limited liability **N** *(Brit)* responsabilité *f* limitée ◆ **~ liability company** société *f* à responsabilité limitée
limited partnership **N** société *f* en commandite simple
limited-stop bus **N** autobus *m* semi-direct

limiting /ˈlɪmɪtɪŋ/ **ADJ** restrictif, contraignant

limitless /ˈlɪmɪtlɪs/ **ADJ** *[power]* sans borne(s), illimité ; *[opportunities]* illimité

limo * /ˈlɪməʊ/ **N** (abbrev of **limousine**) limousine *f*

limousine /ˈlɪməziːn/ **N** *(gen)* limousine *f* ; *(US: from airport etc)* (voiture-)navette *f* **COMP** **limousine liberal** * **N** *(US)* libéral *m* de salon

limp¹ /lɪmp/ **ADJ** [1] (= *not firm*) *[hand, handshake, hair, penis]* mou (molle *f*) ; *[lettuce, flowers]* plus très frais (fraîche *f*) ◆ **to go ~** devenir mou ◆ **his body went ~** tous les muscles de son corps se sont relâchés ◆ **to let one's body go ~** laisser son corps se relâcher ◆ **let your arm go ~** laissez aller votre bras ◆ **his arms hung ~ by his sides** il avait les bras ballants ◆ **he was ~ with exhaustion** il était épuisé ◆ **I feel very ~ in this hot weather** je me sens tout ramolli *or* avachi par cette chaleur ◆ **to have a ~ wrist*** *(fig = be effeminate)* avoir des manières efféminées [2] *(fig = feeble) [excuse]* faible ; *[style]* mou (molle *f*) [3] *(Publishing)* ◆ **~ cover(s)** reliure *f* souple **COMP** **limp-wristed** **ADJ** *(pej = effeminate)* efféminé

limp² /lɪmp/ **VI** *[person]* boiter ; *(fig) [vehicle etc]* marcher tant bien que mal ◆ **to ~ in/out** *etc* entrer/sortir *etc* en boitant ◆ **to ~ along** avancer en boitant, aller clopin-clopant* ◆ **he ~ed to the door** il est allé à la porte en boitant, il a clopiné jusqu'à la porte ◆ **the plane managed to ~ home** l'avion a réussi à regagner sa base tant bien que mal **N** claudication *f*, boiterie *f* ◆ **to have a ~, to walk with a ~** boiter, clopiner

limpet /ˈlɪmpɪt/ **N** [1] (= *shellfish*) patelle *f*, bernique *f* ; *(fig = person)* crampon *m* ◆ **to cling** *or* **stick to sth like a ~** s'accrocher à qch comme une moule au rocher [2] *(Mil:* also **limpet mine***)* mine-ventouse *f*

limpid /ˈlɪmpɪd/ *(liter)* **ADJ** limpide

limply /ˈlɪmplɪ/ **ADV** [1] *(lit)* mollement ◆ **his arms hung ~ by his side** il avait les bras ballants ◆ **the flag hung ~ from the mast** le drapeau pendait mollement [2] *(fig) [say, express]* mollement

limpness /ˈlɪmpnɪs/ **N** [1] *(lit)* mollesse *f* [2] *(fig) [of style]* mollesse *f* ; *[of excuse]* faiblesse *f*

limy /ˈlaɪmɪ/ **ADJ** [1] (= *chalky*) *[soil, water]* calcaire [2] (also **limy green**) d'un vert acide

linage /ˈlaɪnɪdʒ/ **N** *(Press)* lignage *m*, nombre *m* de lignes ◆ **advertising ~** nombre *m* de lignes de publicité **COMP** **linage advertisement** **N** petite annonce *f* ordinaire *(sans encadrement)*

linchpin /ˈlɪntʃpɪn/ **N** [1] *(in car)* esse *f* [2] *(fig)* (= *person*) pilier *m*, cheville *f* ouvrière ; (= *thing*) élément *m* central, pilier *m*

Lincs. /lɪŋks/ abbrev of **Lincolnshire**

linctus /ˈlɪŋktəs/ **N** (pl **linctuses**) sirop *m* (contre la toux)

linden /ˈlɪndən/ **N** (also **linden tree**) tilleul *m*

line¹ /laɪn/

LANGUAGE IN USE 27

1 NOUN	3 COMPOUNDS
2 TRANSITIVE VERB	4 PHRASAL VERB

1 - NOUN

[1] = mark ligne *f*, trait *m* ; *(Math, TV, Sport)* ligne *f* ; (= *pen stroke*) trait *m* ; *(on palm)* ligne *f* ◆ **a straight ~** une (ligne) droite ◆ **a curved ~** une (ligne) courbe ◆ **to put a ~ through sth** barrer *or* rayer qch ◆ **the teacher put a red ~ through my translation** le professeur a barré *or* rayé ma traduction au stylo rouge ◆ **to draw a ~ under sth** *(in exercise book)* tirer un trait sous qch ; *(fig: episode, event)* tirer un trait sur qch ◆ **~ by ~** ligne par ligne ◆ **above the ~** *(Bridge)* (marqué) en points d'honneur ◆ **below the ~** *(Bridge)* (marqué) en points de marche ; *(Accounting)* hors bilan ◆ **on the ~** *(Mus)* sur la ligne ; → **bottom, dotted, draw, state**

[2] = boundary frontière *f* ◆ **there's a thin** *or* **fine ~ between genius and madness** il n'y a qu'un pas du génie à la folie, peu de choses séparent génie et folie

[3] Geog **the Line** (= *equator*) la ligne

[4] = wrinkle ride *f* ◆ **the ~s on her face were now deeper** les rides de son visage s'étaient creusées

[5] = shape ◆ **the rounded ~s of this car** les contours *mpl* arrondis de cette voiture ◆ **clothes that follow the ~s of the body** des vêtements *mpl* moulants *or* qui épousent les contours du corps

[6] = rope corde *f* ; (= *wire*) fil *m* ; *(Fishing)* ligne *f*, fil *m* ; *[of diver]* corde *f* (de sûreté) ; (also **clothes line, washing line**) corde *f* (à linge) ◆ **they threw a ~ to the man in the sea** ils ont lancé une corde à l'homme qui était tombé à la mer

[7] = pipe tuyau *m* ; *(larger: esp for oil, gas)* pipeline *m*

[8] Telec, *also* Elec = cable ligne *f* ◆ **"663-1111 five lines"** "663.11.11 cinq lignes groupées" ◆ **it's a bad ~** la ligne est mauvaise ◆ **the ~'s gone dead** *(during conversation)* on nous a coupés ; *(before dialling)* la ligne est en dérangement ◆ **the ~s are down** les lignes ont été coupées ◆ **the ~ is engaged** *or (US)* **busy** la ligne est occupée, c'est occupé ◆ **Mr Smith is on the ~ (for you)** j'ai M. Smith à l'appareil (pour vous) ◆ **he's on the ~ to the manager** il est en ligne avec le directeur ◆ **the ~s are open from 6 o'clock onwards** on peut téléphoner *or* appeler à partir de 6 heures

[9] of print, writing ligne *f* ; *[of poem]* vers *m* ; (* = *letter*) mot *m* ◆ **page 20, ~ 18** page 20, ligne 18 ◆ **new ~** *(in dictation)* à la ligne ◆ **a six-~ stanza**

une strophe de six vers ◆ **it's one of the best ~s in "Hamlet"** c'est l'un des meilleurs vers de "Hamlet" ◆ **drop me a ~** * envoyez-moi un (petit) mot ◆ **to read between the ~s** lire entre les lignes ◆ **~s** *(Scol = punishment)* lignes *fpl* à copier ◆ **to learn/forget one's ~s** *(Theat)* apprendre/oublier son texte

10 [*esp US* = queue] file *f*, queue *f* ◆ **to form a ~** faire la queue ◆ **to stand** *or* **wait in ~** faire la queue

11 [= row, column] *[of trees, parked cars, hills]* rangée *f* ; *[of cars in traffic jam]* file *f* ; *[of people] (side by side)* rang *m*, rangée *f* ; *(one behind another)* file *f*, colonne *f* ; (also **assembly line**) chaîne *f* ◆ **the new recruits marched in a ~** les nouvelles recrues avançaient en file ◆ **they sat in a ~ in front of him** ils se sont assis en rang devant lui ◆ **a ~ of winning numbers** une série de numéros gagnants ◆ **the first ~ of defence** le premier moyen de défense ◆ **the first ~ of treatment** le premier traitement à suivre

12 [= succession] série *f* ; *(= descent)* ligne *f*, lignée *f* ◆ **the latest in a long ~ of tragedies** la dernière d'une longue série de tragédies ◆ **in a direct ~ from** en droite ligne de, en ligne directe de ◆ **he comes from a long ~ of artists** il est issu d'une longue lignée d'artistes ◆ **the royal ~** la lignée royale ◆ **succession passes through the male ~** la succession se fait par les hommes

13 [also **shipping line**] *(= company)* compagnie *f* maritime ; *(= route)* ligne *f* (maritime) ◆ **the Cunard Line** la compagnie Cunard ◆ **the New York-Southampton ~** la ligne New York-Southampton

14 [Rail *etc*] *(= route)* ligne *f* (de chemin de fer) ; *[of underground]* ligne *f* (de métro) ; *[of bus]* ligne *f* ; *(= track)* voie *f* ◆ **the Brighton ~** la ligne de Brighton ◆ **the ~ was blocked for several hours** la voie a été bloquée plusieurs heures ◆ **cross the ~ by the footbridge** empruntez la passerelle pour traverser la voie ◆ **the train left the ~** le train a déraillé

15 [= direction] ◆ **the main** *or* **broad ~s** *[of story, plan]* les grandes lignes *fpl* ◆ **~ of argument** raisonnement *m* ◆ **the next chapter continues this ~ of thinking** le chapitre suivant développe cet argument ◆ **~ of research** ligne *f* de recherche ◆ **you're on the right ~s** vous êtes sur la bonne voie ◆ **on ethnic/geographical ~s** selon des critères ethniques/géographiques ; → **inquiry, resistance**

16 [= stance] position *f* ; *(= argument)* argument *m* ◆ **they voted against the government ~** ils ont voté contre la position adoptée par le gouvernement ◆ **they came out with their usual ~** ils ont sorti leur argument habituel ◆ **to take a strong ~ on ...** se montrer ferme sur ...

17 [* = field] ◆ **~ of business** *or* **work** activité *f* ◆ **you must be very aware of that in your ~ of business** vous devez en être très conscient dans votre métier ◆ **what's your ~ (of business** *or* **work)?** que faites-vous dans la vie ? ◆ **we're in the same ~ (of business)** *(of companies)* nous sommes dans la même branche ◆ **most kids can do something in the art ~** la plupart des gosses ont un certain don artistique ◆ **cocktail parties are not (in) my ~** les cocktails ne sont pas mon genre ◆ **fishing's more (in) my ~ (of country)** la pêche est davantage mon truc* ◆ **he's got a nice ~ in rude jokes** il connaît plein d'histoires cochonnes*

18 [= product] ◆ **this lager is the shop's best selling ~** cette bière blonde est ce qui se vend le mieux (dans le magasin)

19 [= course] ◆ **in the ~ of duty** dans l'exercice de ses (*or* mes *etc*) fonctions ◆ **it's all in the ~ of duty*** *(fig)* ça fait partie du boulot*

20 [* = idea] ◆ **... but I really don't have a ~ on what's going to happen** ... mais je n'ai vraiment aucune idée de ce qui va se passer ◆ **we've got a ~ on where he's gone to** nous croyons savoir où il est allé

21 [= spiel] **to give sb a ~*** baratiner* qn ◆ **to feed** *or* **hand sb a ~ about sth** ⁑ raconter des bobards* à qn sur qch

22 [Mil] ligne *f* ◆ **in the front ~** *(Mil, fig)* en première ligne ◆ **behind (the) enemy ~s** derrière les lignes ennemies ◆ **~ of battle** ligne *f* de combat ◆ **regiment of the ~** *(Brit Mil)* ≃ régiment *m* d'infanterie ◆ **~ abreast** *(Navy)* ligne *f* de front ◆ **~ astern** *(Navy)* ligne *f* de file ◆ **ship of the ~** vaisseau *m* de ligne, navire *m* de haut bord ◆ **the (battle) ~s are drawn** *(fig)* les hostilités *fpl* sont engagées

23 [Drugs] *[of cocaine etc]* ligne *f*

24 [set structures]

◆ **along the line** ◆ **somewhere along the ~ he got an engineering degree** je ne sais pas exactement quand, il a décroché son diplôme d'ingénieur ◆ **all along the ~** *(= constantly)* toujours ; *(= everywhere)* partout ◆ **didn't I tell you that all along the ~?** c'est ce que je n'ai pas arrêté de te dire ◆ **they've been involved all along the ~** ils ont participé depuis le début ◆ **the effects will be felt all along the ~** les effets en seront ressentis à tous les niveaux

◆ **all (the way)** *or* **right down the line** ⇒ **all along the line**

◆ **along those/the same** *etc* **lines** ◆ **he'd already said something along those ~s** il avait déjà dit quelque chose du même genre ◆ **we are all thinking along the same ~s** nous pensons tous de la même façon, nous sommes tous d'accord *or* du même avis ◆ **several projects were suggested, all along the same ~s** plusieurs projets avaient été suggérés et tous étaient du même genre ◆ **I hope we'll continue along the same ~s** j'espère que nous continuerons sur cette lancée ◆ **along** *or* **on political/racial ~s** *[decide, divide]* selon des critères politiques/raciaux ; *[organize, plan]* dans une optique politique/raciale ◆ **factories now work along Japanese ~s** les usines emploient maintenant des méthodes japonaises

◆ **in line** ◆ **to keep sb in ~** faire tenir qn tranquille ◆ **if the Prime Minister fails to keep the rebels in ~** si le Premier ministre ne réussit pas à maîtriser les éléments rebelles ◆ **to be in ~ for a job** être sur les rangs pour un emploi ◆ **public sector pay is in ~ to rise** les salaires des fonctionnaires devraient augmenter ◆ **Earth was in ~ with Venus and the Sun** la Terre était alignée avec Vénus et le Soleil ◆ **the law is now in ~ with most medical opinion** la loi va maintenant dans le sens de l'avis de la plupart des médecins ◆ **our system is broadly in ~ with that of other countries** notre système correspond plus ou moins à celui d'autres pays

◆ **into line** ◆ **to come** *or* **fall** *or* **step into ~** *[person, group]* se conformer (*with* à) ◆ **to come** *or* **fall into ~** *[plans, proposals]* concorder (*with* avec) ◆ **to fall into ~ with sb** *(fig)* se ranger *or* se conformer à l'avis de qn ◆ **to bring sth into ~ with sth** *(lit, fig)* aligner qch sur qch ◆ **attempts to bring the system into ~ with that of Germany** des tentatives pour aligner le système sur celui de l'Allemagne

◆ **on line** *(= on computer)* en ligne ◆ **they can order their requirements on ~** ils peuvent passer leurs commandes en ligne ◆ **to come on ~** *(= in or into service) [power station, machine]* entrer en service

◆ **on the line** *(* = at stake)* en jeu ◆ **my reputation/job is on the ~** ma réputation/ mon emploi est en jeu ◆ **to put one's reputation/job on the ~** mettre sa réputation/son emploi en jeu ◆ **to put o.s. on the ~** prendre de gros risques ◆ **to put one's neck*** *or* **ass**⁑ *(US)* **on the ~** risquer sa peau*

◆ **out of line*** *(= unreasonable)* ◆ **to be out of ~** ◆ **he was completely out of ~ to suggest that ...** il n'aurait vraiment pas dû suggérer que ... ◆ **he is out of ~ with his own party** *(= in conflict)* il est en décalage par rapport à son parti ◆ **their debts are completely out of ~ with their incomes** leurs dettes sont tout à fait disproportionnées par rapport à leurs revenus ◆ **this result is out of ~ with the trend** ce résultat ne s'inscrit pas dans la tendance générale

2 - TRANSITIVE VERB

[= mark] *[+ face]* rider, marquer ◆ **his face was ~d with exhaustion** il avait le visage marqué par la fatigue ◆ **~d paper** papier *m* réglé

3 - COMPOUNDS

line dancing N danse de style country
line drawing N *(Art)* dessin *m* (au trait)
line feed N *(Comput)* saut *m or* changement *m* de ligne
line fishing N *(Sport)* pêche *f* à la ligne
line judge N *(Tennis)* juge *m* de ligne
line manager N *(Brit)* supérieur *m* hiérarchique *or* direct
line of attack N *(Mil)* plan *m* d'attaque ; *(fig)* plan *m* d'action
line of communication N ligne *f* de communication ◆ **to keep the ~s of communication open with sb** ne pas rompre le dialogue avec qn
line of descent N *(lit, fig)* lignée *f* ◆ **an ancient family who trace their ~ of descent back more than a thousand years** *(lit)* une vieille famille dont les origines remontent à plus de mille ans ◆ **in a direct ~ of descent from sth** *(fig)* dans la lignée directe de qch
line of fire N *(Mil)* ligne *f* de tir ◆ **right in the ~ of fire** en plein dans la ligne de tir *or* de feu
line of flight N *[of bird etc]* ligne *f* de vol ; *[of object]* trajectoire *f*
line of latitude N ligne *f* de latitude
line of longitude N ligne *f* de longitude
line of sight N *(Mil)* ligne *f* de visée
line of vision N champ *m* de vue
line-out N *(Rugby)* touche *f*
line printer N *(Comput)* imprimante *f* ligne par ligne
line spacing N *(Typ, Comput)* interligne *m*
line storm N *(US)* ouragan *m*
line-up N *[of people etc] (= row)* file *f* ; *(Police = identity parade)* séance *f* d'identification (d'un suspect) ; *(Ftbl etc)* (composition *f* de l')équipe *f* ◆ **the new ~-up** *(fig, Pol etc)* la nouvelle composition du Parlement (*or* du Congrès *etc*) ◆ **the President chose his ~-up** le Président a choisi son équipe *or* ses collaborateurs ◆ **the ~-up of African powers** le front des puissances africaines

4 - PHRASAL VERB

► **line up**

VI 1 *(= stand in row)* se mettre en rang(s), s'aligner ; *(= stand in queue)* faire la queue ◆ **the teams ~d up and waited for the whistle** les équipes se sont alignées et ont attendu le coup de sifflet

2 *(fig = align o.s.)* **to ~ up against sb/sth** se liguer contre qn/qch ◆ **to ~ up behind sth** se rallier à qch ◆ **most senators ~d up in support of the president** la plupart des sénateurs se sont ralliés au président ◆ **black people have ~d up on both sides of the issue** les Noirs se sont ralliés aux deux camps ◆ **to ~ up with** *or* **behind** *or* **alongside sb** se ranger du côté de qn, se rallier à qn

VT SEP 1 *[+ people, objects]* aligner, mettre en ligne ◆ **~ them up against the wall** alignez-les contre le mur ◆ **they were ~d up and shot** on les a alignés pour les fusiller ◆ **to be all ~d up*** *(= ready)* être fin prêt (*for* pour ; *to do sth* pour faire qch)

[2] * *(= organize)* *[+ party, trip]* organiser ; *(= find)* trouver ◆ **we must ~ up a chairman for the meeting** il faut que nous trouvions un président pour la réunion ◆ **to have sth ~d up** avoir prévu qch ◆ **to have sb ~d up** avoir qn en vue ◆ **have you got something ~d up for this evening?** est-ce que tu as prévu quelque chose pour ce soir ? ◆ **have you got someone ~d up?** avez-vous quelqu'un en vue ? ◆ **I wonder what he's got ~d up for us** je me demande ce qu'il nous prépare

line² /laɪn/ VT *[+ clothes, bag, box]* doubler *(with de)* ; *[bird] [+ nest]* garnir, tapisser ; *[+ tank, engine part]* revêtir, chemiser ◆ **to ~ one's pockets** *(fig: esp pej)* se remplir les poches ◆ **eat something to ~ your stomach** ne reste pas l'estomac vide ◆ **the walls were ~d with books and pictures** les murs étaient couverts *or* tapissés de livres et de tableaux ◆ **the streets were ~d with cheering crowds** les rues étaient bordées d'une (double) haie de spectateurs enthousiastes ◆ **cheering crowds ~d the route** une foule enthousiaste faisait la haie tout le long du parcours ◆ **the road was ~d with trees** la route était bordée d'arbres ; → **wool**

lineage /ˈlɪnɪɪdʒ/ N [1] *(= ancestry)* lignage † *m*, famille *f* ; *(= descendants)* lignée *f* ◆ **she can trace her ~ back to the 17th century** sa famille remonte au 17ᵉ siècle [2] ⇒ **linage**

lineal /ˈlɪnɪəl/ ADJ en ligne directe

lineament /ˈlɪnɪəmənt/ N *(liter)* *(= feature)* trait *m*, linéament *m* *(liter)* ◆ **~s** *(= characteristic)* caractéristiques *fpl*, particularités *fpl*

linear /ˈlɪnɪəʳ/ ADJ linéaire
COMP **linear accelerator** N accélérateur *m* linéaire
linear equation N équation *f* linéaire
linear perspective N perspective *f* linéaire
linear programming N programmation *f* linéaire

linebacker /ˈlaɪnbækəʳ/ N *(US Sport)* linebacker *m*, défenseur *m* *(positionné derrière la ligne)*

lineman /ˈlaɪnmən/ N (pl **-men**) *(US)* *(Rail)* poseur *m* de rails ; *(Telec)* ouvrier *m* de ligne

linen /ˈlɪnɪn/ N [1] *(NonC = fabric)* lin *m* [2] *(collective n)* *(= sheets, tablecloths etc:* also **linens:** *esp US)* linge *m* (de maison) ; *(= underwear)* linge *m* (de corps) ◆ **dirty** *or* **soiled** ~ linge *m* sale ; → **household, wash**
COMP *[sheet]* de fil, pur fil ; *[suit, thread]* de lin
linen basket N panier *m* à linge
linen closet, linen cupboard N armoire *f or* placard *m* à linge
linen paper N papier *m* de lin

liner /ˈlaɪnəʳ/ N [1] *(= ship)* paquebot *m* ; → **airliner, Atlantic** [2] (also **dustbin liner**) sac *m* poubelle [3] → **eyeliner** [4] *(US)* *[of record]* pochette *f* COMP **liner note** N *(US)* texte *m* *(sur pochette de CD)*

linesman /ˈlaɪnzmən/ N (pl **-men**) *(Sport, Tennis)* juge *m* de ligne ; *(Ftbl, Rugby)* juge *m* de touche

ling¹ /lɪŋ/ N *(= heather)* bruyère *f*

ling² /lɪŋ/ N (pl **ling** or **lings**) [1] *(= sea fish)* lingue *f*, julienne *f* [2] *(= freshwater fish)* lotte *f* de rivière

linger /ˈlɪŋgəʳ/ VI (also **linger on**) *[person]* *(= wait behind)* s'attarder ; *(= take one's time)* prendre son temps ; *(= dawdle)* traîner, lambiner* ; *[smell, pain]* persister ; *[tradition, memory]* persister, subsister ; *[doubt]* subsister ◆ **the others had gone, but he ~ed (on)** les autres étaient partis, lui restait en arrière *or* s'attardait ◆ **after the accident he ~ed (on) for several months** *(before dying)* après l'accident il a traîné quelques mois avant de mourir ◆ **he always ~s behind everyone else** il est toujours derrière tout le monde, il est toujours à la traîne ◆ **don't ~ about** *or* **around** ne lambine pas*, ne traîne pas ◆ **to ~ over a meal** rester longtemps à table, manger sans se presser ◆ **I let my eye ~ on the scene** j'ai laissé mon regard s'attarder sur la scène ◆ **to ~ on a subject** s'attarder *or* s'étendre sur un sujet

lingerie /ˈlænʒəriː/ N *(NonC)* lingerie *f*

lingering /ˈlɪŋgərɪŋ/ ADJ *[look]* long (longue *f*), insistant ; *[doubt]* qui subsiste (encore) ; *[hope]* faible ; *[death]* lent

lingo* /ˈlɪŋgəʊ/ N (pl **lingoes**) *(pej)* *(= language)* langue *f* ; *(= jargon)* jargon *m* ◆ **I don't speak the ~** je ne cause* pas la langue

lingua franca /ˈlɪŋgwəˈfræŋkə/ N (pl **lingua francas** or **linguae francae** /ˈlɪŋgwiːˈfrænsiː/) langue *f* véhiculaire, lingua franca *f inv*

linguist /ˈlɪŋgwɪst/ N linguiste *mf* ◆ **I'm no great ~** je ne suis pas vraiment doué pour les langues

linguistic /lɪŋˈgwɪstɪk/ ADJ linguistique
COMP **linguistic atlas** N atlas *m* linguistique
linguistic borrowing N *(= item borrowed)* emprunt *m* ; *(= process)* emprunts *mpl*
linguistic geography N géographie *f* linguistique
linguistic philosophy N philosophie *f* linguistique

linguistically /lɪŋˈgwɪstɪkəlɪ/ ADV linguistiquement

linguistics /lɪŋˈgwɪstɪks/ N *(NonC)* linguistique *f* COMP *[book, degree, professor]* de linguistique ; *[student]* en linguistique

liniment /ˈlɪnɪmənt/ N liniment *m*

lining /ˈlaɪnɪŋ/ N *[of clothes, bag, box]* doublure *f* ; *[of tank, engine part]* revêtement *m* ; *[of brakes]* garniture *f* ; *[of stomach]* paroi *f* ◆ **~ paper** papier *m* d'apprêt ; *(for drawers)* papier *m* à tapisser ; → **silver**

link /lɪŋk/ LANGUAGE IN USE 17.1
N [1] *[of chain]* maillon *m*
[2] *(= connection)* lien *m*, liaison *f* ; *(= interrelation)* rapport *m*, lien *m* ; *(= bonds)* lien *m*, relation *f* ; *(Comput: of hypertext)* lien *m* ◆ **a new rail ~** une nouvelle liaison ferroviaire ◆ **there must be a ~ between the two phenomena** il doit y avoir un lien *or* un rapport entre ces deux phénomènes ◆ **he served as ~ between management and workers** il a servi de lien *or* d'intermédiaire entre la direction et les ouvriers ◆ **cultural ~s** liens *mpl* culturels, relations *fpl* culturelles ◆ **~s of friendship** liens *mpl* d'amitié ◆ **he broke off all ~s with his friends** il a cessé toutes relations avec ses amis, il a rompu tous les liens avec ses amis ; → **cufflink, missing, weak**
VT [1] *(physically)* lier ◆ **to ~ arms** se donner le bras
[2] *(= establish communication between)* relier ; *(fig)* lier ◆ **~ed by rail/by telephone** reliés par (la) voie ferrée/par téléphone ◆ **~ed (together) in friendship** liés d'amitié ◆ **the two companies are now ~ed (together)** ces deux sociétés sont maintenant liées *or* associées
[3] *(= establish logical connection between)* établir un lien *or* rapport entre ◆ **to ~ sth with sb** établir un lien entre qch et qn ◆ **the police are not ~ing him with the murder** la police n'a établi aucun rapport entre lui et le meurtre ◆ **this is closely ~ed to our sales figures** ceci est étroitement lié à nos chiffres de vente ◆ **smoking and lung cancer are closely ~ed** le tabac et le cancer des poumons sont étroitement liés
VI ◆ **to ~ to a site** *(Comput)* proposer des liens avec un site
COMP **linking consonant** N *(Phon)* consonne *f* de liaison
linking verb N *(Ling)* verbe *m* copulatif, copule *f*
link road N *(Brit)* voie *f* de raccordement
link-up N *(gen)* lien *m*, rapport *m* ; *(Rad, TV)* *(= connection)* liaison *f* ; *(= programme)* émission *f* en duplex ; *(Space)* jonction *f* ◆ **there is no apparent ~-up between the two cases** il n'y a pas de rapport apparent *or* de lien apparent entre les deux affaires ◆ **is there any ~-up between our company and theirs?** y a-t-il un lien entre notre entreprise et la leur ?

▸ **link together**
VI s'unir, se rejoindre
VT SEP *[+ two objects]* unir, joindre ; *(by means of a third)* relier

▸ **link up**
VI *[persons]* se rejoindre ; *[firms, organizations etc]* s'associer ; *[spacecraft]* opérer l'arrimage ; *[roads, railway lines]* se rejoindre, se rencontrer ◆ **they ~ed up with the other group** ils ont rejoint l'autre groupe
VT SEP [1] *(Rad, Telec, TV)* relier, assurer la liaison entre
[2] *[+ spacecraft]* opérer l'arrimage de
N ◆ **link-up** → **link**

linkage /ˈlɪŋkɪdʒ/ N [1] *(= connection)* lien *m*, relation *f* [2] *(for regulating mechanism)* tringlerie *f*, transmission *f* par tringlerie [3] *(Bio)* linkage *m*

linkman /ˈlɪŋkmæn/ N (pl **-men**) *(esp US TV, Rad)* présentateur *m*

links /lɪŋks/ NPL (terrain *m* de) golf *m*, links *mpl*

linnet /ˈlɪnɪt/ N linotte *f*

lino* /ˈlaɪnəʊ/ N *(Brit)* (abbrev of **linoleum**) lino *m* ◆ **~ cut** gravure *f* sur linoléum

linoleum /lɪˈnəʊlɪəm/ N linoléum *m*

Linotype ® /ˈlaɪnəʊtaɪp/ N linotype *f*

linseed /ˈlɪnsiːd/ N *(NonC)* graines *fpl* de lin ◆ **~ oil** huile *f* de lin

lint /lɪnt/ N *(NonC)* [1] *(Med)* tissu *m* ouaté *(pour pansements)* ◆ **a small piece of ~** une compresse, un petit pansement ouaté [2] *(US = fluff)* peluches *fpl* ◆ **a piece** *or* **speck of ~** une peluche

lintel /ˈlɪntl/ N linteau *m*

Linus /ˈlaɪnəs/ N *(esp US)* ◆ **~ blanket** * couverture *f* sécurisante *(pour jeune enfant)*

lion /ˈlaɪən/ N lion *m* ; *(fig = person)* personnage *m* en vue, célébrité *f* ◆ **the Lion** *(Astrol, Astron)* le Lion ◆ **to get** *or* **take the ~'s share** se tailler la part du lion ◆ **to put one's head in the ~'s mouth** *(fig)* se jeter *or* se précipiter dans la gueule du loup ◆ **to throw sb to the ~s** *(fig)* abandonner qn à son sort, jeter *or* livrer qn en pâture ; → **beard, mountain, Richard**
COMP **lion cub** N lionceau *m*
lion-hearted ADJ d'un courage de lion
lion-hunter N *(fig)* ◆ **she is a ~-hunter** * elle cherche toujours à avoir des célébrités comme invités
lion-tamer N dompteur *m*, -euse *f* de lions

lioness /ˈlaɪənɪs/ N lionne *f*

lionize /ˈlaɪənaɪz/ VT *[+ person]* aduler, stariser*

lip /lɪp/ N [1] *(Anat)* lèvre *f* ; *[of dog etc]* babine *f* ◆ **on every ~** *or* **everyone's ~s** sur toutes les lèvres
[2] *(= edge)* *[of jug]* bec *m* ; *[of cup, saucer]* rebord *m* ; *[of crater]* bord *m* ; *[of wound]* bord *m*, lèvre *f*
[3] (* *= insolence*) culot* *m*, insolences *fpl* ◆ **less of your ~!** ne sois pas insolent ! ; → **bite, button, stiff**
COMP **lip balm** N *(esp US)* ⇒ **lip salve**
lip gloss N brillant *m* à lèvres
lip pencil N crayon *m* à lèvres
lip-read VT lire sur les lèvres
lip-reading N lecture *f* sur les lèvres
lip salve N *(Brit)* baume *m* pour les lèvres
lip service N ◆ **to pay ~ service to sth** manifester un intérêt de pure forme pour qch ◆ **~-service paid by politicians to family needs**

l'intérêt de pure forme manifesté par la classe politique à l'égard de la famille ◆ **they only pay ~-service to human rights when it suits them** ils ne manifestent un intérêt pour les droits de l'homme que lorsque cela les arrange ◆ **he only pays ~ service to socialism** il n'est socialiste qu'en paroles
lip-smacking * ADJ *[pleasure, satisfaction, relish]* vif ; *[food]* délicieux
lip-sync(h) VI *(= sing)* chanter en play-back ; *(= speak)* doubler des films VT *(= sing)* chanter en play-back ; *(= speak)* doubler ◆ **to ~-sync(h) sb's words** doubler qn N play-back *m*

lipase /'laɪpeɪs/ N lipase *f*

lipid /'laɪpɪd/ N lipide *m*

lipoprotein /,lɪpəʊ'prəʊtiːn/ N lipoprotéine *f*

liposuction /'lɪpəʊ,sʌkʃən/ N lipo-aspiration *f*, liposuccion *f*

-lipped /lɪpt/ ADJ *(in compounds)* ◆ **dry-lipped** aux lèvres sèches ; → **thick**

lippy * /'lɪpɪ/ ADJ insolent N *(= lipstick)* rouge *m* à lèvres

lipstick /'lɪpstɪk/ N *(NonC) (= substance)* rouge *m* à lèvres ; *(= stick)* (bâton *m* or tube *m* de) rouge *m* à lèvres

liquefaction /,lɪkwɪ'fækʃən/ N liquéfaction *f*

liquefied /'lɪkwɪfaɪd/ ADJ liquéfié COMP **liquefied natural gas** N gaz *m* naturel liquéfié

liquefy /'lɪkwɪfaɪ/ VT liquéfier VI se liquéfier

liqueur /lɪ'kjʊə^r/ N liqueur *f*
COMP **liqueur brandy** N fine (champagne) *f*
liqueur chocolates NPL chocolats *mpl* à la liqueur
liqueur glass N verre *m* à liqueur

liquid /'lɪkwɪd/ ADJ 1 *(= not solid etc) [substance]* liquide ; *[container]* pour (les) liquides ◆ **~ air/oxygen** air *m*/oxygène *m* liquide ◆ **~ ammonia** ammoniaque *m* (liquide) ◆ **~ crystal** cristal *m* liquide ◆ **~ crystal display** affichage *m* à cristaux liquides ◆ **~ diet** régime *m* (exclusivement) liquide ◆ **to have a ~ lunch** *(hum)* boire de l'alcool en guise de déjeuner ◆ **~ measure** mesure *f* de capacité pour les liquides ◆ **Liquid Paper** ® *(for corrections)* correcteur *m* liquide ◆ **~ paraffin** *(Pharm)* huile *f* de paraffine or de vaseline ◆ **~ petroleum gas** GPL *m*, gaz *m* de pétrole liquéfié 2 *(fig) [eyes, sky]* limpide, clair ; *[sound, voice]* limpide, harmonieux ; *(Phon)* liquide ◆ **~ assets** *(Fin)* liquidités *fpl*, disponibilités *fpl* N *(= fluid)* liquide *m* ; *(Ling)* liquide *f*

liquidate /'lɪkwɪdeɪt/ VT 1 *(Fin, Jur)* liquider ◆ **~d damages** *(Jur)* dommages-intérêts *mpl* préalablement fixés (par les parties) 2 (* = *kill)* liquider *

liquidation /,lɪkwɪ'deɪʃən/ N *(Fin, Jur)* liquidation *f* ; *[of debt]* remboursement *m* ◆ **to go into ~** déposer son bilan

liquidator /'lɪkwɪ,deɪtə^r/ N *(Jur)* ≈ liquidateur *m*

liquidity /lɪ'kwɪdɪtɪ/ N *(Econ)* liquidité *f* ; *(Fin)* disponibilités *fpl* de trésorerie COMP **liquidity cushion** N *(Fin)* volant *m* de trésorerie

liquidize /'lɪkwɪdaɪz/ VT liquéfier ; *(Culin)* passer au mixer or mixeur

liquidizer /'lɪkwɪdaɪzə^r/ N *(Brit Culin)* mixer *m*, mixeur *m*

liquor /'lɪkə^r/ N 1 *(esp US) (= alcoholic drink)* boissons *fpl* alcoolisées ; *(= spirits)* spiritueux *m*, alcool *m* ◆ **to be the worse for ~** *(US)* être soûl or ivre ◆ **he can't hold his ~** il ne supporte pas l'alcool 2 *(Culin)* liquide *m*
COMP **liquor license** N *(US)* licence *f* de débit de boissons
liquor store N *(US)* magasin *m* de vins et spiritueux ; → LICENSING LAWS
► **liquor up** ‡ *(US)* VI se pinter ‡ VT SEP ◆ **to liquor sb up** faire trop boire qn, soûler * qn

liquorice /'lɪkərɪs/ *(Brit)* N *(= plant)* réglisse *f* ; *(= sweet)* réglisse *m*
COMP **liquorice all-sorts** NPL *(gen Brit)* bonbons *mpl* assortis au réglisse
liquorice root N bois *m* de réglisse
liquorice stick N bâton *m* de réglisse

lira /'lɪərə/ N (pl **lire** /'lɪərɪ/) lire *f*

Lisbon /'lɪzbən/ N Lisbonne

lisle /laɪl/ N (also **lisle thread**) fil *m* d'Écosse

lisp /lɪsp/ VI zézayer, zozoter * VT (also **lisp out**) dire en zézayant ◆ **"please don't say that," she ~ed coyly** "s'il vous plaît, ne dites pas cela", dit-elle en minaudant N zézaiement *m* ◆ **... she said with a ~** ... dit-elle en zézayant ◆ **to speak with** or **have a ~** zézayer, avoir un cheveu sur la langue *

lissom(e) /'lɪsəm/ ADJ souple, agile

list[1] /lɪst/ N liste *f* ; *(= catalogue)* catalogue *m* ◆ **your name isn't on the ~** votre nom ne figure pas sur la liste ◆ **you can take me off the ~** vous pouvez me rayer de la liste ◆ **you're (at the) top/bottom of the ~** *(lit)* vous êtes en tête/en fin de liste ◆ **that's at the top of my ~** je le ferai en priorité ; → **active, civil, danger**
VT 1 *(= make list of)* faire or dresser la liste de ; *(= write down)* inscrire ; *(= produce list of: Comput)* lister ; *(= enumerate)* énumérer ◆ **your name isn't ~ed** votre nom n'est pas inscrit, votre nom n'est pas sur la liste ◆ **it isn't ~ed** *(not in catalogue)* cela ne figure pas au catalogue ◆ **"airgun" is ~ed under "air"** "airgun" se trouve sous "air" ◆ **the shares are ~ed at €15** les actions sont cotées 15 € ◆ **~ed on the Stock Exchange** coté en Bourse
2 *(= categorize)* répertorier, classer ◆ **the deaths were ~ed as homicides** les décès ont été répertoriés or classés parmi les homicides ◆ **an airgun is ~ed as a weapon** les fusils à air comprimé sont classés parmi les armes
COMP **listed building** N *(Brit)* monument *m* classé or historique
listed company N société *f* cotée en Bourse
listed securities NPL valeurs *fpl* inscrites or admises à la cote officielle, valeurs *fpl* cotées en Bourse
list price N prix *m* catalogue

list[2] /lɪst/ VI *(= lean)* donner de la bande, gîter ◆ **the ship is ~ing badly** le bateau gîte dangereusement ◆ **to ~ to port** gîter or donner de la bande sur bâbord N inclinaison *f* ◆ **to have a ~** gîter ◆ **to have a ~ of 20°** gîter de 20°, donner 20° de gîte or de bande

listen /'lɪsn/ VI 1 écouter ◆ **~ to me** écoute-moi ; see also **2** ◆ **~!** écoute ! ◆ **you never ~ to a word I say!** tu n'écoutes jamais ce que je dis ! ◆ **to ~ to the radio** écouter la radio ◆ **you are ~ing to the BBC** vous êtes à l'écoute de la BBC ◆ **to ~ for** *[+ voice, remark, sign]* guetter ; *[+ footsteps]* guetter le bruit de ◆ **~ for the telephone while I'm out** réponds au téléphone pendant mon absence ; → **half**
2 *(= heed)* écouter ◆ **~ to your father** écoute ton père ◆ **~ to me!** *(as threat)* écoute-moi bien ! ◆ **~ *, I can't stop to talk now but ...** écoute, je n'ai pas le temps de parler tout de suite mais ... ◆ **he wouldn't ~ to reason** il n'a pas voulu entendre raison ◆ **when I asked him to stop, he would not ~** quand je lui ai demandé d'arrêter, il n'a rien voulu entendre
N ◆ **to have a ~** * écouter *(to sth* qch)
► **listen in** VI 1 *(Rad †)* être à l'écoute, écouter
2 *(= eavesdrop)* écouter ◆ **to ~ in on sth** or **to sth** *(secretly)* écouter qch secrètement ◆ **I should like to ~ in to your discussion** j'aimerais assister à votre discussion
► **listen out for** VT FUS *[+ voice, remark, sign]* guetter ; *[+ footsteps]* guetter le bruit de
► **listen up** VI *(esp US)* écouter

listenable /'lɪsənəbl/ ADJ agréable à écouter

listener /'lɪsnə^r/ N *(gen)* personne *f* qui écoute ; *(to speaker, radio etc)* auditeur *m*, -trice *f* ◆ **the ~s** l'auditoire *m*, le public ◆ **she's a good ~** elle sait écouter

listening /'lɪsnɪŋ/ N écoute *f* ◆ **good ~ is good parenting** il faut savoir écouter ses enfants ◆ **he did all the talking, I did all the ~** il a monopolisé la parole et moi, je me suis contenté d'écouter
COMP **listening device** N dispositif *m* d'écoute
listening post N *(Mil)* poste *m* d'écoute

listeria /lɪ'stɪərɪə/ N listeria *f*

listeriosis /lɪ,stɪərɪ'əʊsɪs/ N listériose *f*

listing /'lɪstɪŋ/ N *(gen, also Comput)* listage *m* ; *(Stock Exchange)* inscription *f* à la cote officielle ◆ **the TV ~s** les programmes *mpl* de télévision
COMP **listings magazine** N *(gen)* guide *m* des sorties ; *(TV)* magazine *m* de télévision

listless /'lɪstlɪs/ ADJ *(= without energy)* sans énergie, mou (molle *f*) ◆ **to feel ~** se sentir sans énergie or ressort ◆ **the heat made him ~** la chaleur lui enlevait son énergie ◆ **a day of ~ trading on the world's stock markets** une journée morose sur les marchés financiers mondiaux

listlessly /'lɪstlɪslɪ/ ADV *[say, behave]* avec apathie

listlessness /'lɪstlɪsnɪs/ N manque *m* d'énergie

lists /lɪsts/ NPL *(Hist)* lice *f* ◆ **to enter the ~** *(lit, fig)* entrer en lice

lit /lɪt/ VB pt, ptp of **light**[1] ADJ éclairé, illuminé ◆ **the street was very badly ~** la rue était très mal éclairée ◆ **~ up** * *(= drunk)* parti *, paf ‡ inv

lit.[1] * /lɪt/ N 1 abbrev of **literature** 2 (abbrev of **literary**) littér. ◆ **lit crit** critique *f* littéraire

lit.[2] (abbrev of **literal(ly)**) lit.

litany /'lɪtənɪ/ N litanie *f* ◆ **the Litany** *(Rel)* les litanies

litchi /,laɪ'tʃiː/ N ⇒ **lychee**

lite /laɪt/ * ADJ *(= low-fat)* allégé

liter /'liːtə^r/ N *(US)* ⇒ **litre**

literacy /'lɪtərəsɪ/ N *[of person]* fait *m* de savoir lire et écrire ; *[of population]* degré *m* d'alphabétisation ◆ **his ~ was not in doubt** personne ne doutait du fait qu'il savait lire et écrire ◆ **universal ~ is one of the principal aims** l'un des buts principaux est de donner à tous la capacité de lire et d'écrire ◆ **there is a high/low degree of ~ in that country** le degré d'alphabétisation est élevé/bas dans ce pays ◆ **many adults have problems with ~** de nombreux adultes ont du mal à lire et à écrire
COMP **literacy campaign** N campagne *f* d'alphabétisation or contre l'illettrisme
literacy project, literacy scheme N projet *m* d'alphabétisation
literacy test N test *m* mesurant le niveau d'alphabétisation

literal /'lɪtərəl/ ADJ 1 *(= basic) [meaning]* littéral ◆ **in the ~ sense (of the word)** au sens propre du terme 2 *(= verbatim) [translation]* littéral, mot pour mot ; *[interpretation]* littéral ◆ **to be very ~ about sth** prendre qch au pied de la lettre ; see also **literal-minded** 3 *(= absolute)* **the ~ truth** l'entière or la pure vérité ◆ **it was a ~ fact** c'était un fait ◆ **the drought has meant ~ starvation for millions** la sécheresse a réduit littéralement à la famine des millions de gens
COMP **literal-minded** ADJ prosaïque, sans imagination
literal-mindedness N manque *m* d'imagination

literally /'lɪtərəlɪ/ ADV *[translate, believe, understand]* littéralement ◆ **to take sb/sth ~** prendre qn/qch au pied de la lettre ◆ **he interpreted the message ~** il a interprété le message au pied de la lettre or dans son sens littéral ◆ **I'm ~ * dumbstruck by the news** je suis littéralement * assommé par cette nouvelle

literary /ˈlɪtərərɪ/ ADJ littéraire ◆ **a ~ man** un lettré ◆ **~ types** * amateurs *mpl* de littérature
COMP **literary agent** N agent *m* littéraire
literary critic N critique *mf* littéraire
literary criticism N critique *f* littéraire
literary editor N rédacteur *m*, -trice *f* littéraire
literary theory N théorie *f* littéraire

literate /ˈlɪtərɪt/ ADJ 1 *(= able to read etc)* qui sait lire et écrire ; *(= educated)* instruit ; *(= cultured)* cultivé ◆ **few of them are ~** peu d'entre eux savent lire et écrire ◆ **highly ~** très instruit *or* cultivé 2 *(fig = competent)* ◆ **to be economically/scientifically** *etc* **~** avoir des connaissances de base en économie/sciences *etc* ; → **computer**

literati /ˌlɪtəˈrɑːtiː/ NPL gens *mpl* de lettres, lettrés *mpl*

literature /ˈlɪtərɪtʃəʳ/ N *(NonC)* 1 *(= literary works)* littérature *f* ◆ **18th-century French ~** la littérature française du 18e siècle ◆ **the ~ of ornithology** la littérature *or* la bibliographie de l'ornithologie 2 *(= documentation)* documentation *f* ◆ **travel/educational ~** documentation *f* sur les voyages/pédagogiques ◆ **sales ~** brochures *fpl* publicitaires

lithe /laɪð/ ADJ *[person, body, movement]* souple, agile

lithium /ˈlɪθɪəm/ N lithium *m*

litho * /ˈlaɪθəʊ/ N (abbrev of **lithograph**) litho * *f*

lithograph /ˈlɪθəʊgrɑːf/ N lithographie *f (estampe)* VT lithographier

lithographer /lɪˈθɒgrəfəʳ/ N lithographe *mf*

lithographic /ˌlɪθəˈgræfɪk/ ADJ lithographique

lithography /lɪˈθɒgrəfɪ/ N *(NonC)* lithographie *f (procédé)*

Lithuania /ˌlɪθjʊˈeɪnɪə/ N Lituanie *f*

Lithuanian /ˌlɪθjʊˈeɪnɪən/ ADJ lituanien N 1 Lituanien(ne) *m(f)* 2 *(= language)* lituanien *m*

litigant /ˈlɪtɪgənt/ N *(Jur)* plaideur *m*, -euse *f*

litigate /ˈlɪtɪgeɪt/ VI plaider VT mettre en litige, contester

litigation /ˌlɪtɪˈgeɪʃən/ N litige *m*, procès *m*

litigator /ˈlɪtɪgeɪtəʳ/ N *(Jur)* avocat-conseil *m*

litigious /lɪˈtɪdʒəs/ ADJ *(Jur)* litigieux ; *[person] (= given to litigation)* procédurier, chicaneur ; *(= argumentative etc)* chicanier

litmus /ˈlɪtməs/ N *(Chem)* tournesol *m* ◆ **~ (paper)** papier *m* de tournesol COMP **litmus test** N *(lit)* réaction *f* au (papier de) tournesol ; *(fig)* test *m* décisif

litre, liter *(US)* /ˈliːtəʳ/ N litre *m* ◆ **~ bottle** (bouteille *f* d'un) litre *m*

litter /ˈlɪtəʳ/ N 1 *(NonC)* *(= rubbish)* détritus *mpl* ; *(dirtier)* ordures *fpl* ; *(= papers)* vieux papiers *mpl* ; *(left after picnic etc)* papiers *mpl* gras ◆ **"litter"** *(on basket etc)* "papiers (SVP)" ◆ **"(leave) no litter"** *(on notice)* "prière de ne pas laisser de détritus"
2 *(= untidy mass)* fouillis *m* ◆ **a ~ of papers** un fouillis *or* un fatras de papiers
3 *(= offspring)* portée *f*
4 *(= bedding)* litière *f*
5 *(= stretcher)* civière *f* ; *(= couch)* litière *f*
6 ◆ **cat ~** litière *f* (pour chats)
VT 1 *[person] [+ room]* mettre du désordre dans, mettre en désordre ; *[+ countryside]* laisser des détritus dans ◆ **he ~ed the floor with all his football gear** il a éparpillé ses affaires de football par terre
2 *(gen pass) [rubbish, papers]* joncher *(with* de) ◆ **the floor was ~ed with paper** des papiers jonchaient le sol ◆ **glass from broken bottles ~ed the pavements, the pavements were ~ed with glass from broken bottles** les trottoirs étaient jonchés de tessons de bouteilles ◆ **~ed with mistakes** bourré de fautes ◆ **the desk was ~ed with books** le bureau était couvert *or* encombré de livres ◆ **the streets were ~ed with corpses** les rues étaient jonchées de cadavres ◆ **the road is ~ed with obstacles** cette route est parsemée d'obstacles ◆ **a field ~ed with mines** un champ truffé de mines
VI *(= give birth)* mettre bas
COMP **litter basket, litter bin** N *(Brit)* poubelle *f*
litter box N *(US)* ⇒ **litter tray**
litter tray N *(esp Brit)* caisse *f* à litière

litterbug * /ˈlɪtəbʌg/, **litter-lout** * /ˈlɪtəlaʊt/ N *(pej)* personne qui jette des détritus par terre ◆ **~s should be fined** on devrait mettre à l'amende ces cochons * qui jettent des détritus n'importe où ◆ **all these ~s who foul up camp sites** tous ces cochons * qui jettent leurs détritus dans les campings

little[1] /ˈlɪtl/ ADJ petit ◆ **a ~ present** un petit cadeau ◆ **a ~ cat** un petit chat ◆ **when I was ~** quand j'étais petit ◆ **she had a ~ girl yesterday** elle a eu une petite fille hier ◆ **here's a ~ something for yourself** * voilà un petit quelque chose * pour vous ◆ **a ~ old woman** une petite vieille ◆ **poor ~ thing!** pauvre petit(e) ! ◆ **she's a dear ~ thing** *(patronizing)* c'est une jolie petite fille ◆ **what an annoying ~ man!** ce qu'il est agaçant, ce type ! ◆ **the ~ ones** *(= children)* les petits *mpl* ◆ **the ~ woman** *(hum, gen patronizing = wife)* ma *(or* ta *etc)* petite femme * ◆ **it's always the ~ man who suffers** *(= small trader)* ce sont toujours les petits (commerçants) qui paient ◆ **he's quite a** *or* **the ~ gentleman!** qu'il est bien élevé ce petit ! ◆ **we went for a ~ holiday** on s'est pris des petites vacances ◆ **I'll pay you a ~ visit** je passerai rapidement te voir ◆ **who knows what's going on in his ~ mind** *(pej)* qui sait ce qui se passe dans sa petite tête ◆ **all his dirty ~ jokes** toutes ses plaisanteries cochonnes *
COMP **little auk** N mergule *m* (nain)
little end N *(in car)* pied *m* de bielle
Little Englander N *(Brit)*
1 *(Hist) Anglais opposé à l'expansion de l'empire britannique* 2 *(= chauvinistic)* Anglais(e) *m(f)* chauvin(e) et insulaire ; *(= anti-European)* Anglais(e) *m(f)* anti-européen(ne)
little finger N petit doigt *m*, auriculaire *m*
little green men * NPL *(hum = aliens)* petits hommes *mpl* verts, extraterrestres *mpl*
little hand N *[of clock]* petite aiguille *f*
Little League N *(US Sport) championnat de base-ball pour les moins de 12 ans*
little owl N (chouette *f*) chevêche *f*
the little people NPL *(Ir = fairies)* les fées *fpl*, les lutins *mpl*
little toe N petit orteil *m*

little[2] /ˈlɪtl/

compar **less**, superl **least**

1 ADJECTIVE
2 PRONOUN
3 ADVERB
4 SET STRUCTURES

1 - ADJECTIVE

= not much peu de ◆ **there is ~ hope of finding survivors** il y a peu d'espoir de retrouver des survivants ◆ **I have very ~ money** j'ai très peu d'argent ◆ **he gave me too ~ money** il m'a donné trop peu d'argent ◆ **I have ~ money left** il me reste peu d'argent, il ne me reste pas beaucoup d'argent ◆ **so ~ time** si peu de temps ◆ **I have ~ time for reading** je n'ai pas beaucoup *or* je n'ai guère le temps de lire ◆ **with no ~ trouble/difficulty/satisfaction** avec beaucoup de mal/difficulté/satisfaction

◆ **a little ...** *(= some)* un peu de ... ◆ **I have a ~ money left** il me reste un peu d'argent ◆ **would you like a ~ milk in your tea?** voulez-vous une goutte de lait dans votre thé ? ◆ **a ~ bit (of)** un peu (de) ◆ **we're having a ~ (bit of) trouble** nous avons un petit problème *or* quelques difficultés

2 - PRONOUN

1 = not much peu, pas grand-chose ◆ **he reads ~** il lit peu ◆ **so ~ of what he says is true** il y a si peu de vrai dans ce qu'il dit ◆ **he lost weight because he ate so ~** il a perdu du poids parce qu'il mangeait très peu ◆ **so ~ of the population is literate** une proportion si infime de la population est alphabétisée, la population est si peu alphabétisée ◆ **I know too ~ about him to have an opinion** je le connais trop mal pour me former une opinion ◆ **there was ~ anyone could do** il n'y avait pas grand-chose à faire ◆ **he did ~ to help** il n'a pas fait grand-chose pour aider ◆ **he did very ~** il n'a vraiment pas fait grand-chose ◆ **he had ~ to say** il n'avait pas grand-chose à dire ◆ **I had ~ to do with it** je n'ai pas eu grand-chose à voir là-dedans ◆ **that has very ~ to do with it!** ça n'a pas grand-chose à voir ! ◆ **however ~ you give, we'll be grateful** même si vous ne donnez pas grand-chose, nous vous serons reconnaissants ◆ **I see ~ of her nowadays** je ne la vois plus beaucoup ◆ **he had ~ or nothing to say about it** il n'avait pratiquement rien à dire là-dessus

2 = small amount ◆ **the ~ I have seen is excellent** le peu que j'en ai vu est excellent ◆ **I did what ~ I could** j'ai fait ce que j'ai pu ◆ **every ~ helps** *(= gift)* tous les dons sont les bienvenus ◆ **it's all I can do – every ~ helps!** c'est tout ce que je peux faire – c'est toujours ça !

◆ **a little** *(= a certain amount)* un peu ◆ **give me a ~** donne-m'en un peu ◆ **I'd like a ~ of everything** je voudrais un peu de tout ◆ **I know a ~ about stamp collecting** je m'y connais un peu en philatélie ◆ **they'll have to wait a ~** *(= a certain time)* ils vont devoir attendre un moment ◆ **after/for a ~ (time** *or* **while)** au bout d'un/pendant un moment

3 - ADVERB

1 = hardly, scarcely, not much ◆ **they spoke very ~ on the way home** ils n'ont pas dit grand-chose sur le chemin du retour ◆ **it's ~ better now he's rewritten it** ça n'est pas beaucoup *or* ça n'est guère mieux maintenant qu'il l'a récrit ◆ **it's ~ short of folly** ça frise la folie ◆ **~ more than a month ago** il y a à peine plus d'un mois ◆ **a ~-known work by Corelli** un morceau peu connu de Corelli ◆ **his work is ~ performed these days** on ne joue plus beaucoup ses œuvres aujourd'hui ◆ **however ~ you like it you'll have to go** même si ça ne te plaît pas, il va falloir que tu y ailles ◆ **~ as I like him, I must admit that...** bien que je ne l'aime pas beaucoup, je dois admettre que...

◆ **a little ...** *(= slightly, somewhat)* un peu ... ◆ **she is a ~ tired** elle est un peu fatiguée ◆ **a ~ too big** un peu trop grand ◆ **a ~ more** un peu plus, encore un peu ◆ **a ~ less** un peu moins ◆ **a ~ more slowly** un peu plus lentement ◆ **a ~ later** un peu plus tard ◆ **a ~ more/less cream** un peu plus de/moins de crème ◆ **he was not a ~ surprised** *(frm or hum)* il a été pour le moins surpris ◆ **he spoke a ~ harshly** il a eu des propos un peu trop durs ◆ **she reacted a ~ unreasonably** elle ne s'est pas montrée très raisonnable

2 = not at all **he ~ imagined that ...** il était loin de s'imaginer que ... ◆ **~ did he think that ...** il était loin de se douter que ...

3 = rarely rarement, peu souvent ◆ **I see him/it happens very ~** je le vois/cela arrive très rarement *or* très peu souvent ◆ **I watch**

television very ~ nowadays je ne regarde plus beaucoup *or* plus très souvent la télévision

4 - SET STRUCTURES

♦ **as little as** ♦ **as ~ as possible** le moins possible ♦ **you could get one for as ~ as $20** on peut en trouver un pour (seulement) 20 dollars ♦ **you can eat well for as ~ as 8 euros** on peut bien manger pour 8 euros ♦ **I like him as ~ as you do** je ne l'aime pas plus que toi ♦ **as ~ as I like him, I must admit that …** bien que je ne l'aime pas beaucoup, je dois admettre que …

♦ **little by little** petit à petit, peu à peu

♦ **to make little of sth** *(= accomplish easily)* faire qch sans aucun mal ; *(= play down)* minimiser qch ; *(= underestimate)* sous-estimer qch ♦ **the sailors made ~ of loading the huge boxes** les marins chargeaient les énormes caisses sans aucun mal ♦ **it's hard work, but the scouts make ~ of it** c'est dur mais les scouts ne s'arrêtent pas à ça ♦ **government spokesmen have made ~ of the latest setback** les porte-parole du gouvernement ont minimisé les implications de ce dernier revers ♦ **we've made ~ of the link between women's health and work** nous avons sous-estimé le lien entre la santé et le travail des femmes ♦ **he made ~ of his opportunities** *(= fail to exploit)* il n'a pas tiré parti des possibilités qu'il avait

♦ **to say little for sb/sth** *(= reflect badly on)* ♦ **it says (very) ~ for him** cela n'est pas vraiment à son honneur ♦ **it says ~ for his honesty** cela en dit long sur son honnêteté *(iro)*

littleness /ˈlɪtlnɪs/ **N** petitesse *f*

littoral /ˈlɪtərəl/ **ADJ, N** littoral *m*

liturgical /lɪˈtɜːdʒɪkəl/ **ADJ** liturgique

liturgy /ˈlɪtədʒɪ/ **N** liturgie *f*

livable /ˈlɪvəbl/ **ADJ** *[climate, life]* supportable ; *[pain]* supportable, tolérable ; *[house]* habitable ♦ **this house is not ~ (in)*** cette maison est inhabitable ♦ **he is/is not ~ (with)*** il est facile à vivre/insupportable *or* invivable* ♦ **her life is not ~** elle mène une vie impossible *or* insupportable

live[1] /lɪv/ **VI** 1 *(= be alive)* vivre ; *(= survive)* survivre ; *(after illness, accident)* s'en sortir ♦ **she has only six months to ~** il ne lui reste plus que six mois à vivre ♦ **she'll never ~ to see it** elle ne vivra pas assez longtemps pour le voir ♦ **the doctor said she would ~** le docteur a dit qu'elle s'en sortirait ♦ **nothing could ~ in such a hostile environment** rien ne pourrait survivre dans un environnement si hostile ♦ **he didn't ~ long after his wife died** il n'a pas survécu longtemps à sa femme ♦ **he won't ~ long** *(gen)* il n'en a plus pour longtemps ; *[young person]* il ne fera pas de vieux os ♦ **as long as I ~ I shall never leave you** je ne te quitterai pas tant que je vivrai ♦ **I shall remember it as long as I ~** je m'en souviendrai jusqu'à mon dernier jour ♦ **he was still living when his daughter got married** il était encore en vie quand sa fille s'est mariée ♦ **are your parents still living?** vous avez encore vos parents ? ♦ **while his uncle ~d** du vivant de son oncle ♦ **to ~ to be 90** vivre jusqu'à (l'âge de) 90 ans ♦ **you'll ~ to be a hundred** vous serez centenaire ♦ **you'll ~!*** *(hum, iro)* tu n'en mourras pas !

♦ **to live for sb** *or* **sth** ne vivre que pour qn *or* qch ♦ **she ~s for her children/her work** elle ne vit que pour ses enfants/son travail ♦ **he is living for the day when he will see his son again** il ne vit que pour le jour où il reverra son fils ♦ **he just ~d for football** il ne vivait que pour le football, il n'y avait que le football dans sa vie ♦ **I've got nothing left to ~ for** je n'ai plus de raison de vivre

♦ **to live with sth** *[+ illness, grief]* vivre avec qch ♦ **people living with HIV and AIDS** ceux qui vivent avec la séropositivité et le sida ♦ **he will have to ~ with that awful memory all his life** il lui faudra vivre avec cet horrible souvenir jusqu'à la fin de ses jours ♦ **it's unjust and we can't ~ with that** c'est injuste et nous ne pouvons pas le tolérer *or* l'accepter ♦ **you must learn to ~ with it** il faut que tu t'y fasses *or* que tu t'en accommodes *subj* ♦ **OK, I can ~ with that** *(= it's not a problem)* d'accord, je ferai avec ♦ **if you can ~ with that** si ça ne te dérange pas

2 *(fig = live on)* ♦ **her voice will ~ with me forever** je garderai toujours le souvenir de sa voix ♦ **this night will ~ in history** cette nuit fera date (dans l'histoire)

3 *(= have lifestyle)* vivre ♦ **to ~ honestly** vivre honnêtement, mener une vie honnête ♦ **to ~ in luxury** vivre dans le luxe ♦ **to ~ like a king** *or* **a lord** mener grand train ♦ **to ~ by an ideal/a principle** *etc* vivre en accord avec un idéal/un principe *etc* ♦ **to ~ in fear/terror (of)** vivre dans la peur/la terreur (de) ♦ **you** *or* **we ~ and learn** on apprend à tout âge ♦ **~ and let ~** *(Prov)* il faut se montrer tolérant ♦ **let's ~ a little!*** il faut profiter de la vie ! ♦ **if you haven't been to London you haven't ~d!*** si tu n'as pas vu Londres, tu n'as rien vu ! ♦ **you haven't ~d until you've used their new software*** leur nouveau logiciel, c'est vraiment quelque chose ; → **hand, hope, style, well**[2]

4 *(= earn one's living)* gagner sa vie ♦ **to ~ by journalism** gagner sa vie en tant que *or* comme journaliste ♦ **to ~ by buying and selling used cars** gagner sa vie en achetant et vendant des voitures d'occasion

5 *(= reside)* habiter, vivre ♦ **where do you ~?** où habitez-vous ? ♦ **to ~ in London** habiter (à) Londres, vivre à Londres ♦ **to ~ in a flat** habiter un appartement ♦ **she ~s in Station Road** elle habite (dans) Station Road ♦ **this is a nice place to ~** il fait bon vivre ici ♦ **he ~s with his mother** il vit *or* habite avec sa mère ; *(in her house)* il vit chez sa mère ♦ **he's living with Ann** *(as man and wife)* il vit avec Ann ♦ **he's not an easy person to ~ with** il n'est pas facile à vivre ♦ **a house fit for a queen to ~ in** une maison princière ; see also **fit**[1], **unfit** ♦ **to ~ under occupation** être occupé ; → **sin**

VT vivre, mener ♦ **to ~ a life of luxury/crime** vivre dans le luxe/le crime ♦ **to ~ a healthy life** mener une vie saine ♦ **to ~ a life of ease** avoir une vie facile ♦ **to ~ life to the full** vivre pleinement sa vie, profiter au maximum de la vie ♦ **he has ~d and breathed football since he was seven** il ne vit que pour le football depuis qu'il a sept ans ♦ **to ~ a lie** vivre dans le mensonge ♦ **to ~ the part** *(Theat, fig)* entrer dans la peau du personnage ; → **life**

COMP lived-in ADJ *(lit = inhabited) [house, flat etc]* habité ; *(fig = well-worn) [+ face]* marqué par le temps

live-in ADJ *(gen) [housekeeper etc]* à demeure ♦ **~-in lover** petit(e) ami(e) *m(f)* avec qui l'on vit ♦ **~-in partner** compagnon *m*, compagne *f*

► **live down VT SEP** *[+ disgrace, scandal]* faire oublier (avec le temps) ♦ **you'll never ~ it down!** jamais tu ne feras oublier ça !

► **live in VI** *[servant]* être logé et nourri ; *[student, doctor]* être interne

ADJ ♦ **lived-in** → **live**[1]

ADJ ♦ **live-in** → **live**[1]

► **live off VT FUS** 1 *[+ fruit, rice]* vivre de, se nourrir de ♦ **to ~ off the land** vivre des ressources naturelles

2 *(= depend financially on) [+ person]* vivre aux dépens *or* aux crochets de

► **live on VI** *[person]* continuer à vivre ; *[tradition, memory]* rester, survivre

VT FUS 1 *(= feed on) [+ fruit, rice]* vivre de, se nourrir de ♦ **you can't ~ on air*** on ne vit pas de l'air du temps ♦ **she absolutely ~s on chocolate*** elle se nourrit exclusivement de chocolat ♦ **to ~ on hope** vivre d'espérance

2 *(= subsist on)* ♦ **to live on $10,000 a year** vivre avec 10 000 dollars par an ♦ **we have just enough to ~ on** nous avons juste de quoi vivre ♦ **what does he ~ on?** de quoi vit-il ?, qu'est-ce qu'il a pour vivre ? ♦ **to ~ on one's salary** vivre de son salaire ♦ **to ~ on one's capital** vivre de *or* manger son capital ♦ **to ~ on borrowed time** être en sursis *(fig)*

3 *(= depend financially on) [+ person]* vivre aux dépens *or* aux crochets de

► **live out VI** *[servant]* ne pas être logé ; *[student, doctor]* être externe

VT SEP passer ♦ **she won't ~ the year out** elle ne passera pas l'année ♦ **he ~d out the war in the country** il a passé la durée de la guerre à la campagne

VT FUS *(frm) [+ one's destiny]* accomplir, réaliser ; *[+ one's beliefs]* mettre en pratique, vivre en accord avec

► **live through VT FUS** 1 *(= experience)* vivre, voir ♦ **she has ~d through two world wars** elle a vu deux guerres mondiales ♦ **the difficult years he has ~d through** les années difficiles qu'il a vécues

2 *(= survive)* supporter ♦ **he can't ~ through the winter** il ne passera pas l'hiver ♦ **I couldn't ~ through another day like that** je ne pourrais pas supporter *or* passer une deuxième journée comme ça

► **live together VI** *(as man and wife)* vivre ensemble ; *(as flatmates)* partager un appartement

► **live up VT SEP** ♦ **to live it up** * *(= live in luxury)* mener la grande vie ; *(= have fun)* faire la fête

► **live up to VT FUS** 1 *(= be true to) [+ one's principles]* vivre en accord avec, vivre selon ; *[+ one's promises]* être fidèle à, respecter

2 *(= be equal to)* être *or* se montrer à la hauteur de ; *(= be worthy of)* répondre à, se montrer digne de ♦ **to ~ up to sb's expectations** être *or* se montrer à la hauteur des espérances de qn ♦ **the holiday didn't ~ up to expectations** les vacances n'ont pas été ce qu'on avait espéré ♦ **sales have not ~d up to expectations this year** les ventes ont été décevantes cette année ♦ **his brother's success will give him something to ~ up to** la réussite de son frère lui servira de modèle

live[2] /laɪv/ **ADJ** 1 *[person, animal]* vivant, en vie ; *(fig)* dynamique ♦ **a ~ birth** une naissance viable ♦ **~ bait** *(Fishing)* vif *m (appât)* ♦ **a real ~ spaceman** un astronaute en chair et en os

2 *(Rad, TV)* (transmis *or* diffusé) en direct ♦ **the programme was ~** cette émission était (transmise *or* diffusée) en direct ♦ **performed before a ~ audience** joué en public ♦ **they're a great ~ act** ils font un excellent numéro sur scène ♦ **a CD featuring ~ recordings from her New York concert** un CD avec des morceaux du concert qu'elle a donné à New York ♦ **"recorded live"** "enregistré en public"

3 *[coal]* ardent ; *[ammunition, shell, cartridge]* de combat ; *(= unexploded)* non explosé

4 *(Elec)* **that's ~!** c'est branché ! ♦ **the switch/hair-dryer was ~** l'interrupteur/le séchoir à cheveux était mal isolé (et dangereux) ; see also **comp**

ADV *(Rad, TV)* en direct ♦ **to play ~** *(= on stage)* jouer sur scène ♦ **it was broadcast ~** c'était (transmis *or* diffusé) en direct ♦ **the match is brought to you ~ from …** le match vous est transmis en direct depuis … ♦ **here, ~ from New York, is our reporter Guy Pugh** voici, en direct de New York, notre envoyé spécial Guy Pugh ♦ **to go ~** *(Brit)* prendre l'antenne

COMP **live rail** N (Elec) rail *m* conducteur
live wire N (Elec) fil *m* sous tension ◆ **he's a (real) ~ wire** * il a un dynamisme fou
live yoghurt N yaourt *m* fermenté

liveable /ˈlɪvəbl/ ADJ ⇒ **livable**

livelihood /ˈlaɪvlɪhʊd/ N (NonC) moyens *mpl* d'existence, gagne-pain *m inv* ◆ **to earn a** *or* **one's ~** gagner sa vie ◆ **his ~ depends on ...** son gagne-pain dépend de ... ◆ **their principal ~ is tourism/rice** leur principale source de revenu est le tourisme/la culture du riz

liveliness /ˈlaɪvlɪnɪs/ N 1 (= *lively nature*) *[of person, animal, mind, language]* vivacité *f*, vitalité *f* ; *[of eyes]* éclat *m* ; *[of voice]* enjouement *m* 2 (= *lively mood*) *[of party, bar, street, debate]* animation *f* ; *[of person]* entrain *m* ; *[of song, tune]* gaieté *f*

livelong /ˈlɪvlɒŋ/ ADJ (liter) ◆ **all the ~ day** tout au long du jour *(liter)*, toute la journée

lively /ˈlaɪvlɪ/ ADJ 1 *(by nature) [person, animal, personality]* vif, plein de vitalité ; *[mind, imagination]* vif ◆ **she took a ~ interest in everything** elle manifestait un vif intérêt pour tout 2 *(in mood) [party, bar, street, atmosphere, debate]* animé ; *[person]* plein d'entrain ; *[description, language, style]* vivant ; *[song, tune]* entraînant, gai ◆ **the meeting promises to be a ~ affair** la réunion va sûrement être mouvementée ◆ **things were getting quite ~** *(hum)* ça commençait à chauffer* ◆ **at a ~ pace** *or* **speed** à vive allure 3 * ◆ **to look ~** se remuer* ◆ **come on, look ~!** allez, remue-toi !*

liven /ˈlaɪvn/ VT ◆ **to ~ up** *[+ person]* égayer ; *[+ evening, discussion, party etc]* animer ◆ **a bit of paint should ~ the room up** un peu de peinture égayerait la pièce VI ◆ **to ~ up** s'animer ◆ **things are beginning to ~ up** ça commence à s'animer

liver /ˈlɪvəʳ/ N foie *m* ; → **lily**
COMP **liver complaint** N problème *m* de foie
liver fluke N douve *f* du foie
liver paste N ≈ pâté *m* de foie
liver pâté N pâté *m* de foie
liver salts NPL ≈ Alka-Seltzer ® *m*
liver sausage N saucisse *f* au pâté de foie
liver spot N *(on skin)* tache *f* brune *or* de vieillesse

liveried /ˈlɪvərɪd/ ADJ en livrée

liverish /ˈlɪvərɪʃ/ ADJ 1 (= *bilious*) qui a mal au foie 2 (= *irritable*) de mauvais poil*, grincheux

Liverpudlian /ˌlɪvəˈpʌdlɪən/ N ◆ **he's a ~** il est de Liverpool ADJ de Liverpool

liverwort /ˈlɪvəwɜːt/ N hépatique *f*, herbe *f* de la Trinité

liverwurst /ˈlɪvəwɜːst/ N *(esp US)* ⇒ **liver sausage** ; → **liver**

livery /ˈlɪvərɪ/ N 1 *[of servant]* livrée *f* 2 *[of company, product, train]* couleurs *fpl* 3 ◆ **to keep a horse at ~** avoir un cheval en pension *or* en garde
COMP **livery company** N *(Brit)* corporation *f* londonienne
livery man N *(pl* **livery men***)* *(in London)* membre *m* d'une corporation ; (†† = *retainer*) serviteur *m*
livery stable N *(boarding)* pension *f* pour chevaux ; *(hiring out)* écurie *f* de louage

lives /laɪvz/ NPL of **life**

livestock /ˈlaɪvstɒk/ N *(NonC)* animaux *mpl* d'élevage

livid /ˈlɪvɪd/ ADJ 1 (* = *furious*) *[person, expression, glare]* furieux *(at or about sth* à propos de qch) ◆ **to be ~ at** *or* **about having to do sth** être furieux de devoir faire qch ◆ **to be ~ that ...** être furieux que ... 2 (= *purple*) *[bruise, scar]* violet ; *[shade, hue]* livide *(liter)* ; *[sky]* plombé, de plomb ◆ **~ red** rouge plombé 3 *(liter = pale, greyish) [face]* livide, blême ◆ **to be ~ with rage (at sth)** être livide *or* blême de colère (contre qch)

living /ˈlɪvɪŋ/ ADJ *[person]* vivant, en vie ; *[language, example, faith]* vivant ; *[water]* vif ◆ **~ or dead** mort ou vif ◆ **the (world's) greatest ~ pianist** le plus grand pianiste vivant ◆ **a ~ death** un enfer, un calvaire ◆ **"the Living Desert"** "le désert vivant" ◆ **the ~ rock** le roc ◆ **carved out of the ~ rock** taillé à même le *or* dans le roc ◆ **~ fossil** fossile *m* vivant ◆ **a ~ skeleton** *(fig)* un cadavre ambulant ◆ **in** *or* **within ~ memory** de mémoire d'homme ; → **daylight, image, proof, soul**

N 1 (= *livelihood*) vie *f* ◆ **to earn** *or* **make a ~ by painting portraits/as an artist** gagner sa vie en peignant des portraits/en tant qu'artiste ◆ **to work for one's ~** travailler pour gagner sa vie ◆ **what does he do for a ~?** que fait-il dans la vie ? ◆ **he thinks the world owes him a ~** il croit que tout lui est dû ; → **cost**
2 *(NonC = way of life)* vie *f* ◆ **gracious ~** vie *f* élégante *or* raffinée ◆ **healthy ~** vie *f* saine ◆ **~ was not easy in those days** la vie n'était pas facile en ce temps-là ; → **loose, standard**
3 *(Brit Rel)* cure *f*, bénéfice *m*

NPL **the living** les vivants *mpl* ; → **land**

COMP **living conditions** NPL conditions *fpl* de vie
the living dead NPL *(in horror films etc)* les morts *mpl* vivants ; (= *dying people*) les morts *mpl* en sursis
living expenses NPL frais *mpl* de subsistance
living quarters NPL quartiers *mpl*, logement(s) *m(pl)*
living room N salon *m*, salle *f* de séjour
living space N espace *m* vital
living standards NPL niveau *m* de vie
living wage N ◆ **they were asking for a ~ wage** ils demandaient un salaire décent ◆ **£50 a week isn't a ~ wage** on ne peut pas vivre avec 50 livres par semaine
living will N testament *m* de vie

Livorno /lɪˈvɔːnəʊ/ N Livourne

Livy /ˈlɪvɪ/ N Tite-Live *m*

Lizard /ˈlɪzəd/ N *(Brit Geog)* ◆ **the ~** le cap Lizard

lizard /ˈlɪzəd/ N lézard *m* ; (also **lizardskin**) (peau *f* de) lézard *m* COMP *[bag etc]* en lézard

llama /ˈlɑːmə/ N lama *m* (= *animal*)

LLB /ˌelelˈbiː/ N (abbrev of **Legum Baccalaureus**) (= *Bachelor of Laws*) ≈ licence *f* de droit

LLD /ˌelelˈdiː/ N (abbrev of **Legum Doctor**) (= *Doctor of Laws*) ≈ doctorat *m* de droit

LM /elˈem/ N (abbrev of **lunar module**) → **lunar**

LMS /ˌelemˈes/ N (abbrev of **local management of schools**) → **local**

LMT /ˌelemˈtiː/ (US) (abbrev of **local mean time**) heure *f* locale

LNG /ˌelenˈdʒiː/ N (abbrev of **liquefied natural gas**) GNL *m*

lo /ləʊ/ EXCL *(liter or hum)* regardez ! ◆ **... when ~ and behold, in he walked!** ... et c'est alors qu'il est entré ! ◆ **~ and behold the result!** et voilà le résultat !

loach /ləʊtʃ/ N loche *f* (de rivière)

load /ləʊd/ N 1 (= *cargo, weight*) *[of person, animal, washing machine]* charge *f* ; *[of lorry]* chargement *m*, charge *f* ; *[of ship]* cargaison *f* ; (= *weight*) (gros) poids *m* ; (= *pressure*) poids *m*, pression *f* ◆ **he was carrying a heavy ~** il était lourdement chargé ◆ **the ~ slipped off the lorry** le chargement *or* la charge a glissé du camion ◆ **the lorry had a full ~** le camion avait un chargement complet ◆ **the ship had a full ~** le navire avait une cargaison complète ◆ **under (full) ~** chargé (à plein) ◆ **I had three ~s of coal (delivered) last autumn** on m'a livré trois fois du charbon l'automne dernier ◆ **I put another ~ in the washing machine** j'ai mis une autre charge de linge dans la machine à laver ◆ **he was buckling under the ~ of his rucksack** il pliait sous le poids de son sac à dos
2 *(fig)* (= *burden*) fardeau *m*, charge *f* ; (= *mental strain*) poids *m* ◆ **supporting his brother's family was a heavy ~ for him** c'était pour lui une lourde charge (que) de faire vivre la famille de son frère ◆ **he finds his new responsibilities a heavy ~** il trouve ses nouvelles responsabilités pesantes *or* lourdes ◆ **to take a ~ off sb's mind** débarrasser qn de ce qui lui pèse *(fig)* ◆ **that's a ~ off my mind!** c'est un poids en moins !, quel soulagement ! ; → **busload, payload, shed², work**
3 *(Constr, Elec, Tech, also of firearm)* charge *f*
4 * ◆ **a ~ of** un tas de, des masses de* ◆ **~s of** des tas de*, des masses de* ◆ **that's a ~ of rubbish!** tout ça c'est de la blague !* ◆ **we've got ~s of time** on a tout notre temps, on a largement le temps ◆ **he's got ~s of money** il est plein de fric* ◆ **we've got ~s (of them) at home** nous en avons des tas* *or* des tonnes* à la maison ◆ **there were ~s of people there** il y avait des tas de gens* ◆ **get a ~ of this!**⁑ (= *look*) vise⁑ un peu ça !, regarde voir !* ; (= *listen*) écoute un peu ça !, écoute voir !*

VT 1 *[+ lorry, ship, washing machine etc]* charger *(with* de) ; *[+ person]* charger ; (= *overwhelm*) accabler ◆ **the branch was ~ed (down) with pears** la branche était chargée de poires, la branche ployait sous les poires ◆ **she was ~ed (down) with shopping** elle pliait sous le poids de ses achats ◆ **his pockets were ~ed with sweets and toys** ses poches étaient bourrées de bonbons et de jouets ◆ **they arrived ~ed (down) with presents for us** ils sont arrivés chargés de cadeaux pour nous ◆ **to ~ sb (down) with gifts** couvrir qn de cadeaux ◆ **to ~ sb with honours** combler *or* couvrir qn d'honneurs ◆ **we are ~ed (down) with debts** nous sommes couverts *or* criblés de dettes ◆ **~ed (down) with cares** accablé de soucis ◆ **a heart ~ed (down) with sorrow** un cœur lourd *or* accablé de chagrin ◆ **the whole business is ~ed with problems** toute cette affaire présente d'énormes difficultés
2 (= *take on cargo of*) **to ~ coal/grain** *etc [ship etc]* charger du charbon/du grain *etc* ◆ **to be ~ed for bear** * (US: = *eager*) être gonflé à bloc*
3 (= *refill*) *[+ gun, camera, computer, file, disk]* charger *(with* de, avec)
4 (= *weight*) *[+ cane etc]* plomber ; *[+ dice]* piper ◆ **to ~ the dice against sb** défavoriser qn ◆ **his lack of experience ~s the dice against him** son manque d'expérience joue contre lui ; see also **loaded**
5 *[+ insurance premium]* majorer

VI *[lorry, ship, camera, gun] (also Comput)* se charger

COMP **load-bearing** ADJ *[beam, structure]* porteur
load factor N *(Elec)* facteur *m* d'utilisation ; *[of plane]* coefficient *m* de remplissage
load line N *[of ship]* ligne *f* de charge
load-shedding N *(Elec)* délestage *m*

► **load down** VT SEP charger *(with* de) → **load vt 1**

► **load up** VI *[ship, lorry]* se charger ; *[person]* charger, ramasser son chargement ◆ **to ~ up with sth** charger qch ◆ **to ~ up with** *or* **on**⁑ *(US fig) [+ food, drink]* se bourrer de*
VT SEP *[+ truck, animal, person]* charger *(with* de, avec)

...load /ləʊd/ N *(in compounds)* → **carload, planeload**

loaded /ˈləʊdɪd/ ADJ 1 (= *full*) *[lorry, shelf, gun, camera]* chargé *(with sth* de qch) ◆ **she was ~ (down) with parcels** elle avait les bras chargés de colis ◆ **to be ~ for bear** (US) être prêt à intervenir ◆ **~ software** *(Comput)* logiciel *m* chargé ; see also **load** 2 (= *rich*) ◆ **to be ~**⁑ **(with**

money) être friqué*, être plein aux as* [3] (* = drunk) bourré* ; (through drugs) défoncé* [4] (= tendentious) [word, term, statement] lourd de sens ◆ **that's a ~ question!** c'est une question tendancieuse ! [5] (= weighted) [cane etc] plombé ; [dice] pipé ◆ **the dice were ~** (lit, fig) les dés étaient pipés ◆ **the dice were ~ against him** il avait peu de chances de réussir ◆ **the dice were ~ in his favour** tout jouait en sa faveur ◆ **the situation is ~ in our favour** les faits jouent en notre faveur [6] (US Baseball) [bases] occupé

loader /ˈləʊdəʳ/ N (= person, instrument) chargeur m ; (Constr) chargeuse f ; → **low**[1]

loading /ˈləʊdɪŋ/ N chargement m ◆ **"no loading or unloading"** (street sign) "interdiction de charger et de décharger" COMP **loading bay** N aire f de chargement

loadstar /ˈləʊdstɑːʳ/ N ⇒ **lodestar**

loadstone /ˈləʊdstəʊn/ N ⇒ **lodestone**

loaf[1] /ləʊf/ N (pl **loaves**) [1] (also **loaf of bread**) pain m ; (= round loaf) pain m rond, miche f de pain ◆ **half a ~ is better than no bread** (Prov) faute de grives on mange des merles (Prov) ◆ **use your ~!*** (Brit) réfléchis un peu !, fais marcher tes méninges !* ; → **cottage, sandwich, slice** [2] ◆ **sugar ~** pain m de sucre ; → **meat**

COMP **loaf pan** N (US) ⇒ **loaf tin**
loaf sugar N sucre m en pain
loaf tin N moule m à pain

loaf[2] /ləʊf/ VI (also **loaf about, loaf around**) traîner, fainéanter

loafer /ˈləʊfəʳ/ N [1] (= person) flemmard(e)* m(f), tire-au-flanc* m inv [2] (= shoe) mocassin m

loam /ləʊm/ N (NonC) [1] (= soil) terreau m [2] (for moulds) terre f de moulage

loamy /ˈləʊmɪ/ ADJ [soil] riche en terreau

loan /ləʊn/ N [1] (= money) (lent) prêt m ; (borrowed) emprunt m ◆ **to take out a ~** contracter un emprunt ◆ **can I ask you for a ~?** pouvez-vous m'accorder un prêt ? ◆ **~s and deposits** (Banking) emplois mpl et ressources fpl ; → **raise**

[2] prêt m ◆ **I asked Barbara for the ~ of her car** j'ai demandé à Barbara de me prêter sa voiture ◆ **may I have the ~ of your lawnmower?** pouvez-vous me prêter votre tondeuse à gazon ? ◆ **I can give you the ~ of it for a few days** je peux vous le prêter pour quelques jours ◆ **he had offered the ~ of his villa at Cavalaire** il avait offert de prêter sa villa à Cavalaire

◆ **on loan** ◆ **this picture is on ~ from the city museum** ce tableau est prêté par le or est un prêt du musée municipal ◆ **I have a car on ~ from the company** la compagnie me prête une voiture or met une voiture à ma disposition ◆ **my assistant is on ~ to another department at the moment** mon assistant est détaché dans un autre service en ce moment ◆ **the book is out on ~** (in library) le livre est sorti ◆ **I have this book out on ~ from the library** j'ai emprunté ce livre à la bibliothèque

VT prêter (sth to sb qch à qn)

COMP **loan agreement** N (Fin) convention f de prêt
loan capital N capital m d'emprunt
loan collection N (Art etc) collection f de tableaux (or d'objets etc) en prêt
loan investment N (Fin) investissement m sous forme de prêt
loan office N bureau m de prêt
loan officer N [of bank] gestionnaire mf de crédit
loan shark* N (pej) usurier m, -ière f
loan translation N (Ling) calque m
loan word N (Ling) (mot m d') emprunt m

loath /ləʊθ/ ADJ (frm) ◆ **to be (very) ~ to do sth** répugner à faire qch ◆ **he was ~ to see her again** il n'était pas du tout disposé à la revoir ◆ **I am ~ to add to your difficulties but ...** je ne voudrais surtout pas ajouter à vos difficultés mais ... ◆ **nothing ~** très volontiers

loathe /ləʊð/ LANGUAGE IN USE 7.3 VT [+ person] détester, haïr ; [+ thing] avoir en horreur ◆ **to ~ doing sth** avoir horreur de faire qch ◆ **he ~s being criticized** il a horreur d'être critiqué

loathing /ˈləʊðɪŋ/ N (NonC) dégoût m, répugnance f ◆ **he/it fills me with ~** il/cela me répugne or dégoûte

loathsome /ˈləʊðsəm/ ADJ détestable

loathsomeness /ˈləʊðsəmnɪs/ N caractère m répugnant, nature f détestable or écœurante

loaves /ləʊvz/ NPL of **loaf**

lob /lɒb/ VT [+ stone etc] lancer (haut or en chandelle) ◆ **to ~ a ball** (Tennis) faire un lob, lober ◆ **he ~bed the book (over) to me** il m'a lancé or balancé* le livre ◆ **to ~ the goalkeeper** (Ftbl) lober le gardien de but VI (Tennis) lober, faire un lob N (Tennis) lob m

lobby /ˈlɒbɪ/ N [1] (= entrance hall) [of hotel] hall m ; (smaller) vestibule m, entrée f ; [of private house] vestibule m, entrée f ; [of theatre] foyer m (des spectateurs) [2] (Brit Parl) (where MPs meet public) hall m (de la Chambre des communes où les députés rencontrent le public), ≃ salle f des pas perdus ; (where MPs vote: also **division lobby**) vestibule m (où les députés se répartissent pour voter) [3] (Pol = pressure group) groupe m de pression, lobby m ◆ **the anti-vivisection ~** le groupe de pression or le lobby antivivisection VT (Parl, also gen) [+ person] faire pression sur ; (esp US) [+ proposal, cause] faire pression en faveur de, soutenir activement VI (Pol) ◆ **to ~ for sth** faire pression pour obtenir qch COMP **lobby correspondent** N (Brit Press) journaliste mf parlementaire

lobbyer /ˈlɒbɪəʳ/ N (US) ⇒ **lobbyist**

lobbying /ˈlɒbɪɪŋ/ N (Pol) lobbying m

lobbyism /ˈlɒbɪɪzəm/ N (US) ⇒ **lobbying**

lobbyist /ˈlɒbɪɪst/ N (Pol) lobbyiste mf

lobe /ləʊb/ N lobe m

lobelia /ləʊˈbiːlɪə/ N lobélie f

lobotomize /ləʊˈbɒtəmaɪz/ VT lobotomiser

lobotomy /ləʊˈbɒtəmɪ/ N lobotomie f

lobster /ˈlɒbstəʳ/ N (pl **lobsters** or **lobster**) homard m

COMP **lobster nets** NPL filets mpl à homards
lobster pot N casier m à homards

lobule /ˈlɒbjuːl/ N lobule m

local /ˈləʊkəl/ ADJ [custom, saying, weather forecast, newspaper, currency, train, branch, fog] local ; [shops, library] du or de quartier ; [wine, speciality] du pays, local ; (Med) [pain] localisé ◆ **he's a ~ man** il est du pays or du coin* ◆ **the ~ doctor** (gen) le médecin le plus proche ; (in town) le médecin du quartier ◆ **what is the ~ situation?** (here) quelle est la situation ici ? ; (there) quelle est la situation là-bas ? ◆ **it adds a bit of ~ colour** ça met un peu de couleur locale ◆ **of ~ interest** d'intérêt local ◆ **a ~ call** (Telec) une communication locale ◆ **~ management of schools** (Brit) gestion f des établissements scolaires par les administrations locales

N [1] (* = person) personne f du pays or du coin* ◆ **the ~s** les gens du pays or du coin* ◆ **he's one of the ~s** il est du pays or du coin*

[2] (Brit * = pub) café m du coin, bistro(t)* m du coin ◆ **my ~** le café du coin, le pub où je vais

[3] (US Rail) (train m) omnibus m

[4] * ⇒ **local anaesthetic**

[5] (US = trade union branch) section f syndicale

COMP **local anaesthetic** N anesthésie f locale
local area network N (Comput) réseau m local
local authority N autorité f locale ADJ des autorités locales
local education authority N autorité locale chargée de l'enseignement
local government N administration f locale ◆ **~ government elections** élections fpl municipales
local government officer, local government official N ≃ fonctionnaire mf (de l'administration locale)
local radio N radio f locale ◆ **she works in ~ radio** elle travaille dans une radio locale
local time N heure f locale

locale /ləʊˈkɑːl/ N endroit m

locality /ləʊˈkælɪtɪ/ N [1] (= neighbourhood) environs mpl, voisinage m ; (= district) région f ◆ **in the ~** dans les environs, dans la région ◆ **in the immediate ~ of** tout près de [2] (= place, position) lieu m ◆ **the ~ of the murder** le lieu du meurtre ; → **bump**

localization /ˌləʊkəlaɪˈzeɪʃən/ N localisation f

localize /ˈləʊkəlaɪz/ VT localiser ◆ **~d pain** douleur f localisée

locally /ˈləʊkəlɪ/ ADV (gen) localement ◆ **to live ~** habiter dans le coin ◆ **both nationally and ~** à l'échelon tant national que local ◆ **to be available ~** être disponible sur place ◆ **to produce/buy sth ~** produire/acheter qch sur place ◆ **~ grown** cultivé localement ◆ **we deliver free ~** nous livrons gratuitement dans les environs ◆ **this is Cirencester, known ~ as "Ciren"** c'est Cirencester, que l'on appelle ici "Ciren" ◆ **an ugly concrete building known ~ as "the Gulag"** un bâtiment en béton très laid que les gens du coin surnomment "le goulag"

locate /ləʊˈkeɪt/ VT [1] (= find) [+ place, person] repérer, trouver ; [+ noise, leak, cause] localiser ◆ **I can't ~ the school on this map** je n'arrive pas à repérer or à trouver l'école sur cette carte ◆ **have you ~d the briefcase I left yesterday?** avez-vous retrouvé la serviette que j'ai oubliée hier ? ◆ **the doctors have ~d the cause of the pain/the source of the infection** les médecins ont localisé la cause de la douleur/la source de l'infection

[2] (= situate) [+ factory, school etc] situer ◆ **they decided to ~ the factory in Manchester** ils ont décidé d'implanter or de construire l'usine à Manchester ◆ **where is the hospital to be ~d?** où va-t-on construire l'hôpital ? ◆ **the college is ~d in London** le collège est situé or se trouve à Londres

[3] (= assume to be) situer, placer ◆ **many scholars ~ the Garden of Eden there** c'est là que de nombreux érudits situent or placent le Paradis terrestre

[4] (US = have place to live) ◆ **to be ~d** être installé

VI (US *) s'installer

location /ləʊˈkeɪʃən/ N [1] (= position) emplacement m ◆ **a hotel set in a beautiful ~** un hôtel situé dans un endroit magnifique ◆ **what's your ~?** où vous trouvez-vous ?

[2] (Cine) extérieur m ◆ **to film in foreign ~s** tourner en extérieur à l'étranger

◆ **on location** en décor naturel, en extérieur

[3] (NonC = finding) [of person, object] repérage m

COMP (Cine) [scene, shot] en extérieur

> ⚠ **location** is not translated by the French word **location**, which means 'rental'.

locative /ˈlɒkətɪv/ ADJ, N locatif m

loch /lɒx/ N (Scot) lac m, loch m ◆ **Loch Lomond** le loch Lomond ; → **sea**

loci /ˈləʊsaɪ/ NPL of **locus**

lock[1] /lɒk/ N [1] [of door, box etc] serrure f ; (on steering wheel, bicycle, motorbike) antivol m

◆ **under lock and key** [possessions] sous clé ; [prisoner] sous les verrous ◆ **to put/keep sth under ~ and key** mettre/garder qch sous clé ◆ **to put sb under ~ and key** enfermer qn à clé ; [prisoner] mettre qn sous les verrous ◆ **to**

keep sb under ~ and key garder qn enfermé à clé ; *[prisoner]* garder qn sous les verrous

2 *[of gun]* (also **safety lock**) cran *m* de sûreté ; (also **gunlock**) percuteur *m*

♦ **lock, stock and barrel** en bloc ♦ **he sold the factory ~, stock and barrel** il a vendu l'usine en bloc ♦ **they rejected the proposals ~, stock and barrel** ils ont rejeté les suggestions en bloc *or* toutes les suggestions sans exception ♦ **I'll be moving my family, ~, stock and barrel** ma famille et moi allons déménager avec tout notre fourbi *

3 *(Comput)* verrouillage *m*

4 *[of canal]* écluse *f* ; → **airlock**

5 *(Wrestling)* immobilisation *f* ♦ **to hold sb in a ~** immobiliser qn

6 *[of car steering]* rayon *m* de braquage ♦ **this car has a good ~** cette voiture braque bien *or* a un bon rayon de braquage ♦ **3.5 turns from ~ to ~** 3,5 tours d'une butée à l'autre

7 (*Rugby:* also **lock forward**) (avant *m* de) deuxième ligne *f*

VT 1 (*= fasten*) *[+ door, suitcase, car, safe]* fermer à clé, verrouiller ♦ **behind ~ed doors** à huis clos ♦ **to ~ the stable door after the horse has bolted** *(fig)* prendre ses précautions trop tard ♦ **to ~ horns** *(lit) [animals]* se mettre à lutter cornes contre cornes ; *(fig)* se disputer ♦ **to ~ horns with sb** avoir une prise de bec avec qn

2 *[+ person]* enfermer (*in* dans) ♦ **he got ~ed in the bathroom** il s'est trouvé enfermé dans la salle de bains

3 (*= prevent use of*) *[+ mechanism]* bloquer ; *[+ computer]* verrouiller ♦ **he ~ed the steering wheel on his car** il a bloqué la direction de sa voiture ♦ **to ~ the wheels** *(by braking)* bloquer les roues

4 (*= grip, also fig*) *[+ person]* étreindre, serrer ♦ **she was ~ed in his arms** elle était serrée dans ses bras ♦ **they were ~ed in a close embrace** ils étaient unis dans une étreinte passionnée ♦ **the two armies were ~ed in combat** les deux armées étaient aux prises

VI 1 *[door]* fermer à clé

2 *[wheel, elbow, knee]* se bloquer

COMP **lock gate** N porte *f* d'écluse
lock keeper N éclusier *m*, -ière *f*
lock-up N (*Brit = garage*) box *m* ; (*Brit = shop*) boutique *f* *(sans logement)* ; (*US * = prison*) prison *f*, lieu *m* de détention provisoire ; (** = cell*) cellule *f* provisoire

► **lock away** VT SEP *[+ object, jewels]* mettre sous clé ; *[+ criminal]* mettre sous les verrous ; *[+ mental patient etc]* enfermer

► **lock in** VT SEP 1 *[+ person, dog]* enfermer (à l'intérieur) ♦ **to ~ o.s. in** s'enfermer (à l'intérieur)

2 *(Fin) [+ assets, loans]* engager (à plus d'un an)

► **lock on** VI *[spacecraft]* s'arrimer (*to* à) ♦ **to ~ on to sth** *[radar]* capter qch

► **lock out** VT SEP 1 *[+ person]* *(deliberately)* mettre à la porte ; *(by mistake)* enfermer dehors, laisser dehors (sans clé) ♦ **to find o.s. ~ed out** *(by mistake)* se trouver enfermé dehors, se retrouver à la porte ; *(as punishment)* se trouver mis à la porte ♦ **to ~ o.s. out** s'enfermer dehors ♦ **to ~ o.s. out of one's car** fermer la voiture en laissant les clés à l'intérieur

2 *[+ workers]* *(during dispute)* fermer l'usine à, lockouter

► **lock up** VI fermer (toutes les portes) à clé ♦ **will you ~ up when you leave?** voulez-vous tout fermer en partant ? ♦ **to ~ up for the night** tout fermer pour la nuit

VT SEP 1 *[+ object, jewels]* enfermer, mettre sous clé ; *[+ house]* fermer (à clé) ; *[+ criminal]* mettre sous les verrous *or* en prison ; *[+ mental patient etc]* enfermer ♦ **you ought to be ~ed up!** * on devrait t'enfermer !, il faut te faire soigner !

2 *[+ capital, funds]* immobiliser, bloquer (*in* dans)

N ♦ **lock-up** → **lock[1]**

lock[2] /lɒk/ N *[of hair]* mèche *f* ; (*= ringlet*) boucle *f* ♦ **his ~s** sa chevelure, ses cheveux *mpl* ♦ **her curly ~s** ses boucles *fpl*

lockaway /ˈlɒkəˌweɪ/ N *(Fin)* titre *m* à long terme

locker /ˈlɒkəʳ/ N casier *m* *(fermant à clé)* ♦ **the left-luggage ~s** la consigne (automatique)

COMP **locker-room** N vestiaire *m* ADJ *(fig) [joke etc]* de corps de garde, paillard

locket /ˈlɒkɪt/ N médaillon *m* *(bijou)*

locking /ˈlɒkɪŋ/ ADJ *[door, container, cupboard]* qui ferme à clé, verrouillable ♦ **~ petrol cap** bouchon *m* antivol *(pour réservoir)* N *(gen, Comput)* verrouillage *m* ; *[of car door]* verrouillage *m*, condamnation *f*, → **central**

lockjaw /ˈlɒkdʒɔː/ N *(Med)* tétanos *m*

locknut /ˈlɒknʌt/ N (*= washer*) contre-écrou *m* ; *(self-locking)* écrou *m* autobloquant

lockout /ˈlɒkaʊt/ N *(at factory)* lock-out *m inv*

locksmith /ˈlɒksmɪθ/ N serrurier *m*

loco[1] * /ˈləʊkəʊ/ ADJ *(esp US)* dingue *

loco[2] * /ˈləʊkəʊ/ N (abbrev of **locomotive**) loco † *f*, locomotive *f*

locomotion /ˌləʊkəˈməʊʃən/ N locomotion *f*

locomotive /ˌləʊkəˈməʊtɪv/ N *(Rail)* locomotive *f* ADJ *[engine, power]* locomotif ; *[muscle]* locomoteur (-trice *f*)

COMP **locomotive driver, locomotive engineer** N mécanicien *m*
locomotive shed N hangar *m* à locomotives
locomotive workshop N (*= factory*) usine *f* de construction de locomotives ; *(for repairs)* atelier *m* de réparation de locomotives

locoweed /ˌləʊkəʊˈwiːd/ N oxytrope *m*

locum /ˈləʊkəm/ N (also **locum tenens :** *esp Brit*) suppléant(e) *m(f)* *(de prêtre ou de médecin etc)*

locus /ˈlɒkəs/ N (pl **loci**) lieu *m*, point *m* ; *(Math)* lieu *m* géométrique

locust /ˈləʊkəst/ N locuste *f*, sauterelle *f*

COMP **locust bean** N caroube *f*
locust tree N caroubier *m*

locution /ləˈkjuːʃən/ N locution *f*

lode /ləʊd/ N *(Miner)* filon *m*, veine *f*

lodestar /ˈləʊdstɑːʳ/ N 1 *(Astron)* étoile *f* polaire 2 *(fig)* principe *m* directeur

lodestone /ˈləʊdstəʊn/ N magnétite *f*, aimant *m* naturel

lodge /lɒdʒ/ N (*= small house in grounds*) maison *f* *or* pavillon *m* de gardien ; (*= porter's room in building*) loge *f* ; *(Freemasonry)* loge *f* ; (*US: of union*) section *f* syndicale ; *[of beaver]* abri *m*, gîte *m* ; → **hunting** VT 1 *[+ person]* loger, héberger 2 *[+ bullet]* loger 3 *(Admin, Jur)* (*= leave*) *[+ money]* déposer ; *[+ statement, report]* présenter (*with sb* à qn) déposer (*with sb* chez qn) ♦ **to ~ an appeal** *(Jur)* interjeter appel, se pourvoir en cassation ♦ **to ~ a complaint against** *(Jur)* porter plainte contre ♦ **documents ~d by the parties** *(Jur)* pièces *fpl* versées aux débats par les parties VI *[person]* être logé, être en pension (*with* chez) ; *[bullet]* se loger

lodger /ˈlɒdʒəʳ/ N *(Brit) (room only)* locataire *mf* ; *(room and meals)* pensionnaire *mf* ♦ **to take (in) ~s** *(room only)* louer des chambres ; *(room and meals)* prendre des pensionnaires

lodging /ˈlɒdʒɪŋ/ N (*NonC = accommodation*) logement *m*, hébergement *m* ♦ **they gave us a night's ~** ils nous ont logés *or* hébergés une nuit ; → **board** NPL **lodgings** (*= room*) chambre *f* ; (*= flatlet*) logement *m* ♦ **he took ~s with Mrs Smith** † *(with meals)* il a pris pension chez Mme Smith ; *(without meals)* il a pris une chambre *or* un logement chez Mme Smith ♦ **he's in ~s** il vit en meublé *or* en garni † ♦ **to look for ~s** *(room)* chercher une chambre meublée ; *(flatlet)* chercher un logement meublé ; *(with meals)* chercher à prendre pension ♦ **we took him back to his ~s** nous l'avons ramené chez lui

COMP **lodging house** N pension *f*

loess /ˈləʊɪs/ N lœss *m*

loft /lɒft/ N 1 *[of house, stable, barn]* grenier *m* ; → **hayloft, pigeon** 2 *[of church, hall]* galerie *f* ; → **organ** 3 (*= converted living space*) loft *m* VT 1 *(Golf) [+ ball]* lancer en chandelle 2 (*= send very high*) lancer très haut

COMP **loft conversion** N *(Brit)* (*= accommodation*) grenier *m* aménagé ; (*NonC = process, activity*) aménagement *m* de grenier

loftily /ˈlɒftɪlɪ/ ADV *[say, declare, look at]* avec hauteur ♦ **his ~ dismissive attitude** son attitude hautaine et dédaigneuse ♦ **to be ~ indifferent to sb/sth** être d'une indifférence hautaine vis-à-vis de qn/qch

loftiness /ˈlɒftɪnɪs/ N 1 (*= great height*) hauteur *f* 2 (*fig = nobility*) noblesse *f* 3 (*pej = haughtiness*) hauteur *f*

lofty /ˈlɒftɪ/ ADJ 1 (*= high*) *[building, ceiling, mountain]* haut ; *[room]* haut de plafond ♦ **to rise to a ~ position in government** atteindre un poste élevé au gouvernement 2 (*= noble*) *[aim, ideal, idea]* noble 3 (*pej = haughty*) hautain 4 (*= elevated*) *[style, rhetoric]* élevé, noble

log[1] /lɒg/ N 1 (*= felled tree trunk*) rondin *m* ; *(for fire)* bûche *f* ; → **sleep**

2 (*= device on boat*) loch *m*

3 (*= logbook*) journal *m* de bord ; *[of lorry driver etc]* carnet *m* de route ; *(gen)* registre *m* ; *(Comput)* fichier *m* compte-rendu ♦ **to keep the ~** tenir le journal de bord ♦ **to write up the ~** rédiger le journal de bord

VT 1 *[+ trees]* tronçonner, débiter *or* tailler en rondins

2 (*= record*) *(gen)* noter, consigner ; (*Aviat, Naut:* also **log up**) inscrire au journal de bord ♦ **details of the crime are ~ged in the computer** les données concernant le crime sont entrées dans l'ordinateur

3 *(speed)* ♦ **the ship was ~ging 18 knots** le navire filait 18 nœuds ♦ **the plane was ~ging 300mph** l'avion volait à 500 km/h

4 (*= clock up*) (also **log up**) **he has ~ged 5,000 hours' flying time** il a à son actif *or* il compte 5 000 heures de vol ♦ **sailors often ~ 5,000 sea miles in a year** les marins font souvent 5 000 milles marins par an ♦ **I ~ged eight hours' work each day** j'ai travaillé huit heures par jour

COMP **log cabin** N cabane *f* en rondins
log file N fichier *m* compte-rendu
log fire N feu *m* de bois
log jam N *(lit)* train *m* de flottage bloqué ; *(fig)* impasse *f* *(fig)*
log-rolling N *(Sport) sport de bûcheron, consistant à faire tourner avec les pieds, sans tomber, un tronc d'arbre flottant* ; *(fig pej) échange de concessions ou de faveurs*

► **log in** *(Comput)* ⇒ **log on**

► **log off** *(Comput)* VI sortir
VT SEP déconnecter

► **log on** *(Comput)* VI entrer
VT SEP connecter, faire entrer dans le système

► **log out** *(Comput)* ⇒ **log off**

► **log up** VT SEP → **log[1]** vt 2, 4

log[2] /lɒg/ N *(Math)* (abbrev of **logarithm**) log * *m* ♦ **~ tables** tables *fpl* de logarithmes

loganberry /ˈləʊgənbərɪ/ N framboise *f* de Logan

logarithm /ˈlɒgərɪθəm/ N logarithme *m*

logbook /ˈlɒgbʊk/ N 1 *(on plane, ship)* ⇒ **log[1]** noun 3 2 *(Brit: for driver)* ≃ carte *f* grise

loge /ləʊʒ/ N *(Theat)* loge *f*

logger /ˈlɒɡəʳ/ **N** *(US)* bûcheron *m*

loggerheads /ˈlɒɡəhedz/ **NPL** ◆ **to be at ~ (with)** être en désaccord *or* à couteaux tirés (avec)

loggia /ˈlɒdʒɪə/ **N** (pl **loggias** *or* **loggie** /ˈlɒdʒe/) loggia *f*

logging /ˈlɒɡɪŋ/ **N** exploitation *f* du bois

logic /ˈlɒdʒɪk/ **N** logique *f* ◆ **I can't see the ~ of it** ça ne me paraît pas rationnel ◆ **to chop ~** *(Brit fig)* discutailler *(pej)*, ergoter *(with sb* avec qn)
COMP **logic-chopping N** *(Brit fig)* ergoterie *f*, ergotage *m*
logic circuit N *(Comput)* circuit *m* logique

logical /ˈlɒdʒɪkəl/ **ADJ** logique ◆ **capable of ~ thinking** capable de penser logiquement
COMP **logical positivism N** positivisme *m* logique, logicopositivisme *m*
logical positivist N logicopositiviste *mf*

logically /ˈlɒdʒɪkəlɪ/ **ADV** *[possible, consistent]* logiquement ; *[consider, examine, discuss]* rationnellement ◆ **it follows ~ (from this) that ...** il s'ensuit logiquement que ... ◆ **the keyboard is laid out ~** le clavier est logiquement conçu *or* conçu avec logique ◆ **~, I should have taken this into consideration** logiquement, j'aurais dû en tenir compte

logician /lɒˈdʒɪʃən/ **N** logicien(ne) *m(f)*

logistic /lɒˈdʒɪstɪk/ **ADJ** logistique **NPL logistics** logistique *f*

logistical /lɒˈdʒɪstɪkəl/ **ADJ** logistique

logistically /lɒˈdʒɪstɪkəlɪ/ **ADV** sur le plan logistique

logo /ˈləʊɡəʊ/ **N** logo *m*

logy * /ˈləʊɡɪ/ **ADJ** *(US)* apathique, léthargique

loin /lɔɪn/ **N** *(Culin: gen)* filet *m* ; *[of veal, venison]* longe *f* ; *[of beef]* aloyau *m* **NPL loins** 1 (= *lower back)* reins *mpl*, lombes *mpl* 2 (= *groin)* aine *f* ; *(euph)* (= *genitals)* bas-ventre *m (euph)* ; → **gird**
COMP **loin chop N** *(Culin)* côte *f* première

loincloth /ˈlɔɪnklɒθ/ **N** pagne *m (d'étoffe)*

Loire /lwaʳ/ **N** Loire *f* ◆ **the ~ Valley** la vallée de la Loire ; *(between Orléans and Tours)* le Val de Loire

loiter /ˈlɔɪtəʳ/ **VI** 1 (also **loiter about** = *stand around)* traîner ; *(suspiciously)* rôder 2 *(Jur)* **to ~ with intent** ≈ commettre un délit d'intention ◆ **to be charged with ~ing with intent** être accusé d'un délit d'intention

loll /lɒl/ **VI** *[person]* se prélasser ; *[head]* pendre
► **loll about, loll around VI** fainéanter, flâner
► **loll back VI** *[person]* se prélasser ; *[head]* pendre en arrière ◆ **to ~ back in an armchair** se prélasser dans un fauteuil
► **loll out** 1 **VI** *[tongue]* pendre
2 **VT SEP** *[+ tongue]* laisser pendre

lollapalooza‡ /ˌlɒləpəˈluːzəʳ/, **lollapaloosa**‡ /ˌlɒləpəˈluːsəʳ/ **N** *(US)* *(amazing)* truc* *m* génial ; *(large)* truc *m* maous*

Lollards /ˈlɒlədz/ **NPL** *(Hist)* Lollards *mpl*

lollipop /ˈlɒlɪpɒp/ **N** sucette *f (bonbon)* COMP **lollipop lady***, **lollipop man*** (pl **lollipop men**) **N** *(Brit) personne chargée d'aider les écoliers à traverser la rue*

LOLLIPOP LADY, LOLLIPOP MAN

On appelle respectivement **lollipop lady** et **lollipop man** une femme ou un homme placé à proximité d'une école et chargé d'aider les écoliers à traverser la rue. Vêtues d'un manteau blanc ou jaune fluorescent, ces personnes arrêtent la circulation à l'aide d'un grand panneau rond indiquant "stop" et qui rappelle par sa forme les sucettes appelées "lollipops".

lollop /ˈlɒləp/ **VI** *[animal]* galoper ; *[person]* courir gauchement *or* à grandes enjambées maladroites ◆ **to ~ in/out** *etc* entrer/sortir *etc* à grandes enjambées maladroites

lolly /ˈlɒlɪ/ **N** *(Brit)* 1 * sucette *f* ; → **ice** 2 *(NonC:* ‡ = *money)* fric‡ *m*, pognon‡ *m*

lollygag‡ /ˈlɒlɪɡæɡ/ **VI** *(US)* 1 (= *waste time)* glander‡ 2 (= *kiss and cuddle)* se peloter‡

Lombard /ˈlɒmbəd/ **N** Lombard(e) *m(f)* **ADJ** lombard

Lombardy /ˈlɒmbədɪ/ **N** Lombardie *f* COMP **Lombardy poplar N** peuplier *m* d'Italie

London /ˈlʌndən/ **N** Londres
COMP *[life]* londonien, à Londres ; *[person, accent, street]* londonien, de Londres ; *[taxi]* londonien
London Bridge N pont *m* de Londres
London pride N (= *plant)* saxifrage *f* ombreuse, désespoir *m* des peintres

Londoner /ˈlʌndənəʳ/ **N** Londonien(ne) *m(f)*

lone /ləʊn/ **ADJ** *[gunman]* isolé ; *[piper, rider]* solitaire ; *[survivor]* unique ◆ **a ~ figure** une silhouette solitaire ◆ **to fight a ~ battle for sth** être seul à se battre pour qch ◆ **she was a ~ voice** elle était la seule à être de cet avis
COMP **lone father N** père *m* célibataire
lone mother N mère *f* célibataire
lone parent N *père ou mère qui élève seul ses enfants*
lone-parent family N *(Brit)* famille *f* monoparentale
the lone star state N *(US)* le Texas
lone wolf N ◆ **he's a ~ wolf** c'est un (loup) solitaire

loneliness /ˈləʊnlɪnɪs/ **N** *[of person, atmosphere, life]* solitude *f* ; *[of house, road]* (= *isolated position)* isolement *m*

lonely /ˈləʊnlɪ/ **ADJ** *[person, time, life, journey, job]* solitaire ; *[village, house]* isolé ; *[road]* peu fréquenté ◆ **it's ~ at the top** le pouvoir isole ◆ **to feel ~** se sentir seul ◆ **you might find London a ~ place** il se peut que vous vous sentiez seul *or* que vous souffriez de solitude à Londres **NPL** ◆ **the ~** les personnes *fpl* seules
COMP **lonely hearts ad* N** petite annonce *f* de rencontre
lonely hearts club* N club *m* de rencontres (pour personnes seules)
lonely hearts column* N petites annonces *fpl* de rencontres

loner /ˈləʊnəʳ/ **N** solitaire *mf*

lonesome /ˈləʊnsəm/ **ADJ** *(esp US)* ⇒ **lonely N** ◆ **all on my** (*or* **your** *etc*) **~** * tout seul, toute seule

long¹ /lɒŋ/

1 ADJECTIVE	3 NOUN
2 ADVERB	4 COMPOUNDS

1 - ADJECTIVE

1 in size *[dress, hair, rope, distance, journey, book etc]* long (longue *f*) ◆ **the wall is 10 metres ~** le mur fait *or* a 10 mètres de long ◆ **a wall 10 metres ~** un mur de 10 mètres de long ◆ **how ~ is the swimming pool?** quelle est la longueur de la piscine ? ◆ **to get ~er** *[queue]* s'allonger ; *[hair]* pousser ◆ **the document is ~ on generalities and short on practicalities** le document fait une large place aux généralités et ne donne pas beaucoup de détails pratiques ◆ **the cooking wasn't exactly ~ on imagination** * la cuisine n'était pas très originale ◆ **to have a ~ arm** *(fig)* avoir le bras long ◆ **they were eventually caught by the ~ arm of the law** ils ont fini par être rattrapés par la justice ◆ **a string of degrees as ~ as your arm** * (= *masses of degrees)* des diplômes à n'en plus finir ◆ **to have a ~ face** *(fig)* avoir la mine allongée, faire triste mine ◆ **to make** *or* **pull a ~ face** faire la grimace ◆ **to be ~ in the leg** *(of person)* avoir de longues jambes ; *(of trousers)* être trop long ◆ **he's getting a bit ~ in the tooth*** il n'est plus tout jeune, il n'est plus de la première jeunesse ◆ **not by a ~ chalk** *or* **shot** * loin de là ◆ **it's a ~ shot but we might be lucky** *(fig)* c'est très risqué mais nous aurons peut-être de la chance ◆ **it was just a ~ shot** *(fig)* il y avait peu de chances pour que cela réussisse ; see also **compounds**

2 in distance ◆ **it's a ~ way** c'est loin ◆ **it's a ~ way to the shops** les magasins sont loin ◆ **we walked a ~ way** nous avons beaucoup marché ◆ **it was a ~ 3 miles to the nearest pub** le pub le plus proche était à 5 bons kilomètres

3 in time *[visit, wait, weekend, look, film]* long (longue *f*) ; *[delay]* important ◆ **I find the days very ~** je trouve les jours bien longs ◆ **the days are getting ~er** les jours rallongent ◆ **to be six months ~** durer six mois ◆ **at ~ last** enfin ◆ **he took a ~ drink of water** il a bu beaucoup d'eau ; see also **compounds** ◆ **it will be a ~ job** ça va prendre du temps ◆ **to have a ~ memory** ne pas oublier vite ◆ **in the ~ run** à la longue ◆ **in the ~ term** à long terme ; see also **long-term** ◆ **~ time no see!**‡ tiens, un revenant !*, ça fait une paye !* ◆ **to take the ~ view** penser à l'avenir ◆ **he's not ~ for this world** * il n'en a plus pour longtemps ◆ **the reply was not ~ in coming** la réponse n'a pas tardé à venir

◆ **a long time** longtemps ◆ **a ~ time ago** il y a longtemps ◆ **that was a ~, ~ time ago** il y a bien longtemps de cela ◆ **what a ~ time you've been!** tu en as mis du temps !* ◆ **it will be a ~ time before I see her again** je ne la reverrai pas de si tôt *or* pas avant longtemps ◆ **it will be remembered for a ~ time to come** on s'en souviendra longtemps ◆ **it'll be a ~ time before I do that again!** je ne recommencerai pas de si tôt ! ◆ **for a ~ time I had to stay in bed** j'ai dû longtemps garder le lit ◆ **have you been studying English for a ~ time?** il y a longtemps que vous étudiez l'anglais ? ◆ **it's a ~ time since I last saw him** ça fait longtemps que je ne l'ai pas vu ◆ **he has not been seen for a ~ time** on ne l'a pas vu depuis longtemps, cela fait longtemps qu'on ne l'a pas vu ◆ **for a ~ time now he has been unable to work** voilà longtemps qu'il est dans l'incapacité de travailler ◆ **you took a ~ time to get here** *or* **getting here** tu as mis longtemps pour *or* à venir ◆ **it takes a ~ time for the drug to act** ce médicament met du temps à agir ◆ **it took a ~ time for the truth to be accepted** les gens ont mis très longtemps à accepter la vérité

4 Ling *[vowel]* long (longue *f*)

2 - ADVERB

1 = a long time longtemps ◆ **they didn't stay ~** ils ne sont pas restés longtemps ◆ **he didn't live ~ after that** il n'a pas survécu longtemps ◆ **he hasn't been gone ~** il n'y a pas longtemps qu'il est parti ◆ **it didn't take him ~ to realize that ...** il n'a pas mis longtemps à se rendre compte que ... ◆ **are you going away for ~?** vous partez pour longtemps ? ◆ **not for ~** pas pour longtemps ◆ **not for much ~er** plus pour très longtemps ◆ **will you be ~?** tu en as pour longtemps ? ◆ **I won't be ~** je n'en ai pas pour longtemps ◆ **don't be ~** dépêche-toi ◆ **he hasn't ~ to live** il n'en a plus pour longtemps ◆ **women live ~er than men** les femmes vivent plus longtemps que les hommes ◆ **this method has ~ been used in industry** cette méthode est employée depuis longtemps dans l'industrie ◆ **have you been here/been waiting ~?** vous êtes ici/vous attendez depuis longtemps ?, il y a longtemps que vous êtes ici/que vous attendez ? ◆ **these are ~-needed changes** ce sont des changements qui s'imposent depuis longtemps ◆ **his ~-awaited reply** sa réponse (si) longtemps attendue ◆ **I have ~**

wished to say ... il y a longtemps que je souhaite dire ... ♦ **~ may this situation continue** espérons que cela continuera ♦ **~ live the King!** vive le roi ! ♦ **I only had ~ enough to buy a paper** je n'ai eu que le temps d'acheter un journal ♦ **six months at (the) ~est** six mois au plus ♦ **so ~!** * à bientôt !

2 [= through] ♦ **all night ~** toute la nuit ♦ **all summer ~** tout l'été ♦ **his whole life ~** toute sa vie

3 [set structures]

♦ **before long** (+ *future*) sous peu, dans peu de temps ; (+ *past*) peu après

♦ **how long ?** (*in time*) ♦ **how ~ will you be?** ça va te demander combien de temps ?, tu vas mettre combien de temps ? ♦ **how ~ did they stay?** combien de temps sont-ils restés ? ♦ **how ~ is it since you saw him?** cela fait combien de temps que tu ne l'as pas vu ? ♦ **how ~ are the holidays?** les vacances durent combien de temps ?

In the following **depuis** + present/imperfect translates English perfect/pluperfect continuous.

♦ **how ~ have you been learning Greek?** depuis combien de temps apprenez-vous le grec ? ♦ **how ~ had you been living in Paris?** depuis combien de temps viviez-vous à Paris ?, cela faisait combien de temps que vous viviez à Paris ?

♦ **long ago** il y a longtemps ♦ **how ~ ago was it?** il y a combien de temps de ça ? ♦ **as ~ ago as 1930** déjà en 1930 ♦ **of ~ ago** d'il y a longtemps ♦ **not ~ ago** il n'y a pas longtemps, il y a peu de temps ♦ **he arrived not ~ ago** il n'y a pas longtemps qu'il est arrivé, il vient d'arriver

♦ **long after** longtemps après ♦ **~ after he died** longtemps après sa mort ♦ **he died ~ after his wife** il est mort longtemps après sa femme

♦ **long before** ♦ **~ before the war** bien avant la guerre ♦ **~ before his wife's death** bien avant la mort de sa femme, bien avant que sa femme ne meure ♦ **his wife had died ~ before** sa femme était morte depuis longtemps, il y avait longtemps que sa femme était morte ♦ **you should have done it ~ before now** vous auriez dû le faire il y a longtemps ♦ **not ~ before the war** peu (de temps) avant la guerre ♦ **not ~ before his wife died** peu (de temps) avant la mort de sa femme, peu avant que sa femme ne meure ♦ **she had died not ~ before** elle était morte peu de temps avant *or* auparavant

♦ **long since** ♦ **it's not ~ since he died** ♦ **he died not ~ since** * il est mort il y a peu *or* il n'y a pas longtemps ♦ **~ since** il y a longtemps ♦ **he thought of friends ~ since dead** il a pensé à des amis morts depuis longtemps

♦ **any/no/a little longer** ♦ **I can't stay any ~er** je ne peux pas rester plus longtemps ♦ **she no ~er wishes to do it** elle ne veut plus le faire ♦ **he is no ~er living there** il n'y habite plus ♦ **wait a little ~er** attendez encore un peu

♦ **as long as** (*relating to time*) ♦ **as ~ as necessary** le temps qu'il faudra ♦ **stay (for) as ~ as you like** restez autant que *or* aussi longtemps que vous voulez ♦ **as** *or* **so ~ as this crisis lasts** tant que durera cette crise ♦ **as** *or* **so ~ as the war lasted** tant que dura la guerre

♦ **as** *or* **so long as** (*conditional*) à condition que + *subj* ♦ **you can borrow it as ~ as** *or* **so ~ as John doesn't mind** vous pouvez l'emprunter à condition que John n'y voie pas d'inconvénient

3 - NOUN

1 ♦ **the ~ and the short of it is that ...** le fin mot de l'histoire, c'est que ...

2 [= syllable, beat] longue *f*

4 - COMPOUNDS

long-acting ADJ [*drug*] à effet lent et à action longue

long-chain ADJ (*Chem*) à chaîne longue

long-dated ADJ (*Fin*) à longue échéance

long-distance ADJ [*race, runner*] de fond ♦ **~-distance call** (*Telec*) appel *m* (à) longue distance ♦ **~-distance flight** vol *m* long-courrier ♦ **~-distance lorry driver** (*Brit*) routier *m* ♦ **~-distance skier** fondeur *m*, -euse *f* ADV ♦ **to call sb ~-distance** appeler qn à longue distance

long division N (*Math*) division *f* écrite complète (*avec indication des restes partiels*)

long-drawn-out ADJ interminable, qui n'en finit pas

long drink N long drink *m*

long-eared ADJ aux longues oreilles

long-established ADJ [*business, company*] qui existe depuis longtemps ; [*habit*] vieux (vieille *f*)

long fin tuna, long fin tunny N thon *m* blanc

long-forgotten ADJ oublié depuis longtemps

long-grain rice N riz *m* long

long green * N (*US = money*) argent *m*, fric * *m*

long-haired ADJ [*person*] aux cheveux longs ; [*animal*] à longs poils

long-haul N transport *m* à longue distance ♦ **~-haul airline/flight** ligne *f*/vol *m* long-courrier

long-headed ADJ (*fig*) avisé, perspicace, prévoyant

long johns * NPL caleçon *m* long

long jump N (*Sport*) saut *m* en longueur

long jumper N sauteur *m*, -euse *f* en longueur

long-lasting ADJ durable ♦ **to be longer-lasting** *or* **more ~-lasting** durer plus longtemps

long-legged ADJ [*person, horse*] aux jambes longues ; [*other animal, insect*] à longues pattes

long-life ADJ [*milk*] longue conservation ; [*batteries*] longue durée

long-limbed ADJ aux membres longs

long list N première liste *f*, liste *f* préliminaire

long-lived ADJ d'une grande longévité ♦ **women are longer-lived** *or* **more ~-lived than men** les femmes vivent plus longtemps que les hommes

long-lost ADJ [*person*] perdu de vue depuis longtemps ; [*thing*] perdu depuis longtemps

long-nosed ADJ au nez long

long play N (*US*) ⇒ **long-playing record**

long-playing record N 33 tours *m inv*

long-range ADJ [*missile, rocket, gun*] à longue portée ; [*planning etc*] à long terme ♦ **~-range plane** (*Mil*) avion *m* à grand rayon d'action ; (*civil*) long-courrier *m* ♦ **~-range weather forecast** prévisions *fpl* météorologiques à long terme

long-running ADJ [*play*] qui tient l'affiche depuis longtemps ; [*TV programme*] qui est diffusé depuis longtemps ♦ **~-running series** (*TV*) série-fleuve *f* ; [*dispute*] qui dure depuis longtemps

long shot N (*Cine*) plan *m* général *or* d'ensemble ; see also **adjective 1**

long-sighted ADJ (*Brit*) (*lit*) hypermétrope ; (*in old age*) presbyte ; (*fig*) [*person*] prévoyant, qui voit loin ; [*decision*] pris avec prévoyance ; [*attitude*] prévoyant

long-sightedness N (*lit*) hypermétropie *f* ; (*in old age*) presbytie *f* ; (*fig*) prévoyance *f*

long-sleeved ADJ à manches longues

long-standing ADJ de longue date ♦ **~-standing links** des liens de longue date ♦ **their ~-standing dispute** le conflit qui les oppose depuis longtemps ♦ **the city's ~-standing policy** la politique déjà ancienne de la ville

long-stay car park N parking *m or* parc *m* de stationnement de longue durée

long stop N (*fig*) garde-fou *m*

long-suffering ADJ très patient, d'une patience à toute épreuve

long-tailed ADJ à longue queue ♦ **~-tailed tit** mésange *f* à longue queue

long-term ADJ → **long-term**

long-time ADJ de longue date, vieux (vieille *f*)

long trousers NPL (*as opposed to shorts*) pantalon *m* ♦ **when I was old enough to wear ~ trousers** quand j'ai passé l'âge des culottes courtes

the long vacation, the long vac * N (*Brit Univ*) les grandes vacances *fpl*

long wave N (*Rad*) grandes ondes *fpl* ♦ **on (the) ~ wave** sur les grandes ondes

long-wearing ADJ (*US*) solide, résistant

long-winded ADJ [*person*] intarissable, prolixe ; [*speech*] interminable

long-windedly ADV intarissablement

long-windedness N prolixité *f*

long² /lɒŋ/ VI ♦ **to ~ to do sth** (= *hope to*) avoir très envie de faire qch ; (= *dream of*) rêver de faire qch ♦ **I'm ~ing to meet her** j'ai très envie de la rencontrer ♦ **to ~ for sth** (= *hope for*) avoir très envie de qch ; (= *dream of*) rêver de qch ♦ **the ~ed-for baby** le bébé tant attendu ♦ **to ~ for sb to do sth** mourir d'envie que qn fasse qch ♦ **she ~ed for her friends** ses amis lui manquaient beaucoup *or* terriblement

longboat /ˈlɒŋbəʊt/ N (grande) chaloupe *f*

longbow /ˈlɒŋbəʊ/ N arc *m* (anglais)

longevity /lɒnˈdʒevɪtɪ/ N longévité *f*

longhair * /ˈlɒŋhɛəʳ/ N (*US*) intello * *m*

longhand /ˈlɒŋhænd/ N écriture *f* normale *or* courante ♦ **in ~** (*not shorthand*) en clair ; (*not typed*) à la main ADJ en clair

longhorn cattle /ˈlɒŋhɔːnˈkætl/ N (*NonC*) bovins *mpl* longhorn *inv or* à longues cornes

longing /ˈlɒŋɪŋ/ N 1 (= *urge*) désir *m*, envie *f* (*for sth* de qch) ; (= *craving*) (*for food etc*) envie *f* ♦ **to have a sudden ~ to do sth** avoir un désir soudain *or* une envie soudaine de faire qch 2 (= *nostalgia*) nostalgie *f* ♦ **his ~ for the happy days of his childhood** la nostalgie qu'il avait des jours heureux de son enfance ADJ [*look, glance*] (*for sth*) plein d'envie ; (*for sb*) plein de désir

longingly /ˈlɒŋɪŋlɪ/ ADV ♦ **to look ~ at sb** regarder qn d'un air enamouré ♦ **to look ~ at sth** regarder qch avec convoitise, dévorer qch des yeux ♦ **to think ~ of sb** penser amoureusement à qn ♦ **to think ~ of sth** penser avec envie à qch

longish /ˈlɒŋɪʃ/ ADJ [*hair, period, distance*] assez long (longue *f*) ; [*book, play*] assez long (longue *f*), longuet * (*slightly pej*) ♦ **(for) a ~ time** assez longtemps

longitude /ˈlɒŋgɪtjuːd/ N longitude *f* ♦ **at a ~ of 48°** par 48° de longitude

longitudinal /ˌlɒŋgɪˈtjuːdɪnl/ ADJ longitudinal

longitudinally /ˌlɒŋgɪˈtjuːdɪnəlɪ/ ADV longitudinalement

longlist /ˈlɒŋlɪst/ VT ♦ **to be ~ed** figurer sur une première liste de sélection

longship /ˈlɒŋʃɪp/ N (*Vikings*) drakkar *m*

longshoreman /ˈlɒŋʃɔːmən/ N (pl **-men**) (*US*) débardeur *m*, docker *m*

longshoring /ˈlɒŋʃɔːrɪŋ/ N (*US*) débardage *m*

long-term /ˈlɒŋˈtɜːm/ ADJ [*loan, policy, investment, effects, solution, view, interests, future*] à long terme ; [*resident*] de longue durée ♦ **~ political prisoners** prisonniers politiques de longue durée ♦ **no amount of aid will solve the long term problems of the people** quelle que soit l'aide fournie, elle ne résoudra pas les problèmes persistants des gens ♦ **the side-effects of long term injections of growth hormone** les effets secondaires des injections d'hormone de croissance sur une longue période ♦ **a ~ project** un projet de longue haleine ♦ **I'm looking for a ~ relationship** je recherche une relation qui dure *or* durable ♦ **he's in a ~**

relationship *(going out with sb)* il sort avec la même personne depuis longtemps ; *(living with)* il vit avec la même personne depuis longtemps ◆ **they're in a ~ relationship** *(going out)* ils sortent ensemble depuis longtemps ; *(living together)* ils vivent ensemble depuis longtemps

COMP **long-term care** N prise *f* en charge de longue durée

long-term car park N parc *m* de stationnement *(avec forfait à la journée/à la semaine etc)*

long-term health care N ⇒ **long-term care**

long-term memory N mémoire *f* à long terme

the long-term unemployed NPL les chômeurs *mpl* de longue durée ; see also **long**[1]

longways /ˈlɒŋweɪz/ ADV en longueur, en long ◆ **~ on** dans le sens de la longueur

loo * /luː/ N *(Brit)* toilettes *fpl*, W.-C. *mpl* ◆ **he's in the ~** il est au petit coin * *or* aux toilettes

loofah /ˈluːfəʳ/ N luffa *m*, loofa *m*

look /lʊk/

LANGUAGE IN USE 16.2

1 NOUN
2 PLURAL NOUN
3 INTRANSITIVE VERB
4 TRANSITIVE VERB
5 COMPOUNDS
6 PHRASAL VERBS

1 - NOUN

1 [at sth, sb] ◆ **do you want a ~ ?** tu veux regarder *or* jeter un coup d'œil ? ◆ **and now for a quick ~ at the papers** et maintenant, les grands titres de vos journaux

◆ **to have/take + a look** ◆ **let me have a ~** *(= may I)* fais voir ; *(= I'm going to)* je vais voir ◆ **let me have another ~** *(= may I)* je peux regarder encore une fois ? ◆ **to have** *or* **take a ~ at sth** regarder qch, jeter un coup d'œil à qch ◆ **take** *or* **have a ~ at this!** regarde-moi ça !, regarde ! ◆ **to take another** *or* **a second ~ at sth** examiner qch de plus près ◆ **to take a good ~ at sth** bien regarder qch ◆ **to take a good ~ at sb** regarder qn avec attention ◆ **take a good ~!** regarde bien ! ◆ **to take a long ~ at sb** regarder longuement qn, bien regarder qn ◆ **to take a long hard ~ at sth** *(fig)* examiner qch de près ◆ **to take a long (hard) ~ at o.s.** *(fig)* faire son autocritique ◆ **to have a ~ round the house** visiter la maison ◆ **I just want to have a ~ round** *(in town)* je veux simplement faire un tour ; *(in a shop)* est-ce que je peux regarder ? ◆ **have a ~ through the telescope** regarde dans le télescope

2 [= expression] regard *m* ◆ **an inquiring ~** un regard interrogateur ◆ **with a nasty ~ in his eye** avec un regard méchant ◆ **he gave me a furious ~** il m'a jeté un regard furieux, il m'a regardé d'un air furieux ◆ **we got some very odd ~s** les gens nous ont regardé d'un drôle d'air ◆ **I told her what I thought and if ~s could kill*, I'd be dead** je lui ai dit ce que je pensais et elle m'a fusillé *or* foudroyé du regard ; see also **black, dirty, long**[1]

3 [= search] **to have a ~ for sth** chercher qch ◆ **have another ~!** cherche bien ! ◆ **I've had a good ~ for it already** je l'ai déjà cherché partout

4 [= appearance] air *m* ◆ **there was a sad ~ about him** il avait l'air plutôt triste ◆ **I like the ~ of her** * je trouve qu'elle a l'air sympathique *or* qu'elle a une bonne tête * ◆ **I don't like the ~(s) of him** * il a une tête qui ne me revient pas * ◆ **he had the ~ of a sailor (about him)** il avait l'air d'un marin ◆ **she has a ~ of her mother (about her)** elle a quelque chose de sa mère ◆ **by the ~(s) of him** * à le voir ◆ **by the ~(s) of it** *or* **things** * de toute évidence ◆ **you can't go by ~s** il ne faut pas se fier aux apparences *(Prov)* ◆ **I don't like the ~ of this at all** * ça ne me dit rien qui vaille

5 [Fashion = style] look *m* ◆ **I need a new ~** il faut que je change *subj* de look

2 - PLURAL NOUN

looks * beauté *f* ◆ **~s aren't everything** la beauté n'est pas tout ◆ **she has kept her ~s** elle est restée belle ◆ **she's losing her ~s** elle n'est plus aussi belle qu'autrefois, sa beauté se fane

3 - INTRANSITIVE VERB

1 [= see, glance] regarder ◆ **~ over there!** regarde là-bas ! ◆ **~!** regarde ! ◆ **just ~!** regarde un peu ! ◆ **~ and see if he's still there** regarde s'il est encore là ◆ **~ what a mess you've made!** regarde le gâchis que tu as fait ! ◆ **~ who's here!** * regarde qui est là ! ◆ **let me ~** *(= may I)* fais voir ; *(= I'm going to)* je vais voir ◆ **to ~ the other way** *(lit = avert one's eyes)* détourner le regard ; *(fig)* fermer les yeux *(fig)* ◆ **~ before you leap** *(Prov)* il faut réfléchir avant d'agir

◆ **to look** + *adverb/preposition* ◆ **he ~ed around him for an ashtray** il a cherché un cendrier des yeux ◆ **to ~ down one's nose at sb** * regarder qn de haut ◆ **she ~s down her nose at** * **romantic novels** elle méprise les romans à l'eau de rose ◆ **to ~ down the list** parcourir la liste ◆ **~ here***, **we must discuss it first** écoutez, il faut d'abord en discuter ◆ **~ here***, **that isn't what I said!** dites donc, ce n'est pas (du tout) ce que j'ai dit ! ◆ **she ~ed into his eyes** *(gen)* elle l'a regardé droit dans les yeux ; *(romantically)* elle a plongé son regard dans le sien ◆ **(you must) ~ on the bright side (of life)** il faut être optimiste, il faut voir le bon côté des choses ◆ **to ~ over sb's shoulder** *(lit)* regarder par-dessus l'épaule de qn ; *(fig)* être constamment sur le dos de qn, surveiller qn constamment ◆ **to be ~ing over one's shoulder** *(fig)* être sur ses gardes ◆ **he ~ed right through me** * *(fig)* il a fait comme s'il ne me voyait pas

2 [= face] *[building]* donner ◆ **the house ~s east** la maison donne à l'est ◆ **the house ~s onto the main street** la maison donne sur la rue principale

3 [= search] chercher ◆ **you should have ~ed more carefully** tu aurais dû chercher un peu mieux ◆ **you can't have ~ed far** tu n'as pas dû beaucoup chercher

4 [= seem] avoir l'air ◆ **he doesn't ~ himself, he's not ~ing himself** il n'a pas l'air dans son assiette, il n'a pas l'air en forme ◆ **he ~s about 40** il doit avoir la quarantaine ◆ **he ~s about 75 kilos/1 metre 80** il doit faire environ 75 kilos/1 mètre 80 ◆ **she's tired and she ~s it** elle est fatiguée et ça se voit ◆ **he's 50 and he ~s it** il a 50 ans et il les fait ◆ **how did she ~?** *(health)* elle avait l'air en forme ? ; *(on hearing news)* quelle tête elle a fait ? ◆ **how do I ~?** comment me trouves-tu ? ◆ **how does it ~ to you?** qu'en pensez-vous ?

◆ **to look as if** ◆ **try to ~ as if you're glad to see them!** essaie d'avoir l'air content de les voir ! ◆ **it ~s as if it's going to snow** on dirait qu'il va neiger ◆ **it ~s as if he isn't coming, it doesn't ~ as if he's coming** on dirait qu'il ne va pas venir ◆ **it ~s to me as if he isn't coming, it doesn't ~ to me as if he's coming** j'ai l'impression qu'il ne va pas venir

◆ **to look** + *adjective/noun* ◆ **she ~s her age** elle fait son âge ◆ **~ alive** *or* **lively!** * remue-toi ! * ◆ **it will ~ bad** ça va faire mauvais effet ◆ **she ~s her best in blue** c'est le bleu qui lui va le mieux ◆ **you must ~ your best for this interview** il faut que tu présentes bien pour cet entretien ◆ **he just does it to ~ big** * il fait ça uniquement pour se donner de l'importance ◆ **they made me ~ foolish** *or* **a fool** ils m'ont ridiculisé ◆ **he ~s good in uniform** l'uniforme lui va bien ◆ **that dress ~s good** *or* **well on her** cette robe lui va bien ◆ **that hat/necklace ~s good on you** ce chapeau/collier te va bien ◆ **that pie ~s good** cette tarte a l'air bonne ◆ **how are you getting on with your autobiography? – it's ~ing good** comment avance ton autobiographie ? – elle avance bien ◆ **it ~s good on paper** c'est très bien en théorie *or* sur le papier ◆ **that story ~s interesting** cette histoire a l'air intéressante *or* semble intéressante ◆ **that hairstyle makes her ~ old** cette coiffure la vieillit ◆ **it makes him ~ ten years older/younger** ça le vieillit/rajeunit de dix ans ◆ **he ~s older than that** il a l'air plus âgé que ça ◆ **to ~ the part** *(fig)* avoir le physique *or* avoir la tête de l'emploi * ◆ **how pretty you ~!** comme vous êtes jolie ! ◆ **it ~s promising** c'est prometteur ◆ **it doesn't ~ right** il y a quelque chose qui ne va pas ◆ **it ~s all right to me** ça m'a l'air d'aller ◆ **to make sb ~ small** *(fig)* rabaisser qn, diminuer qn ◆ **she ~s tired** elle a l'air fatigué(e) ◆ **you ~ or you're ~ing well** vous avez bonne mine ◆ **she doesn't ~ well** elle n'a pas bonne mine, elle a mauvaise mine

◆ **to look like** *(= be in appearance)* ◆ **what does he ~ like ?** comment est-il ? ◆ **you can see what the house used to ~ like** on voit comment était la maison ◆ **he ~s like his father** *(= resemble)* il ressemble à son père ◆ **the picture doesn't ~ like him at all** on ne le reconnaît pas du tout sur cette photo ◆ **he ~s like a soldier** il a l'air d'un soldat ◆ **she ~ed like nothing on earth** (‡, *pej ill, depressed*) elle avait une tête épouvantable ◆ **it ~s like salt** *(= seem)* on dirait du sel ◆ **this ~s to me like the right shop** cela m'a l'air d'être le bon magasin ◆ **it ~s like rain** * on dirait qu'il va pleuvoir ◆ **the rain doesn't ~ like stopping** la pluie n'a pas l'air de (vouloir) s'arrêter ◆ **it certainly ~s like it** ça m'en a tout l'air ◆ **the evening ~ed like being interesting** la soirée promettait d'être intéressante

4 - TRANSITIVE VERB

1 [= look at] regarder ◆ **to ~ sb in the face** *or* **in the eye(s)** regarder qn en face *or* dans les yeux ◆ **I could never ~ him in the face** *or* **in the eye(s) again** *(fig)* je ne pourrais plus le regarder en face ◆ **to ~ sb up and down** toiser qn

2 [= pay attention to] regarder, faire attention à ◆ **~ where you're going!** regarde où tu vas ! ◆ **~ what you've done now!** regarde ce que tu as fait !

5 - COMPOUNDS

look-alike * N sosie *m* ◆ **a Churchill ~-alike** un sosie de Churchill

looked-for ADJ *[result]* attendu, prévu ; *[effect]* escompté, recherché

look-in * N *(= visit)* ◆ **to give sb a ~-in** passer voir qn, faire une visite éclair *or* un saut chez qn ◆ **with such competition we won't get a ~-in** *(Brit = chance)* avec de tels concurrents nous n'avons pas la moindre chance ◆ **our team didn't have** *or* **get a ~-in** notre équipe n'a jamais eu le moindre espoir *or* la moindre chance de gagner

looking-glass † N glace *f*, miroir *m*

look-out N → **look-out**

look-see ‡ N ◆ **to have** *or* **to take a ~-see** jeter un coup d'œil, jeter un œil *

look-up *(Comput)* N consultation *f* ADJ *[list etc]* à consulter

6 - PHRASAL VERBS

► **look about** VI regarder autour de soi ◆ **to ~ about for sb/sth** chercher qn/qch (des yeux)

► **look after** VT FUS 1 *(= take care of) [+ invalid, animal, plant]* s'occuper de ; *[+ one's possessions]* prendre soin de ; *[+ finances]* gérer ◆ **she doesn't ~ after herself properly** elle se néglige ◆ ~ **after yourself!** * prends soin de toi !, fais bien attention à toi ! * ◆ **she's quite old enough to ~ after herself** elle est assez grande pour se débrouiller * toute seule ◆ **he certainly ~s after his car** il bichonne sa voiture ◆ **we're well ~ed after here** on s'occupe bien de nous ici, on nous soigne ici

2 (= *mind*) [+ *child*] garder, s'occuper de ; [+ *shop, business*] s'occuper de ; [+ *luggage, house*] (= *watch over*) surveiller ; (= *keep temporarily*) garder (*sth for sb* qch pour qn) ◆ **to ~ after one's own interests** protéger ses propres intérêts

► **look ahead** VI (= *in front*) regarder devant soi ; (= *to future*) penser à l'avenir ◆ **I'm ~ing ahead at what might happen** j'essaie d'imaginer ce qui pourrait se passer

► **look around** VI ⇒ **look about**

► **look at** VT FUS 1 (= *observe*) [+ *person, object*] regarder ◆ **to ~ hard at** [+ *person*] dévisager ; [+ *thing*] regarder *or* examiner de très près ◆ **just ~ at this mess!** regarde un peu ce fouillis ! ◆ **just ~ at you!** * regarde de quoi tu as l'air !, regarde-toi ! ◆ **to ~ at him you would never think (that)** … à le voir, on n'imaginerait pas que … ◆ **it isn't much to ~ at** *, **it's nothing to ~ at** * ça ne paie pas de mine

2 (= *consider*) [+ *situation, problem*] examiner ◆ **let's ~ at the facts** considérons *or* examinons les faits ◆ **they wouldn't ~ at my proposal** ils n'ont même pas pris ma proposition en considération, ils ont d'emblée rejeté ma proposition ◆ **he now ~ed at her with new respect** il commença à la considérer avec respect ◆ **that's one way of ~ing at it** c'est un point de vue, mais pas le mien ◆ **it depends (on) how you ~ at it** tout dépend comment on voit *or* envisage la chose ◆ **just ~ at him now!** (*what's become of him*) regarde où il en est aujourd'hui !

3 (= *check*) vérifier ; (= *see to*) s'occuper de ◆ **will you ~ at the carburettor?** pourriez-vous vérifier le carburateur ? ◆ **I'll ~ at it tomorrow** je m'en occuperai demain

4 (* = *have in prospect*) **you're ~ing at a minimum of £65** ça va vous coûter 65 livres au minimum ◆ **they are ~ing at savings of £3m** il s'agit d'économies qui pourraient atteindre 3 millions de livres

► **look away** VI (*lit*) détourner les yeux *or* le regard (*from* de) ; (*fig*) fermer les yeux

► **look back** VI 1 (*lit*) regarder derrière soi ◆ **she ~ed back at Marie and smiled** elle se retourna pour regarder Marie et lui sourit

2 (*fig: in memory*) revenir sur le passé ◆ **after that he never ~ed back** * après, ça n'a fait qu'aller de mieux en mieux pour lui ◆ **there's no point ~ing back** ça ne sert à rien de revenir sur le passé ◆ **~ing back, I'm surprised I didn't suspect anything** rétrospectivement *or* avec le recul, je suis étonné de n'avoir rien soupçonné ◆ **to ~ back on** *or* **at** *or* **over sth** (= *remember, evaluate*) repenser à qch ◆ **when they ~ back on** *or* **at this match** … lorsqu'ils repenseront à ce match … ◆ **we can ~ back on** *or* **over 20 years of happy marriage** nous avons derrière nous 20 ans de bonheur conjugal

► **look behind** VI regarder en arrière

► **look down** VI baisser les yeux ◆ **to ~ down at the ground** regarder par terre ◆ **don't ~ down or you'll fall** ne regarde pas en bas, sinon tu vas tomber ◆ **he ~ed down at** *or* **on the town from the hilltop** il a regardé la ville du haut de la colline

► **look down on** VT FUS 1 (= *despise*) mépriser ◆ **to ~ down on sb** regarder qn de haut, mépriser qn

2 (= *overlook*) dominer ◆ **the castle ~s down on the valley** le château domine la vallée

► **look for** VT FUS 1 (= *seek*) [+ *object, work*] chercher ◆ **to be ~ing for trouble** * chercher les ennuis

2 (= *expect*) [+ *praise, reward*] attendre, espérer

► **look forward to** VT FUS [+ *event, meal, trip, holiday*] attendre avec impatience ◆ **I'm ~ing forward to seeing them** j'ai hâte de les voir ◆ **I ~ forward to meeting you on the 5th** (*frm*) je vous verrai donc le 5 ◆ **~ing forward to hearing from you** (*in letter*) en espérant avoir bientôt de vos nouvelles, dans l'attente de votre réponse (*frm*) ◆ **I ~ forward to the day when** … j'attends avec impatience le jour où … ◆ **are you ~ing forward to your birthday?** tu attends ton anniversaire avec impatience ? ◆ **we'd been ~ing forward to it for weeks** on attendait ça depuis des semaines ◆ **I'm really ~ing forward to it** je m'en fais déjà une fête, je m'en réjouis à l'avance ◆ **they are ~ing forward to an increase in sales** ils anticipent une augmentation des ventes

► **look in** VI 1 (*lit*) regarder à l'intérieur ◆ **to ~ in at the window** regarder par la fenêtre

2 (* = *pay visit*) passer ◆ **we ~ed in at Robert's** nous sommes passés chez Robert, nous avons fait un saut chez Robert ◆ **to ~ in on sb** passer voir qn ◆ **the doctor will ~ in again tomorrow** le docteur repassera demain

► **look into** VT FUS (= *examine*) [+ *possibility, problem, situation*] examiner, étudier ◆ **they are going to ~ into other possibilities** ils vont examiner d'autres solutions ◆ **there's obviously been a mistake. I'll ~ into it** il y a dû y avoir une erreur. Je vais m'en occuper ◆ **we must ~ into what happened to the money** il va falloir que nous enquêtions pour voir ce qu'est devenu cet argent

► **look on**

VI regarder (faire) ◆ **they just ~ed on while the raiders escaped** quand les bandits se sont enfuis, ils se sont contentés de regarder ◆ **he wrote the letter while I ~ed on** il a écrit la lettre tandis que je le regardais faire

VT FUS considérer ◆ **many ~ on him as a hero** beaucoup le considèrent comme un héros ◆ **to ~ kindly (up)on sth/sb** (*frm*) approuver qch/qn ◆ **I do not ~ on the matter in that way** (*frm*) je ne vois *or* n'envisage pas la chose de cette façon(-là)

► **look out**

VI 1 (*lit = look outside*) regarder dehors ◆ **to ~ out of the window** regarder par la fenêtre

2 (= *take care*) faire attention, prendre garde ◆ **I told you to ~ out!** je t'avais bien dit de faire attention ! ◆ **~ out!** attention !

VT SEP (*Brit*) (= *look for*) chercher ; (= *find*) trouver ◆ **I'll ~ out some old magazines** je vais essayer de trouver *or* vais chercher des vieux magazines ◆ **I've ~ed out the minutes of the meeting** j'ai trouvé le procès-verbal de la réunion

► **look out for** VT FUS 1 (= *look for*) chercher, être à la recherche de ; (= *watch out for*) [+ *sth good*] essayer de repérer ; [+ *danger*] se méfier de, faire attention à ◆ **~ out for special deals** soyez à l'affût des bonnes affaires ◆ **~ out for ice on the road** méfiez-vous du *or* faites attention au verglas

2 (* = *look after*) [+ *person*] s'occuper de ◆ **to ~ out for oneself** se débrouiller tout seul ◆ **we ~ out for each other** on se tient les coudes

► **look over** VT SEP [+ *document, list*] parcourir ; [+ *goods, produce*] inspecter ; [+ *town, building*] visiter ; [+ *person*] (*quickly*) jeter un coup d'œil à ; (*slowly*) regarder de la tête aux pieds, toiser

► **look round**

VI 1 (= *glance about*) regarder (autour de soi) ◆ **we're just ~ing round** (*in shop*) on regarde

2 (= *search*) chercher ◆ **I ~ed round for you after the concert** je vous ai cherché après le concert ◆ **I'm ~ing round for an assistant** je cherche un assistant, je suis à la recherche d'un assistant

3 (= *look back*) se retourner ◆ **I ~ed round to see where he was** je me suis retourné pour voir où il était ◆ **don't ~ round!** ne vous retournez pas !

VT FUS [+ *town, factory*] visiter, faire le tour de

► **look through** VT FUS 1 (= *scan*) [+ *mail*] regarder ; (*thoroughly*) [+ *papers, book*] examiner ; (*briefly*) [+ *papers*] parcourir ; [+ *book*] parcourir, feuilleter

2 (= *revise*) [+ *lesson*] réviser, repasser ; (= *reread*) [+ *notes*] relire

3 (= *ignore*) ◆ **he just looked right through me** * il a fait comme s'il ne me voyait pas

► **look to** VT FUS 1 (= *seek help from*) se tourner vers ◆ **many sufferers ~ to alternative therapies** de nombreux malades se tournent vers les médecines parallèles ◆ **I ~ to you for help** je compte sur votre aide

2 (= *think of*) penser à ◆ **to ~ to the future** penser à l'avenir

3 (= *seek to*) chercher à ◆ **they are ~ing to make a profit** ils cherchent à réaliser un bénéfice

► **look up**

VI 1 (= *glance upwards*) regarder en haut ; (*from reading etc*) lever les yeux

2 (* = *improve*) [*prospects, weather*] s'améliorer ; [*business*] reprendre ◆ **things are ~ing up** ça va mieux, ça s'améliore ◆ **oil shares are ~ing up** les actions pétrolières remontent *or* sont en hausse

VT SEP 1 (* = *seek out*) [+ *person*] passer voir ◆ **~ me up the next time you are in London** venez *or* passez me voir la prochaine fois que vous serez à Londres

2 (*in reference book*) [+ *name, word*] chercher ◆ **to ~ up a word in the dictionary** chercher un mot dans le dictionnaire ◆ **you'll have to ~ that one up** [+ *word*] il va falloir que tu cherches *subj* dans le dictionnaire

VT FUS [+ *reference book*] consulter, chercher dans *or* vérifier dans

► **look upon** VT FUS ⇒ **look on vt fus**

► **look up to** VT FUS (= *admire*) admirer

looker /ˈlʊkəʳ/ N * ◆ **she's a (real) ~** c'est une belle plante *, elle est vraiment canon * ◆ **he's a (real) ~** c'est un beau mec * COMP **looker-on** N badaud(e) *m(f)*

-looking /ˈlʊkɪŋ/ ADJ (*in compounds*) ◆ **ugly-looking** laid (d'aspect) ◆ **sinister-looking** à l'air sinistre ; → **good**

look-out /ˈlʊkaʊt/ N 1 (= *observation*) surveillance *f*, guet *m* ◆ **to keep a ~, to be on the ~** faire le guet, guetter ◆ **to keep a** *or* **be on the ~ for sb/sth** guetter qn/qch ◆ **to be on the ~ for bargains** être à l'affût des bonnes affaires ◆ **to be on the ~ for danger** être sur ses gardes ◆ **to be on ~ (duty)** (*Mil*) être au guet ; (*Naut*) être en vigie ; → **sharp**

2 (= *observer*) (*gen*) guetteur *m* ; (*Mil*) homme *m* de guet, guetteur *m* ; (*Naut*) homme *m* de veille *or* de vigie, vigie *f*

3 (= *observation post*) (*gen, Mil*) poste *m* de guet ; (*Naut*) vigie *f*

4 (*esp Brit: * = outlook*) perspective *f* ◆ **it's a poor ~ for cotton** les perspectives pour le coton ne sont pas brillantes ◆ **it's a grim ~ for people like us** la situation *or* ça s'annonce mal pour les gens comme nous ◆ **that's your ~!** cela vous regarde !, c'est votre affaire !

COMP [*tower*] d'observation **look-out post** N (*Mil*) poste *m* de guet *or* d'observation

loom¹ /luːm/ VI (also **loom up** = *appear*) [*building, mountain*] apparaître indistinctement, se dessiner ; [*figure, ship*] surgir ; (*fig*) [*danger, crisis*] menacer ; [*event*] être imminent ◆ **the ship**

~ed (up) out of the mist le navire a surgi de *or* dans la brume ◆ **the dark mountains ~ed (up) in front of us** les sombres montagnes sont apparues *or* se sont dressées menaçantes devant nous ◆ **the possibility of defeat ~ed (up) before him** la possibilité de la défaite s'est présentée à son esprit ◆ **a recession is ~ing in the United States** une récession menace sérieusement les États-Unis ◆ **the threat of war ~s ahead** la guerre menace d'éclater ◆ **the threat of an epidemic ~ed large in their minds** la menace d'une épidémie était au premier plan de leurs préoccupations ◆ **the exams are ~ing large** les examens sont dangereusement proches

loom² /luːm/ **N** *(for weaving)* métier *m* à tisser

loon /luːn/ **N** 1 *(* = fool)* imbécile *m*, idiot *m* 2 *(US = bird)* plongeon *m* arctique, huard *m or* huart *m*

loon pants /ˈluːnpænts/, **loons** /luːnz/ **NPL** *pantalon moulant à taille basse et pattes d'éléphant*

loony⁑ /ˈluːnɪ/ **N** timbré(e)* *m(f)*, cinglé(e)* *m(f)* **ADJ** timbré*, cinglé*

COMP **loony bin** **N** maison *f* de fous, asile *m* ◆ **in the ~ bin** chez les fous

loony left * *(Brit Pol: pej)* **N** ◆ **the ~ left** *l'aile extrémiste du parti travailliste* **ADJ** *de l'aile extrémiste du parti travailliste*

loop /luːp/ **N** 1 *(in string, ribbon, writing)* boucle *f* ; *(in river)* méandre *m*, boucle *f* ◆ **the string has a ~ in it** la ficelle fait une boucle ◆ **to put a ~ in sth** faire une boucle à qch ◆ **to knock** *or* **throw sb for a ~** * *(esp US)* sidérer* qn ◆ **to be in/out of the ~** * être/ne pas être au courant ◆ **keep me in the ~** * tiens-moi au courant

2 *(Elec)* circuit *m* fermé ; *(Comput)* boucle *f* ; *(Rail:* also **loop line***)* voie *f* d'évitement ; *(by motorway etc)* bretelle *f*

3 *(Med)* **the ~** *(= contraceptive)* le stérilet

4 *(= curtain fastener)* embrasse *f*

VT *[+ string etc]* faire une boucle à, boucler ◆ **he ~ed the rope round the post** il a passé la corde autour du poteau ◆ **to ~ the loop** *(in plane)* faire un looping, boucler la boucle

VI former une boucle

► **loop back** **VI** *[road, river]* former une boucle ; *(Comput)* se reboucler

VT SEP (also **loop up**) *[+ curtain]* retenir *or* relever avec une embrasse

loophole /ˈluːphəʊl/ **N** *(in law, regulations)* faille *f* , lacune *f* ; *(Archit)* meurtrière *f* ◆ **a ~ in the law** une faille *or* une lacune de la législation, un vide juridique ◆ **they're going to change the rules and close the ~** ils vont changer le règlement et combler la faille *or* lacune ◆ **we must try to find a ~** *(fig)* il faut que nous trouvions une échappatoire *or* une porte de sortie*

loopy⁑ /ˈluːpɪ/ **ADJ** cinglé* ◆ **to go ~** perdre les pédales*

loose /luːs/ **ADJ** 1 *(= not tied up) [animal] (= free)* en liberté ; *(= escaped)* échappé ; *(= freed)* lâché ; *[hair]* dénoué, flottant ; *(= not attached) [page from book]* détaché ◆ **~ chippings** *(on roadway)* gravillons *mpl* ◆ **write it on a ~ sheet of paper** écrivez-le sur une feuille volante ; *(to pupil)* écrivez-le sur une (feuille de) copie ◆ **the ~ end of a rope** le bout libre d'une corde ◆ **to let** *or* **set** *or* **turn an animal ~** libérer *or* lâcher un animal ◆ **to tear (o.s.) ~** se dégager ◆ **to tear sth ~** détacher qch (en déchirant)

◆ **to be coming** *or* **getting** *or* **working loose** *[knot]* se desserrer, se défaire ; *[screw]* se desserrer, avoir du jeu ; *[stone, brick]* branler ; *[tooth]* branler, bouger ; *[page]* se détacher ; *[hair]* se dénouer, se défaire

◆ **to cut loose** *(= liberate oneself)* se laisser aller ; *(Naut)* couper les amarres ◆ **you need to cut ~ and just relax** il faut que tu te laisses aller et que tu te détendes un peu ◆ **she feels she has cut ~ from Japanese culture** elle sent qu'elle a pris de la distance par rapport à la culture japonaise ◆ **he cut ~ (from his family)** il a coupé les ponts (avec sa famille)

◆ **to get loose** *[animal]* s'échapper

◆ **to have come loose** *[page]* s'être détaché ; *[hair]* s'être dénoué ; *[knot]* s'être défait ; *[screw]* s'être desserré ; *[stone, brick]* branler ; *[tooth]* branler, bouger

◆ **to let + loose on** ◆ **to let the dogs ~ on sb** lâcher les chiens sur qn ◆ **we can't let him ~ on that class** on ne peut pas le lâcher dans cette classe ; → **break, hell**

2 *(= not firmly in place) [screw]* desserré, qui a du jeu ; *[stone, brick]* branlant ; *[tooth]* qui branle, qui bouge ; *[knot, shoelace]* qui se défait, desserré ◆ **one of your buttons is very ~** l'un de tes boutons va tomber *or* se découd ◆ **a ~ connection** *(Elec)* un mauvais contact ◆ **the reins hung ~** les rênes n'étaient pas tenues *or* tendues, les rênes étaient sur le cou ◆ **hang** *or* **stay ~!**⁑ relax !* ; → **screw**

3 *(= not pre-packed) [biscuits, carrots etc]* en vrac ; *[butter, cheese]* à la coupe ◆ **the potatoes were ~ in the bottom of the basket** les pommes de terre étaient à même au fond du panier ◆ **just put them ~ into the basket** mettez-les à même *or* tels quels dans le panier

4 *(= not tight) [skin]* flasque, mou (molle *f*) ; *[coat, dress] (= not close-fitting)* ample, vague ; *(= not tight enough)* lâche, large ; *[collar]* lâche ◆ **these trousers are too ~ round the waist** ce pantalon est trop large *or* lâche à la taille ◆ **~ clothes are better for summer wear** l'été il vaut mieux porter des vêtements amples *or* pas trop ajustés ◆ **the rope round the dog's neck was quite ~** la corde passée au cou du chien était toute lâche ◆ **a ~ weave** un tissu lâche ; see also **comp** ◆ **he's got a ~ tongue** il ne sait pas tenir sa langue ◆ **his bowels are ~** ses intestins sont relâchés ; → **play**

5 *(= not strict) [discipline]* relâché ; *[organization]* peu structuré ; *[translation]* approximatif, assez libre ; *[style]* lâche, relâché ; *(= vague) [reasoning, thinking]* imprécis ; *[association, link]* vague ◆ **a ~ interpretation of the rules** une interprétation peu rigoureuse du règlement ◆ **a ~ coalition of left-wing forces** une coalition informelle de mouvements de gauche ◆ **there is a ~ connection between the two theories** il y a un vague lien entre les deux théories

6 *(pej) (= dissolute) [woman]* facile, de mœurs légères ; *[morals]* relâché, douteux ◆ **~ living** vie *f* dissolue *or* de débauche ◆ **~ talk** *(= careless)* propos *mpl* inconsidérés

7 *(= available) [funds]* disponible, liquide

8 *(= not compact) [soil]* meuble ◆ **~ scrum** *(Rugby)* mêlée *f* ouverte

N *(of prisoner)* ◆ **on the ~** * en cavale ◆ **there was a crowd of kids on the ~ * in the town** il y avait une bande de jeunes qui traînait dans les rues sans trop savoir quoi faire ◆ **a gang of hooligans on the ~** * une bande de voyous déchaînés ◆ **in the ~** *(Rugby)* dans la mêlée ouverte

VT 1 *(= undo)* défaire ; *(= untie)* délier, dénouer ; *[+ screw etc]* desserrer ; *(= free) [+ animal]* lâcher ; *[+ prisoner]* relâcher, mettre en liberté ◆ **to ~ a boat (from its moorings)** démarrer une embarcation, larguer les amarres ◆ **they ~d the dogs on him** ils ont lâché les chiens après *or* sur lui

2 (also **loose off**) *[+ gun]* décharger *(on or at sb* sur qn) ; *[+ arrow]* tirer *(on or at sb* sur qn) ; *[+ violence etc]* déclencher *(on contre)* ◆ **to ~ (off) a volley of abuse at sb** *(fig)* déverser un torrent *or* lâcher une bordée d'injures sur qn

COMP **loose box** **N** *(Brit: for horses)* box *m*

loose cannon * **N** franc-tireur *m*

loose change **N** petite *or* menue monnaie *f*

loose covers **NPL** *(Brit: of furniture)* housses *fpl*

loose end **N** détail *m* inexpliqué ◆ **there are some ~ ends in the plot** il y a des détails inexpliqués dans le scénario ◆ **to tie up (the) ~ ends** *(fig)* régler les détails qui restent ◆ **to be at a ~ end** ne pas trop savoir quoi faire, ne pas savoir quoi faire de sa peau*

loose-fitting **ADJ** ample, vague

loose-leaf **ADJ** à feuilles volantes, à feuilles *or* feuillets mobiles

loose-leaf binder **N** classeur *m* (à feuilles mobiles)

loose-leafed **ADJ** ⇒ **loose-leaf**

loose-limbed **ADJ** agile

loose-weave **ADJ** *[material]* lâche ; *[curtains]* en tissu lâche

► **loose off** **VI** *(= shoot)* tirer *(at sb* sur qn)

VT SEP ⇒ **loose vt 2**

loosely /ˈluːslɪ/ **ADV** 1 *(= not tightly) [hold]* sans serrer ; *[tie]* lâchement ◆ **stand with your arms hanging ~ by your sides** tenez-vous debout, les bras relâchés le long du corps ◆ **a ~ woven mesh** des mailles lâches 2 *(= imprecisely, not strictly) [translated]* librement ; *[connected]* vaguement ◆ **~ defined** mal défini ◆ **~ organized** peu structuré ◆ **~ knit** *[association, grouping]* peu structuré ◆ **a character ~ based on Janis Joplin** un personnage librement inspiré de Janis Joplin ◆ **~ speaking** grosso modo ◆ **that word is ~ used to mean ...** on emploie couramment ce mot pour dire ... **COMP** **loosely-knit** **ADJ** aux mailles lâches

loosen /ˈluːsn/ **VT** 1 *(= slacken) [+ screw, belt, knot]* desserrer ; *[+ rope]* détendre, relâcher ; *(= untie) [+ knot, shoelace]* défaire ; *(fig) [+ emotional ties]* distendre ; *[+ laws, restrictions]* assouplir ◆ **first ~ the part then remove it gently** il faut d'abord dégager la pièce puis l'enlever doucement ◆ **to ~ one's grip (on sth)** *(lit)* desserrer sa prise *or* son étreinte (sur qch) ; *(fig = be less strict with)* perdre son emprise (sur qch) ◆ **to ~ sb's tongue** délier la langue à qn

2 *(Agr) [+ soil]* rendre meuble, ameublir ◆ **to ~ the bowels** *(Med)* relâcher les intestins

VI *[fastening]* se défaire ; *[screw]* se desserrer, jouer ; *[knot] (= slacken)* se desserrer ; *(= come undone)* se défaire ; *[rope]* se détendre

► **loosen up** **VI** 1 *(= limber up)* faire des exercices d'assouplissement ; *(before race etc)* s'échauffer

2 *(= become less shy)* se dégeler, perdre sa timidité

3 *(= become less strict with)* **to ~ up on sb** * se montrer plus coulant* *or* moins strict envers qn

VT SEP ◆ **to loosen up one's muscles** faire des exercices d'assouplissement ; *(before race etc)* s'échauffer

looseness /ˈluːsnɪs/ **N** 1 *(= immorality) [of behaviour]* immoralité *f* ; *[of morals]* relâchement *m* 2 *[of translation]* imprécision *f* ; *[of style]* manque *m* de rigueur *or* de précision 3 *[of soil]* ameublissement *m* ◆ **~ of the bowels** *(Med)* relâchement *m* des intestins *or* intestinal

loot /luːt/ **N** 1 *(= plunder)* butin *m* 2 ⁑ *(fig) (= prizes, gifts etc)* butin *m* ; *(= money)* pognon⁑ *m*, fric⁑ *m* **VT** *[+ town]* piller, mettre à sac ; *[+ shop, goods]* piller **VI** ◆ **to go ~ing** se livrer au pillage

looter /ˈluːtəʳ/ **N** pillard *m*

looting /ˈluːtɪŋ/ **N** pillage *m*

lop /lɒp/ **VT** *[+ tree]* tailler ; *[+ branch]* couper

► **lop off** **VT SEP** *[+ branch, piece]* couper ; *[+ head]* trancher

lope /ləʊp/ **VI** courir en bondissant ◆ **to ~ along/in/out** *etc* avancer/entrer/sortir *etc* en bondissant

lop-eared /ˈlɒp,ɪəd/ **ADJ** aux oreilles pendantes

lopsided /ˈlɒpˈsaɪdɪd/ **ADJ** 1 *(= not straight)* de travers, de guingois* ; *[smile]* de travers ;

(= asymmetric) disproportionné 2 (fig = unequal) [contest etc] inégal

loquacious /lǝ'kweɪʃǝs/ ADJ loquace, bavard

loquacity /lǝ'kwæsɪtɪ/ N loquacité f, volubilité f

lord /lɔːd/ N 1 seigneur m ◆ **~ of the manor** châtelain m ◆ **~ and master** (hum) seigneur m et maître m (hum) ◆ **Lord (John) Russel** (Brit) lord (John) Russel ◆ **the (House of) Lords** la Chambre des lords ◆ **my Lord Bishop of Tooting** (Monseigneur) l'évêque de Tooting ◆ **my Lord** Monsieur le baron (or comte etc) ; (to judge) Monsieur le Juge ; (to bishop) Monseigneur, Excellence ; → **law, live¹, sea**

2 (Rel) **the Lord** le Seigneur ◆ **Our Lord** Notre Seigneur ◆ **the Lord Jesus** le Seigneur Jésus ◆ **the Lord's supper** l'Eucharistie f, la sainte Cène ◆ **the Lord's prayer** le Notre-Père ◆ **the Lord's day** le jour du Seigneur

3 (in exclamations) **good Lord!*** mon Dieu !, bon sang !* ◆ **oh Lord!*** Seigneur !, zut !* ◆ **Lord knows*** **(what/who etc)** Dieu sait (quoi/qui etc)

VT * ◆ **to ~ it** vivre en grand seigneur, mener la grande vie ◆ **to ~ it over sb** traiter qn avec arrogance or de haut

COMP **Lord Advocate** N (Scot) ≃ procureur m de la République

Lord Chamberlain N (Brit) grand chambellan m

Lord Chancellor N ⇒ **Lord High Chancellor**

Lord Chief Justice (of England) N président m de la Haute Cour de justice

Lord High Chancellor N grand chancelier m d'Angleterre

Lord High Commissioner N représentant de la Couronne à l'Assemblée générale de l'église d'Écosse

Lord Justice of Appeal N juge m à la cour d'appel

Lord Lieutenant N représentant de la Couronne dans un comté

Lord Mayor N lord-maire m (titre du maire des principales villes anglaises et galloises) ; voir aussi **mayor**

Lord of Appeal (in Ordinary) N juge m de la Cour de cassation (siégeant à la Chambre des lords)

Lord President of the Council N président m du Conseil privé de la reine

Lord Privy Seal N lord m du Sceau privé

Lord Provost N titre du maire des principales villes écossaises

lords-and-ladies N (= plant) pied-de-veau m

Lord spiritual N (Brit) membre ecclésiastique de la Chambre des lords

Lord temporal N (Brit) membre laïque de la Chambre des lords

lordliness /'lɔːdlɪnɪs/ N (frm) 1 (pej = haughtiness) morgue f (liter) 2 (= dignity) [of person, bearing] dignité f ; (= impressiveness) [of mansion, palace] magnificence f

lordly /'lɔːdlɪ/ ADJ (frm) 1 (pej = haughty) [person, expression, sneer] hautain, arrogant ; [behaviour, indifference] souverain 2 (= dignified) [person] noble, digne ; [bearing] noble, majestueux 3 (= impressive) [mansion, palace] seigneurial

lordship /'lɔːdʃɪp/ N (= rights, property) seigneurie f ; (= power) autorité f (over sur) ◆ **your Lordship** Monsieur le comte (or le baron etc) ; (to judge) Monsieur le Juge ; (to bishop) Monseigneur, Excellence

lore /lɔːʳ/ N (NonC) 1 (= traditions) tradition(s) f(pl), coutumes fpl, usages mpl ; → **folklore** 2 (= knowledge: gen in compounds) ◆ **his bird/wood ~** sa (grande) connaissance des oiseaux/de la vie dans les forêts

Lorenzo /lǝ'renzǝʊ/ N ◆ **~ the Magnificent** Laurent m le Magnifique

lorgnette /lɔː'njet/ N (= eyeglasses) face-à-main m ; (= opera glasses) lorgnette f, jumelles fpl de spectacle

Lorraine /lɒ'reɪn/ N Lorraine f ◆ **Cross of ~** croix f de Lorraine

lorry /'lɒrɪ/ (Brit) N camion m, poids m lourd ◆ **to transport sth by ~** transporter qch par camion, camionner qch ◆ **it fell off the back of a ~*** (Brit) ça sort pas d'un magasin*, c'est de la fauche* ; → **articulate**

COMP **lorry driver** N camionneur m, conducteur m de poids lourd ; (long-distance) routier m

lorry load N chargement m (de camion)

Los Angeles /lɒs'ændʒɪˌliːz/ N Los Angeles

lose /luːz/ (pret, ptp **lost**) VT 1 (= mislay, fail to find) [+ object] perdre ◆ **I lost him in the crowd** je l'ai perdu dans la foule ◆ **you've lost me there*** je ne vous suis plus, je n'y suis plus

♦ **to get lost** ◆ **he got lost in the wood** il s'est perdu or égaré dans la forêt ◆ **some of our boxes got lost in the move** nous avons perdu quelques cartons pendant le déménagement ◆ **to get lost in the post** être égaré par la poste ◆ **get lost!**‡ (= go away) barre-toi !‡ ; (= forget it) va te faire voir !‡

2 (= not win) [+ game, match, money, bet] perdre ◆ **how much did you ~?** (in gambling etc) combien avez-vous perdu ?

3 (= be deprived of) [+ person, money, possessions, job, one's sight, limb, enthusiasm] perdre ◆ **he lost $1,000 on that deal** il a perdu 1 000 dollars dans cette affaire ◆ **7,000 jobs lost** 7 000 suppressions fpl d'emploi ◆ **they lost 100 planes in one battle** ils ont perdu 100 avions en une seule bataille ◆ **he's lost his licence** [driver] on lui a retiré or il s'est fait retirer son permis de conduire ◆ **I lost my father when I was ten** j'ai perdu mon père à l'âge de dix ans ◆ **to ~ a patient** [doctor] perdre un malade ◆ **100 men were lost** 100 hommes ont perdu la vie, 100 hommes ont péri (liter) ◆ **to be lost at sea** [person] être perdu en mer, périr (liter) en mer ◆ **the ship was lost with all hands** le navire a disparu or a sombré corps et biens ◆ **to ~ one's life** perdre la vie ◆ **20 lives were lost in the explosion** 20 personnes ont trouvé la mort or ont péri (liter) dans l'explosion ◆ **to ~ one's breath** s'essouffler ◆ **to have lost one's breath** être hors d'haleine, être à bout de souffle ◆ **he didn't ~ any sleep over it** il n'en a pas perdu le sommeil pour autant, ça ne l'a pas empêché de dormir ◆ **don't ~ any sleep over it!** ne vous en faites pas !, dormez sur vos deux oreilles ! ◆ **to ~ one's voice** (because of a cold) avoir une extinction de voix ◆ **to have lost one's voice** avoir une extinction de voix, être aphone ◆ **she's lost her figure** elle a perdu sa ligne ◆ **she's losing her looks** elle n'est plus aussi belle qu'autrefois, sa beauté se fane ◆ **to ~ interest in sth** se désintéresser de qch ◆ **to ~ the use of an arm** perdre l'usage d'un bras ◆ **the poem ~s a lot in translation** la traduction n'a pas su rendre les subtilités de ce poème ◆ **you've got nothing to ~ (by it)** tu n'as rien à perdre ◆ **you've got nothing to ~ by helping him** tu n'as rien à perdre à l'aider ◆ **he's lost it*** (= doesn't know what he's doing) il déraille *; (= has lost his touch) il n'est plus à la hauteur; see also **lost** ; → **balance, consciousness, cool, heart**

4 (= miss, waste) [+ opportunity] manquer, perdre ◆ **what he said was lost in the applause** ses paroles se sont perdues dans les applaudissements ◆ **this was not lost on him** cela ne lui a pas échappé ◆ **there's no time to ~** or **to be lost** il n'y a pas de temps à perdre ◆ **there's not a minute to ~** il n'y a pas une minute à perdre

5 [watch, clock] ◆ **to ~ ten minutes a day** retarder de dix minutes par jour

6 (= get rid of) [+ unwanted object] renoncer à, se débarrasser de ; (= shake off) [+ competitors, pursuers] distancer, semer ◆ **to ~ weight** perdre du poids, maigrir ◆ **I lost 2 kilos** j'ai maigri de or j'ai perdu 2 kilos ◆ **they had to ~ 100 workers** ils ont dû licencier 100 employés ◆ **he managed to ~ the detective who was following him** il a réussi à semer le détective qui le suivait ◆ **try to ~ him* before you come to see us** essaie de le semer avant de venir nous voir

7 (= cause to lose) faire perdre, coûter ◆ **that will ~ you your job** cela va vous faire perdre or vous coûter votre place ◆ **that lost us the war/the match** cela nous a fait perdre la guerre/le match

VI 1 [player, team] perdre ◆ **they lost 6-1** (Ftbl etc) ils ont perdu or ils se sont fait battre 6 à 1 ◆ **they lost to the new team** ils se sont fait battre par la nouvelle équipe ◆ **our team is losing today** notre équipe est en train de perdre aujourd'hui

2 (fig) **he lost on the deal** il a été perdant dans l'affaire ◆ **you can't ~!*** tu n'as rien à perdre (mais tout à gagner) ◆ **it ~s in translation** cela perd à la traduction ◆ **the story did not ~ in the telling** l'histoire n'a rien perdu à être racontée

3 [watch, clock] retarder

► **lose out** VI être perdant ◆ **to ~ out on a deal** être perdant dans une affaire ◆ **he lost out on it** il y a été perdant

loser /'luːzǝʳ/ N 1 (Sport etc) perdant(e) m(f) ◆ **good/bad ~** bon/mauvais joueur m, bonne/mauvaise joueuse f ◆ **to come off the ~** être perdant ◆ **he is the ~ by it** il y perd 2 (* pej) loser* or looser* m ◆ **he's a born ~** c'est un loser* or looser* ; → **back**

losing /'luːzɪŋ/ ADJ [team, party, candidate] perdant ◆ **(to fight) a ~ battle** (fig) (livrer) une bataille perdue d'avance ◆ **to be on the ~ side** être du côté des perdants ◆ **(to be on) a ~ streak*** (être dans) une période de déveine* ◆ **to be on a ~ wicket*** (Brit fig) ne pas être en veine* NPL **losings** (= money losses) pertes fpl

loss /lɒs/ LANGUAGE IN USE 24.4

N 1 (gen) perte f ◆ **a ~ of confidence/control/interest** une perte de confiance/de contrôle/d'intérêt ◆ **the ~ of a limb/one's eyesight** la perte d'un membre/de la vue ◆ **our sadness at the ~ of a loved one** notre tristesse après la perte d'un être aimé ◆ **after the ~ of his wife, he ...** après avoir perdu sa femme, il ... ◆ **it was a comfort to her in her great ~** c'était un réconfort pour elle dans son grand malheur or sa grande épreuve ◆ **his death was a great ~ to the company** sa mort a été or a représenté une grande perte pour la société ◆ **he's no great ~*** ce n'est pas une grande or une grosse perte ◆ **to feel a sense of ~** éprouver un sentiment de vide ◆ **~es amounting to $2 million** des pertes qui s'élèvent (or s'élevaient etc) à 2 millions de dollars ◆ **to suffer heavy ~es** subir des pertes importantes or de lourdes pertes ◆ **enemy ~es were high** l'ennemi avait subi de lourdes pertes ◆ **Conservative ~es in the North** (in election) les sièges perdus par les conservateurs dans le nord ◆ **to sell at a ~** [salesman] vendre à perte ; [goods] se vendre à perte ◆ **to cut one's ~es** faire la part du feu, sauver les meubles*

♦ **to be at a loss** être perplexe or embarrassé ◆ **to be at a ~ to explain sth** être incapable d'expliquer qch, être embarrassé pour expliquer qch ◆ **we are at a ~ to know why he did it** nous ne savons absolument pas pourquoi il l'a fait ◆ **to be at a ~ for words** chercher or ne pas trouver ses mots ◆ **he's never at a ~ for words** il a toujours quelque chose à dire

2 **~ of appetite, appetite ~** perte f d'appétit ◆ **~ of blood, blood ~** perte f de sang ; (more serious) hémorragie f ◆ **hair ~** perte f de cheveux ◆ **weight ~, ~ of weight** perte f de poids ◆ **there was great ~ of life** il y a eu beaucoup de victimes or de nombreuses victimes ◆ **the coup succeeded without ~ of life** le coup (d'État) a réussi sans faire de victimes ◆ **~ of heat, heat ~** perte f de chaleur ◆ **~ of earnings** or **income** perte f de revenus ◆ **job ~es** suppressions fpl d'emploi ◆ **the factory closed**

with the ~ of 300 jobs l'usine a fermé et 300 emplois ont été supprimés ◆ **without ~ of time** sans perte *or* sans perdre de temps ◆ **to suffer a ~ of face** perdre la face ; → **dead, profit**

COMP **loss adjuster** N *(Brit Insurance)* expert *m* en sinistres

loss leader N *(= product)* article *m* pilote *(vendu à perte pour attirer les clients)*

loss maker N *(= product)* article *m* vendu à perte ; *(= firm)* entreprise *f* en déficit chronique

loss-making ADJ *[product]* vendu à perte ; *[firm]* déficitaire

loss ratio N *(Insurance)* ratio *m* sinistres-pertes

lost /lɒst/ VB pt, ptp of **lose**

ADJ [1] *(= mislaid, not found)* perdu, égaré ◆ **several ~ children were reported** on a signalé plusieurs cas d'enfants qui s'étaient perdus *or* égarés ◆ **the ~ sheep** *(Rel)* la brebis égarée

[2] *(= bewildered, uncomprehending)* perdu ◆ **it was too difficult for me, I was ~** c'était trop compliqué pour moi, j'étais perdu ◆ **after his death I felt ~** après sa mort j'étais complètement perdu *or* désorienté ◆ **he had a ~ look in his eyes** *or* **a ~ expression on his face** il avait l'air complètement perdu *or* désorienté ◆ **to be ~ for words** chercher *or* ne pas trouver ses mots

[3] *(= gone, disappeared, departed) [person, job, limb, enthusiasm, interest]* perdu ◆ **to give sb/sth up for ~** considérer qn/qch comme perdu ◆ **the ~ generation** la génération perdue ◆ **songs that reminded him of his ~ youth** des chansons qui lui rappelaient sa jeunesse passée ◆ **a mother mourning for her ~ child** une mère pleurant son enfant (disparu) ◆ **he was ~ to British science forever** ses dons ont été perdus à jamais pour la science britannique ◆ **to regain one's ~ confidence** retrouver confiance en soi

[4] *(= beyond hope)* ◆ **~ cause** cause *f* perdue ◆ **a ~ soul** *(Rel fig)* une âme en peine ◆ **all is not ~!** tout n'est pas perdu ! ◆ **he is ~ to all finer feelings** tous les sentiments délicats le dépassent

[5] *(= wasted) [+ opportunity]* manqué, perdu ◆ **my advice was ~ on him** il n'a pas écouté mes conseils, mes conseils ont été en pure perte ◆ **modern music is ~ on me** *(= don't understand it)* je ne comprends rien à la musique moderne ; *(= don't enjoy it)* la musique moderne me laisse froid ◆ **the remark was ~ on him** il n'a pas compris la remarque ◆ **to make up for ~ time** rattraper le temps perdu

[6] *(= absorbed)* perdu, plongé *(in* dans) absorbé *(in* par) ◆ **to be ~ in one's reading** être plongé dans sa lecture, être absorbé par sa lecture ◆ **he was ~ in thought** il était perdu dans *or* absorbé par ses pensées ◆ **she is ~ to the world** * elle est ailleurs, plus rien n'existe pour elle

COMP **lost and found** N *(US)* ⇒ **lost property**

lost-and-found columns NPL *(Press)* (page *f* des) objets *mpl* perdus et trouvés

lost-and-found department N *(US)* ⇒ **lost property office**

lost property N objets *mpl* trouvés

lost property office N (bureau *m* des) objets *mpl* trouvés

Lot /lɒt/ N *(Bible)* Lot(h) *m*

lot[1] /lɒt/ N ◆ **a ~** *(= a great deal)* beaucoup ◆ **I'd give a ~ to know ...** je donnerais cher pour savoir ... ◆ **there wasn't a ~ we could do/say** nous ne pouvions pas faire/dire grand-chose ◆ **a ~ of** beaucoup de ◆ **a ~ of time/money** beaucoup de temps/d'argent ◆ **there were a ~ of people** il y avait beaucoup de monde ◆ **a ~ of people think that ...** beaucoup de gens pensent que ... ◆ **quite a ~ of** *[of people, cars]* un assez grand nombre de, pas mal de ; *[of honey, cream]* une assez grande quantité de, pas mal de ◆ **such a ~ of ...** tellement de ..., tant de ... ◆ **what a ~!** quelle quantité ! ◆ **what a ~ of people!** que de monde *or* de gens ! ◆ **what a ~ of time you take to get dressed!** tu en mets du temps à t'habiller ! ◆ **we don't go out a ~** nous ne sortons pas beaucoup *or* pas souvent ◆ **we see a ~ of her** nous la voyons souvent *or* beaucoup ◆ **things have changed quite a ~** les choses ont beaucoup *or* pas mal changé ◆ **he cries such a ~** il pleure tellement ◆ **he's a ~ better** il va beaucoup *or* bien mieux ◆ **that's a ~ better** c'est beaucoup *or* bien mieux ◆ **a ~ you care!** * *(iro)* comme si ça te faisait quelque chose ! ◆ **thanks a ~!** * merci beaucoup ! ; *(iro)* merci (bien) ! *(iro)* ; → **awful, fat**

NPL **lots** * *(= plenty)* beaucoup, des tas * ◆ **~s of** beaucoup de, plein de * ◆ **~s and ~s (of)** *[of people, cars]* des tas * (de) ; *[of flowers]* des masses * (de) ; *[of butter, honey]* des tonnes * (de) ◆ **I've got ~s** j'en ai plein * ◆ **there's ~s (of it)** il y en a plein * ◆ **there were ~s (of them)** il y en avait plein * ◆ **~s better/bigger/easier** bien mieux/plus grand/plus facile

lot[2] /lɒt/ N [1] *(= destiny)* sort *m*, lot *m (liter)* ◆ **the hardships that are the ~ of the poor** la dure vie qui est lot des pauvres ◆ **it is the common ~** *(liter)* c'est le sort *or* le lot commun ◆ **she is content with her ~** elle est contente de son sort ◆ **a woman's/soldier's ~ is not always a happy one** ce n'est pas toujours facile d'être une femme/d'être soldat ◆ **her ~ (in life) had not been a happy one** elle n'avait pas eu une vie heureuse ◆ **it was not his ~ to make a fortune** il n'était pas destiné à faire fortune, le sort n'a pas voulu qu'il fasse fortune ◆ **it fell to my ~ to break the news to her** il m'incomba de *or* il me revint de lui annoncer la nouvelle ◆ **to improve one's ~** améliorer sa condition ◆ **to throw in** *or* **cast in one's ~ with sb** partager (volontairement) le sort de qn, unir sa destinée à celle de qn

[2] *(= random selection)* tirage *m* au sort, sort *m* ◆ **by ~** par tirage au sort ◆ **to draw** *or* **cast ~s** tirer au sort

[3] *(= batch) [of goods]* lot *m* ; *[of shares]* paquet *m* ◆ **there was only one ~ of recruits still to arrive** il ne manquait plus qu'un lot de recrues ◆ **~ no. 69 is an antique table** *(at auction)* le lot no. 69 est une table ancienne ◆ **are you coming, you ~?** * bon vous venez, vous autres ? * ◆ **us ~‡ should stick together** il faut qu'on se serre *subj* les coudes ◆ **he's a bad ~** * il ne vaut pas cher * ◆ **you rotten ~!** * vous êtes vaches !‡ ; → **job**

[4] *(noun phrase)* ◆ **the ~** * *(= everything)* (le) tout ; *(= everyone)* tous *mpl*, toutes *fpl* ◆ **that's the ~** c'est tout, tout y est ◆ **here are some apples, take the (whole) ~** voici des pommes, prends-les toutes ◆ **here's some money, just take the ~** voici de l'argent, prends tout ◆ **the (whole) ~ cost me £1** ça m'a coûté une livre en tout ◆ **big ones, little ones, the ~!** les grands, les petits, tous ! ◆ **the ~ of you** vous tous ◆ **they went off, the whole ~ of them** ils sont tous partis, ils sont partis tous tant qu'ils étaient

[5] *(esp US) (= plot of land)* lot *m* (de terrain), parcelle *f* ; *(= film studio)* enceinte *f* des studios ◆ **building ~** terrain *m* à bâtir ◆ **vacant** *or* **empty ~** terrain *m* disponible ; → **parking** ◆ **all over the ~** * *(US) (= everywhere)* partout ; *(= in confusion)* en désordre, bordélique *

loth /ləʊθ/ ADJ ⇒ **loath**

Lothario /ləʊ'θɑːrɪ,əʊ/ N *(liter or hum)* don Juan *m*

lotion /'ləʊʃən/ N lotion *f* ; → **hand**

lotos /'ləʊtəs/ N ⇒ **lotus**

lottery /'lɒtərɪ/ N *(lit, fig)* loterie *f* ◆ **~ ticket** billet *m* de loterie

lotto /'lɒtəʊ/ N loto *m*

lotus /'ləʊtəs/ N lotus *m*

COMP **lotus-eater** N *(Myth)* mangeur *m*, -euse *f* de lotus, lotophage *m*

lotus position N *(Yoga)* position *f* du lotus

louche /luːʃ/ ADJ *[person, place]* louche

loud /laʊd/ ADJ [1] *(= noisy) [voice]* fort, sonore ; *[laugh]* bruyant, sonore ; *[noise, cry]* grand ; *[music]* fort, bruyant ; *[thunder]* fracassant ; *[protests]* vigoureux ; *(pej) [behaviour]* tapageur ◆ **the orchestra is too ~** l'orchestre joue trop fort ◆ **the music is too ~** la musique est trop bruyante ◆ **in a ~ voice** d'une voix forte ◆ **... he said in a ~ whisper** ... chuchota-t-il bruyamment ◆ **this remark was greeted by ~ applause** un tonnerre d'applaudissements a accueilli cette remarque ◆ **to be ~ in one's support/condemnation of sth** soutenir/condamner qch avec force *or* virulence ◆ **~ pedal** *(Mus)* pédale *f* forte

[2] *(pej = gaudy) [colour]* voyant, criard ; *[clothes]* voyant, tapageur

ADV *[speak etc]* fort, haut ◆ **turn the radio up a little ~er** mets la radio un peu plus fort, augmente le volume (de la radio)

◆ **loud and clear** ◆ **I am reading** *or* **receiving you ~ and clear** je vous reçois cinq sur cinq ◆ **the president's message was received ~ and clear** le message du président a été reçu cinq sur cinq ◆ **we could hear it ~ and clear** nous l'entendions clairement

◆ **out loud** tout haut ◆ **to laugh out ~** rire tout haut

COMP **loud-mouth** * N *(pej)* grande gueule‡ *f*

loud-mouthed ADJ *(pej)* braillard, fort en gueule *

loudhailer /,laʊd'heɪləʳ/ N *(Brit)* porte-voix *m inv*, mégaphone *m*

loudly /'laʊdlɪ/ ADV [1] *(= noisily, in a loud voice) [say]* d'une voix forte ; *[talk, speak, shout]* fort ; *[laugh, clear one's throat, knock, applaud, quarrel, complain]* bruyamment ; *[proclaim]* haut et fort [2] *(fig = vociferously) [complain, protest]* vigoureusement [3] *(pej = garishly) [dress]* d'une façon voyante *or* tapageuse

loudness /'laʊdnɪs/ N *[of voice, tone, music, thunder]* force *f* ; *[of applause]* bruit *m* ; *[of protests]* vigueur *f*

loudspeaker /,laʊd'spiːkəʳ/ N *(for PA system, musical instruments)* haut-parleur *m*, enceinte *f* ; *[of stereo]* baffle *m*, enceinte *f*

lough /lɒx/ N *(Ir)* lac *m* ◆ **Lough Corrib** le lough Corrib

Louis /'luːɪ/ N Louis *m* ◆ **~ XIV** Louis XIV

louis /'luːɪ/ N *(pl inv)* louis *m* (d'or)

Louisiana /luː,iːzɪ'ænə/ N Louisiane *f* ◆ **in ~** en Louisiane

lounge /laʊndʒ/ N *(esp Brit) [of house, hotel]* salon *m* ; → **airport, arrival, departure, sun, television** VI *(= recline) (on bed, chair)* se prélasser ; *(pej) (= sprawl)* être allongé paresseusement ◆ **to ~ against a wall** s'appuyer paresseusement contre un mur

COMP **lounge bar** N *[of pub]* ≈ salon *m* ; *[of hotel]* ≈ bar *m*

lounge jacket N *(US)* veste *f* d'intérieur *or* d'appartement

lounge lizard † * N *(pej)* salonnard *m (pej)*

lounge suit N *(Brit)* complet(-veston) *m* ; *(US)* tenue *f* d'intérieur (de femme) ◆ **"lounge suit"** *(Brit: on invitation)* "tenue de ville"

► **lounge about, lounge around** VI paresser, flâner, flemmarder *

► **lounge back** VI ◆ **to lounge back in a chair** se prélasser dans un fauteuil

lounger /'laʊndʒəʳ/ N [1] *(= bed)* lit *m* de plage [2] *(pej = person)* fainéant(e) *m(f)*, flemmard(e) * *m(f)*

louse /laʊs/ N *(pl* **lice)** [1] *(= insect)* pou *m* [2] *(‡ pej = person)* salaud‡ *m*, (peau *f* de) vache‡ *f* *("louse" dans ce sens est utilisé au singulier seulement)*

► **louse up**‡ VT SEP *[+ deal, event]* bousiller *, foutre en l'air‡

lousy /ˈlaʊzɪ/ ADJ 1 (* = terrible) [car, day, weather] pourri* ; [idea, film, book, pay] nul, minable ; [food] infect, dégueulasse‡ ; [headache] fichu* before n ; [mood] massacrant ◆ **to be a ~ secretary/teacher** être nul en tant que secrétaire/professeur ◆ **she's a ~ driver** elle conduit comme un pied* ◆ **to be ~ in bed, to be a ~ lover** être nul au lit ◆ **to be ~ at sth** être nul en qch ◆ **she's been having a ~ time lately** la vie n'est pas drôle pour elle en ce moment ◆ **we had a ~ time on holiday** nos vacances ont été un vrai cauchemar ◆ **to be ~ to sb** être infect avec qn

2 (*: expressing displeasure) malheureux ◆ **10 ~ pounds!** 10 malheureuses livres ! ◆ **a ~ trick** une vacherie* ◆ **you can keep your ~ job, I don't want it!** votre boulot minable or votre boulot de merde‡, je n'en veux pas !

3 (= ill) ◆ **to feel ~*** être mal fichu*

4 (esp US: * = teeming) ◆ **this place is ~ with cops** c'est infesté de flics* ici ◆ **he is ~ with money** il est bourré de fric*

5 (= infested with lice) [person, blanket] pouilleux

lout /laʊt/ N rustre m, butor m ; → **litterbug**

loutish /ˈlaʊtɪʃ/ ADJ [manners] de rustre, de butor ◆ **his ~ behaviour** la grossièreté de sa conduite

louvre, louver (US) /ˈluːvəʳ/ N (in roof) lucarne f ; (on window) persienne f, jalousie f

louvred door, louvered door (US) /ˈluːvəddɔːʳ/ N porte f à claire-voie

lovable /ˈlʌvəbl/ ADJ [person] très sympathique ; [child, animal] adorable

love /lʌv/ LANGUAGE IN USE 21.2

N 1 (for person) amour m (of de, pour ; for pour) ; (for country, music, horses) amour m (of de ; for pour) ; (stronger) passion f (of de ; for pour) ◆ **her ~ for or of her children** son amour pour ses enfants, l'amour qu'elle porte (or portait etc) à ses enfants ◆ **her children's ~ (for her)** l'amour que lui portent (or portaient etc) ses enfants ◆ **he did it out of ~ for his children** il l'a fait par amour pour ses enfants ◆ **I feel no ~ for or towards him any longer** je n'éprouve plus d'amour pour lui ◆ **it was ~ at first sight** ça a été le coup de foudre ◆ **there's no ~ lost between them** ils ne peuvent pas se sentir* ◆ **I won't do it for ~ nor money** je ne le ferai pour rien au monde ◆ **it wasn't to be had for ~ nor money** c'était introuvable, on ne pouvait se le procurer à aucun prix ; → **brotherly, labour, lady**

◆ **for + love** ◆ **don't give me any money, I'm doing it for ~** ne me donnez pas d'argent, je le fais gratuitement or pour l'amour de l'art ◆ **to marry for ~** faire un mariage d'amour ◆ **for ~ of her son** par amour pour son fils ◆ **for the ~ of God** pour l'amour de Dieu ◆ **he studies history for the ~ of it** il étudie l'histoire pour son or le plaisir

◆ **to fall in love** tomber amoureux ◆ **we fell madly in ~** nous sommes tombés amoureux fous l'un de l'autre

◆ **to fall in love with sb** or **sth** tomber amoureux de qn or qch ◆ **I immediately fell in ~ with him** je suis tout de suite tombée amoureuse de lui ◆ **I fell in ~ with the cinema** je suis tombé amoureux du cinéma

◆ **to be in love** être amoureux ◆ **she's in ~** elle est amoureuse ◆ **we were madly in ~ for two years** nous nous sommes aimés passionnément pendant deux ans ◆ **they are in ~** ils s'aiment ◆ **my mother has always been in ~ with France** ma mère a toujours été amoureuse de la France

◆ **to make love** faire l'amour (with avec ; to à)

2 (in formulae: in letter) **(with) ~ (from) Jim** affectueusement, Jim ◆ **all my ~, Jim** bises, Jim ◆ **give her my ~** dis-lui bien des choses de ma part ; (stronger) embrasse-la pour moi ◆ **~ and kisses** bisous mpl, grosses bises fpl ◆ **he sends (you) his ~** il t'envoie ses amitiés ; (stronger) il t'embrasse

3 (= object of affections) [of thing, object] passion f ; [of person] amour m ◆ **the theatre was her great ~** le théâtre était sa grande passion ◆ **he's a little ~!*** il est adorable ! ◆ **his first ~ was football** sa première passion a été le football ◆ **he thought of his first ~** il pensait à son premier amour ◆ **he/she is the ~ of my life** c'est l'homme/la femme de ma vie ◆ **football is the ~ of her life** le football est sa grande passion

4 (Brit *: term of address: in shop etc, to man) monsieur ; (to woman) ma jolie* ; (to child) mon petit, ma petite ◆ **(my) ~** (to man) mon chéri ; (to woman) ma chérie

5 (Tennis etc) rien m, zéro m ◆ **~ 30** rien à 30, zéro 30

VT 1 (= feel affection for) [+ partner, spouse, child] aimer ; [+ relative, friend] aimer (beaucoup) ◆ **he didn't just like her, he ~d her** il ne l'aimait pas d'amitié, mais d'amour ◆ **they ~ each other** ils s'aiment ◆ **~ me, ~ my dog** (Prov) qui m'aime aime mon chien ◆ **I must ~ you and leave you*** malheureusement, il faut que je vous quitte ◆ **~ thy neighbour as thyself** (Bible) tu aimeras ton prochain comme toi-même ◆ **she ~s me, she ~s me not** (counting etc) elle m'aime, un peu, beaucoup, passionnément, à la folie, pas du tout

2 (= appreciate, enjoy) [+ music, food, activity, place] aimer (beaucoup) ; (stronger) adorer ◆ **to ~ to do or doing sth** aimer (beaucoup) or adorer faire qch ◆ **he ~s reading/knitting/photography** il est passionné de lecture/tricot/photographie, il aime or adore lire/tricoter/la photographie ◆ **she ~s singing/swimming** elle aime or adore chanter/nager ◆ **I'd ~ to come** j'aimerais beaucoup venir, je serais enchanté or ravi de venir ◆ **I'd ~ to!** (in answer to question) avec plaisir ! ◆ **I'd ~ to but unfortunately ...** j'aimerais bien, malheureusement ... ◆ **I ~ the way she smiles** j'adore son sourire ◆ **I ~ the way he leaves us to do all the work!** (iro) il nous laisse tout le travail, vraiment j'apprécie (iro) ◆ **she's going to ~ you!** (iro) elle va te bénir ! (iro) ◆ **she's going to ~ that!** (iro) elle va être ravie ! (iro)

COMP **love affair** N (lit) liaison f (amoureuse) ; (fig) passion f (with pour)
love apple † N (= tomato) pomme f d'amour †
love child* N enfant mf de l'amour, enfant mf illégitime or naturel(le)
loved ones NPL êtres mpl chers ◆ **my ~d ones** les êtres qui me sont chers
love feast N (among early Christians) agape f ; (= banquet) banquet m ; (iro) agapes fpl
love game N (Tennis) jeu m blanc
love handles* NPL poignées fpl d'amour*
love-hate relationship N rapport m amour-haine ◆ **they have a ~-hate relationship** ils s'aiment et se détestent à la fois
love-in-a-mist N (= plant) nigelle f de Damas
love-knot N lacs mpl d'amour
love letter N lettre f d'amour, billet m doux (often hum)
love life* N ◆ **how's your ~ life (these days)?** comment vont les amours ? ◆ **his ~ life is bothering him** il a des problèmes de cœur or sentimentaux
love match N mariage m d'amour
love nest* N nid m d'amoureux or d'amour
love scene N scène f d'amour
love seat N causeuse f (siège)
love story N histoire f d'amour
love-stricken ADJ ⇒ **lovestruck**
love token N gage m d'amour
love triangle N triangle m amoureux

lovebirds /ˈlʌvbɜːdz/ NPL 1 (= birds) perruches fpl inséparables 2 (fig = lovers) tourtereaux mpl

lovebite /ˈlʌvbaɪt/ N suçon m

-loved /lʌvd/ ADJ (in compounds) ◆ **much-loved** adoré ◆ **best-loved** préféré

loveless /ˈlʌvlɪs/ ADJ [life, family, marriage] sans amour ; [person] (= unloved) qui manque d'affection ; (= unloving) incapable d'aimer

loveliness /ˈlʌvlɪnɪs/ N beauté f, charme m

lovelorn /ˈlʌv,lɔːn/ ADJ († or hum) qui languit d'amour

lovely /ˈlʌvlɪ/ ADJ 1 (= beautiful) [woman, place, clothes, flower] ravissant ; [baby, animal, picture, voice] beau (belle f) ◆ **you look ~** tu es ravissante ◆ **this dress looks ~ on you** cette robe te va à ravir

2 (= pleasant) [person] charmant ; [day, weekend, flavour, meal, surprise] merveilleux ; [weather, holiday] beau (belle f), merveilleux ; [food, smell] délicieux ; [idea, suggestion] excellent ◆ **~!** formidable ! ◆ **thanks, that's ~*** (= fine) merci, c'est très bien comme ça ◆ **it's ~ to see you again** ça me fait bien plaisir de te revoir ◆ **it's been ~ seeing or to see you** j'ai été vraiment content de vous voir ◆ **we had a ~ time** nous nous sommes bien amusés ◆ **he made a ~ job of it** il a fait du bon travail ◆ **the water's ~ and warm** l'eau est bonne ◆ **it was ~ and hot outside** il faisait agréablement chaud dehors ◆ **we're ~ and early*** c'est bien, on est en avance

N (* = girl) belle fille f, beau brin m de fille, mignonne f ◆ **my ~** ma jolie, ma mignonne

lovemaking /ˈlʌv,meɪkɪŋ/ N (NonC) amour m, rapports mpl (sexuels) ◆ **after ~** après l'amour

lover /ˈlʌvəʳ/ N 1 amant m ; († = suitor) amoureux m ◆ **~s' vows** promesses fpl d'amoureux ◆ **they are ~s** ils ont une liaison, ils couchent* ensemble ◆ **they have been ~s for two years** leur liaison dure depuis deux ans ◆ **she took a ~** elle a pris un amant ◆ **Casanova was a great ~** Casanova fut un grand séducteur

2 [of hobby, wine etc] amateur m ◆ **he's a ~ of good food** il est grand amateur de bonne cuisine, il aime beaucoup la bonne cuisine ◆ **he's a great ~ of Brahms** or **a great Brahms ~** c'est un fervent de Brahms, il aime beaucoup (la musique de) Brahms ◆ **art/theatre ~** amateur m d'art/de théâtre ◆ **music ~** amateur m de musique, mélomane mf ◆ **he's a nature ~** il aime la nature, c'est un amoureux de la nature ◆ **football ~s everywhere** tous les amateurs or passionnés de football

COMP **lover boy*** N (hum or iro = womanizer) don Juan m, tombeur* m ◆ **come on ~ boy!** allez, beau gosse !*

lovesick /ˈlʌvsɪk/ ADJ amoureux, qui languit d'amour

lovesong /ˈlʌvsɒŋ/ N chanson f d'amour

lovestruck /ˈlʌvstrʌk/ ADJ éperdument amoureux

lovey* /ˈlʌvɪ/ N chéri(e) m(f) COMP **lovey-dovey*** ADJ (hum) (trop) tendre

loving /ˈlʌvɪŋ/ ADJ [person, child, couple, relationship] affectueux ; [marriage] heureux ; [wife, husband, parent] aimant ; [family] uni ; [kiss] tendre ; [smile] plein de tendresse ◆ **~ kindness** bonté f, charité f ◆ **with ~ care** avec le plus grand soin ◆ **"from your loving son, Martin"** "ton fils qui t'aime, Martin" COMP **loving cup** N coupe f de l'amitié

-loving /ˈlʌvɪŋ/ ADJ (in compounds) ◆ **art-loving** qui aime l'art, qui est amateur d'art ◆ **money-loving** qui aime l'argent

lovingly /ˈlʌvɪŋlɪ/ ADV 1 [look at] (= with affection) tendrement, avec tendresse ; (= with love) amoureusement 2 (= carefully) [restored, maintained] avec amour

low¹ /ləʊ/ ADJ 1 [wall, shelf, seat, ceiling, level, tide] bas (basse f) ◆ **a dress with a ~ neck** une robe décolletée ◆ **to make a ~ bow** saluer bien bas ◆ **~ cloud** nuages mpl bas ◆ **fog on ~ ground**

brouillard *m* à basse altitude ◆ **the ~ ground near the sea** les basses terres *fpl* près de la mer ◆ **the house/town is on ~ ground** la maison/ville est bâtie dans une dépression ◆ **the river is very ~ just now** la rivière est très basse en ce moment ◆ **the sun is ~ in the sky** le soleil est bas dans le ciel *or* bas sur l'horizon ◆ **at ~ tide** à marée basse ◆ **~ water** marée *f* basse, basses eaux *fpl* ◆ **the ~ point** *[of sb's career]* le creux de la vague ;

2 *[voice]* (= *soft*) bas (basse *f*) ; (= *deep*) bas (basse *f*), profond ; *(Mus) [note]* bas (basse *f*) ◆ **in a ~ voice** (= *softly*) à voix basse ; (= *in deep tones*) d'une voix basse *or* profonde ◆ **a ~ murmur** un murmure sourd *or* étouffé ◆ **they were talking in a ~ murmur** ils chuchotaient ◆ **he gave a ~ groan** il a gémi faiblement, il a poussé un faible gémissement ◆ **it's a bit ~** *[radio etc]* on n'entend pas, ce n'est pas assez fort ; see also **comp**

3 *[wage, rate]* bas (basse *f*), faible ; *[price]* bas (basse *f*), modéré ◆ **people on ~ incomes** les gens à faibles revenus ◆ **at the ~est price** au meilleur prix

4 *[latitude, number, frequency]* bas (basse *f*) ; *(Scol) [mark]* bas (basse *f*), faible ; *(Chem, Phys) [density]* faible ; *[temperature]* bas (basse *f*), peu élevé ; *[speed]* petit *before n*, faible ; *[lights]* faible, bas (basse *f*) ; *[visibility]* mauvais, limité ◆ **in ~ gear** en première ou en seconde (vitesse) ◆ **the temperature never falls below 20° at the ~est** la température ne tombe jamais en dessous de 20° ◆ **the temperature is in the ~ thirties** il fait entre 30 et 35 degrés ◆ **the fire is getting ~ /is ~** le feu baisse/est bas ◆ **at** *or* **on a ~ heat** *(Culin)* à feu doux ◆ **cook in a ~ oven** cuire au four à feu doux

5 *[standard]* bas (basse *f*), faible ; *[quality]* inférieur (-eure *f*) ◆ **activity is at its ~est in the summer** c'est en été que l'activité est particulièrement réduite ◆ **people of ~ intelligence** les gens peu intelligents ◆ **to have a ~ opinion of sb** ne pas avoir bonne opinion de qn, avoir une piètre opinion de qn ◆ **to have a ~ opinion of sth** ne pas avoir bonne opinion de qch ◆ **their stock of soap was very ~** *(shop)* leur stock de savon était presque épuisé ◆ **supplies are getting** *or* **running ~** les provisions diminuent ;

6 ◆ **~ in fat** à faible teneur en matières grasses ◆ **~ in nitrogen** contenant peu d'azote ◆ **we're a bit ~ on petrol** nous n'avons plus beaucoup *or* il ne nous reste plus beaucoup d'essence ◆ **they were ~ on water** ils étaient à court d'eau ◆ **I'm ~ on funds** * je suis à court (d'argent)

7 *(Cards)* **a ~ card** une basse carte ◆ **a ~ diamond** un petit carreau

8 (= *feeble*) *[person]* faible, affaibli ; *[health]* mauvais ; (= *depressed*) déprimé ◆ **to be in ~ spirits, to be** *or* **feel ~** être déprimé, ne pas avoir le moral ◆ **the patient is very ~** le malade est bien bas ; see also **comp**

9 (= *primitive*) *[animals, plants]* inférieur (-eure *f*), peu évolué ◆ **the ~ forms of life** les formes *fpl* de vie inférieures *or* les moins évoluées

10 (= *humble*) *[rank, origin]* bas (basse *f*) ; (= *vulgar*) *[company, taste]* mauvais ; *[character]* grossier, bas (basse *f*) ; *[café etc]* de bas étage ; (= *shameful*) *[behaviour]* ignoble, odieux ◆ **the ~est of the ~** le dernier des derniers ◆ **that's a ~ trick** c'est un sale tour * ◆ **with ~ cunning** avec une ruse ignoble ; see also **comp, lower¹**

ADV 1 (= *in low position*) *[aim, fly]* bas ◆ **to bow ~** saluer bien bas ◆ **a dress cut ~ in the back** une robe très décolletée dans le dos ◆ **she is rather ~ down in that chair** elle est bien bas dans ce fauteuil, elle est assise bien bas ◆ **~er down the wall/the page** plus bas sur le mur/la page ◆ **~er down the hill** plus bas sur la colline, en contrebas ◆ **the plane came down ~ over the town** l'avion est descendu et a survolé la ville à basse altitude ◆ **the plane flew ~ over the town** l'avion a survolé la ville à basse altitude ◆ **to fall** *or* **sink ~** tomber bien bas ◆ **I wouldn't stoop so ~ as to do that** je ne m'abaisserais pas à faire cela ; → **lay¹, lie¹**

2 (= *at low volume, intensity, cost*) ◆ **to turn the heating/lights/music/radio down ~** baisser le chauffage/la lumière/la musique/la radio ◆ **the fire was burning ~** le feu était bas ◆ **to speak ~** parler à voix basse *or* doucement ◆ **to sing ~** chanter bas ◆ **the song is pitched too ~ for me** le ton de cette chanson est trop bas pour moi ◆ **I can't get as ~ as that** *(in singing)* ma voix ne descend pas si bas ◆ **to buy ~** *(on Stock Exchange)* acheter quand le cours est bas ◆ **to play ~** *(Cards)* jouer une basse carte

N 1 *(Weather)* dépression *f*

2 ◆ **in low** (= *in low gear*) en première ou en seconde (vitesse)

3 (= *low point: esp Fin*) minimum *m* ◆ **prices/temperatures have reached a new ~** *or* **an all-time ~** les prix/les températures ont atteint leur niveau le plus bas *or* n'ont jamais été aussi bas(ses) ◆ **the pound has sunk** *or* **fallen to a new ~** la livre a atteint son niveau le plus bas ◆ **this is really a new ~ in vulgarity** cela bat tous les records de vulgarité

COMP **low-alcohol** ADJ *[lager, wine, beer]* à faible teneur en alcool, peu alcoolisé

low-angle shot N *(Phot)* contre-plongée *f*

low blow N *(Boxing, fig)* coup *m* bas

low-budget ADJ *[film, project]* à petit budget ; *[car etc]* pour les petits budgets

low-calorie, low-cal * ADJ *[food, diet]* à basses calories, hypocalorique

Low Church N *tendance évangéliste de l'Église anglicane*

low-cost ADJ (à) bon marché, pas cher ◆ **~-cost housing** *(NonC)* habitations *fpl* à loyer modéré, HLM *mpl*

the Low Countries NPL les Pays-Bas *mpl*

low-cut ADJ *[dress etc]* décolleté

low-down N → **low-down**

lowest common denominator N *(Math)* plus petit dénominateur *m* commun ◆ **these papers pander to the ~est common denominator** ces journaux flattent les instincts les plus triviaux du public

lowest common multiple N *(Math)* plus petit commun multiple *m*

low-fat ADJ *[diet]* pauvre en matières grasses ; *[milk, cheese etc]* allégé

low flying N *(NonC)* vol(s) *m(pl)* à basse altitude

low-flying ADJ volant à basse altitude

low-frequency ADJ *(Elec)* basse fréquence *inv*

Low German N bas allemand *m*

low-grade ADJ de qualité *or* de catégorie inférieure

low-heeled ADJ à talon(s) plat(s), plat

low-impact ADJ *[aerobics, exercise]* low-impact *inv*

low-key ADJ discret (-ète *f*) ◆ **it was a ~-key operation** l'opération a été conduite de façon très discrète ◆ **to keep sth ~-key** faire qch de façon discrète ◆ **the wedding will be a ~-key affair** ce sera un mariage tout simple ◆ **he wanted to keep the meeting ~-key** il ne voulait pas faire toute une affaire de cette réunion ◆ **the ~-key approach to the incident taken by the prison authorities** l'approche prudente adoptée par les autorités carcérales à la suite de l'incident

Low Latin N bas latin *m*

low-level ADJ *(gen)* bas (basse *f*) ; *[job]* subalterne ; *[talks, discussions]* à bas niveau ◆ **~-level flying** vol *m* or navigation *f* à basse altitude ◆ **~-level language** *(Comput)* langage *m* de bas niveau ◆ **~-level waste** *(Nucl Phys)* déchets *mpl* de faible activité

low-loader N (= *lorry*) semi-remorque *f* à plateforme surbaissée ; (= *train wagon*) wagon *m* (de marchandises) à plateforme surbaissée

low-lying ADJ à basse altitude

Low Mass N *(Rel)* messe *f* basse

low-minded ADJ vulgaire, grossier

low-necked ADJ décolleté

low-paid ADJ *[job]* mal payé, qui paie mal ; *[worker]* mal payé, qui ne gagne pas beaucoup ◆ **the ~-paid** les petits salaires *mpl*, les petits salariés *mpl* ; see also **lower¹**

low-pitched ADJ *[ball]* bas (basse *f*) ; *[sound]* bas (basse *f*), grave

low-powered ADJ de faible puissance

low-pressure ADJ à *or* de basse pression

low-priced ADJ à bas prix, (à) bon marché *inv*

low-principled ADJ sans grands principes

low-profile ADJ *(gen)* discret (-ète *f*) ◆ **to keep a ~ profile** rester discret ◆ **the police deliberately kept a ~ profile** la police est volontairement restée discrète ◆ **~-profile tyre** pneu *m* taille basse

low-quality ADJ *[goods]* de qualité inférieure

low-rent ADJ *(lit) [housing, flat]* à loyer modéré ; *(fig)* de bas étage

low-rise ADJ *(Archit)* à *or* de hauteur limitée, bas (basse *f*)

low-scoring ADJ *où peu de points ou buts sont marqués*

low season N *(esp Brit)* basse *or* morte-saison *f* ADJ *[rates, holiday]* pendant la basse *or* morte-saison

low-slung ADJ *[chair]* bas (basse *f*) ; *[sports car]* surbaissé

low-spirited ADJ déprimé, démoralisé

low-start mortgage N *(Brit) emprunt hypothécaire à faibles remboursements initiaux*

low-sulphur ADJ *[diesel, petrol, fuel]* à faible teneur en soufre

Low Sunday N dimanche *m* de Quasimodo

low-tar ADJ *[cigarette]* à faible teneur en goudron

low-tech ADJ *[machinery]* rudimentaire ; *[design]* sommaire

low-tension ADJ à basse tension

low vowel N *(Ling)* voyelle *f* basse

low-water mark N *(lit)* laisse *f* de basse mer ◆ **their morale had reached ~-water mark** leur moral était on ne peut plus bas, ils avaient le moral à zéro * ◆ **sales had reached ~-water mark** les ventes n'avaient jamais été aussi mauvaises

low² /ləʊ/ VI *[cattle]* meugler, beugler, mugir

lowborn /ˈləʊbɔːn/ ADJ de basse extraction

lowboy /ˈləʊbɔɪ/ N *(US)* commode *f* basse

lowbrow * /ˈləʊbraʊ/ N (= *person*) personne *f* peu intellectuelle *or* sans prétentions intellectuelles ADJ *[person, book, film, programme]* sans prétentions intellectuelles

low-down * /ˈləʊdaʊn/ ADJ *(esp US pej) [person]* méprisable ◆ **a ~ trick** un sale tour N ◆ **to get the ~ on sb/sth** se renseigner sur qn/qch ◆ **to give sb the ~ on sth** mettre qn au courant *or* au parfum ‡ de qch

lower¹ /ˈləʊəʳ/ (compar of **low¹**) ADJ inférieur (-eure *f*) ◆ **the ~ half of the body** le bas du corps ◆ **Annapurna is the ~ of the two** l'Annapurna est la moins haute (des deux) ◆ **the ~ shelf** l'étagère *f* du bas ; see also **low¹** ; → **reach**

COMP **the lower abdomen** N le bas-ventre

the lower animals NPL les animaux *mpl* inférieurs

the lower back N le bas du dos

lower-back pain N douleurs *fpl* lombaires

lower case N *(Typ)* bas *m* de casse ◆ **in ~ case** en bas de casse

lower-case ADJ minuscule

the lower chamber N *(Parl)* la Chambre basse

lower class N classes *fpl* inférieures, classe *f* populaire ◆ **~-class family** famille *f* prolétarienne *or* ouvrière

lower classes NPL ⇒ **lower class**

lower court N *(Jur)* instance *f* inférieure

lower deck N *[of bus]* étage *m* inférieur ; *(Naut)* (= *part of ship*) pont *m* inférieur ◆ **the ~ deck** *

(= personnel) les sous-officiers *mpl* et les matelots *mpl*
Lower Egypt N Basse-Égypte *f*
the Lower House N *(Parl) (gen)* la Chambre basse ; *(Brit)* la Chambre basse, la Chambre des communes
lower-income ADJ *[group, family]* économiquement faible
lower jaw N mâchoire *f* inférieure
the lower leg N la partie inférieure de la jambe
lower limbs NPL membres *mpl* inférieurs
lower lip N lèvre *f* inférieure
the lower mammals NPL les mammifères *mpl* inférieurs
lower middle class N petite bourgeoisie *f*, (petite) classe *f* moyenne ◆ **a ~ middle-class family** une famille de la classe moyenne *or* de la petite bourgeoisie ◆ **a ~ middle-class background** un milieu petit bourgeois
the lower paid NPL les personnes *fpl* à faible revenu
the lower ranks NPL *(Mil)* les grades *mpl* inférieurs ; *(fig)* les rangs *mpl* inférieurs
the Lower Rhine N le Bas-Rhin
Lower Saxony N Basse-Saxe *f*
the lower school N ≈ le collège
lower sixth (form) N *(Brit Scol)* ≈ classe *f* de première
the lower vertebrates NPL les vertébrés *mpl* inférieurs ; see also **second**[1]

lower[2] /ˈləʊəʳ/ VT 1 *[+ blind, window, construction]* baisser, abaisser ; *[+ sail, flag]* abaisser, amener ; *[+ boat, lifeboat]* mettre à la mer ◆ **to ~ the boats** mettre les embarcations à la mer ◆ **to ~ sb/sth on a rope** (faire) descendre qn/descendre qch au bout d'une corde ◆ **to ~ one's guard** baisser sa garde ◆ **to ~ the boom on sb** *(fig)* serrer la vis* à qn
2 *[+ pressure, heating, price, voice]* baisser ◆ **to ~ sb's resistance** *(Med)* diminuer la résistance de qn ◆ **to ~ sb's morale** démoraliser qn, saper le moral de qn ◆ **~ your voice!** baisse la voix !, (parle) moins fort ! ◆ **he ~ed his voice to a whisper** il a baissé la voix jusqu'à en chuchoter, il s'est mis à chuchoter ◆ **to ~ o.s. to do sth** s'abaisser à faire qch ◆ **I refuse to ~ myself** je refuse de m'abaisser *or* de m'avilir ainsi
VI *(lit)* baisser ; *[pressure, price etc]* baisser, diminuer

lower[3] /ˈlaʊəʳ/ VI *[sky]* se couvrir, s'assombrir ; *[clouds]* être menaçant ; *[person]* prendre un air sombre *or* menaçant ◆ **to ~ at sb** jeter un regard menaçant à qn, regarder qn de travers

lowering[1] /ˈləʊərɪŋ/ N 1 *[of window, flag]* abaissement *m* ; *[of boat]* mise *f* à la mer 2 *[of temperature]* baisse *f*, abaissement *m* ; *[of price, value]* baisse *f*, diminution *f* ; *[of pressure]* baisse *f* ; *(Med) [of resistance]* diminution *f* ◆ **the ~ of morale** la baisse du moral, la démoralisation
ADJ abaissant, dégradant, humiliant

lowering[2] /ˈlaʊərɪŋ/ ADJ *[look, sky]* sombre, menaçant

lowing /ˈləʊɪŋ/ N *[of cattle]* meuglement *m*, beuglement *m*, mugissement *m*

lowland /ˈləʊlənd/ N plaine *f* ◆ **the Lowlands (of Scotland)** la Basse Écosse, les Basses-Terres *fpl* (d'Écosse) COMP *(in Scot) [town, people, culture]* de Basse-Écosse **Lowland Scots** N *(Ling)* ⇒ **Lallans noun**

lowlander /ˈləʊləndəʳ/ N *(gen)* habitant(e) *m(f)* de la (*or* des) plaine(s) ◆ **Lowlander** *(in Scot)* habitant(e) *m(f) or* originaire *mf* de la Basse-Écosse

lowlife* /ˈləʊlaɪf/ ADJ *(esp US)* ◆ **his ~ friends** les voyous qu'il fréquente

lowlights /ˈləʊlaɪts/ NPL 1 *(Hairdressing)* mèches *fpl* sombres 2 *(hum)* ◆ **one of the ~*** of the sporting season un des moments les moins glorieux de la saison sportive

lowliness /ˈləʊlɪnɪs/ N humilité *f*

lowly /ˈləʊlɪ/ ADJ humble

lowness /ˈləʊnɪs/ N *(in height)* manque *m* de hauteur ; *[of price, wages]* modicité *f* ; *[of temperature]* peu *m* d'élévation ◆ **the ~ of the ceiling made him stoop** la maison était si basse de plafond qu'il a dû se baisser

lox /lɒks/ N *(US)* saumon *m* fumé

loyal /ˈlɔɪəl/ ADJ *[friend, ally, supporter]* loyal, fidèle ; *[wife, customer, reader]* fidèle ; *[employee, servant]* fidèle, dévoué ◆ **he has a ~ following** il a des partisans fidèles ◆ **the Queen's ~ subjects** les loyaux sujets de la reine ◆ **the ~ toast** *(Brit)* le toast porté au souverain ◆ **to be/remain** *or* **stay ~ to sb/sth** être/rester fidèle à qn/qch

loyalist /ˈlɔɪəlɪst/ ADJ, N loyaliste *mf*

loyally /ˈlɔɪəlɪ/ ADV *[serve, support]* fidèlement ; *[say]* en toute loyauté

loyalty /ˈlɔɪəltɪ/ N *(to person)* loyauté *f (to* envers) ; *(to cause)* dévouement *m (to* à) ; *(to political party)* loyauté *f*, loyalisme *m (to* envers) ◆ **my first ~ is to my family** ma famille passe avant tout ◆ **to pledge one's ~ to sb/sth** promettre d'être loyal envers qn/d'être dévoué à qch ◆ **to decide where one's loyalties lie** choisir son camp ◆ **to suffer from** *or* **have divided loyalties** être partagé, se sentir écartelé ◆ **a man of fierce loyalties** un homme d'une loyauté farouche COMP **loyalty card** N *(Brit Comm)* carte *f* de fidélité

lozenge /ˈlɒzɪndʒ/ N 1 *(= throat tablet)* pastille *f* 2 *(= shape, heraldic device)* losange *m*

LP /elˈpiː/ N *(Mus)* (abbrev of **long-playing (record)**) → **long**[1]

LPG /elpiːˈdʒiː/ N (abbrev of **liquified petroleum gas**) GPL *m*

LPN /elpiːˈen/ N *(US Med)* (abbrev of **Licensed Practical Nurse**) → **license**

LRAM /elɑːreɪˈem/ N *(Brit)* (abbrev of **Licentiate of the Royal Academy of Music**) *diplôme d'un des Conservatoires de musique*

LRCP /elɑːsiːˈpiː/ N *(Brit)* (abbrev of **Licentiate of the Royal College of Physicians**) ≈ agrégation *f* de médecine

LRCS /elɑːsiːˈes/ N *(Brit)* (abbrev of **Licentiate of the Royal College of Surgeons**) ≈ agrégation *f* de médecine (opératoire)

LRP /ˌelɑːˈpiː/ N (abbrev of **lead replacement petrol**) → **lead**[2]

LSAT /eleseɪˈtiː/ N *(US Univ)* (abbrev of **Law School Admission Test**) *examen d'entrée à une faculté de droit*

LSD[1] /elesˈdiː/ N *(Drugs)* (abbrev of **lysergic acid diethylamide**) LSD *m*

LSD[2] /elesˈdiː/ N *(Brit)* (abbrev of **librae, solidi, denarii**) *(= pounds, shillings and pence) ancien système monétaire britannique*

LSE /ˌelesˈiː/ N *(Brit)* 1 abbrev of **London School of Economics** 2 abbrev of **London Stock Exchange**

LT /elˈtiː/ *(Elec)* (abbrev of **low tension**) → **low**[1]

Lt (abbrev of **Lieutenant**) *(on envelope etc)* **~. J. Smith** Lieutenant J. Smith ◆ **~.-Col** (abbrev of **Lieutenant-Colonel**) → **lieutenant** ◆ **~.-Gen** (abbrev of **Lieutenant-General**) → **lieutenant**

Ltd *(Brit)* (abbrev of **Limited (Liability)**) **Smith & Co. ~** Smith & Cie SA *or* Ltée *(Can)*

lube* /luːb/ N 1 *(= oil)* huile *f* de graissage 2 *(= gel)* lubrifiant *m* (intime) VT graisser, lubrifier

lubricant /ˈluːbrɪkənt/ ADJ, N lubrifiant *m* ◆ **alcohol is a great (social) ~** l'alcool facilite beaucoup les contacts

lubricate /ˈluːbrɪkeɪt/ VT 1 *(lit)* lubrifier ; *(with grease)* graisser 2 *(fig = facilitate)* faciliter COMP

lubricating oil N huile *f* (de graissage), lubrifiant *m*

lubricated‡ /ˈluːbrɪkeɪtɪd/ ADJ *(hum = drunk)* paf‡ inv, beurré‡

lubrication /ˌluːbrɪˈkeɪʃən/ N lubrification *f* ; *(with grease)* graissage *m*

lubricator /ˈluːbrɪkeɪtəʳ/ N *(= person, device)* graisseur *m*

lubricious /luːˈbrɪʃəs/ ADJ *(frm = lewd)* lubrique

lubricity /luːˈbrɪsɪtɪ/ N *(frm = lewdness)* lubricité *f*

lucerne /luːˈsɜːn/ N *(esp Brit)* luzerne *f*

lucid /ˈluːsɪd/ ADJ 1 *(= clear) [style, explanation, account]* clair 2 *(= clear-headed) [person]* lucide ; *[moment, interval]* de lucidité 3 *(liter = bright) [air, light]* lucide † *(also liter)*
COMP **lucid dream** N *(Psych)* rêve *m* lucide
lucid dreamer N *(Psych)* rêveur *m*, -euse *f* lucide
lucid dreaming N *(Psych)* rêverie *f* lucide

lucidity /luːˈsɪdɪtɪ/ N 1 *(= clarity) [of style, explanation, book]* clarté *f* 2 *(= clear-headedness) [of mind]* lucidité *f* 3 *(liter = brightness)* éclat *m*

lucidly /ˈluːsɪdlɪ/ ADV *[explain, write, argue]* clairement ; *[think]* lucidement, avec lucidité

Lucifer /ˈluːsɪfəʳ/ N Lucifer *m*

luck /lʌk/ LANGUAGE IN USE 23.5 N 1 *(= chance, fortune)* chance *f*, hasard *m* ◆ **good health is not simply a matter of ~** si l'on est en bonne santé, ce n'est pas simplement une question de hasard ◆ **it's the ~ of the draw** *(fig)* c'est une question de chance ◆ **(it's) just my ~!*** c'est bien ma chance *or* ma veine !* ◆ **it was just his ~* to meet the boss** il a eu la malchance *or* le malheur de rencontrer le patron ◆ **~ favoured him, ~ was with him, ~ was on his side** la chance lui souriait ◆ **as ~ would have it** comme par hasard ◆ **better ~ next time!** * ça ira mieux la prochaine fois ! ◆ **any ~?*** *(gen)* alors (ça a marché) ?* ; *(= did you find it?)* tu as trouvé ? ◆ **no ~?*** *(gen)* ça n'a pas marché ? ; *(= didn't you find it?)* tu n'as pas trouvé ?
◆ **good luck** chance *f* ◆ **by good ~ the first man I ran into was Dan** la chance a voulu que la première personne que je rencontre soit Dan ◆ **to have the good ~ to do sth** avoir la chance de faire qch
◆ **to be** *or* **bring good luck** porter bonheur ◆ **it's good ~ to see a black cat** cela porte bonheur de voir un chat noir ◆ **he brought me good ~** il m'a porté bonheur
◆ **good luck !** bonne chance ! ◆ **good ~ with your exams!** bonne chance pour tes examens !
◆ **bad luck** malchance *f*, malheur *m* ◆ **I had a lot of bad ~ at the start of the season** j'ai eu beaucoup de malchance *or* j'ai joué de malchance en début de saison ◆ **to have the bad ~ to do sth** avoir la malchance de faire qch
◆ **to be** *or* **bring bad luck** porter malheur ◆ **it's bad ~ to walk under a ladder** ça porte malheur de passer sous une échelle ◆ **she believed the colour green brought bad ~** elle croyait que le vert était une couleur qui portait malheur ◆ **it brought us nothing but bad ~** cela ne nous a vraiment pas porté chance
◆ **bad** *or* **hard** *or* **tough luck !*** pas de veine !*
◆ **worse luck !*** malheureusement ! ◆ **she's not here, worse ~** elle n'est pas là, malheureusement
◆ **to push one's luck*** y aller fort, exagérer ◆ **I didn't dare push my ~ too far** je n'ai pas osé y aller trop fort ◆ **he's pushing his ~** il y va un peu fort, il exagère ◆ **don't push your ~!** n'exagère pas !
◆ **to be down on one's luck*** *(= be going through bad patch)* traverser une mauvaise passe ◆ **she seemed down on her ~** elle avait l'air de traverser une mauvaise passe ◆ **I seem**

to attract people who are down on their ~ j'ai l'impression que j'attire les gens à problèmes ; → **beginner, chance**

2 *(= good fortune)* bonheur *m*, chance *f* ◆ **you're in ~, the doctor's still here** tu as de la veine* *or* du pot*, le docteur est encore là ◆ **it looks like your ~'s in tonight** c'est ta soirée, on dirait ◆ **you're out of ~** * ◆ **your ~'s out** * tu n'as pas de veine* *or* de pot* ◆ **that's a bit** *or* **a stroke of ~!** * quelle veine !*, coup de pot !* ◆ **he had the ~ to meet her in the street** il a eu la chance de la rencontrer dans la rue ◆ **here's (wishing you) ~!** bonne chance ! ◆ **no such ~!** * ç'aurait été trop beau !, penses-tu ! ◆ **with any ~ ...** avec un peu de chance *or* de veine* ... ◆ **to keep a horseshoe for ~** avoir un fer à cheval comme porte-bonheur ◆ **and the best of (British) ~!*** *(iro)* je vous (*or* leur *etc*) souhaite bien du plaisir !* *(iro)* ◆ **he's got the ~ of the devil*, he's got the devil's own ~*** il a une veine de cocu*

► **luck out*** VI *(US)* avoir de la veine* *or* du pot*

luckily /ˈlʌkɪlɪ/ ADV heureusement ◆ **~ for me ...** heureusement pour moi ...

luckless /ˈlʌklɪs/ *(liter)* ADJ *[person, journey]* infortuné *(liter)* ; *[week, year]* d'infortune *(liter)*

lucky /ˈlʌkɪ/ ADJ 1 *[person] (= having luck) (always)* qui a de la chance, chanceux ; *(on one occasion)* qui a de la chance ◆ **we were ~ with the weather** on a eu de la chance avec le temps ◆ **he is ~ to be alive** il a de la chance d'être en vie ◆ **he's ~ that I didn't run him over** il a eu de la chance, j'aurais pu l'écraser ◆ **it was ~ that you got here in time** heureusement que vous êtes arrivé à temps ◆ **it was ~ for him that he got out of the way** heureusement (pour lui), il s'est écarté ◆ **to be ~ in life** avoir de la chance dans la vie ◆ **to be ~ in love** être heureux en amour ◆ **I'm ~ in having an excellent teacher** j'ai la chance d'avoir un excellent professeur ◆ **to count o.s. ~** s'estimer heureux ◆ **some people are born ~** il y a des gens qui ont de la chance ◆ **~ winner** heureux gagnant *m*, heureuse gagnante *f* ◆ **who's the ~ man/woman?** *(hum)* comment s'appelle l'heureux élu/l'heureuse élue ? ◆ **(you) ~ thing*** *or* **devil*** *or* **dog*!** veinard(e) !* ◆ **he's a ~ thing*** *or* **devil*** *or* **dog*!** quel veinard !* ◆ **~ (old) you!** * tu en as de la veine !* ◆ **~ old Thomson!** * quel veinard*, ce Thomson ! ◆ **if you're ~** avec un peu de chance ◆ **you'll be ~!** ⁑ *(= not likely)* tu peux toujours courir !* ◆ **you'll be ~*** **if you get any breakfast** tu pourras t'estimer heureux si tu as un petit déjeuner ◆ **you'll be ~ to get $5 for that** tu auras du mal à en tirer 5 dollars ◆ **I should be so ~**⁑ tu parles !*, ce serait trop beau !* ◆ **to get ~**⁑ **(with sb)** *(= be allowed sex)* arriver à ses fins (avec qn) ; → **strike, third**

2 *(= fortunate, resulting from luck) [coincidence, shot]* heureux ◆ **how ~!, that was ~!** quelle chance ! ◆ **to have a ~ escape** l'échapper belle, s'en tirer de justesse ◆ **a ~ chance** un coup de chance ◆ **a ~ break*** un coup de bol* ◆ **how did you know? – it was just a ~ guess** comment as-tu deviné ? – par hasard *or* j'ai dit ça au hasard ◆ **it's your ~ day** * c'est ton jour de chance

3 *(= bringing luck) [number, horseshoe]* porte-bonheur *inv* ◆ **a ~ charm** un porte-bonheur ◆ **a ~ rabbit's foot** une patte de lapin porte-bonheur ; → **star**

COMP **lucky bag** N pochette-surprise *f*

lucky dip N *(Brit: at fair)* ≃ pêche *f* à la ligne ; *(fig)* loterie *f (fig)*

lucrative /ˈluːkrətɪv/ ADJ lucratif

lucre /ˈluːkəʳ/ N 1 *(NonC: pej = gain)* lucre *m* 2 *(* hum = money:* also **filthy lucre**) fric* *m*

Lucretia /luːˈkriːʃɪə/ N Lucrèce *f*

Lucretius /luːˈkriːʃɪəs/ N Lucrèce *m*

Luddite /ˈlʌdaɪt/ ADJ, N luddite *mf*

ludic /ˈluːdɪk/ ADJ *(liter)* ludique

ludicrous /ˈluːdɪkrəs/ ADJ ridicule

ludicrously /ˈluːdɪkrəslɪ/ ADV ridiculement

ludo /ˈluːdəʊ/ N *(Brit)* jeu *m* des petits chevaux

luff /lʌf/ *(Naut)* N aulof(f)ée *f* VI lofer, venir au lof

luffa /ˈlʌfə/ N *(US)* ⇒ **loofah**

lug¹ /lʌg/ N 1 *(Constr)* tenon *m* ; *[of dish, saucepan etc]* oreille *f (d'une casserole etc)* 2 *(Brit* ⁑ *= ear)* oreille *f*, portugaise⁑ *f* COMP **lug screw** N vis *f* sans tête

lug²* /lʌg/ VT traîner, tirer ◆ **to ~ sth up/down** monter/descendre qch en le traînant ◆ **to ~ sth out** traîner qch dehors ◆ **why are you ~ging that parcel around?** pourquoi est-ce que tu trimballes* ce paquet ? ◆ **they ~ged him off to the theatre** ils l'ont traîné *or* embarqué* au théâtre (malgré lui)

luge /luːʒ/ N luge *f* VI faire de la luge

luggage /ˈlʌgɪdʒ/ N *(NonC)* bagages *mpl* ◆ **~ in advance** *(Rail)* bagages *mpl* non accompagnés ; → **hand, left¹, piece**

COMP **luggage boot** N *(Brit: in car)* coffre *m*

luggage carrier N porte-bagages *m inv*

luggage handler N *(at airport etc)* bagagiste *m*

luggage insurance N assurance *f* bagages

luggage label N étiquette *f* à bagages

luggage locker N (casier *m* de) consigne *f* automatique

luggage rack N *(in train)* porte-bagages *m inv*, filet *m* ; *(on car)* galerie *f*

luggage van N *(esp Brit Rail)* fourgon *m* (à bagages)

lugger /ˈlʌgəʳ/ N lougre *m*

lughole⁑ /ˈlʌghəʊl/ N *(Brit = ear)* oreille *f*

lugubrious /lʊˈguːbrɪəs/ ADJ *(liter)* lugubre

lugubriously /lʊˈguːbrɪəslɪ/ ADV *(liter)* lugubrement

lugworm /ˈlʌgwɜːm/ N arénicole *f*

Luke /luːk/ N Luc *m*

lukewarm /ˈluːkwɔːm/ ADJ 1 *(in temperature)* tiède 2 *(= unenthusiastic) [response, reception, applause]* peu enthousiaste ◆ **to be ~ about sb/sth** ne pas être enthousiasmé par qn/qch ◆ **to be ~ about (doing) sth** ne pas être très chaud pour (faire) qch

lull /lʌl/ N *[of storm]* accalmie *f* ; *[of hostilities, shooting]* arrêt *m* ; *[of conversation]* arrêt *m*, pause *f* ◆ **it's just the ~ before the storm** *(fig)* c'est le calme avant la tempête VT *[+ person, fear]* apaiser, calmer ◆ **to ~ a child to sleep** endormir un enfant en le berçant ◆ **to be ~ed into a false sense of security** s'endormir dans une fausse sécurité

lullaby /ˈlʌləbaɪ/ N berceuse *f* ◆ **~ my baby** dors (mon) bébé, dors

lulu* /ˈluːluː/ N *(esp US)* ◆ **it's a ~!** c'est super !* ; *(iro)* c'est pas de la tarte !⁑

lumbago /lʌmˈbeɪgəʊ/ N lumbago *m*

lumbar /ˈlʌmbəʳ/ ADJ lombaire COMP **lumbar puncture** N ponction *f* lombaire

lumber¹ /ˈlʌmbəʳ/ N *(NonC)* 1 *(= wood)* bois *m* de charpente 2 *(* = junk)* bric-à-brac *m inv* VT 1 *(Brit * = burden)* **to ~ sb with a task** refiler un boulot à qn* ◆ **she was ~ed with a bill for £90** elle s'est pris une facture de 90 livres ◆ **he got ~ed with the job of making the list** il s'est tapé* *or* farci* le boulot de dresser la liste ◆ **I got ~ed with the girl for the evening** j'ai dû me coltiner* *or* m'appuyer* la fille toute la soirée ◆ **now (that) we're ~ed with it ...** maintenant qu'on a ça sur les bras *or* qu'on nous a collé* ça ... 2 *(US Forestry) (= fell)* abattre ; *(= saw up)* débiter

COMP **lumber jacket** N grosse veste *f* (de bûcheron)

lumber mill N scierie *f*

lumber room N *(Brit)* (cabinet *m* de) débarras *m*

lumber yard N dépôt *m* de bois d'œuvre et de construction

lumber² /ˈlʌmbəʳ/ VI (also **lumber about, lumber along**) *[person, animal]* marcher pesamment ; *[vehicle]* rouler lentement ◆ **to ~ in/out** *etc* *[person]* entrer/sortir *etc* d'un pas pesant *or* lourd

lumbering¹ /ˈlʌmbərɪŋ/ N *(US)* débit *m or* débitage *m or* tronçonnage *m* de bois

lumbering² /ˈlʌmbərɪŋ/ ADJ *[step]* lourd, pesant ; *[person]* mal dégrossi

lumberjack /ˈlʌmbədʒæk/ N bûcheron *m* COMP **lumberjack shirt** N *épaisse chemise à carreaux*

lumberman /ˈlʌmbəmən/ N (pl **-men**) ⇒ **lumberjack**

luminary /ˈluːmɪnərɪ/ N *(= person)* lumière *f*, sommité *f*

luminescence /ˌluːmɪˈnesns/ N luminescence *f*

luminosity /ˌluːmɪˈnɒsɪtɪ/ N luminosité *f*

luminous /ˈluːmɪnəs/ ADJ lumineux ◆ **my watch is ~** le cadran de ma montre est lumineux

lumme †⁑ /ˈlʌmɪ/ EXCL *(Brit)* ⇒ **lummy**

lummox /ˈlʌməks/ N *(US)* lourdaud(e) *m(f)*

lummy †⁑ /ˈlʌmɪ/ EXCL *(Brit)* ça alors !, sapristi !*

lump¹ /lʌmp/ N 1 *(= piece) (gen)* morceau *m* ; *(larger)* gros morceau *m*, masse *f* ; *[of metal, stone]* morceau *m*, masse *f* ; *[of coal, cheese, sugar]* morceau *m* ; *[of clay, earth]* motte *f* ; *(in sauce etc)* grumeau *m* ◆ **meteorites are ~s of rock** les météorites sont des amas rocheux

2 *(cancerous)* grosseur *f* ; *(= swelling)* protubérance *f* ; *(from bump etc)* bosse *f* ◆ **to have a ~ in one's throat** *(fig)* avoir une boule dans la gorge, avoir la gorge serrée

3 *(* pej = person)* lourdaud(e) *m(f)*, empoté(e)* *m(f)* ◆ **fat ~!** gros lourdaud !, espèce d'empoté(e) !*

VT (also **lump together**) *[+ books, objects]* réunir, mettre en tas ; *[+ persons]* réunir ; *[+ subjects]* réunir, considérer en bloc

COMP **lump sugar** N sucre *m* en morceaux

lump sum N *(Fin etc)* montant *m* forfaitaire ; *(= payment)* paiement *m* unique ◆ **he was working for a ~ sum** il travaillait à forfait ◆ **to pay a ~ sum** *(Insurance etc)* verser un capital

► **lump together** VT SEP réunir ; *(fig) [+ people, cases]* mettre dans la même catégorie *or* dans le même sac* *(pej)*, considérer en bloc ; see also **lump¹**

lump²* /lʌmp/ VT *(Brit = endure)* ◆ **(if you don't like it) you'll just have to ~ it** que ça te plaise ou pas, t'as pas le choix* ◆ **like it or ~ it*, you'll have to go** que tu le veuilles ou non *or* que ça te plaise ou non il faudra que tu y ailles

lumpectomy /lʌmˈpektəmɪ/ N ablation *f* d'une tumeur mammaire

lumpen /ˈlʌmpən/ ADJ *(esp Brit)* 1 *(liter = shapeless)* informe 2 *(= dull) [person]* terne

lumpenproletariat /ˌlʌmpənprəʊləˈtɛərɪət/ N sous-prolétariat *m*, lumpenprolétariat *m*

lumpfish /ˈlʌmpfɪʃ/ N (pl **lumpfish** *or* **lumpfishes**) lump *m*, lompe *m* ◆ **~ roe** œufs *mpl* de lump

lumpish /ˈlʌmpɪʃ/ ADJ 1 * *(= clumsy)* gauche, maladroit, pataud ; *(= stupid)* idiot, godiche* 2 *(= shapeless) [mass, piece]* informe

lumpsucker /ˈlʌmpˌsʌkəʳ/ N lump *m*, lompe *m*

lumpy /ˈlʌmpɪ/ ADJ *[mattress, bed]* plein de bosses ; *[gravy, sauce, mixture]* grumeleux, plein de grumeaux ; *[person, face, thighs]* plein de bourrelets ; *[surface, ground]* plein de bosses, inégal ◆ **to become** *or* **go ~** *[sauce]* faire des grumeaux

lunacy /ˈluːnəsɪ/ N (*Med*) aliénation *f* mentale, folie *f*, démence *f* ; (*Jur*) démence *f* ; (*fig*) folie *f*, démence *f* ◆ **that's sheer ~!** c'est de la pure folie !, c'est démentiel *or* de la démence !

lunar /ˈluːnəʳ/ ADJ [*month, rock, year*] lunaire ; [*eclipse*] de lune
COMP **lunar landing** N (*Space*) alunissage *m*
lunar module N (*Space*) module *m* lunaire
lunar orbit N (*Space*) ◆ **in ~ orbit** en orbite lunaire *or* autour de la lune

lunatic /ˈluːnətɪk/ N (*Med*) aliéné(e) *m(f)* ; (*Jur*) dément(e) *m(f)* ; (*fig*) fou *m*, folle *f*, cinglé(e)* *m(f)* ◆ **he's a ~!** il est fou à lier !, il est cinglé !*
ADJ (*Med*) [*person*] (*also fig*) fou (folle *f*), dément ; [*idea, action*] absurde, extravagant, démentiel
◆ **~ asylum** asile *m* d'aliénés ◆ **the ~ fringe** les enragés* *mpl*, les extrémistes *mpl* fanatiques

lunch /lʌntʃ/ N déjeuner *m* ◆ **light/quick ~** déjeuner *m* léger/rapide ◆ **we're having pork for ~** nous avons du porc pour déjeuner *or* à midi ◆ **to have ~** déjeuner ◆ **he is at** *or* **out to ~** (= *away from office etc*) il est parti déjeuner ; (*Brit* = *having lunch*) il est en train de déjeuner ◆ **to be out to ~**‡ (*fig, hum*) débloquer‡ ◆ **come to** *or* **for ~ on Sunday** venez déjeuner dimanche ◆ **we had him to ~ yesterday** il est venu déjeuner (chez nous) hier ; → **school¹, working**
VI déjeuner ◆ **we ~ed on sandwiches** nous avons déjeuné de sandwiches, nous avons eu des sandwiches pour déjeuner ◆ **to ~ out** déjeuner à l'extérieur *or* en ville
COMP **lunch break** N pause *f* de midi, heure *f* du déjeuner
lunch hour N ◆ **it's his ~ hour just now** c'est l'heure à laquelle il déjeune, c'est l'heure de son déjeuner ◆ **during one's ~ hour** à l'heure du déjeuner ; see also **lunchtime**

lunchbox /ˈlʌntʃbɒks/ N 1 (= *box*) boîte *f* à sandwichs 2 ‡ (*Brit:* = *genitals*) attributs *mpl* virils

luncheon /ˈlʌntʃən/ N (*frm*) déjeuner *m*
COMP **luncheon basket** N panier-repas *m*
luncheon meat N viande de porc en conserve
luncheon voucher N (*in Brit*) chèque-repas *m*, ticket-repas *m*, ticket-restaurant *m*

luncheonette /ˌlʌntʃəˈnet/ N (*US*) ≃ snack-bar *m*

lunchpail /ˈlʌntʃpeɪl/ N (*US*) ⇒ **lunchbox**

lunchtime /ˈlʌntʃtaɪm/ N ◆ **it's his ~ just now** c'est l'heure à laquelle il déjeune, c'est l'heure de son déjeuner ◆ **it's ~** c'est l'heure de déjeuner ◆ **at ~** à l'heure du déjeuner

lung /lʌŋ/ N poumon *m* ◆ **at the top of one's ~s** à pleins poumons, à tue-tête ; → **iron**
COMP [*disease, infection*] pulmonaire
lung cancer N cancer *m* du poumon
lung specialist N pneumologue *mf*
lung transplant N greffe *f* du poumon

lunge /lʌndʒ/ N 1 (= *thrust*) (brusque) coup *m* *or* mouvement *m* en avant ; (*Fencing*) botte *f* 2 (*also* **lunge rein**) longe *f* VI 1 (= *move: also* **lunge forward**) faire un mouvement brusque en avant ; (*Fencing*) se fendre 2 (= *attack*) ◆ **to ~ at sb** envoyer *or* assener un coup à qn ; (*Fencing*) porter *or* allonger une botte à qn VT [+ *horse*] mener à la longe

lunula /ˈluːnjʊlə/ N (pl **lunulae** /ˈluːnjʊˌliː/) (*Anat*) lunule *f*

lupin /ˈluːpɪn/ N lupin *m*

lupus /ˈluːpəs/ N (*Med*) lupus *m* ◆ **~ erythematosus** lupus *m* érythémateux

lurch¹ /lɜːtʃ/ N 1 [*of person*] écart *m* brusque, vacillement *m* ; [*of car, ship*] embardée *f* ◆ **to give a ~** [*car, ship*] faire une embardée ; [*person*] vaciller, tituber ◆ **my stomach gave a ~** (*from disgust, sickness*) j'ai eu un haut-le-cœur ◆ **my heart gave a ~** (*from misery*) mon cœur s'est serré ◆ **my heart** *or* **stomach gave a ~** (*from fear*) mon sang n'a fait qu'un tour
2 (*fig: Pol*) **the party's ~ to the right** le virage à droite du parti ◆ **they fear a ~ into recession** ils craignent que l'on ne sombre *subj* dans la récession
VI 1 [*person*] vaciller, tituber ; [*car, ship*] faire une embardée ◆ **to ~ in/out/along** *etc* [*person*] entrer/sortir/avancer *etc* en titubant ◆ **the car ~ed along** *or* **forwards** la voiture avançait en faisant des embardées ◆ **the ship ~ed from side to side** le bateau se mit à rouler violemment ◆ **he ~ed to his feet** il s'est levé en titubant ◆ **my stomach ~ed** (*from disgust, sickness*) j'ai eu un haut-le-cœur ◆ **my heart ~ed** (*from misery*) mon cœur s'est serré ◆ **my heart** *or* **stomach ~ed** (*from fear*) mon sang n'a fait qu'un tour
2 (*fig*) **to ~ towards crisis/into turmoil** sombrer dans la crise/le chaos ◆ **the government ~es from one crisis to the next** le gouvernement navigue entre les écueils

lurch² /lɜːtʃ/ N ◆ **to leave sb in the ~** laisser qn en plan*

lure /ljʊəʳ/ N 1 (*NonC*) (= *charm*) [*of sea, travel etc*] attrait *m*, charme *m* ◆ **the ~ of money/drugs** (*fig* = *false attraction*) l'attrait *m* exercé par l'argent/la drogue ◆ **the ~ of profit** l'appât *m* du gain 2 (*Hunting* = *decoy*) leurre *m* VT tromper, attirer *or* persuader par la ruse ◆ **to ~ sb in/out** *etc* persuader qn par la ruse d'entrer/de sortir *etc* ◆ **clever advertising to ~ customers in** de la publicité accrocheuse pour faire entrer les clients ◆ **to ~ sb into a trap** attirer qn dans un piège ◆ **to ~ sb into a house** attirer qn dans une maison

► **lure away** VT SEP ◆ **to lure sb away from the house** éloigner qn *or* faire sortir qn de la maison par la ruse ◆ **to ~ customers away from one's competitors** attirer les clients de ses concurrents

► **lure on** VT SEP entraîner par la ruse, séduire

lurex /ˈlʊəreks/ N lurex *m*

lurgy‡ /ˈlɜːgɪ/ N (*Brit hum*) ◆ **to have the (dreaded) ~** (= *cold, flu*) avoir la crève* ; (= *infectious illness*) avoir chopé* un microbe

lurid /ˈljʊərɪd/ ADJ 1 (= *graphic, sensational*) [*story*] horrible, cru ; [*image, photo*] horrible ; [*headlines*] à sensation ; [*scandal, rumour*] épouvantable ◆ **in ~ detail** avec un luxe de détails choquants ◆ **~ details of their relationship** les détails les plus scabreux de leur liaison 2 (= *garish*) [*colour*] criard ; [*shirt, skirt*] aux couleurs criardes 3 (= *glowing*) [*sky, sunset*] empourpré ; [*glow*] sanglant 4 (*liter* = *pallid*) [*light*] blafard

luridly /ˈljʊərɪdlɪ/ ADV (= *garishly*) [*lit*] de façon tapageuse ◆ **~ coloured** (*one colour*) criard ; (*two or more colours*) aux couleurs criardes

lurk /lɜːk/ VI [*person*] se cacher (*dans un but malveillant*), se tapir ; [*danger*] menacer ; [*doubt*] persister ◆ **he was ~ing behind the bush** il se cachait *or* il était tapi derrière le buisson ◆ **there's someone ~ing (about) in the garden** quelqu'un rôde dans le jardin, il y a un rôdeur dans le jardin

lurking /ˈlɜːkɪŋ/ ADJ [*fear, doubt*] vague ◆ **a ~ idea** une idée de derrière la tête

luscious /ˈlʌʃəs/ ADJ 1 (* = *beautiful*) [*woman, blonde, lips*] pulpeux ; [*fabrics*] somptueux 2 (= *delicious*) [*food, wine*] succulent

lush /lʌʃ/ ADJ 1 (= *luxuriant*) [*field, vegetation*] luxuriant ; [*pasture*] riche ◆ **~ green meadows** de luxuriantes prairies *fpl* 2 (= *opulent*) [*hotel, surroundings, fabric*] luxueux 3 (*Mus*) [*harmonies, sound*] riche N (* = *alcoholic*) alcoolo* *m*, poivrot(e)* *m(f)*

lushness /ˈlʌʃnɪs/ N 1 [*of vegetation*] luxuriance *f* 2 (= *opulence*) luxe *m*

lust /lʌst/ N (*sexual*) désir *m* (sexuel) ; (*Rel* = *one of the seven sins*) luxure *f* ; (*for fame, power etc*) soif *f* (*for* de) ◆ **the ~ for life** la soif *or* la rage de vivre

► **lust after, lust for** VT FUS [+ *woman*] désirer, convoiter ; [+ *revenge, power*] avoir soif de ; [+ *riches*] convoiter

luster /ˈlʌstəʳ/ N (*US*) ⇒ **lustre**

lustful /ˈlʌstfʊl/ ADJ (= *lecherous*) lascif

lustfully /ˈlʌstfəlɪ/ ADV lascivement

lustfulness /ˈlʌstfʊlnɪs/ N lubricité *f*, lascivité *f*

lustily /ˈlʌstɪlɪ/ ADV vigoureusement

lustre, luster (*US*) /ˈlʌstəʳ/ N (– *gloss*) lustre *m*, brillant *m* ; (= *substance*) lustre *m* ; (*fig*) (= *renown*) éclat *m* VT lustrer

lustreless /ˈlʌstəlɪs/ ADJ (*liter*) terne

lustreware /ˈlʌstəwɛəʳ/ N poterie *f* mordorée

lustrous /ˈlʌstrəs/ ADJ (= *shining*) [*material*] lustré, brillant ; [*eyes*] brillant ; [*pearls*] chatoyant ; (*fig*) (= *splendid*) splendide, magnifique

lusty /ˈlʌstɪ/ ADJ (= *healthy*) [*person, infant*] vigoureux, robuste ; (= *hearty*) [*cheer, voice*] vigoureux, vif

lute /luːt/ N luth *m*

Lutetia /luːˈtiːʃə/ N Lutèce *f*

lutetium /luˈtiːʃɪəm/ N lutécium *m*

Luther /ˈluːθəʳ/ N Luther *m*

Lutheran /ˈluːθərən/ N Luthérien(ne) *m(f)* ADJ luthérien

Lutheranism /ˈluːθərənɪzəm/ N luthéranisme *m*

luv* /lʌv/ (*Brit*) ⇒ **love**

luvvie‡ /ˈlʌvɪ/ N (*Brit*) 1 (*term of address* = *darling*) chéri(e) *m(f)* 2 (*hum, gen pej* = *actor, actress*) acteur *m* (prétentieux), actrice *f* (prétentieuse)

Luxemb(o)urg /ˈlʌksəmbɜːg/ N Luxembourg *m* ◆ **in ~** au Luxembourg ◆ **the Grand Duchy of Luxemb(o)urg** le grand-duché de Luxembourg ◆ **the Luxemb(o)urg Embassy, the Embassy of Luxemb(o)urg** l'ambassade *f* du Luxembourg

Luxemb(o)urger /ˈlʌksəmbɜːgəʳ/ N Luxembourgeois(e) *m(f)*

Luxor /ˈlʌksɔːʳ/ N Louxor

luxuriance /lʌgˈzjʊərɪəns/ N 1 [*of foliage, garden*] luxuriance *f* ; [*of hair*] abondance *f* 2 [*of style, language*] exubérance *f*

luxuriant /lʌgˈzjʊərɪənt/ ADJ 1 [*foliage, leaves, garden, forest, plants*] luxuriant ; [*beard*] touffu ; [*hair, moustache*] abondant 2 [*style, imagery*] exubérant

luxuriantly /lʌgˈzjʊərɪəntlɪ/ ADV 1 (= *in profusion*) ◆ **to grow ~** [*flowers, hair*] pousser en abondance ; [*tropical vegetation*] pousser avec exubérance ◆ **his ~ silky beard** sa barbe épaisse et soyeuse 2 (= *richly*) ◆ **~ poetic writing** des écrits d'une poésie exubérante

luxuriate /lʌgˈzjʊərɪeɪt/ VI 1 (= *revel*) **to ~ in sth** s'abandonner *or* se livrer avec délices à qch 2 (= *grow profusely*) pousser avec exubérance *or* à profusion

luxurious /lʌgˈzjʊərɪəs/ ADJ 1 (= *comfortable*) [*hotel, surroundings*] luxueux, somptueux ; [*car, fabric, lifestyle*] luxueux ; [*tastes*] de luxe 2 (= *sensuous*) [*sigh, yawn*] voluptueux

luxuriously /lʌgˈzjʊərɪəslɪ/ ADV 1 (= *comfortably*) [*furnished, appointed, decorated*] luxueusement ◆ **to live ~** vivre dans le luxe 2 (= *sensuously*) [*sigh, yawn, stretch*] voluptueusement

luxuriousness /lʌgˈzjʊərɪəsnɪs/ N [*of hotel, car, surroundings*] luxe *m*

luxury /ˈlʌkʃərɪ/ N 1 (*NonC*) luxe *m* ◆ **to live in ~** vivre dans le luxe ; → **lap¹** 2 (= *luxurious item*) luxe *m* ◆ **good bread is becoming a ~** le bon pain devient un (produit de) luxe ◆ **it's quite a**

~ **for me to go to the theatre** c'est du luxe pour moi que d'aller au théâtre ◆ **what a ~ to have** *or* **take a bath at last!** quel luxe de pouvoir enfin prendre un bain ! ADJ *[goods, article, item]* de luxe ; *[flat, hotel]* de grand luxe, de grand standing ◆ **a ~ car** une voiture de luxe

LV (abbrev of **luncheon voucher**) → **luncheon**

LW *(Rad)* (abbrev of **long wave**) GO *fpl*

lycanthropy /laɪˈkænθrəpɪ/ N lycanthropie *f*

lyceum /laɪˈsiːəm/ N ≈ maison *f* de la culture

lychee /ˈlaɪtʃiː/ N litchi *m*

lychgate /ˈlɪtʃgeɪt/ N ⇒ **lichgate**

Lycra ® /ˈlaɪkrə/ N Lycra ® *m* COMP en Lycra

lye /laɪ/ N lessive *f (substance)*

lying¹ /ˈlaɪɪŋ/ N *(NonC)* mensonge(s) *m(pl)* ◆ ~ **will get you nowhere** ça ne te servira à rien de mentir ADJ *[person]* menteur ; *[statement, story]* mensonger ◆ **you ~ bastard!** ** sale menteur ! *

lying² /ˈlaɪɪŋ/ N *[of body]* ◆ ~ **in state** exposition *f* (solennelle)
COMP **lying-in** † N (pl **lyings-in**) *(Med)* accouchement *m*, couches *fpl*
lying-in ward N salle *f* de travail *or* d'accouchement

lymph /lɪmf/ N *(Anat)* lymphe *f*
COMP **lymph gland** † N ⇒ **lymph node**
lymph node N ganglion *m* lymphatique

lymphatic /lɪmˈfætɪk/ ADJ lymphatique

lymphocyte /ˈlɪmfəʊˌsaɪt/ N lymphocyte *m*

lymphoid /ˈlɪmfɔɪd/ ADJ lymphoïde

lymphoma /lɪmˈfəʊmə/ N lymphome *m*

lymphosarcoma /ˌlɪmfəʊsɑːˈkəʊmə/ N lymphosarcome *m*

lynch /lɪntʃ/ VT *(= hang)* exécuter sommairement *(par pendaison)* ; *(= kill)* lyncher
COMP **lynch law** N loi *f* de Lynch
lynch mob N lyncheurs *mpl*

lynching /ˈlɪntʃɪŋ/ N *(= action, result)* lynchage *m*

lynchpin /ˈlɪntʃpɪn/ N ⇒ **linchpin**

lynx /lɪŋks/ N (pl **lynxes** *or* **lynx**) lynx *m inv* COMP **lynx-eyed** ADJ aux yeux de lynx

Lyons /ˈlaɪənz/ N Lyon

lyophilize /laɪˈɒfɪˌlaɪz/ VT lyophiliser

lyre /ˈlaɪəʳ/ N lyre *f*

lyrebird /ˈlaɪəbɜːd/ N oiseau-lyre *m*, ménure *m*

lyric /ˈlɪrɪk/ N 1 *(= poem)* poème *m* lyrique 2 *(= words of song)* ~**(s)** paroles *fpl* ADJ *[poem, poet]* lyrique COMP **lyric writer** N parolier *m*, -ière *f*

lyrical /ˈlɪrɪkəl/ ADJ 1 *(Poetry)* lyrique 2 * → **wax²**

lyrically /ˈlɪrɪkəlɪ/ ADV *(= poetically) [speak, write, describe]* avec lyrisme ◆ ~ **beautiful** d'une beauté lyrique

lyricism /ˈlɪrɪsɪzəm/ N lyrisme *m*

lyricist /ˈlɪrɪsɪst/ N *(= poet)* poète *m* lyrique ; *(= song-writer)* parolier *m*, -ière *f*

lysergic /laɪˈsɜːdʒɪk/ ADJ lysergique COMP **lysergic acid** N acide *m* lysergique

Mm

M, m /em/ N [1] *(= letter)* M, m *m* ◆ **M for Mike, M for Mother** ≈ M comme Marie [2] *(Brit)* (abbrev of **motorway**) ◆ **on the M6** sur l'autoroute M6 [3] (abbrev of **million(s)**) → **million** [4] (abbrev of **medium**) moyen [5] (abbrev of **metre(s)**) m [6] (abbrev of **mile(s)**) → **mile**

MA /ˌemˈeɪ/ [1] *(Univ)* (abbrev of **Master of Arts**) ◆ **to have an ~ in French** ≈ avoir une maîtrise de français ; → **master** ; → DEGREE [2] abbrev of **Massachusetts** [3] *(US)* (abbrev of **Military Academy**) → **military**

ma * /mɑː/ N maman *f* ◆ **Ma Smith** *(pej)* la mère Smith

ma'am /mæm/ N (abbrev of **madam**) *(gen: esp US)* Madame *f*, Mademoiselle *f* ; *(to royalty)* Madame *f*

Maastricht Treaty /ˈmɑːstrɪktˈtriːtɪ/ N ◆ **the ~** le traité de Maastricht

mac /mæk/ N [1] *(Brit *)* (abbrev of **mackintosh**) imperméable *m*, imper * *m* [2] *(esp US *: form of address)* **hurry up Mac!** hé ! dépêchez-vous ! ; *(to friend)* dépêche-toi mon vieux *or* mon pote ! *

macabre /məˈkɑːbrə/ ADJ macabre

macadam /məˈkædəm/ N macadam *m* ; → **tar¹**
COMP *[surface]* en macadam ; *[road]* macadamisé

macadamize /məˈkædəmaɪz/ VT macadamiser

macaroni /ˌmækəˈrəʊnɪ/ N (pl **macaronis** *or* **macaronies**) macaroni(s) *m(pl)* COMP **macaroni cheese** N gratin *m* de macaroni(s)

macaronic /ˌmækəˈrɒnɪk/ ADJ macaronique N vers *m* macaronique

macaroon /ˌmækəˈruːn/ N macaron *m*

macaw /məˈkɔː/ N ara *m*

Mace ® /meɪs/ N *(= gas)* gaz *m* incapacitant, mace *m* VT attaquer au gaz incapacitant *or* au mace

mace¹ /meɪs/ N *(NonC = spice)* macis *m*

mace² /meɪs/ N *(= weapon)* massue *f* ; *(= ceremonial staff)* masse *f*

macebearer /ˈmeɪsbeərəʳ/ N massier *m*

Macedonia /ˌmæsɪˈdəʊnɪə/ N Macédoine *f*

Macedonian /ˌmæsɪˈdəʊnɪən/ ADJ macédonien N *(= person)* Macédonien(ne) *m(f)*

macerate /ˈmæsəreɪt/ VTI macérer

Mach /mæk/ N (also **Mach number**) (nombre *m* de) Mach *m* ◆ **to fly at ~ 2** voler à Mach 2

machete /məˈʃetɪ/ N machette *f*

Machiavelli /ˌmækɪəˈvelɪ/ N Machiavel *m*

Machiavellian /ˌmækɪəˈvelɪən/ ADJ machiavélique

machination /ˌmækɪˈneɪʃən/ N machination *f*, intrigue *f*, manœuvre *f*

machine /məˈʃiːn/ N [1] *(lit)* machine *f* ◆ **bread-making/cigarette-making** *etc* **~** machine *f* à fabriquer du pain/à fabriquer des cigarettes *etc* ◆ **shredding ~** broyeur *m*, broyeuse *f* ◆ **milking ~** trayeuse *f* ◆ **by ~** à la machine ; → **flying, knitting, washing**

[2] *(fig)* machine *f* ◆ **the company is a real money-making ~** cette société est une vraie machine à fabriquer de l'argent ◆ **the military ~** la machine *or* l'appareil *m* militaire ◆ **publicity/propaganda ~** appareil *m* publicitaire/de propagande ◆ **the political ~** la machine *or* l'appareil *m* politique ◆ **the Democratic ~** *(US Pol)* la machine administrative *or* l'appareil *m* du parti démocrate ; → **party**

[3] *(pej = soulless person)* machine *f*, automate *m*
VT *(Tech)* façonner à la machine, usiner ; *(Sewing)* coudre à la machine, piquer (à la machine)
COMP *(gen)* de la machine, des machines ; *(Comput)* machine

machine age N siècle *m* de la machine *or* des machines

machine-assisted translation N traduction *f* assistée par ordinateur

machine code N *(Comput)* code *m* machine

machine error N erreur *f* technique

machine gun N mitrailleuse *f*

machine-gun VT mitrailler

machine gunner N mitrailleur *m*

machine-gunning N mitraillage *m*

machine intelligence N intelligence *f* artificielle

machine language N langage *m* machine

machine-made ADJ fait à la machine

machine operator N *(in factory)* opérateur *m*, -trice *f* (sur machines) ; *(Comput)* opérateur *m*, -trice *f*

machine-readable ADJ *(Comput)* exploitable par un ordinateur ◆ **in ~-readable form** sous (une) forme exploitable par ordinateur

machine shop N atelier *m* d'usinage

machine stitch N point *m* (de piqûre) à la machine

machine-stitch VT piquer à la machine

machine time N temps *m* d'opération (d'une machine)

machine tool N machine-outil *f* ◆ **~-tool operator** opérateur *m* sur machine-outil, usineur *m*

machine translation N traduction *f* automatique

machine washable ADJ lavable à la *or* en machine

machinery /məˈʃiːnərɪ/ N *(NonC)* [1] *(= machines collectively)* machinerie *f*, machines *fpl* ; *(= parts of machine)* mécanisme *m*, rouages *mpl* ◆ **a piece of ~** un mécanisme ◆ **to get caught in the ~** être pris dans la machine ◆ **agricultural ~** machines *fpl* agricoles ◆ **electrical ~** appareils *mpl* électriques ◆ **industrial ~** équipements *mpl* industriels [2] *(fig)* **the ~ of government** l'appareil *m* étatique ◆ **the ~ to enforce this legislation simply doesn't exist** aucun dispositif d'application n'a été mis en place pour cette législation

machinist /məˈʃiːnɪst/ N machiniste *mf*, opérateur *m*, -trice *f* (sur machine) ; *(on sewing, knitting machines)* mécanicienne *f*

machismo /mæˈtʃiːzməʊ/ N *(NonC)* machisme *m*, phallocratie *f*

macho /ˈmætʃəʊ/ N macho *m*, phallocrate *m*
ADJ macho *inv*

mackerel /ˈmækrəl/ N (pl **mackerel** *or* **mackerels**) maquereau *m* COMP **mackerel sky** N ciel *m* pommelé

Mackinaw /ˈmækɪˌnɔː/ N *(US)* (also **Mackinaw coat**) grosse veste *f* de laine à carreaux ; (also **Mackinaw blanket**) grosse couverture *f* de laine à carreaux

mackintosh /ˈmækɪntɒʃ/ N imperméable *m*

macramé /məˈkrɑːmɪ/ N macramé *m* COMP *[plant holder etc]* en macramé

macro /ˈmækrəʊ/ N *(Comput)* macro *f* COMP *(Phot)* **macro lens** N *(Phot)* objectif *m* macro

macrobiotic /ˌmækrəʊbaɪˈɒtɪk/ ADJ macrobiotique

macrobiotics /ˌmækrəʊbaɪˈɒtɪks/ N *(NonC)* macrobiotique *f*

macrocosm /ˈmækrəʊkɒzəm/ N macrocosme *m*

macroeconomics /ˌmækrəʊˌiːkəˈnɒmɪks/ N *(NonC)* macroéconomie *f*

macro-instruction /ˌmækrəʊɪnˈstrʌkʃən/ N macro-instruction *f*

macrolinguistics /ˌmækrəʊlɪŋˈgwɪstɪks/ N *(NonC)* macrolinguistique *f*

macromarketing /ˌmækrəʊˈmɑːkɪtɪŋ/ N macromarketing *m*

macromolecule /ˈmækrəʊˌmɒlɪkjuːl/ N macromolécule *f*

macron /ˈmækrɒn/ N macron *m*

macrophotography /ˌmækrəʊfəˈtɒgrəfɪ/ N macrophotographie *f*

macroscopic /ˌmækrəˈskɒpɪk/ ADJ macroscopique

MAD /ˌemeɪˈdiː/ N (US Mil) (abbrev of **mutual(ly) assured destruction**) → **mutual**

mad /mæd/ ADJ 1 [person] (= deranged) fou (folle f) ; (= rash, crazy) fou (folle f), insensé ; [hope, plan, idea] insensé ; [race, gallop] effréné ; [bull] furieux ; [dog] enragé ◆ **to go ~** devenir fou ◆ **this is idealism gone ~** c'est de l'idéalisme qui dépasse les bornes ; (stronger) c'est de l'idéalisme qui vire à la folie ◆ **to drive sb ~** (lit, fig) rendre qn fou ; see also **2** ◆ **as ~ as a hatter** or **a March hare** * ◆ **(stark) raving ~** * ◆ **stark staring ~** * fou à lier ◆ **~ with grief** fou de chagrin ◆ **that was a ~ thing to do** il fallait être fou pour faire cela ◆ **you're ~ to think of it!** tu es fou d'y songer ! ◆ **are you ~?** ça ne va pas ?* (iro) ◆ **you must be ~!** ça ne va pas, non !* ◆ **you must be ~ to cycle in this weather!, you must be ~, cycling in this weather!** il faut vraiment que tu sois fou pour faire du vélo par ce temps !, tu es fou de faire du vélo par ce temps ! ◆ **we had a ~ dash for the bus** nous avons dû foncer* pour attraper le bus ◆ **I'm in a ~ rush** * je suis à la bourre*

◆ **like mad** * (Brit = happy) ◆ **to pedal/push** etc **like ~** pédaler/appuyer etc comme un fou ◆ **to run like ~** courir comme un fou or un dératé ◆ **to cry like ~** pleurer comme une Madeleine ◆ **to laugh like ~** rire comme une baleine* ◆ **the phone has been ringing like ~ all morning** le téléphone n'a pas arrêté de sonner ce matin ◆ **to work/shout like ~** travailler/crier comme un fou or un forcené ◆ **this plant grows like ~** cette plante pousse comme du chiendent

2 (esp US * = angry) furieux ◆ **to be ~ at** or **with sb** être furieux contre qn ◆ **to get ~ at** or **with sb** s'emporter contre qn ◆ **don't get ~ at** or **with me!** ne te fâche pas contre moi ! ◆ **he was ~ at** or **with me for spilling the tea** il était furieux contre moi parce que j'avais renversé le thé ◆ **he was really ~ about my mistake** mon erreur l'a mis hors de lui ◆ **he makes me ~!** ce qu'il peut m'agacer or m'énerver ! ◆ **to drive sb ~** faire enrager qn, mettre qn en fureur ◆ **he's hopping** or **spitting ~** il est fou furieux ◆ **~ as a hornet** * (US) furibard*

3 (* = enthusiastic: also **mad keen**) ◆ **to go ~ on sth** devenir dingue* de qch ◆ **~ on** or **about sth** mordu* or dingue* de qch ◆ **to be ~ on** or **about sb** être fou de qn ◆ **I'm not ~ on** or **about him** je ne l'aime pas trop ◆ **to be ~ on** or **about swimming/football/computers, to be swimming-/football-/computer-~** être mordu* or dingue* de natation/de football/d'informatique ◆ **I'm not ~ about it** ça ne m'emballe pas*

4 (* = excited) ◆ **the audience went ~** la folie a gagné le public ◆ **the dog went ~ when he saw his master** le chien est devenu comme fou quand il a vu son maître ◆ **I went ~ and finished everything in an hour** sur un coup de tête or de folie, j'ai tout fini en une heure

COMP **mad cow disease** N maladie f de la vache folle

mad money * N (NonC: US) ◆ **this is my ~ money** cet argent-là, c'est pour mes petits plaisirs

Madagascan /ˌmædəˈgæskən/ ADJ malgache N (= person) Malgache mf

Madagascar /ˌmædəˈgæskəʳ/ N (= island) Madagascar f ; (= country) Madagascar m ◆ **the Democratic Republic of ~** la République démocratique de Madagascar ◆ **in ~** à Madagascar

madam /ˈmædəm/ N (pl **madams** or **mesdames** /ˈmeɪdæm/) 1 madame f ; (unmarried) mademoiselle f ◆ **Dear Madam** (in letters) Madame, Mademoiselle ◆ **Madam Chairman** (frm) Madame la Présidente 2 (Brit) ◆ **she's a little ~** * c'est une petite pimbêche or mijaurée 3 (= brothelkeeper) sous-maîtresse f, tenancière f de maison close

madcap /ˈmædkæp/ ADJ, N écervelé(e) m(f)

madden /ˈmædn/ VT rendre fou ; (= infuriate) exaspérer ◆ **~ed by pain** fou de douleur

maddening /ˈmædnɪŋ/ ADJ exaspérant

maddeningly /ˈmædnɪŋlɪ/ ADV [say, smile] d'une façon exaspérante ◆ **to be ~ cautious/slow** être d'une prudence/lenteur exaspérante

made /meɪd/ VB pt, ptp of **make**

COMP **made-to-measure** ADJ (fait) sur mesure

made-to-order ADJ (fait) sur commande

made-up ADJ 1 (= invented) [story] inventé, fabriqué ; (pej) faux (fausse f) ; (with cosmetics) [face, eyes] maquillé ; [nails] fait ◆ **she is too ~-up** elle est trop maquillée 2 * (Brit = happy, delighted) ravi

-made /meɪd/ ADJ ENDING IN COMPS ◆ **British/French-made** fabriqué en Grande-Bretagne/France

Madeira /məˈdɪərə/ N (Geog) (l'île f de) Madère f ; (= wine) (vin m de) madère m

COMP **Madeira cake** N ≈ quatre-quarts m

Madeira sauce N sauce f madère

madhouse * /ˈmædhaʊs/ N (lit, fig) maison f de fous

Madison Avenue /ˈmædɪsənˈævənjuː/ N (US) le monde de la publicité

madly /ˈmædlɪ/ ADV 1 [scream, grin] comme un fou ◆ **to be/fall ~ in love with sb** être/tomber éperdument amoureux de qn ◆ **to love sb ~** aimer qn à la folie ◆ **we were ~ rushing for the train** (= furiously) c'était la course pour attraper le train ◆ **I was ~ trying to open it** j'essayais désespérément de l'ouvrir 2 [attractive, exciting] follement ; [irritating] extrêmement ◆ **~ impatient** piaffant d'impatience ◆ **~ jealous** fou de jalousie

madman /ˈmædmən/ N (pl **-men**) fou m

madness /ˈmædnɪs/ N (gen, Med) folie f ; (in animals = rabies) rage f ; (= rashness) folie f, démence f ◆ **it is sheer ~ to say so** c'est de la pure folie or de la démence de le dire ◆ **what ~!** c'est de la pure folie !, il faut être fou !

Madonna /məˈdɒnə/ N (Rel) Madone f ; (fig) madone f COMP **Madonna lily** N lis m blanc

Madras /məˈdrɑːs/ N (Geog) Madras

madras /məˈdrɑːs/ N 1 (Culin = curry) curry très épicé ◆ **beef/chicken ~** curry de bœuf/poulet très épicé 2 (also **madras cotton**) madras m

Madrid /məˈdrɪd/ N Madrid

madrigal /ˈmædrɪgəl/ N madrigal m

madwoman /ˈmædwʊmən/ N (pl **-women**) folle f

maelstrom /ˈmeɪlstrəʊm/ N (lit, fig) tourbillon m, maelström m

maestro /ˈmaɪstrəʊ/ N (pl **maestros** or **maestri** /ˈmaɪstrɪ/) maestro m

Mae West †* /ˌmeɪˈwest/ N gilet m de sauvetage (gonflable)

MAFF N (Brit: formerly) (abbrev of **Ministry of Agriculture, Fisheries and Food**) ministère m de l'Agriculture, de la Pêche et de l'Alimentation

mafia /ˈmæfɪə/ N (lit, fig) mafia f ◆ **it's a real ~** c'est une véritable mafia ◆ **a literary ~** une coterie littéraire ◆ **~ links** relations mafieuses

mafioso /ˌmæfɪˈəʊsəʊ/ N maf(f)ioso m, maf(f)ieux

mag * /mæg/ N (abbrev of **magazine**) revue f, magazine m

magazine /ˌmægəˈziːn/ N 1 (Press) revue f, magazine m ; (Rad, TV: also **magazine programme**) magazine m 2 (Mil = store) magasin m (du corps) 3 (in gun) (= compartment) magasin m ; (= cartridges) chargeur m ; (in slide projector etc) magasin m

Magellan /məˈgelən/ N Magellan m ◆ **~ Strait** détroit m de Magellan

magenta /məˈdʒentə/ N magenta m ADJ magenta inv

Maggiore /ˌmædʒɪˈɔːrɪ/ N ◆ **Lake ~** le lac Majeur

maggot /ˈmægət/ N ver m, asticot m

maggoty /ˈmægətɪ/ ADJ [fruit] véreux

Maghreb /ˈmʌgrəb/ N Maghreb m

Magi /ˈmeɪdʒaɪ/ NPL (rois mpl) mages mpl

magic /ˈmædʒɪk/ N (NonC) magie f, enchantement m ◆ **as if by ~, like ~** comme par enchantement or magie ◆ **the ~ of that moment** la magie de cet instant

ADJ 1 (= supernatural) magique, enchanté ; (fig) merveilleux, prodigieux ◆ **to say the ~ word** prononcer la formule magique ◆ **the Magic Flute** la Flûte enchantée

2 (esp Brit * = brilliant) super*, génial*

COMP **magic bullet** N (= miracle cure) médicament m miracle ; (US * = solution) solution f miracle

magic carpet N tapis m volant

magic circle N cercle m magique

magic lantern N lanterne f magique

magic mushroom * N champignon m hallucinogène

magic realism N réalisme m magique

magic spell N sort m sortilège m

magic square N carré m magique

► **magic away** VT SEP faire disparaître comme par enchantement

► **magic up** VT SEP faire apparaître comme par enchantement

magical /ˈmædʒɪkəl/ ADJ 1 (= supernatural) [powers, properties] magique 2 (= wonderful) [story, tale, experience] merveilleux ; [place, moment] magique

COMP **magical mystery tour** N voyage m enchanté

magical realism N réalisme m magique

magically /ˈmædʒɪkəlɪ/ ADV [disappear, transform, produce] comme par magie or enchantement

magician /məˈdʒɪʃən/ N (lit, fig) magicien(ne) m(f) ; (Theat etc) illusionniste mf

magisterial /ˌmædʒɪsˈtɪərɪəl/ ADJ (lit) de magistrat ; (fig) magistral, formidable

magisterially /ˌmædʒɪsˈtɪərɪəlɪ/ ADV magistralement

magistracy /ˈmædʒɪstrəsɪ/ N (NonC) magistrature f

magistrate /ˈmædʒɪstreɪt/ N magistrat m ; (dealing with minor crimes) juge mf d'instance ◆ **~s' court** ≈ tribunal m d'instance

magma /ˈmægmə/ N (pl **magmas** or **magmata** /ˈmægmətə/) magma m

Magna C(h)arta /ˌmægnəˈkɑːtə/ N (Brit Hist) ◆ **(the) ~** la Grande Charte f

magna cum laude /ˈmægnəkʌmˈlaʊdeɪ/ ADV (US Univ) ◆ **to graduate ~** ≈ obtenir la mention très bien

magnanimity /ˌmægnəˈnɪmɪtɪ/ N magnanimité f

magnanimous /mægˈnænɪməs/ ADJ [person, gesture] magnanime (to sb envers qn) ◆ **to be ~ in victory** se montrer magnanime dans la victoire, être un vainqueur magnanime

magnanimously /mægˈnænɪməslɪ/ ADV magnanimement

magnate /ˈmægneɪt/ N magnat m, roi m ◆ **industrial/financial ~** magnat m de l'industrie/de la finance ◆ **oil ~** magnat m or roi m du pétrole

magnesia /mægˈniːʃə/ N magnésie f ; → **milk**

magnesium /mægˈniːzɪəm/ N magnésium m

magnet /ˈmægnɪt/ N (lit, fig) aimant m COMP **magnet school** N (US) école, généralement si-

tuée dans un quartier défavorisé, qui bénéficie d'avantages particuliers destinés à attirer des élèves d'autres quartiers

magnetic /mæg'netɪk/ **ADJ** (lit, fig) magnétique **COMP** **magnetic card reader** **N** lecteur *m* de cartes magnétiques
magnetic disk **N** disque *m* magnétique
magnetic field **N** champ *m* magnétique
magnetic needle **N** aiguille *f* aimantée
magnetic north **N** nord *m* magnétique
magnetic resonance imager **N** imageur *m* à résonance magnétique
magnetic resonance imaging **N** imagerie *f* par résonance magnétique
magnetic storm **N** orage *m* magnétique
magnetic strip, magnetic stripe **N** (on credit card etc) piste *f* magnétique
magnetic tape **N** bande *f* magnétique

magnetically /mæg'netɪkəlɪ/ **ADV** 1 (Phys) [attach] magnétiquement 2 (fig) ◆ **to be ~ drawn to sb/sth** être attiré par qn/qch comme par un aimant

magnetism /'mægnɪtɪzəm/ **N** (lit, fig) magnétisme *m*

magnetize /'mægnɪtaɪz/ **VT** (lit) aimanter, magnétiser ; (fig) magnétiser

magneto /mæg'niːtəʊ/ **N** magnéto *f*

magnetometer /,mægnɪ'tɒmɪtəʳ/ **N** magnétomètre *m*

magnetosphere /mæg'niːtəʊ,sfɪəʳ/ **N** magnétosphère *f*

Magnificat /mæg'nɪfɪ,kæt/ **N** (Rel) Magnificat *m inv*

magnification /,mægnɪfɪ'keɪʃən/ **N** 1 (Opt) grossissement *m* ◆ **under ~** au microscope 2 (fig = amplification) amplification *f* 3 (Rel) glorification *f* **COMP** **magnification factor** **N** coefficient *m* de grossissement

magnificence /mæg'nɪfɪsəns/ **N** magnificence *f*, splendeur *f*, somptuosité *f*

magnificent /mæg'nɪfɪsənt/ **ADJ** (gen) magnifique ; [food, meal] splendide

magnificently /mæg'nɪfɪsəntlɪ/ **ADV** magnifiquement

magnify /'mægnɪfaɪ/ **VT** 1 [+ image] grossir ; [+ sound] amplifier ; [+ incident] exagérer, grossir ◆ **to ~ sth four times** grossir qch quatre fois ◆ **a severe lack of information is ~ing their confusion** un grave manque d'information ajoute à leur confusion ◆ **adolescence is a time when all your insecurities are magnified** l'adolescence est une période où tous nos sentiments d'insécurité sont amplifiés ◆ **poverty magnifies the effects of disasters** la pauvreté amplifie les effets des catastrophes naturelles ◆ **signs of discontent are often magnified** les signes de mécontentement sont souvent exagérés ◆ **the dispute has been magnified out of all proportion** l'importance du conflit a été démesurément exagérée ◆ **companies that use bank loans to ~ their buying power** les sociétés qui ont recours aux prêts bancaires pour augmenter leur pouvoir d'achat
2 (Rel = praise) glorifier
COMP **magnifying glass** **N** loupe *f*, verre *m* grossissant

magnitude /'mægnɪtjuːd/ **N** ampleur *f* ; (Astron) magnitude *f* ◆ **of the first ~** (fig) de première grandeur

magnolia /mæg'nəʊlɪə/ **N** 1 (also **magnolia tree**) magnolia *m*, magnolier *m* 2 (= colour) rose *m* pâle **ADJ** rose pâle *inv* **COMP** **the Magnolia State** **N** (US) le Mississippi

magnox /'mægnɒks/ **N** magnox *m* ◆ **~ reactor** réacteur *m* au magnox

magnum /'mægnəm/ **N** (pl **magnums**) magnum *m* **COMP** **magnum opus** **N** (Art, Literat, fig) œuvre *f* maîtresse

magpie /'mægpaɪ/ **N** 1 (= bird) pie *f* ◆ **to chatter like a ~** jacasser comme une pie, être un vrai moulin à paroles * 2 (fig = collector) **he's a real ~** c'est un collectionneur invétéré

Magyar /'mægjɑːʳ/ **ADJ** magyar **N** Magyar(e) *m(f)*

maharaja(h) /,mɑːhə'rɑːdʒə/ **N** mahara(d)jah *m*

maharanee, maharani /,mɑːhə'rɑːniː/ **N** maharani *f*

maharishi /,mɑːhɑː'riːʃɪ/ **N** maharishi *m*

mahatma /mə'hɑːtmə/ **N** mahatma *m*

mahjong(g) /,mɑː'dʒɒŋ/ **N** ma(h)-jong *m*

mahogany /mə'hɒgənɪ/ **N** acajou *m* **COMP** (= made of mahogany) en acajou ; (= mahogany-coloured) acajou *inv*

Mahomet /mə'hɒmɪt/ **N** Mahomet *m*

Mahometan † /mə'hɒmɪtən/ **ADJ** mahométan **N** mahométan(e) *m(f)*

Mahometanism † /mə'hɒmɪtənɪzəm/ **N** mahométisme *m*

mahout /mə'haʊt/ **N** cornac *m*

maid /meɪd/ **N** 1 (= servant) domestique *f* ; (in hotel) femme *f* de chambre ; → **barmaid, housemaid, lady** 2 †† (= young girl) jeune fille *f* ; (= virgin) vierge *f* ◆ **the Maid (of Orleans)** (Hist) la Pucelle (d'Orléans) ; → **old**
COMP **maid-of-all-work** **N** bonne *f* à tout faire
maid of honour **N** (esp US) demoiselle *f* d'honneur

maiden /'meɪdn/ **N** (liter) (= girl) jeune fille *f* ; (= virgin) vierge *f*
COMP [flight, voyage] premier *before n*, inaugural
maiden aunt **N** tante *f* célibataire, tante *f* restée vieille fille (pej)
maiden lady **N** († or hum) demoiselle *f*
maiden name **N** nom *m* de jeune fille
maiden over **N** (Cricket) *série de six balles où aucun point n'est marqué*
maiden speech **N** (Parl) premier discours *m* (d'un député etc)

maidenhair /'meɪdnheəʳ/ **N** (also **maidenhair fern**) capillaire *m*, cheveu-de-Vénus *m*

maidenhead /'meɪdnhed/ **N** 1 (Anat) hymen *m* 2 (= virginity) virginité *f*

maidenhood /'meɪdnhʊd/ **N** virginité *f*

maidenly /'meɪdnlɪ/ **ADJ** de jeune fille, virginal, modeste

maidservant † /'meɪdsɜːvənt/ **N** servante *f*

mail[1] /meɪl/ **N** 1 (NonC = postal system) poste *f* ◆ **by ~** par la poste
2 (NonC = letters) courrier *m* ◆ **here's your ~** voici votre courrier
3 (Comput: also **e-mail, electronic mail**) courrier *m* électronique, e-mail *m* ◆ **to send sb a ~** envoyer un message à qn (par courrier électronique), envoyer un courrier électronique *or* un e-mail à qn
VT 1 (esp US = post) envoyer *or* expédier (par la poste), poster
2 (Comput: also **e-mail**) [+ message, memo etc] envoyer par courrier électronique ◆ **to ~ sb** envoyer un message à qn (par courrier électronique), envoyer un courrier électronique à qn (about à propos de)
COMP **mail bomb** **N** (US) colis *m* piégé
mail car **N** (US Rail) wagon *m* postal
mail carrier **N** (US) facteur *m*, préposé(e) *m(f)*
mail clerk **N** (employé(e) *m(f)*) préposé(e) *m(f)* au courrier
mail coach **N** (Rail) wagon-poste *m* ; (horse-drawn) malle-poste *f*
mailing list **N** (Comm) liste *f* d'adresses
mail-merge **N** (Comput) publipostage *m*
mail order **N** vente *f* par correspondance ◆ **we got it by ~ order** nous l'avons acheté par correspondance
mail-order **ADJ** ◆ **~-order catalogue** catalogue *m* de vente par correspondance ◆ **~-order firm, ~-order house** maison *f* de vente par correspondance
mail room **N** (esp US) service *m* courrier
mail slot **N** (US) fente *f* de la *or* d'une boîte aux lettres
mail train **N** train *m* postal
mail truck **N** (US) camionnette *f or* fourgon *m* des postes
mail van **N** (Brit) (= vehicle) camionnette *f or* fourgon *m* des postes ; (= train wagon) wagon *m* postal

mail[2] /meɪl/ **N** (NonC) mailles *fpl* ◆ **coat of ~** cotte *f* de mailles ◆ **the ~ed fist** (fig) la manière forte ; → **chain**

mailbag /'meɪlbæg/ **N** sac *m* postal

mailboat /'meɪlbəʊt/ **N** paquebot(-poste) *m*

mailbox /'meɪlbɒks/ **N** (Comput, US Post) boîte *f* aux lettres

Mailgram ® /'meɪlgræm/ **N** (US) télégramme *m* (distribué avec le courrier)

mailing /'meɪlɪŋ/ **N** publipostage *m*, mailing *m* ◆ **~ list** fichier *m or* liste *f* d'adresses **COMP** **mailing address** **N** (US) adresse *f* postale

mailman /'meɪlmæn/ **N** (pl **-men**) (US) facteur *m*, préposé *m*

mailshot /'meɪlʃɒt/ **N** (Brit) mailing *m*, publipostage *m*

maim /meɪm/ **VT** estropier, mutiler ◆ **to be ~ed for life** être estropié pour la vie *or* à vie

Main /meɪn/ **N** (= river) Main *m*

main /meɪn/ **ADJ** 1 [door, entrance, shop, feature, idea, objective] principal ; [pipe, beam] maître (maîtresse *f*) ◆ **the ~ body of the army/the crowd** le gros de l'armée/de la foule ◆ **one of his ~ ideas was ...** une de ses principales idées *or* idées maîtresses consistait à ... ◆ **my ~ idea was to establish ...** mon idée directrice était d'établir ... ◆ **the ~ point of his speech** le point fondamental de son discours ◆ **the ~ point** *or* **object** *or* **objective of the meeting** l'objet principal de cette réunion ◆ **the ~ thing is to keep quiet** l'essentiel est de se taire ◆ **the ~ thing to remember is ...** ce qu'il ne faut surtout pas oublier c'est ... ◆ **to have an eye to the ~ chance** tirer profit de toutes les situations ◆ **one of the ~ tourist areas of Amsterdam** l'un des grands quartiers touristiques d'Amsterdam ◆ **my ~ concern is to protect the children** ma préoccupation première *or* essentielle est de protéger les enfants ; see also **comp** ; → **drag, eye, issue**
2 ◆ **by ~ force** de vive force
N 1 (= principal pipe, wire) canalisation *f or* conduite *f* maîtresse ◆ **(electricity) ~** conducteur *m* principal ◆ **(gas) ~** (in street) conduite *f* principale ; (in house) conduite *f* de gaz ◆ **~ (sewer)** (égout *m*) collecteur *m* ◆ **(water) ~** (in street or house) conduite *f* d'eau de la ville ◆ **the water in this tap comes from the ~s** l'eau de ce robinet vient directement de la conduite ◆ **the ~s** (Elec) le secteur ◆ **connected to the ~s** branché sur (le) secteur ◆ **this radio works by battery or from the ~s** ce poste de radio marche sur piles ou sur (le) secteur ◆ **to turn off the electricity/gas/water at the ~(s)** couper le courant/le gaz/l'eau au compteur
2 (set structure)
◆ **in the main** dans l'ensemble, en général
3 (liter) ◆ **the ~** (= sea) l'océan *m*, le (grand) large ; → **Spanish**
COMP **main beam** **N** (Archit) poutre *f* maîtresse
main bearing **N** (in mechanism, car) palier *m*
main clause **N** (Gram) proposition *f* principale
main course **N** (Culin) plat *m* principal
main deck **N** (Naut) pont *m* principal

main door (flat) N *(Brit)* appartement *m* avec porte d'entrée particulière sur la rue
main line N *(Rail)* grande ligne *f*
main man* N (pl **main men**) *(US)* meilleur pote* *m*
main memory N *(Comput)* mémoire *f* centrale
main office N *[of company]* bureau *m* principal ; *[of political party, newspaper, agency etc]* siège *m* (social)
main road N grande route *f*, route *f* à grande circulation ◆ **the ~ road** la grand-route ◆ **it is one of the ~ roads into Edinburgh** c'est une des grandes voies d'accès à Édimbourg
main sheet N *(Naut)* écoute *f* de (la) grand-voile
mains set N *(radio, tape recorder etc)* appareil *m* fonctionnant sur secteur
mains supply N ◆ **to be on the ~s supply** *(for electricity/gas/water)* être raccordé au réseau (de distribution) d'électricité/de gaz/d'eau
main street N grand-rue *f*, rue *f* principale
mains water N eau *f* de la ville

mainbrace /ˈmeɪnbreɪs/ N *(Naut)* bras *m* (de grand-vergue) ; → **splice**

Maine /meɪn/ N Maine *m* ◆ **in ~** dans le Maine

mainframe /ˈmeɪnfreɪm/ N (also **mainframe computer**) *(= central computer)* unité *f* centrale, processeur *m* central ; *(= large computer)* gros ordinateur *m*

mainland /ˈmeɪnlænd/ N continent *m (opposé à une île)* ◆ **the ~ of Greece, the Greek ~** la Grèce continentale ◆ **the Mainland** *(Brit) (not Northern Ireland)* la Grande-Bretagne *(l'Angleterre, l'Écosse et le pays de Galles)* ; *(not Hong Kong)* la Chine continentale ADJ /ˈmeɪnlənd/ continental ◆ **~ Greece** la Grèce continentale

mainline /ˈmeɪnlaɪn/ ADJ 1 *(= principal)* → **mainstream** 2 *[station, train]* de grande ligne VI *(* Drugs)* se shooter VT * *(= inject)* ◆ **to ~ heroin** se shooter* à l'héroïne

mainliner* /ˈmeɪnlaɪnəʳ/ N *(Drugs)* junkie *mf* qui se shoote*

mainly /ˈmeɪnlɪ/ ADV surtout, principalement ◆ **~ because** surtout parce que

mainmast /ˈmeɪnmɑːst/ N *(Naut)* grand mât *m*

mainsail /ˈmeɪnseɪl/ N *(Naut)* grand-voile *f*

mainspring /ˈmeɪnsprɪŋ/ N *[of clock etc]* ressort *m* principal ; *(fig)* mobile *m* principal

mainstay /ˈmeɪnsteɪ/ N *(Naut)* étai *m* (de grand mât) ; *(fig)* soutien *m*, point *m* d'appui ◆ **he was the ~ of the organization** c'était lui le pilier *or* le pivot de l'organisation

mainstream /ˈmeɪnstriːm/ ADJ *[political party, denomination]* grand, dominant ; *[media]* principal ; *[press]* traditionnel ; *[culture]* grand public *inv* ; *[film, music]* conventionnel, mainstream* ; *[audience]* moyen ◆ **fascism has never been part of ~ politics in Britain** le fascisme n'a jamais fait partie des grands courants politiques en Grande-Bretagne N *[of politics etc]* courant *m* dominant VT *(US Scol)* intégrer dans la vie scolaire normale

mainstreaming /ˈmeɪnstriːmɪŋ/ N *(US)* 1 *(Scol) intégration (d'enfants retardés ou surdoués) dans la vie scolaire normale* 2 *[of social group] fait de faire sortir (un groupe social) de la marginalité*

maintain /meɪnˈteɪn/ LANGUAGE IN USE 26.2
VT 1 *(= continue, keep up) [+ rate, level, order, progress, stability, sanctions, temperature, speed, value, standard, quality]* maintenir ; *[+ friendship, correspondence, diplomatic relations]* entretenir ; *[+ silence]* garder ; *[+ attitude, advantage]* conserver, garder ◆ **to ~ the status quo** maintenir le statu quo ◆ **to ~ sth at a constant temperature** maintenir qch à une température constante ◆ **to ~ radio silence** maintenir le silence radio ◆ **to ~ control** garder le contrôle ◆ **~ the pressure on the wound** continuez à comprimer la blessure ◆ **to ~ one's living standards** maintenir son niveau de vie ◆ **the government has failed to ~ standards of health care in this country** le gouvernement n'a pas réussi à maintenir la qualité des soins médicaux dans notre pays ◆ **pupils who manage to ~ their high standards throughout their school career** des élèves qui arrivent à rester parmi les meilleurs pendant toute leur scolarité ◆ **he ~ed his opposition to ...** il continua à s'opposer à ... ◆ **if the improvement is ~ed** si l'on *(or* s'il *etc)* continue à faire des progrès ◆ **products which help to ~ healthy skin and hair** des produits qui aident à garder une peau et des cheveux en bonne santé ◆ **to ~ one's weight (at the same level)** garder le même poids ◆ **he wants to ~ his weight at 150 pounds** il veut rester à 68 kilos
2 *(= support, finance) [+ family, wife, child, army]* entretenir
3 *(= assure upkeep of) [+ road, building, car, machine]* entretenir ; *[+ child]* élever ◆ **a husband should pay and ~ his wife** le mari devrait payer sa femme et subvenir à ses besoins
4 *(= assert) [+ opinion, fact]* soutenir, maintenir ◆ **to ~ one's innocence** clamer son innocence ◆ **I ~ that ...** je soutiens *or* maintiens que ... ◆ **"I wasn't there," she ~ed** "je n'y étais pas", insista-t-elle ◆ **he ~ed the money was donated for humanitarian aid** il a maintenu que l'argent avait été donné à des fins d'aide humanitaire ◆ **"life doesn't have to be like this," she ~s** "on n'est pas forcé de vivre comme ça", maintient-elle
COMP **maintained school** N *(Brit)* école *f* publique

maintenance /ˈmeɪntɪnəns/ N *(NonC)* 1 *(= continuation, preservation) [of rate, level, order, progress, stability, sanctions, temperature, speed, value, standard, quality]* maintien *m*
2 *(= upkeep) [of road, building, car, machine]* entretien *m*, maintenance *f (Tech)* ◆ **car ~** mécanique *f* (auto) ◆ **they are responsible for ~ on long haul flights** ils sont chargés de l'entretien *or* de la maintenance sur les vols long-courriers
3 *(= financing) [of family, wife, child, army]* entretien *m* ◆ **parents are liable for the ~ of their children** les parents doivent subvenir aux besoins de leurs enfants
4 *(Jur)* pension *f* alimentaire ◆ **he pays £50 per week ~** il verse une pension alimentaire de 50 livres par semaine ◆ **plans to make absent fathers pay ~ for their children** un projet visant à obliger les pères absents à payer la pension alimentaire de leurs enfants
COMP **maintenance allowance** N *[of student]* bourse *f* (d'études) ; *[of worker away from home]* indemnité *f* (pour frais) de déplacement
maintenance contract N contrat *m* d'entretien
maintenance costs NPL frais *mpl* d'entretien
maintenance crew N équipe *f* d'entretien
maintenance grant N ⇒ **maintenance allowance**
maintenance man N (pl **maintenance men**) *(Tech etc)* employé *m* chargé de l'entretien
maintenance order N *(Jur)* ordonnance *f* de versement de pension alimentaire

maisonette /ˌmeɪzəˈnet/ N *(esp Brit)* (appartement *m* en) duplex *m*

maître d'hôtel /ˌmetrədəʊˈtel/ N (pl **maîtres d'hôtel**) (also **maître d'**) maître *m* d'hôtel

maize /meɪz/ N *(Brit)* maïs *m* ◆ **~ field** champ *m* de maïs

Maj. (abbrev of **Major**) *(on envelope)* ◆ **~ J. Smith** Monsieur le Major J. Smith

majestic /məˈdʒestɪk/ ADJ majestueux

majestically /məˈdʒestɪkəlɪ/ ADV majestueusement

majesty /ˈmædʒɪstɪ/ N majesté *f* ◆ **His Majesty the King** Sa Majesté le Roi ◆ **Your Majesty** Votre Majesté ◆ **His** *or* **Her Majesty's Government** *(Brit)* le gouvernement britannique ◆ **on His** *or* **Her Majesty's service** *(Brit)* au service du gouvernement britannique ◆ **His** *or* **Her Majesty's Stationery Office** *(Brit)* ≃ l'Imprimerie *f* nationale ; → **ship**

major /ˈmeɪdʒəʳ/ ADJ majeur ◆ **of ~ importance** d'importance majeure ◆ **to play a ~ part in sth** jouer un rôle majeur dans qch ◆ **of ~ interest** d'intérêt majeur ◆ **the ~ factor in his decision to stay was ...** le facteur principal qui l'a poussé à rester est ... ◆ **a ~ operation** *(Med)* une grosse opération ◆ **~ repairs** grosses réparations *fpl*, gros travaux *mpl* ◆ **a ~ portion of funding comes from the trade unions** la majeure partie du financement provient des syndicats ◆ **~ road** route *f* principale ◆ **it was a ~ success** cela a eu un succès considérable ◆ **Smith Major** *(Brit Scol)* Smith aîné
N 1 *[of army and US Air Force]* commandant *m* ; *[of cavalry]* chef *m* d'escadron ; *[of infantry]* chef *m* de bataillon
2 *(Jur)* majeur(e) *m(f)*
3 *(US Univ)* matière *f* principale
4 *(esp US Univ)* ◆ **music/psychology** *etc* **~** étudiant(e) *m(f)* en musique/psychologie *etc*
VI *(US Univ)* ◆ **to ~ in chemistry** se spécialiser en chimie
COMP **major-general** N *(Mil)* général *m* de division ; *(US Air Force)* général *m* de division aérienne
major key N *(Mus)* ton *m* majeur ◆ **in the ~ key** en majeur
major league N *(US Sport)* première division *f*
major suit N *(Cards)* majeure *f*

Majorca /məˈjɔːkə/ N Majorque *f* ◆ **in ~** à Majorque

Majorcan /məˈjɔːkən/ ADJ majorquin N Majorquin(e) *m(f)*

majordomo /ˌmeɪdʒəˈdəʊməʊ/ N majordome *m*

majorette /ˌmeɪdʒəˈret/ N majorette *f*

majority /məˈdʒɒrɪtɪ/ N 1 *(= greater part)* majorité *f* ◆ **to be in the** *or* **a ~** être majoritaire *or* en majorité ◆ **elected by a ~ of nine** élu avec une majorité de neuf voix ◆ **a four-fifths ~** une majorité des quatre cinquièmes ◆ **in the ~ of cases** dans la majorité *or* la plupart des cas ◆ **the ~ of people think that ...** la plupart *or* la majorité des gens pensent que ... ◆ **the vast ~ of them believe ...** dans leur immense majorité ils croient ... ; → **silent** 2 *(in age)* majorité *f* ◆ **the age of ~** l'âge *m* de la majorité ◆ **to reach one's ~** atteindre sa majorité
COMP *(Pol) [government, rule]* majoritaire
majority opinion N *(US Jur)* arrêt *m* rendu à la majorité *(des votes des juges)*
majority verdict N *(Jur)* verdict *m* majoritaire *or* rendu à la majorité

make /meɪk/
vb : pret, ptp **made**

1 TRANSITIVE VERB	4 COMPOUNDS
2 INTRANSITIVE VERB	5 PHRASAL VERBS
3 NOUN	

1 - TRANSITIVE VERB

When **make** is part of a set combination, eg **make a case, make an attempt, make a bow, make sure, make bold**, look up the other word.

1 *= create, produce [+ bed, cake, clothes, coffee, fire, noise, remark, one's will]* faire ; *[+ shelter]* construire ; *[+ toys, tools, machines]* fabriquer, faire ◆ **I'm going to ~ a cake** je vais faire un gâteau

◆ **he made it himself** il l'a fait lui-même ◆ **two and two ~ four** deux et deux font *or* égalent quatre ◆ **how much does that ~ (altogether)?** combien ça fait (en tout) ? ◆ **that ~s the third time I've rung him** ça fait la troisième fois *or* trois fois que je l'appelle ◆ **to ~ a payment** effectuer un paiement ◆ **God made Man** Dieu a créé l'homme ◆ **he's as clever as they ~ 'em** * il est malin comme pas un*, il est malin comme tout*

♦ **to make the/a total** ◆ **I ~ the total 15 euros** selon mes calculs ça fait 15 € ◆ **that ~s a total of 18 points** ça fait 18 points en tout

♦ **to make sth into sth** transformer qch en qch

♦ **made** + *preposition* ◆ **they were made for each other** ils étaient faits l'un pour l'autre ◆ **her shoes weren't made for walking** elle n'avait pas les chaussures adaptées pour la marche ◆ **made in France** *(on label)* fabriqué en France, "made in France" ◆ **the frames are made of plastic** la monture est en plastique ◆ **to show what one is made of** montrer ce dont on est capable ◆ **this car wasn't made to carry eight people** cette voiture n'est pas faite pour transporter huit personnes

2 = earn [+ *money*] *[person]* gagner, se faire ; *[company, firm]* réaliser un bénéfice net de ; *[product, deal]* rapporter ◆ **he ~s $400 a week** il gagne *or* se fait 400 dollars par semaine ◆ **how much do you ~?** combien gagnez-vous ? ◆ **how much do you stand to ~?** combien pensez-vous pouvoir gagner ? ◆ **the company made 1.4 million pounds last year** la société a réalisé un bénéfice net de 1,4 million de livres l'année dernière ◆ **the film made millions** le film a rapporté des millions ◆ **the deal made him $500** cette affaire lui a rapporté 500 dollars ◆ **what did you ~ by** *or* **on it?** combien est-ce que ça t'a rapporté ?

3 = score marquer ◆ **Lara made a hundred** Lara a marqué cent points

4 = reach, attain [+ *destination*] arriver à ; (= *catch*) [+ *train, plane*] attraper, avoir ◆ **will we ~ Paris before lunch?** est-ce que nous arriverons à Paris avant le déjeuner ? ◆ **we made good time** *(on foot)* nous avons bien marché ; *(in vehicle)* nous avons bien roulé ◆ **he made the list of ...** * son nom a figuré sur la liste de ...

réussir à/arriver à + infinitive are used in the following to translate **make** + noun:

◆ **do you think he'll ~ (it to) university?** croyez-vous qu'il arrivera à entrer à l'université ? ◆ **the novel made the bestseller list** le roman a réussi à se placer sur la liste des best-sellers ◆ **he made (it into) the first team** il a réussi à être sélectionné dans l'équipe première

5 = force obliger, forcer ◆ **you can't ~ me!** tu ne peux pas m'y forcer *or* obliger ! ; see also **10**

6 = reckon ◆ **how many do you ~ it?** combien en comptes-tu ? ◆ **I ~ it 100km from here to Paris** d'après moi *or* selon moi il y a 100 km d'ici à Paris ◆ **what time do you ~ it?** quelle heure as-tu ?

7 = ensure success of ◆ **the beautiful pictures ~ the book** ce livre doit beaucoup à ses magnifiques images ◆ **that film made her** ce film l'a consacrée ◆ **he was made for life** * son avenir était assuré ◆ **you're made!** * ton avenir est assuré, tu n'as pas de soucis à te faire pour ton avenir ! ◆ **he's got it made** * son avenir est assuré, il n'a pas à s'en faire pour son avenir ◆ **to ~ or break sb** assurer ou briser la carrière de qn ◆ **his visit made my day!** * sa visite m'a fait un plaisir fou ! * ◆ **go ahead, ~ my day!** * *(iro)* vas-y, qu'est-ce que tu attends ?

8 = be, constitute faire ◆ **he'll ~ a good footballer** il fera un bon joueur de football ◆ **he'll ~ somebody a good husband** il fera un bon mari ◆ **to ~ a fourth** *(in game)* faire le quatrième ◆ **I made one of their group** je faisais partie de leur groupe ◆ **they ~ good cooking apples** ce sont *or* elles font de bonnes pommes à cuire ◆ **she made him a good wife** elle a été une bonne épouse pour lui ◆ **they ~ a handsome pair** ils forment un beau couple ◆ **these books ~ a set** ces livres forment une collection ◆ **the latest report doesn't ~ pleasant reading** le dernier compte-rendu n'est pas très réjouissant

9 Cards ◆ **to ~ the cards** battre les cartes ◆ **to ~ a trick** faire un pli ◆ **he made ten and lost three (tricks)** il a fait dix plis et en a perdu trois ◆ **to bid and ~ three hearts** *(Bridge)* demander et faire trois cœurs ◆ **he managed to ~ his queen of diamonds** il a réussi à faire un pli avec sa dame de carreau

10 set structures

♦ **to make sb do sth** (= *cause to*) faire faire qch à qn ; (= *force*) obliger *or* forcer qn à faire qch ◆ **to ~ o.s. do sth** s'obliger à faire qch ◆ **to ~ sb laugh** faire rire qn ◆ **what made you believe that ...?** qu'est-ce qui vous a fait croire que ... ? ◆ **the author ~s him die in the last chapter** l'auteur le fait mourir au dernier chapitre ◆ **I was made to wait for an hour** on m'a fait attendre une heure ◆ **they made him tell them the password** ils l'ont obligé *or* forcé à leur dire le mot de passe ◆ **I don't know what ~s him do it** je ne sais pas ce qui le pousse à faire ça

♦ **to make sb sth** (= *choose as*) ◆ **to ~ sb king** mettre qn sur le trône ◆ **he made John his assistant** il a fait de John son assistant ◆ **he made her his wife** il l'a épousée ◆ **this actor ~s the hero a tragic figure** cet acteur fait du héros un personnage tragique

♦ **to make + of** ◆ **what did you ~ of the film?** que penses-tu de ce film ? ◆ **what do you ~ of him?** qu'est-ce que tu penses de lui ? ◆ **I don't know what to ~ of it all** je ne sais pas quoi penser de tout ça ◆ **I can't ~ anything of this letter, I can ~ nothing of this letter** je ne comprends rien à cette lettre ◆ **to make sth of o.s.** *or* **of one's life** faire qch de sa vie

♦ **to make ...** + *adjective* ◆ **to ~ o.s. useful/ill** se rendre utile/malade ◆ **to ~ sb happy/unhappy** rendre qn heureux/malheureux ◆ **~ yourself comfortable** mettez-vous à l'aise

Look up other combinations, eg **to make sb thirsty, to make o.s. ridiculous**, at the adjective.

♦ **to make believe** (= *pretend*) faire semblant ; (= *imagine*) imaginer ◆ **he made believe he couldn't understand** il a fait semblant de ne pas comprendre ◆ **let's ~ believe we're on a desert island** imaginons que nous sommes sur une île déserte

♦ **to make do** (= *manage*) se débrouiller ◆ **I'll ~ do with what I've got** je vais me débrouiller avec ce que j'ai ◆ **she had to ~ do and mend for many years** elle a dû se débrouiller pendant des années avec ce qu'elle avait ◆ **he can't come, you'll have to ~ do with me** (= *be satisfied*) il ne peut pas venir, tu vas devoir te contenter de moi

♦ **to make it** (= *come*) venir ; (= *arrive*) arriver ; (= *succeed*) réussir, y parvenir, y arriver ◆ **sorry, I can't ~ it** désolé, je ne peux pas venir ◆ **he made it just in time** il est arrivé juste à temps ◆ **you've got the talent to ~ it** tu as tout pour réussir ◆ **he tried for months to get into the team and eventually made it** il a essayé pendant des mois d'intégrer l'équipe et a fini par y parvenir *or* y arriver ◆ **can you ~ it by 3 o'clock?** est-ce que tu peux y être pour 3 heures ? ◆ **they're making it (together)** ‡ ils couchent * ensemble

♦ **to make it with sb** (* = *be accepted*) être accepté par qn ; (‡ = *have sex with*) s'envoyer ‡ *or* se taper ‡ qn ◆ **he'll never ~ it with them** * il ne réussira jamais à se faire accepter d'eux

♦ **to make it** + *time, date, amount* ◆ **let's ~ it 5 o'clock/$30** si on disait 5 heures/30 dollars ? ◆ **I'm coming tomorrow – okay, can you ~ it the afternoon?** je viendrai demain – d'accord, mais est-ce que tu peux venir dans l'après-midi ?

2 – INTRANSITIVE VERB

1 = act

♦ **to make as if, to make like** * ◆ **he made as if to strike me** il fit mine de me frapper ◆ **she made as if to protest, then hesitated** elle parut sur le point de protester, puis hésita ◆ **he was making like he didn't have any money** il faisait mine de ne pas avoir d'argent

2 tide, flood monter

3 – NOUN

1 Comm (= *brand*) marque *f* ; (= *manufacture*) fabrication *f* ◆ **it's a good ~** c'est une bonne marque ◆ **the cars were mainly of French ~** les voitures étaient pour la plupart de fabrication française ◆ **what ~ of car do you drive?** qu'est-ce que vous avez comme (marque de) voiture ? BUT **these are our own ~** *(industrial products)* ceux-là sont fabriqués par nous ; *(confectionery, food)* ceux-là sont faits maison ◆ **it's my own ~** je l'ai fait moi-même

2 set structure

♦ **to be on the make** * *(pej) [person]* (= *trying to make money*) chercher à se remplir les poches ; (= *trying to get power*) avoir une ambition dévorante ; *(US) [person, thing]* (= *to be successful*) avoir du succès ; *[tide]* (= *to be rising*) monter ◆ **some politicians are on the ~** certains hommes politiques cherchent à se remplir les poches ◆ **a brilliant young man on the ~** un jeune homme brillant à l'ambition dévorante ◆ **it's on the ~** ça a du succès ◆ **the tide is on the ~** la marée monte

4 – COMPOUNDS

make-believe N ◆ **to play at ~-believe** jouer à faire semblant ◆ **the land of ~-believe** le pays des chimères ◆ **theatre is a world of ~-believe** le théâtre est un monde d'illusions ADJ ◆ **his story is pure ~-believe** son histoire est de l'invention pure *or* (de la) pure fantaisie ◆ **they were on a ~-believe island** ils faisaient semblant d'être sur une île ◆ **the child made a ~-believe boat out of the chair** l'enfant faisait de la chaise un bateau imaginaire

make-or-break * ADJ décisif *(for sb/sth* pour qn/qch)

make-up N → **make-up**

5 – PHRASAL VERBS

► **make after** VT FUS se lancer à la poursuite de ◆ **they made after him** ils se sont lancés à sa poursuite

► **make at** VT FUS se jeter sur ◆ **he made at me with a knife** il s'est jeté sur moi avec un couteau

► **make away** VI ⇒ **make off**

► **make away with** VT FUS (= *murder*) supprimer ◆ **to ~ away with o.s.** se supprimer

► **make for** VT FUS 1 (= *go to*) ◆ **where are you making for?** où allez-vous ? ◆ **he made for the door** il se dirigea vers la porte ◆ **the ship is making for Cyprus** le navire fait route vers Chypre ◆ **to ~ for home** rentrer (chez soi) 2 (= *produce*) produire ; (= *contribute to*) contribuer à ◆ **controversy ~s for eye-catching headlines** toute controverse produit des gros titres accrocheurs ◆ **a good education system ~s for a successful economy** un bon système éducatif contribue à la prospérité de l'économie ◆ **happy parents ~ for a happy child** quand les parents sont heureux, l'enfant l'est aussi, à parents heureux, enfant heureux

▸ **make off** VI se tirer * ◆ **to ~ off with sth** se tirer * avec qch

▸ **make out** VI ① (* = *manage*) se débrouiller ◆ **they're making out fairly well** ils se débrouillent assez bien ◆ **how are you making out?** comment ça marche ?, comment te débrouilles-tu ? ◆ **how are you making out with your research?** comment avancent tes recherches ? ◆ **the firm is making out all right** l'entreprise marche bien ② (*US* ⁑ = *have sex*) s'envoyer en l'air⁑ ◆ **to ~ out with sb** s'envoyer⁑ qn VT SEP ① (= *draw up, write*) *[+ list, bill]* faire, dresser ; *[+ cheque]* libeller ; *[+ will]* faire, rédiger ◆ **cheques made out to ...** chèques *mpl* libellés à l'ordre *or* au nom de ... ◆ **who shall I ~ it out to?** je le fais à l'ordre de qui ?, c'est à quel ordre ? ② (= *put forward*) ◆ **he made out a good case for not doing it** il a présenté de bons arguments pour ne pas le faire ③ (= *see, distinguish*) *[+ object, person]* discerner, distinguer ; (= *hear*) distinguer, comprendre ; (= *understand*) comprendre ; (= *decipher*) *[+ handwriting]* déchiffrer ◆ **I could just ~ out three figures in the distance** j'arrivais tout juste à discerner *or* distinguer trois silhouettes au loin ◆ **I can't ~ it out at all** je n'y comprends rien ◆ **how do you ~ that out?** qu'est-ce qui vous fait penser cela ? ◆ **I can't ~ out what he wants/why he is here** je n'arrive pas à comprendre ce qu'il veut/pourquoi il est ici ④ (= *claim, pretend*) prétendre *(that* que) ; (= *portray as*) présenter comme ◆ **he's not as stupid as he ~s out** il n'est pas aussi stupide qu'il le prétend ◆ **he isn't as rich as people ~ out** il n'est pas aussi riche que les gens le prétendent ◆ **the programme made her out to be naive** l'émission la présentait comme une femme naïve ◆ **the biography ~s her out to be ruthless** cette biographie la décrit comme une femme impitoyable ◆ **they made him out to be a fool** ils disaient que c'était un imbécile ◆ **he made out that he was a doctor** il se faisait passer pour (un) médecin

▸ **make over** VT SEP ① (= *assign*) *[+ money, land]* céder, transférer *(to* à) ② (= *remake*) *[+ garment, story]* reprendre ; (= *convert*) *[+ building]* convertir ◆ **she made the jacket over to fit her son** elle a repris la veste pour (qu'elle aille à) son fils

▸ **make up** VI ① (= *become friends again*) se réconcilier, se rabibocher * ② (= *apply cosmetics*) se maquiller ; *(Theat)* se maquiller ; *(heavily)* se grimer VT SEP ① (= *invent*) *[+ story, excuse, explanation]* inventer, fabriquer ◆ **you're making it up!** tu l'inventes (de toutes pièces) ! ② (= *put together*) *[+ packet, parcel]* faire ; *[+ dish, medicine, solution]* préparer ; *[+ garment]* assembler ; *[+ list]* faire, dresser ◆ **to ~ sth up into a bundle** faire un paquet de qch ◆ **to ~ up a book** *(Typ)* mettre un livre en pages ◆ **to ~ up a prescription** *(Pharm)* exécuter *or* préparer une ordonnance ◆ **she made up a bed for him on the sofa** elle lui a fait *or* préparé un lit sur le canapé ◆ **have you made up the beds?** as-tu fait les lits ? ◆ **customers' accounts are made up monthly** les relevés de compte des clients sont établis chaque mois ◆ **they sell material and also ~ up clothes** ils vendent du tissu et font aussi des vêtements ◆ **"customers' own material made up"** "travail à façon" ③ (= *counterbalance, replace*) *[+ loss, deficit]* combler, compenser ; *[+ sum of money, numbers, quantity, total]* compléter ◆ **to ~ up the difference** mettre la différence ◆ **they made up the number with five amateurs** ils ont complété l'équipe en faisant appel à cinq amateurs ◆ **he made it up to $100** il a complété les 100 dollars ◆ **to ~ up lost time** rattraper le temps perdu ◆ **to ~ up lost ground** regagner le terrain perdu ◆ **to ~ up ground on sb** gagner du terrain sur qn ④ (= *repay*) ◆ **to make sth up to sb, to make it up to sb for sth** revaloir qch à qn ◆ **I'll ~ it up to you I promise** je te revaudrai ça, je te le promets ◆ **I must ~ it up to him for my stupid mistake** je dois me faire pardonner auprès de lui pour mon erreur stupide ⑤ (= *settle*) *[+ dispute]* mettre fin à ; *[+ differences]* régler ◆ **to ~ up one's quarrel, to ~ it up** se réconcilier, se rabibocher * ◆ **let's ~ it up** faisons la paix ⑥ (= *apply cosmetics to*) *[+ person]* maquiller ; *(Theat)* maquiller ; *(heavily)* grimer ◆ **to ~ o.s. up, to ~ up one's face** se maquiller ; *(Theat)* se maquiller ; *(heavily)* se grimer ◆ **she was making up her eyes** elle se maquillait les yeux ⑦ (= *compose, form*) composer, constituer ; (= *represent*) constituer, représenter ◆ **the group was made up of six teachers** le groupe était composé *or* constitué de six professeurs ◆ **how many people ~ up the team?** combien y a-t-il de personnes dans l'équipe ? ◆ **they ~ up 6% of ...** ils représentent *or* constituent 6% de ...

▸ **make up for** VT FUS compenser ◆ **he has made up for last year's losses** il a comblé les pertes de l'année dernière ◆ **money can't ~ up for what we've suffered** l'argent ne peut compenser ce que nous avons souffert ◆ **he tried to ~ up for all the trouble he'd caused** il essaya de se faire pardonner les ennuis qu'il avait causés ◆ **he made up for all the mistakes he'd made** il s'est rattrapé pour toutes les erreurs qu'il avait commises ◆ **she said that nothing could ~ up for her husband's death** elle dit que rien ne la consolerait de la mort de son mari ◆ **to ~ up for lost time** rattraper le temps perdu

▸ **make up on** VT FUS (= *catch up with*) rattraper

▸ **make up to** * VT FUS (= *curry favour with*) passer de la pommade * à qn

makefast /ˈmeɪkfɑːst/ N *(US)* point *m* d'amarre

makeover /ˈmeɪkəʊvəʳ/ N *(lit, fig)* changement *m* de look *

Maker /ˈmeɪkəʳ/ N *(Rel)* ◆ **our ~** le Créateur ◆ **he's gone to meet his ~** *(hum)* il est allé ad patres *(hum)*

-maker /ˈmeɪkəʳ/ N *(in compounds)* ① (= *manufacturer: gen)* fabricant(e) *m(f)* de ... ◆ **tyre/furniture-maker** fabricant *m* de pneus/de meubles ◆ **film-maker** cinéaste *mf* ; see also **watchmaker** ② (= *machine*) ◆ **coffee-maker** cafetière *f* électrique ◆ **yoghurt-maker** yaourtière *f*

makeshift /ˈmeɪkʃɪft/ N expédient *m*, moyen *m* de fortune ADJ de fortune ◆ **~ shelters** des abris de fortune

make-up /ˈmeɪkʌp/ N ① *(NonC* = *nature)* *[of object, group etc]* constitution *f* ; *[of person]* tempérament *m*, caractère *m* ② *(NonC* = *cosmetics)* maquillage *m* ◆ **she wears too much ~** elle se maquille trop, elle est trop maquillée ③ *(US Scol etc: *)* examen *m* de rattrapage

COMP **make-up artist** N maquilleur *m*, -euse *f*
make-up bag N trousse *f* de maquillage
make-up base N base *f* (de maquillage)
make-up case N nécessaire *m* *or* boîte *f* de maquillage
make-up class N *(US Scol)* cours *m* de rattrapage
make-up girl N maquilleuse *f*
make-up man N (pl **make-up men**) maquilleur *m*
make-up remover N démaquillant *m*

makeweight /ˈmeɪkweɪt/ N ① *(lit)* (= *weight, object)* tare *f* ② *(fig* = *person)* bouche-trou *m*

making /ˈmeɪkɪŋ/ N ① *(NonC)* *(gen)* fabrication *f* ; *[of dress]* façon *f*, confection *f* ; *[of machines]* fabrication *f*, construction *f* ; *[of food]* *(by machine)* fabrication *f* ◆ **rennet is used in the ~ of cheese** on utilise la présure dans la fabrication du fromage ◆ **bread-/cheese-/wine- etc ~** fabrication *f* du pain/du fromage/du vin *etc* ◆ **she does her own wine-~** elle fait son vin elle-même ◆ **all his troubles are of his own ~** tous ses ennuis sont de sa faute ◆ **decision-~** prise *f* de décisions ◆ **he wrote a book on the ~ of the film** il a écrit un livre sur la genèse de ce film

◆ **in the making** ◆ **the film was three months in the ~** il a fallu trois mois pour faire ce film ◆ **a new system/society is in the ~** un nouveau système/une nouvelle société est en train de se créer ◆ **a compromise may be in the ~** il se peut que l'on soit sur le point d'arriver à un compromis ◆ **a genius/star in the ~** un génie/une star en herbe ◆ **a dictator/criminal in the ~** de la graine de dictateur/criminel ◆ **it's a disaster in the ~** ça risque de tourner au désastre ◆ **it's history in the ~** c'est l'histoire en train de se faire ◆ **it's still in the ~** *[product, film]* c'est encore en chantier

② (= *forming*) ◆ **it was the ~ of him** *(gen)* c'est ce qui a formé son caractère ; (= *made him successful)* son succès est parti de là

NPL **makings** éléments *mpl* essentiels ◆ **he has the ~s of a footballer** il a l'étoffe d'un footballeur ◆ **the situation has the ~s of a civil war** cette situation laisse présager une guerre civile ◆ **we have all the ~s of a great movie** il y a tous les ingrédients pour faire un grand film

Malachi /ˈmæləˌkaɪ/ N Malachie *m*

malachite /ˈmæləˌkaɪt/ N malachite *f*

maladjusted /ˌmæləˈdʒʌstɪd/ ADJ ① *(Psych)* inadapté ② *[mechanism]* mal ajusté, mal réglé

maladjustment /ˌmæləˈdʒʌstmənt/ N ① *(Psych)* inadaptation *f* ② *[of mechanism]* mauvais ajustement *m*

maladministration /ˈmæləd,mɪnɪsˈtreɪʃən/ N mauvaise gestion *f*

maladroit /ˌmæləˈdrɔɪt/ ADJ *(frm)* inhabile, maladroit

maladroitly /ˌmæləˈdrɔɪtlɪ/ ADV *(frm)* maladroitement

maladroitness /ˌmæləˈdrɔɪtnɪs/ N *(frm)* maladresse *f*

malady /ˈmælədɪ/ N *(frm)* maladie *f*, mal *m*

Malagasy /ˈmæləˈgɑːzɪ/ N ① Malgache *mf* ② (= *language)* malgache *m* ADJ *(Hist)* malgache ◆ **the ~ Republic** la République malgache

malaise /mæˈleɪz/ N *(frm)* malaise *m*

malapropism /ˈmæləprɒpɪzəm/ N impropriété *f* (de langage)

malaria /məˈlɛərɪə/ N paludisme *m*, malaria *f*

malarial /məˈlɛərɪəl/ ADJ *[parasite]* du paludisme ; *[mosquito]* porteur de paludisme ; *[region]* impaludé ◆ **~ fever** paludisme *m*, malaria *f*

malark(e)y ⁑ /məˈlɑːkɪ/ N *(NonC)* âneries *fpl*

Malawi /məˈlɑːwɪ/ N Malawi *m* ◆ **in ~** au Malawi

Malawian /məˈlɑːwɪən/ N Malawien(ne) *m(f)* ADJ malawien

Malay /məˈleɪ/ ADJ *[language, community, culture]* malais ◆ **the ~ mainland** la Malaisie continentale N ① (= *person)* Malais(e) *m(f)* ② (= *language)* malais *m*

COMP **the Malay Archipelago** N l'archipel *m* malais
the Malay Peninsula N la péninsule malaise
Malay States NPL *(Hist)* États *mpl* malais

Malaya /məˈleɪə/ N Malaisie *f* occidentale

Malayan /məˈleɪən/ ADJ, N ⇒ **Malay**

Malaysia /məˈleɪzɪə/ N Malaisie *f*, Malaysia *f*

Malaysian /məˈleɪzɪən/ ADJ malais N Malais(e) *m(f)*

malcontent /ˈmælkənˌtent/ ADJ, N mécontent(e) *m(f)*

Maldives /ˈmɔːldaɪvz/ NPL Maldives *fpl*

male /meɪl/ ADJ (Anat, Bio, Tech etc) mâle ; (fig) (= manly) mâle, viril (virile f) ◆ ~ **child** enfant m mâle ◆ **the ~ sex** le sexe masculin ; → **chauvinist, menopause, model** N (= animal) mâle m ; (= man) homme m

COMP **male bonding** N fraternisation f masculine

male-dominated ADJ dominé par les hommes

male-voice choir N chœur m d'hommes, chœur m de voix mâles

malediction /ˌmælɪˈdɪkʃən/ N malédiction f

malefactor /ˈmælɪfæktəʳ/ N malfaiteur m, -trice f

maleness /ˈmeɪlnɪs/ N (= being male) fait m d'être mâle ; (= masculinity) masculinité f

malevolence /məˈlevələns/ N malveillance f (towards envers)

malevolent /məˈlevələnt/ ADJ malveillant

malevolently /məˈlevələntlɪ/ ADV avec malveillance

malformation /ˌmælfɔːˈmeɪʃən/ N malformation f, difformité f

malformed /ˌmælˈfɔːmd/ ADJ [baby] malformé ◆ **to have a ~ heart/foot** avoir une malformation cardiaque/du pied

malfunction /ˌmælˈfʌŋkʃən/ N mauvais fonctionnement m, défaillance f VI mal fonctionner

Mali /ˈmɑːlɪ/ N Mali m ◆ **in ~** au Mali

Malian /ˈmɑːlɪən/ N Malien(ne) m(f) ADJ malien

malice /ˈmælɪs/ N méchanceté f ; (stronger) malveillance f ◆ **to bear sb ~** vouloir du mal à qn ◆ **a man without ~** un homme sans malice ◆ **with ~ aforethought** (Jur) avec préméditation, avec intention criminelle or délictueuse

malicious /məˈlɪʃəs/ ADJ [person] méchant ; [talk, rumour, attack, phone call] malveillant ; [smile] mauvais ◆ **~ gossip** médisances fpl ◆ **with ~ intent** avec l'intention de nuire

COMP **malicious falsehood** N (Jur) diffamation f

malicious wounding N (Jur) ≃ coups mpl et blessures fpl volontaires

> ⚠ **malicieux** means 'mischievous', not **malicious.**

maliciously /məˈlɪʃəslɪ/ ADV [say, smile] méchamment ; (stronger) avec malveillance ; (Jur) avec préméditation, avec intention criminelle

malign /məˈlaɪn/ ADJ pernicieux VT calomnier, diffamer ◆ **you ~ me** vous me calomniez

malignancy /məˈlɪgnənsɪ/ N 1 malveillance f, malfaisance f 2 (Med) malignité f

malignant /məˈlɪgnənt/ ADJ 1 (= malevolent) [influence, effect] nocif ; [plot, look, person] malveillant 2 (Med) malin (-igne f)

malignantly /məˈlɪgnəntlɪ/ ADV [speak, say] avec malveillance

malignity /məˈlɪgnɪtɪ/ N ⇒ **malignancy**

malinger /məˈlɪŋgəʳ/ VI faire le (or la) malade

malingerer /məˈlɪŋgərəʳ/ N faux malade m, fausse malade f ; (Admin, Mil etc) simulateur m, -trice f ◆ **he's a ~** il se fait passer pour malade

mall /mɔːl, (US) mæl/ N 1 (gen) allée f, mail m 2 (US = pedestrianized street) rue f piétonnière ; (also **shopping mall**) centre m commercial COMP **mall rat*** N jeune qui traîne dans les centres commerciaux

mallard /ˈmæləd/ N (pl **mallard(s)**) (also **mallard duck**) colvert m

malleability /ˌmælɪəˈbɪlɪtɪ/ N malléabilité f

malleable /ˈmælɪəbl/ ADJ 1 (lit) [material] malléable 2 (fig) [person] malléable, influençable

mallet /ˈmælɪt/ N maillet m

malleus /ˈmælɪəs/ N (pl **mallei** /ˈmælɪˌaɪ/) marteau m

mallow /ˈmæləʊ/ N (= plant) mauve f ; → **marshmallow**

malnourished /ˌmælˈnʌrɪʃt/ ADJ [person] qui souffre de malnutrition

malnutrition /ˌmælnjʊˈtrɪʃən/ N malnutrition f

malodorous /mælˈəʊdərəs/ ADJ (liter) malodorant

malpractice /ˌmælˈpræktɪs/ N (= wrongdoing) faute f professionnelle ; (= neglect of duty) négligence f or incurie f professionnelle

COMP **malpractice suit** N (US Jur) procès m pour faute professionnelle ◆ **to bring a ~ suit against sb** poursuivre qn pour faute professionnelle

malt /mɔːlt/ N malt m VT malter

COMP [vinegar] de malt

malt extract N extrait m de malt

malt liquor N (US) bière f

malt whisky N (whisky m) pur malt m

Malta /ˈmɔːltə/ N (island) Malte f ; (state) Malte m ◆ **in ~** à Malte

maltase /ˈmɔːlteɪz/ N maltase f

malted /ˈmɔːltɪd/ ADJ malté

COMP **malted barley** N orge f maltée

malted milk N lait m malté

Maltese /ˌmɔːlˈtiːz/ ADJ maltais ◆ **~ cross** croix f de Malte ◆ **~ fever** fièvre f de Malte N 1 (pl inv) Maltais(e) m(f) 2 (= language) maltais m NPL **the Maltese** les Maltais mpl

Malthus /ˈmælθəs/ N Malthus m

Malthusianism /mælˈθjuːzɪəˌnɪzəm/ N malthusianisme m

maltreat /ˌmælˈtriːt/ VT maltraiter, malmener

maltreatment /ˌmælˈtriːtmənt/ N mauvais traitement m ◆ **sexual ~** sévices mpl sexuels

malware /ˌmælˈwɛə/ N (Comput) malware m, logiciel m néfaste

mam* /mæm/ N (Brit dial) maman f ◆ **my ~** maman

mama /məˈmɑː/ N (esp US) mère f, maman f ◆ **he's a mam(m)a's boy** (pej) c'est un fils à sa mère (pej)

mamba /ˈmæmbə/ N (= snake) mamba m ◆ **black/green ~** mamba m noir/vert

mamma /məˈmɑː/ N ⇒ **mama**

mammal /ˈmæməl/ N mammifère m

mammalian /mæˈmeɪlɪən/ ADJ mammalien

mammary /ˈmæmərɪ/ ADJ mammaire

COMP **mammary gland** N glande f mammaire

mammogram /ˈmæməgræm/ N (Med) mammographie f

mammography /mæˈmɒgrəfɪ/ N mammographie f

Mammon /ˈmæmən/ N le dieu Argent, Mammon m

mammoth /ˈmæməθ/ N mammouth m ADJ colossal

mammy /ˈmæmɪ/ N 1 (* =mother) maman f 2 (US = Black nurse) nourrice f noire

Man /mæn/ N ⇒ **Isle of Man**

man /mæn/ N (pl **men**) 1 (gen) homme m ; (= servant) domestique m ; (in factory etc) ouvrier m ; (in office, shop etc) employé m ; (Sport = player) joueur m, équipier m ; (= husband) homme m ◆ **men and women** les hommes mpl et les femmes fpl ◆ **he's a nice ~** c'est un homme sympathique ◆ **an old ~** un vieil homme, un vieillard ◆ **a blind ~** un aveugle ◆ **a medical ~** un docteur ◆ **a ~ of God** un homme de Dieu ◆ **I don't like the ~** je n'aime pas cet homme or ce type* ◆ **the ~'s an idiot** c'est un imbécile ◆ **that ~ Smith** ce (type*) Smith ◆ **the ~ Jones** † le dénommé or le nommé Jones ◆ **the ~ in the moon** le visage que l'on peut imaginer en regardant la lune ◆ **as one ~** (= in unison) comme un seul homme ◆ **as one ~ to another** d'homme à homme ◆ **they're communists to a ~** or **to the last ~** ils sont tous communistes sans exception ◆ **they perished to a ~** pas un seul d'entre eux n'a survécu ◆ **he's been with this firm ~ and boy for 30 years** cela fait 30 ans qu'il est entré tout jeune encore dans la maison ◆ **the employers and the men** les patrons mpl et les ouvriers mpl ◆ **~ and wife** mari m et femme f ◆ **to live as ~ and wife** vivre maritalement ◆ **her ~*** son homme* ◆ **my old ~*** (= father) mon paternel* ; (= husband) mon homme* ◆ **her young ~** †* son amoureux †, son futur (hum) ◆ **it will make a ~ of him** cela fera de lui un homme ◆ **be a ~!** sois un homme ! ◆ **he took it like a ~** il a pris ça vaillamment ◆ **he was ~ enough to apologise** il a eu le courage de s'excuser ◆ **he's his own ~ again** (= not subordinate to anyone) il est redevenu son propre maître ; (= in control of his emotions etc) il est de nouveau maître de lui ; → **best, estate, jack**

2 (in Army) homme m (de troupe), soldat m ; (in Navy) homme m (d'équipage), matelot m ◆ **officers and men** (in Airforce, Army) officiers mpl et soldats mpl, officiers mpl et hommes mpl de troupe ; (in Navy) officiers mpl et matelots mpl ◆ **the corporal and his men** le caporal et ses hommes ◆ **they fought to the last ~** ils se sont battus jusqu'au dernier

3 (= sort, type) ◆ **I'm not a drinking ~** je ne bois pas (beaucoup) ◆ **I'm not a gambling ~** je ne suis pas joueur ◆ **he's not a football ~** ce n'est pas un amateur de football ◆ **I'm a whisky ~ myself** personnellement, je préfère le whisky ◆ **a leg/tit**/bum** ~** un homme attiré par les belles jambes/les beaux nichons**/les belles fesses ◆ **he's a man's ~** c'est un homme qui est plus à l'aise avec les hommes ◆ **he's a Leeds ~** (= native) il est or vient de Leeds ; (= football supporter) c'est un supporter de Leeds ◆ **he's not the ~ to fail** il n'est pas homme à échouer ◆ **he's not the ~ for that** il n'est pas fait pour cela ◆ **he's the ~ for the job** c'est l'homme qu'il nous (or leur etc) faut ◆ **if you're looking for someone to help you, then I'm your ~** si vous cherchez quelqu'un pour vous aider, je suis votre homme ◆ **the ~ in the street** l'homme m de la rue, Monsieur Tout-le-monde ◆ **a ~ of the world** un homme d'expérience ◆ **a ~ about town** un homme du monde ◆ **the ~ of the hour** or **the moment** le héros du jour, l'homme m du moment ; → **destiny, idea, lady, letter, local, property**

4 (in compounds) ◆ **the ice-cream ~** le marchand de glaces ◆ **the TV ~** l'installateur m (or le dépanneur) de télé ◆ **the gas ~** l'employé m du gaz ◆ **it's the green/red ~** (Brit: at crossing) le feu pour les piétons est au vert/au rouge ; → **repair¹**

5 (= humanity in general) ◆ **Man** l'homme m ◆ **that's no use** or **good to ~ (n)or beast** cela ne sert strictement à rien ◆ **Man proposes, God disposes** (Prov) l'homme propose et Dieu dispose (Prov)

6 (= person) homme m ◆ **all men must die** tous les hommes sont mortels, nous sommes tous mortels ◆ **men say that ...** on dit que ..., certains disent que ... ◆ **any ~ would have done the same** n'importe qui aurait fait de même ◆ **no ~ could blame him** personne ne pouvait le lui reprocher ◆ **what else could a ~ do?** qu'est-ce qu'on aurait pu faire d'autre ?

7 (in direct address) **hurry up, ~!** * dépêchez-vous !, magnez-vous donc !* ; (to friend etc) magne-toi, mon vieux !* ◆ **~*, was I terrified!** quelle frousse* j'ai eue ! ◆ **look here young ~!** dites donc, jeune homme ! ◆ **(my) little ~!** mon grand ! ◆ **old ~** †* mon vieux* ◆ **my (good) ~** † mon brave † ◆ **good ~!** bravo !

8 (Chess) pièce f ; (Draughts) pion m

9 (US) ◆ **the Man**** (= white man) le blanc ; (= boss) le patron ; (= police) les flics* mpl

VT 1 *(= provide staff for)* assurer une permanence à ; *(= work at)* être de service à ◆ **they haven't enough staff to ~ the office every day** ils n'ont pas assez de personnel pour assurer une permanence au bureau tous les jours ◆ **who will ~ the enquiry desk?** qui sera de service au bureau des renseignements ? ◆ **the telephone is ~ned twelve hours per day** il y a une permanence téléphonique douze heures par jour

2 *(Mil) [+ post]* être en faction à ; *[+ fortress]* être en garnison à ◆ **to ~ a ship** équiper un navire en personnel ◆ **the ship was ~ned mainly by Chinese** l'équipage était composé principalement de Chinois ◆ **the troops who ~ned the look-out posts** les troupes en faction au poste ◆ **the soldiers ~ning the fortress** les soldats qui étaient en garnison dans la forteresse ◆ **to ~ the boats** *(Naut)* armer les bateaux ◆ **to ~ the guns** *(Mil)* servir les canons ◆ **to ~ the pumps** armer les pompes ; see also **manned**

COMP **man-at-arms** **N** (pl **men-at-arms**) homme *m* d'armes, cuirassier *m*

man-child **N** *(liter)* enfant *m* mâle

man-day **N** *(= time worked)* jour-homme *m*, jour *m* de travail

man-eater **N** *(= animal)* mangeur *m* d'hommes ; *(= cannibal)* cannibale *m*, anthropophage *m* ; *(fig hum = woman)* dévoreuse *f* d'hommes, mante *f* religieuse

man-eating **ADJ** *[animal]* mangeur d'hommes ; *[tribe etc]* anthropophage

man Friday **N** *(in Robinson Crusoe)* Vendredi *m* ; *(fig) (= retainer)* fidèle serviteur *m* ; *(= assistant)* aide *m* de bureau

man-hater **N** ◆ **to be a ~-hater** *[woman]* avoir les hommes en horreur

man-hour **N** *(= time worked)* heure-homme *f*, heure *f* de travail

man-made **ADJ** *[fibre, fabric]* synthétique ; *[lake, barrier]* artificiel

man management **N** ◆ **he's not very good at ~ management** il ne sait pas très bien diriger une équipe ◆ **~ management is an important skill** il faut savoir bien diriger une équipe

man-of-war, man-o'-war **N** (pl **men-of-war**) *(Naut)* vaisseau *m* or navire *m* or bâtiment *m* de guerre ; → **Portuguese**

man-sized * **ADJ** *(fig)* grand, de taille, de grande personne *

man-to-man **ADJ, ADV** d'homme à homme

man-to-man marking **N** *(Brit Ftbl)* marquage *m* individuel

manacle /ˈmænəkl/ **N** *(gen pl)* menottes *fpl* **VT** mettre les menottes à ◆ **~d** les menottes aux poignets

manage /ˈmænɪdʒ/ LANGUAGE IN USE 15.4, 16.4

VT 1 *(= direct) [+ business, estate, theatre, restaurant, hotel, shop, time, capital]* gérer ; *[+ institution, organization]* administrer, diriger ; *[+ football team, boxer etc]* être le manager de ; *[+ actor, singer etc]* être le manager or l'imprésario de ; *[+ farm]* exploiter

2 *(= handle, deal with) [+ boat, vehicle]* manœuvrer, manier ; *[+ animal, person]* savoir s'y prendre avec ◆ **you ~d the situation very well** tu as très bien géré la situation

3 *(= succeed, contrive)* ◆ **to ~ to do sth** réussir or arriver à faire qch ◆ **how did you ~ to do it?** comment as-tu réussi à le faire ?, comment y es-tu arrivé ? ◆ **how did you ~ not to spill it?** comment as-tu fait pour ne pas le renverser ? ◆ **he ~d not to get his feet wet** il a réussi à ne pas se mouiller les pieds ◆ **he ~d to annoy everybody** *(iro)* il a trouvé le moyen de mécontenter tout le monde ◆ **you'll ~ it next time!** tu réussiras or tu y arriveras la prochaine fois ! ◆ **will you come? – I can't ~ (it) just now** tu viendras ? – je ne peux pas pour l'instant

4 *(= manage to do, pay, eat etc)* ◆ **how much will you give? – I can ~ 10 euros** combien allez-vous donner ? – je peux aller jusqu'à 10 € or je peux mettre 10 € ◆ **surely you could ~ another biscuit?** tu mangeras bien encore un autre biscuit ? ◆ **I couldn't ~ another thing!** * je n'en peux plus ! ◆ **can you ~ the suitcases?** pouvez-vous porter les valises ? ◆ **can you ~ 8 o'clock?** 8 heures, ça vous convient ? ◆ **can you ~ two more in the car?** peux-tu encore en prendre deux or as-tu de la place pour deux de plus dans la voiture ? ◆ **I ~d a smile/a few words of greeting** *etc* j'ai quand même réussi à sourire/à dire quelques mots de bienvenue *etc*

VI *(= succeed, get by)* se débrouiller ◆ **can you ~?** tu y arrives or arriveras ? ◆ **thanks, I can ~** merci, ça va ◆ **I can ~ without him** je peux me débrouiller sans lui ◆ **she ~s on her pension/on £60 a week** elle se débrouille avec seulement sa retraite/avec seulement 60 livres par semaine ◆ **how will you ~?** comment allez-vous faire or vous débrouiller ?

COMP **managed competition** **N** *(US)* concurrence *f* réglementée or encadrée

managed economy **N** économie *f* dirigée

managed forests **NPL** forêts *fpl* gérées

managed funds **NPL** fonds *mpl* gérés

managed trade **N** commerce *m* dirigé

manageable /ˈmænɪdʒəbl/ **ADJ** *[size, amount, number, proportions]* raisonnable ; *[problem]* soluble ; *[task]* faisable ; *[person]* souple ; *[child, animal]* docile ; *[hair]* facile à coiffer ; *[vehicle, boat]* maniable ◆ **the situation is ~** la situation est gérable

management /ˈmænɪdʒmənt/ **N** 1 *(NonC = managing) [of company, estate, theatre]* gestion *f* ; *[of institution, organization]* administration *f*, direction *f* ; *[of farm]* exploitation *f* ◆ **his skilful ~ of his staff** l'habileté avec laquelle il dirige son personnel

2 *(= people in charge) [of business, hotel, theatre etc]* direction *f* ◆ **by order of the ~** par ordre de la direction ◆ **the ~ and the workers** la direction et les travailleurs ◆ **~ and labour** or **unions** les partenaires *mpl* sociaux ◆ **he's (one of the) ~ now** il fait partie des cadres (supérieurs) maintenant ◆ **"under new management"** "changement de propriétaire"

COMP **management accounting** **N** comptabilité *f* de gestion

management buyout **N** rachat *m* d'une entreprise par ses cadres or sa direction

management chart **N** organigramme *m*

management committee **N** comité *m* de direction

management company **N** société *f* de gestion

management consultancy **N** *(= business)* cabinet *m* de conseil ; *(= advice)* conseil *m* en gestion d'entreprise

management consultant **N** conseiller *m* en gestion (d'entreprise)

management information system **N** système *m* intégré de gestion

management selection procedures **NPL** (procédure *f* de) sélection *f* des cadres

management studies **NPL** *(Educ)* (études *fpl* de) gestion *f*

management style **N** mode *m* de gestion

management trainee **N** cadre *m* stagiaire

manager /ˈmænɪdʒəʳ/ **N** *[of company, business]* directeur *m*, administrateur *m* ; *[of theatre, cinema]* directeur *m* ; *[of restaurant, hotel, shop]* gérant *m* ; *[of farm]* exploitant *m* ; *[of actor, singer, boxer etc]* manager *m* ; *[of sports team]* directeur *m* sportif ; *(Fin)* chef *m* de file ◆ **school ~** *(Brit)* ≃ membre *m* du conseil d'établissement ◆ **general ~** directeur *m* général ◆ **to be a good ~** être bon gestionnaire ; → **business, sale**

manageress /ˌmænɪdʒəˈres/ **N** *[of hotel, café, shop]* gérante *f* ; *[of theatre, cinema]* directrice *f*

managerial /ˌmænəˈdʒɪərɪəl/ **ADJ** *[responsibilities, staff]* d'encadrement ; *[job, position]* d'encadrement, de cadre ; *(Ftbl) [career]* de directeur sportif ◆ **the ~ class** les cadres *mpl* (supérieurs) ◆ **proven ~ skills** des compétences *fpl* confirmées en matière de gestion ◆ **his ~ style** son style de gestion ◆ **a ~ decision** une décision de la direction

managership /ˈmænɪdʒəʃɪp/ **N** directorat *m*

managing /ˈmænɪdʒɪŋ/ **ADJ** *(Brit = bossy)* autoritaire

COMP **managing bank** **N** banque *f* chef de file

managing director **N** *(Brit)* directeur *m* général, PDG *m*

managing editor **N** directeur *m* de la rédaction

manatee /ˌmænəˈtiː/ **N** lamantin *m*

Manchu /mænˈtʃuː/ **N** 1 *(= person)* Mandchou(e) *m(f)* 2 *(Ling)* mandchou *m* **ADJ** mandchou

Manchuria /mænˈtʃʊərɪə/ **N** Mandchourie *f*

Manchurian /mænˈtʃʊərɪən/ **ADJ** mandchou **N** Mandchou(e) *m(f)*

Mancunian /mæŋˈkjuːnɪən/ **N** ◆ **he's a ~** il est de Manchester **ADJ** de Manchester

mandala /ˈmændələ/ **N** mandala *m*

Mandarin /ˈmændərɪn/ **N** (also **Mandarin Chinese**) Mandarin *m*

mandarin /ˈmændərɪn/ **N** 1 *(= person: lit, fig)* mandarin *m* 2 (also **mandarin orange**) mandarine *f* 3 (also **mandarin duck**) canard *m* mandarin

mandate /ˈmændeɪt/ **N** 1 *(= authority)* mandat *m* ◆ **they have no ~ to govern** ils n'ont pas le mandat du peuple ◆ **with such a small majority, how can the government claim to have a ~?** avec une majorité si infime, le gouvernement ne peut pas prétendre avoir reçu le mandat du peuple ◆ **the union has a ~ to ...** le syndicat est mandaté pour ... ◆ **the ICRC's ~ is to provide impartial assistance to victims of conflict** le CICR a pour mandat de fournir une assistance impartiale aux victimes de conflits

2 *(= country)* pays *m* sous mandat ◆ **under French ~** sous mandat français

VT 1 *(= give authority to)* donner mandat *(sb to do sth* à qn de faire qch)

2 *(US) (= make obligatory)* rendre obligatoire ; *(= entail) [act, decision]* entraîner, comporter

3 *(= place under mandate) [+ territory]* mettre sous le mandat *(to de)*

mandatory /ˈmændətərɪ/ **ADJ** 1 *(= obligatory)* obligatoire *(for sb/sth* pour qn/qch) ◆ **to be ~ (for sb) to do sth** être obligatoire (pour qn) de faire qch ◆ **the ~ retirement age** l'âge *m* de la retraite obligatoire 2 *(Jur = not discretionary) [life sentence, death penalty, ban, fine]* automatique 3 *(Pol) [state, functions]* mandataire ◆ **to be a ~ power** être une puissance mandataire ◆ **to have ~ powers** avoir des pouvoirs conférés par mandat

mandible /ˈmændɪbl/ **N** *[of bird, insect]* mandibule *f* ; *[of mammal, fish]* mâchoire *f* (inférieure)

mandolin(e) /ˈmændəlɪn/ **N** mandoline *f*

mandrake /ˈmændreɪk/, **mandragora** /mænˈdrægərə/ **N** mandragore *f*

mandrill /ˈmændrɪl/ **N** mandrill *m*

mane /meɪn/ **N** *(lit, fig)* crinière *f*

maneuver *etc* /məˈnuːvəʳ/ *(US)* ⇒ **manoeuvre** *etc*

manful /ˈmænfʊl/ **ADJ** *[attempt]* vaillant

manfully /ˈmænfəlɪ/ **ADV** *[struggle, battle, cope]* vaillamment

manga /ˈmæŋgə/ **N** (pl **manga**) manga *m*

manganese /ˌmæŋgəˈniːz/ **N** manganèse *m*

COMP **manganese bronze** **N** bronze *m* au manganèse

manganese oxide **N** oxyde *m* de manganèse

manganese steel **N** acier *m* au manganèse

mange /meɪndʒ/ **N** gale *f*

mangel(-wurzel) /ˈmæŋgl(ˌwɜːzl)/ N betterave f fourragère

manger /ˈmeɪndʒəʳ/ N *(Agr)* mangeoire f ; *(Rel)* crèche f ; → **dog**

mangetout /ˈmɒnʒtuː/ N *(pl inv)* (also **mangetout pea**) mange-tout m inv

mangle¹ /ˈmæŋgl/ N *(for wringing)* essoreuse f à rouleaux ; *(for smoothing)* calandre f VT essorer, calandrer

mangle² /ˈmæŋgl/ VT (also **mangle up**) *[+ object, body]* déchirer, mutiler ; *(fig) [+ text]* mutiler ; *[+ quotation]* estropier ; *[+ message]* estropier, mutiler

mango /ˈmæŋgəʊ/ N (pl **mango(e)s**) *(= fruit)* mangue f ; *(= tree)* manguier m COMP **mango chutney** N condiment m à la mangue

mangold(-wurzel) /ˈmæŋgəld(ˌwɜːzl)/ N ⇒ **mangel(-wurzel)**

mangosteen /ˈmæŋgəˌstiːn/ N mangoustan m

mangrove /ˈmæŋgrəʊv/ N palétuvier m, manglier m COMP **mangrove swamp** N mangrove f

mangy /ˈmeɪndʒɪ/ ADJ 1 *(= diseased) [animal]* galeux 2 * *(= shabby) [coat, wig, rug, blanket]* miteux ◆ **what a ~ trick!** quel tour de cochon ! *

manhandle /ˈmænˌhændl/ VT *(= treat roughly)* malmener ; *(esp Brit) (= move by hand) [+ goods etc]* manutentionner

Manhattan /mænˈhætən/ N 1 *(Geog)* Manhattan 2 *(= drink)* manhattan m *(cocktail de whisky et de vermouth doux)*

manhole /ˈmænhəʊl/ N bouche f d'égout COMP **manhole cover** N plaque f d'égout

manhood /ˈmænhʊd/ N 1 *(= age, state)* âge m d'homme, âge m viril ◆ **to reach ~** atteindre l'âge d'homme ◆ **during his early ~** quand il était jeune homme 2 *(= manliness)* virilité f ◆ **a threat to his ~** une menace pour sa virilité 3 *(= men collectively)* hommes mpl 4 *(euph = penis)* membre m viril

manhunt /ˈmænhʌnt/ N chasse f à l'homme

mania /ˈmeɪnɪə/ N *(Psych, fig)* manie f ◆ **persecution ~** manie f or folie f de la persécution ◆ **to have a ~ for (doing) sth** * avoir la manie de (faire) qch

maniac /ˈmeɪnɪæk/ N *(Psych)* maniaque mf ; * fou m, folle f ; *(Jur)* dément(e) m(f) ◆ **a self-confessed golf ~** * un mordu * du golf, de son propre aveu ◆ **he drives like a ~** * il conduit comme un fou ◆ **he's a ~!** * il est fou à lier !, il est bon à enfermer ! ADJ *(Psych)* maniaque ; * fou (folle f) ; *(Jur)* dément

maniacal /məˈnaɪəkəl/ ADJ *[person]* maniaque ; *[laughter]* hystérique ; *[expression, eyes]* de fou (folle f)

maniacally /məˈnaɪəkəlɪ/ ADV *[grin]* comme un(e) dément(e) ◆ **he laughed ~** il a ri d'un rire hystérique

manic /ˈmænɪk/ ADJ *(Psych) [person]* maniaque ; *(fig) [person]* survolté * ; *[activity, energy]* frénétique ; *[grin, smile]* de dément(e) ; *[laughter]* hystérique

COMP **manic depression** N psychose f maniacodépressive, cyclothymie f

manic-depressive ADJ, N maniacodépressif m, -ive f, cyclothymique mf

Manich(a)ean /ˌmænɪˈkiːən/ ADJ, N manichéen(ne) m(f) ◆ **the Manich(a)ean heresy** l'hérésie f manichéenne

Manich(a)eism /ˈmænɪkiːˌɪzəm/ N *(Hist, fig)* manichéisme m

manicure /ˈmænɪˌkjʊəʳ/ N *(= act)* soin m des mains, manucure f ◆ **to have a ~** se faire faire les mains, se faire manucurer ◆ **to give sb a ~** faire les mains à qn, manucurer qn VT *[+ person]* faire les mains à, manucurer ; *[+ sb's nails]* faire ◆ **to ~ one's nails** se faire les ongles

COMP **manicure case** N trousse f à ongles or de manucure

manicure scissors NPL ciseaux mpl de manucure or à ongles

manicure set N ⇒ **manicure case**

manicured /ˈmænɪkjʊəd/ ADJ *[nails, hands]* manucuré ; *[person]* aux mains manucurées ; *(fig) [lawn, garden]* impeccable

manicurist /ˈmænɪˌkjʊərɪst/ N manucure mf

manifest /ˈmænɪfest/ ADJ manifeste

VT manifester ◆ **the virus needs two weeks to ~ itself** il faut deux semaines avant que le virus ne se manifeste ◆ **he ~ed a pleasing personality on stage** sur scène il présentait une personnalité agréable ◆ **a problem ~ed itself** un problème s'est présenté

N *(for ship, plane)* manifeste m

COMP **Manifest Destiny** N *(US Hist)* destinée f manifeste

Manifest Destiny

Au 19ᵉ siècle, les Américains estimaient que les États-Unis avaient pour « destinée manifeste », voulue par Dieu, d'étendre leur territoire et leur influence à travers le continent nord-américain. Ce principe a servi à justifier l'avance des colons vers le Mexique ainsi que la guerre hispano-américaine de 1898, à l'issue de laquelle les États-Unis ont annexé Porto Rico et les Philippines. Rarement évoqué aujourd'hui, ce sentiment demeure sous-jacent chez beaucoup d'Américains qui trouvent naturelle la suprématie de leur pays en Amérique et sur le pourtour de l'océan Pacifique.

manifestation /ˌmænɪfesˈteɪʃən/ N manifestation f

manifestly /ˈmænɪfestlɪ/ ADV *(frm)* manifestement

manifesto /ˌmænɪˈfestəʊ/ N (pl **manifesto(e)s**) *(Pol etc)* manifeste m

manifold /ˈmænɪfəʊld/ ADJ *(frm) [difficulties, benefits]* multiple ; *[effects]* divers ; *[shortcomings, duties]* nombreux ; *[collection]* divers, varié ◆ **in ~ forms** sous diverses formes ◆ **~ wisdom** sagesse f infinie N ◆ **inlet/exhaust ~** collecteur m or tubulure f d'admission/d'échappement

manikin /ˈmænɪkɪn/ N ⇒ **mannikin**

Manila /məˈnɪlə/ N Manille, Manila

mani(l)la envelope /məˌnɪləˈenvələʊp/ N enveloppe f en papier kraft

mani(l)la paper /məˌnɪləˈpeɪpəʳ/ N papier m kraft

manioc /ˈmænɪɒk/ N manioc m

manipulate /məˈnɪpjʊleɪt/ VT 1 *[+ tool etc]* manipuler ◆ **they use computers to ~ images** ils utilisent l'ordinateur pour manipuler des images 2 *(pej) [+ facts, figures, accounts]* tripoter, trafiquer * ; *[+ events]* agir sur ; *[+ person]* manipuler, manœuvrer ◆ **to ~ a situation** faire son jeu des circonstances ◆ **to ~ sb into doing sth** manipuler qn pour lui faire faire qch

manipulation /məˌnɪpjʊˈleɪʃən/ N *(gen, Med)* manipulation f ◆ **market ~** *(Fin)* manœuvre(s) f(pl) boursière(s)

manipulative /məˈnɪpjʊlətɪv/ ADJ 1 *(pej = controlling) [person, behaviour, film, speech]* manipulateur (-trice f) 2 *(Physiotherapy)* ◆ **~ therapy** or **treatment** (traitement m par) manipulations fpl ◆ **~ therapist** thérapeute mf qui soigne par manipulations

manipulator /məˈnɪpjʊleɪtəʳ/ N manipulateur m, -trice f

Manitoba /ˌmænɪˈtəʊbə/ N Manitoba m ◆ **in ~** dans le Manitoba

mankind /mænˈkaɪnd/ N *(NonC) (= the human race)* le genre humain, l'humanité f ; *(= the male sex)* les hommes mpl

manky * /ˈmæŋkɪ/ *(Brit)* ADJ cradingue *

manlike /ˈmænlaɪk/ ADJ *[form, figure, qualities]* humain ; *(pej) [woman]* hommasse *(pej)*

manliness /ˈmænlɪnɪs/ N virilité f, caractère m viril

manly /ˈmænlɪ/ ADJ *[man, boy, chest, shoulders, sport]* viril (virile f) ; *[pride, virtue]* mâle

manna /ˈmænə/ N manne f ◆ **~ from heaven** manne f tombée du ciel or providentielle

manned /mænd/ ADJ *[spacecraft, flight]* habité ; *[mission]* habité, humain ; see also **man**

mannequin /ˈmænɪkɪn/ N mannequin m

manner /ˈmænəʳ/ N 1 *(= mode, way)* manière f, façon f ◆ **the ~ in which he did it** la manière or façon dont il l'a fait ◆ **in such a ~ that ...** *(frm)* de telle sorte que ... + *indic (actual result)* or + *subj (intended result)* ◆ **in this ~, after this ~** *(frm)* de cette manière or façon ◆ **in** or **after the ~ of Van Gogh** à la manière de Van Gogh ◆ **in the same ~, in like ~** *(frm)* de la même manière ◆ **in a (certain) ~** en quelque sorte ◆ **in such a ~ as to ...** de façon à ... ◆ **in a ~ of speaking** pour ainsi dire ◆ **it's a ~ of speaking** c'est une façon de parler ◆ **~ of payment** mode m de paiement ◆ **(as) to the ~ born** comme s'il (or elle etc) avait cela dans le sang

2 *(= behaviour, attitude)* attitude f, comportement m ◆ **his ~ to his mother** son attitude envers sa mère, sa manière de se conduire avec sa mère ◆ **I don't like his ~** je n'aime pas son attitude ◆ **there's something odd about his ~** il y a quelque chose de bizarre dans son comportement

3 *(= class, sort, type)* sorte f, genre m ◆ **all ~ of birds** toutes sortes d'oiseaux ◆ **no ~ of doubt** aucun doute ; → **means**

NPL **manners** 1 *(= social behaviour)* manières fpl ◆ **good ~s** bonnes manières fpl, savoir-vivre m ◆ **bad ~s** mauvaises manières fpl ◆ **it's good/bad ~s (to do that)** ça se fait/ne se fait pas (de faire ça) ◆ **he has no ~s, his ~s are terrible** il a de très mauvaises manières, il n'a aucun savoir-vivre ◆ **aren't you forgetting your ~s?** *(to child)* est-ce que c'est comme ça qu'on se tient ? ◆ **road ~s** politesse f au volant

2 *(= social customs)* mœurs fpl, usages mpl ◆ **novel of ~s** roman m de mœurs ; → **comedy**

mannered /ˈmænəd/ ADJ 1 *(pej = affected) [voice, gesture, writing, painting]* maniéré ; *[style]* maniéré, précieux 2 *(= polite) [person]* bien élevé ; *[society]* civilisé ◆ **beautifully** or **impeccably ~** qui a des manières exquises

-mannered /ˈmænəd/ ADJ *(in compounds)* ◆ **rough-mannered** aux manières rudes ; → **bad, mild, well²**

mannerism /ˈmænərɪzəm/ N 1 *(= habit, trick of speech etc)* trait m particulier ; *(pej)* tic m, manie f 2 *(NonC: Art, Literat etc)* maniérisme m

mannerist /ˈmænərɪst/ ADJ, N maniériste mf

mannerliness /ˈmænəlɪnɪs/ N *(= civility)* savoir-vivre m

mannerly /ˈmænəlɪ/ ADJ bien élevé

mannikin /ˈmænɪkɪn/ N 1 *(Art, Dressmaking)* mannequin m *(objet)* 2 *(= dwarf etc)* homoncule m, nabot m

manning /ˈmænɪŋ/ N *(Mil)* armement m ; *(= employees)* effectifs mpl ◆ **~ levels** niveau m des effectifs

mannish /ˈmænɪʃ/ ADJ *[woman]* masculin, hommasse *(pej)* ; *[behaviour, clothes]* masculin ◆ **in a ~ way** comme un homme, d'une façon masculine

mannishly /ˈmænɪʃlɪ/ ADV *[dress]* comme un homme

manoeuvrability, maneuverability (US) /məˌnuːvrəˈbɪlɪtɪ/ N manœuvrabilité *f*, maniabilité *f*

manoeuvrable, maneuverable (US) /məˈnuːvrəbl/ ADJ *[car, ship]* maniable, manœuvrable

manoeuvre, maneuver (US) /məˈnuːvəʳ/ N (*all senses*) manœuvre *f* ◆ **to be on ~s** (*Mil etc*) faire des *or* être en manœuvres ◆ **it doesn't leave much room for ~** (*fig*) cela ne laisse pas une grande marge de manœuvre

VT (*all senses*) manœuvrer ◆ **to ~ sth out/in/through** *etc* faire sortir/entrer/traverser *etc* qch en manœuvrant ◆ **they ~d the gun into position** ils ont manœuvré le canon pour le mettre en position ◆ **he ~d the car through the gate** il a pu à force de manœuvres faire passer la voiture par le portail ◆ **to ~ sb into doing sth** manœuvrer qn pour qu'il fasse qch ◆ **the government tried to ~ itself into a stronger position** le gouvernement a essayé de manœuvrer pour renforcer ses positions

VI (*all senses*) manœuvrer

manoeuvring /məˈnuːvərɪŋ/ N (*NonC: pej = scheming*) magouille* *f*

manometer /mæˈnɒmɪtəʳ/ N manomètre *m*

manor /ˈmænəʳ/ N 1 (also **manor house**) manoir *m*, gentilhommière *f* 2 (*Hist = estate*) domaine *m* seigneurial ; → **lord** 3 (*Brit Police etc:* *) fief *m*

manorial /məˈnɔːrɪəl/ ADJ seigneurial

manpower /ˈmænˌpaʊəʳ/ N (*NonC*) 1 (*= workers available*) main-d'œuvre *f* ; (*in armed forces*) effectifs *mpl* ◆ **the shortage of skilled ~** la pénurie de main-d'œuvre qualifiée 2 (*= physical exertion*) force *f* physique COMP **Manpower Services Commission** N (*Brit: formerly*) ≃ Agence *f* nationale pour l'emploi

mansard /ˈmænsɑːd/ N (also **mansard roof**) mansarde *f*, comble *m* brisé

manse /mæns/ N presbytère *m* (*d'un pasteur presbytérien*)

manservant /ˈmænsɜːvənt/ N (pl **menservants** *or* **manservants**) valet *m* de chambre

mansion /ˈmænʃən/ N (*in town*) hôtel *m* particulier ; (*in country*) château *m*, manoir *m* COMP **the Mansion House** N *résidence officielle du Lord Mayor de Londres*

manslaughter /ˈmænslɔːtəʳ/ N (*Jur*) homicide *m* (involontaire *or* par imprudence)

mansuetude †† /ˈmænswɪtjuːd/ N mansuétude *f*, douceur *f*

mantel /ˈmæntl/ N 1 (also **mantelpiece, mantelshelf**) (dessus *m or* tablette *f* de) cheminée *f* 2 (*= structure round fireplace*) manteau *m*, chambranle *m* (de cheminée)

mantes /ˈmæntiːz/ NPL of **mantis**

mantilla /mænˈtɪlə/ N mantille *f*

mantis /ˈmæntɪs/ N (pl **mantises** *or* **mantes**) mante *f* ; → **praying**

mantle /ˈmæntl/ N 1 † (*= cloak*) cape *f* ; [*of lady*] mante †† *f* ◆ **~ of snow** (*liter*) manteau *m* de neige ◆ **since taking on the ~ of European City of Culture in 1990 Glasgow ...** depuis qu'elle a assumé, en 1990, le rôle de ville européenne de la culture, Glasgow ... ◆ **she has the intellectual form to take up the ~ of party leader** elle a les capacités intellectuelles nécessaires pour prendre la tête du parti 2 [*of gas lamp*] manchon *m* ; → **gas** 3 (*Geol: of earth*) manteau *m* VT (*liter*) (re)couvrir

mantra /ˈmæntrə/ N 1 (*lit*) mantra *m* 2 (*fig*) litanie *f*

mantrap /ˈmæntræp/ N piège *m* à hommes

manual /ˈmænjʊəl/ ADJ [*work, worker, lens, method, dexterity, gearbox*] manuel ; [*transmission, typewriter*] mécanique ; [*pump*] à main ◆ **~ labour** main-d'œuvre *f* ◆ **~ controls** commandes *fpl* manuelles N 1 (*= book*) manuel *m* 2 [*of organ*] clavier *m*

manually /ˈmænjʊəlɪ/ ADV à la main, manuellement ◆ **~ operated** à main, manuel

manufacture /ˌmænjʊˈfæktʃəʳ/ N (*NonC*) fabrication *f* ; [*of clothes*] confection *f* NPL **manufactures** produits *mpl* manufacturés VT (*gen*) fabriquer ; [*+ clothes*] confectionner ; (*fig*) [*+ story, excuse*] fabriquer ◆ **~d goods** produits *mpl* manufacturés

manufacturer /ˌmænjʊˈfæktʃərəʳ/ N fabricant *m*

COMP **manufacturers' recommended price** N prix *m* public

manufacturing /ˌmænjʊˈfæktʃərɪŋ/ N fabrication *f*

COMP [*town, city, job, output, sector*] industriel ; [*industry*] de transformation

manufacturing base N base *f* industrielle

manufacturing company N manufacture *f*

manufacturing plant N usine *f*

manure /məˈnjʊəʳ/ N (*NonC*) (also **farmyard manure**) fumier *m* ; (also **artificial manure**) engrais *m* ◆ **liquid ~** (*organic*) purin *m*, lisier *m* ; (*artificial*) engrais *m* liquide ; → **horse** VT (*with farmyard manure*) fumer ; (*with artificial manure*) répandre des engrais sur COMP **manure heap** N (tas *m* de) fumier *m*

manuscript /ˈmænjʊskrɪpt/ N manuscrit *m* ◆ **in ~** (*= not yet printed*) sous forme de manuscrit ; (*= handwritten*) écrit à la main ADJ manuscrit, écrit à la main

Manx /mæŋks/ ADJ de l'île de Man, mannois N (*= language*) mannois *m* NPL **the Manx** les Mannois *mpl* COMP **Manx cat** N chat *m* de l'île de Man

Manxman /ˈmæŋksmən/ N (pl **-men**) Mannois *m*

Manxwoman /ˈmæŋkswʊmən/ N (pl **-women**) Mannoise *f*

many /ˈmenɪ/ ADJ, PRON (compar **more**, superl **most**) beaucoup (de), un grand nombre (de) ◆ **~ books** beaucoup de livres, un grand nombre de livres ◆ **very ~ books** un très grand nombre de livres, de très nombreux livres ◆ **~ of those books** un grand nombre de ces livres ◆ **~ of them** un grand nombre d'entre eux, beaucoup d'entre eux ◆ **a good ~ of those books** (un) bon nombre de ces livres ◆ **~ people** beaucoup de gens *or* de monde, bien des gens ◆ **~ came** beaucoup sont venus ◆ **~ believe that to be true** bien des gens croient que c'est vrai ◆ **the ~** (*liter*) la multitude, la foule ◆ **the ~ who admire him** le grand nombre de gens qui l'admirent ◆ **~ times** bien des fois ◆ **~ a time, ~'s the time*** maintes fois, souvent ◆ **I've lived here for ~ years** j'habite ici depuis des années ◆ **he lived there for ~ years** il vécut là de nombreuses années *or* de longues années ◆ **people of ~ kinds** des gens de toutes sortes ◆ **a good** *or* **great ~ things** beaucoup de choses ◆ **in ~ cases** dans bien des cas, dans de nombreux cas ◆ **~ a man would be grateful** il y en a plus d'un qui serait reconnaissant ◆ **a woman of ~ moods** une femme d'humeur changeante ◆ **a man of ~ parts** un homme qui a des talents très divers ◆ **~ happy returns (of the day)!** bon *or* joyeux anniversaire !

◆ **as many** ◆ **I have as ~ problems as you** j'ai autant de problèmes que vous ◆ **I have as ~ as you** j'en ai autant que vous ◆ **as ~ as wish to come** tous ceux qui désirent venir ◆ **as ~ as 100 people are expected** on attend jusqu'à 100 personnes ◆ **there were as ~ again outside the hall** il y en avait encore autant dehors que dans la salle

◆ **how many** ◆ **how ~ people?** combien de gens ? ◆ **how ~?** combien ? ◆ **how ~ there are!** qu'ils sont nombreux !

◆ **however many** ◆ **however ~ books you have** quel que soit le nombre de livres que vous ayez ◆ **however ~ there may be** quel que soit leur nombre

◆ **so many** ◆ **so ~ have said it** il y en a tant qui l'ont dit ◆ **I've got so ~ already (that ...)** j'en ai déjà tant (que ...) ◆ **there were so ~ (that ...)** il y en avait tant (que ...) ◆ **so ~ dresses** tant de robes ◆ **ever so ~ times*** je ne sais combien de fois, tant de fois ◆ **the people far below, like so ~ ants** les gens tout en bas comme autant de fourmis ◆ **he did not say that in so ~ words** il n'a pas dit cela explicitement

◆ **too many** trop ◆ **there were too ~** il y en avait trop ◆ **too ~ cakes** trop de gâteaux ◆ **three too ~** trois de trop ◆ **20 would not be too ~** il n'y en aurait pas trop de 20 ◆ **he's had one too ~*** (*drinks*) il a bu un coup de trop ◆ **I've got too ~ already** j'en ai déjà trop ◆ **there are too ~ of you** vous êtes trop nombreux ◆ **too ~ of these books** trop de ces livres ◆ **too ~ of us know that ...** nous sommes trop (nombreux) à savoir que ...

COMP **many-coloured, many-hued** ADJ (*liter*) multicolore

many-sided ADJ [*object*] qui a de nombreux côtés ; (*fig*) [*person*] aux intérêts (*or* talents) variés *or* multiples ; [*problem*] complexe, qui a de nombreuses facettes

Maoism /ˈmaʊɪzəm/ N maoïsme *m*

Maoist /ˈmaʊɪst/ ADJ, N maoïste *mf*

Maori /ˈmaʊrɪ/ ADJ maori N 1 (*= person*) Maori(e) *m(f)* 2 (*= language*) maori *m*

Mao (Tse Tung) /ˈmaʊ(tseɪˈtʊŋ)/ N Mao (Tsê-Tung) *m*

map /mæp/ N (*gen*) carte *f* ; [*of town, bus, tube, subway*] plan *m* ◆ **geological/historical/linguistic ~** carte *f* géologique/historique/linguistique ◆ **~ of Paris/the Underground** plan *m* de Paris/du métro ◆ **~ of France** carte *f* de la France ◆ **this will put Bishopbriggs on the ~** (*fig*) cela fera connaître Bishopbriggs ◆ **the whole town was wiped off the ~** la ville entière a été rayée de la carte ◆ **off the ~*** (*fig*) (*= unimportant*) perdu ; (*= distant*) à l'autre bout du monde ; → **relief**

VT [*+ country, district etc*] faire *or* dresser la carte (*or* le plan) de ; [*+ route*] tracer

COMP **map-reading** N lecture *f* des cartes

▸ **map out** VT SEP [*+ route, plans*] tracer ; [*+ book, essay*] établir les grandes lignes de ; [*+ one's time, career, day*] organiser ; [*+ strategy, plan*] élaborer ◆ **he hasn't yet ~ped out what he will do** il n'a pas encore de plan précis de ce qu'il va faire

maple /ˈmeɪpl/ N érable *m*

COMP **maple leaf** N (pl **maple leaves**) feuille *f* d'érable

maple sugar N sucre *m* d'érable

maple syrup N sirop *m* d'érable

mapmaker /ˈmæpmeɪkəʳ/ N cartographe *mf*

mapmaking /ˈmæpmeɪkɪŋ/ N cartographie *f*

mapping /ˈmæpɪŋ/ N (*Math*) application *f* ; (*Comput*) mappage *m* COMP **mapping pen** N plume *f* de dessinateur *or* à dessin

mar /mɑːʳ/ VT gâter, gâcher ◆ **to make or ~ sth** assurer le succès ou l'échec de qch

Mar. abbrev of **March**

maracas /məˈrækəz/ NPL maracas *mpl*

maraschino /ˌmærəsˈkiːnəʊ/ N marasquin *m* COMP **maraschino cherry** N cerise *f* au marasquin

Marathon /ˈmærəθən/ N (*Geog, Hist*) Marathon

marathon /ˈmærəθən/ N (*Sport, fig*) marathon *m* ADJ 1 (*Sport*) [*runner*] de marathon 2 (*fig = very long*) marathon *inv* ◆ **a ~ session** une séance-marathon

maraud /məˈrɔːd/ VI marauder, être en maraude ◆ **to go ~ing** aller à la maraude

marauder /məˈrɔːdəʳ/ N maraudeur *m*, -euse *f*

marauding /məˈrɔːdɪŋ/ ADJ en maraude N maraude *f*

marble /ˈmɑːbl/ N 1 *(= stone, sculpture)* marbre *m* 2 *(= toy)* bille *f* ◆ **to play ~s** jouer aux billes ◆ **to lose one's ~s** * perdre la boule * ◆ **to pick up one's ~s and go home** * *(US)* reprendre ses billes VT marbrer
COMP *[staircase, statue]* de *or* en marbre ; *[industry]* marbrier
marble cake N gâteau *m* marbré
marble quarry N marbrière *f*

March /mɑːtʃ/ N mars *m* ; → **mad** ; *for other phrases see* **September**

march /mɑːtʃ/ N 1 *(Mil etc)* marche *f* ◆ **on the ~** en marche ◆ **quick/slow ~** marche *f* rapide/lente ◆ **a day's ~** une journée de marche ◆ **a 10km ~, a ~ of 10km** une marche de 10 km ◆ **the ~ on Rome** la marche sur Rome ◆ **the ~ of time/progress** la marche du temps/progrès ; → **forced, route, steal**
2 *(= demonstration)* manifestation *f* *(against* contre ; *for* pour)
3 *(Mus)* marche *f* ; → **dead**
VI 1 *(Mil etc)* marcher au pas ◆ **the army ~ed in/out** l'armée entra/sortit (au pas) ◆ **to ~ into battle** marcher au combat ◆ **to ~ past** défiler ◆ **to ~ past sb** défiler devant qn ◆ **~!** marche ! ; → **forward, quick**
2 *(gen)* **to ~ in/out/up** *etc (briskly)* entrer/sortir/monter *etc* d'un pas énergique ; *(angrily)* entrer/sortir/monter *etc* d'un air furieux ◆ **he ~ed up to me** il s'est approché de moi d'un air décidé ◆ **to ~ up and down the room** faire les cent pas dans la pièce, arpenter la pièce
3 *(= demonstrate)* manifester *(against* contre ; *for* pour)
VT 1 *(Mil)* faire marcher (au pas) ◆ **to ~ troops in/out** *etc* faire entrer/faire sortir *etc* des troupes (au pas)
2 *(fig)* **to ~ sb in/out/away** faire entrer/faire sortir/emmener qn tambour battant ◆ **to ~ sb off to prison** * embarquer qn en prison *
COMP **march-past** N *(Mil etc)* défilé *m*

marcher /ˈmɑːtʃəʳ/ N *(in demo etc)* manifestant(e) *m(f)*

marches /ˈmɑːtʃɪz/ NPL *(= border)* frontière *f* ; *(= borderlands)* marche *f*

marching /ˈmɑːtʃɪŋ/ N marche *f*
COMP **marching band** N *(US)* orchestre *m* d'école (avec majorettes)
marching orders NPL *(Mil)* feuille *f* de route ◆ **to give sb his ~ orders** * *(fig)* flanquer * qn à la porte, envoyer promener * qn ◆ **to get one's ~ orders** * *(fig)* se faire mettre à la porte
marching song N chanson *f* de route

marchioness /ˈmɑːʃənɪs/ N marquise *f* *(personne)*

Marco Polo /ˈmɑːkəʊˈpəʊləʊ/ N Marco Polo *m*

Marcus Aurelius /ˈmɑːkəsɔːˈriːlɪəs/ N Marc Aurèle *m*

Mardi Gras /ˈmɑːdɪˈgrɑː/ N mardi gras *m inv*, carnaval *m*

mare /meəʳ/ N jument *f* COMP **mare's nest** N ◆ **his discovery turned out to be a ~'s nest** sa découverte s'est révélée très décevante

marg * /mɑːdʒ/ N *(Brit)* abbrev of **margarine**

Margaret /ˈmɑːgərɪt/ N Marguerite *f*

margarine /ˌmɑːdʒəˈriːn/ N margarine *f*

margarita /ˌmɑːgəˈriːtə/ N margarita *f*

marge * /mɑːdʒ/ N *(Brit)* abbrev of **margarine**

margin /ˈmɑːdʒɪn/ N *[of book, page]* marge *f* ; *[of river, lake]* bord *m* ; *[of wood]* lisière *f* ; *(fig: Comm, Econ, gen)* marge *f* ◆ **notes in the ~** notes en marge *or* marginales ◆ **do not write in the ~** n'écrivez rien dans la marge ◆ **wide/narrow ~** *(Typ)* grande/petite marge *f* ◆ **to win by a wide/narrow ~** gagner de loin/de peu ◆ **elected by a narrow ~** élu de justesse *or* avec peu de voix de majorité ◆ **on the ~(s) of society** en marge de la société ◆ **to allow a ~ for ...** laisser une marge pour ... ◆ **to allow for a ~ of error** prévoir une marge d'erreur ◆ **profit ~, ~ of profit** marge *f* (bénéficiaire) ◆ **~ of safety, safety ~** marge *f* de sécurité

marginal /ˈmɑːdʒɪnl/ ADJ 1 *(= unimportant) [importance, significance, role, writer, business]* marginal *(to sth* par rapport à qch) ; *[existence]* de marginal(e) ; *[issue]* insignifiant ; *[benefit]* minime ◆ **a ~ case** un cas limite ◆ **the effect will be ~** l'effet sera négligeable ◆ **this is a ~ improvement on October** ceci constitue une amélioration négligeable *or* minime par rapport au mois d'octobre ◆ **the role of the opposition party proved ~** le rôle du parti d'opposition s'est révélé minime *or* insignifiant
2 *(Brit Parl) [seat, constituency]* très disputé
3 *(Sociol) [people, groups]* marginal
4 *(Agr) [land]* à faible rendement
5 *(= written in margin) [comments, notes]* en marge, marginal
N *(Brit Parl)* siège *m* à faible majorité

MARGINAL SEAT

En Grande-Bretagne, siège de député obtenu à une faible majorité et qui ne peut donc être considéré comme solidement acquis à un parti, contrairement au « safe seat » (siège sûr). Les circonscriptions à faible majorité appelées « marginal constituencies », intéressent particulièrement les médias en cas d'élection partielle, car elles constituent un bon baromètre de la popularité du parti au pouvoir.

marginalize /ˈmɑːdʒɪnəlaɪz/ VT marginaliser

marginally /ˈmɑːdʒɪnəlɪ/ ADV légèrement

marguerita /ˌmɑːgəˈriːtə/ N ⇒ **margarita**

marguerite /ˌmɑːgəˈriːt/ N marguerite *f*

Maria /məˈraɪə/ N Marie *f* ; → **black**

marigold /ˈmærɪgəʊld/ N *(= plant)* souci *m*

marijuana, marihuana /ˌmærɪˈhwɑːnə/ N marihuana *f or* marijuana *f*

marimba /məˈrɪmbə/ N marimba *m*

marina /məˈriːnə/ N marina *f*

marinade /ˌmærɪˈneɪd/ N marinade *f* VT /ˈmærɪneɪd/ mariner

marinate /ˈmærɪneɪt/ VT mariner

marine /məˈriːn/ ADJ *(= in the sea) [plant, animal]* marin ; *(= from the sea) [products]* de la mer ; *(= by the sea) [vegetation, forces]* maritime N 1 *(Naut)* **mercantile** *or* **merchant ~** marine *f* marchande 2 *(Mil)* fusilier *m* marin ; *(US)* marine *m* (américain) ◆ **the Marines** *(Brit)* ◆ **the Marine Corps** *(US)* les fusiliers *mpl* marins, les marines *mpl* ◆ **tell that to the ~s!** ‡ † à d'autres ! *
COMP **marine biologist** N océanographe *mf* biologiste
marine biology N océanographie *f* biologique
marine engineer N ingénieur *m* du génie maritime
marine engineering N génie *m* maritime
marine insurance N assurance *f* maritime
marine life N vie *f* marine
marine science N sciences *fpl* marines *or* de la mer
marine underwriter N assureur *m* maritime

mariner /ˈmærɪnəʳ/ N *(liter)* marin *m* COMP **mariner's compass** N boussole *f*, compas *m* ; → **master**

Mariolatry /ˌmeərɪˈɒlətrɪ/ N *(Rel: pej)* vénération *f* excessive de la Vierge

Mariology /ˌmeərɪˈɒlədʒɪ/ N mariologie *f*

marionette /ˌmærɪəˈnet/ N marionnette *f*

marital /ˈmærɪtl/ ADJ 1 *(= relating to marriage)* conjugal ◆ **~ breakdown** rupture *f* des rapports conjugaux ◆ **to commit ~ rape** violer son épouse 2 *(= relating to husband)* marital
COMP **marital relations** NPL rapports *mpl* conjugaux
marital status N *(frm)* situation *f* de famille, état *m* civil

maritime /ˈmærɪtaɪm/ ADJ maritime
COMP **maritime law** N droit *m* maritime
the Maritime Provinces NPL *(in Canada)* les provinces *fpl* maritimes

marjoram /ˈmɑːdʒərəm/ N marjolaine *f*

Mark /mɑːk/ N Marc *m* ◆ **~ Antony** Marc Antoine *m*

mark¹ /mɑːk/ N *(= currency)* mark *m*

mark² /mɑːk/ N 1 *(= physical marking)* marque *f* ; *(= stain)* marque *f*, tache *f* ; *(= written symbol on paper, cloth etc)* signe *m* ; *(as signature)* marque *f*, croix *f* ; *(= footprint, animal track, tyre track etc)* empreinte *f* ; *(= marking on animal, bird)* tache *f* ◆ **that will leave a ~** *(gen)* cela laissera une marque ; *(= stain)* cela laissera une tache ◆ **to make one's ~** *(as signature)* faire une marque *or* une croix ; see also **4** ◆ **he was found without a ~ on his body** quand on l'a trouvé, son corps ne portait aucune trace de blessure ◆ **the ~s of violence were visible everywhere** on voyait partout des marques *or* traces de violence ◆ **the city still bears the ~s of occupation** la ville porte encore les marques *or* traces de son occupation ; see also **3** ; → **finger, punctuation**
2 *(fig = sign)* signe *m* ◆ **a ~ of strength/success** un signe de force/de réussite (sociale) ◆ **the tendency to drink in secret is a ~ of addiction** la propension à boire en cachette est un signe d'alcoolisme ◆ **a ~ of shame** un objet de honte ◆ **as a ~ of protest/defiance** en signe de protestation/défi ◆ **as a ~ of respect** en signe de respect ◆ **as a ~ of my gratitude** en témoignage de ma gratitude ◆ **as a ~ of his confidence in/disapproval of ...** pour marquer sa confiance en/sa désapprobation de ...
3 *(fig = hallmark)* marque *f* ◆ **it bears the ~(s) of genius** cela porte la marque du génie ◆ **the attack bore the ~s of a terrorist organization** cet attentat portait la marque d'une organisation terroriste ◆ **it is the ~ of a good teacher** c'est le signe d'un bon professeur ◆ **the ~ of a true teacher/architect is the ability to ...** on reconnaît le véritable professeur/architecte à sa capacité à ... ◆ **to react the way he did was the ~ of a true hero** il s'est montré *or* révélé un véritable héros en réagissant comme il l'a fait
4 *(fig = lasting impression)* ◆ **to leave one's ~ on sth** laisser son empreinte sur qch ◆ **he has certainly made his ~** il s'est certainement imposé ◆ **he has certainly made a** *or* **his ~ in British politics** il a certainement marqué la politique britannique de son empreinte ◆ **to make one's ~ as a politician** s'imposer comme homme politique ◆ **to make one's ~ as a poet/writer** se faire un nom en tant que poète/qu'écrivain
5 *(Scol) (= grade: in exam, essay, overall assessment)* note *f* ; *(= point)* point *m* ◆ **good/bad ~** bonne/mauvaise note *f* ◆ **she got a good ~** *or* **good ~s in French** elle a eu une bonne note en français ◆ **~s for effort/conduct** *etc (Brit)* note *f* d'application/de conduite *etc* ◆ **the ~ is out of 20** c'est une note sur 20 ◆ **you need 50 ~s to pass** il faut avoir 50 points pour être reçu ◆ **to fail by two ~s** échouer à deux points près ◆ **he got full ~s** *(Brit Scol)* il a eu dix sur dix (*or* vingt sur vingt *etc*) ◆ **he deserves full ~s** *(Brit fig)* il mérite vingt sur vingt ◆ **full ~s to him for achieving so much** *(Brit: fig)* on ne peut que le féliciter de tout ce qu'il a accompli ◆ **(I give**

him) full ~s for trying c'est bien d'avoir essayé ◆ **full ~s for honesty** bravo pour l'honnêteté ◆ **there are no ~s * for guessing his name** *(hum)* il n'y a pas besoin d'être un génie pour savoir de qui je parle

6 *(= target)* cible *f* ◆ **to hit the ~** *(lit)* faire mouche ; *(fig)* faire mouche, mettre dans le mille ◆ **to be right on the ~** *[comment, observation]* être très pertinent ◆ **she's normally right on the ~** d'habitude, ses observations sont très pertinentes ◆ **to miss the ~** *(lit)* manquer le but ◆ **to miss the ~, to be wide of the ~** *or* **off the ~** *or* **far from the ~** *(fig)* être loin de la vérité ◆ **it's way off the ~** * *[forecast, estimate]* c'est complètement à côté de la plaque* ◆ **to be an easy ~** *(pej)* être une cible facile ; → **overshoot, overstep**

7 *(Sport)* ligne *f* de départ ; *(Rugby)* arrêt *m* de volée ◆ **on your ~s! get set! go!** à vos marques ! prêts ! partez ! ◆ **to get off the ~** *(lit, fig)* démarrer ◆ **to be quick off the ~** *(= quick on the uptake)* avoir l'esprit vif ; *(= quick in reacting)* avoir des réactions rapides ◆ **to be quick off the ~ in doing sth** ne pas perdre de temps pour faire qch ◆ **to be slow off the ~** *(fig)* être lent (à la détente*) ◆ **I don't feel up to the ~** je ne suis pas dans mon assiette, je ne suis pas en forme ◆ **he isn't up to the ~ for this job** il n'est pas à la hauteur de ce travail ◆ **his work isn't up to the ~, his work doesn't come up to the ~** son travail n'est pas satisfaisant, son travail laisse à désirer ◆ **this film came well up to the ~** ce film ne m'a pas déçu

8 *(Econ = level, point)* barre *f* ◆ **the number of unemployed has reached the 2 million ~/fallen below the 2 million ~** le chiffre du chômage a atteint la barre des 2 millions/est descendu en dessous de la barre des 2 millions

9 *(= brand name)* marque *f*

10 *(Mil, Tech = model, type)* série *f* ◆ **Concorde Mark 1** Concorde *m* première série

11 *(= oven temperature)* **(gas) ~ 6** thermostat *m* 6

VT 1 *(= make a mark on)* marquer, mettre une marque à *or* sur ; *[+ paragraph, item, linen, suitcase]* marquer ; *(= stain)* tacher, marquer ◆ **I hope your dress isn't ~ed** j'espère que ta robe n'est pas tachée ◆ **to ~ the cards** *(lit)* marquer les cartes

2 *[animal, bird]* ◆ **a bird ~ed with red** un oiseau tacheté de rouge

3 *(fig = scar)* marquer ◆ **the accident ~ed him for life** l'accident l'a marqué pour la vie ◆ **suffering had ~ed him** la douleur l'avait marqué ◆ **his reign was ~ed by civil wars** son règne fut marqué par des guerres civiles

4 *(= indicate)* marquer ; *[+ price etc]* marquer, indiquer ; *(Stock Exchange)* coter ; *(Sport)* *[+ score]* marquer ◆ **this flag ~s the frontier** ce drapeau marque la frontière ◆ **they ~ed his grave with a cross** ils ont mis une croix sur sa tombe ◆ **it ~s a change of policy** cela indique un changement de politique ◆ **in order to ~ the occasion** pour marquer l'occasion ◆ **this ~s him as a future manager** ceci fait présager pour lui une carrière de cadre ◆ **to ~ time** *(Mil)* marquer le pas ; *(fig) (= wait)* faire du sur place, piétiner ; *(by choice, before doing sth)* attendre son heure ; → **X** ; see also **marked**

5 *[+ essay, exam]* corriger, noter ; *[+ candidate]* noter, donner une note à ◆ **to ~ sth right/wrong** marquer qch juste/faux

6 *(= note, pay attention to)* bien écouter ◆ **(you) ~ my words!** crois-moi ! ; *(predicting)* tu verras ! ◆ **~ you, he may have been right** remarquez qu'il avait peut-être raison ◆ **~ him well** †† écoutez bien ce qu'il dit

7 *(Sport) [+ opposing player]* marquer

VI se tacher

COMP mark reader N lecteur *m* optique
mark reading N lecture *f* optique
mark scanner N lecteur *m* de marques
mark scanning N lecture *f* de marques

mark-up N *(= price increase)* hausse *f*, majoration *f* de prix ; *(= profit margin)* bénéfice *m* ◆ **~-up on a bill** majoration *f* sur une facture ◆ **there's a 50% ~-up on this product** ils ont une marge *or* ils font un bénéfice de 50% sur ce produit

► **mark down VT SEP** 1 *(= write down)* inscrire, noter

2 *(= reduce) [+ price]* baisser ; *[+ goods]* démarquer, baisser le prix de ◆ **all these items have been ~ed down for the sales** tous ces articles ont été démarqués pour les soldes ◆ **to be ~ed down** *(Stock Exchange)* s'inscrire en baisse, reculer

3 *(Scol) [+ exercise, pupil]* baisser la note de

4 *(= single out) [+ person]* désigner, prévoir *(for* pour)

► **mark off VT SEP** 1 *(= separate)* séparer, distinguer *(from* de)

2 *[+ area]* délimiter ; *[+ distance]* mesurer ; *[+ road, boundary]* tracer

3 *[+ items on list etc]* cocher ◆ **he ~ed the names off as the people went in** il cochait les noms (sur la liste) à mesure que les gens entraient

► **mark out VT SEP** 1 *[+ zone etc]* délimiter, tracer les limites de ; *[+ field]* borner ; *[+ route, footpath]* baliser ; *(with stakes)* jalonner ◆ **to ~ out a tennis court** tracer les lignes d'un court de tennis ◆ **the route is ~ed out with flags** l'itinéraire est jalonné de drapeaux

2 *(= single out)* désigner, distinguer ◆ **to ~ sb out for promotion** désigner qn pour l'avancement ◆ **he was ~ed out long ago for that job** il y a longtemps qu'on l'avait prévu pour ce poste ◆ **his red hair ~ed him out from the others** ses cheveux roux le distinguaient des autres

► **mark up VT SEP** 1 *(on board, wall etc) [+ price, score]* marquer

2 *(= put a price on)* indiquer *or* marquer le prix de ◆ **these items have not been ~ed up** le prix n'est pas marqué sur ces articles

3 *(= increase) [+ price]* majorer ; *[+ goods]* majorer le prix de ◆ **all these chairs have been ~ed up** toutes ces chaises ont augmenté ◆ **to be ~ed up** s'inscrire en hausse, avancer

4 *[+ exercise, pupil]* surnoter, gonfler la note de

N ◆ **mark-up** → **comp**

markdown /ˈmɑːkdaʊn/ **N** *(= price reduction)* remise *f*, réduction *f*

marked /mɑːkt/ **ADJ** 1 *(= noticeable) [improvement, increase, decline, change, effect]* sensible ; *[lack]* net ; *[preference, tendency, difference]* net, marqué ; *[reluctance]* vif, marqué ; *[contrast]* frappant ; *[bias]* manifeste ; *[accent]* prononcé ◆ **it is becoming more ~** cela s'accentue ◆ **in ~ contrast (to ...)** en contraste frappant (avec ...) 2 ◆ **to be a ~ man** être un homme marqué 3 *(= signposted) [path, trail]* balisé 4 *(Ling)* marqué ◆ **~ form** forme *f* marquée ◆ **to be ~ for number/gender** porter la marque du nombre/du genre 5 *(Stock Exchange)* ◆ **~ shares** actions *fpl* estampillées

markedly /ˈmɑːkɪdlɪ/ **ADV** *[improve, differ, contrast, change]* sensiblement ◆ **to be ~ better/worse** être nettement mieux/moins bien

marker /ˈmɑːkər/ **N** 1 (also **marker pen**) marqueur *m* indélébile ; *(for laundry etc)* marquoir *m* 2 *(= flag, stake)* marque *f*, jalon *m* ; *(= light etc)* balise *f* ◆ **to put** *or* **lay down a ~ for sth** *(fig)* révéler ses intentions pour qch 3 *(= bookmark)* signet *m* 4 *(Sport etc = person)* marqueur *m*, -euse *f* ◆ **to lose** *or* **shake off one's ~** *(Ftbl)* se démarquer 5 *(Scol = person)* correcteur *m*, -trice *f* 6 *(Tech: showing sth is present)* indicateur *m* *(for sth* de qch) 7 *(Ling)* marqueur *m*

market /ˈmɑːkɪt/ **N** 1 *(= trade, place)* marché *m* ◆ **to go to ~** aller au marché ◆ **the wholesale ~** le marché de gros ◆ **cattle ~** marché *m or* foire *f* aux bestiaux ◆ **the sugar ~, the ~ in sugar** le marché du sucre ◆ **the world coffee ~** le marché mondial du *or* des café(s) ◆ **free ~** marché *m* libre ◆ **a dull/lively ~** *(Stock Exchange)* un marché lourd/actif ◆ **the ~ is rising/falling** *(Stock Exchange)* les cours *mpl* sont en hausse/en baisse ◆ **the company intends to go to the ~** *(Stock Exchange)* la société a l'intention d'entrer en Bourse ; → **black, buyer, common**

2 *(fig)* marché *m* ◆ **home/overseas/world ~** marché *m* intérieur/d'outre-mer/mondial ◆ **to have a good ~ for sth** avoir une grosse demande pour qch ◆ **to find a ready ~ for sth** trouver facilement un marché *or* des débouchés pour qch ◆ **there is a ready ~ for small cars** les petites voitures se vendent bien ◆ **there's no ~ for pink socks** les chaussettes roses ne se vendent pas ◆ **this appeals to the French ~** cela plaît à la clientèle française, cela se vend bien en France ◆ **our competitors control 72% of the ~** nos concurrents contrôlent 72% du marché ◆ **to be in the ~ for sth** être acheteur de qch ◆ **to put sth/to be on the ~** mettre qch/être en vente *or* dans le commerce *or* sur le marché ◆ **to come on to the ~** arriver sur le marché ◆ **it's the dearest car on the ~** c'est la voiture la plus chère sur le marché ◆ **on the open ~** en vente libre ; → **flood**

VT *(= promote)* commercialiser ; *(= sell)* vendre ; *(= find outlet for)* trouver un *or* des débouché(s) pour

VI *(esp US: also* **to go marketing***)* aller faire des commissions

COMP market analysis N analyse *f* de marché
market cross N croix *f* sur la place du marché
market day N jour *m* de *or* du marché ; *(Stock Exchange)* jour *m* de bourse
market-driven ADJ *[innovation]* répondant *inv* à la demande du marché
market economy N économie *f* de marché
market forces NPL forces *fpl* du marché
market garden N *(Brit)* jardin *m* maraîcher
market gardener N *(Brit)* maraîcher *m*, -ère *f*
market gardening N *(Brit)* culture *f* maraîchère
market leader N *(= company, product)* leader *m* du marché
market opportunity N créneau *m*
market place N *(lit)* place *f* du marché ◆ **in the ~ place** *(lit)* au marché ; *(fig: Econ)* sur le marché
market price N prix *m* du marché ◆ **at ~ price** au cours, au prix courant ◆ **~ prices** *(Stock Exchange)* cours *m* du marché
market rates NPL taux *m* du cours libre
market research N étude *f* de marché *(in* de) ◆ **to do some ~ research** faire une étude de marché ◆ **I work in ~ research** je travaille pour un consultant en études de marché *or* une société de marketing ◆ **~ research institute** *or* **organization** institut *m* de marketing
market researcher N enquêteur *m*, -trice *f* *(qui fait des études de marché)*
market share N part *f* du marché
market square N place *f* du marché
market-test VT tester sur le marché **N** test *m* de marché
market town N *(Brit)* bourg *m*
market trader N *(Brit)* commerçant(e) *m(f)* *(qui vend sur les marchés)*
market trends NPL tendances *fpl* du marché
market value N valeur *f* marchande

marketability /ˌmɑːkɪtəˈbɪlɪtɪ/ **N** possibilité *f* de commercialisation

marketable /ˈmɑːkɪtəbl/ **ADJ** 1 *[commodity, product, skill]* facilement commercialisable ; *[securities]* négociable ◆ **of ~ quality** d'une bonne qualité marchande 2 *(fig) [person]* coté

marketeer /ˌmɑːkəˈtɪər/ **N** 1 → **black** 2 *(Brit Pol)* ◆ **(pro-)Marketeers** ceux qui sont en faveur du Marché commun ◆ **anti-Marketeers** ceux qui s'opposent au Marché commun

marketing /ˈmɑːkɪtɪŋ/ N 1 *[of product, goods]* commercialisation *f*, marketing *m* 2 *(= field of activity)* marketing *m*, mercatique *f* 3 *(= department)* service *m* du marketing, département *m* marketing

COMP *[concept, plan]* de commercialisation
marketing arrangement N accord *m* de commercialisation
marketing department N service *m* du marketing, département *m* marketing
marketing intelligence N informations *fpl* commerciales
marketing manager N directeur *m*, -trice *f* du marketing
marketing mix N marketing mix *m*, plan *m* de marchéage
marketing people NPL ◆ **one of our ~ people** l'un de nos commerciaux
marketing strategy N stratégie *f* marketing

marking /ˈmɑːkɪŋ/ N 1 (NonC) *[of animals, trees, goods]* marquage *m* 2 *(Brit Scol) (gen = correcting)* correction *f* (des copies) ; *(= giving of marks)* attribution *f* de notes, notation *f* ; *(= marks given)* notes *fpl* 3 (also **markings**) *(on animal)* marques *fpl*, taches *fpl* ; *(on road)* signalisation *f* horizontale 4 *(Ftbl)* marquage *m* (d'un joueur)

COMP **marking ink** N encre *f* indélébile
marking scheme N barème *m*

marksman /ˈmɑːksmən/ N (pl **-men**) tireur *m* ; *(Police)* tireur *m* d'élite

marksmanship /ˈmɑːksmənʃɪp/ N adresse *f* au tir

marl /mɑːl/ *(Geol)* N marne *f* VT marner

marlin /ˈmɑːlɪn/ N 1 (pl **marlin** or **marlins**) *(= fish)* marlin *m*, makaire *m* 2 ⇒ **marline**

marline /ˈmɑːlɪn/ N *(Naut)* lusin *m* COMP **marlin(e) spike** N *(Naut)* épissoir *m*

marly /ˈmɑːlɪ/ ADJ marneux

marmalade /ˈmɑːməleɪd/ N confiture *f* or marmelade *f* (d'agrumes) COMP **marmalade orange** N orange *f* amère, bigarade *f*

Marmara, Marmora /ˈmɑːmərə/ N ◆ **the Sea of ~** la mer de Marmara

marmoreal /mɑːˈmɔːrɪəl/ ADJ *(liter)* marmoréen

marmoset /ˈmɑːməʊzet/ N ouistiti *m*

marmot /ˈmɑːmət/ N marmotte *f*

maroon¹ /məˈruːn/ ADJ *(= colour)* bordeaux *inv*

maroon² /məˈruːn/ N *(= distress signal)* fusée *f* de détresse

maroon³ /məˈruːn/ VT *(lit) [+ castaway]* abandonner (sur une île or une côte déserte) ; *(fig) [sea, traffic, strike etc]* bloquer ◆ **to be ~ed** *(fig)* être abandonné or délaissé

marque /mɑːk/ N *(= brand)* marque *f*

marquee /mɑːˈkiː/ N 1 *(esp Brit) (= tent)* grande tente *f* ; *(in circus)* chapiteau *m* 2 *(= awning)* auvent *m* ; *(US) [of theatre, cinema]* marquise *f*, fronton *m*

Marquesas Islands /mɑːˈkeɪsəsˈaɪləndz/ NPL îles *fpl* Marquises

marquess /ˈmɑːkwɪs/ N marquis *m*

marquetry /ˈmɑːkɪtrɪ/ N marqueterie *f* COMP *[table etc]* de or en marqueterie

marquis /ˈmɑːkwɪs/ N ⇒ **marquess**

Marrakesh, Marrakech /ˈməˈrækeʃ, mærəˈkeʃ/ N Marrakech

marriage /ˈmærɪdʒ/ LANGUAGE IN USE 24.3

N mariage *m* ; *(fig)* mariage *m*, alliance *f* ◆ **to give sb in ~** donner qn en mariage ◆ **to take sb in ~** † *(gen)* épouser qn ; *(in actual wording of service)* prendre qn comme époux (or épouse) ◆ **civil ~** mariage *m* civil ◆ **aunt by ~** tante *f* par alliance ◆ **they are related by ~** ils sont parents par alliance ; → **offer, shotgun**

COMP **marriage bed** N lit *m* conjugal
marriage bonds NPL liens *mpl* conjugaux
marriage broker N agent *m* matrimonial
marriage bureau N agence *f* matrimoniale
marriage ceremony N (cérémonie *f* de) mariage *m*
marriage certificate N (extrait *m* d')acte *m* de mariage
marriage customs NPL coutumes *fpl* matrimoniales
marriage guidance N consultation *f* conjugale
marriage guidance counsellor N conseiller *m*, -ère *f* conjugal(e)
marriage licence N certificat *m* de publication des bans
marriage lines NPL *(Brit)* ⇒ **marriage certificate** ~ **of convenience** mariage *m* de convenance
marriage partner N conjoint(e) *m(f)*
marriage rate N taux *m* de nuptialité
marriage settlement N ≈ contrat *m* de mariage
marriage vows NPL vœux *mpl* de mariage

marriageable † /ˈmærɪdʒəbl/ ADJ *[person]* mariable ◆ **of ~ age** en âge de se marier ◆ **he's very ~** c'est un très bon parti

married /ˈmærɪd/ ADJ 1 *(= wedded) [person, couple]* marié (*to* à, avec) ◆ **twice-~** marié deux fois ◆ **"just married"** "jeunes mariés" ◆ **the newly ~ couple** les (nouveaux) mariés *mpl* ◆ **he is a ~ man** c'est un homme marié ◆ **to be happily ~** être heureux en ménage ◆ **~ life** vie *f* conjugale ; see also **happily** 2 *(fig)* ◆ **to be ~ to one's job** or **work** ne vivre que pour son travail

COMP **married name** N nom *m* de femme mariée
married quarters NPL *(Mil)* quartiers *mpl* des personnes mariées ; → **marry**

marrow /ˈmærəʊ/ N 1 *[of bone]* moelle *f* ; *(fig)* essence *f* ◆ **to be chilled** or **frozen to the ~** être gelé jusqu'à la moelle des os 2 *(Brit = vegetable)* courge *f* ◆ **baby ~** courgette *f*

marrowbone /ˈmærəʊbəʊn/ N os *m* à moelle

marrowfat /ˈmærəʊfæt/ N (also **marrowfat pea**) *pois de grande taille*

marry /ˈmærɪ/ LANGUAGE IN USE 24.3

VT 1 *(= take in marriage)* épouser, se marier avec ◆ **will you ~ me?** veux-tu or voulez-vous m'épouser ? ◆ **to get** or **be married** se marier ◆ **they've been married for ten years** ils sont mariés depuis dix ans ◆ **to ~ money** épouser une grosse fortune

2 *(= give or join in marriage) [priest, parent]* marier ◆ **he has three daughters to ~ (off)** il a trois filles à marier ◆ **she married (off) her daughter to a lawyer** elle a marié sa fille avec or à un avocat

VI se marier ◆ **to ~ for money/love** faire un mariage d'argent/d'amour ◆ **to ~ into a family** s'allier à une famille par le mariage, s'apparenter à une famille ◆ **to ~ into money** épouser une grosse fortune ◆ **to ~ beneath o.s.** † se mésallier, faire une mésalliance ◆ **to ~ again** se remarier

► **marry off** VT SEP *[parent etc]* marier ; → **marry** vt 2

► **marry up** VT SEP *[pattern etc]* faire coïncider

Mars /mɑːz/ N *(Myth)* Mars *m* ; *(Astron)* Mars *f*

Marseillaise /ˌmɑːsəˈleɪz/ N Marseillaise *f*

Marseilles /mɑːˈseɪlz/ N Marseille

marsh /mɑːʃ/ N marais *m*, marécage *m* ; → **salt**

COMP **marsh fever** N paludisme *m*, fièvre *f* des marais
marsh gas N gaz *m* des marais
marsh marigold N renoncule *f* des marais
marsh warbler N rousserolle *f*

marshal /ˈmɑːʃəl/ N 1 *(Mil etc)* maréchal *m* ◆ **Marshal of the Royal Air Force** *(Brit)* maréchal de la RAF ; → **air, field** 2 *(Brit: at demonstration, sports event etc)* membre *m* du service d'ordre 3 *(in US, in police/fire department)* ≈ capitaine *m* de gendarmerie/des pompiers ; *(= law officer)* marshal *m (magistrat et officier de police fédérale)* 4 *(in Brit: at Court etc)* chef *m* du protocole VT 1 *(Mil, Police) [+ troops, forces]* rassembler ; *[+ crowd, traffic]* canaliser ; *(Rail) [+ wagons]* trier ◆ **the police ~led the procession into the town** la police a fait entrer le cortège en bon ordre dans la ville 2 *(fig) [+ facts]* organiser ; *[+ evidence]* rassembler ; *[+ resources]* mobiliser ; *[+ support]* obtenir, rallier ◆ **to ~ one's thoughts** rassembler ses idées

marshalling /ˈmɑːʃəlɪŋ/ N 1 *[of crowd, demonstrators]* maintien *m* de l'ordre *(of* parmi*)* 2 *(Rail)* triage *m* COMP **marshalling yard** N gare *f* or centre *m* de triage

marshland /ˈmɑːʃlænd/ N région *f* marécageuse, marécage *m*

marshmallow /mɑːʃˈmæləʊ/ N 1 *(= plant)* guimauve *f* 2 *(= sweet)* marshmallow *m*

marshy /ˈmɑːʃɪ/ ADJ marécageux

marsupial /mɑːˈsuːpɪəl/ ADJ, N marsupial *m*

mart /mɑːt/ N *(esp US) (= trade centre)* centre *m* commercial ; *(= market)* marché *m* ; *(= auction room)* salle *f* des ventes ; → **property**

marten /ˈmɑːtɪn/ N (pl **martens** or **marten**) martre *f* or marte *f*

martial /ˈmɑːʃəl/ ADJ *[music]* militaire ; *[spirit]* guerrier ; *[behaviour]* martial ; → **court martial**

COMP **martial art** N art *m* martial
martial artist N expert *m* en arts martiaux
martial law N loi *f* martiale ◆ **to be under ~ law** être soumis à la loi martiale
martial rule N domination *f* militaire

Martian /ˈmɑːʃən/ N martien(ne) *m(f)* ADJ martien

martin /ˈmɑːtɪn/ N *(= bird)* ◆ **house ~** hirondelle *f* de fenêtre ◆ **sand ~** hirondelle *f* de rivage

martinet /ˌmɑːtɪˈnet/ N ◆ **to be a (real) ~** être impitoyable or intraitable en matière de discipline

martingale /ˈmɑːtɪngeɪl/ N *(Horse-riding, Gambling)* martingale *f*

Martini ® /mɑːˈtiːnɪ/ N Martini ® *m* ; *(US = cocktail)* Martini *m* américain ◆ **sweet ~** Martini *m* rouge

Martinique /ˌmɑːtɪˈniːk/ N Martinique *f* ◆ **in ~** à la Martinique, en Martinique

Martinmas /ˈmɑːtɪnməs/ N la Saint-Martin

martyr /ˈmɑːtəʳ/ N *(Rel, fig)* martyr(e) *m(f)* (*to* de) ◆ **a ~'s crown** la couronne du martyre ◆ **he is a ~ to migraine(s)** ses migraines lui font souffrir le martyre ◆ **don't be such a ~!** *, **stop acting like a ~!** arrête de jouer les martyrs ! VT *(Rel, fig)* martyriser

martyrdom /ˈmɑːtədəm/ N (NonC) *(Rel)* martyre *m* ; *(fig)* martyre *m*, calvaire *m*

martyrize /ˈmɑːtɪraɪz/ VT *(Rel, fig)* martyriser

marvel /ˈmɑːvəl/ N *(= thing)* merveille *f* ; *(= wonder)* prodige *m*, miracle *m* ◆ **the ~s of modern science** les prodiges *mpl* de la science moderne ◆ **plastics were hailed as a ~ of modern science** on a salué les matières plastiques comme un prodige de la science moderne ◆ **the cathedral is a ~ of Gothic architecture** la cathédrale est un joyau de l'architecture gothique ◆ **if he gets there it will be a ~** ce sera (un) miracle s'il y arrive ◆ **she's a ~** * c'est une perle ◆ **it's a ~ to me * how he does it** je ne sais vraiment pas comment il y arrive ◆ **it's a ~ to me * that ...** cela me paraît un miracle que ... + *subj*, je n'en reviens pas que ... + *subj* ◆ **it's a ~ that ...** c'est un miracle que ... + *subj* ; → **work**

VI s'émerveiller, s'étonner (*at* de)

VT s'étonner (*that* de ce que + *indic or* + *subj*)

marvellous, marvelous (US) /ˈmɑːvələs/ ADJ merveilleux ◆ **(isn't it) ~!** (iro) c'est vraiment extraordinaire ! (iro) ◆ **to have a ~ time** s'amuser énormément ◆ **it's ~ to see you** je suis si content de te voir

marvellously, marvelously (US) /ˈmɑːvələslɪ/ ADV merveilleusement

Marxian /ˈmɑːksɪən/ ADJ marxien

Marxism /ˈmɑːksɪzəm/ N marxisme *m* COMP **Marxism-Leninism** N marxisme-léninisme *m*

Marxist /ˈmɑːksɪst/ ADJ, N marxiste *mf* ◆ **with ~ tendencies** marxisant COMP **Marxist-Leninist** ADJ, N marxiste-léniniste *mf*

Mary /ˈmeərɪ/ N Marie *f* ◆ **~ Magdalene** Marie-Madeleine *f* ◆ **~ Queen of Scots, ~ Stuart** Marie Stuart(, reine d'Écosse) ◆ **~ Jane*** (Drugs) marie-jeanne* *f*, marijuana *f* ; → **bloody**

Maryland /ˈmeərɪlænd/ N Maryland *m* ◆ **in ~** dans le Maryland

marzipan /ˈmɑːzɪ,pæn/ N pâte *f* d'amandes, massepain *m* COMP [sweet etc] à la pâte d'amandes

masc. abbrev of **masculine**

mascara /mæsˈkɑːrə/ N mascara *m*

mascaraed /mæsˈkɑːrəd/ ADJ maquillé (au mascara)

mascarpone /,mæskəˈpəʊneɪ/ N mascarpone *m*

mascot /ˈmæskət/ N mascotte *f*

masculine /ˈmæskjʊlɪn/ ADJ masculin N (Gram) masculin *m* ◆ **in the ~** au masculin

masculinist /ˈmæskjʊlɪnɪst/, **masculist** /ˈmæskjʊlɪst/ ADJ masculin ; (*pej*) phallocrate, machiste

masculinity /,mæskjʊˈlɪnɪtɪ/ N masculinité *f*

masculinize /ˈmæskjʊlɪnaɪz/ VT masculiniser

masculist /ˈmæskjʊlɪst/ N ⇒ **masculinist**

maser /ˈmeɪzəʳ/ N maser *m*

MASH /mæʃ/ N (US) (abbrev of **mobile army surgical hospital**) unité *f* chirurgicale mobile de campagne

COMP **MASH team** N équipe *f* chirurgicale mobile de campagne

MASH unit N unité *f* chirurgicale mobile de campagne

mash /mæʃ/ N 1 (= *pulp*) pulpe *f* 2 (*Brit Culin* * = *potatoes*) purée *f* (de pommes de terre) ; → **banger** 3 (*Agr*) (*for pigs, hens etc*) pâtée *f* ; (*for horses*) mash *m* 4 (*Brewing*) pâte *f* VT 1 (= *crush*) (also **mash up**) écraser, broyer ; (*Culin*) [+ *potatoes, bananas*] faire une purée de ◆ **~ed potatoes** purée *f* (de pommes de terre) 2 (= *injure, damage*) écraser 3 (*Brewing*) brasser

masher /ˈmæʃəʳ/ N (*Tech*) broyeur *m* ; (*in kitchen*) presse-purée *m inv*

mashie /ˈmæʃɪ/ N (*Golf*) mashie *m*

mask /mɑːsk/ N (*gen*) masque *m* ; (*for eyes: in silk or velvet*) masque *m*, loup *m* ; (*Comput*) masque *m* de saisie ; → **death, gasmask, iron** VT 1 [+ *person, face*] masquer 2 (= *hide*) [+ *object, truth, fact, differences*] masquer, cacher ; [+ *motives, pain*] cacher, dissimuler ; [+ *taste, smell*] masquer ◆ **to ~ sth from sb** (*fig*) cacher qch à qn VI [*surgeon etc*] se masquer

COMP **masked ball** N bal *m* masqué

masking tape N ruban *m* de masquage

masochism /ˈmæsəʊkɪzəm/ N masochisme *m*

masochist /ˈmæsəʊkɪst/ N masochiste *mf*

masochistic /,mæsəʊˈkɪstɪk/ ADJ masochiste

mason /ˈmeɪsn/ N 1 (= *stoneworker*) maçon *m* ; → **monumental** 2 (also **freemason**) (franc-)maçon *m*

COMP **the Mason-Dixon Line** N (*US Hist*) la ligne Mason-Dixon

Mason jar N (*US*) bocal *m* à conserves (étanche)

> **MASON-DIXON LINE**
>
> La **ligne Mason-Dixon** est la frontière symbolique (longue de 375 km) qui, au 18ᵉ siècle, séparait le nord du sud des États-Unis, c'est-à-dire les États esclavagistes des États anti-esclavagistes. L'expression est encore utilisée de nos jours. De même, les chanteurs de musique country parlent souvent avec nostalgie de traverser la **ligne Mason-Dixon** pour évoquer leur désir de rentrer chez eux dans le Sud.

masonic /məˈsɒnɪk/ ADJ (franc-)maçonnique

Masonite ® /ˈmeɪsənaɪt/ N (*US*) aggloméré *m*

masonry /ˈmeɪsənrɪ/ N (*NonC*) 1 (= *stonework*) maçonnerie *f* 2 (= *freemasonry*) (franc-)maçonnerie *f*

masque /mɑːsk/ N (*Theat*) mascarade *f*, comédie-masque *f*

masquerade /,mæskəˈreɪd/ N (*lit, fig*) mascarade *f* VI ◆ **to ~ as ...** se faire passer pour ...

mass¹ /mæs/ N 1 (*NonC: Art, Phys*) masse *f*

2 [*of matter, dough, rocks, air, snow, water etc*] masse *f* ◆ **a ~ of daisies** une multitude de pâquerettes ◆ **the garden was a (solid) ~ of colour** le jardin n'était qu'une profusion de couleurs ◆ **he was a ~ of bruises** il était couvert de bleus ◆ **in the ~** dans l'ensemble ◆ **the great ~ of people** la (grande) masse des gens, la (grande) majorité des gens

3 (= *people*) ◆ **the ~(es)** les masses (populaires) ◆ **Shakespeare for the ~es** Shakespeare à l'usage des masses

NPL **masses** * ◆ **~es (of ...)** des masses* (de ...), des tas* (de ...) ◆ **I've got ~es** j'en ai plein*

ADJ 1 (= *en masse*) [*support, unemployment, opposition, destruction*] massif ; [*rally*] massif, de masse ; [*resignations, desertions, sackings*] en masse ; [*hysteria, hypnosis*] collectif ◆ **~ executions** exécutions *fpl* systématiques

2 (= *for the masses*) [*culture, movement*] (also *Comput*) [*memory*] de masse ; (= *relating to the masses*) [*psychology, education*] des masses

VT ◆ **~ed bands/troops** fanfares *fpl*/troupes *fpl* regroupées

VI [*troops, people*] se masser ; [*clouds*] s'amonceler

COMP **mass cult*** N (*US*) culture *f* populaire *or* de masse

mass funeral N obsèques *fpl* collectives

mass grave N charnier *m*

mass mailing N publipostage *m*

mass-market ADJ grand public *inv*

mass marketing N commercialisation *f* de masse

mass media NPL (mass-)médias *mpl*

mass meeting N grand rassemblement *m*

mass murder N tuerie *f*, massacre *m*

mass murderer N (*lit, fig*) boucher *m*, auteur *m* d'un massacre

mass noun N (*Ling*) nom *m* massif

mass-produce VT fabriquer en série

mass production N production *f or* fabrication *f* en série

mass² /mæs/ N (*Rel, Mus*) messe *f* ◆ **to say ~** dire la messe ◆ **to go to ~** aller à la messe ; → **black**

Mass. abbrev of **Massachusetts**

Massachusetts /,mæsəˈtʃuːsɪts/ N Massachusetts *m* ◆ **in ~** dans le Massachusetts

massacre /ˈmæsəkəʳ/ N (*lit, fig*) massacre *m* ◆ **a ~ on the roads** une hécatombe sur les routes VT (*lit, fig*) massacrer

massage /ˈmæsɑːʒ/ N massage *m* ; (*euph*) massage *m* thaïlandais VT masser ; (*fig*) [+ *figures*] manipuler

COMP **massage glove** N gant *m* de crin

massage parlour N institut *m* de massage (spécialisé)

masseur /mæˈsɜːʳ/ N masseur *m*

masseuse /mæˈsɜːz/ N masseuse *f*

massicot /ˈmæsɪkɒt/ N massicot *m*

massif /mæˈsiːf/ N massif *m* COMP **the Massif Central** N le Massif central

massive /ˈmæsɪv/ ADJ 1 (= *imposing, solid*) [*features, physique, building, furniture, rock face*] massif 2 (= *large-scale*) [*dose, explosion, increase*] massif ; [*majority*] écrasant ; [*heart attack, stroke*] foudroyant ◆ **on a ~ scale** à très grande échelle 3 (* = *huge*) [*suitcase, car, house etc*] énorme, gigantesque ◆ **he weighs in at a ~ 100 kilos** il fait le poids imposant de 100 kilos, c'est un colosse de 100 kilos

massively /ˈmæsɪvlɪ/ ADV [*invest, borrow, increase*] massivement ; [*reduce*] énormément ; [*successful, popular*] extrêmement ◆ **~ overloaded** beaucoup trop chargé ◆ **~ overweight** obèse

massiveness /ˈmæsɪvnɪs/ N 1 [*of building, features, dose, increase*] aspect *m or* caractère *m* massif ; [*of majority*] ampleur *f* 2 * [*of suitcase, car, house etc*] taille *f* gigantesque

mast¹ /mɑːst/ N (*on ship, also flagpole*) mât *m* ; (*for radio*) pylône *m* ◆ **the ~s of a ship** la mâture d'un navire ◆ **to sail before the ~** (*Naut*) servir comme simple matelot

mast² /mɑːst/ N (*Bot*) → **beechmast**

mastectomy /mæˈstektəmɪ/ N mastectomie *f*

-masted /ˈmɑːstɪd/ ADJ (*in compounds*) ◆ **three-masted** à trois mâts

master /ˈmɑːstəʳ/ N 1 [*of household, institution, animal*] maître *m* ◆ **the ~ of the house** le maître de maison ◆ **to be ~ in one's own house** être maître chez soi ◆ **the ~ is not at home** † Monsieur n'est pas là ◆ **like ~ like man** (*Prov*) tel maître tel valet (*Prov*) ◆ **old ~s** (*Art* = *pictures*) tableaux *mpl* de maître ◆ **I am the ~ now** c'est moi qui commande *or* qui donne les ordres maintenant ◆ **he has met his ~** (*fig*) il a trouvé son maître ◆ **to be one's own ~** être son (propre) maître ◆ **to be ~ of o.s./of the situation** être maître de soi/de la situation ◆ **to be (the) ~ of one's destiny** *or* **fate** être maître de sa destinée ◆ **he is a ~ of the violin** c'est un virtuose du violon ◆ **the Master** (*Bible*) le Seigneur ; → **old, past**

2 († : also **schoolmaster**) (*in secondary school*) professeur *m* ; (*in primary school*) instituteur *m*, maître *m* ◆ **music ~** (*in school*) professeur *m* de musique ; (*private tutor*) professeur *m or* maître *m* de musique ; → **fencing**

3 (*Naut*) [*of ship*] capitaine *m* ; [*of liner*] (capitaine) commandant *m* ; [*of fishing boat*] patron *m*

4 (*Univ*) **Master of Arts/Science** *etc* ≈ titulaire *mf* d'une maîtrise en lettres/sciences *etc* ; → DEGREE ◆ **a ~'s (degree)** ≈ une maîtrise ◆ **~'s essay** *or* **paper** *or* **thesis** (*US*) ≈ mémoire *m* (de maîtrise)

5 (*Brit Univ*) [*of Oxbridge college etc*] ≈ directeur *m*, principal *m*

6 (*Brit: title for boys*) monsieur *m*

7 ⇒ **master tape, master disk**

8 (*Golf*) **the (US) Masters** les Masters *mpl*

VT 1 [+ *person*] mater ; [+ *animal*] dompter ; [+ *emotion*] maîtriser ; [+ *difficulty, crisis, problem*] gérer, surmonter ; [+ *situation*] se rendre maître de

2 (= *understand, learn*) [+ *theory*] saisir ; [+ *language, skill*] maîtriser ◆ **he has ~ed Greek** il connaît *or* possède le grec à fond ◆ **he'll never ~ the violin** il ne saura jamais bien jouer du violon ◆ **he has ~ed the trumpet** il est devenu très bon trompettiste *or* un trompettiste accompli ◆ **it's so difficult that I'll never ~ it** c'est si difficile que je n'y parviendrai jamais

COMP [beam] maître (maîtresse f) ; [control, cylinder, switch] principal

master-at-arms N (pl **masters-at-arms**) (Naut) capitaine m d'armes

master baker N maître m boulanger

master bedroom N chambre f principale

master builder N entrepreneur m en bâtiment

master butcher N maître m boucher

master card N (Cards, fig) carte f maîtresse

master chief petty officer N (US Naut) major m

master class N cours m de (grand) maître

master copy N original m

master cylinder N (in car engine) maître cylindre m

master disk N (Comput) disque m d'exploitation

master file N (Comput) fichier m maître or permanent

master hand N (= expert) maître m ◆ **to be a ~ hand at (doing) sth** être passé maître dans l'art de (faire) qch ◆ **the work of a ~ hand** un travail exécuté de main de maître

master key N passe-partout m inv

master mariner N (Naut) (foreign-going) ≈ capitaine m au long cours ; (home trade) ≈ capitaine m de la marine marchande

master of ceremonies N maître m des cérémonies ; (TV etc) animateur m

master of (fox)hounds N grand veneur m

Master of the Rolls N (Brit Jur) ≈ premier président m de la Cour de cassation

master plan N schéma m directeur

master print N (Cine) copie f étalon

master race N race f supérieure

master sergeant N (US) adjudant m ; (US Aviat) ≈ sergent-chef m

master stroke N coup m magistral or de maître

master tape N bande f mère

MasterCard ® /ˈmɑːstəkɑːd/ N MasterCard ® f

masterful /ˈmɑːstəfʊl/ ADJ 1 (= dominant) [person] à l'autorité naturelle 2 (= skilful) [performance, job, display] magistral ◆ **to be ~ at doing sth** réussir remarquablement à faire qch

masterfully /ˈmɑːstəfəlɪ/ ADV 1 (= imperiously) [act, decide] en maître ; [speak, announce] d'un ton décisif, sur un ton d'autorité 2 (= expertly) magistralement, de main de maître

masterly /ˈmɑːstəlɪ/ ADJ [performance, analysis] magistral ; [actor, player, politician] de grande classe ◆ **in ~ fashion** avec maestria ◆ **to say sth with ~ understatement** dire qch avec un art consommé de la litote

mastermind /ˈmɑːstəmaɪnd/ N (= genius) génie m, cerveau m ; [of plan, crime etc] cerveau m VT [+ operation etc] diriger, organiser

masterpiece /ˈmɑːstəpiːs/ N chef-d'œuvre m

masterwork /ˈmɑːstəwɜːk/ N chef-d'œuvre m

mastery /ˈmɑːstərɪ/ N (gen) maîtrise f (of de) ◆ **to gain ~ over** [+ person] avoir le dessus sur, l'emporter sur ; [+ animal] dompter ; [+ nation, country] s'assurer la domination de ; [+ the seas] s'assurer la maîtrise de

masthead /ˈmɑːsthed/ N [of ship] tête f de mât ; [of newspaper] (= title) titre m ; (= staff etc) ours* m (Press)

mastic /ˈmæstɪk/ N (= resin, adhesive) mastic m

masticate /ˈmæstɪkeɪt/ VTI mastiquer, mâcher

mastiff /ˈmæstɪf/ N mastiff m

mastitis /mæˈstaɪtɪs/ N mastite f

mastodon /ˈmæstədɒn/ N mastodonte m (lit)

mastoid /ˈmæstɔɪd/ ADJ mastoïdien N (= bone) apophyse f mastoïde

mastoiditis /ˌmæstɔɪˈdaɪtɪs/ N mastoïdite f

masturbate /ˈmæstəbeɪt/ VI se masturber VT masturber

masturbation /ˌmæstəˈbeɪʃən/ N masturbation f

masturbatory /ˌmæstəˈbeɪtərɪ/ ADJ masturbatoire, masturbateur (-trice f)

MAT /ˌemeɪˈtiː/ N (abbrev of **machine-assisted translation**) TAO f

mat¹ /mæt/ N 1 (for floors etc) (petit) tapis m, carpette f ; [of straw etc] natte f ; (at door) paillasson m ; (in car, gymnasium) tapis m ◆ **to have sb on the ~*** (fig) passer un savon à qn* ◆ **a ~ of hair** des cheveux emmêlés ◆ **to go to the ~ for sb/to do sth** (US) monter au créneau pour qn/pour faire qch ; → **rush²** 2 (on table, heat-resistant) dessous-de-plat m inv ; (decorative) set m (de table) ; (embroidered linen) napperon m ; → **drip, place** VI (= become matted) [hair etc] s'emmêler ; [woollens] (se) feutrer ; → **matted**

mat² /mæt/ ADJ → **matt(e)**

matador /ˈmætədɔːʳ/ N matador m

match¹ /mætʃ/ N allumette f ◆ **box/book of ~es** boîte f/pochette f d'allumettes ◆ **have you got a ~?** avez-vous une allumette or du feu ? ◆ **to strike** or **light a ~** gratter or frotter or faire craquer une allumette ◆ **to put** or **set a ~ to sth** mettre le feu à qch ; → **safety**

match² /mætʃ/ N 1 (Sport) match m ; (esp Brit) (= game) partie f ◆ **to play a ~ against sb** disputer un match contre qn, jouer contre qn ◆ **international ~** match m international, rencontre f internationale ◆ **~ abandoned** match m suspendu ; → **away, home, return**

2 (= equal) égal(e) m(f) ◆ **to meet one's ~ (in sb)** trouver à qui parler (avec qn), avoir affaire à forte partie (avec qn) ◆ **he's a ~ for anybody** il est de taille à faire face à n'importe qui ◆ **he's no ~ for Paul** il n'est pas de taille à lutter contre Paul, il ne fait pas le poids contre Paul ◆ **he was more than a ~ for Simon** Simon n'était pas à sa mesure or ne faisait pas le poids contre lui

3 **to be a good ~** [clothes, colours etc] aller bien ensemble, s'assortir bien ◆ **I'm looking for a ~ for these curtains** je cherche quelque chose pour aller avec ces rideaux

4 (= comparison) adéquation f ◆ **a poor ~ between our resources and our objectives** une mauvaise adéquation entre nos ressources et nos objectifs

5 († = marriage) mariage m ◆ **he's a good ~ for her** c'est un bon parti (pour elle) ◆ **they're a good ~** ils sont bien assortis ; see also **love**

VT 1 (= be equal to) (also **match up to**) égaler, être l'égal de ◆ **his essay didn't ~ (up to) Jason's in originality** sa dissertation n'égalait pas or ne valait pas celle de Jason en originalité ◆ **she doesn't ~ (up to) her sister in intelligence** elle n'a pas l'intelligence de sa sœur ◆ **the result didn't ~ (up to) our hopes** le résultat a déçu nos espérances ◆ **he didn't ~ (up to) his father's expectations** il n'a pas été à la hauteur des espérances de son père

2 (= produce equal to) **to ~ sb's offer/proposal** faire une offre/une proposition équivalente à celle de qn ◆ **I can ~ any offer** je peux offrir autant que n'importe qui ◆ **to ~ sb's price/terms** offrir le même prix/des conditions aussi favorables que qn ◆ **this is ~ed only by ...** cela n'a d'égal que ...

3 [clothes, colours etc] (intended as a set) être assorti à ; (a good match) aller bien avec ◆ **his tie doesn't ~ his shirt** sa cravate ne va pas avec sa chemise

4 (= find similar piece etc to: also **match up**) **can you ~ (up) this material?** (exactly same) avez-vous du tissu identique à celui-ci ? ; (going well with) avez-vous du tissu assorti à celui-ci ?

5 (= pair off) **to ~ sb against sb** opposer qn à qn ◆ **she ~ed her wits against his strength** elle opposait son intelligence à sa force ◆ **evenly ~ed** de force égale ◆ **they are well ~ed** [opponents] ils sont de force égale ; [married couple etc] ils sont bien assortis

VI [colours, materials] être bien assortis, aller bien ensemble ; [cups] être appareillés ; [gloves, socks] faire la paire ; [two identical objects] se faire pendant ◆ **with (a) skirt to ~** avec (une) jupe assortie

COMP **match day** N (Brit Sport) jour m de match

match-fit ADJ (Brit Sport) en état de jouer (un match)

match fitness N (Brit Sport) ◆ **to regain ~ fitness** retrouver la forme pour jouer (un match)

match-fixing N ◆ **there were allegations of ~-fixing** selon certains, le match aurait été truqué

match play N (Golf) match-play m

match point N (Tennis) balle f de match

► **match up** VI [colours etc] aller bien ensemble, être assortis

VT SEP ⇒ **match²** vt 4

► **match up to** VT FUS ⇒ **match²** vt 1

matchbook /ˈmætʃbʊk/ (esp US) N pochette f d'allumettes

matchbox /ˈmætʃbɒks/ N boîte f d'allumettes

matching /ˈmætʃɪŋ/ ADJ [clothes, accessories, earrings, curtains] assorti ◆ **he was dressed in a smart grey suit and ~ tie** il était vêtu d'un élégant costume gris avec une cravate assortie ◆ **her ~ blue sweater and skirt** son pull bleu et sa jupe assortie ◆ **a ~ pair** une paire

matchless /ˈmætʃlɪs/ ADJ (liter) sans égal

matchmake* /ˈmætʃmeɪk/ VI jouer les entremetteurs

matchmaker /ˈmætʃmeɪkəʳ/ N entremetteur m, -euse f, marieur* m, -euse* f ◆ **she is a great ~** elle aime jouer les entremetteuses

matchstick /ˈmætʃstɪk/ N allumette f COMP (= thin) [limbs, body] filiforme

matchwood /ˈmætʃwʊd/ N (for matches) bois m d'allumettes ◆ **to smash sth to ~** (= debris) réduire qch en miettes, pulvériser qch

mate¹ /meɪt/ N 1 (at work) camarade mf 2 * (Brit = friend) copain* m, copine* f ◆ **he's a good ~** c'est un bon copain ◆ **cheers ~!*** merci, mon vieux !* ; → **classmate, playmate, workmate** 3 (= assistant) aide mf ◆ **plumber's ~** aide-plombier m 4 [of animal] mâle m, femelle f ; (* hum) [of human] (= spouse etc) compagnon m, compagne f 5 (Brit Merchant Navy) ≈ second m (capitaine m) ; (US Naut) maître m (dans la marine) ; → **first** VT accoupler (with à) VI s'accoupler (with à, avec)

mate² /meɪt/ (Chess) N mat m ; → **checkmate, stalemate** VT mettre échec et mat, mater

material /məˈtɪərɪəl/ ADJ (esp Jur) 1 (= physical) matériel ◆ **~ damage** dommage m matériel ◆ **~ evidence** preuves fpl matérielles

2 (= relevant) pertinent (to sth pour qch) ◆ **~ information** informations fpl pertinentes ◆ **~ witness** témoin m de fait

N 1 (= substance) substance f, matière f ◆ **chemical/dangerous ~s** substances fpl or matières fpl chimiques/dangereuses ; → **waste**

2 (= cloth, fabric) tissu m ◆ **dress ~** tissu m pour robes

3 (= substances from which product is made) matériau m ◆ **building ~s** matériaux mpl de construction ◆ **he's officer ~** il a l'étoffe d'un officier ◆ **he's not university ~** il n'est pas capable d'entreprendre des études supérieures ; → **raw**

4 (= necessary tools, supplies) matériel m ◆ **the desk held all his writing ~s** le bureau contenait tout son matériel nécessaire pour écrire ◆ **have you got any writing ~s?** avez-vous de quoi écrire ? ◆ **reading ~** (gen) de quoi lire, de la lecture ; (for studies) des ouvrages mpl (et des

articles *mpl*) à consulter ◆ **play ~s** le matériel de jeu ◆ **teaching** *or* **course ~(s)** *(Scol etc)* matériel *m* pédagogique

5 *(NonC = facts, data)* matériaux *mpl* ◆ **they had all the ~ necessary for a biography** ils avaient tous les matériaux *or* toutes les données nécessaires pour une biographie ◆ **I had all the ~ I needed for my article** j'avais tout ce qu'il me fallait pour mon article ◆ **the amount of ~ to be examined** la quantité de matériaux *or* de documents à examiner ◆ **all the background ~** toute la documentation d'appui ◆ **reference ~** ouvrages *mpl* de référence

6 *(NonC = sth written, composed etc)* **she writes her own ~** *[singer]* elle écrit ses propres chansons ; *[comic]* elle écrit ses propres sketches ◆ **an album of original ~** un album de titres inédits ◆ **she has written some very funny ~** elle a écrit des choses très amusantes ◆ **we cannot publish this ~** nous ne pouvons pas publier ce texte ◆ **in my version of the story, I added some new ~** dans ma version de l'histoire, j'ai ajouté des éléments nouveaux ◆ **publicity ~** matériel *m* publicitaire *or* promotionnel ◆ **video ~** enregistrements *mpl* vidéo ◆ **30% of the programme was recorded ~** 30% de l'émission avait été préenregistrée

materialism /məˈtɪərɪəlɪzəm/ **N** matérialisme *m*

materialist /məˈtɪərɪəlɪst/ **ADJ, N** matérialiste *mf*

materialistic /məˌtɪərɪəˈlɪstɪk/ **ADJ** *(pej)* matérialiste

materialize /məˈtɪərɪəlaɪz/ **VI** 1 *(= take shape) [plan, wish]* se matérialiser, se réaliser ; *[offer, loan etc]* se concrétiser, se matérialiser ; *[idea]* prendre forme 2 *(= appear, happen)* ◆ **the promised cash didn't ~** l'argent promis ne s'est pas concrétisé *or* matérialisé ◆ **a rebellion by radicals failed to ~** il n'y a pas eu de rébellion des radicaux ◆ **none of the anticipated difficulties ~d** les difficultés auxquelles on s'attendait ne se sont pas présentées 3 *(Spiritualism etc)* prendre une forme matérielle, se matérialiser ◆ **Derek ~d at her side** *(hum)* Derek est soudain apparu à ses côtés **VT** matérialiser, concrétiser

materially /məˈtɪərɪəlɪ/ **ADV** matériellement

maternal /məˈtɜːnl/ **ADJ** maternel ◆ **~ smoking can damage the unborn child** en fumant, les femmes enceintes risquent de compromettre la santé de leur bébé

COMP **maternal death** **N** mort *f* en couches

maternal deprivation **N** *(Psych)* dépression *f* anaclitique

maternal health care **N** soins *mpl* aux jeunes mères

maternal instinct **N** instinct *m* maternel

maternity /məˈtɜːnɪtɪ/ **N** maternité *f*

COMP *[services etc]* obstétrique ; *[clothes]* de grossesse **maternity allowance, maternity benefit** **N** *(Brit)* allocation *f* de maternité

maternity dress **N** robe *f* de grossesse

maternity home, maternity hospital **N** maternité *f* ; *(private)* clinique *f* d'accouchement

maternity leave **N** congé *m* de maternité

maternity pay **N** *(Brit) indemnités versées pendant le congé de maternité*

maternity ward **N** (service *m* de) maternité *f*

matey /ˈmeɪtɪ/ *(Brit)* **ADJ** * *[person]* copain * (copine * *f*) *(with sb* avec qn) ; *[tone]* copain-copain * *f inv* ; *[charm]* familier **N** *(as term of address)* ◆ **sorry, ~ !** ‡ désolé, mon vieux ! *

math * /mæθ/ **N** *(US)* (abbrev of **mathematics**) math(s) * *fpl*

mathematical /ˌmæθəˈmætɪkəl/ **ADJ** *[formula, equation, model, calculations]* mathématique ; *[skills, ability]* en mathématiques ◆ **I'm not ~** * je ne suis pas un matheux *, je n'ai pas la bosse * des maths ◆ **I haven't got a ~ mind** je n'ai pas l'esprit mathématique ◆ **she was a ~ genius** c'était une mathématicienne de génie, c'était un génie en mathématiques

mathematically /ˌmæθəˈmætɪkəlɪ/ **ADV** *(gen)* mathématiquement ◆ **~ gifted** doué en mathématiques ◆ **~ precise** avec une précision mathématique ◆ **to be ~ inclined** *or* **minded** avoir l'esprit mathématique

mathematician /ˌmæθəməˈtɪʃən/ **N** mathématicien(ne) *m(f)*

mathematics /ˌmæθəˈmætɪks/ **N** *(NonC)* mathématiques *fpl* ◆ **I don't understand the ~ of it** je ne vois pas comment on arrive à ce chiffre *or* à ce résultat

maths * /mæθs/ **N** *(Brit)* (abbrev of **mathematics**) math(s) * *fpl*

matinée /ˈmætɪneɪ/ **N** *(Theat)* matinée *f*

COMP **matinée coat** **N** *(Brit)* veste *f* (de bébé)

matinée idol **N** *(Theat)* idole *f* du public féminin

matinée jacket **N** ⇒ **matinée coat**

mating /ˈmeɪtɪŋ/ **N** *[of animals]* accouplement *m*

COMP **mating call** **N** appel *m* du mâle

mating season **N** saison *f* des amours

matins /ˈmætɪnz/ **N** *(Rel)* matines *fpl*

matriarch /ˈmeɪtrɪɑːk/ **N** matrone *f*, femme *f* chef de tribu *or* de famille

matriarchal /ˌmeɪtrɪˈɑːkl/ **ADJ** matriarcal

matriarchy /ˈmeɪtrɪɑːkɪ/ **N** matriarcat *m*

matric * /məˈtrɪk/ **N** *(Brit Scol: formerly)* abbrev of **matriculation noun 2**

matrices /ˈmeɪtrɪsiːz/ **NPL** of **matrix**

matricide /ˈmeɪtrɪsaɪd/ **N** *(= crime)* matricide *m* ; *(= person)* matricide *mf*

matriculate /məˈtrɪkjʊleɪt/ **VI** 1 s'inscrire, se faire immatriculer 2 *(Brit Scol: formerly) être reçu à l'examen de "matriculation"*

matriculation /məˌtrɪkjʊˈleɪʃən/ **N** 1 *(Univ)* inscription *f*, immatriculation *f* 2 *(Brit Scol: formerly) examen donnant droit à l'inscription universitaire* **COMP** *(Univ) [card, fee]* d'inscription

matrimonial /ˌmætrɪˈməʊnɪəl/ **ADJ** *(frm) [bed, problems]* matrimonial ; *[law]* sur le mariage ◆ **the ~ home** le domicile conjugal

matrimony /ˈmætrɪmənɪ/ **N** *(NonC)* mariage *m* ; → **holy**

matrix /ˈmeɪtrɪks/ **N** (pl **matrixes** *or* **matrices**) matrice *f*

matron /ˈmeɪtrən/ **N** 1 *(† = woman)* matrone † *f* 2 *(Med) [of hospital]* surveillante *f* générale ; *(in school)* infirmière *f* ; *[of orphanage, old people's home etc]* directrice *f* ◆ **yes ~** oui madame *(or* mademoiselle) **COMP** **matron of honour** **N** dame *f* d'honneur

matronly /ˈmeɪtrənlɪ/ **ADJ** *[figure]* imposant ; *[manner, clothes]* de matrone ◆ **a ~ woman** une matrone

matt(e) /mæt/ **ADJ** mat

COMP **matt emulsion** **N** peinture *f* mate

matt finish **N** finition *f* mate

matt paint **N** peinture *f* mate

matted /ˈmætɪd/ **ADJ** *[hair, beard, fur]* emmêlé ; *[fibres, wool]* feutré ◆ **to become ~** *[hair, beard, fur]* s'emmêler ; *[fibres, wool]* feutrer ◆ **~ together** emmêlé ◆ **~ with blood/mud** mêlé de sang/boue, collé par le sang/la boue

matter /ˈmætəʳ/ **LANGUAGE IN USE 7.5**

N 1 *(NonC) (= physical substance)* matière *f*, substance *f* ; *(Philos, Phys)* matière *f* ; *(Typ)* matière *f*, copie *f* ; *(Med) (= pus)* pus *m* ◆ **vegetable/inanimate ~** matière *f* végétale/inanimée ◆ **colouring ~** colorant *m* ◆ **advertising ~** publicité *f*, réclames *fpl* ; → **grey, mind, reading**

2 *(NonC = content) [of book etc]* fond *m*, contenu *m* ◆ **~ and form** le fond et la forme ◆ **the ~ of his essay was good but the style poor** le contenu de sa dissertation était bon mais le style laissait à désirer

3 *(= affair, concern)* affaire *f*, question *f* ◆ **the ~ in hand** l'affaire en question ◆ **the ~ is closed** l'affaire est close *or* classée ◆ **she placed the ~ in the hands of her solicitor** elle a remis l'affaire entre les mains de son avocat ◆ **it's a small ~** c'est un détail ◆ **in this ~** à cet égard ◆ **in the ~ of ...** en matière de ..., en ce qui concerne ... ◆ **he doesn't see this as a resigning ~** il n'y a pas là, selon lui, de quoi démissionner ◆ **this is no joking ~** c'est très sérieux ; → **laughing** ◆ **it will be no easy ~** cela ne sera pas une mince affaire ◆ **for that ~** d'ailleurs ◆ **there's the ~ of my expenses** il y a la question de mes frais ◆ **there's the small ~ of that £200 I lent you** il y a le petit problème des 200 livres que je vous ai prêtées ◆ **in all ~s of education** pour tout ce qui touche à *or* concerne l'éducation ◆ **it is a ~ of great concern** c'est extrêmement inquiétant ◆ **it's a ~ of habit** c'est une question *or* une affaire d'habitude ◆ **it took a ~ of days** cela a été l'affaire de quelques jours ◆ **in a ~ of ten minutes** en l'espace de dix minutes ◆ **it's a ~ of $200 or so** il s'agit de quelque 200 dollars ◆ **as a ~ of course** automatiquement ◆ **as a ~ of fact** à vrai dire, en fait ; see also **matter-of-fact** ◆ **it's a ~ of life and death** c'est une question de vie ou de mort ◆ **that's a ~ of opinion!** c'est discutable ! ◆ **it is only a ~ of time** ce n'est qu'une question de temps ◆ **it is only a ~ of time before the bridge collapses** le pont va s'écrouler, ce n'est qu'une question de temps

4 *(= importance)* **no ~!** peu importe !, tant pis ! ◆ **what ~ (if ...)?** *(liter)* qu'importe (si ...) ? ◆ **(it is of) no ~ whether ...** *(liter)* peu importe si ... ◆ **it is (of) no great ~** c'est peu de chose, cela n'a pas grande importance ◆ **get one, no ~ how** débrouille-toi (comme tu peux) pour en trouver un ◆ **it must be done, no ~ how** cela doit être fait par n'importe quel moyen ◆ **ring me no ~ how late** téléphonez-moi même tard *or* à n'importe quelle heure ◆ **no ~ how you use it** peu importe comment vous l'utilisez ◆ **no ~ when he comes** quelle que soit l'heure à laquelle il arrive ◆ **no ~ how big it is** aussi grand qu'il soit ◆ **no ~ what he says** quoi qu'il dise ◆ **no ~ where/who** où/qui que ce soit

5 *(NonC) (= difficulty, problem)* ◆ **what's the ~?** qu'est-ce qu'il y a ?, qu'y a-t-il ? ◆ **what's the ~ with him?** qu'est-ce qu'il a ?, qu'est-ce qui lui prend ? ◆ **what's the ~ with your hand?** qu'est-ce que vous avez à la main ? ◆ **what's the ~ with my hat?** qu'est-ce qu'il a, mon chapeau ? * ◆ **what's the ~ with trying to help him?** quel inconvénient *or* quelle objection y a-t-il à ce qu'on l'aide *subj* ? ◆ **is anything the ~?** quelque chose ne va pas ? ◆ **there's something the ~ with my arm** j'ai quelque chose au bras ◆ **there's something the ~ with the engine** il y a quelque chose qui ne va pas dans le moteur ◆ **as if nothing was the ~** comme si de rien n'était ◆ **nothing's the ~** * il n'y a rien ◆ **there's nothing the ~ with me!** moi, je vais tout à fait bien ! ◆ **there's nothing the ~ with the car** la voiture marche très bien ◆ **there's nothing the ~ with that idea** il n'y a rien à redire à cette idée

VI importer *(to* à) ◆ **it doesn't ~** ça n'a pas d'importance, ça ne fait rien ◆ **it doesn't ~ whether ...** peu importe que ... + *subj*, cela ne fait rien si ..., peu importe si ... ◆ **it doesn't ~ who/where** *etc* peu importe qui/où *etc* ◆ **it ~s little** *(frm)* peu importe ◆ **what does it ~?** qu'est-ce que cela peut faire ? ◆ **what does it ~ to you (if ...)?** qu'est-ce que cela peut bien vous faire (si ...) ? ◆ **why should it ~ to me?** pourquoi est-ce que cela me ferait quelque chose ? ◆ **some things ~ more than others** il y a des choses qui importent plus que d'autres ◆ **nothing else ~s** le reste n'a aucune importance

Matterhorn /ˈmætəhɔːn/ N ◆ **the ~** le Cervin

matter-of-fact /ˌmætərəvˈfækt/ ADJ *[tone, voice]* neutre ; *[style]* prosaïque ; *[attitude, person]* terre à terre *or* terre-à-terre ; *[assessment, account]* neutre, qui se limite aux faits

matter-of-factly /ˌmætərəvˈfæktlɪ/ ADV *[say, explain]* d'un ton neutre

Matthew /ˈmæθjuː/ N Matthieu *m*

matting /ˈmætɪŋ/ N *(NonC)* sparterie *f*, pièces *fpl* de natte ; → **rush**[1]

mattins /ˈmætɪnz/ N ⇒ **matins**

mattock /ˈmætək/ N pioche *f*

mattress /ˈmætrɪs/ N matelas *m* COMP **mattress cover** N alèse *f*

maturation /ˌmætjʊəˈreɪʃən/ N maturation *f*

mature /məˈtjʊəʳ/ ADJ 1 *[person]* mûr ; *(euph = old)* d'âge mûr ◆ **she was ~ enough to take on these responsibilities** elle était assez mûre pour assumer ces responsabilités ◆ **he behaves like a ~ adult** il se comporte en adulte ◆ **he's got much more ~ since then** il a beaucoup mûri depuis

2 *[age, reflection, plan]* mûr ; *[tree, democracy]* adulte ; *[market]* arrivé à maturité, mûr ; *[wine]* à maturité ; *[cheese]* affiné ; *[style, writing]* abouti ; *[cell]* mature

VT affiner

VI *[person]* *(psychologically)* mûrir ; *[child, animal]* se développer ; *[cheese]* s'affiner ; *[wine]* *(= reach maturity)* arriver à maturité ; *(Fin)* *[policy, pension plan]* venir à échéance

COMP **mature student** N *(Univ)* *(gen)* étudiant(e) *m(f)* plus âgé(e) que la moyenne ; *(Brit Admin)* étudiant(e) *m(f)* de plus de 26 ans *(ou de 21 ans dans certains cas)*

⚠ The word **mature** exists in French, but 'mûr' is much commoner in everyday contexts.

maturely /məˈtjʊəlɪ/ ADV *[think, behave]* en adulte

maturity /məˈtjʊərɪtɪ/ N maturité *f* ◆ **date of ~** *(Fin)* échéance *f*

matzo /ˈmɒtsə/ N pain *m* azyme

COMP **matzo balls** NPL boulettes *fpl* de pain azyme

matzo cracker N cracker *m* de pain azyme

matzo meal N farine *f* de pain azyme

maudlin /ˈmɔːdlɪn/ ADJ larmoyant ◆ **to get ~ about sth** devenir excessivement sentimental à propos de qch

maul /mɔːl/ VT 1 *(= attack)* *[tiger etc]* mutiler, lacérer ; *(fatally)* déchiqueter 2 *(= manhandle)* malmener 3 *(* = paw at: sexually)* tripoter ◆ **stop ~ing me!** arrête de me tripoter ! N *(Rugby)* maul *m*

mauling /ˈmɔːlɪŋ/ N ◆ **to get a ~** *[player, team]* être battu à plate(s) couture(s) ; *[author, book]* être éreinté par la critique

maulstick /ˈmɔːlstɪk/ N appuie-main *m*

maunder /ˈmɔːndəʳ/ VI *(= talk)* divaguer ; *(= move)* errer ; *(= act)* agir de façon incohérente

Maundy money /ˈmɔːndɪˌmʌnɪ/ N *(Brit)* aumône *f* royale du jeudi saint

Maundy Thursday /ˌmɔːndɪˈθɜːzdɪ/ N le jeudi saint

Mauritania /ˌmɒrɪˈteɪnɪə/ N Mauritanie *f*

Mauritanian /ˌmɒrɪˈteɪnɪən/ ADJ mauritanien N Mauritanien(ne) *m(f)*

Mauritian /məˈrɪʃən/ ADJ *(gen)* mauricien ; *[ambassador, embassy]* de l'île Maurice N Mauricien(ne) *m(f)*

Mauritius /məˈrɪʃəs/ N (l'île *f*) Maurice *f* ◆ **in ~** à (l'île) Maurice

mausoleum /ˌmɔːsəˈlɪəm/ N (pl **mausoleums** or **mausolea** /ˌmɔːsəˈlɪə/) mausolée *m*

mauve /məʊv/ ADJ, N mauve *m*

maverick /ˈmævərɪk/ N 1 *(= unmarked calf)* veau *m* non marqué 2 *(fig = person)* franc-tireur *m (fig)*, indépendant(e) *m(f)* ADJ dissident, non-conformiste

maw /mɔː/ N *(= mouth: lit, fig)* gueule *f*

mawkish /ˈmɔːkɪʃ/ ADJ *(= sentimental)* mièvre

mawkishness /ˈmɔːkɪʃnɪs/ N *[of film, poem]* mièvrerie *f*

max /mæks/ (abbrev of **maximum**) ADV ◆ **a couple of weeks, ~** * quinze jours, max * N max * *m* ◆ **to do sth to the ~** * faire qch à fond

maxi ^ /ˈmæksɪ/ N *(= coat/skirt)* (manteau *m*/jupe *f*) maxi *m*

COMP **maxi single** N disque *m* double durée

maxilla /mækˈsɪlə/ N (pl **maxillae** /mækˈsɪliː/) *(Anat)* maxillaire *m*

maxillary /mækˈsɪlərɪ/ ADJ *(Anat)* maxillaire

maxim /ˈmæksɪm/ N maxime *f*

maxima /ˈmæksɪmə/ NPL of **maximum**

maximal /ˈmæksɪməl/ ADJ maximal

maximization /ˌmæksɪmaɪˈzeɪʃən/ N maximalisation *f*, maximisation *f* ◆ **~ of profits** maximalisation *or* maximisation *f* des bénéfices

maximize /ˈmæksɪmaɪz/ VT *(= increase)* porter *or* développer au maximum ; *[+ profits]* maximiser ◆ **to ~ the advantages of sth** exploiter au maximum les avantages de qch

maximum /ˈmæksɪməm/ N (pl **maximums** or **maxima**) maximum *m* ◆ **a ~ of $8** un maximum de 8 dollars, 8 livres au maximum ◆ **at the ~** au maximum ◆ **to the ~** au maximum, à fond ADJ maximum ◆ **~ prices** prix *mpl* maximums *or* maxima ◆ **~ security jail** *or* **prison** prison *f* de haute sécurité ; see also **security** ◆ **~ speed** *(= highest permitted)* vitesse *f* limite, vitesse *f* maximale autorisée ; *(= highest possible)* plafond *m* ◆ **~ load** *(on truck)* charge *f* limite ◆ **~ temperatures** températures *fpl* maximales ADV (au) maximum ◆ **twice a week ~** deux fois par semaine (au) maximum

May /meɪ/ N mai *m* ◆ **the merry month of ~** *(liter)* le joli mois de mai ; see also **September**

COMP **May beetle, May bug** N hanneton *m*

May Day N le Premier Mai *(fête du Travail)*

May queen N reine *f* de mai

may[1] /meɪ/ LANGUAGE IN USE 9.1 MODAL AUX VB 1 *(= might)*

When **may** expresses present, past or future possibility, it is often translated by **peut-être**, with the appropriate tense of the French verb.

◆ **he ~ arrive late** il arrivera peut-être en retard, il pourrait arriver en retard ◆ **you ~ be making a big mistake** tu es peut-être en train de faire une grosse erreur ◆ **I ~ have left it behind** il se peut que je l'aie oublié, je l'ai peut-être oublié ◆ **a vegetarian diet ~ not provide enough iron** il se peut qu'un régime végétarien ne soit pas assez riche en fer ◆ **it ~ rain later** il se peut qu'il pleuve plus tard ◆ **be that as it ~** *(frm)* quoi qu'il en soit ◆ **that's as ~ be but** ... peut-être bien *or* c'est bien possible mais ...

◆ **may as well** ◆ **one ~ as well say £5 million** autant dire 5 millions de livres ◆ **I ~ as well tell you all about it** je ferais aussi bien de tout vous dire ◆ **you ~ as well leave now** vous feriez aussi bien de partir tout de suite ◆ **can I tell her? – you ~ as well** est-ce que je peux le lui dire ? – oui, pourquoi pas ?

◆ **may well** ◆ **this ~ well be his last chance** c'est peut-être bien sa dernière chance ◆ **that ~ well be so** c'est bien possible ◆ **one ~ well ask if this is a waste of money** on est en droit de se demander si c'est une dépense inutile

2 *(= can)* pouvoir ◆ **the sleeping bag ~ be used as a bedcover** le sac de couchage peut servir de couvre-lit ◆ **you ~ go now** *(permission, also polite order)* vous pouvez partir ; *(to subordinate)* vous pouvez disposer ◆ **if I ~ say so** si je puis me permettre ◆ **as soon as ~ be** aussitôt que possible

◆ **may I ?** vous permettez ?

◆ **may I ... ?** ◆ **~ I interrupt for a moment?** je peux vous interrompre une seconde ? ◆ **~ I help you?** puis-je *or* est-ce que je peux vous aider ? ; *(in shop)* vous désirez (quelque chose) ? ◆ **~ I sit here?** vous permettez que je m'assoie ici ? ◆ **~ I have a word with you? – of course you ~** puis-je vous parler un instant ? – mais oui *or* bien sûr ◆ **~ I call? – no, you ~ not** puis-je passer vous voir ? – non

3 *(in prayers, wishes)* ◆ **God bless you!** (que) Dieu vous bénisse ! ◆ **~ he rest in peace** qu'il repose *subj* en paix ◆ **much good ~ it do you!** *(iro)* grand bien vous fasse ! ◆ **O Lord, grant that we ~ always obey** Seigneur, accordenous de toujours obéir ◆ **in order that they ~ know** afin qu'ils sachent

may[2] /meɪ/ N *(= hawthorn)* aubépine *f*

COMP **may blossom** N fleurs *fpl* d'aubépine

may tree N *(Brit)* aubépine *f*

Maya /ˈmaɪjə/ NPL ◆ **the ~** les Mayas *mpl*

Mayan /ˈmaɪən/ *(in South America)* ADJ maya N 1 Maya *mf* 2 *(= language)* maya *m*

maybe /ˈmeɪbiː/ LANGUAGE IN USE 15.3 ADV peut-être ◆ **~ he'll be there** peut-être qu'il sera là, il sera peut-être là ◆ **~, ~ not** peut-être que oui, peut-être que non ◆ **that's as ~** peut-être bien

mayday /ˈmeɪdeɪ/ N SOS *m*

Mayfair /ˈmeɪfɛəʳ/ N *(Brit)* Mayfair *(quartier chic de Londres)*

mayfly /ˈmeɪflaɪ/ N éphémère *mf*

mayhem /ˈmeɪhem/ N 1 *(Jur ††, also US)* mutilation *f* du corps humain 2 *(= havoc)* grabuge * *m* ; *(= destruction)* destruction *f*

mayn't /meɪnt/ ⇒ **may not** ; → **may**[1]

mayo * /ˈmeɪəʊ/ N *(US)* abbrev of **mayonnaise**

mayonnaise /ˌmeɪəˈneɪz/ N mayonnaise *f*

mayor /mɛəʳ/ N maire *m*; *(in London)* maire *m* exécutif *(élu au suffrage universel)* ◆ **Mr/Madam Mayor** Monsieur/Madame le maire ; → **lord**

mayoral /ˈmɛərəl/ ADJ de (or du) maire ◆ **the ~ residence/limousine** *etc* la résidence/limousine *etc* du maire

mayoralty /ˈmɛərəltɪ/ N mandat *m* de maire

mayoress /ˈmɛəres/ N *(esp Brit)* 1 *(= female mayor)* maire *m* 2 *(= wife of mayor)* femme *f* du maire ; → **lady**

maypole /ˈmeɪpəʊl/ N mât *m* enrubanné

maze /meɪz/ N labyrinthe *m*, dédale *m* ◆ **a ~ of little streets** un labyrinthe *or* un dédale de ruelles

mazuma ‡ /məˈzuːmə/ N *(US = money)* fric ‡ *m*, pognon ‡ *m*

mazurka /məˈzɜːkə/ N mazurka *f*

MB /emˈbiː/ N 1 *(Comput)* (abbrev of **megabyte**) Mo 2 *(Brit Univ)* (abbrev of **Bachelor of Medicine**) *diplôme de médecine*

MBA /ˈembiːˈeɪ/ N *(Univ)* (abbrev of **Master of Business Administration**) *mastère de gestion*

MBBS, MBChB *(Univ)* (abbrev of **Bachelor of Medicine and Surgery**) *diplôme de chirurgie*

MBE /ˌembiːˈiː/ N *(Brit)* (abbrev of **Member of the Order of the British Empire**) *titre honorifique* ; → HONOURS LIST

MBO /ˌembiːˈəʊ/ N (abbrev of **management buyout**) RES *m*

MC /emˈsiː/ N [1] (abbrev of **Master of Ceremonies**) → **master** [2] (US) (abbrev of **Member of Congress**) → **member** [3] (Brit Mil) (abbrev of **Military Cross**) ≈ Croix *f* de la valeur militaire

MCAT /ˌemsiːeiˈtiː/ N (US Univ) (abbrev of **Medical College Admissions Test**) → **medical**

McCarthyism /məˈkɑːθɪˌɪzəm/ N (US Pol: *gen pej*) maccarthysme *m*

MCP* /ˌemsiːˈpiː/ N (abbrev of **male chauvinist pig**) → **chauvinist**

MD /emˈdiː/ N [1] (Univ) (abbrev of **Doctor of Medicine**) → **medicine** [2] (US) **the ~** * le médecin [3] (Brit) (abbrev of **Managing Director**) PDG *m* [4] abbrev of **Maryland** [5] (Mus) (abbrev of **minidisc**) MD *m* COMP **MD-player** N lecteur *m* (de) MD

Md. abbrev of **Maryland**

MDF /ˌemdiːˈef/ N (abbrev of **medium-density fibreboard**) médium *m*, MDF *m*

MDT /ˌemdiːˈtiː/ (US) (abbrev of **Mountain Daylight Time**) → **mountain**

ME /ˌemˈiː/ N [1] (Med) (abbrev of **myalgic encephalomyelitis**) SFC *m*, syndrome *m* de fatigue chronique, encéphalomyélite *f* myalgique [2] abbrev of **Maine** [3] (US) (abbrev of **medical examiner**) médecin *m* légiste

me¹ /miː/ PERS PRON [1] (*direct, unstressed*) me ; (*before vowel*) m' ; (*stressed*) moi ◆ **he can see ~** il me voit ◆ **he saw ~** il m'a vu ◆ **you don't like jazz? me, I love it** * tu n'aimes pas le jazz ? moi, j'adore [2] (*indirect*) me, moi ; (*before vowel*) m' ◆ **he gave ~ the book** il me donna *or* m'a donné le livre ◆ **give it to ~** donnez-le-moi ◆ **he was speaking to ~** il me parlait [3] (*after prep etc*) moi ◆ **without ~** sans moi ◆ **I'll take it with ~** je l'emporterai avec moi ◆ **it's ~** c'est moi ◆ **it's ~ he's speaking to** c'est à moi qu'il parle ◆ **you're smaller than ~** tu es plus petit que moi ◆ **if you were ~** à ma place ◆ **poor (little) ~!*** pauvre de moi ! ◆ **dear ~!*** mon Dieu !, oh là là !*

me² /miː/ N (Mus) mi *m*

Me. abbrev of **Maine**

mead¹ /miːd/ N (= *drink*) hydromel *m*

mead² /miːd/ N (*liter* = *meadow*) pré *m*, prairie *f*

meadow /ˈmedəʊ/ N pré *m*, prairie *f* ; → **water**

meadowlark /ˈmedəʊlɑːk/ N sturnelle *f*

meadowsweet /ˈmedəʊswiːt/ N reine *f* des prés

meagre, meager (US) /ˈmiːgəʳ/ ADJ maigre *before n* ◆ **he eked out a ~ existence (as a labourer)** il gagnait péniblement sa vie (en tant qu'ouvrier) ◆ **his salary is a ~ £350 a month** il gagne un salaire de misère : 350 livres par mois

meal¹ /miːl/ N repas *m* ◆ **to have a ~** prendre un repas, manger ◆ **to have a good ~** bien manger ◆ **to have one ~ a day** manger une fois par jour ◆ **we had a ~ at the Sea Crest Hotel** nous avons déjeuné (*or* dîné) au Sea Crest Hotel ◆ **midday ~** déjeuner *m* ◆ **evening ~** dîner *m* ◆ **that was a lovely ~!** nous avons très bien déjeuné (*or* dîné) ! ◆ **he made a ~ of bread and cheese** il a déjeuné (*or* dîné) de pain et de fromage ◆ **to make a ~ of sth** * (*fig*) faire tout un plat de qch * ; → **square**

COMP **meals on wheels** NPL *repas livrés à domicile aux personnes âgées ou handicapées*

meal ticket N (*lit*) ticket-repas *m*, coupon-repas *m* ; (* *fig*) (= *job*) gagne-pain *m inv* ◆ **(don't forget) she's your ~ ticket** (= *person*) (n'oublie pas que) sans elle tu crèverais de faim

meal² /miːl/ N (NonC = *flour etc*) farine *f* (*d'avoine, de seigle, de maïs etc*) ; → **oatmeal, wheatmeal**

mealie meal /ˈmiːlimiːl/ N (*in South Africa*) farine *f* de maïs

mealies /ˈmiːlɪz/ NPL maïs *m*

mealtime /ˈmiːltaɪm/ N heure *f* du repas ◆ **at ~s** aux heures des repas

mealworm /ˈmiːlwɜːm/ N ver *m* de farine

mealy /ˈmiːlɪ/ ADJ [*substance, mixture, texture, potato*] farineux ; [*complexion*] blême COMP **mealy-mouthed** ADJ ◆ **to be ~-mouthed** ne pas s'exprimer franchement, tourner autour du pot *

mean¹ /miːn/ LANGUAGE IN USE 26.3 (pret, ptp **meant**) VT [1] (= *signify*) vouloir dire, signifier ; (= *imply*) vouloir dire ◆ **what does "media" ~?, what is meant by "media"?** que veut dire *or* que signifie "media" ? ◆ **"homely" ~s something different in America** "homely" a un sens différent en Amérique ◆ **what do you ~ (by that)?** que voulez-vous dire (par là) ?, qu'entendez-vous par là ? ◆ **is he honest? – how** *or* **what do you ~, honest?** est-il honnête ? – que voulez-vous dire *or* qu'entendez-vous par "honnête" ? ◆ **see what I ~?** * tu vois ce que je veux dire ? ◆ **this is John, I ~ Jim** voici John, pardon (je veux dire) Jim ◆ **the name ~s nothing to me** ce nom ne me dit rien ◆ **the play didn't ~ a thing to her** la pièce n'avait aucun sens pour elle ◆ **what does this ~?** qu'est-ce que cela signifie *or* veut dire ? ◆ **it ~s he won't be coming** cela veut dire qu'il ne viendra pas ◆ **this ~s war** c'est la guerre à coup sûr ◆ **it ~s trouble** cela nous annonce des ennuis ◆ **it will ~ a lot of expense** cela entraînera beaucoup de dépenses ◆ **catching the train ~s getting up early** pour avoir ce train il faut se lever tôt ◆ **a pound ~s a lot to him** une livre représente une grosse somme pour lui ◆ **holidays don't ~ much to me** les vacances comptent peu pour moi ◆ **I can't tell you what your gift has meant to me!** je ne saurais vous dire à quel point votre cadeau m'a touché ! ◆ **don't I ~ anything to you at all?** je ne suis donc rien pour toi ? ◆ **you ~ everything to me, darling** tu es tout pour moi, mon amour ◆ **what it ~s to be free!** quelle belle chose que la liberté ! ◆ **money doesn't ~ happiness** l'argent ne fait pas le bonheur ◆ **you don't really ~ that?** (= *fully intend*) vous n'êtes pas sérieux ?, vous plaisantez ? ◆ **I really ~ it** je ne plaisante pas, je suis sérieux ◆ **he said it as if he meant it** il l'a dit d'un air sérieux *or* sans avoir l'air de plaisanter ◆ **I always ~ what I say** quand je dis quelque chose c'est que je le pense ◆ **I ~, it's not difficult** * (*as conversational filler*) après tout, ce n'est pas difficile ; → **know, world**

[2] (= *intend, purpose*) avoir l'intention (*to do sth* de faire qch), compter (*to do sth* faire qch) ; (= *intend, destine*) [+ *gift etc*] destiner (*for* à) ; [+ *remark*] adresser (*for* à) ◆ **I meant to come yesterday** j'avais l'intention de *or* je comptais venir hier ◆ **what does he ~ to do now?** qu'a-t-il l'intention de faire maintenant ?, que compte-t-il faire maintenant ? ◆ **I didn't ~ to break it** je n'ai pas fait exprès de le casser, je ne l'ai pas cassé exprès ◆ **I didn't ~ to!** je ne l'ai pas fait exprès ! ◆ **I touched it without ~ing to** je l'ai touché sans le vouloir ◆ **I ~ to succeed** j'ai bien l'intention de réussir ◆ **despite what he says I ~ to go** je partirai quoi qu'il dise ◆ **I ~ you to leave, I ~ for you to leave** (US) je veux que vous partiez *subj* ◆ **I'm sure he didn't ~ it** je suis sûr que ce n'était pas intentionnel *or* délibéré ◆ **he didn't ~ anything by it** il l'a fait (*or* dit) sans penser à mal ◆ **I meant it as a joke** j'ai dit (*or* fait) cela par plaisanterie *or* pour rire ◆ **we were meant to arrive at six** nous étions censés arriver *or* nous devions arriver à six heures ◆ **she ~s well** ce qu'elle fait (*or* dit *etc*) part d'un bon sentiment, elle est pleine de bonnes intentions ◆ **he looks as if he ~s trouble** * il a une mine qui n'annonce rien qui vaille *or* de bon ◆ **do you ~ me?** (= *are you speaking to me*) c'est à moi que vous parlez ? ; (= *are you speaking about me*) c'est de moi que vous parlez ? ◆ **he meant you when he said ...** c'est vous qu'il visait *or* c'est à vous qu'il faisait allusion lorsqu'il disait ... ◆ **I meant the book for Douglas** je destinais le livre à Douglas ◆ **that book is meant for children** ce livre est destiné aux enfants *or* s'adresse aux enfants ◆ **perhaps you're not meant to be a doctor** peut-être n'êtes-vous pas fait pour être médecin ◆ **it was meant to be** le destin en avait décidé ainsi ◆ **the poem is not ~t to be read silently** le poème n'est pas fait pour *or* n'est pas censé être lu silencieusement ◆ **this portrait is meant to be Anne** ce portrait est censé être celui d'Anne *or* représenter Anne ◆ **it's ~t to be like that** c'est fait exprès ; → **business, harm, offence**

[3] (*modal usage in passive*) **it's meant to be good** (= *considered to be*) on dit que c'est bien ; (= *supposed to be*) c'est censé être bien

mean² /miːn/ N (= *middle term*) milieu *m*, moyen terme *m* ; (Math) moyenne *f* ◆ **the golden** *or* **happy ~** le juste milieu ; → **geometric(al), means** ADJ (= *average*) [*distance, temperature, price*] moyen ◆ **~ life** (Phys) vie *f* moyenne

mean³ /miːn/ ADJ [1] (*Brit* = *stingy*) avare, mesquin ◆ **~ with one's time/money** avare de son temps/argent ◆ **don't be so ~!** ne sois pas si radin !*

[2] (= *unpleasant, unkind*) [*person, behaviour*] mesquin, méchant ◆ **a ~ trick** un sale tour, une crasse * ◆ **you ~ thing!*** chameau !* ; (*to a child*) méchant ! ◆ **you were ~ to me** tu n'as vraiment pas été chic * *or* sympa * avec moi ◆ **that was ~ of them** c'était bien mesquin de leur part, ce n'était pas chic * de leur part ◆ **to feel ~ about sth** avoir un peu honte de qch, ne pas être très fier de qch

[3] (*US* * = *vicious*) [*horse, dog etc*] méchant, vicieux

[4] (= *inferior, poor*) [*appearance, existence*] misérable, minable ◆ **the ~est citizen** le dernier des citoyens ◆ **the ~est intelligence** l'esprit le plus borné ◆ **he is no ~ scholar** c'est un grand savant ◆ **he's no ~ singer** c'est un chanteur de talent ◆ **it was no ~ feat** cela a été un véritable exploit, ce n'a pas été un mince exploit ◆ **to have no ~ opinion of o.s.** avoir une (très) haute opinion de soi-même

[5] (* = *excellent*) super * ◆ **she plays a ~ game of tennis** elle joue super * bien au tennis

COMP **mean-spirited** ADJ mesquin

mean-spiritedness N mesquinerie *f*

meander /mɪˈændəʳ/ VI [1] [*river*] faire des méandres, serpenter [2] [*person*] (= *aimlessly*) errer, vagabonder ; (= *leisurely*) flâner N méandre *m*

meandering /mɪˈændərɪŋ/ ADJ [1] (= *winding*) [*river, stream, road, path, route*] sinueux [2] (*pej* = *rambling*) [*speech, account, article*] plein de méandres

meanie * /ˈmiːnɪ/ N [1] (*Brit* = *stingy person*) radin(e) * *m(f)*, pingre *m* [2] (*US* = *unpleasant person*) sale type *m*, mégère *f*

meaning /ˈmiːnɪŋ/ N [*of word*] sens *m*, signification *f* ; [*of phrase, action*] signification *f* ; (Ling) signification *f* ◆ **with a double ~** à double sens ◆ **literal ~** sens *m* propre *or* littéral ◆ **what is the ~ of this word?** quel est le sens de ce mot ?, que signifie ce mot ? ◆ **he doesn't know the ~ of the word "fear"** il ne sait pas ce que le mot "peur" veut dire, il ignore le sens du mot "peur" ◆ **she doesn't know the ~ of love/kindness** elle ne sait pas ce qu'est l'amour/la gentillesse ◆ **what is the ~ of this?** (*in anger, disapproval etc*) qu'est-ce que cela signifie ? ◆ **within the ~ of this Act** (Jur) au sens de la présente loi ◆ **... if you get my ~** * ... vous voyez ce que je veux dire ? ◆ **look/gesture full of ~** regard *m*/geste *m* éloquent ◆ **his speech had ~ for many people** beaucoup de gens se sentaient concernés par son discours ◆ **"re-**

ally?" he said with ~ son "vraiment ?" était éloquent

ADJ *[look etc]* éloquent, expressif ; → **well²**

meaningful /ˈmiːnɪŋfʊl/ ADJ 1 *(= worthwhile) [relationship, discussion, dialogue]* sérieux ; *[experience]* riche ; *[role]* important ; *[contribution]* important, significatif ◆ **a** ~ **life** une vie qui a *(ou* avait) un sens 2 *(= comprehensible, not spurious) [response, results, statement, gesture]* significatif ; *[explanation]* sensé 3 *(= eloquent) [look, glance, smile]* éloquent 4 *(Ling) [phrase]* sémantique

meaningfully /ˈmiːnɪŋfəlɪ/ ADV 1 *(= eloquently, pointedly) [say]* d'un ton qui en dit *(ou* disait) long ◆ **he looked/smiled at her** ~ il lui jeta un regard éloquent/fit un sourire qui en disait long 2 *(= usefully) [participate, spend time]* utilement 3 *(= comprehensibly) [explain]* clairement

meaningless /ˈmiːnɪŋlɪs/ ADJ 1 *(= without meaning) [words, song, action, gesture]* dénué de sens ; *[distinction]* insignifiant ◆ **to be** ~ **(to sb)** ne pas avoir de sens (pour qn), ne rien vouloir dire (pour qn) 2 *(= futile) [life, existence, victory]* futile, vain ; *[waste, suffering]* insensé

meanly /ˈmiːnlɪ/ ADV 1 *(= spitefully)* méchamment 2 *(= stingily)* mesquinement

meanness /ˈmiːnnɪs/ N 1 *(= stinginess) [of person]* avarice *f* 2 *(= unkindness) [of person]* méchanceté *f* ◆ ~ **of spirit** mesquinerie *f* 3 *(US = viciousness) [of animal]* comportement *m* sauvage 4 *(= wretchedness) [of place]* misère *f*

means /miːnz/ N 1 *(= method, way)* moyen(s) *m(pl)* ◆ **to find the** ~ **to do sth** *or* **of doing sth** trouver le(s) moyen(s) de faire qch ◆ **to find (a)** ~ **of doing sth** trouver moyen de faire qch ◆ **the only** ~ **of contacting him is ...** le seul moyen de le joindre, c'est ... ◆ **there's no** ~ **of getting in** il n'y a pas moyen d'entrer ◆ **the** ~ **to an end** le moyen d'arriver à ses fins ◆ **by illegal/political/military** ~ par des moyens illégaux/politiques/militaires ◆ **the** ~ **of salvation** *(Rel)* les voies *fpl* du salut ◆ **by some** ~ **or (an)other** d'une façon ou d'une autre ◆ **by this** ~ de cette façon

◆ **by all means** ◆ **come in by all** ~**!** je vous en prie, entrez ! ◆ **by all** ~**!** *(= of course)* mais certainement !, bien sûr ! ◆ **read them if you like, by all** ~ vous pouvez les lire si vous voulez ◆ **by all** ~ **consult your physician about this** vous pouvez en parler à votre médecin si vous voulez ◆ **by all manner of** ~ par tous les moyens

◆ **by any means** ◆ **the military collapse is not imminent by any** ~ la débâcle militaire est loin d'être imminente ◆ **I'm not a country person by any (manner of)** ~ je ne suis vraiment pas attiré par la (vie à la) campagne ◆ **I don't think we're leading the field by any (manner of)** ~ je suis loin de penser que nous sommes les leaders dans ce domaine

◆ **by no means** nullement, pas le moins du monde ◆ **she is by no** ~ **stupid** elle est loin d'être stupide ◆ **they were by no** ~ **the poorest residents of their neighbourhood** ils étaient loin d'être les plus pauvres de leur quartier

◆ **by means of ...** *(gen)* au moyen de ... ◆ **by** ~ **of a penknife/binoculars** au moyen d'un *or* à l'aide d'un canif/au moyen de *or* à l'aide de jumelles ◆ **by** ~ **of the telephone/a ballot** par le moyen du téléphone/d'un scrutin ◆ **he taught English by** ~ **of play** il enseignait l'anglais par le jeu *or* par le biais du jeu ◆ **by** ~ **of hard work** à force de travail

2 *(= wealth)* moyens *mpl*, ressources *fpl* ◆ **he is a man of** ~ il a une belle fortune *or* de gros moyens* ◆ **to live within/beyond one's** ~ vivre selon ses moyens/au-dessus de ses moyens ◆ **to have private** ~ avoir une fortune personnelle ◆ **slender** ~ ressources *fpl* très modestes

COMP **means test** N *(Admin)* examen *m* des ressources *(d'une personne qui demande une aide pécuniaire)*

means-test VT *(Admin)* ◆ **to ~-test sb** examiner les ressources de qn *(avant d'accorder certaines prestations sociales)* ◆ **the grant is not ~-tested** cette allocation ne dépend pas des ressources familiales (ou personnelles)

meant /ment/ VB pt, ptp of **mean¹**

meantime /ˈmiːntaɪm/, **meanwhile** /ˈmiːnwaɪl/ ADV ◆ **(in the)** ~ en attendant, pendant ce temps, dans l'intervalle ◆ **for the** ~ en attendant

meany* /ˈmiːnɪ/ N ⇒ **meanie**

measles /ˈmiːzlz/ N rougeole *f* ; → **German**

measly* /ˈmiːzlɪ/ ADJ misérable ◆ **a** ~ **£5!** 5 misérables livres !

measurable /ˈmeʒərəbl/ ADJ mesurable

measure /ˈmeʒəʳ/ N 1 *(= system, unit)* mesure *f* ; *(fig)* mesure *f* ; *[of alcohol]* dose *f* ◆ **to give good** *or* **full** ~ faire bonne mesure *or* bon poids ◆ **to give short** ~ voler *or* rogner sur la quantité ◆ **for good** ~ *(fig)* pour faire bonne mesure ◆ **suit made to** ~ complet *m* fait sur mesure ◆ **liquid** ~ mesure *f* de capacité pour les liquides ◆ **a pint** ~ ≈ une mesure d'un demi-litre ◆ **happiness beyond** ~ bonheur *m* sans bornes ◆ **in some** ~ dans une certaine mesure, jusqu'à un certain point ◆ **in great** *or* **large** ~ dans une large mesure, en grande partie ◆ **the audience laughed and cried in equal** ~ le public a ri autant qu'il a pleuré ◆ **to take the** ~ **of sth** *(fig)* évaluer qch ◆ **I've got his** ~ † je sais ce qu'il vaut ◆ **it had a** ~ **of success** cela a eu un certain succès

2 *(sth for measuring) (= ruler)* règle *f* ; *(folding)* mètre *m* pliant ; *(= tape) (steel)* mètre *m* à ruban ; *(fabric)* centimètre *m* ; *(= jug, glass)* verre *m* gradué *or* mesureur ; *(= post)* toise *f* ◆ **to be the** ~ **of sth** *(fig)* donner la mesure de qch ◆ **this exam is just a** ~ **of how you're getting on** *(fig)* cet examen sert simplement à évaluer votre progression ; → **tape**

3 *(= step)* mesure *f*, démarche *f* ; *(Parl) (= bill)* projet *m* de loi ; *(= act)* loi *f* ◆ **strong/drastic ~s** mesures *fpl* énergiques/draconiennes ◆ **precautionary/preventive ~s** mesures *fpl* de précaution/de prévention ◆ **temporary** *or* **interim ~s** mesures *fpl* temporaires *or* provisoires ◆ **to take ~s against** prendre des mesures contre ◆ **~s aimed at building confidence between states** des mesures *fpl* visant à créer un climat de confiance entre États

4 *(Mus, Poetry etc)* mesure *f*

VT *(lit) [+ child, length, time]* mesurer ; *(fig) [+ strength, courage]* mesurer ; *[+ success, performance]* évaluer, juger ◆ **to** ~ **the height of sth** mesurer *or* prendre la hauteur de qch ◆ **to be ~d for a dress** faire prendre ses mesures pour une robe ◆ **what does it** ~**?** quelles sont ses dimensions ? ◆ **the room ~s 4 metres across** la pièce fait *or* mesure 4 mètres de large ◆ **the carpet ~s 3 metres by 2** le tapis fait *or* mesure 3 mètres sur 2 ◆ **to be ~d against** *(fig)* être comparé avec *or* à ◆ **to** ~ **one's strength against sb** se mesurer à qn ; see also **length**

► **measure off** VT SEP *[+ lengths of fabric etc]* mesurer

► **measure out** VT SEP 1 *[+ ingredients, piece of ground]* mesurer 2 *(= issue)* distribuer

► **measure up** VT SEP *[+ wood]* mesurer ; *[+ sb's intentions]* jauger ; *[+ person]* évaluer, jauger VI *(fig) [person]* être à la hauteur

► **measure up to** VT FUS *[+ task]* être au niveau de, être à la hauteur de ; *[+ person]* être l'égal de

measured /ˈmeʒəd/ ADJ 1 *[amount, dose, distance, time]* mesuré ◆ **over a** ~ **kilometre** sur un kilomètre exactement 2 *(= even, calm) [look, gaze]* posé ; *[pace, words, language, statement]* modéré, mesuré ◆ **to make a** ~ **response to sth** réagir de façon modérée à qch ◆ **with** ~ **steps** à pas comptés *or* mesurés ◆ **to speak in** ~ **tones** parler d'un ton mesuré

measureless /ˈmeʒəlɪs/ ADJ *(liter)* incommensurable

measurement /ˈmeʒəmənt/ N 1 *(= dimension: gen pl)* ◆ **~s** mesures *fpl*, dimensions *fpl* ; *[of piece of furniture etc]* encombrement *m* au sol ◆ **to take the ~s of a room** prendre les mesures d'une pièce ◆ **what are your ~s?** quelles sont vos mesures ? 2 *(NonC) (= activity)* mesurage *m* 3 *(Comm) [of freight]* cubage *m* ◆ **to pay by** ~ **for freight** payer la cargaison au cubage

measuring /ˈmeʒərɪŋ/ N *(NonC)* mesurage *m*, mesure *f*

COMP **measuring chain** N chaîne *f* d'arpenteur

measuring device N appareil *m* de mesure *or* de contrôle

measuring glass N verre *m* gradué *or* mesureur

measuring jug N pot *m* gradué

measuring rod N règle *f*, mètre *m*

measuring spoon N cuiller *f* à mesurer

measuring tape N *(fabric)* centimètre *m* ; *(steel)* mètre *m* (à) ruban

meat /miːt/ N 1 *(fresh)* viande *f* ; *(†† = food)* nourriture *f*, aliment *m* ◆ **cold** ~ viande *f* froide ◆ **cold** ~ **platter** assiette *f* anglaise ◆ ~ **and two veg** * *de la viande avec des pommes de terre et un légume* ◆ **remove the** ~ **from the bone** ôter la chair de l'os ◆ ~ **and drink** *(lit)* de quoi manger et boire ◆ **this is** ~ **and drink to them** *(fig)* ils se régalent *(fig)* ◆ **that's my** ~**!*** *(US)* ça me botte vachement !* ◆ **one man's** ~ **is another man's poison** *(Prov)* le malheur des uns fait le bonheur des autres *(Prov)*

2 *(fig)* substance *f* ◆ **there's not much** ~ **in his book** son livre n'a pas beaucoup de substance

COMP **meat axe** N *(US)* ⇒ **meat axe**

meat axe N couperet *m*

meat cleaver N ⇒ **meat axe**

meat diet N régime *m* carné

meat-eater N *(= animal)* carnivore *m* ◆ **he's a big ~-eater** c'est un gros mangeur de viande

meat-eating ADJ carnivore

meat extract N concentré *m* de viande

meat grinder N *(US)* hachoir *m* (à viande)

meat hook N crochet *m* de boucherie, allonge *f*

meat loaf N pain *m* de viande

meat market N 1 *(for animals)* halle *f* aux viandes 2 *(* pej: for people)* lieu *m* de drague*

meat pie N tourte *f* à la viande

meat products NPL produits *mpl* à base de viande

meat safe N *(Brit)* garde-manger *m inv*

meatball /ˈmiːtbɔːl/ N boulette *f* de viande

meathead* /ˈmiːthed/ N *(US)* andouille* *f*

meatless /ˈmiːtlɪs/ ADJ sans viande

meatpacker /ˈmiːtpækəʳ/ N *(US Comm)* ouvrier *m*, -ière *f* d'abattoir

meatpacking /ˈmiːtpækɪŋ/ N *(US Comm)* abattage *m*

meatus /mɪˈeɪtəs/ N (pl **meatus** *or* **meatuses**) *(Anat)* conduit *m*, méat *m*

meaty /ˈmiːtɪ/ ADJ 1 *(= like meat) [flavour]* de viande ; *[soup]* plein de viande ◆ **a** ~ **sauce** une sauce qui contient beaucoup de viande ◆ **to have a** ~ **texture** avoir la consistance de la viande ◆ **shark is a** ~ **fish** la chair du requin ressemble à de la viande 2 *(* = containing meat, meat-based) [diet]* carné ; *[sauce, stock]* à base de viande ◆ **nothing** ~ **for me, thanks** pas de viande pour moi, merci 3 *(= fleshy) [hands]* épais (-aisse *f*) ; *[arms, legs]* gros (grosse *f*) *before n* ; *[lips]* charnu 4 *(* = satisfying, chewy)* ◆ ~ **chunks** gros morceaux *mpl* ◆ **a nice** ~ **steak** un bon steak bien épais ◆ a ~ wine un vin qui a du corps 5 (* = substantial) [story, report, book] où il y a de quoi lire ; [role] substantiel

Mecca /ˈmekə/ N (Geog) La Mecque ◆ **a ~ for Japanese tourists** la Mecque des touristes japonais

Meccano ® /mɪˈkɑːnəʊ/ N (Brit) Meccano ® m

mechanic /mɪˈkænɪk/ N mécanicien m ◆ **motor ~** mécanicien m garagiste

mechanical /mɪˈkænɪkəl/ ADJ 1 [device, means, problem, process] mécanique ◆ **a ~ failure** une panne (mécanique) 2 (= mechanically minded) ◆ **to be ~** avoir le sens de la mécanique 3 (= unthinking) [behaviour, action, reply] machinal, mécanique 4 (= stilted) [style, painting] qui manque de naturel ◆ **his dancing is ~** il danse d'une manière guindée

COMP **mechanical digger** N pelleteuse f, pelle f mécanique
mechanical drawing N dessin m à l'échelle
mechanical engineer N ingénieur m mécanicien
mechanical engineering N (= theory) mécanique f ; (= practice) construction f mécanique
mechanical shovel N pelle f mécanique

mechanically /mɪˈkænɪkəlɪ/ ADV 1 [operate, work, harvest] mécaniquement ◆ **to be ~ minded** or **inclined** avoir le sens de la mécanique 2 (= unthinkingly) [eat, drink, say, reply, shake hands] machinalement, mécaniquement

COMP **mechanically recovered meat** N viande f obtenue par désossement mécanique

mechanics /mɪˈkænɪks/ N (NonC = science) mécanique f NPL (= technical aspect) mécanisme m, processus m ; (= mechanism, working parts) mécanisme m, mécanique f ◆ **we'll discuss the ~ of organizing your accounts** nous discuterons de l'aspect pratique or des détails pratiques de votre comptabilité ◆ **the ~ of government** les mécanismes mpl du gouvernement

mechanism /ˈmekənɪzəm/ N (all senses) mécanisme m ◆ **defence ~** mécanisme m de défense ; → **safety**

mechanistic /ˌmekəˈnɪstɪk/ ADJ mécaniste

mechanization /ˌmekənaɪˈzeɪʃən/ N mécanisation f

mechanize /ˈmekənaɪz/ VT [+ process, production] mécaniser ; [+ army] motoriser ◆ **~d industry** industrie f mécanisée

MEd /emˈed/ N (Univ) (abbrev of **Master of Education**) ≃ CAPES m

Med * /med/ N 1 (abbrev of **Mediterranean Sea**) ◆ **the ~** la Méditerranée 2 (= region) région f méditerranéenne

med. ADJ abbrev of **medium**

medal /ˈmedl/ N (Mil, Sport, gen) médaille f ◆ **swimming/athletics ~** médaille f de natation/d'athlétisme ◆ **(Congressional) Medal of Honor** (in US) Médaille f d'honneur (la plus haute décoration militaire)

medalist /ˈmedəlɪst/ N (US) ⇒ **medallist**

medallion /mɪˈdæljən/ N (gen, Archit) médaillon m

medallist, medalist (US) /ˈmedəlɪst/ N ◆ **he's a gold/silver ~** il a eu la médaille d'or/d'argent ◆ **the three ~s on the podium** les trois médaillés mpl or vainqueurs mpl sur le podium

meddle /ˈmedl/ VI 1 (= interfere) se mêler, s'occuper (in de), s'ingérer (frm) (in dans) ◆ **stop meddling!** cesse de t'occuper or de te mêler de ce qui ne te regarde pas ! 2 (= tamper) toucher (with à)

meddler /ˈmedləʳ/ N 1 (= busybody) ◆ **he's a compulsive ~** il faut toujours qu'il fourre son nez partout 2 (touching things) touche-à-tout m inv

meddlesome /ˈmedlsəm/, **meddling** /ˈmedlɪŋ/ ADJ (pej) [person] qui fourre son nez partout

Medevac /ˈmedɪˌvæk/ N (= helicopter) hélicoptère m sanitaire de l'armée

media /ˈmiːdɪə/ NPL of **medium** ◆ **the ~** les médias mpl ◆ **the ~ is** or **are state-controlled** les médias sont étatisés ◆ **the ~ have welcomed her visit** les médias ont salué sa visite ◆ **they issued a statement to the ~ assembled outside** ils ont fait une déclaration à l'intention des journalistes qui attendaient à l'extérieur

COMP [attention, reaction] des médias ; [event, coverage] médiatique
media circus * N (pej = event) cirque m médiatique
media man N (pl **media men**) (Press, Rad, TV) journaliste m, reporter m ; (Advertising) publicitaire m
media person N (Press, Rad, TV) journaliste mf ; (Advertising) publicitaire mf
media-shy ADJ qui n'aime pas être interviewé
media star N vedette f des médias
media studies NPL (Univ etc) études fpl de communication

mediaeval etc /ˌmedɪˈiːvəl/ ⇒ **medieval**

medial /ˈmiːdɪəl/ ADJ 1 (= middle) (gen) médian ; (Phon) médial, médian 2 (= mid-point) moyen N (Phon) médiane f

median /ˈmiːdɪən/ ADJ (= mid value) médian ◆ **~ income** revenu m médian N 1 (Math, Stat) médiane f 2 (US Aut) (also **median strip**) terre-plein m central

COMP **median nerve** N (Anat) nerf m médian
median strip N (US Aut) terre-plein m central

mediant /ˈmiːdɪənt/ N médiante f

mediate /ˈmiːdɪeɪt/ VI servir d'intermédiaire (between entre ; in dans) VT 1 (= arbitrate) [+ peace, settlement] obtenir par médiation ; [+ dispute] arbitrer 2 (frm, lit = change) modifier (légèrement)

mediating /ˈmiːdɪeɪtɪŋ/ ADJ médiateur (-trice f)

mediation /ˌmiːdɪˈeɪʃən/ N médiation f ◆ **through the ~ of sb** par l'entremise f de qn

mediator /ˈmiːdɪeɪtəʳ/ N médiateur m, -trice f

Medibank /ˈmedɪbæŋk/ N (Austral) Sécurité sociale australienne

medic * /ˈmedɪk/ N (abbrev of **medical**) (= student) carabin * m ; (= doctor) toubib * m

Medicaid /ˈmedɪˌkeɪd/ N (US Med) Medicaid m

MEDICAID, MEDICARE

Medicaid est un organisme américain, administré conjointement par le gouvernement fédéral et par les États, qui prend en charge les traitements hospitaliers et les soins médicaux des personnes de moins de 65 ans vivant en dessous du seuil de pauvreté officiel. Les critères pour bénéficier de ces soins gratuits varient selon les États.

Medicare est un régime d'assurance maladie, financé par le gouvernement fédéral, qui prend en charge une partie des coûts d'hospitalisation et de traitement des personnes âgées de plus de 65 ans, des insuffisants rénaux et de certains handicapés. Les bénéficiaires de ce régime paient une cotisation mensuelle et doivent se faire soigner dans certains hôpitaux et par certains médecins agréés. Il existe parallèlement une assurance complémentaire privée appelée « Medigap ». Toute personne non couverte par **Medicare** ou **Medicaid** doit prendre en charge personnellement ses soins de santé par le biais d'une assurance maladie privée.

medical /ˈmedɪkəl/ ADJ [subject, certificate, treatment] médical

N (also **medical examination**) (in hospital, school, army etc) visite f médicale ; (private) examen m médical

COMP **medical board** N commission f médicale, conseil m de santé ; (Mil) conseil m de révision
medical care N soins mpl médicaux
Medical College Admissions Test N (US Univ) examen d'entrée en faculté de médecine
medical doctor N docteur m en médecine
medical examination N ⇒ **medical noun**
medical examiner N (US Med) médecin m légiste
medical history N 1 [of person] (= record) dossier m médical ; (= background) antécédents mpl médicaux 2 (= history of medicine) histoire f de la médecine
medical insurance N assurance f maladie
medical jurisprudence N médecine f légale
medical librarian N (US) bibliothécaire mf médical(e)
medical man * N (pl **medical men**) médecin m
medical officer N (at work) médecin m du travail ; (in armed forces) médecin-major m (or -colonel etc)
Medical Officer of Health N directeur m de la santé publique
medical practitioner N médecin m (de médecine générale), généraliste mf
the medical profession N (= career) la carrière médicale ; (= personnel) le corps médical
the Medical Research Council N (Brit) organisme d'aide à la recherche médicale
medical school N (Univ) école f or faculté f de médecine
medical social worker N (Brit) assistant(e) m(f) social(e) (dans un hôpital)
medical student N étudiant(e) m(f) en médecine
medical studies NPL études fpl de médecine or médicales
medical technician N technicien(ne) m(f) de laboratoire
medical unit N service m de médecine générale
medical ward N salle f de médecine générale

medically /ˈmedɪkəlɪ/ ADV [treat] médicalement ; [prove, explain, recognize] d'un point de vue médical ◆ **to examine sb ~** faire subir un examen médical à qn ◆ **to be ~ fit for sth** être en état de faire qch ◆ **to be ~ qualified** être diplômé en médecine ◆ **to be ~ safe** être sans danger pour la santé ◆ **to be ~ trained** avoir suivi une formation médicale

medicament /meˈdɪkəmənt/ N médicament m

Medicare /ˈmedɪkeəʳ/ N (US) Medicare m ; → **MEDICAID, MEDICARE**

medicate /ˈmedɪkeɪt/ VT [+ patient] traiter avec des médicaments ; [+ substance] ajouter une substance médicinale à

medicated /ˈmedɪkeɪtɪd/ ADJ [soap] médical ; [shampoo] traitant ◆ **~ sweet** pastille f médicamenteuse

medication /ˌmedɪˈkeɪʃən/ N médication f

Medici /ˈmedɪtʃɪ/ NPL Médicis mpl

medicinal /meˈdɪsɪnl/ ADJ [plant, herb, value] médicinal ; [property, quality] thérapeutique ◆ **~ drug** médicament m ◆ **for ~ purposes** or **use** (lit) à des fins thérapeutiques ◆ **"medicinal use only"** "pour usage médical"

medicinally /meˈdɪsɪnəlɪ/ ADV [use, prescribe] comme médicament

medicine /ˈmedsn, ˈmedɪsn/ N 1 (NonC = science) médecine f ◆ **to study ~** faire (sa) médecine ◆ **Doctor of Medicine** (Univ) docteur m en médecine ; → **forensic** 2 (= drug etc) médicament m ◆ **it's a very good ~ for colds** c'est un remède souverain contre les rhumes ◆ **to take one's ~** (lit) prendre son médicament ; (fig) avaler la pilule ◆ **let's give him a taste** or **dose**

of his own ~ on va lui rendre la monnaie de sa pièce ; → **patent**
COMP **medicine ball** N médecine-ball *m*
medicine box N pharmacie *f* (portative)
medicine cabinet N (armoire *f* à) pharmacie *f*
medicine chest N (= *box*) pharmacie *f* (portative) ; (= *cupboard*) (armoire *f* à) pharmacie *f*
medicine cupboard N ⇒ **medicine cabinet**
medicine man N (pl **medicine men**) sorcier *m*

medico * /ˈmedɪkəʊ/ N ⇒ **medic**

medieval /ˌmedrˈiːvəl/ ADJ 1 *(Hist) [period, building, town, streets, art, architecture, manuscript]* médiéval ; *[knight, lady, peasant]* du Moyen Âge ; *[atmosphere, charm]* moyenâgeux ◆ **Europe/England** l'Europe *f*/l'Angleterre *f* médiévale *or* du Moyen Âge ◆ ~ **German literature** la littérature allemande médiévale ◆ **in ~ times** à l'époque médiévale 2 *(pej = primitive) [plumbing, facilities]* moyenâgeux *(pej)*
COMP **Medieval History** N histoire *f* médiévale
Medieval Latin N latin *m* médiéval
medieval studies NPL études *fpl* médiévales

medievalism /ˌmedrˈiːvəlɪzəm/ N médiévisme *m*

medievalist /ˌmedrˈiːvəlɪst/ N médiéviste *mf*

Medina /meˈdiːnə/ N *(Geog, Rel)* Médine

mediocre /ˌmiːdɪˈəʊkəʳ/ ADJ médiocre

mediocrity /ˌmiːdɪˈɒkrɪtɪ/ N médiocrité *f*

meditate /ˈmedɪteɪt/ VI méditer *(on, about* sur), réfléchir *(on, about* à)

meditation /ˌmedɪˈteɪʃən/ N méditation *f (on, about* sur) ◆ **the fruit of long ~** le fruit de longues méditations ◆ **~s** *(Literat, Rel etc)* méditations *fpl (on* sur)

meditative /ˈmedɪtətɪv/ ADJ *[person, mood, techniques, music]* méditatif ; *[exercises, state]* de méditation ◆ **the ~ calm of churches** le calme des églises qui incite à la méditation

meditatively /ˈmedɪtətɪvlɪ/ ADV d'un air méditatif

Mediterranean /ˌmedɪtəˈreɪnɪən/ ADJ *[country, town, coast, culture, climate, diet, species]* méditerranéen ; *[island]* de la Méditerranée ; *[holiday]* au bord de la Méditerranée ; *[cruise]* en Méditerranée ◆ **the ~ Sea** la mer Méditerranée ◆ **~ people** les Méditerranéens *mpl* ◆ **the ~ type** le type méditerranéen N 1 ◆ **the ~** (= *sea*) la Méditerranée ; (= *region*) la région méditerranéenne 2 (= *person*) Méditerranéen *m*, -enne *f*

medium /ˈmiːdɪəm/ N (pl **media** *or* **mediums**) 1 *(Bio, Chem, gen)* (= *substance*) substance *f* ◆ **blood is the ~ in which oxygen is carried all over the body** le sang est la substance qui sert au transport de l'oxygène à travers le corps ◆ **water-based ~s like gouache and acrylics** les substances à base d'eau telles que la gouache et les peintures acryliques ; → **culture**
2 (= *means of expression*) véhicule *m* ; *[of artist]* moyen *m* d'expression ; (= *branch of art*) discipline *f* ◆ **English is used as the ~ of instruction** l'anglais est utilisé comme véhicule de l'enseignement ◆ **he chose sculpture as his ~** il a choisi la sculpture comme moyen d'expression ◆ **video is his favourite ~** la vidéo est son moyen d'expression favori *or* sa discipline favorite ◆ **water-colour painting is a difficult ~** l'aquarelle est une technique difficile ◆ **through the ~ of the press** par voie de presse ◆ **advertising ~** support *m* publicitaire ◆ **television is the best ~ for this type of humour** c'est à la télévision que ce genre d'humour passe le mieux, la télévision est le meilleur véhicule pour ce genre d'humour
3 (= *mid-point*) milieu *m* ◆ **the happy ~** le juste milieu
4 (pl **mediums**) *(Spiritualism)* médium *m*
ADJ *(gen)* moyen ; *[pen]* à pointe moyenne ◆ **"medium"** *(on garment labels)* "moyen" ; see also **comp**
COMP **medium close shot** N *(Cine)* plan *m* américain
medium-dry ADJ *[wine, sherry, cider]* demi-sec
medium-fine pen N stylo *m or* feutre *m* à pointe moyenne
medium-priced ADJ à prix moyen
medium range missile N missile *m* à moyenne portée
medium rare ADJ *(of steaks)* à point
medium-sized ADJ de grandeur *or* de taille moyenne
medium-sweet ADJ *[wine, sherry, cider]* demi-doux
medium-term ADJ à moyen terme
medium-wave ADJ *(Rad)* sur ondes moyennes ◆ **on ~ wave** sur les ondes moyennes

mediumship /ˈmiːdɪəmʃɪp/ N médiumnité *f*

medlar /ˈmedləʳ/ N (= *fruit*) nèfle *f* ; (also **medlar tree**) néflier *m*

medley /ˈmedlɪ/ N mélange *m* ; *(Mus)* pot-pourri *m* ◆ **400 metres ~** *(Sport)* le 4 x 100 mètres quatre nages

medulla /meˈdʌlə/ N (pl **medullas** *or* **medullae** /meˈdʌliː/) *(Anat)* moelle *f*

Medusa /mɪˈdjuːzə/ N Méduse *f*

meek /miːk/ ADJ *[person]* docile, bonasse *(pej)* ; *[voice]* doux (douce *f*) ◆ **~ and mild** doux et docile ◆ **as ~ as a lamb** doux comme un agneau NPL **the meek** *(Bible)* les débonnaires *mpl*

meekly /ˈmiːklɪ/ ADV *[listen, accept, sit, stand]* docilement ; *[say]* humblement

meekness /ˈmiːknɪs/ N humilité *f*

meerschaum /ˈmɪəʃəm/ N 1 *(NonC = clay)* écume *f* (de mer) 2 (= *pipe*) pipe *f* en écume (de mer)

meet¹ /miːt/ (pret, ptp **met**) VT 1 *[+ person] (by chance)* rencontrer, tomber sur ; *(coming in opposite direction)* croiser ; *(by arrangement)* retrouver ; (= *go to meet*) aller chercher ; (= *come to meet*) venir chercher ◆ **to arrange to ~ sb at 3 o'clock** donner rendez-vous à qn pour 3 heures ◆ **I am ~ing the chairman at the airport** je vais chercher le président à l'aéroport ◆ **I am being met at the airport** on doit venir me chercher à l'aéroport ◆ **I'll ~ you outside the cinema** je te *or* on se retrouve devant le cinéma ◆ **don't bother to ~ me** ne prenez pas la peine de venir me chercher ◆ **he went to ~ them** il est allé à leur rencontre, il est allé au-devant d'eux ◆ **she came down the steps to ~ me** elle a descendu les escaliers et est venue à ma rencontre, elle a descendu les escaliers pour venir à ma rencontre ◆ **candidates will be required to ~ the committee** les candidats devront se présenter devant les membres du comité ; → **halfway, match²**
2 *[+ river, sea]* rencontrer ◆ **the bus for Aix ~s the 10 o'clock train** l'autobus d'Aix assure la correspondance avec le train de 10 heures ◆ **a car met his train at King's Cross** une voiture l'attendait à l'arrivée de son train en gare de King's Cross ◆ **I'm due back at 10 o'clock, can you be there to ~ my plane?** je reviens à 10 heures, peux-tu venir me chercher à l'aéroport ?
3 (= *make acquaintance of*) rencontrer, faire la connaissance de ◆ **~ Mr Martin** je vous présente M. Martin ◆ **I am very pleased to ~ you** enchanté de faire votre connaissance ◆ **glad** *or* **pleased to ~ you!** enchanté !
4 (= *encounter*) *[+ opponent, opposing team, obstacle]* rencontrer ; (= *face*) *[+ enemy, danger]* faire face à, affronter ; *(in duel)* se battre avec ◆ **he met his death** *or* **his end in 1880** il trouva la mort en 1880 ◆ **to ~ death calmly** affronter la mort avec calme *or* sérénité ; → **halfway**
5 (= *satisfy, settle*) *[+ expenses, bill]* régler, payer ; *[+ responsibilities, debt]* faire face à, s'acquitter de ; *[+ deficit]* combler ; *[+ goal, aim]* atteindre ; *[+ demand, need, want]* satisfaire, répondre à ; *[+ condition, stipulation]* remplir ; *[+ charge, objection]* réfuter ; *(Comm) [+ orders]* satisfaire, assurer ◆ **to ~ the cost of sth** prendre en charge les frais de qch ◆ **he offered to ~ the full cost of the repairs** il a proposé de payer la totalité des réparations ◆ **to ~ payments** faire face à ses obligations financières ◆ **to ~ the payments on a washing machine** payer les traites d'une machine à laver ◆ **this ~s our requirements** cela correspond à nos besoins ◆ **it did not ~ our expectations** nous n'en avons pas été satisfaits
6 *(seeing, hearing)* ◆ **the sound which met his ears** le bruit qui frappa ses oreilles ◆ **the sight which met my eye(s)** le spectacle qui s'offrit à mes yeux ◆ **I met his eye** mon regard rencontra le sien, nos regards se croisèrent ◆ **I dared not** *or* **couldn't ~ her eye** je n'osais pas la regarder en face ◆ **there's more to this than ~s the eye** *(sth suspicious)* on ne voit pas *or* on ne connaît pas les dessous de cette affaire ; *(more difficult than it seems)* c'est moins simple que cela n'en a l'air
VI 1 *[people] (by chance)* se rencontrer ; *(by arrangement)* se retrouver ; *(more than once)* se voir ; (= *become acquainted*) se rencontrer, faire connaissance ◆ **to ~ again** se revoir ◆ **until we ~ again!** au revoir !, à la prochaine fois ! ◆ **keep it until we ~ again** *or* **until we next ~** garde-le jusqu'à la prochaine fois ◆ **have you met before?** vous vous connaissez déjà ? ◆ **they arranged to ~ at 10 o'clock** ils se sont donné rendez-vous pour 10 heures
2 *[Parliament etc]* se réunir, tenir séance ; *[committee, society etc]* se réunir ◆ **the class ~s in the art room** le cours a lieu dans la salle de dessin
3 *[armies]* se rencontrer, s'affronter ; *[opposing teams]* se rencontrer
4 *[lines, roads etc]* (= *join*) se rencontrer ; (= *cross*) se croiser ; *[rivers]* se rencontrer, confluer ◆ **our eyes met** nos regards se croisèrent ; → **end**
N 1 *(Brit Hunting)* rendez-vous *m* de chasse *(au renard)* ; (= *huntsmen collectively*) chasse *f*
2 *(Sport etc)* meeting *m*
COMP **meet-and-greet** (US) VT accueillir, recevoir N réception *f*

► **meet up** VI *(by chance)* se rencontrer ; *(by arrangement)* se retrouver ◆ **to ~ up with sb** *(by chance)* rencontrer qn ; *(by arrangement)* retrouver qn ◆ **this road ~s up with the motorway** cette route rejoint l'autoroute

► **meet with** VT FUS 1 *[+ difficulties, resistance, obstacles]* rencontrer ; *[+ refusal, losses, storm, gale]* essuyer ; *[+ welcome, reception]* recevoir ◆ **he met with an accident** il lui est arrivé un accident ◆ **to ~ with failure** échouer ◆ **only 59 out of 238 applicants met with success** seuls 59 des 238 candidats ont vu leur demande acceptée ◆ **I'm delighted this approach has met with success** je suis ravi que cette approche ait été couronnée de succès ◆ **this suggestion was met with angry protests** de vives protestations ont accueilli cette suggestion ◆ **this met with no response** *(in writing)* il n'y a pas eu de réponse ; *(in person)* il (*or* elle) n'a pas réagi ◆ **we hope our offer ~s with your approval** *(frm)* nous espérons que notre proposition vous conviendra
2 (US) *[+ person] (by chance)* rencontrer, tomber sur ; *(coming in opposite direction)* croiser ; *(by arrangement)* retrouver

meet² †† /miːt/ ADJ (= *fitting*) convenable, séant †

meeting /ˈmiːtɪŋ/ N 1 *(of group of people, political party, club etc)* réunion *f* ; *(large, formal)* assemblée *f* ; *(Pol, Sport)* meeting *m* ◆ **business ~** réunion *f* d'affaires *or* de travail ◆ **he's in a ~** il est en réunion ◆ **I've got ~s all afternoon** je suis pris par des réunions tout l'après-midi ◆ **to call a ~ of shareholders** convoquer les actionnaires ◆ **to call a ~ to discuss sth** convoquer une réunion pour débattre qch ◆ **to address a ~** prendre la parole à une réunion (*or* un meeting) ; → **annual, mass¹, open**

2 *(between individuals)* rencontre *f* ; *(arranged)* rendez-vous *m* ; *(formal)* entrevue *f* ◆ **the minister had a ~ with the ambassador** le ministre s'est entretenu avec l'ambassadeur, le ministre a eu une entrevue avec l'ambassadeur ◆ **a ~ of minds** une entente profonde

3 *(Quakers)* culte *m* ◆ **to go to ~** aller au culte

COMP **meeting house** N (also **Quakers' meeting house**) temple *m* (des Quakers)
meeting place N lieu *m* de réunion

meg * /meg/ N (pl **meg** *or* **megs**) *(Comput = megabyte)* méga * *m* ; *(= megahertz)* mégahertz *m*

mega ‡ /'megə/ ADJ hypergénial *

megabuck * /'megə,bʌk/ N 1 *(US = million dollars)* million *m* de dollars 2 *(fig)* **~s** des sommes astronomiques ◆ **it's worth ~s** ça vaut la peau des fesses *

megabyte /'megə,baɪt/ N *(Comput)* méga-octet *m*, Mo *m*

megacycle /'megə,saɪkl/ N mégacycle *m*

megadeath /'megə,deθ/ N million *m* de morts

megahertz /'megə,hɜːts/ N (pl **megahertz**) mégahertz *m*

megalith /'megəlɪθ/ N mégalithe *m*

megalithic /,megə'lɪθɪk/ ADJ mégalithique

megalomania /,megələʊ'meɪnɪə/ N mégalomanie *f*

megalomaniac /,megələʊ'meɪnɪæk/ ADJ, N mégalomane *mf*

megalopolis /,megə'lɒpəlɪs/ N mégalopole *f*

megaphone /'megəfəʊn/ N porte-voix *m inv*

megastar /'megəstaːʳ/ N mégastar *f*

megaton /'megətʌn/ N mégatonne *f* ◆ **a five-~ bomb** une bombe de cinq mégatonnes

megavolt /'megəvɒlt/ N mégavolt *m*

megawatt /'megəwɒt/ N mégawatt *m*

megillah ‡ /mə'gɪlə/ N *(US)* grand laïus *m*, longues explications *fpl* ◆ **the whole ~** tout le tremblement *

meiosis /maɪ'əʊsɪs/ N (pl **meioses** /maɪ'əʊ,siːz/) 1 *(Bio)* méiose *f* 2 *(Literat)* litote *f*

Mekong /,miː'kɒŋ/ N Mékong *m* COMP **Mekong Delta** N delta *m* du Mékong

melamine /'meləmiːn/ N mélamine *f*
COMP *[cup, surface]* de *or* en mélamine
melamine-coated, melamine-faced ADJ mélaminé

melancholia /,melən'kəʊlɪə/ N *(Psych)* mélancolie *f*

melancholic † /,melən'kɒlɪk/ ADJ *[person, nature, mood, song]* mélancolique ◆ **the ~ temperament** *(Med)* le tempérament mélancolique

melancholically /,melən'kɒlɪklɪ/ ADV mélancoliquement

melancholy /'melənkəlɪ/ N *(NonC)* mélancolie *f* ADJ *[person, place, look, smile, thoughts, sound, song]* mélancolique ; *[news, event, duty]* triste ◆ **to be in a ~ mood** être d'humeur mélancolique ◆ **the ~ truth** la triste vérité

Melanesia /,melə'niːzɪə/ N Mélanésie *f*

Melanesian /,melə'niːzɪən/ ADJ mélanésien N 1 *(= person)* Mélanésien(ne) *m(f)* 2 *(= language)* mélanésien *m*

melange, mélange /meɪ'lɑːnʒ/ N *(esp liter)* mélange *m*

melanic /mə'lænɪk/ ADJ mélanique

melanin /'melənɪn/ N mélanine *f*

melanism /'melənɪzəm/ N mélanisme *m*

melanoma /,melə'nəʊmə/ N (pl **melanomas** *or* **melanomata** /,melə'nəʊmətə/) *(Med)* mélanome *m*

melatonin /,melə'təʊnɪn/ N mélatonine *f*

Melba toast /'melbə'təʊst/ N *(Culin)* biscotte *f* très fine

Melbourne /'melbən/ N Melbourne

melee, mêlée /'meleɪ/ N mêlée *f*

mellifluous /me'lɪflʊəs/ ADJ mélodieux

mellow /'meləʊ/ ADJ 1 *(= soft, smooth) [light, colour, music, voice]* doux (douce *f*) ; *[brick, stone]* patiné ; *[wine, flavour, cheese, fruit]* moelleux ; *[brandy, whisky]* velouté 2 *(= genial, serene) [person]* serein 3 *(* = relaxed) [person, mood, feeling]* relax * *inv* VT *[+ wine]* rendre moelleux, donner du moelleux à ; *[+ voice, sound]* adoucir, rendre plus moelleux ; *[+ colour]* fondre, velouter ; *[+ person, character]* adoucir ◆ **the years have ~ed him** les angles de son caractère se sont arrondis avec l'âge, il s'est adouci *or* assagi avec les années VI *[fruit]* mûrir ; *[wine]* se velouter ; *[colour]* se velouter, se patiner ; *[voice]* prendre du moelleux, se velouter ; *[person, character]* s'adoucir

mellowing /'meləʊɪŋ/ N *[of fruit, wine]* maturation *f* ; *[of voice, colours, person, attitude]* adoucissement *m* ADJ *[effect etc]* adoucissant

mellowness /'meləʊnɪs/ N *[of light, colour, music, voice]* douceur *f* ; *[of wine, flavour, cheese, fruit]* moelleux *m* ; *[of brick, stone]* patine *f*

melodic /mɪ'lɒdɪk/ ADJ 1 *(= melodious) [music, song, voice]* mélodieux 2 *(Mus) [line, theme, structure, invention]* mélodique COMP **melodic minor (scale)** N *(Mus)* gamme *f* mineure mélodique

melodically /mɪ'lɒdɪkəlɪ/ ADV mélodiquement

melodious /mɪ'ləʊdɪəs/ ADJ mélodieux

melodiously /mɪ'ləʊdɪəslɪ/ ADV mélodieusement

melodrama /'meləʊ,drɑːmə/ N *(lit, fig)* mélodrame *m*

melodramatic /,meləʊdrə'mætɪk/ ADJ mélodramatique NPL **melodramatics** mélo * *m* ◆ **I've had enough of your ~s** j'en ai assez de ton cinéma *

melodramatically /,meləʊdrə'mætɪkəlɪ/ ADV d'une façon mélodramatique

melody /'melədɪ/ N mélodie *f*

melon /'melən/ N 1 *(Bot, Culin)* melon *m* ◆ **to cut a ~** * *(US fig)* se partager le gâteau ; → **watermelon** 2 ◆ **~s** ‡ *(= breasts)* roberts ‡ *mpl*

melt /melt/ VI 1 *[ice, butter, metal]* fondre ; *[solid in liquid]* fondre, se dissoudre ◆ **these cakes ~ in the mouth** ces pâtisseries fondent dans la bouche ◆ **he looks as if butter wouldn't ~ in his mouth** on lui donnerait le bon Dieu sans confession * ; see also **melting**

2 *(fig) [colours, sounds]* se fondre, s'estomper *(into dans)* ; *[person]* se laisser attendrir ; *[anger]* tomber ; *[resolution, determination]* fléchir, fondre ◆ **to ~ into tears** fondre en larmes ◆ **her heart ~ed with pity** son cœur a fondu de pitié ◆ **night ~ed into day** la nuit a fait insensiblement place au jour ◆ **one colour ~ed into another** les couleurs se fondaient les unes dans les autres ◆ **the thief ~ed into the crowd** le voleur s'est fondu *or* a disparu dans la foule

3 *(= be too hot)* **to be ~ing** * fondre, être en nage

VT *[+ ice, butter]* (faire) fondre ; *[+ metal]* fondre ◆ **to ~ sb's heart** attendrir *or* émouvoir (le cœur de) qn ◆ **~ed butter** *(Culin)* beurre *m* fondu ; see also **melting**

► **melt away** VI 1 *[ice etc]* fondre complètement, disparaître

2 *(fig) [money, savings]* fondre ; *[anger]* se dissiper, tomber ; *[confidence]* disparaître ; *[fog]* se dissiper ; *[crowd]* se disperser ; *[person]* se volatiliser

► **melt down** VT SEP fondre ; *[+ scrap iron, coins]* remettre à la fonte
N ◆ **meltdown** → **meltdown**

meltdown /'meltdaʊn/ N 1 *(Nucl Phys)* fusion *f* *(du cœur d'un réacteur nucléaire)* 2 *(fig) (= disaster)* effondrement *m*

melting /'meltɪŋ/ ADJ *[snow]* fondant ; *(fig) [voice, look]* attendri ; *[words]* attendrissant N *[of snow]* fonte *f* ; *[of metal]* fusion *f*, fonte *f*
COMP **melting point** N point *m* de fusion
melting pot N *(fig)* melting-pot *m* ◆ **the country was a ~ pot of many nationalities** ce pays fut un melting-pot *or* fut un creuset ethnique ◆ **the scheme was back in the ~ pot again** *(Brit)* le projet a été remis en question une fois de plus ◆ **it's still all in the ~ pot** *(Brit)* c'est encore en pleine discussion *or* au stade des discussions

member /'membəʳ/ N 1 *[of society, political party etc]* membre *m*, adhérent(e) *m(f)* ; *[of family, tribe]* membre *m* ◆ **"members only"** *(on notice etc)* "réservé aux adhérents" ◆ **a ~ of the audience** un membre de l'assistance ; *(= hearer)* un auditeur ; *(= spectator)* un spectateur ◆ **Member of Congress** *(US Pol)* membre *m* du Congrès, ≃ député *m* ◆ **a ~ of the congress** un(e) congressiste ◆ **they treated her like a ~ of the family** ils l'ont traitée comme si elle faisait partie de *or* était de la famille ◆ **Member of Parliament** *(Brit Pol)* ≃ député *m* ◆ **the Member (of Parliament) for Woodford** le député de Woodford ◆ **Member of the European Parliament** *(Brit)* député *m* européen ◆ **a ~ of the public** un particulier ◆ **~s of the public were not allowed in** le public n'était pas admis ◆ **a ~ of the staff, an ordinary ~ of the public** un(e) simple citoyen(e) ; *(of firm, organization)* un(e) employé(e) ◆ **a ~ of staff** *(Scol, Univ)* un professeur ; → **full, honorary, private**

2 *(Anat, Bot, Math etc)* membre *m* ◆ **(male) ~** *(= penis)* membre *m* (viril)

COMP **member countries, member nations, member states** NPL États *mpl or* pays *mpl* membres

membership /'membəʃɪp/ N 1 *(= position as member)* appartenance *f* ; *(= admission as member)* adhésion *f* ◆ **Britain's ~ of the EU** l'appartenance de la Grande-Bretagne à l'UE ◆ **when I applied for ~ of the club** quand j'ai fait ma demande d'adhésion au club ◆ **the application by Namibia for ~ of the United Nations** la demande d'adhésion de la Namibie aux Nations unies ◆ **he has given up his ~ of the party** il a rendu sa carte du parti ◆ **~ carries certain privileges** les membres jouissent de certains privilèges ◆ **temporary ~** (système *m* d') adhésion *f* provisoire ◆ **he was charged with ~ of the IRA** il a été accusé d'appartenir à l'IRA

2 *(= number of members)* nombre *m* d'adhérents ◆ **organizations with huge ~s** des organismes qui ont un nombre d'adhérents énorme ◆ **this society has a ~ of over 800** cette société a plus de 800 membres

3 *(= members)* membres *mpl*

COMP **membership card** N carte *f* d'adhérent *or* de membre
membership fee N cotisation *f*, droits *mpl* d'inscription
membership qualifications NPL conditions *fpl* d'adhésion

membrane /'membreɪn/ N membrane *f*

membranous /mem'breɪnəs/ ADJ membraneux

memento /mə'mentəʊ/ N (pl **mementos** *or* **mementoes**) *(= keepsake)* souvenir *m* ; *(= note, mark etc)* mémento *m* ; *(= scar)* souvenir *m* ◆ **as a ~ of** en souvenir de

memo /ˈmeməʊ/ **N** (abbrev of **memorandum**) note *f* (de service) **COMP** **memo pad N** bloc-notes *m*

memoir /ˈmemwɑːʳ/ **N** *(= essay)* mémoire *m*, étude *f* (on sur) ; *(= short biography)* notice *f* biographique ◆ **~s** *(autobiographical)* mémoires *mpl* ; *[of learned society]* actes *mpl*

memorabilia /ˌmemərəˈbɪlɪə/ **N** souvenirs *mpl* *(objets)*

memorable /ˈmemərəbl/ **ADJ** mémorable ◆ **one of his more ~ films** un de ses films dont on se souvient mieux

memorably /ˈmemərəblɪ/ **ADV** mémorablement

memorandum /ˌmeməˈrændəm/ **N** (pl **memorandums** or **memoranda** /ˌmeməˈrændə/) 1 *(= reminder, note)* note *f* ◆ **to make a ~ of sth** prendre note de qch, noter qch 2 *(= communication within company etc)* note *f* (de service) ◆ **he sent a ~ round about the drop in sales** il a fait circuler une note *or* il a fait passer une circulaire à propos de la baisse des ventes 3 *(Diplomacy)* mémorandum *m* 4 *(Jur)* sommaire *m* des articles (d'un contrat) ◆ **~ of agreement** protocole *m* d'accord

memorial /mɪˈmɔːrɪəl/ **ADJ** *[plaque]* commémoratif **N** 1 *(= sth serving as reminder)* **this scholarship is a ~ to John F. Kennedy** cette bourse d'études a été créée en mémoire de John F. Kennedy 2 *(= monument)* monument *m* (commémoratif), mémorial *m* ; *(over grave)* monument *m* (funéraire) ◆ **a ~ to the victims** un monument aux victimes 3 (also **war memorial**) monument *m* aux morts 4 *(Hist)* **~s** *(= chronicles)* chroniques *fpl*, mémoires *mpl*, mémorial *m* 5 *(Admin etc = petition)* pétition *f*, requête *f* (officielle)
COMP **Memorial Day N** *(US)* le jour des morts au champ d'honneur *(dernier lundi de mai)*
memorial park N *(US = cemetery)* cimetière *m*
memorial service N ≃ messe *f* de souvenir

memorialize /mɪˈmɔːrɪəlaɪz/ **VT** commémorer

memorize /ˈmeməraɪz/ **VT** *[+ facts, figures, names]* mémoriser, retenir ; *[+ poem, speech]* apprendre par cœur

memory /ˈmemərɪ/ **N** 1 *(= faculty: also Comput)* mémoire *f* ◆ **to have a good/bad ~** avoir (une) bonne/mauvaise mémoire ◆ **to have a ~ for faces** avoir la mémoire des visages, être physionomiste *mf* ◆ **to play/quote from ~** jouer/citer de mémoire ◆ **to have a long ~** ne pas oublier facilement ◆ **to commit to ~** *[+ poem]* apprendre par cœur ; *[+ facts, figures]* mémoriser, retenir ◆ **to the best of my ~** autant que je m'en souvienne ◆ **loss of ~, ~ loss** perte *f* de mémoire ; *(Med)* amnésie *f* ◆ **additional** *or* **back-up ~** *(Comput)* mémoire *f* auxiliaire ; → **fresh, living**
2 *(= recollection)* souvenir *m* ◆ **childhood memories** souvenirs *mpl* d'enfance ◆ **he had happy memories of his father** il avait de bons souvenirs de son père ◆ **"Memories of a country childhood"** "Souvenirs d'une enfance à la campagne" ◆ **the ~ of the accident remained with him all his life** il a conservé toute sa vie le souvenir de l'accident, le souvenir de l'accident est resté gravé dans sa mémoire toute sa vie ◆ **to keep sb's ~ alive** *or* **green** garder vivant le souvenir de qn, entretenir la mémoire de qn ◆ **in ~ of** en souvenir de, à la mémoire de ◆ **sacred to the ~ of** à la mémoire de ◆ **of blessed ~** de glorieuse mémoire
COMP **memory bank N** bloc *m* de mémoire
memory capacity N *(Comput)* capacité *f* de mémoire
memory card N *(Comput)* carte *f* d'extension mémoire
memory chip N *(Comput)* puce *f* mémoire
memory lane N ◆ **it was a trip down ~ lane** c'était un retour en arrière *or* un retour aux sources

memsahib /ˈmemˌsɑːhɪb/ **N** Madame *f* *(aux Indes)*

men /men/ **NPL** of **man** ◆ **that'll separate the ~ from the boys** *(hum)* cela fera la différence (entre les hommes et les mauviettes*) **COMP** **men's room N** *(US)* toilettes *fpl* pour hommes

menace /ˈmenɪs/ **N** menace *f* ◆ **he drives so badly he's a ~ to the public** il conduit si mal qu'il est un danger public ◆ **that child/dog/motorbike is a ~*** cet enfant/ce chien/cette moto est une plaie* ◆ **to demand money with ~s** *(Brit Jur)* extorquer de l'argent **VT** menacer

menacing /ˈmenɪsɪŋ/ **ADJ** menaçant

menacingly /ˈmenɪsɪŋlɪ/ **ADV** *[act]* d'un air menaçant ; *[say]* d'un ton menaçant

ménage /meˈnɑːʒ/ **N** *(pej)* ménage *m* ◆ **~ à trois** ménage *m* à trois

menagerie /mɪˈnædʒərɪ/ **N** ménagerie *f*

mend /mend/ **VT** 1 *(= repair)* *[+ watch, wall, vehicle, shoes etc]* réparer ; *[+ clothes etc]* raccommoder ; *(= darn)* *[+ sock, stocking]* repriser ; *[+ laddered stocking]* remmailler ; → **fence** 2 *(fig)* *[+ marriage]* sauver ◆ **to ~ relations with sb** renouer de bonnes relations avec qn ◆ **that won't ~ matters** cela ne va pas arranger les choses ◆ **to ~ one's ways, to ~ one's manners** s'amender ; → **least** **VI** 1 *(= darn etc)* faire le raccommodage 2 * ⇒ **to be on the mend** **N** 1 *(on clothes)* raccommodage *m* ; *(= patch)* pièce *f* ; *(= darn)* reprise *f* 2 ◆ **to be on the ~** *[invalid]* être en voie de guérison, aller mieux ; *[business, sales]* reprendre, s'améliorer ; *[conditions, situation, weather]* s'améliorer

mendacious /menˈdeɪʃəs/ **ADJ** *(frm)* *[statement, report]* mensonger ; *[person]* menteur

mendacity /menˈdæsɪtɪ/ **N** 1 *(NonC, habit)* fausseté *f*, habitude *f* de mentir ; *(tendency)* propension *f* au mensonge ; *[of report]* caractère *m* mensonger 2 *(= lie)* mensonge *m*

mendelevium /ˌmendɪˈliːvɪəm/ **N** mendélévium *m*

Mendelian /menˈdiːlɪən/ **ADJ** mendélien

Mendelism /ˈmendəlɪzəm/ **N** mendélisme *m*

mendicancy /ˈmendɪkənsɪ/ **N** mendicité *f*

mendicant /ˈmendɪkənt/ **ADJ, N** mendiant(e) *m(f)*

mendicity /menˈdɪsɪtɪ/ **N** mendicité *f*

mending /ˈmendɪŋ/ **N** *(= act)* raccommodage *m* ; *(= clothes to be mended)* vêtements *mpl* à raccommoder ; → **invisible**

Menelaus /ˌmenɪˈleɪəs/ **N** Ménélas *m*

menfolk /ˈmenfəʊk/ **NPL** ◆ **the ~** les hommes *mpl*

menhir /ˈmenhɪəʳ/ **N** menhir *m*

menial /ˈmiːnɪəl/ **ADJ** *[person]* servile ; *[task]* de domestique, inférieur (-eure *f*) ; *[position]* subalterne **N** domestique *mf*, laquais *m* *(pej)*

meninges /mɪˈnɪndʒiːz/ **NPL** méninges *fpl*

meningitis /ˌmenɪnˈdʒaɪtɪs/ **N** méningite *f*

meniscus /mɪˈnɪskəs/ **N** (pl **meniscuses** or **menisci** /mɪˈnɪsaɪ/) ménisque *m*

menopausal /ˈmenəʊpɔːzəl/ **ADJ** *[symptom]* de la ménopause ; *[woman]* ménopausée

menopause /ˈmenəʊpɔːz/ **N** ménopause *f* ◆ **the male ~** l'andropause *f*

Menorca /mɪˈnɔːkə/ **N** Minorque *f* ◆ **in ~** à Minorque

menorrhagia /ˌmenɔːˈreɪdʒɪə/ **N** ménorragie *f*

Mensa /ˈmensə/ **N** Mensa *f* *(association de personnes ayant un QI supérieur à la moyenne)*

mensch* /menʃ/ **N** *(US)* *(= man)* type *m* vraiment bien ; *(= woman)* fille *f* vraiment bien ◆ **be a ~!** comporte-toi en adulte !

menses /ˈmensiːz/ **NPL** menstrues *fpl*

Menshevik /ˈmenʃɪvɪk/ **N, ADJ** menchevik *m*

menstrual /ˈmenstrʊəl/ **ADJ** menstruel
COMP **menstrual cramps NPL** dysménorrhée *f*, règles *fpl* douloureuses
menstrual cycle N cycle *m* (menstruel)
menstrual period N règles *fpl*, menstruation *f*

menstruate /ˈmenstrʊeɪt/ **VI** avoir ses règles

menstruation /ˌmenstrʊˈeɪʃən/ **N** menstruation *f*

mensuration /ˌmensjʊəˈreɪʃən/ **N** *(also Math)* mesurage *m*

menswear /ˈmenzweəʳ/ **N** *(NonC)* *(= clothing)* habillement *m* masculin ; *(= department)* rayon *m* hommes

mental /ˈmentl/ **ADJ** 1 *(= not physical)* mental ◆ **I made a ~ note of her phone number** j'ai noté mentalement son numéro de téléphone ◆ **I made a ~ note to get petrol** je me suis dit que je devais faire le plein
2 (* = *mad*) cinglé* ◆ **to go ~** perdre la boule*
COMP **mental age N** âge *m* mental
mental arithmetic N calcul *m* mental
mental block N blocage *m* (psychologique)
mental cruelty N *(Jur)* cruauté *f* mentale
mental defective N débile *mf* mental(e)
mental deficiency N débilité *f* or déficience *f* mentale
mental disability, mental handicap N handicap *m* mental
mental healing N *(US Med)* thérapeutique *f* par la suggestion
mental health N *(of person)* santé *f* mentale ; *(= activity, profession)* psychiatrie *f*
mental home N clinique *f* psychiatrique
mental hospital N hôpital *m* psychiatrique
mental illness N maladie *f* mentale
mental institution N institution *f* psychiatrique
mental patient N malade *mf* mental(e)
mental powers NPL facultés *fpl* intellectuelles
mental reservation N restriction *f* mentale
mental retardation N arriération *f* mentale
mental strain N *(= tension)* tension *f* nerveuse ; *(= overwork)* surmenage *m* (intellectuel) ◆ **she's been under a great deal of ~ strain** ses nerfs ont été mis à rude épreuve

mentality /menˈtælɪtɪ/ **N** mentalité *f*

mentally /ˈmentəlɪ/ **ADV** *[calculate, formulate]* mentalement ◆ **~ handicapped** handicapé mental ◆ **a ~ handicapped son/child** un fils/enfant handicapé mental ◆ **he is ~ handicapped** c'est un handicapé mental ◆ **~ ill** *or* **sick** malade mental ◆ **a ~ ill** *or* **sick person** un(e) malade mental(e) ◆ **the ~ ill** les malades *mpl* mentaux ◆ **~ retarded** † débile mental ◆ **~ subnormal** † débile léger ◆ **~ disturbed** *or* **disordered** *or* **unstable** *or* **unbalanced** déséquilibré ◆ **~ defective** *or* **deficient** † mentalement déficient

mentee /menˈtiː/ **N** filleul(e) *m(f)*

menthol /ˈmenθɒl/ **N** menthol *m* **COMP** **menthol cigarettes NPL** cigarettes *fpl* mentholées

mentholated /ˈmenθəleɪtɪd/ **ADJ** mentholé

mention /ˈmenʃən/ LANGUAGE IN USE 26.2
VT *(gen)* mentionner ; *[+ dates, figures]* citer ◆ **he ~ed to me that you were coming** il m'a dit que vous alliez venir ◆ **I'll ~ it to him** je lui en toucherai un mot, je le lui signalerai ◆ **I've never heard him ~ his father** je ne l'ai jamais entendu parler de son père ◆ **to ~ sb in one's will** coucher qn sur son testament ◆ **he didn't ~ the accident** il n'a pas fait mention de l'accident, il n'a pas soufflé mot de l'accident ◆ **just ~ my name** dites que c'est de ma part ◆ **he ~ed several names** il a cité plusieurs noms ◆ **without ~ing any names** sans nommer *or* citer personne ◆ **I ~ this fact only because ...** je relève ce fait uniquement parce que ... ◆ **they are too numerous to ~** ils sont

trop nombreux pour qu'on les mentionne *subj* or cite *subj* tous ◆ **don't ~ it!** il n'y a pas de quoi !, je vous en prie ! ◆ **I need hardly ~ that ...** il va sans dire que ... ◆ **it is not worth ~ing** cela ne vaut pas la peine d'en parler ◆ **I have no jazz records worth ~ing** je n'ai pour ainsi dire pas de disques de jazz ; → **dispatch**

◆ **not to mention** sans parler de ◆ **a lot of time, not to ~ the expense and anxiety** beaucoup de temps, sans parler du coût et du stress

N mention *f* ◆ **to make ~ of sth** *(frm)* faire mention de qch, signaler qch ◆ **honourable ~** mention *f* honorable ◆ **it got a ~ in the news** on en a parlé *or* on l'a mentionné aux informations

mentor /ˈmentɔːʳ/ N ◆ **he has been my ~ and friend for 8 years** voilà 8 ans qu'il est mon guide *or* conseiller et mon ami ◆ **their spiritual ~** leur guide spirituel

menu /ˈmenjuː/ N *(in restaurant etc)* menu *m* ; *(printed, written)* menu *m*, carte *f* ; *(Comput)* menu *m* ◆ **on the ~** au menu ; → **fixed**

COMP **menu bar** N *(Comput)* barre *f* de menu

menu-driven ADJ *(Comput)* dirigé *or* piloté par menu

meow /miːˈaʊ/ N, VI ⇒ **miaow**

MEP /ˌemiːˈpiː/ N *(Brit)* (abbrev of **Member of the European Parliament**) → **member**

Mephistopheles /ˌmefɪsˈtɒfɪliːz/ N Méphistophélès *m*

mephistophelian /ˌmefɪstəˈfiːlɪən/ ADJ méphistophélique

mercantile /ˈmɜːkəntaɪl/ ADJ 1 *[class, tradition, navy, vessel]* marchand ; *[affairs]* commercial ; *[nation]* commerçant ; *[firm, establishment, court]* de commerce 2 *(pej)* *[person, attitude]* mercantile

COMP **mercantile law** N droit *m* commercial

mercantile marine N *(Brit)* marine *m* marchande

mercantilism /ˈmɜːkəntɪlɪzəm/ N *(Econ, also pej)* mercantilisme *m*

mercantilist /ˈmɜːkəntɪlɪst/ ADJ, N *(Econ)* mercantiliste *m*

Mercator /mɜːˈkeɪtəʳ/ N ◆ **~ projection** projection *f* de Mercator

mercenary /ˈmɜːsɪnərɪ/ ADJ 1 *(pej)* *[person, attitude]* intéressé, mercenaire 2 *(Mil)* mercenaire N *(Mil)* mercenaire *m*

mercer /ˈmɜːsəʳ/ N *(Brit)* marchand *m* de tissus

merchandise /ˈmɜːtʃəndaɪz/ N *(NonC)* marchandises *fpl* VI commercer, faire du commerce VT promouvoir la vente de

merchandizer /ˈmɜːtʃəndaɪzəʳ/ N spécialiste *mf* du marchandisage *or* merchandising

merchandizing /ˈmɜːtʃəndaɪzɪŋ/ N marchandisage *m*, merchandising *m*

merchant /ˈmɜːtʃənt/ N *(= trader, dealer)* négociant *m* ; *(= wholesaler)* marchand *m* en gros, grossiste *m* ; *(= retailer)* marchand *m* au détail, détaillant *m* ; *(= shopkeeper)* commerçant *m* ◆ **builders'/plumbers' ~** fournisseur *m* de *or* en matériaux de construction/en sanitaires ◆ **timber/cloth/spice ~** marchand *m* de bois/de tissu/d'épices ◆ **"The Merchant of Venice"** "le Marchand de Venise" ◆ **a doom-and-gloom ~** * un oiseau de mauvais augure ◆ **a rip-off ~** ⁎ un arnaqueur * ; → **coal, speed, wine**

COMP **merchant bank** N *(Brit)* banque *f* d'affaires

merchant banker N *(Brit)* banquier *m* d'affaires

merchant marine N *(US)* ⇒ **merchant navy**

merchant navy N *(Brit)* marine *f* marchande

merchant seaman N (pl **merchant seamen**) marin *m* de la marine marchande

merchant ship N navire *m* marchand *or* de commerce

merchant shipping N *(NonC)* navires *mpl* marchands *or* de commerce

merchant vessel N navire *m* marchand *or* de commerce

merchantability /ˌmɜːtʃəntəˈbɪlɪtɪ/ N *(Comm)* valeur *f* commerciale ; *(Jur)* qualité *f* loyale et marchande

merchantable /ˈmɜːtʃəntəbl/ ADJ 1 *(Comm)* commercialisable, vendable 2 *(Jur)* (also **of merchantable quality**) d'une bonne qualité marchande

merchantman /ˈmɜːtʃəntmən/ N (pl **-men**) *(Naut)* ⇒ **merchant ship** ; → **merchant**

merciful /ˈmɜːsɪfʊl/ ADJ 1 *(= compassionate)* *[person, judge, court]* clément *(to or towards sb* envers qn) ; *[God]* miséricordieux *(to or towards sb* envers qn) 2 *(= welcome)* ◆ **death came as a ~ release** la mort fut une délivrance ◆ **his death came with ~ suddenness** heureusement pour lui, la mort a été rapide

mercifully /ˈmɜːsɪfəlɪ/ ADV 1 *[judge, act]* *(person)* avec clémence ; *(God)* miséricordieusement 2 *(= fortunately)* ◆ **~ it didn't rain** Dieu merci *or* par bonheur il n'a pas plu

merciless /ˈmɜːsɪlɪs/ ADJ *[person, attack, treatment]* impitoyable *(towards sb* envers qn) ; *[sun, heat, rain, scrutiny]* implacable ◆ **to be a ~ critic of sb/sth** critiquer qn/qch impitoyablement

mercilessly /ˈmɜːsɪlɪslɪ/ ADV *[behave, attack, treat, criticize]* impitoyablement, sans pitié ◆ **the sun beat down ~** le soleil était implacable

mercurial /mɜːˈkjʊərɪəl/ ADJ 1 *(liter)* *(= changeable)* *[person, temperament, nature]* versatile, lunatique *(pej)* ; *[moods]* changeant ; *(= lively)* *[wit]* vif 2 *(Chem)* mercuriel

mercury /ˈmɜːkjʊrɪ/ N 1 *(Chem)* mercure *m* 2 ◆ **Mercury** *(Myth)* Mercure *m* ; *(Astron)* Mercure *f*

mercy /ˈmɜːsɪ/ N 1 *(gen)* miséricorde *f* ; *(= clemency)* clémence *f* ; *(= pity)* pitié *f* ◆ **God in his ~** Dieu en sa miséricorde ◆ **to have ~ on sb, to show ~ to sb** † faire preuve de clémence envers qn, avoir pitié de qn ◆ **have ~ on me!** ayez pitié de moi ! ◆ **to beg for ~** demander grâce ◆ **with a recommendation for** *or* **of ~** *(Jur)* ≃ avec avis en faveur d'une commutation de peine ◆ **a cruelty without ~** une cruauté impitoyable ◆ **he was beaten without ~** il a été battu impitoyablement ◆ **no ~ was shown to them** ils furent impitoyablement traités *or* traités sans merci ◆ **to throw o.s. on sb's ~** *(liter)* s'en remettre à la merci de qn ◆ **at the ~ of sb/the weather** *etc* à la merci de qn/du temps *etc* ◆ **to leave sb to the ~ of** *or* **to the tender mercies of ...** *(iro)* livrer qn à ..., abandonner qn à la merci de ... ◆ **~ (me)!** †* Seigneur !, miséricorde ! ◆ **for ~'s sake!** † par pitié ! ; → **errand**

2 *(= piece of good fortune)* **it's a ~ that ...** heureusement que ... + *indic*, c'est une chance que ... + *subj* ◆ **his death was a ~** sa mort a été une délivrance

COMP *[flight, dash]* ◆ **a helicopter arrived for the ~ dash** *or* **flight to hospital** un hélicoptère est arrivé pour la transporter d'urgence à l'hôpital

mercy killing N euthanasie *f*

mere[1] /mɪəʳ/ N étang *m*, (petit) lac *m*

mere[2] /mɪəʳ/ ADJ 1 *(= least, even)* simple *before n* ◆ **the ~ mention of sth** le simple fait de mentionner qch ◆ **the ~ existence of neo-Nazis is an outrage** le simple fait que les néonazis existent est un scandale, la simple existence des néonazis constitue un scandale ◆ **the ~ possibility of rain was enough to put him off** le fait qu'il risquait de pleuvoir a suffi à le décourager ◆ **the ~ sight of him makes me shiver** sa seule vue me fait frissonner, rien qu'à le voir je frissonne ◆ **the ~st suggestion of sth** *(= mention)* le simple fait d'évoquer qch ◆ **the ~st hint** *or* **suspicion of sth** le moindre soupçon de qch

2 *(= simple, slight)* *[coincidence, formality]* simple *before n* ◆ **a ~ mortal** un(e) simple mortel(le) ◆ **he's a ~ clerk** c'est un simple employé de bureau ◆ **I was a ~ child when I married him** je n'étais qu'une enfant quand je l'ai épousé ◆ **by a ~ chance** par pur hasard ◆ **he's a ~ nobody** c'est un moins que rien ◆ **a ~ nothing** trois fois rien ◆ **they quarrelled over a ~ nothing** ils se sont disputés pour une vétille ◆ **his voice was the merest whisper** sa voix n'était qu'un murmure ◆ **it's a ~ kilometre away** ce n'est qu'à un kilomètre (de distance) ◆ **in a ~ 17 minutes** en 17 minutes seulement ◆ **a ~ $45** 45 dollars seulement

merely /ˈmɪəlɪ/ ADV simplement ◆ **I ~ said that she was coming** j'ai tout simplement dit *or* je n'ai fait que dire qu'elle arrivait ◆ **he ~ nodded** il se contenta de faire un signe de tête ◆ **he's ~ a good friend** c'est un ami, c'est tout ◆ **I did it ~ to please her** je ne l'ai fait que pour lui faire plaisir ◆ **~ to look at him makes me shiver** rien que de le regarder me fait frissonner ◆ **it's ~ a formality** c'est une simple formalité ◆ **it's not ~ dirty, it's filthy** ce n'est pas seulement sale, c'est dégoûtant

meretricious /ˌmerɪˈtrɪʃəs/ ADJ *(frm)* *[charm, attraction]* factice ; *[style]* ampoulé

merge /mɜːdʒ/ VI 1 *[colours, shapes]* se mêler *(into, with* à), se fondre *(into, with* dans) ; *[sounds]* se mêler *(into, with* à), se perdre *(into, with* dans) ; *[roads]* se rencontrer *(with* avec), se joindre *(with* à) ; *[river]* confluer *(with* avec) ◆ **to ~ into** *(also fig)* *[+ darkness, background etc]* se fondre dans ◆ **the colours ~d into one another** les couleurs se mélangeaient 2 *(Comm, Fin)* fusionner *(with* avec) VT 1 unifier ◆ **the states were ~d (into one) in 1976** ces États se sont unifiés en 1976, l'unification de ces États s'est réalisée en 1976 2 *(Comm, Fin, Comput)* fusionner ◆ **the firms were ~d** les entreprises ont fusionné ◆ **they decided to ~ the companies into a single unit** ils décidèrent de fusionner les deux sociétés

merger /ˈmɜːdʒəʳ/ N *(Comm, Fin)* fusion *f*, fusionnement *m*

meridian /məˈrɪdɪən/ N *(Astron, Geog)* méridien *m* ; *(fig)* apogée *m*, zénith *m* ADJ méridien

meridional /məˈrɪdɪənl/ ADJ méridional N *(= person)* méridional(e) *m(f)*

meringue /məˈræŋ/ N meringue *f*

merino /məˈriːnəʊ/ N mérinos *m*

merit /ˈmerɪt/ LANGUAGE IN USE 13

N mérite *m*, valeur *f* ◆ **people of ~** gens *mpl* de valeur *or* de mérite ◆ **a work of great ~** un travail de grande valeur ◆ **the great ~ of this scheme** le grand mérite de ce projet ◆ **there is little ~ in continuing with this policy** il n'y a pas grand intérêt à poursuivre cette politique ◆ **he sees little ~ in ...** il ne voit pas vraiment l'intérêt de ... ◆ **to treat sb according to his ~s** traiter qn selon ses mérites ◆ **to judge sth on its own ~s** juger qch en fonction de ses mérites ◆ **to judge sb on their own ~s** juger qn selon ses mérites ◆ **to take** *or* **judge each case on its own ~s** décider au cas par cas ◆ **whatever its ~s, their work will never be used** quelle que soit leur validité, leurs travaux ne seront jamais utilisés ◆ **certificate of ~** prix *m*

◆ **the merits of sth** *(= good points)* les avantages de qch ◆ **they have been persuaded of the ~s of these proposals** ils sont convaincus des avantages de ces propositions ◆ **they went into the ~s of the new plan** ils ont discuté le pour et le contre de ce nouveau projet

VT mériter ◆ **this ~s fuller discussion** ceci mérite plus ample discussion

COMP **merit list** N *(Scol etc)* tableau *m* d'honneur ◆ **to get one's name on the ~ list** être inscrit au tableau d'honneur
merit system N *(US Admin)* système *m* de recrutement et de promotion par voie de concours

meritocracy /ˌmerɪˈtɒkrəsɪ/ N méritocratie *f*

meritocrat /ˈmerɪtəʊkræt/ N membre *m* de la méritocratie

meritocratic /ˌmerɪtəʊˈkrætɪk/ ADJ méritocratique

meritorious /ˌmerɪˈtɔːrɪəs/ ADJ *(frm) [performance, victory, work, deed]* méritoire ; *[person]* méritant ◆ **for ~ conduct** pour conduite exemplaire

meritoriously /ˌmerɪˈtɔːrɪəslɪ/ ADV d'une façon méritoire

Merlin /ˈmɜːlɪn/ N *(Myth)* Merlin *m* l'Enchanteur

merlin /ˈmɜːlɪn/ N *(= bird)* émerillon *m*

mermaid /ˈmɜːmeɪd/ N *(Myth)* sirène *f*

merman /ˈmɜːmæn/ N (pl **-men**) *(Myth)* triton *m*

Merovingian /ˌmerəʊˈvɪndʒɪən/ ADJ mérovingien N Mérovingien(ne) *m(f)*

merrie † /ˈmerɪ/ ADJ ◆ **Merrie England** l'Angleterre *f* du bon vieux temps

merrily /ˈmerɪlɪ/ ADV 1 *(= jovially) [laugh, say]* gaiement, joyeusement 2 *(= cheeringly) [burn, boil, bubble, ring]* gaiement 3 *(* = obliviously, inconsiderately)* gaiement ◆ **I was chattering away ~, without realizing that ...** je bavardais gaiement sans me rendre compte que ...

merriment /ˈmerɪmənt/ N *(NonC)* gaieté *or* gaîté *f*, joie *f* ; *(= laughter)* hilarité *f* ◆ **this remark caused a lot of ~** cette remarque a provoqué l'hilarité générale

merry /ˈmerɪ/ LANGUAGE IN USE 23.2 ADJ 1 *(= cheerful) [laughter, mood, face, sound, tune]* joyeux ; *[eyes]* rieur ◆ **Merry Christmas** Joyeux Noël ◆ **a Merry Christmas to all our readers** Joyeux Noël à tous nos lecteurs ◆ **Robin Hood and his ~ men** Robin des Bois et ses joyeux compagnons ◆ **to make ~** *(liter)* se divertir ; → **May, more** 2 *(pej, iro)* ◆ **to go on one's ~ way** poursuivre son petit bonhomme de chemin ◆ **to lead sb a ~ dance** † *(Brit)* donner du fil à retordre à qn ; → **hell** 3 *(Brit *: euph = tipsy)* éméché*, gris* ◆ **to get ~** être éméché* COMP **merry-go-round** N *(in fairground)* manège *m* ; *(fig)* tourbillon *m*

merrymaker /ˈmerɪmeɪkəʳ/ N fêtard *m*

merrymaking /ˈmerɪmeɪkɪŋ/ N *(NonC)* réjouissances *fpl*

mesa /ˈmeɪsə/ N *(US)* mesa *f*, plateau *m*

mescaline /ˈmeskəlɪn/ N mescaline *f*

mesh /meʃ/ N 1 *[of net, sieve etc] (= space)* maille *f* ; *(fig = network)* réseau *m*, rets *mpl* ; *(= snare)* rets *mpl*, filets *mpl* ◆ **netting with a 5cm ~** filet *m* à mailles de 5 cm ◆ **~es** *(= threads)* mailles *fpl* ; *[of spider's web]* fils *mpl*, toile *f* ◆ **a ~ of lies** un tissu de mensonges ◆ **caught in the ~es of the law** pris dans les mailles de la justice ◆ **the ~(es) of intrigue** le réseau d'intrigues ; → **micromesh stockings**
2 *(NonC = fabric)* tissu *m* à mailles ◆ **nylon ~** tulle *m* de nylon ® ◆ **wire ~** treillis *m*, grillage *m*
3 *[of gears etc]* engrenage *m* ◆ **in ~** en prise
VI *[wheels, gears]* s'engrener ; *[dates, plans]* concorder, cadrer ; *(fig) [two people, their characters etc]* avoir des affinités
VT *[+ fish etc]* prendre au filet
COMP **mesh bag** N filet *m* (à provisions)
mesh stockings NPL *(non-run)* bas *mpl* indémaillables ; *(in cabaret, circus etc)* bas *mpl* résille

meshug(g)a, meshuggah /mɪˈʃʊgə/ ADJ *(US)* cinglé*, maboul*

mesmeric /mezˈmerɪk/ ADJ *(lit, fig)* hypnotique, magnétique

mesmerism /ˈmezmərɪzəm/ N mesmérisme *m*

mesmerize /ˈmezməraɪz/ VT *(lit, fig)* hypnotiser, magnétiser ; *[snake]* fasciner ◆ **I was ~d** *(fig)* je ne pouvais pas détourner mon regard, j'étais comme hypnotisé

mesomorph /ˈmesəʊˌmɔːf/ N mésomorphe *mf*

meson /ˈmiːzɒn/ N *(Phys)* méson *m*

Mesopotamia /ˌmesəpəˈteɪmɪə/ N Mésopotamie *f*

Mesozoic /ˌmesəʊˈzəʊɪk/ ADJ, N mésozoïque *m*

mess /mes/ N 1 *(= confusion of objects etc)* pagaille* *f*, pagaïe* *f*, fouillis *m* ; *(= dirt)* saleté *f* ; *(= muddle)* gâchis *m* ◆ **get this ~ cleared up at once!** range-moi ce fouillis tout de suite ! ◆ **the result is a political/legal** *etc* **~** politiquement/juridiquement *etc* on aboutit à un vrai gâchis ◆ **a financial/an administrative ~** une pagaille* financière/administrative ◆ **what a ~ it all is!** quel gâchis ! ◆ **this page is a ~, rewrite it** cette page est un vrai torchon, recopiez-la ◆ **you look a ~, you're a ~** tu n'es pas présentable ◆ **he's a ~** * *(emotionally, psychologically)* il est complètement déboussolé* ; *(US) (= no use)* il n'est bon à rien ◆ **to get (o.s.) out of a ~** se sortir d'un mauvais pas, se dépatouiller* ◆ **to get sb out of a ~** sortir qn d'un mauvais pas

◆ **in a mess** ◆ **the house was in a terrible ~** *(= untidy)* la maison était dans un désordre épouvantable ; *(= dirty)* la maison était d'une saleté épouvantable ; *(after bombing etc)* la maison était dans un état épouvantable ◆ **the toys were in a ~** les jouets étaient en pagaille* *or* en désordre ◆ **they left everything in a ~** ils ont tout laissé en désordre ◆ **his face was in a dreadful ~** *(after fight, accident etc)* il avait le visage dans un état épouvantable ◆ **to be/get (o.s.) in a ~** *(fig = difficulties)* être/se mettre dans de beaux draps ◆ **his life is in a ~** sa vie est un vrai gâchis

◆ **to make a mess** ◆ **she made a ~ of her new skirt** *(= dirtied it)* elle a sali *or* tout taché sa jupe neuve ; *(= damaged it)* elle a déchiré sa jupe neuve ◆ **the dog has made a ~ of the flower-beds** le chien a saccagé les plates-bandes ◆ **your boots have made an awful ~ on the carpet** tu as fait des saletés sur le tapis avec tes bottes ◆ **the cat has made a ~ in the kitchen** *(euph)* le chat a fait des saletés dans la cuisine ◆ **what a ~ they've made!** ils ont mis une de ces pagailles !* ◆ **to make a ~ of one's life/career** gâcher sa vie/sa carrière ◆ **to make a ~ of things*** tout bousiller*, tout gâcher
2 *(Mil) (= place)* mess *m*, cantine *f* ; *(Naut)* carré *m*, gamelle *f* ; *(= food)* ordinaire *m*, gamelle *f* ; *(= members collectively)* mess *m*
3 *(= animal food)* pâtée *f* ; *(†† = dish)* mets *m*, plat *m* ◆ **a ~ of pottage** *(Bible)* un plat de lentilles
VT salir, souiller
VI *(Mil etc)* manger au mess, manger en commun *(with* avec) ◆ **no ~ing!*** *(fig)* sans blague !*
COMP **mess deck** N *(Naut)* poste *m* d'équipage
mess dress, mess gear* *(Brit)* N *(Mil etc)* tenue *f* de soirée
mess hall N *(US)* ⇒ **mess room**
mess jacket N *(Mil etc)* veston *m* de tenue de soirée ; *[of civilian waiter]* veste *f* courte
mess kit N *(US)* gamelle *f* ; *(Brit *)* tenue *f* de soirée
mess mate N *(Mil)* camarade *mf* de mess
mess room N *(Mil)* mess *m* ; *(Naut)* carré *m*
mess tin N *(Mil)* gamelle *f*
mess-up* N gâchis *m*

► **mess about*** VI 1 *(= play in water, mud)* patouiller* ; *(= act the fool)* faire l'imbécile *or* le fou ◆ **we were ~ing about playing with paint** on faisait les fous en jouant avec de la peinture ◆ **stop ~ing about!** arrête tes bêtises ! ◆ **I love ~ing about in boats** *(= have fun)* j'aime (m'amuser à) faire du bateau
2 *(= waste time)* gaspiller *or* perdre son temps ; *(= dawdle)* lambiner, lanterner ◆ **he was ~ing about with his friends** il traînait avec ses copains ◆ **what were you doing? – just ~ing about** que faisais-tu ? – rien de particulier *or* de spécial
VT SEP *(Brit = disturb, upset) [+ person]* créer des complications à, embêter* ; *[+ plans, arrangements]* chambarder*, chambouler* ◆ **stop ~ing me about** arrête de me traiter par-dessus la jambe* comme ça

► **mess about with*** VT FUS 1 *(= fiddle with) [+ pen etc]* s'amuser avec, tripoter
2 *(= amuse o.s. with)* **they were ~ing about with a ball** ils s'amusaient à taper dans un ballon
3 ⇒ **mess about vt sep**
4 *(sexually)* peloter*

► **mess around** ⇒ **mess about**

► **mess around with*** VT FUS ⇒ **mess about with**

► **mess together** VI *(Mil etc)* manger ensemble au mess ; *(* gen)* faire popote* ensemble

► **mess up** VT SEP *[+ clothes]* salir, gâcher ; *[+ room]* mettre en désordre, semer la pagaille dans* ; *[+ hair]* ébouriffer ; *[+ task, situation, plans, life etc]* gâcher ◆ **to ~ sb's hair up** décoiffer qn ◆ **that's ~ed everything up!** ça a tout gâché ! ◆ **to ~ sb up*** *(fig) (psychologically)* perturber *or* traumatiser qn ; *(US = beat up)* abîmer le portrait de qn*
N ◆ **mess-up*** → **mess**

► **mess with*** VT FUS *[+ people]* se frotter à* ; *[+ drugs, drinks etc]* toucher à* ◆ **if you ~ with me ...** *(threatening)* si tu m'embêtes ...

message /ˈmesɪdʒ/ LANGUAGE IN USE 27.3
N 1 *(= communication)* message *m* ◆ **telephone ~** message *m* téléphonique ◆ **to leave a ~ (for sb)** laisser un message (pour *or* à qn) ◆ **would you give him this ~?** voudriez-vous lui transmettre ce message ? ◆ **I'll give him the ~** je lui ferai la commission ◆ **to send sb a ~** envoyer un message à qn ◆ **the President's ~ to Congress** le message du Président au Congrès ◆ **to send the wrong ~** être trompeur *or* ambigu ◆ **the jury's verdict sends out the wrong ~ to the community** le verdict du jury est susceptible d'être mal interprété par le public
2 *(= meaning) [of prophet, writer, artist, book etc]* message *m* ◆ **to get the ~*** comprendre, saisir* ◆ **to get the** *or* **one's ~ across to sb** se faire comprendre de qn ◆ **I get the ~!*** (c'est) compris !, je pige !*
3 *(Scot = errand)* course *f*, commission *f* ◆ **to go on a ~ for sb** faire une course pour qn ◆ **to go for** *or* **get the ~s** faire les courses *or* les commissions
VI *(= send text messages)* envoyer des télémessages
COMP **message bag** N *(Scot)* sac *m* à provisions
message board N *(Comput)* forum *m*
message-boy N garçon *m* de courses
message switching N *(Comput)* commutation *f* des messages

messaging /ˈmesɪdʒɪŋ/ N *(Comput)* messagerie *f*

messenger /ˈmesɪndʒəʳ/ N messager *m*, -ère *f* ; *(in office)* commissionnaire *m*, coursier *m* ; *(in hotel etc)* chasseur *m*, coursier *m* ; *(Post)* (petit) télégraphiste *m* ; → **king** COMP **messenger boy** N garçon *m* de courses

Messiah /mɪˈsaɪə/ N Messie *m*

messiah /mɪˈsaɪə/ N messie *m*

messianic /ˌmesɪˈænɪk/ ADJ messianique

messily /ˈmesɪlɪ/ ADV *[play, eat, work]* salement, de manière peu soignée ◆ **my parents divorced very** ~ le divorce de mes parents a été très pénible *or* difficile

Messrs /ˈmesəz/ NPL *(Brit)* (abbrev of **Messieurs**) MM., messieurs *mpl* ◆ ~ **Smith & Co** MM. Smith & Cie

messy /ˈmesɪ/ ADJ 1 *(= producing mess) [person]* désordonné ; *[activity, job]* salissant ◆ **to be** ~ *[animal]* salir ◆ **to be a** ~ **eater** manger salement 2 *(= dirty) [nappy]* sale 3 *(= untidy) [place, room, desk]* en désordre ; *[clothes]* négligé ; *[hair]* en bataille ; *[work, job]* bâclé ; *[handwriting]* peu soigné 4 *(= complicated, awkward) [situation, business, compromise]* embrouillé ; *[process]* délicat ; *[dispute, relationship, love affair]* compliqué ◆ **he had been through a** ~ **divorce** son divorce a été difficile

mestizo /mɪˈstiːzəʊ/ N (pl **mestizos** *or* **mestizoes**) *(US)* métis(se) *m(f) (né d'un parent espagnol ou portugais et d'un parent indien)*

Met * /met/ N ◆ **the** ~ 1 *(US)* (abbrev of **Metropolitan Opera Company**) *principal opéra de New York* 2 *(US)* (abbrev of **Metropolitan Museum of Art**) *principal musée d'art de New York* 3 *(Brit)* (abbrev of **Metropolitan Police**) → **metropolitan**

met¹ /met/ VB pt, ptp of **meet¹**

met² /met/ ADJ *(Brit)* (abbrev of **meteorological**) météo *inv*

COMP **the Met Office** N *(Brit)* ≃ la Météorologie nationale
met report N bulletin *m* (de la) météo

metabolic /ˌmetəˈbɒlɪk/ ADJ *[process, activity]* métabolique ; *[disorder]* du métabolisme COMP
metabolic rate N métabolisme *m* basal *or* de base

metabolically /ˌmetəˈbɒlɪklɪ/ ADV métaboliquement

metabolism /meˈtæbəlɪzəm/ N métabolisme *m*

metabolize /meˈtæbəlaɪz/ VT métaboliser

metacarpal /ˌmetəˈkɑːpl/ ADJ, N métacarpien *m*

metacarpus /ˌmetəˈkɑːpəs/ N (pl **metacarpi** /ˌmetəˈkɑːpaɪ/) métacarpe *m*

metal /ˈmetl/ N 1 *(Chem, Miner)* métal *m* 2 *(Brit) (for road)* empierrement *m*, cailloutis *m* ; *(for railway)* ballast *m* 3 ⇒ **mettle** VT 1 *(= cover with metal)* métalliser 2 *(Brit) [+ road]* empierrer, caillouter

COMP de métal, en métal
metal detector N détecteur *m* de métaux
metal fatigue N fatigue *f* du métal
metal polish N produit *m* d'entretien *(pour métaux)*

metalanguage /ˈmetəlæŋgwɪdʒ/ N métalangue *f*, métalangage *m*

metalinguistic /ˌmetəlɪŋˈgwɪstɪk/ ADJ métalinguistique

metalinguistics /ˌmetəlɪŋˈgwɪstɪks/ N *(NonC)* métalinguistique *f*

metallic /mɪˈtælɪk/ ADJ *[object, element, mineral, sound, colour, taste]* métallique ; *[paint, finish]* métallisé ; *[dish]* en métal ◆ **a** ~ **blue Ford** une Ford bleu métallisé

metallurgic(al) /ˌmetəˈlɜːdʒɪk(əl)/ ADJ métallurgique

metallurgist /meˈtælədʒɪst/ N métallurgiste *m*

metallurgy /meˈtælədʒɪ/ N métallurgie *f*

metalwork /ˈmetlwɜːk/ N *(NonC)* 1 *(= structure, articles)* ferronnerie *f* ; *[of car]* carrosserie *f* 2 *(= craft)* (also **metalworking**) travail *m* des métaux 3 *(Scol)* travail *m* des métaux

metalworker /ˈmetlwɜːkəʳ/ N ferronnier *m* ; *(in foundry)* (ouvrier *m*) métallurgiste *m*

metamorphic /ˌmetəˈmɔːfɪk/ ADJ métamorphique

metamorphism /ˌmetəˈmɔːfɪzəm/ N 1 *(Geol)* métamorphisme *m* 2 *(= metamorphosis)* métamorphose *f*

metamorphose /ˌmetəˈmɔːfəʊz/ VT métamorphoser, transformer *(into* en) VI se métamorphoser *(into* en)

metamorphosis /ˌmetəˈmɔːfəsɪs/ N (pl **metamorphoses** /ˌmetəˈmɔːfəˌsiːz/) métamorphose *f*

metamorphous /ˌmetəˈmɔːfəs/ ADJ ⇒ **metamorphic**

metaphor /ˈmetəfəʳ/ N métaphore *f* ; → **mix, mixed**

metaphorical /ˌmetəˈfɒrɪkəl/ ADJ *[language]* métaphorique ◆ **to talk** *or* **speak in** ~ **terms** parler par métaphores ◆ **to express sth in** ~ **terms** exprimer qch en termes métaphoriques

metaphorically /ˌmetəˈfɒrɪkəlɪ/ ADV *[speak]* métaphoriquement ◆ ~ **speaking** métaphoriquement

metaphysical /ˌmetəˈfɪzɪkəl/ ADJ métaphysique ◆ **the Metaphysical poets** les poètes *mpl* métaphysiques

metaphysics /ˌmetəˈfɪzɪks/ N *(NonC)* métaphysique *f*

metastasis /mɪˈtæstəsɪs/ N (pl **metastases** /mɪˈtæstəˌsiːz/) métastase *f*

metatarsal /ˌmetəˈtɑːsl/ ADJ, N métatarsien *m*

metatarsus /ˌmetəˈtɑːsəs/ N (pl **metatarsi** /ˌmetəˈtɑːsaɪ/) métatarse *m*

metathesis /meˈtæθəsɪs/ N (pl **metatheses** /meˈtæθəˌsiːz/) métathèse *f*

metazoan /ˌmetəˈzəʊən/ N, ADJ métazoaire *m*

mete /miːt/ VT ◆ **to** ~ **out** *[+ punishment]* infliger, donner ; *[+ reward]* décerner ◆ **to** ~ **out justice** rendre la justice

meteor /ˈmiːtɪəʳ/ N météore *m*

COMP **meteor crater** N cratère *m* météorique
meteor shower N averse *f* météorique

meteoric /ˌmiːtɪˈɒrɪk/ ADJ 1 *(= rapid) [career]* fulgurant ◆ **his** ~ **rise to power/to fame** sa fulgurante ascension au pouvoir/à la célébrité 2 *(Astron) [dust, impact]* météorique

meteorite /ˈmiːtɪəraɪt/ N météorite *m or f*

meteorological /ˌmiːtɪərəˈlɒdʒɪkəl/ ADJ *[conditions, data, station, centre]* météorologique COMP
the Meteorological Office N *office météorologique britannique*, ≃ la Météorologie nationale

meteorologically /ˌmiːtɪərəˈlɒdʒɪklɪ/ ADV météorologiquement

meteorologist /ˌmiːtɪəˈrɒlədʒɪst/ N météorologiste *mf*, météorologue *mf*

meteorology /ˌmiːtɪəˈrɒlədʒɪ/ N météorologie *f*

meter /ˈmiːtəʳ/ N 1 *(gen = measuring device)* compteur *m* ◆ **electricity/gas/water** ~ compteur *m* d'électricité/à gaz/à eau ◆ **to turn water/gas/electricity off at the** ~ fermer l'eau/le gaz/l'électricité au compteur ; → **light¹** 2 (also **parking meter**) parcmètre *m* 3 *(US)* ⇒ **metre**

COMP **meter maid** * N contractuelle *f*
meter reader N releveur *m* de compteurs

meterage /ˈmiːtərɪdʒ/ N métrage *m*

methadone /ˈmeθəˌdəʊn/ N méthadone *f*

methamphetamine /ˌmeθæmˈfetəmiːn/ N méthamphétamine *f*

methane /ˈmiːθeɪn/ N (also **methane gas**) méthane *m*

methanol /ˈmeθənɒl/ N méthanol *m*

methinks /mɪˈθɪŋks/ (pret **methought**) VB († † *or hum*) ce me semble

method /ˈmeθəd/ N 1 *(NonC = orderliness)* méthode *f*, ordre *m* ◆ **lack of** ~ manque *m* de méthode ◆ **there's** ~ **in his madness** il n'est pas si fou qu'il en a l'air 2 *(= manner, fashion)* méthode *f* ◆ **his** ~ **of working** sa méthode de travail ◆ **there are several** ~**s of doing this** il a plusieurs méthodes pour faire cela ◆ ~ **of assessment** *(Scol etc)* modalités *fpl* de contrôle ◆ **teaching** ~**s** la didactique 3 *(Cine, Theat)* **the Method** le système *or* la méthode de Stanislavski

COMP **method acting** N *(Cine, Theat)* système *m or* méthode *f* de Stanislavski
method actor, method actress N *(Cine, Theat)* adepte *mf* du système *or* de la méthode de Stanislavski

methodical /mɪˈθɒdɪkəl/ ADJ méthodique

methodically /mɪˈθɒdɪkəlɪ/ ADV méthodiquement

Methodism /ˈmeθədɪzəm/ N méthodisme *m*

Methodist /ˈmeθədɪst/ ADJ, N méthodiste *mf*

methodological /ˌmeθədəˈlɒdʒɪkəl/ ADJ méthodologique

methodologically /ˌmeθədəˈlɒdɪkəlɪ/ ADV méthodologiquement

methodology /ˌmeθəˈdɒlədʒɪ/ N méthodologie *f*

methought † † /mɪˈθɔːt/ VB pret of **methinks**

meths * /meθs/ *(Brit)* N abbrev of **methylated spirit(s)** COMP **meths drinker** N alcoolo * *mf (qui se soûle à l'alcool à brûler)*

Methuselah /məˈθuːzələ/ N *(Bible)* Mathusalem *m* ◆ **he's as old as** ~ il est vieux comme Mathusalem

methyl /ˈmeθɪl/ N méthyle *m* ◆ ~ **acetate/bromide/chloride** acétate *m*/bromure *m*/chlorure *m* de méthyle

methylated spirit(s) /ˈmeθɪleɪtɪdˈspɪrɪt(s)/ N(PL) alcool *m* à brûler *or* dénaturé

methylene /ˈmeθɪliːn/ N méthylène *m*

meticulous /mɪˈtɪkjʊləs/ ADJ méticuleux ◆ **to be** ~ **about sth** apporter un soin méticuleux à qch ◆ ~ **attention to detail** souci *m* minutieux du détail

meticulously /mɪˈtɪkjʊləslɪ/ ADV méticuleusement ◆ **to be** ~ **clean** être d'une propreté méticuleuse ◆ ~ **precise** d'une exactitude scrupuleuse

meticulousness /mɪˈtɪkjʊləsnɪs/ N soin *m* méticuleux

métier /ˈmeɪtɪeɪ/ N 1 *(= calling)* métier *m* 2 *(= strong point)* point *m* fort

metonymy /mɪˈtɒnɪmɪ/ N métonymie *f*

metre /ˈmiːtəʳ/ N *(Measure, Poetry)* mètre *m* ; *(Mus)* mesure *f*

metric /ˈmetrɪk/ ADJ *[measurement, weights and measures]* du système métrique ; *[equivalent, size]* dans le système métrique ◆ **Britain went** ~ * **in 1971** la Grande-Bretagne a adopté le système métrique en 1971

COMP **the metric system** N le système métrique
metric ton, metric tonne N tonne *f*

metrical /ˈmetrɪkəl/ ADJ *(Literat, Mus)* métrique COMP **metrical psalm** N psaume *m* versifié

metricate /ˈmetrɪˌkeɪt/ VT convertir au système métrique

metrication /ˌmetrɪˈkeɪʃən/ N conversion *f* au *or* adoption *f* du système métrique

metrics /ˈmetrɪks/ N *(NonC)* métrique *f*

metro /ˈmetrəʊ/ N métro *m*

metrological /ˌmetrəˈlɒdʒɪkəl/ ADJ métrologique

metrology /mɪˈtrɒlədʒɪ/ N métrologie *f*

metronome /ˈmetrənəʊm/ N métronome *m*

metronomic /ˌmetrəˈnɒmɪk/ ADJ métronomique

metropolis /mɪˈtrɒpəlɪs/ N (pl **metropolises**) métropole *f (ville)*

metropolitan /ˌmetrəˈpɒlɪtən/ **ADJ** *(Geog, Rel)* métropolitain **N** *(Rel)* métropolitain *m* ; *(in Orthodox Church)* métropolite *m* **COMP** **the Metropolitan Police** **N** *(Brit)* la police de Londres

metrosexual /ˌmetrəˈsɛksjʊəl/ **ADJ, N** métrosexuel(le) *m(f)*

mettle /ˈmetl/ **N** *[of person]* courage *m* ; *[of horse]* fougue *f* ◆ **to be on one's ~** être prêt à donner le meilleur de soi-même ◆ **to prove** *or* **show one's ~** montrer de quoi on est capable, faire ses preuves ◆ **to test sb's ~** mettre qn à l'épreuve ◆ **to be a test of sb's ~** être un test pour qn

mettlesome /ˈmetlsəm/ **ADJ** ardent, fougueux

mew /mjuː/ **N** *[of cat etc]* (also **mewing**) miaulement *m* **VI** miauler

mewl /mjuːl/ **VI** vagir

mews /mjuːz/ *(Brit)* **N** [1] *(= small street)* ruelle *f*, venelle *f* [2] *(= stables)* écuries *fpl* **COMP** **mews flat** **N** *petit appartement aménagé dans une ancienne écurie, remise etc*

Mexican /ˈmeksɪkən/ **ADJ** *(gen)* mexicain ; *[ambassador, embassy]* du Mexique **N** Mexicain(e) *m(f)*
COMP **Mexican jumping bean** **N** fève *f* sauteuse
Mexican standoff **N** *(US fig)* impasse *f* ; *(Hist)* **the Mexican War** la guerre du Mexique
Mexican wave **N** hola *f (vague déferlante produite dans un stade par les spectateurs qui se lèvent tour à tour)*

Mexico /ˈmeksɪkəʊ/ **N** Mexique *m* ◆ **in ~** au Mexique **COMP** **Mexico City** **N** Mexico

mezcaline /ˈmezkəlɪn/ **N** ⇒ **mescaline**

mezzanine /ˈmezəniːn/ **N** [1] *(= floor)* entresol *m* [2] *(Theat) (Brit)* dessous *m* de scène ; *(US)* mezzanine *f*, corbeille *f*

mezzo(-soprano) /ˈmetsəʊ(səˈprɑːnəʊ)/ **N** *(= voice)* mezzo-soprano *m* ; *(= singer)* mezzo (-soprano) *f*

mezzotint /ˈmetsəʊtɪnt/ **N** mezzo-tinto *m inv*

MF /emˈef/ **N** (abbrev of **medium frequency**) OM

MFA /ˌemefˈeɪ/ **N** *(US Univ)* (abbrev of **Master of Fine Arts**) *diplôme des beaux-arts*

MFH /ˌemefˈeɪtʃ/ **N** *(Brit)* (abbrev of **Master of Foxhounds**) → **master**

mfrs. *(Comm)* (abbrev of **manufacturers**) → **manufacturer**

mg **N** (abbrev of **milligram(s)**) mg

Mgr abbrev of **Monseigneur** *or* **Monsignor**

mgr abbrev of **manager**

MHR /ˌemeɪtʃˈɑːʳ/ **N** *(in US)* (abbrev of **Member of the House of Representatives**) ≈ député *m*

MHz *(Rad etc)* (abbrev of **megahertz**) MHz

MI **N** [1] abbrev of **Michigan** [2] (abbrev of **machine intelligence**) IA *f*

mi /miː/ **N** *(Mus)* mi *m*

MI5 /ˌemaɪˈfaɪv/ **N** *(Brit)* (abbrev of **Military Intelligence 5**) *service britannique chargé de la surveillance du territoire*, ≈ DST *f*

MI6 /ˌemaɪˈsɪks/ **N** *(Brit)* (abbrev of **Military Intelligence 6**) *services britanniques d'espionnage et de contre-espionnage*, ≈ DGSE *f*

MIA /ˌemaɪˈeɪ/ *(Mil)* (abbrev of **missing in action**) → **missing**

miaow /miːˈaʊ/ **N** miaulement *m*, miaou *m* ◆ **~!** miaou ! **VI** miauler

miasma /mɪˈæzmə/ **N** (pl **miasmas** *or* **miasmata** /mɪˈæzmətə/) miasme *m*

mica /ˈmaɪkə/ **N** mica *m* **COMP** **mica-schist** **N** micaschiste *m*

mice /maɪs/ **NPL** of **mouse**

Mich. abbrev of **Michigan**

Michael /ˈmaɪkl/ **N** Michel *m*

Michaelmas /ˈmɪklməs/ **N** (also **Michaelmas Day**) la Saint-Michel
COMP **Michaelmas daisy** **N** aster *m* d'automne
Michaelmas term **N** *(Brit Jur, Univ)* trimestre *m* d'automne

Michelangelo /ˌmaɪkəlˈændʒɪləʊ/ **N** Michel-Ange *m*

Michigan /ˈmɪʃɪgən/ **N** Michigan *m* ◆ **in ~** dans le Michigan ◆ **Lake ~** le lac Michigan

Mick /mɪk/ **N** [1] dim of **Michael** [2] (*✻ pej*) Irlandais *m* [3] *(Brit)* **to take the ~** * se moquer ◆ **to take the ~ out of sb** * se payer la tête de qn

Mickey /ˈmɪkɪ/ **N** dim of **Michael**
COMP **Mickey Finn** **N** boisson *f* droguée
Mickey Mouse **N** *(= cartoon character)* Mickey *m* **ADJ** (* *pej:* also **mickey-mouse**) *[car, penknife, regulations]* à la noix * ; *[job, courses]* pas sérieux, enfantin ; *[degree]* sans valeur, à la noix *

mickey /ˈmɪkɪ/ **N** *(Brit)* ◆ **to take the ~ * out of sb** se payer la tête de qn ◆ **he's always taking the ~ *** il n'arrête pas de se payer la tête des gens
COMP **mickey finn** **N** ⇒ **Mickey Finn** ; → **Mickey**
mickey-mouse **ADJ** → **Mickey**

micra /ˈmaɪkrə/ **NPL** of **micron**

micro * /ˈmaɪkrəʊ/ **N** abbrev of **microcomputer**

microanalysis /ˌmaɪkrəʊəˈnælɪsɪs/ **N** microanalyse *f*

microanalytical /ˌmaɪkrəʊˌænəˈlɪtɪkl/ **ADJ** microanalytique

microbe /ˈmaɪkrəʊb/ **N** microbe *m*

microbial /maɪˈkrəʊbɪəl/, **microbian** /maɪˈkrəʊbɪən/, **microbic** /maɪˈkrəʊbɪk/ **ADJ** microbien

microbiological /ˌmaɪkrəʊbaɪəʊˈlɒdʒɪkəl/ **ADJ** microbiologique

microbiologist /ˌmaɪkrəʊbaɪˈɒlədʒɪst/ **N** microbiologiste *mf*

microbiology /ˌmaɪkrəʊbaɪˈɒlədʒɪ/ **N** microbiologie *f*

micro-brewery, microbrewery /ˈmaɪkrəʊbruːərɪ/ **N** microbrasserie *f*

microbus /ˈmaɪkrəʊˌbʌs/ **N** *(US)* microbus *m*

microcapsule /ˈmaɪkrəʊˌkæpsjʊl/ **N** microcapsule *f*

microcassette /ˈmaɪkrəʊkəˈset/ **N** microcassette *f*

microcephalic /ˌmaɪkrəʊsɪˈfælɪk/ **ADJ** microcéphale

microcephaly /ˌmaɪkrəʊˈsefəlɪ/ **N** microcéphalie *f*

microchip /ˈmaɪkrəʊˌtʃɪp/ **N** puce *f* (électronique) **VT** *[+ dog, cat etc]* implanter *or* mettre une micropuce à

microcircuit /ˈmaɪkrəʊˌsɜːkɪt/ **N** microcircuit *m*

microcircuitry /ˈmaɪkrəʊˈsɜːkətrɪ/ **N** microcircuit *m*

microclimate /ˈmaɪkrəʊklaɪmɪt/ **N** microclimat *m*

micrococcus /ˌmaɪkrəʊˈkɒkəs/ **N** microcoque *m*

microcomputer /ˈmaɪkrəʊkəmˈpjuːtəʳ/ **N** micro-ordinateur *m*

microcomputing /ˈmaɪkrəʊkəmˈpjuːtɪŋ/ **N** micro-informatique *f*

microcopy /ˈmaɪkrəʊˌkɒpɪ/ **N** microcopie *f* **VT** microcopier

microcosm /ˈmaɪkrəʊˌkɒzəm/ **N** microcosme *m* ◆ **a ~ of ...** un microcosme de ... ◆ **in ~** en microcosme

microcosmic /ˈmaɪkrəʊˈkɒzmɪk/ **ADJ** microcosmique

microcredit /ˈmaɪkrəʊˌkredɪt/ **N** microcrédit *m*

microcrystal /ˌmaɪkrəʊˈkrɪstəl/ **N** microcristal *m*

microcrystalline /ˈmaɪkrəʊˈkrɪstəˌlaɪn/ **ADJ** microcristallin

microculture /ˈmaɪkrəʊˌkʌltʃəʳ/ **N** microculture *f*

microdissection /ˈmaɪkrəʊdɪˈsekʃən/ **N** microdissection *f*

microdot /ˈmaɪkrəʊˌdɒt/ **N** microcopie *f*

microeconomic /ˈmaɪkrəʊˌiːkəˈnɒmɪk/ **ADJ** microéconomique

microeconomics /ˈmaɪkrəʊˌiːkəˈnɒmɪks/ **N** *(NonC)* microéconomie *f*

microelectrode /ˈmaɪkrəʊɪˈlektrəʊd/ **N** microélectrode *f*

microelectronic /ˈmaɪkrəʊɪlekˈtrɒnɪk/ **ADJ** microélectronique

microelectronically /ˈmaɪkrəʊɪlekˈtrɒnɪklɪ/ **ADV** microélectroniquement

microelectronics /ˈmaɪkrəʊɪlekˈtrɒnɪks/ **N** *(NonC)* microélectronique *f*

microenvironment /ˈmaɪkrəʊɪnˈvaɪərənmənt/ **N** microenvironnement *m*

microfauna /ˈmaɪkrəʊˌfɔːnə/ **N** microfaune *f*

microfibre *(Brit)*, **microfiber** *(US)* /ˈmaɪkrəʊˌfaɪbəʳ/ **N** microfibre *f*

microfiche /ˈmaɪkrəʊˌfiːʃ/ **N** microfiche *f* **COMP** **microfiche reader** **N** microlecteur *m* (pour microfiches)

microfilm /ˈmaɪkrəʊˌfɪlm/ **N** microfilm *m* **VT** microfilmer **COMP** **microfilm reader** **N** microlecteur *m*

microflora /ˈmaɪkrəʊˌflɔːrə/ **N** microflore *f*

microform /ˈmaɪkrəʊˌfɔːm/ **N** microforme *f*

microgram /ˈmaɪkrəʊˌgræm/ **N** microgramme *m*

micrographic /ˌmaɪkrəʊˈgræfɪk/ **ADJ** micrographique

micrographically /ˌmaɪkrəʊˈgræfɪklɪ/ **ADV** micrographiquement

micrographics /ˌmaɪkrəʊˈgræfɪks/ **N** *(NonC)* micrographie *f*

micrography /maɪˈkrɒgrəfɪ/ **N** micrographie *f*

microgravity /ˈmaɪkrəʊˈgrævɪtɪ/ **N** *(Phys)* microgravité *f*

microgroove /ˈmaɪkrəʊˌgruːv/ **N** microsillon *m*

microhabitat /ˈmaɪkrəʊˈhæbɪtæt/ **N** microhabitat *m*

microlight /ˈmaɪkrəʊˌlaɪt/ **N** *(= aircraft)* ULM *m*, ultra-léger-motorisé *m*

microlinguistics /ˈmaɪkrəʊlɪŋˈgwɪstɪks/ **N** *(NonC)* microlinguistique *f*

microlitre, microliter *(US)* /ˈmaɪkrəʊˈliːtəʳ/ **N** microlitre *m*

micromesh stockings /ˈmaɪkrəʊmeʃ ˈstɒkɪŋz/ **NPL** bas *mpl* superfins

micrometeorite /ˈmaɪkrəʊˈmiːtɪəˌraɪt/ **N** micrométéorite *f or m*

micrometeorologist /ˈmaɪkrəʊmiːtɪəˈrɒlədʒɪst/ **N** micrométéorologue *mf*

micrometeorology /ˈmaɪkrəʊmiːtɪəˈrɒlədʒɪ/ **N** micrométéorologie *f*

micrometer /maɪˈkrɒmɪtəʳ/ **N** [1] *(= instrument)* palmer *m* [2] *(US = unit)* micromètre *m*

micrometry /maɪˈkrɒmɪtrɪ/ **N** micrométrie *f*

microminiature /ˌmaɪkrəʊˈmɪnɪtʃəʳ/ **N** microminiature *f*

microminiaturization /ˈmaɪkrəʊˌmɪnɪtʃəraɪˈzeɪʃən/ **N** microminiaturisation *f*

microminiaturize /ˈmaɪkrəʊˈmɪnɪtʃəraɪz/ **VT** microminiaturiser

micron /ˈmaɪkrɒn/ **N** (pl **microns** *or* **micra** /ˈmaɪkrə/) micron *m*

microorganism /ˈmaɪkrəʊˈɔːgəˌnɪzəm/ **N** micro-organisme *m*

microphone /ˈmaɪkrəʊˌfəʊn/ **N** microphone *m*

microphotograph /ˈmaɪkrəʊˈfəʊtəˌgrɑːf/ **N** microphotographie *f* **VT** microphotographier

microphotographic /ˈmaɪkrəʊˌfəʊtəˈgræfɪk/ **ADJ** microphotographique

microphotography /ˈmaɪkrəʊfəˈtɒgrəfɪ/ **N** microphotographie *f*

microphotometer /ˈmaɪkrəʊfəˈtɒmɪtəʳ/ **N** microphotomètre *m*

microphotometric /ˈmaɪkrəʊfəʊtəˈmetrɪk/ **ADJ** microphotométrique

microphotometry /ˈmaɪkrəʊfəˈtɒmɪtrɪ/ **N** microphotométrie *f*

microphysical /ˈmaɪkrəʊˈfɪzɪkəl/ **ADJ** microphysique

microphysicist /ˈmaɪkrəʊˈfɪzɪsɪst/ **N** microphysicien(ne) *m(f)*

microphysics /ˈmaɪkrəʊˌfɪzɪks/ **N** *(NonC)* microphysique *f*

microprism /ˈmaɪkrəʊˌprɪzəm/ **N** microprisme *m*

microprobe /ˈmaɪkrəʊˌprəʊb/ **N** microsonde *f*

microprocessor /ˌmaɪkrəʊˈprəʊsesəʳ/ **N** microprocesseur *m*

microprogram /ˈmaɪkrəʊˌprəʊgræm/ **N** microprogramme *m*

microprogramming /ˈmaɪkrəʊˌprəʊgræmɪŋ/ **N** *(Comput)* microprogrammation *f*

microreader /ˈmaɪkrəʊˌriːdəʳ/ **N** lecteur *m* de microforme, microlecteur *m*

microreproduction /ˈmaɪkrəʊˌriːprəˈdʌkʃən/ **N** microreproduction *f*

micro-scooter /ˈmaɪkrəʊˌskuːtəʳ/ **N** trottinette *f*

microscope /ˈmaɪkrəskəʊp/ **N** microscope *m* ◆ **under the** ~ au microscope

microscopic /ˌmaɪkrəˈskɒpɪk/ **ADJ** 1 *(= visible with, using microscope) [cell, fibre, particle, organism]* microscopique ; *[examination, analysis]* au microscope ◆ ~ **section** coupe *f* histologique 2 *(= minute) [amount]* minuscule ; *[writing]* microscopique, minuscule ◆ **to be ~ in size** être d'une taille microscopique *or* minuscule 3 *(= meticulous)* ◆ **with ~ care** avec un soin minutieux ◆ **with ~ precision** avec une précision minutieuse

microscopical /ˌmaɪkrəˈskɒpɪkəl/ **ADJ** ⇒ **microscopic**

microscopically /ˌmaɪkrəˈskɒpɪkəlɪ/ **ADV** 1 *(= with microscope) [examine, detect]* au microscope 2 *(= minutely)* ◆ ~ **small** microscopique

microscopy /maɪˈkrɒskəpɪ/ **N** microscopie *f*

microsecond /ˈmaɪkrəʊˌsekənd/ **N** microseconde *f*

microstructural /ˌmaɪkrəʊˈstrʌktʃərəl/ **ADJ** microstructurel

microstructure /ˈmaɪkrəʊˌstrʌktʃəʳ/ **N** microstructure *f*

microsurgery /ˈmaɪkrəʊˌsɜːdʒərɪ/ **N** microchirurgie *f*

microsurgical /ˌmaɪkrəʊˈsɜːdʒɪkəl/ **ADJ** microchirurgical

microtransmitter /ˌmaɪkrəʊtrænzˈmɪtəʳ/ **N** microémetteur *m*

microvolt /ˈmaɪkrəʊˌvəʊlt/ **N** microvolt *m*

microwatt /ˈmaɪkrəʊˌwɒt/ **N** microwatt *m*

microwave /ˈmaɪkrəʊˌweɪv/ **N** 1 *(Phys, Rad)* micro-onde *f* 2 *(also* **microwave oven***)* (four *m* à) micro-ondes *m* **VT** faire cuire au micro-ondes **COMP** **microwave spectroscopy** **N** spectroscopie *f* à ondes courtes

microwavable /ˈmaɪkrəʊˌweɪvəbl/ **ADJ** qui peut être cuit au micro-ondes

micturate /ˈmɪktjʊəreɪt/ **VI** uriner

micturition /ˌmɪktjʊəˈrɪʃən/ **N** miction *f*

mid¹ /mɪd/ **PREF** ◆ ~ **May** la mi-mai ◆ **in ~ May** à la mi-mai, au milieu (du mois) de mai ◆ ~ **morning** au milieu de la matinée ◆ ~**-morning coffee break** pause-café *f* du matin ◆ **to take a ~-career break** interrompre sa carrière ◆ **in ~ course** à mi-course ◆ **in ~ ocean** en plein océan, au milieu de l'océan ◆ **in ~ Atlantic** en plein Atlantique, au milieu de l'Atlantique ◆ **a ~-Channel collision** une collision au milieu de la Manche ◆ **in ~ discussion** *etc* au beau milieu de la discussion *etc* ◆ **she's in her ~ forties** elle a dans les quarante-cinq ans ◆ **Mid Wales** *la région centrale du pays de Galles ;* → **midday, midstream, mid-term, mid-Victorian** **COMP** **mid heavyweight** **N** *(Wrestling)* lourd-léger *m*

mid² /mɪd/ **PREP** *(liter)* ⇒ **amid**

midair /ˌmɪdˈɛəʳ/ **N** *(lit)* ◆ **in ~** en plein ciel ◆ **to leave sth in ~** laisser qch en suspens **ADJ** *[collision etc]* en plein ciel

Midas /ˈmaɪdəs/ **N** Midas *m* ◆ **to have the ~ touch** avoir le don de tout transformer en or

mid-Atlantic /ˌmɪdətˈlæntɪk/ **ADJ** *[accent]* mi-britannique, mi-américain

midbrain /ˈmɪdˌbreɪn/ **N** mésencéphale *m*

midday /ˌmɪdˈdeɪ/ **N** midi *m* ◆ **at ~** à midi **COMP** /ˈmɪddeɪ/ *[sun, heat]* de midi

midden /ˈmɪdn/ **N** *(= dunghill)* fumier *m* ; *(= refuse-heap)* tas *m* d'ordures ◆ **this place is (like) a ~!*** c'est une vraie écurie *or* porcherie ici !, on se croirait dans une écurie *or* porcherie ici !

middie /ˈmɪdɪ/ **N** ⇒ **middy**

middle /ˈmɪdl/ **ADJ** *[chair, period etc]* du milieu ◆ **the ~ button of his jacket** le bouton du milieu de sa veste ◆ **she's in her ~ forties** elle a dans les quarante-cinq ans ◆ **the ~ way** *(fig) (= compromise)* la solution intermédiaire ; *(= happy medium)* le juste milieu ◆ **to take the ~ course** choisir le moyen terme *or* la solution intermédiaire ◆ **he was of (less than) ~ height** il était d'une taille (inférieure à la) moyenne ◆ **I'm the ~ child of three** * je suis la deuxième de trois enfants ◆ **the ~ fortnight in May** les deuxième et troisième semaines de mai ; see also **comp**

N 1 milieu *m* ◆ **in the ~ of the morning/year/century** au milieu de la matinée/de l'année/du siècle ◆ **in the ~ of the room** au milieu de la pièce ◆ **in the very ~ (of ...), right in the ~ (of ...)** au beau milieu (de ...) ◆ **to cut sth down the ~** couper qch en deux ◆ **the bullet hit him in the ~ of his chest** le coup de feu l'a atteint en pleine poitrine ◆ **in the ~ of June** au milieu (du mois) de juin, à la mi-juin ◆ **by the ~ of the 19th century** vers le milieu du 19ᵉ siècle ◆ **they are all due to leave by the ~ of next year** ils doivent tous partir d'ici le milieu de l'année prochaine ◆ **it's in the ~ of nowhere*** c'est dans un bled perdu* *or* en pleine brousse* ◆ **a village in the ~ of nowhere*** un petit trou perdu* ◆ **I was in the ~ of my work** j'étais en plein travail ◆ **I'm in the ~ of reading it** je suis justement en train de le lire ; → **split**

2 *(* = waist)* taille *f* ◆ **he wore it round his ~** il le portait à la taille *or* autour de la taille ◆ **in the water up to his ~** dans l'eau jusqu'à la taille

COMP **middle age** **N** ≈ la cinquantaine ◆ **he's reached ~ age** il a la cinquantaine ◆ **during his ~ age** lorsqu'il avait la cinquantaine

middle-aged **ADJ** *[person]* d'âge moyen ; *[outlook, attitude]* vieux jeu *inv* ◆ **the ~-aged** les gens d'âge moyen

the Middle Ages **NPL** le Moyen Âge *or* moyen âge

Middle America **N** les Américains *mpl* moyens

middle C **N** *(Mus)* do *m* du milieu du piano

middle class **N** ◆ **the ~ class(es)** les classes *fpl* moyennes, la classe moyenne

middle-class **ADJ** des classes moyennes

middle distance **N** ◆ **in the ~ distance** *(Art etc)* au second plan ; *(gen)* à mi-distance

middle-distance race **N** *(Sport)* course *f* de demi-fond

middle-distance runner **N** *(Sport)* coureur *m*, -euse *f* de demi-fond

middle ear **N** *(Anat)* oreille *f* moyenne

Middle East **N** Moyen-Orient *m*

Middle Eastern **ADJ** du Moyen-Orient

Middle England **N** *(fig)* l'Angleterre *f* moyenne

Middle English **N** *(= language)* moyen anglais *m*

middle finger **N** majeur *m*, médius *m*

Middle French **N** *(= language)* moyen français *m*

middle-grade manager **N** *(US)* cadre *m* moyen

middle ground **N** terrain *m* d'entente

Middle High German **N** *(= language)* moyen haut allemand *m*

the Middle Kingdom **N** *(Hist) (of Egypt)* le Moyen Empire ; *(of China)* l'Empire *m* du Milieu

middle management **N** *(NonC)* cadres *mpl* moyens ◆ **to be in ~ management** être cadre moyen

middle manager **N** cadre *m* moyen

middle name **N** deuxième prénom *m* ◆ **discretion is my ~ name** la discrétion est ma plus grande vertu *or* qualité

middle-of-the-road **ADJ** *(fig) [politics, approach, group]* modéré, centriste ; *[solution]* moyen, du juste milieu ; *[music]* grand public *inv* ; *[fashion]* passe-partout *inv*

middle-of-the-roader **N** modéré(e) *m(f)*, centriste *mf*, partisan(e) *m(f)* du juste milieu

middle school **N** ≈ premier cycle *m* du secondaire

middle-sized **ADJ** *[tree, building]* de grandeur moyenne ; *[parcel]* de grosseur moyenne ; *[person]* de taille moyenne

middle voice **N** *(Ling)* voix *f* moyenne

the Middle West **N** *(US)* le Middle West, le Midwest

middlebrow* /ˈmɪdlbraʊ/ **N** personne *f* sans grandes prétentions intellectuelles **ADJ** intellectuellement moyen

middleman /ˈmɪdlmæn/ **N** (pl **-men**) *(gen)* intermédiaire *m* ; *(Comm)* intermédiaire *m*, revendeur *m* ◆ **to cut out the ~** se passer d'intermédiaire

middlemost /ˈmɪdlməʊst/ **ADJ** ⇒ **midmost**

middleweight /ˈmɪdlweɪt/ *(Boxing)* **N** (poids *m*) moyen *m* **ADJ** *[championship, boxer]* de poids moyen

middling* /ˈmɪdlɪŋ/ **ADJ** *[performance, result]* moyen, passable ; *[success]* moyen ◆ **business is only ~** les affaires vont comme ci comme ça *or* moyennement ◆ **how are you? – ~** comment ça va ? – couci-couça* ; → **fair¹** **ADV** * assez, moyennement ◆ ~ **well** assez bien ◆ ~ **big** assez grand

Middx abbrev of **Middlesex**

middy* /ˈmɪdɪ/ **N** *(Naut)* (abbrev of **midshipman**) midship* *m*

Mideast /mɪdˈiːst/ *(US)* **N** ◆ **the ~** le Moyen-Orient **ADJ** du Moyen-Orient

midfield /ˈmɪdˌfiːld/ **N** *(Ftbl = place, player)* milieu *m* de terrain

midfielder /mɪdˈfiːldəʳ/ **N** (*Ftbl*) milieu *m* de terrain

midge /mɪdʒ/ **N** moucheron *m*

midget /ˈmɪdʒɪt/ **N** nain(e) *m(f)* ; (*fig*) puce *f* **ADJ** minuscule

MIDI /ˈmɪdɪ/ (abbrev of **musical instrument digital interface**) **N** interface *f* MIDI **ADJ** MIDI *inv*
COMP **MIDI system N** chaîne *f* (hi-fi) midi

midi /ˈmɪdɪ/ **N** (= *skirt*) jupe *f* mi-longue

midland /ˈmɪdlənd/ **N** (*Brit Geog*) ♦ **the Midlands** les Midlands (*les comtés du centre de l'Angleterre*) **COMP** du centre (du pays) **midland regions NPL** régions *fpl* centrales (de l'Angleterre)

midlife /ˌmɪdˈlaɪf/ **ADJ** de la cinquantaine **ADV** autour de la cinquantaine **N** ♦ **in ~** autour de la cinquantaine **COMP** **midlife crisis N** crise *f* de la cinquantaine

midmost /ˈmɪdməʊst/ **ADJ** le plus proche du milieu *or* centre

midnight /ˈmɪdnaɪt/ **N** minuit *m* ♦ **at ~** à minuit
COMP de minuit
midnight blue N bleu *m* nuit
midnight-blue ADJ bleu nuit *inv*
midnight oil N ♦ **to burn the ~ oil** travailler très tard dans la nuit ♦ **his essay smells of the ~ oil*** on dirait qu'il a passé la moitié de la nuit sur sa dissertation
midnight sun N soleil *m* de minuit

midpoint /ˈmɪdpɔɪnt/ **N** milieu *m* ♦ **at ~** à mi-course, à mi-parcours

mid-price /ˌmɪdpraɪs/ **ADJ** milieu de gamme *inv*

mid-range /mɪdˈreɪndʒ/ **ADJ** [*product, car*] de milieu de gamme ; [*hotel, restaurant*] à prix modérés

midriff /ˈmɪdrɪf/ **N** [*of person*] ventre *m* ; [*of dress*] taille *f* ♦ **dress with a bare ~** robe *f* découpée à la taille, robe *f* (deux-pièces) laissant voir le ventre

mid-sentence /ˌmɪdˈsentəns/ **N** ♦ **in ~** au beau milieu d'une phrase

midshipman /ˈmɪdʃɪpmən/ **N** (pl **-men**) (*Naut*) midshipman *m*, ≃ enseigne *m* de vaisseau de deuxième classe, aspirant *m*

midships /ˈmɪdʃɪps/ **ADV** ⇒ **amidships**

midsize /ˈmɪdˌsaɪz/ **ADJ** de taille moyenne

midst /mɪdst/ **N** ♦ **in the ~ of** (= *in the middle of*) au milieu de ; (= *surrounded by*) entouré de ; (= *among*) parmi ; (= *during*) pendant, au milieu de ♦ **we are in the ~ of an economic crisis** nous sommes en pleine crise économique ♦ **he's in the ~ of revising for his exams** il est en plein dans ses révisions ♦ **in our ~** parmi nous ♦ **in the ~ of plenty** (*liter*) dans l'abondance ♦ **in the ~ of life** au milieu de la vie **PREP** (*liter*) ⇒ **amidst**

midstream /ˈmɪdˈstriːm/ **N** ♦ **in ~** (*lit*) au milieu du courant ; (*fig*) en plein milieu ; (*when speaking*) au beau milieu d'une phrase ♦ **to change course in ~** (*fig*) changer d'avis en cours de route *or* à mi-parcours ; (*Sport*) changer de tactique en milieu de match ; → **horse**
ADV ⇒ **in midstream noun**

midsummer /ˈmɪdˌsʌməʳ/ **N** (= *height of summer*) milieu *m or* cœur *m* de l'été ; (= *solstice*) solstice *m* d'été ♦ **in ~** au cœur de l'été, en plein été ♦ **at ~** à la Saint-Jean
COMP [*heat, weather, storm etc*] estival, de plein été
Midsummer Day N la Saint-Jean
midsummer madness N ♦ **it's ~ madness** c'est de la folie pure

midterm /ˈmɪdˈtɜːm/ **N** 1 le milieu du trimestre 2 (also **midterm holiday**) ≃ vacances *fpl* de (la) Toussaint (*or* de février *or* de Pentecôte)
COMP **midterm elections NPL** ≃ élections *fpl* législatives (*intervenant au milieu du mandat présidentiel*)
midterm exams NPL examens *mpl* de milieu de trimestre

mid-term /ˌmɪdˈtɜːm/ **ADJ** ♦ **~ blues** (*Brit Pol*) *désenchantement de l'électorat en milieu de mandat*

midtown /ˈmɪdtaʊn/ (*US*) **N** centre-ville *m* **ADJ** du centre-ville

mid-Victorian /ˈmɪdvɪkˈtɔːrɪən/ **ADJ** (*Brit*) du milieu de l'époque victorienne

midway /ˌmɪdˈweɪ/ **ADJ** [*place*] (situé) à mi-chemin **ADV** [*stop, pause*] à mi-chemin, à mi-route ♦ **~ between** à mi-chemin entre **N** (*US: in fair*) emplacement *m* d'attractions foraines

midweek /ˌmɪdˈwiːk/ **ADJ** [*flight, performance, match*] en milieu de semaine ♦ **~ return (ticket)** (*Rail*) (billet *m*) aller et retour *m* en semaine (*meilleur marché*) **ADV** en milieu de semaine

Midwest /ˌmɪdˈwest/ **N** (*in US*) ♦ **the ~** le Middle West, le Midwest

Midwestern /ˌmɪdˈwestən/ **ADJ** du Middle West, du Midwest

Midwesterner /mɪdˈwestənəʳ/ **N** natif *m*, -ive *f or* habitant(e) *m(f)* du Middle West

midwife /ˈmɪdwaɪf/ **N** (pl **-wives**) sage-femme *f*, maïeuticien *m*

midwifery /ˈmɪdwɪfərɪ/ **N** (*NonC* = *profession*) profession *f* de sage-femme ♦ **she's studying ~** elle fait des études de sage-femme

midwinter /ˌmɪdˈwɪntəʳ/ **N** (= *heart of winter*) milieu *m or* fort *m* de l'hiver ; (= *solstice*) solstice *m* d'hiver ♦ **in ~** au cœur de l'hiver, en plein hiver ♦ **at ~** au solstice d'hiver **COMP** [*cold, snow, temperature*] hivernal, de plein hiver

mien /miːn/ **N** (*frm, liter*) contenance *f*, air *m*, mine *f*

miff* /mɪf/ **N** (= *quarrel*) fâcherie *f* ; (= *sulks*) bouderie *f* **VT** fâcher, mettre en boule* ♦ **to be ~ed about** *or* **at sth** être fâché *or* vexé de qch

might[1] /maɪt/ **LANGUAGE IN USE 15.3**
MODAL AUX VB 1

> When **might** expresses present, past or future possibility, it is often translated by **peut-être**, with the appropriate tense of the French verb.

♦ **you ~ be right** tu as peut-être raison ♦ **he ~ still be alive** il est peut-être encore vivant ♦ **you ~ be making a big mistake** tu es peut-être en train de faire une grosse erreur ♦ **he ~ arrive late** il se peut qu'il arrive *subj* en retard, il arrivera peut-être en retard ♦ **I ~ have left it behind** il se peut que je l'aie oublié, je l'ai peut-être oublié ♦ **~ they have left already?** se peut-il qu'ils soient déjà partis ? ♦ **I heard what ~ have been an explosion** j'ai entendu ce qui était peut-être une explosion ♦ **they ~ not come** ils ne viendront peut-être pas ♦ **you ~ not have heard of it** vous n'en avez peut-être pas entendu parler

> When **might** expresses a future possibility, the conditional of **pouvoir** can also be used.

♦ **the two countries ~ go to war** les deux pays pourraient entrer en guerre ♦ **you ~ regret it later** tu pourrais le regretter plus tard ♦ **I said that he ~ arrive late** j'ai dit qu'il arriverait peut-être en retard

♦ **might as well** ♦ **I ~ as well tell you all about it** je ferais aussi bien de tout vous dire ♦ **you ~ as well leave now** vous feriez aussi bien de partir tout de suite ♦ **we ~ as well not buy the paper, since no one reads it** je me demande bien pourquoi nous achetons le journal puisque personne ne le lit ♦ **they ~ (just) as well not have gone** ils auraient tout aussi bien pu ne pas y aller

♦ **might well** ♦ **why did he give her his credit card? – you ~ well ask!** mais pourquoi lui a-t-il donné sa carte de crédit ? – va savoir ! ♦ **one ~ well ask whether ...** on est en droit de se demander si ... ♦ **crime levels in other countries ~ well be higher** il se pourrait bien que le taux de criminalité soit plus élevé dans d'autres pays

2 (= *could*)

> When **might** means 'could', and refers to the future, or the present, it is often translated by the conditional of **pouvoir**.

♦ **the sort of people who ~ be interested** le genre de personnes qui pourraient être intéressées ♦ **you ~ at least say thank you** tu pourrais au moins dire merci ♦ **you ~ give me a lift home if you've got time** tu pourrais peut-être me ramener si tu as le temps ♦ **~n't it be an idea to go and see him?** on ferait (*or* tu ferais *etc*) peut-être bien d'aller le voir ♦ **it might be an idea** c'est une idée

> When **might** indicates permission given in the past, it is often translated by a past tense of **pouvoir**.

♦ **he said I ~ leave** il a dit que je pouvais partir ♦ **he wrote to ask if he ~ stay with her for a week** il a écrit pour demander s'il pouvait loger chez elle pendant une semaine

♦ **you might ...** (*offering advice*) tu devrais *or* pourrais peut-être ... ♦ **you ~ try writing to him** tu devrais *or* pourriez peut-être essayer de lui écrire ♦ **you ~ want to consider other options** vous devriez *or* pourriez peut-être envisager d'autres options

♦ **might I ... ?** (*frm*) ♦ **~ I see it?** est-ce que je pourrais le voir ?, vous permettez que je le voie ? ♦ **~ I suggest that ...?** puis-je me permettre de suggérer que ... ?

♦ **might have** (*recriminatory*) ♦ **you ~ have told me you weren't coming!** tu aurais (tout de même) pu me prévenir que tu ne viendrais pas ! ♦ **you ~ have killed me!** tu aurais pu me tuer !

3 (= *should*) **you ~ be more careful!** tu pourrais faire attention ! ♦ **I ~ have known** j'aurais dû m'en douter ♦ **she blushed, as well she ~!** elle a rougi, et pour cause !

4 (*emphatic*) **and, I ~ add, it was entirely his fault** et j'ajouterais que c'était entièrement de sa faute ♦ **try as he ~, he couldn't do it** il a eu beau essayer, il n'y est pas arrivé ♦ **what ~ your name be?** et vous, comment vous appelez-vous ? ♦ **who ~ you be?** qui êtes-vous, sans indiscrétion ?

COMP **might-have-been N** ce qui aurait pu être, espoir *m* déçu ; (= *person*) raté(e) *m(f)*

might[2] /maɪt/ **N** (*NonC*) puissance *f*, force(s) *f(pl)* ♦ **~ is right** (*Prov*) la force prime le droit ♦ **with ~ and main, with all one's ~** de toutes ses forces

mightily /ˈmaɪtɪlɪ/ **ADV** 1 († = *greatly*) considérablement ♦ **to deem sth ~ important** donner une importance considérable à qch 2 (*liter* = *powerfully*) [*strike, hit*] vigoureusement

mightiness /ˈmaɪtɪnɪs/ **N** puissance *f*, pouvoir *m*, grandeur *f*

mightn't /ˈmaɪtnt/ ⇒ **might not** ; → **might**

mighty /ˈmaɪtɪ/ **ADJ** (*liter*) [*nation, king, river, effort, blow, bang*] puissant ; [*oak, redwood*] imposant, majestueux ; [*power*] formidable ♦ **the ~ ocean** le vaste océan ; → **high** **ADV** (*esp US* *) vachement* **NPL** **the mighty** les puissants *mpl* ♦ **how are the ~ fallen** (*Bible*) ils sont tombés les héros

mignonette /ˌmɪnjəˈnet/ **N** (= *plant*) réséda *m*

migraine /ˈmiːgreɪn/ **N** migraine *f* ♦ **it gives me a ~** ça me donne la migraine ♦ **to get** *or* **suffer from ~s** souffrir de migraines

migrant /ˈmaɪgrənt/ **ADJ** 1 [*worker, labour*] (*gen*) itinérant ; (= *immigrant*) immigré ; (= *seasonal*) saisonnier ; [*family, child*] (*gen*) itinérant ;

(= nomadic) nomade ; *(= immigrant)* d'immigrés 2 *[animal, bird]* migrateur (-trice *f*) N 1 *(= bird, animal)* migrateur *m* ; *(= person)* migrant(e) *m(f)* 2 (also **migrant worker**) *(gen)* travailleur *m* itinérant ; *(immigrant)* travailleur *m* immigré ; *(seasonal)* travailleur *m* saisonnier ; → **economic**

migrate /maɪˈgreɪt/ VI migrer VT faire migrer

migration /maɪˈgreɪʃən/ N migration *f*

migratory /maɪˈgreɪtərɪ/ ADJ 1 *[bird, animal, fish, locust]* migrateur (-trice *f*) ; *[habits, movement, journey]* migratoire 2 *[labour] (gen)* itinérant ; *(= immigrant)* immigré ; *(= seasonal)* saisonnier ; *[population] (gen)* itinérant ; *(= nomadic)* nomade ; *(= immigrant)* d'immigrés ◆ **~ pressures** les pressions *fpl* qui obligent les gens à migrer

mikado /mɪˈkɑːdəʊ/ N mikado *m*

Mike /maɪk/ N 1 dim of **Michael** 2 **for the love of ~**‡ pour l'amour du ciel

mike * /maɪk/ N (abbrev of **microphone**) micro *m*

► **mike up** * VT SEP ◆ **to be miked up** porter un micro

mil² * /mɪl/ N abbrev of **million(s)**

milady † /mɪˈleɪdɪ/ N madame la comtesse *etc*

Milan /mɪˈlæn/ N Milan

Milanese /ˌmɪləˈniːz/ ADJ *(gen, also Culin)* milanais

milch cow /ˈmɪltʃkaʊ/ N 1 *(Agr †)* vache *f* laitière 2 *(fig)* vache *f* à lait

mild /maɪld/ ADJ *[climate, winter, voice, flavour, cheese, soap, shampoo]* doux (douce *f*) ; *[tobacco, reproach, punishment]* léger ; *[exercise, effect, protest]* modéré ; *[sauce]* peu épicé *or* relevé ; *[medicine]* bénin (-igne *f*), anodin ; *[illness]* bénin (-igne *f*) ◆ **it's ~ today** il fait doux aujourd'hui ◆ **a ~ spell** *(gen)* une période clémente ; *(after frost)* un redoux ◆ **he had a ~ form of polio** il a eu la poliomyélite sous une forme bénigne *or* atténuée ◆ **a ~ sedative** un sédatif léger ◆ **a ~ curry** *(Culin)* un curry pas trop fort *or* pimenté N *(Brit)* (also **mild ale**) *bière brune faiblement alcoolisée* COMP **mild-mannered** ADJ doux (douce *f*), d'un naturel doux

mildew /ˈmɪldjuː/ N *(NonC, gen)* moisissure *f* ; *(on wheat, roses etc)* rouille *f* ; *(on vine)* mildiou *m* VT *[+ plant]* piquer de rouille ; *[+ vine]* frapper de mildiou ; *[+ paper, cloth]* piquer (d'humidité) VI *[roses, wheat etc]* se rouiller ; *[vine]* devenir mildiousé, être attaqué par le mildiou ; *[paper, cloth]* se piquer

mildewed /ˈmɪlˌdjuːd/ ADJ *[carpet, mattress, wallpaper, wall, wood]* moisi ; *[cloth, paper]* piqué (par l'humidité) ; *[wheat, roses]* piqué de rouille ; *[vine]* mildiousé

mildly /ˈmaɪldlɪ/ ADV 1 *(= gently) [say, reply, ask]* doucement, avec douceur ◆ **to protest ~** protester faiblement *or* timidement ◆ **that's putting it ~** *(= euphemistically)* c'est le moins que l'on puisse dire ◆ **to call him naïve is putting it ~** le qualifier de naïf est un euphémisme 2 *(= moderately) [interested, amusing]* modérément ; *[surprised, irritated, encouraging]* légèrement ◆ **to be ~ critical of sb/sth** critiquer légèrement qn/qch

mildness /ˈmaɪldnɪs/ N *[of person, manner, response, weather, soap]* douceur *f* ; *[of flavour, food, tobacco, cigarette]* légèreté *f* ; *[of punishment, sentence]* clémence *f* ; *(Med) [of illness]* bénignité *f*

mile /maɪl/ N 1 mile *m* (= 1 609,33 *m*) ; (also **nautical mile**) mille *m* ◆ **a 50-~ journey** ≈ un trajet de 80 km ◆ **it's 12 ~s to Manchester** ≈ il y a vingt kilomètres d'ici à Manchester ◆ **30 ~s per gallon** ≈ huit litres aux cent ◆ **50 ~s per hour** ≈ 80 kilomètres à l'heure ◆ **there was nothing but sand for ~s and ~s** il n'y avait que du sable sur des kilomètres (et des kilomètres) ◆ **they live ~s away** ils habitent à cent lieues d'ici ◆ **we've walked (for) ~s!** on a marché pendant des kilomètres !, on a fait des kilomètres ! ; → IMPERIAL SYSTEM ◆ **not a million ~s from here** sans aller chercher bien loin ◆ **you could see/smell it a ~ off** ça se voyait/se sentait à un kilomètre ◆ **it sticks** *or* **stands out a ~** * ça se voit comme le nez au milieu de la figure ◆ **you were ~s off (the) target** * *(lit)* vous n'étiez pas près de toucher la cible ; *(fig)* vous étiez bien loin du but ◆ **sorry, I was ~s away** * *(= day-dreaming)* désolé, j'étais ailleurs ◆ **the President is willing to go the extra ~ for peace** *or* **to achieve peace** le président est prêt à faire un effort supplémentaire pour ramener la paix

2 ◆ **~s** * *(= lots)* **she's ~s better than I am at maths** elle est bien plus calée que moi en maths * ◆ **he's ~s bigger than you** il est bien plus grand que toi

mileage /ˈmaɪlɪdʒ/ N 1 *(= distance covered)* distance *f or* parcours *m* en miles, ≈ kilométrage *m* ◆ **the indicator showed a very low ~** le compteur marquait peu de kilomètres ◆ **the car had a low ~** la voiture avait peu roulé *or* avait peu de kilomètres ◆ **what ~ has this car done?** quel est le kilométrage de cette voiture ?, combien de kilomètres a cette voiture ? ◆ **most of our ~ is in and around town** nous roulons surtout en ville et dans les alentours

2 *(= miles per gallon or litre)* ≈ consommation *f* (de carburant) aux cent (km) ◆ **for a car of that size the ~ was very good** pour une voiture aussi puissante elle consommait peu ◆ **you'll get a better ~ from this car** vous consommerez moins (d'essence) avec cette voiture ; → **gas**

3 (* fig = potential, profit) ◆ **he got a lot of ~ out of it** *(of idea, story, event)* il en a tiré le maximum ◆ **there's still some ~ left in it** *(idea etc)* on peut encore en tirer quelque chose ◆ **he decided there was no ~ in provoking a row with his boss** il a décidé que cela ne servirait à rien de se disputer avec son patron

COMP **mileage allowance** N ≈ indemnité *f* kilométrique

mileage indicator N ≈ compteur *m* kilométrique

mileometer /maɪˈlɒmɪtəʳ/ N ⇒ **milometer**

milepost /ˈmaɪlpəʊst/ N ≈ borne *f* kilométrique

miler * /ˈmaɪləʳ/ N *(= person, horse) athlète ou cheval qui court le mile*

milestone /ˈmaɪlstəʊn/ N *(lit)* borne *f* (milliaire), ≈ borne *f* kilométrique ; *(fig: in life, career etc)* jalon *m*, événement *m* marquant *or* déterminant

milieu /ˈmiːljɜː/ N (pl **milieus**) *(frm)* milieu *m* (social)

militancy /ˈmɪlɪtənsɪ/ N militantisme *m*

militant /ˈmɪlɪtənt/ ADJ militant N *(all senses)* militant(e) *m(f)* COMP **Militant Tendency** N *(Brit Pol) ex-faction trotskiste du parti travailliste britannique*

militantly /ˈmɪlɪtəntlɪ/ ADV *[act]* de façon militante ◆ **to be ~ opposed to sb/sth** s'opposer activement à qn/qch ◆ **~ nationalist/Catholic** d'un nationalisme/catholicisme militant

militarily /ˌmɪlɪˈtərɪlɪ/ ADV *[significant, useful, sensitive, effective]* d'un point de vue militaire ; *[strong, powerful]* militairement ◆ **to intervene/respond ~** intervenir/répondre militairement

militarism /ˈmɪlɪtərɪzəm/ N militarisme *m*

militarist /ˈmɪlɪtərɪst/ ADJ, N militariste *mf*

militaristic /ˌmɪlɪtəˈrɪstɪk/ ADJ *(pej)* militariste

militarize /ˈmɪlɪtəraɪz/ VT militariser

military /ˈmɪlɪtərɪ/ ADJ *[government, life, uniform]* militaire ; *[family]* de militaires ◆ **of ~ age** en âge de faire son service (militaire *or* national) NPL **the military** l'armée *f*, le(s) militaire(s) *m(pl)*

COMP **military academy** N *(US)* école *f* (spéciale) militaire

military attaché N attaché *m* militaire

military band N musique *f* militaire

military-industrial complex N complexe *m* militaro-industriel

military police N police *f* militaire

military policeman N agent *m* de la police militaire

military service N service *m* (militaire *or* national) ◆ **to do one's ~ service** faire son service (militaire *or* national)

military superiority N supériorité *f* militaire

military training N préparation *f* militaire

militate /ˈmɪlɪteɪt/ VI militer (*against* contre ; *for, in favour of* pour) ◆ **his attitude ~s against him** son attitude le dessert *or* joue contre lui

militia /mɪˈlɪʃə/ COLLECTIVE N *(gen)* milice(s) *f(pl)* ◆ **the ~** *(US)* la réserve (territoriale) ; → **state**

militiaman /mɪˈlɪʃəmən/ N (pl **-men**) milicien *m*

milk /mɪlk/ N *(also Cosmetics)* lait *m* ◆ **coconut ~** lait *m* de coco ◆ **moisturising ~** lait *m* hydratant ◆ **the ~ of human kindness** le lait de la tendresse humaine ◆ **a land flowing with ~ and honey** un pays de cocagne ◆ **he came home with the ~** * *(hum)* il est rentré avec le jour *or* à potron-minet * ◆ **he dismissed the report as ~ and water** il a déclaré que le rapport n'était ni fait ni à faire ; → **cleansing, condense, cry, skim**

VT 1 *[+ cow]* traire

2 *(fig = rob)* dépouiller (*of* de), exploiter ◆ **his son ~ed him of all his savings** son fils l'a dépouillé de toutes ses économies ◆ **it ~ed (him of) his strength** cela a sapé *or* miné ses forces ◆ **to ~ sb of ideas/information** soutirer des idées/des renseignements à qn ◆ **to ~ sb dry** exploiter qn à fond, épuiser les forces créatrices de qn

3 *[performer]* ◆ **to ~ the applause** tout faire pour que les gens continuent d'applaudir

VI ◆ **to go ~ing** (s'en) aller traire ses vaches

COMP **milk-and-water** ADJ *(fig pej)* à la manque *

milk bar N milk-bar *m*

milk can N pot *m* à lait ; *(larger)* bidon *m* à lait

milk chocolate N chocolat *m* au lait

milk churn N bidon *m* à lait

milk diet N régime *m* lacté

milk duct N *(Anat)* canal *m* galactophore

milk fever N fièvre *f* lactée

milk float N *(Brit)* voiture *f* de laitier

milk gland N *(Anat)* glande *f* galactogène

milk jug N (petit) pot *m* à lait

milk of magnesia N lait *m* de magnésie, magnésie *f* hydratée

milk pan N petite casserole *f* pour le lait

milk powder N lait *m* en poudre

milk products NPL produits *mpl* laitiers

milk pudding N entremets *m* au lait

milk round N *(Brit)* tournée *f* (du laitier) ; *(Brit Univ *) tournée de recrutement dans les universités* ◆ **to do a ~ round** *[child etc]* livrer le lait

milk run * N *(= flight)* vol *m* sans accroc

milk saucepan N petite casserole *f* pour le lait

milk shake N milk-shake *m*

milk stout N *(Brit)* bière *f* brune douce

milk tooth N dent *f* de lait

the milk train N *(fig hum)* le tout premier train (du matin)

milk-white ADJ *(liter)* d'une blancheur de lait, blanc (blanche *f*) comme le *or* du lait, laiteux

milking /ˈmɪlkɪŋ/ N traite *f* ◆ **to do the ~** traire les vaches

COMP *[pail, stool]* à traire **milking machine** N trayeuse *f* (mécanique)

milking time N heure *f* de la traite

milkmaid /ˈmɪlkmeɪd/ N trayeuse *f (personne)*

milkman /ˈmɪlkmən/ N (pl **-men**) laitier *m*

milksop* /ˈmɪlksɒp/ N chiffe *f* molle* *(fig)*, lavette* *f (fig)*, mollusque* *m (fig)*

milkweed /ˈmɪlkwiːd/ N laiteron *m*

milky /ˈmɪlkɪ/ ADJ 1 *(in colour)* laiteux 2 *[drink]* à base de lait ; *[coffee, tea]* avec beaucoup de lait

COMP **the Milky Way** N la Voie lactée

milky-white ADJ d'un blanc laiteux

mill /mɪl/ N 1 (also **windmill** *or* **water mill**) moulin *m* ; *(= industrial grain mill)* minoterie *f* ; *(small: for coffee etc)* moulin *m* ◆ **pepper-~** moulin *m* à poivre ◆ **to go through the ~** *(fig)* passer par de dures épreuves, en voir de dures* ◆ **to put sb through the ~** *(fig)* mettre qn à l'épreuve, en faire voir de dures à qn* ; → **coffee, run, windmill**

2 *(= factory: gen)* usine *f*, fabrique *f* ; (also **spinning mill**) filature *f* ; (also **weaving mill**) tissage *m* ; (also **steel mill**) aciérie *f* ◆ **paper ~** (usine *f* de) papeterie *f* ◆ **cotton ~** filature *f* de coton ; → **sawmill**

VT 1 *[+ flour, coffee, pepper]* moudre

2 *[+ screw, nut]* moleter ; *[+ wheel, edge of coin]* créneler ◆ **~ed edge** *[of coin]* tranche *f* cannelée

VI ◆ **to ~ round sth** *[crowd etc]* grouiller autour de qch

COMP **mill girl** N *(in factory)* ouvrière *f* des filatures (*or* des tissages *or* des aciéries)

mill owner N *(= owner of factory)* industriel *m* (du textile)

mill race N bief *m* d'amont *or* de moulin

mill stream N courant *m* du bief

mill wheel N roue *f* de moulin

mill worker N *(in factory)* ouvrier *m*, -ière *f* des filatures (*or* des tissages *or* des aciéries)

► **mill about, mill around** VI *[crowd]* grouiller, fourmiller ; *[cattle etc]* tourner sur place *or* en rond

millboard /ˈmɪlbɔːd/ N carton *m* pâte

millenarian /ˌmɪləˈneərɪən/ ADJ, N millénariste *mf*

millenary /mɪˈlenərɪ/, **millennial** /mɪˈlenɪəl/ ADJ, N millénaire *m*

millennium /mɪˈlenɪəm/ N (pl **millenniums** *or* **millennia** /mɪˈlenɪə/) millénaire *m* ◆ **the ~** *(Rel, also fig)* le millénium

COMP **the millennium bug** N *(Comput)* le bogue de l'an 2000

the Millennium Dome N *(Brit)* le Dôme du millénaire

millepede /ˈmɪlɪpiːd/ N ⇒ **millipede**

miller /ˈmɪlər/ N meunier *m* ; *(large-scale)* minotier *m*

millet /ˈmɪlɪt/ N *(NonC)* millet *m*

millhand /ˈmɪlhænd/ N *(Ind)* ⇒ **mill worker** ; → **mill**

milliard /ˈmɪlɪɑːd/ N *(Brit)* milliard *m*

millibar /ˈmɪlɪbɑːr/ N millibar *m*

milligram(me) /ˈmɪlɪgræm/ N milligramme *m*

millilitre, milliliter *(US)* /ˈmɪlɪˌliːtər/ N millilitre *m*

millimetre, millimeter *(US)* /ˈmɪlɪˌmiːtər/ N millimètre *m*

milliner /ˈmɪlɪnər/ N modiste *f*, chapelier *m*, -ière *f*

millinery /ˈmɪlɪnərɪ/ N *(NonC)* chapellerie *f* féminine

milling /ˈmɪlɪŋ/ N *(NonC)* *[of flour etc]* mouture *f* ; *[of screw etc]* moletage *m* ; *[of coin]* crénelage *m* ADJ *[crowd, people]* grouillant

million /ˈmɪljən/ N million *m* ◆ **a ~ men** un million d'hommes ◆ **he's one in a ~*** c'est la crème des hommes *or* la perle des hommes ◆ **it's a chance** *etc* **in a ~** c'est une occasion *etc* unique ◆ **~s of ...*** des milliers de ... ◆ **thanks a ~!*** merci mille fois ! ◆ **to feel (like) a ~ dollars** *or (esp US)* **bucks*** se sentir dans une forme époustouflante* ◆ **she looked (like) a ~ dollars** *or (esp US)* **bucks in her new outfit*** elle était absolument superbe dans sa nouvelle tenue

millionaire /ˌmɪljəˈneər/ N millionnaire *m*, ≃ milliardaire *m*

millionairess /ˌmɪljəˈneərɪs/ N millionnaire *f*

millionth /ˈmɪljənθ/ ADJ millionième N millionième *mf* ; *(= fraction)* millionième *m*

millipede /ˈmɪlɪpiːd/ N mille-pattes *m inv*

millisecond /ˈmɪlɪˌsekənd/ N milliseconde *f*

millpond /ˈmɪlpɒnd/ N bief *m or* retenue *f* d'un moulin ◆ **the sea was like a ~** c'était une mer d'huile

Mills bomb /ˈmɪlzˌbɒm/ N grenade *f* à main

millstone /ˈmɪlstəʊn/ N *(lit)* meule *f* ◆ **it's a ~ round his neck** c'est un boulet qu'il traîne avec lui

millwright /ˈmɪlraɪt/ N constructeur *m or* installateur *m* de moulins

milometer /maɪˈlɒmɪtər/ N *(Brit)* compteur *m* de miles, ≃ compteur *m* kilométrique

milord /mɪˈlɔːd/ N milord *m*

milt /mɪlt/ N laitance *f*, laite *f*

mime /maɪm/ N 1 *(= skill, classical play)* mime *m* ; *(= modern play)* mimodrame *m* ; *(fig) (= gestures etc)* mimique *f* 2 *(= actor)* mime *m* VTI mimer ◆ **to ~ to a tape** *(= sing etc)* chanter *etc* en play-back COMP **mime artist** N mime *mf*

mimeo /ˈmɪmɪəʊ/ (abbrev of **mimeograph**) N ronéo ® *f* VT ronéoter*

Mimeograph ® /ˈmɪmɪəgrɑːf/ N *(= machine)* ronéo ® *f* ; *(= copy)* polycopié *m* VT ◆ **mimeograph** ronéotyper, ronéoter*

mimetic /mɪˈmetɪk/ ADJ mimétique

mimic /ˈmɪmɪk/ N imitateur *m*, -trice *f* ADJ 1 *(= imitating)* imitateur (-trice *f*) 2 *(= sham)* factice, simulé VT *(= copy)* imiter ; *(= burlesque)* imiter, singer ◆ **computers that ~ human intelligence** des ordinateurs qui cherchent à reproduire l'intelligence humaine

mimicry /ˈmɪmɪkrɪ/ N *(NonC)* imitation *f* ; *(in animals)* mimétisme *m*

mimosa /mɪˈməʊzə/ N 1 *(= tree)* mimosa *m* 2 *(US = cocktail)* mimosa *m* *(champagne-jus d'orange)*

Min. *(Brit)* abbrev of **Ministry**

min. 1 (abbrev of **minute**[1]) min. 2 (abbrev of **minimum**) min.

mina /ˈmaɪnə/ N ⇒ **mynah**

minaret /ˈmɪnəret/ N minaret *m*

minatory /ˈmɪnətərɪ/ ADJ *(frm)* *[silence, place]* menaçant

mince /mɪns/ N *(Brit Culin)* bifteck *m* haché, hachis *m* de viande VT 1 *[+ meat, vegetables]* hacher ◆ **~d beef** bœuf *m* haché 2 *(fig)* **he didn't ~ (his) words** il n'a pas mâché ses mots, il n'y est pas allé par quatre chemins ◆ **never one to ~ words, he ...** n'ayant pas l'habitude de mâcher ses mots, il ... VI *(in talking)* parler du bout des lèvres ; *(in walking)* marcher en minaudant ◆ **to ~ in/out** entrer/sortir en minaudant COMP **mince pie** N *(Culin)* tartelette *f* de Noël (aux fruits secs)

► **mince up** VT SEP *(Culin etc)* hacher

mincemeat /ˈmɪnsmiːt/ N *(Culin)* *hachis de fruits secs, de pommes et de graisse* ; *(US)* ⇒ **mince noun** ◆ **to make ~ of** *(fig)* *[+ opponent, enemy]* battre à plate(s) couture(s)*, pulvériser ; *[+ theories, arguments]* pulvériser

mincer /ˈmɪnsər/ N hachoir *m (appareil)*

mincing /ˈmɪnsɪŋ/ ADJ *(pej)* *[steps, gait, voice]* affecté COMP **mincing machine** N hachoir *m*

mincingly /ˈmɪnsɪŋlɪ/ ADV *(pej)* *[say, walk]* en minaudant

mind /maɪnd/

LANGUAGE IN USE 4, 7.5, 8.2, 9.1

1 NOUN	4 COMPOUNDS
2 TRANSITIVE VERB	5 PHRASAL VERB
3 INTRANSITIVE VERB	

1 - NOUN

1 = brain esprit *m* ◆ **a logical/an analytical/a creative ~** un esprit logique/d'analyse/créateur *or* créatif ◆ **he is one of the great ~s of the century** c'est un des grands esprits de son siècle ◆ **great ~s think alike** *(Prov)* les grands esprits se rencontrent ◆ **he has the ~ of a five-year-old** il a cinq ans d'âge mental ◆ **~ over matter** victoire de l'esprit sur la matière ◆ **his ~ went blank** il a eu un trou *or* un passage à vide ◆ **his ~ is going** il n'a plus toute sa tête ◆ **at the back of my ~ I had the feeling that ...** je sentais confusément que ... ◆ **of sound ~** sain d'esprit ◆ **to be of unsound ~** ne plus avoir toutes ses facultés (mentales) ◆ **that's a load** *or* **a weight off my ~*** c'est un gros souci de moins, cela m'ôte un poids ◆ **what's on your ~?** qu'est-ce qui vous préoccupe *or* vous tracasse ? ◆ **it came (in)to** *or* **entered my ~ that ...** il m'est venu à l'esprit que ..., l'idée m'est venue que ... ◆ **to come** *or* **spring to ~** venir à l'esprit ◆ **she wanted to get into the ~ of this woman** elle voulait se mettre dans la peau de cette femme ◆ **I can't get it out of my ~** je ne peux pas m'empêcher d'y penser ◆ **I can't get him/her out of my ~** je ne peux pas m'empêcher de penser à lui/elle ◆ **you can put that right out of your ~!** tu peux faire une croix dessus ! ◆ **try to put it out of your ~** essayez de ne plus y penser ◆ **to let one's ~ run on sth** se laisser aller à penser à qch ◆ **to read** *or* **see into sb's ~** lire dans les pensées de qn ◆ **to set** *or* **put sb's ~ at ease** *or* **rest** rassurer qn ◆ **it's all in the ~** tout ça, c'est dans la tête* ◆ **nobody in their right ~ would do that** aucun être sensé ne ferait cela

◆ **in mind** ◆ **to bear sth in ~** *(= take account of)* tenir compte de qch ; *(= remember)* ne pas oublier qch ◆ **bear it in ~!** songez-y bien ! ◆ **I'll bear you in ~** je songerai *or* penserai à vous ◆ **to keep sth in ~** ne pas oublier qch ◆ **we must keep in ~ that ...** n'oublions pas que ... ◆ **have you (got) anything particular in ~?** avez-vous quelque chose de particulier en tête ? ◆ **do you have somebody in ~ for the job?** vous avez quelqu'un en vue pour ce poste ? ◆ **to have (it) in ~ to do sth** penser faire qch ◆ **that puts me in ~ of ...** cela me rappelle ...

◆ **in one's mind** ◆ **I'm not clear in my own ~ about it** je ne sais pas qu'en penser moi-même ◆ **to be easy in one's ~ (about sth)** avoir l'esprit tranquille (à propos de qch) ◆ **to be uneasy in one's ~ (about sth)** être inquiet (au sujet de qch) ◆ **to be in one's right ~** avoir toute sa raison *or* sa tête ◆ **in one's ~'s eye** en imagination

◆ **out of one's mind** ◆ **to be out of one's ~* (with worry/jealousy)** être fou (d'inquiétude/de jalousie) ◆ **to go out of one's ~ with worry/jealousy** devenir fou d'inquiétude/de jalousie ◆ **he's out of his ~!** il est complètement fou ! ◆ **you must be out of your ~!** tu es complètement fou !, ça ne va pas ! * ◆ **he went out of his ~** il a perdu la tête *or* la raison

2 = attention, concentration ◆ **to have one's ~ on sth** être préoccupé par qch ◆ **to have one's ~ on something else** avoir la tête ailleurs ◆ **to let one's ~ wander** relâcher son attention ◆ **it went quite** *or* **right** *or* **clean* out of my ~** ça

m'est complètement sorti de la tête* ◆ **to bring one's ~ to bear on sth** porter *or* concentrer son attention sur qch ◆ **to give one's ~ to sth** bien réfléchir à qch ◆ **I haven't had time to give my ~ to it** je n'ai pas eu le temps de bien y réfléchir ◆ **he can't give his whole ~ to his work** il n'arrive pas à se concentrer sur son travail ◆ **to keep one's ~ on sth** se concentrer sur qch ◆ **to put** *or* **set one's ~ to a problem** s'attaquer à un problème ◆ **you can do it if you put** *or* **set your ~ to it** tu peux le faire si tu le veux vraiment ◆ **this will take her ~ off her troubles** cela lui changera les idées

3 = opinion avis *m*, idée *f* ◆ **to my ~** à mon avis ◆ **to have a closed ~ (on** *or* **about sth)** avoir des idées *or* opinions arrêtées (sur *or* au sujet de qch) ◆ **to have a ~ of one's own** *[person]* avoir ses idées ; *[machine]* avoir des caprices ◆ **they were of one ~** *or* **like ~** *or* **the same ~** ils étaient d'accord *or* du même avis ◆ **I'm still of the same ~** je n'ai pas changé d'avis ◆ **they thought with one ~** ils étaient unanimes ◆ **to know one's own ~** savoir ce que l'on veut

◆ **to make up one's mind** ◆ **we can't make up our ~s about the house** nous ne savons pas quelle décision prendre pour la maison ◆ **I can't make up my ~ about him** je ne sais pas vraiment que penser de lui ◆ **have you made your ~ up?** avez-vous pris votre décision ? ◆ **to make up one's ~ to do sth** décider de faire qch

4 = inclination, intention **you can do it if you have a ~ (to)** vous pouvez le faire si vous en avez envie ◆ **I have no ~ to offend him** † je n'ai aucune envie de l'offenser ◆ **I've a good ~ to do it*** j'ai bien envie de le faire ◆ **I've a good ~ to tell him everything!** * j'ai bien envie de tout lui dire ! ◆ **I've half a ~ to do it*** j'ai presque envie de le faire ◆ **nothing is further from my ~!** (bien) loin de moi cette pensée ! ◆ **nothing was further from my ~ than going to see her** je n'avais nullement l'intention d'aller la voir ◆ **I was of a ~ to go and see him** j'avais l'intention d'aller le voir ◆ **to set one's ~ on doing sth** avoir fermement l'intention de faire qch

◆ **in two minds** ◆ **to be in two ~s about doing sth** hésiter à faire qch ◆ **I'm in two ~s about it** j'hésite, je me tâte*

5 = memory **to stick in sb's ~** rester gravé dans la mémoire de qn ◆ **to bring** *or* **call sth to ~** rappeler qch ◆ **to pass out of ~** *(liter)* tomber dans l'oubli

2 - TRANSITIVE VERB

1 = pay attention to faire *or* prêter attention à ; (= *beware of*) prendre garde à ; (*US* = *listen to*) écouter ◆ **~ what you're doing!** (fais) attention à ce que tu fais ! ◆ **~ you don't fall!** prenez garde de ne pas tomber ! ◆ **~ what I say!** écoute bien ce que je te dis !, fais bien attention à ce que je te dis ! ◆ **~ the step!** attention à la marche ! ◆ **~ your head!** attention à votre tête ! ◆ **~ your backs!** * gare à vous !, dégagez !* ◆ **~ yourself!, ~ your eye!** ⁑ prends garde !, fais gaffe !⁑ ◆ **~ your language/your manners!** surveille ton langage/tes manières ! ◆ **~ how you go*** prends bien soin de toi ◆ **don't ~ him!** ne t'occupe pas de lui !, ne fais pas attention à lui ! ◆ **don't ~ me!*** *(iro)* ne vous gênez surtout pas (pour moi) !* *(iro)*

2 = dislike, object to **I don't ~ ironing/travelling alone** ça ne me dérange pas de faire le repassage/de voyager seul ◆ **I don't ~ wet weather** la pluie ne me dérange pas ◆ **I don't ~ him but she's awful!** * lui, passe encore *or* lui, ça va, mais elle, je la trouve vraiment horrible ! ◆ **I wouldn't ~ a cup of coffee** * une tasse de café ne serait pas de refus*, je prendrais bien une tasse de café ◆ **if you don't ~ my** *(frm)* *or* **me saying (so)** si je puis me permettre ◆ **I don't ~ telling you*, I was shocked** inutile de dire que j'ai été vraiment choqué ◆ **I don't ~ going with you** je veux bien vous accompagner ◆ **cigarette? – I don't ~** if I do une cigarette ? – ce n'est pas de refus !*

◆ **would you mind** + *gerund* ◆ **would you ~ opening the door?** cela vous ennuierait d'ouvrir la porte ? ◆ **would you ~ coming with me?** cela vous dérangerait de m'accompagner ? ; *(abruptly)* suivez-moi, s'il vous plaît

3 = care ◆ **I don't ~ what people say** je me moque du qu'en-dira-t-on ◆ **I don't ~ where we go** peu importe où nous allons

4 = take charge of *[+ children, animals]* garder ; *[+ shop, business]* garder, tenir ◆ **to ~ the shop*** *or* **the store*** *(US)* *(fig)* veiller au grain

5 dial **I ~ the day when ...** (= *remember*) je me rappelle le jour où ...

3 - INTRANSITIVE VERB

1 = object **if you don't ~** si cela ne vous fait rien ◆ **if you don't ~!** *(iro indignantly)* non, mais ! ◆ **do you ~ if I take this book? – I don't ~ at all** ça ne vous ennuie pas que je prenne ce livre ? – mais non, je vous en prie ◆ **I'm sure they won't ~ if you don't come** je suis sûre qu'ils ne seront pas trop contrariés si tu ne viens pas

2 = care ◆ **which do you want? – I don't ~** lequel voulez-vous ? – ça m'est égal

◆ **never + mind** (= *don't worry*) ne t'en fais pas !, ne t'inquiète pas ! ; (= *it makes no odds*) ça ne fait rien !, peu importe ! ◆ **never ~ that now!** *(soothingly)* n'y pense plus ! ; *(irritably)* ça peut très bien attendre ! ◆ **he can't walk, never ~* run** il ne peut pas marcher, encore moins courir ◆ **never you ~!*** ça ne te regarde pas !, ce ne sont pas tes oignons !*

3 = be sure ◆ **~ you tell her!** n'oubliez pas de le lui dire ! ◆ **~ and come to see us!*** n'oublie pas de venir nous voir ! ◆ **be there at ten, ~*** sois là à 10 heures sans faute

◆ **mind you*** ◆ **~ you, I didn't know he was going to Paris** remarquez, je ne savais pas qu'il allait à Paris ◆ **~ you, it won't be easy** mais ce ne sera pas facile pour autant ◆ **~ you, he could be right, he could be right, ~ you** peut-être qu'il a raison après tout ◆ **I got substantial damages. It took two years, ~ you** je me suis fait largement dédommager mais ça a quand même pris deux ans

4 - COMPOUNDS

mind-altering ADJ *[drug, substance]* psychotrope
mind-bender* N *(US)* révélation *f*
mind-bending*, **mind-blowing*** ADJ *[drug]* hallucinogène ; *[experience, news, scene]* hallucinant
mind-boggling* ADJ époustouflant*, ahurissant
mind-expanding ADJ *[drug etc]* hallucinogène
mind game N manœuvre *f* psychologique ◆ **to play ~ games with sb** chercher à manœuvrer qn psychologiquement
mind-numbing* ADJ ennuyeux à mourir
mind-numbingly* ADV ◆ **~-numbingly boring** ennuyeux à mourir ◆ **~-numbingly simple** d'une simplicité enfantine ◆ **~-numbingly banal** d'une banalité affligeante
mind reader N *(lit)* télépathe *mf* ◆ **he's a ~ reader!** il lit dans la pensée des gens ! ◆ **I'm not a ~ reader!*** je ne suis pas devin !*
mind reading N télépathie *f*
mind-set N mentalité *f*

5 - PHRASAL VERB

► **mind out*** VI faire attention, faire gaffe* ◆ **~ out!** attention ! ◆ **~ out of the way!** ôtez-vous de là !, dégagez !* ◆ **~ out or you'll break it** fais attention de ne pas le casser

minded /ˈmaɪndɪd/ ADJ *(frm)* ◆ **if you are so ~** si le cœur vous en dit ◆ **to be ~ to do sth** être disposé à faire qch

-minded /ˈmaɪndɪd/ ADJ *(in compounds)* 1 *(describing mental faculties)* qui est ... d'esprit ◆ **feeble-minded** faible d'esprit ; → **high, strong-minded** 2 *(describing interests)* qui s'intéresse à ... ◆ **business-minded** qui a le sens des affaires ◆ **he's become very ecology-minded** il est devenu très sensible aux problèmes écologiques ◆ **an industrially-minded nation** une nation tournée vers l'industrie ◆ **a romantically-minded girl** une jeune fille aux idées romantiques ; → **family, like**

minder /ˈmaɪndəʳ/ N 1 *(Brit:* also **baby-minder, child-minder***)* gardienne *f* 2 (* = *bodyguard etc*) ange *m* gardien *(fig)*

mindful /ˈmaɪndfʊl/ ADJ *(frm)* ◆ **to be ~ of sth** être attentif à qch ◆ **to be ~ that...** être attentif au fait que ... ◆ **I am ever ~ of how much I am indebted to you** je n'oublie pas à quel point je vous suis obligé ◆ **be ~ of what I said** songez à ce que j'ai dit

mindless /ˈmaɪndlɪs/ ADJ 1 *(Brit* = *senseless)* *[violence, brutality, vandalism, killing]* gratuit 2 (= *stupid*) *[work, routine, film, entertainment]* bêtifiant ; *[person]* stupide ◆ **a ~ idiot** un(e) idiot(e) fini(e) 3 *(frm* = *unmindful)* ◆ **to be ~ of sth** être oublieux *or* insouciant de qch

mine¹ /maɪn/ POSS PRON le mien, la mienne, les miens *mpl*, les miennes *fpl* ◆ **that book is ~** ce livre m'appartient *or* est à moi ◆ **this poem is ~** ce poème est de moi ◆ **will you be ~?** † voulez-vous m'épouser ? ◆ **the house became ~** la maison est devenue (la) mienne ◆ **no it's ~** non, c'est à moi *or* le mien ◆ **which dress do you prefer, hers or ~?** quelle robe préférez-vous, la sienne ou la mienne ? ◆ **what is ~ is yours** ce qui est à moi est à toi, ce qui m'appartient t'appartient ◆ **it is not ~ to decide** *(frm)* ce n'est pas à moi de décider, il ne m'appartient pas de décider ◆ **~ is a specialized department** le service où je suis est spécialisé

◆ **... of mine** ◆ **no advice of ~ could prevent him** aucun conseil de ma part ne pouvait l'empêcher ◆ **a friend of ~** un de mes amis, un ami à moi ◆ **I think that cousin of ~* is responsible** je pense que c'est mon cousin qui est responsable ◆ **it's no fault of ~** ce n'est pas (de) ma faute

POSS ADJ †† mon, ma, mes ; → **host¹**

mine² /maɪn/ N 1 *(Min)* mine *f* ◆ **coalmine** mine *f* de charbon ◆ **to go down the ~(s)** travailler *or* descendre à la mine ◆ **to work a ~** exploiter une mine

2 *(fig* = *rich source)* ◆ **a (real) ~ of information** une véritable mine de renseignements, une source inépuisable de renseignements ◆ **she's a ~ of celebrity gossip** elle connaît tous les potins sur les célébrités

3 *(Mil, Naut* = *bomb)* mine *f* ◆ **to lay a ~** mouiller *or* poser une mine ◆ **to clear a beach of ~s** déminer une plage ; → **landmine**

VT 1 *(Min)* *[+ coal, ore]* extraire

2 *(Mil, Naut etc)* *[+ sea, beach]* miner, semer de mines ; *[+ ship, tank]* miner

VI exploiter un gisement ◆ **to ~ for coal** extraire du charbon, exploiter une mine (de charbon)

COMP **mine-clearing** N *(Mil, Naut)* déminage *m*
mine detector N *(Mil)* détecteur *m* de mines
mine disposal N *(Mil, Naut)* déminage *m*
mine-sweeping N *(Mil, Naut)* dragage *m* de mines, déminage *m*

minefield /ˈmaɪnfiːld/ N 1 *(Mil, Naut)* champ *m* de mines 2 *(fig* = *problematic area)* **it's a legal/political ~** c'est un terrain politiquement/juridiquement miné

minehunter /ˈmaɪnhʌntəʳ/ N *(Mil, Naut)* chasseur *m* de mines

minelayer /ˈmaɪnˌleɪəʳ/ N (Mil, Naut) mouilleur m de mines

minelaying /ˈmaɪnleɪɪŋ/ N (Mil, Naut) mouillage m de mines

miner /ˈmaɪnəʳ/ N mineur m ◆ **the ~s' strike** la grève des mineurs ◆ **~'s lamp** lampe f de mineur

mineral /ˈmɪnərəl/ N (Geol) minéral m NPL **minerals** (Brit = soft drinks) boissons fpl gazeuses ADJ minéral
COMP **mineral deposits** NPL gisements mpl miniers
the mineral kingdom N le règne minéral
mineral oil N (Brit) huile f minérale ; (US) huile f de paraffine
mineral rights NPL droits mpl miniers
mineral water N eau f minérale

mineralogical /ˌmɪnərəˈlɒdʒɪkl/ ADJ minéralogique

mineralogist /ˌmɪnəˈrælədʒɪst/ N minéralogiste mf

mineralogy /ˌmɪnəˈrælədʒɪ/ N minéralogie f

Minerva /mɪˈnɜːvə/ N Minerve f

mineshaft /ˈmaɪnʃɑːft/ N puits m de mine

minestrone /ˌmɪnɪˈstrəʊnɪ/ N minestrone m

minesweeper /ˈmaɪnswiːpəʳ/ N (Mil, Naut) dragueur m de mines

minging‡ /ˈmɪŋɪŋ/ ADJ horrible

mingle /ˈmɪŋgl/ VT mêler, mélanger (with avec) VI (= mix) se mêler, se mélanger ; (at party etc) se mêler aux invités or à la fête ; (= become indistinguishable) se confondre (with avec) ◆ **to ~ with the crowd** se mêler à la foule ◆ **he ~s with all sorts of people** il fraye avec toutes sortes de gens ◆ **guests ate and ~d** les invités ont mangé et ont discuté les uns avec les autres ◆ **she ~d for a while and then sat down with her husband** elle s'est mêlée aux autres invités pour discuter puis s'est assise avec son mari

mingy* /ˈmɪndʒɪ/ ADJ (Brit) 1 (= mean) [person] radin* (about sth en ce qui concerne qch) 2 (= measly) [amount] misérable

Mini ® /ˈmɪnɪ/ N (= car) Mini (Cooper) ® f

mini /ˈmɪnɪ/ N (= fashion) mini f ADJ ◆ **~ system** (= hi-fi) chaîne f (hi-fi) mini

mini... /ˈmɪnɪ/ PREF mini... ◆ **he's a kind of mini-dictator*** c'est une sorte de minidictateur

miniature /ˈmɪnɪtʃəʳ/ N 1 (Art) miniature f ◆ **in ~** (lit, fig) en miniature 2 (of whisky etc) mignonnette f ADJ [rose, railway, car, camera, version] miniature ; [dog, tree] nain ◆ **submarine** sous-marin m de poche ◆ **~ bottle of whisky** mignonnette f de whisky
COMP **miniature golf** N minigolf m
miniature poodle N caniche m nain

miniaturist /ˈmɪnɪtʃərɪst/ N miniaturiste mf

miniaturization /ˌmɪnɪtʃəraɪˈzeɪʃən/ N miniaturisation f

miniaturize /ˈmɪnɪtʃəraɪz/ VT miniaturiser

minibar /ˈmɪnɪbɑːʳ/ N (= fridge) minibar m

mini-boom /ˈmɪnɪbuːm/ N miniboom m

mini-break /ˈmɪnɪbreɪk/ N petit voyage m, mini-séjour m

minibudget /ˈmɪnɪˌbʌdʒɪt/ N (Pol) collectif m budgétaire

minibus /ˈmɪnɪˌbʌs/ N minibus m ◆ **by ~** en minibus

minicab /ˈmɪnɪˌkæb/ N (Brit) taxi m (qu'il faut commander par téléphone) ◆ **by ~** en taxi

minicalculator † /ˈmɪnɪˈkælkjʊˌleɪtəʳ/ N calculette f, calculatrice f de poche

minicam /ˈmɪnɪkæm/ N minicam f

minicar /ˈmɪnɪˌkɑːʳ/ N toute petite voiture f

minicomputer /ˈmɪnɪkəmˈpjuːtəʳ/ N mini-ordinateur m

mini-course /ˈmɪnɪˌkɔːs/ N (US Scol) cours m extrascolaire

minidisc /ˈmɪnɪdɪsk/ N (= system, disc) MiniDisc m COMP **minidisc player** N lecteur m de MiniDisc

minidress /ˈmɪnɪˌdres/ N minirobe f

minim /ˈmɪnɪm/ N 1 (Brit Mus) blanche f 2 (Measure = 0.5ml) ≈ goutte f COMP **minim rest** N demi-pause f

minima /ˈmɪnɪmə/ NPL of **minimum**

minimal /ˈmɪnɪml/ ADJ [risk, role, resources, effect, change] minime ; [level, requirements] minimal, minimum ◆ **the money saved is ~** la somme d'argent économisée est minime ◆ **~ publicity/disruption** un minimum de publicité/perturbation ◆ **a ~ amount of effort** un minimum d'effort, un effort minime ◆ **to have ~ impact on sth** n'avoir qu'un très faible impact sur qch ◆ **damage was ~** les dégâts étaient minimes ◆ **~ loss of life** des pertes minimums en vies humaines ◆ **at ~ cost** pour un coût minimum ◆ **with ~ effort** avec un minimum d'effort
COMP **minimal art** N art m minimal
minimal free form N (Ling) forme f libre minimale
minimal pair N (Ling) paire f minimale

minimalism /ˈmɪnɪməlɪzəm/ N (Art etc) minimalisme m

minimalist /ˈmɪnɪməlɪst/ ADJ, N (Art etc) minimaliste mf

minimally /ˈmɪnɪməlɪ/ ADV à peine

minimarket /ˈmɪnɪˌmɑːkɪt/, **minimart** /ˈmɪnɪˌmɑːt/ N supérette f

minimize /ˈmɪnɪmaɪz/ VT 1 (= reduce to minimum) [+ amount, risk, losses] réduire au minimum 2 (= play down) [+ risk, losses, sb's contribution, help] minimiser

minimum /ˈmɪnɪməm/ N (pl **minimums** or **minima**) minimum m ◆ **a ~ of $100** un minimum de 100 dollars ◆ **$100 (at the) ~** au moins 100 dollars ◆ **to do the ~** faire le minimum ◆ **to reduce to a** or **the ~** réduire au minimum ◆ **keep interruptions to a** or **the ~** limitez les interruptions autant que possible ◆ **to keep costs to a ~** maintenir les coûts au plus bas ◆ **with a ~ of commonsense one could ...** avec un minimum de bon sens on pourrait ...
ADJ minimum f inv, minimal ◆ **with ~ effort** avec un minimum d'effort ◆ **at ~ cost** pour un coût minimum
COMP **minimum iron fabric** N tissu m ne demandant qu'un repassage minimum
minimum lending rate N taux m de base bancaire
minimum security prison N (esp US) établissement m pénitentiaire à régime assoupli or souple
minimum wage N salaire m minimum, ≈ SMIC m

mining /ˈmaɪnɪŋ/ N (NonC) 1 (Min) exploitation f minière 2 (Mil, Naut) pose f or mouillage m de mines
COMP [village, company, industry, rights] minier ; [family] de mineurs
mining area N région f (d'industrie) minière
mining engineer N ingénieur m des mines
mining engineering N génie m minier ◆ **to study ~ engineering** ≈ faire des études à l'école des Mines

minion /ˈmɪnjən/ N (lit = servant) laquais m ; (fig, hum) sous-fifre* m ◆ **she delegated the job to one of her ~s** elle a donné ce travail à l'un de ses sous-fifres*

minipill /ˈmɪnɪpɪl/ N minipilule f

miniscule /ˈmɪnɪˌskjuːl/ ADJ ⇒ **minuscule**

miniseries /ˈmɪnɪsɪərɪz/ N (TV) minifeuilleton m

mini-ski /ˈmɪnɪˌskiː/ N (Ski) miniski m

miniskirt /ˈmɪnɪˌskɜːt/ N minijupe f

minister /ˈmɪnɪstəʳ/ N 1 (Brit Govt) ministre m 2 (Rel: also **minister of religion**) pasteur m, ministre m VI ◆ **to ~ to sb's needs** pourvoir aux besoins de qn ◆ **to ~ to sb** secourir qn ◆ **to ~ to a parish** (Rel) desservir une paroisse
COMP **ministering angel** N (fig) ange m de bonté
Minister for Education and Employment N (Brit) ministre mf de l'Éducation et de l'Emploi
Minister of Health N ministre m de la Santé
Minister of State N (Brit Govt) ≈ secrétaire m d'État ; (gen) ministre m
minister plenipotentiary N ministre m plénipotentiaire
minister resident N ministre m résident ; → **defence, foreign**

ministerial /ˌmɪnɪsˈtɪərɪəl/ ADJ 1 (Govt) [meeting, team, reshuffle, approval, decision] ministériel ; [post, career, duties] de ministre ; [resignation] d'un ministre ◆ **the ~ benches** le banc des ministres ◆ **a ~ colleague** un(e) collègue ministre ◆ **the rules governing ~ conduct** le règlement régissant la conduite des ministres ◆ **at ~ level** à niveau ministériel ◆ **to hold ~ office** occuper des fonctions ministérielles 2 (Rel) ◆ **his ~ duties** les obligations de son ministère ◆ **a ~ friend of his in Glasgow** un de ses amis, ministre du culte à Glasgow

ministration /ˌmɪnɪsˈtreɪʃən/ N 1 ◆ **~s** (= services, help) soins mpl 2 (Rel) ministère m

ministry /ˈmɪnɪstrɪ/ N 1 (= government department) ministère m ◆ **Ministry of Health/Defence** ministère m de la Santé/Défense ◆ **to form a ~** (Parl) former un ministère or un gouvernement ◆ **the coalition ~ lasted two years** le ministère de coalition a duré deux ans 2 (= period of office) ministère m 3 (= clergy) **the ~** le saint ministère ◆ **to go into** or **enter the ~** devenir or se faire pasteur or ministre

minium /ˈmɪnɪəm/ N minium m

miniver /ˈmɪnɪvəʳ/ N menu-vair m

mink /mɪŋk/ N (pl **mink** or **minks**) (= animal, fur) vison m COMP [coat etc] de vison

minke /ˈmɪŋkɪ/ N ◆ **~ (whale)** baleine f minke

Minn. abbrev of **Minnesota**

minneola /ˌmɪnɪˈəʊlə/ N minnéola m

Minnesota /ˌmɪnɪˈsəʊtə/ N Minnesota m ◆ **in ~** dans le Minnesota

minnow /ˈmɪnəʊ/ N 1 (= specific species of fish) vairon m ; (= any small fish) fretin m 2 (fig = unimportant person) menu fretin m pl inv

Minoan /mɪˈnəʊən/ ADJ minoen

minor /ˈmaɪnəʳ/ ADJ [change, consideration, defect] (also Jur, Mus, Philos, Rel) mineur (-eure f) ; [detail, expenses, repairs] petit, menu ; [importance, interest, position, role] secondaire, mineur ◆ **~ poet** poète m mineur ◆ **~ problem/worry** problème m/souci m mineur ◆ **G ~** (Mus) sol mineur ◆ **~ key** (Mus) ton m mineur ◆ **in the ~ key** (Mus) en mineur ◆ **~ offence** (Jur) ≈ délit m mineur ◆ **~ operation** (Med) opération f bénigne ◆ **to play a ~ part** (Theat, fig) jouer un rôle accessoire or un petit rôle ◆ **~ planet** petite planète f, astéroïde m ◆ **~ suit** (Cards) (couleur f) mineure f ◆ **Smith ~** (Brit Scol) Smith junior N 1 (Jur) mineur(e) m(f) 2 (US Univ) matière f secondaire VI (US Univ) ◆ **to ~ in chemistry** étudier la chimie comme matière secondaire or sous-dominante

Minorca /mɪˈnɔːkə/ N Minorque f ◆ **in ~** à Minorque

minority /maɪˈnɒrɪtɪ/ N (also Jur) minorité f ◆ **in a** or **the ~** en minorité ◆ **you are in a ~ of one** (hum) vous êtes le seul à penser ainsi, personne ne partage vos vues or votre opinion ◆ **the reforms will affect only a small ~ of the**

population les réformes ne toucheront qu'une petite minorité de la population
COMP *[party, opinion, government]* minoritaire
minority president N *(US Pol) président n'ayant pas la majorité absolue au Congrès*
minority programme N *(Rad, TV)* émission *f* destinée à un public restreint
minority report N *(Admin)* rapport *m* soumis par un groupe minoritaire

Minos /'maɪnɒs/ N Minos *m*

Minotaur /'maɪnətɔːʳ/ N Minotaure *m*

minster /'mɪnstəʳ/ N cathédrale *f* ; *[of monastery]* église *f* abbatiale ◆ **York Minster** cathédrale *f* d'York

minstrel /'mɪnstrəl/ N *(Hist etc)* ménestrel *m*
COMP **minstrel gallery** N *(Archit)* tribune *f* des musiciens
minstrel show N *(Theat)* spectacle *m* de chanteurs et musiciens blancs déguisés en noirs

minstrelsy /'mɪnstrəlsɪ/ N *(NonC)* *(= art)* art *m* du ménestrel *or* trouvère *or* troubadour ; *(= songs)* chants *mpl*

mint¹ /mɪnt/ N 1 *(also Brit:* also **Royal Mint**) Monnaie *f*, hôtel *m* de la Monnaie 2 *(fig = large sum)* une *or* des somme(s) folle(s) ◆ **to make a ~ (of money)** faire fortune ◆ **he made a ~ in oil** * il a fait fortune dans le pétrole VT *[+ coins]* battre ; *[+ gold]* monnayer *(into* pour obtenir) ; *(fig)* *[+ word, expression]* forger, inventer ◆ **he ~s money** * il fait des affaires d'or, il ramasse l'argent à la pelle
COMP **mint condition** N ◆ **in ~ condition** à l'état (de) neuf, en parfaite condition
mint stamp N *(Philat)* timbre *m* non oblitéré

mint² /mɪnt/ N *(= plant, leaves, extract)* menthe *f* ; *(= sweet)* bonbon *m* à la menthe
COMP *[chocolate, sauce]* à la menthe
mint julep N *(US)* whisky *m etc* glacé à la menthe
mint sauce N sauce *f* à la menthe
mint tea N *(= herbal tea)* infusion *f* de menthe ; *(= tea with mint)* thé *m* à la menthe

-minted /'mɪntɪd/ ADJ *(in compounds)* ◆ **newly-minted** *[coin]* tout neuf

minuet /,mɪnjʊ'et/ N menuet *m*

minus /'maɪnəs/ PREP 1 *(Math)* moins ◆ **five ~ three equals two** cinq moins trois égale(nt) deux ◆ **A/B ~** *(Scol)* ≃ A/B moins
2 *(* = without)* sans, avec ... en *or* de moins ◆ **he arrived ~ his coat** il est arrivé sans son manteau ◆ **they found his wallet ~ the money** ils ont retrouvé son portefeuille mais sans l'argent ◆ **~ a finger** avec un doigt en *or* de moins
N *(Math)* *(= sign)* moins *m* ; *(= amount)* quantité *f* négative ◆ **the ~es** *(fig: of situation etc)* les inconvénients *mpl* ◆ **the ~es far outweigh any possible gain** les inconvénients l'emportent largement sur les avantages éventuels ◆ **the plusses and ~es were about equal** les avantages et les inconvénients s'équilibraient plus ou moins
COMP **minus quantity** N *(Math)* quantité *f* négative ; *(* fig)* quantité *f* négligeable
minus sign N *(Math)* (signe *m*) moins *m*

minuscule /'mɪnə,skjuːl/ ADJ minuscule

minute¹ /'mɪnɪt/ N 1 *(fig, of time)* minute *f* ◆ **it is 23 ~s past 2** il est 2 heures 23 (minutes) ◆ **at 4 o'clock to the ~** à 4 heures pile *or* tapant(es) ◆ **we got the train without a ~ to spare** une minute de plus et nous manquions le train ◆ **I'll do it in a ~** je le ferai dans une minute ◆ **I'll do it the ~ he comes** je le ferai dès qu'il arrivera ◆ **do it this ~!** * fais-le tout de suite *or* à la minute ! ◆ **he went out this (very) ~** * il vient tout juste de sortir ◆ **I've just this ~ heard of it** * je viens de l'apprendre à la minute ◆ **at any ~** à tout moment, d'une minute *or* d'un instant à l'autre ◆ **any ~ now** * d'une minute à l'autre ◆ **at the last ~** à la dernière minute ◆ **to leave things till the last ~** tout faire à la dernière minute ◆ **I'll just be a ~, I shan't be a ~** * j'en ai pour deux secondes ◆ **it won't take five ~s** ce sera fait en un rien de temps ◆ **I'm not suggesting for a ~ that he's lying** loin de moi l'idée qu'il ment ◆ **one ~ he's there, the next he's gone** une minute il est là, la minute d'après il est parti ◆ **one ~ you say you love me, the next you're threatening to leave** tu dis que tu m'aimes et deux minutes plus tard tu menaces de me quitter ◆ **it's a few ~s' walk from the station** c'est tout près de la gare, c'est à quelques minutes à pied de la gare ◆ **wait a ~, just a ~** attendez une minute *or* un instant *or* un moment ; *(indignantly)* minute ! ◆ **half a ~!** † une petite minute ! ◆ **there's one born every ~!** * il faut vraiment le faire ! *
2 *(Geog, Math = part of degree)* minute *f*
3 *(= official record)* compte rendu *m*, procès-verbal *m* ; *(Comm etc)* *(= memorandum)* note *f* ◆ **to take the ~s of a meeting** rédiger le procès-verbal *or* le compte rendu d'une réunion ◆ **who will take the ~s?** qui se charge du compte rendu ?
VT 1 *(= note etc)* *[+ fact, detail]* prendre note de ; *[+ meeting]* rédiger le compte rendu de, dresser le procès-verbal de
2 *(= send minute to)* *[+ person]* faire passer une note à *(about* au sujet de)
COMP **minute book** N *(Admin, Comm etc)* registre *m* des délibérations
minute hand N *[of clock etc]* grande aiguille *f*
minute steak N *(Culin)* entrecôte *f* minute

minute² /maɪ'njuːt/ ADJ *(= tiny)* *[object, amount, variation, trace]* minuscule ; *(= detailed)* *[examination, analysis]* minutieux ◆ **in ~ or the ~st detail** jusque dans les moindres *or* plus infimes détails

minutely /maɪ'njuːtlɪ/ ADV 1 *(= in detail)* *[examine, describe]* minutieusement, dans les moindres détails ◆ **a ~ detailed account** un compte rendu extrêmement détaillé *or* circonstancié 2 *(= slightly)* *[move, change, differ]* très légèrement ◆ **anything ~ resembling a fish** quelque chose ayant très vaguement l'apparence d'un poisson 3 *(= very small)* *[write, fold]* en tout petit

minutiae /mɪ'njuːʃɪiː/ NPL menus détails *mpl*

minx /mɪŋks/ N (petite) espiègle *f*

Miocene /'maɪə,siːn/ ADJ, N miocène *m*

MIPS, mips /mɪps/ N (abbrev of **millions of instructions per second**) MIPS

miracle /'mɪrəkl/ N miracle *m* ◆ **by a ~, by some ~** par miracle ◆ **it is a ~ of ingenuity** c'est un miracle *or* une merveille d'ingéniosité ◆ **it is a ~ that** ... c'est miracle que ... + *subj* ◆ **it will be a ~ if** ... ce sera (un) miracle si ...
COMP **miracle cure, miracle drug** N remède *m* miracle
miracle-man N (pl **miracle-men**) faiseur *m* de miracles
miracle play N *(Rel, Theat)* miracle *m*
miracle worker N *(fig)* ◆ **I'm not a ~ worker!** * je ne sais pas faire de miracles !

miraculous /mɪ'rækjʊləs/ ADJ *(Rel, fig)* miraculeux ◆ **to make a ~ escape** en réchapper miraculeusement ◆ **to make a ~ recovery** guérir miraculeusement ◆ **to be little** *or* **nothing short of ~** être tout bonnement miraculeux

miraculously /mɪ'rækjʊləslɪ/ ADV 1 *(= as if by miracle)* *[survive, escape, transform]* miraculeusement, par miracle ◆ **to be ~ intact/unharmed** être miraculeusement intact/indemne ◆ **~ the baby appeared to be unhurt** par miracle, il semblait que le bébé était indemne 2 *(= extremely)* *[beautiful]* merveilleusement

mirage /'mɪrɑːʒ/ N *(lit, fig)* mirage *m*

MIRAS /'maɪræs/ N *(Brit Fin)* (abbrev of **mortgage interest relief at source**) *exonération fiscale à la source sur les intérêts d'emprunts hypothécaires*

mire /'maɪəʳ/ N *(liter)* *(= mud)* fange *f* *(liter)* ; *(= swampy ground)* bourbier *m* ◆ **to drag sb's name through the ~** traîner (le nom de) qn dans la fange *or* la boue

mired /'maɪəd/ ADJ *(esp liter)* 1 *(= dirtied)* ◆ **~ in mud** *[vehicle]* embourbé ; *[road]* recouvert de boue 2 *(= involved)* ◆ **~ in debt** endetté jusqu'au cou ◆ **~ in scandal** fortement compromis dans un scandale

mirror /'mɪrəʳ/ N miroir *m*, glace *f* ; *[of vehicle]* rétroviseur *m* ; *(fig)* miroir *m* ◆ **hand ~** miroir *m* à main ◆ **pocket ~** miroir *m* de poche ◆ **to look at o.s. in the ~** se regarder dans le miroir *or* dans la glace ◆ **it holds a ~ (up) to ...** *(fig)* cela reflète ... VT *(lit, fig)* refléter ◆ **to be ~ed in** *or* **by sth** se refléter dans qch
COMP **mirror image** N image *f* inversée
mirror site N *(Comput)* site *m* miroir
mirror writing N écriture *f* en miroir

mirth /mɜːθ/ N *(NonC)* hilarité *f* ◆ **this remark caused some ~** cette remarque a déclenché une certaine hilarité

mirthful /'mɜːθfʊl/ ADJ *(liter)* gai, joyeux

mirthless /'mɜːθlɪs/ ADJ sans joie

mirthlessly /mɜːθlɪslɪ/ ADV sans joie

MIRV /mɜːv/ (abbrev of **Multiple Independently Targeted Re-entry Vehicle**) MIRV *m*

miry /'maɪərɪ/ ADJ *(liter)* fangeux *(liter)*, bourbeux

MIS /,emaɪ'es/ N (abbrev of **management information system**) SIG *m*

misadventure /,mɪsəd'ventʃəʳ/ N mésaventure *f* ; *(less serious)* contretemps *m* ◆ **death by ~** *(Jur)* mort *f* accidentelle

misalignment /mɪsə'laɪnmənt/ N mauvais alignement *m* ◆ **the dollar ~** le mauvais alignement du dollar

misalliance /,mɪsə'laɪəns/ N mésalliance *f*

misanthrope /'mɪzənθrəʊp/ N misanthrope *mf*

misanthropic /,mɪzən'θrɒpɪk/ ADJ *[person]* misanthrope ; *[feeling, mood, view]* de misanthrope

misanthropist /mɪ'zænθrəpɪst/ N misanthrope *mf*

misanthropy /mɪ'zænθrəpɪ/ N misanthropie *f*

misapplication /,mɪsæplɪ'keɪʃən/ N *[of knowledge]* usage *m* impropre ; *[of funds]* détournement *m*

misapply /'mɪsə'plaɪ/ VT *[+ discovery, knowledge]* mal employer, mal appliquer ; *[+ abilities, intelligence]* mal employer ; *[+ money, funds]* détourner

misapprehend /'mɪs,æprɪ'hend/ VT mal comprendre, se faire une idée fausse de *or* sur

misapprehension /'mɪs,æprɪ'henʃən/ N malentendu *m*, méprise *f* ◆ **there seems to be some ~** il semble y avoir malentendu *or* méprise

misappropriate /'mɪsə'prəʊprɪeɪt/ VT *[+ money, funds]* détourner

misappropriation /'mɪsə,prəʊprɪ'eɪʃən/ N détournement *m*

misbegotten /'mɪsbɪ'gɒtn/ ADJ 1 *(lit: liter)* illégitime, bâtard 2 *(fig = misguided)* *[plan, scheme]* mal conçu, malencontreux

misbehave /'mɪsbɪ'heɪv/ VI se conduire mal ; *[child]* ne pas être sage, se tenir mal

misbehaviour, misbehavior (US) /'mɪsbɪ'heɪvjəʳ/ N *[of person, child]* mauvaise conduite *f* ; *(stronger)* inconduite *f*

misbelief /'mɪsbɪ'liːf/ N *(Rel)* croyance *f* fausse

misbeliever /'mɪsbɪ'liːvəʳ/ N *(Rel)* mécréant(e) *m(f)*

misc. ADJ (abbrev of **miscellaneous**) divers

miscalculate /ˈmɪsˈkælkjʊleɪt/ VT mal calculer VI (fig) se tromper

miscalculation /ˈmɪsˌkælkjʊˈleɪʃən/ N (lit, fig) erreur f de calcul, mauvais calcul m

miscall /ˈmɪsˈkɔːl/ VT mal nommer, appeler à tort

miscarriage /ˈmɪsˈkærɪdʒ/ N 1 [of plan etc] insuccès m, échec m ; [of letter, goods] perte f ◆ **~ of justice** erreur f judiciaire 2 (Med) fausse couche f ◆ **to have a ~** faire une fausse couche

miscarry /ˌmɪsˈkærɪ/ VI 1 [plan, scheme] échouer, avorter ; [letter, goods] s'égarer, ne pas arriver à destination 2 (Med) faire une fausse couche

miscast /ˈmɪsˈkɑːst/ (pret, ptp **miscast**) VT (Cine, Theat etc) ◆ **the play has been ~** la distribution est mauvaise ◆ **he was ~** on n'aurait pas dû lui donner or attribuer ce rôle

miscegenation /ˌmɪsɪdʒɪˈneɪʃən/ N croisement m entre races (humaines)

miscellaneous /ˌmɪsɪˈleɪnɪəs/ ADJ [people, objects, writings, costs] divers ; [collection] hétéroclite ◆ **categorized** or **classified as "miscellaneous"** classé "divers" ◆ **"miscellaneous"** (on agenda) "divers"

COMP **miscellaneous expenses** NPL frais mpl divers

miscellaneous items NPL (Comm) articles mpl divers ; (Press) faits mpl divers

miscellany /mɪˈselənɪ/ N [of objects etc] collection f hétéroclite ; (Literat) sélection f, anthologie f ; (Rad, TV) sélection f, choix m ◆ **miscellanies** (Literat) miscellanées fpl, (volume m de) mélanges mpl

mischance /ˌmɪsˈtʃɑːns/ N mésaventure f, malchance f ◆ **by (a) ~** par malheur

mischief /ˈmɪstʃɪf/ N 1 (NonC) (= roguishness) malice f, espièglerie f ; (= naughtiness) sottises fpl, polissonnerie f ; (= maliciousness) méchanceté f ◆ **he's up to (some) ~** [child] il (nous) prépare une sottise ; [adult] (in fun) il (nous) prépare une farce or niche ; (from malice) il médite un mauvais tour or coup ◆ **he's always up to some ~** il trouve toujours une sottise or niche à faire ◆ **to get into ~** [child only] faire des sottises, faire des siennes ◆ **to keep sb out of ~** empêcher qn de faire des sottises or des bêtises, garder qn sur le droit chemin (hum) ◆ **the children managed to keep out of ~** les enfants sont arrivés à ne pas faire de sottises, les enfants ont même été sages ◆ **he means ~** [child] il va sûrement faire une sottise ; [adult] (in fun) il va sûrement faire une farce ; (from malice) il est mal intentionné ◆ **out of sheer ~** (for fun) par pure espièglerie ; (from malice) par pure méchanceté ◆ **full of ~** espiègle, plein de malice ◆ **bubbling over with ~** pétillant de malice ◆ **to make ~ (for sb)** créer des ennuis (à qn) ◆ **to make ~ between two people** semer la zizanie or la discorde entre deux personnes

2 (* = child) polisson(ne) m(f), petit(e) vilain(e) m(f)

3 (= injury, damage) mal m ; (to ship, building etc) dommage m, dégât(s) m(pl) ◆ **to do sb a ~** * faire mal à qn ◆ **to do o.s. a ~** se faire mal

COMP **mischief-maker** N semeur m, -euse f de discorde, faiseur m, -euse f d'histoires ; (esp gossip) mauvaise langue f

mischievous /ˈmɪstʃɪvəs/ ADJ 1 (= impish) [person, nature, smile, glance] malicieux ; (= naughty) [child, trick] vilain ; [kitten, behaviour] espiègle 2 (= malicious) [person, behaviour, attempt, suggestion, rumour] malveillant

mischievously /ˈmɪstʃɪvəslɪ/ ADV 1 (= impishly) [say, smile] malicieusement ; (= naughtily) [behave] mal 2 (= maliciously) [suggest, claim, attempt] avec malveillance

mischievousness /ˈmɪstʃɪvəsnɪs/ N (= roguishness) malice f, espièglerie f ; (= naughtiness) polissonnerie f

misconceive /ˈmɪskənˈsiːv/ VT mal comprendre, mal interpréter VI se tromper, se méprendre (of sur)

misconceived /ˌmɪskənˈsiːvd/ ADJ [policy, plan, approach] peu judicieux ; [idea] faux (fausse f), erroné

misconception /ˈmɪskənˈsepʃən/ N 1 (= wrong idea/opinion) idée f/opinion f fausse or erronée 2 (= misunderstanding) malentendu m, méprise f

misconduct /ˌmɪsˈkɒndʌkt/ N 1 (= bad behaviour) mauvaise conduite f ; (Jur: sexual) adultère m ; (Sport) mauvaise conduite f ◆ **to be sacked for ~** être licencié pour faute professionnelle ◆ **gross ~** faute f (professionnelle) grave ◆ **professional ~** faute f professionnelle ◆ **allegations of police ~** des allégations fpl selon lesquelles la police aurait commis des abus 2 (= bad management) [of business etc] mauvaise administration f or gestion f VT /ˌmɪskənˈdʌkt/ [+ business] mal diriger, mal gérer ◆ **to ~ o.s.** † se conduire mal

misconstruction /ˈmɪskənˈstrʌkʃən/ N (= misinterpretation) fausse interprétation f ◆ **words open to ~** mots qui prêtent à méprise or contresens

misconstrue /ˈmɪskənˈstruː/ VT [+ acts, words] mal interpréter

miscount /ˈmɪsˈkaʊnt/ N (gen) mécompte m ; (Pol: during election) erreur f de comptage or dans le décompte des voix VTI mal compter

miscreant /ˈmɪskrɪənt/ N (frm) scélérat(e) m(f), gredin(e) m(f)

misdeal /ˈmɪsˈdiːl/ (vb : pret, ptp **misdealt**) (Cards) N maldonne f VTI ◆ **to ~ (the cards)** faire maldonne

misdeed /ˈmɪsˈdiːd/ N méfait m, mauvaise action f ; (stronger) crime m

misdemeanour, misdemeanor (US) /ˌmɪsdɪˈmiːnəʳ/ N 1 (= misdeed) incartade f, écart m de conduite ; (more serious) méfait m 2 (Jur) (Brit) infraction f, contravention f ; (US) délit m

misdescribe /ˌmɪsdɪˈskraɪb/ VT [+ goods for sale] décrire de façon mensongère

misdiagnose /ˈmɪsdaɪəgnəʊz/ VT 1 (Med) [+ illness] faire une erreur de diagnostic au sujet de ; [+ patient] faire une erreur de diagnostic sur 2 (= analyse wrongly) [+ problem, situation] faire une erreur d'analyse quant à

misdiagnosis /ˌmɪsdaɪəgˈnəʊsɪs/ N (pl **misdiagnoses** /ˌmɪsdaɪəgˈnəʊsiːz/) 1 (Med) [of illness] erreur f de diagnostic 2 (= wrong analysis) [of problem, situation] erreur f d'analyse

misdirect /ˈmɪsdɪˈrekt/ VT [+ letter etc] mal acheminer ; [+ person] mal renseigner ; [+ blow, efforts] mal diriger, mal orienter ; [+ operation, scheme] mener mal ◆ **to ~ the jury** (Jur) mal instruire le jury

misdirection /ˈmɪsdɪˈrekʃən/ N [of letter etc] erreur f d'acheminement ; [of blow, efforts] mauvaise orientation f ; [of operation, scheme] mauvaise conduite f

miser /ˈmaɪzəʳ/ N avare mf, grippe-sou m

miserable /ˈmɪzərəbl/ ADJ 1 (= unhappy) [person, face, look, experience] malheureux ◆ **to feel ~** (= unhappy) ne pas avoir le moral ; (= unwell) être mal en point ◆ **to make sb's life ~, to make life ~ for sb** [person] mener la vie dure à qn ; [illness] gâcher la vie à qn ◆ **don't look so ~!** ne fais pas cette tête ! ◆ **she's been having a ~ time recently** la vie n'est pas drôle pour elle en ce moment ◆ **we had a ~ time on holiday** nos vacances ont été un vrai cauchemar

2 ◆ **~ weather** * (= awful) un temps affreux, un très sale temps ; (= depressing, overcast) un temps maussade

3 (= wretched, abject) [person, place, conditions, life, existence] misérable ; [sight] lamentable, déplorable ; [failure] lamentable

4 (= paltry) [number, amount] dérisoire ; [offer] minable ; [salary] dérisoire, de misère ; [meal] piteux ; [gift] miteux ◆ **a ~ 10 euros** la somme dérisoire de 10 euros

miserably /ˈmɪzərəblɪ/ ADV 1 (= unhappily) [say, look, smile, nod] d'un air malheureux ◆ **a ~ unhappy family** une famille des plus misérables et malheureuses ◆ **it was ~ cold and wet** il faisait désagréablement froid et humide 2 (= wretchedly, horribly) [live] misérablement ; [perform, fail] lamentablement ◆ **a ~ low wage** un salaire de misère ◆ **they played ~** ils ont été minables, ils ont joué d'une façon minable

misère /mɪˈzeəʳ/ N (Cards) misère f

miserliness /ˈmaɪzəlɪnɪs/ N avarice f

miserly /ˈmaɪzəlɪ/ ADJ 1 (= mean) [person] avare (with sth de qch) 2 (= parsimonious) [sum, amount, offer] dérisoire ◆ **a ~ 8 dollars** 8 malheureux dollars

misery /ˈmɪzərɪ/ N 1 (= unhappiness) tristesse f, douleur f ; (= suffering) souffrances fpl, supplice m ; (= wretchedness) misère f, détresse f ◆ **the miseries of mankind** la misère de l'homme ◆ **a life of ~** une vie de misère ◆ **to make sb's life a ~** [person] mener la vie dure à qn ; [illness] gâcher la vie de qn ◆ **to put an animal out of its ~** achever un animal ◆ **put him out of his ~** * **and tell him the results** abrégez son supplice et donnez-lui les résultats 2 (Brit * = gloomy person) (child) pleurnicheur m, -euse f ; (adult) grincheux m, -euse f, rabat-joie m inv ◆ **what a ~ you are!** ce que tu peux être grincheux or rabat-joie ! COMP **misery-guts** N râleur * m, -euse * f, rabat-joie m inv

misfire /ˈmɪsˈfaɪəʳ/ VI [gun] faire long feu, rater ; [plan] rater, foirer * ; [joke] tomber à plat ; [car engine] avoir des ratés

misfit /ˈmɪsfɪt/ N 1 (Dress) vêtement m mal réussi or qui ne va pas bien 2 (fig = person) inadapté(e) m(f) ◆ **he's always been a ~ here** il ne s'est jamais intégré ici, il n'a jamais su s'adapter ici ; → **social**

misfortune /mɪsˈfɔːtʃən/ N (single event) malheur m ; (NonC = bad luck) malchance f, infortune f (liter) ◆ **~s never come singly** un malheur n'arrive jamais seul ◆ **~ dogs his footsteps** (liter) il joue de malchance ◆ **he'd had more than his fair share of ~** il avait eu plus que sa part de malheur ◆ **companion in ~** compagnon m or compagne f d'infortune ◆ **it is his ~ that he is deaf** pour son malheur il est sourd ◆ **I had the ~ to meet him** par malheur or par malchance je l'ai rencontré ◆ **that's your ~!** tant pis pour toi !

misgiving /mɪsˈgɪvɪŋ/ N (= worries) inquiétude f ; (= doubts) doutes mpl ◆ **to have ~s about sb/sth** avoir des doutes au sujet de qn/qch ◆ **her son is already having ~s about religion** son fils se pose déjà des questions sur la religion ◆ **not without some ~(s)** non sans hésitation

misgovern /ˈmɪsˈgʌvən/ VTI mal gouverner, mal administrer

misgovernment /ˈmɪsˈgʌvənmənt/ N mauvaise gestion f

misguided /ˈmɪsˈgaɪdɪd/ ADJ [person] dans l'erreur ; [attempt] peu judicieux ; [patriotism, idealism] fourvoyé ; [belief, view, policy] erroné ◆ **to be ~ in sth/in doing sth** faire erreur en ce qui concerne qch/en faisant qch ◆ **it would be ~ to do that** ce serait une erreur de faire cela

misguidedly /ˈmɪsˈgaɪdɪdlɪ/ ADV malencontreusement, peu judicieusement, à mauvais escient

mishandle /ˈmɪsˈhændl/ VT 1 (= treat roughly) [+ object] manier or manipuler sans précaution 2 *(= mismanage) [+ person]* mal prendre, mal s'y prendre avec ; *[+ problem]* mal traiter, mal aborder ◆ **he ~d the whole situation** il a mal géré l'ensemble de la situation

mishap /ˈmɪshæp/ N mésaventure *f* ◆ **slight ~** contretemps *m*, anicroche *f* ◆ **without ~** sans encombre ◆ **he had a ~** il lui est arrivé une (petite) mésaventure

mishear /mɪsˈhɪəʳ/ (pret, ptp **misheard** /mɪsˈhɜːd/) VT mal entendre

mishit /mɪsˈhɪt/ N coup *m* manqué VT *[+ ball]* mal jouer

mishmash* /ˈmɪʃmæʃ/ N méli-mélo* *m*

misinform /ˈmɪsɪnˈfɔːm/ VT mal renseigner

misinformation /ˌmɪsɪnfəˈmeɪʃən/ N désinformation *f*

misinterpret /ˈmɪsɪnˈtɜːprɪt/ VT mal interpréter, prendre à contresens

misinterpretation /ˈmɪsɪnˌtɜːprɪˈteɪʃən/ N interprétation *f* erronée *(of* de), contresens *m* ◆ **open to ~** qui prête à confusion

misjudge /ˈmɪsˈdʒʌdʒ/ VT *[+ amount, numbers, time]* mal évaluer ; *(= underestimate)* sous-estimer ; *[+ person]* méjuger, se méprendre sur le compte de

misjudg(e)ment /ˌmɪsˈdʒʌdʒmənt/ N *[of person, situation, mood, attitude]* appréciation *f* erronée ; *[of time, distance, speed, amount]* mauvaise évaluation *f* ◆ **the government's economic misjudg(e)ments** les erreurs de jugement du gouvernement en matière d'économie

miskick /ˌmɪsˈkɪk/ VT ◆ **to ~ the ball** rater son coup de pied N coup *m* de pied raté

mislay /ˌmɪsˈleɪ/ (pret, ptp **mislaid**) VT égarer

mislead /ˌmɪsˈliːd/ (pret, ptp **misled**) VT *(accidentally)* induire en erreur, tromper ; *(deliberately)* tromper, fourvoyer

misleading /ˌmɪsˈliːdɪŋ/ ADJ *[information, report, statement]* trompeur ◆ **~ advertising** publicité *f* mensongère ◆ **it would be ~ to suggest that ...** il serait trompeur de suggérer que ...

misleadingly /ˌmɪsˈliːdɪŋlɪ/ ADV *[describe]* de façon trompeuse

misled /ˌmɪsˈled/ VB pt, ptp of **mislead**

mislike † /mɪsˈlaɪk/ VT ne pas aimer, détester

mismanage /ˈmɪsˈmænɪdʒ/ VT *[+ business, estate, shop]* mal gérer, gérer en dépit du bon sens ; *[+ institution, organization]* mal administrer ◆ **the whole situation has been ~d** l'affaire a été mal gérée d'un bout à l'autre

mismanagement /ˈmɪsˈmænɪdʒmənt/ N mauvaise gestion *f* or administration *f*

mismatch /mɪsˈmætʃ/ N *[of objects]* disparité *f* ; *[of colours, styles]* dissonance *f*

mismatched /mɪsˈmætʃt/ ADJ *[people, things]* mal assortis

misname /ˈmɪsˈneɪm/ VT donner un nom inexact or impropre à, mal nommer

misnomer /ˈmɪsˈnəʊməʳ/ N terme *m* impropre ◆ **that is a ~** c'est un terme qui ne convient guère

misogamist /mɪˈsɒgəmɪst/ N misogame *mf*

misogamy /mɪˈsɒgəmɪ/ N misogamie *f*

misogynist /mɪˈsɒdʒɪnɪst/ N misogyne *mf* ADJ *(= misogynistic)* misogyne

misogynistic /mɪˌsɒdʒɪˈnɪstɪk/ ADJ misogyne

misogyny /mɪˈsɒdʒɪnɪ/ N misogynie *f*

misplace /ˈmɪsˈpleɪs/ VT 1 *[+ object, word]* mal placer, ne pas mettre où il faudrait ; *[+ affection, trust]* mal placer 2 *(= lose)* égarer

misplaced /ˈmɪsˈpleɪst/ ADJ *[remark, humour]* déplacé

misprint /ˈmɪsprɪnt/ N faute *f* d'impression or typographique, coquille *f* VT /mɪsˈprɪnt/ imprimer mal or incorrectement

mispronounce /ˈmɪsprəˈnaʊns/ VT prononcer de travers, écorcher

mispronunciation /ˈmɪsprəˌnʌnsɪˈeɪʃən/ N prononciation *f* incorrecte *(of* de), faute(s) *f(pl)* de prononciation

misquotation /ˈmɪskwəʊˈteɪʃən/ N citation *f* inexacte

misquote /ˈmɪsˈkwəʊt/ VT citer faussement or inexactement ◆ **he was ~d in the press** la presse a déformé ses propos ◆ **he was ~d as having said ...** on lui a incorrectement fait dire que ... ◆ **he said that he had been ~d** il a dit qu'on avait déformé ses propos

misread /ˈmɪsˈriːd/ (pret, ptp **misread** /ˈmɪsˈred/) VT 1 *(lit) [+ word]* mal lire ◆ **he misread "bat" as "rat"** il s'est trompé et a lu "rat" au lieu de "bat" 2 *(fig = misinterpret) [+ sb's reply, signs etc]* mal interpréter, se tromper sur ◆ **he misread the statements as promises of ...** il s'est mépris sur les déclarations en y voyant des promesses de ..., il a vu à tort dans ces déclarations des promesses de ... ◆ **he misread the whole situation** il a interprété la situation de façon tout à fait incorrecte

misremember /mɪsrɪˈmembəʳ/ VT *(esp US: frm)* se tromper (dans son souvenir) sur

misrepresent /ˈmɪsˌreprɪˈzent/ VT *[+ facts]* dénaturer, déformer ; *[+ person]* présenter sous un faux jour, donner une impression incorrecte de ◆ **he was ~ed in the press** *(= wrongly portrayed)* la presse a donné de lui une image inexacte ; *(= misquoted)* la presse a déformé ses propos

misrepresentation /ˈmɪsˌreprɪzenˈteɪʃən/ N déformation *f*, présentation *f* déformée ◆ **their ~ of the facts ...** le fait qu'ils aient déformé les faits ... ◆ **the programme is guilty of bias and ~** l'émission véhicule des préjugés et déforme la réalité

misrule /ˈmɪsˈruːl/ N 1 *(= bad government)* mauvaise administration *f* 2 *(= disorder)* désordre *m*, anarchie *f* VT gouverner mal

miss¹ /mɪs/ N 1 *(= shot etc)* coup *m* manqué or raté ; *(* = omission)* manque *m*, lacune* *f* ; *(* = mistake)* erreur *f*, faute *f* ◆ **a ~ is as good as a mile** *(Prov)* rater c'est rater (même de justesse) ; → **hit, near**

◆ **to give sth a miss*** se passer de qch ◆ **to give a concert/a lecture/the Louvre a ~*** se passer d'aller à un concert/à une conférence/au Louvre ◆ **I'll give the wine a ~ this evening*** je me passerai de vin ce soir ◆ **I'll give my evening class a ~ this week*** tant pis pour mon cours du soir cette semaine ◆ **oh give it a ~!*** ça suffit !, arrête !

2 *(= failure)* four *m*, bide* *m* ◆ **they voted the record a ~*** le disque a été jugé minable*

VT 1 *(= fail to hit) [+ target, goal]* manquer ◆ **the shot just ~ed me** la balle m'a manqué de justesse or d'un cheveu ◆ **the plane just ~ed the tower** l'avion a failli toucher la tour

2 *(= fail to find, catch, use etc) [+ vocation, opportunity, appointment, train, person to be met, cue, road, turning]* manquer, rater ; *[+ house, thing looked out for, solution]* ne pas trouver, ne pas voir ; *[+ meal]* sauter ; *[+ class, lecture]* manquer ◆ **you haven't ~ed much!** *(iro)* vous n'avez pas manqué or perdu grand-chose ! ◆ **we ~ed the tide** nous avons manqué la marée ◆ **you ~ed your vocation** vous avez raté votre vocation ◆ **to ~ the boat* or the bus*** louper le coche* ◆ **to ~ one's cue** *(Theat)* manquer sa réplique ; *(fig)* rater l'occasion, manquer le coche* ◆ **to ~ one's footing** glisser ◆ **she doesn't ~ much** or **a trick*** rien ne lui échappe ◆ **to ~ one's way** perdre son chemin, s'égarer ◆ **you can't ~ our house** vous trouverez tout de suite notre maison ◆ **you mustn't ~ (seeing) this film** ne manquez pas (de voir) or ne ratez pas ce film, c'est un film à ne pas manquer or rater ◆ **don't ~ the Louvre** ne manquez pas d'aller au Louvre ◆ **if we go that way we'll ~ Bourges** si nous prenons cette route nous ne verrons pas Bourges ◆ **I ~ed him at the station by five minutes** je l'ai manqué or raté de cinq minutes à la gare ◆ **to ~ a payment (on sth)** sauter un versement (pour qch) ◆ **I've never ~ed a payment on my mortgage** je n'ai jamais sauté de versement pour mon emprunt immobilier

3 *[+ remark, joke, meaning] (= not hear)* manquer, ne pas entendre ; *(= not understand)* ne pas comprendre, ne pas saisir ◆ **I ~ed what you said** je n'ai pas entendu ce que vous avez dit ◆ **I ~ed that** je n'ai pas entendu, je n'ai pas compris ◆ **I ~ed the point of that joke** je n'ai pas compris ce que ça avait de drôle, je n'ai pas saisi l'astuce ◆ **you've ~ed the whole point!** vous n'avez rien compris !, vous avez laissé passer l'essentiel !

4 *(= escape, avoid) [+ accident, bad weather]* échapper à ◆ **he narrowly ~ed being killed** il a manqué or il a bien failli se (faire) tuer

5 *(= long for) [+ person]* regretter (l'absence de) ◆ **I do ~ Paris** Paris me manque beaucoup ◆ **we ~ you very much** nous regrettons beaucoup ton absence, tu nous manques beaucoup ◆ **are you ~ing me?** est-ce que je te manque ? ◆ **they're ~ing one another** ils se manquent l'un à l'autre ◆ **he will be greatly ~ed** on le regrettera beaucoup ◆ **he won't be ~ed** personne ne le regrettera, bon débarras ◆ **I ~ the old trams** je regrette les vieux trams ◆ **I ~ the sunshine/the freedom** le soleil/la liberté me manque ◆ **I ~ going to concerts** les concerts me manquent

6 *(= notice loss of) [+ money, valuables]* remarquer l'absence or la disparition de ◆ **I suddenly noticed I was ~ing my wallet** tout d'un coup je me suis aperçu que je n'avais plus mon portefeuille ◆ **I'm ~ing 8 dollars*** il me manque 8 dollars ◆ **here's your hat back – I hadn't even ~ed it!** je vous rends votre chapeau – je ne m'étais même pas aperçu or n'avais même pas remarqué que je ne l'avais plus ! ◆ **you can keep that pen, I won't ~ it** vous pouvez garder ce stylo, je n'en aurai pas besoin

VI *[shot, person]* manquer son coup, rater ◆ **you can't ~!** *(fig)* vous ne pouvez pas ne pas réussir ! ; see also **missing**

▸ **miss out** VT SEP *(esp Brit)* 1 *(accidentally) [+ name, word, line of verse, page]* sauter, oublier ; *(in distributing sth) [+ person]* sauter, oublier

2 *(on purpose) [+ course at meal]* ne pas prendre, sauter ; *[+ name on list]* omettre ; *[+ word, line of verse, page]* laisser de côté, sauter ; *[+ concert, lecture, museum]* ne pas aller à ; *(in distributing sth) [+ person]* omettre

VI *(= lose out)* ◆ **I feel my children ~ out because we don't have much money** j'ai l'impression que mes enfants sont désavantagés parce que nous n'avons pas beaucoup d'argent ◆ **I feel I ~ed out by not having my father around when I was growing up** j'ai le sentiment que l'absence de mon père pendant mon enfance m'a privé de quelque chose d'important

▸ **miss out on*** VT FUS 1 *(= fail to benefit from) [+ opportunity, bargain]* rater, louper* ; *[+ one's share]* ne pas recevoir, perdre ◆ **he ~ed out on several good deals** il a raté or loupé* plusieurs bonnes affaires

2 *(= come off badly)* **he ~ed out on the deal** il n'a pas obtenu tout ce qu'il aurait pu de l'affaire ◆ **make sure you don't ~ out on anything** vérifie que tu reçois ton dû

miss² /mɪs/ N 1 Mademoiselle *f* ◆ **Miss Smith** Mademoiselle Smith, Mlle Smith ◆ **the Misses Smith** † les demoiselles *fpl* Smith ; *(on letter)* Mesdemoiselles Smith ◆ **Dear Miss**

Smith *(in letter)* Chère Mademoiselle ◆ **yes Miss Smith** oui, Mademoiselle ◆ **yes, ~*** oui, Mademoiselle ◆ **Miss France 2000** Miss France 2000 [2] †* petite *or* jeune fille *f* ◆ **the modern ~** la jeune fille moderne ◆ **she's a cheeky little ~** c'est une petite effrontée

Miss. abbrev of **Mississippi**

missal /ˈmɪsəl/ N missel *m*

mis-sell /mɪsˈsel/ (pt, pp **mis-sold**) VT ◆ **to ~ pensions** vendre des contrats de retraite lésant les souscripteurs *or* des contrats de retraite inadaptés ◆ **to be mis-sold a pension** souscrire un contrat de retraite inadapté

mis-selling /mɪsˈselɪŋ/ N ◆ **the ~ of pensions** la vente de contrats de retraite lésant les souscripteurs *or* de contrats de retraite inadaptés

misshapen /ˈmɪsˈʃeɪpən/ ADJ difforme

missile /ˈmɪsaɪl/ N *(Mil)* missile *m* ; *(= stone etc thrown)* projectile *m* ; → **ballistic, ground¹, guided**

COMP **missile base** N base *f* de missiles *(or* fusées*)*

missile launcher N lance-missiles *m inv*

missing /ˈmɪsɪŋ/ ADJ [1] *(= lost)* ◆ **to be ~** *[person, object]* avoir disparu *(from sth* de qch*)* ◆ **to go ~** disparaître ◆ **there is one plate ~, one plate has gone** *or* **is ~** il manque une assiette ◆ **~ luggage** bagages *mpl* égarés

[2] *(= lacking)* ◆ **to be ~** *[person, object, details, information]* manquer *(from sth* à qch*)* ◆ **two pieces are ~** il manque deux pièces ◆ **how many are ~?** combien en manque-t-il ? ◆ **there's nothing ~** il ne manque rien, tout y est ◆ **there's a button ~ on** *or* **from my jacket** il manque un bouton à ma veste ◆ **he had a tooth ~** il lui manquait une dent, il avait une dent en moins ◆ **fill in the ~ words** trouvez les mots manquants *or* qui manquent

[3] *[serviceman, fisherman, plane]* porté disparu ◆ **~ in action** ADJ porté disparu N soldat *m etc* porté disparu ◆ **~ (and) presumed dead, ~ believed killed** *or* **presumed dead, reported ~** porté disparu ◆ **one of our aircraft is ~** un de nos avions n'est pas rentré

COMP **the missing link** N *(Anthropology)* le chaînon manquant ; *(detail)* l'élément *m* manquant

missing person N personne *f* disparue ◆ **~ persons file** fichier *m* des personnes disparues

Missing Persons* N *(US)* ⇒ **Missing Persons Bureau**

Missing Persons Bureau N *service de police enquêtant sur les personnes disparues*

mission /ˈmɪʃən/ N *(all senses)* mission *f* ◆ **foreign ~s** *(Rel)* missions *fpl* étrangères ◆ **to send sb on a ~ to sb** envoyer qn en mission auprès de qn ◆ **his ~ in life is to help others** il s'est donné pour mission d'aider autrui ; → **trade**

COMP **mission control** N *(Space etc)* centre *m* de contrôle

mission controller N ingénieur *m* du centre de contrôle

mission statement N *(= description of work to be done)* cahier *m* des charges

missionary /ˈmɪʃənrɪ/ N missionnaire *mf* COMP *[work, duties]* missionnaire ; *[society]* de missionnaires

missionary position N *(sex)* position *f* du missionnaire

missis‡ /ˈmɪsɪz/ N ◆ **the/my ~** *(= wife)* la/ma bourgeoise‡ ◆ **the ~** *(= boss)* la patronne‡ ◆ **hey ~!** eh, Madame !*

Mississippi /ˌmɪsɪˈsɪpɪ/ N *(= state, river)* Mississippi *m* ◆ **in ~** dans le Mississippi ◆ **the ~ Delta** le delta du Mississippi

missive /ˈmɪsɪv/ N missive *f*

Missouri /mɪˈzʊərɪ/ N *(= state, river)* Missouri *m* ◆ **in ~** dans le Missouri ◆ **I'm from ~*** *(US fig)* je veux des preuves

misspell /ˈmɪsˈspel/ (pret, ptp **misspelled** *or* **misspelt**) VT mal écrire, mal orthographier

misspelling /ˈmɪsˈspelɪŋ/ N [1] *(= mistake)* faute *f* d'orthographe [2] *(= mistakes)* fautes *fpl* d'orthographe

misspend /ˈmɪsˈspend/ (pret, ptp **misspent**) VT *[+ money]* dépenser à mauvais escient, gaspiller ; *[+ time, strength, talents]* mal employer, gaspiller

misspent /ˌmɪsˈspent/ VB pret, ptp of **misspend** ADJ ◆ **~ youth** folle jeunesse *f*

misstate /ˈmɪsˈsteɪt/ VT rapporter incorrectement

misstatement /ˈmɪsˈsteɪtmənt/ N rapport *m* inexact

missus‡ /ˈmɪsɪz/ N ⇒ **missis**

missy †* /ˈmɪsɪ/ N ma petite demoiselle*

mist /mɪst/ N *(Weather)* brume *f* ; *(on glass)* buée *f* ; *(before eyes)* brouillard *m* ; *[of perfume, dust etc]* nuage *m* ; *[of ignorance, tears]* voile *m* ◆ **morning/sea ~** brume *f* matinale/de mer ◆ **lost in the ~s of time** *(fig liter)* perdu dans la nuit des temps ; → **Scotch** VT (also **mist over, mist up**) *[+ mirror, windscreen, eyes]* embuer VI (also **mist over, mist up**) *[scene, landscape, view]* se couvrir de brume, devenir brumeux ; *[mirror, windscreen, eyes]* s'embuer

mistakable /mɪsˈteɪkəbl/ ADJ facile à confondre *(with, for* avec*)*

mistake /mɪsˈteɪk/ LANGUAGE IN USE 26.3 (vb : pret **mistook**, ptp **mistaken**)

N *(= error) (in judgment, calculation, procedure)* erreur *f* ; *(in spelling, typing etc)* faute *f* ; *(= misunderstanding)* méprise *f* ◆ **there must be** *or* **let there be no ~ about it** qu'on ne s'y méprenne pas *or* ne s'y trompe *subj* pas ◆ **it was a ~ to do that** c'était une erreur de faire cela ◆ **turning down that job was the biggest ~ of his life** en refusant ce poste il a fait la plus grosse erreur *or* bêtise de sa vie ◆ **my ~ was to do ...** *or* **in doing ...** mon erreur a été de faire ... ◆ **my ~!** c'est (de) ma faute !, mea culpa ! ◆ **there must be some ~** il doit y avoir erreur ◆ **I took his keys in ~ for mine** j'ai pris ses clés par erreur *or* en croyant prendre les miennes ◆ **they arrested him in ~ for his brother** ils l'ont pris pour son frère *or* l'ont confondu avec son frère et l'ont arrêté ◆ **that's a surprise and no ~!** pour une surprise c'est une surprise ! ◆ **by ~** par erreur

◆ **to make + mistake(s)** faire une erreur *or* une faute ; *(= misunderstand)* se tromper ◆ **you're making a big ~** tu fais une grave *or* lourde erreur ◆ **she doesn't want her daughters to make the same ~s she did** elle ne veut pas que ses filles fassent les mêmes erreurs qu'elle ◆ **to make the ~ of thinking/doing sth** faire l'erreur de penser/faire qch ◆ **to make a ~ in a calculation** faire une erreur de calcul ◆ **to make a ~ in a dictation** faire une faute dans une dictée ◆ **I made a ~ about the book/about him** je me suis trompé sur le livre/sur son compte ◆ **I made a ~ about** *or* **over the dates** je me suis trompé de dates ◆ **I made a ~ about the** *or* **over the** *or* **which road to take** je me suis trompé de route ◆ **make no ~ about it** ne vous y trompez pas

VT *[+ meaning]* mal comprendre, mal interpréter ; *[+ intentions]* se méprendre sur ; *[+ time, road]* se tromper de ◆ **to ~ A for B** prendre A pour B, confondre A avec B

◆ **no mistaking** ◆ **there's no mistaking her voice** il est impossible de ne pas reconnaître sa voix ◆ **there's no mistaking that ...** il est indubitable que ... ◆ **there's no mistaking it, he ...** il ne faut pas s'y tromper, il ... ; see also **mistaken**

mistaken /mɪsˈteɪkən/ LANGUAGE IN USE 12.1

VB ptp of **mistake**

ADJ [1] *(= wrong)* ◆ **to be ~ (about sb/sth)** se tromper (à propos de qn/qch) ◆ **to be ~ in thinking that ...** se tromper en croyant que ... ◆ **I knew I wasn't ~!** je savais bien que je ne me trompais pas ! ◆ **unless I'm (very much) ~, if I'm not (very much) ~** si je ne me trompe, sauf erreur de ma part ◆ **if they think that, then they are very much ~** si c'est ce qu'ils croient, eh bien ils se trompent lourdement ◆ **that's just where you're ~!** c'est là que vous vous trompez ! ◆ **you couldn't be more ~!** vous vous trompez du tout au tout !

[2] *(= erroneous) [belief, idea, opinion, conclusion]* erroné ◆ **to do sth in the ~ belief that ...** faire qch en croyant à tort que ... ◆ **to be under** *or* **have the ~ impression that ...** avoir l'impression fausse que ... ; → **identity**

mistakenly /mɪsˈteɪkənlɪ/ ADV [1] *(= wrongly) [believe, think, assume]* à tort [2] *(= accidentally) [kill, attack]* par erreur

mister /ˈmɪstəʳ/ N [1] *(gen shortened to Mr)* monsieur *m* ◆ **Mr Smith** Monsieur Smith, M. Smith ◆ **yes Mr Smith** oui, Monsieur ◆ **Mr Chairman** monsieur le président ◆ **Mister Big*** *(fig)* le caïd‡, le gros bonnet* ◆ **Mister Right*** *(fig)* l'homme idéal *or* de ses *(or* mes *etc)* rêves [2] **hey ~!** ‡ eh, Monsieur !*

mistime /ˈmɪsˈtaɪm/ VT *[+ act, blow, kick]* mal calculer ◆ **~d remark** remarque *f* inopportune ◆ **he ~d it** il a choisi le mauvais moment ◆ **he ~d his entrance** *[actor]* il a raté son entrée ◆ **to ~ one's arrival** *(= arrive inopportunely)* arriver au mauvais moment ; *(= miscalculate time)* se tromper sur *or* mal calculer son (heure d')arrivée

mistiming /ˌmɪsˈtaɪmɪŋ/ N ◆ **the ~ of his arrival** son arrivée malencontreuse ◆ **the ~ of the announcement** le moment mal choisi de cette annonce

mistiness /ˈmɪstɪnɪs/ N *[of morning etc]* bruine *f*, état *m* brumeux ; *(on mirror, window pane)* buée *f*

mistlethrush /ˈmɪslθrʌʃ/ N draine *f or* drenne *f*

mistletoe /ˈmɪsltəʊ/ N (NonC) gui *m*

mistook /mɪsˈtʊk/ VB pt of **mistake**

mistranslate /ˈmɪstrænzˈleɪt/ VT mal traduire, faire un (or des) contresens en traduisant

mistranslation /ˈmɪstrænzˈleɪʃən/ N [1] erreur *f* de traduction, contresens *m* [2] (NonC) *[of text etc]* mauvaise traduction *f*, traduction *f* inexacte

mistreat /ˌmɪsˈtriːt/ VT maltraiter

mistreatment /ˌmɪsˈtriːtmənt/ N mauvais traitement *m*

mistress /ˈmɪstrɪs/ N [1] *(= lover)* maîtresse *f* ; *(†† = sweetheart)* amante † *f* [2] *[of household, institution etc]* maîtresse *f* ◆ **is your** *or* **the ~ at home?** † *(to servant)* Madame est-elle là ? ◆ **to be one's own ~** être sa propre maîtresse, être indépendante [3] *(Brit † = teacher) (in primary school)* maîtresse *f*, institutrice *f* ; *(in secondary school)* professeur *m* ◆ **the English ~** le professeur d'anglais [4] *(††: term of address)* madame *f*

mistrial /ˌmɪsˈtraɪəl/ N *(Brit, US Jur)* procès *m* entaché d'un vice de procédure ; *(US)* procès *m* ajourné pour défaut d'unanimité dans le jury

mistrust /ˈmɪsˈtrʌst/ N méfiance *f*, défiance *f* *(of* à l'égard de*)* VT *[+ person, sb's motives, suggestion]* se méfier de, se défier de *(liter)* ; *[+ abilities]* douter de, ne pas avoir confiance en

mistrustful /mɪsˈtrʌstfʊl/ ADJ *[person, look, glance]* méfiant ◆ **to be ~ of sb/sth** se méfier de qn/qch

mistrustfully /mɪsˈtrʌstfəlɪ/ ADV avec méfiance ; *[look, say]* d'un air méfiant

misty /ˈmɪstɪ/ ADJ *[weather]* brumeux ; *[day]* de brume, brumeux ; *[mirror, windowpane]* embué ; *(fig) [eyes, look]* embrumé, embué ; *(fig) [outline, recollection, idea]* nébuleux, flou ◆ **~ blue/grey/green** bleu/gris/vert vaporeux *or* fondu COMP **misty-eyed** ADJ *(= near tears)* qui a les yeux embués de larmes ; (= *sentimental*) qui a la larme à l'œil

misunderstand /ˈmɪsʌndəˈstænd/ (pret, ptp **misunderstood**) VT [+ *words, action, reason*] mal comprendre, comprendre de travers ◆ **you ~ me** vous m'avez mal compris ◆ **she was misunderstood all her life** toute sa vie elle est restée incomprise *or* méconnue

misunderstanding /ˈmɪsʌndəˈstændɪŋ/ N malentendu *m*, méprise *f* ◆ **there must be some ~** il doit y avoir méprise *or* une erreur ◆ **they had a slight ~** (= *disagreement*) il y a eu un léger malentendu entre eux

misunderstood /ˈmɪsʌndəˈstʊd/ VB pt, ptp of **misunderstand**

misuse /ˈmɪsˈjuːs/ N [*of power, authority*] abus *m* ; [*of word, tool*] usage *m* impropre *or* abusif ; [*of money, resources, energies, one's time*] mauvais emploi *m* ◆ **~ of funds** (*Jur*) détournement *m* de fonds VT /ˈmɪsˈjuːz/ [+ *power, authority*] abuser de ; [+ *word*] employer improprement *or* abusivement ; [+ *tool, money, resources, energies, one's time*] mal employer ; [+ *funds*] détourner

MIT /ˌemaɪˈtiː/ N (*US Univ*) abbrev of **Massachusetts Institute of Technology**

mite /maɪt/ N 1 (= *ancient coin*) denier *m* ; (*as contribution*) obole *f* ◆ **the widow's ~** le denier de la veuve ◆ **he gave his ~ to the collection** il a apporté son obole à la souscription 2 (= *small amount*) ◆ **there's not a ~ of bread left** il ne reste plus une miette de pain ◆ **not a ~ of truth** pas une parcelle *or* un atome de vérité ◆ **a ~ of consolation** une toute petite consolation ◆ **well, just a ~ then** bon, mais alors un tout petit peu seulement ◆ **we were a ~ surprised** * nous avons été un tantinet *or* un rien surpris 3 (= *small child*) petit(e) *m(f)* ◆ **poor little ~** (le) pauvre petit 4 (= *animal*) acarien *m* ◆ **cheese ~** acarien *m* ou mite *f* du fromage

miter /ˈmaɪtəʳ/ (*US*) ⇒ **mitre**

Mithraic /mɪθˈreɪɪk/ ADJ mithriaque

Mithras /ˈmɪθræs/ N Mithra *m*

mitigate /ˈmɪtɪgeɪt/ VT [+ *punishment, sentence, suffering, sorrow*] alléger, atténuer ; [+ *effect, evil*] atténuer COMP **mitigating circumstances** NPL circonstances *fpl* atténuantes

mitigation /ˌmɪtɪˈgeɪʃən/ N 1 (*Jur*) [*of sentence*] réduction *f*, allègement *m* 2 (= *excuse for crime, behaviour*) circonstances *fpl* atténuantes (*for* pour) ◆ **in ~** en guise de circonstances atténuantes ◆ **to tender a plea in ~** plaider les circonstances atténuantes 3 (= *alleviation*) [*of problem, illness, suffering*] atténuation *f* ; [*of situation*] apaisement *m*

mitral /ˈmaɪtrəl/ ADJ mitral ◆ **~ valve** valvule *f* mitrale

mitre, miter (*US*) /ˈmaɪtəʳ/ N (*Rel*) mitre *f* ; (*Carpentry*) onglet *m* VT (*Carpentry*) (= *join*) [+ *frame etc*] assembler à *or* en onglet ; (= *cut*) [+ *corner, end*] tailler à onglet
COMP **mitre box** N (*Carpentry*) boîte *f* à onglets
mitre joint N (assemblage *m* à) onglet *m*

mitt /mɪt/ N 1 ⇒ **mitten** 2 (*Baseball:* also **catcher's mitt**) gant *m* de baseball 3 (* = *hand*) patte * *f*, paluche * *f*

mitten /ˈmɪtn/ N (*with cut-off fingers*) mitaine *f* ; (*with no separate fingers*) moufle *f* ; (*Boxing* *) gant *m*, mitaine * *f*

mix /mɪks/ N 1 (= *combination*) [*of styles, types, cultures, emotions*] mélange *m* ◆ **a ~ of modern and traditional styles** un mélange de styles modernes et traditionnels ◆ **the company's product ~** les différents articles produits par l'entreprise ◆ **a real ~ of people** toutes sortes de gens ◆ **schools which have an ethnic or religious ~** des écoles qui ont des élèves d'origines ethniques ou religieuses variées ◆ **the broad racial ~ in this country** le melting-pot *or* le brassage des races dans ce pays ◆ **the candidate with the correct ~ of skills for this job** le candidat possédant la diversité des compétences requises pour cet emploi ◆ **pupils study a broad ~ of subjects at this school** les élèves étudient des matières diverses dans cette école ◆ **a ~ of plants including roses and lavender** un assortiment de plantes comprenant (notamment) des roses et des lavandes ◆ **shirt in a linen and cotton ~** chemise *f* en mélange lin et coton ◆ **a wool ~ pullover** un pull-over en laine mélangée

2 (*Culin etc*) ◆ **(packet) cake/bread/pizza ~** préparation *f* pour gâteau/pain/pizza ◆ **cement ~** mortier *m*

3 (*Mus*) (= *track*) version *f* mixée ; (= *mixing process*) mixage *m*

VT 1 [+ *liquids, ingredients, colours*] mélanger (*with* avec, à) ; [+ *small objects*] mêler, mélanger (*with* avec, à) ; [+ *metals*] allier, amalgamer ; [+ *cement, mortar*] malaxer, préparer ; [+ *cake, sauce*] préparer, faire ; [+ *salad*] remuer, retourner ◆ **to ~ one thing with another** mélanger une chose à *or* avec une autre ◆ **to ~ sth to a smooth paste** (bien) mélanger qch pour obtenir une pâte homogène ◆ **~ the eggs into the sugar** incorporez les œufs au sucre ◆ **he ~ed the drinks** il a préparé les boissons ◆ **can I ~ you a drink?** je vous sers un verre ? ◆ **never ~ your drinks!** évitez toujours les mélanges ! ◆ **to ~ business and** *or* **with pleasure** mélanger le travail et l'agrément, joindre l'utile à l'agréable ◆ **to ~ one's metaphors** faire des métaphores incohérentes ◆ **to ~ and match** mélanger différents types de

2 (*Mus*) [+ *track, album*] mixer

3 (*Brit fig*) **to ~ it** * (= *cause trouble*) causer des ennuis ; (= *quarrel, fight*) se bagarrer *

VI 1 [*liquids, ingredients, colours*] se mélanger ◆ **oil and water don't ~** (*lit*) l'huile et l'eau ne se mélangent pas ; (*fig*) l'eau et le feu ne se marient pas ◆ **these colours just don't ~** ces couleurs ne s'harmonisent pas *or* ne vont pas bien ensemble ◆ **to ~ and match** faire des mélanges

2 (*socially*) ◆ **he ~es with all kinds of people** il fréquente toutes sortes de gens ◆ **he doesn't ~ well** il est peu sociable ◆ **children from different social backgrounds don't often ~** les enfants d'origines sociales différentes ne se fréquentent *or* ne se mélangent pas souvent ◆ **they don't ~ (with each other) socially** [*work colleagues*] ils ne se voient pas en dehors du bureau

COMP **mix-and-match** ADJ composite
mix-up N (= *confusion*) confusion *f* ; (= *trouble*) démêlé *m* ◆ **there was a ~-up over tickets** il y a eu confusion en ce qui concerne les billets ◆ **we got in a ~-up over the dates** nous nous sommes embrouillés dans les dates ◆ **he got into a ~-up with the police** il a eu un démêlé avec la police

► **mix in** VI ◆ **he doesn't want to mix in** il préfère rester à l'écart ◆ **you must try to ~ in** il faut essayer de vous mêler un peu aux autres
VT SEP ◆ **mix in the eggs with ...** incorporez les œufs à ... ◆ **the producer used archive news footage ~ed in with interviews** le producteur a combiné documents d'archives et interviews

► **mix round** VT SEP mélanger, remuer

► **mix together** VT SEP mélanger, amalgamer

► **mix up** VT SEP 1 (= *prepare*) [+ *drink, medicine*] préparer

2 (= *put in disorder*) [+ *documents, garments*] mêler, mélanger

3 (= *confuse*) [+ *two objects, two people*] confondre ◆ **he ~ed her up with Jane** il l'a confondue avec Jane

4 ◆ **to mix sb up in sth** impliquer qn dans qch ◆ **to be/get ~ed up in an affair** être/se trouver mêlé à une affaire ◆ **don't get ~ed up in it!** restez à l'écart ! ◆ **he is/he has got ~ed up with a lot of criminals** il fréquente/il s'est mis à fréquenter un tas de malfaiteurs * ◆ **to ~ it up** * (*US*) (= *cause trouble*) causer des ennuis ; (= *quarrel, fight*) se bagarrer *

5 (= *muddle*) [+ *person*] embrouiller ◆ **to be ~ed up** [*person*] être (tout) désorienté *or* déboussolé * ; [*account, facts*] être embrouillé *or* confus ◆ **I'm all ~ed up about it** je ne sais plus où j'en suis, je ne m'y reconnais plus ◆ **you've got me all ~ed up** vous m'avez embrouillé

N ◆ **mix-up** → **mix**

ADJ ◆ **mixed-up** → **mixed**

mixed /mɪkst/ ADJ 1 (*gen*) [*school, education, bathing*] mixte ; [*neighbourhood*] mélangé, hétérogène ; [*vegetables, herbs, biscuits*] assorti ◆ **a man/woman of ~ blood** un/une sang-mêlé ◆ **in ~ company** en présence d'hommes et de femmes ◆ **you shouldn't swear in ~ company** tu ne devrais pas jurer devant des dames ◆ **~ nuts** noix *fpl* et noisettes *fpl* assorties ◆ **to be of ~ parentage** être issu d'un mariage mixte

2 (= *varying*) [*reviews, emotions, messages, signals*] contradictoire ; [*results, reaction*] inégal ; [*weather*] inégal, variable ; [*success, reception*] mitigé ; [*year*] avec des hauts et des bas ◆ **she had ~ feelings about it** elle était partagée à ce sujet ◆ **to have had ~ fortunes** avoir connu un sort inégal ◆ **to have ~ motives** ne pas être complètement désintéressé

COMP **mixed ability** N (*Scol*) ◆ **a class of ~ ability** une classe sans groupes de niveau ◆ **~-ability group** classe *f* sans groupes de niveau ◆ **~-ability teaching** enseignement *m* sans groupes de niveau
mixed bag N ◆ **to be a ~ bag (of sth)** être un mélange (de qch) ◆ **the students are a bit of a ~ bag** il y a un peu de tout parmi les étudiants ◆ **it's very much a ~ bag of activities** c'est un pot-pourri d'activités, c'est tout un mélange d'activités
mixed blessing N ◆ **to be a ~ blessing** avoir du bon et du mauvais ◆ **children can be a ~ blessing!** les enfants, ça peut avoir du bon et du mauvais !
mixed bunch N ◆ **a ~ bunch** [*of people*] un groupe hétérogène *or* disparate ; [*of products*] un ensemble hétéroclite ; [*of flowers*] un bouquet composé
mixed doubles NPL (*Sport*) double *m* mixte
mixed economy N (*Pol, Econ*) économie *f* mixte
mixed farm N exploitation *f* en polyculture et élevage
mixed farming N polyculture *f* et élevage *m*
mixed grill N (*Brit*) assortiment *m* de grillades, mixed-grill *m*
mixed marriage N mariage *m* mixte
mixed media ADJ multimédia
mixed metaphor N mélange *m* de métaphores
mixed race N ◆ **to be of ~ race** être métis (-isse *f*) ◆ **people of ~ race** des métis
mixed-race ADJ [*couple, neighbourhood*] mixte ; [*child*] métis (-isse *f*) ◆ **a ~-race marriage** un mariage interracial
mixed spice N mélange *m* d'épices
mixed-up ADJ [*person*] désorienté, déboussolé * ; [*report etc*] embrouillé, confus ◆ **he's a ~-up kid** * c'est un gosse * qui a des problèmes

mixer /ˈmɪksəʳ/ N 1 (*Culin*) **hand ~** batteur *m* à main ◆ **electric ~** batteur *m* électrique, mixer *or* mixeur *m* 2 [*of cement, mortar etc*] malaxeur *m* ; [*of industrial liquids*] agitateur *m* 3 (*Cine etc:* also **sound mixer**) (= *person*) ingénieur *m* du son ; (= *machine*) mélangeur *m* de signaux, mixeur *m* 4 (*socially*) ◆ **he's a good ~** il est très sociable *or* liant 5 (*US* = *social gathering*) soirée-rencontre *f*, réunion-rencontre *f* 6 (= *drink*) boisson *f* gazeuse (*servant à couper un alcool*) COMP
mixer tap N (*Brit*) (robinet *m*) mélangeur *m*

mixing /ˈmɪksɪŋ/ N 1 *(gen) [of ingredients, substances, sexes, generations, races]* mélange *m* ; *[of cocktails, cake, sauce]* préparation *f* ; *[of cement, mortar]* malaxage *m* ◆ **the ~ of charcoal with clay** le mélange de charbon de bois et d'argile ◆ **the ~ of the eggs into the flour** l'incorporation *f* des œufs dans la farine ◆ **colour ~** mélange *m* de couleurs 2 *(Cine, Audio, Video)* mixage *m* ◆ **audio ~** mixage *m* audio
COMP **mixing bowl** N *(Culin)* saladier *m* (de cuisine)
mixing faucet N *(US)* (robinet *m*) mélangeur *m*

mixture /ˈmɪkstʃəʳ/ N 1 *(= combination) [of colours, flavours, ingredients, styles, types, reasons, emotions]* mélange *m* ◆ **they spoke in a ~ of French, Italian and English** ils parlaient un mélange de français, d'italien et d'anglais ◆ **the family is an odd ~** cette famille est un mélange bizarre *or* curieux ◆ **a ~ of people** toutes sortes de gens ◆ **the course offers a ~ of subjects** le cours propose des matières diverses ◆ **it's just the ~ as before** *(fig)* c'est toujours la même chose, il n'y a rien de nouveau 2 *(Med)* préparation *f*, mixture *f* ; *(Culin: for cake, dough, batter etc)* mélange *m* ◆ **fold the eggs into the cheese ~** incorporez les œufs dans le mélange à base de fromage ; → **cough**

miz(z)en /ˈmɪzn/ N *(Naut)* artimon *m*

miz(z)enmast /ˈmɪznmɑːst/ N *(Naut)* mât *m* d'artimon

mizzle * /ˈmɪzl/ *(dial)* VI bruiner N bruine *f*

mk (abbrev of **mark**) DM *m*

ml N (abbrev of **millilitre(s)**) ml

MLA /ˌemelˈeɪ/ N (pl **MLAs**) *(Brit Pol)* (abbrev of **Member of the Legislative Assembly**) député *m*

MLitt /ˈemˈlɪt/ N (abbrev of **Master of Literature** *or* **Master of Letters**) ≈ doctorat *m* de troisième cycle

MLR /ˌemelˈɑːʳ/ N (abbrev of **minimum lending rate**) → **minimum**

MLS /ˌemelˈes/ N *(US Univ)* (abbrev of **Master of Library Science**) *diplôme supérieur de bibliothécaire*

M'lud /məˈlʌd/ N *(Brit Jur)* (abbrev of **My Lord**) Monsieur le Juge

mm¹ /əm/ EXCL mmm !

mm² (abbrev of **millimetre(s)**) mm

MMC /ˌememˈsiː/ N (abbrev of **Monopolies and Mergers Commission**) → **monopoly**

MME /ˌememˈiː/ N *(US Univ)* 1 abbrev of **Master of Mechanical Engineering** 2 abbrev of **Master of Mining Engineering**

MMR /ˌememˈɑːʳ/ N (abbrev of **measles, mumps, rubella**) ROR *m* COMP **MMR vaccine** vaccin *m* ROR

MMS /ememˈes/ N (abbrev of **multimedia messaging service**) MMS *m*

MN /emˈen/ N 1 *(Brit)* (abbrev of **Merchant Navy**) → **merchant** 2 abbrev of **Minnesota**

mnemonic /nɪˈmɒnɪk/ ADJ, N mnémotechnique *f*, mnémonique *f*

mnemonics /nɪˈmɒnɪks/ N *(NonC)* mnémotechnique *f*

MO /emˈəʊ/ N 1 (abbrev of **medical officer**) → **medical** 2 abbrev of **Missouri** 3 *(esp US *)* (abbrev of **modus operandi**) méthode *f*, truc * *m*

Mo. abbrev of **Missouri**

mo' * /məʊ/ N (abbrev of **moment**) moment *m*, instant *m* ◆ **half** *or* **just a ~!** un instant ! ; *(interrupting)* minute ! *

m.o. /ˈemˈəʊ/ N (abbrev of **money order**) → **money**

moan /məʊn/ N 1 *(= groan)* gémissement *m*, plainte *f* ◆ **I'm fed up with all your ~s** * *(= complaint)* j'en ai marre de tes récriminations *or* de t'entendre râler * ◆ **one of my biggest ~s is that ...** une des choses qui me fait le plus râler *, c'est que ... VI *(= groan)* gémir, geindre ; *[wind etc]* gémir ; *(* = complain)* récriminer, râler * VT dire en gémissant ◆ **they ~ that they're underpaid** ils se plaignent d'être sous-payés

moaner * /ˈməʊnəʳ/ N rouspéteur * *m*, -euse * *f*, râleur * *m*, -euse * *f*

moaning /ˈməʊnɪŋ/ N gémissements *mpl*, plainte(s) *f(pl)* ; *(* = complaints)* plaintes *fpl*, récriminations *fpl* ADJ gémissant ; *(* = complaining)* rouspéteur *, râleur *

moat /məʊt/ N douves *fpl*, fossés *mpl*

moated /ˈməʊtɪd/ ADJ *[castle etc]* entouré de douves *or* de fossés

mob /mɒb/ N 1 *(= crowd)* foule *f* ◆ **they went in a ~ to the town hall** ils se rendirent en foule *or* en masse à la mairie ◆ **the embassy was set on fire by the ~** la foule a incendié l'ambassade ◆ **an angry ~** une foule en colère 2 *(* = group)* bande *f*, clique *f (pej)* ◆ **Paul and his ~** Paul et sa bande, Paul et sa clique *(pej)* 3 *(= gang) [of criminals, bandits etc]* gang *m* 4 *(= Mafia)* ◆ **the Mob** * la Maf(f)ia 5 *(pej)* ◆ **the ~** *(= the common people)* la populace VT *[+ person] (= surround)* se presser en foule autour de ; *(= attack)* assaillir ; *[+ place]* assiéger ◆ **the shops were ~bed** * les magasins étaient pris d'assaut *
COMP **mob-handed** * ADV en force
mob hysteria N hystérie *f* collective
mob oratory N éloquence *f* démagogique
mob rule N *(pej)* la loi de la populace *or* de la rue
mob violence N violence *f* collective

mobcap /ˈmɒbkæp/ N charlotte *f (bonnet)*

mobile /ˈməʊbaɪl/ ADJ *(gen, also Sociol)* mobile ◆ **I'm not ~ this week** * *(fig)* je ne suis pas motorisé * cette semaine ; → **shop, upwardly mobile** N 1 (also **mobile phone**) portable *m* 2 *(Art, toy)* mobile *m*
COMP **mobile canteen** N (cuisine *f*) roulante *f*
mobile data system N système *m* de données mobile
mobile home N mobile home *m*
mobile library N bibliobus *m*
mobile phone N (téléphone *m*) portable *m*
mobile police unit N unité *f* mobile de police
mobile studio N *(Rad, TV)* car *m* de reportage

mobility /məʊˈbɪlɪtɪ/ N mobilité *f* COMP **mobility allowance** N allocation *f* or indemnité *f* de transport *(pour handicapés)* ; → **upward**

mobilization /ˌməʊbɪlaɪˈzeɪʃən/ N *(all senses)* mobilisation *f*

mobilize /ˈməʊbɪlaɪz/ VTI *(gen, also Mil)* mobiliser ◆ **to ~ sb into doing sth** mobiliser qn pour faire qch ◆ **they were ~d into a group which ...** on les a mobilisés pour constituer un groupe qui ...

mobster /ˈmɒbstəʳ/ N membre *m* du milieu, truand *m*

moccasin /ˈmɒkəsɪn/ N mocassin *m*

mocha /ˈmɒkə/ N moka *m*

mock /mɒk/ N ◆ **to make a ~ of sth/sb** tourner qch/qn en ridicule NPL **mocks** * *(Brit Scol)* examens *mpl* blancs ADJ 1 *(= imitation) [leather etc]* faux (fausse *f*) *before n*, imitation *inv before n*, simili- *inv* 2 *(= pretended) [anger, modesty]* simulé, feint ◆ **a ~ battle/trial** un simulacre de bataille/de procès 3 *(Literat)* burlesque ; see also **comp** VT 1 *(= ridicule)* ridiculiser ; *(= scoff at)* se moquer de, railler ; *(= mimic, burlesque)* singer, parodier 2 *(liter = defy) [+ sb's plans, attempts]* narguer VI se moquer *(at* de*)*
COMP **mock examination** N examen *m* blanc
mock-heroic ADJ *(gen)* burlesque ; *(Literat)* héroïcomique, burlesque
mock orange N *(= plant)* seringa(t) *m*
mock-serious ADJ à demi sérieux
mock turtle soup N consommé *m* à la tête de veau
mock-up N maquette *f*

► **mock up** VT SEP faire la maquette de N ◆ **mock-up** → **mock**

mocker /ˈmɒkəʳ/ N moqueur *m*, -euse *f*

mockers ‡ /ˈmɒkəz/ NPL ◆ **to put the ~ on sth** ficher qch en l'air ‡

mockery /ˈmɒkərɪ/ N 1 *(= mocking)* moquerie *f*, raillerie *f* ; *(= person, thing)* sujet *m* de moquerie *or* de raillerie, objet *m* de risée ◆ **to make a ~ of sb/sth** tourner qn/qch en dérision, bafouer qn/qch ◆ **he had to put up with a lot of ~** il a dû endurer beaucoup de railleries *or* de persiflages 2 *(= travesty)* ◆ **it is a ~ of justice** c'est une parodie de justice ◆ **a ~ of a trial** une parodie *or* une caricature de procès ◆ **what a ~ it was!** c'était grotesque !

mocking /ˈmɒkɪŋ/ N *(NonC)* moquerie *f*, raillerie *f* ADJ *(gen)* moqueur, railleur ; *(maliciously)* narquois

mockingbird /ˈmɒkɪŋˌbɜːd/ N oiseau *m* moqueur

mockingly /ˈmɒkɪŋlɪ/ ADV *[say] (gen)* d'un ton moqueur *or* railleur ; *(= maliciously)* d'un ton narquois ; *[smile] (gen)* d'une façon moqueuse ; *(= maliciously)* d'une façon narquoise

MOD /ˌeməʊˈdiː/ N *(Brit)* (abbrev of **Ministry of Defence**) → **defence**

mod¹ /mɒd/ (abbrev of **modern**) ADJ *(Brit)* ◆ **~ cons** * ⇒ **modern conveniences** ; → **modern** NPL **mods** mods * *mpl*

mod² /mɒd/ N *(Scot)* concours *m* de musique et de poésie *(en gaélique)*

modal /ˈməʊdl/ ADJ *(Ling, Mus etc)* modal ◆ **~ auxiliary** *or* **verb** auxiliaire *m* modal

modality /məʊˈdælɪtɪ/ N modalité *f*

mode /məʊd/ N 1 *(= way, manner)* mode *m*, façon *f*, manière *f* ◆ **~ of life** façon *f* or manière *f* de vivre, mode *m* de vie 2 *(Comput, Ling, Mus, Philos etc)* mode *m* ◆ **in interactive** *etc* **~** *(Comput)* en mode conversationnel *etc*

model /ˈmɒdl/ N 1 *(= small-scale representation) [of boat etc]* modèle *m* (réduit) ; *(Archit, Tech, Town Planning etc)* maquette *f* ; → **scale¹**
2 *(= standard, example)* modèle *m*, exemple *m* ◆ **he was a ~ of discretion** c'était un modèle de discrétion ◆ **on the ~ of** sur le modèle de, à l'image de ◆ **to take sb/sth as one's ~** prendre modèle *or* exemple sur qn/qch ◆ **to hold sb out** *or* **up as a ~** citer *or* donner qn en exemple
3 *(= person) (for artist)* modèle *m* ; *(= fashion model)* mannequin *m* ◆ **male ~** mannequin *m* masculin
4 *[of product, car, clothing]* modèle *m* ◆ **the latest ~s** *(= garments, hats)* les derniers modèles *mpl* ◆ **a 1998 ~** un modèle 1998 ◆ **sports ~** modèle *m* sport ◆ **four-door ~** version *f* quatre portes ◆ **factory ~** modèle *m* de fabrique
5 *(Ling)* modèle *m*
ADJ 1 *(= exemplary, designed as model)* modèle
2 *(= miniature) [railway, theatre, village]* miniature ◆ **~ aeroplane/boat/train** maquette *f* d'avion/de bateau/de train, modèle *m* réduit d'avion/de bateau/de train ◆ **~ car** modèle *m* réduit de voiture
VT 1 *(= make model of)* modeler *(in* en*)*
2 *(= base)* ◆ **to ~ sth on sth** modeler qch sur qch ◆ **to ~ o.s. on sb** se modeler sur qn, prendre modèle *or* exemple sur qn
3 *(Fashion)* **to ~ clothes** être mannequin, présenter les modèles de collection ◆ **she was ~ling swimwear** elle présentait les modèles de maillots de bain
4 *(= describe, map out) [+ system, process]* modéliser
VI *(for artist)* poser *(for* pour*)* ; *(for fashion designer)* être mannequin *(for* chez*)*

modeller, modeler (US) /ˈmɒdləʳ/ N modeleur m, -euse f

modelling, modeling (US) /ˈmɒdlɪŋ/ N [1] (Art etc) modelage m ; (= model making) modélisme m ◆ **she does ~** (fashion) elle travaille comme mannequin ; (for artist) elle travaille comme modèle [2] [of system, process] modélisation f COMP **modelling clay** N pâte f à modeler

modem /ˈməʊdem/ N modem m

Modena /ˈmɔːdena/ N Modène

moderate /ˈmɒdərɪt/ ADJ [1] (also Pol = not extreme) [person, behaviour, views, demands] modéré ; [language, terms] mesuré ◆ **he was ~ in his demands** ses exigences étaient raisonnables or n'avaient rien d'excessif ◆ **to be a ~ drinker** boire modérément ◆ **to take ~ exercise** faire de l'exercice avec modération
[2] (= average, middling) [size] moyen, modéré ; [amount, appetite, speed] modéré ; [improvement, reduction, success, benefit] léger ; [price] modéré, raisonnable ◆ **over a ~ heat** (Culin) à or sur feu moyen ◆ **in a ~ oven** à four moyen
[3] [climate] tempéré
N (esp Pol) modéré(e) m(f)
VT /ˈmɒdəreɪt/ [1] (= restrain, diminish) modérer ◆ **moderating influence** influence f modératrice
[2] (= preside over) présider
VI [storm, wind etc] se modérer, se calmer
COMP /ˈmɒdərɪt/ **moderate-sized** ADJ de grandeur or de grosseur or de taille moyenne

moderately /ˈmɒdərɪtlɪ/ ADV [1] [wealthy, pleased, expensive, difficult] relativement, moyennement ◆ **to make a ~ good attempt to do sth** essayer tant bien que mal de faire qch ◆ **~ priced** d'un prix raisonnable ◆ **~ quickly** assez or relativement vite ◆ **to be ~ successful** réussir moyennement ◆ **she did ~ well in her exams** elle s'en est relativement bien tirée à ses examens [2] [increase, decline] quelque peu ◆ **the dollar has gained ~ against the yen** le dollar a enregistré une hausse modérée par rapport au yen [3] [act] avec modération ; [eat, drink] modérément, avec modération ◆ **to exercise ~** faire de l'exercice avec modération

moderation /ˌmɒdəˈreɪʃən/ N (NonC) modération f, mesure f ◆ **in ~** [eat, drink, exercise] avec modération, modérément ◆ **it's all right in ~** c'est très bien à petites doses or à condition de ne pas en abuser ◆ **with ~** avec mesure or modération ◆ **to advise ~ in drinking** conseiller la modération en matière de consommation d'alcool, conseiller de boire modérément or avec modération

moderator /ˈmɒdəreɪtəʳ/ N [1] (Rel) **Moderator** président m (de l'Assemblée générale de l'Église presbytérienne) [2] (in assembly, council, discussion) président(e) m(f) [3] (Brit Univ = examiner) examinateur m, -trice f [4] (Phys, Tech) modérateur m

modern /ˈmɒdən/ ADJ moderne ◆ **house with all ~ conveniences** maison f tout confort ◆ **it has all ~ conveniences** il y a tout le confort (moderne) ◆ **~ languages** langues fpl vivantes ◆ **in ~ times** dans les temps modernes, à l'époque moderne ◆ **~-day** des temps modernes N (= artist, poet etc) moderne mf

modernism /ˈmɒdənɪzəm/ N [1] (NonC: Art, Rel) modernisme m [2] (= word) néologisme m

modernist /ˈmɒdənɪst/ ADJ, N moderniste mf

modernistic /ˌmɒdəˈnɪstɪk/ ADJ [building, room, architecture, design] moderniste

modernity /mɒˈdɜːnɪtɪ/ N modernité f

modernization /ˌmɒdənaɪˈzeɪʃən/ N modernisation f

modernize /ˈmɒdənaɪz/ VT moderniser VI se moderniser

modest /ˈmɒdɪst/ ADJ [1] (= not boastful) [person] modeste ◆ **to be ~ about sth** être modeste à propos de qch ◆ **to be ~ about one's achievements** ne pas se faire gloire de ses réussites or exploits [2] (= small, unostentatious) [amount, size, house, income, proposal, ambition] modeste ◆ **his ~ beginnings/origins** ses modestes débuts/origines ◆ **a family of ~ means** une famille aux moyens modestes ◆ **he was ~ in his demands** ses exigences étaient modestes ◆ **on a ~ scale** à une échelle modeste ◆ **the book was a ~ success** le livre a eu un succès modeste [3] (= decorous) [person] pudique ; [clothes] décent

modestly /ˈmɒdɪstlɪ/ ADV [1] (= in moderation) [gamble] avec modération ; [drink] modérément, avec modération ◆ **to live ~** vivre simplement ◆ **~ furnished** modestement meublé ◆ **~ priced** d'un prix raisonnable ◆ **~ sized** de taille modeste ◆ **his ~ successful paintings** ses tableaux au succès modeste [2] (= not boastfully) [talk, smile] modestement, avec modestie [3] (= decorously) [behave] pudiquement ; [dress] avec pudeur

modesty /ˈmɒdɪstɪ/ N [1] (gen) modestie f ; († = chasteness) pudeur f, modestie f ◆ **false ~** fausse modestie f ◆ **may I say with all due ~ ...** soit dit en toute modestie ... [2] [of request etc] modération f ; [of sum of money, price] modicité f

modicum /ˈmɒdɪkəm/ N ◆ **a ~ of ...** un minimum de ...

modifiable /ˈmɒdɪfaɪəbl/ ADJ modifiable

modification /ˌmɒdɪfɪˈkeɪʃən/ N modification f (to, in à) ◆ **to make ~s (in or to)** faire or apporter des modifications (à)

modifier /ˈmɒdɪfaɪəʳ/ N modificateur m ; (Gram) modificatif m

modify /ˈmɒdɪfaɪ/ VT [1] (= change) [+ plans, design] modifier, apporter des modifications à ; [+ customs, society] transformer, modifier ; (Gram) modifier [2] (= make less strong) modérer ◆ **he'll have to ~ his demands** il faudra qu'il modère subj ses exigences ◆ **he modified his statement** il modéra les termes de sa déclaration

modifying /ˈmɒdɪfaɪɪŋ/ N modification f ADJ [note, term] modificatif (also Gram) ; [factor] modifiant

modish /ˈməʊdɪʃ/ ADJ à la mode

modishly /ˈməʊdɪʃlɪ/ ADV à la mode

modiste /məʊˈdiːst/ N modiste f

Mods * /mɒdz/ N (at Oxford university) (abbrev of **moderations**) premier examen du cursus universitaire

modular /ˈmɒdjʊləʳ/ ADJ [1] (Constr) modulaire [2] (esp Brit Univ) [course, programme, curriculum] par modules or unités de valeur ◆ **the course is ~ in structure** l'enseignement est organisé en modules or unités de valeur ◆ **a six-week ~ course** une unité de valeur or un module de six semaines ◆ **~ degree** licence f (par modules ou unités de valeur)

modulate /ˈmɒdjʊleɪt/ VT (all senses) moduler VI (Mus) moduler

modulation /ˌmɒdjʊˈleɪʃən/ N modulation f ◆ **amplitude ~** modulation f d'amplitude ◆ **frequency ~** modulation f de fréquence

module /ˈmɒdjuːl/ N (gen) module m ; (esp Brit Univ) module m, ≃ unité f de valeur, UV f ◆ **~ learning** (US) enseignement m par groupes de niveaux ; → **lunar**

modulus /ˈmɒdjʊləs/ N (pl **moduli** /ˈmɒdjʊˌlaɪ/) (Math, Phys) module m, coefficient m

modus /ˈməʊdəs/ N ◆ **~ operandi** modus operandi m inv ◆ **~ vivendi** (between people) modus vivendi m inv ; (= way of life) mode m de vie

Mogadishu /mɒgəˈdɪʃuː/ N (Geog) Mogadiscio

moggie *, **moggy** * /ˈmɒgɪ/ N (Brit = cat) minou * m

Mogul /ˈməʊgəl/ ADJ mog(h)ol N Mog(h)ol m

mogul /ˈməʊgəl/ N [1] (fig = powerful person) nabab m ◆ **a ~ of the film industry** un nabab du cinéma [2] (Ski) bosse f

MOH /ˌeməʊˈeɪtʃ/ N (Brit) (abbrev of **Medical Officer of Health**) → **medical**

mohair /ˈməʊhɛəʳ/ N mohair m COMP en or de mohair

Mohammed /məʊˈhæmed/ N Mohammed m, Mahomet m

Mohammedan † /məʊˈhæmɪdən/ ADJ mahométan N mahométan(e) m(f)

Mohammedanism † /məʊˈhæmɪdənɪzəm/ N mahométisme m

Mohican /ˈməʊhɪkən/ N (pl **Mohicans** or **Mohican**) (also **Mohican Indian**) Mohican mf ◆ **mohican (hairdo)** iroquoise f

moire /mwɑː/ N moire f

moiré /ˈmwɑːreɪ/ ADJ, N moiré(e) m(f)

moist /mɔɪst/ ADJ [air, atmosphere, heat, skin] (gen) humide ; (unpleasantly) moite ; [place, climate, soil, eyes] humide ; [cake, texture] moelleux ◆ **a plant which likes ~ conditions** une plante qui aime l'humidité ◆ **~ with tears** mouillé de larmes

moisten /ˈmɔɪsn/ VT humecter, mouiller légèrement ; (Culin) mouiller légèrement ◆ **to ~ one's lips** s'humecter les lèvres VI devenir humide or moite

moistness /ˈmɔɪstnɪs/ N [of air, atmosphere, heat, skin] (gen) humidité f ; (unpleasant) moiteur f ; [of soil] humidité f ; [of cake, texture] moelleux m ◆ **she tried to hide the ~ in her eyes** elle essaya de cacher ses yeux embués de larmes

moisture /ˈmɔɪstʃəʳ/ N humidité f ; (on glass etc) buée f

moisturize /ˈmɔɪstʃəraɪz/ VT [+ skin] hydrater ; [+ air, atmosphere] humidifier

moisturizer /ˈmɔɪstʃəraɪzəʳ/ N crème f hydratante, lait m hydratant

mojahedin /ˌmɒdʒəˈhediːn/ NPL ⇒ **mujaheddin**

moke ‡ /məʊk/ N (Brit) bourricot m, baudet m

molar /ˈməʊləʳ/ N (= tooth) molaire f ADJ (Dentistry, Phys) molaire

molasses /məʊˈlæsɪz/ N (NonC) mélasse f ◆ **to be as slow as ~ in winter** * (US) être lent comme une tortue

mold /məʊld/ (US) ⇒ **mould**

Moldavia /mɒlˈdeɪvɪə/ N (formerly) Moldavie f

Moldavian /mɒlˈdeɪvɪən/ (formerly) N Moldave mf ADJ moldave

Moldova /mɒlˈdəʊvə/ N Moldova f

Moldovan /mɒlˈdəʊvən/ ADJ moldave N Moldave mf

mole[1] /məʊl/ N taupe f (also fig) COMP **molecatcher** N taupier m

mole[2] /məʊl/ N (on skin) grain m de beauté

mole[3] /məʊl/ N (= breakwater) môle m, digue f

molecular /məʊˈlekjʊləʳ/ ADJ [structure] moléculaire
COMP **molecular biologist** N biologiste mf moléculaire
molecular biology N biologie f moléculaire
molecular geneticist N chercheur m en génétique moléculaire
molecular genetics N (NonC) génétique f moléculaire

molecule /ˈmɒlɪkjuːl/ N molécule f

molehill /ˈməʊlhɪl/ N taupinière f ; → **mountain**

moleskin /ˈməʊlskɪn/ N (lit) (peau f de) taupe f ; (Brit = fabric) moleskine f ADJ (lit) de or en (peau de) taupe ; (Brit) [trousers etc] de or en moleskine

molest /məʊ'lest/ VT (= attack) attaquer ; (Jur: sexually) attenter à la pudeur de ; [dog] s'attaquer à ; († = trouble) importuner, harceler

molestation /,məʊles'teɪʃən/ N [1] (Jur) brutalités fpl ♦ **child** ~ maltraitance f à enfant ♦ **sexual** ~ agression f sexuelle [2] († = annoyance) importunité † f ♦ **I was allowed to work without hindrance or** ~ on m'a laissé travailler sans me gêner ni m'importuner

molester /məʊ'lestə^r/ N satyre m

Moley /'məʊlɪ/ → **holy**

moll* /mɒl/ N (pej) nana* f (de gangster)

mollify /'mɒlɪfaɪ/ VT apaiser, calmer ♦ **~ing remarks** propos mpl lénifiants

mollusc, mollusk (US) /'mɒləsk/ N mollusque m

mollycoddle /'mɒlɪkɒdl/ VT (gen) élever dans du coton, chouchouter* ; [+ pupil] materner

mollycoddling /'mɒlɪkɒdlɪŋ/ N (pej) chouchoutage m, maternage m

Molotov /'mɒlətɒf/ N ♦ ~ **cocktail** cocktail m Molotov

molt /məʊlt/ (US) ⇒ **moult**

molten /'məʊltən/ ADJ en fusion

Molucca /məʊ'lʌkə/ N ♦ **the ~ Islands** or **the ~s** les Moluques fpl

Moluccan /məʊ'lʌkən/ N → **south**

molybdenum /mɒ'lɪbdɪnəm/ N molybdène m

mom* /mɒm/ N (US) maman f ♦ ~ **and pop store*** petite boutique f familiale, petit commerce m

moment /'məʊmənt/ N [1] moment m, instant m ♦ **man of the** ~ homme m du moment ♦ **wait a ~!, just a ~!, one ~!** (attendez) un instant or une minute ! ; (objecting to sth) minute !, pas si vite !* ♦ **I shan't be a ~, I'll just** or **only be a** ~ j'en ai pour un instant ♦ **a** ~ **ago** il y a un instant ♦ **a ~ later** un instant plus tard ♦ **that very** ~ à cet instant or ce moment précis ♦ **the ~ he arrives** dès or aussitôt qu'il arrivera ♦ **the ~ he arrived** dès or aussitôt qu'il arriva, dès son arrivée ♦ **do it this ~!** fais-le à l'instant or tout de suite ! ♦ **I've just this ~ heard of it** je viens de l'apprendre à l'instant (même) ♦ **it won't take a** ~ c'est l'affaire d'un instant ♦ **at the (present) ~, at this ~ in time** en ce moment (même), à l'heure qu'il est ♦ **any ~ now** d'une minute à l'autre ♦ **at that** ~ à ce moment(-là) ♦ **(at) any** ~ d'un moment or instant à l'autre ♦ **at every** ~ à chaque instant, à tout moment ♦ **at the right** ~ au bon moment, à point nommé ♦ **at the last** ~ au dernier moment ♦ **to leave things till the last** ~ attendre le dernier moment ♦ **for a** ~ un instant ♦ **for a brief** ~ l'espace d'un instant ♦ **not for a ~!** jamais de la vie ! ♦ **I don't think for a** or **one ~ (that) he believed my story** je ne crois or pense pas un (seul) instant qu'il ait cru mon histoire ♦ **for the** ~ pour le moment ♦ **that's enough for the** ~ ça suffit pour le moment ♦ **from the ~ I saw him** dès l'instant où je l'ai vu ♦ **from that** ~ dès ce moment, dès cet instant ♦ **she changes her mind from one ~ to the next** elle n'arrête pas de changer d'avis ♦ **I'll come in a** ~ j'arrive dans un instant ♦ **it was all over in a** ~ ça n'a duré qu'un instant ♦ **the ~ of truth** la minute or l'heure f de vérité ♦ **he has his ~s** (fig) il a ses bons côtés ♦ **it has its ~s** (of film) il y a de bons moments ; (of book) il y a de bons passages ; (of essay) il y a de bonnes choses ♦ **the psychological** ~ le moment psychologique ; → **spur**

[2] († = importance) importance f ♦ **of little** ~ de peu d'importance ♦ **of (great)** ~ de grande or haute importance

[3] (Phys) moment m ♦ ~ **of inertia** moment m d'inertie

momentarily /'məʊməntərɪlɪ/ ADV [1] (= temporarily) [distracted, blinded] momentanément ♦ **I had ~ forgotten** j'avais momentanément oublié ♦ **to be ~ lost for words** ne pas savoir quoi dire pendant un moment ♦ **to pause** ~ s'arrêter un instant [2] (US = shortly) dans un instant

momentary /'məʊməntərɪ/ ADJ [lapse, lull, weakness, silence] momentané ; [feeling, relief, panic, hesitation] passager ♦ **I caught a ~ glimpse of him** je l'ai entrevu rapidement or l'espace d'un instant ♦ **a ~ lapse of concentration** un moment d'inattention ♦ **she experienced a ~ loss of confidence** elle perdit momentanément confiance

momentous /məʊ'mentəs/ ADJ [event, occasion, day] de grande importance ; [decision, change] capital

momentousness /məʊ'mentəsnɪs/ N (NonC) importance f capitale, portée f

momentum /məʊ'mentəm/ N (pl **momentums** or **momenta** /məʊ'mentə/) (gen) vitesse f (acquise) ; (Phys etc) moment m (des quantités de mouvement) ; [of political movement etc] dynamisme m ♦ **to gain** or **gather** ~ [spacecraft, car etc] prendre de la vitesse ; (fig) gagner du terrain ♦ **to lose** ~ (lit, fig) être en perte de vitesse ♦ **to have** ~ [politician, party etc] avoir le vent en poupe ♦ **the Bush** ~ la dynamique or l'effet m Bush

momma* /'mɒmə/ N (US) ⇒ **mom**

mommy* /'mɒmɪ/ N (US) ⇒ **mom**

Mon. abbrev of **Monday**

Monacan /mɒ'nɑːkən/ ADJ monégasque N Monégasque mf

Monaco /'mɒnəkəʊ/ N Monaco m ♦ **in** ~ à Monaco

monad /'mɒnæd/ N (Chem, Philos) monade f

Mona Lisa /'məʊnə'liːzə/ N ♦ **the** ~ la Joconde

monarch /'mɒnək/ N (lit, fig) monarque m

monarchic(al) /mɒ'nɑːkɪk(əl)/ ADJ monarchique

monarchism /'mɒnəkɪzəm/ N monarchisme m

monarchist /'mɒnəkɪst/ ADJ, N monarchiste mf

monarchy /'mɒnəkɪ/ N monarchie f

monastery /'mɒnəstərɪ/ N monastère m

monastic /mə'næstɪk/ ADJ [1] (Rel) [life] monacal, monastique ; [community, building, vows] monastique [2] (= austere) [life, existence] monacal ; [room] austère

monasticism /mə'næstɪsɪzəm/ N monachisme m

monaural /,mɒn'ɔːrəl/ ADJ [instrument] monophonique, monaural ; [hearing] monauriculaire

Monday /'mʌndɪ/ N lundi m ; → **Easter, Whit** ; for other phrases see **Saturday** COMP **Monday-morning** ADJ (fig) ♦ **that ~-morning feeling** la déprime* du lundi matin ♦ **~-morning quarterback*** (US fig) spécialiste mf du je-vous-l'avais-bien-dit

Monegasque /mɒnə'gæsk/ ADJ monégasque N Monégasque mf

monetarism /'mʌnɪtərɪzəm/ N monétarisme m

monetarist /'mʌnɪtərɪst/ ADJ, N monétariste mf

monetary /'mʌnɪtərɪ/ ADJ [cooperation, policy, control, value] monétaire ; [gain] financier ♦ **economic and ~ union** union f économique et monétaire ♦ ~ **school** école f monétaire or monétariste ; → **international**

money /'mʌnɪ/ N [1] (NonC) argent m ; (Fin) monnaie f ♦ **French/Swedish** ~ argent m français/suédois ♦ **paper** ~ papier-monnaie m, monnaie f de papier (often pej) ♦ **to make** ~ [person] gagner de l'argent ; [business etc] rapporter, être lucratif ; see also **noun 2** ♦ **he made his ~ by dealing in cotton** il s'est enrichi avec le coton ♦ **the government's answer to the problem has been to throw ~ at it** le gouvernement n'a pas trouvé d'autre solution pour résoudre le problème que d'y injecter de l'argent ♦ **to come into** ~ (by inheritance) hériter (d'une somme d'argent) ; (gen) recevoir une somme d'argent ♦ **I paid** or **gave good ~ for it** ça m'a coûté de l'argent ♦ **he's earning good** ~ il gagne bien sa vie ; see also **noun 2** ♦ **he's earning big** ~ il gagne gros ♦ **that's big** ~ c'est une grosse somme ♦ **the deal involves big** ~ de grosses sommes sont en jeu dans cette transaction ; see also **noun 2** ♦ **he gets his ~ on Fridays** il touche son argent or sa paie le vendredi, il est payé le vendredi ♦ **when do I get my ~?** quand est-ce que j'aurai mon argent ? ♦ **to get one's ~'s worth** (lit, fig) en avoir pour son argent ♦ **to get one's ~ back** se faire rembourser ; (with difficulty) récupérer son argent ♦ **I want my ~ back!** remboursez ! ♦ **to put ~ into sth** placer son argent dans qch ♦ **is there ~ in it?** est-ce que ça rapporte ?, est-ce que c'est lucratif ? ♦ **it was ~ well spent** j'ai (or nous avons etc) fait une bonne affaire ; → **coin, counterfeit, ready**

[2] (phrases) ♦ **it's a bargain for the ~!** à ce prix-là c'est une occasion ! ♦ **that's the one for my ~!** c'est juste ce qu'il me faut ! ♦ **that's the team for my** ~ je serais prêt à parier pour cette équipe ♦ **for my ~ we should do it now** à mon avis nous devrions le faire maintenant ♦ **it's ~ for jam*** or **old rope*** (Brit) c'est de l'argent vite gagné or gagné sans peine, c'est être payé à ne rien faire ♦ **he's made of ~*** ♦ **he's rolling in ~*** ♦ **he has pots of ~*** il est cousu d'or, il roule sur l'or* ♦ **he's got ~ to burn** il a de l'argent à ne savoir qu'en faire or à jeter par la fenêtre ♦ **we're in the ~ now!*** nous roulons sur l'or* maintenant ♦ **he's in the big ~*** il récolte un fric fou* ♦ ~ **makes** ~ (Prov) l'argent attire l'argent ♦ ~ **is the root of all evil** (Prov) l'argent est la racine de tous les maux ♦ ~ **talks** (Prov) l'argent est roi ♦ ~ **doesn't grow on trees** l'argent ne tombe pas du ciel ♦ **to put one's ~ where one's mouth is** joindre l'acte à la parole (en déboursant une somme d'argent) ♦ **to throw** or **send good ~ after bad** dépenser de l'argent pour rien ♦ **bad ~ drives out good** les capitaux douteux font fuir les investissements sains ♦ **your ~ or your life!** la bourse ou la vie ! ♦ ~ **runs through his fingers like water, he spends ~ like water** l'argent lui fond dans les mains ♦ **it's ~ from home*** (US fig) c'est du tout cuit* ♦ **his analysis was right on the** ~ (US) son analyse était tout à fait juste ; → **even²**

[3] (Jur) **~s, monies** sommes fpl d'argent ♦ **~s paid out** versements mpl ♦ **~s received** recettes fpl, rentrées fpl ♦ **public ~s** deniers mpl publics

COMP [difficulties, problems, questions] d'argent, financier

money belt N ceinture-portefeuille f

money expert N expert m en matières financières

money laundering N blanchiment m d'argent

money-loser N affaire f non rentable or qui perd de l'argent

money market N (Econ) marché m monétaire

money matters NPL questions fpl d'argent or financières

money order N (US) mandat m postal, mandat-poste m

money spider* N araignée f porte-bonheur inv

money spinner* N (Brit) mine f d'or (fig)

money-spinning* ADJ (Brit) [idea] qui peut rapporter de l'or

money supply N (Econ) masse f monétaire

moneybag /ˈmʌnɪbæɡ/ N sac *m* d'argent ◆ **he's a ~s⁑** il est plein aux as⁑

moneybox /ˈmʌnɪbɒks/ N tirelire *f*

moneychanger /ˈmʌnɪ,tʃeɪndʒəʳ/ N *(= person)* changeur *m* ; *(= change machine)* distributeur *m* de monnaie, monnayeur *m*

moneyed /ˈmʌnɪd/ ADJ riche, aisé ◆ **the ~ classes** les classes *fpl* possédantes, les nantis *mpl*

moneygrubber /ˈmʌnɪɡrʌbəʳ/ N *(pej)* grippe-sou *m*

moneygrubbing /ˈmʌnɪɡrʌbɪŋ/ N *(pej)* thésaurisation *f*, rapacité *f* ADJ rapace, grippe-sou *inv*

moneylender /ˈmʌnɪlendəʳ/ N prêteur *m*, -euse *f* sur gages

moneylending /ˈmʌnɪlendɪŋ/ N prêt *m* à intérêt ADJ prêteur

moneymaker /ˈmʌnɪmeɪkəʳ/ N ◆ **to be a ~** *[scheme]* être une affaire lucrative ; *[person]* gagner beaucoup d'argent

moneymaking /ˈmʌnɪmeɪkɪŋ/ N acquisition *f* d'argent ADJ lucratif, qui rapporte

moneyman * /ˈmʌnɪmæn/ N (pl **-men**) *(US)* financier *m*

moneywort /ˈmʌnɪwɜːt/ N souci *m* d'eau, lysimaque *f*

...monger /ˈmʌŋɡəʳ/ SUF marchand *m* de... ; → **fishmonger, scandalmonger, warmonger**

Mongol /ˈmɒŋɡəl/ ADJ mongol N [1] Mongol(e) *m(f)* [2] *(= language)* mongol *m*

mongol † /ˈmɒŋɡəl/ ADJ *(= with/of Down's syndrome)* mongolien N *(= person with Down's syndrome)* mongolien(ne) *m(f)*

Mongolia /mɒŋˈɡəʊlɪə/ N Mongolie *f*

Mongolian /mɒŋˈɡəʊlɪən/ N Mongol(e) *m(f)* ADJ mongol ◆ **the ~ People's Republic** la République populaire de Mongolie

mongolism † /ˈmɒŋɡəlɪzəm/ N *(= Down's syndrome)* mongolisme *m*

Mongoloid /ˈmɒŋɡə,lɔɪd/ ADJ, N ⇒ **Mongol adj, noun 1, mongol noun**

mongoose /ˈmɒŋɡuːs/ N (pl **mongooses**) mangouste *f*

mongrel /ˈmʌŋɡrəl/ N *(= dog)* (chien *m*) bâtard *m* ; *(= animal, plant)* hybride *m*, métis(se) *m(f)* ADJ hybride, bâtard, (de race) indéfinissable

monied /ˈmʌnɪd/ ADJ ⇒ **moneyed**

monies /ˈmʌnɪz/ NPL of **money noun 3**

moniker⁑ /ˈmɒnɪkəʳ/ N *(= name)* nom *m* ; *(= nickname)* surnom *m*

monitor /ˈmɒnɪtəʳ/ N [1] *(= device)* moniteur *m* ◆ **heart rate ~** moniteur *m* cardiaque [2] *(= person: Rad)* rédacteur *m*, -trice *f* d'un service d'écoute [3] *(Scol)* ≈ chef *m* de classe [4] *(= official)* observateur *m*, -trice *f* VT [1] *[+ person, pupil, work, progress, system]* suivre de près ; *[+ equipment etc]* contrôler (les performances de) ; *[+ machine]* contrôler ◆ **a nurse ~s the patient's progress** une infirmière suit de près *or* surveille l'évolution de l'état du malade ◆ **a machine ~s the patient's progress** une machine contrôle l'évolution de l'état du malade ◆ **to ~ the situation** surveiller l'évolution des choses ◆ **UN officials are ~ing the voting** les délégués de l'ONU surveillent le déroulement du scrutin [2] *(Rad) [+ foreign broadcasts, station]* être à l'écoute de

monitoring /ˈmɒnɪtərɪŋ/ N [1] *(gen, by person)* surveillance *f* ; *(by machine)* contrôle *m* ; *(Med, Tech)* monitorage *m* ; *(Univ, Scol)* contrôle *m* continu (des connaissances) [2] *(Rad)* (service *m* d')écoute *f*

monitory /ˈmɒnɪtərɪ/ ADJ monitoire, d'admonition

monk /mʌŋk/ N moine *m*, religieux *m*

monkey /ˈmʌŋkɪ/ N singe *m* ; *(= naughty child)* galopin(e) *m(f)*, polisson(ne) *m(f)* ; *(Brit ⁑ = £500)* cinq cents livres ◆ **to make a ~ out of sb** tourner qn en ridicule ◆ **to have a ~ on one's back** * *(US Drugs)* être esclave de la drogue ◆ **I don't give a ~'s⁑** *or* **a ~'s cuss** †⁑ **(about football)** *(Brit)* je n'en ai rien à foutre⁑ (du football) ◆ **as clever as a cartload** *or* **barrel (load) of ~s** † * *(Brit)* malin (-igne *f*) comme un singe

COMP **monkey bars** NPL *(for climbing on)* cage *f* à poules

monkey business * N *(fig) (dishonest)* affaire *f* louche, combine(s) *f(pl)* ; *(mischievous)* singeries *fpl* ◆ **no ~ business now!** * pas de blagues ! *

monkey house N cage *f* des singes, singerie *f*

monkey jacket N *(Naut)* vareuse *f* ajustée

monkey nut N *(Brit)* cacahouète *or* cacahuète *f*

monkey puzzle N *(= tree)* araucaria *m*

monkey suit * N *(esp US: pej)* costume *m* de pingouin *, smoking *m*

monkey tricks * NPL *(fig) (dishonest)* manœuvres *fpl*, combine(s) *f(pl)* ; *(mischievous)* singeries *fpl* ◆ **no ~ tricks now!** * pas de blagues ! *

monkey wrench N clé *f* anglaise *or* à molette ◆ **to throw a ~ wrench into the works** * *(US fig)* flanquer la pagaille *

► **monkey about** *, **monkey around** * VI [1] *(= waste time)* perdre son temps ◆ **stop ~ing about and get on with your work** cesse de perdre ton temps et fais ton travail

[2] *(= play the fool)* faire l'idiot *or* l'imbécile ◆ **to ~ about with sth** tripoter qch, faire l'imbécile avec qch

monkeyshines * /ˈmʌŋkɪʃaɪnz/ NPL *(US)* pitreries *fpl*

monkfish /ˈmʌŋkfɪʃ/ N (pl **monkfish** *or* **monkfishes**) *(= angler fish)* lotte *f* ; *(= angel fish)* ange *m* de mer

monkish /ˈmʌŋkɪʃ/ ADJ de moine

monkshood /ˈmʌŋkshʊd/ N *(= plant)* aconit *m*

mono /ˈmɒnəʊ/ ADJ (abbrev of **monophonic**) mono *inv* N [1] ◆ **recorded in ~** enregistré en mono [2] (also **mono record**) disque *m* mono

monobasic /mɒnəʊˈbeɪsɪk/ ADJ monobasique

monochromatic /mɒnəʊkrəʊˈmætɪk/ ADJ monochromatique

monochrome /ˈmɒnəkrəʊm/ N *(gen, also Art)* monochrome *m* ; *(Phot, TV)* noir *m* et blanc *m* ◆ **landscape in ~** paysage *m* en camaïeu ADJ *(gen)* monochrome ; *(Art)* en camaïeu ; *(Phot, TV)* en noir et blanc

monocle /ˈmɒnəkl/ N monocle *m*

monocled /ˈmɒnəkld/ ADJ qui porte un monocle

monocoque /ˈmɒnəkɒk/ ADJ monocoque N *(= car)* monocoque *f* ; *(= boat, bicycle)* monocoque *m*

monocracy /mɒˈnɒkrəsɪ/ N monocratie *f*

monocrat /ˈmɒnəkræt/ N monocrate *m*

monocratic /mɒnəˈkrætɪk/ ADJ monocratique

monocular /mɒˈnɒkjʊləʳ/ ADJ monoculaire

monoculture /ˈmɒnəʊkʌltʃəʳ/ N monoculture *f*

monocyte /ˈmɒnəʊsaɪt/ N monocyte *m*

monody /ˈmɒnədɪ/ N monodie *f*

monogamist /mɒˈnɒɡəmɪst/ N monogame *mf*

monogamous /mɒˈnɒɡəməs/ ADJ monogame

monogamy /mɒˈnɒɡəmɪ/ N monogamie *f*

monogenetic /mɒnəʊdʒɪˈnetɪk/ ADJ monogénétique

monogram /ˈmɒnəɡræm/ N monogramme *m* VT marquer de son (*or* mon *etc*) monogramme *or* de son (*or* mon *etc*) chiffre

monogrammed, monogramed *(US)* /ˈmɒnəɡræmd/ ADJ portant un (*or* son *etc*) monogramme, à son (*or* mon *etc*) chiffre

monograph /ˈmɒnəɡræf/ N monographie *f*

monogynous /mɒˈnɒdʒɪnəs/ ADJ monogame

monogyny /mɒˈnɒdʒɪnɪ/ N monogamie *f*

monohull /ˈmɒnəʊhʌl/ N monocoque *m (Naut)*

monokini /ˈmɒnəʊkiːnɪ/ N monokini *m*

monolingual /,mɒnəʊˈlɪŋɡwəl/ ADJ monolingue

monolith /ˈmɒnəlɪθ/ N [1] *(lit = stone)* monolithe *m* [2] *(fig = organization etc)* mastodonte *m*

monolithic /,mɒnəˈlɪθɪk/ ADJ *[system, structure, building, state, party]* monolithique ; *(Archeol)* monolithe

monolog /ˈmɒnə,lɒɡ/ N *(US)* ⇒ **monologue**

monologist /ˈmɒnə,lɒɡɪst/ N monologueur *m*

monologue, monolog *(also US)* /ˈmɒnəlɒɡ/ N monologue *m*

monomania /,mɒnəʊˈmeɪnɪə/ N monomanie *f*

monomaniac /mɒnəʊˈmeɪnɪæk/ N, ADJ monomane *mf*, monomaniaque *mf*

monometallism /,mɒnəʊˈmetəlɪzəm/ N monométallisme *m*

monometer /mɒˈnɒmɪtəʳ/ N monomètre *m*

monomial /mɒˈnəʊmɪəl/ N monôme *m* ADJ de *or* en monôme

monomorphic /mɒnəʊˈmɔːfɪk/ ADJ monomorphe

monomorphism /mɒnəʊˈmɔːfɪzəm/ N monomorphisme *m*

mononuclear /mɒnəʊˈnjuːklɪəʳ/ ADJ mononucléaire

mononucleosis /,mɒnəʊnjuːklɪˈəʊsɪs/ N mononucléose *f*

monophonic /,mɒnəʊˈfɒnɪk/ ADJ monophonique, monaural

monophony /mɒˈnɒfənɪ/ N monophonie *f*

monophthong /ˈmɒnəfθɒŋ/ N monophthongue *f*

monoplane /ˈmɒnəʊpleɪn/ N monoplan *m*

monopolist /məˈnɒpəlɪst/ N monopoliste *mf*

monopolistic /mənɒpəˈlɪstɪk/ ADJ monopolistique

monopolization /mənɒpəlaɪˈzeɪʃən/ N monopolisation *f*

monopolize /məˈnɒpəlaɪz/ VT *(Comm)* monopoliser, avoir le monopole de ; *(fig)* monopoliser, accaparer

monopoly /məˈnɒpəlɪ/ N [1] monopole *m (of, in de)* [2] *(= game)* **Monopoly** ® Monopoly ® *m*

COMP **Monopolies and Mergers Commission** N *(Brit)* Commission *f* d'enquête sur les monopoles Commission *f* de la concurrence

Monopoly money * N *(NonC) (= large amount)* somme *f* mirobolante * ; *(pej) (= foreign currency)* ≈ monnaie *f* de singe

monorail /ˈmɒnəʊreɪl/ N monorail *m*

monoski /ˈmɒnəʊ,skiː/ N monoski *m*

monosodium glutamate /mɒnəʊˈsəʊdɪəm ˈɡluːtəmeɪt/ N glutamate *m* (de sodium)

monosyllabic /ˈmɒnəʊsɪˈlæbɪk/ ADJ *[word, reply]* monosyllabique ◆ **she was ~** elle ne s'exprimait que par monosyllabes ◆ **his English was fairly ~** son anglais était plutôt rudimentaire

monosyllable /ˈmɒnə,sɪləbl/ N monosyllabe *m* ◆ **to answer in ~s** répondre par monosyllabes

monotheism /ˈmɒnəʊ,θiːɪzəm/ N monothéisme *m*

monotheist /ˈmɒnəʊ,θiːɪst/ N monothéiste *mf*

monotheistic /,mɒnəʊθiːˈɪstɪk/ ADJ monothéiste

monotone /'mɒnətəʊn/ **N** *(= voice/tone etc)* voix *f*/ton *m etc* monocorde ◆ **to speak in a ~** parler sur un ton monocorde

monotonous /mə'nɒtənəs/ **ADJ** monotone

monotonously /mə'nɒtənəslɪ/ **ADV** *[predictable]* de façon monotone ◆ **the rain dripped ~ from the trees** la pluie ruisselait des arbres avec monotonie ◆ **the sky was ~ grey** le ciel était d'un gris monotone

monotony /mə'nɒtənɪ/ **N** monotonie *f*

monotype /'mɒnəʊtaɪp/ **N** *(Art, Engraving)* monotype *m* ◆ **Monotype** ® *(Typ = machine)* Monotype ® *f*

monoxide /mɒ'nɒksaɪd/ **N** monoxyde *m*

Monroe doctrine /mən'rəʊ'dɒktrɪn/ **N** doctrine *f* de Monroe

monseigneur /,mɒnsen'jɜː^r/ **N** monseigneur *m*

monsignor /mɒn'siːnjə^r/ **N** (pl **monsignors** or **monsignori**) *(Rel)* monsignor *m*

monsoon /mɒn'suːn/ **N** mousson *f* ◆ **the ~s** la mousson ◆ **the ~ season** la mousson d'été

mons pubis /'mɒnz'pjuːbɪs/ **N** (pl **montes pubis** /'mɒntiːz'pjuːbɪs/) mont *m* de Vénus, pénil *m (chez l'homme)*

monster /'mɒnstə^r/ **N** *(all senses)* monstre *m* **ADJ** * colossal, monstre *

monstrance /'mɒnstrəns/ **N** ostensoir *m*

monstrosity /mɒn'strɒsɪtɪ/ **N** *(= thing)* monstruosité *f* ; *(= person)* monstre *m*

monstrous /'mɒnstrəs/ **ADJ** monstrueux ◆ **it is ~ that ...** c'est monstrueux que ... + *subj*

monstrously /'mɒnstrəslɪ/ **ADV** monstrueusement

mons veneris /'mɒnz'venərɪs/ **N** (pl **montes veneris** /'mɒntiːz'venərɪs/) mont *m* de Vénus

Mont. abbrev of **Montana**

montage /mɒn'tɑːʒ/ **N** *(Cine, Phot)* montage *m*

Montana /mɒn'tænə/ **N** Montana *m* ◆ **in ~** dans le Montana

Mont Blanc /mɔ̃blɑ̃/ **N** le mont Blanc

monte * /'mɒntɪ/ **N** ⇒ **monty**

Monte Carlo /'mɒntɪ'kɑːləʊ/ **N** Monte-Carlo

Montenegrin /,mɒntɪ'niːgrɪn/, **Montenegran** /,mɒntɪ'niːgrən/ **ADJ** monténégrin **N** Monténégrin(e) *m(f)*

Montenegro /,mɒntɪ'niːgrəʊ/ **N** Monténégro *m* ◆ **in ~** au Monténégro

Montezuma /mɒntɪ'zuːmə/ **N** Montezuma *m*, Moctezuma II *m* ◆ **~'s revenge** * turista *f*

month /mʌnθ/ **N** mois *m* ◆ **it went on for ~s** *or* **for ~ after ~** cela a duré des mois (et des mois) ◆ **in the ~ of May** au mois de mai, en mai ◆ **to be paid by the ~** être payé au mois, être mensualisé ◆ **every ~** *[happen]* tous les mois ; *[pay]* mensuellement ◆ **~ by ~** de mois en mois ◆ **~ on ~** *(+ noun)* mensuel ◆ **output climbed by 0.3% ~ on ~ in March** en mars, la production a augmenté de 0,3% par rapport au mois précédent ◆ **which day of the ~ is it?** le combien sommes-nous ? ◆ **at the end of this ~** à la fin du *or* de ce mois ◆ **at the end of the current ~** *(Comm)* fin courant * ◆ **he owes his landlady two ~s' rent** il doit deux mois à sa propriétaire ◆ **six ~s pregnant** enceinte de six mois ◆ **he'll never do it in a ~ of Sundays** * il le fera la semaine des quatre jeudis * *or* à la saint-glinglin * ; → **calendar, lunar**

monthly /'mʌnθlɪ/ **ADJ** mensuel ◆ **on a ~ basis** *[pay]* par mensualités *[happen, do sth]* tous les mois ◆ **~ payment** *or* **instalment** mensualité *f* ◆ **~ period** *(= menstruation)* règles *fpl* ◆ **~ ticket** carte *f* (d'abonnement) mensuelle **N** *(Press)* mensuel *m* **ADV** *[publish]* mensuellement ; *[pay]* au mois ; *[happen]* tous les mois ◆ **~ paid staff** employés *mpl* mensualisés

Montreal /,mɒntrɪ'ɔːl/ **N** Montréal

monty * /'mɒntɪ/ **N** *(Brit)* ◆ **the full ~** la totale *

monument /'mɒnjʊmənt/ **N** *(all senses)* monument *m (to, of à)* ◆ **Monty Python films are a ~ to British eccentricity** les films de Monty Python sont un monument d'excentricité britannique

monumental /,mɒnjʊ'mentl/ **ADJ** 1 *(= huge) [object, task, achievement, blunder]* monumental ; *[effort, success]* prodigieux ◆ **on a ~ scale** *[build]* sur une très grande *or* une vaste échelle ◆ **he was stupid on a ~ scale** il était d'une bêtise monumentale 2 *[art, sculpture]* monumental **COMP** **monumental mason** **N** marbrier *m (funéraire)*

monumentally /,mɒnjʊ'mentəlɪ/ **ADV** *[dull, boring]* prodigieusement ◆ **~ important** d'une importance capitale *or* monumentale ◆ **it was ~ successful** ça a eu un succès foudroyant

moo /muː/ **N** meuglement *m* ◆ **~!** meuh ! ◆ **silly ~** * pauvre cloche * *f* **VI** meugler **COMP** **moo-cow** **N** *(baby talk)* meuh-meuh *f (baby talk)*

mooch * /muːtʃ/ **VT** *(US)* ◆ **to ~ sth from sb** *(= cadge)* taper qn de qch * **VI** ◆ **to ~ in/out** *etc* entrer/sortir *etc* en traînant

► **mooch about** *, **mooch around** * **VI** traînasser, flemmarder *

mood /muːd/ **N** 1 humeur *f* ◆ **to be in a good/bad ~** être de bonne/mauvaise humeur, être de bon/mauvais poil * ◆ **to be in a ~** être de mauvaise humeur ◆ **to be in an ugly ~** *[person]* être d'une humeur massacrante *or* exécrable ; *[crowd]* être menaçant ◆ **to be in a forgiving ~** être en veine de générosité *or* d'indulgence ◆ **that depends on his ~** cela dépend de son humeur ◆ **he's in one of his ~s** il est encore mal luné ◆ **she has ~s** elle a des sautes d'humeur, elle est lunatique ◆ **the ~ of the meeting** l'état d'esprit de l'assemblée ◆ **they misread the ~ of the electorate** ils ont mal interprété l'état d'esprit des électeurs ◆ **the government is in tune with the ~ of the people** le gouvernement est en phase avec la population ◆ **the political ~ in the country** le climat politique du pays ◆ **she set the ~ with music and candlelight** elle a créé une ambiance avec de la musique et des bougies ◆ **as the ~ takes him** selon son humeur, comme ça lui chante *

◆ **in the mood** ◆ **I'm in the ~ for a dance** j'ai envie de danser ◆ **I'm not in the ~ for laughing** je ne suis pas d'humeur à rire, je n'ai aucune envie de rire ◆ **are you in the ~ for chess?** une partie d'échecs, ça vous dit * ? ◆ **he plays well when he's in the ~** quand il veut *or* quand ça lui chante * il joue bien ◆ **I'm not in the ~** ça ne me dit rien

◆ **in no mood** ◆ **I'm in no ~ to listen to him** je ne suis pas d'humeur à l'écouter ◆ **they were in no ~ for compromise** ils n'étaient nullement disposés à faire des compromis

2 *(Ling, Mus)* mode *m*

COMP **mood disorder** **N** *(Psych)* trouble *m* de l'humeur

mood music **N** musique *f* d'ambiance

mood swing **N** saute *f* d'humeur

moodily /'muːdɪlɪ/ **ADV** *(= bad-temperedly) [reply]* d'un ton maussade, maussadement ; *(= gloomily) [stare at]* d'un air morose

moodiness /'muːdɪnɪs/ **N** *(= sulkiness)* humeur *f* maussade ; *(= changeability)* humeur *f* changeante

moody /'muːdɪ/ **ADJ** 1 *(= sulky) [person]* de mauvaise humeur *(with sb* avec qn) ◆ **Elvis's ~ looks** la beauté ténébreuse d'Elvis 2 *(= temperamental) [person]* d'humeur changeante, lunatique ◆ **to be ~** être lunatique 3 *(= atmospheric) [music, film, picture]* sombre

moola(h) * /'muːlɑː/ **N** *(US = money)* pèze * *m*, fric * *m*

moon /muːn/ **N** lune *f* ◆ **there was no ~** c'était une nuit sans lune ◆ **there was a ~ that night** il y avait clair de lune cette nuit-là ◆ **when the ~ is full** à la pleine lune ◆ **by the light of the ~** à la clarté de la lune, au clair de lune ◆ **the ~s of Jupiter** les lunes de Jupiter ◆ **many ~s ago** *(hum)* il y a de cela bien longtemps ◆ **to ask for the ~** demander la lune ◆ **he's over the ~** * **(about it)** il est aux anges ; → **blue, half, land, man, new, shoot** **VI** (* *= exhibit buttocks)* montrer son cul * *

COMP **moon buggy** **N** jeep ® *f* lunaire

moon landing **N** alunissage *m*

moon rock **N** roche *f* lunaire

moon shot **N** *(Space)* lancement *m* d'une fusée lunaire

moon walk **N** marche *f* sur la lune

► **moon about, moon around** **VI** musarder en rêvassant

► **moon over** **VT FUS** ◆ **to moon over sb** soupirer pour qn

moonbeam /'muːnbiːm/ **N** rayon *m* de lune

moonboots /'muːnbuːts/ **NPL** après-skis *mpl*, moonboots *fpl*

mooncraft /'muːnkrɑːft/ **N** *(Space)* module *m* lunaire

moonfaced /'muːnfeɪst/ **ADJ** au visage rond

Moonie /'muːnɪ/ **N** mooniste *mf*, adepte *mf* de la secte Moon

moonless /'muːnlɪs/ **ADJ** sans lune

moonlight /'muːnlaɪt/ **N** clair *m* de lune ◆ **by ~, in the ~** au clair de lune **VI** (* *= work extra)* travailler au noir

COMP *[walk, encounter]* au clair de lune

moonlight flit **N** *(Brit fig)* ◆ **to do a ~ flit** déménager à la cloche de bois

moonlight night **N** nuit *f* de lune

moonlighting * /'muːnlaɪtɪŋ/ **N** *(NonC)* travail *m* au noir

moonlit /'muːnlɪt/ **ADJ** éclairé par la lune ◆ **a ~ night** une nuit de lune

moonrise /'muːnraɪz/ **N** lever *m* de (la) lune

moonscape /'muːnskeɪp/ **N** paysage *m* lunaire

moonshine * /'muːnʃaɪn/ **N** *(fig = nonsense)* sornettes *fpl* ; *(US = illegal spirits)* alcool *m* de contrebande

moonshiner /'muːnʃaɪnə^r/ **N** *(US) (= distiller)* bouilleur *m* de cru clandestin ; *(= smuggler)* contrebandier *m* d'alcool

moonshining /'muːnʃaɪnɪŋ/ **N** *(US)* distillation *f* clandestine

moonship /'muːnʃɪp/ **N** *(Space)* module *m* lunaire

moonstone /'muːnstəʊn/ **N** pierre *f* de lune

moonstruck /'muːnstrʌk/ **ADJ** ◆ **he's ~** il n'a pas toute sa tête

moony * /'muːnɪ/ **ADJ** dans la lune

Moor /mʊə^r/ **N** Maure *m or* More *m*, Mauresque *f or* Moresque *f*

moor[1] /mʊə^r/ **N** *(esp Brit)* lande *f*

moor[2] /mʊə^r/ **VT** *[+ ship]* amarrer **VI** mouiller

moorhen /'mʊəhen/ **N** poule *f* d'eau

mooring /'mʊərɪŋ/ **N** *(Naut) (= place)* mouillage *m* ; *(= ropes etc)* amarres *fpl* ◆ **at her ~s** sur ses amarres ◆ **~ buoy** coffre *m* (d'amarrage), bouée *f* de corps-mort

Moorish /'mʊərɪʃ/ **ADJ** *[person, culture, influence, invasion]* maure ; *[architecture]* mauresque

moorland /'mʊələnd/ **N** lande *f* ; *(boggy)* terrain *m* tourbeux

moose /muːs/ **N** *(pl inv, in Canada)* orignal *m* ; *(in Europe)* élan *m*

moot /muːt/ **ADJ** *[question]* discutable, controversé ◆ **it's a ~ point** c'est discutable **VT**

[+ question] soulever, mettre sur le tapis ◆ **it has been ~ed that** ... on a suggéré que ...
COMP **moot case** N *(Jur)* hypothèse *f* d'école
moot court N *(US) tribunal fictif permettant aux étudiants de s'exercer*

mop /mɒp/ N 1 *(for floor)* balai *m* à franges ; *(for dishes)* lavette *f* (à vaisselle) ; *(Naut)* faubert *m* 2 (also **mop of hair**) tignasse *f* ◆ **a ~ of curls** crinière* *f* bouclée VT *[+ floor, surface]* essuyer ◆ **to ~ one's brow** s'éponger le front COMP **mopping-up operation, mop-up** N *(Mil)* (opération *f* de) nettoyage *m*
► **mop down** VT SEP passer un coup de balai à
► **mop up** VT SEP 1 *[+ liquid]* éponger ; *[+ floor, surface]* essuyer ◆ **she ~ped up the sauce with a piece of bread** elle a saucé son assiette avec un morceau de pain 2 *[+ profits]* rafler, absorber 3 *(Mil) [+ terrain]* nettoyer ; *[+ remnants of enemy]* éliminer ADJ ◆ **mopping-up** → **mop**

mopboard /ˈmɒpbɔːd/ N *(US)* plinthe *f*

mope /məʊp/ VI se morfondre, avoir le cafard* *or* des idées noires ◆ **she ~d about it all day** toute la journée elle a broyé du noir en y pensant
► **mope about, mope around** VI passer son temps à se morfondre, traîner son ennui

moped /ˈməʊped/ N *(esp Brit)* vélomoteur *m*, mobylette ®*f*

moppet* /ˈmɒpɪt/ N chéri(e) *m(f)*

moquette /mɒˈket/ N moquette *f (étoffe)*

MOR ADJ *(Mus)* (abbrev of **middle-of-the-road**) grand public *inv*

moraine /mɒˈreɪn/ N moraine *f*

moral /ˈmɒrəl/ ADJ *(all senses)* moral ◆ **it is a ~ certainty** c'est une certitude morale ◆ **to be under** *or* **have a ~ obligation to do sth** être moralement obligé de faire qch, être dans l'obligation morale de faire qch ◆ **~ support** soutien *m* moral ◆ **I'm going along as ~ support for him** j'y vais pour le soutenir moralement ◆ **the Moral Majority** *(US Pol)* les néoconservateurs *mpl* (américains) ◆ **~ philosopher** moraliste *mf* ◆ **~ philosophy** la morale, l'éthique *f* ◆ **Moral Rearmament** *(Rel)* Réarmement *m* moral ◆ **to raise ~ standards** relever le niveau moral ◆ **~ standards are falling** le sens moral se perd ◆ **~ suasion** pression *f* morale ◆ **a ~ victory** une victoire morale
N *[of story]* morale *f* ◆ **to point the ~** tirer la morale
NPL **morals** *[of person, act, attitude]* moralité *f* ◆ **of loose ~s** de mœurs relâchées ◆ **he has no ~s** il est sans moralité

morale /mɒˈrɑːl/ N (NonC) moral *m* ◆ **high ~** bon moral *m* ◆ **his ~ was very low** il avait le moral très bas *or* à zéro ◆ **to raise sb's ~** remonter le moral à qn ◆ **to lower** *or* **undermine sb's ~** démoraliser qn
COMP **morale booster** N ◆ **to be a ~ booster for sb** remonter le moral de qn
morale-boosting ADJ qui regonfle le moral

moralist /ˈmɒrəlɪst/ N moraliste *mf*

moralistic /mɒrəˈlɪstɪk/ ADJ *(pej)* moralisateur (-trice *f*) *(pej)*

morality /məˈrælɪtɪ/ N 1 (NonC) *(= ethics)* morale *f* ◆ **an effort to preserve traditional ~** des efforts pour préserver la morale traditionnelle ◆ **they've got no ~** ils n'ont aucun sens moral 2 *(= value system)* morale *f* ◆ **you have the typical bourgeois ~** vous avez une morale typiquement bourgeoise 3 *(= rightness)* moralité *f* 4 *(Theat:* also **morality play**) moralité *f*

moralize /ˈmɒrəlaɪz/ VI moraliser *(about* sur) VT moraliser, faire la morale à

moralizing /ˈmɒrəlaɪzɪŋ/ ADJ moralisateur (-trice *f*) N leçons *fpl* de morale

morally /ˈmɒrəlɪ/ ADV 1 *(= ethically)* moralement ◆ **~ wrong** contraire à la morale ◆ **~ right** conforme à la morale ◆ **she was ~ right** elle avait raison d'un point de vue moral ◆ **~ the situation is a minefield** d'un point de vue moral la situation est épineuse 2 *(frm = virtually)* ◆ **~ certain** pratiquement sûr

morass /məˈræs/ N marais *m*, marécage *m* ◆ **a ~ of problems** des problèmes à ne plus s'y retrouver *or* à ne plus s'en sortir ◆ **a ~ of figures** un fatras de chiffres ◆ **a ~ of paperwork** de la paperasserie, un monceau de paperasserie

moratorium /ˌmɒrəˈtɔːrɪəm/ N (pl **moratoriums** *or* **moratoria** /ˌmɒrəˈtɔːrɪə/) moratoire *m*, moratorium *m*

Moravia /məˈreɪvɪə/ N Moravie *f*

Moravian /məˈreɪvɪən/ ADJ morave ◆ **the ~ Church** l'Église *f* morave N Morave *mf*

moray eel /mɒˈreɪˈiːl/ N murène *f*

morbid /ˈmɔːbɪd/ ADJ *(= ghoulish) [person, thoughts, interest]* morbide ; *[fear, dislike]* maladif ◆ **don't be so ~!** cesse donc de broyer du noir ! COMP **morbid anatomy** N anatomie *f* pathologique

morbidity /mɔːˈbɪdɪtɪ/ N *(also Med)* morbidité *f*
COMP **morbidity rate** N taux *m* de morbidité

morbidly /ˈmɔːbɪdlɪ/ ADV ◆ **to be ~ curious about sb/sth** être animé d'une curiosité malsaine pour qn/qch ◆ **to be ~ fascinated by sb/sth** avoir une fascination malsaine pour qn/qch ◆ **to be ~ obsessed by sth** avoir la hantise de qch

morbidness /ˈmɔːbɪdnɪs/ N ⇒ **morbidity**

mordacious /mɔːˈdeɪʃəs/ ADJ mordant, caustique

mordacity /mɔːˈdæsɪtɪ/ N mordacité *f (liter)*, causticité *f*

mordant /ˈmɔːdənt/ ADJ *(frm)* mordant

mordent /ˈmɔːdənt/ N *(Mus)* ◆ **(lower) ~** mordant *m*, pincé *m* ◆ **upper** *or* **inverted ~** pincé *m* renversé

more /mɔːʳ/ LANGUAGE IN USE 5.1 (compar of **many, much**)
ADJ, PRON *(= greater in number or quantity)* plus (de), davantage (de) ; *(= additional)* encore (de) ; *(= other)* d'autres ◆ **many came but ~ stayed away** beaucoup de gens sont venus mais davantage *or* un plus grand nombre se sont abstenus ◆ **many ~** *or* **a lot ~ books/time** beaucoup plus de livres/de temps ◆ **I need a lot ~** il m'en faut beaucoup plus *or* bien davantage ◆ **I need a few ~ books** il me faut encore quelques livres *or* quelques livres de plus ◆ **some were talking and a few ~ were reading** il y en avait qui parlaient et d'autres qui lisaient ◆ **a little ~** un peu plus (de) ◆ **several ~ days** quelques jours de plus, encore quelques jours ◆ **I'd like (some) ~ meat** je voudrais encore de la viande ◆ **there's no ~ meat** il n'y a plus de viande ◆ **is there (any) ~ wine?** y a-t-il encore du vin ?, est-ce qu'il reste du vin ? ◆ **have some ~ ice cream** reprenez de la glace ◆ **has she any ~ children?** a-t-elle d'autres enfants ? ◆ **no ~ shouting!** assez de cris !, arrêtez de crier ! ◆ **I've got no ~, I haven't any ~** je n'en ai plus, il ne m'en reste plus ◆ **I've no ~ time** je n'ai plus le temps ◆ **I shan't say any ~, I shall say no ~** je n'en dirai pas davantage ; *(threat)* tenez-le-vous pour dit ◆ **have you heard any ~ about him?** avez-vous d'autres nouvelles de lui ? ◆ **I've got ~ like these** j'en ai d'autres comme ça ◆ **you couldn't ask for ~** on ne peut guère en demander plus *or* davantage ◆ **we must see ~ of her** il faut que nous la voyions *subj* davantage *or* plus souvent ◆ **I want to know ~ about it** je veux en savoir plus long, je veux en savoir davantage ◆ **there's ~ where that came from** ce n'est qu'un début ◆ **the ~ the merrier** plus on est de fous plus on rit *(Prov)* ◆ **and what's ~** ... et qui plus est ... ◆ **his speech, of which ~ later, ...** son discours, sur lequel nous reviendrons, ... ◆ **let's say no ~ about it** n'en parlons plus ◆ **I shall have ~ to say about that** je reviendrai sur ce sujet (plus tard) ◆ **I've nothing ~ to say** je n'ai rien à ajouter ◆ **nothing ~** rien de plus ◆ **something ~** autre chose, quelque chose d'autre *or* de plus
◆ **more ... than** plus ... que ; *(before a number)* plus de ... que ◆ **I've got ~ money/books than you** j'ai plus d'argent/de livres que vous ◆ **he's got ~ than you** il en a plus que vous ◆ **~ people than seats** plus de gens que de places ◆ **~ people than usual/than we expected** plus de gens que de coutume/que prévu ◆ **it cost ~ than I expected** c'était plus cher que je ne pensais ◆ **~ than half the audience** plus de la moitié de l'assistance *or* des auditeurs ◆ **not ~ than a kilo** pas plus d'un kilo ◆ **~ than 20 came** plus de 20 personnes sont venues ◆ **no ~ than a dozen** une douzaine au plus ◆ **~ than enough** plus que suffisant, amplement *or* bien suffisant ◆ **he can't afford ~ than a small house** il ne peut se payer qu'une petite maison
ADV plus *[exercise, sleep etc]* plus, davantage ◆ **~ difficult** plus difficile ◆ **~ easily** plus facilement ◆ **~ and ~ difficult** de plus en plus difficile ◆ **even ~ difficult** encore plus difficile ◆ **you must rest ~** vous devez vous reposer davantage ◆ **he sleeps ~ and ~** il dort de plus en plus ; → **never**
◆ **more than** plus que ◆ **he talks ~ than I do** il parle plus *or* davantage que moi ◆ **she talks even ~ than he does** elle parle encore plus *or* davantage que lui ◆ **I like apples ~ than oranges** je préfère les pommes aux oranges ◆ **no** *or* **nothing ~ than ...** rien (de plus) que ... ◆ **not much ~ than ...** pas beaucoup plus que ... ◆ **it will ~ than cover the cost** cela couvrira largement *or* amplement les frais ◆ **the house is ~ than half built** la maison est plus qu'à moitié bâtie ◆ **I had ~ than kept my promise** j'avais fait plus que tenir ma promesse
◆ **more ... than** plus ... que ◆ **~ amused than annoyed** plus amusé que fâché ◆ **he was ~ frightened than hurt** il a eu plus de peur que de mal ◆ **each ~ beautiful than the next** *or* **the other** tous plus beaux les uns que les autres ◆ **it's ~ a short story than a novel** c'est une nouvelle plus qu'un roman ◆ **he's no ~ a duke than I am** il n'est pas plus duc que moi ◆ **he could no ~ pay me than fly in the air*** il ne pourrait pas plus me payer que devenir pape*
◆ **... any more** *(= any longer, again)* ◆ **I won't do it any ~** je ne le ferai plus ◆ **don't do it any ~!** ne recommence pas ! ◆ **he doesn't live here any ~** il n'habite plus ici ◆ **I can't stay any ~** je ne peux pas rester plus longtemps *or* davantage
◆ **more or less** plus ou moins
◆ **no more and no less** ni plus ni moins
◆ **neither more nor less (than ...)** ni plus ni moins (que ...)
◆ **no more ...** † *(= neither)* ◆ **I can't bear him! – no ~ can I!** je ne peux pas le souffrir ! – ni moi non plus ! ◆ **I shan't go there again! – no ~ you shall** je ne veux pas y retourner ! – c'est entendu
◆ **... no more** *(liter) (= no longer)* ◆ **we shall see him no ~** nous ne le reverrons jamais plus *or* plus jamais ◆ **he is no ~** il n'est plus
◆ **... only more so*** ◆ **he's like his father, only ~ so** *(= worse)* il est comme son père, mais en pire ◆ **it's like that in Canada, only ~ so** *(= better)* c'est comme ça au Canada, mais en mieux
◆ **once more** une fois de plus, encore une fois ◆ **only once ~** une dernière fois
◆ **the more ...** ◆ **the ~ you rest the quicker you'll get better** plus vous vous reposerez plus vous vous rétablirez rapidement ◆ **the ~ I think of it the ~ ashamed I feel** plus j'y pense plus j'ai honte ◆ **he is all the ~ happy** il est d'autant plus heureux *(as* que) ◆ **(all) the ~ so**

as *or* because ... d'autant plus que ... ♦ **I love him all the ~ for it** je l'aime d'autant plus ♦ **she respected him all the ~ for his frankness** elle l'a respecté d'autant plus pour sa franchise

moreish* /ˈmɔːrɪʃ/ ADJ ♦ **these cakes are very ~** ces gâteaux ont un goût de revenez-y *

moreover /mɔːˈrəʊvəʳ/ LANGUAGE IN USE 26.2, 26.3 ADV *(frm)* de plus, en outre

mores /ˈmɔːreɪz/ NPL mœurs *fpl*

morganatic /ˌmɔːgəˈnætɪk/ ADJ morganatique

morganatically /ˌmɔːgəˈnætɪkəlɪ/ ADV morganatiquement

morgue /mɔːg/ N *(= mortuary)* morgue *f* ; (*: *of newspaper)* archives *fpl (d'un journal)*

MORI /ˈmɒrɪ/ N (abbrev of **Market and Opinion Research Institute**) ♦ **~ poll** sondage *m* d'opinion

moribund /ˈmɒrɪbʌnd/ ADJ *(frm: lit, fig)* moribond

Mormon /ˈmɔːmən/ N mormon(e) *m(f)* ADJ mormon

Mormonism /ˈmɔːmənɪzəm/ N mormonisme *m*

morn /mɔːn/ N *(liter) (= morning)* matin *m* ; *(= dawn)* aube *f*

morning /ˈmɔːnɪŋ/ N *(= point in time)* matin *m* ; *(= duration)* matinée *f* ♦ **on the ~ of 23 January** le 23 janvier au matin, le matin du 23 janvier ♦ **during (the course of) the ~** pendant la matinée ♦ **I was busy all ~** j'ai été occupé toute la matinée ♦ **good ~!** *(= hello)* bonjour ! ; *(† = goodbye)* au revoir ! ♦ **he came in the ~** il est arrivé dans la matinée ♦ **I'll do it in the ~** je le ferai le matin *or* dans la matinée ; *(= tomorrow)* je le ferai demain matin ♦ **it happened first thing in the ~** c'est arrivé tout au début de la matinée ♦ **I'll do it first thing in the ~** je le ferai demain à la première heure ♦ **at 7 (o'clock) in the ~** à 7 heures du matin ♦ **in the early ~** au (petit) matin ♦ **to get up very early in the ~** se lever de très bonne heure *or* très tôt le matin, se lever de bon *or* de grand matin ♦ **I work in the ~(s)** je travaille le matin ♦ **she's working ~s** *or* **she's on ~s*** **this week** elle travaille le matin, cette semaine ♦ **a ~'s work** une matinée de travail ♦ **she's got the ~ off (today)** elle a congé ce matin ♦ **I have a ~ off every week** j'ai un matin *or* une matinée (de) libre par semaine ♦ **what a beautiful ~!** quelle belle matinée ! ♦ **this ~** ce matin ♦ **tomorrow ~** demain matin ♦ **the ~ before** la veille au matin ♦ **yesterday ~** hier matin ♦ **the next** *or* **following ~, the ~ after** le lendemain matin ♦ **the ~ after (the night before)*** un lendemain de cuite* ♦ **every Sunday ~** tous les dimanches matin ♦ **one summer ~** (par) un matin d'été ; → **Monday**

ADJ *[walk, swim]* matinal, du matin ♦ **a ~ train** un train le matin *or* dans la matinée ♦ **the ~ train** le train du matin

COMP **morning-after pill** N *(= contraceptive)* pilule *f* du lendemain

morning coat N jaquette *f*

morning coffee N pause-café *f* (dans la matinée) ♦ **we have ~ coffee together** nous prenons un café ensemble le matin

morning dress N jaquette *f* (et pantalon *m* rayé)

morning-glory N *(= flower)* belle-de-jour *f*

morning paper N journal *m* (du matin)

morning prayer(s) N(PL) prière(s) *f(pl)* du matin

morning room † N petit salon *m (conçu pour recevoir le soleil le matin)*

morning service N office *m* du matin

morning sickness N nausée *f* (du matin), nausées *fpl* matinales

morning star N étoile *f* du matin

morning watch N *(on ship)* premier quart *m* du jour

Moroccan /məˈrɒkən/ ADJ *(gen)* marocain ; *[ambassador, embassy]* du Maroc N Marocain(e) *m(f)*

Morocco /məˈrɒkəʊ/ N 1 Maroc *m* ♦ **in ~** au Maroc 2 ♦ **morocco (leather)** maroquin *m* ♦ **morocco-bound** relié en maroquin

moron /ˈmɔːrɒn/ N (* *= idiot)* crétin (e) *m(f)* * ; *(Med)* débile *m* léger, débile *f* légère

moronic /məˈrɒnɪk/ ADJ crétin *

morose /məˈrəʊs/ ADJ morose

morosely /məˈrəʊslɪ/ ADV *[look at]* d'un air morose ; *[say]* d'un ton morose

morph¹ /mɔːf/ N *(Ling)* morphe *m*

morph²* /mɔːf/ VI ♦ **to ~ into sth** se transformer en qch

morpheme /ˈmɔːfiːm/ N *(Ling)* morphème *m*

morphemics /mɔːˈfiːmɪks/ N *(NonC) (Ling)* morphématique *f*

Morpheus /ˈmɔːfɪəs/ N Morphée *m* ; → **arm¹**

morphia /ˈmɔːfɪə/ N ⇒ **morphine**

morphine /ˈmɔːfiːn/ N morphine *f*

COMP **morphine addict** N morphinomane *mf*

morphine addiction N morphinomanie *f*

morphing /ˈmɔːfɪŋ/ N *(Cine, Comput)* morphing *m*

morphological /ˌmɔːfəˈlɒdʒɪkəl/ ADJ morphologique

morphologically /ˌmɔːfəˈlɒdʒɪkəlɪ/ ADV morphologiquement

morphologist /mɔːˈfɒlədʒɪst/ N morphologue *mf*

morphology /mɔːˈfɒlədʒɪ/ N morphologie *f*

morphophonemics /ˌmɔːfəʊfəʊˈniːmɪks/ N *(NonC)* morphophonémique *f*

morphophonology /ˌmɔːfəʊfəˈnɒlədʒɪ/ N morphophonologie *f*

morphosyntax /ˌmɔːfəʊˈsɪntæks/ N morphosyntaxe *f*

morris /ˈmɒrɪs/ N *(US)* ⇒ **morris dance**

COMP **morris dance** N *danse folklorique anglaise*

morris dancer N *danseur de "morris dance"*

morris dancing N *danse folklorique anglaise*

morris men NPL *danseurs de "morris dance"*

> **MORRIS DANCING**
>
> Le Morris dancing est une danse folklorique anglaise traditionnellement réservée aux hommes. Habillés tout en blanc et portant des clochettes, ils exécutent différentes figures avec des mouchoirs et de longs bâtons. Cette danse est très populaire dans les fêtes de village.

morrow /ˈmɒrəʊ/ N *(† or liter) (= morning)* matin *m* ; *(= next day)* lendemain *m* ♦ **he said he would leave on the ~** il a dit qu'il partirait le lendemain

Morse /mɔːs/ N morse *m*

COMP **Morse alphabet** N alphabet *m* morse

Morse Code N morse *m*

Morse signals NPL signaux *mpl* en morse

morsel /ˈmɔːsl/ N *(gen)* (petit) bout *m* ♦ **she ate only a ~ of fish** elle n'a mangé qu'une bouchée de poisson ♦ **choice ~** morceau *m* de choix

mortadella /ˌmɔːtəˈdelə/ N mortadelle *f*

mortal /ˈmɔːtl/ ADJ *[life, hatred, enemy, fear]* mortel ; *[injury]* mortel, fatal ♦ **~ combat** combat *m* à mort ♦ **~ remains** dépouille *f* mortelle ♦ **~ sin** péché *m* mortel ♦ **it's no ~ good to him*** cela ne lui sert strictement à rien N mortel(le) *m(f)*

mortality /mɔːˈtælɪtɪ/ N mortalité *f* ♦ **infant ~** (taux *m* de) mortalité *f* infantile

mortally /ˈmɔːtəlɪ/ ADV *[wounded, offended]* mortellement ; *[embarrassed]* horriblement ♦ **~ ill** condamné ♦ **~ afraid** mort de peur

mortar /ˈmɔːtəʳ/ N *(= substance, weapon)* mortier *m*

mortarboard /ˈmɔːtəbɔːd/ N *toque portée par les enseignants et les étudiants pendant la cérémonie de remise de diplômes universitaires*

mortgage /ˈmɔːgɪdʒ/ N *(in house buying etc)* emprunt *m* immobilier ; *(= second loan etc)* hypothèque *f* ♦ **to take out** *or* **raise a ~** contracter un emprunt immobilier *(on, for* pour), prendre une hypothèque ♦ **to pay off** *or* **clear a ~** rembourser un emprunt immobilier, purger une hypothèque ♦ **to carry a ~** être grevé d'une hypothèque VT *[+ house, one's future]* hypothéquer

COMP **mortgage broker** N courtier *m* en prêts hypothécaires

mortgage payment N remboursement *m* d'un emprunt immobilier

mortgage rate N taux *m* d'emprunt hypothécaire

mortgage relief N *(Brit) exonération fiscale sur les emprunts immobiliers*

mortgageable /ˈmɔːgədʒɪbl/ ADJ hypothécable

mortgagee /ˌmɔːgəˈdʒiː/ N créancier *m*, -ière *f* hypothécaire

mortgagor /ˌmɔːgəˈdʒɔːʳ/ N débiteur *m*, -trice *f* hypothécaire

mortice /ˈmɔːtɪs/ N ⇒ **mortise**

mortician /mɔːˈtɪʃən/ N *(US)* entrepreneur *m* de pompes funèbres

mortification /ˌmɔːtɪfɪˈkeɪʃən/ N *(gen)* grande honte *f* ; *(Rel)* mortification *f*

mortified /ˈmɔːtɪfaɪd/ ADJ ♦ **I was ~ to learn that ...** j'ai été morte de honte en apprenant que ...

mortify /ˈmɔːtɪfaɪ/ VT *(gen)* faire honte à, rendre honteux ; *(Rel)* mortifier ♦ **to ~ the flesh** se mortifier, mortifier sa chair

mortifying /ˈmɔːtɪfaɪɪŋ/ ADJ très gênant *(to sb* pour qn)

mortise /ˈmɔːtɪs/ N mortaise *f* VT mortaiser

COMP **mortise and tenon joint** N assemblage *m* à tenon et mortaise

mortise lock N serrure *f* encastrée

mortuary /ˈmɔːtjʊərɪ/ N morgue *f*, dépôt *m* mortuaire ADJ mortuaire

Mosaic /məʊˈzeɪɪk/ ADJ *(= of Moses)* mosaïque, de Moïse

mosaic /məʊˈzeɪɪk/ N mosaïque *f* COMP en mosaïque

Moscow /ˈmɒskəʊ/ N Moscou ♦ **the ~ team** l'équipe *f* moscovite

Moselle /məʊˈzel/ N 1 *(Geog)* Moselle *f* 2 *(= wine)* (vin *m* de) Moselle *m*

Moses /ˈməʊzɪz/ N Moïse *m* ♦ **Holy ~!*** mince alors !* COMP **Moses basket** N moïse *m*

mosey* /ˈməʊzɪ/ *(US)* VI ♦ **to ~ along** (se) baguenauder*, aller *or* marcher sans (trop) se presser ♦ **they ~ed over to Joe's** ils sont allés faire un tour chez Joe ♦ **I'll just ~ on down** je vais y aller doucement N ♦ **to have a ~ round somewhere** faire une balade* *or* un tour quelque part

Moslem /ˈmɒzləm/ N, ADJ ⇒ **Muslim**

mosque /mɒsk/ N mosquée *f*

mosquito /mɒsˈkiːtəʊ/ N (pl **mosquito(e)s**) moustique *m*

COMP **mosquito bite** N piqûre *f* de moustique

mosquito coil N serpentin *m* antimoustique

mosquito net N moustiquaire *f*

mosquito netting N mousseline *f or* gaze *f* pour moustiquaire

moss /mɒs/ N mousse *f* (*Bot*) ; → **rolling**
COMP **moss green** ADJ vert mousse *inv* N vert *m* mousse *inv*
moss rose N rose *f* mousseuse
moss stitch N (*Knitting*) point *m* de riz

Mossad /ˈmɒsæd/ N Mossad *m*

mossback * /ˈmɒsbæk/ N (*US fig*) conservateur *m* à tout crin

mossy /ˈmɒsɪ/ ADJ [*wall, stone*] moussu ◆ **~ green** ADJ vert mousse *inv* N vert *m* mousse

most /məʊst/ LANGUAGE IN USE 7.2 (superl of **many, much**)
ADJ, PRON 1 (= *greatest in amount, number*) le plus (de) ◆ **he earns (the) ~ money** c'est lui qui gagne le plus d'argent ◆ **I've got (the) ~ records** c'est moi qui ai le plus (grand nombre) de disques ◆ **(the) ~** le plus, le maximum ◆ **who has got (the) ~?** qui en a le plus ? ◆ **at (the) ~, at the very ~** au maximum, (tout) au plus ◆ **they're the ~!**‡ ils sont champions ! *
◆ **to make the most of** [*+ one's time*] ne pas perdre, bien employer ; [*+ opportunity, sunshine, sb's absence*] profiter (au maximum) de ; [*+ one's talents, business offer, money*] tirer le meilleur parti de ; [*+ one's resources, remaining food*] utiliser au mieux, faire durer ◆ **make the ~ of it!** profitez-en bien !, tâchez de bien en profiter ! ◆ **he certainly made the ~ of the story** il a vraiment exploité cette histoire à fond ◆ **to make the ~ of o.s.** se faire valoir, se mettre en valeur
2 (= *largest part*) la plus grande partie (de), la majeure partie (de) ; (= *greatest number*) la majorité (de), la plupart (de) ◆ **~ (of the) people/books** *etc* la plupart *or* la majorité des gens/des livres *etc* ◆ **~ cars are bought on credit** la plupart *or* la majorité des voitures sont achetées à crédit ◆ **~ of the butter** presque tout le beurre ◆ **~ of the money** la plus grande *or* la majeure partie de l'argent, presque tout l'argent ◆ **~ of it** presque tout ◆ **~ of them** la plupart d'entre eux ◆ **~ of the day** la plus grande *or* la majeure partie de la journée ◆ **~ of the time** la plupart du temps ◆ **for the ~ part** pour la plupart, en général ◆ **in ~ cases** dans la plupart *or* la majorité des cas
ADV 1 (*forming superl of adjs and advs*) le plus ◆ **the ~ intelligent boy** le garçon le plus intelligent ◆ **the ~ beautiful woman of all** la plus belle femme *or* la femme la plus belle de toutes ◆ **~ easily** le plus facilement
2 [*work, sleep etc*] le plus ◆ **he talked ~** c'est lui qui a le plus parlé *or* parlé le plus ◆ **what he wants ~ (of all)** ce qu'il veut par-dessus tout *or* avant tout ◆ **the book he wanted ~ (of all)** le livre qu'il voulait le plus *or* entre tous ◆ **that's what annoyed me ~ (of all)** c'est ce qui m'a contrarié le plus *or* par-dessus tout
3 (= *very*) bien, très, fort ◆ **~ likely** très probablement ◆ **a ~ delightful day** une journée on ne peut plus agréable *or* des plus agréables ◆ **you are ~ kind** vous êtes (vraiment) très aimable ◆ **it's a ~ useful gadget** c'est un gadget des plus utiles *or* tout ce qu'il y a de plus utile ◆ **the Most High** le Très-Haut ◆ **Most Reverend** révérendissime
4 (*US* * = *almost*) presque

...most /məʊst/ SUF le plus ◆ **northernmost** le plus au nord ; → **foremost, inmost**

mostly /ˈməʊstlɪ/ ADV 1 (= *chiefly*) principalement, surtout ◆ **he now works ~ in Hollywood** à présent, il travaille principalement *or* surtout à Hollywood ◆ **the human body is ~ water** le corps humain est presque entièrement composé d'eau ◆ **it is ~ a book about nature** c'est avant tout un livre sur la nature 2 (= *almost all*) pour la plupart ◆ **the men were ~ fairly young** les hommes étaient, pour la plupart, assez jeunes ◆ **more than one hundred people, ~ women** plus de cent personnes, pour la plupart des femmes 3 (= *usually*) en général ◆ **he ~ comes on Mondays** il vient en général le lundi

MOT /ˌeməʊˈtiː/ (*Brit*) N 1 abbrev of **Ministry of Transport** 2 (also **MOT test**) ≃ contrôle *m* technique ◆ **the car has passed/failed its ~ (test)** la voiture a obtenu/n'a pas obtenu le certificat de contrôle technique ◆ **the ~ (certificate) runs out in April** le certificat de contrôle technique expire en avril VT ◆ **to get one's car ~'d** faire passer sa voiture au contrôle technique ◆ **car for sale, ~'d till June** voiture à vendre, certificat de contrôle technique valable jusqu'en juin

mote /məʊt/ N atome *m* ; [*of dust*] grain *m* ◆ **the ~ in thy brother's eye** (*Bible*) la paille dans l'œil de ton frère

motel /məʊˈtel/ N motel *m*

motet /məʊˈtet/ N motet *m*

moth /mɒθ/ N papillon *m* de nuit, phalène *m or f* ; (also **clothes-moth**) mite *f* ◆ **to be attracted like a ~ to a flame** être irrésistiblement attiré
COMP **moth-eaten** ADJ mangé par les mites, mité ; (* fig) mangé aux mites * ◆ **to become ~-eaten** se miter
moth-hole N trou *m* de mite

mothball /ˈmɒθbɔːl/ N boule *f* de naphtaline ◆ **in ~s** * (*fig*) [*object*] au placard (*hum*) ; [*ship*] en réserve ◆ **to put sth in ~s** (*fig*) [*+ project*] mettre *or* remiser qch au placard VT [*+ ship*] mettre en réserve ; [*+ factory*] fermer provisoirement ; (*fig*) [*+ project*] mettre *or* remiser au placard

mother /ˈmʌðəʳ/ N 1 (*lit, fig*) mère *f* ◆ **yes, Mother** (*as form of address*) oui, mère ◆ **she was (like) a ~ to me** elle était une vraie mère pour moi ◆ **a ~ of three** une mère de trois enfants ◆ **~'s milk** lait *m* maternel ◆ **the Reverend Mother** (*Rel*) la Révérende Mère ◆ **she's her ~'s daughter** c'est (bien) la fille de sa mère ◆ **every ~'s son of them** * tous sans exception ◆ **shall I be ~?** (*Brit hum = shall I serve*) je fais le service *or* la mère de famille ? ; → **foster, housemother, necessity, single**
2 * **the ~ of all battles** une bataille homérique *or* sans précédent ◆ **the ~ of all controversies/confrontations** une controverse/une confrontation homérique *or* sans précédent ◆ **the ~ of all traffic jams** un énorme bouchon
3 († *or liter*) **old Mother Jones** la mère Jones ; see also **comp**
4 (*US* *‡*) ⇒ **motherfucker**
VT (= *act as mother to*) s'occuper de ; (= *indulge, protect*) dorloter, chouchouter ; (*Psych*) materner ; († † = *give birth to*) donner naissance à ◆ **she always ~s her lodgers** c'est une vraie mère pour ses locataires ◆ **why do men so often want their girlfriends to ~ them?** pourquoi les hommes veulent-ils si souvent être maternés par leur petite amie ?
COMP **Mother Church** N ◆ **our Mother Church** notre sainte mère l'Église
mother country N mère patrie *f*
mother craft N (*Space*) vaisseau *m* amiral
Mother Earth N notre mère *f* la Terre, la Terre mère
Mother Goose N ma Mère l'Oye
mother hen N mère *f* poule
mother-in-law N (pl **mothers-in-law**) belle-mère *f*
mother love N amour *m* maternel
mother-naked ADJ nu comme un ver
Mother Nature N Dame Nature *f*
Mother of God N Marie, mère *f* de Dieu
mother-of-pearl N nacre *f* (*de perle*)
mother-of-thousands N (= *plant*) chlorophytum *m*
Mother's Day N la fête des Mères
mother's help, mother's helper (*US*) N aide *f* maternelle
mother ship N (*Naut*) ravitailleur *m*
Mother Superior N (pl **Mother Superiors** *or* **Mothers Superior**) (*Rel*) Mère *f* supérieure
mother-to-be N (pl **mothers-to-be**) future maman *f*
mother tongue N langue *f* maternelle
mother wit N bon sens *m* inné

motherboard /ˈmʌðəbɔːd/ N (*Comput*) carte *f* mère

mothercraft /ˈmʌðəkrɑːft/ N puériculture *f*

motherfucker *‡/ˈmʌðəfʌkəʳ/ N (*esp US*) (= *person*) enfoiré(e) *‡ *m(f)*, enculé(e) *‡ *m(f)* ; (= *thing*) saloperie ‡ *f*

motherfucking *‡ /ˈmʌðəfʌkɪŋ/ ADJ (*esp US*) ◆ **that ~ car !** cette putain de bagnole ! ‡ ◆ **get your ~ ass in gear!** magne-toi le cul ! *‡ ◆ **you ~ son-of-a-bitch!** espèce de fils de pute ! *‡

motherhood /ˈmʌðəhʊd/ N maternité *f*

mothering /ˈmʌðərɪŋ/ N soins *mpl* maternels ; (*fig*) maternage *m* ◆ **he needs ~** il a besoin d'être materné COMP **Mothering Sunday** N (*Brit*) la fête des Mères

motherland /ˈmʌðəlænd/ N patrie *f*

motherless /ˈmʌðəlɪs/ ADJ sans mère

motherly /ˈmʌðəlɪ/ ADJ maternel

mothproof /ˈmɒθpruːf/ ADJ traité à l'antimite VT traiter à l'antimite

motif /məʊˈtiːf/ N (*Art, Mus*) motif *m*

motion /ˈməʊʃən/ N 1 (*NonC*) mouvement *m*, marche *f* ; (*Mus*) mouvement *m* ◆ **perpetual ~** mouvement *m* perpétuel ◆ **to be in ~** [*vehicle*] être en marche ; [*machine*] être en mouvement *or* en marche ◆ **to set in ~** [*+ machine*] mettre en mouvement *or* en marche ; [*+ vehicle*] mettre en marche ; (*fig*) [*+ process etc*] mettre en branle ◆ **to put** *or* **set the wheels in ~** (*fig: of process etc*) lancer le processus, mettre les choses en branle ◆ **the ~ of the car made him ill** le mouvement de la voiture l'a rendu malade
2 (= *gesture etc*) mouvement *m*, geste *m* ◆ **he made a ~ to close the door** il a esquissé le geste d'aller fermer la porte ◆ **to go through the ~s of doing sth** (*fig*) (*mechanically*) faire qch machinalement *or* en ayant l'esprit ailleurs ; (*insincerely*) faire mine *or* semblant de faire qch
3 (*at meeting etc*) motion *f* ; (*Parl*) proposition *f* ◆ **to propose a ~** proposer une motion ◆ **~ carried/rejected** motion *f* adoptée/rejetée ◆ **meeting convened of its own ~** (*Admin, Jur*) réunion *f* convoquée d'office
4 (*Brit:* also **bowel motion**) selles *fpl* ◆ **to have** *or* **pass a ~** aller à la selle
5 [*of watch*] mouvement *m*
VTI ◆ **to ~ (to) sb to do sth** faire signe à qn de faire qch ◆ **he ~ed me in/out/to a chair** il m'a fait signe d'entrer/de sortir/de m'asseoir
COMP **motion picture** N (*esp US Cine*) film *m* (*de cinéma*) ◆ **~-picture camera** caméra *f* ◆ **the ~-picture industry** l'industrie *f* cinématographique, le cinéma
motion sickness N mal *m* des transports
motion study N (*Ind etc*) étude *f* des cadences

motionless /ˈməʊʃənlɪs/ ADJ [*person, body*] immobile ◆ **to remain ~** rester immobile ◆ **to stand/sit/lie ~** rester debout/assis/étendu sans bouger

motivate /ˈməʊtɪveɪt/ VT [*+ act, decision*] motiver ; [*+ person*] pousser, inciter (*to do sth* à faire qch)

motivated /ˈməʊtɪveɪtɪd/ ADJ motivé (*to do sth* pour faire qch) ◆ **to keep sb ~** faire en sorte que qn reste *subj* motivé ◆ **highly ~** extrêmement motivé ◆ **he's not very politically ~** il ne s'intéresse pas beaucoup à la politique ◆ **the violence was racially ~** c'est le racisme qui a motivé les violences

motivation /ˌməʊtɪˈveɪʃən/ N 1 (= *motive*) mobile *m* ◆ **he did not tell them the true ~ for**

the killings il ne leur a pas révélé le véritable mobile des assassinats ◆ **the primary ~ behind the deal was political** la raison principale de l'accord était politique ◆ **money is my ~** je fais ça pour l'argent 2 *[of worker, student]* motivation *f* ◆ **he lacks ~** il n'est pas assez motivé, il manque de motivation COMP **motivation research** N études *fpl* de motivation

motivational research /ˌməʊtɪˈveɪʃənəl rɪˈsɜːtʃ/ N ⇒ **motivation research** ; → **motivation**

motive /ˈməʊtɪv/ N 1 *(= reason)* intention *f*, raison *f* ; *(= motivation) [of person]* motivations *fpl* ; *(for action)* motifs *mpl* ; *(Jur)* mobile *m* ◆ **I did it from the best ~s** je l'ai fait avec les meilleures intentions *or* avec les motifs les plus louables ◆ **his ~ for saying that** la raison pour laquelle il a dit cela ◆ **what were his ~s?** quelles étaient ses motivations ? ◆ **what was the ~ for his behaviour?** quels étaient les motifs de sa conduite ? ◆ **he had no ~ for killing her** il n'avait aucune raison de la tuer ◆ **what was the ~ for the murder?** quel était le mobile du meurtre ? ◆ **the only suspect with a ~** le seul suspect à avoir un mobile ; → **profit, ulterior** 2 ⇒ **motif** ADJ moteur (-trice *f*) ◆ **~ power** force *f* motrice

motiveless /ˈməʊtɪvlɪs/ ADJ *[act, crime]* immotivé, gratuit

motley /ˈmɒtlɪ/ ADJ 1 *(pej = ill-assorted) [collection, assortment]* disparate ◆ **what a ~ crew!** en voilà une belle équipe ! * 2 *(= multicoloured)* (also **motley coloured**) bariolé N *(= garment)* habit *m* bigarré *(du bouffon)*

motocross /ˈməʊtəkrɒs/ N moto-cross *m*

motor /ˈməʊtəʳ/ N 1 *(= engine)* moteur *m*
2 *(Brit *)* voiture *f*, bagnole * *f*
ADJ *[muscle, nerve]* moteur (-trice *f*) ; see also **comp**
VI † aller en auto ◆ **to go ~ing** faire de l'auto ◆ **we ~ed downriver** *(in boat)* nous avons descendu la rivière en bateau à moteur
VT *(Brit †)* conduire en auto ◆ **to ~ sb away/back** *etc* emmener/ramener *etc* qn en auto
COMP *[accident]* de voiture
motor-assisted ADJ à moteur
motor bus † N autobus *m*
motor coach N *(Brit)* car *m*
motor drive N *(Tech)* entraînement *m* par moteur
motor-driven ADJ à entraînement par moteur
motor home N *(US)* camping-car *m*
motor industry N industrie *f* automobile
motor inn N *(US)* ⇒ **motor lodge**
motor insurance N assurance-automobile *f*
motor launch N *(Naut)* vedette *f*
motor lodge N *(US)* motel *m*
motor lorry N *(Brit)* ⇒ **motor truck**
motor mechanic N mécanicien *m* garagiste
motor mower N tondeuse *f* (à gazon) à moteur
motor neuron disease N *(Med)* sclérose *f* latérale amyotrophique
motor oil N huile *f* (de graissage)
motor racing N *(NonC)* course *f* automobile
motor road † N route *f* carrossable
motor scooter N scooter *m*
motor ship N ⇒ **motor vessel**
motor show N exposition *f* de voitures ◆ **the Motor Show** *(Brit)* le Salon de l'automobile
motor torpedo boat N vedette *f* lance-torpilles
the motor trade N (le secteur de) l'automobile *f*
motor truck N camion *m* (automobile)
motor vehicle N véhicule *m* automobile
motor vessel N *(Naut)* navire *m* à moteur (diesel), motorship *m*

motorail /ˈməʊtəreɪl/ N train *m* auto-couchettes

motorbike /ˈməʊtəbaɪk/ N moto *f* ◆ **~ gang** bande *f* de motards *

motorboat /ˈməʊtəbəʊt/ N canot *m* automobile, bateau *m* à moteur

motorcade /ˈməʊtəkeɪd/ N cortège *m* de voitures

motorcar /ˈməʊtəkɑːʳ/ N *(Brit)* automobile *f*, voiture *f*

motorcycle /ˈməʊtəsaɪkl/ N moto(cyclette) *f*
COMP **motorcycle club** N club *m* de moto
motorcycle combination N (motocyclette *f* à) side-car *m*
motorcycle engine N moteur *m* de moto

motorcycling /ˈməʊtəsaɪklɪŋ/ N motocyclisme *m*

motorcyclist /ˈməʊtəsaɪklɪst/ N motocycliste *mf*

-motored /ˈməʊtəd/ ADJ *(in compounds)* ◆ **four-motored** quadrimoteur (-trice *f*)

motoring /ˈməʊtərɪŋ/ N promenades *fpl* en voiture
COMP *[accident]* de voiture, d'auto ; *[holiday]* en voiture, en auto
motoring correspondent N *(Brit Press)* chroniqueur *m* automobile
motoring magazine N revue *f* automobile
motoring public N automobilistes *mpl*
motoring school N auto-école *f*

motorist /ˈməʊtərɪst/ N automobiliste *mf*

motorization /ˌməʊtəraɪˈzeɪʃən/ N motorisation *f*

motorize /ˈməʊtəraɪz/ VT *(esp Mil)* motoriser ◆ **~d bicycle** *or* **bike** * cyclomoteur *m*

motorman /ˈməʊtəmən/ N (pl **-men**) *(US)* conducteur *m* ; *[of train]* conducteur *m*, mécanicien *m*

motormouth ‡ /ˈməʊtəmaʊθ/ N moulin *m* à paroles *

motorway /ˈməʊtəweɪ/ *(Brit)* N autoroute *f* ; → ROADS
COMP *[bridge, exit, junction]* d'autoroute **motorway restaurant** N restoroute *m* ®

Motown /ˈməʊtaʊn/ N *(US)* 1 Detroit 2 *(Mus)* Motown *m*

mottle /ˈmɒtl/ VT marbrer *(with* de)

mottled /ˈmɒtld/ ADJ *[leaf, skin, colour, porcelain]* marbré *(with sth* de qch) ; *[horse]* moucheté ; *[sky]* pommelé ; *[material]* chiné ◆ **~ complexion** teint *m* brouillé ◆ **~ blue and white** marbré de bleu et de blanc

motto /ˈmɒtəʊ/ N (pl **mottoes** *or* **mottos**) 1 *[of family, school etc]* devise *f* 2 *(in cracker) (= riddle)* devinette *f* ; *(= joke)* blague *f* 3 *(Mus)* **~ theme** leitmotiv *m*

mould¹, mold¹ *(US)* /məʊld/ N *(Art, Culin, Metal, Tech etc) (= container, core, frame)* moule *m* ; *(= model for design)* modèle *m*, gabarit *m* ◆ **rice ~** *(Culin)* gâteau *m* de riz ◆ **to cast metal in a ~** couler *or* jeter du métal dans un moule ◆ **to cast a figure in a ~** jeter une figure en moule, mouler une figure ; *(fig)* ◆ **to break the ~** *(= reorganize)* rompre avec la tradition ◆ **they broke the ~ when they made him** il n'y a pas deux comme lui ◆ **cast in a heroic ~** de la trempe des héros ◆ **cast in the same ~** fait sur *or* coulé dans le même moule ◆ **men of his ~** des hommes de sa trempe *or* de son calibre * VT *(= cast) [+ metals]* fondre, mouler ; *[+ plaster, clay]* mouler ; *(= fashion) [+ figure etc]* modeler *(in, out of* en) ; *(fig) [+ sb's character, public opinion etc]* former, façonner

mould², mold² *(US)* /məʊld/ N *(= fungus)* moisissure *f* VI moisir

mould³, mold³ *(US)* /məʊld/ N *(= soil)* humus *m*, terreau *m* ; → **leaf**

moulder, molder *(US)* /ˈməʊldəʳ/ VI *(gen)* moisir ; (also **moulder away**) *[building]* tomber en poussière, se désagréger ; (* *fig*) *[person, object]* moisir

moulding, molding *(US)* /ˈməʊldɪŋ/ N 1 *(Archit)* moulure *f* 2 *(on car body)* baguette *f* 3 *(= moulded object)* objet *m* moulé, moulage *m* ; *(= process) (gen)* moulage *m* ; *[of metal]* coulée *f* ; *[of statue]* coulage *m* 4 *(NonC = influencing) [of character, public opinion]* formation *f*
COMP **moulding machine** N machine *f* à moulures
moulding process N procédé *m* de moulage
moulding technique N technique *f* de moulage

mouldy, moldy *(US)* /ˈməʊldɪ/ ADJ 1 *(= with mould) [food, mattress, wallpaper, clothes]* moisi ◆ **to go ~** moisir ◆ **to smell ~** sentir le moisi ◆ **to taste ~** avoir goût de moisi 2 *(Brit * = paltry)* minable ◆ **all he gave me was a ~ £5** il m'a juste refilé un malheureux billet de 5 livres

moult, molt *(US)* /məʊlt/ N mue *f* VI *[bird]* muer ; *[dog, cat]* perdre ses poils VT *[+ feathers, hair]* perdre

mound /maʊnd/ N 1 *[of earth] (natural)* monticule *m* ; *(artificial)* levée *f* de terre, remblai *m* ; *(Archeol)* (also **burial mound**) tumulus *m* 2 *(= pile)* tas *m*, monceau *m*

mount /maʊnt/ N 1 *(liter)* mont *m*, montagne *f* ◆ **Mount Carmel** le mont Carmel ◆ **the Mount of Olives** le mont des Oliviers ; → **sermon**
2 *(= horse)* monture *f*
3 *(= support) [of machine]* support *m* ; *[of jewel, lens, specimen]* monture *f* ; *[of microscope slide]* lame *f* ; *[of transparency]* cadre *m* ; *[of painting, photo]* carton *m* de montage ; *[of stamp in album]* charnière *f*
VT 1 *(frm: = climb on or up) [+ hill, stairs]* monter ; *(with effort)* gravir ; *[+ horse, ladder]* monter à ; *[+ cycle]* monter sur, enfourcher ; *[+ platform, throne]* monter sur ◆ **the car ~ed the pavement** la voiture est montée sur le trottoir
2 *[male animal]* monter
3 *[+ machine, specimen, jewel]* monter *(on, in* sur) ; *[+ map]* monter, entoiler ; *[+ picture, photo]* monter *or* coller sur un carton ; *[+ exhibit]* fixer sur un support ; *[+ gun]* mettre en position ◆ **to ~ stamps in an album** coller *or* mettre des timbres dans un album ◆ **~ing press** *(Phot)* colleuse *f*
4 *(= stage, orchestrate) [+ play, demonstration, plot, campaign, rescue operation etc]* monter ◆ **to ~ guard** *(Mil)* monter la garde *(on* sur ; *over* auprès de) ◆ **to ~ an offensive** monter une attaque ◆ **she ~ed a challenge to the Prime Minister's leadership** elle s'est posée en successeur du Premier ministre, en contestant son autorité ◆ **she ~ed a title challenge to the reigning World Champion** elle a essayé de ravir son titre au champion du monde ◆ **they ~ed a legal challenge to the directive** ils ont essayé de contester cette directive devant les tribunaux
5 *(= provide with horse)* monter ; → **mounted**
VI 1 *[prices, temperature]* monter, augmenter ; *[pressure, tension]* monter ; *[concern]* grandir, monter ; *[debts, losses]* augmenter ◆ **the death toll has ~ed to 8,000** le nombre de morts se monte maintenant à 8 000 ◆ **opposition to the treaty is ~ing** l'opposition au traité grandit *or* prend de l'ampleur ◆ **pressure is ~ing on him to resign** la pression s'accentue sur lui pour qu'il démissionne ◆ **evidence is ~ing that …** il y a de plus en plus de raisons de penser que … ◆ **speculation was ~ing that she was about to resign** on se perdait en conjectures sur sa démission éventuelle
2 *(= get on horse)* se mettre en selle

► **mount up** VI *(= increase)* monter, s'élever ; *(= accumulate)* s'accumuler ◆ **it all ~s up** tout cela finit par chiffrer

mountain /ˈmaʊntɪn/ N montagne *f* ◆ **to go to/live in the ~s** aller à/habiter la montagne ◆ **to make a ~ out of a molehill** (se) faire une montagne d'une taupinière ◆ **beef/butter ~**

(Econ) montagne f de bœuf/de beurre ♦ **debt ~** montagne f de dettes ♦ **faith can move ~s** la foi soulève des montagnes ♦ **we have a ~ to climb** (esp Brit fig) nous allons devoir soulever des montagnes ♦ **if Mohammed won't go to the ~, the ~ must come to Mohammed** si la montagne ne vient pas à Mahomet, Mahomet ira à la montagne ♦ **a ~ of** (fig) une montagne de ♦ **a ~ of dirty washing** un monceau de linge sale ♦ **a ~ of work** un travail fou or monstre

COMP [tribe, people] montagnard ; [animal, plant] de(s) montagne(s) ; [air] de la montagne ; [path, scenery, shoes, chalet] de montagne

mountain ash N sorbier m (des oiseleurs)

mountain bike N VTT m, vélo m tout terrain

mountain cat N puma m, couguar m

mountain chain N chaîne f de montagnes

mountain climber N grimpeur m, alpiniste mf

Mountain Daylight Time N (US) heure f d'été des montagnes Rocheuses

mountain dew * N whisky m (en général illicitement distillé)

mountain goat N chèvre f de montagne

mountain guide N (Climbing) guide m de montagne

mountain lion N (US) ⇒ **mountain cat**

mountain pass N col m

mountain range N chaîne f de montagnes

mountain sickness N mal m des montagnes

Mountain Standard Time N (US) heure f d'hiver des montagnes Rocheuses

the Mountain State N (US) la Virginie occidentale

Mountain Time N (US) heure f des montagnes Rocheuses

mountain top N sommet m de la (or d'une) montagne, cime f

mountaineer /ˌmaʊntɪˈnɪəʳ/ N alpiniste mf VI faire de l'alpinisme

mountaineering /ˌmaʊntɪˈnɪərɪŋ/ N alpinisme m

mountainous /ˈmaʊntɪnəs/ ADJ 1 (= hilly) montagneux 2 (= immense) colossal 3 [seas] démonté ; [waves] énorme

mountainside /ˈmaʊntɪnsaɪd/ N flanc m or versant m d'une (or de la) montagne

mountebank /ˈmaʊntɪbæŋk/ N charlatan m

mounted /ˈmaʊntɪd/ ADJ [soldiers, troops] à cheval

COMP **mounted police** N police f montée

mounted policeman N (pl **mounted policemen**) policier m à cheval

Mountie * /ˈmaʊntɪ/ N (Can) membre m de la police montée ♦ **the ~s** la police montée

mounting /ˈmaʊntɪŋ/ N ⇒ **mount vt 3**

mourn /mɔːn/ VI pleurer ♦ **to ~ for sb** pleurer qn ♦ **to ~ for sth** pleurer la perte de qch VT [+ person] pleurer ; (sth gone) pleurer la perte de ; (sth sad) déplorer (frm) ♦ **he was still ~ing the loss of his son** il pleurait encore son fils ♦ **he is still ~ing the break-up of his relationship** il ne s'est pas encore remis de leur rupture

mourner /ˈmɔːnəʳ/ N parent(e) m(f) or ami(e) m(f) du défunt ♦ **the ~s** le convoi or le cortège funèbre ♦ **to be the chief ~** mener le deuil

mournful /ˈmɔːnfʊl/ ADJ [person, face, voice, sound, music] mélancolique ; [howl] lugubre ; [occasion] triste

mournfully /ˈmɔːnfəlɪ/ ADV mélancoliquement

mournfulness /ˈmɔːnfʊlnɪs/ N [of person] tristesse f, mélancolie f

mourning /ˈmɔːnɪŋ/ N deuil m ; (= clothes) vêtements mpl de deuil ♦ **in deep ~** en grand deuil ♦ **to be in ~ (for sb)** porter le deuil (de qn), être en deuil (de qn) ♦ **to go into/come out of ~** prendre/ quitter le deuil

COMP **mourning band** N crêpe m

mourning clothes NPL habits mpl de deuil

mouse /maʊs/ N (pl **mice**) 1 souris f ; (fig) timide mf, souris f ; → **fieldmouse** 2 (Comput) souris f ADJ [hair] châtain terne inv ♦ **~ brown** brun terne inv VI chasser les souris COMP **mouse mat, mouse pad** N (Comput) tapis m (pour souris)

mousehole /ˈmaʊshəʊl/ N trou m de souris

mouser /ˈmaʊsəʳ/ N souricier m

mousetrap /ˈmaʊstræp/ N souricière f ♦ **~ (cheese)** * (pej) fromage m ordinaire

mousey /ˈmaʊsɪ/ ADJ ⇒ **mousy**

moussaka /mʊˈsɑːkə/ N moussaka f

mousse /muːs/ N (Culin) mousse f ♦ **chocolate ~** mousse f au chocolat ♦ **(styling) ~** (for hair) mousse f coiffante or de coiffage

moustache /məsˈtɑːʃ/, **mustache** (US) /ˈmʌstæʃ/ N moustache(s) f(pl) ♦ **man with a ~** homme m moustachu or à moustache

moustachio /məsˈtɑːʃɪəʊ/ N moustache f à la gauloise

moustachioed /məsˈtɑːʃɪəʊd/ ADJ moustachu

mousy /ˈmaʊsɪ/ ADJ (pej) (= nondescript) [person] effacé ; (= brownish) [hair] châtain terne inv ♦ **~ brown** brun terne inv

mouth /maʊθ/ N (pl **mouths** /maʊðz/) 1 [of person, horse, sheep, cow] bouche f ; [of dog, cat, lion, tiger, bear, snake, whale] gueule f ♦ **to be taken by ~** (Pharm) à prendre par voie orale ♦ **with one's ~ wide open** la bouche grand ouverte ♦ **it makes my ~ water** (lit, fig) cela me met l'eau à la bouche ♦ **she didn't dare open her ~** elle n'a pas osé ouvrir la bouche ♦ **he never opened his ~ all evening** il n'a pas ouvert la bouche or il n'a pas desserré les dents de la soirée ♦ **he kept his ~ shut (about it)** il n'a pas soufflé mot ♦ **keep your ~ shut about this!** n'en parle à personne !, garde-le pour toi ! ♦ **shut your ~!** ‡ ferme-la !‡, boucle-la !‡ ♦ **to shut sb's ~ (for him)** * (fig) (= silence) clouer le bec à qn * ; (= kill) supprimer qn ♦ **he's a big ~** * c'est un fort en gueule‡, c'est une grande gueule‡ ♦ **(you've got a) big ~!** * tu ne pouvais pas la fermer ! * ♦ **me and my big ~!** * j'ai encore perdu une occasion de me taire ! ♦ **to speak or talk out of both sides of one's ~** (US) retourner sa veste sans arrêt ♦ **he's all ~** * (Brit) c'est un fort en gueule‡ ♦ **watch your ~!** * sois poli !, surveille ton langage ! ; → **down¹, feed, heart, word**

2 [of river] embouchure f ; [of bag] ouverture f ; [of hole, cave, harbour] entrée f ; [of bottle] goulot m ; [of cannon, gun] bouche f, gueule f ; [of well] trou m ; [of volcano] bouche f ; [of letterbox] ouverture f, fente f

VT /maʊð/ 1 (soundlessly: gen) articuler en silence ; (during spoken voice-over) faire semblant de prononcer ; (during singing) faire semblant de chanter ♦ **"go away!" she ~ed at him** "va-t'en !" lui dit-elle en remuant les lèvres silencieusement

2 (insincerely) [+ platitudes, slogans, rhetoric] débiter ♦ **to ~ apologies/promises** se répandre en plates excuses/en fausses promesses

COMP **mouth organ** N (esp Brit) harmonica m

mouth-to-mouth (resuscitation) N bouche-à-bouche m inv

mouth ulcer N aphte m

mouth-watering ADJ appétissant, alléchant

► **mouth off** * VI (= talk boastfully) en avoir plein la bouche * (about de) ; (US) (= talk insolently) dégoiser‡

-mouthed /maʊðd/ ADJ (in compounds) ♦ **wide-mouthed** [person] qui a une grande bouche ; [river] à l'embouchure large ; [cave] avec une vaste entrée ; [bottle] au large goulot ; → **loud, mealy**

mouthful /ˈmaʊθfʊl/ N [of food] bouchée f ; [of drink] gorgée f ♦ **he swallowed it in one ~** [+ food] il n'en a fait qu'une bouchée ; [+ drink] il l'a avalé d'un trait ♦ **it's a real ~ of a name!** * quel nom à coucher dehors ! ♦ **you said a ~!** * (fig) c'est vraiment le cas de le dire ! ♦ **to give sb a ~** * (fig) passer un savon * à qn, enguirlander * qn

mouthpiece /ˈmaʊθpiːs/ N [of wind instrument, brass instrument] embouchoir m ; [of recorder] bec m ; [of telephone] microphone m ; (fig = spokesman) porte-parole m inv

mouthwash /ˈmaʊθwɒʃ/ N bain m de bouche ; (for gargling) gargarisme m

mouthy * /ˈmaʊθɪ/ ADJ ♦ **to be ~** être grande gueule‡

movable /ˈmuːvəbl/ ADJ mobile ♦ **~ feast** (Rel) fête f mobile ♦ **it's a ~ feast** il n'y a pas de date fixe NPL **movables** (Jur) biens mpl meubles

move /muːv/

1 NOUN	3 INTRANSITIVE VERB
2 TRANSITIVE VERB	4 PHRASAL VERBS

1 - NOUN

1 = movement mouvement m ♦ **get a ~ on!** * remue-toi ! *, grouille-toi !‡

♦ **on the move** ♦ **to be on the ~** [troops, army] être en marche or en mouvement ♦ **he's on the ~ the whole time** (= moving around) il se déplace constamment, il est sans arrêt en déplacement ♦ **to be always on the ~** [gipsies etc] se déplacer continuellement, être sans cesse par monts et par vaux ; [military or diplomatic personnel etc] être toujours en déplacement ; [child, animal] ne pas tenir en place ; (* = be busy) ne jamais (s')arrêter ♦ **the circus is on the ~ again** le cirque a repris la route ♦ **the police were after him and he had to stay on the ~** recherché par la police, il était obligé de se déplacer constamment or de déménager constamment ♦ **it's a country on the ~** c'est un pays en marche

♦ **to make a move** (= leave) manifester l'intention de partir ; (= act) faire quelque chose, agir ♦ **it's time we made a ~** (= that we left) il est temps que nous partions ; (= acted, did sth) il est temps que nous fassions quelque chose ♦ **it was midnight and no one had made a ~** il était minuit et personne n'avait manifesté l'intention de partir ♦ **he made a ~ towards the door** il esquissa un mouvement vers la porte

2 = change (of house) déménagement m ; (of job) changement m d'emploi ♦ **it's our third ~ in two years** c'est notre troisième déménagement en deux ans ♦ **it's time he had a ~** il a besoin de changer d'air or d'horizon

3 Chess, Draughts etc [of chessman etc] coup m ; (= player's turn) tour m ; (fig) pas m, démarche f, manœuvre f, mesure f ♦ **knight's ~** marche f du cavalier ♦ **that was a silly ~** (in game) c'était un coup stupide ; (fig) c'était une démarche or une manœuvre stupide ♦ **it's your ~** (c'est) à vous de jouer ♦ **to have the first ~** jouer en premier ; (Chess, Draughts) avoir le trait ♦ **he knows every ~ in the game** (fig) il connaît toutes les astuces ♦ **his first ~ after his election was to announce …** la première mesure qu'il a prise après son élection a été d'annoncer … ♦ **what's our or the next ~?** et maintenant, qu'est-ce qu'on fait ? ♦ **let him make the first ~** laisse-lui faire les premiers pas ♦ **we must watch his every ~** il nous faut surveiller tous ses faits et gestes ♦ **there was a ~ to defeat the proposal** on a tenté de faire échec à la proposition

4 [Climbing] (*= step etc*) pas *m* ; (*= section of pitch*) passage *m*

2 - TRANSITIVE VERB

1 [= change position of] [*+ object, furniture*] déplacer ; [*+ limbs*] remuer ; [*+ troops, animals*] transporter ◆ **you've ~d the stick!** tu as bougé le bâton ! ◆ **he hadn't ~d his chair** il n'avait pas déplacé sa chaise *or* changé sa chaise de place ◆ **~ your chair nearer the fire** approchez votre chaise du feu ◆ **~ your books over here** mets tes livres par ici ◆ **can you ~ your fingers?** pouvez-vous remuer vos doigts ? ◆ **he ~d his family out of the war zone** il a évacué sa famille hors de la zone des conflits ◆ **they ~d the crowd off the grass** ils ont fait dégager la foule de la pelouse ◆ **~ your feet off the table** enlève tes pieds de la table ◆ **the wind ~s the leaves** le vent agite *or* fait remuer les feuilles ◆ **to ~ house** (*Brit*) déménager ◆ **to ~ one's job** changer d'emploi ◆ **his firm want to ~ him** son entreprise veut l'envoyer ailleurs ; (*Admin*) son entreprise veut le muter ◆ **he's asked to be ~d to London/to a different department** il a demandé à être muté à Londres/affecté à *or* muté dans un autre service ◆ **to ~ heaven and earth to do sth** remuer ciel et terre pour faire qch, se mettre en quatre pour faire qch ◆ **to ~ a piece** (*Chess*) jouer une pièce

2 [= change timing of] **to ~ sth (forward/back)** [*+ event, date*] avancer/reculer qch

3 [= remove] [*+ stain, mark*] enlever, faire partir

4 [Med] ◆ **to ~ one's bowels** aller à la selle

5 [Comm] [*+ stock*] écouler

6 [emotionally] émouvoir, attendrir ◆ **she's easily ~d** elle est facilement émue *or* attendrie ◆ **this did not ~ him** ceci n'a pas réussi à l'émouvoir *or* à l'attendrir ◆ **to ~ sb to tears** émouvoir qn jusqu'aux larmes ◆ **to ~ sb to laughter** faire rire qn ◆ **to ~ sb to anger** mettre qn en colère ◆ **to ~ sb to pity** apitoyer qn

7 [= stimulate, persuade] pousser, inciter (*sb to do sth* qn à faire qch) ◆ **I am ~d to ask why ...** je suis incité à demander pourquoi ... ◆ **if I feel ~d to do it, if the spirit ~s me** (*hum*) si le cœur m'en dit ◆ **he won't be ~d** il est inébranlable ◆ **even this did not ~ him** même ceci n'a pas réussi à l'ébranler

8 [Admin, Parl *etc* = propose] proposer ◆ **to ~ a resolution** proposer une motion ◆ **to ~ that sth be done** proposer que qch soit fait ◆ **he ~d that the meeting be adjourned** il a proposé que la séance soit levée

3 - INTRANSITIVE VERB

1 [person, animal] (*= stir*) bouger, remuer ; (*= go*) aller, se déplacer ; [*limb, lips, trees, leaves, curtains, door*] bouger, remuer ; [*clouds*] passer, avancer ; [*vehicle, ship, plane, procession*] aller, passer ; [*troops, army*] se déplacer ◆ **don't ~!** ne bougez pas ! ◆ **troops are moving near the frontier** il y a des mouvements de troupes près de la frontière ◆ **the procession ~d slowly out of sight** petit à petit la procession a disparu ◆ **I saw something moving over there** j'ai vu quelque chose bouger là-bas ◆ **keep moving!** (*to keep warm etc*) ne restez pas sans bouger ! ; (*= pass along etc*) circulez ! ◆ **to ~ freely** [*mechanical part*] jouer librement ; [*people, cars*] circuler aisément ; [*traffic*] être fluide ◆ **to keep the traffic moving** assurer la circulation ininterrompue des véhicules ◆ **the car in front isn't moving** la voiture devant nous est à l'arrêt ◆ **do not get out while the bus is moving** ne descendez pas de l'autobus en marche, attendez l'arrêt complet de l'autobus pour descendre ◆ **the coach was moving at 30km/h** le car faisait du 30 km/h *or* roulait à 30 (km) à l'heure ◆ **to ~ in high society** (*fig*) fréquenter la haute société ◆ **he was certainly moving!** il ne traînait pas ! ◆ **that horse can certainly ~** quand il s'agit de foncer ce cheval se défend !* ◆ **you can't ~ for books in that room*** on ne peut plus se retourner dans cette pièce tellement il y a de livres

◆ **to move** + *preposition* ◆ **they ~d rapidly across the lawn** ils ont traversé la pelouse rapidement ◆ **I'll not ~ from here** je ne bougerai pas d'ici ◆ **he has ~d into another class** il est passé dans une autre classe ◆ **let's ~ into the garden** passons dans le jardin ◆ **the car ~d round the corner** la voiture a tourné au coin de la rue ◆ **he ~d slowly towards the door** il se dirigea lentement vers la porte

2 [= depart] **it's time we were moving** il est temps que nous partions *subj*, il est temps de partir ◆ **let's ~!** partons !, en route !

3 [= move house etc] [*person, family*] déménager ; [*office, shop, business*] être transféré ◆ **to ~ to a bigger house** emménager dans une maison plus grande ◆ **to ~ to the country** aller habiter (à) la campagne, aller s'installer à la campagne

4 [= progress] [*plans, talks etc*] progresser, avancer ◆ **things are moving at last!** enfin ça avance *or* ça progresse ! ◆ **he got things moving** avec lui ça a bien démarré *or* c'est bien parti

5 [= act, take steps] agir ◆ **the government won't ~ until ...** le gouvernement ne bougera pas *or* ne fera rien tant que ... ◆ **we must ~ first** nous devons prendre l'initiative ◆ **we'll have to ~ quickly if we want to avoid ...** il nous faudra agir sans tarder si nous voulons éviter ... ◆ **the committee ~d to stop the abuse** le comité a pris des mesures pour mettre fin aux abus

6 [in games] [*player*] jouer ; [*chesspiece*] avancer, se déplacer ◆ **it's you to ~** (c'est) votre tour de jouer ◆ **white ~s** (*Chess*) les blancs jouent ◆ **the knight ~s like this** (*Chess*) le cavalier avance *or* se déplace comme cela

7 [Comm] [*goods*] se vendre

4 - PHRASAL VERBS

► **move about** VI (*gen*) se déplacer ; (*= fidget*) remuer ; (*= travel*) voyager ◆ **he can ~ about only with difficulty** il ne se déplace qu'avec peine ◆ **stop moving about!** tiens-toi tranquille ! ◆ **we've ~d about a good deal** (*= change residence*) nous ne sommes jamais restés longtemps au même endroit, nous avons souvent déménagé VT SEP [*+ object, furniture, employee*] déplacer

► **move along** VI [*people or vehicles in line*] avancer, circuler ◆ **~ along there!** (*on bus*) avancez un peu, ne restez pas près des portes ! ; (*policeman*) circulez ! ◆ **can you ~ along a few places?** (*on bench etc*) pouvez-vous vous pousser un peu ? VT SEP [*+ crowd*] faire circuler, faire avancer ; [*+ animals*] faire avancer

► **move around** ⇒ **move about**

► **move away** VI 1 (*= depart*) partir, s'éloigner (*from* de) 2 (*= move house*) déménager ◆ **they've ~d away from here** ils n'habitent plus ici VT SEP [*+ person, object*] éloigner, écarter (*from* de)

► **move back** VI 1 (*= withdraw*) reculer 2 (*to original position*) (*= go back*) retourner ; (*= come back*) revenir ◆ **he ~d back to the desk** il retourna au bureau 3 (*= move house*) **they've ~d back to London** (*= gone back*) ils sont retournés habiter (à) Londres ; (*= come back*) ils sont revenus habiter (à) Londres VT SEP 1 (*backwards*) [*+ person, crowd, animals*] faire reculer ; [*+ troops*] replier ; [*+ object, furniture*] reculer 2 (*to original position*) [*+ person*] faire revenir *or* retourner ; [*+ object*] remettre ◆ **his firm ~d him back to London** (*= go back*) son entreprise l'a fait retourner à Londres ; (*= come back*) son entreprise l'a fait revenir à Londres ◆ **~ the table back to where it was before** remets la table là où elle était

► **move down** VI 1 [*person, object, lift*] descendre ◆ **he ~d down from the top floor** il est descendu du dernier étage ◆ **can you ~ down a few places?** (*on bench etc*) pouvez-vous vous pousser un peu ? 2 (*Sport: in league*) reculer VT SEP 1 [*+ person*] faire descendre ; [*+ object*] descendre 2 (*= demote*) [*+ pupil*] faire descendre (dans une classe inférieure) ; [*+ employee*] rétrograder

► **move forward** VI [*person, animal, vehicle*] avancer ; [*troops*] se porter en avant VT SEP [*+ person, vehicle*] faire avancer ; [*+ troops*] porter en avant ; [*+ object, chair*] avancer

► **move in** VI 1 (*= approach*) [*police etc*] avancer, intervenir 2 (*to a house*) emménager VT SEP [*+ person*] faire entrer ; [*+ furniture etc*] rentrer, mettre *or* remettre à l'intérieur ; (*on removal day*) installer

► **move in on*** VT FUS (*= advance on*) (*Mil etc*) marcher sur, avancer sur ; [*police*] faire une descente dans ; (*= attempt takeover of*) [*+ firm*] essayer de mettre la main sur ◆ **to ~ in on sb (for the night)** se faire héberger par qn (pour la nuit)

► **move off** VI [*person*] s'en aller, partir ; [*car*] démarrer ; [*train, army, procession*] s'ébranler, partir VT SEP [*+ object*] enlever

► **move on** VI [*person, vehicle*] avancer ; (*after stopping*) se remettre en route ; [*time*] passer, s'écouler ◆ **the gipsies ~d on to another site** les gitans sont allés s'installer plus loin ◆ **~ on (now) please!** (*policeman etc*) circulez s'il vous plaît ! ◆ **moving on now to ...** (*in discussion etc*) passons maintenant à ... VT SEP [*+ person, onlookers*] faire circuler ; [*+ clock*] avancer

► **move out** VI (*of house, office, room etc*) déménager ◆ **to ~ out of a flat** déménager d'un appartement, quitter un appartement VT SEP [*+ person, animal*] faire sortir ; [*+ troops*] retirer ; [*+ object, furniture*] sortir ; (*on removal day*) déménager

► **move over** VI s'écarter, se pousser ◆ **~ over!** pousse-toi ! ◆ **if he can't do the job he should ~ over and let someone else who can** (*in job*) s'il n'est pas capable de faire ce travail, il n'a qu'à céder la place à quelqu'un de plus compétent ◆ **to ~ over to sth new** (*= change over*) adopter qch de nouveau VT SEP [*+ object*] déplacer

► **move up** VI 1 [*person, flag etc*] monter ◆ **can you ~ up a few seats?** pouvez-vous vous pousser un peu *or* vous décaler de quelques sièges ? ◆ **I want to ~ up nearer the stage** je veux m'approcher de la scène 2 [*employee*] avoir de l'avancement ; (*Sport: in league*) progresser dans le classement ◆ **to ~ up a class** [*pupil*] passer dans la classe supérieure VT SEP 1 [*+ person*] faire monter ; [*+ object*] monter 2 (*= promote*) [*+ pupil*] faire passer dans une classe supérieure ; [*+ employee*] donner de l'avancement à

moveable /ˈmuːvəbl/ ADJ ⇒ **movable**

movement /ˈmuːvmənt/ N 1 [*of person, troops, army, population, vehicles, goods, capital*] mouvement *m* ; (*= gesture*) mouvement *m*, geste *m* ◆ **massage the skin using small circular ~s** massez la peau en faisant de petits mouvements circulaires ◆ **hand ~s** mouvements *mpl* *or* gestes *mpl* de la main ◆ **eye ~s** (*during sleep*) mouvements *mpl* oculaires ◆ **her eye ~s were furtive and suspicious** elle jetait des coups d'œil furtifs et soupçonneux ◆ **there was a ~ towards the exit** il y eut un mouvement vers la sortie, on se dirigea vers la sortie ◆ **the accident disrupted the ~ of traffic** l'accident a perturbé la circulation ◆ **the free ~ of labour, capital and goods** la libre circulation de la main-d'œuvre, des capitaux et des marchandises

2 ◆ ~s (= *comings and goings*) allées *fpl* et venues *fpl* ◆ **the police know very little about the suspect's ~s** la police ne sait pas grand-chose sur les allées et venues du suspect

3 (= *action, impetus*) [*of prices, shares, market, situation*] mouvement *m* ◆ **an upward/downward ~ in the economy** une progression/régression économique ◆ **an upward/downward ~ in share prices** un mouvement *or* une tendance à la hausse/à la baisse du prix des actions ◆ **there has been little ~ in the political situation** la situation politique demeure à peu près inchangée ◆ **there has been some ~ towards fewer customs restrictions** il semble que l'on aille vers une réduction des restrictions douanières ◆ **a ~ towards multimedia products** un intérêt grandissant pour les produits multimédia

4 (*Pol = group, party*) mouvement *m* ◆ **peace ~** mouvement *m* en faveur de la paix ◆ **separatist/resistance ~** mouvement *m* séparatiste/de résistance

5 (*Mus*) [*of symphony, concerto etc*] mouvement *m* ◆ **in four ~s** en quatre mouvements

6 (= *mechanism*) [*of machine, clock, watch etc*] mouvement *m*

7 (*Med:* also **bowel movement**) selles *fpl* ◆ **to have a (bowel) ~** aller à la selle

mover /ˈmuːvəʳ/ N 1 (*Admin, Parl etc*) [*of motion*] motionnaire *mf*, auteur *m* d'une motion ; → **prime** 2 (*US = removal person*) déménageur *m* 3 ◆ **she's a lovely ~** * elle a une chouette façon de danser (*or de marcher etc*) * 4 ◆ **the ~s and shakers** * les personnages *mpl* influents

movie /ˈmuːvɪ/ (*esp US*) N film *m* (*de cinéma*) ◆ **the ~s** * le ciné * ◆ **to go to the ~s** * aller au ciné *

COMP **movie actor** N acteur *m* de cinéma
movie actress N actrice *f* de cinéma
movie camera N caméra *f*
movie director N cinéaste *mf*
movie-going N la fréquentation des salles de cinéma
movie house N cinéma *m* (*salle*)
the movie industry N l'industrie *f* cinématographique, le cinéma
movie maker N (*US*) cinéaste *mf*
movie rating N (*US*) *système de classification des films*
movie star N star *f or* vedette *f* (*de cinéma*)
movie theater N (*US*) cinéma *m* (*salle*)

Movie Rating, Film Rating

En Grande-Bretagne, l'organisme chargé d'autoriser la diffusion des films et vidéos est le British Board of Classification. Le système de classification adopté est le suivant : « U » (Universal) : pour tous publics ; « PG » (Parental Guidance) : certaines scènes peuvent heurter les jeunes enfants ; « 12 », « 15 » ou « 18 » : interdiction aux moins de 12, 15 ou 18 ans ; « Restricted 18 » : pour adultes seulement, le film ne pouvant être diffusé que dans des salles disposant d'une licence spéciale.

Aux États-Unis, ces fonctions de contrôle sont assumées par la Motion Picture Association of America, et la classification est la suivante : « G » (General) : pour tous publics ; « PG » (Parental Guidance) : certaines scènes peuvent heurter la sensibilité des jeunes enfants ; « PG13 » : certaines scènes sont déconseillées aux moins de 13 ans ; « R » (Restricted) : toute personne de moins de 17 ans doit être accompagnée d'un adulte ; « NC-17 » ou « X » : strictement interdit aux moins de 17 ans.

moviegoer /ˈmuːvɪgəʊəʳ/ N (*gen*) amateur *m* de cinéma, cinéphile *mf* ◆ **I'm an occasional ~** je vais de temps en temps au cinéma

movieland * /ˈmuːvɪlænd/ N le (monde du) cinéma

moving /ˈmuːvɪŋ/ ADJ 1 (= *in motion*) [*vehicle, train*] en marche ; [*object, crowd*] en mouvement ; [*picture, image, graphics*] animé ◆ **~ part** (*in machine*) pièce *f* mobile ◆ **~ target** cible *f* mouvante *or* mobile ◆ **~ traffic** circulation *f* 2 (*emotionally*) [*sight, plea*] émouvant, touchant ; [*book, film, story, account*] émouvant ◆ **it was a deeply ~ moment** c'était un moment vraiment très émouvant 3 (= *motivating*) ◆ **he was the ~ force** *or* **spirit in the whole affair** il était l'âme de toute l'affaire

COMP **moving belt** N tapis *m* roulant
the moving party N (*Jur*) la partie demanderesse
moving pavement N trottoir *m* roulant
moving picture † N (*Cine*) film *m* (*de cinéma*)
moving sidewalk N (*US*) trottoir *m* roulant
moving staircase N escalier *m* mécanique *or* roulant
moving walkway N trottoir *m* roulant

movingly /ˈmuːvɪŋlɪ/ ADV d'une manière émouvante *or* touchante

mow /məʊ/ (pret **mowed**, ptp **mowed** *or* **mown**) VT [+ *corn*] faucher ◆ **to ~ the lawn** tondre le gazon

► **mow down** VT SEP [+ *people, troops*] faucher

mower /ˈməʊəʳ/ N 1 (= *machine: Agr*) faucheuse *f* ; (also **lawnmower**) tondeuse *f* (à gazon) ; → **motor** 2 (= *person*) faucheur *m*, -euse *f*

mowing /ˈməʊɪŋ/ N (*Agr*) fauchage *m* ◆ **~ machine** (*Agr*) faucheuse *f* ; (*in garden*) tondeuse *f* (à gazon)

mown /məʊn/ VB ptp of **mow**

moxie * /ˈmɒksɪ/ N (*US*) couilles *‡ *fpl*, cran *m*

Mozambican /məʊzəmˈbiːkən/ ADJ mozambicain N Mozambicain(e) *m(f)*

Mozambique /məʊzəmˈbiːk/ N Mozambique *m* in Mozambique, au Mozambique

Mozart /ˈməʊtsɑːt/ N Mozart *m*

Mozartian /məʊˈtsɑːtɪən/ ADJ mozartien

mozzarella /mɒtsəˈrelə/ N (= *cheese*) mozzarella *f*

MP /emˈpiː/ N 1 (*Brit*) (abbrev of **Member of Parliament**) → **member** 2 (abbrev of **Military Police**) → **military** 3 (*Can*) (abbrev of **Mounted Police**) → **mounted**

MP3 /ˌempiːˈθriː/ N mp3 *m* COMP **MP3-player** N lecteur *m* mp3

mpg /ˌempiːˈdʒiː/ N (abbrev of **miles per gallon**) → **mile**

mph /ˌempiːˈeɪtʃ/ N (abbrev of **miles per hour**) ≃ km/h

MPhil /ˌemˈfɪl/ N (*Univ*) (abbrev of **Master of Philosophy**) *diplôme de fin de deuxième cycle universitaire en lettres*, ≃ DEA *m*

MPS /ˌempiːˈes/ N (*Brit*) (abbrev of **Member of the Pharmaceutical Society**) *diplôme de pharmacie*

MPV /ˌempiːˈviː/ N (abbrev of **multipurpose vehicle**) → **multipurpose**

Mr /ˈmɪstəʳ/ N (pl **Messrs**) M., Monsieur ; → **mister**

MRC /ˌemɑːˈsiː/ N (*Brit*) (abbrev of **Medical Research Council**) → **medical**

MRCP /ˌemɑːsiːˈpiː/ N (*Brit*) (abbrev of **Member of the Royal College of Physicians**) *diplôme supérieur de médecine générale*

MRCS /ˌemɑːsiːˈes/ N (*Brit*) (abbrev of **Member of the Royal College of Surgeons**) *diplôme supérieur de chirurgie*

MRCVS /ˌemɑːsiːviːˈes/ N (*Brit*) (abbrev of **Member of the Royal College of Veterinary Surgeons**) *diplôme de médecine vétérinaire*

MRI /ˌemɑːrˈaɪ/ N (abbrev of **magnetic resonance imaging**) IRM *f*, imagerie *f* par résonance magnétique

MRM /ˌemɑːrˌem/ N (abbrev of **mechanically recovered meat**) → **mechanically**

MRP /ˌemɑːˈpiː/ N (abbrev of **manufacturers' recommended price**) → **manufacturer**

Mrs /ˈmɪsɪz/ N (*pl inv*) Mme COMP **Mrs Mop** * N (*Brit hum*) femme *f* de ménage

MS /ˌemˈes/ N 1 (also **ms**) abbrev of **manuscript** 2 (abbrev of **multiple sclerosis**) → **multiple** 3 abbrev of **Mississippi** 4 (*US Univ*) (abbrev of **Master of Science**) *maîtrise de sciences* ; → DEGREE

Ms /mɪz, məz/ N ≃ Mme

Ms

Ms est un titre utilisé à la place de « Mrs » (Mme) ou de « Miss » (Mlle) pour éviter la distinction traditionnelle entre femmes mariées et femmes non mariées. Il se veut ainsi l'équivalent du « Mr » (M.) pour les hommes. Souvent tourné en dérision à l'origine comme étant l'expression d'un féminisme exacerbé, ce titre est aujourd'hui couramment utilisé.

MSA /ˌemesˈeɪ/ N (*US Univ*) (abbrev of **Master of Science in Agriculture**) *diplôme d'ingénieur agronome*

MSC /ˌemesˈsiː/ N (*Brit: formerly*) (abbrev of **Manpower Services Commission**) → **manpower**

MSc /ˌemesˈsiː/ N (*Brit Univ*) (abbrev of **Master of Science**) ◆ **to have an ~ in Biology** avoir une maîtrise de biologie ; → **master** ; → DEGREE

MSF N (*Brit*) (abbrev of **Manufacturing, Science, Finance**) *syndicat*

MSG /ˈemesˈdʒiː/ N abbrev of **monosodium glutamate**

Msgr abbrev of **monsignor**

MSP /ˌemesˈpiː/ (pl **MSPs**) N (*Brit Pol*) (abbrev of **Member of the Scottish Parliament**) député *m* au Parlement écossais

MSS, mss NPL abbrev of **manuscripts**

MST /ˌemesˈtiː/ N (*US*) (abbrev of **Mountain Standard Time**) → **mountain**

MT /emˈtiː/ N 1 (abbrev of **machine translation**) → **machine** 2 abbrev of **Montana** 3 (*US*) (abbrev of **Mountain Time**) → **mountain**

Mt (*Geog*) (abbrev of **Mount**) Mt ◆ **~ Pelat** Mt Pelat ◆ **~ Everest** l'Everest *m*

mth abbrev of **month**

MTV /ˌemtiːˈviː/ N (abbrev of **music television**) MTV

much /mʌtʃ/
compar **more**, superl **most**

1 PRONOUN | 3 ADVERB
2 ADJECTIVE

1 - PRONOUN

1 = a great deal, a lot ◆ **~ has happened since then** beaucoup de choses se sont passées depuis ◆ **~ will depend on the state of the economy** cela va dépendre en grande partie de l'état de l'économie ◆ **~ has been written about this phenomenon** on a écrit beaucoup de choses sur ce phénomène ◆ **we have ~ to be thankful for** nous avons tout lieu d'être reconnaissants ◆ **does it cost ~?** est-ce que ça coûte cher ? ◆ **is it worth ~?** est-ce que ça a de la valeur ?

◆ **much of** (*= a large part of*) une bonne partie de ◆ **~ of the town/night** une bonne partie de la ville/de la nuit ◆ **~ of what you say** une bonne partie de ce que vous dites

◆ **to make + much of sth** (*= emphasize*) faire grand cas de qch, attacher beaucoup d'importance à qch ◆ **he made ~ of the fact that ...** il a fait grand cas du fait que ..., il a attaché beaucoup d'importance au fait que ... ◆ **he made too ~ of it** il y attachait trop d'importance ◆ **I couldn't make ~ of what he was saying** (*= understand*) je n'ai pas bien compris *or* saisi ce qu'il disait

2 in negative sentences

◆ **not ... much** (*= a small amount*) pas grand-chose, pas beaucoup

When the sense is **not much of it**, **en** is required with **pas beaucoup**, but not with **pas grand-chose**.

◆ **I haven't got ~ left** il ne m'en reste pas beaucoup, il ne me reste pas grand-chose ◆ **what was stolen? – nothing ~** qu'est-ce qui a été volé ? – pas grand-chose ◆ **he hadn't ~ to say about it** il n'avait pas grand-chose à en dire ◆ **there's not ~ anyone can do about it** personne n'y peut grand-chose ◆ **I haven't heard ~ of him lately** je n'ai pas eu beaucoup de nouvelles de lui ces derniers temps ◆ **we don't see ~ of each other** nous ne nous voyons pas beaucoup BUT **he's/it's not ~ to look at** * il/ça ne paie pas de mine ◆ **it isn't up to ~** * ce n'est pas terrible * ◆ **she won but there wasn't ~ in it** elle a gagné mais de justesse

Constructions with **valoir** are often used when assessing value or merit.

◆ **I don't think ~ of that film** à mon avis ce film ne vaut pas grand-chose, je ne trouve pas ce film très bon ◆ **there isn't ~ to choose between them** ils se valent plus ou moins ◆ **there isn't ~ in it** (*in choice, competition*) ça se vaut

2 – ADJECTIVE

beaucoup de ◆ **~ money** beaucoup d'argent ◆ **~ crime goes unreported** beaucoup de crimes ne sont pas signalés ◆ **he hasn't (very) ~ time** il n'a pas beaucoup de temps ◆ **~ "antique" furniture is not genuine** beaucoup de *or* bien des meubles dits "anciens" ne le sont pas ◆ **without ~ money** avec peu d'argent ; (*iro*) ◆ **and ~ good may it do you** grand bien t'en fasse ◆ **it's a bit ~!** * c'est un peu fort !

3 – ADVERB

1 = to a great degree beaucoup ◆ **he hasn't changed ~** il n'a pas beaucoup changé ◆ **she doesn't go out ~** elle ne sort pas beaucoup *or* pas souvent ◆ **~ bigger** beaucoup plus grand ◆ **~ more easily** beaucoup plus facilement ◆ **~ the cleverest** de beaucoup *or* de loin le plus intelligent ◆ **it doesn't ~ matter** ça n'a pas grande importance ◆ **he ~ regrets that ...** (*frm*) il regrette beaucoup *or* vivement que ... ◆ **~ to my amazement** à ma grande stupéfaction

◆ **very much** ◆ **thank you very ~** merci beaucoup ◆ **I very ~ hope that ...** j'espère de tout cœur que ... ◆ **something was very ~ the matter** quelque chose n'allait pas du tout ◆ **this is very ~ the case** c'est tout à fait le cas

◆ **much +** *past participle* ◆ **the ~-improved program will be introduced next year** le logiciel, qui a subi de nombreuses améliorations, sera introduit l'année prochaine ◆ **they would lose ~-needed development funds** ils perdraient des fonds de développement dont ils ont le plus grand besoin ◆ **estate agents are ~ maligned** on dit beaucoup de mal des agents immobiliers ◆ **potatoes are a ~-maligned vegetable** la pomme de terre est un légume méconnu ◆ **he was ~ displeased** (*frm*) il était très mécontent

2 = more or less ◆ **it's (very** *or* **pretty) ~ the same** c'est presque la même chose ◆ **the town is (pretty) ~ the same as it was ten years ago** la ville n'a pas beaucoup changé en dix ans ◆ **they are (very** *or* **pretty) ~ of an age** ils sont à peu près du même âge

3 set structures

◆ **as much** (*= that quantity*) ◆ **as ~ again** encore autant ◆ **twice as ~** deux fois plus *or* autant ◆ **half as ~ again** la moitié de plus ◆ **I thought as ~!** (*= that*) c'est bien ce que je pensais !, je m'y attendais ! ◆ **it was his fault, and he admitted as ~ later** c'était de sa faute et il l'a admis par la suite

◆ **as much ... as** (*in comparisons of equality*) ◆ **as ~ as possible** autant que possible ◆ **as ~ time as ...** autant de temps que ... ◆ **I've got as ~ as you** j'en ai autant que toi ◆ **I need it as ~ as you do** j'en ai autant besoin que toi ◆ **I love him as ~ as ever** je l'aime toujours autant ◆ **twice as ~ money as ...** deux fois plus d'argent que ... ◆ **I didn't enjoy it as ~ as all that** je ne l'ai pas aimé tant que ça ◆ **it's as ~ as he can do to stand up** c'est tout juste s'il peut se lever

◆ **as much as** + *amount* ◆ **you could pay as ~ as 60 euros for that** ça va chercher jusqu'à 60 euros ◆ **they hope to raise as ~ as $5 million** ils espèrent collecter près de *or* jusqu'à 5 millions de dollars

◆ **however much** ◆ **however ~ you protest ...** on a beau protester ... ◆ **however ~ you like him ...** quelle que soit votre affection pour lui, ...

◆ **how much** combien ◆ **how ~ does it cost?** combien ça coûte ? ◆ **how ~ money have you got?** combien d'argent as-tu ? ◆ **you know how ~ I wanted to go** tu sais à quel point je voulais y aller ◆ **I didn't realise how ~ she loved me** je ne me rendais pas compte à quel point elle m'aimait

◆ **much as** ◆ **~ as I like him, I don't trust him** ce n'est pas que je ne l'aime pas mais je ne lui fais pas confiance ◆ **~ as I dislike doing this, ...** bien que je n'aime pas du tout faire cela, ...

◆ **much less** (*= and even less*) ◆ **he couldn't understand the question, ~ less answer it** il ne pouvait pas comprendre la question et encore moins y répondre

◆ **much though** ◆ **~ though she loves them both** bien qu'elle les aime *subj* tous deux profondément

◆ **not much of a** * (*= not a great*) ◆ **he is not ~ of a writer** ce n'est pas un très bon écrivain, comme écrivain il y a mieux ◆ **I'm not ~ of a drinker** je ne bois pas beaucoup ◆ **it wasn't ~ of an evening** ce n'était pas une soirée très réussie

◆ **so much** (*= a lot*) tellement, tant ◆ **he'd drunk so ~ that ...** il avait tellement *or* tant bu que ... ◆ **so ~ of what he says is untrue** il y a tellement *or* tant de mensonges dans ce qu'il dit ◆ **so ~ pleasure** tant de plaisir ◆ **you spend so ~ of your time worrying that ...** tu passes tellement de temps à te faire du souci que ... ◆ **he beat me by so ~** il m'a battu de ça ◆ **do you want water in your whisky ? – about so ~** vous voulez de l'eau dans votre whisky ? – à peu près comme ça ◆ **so ~ so that ...** à tel point que ... ◆ **without so ~ as a word** sans même (dire) un mot

◆ **not so much ... as** ◆ **the problem is not so ~ one of money as of staff** il ne s'agit pas tant d'un problème d'argent que d'un problème de personnel ◆ **I think of her not so ~ as a doctor but as a friend** je la considère plus comme une amie que comme un médecin

◆ **so much for** ◆ **so ~ for the producers, what of the consumers?** nous avons examiné le cas des producteurs mais qu'en est-il des consommateurs ? ◆ **so ~ for his help!** c'est ça qu'il appelle aider ! ◆ **so ~ for his promises!** voilà ce que valaient ses promesses ! ◆ **so ~ for that!** tant pis !

◆ **so much the** + *comparative* ◆ **so ~ the better!** tant mieux ! ◆ **that leaves so ~ the less to do** c'est toujours ça de moins à faire

◆ **this/that much** ◆ **this ~?** (ça ira) comme ça ? ◆ **it's that ~ too long** c'est trop long de ça ◆ **he was at least this ~ taller than me** il était plus grand que moi d'au moins ça ◆ **I can't carry this ~** je ne peux pas porter (tout) ceci ◆ **I know this ~** je sais tout au moins ceci ◆ **this ~ we do know: ...** tout au moins nous savons ceci : ... ◆ **he has left, this ~ we do know** il est parti, ça nous le savons déjà ◆ **this ~ is certain ...** un point est acquis ... ◆ **this ~ is true** il y a ceci de vrai

◆ **too much** trop ◆ **I've eaten too ~** j'ai trop mangé ◆ **he talks too ~** il parle trop ◆ **$500 is too ~** 500 dollars, c'est trop ◆ **that was too ~ for me** c'en était trop pour moi ◆ **too ~ sugar** trop de sucre ◆ **that's too ~!** (*lit*) c'est trop ! ; (*protesting*) (ça) c'est trop fort ! ◆ **too ~!** * c'est dingue * ! ◆ **he was too ~ for his opponent** il était trop fort pour son adversaire ◆ **the stress was too ~ for me** je n'arrivais plus à supporter le stress ; (*disapproving*) ◆ **that film was really too ~** *or* **a bit ~ for me** j'ai trouvé que le film dépassait vraiment *or* un peu les bornes

---

muchness * /ˈmʌtʃnɪs/ **N** ◆ **they're much of a ~** c'est blanc bonnet et bonnet blanc

mucilage /ˈmjuːsɪlɪdʒ/ **N** mucilage *m*

mucilaginous /ˌmjuːsɪˈlædʒɪnəs/ **ADJ** mucilagineux

muck /mʌk/ **N** 1 (*= dirt*) saletés *fpl* ; (*= mud*) boue *f*, gadoue *f* ◆ **where there's ~ there's brass** (*Prov*) * l'argent n'a pas d'odeur ; → **lady**

2 (*= excrement*) [*of dog*] crotte *f* ; [*of horse*] crottin *m* ; [*of cow*] bouse *f* ; [*of bird*] fiente *f* ; (*= manure*) fumier *m*

3 (*fig: describing food, film, book, conversation etc*) saleté(s) *f(pl)*, cochonnerie(s) * *f(pl)*

4 (*= bungle*) ◆ **to make a ~** * of sth saloper * qch

COMP **muck heap** **N** tas *m* de fumier *or* d'ordures

muck-up * **N** (*= bungle*) gâchis *m*

► **muck about** *, **muck around** * (*Brit*) **VI** 1 (*= spend time aimlessly*) perdre son temps ◆ **stop ~ing about and get on with your work** cesse de perdre ton temps et fais ton travail

2 (*= potter around*) ◆ **he enjoys mucking about in the garden** il aime bricoler dans le jardin

3 (*= play the fool*) faire l'idiot *or* l'imbécile ◆ **to ~ about with sth** (*= fiddle with*) jouer avec qch, tripoter qch

VT SEP [*+ person*] traiter par-dessus la jambe *

► **muck in** * **VI** (*Brit*) (*= share money etc*) faire bourse commune (*with* avec) ◆ **to ~ in with sb** (*= share room*) crécher * avec qn ◆ **everyone ~s in here** tout le monde met la main à la pâte * ici

► **muck out** **VT SEP** (*Brit*) [*+ stable*] nettoyer, curer

► **muck up** * (*Brit*) **VT SEP** 1 (*= ruin*) [*+ task*] saloper * ; [*+ plans, deal*] chambouler * ; [*+ life*] gâcher ; [*+ mechanism*] bousiller * ◆ **he's really ~ed things up!** il a vraiment tout flanqué par terre ! *

2 (*= make untidy*) [*+ room*] semer la pagaille * dans ; [*+ hair*] emmêler ; [*+ hairstyle*] abîmer ; (*= make dirty*) [*+ room, clothes*] salir

N ◆ **muck-up** → **muck**

muckiness /ˈmʌkɪnɪs/ **N** saleté *f*, malpropreté *f*

muckraker /ˈmʌkreɪkəʳ/ N *(fig)* fouineur *m*, -euse *f (qui déterre des scandales)*, fouille-merde* *mf*

muckraking /ˈmʌkreɪkɪŋ/ N mise *f* au jour de scandales

mucky* /ˈmʌkɪ/ ADJ *(Brit)* 1 *(= dirty) [person, animal, place, object]* boueux ; *[job]* crasseux ◆ **to get ~** se salir ◆ **to get sth ~** salir qch ◆ **keep your ~ paws off!** *(hum)* touche pas avec tes pattes sales ! ◆ **you ~ pup!** *(hum)* petit(e) cochon(ne) ! 2 *(= smutty) [book, magazine, film]* cochon 3 *(= unpleasant) [weather]* sale

mucous /ˈmjuːkəs/ ADJ muqueux ◆ **~ membrane** (membrane *f*) muqueuse *f*

mucus /ˈmjuːkəs/ N mucus *m*, mucosités *fpl*

mud /mʌd/ N boue *f* ; *(in river, sea)* boue *f*, vase *f* ; *(in swamp)* boue *f*, bourbe *f* ◆ **car stuck in the ~** voiture *f* embourbée ◆ **to drag sb's (good) name through the ~** *or* **drag sb through the ~** calomnier qn ◆ **to throw** *or* **sling ~ at sb** *(fig)* couvrir qn de boue ◆ **~ sticks** *(esp Brit)* il est difficile de se laver de tout soupçon ◆ **here's ~ in your eye!*** *(hum)* à la tienne Étienne !* *(hum)* ; → **clear, name, stick**

COMP **mud-caked** ADJ tout crotté
mud flap N *[of car, motorcycle]* pare-boue *m inv* ; *[of truck]* bavette *f*
mud flat(s) N(PL) laisse *f* de vase
mud hut N hutte *f* de terre
mud pie N pâté *m (de sable, de terre)*
mud-slinging N *(NonC)* médisance *f*, dénigrement *m*
mud wrestling N catch *m* dans la boue *(généralement féminin)*

mudbank /ˈmʌdbæŋk/ N banc *m* de vase

mudbath /ˈmʌdbæθ/ N bain *m* de boue

muddle /ˈmʌdl/ N *(= disorder)* désordre *m* ; *(= tangle of objects)* fouillis *m* ; *(fig)* confusion *f* ◆ **the ~ of notebooks and papers on her desk** le fouillis de bloc-notes et de papiers sur son bureau ◆ **her office was a ~ of files and papers** il y avait un vrai fouillis de dossiers et de papiers dans son bureau ◆ **there's been a ~ over the seats** il y a eu confusion en ce qui concerne les places ◆ **a legal/financial/bureaucratic ~** un imbroglio juridique/financier/bureaucratique ◆ **what a ~!** *(= disorder)* quel fouillis ! ; *(= mix-up)* quelle confusion !, quelle pagaille !* ◆ **to be in a ~** *[room, books, clothes]* être en désordre, être sens dessus dessous ; *[person]* ne plus s'y retrouver *(over sth* dans qch) ; *[ideas]* être embrouillé *or* confus ; *[plans, arrangements]* être confus *or* incertain ◆ **to get into a ~** *[person]* s'embrouiller *(over sth* dans qch, au sujet de qch) ; *[ideas]* s'embrouiller ◆ **the files have got into a real ~** les dossiers sont sens dessus dessous

VT (also **muddle up**) 1 ◆ **to ~ (up) A and** *or* **with B** confondre A avec B

2 *(= perplex) [+ person]* embrouiller ; *[+ sb's ideas]* brouiller, embrouiller ◆ **to be ~d (up)** être embrouillé ◆ **I got rather ~d by her explanation** son explication m'a plutôt embrouillé ◆ **to get ~d (up)** *[person, ideas]* s'embrouiller ; see also **muddled**

3 *[+ facts, story, details]* brouiller, embrouiller ; see also **muddled**

COMP **muddle-headed** ADJ *[person]* aux idées confuses, brouillon ; *[plan, ideas]* confus
muddle-up N confusion *f*, embrouillamini* *m*

► **muddle along** VI se débrouiller tant bien que mal

► **muddle on** VI se débrouiller tant bien que mal

► **muddle through** VI se tirer d'affaire *or* s'en sortir tant bien que mal ◆ **I expect we'll ~ through** je suppose que nous nous en sortirons d'une façon ou d'une autre

► **muddle up** VT SEP ⇒ **muddle vt**

N ◆ **muddle-up** → **muddle**

muddled /ˈmʌdəld/ ADJ *[message, effort, attempt, situation, storyline]* confus

muddler /ˈmʌdləʳ/ N esprit *m* brouillon *(personne)*

muddy /ˈmʌdɪ/ ADJ 1 *(= dirty) [clothes, object]* boueux, couvert de boue ; *[person]* couvert de boue 2 *(= dull) [colour]* terne ; *[skin, complexion]* terreux ; *[liquid]* trouble ◆ **~ brown** brun terne *inv* 3 *(= confused) [ideas, thinking]* confus VT *[+ hands, clothes, shoes]* crotter, salir ; *[+ road]* rendre boueux ; *[+ water, river]* troubler ◆ **to ~ the waters** *(fig)* brouiller les pistes

mudguard /ˈmʌdgɑːd/ N *(Brit) [of car etc]* pare-boue *m inv* ; *[of bicycle]* garde-boue *m inv*

mudlark † /ˈmʌdlɑːk/ N gamin(e) *m(f)* des rues

mudpack /ˈmʌdpæk/ N masque *m* (de beauté) à l'argile

mudslide /ˈmʌdslaɪd/ N coulée *f* de boue

muesli /ˈmjuːzlɪ/ N muesli *m*

muezzin /muːˈezɪn/ N muezzin *m*

muff /mʌf/ N *(Dress, Tech)* manchon *m* VT * rater, louper* ; *(Sport) [+ ball, shot]* rater, louper* ; *[+ chance, opportunity]* rater, laisser passer ◆ **to ~ one's lines** *(Theat)* se tromper dans son texte ◆ **to ~ it*** rater son coup VI * rater son coup

muffin /ˈmʌfɪn/ N *(Brit)* muffin *m (petit pain rond et plat)* ; *(US) petit gâteau au chocolat ou aux fruits*

muffle /ˈmʌfl/ VT 1 *[+ sound, noise]* assourdir, étouffer ; *[+ noisy thing, bell, drum]* assourdir ◆ **to ~ the oars** assourdir les avirons ◆ **in a ~d voice** d'une voix sourde *or* étouffée 2 (also **muffle up**) *(= wrap up) [+ object]* envelopper ; *[+ person]* emmitoufler ◆ **to ~ o.s. (up)** s'emmitoufler ◆ **he was all ~d up** il était emmitouflé des pieds à la tête

► **muffle up** VI s'emmitoufler VT SEP ⇒ **muffle 2**

muffler /ˈmʌfləʳ/ N 1 *(= scarf)* cache-nez *m inv*, cache-col *m inv* 2 *(US: in car)* silencieux *m*

mufti /ˈmʌftɪ/ N 1 *(Brit *)* tenue *f* civile ◆ **in ~** en civil, en pékin* *(Mil)* 2 *(Muslim)* mufti *or* muphti *m*

mug /mʌg/ N 1 *(= cup)* tasse *f* (américaine), grande tasse *f* ; *(= glass: for beer etc)* chope *f* ◆ **a ~ of coffee** *(= amount)* un grand café 2 (*‡* *= face)* bouille* *f*, bille‡ *f* ◆ **ugly ~** sale gueule *f* 3 *(Brit* *‡* *= fool)* andouille‡ *f*, poire* *f* ◆ **what sort of a ~ do you take me for?** tu me prends pour une andouille ?‡ ◆ **they're looking for a ~ to help** ils cherchent une bonne poire* pour aider ◆ **it's a ~'s game** c'est un piège à con‡ VT *(= assault)* agresser VI * 1 *(= pull faces)* faire des grimaces 2 *(= overact, act up)* charger son rôle

COMP **mug shot*** N *(Police)* photo *f* d'identité judiciaire ; *(gen)* photo *f* d'identité

► **mug up*** VT SEP 1 *(Brit = swot up)* bûcher*, potasser* 2 *(US)* **to ~ it up‡** faire des grimaces VI *(Brit)* ◆ **to ~ up for an exam** bûcher* pour un examen

mugger /ˈmʌgəʳ/ N agresseur *m*

mugging /ˈmʌgɪŋ/ N 1 *(= assault)* agression *f* 2 *(= overacting)* jeu *m* forcé

muggins‡ /ˈmʌgɪnz/ N *(Brit)* idiot(e) *m(f)*, niais(e) *m(f)* ◆ **~ had to pay for it** *(= oneself)* c'est encore ma pomme‡ qui a payé

muggy /ˈmʌgɪ/ ADJ *[weather, air, heat]* lourd ; *[climate]* chaud et humide ; *[summer, day, evening]* lourd, chaud et humide ◆ **it's very ~ today** il fait très lourd aujourd'hui

mugwump /ˈmʌgwʌmp/ N *(US Pol)* non-inscrit *m*, indépendant *m*

mujaheddin, mujahedeen /ˌmuːdʒəhəˈdiːn/ NPL ◆ **the ~** les moudjahiddin *mpl*

mulatto /mjuːˈlætəʊ/ N (pl **mulattos** *or* **mulattoes**) mulâtre(sse) *m(f)* ADJ mulâtre *f inv*

mulberry /ˈmʌlbərɪ/ N *(= fruit)* mûre *f* ; (also **mulberry tree**) mûrier *m*

mulch /mʌltʃ/ N paillis *m*, mulch *m* VT pailler, couvrir

mulct /mʌlkt/ N *(= fine)* amende *f* VT 1 *(= fine)* frapper d'une amende 2 *(by fraud etc)* ◆ **to ~ sb of sth, to ~ sth from sb** extorquer qch à qn

mule¹ /mjuːl/ N 1 *(= animal)* mulet *m* ; *(female)* mule *f* ; *(fig) (= person)* mule *f* ◆ **obstinate** *or* **stubborn as a ~** têtu comme une mule *or* un mulet 2 *(Spinning)* renvideur *m* 3 *(Drugs * = courier)* fourmi* *f*

COMP **mule driver, mule skinner*** *(US)* N muletier *m*, -ière *f*
mule track N chemin *m* muletier

mule² /mjuːl/ N *(= slipper)* mule *f*

muleteer /ˌmjuːlɪˈtɪəʳ/ N muletier *m*, -ière *f*

mulish /ˈmjuːlɪʃ/ ADJ *(pej) [person]* têtu ; *[look]* buté, têtu ; *[attitude]* buté

mulishness /ˈmjuːlɪʃnɪs/ N entêtement *m*

mull /mʌl/ VT *[+ wine, ale]* chauffer et épicer ; see also **mulled**

► **mull over** VT SEP retourner dans sa tête

mullah /ˈmʌlə/ N mollah *m*

mulled /mʌld/ ADJ ◆ **(a glass of) ~ wine** (un) vin chaud

mullet /ˈmʌlɪt/ N ◆ **grey ~** mulet *m* ◆ **red ~** rouget *m*

mulligan stew‡ /ˈmʌlɪgən stjuː/ N *(US)* ragoût *m* grossier

mulligatawny /ˌmʌlɪgəˈtɔːnɪ/ N soupe *f* au curry

mullion /ˈmʌlɪən/ N meneau *m* ◆ **~ed window** fenêtre *f* à meneaux

multi... /ˈmʌltɪ/ PREF multi... ◆ **multi-family accommodation** résidence *f* pour *or* destinée à plusieurs familles ◆ **multi-journey ticket** abonnement *m* (pour un nombre déterminé de trajets) ◆ **multi-person vehicle** véhicule *m* pour plusieurs personnes ◆ **multistage rocket** fusée *f* à plusieurs étages

multi-access /ˌmʌltɪˈækses/ N *(Comput)* multivoie *f* ◆ **~ system** système *m* à multivoie

multicellular /ˌmʌltɪˈseljʊləʳ/ ADJ multicellulaire

multichannel /ˌmʌltɪˈtʃænl/ ADJ ◆ **~ TV** télévision *f* à canaux multiples

multicoloured, multicolored *(US)* /ˈmʌltɪˌkʌləd/ ADJ multicolore

multicultural /ˌmʌltɪˈkʌltʃərəl/ ADJ multiculturel, pluriculturel

multiculturalism /ˌmʌltɪˈkʌltʃərəlɪzəm/ N multiculturalisme *m*, pluriculturalisme *m*

multidimensional /ˌmʌltɪdaɪˈmenʃənl/ ADJ multidimensionnel

multidirectional /ˌmʌltɪdɪˈrekʃənl/ ADJ multidirectionnel

multidisciplinary /ˌmʌltɪˈdɪsɪplɪnərɪ/ ADJ pluridisciplinaire, multidisciplinaire ◆ **~ system** pluridisciplinarité *f*

multifaceted /ˌmʌltɪˈfæsɪtɪd/ ADJ *(fig)* qui présente de nombreux aspects, à multiples facettes

multifarious /ˌmʌltɪˈfeərɪəs/ ADJ *(frm)* multiple

multiflora /ˌmʌltɪˈflɔːrə/ ADJ *[rose etc]* multiflore

multiform /ˈmʌltɪfɔːm/ ADJ multiforme

multi-function /ˈmʌltɪˈfʌŋkʃən/ ADJ multifonctionnel, polyvalent

multigym /ˈmʌltɪˌdʒɪm/ N banc *m* de musculation

multihull /ˈmʌltɪhʌl/ N multicoque *m*

multilateral /ˌmʌltɪˈlætərəl/ ADJ multilatéral

multilateralist /ˌmʌltɪˈlætərəlɪst/ (Pol) ADJ en faveur des accords multilatéraux sur le désarmement nucléaire N partisan(e) m(f) des accords multilatéraux sur le désarmement nucléaire

multi-level /ˈmʌltɪlevl/ ADJ (US) à plusieurs niveaux

multilingual /ˌmʌltɪˈlɪŋgwəl/ ADJ [person] polyglotte ; [society, country, dictionary] multilingue, plurilingue ; [pamphlet, announcement, sign] en plusieurs langues

multilingualism /ˌmʌltɪˈlɪŋgwəlɪzəm/ N multilinguisme m, plurilinguisme m

multimedia /ˈmʌltɪˈmiːdɪə/ ADJ [product, system, market, CD] multimédia f inv

multimillion /ˈmʌltɪˈmɪljən/ ADJ ◆ **a ~ pound deal** une affaire qui vaut plusieurs millions de livres ◆ **a ~ dollar investment** un investissement de plusieurs millions de dollars

multimillionaire /ˌmʌltɪˌmɪljəˈnɛəʳ/ N multimillionnaire mf, multimilliardaire mf

multi-nation /ˈmʌltɪˈneɪʃən/ ADJ [treaty, agreement] multinational

multinational /ˌmʌltɪˈnæʃənl/ N multinationale f ADJ multinational

multipack /ˈmʌltɪpæk/ N pack m

multiparous /mʌlˈtɪpərəs/ ADJ multipare

multipartite /ˌmʌltɪˈpɑːtaɪt/ ADJ divisé en plusieurs parties

multiparty /ˌmʌltɪˈpɑːtɪ/ ADJ (Pol) pluripartite

multiple /ˈmʌltɪpl/ N (Math) multiple m ; → **low**¹ ADJ multiple ◆ **~ crash** or **pileup** carambolage m

COMP **multiple choice** N (Scol, Univ) (also **multiple-choice exam** or **test**) QCM m, questionnaire m à choix multiple ; (also **multiple-choice question**) question f à choix multiple

multiple entry visa N visa autorisant à entrer plusieurs fois dans un pays

multiple exposure N (Phot) exposition f multiple

multiple ownership N multipropriété f

multiple personality N (Psych) dédoublement m de la personnalité

multiple-risk insurance N assurance f multirisque

multiple sclerosis N (Med) sclérose f en plaques

multiple store N (Brit) grand magasin m à succursales multiples

multiplex /ˈmʌltɪpleks/ ADJ multiplex ◆ **~ cinema** complexe m multisalle N multiplex m ; (Cine) complexe m multisalle VT communiquer en multiplex

multiplexer /ˈmʌltɪpleksəʳ/ N multiplexeur m

multiplexing /ˈmʌltɪpleksɪŋ/ N multiplexage m

multipliable /ˈmʌltɪˌplaɪəbl/, **multiplicable** /ˈmʌltɪˌplɪkəbl/ ADJ multipliable

multiplicand /ˌmʌltɪplɪˈkænd/ N multiplicande m

multiplication /ˌmʌltɪplɪˈkeɪʃən/ N multiplication f

COMP **multiplication sign** N signe m de multiplication

multiplication tables NPL tables fpl de multiplication

multiplicative /ˈmʌltɪplɪˌkeɪtɪv/ ADJ (Math, Gram) multiplicatif

multiplicity /ˌmʌltɪˈplɪsɪtɪ/ N multiplicité f

multiplier /ˈmʌltɪplaɪəʳ/ N multiplicateur m

COMP **multiplier effect** N effet m multiplicateur

multiply /ˈmʌltɪplaɪ/ VT multiplier (by par) VI se multiplier

multiplying /ˈmʌltɪplaɪɪŋ/ ADJ multiplicateur (-trice f), multiplicatif

multipolar /ˈmʌltɪˈpəʊləʳ/ ADJ multipolaire

multiprocessing /ˌmʌltɪˈprəʊsesɪŋ/ N (Comput) multitraitement m

multiprocessor /ˌmʌltɪˈprəʊsesəʳ/ N (Comput) multiprocesseur m

multiprogramming /ˌmʌltɪˈprəʊgræmɪŋ/ N (Comput) multiprogrammation f

multipurpose /ˌmʌltɪˈpɜːpəs/ ADJ polyvalent, à usages multiples COMP **multipurpose vehicle** N (= off-roader) tout-terrain m ; (= people-carrier) monospace m

multiracial /ˌmʌltɪˈreɪʃəl/ ADJ multiracial

multirisk /ˌmʌltɪˈrɪsk/ ADJ (Insurance) multirisque

multisensory /ˌmʌltɪˈsensərɪ/ ADJ multisensoriel

multistandard /ˌmʌltɪˈstændəd/ ADJ (TV) [set, video etc] multistandard inv

multistorey /ˌmʌltɪˈstɔːrɪ/, **multistoreyed, multistoried** (US) /ˌmʌltɪˈstɔːrɪd/ ADJ à étages ◆ **~ car park** parking m à étages or à niveaux multiples

multitasking, multi-tasking /ˌmʌltɪˈtɑːskɪŋ/ N (Comput) traitement m multitâche; (by person) capacité f à mener plusieurs tâches de front

multitrack /ˌmʌltɪˈtræk/ ADJ à plusieurs pistes

multitude /ˈmʌltɪtjuːd/ N multitude f ◆ **the ~** la multitude, la foule ◆ **for a ~ of reasons** pour une multitude or une foule de raisons ◆ **that covers** or **hides a ~ of sins** c'est un véritable cache-misère

multitudinous /ˌmʌltɪˈtjuːdɪnəs/ ADJ innombrable

multiuser /ˌmʌltɪˈjuːzəʳ/ ADJ (Comput) ◆ **~ system** configuration f multiposte

multivalence /ˌmʌltɪˈveɪləns/ N polyvalence f

multivalent /ˌmʌltɪˈveɪlənt/ ADJ polyvalent

multivitamin /ˌmʌltɪˈvɪtəmɪn/ N complexe m vitaminé ◆ **~ tablet** comprimé m de multivitamines

mum¹ * /mʌm/ N (Brit = mother) maman f, mère f ◆ **hello ~!** bonjour, maman ! ◆ **she's a teacher and her ~'s a doctor** elle est enseignante et sa mère est médecin

mum² /mʌm/ ADJ ◆ **to keep ~ (about sth)** ne pas piper mot (de qch), ne pas souffler mot (de qch) ◆ **~'s the word!** motus !, bouche cousue !

mum³ * /mʌm/ N (abbrev of **chrysanthemum**) ◆ **~s** chrysanthèmes mpl

Mumbai /mumˈbaɪ/ N Mumbai (nouveau nom de Bombay)

mumble /ˈmʌmbl/ VI marmotter ◆ **stop mumbling!** arrête de marmotter or de parler entre tes dents ! VT marmonner, marmotter ◆ **to ~ one's words** manger ses mots ◆ **to ~ an answer** répondre entre ses dents, marmonner une réponse ◆ **to ~ that ...** marmonner que ... N marmonnement m, marmottement m ◆ **... he said in a ~** ... dit-il entre ses dents

mumbo jumbo /ˌmʌmbəʊˈdʒʌmbəʊ/ N (= nonsense) baragouin * m, charabia * m ; (= pretentious words) jargon m obscur ; (= pretentious ceremony etc) tralala * m, salamalecs * mpl

mummer /ˈmʌməʳ/ N (Theat) mime mf

mummery /ˈmʌmərɪ/ N (Theat, fig) momerie f

mummification /ˌmʌmɪfɪˈkeɪʃən/ N momification f

mummify /ˈmʌmɪfaɪ/ VT momifier

mummy¹ /ˈmʌmɪ/ N (= embalmed) momie f

mummy² * /ˈmʌmɪ/ N (Brit = mother) maman f ◆ **~'s boy** (pej) fils m à sa maman *

mump /mʌmp/ VI grogner, grommeler

mumps /mʌmps/ N (NonC) oreillons mpl

munch /mʌntʃ/ VTI (gen) croquer ; (= chew noisily) mastiquer bruyamment ◆ **to ~ (away) on** or **at sth** dévorer qch à belles dents

Münchhausen's syndrome /ˈmʌntʃaʊzənzˈsɪndrəʊm/ N (Med) syndrome m de Münchhausen

munchies * /ˈmʌntʃɪz/ NPL 1 (= snack) quelque chose à grignoter 2 ◆ **to have the ~** (= be hungry) avoir un creux

munchkin * /ˈmʌntʃkɪn/ N (esp US = small person, child) lilliputien m

mundane /ˌmʌnˈdeɪn/ ADJ [matter, issue, problem, object] banal ; [task] courant ; [explanation, concern] terre-à-terre ◆ **on a more ~ level** au niveau pratique

mung bean /ˈmʌŋbiːn/ N haricot m mung

Munich /ˈmjuːnɪk/ N Munich

municipal /mjuːˈnɪsɪpəl/ ADJ municipal COMP **municipal court** N (US Jur) tribunal local de première instance

municipality /mjuːˌnɪsɪˈpælɪtɪ/ N municipalité f

munificence /mjuːˈnɪfɪsns/ N munificence f

munificent /mjuːˈnɪfɪsnt/ ADJ (frm) munificent (liter)

muniments /ˈmjuːnɪmənts/ NPL (Jur) titres mpl (concernant la propriété d'un bien-fonds)

munitions /mjuːˈnɪʃənz/ NPL munitions fpl COMP **munitions dump** N dépôt m de munitions

munitions factory N fabrique f de munitions

muon /ˈmjuːɒn/ N (Phys) muon m

mural /ˈmjʊərəl/ ADJ mural N peinture f murale ; (in Modern Art) mural m

murder /ˈmɜːdəʳ/ N 1 (gen) meurtre m ; (Jur) meurtre m ; (premeditated) assassinat m ◆ **four ~s in one week** quatre meurtres en une semaine ◆ **~!** au meurtre !, à l'assassin ! ◆ **~ will out** (Prov) tôt ou tard la vérité se fait jour ◆ **he was screaming** or **shouting blue ~** * il criait comme un putois or comme si on l'écorchait ◆ **she lets the children get away with ~** * elle passe tout aux enfants ◆ **they get away with ~** * ils peuvent tout se permettre

2 * **the noise/heat in here is ~** le bruit/la chaleur ici est infernal(e) ◆ **the exam was ~** l'examen était épouvantable or coton * ◆ **did you have a good holiday? – no, it was ~** avez-vous passé de bonnes vacances ? – non, c'était l'enfer ◆ **the roads were ~** les routes étaient un cauchemar

VT [+ person] assassiner ; (fig) [+ song, music, language] massacrer ; [+ opponent, team] battre à plates coutures, écraser ◆ **the ~ed man** (or **woman etc**) la victime

COMP **murder case** N (Jur) procès m pour meurtre ; (Police) affaire f de meurtre

murder hunt N chasse f à l'homme pour retrouver le (or un) meurtrier

Murder Squad N (Police) ≈ brigade f criminelle (de la police judiciaire)

murder trial N ≈ procès m pour homicide

murder weapon N arme f du crime

murderer /ˈmɜːdərəʳ/ N meurtrier m, assassin m

murderess /ˈmɜːdərɪs/ N meurtrière f

murderous /ˈmɜːdərəs/ ADJ 1 (= homicidal) meurtrier ◆ **a ~-looking individual** un individu à tête d'assassin 2 (* = awful) [heat] effroyable

murk /mɜːk/, **murkiness** /ˈmɜːkɪnɪs/ N obscurité f

murky /ˈmɜːkɪ/ ADJ [room, street, day, sky] sombre ; [fog, night, darkness] épais (épaisse f) ; [water, depths] trouble ; [colour] terne, terreux ◆ **~ brown/green** brun inv/vert inv sale ◆ **the room**

was ~ with smoke la pièce était obscurcie par la fumée ◆ **his ~ past** son passé trouble ◆ **the ~ world of the arms trade** le monde trouble des trafiquants d'armes

murmur /ˈmɜːməʳ/ N 1 *[of voice(s)]* murmure *m* ; *[of bees, traffic etc]* bourdonnement *m* ; *(fig = protest)* murmure *m* ◆ **there wasn't a ~ in the classroom** il n'y avait pas un murmure dans la classe ◆ **to speak in a ~** parler à voix basse, chuchoter ◆ **a ~ of conversation** un bourdonnement de voix ◆ **there were ~s of disagreement** il y eut des murmures de désapprobation ◆ **he agreed without a ~** il accepta sans murmure 2 *(Med)* ◆ **a heart ~** un souffle au cœur VT murmurer VI *[person, stream]* murmurer ; *(= complain)* murmurer *(against, about* contre*)*

murmuring /ˈmɜːmərɪŋ/ N *[of people, stream]* *(also fig)* *[of protests]* murmures *mpl* ; *[of bees etc]* bourdonnement *m* ADJ *[stream]* murmurant, qui murmure

Murphy /ˈmɜːfɪ/ N *(US, Ir* * *= potato)* pomme *f* de terre
COMP **Murphy bed** N *(US)* lit *m* escamotable
Murphy's law N *(hum)* loi *f* de l'emmerdement‡ maximum

MusBac N (abbrev of **Bachelor of Music**) *diplôme d'études musicales*

muscat /ˈmʌskət/ N 1 (also **muscat grape**) (raisin *m*) muscat *m* 2 *(= wine)* (vin *m*) muscat *m*

muscatel /ˌmʌskəˈtel/ N *(= grape, wine)* muscat *m*

muscle /ˈmʌsl/ N 1 *(Anat)* muscle *m* ◆ **he didn't move a ~** il n'a pas levé *or* remué le petit doigt *(to help etc* pour aider *etc)* ; *(= didn't flinch)* il n'a pas bronché, il n'a pas sourcillé ◆ **put some ~ into it** * *(= energy)* vas-y avec un peu plus de nerf * *or* de force 2 *(= power)* pouvoir *m* effectif, impact *m* ◆ **political ~** pouvoir *m* politique effectif, moyens *mpl* politiques ◆ **this union hasn't much ~** ce syndicat n'a pas beaucoup d'impact *or* de poids COMP **muscle-bound** ADJ *(lit)* aux muscles hypertrophiés ; *(fig)* raide

► **muscle in** * VI 1 *(Brit: into group etc)* intervenir, s'immiscer ◆ **to ~ (one's way) in on a group/a discussion** essayer de s'imposer dans un groupe/une discussion ◆ **stop muscling in!** occupe-toi de tes oignons ! * 2 *(US = force one's way inside)* entrer violemment

muscleman /ˈmʌslmæn/ N (pl **-men**) *(= strong man)* hercule *m* ; *(= gangster etc)* homme *m* de main, sbire *m*

muscl(e)y /ˈmʌsəlɪ/ ADJ musclé

Muscovite /ˈmʌskəvaɪt/ ADJ moscovite N Moscovite *mf*

muscular /ˈmʌskjʊləʳ/ ADJ 1 *(= brawny)* musclé ◆ **to be of ~ build** être musclé 2 *(Med, Physiol)* musculaire COMP **muscular dystrophy** N dystrophie *f* musculaire, myopathie *f* musculaire progressive

musculature /ˈmʌskjʊlətjʊəʳ/ N musculature *f*

MusDoc N (abbrev of **Doctor of Music**) ≈ doctorat *m* de musique

muse /mjuːz/ VI méditer *(on, about, over* sur*)*, songer, réfléchir *(on, about, over* à*)* VT ◆ **"they might accept," he ~d** *(= said)* "il se pourrait qu'ils acceptent", dit-il d'un ton songeur ; *(= thought)* "il se pourrait qu'ils acceptent", songeait-il N *(Myth, fig:* also **Muse***)* muse *f*

museum /mjuːˈzɪəm/ N musée *m* COMP **museum piece** N *(lit, fig)* pièce *f* de musée

mush¹ /mʌʃ/ N *(NonC)* bouillie *f* ; *(fig)* sentimentalité *f* de guimauve *or* à l'eau de rose

mush²‡ /mʊʃ/ N *(Brit)* 1 *(= face)* tronche * *f* 2 *(= person)* ◆ **hey, ~ !** hé, machin ! *

mushroom /ˈmʌʃrʊm/ N champignon *m* (comestible) ◆ **to spring up** *or* **sprout like ~s** pousser comme des champignons
VI 1 *(= grow quickly)* *[town]* pousser comme un champignon ; *[sales, debts, investment]* augmenter rapidement ; *[market]* connaître une expansion rapide ; *[population]* connaître une croissance rapide ◆ **this small town ~ed into a large city** cette petite ville a poussé comme un champignon ◆ **the dispute ~ed into a serious political crisis** le contentieux a pris de l'ampleur et s'est vite transformé en une grave crise politique ◆ **unemployment has ~ed** le chômage monte en flèche ◆ **his debts have ~ed into thousands of dollars** ses dettes se montent maintenant à des milliers de dollars
2 *(= appear, spring up)* apparaître un peu partout ; *(= multiply)* proliférer, se multiplier ◆ **voluntary groups have ~ed in recent years** les groupes de bénévoles se sont multipliés ces dernières années
3 *(= gather mushrooms)* ◆ **to go ~ing** aller aux champignons
COMP *[soup, omelette]* aux champignons ; *[flavour]* de champignons ; *(= colour)* *[carpet etc]* beige rosé *inv*
mushroom cloud N champignon *m* atomique
mushroom growth N poussée *f* soudaine
mushroom town N ville *f* champignon *inv*

mushrooming /ˈmʌʃrʊmɪŋ/ N 1 *(= picking mushrooms)* cueillette *f* des champignons ; → **mushroom vi 3** 2 *(fig = growth)* *[of town etc]* poussée *f* rapide ; *[of sales, debts, investment]* montée *f* en flèche ; *[of market]* expansion *f or* essor *m* rapide ◆ **the ~ of new shopping centres in the suburbs** *(= proliferation)* la prolifération des centres commerciaux en périphérie des villes ADJ *(= fast-growing)* *[unemployment]* qui monte en flèche ; *[problem]* de plus en plus présent ; *[number]* croissant ; *[growth]* très rapide ; *[population]* qui connaît une croissance rapide

mushy /ˈmʌʃɪ/ ADJ 1 *(= soft)* *[vegetables, fish]* en bouillie ; *[fruit]* blet ; *[snow]* à demi fondu ◆ **to become** *or* **get** *or* **go ~** se ramollir 2 *(pej = sentimental)* *[film, book, sentimentality]* à l'eau de rose COMP **mushy peas** NPL *(Brit)* purée *f* de petits pois

music /ˈmjuːzɪk/ N *(all senses)* musique *f* ◆ **to set to ~** mettre en musique ◆ **it was ~ to his ears** c'était doux à son oreille ◆ **the Faculty of Music** *(Univ)* la faculté de musique ; → **ear¹, face, pop²**
COMP *[teacher, lesson, exam]* de musique
music box N boîte *f* à musique
music case N porte-musique *m inv*
music centre N *(= equipment)* chaîne *f* (stéréo) ; *(= shop)* magasin *m* de hi-fi
music critic N *(Press)* critique *m* musical
music director N directeur *m* musical
music festival N festival *m* de musique
music hall *(Brit)* N music-hall *m* ADJ de music-hall
music lover N mélomane *mf*
music paper N papier *m* à musique
music stand N pupitre *m* à musique
music stool N tabouret *m* *(de musicien)*
music video N *(for single)* vidéoclip *m* ; *(for album)* série *f* de vidéoclips ; *(for concert)* concert *m* en vidéo

musical /ˈmjuːzɪkəl/ ADJ *(lit, fig)* *[voice, sound, criticism, studies]* musical ; *[family, person]* musicien ◆ **he comes from a ~ family** ils sont très musiciens dans sa famille ◆ **she's very ~** *(= gifted)* elle est musicienne, elle est très douée pour la musique ; *(= fond of it)* elle est mélomane N *(Cine, Theat)* comédie *f* musicale
COMP **musical box** N boîte *f* à musique
musical chairs NPL chaises *fpl* musicales ◆ **they were playing at ~ chairs** *(fig)* ils changeaient tout le temps de place
musical comedy N comédie *f* musicale, opérette *f*
musical director N directeur *m* musical
musical evening N soirée *f* musicale
musical instrument N instrument *m* de musique

musically /ˈmjuːzɪkəlɪ/ ADV musicalement ; *[develop]* du point de vue musical ; *(melodiously)* ◆ **she laughed ~** elle a eu un rire mélodieux ◆ **I'm ~ trained** j'ai pris des leçons de musique ◆ **there's a lot going on ~ in London** il se passe beaucoup de choses d'un point de vue musical à Londres ◆ **~ (speaking) this piece is beautiful** musicalement parlant, ce morceau est magnifique

musician /mjuːˈzɪʃən/ N musicien(ne) *m(f)*

musicianship /mjuːˈzɪʃənʃɪp/ N maestria *f* (de musicien), sens *m* de la musique

musicologist /ˌmjuːzɪˈkɒlədʒɪst/ N musicologue *mf*

musicology /ˌmjuːzɪˈkɒlədʒɪ/ N musicologie *f*

musing /ˈmjuːzɪŋ/ ADJ songeur, pensif N songerie *f* ◆ **idle ~s** rêvasseries *fpl*

musingly /ˈmjuːzɪŋlɪ/ ADV d'un air songeur, pensivement

musk /mʌsk/ N musc *m*
COMP **musk ox** N bœuf *m* musqué
musk rose N rose *f* muscade

muskeg /ˈmʌskeg/ N *(US = bog)* tourbière *f*

musket /ˈmʌskɪt/ N mousquet *m*

musketeer /ˌmʌskɪˈtɪəʳ/ N mousquetaire *m* ◆ **the Three Musketeers** les Trois Mousquetaires

musketry /ˈmʌskɪtrɪ/ N tir *m* (au fusil *etc*) COMP *[range, training]* de tir (au fusil *etc*)

muskmelon /ˈmʌskmelən/ N cantaloup *m*

muskrat /ˈmʌskræt/ N rat *m* musqué, ondatra *m*

musky /ˈmʌskɪ/ ADJ musqué

Muslim /ˈmʊzlɪm/ N (pl **Muslims** *or* **Muslim**) musulman(e) *m(f)* ; → **black** ADJ musulman

muslin /ˈmʌzlɪn/ N mousseline *f* COMP de *or* en mousseline

muso * /ˈmjuːzəʊ/ N *(= musician)* musicien(ne) *m(f)* ADJ musical

musquash /ˈmʌskwɒʃ/ N *(= animal)* rat *m* musqué, ondatra *m* ; *(= fur)* rat *m* d'Amérique, ondatra *m* COMP *[coat]* d'ondatra

muss * /mʌs/ VT (also **muss up**) *[+ dress, clothes]* chiffonner, froisser ◆ **to ~ sb's hair** décoiffer qn

mussel /ˈmʌsl/ N moule *f* ◆ **~ bed** parc *m* à moules, moulière *f*

must¹ /mʌst/ LANGUAGE IN USE 10, 15.2
MODAL AUX VB 1 *(obligation)*

> When **must** expresses obligation, it is translated either by the impersonal expression **il faut que**, followed by the subjunctive, or by **devoir**, followed by the infinitive.

◆ **I ~ be going** il faut que j'y aille ◆ **I ~ phone my mother** il faut que j'appelle ma mère ◆ **I ~ see him!** il faut absolument que je le voie ! ◆ **you ~ get your brakes checked** tu dois absolument faire vérifier tes freins, il faut absolument que tu fasses vérifier tes freins ◆ **you ~ hand in your work on time** tu dois rendre ton travail à temps, il faut que tu rendes ton travail à temps ◆ **why ~ you always be so pessimistic?** pourquoi faut-il toujours que tu sois si pessimiste ? ◆ **this is what ~ be done now** voici ce qu'il faut faire maintenant ◆ **how long ~ I continue with the tablets?** pendant combien de temps dois-je continuer à prendre les comprimés ? ◆ **I ~ ask you not to touch that** *(frm)* je dois vous prier *or* je vous prie de ne pas toucher à cela ◆ **you ~ know that ...** *(frm: = I must tell you)* il faut que vous sachiez que ...
◆ **must not** *(= should not)* ◆ **we ~ not repeat the mistakes of the 20th century** nous devons

éviter de reproduire les erreurs commises au 20e siècle ◆ **you ~ not forget this** n'oubliez pas ceci ◆ **patients ~ not be put at risk** il ne faut pas mettre en danger la santé des patients ◆ **"the windows must not be opened"** *(on notice)* "défense d'ouvrir les fenêtres"

◆ **it must be +** *past participle* ◆ **it ~ be noted that not all officers obeyed orders** notez que tous les officiers n'ont pas obéi aux ordres ◆ **it ~ be remembered that this is a serious disease** il ne faut pas oublier qu'il s'agit d'une maladie grave ◆ **it ~ not be forgotten that ...** il ne faut pas oublier que ...

◆ **if I** (*or* **you** *or* **we) must** s'il le faut, si c'est nécessaire ◆ **(well), if I ~** eh bien, s'il le faut vraiment *or* si c'est vraiment nécessaire ◆ **we'll handle them by ourselves if we ~** nous nous occuperons d'eux tout seuls s'il le faut *or* si c'est nécessaire ◆ **kill me if you ~, not him** si vous devez tuer quelqu'un, tuez-moi, pas lui

◆ **if you must know** si tu tiens vraiment à le savoir, si tu veux vraiment le savoir ◆ **I've been to Jan's for dinner, if you ~ know** je suis allé dîner chez Jan, si tu tiens vraiment à le savoir *or* si tu veux vraiment le savoir

◆ **I must say** *or* **admit** je dois avouer ◆ **this came as a surprise, I ~ say** je dois avouer que cela m'a surpris ◆ **I ~ admit I'm envious** je dois avouer que je suis jaloux ◆ **I ~ say, he's very irritating** il est vraiment très agaçant ◆ **it took a long time, I ~ say!** ça a pris drôlement longtemps ! ◆ **well, you've got a nerve, I ~ say!** eh bien, tu es drôlement culotté !

2 *(invitations, suggestions)*

When **you must** is used to make invitations and suggestions more forceful, the imperative may be used in French.

◆ **you ~ come and have dinner some time** venez dîner à la maison un de ces jours ◆ **you ~ be very careful** faites bien attention ◆ **you ~ stop being so negative** ne sois pas si négatif

◆ **you mustn't** *(= don't)* ◆ **you mustn't touch it** n'y touche pas ◆ **you mustn't forget to send her a card** n'oublie pas de lui envoyer une carte

3 *(indicating certainty)* **he ~ be wrong** il doit se tromper, il se trompe certainement ◆ **you ~ know my aunt** vous devez connaître ma tante, vous connaissez sans doute ma tante ◆ **that ~ be Paul** ça doit être Paul ◆ **he ~ be regretting it, mustn't he?** il le regrette sûrement ◆ **he ~ be clever, mustn't he?** il faut croire qu'il est intelligent, non ? ◆ **he ~ be mad!** il est fou, ma parole ! ◆ **you ~ be joking!** vous plaisantez !

When **must** indicates certainty in the past, it is translated by the imperfect of **devoir**.

◆ **I thought he ~ be really old** je me suis dit qu'il devait être très vieux ◆ **he said there ~ be some mistake** il a dit qu'il devait y avoir une erreur

◆ **must have made/had/been** *etc*

The perfect tense of **devoir** + infinitive is generally used to translate **must have** + past participle.

◆ **I ~ have made a mistake** j'ai dû me tromper ◆ **you ~ have had some idea of the situation** tu as dû te rendre compte de la situation ◆ **was he disappointed? – he ~ have been!** est-ce qu'il a été déçu ? – sûrement ! ◆ **I realized she ~ have heard what we'd said** j'ai compris qu'elle avait dû nous entendre

N * chose *f* indispensable, must* *m* ◆ **a ~ for all housewives!** un must* pour toutes les ménagères !, indispensable pour toutes les ménagères ! ◆ **this concert is a ~ for all Barry Manilow fans** ce concert est un must* pour tous les fans de Barry Manilow ◆ **this book is a ~** c'est un livre à lire absolument ◆ **a car is a ~ in the country** une voiture est absolument indispensable à la campagne

must² /mʌst/ N *[of fruit]* moût *m*

must- * /mʌst/ PREF ◆ **a ~see movie** un film à ne pas manquer ◆ **Machu Picchu is a ~see for any visitor to Peru** le Machu Picchu est LE site à visiter au Pérou ◆ **a ~read** un livre à lire absolument ◆ **the ~have fashion item of the season** le must* de la saison ◆ **it was a ~win match** c'était un match qu'ils devaient gagner

mustache /ˈmʌstæʃ/ N *(US)* ⇒ **moustache**

mustang /ˈmʌstæŋ/ N mustang *m*

mustard /ˈmʌstəd/ N *(= plant, condiment)* moutarde *f* ◆ **to cut the ~** * faire le poids, être à la hauteur ; → **keen¹** ADJ moutarde

COMP **mustard and cress** N *salade de cresson alénois et de pousses de moutarde blanche*
mustard bath N bain *m* sinapisé *or* à la moutarde
mustard gas N ypérite *f*, gaz *m* moutarde
mustard plaster N sinapisme *m*, cataplasme *m* sinapisé
mustard pot N moutardier *m*, pot *m* à moutarde
mustard powder N farine *f* de moutarde

muster /ˈmʌstəʳ/ N *(= gathering)* assemblée *f* ; *(Mil, Naut:* also **muster roll**) rassemblement *m* ; *(= roll-call)* appel *m* ◆ **to pass ~** *(fig)* (pouvoir) passer, être acceptable VT 1 *(= assemble, collect)* *[+ helpers, number, sum]* réunir ; (also **muster up**) *[+ strength, courage, energy]* rassembler ◆ **I couldn't ~ (up) enough energy to protest** je n'ai pas trouvé l'énergie de protester ◆ **they could only ~ five volunteers** ils n'ont trouvé que cinq volontaires ◆ **the club can only ~ 20 members** le club ne compte que 20 membres 2 *(= call roll of)* battre le rappel de VI *(= gather, assemble)* se réunir, se rassembler COMP **muster station** N *(on ship)* point *m* de rassemblement

mustiness /ˈmʌstɪnɪs/ N *(= stale taste)* goût *m* de moisi ; *(= stale smell)* odeur *f* de renfermé ; *(= damp smell)* odeur *f* de moisi

mustn't /ˈmʌsnt/ ⇒ **must not ;** → **must**

musty /ˈmʌstɪ/ ADJ 1 *[taste]* de moisi ; *[smell] (= stale)* de renfermé ; *(= damp)* de moisi ; *[book, clothes]* moisi ◆ **to grow ~** moisir ◆ **to smell ~** *[room]* sentir le renfermé ; *[book, clothes]* avoir une odeur de moisi 2 *(= hackneyed) [ideas, methods]* suranné

mutability /ˌmjuːtəˈbɪlɪtɪ/ N mutabilité *f*

mutable /ˈmjuːtəbl/ ADJ sujet à mutation ; *[virus, gene]* mutable ; *(Ling)* sujet à la mutation

mutagen /ˈmjuːtədʒən/ N mutagène *m*

mutagenic /mjuːtəˈdʒenɪk/ ADJ mutagène

mutant /ˈmjuːtənt/ ADJ, N mutant (e) *m(f)*

mutate /mjuːˈteɪt/ VI 1 *(lit = undergo mutation)* subir une mutation 2 *(fig = change)* se transformer *(into sth* en qch) VT faire subir une mutation à

mutation /mjuːˈteɪʃən/ N *(gen, Ling)* mutation *f*

mutatis mutandis /muːˈtɑːtɪsmuːˈtændɪs/ ADV mutatis mutandis

mute /mjuːt/ ADJ 1 *[person, reproach]* muet ; *[consent]* tacite ◆ **~ with admiration, in ~ admiration** muet d'admiration ◆ **he turned to her in ~ appeal** il lui lança un regard suppliant ◆ **to be** *or* **bear ~ testimony** *or* **witness to sth** être un témoin silencieux *or* muet de qch 2 *(Ling)* **H ~** H muet ◆ **~ "e"** "e" muet N 1 *(Med † = deaf person)* muet(te) *m(f)* ; → **deaf** 2 *(Mus)* sourdine *f* VT 1 *(Mus) [+ trumpet, violin etc]* mettre la sourdine à 2 *[+ sound]* assourdir, rendre moins sonore ; *[+ colour]* adoucir, atténuer 3 *[+ feelings, emotions, enthusiasm]* tempérer, modérer ◆ **to ~ one's criticism of sth** tempérer *or* modérer ses critiques de qch COMP **mute swan** N cygne *m* tuberculé *or* muet

muted /ˈmjuːtɪd/ ADJ *[voice, sound]* sourd, assourdi ; *[colour]* sourd ; *(Mus) [violin]* en sourdine ; *[criticism, protest, feelings, enthusiasm]* tempéré

mutilate /ˈmjuːtɪleɪt/ VT *[+ person, limb]* mutiler, estropier ; *[+ object]* mutiler, dégrader ; *(fig) [+ text]* mutiler, tronquer

mutilation /ˌmjuːtɪˈleɪʃən/ N mutilation *f*

mutineer /ˌmjuːtɪˈnɪəʳ/ N *(Mil, Naut)* mutiné *m*, mutin *m*

mutinous /ˈmjuːtɪnəs/ ADJ *[crew, soldiers]* prêt à se mutiner, mutin ; *[workers, prisoners]* rebelle ; *[feelings]* de rébellion ; *[attitude, mood]* rebelle ; *[look]* de défi ◆ **the children were already fairly ~** les enfants regimbaient déjà

mutiny /ˈmjuːtɪnɪ/ N *(Mil, Naut)* mutinerie *f* ; *(fig)* révolte *f* VI se mutiner ; *(fig)* se révolter

mutt ‡ /mʌt/ N 1 *(= fool)* corniaud* *m*, crétin(e)* *m(f)* 2 *(= dog)* clebs* *m*, corniaud *m*

mutter /ˈmʌtəʳ/ N marmonnement *m* ; *(= grumbling)* grommellement *m*

VT *[+ word, excuse, threat, prayer]* marmonner, marmotter ; *[+ curses, obscenities]* marmonner, grommeler ◆ **"no", he ~ed** "non" marmonna-t-il *or* dit-il entre ses dents ◆ **he ~ed something to himself** il a marmonné *or* marmotté quelque chose entre ses dents ◆ **a ~ed conversation** une conversation à voix basse ◆ **to ~ that** marmonner que

VI marmonner, murmurer ; *(= grumble)* grommeler, grogner ◆ **to ~ to oneself** *(talking)* marmonner *or* marmotter entre ses dents ; *(complaining)* grommeler entre ses dents ◆ **she was ~ing about the bad weather** elle maugréait contre le mauvais temps ◆ **to ~ about doing sth** parler de faire qch ◆ **the man who dared to say what others only ~ed about** l'homme qui osait dire tout haut ce que les autres pensaient tout bas

muttering /ˈmʌtərɪŋ/ N grommellement *m*

mutton /ˈmʌtn/ N *(Culin)* mouton *m* ◆ **leg of ~** gigot *m* ◆ **shoulder of ~** épaule *f* de mouton ◆ **she's ~ dressed (up) as lamb** * elle s'habille trop jeune pour son âge ; → **dead, leg**

COMP **mutton chop** N côtelette *f* de mouton
mutton chops * NPL *(= whiskers)* favoris *mpl (bien fournis)*, rouflaquettes *fpl*

muttonhead ‡ /ˈmʌtnhed/ N cornichon* *m*

mutual /ˈmjuːtjʊəl/ ADJ 1 *(= reciprocal) [support, hatred, respect, need, destruction]* mutuel ◆ **~ aid** entraide *f*, aide *f* mutuelle ◆ **I didn't like him and the feeling was ~** je ne l'aimais pas et c'était réciproque 2 *(= common) [interest, friend]* commun ◆ **it is to our ~ benefit** *or* **advantage** c'est dans notre intérêt commun ◆ **by ~ consent** par consentement mutuel

COMP **mutual assured destruction** N *(US Mil)* destruction *f* mutuelle assurée
mutual fund (company) N *(US)* société *f* d'investissement *(de type SICAV)*
mutual insurance (company) N mutuelle *f*
mutual masturbation N masturbation *f* mutuelle
mutual society N mutuelle *f*

mutuality /ˌmjuːtjʊˈælɪtɪ/ N mutualité *f*

mutually /ˈmjuːtjʊəlɪ/ ADV *[convenient, acceptable, beneficial]* mutuellement ◆ **a ~ agreed goal** un objectif convenu ◆ **~ contradictory** contradictoire ◆ **the two things are not ~ exclusive** ces deux choses ne sont pas incompatibles COMP **mutually assured destruction** N ⇒ **mutual assured destruction ;** → **mutual**

Muzak ® /ˈmjuːzæk/ N musique *f* (d'ambiance) enregistrée

muzzle /ˈmʌzl/ **N** 1 *[of dog, fox etc]* museau *m* ; *[of gun]* bouche *f*, gueule *f* 2 *(= anti-biting device)* muselière *f* ; *(fig)* muselière *f*, bâillon *m* **VT** *[+ dog]* museler ; *(fig)* museler, bâillonner
COMP **muzzle loader** **N** arme *f* qu'on charge par le canon
muzzle velocity **N** vitesse *f* initiale

muzzy /ˈmʌzɪ/ **ADJ** *(Brit)* 1 *(= groggy, confused)* *[brain]* brouillé ; *[feeling]* de confusion ; *[ideas]* confus, nébuleux ◆ **to be** *or* **feel ~** *[person]* avoir le cerveau brouillé 2 *(= blurred)* *[TV picture]* flou ; *[outline]* estompé, flou

MVP **N** *(US Sport)* (abbrev of **most valuable player**) *(= person)* meilleur joueur *m*, meilleure joueuse *f* ; *(= title)* titre *m* de meilleur joueur

MW **N** 1 *(Rad)* (abbrev of **medium wave**) PO 2 *(Elec)* (abbrev of **megawatt(s)**) MW

my /maɪ/ **POSS ADJ** mon, ma, mes ◆ **~ book** mon livre ◆ **~ table** ma table ◆ **~ friend** mon ami(e) ◆ **~ clothes** mes vêtements ◆ **MY book** mon livre à moi ◆ **I've broken ~ leg** je me suis cassé la jambe **EXCL** ◆ **(oh) ~ !** * ◆ **~, ~ !*** ça, par exemple !

myalgia /maɪˈældʒə/ **N** myalgie *f*

myalgic encephalomyelitis /maɪˈældʒɪkenˌsefələʊmaɪəˈlaɪtɪs/ **N** *(Med)* encéphalomyélite *f* myalgique

Myanmar /ˈmaɪænmɑːʳ/ **N** Myanmar *m* ◆ **in ~** au Myanmar

mycology /maɪˈkɒlədʒɪ/ **N** mycologie *f*

mycosis /maɪˈkəʊsɪs/ **N** mycose *f*

mynah /ˈmaɪnə/ **N** (also **mynah bird**) mainate *m*

myocardial infarction /ˈmaɪəʊˌkɑːdɪəl ɪnˈfɑːkʃən/ **N** infarctus *m* du myocarde

myopia /maɪˈəʊpɪə/ **N** myopie *f*

myopic /maɪˈɒpɪk/ **ADJ** *(Opt)* myope ; *(fig)* *[attitude]* peu prévoyant, à courte vue ◆ **this is a somewhat ~ view** c'est une vision à court terme

myriad /ˈmɪrɪəd/ **N** myriade *f* ◆ **a ~ of** une myriade de **ADJ** *(liter)* innombrable, sans nombre

myrmidon /ˈmɜːmɪdən/ **N** *(pej hum)* sbire *m*

myrrh /mɜːʳ/ **N** myrrhe *f*

myrtle /ˈmɜːtl/ **N** myrte *m*

myself /maɪˈself/ **PERS PRON** *(reflexive: direct and indirect)* me ; *(emphatic)* moi-même ; *(after prep)* moi ◆ **I've hurt ~** je me suis blessé ◆ **I said to ~** je me suis dit ◆ **I spoke to him ~** je lui ai parlé moi-même ◆ **people like ~** des gens comme moi ◆ **I've kept one for ~** j'en ai gardé un pour moi ◆ **he asked me for a photo of ~** il m'a demandé une photo de moi ◆ **I told him ~** je le lui ai dit moi-même ◆ **I'm not ~ today** je ne suis pas dans mon assiette aujourd'hui
◆ **(all) by myself** tout seul

mysterious /mɪsˈtɪərɪəs/ **ADJ** *[person, object, disappearance, illness, power]* mystérieux ; *[smile]* mystérieux, énigmatique ◆ **why are you being so ~?** pourquoi tous ces mystères ? ◆ **God moves in ~ ways** les voies du Seigneur sont impénétrables

mysteriously /mɪsˈtɪərɪəslɪ/ **ADV** mystérieusement

mystery /ˈmɪstərɪ/ **N** 1 *(gen, Rel)* mystère *m* ◆ **there's no ~ about it** ça n'a rien de mystérieux ◆ **it's a ~ to me how he did it** je n'arrive pas à comprendre comment il l'a fait ◆ **to make a great ~ of sth** faire grand mystère de qch 2 *(Theat:* also **mystery play**) mystère *m* 3 *(Literat:* also **mystery story**) roman *m* à énigmes
COMP *[ship, man]* mystérieux
mystery play **N** *(Theat)* mystère *m*
mystery tour **N** *(in coach etc)* voyage *m* surprise *(dont on ne connaît pas la destination)*

mystic /ˈmɪstɪk/ **ADJ** *(Rel)* mystique ; *[power]* occulte ; *[rite]* ésotérique ; *[truth]* surnaturel ; *[formula]* magique **N** mystique *mf*

mystical /ˈmɪstɪkəl/ **ADJ** mystique

mysticism /ˈmɪstɪsɪzəm/ **N** mysticisme *m*

mystification /ˌmɪstɪfɪˈkeɪʃən/ **N** 1 *(= bewilderment)* perplexité *f* 2 *[of issue, subject]* mystification *f*

mystify /ˈmɪstɪfaɪ/ **VT** rendre *or* laisser perplexe ; *(= deliberately deceive)* mystifier

mystique /mɪsˈtiːk/ **N** mystique *f*

myth /mɪθ/ **N** *(lit, fig)* mythe *m*

mythic /ˈmɪθɪk/ **ADJ** *[figure, symbol, status]* mythique ; *[proportions]* fabuleux

mythical /ˈmɪθɪkəl/ **ADJ** *[beast, creature, figure]* mythique ; *[world]* fictif, mythique

mythological /ˌmɪθəˈlɒdʒɪkəl/ **ADJ** mythologique

mythology /mɪˈθɒlədʒɪ/ **N** mythologie *f*

myxomatosis /ˌmɪksəʊməˈtəʊsɪs/ **N** myxomatose *f*

Nn

N, n /en/ **N** ① (= *letter*) N, n *m* ◆ **N for Nancy** ≈ N comme Noémie ② (*Math*) **to the nth (power)** à la puissance n ◆ **to the nth degree** (*fig*) à la puissance mille ◆ **I told him for the nth time* to stop talking** je lui ai dit pour la énième fois de se taire ◆ **there are n ways of doing it** il y a mille *or* des tas de* façons de le faire ③ (abbrev of **north**) N ④ (*Elec*) (abbrev of **neutral**) N

'n'⁑ /ən/ **CONJ** ⇒ **and**

n/a ① (abbrev of **not applicable**) ne s'applique pas ② (*Banking*) (abbrev of **no account**) pas de compte

NAACP /eneɪˌeɪsiːˈpiː/ **N** (*US*) (abbrev of **National Association for the Advancement of Colored People**) *organisation de défense des droits civiques des Noirs*

NAAFI /ˈnæfɪ/ **N** (*Brit Mil*) (abbrev of **Navy, Army and Air Force Institute**) coopérative *f* militaire

nab* /næb/ **VT** ① (= *catch in wrongdoing*) pincer*, choper⁑ ② (= *catch to speak to etc*) attraper, coincer* ③ (= *take*) [*+ sb's pen, chair*] piquer*

nabob /ˈneɪbɒb/ **N** (*lit, fig*) nabab *m*

nacelle /næˈsel/ **N** (*of aircraft*) nacelle *f*

nacho /ˈnɑːtʃəʊ/ **N** (pl **nachos**) (*Culin*) nacho *m*

nacre /ˈneɪkəʳ/ **N** nacre *f*

nacred /ˈneɪkəd/, **nacreous** /ˈneɪkrɪəs/ **ADJ** nacré

nada* /ˈnɑːdə/ **PRON** (*US*) rien

Naderism /ˈneɪdərɪzəm/ **N** consumérisme *m*, défense *f* du consommateur

nadir /ˈneɪdɪəʳ/ **N** (*Astron*) nadir *m* ; (*fig*) point *m* le plus bas ◆ **in the ~ of despair** dans le plus profond désespoir ◆ **his fortunes reached their ~ when ...** il atteignit le comble de l'infortune quand ...

naevus, nevus (*US*) /ˈniːvəs/ **N** (pl **naevi**, (*US*) **nevi** /ˈniːvaɪ/) nævus *m*

naff⁑ /næf/ (*Brit*) **ADJ** tarte*, ringard*

► **naff off**⁑ **VI** foutre le camp⁑

naffing⁑ /ˈnæfɪŋ/ **ADJ** (*Brit*) foutu⁑

NAFTA /ˈnæftə/ **N** (abbrev of **North American Free Trade Agreement**) ALENA *f*

nag¹ /næg/ **VT** (also **nag at**) [*person*] harceler, asticoter* ; [*worries*] harceler, accabler ; [*doubt*] harceler, assaillir ; [*anxiety*] tenailler ◆ **he was ~ging (at) me to tidy my room** il me harcelait *or* m'asticotait* pour que je range *subj* ma chambre ◆ **to ~ sb into doing sth** harceler *or* asticoter* qn jusqu'à ce qu'il fasse qch ◆ **to ~ sb about sth** embêter* qn avec qch ◆ **to ~ sb to do sth** *or* **about doing sth** harceler *or* asticoter* qn pour qu'il fasse qch ◆ **she ~ged him about never being home** elle lui reprochait de ne jamais être à la maison ◆ **his conscience was ~ging (at) him** sa conscience le travaillait ◆ **~ged by doubts** rongé par le doute

VI [*person*] (= *scold*) ne pas arrêter de faire des remarques ; [*pain, doubts*] être harcelant ◆ **to ~ at sb** ⇒ **vt**

N ◆ **he's a dreadful ~** * (*scolding*) il n'arrête pas de faire des remarques ; (*pestering*) il n'arrête pas de nous (*or* le *etc*) harceler

nag²* /næg/ **N** (= *horse*) cheval *m* ; (*pej*) canasson* *m* (*pej*)

Nagasaki /ˌnɑːgəˈsɑːkɪ/ **N** Nagasaki

nagger /ˈnægəʳ/ **N** ⇒ **nag¹ noun**

nagging /ˈnægɪŋ/ **ADJ** ① [*doubt, feeling, fear, worry, question*] persistant ; [*pain*] tenace ② [*voice*] insistant ◆ **she lost patience with her ~ mother** les remarques continuelles de sa mère lui ont fait perdre patience **N** (*NonC*) remarques *fpl* continuelles

NAHT /ˌeneɪeɪtʃˈtiː/ **N** (*Brit*) (abbrev of **National Association of Head Teachers**) *association nationale des chefs d'établissements*

naiad /ˈnaɪæd/ **N** (pl **naiads** *or* **naiades** /ˈnaɪədiːz/) naïade *f*

nail /neɪl/ **N** ① [*of finger, toe*] ongle *m* ; → **bite, fingernail, toenail, tooth**

② (= *spike*) clou *m* ◆ **to pay on the ~** payer rubis sur l'ongle ◆ **to demand cash on the ~** demander à être payé rubis sur l'ongle ◆ **that decision was a** *or* **another ~ in his coffin** cette décision a été un nouveau coup dur pour lui ◆ **to be as hard** *or* **tough as ~s** (= *resilient*) être coriace ; (*towards other people*) être impitoyable ; → **bed, hit**

VT ① (= *fix with nails*) clouer ◆ **to ~ the lid on(to) a crate** clouer le couvercle d'une caisse ◆ **to be ~ed to the spot** *or* **ground** rester cloué sur place ◆ **to ~ one's colours to the mast** proclamer une fois pour toutes sa position ◆ **the Prime Minister has ~ed his colours firmly to the European mast** le Premier ministre a proclamé une fois pour toutes qu'il était pro-européen ◆ **it's like trying to ~ Jell-O® to the wall*** (*US*) autant essayer de vider la mer avec une petite cuiller

② (= *put nails into*) clouter ◆ **~ed shoes** chaussures *fpl* cloutées

③ * (= *catch in crime etc*) [*+ person*] pincer*, choper* ; (= *expose*) [*+ lie*] démasquer ; [*+ rumour*] démentir

④ (* = *hit with shot etc*) descendre*, abattre

COMP **nail-biting** **N** habitude *f* de se ronger les ongles **ADJ** [*film*] à suspense, angoissant ; [*finish, match*] serré

nail bomb **N** ≈ bombe *f* de fabrication artisanale

nail clippers **NPL** coupe-ongles *m inv*, pince *f* à ongles

nail enamel **N** (*US*) ⇒ **nail lacquer**

nail lacquer, nail polish **N** vernis *m* à ongles

nail polish remover **N** dissolvant *m*

nail scissors **NPL** ciseaux *mpl* à ongles

nail varnish **N** (*Brit*) ⇒ **nail polish**

nail varnish remover **N** (*Brit*) ⇒ **nail polish remover**

► **nail down** **VT SEP** ① [*+ lid*] clouer

② (*fig*) [*+ hesitating person*] obtenir une décision de ; [*+ agreement, policy*] établir, arrêter ◆ **I ~ed him down to coming at 6 o'clock** je l'ai réduit *or* contraint à accepter de venir à 6 heures

► **nail up** **VT SEP** ① [*+ picture etc*] fixer par des clous

② [*+ door, window*] condamner (en clouant)

③ [*+ box, crate*] clouer ◆ **to ~ up goods in a crate** empaqueter des marchandises dans une caisse clouée

nailbrush /ˈneɪlbrʌʃ/ **N** brosse *f* à ongles

nailfile /ˈneɪlfaɪl/ **N** lime *f* à ongles

Nairobi /naɪˈrəʊbɪ/ **N** Nairobi

naïve, naive /naɪˈiːv/ **ADJ** ① (*pej* = *unrealistic*) [*person, belief, optimism*] naïf (naïve *f*) ◆ **politically ~** naïf sur le plan politique ◆ **it is ~ to think that ...** il faut être naïf pour croire que ... ② (= *innocent*) [*person, charm*] ingénu ③ (*Art*) [*painting, style*] naïf (naïve *f*)

naïvely, naively /naɪˈiːvlɪ/ **ADV** [*think, assume, expect, believe*] naïvement ◆ **to be ~ idealistic** être d'un idéalisme naïf

naïveté, naiveté /naɪˈiːvteɪ/, **naivety** /naɪˈiːvtɪ/ **N** naïveté *f*, ingénuité *f*

naked /ˈneɪkɪd/ **ADJ** ① [*person, body, flesh, animal, light bulb, sword*] nu ; [*wire*] dénudé ◆ **to go ~** être (tout) nu ◆ **to sunbathe ~** se bronzer (tout) nu, faire du bronzage intégral ◆ **~ to the waist** torse nu ◆ **~ except for his socks** tout nu à part ses chaussettes, avec ses chaussettes pour seul vêtement ◆ **to feel ~ without sth** se sentir nu sans qch ◆ **(as) ~ as the day he/she was born** nu/nue comme un ver, en costume d'Adam/d'Ève ◆ **to see sth with the ~ eye** voir qch à l'œil nu ◆ **visible/invisible to the ~ eye** visible/invisible à l'œil nu ◆ **a ~ flame** une flamme (nue) ; → **stark, strip** ② (= *pure*) [*hatred*] non déguisé ; [*greed*] éhonté ; [*attempt*] flagrant ; [*ambition, aggression*] pur ; [*facts*] brut

♦ **the ~ truth** la vérité toute nue [3] *(liter = defenceless) [person]* sans défense

nakedly /ˈneɪkɪdlɪ/ ADV ouvertement ♦ **he was ~ ambitious** il ne cachait pas son ambition

nakedness /ˈneɪkɪdnɪs/ N nudité *f*

namby-pamby * /ˈnæmbɪˈpæmbɪ/ *(pej)* N gnangnan * *mf* ADJ gnangnan * *inv*

name /neɪm/ N [1] nom *m* ♦ **what's your ~?** comment vous appelez-vous ?, quel est votre nom ? ♦ **my ~ is Robert** je m'appelle Robert, mon nom est Robert ♦ **his real ~ is Piers Knight** il s'appelle Piers Knight de son vrai nom, son vrai nom est Piers Knight ♦ **what ~ are they giving the child?** comment vont-ils appeler l'enfant ? ♦ **they married to give the child a ~** ils se sont mariés pour que l'enfant soit légitime ♦ **what ~ shall I say?** *(on telephone)* c'est de la part de qui ? ; *(announcing arrival)* qui dois-je annoncer ? ♦ **please fill in your ~ and address** prière d'inscrire vos nom, prénom et adresse ♦ **to take sb's ~ and address** noter le nom et l'adresse *or* les coordonnées de qn ♦ **to put one's ~ down for a job** poser sa candidature à un poste ♦ **to put one's ~ down for a competition/for a class** s'inscrire à un concours/à un cours ♦ **we've put our ~ down for a council house** on a fait une demande pour avoir un logement social ♦ **to have one's ~ taken** *(Sport)* recevoir un avertissement ♦ **to name ~s** donner des noms ♦ **to name** *or* **mention no ~s, naming** *or* **mentioning no ~s** pour ne nommer personne ♦ **without mentioning any ~s** sans nommer *or* citer personne ♦ **that's the ~ of the game** *(= that's what matters)* c'est ce qui compte ; *(= that's how it is)* c'est comme ça ♦ **I'll do it or my ~'s not Robert Smith!** * je le ferai, foi de Robert Smith ! ; → **first, know, maiden, pet¹**

♦ **by + name** ♦ **to refer to sb by ~** désigner qn par son nom ♦ **this man, Smith by ~** *or* **by the ~ of Smith** cet homme, qui répond au nom de Smith ♦ **he goes by the ~ of ...** il est connu sous le nom de ... ♦ **we know him by the ~ of ...** on le connaît sous le nom de ... ♦ **to go by the ~ of ...** se faire appeler ...

♦ **in + name** ♦ **in ~ only** *or* **alone** de nom seulement ♦ **to exist in ~ only** *or* **in ~ alone** n'exister que de nom ; *[power, rights]* être nominal ♦ **a marriage in ~ only** un mariage qui n'en est pas un ♦ **he is king in ~ only** il n'est roi que de nom, il n'a de roi que le nom ♦ **she's the boss in all but ~** elle est le patron sans en avoir le titre

♦ **in the name of ...** au nom de ... ♦ **terrible crimes were committed in the ~ of patriotism** des crimes atroces ont été commis au nom du patriotisme ♦ **in God's ~** pour l'amour du ciel *or* de Dieu ♦ **in the king's ~** au nom du roi, de par le roi ♦ **what in Heaven's** * *or* **God's** * **~ are you doing?** mais qu'est-ce que tu fais, pour l'amour du ciel ? ♦ **what in Heaven's** * *or* **God's** * **~ does that mean?** mais qu'est-ce que ça peut bien vouloir dire ?

♦ **to one's name** ♦ **she has five bestsellers/gold medals to her ~** elle a cinq best-sellers/médailles d'or à son actif ♦ **she only has one pair of shoes to her ~** elle n'a qu'une seule paire de chaussures ♦ **I haven't a penny to my ~** * je n'ai pas un sou, je suis sans le sou

♦ **under the name of** sous le nom de ♦ **the drug is sold under the ~ of ...** le médicament est vendu sous le nom de ... ♦ **he goes under the ~ of Steve Jones** il se fait appeler Steve Jones ♦ **he writes under the ~ of John Smith** il écrit sous le pseudonyme de John Smith

[2] *(= reputation)* réputation *f*, renom *m* ♦ **he has a ~ for honesty** il est réputé honnête, il a la réputation d'être honnête ♦ **he has a ~ for stubbornness** il a la réputation d'être têtu ♦ **to protect one's (good) ~** protéger sa réputation ♦ **this firm has a good ~** cette maison a (une) bonne réputation ♦ **to have a bad ~** avoir (une) mauvaise réputation ♦ **to get a bad ~** se faire une mauvaise réputation ♦ **my ~ is mud** * **in this place** je ne suis pas en odeur de sainteté ici, je suis grillé * ici ♦ **if I do that my ~ will be mud** * **in the office** si je fais ça, c'en est fini de ma réputation *or* je suis grillé * au bureau ; → **dog, vain**

♦ **to make + name** ♦ **this book made his ~** ce livre l'a rendu célèbre ♦ **to make a ~ for o.s. (as)** se faire une réputation *or* un nom (comme *or* en tant que) ♦ **he made his ~ as a singer** il s'est fait un nom en tant que chanteur

[3] *(= famous person)* **all the great** *or* **big ~s were there** toutes les célébrités étaient là ♦ **he's one of the big ~s in show business** c'est un des grands noms du show-business

[4] *(= insult)* **to call sb ~s** injurier qn, traiter qn de tous les noms ♦ **he called me ~s!** il m'a traité de tous les noms ! ♦ **~s can't hurt me** les injures ne me touchent pas

[5] *(Fin)* (also **Lloyd's name**) *membre de la Lloyd's*

VT [1] *(= call by a name, give a name to)* nommer, appeler ; *[+ ship]* baptiser ; *[+ comet, star, mountain]* donner un nom à ♦ **a person ~d Smith** un(e) nommé(e) Smith ♦ **the child was ~d Isobel** on a appelé l'enfant Isobel ♦ **to ~ a child after** *or* **for sb** donner à un enfant le nom de qn ♦ **the child was ~d after his father** l'enfant a reçu le nom de son père ♦ **they ~d him Winston after Churchill** ils l'ont appelé Winston en souvenir de Churchill ♦ **tell me how plants are ~d** expliquez-moi l'appellation des plantes

[2] *(= give name of)* nommer ; *(= list)* nommer, citer ; *(= fix) [+ date, price]* fixer ♦ **he was ~d for the chairmanship** son nom a été avancé pour la présidence ♦ **he ~d his son (as) his heir** il a désigné son fils comme héritier ♦ **he refused to ~ his accomplices** il a refusé de nommer ses complices *or* de révéler les noms de ses complices ♦ **my collaborators are ~d in the preface** mes collaborateurs sont mentionnés dans l'avant-propos ♦ **~ the presidents** donnez le nom des présidents, nommez les présidents ♦ **~ the chief works of Shakespeare** citez les principaux ouvrages de Shakespeare ♦ **~ your price** fixez votre prix ♦ **to ~ the day** *(for wedding)* fixer la date du mariage ♦ **you ~ it, they have it!** * *[shop]* ils ont tous les produits possibles et imaginables ; *[family]* ils ont tous les gadgets ♦ **he was ~d as chairman** il a été nommé président ♦ **he has been ~d as the leader of the expedition** on l'a désigné pour diriger l'expédition ♦ **he was ~d as the thief** on a dit que c'était lui le voleur ♦ **they have been ~d as witnesses** ils ont été cités comme témoins ♦ **to ~ and shame sb** * désigner qn du doigt *(fig)*

COMP **name-calling** N injures *fpl*

name-check → **name-check**

name day N fête *f*

name-drop VI émailler sa conversation de noms de gens en vue

name-dropper * N ♦ **he's a dreadful ~-dropper** il émaille toujours sa conversation de noms de gens en vue, à l'entendre il connaît la terre entière

name-dropping * N ♦ **there was so much ~-dropping in his speech** son discours était truffé de noms de gens en vue

name part N *(Theat)* rôle-titre *m*

name tape N marque *f (sur du linge ou des vêtements)*

name-check /ˈneɪmtʃek/ N mention *f* ♦ **to get a ~** être nommément cité VT citer nommément

-named /neɪmd/ ADJ *(in compounds)* ♦ **the first-named** le premier, la première ♦ **the last-named** ce dernier, cette dernière

nameless /ˈneɪmlɪs/ ADJ [1] *(= unnamed) [person, grave]* anonyme ; *[baby, town, island]* sans nom ♦ **to remain ~** *(= anonymous)* garder l'anonymat ♦ **a certain person, who shall be** *or* **remain ~** une certaine personne, que je ne nommerai pas [2] *(= indefinable) [terror, sensation, emotion]* indéfinissable ; *(= unmentionable) [vice, crime]* innommable

namely /ˈneɪmlɪ/ ADV à savoir ♦ **two of them, ~ Emma and Harry** deux d'entre eux, (à savoir) Emma et Harry ♦ **~ that ...** à savoir que ...

nameplate /ˈneɪmpleɪt/ N *(on door etc)* plaque *f* ; *(on manufactured goods)* plaque *f* du fabricant *or* du constructeur

namesake /ˈneɪmseɪk/ N homonyme *m*

Namibia /nɑːˈmɪbɪə/ N Namibie *f*

Namibian /nɑːˈmɪbɪən/ ADJ namibien N Namibien(ne) *m(f)*

nan¹ /nɑːn/ N (also **nan bread**) nan *m (pain indien)*

nan² * /næn/, **nana** * /ˈnænə/ N *(Brit = grandmother)* mamie *f*, mémé *f*

nance ‡ /næns/, **nancy** ‡ /ˈnænsɪ/, **nancy-boy** ‡ /ˈnænsɪbɔɪ/ N *(Brit pej)* tante ‡ *f (pej)*, tapette ‡ *f (pej)*

nandrolone /ˈnændrələʊn/ N nandrolone *f*

nankeen /nænˈkiːn/ N *(= fabric)* nankin *m*

nanny /ˈnænɪ/ N [1] *(= live-in carer)* bonne *f* d'enfants, nurse *f* ; *(= daytime carer)* garde *f* d'enfants, nourrice *f* ♦ **yes ~** oui nounou *(baby talk)* [2] *(* = grandmother)* mamie *f*, mémé *f*

COMP **nanny-goat** N chèvre *f*, bique * *f*

nanny state N *(esp Brit)* État-providence *m*

nannying /ˈnænɪɪŋ/ N [1] *(= job)* garde *f* d'enfants [2] *(pej = mollycoddling)* maternage *m* (excessif)

nanometre /ˈnænəʊˌmiːtəʳ/ N nanomètre *m*

nanoscience /ˈnænəʊˌsaɪəns/ N nanoscience *f*

nanotechnology /ˌnænəʊtekˈnɒlədʒɪ/ N nanotechnologie *f*

nap¹ /næp/ N *(= sleep)* petit somme *m* ♦ **afternoon ~** sieste *f* ♦ **to have** *or* **take a ~** faire un petit somme ; *(after lunch)* faire la sieste VI faire un (petit) somme, sommeiller ♦ **to catch sb ~ping** *(= unawares)* prendre qn à l'improviste *or* au dépourvu ; *(= in error etc)* surprendre qn en défaut

nap² /næp/ N *[of fabric]* poil *m* ♦ **cloth that has lost its ~** tissu *m* râpé *or* élimé ♦ **with/without ~** *(on sewing pattern)* avec/sans sens

nap³ /næp/ N *(Cards)* ≈ manille *f* aux enchères

nap⁴ /næp/ VT *(Brit Racing)* ♦ **to ~ the winner** donner le cheval gagnant

napalm /ˈneɪpɑːm/ N napalm *m* VT attaquer au napalm

COMP **napalm bomb** N bombe *f* au napalm

napalm bombing N bombardement *m* au napalm

nape /neɪp/ N (also **nape of the neck**) nuque *f*

naphtha /ˈnæfθə/ N *(gen)* naphte *m* ♦ **petroleum ~** naphta *m*

naphthalene /ˈnæfθəliːn/ N naphtaline *f*

napkin /ˈnæpkɪn/ N [1] serviette *f* (de table) [2] *(Brit † : for babies)* couche *f*

COMP **napkin ring** N rond *m* de serviette

Naples /ˈneɪplz/ N Naples

Napoleon /nəˈpəʊlɪən/ N [1] Napoléon *m* [2] *(= coin)* **napoleon** napoléon *m* [3] *(US)* **napoleon** *(= pastry)* millefeuille *m*

Napoleonic /nəˌpəʊlɪˈɒnɪk/ ADJ napoléonien

napper † ‡ /ˈnæpəʳ/ N *(= head)* caboche ‡ *f*

nappy /ˈnæpɪ/ *(Brit)* N couche *f*

COMP **nappy liner** N protège-couche *m*

nappy rash N érythème *m* (fessier) *(Med frm)* ♦ **to have ~ rash** *(gen)* avoir les fesses rouges

narc ‡ /nɑːk/ N *(US)* (abbrev of **narcotics agent**) agent *m* de la brigade des stupéfiants, stup ‡ *m*

narcissi /nɑːˈsɪsaɪ/ NPL of **narcissus**

narcissism /nɑːˈsɪsɪzəm/ N narcissisme *m*

narcissist /ˈnɑːsɪsɪst/ N narcissique *mf*

narcissistic /ˌnɑːsɪˈsɪstɪk/ ADJ *[person]* narcissique COMP **narcissistic personality disorder** N *(Psych)* névrose *f* narcissique

narcissus /nɑːˈsɪsəs/ N (pl **narcissi** or **narcissuses**) 1 *(= flower)* narcisse *m* 2 ◆ **Narcissus** Narcisse *m*

narco- /ˈnɑːkəʊ/ PREF narco-

narcolepsy /ˈnɑːkəʊlepsɪ/ N narcolepsie *f*

narcosis /nɑːˈkəʊsɪs/ N narcose *f*

narco-terrorism /ˌnɑːkəʊˈterəˌrɪzəm/ N narco-terrorisme *m*

narcotic /nɑːˈkɒtɪk/ ADJ 1 *(Med) [effect]* narcotique ◆ ~ **drug** narcotique *m* 2 *(esp US Drugs) [industry]* des stupéfiants N 1 *(Med)* narcotique *m* 2 *(esp US Drugs)* stupéfiant *m*
COMP **narcotics agent** N agent *m* de la brigade des stupéfiants
narcotics charge N ◆ **to be on a ~s charge** être mis en examen pour une affaire de stupéfiants
Narcotics Squad N brigade *f* des stupéfiants

narcotism /ˈnɑːkəˌtɪzəm/ N narcotisme *m*

narcotize /ˈnɑːkətaɪz/ VT donner *or* administrer un narcotique à, narcotiser

nark* /nɑːk/ VT 1 *(Brit = infuriate)* ficher en boule*, foutre en rogne‡ ; see also **narked** 2 ◆ **to ~ it** arrêter (de faire qch) ◆ ~ **it!** suffit !*, écrase !‡ VI *(Brit = inform police)* moucharder* N 1 *(Brit:* also **copper's nark**) indic‡ *m*, mouchard* *m* 2 *(US)* ⇒ **narc**

narked* /nɑːkt/ ADJ de mauvais poil* ◆ **to get ~** se mettre *or* se foutre‡ en rogne* *(about* à propos de)

narky‡ /ˈnɑːkɪ/ ADJ *(Brit)* grognon(ne), mal embouché ; *(on one occasion)* de mauvais poil*, en rogne*

narrate /nəˈreɪt/ VT raconter, narrer *(liter)* ◆ **~d by Richard Briers** narrateur : Richard Briers

narration /nəˈreɪʃən/ N narration *f* ◆ **a film about dolphins, with ~ by Jacques Cousteau** un film sur les dauphins avec un commentaire de Jacques Cousteau

narrative /ˈnærətɪv/ N 1 *(= story, account)* récit *m*, narration *f* 2 *(NonC)* narration *f* ◆ **he has a gift for ~** il est doué pour la narration ADJ *[poem, painting, structure, style]* narratif ; *[skill]* de conteur ◆ **Jane Austen's ~ voice** le ton narratif de Jane Austen

narrator /nəˈreɪtəʳ/ N narrateur *m*, -trice *f* ; *(Mus)* récitant(e) *m(f)*

narrow /ˈnærəʊ/ ADJ 1 *[road, path, passage, stream, garment, limits]* étroit ; *[valley]* étroit, encaissé ◆ **within a ~ compass** dans d'étroites limites, dans un champ restreint
2 *[mind]* étroit, borné ; *[majority]* faible, petit ; *[advantage]* petit ◆ **his outlook is too ~** ses vues sont trop étroites ◆ **in the ~est sense (of the word)** au sens le plus restreint (du terme) ◆ **a ~ victory** une victoire remportée de justesse ◆ **to have a ~ escape** s'en tirer de justesse, l'échapper belle ◆ **that was a ~ shave*** *or* **squeak!*** on l'a échappé belle !, il était moins une !* ◆ ~ **vowel** *(Ling)* voyelle *f* tendue
NPL **narrows** passage *m* étroit ; *[of harbour]* passe *f*, goulet *m* ; *[of river]* pertuis *m*, étranglement *m*
VI 1 *[road, path, river, valley]* se rétrécir ◆ **his eyes ~ed** il plissa les yeux
2 *(fig) [majority]* s'amenuiser, se rétrécir ◆ **the search has now ~ed (down) to Soho** les recherches se concentrent maintenant sur Soho ◆ **the choice has ~ed (down) to five candidates** il ne reste maintenant que cinq candidats en lice ◆ **the field of inquiry has ~ed (down) to five people** ils concentrent maintenant leurs recherches sur cinq personnes ◆ **his outlook has ~ed considerably since then** son horizon s'est beaucoup restreint *or* rétréci depuis ◆ **Britain's trade deficit ~ed a little last month** le déficit commercial de la Grande-Bretagne s'est légèrement réduit le mois dernier ◆ **the gap between Labour and the Conservatives is ~ing** l'écart entre les travaillistes et les conservateurs se réduit ◆ **"road narrows"** "chaussée rétrécie"
VT 1 *(= make narrower) [+ road, piece of land]* rétrécir, réduire la largeur de ; *[+ skirt]* rétrécir, resserrer ◆ **with ~ed eyes** en plissant les yeux
2 *(fig) [+ choice]* réduire, restreindre ; *[+ ideas]* rétrécir ; *[+ differences]* réduire ◆ **they decided to ~ the focus of their investigation** ils ont décidé de restreindre le champ de leur enquête ◆ **to ~ the field (down)** restreindre le champ ◆ **they are hoping to ~ the gap between rich and poor nations** ils espèrent réduire l'écart entre pays riches et pays pauvres
COMP **narrow boat** N *(Brit)* péniche *f*
narrow-gauge line, narrow-gauge track N *(Rail)* voie *f* étroite
narrow-minded ADJ *[person]* à l'esprit étroit, borné ; *[ideas, outlook]* étroit, borné
narrow-mindedness N étroitesse *f* d'esprit
narrow-shouldered ADJ étroit de carrure

► **narrow down** VI 1 *[road, path, valley]* se rétrécir
2 *(fig)* ⇒ **narrow vt 2**
VT SEP *[+ choice]* réduire, restreindre ; *[+ meaning, interpretation]* restreindre, limiter ; see also **narrow vt**

narrowcasting /ˈnærəʊˌkæstɪŋ/ N *(Telec, TV)* câblodistribution *f (sur une zone réduite)*

narrowing /ˈnærəʊɪŋ/ N *(NonC) (lit)* rétrécissement *m* ; *(fig) (= reduction)* réduction *f*

narrowly /ˈnærəʊlɪ/ ADV 1 *(= barely) [escape, avoid, defeat]* de justesse ; *[miss, fail]* de peu 2 *[defined] (= strictly)* rigoureusement ; *(= restrictively)* d'une manière restrictive ; *[technical, vocational]* strictement ◆ **a ~ based curriculum** un programme d'enseignement restreint ◆ **to focus too ~ on sth** trop se focaliser sur qch ◆ **to interpret a rule ~** interpréter une règle de manière restrictive, donner une interprétation restrictive d'une règle 3 *(= closely) [look at, watch]* de près

narrowness /ˈnærəʊnɪs/ N étroitesse *f*

narwhal /ˈnɑːwəl/ N narval *m*

NAS /ˌeneɪˈes/ N *(US)* (abbrev of **National Academy of Sciences**) *académie des sciences*

NASA /ˈnæsə/ N *(US)* (abbrev of **National Aeronautics and Space Administration**) NASA *f*

nasal /ˈneɪzəl/ ADJ *(Anat)* nasal ; *(Ling) [sound, vowel, pronunciation]* nasal ; *[accent]* nasillard ◆ **to speak in a ~ voice** parler du nez, nasiller N *(Ling)* nasale *f*

nasality /neɪˈzælɪtɪ/ N nasalité *f*

nasalization /ˌneɪzəlaɪˈzeɪʃən/ N nasalisation *f*

nasalize /ˈneɪzəlaɪz/ VT nasaliser

nasally /ˈneɪzəlɪ/ ADV *[whine, complain]* d'une voix nasillarde ◆ **to speak ~** nasiller

nascent /ˈnæsnt/ ADJ 1 *(frm = developing) [democracy, science, industry]* naissant 2 *(Chem)* naissant

Nassau /ˈnæsɔː/ N *(Bahamas)* Nassau

nastily /ˈnɑːstɪlɪ/ ADV 1 *(= spitefully) [say, laugh]* méchamment 2 *(= badly) [injured]* gravement ◆ **to cough ~** avoir une vilaine toux ◆ **her marriage ended rather ~** son mariage s'est mal terminé

nastiness /ˈnɑːstɪnɪs/ N 1 *[of person, behaviour, remark]* méchanceté *f* 2 *(= trouble)* troubles *mpl* ◆ **the recent ~ in the West Bank** les récents troubles en Cisjordanie

nasturtium /nəsˈtɜːʃəm/ N *(Bot)* capucine *f* ◆ **climbing/dwarf ~** capucine *f* grimpante/naine

nasty /ˈnɑːstɪ/ ADJ 1 *(= unkind, spiteful) [person, remark, joke]* méchant ◆ **to get** *or* **turn ~** *[person]* devenir méchant ◆ **to be ~ to sb** être méchant avec qn ◆ **to be ~ about sb/sth** dire du mal de qn/qch ◆ **she never said a ~ word about anybody** elle n'a jamais dit de mal de personne ◆ **a ~ little man** un type* désagréable ◆ **he's/she's a ~ piece of work** c'est un sale type*/une sale bonne femme* ◆ **to have a ~ look in one's eye** avoir une lueur mauvaise dans le regard ◆ **to have a ~ temper** avoir un sale caractère ◆ **to have a ~ mind** toujours voir le mal partout ◆ **a ~ trick** un sale tour
2 *(= unpleasant) [habit, rumour]* vilain ; *[bend, corner]* dangereux ; *[smell, taste, moment]* mauvais *before n*, désagréable ; *[feeling, situation, experience]* désagréable ; *[problem]* épineux ; *[weather]* affreux, vilain ; *[book, story]* ignoble ; *[life]* dur ◆ **a ~ business** une sale affaire ◆ **a ~ job** un sale travail ◆ **what a ~ mess!** *(lit)* quel pagaille épouvantable ! ; *(fig)* quel gâchis ! ◆ **a ~ shock** *or* **surprise** une mauvaise surprise ◆ **to turn ~** *[situation]* mal tourner ; *[weather]* se gâter ◆ **events took a ~ turn** les choses ont mal tourné ◆ **to smell ~** sentir mauvais, avoir une mauvaise odeur ◆ **to taste ~** avoir un goût désagréable ; see also **taste** ◆ **he had a ~ time of it!** *(short spell)* il a passé un mauvais quart d'heure ! ; *(longer period)* il a traversé une période très éprouvante !
3 *(= serious) [accident, disease]* grave ; *[fall, wound]* vilain, mauvais ◆ **a ~ cold** un gros rhume ◆ **a ~ bout of flu** une mauvaise grippe ◆ **a ~ case of food poisoning** une grave intoxication alimentaire
NPL **nasties** * *(= nasty things)* saletés *fpl*, saloperies‡ *fpl* ; → **video**

NAS/UWT /ˌeneɪˈesˌjuːdʌbljʊˈtiː/ *(Brit)* (abbrev of **National Association of Schoolmasters/Union of Women Teachers**) *syndicat*

Nat* /næt/ N *(= nationalist)* nationaliste *mf*

Natal /nəˈtæl/ N Natal *m* ◆ **in ~** au Natal

natal /ˈneɪtl/ ADJ natal ◆ ~ **day** *(liter)* jour *m* de (la) naissance ; → **antenatal, postnatal**

natality /nəˈtælɪtɪ/ N natalité *f*

natch‡ /nætʃ/ EXCL (abbrev of **naturally**) naturellement

NATFHE /ˌeneɪˈtiːˌefeɪtʃˈiː/ N *(Brit)* (abbrev of **National Association of Teachers in Further and Higher Education**) *syndicat*

nation /ˈneɪʃən/ N nation *f* ◆ **the French ~** la nation française ◆ **people of all ~s** des gens de toutes les nationalités ◆ **the voice of the ~** la voix de la nation *or* du peuple ◆ **in the service of the ~** au service de la nation ◆ **the whole ~ watched while he did it** il l'a fait sous les yeux de la nation tout entière ; → **league¹, united**
COMP **nation-state** N État-nation *m*

national /ˈnæʃənl/ ADJ national ◆ **on a ~ scale** à l'échelon national ◆ **they won 20% of the ~ vote** ils ont obtenu 20% des voix à l'échelle nationale
N 1 *(= person)* ressortissant(e) *m(f)* ◆ **he's a French ~** il est de nationalité française, c'est un ressortissant français ◆ **foreign ~s** ressortissants *mpl* étrangers
2 *(Brit Racing)* **the (Grand) National** le Grand National *(course d'obstacles qui se tient annuellement à Liverpool)*
3 (also **national newspaper**) quotidien *m* national
COMP **National Aeronautics and Space Administration** N *(US Admin)* Agence *f* nationale de l'aéronautique et de l'espace
national anthem N hymne *m* national
National Assembly N Assemblée *f* nationale

National Assistance N *(Brit Admin: formerly)* ≃ Sécurité *f* sociale
national bank N *(US)* banque *f* fédérale
national costume N ⇒ **national dress**
National Criminal Intelligence Service N *(Brit)* services *mpl* de renseignements
National Curriculum N *(Brit)* programme *m* d'enseignement obligatoire
national debt N dette *f* publique *or* nationale
national dress N costume *m* national *or* du pays
National Economic Development Council N *(Brit: formerly)* ≃ Agence *f* nationale d'information économique
National Enterprise Board N *(Brit)* ≃ Institut *m* de développement industriel
National Executive Committee N bureau *m* exécutif *or* national
National Extension College N *(Brit Scol)* ≃ Centre *m* national d'enseignement par correspondance
national flag N drapeau *m* national ; *(Naut)* pavillon *m* national
National Foundation of the Arts and the Humanities N *(US)* ≃ ministère *m* de la Culture
National Front N *(Brit Pol) parti britannique d'extrême droite*
national government N *(= not local)* gouvernement *m* (central) ; *(= coalition)* gouvernement *m* de coalition
national grid N *(Brit Elec)* réseau *m* national
National Guard N *(US)* garde *f* nationale *(milice de volontaires intervenant en cas de catastrophe naturelle et pouvant prêter main forte à l'armée en cas de crise)*
National Guardsman N (pl **National Guardsmen**) *(US)* membre *m* de la garde nationale ; see also **National Guard**
National Health N ◆ **I got it on the National Health** * ≃ je l'ai eu par la Sécurité sociale, ça m'a été remboursé par la Sécurité sociale
National Health Service N *(Brit)* ≃ Sécurité *f* sociale ; → **NHS, NATIONAL INSURANCE**
national holiday N fête *f* nationale
National Hunt racing N *(NonC: Brit)* courses *fpl* d'obstacles
national income N revenu *m* national
National Insurance N *(Brit)* ≃ Sécurité *f* sociale
National Insurance benefits NPL *(Brit)* ≃ prestations *fpl* de la Sécurité sociale
National Insurance contributions NPL *(Brit)* ≃ cotisations *fpl* de Sécurité sociale
National Insurance number N *(Brit)* ≃ numéro *m* de Sécurité sociale
National Labor Relations Board N *(US Admin) commission d'arbitrage du ministère du travail*
National League N *(US Sport) l'une des deux principales divisions de base-ball aux États-Unis*
National Liberation Front N Front *m* de libération nationale
the National Lottery N *(Brit)* ≃ la Loterie nationale
national monument N monument *m* national
national park N parc *m* national
National Rifle Association N *(US) organisation américaine militant pour le droit du port d'armes* ; → **GUN CONTROL**
National Safety Council N *(Brit)* Protection *f* civile
National Savings N *(Brit)* épargne *f* nationale
National Savings Bank N *(Brit)* ≃ Caisse *f* nationale d'épargne
National Savings Certificate N *(Brit)* bon *m* d'épargne
National Security Council N *(US Pol)* Conseil *m* national de sécurité
national service N *(Brit Mil)* service *m* national *or* militaire ◆ **to do one's ~ service** faire son service national *or* militaire
national serviceman N (pl **national servicemen**) *(Brit Mil)* appelé *m*, conscrit *m*
National Socialism N national-socialisme *m*
national status N nationalité *f*
National Trust N *(Brit)* ≃ Caisse *f* nationale des monuments historiques et des sites

NATIONAL CURRICULUM

Le **National Curriculum** est le programme d'enseignement obligatoire pour tous les élèves des écoles en Angleterre, au pays de Galles et en Irlande du Nord. Il comprend les matières suivantes : anglais, mathématiques, sciences, technologie, histoire, géographie, musique, art, éducation physique et une langue vivante étrangère (et le gallois dans les écoles du pays de Galles). Tous les établissements primaires et secondaires doivent proposer un enseignement religieux, et les écoles secondaires une éducation sexuelle, mais les parents sont libres, s'ils le veulent, d'en dispenser leurs enfants.

NATIONAL INSURANCE

La **National Insurance** est le régime de sécurité sociale britannique auquel cotisent les salariés, leurs employeurs et les travailleurs indépendants. Une partie de ces contributions finance l'assurance maladie (National Health Service), mais l'essentiel sert à payer les pensions de retraite, l'assurance chômage et les allocations de veuvage, d'invalidité et de maternité. Pour avoir droit à ces dernières prestations, il faut avoir cotisé à la **National Insurance** pendant un certain nombre d'années. → **NHS**

nationalism /ˈnæʃnəlɪzəm/ N nationalisme *m* ; → **Scottish**
nationalist /ˈnæʃnəlɪst/ ADJ nationaliste ◆ **Nationalist China** la Chine nationaliste N nationaliste *mf* → **Scottish**
nationalistic /ˌnæʃnəˈlɪstɪk/ ADJ *(esp pej)* nationaliste
nationality /ˌnæʃəˈnælɪtɪ/ N nationalité *f* ; → **dual**
nationalization /ˌnæʃnəlaɪˈzeɪʃən/ N 1 *[of industry]* nationalisation *f* 2 *[of person]* ⇒ **naturalization 1**
nationalize /ˈnæʃnəlaɪz/ VT 1 *[+ industry]* nationaliser 2 *[+ person]* ⇒ **naturalize vt 1**
nationally /ˈnæʃnəlɪ/ ADV *[distribute, make available]* dans l'ensemble du pays ; *[broadcast]* sur l'ensemble du pays ; *[organize]* à l'échelon national ◆ **a ~ recognized qualification** une qualification reconnue dans tout le pays
nationhood /ˈneɪʃənhʊd/ N *(= existence as a nation)* statut *m* de nation ; *(= national identity)* identité *f* nationale ◆ **to achieve ~** accéder au statut de nation ◆ **a strong sense of ~** un sentiment très fort d'identité nationale ◆ **the idea of Macedonian ~** l'idée d'une nation macédonienne
nationwide /ˈneɪʃənwaɪd/ ADJ *[strike, protest etc]* à l'échelle nationale, national ADV à l'échelle nationale ◆ **there was a ~ search for the killers** on a organisé une chasse à l'homme dans tout le pays pour retrouver les assassins
native /ˈneɪtɪv/ ADJ 1 *(= original) [country, town]* natal ; *[language]* maternel ◆ **~ land** pays *m* natal, patrie *f* ◆ **French ~ speaker** personne *f* de langue maternelle française, francophone *mf* ◆ **you should ask a ~ speaker** *(Ling)* il faudrait demander à un locuteur natif ◆ **~ son** *(fig)* enfant *m* du pays ; → **informant**
2 *(= innate) [charm, talent, ability]* inné, naturel ◆ **~ wit** bon sens *m* inné
3 *(= indigenous) [plant, animal]* indigène ; *[product, resources] (= of country)* du pays ; *(= of region)* de la région ◆ **plant/animal ~ to ...** plante *f*/animal *m* originaire de ...
4 *(= of the natives) [customs, costume]* du pays ; *[matters, rights, knowledge]* du pays, des autochtones ◆ **Minister of Native Affairs** ministre *m* chargé des Affaires indigènes ◆ **Ministry of Native Affairs** ministère *m* des Affaires indigènes ◆ **~ labour** main-d'œuvre *f* indigène ◆ **~ quarter** quartier *m* indigène ◆ **to go ~** * adopter le mode de vie indigène
N 1 *(= person)* autochtone *mf* ; *(esp of colony)* indigène *mf* ◆ **a ~ of the country** un(e) autochtone ◆ **a ~ of France** un(e) Français(e) de naissance ◆ **he is a ~ of Bourges** il est originaire de *or* natif de Bourges ◆ **she speaks French like a ~** elle parle français comme si c'était sa langue maternelle ◆ **the ~s** *(hum or pej)* les autochtones *mpl* les indigènes *mpl*
2 *(= plant, animal)* indigène *mf* ◆ **this plant/animal is a ~ of Australia** cette plante/cet animal est originaire d'Australie
COMP **Native American** N Indien(ne) *m(f)* d'Amérique, Amérindien(ne) *m(f)* ADJ amérindien
native-born ADJ de souche ◆ **he's a ~-born Scot** il est écossais de souche

NATIVE AMERICAN

Aux États-Unis, l'expression **Native Americans** désigne les populations autochtones, par opposition aux Américains d'origine européenne, africaine ou asiatique. On peut aussi parler d'« American Indian » (Indien d'Amérique), mais l'on évite les dénominations « Red Indian » ou « redskin » (Peau-Rouge), considérées comme méprisantes ou insultantes.

nativism /ˈneɪtɪˌvɪzəm/ N *(US)* hostilité *f* aux immigrants
nativity /nəˈtɪvɪtɪ/ N 1 *(Rel)* **Nativity** Nativité *f* 2 *(Astrol)* horoscope *m* COMP **nativity play** N pièce *f* représentant la Nativité
NATO /ˈneɪtəʊ/ N (abbrev of **North Atlantic Treaty Organization**) OTAN *f*
Nats * /ˈnæts/ NPL *(Pol)* nationalistes *mpl*
NATSOPA /ˌnætˈsəʊpə/ N *(Brit)* (abbrev of **National Society of Operative Printers, Graphical and Media Personnel**) *syndicat*
natter * /ˈnætəʳ/ *(Brit)* VI *(= chat)* causer, bavarder ; *(= chatter)* bavarder, jacasser ◆ **we ~ed (away) for hours** nous avons bavardé pendant des heures ◆ **she does ~!** elle n'arrête pas de jacasser ! N 1 *(= chat)* causerie *f*, causette * *f* ◆ **we had a good ~** nous avons bien bavardé, nous avons taillé une bonne bavette * 2 *(= chatterbox)* moulin *m* à paroles *
natterer * /ˈnætərəʳ/ N ⇒ **natter noun 2**
natty * /ˈnætɪ/ ADJ 1 *(= smart) [person]* chic *inv* ◆ **to be a ~ dresser** être toujours bien sapé * ◆ **to look ~** être très chic 2 *(= handy) [gadget]* pratique
natural /ˈnætʃrəl/ ADJ 1 *(= normal)* naturel, normal ◆ **it's only ~** c'est tout naturel, c'est bien normal ◆ **it seems quite ~ to me** ça me semble tout à fait naturel *or* normal ◆ **there's a perfectly ~ explanation for the sound** le bruit s'explique tout à fait naturellement ◆ **it is ~ for this animal to hibernate** il est dans la nature de cet animal d'hiberner, il est naturel *or* normal que cet animal hiberne *subj* ◆ **it is ~ for you to think ..., it is ~ that you should think ...** il est naturel *or* normal que vous pensiez *subj* ... ◆ **~ break** *(in television programme)* interruption *f* normale ◆ **death from ~ causes** *(Jur)* mort *f* naturelle ◆ **to die of *or* from ~ causes** *(Jur)* mourir de mort naturelle ◆ **to die a ~ death** mourir de sa belle mort ◆ **for (the**

rest of) his ~ life *(Jur)* à vie ◆ **~ size** grandeur *f* nature
2 *(= of or from nature)* naturel ◆ **~ resources** ressources *fpl* naturelles ◆ **her hair is a ~ blonde** ses cheveux sont naturellement blonds
3 *(= inborn)* inné, naturel ◆ **to have a ~ talent for** être naturellement doué pour, avoir un don (inné) pour ◆ **he's a ~** or *(US)* **~-born painter** c'est un peintre né
4 *(= unaffected) [person, manner]* simple, naturel
5 *(Mus)* naturel ◆ **B ~** si *m* naturel ◆ **~ horn** cor *m* d'harmonie ◆ **~ key** ton *m* naturel ◆ **~ trumpet** trompette *f* naturelle
6 *(= biological) [parents, child]* biologique
7 (†† *= illegitimate) [child]* naturel
ADV * ◆ **playing the piano comes ~ to her** elle est naturellement douée pour le piano ◆ **try to act ~!** essaie d'avoir l'air naturel !, fais comme si de rien n'était !
N 1 *(Mus) (= sign)* bécarre *m* ; *(= note)* note *f* naturelle
2 (* *= ideal)* **he's a ~ for this part** il est fait pour ce rôle ◆ **did you hear her play the piano? she's a ~!** est-ce que vous l'avez entendue jouer ? c'est une pianiste née ! ◆ **it's a ~** *(US)* ça coule de source
3 (†† *= simpleton)* idiot(e) *m(f)* (de naissance), demeuré(e) *m(f)*
COMP **natural-born** ADJ ◆ **he's not a ~-born orator** ce n'est pas un orateur-né
natural (child)birth N accouchement *m* sans douleur
natural disaster N catastrophe *f* naturelle
natural gas N gaz *m* naturel
natural history N histoire *f* naturelle
natural justice N *(NonC)* principes *mpl* élémentaires du droit
natural language N langage *m* naturel
natural language processing N *(Comput)* traitement *m* automatique de la langue, traitement *m* de la langue naturelle
natural law N loi *f* naturelle *or* de la nature
natural logarithm N logarithme *m* népérien *or* naturel
natural monopoly N *(Econ)* monopole *m* naturel
natural number N *(Math)* nombre *m* naturel
natural philosopher N physicien(ne) *m(f)*
natural philosophy N physique *f*
natural science N *(NonC)* sciences *fpl* naturelles
natural selection N sélection *f* naturelle
natural theology N théologie *f* naturelle, théodicée *f*
natural wastage N *(= employees leaving)* départs *mpl* naturels ◆ **to reduce the staff by ~ wastage** *(esp Brit)* réduire le personnel par départs naturels

naturalism /ˈnætʃrəlɪzəm/ N naturalisme *m*

naturalist /ˈnætʃrəlɪst/ ADJ, N naturaliste *mf*

naturalistic /ˌnætʃrəˈlɪstɪk/ ADJ *(Art, Literat) [artist, writer, novel, painting]* naturaliste ◆ **a ~ environment** *(= simulating nature)* un environnement qui reproduit les conditions naturelles

naturalization /ˌnætʃrəlaɪˈzeɪʃən/ N 1 *[of person]* naturalisation *f* 2 *[of plant, animal]* acclimatation *f* **COMP** **naturalization papers** NPL *(Brit)* déclaration *f* de naturalisation

naturalize /ˈnætʃrəlaɪz/ VT 1 *[+ person]* naturaliser ◆ **to be ~d** se faire naturaliser 2 *[+ animal, plant]* acclimater ; *[+ word, sport]* naturaliser VI *[plant, animal]* s'acclimater

naturally /ˈnætʃrəlɪ/ ADV 1 *(= as is normal) [happen, develop, follow from, lead to, give birth]* naturellement ; *[die]* de mort naturelle
2 *(= of course)* naturellement ◆ **~, I understand your feelings** naturellement, je comprends vos sentiments ◆ **~, I'll do all I can to help you** je ferai naturellement tout mon possible pour vous aider, il va de soi que je ferai tout mon possible pour vous aider ◆ **~ enough** bien naturellement
3 *(= unaffectedly) [behave, talk, smile]* avec naturel, naturellement
4 *(= by nature) [cautious, cheerful, lazy]* de nature ◆ **her hair is ~ blond** c'est une vraie blonde ◆ **her hair is ~ curly** elle frise naturellement ◆ **a ~ optimistic person** un(e) optimiste né(e) ◆ **to do what comes ~ (to one)** faire ce qui (vous) semble naturel ◆ **caution comes ~ to him** il est prudent de nature ◆ **cynicism doesn't come ~ to her** elle n'est pas du genre cynique ◆ **playing the piano comes ~ to her** elle a un don (inné) pour le piano

naturalness /ˈnætʃrəlnɪs/ N naturel *m*

nature /ˈneɪtʃəʳ/ **N** 1 *(NonC:* also **Nature)** nature *f* ◆ **he loves ~** il aime la nature ◆ **in ~** dans la nature ◆ **~ versus nurture** l'inné *m* et l'acquis *m* ◆ **let ~ take its course** laissez faire la nature ◆ **a freak of ~** un caprice de la nature ◆ **to paint from ~** peindre d'après nature ◆ **against ~** contre nature ◆ **~ abhors a vacuum** la nature a horreur du vide ◆ **in a state of ~** *(hum)* à l'état naturel, dans le costume d'Adam * ◆ **to go back** or **return to ~** *[person]* retourner à la nature ; *[land]* retourner à la nature *or* l'état sauvage ◆ **a return to ~** *[of garden, land]* un retour à la nature *or* l'état sauvage ; *[of person]* un retour à la nature ; → **law, mother**
2 *(= character) [of person, animal]* nature *f*, naturel *m* ◆ **by ~** de nature, par tempérament ; see also **3** ◆ **he has a nice ~** c'est quelqu'un de très gentil ◆ **it is in the ~ of human beings to contradict themselves** la contradiction est le propre de l'homme ◆ **it is in the ~ of young people to want to travel** il est naturel de vouloir voyager quand on est jeune ◆ **it is not in his ~ to lie** il n'est pas de nature à mentir, il n'est pas dans sa nature de mentir ◆ **that's very much in his ~** c'est tout à fait dans sa nature ◆ **the ~ of the soil** la nature du sol ◆ **it is in the ~ of things** c'est dans l'ordre des choses, c'est dans la nature des choses ◆ **the true ~ of things** l'essence des choses ◆ **in the ~ of this case it is clear that ...** vu la nature de ce cas il est clair que ... ◆ **cash is, by its (very) ~, easy to steal** l'argent est, par nature *or* de par sa nature, facile à voler ◆ **that's the ~ of the beast** *(fig)* ça fait partie (des règles) du jeu ; → **better¹, good, human, second¹**
3 *(= type, sort)* nature *f*, genre *m* ◆ **things of this ~** ce genre de chose ◆ **I will have nothing to do with anything of that ~** je refuse d'être mêlé à ce genre de chose ◆ **his comment was in the ~ of a compliment** sa remarque était en quelque sorte un compliment ◆ **something in the ~ of an apology** une sorte d'excuse, une vague excuse ◆ **ceremonies of a religious/solemn** *etc* **~** cérémonies *fpl* religieuses/solennelles *etc*
COMP **nature conservancy** N protection *f* de la nature
Nature Conservancy Board N *(Brit)* ≃ Direction *f* générale de la protection de la nature et de l'environnement
nature cure N *(NonC: Med)* naturopathie *f*
nature lover N amoureux *m*, -euse *f* de la nature
nature reserve N réserve *f* naturelle
nature study N histoire *f* naturelle ; *(Scol)* sciences *fpl* naturelles
nature trail N sentier *m* de découverte de la nature
nature worship N adoration *f* de la nature

-natured /ˈneɪtʃəd/ ADJ *(in compounds)* de nature ◆ **jealous-natured** jaloux de nature, d'un naturel jaloux ; → **good, ill**

naturism /ˈneɪtʃərɪzəm/ N *(esp Brit)* naturisme *m*

naturist /ˈneɪtʃərɪst/ N *(esp Brit)* naturiste *mf*

naturopath /ˈneɪtʃərəˌpæθ/ N naturopathe *mf*

naturopathy /ˌneɪtʃəˈrɒpəθɪ/ N naturopathie *f*

naught /nɔːt/ N 1 *(esp Brit Math)* zéro *m* ◆ **~s and crosses** *(Brit)* ≃ morpion *m (jeu)* 2 († *or liter = nothing)* rien *m* ◆ **to bring sth to ~** faire échouer qch, faire avorter qch ◆ **to come to ~** échouer, n'aboutir à rien ◆ **to care ~ for, to set at ~** ne faire aucun cas de, ne tenir aucun compte de

naughtily /ˈnɔːtɪlɪ/ ADV 1 *[say, remark]* avec malice ◆ **to behave ~** se conduire mal ; *[child]* être vilain 2 *(= suggestively)* d'une manière osée

naughtiness /ˈnɔːtɪnɪs/ N 1 *[of child etc]* désobéissance *f*, mauvaise conduite *f* ◆ **it was just a young boy's natural ~** il était désobéissant, comme tous les enfants de son âge 2 *(= suggestiveness) [of story, joke, play]* grivoiserie *f* ◆ **a writer who shocked the bourgeoisie with his sexual ~** un écrivain qui a choqué la bourgeoisie avec ses grivoiseries

naughty /ˈnɔːtɪ/ **ADJ** 1 *(= badly behaved)* ◆ **a ~ boy/girl** un vilain garçon/une vilaine (petite) fille ◆ **(you) ~ boy/girl!** vilain/vilaine ! ◆ **he's ~** c'est un vilain garçon ◆ **girls, you're being very ~** les filles, vous êtes très vilaines ◆ **that was a ~ thing to do!** c'est vilain d'avoir fait ça ! 2 *(esp Brit hum = slightly immoral) [person]* culotté * ◆ **it was ~ of us, but it solved the problem** on n'aurait peut-être pas dû, mais ça a résolu le problème * ◆ **a wonderfully ~ chocolate cake** un gâteau au chocolat à se mettre à genoux devant * 3 *(Brit = suggestive) [joke]* grivois, leste ; *[book, magazine, story]* osé
COMP **naughty bits** NPL *(euph = genitals)* parties *fpl* intimes
the Naughty Nineties NPL *(Brit)* ≃ la Belle Époque
naughty word N *(esp baby talk)* vilain mot *m*

nausea /ˈnɔːsɪə/ N *(lit)* nausée *f* ; *(fig)* dégoût *m*, écœurement *m* ◆ **she looked at the plate with a feeling of ~** l'assiette de nourriture lui soulevait le cœur

nauseate /ˈnɔːsɪeɪt/ VT *(lit, fig)* écœurer

nauseating /ˈnɔːsɪeɪtɪŋ/ ADJ *(lit, fig)* écœurant

nauseatingly /ˈnɔːsɪeɪtɪŋlɪ/ ADV d'une façon dégoûtante *or* écœurante ◆ **she was ~ beautiful/thin** elle était d'une beauté/minceur écœurante

nauseous /ˈnɔːsɪəs/ ADJ 1 *(= queasy)* ◆ **to be** *or* **feel ~ (at the sight/thought of sth)** avoir la nausée (à la vue/pensée de qch) ◆ **to make sb (feel) ~** donner la nausée à qn 2 *(= nauseating) [smell]* écœurant

nautical /ˈnɔːtɪkəl/ **ADJ** *[chart]* nautique, marin ; *[theme, look, feel]* marin ; *[term]* de marine ; *[uniform]* de marin ; *[book]* sur la navigation maritime ◆ **he's a ~ man** c'est un marin
COMP **nautical almanac** N almanach *m* marin
nautical mile N mille *m* marin *or* nautique

nautilus /ˈnɔːtɪləs/ N (pl **nautiluses** *or* **nautili** /ˈnɔːtɪˌlaɪ/) *(= animal)* nautile *m*

Navaho /ˈnævəhəʊ/ N (also **Navaho Indian**) Navaho *or* Navajo *mf*

naval /ˈneɪvəl/ **ADJ** *[battle, blockade, operation, unit]* naval ; *[affairs, matters]* de la marine ; *[commander]* de marine ◆ **~ forces** forces *fpl* navales ◆ **to have a ~ presence in a region** avoir des forces navales dans une région ◆ **~ warfare** combats *mpl* navals
COMP **naval air station** N station *f* aéronavale
naval architect N architecte *m(f)* naval(e)
naval architecture N architecture *f* navale
naval aviation N aéronavale *f*
naval barracks NPL caserne *f* maritime
naval base N base *f* navale
naval college N école *f* navale
naval dockyard N arsenal *m* (maritime)

naval hospital N hôpital *m* maritime
naval officer N officier *m* de marine
naval station N ⇒ **naval base**
naval stores NPL entrepôts *mpl* maritimes

Navarre /nə'vɑːr/ N Navarre *f*

nave[1] /neɪv/ N *[of church]* nef *f*

nave[2] /neɪv/ N *[of wheel]* moyeu *m* COMP **nave plate** N enjoliveur *m*

navel /'neɪvəl/ N *(Anat)* nombril *m*
COMP **navel-gazing** N *(pej)* nombrilisme* *m*
navel orange N (orange *f*) navel *f inv*

navigable /'nævɪgəbl/ ADJ *[river, canal, channel]* navigable ; *[missile, balloon, airship]* dirigeable

navigate /'nævɪgeɪt/ VI naviguer ◆ **you drive, I'll ~** *(in car)* tu prends le volant, moi je lis la carte (*or* le plan) ◆ **the Government is trying to ~ through its present difficulties** le gouvernement essaie actuellement de naviguer entre les écueils VT ① *(= plot course of)* **to ~ a ship** (*or* **a plane**) naviguer ② *(= steer) [+ boat]* être à la barre de ; *[+ aircraft]* piloter ; *[+ missile]* diriger ◆ **he ~d the ship through the dangerous channel** il a dirigé le navire dans ce dangereux chenal ③ *(= sail) [+ seas, ocean]* naviguer sur ④ *(fig)* ◆ **he ~d his way through to the bar** il s'est frayé un chemin jusqu'au bar ◆ **he ~d the maze of back streets** il a réussi à retrouver son chemin dans le dédale des petites rues

navigation /,nævɪ'geɪʃən/ N navigation *f* ; → **coastal**
COMP **navigation laws** NPL code *m* maritime
navigation lights NPL feux *mpl* de bord

navigational /,nævɪ'geɪʃənl/ ADJ *[instrument, techniques]* de navigation ◆ **it is a ~ hazard** c'est un danger pour la navigation

navigator /'nævɪgeɪtər/ N ① *(in plane, ship)* navigateur *m* ; *(in car)* copilote *mf* ◆ **I'm a useless ~** *(in car)* je suis incapable de lire une carte ② *(= sailor-explorer)* navigateur *m*, marin *m*

navvy /'nævɪ/ N *(Brit)* terrassier *m*

navy /'neɪvɪ/ N ① marine *f* (militaire *or* de guerre) ◆ **he's in the ~** il est dans la marine ◆ **Department of the Navy, Navy Department** *(US)* ministère *m* de la Marine ◆ **Secretary for the Navy** *(US)* ministre *m* de la Marine ◆ **to serve in the ~** servir dans la marine ; → **merchant, royal** ② *(= colour)* ⇒ **navy-blue**
ADJ ⇒ **navy-blue**
COMP **navy bean** N *(US)* haricot *m* blanc
navy-blue N, ADJ bleu marine *m inv*
Navy Register N *(US)* liste *f* navale
navy yard N *(US)* arsenal *m* (maritime)

nay /neɪ/ (†† *or liter*) PARTICLE non ◆ **do not say me ~** ne me dites pas non ; → **yea** ADV ou plutôt ◆ **surprised, ~ astonished** surpris, ou plutôt abasourdi

naysayer /'neɪseɪər/ N *(US)* opposant(e) *m(f)* systématique

Nazareth /'næzərɪθ/ N Nazareth

Nazi /'nɑːtsɪ/ N Nazi(e) *m(f)* ADJ nazi

Nazism /'nɑːtsɪzəm/ N nazisme *m*

NB /en'biː/ (abbrev of **nota bene**) NB

NBA /,enbiː'eɪ/ N ① *(US)* (abbrev of **National Basketball Association**) *association nationale de basket-ball* ② *(Brit)* (abbrev of **Net Book Agreement**) → **net[2]**

NBC /,enbiː'siː/ N *(US)* (abbrev of **National Broadcasting Company**) NBC *f (chaîne de télévision américaine)*

NC ① (abbrev of **no charge**) gratuit ② abbrev of **North Carolina**

NCB /,ensiː'biː/ N *(Brit: formerly)* (abbrev of **National Coal Board**) Charbonnages *mpl* de Grande-Bretagne

NCCL /,ensiːsiː'el/ N *(Brit Hist)* (abbrev of **National Council for Civil Liberties**) ≈ ligue *f* des droits de l'homme

NCIS /'ensɪs/ N *(Brit)* (abbrev of **National Criminal Intelligence Service**) → **national**

NCO /,ensiː'əʊ/ N *(Mil)* (abbrev of **non-commissioned officer**) sous-officier *m*

ND abbrev of **North Dakota**

NDP /,endiː'piː/ N (abbrev of **net domestic product**) → **net[2]**

NE ① (abbrev of **north-east**) N-E ② abbrev of **Nebraska**

Neanderthal /nɪ'ændətɑːl/ N ① *(lit: Geog)* Neandertal *or* Néanderthal *m* ② *(fig) (= unreconstructed male)* primaire *m (pej)*, primate* *m (pej)* ; *(= brute)* brute *f* épaisse ADJ ① *(= primitive) [age, times]* de Neandertal *or* de Néanderthal ; *[skeleton, grave]* de l'époque de Neandertal *or* de Néanderthal ② *(pej = primitive) [person, attitude, approach]* primitif *(pej)* ; *[system, method]* primitif, archaïque ③ *(hum = brutish) [person]* fruste ; *[grunt]* de sauvage ; *[appearance]* d'homme des cavernes COMP **Neanderthal man** N (pl **Neanderthal men**) homme *m* de Neandertal *or* de Néanderthal

neap /niːp/ N (also **neaptide**) marée *f* de morte-eau COMP **neap season** N (also **neaptide season**) époque *f* des mortes-eaux

Neapolitan /nɪə'pɒlɪtən/ ADJ napolitain ◆ **a ~ ice (cream)** une tranche napolitaine N Napolitain(e) *m(f)*

near /nɪər/ ADV ① *(in space)* tout près, à proximité ; *(in time)* près, proche ◆ **he lives quite ~** il habite tout près ◆ **~ at hand** *[object]* à portée de (la) main ; *[event]* tout proche ◆ **the shops are ~ at hand** les magasins sont tout près ◆ **to draw** *or* **come ~ (to)** s'approcher (de) ◆ **to draw** *or* **bring sth ~er** rapprocher qch ◆ **it was drawing** *or* **getting ~ to Christmas, Christmas was drawing** *or* **getting ~** Noël approchait ◆ **the ~er it gets to the election, the more they look like losing** plus les élections approchent, plus leur défaite semble certaine ◆ **it was ~ to 6 o'clock** il était près de *or* presque 6 heures ◆ **~ to where I had seen him** près de l'endroit où je l'avais vu ◆ **she was ~ to tears** elle était au bord des larmes ◆ **so ~ and yet so far!** on était pourtant si près du but !
② (also **nearly** : *in degree*) presque; → **nowhere**
③ *(= close)* **as ~ as I can judge** pour autant que je puisse en juger ◆ **you won't get any ~er than that to what you want** vous ne trouverez pas mieux ◆ **that's ~ enough*** ça pourra aller ◆ **there were 60 people, ~ enough*** il y avait 60 personnes à peu près *or* grosso modo ◆ **as ~ as dammit*** ou presque, ou c'est tout comme*
④ *(Naut)* près du vent, en serrant le vent ◆ **as ~ as she can** au plus près
PREP ① *(in space)* près de, auprès de ; *(in time)* près de, vers ◆ **~ here/there** près d'ici/de là ◆ **~ the church** près de l'église ◆ **he was standing ~ the table** il se tenait près de la table ◆ **regions ~ the Equator** les régions *fpl* près de *or* avoisinant l'équateur ◆ **stay ~ me** restez près de moi ◆ **don't come ~ me** ne vous approchez pas de moi ◆ **the sun was ~ to setting** le soleil était près *or* sur le point de se coucher ◆ **the passage is ~ the end of the book** le passage se trouve vers la fin du livre ◆ **her birthday is ~ mine** son anniversaire est proche du mien ◆ **he won't go ~ anything illegal** il ne se risquera jamais à faire quoi que ce soit d'illégal
② *(= on the point of)* près de, sur le point de ◆ **~ tears** au bord des larmes ◆ **~ death** près de *or* sur le point de mourir
③ *(= on the same level, in the same degree)* au niveau de, près de ◆ **to be ~ sth** se rapprocher de qch ; *(fig)* ressembler à qch ◆ **French is ~er Latin than English is** le français ressemble plus au latin *or* est plus près du latin que l'anglais ◆ **it's the same thing or ~ it** c'est la même chose ou presque ◆ **it was of a quality as ~ perfection as makes no difference** c'était d'une qualité proche de la perfection ◆ **nobody comes anywhere ~ him at swimming** personne ne lui arrive à la cheville en natation ◆ **that's ~er it, that's ~er the thing*** voilà qui est mieux ; → **nowhere**
ADJ ① *(= close in space) [building, town, tree]* proche, voisin ; *[neighbour]* proche ◆ **these glasses make things look ~er** ces lunettes rapprochent les objets ◆ **to the ~est decimal place** *(Math)* à la plus proche décimale près ◆ **to the ~est pound** à une livre près ◆ **the ~est route** l'itinéraire le plus court *or* le plus direct ; see also **comp**
② *(= close in time)* proche, prochain ◆ **the hour is ~ (when ...)** l'heure est proche (où ...) ◆ **in the ~ future** dans un proche avenir, dans un avenir prochain ◆ **these events are still very ~** ces événements sont encore très proches *or* très rapprochés de nous
③ *(fig) [relative]* proche ; *[race, contest, result]* serré ◆ **my ~est and dearest*** les êtres qui me sont chers ◆ **the ~est equivalent** ce qui s'en rapproche le plus ◆ **his ~est rival/challenger** son plus dangereux rival/challenger ◆ **that was a ~ thing** *(gen)* il s'en est fallu de peu *or* d'un cheveu ; *[of shot]* c'est passé très près ◆ **it was a ~ thing** *(of election, race result)* ça a été très juste ◆ **the translation is fairly ~** la traduction est assez fidèle ◆ **that's the ~est thing to a compliment** ça pourrait passer pour un compliment, de sa *etc* part c'est un compliment
④ ⇒ **nearside**
⑤ (* *= mean*) radin*, pingre
VT *[+ place]* approcher de ; *[+ person]* approcher, s'approcher de ◆ **to be ~ing one's goal** toucher au but ◆ **my book is ~ing completion** mon livre est près d'être achevé ◆ **the book is ~ing publication** la date de publication du livre approche ◆ **the country is ~ing disaster** le pays est au bord de la catastrophe ◆ **to be ~ing one's end** *(= dying)* toucher à *or* être près de sa fin
COMP **near beer** N *(US)* bière *f* légère
near-death experience N état *m* de mort imminente
the Near East N le Proche-Orient
near gold N similor *m*
near letter quality N qualité *f* pseudo-courrier ADJ de qualité pseudo-courrier
near miss N *(in plane, ship)* quasi-collision *f* ; *(in shooting)* tir *m* très près du but ; *(in football)* tir *m* raté de peu ◆ **we had a ~ miss with that truck** on a frôlé l'accident *or* on l'a échappé belle avec ce camion ◆ **that was a ~ miss** *or* **a ~ thing** *(gen)* il s'en est fallu de peu *or* d'un cheveu ; *[of shot]* c'est passé très près ◆ **he made up for his ~ miss the previous day with a stunning victory** il a compensé par une victoire éclatante le fait qu'il l'avait manquée de très peu la veille
near money N *(Fin)* quasi-monnaie *f*
near-nudity N nudité *f* presque totale, quasi-nudité *f*
near-sighted ADJ *(esp US)* ◆ **to be ~-sighted** être myope, avoir la vue basse
near-sightedness N *(esp US)* myopie *f*
near silk N soie *f* artificielle

nearby /,nɪə'baɪ/ ADV tout près, à proximité ADJ voisin ◆ **the house is ~** la maison est tout près ◆ **a ~ house** une maison voisine

nearly /'nɪəlɪ/ ADV ① *(= almost)* presque ◆ **it's ~ complete** c'est presque terminé ◆ **~ black** presque noir ◆ **I've ~ finished** j'ai presque fini ◆ **we are ~ there** nous sommes presque arrivés ◆ **it's ~ 2 o'clock** il est près de *or* presque 2 heures ◆ **it's ~ time to go** il est presque l'heure de partir ◆ **she is ~ 60** elle a près de 60 ans, elle va sur ses 60 ans ◆ **their marks are ~ the same** leurs notes sont à peu près les mêmes ◆ **~ all my money** presque tout mon argent, la presque totalité de mon argent ◆ **he ~ laughed** il a failli rire ◆ **I very ~ lost my place** j'ai bien failli perdre ma place ◆ **she was ~ crying** elle était sur le point de pleurer, elle était au bord des larmes ◆ **it's the same or very ~ so** c'est la même chose ou presque

2 ◆ **not ~** loin de ◆ **she is not ~ so old as you** elle est loin d'être aussi âgée que vous ◆ **that's not ~ enough** c'est loin d'être suffisant ◆ **it's not ~ good enough** c'est loin d'être satisfaisant

3 *(= closely)* près, de près ◆ **this concerns me very ~** cela me touche de très près

COMP **nearly-new** ADJ *[clothes]* d'occasion *(en bon état)*
nearly-new shop N *(Brit)* magasin *m* d'articles d'occasion

nearness /ˈnɪənɪs/ N 1 *(in time, place)* proximité *f* ; *[of relationship]* intimité *f* ; *[of translation]* fidélité *f* ; *[of resemblance]* exactitude *f* 2 *(* = meanness)* parcimonie *f*, radinerie * *f*

nearside /ˈnɪəˌsaɪd/ *(Driving, Horse-riding etc)* N *(in Britain)* côté *m* gauche ; *(in France, US etc)* côté *m* droit ADJ *(in Brit)* de gauche ; *(in France, US etc)* de droite

neat /niːt/ ADJ 1 *(= ordered) [house, room, desk]* bien rangé ; *[garden]* bien entretenu ; *[hair]* bien coiffé ; *[handwriting, clothes, notes, work, appearance, sewing, stitches]* soigné ◆ **everything was ~ and tidy** tout était bien rangé ◆ **she put her clothes in a ~ pile** elle a soigneusement empilé ses vêtements ◆ **in ~ rows** en rangées régulières ◆ **a ~ hairstyle** une coiffure nette ◆ **a ~ little suit** un petit tailleur bien coupé ◆ **she is very ~ in her dress** elle est toujours impeccable *or* tirée à quatre épingles ◆ **he is a ~ worker** il est soigneux dans son travail

2 *(= trim) [waist, waistline, ankles]* fin ; *[legs]* bien fait ◆ **she has a ~ figure** elle est bien faite ◆ **a ~ little car** une jolie petite voiture

3 *(= skilful and effective) [solution]* ingénieux ; *[plan]* habile, ingénieux ; *[division, category]* net, bien défini ; *[explanation] (= clever)* astucieux ; *(= devious)* habile ; *[phrase]* bien tourné ◆ **to make a ~ job of sth** bien faire qch, réussir qch

4 *(US * = good) [car, apartment, idea]* super* ◆ **he's a really ~ guy** c'est un mec super* ◆ **it would be ~ to do that** ce serait chouette* (de faire ça)

5 *(= undiluted) [whisky, brandy, vodka]* sec (sèche *f*), sans eau

neaten /ˈniːtn/ VT *[+ dress]* ajuster ; *[+ desk]* ranger ◆ **to ~ one's hair** se recoiffer

'neath /niːθ/ PREP *(liter)* ⇒ **beneath prep**

neatly /ˈniːtlɪ/ ADV 1 *(= carefully) [write, type, dress, fold]* soigneusement ◆ **to put sth away ~** ranger qch soigneusement *or* avec soin 2 *(= skilfully) [summarize]* habilement ◆ **he avoided the question very ~** il a éludé la question très habilement ◆ **as you so ~ put it** comme vous le dites si bien ◆ **a ~ turned sentence** une phrase bien tournée *or* joliment tournée ◆ **you got out of that very ~** vous vous en êtes très habilement tiré 3 *(= conveniently) [fit, work out]* parfaitement

neatness /ˈniːtnɪs/ N 1 *(= tidiness) [of person, clothes, house]* netteté *f*, belle ordonnance *f* ; *[of garden, sewing]* aspect *m* soigné ◆ **the ~ of her work/appearance** son travail/sa tenue soigné(e), le soin qu'elle apporte à son travail/à sa tenue 2 *[of ankles]* finesse *f* ; *[of figure]* sveltesse *f* 3 *(= skilfulness)* adresse *f*, habileté *f*

NEB /ˌeniːˈbiː/ N 1 *(Brit)* (abbrev of **National Enterprise Board**) → **national** 2 (abbrev of **New English Bible**) → **new comp**

nebbish* /ˈnebɪʃ/ ADJ *(US)* empoté* ◆ **your ~ brother** ton empoté de frère N ballot* *m*, empoté(e) *m(f)*

Nebraska /nɪˈbræskə/ N Nebraska *m* ◆ **in ~** dans le Nebraska

Nebuchadnezzar /ˌnebjʊkədˈnezəʳ/ N Nabuchodonosor *m*

nebula /ˈnebjʊlə/ N (pl **nebulas** *or* **nebulae** /ˈnebjʊliː/) nébuleuse *f*

nebulizer /ˈnebjʊlaɪzəʳ/ N *(Med)* nébuliseur *m*

nebulous /ˈnebjʊləs/ ADJ *(= vague) [notion, concept]* nébuleux, vague ; *(Astron)* nébuleux

NEC /ˌeniːˈsiː/ N (abbrev of **National Executive Committee**) → **national**

necessarily /ˈnesɪsərɪlɪ/ LANGUAGE IN USE 16.1
ADV 1 *(= automatically)* ◆ **not ~** pas forcément ◆ **this is not ~ the case** ce n'est pas forcément le cas ◆ **you don't ~ have to believe it** vous n'êtes pas forcé *or* obligé de le croire ◆ **he was lying, of course – not ~** bien entendu, il mentait – pas forcément 2 *(= inevitably) [slow, short]* forcément, nécessairement ◆ **at this stage the plan ~ lacks detail** à ce stade, le plan n'est forcément pas très détaillé

necessary /ˈnesɪsərɪ/ LANGUAGE IN USE 10.3
ADJ 1 *(= required) [skill, arrangements]* nécessaire, requis *(to, for sth* à qch*)* ◆ **all the qualifications ~ for this job** toutes les qualifications requises pour ce poste ◆ **if ~** le cas échéant, si nécessaire ◆ **when** *or* **where ~** lorsque c'est nécessaire ◆ **to do more than is ~** en faire plus qu'il n'est nécessaire ◆ **to do no more than is strictly ~** ne faire que le strict nécessaire ◆ **to do whatever is** *or* **everything ~ (for)** faire le nécessaire (pour) ◆ **to make it ~ for sb to do sth** mettre qn dans la nécessité de faire qch ◆ **it is ~ to do this** il est nécessaire de le faire ◆ **it is ~ for him to do this** il est nécessaire qu'il le fasse ◆ **it is ~ that ...** il est nécessaire que ... *+ subj*

2 *(= inevitable) [consequence]* inéluctable ; *[corollary]* nécessaire ; *[result]* inévitable ◆ **there is no ~ connection between ...** il n'y a pas nécessairement de rapport entre ... ◆ **a ~ evil** un mal nécessaire

N 1 ◆ **to do the ~** * faire le nécessaire
2 *(= money)* ◆ **the ~** * le fric*
3 *(Jur)* ◆ **necessaries** *(= necessities)* les choses *fpl* nécessaires

necessitate /nɪˈsesɪteɪt/ VT nécessiter, rendre nécessaire ◆ **the situation ~d his immediate return** la situation l'a obligé à revenir immédiatement, la situation a nécessité son retour immédiat ◆ **the situation ~s our abandoning the plan** la situation exige que nous abandonnions le projet

necessitous /nɪˈsesɪtəs/ ADJ *(frm)* nécessiteux ◆ **in ~ circumstances** dans le besoin, dans la nécessité

necessity /nɪˈsesɪtɪ/ N 1 *(NonC) (= compelling circumstances)* nécessité *f* ; *(= need, compulsion)* besoin *m*, nécessité *f* ◆ **the ~ of doing sth** le besoin *or* la nécessité de faire qch ◆ **she realized the ~ of going to see him** elle a compris qu'il était nécessaire d'aller le voir *or* qu'il fallait aller le voir ◆ **she questioned the ~ of buying a brand new car** elle mettait en doute la nécessité d'acheter une voiture neuve ◆ **she regretted the ~ of making him redundant** elle regrettait d'avoir à le licencier ◆ **is there any ~?** est-ce nécessaire ? ◆ **there's no ~ for tears/apologies** il n'est pas nécessaire de pleurer/s'excuser ◆ **there is no ~ for you to do that** il n'est pas nécessaire que vous fassiez cela ◆ **from** *or* **out of ~** par nécessité, par la force des choses ◆ **of ~** par nécessité ◆ **to be born of ~** être dicté par les circonstances ◆ **to be under the ~ of doing sth** *(frm)* être dans la nécessité *or* dans l'obligation de faire qch ◆ **a case of absolute ~** un cas de force majeure ◆ **in case of ~** au besoin, en cas de besoin ◆ **~ knows no law** *(Prov)* nécessité fait loi *(Prov)* ◆ **~ is the mother of invention** *(Prov)* la nécessité rend ingénieux, nécessité est mère d'invention † ; → **virtue**

2 *(NonC = poverty)* besoin *m*, nécessité † *f*

3 *(= necessary object etc)* chose *f* indispensable ◆ **a dishwasher is a ~ nowadays** un lave-vaisselle est indispensable de nos jours, de nos jours, il est indispensable d'avoir un lave-vaisselle ◆ **a basic ~** *(= product)* un produit de première nécessité ◆ **water is a basic ~ of life** l'eau est indispensable à la vie ◆ **a political/economic ~** un impératif politique/économique ; → **bare**

neck /nek/ N 1 cou *m* ; *[of horse, cow, swan]* encolure *f* ◆ **to have a sore ~** avoir mal au cou ◆ **to fling one's arms round sb's ~, to fall on sb's ~** *(liter)* se jeter *or* sauter au cou de qn ◆ **to win by a ~** *(Racing)* gagner d'une encolure ◆ **I don't want (to have) him (hanging) round my ~** * je ne veux pas l'avoir sur le dos ◆ **to risk one's ~** risquer sa vie *or* sa peau* ◆ **he's up to his ~ in it** * *(in crime, plot, conspiracy)* il est mouillé jusqu'au cou* ◆ **to be up to one's ~ in work** * être débordé (de travail) ◆ **he's up to his ~ in debt** * il est endetté jusqu'au cou ◆ **he's up to his ~ in drug dealing** * il est mouillé jusqu'au cou dans des affaires de trafic de stupéfiants ◆ **the government is up to its ~ in new allegations of corruption** * le gouvernement a fort à faire avec ces nouvelles allégations de corruption ◆ **he got it in the ~** * *(= got told off)* il en a pris pour son grade* ; *(= got beaten up)* il a dérouillé* ; *(= got killed)* il s'est fait descendre* ◆ **to stick one's ~ out** * se mouiller* ◆ **to throw sb out ~ and crop** jeter qn dehors avec violence ◆ **it's ~ or nothing** * *(Brit)* il faut jouer *or* risquer le tout pour le tout ; → **breakneck, breathe, pain, save¹, stiff**

2 *(Culin)* ◆ **~ of mutton** collet *m or* collier *m* de mouton ◆ **~ of beef** collier *m* de bœuf ◆ **best end of ~** côtelettes *fpl* premières

3 *[of dress, shirt etc]* encolure *f* ◆ **high ~** col *m* montant ◆ **square ~** col *m* carré ◆ **a dress with a low ~** une robe décolletée ◆ **a shirt with a 38cm ~** une chemise qui fait 38 cm d'encolure *or* de tour de cou ; → **polo, roll**

4 *[of bottle]* goulot *m* ; *[of vase]* col *m* ; *[of tooth, screw]* collet *m* ; *[of land]* isthme *m* ; *[of guitar, violin]* manche *m* ; *[of uterus, bladder]* col *m* ◆ **in our** *or* **this ~ of the woods** par ici ◆ **she's from your ~ of the woods** elle vient du même coin que vous ; → **bottleneck**

5 *(Brit * = impertinence)* toupet* *m*, culot* *m*

VI *(esp US *) [couple]* se peloter* ◆ **to ~ with sb** peloter* qn

VT * *(= drink)* s'enfiler*

COMP **neck and neck** ADJ à égalité

neckband /ˈnekbænd/ N *(= part of garment)* col *m* ; *(= choker)* tour *m* de cou

-necked /nekt/ ADJ *(in compounds)* → **low¹, round, stiff**

neckerchief /ˈnekətʃiːf/ N *(= scarf)* foulard *m*, tour *m* de cou ; *(on dress)* fichu *m*

necking * /ˈnekɪŋ/ N *(esp US)* pelotage* *m*

necklace /ˈneklɪs/ N collier *m* ; *(long)* sautoir *m* ◆ **ruby/pearl ~** collier *m* de rubis/de perles ◆ **diamond ~** collier *m or* rivière *f* de diamants
VT *(* = kill with burning tyre)* faire subir le supplice du collier à COMP **necklace killing** N supplice *m* du collier

necklacing /ˈneklɪsɪŋ/ N ⇒ **necklace killing** ; → **necklace**

necklet /ˈneklɪt/ N collier *m*

neckline /ˈneklaɪn/ N encolure *f*

neckshot /ˈnekʃɒt/ N ≈ balle *f* dans la nuque

necktie /ˈnektaɪ/ N *(esp US)* cravate *f*

necrological /ˌnekrəʊˈlɒdʒɪkəl/ ADJ nécrologique

necrologist /neˈkrɒlədʒɪst/ N nécrologue *m*

necrology /neˈkrɒlədʒɪ/ N nécrologie *f*

necromancer /ˈnekrəʊmænsəʳ/ N nécromancien(ne) *m(f)*

necromancy /ˈnekrəʊmænsɪ/ N nécromancie *f*

necrophile /ˈnekrəʊˌfaɪl/ N nécrophile *mf*

necrophilia /ˌnekrəʊˈfɪlɪə/ N nécrophilie *f*

necrophiliac /ˌnekrəʊˈfɪlɪˌæk/ N nécrophile *mf*

necrophilic /ˌnekrəʊˈfɪlɪk/ ADJ nécrophile

necrophilism /neˈkrɒfɪlɪzəm/ N ⇒ **necrophilia**

necrophobe /ˈnekrəʊˌfəʊb/ N nécrophobe *mf*

necrophobia /ˌnekrəʊˈfəʊbɪə/ N nécrophobie *f*

necrophobic /ˌnekrəʊˈfəʊbɪk/ ADJ nécrophobe

necropolis /neˈkrɒpəlɪs/ N (pl **necropolises** *or* **necropoleis** /neˈkrɒpəˌleɪs/) nécropole *f*

necrosis /neˈkrəʊsɪs/ N nécrose *f*

necrotising fasciitis, necrotizing fasciitis (US) /ˈnekrəʊtaɪzɪŋfæʃɪˈaɪtɪs/ N (*Med*) fasciite *f* nécrosante *or* gangreneuse

nectar /ˈnektəʳ/ N nectar *m*

nectarine /ˈnektərɪn/ N (*= fruit*) brugnon *m*, nectarine *f* ; (*= tree*) brugnonier *m*

ned ⁑ /ned/ N (*esp Scot*) voyou *m*

NEDC /ˌeniːdiːˈsiː/ N (*Brit: formerly*) (abbrev of **National Economic Development Council**) → **national**

Neddy * /ˈnedɪ/ N (*Brit: formerly*) (abbrev of **National Economic Development Council**) → **national**

née /neɪ/ ADJ née ◆ **Mrs Gautier, ~ Buchanan** Mme Gautier, née Buchanan

need /niːd/ LANGUAGE IN USE 10.2

N 1 (*NonC = necessity, obligation*) besoin *m* ◆ **in case of ~** en cas de besoin ◆ **I can't see the ~ for it** je n'en vois pas la nécessité

◆ **if need be** si besoin est, s'il le faut

◆ **no need** ◆ **there's no ~ to hurry** il n'y a pas besoin *or* lieu de se dépêcher ◆ **no ~ to rush!** il n'y a pas le feu ! ◆ **no ~ to worry!** inutile de s'inquiéter ! ◆ **no ~ to tell him** pas besoin de lui dire ◆ **to have no ~ to do sth** ne pas avoir besoin de faire qch ◆ **there's no ~ for you to come, you have no ~ to come** vous n'êtes pas obligé de venir ◆ **should I call him? – no, there's no ~** dois-je l'appeler ? – non, ce n'est pas la peine

2 (*NonC*) (*= want, lack, poverty*) besoin *m* ◆ **there is much ~ of food** il y a un grand besoin de vivres ◆ **when the ~ arises** quand le besoin se présente *or* s'en fait sentir ◆ **your ~ is greater than mine** vous êtes plus dans le besoin que moi ; (* *hum*) vous en avez plus besoin que moi ; → **serve**

◆ **to be in need of, to have need of** avoir besoin de ◆ **to be badly** *or* **greatly in ~ of** avoir grand besoin de ◆ **I'm in ~ of a drink** j'ai besoin de prendre un verre ◆ **the house is in ~ of repainting** la maison a besoin d'être repeinte ◆ **those most in ~ of help** ceux qui ont le plus besoin d'aide ◆ **I have no ~ of advice** je n'ai pas besoin de conseils

3 (*NonC*) (*= misfortune*) adversité *f*, difficulté *f* ; (*= poverty*) besoin *m* ◆ **in times of ~** aux heures *or* aux moments difficiles ◆ **do not fail me in my hour of ~** ne m'abandonnez pas dans l'adversité

◆ **in need** ◆ **to be in ~** être dans le besoin ; → **friend**

4 (*= thing needed*) besoin *m* ◆ **to supply sb's ~s** subvenir aux besoins de qn ◆ **his ~s are few** il a peu de besoins ◆ **give me a list of your ~s** donnez-moi une liste de ce dont vous avez besoin *or* de ce qu'il vous faut ◆ **the greatest ~s of industry** ce dont l'industrie a le plus besoin

VT 1 (*= require*) [*person, thing*] avoir besoin de ◆ **they ~ one another** ils ont besoin l'un de l'autre ◆ **I ~ money** j'ai besoin d'argent, il me faut de l'argent ◆ **I ~ more money** il me faut plus d'argent ◆ **I ~ it** j'en ai besoin ◆ **do you ~ more time?** avez-vous besoin qu'on vous accorde *subj* plus de *or* davantage de temps ? ◆ **have you got all that you ~?** vous avez tout ce qu'il vous faut ? ◆ **it's just what I ~ed** c'est tout à fait ce qu'il me fallait ◆ **I ~ two more to complete the series** il m'en faut encore deux pour compléter la série ◆ **he ~ed no second invitation** il n'a pas eu besoin qu'on lui répète *subj* l'invitation ◆ **the house ~s repainting** *or* **to be repainted** la maison a besoin d'être repeinte ◆ **her hair ~s brushing** *or* **to be brushed** ses cheveux ont besoin d'un coup de brosse ◆ **a visa is ~ed** il faut un visa ◆ **a much ~ed holiday** des vacances dont on a (*or* j'ai *etc*) grand besoin ◆ **I gave it a much ~ed wash** je l'ai lavé, ce dont il avait grand besoin ◆ **it ~ed a war to alter that** il a fallu une guerre pour changer ça ◆ **it** *or* **he doesn't ~ me to tell him** il n'a pas besoin que je le lui dise ◆ **she ~s watching** *or* **to be watched** elle a besoin d'être surveillée ◆ **he ~s to have everything explained to him in detail** il faut tout lui expliquer en détail ◆ **you will hardly ~ to be reminded that ...** vous n'avez sûrement pas besoin qu'on (*or* que je *etc*) vous rappelle *subj* que ... ◆ **you only ~ed to ask** tu n'avais qu'à demander ◆ **who ~s it?** * (*fig*) on s'en fiche ! * ◆ **who ~s politicians (anyway)?** * (*fig*) (de toutes façons) les hommes politiques, à quoi ça sert* *or* qu'est-ce qu'on en a à faire ?* ; → **hole**

2 (*= demand*) demander ◆ **this book ~s careful reading** ce livre demande à être lu attentivement *or* nécessite une lecture attentive ◆ **this coat ~s to be cleaned regularly** ce manteau doit être nettoyé régulièrement ◆ **this plant ~s care** il faut prendre soin de cette plante ◆ **the situation ~s detailed consideration** la situation doit être considérée dans le détail ◆ **this will ~ some explaining** il va falloir fournir de sérieuses explications là-dessus

MODAL AUX VB 1 (*indicating obligation*) ◆ **he go?, does he ~ to go?** a-t-il besoin *or* est-il obligé d'y aller ?, faut-il qu'il y aille ? ◆ **you needn't wait** vous n'avez pas besoin *or* vous n'êtes pas obligé d'attendre ◆ **you needn't bother to write to me** ce n'est pas la peine *or* ne vous donnez pas la peine de m'écrire ◆ **I told her she needn't reply** *or* **she didn't ~ to reply** je lui ai dit qu'elle n'était pas obligée *or* forcée de répondre ◆ **we needn't have hurried** ce n'était pas la peine de nous presser ◆ **~ I finish the book now?** faut-il que je termine *subj* le livre maintenant ? ◆ **~ we go into all this now?** est-il nécessaire de *or* faut-il discuter de tout cela maintenant ? ◆ **I ~ hardly say that ...** je n'ai guère besoin de dire que ..., inutile de dire que ... ◆ **~ I say more?** ai-je besoin d'en dire plus (long) ? ◆ **you needn't say any more** inutile d'en dire plus ◆ **no one ~ go** *or* **~s to go hungry nowadays** de nos jours personne ne devrait souffrir de la faim ◆ **why ~ you always remind me of that?, why do you always ~ to remind me of that?** pourquoi faut-il toujours que tu me rappelles *subj* cela ?

2 (*indicating logical necessity*) ◆ **~ that be true?** est-ce nécessairement vrai ? ◆ **that needn't be the case** ce n'est pas nécessairement *or* forcément le cas ◆ **it ~ not follow that they are all affected** il ne s'ensuit pas nécessairement *or* forcément qu'ils soient tous affectés

COMP **need-to-know** ADJ ◆ **to access information on a ~-to-know basis** avoir accès à des renseignements de manière ponctuelle

needful /ˈniːdfʊl/ ADJ nécessaire ◆ **to do what is ~** faire ce qui est nécessaire, faire le nécessaire ◆ **as much as is ~** autant qu'il en faut N ◆ **to do the ~** * faire ce qu'il faut

neediness /ˈniːdɪnɪs/ N indigence *f*

needle /ˈniːdl/ N 1 aiguille *f* ◆ **knitting/darning** *etc* **~** aiguille *f* à tricoter/à repriser *etc* ◆ **record-player ~** pointe *f* de lecture, saphir *m* ◆ **gramophone ~** aiguille *f* de phonographe ◆ **pine ~** aiguille *f* de pin ◆ **it's like looking for a ~ in a haystack** autant chercher une aiguille dans une botte de foin ◆ **to be on the ~** ⁑ (*Drugs*) se shooter⁑ ; → **pin, sharp**

2 (*Brit* *) **he gives me the ~** (*= teases me*) il me charrie⁑ ; (*= annoys me*) il me tape sur les nerfs* *or* sur le système* ◆ **to get the ~** se ficher en boule⁑

VT 1 * (*= annoy*) asticoter, agacer ; (*= sting*) piquer *or* toucher au vif ; (*= nag*) harceler ◆ **she was ~d into replying sharply** touchée au vif *or* agacée elle a répondu avec brusquerie

2 (*US*) **to ~ a drink** ⁑ corser une boisson

COMP **needle book, needle case** N porte-aiguilles *m inv*

needle exchange N (*= needle swapping*) échange *m* de seringues ; (*= place*) centre *m* d'échange de seringues

needle match N (*Brit Sport*) règlement *m* de comptes

needle-sharp ADJ (*fig*) (*= alert*) malin (-igne *f*) comme un singe ; (*= penetrating*) perspicace

needlecord /ˈniːdlkɔːd/ N velours *m* mille-raies

needlecraft /ˈniːdlkrɑːft/ N travaux *mpl* d'aiguille

needlepoint /ˈniːdlpɔɪnt/ N tapisserie *f* (à l'aiguille)

needless /ˈniːdlɪs/ ADJ [*death, suffering, sacrifice, repetition*] inutile ; [*cruelty, destruction*] gratuit ; [*expense, risk*] inutile, superflu ; [*remark, sarcasm, rudeness*] déplacé ◆ ◆ **to say, ...** inutile de dire que ..., il va sans dire que ...

needlessly /ˈniːdlɪslɪ/ ADV [*repeat, prolong*] inutilement ; [*die*] en vain ; [*suffer*] pour rien ◆ **you're worrying quite ~** vous vous inquiétez sans raison ◆ **he was ~ rude** il a été d'une impolitesse tout à fait déplacée

needlessness /ˈniːdlɪsnɪs/ N inutilité *f* ; [*of remark*] inopportunité *f*

needlestick /ˈniːdlstɪk/ N ◆ **~ injury** blessure *f* causée par une seringue

needlewoman /ˈniːdlwʊmən/ N (pl **-women**) ◆ **she is a good ~** elle est douée pour les travaux d'aiguille

needlework /ˈniːdlwɜːk/ N (*gen*) travaux *mpl* d'aiguille ; (*= mending etc*) (*also Scol*) couture *f* ◆ **bring your ~ with you** apportez votre ouvrage

needn't /ˈniːdnt/ ⇒ **need not** ; → **need modal aux vb**

needs /niːdz/ ADV (*liter*) ◆ **I must ~ leave tomorrow** il me faut absolument partir demain, je dois de toute nécessité partir demain ◆ **if ~ must** s'il le faut absolument, si c'est absolument nécessaire ◆ ◆ **~ must when the devil drives** (*Prov*) nécessité fait loi (*Prov*)

needy /ˈniːdɪ/ ADJ [*person*] indigent, dans le besoin ; [*area*] sinistré ◆ **he's very ~ at the moment** (*emotionally*) il a besoin de beaucoup d'attention en ce moment NPL **the needy** les nécessiteux *mpl*

neep /niːp/ N (*Scot*) rutabaga *m*

ne'er /neəʳ/ ADV (*liter*) ⇒ **never adv** COMP **ne'er-do-well** N bon(ne) *m(f)* *or* propre *mf* à rien ADJ bon *or* propre à rien

ne'ertheless /ˈneəðəles/ ADV (*liter*) ⇒ **nevertheless**

nefarious /nɪˈfeərɪəs/ ADJ (*frm*) vil (vile *f*) (*liter*)

nefariousness /nɪˈfeərɪəsnɪs/ N (*frm*) scélératesse *f*

neg. (abbrev of **negative**) nég.

negate /nɪˈgeɪt/ VT *(frm)* *(= nullify)* annuler ; *(= deny truth of)* nier la vérité de ; *(= deny existence of)* nier (l'existence de) ◆ **this ~d all the good that we had achieved** cela a réduit à rien tout le bien que nous avions fait

negation /nɪˈgeɪʃən/ N *(all senses)* négation *f*

negative /ˈnegətɪv/ ADJ *(gen, Elec, Ling, Phys etc)* négatif *(about sb/sth* à l'égard de qn/qch) ; *(= harmful) [effect, influence]* néfaste ◆ **he's a very ~ person** c'est quelqu'un de très négatif

N 1 réponse *f* négative ◆ **his answer was a curt ~** il a répondu par un non fort sec ◆ **the answer was in the ~** la réponse était négative ◆ **to answer in the ~** répondre négativement *or* par la négative, faire une réponse négative ◆ **"negative"** *(as answer, gen)* "négatif" ; *(computer voice)* "réponse négative"

2 *(Ling)* négation *f* ◆ **double ~** double négation *f* ◆ **two ~s make a positive** deux négations équivalent à une affirmation ◆ **in(to) the ~** à la forme négative

3 *(Phot)* négatif *m*, cliché *m*

4 *(Elec)* (pôle *m*) négatif *m*

VT 1 *(= veto) [+ plan]* rejeter, repousser ◆ **the amendment was ~d** l'amendement fut repoussé

2 *(= contradict, refute) [+ statement]* contredire, réfuter

3 *(= nullify) [+ effect]* neutraliser

COMP **negative campaigning** N *(NonC: Pol)* campagne *f* négative

negative charge N *(Phys)* charge *f* négative

negative equity N moins-value *f*

negative feedback N *(NonC)* 1 *(= criticism)* réactions *fpl* négatives ◆ **to give sb/get ~ feedback (about sb/sth)** faire part à qn de ses/recevoir des réactions négatives (au sujet de qn/qch) 2 *(Elec)* contre-réaction *f*

negative income tax N impôt *m* négatif

negative number N nombre *m* négatif

negative particle N *(Ling, Phys)* particule *f* négative

negative pole N *(Phys)* pôle *m* négatif

negative sign N *(Math)* signe *m* moins

negative tax N ⇒ **negative income tax**

negatively /ˈnegətɪvlɪ/ ADV *[respond]* négativement ; *[affect]* d'une manière défavorable ◆ **to look at things ~** voir les choses de façon négative

Negev Desert /ˈnegevˈdezət/ N désert *m* du Néguev

neglect /nɪˈglekt/ VT *[+ person, animal]* négliger, délaisser ; *[+ garden, house, car, machinery]* ne pas entretenir ; *[+ rule, law]* ne tenir aucun compte de, ne faire aucun cas de ; *[+ duty, obligation, promise]* manquer à ; *[+ business, work, hobby]* négliger ; *[+ opportunity]* laisser passer ; *[+ one's health]* négliger ; *[+ advice]* ne tenir aucun compte de, ne faire aucun cas de *(frm)* ◆ **to ~ o.s.** *or* **one's appearance** se négliger ◆ **to ~ to do sth** négliger *or* omettre de faire qch ; see also **neglected**

N *(NonC)* *[of duty]* manquement *m* (*of* à) ; *[of work]* manque *m* d'intérêt *m* (*of* pour) ; *[of building]* manque *m* d'entretien ◆ **~ of one's appearance** manque *m* de soin apporté à son apparence ◆ **his ~ of his promise** son manquement à sa promesse, le fait de ne pas tenir sa promesse ◆ **his ~ of his children** la façon dont il a négligé *or* délaissé ses enfants ◆ **his ~ of his house/garden/car** le fait qu'il ne s'occupe pas de sa maison/de son jardin/de sa voiture ◆ **the garden was in a state of ~** le jardin était mal tenu *or* était à l'abandon ◆ **after years of ~, the building is being renovated** après être resté des années à l'abandon, l'immeuble est en train d'être rénové

neglected /nɪˈglektɪd/ ADJ 1 *(= uncared-for) [person, district]* délaissé ; *[house, garden]* mal entretenu ; *[appearance]* négligé 2 *(= forgotten) [play]* méconnu, ignoré ◆ **a ~ area of scientific research** un domaine négligé de la recherche scientifique

neglectful /nɪˈglektfʊl/ ADJ négligent ◆ **to be ~ of sth** négliger qch

neglectfully /nɪˈglektfəlɪ/ ADV avec négligence

négligé, negligee, negligée /ˈneglɪʒeɪ/ N négligé *m*, déshabillé *m*

negligence /ˈneglɪdʒəns/ N *(NonC)* négligence *f*, manque *m* de soins *or* de précautions ◆ **through ~** par négligence ◆ **sin of ~** *(Rel)* faute *f or* péché *m* d'omission ; → **contributory**

negligent /ˈneglɪdʒənt/ ADJ 1 *(= careless)* négligent ◆ **he was ~ in his work** il a fait preuve de négligence dans son travail ◆ **to be ~ in doing sth** faire preuve de négligence en faisant qch ◆ **to be ~ of sth** négliger qch 2 *(= nonchalant)* nonchalant COMP **negligent homicide** N *(US)* ≃ homicide *m* involontaire

negligently /ˈneglɪdʒəntlɪ/ ADV 1 *(= carelessly)* ◆ **to behave ~** faire preuve de négligence 2 *(= nonchalantly, offhandedly)* négligemment ◆ **... she answered ~** ... répondit-elle négligemment

negligible /ˈneglɪdʒəbl/ ADJ *[amount, effect]* négligeable ; *[risk, impact]* négligeable, insignifiant ; *[support, cost]* insignifiant

negotiable /nɪˈgəʊʃɪəbl/ ADJ 1 *(esp Fin) [price, salary]* à débattre ; *[rates, conditions, contract, bonds]* négociable ◆ **not ~** non négociable 2 *(= passable) [road, valley]* praticable ; *[mountain, obstacle]* franchissable ; *[river] (= can be sailed)* navigable ; *(= can be crossed)* franchissable COMP **negotiable securities** NPL fonds *mpl* négociables

negotiant /nɪˈgəʊʃɪənt/ N négociateur *m*, -trice *f*

negotiate /nɪˈgəʊʃɪeɪt/ VT 1 *[+ sale, loan, settlement, salary]* négocier 2 *[+ obstacle, hill]* franchir ; *[+ river] (= sail on)* naviguer ; *(= cross)* franchir, traverser ; *[+ rapids, falls]* franchir ; *[+ bend in road]* prendre, négocier ; *[+ difficulty]* surmonter, franchir 3 *[+ bill, cheque, bond]* négocier VI négocier, traiter *(with sb for sth* avec qn pour obtenir qch) ◆ **they are negotiating for more pay** ils sont en pourparler(s) *or* ils ont entamé des négociations pour obtenir des augmentations

negotiation /nɪˌgəʊʃɪˈeɪʃən/ N *(= discussion)* négociation *f* ◆ **to begin ~s with** engager *or* entamer des négociations *or* des pourparlers avec ◆ **to be in ~ with** être en pourparlers avec ◆ **the deal is under ~** l'affaire est en cours de négociation ◆ **~s are proceeding** des négociations *or* des pourparlers sont en cours ◆ **to solve sth by ~** résoudre qch par la négociation

negotiator /nɪˈgəʊʃɪeɪtəʳ/ N négociateur *m*, -trice *f*

Negress /ˈniːgres/ N Noire *f*

Negro /ˈniːgrəʊ/ ADJ noir ; *(Anthropology)* négroïde ; → **spiritual** N *(pl* **Negroes**) Noir *m*

Negroid /ˈniːgrɔɪd/ ADJ négroïde

Nehemiah /ˌniːɪˈmaɪə/ N Néhémie *m*

neigh /neɪ/ VI hennir N hennissement *m*

neighbour, neighbor *(US)* /ˈneɪbəʳ/ N voisin(e) *m(f)* ; *(Bible etc)* prochain(e) *m(f)* ◆ **she is my ~** c'est ma voisine ◆ **she is a good ~** c'est une bonne voisine ◆ **Good Neighbor Policy** *(US Pol)* politique *f* de bon voisinage ◆ **Britain's nearest ~ is France** la France est la plus proche voisine de la Grande-Bretagne ; → **next door** VI *(US)* ◆ **to neighbor with sb** se montrer bon voisin envers qn COMP **neighbor states** NPL *(US)* États *mpl* voisins

neighbourhood, neighborhood *(US)* /ˈneɪbəhʊd/ N *(= district)* quartier *m* ; *(= area nearby)* voisinage *m*, environs *mpl* ◆ **all the children of the ~** tous les enfants du voisinage *or* du quartier ◆ **it's not a nice ~** c'est un quartier plutôt mal famé ◆ **the whole ~ knows him** tout le quartier le connaît ◆ **is there a cinema in your ~?** y a-t-il un cinéma près de chez vous ? ◆ **in the ~ of the church** dans le voisinage de l'église, du côté de l'église ◆ **(something) in the ~ of $100** dans les 100 dollars, environ 100 dollars ◆ **anyone in the ~ of the crime** toute personne se trouvant dans les parages du crime

ADJ *[doctor, shops]* du quartier ; *[café]* du coin ◆ **our/your friendly ~ dentist** *(fig, often iro)* le gentil dentiste de notre/votre quartier

COMP **neighbourhood TV** N télévision *f* locale

neighbourhood watch N *système de surveillance assuré par les habitants d'un quartier*

neighbouring, neighboring *(US)* /ˈneɪbərɪŋ/ ADJ *[country, area, building]* voisin, avoisinant ; *[state, town]* voisin ◆ **in ~ Italy** dans l'Italie voisine

neighbourliness, neighborliness *(US)* /ˈneɪbəlɪnɪs/ N ◆ **(good) ~** rapports *mpl* de bon voisinage

neighbourly, neighborly *(US)* /ˈneɪbəlɪ/ ADJ *[person]* aimable *(to sb* avec qn), amical ; *[feeling]* amical ; *[behaviour, gesture]* de bon voisin ◆ **they are ~ people** ils sont bons voisins ◆ **~ relations** rapports *mpl* de bon voisinage ◆ **to behave in a ~ way** se conduire en bon voisin ◆ **that's very ~ of you** c'est très aimable (de votre part)

neighing /ˈneɪɪŋ/ N hennissement(s) *m(pl)* ADJ hennissant

neither /ˈnaɪðəʳ, ˈniːðəʳ/ ADV ni ◆ **~ ... nor** ni ... ni + *ne before vb* ◆ **~ good nor bad** ni bon ni mauvais ◆ **I've seen ~ him nor her** je ne les ai vus ni l'un ni l'autre ◆ **he can ~ read nor write** il ne sait ni lire ni écrire ◆ **the house has ~ water nor electricity** la maison n'a ni eau ni électricité ◆ **~ you nor I know** ni vous ni moi ne (le) savons ◆ **he ~ knows nor cares** il n'en sait rien et ça lui est égal

◆ **neither here nor there** ◆ **that's ~ here nor there** ce n'est pas la question ◆ **the fact that she needed the money is ~ here nor there, it's still stealing** peu importe qu'elle ait eu besoin de cet argent, il n'en reste pas moins que c'est du vol ◆ **an extra couple of miles is ~ here nor there** on n'en est pas à deux ou trois kilomètres près

CONJ 1 **if you don't go, ~ shall I** si tu n'y vas pas je n'irai pas non plus ◆ **I'm not going – ~ am I** je n'y vais pas – moi non plus ◆ **he didn't do it – ~ did his brother** il ne l'a pas fait – son frère non plus

2 *(liter – moreover ... not)* d'ailleurs ... ne ... pas ◆ **I can't go, ~ do I want to** je ne peux pas y aller et d'ailleurs je n'en ai pas envie

ADJ ◆ **~ story is true** ni l'une ni l'autre des deux histoires n'est vraie, aucune des deux histoires n'est vraie ◆ **~ candidate got the job** les candidats n'ont eu le poste ni l'un ni l'autre ◆ **in ~ way** ni d'une manière ni de l'autre ◆ **in ~ case** ni dans un cas ni dans l'autre

PRON aucun(e) *m(f)*, ni l'un(e) ni l'autre + *ne before vb* ◆ **~ of them knows** ni l'un ni l'autre ne le sait, ils ne le savent ni l'un ni l'autre ◆ **I know ~ of them** je ne (les) connais ni l'un ni l'autre ◆ **which (of the two) do you prefer? – ~** lequel (des deux) préférez-vous ? – ni l'un ni l'autre

Nelly /ˈnelɪ/ N (dim of **Helen, Ellen**) Hélène *f*, Éléonore *f* ◆ **not on your ~!**✻ jamais de la vie !

nelson /ˈnelsən/ N *(Wrestling)* ◆ **full ~** nelson *m* ◆ **half-~** clef *f* au cou ◆ **to put a half-~ on sb** * *(fig)* attraper qn *(pour l'empêcher de faire qch)*

nematode /ˈnemətəʊd/ N (also **nematode worm**) nématode *m*

nem. con. (abbrev of **nemine contradicente**) *(= no one contradicting)* à l'unanimité

nemesia /nɪˈmiːʒə/ N némésia *m (fleur)*

Nemesis /ˈnemɪsɪs/ N (pl **Nemeses**) 1 *(Myth)* Némésis *f* 2 (also **nemesis**) némésis *f*, instrument *m* de vengeance ◆ **it's ~** c'est un juste retour des choses ◆ **she's my ~** *(esp US)* je suis vaincu d'avance avec elle

neo... /ˈniːəʊ/ PREF néo...

Neocene /ˈniːəˌsiːn/ N néogène *m*

neoclassical /ˌniːəʊˈklæsɪkəl/ ADJ néoclassique

neoclassicism /ˌniːəʊˈklæsɪˌsɪzəm/ N néoclassicisme *m*

neocolonial /ˌniːəʊkəˈləʊnɪəl/ ADJ néocolonial

neocolonialism /ˌniːəʊkəˈləʊnɪəlɪzəm/ N néocolonialisme *m*

neodymium /ˌniːəʊˈdɪmɪəm/ N néodyme *m*

neofascism /ˌniːəʊˈfæʃɪzəm/ N néofascisme *m*

neofascist /ˌniːəʊˈfæʃɪst/ ADJ, N néofasciste *mf*

Neogene /ˈniːəˌdʒiːn/ N néogène *m*

neolith /ˈniːəlɪθ/ N *(Archeol)* pierre *f* polie

neolithic /ˌniːəʊˈlɪθɪk/ ADJ *[site, tomb]* néolithique ; *[person]* du néolithique COMP **the Neolithic Age, the Neolithic Period** N le néolithique

neological /ˌnɪəˈlɒdʒɪkəl/ ADJ néologique

neologism /nɪˈɒləˌdʒɪzəm/ N néologisme *m*

neologize /nɪˈɒlədʒaɪz/ VI faire un (or des) néologisme(s)

neology /nɪˈɒlədʒɪ/ N ⇒ **neologism**

neomycin /ˌniːəʊˈmaɪsɪn/ N néomycine *f*

neon /ˈniːɒn/ N (gaz *m*) néon *m* COMP *[lamp, lighting]* au néon **neon sign** N enseigne *f* (lumineuse) au néon

neonatal /ˌniːəʊˈneɪtəl/ ADJ néonatal ◆ **~ care** soins *mpl* néonatals ◆ **~ unit** service *m* de nouveaux-nés *or* de néonatalité

neonate /ˈniːəʊˌneɪt/ N *(frm)* nouveau-né *m*

neonazi /ˌniːəʊˈnɑːtsɪ/ ADJ, N néonazi(e) *m(f)*

neophyte /ˈniːəʊˌfaɪt/ N néophyte *mf*

neoplasm /ˈniːəʊˌplæzəm/ N néoplasme *m*

Neo-Platonic, neoplatonic /ˌniːəʊpləˈtɒnɪk/ ADJ néoplatonicien

Neo-Platonism, neoplatonism /ˌniːəʊˈpleɪtəˌnɪzəm/ N néoplatonisme *m*

Neo-Platonist, neoplatonist /ˌniːəʊˈpleɪtəˌnɪst/ N néoplatonicien(ne) *m(f)*

Neozoic /ˌniːəʊˈzəʊɪk/ ADJ néozoïque

Nepal /nɪˈpɔːl/ N Népal *m* ◆ **in ~** au Népal

Nepalese /ˌnepɔːˈliːz/, **Nepali** /nɪˈpɔːlɪ/ ADJ népalais N 1 *(pl inv)* Népalais(e) *m(f)* 2 *(= language)* népalais *m*

nephew /ˈnefjuː/ N neveu *m*

nephralgia /nɪˈfrældʒɪə/ N néphralgie *f*

nephrectomy /nɪˈfrektəmɪ/ N néphrectomie *f*

nephritic /neˈfrɪtɪk/ ADJ néphrétique

nephritis /neˈfraɪtɪs/ N néphrite *f*

nephrology /nɪˈfrɒlədʒɪ/ N néphrologie *f*

nephrosis /nɪˈfrəʊsɪs/ N néphrose *f*

nephrotomy /nɪˈfrɒtəmɪ/ N néphrotomie *f*

nepotism /ˈnepətɪzəm/ N népotisme *m*

Neptune /ˈneptjuːn/ N *(Myth)* Neptune *m* ; *(Astron)* Neptune *f*

neptunium /nepˈtjuːnɪəm/ N neptunium *m*

nerd‡ /nɜːd/ N 1 *(= pathetic person)* pauvre mec* *m*, ringard* *m* 2 *(= enthusiast)* ◆ **a computer/science ~** un fou d'informatique/de sciences

nerdish‡ /ˈnɜːdɪʃ/, **nerdy**‡ /ˈnɜːdɪ/ ADJ ringard*

nereid /ˈnɪərɪɪd/ N *(Myth, Zool)* néréide *f*

Nero /ˈnɪərəʊ/ N Néron *m*

nerve /nɜːv/ N 1 *(Anat, Dentistry)* nerf *m* ; *(Bot)* nervure *f* ◆ **to kill the ~ of a tooth** dévitaliser une dent ◆ **his speech touched** *or* **struck a (raw) ~** son discours a touché un point sensible

2 *(NonC: fig)* sang-froid *m* ◆ **it was a test of ~ and stamina for the competitors** le sang-froid et l'endurance des concurrents furent mis à l'épreuve ◆ **to hold** *or* **keep one's ~** garder son sang-froid ◆ **he held his ~ to win the race** *(Sport)* il a gardé son sang-froid et il a gagné la course ◆ **he never got his ~ back** *or* **never regained his ~** il n'a jamais repris confiance en lui ◆ **I haven't the ~ to do that** je n'ai pas le courage *or* le cran* de faire ça ◆ **did you tell him? – I didn't/wouldn't have the ~!** le lui as-tu dit ? – je n'en ai pas eu/je n'en aurais pas le courage ! ◆ **his ~ failed him, he lost his ~** le courage lui a manqué, il s'est dégonflé*

3 *(* = cheek)* toupet* *m*, culot* *m* ◆ **you've got a ~!** tu es gonflé !*, tu as du culot* *or* du toupet* ! ◆ **you've got a bloody**‡ **~!** *(Brit)* tu charries !‡ ◆ **what a ~!, of all the ~!, the ~ of it!** quel toupet !*, quel culot !* ◆ **he had the ~ to say that ...** il a eu le toupet* *or* le culot* de dire que ...

NPL **nerves** *(fig = nervousness)* nerfs *mpl*, nervosité *f* ◆ **her ~s are bad, she suffers from ~s** elle a les nerfs fragiles ◆ **to have a fit** *or* **an attack of ~s** *(before performance, exam etc)* avoir le trac* ◆ **it's only ~s** c'est de la nervosité ◆ **to be all ~s, to be a bundle of ~s** être un paquet de nerfs ◆ **he was in a state of ~s, his ~s were on edge** il était sur les nerfs, il avait les nerfs tendus *or* à vif ◆ **he/the noise gets on my ~s** il/ce bruit me tape sur les nerfs* *or* sur le système* ◆ **to live on one's ~s** vivre sur les nerfs ◆ **to have ~s of steel** avoir les nerfs solides *or* des nerfs d'acier ◆ **war of ~s** guerre *f* des nerfs ; → **strain**[1]

VT ◆ **to ~ o.s. to do sth** prendre son courage à deux mains *or* s'armer de courage pour faire qch ◆ **I can't ~ myself to do it** je n'ai pas le courage de le faire

COMP **nerve agent** N substance *f* neurotoxique

nerve cell N cellule *f* nerveuse

nerve centre N *(Anat)* centre *m* nerveux ; *(fig)* centre *m* d'opérations *(fig)*

nerve ending N terminaison *f* nerveuse

nerve gas N gaz *m* neurotoxique

nerve-racking ADJ angoissant, très éprouvant pour les nerfs

nerve specialist N neurologue *mf*

nerve-wracking ADJ ⇒ **nerve-racking**

nerveless /ˈnɜːvlɪs/ ADJ 1 *(= weak) [fingers, hands]* inerte ◆ **the dagger fell from his ~ grasp** sa main inerte a lâché le poignard 2 *(= brave)* intrépide ; *(= calm, collected)* impassible 3 *(pej = cowardly)* lâche, dégonflé* ◆ **he's ~** c'est un dégonflé* 4 *(Anat)* peu innervé ; *(Bot)* sans nervures

nervelessness /ˈnɜːvlɪsnɪs/ N *(fig)* 1 *(= calmness)* sang-froid *m* 2 *(= cowardice)* lâcheté *f*

nerviness* /ˈnɜːvɪnɪs/ N 1 nervosité *f* 2 *(US = cheek)* culot* *m*, toupet* *m*

nervous /ˈnɜːvəs/ ADJ 1 *[person] (= tense)* nerveux, tendu ; *(by nature)* nerveux ◆ **to be ~ about sth** appréhender qch ◆ **I was ~ about him** *or* **on his account** j'étais inquiet pour lui ◆ **to be ~ of sth** appréhender qch ◆ **to be ~ of** *or* **about doing sth** hésiter à faire qch ◆ **don't be ~, it'll be all right** ne t'inquiète pas, tout se passera bien ◆ **people of a ~ disposition** les personnes sensibles ◆ **to feel ~** être nerveux ; *(before performance, exam etc)* avoir le trac* ◆ **he makes me (feel) ~** il m'intimide

2 *(Med) [disorder, tension]* nerveux ◆ **on the verge of ~ collapse** au bord de la dépression nerveuse

COMP **nervous breakdown** N dépression *f* nerveuse ◆ **to have a ~ breakdown** avoir *or* faire une dépression nerveuse

nervous energy N vitalité *f*, énergie *f*

nervous exhaustion N fatigue *f* nerveuse ; *(serious)* surmenage *m*

nervous Nellie‡ N *(esp US)* timoré(e) *m(f)*, trouillard(e)‡ *m(f)*

nervous system N système *m* nerveux

nervous wreck* N ◆ **to be a ~ wreck** être à bout de nerfs ◆ **to turn sb into** *or* **make sb a ~ wreck** pousser qn à bout

nervously /ˈnɜːvəslɪ/ ADV nerveusement

nervousness /ˈnɜːvəsnɪs/ N nervosité *f*

nervy* /ˈnɜːvɪ/ ADJ 1 *(= nervous)* nerveux ◆ **to be in a ~ state** avoir les nerfs à vif 2 *(US = cheeky)* ◆ **to be ~** avoir du toupet* *or* du culot*

nest /nest/ N 1 *[of birds, mice, turtles, ants etc]* nid *m* ; *(= contents)* nichée *f* ◆ **to leave** *or* **fly the ~** *(lit, fig)* quitter le nid ; → **hornet, love** 2 *(fig)* nid *m* ◆ **~ of spies/machine guns** nid *m* d'espions/de mitrailleuses 3 *[of boxes etc]* jeu *m* ◆ **~ of tables** tables *fpl* gigognes VI 1 *[bird etc]* (se) nicher, faire son nid 2 ◆ **to go (bird) ~ing** aller dénicher les oiseaux *or* les œufs 3 *[boxes etc]* s'emboîter COMP **nest egg** N *(= money)* pécule *m*

nested /ˈnestɪd/ ADJ 1 *[tables]* gigognes 2 *(Gram)* emboîté

nesting /ˈnestɪŋ/ N 1 *[of birds]* nidification *f* ◆ **~ box** nichoir *m* ; *(gen: for hens)* pondoir *m* 2 *(Gram)* emboîtement *m*

nestle /ˈnesl/ VI *[person]* se blottir, se pelotonner *(up to, against* contre) ; *[house etc]* se nicher ◆ **to ~ down in bed** se pelotonner dans son lit ◆ **to ~ against sb's shoulder** se blottir contre l'épaule de qn ◆ **a house nestling among the trees** une maison nichée parmi les arbres *or* blottie dans la verdure

nestling /ˈnesflɪŋ/ N oisillon *m*

net[1] /net/ N 1 *(gen, Ftbl, Tennis etc)* filet *m* ◆ **to come up to the ~** *(Tennis)* monter au filet ◆ **the ball's in the ~!** *(Ftbl etc)* c'est un but !

2 *(fig)* filet *m* ◆ **to slip through the ~** passer à travers les mailles du filet ◆ **to be caught in the ~** être pris au piège ◆ **to walk into the ~** donner *or* tomber dans le panneau ◆ **to cast one's ~ wider** élargir son horizon *or* ses perspectives ; → **butterfly, hairnet, mosquito, safety**

3 *(NonC = fabric)* tulle *m*, voile *m*

4 *(Internet)* ◆ **the Net** le Net

VT 1 *(= catch) [+ fish, game]* prendre au filet ◆ **the police ~ted several wanted men** un coup de filet de la police a permis d'arrêter plusieurs personnes recherchées

2 *[+ river]* tendre des filets dans ; *[+ fruit bushes]* poser un filet sur

3 *(Sport)* ◆ **to ~ the ball** envoyer la balle dans le filet ◆ **to ~ a goal** marquer un but

COMP **net cord** N *(Tennis)* bande *f* du filet

net curtains NPL voilage *m* ; *(half-length)* brise-bise *m inv*

net fishing N pêche *f* au filet

net play N *(Tennis etc)* jeu *m* au filet

Net surfer N *(Comput)* internaute *mf*

net[2] /net/ ADJ 1 *[income, assets, worth, price, loss]* net ◆ **the price is $15 ~** le prix net est de 15 dollars ◆ **"terms strictly net"** "prix nets" 2 *[result, effect]* final VT *[business deal etc]* rapporter *or* produire net ; *[person]* gagner *or* toucher net

COMP **the Net Book Agreement** N *(Brit: formerly) accord de maintien des prix publics des livres (entre les éditeurs et les libraires)*

net domestic product N produit *m* intérieur net

net national product N produit *m* national net

net present value N valeur *f* actuelle nette

net profit N bénéfice *m* net

net realizable value N valeur *f* nette réalisable

net weight N poids *m* net

netball /ˈnetbɔːl/ N (*Brit*) netball *m*

nethead* /ˈnethed/ N accro *mf* du Net

nether †† /ˈneðəʳ/ ADJ ◆ ~ **lip** lèvre *f* inférieure ◆ ~ **garments** (*also hum*) sous-vêtements *mpl* ◆ **the** ~ **regions** (= *Hell*) les enfers *mpl* ; (*hum euph* = *genitals*) les parties *fpl* intimes ◆ **the** ~ **regions of the company** (*hum*) les coulisses *fpl* de l'entreprise ◆ **the** ~ **world** les enfers *mpl*

Netherlander /ˈneðəˌlændəʳ/ N Néerlandais(e) *m(f)*

Netherlands /ˈneðələndz/ NPL ◆ **the** ~ les Pays-Bas *mpl* ◆ **in the** ~ aux Pays-Bas ADJ néerlandais

nethermost †† /ˈneðəməʊst/ ADJ le plus bas, le plus profond

netiquette /ˈnetɪket/ N netiquette *f*

netspeak /ˈnetspiːk/ N jargon *m* du Net

netsurfer /ˈnetsɜːfəʳ/ N surfeur *m* -euse *f*

netsurfing /ˈnetsɜːfɪŋ/ N surfing *m*

nett /net/ ADJ, VT ⇒ **net²**

netting /ˈnetɪŋ/ N (*NonC*) 1 (= *nets*) filets *mpl* ; (= *mesh*) mailles *fpl* ; (*for fence etc*) treillis *m* métallique ; (= *fabric*) voile *m*, tulle *m* (*pour rideaux*) ; → **mosquito, wire** 2 (= *net-making*) fabrication *f* de filets 3 (= *action: Fishing*) pêche *f* au filet

nettle /ˈnetl/ N (= *plant*) ortie *f* ◆ **stinging** ~ ortie *f* brûlante *or* romaine ◆ **dead** ~ ortie *f* blanche ◆ **to grasp the** ~ (*Brit*) prendre le taureau par les cornes VT (= *annoy*) agacer, irriter ◆ **he was ~d into replying sharply** agacé, il a répondu avec brusquerie COMP **nettle sting** N piqûre *f* d'ortie

nettlerash /ˈnetlræʃ/ N urticaire *f*

nettlesome /ˈnetlsəm/ ADJ (= *annoying*) irritant ; (= *touchy*) susceptible

network /ˈnetwɜːk/ N réseau *m* ◆ **rail** ~ réseau *m* ferré *or* ferroviaire *or* de chemin de fer ◆ **road** ~ réseau *m* or système *m* routier ◆ **a** ~ **of narrow streets** un lacis (*liter*) *or* enchevêtrement de ruelles ◆ ~ **of veins** réseau *m* or lacis *m* de veines ◆ **a** ~ **of spies/contacts/salesmen** un réseau d'espions/de relations/de représentants ◆ **the programme went out over the whole** ~ le programme a été diffusé sur l'ensemble du réseau ◆ **the** ~**s** (*TV*) les chaînes *fpl* ; → **old**

VT [+ *radio or TV programmes*] diffuser sur l'ensemble du réseau ; [+ *computers*] mettre en réseau

VI 1 (= *form business contacts*) prendre des contacts ◆ **these parties are a good opportunity to** ~ ces soirées permettent de prendre des contacts

2 (= *work as a network*) travailler en réseau

COMP **network provider** N (*for mobile phone*) opérateur *m* (de téléphonie mobile)

Network Standard N (*US Ling*) américain *m* standard ; → ENGLISH

networking /ˈnetˌwɜːkɪŋ/ N 1 (= *making contacts*) établissement *m* d'un réseau de relations ◆ **these seminars make** ~ **very easy** ces séminaires facilitent les prises de contact 2 (= *working as part of network*) travail *m* en réseau ◆ ~ **software** logiciels *mpl* de gestion de réseau

neural /ˈnjʊərəl/ ADJ [*tube*] neural ; [*system*] nerveux

COMP **neural cell** N cellule *f* nerveuse, neurone *m*

neural network N (*Comput*) réseau *m* neuronal

neuralgia /njʊˈrældʒə/ N névralgie *f*

neuralgic /njʊˈrældʒɪk/ ADJ névralgique

neurasthenia /ˌnjʊərəsˈθiːnɪə/ N neurasthénie *f*

neurasthenic /ˌnjʊərəsˈθenɪk/ ADJ, N neurasthénique *mf*

neuritis /njʊəˈraɪtɪs/ N névrite *f*

neurogenic /ˌnjʊərəʊˈdʒenɪk/ ADJ neurogène

neurolinguistic programming /ˈnjʊərəʊlɪŋˈgwɪstɪkˈprəʊgræmɪŋ/ N programmation *f* neurolinguistique

neurological /ˌnjʊərəˈlɒdʒɪkəl/ ADJ [*disease, disorder, damage*] neurologique ◆ ~ **surgeon** neurochirurgien *m* ◆ ~ **department** (service *m* de) neurologie *f*

neurologist /njʊəˈrɒlədʒɪst/ N neurologue *mf*

neurology /njʊəˈrɒlədʒɪ/ N neurologie *f*

neuroma /njʊˈrəʊmə/ N (pl **neuromas** *or* **neuromata** /njʊˈrəʊmətə/) névrome *m*, neurome *m*

neuromuscular /ˌnjʊərəʊˈmʌskjʊləʳ/ ADJ neuromusculaire

neuron /ˈnjʊərɒn/, **neurone** /ˈnjʊərəʊn/ N neurone *m*

neuropath /ˈnjʊərəpæθ/ N névropathe *mf*

neuropathic /ˌnjʊərəˈpæθɪk/ ADJ névropathique

neuropathology /ˌnjʊərəʊpəˈθɒlədʒɪ/ N neuropathologie *f*

neuropathy /njʊˈrɒpəθɪ/ N névropathie *f*

neurophysiological /ˌnjʊərəʊˌfɪzɪəˈlɒdʒɪkəl/ ADJ neurophysiologique

neurophysiologist /ˌnjʊərəʊˌfɪzɪˈɒlədʒɪst/ N neurophysiologiste *mf*

neurophysiology /ˌnjʊərəʊˌfɪzɪˈɒlədʒɪ/ N neurophysiologie *f*

neuropsychiatric /ˌnjʊərəʊˌsaɪkɪˈætrɪk/ ADJ neuropsychiatrique

neuropsychiatrist /ˌnjʊərəʊsaɪˈkaɪətrɪst/ N neuropsychiatre *mf*

neuropsychiatry /ˌnjʊərəʊsaɪˈkaɪətrɪ/ N neuropsychiatrie *f*

neurosis /njʊˈrəʊsɪs/ N (pl **neuroses** /njʊˈrəʊsiːz/) (*Psych, fig*) névrose *f*

neurosurgeon /ˌnjʊərəʊˈsɜːdʒən/ N neurochirurgien(ne) *m(f)*

neurosurgery /ˌnjʊərəʊˈsɜːdʒərɪ/ N neurochirurgie *f*

neurosurgical /ˌnjʊərəʊˈsɜːdʒɪkəl/ ADJ neurochirurgical

neurotic /njʊˈrɒtɪk/ ADJ 1 (*Psych*) [*person*] névrosé ; [*behaviour, personality, disorder*] névrotique 2 (*pej* = *unreasonably anxious*) [*person*] parano* ; [*obsession*] maladif ◆ **he's getting** ~ **about the whole business** toute cette histoire le rend complètement parano* N (*Psych*) névrosé(e) *m(f)* ; (*fig pej*) parano* *mf*

neurotically /njʊˈrɒtɪkəlɪ/ ADV de façon obsessionnelle, jusqu'à la névrose

neuroticism /njʊˈrɒtɪsɪzəm/ N tendances *fpl* à la névrose

neurotomy /njʊˈrɒtəmɪ/ N neurotomie *f*

neurotransmitter /ˌnjʊərəʊtrænzˈmɪtəʳ/ N neurotransmetteur *m*

neurovascular /ˈnjʊərəʊˈvæskjʊləʳ/ ADJ neurovasculaire

neuter /ˈnjuːtəʳ/ ADJ 1 (*gen*) neutre 2 (= *castrated*) châtré N 1 (*Gram*) neutre *m* ◆ **in the** ~ au neutre 2 (= *animal*) animal *m* châtré VT 1 [+ *animal*] châtrer 2 (*esp Brit fig* = *render ineffective*) neutraliser

neutral /ˈnjuːtrəl/ ADJ neutre ◆ **let's meet on** ~ **territory** rencontrons-nous en terrain neutre ◆ **let's try to find some** ~ **ground** essayons de trouver un terrain d'entente ◆ ~ **policy** politique *f* neutraliste *or* de neutralité N 1 (*Pol*) habitant(e) *m(f)* d'un pays neutre 2 (*Driving*) point *m* mort ◆ **in** ~ au point mort

neutralism /ˈnjuːtrəlɪzəm/ N neutralisme *m*

neutralist /ˈnjuːtrəlɪst/ ADJ, N neutraliste *mf*

neutrality /njuːˈtrælɪtɪ/ N (*gen, Chem, Pol etc*) neutralité *f* ; → **armed**

neutralization /ˌnjuːtrəlaɪˈzeɪʃən/ N neutralisation *f*

neutralize /ˈnjuːtrəlaɪz/ VT (*also Chem*) neutraliser

neutrino /njuːˈtriːnəʊ/ N neutrino *m*

neutron /ˈnjuːtrɒn/ N neutron *m*

COMP **neutron bomb** N bombe *f* à neutrons

neutron number N nombre *m* de neutrons

neutron star N étoile *f* à neutrons

Nevada /nɪˈvɑːdə/ N Nevada *m* ◆ **in** ~ dans le Nevada

never /ˈnevəʳ/ ADV 1 ne ... jamais ◆ **I** ~ **eat fish** je ne mange jamais de poisson ◆ **I have** ~ **seen him** je ne l'ai jamais vu ◆ **he will** ~ **come back** il ne reviendra jamais *or* plus (jamais) ◆ ~ **more** (*liter*) (ne ...) plus jamais, (ne ...) jamais plus ◆ ~ **in all my life** jamais de ma vie ◆ **I** ~ **heard such a thing!** je n'ai jamais entendu une chose pareille !

◆ **never (...) again** ◆ ~ **say that again** ne répète jamais ça ◆ **you must** ~ **ever come here again** tu ne dois jamais plus revenir ici ◆ **we shall** ~ **see her again** on ne la reverra (plus) jamais ◆ ~ **again!** plus jamais !, jamais plus !

◆ **never (...) before** ◆ **I'd** ~ **seen him before** je ne l'avais jamais vu auparavant ◆ ~ **before had there been such a disaster** jamais on n'avait connu tel désastre

◆ **never yet** ◆ **I have** ~ **yet been able to find** ... je n'ai encore jamais pu trouver ..., jusqu'ici je n'ai jamais pu trouver ...

2 (*emphatic*) **that will** ~ **do!** c'est inadmissible ! ◆ **I** ~ **slept a wink** je n'ai pas fermé l'œil ◆ **he** ~ **so much as smiled** il n'a pas même souri ◆ **he** ~ **said a word, he said** ~ **a word** (*liter*) il n'a pas pipé mot ◆ ~ **a one** pas un seul ◆ ~ **was a child more loved** jamais enfant ne fut plus aimé ◆ **(surely) you've** ~ **left it behind!*** ne me dites pas que vous l'avez oublié ! ◆ **I've left it behind!** – ~**!** je l'ai oublié ! – ça n'est pas vrai *or* pas possible ! ◆ **well I** ~ **(did)!*** ça par exemple !*, ça alors !* ◆ ~ **fear!** n'ayez pas peur !, soyez tranquille ! ; → **mind**

COMP **never-ending** ADJ interminable

never-failing ADJ [*method*] infaillible ; [*source, spring*] inépuisable, intarissable

never-never* N (*Austral* = *outback*) régions *désertiques d'Australie* ; (*Brit*) ◆ **to buy on the never-never** acheter à crédit *or* à tempérament

never-never land N pays *m* imaginaire

never-outs NPL (*Comm*) articles *mpl* toujours en stock

never-to-be-forgotten ADJ inoubliable, qu'on n'oubliera jamais

nevermore /ˈnevəmɔːʳ/ ADV ne ... plus jamais, ne ... jamais plus ◆ ~**!** jamais plus !, plus jamais !

nevertheless /ˌnevəðəˈles/ LANGUAGE IN USE 26.2, 26.3 ADV néanmoins ◆ **it wasn't my fault. Nevertheless, I felt guilty** ce n'était pas ma faute ; néanmoins *or* cependant, je me suis senti coupable ◆ **it is** ~ **true that** ... cependant, il est vrai que ..., il est néanmoins vrai que ... ◆ **I shall go** ~ j'irai néanmoins *or* malgré tout ◆ **he is** ~ **my brother** il n'en reste pas moins mon frère ◆ **she has had no news, (yet)** ~ **she goes on hoping** elle n'a pas eu de nouvelles, et pourtant *or* et malgré tout elle continue d'espérer

nevus /ˈniːvəs/ N (*US*) ⇒ **naevus**

new /njuː/ ADJ 1 *(= not previously known etc)* nouveau (nouvelle *f*), nouvel *m before vowel* ; (also **brand-new**) neuf (neuve *f*) ◆ **I've got a ~ car** *(= different)* j'ai une nouvelle *or* une autre voiture ; *(= brand-new)* j'ai une voiture neuve ◆ **he has written a ~ book/article** il a écrit un nouveau livre/un nouvel article ◆ **this is Juliette's ~ book** c'est le nouveau *or* dernier livre de Juliette ◆ **~ carrots** carottes *fpl* de primeur *or* nouvelles ◆ **there are several ~ plays on in London** on donne plusieurs nouvelles pièces à Londres ◆ **it's the ~ fashion** c'est la dernière *or* la nouvelle mode *f* ◆ **a ~ theory/invention** une nouvelle théorie/invention ◆ **the ~ moon** la nouvelle lune ◆ **there's a ~ moon tonight** c'est la nouvelle lune ce soir ◆ **I need a ~ notebook** il me faut un nouveau carnet *or* un carnet neuf ◆ **don't get your ~ shoes wet** ne mouille pas tes chaussures neuves ◆ **dressed in ~ clothes** vêtu *or* habillé de neuf ◆ **as good as ~** comme neuf, à l'état de neuf ◆ **he made the bike as good as ~** il a remis le vélo à neuf ◆ **"as new"** "état neuf" ◆ **I don't like all these ~ paintings** je n'aime pas tous ces tableaux modernes ◆ **I've got several ~ ideas** j'ai plusieurs idées nouvelles *or* neuves ◆ **this idea is not ~** ce n'est pas une idée nouvelle *or* neuve ◆ **the ~ nations** les pays *mpl* neufs ◆ **this is a completely ~ subject** c'est un sujet tout à fait neuf ◆ **this sort of work is ~ to me** ce genre de travail est (quelque chose de) nouveau pour moi ◆ **a ~ deal** *(Pol etc)* une nouvelle donne ◆ **the ~ diplomacy** la nouvelle diplomatie ◆ **~ style** nouveau style *m* ; see also **comp** ◆ **the New Left** *(Pol)* la nouvelle gauche ◆ **the ~ rich** les nouveaux riches *mpl*

2 *(= recently arrived)* **he came ~ to the firm last year** il est arrivé (dans l'entreprise) l'an dernier ◆ **I'm ~ to this kind of work** je n'ai jamais fait ce genre de travail, je suis novice dans ce genre de travail ◆ **he's ~ to the trade** il est nouveau dans le métier ◆ **he's quite ~ to the town** il est tout nouvellement arrivé dans la ville ◆ **she's ~ to this game** * elle fait ses premières armes ◆ **the ~ people at number five** les gens qui viennent d'emménager au numéro cinq ◆ **~ recruit** nouvelle recrue *f*, bleu * *m* ◆ **the ~ students** les nouveaux *mpl*, les nouvelles *fpl* ◆ **a ~ boy** *(Scol)* un nouveau ◆ **a ~ girl** *(Scol)* une nouvelle ◆ **she's ~, poor thing** elle est nouvelle, la pauvre ◆ **are you ~ here?** *(gen)* vous venez d'arriver ici ? ; *(in school, firm etc)* vous êtes nouveau ici ?

3 *(= different)* **bring me a ~ glass, this one is dirty** apportez-moi un autre verre, celui-ci est sale ◆ **there was a ~ waiter today** il y avait un autre *or* un nouveau serveur aujourd'hui ◆ **he's a ~ man since he remarried** il est transformé *or* c'est un autre homme depuis qu'il s'est remarié ; see also **comp** ◆ **there's nothing ~ under the sun** *(Prov)* il n'y a rien de nouveau sous le soleil *(Prov)* ◆ **that's nothing ~!** ce *or* ça n'est pas nouveau !, il n'y a rien de neuf là-dedans ! ◆ **that's a ~ one on me!** * première nouvelle ! *, on en apprend tous les jours ! *(iro)* ◆ **that's something ~!** ça c'est nouveau ! ◆ **what's ~?** * quoi de neuf ? * ; see also **comp** ; → **brand, broom, leaf, split**

4 *(= fresh)* *[bread]* frais (fraîche *f*) ; *[milk]* frais (fraîche *f*), fraîchement trait ; *[cheese]* frais (fraîche *f*), pas (encore) fait ; *[wine]* nouveau (nouvelle *f*), nouvel *m before vowel*

ADV *(gen in compounds)* nouvellement ◆ **he's ~ out of college** il sort tout juste de l'université ; → **comp**

COMP **New Age** N New Age *m* ADJ New Age *inv*
New Ager * N adepte *mf* du New Age
New Age travellers NPL voyageurs *mpl* New Age *(personnes vivant en marge de la société, selon un mode de vie nomade)*
New Amsterdam N La Nouvelle-Amsterdam
New Brunswick N Nouveau-Brunswick *m*
New Caledonia N Nouvelle-Calédonie *f*
New Caledonian N Néo-Calédonien(ne) *m(f)*
New Delhi N New Delhi
New England N Nouvelle-Angleterre *f*
New Englander N habitant(e) *m(f)* de la Nouvelle-Angleterre
New English Bible N *traduction moderne de la Bible en anglais*
new face N nouveau visage *m*
new-fangled ADJ *(pej)* ultramoderne
new-found ADJ *[happiness etc]* de fraîche date
New Guinea N Nouvelle-Guinée *f*
New Hampshire N New Hampshire *m* ◆ **in New Hampshire** dans le New Hampshire
the New Hebrides NPL les Nouvelles-Hébrides *fpl*
New Jersey N New Jersey *m* ◆ **in New Jersey** dans le New Jersey
New Jerusalem N la Nouvelle Jérusalem
New Labour N SG *(Brit Pol)* le New Labour
New Lad * N *(Brit)* macho *m* nouvelle manière
new-laid egg N œuf *m* du jour *or* tout frais (pondu)
New Latin N latin *m* moderne
new look N new-look *m*
new-look ADJ new-look *inv*
New Man N *(Brit)* ≃ homme *m* moderne *(qui partage les tâches ménagères, s'occupe des enfants etc)*
new maths N mathématiques *fpl or* maths * *fpl* modernes
New Mexico N Nouveau-Mexique *m*
new-mown ADJ *[grass]* frais coupé ; *[hay]* frais fauché
New Orleans N La Nouvelle-Orléans ◆ **in New Orleans** à La Nouvelle-Orléans
new potato N pomme *f* (de terre) nouvelle
new product development N développement *m* de nouveaux produits
New Scotland Yard N Scotland Yard *m*
New South Wales N Nouvelle-Galles du Sud *f*
new-speak N *(Pol)* langue *f* de bois ; *(Literat)* novlangue *f*
the new-style calendar N le nouveau calendrier, le calendrier grégorien
New Testament N Nouveau Testament *m*
new town N *(Brit)* ville *f* nouvelle
New Wave ADJ *[film]* de la nouvelle vague ; *[music]* New Wave *inv* N *(Cine)* nouvelle vague *f* ; *(Mus)* New Wave *f*
the New World N le Nouveau Monde ◆ **the New World Symphony, the Symphony from the New World** la Symphonie du Nouveau Monde
New Year N → **New Year**
New Year's * N *(US)* ⇒ **New Year's Day, New Year's Eve** ; → **New Year**
New York N *(= state)* (l'État *m* de) New York *m* ; *(= city)* New York ◆ **in New York (State)** dans l'État de New York ADJ new-yorkais
New Yorker N New-Yorkais(e) *m(f)*
New Zealand N Nouvelle-Zélande *f* ADJ néo-zélandais
New Zealander N Néo-Zélandais(e) *m(f)*

newbie * /ˈnjuːbɪ/ N nouveau *m*, nouvelle *f* ; *(Internet)* newbie *m*

newborn /ˈnjuːbɔːn/ ADJ 1 *(lit)* *[child, animal]* nouveau-né ◆ **a ~ babe** un(e) nouveau-né(e) *m(f)* 2 *(fig)* *[nation, organization]* tout jeune NPL **the newborn** les nouveaux-nés *mpl* N nouveau-né(e) *m(f)* ; → **innocent**

newcomer /ˈnjuːkʌməʳ/ N nouveau venu *m*, nouvelle venue *f* ◆ **they are ~s to this town** ils viennent d'arriver dans cette ville

newel /ˈnjuːəl/ N noyau *m* (d'escalier)

Newfoundland /ˈnjuːfəndlənd/ N Terre-Neuve *f* ADJ terre-neuvien ◆ **~ fisherman** terre-neuvas *m* COMP **Newfoundland dog** N chien *m* de Terre-Neuve, terre-neuve *m inv*

Newfoundlander /njuːˈfaʊndləndəʳ/ N habitant(e) *m(f)* de Terre-Neuve, Terre-Neuvien(ne) *m(f)*

newish /ˈnjuːɪʃ/ ADJ assez neuf (neuve *f*)

newly /ˈnjuːlɪ/ ADV nouvellement ◆ **the ~-elected members** les membres nouvellement élus ◆ **her ~-awakened curiosity** sa curiosité récemment éveillée ◆ **~ arrived** récemment arrivé ◆ **~ rich** nouveau riche ◆ **~ shaved** rasé de frais ◆ **a ~-dug grave** une tombe fraîchement creusée *or* ouverte ◆ **a ~-formed friendship** une amitié de fraîche date ◆ **his ~-found happiness** son bonheur tout neuf ◆ **~-made wine** vin *m* qu'on vient de faire ◆ **her ~-made friends** ses nouveaux amis ◆ **when I was ~ married** quand j'étais jeune marié

COMP **newly industrialized country, newly industrializing country** N nouveau pays *m* industrialisé, pays *m* nouvellement industrialisé
newly-weds NPL jeunes mariés *mpl*

newness /ˈnjuːnɪs/ N *[of fashion, ideas etc]* nouveauté *f* ; *[of clothes etc]* état *m* (de) neuf ; *[of bread]* fraîcheur *f* ; *[of cheese]* manque *m* de maturité ; *[of wine]* jeunesse *f*

news /njuːz/ N *(NonC)* 1 nouvelle(s) *f(pl)* ◆ **a piece** *or* **an item of ~** *(gen)* une nouvelle ; *(Press)* une information ◆ **have you heard the ~?** tu es au courant ? ◆ **have you heard the ~ about Paul?** vous savez ce qui est arrivé à Paul ? ◆ **have you any ~ of him?** *(= heard from him)* avez-vous de ses nouvelles ? ◆ **I have no ~ of her** je ne sais pas ce qu'elle est devenue ◆ **do let me have your ~** surtout donnez-moi de vos nouvelles ◆ **what's your ~?** quoi de neuf *or* de nouveau (chez vous) ? ◆ **is there any ~?** y a-t-il du nouveau ? ◆ **I've got ~ for you!** j'ai du nouveau à vous annoncer ! ◆ **this is ~ to me!** * première nouvelle ! *, on en apprend tous les jours ! *(iro)* ◆ **it will be ~ to him * that we are here** ça va le surprendre de nous savoir ici ◆ **good ~** bonnes nouvelles *fpl* ◆ **bad** *or* **sad ~** mauvaises *or* tristes nouvelles *fpl* ◆ **he's/it's bad ~** * on a toujours des ennuis avec lui/ça ◆ **she/it made ~** on a parlé d'elle/on en a parlé dans le journal ◆ **bad ~ travels fast** les malheurs s'apprennent vite ◆ **no ~ is good ~!** *(Prov)* pas de nouvelles, bonnes nouvelles ! ◆ **when the ~ broke** quand on a su la nouvelle ◆ **"dog bites man" isn't ~** "un homme mordu par un chien" n'est pas (ce qu'on peut appeler) une nouvelle ◆ **he's in the ~ again** *(fig)* le voilà qui refait parler de lui ; → **break**

2 *(Press, Rad)* informations *fpl* ; *(TV)* informations *fpl*, journal *m* télévisé ◆ **official ~** communiqué *m* officiel ◆ **financial/sporting** *etc* **~** chronique *f or* rubrique *f* financière/sportive *etc* ◆ **"news in brief"** *(Press)* "nouvelles brèves"

COMP **news agency** N agence *f* de presse
news analyst N *(US Rad, TV)* commentateur *m*
news blackout N black-out *m*
news broadcast, news bulletin N (bulletin *m* d')informations *fpl*, journal *m* télévisé
news conference N conférence *f* de presse
news desk N service *m* des informations
news editor N rédacteur *m*
news film N film *m* d'actualités
news flash N flash *m* (d'information)
news gathering N *(NonC)* collecte *f* des informations
news headlines NPL titres *mpl* de l'actualité
news item N *(Press etc)* information *f*
news magazine N magazine *m* d'actualités
news photographer N reporter *m* photographe
news pictures NPL reportage *m* photographique
news release N *(esp US)* communiqué *m* de presse
news service N agence *f* de presse
news sheet N feuille *f* d'informations
news stand N kiosque *m* (à journaux)
news theatre N cinéma *m or* salle *f* d'actualités

news value N ◆ **to have ~ value** présenter un intérêt pour le public
news weekly N hebdomadaire *m* d'actualités

newsagent /ˈnjuːzˌeidʒənt/ N (*Brit*) marchand(e) *m(f)* de *or* dépositaire *mf* de journaux
COMP **newsagent's (shop)** N (*Brit*) maison *f* de la presse

newsboy /ˈnjuːzbɔɪ/ N vendeur *m or* crieur *m* de journaux

newsbreak /ˈnjuːzbreɪk/ N (*US*) nouvelle *f* digne d'intérêt

newscast /ˈnjuːzkɑːst/ N (*US*) (bulletin *m* d')informations *fpl*

newscaster /ˈnjuːzkɑːstəʳ/ N (*Rad, TV*) présentateur *m*, -trice *f* (de journal télévisé)

newsclip /ˈnjuːzklɪp/ N (*US Press*) coupure *f* de journal

newsdealer /ˈnjuːzdiːləʳ/ N (*US*) → **newsagent**

newsgroup /ˈnjuːzgruːp/ N (*on Internet*) forum *m* de discussion

newshound /ˈnjuːzhaʊnd/, **newshawk** /ˈnjuːzhɔːk/ N reporter *m* ◆ **there was a crowd of ~s around him** (*pej*) il était aux prises avec une meute de journalistes

newsletter /ˈnjuːzletəʳ/ N bulletin *m* (*d'une entreprise*)

newsmaker /ˈnjuːzmeɪkəʳ/ N (*US*) (= *event*) sujet *m* d'actualité ; (= *person*) vedette *f* de l'actualité

newsman /ˈnjuːzmən/ N (pl **-men**) journaliste *m*

newsmonger /ˈnjuːzmʌŋgəʳ/ N (*pej*) pipelette* *f*, commère *f*

newspaper /ˈnjuːzˌpeɪpəʳ/ N journal *m* ◆ **daily ~** quotidien *m* ◆ **weekly ~** hebdomadaire *m* ◆ **he works for** *or* **on a ~** il travaille pour un journal
COMP **newspaper advertising** N publicité-presse *f*
newspaper clipping, newspaper cutting N coupure *f* de journal *or* de presse
newspaper office N (bureaux *mpl* de la) rédaction *f*
newspaper photographer N reporter *m* photographe
newspaper report N reportage *m*

newspaperman /ˈnjuːzˌpeɪpəmæn/ N (pl **-men**) journaliste *m*

newspaperwoman /ˈnjuːzˌpeɪpəwʊmən/ N (pl **-women**) journaliste *f*

newsprint /ˈnjuːzprɪnt/ N (*NonC*) (= *paper*) papier *m* (journal) ; (= *ink*) encre *f* d'imprimerie

newsreader /ˈnjuːzriːdəʳ/ N (*Brit Rad, TV*) présentateur *m*, -trice *f* (de journal)

newsreel /ˈnjuːzriːl/ N actualités *fpl* (filmées)

newsroom /ˈnjuːzrʊm/ N salle *f* de rédaction

newsvendor /ˈnjuːzvendəʳ/ N vendeur *m* de journaux

newsworthy /ˈnjuːzwɜːðɪ/ ADJ ◆ **to be ~** valoir la peine d'être publié

newsy* /ˈnjuːzɪ/ ADJ (= *full of news*) [*letter*] plein de nouvelles

newt /njuːt/ N triton *m*

newton /ˈnjuːtən/ N (*Phys*) newton *m*

Newtonian /njuːˈtəʊnɪən/ ADJ newtonien

New Year /ˈnjuːˈjɪəʳ/ LANGUAGE IN USE 23.2 N nouvel an *m*, nouvelle année *f* ◆ **to bring in** *or* **see in the ~** réveillonner (à la Saint-Sylvestre), fêter le nouvel an ◆ **Happy ~!** bonne année ! ◆ **to wish sb a happy ~** souhaiter une *or* la bonne année à qn
COMP **New Year gift** N étrennes *fpl*
New Year resolution N bonne résolution *f* (de nouvel an)
New Year's Day N jour *m or* premier *m* de l'an, nouvel an *m*
New Year's Eve N la Saint-Sylvestre
New Year's Honours List N (*Brit*) ⇒ **Honours List** ; → **honour**

next /nekst/ ADJ [1] (*in time, in future*) prochain ; (*in past*) suivant ◆ **come back ~ week/month** revenez la semaine prochaine/le mois prochain ◆ **he came back the ~ week** il est revenu la semaine suivante *or* d'après ◆ **he came back the ~ day** il est revenu le lendemain *or* le jour suivant ◆ **the ~ day but one** le surlendemain ◆ **during the ~ five days he did not go out** il n'est pas sorti pendant les cinq jours qui ont suivi ◆ **I will finish this in the ~ five days** je finirai ceci dans les cinq jours qui viennent *or* à venir ◆ **the ~ morning** le lendemain matin ◆ **(the) ~ time I see him** la prochaine fois que je le verrai ◆ **the ~ time I saw him** la première fois où *or* que je l'ai revu, quand je l'ai revu ◆ **I'll come back ~ week and the ~ again** je reviendrai la semaine prochaine et la suivante ◆ **this time ~ week** d'ici huit jours ◆ **the ~ moment** l'instant d'après ◆ **from one moment to the ~** d'un moment à l'autre ◆ **the year after ~** dans deux ans ◆ **~ Wednesday, Wednesday ~*** mercredi prochain ◆ **~ March** en mars prochain ◆ **~ year** l'année prochaine, l'an prochain
[2] (*in series, list etc*) (= *following*) [*page, case*] suivant ; (= *which is to come*) prochain ◆ **he got off at the ~ stop** il est descendu à l'arrêt suivant ◆ **you get off at the ~ stop** vous descendez au prochain arrêt ◆ **who's ~?** à qui le tour ?, c'est à qui ? ◆ **you're ~** c'est votre tour, c'est à vous (maintenant) ◆ **~ please!** au suivant ! ◆ **I was the ~ person** *or* **I was ~ to speak** ce fut ensuite à mon tour de parler ; see also **noun 1** ◆ **I'll ask the very ~ person I see** je vais demander à la première personne que je verrai ◆ **in the ~ place** ensuite ◆ **on the ~ page** à la page suivante ◆ **"continued in the next column"** "voir colonne ci-contre" ◆ **the ~ thing to do is ...** la première chose à faire maintenant est de ... ◆ **he saw that the ~ thing to do was ...** il a vu que ce qu'il devait faire ensuite (c')était ... ◆ **(the) ~ thing I knew, he had gone*** et tout d'un coup, il a disparu ◆ **I'll try the ~ size up** je vais essayer la taille au-dessus ◆ **the ~ size down** la taille au-dessous
[3] (= *immediately adjacent*) [*house, street, room*] d'à côté
ADV (*in time*) ensuite, après ◆ **~ we had lunch** ensuite *or* après nous avons déjeuné ◆ **what shall we do ~?** qu'allons-nous faire maintenant ? ◆ **when you ~ come to see us** la prochaine fois que vous viendrez nous voir ◆ **when I ~ saw him, when ~ I saw him** (*frm*) quand je l'ai revu (la fois suivante) ◆ **when shall we meet ~?** quand nous reverrons-nous ? ◆ **a new dress! what(ever) ~?** une nouvelle robe ! et puis quoi encore ?
◆ **next** + *superlative* ◆ **the ~ best thing would be to speak to his brother** à défaut le mieux serait de parler à son frère ◆ **she's my ~ best friend** à part une autre c'est ma meilleure amie ◆ **this is my ~ oldest daughter after Marie** c'est la plus âgée de mes filles après Marie ◆ **she's the ~ youngest** elle suit (par ordre d'âge) ◆ **who's the ~ tallest (boy)?** qui est le plus grand après ?
◆ **next to** (= *beside*) à côté de ; (= *almost*) presque ◆ **his room is ~ to mine** sa chambre est à côté de la mienne ◆ **the church stands ~ to the school** l'église est à côté de l'école ◆ **he was sitting ~ to me** il était assis à côté de moi ◆ **to wear wool ~ to the skin** porter de la laine à même la peau ◆ **the thing ~ to my heart** la chose qui me tient le plus à cœur ◆ **~ to France, what country do you like best?** après la France, quel est votre pays préféré ? ◆ **to get ~ to sb*** (*US*) se mettre bien* avec qn ◆ **the ~ to last row** l'avant-dernier *or* le pénultième rang ◆ **he was ~ to last** il était avant-dernier ◆ **~ to nothing*** presque rien ◆ **I got it for ~ to nothing*** je l'ai payé trois fois rien ◆ **~ to nobody*** presque personne ◆ **there's ~ to no news*** il n'y a presque rien de neuf ◆ **the ~ to top/bottom shelf** le deuxième rayon (en partant) du haut/du bas
PREP (*Brit* †) à côté de
N prochain(e) *m(f)* ◆ **the ~ to speak is Paul** c'est Paul qui parle ensuite, c'est Paul qui est le prochain à parler ◆ **the ~ to arrive was Robert** c'est Robert qui est arrivé ensuite *or* le suivant ◆ **I hope my ~* will be a boy** (= *baby*) j'espère que mon prochain (enfant) sera un garçon ◆ **to be continued in our ~** (= *edition*) suite au prochain numéro
COMP **next door** N, ADV → **next door**
next of kin N (*on forms etc*) "nom et prénom de votre plus proche parent" ◆ **who is your ~ of kin?** qui est votre plus proche parent ? ◆ **the police will inform the ~ of kin** la police préviendra la famille

next door /ˈneksˈdɔːʳ/ N la maison (*or* l'appartement *etc*) d'à côté ◆ **it's the man from ~** c'est le monsieur d'à côté *or* qui habite à côté
ADV [1] (= *in or to next house, room*) [*live, go*] à côté ◆ **she lived ~ to me** elle habitait à côté de chez moi ◆ **we live ~ to each other** nous sommes voisins ◆ **he has the room ~ to me at the hotel** il a la chambre à côté de la mienne à l'hôtel ◆ **the house ~** la maison d'à côté ◆ **the boy/girl ~** (*lit*) le garçon/la fille d'à côté ◆ **he's the boy ~ type** (*fig*) c'est quelqu'un de très simple ◆ **she married the boy ~** (*fig*) elle s'est mariée avec un bon gars* ◆ **at the table ~*** à la table d'à côté
[2] (* *fig* = *almost*) ◆ **that is ~ to madness** cela frise la folie ◆ **if he isn't mad he's ~ to it** s'il n'est pas fou il s'en faut de peu *or* c'est tout comme* ◆ **we were ~ to being ruined** nous avons été au bord de la ruine, nous avons frôlé la ruine
ADJ ◆ **next-door** [*neighbour, building, room, table*] d'à côté

nexus /ˈneksəs/ N (*pl inv*) (= *connection*) lien *m* ; (= *series of connections*) liaison *f*

NF /enˈef/ N (*Brit Pol*) (abbrev of **National Front**) → **national**

n/f (*Banking*) (abbrev of **no funds**) défaut *m* de provision

NFL /ˌenefˈel/ N (*US*) (abbrev of **National Football League**) Fédération *f* américaine de football

NFU /ˌenefˈjuː/ N (*Brit*) (abbrev of **National Farmers' Union**) *syndicat*

NG /enˈdʒiː/ N (*US*) (abbrev of **National Guard**) → **national**

NGA /ˌendʒiːˈeɪ/ N (*Brit: formerly*) (abbrev of **National Graphical Association**) *ancien syndicat*

NGO /ˌendʒiːˈəʊ/ N (abbrev of **non-governmental organization**) ONG *f*

NH abbrev of **New Hampshire**

NHL /ˌeneɪtʃˈel/ N (*US*) (abbrev of **National Hockey League**) Fédération *f* américaine de hockey sur glace

NHS /ˌeneɪtʃˈes/ N (*Brit*) (abbrev of **National Health Service**) ≈ Sécurité *f* sociale

NHS

Le **National Health Service**, ou **NHS**, est la branche maladie du régime de sécurité sociale, qui, depuis 1948, assure des soins médicaux gratuits à toute personne résidant en Grande-Bretagne. Le **NHS** est essentiellement financé par l'impôt, mais aussi par les charges et les cotisations sociales et, enfin, par la quote-part à la charge de l'assuré sur les médicaments prescrits. Les soins dentaires ne sont pas gratuits. → **PRESCRIPTION CHARGE**

NI 1 (abbrev of **Northern Ireland**) → **northern** 2 *(Brit)* (abbrev of **National Insurance**) → **national**

niacin /ˈnaɪəsɪn/ N acide *m* nicotinique

Niagara /naɪˈægrə/ N Niagara *m* COMP **Niagara Falls** NPL les chutes *fpl* du Niagara

nib /nɪb/ N 1 *[of pen]* (bec *m* de) plume *f* ◆ **fine ~** plume *f* fine *or* à bec fin ◆ **broad ~** grosse plume *f*, plume *f* à gros bec 2 *[of tool]* pointe *f*

-nibbed /nɪbd/ ADJ *(in compounds)* ◆ **fine-nibbed** à plume fine ◆ **gold-nibbed** à plume en or

nibble /ˈnɪbl/ VTI *[person]* *[+ food]* grignoter ; *[+ pen, finger, ear]* mordiller ; *[sheep, goats etc]* brouter ; *[fish]* mordre, mordiller ◆ **to ~ (at) one's food** chipoter ◆ **she was nibbling (at) some chocolate** elle grignotait un morceau de chocolat ◆ **he was nibbling (at) her ear** il lui mordillait l'oreille ◆ **she ~d (on) her pencil** elle mordillait son crayon ◆ **to ~ at an offer** se montrer tenté par une offre N 1 *(Fishing)* touche *f* 2 *(= snack)* ◆ **I feel like a ~** * je grignoterais bien quelque chose NPL **nibbles** amuse-gueule(s) *m(pl)*

niblick /ˈnɪblɪk/ N *(Golf)* niblick *m*

nibs /nɪbz/ N *(hum)* ◆ **his ~** ‡ Son Altesse *(iro)*, sézigue *

NIC /ˌenaɪˈsiː/ N 1 (abbrev of **newly industrialized** *or* **industrializing country**) NPI *m* 2 *(Brit)* (abbrev of **National Insurance Contribution**) → **national**

nicad /ˈnaɪkæd/ ADJ *[battery]* NiCad *inv*

NICAM /ˈnaɪkæm/ (abbrev of **near-instantaneous companded audio multiplex**) NICAM

Nicaragua /ˌnɪkəˈrægjʊə/ N Nicaragua *m*

Nicaraguan /ˌnɪkəˈrægjʊən/ ADJ nicaraguayen N Nicaraguayen(ne) *m(f)*

nice /naɪs/ ADJ 1 *(= pleasant, likeable)* *[person]* sympathique ; *[place, manners]* agréable ; *[view]* beau (belle *f*) ; *[holiday]* beau (belle *f*), agréable ; *[smell, taste]* bon, agréable ; *[meal, idea]* bon ; *[dress, face, voice, smile, ring, photo]* joli ; *[car]* *(to look at)* beau (belle *f*) ; *(to drive)* bon ◆ **he seems like a ~ person** il a l'air sympathique ◆ **it's ~ here** on est bien ici ◆ **to smell ~** sentir bon ◆ **to taste ~** avoir bon goût ◆ **you look very ~** tu es très bien ◆ **you look ~ in that dress** cette robe te va bien ◆ **a ~ little house** une jolie petite maison ◆ **it would be ~ if ...** ce serait bien si ... ◆ **it would be ~ to know what they intend to do** j'aimerais bien savoir ce qu'ils ont l'intention de faire ◆ **(it's) ~ to see you** ça fait plaisir de vous voir ◆ **(it's been) ~ meeting you** *or* **to have met you** ça m'a fait plaisir de faire votre connaissance ◆ **~ to meet you!** * enchanté ! ◆ **a ~ cup of coffee** un bon petit café ◆ **~ one!** * *(Brit)*, **~ work!** * *(lit)* bien joué ! * ; *(also iro)* bravo ! ◆ **have a ~ day!** bonne journée ! ◆ **we had a ~ evening** nous avons passé une bonne soirée *or* une soirée agréable ◆ **did you have a ~ time at the party?** vous vous êtes bien amusés à la soirée ?

2 *(= kind, friendly)* *[person]* gentil *(to sb* avec qn*)*, aimable *(to sb* envers qn*)* ◆ **he was perfectly ~ about it** il a bien pris la chose ◆ **that wasn't ~ of you** ce n'était pas gentil à vous *or* de votre part ◆ **it's ~ of you to do that** c'est gentil à vous de faire cela ◆ **to say ~ things about sb/sth** dire du bien de qn/sur qch ◆ **to be as ~ as pie * (to sb)** être gentil comme tout (avec qn) ◆ **to be as ~ as pie * about sth** très bien prendre qch ◆ **no more Mr Nice Guy!** * *(hum)* finis les ronds de jambe !

3 *(often iro = respectable, refined)* *[person, behaviour, expression, book, film]* convenable, comme il faut ◆ **not ~** peu convenable, pas comme il faut ◆ **that's not ~!** ça ne se fait pas ! ◆ **~ girls don't do that** les filles bien élevées ne font pas ce genre de chose

4 *(= fine)* *[weather, day]* beau (belle *f*) ◆ **~ weather we're having!** * beau temps, n'est-ce pas ?

5 *(*: used as intensifier)* **a ~ bright colour** une belle couleur vive ◆ **to have a ~ cold drink** boire quelque chose de bien frais ◆ **he gets ~ long holidays** il a la chance d'avoir de longues vacances ◆ **we had a ~ long chat** nous avons bien bavardé

◆ **nice and ...** ◆ **to get up ~ and early** se lever de bonne heure ◆ **we'll take it ~ and easy** on va y aller doucement ◆ **it's so ~ and peaceful here** c'est tellement paisible ici ◆ **I like my coffee ~ and sweet** j'aime mon café bien sucré ◆ **it's ~ and warm outside** il fait bon dehors

6 *(iro)* joli ◆ **you're in a ~ mess** vous voilà dans un joli pétrin * *or* dans de beaux draps ◆ **here's a ~ state of affairs!** c'est du joli ! ◆ **that's a ~ way to talk!** c'est sympa * ce que tu dis ! *(iro)* ◆ **you're so stupid! – oh that's ~!** ce que tu peux être stupide ! – merci pour le compliment ! ◆ **~ friends you've got!** ils sont bien, tes amis !

7 *(frm = subtle, fastidious)* *[distinction, judgement, point]* subtil ◆ **he has a ~ taste in wine** il est difficile en ce qui concerne le vin ◆ **she's not very ~ in her methods** elle n'a pas beaucoup de scrupules quant à ses méthodes

COMP **nice-looking** ADJ joli, beau (belle *f*) ◆ **he's ~-looking** il est joli *or* beau garçon

nicely /ˈnaɪslɪ/ ADV 1 *(= well)* *[manage, function, work, progress]* bien ◆ **to dress ~** être bien habillé ◆ **~ done** bien fait ◆ **that will do ~!** * c'est parfait ! ◆ **to be doing very ~ (for oneself)** * s'en sortir très bien ◆ **to be coming along ~** * bien se présenter ◆ **to be ~ placed to do sth** être bien placé pour faire qch 2 *(= politely)* *[eat, thank]* poliment ; *[ask]* gentiment, poliment ◆ **a ~ behaved child** un enfant bien élevé 3 *(frm = subtly)* *[differentiated]* subtilement

Nicene /ˈnaɪsiːn/ ADJ ◆ **the ~ Creed** le Credo *or* le symbole de Nicée

niceness /ˈnaɪsnɪs/ N 1 *(= pleasantness)* *[of person]* gentillesse *f*, amabilité *f* ; *[of place, thing]* agrément *m*, caractère *m* agréable 2 *(frm = subtlety)* délicatesse *f* ; *[of distinction, point, taste etc]* subtilité *f*

nicety /ˈnaɪsɪtɪ/ N 1 *(of one's judgement)* justesse *f*, précision *f* ◆ **to a ~** à la perfection 2 ◆ **niceties** *(= subtleties, fine details)* *[of system, process, legislation, diplomacy]* subtilités *fpl* ; *(= refinements)* *[of clothes, fashion etc]* raffinements *mpl* ◆ **legal/diplomatic niceties** subtilités *fpl* légales/diplomatiques ◆ **social niceties** mondanités *fpl* ◆ **the niceties of dinner party conversation** les mondanités qui s'échangent lors des dîners

niche /niːʃ/ N *(gen)* niche *f* ; *(in market)* créneau *m* ◆ **to find one's ~ (in life)** trouver sa voie (dans la vie) COMP **niche marketing** N marketing *m* du créneau

Nicholas /ˈnɪkələs/ N Nicolas *m*

Nick /nɪk/ N 1 dim of **Nicholas** 2 ◆ **Old ~** * le diable, le malin

nick /nɪk/ N 1 *(in wood)* encoche *f* ; *(in blade, dish)* ébréchure *f* ; *(on face, skin)* (petite) coupure *f* ◆ **in the ~ of time** juste à temps

2 *(Brit ‡)* taule * *f* ; *(= police station)* poste *m* de police ◆ **to be in the ~** être en taule *

3 *(Brit * = condition)* état *m*, condition *f* ◆ **in good ~** en bon état ◆ **in bad ~** en mauvais état, nase ‡ ◆ **his car's in better ~ than mine** sa voiture est en meilleur état que la mienne

VT 1 *[+ plank, stick]* faire une *or* des encoche(s) sur ; *[+ blade, dish]* ébrécher ; *[+ cards]* biseauter ◆ **he ~ed his chin while shaving** il s'est fait une (petite) coupure au menton en se rasant

2 *(Brit ‡ = arrest)* pincer *, choper * ◆ **to get ~ed** se faire pincer * *or* choper * ◆ **to ~ sb for sth** pincer * qn pour qch ◆ **all right mate, you're ~ed!** allez, mon gars, tu es fait ! *

3 *(Brit ‡ = steal)* piquer *, faucher *

4 *(US)* ◆ **how much did they ~ you for that suit ?** ‡ tu t'es fait avoir * de combien pour *or* sur ce costume ?

nickel /ˈnɪkl/ N 1 *(NonC = metal)* nickel *m* 2 *(in Can, US = coin)* pièce *f* de cinq cents VT nickeler COMP **nickel-and-dime** * ADJ *(US = cheap and nasty)* de camelote, au rabais
nickel-in-the-slot machine † N *(US)* machine *f* à sous
nickel-plated ADJ nickelé
nickel-plating N nickelage *m*
nickel silver N argentan *m*, maillechort *m*

nickelodeon /ˌnɪkəˈləʊdɪən/ N *(US)* *(= cinema)* cinéma *m* à cinq sous ; *(= jukebox)* juke-box *m*

nicker /ˈnɪkəʳ/ VI 1 *[horse]* hennir doucement 2 *(= snigger)* ricaner N *(pl inv: Brit ‡)* livre *f*

nickname /ˈnɪkneɪm/ N surnom *m* ; *(esp humorous or malicious)* sobriquet *m* ; *(= short form of name)* diminutif *m* VT surnommer, donner un sobriquet à ◆ **John, ~d "Taffy"** John, surnommé "Taffy" ◆ **they ~d their teacher "Goggles"** ils ont surnommé leur professeur "Goggles", ils ont donné à leur professeur le sobriquet de "Goggles"

Nicodemus /ˌnɪkəˈdiːməs/ N Nicodème *m*

Nicosia /ˌnɪkəˈsiːə/ N Nicosie

nicotiana /nɪˌkəʊʃɪˈɑːnə/ N nicotiana *m*

nicotine /ˈnɪkətiːn/ N nicotine *f* COMP **nicotine patch** N patch *m* de nicotine, timbre *m* à la nicotine *or* antitabac
nicotine poisoning N nicotinisme *m*
nicotine-stained ADJ jauni *or* taché de nicotine

nicotinic /ˌnɪkəˈtɪnɪk/ ADJ ◆ **~ acid** acide *m* nicotinique

nicotinism /ˈnɪkətiːˌnɪzəm/ N nicotinisme *m*, tabagisme *m*

niece /niːs/ N nièce *f*

Nielsen rating /ˈniːlsənreɪtɪŋ/ N *(TV)* ≈ audimat ® *m*

Nietzschean /ˈniːtʃɪən/ ADJ nietzschéen

niff ‡ /nɪf/ N *(Brit)* puanteur *f* ◆ **what a ~!** ce que ça cocotte ‡ *or* (s)chlingue ‡ !

niffy * /ˈnɪfɪ/ ADJ *(Brit)* puant ◆ **it's ~ in here** ça cocotte ‡ *or* (s)chlingue ‡ ici !

nifty * /ˈnɪftɪ/ ADJ 1 *(= excellent)* *[person, place, idea, gadget, car]* chouette * 2 *(= skilful)* *[player]* habile ◆ **he's pretty ~ with a screwdriver** il manie drôlement bien le tournevis 3 *(= quick)* ◆ **you'd better be ~ about it !** tu as intérêt à te magner ! * 4 *(= stylish)* *[outfit]* coquet, chic *inv*

Niger /ˈnaɪdʒəʳ/ N *(= country, river)* Niger *m* ◆ **in ~** au Niger COMP nigérien ; *[embassy, capital]* du Niger

Nigeria /naɪˈdʒɪərɪə/ N Nigeria *m* ◆ **in ~** au Nigeria

Nigerian /naɪˈdʒɪərɪən/ N Nigérian(e) *m(f)* ADJ *(gen)* nigérian ; *[ambassador, embassy]* du Nigeria

Nigerien /niːˈʒeərɪən/ N Nigérien(enne) *m(f)* ADJ *(gen)* nigérien ; *[ambassador, embassy]* du Niger

niggardliness /ˈnɪgədlɪnɪs/ N avarice *f*, pingrerie *f*

niggardly /ˈnɪgədlɪ/ ADJ *[person]* pingre, avare ; *[amount, portion]* mesquin, piètre ; *[salary]* piètre ◆ **a ~ £50** 50 malheureuses livres ADV chichement, mesquinement

nigger *‡ /ˈnɪgəʳ/ N *(pej)* nègre *m*, négresse *f* ◆ **there's a ~ in the woodpile** il se trame quelque chose ◆ **to be the ~ in the woodpile** *(Brit)* faire le trouble-fête COMP **nigger brown** † ADJ *(Brit)* tête-de-nègre *inv*

niggle /ˈnɪgl/ VI [person] (= go into detail) couper les cheveux en quatre ; (= find fault) trouver toujours à redire VT ◆ **his conscience was niggling him** sa conscience le travaillait N (= doubt, query) ◆ **your report is excellent, I just have one little ~** * votre rapport est excellent, j'ai juste une petite remarque

niggling /ˈnɪglɪŋ/ ADJ (= trivial but annoying) [doubt, suspicion] obsédant ; (= finicky) [person] tatillon ; (= petty) [details] insignifiant ◆ **a ~ injury** une vieille blessure qui se réveille de temps en temps ◆ **a ~ little pain** une petite douleur tenace ◆ **I've got a ~ worry about it** il y a quelque chose qui me tracasse (là-dedans) N (NonC) chicanerie f

nigh /naɪ/ ADV (liter) ⇒ **near**

night /naɪt/ N 1 (= night-time) nuit f ◆ **~ after ~** des nuits durant ◆ **~ and day** nuit et jour ◆ **all ~ (long)** toute la nuit ◆ **to sit up all ~ talking** passer la nuit (entière) à bavarder ◆ **at ~, in the ~** la nuit ◆ **by ~, in the ~** de nuit ◆ **during the ~, in the ~** pendant la nuit ◆ **far into the ~** jusqu'à une heure avancée de la nuit, (très) tard dans la nuit ◆ **to spend the ~ (with sb)** passer la nuit (avec qn) ◆ **to have a good/bad ~** bien/mal dormir, passer une bonne/mauvaise nuit ◆ **I've had several bad ~s in a row** j'ai mal dormi plusieurs nuits de suite ◆ **he needs a good ~'s sleep** il a besoin d'une bonne nuit de sommeil ◆ **a ~'s lodging** un toit or un gîte pour la nuit ◆ **he's on ~s this week** il est de nuit cette semaine ◆ **to work ~s** travailler de nuit ; (US) ◆ **I can't sleep (at) ~s** je ne peux pas dormir la nuit ; → **Arabian, early, goodnight**

2 (= evening) soir m ◆ **6 o'clock at ~** 6 heures du soir ◆ **to have a ~ out** sortir le soir ◆ **a ~ at the opera** une soirée à l'opéra ◆ **to make a ~ of it** * prolonger la soirée ◆ **I've had too many late ~s** je me suis couché tard trop souvent ◆ **she's used to late ~s** elle a l'habitude de se coucher tard

3 (specifying) **last ~** (= night-time) la nuit dernière, cette nuit ; (= evening) hier soir ◆ **tomorrow ~** demain soir ◆ **the ~ before** la veille au soir ◆ **the ~ before last** avant-hier soir m ◆ **Monday ~** (= evening) lundi soir ; (= night-time) dans la nuit de lundi à mardi

4 (NonC = darkness) nuit f ◆ **~ is falling** la nuit or le soir tombe ◆ **he went out into the ~** il partit dans la nuit ◆ **he's afraid of the ~** il a peur du noir ◆ **a creature of the ~** (lit, fig) une créature de la nuit

5 (Theat) soirée f, représentation f ◆ **the last three ~s of ...** les trois dernières (représentations) de ... ◆ **Mozart ~** soirée f (consacrée à) Mozart ; → **first**

COMP [clothes, flight] de nuit

night-bird N (lit) oiseau m de nuit, nocturne m ; (fig) couche-tard mf inv, noctambule mf (hum)

night-blind ADJ héméralope

night blindness N héméralopie f

night editor N (Press) secrétaire mf de rédaction de nuit

night-fighter N (= plane) chasseur m de nuit

night letter N (US) télégramme à tarif réduit, livré le lendemain matin

night light N (child's) veilleuse f ; (Naut) feu m de position

night-night * EXCL (= goodnight) bonne nuit

night nurse N infirmier m, -ière f de nuit

night owl * N (fig) couche-tard mf inv, noctambule mf (hum)

night porter N gardien m de nuit, concierge mf de service la nuit

night safe N coffre m de nuit

night school N cours mpl du soir

night shelter N asile m de nuit

night shift N (= workers) équipe f de nuit ; (= work) poste m de nuit ◆ **to be or to work on (the) ~ shift** être (au poste) de nuit

the night sky N (gen) le ciel la nuit ; (liter) la voûte céleste

night soil † N selles fpl (nocturnes)

night stand N (US) table f de nuit

night stick N (US Police) matraque f (d'agent de police)

night storage heater N radiateur m par accumulation (fonctionnant au tarif de nuit)

night storage heating N chauffage m par accumulation (fonctionnant au tarif de nuit)

night table N table f de nuit

night-time N (NonC) nuit f ◆ **at ~-time** la nuit ◆ **in the ~-time** pendant la nuit, de nuit

night vision N vision f nocturne

night-vision ADJ [equipment, goggles] pour la vision nocturne

night watch N (= activity, period of time) veille f or garde f de nuit ; (= group of guards) équipe f des veilleurs or gardiens de nuit ; (= one man) ⇒ **night watchman**

night watchman N (pl **night watchmen**) veilleur m or gardien m de nuit

night work N travail m de nuit ; see also **black, deadly, woody**

nightcap /ˈnaɪtkæp/ N 1 (= hat) bonnet m de nuit 2 (= drink) boisson f (généralement alcoolisée, prise avant le coucher) ◆ **would you like a ~?** voulez-vous boire quelque chose avant d'aller vous coucher ?

nightclothes /ˈnaɪtkləʊðz/ NPL vêtements mpl de nuit

nightclub /ˈnaɪtklʌb/ N boîte f (de nuit)

nightclubber /ˈnaɪtklʌbəʳ/ N night-clubber mf noctambule mf

nightclubbing /ˈnaɪtklʌbɪŋ/ N sorties fpl en boîte (de nuit), clubbing m ◆ **to go ~** sortir en boîte

nightdress /ˈnaɪtdres/ N (esp Brit) chemise f de nuit

nightfall /ˈnaɪtfɔːl/ N tombée f du jour or de la nuit ◆ **at ~** à la tombée du jour, à la nuit tombante

nightgown /ˈnaɪtgaʊn/ N chemise f de nuit

nighthawk /ˈnaɪthɔːk/ N 1 (= bird) engoulevent m (d'Amérique) 2 (US fig = person) couche-tard mf inv, noctambule mf (hum)

nightie * /ˈnaɪtɪ/ N chemise f de nuit

nightingale /ˈnaɪtɪŋgeɪl/ N rossignol m

nightjar /ˈnaɪtdʒɑːʳ/ N engoulevent m (d'Europe)

nightlife /ˈnaɪtlaɪf/ N vie f nocturne ◆ **the Parisian/Roman ~** la vie nocturne à Paris/Rome

nightlong /ˈnaɪtlɒŋ/ ADJ (gen) de toute une nuit ; [festivities, vigil] qui dure toute la nuit

nightly /ˈnaɪtlɪ/ ADJ ◆ **muggings are a ~ occurrence** les agressions nocturnes sont devenues quotidiennes ◆ **~ performance** (Theat) représentation f tous les soirs ADV (= every evening) tous les soirs ; (= every night) toutes les nuits ◆ **performances ~** (Theat) représentations fpl tous les soirs

nightmare /ˈnaɪtmeəʳ/ N cauchemar m ◆ **what a ~!** * quel cauchemar ! ◆ **to be sb's worst ~** être la pire hantise de qn COMP **nightmare scenario** N scénario m catastrophe

nightmarish /ˈnaɪtmeərɪʃ/ ADJ de cauchemar, cauchemardesque

nightshade /ˈnaɪtʃeɪd/ N (Bot) ◆ **the ~ family** les solanacées fpl ; → **deadly, woody**

nightshirt /ˈnaɪtʃɜːt/ N chemise f de nuit

nightspot * /ˈnaɪtspɒt/ N ⇒ **nightclub**

nightwear /ˈnaɪtweəʳ/ N (NonC) vêtements mpl de nuit

nihilism /ˈnaɪɪlɪzəm/ N nihilisme m

nihilist /ˈnaɪɪlɪst/ N nihiliste mf

nihilistic /ˌnaɪɪˈlɪstɪk/ ADJ nihiliste

Nikkei index /nɪˌkeɪˈɪndeks/, **Nikkei average** /nɪˌkeɪˈævərɪdʒ/ N (Fin) indice m Nikkei

nil /nɪl/ N (Sport) zéro ; → ZERO (in form-filling etc) néant ◆ **my morale was ~** j'avais le moral à zéro * ◆ **his motivation was ~** il n'était pas du tout motivé ◆ **"nil by mouth"** (in hospital) "à jeun"

Nile /naɪl/ N Nil m ◆ **the ~ Delta/Valley** le Delta/la Vallée du Nil ◆ **~ cruise** croisière f sur le Nil ◆ **the Battle of the ~** (Hist) la bataille d'Aboukir

nimbi /ˈnɪmbaɪ/ NPL of **nimbus**

nimble /ˈnɪmbl/ ADJ [person, fingers, feet] agile ; [mind] vif ; [car] maniable

COMP **nimble-fingered** ADJ aux doigts agiles

nimble-footed ADJ au pied léger

nimble-minded, nimble-witted ADJ à l'esprit vif

nimbleness /ˈnɪmblnɪs/ N [of person, fingers, limbs etc] agilité f ; [of mind] vivacité f

nimbly /ˈnɪmblɪ/ ADV [move, jump] lestement

nimbostratus /ˌnɪmbəʊˈstreɪtəs/ N (pl **nimbostrati** /ˌnɪmbəʊˈstreɪtaɪ/) nimbostratus m

nimbus /ˈnɪmbəs/ N (pl **nimbi** or **nimbuses**) 1 (= halo) nimbe m 2 (= cloud) nimbus m

Nimby * /ˈnɪmbɪ/ N (abbrev of **not in my back yard**) riverain(e) m(f) contestataire (s'opposant à toute installation gênante près de chez lui)

nincompoop †* /ˈnɪŋkəmpuːp/ N cornichon * m, gourde * f

nine /naɪn/ ADJ neuf inv ◆ **~ times out of ten** neuf fois sur dix ◆ **cats have ~ lives** un chat retombe toujours sur ses pattes ◆ **he's got ~ lives** (hum) [person] un ange gardien veille sur lui N neuf m inv ◆ **dressed (up) to the ~s** * sur son trente et un ; for other phrases see **six** PRON neuf ◆ **there are ~** il y en a neuf

COMP **nine-day wonder** N merveille f d'un jour

Nine-Eleven, 9-11 N le 11 septembre

nine-hole ADJ ◆ **~-hole golf course** (parcours m de) neuf trous

nine-nine-nine N le numéro des urgences, en Grande-Bretagne ◆ **to call or ring or dial 999** appeler les urgences

nine-to-five * ADJ ◆ **~-to-five job** travail m de bureau ◆ **he's got a ~-to-five mentality or attitude** il a une mentalité de fonctionnaire

ninepins /ˈnaɪnpɪnz/ NPL (jeu m de) quilles fpl ◆ **they went down like ~** ils sont tombés comme des mouches

nineteen /ˈnaɪnˈtiːn/ ADJ dix-neuf inv N dix-neuf m inv ◆ **he talks ~ to the dozen** * (Brit) c'est un vrai moulin à paroles ◆ **they were talking ~ to the dozen** * ils jacassaient à qui mieux mieux ; for other phrases see **six** PRON dix-neuf ◆ **there are ~** il y en a dix-neuf

nineteenth /ˈnaɪnˈtiːnθ/ ADJ dix-neuvième ◆ **the ~ (hole)** (Golf hum) le bar, la buvette N dix-neuvième mf ; (= fraction) dix-neuvième m ; for phrases see **sixth**

ninetieth /ˈnaɪntɪɪθ/ ADJ quatre-vingt-dixième N quatre-vingt-dixième mf ; (= fraction) quatre-vingt-dixième m ; for phrases see **sixth**

ninety /ˈnaɪntɪ/ ADJ quatre-vingt-dix inv N quatre-vingt-dix m inv ◆ **~-one** quatre-vingt-onze ◆ **~-nine** quatre-vingt-dix-neuf ◆ **~-nine times out of a hundred** quatre-vingt dix-neuf fois sur cent ◆ **to be in one's nineties** être nonagénaire, avoir passé quatre-vingt-dix ans ◆ **"say ninety-nine!"** (at doctor's) ≃ "dites trente-trois !" ; → **naughty** ; for other phrases see **sixty** PRON quatre-vingt-dix ◆ **there are ~** il y en a quatre-vingt-dix

ninny * /ˈnɪnɪ/ N cornichon * m, serin(e) * m(f), gourde * f

ninth /naɪnθ/ ADJ neuvième N neuvième mf ; (= fraction) neuvième m ; for phrases see **sixth**

niobium /naɪˈəʊbɪəm/ N niobium m

Nip** /nɪp/ N (pej) Nippon m, -on(n)e f, Jap* m (pej)

nip¹ /nɪp/ N (= pinch) pinçon m ; (= bite) morsure f ◆ **the dog gave him a ~** le chien lui a donné un (petit) coup de dent ◆ **there's a ~ in the air today** (= chill) il fait frisquet aujourd'hui
VT (= pinch) pincer ; (= bite) donner un (petit) coup de dent à ; [cold, frost] [+ plants] brûler ; (= prune) [+ bud, shoot] pincer ; (fig) [+ plan, ambition] faire échec à ◆ **the cold air ~ped our faces** l'air froid nous piquait or pinçait le or au visage ◆ **to ~ sth in the bud** faire avorter qch, tuer or écraser qch dans l'œuf
VI 1 (Brit *) **to ~ up/down/out** monter/descendre/sortir en courant ◆ **he ~ped into the café** il a fait un saut au café
2 (= bite) **the dog ~ped at his feet** le chien lui a mordillé le pied
COMP **nip and tuck*** ADV (= neck and neck) **it was ~ and tuck** [race] la course a été serrée, ils sont arrivés dans un mouchoir de poche N (= plastic surgery) lifting m

► **nip along*** VI (Brit) [person] aller d'un bon pas ; [car] filer ◆ **~ along to Anne's house** cours vite or fais un saut chez Anne

► **nip in*** VI (Brit) entrer en courant, entrer un instant ◆ **I've just ~ped in for a minute** je ne fais qu'entrer et sortir ◆ **to ~ in and out of the traffic** se faufiler entre les voitures
VT SEP (Sewing) faire une (or des) pince(s) à ◆ **dress ~ped in at the waist** robe f pincée à la taille

► **nip off** VI (Brit *) filer*, se sauver*
VT SEP [+ bud, shoot] pincer ; [+ top of sth] couper

nip² /nɪp/ N (= drink) goutte f, petit verre m ◆ **to take a ~** boire une goutte or un petit verre ◆ **have a ~ of whisky!** une goutte de whisky ?

nipper /ˈnɪpəʳ/ N 1 (Brit *) gosse* mf, mioche* mf 2 (= tool) ◆ **(pair of) ~s** pince f, tenaille(s) f(pl) 3 [of crab etc] pince f

nipple /ˈnɪpl/ N 1 (Anat) mamelon m, bout m de sein 2 [of baby's bottle] tétine f ; (Geog) mamelon m 3 (for grease etc) graisseur m

Nippon /ˈnɪpɒn/ N (= Japan) Japon m

Nipponese /ˌnɪpəˈniːz/ ADJ nippon (-on(n)e f) N Nippon m, -on(n)e f

nippy* /ˈnɪpɪ/ ADJ 1 (= chilly) [weather, wind] frisquet ◆ **it's a bit ~ today** il fait frisquet aujourd'hui ◆ **a ~ autumn day** une fraîche journée d'automne 2 (Brit = brisk) [person] rapide ◆ **a ~ little car** une petite voiture rapide et nerveuse 3 (US = piquant) [cheese, flavour] piquant

NIREX /ˈnaɪreks/ (abbrev of **Nuclear Industry Radioactive Waste Executive**) → **nuclear**

nirvana /nɪəˈvɑːnə/ N nirvana m

Nisei /ˈniːseɪ/ N (pl **Nisei** or **Niseis**) (US) Américain né d'immigrants japonais

nisi /ˈnaɪsaɪ/ ADJ → **decree**

Nissen hut /ˈnɪsnˌhʌt/ N hutte f préfabriquée (en tôle, en forme de tunnel)

nit /nɪt/ N 1 (= louse-egg) lente f 2 (Brit * = fool) crétin(e)* m(f)
COMP **nit-pick*** VI ◆ **he's always ~-picking** il est très tatillon
nit-picker* N tatillon m, -onne f

nite* /naɪt/ N ⇒ **night**

niter /ˈnaɪtəʳ/ N (US) ⇒ **nitre**

nitrate /ˈnaɪtreɪt/ N nitrate m

nitration /naɪˈtreɪʃən/ N nitration f

nitre, niter (US) /ˈnaɪtəʳ/ N nitre m, salpêtre m

nitric /ˈnaɪtrɪk/ ADJ nitrique
COMP **nitric acid** N acide m nitrique
nitric oxide N oxyde m nitrique

nitrite /ˈnaɪtraɪt/ N nitrite m

nitro* /ˈnaɪtrəʊ/ N abbrev of **nitroglycerin(e)**

nitro... /ˈnaɪtrəʊ/ PREF nitro...

nitrogen /ˈnaɪtrədʒən/ N azote m
COMP **nitrogen cycle** N cycle m de l'azote
nitrogen dioxide N dioxyde m d'azote
nitrogen gas N (gaz m) azote m

nitrogenous /naɪˈtrɒdʒɪnəs/ ADJ azoté

nitroglycerin(e) /ˈnaɪtrəʊˈglɪsəriːn/ N nitroglycérine f

nitrous /ˈnaɪtrəs/ ADJ nitreux, d'azote
COMP **nitrous acid** N acide m nitreux
nitrous oxide N oxyde m d'azote

nitty-gritty* /ˈnɪtɪˈgrɪtɪ/ N ◆ **to get down to the ~** passer aux choses sérieuses ◆ **the ~ of life** (= hard facts) la dure réalité ◆ **the ~ of motherhood** (les difficultés de) la vie quotidienne d'une mère de famille ◆ **the ~ of everyday politics** la dure réalité quotidienne de la vie politique ADJ [details] pratique ; [problems] concret

nitwit** /ˈnɪtwɪt/ N crétin(e) m(f)

nix** /nɪks/ N (esp US = nothing) que dalle** VT (US) mettre son veto à

nixie mail* /ˈnɪksɪmeɪl/ N (US) courrier difficile à faire parvenir en raison d'une adresse illisible, incomplète etc

NJ abbrev of **New Jersey**

NLF /ˈenelˈef/ N (abbrev of **National Liberation Front**) FLN m

NLP /ˌenelˈpiː/ N (abbrev of **neurolinguistic programming**) PNL f

NLQ /ˌenelˈkjuː/ (abbrev of **near letter quality**) → **near**

NM, N Mex abbrev of **New Mexico**

NMR /ˌenemˈɑːʳ/ N (abbrev of **nuclear magnetic resonance**) RMN f

no /nəʊ/ PARTICLE non ◆ **oh ~!** (denying) mais non ! ; (disappointed) oh non ! ◆ **to say/answer ~** dire/répondre non ◆ **the answer is ~** la réponse est non or négative ◆ **I won't take ~ for an answer** * j'insiste ◆ **I wouldn't do it, no not for $1,000** je ne le ferais pas, même pas pour 1 000 dollars ◆ **~ to nuclear power!** non au nucléaire ! ; see also **say**
N (pl **noes**) non m inv ◆ **the noes have it** les non l'emportent, les voix contre l'emportent ◆ **there were seven noes** il y avait sept non or sept voix contre ; → **ay**
ADJ 1 (= not any) pas de used with ne, aucun used with ne ◆ **she had ~ coat** elle n'avait pas de manteau ◆ **I have ~ idea** je n'ai aucune idée ◆ **I have ~ more money** je n'ai plus d'argent ◆ **~ man could do more** (liter) aucun homme ne pourrait faire davantage ◆ **~ one man could do it** aucun homme ne pourrait le faire (à lui) seul ◆ **~ two men would agree on this** il n'y a pas deux hommes qui seraient d'accord là-dessus ◆ **~ two are alike** il n'y en a pas deux pareils ◆ **~ sensible man would have done that** un homme sensé n'aurait pas fait ça, aucun homme sensé n'aurait fait ça ◆ **~ Frenchman would say that** aucun Français ne dirait ça, un Français ne dirait jamais ça ◆ **there's ~ whisky like Scotch whisky** il n'y a pas de meilleur whisky que le whisky écossais ◆ **there's ~ Catholic like a converted Catholic** il n'y a pas plus catholique qu'un catholique converti ◆ **it's of ~ interest** ça n'a aucun intérêt, c'est sans intérêt ◆ **a man of ~ intelligence** un homme sans intelligence, un homme dénué d'intelligence ◆ **~ win ~ fee** (US) le client ne paie les honoraires que s'il a gain de cause ◆ **~ way!***, **~ go!*** pas question !* ; see also **comp** ◆ **it's ~ good waiting for him** cela ne sert à rien or ce n'est pas la peine de l'attendre ◆ **it's ~ wonder (that ...)** (ce n'est) pas étonnant (que ... + subj or si ... + indic) ◆ **~ wonder!*** pas étonnant !*
2 (emphatic) ◆ **by ~ means** pas du tout, absolument pas ◆ **he's ~ friend of mine** il n'est pas de mes amis ◆ **he's ~ genius** ce n'est certes pas un génie, il n'a rien d'un génie ◆ **this is ~ place for children** ce n'est pas un endroit pour les enfants ◆ **in ~ time (at all)** en un rien de temps ◆ **it's ~ small matter** (frm) ce n'est pas rien ◆ **headache or ~ headache, you'll have to do it** * migraine ou pas (migraine), tu vas devoir le faire ◆ **theirs is ~ easy task** ils n'ont pas la tâche facile, leur tâche n'est pas facile ◆ **there's ~ such thing** cela n'existe pas ; → **end, mistake**
3 (forbidding) **~ smoking** défense de fumer ◆ **~ entry** entrée f interdite, défense d'entrer ◆ **~ parking** stationnement m interdit ◆ **~ surrender!** on ne se rend pas ! ◆ **no nonsense!** pas d'histoires !, pas de blagues !* ; see also **comp**
4 (with gerund) **there's ~ saying** or **knowing what he'll do next** impossible de dire ce qu'il fera après ◆ **there's ~ pleasing him** (quoi qu'on fasse) il n'est jamais satisfait
ADV 1 non ◆ **whether he comes or ~** qu'il vienne ou non ◆ **hungry or ~, you'll eat your soup** que tu aies faim ou non, tu vas manger ta soupe
2 (with compar) ne ... pas ◆ **the patient is ~ better** le malade ne va pas mieux ◆ **I can go ~ further** je ne peux pas aller plus loin, je n'en peux plus ◆ **I can bear it ~ longer** je ne peux plus le supporter, je n'en peux plus ◆ **she took ~ less than four weeks to do it** il lui a fallu pas moins de quatre semaines pour le faire ◆ **he returned with a bottle of champagne, ~ less!** il est revenu avec une bouteille de champagne, excusez du peu !* ◆ **~ sooner said than done** aussitôt dit aussitôt fait
COMP **no-account*** ADJ, N (US) bon(ne) m(f) à rien
no ball N (Cricket) balle f nulle
no-brainer N (esp US: pej) (= person) débile mf ; (= film, book) nullité f ◆ **it's a no-brainer** (= obvious) c'est une évidence, ça tombe sous le sens
no-claim(s) bonus N (Insurance) bonus m
no-fault divorce N (Jur) ≈ divorce m par consentement mutuel (sans torts prononcés)
no-fault insurance N (esp US Jur) assurance f automobile à remboursement automatique
no-fly zone N zone f d'exclusion aérienne
no-frills ADJ avec service (réduit au strict) minimum or simplifié
no-go ADJ ◆ **it's no-go** * ça ne marche pas ◆ **~-go area** zone f interdite
no-good* ADJ nul (nulle f), propre or bon à rien N propre mf à rien
no-holds-barred ADJ (lit, fig) où tous les coups sont permis ; see also **hold**
no-hoper* N raté(e) m(f), nullard(e)* m(f), zéro* m
no jump N (Sport) saut m annulé
no-knock raid N (US) perquisition-surprise f
no-man's-land N (Mil) no man's land m ; (= wasteland) terrain m vague ; (= indefinite area) zone f mal définie
no-no* N ◆ **it's a no-no** (= forbidden) ça ne se fait pas ; (= impossible) c'est impossible
no-nonsense ADJ [approach, attitude] raisonnable, plein de bon sens
no one N ⇒ **nobody pron**
no place* ADV (esp US) ⇒ **nowhere**
no sale N (Comm) non-vente f
no-score draw N (Brit Ftbl) match m nul sans but marqué
no-show N (esp US: on plane/at show etc) passager m/spectateur m etc qui ne se présente pas
no throw N (Sport) lancer m annulé
no-trump(s) N sans-atout m inv ◆ **to call no-trump(s)** annoncer sans-atout ◆ **three tricks in no-trump(s)** trois sans-atout
no-win situation N situation f inextricable

no. (abbrev of **number**) n°

Noah /ˈnəʊə/ N Noé m ◆ **~'s ark** l'arche f de Noé

nob¹ †* /nɒb/ N (esp Brit) aristo* mf, richard(e)* m(f) (pej) ◆ **the ~s** (les gens de) la haute*, les rupins* mpl

nob² ‡ /nɒb/ N (= head) caboche* f, fiole‡ f

nobble * /ˈnɒbl/ VT (Brit) 1 (= corrupt) [+ person, jury etc] (by bribery) acheter, soudoyer ; (by intimidation) intimider 2 (Racing) [+ horse, dog] droguer (pour l'empêcher de gagner) 3 (= thwart) [+ plan etc] contrecarrer 4 (= obtain dishonestly) [+ votes etc] acheter 5 (= catch) [+ wrongdoer] pincer‡, choper‡ ◆ **the reporters ~d him as he left his hotel** les reporters l'ont happé or lui ont mis la main dessus au moment où il quittait son hôtel

Nobel /nəʊˈbel/ N ◆ **~ prize** prix m Nobel ◆ **~ prizewinner** or **laureate** (lauréat(e) m(f) du) prix m Nobel

nobelium /nəʊˈbiːlɪəm/ N nobélium m

nobility /nəʊˈbɪlɪtɪ/ N (NonC) 1 (= nobles) (haute) noblesse f 2 (= quality) noblesse f ◆ **~ of mind** grandeur f d'âme, magnanimité f

noble /ˈnəʊbl/ ADJ 1 (= aristocratic, admirable) [person, family, cause, attempt, sentiment] noble ; [wine] grand, noble ; [brandy] grand ; [monument, edifice] majestueux, imposant ◆ **to be of ~ birth** être de naissance noble ◆ **the ~ art** le noble art, la boxe ; see also **comp** 2 (* = unselfish) généreux, magnanime ◆ **I was very ~ and gave her my share** dans un geste magnanime je lui ai donné ma part, je lui ai généreusement donné ma part ◆ **it's very ~ of you to give up your day off to help** c'est très généreux de ta part de te priver de ton jour de congé pour aider 3 (Chem) [metal] noble ; see also **comp** N noble mf

COMP **noble gas** N gaz m noble
noble-minded ADJ magnanime, généreux
noble savage N bon sauvage m

nobleman /ˈnəʊblmən/ N (pl **-men**) noble m, aristocrate m

nobleness /ˈnəʊblnɪs/ N [of person, birth] noblesse f ; [of spirit, action etc] noblesse f, magnanimité f, générosité f ; [of animal, statue etc] belles proportions fpl, noblesse f de proportions ; [of building etc] majesté f ◆ **~ of mind** grandeur f d'âme, magnanimité f

noblewoman /ˈnəʊblwʊmən/ N (pl **-women**) aristocrate f, noble f

nobly /ˈnəʊblɪ/ ADV 1 (= aristocratically, admirably) [behave] noblement ◆ **~ born** de naissance noble 2 (* = selflessly) [volunteer, offer] généreusement ◆ **he ~ did the washing up** généreux, il a fait la vaisselle 3 (= imposingly) [stand, rise] majestueusement

nobody /ˈnəʊbədɪ/ PRON personne + ne before vb ◆ **I saw ~** je n'ai vu personne ◆ **~ knows** personne or nul ne le sait ◆ **~ spoke to me** personne ne m'a parlé ◆ **who saw him? – ~** qui l'a vu ? – personne ◆ **~ knows better than I** personne ne sait mieux que moi ◆ **~ (that was) there will ever forget ...** personne parmi ceux qui étaient là n'oubliera jamais ... ◆ **it is ~'s business** cela ne regarde personne ◆ **it's ~'s business what I do, what I do is ~'s business** ce que je fais ne regarde personne ◆ **like ~'s business** ‡ [run etc] à toutes jambes, comme un dératé* ; [work etc] d'arrache-pied, sans désemparer ◆ **he's ~'s fool** il n'est pas né d'hier, c'est loin d'être un imbécile ; → **else**
N moins que rien mf inv, rien du tout m ◆ **he's a mere ~, he's just a ~** c'est un moins que rien or un rien du tout ◆ **they are nobodies** ce sont des moins que rien or des riens du tout ◆ **I worked with him when he was ~** j'ai travaillé avec lui alors qu'il était encore inconnu

nocturnal /nɒkˈtɜːnl/ ADJ [animal, activity, habits] nocturne ; [raid] de nuit COMP **nocturnal emission** † N (Med) pollutions fpl nocturnes

nocturne /ˈnɒktɜːn/ N (Mus) nocturne m

nod /nɒd/ N 1 signe m (affirmatif) or inclinaison f de (la) tête ◆ **he gave me a ~** (gen) il m'a fait un signe de (la) tête ; (in greeting) il m'a salué de la tête ; (signifying "yes") il m'a fait signe que oui de la tête ◆ **he rose with a ~ of agreement** il s'est levé, signifiant son accord d'un signe de (la) tête ◆ **to answer with a ~** répondre d'un signe de (la) tête ◆ **to get the ~** * [project etc] avoir le feu vert ◆ **on the ~** * (Brit) [pass, approve] sans discussion, d'un commun accord ◆ **to give sb the ~** (lit) faire un signe de tête à qn ; (= give approval) accepter qn ; (= give permission) donner le feu vert à qn ◆ **a ~ and a wink** * un clin d'œil entendu ◆ **to give sb a ~ and a wink** * faire un clin d'œil entendu à qn ◆ **a ~ is as good as a wink (to a blind horse)** (Prov) l'allusion est claire
2 ◆ **Land of Nod** → **land**
VI 1 (= move head) faire un signe de (la) tête, incliner la tête ; (as sign of assent) hocher la tête, faire signe que oui ◆ **to ~ to sb** faire un signe de tête à qn ; (in greeting) saluer qn d'un signe de tête, saluer qn de la tête ◆ **"does it work?" he asked, ~ding at the piano** "est-ce qu'il marche ?" demanda-t-il, montrant le piano d'un signe de (la) tête ◆ **he ~ded to me to go** de la tête il m'a fait signe de m'en aller ◆ **we're on ~ding terms, we have a ~ding acquaintance** nous nous disons bonjour, nous nous saluons ◆ **he has a ~ding acquaintance with German/Montaigne** il connaît vaguement l'allemand/Montaigne
2 (= doze) sommeiller, somnoler ◆ **he was ~ding over a book** il dodelinait de la tête or il somnolait sur un livre ◆ **to catch sb ~ding** (fig) prendre qn en défaut
3 [flowers, plumes] se balancer, danser
VT ◆ **to ~ one's head** (= move head down) faire un signe de (la) tête, incliner la tête ; (as sign of assent) faire un signe de tête affirmatif ◆ **to ~ one's agreement/approval** manifester son assentiment/son approbation par un or d'un signe de tête ◆ **to ~ assent** faire signe que oui ◆ **they ~ded goodnight to Jane** ils ont dit bonsoir à Jane d'un signe de tête ◆ **Taylor leapt up to ~ the ball home** (Ftbl) Taylor a bondi pour marquer un but de la tête

► **nod off** * VI s'endormir ◆ **I ~ded off for a moment** je me suis endormi un instant

nodal /ˈnəʊdl/ ADJ nodal

noddle †‡ /ˈnɒdl/ N (= head) caboche* f, fiole‡ f

Noddy /ˈnɒdɪ/ N (= children's character) Oui-Oui m

node /nəʊd/ N (gen) nœud m ; (Bot) nœud m, nodosité f ; (Anat) nodus m, nodosité f ◆ **remote/network** ~ (Comput) nœud m distant/de réseau ; → **lymph**

nodular /ˈnɒdjʊləʳ/ ADJ nodulaire

nodule /ˈnɒdjuːl/ N (Anat, Bot, Geol) nodule m

Noel /nəʊˈel/ N Noël m

noggin /ˈnɒgɪn/ N 1 (= container) (petit) pot m ; (= amount) quart m (de pinte) ◆ **let's have a ~** (Brit = drink) allons boire or prendre un pot 2 (US ‡ = head) caboche* f, tête f

nohow * /ˈnəʊhaʊ/ ADV (esp US = no way) pas du tout

noise /nɔɪz/ N 1 (= sound) bruit m ◆ **I heard a small ~** j'ai entendu un petit bruit ◆ **the ~ of the traffic** le bruit de la circulation ◆ **to make a ~** faire du bruit ◆ **stop that ~!** arrêtez(-moi) tout ce bruit ! ◆ **~s in the ears** bourdonnements mpl (d'oreilles) ◆ **a hammering ~** un martèlement ◆ **a clanging ~** un bruit métallique ◆ **~s off** (Theat) bruits mpl dans les coulisses
2 (fig) **to make reassuring/placatory ~s** tenir des propos rassurants/apaisants ◆ **to make (all) the right ~s** * se montrer complaisant ◆ **the book made a lot of ~ when it came out** le livre a fait beaucoup de bruit quand il est sorti ◆ **to make a lot of ~ about sth** * faire du tapage autour de qch ◆ **she made ~s* about wanting to go home early** elle a laissé entendre qu'elle voulait rentrer tôt ; → **big**
3 (NonC) (Rad, TV) interférences fpl, parasites mpl ; (on phone) friture f ; (Comput) bruit m
VT (frm) ◆ **to ~ sth about** or **abroad** ébruiter qch

COMP **noise abatement** N lutte f antibruit ◆ **~-abatement campaign/society** campagne f/ligue f antibruit or pour la lutte contre le bruit
noise pollution N nuisances fpl sonores
noise prevention N mesure f antibruit or contre le bruit

noiseless /ˈnɔɪzlɪs/ ADJ [person, machine] silencieux

noiselessly /ˈnɔɪzlɪslɪ/ ADV sans bruit

noiselessness /ˈnɔɪzlɪsnɪs/ N silence m, absence f de bruit

noisily /ˈnɔɪzɪlɪ/ ADV bruyamment

noisiness /ˈnɔɪzɪnɪs/ N caractère m bruyant ; [of child] turbulence f

noisome /ˈnɔɪsəm/ ADJ (liter) 1 (= malodorous) [smell, odour, vapours] méphitique (liter) 2 (= unpleasant) [person] immonde ; (= harmful) [environment] néfaste

noisy /ˈnɔɪzɪ/ ADJ 1 (= loud) bruyant ◆ **to be ~** [person, car] être bruyant, faire beaucoup de bruit 2 (= garish) [colour] criard, voyant

nomad /ˈnəʊmæd/ N nomade mf

nomadic /nəʊˈmædɪk/ ADJ (lit, fig) nomade

nomadism /ˈnəʊmədɪzəm/ N nomadisme m

nom de plume † /ˈnɒmdəˈpluːm/ N (pl **noms de plume**) (Literat) pseudonyme m

nomenclature /nəʊˈmenklətʃəʳ/ N nomenclature f

nomenklatura /ˌnəʊmenkləˈtʊərə/ N (Pol: formerly in Eastern Europe) ◆ **the ~** la nomenklatura

nominal /ˈnɒmɪnl/ ADJ 1 (= in name only) [agreement, power, rights, control, leader, value] nominal ◆ **he's a ~ socialist/Christian** il n'a de socialiste/chrétien que le nom 2 (= minimal) [fee, charge, sum] minimal, insignifiant ; [wage, salary, rent] insignifiant ; [fine, penalty] symbolique ◆ **~ damages** (Jur) dommages-intérêts mpl symboliques 3 (Gram) [clause] nominal N (Gram) expression f nominale

nominalism /ˈnɒmɪnəlɪzəm/ N nominalisme m

nominalist /ˈnɒmɪnəlɪst/ N, ADJ nominaliste mf

nominalization /ˌnɒmɪnəlaɪˈzeɪʃən/ N (Ling) nominalisation f

nominalize /ˈnɒmɪnəlaɪz/ VT (Ling) nominaliser

nominally /ˈnɒmɪnəlɪ/ ADV [independent] théoriquement, en théorie ◆ **~ in charge** théoriquement responsable ◆ **~, they are on the same side, but ...** en principe, ils sont du même bord, mais ... ◆ **~ socialist/Christian** qui n'a de socialiste/chrétien que le nom

nominate /ˈnɒmɪneɪt/ VT 1 (= appoint) nommer, désigner ◆ **he was ~d chairman, he was ~d to the chairmanship** il a été nommé président ◆ **~d and elected members of a committee** membres mpl désignés et membres élus d'un comité 2 (= propose) proposer, présenter ◆ **he was ~d for the presidency** il a été proposé comme candidat à la présidence ◆ **they ~d Mr Lambotte for mayor** ils ont proposé M. Lambotte comme candidat à la mairie ◆ **to ~ sb for an Oscar** proposer or nominer qn pour un Oscar

nomination /ˌnɒmɪˈneɪʃən/ N 1 (= appointment) nomination f (to à) 2 (for job, political office etc) proposition f de candidat ◆ **~s must be received by ...** toutes propositions de candidats doivent être reçues avant ... 3 (Cine: for *award)* nomination *f* COMP **nomination paper** N *(Pol)* feuille *f* de candidature, nomination *f*

nominative /ˈnɒmɪnətɪv/ ADJ *(gen)* nominatif ; *[ending]* du nominatif N nominatif *m* ◆ **in the ~** au nominatif, au cas sujet

nominator /ˈnɒmɪneɪtəʳ/ N présentateur *m*

nominee /ˌnɒmɪˈniː/ N *(for post)* personne *f* désignée *or* nommée ; *(in election)* candidat(e) *m(f)* désigné(e) ; *(for annuity etc)* personne *f* dénommée ; *(Stock Exchange)* mandataire *mf* ◆ **~ company** *(Stock Exchange)* société *f* prête-nom

non- /nɒn/ PREF non- ◆ **strikers and ~strikers** grévistes *mpl* et non-grévistes *mpl* ◆ **believers and ~believers** ceux qui croient et ceux qui ne croient pas, (les) croyants *mpl* et (les) non-croyants *mpl*

COMP **non-absorbent** ADJ non absorbant
non-accidental injury N *(NonC)* maltraitance *f*
non-accountable ADJ non responsable
non-achievement N échec *m*
non-achiever N personne *f* qui ne réussit pas
non-addictive ADJ qui ne crée pas de dépendance
non-affiliated ADJ *[business]* non affilié ; *[industry]* non confédéré
non-aggression N non-agression *f* ◆ **~aggression pact** *or* **treaty** pacte *m* de non-agression
non-alcoholic ADJ non alcoolisé, sans alcool
non-aligned ADJ *(Pol)* non aligné
non-alignment N *(Pol)* non-alignement *m* ◆ **~alignment policy** politique *f* de non-alignement
non-appearance N *(Jur)* non-comparution *f*
non-arrival N non-arrivée *f*
non-assertive ADJ qui manque d'assurance, qui ne se met pas en avant
non-attendance N absence *f*
non-availability N non-disponibilité *f*
non-believer N *(Rel)* incroyant(e) *m(f)*
non-biological ADJ *[solution, parent]* non biologique ; *[washing powder]* sans enzymes
non-Catholic ADJ, N non catholique *mf*
non-Christian ADJ non chrétien
non-classified ADJ qui n'est pas classé secret
non-collegiate ADJ *[student]* qui n'appartient à aucun collège ◆ **~collegiate university** université *f* qui n'est pas divisée en collèges
non-com* N (abbrev of **non-commissioned officer**)*(US Mil)* sous-off* *m*
non-communication N manque *m* de communication
non-completion N *[of work]* non-achèvement *m* ; *[of contract]* non-exécution *f*
non-compliance N refus *m* d'obéissance *(with* à)
non compos mentis ADJ qui n'a pas toute sa raison
non-contagious ADJ non contagieux
non-contributory ADJ ◆ **~contributory pension scheme** régime *m* de retraite sans retenues *or* cotisations
non-controversial ADJ ⇒ **uncontroversial**
non-conventional ADJ non conventionnel
non-cooperation N refus *m* de coopérer, non-coopération *f*
non-cooperative ADJ peu coopératif
non-crush(able) ADJ infroissable
non-cumulative ADJ non cumulatif
non-custodial ADJ *(Jur)* ◆ **~custodial sentence** peine *f* non privative de liberté
non-dairy ADJ qui n'est pas à base de lait
non-degradable ADJ qui n'est pas biodégradable
non-democratic ADJ non démocratique
non-denominational ADJ œcuménique
non-drinker N personne *f* qui ne boit pas d'alcool
non-drip ADJ *[paint]* qui ne coule pas
non-driver N personne *f* qui n'a pas le permis de conduire
non-EU ADJ *[citizens, passports]* des pays qui n'appartiennent pas à l'UE ; *[imports]* hors Union européenne
non-executive ADJ non-exécutif N non-exécutif *m*
non-governmental organization N organisation *f* non gouvernementale
non-greasy ADJ *[ointment, lotion]* qui ne graisse pas ; *[skin, hair]* normal, qui n'est pas gras (grasse *f*)
non-hero N antihéros *m*
non-interference N non-intervention *f*
non-iron ADJ qui ne nécessite aucun repassage ◆ **"non-iron"** *(on label)* "ne pas repasser"
non-Jew N non-juif *m*, -ive *f*
non-Jewish ADJ non juif
non-league ADJ *(Brit Sport)* hors division
non-manual worker N col *m* blanc
non-Muslim ADJ non musulman N non-musulman(e) *m(f)*
non-negotiable ADJ non négociable
non-nuclear ADJ *[weapon]* conventionnel ; *[country]* non nucléaire
non-nutritious ADJ sans valeur nutritive
non-party ADJ *(Pol)* *[vote, decision]* indépendant, neutre
non-penetrative ADJ *[sex]* sans pénétration
non-person N *(= stateless etc)* personne *f* sans identité juridique
non-practising ADJ *[Christian, Muslim etc]* non pratiquant
non-productive ADJ non productif
non-professional ADJ *[player etc]* amateur ◆ **~professional conduct** manquement *m* aux devoirs de sa profession N *(Sport etc)* amateur *mf*
non-punitive ADJ dont l'intention n'est pas de punir
non-racial ADJ non racial
non-refillable ADJ *[pen, bottle]* non rechargeable
non-reflective ADJ *[glass]* non réfléchissant, antireflet *f inv*
non-religious ADJ non croyant
non-resident ADJ *(gen)* non résident ◆ **~resident course** stage *m* sans hébergement ◆ **~resident doctor** attaché(e) *m(f)* de consultations ◆ **~resident student** *(US)* *étudiant(e) d'une université d'État dont le domicile permanent est situé en dehors de cet État* N non-résident(e) *m(f)* ; *(Brit: in hotel)* client(e) *m(f)* de passage *(qui n'a pas de chambre)*
non-sexist ADJ qui n'est pas sexiste, non sexiste
non-student N non-étudiant(e) *m(f)*
non-threatening ADJ qui n'est pas menaçant
non-traditional ADJ non traditionnel
non-union ADJ *[company, organization]* qui n'emploie pas de personnel syndiqué
non-unionized ADJ ⇒ **non-union**
non-white N personne *f* de couleur ADJ de couleur

nonacademic /ˌnɒnækəˈdemɪk/ ADJ 1 *(= extra-curricular)* extrascolaire 2 *(= non-educational)* *[staff]* non enseignant ; *[career]* en dehors de l'enseignement 3 *(= not academically gifted)* *[child, pupil]* peu doué pour les études

nonage /ˈnəʊnɪdʒ/ N *(Jur)* minorité *f*

nonagenarian /ˌnɒnədʒɪˈneərɪən/ ADJ, N nonagénaire *mf*

nonbreakable /ˌnɒnˈbreɪkəbl/ ADJ incassable

nonce /nɒns/ N 1 ◆ **for the ~** pour la circonstance, pour l'occasion 2 ⁑ pointeur* *m* COMP **nonce-bashing*** N chasse *f* aux pointeurs*

nonchalance /ˈnɒnʃələns/ N nonchalance *f*

nonchalant /ˈnɒnʃələnt/ ADJ nonchalant ◆ **to be ~ about sth** prendre qch avec nonchalance

nonchalantly /ˈnɒnʃələntlɪ/ ADV nonchalamment, avec nonchalance

noncombatant /ˌnɒnˈkɒmbətənt/ ADJ, N noncombattant(e) *m(f)*

noncombustible /ˌnɒnkəmˈbʌstɪbl/ ADJ non combustible

noncommercial /ˌnɒnkəˈmɜːʃəl/ ADJ sans but lucratif

noncommissioned /ˈnɒnkəˈmɪʃənd/ ADJ *(Mil)* non breveté, sans brevet ◆ **~ officer** sous-officier *m*

noncommittal /ˈnɒnkəˈmɪtl/ ADJ *[person]* qui ne s'engage pas ; *[letter, statement]* qui n'engage à rien, évasif ; *[grunt]* évasif ; *[expression, attitude]* réservé ◆ **he gave a ~ answer** il fit une réponse évasive *or* qui ne l'engageait pas ◆ **I'll be very ~** je ne m'engagerai pas ◆ **he was very ~ about it** il ne s'est pas prononcé là-dessus

noncommittally /ˌnɒnkəˈmɪtəlɪ/ ADV *[say, answer]* évasivement, sans s'engager

noncommunicant /ˈnɒnkəˈmjuːnɪkənt/ ADJ, N *(Rel)* non-communiant(e) *m(f)*

nonconductor /ˈnɒnkənˈdʌktəʳ/ N *(Phys)* non-conducteur *m*, mauvais conducteur *m* ; *[of heat]* isolant *m*, calorifuge *m* ; *(Elec)* isolant *m*

nonconformism /ˈnɒnkənˈfɔːmɪzəm/ N non-conformisme *m*

nonconformist /ˈnɒnkənˈfɔːmɪst/ N non-conformiste *mf* ADJ non conformiste

Nonconformity /ˈnɒnkənˈfɔːmɪtɪ/ N *(Rel)* non-conformité *f*

nondazzle /ˈnɒnˈdæzl/ ADJ antiéblouissant

nondescript /ˈnɒndɪskrɪpt/ ADJ *[person, face, building]* quelconque ; *[appearance]* insignifiant, quelconque ; *[colour]* indéfinissable

nondestructive /ˈnɒndɪsˈtrʌktɪv/ ADJ *(Tech)* *[testing]* non destructeur (-trice *f*)

nondetachable /ˈnɒndɪˈtætʃəbl/ ADJ *[handle etc]* fixe, indémontable ; *[lining, hood]* non détachable

nondirectional /ˈnɒnˈdɪrekʃənl/ ADJ omnidirectionnel

nondirective therapy /ˈnɒndɪˌrektɪvˈθerəpɪ/ N *(Psych)* psychothérapie *f* non directive, non-directivisme *m*

nondistinctive /ˈnɒndɪsˈtɪŋktɪv/ ADJ *(Ling)* non distinctif

none /nʌn/ PRON 1

When **none** refers to a noun in the plural, it is generally translated by **aucun(e)**. The verb that follows is preceded by **ne**.

◆ **I tried four jackets on, but ~ fitted me** j'ai essayé quatre vestes, mais aucune ne m'allait ◆ **the police interviewed ten men, but ~ admitted seeing her** la police a interrogé dix hommes, mais aucun n'a avoué l'avoir vue

Note the possible translations when **none** refers to an uncountable noun or a noun in the singular.

◆ **I looked for butter, but there was ~** j'ai cherché du beurre mais il n'y en avait pas ◆ **I asked her for an answer, but she gave ~** je lui ai demandé une réponse, mais elle n'en a pas donné ◆ **he tried to hire a car but there were ~ available** il a essayé de louer une voiture mais il n'y en avait pas de disponible ◆ **there's ~ left** il n'y en a plus, il n'en reste plus

♦ **none at all** ◆ **there was no evidence, ~ at all** il n'y avait aucune preuve, absolument aucune ◆ **we had no notice of it, ~ at all** nous n'en avons pas été prévenus à l'avance, absolument pas ◆ **is there any bread left? – ~ at all** y a-t-il encore du pain ? – pas une miette ◆ **I need money but have ~ at all** j'ai besoin d'argent mais je n'en ai pas du tout

♦ **none of**

When **none of** is followed by a plural, it is generally translated **aucun(e) de**. The verb that follows is preceded by **ne**.

♦ **~ of these problems should affect us** aucun de ces problèmes ne devrait nous toucher ♦ **~ of the band members are well known** aucun des membres du groupe n'est célèbre ♦ **I want ~ of your excuses!** vos excuses ne m'intéressent pas !

When **none of** is followed by an uncountable noun, the negative idea is expressed in various ways.

♦ **she did ~ of the work herself** elle n'a rien fait elle-même ♦ **~ of the food/aid arrived on time** la nourriture/l'aide n'est pas arrivée à temps, toute la nourriture/l'aide est arrivée en retard ♦ **~ of this milk was pasteurized/contained bacteria** ce lait n'était pas pasteurisé/ne contenait aucune bactérie ♦ **~ of this money** pas un centime de cet argent ♦ **~ of this land** pas un mètre carré *or* pas un pouce de ce terrain ♦ **~ of the evidence unequivocally shows that it is harmful** rien ne prouve clairement que c'est nocif ; → **business**

When **none of** is followed by a pronoun, it is generally translated by **aucun(e) de**. When referring to people, it can be translated by **aucun(e) d'entre**. Note the use of **ne** before the verb.

♦ **~ of us** aucun de nous *or* d'entre nous, personne parmi nous ♦ **~ of us knew how to change a wheel** aucun de nous *or* d'entre nous ne savait changer une roue ♦ **~ of them saw him** aucun d'entre eux ne l'a vu ♦ **~ of you knew** aucun d'entre vous ne le savait ♦ **I checked the glasses and ~ of them were broken** j'ai vérifié les verres et aucun n'était cassé

♦ **none of it** ♦ **I read what he'd written but ~ of it made any sense** j'ai lu ce qu'il avait écrit mais c'était complètement incohérent ♦ **~ of it was true** tout était faux ♦ **we tried the wine but ~ of it was drinkable** nous avons goûté le vin mais pas une goutte n'était buvable ♦ **they promised financial aid, but so far ~ of it has arrived** ils ont promis une aide financière, mais jusqu'à maintenant pas un seul centime n'a été versé ♦ **I understood ~ of it** je n'y ai rien compris

♦ **none of this/that** rien de ceci/cela ♦ **~ of that!** pas de ça !

♦ **will have** *or* **is having** *etc* **none of** ♦ **he will have ~ of this kind of talk** il ne tolère pas ce genre de discours ♦ **he would have ~ of it** il ne voulait rien savoir ♦ **she was having ~ of that nonsense** elle refusait d'écouter ces sottises

2 *(= nobody)* personne + *ne before vb* ♦ **I know, ~ better, that ...** je sais mieux que personne que ... ♦ **Dr. Harriman was a specialist, ~ better** le Docteur Harriman était un spécialiste, il n'y en avait pas de meilleur

♦ **none but** *(frm)* seul ♦ **~ but God will ever know what I suffered** seul Dieu saura jamais combien j'ai souffert ♦ **~ but Sarah came** seule Sarah est venue

♦ **none other** ♦ **it was Hillary Clinton, ~ other** c'était Hillary Clinton en personne ♦ **their guest was ~ other than the president himself** leur invité n'était autre que le président en personne ♦ **for this reason and ~ other** pour cette raison très exactement

3 *(in form-filling)* néant *m*

ADV

♦ **none the ...** ♦ **he's ~ the worse for it** il ne s'en porte pas plus mal ♦ **she's looking ~ the worse for her ordeal** cette épreuve ne semble pas l'avoir trop marquée ♦ **I like him ~ the worse for it** je ne l'en aime pas moins pour cela ♦ **the house would be ~ the worse for a coat of paint** une couche de peinture ne ferait pas de mal à cette maison ♦ **he was ~ the wiser** il n'en savait pas plus pour autant, il n'était pas plus avancé

♦ **none too ...** ♦ **it's ~ too warm** il ne fait pas tellement chaud ♦ **and ~ too soon either!** et ce n'est pas trop tôt ! ♦ **I was ~ too sure that he would come** j'étais loin d'être sûr qu'il viendrait ♦ **she was ~ too happy about it** elle était loin d'être contente ♦ **he was ~ too pleased at being disturbed** ça ne l'a pas enchanté qu'on le dérange

nonedible /nɒ'nedɪbl/ ADJ non comestible

nonentity /nɒ'nentɪtɪ/ N personne *f* insignifiante *or* sans intérêt ♦ **he's a complete ~** c'est une nullité

nonessential /,nɒnɪ'senʃl/ ADJ non essentiel, accessoire NPL **nonessentials** accessoires *mpl* ♦ **the ~s** l'accessoire *m*

nonestablished /,nɒnɪs'tæblɪʃt/ ADJ *[church]* non établi

nonesuch /'nʌnsʌtʃ/ N ⇒ **nonsuch**

nonet /nɒ'net/ N *(Mus)* nonet *m*

nonetheless /,nʌnðə'les/ ADV ⇒ **nevertheless**

nonevent * /'nɒnɪ'vent/ N non-événement *m*

nonexamination course /,nɒnɪg'zæmɪ'neɪʃənkɔːs/ N *(Scol etc)* études *fpl* non sanctionnées par un examen

nonexecutive director /,nɒnɪg'zekjʊtɪvdɪ'rektəʳ/ N administrateur *m*

nonexistence /'nɒnɪg'zɪstəns/ N non-existence *f*

nonexistent /'nɒnɪg'zɪstənt/ ADJ inexistant

nonexplosive /'nɒnɪk'spləʊsɪv/ ADJ *[gas]* non explosif

nonfactual /,nɒn'fæktjʊəl/ ADJ qui n'est pas fondé sur des faits

nonfat /'nɒnfæt/ ADJ *[cooking, diet]* sans corps gras *or* matière grasse ; *[meat]* maigre

nonfattening /,nɒn'fætnɪŋ/ ADJ qui ne fait pas grossir

nonferrous /,nɒn'ferəs/ ADJ non ferreux

nonfiction /,nɒn'fɪkʃən/ N littérature *f* non romanesque ♦ **he only reads ~** il ne lit jamais de romans

nonfinite /,nɒn'faɪnaɪt/ ADJ ♦ **~ verb** verbe *m* au mode impersonnel ♦ **~ forms** modes *mpl* impersonnels

nonflammable /,nɒn'flæməbl/ ADJ ⇒ **noninflammable**

nonfulfilment /,nɒnfʊl'fɪlmənt/ N non-exécution *f*, inexécution *f*

nonglare /,nɒn'gleəʳ/ ADJ antiéblouissant

nongovernmental /,nɒngʌvən'mentl/ ADJ non gouvernemental

nongrammatical /,nɒngrə'mætɪkəl/ ADJ non grammatical

non grata * /,nɒn'grɑːtə/ ADJ ♦ **he felt rather ~** il avait l'impression d'être un intrus ; see also **persona**

nonillion /nəʊ'nɪljən/ N *(esp Brit = 10⁵⁴)* nonillion *m* ; *(esp US) (= 10³⁰)* quintillion *m*

noninfectious /,nɒnɪn'fekʃəs/ ADJ non contagieux

noninflammable /,nɒnɪn'flæməbl/ ADJ ininflammable

nonintervention /,nɒnɪntə'venʃən/ N *(Pol etc)* non-intervention *f*, laisser-faire *m*

noninterventionist /,nɒnɪntə'venʃənɪst/ ADJ non interventionniste N *(Pol etc)* non-interventionniste *mf*

noninvolvement /,nɒnɪn'vɒlvmənt/ N *(in war, conflict)* non-engagement *m*, neutralité *f* ; *(in negotiations etc)* non-participation *f* ; *(Psych)* détachement *m*

nonjudg(e)mental /,nɒndʒʌdʒ'mentəl/ ADJ qui ne porte pas de jugement, neutre

nonladdering /,nɒn'lædərɪŋ/ ADJ ⇒ **nonrun**

nonlinear /,nɒn'lɪnɪəʳ/ ADJ non linéaire

nonlinguistic /,nɒnlɪŋ'gwɪstɪk/ ADJ *[communication etc]* non verbal

nonliterate /,nɒn'lɪtərɪt/ ADJ *[tribe, culture]* sans écriture

nonmalignant /,nɒnmə'lɪgnənt/ ADJ *[tumour]* bénin (-igne *f*)

nonmaterial /'nɒnmə'tɪərɪəl/ ADJ immatériel

nonmember /,nɒn'membəʳ/ N *[of club etc]* personne *f* étrangère (au club *etc*) ♦ **open to ~s** ouvert au public

nonmetal /'nɒnmetl/ N *(Chem)* non-métal *m*, métalloïde *m*

nonmetallic /,nɒnmɪ'tælɪk/ ADJ *(= relating to nonmetals)* métalloïdique ; *(= not of metallic quality)* non métallique

nonmilitant /,nɒn'mɪlɪtənt/ ADJ non militant

nonmilitary /,nɒn'mɪlɪtərɪ/ ADJ non militaire

nonobservance /,nɒnəb'zɜːvəns/ N *(gen)* non-observation *f*, inobservation *f* ; *(Rel)* non-observance *f*

non obst. PREP (abbrev of **non obstante**) *(= notwithstanding)* nonobstant

nonoperational /,nɒnɒpə'reɪʃənl/ ADJ non opérationnel

nonpareil /'nɒnpərəl/ *(liter)* N personne *f or* chose *f* sans pareille ADJ incomparable, sans égal

nonpartisan /'nɒn,pɑːtɪ'zæn/ ADJ impartial

nonpaying /,nɒn'peɪɪŋ/ ADJ *[visitor etc]* qui ne paie pas, admis à titre gracieux

nonpayment /'nɒn'peɪmənt/ N non-paiement *m (of* de*)*

nonplus /'nɒn'plʌs/ VT déconcerter, dérouter ♦ **I was utterly ~sed** j'étais complètement déconcerté *or* dérouté

nonpolitical /'nɒnpə'lɪtɪkəl/ ADJ apolitique

nonpolluting /'nɒnpə'luːtɪŋ/ ADJ non polluant

nonprofitmaking /'nɒn'prɒfɪtmeɪkɪŋ/, **nonprofit** (US) /'nɒn'prɒfɪt/ ADJ à but non lucratif

nonproliferation /'nɒnprə,lɪfə'reɪʃən/ N non-prolifération *f* ♦ **~ treaty** traité *m* de non-prolifération

non-punitive /'nɒn'pjuːnɪtɪv/ ADJ dont l'intention n'est pas de punir

nonreceipt /'nɒnrɪ'siːt/ N *[of letter etc]* non-réception *f*

nonrecurring expenses /'nɒnrɪ'kɜːrɪŋ ɪk'spensɪz/ NPL dépenses *fpl* d'équipement

nonreturnable /'nɒnrɪ'tɜːnəbl/ ADJ *[bottle etc]* non consigné

nonrun /'nɒnrʌn/ ADJ indémaillable

nonrunner /'nɒn'rʌnəʳ/ N non-partant *m*

nonscheduled /'nɒn'ʃedjuːld/ ADJ *[plane, flight]* spécial

nonsectarian /'nɒnsek'teərɪən/ ADJ non confessionnel

nonsegregated /'nɒn'segrɪgeɪtɪd/ ADJ sans ségrégation

nonsense /'nɒnsəns/ N *(NonC)* absurdités *fpl*, idioties *fpl* ♦ **to talk ~** dire n'importe quoi ♦ **that's a piece of ~!** c'est une absurdité !, n'importe quoi ! ♦ **that's (a lot of) ~!** tout ça ce sont des absurdités ♦ **but that's ~!** mais c'est absurde !, mais c'est n'importe quoi ! ♦ **oh, ~!** oh, ne dis pas n'importe quoi ! ♦ **I'm putting on weight** – **~!** je grossis – penses-tu ! ♦ **all**

this ~ about them not being able to pay toutes ces histoires idiotes comme quoi* *or* selon lesquelles ils seraient incapables de payer ◆ **it is ~ to say ...** il est absurde *or* idiot de dire ... ◆ **he will stand no ~ from anybody** il ne se laissera pas faire par qui que ce soit, il ne se laissera marcher sur les pieds par personne ◆ **he won't stand any ~ about that** il ne plaisante pas là-dessus ◆ **I've had enough of this ~!** j'en ai assez de ces histoires *or* idioties ! ◆ **stop this ~!, no more of your ~!** arrête tes idioties ! ◆ **there's no ~ about him** c'est un homme très carré ◆ **to knock the ~ out of sb*** ramener qn à la raison ◆ **to make (a) ~ of** *[+ project, efforts, pledge]* rendre inutile ; *[+ claim]* invalider ◆ **it is an economic ~ to ...** c'est absolument absurde d'un point de vue économique que de ... ; → **stuff**

COMP **nonsense verse** N vers *mpl* amphigouriques

nonsense word N mot *m* inventé de toutes pièces

nonsensical /nɒnˈsensɪkəl/ ADJ *[idea, action]* absurde, dénué de sens ; *[person, attitude, rule, lyrics]* absurde

nonsensically /nɒnˈsensɪkəlɪ/ ADV absurdement

non sequitur /ˌnɒnˈsekwɪtəʳ/ N ◆ **it's a ~** ça manque de suite

nonshrink /ˈnɒnʃrɪŋk/ ADJ irrétrécissable

nonsinkable /ˈnɒnˈsɪŋkəbl/ ADJ insubmersible

nonsked* /ˈnɒnˈsked/ N (US) avion *m* spécial

nonskid /ˈnɒnˈskɪd/ ADJ antidérapant

nonskilled /ˈnɒnˈskɪld/ ADJ ⇒ **unskilled**

nonslip /ˈnɒnˈslɪp/ ADJ *[shoe sole, ski]* antidérapant

nonsmoker /ˈnɒnˈsməʊkəʳ/ N (= *person*) non-fumeur *m*, -euse *f*, personne *f* qui ne fume pas ◆ **he is a ~** il ne fume pas

nonsmoking /ˈnɒnˈsməʊkɪŋ/ ADJ *[flight, seat, compartment, area]* non-fumeurs *inv* ; *[office, restaurant]* où il est interdit de fumer ; *[person]* qui ne fume pas, non fumeur ◆ **the ~ population** ceux *mpl* qui ne fument pas, les non-fumeurs *mpl*

nonsolvent /ˈnɒnˈsɒlvənt/ ADJ (Chem) non dissolvant

nonspecialist /ˈnɒnˈspeʃəlɪst/ N (gen) nonspécialiste *mf* ; (Med) généraliste *mf* ADJ *[knowledge, dictionary]* général

nonspecific /ˈnɒnspəˈsɪfɪk/ ADJ 1 (Med) non spécifique 2 (= *imprecise*) général COMP **nonspecific urethritis** N (Med) urétrite *f*

nonstandard /ˈnɒnˈstændəd/ ADJ (Ling) non standard *inv*

nonstarter /ˈnɒnˈstɑːtəʳ/ N 1 (= *horse*) nonpartant *m* 2 (= *person*) nullité *f* 3 (= *idea*) ◆ **it's a ~** c'est voué à l'échec

nonstick /ˈnɒnˈstɪk/ ADJ *[coating]* antiadhésif ; *[saucepan]* qui n'attache pas

nonstop /ˌnɒnˈstɒp/ ADJ *[flight]* sans escale ; *[train]* direct ; *[journey]* sans arrêt ; *[music]* ininterrompu ; (Ski) non-stop ◆ **the movie's two hours of ~ action** les deux heures d'action ininterrompue du film ADV *[talk, work, rain]* sans interruption, sans arrêt ; (Ski) non-stop ◆ **to fly ~ from London to Chicago** faire Londres-Chicago sans escale

nonsuch /ˈnʌnsʌtʃ/ N (liter) personne *f* or chose *f* sans pareille

nonsuit /ˈnɒnˈsuːt/ N (Jur) (gen) ordonnance *f* de non-lieu ; (*on the part of the plaintiff*) cessation *f* de poursuites, retrait *m* de plainte ◆ **to direct a ~** rendre une ordonnance de non-lieu VT † débouter ◆ **to be ~ed** être débouté (de sa demande)

nonsupport /ˈnɒnsəˈpɔːt/ N (US Jur) défaut *m* de pension alimentaire

nonswimmer /ˈnɒnˈswɪməʳ/ N personne *f* qui ne sait pas nager

nontaxable /ˈnɒnˈtæksəbl/ ADJ non imposable

nonteaching staff /ˌnɒnˈtiːtʃɪŋstɑːf/ N (Scol etc) personnel *m* non enseignant

nontoxic /ˌnɒnˈtɒksɪk/ ADJ non toxique

nontransferable /ˈnɒntrænsˈfɜːrəbl/ ADJ *[ticket]* non transmissible ; *[share]* nominatif ; *[pension]* non réversible

non-trivial /ˌnɒnˈtrɪvɪəl/ ADJ non insignifiant

nonverbal /ˌnɒnˈvɜːbəl/ ADJ non verbal

nonviable /ˌnɒnˈvaɪəbl/ ADJ non viable

nonviolence /ˌnɒnˈvaɪələns/ N non-violence *f*

nonviolent /ˌnɒnˈvaɪələnt/ ADJ non violent

nonvocational /ˌnɒnvəʊˈkeɪʃənl/ ADJ *[courses]* non professionnel

nonvoluntary /ˌnɒnˈvɒləntərɪ/ ADJ *[work]* rémunéré

nonvoter /ˌnɒnˈvəʊtəʳ/ N (US Pol) abstentionniste *mf*

nonvoting share /ˌnɒnˈvəʊtɪŋʃeər/ N (Fin) action *f* sans droit de vote

nonworker /ˌnɒnˈwɜːkəʳ/ N personne *f* sans activité professionnelle

nonworking /ˌnɒnˈwɜːkɪŋ/ ADJ sans emploi, qui ne travaille pas

nonwoven /ˌnɒnˈwəʊvən/ ADJ non tissé

noodle /ˈnuːdl/ N 1 (Culin) ◆ **~s** nouilles *fpl* ◆ **~ soup** potage *m* au vermicelle 2 (* = *silly person*) nouille* *f*, nigaud(e) *m(f)* 3 (US, Can ‡ = *head*) caboche* *f*, tête *f*

nook /nʊk/ N (= *corner*) coin *m*, recoin *m* ; (= *remote spot*) retraite *f* ◆ **~s and crannies** coins *mpl* et recoins *mpl* ◆ **breakfast ~** coin-repas *m* ◆ **a shady ~** une retraite ombragée, un coin ombragé

nookie‡, nooky‡ /ˈnʊkɪ/ N (Brit: *esp hum*) la fesse‡ ◆ **to have a bit of ~** se faire une partie de jambes en l'air‡

noon /nuːn/ N midi *m* ◆ **at/about ~** à/vers midi ; → **high**

noonday /ˈnuːndeɪ/, **noontide** †† /ˈnuːntaɪd/, **noontime** (*esp US*) /ˈnuːntaɪm/ N midi *m* ◆ **at the ~ of his fame** (*fig, liter*) à l'apogée de sa gloire ADJ de midi

noose /nuːs/ N nœud *m* coulant ; (*in animal trapping*) collet *m* ; *[of cowboy]* lasso *m* ; *[of hangman]* corde *f* ◆ **to put one's head in the ~, to put a ~ round one's neck** (*fig*) se jeter dans la gueule du loup VT 1 *[+ rope]* faire un nœud coulant à 2 (*in trapping*) prendre au collet ; *[cowboy]* prendre *or* attraper au lasso

nope‡ /nəʊp/ PARTICLE non

nor /nɔːʳ/ CONJ 1 (*following "neither"*) ni ◆ **neither you ~ I can do it** ni vous ni moi (nous) ne pouvons le faire ◆ **she neither eats ~ drinks** elle ne mange ni ne boit ◆ **neither here ~ elsewhere does he stop working** ici comme ailleurs il ne cesse pas de travailler ; → **neither**

2 (= *and not*) **I don't know, ~ do I care** je ne sais pas et d'ailleurs je m'en moque ◆ **that's not funny, ~ is it true** ce n'est ni drôle ni vrai ◆ **that's not funny, ~ do I believe it's true** cela n'est pas drôle et je ne crois pas non plus que ce soit vrai ◆ **I shan't go and ~ will you** je n'irai pas et toi non plus ◆ **I don't like him – ~ do I** je ne l'aime pas – moi non plus ◆ **~ was this all** et ce n'était pas tout ◆ **~ will I deny that ...** et je ne nie pas non plus que ... + *subj* ◆ **~ was he disappointed** et il ne fut pas déçu non plus ; → **yet**

nor' /nɔːʳ/ ADJ (Naut: *in compounds*) ⇒ **north** ◆ **~east** *etc* ⇒ **north-east** ; → **north**

noradrenalin(e) /ˈnɔːrəˈdrenəlɪn, iːn/ N noradrénaline *f*

Nordic /ˈnɔːdɪk/ ADJ nordique

COMP **Nordic skier** N skieur *m*, -euse *f* nordique

Nordic skiing N ski *m* nordique

norm /nɔːm/ N norme *f* ◆ **to differ from the ~** s'écarter de la norme

normal /ˈnɔːməl/ ADJ 1 (gen) normal ; (= *usual*) habituel ◆ **traffic was ~ for a bank holiday weekend** la circulation était normale pour un long week-end ◆ **a higher than ~ risk of infection** un risque d'infection plus élevé que la normale ◆ **it's perfectly ~ to feel that way** il est tout à fait normal de ressentir cela ◆ **it was quite ~ for him to be late** c'était tout à fait dans ses habitudes d'arriver en retard ◆ **as ~** comme d'habitude ◆ **it's ~ practice to do that** il est normal de faire cela ◆ **to buy sth for half the ~ price** acheter qch à moitié prix ◆ **~ service will be resumed as soon as possible** (TV) nous vous prions de nous excuser pour cette interruption momentanée de l'image ◆ **the factory is back to ~ working** le travail a repris normalement à l'usine

2 (Math) normal, perpendiculaire

3 (Chem) neutre

N 1 normale *f* ◆ **above/below ~** au-dessus/en dessous de la normale ◆ **temperatures below ~** des températures au-dessous de la normale ◆ **to return** *or* **get back to ~** revenir à la normale

2 (Math) normale *f*, perpendiculaire *f*

COMP **normal school** N (US: *formerly*) *institut universitaire de formation des maîtres*, ≃ école *f* normale

normal time N (Sport) temps *m* réglementaire ◆ **at the end of ~ time** à l'issue du temps réglementaire

normality /nɔːˈmælɪtɪ/, **normalcy** (*esp US*) /ˈnɔːməlsɪ/ N normalité *f*

normalization /ˌnɔːməlaɪˈzeɪʃən/ N normalisation *f*

normalize /ˈnɔːməlaɪz/ VT normaliser, régulariser VI se normaliser, se régulariser

normally /ˈnɔːməlɪ/ ADV (= *usually*) généralement, d'habitude ; (= *as normal*) normalement ◆ **he ~ arrives at about 10 o'clock** d'habitude il arrive vers 10 heures ◆ **the trains are running ~** les trains circulent normalement

Norman /ˈnɔːmən/ ADJ normand ; (Archit) roman ◆ **the ~ Conquest** la conquête normande ◆ **~ French** (= *language*) anglo-normand *m* N Normand(e) *m(f)*

Normandy /ˈnɔːməndɪ/ N Normandie *f* ; → **landing¹**

normative /ˈnɔːmətɪv/ ADJ normatif

Norse /nɔːs/ ADJ (Hist) nordique, scandinave ◆ **~man** Scandinave *m* N (= *language*) nordique *m*, norrois *m* ◆ **Old ~** vieux norrois *m*

north /nɔːθ/ N nord *m* ◆ **magnetic ~** Nord *m* or pôle *m* magnétique ◆ **to the ~ of ...** au nord de ... ◆ **house facing the ~** maison *f* exposée au nord ◆ **to veer to the ~, to go into the ~** *[wind]* tourner au nord, anordir (Naut) ◆ **the wind is in the ~** le vent est au nord ◆ **the wind is (coming** *or* **blowing) from the ~** le vent vient *or* souffle du nord ◆ **to live in the ~** habiter dans le Nord ◆ **in the ~ of Scotland** dans le nord de l'Écosse ◆ **the North** (US Hist) les États *mpl* antiesclavagistes *or* du Nord

ADJ *[side, coast, slope, end]* nord *inv* ; *[region, area]* septentrional (*frm*) ◆ **~ wind** vent *m* du nord ◆ **(in) ~ Wales/London** (dans) le nord du pays de Galles/de Londres ◆ **on the ~ side** du côté nord ◆ **studio with a ~ light** atelier *m* exposé au nord ◆ **a ~ aspect** une exposition au nord ◆ **room with a ~ aspect** pièce *f* exposée au nord ◆ ~ **wall** mur *m* (exposé au) nord ◆ ~ **transept/door** *(Archit)* transept *m*/portail *m* nord ; see also **comp**

ADV *[lie, be]* au nord (*of* de) ; *[go]* vers le nord, en direction du nord ◆ **further** ~ plus au nord ◆ ~ **of the island** au nord de l'île ◆ **the town lies** ~ **of the border** la ville est (située) au nord de la frontière ◆ **we drove** ~ **for 100km** nous avons roulé pendant 100 km en direction du nord *or* vers le nord ◆ **go** ~ **till you get to Oxford** allez en direction du nord *or* vers le nord jusqu'à Oxford ◆ **to sail due** ~ aller droit vers le nord ; *(Naut)* avoir le cap au nord ◆ ~ **by** ~**-east** nord quart nord-est

COMP **North Africa** N Afrique *f* du Nord
North African ADJ nord-africain, d'Afrique du Nord N Africain(e) *m(f)* du Nord, Nord-Africain(e) *m(f)*
North America N Amérique *f* du Nord
North American ADJ nord-américain, d'Amérique du Nord N Nord-Américain(e) *m(f)*
the North Atlantic N l'Atlantique *m* nord
North Atlantic Drift N dérive *f* nord-atlantique
North Atlantic Treaty Organization N Organisation *f* du traité de l'Atlantique nord
North Carolina N Caroline *f* du Nord ◆ **in North Carolina** en Caroline du Nord
the North Country N *(Brit)* le Nord de l'Angleterre
north-country ADJ du Nord (de l'Angleterre)
North Dakota N Dakota *m* du Nord ◆ **in North Dakota** dans le Dakota du Nord
north-east N nord-est *m* ADJ (du *or* au) nord-est *inv* ADV vers le nord-est
north-easter N nordet *m* *(Naut)*, vent *m* du nord-est
north-easterly ADJ *[wind, direction]* du nord-est ; *[situation]* au nord-est ADV vers le nord-est
north-eastern ADJ (du) nord-est *inv*
north-eastward(s) ADV vers le nord-est
north-facing ADJ exposé au nord
North Island N *(of New Zealand)* l'île *f* du Nord *(de la Nouvelle-Zélande)*
North Korea N Corée *f* du Nord
North Korean ADJ nord-coréen N Nord-Coréen(ne) *m(f)*
north-north-east N nord-nord-est *m* ADJ (du *or* au) nord-nord-est *inv* ADV vers le nord-nord-est
north-north-west N nord-nord-ouest *m* ADJ (du *or* au) nord-nord-ouest *inv* ADV vers le nord-nord-ouest
North Pole N pôle *m* Nord
North Sea N mer *f* du Nord
North Sea gas N *(Brit)* gaz *m* naturel de la mer du Nord
North Sea oil N pétrole *m* de la mer du Nord
North Star N étoile *f* polaire
North Vietnam N Vietnam *m* du Nord
North Vietnamese ADJ nord-vietnamien N Nord-Vietnamien(ne) *m(f)*
north-wall hammer N *(Climbing)* marteau-piolet *m*
north-west N nord-ouest *m* ADJ (du *or* au) nord-ouest *inv* ADV vers le nord-ouest
north-wester N noroît *m* *(Naut)*, vent *m* du nord-ouest
north-westerly ADJ *[wind, direction]* du nord-ouest ; *[situation]* au nord-ouest ADV vers le nord-ouest
north-western ADJ nord-ouest *inv*, du nord-ouest
North-West Frontier N frontière *f* du Nord-Ouest
North-West Passage N passage *m* du Nord-Ouest
north-westward(s) ADV vers le nord-ouest

Northants /nɔːˈθænts/ abbrev of **Northamptonshire**

northbound /ˈnɔːθbaʊnd/ ADJ *[traffic]* en direction du nord ; *[vehicle]* qui va vers le nord ; *[carriageway]* nord *inv*

Northd abbrev of **Northumberland**

northerly /ˈnɔːðəlɪ/ ADJ *[wind]* du nord ; *[situation]* au nord ; *[direction]* vers le nord ◆ ~ **latitudes** latitudes *fpl* boréales ◆ ~ **aspect** exposition *f* au nord ◆ **in a** ~ **direction** en direction du nord, vers le nord ADV vers le nord

northern /ˈnɔːðən/ ADJ *[province, state, neighbour]* du nord ; *[border, suburbs]* nord *inv* ◆ **the** ~ **coast** le littoral nord *or* septentrional ◆ **house with a** ~ **outlook** maison *f* exposée au nord ◆ ~ **wall** mur *m* exposé au nord ◆ **in** ~ **Spain** dans le nord de l'Espagne ◆ ~ **hemisphere** hémisphère *m* Nord *or* boréal ◆ **in the** ~ **town of Lille** à Lille, dans le Nord

COMP **Northern Ireland** N Irlande *f* du Nord
Northern Irish ADJ d'Irlande du Nord NPL Irlandais *mpl* du Nord
northern lights NPL aurore *f* boréale
the Northern Territory N *(of Australia)* le Territoire du Nord

northerner /ˈnɔːðənəʳ/ N 1 homme *m* or femme *f* du Nord, habitant(e) *m(f)* du Nord ◆ **he is a** ~ il vient du Nord ◆ **the** ~**s** les gens *mpl* du Nord, les septentrionaux *mpl* 2 *(US Hist)* Nordiste *mf*

northernmost /ˈnɔːðənməʊst/ ADJ le plus au nord, à l'extrême nord

Northlands /ˈnɔːθləndz/ NPL pays *mpl* du Nord

Northman /ˈnɔːθmən/ N (pl **-men**) *(Hist)* Viking *m*

Northumb abbrev of **Northumberland**

Northumbria /nɔːˈθʌmbrɪə/ N Northumbrie *f*

Northumbrian /nɔːˈθʌmbrɪən/ ADJ de Northumbrie N habitant(e) *m(f)* or natif *m*, -ive *f* de Northumbrie

northward /ˈnɔːθwəd/ ADJ au nord ADV (also **northwards**) vers le nord

Northwest Territories /ˌnɔːθwestˈterɪtərɪz/ NPL *(Can)* (Territoires *mpl* du) Nord-Ouest *m*

Northwest Territory /ˌnɔːθwestˈterɪtərɪ/ N *(US Hist)* Territoire *m* du Nord-Ouest

Norway /ˈnɔːweɪ/ N Norvège *f*

Norwegian /nɔːˈwiːdʒən/ ADJ *(gen)* norvégien ; *[ambassador, embassy]* de Norvège N 1 *(= person)* Norvégien(ne) *m(f)* 2 *(= language)* norvégien *m*

Nos, nos (abbrev of **numbers**) nº

nose /nəʊz/ N 1 *[of person, animal]* nez *m* ; *[of dog, cat]* museau *m* ◆ **he has a nice** ~ il a un joli nez ◆ **his** ~ **was bleeding** il saignait du nez ◆ **the horse won by a** ~ le cheval a gagné d'une demi-tête ◆ **to speak through one's** ~ nasiller, parler du nez

2 *(= sense of smell)* odorat *m*, nez *m* ◆ **to have a good** ~ avoir l'odorat *or* le nez fin

3 *(= instinct)* ◆ **to have a (good)** ~ **for sth** savoir flairer qch ◆ **he's got a (good)** ~ **for a bargain/for danger/for a story** il sait flairer les bonnes affaires/le danger/les scoops

4 *[of wine etc]* arôme *m*, bouquet *m*

5 *(in phrases: fig)* ◆ **with one's** ~ **in the air** d'un air hautain ◆ **she's always got her** ~ **in a book** * elle a toujours le nez fourré dans un livre * ◆ **it was there under his very** ~ *or* **right under his** ~ **all the time** c'était là juste *or* en plein sous son nez ◆ **she did it under his very** ~ *or* **right under his** ~ elle l'a fait à sa barbe *or* sous son nez ◆ **to look down one's** ~ **at sb/sth** prendre qn/qch de haut ◆ **he can't see beyond** *or* **further than (the end of) his** ~ il ne voit pas plus loin que le bout de son nez ◆ **to turn one's** ~ **up (at sth)** faire le dégoûté (devant qch) ◆ **to keep one's** ~ **out of sth** ne pas se mêler de qch ◆ **to poke** *or* **stick one's** ~ **into sth** mettre *or* fourrer * son nez dans qch ◆ **you'd better keep your** ~ **clean** * il vaut mieux que tu te tiennes à carreau * ◆ **to lead sb by the** ~ mener qn par le bout du nez ◆ **it gets up my** ~ * ça me pompe l'air *, ça me tape sur les nerfs * ; *(US)* ◆ **right on the** ~‡ en plein dans le mille ; → **blow¹, end, follow, grindstone, joint, pay, rub, thumb**

VT 1 *(= smell)* flairer, renifler

2 ◆ **a van** ~**d its way past** *or* **through** une camionnette est passée lentement

VI *[ship, vehicle]* avancer lentement

COMP **nose cone** N *[of missile]* ogive *f*
nose drops NPL gouttes *fpl* nasales, gouttes *fpl* pour le nez
nose job * N *(plastic surgery)* ◆ **to have a** ~ **job** se faire refaire le nez
nose ring N anneau *m* de nez
nose wheel N *[of plane]* roue *f* avant du train d'atterrissage

► **nose about** *, **nose around** * VI fouiner *, fureter

► **nose at** VT FUS flairer, renifler

► **nose in** VI 1 *[car]* se glisser dans une file 2 * *[person]* s'immiscer *or* s'insinuer (dans un groupe)

► **nose out** VI *[car]* déboîter prudemment

VT SEP 1 *[dog]* flairer

2 ◆ **to nose out a secret** découvrir *or* flairer un secret ◆ **to** ~ **sb out** dénicher *or* dépister qn

nosebag /ˈnəʊzbæg/ N musette *f*

noseband /ˈnəʊzbænd/ N *[of horse]* muserolle *f*

nosebleed /ˈnəʊzbliːd/ N saignement *m* de nez ◆ **to have a** ~ saigner du nez

-nosed /nəʊzd/ ADJ *(in compounds)* au nez ... ◆ **red-nosed** au nez rouge ; → **long¹, snub²**

nosedive /ˈnəʊzdaɪv/ N 1 *[of plane]* piqué *m* 2 *(fig) [of stocks, prices]* chute *f* libre, plongeon *m* ◆ **to take a** ~ ⇒ **vi 2** VI 1 *[plane]* descendre en piqué 2 *(fig) [stocks]* baisser rapidement ; *[prices, sales]* chuter ; *[career]* s'effondrer

nosegay /ˈnəʊzgeɪ/ N petit bouquet *m*

nosepiece /ˈnəʊzpiːs/ N *(on spectacles)* pont *m* ; *(on microscope)* porte-objectif *m*

nosey * /ˈnəʊzɪ/ ADJ fouineur *, curieux ◆ **to be** ~ mettre *or* fourrer * son nez partout ◆ **don't be (so)** ~! mêlez-vous de vos affaires *or* de ce qui vous regarde ! ◆ **Nosey Parker** *(pej)* fouineur * *m*, -euse * *f*

nosh ‡ /nɒʃ/ N 1 *(Brit = food)* bouffe ‡ *f* ◆ **to have some** ~ boulotter *, bouffer ‡ 2 *(US = snack)* casse-croûte *m* VI 1 *(Brit = eat)* boulotter *, bouffer ‡ 2 *(US = have a snack)* manger *or* grignoter entre les repas COMP **nosh-up** ‡ N *(Brit)* bouffe ‡ *f* ◆ **to have a** ~**-up** bouffer ‡, bâfrer ‡

nosily * /ˈnəʊzɪlɪ/ ADV indiscrètement

nosiness * /ˈnəʊzɪnɪs/ N curiosité *f*

nosing /ˈnəʊzɪŋ/ N *[of stair]* rebord *m*

nosography /nɒˈsɒgrəfɪ/ N nosographie *f*

nosological /ˌnɒsəˈlɒdʒɪkəl/ ADJ nosologique

nosologist /nɒˈsɒlədʒɪst/ N nosologiste *mf*

nosology /nɒˈsɒlədʒɪ/ N nosologie *f*

nostalgia /nɒsˈtældʒɪə/ N nostalgie *f*

nostalgic /nɒsˈtældʒɪk/ ADJ nostalgique ◆ **to be** ~ **for** *or* **about sth** avoir la nostalgie de qch

nostalgically /nɒˈstældʒɪkəlɪ/ ADV avec nostalgie

Nostradamus /ˌnɒstrəˈdɑːməs/ N Nostradamus *m*

nostril /ˈnɒstrəl/ N *[of person, dog etc]* narine *f* ; *[of horse etc]* naseau *m*

nostrum /ˈnɒstrəm/ N *(= patent medicine, also fig)* panacée *f*, remède *m* universel ; *(= quack medicine)* remède *m* de charlatan

nosy * /ˈnəʊzɪ/ ADJ ⇒ **nosey**

not /nɒt/ ADV 1 *(with vb)* ne ... pas ◆ **he is** ~ **here** il n'est pas ici ◆ **he has** ~ *or* **hasn't come** il n'est pas venu ◆ **he will** ~ *or* **won't stay** *(prediction)* il ne restera pas ; *(refusal)* il ne veut pas rester ◆ **is it** ~**?, isn't it?** non ?, n'est-ce pas ?

◆ **you have got it, haven't you?** vous l'avez (bien), non *or* n'est-ce pas ? ◆ **he told me ~ to come** il m'a dit de ne pas venir ◆ **~ wanting to be heard, he removed his shoes** ne voulant pas qu'on l'entende, il ôta ses chaussures ; → **mention**

♦ **not only … but also …** non seulement … mais également …

[2] *(as substitute for clause)* non ◆ **is he coming? – I believe ~** est-ce qu'il vient ? – je crois que non ◆ **it would appear ~** il semble que non ◆ **I am going whether he comes or ~** j'y vais qu'il vienne ou non

[3] *(elliptically)* **I wish it were ~ so** *(frm)* je voudrais bien qu'il en soit autrement ◆ **for the young and the ~ so young** pour les jeunes et les moins jeunes ◆ **big, ~ to say enormous** gros pour ne pas dire énorme ◆ **will he come? – as likely as ~** est-ce qu'il viendra ? – ça se peut ◆ **as likely as ~ he'll come** il y a une chance sur deux *or* il y a des chances (pour) qu'il vienne

♦ **not at all** pas du tout ◆ **are you cold? – ~ at all** avez-vous froid ? – pas du tout ◆ **thank you very much – ~ at all** merci beaucoup – je vous en prie *or* de rien *or* il n'y a pas de quoi

♦ **not in the least** pas du tout, nullement

♦ **not that …** ◆ **~ that I care** non pas que cela me fasse quelque chose ◆ **~ that I know of** pas (autant) que je sache ◆ **~ that they haven't been useful** on ne peut pas dire qu'ils *or* ce n'est pas qu'ils n'aient pas été utiles

♦ **why not ?** pourquoi pas ?

[4] *(understatement)* **~ a few …** bien des …, pas mal de … ◆ **~ without reason** non sans raison ◆ **~ without some regrets** non sans quelques regrets ◆ **I shall ~ be sorry to …** je ne serai pas mécontent de … ◆ **it is ~ unlikely that …** il n'est pas du tout impossible que … ◆ **a ~ inconsiderable number of …** un nombre non négligeable de …

[5] *(with pron etc)* **~ me** *or* *(frm)* **I!** moi pas !, pas moi ! ◆ **~ one book** pas un livre ◆ **~ one man knew** pas un (homme) ne savait ◆ **~ everyone can do that** tout le monde n'en est pas capable, ce n'est pas donné à tout le monde ◆ **~ any more** plus (maintenant) ◆ **~ yet** pas encore

[6] *(with adj)* non, pas ◆ **~ guilty** non coupable ◆ **~ negotiable** non négociable

notability /ˌnəʊtəˈbɪlɪtɪ/ **N** [1] *(NonC)* *[of quality]* prééminence *f* [2] *[of person]* notabilité *f*, notable *m*

notable /ˈnəʊtəbl/ **ADJ** *[designer, philosopher, example]* éminent ; *[fact]* notable, remarquable ; *[success]* remarquable ◆ **with a few ~ exceptions** à quelques notables exceptions près ◆ **to be ~ for sth** se distinguer par qch ◆ **it is ~ that …** il est remarquable que … + *subj* **N** notable *m*

notably /ˈnəʊtəblɪ/ LANGUAGE IN USE 26.2 **ADV** [1] *(= in particular)* notamment [2] *(= noticeably)* notablement ◆ **~, she failed to mention …** il est significatif *or* intéressant qu'elle n'ait pas mentionné …

notarial /nəʊˈtɛərɪəl/ **ADJ** *[seal]* notarial ; *[deed]* notarié ; *[style]* de notaire

notarize /ˈnəʊtəˌraɪz/ **VT** *(US)* *[notary]* authentifier, certifier conforme

notary /ˈnəʊtərɪ/ **N** (also **notary public**) notaire *m* ◆ **before a ~** par-devant notaire

notate /nəʊˈteɪt/ **VT** *(Mus)* noter, transcrire

notation /nəʊˈteɪʃən/ **N** *(Mus, Ling, Math)* notation *f*

notch /nɒtʃ/ **N** *(in wood, stick etc)* entaille *f*, encoche *f* ; *(in belt etc)* cran *m* ; *(in wheel, board etc)* dent *f*, cran *m* ; *(in saw)* dent *f* ; *(in blade)* ébréchure *f* ; *(US Geog)* défilé *m* ; *(Sewing)* cran *m* ◆ **he pulled his belt in one ~** il a resserré sa ceinture d'un cran **VT** *[+ stick etc]* encocher ; *[+ wheel etc]* cranter, denteler ; *[+ blade]* ébrécher ; *(Sewing)* *[+ seam]* cranter

► **notch together VT SEP** *(Carpentry)* assembler à entailles

► **notch up VT SEP** *[+ score, point, win, success]* marquer

notchback /ˈnɒtʃbæk/ **N** *(US = car)* tricorps *f*, trois-volumes *f*

note /nəʊt/ LANGUAGE IN USE 26.1, 26.2

N [1] *(= short record of facts, things to do etc)* note *f* ◆ **to take** *or* **make a ~ of sth** prendre qch en note, prendre note de qch ◆ **I must make a mental ~ to buy some more** il faut que je me souvienne d'en racheter ◆ **to take** *or* **make ~s** *[student, policeman, secretary etc]* prendre des notes ◆ **lecture ~s** notes *fpl* de cours ◆ **to speak from ~s** parler en consultant ses notes ◆ **to speak without ~s** parler sans notes *or* papiers ; → **compare**

[2] *(= short commentary)* note *f*, annotation *f* ◆ **author's ~** note *f* de l'auteur ◆ **translator's ~s** *(= footnotes etc)* remarques *fpl* *or* notes *fpl* du traducteur ; *(= foreword)* préface *f* du traducteur ◆ **"Notes on Molière"** "Notes sur Molière" ◆ **~s on a literary work** commentaire *m* sur un ouvrage littéraire ◆ **to put ~s into a text** annoter un texte

[3] *(= informal letter)* mot *m* ◆ **take a ~ to Mr Jones** *(to secretary)* je vais vous dicter un mot pour M. Jones ◆ **just a quick ~ to tell you …** un petit mot à la hâte *or* en vitesse pour te dire …

[4] *(Diplomacy)* note *f* ◆ **diplomatic ~** note *f* diplomatique, mémorandum *m* ◆ **official ~ from the government** note *f* officielle du gouvernement

[5] *(Mus)* note *f* ; *[of piano]* touche *f* ; *[of bird]* note *f* ◆ **to hold a ~** tenir *or* prolonger une note ◆ **to play a false ~, to sing a false ~** faire une fausse note

[6] *(fig = tone)* note *f* ◆ **on an optimistic/positive ~** sur une note optimiste/positive ◆ **on a personal/practical ~** d'un point de vue personnel/pratique ◆ **if I could add just a personal ~** si je peux me permettre une remarque personnelle ◆ **on a more positive ~ …** pour continuer sur une note plus optimiste … ◆ **peace talks ended on a high/a more positive ~** les pourparlers de paix se sont terminés sur une note optimiste/plus positive ◆ **on a more serious ~ …** plus sérieusement *or* pour passer aux choses sérieuses … ◆ **the talks began on a friendly ~** les négociations ont débuté sur une note amicale ◆ **his speech struck the right/wrong ~** son discours était bien dans la note/n'était pas dans la note ◆ **several speakers struck a pessimistic ~** plusieurs orateurs se sont montrés pessimistes

[7] *(= quality, implication)* note *f*, accent *m* ◆ **with a ~ of anxiety in his voice** avec une note d'anxiété dans la voix ◆ **his voice held a ~ of desperation** sa voix avait un accent de désespoir ◆ **a ~ of nostalgia** une note *or* touche nostalgique ◆ **a ~ of warning** un avertissement discret

[8] *(Brit:* also **banknote**) billet *m* (de banque) ◆ **ten-pound ~** billet *m* de dix livres (sterling)

[9] *(Comm)* *(= promise to pay)* effet *m*, billet *m* ; *(= voucher)* bon *m* ◆ **~ of hand** reconnaissance *f* (de dette) ◆ **~s payable** *(Fin)* effets *mpl* à payer ; → **advice, promissory note**

[10] *(NonC: frm = notability)* ◆ **a man of ~** un homme éminent *or* de marque ◆ **a family of ~** une famille éminente ◆ **all the people of ~** toutes les personnes importantes ◆ **nothing of ~** rien d'important

[11] *(NonC = notice)* **to take ~ of** prendre (bonne) note de, remarquer ◆ **take ~!** prenez bonne note ! ◆ **the critics took ~ of the book** les critiques ont remarqué le livre ◆ **they will take ~ of what you say** ils feront *or* prêteront attention à ce que vous dites ◆ **worthy of ~** *(frm)* remarquable, digne d'attention

VT [1] *(gen)* noter, prendre (bonne) note de *(frm)* ; *(Jur)* prendre acte de ◆ **to ~ a fact** *(gen)* prendre note d'un fait ; *(Jur)* prendre acte d'un fait ◆ **which fact is duly ~d** *(Jur)* dont acte ◆ **we have ~d your remarks** nous avons pris (bonne) note de vos remarques

[2] *(= notice)* constater ◆ **to ~ an error** constater une erreur ◆ **I ~ that …** je constate que … ◆ **~ that the matter is not yet closed** notez bien que l'affaire n'est pas encore close

[3] (also **note down**) noter ◆ **let me ~ it (down)** laissez-moi le noter ◆ **to ~ (down) sb's remarks** noter les remarques de qn ◆ **to ~ (down) an appointment in one's diary** noter un rendez-vous dans son agenda

COMP note-case N *(Brit)* portefeuille *m*, porte-billets *m inv*

note issue N émission *f* fiduciaire

► **note down VT SEP** ⇒ **note vt 3**

notebook /ˈnəʊtbʊk/ **N** [1] *(= notepad)* carnet *m*, calepin *m* ; *(Scol)* cahier *m* ; *(tear-off)* bloc-notes *m* [2] *(Comput:* also **notebook computer**) notebook *m*

noted /ˈnəʊtɪd/ **ADJ** *[historian, writer]* éminent, célèbre ; *[thing, fact]* célèbre ◆ **to be ~ for sth/for doing sth** être connu pour qch/pour avoir fait qch ◆ **a man not ~ for his generosity** *(iro)* un homme qui ne passe pas pour être particulièrement généreux

notelet /ˈnəʊtlɪt/ **N** carte-lettre *f*

notepad /ˈnəʊtpæd/ **N** bloc-notes *m*

notepaper /ˈnəʊtpeɪpəʳ/ **N** papier *m* à lettres

noteworthiness /ˈnəʊtwɜːðɪnɪs/ **N** importance *f*

noteworthy /ˈnəʊtwɜːðɪ/ **ADJ** *(frm)* remarquable, notable ◆ **it is ~ that …** il convient de noter que …

nothing /ˈnʌθɪŋ/ **N** [1] rien *m* + *ne before vb* ◆ **I saw ~** je n'ai rien vu ◆ **~ happened** il n'est rien arrivé, il ne s'est rien passé ◆ **to eat ~** ne rien manger ◆ **~ to eat/read** rien à manger/à lire ◆ **he's had ~ to eat yet** il n'a encore rien mangé ◆ **~ could be easier** rien de plus simple ◆ **~ pleases him** rien ne le satisfait, il n'est jamais content

[2] *(+ adj)* rien de ◆ **~ new/interesting** *etc* rien de nouveau/d'intéressant *etc*

[3] *(in phrases)*

For set expressions such as **nothing doing**, **nothing else**, **nothing like** *etc*, look up the other word

he's five foot ~ * il ne fait qu'un (petit) mètre cinquante deux ◆ **as if ~ had happened** comme si de rien n'était ◆ **I can do ~ (about it)** je n'y peux rien ◆ **he got ~ out of it** il n'en a rien retiré, il n'y a rien gagné ◆ **all his fame was as ~, all his fame counted for ~** toute sa gloire ne comptait pour rien ◆ **~ of the kind!** absolument pas !, (mais) pas du tout ! ◆ **don't apologize, it's ~** ne vous excusez pas, ce n'est rien ◆ **her secretarial skills are ~ compared with** *or* **to her sister's** elle est beaucoup moins bonne secrétaire que sa sœur ◆ **that is ~ to you** *(= it's easy for you)* pour vous ce n'est rien ◆ **£500 is ~ to her** 500 livres, c'est une bricole pour elle, elle n'en est pas à 500 livres près ◆ **she is** *or* **means ~ to him** elle n'est rien pour lui ◆ **it's** *or* **it means ~ to me whether he comes or not** il m'est indifférent qu'il vienne ou non ◆ **that's ~ to what is to come** ce n'est rien à côté de ce qui nous attend ◆ **I can make ~ of it** je n'y comprends rien ◆ **there's ~ to it** * c'est facile (comme tout *) ◆ **you get ~ for ~** on n'a rien pour rien ◆ **to come to ~** ne pas aboutir, ne rien donner, faire fiasco ◆ **to be reduced to ~** être réduit à néant ◆ **there is ~ to laugh at** il n'y a pas de quoi rire ◆ **I've got ~ to say** je n'ai rien à dire ◆ **he had ~ to say for himself** *(= no* *explanation)* il ne trouvait aucune excuse ; *(= no conversation)* il n'avait pas de conversation ◆ **in ~ flat** * *(= very quickly)* en un rien de temps, en cinq sec *

◆ **for nothing** *(= in vain)* en vain, inutilement ; *(= without payment)* pour rien, gratuitement ; *(= for no reason)* sans raison ◆ **he was working for ~** il travaillait gratuitement *or* sans se faire payer ◆ **I'm not Scottish for ~** * *(hum)* ce n'est pas pour rien que je suis écossais

◆ **nothing but** ◆ **he does ~ but eat** il ne fait que manger ◆ **he does ~ but complain** il ne fait que se plaindre, il n'arrête pas de se plaindre ◆ **I get ~ but complaints all day** je n'entends que des plaintes à longueur de journée

◆ **nothing for it** *(Brit)* ◆ **there's ~ for it but to go** il n'y a qu'à *or* il ne nous reste qu'à partir ◆ **there was nothing for it, he would have to tell her** rien à faire, il fallait qu'il le lui dise

◆ **nothing in ...** ◆ **there's ~ in it** *(= not interesting)* c'est sans intérêt ; *(= not true)* ce n'est absolument pas vrai ; *(= no difference)* c'est du pareil au même ; *(in contest = very close)* c'est très serré ◆ **there's ~ in these rumours** il n'y a rien de vrai *or* pas un grain de vérité dans ces rumeurs ◆ **there's ~ in it** * **for us** nous n'avons rien à y gagner ◆ **Oxford is leading, but there's ~ in it** Oxford est en tête, mais c'est très serré

◆ **nothing on** ◆ **to have ~ on** *(= be naked)* être nu ; *(= have no plans)* être libre ◆ **I have ~ on (for) this evening** je suis libre ce soir, je n'ai rien de prévu ce soir ◆ **the police have ~ on him** la police n'a rien pu retenir contre lui ◆ **he has ~ on her** * *(fig = isn't as good as)* il ne lui arrive pas à la cheville

◆ **nothing to do with** ◆ **that has ~ to do with us** nous n'avons rien à voir là-dedans ◆ **I've got ~ to do with it** je n'y suis pour rien ◆ **have ~ to do with it!** ne vous en mêlez pas ! ◆ **that has ~ to do with it** cela n'a rien à voir

◆ **to say nothing of ...** sans parler de ... ◆ **the tablecloth was ruined, to say ~ of my shirt** la nappe était fichue *, sans parler de ma chemise

4 *(Math *)* zéro *m*

5 *(NonC = nothingness)* néant *m*, rien *m*

6 *(= person)* nullité *f* ; *(= thing)* vétille *f*, rien *m* ◆ **it's a mere ~ compared with what he spent last year** ça n'est rien en comparaison de ce qu'il a dépensé l'an dernier ◆ **he's a ~** c'est une nullité

ADV aucunement, nullement ◆ **~ less than** rien moins que ◆ **it was ~ like as big as we thought** c'était loin d'être aussi grand qu'on avait cru ◆ **~ daunted, he ...** nullement *or* aucunement découragé, il ..., sans se (laisser) démonter, il ... ; → **loath**

ADJ *(US ⁎ pej)* minable, de rien du tout

nothingness /ˈnʌθɪŋnɪs/ **N** (NonC) néant *m*

notice /ˈnəʊtɪs/ **N** 1 (NonC) *(= warning, intimation)* avis *m*, notification *f* ; *(Jur = official personal communication)* mise *f* en demeure ; *(= period)* délai *m* ; *(= end of work contract) (by employer)* congé *m* ; *(by employee)* démission *f* ◆ **I must have (some) ~ of what you intend to do** il faut que je sois prévenu *or* avisé à l'avance de ce que vous avez l'intention de faire ◆ **we require six days' ~** nous demandons un préavis de six jours ◆ **a week's ~** une semaine de préavis, un préavis d'une semaine ◆ **I must have at least a week's ~ if you want to ...** il faut me prévenir *or* m'avertir au moins une semaine à l'avance si vous voulez ... ◆ **we had no ~ (of it)** nous n'avons pas été prévenus à l'avance ◆ **advance** *or* **previous ~** préavis *m* ◆ **final ~** dernier avertissement *m* ◆ **to get one's ~** *(from job)* recevoir son congé, être licencié ◆ **to give ~ to** *[+ tenant]* donner congé à ; *[+ landlord etc]* donner un préavis de départ à ◆ **to give ~ that ...** faire savoir que ... ; *(Admin etc: officially)* donner acte que ... ◆ **to give ~ of sth** annoncer qch ◆ **~ is hereby given that ...** il est porté à la connaissance du public par la présente que ... ◆ **to give sb ~ of sth** avertir *or* prévenir qn de qch ; *(Admin etc: officially)* donner acte à qn de qch ◆ **to give sb ~ that ...** aviser qn que ..., faire savoir à qn que ... ◆ **he gave her ~ to ...** il l'a avisée qu'elle devait ... ◆ **to give sb ~ (of dismissal)** *[+ employee]* licencier qn, renvoyer qn ; *[+ servant etc]* donner son congé à qn, congédier qn ◆ **to give in** *or* **hand in one's ~** *[professional or office worker]* donner sa démission ; *[servant]* donner ses huit jours ◆ **to serve ~ on sb that ...** aviser qn que ..., faire savoir à qn que ...

2 *(Jur)* ◆ **~ to appear** assignation *f* (à comparaître) ◆ **~ of calls** *(Jur, Fin)* (avis *m* d')appel *m* de fonds ◆ **~ to pay** avis *m* d'avoir à payer ◆ **~ to quit** *(to tenant etc)* congé *m* ◆ **~ of receipt** *(Comm)* avis *m* de réception ◆ **~ of termination** *(Jur)* avis *m* de clôture (d'une procédure)

3 ◆ **at short ~** *(Fin)* à court terme ◆ **he rang me up at short ~** il m'a téléphoné à la dernière minute ◆ **you must be ready to leave at very short ~** il faut que vous soyez prêt à partir dans les plus brefs délais ◆ **I know it's short ~, but can I come this evening?** je sais que je préviens un peu tard, mais est-ce que je peux venir ce soir ? ◆ **at a moment's ~** sur-le-champ, immédiatement ◆ **at three days' ~** dans un délai de trois jours ◆ **he's under ~ (to leave)** *(from job)* il a reçu son congé ◆ **until further ~** jusqu'à nouvel ordre ◆ **without (previous) ~** *(Admin frm)* sans préavis, sans avis préalable ◆ **he was dismissed without (any) ~** il a été renvoyé sans préavis

4 *(= announcement)* avis *m*, annonce *f* ; *(in newspaper) (= advert etc)* annonce *f* ; *(= short article)* entrefilet *m* ; *(= poster)* affiche *f*, placard *m* ; *(= sign)* pancarte *f*, écriteau *m* ◆ **birth/marriage/death ~** annonce *f* de naissance/mariage/décès ◆ **public ~** avis *m* au public ◆ **to put a ~ in the paper** mettre *or* faire insérer une annonce dans le journal ◆ **I saw a ~ in the paper about the concert** *(Press)* j'ai vu une annonce *or* un entrefilet dans le journal à propos du concert ◆ **the ~ says "keep out"** l'écriteau porte l'inscription "défense d'entrer" ◆ **the ~ of the meeting was published in ...** l'annonce de la réunion a été publiée dans ...

5 *(= review) [of book, film, play etc]* compte rendu *m*, critique *f* ◆ **the book/film/play got good ~s** le livre/le film/la pièce a eu de bonnes critiques

6 *(= attention)* **it escaped his ~ that ...** il ne s'est pas aperçu que ... ◆ **nothing escapes their ~** rien ne leur échappe ◆ **to attract ~** se faire remarquer ; *(deliberately = show off)* s'afficher *(pej)* ◆ **it has attracted a lot of ~** cela a suscité un grand intérêt ◆ **to avoid ~** (essayer de) passer inaperçu ◆ **to bring sth to sb's ~** faire observer *or* remarquer qch à qn, porter qch à la connaissance de qn ◆ **it has come** *or* **it has been brought to my ~ that ...** *(frm)* il a été porté à ma connaissance que ..., on m'a signalé que ...

◆ **to take notice** ◆ **I wasn't taking much ~ at the time** je ne faisais pas très attention à ce moment-là ◆ **we should take ~ when things like this happen** de tels événements devraient nous interpeller ◆ **recent events have made the government sit up and take ~** les récents événements ont fait réagir le gouvernement ◆ **to take ~ of sb/sth** remarquer qn/qch ◆ **he got talking to me and started really taking ~ of me for the first time** il s'est mis à me parler et c'est là qu'il m'a vraiment remarqué pour la première fois ◆ **as for Henry, he took little ~ of me** quant à Henry, il ne faisait guère attention à moi *or* il ne me prêtait guère attention ◆ **a lot of ~ he takes of me!** * *(= he ignores my advice)* il ne fait absolument pas attention à ce que je lui dis !

◆ **to take no notice** ne pas faire attention ◆ **take no ~!** ne faites pas attention ! ◆ **to take no ~ of sb/sth** ne pas faire attention à qn/qch ◆ **he took no ~ of her** il n'a absolument pas fait attention à elle ◆ **he took no ~ of her remarks** il n'a absolument pas tenu compte de ses remarques ; *(iro)*

VT 1 *(= perceive)* s'apercevoir de, remarquer ; *(= heed)* faire attention à ◆ **I ~d a tear in his coat** j'ai remarqué un accroc dans son manteau ◆ **when he ~d me he called out to me** quand il m'a vu, il m'a appelé ◆ **to ~ a mistake** remarquer une faute, s'apercevoir d'une faute ◆ **without my noticing it** sans que je le remarque *subj or* que je m'en aperçoive ◆ **I'm afraid I didn't ~** malheureusement je n'ai pas remarqué ◆ **did you ~ what he said/when he arrived?** avez-vous remarqué ce qu'il a dit/à quelle heure il est arrivé ? ◆ **I never ~ such things** je ne remarque jamais ce genre de chose ◆ **I ~d her hesitating** j'ai remarqué *or* je me suis aperçu qu'elle hésitait ◆ **I ~ you have a new dress** je vois que vous avez une nouvelle robe ◆ **yes, so I've ~d!** je m'en suis aperçu !, j'ai remarqué !

2 *(= review) [+ book, film, play]* faire le compte rendu *or* la critique de

COMP **notice board** **N** *(esp Brit) (printed or painted sign)* écriteau *m*, pancarte *f* ; *(for holding announcements)* panneau *m* d'affichage

> ⚠ The French word **notice** means a short note in a book or leaflet.

noticeable /ˈnəʊtɪsəbl/ LANGUAGE IN USE 26.3 **ADJ** *[effect, difference, improvement]* visible, sensible ; *[lack]* évident, sensible ◆ **it isn't really ~** ça ne se voit pas vraiment ◆ **to be ~ by one's absence** briller par son absence

◆ **it is noticeable that ...** *(= noteworthy)* on remarque que ... ; *(= easily visible)* on voit bien que ... ◆ **it is ~ that mature students generally get better marks** on remarque que les étudiants adultes ont généralement de meilleures notes ◆ **it was ~ that his hands were shaking** on voyait bien que ses mains tremblaient

noticeably /ˈnəʊtɪsəblɪ/ **ADV** *[better, worse, higher, lower]* nettement ◆ **to be ~ absent** briller par son absence ◆ **~ lacking** manquant visiblement ◆ **to improve ~** s'améliorer sensiblement ◆ **he shuddered ~** il frissonna de façon visible

◆ **most noticeably** *(= particularly)* notamment, en particulier ◆ **some industries, most ~ construction ...** certaines industries, notamment *or* en particulier le bâtiment ...

notifiable /ˈnəʊtɪfaɪəbl/ **ADJ** *(frm, Admin) [disease]* à déclarer obligatoirement ; *[offence]* à signaler ◆ **all changes of address are ~ immediately** tout changement d'adresse doit être signalé immédiatement aux autorités

notification /ˌnəʊtɪfɪˈkeɪʃən/ **N** (NonC) avis *m* ; *(Jur, Admin)* notification *f* ; *[of marriage, engagement]* annonce *f* ; *[of birth, death]* déclaration *f* ◆ **written ~** *(Press)* notification *f* écrite

notify /ˈnəʊtɪfaɪ/ **VT** ◆ **to ~ sth to sb** signaler *or* notifier qch à qn ◆ **to ~ sb of sth** aviser *or* avertir qn de qch ◆ **any change of address must be notified** tout changement d'adresse doit être signalé *or* notifié ◆ **you will be notified later of the result** on vous communiquera le résultat ultérieurement *or* plus tard

notion /ˈnəʊʃən/ **N** 1 *(= thought, project)* idée *f* ◆ **I've got a ~ for a play** j'ai l'idée d'une pièce ◆ **I hit (up)on the ~ of going to see her** tout à coup l'idée m'est venue d'aller la voir ◆ **the ~ never entered my head!** cette idée ne m'est jamais venue à l'esprit *or* ne m'a jamais effleuré ! ◆ **he got the ~ (into his head)** *or* **he somehow got hold of the ~ that she wouldn't help him** il s'est mis en tête (l'idée) qu'elle ne l'aiderait pas ◆ **where did you get the ~** *or* **what gave you the ~ that I couldn't come?**

qu'est-ce qui t'a fait penser que je ne pourrais pas venir ? ♦ **to put ~s into sb's head***, **to give sb ~s*** mettre *or* fourrer* des idées dans la tête de qn ♦ **that gave me the ~ of inviting her** c'est ce qui m'a donné l'idée de l'inviter ♦ **I'd had a few ~s about being a journalist** j'avais songé à devenir journaliste

2 *(= opinion)* idée *f*, opinion *f* ; *(= way of thinking)* façon *f* de penser ♦ **he has some odd ~s** il a de drôles d'idées ♦ **she has some odd ~s about how to bring up children** elle a de drôles d'idées sur la façon d'élever les enfants ♦ **according to his ~** selon sa façon de penser ♦ **if that's your ~ of fun ...** si c'est ça que tu appelles t'amuser ... ♦ **it wasn't my ~ of a holiday** ce n'était pas ce que j'appelle des vacances

3 *(= vague knowledge)* idée *f*, notion *f* ♦ **I've got some ~ of physics** j'ai quelques notions de physique ♦ **have you any ~ of what he meant to do?** avez-vous la moindre idée de ce qu'il voulait faire ? ♦ **I haven't the least** † *or* **slightest** *or* **foggiest*** **~** je n'en ai pas la moindre idée ♦ **I have a ~ that he was going to Paris** j'ai dans l'idée qu'il allait à Paris ♦ **I had no ~ they knew each other** je n'avais aucune idée *or* j'ignorais absolument qu'ils se connaissaient ♦ **he has no ~ of time** il n'a pas la notion du temps

NPL **notions** *(US = ribbons, thread etc)* (articles *mpl* de) mercerie *f*

notional /ˈnəʊʃənl/ ADJ 1 *(= hypothetical) [value, profit, amount]* théorique, hypothétique ; *[time, line]* imaginaire 2 *(Philos)* notionnel, conceptuel 3 *(Ling) [grammar]* notionnel ♦ **~ word** mot *m* plein 4 *(US = whimsical) [person]* capricieux, fantasque

notionally /ˈnəʊʃənəlɪ/ ADV *(= hypothetically)* théoriquement

notoriety /ˌnəʊtəˈraɪətɪ/ N 1 *(NonC)* (triste) notoriété *f*, triste réputation *f* 2 *(= person)* individu *m* au nom tristement célèbre

notorious /nəʊˈtɔːrɪəs/ ADJ *[criminal, liar, womaniser, meanness, brothel]* notoire ; *[crime, case]* célèbre ; *[person, prison]* tristement célèbre ♦ **the ~ Richard** le tristement célèbre Richard ♦ **to be ~ for one's meanness** être d'une mesquinerie notoire ♦ **to be ~ for one's racism** être bien connu pour ses idées racistes ♦ **he's ~ as a womanizer** c'est un coureur de jupons notoire ♦ **he's ~ for murdering his wife** il est tristement célèbre pour avoir assassiné sa femme ♦ **it is ~ that ...** il est notoire que ...

notoriously /nəʊˈtɔːrɪəslɪ/ ADV *[slow, unreliable, fickle]* notoirement ♦ **~ cruel/inefficient** d'une cruauté/incompétence notoire ♦ **it is ~ difficult to do that** chacun sait à quel point c'est difficile à faire

Notts abbrev of **Nottinghamshire**

notwithstanding /ˌnɒtwɪθˈstændɪŋ/ PREP malgré, en dépit de ; *(Jur)* nonobstant ADV néanmoins, malgré tout CONJ (also **notwithstanding that**) quoique + *subj*, bien que + *subj*

nougat /ˈnuːgɑː, ˈnʌgət/ N nougat *m*

nought /nɔːt/ N ⇒ **naught** ; → ZERO

noun /naʊn/ N nom *m*, substantif *m*

COMP **noun clause** N proposition *f*

noun phrase N syntagme *m* nominal

nourish /ˈnʌrɪʃ/ VT *[+ person]* nourrir *(with* de*)* ; *[+ leather etc]* entretenir ; *(fig) [+ hopes etc]* nourrir, entretenir ; → **ill, undernourish, well²**

nourishing /ˈnʌrɪʃɪŋ/ ADJ *(= nutritious) [food]* nourrissant, nutritif ; *(Cosmetics) [cream]* qui nourrit la peau

nourishment /ˈnʌrɪʃmənt/ N *(NonC = food)* nourriture *f*, aliments *mpl* ♦ **to take ~** *(frm)* se nourrir, s'alimenter ♦ **he has taken (some) ~** *(frm)* il s'est alimenté ♦ **sugar provides no real ~, there's no real ~ in sugar** le sucre n'est pas vraiment nourrissant

nous* /naʊs/ N *(NonC: Brit)* bon sens *m* ♦ **he's got a lot of ~** il a du plomb dans la cervelle*

Nov. abbrev of **November**

nova /ˈnəʊvə/ N (pl **novas** *or* **novae** /ˈnəʊviː/) nova *f*

Nova Scotia /ˈnəʊvəˈskəʊʃə/ N Nouvelle-Écosse *f*

Nova Scotian /ˈnəʊvəˈskəʊʃən/ ADJ néo-écossais N Néo-Écossais(e) *m(f)*

novel /ˈnɒvəl/ N *(Literat)* roman *m* ADJ original

novelette /ˌnɒvəˈlet/ N *(Literat)* nouvelle *f* ; *(trivial)* roman *m* de quatre sous *(pej)* ; *(= love story)* roman *m* à l'eau de rose

novelist /ˈnɒvəlɪst/ N romancier *m*, -ière *f*

novella /nəʊˈvelə/ N (pl **novellas** *or* **novelle** /nəʊˈveleɪ/) roman *m* court

novelty /ˈnɒvəltɪ/ N 1 *(NonC) (= newness)* nouveauté *f* ; *(= unusualness)* étrangeté *f* ♦ **once** *or* **when the ~ has worn off** une fois passé l'attrait de la nouveauté ♦ **the game sold well because of its ~ value** le jeu s'est bien vendu parce que c'était quelque chose de nouveau ♦ **it's fun at first, but it soon loses its ~ value** au début c'est amusant mais ça perd vite son attrait 2 *(= idea, thing)* innovation *f* ♦ **it was quite a ~** c'était assez nouveau 3 *(= gadget)* gadget *m* ADJ fantaisie *inv* ♦ **a ~ keyring/mug** un porte-clés/une tasse fantaisie ♦ **~ cushions/jewellery** des coussins/des bijoux fantaisie

November /nəʊˈvembəʳ/ N novembre *m* ; *for phrases see* **September**

novena /nəʊˈviːnə/ N (pl **novenae** /nəʊˈviːniː/) neuvaine *f*

novice /ˈnɒvɪs/ N 1 *(= beginner)* novice *mf*, débutant(e) *m(f)* ♦ **to be a ~ at sth** être novice en qch ♦ **he's a ~ in politics, he's a political ~** c'est un novice *or* débutant en politique ♦ **he's no ~** il n'est pas novice, il n'en est pas à son coup d'essai 2 *(Sport) (= person)* débutant(e) *m(f) (sportif qui n'a pas remporté de titre important)* ; *(= racehorse) cheval qui n'a pas remporté suffisamment de courses* 3 *(Rel)* novice *mf* ADJ *[worker, writer etc]* novice, débutant

noviciate, novitiate /nəʊˈvɪʃɪɪt/ N 1 *(Rel) (= period)* (temps *m* du) noviciat *m* ; *(= place)* maison *f* des novices, noviciat *m* 2 *(fig)* noviciat *m*, apprentissage *m*

Novocain(e) ® /ˈnəʊvəʊkeɪn/ N novocaïne *f*

NOW /naʊ/ N *(in US)* (abbrev of **National Organization for Women**) *organisation féministe*

now /naʊ/ ADV 1 *(= at this time)* maintenant ; *(= these days, at the moment)* actuellement, en ce moment ; *(= at that time)* alors, à ce moment-là ♦ **~ I'm ready** je suis prêt maintenant ♦ **~ is the best time to go to Scotland** c'est maintenant le meilleur moment pour aller en Écosse ♦ **she's a widow ~** elle est maintenant veuve ♦ **the couple, who ~ have three children ...** ce couple, qui a maintenant trois enfants ... ♦ **they won't be long ~** ils ne vont plus tarder (maintenant) ♦ **what are you doing ~?** qu'est-ce que tu fais actuellement *or* en ce moment ? ♦ **strawberries are in season ~** c'est la saison des fraises ♦ **he ~ understood why she had left him** alors il comprit *or* il comprit alors pourquoi elle l'avait quitté ♦ **~ is the time to do it** c'est le moment de le faire ♦ **I'll do it (right) ~** je vais le faire dès maintenant *or* à l'instant ♦ **I am doing it (right) ~** je suis (justement) en train de le faire, je le fais à l'instant même ♦ **~ for the question of your expenses** et maintenant en ce qui concerne la question de vos dépenses ♦ **how can I believe you ~?** comment puis-je te croire maintenant ? ♦ **(every) ~ and again, (every) ~ and then** de temps en temps, de temps à autre ♦ **it's ~ or never!** c'est le moment ou jamais !

♦ **even now** ♦ **even ~ there's time to change your mind** il est encore temps (maintenant) de changer d'avis ♦ **even ~ he doesn't believe me** il ne me croit toujours pas ♦ **people do that even ~** les gens font ça encore aujourd'hui *or* maintenant ♦ **even ~ we are very short of money** encore actuellement *or* à l'heure actuelle nous avons très peu d'argent

2 *(with prep)* **between ~ and next Tuesday** d'ici (à) mardi prochain ♦ **that will do for ~** ça ira pour l'instant *or* pour le moment ♦ **till ~, until ~, up to ~** *(= till this moment)* jusqu'à présent, jusqu'ici ; *(= till that moment)* jusque-là

♦ **before now** ♦ **you should have done that before ~** vous auriez déjà dû l'avoir fait ♦ **before ~ people thought that ...** auparavant les gens pensaient que ... ♦ **you should have finished long before ~** il y a longtemps que vous auriez dû avoir fini ♦ **long before ~ it was realized that ...** il y a longtemps déjà, on comprenait que ...

♦ **by now** ♦ **they should have arrived by ~** ils devraient être déjà arrivés, ils devraient être arrivés à l'heure qu'il est ♦ **haven't you finished by ~?** vous n'avez toujours pas fini ?, vous n'avez pas encore fini ? ♦ **by ~ it was clear that ...** dès lors, il était évident que ...

♦ **from now** ♦ **(in) three weeks from ~** dans trois semaines ♦ **from ~ until then** d'ici là ♦ **from ~ on(wards)** *(with present tense)* à partir de maintenant ; *(with future tense)* à partir de maintenant, dorénavant, désormais ; *(with past tense)* dès lors, dès ce moment-là

3 *(showing alternation)* **~ walking, ~ running** tantôt (en) marchant tantôt (en) courant ♦ **~ here, ~ there** tantôt par ici tantôt par là

4 *(without temporal implication)* **~!** bon !, alors ! ♦ **~, ~!** allons, allons ! ♦ **~, Simon!** *(warning)* allons, Simon ! ♦ **come ~!** allons ! ♦ **well, ~!** eh bien ! ♦ **~ then, let's start!** bon, commençons ! ♦ **~ then, what's all this?** alors, qu'est-ce que c'est que ça ? ♦ **~, they had been looking for him all morning** or, ils avaient passé toute la matinée à sa recherche ♦ **~, he was a fisherman** or, il était pêcheur ♦ **~ do be quiet for a minute** allons, taisez-vous une minute

CONJ maintenant que ♦ **~ (that) you've seen him** maintenant que vous l'avez vu

ADJ 1 *(esp US = present)* actuel ♦ **the ~ president** le président actuel

2 * *(= exciting and new) [clothes]* du dernier cri ; *(= interested in new things) [people]* branché*, dans le vent

N → **here**

nowadays /ˈnaʊədeɪz/ ADV *(in contrast to past years)* de nos jours, aujourd'hui ; *(in contrast to recently)* ces jours-ci ♦ **rents are very high ~** les loyers sont très élevés de nos jours ♦ **why don't we ever see Jim ~?** pourquoi ne voit-on plus jamais Jim ces jours-ci ?

noway(s) /ˈnəʊweɪ(z)/ ADV *(US) (after request for favour)* pas question ; *(= not at all)* pas du tout

nowcast /ˈnaʊkɑːst/ N prévision *f* en temps réel

nowhere /ˈnəʊweəʳ/, **nowheres*** *(US)* /ˈnəʊweəz/ ADV 1 *(lit = no place)* nulle part ♦ **they have ~ to go** ils n'ont nulle part où aller ♦ **there was ~ to hide** il n'y avait aucun endroit où se cacher ♦ **from (out of) ~** de nulle part ♦ **there's ~ I'd rather be** je me sens vraiment bien ici ♦ **there is ~ more romantic than Paris** il n'y a pas d'endroit plus romantique que Paris ♦ **it's ~ you know** ce n'est pas un endroit que tu connais ♦ **it's ~ you'll ever find it** tu n'arriveras jamais à le trouver ♦ **where are you going? – ~ special** *or* **~ in particular** où vas-tu ? – nulle part ♦ **she was ~ to be found** elle était introuvable ♦ **he was ~ in**

sight *or* ~ **to be seen** il avait disparu ; → **else, middle**

2 *(fig)* ◆ **without him I would be** ~ sans lui, je ne serais arrivé à rien ◆ **to come** ~ * *(Sport)* n'arriver à rien ◆ **he came from** ~ **to take the lead from Coe** contre toute attente, il a dépassé Coe ◆ **he came from** ~ **to win the election** cet outsider a remporté l'élection ◆ **the enquiry was getting** ~ l'enquête piétinait ◆ **threatening me will get you** ~ vous n'obtiendrez rien en me menaçant ◆ **lying will get you** ~ ça ne te servira à rien de mentir ◆ **we're getting** *or* **this is getting us** ~ **(fast)** * ça ne nous mène à rien, on tourne en rond ◆ **to be going** ~ **(fast)** * *[person]* n'arriver à rien ; *[talks]* être dans l'impasse ◆ **to get** ~ **with sb** n'arriver à rien avec qn ◆ **a fiver goes** ~ **these days** on ne va pas loin avec un billet de cinq livres (*or* dollars) aujourd'hui

◆ **nowhere near** ◆ **his house is** ~ **near the church** sa maison n'est pas près de l'église du tout ◆ **you are** ~ **near the truth** vous êtes à mille lieues de la vérité ◆ **you're** ~ **near it!, you're** ~ **near right!** tu n'y es pas du tout ! ◆ **we're** ~ **near finding a cure** nous sommes loin d'avoir trouvé un traitement ◆ **she is** ~ **near as clever as he is** elle est nettement moins intelligente que lui ◆ **£10 is** ~ **near enough** 10 livres sont loin de suffire

nowise /ˈnəʊwaɪz/ ADV (US) ⇒ **noway(s)**

nowt /naʊt/ N (Brit dial) ⇒ **nothing**

noxious /ˈnɒkʃəs/ ADJ *(= toxic) [gas, substance]* nocif ; *(= unpleasant) [smell]* infect, nauséabond ; *(= repugnant) [attitude, behaviour]* odieux ; *[influence, habit]* nocif ◆ **to have a** ~ **effect on** avoir un effet nocif sur

nozzle /ˈnɒzl/ N 1 *[of hose etc]* ajutage *m*, jet *m* ; *[of syringe]* canule *f* ; *(for icing)* douille *f* ; *[of bellows]* bec *m* ; *[of vacuum cleaner]* suceur *m* ; *[of flamethrower]* ajutage *m* 2 (‡ *= nose)* pif‡ *m*, blair‡ *m*

NPD /ˌenpiːˈdiː/ N (abbrev of **new product development**) → **new**

NPV /ˌenpiːˈviː/ N (abbrev of **net present value**) VAN *f*

nr PREP abbrev of **near**

NRA /ˌenɑːrˈeɪ/ N 1 (US) (abbrev of **National Rifle Association**) → **national** 2 (Brit) (abbrev of **National Rivers Authority**) *administration nationale des cours d'eau*

NRV /ˌenɑːˈviː/ N (abbrev of **net realizable value**) → **net²**

NS abbrev of **Nova Scotia**

n/s N abbrev of **nonsmoker** ADJ abbrev of **nonsmoking**

NSB /ˌenesˈbiː/ N (Brit) (abbrev of **National Savings Bank**) → **national**

NSC /ˌenesˈsiː/ N 1 (US) (abbrev of **National Security Council**) → **national** 2 (Brit) (abbrev of **National Safety Council**) → **national**

NSPCC /ˌenesˌpiːsiːˈsiː/ N (Brit) (abbrev of **National Society for the Prevention of Cruelty to Children**) *société pour la protection de l'enfance*

NSU /ˌenesˈjuː/ N (abbrev of **nonspecific urethritis**) → **nonspecific**

NSW (abbrev of **New South Wales**) → **new**

NT 1 (abbrev of **New Testament**) → **new** 2 (Brit) (abbrev of **National Trust**) → **national**

nth /enθ/ ADJ → **N 2**

NUAAW N (Brit) (abbrev of **National Union of Agricultural and Allied Workers**) *syndicat*

nuance /ˈnjuːɑːns/ N nuance *f* VT nuancer

nub /nʌb/ N *(= small lump)* petit morceau *m* ◆ **the** ~ **of the matter** *(fig)* l'essentiel *m* ◆ **to get to the** ~ **of the matter** entrer dans le vif du sujet

Nubia /ˈnjuːbɪə/ N Nubie *f*

Nubian /ˈnjuːbɪən/ ADJ nubien N Nubien(ne) *m(f)*

nubile /ˈnjuːbaɪl/ ADJ *(frm or hum) [young woman]* nubile

nubility /njuːˈbɪlɪtɪ/ N nubilité *f*

nuclear /ˈnjuːklɪəʳ/ ADJ nucléaire ◆ **to go** ~ *[country]* acquérir l'arme nucléaire, se nucléariser ; *[conflict]* dégénérer en guerre nucléaire ; *(esp Brit *) [person]* piquer une crise*, exploser*

COMP **nuclear bomb** N bombe *f* atomique *or* nucléaire
nuclear capability N capacité *f* nucléaire
nuclear deterrent N force *f* de dissuasion nucléaire
nuclear disarmament N désarmement *m* nucléaire
nuclear energy N énergie *f* nucléaire
nuclear family N *(Sociol)* famille *f* nucléaire
nuclear fission N fission *f* nucléaire
nuclear-free ADJ *[zone, world]* dénucléarisé
nuclear fuel N combustible *m* nucléaire
nuclear fusion N fusion *f* nucléaire
nuclear industry N industrie *f* nucléaire
Nuclear Industry Radioactive Waste Executive N *(Brit) organisme de décision en matière de politique concernant les déchets radioactifs*
nuclear magnetic resonance N résonance *f* magnétique nucléaire
nuclear medicine N médecine *f* nucléaire
the Nuclear Non-Proliferation Treaty N le Traité de non-prolifération des armes nucléaires
nuclear physicist N physicien(ne) *m(f)* nucléaire
nuclear physics N physique *f* nucléaire
nuclear plant N centrale *f* nucléaire
nuclear power N puissance *f* nucléaire
nuclear-powered ADJ (à propulsion) nucléaire
nuclear power station N centrale *f* nucléaire
nuclear reaction N réaction *f* nucléaire
nuclear reactor N réacteur *m* nucléaire
nuclear reprocessing plant N usine *f* de retraitement des déchets nucléaires
nuclear scientist N chercheur *m* en physique nucléaire
nuclear submarine N sous-marin *m* nucléaire
nuclear test N essai *m* nucléaire
nuclear testing N essais *mpl* nucléaires
nuclear umbrella N parapluie *m* nucléaire
nuclear warhead N ogive *f or* tête *f* nucléaire
nuclear waste N déchets *mpl* nucléaires
nuclear weapon N arme *f* nucléaire
nuclear winter N hiver *m* nucléaire

nuclei /ˈnjuːklɪaɪ/ NPL of **nucleus**

nucleic acid /njuːˈkliːɪkˈæsɪd/ N acide *m* nucléique

nucleotide /ˈnjuːklɪəˌtaɪd/ N nucléotide *m*

nucleus /ˈnjuːklɪəs/ N (pl **nuclei** *or* **nucleuses**) noyau *m* ; *[of cell]* nucléus *m*, noyau *m* ◆ **atomic** ~ noyau *m* atomique ◆ **the** ~ **of a library/university/crew** les principaux éléments *mpl* d'une bibliothèque/d'une université/d'un équipage ◆ **these three great footballers form the** ~ **of the side** ces trois grands footballeurs forment la base de l'équipe ◆ **this group could be the** ~ **of a future centrist party** ce groupe pourrait servir de base à un futur parti centriste

nude /njuːd/ ADJ *[person, body]* nu ; *[photograph]* de nu ◆ **to bathe** ~ se baigner nu ◆ **to sunbathe** ~ bronzer nu ◆ ~ **scene** *(Cine)* scène *f* déshabillée ◆ ~ **figures** *or* **studies** *(Art)* nus *mpl*
N 1 *(Art)* nu *m* ◆ **a Goya** ~ un nu de Goya 2 ◆ **in the** ~ nu

nudge /nʌdʒ/ VT 1 *(lit)* pousser du coude, donner un (petit) coup de coude à ◆ **she ~d him forward** elle l'a (légèrement) poussé en avant 2 *(fig = approach)* **she's nudging fifty** elle approche de la cinquantaine ◆ **the temperature was nudging 35°C** la température approchait *or* frôlait les 35° 3 *(= encourage)* encourager ◆ **to** ~ **sb into doing sth** amener qn à faire qch N *(lit)* coup *m* de coude ; *(fig)* coup *m* de pouce ◆ **a** ~ **and a wink** *(fig)* un clin d'œil ◆ **she made me an offer I couldn't refuse,** ~-~ **wink-wink (say no more)!** ‡ elle m'a fait une proposition très intéressante, si vous voyez ce que je veux dire

▸ **nudge up** VT SEP *[+ prices]* donner un coup de pouce à

nudie * /ˈnjuːdɪ/ ADJ ◆ ~ **calendar** calendrier *m* avec des photos de femmes nues ◆ ~ **magazine** *(gen)* magazine *m* de charme ; *(= pornographic)* revue *f* porno*

nudism /ˈnjuːdɪzəm/ N nudisme *m*

nudist /ˈnjuːdɪst/ ADJ, N nudiste *mf*

COMP **nudist camp** N camp *m* de nudistes
nudist colony N colonie *f* de nudistes

nudity /ˈnjuːdɪtɪ/ N nudité *f*

nudnik ‡ /ˈn(j)ʊdnɪk/ N (US) casse-pieds *mf inv*

nugatory /ˈnjuːgətərɪ/ ADJ *(frm) (= worthless)* futile, sans valeur ; *(= trivial)* insignifiant ; *(= ineffectual)* inefficace, inopérant ; *(= not valid)* non valable

nugget /ˈnʌgɪt/ N pépite *f* ◆ **gold** ~ pépite *f* d'or

NUGMW N (Brit) (abbrev of **National Union of General and Municipal Workers**) *syndicat*

nuisance /ˈnjuːsns/ N 1 *(= annoying thing or event)* ◆ **what a** ~ **he can't come** comme c'est ennuyeux *or* embêtant qu'il ne puisse pas venir ◆ **it's a** ~ **having to shave** c'est agaçant d'avoir à se raser ◆ **the** ~ **of having to shave each morning** la corvée de devoir se raser tous les matins ◆ **these weeds are a** ~ ces mauvaises herbes sont une vraie plaie*, quel fléau, ces mauvaises herbes ◆ **these mosquitoes are a** ~ ces moustiques sont un vrai fléau *or* une plaie* ◆ **what a** ~**!** c'est vraiment ennuyeux !, quelle barbe !*

2 *(= annoying person)* peste *f*, fléau *m* ◆ **that child is a** ~ cet enfant est une peste *or* un fléau ◆ **what a** ~ **you are!** ce que tu peux être agaçant *or* casse-pieds* ! ◆ **he could be a bit of a** ~ **when he was drunk** il pouvait être un peu casse-pieds* quand il était ivre ◆ **you're being a** ~ tu es agaçant ◆ **sorry to be a** ~ désolé de vous déranger *or* importuner ◆ **to make a** ~ **of o.s.** embêter le monde*, être une peste *or* un fléau ; → **public**

3 *(Jur)* infraction *f* simple, dommage *m* simple ; → **public**

COMP **nuisance call** N appel *m* anonyme
nuisance caller N auteur *m* d'un appel anonyme
nuisance value N ◆ **it has a certain** ~ **value** cela sert à gêner *or* embêter* le monde

NUJ /ˌenjuːˈdʒeɪ/ N (Brit) (abbrev of **National Union of Journalists**) *syndicat*

nuke * /njuːk/ VT *(= attack) [+ city]* lancer une bombe atomique sur ; *[+ nation, enemy]* lancer une attaque nucléaire contre ; *(= destroy)* détruire à l'arme atomique *or* nucléaire N 1 *(= weapon)* arme *f* atomique *or* nucléaire ◆ **"no nukes!"** * *(slogan)* "à bas les armes nucléaires !", "non au nucléaire !" 2 *(US = power station)* centrale *f* nucléaire

null /nʌl/ ADJ 1 *(Jur) [act, decree]* nul (nulle *f*), invalide ; *[legacy]* caduc (-uque *f*) ◆ ~ **and void** nul et non avenu ◆ **to render** ~ annuler, frapper de nullité 2 *(= ineffectual) [person]* insignifiant ; *[influence]* inexistant COMP **null hypothesis** N hypothèse *f* nulle

nullification /ˌnʌlɪfɪˈkeɪʃən/ N 1 infirmation *f*, invalidation *f* 2 *(US Hist)* invalidation *f* par un État d'une loi fédérale

nullify /ˈnʌlɪfaɪ/ VT infirmer, invalider

nullity /'nʌlɪtɪ/ **N** (*NonC: Jur*) [*of act, decree*] nullité *f*, invalidité *f* ; [*of legacy*] caducité *f* **COMP** **nullity suit N** (*Jur*) demande *f* en nullité de mariage

NUM /ˌenju:'em/ **N** (*Brit*) (abbrev of **National Union of Mineworkers**) *syndicat*

numb /nʌm/ **ADJ** 1 (*= without sensation*) [*person, limb, face, lip*] engourdi ◆ **to go ~** s'engourdir ◆ **~ with cold** [*person, body*] transi, engourdi par le froid ; [*face, hands, feet*] engourdi par le froid 2 (*= stunned*) [*person*] hébété ◆ **~ with disbelief** figé d'incrédulité ◆ **~ with fright** paralysé par la peur, transi *or* glacé de peur ◆ **~ with grief** muet de douleur ◆ **~ with shock** abasourdi par le choc **VT** engourdir ; (*fig*) [*fear etc*] transir, glacer ◆ **~ed with grief** muet de douleur ◆ **~ed with fear** paralysé par la peur, transi *or* glacé de peur ◆ **it ~s the pain** cela endort la douleur

number /'nʌmbəʳ/ **LANGUAGE IN USE 27**

N 1 (*gen*) nombre *m* ; (*= actual figure: when written etc*) chiffre *m* ◆ **even/odd/whole/cardinal/ordinal ~** nombre *m* pair/impair/entier/cardinal/ordinal ◆ **(the Book of) Numbers** (*Bible*) les Nombres *mpl* ◆ **to paint by ~s** peindre selon des indications chiffrées ◆ **to do sth by ~s** *or* **by the ~s** (*US*) (*fig*) faire qch mécaniquement *or* bêtement ◆ **to play the ~s** *or* **the ~s game** *or* **the ~s racket*** (*US Gambling*) faire des paris clandestins, jouer à une loterie clandestine ; → **lucky, round**

2 (*= quantity, amount*) nombre *m*, quantité *f* ◆ **a ~ of people** de nombreuses personnes ◆ **large ~s of people** un grand nombre de personnes ◆ **a great ~ of books/chairs** une grande quantité de livres/chaises ◆ **in a small ~ of cases** dans un petit nombre de cas ◆ **on a ~ of occasions** à plusieurs occasions, à maintes occasions ◆ **there were a ~ of faults in the machine** la machine avait un (certain) nombre de défauts ◆ **there are a ~ of things which ...** il y a un certain nombre de choses *or* pas mal* de choses qui ... ◆ **a fair ~** un assez grand nombre, un nombre assez important ◆ **boys and girls in equal ~s** garçons et filles en nombre égal ◆ **~s being equal ...** à nombre égal ... ◆ **ten in ~** au nombre de dix ◆ **they were ten in ~** ils étaient (au nombre de) dix ◆ **to the ~ of some 200** au nombre de 200 environ ◆ **few in ~, in small ~s** en petit nombre ◆ **many in ~, in large ~s** en grand nombre ◆ **in vast** *or* **huge ~s** en très grand nombre ◆ **to swell the ~ of ...** grossir le nombre de ... ◆ **he was brought in to swell the ~s** on l'a amené pour grossir l'effectif ◆ **without** *or* **beyond ~** innombrable, sans nombre ◆ **times without ~** à maintes reprises, mille et mille fois ◆ **any ~ can play** le nombre de joueurs est illimité ◆ **there were any ~ of* cards in the box** il y avait une quantité *or* un tas* de cartes dans la boîte ◆ **I've told you any ~ of* times** je te l'ai dit mille fois ◆ **they are found in ~s in Africa** on les trouve en grand nombre en Afrique ◆ **they came in their ~s** ils sont venus en grand nombre ◆ **there were flies in such ~s that ...** les mouches étaient en si grand nombre que ... ◆ **the power of ~s** le pouvoir du nombre ◆ **to win by force of ~s** *or* **by sheer ~s** l'emporter par le nombre *or* par la force du nombre ◆ **one of their ~** un d'entre eux ◆ **one of our ~** un des nôtres ◆ **he was of our ~** il était des nôtres, il était avec nous

3 (*in series*) (*Telec*) numéro *m* ◆ **wrong ~** (*Telec*) faux numéro ◆ **to get a wrong ~** se tromper de numéro ◆ **that's the wrong ~** ce n'est pas le bon numéro ◆ **at ~ four** au (numéro) quatre ◆ **Number 10** (*Brit Pol*) 10 Downing Street (*résidence du Premier ministre*) ; → **Downing Street** ◆ **reference ~** numéro *m* de référence ◆ **(registration) ~** (numéro *m* d')immatriculation *f*, numéro *m* minéralogique ◆ **to take a car's ~** relever le numéro d'une voiture ◆ **I've got his ~!** * (*fig*) je l'ai repéré ! ◆ **their ~ came up*** ça a été leur tour d'y passer*, il a fallu qu'ils y passent* aussi ◆ **his ~'s up*** il est fichu*, son compte est bon ◆ **that bullet had his ~ on it!*** cette balle était pour lui ! ◆ **he only thinks of ~ one*** il ne pense qu'à lui *or* qu'à sa pomme* ◆ **to look after** *or* **take care of ~ one*** penser avant tout à soi ◆ **to be ~ one (in the charts)** être numéro un (au hit-parade) ◆ **the ~ one English player** le meilleur *or* premier joueur anglais ◆ **he's the ~ one there** c'est lui qui dirige tout là-dedans ◆ **this is the ~ one issue at the moment** c'est le problème numéro un en ce moment ◆ **he's my ~ two*** il est mon second ; → **opposite**

4 (*= model, issue*) [*of manufactured goods, clothes, car*] modèle *m* ; [*of newspaper, journal*] numéro *m* ◆ **the January ~** (*Press*) le numéro de janvier ◆ **this car's a nice little ~*** c'est une chouette* petite voiture ◆ **this wine is a nice little ~*** c'est un bon petit vin ◆ **a little ~ in black** (*= dress*) une petite robe noire (toute simple) ; → **back**

5 [*of music hall, circus*] numéro *m* ; [*of pianist, dance band*] morceau *m* ; [*of singer*] chanson *f* ; [*of dancer*] danse *f* ◆ **there were several dance ~s on the programme** le programme comprenait plusieurs numéros de danse ◆ **my next ~ will be ...** (*singer*) je vais maintenant chanter ...

6 (*NonC: Gram*) nombre *m* ◆ **~ is one of the basic concepts** le nombre est un des concepts de base ◆ **to agree in ~** s'accorder en nombre

7 (*Mus*) rythme *m* ◆ **~s** (*Poetry*) vers *mpl*, poésie *f* ; (*Mus*) mesures *fpl*

VT 1 (*= give a number to*) numéroter ◆ **they are ~ed from one to ten** ils sont numérotés de un à dix ◆ **the houses are not ~ed** les maisons n'ont pas de numéro ◆ **~ed (bank) account** compte *m* (en banque) numéroté

2 (*= include*) compter, comprendre ◆ **the library ~s 30,000 volumes** la bibliothèque compte *or* comporte 30 000 volumes ◆ **I ~ him among my friends** je le compte parmi mes amis ◆ **to be ~ed with the heroes** compter au nombre des *or* parmi les héros

3 (*= amount to*) compter ◆ **the crew ~s 50 men** l'équipage compte 50 hommes ◆ **they ~ed 700** leur nombre s'élevait *or* se montait à 700, ils étaient au nombre de 700

4 (*= count*) compter ◆ **his days were ~ed** ses jours étaient comptés ◆ **your chances of trying again are ~ed** il ne te reste plus beaucoup d'occasions de tenter ta chance ◆ **he was ~ing the hours till the attack began** il comptait les heures qui le séparaient de l'assaut

VI (*Mil etc*: also **number off**) se numéroter ◆ **to ~ (off) from the right** se numéroter en partant de la droite

COMP **number-cruncher*** **N** (*= machine*) calculatrice *f* ◆ **he's the ~-cruncher*** c'est le comptable, c'est le préposé aux chiffres (*hum*)
number-crunching* **N** calcul *m*
number plate N (*Brit*) plaque *f* minéralogique *or* d'immatriculation *or* de police ◆ **a car with French ~ plates** une voiture immatriculée en France
numbers game N
1 (*US Gambling*: also **numbers racket**) ⇒ **number noun 1** 2 (*= focusing on numbers*) *usage trompeur de chiffres* ◆ **to play the ~s game** jouer sur les chiffres
number theory N théorie *f* des nombres

numbering /'nʌmbərɪŋ/ **N** (*NonC*) [*of houses, seats etc*] numérotage *m* **COMP** **numbering machine N** machine *f* à numéroter

numberless /'nʌmbəlɪs/ **ADJ** (*liter*) innombrable

numbhead* /'nʌmhed/ **N** (*US*) imbécile *mf*, gourde* *f*

numbly /'nʌmlɪ/ **ADV** [*say, look at*] d'un air hébété ; [*walk*] l'air hébété

numbness /'nʌmnɪs/ **N** [*of hand, finger, senses*] engourdissement *m* ; [*of mind*] torpeur *f*, engourdissement *m*

numbskull* /'nʌmskʌl/ **N** imbécile *mf*, gourde* *f*

numerable /'nju:mərəbl/ **ADJ** nombrable, dénombrable

numeracy /'nju:mərəsɪ/ **N** (*NonC*) notions *fpl* de calcul, capacités *fpl* au calcul

numeral /'nju:mərəl/ **N** chiffre *m*, nombre *m* ◆ **Arabic/Roman ~** chiffre *m* arabe/romain **ADJ** numéral

numerate /'nju:mərɪt/ **ADJ** [*child, graduate*] qui sait compter ◆ **he is barely ~** il sait à peine compter

numeration /ˌnju:mə'reɪʃən/ **N** (*Math*) numération *f*

numerator /'nju:məreɪtəʳ/ **N** (*Math*) numérateur *m* ; (*= instrument*) numéroteur *m*

numerical /nju:'merɪkəl/ **ADJ** [*value, data, superiority, strength*] numérique ; [*majority*] en nombre ◆ **in ~ order** dans l'ordre numérique

numerically /nju:'merɪkəlɪ/ **ADV** numériquement

numeric keypad /nju:'merɪk'ki:pæd/ **N** pavé *m* numérique

numerological /ˌnju:mərə'lɒdʒɪkəl/ **ADJ** numérologique

numerology /ˌnju:mə'rɒlədʒɪ/ **N** numérologie *f*

numerous /'nju:mərəs/ **ADJ** nombreux

numinous /'nju:mɪnəs/ **ADJ** (*liter*) [*power, symbol*] sacré

numismatic /ˌnju:mɪz'mætɪk/ **ADJ** numismatique

numismatics /ˌnju:mɪz'mætɪks/ **N** (*NonC*) numismatique *f*

numismatist /nju:'mɪzmətɪst/ **N** numismate *mf*

numpkin‡ /'nʌmpkɪn/, **numpty‡** /'nʌmptɪ/ **N** (*Brit*) tête *f* de linotte

numskull /'nʌmskʌl/ **N** ⇒ **numbskull**

nun /nʌn/ **N** religieuse *f*, bonne sœur* *f* ◆ **to become a ~** entrer en religion, prendre le voile

Nunavut /'nʊnəvʊt/ **N** Nunavut *m*

nunciature /'nʌnʃɪətjʊəʳ/ **N** nonciature *f*

nuncio /'nʌnʃɪəʊ/ **N** nonce *m* ; → **papal**

nunnery † /'nʌnərɪ/ **N** couvent *m*

NUPE /'nju:pɪ/ **N** (*Brit: formerly*) (abbrev of **National Union of Public Employees**) *ancien syndicat*

nuptial /'nʌpʃəl/ (*liter or hum*) **ADJ** nuptial ◆ **the ~ day** le jour des noces **NPL** **nuptials** noce *f*

NUR /ˌenju:'ɑ:ʳ/ **N** (*Brit: formerly*) (abbrev of **National Union of Railwaymen**) *ancien syndicat*

nurd‡ /nɜ:d/ **N** ⇒ **nerd**

nurse /nɜ:s/ **N** 1 (*in hospital*) infirmier *m*, -ière *f* ; (*at home*) infirmier *m*, -ière *f*, garde-malade *f* ◆ **(male) ~** infirmier *m*, garde-malade *m* ◆ **~'s aide** (*US Med*) aide-soignant(e) *m(f)* ◆ **~s' station** (*US Med*) bureau *m* des infirmières ◆ **the ~s' strike** la grève du personnel soignant *or* des infirmiers ; → **night**

2 († *= children's nurse*) nurse *f*, bonne *f* d'enfants ◆ **yes ~** oui, nounou

3 († : also **wet-nurse**) nourrice *f*

VT 1 (*Med*) [*+ person, illness, injury*] soigner ◆ **she ~d him through pneumonia** elle l'a soigné pendant sa pneumonie ◆ **she ~d him back to health** il a guéri grâce à ses soins ◆ **to ~ a cold** soigner un rhume

2 [*+ baby*] (*= suckle*) nourrir, allaiter ; (*Brit*) (*= cradle in arms*) bercer (dans ses bras)

3 (*fig*) [*+ hope, one's wrath etc*] nourrir, entretenir ; [*+ ambition*] nourrir ; [*+ plan, plot*] mijoter,

couver ; [+ horse, car engine] ménager ; [+ a fire] entretenir ◆ **to ~ one's wounded pride** lécher ses plaies ◆ **to ~ a constituency** *(Brit Pol)* soigner les électeurs ◆ **Jane still ~s the pain of rejection** Jane souffre toujours d'avoir été rejetée ◆ **to ~ the business along** (essayer de) maintenir la compagnie à flot ◆ **to ~ a drink all evening** faire durer un verre toute la soirée

nurseling /ˈnɜːslɪŋ/ N ⇒ **nursling**

nursemaid /ˈnɜːsmeɪd/ N nurse *f*, bonne *f* d'enfants

nursery /ˈnɜːsərɪ/ N 1 *(= room)* nursery *f*, chambre *f* d'enfants ◆ **night ~** chambre *f* des enfants *or* d'enfants ; → **day** 2 *(= institution) (daytime only)* crèche *f*, garderie *f* ; *(daytime or residential)* pouponnière *f* 3 *(Agr)* pépinière *f* 4 *(fig)* pépinière *f* ◆ **a ~ of talent** une pépinière de talents

COMP **nursery education** N enseignement *m* de l'école maternelle
nursery nurse N puéricultrice *f*
nursery rhyme N comptine *f*
nursery school N *(state-run)* école *f* maternelle ; *(gen private)* jardin *m* d'enfants ◆ **~ school teacher** *(state-run)* professeur *m* d'école maternelle ; *(private)* jardinière *f* d'enfants
nursery slopes NPL *(Brit Ski)* pentes *fpl or* pistes *fpl* pour débutants

nurseryman /ˈnɜːsərɪmən/ N (pl **-men**) pépiniériste *m*

nursing /ˈnɜːsɪŋ/ ADJ 1 ◆ **~ mother** mère *f* qui allaite ◆ **room for ~ mothers** salle *f* réservée aux mères qui allaitent
2 ◆ **the ~ staff** [of hospital] le personnel soignant *or* infirmier ; *(all female)* les infirmières *fpl* ; *(male and female)* les infirmiers *mpl*
N 1 *(= profession of nurse)* profession *f* d'infirmière ; *(= care of invalids)* soins *mpl* ◆ **she's going in for ~** elle va être infirmière
2 *(= suckling)* allaitement *m*

COMP **nursing auxiliary** N *(Brit)* aide-soignant(e) *m(f)*
nursing bottle N *(US)* biberon *m*
nursing bra N soutien-gorge *m* d'allaitement
nursing home N *(esp Brit) (for medical, surgical cases)* clinique *f*, polyclinique *f* ; *(for mental cases, disabled etc)* maison *f* de santé ; *(for convalescence/rest cure)* maison *f* de convalescence/de repos ; *(for old people)* maison *f* de retraite
nursing officer N *(Brit Med)* surveillant(e) *m(f)* général(e)
nursing orderly N *(Brit Mil)* infirmier *m* (militaire)
nursing sister N *(Brit Med)* infirmière *f* chef
nursing studies NPL études *fpl* d'infirmière *or* d'infirmier

nursling /ˈnɜːslɪŋ/ N *(liter)* nourrisson *m*

nurture /ˈnɜːtʃəʳ/ N *(frm: lit, fig)* nourriture *f* ; → **nature** VT *(= rear)* élever, éduquer ; *(= feed)* nourrir (*on* de) ; ◆ **she ~s her plants** elle s'occupe bien de ses plantes ◆ **he ~d an ambition to take over the company** il nourrissait l'ambition de prendre le contrôle de l'entreprise ◆ **a nurturing mother** une mère très présente

NUS /ˌenjuːˈes/ N *(Brit)* 1 (abbrev of **National Union of Students**) *syndicat* 2 *(formerly)* (abbrev of **National Union of Seamen**) *ancien syndicat*

NUT /ˌenjuːˈtiː/ N *(Brit)* (abbrev of **National Union of Teachers**) *syndicat*

nut /nʌt/ N 1 *(= hazelnut)* noisette *f* ; *(= walnut)* noix *f* ; *(= almond)* amande *f* ; *(Agr)* fruit *m* (sec) oléagineux, oléagineux *m* ◆ **this chocolate has got ~s in it** c'est du chocolat aux noisettes (*or* aux amandes *etc*) ◆ **a bag of mixed ~s** un sachet de noisettes, cacahouètes, amandes *etc* panachées ◆ **~s and raisins** mendiants *mpl* ◆ **he's a tough ~** c'est un dur à cuire* ◆ **that's a hard ~ to crack*** ce n'est pas un petit problème ◆ **he's a hard ~ to crack*** c'est un dur à cuire* ◆ **he can't paint for ~s⁑** il peint comme un pied⁑ ; → **beechnut, nuts, pistachio**
2 *(for bolt)* écrou *m* ; *(Climbing)* coinceur *m* ◆ **the ~s and bolts of ...** *(fig)* les détails *mpl* pratiques de ... ; see also **comp**
3 ◆ **(coal) ~s, ~ coal** noix *fpl*, tête(s)-de-moineau *f(pl)* or tête(s) de moineau *f(pl)* ◆ **anthracite ~s** noix *fpl or* tête(s)-de-moineau *f(pl)* d'anthracite
4 *(Culin)* → **ginger**
5 *(⁑ = head)* caboche* *f* ◆ **use your ~!** réfléchis donc un peu !, creuse-toi un peu les méninges !⁑ ◆ **to be off one's ~** être tombé sur la tête*, être cinglé* ◆ **you must be off your ~!** mais ça (ne) va pas !*, mais tu es tombé sur la tête !* ◆ **to go off one's ~** perdre la boule⁑ ◆ **to do one's ~** *(Brit)* piquer une crise*
6 **he's a real ~⁑** *(= mad person)* il est cinglé* *or* toqué*
7 *(= enthusiast)* **a movie/football ~⁑** un(e) dingue* de cinéma/football
8 * ◆ **~s !** des clous !⁑ ◆ **~s to you!** va te faire fiche !*
9 **~s** *⁑ *(= testicles)* couilles*⁑ *fpl*, roubignoles*⁑ *fpl* ; see also **nuts**
VT *(* Brit = headbutt)* ◆ **to ~ sb** donner un coup de tête *or* de boule* à qn
COMP *(Culin)* [cutlet, rissoles, roast etc] à base de cacahouètes (*or* noisettes *etc*) hachées **nut-brown** ADJ [eyes] noisette *inv* ; [complexion] brun ; [hair] châtain
nut chocolate N chocolat *m* aux noisettes (*or* aux amandes *etc*)
nuts-and-bolts* ADJ *(= practical)* avant tout pratique ◆ **~s-and-bolts education** enseignement *m* axé sur les matières fondamentales

nutcase⁑ /ˈnʌtkeɪs/ N dingue* *mf*, cinglé(e)* *m(f)* ◆ **he's a ~** il est bon à enfermer*, il est dingue*

nutcracker(s) /ˈnʌtkrækə(z)/ N(PL) casse-noix *m inv*, casse-noisette(s) *m* ◆ **"The Nutcracker"** *(Mus)* "Casse-noisette" COMP **nutcracker chin** N menton *m* en galoche *or* en casse-noisette

nuthatch /ˈnʌthætʃ/ N *(= bird)* sittelle *f*

nuthouse⁑ /ˈnʌthaʊs/ N asile *m* ◆ **he's in the ~** il est à l'asile

nutmeg /ˈnʌtmeg/ N *(= nut)* (noix *f*) muscade *f* ; *(= tree)* muscadier *m*
COMP **nutmeg grater** N râpe *f* à muscade
the Nutmeg State N *(US)* le Connecticut

Nutrasweet ® /ˈnjuːtrəswiːt/ N *(= artificial sweetener)* édulcorant *m* ; *(for tea, coffee)* sucrette ® *f*

nutrient /ˈnjuːtrɪənt/ ADJ nutritif N substance *f* nutritive, nutriment *m*

nutriment /ˈnjuːtrɪmənt/ N élément *m* nutritif, nutriment *m*

nutrition /njuːˈtrɪʃən/ N nutrition *f*, alimentation *f*

nutritional /njuːˈtrɪʃənl/ ADJ [information, advice] nutritionnel ; [value, content, requirements, deficiencies] nutritif

nutritionist /njuːˈtrɪʃənɪst/ N nutritionniste *mf*

nutritious /njuːˈtrɪʃəs/ ADJ nourrissant, nutritif

nutritiousness /njuːˈtrɪʃəsnɪs/ N caractère *m* nutritif

nutritive /ˈnjuːtrɪtɪv/ ADJ nutritif

nuts⁑ /nʌts/ ADJ dingue*, cinglé* ◆ **to go ~** perdre la boule* ◆ **to be ~ about sb/sth** être dingue* de qn/qch ; see also **nut**

nutshell /ˈnʌtʃel/ N coquille *f* de noix *or* de noisette *etc* ◆ **in a ~ ...** en un mot ... ◆ **to put the matter in a ~** résumer l'affaire en un mot

nutter⁑ /ˈnʌtəʳ/ N *(Brit)* cinglé(e)* *m(f)*, dingue* *mf*

nutty /ˈnʌtɪ/ ADJ 1 *(no generic term in French, with hazelnuts)* aux noisettes ; *(with almonds)* aux amandes ; *(with walnuts)* aux noix ; [flavour, taste, smell] de noisette *etc* 2 *(* = mad)* [idea] dingue* ; [person] cinglé*, dingue* ◆ **to be (as) ~ as a fruitcake** *(hum)* être complètement dingue* ◆ **to be ~ about sb/sth** *(= enthusiastic)* être dingue* de qn/qch
COMP **nutty professor*** N professeur Tournesol *m*
nutty slack N *(Brit Min)* déclassés *mpl* des gros

nuzzle /ˈnʌzl/ VI [pig] fouiller du groin, fouiner ◆ **the dog ~d up to my leg** le chien est venu fourrer son nez contre ma jambe ◆ **she ~d up to me** elle est venue se blottir contre moi

NV abbrev of **Nevada**

NVQ /ˌenviːˈkjuː/ N (abbrev of **National Vocational Qualification**) ◆ **NVQ level 1** ≃ CAP *m* ◆ **NVQ level 3** ≃ BTS *m*

NVQ

Les **National Vocational Qualifications**, ou **NVQ**, sont un système de qualifications à la fois théoriques et pratiques destinées essentiellement aux personnes occupant déjà un emploi. Toutefois, certains établissements secondaires préparent à ces examens, en plus ou à la place des examens traditionnels (« GCSE » ou « A levels »). Ce système existe en Angleterre, au pays de Galles et en Irlande du Nord ; en Écosse, il existe une filière comparable qui porte le nom de « Scottish Vocational Qualifications » ou « SVQ ».

NW (abbrev of **north-west**) N-O

NY /enˈwaɪ/ N (abbrev of **New York**) → **new**

Nyasaland /nɪˈæsəˌlænd/ N Nyas(s)aland *m* ◆ **in ~** au Nyas(s)aland

NYC /enwaɪˈsiː/ N abbrev of **New York City**

nylon /ˈnaɪlɒn/ N *(NonC)* nylon ® *m* ADJ [stockings etc] de *or* en nylon ® NPL **nylons** bas *mpl* (*or* collant *m*) de *or* en nylon ®

nymph /nɪmf/ N nymphe *f* ; (also **water nymph**) naïade *f* ; (also **wood nymph**) (hama)dryade *f* ; (also **sea nymph**) néréide *f* ; (also **mountain nymph**) oréade *f*

nymphet /nɪmˈfet/ N nymphette *f*

nympho⁑ /ˈnɪmfəʊ/ ADJ, N abbrev of **nymphomaniac**

nymphomania /ˌnɪmfəʊˈmeɪnɪə/ N nymphomanie *f*

nymphomaniac /ˌnɪmfəʊˈmeɪnɪæk/ ADJ, N nymphomane *f*

NYSE /ˈenwaɪesˈiː/ N *(US)* (abbrev of **New York Stock Exchange**) *Bourse de New York*

NZ, N. Zeal (abbrev of **New Zealand**) → **new**

Oo

O, o[1] /əʊ/ N [1] *(= letter)* O, o *m* ◆ **O for Orange** ≈ O comme Oscar ; see also **OK**[2] [2] *(= number: Telec etc)* zéro *m*
COMP **O Grade** N *(Scot Educ: formerly)* ≈ matière *f* présentée au brevet ◆ **to do an O Grade in French** ≈ passer l'épreuve de français au brevet
O level N *(Brit Educ: formerly)* ≈ matière *f* présentée au brevet ◆ **to do an O level in French** ≈ passer l'épreuve de français au brevet ◆ **O levels** ≈ brevet *m*
O-shaped ADJ en forme de O *or* de cercle

O[2] /əʊ/ EXCL *(liter)* ô

o' /əʊ/ PREP (abbrev of **of**) de ; → **o'clock**

oaf /əʊf/ N *(awkward)* balourd* *m* ; *(bad-mannered)* malotru(e) *m(f)*, mufle *m*

oafish /ˈəʊfɪʃ/ ADJ *(pej)* *[person]* mufle ; *[behaviour, remark]* de mufle

oak /əʊk/ N *(= wood, tree)* chêne *m* ◆ **light/dark ~** chêne *m* clair/foncé ◆ **great ~s from little acorns grow** *(Prov)* les petits ruisseaux font les grandes rivières *(Prov)*
COMP *(= made of oak)* de *or* en (bois de) chêne ; *(= oak-coloured)* (couleur) chêne *inv*
oak-aged ADJ vieilli en fûts de chêne
oak apple N noix *f* de galle, galle *f* du chêne
oak leaf N *(= tree leaf, salad)* feuille *f* de chêne
oak leaf cluster N *(US)* ≈ barrette *f (portée sur le ruban d'une médaille)*
oak-panelled ADJ lambrissé de chêne

oaken /ˈəʊkən/ ADJ *(liter)* de *or* en chêne

oakum /ˈəʊkəm/ N étoupe *f* ◆ **to pick ~** faire de l'étoupe

oakwood /ˈəʊkwʊd/ N [1] *(= forest)* chênaie *f*, forêt *f* de chênes [2] *(NonC = material)* (bois *m* de) chêne *m*

O & M /əʊəndˈem/ (abbrev of **organization and methods**) → **organization**

OAP /ˌəʊeɪˈpiː/ N *(Brit)* (abbrev of **old age pension** *or* **pensioner**) → **old**

oar /ɔːʳ/ N [1] *(gen)* rame *f* ; *(Sport)* aviron *m* ◆ **he always puts** *or* **sticks*** *or* **shoves* his ~ in** il faut toujours qu'il se mêle *subj* de tout *or* qu'il vienne mettre son grain de sel* ; → **rest, ship** [2] *(= person)* rameur *m*, -euse *f*

-oared /ɔːd/ ADJ *(in compounds)* ◆ **four-oared** à quatre avirons

oarlock /ˈɔːlɒk/ N dame *f* (de nage), tolet *m*

oarsman /ˈɔːzmən/ N (pl **-men**) rameur *m*, nageur *m (SPEC)*

oarsmanship /ˈɔːzmənʃɪp/ N *(= art of rowing)* art *m* de ramer ; *(= skill as rower)* qualités *fpl* de rameur

oarswoman /ˈɔːzwʊmən/ N (pl **-women**) rameuse *f*, nageuse *f (SPEC)*

OAS /ˌəʊeɪˈes/ N [1] *(US)* (abbrev of **Organization of American States**) OEA *f* [2] *(Hist: in Algeria)* (abbrev of **Organisation de l'armée secrète**) OAS *f*

oasis /əʊˈeɪsɪs/ N (pl **oases** /əʊˈeɪsiːz/) *(lit, fig)* oasis *f* ◆ **an ~ of peace** un havre *or* une oasis de paix

oast /əʊst/ N four *m* à (sécher le) houblon COMP
oast house N sécherie *f or* séchoir *m* à houblon

oat /əʊt/ NPL *(= plant, food)* ◆ **~s** avoine *f NonC* ◆ **to get one's ~s**‡ *(Brit)* tirer son coup‡ ◆ **to feel one's ~s*** *(US)* *(= feel high-spirited)* avoir la pêche ; *(= feel important)* faire l'important ; → **rolled, wild**

oatcake /ˈəʊtkeɪk/ N biscuit *m* or galette *f* d'avoine

oath /əʊθ/ N (pl **oaths** /əʊðz/) [1] serment *m* ◆ **he took** *or* **swore an ~ promising to uphold the country's laws** il a fait le serment *or* il a juré de faire respecter les lois du pays ◆ **he took** *or* **swore an ~ of loyalty to the government** il a juré loyauté au gouvernement ◆ **he swore on his ~ that he had never been there** il jura n'y avoir jamais été *or* qu'il n'y avait jamais été ◆ **I'll take my ~ on it!** je vous le jure !
[2] *(Jur)* **to take the ~** prêter serment ◆ **on** *or* **under ~** sous serment ◆ **witness on** *or* **under ~** témoin *m* assermenté ◆ **to put sb on** *or* **under ~, to administer the ~ to sb** faire prêter serment à qn ◆ **to put sb on** *or* **under ~ to do sth** faire promettre à qn sous serment de faire qch ; → **allegiance**
[3] *(= bad language)* juron *m* ◆ **to let out** *or* **utter an ~** lâcher *or* pousser un juron
COMP **oath-taking** N *(Jur etc)* prestation *f* de serment

oatmeal /ˈəʊtmiːl/ N *(NonC)* *(= cereal)* flocons *mpl* d'avoine ; *(US)* *(= porridge)* bouillie *f* d'avoine, porridge *m* COMP *(in colour)* *[dress, fabric]* beige, grège

OAU /ˌəʊeɪˈjuː/ N (abbrev of **Organization of African Unity**) OUA *f*

OB N *(Brit)* (abbrev of **outside broadcast**) → **outside**

Obadiah /ˌəʊbəˈdaɪə/ N Abdias *m*

obbligato /ˌɒblɪˈɡɑːtəʊ/ *(Mus)* ADJ obligé N (pl **obbligatos** *or* **obbligati** /ˌɒblɪˈɡɑːtiː/) partie *f* obligée

obduracy /ˈɒbdjʊrəsɪ/ N *(frm)* [1] *(pej = stubbornness)* *[of person]* obstination *f*, entêtement *m* ◆ **the ~ of his behaviour** son comportement obstiné ◆ **the ~ of his silence** son silence obstiné [2] *(= difficulty)* *[of problem, situation]* insolubilité *f*

obdurate /ˈɒbdjʊrɪt/ ADJ *(frm, pej)* *[person]* obstiné, entêté ◆ **her look of ~ stubbornness** son air obstiné et inflexible ◆ **to remain ~** s'obstiner, rester inflexible ◆ **they were ~ in their refusal** ils s'obstinaient dans leur refus

obdurately /ˈɒbdjʊrɪtlɪ/ ADV *(frm)* *(= stubbornly)* obstinément, opiniâtrement ; *(= unyieldingly)*

OBE /ˌəʊbiːˈiː/ N (abbrev of **Officer of the Order of the British Empire**) *titre honorifique* ; → **HONOURS LIST**

obedience /əˈbiːdɪəns/ N *(NonC)* obéissance *f (to à)* ; *(Rel)* obédience *f (to à)* ◆ **in ~ to the law/his orders** conformément à la loi/ses ordres ◆ **to owe ~ to sb** *(frm)* devoir obéissance à qn ◆ **to command ~ (from)** savoir se faire obéir (de)
◆ **~ training** dressage *m* ; → **blind**

> ⚠ **obedience** is rarely translated by the French word **obédience**, which usually means 'allegiance'.

obedient /əˈbiːdɪənt/ ADJ *[person, child]* obéissant ; *[dog]* obéissant, docile ◆ **to be ~ to sb** être obéissant avec qn, obéir à qn ◆ **to be ~ to sb's wishes** obéir aux désirs de qn ◆ **your ~ servant** † *(in letters)* votre très obéissant serviteur † *m*

obediently /əˈbiːdɪəntlɪ/ ADV docilement

obeisance /əʊˈbeɪsəns/ N *(frm)* [1] *(NonC = homage)* hommage *m* [2] *(= bow)* révérence *f*, salut *m* cérémonieux

obelisk /ˈɒbɪlɪsk/ N *(Archit)* obélisque *m*

obese /əʊˈbiːs/ ADJ obèse

obeseness /əʊˈbiːsnɪs/, **obesity** /əʊˈbiːsɪtɪ/ N obésité *f*

obey /əˈbeɪ/ VT *[+ person, instinct, order]* obéir à ; *[+ the law]* se conformer à, obéir à ; *[+ instructions]* se conformer à, observer ; *(Jur)* *[+ summons, order]* obtempérer à ◆ **the plane's engine refused to ~ the computer's commands** le moteur de l'avion refusait de répondre aux commandes de l'ordinateur VI obéir

obfuscate /ˈɒbfəskeɪt/ *(frm)* VT *[+ intentions, figures]* essayer de masquer ◆ **they are obfuscating the issue** ils cherchent des faux-fuyants, ils essaient de noyer le poisson VI chercher des faux-fuyants, chercher à noyer le poisson

obfuscation /ˌɒbfəˈskeɪʃən/ N *(= attempt to confuse)* faux-fuyants *mpl* ◆ **the deliberate ~ of their huge deficit** la tentative délibérée de masquer leur énorme déficit

obit* /ˈəʊbɪt/ N (abbrev of **obituary**) notice *f* nécrologique, nécrologie *f*

obituarist /əˈbɪtjʊərɪst/ N nécrologue *mf*

obituary /əˈbɪtjʊərɪ/ N (also **obituary notice**) notice *f* nécrologique, nécrologie *f*

COMP *[announcement]* nécrologique

obituary column N nécrologie *f*, rubrique *f* nécrologique

object /ˈɒbdʒɪkt/ LANGUAGE IN USE 26.1, 26.3

N 1 *(= thing in general)* objet *m*, chose *f* ; *(Comput)* objet *m* ◆ **what is this ~?** *(pej)* quelle est cette chose ? *(pej)*

2 *(= focus)* ◆ **~ of pity/ridicule** objet *m* de pitié/de risée ◆ **the ~ of one's love** l'objet *m* aimé

3 *(= aim)* but *m* ; *(Philos)* objet *m* ◆ **he has no ~ in life** il n'a aucun but dans la vie ◆ **with this ~ (in view** *or* **in mind)** dans ce but, à cette fin ◆ **with the ~ of doing sth** dans le but de faire qch ◆ **with the sole ~ of doing sth** à seule fin *or* dans le seul but de faire qch ◆ **what ~ is there in** *or* **what's the ~ of doing that?** à quoi bon faire cela ? ; → **defeat**

4 *(= obstacle)* ◆ **distance/money is no ~** la distance/l'argent n'est pas un problème

5 *(Gram)* complément *m* (d'objet) ◆ **direct/indirect ~** complément *m* (d'objet) direct/indirect

6 ◆ **~ of virtu** objet *m* d'art, curiosité *f*

VI /əbˈdʒekt/ élever une objection *(to sb/sth* contre qn/qch) ◆ **I ~!** je proteste ! ◆ **I ~ most strongly!** je proteste catégoriquement *or* énergiquement ! ◆ **if you don't ~** si cela ne vous fait rien, si vous n'y voyez pas d'inconvénient *or* d'objection ◆ **he didn't ~ when ...** il n'a élevé *or* formulé aucune objection quand ... ◆ **I ~ to that remark** je proteste *or* je m'élève contre cette remarque ◆ **I ~ to your rudeness** votre grossièreté est inadmissible ◆ **he ~s to her drinking** cela l'ennuie qu'elle boive ◆ **do you ~ to my smoking?** cela vous ennuie que je fume *subj* ?, est-ce que cela vous gêne si je fume ? ◆ **she ~s to all this noise** elle se plaint de tout ce bruit ◆ **I don't ~ to helping you** je veux bien vous aider ◆ **to ~ to sb** élever des objections contre qn ◆ **I would ~ to Paul but not to Robert as chairman** je ne voudrais pas que Paul soit président mais je n'ai rien contre Robert ◆ **they ~ed to him because he was too young** ils lui ont objecté son jeune âge ◆ **to ~ to a witness** *(Jur)* récuser un témoin ◆ **I wouldn't ~ to a bite to eat*** je mangerais bien un morceau

VT /əbˈdʒekt/ ◆ **to ~ that ...** objecter que ..., faire valoir que ...

COMP **object clause** N *(Gram)* proposition *f* complément d'objet, complétive *f* d'objet

object database N base *f* de données objet

object language N *(Ling)* langage-objet *m*

object lesson N *(fig)* ◆ **it was an ~ lesson in how not to drive a car** c'était une illustration de ce que l'on ne doit pas faire au volant ◆ **it was an ~ lesson in good manners** c'était une démonstration de bonnes manières

object-oriented ADJ *[software, technology, programming]* orienté objet

objection /əbˈdʒekʃən/ LANGUAGE IN USE 9.1, 26.3 N objection *f* ◆ **I have no ~(s)** je n'ai pas d'objection, je ne m'y oppose pas ◆ **if you have no ~(s)** si cela ne vous fait rien, si vous n'y voyez pas d'inconvénient *or* d'objection ◆ **I have no ~ to him** je n'ai rien contre lui ◆ **I have a strong ~ to dogs in shops** je ne supporte pas les chiens dans les magasins ◆ **have you any ~ to my smoking?** cela ne vous ennuie pas que je fume *subj* ?, est-ce que cela vous gêne si je fume ? ◆ **I have no ~ to the idea/to his leaving** je ne vois pas d'objection *or* je ne m'oppose pas à cette idée/à ce qu'il parte ◆ **there is no ~ to our leaving** il n'y a pas d'obstacle *or* d'inconvénient à ce que nous partions *subj* ◆ **to make** *or* **raise an ~** soulever *or* formuler une objection ◆ **to make ~ to an argument** *(Jur)* récuser un argument ◆ **~!** *(Jur)* objection ! ; *(gen)* je proteste ! ◆ **~ overruled!** *(Jur)* objection rejetée !

objectionable /əbˈdʒekʃnəbl/ ADJ *[smell]* nauséabond ; *[behaviour, attitude]* répréhensible ; *[language]* choquant ; *[remark]* désobligeant ◆ **I find him thoroughly ~** il me déplaît souverainement ◆ **I find your tone highly ~** je trouve votre ton tout à fait désagréable ◆ **the language used in the programme was ~ to many viewers** le langage utilisé au cours de l'émission a choqué de nombreux téléspectateurs

objective /əbˈdʒektɪv/ ADJ 1 *(= impartial) [person, report, view]* objectif, impartial ; *[evidence, facts, criteria]* objectif ◆ **to take an ~ look at sth** examiner qch d'une manière objective ◆ **he is very ~ in his reporting** ses reportages sont très objectifs 2 *(Philos)* objectif 3 *(Gram) [pronoun]* complément d'objet ; *[genitive]* objectif ◆ **~ case** (cas *m*) accusatif *m*, cas *m* régime N 1 *(gen, also Phot)* objectif *m* ◆ **to reach** *or* **attain one's ~** atteindre le but qu'on s'était fixé *or* son objectif 2 *(Gram)* accusatif *m*

objectively /əbˈdʒektɪvlɪ/ ADV objectivement

objectivism /əbˈdʒektɪvɪzəm/ N objectivisme *m*

objectivity /ˌɒbdʒɪkˈtɪvɪtɪ/ N objectivité *f*

objector /əbˈdʒektəʳ/ N opposant(e) *m(f)* ◆ **the ~s to this scheme** les opposants au projet, les adversaires du projet ; → **conscientious**

objet d'art /ˈɒbʒeɪˈdɑː/ N (pl **objets d'art**) objet *m* d'art

objet de vertu /ˈɒbʒeɪdəˈvɜːtjuː/ N (pl **objets de vertu**) objet *m* d'art, curiosité *f*

objurgate /ˈɒbdʒɜːgeɪt/ VT *(frm)* réprimander ; *(stronger)* accabler de reproches

objurgation /ˌɒbdʒɜːˈgeɪʃən/ N *(frm)* réprimande *f*

oblate /ˈɒbleɪt/ N *(Rel)* oblat(e) *m(f)* ADJ *(Geom)* aplati aux pôles

oblation /əʊˈbleɪʃən/ N *(Rel)* (= *act*) oblation *f* ; (= *offering*: also **oblations**) oblats *mpl*

obligate /ˈɒblɪgeɪt/ VT obliger, contraindre *(sb to do sth* qn à faire qch) ◆ **to be ~d to do sth** être obligé de *or* contraint à faire qch

obligation /ˌɒblɪˈgeɪʃən/ N 1 *(= duty)* obligation *f* ◆ **to be under an ~ to do sth** être tenu de faire qch, être dans l'obligation de faire qch ◆ **I'm under no ~ to do it** rien ne m'oblige à le faire ◆ **to lay** *or* **put sb under an ~** créer une obligation à qn ◆ **to put** *or* **lay an ~ on sb to do sth** mettre qn dans l'obligation de faire qch ◆ **it is your ~ to see that ...** il vous incombe de veiller à ce que ... + *subj* ◆ **"without obligation"** *(in advert)* "sans engagement" ◆ **"no obligation to buy"** *(in advert)* "aucune obligation d'achat" ; *(in shop)* "entrée libre"

2 *(= commitment)* obligation *f*, engagement *m* ◆ **to meet one's ~s** respecter ses obligations *or* ses engagements ◆ **to fail to meet one's ~s** manquer à ses obligations *or* à ses engagements ◆ **to be under an ~ to sb** devoir de la reconnaissance à qn ◆ **to be under an ~ to sb for sth** être redevable à qn de qch

3 *(= debt)* devoir *m*, dette *f* (de reconnaissance) ◆ **to repay an ~** acquitter une dette de reconnaissance

obligatory /ɒˈblɪgətərɪ/ LANGUAGE IN USE 10.1 ADJ 1 *(= compulsory) [attendance]* obligatoire ◆ **it is not ~ to attend** il n'est pas obligatoire d'y assister ◆ **it is ~ for you to attend** vous êtes dans l'obligation *or* vous êtes tenu d'y assister ◆ **to make it ~ for sb to do sth** obliger qn à faire qch 2 *(= customary) [smile, kiss]* de rigueur ◆ **she was wearing the ~ sweater and pearl necklace** elle portait le pull et le collier de perles de rigueur

oblige /əˈblaɪdʒ/ LANGUAGE IN USE 4, 10, 20.6

VT 1 *(= compel)* obliger *(sb to do sth* qn à faire qch) ◆ **to be ~d to do sth** être obligé de faire qch

2 *(= do a favour to)* rendre service à, obliger *(liter)* ◆ **he did it to ~ us** il l'a fait pour nous rendre service ◆ **can you ~ me with a pen?** *(frm)* auriez-vous l'amabilité *or* l'obligeance de me prêter un stylo ? ◆ **he's always ready to ~ journalists with information** il est toujours prêt à communiquer des informations aux journalistes ◆ **to be ~d to sb for sth** *(Comm)* être reconnaissant *or* savoir gré à qn de qch ◆ **I am much ~d to you** je vous remercie infiniment ◆ **I would be ~d if you would read it to us** je vous serais reconnaissant de bien vouloir nous le lire ◆ **thanks, I'd be ~d** merci, ce serait très gentil (de votre part) ◆ **much ~d!** merci beaucoup !, merci mille fois ! ◆ **much ~d for your assistance!** merci beaucoup *or* merci mille fois de votre aide !

VI ◆ **she is always ready** *or* **willing to ~** elle est toujours prête à rendre service ◆ **anything to ~!*** à votre service ! ◆ **he asked for more time and they ~d by delaying their departure** il a demandé un délai et ils se sont pliés à ses désirs en retardant leur départ ◆ **we asked him the way and he ~d with directions** nous lui avons demandé notre chemin et il nous a très gentiment donné des indications ◆ **a prompt answer will ~** *(Comm †)* une réponse rapide nous obligerait

obligee /ˌɒblɪˈdʒiː/ N *(Jur)* obligataire *m*, créancier *m*

obliging /əˈblaɪdʒɪŋ/ ADJ obligeant, serviable ◆ **it is very ~ of them** c'est très gentil *or* aimable de leur part

obligingly /əˈblaɪdʒɪŋlɪ/ ADV obligeamment

obligor /ˌɒblɪˈgɔːʳ/ N *(Jur)* obligé *m*

oblique /əˈbliːk/ ADJ 1 *(= indirect) [approach, reference, criticism, warning]* indirect 2 *(= slanting) [line, plane, cut]* oblique ; *[look]* en biais, oblique ; *[view]* de biais ; *(Math) [angle] (= acute)* aigu(-guë *f*) ; *(= obtuse)* obtus ◆ **it lies at an ~ angle to the coastline** c'est en biais par rapport à la côte 3 *(Gram)* ◆ **~ case** cas *m* oblique N 1 *(Anat)* oblique *f* 2 *(Brit Typ:* also **oblique stroke**) trait *m* oblique, oblique *f*

obliquely /əˈbliːklɪ/ ADV 1 *(= indirectly) [refer to, answer, approach]* indirectement 2 *(= diagonally) [cut]* obliquement, en biais

obliqueness /əˈbliːknɪs/, **obliquity** /əˈblɪkwɪtɪ/ N 1 *[of approach, reference]* caractère *m* indirect 2 *[of line]* obliquité *f*

obliterate /əˈblɪtəreɪt/ VT 1 *(= destroy)* détruire, anéantir 2 *[+ writing etc] (= erase)* effacer, enlever ; *(= obscure)* rendre illisible ; *(by progressive wear)* oblitérer *(frm)* ; *(fig) [+ memory, impressions]* oblitérer *(frm)* ; *[+ the past]* faire table rase de 3 *(Post) [+ stamp]* oblitérer

obliteration /əˌblɪtəˈreɪʃən/ N 1 *(= destruction) [of person, object, country]* anéantissement *m* ; *[of rainforest]* destruction *f* 2 *(= erasure)* rature *f*, biffure *f* ; *(fig) [of memory]* effacement *m*

oblivion /əˈblɪvɪən/ N (état *m* d')oubli *m* ◆ **to sink** *or* **fall into ~** tomber dans l'oubli

oblivious /əˈblɪvɪəs/ ADJ *(= unaware)* inconscient *(of or to sb/sth* de qn/qch) ; *(= forgetful)* oublieux *(of or to sb/sth* de qn/qch)

oblong /ˈɒblɒŋ/ ADJ *(= rectangular)* oblong (oblongue *f*) ; *(= elongated)* allongé ◆ **an ~ dish** un plat rectangulaire N rectangle *m*

obloquy /ˈɒbləkwɪ/ N opprobre *m*

obnoxious /əbˈnɒkʃəs/ ADJ *[person]* odieux ; *[child, dog, behaviour]* odieux, détestable ; *[smell]* nauséabond ◆ **stop being so ~!** arrête d'être odieux !

obnoxiously /əbˈnɒkʃəslɪ/ ADV odieusement

o.b.o., OBO /əʊbiːˈəʊ/ (abbrev of **or best offer**) à déb., à débattre ; → **offer**

oboe /ˈəʊbəʊ/ N hautbois *m* COMP **oboe d'amore** N hautbois *m* d'amour

oboist /ˈəʊbəʊɪst/ N hautboïste *mf*

obs * /ɒbz/ N 1 abbrev of **obstetrics** 2 abbrev of **observation**

obscene /əbˈsiːn/ ADJ *[act, gesture, language, remark, phone call]* obscène ; *[profit, salary]* indécent ◆ **it is ~ that discrimination of this sort can take place today** c'est une honte *or* un scandale qu'il puisse y avoir une telle discrimination de nos jours ◆ **they spend an ~ amount of money** ils dépensent des sommes scandaleuses

COMP **obscene publication** N *(Jur)* publication *f* obscène

Obscene Publications Act N *(Brit)* loi *f* sur les publications obscènes

Obscene Publications Squad N *(Brit) brigade de répression des publications obscènes*

obscenely /əbˈsiːnlɪ/ ADV ◆ **to talk ~** dire des obscénités ◆ **~ rich** d'une richesse indécente ◆ **she earns ~ large amounts of money** elle gagne tellement d'argent que c'en est indécent ◆ **an ~ expensive house** une maison tellement chère que c'en est indécent

obscenity /əbˈsenɪtɪ/ N *(gen, also Jur)* obscénité *f* ; *(= moral outrage)* infamie *f* ◆ **he was convicted on ~ charges** il a été condamné pour obscénité ◆ **the ~ laws** les lois *fpl* sur l'obscénité ◆ **~ trial** procès *m* pour obscénité

obscurantism /ˌɒbskjʊəˈræntɪzəm/ N obscurantisme *m*

obscurantist /ˌɒbskjʊəˈræntɪst/ ADJ, N obscurantiste *mf*

obscure /əbˈskjʊəʳ/ ADJ 1 *(= not straightforward, not obvious) [word, reference, reason, origins]* obscur 2 *(= not well-known) [writer, artist, book]* obscur, peu connu ; *[village]* peu connu, perdu 3 *(= indistinct) [shape]* indistinct VT 1 *(= hide) [+ sun] (partly)* voiler ; *(completely)* cacher ; *[+ view]* cacher, masquer ◆ **his view was ~d by trees** les arbres lui cachaient la vue 2 *[+ argument, idea]* rendre obscur ; *[+ truth]* masquer, cacher ◆ **to ~ the issue** embrouiller la question

obscurely /əbˈskjʊəlɪ/ ADV obscurément

obscurity /əbˈskjʊərɪtɪ/ N 1 *(= darkness)* obscurité *f*, ténèbres *fpl (liter)* 2 *(fig) [of argument, idea]* obscurité *f*

obsequies /ˈɒbsɪkwɪz/ NPL *(frm)* obsèques *fpl*, funérailles *fpl*

obsequious /əbˈsiːkwɪəs/ ADJ *(pej) [person, manner]* obséquieux, servile *(to sb* devant qn*)* ; *[smile]* obséquieux ◆ **their ~ treatment of the film star** leur obséquiosité *f* à l'égard de la vedette

obsequiously /əbˈsiːkwɪəslɪ/ ADV *(pej)* obséquieusement

obsequiousness /əbˈsiːkwɪəsnɪs/ N obséquiosité *f*, servilité *f*

observable /əbˈzɜːvəbl/ ADJ *[facts, phenomena, pattern]* observable ; *[benefits, consequences, effect]* observable, visible ◆ **the ~ universe** *(Astron)* l'univers *m* observable

observably /əbˈzɜːvəblɪ/ ADV visiblement

observance /əbˈzɜːvəns/ N 1 *(NonC) [of rule, law]* observation *f*, respect *m* ; *[of rite, custom, Sabbath]* observance *f* ; *[of anniversary]* célébration *f* 2 *(= rite, ceremony)* observance *f* ◆ **religious ~s** observances *fpl* religieuses

observant /əbˈzɜːvənt/ ADJ *[person, eye]* observateur (-trice *f*)

observation /ˌɒbzəˈveɪʃən/ N 1 *(NonC)* observation *f* ◆ **~ of birds/bats** observation *f* des oiseaux/des chauves-souris ◆ **his powers of ~** ses facultés *fpl* d'observation ◆ **careful ~ of the movement of the planets** une observation attentive du mouvement des planètes ◆ **to keep sb under ~** *(Med)* garder qn en observation ; *(Police)* surveiller qn ◆ **they kept the house under ~** ils surveillaient la maison ◆ **to be under ~** *(Med)* être en observation ; *(Police)* être sous surveillance ◆ **he came under ~ when ...** *(Police)* on s'est mis à le surveiller quand ... ◆ **to take an ~** *(Astron)* faire une observation

2 *(= remark)* observation *f*, remarque *f* ◆ **this book contains ~s about the causes of addictions** ce livre contient diverses observations *or* remarques sur les causes des dépendances ◆ **his ~s on "Hamlet"** ses réflexions *fpl* sur "Hamlet"

COMP **observation balloon** N ballon *m* d'observation

observation car N *(Rail)* wagon *m or* voiture *f* panoramique

observation deck N terrasse *f* panoramique

observation post N *(Mil)* poste *m* d'observation, observatoire *m*

observation satellite N satellite *m* d'observation

observation tower N mirador *m*, tour *f* de guet

observation ward N *(Med)* salle *f* d'observation

observational /ˌɒbzəˈveɪʃənl/ ADJ *(frm) [skills, faculties, test, device]* d'observation ; *[evidence, data, study]* basé sur l'observation

observatory /əbˈzɜːvətrɪ/ N observatoire *m*

observe /əbˈzɜːv/ LANGUAGE IN USE 26.2, 26.3 VT 1 *(= obey) [+ rule, custom, ceasefire]* observer, respecter ; *[+ silence]* garder ◆ **to ~ a minute's silence** observer une minute de silence ◆ **failure to ~ the law** *(Jur)* inobservation *f* de la loi

2 *(= celebrate) [+ anniversary]* célébrer ; *[+ the Sabbath]* observer ◆ **to ~ Christmas/May Day** fêter Noël/le premier mai

3 *(= take note of)* observer, remarquer ; *(= study)* observer ◆ **to ~ sth closely** observer qch attentivement, scruter qch ◆ **I'm only here to ~** je ne suis ici qu'en tant qu'observateur

4 *(= say, remark)* (faire) remarquer, faire observer ◆ **he ~d that the weather was cold** il a fait observer *or* remarquer qu'il faisait froid ◆ **as I was about to ~ ...** comme j'allais le dire *or* le faire remarquer ... ◆ **I ~d to him that ...** je lui ai fait remarquer *or* observer que ... ◆ **"he's a handsome young man", she ~d** "c'est un beau jeune homme", remarqua-t-elle ◆ **... as Elliot ~d** ... comme l'a remarqué *or* relevé Elliot

observer /əbˈzɜːvəʳ/ N 1 *(= person watching)* observateur *m*, -trice *f*, spectateur *m*, -trice *f* ◆ **the ~ may note ...** les observateurs *or* spectateurs remarqueront ... ◆ **a casual ~ would have assumed they were friends** un simple observateur aurait pensé qu'ils étaient amis 2 *(= official: at meeting etc)* observateur *m*, -trice *f* ◆ **UN ~s will attend the conference** les observateurs de l'ONU assisteront à la conférence 3 *(Pol etc = analyst, commentator)* spécialiste *mf*, expert *m* ◆ **an ~ of Soviet politics** un spécialiste de la politique soviétique ◆ **political ~s believe that ...** les observateurs politiques pensent que ...

COMP **observer force** N *(Mil)* force *f* d'observation

observer mission N *(Mil)* mission *f* d'observation

observer team N *(Mil)* groupe *m* d'observateurs

obsess /əbˈses/ VT obséder ◆ **~ed by** obsédé par VI ◆ **to ~ about** *or* **over sth** être obsédé par qch

obsession /əbˈseʃən/ N *(= state)* obsession *f* ; *(= fixed idea)* obsession *f*, idée *f* fixe ; *(of sth unpleasant)* hantise *f* ◆ **sport is an ~ with him** c'est un obsédé de sport ◆ **he has an ~ about cleanliness** c'est un obsédé de la propreté, il a l'obsession de la propreté ◆ **his ~ with her** la manière dont elle l'obsède ◆ **his ~ with death** *(= fascination)* son obsession de la mort ; *(= fear)* sa hantise de la mort

obsessional /əbˈseʃənl/ ADJ *[behaviour, love, hatred]* obsessionnel ◆ **to be ~** *[person]* souffrir d'une obsession *or* d'obsessions ◆ **to be ~ about tidiness/cleanliness** *etc* être un maniaque de l'ordre/de la propreté *etc*

obsessionally /əbˈseʃənəlɪ/ ADV de façon obsessionnelle ◆ **~ tidy** obsédé par l'ordre, maniaque de l'ordre ◆ **to be ~ jealous of sb** éprouver une jalousie obsessionnelle vis-à-vis de qn

obsessive /əbˈsesɪv/ ADJ *[behaviour, need, desire, love, interest, secrecy]* obsessionnel ; *[memory, thought]* obsédant ◆ **to be ~** *[person]* souffrir d'une obsession *or* d'obsessions ◆ **to be ~ about tidiness/cleanliness** *etc* être un maniaque de l'ordre/de la propreté *etc* ◆ **an ~ gambler** un(e) obsédé(e) du jeu ◆ **his ~ tidiness was driving her crazy** son obsession de l'ordre la rendait folle COMP **obsessive compulsive disorder** N *(Psych)* troubles *mpl* obsessionnels compulsifs

obsessively /əbˈsesɪvlɪ/ ADV *[work, love, hate]* de façon obsessionnelle ◆ **she is ~ tidy** c'est une maniaque de l'ordre ◆ **to be ~ in love with sb** aimer qn d'un amour obsessionnel ◆ **he's ~ worried about her** il se fait tellement de souci pour elle que ça tourne à l'obsession

obsidian /ɒbˈsɪdɪən/ N obsidienne *f*

obsolescence /ˌɒbsəˈlesns/ N 1 *[of machinery, goods, words]* obsolescence *f* ◆ **planned** *or* **built-in ~** obsolescence *f* programmée 2 *(Bio)* atrophie *f*, myopathie *f* COMP **obsolescence clause** N *(Insurance)* clause *f* de vétusté

obsolescent /ˌɒbsəˈlesnt/ ADJ 1 *[machinery, weapon]* obsolescent ; *[word]* désuet 2 *(Bio) [organ]* en voie d'atrophie

obsolete /ˈɒbsəliːt/ ADJ 1 *[weapon, equipment, machine]* obsolète ; *[system, attitude, idea, process, practice]* dépassé ; *[word]* obsolète, tombé en désuétude ; *[law]* caduc (caduque *f*), tombé en désuétude 2 *(Bio)* atrophié

obstacle /ˈɒbstəkl/ N *(lit, fig)* obstacle *m* ◆ **to be an ~ to sth** être un obstacle à qch ◆ **overcrowding remains a serious ~ to improving living conditions** le surpeuplement reste un obstacle important à l'amélioration des conditions de vie ◆ **the main ~ in negotiations is ...** le principal obstacle dans les négociations est ... ◆ **to put an ~ in the way of sth/in sb's way** faire obstacle à qch/qn

COMP **obstacle course** N *(lit)* parcours *m* d'obstacles ; *(fig)* parcours *m* du combattant

obstacle race N *(Sport)* course *f* d'obstacles

obstetric(al) /ɒbˈstetrɪk(əl)/ ADJ *[techniques etc]* obstétrical ; *[clinic]* obstétrique

obstetrician /ˌɒbstəˈtrɪʃən/ N obstétricien(ne) *m(f)*, (médecin *m*) accoucheur *m*

obstetrics /ɒbˈstetrɪks/ N *(NonC)* obstétrique *f*

obstinacy /ˈɒbstɪnəsɪ/ N *[of person]* obstination *f (in doing sth* à faire qch*)* ; *[of illness]* persistance *f* ; *[of resistance, refusal]* obstination *f*

obstinate /ˈɒbstɪnɪt/ ADJ 1 *(= stubborn) [person, refusal, silence, resistance]* obstiné ◆ **to have an ~ streak** être du genre obstiné ◆ **he's very ~ about it** il n'en démord pas ◆ **she was ~ in her refusal** elle s'est obstinée dans son refus 2 *(= persistent) [weeds, stain, cough]* rebelle ; *[pain, illness]* persistant

obstinately /ˈɒbstɪnɪtlɪ/ ADV *[refuse, insist, struggle]* obstinément ◆ **to be ~ uncooperative** refuser obstinément de coopérer ◆ **he was ~ silent** il restait obstinément silencieux ◆ **unemployment figures are remaining ~ high** le taux de chômage reste obstinément élevé ◆ **"no" he said ~** "non" répondit-il d'un air obstiné ◆ **he tried ~ to do it by himself** il s'est obstiné *or* entêté à le faire tout seul

obstreperous /əb'strepərəs/ ADJ (= *noisy*) tapageur, bruyant ; (= *awkward, rebellious*) récalcitrant ; **to get ~** (= *make a fuss*) faire un scandale

obstreperously /əb'strepərəslɪ/ ADV (= *noisily*) bruyamment, tapageusement ; (= *rebelliously*) avec force protestations, en rouspétant*

obstruct /əb'strʌkt/ VT 1 (= *block*) [+ *road*] bloquer (*with* de) ; [+ *pipe*] engorger ; (*Med*) [+ *artery, windpipe*] obstruer ; [+ *view*] boucher, cacher 2 (= *halt*) [+ *traffic*] bloquer ; [+ *progress*] arrêter, enrayer 3 (= *hinder*) [+ *progress, traffic, plan*] entraver ; [+ *person*] gêner, entraver ; (*Sport*) [+ *player*] faire obstruction à ◆ **to ~ the course of justice** entraver le cours de la justice ◆ **to ~ (the passage of) a bill** (*Pol*) faire de l'obstruction parlementaire ◆ **to ~ a policeman in the execution of his duty** (*Jur*) gêner *or* entraver un agent de police dans l'exercice de ses fonctions VI (*Sport*) faire de l'obstruction

obstruction /əb'strʌkʃən/ N 1 (*to plan, progress, view*) obstacle *m* ; (*in pipe*) bouchon *m* ; (*in artery, windpipe*) obstruction *f*, occlusion *f* ◆ **to remove an ~ from a chimney** enlever un objet qui obstrue une cheminée ◆ **the country's ~ of the UN inspection process** l'obstruction du pays au processus d'inspection de l'ONU ◆ **legal ~s** obstacles *mpl* juridiques ◆ **a bowel ~** une occlusion intestinale ◆ **an ~ of the Fallopian tubes** une obturation des trompes de Fallope ◆ **to cause an ~** (*Jur, gen*) encombrer *or* obstruer la voie publique ; (*to traffic*) bloquer la circulation ◆ **~ of justice** (*Jur*) entrave *f* à la justice ◆ **he was charged with ~ of the police in the course of their duties** il a été inculpé pour entrave à l'action de la police dans l'exercice de ses fonctions

2 (*Sport*) obstruction *f*

obstructionism /əb'strʌkʃənɪzəm/ N obstructionnisme *m*

obstructionist /əb'strʌkʃənɪst/ ADJ, N obstructionniste *mf* ◆ **to adopt ~ tactics** faire de l'obstruction, pratiquer l'obstruction

obstructive /əb'strʌktɪv/ ADJ 1 (= *troublesome*) [*bureaucracy*] tracassier (-ière) ◆ **he's intent on being ~** il fait de l'obstruction systématique 2 (*Parl*) [*person, behaviour, policy, tactics, measures*] obstructionniste 3 (*Med*) obstructif, obstruant

obstructiveness /əb'strʌktɪvnɪs/ N tendance *f* à dresser des obstacles *or* à faire obstacle

obtain /əb'teɪn/ VT (*gen*) obtenir ; [+ *goods*] procurer (*for sb* à qn) ; (*for o.s.*) se procurer ; [+ *information, job, money*] obtenir, (se) procurer ; [+ *votes*] obtenir, recueillir ; [+ *prize*] obtenir, remporter ; (*Fin*) [+ *shares*] acquérir ◆ **this gas is ~ed from coal** on obtient ce gaz à partir du charbon ◆ **these goods may be ~ed from any large store** on peut se procurer ces articles dans tous les grands magasins VI (*frm*) [*rule, custom etc*] avoir cours, être en vigueur ; [*fashion*] être en vogue ; [*method*] être courant

obtainable /əb'teɪnəbl/ ADJ [*product*] qu'on peut se procurer, disponible ◆ **the form is ~ from** *or* **at post offices** on peut se procurer ce formulaire dans les bureaux de poste

obtrude /əb'truːd/ (*frm*) VT imposer (*sth on sb* qch à qn) VI [*object*] gêner ; [*person*] s'imposer, imposer sa présence ◆ **the author's opinions do not ~** l'auteur n'impose pas ses opinions

obtrusion /əb'truːʒən/ N intrusion *f*

obtrusive /əb'truːsɪv/ ADJ [*person*] envahissant, qui s'impose ; [*object, building*] trop en évidence ; [*presence*] gênant, envahissant ; [*music, smell*] gênant, envahissant

obtrusively /əb'truːsɪvlɪ/ ADV [*leave, walk out*] ostensiblement ; [*stare*] de façon importune

obtuse /əb'tjuːs/ ADJ 1 [*person*] obtus ◆ **are you just being deliberately ~?** faites-vous exprès de ne pas comprendre ? 2 (*Math*) [*angle*] obtus

obtuseness /əb'tjuːsnɪs/ N stupidité *f*

obverse /'ɒbvɜːs/ N [*of coin*] face *f*, côté *m* face ; [*of statement, truth*] contrepartie *f*, contre-pied *m* ADJ 1 [*side of coin etc*] de face, qui fait face ; (*fig*) correspondant, faisant contrepartie 2 (*in shape*) [*leaf*] renversé, plus large au sommet qu'à la base

obviate /'ɒbvɪeɪt/ VT [+ *difficulty*] obvier à, parer à ; [+ *danger, objection*] prévenir ◆ **it ~s the need to buy new equipment** cela évite de devoir acheter du matériel neuf ◆ **this can ~ the need for surgical intervention** cela peut rendre inutile l'intervention chirurgicale

obvious /'ɒbvɪəs/ LANGUAGE IN USE 26.3

ADJ [*question, solution, danger, reason, disadvantage*] évident (*to sb* pour qn) ; [*good faith*] évident, incontestable ; [*remark*] prévisible ; [*lie*] flagrant ◆ **an ~ injustice** une injustice manifeste *or* patente ◆ **he was the ~ choice for the role** il était tout désigné pour ce rôle ◆ **~ statement** truisme *m*, lapalissade *f* ◆ **it's the ~ thing to do** c'est la chose à faire, cela s'impose ◆ **the ~ thing to do is to leave** la chose à faire c'est évidemment de partir ◆ **that's the ~ one to choose** c'est bien évidemment celui-là qu'il faut choisir ◆ **we mustn't be too ~ about it** il ne faut pas dévoiler notre jeu ◆ **it is ~ that ...** il est évident que ... ◆ **he made it ~ that he didn't like it** il a bien fait comprendre qu'il n'aimait pas cela

N ◆ **you are merely stating the ~** c'est une lapalissade *or* un truisme, vous enfoncez une porte ouverte ◆ **to repeat the ~** répéter des évidences

obviously /'ɒbvɪəslɪ/ LANGUAGE IN USE 15.1 ADV [*angry, upset, happy, pregnant*] visiblement ◆ **it's ~ true that ...** il est manifeste *or* notoire que ... ◆ **that's ~ true!** c'est la vérité ! ◆ **you're ~ not surprised** manifestement, tu n'es pas surpris ◆ **he was not ~ drunk** à le voir, on ne pouvait pas dire s'il était ivre ◆ **it wasn't ~ wrong** l'erreur ne sautait pas aux yeux ◆ **she ~ adores her sister** il est évident qu'elle adore sa sœur ◆ **~ I am delighted** je suis bien entendu ravi ◆ **~!** bien sûr !, évidemment ! ◆ **~ not!** apparemment non !

OC /'əʊ'siː/ N abbrev of **Officer Commanding**

ocarina /ˌɒkə'riːnə/ N ocarina *m*

Occam /'ɒkəm/ N Occam *m* ◆ **~'s razor** le rasoir d'Occam

occasion /ə'keɪʒən/ N 1 (= *particular time, date, occurrence etc*) occasion *f* ◆ **on the ~ of ...** à l'occasion de ... ◆ **(on) the first ~ (that) it happened** la première fois que cela s'est passé ◆ **on that ~** à cette occasion, cette fois-là ◆ **on several ~s** à plusieurs occasions *or* reprises ◆ **on rare ~s** en de rares occasions ◆ **on just such an ~** dans une occasion tout à fait semblable ◆ **on great ~s** dans les grandes occasions ◆ **on a previous** *or* **former ~** précédemment ◆ **I'll do it on the first possible ~** je le ferai à la première occasion (possible) *or* dès que l'occasion se présentera ◆ **on ~(s)** à l'occasion, quand l'occasion se présente (*or* se présentait *etc*) ◆ **should the ~ arise** le cas échéant ◆ **should the ~ so demand** si les circonstances l'exigent ◆ **as the ~ requires** selon le cas ◆ **he has had few ~s to speak Italian** il n'a pas eu souvent l'occasion de parler italien ◆ **he took (the) ~ to say ...** il en a profité pour dire ... ◆ **he was waiting for a suitable ~ to apologize** il attendait une occasion favorable pour *or* l'occasion de présenter ses excuses ◆ **this would be a good ~ to try it out** c'est l'occasion tout indiquée pour l'essayer ◆ **to rise to** *or* **be equal to the ~** être à la hauteur de la situation

2 (= *event, function*) événement *m*, occasion *f* ◆ **a big ~** un grand événement, une grande occasion ◆ **it was quite an ~** c'était un véritable événement ◆ **it was an ~ to remember** c'était un événement mémorable ◆ **he has no sense of ~** il n'a pas le sens de la fête ◆ **flowers add to the sense of ~ at a wedding** pour un mariage, des fleurs ajoutent au caractère exceptionnel de l'événement ◆ **play/music written for the ~** pièce *f* spécialement écrite/musique *f* spécialement composée pour l'occasion

3 (= *reason*) motif *m* ◆ **there is no ~ for alarm** *or* **to be alarmed** il n'y a pas lieu de s'alarmer, il n'y a pas de quoi s'inquiéter ◆ **there was no ~ for it** ce n'était pas nécessaire ◆ **I have no ~ for complaint** je n'ai pas motif à *or* sujet de me plaindre ◆ **you had no ~ to say that** vous n'aviez aucune raison de dire cela ◆ **I had ~ to reprimand him** (*frm*) j'ai eu l'occasion de *or* j'ai eu à le réprimander

4 (*frm*) **to go about one's lawful ~s** vaquer à ses occupations

VT (*frm*) occasionner, causer

occasional /ə'keɪʒənl/ ADJ 1 (= *infrequent*) [*meeting, event*] qui a (*or* avait) lieu de temps en temps ; [*worker, use*] occasionnel ; [*rain, showers*] intermittent ; [*skirmish, gunshot*] sporadique ◆ **I have the ~ drink** je prends un verre de temps en temps ◆ **she made ~ visits to England** elle allait de temps en temps en Angleterre ◆ **they had passed an ~ car on the road** ils avaient croisé quelques rares voitures ◆ **~ series** (*TV*) émission *f* thématique (*non diffusée régulièrement*) 2 (*frm: Literat, Mus*) [*poem, essay, music*] de circonstance COMP **occasional table** N (*Brit*) table *f* d'appoint

occasionally /ə'keɪʒnəlɪ/ ADV [*do, say, think etc*] parfois, de temps en temps, à l'occasion ; [*rude, silly, angry etc*] parfois ◆ **(only) very ~** très rarement, exceptionnellement

occident /'ɒksɪdənt/ N (*liter*) occident *m*, couchant *m* ◆ **the Occident** l'Occident *m*

occidental /ˌɒksɪ'dentl/ ADJ (*liter*) occidental

occipita /ɒk'sɪpɪtə/ NPL of **occiput**

occipital /ɒk'sɪpɪtəl/ ADJ occipital

occiput /'ɒksɪpʌt/ N (pl **occiputs** *or* **occipita**) occiput *m*

occlude /ɒ'kluːd/ VT (*all senses*) occlure VI (*Dentistry*) s'emboîter COMP **occluded front** N (*Weather*) front *m* occlus

occlusion /ɒ'kluːʒən/ N (*all senses*) occlusion *f*

occlusive /ɒ'kluːsɪv/ ADJ (*also Ling*) occlusif N (*Phon*) (consonne *f*) occlusive *f*

occult /ɒ'kʌlt/ ADJ occulte N ◆ **the ~** le surnaturel ◆ **to study the ~** étudier les sciences occultes

occultism /'ɒkəltɪzəm/ N occultisme *m*

occultist /ɒ'kʌltɪst/ N occultiste *mf*

occupancy /'ɒkjʊpənsɪ/ N [*of house, hotel, hospital*] occupation *f* ◆ **~ rates** taux *mpl* d'occupation ◆ **they charge 275 euros for double (room) ~** le prix de la chambre est de 275 euros pour deux personnes ◆ **supplements apply on single ~ bookings** un supplément est payable lorsque la réservation est pour une seule personne

occupant /'ɒkjʊpənt/ N [*of house*] occupant(e) *m(f)*, habitant(e) *m(f)* ; (= *tenant*) locataire *mf* ; [*of land, vehicle etc*] occupant(e) *m(f)* ; [*of job, post*] titulaire *mf*

occupation /ˌɒkjʊ'peɪʃən/ N 1 (*NonC*) [*of house etc*] occupation *f* ; (*Jur*) prise *f* de possession ◆ **unfit for ~** impropre à l'habitation ◆ **the house is ready for ~** la maison est prête à être habitée ◆ **we found them already in ~** nous les avons trouvés déjà installés

② *(NonC: Mil, Pol)* occupation *f* ◆ **army of ~** armée *f* d'occupation ◆ **under (military) ~** sous occupation (militaire) ◆ **during the Occupation** pendant *or* sous l'Occupation

③ *(= trade)* métier *m* ; *(= profession)* profession *f* ; *(= work)* emploi *m*, travail *m* ; *(= activity, pastime)* occupation *f*, passe-temps *m inv* ◆ **he is a plumber by ~** il est plombier de son métier ◆ **he needs some ~ for his spare time** il lui faut une occupation *or* de quoi occuper ses loisirs ◆ **his only ~ was helping his father** sa seule occupation était *or* il avait pour seule occupation d'aider son père ◆ **parachuting is a dangerous ~** le parachutisme est un passe-temps dangereux

COMP *[troops]* d'occupation

occupational /ˌɒkjʊ'peɪʃənl/ ADJ *[training, group]* professionnel ; *[disease, accident]* du travail ; *[safety]* au travail ; *[risk]* professionnel, du métier

COMP **occupational hazard** N *[of job]* risque *m* professionnel *or* du métier ; *[of skiing/sailing etc]* risque *m* encouru par ceux qui font du ski/de la voile *etc* ◆ **it's an ~ hazard of** *or* **in this job** c'est un des risques de ce métier

occupational health N santé *f* du travail ◆ **~ health service** *or* **department** service *m* de médecine du travail

occupational medicine N médecine *f* du travail

occupational pension N retraite *f* complémentaire

occupational psychologist N psychologue *mf* du travail

occupational psychology N psychologie *f* du travail

Occupational Safety and Health Administration N *(US)* ≃ inspection *f* du travail

occupational therapist N ergothérapeute *mf*

occupational therapy N ergothérapie *f* ◆ **~ therapy department** service *m* d'ergothérapie

occupationally /ˌɒkjʊ'peɪʃənəlɪ/ ADV *[acquired, received]* dans l'exercice de sa (*or* leur *etc*) profession ◆ **an ~ induced disease** une maladie professionnelle

occupied /'ɒkjʊpaɪd/ ADJ ① *(= inhabited) [house]* habité

② *[toilet, room]* occupé ; *[seat, bed]* occupé, pris

③ *(= busy, active)* occupé ◆ **to keep sb ~** occuper qn ◆ **how do you keep ~ all day?** que faites-vous pour occuper vos journées ? ◆ **to keep one's mind ~** s'occuper l'esprit ◆ **she was fully ~ packing up** elle était tout occupée à faire les bagages

◆ **to be occupied with** *(= doing)* être occupé à ◆ **I was ~ with other things** *(= doing)* j'étais occupé à autre chose ; *(= thinking about)* je pensais à autre chose ◆ **my mind was ~ with other matters** mon esprit était concentré sur autre chose ◆ **he was fully ~ with the children** les enfants l'accaparaient complètement

④ *(Mil)* occupé ◆ **Nazi-~ Budapest** Budapest sous l'occupation nazie ; → **occupy**

COMP **the Occupied Territories** NPL *(in Middle East)* les territoires *mpl* occupés

occupier /'ɒkjʊpaɪəʳ/ N *[of house]* occupant(e) *m(f)*, habitant(e) *m(f)* ; *(= tenant)* locataire *mf* ; *[of land]* occupant(e) *m(f)* ; → **owner**

occupy /'ɒkjʊpaɪ/ VT ① *(= inhabit) [+ house]* résider dans, habiter ; *(= fill) [+ post]* occuper ② *[troops, demonstrators]* occuper ; → **occupied** ③ *(= take up) [+ attention, mind, person, time, space]* occuper ◆ **occupied with the thought of ...** absorbé par la pensée de ... ◆ **to be occupied in** *or* **with doing sth** être occupé à faire qch ◆ **to ~ o.s.** *or* **one's time (with** *or* **by doing sth)** s'occuper (à faire qch) ◆ **how do you ~ your time/your days?** comment occupez-vous votre temps/vos journées ?

occur /ə'kɜːʳ/ VI ① *[event]* se produire, arriver ; *[word]* se rencontrer, se trouver ; *[difficulty, opportunity]* se présenter ; *[change]* s'opérer ; *[disease, error]* se produire, se rencontrer ; *[plant etc]* se trouver ◆ **if a vacancy ~s** au cas où un poste se libérerait ◆ **should a crisis/problem ~** en cas de crise/de problème

② *(= come to mind)* se présenter *or* venir à l'esprit *(to sb* de qn) ◆ **an idea ~red to me** une idée m'est venue à l'esprit ◆ **it ~red to me that he might be wrong** l'idée m'a traversé l'esprit qu'il pouvait avoir tort ◆ **it ~red to me that we could ...** j'ai pensé *or* je me suis dit que nous pourrions ... ◆ **it didn't ~ to him to refuse** il n'a pas eu l'idée de refuser ◆ **the thought would never ~ to me** ça ne me viendrait jamais à l'idée *or* à l'esprit ◆ **did it never ~ to you to ask?** il ne t'est jamais venu à l'esprit de demander ?, tu n'as jamais eu l'idée de demander ?

occurrence /ə'kʌrəns/ N ① *(= event)* événement *m*, circonstance *f* ◆ **an everyday ~** un fait journalier ◆ **terrorist attacks have become a daily ~** les attentats terroristes sont devenus une réalité quotidienne ◆ **this is a common/rare ~** ceci arrive *or* se produit souvent/rarement ◆ **these attacks have become a regular/frequent ~** ces attaques sont devenues courantes/fréquentes ② fait *m* de se produire *or* d'arriver ◆ **chemicals which are used to prevent the ~ of algae** les produits chimiques utilisés pour empêcher l'apparition d'algues ◆ **the greatest ~ of heart disease is in those over 65** c'est chez les plus de 65 ans que l'on trouve *or* observe le plus grand nombre de cas de maladies cardiaques ③ *(Ling)* occurrence *f*

ocean /'əʊʃən/ N *(lit, fig)* océan *m* ◆ **the ~ deeps** les grands fonds *mpl* ◆ **~s of*** énormément de* ◆ **it's a drop in the ~** c'est une goutte d'eau dans la mer

COMP *[climate, region]* océanique ; *[cruise]* sur l'océan

ocean bed N fond(s) *m(pl)* sous-marin(s)

ocean-going ADJ de haute mer ◆ **~-going ship** navire *m* de haute mer

ocean liner N paquebot *m*

the Ocean State N *(US)* Rhode Island

oceanarium /ˌəʊʃə'nɛərɪəm/ N (pl **oceanariums** *or* **oceanaria** /ˌəʊʃə'nɛərɪə/) parc *m* océanographique

Oceania /ˌəʊʃɪ'eɪnɪə/ N Océanie *f*

Oceanian /ˌəʊʃɪ'eɪnɪən/ ADJ océanien N Océanien(ne) *m(f)*

oceanic /ˌəʊʃɪ'ænɪk/ ADJ océanique

COMP **the oceanic feeling** N *(Psych)* le sentiment océanique

oceanic ridge N dorsale *f* océanique

oceanic trench N fosse *f* océanique

oceanographer /ˌəʊʃə'nɒgrəfəʳ/ N océanographe *mf*

oceanographic /ˌəʊʃənə'græfɪk/ ADJ océanographique

oceanography /ˌəʊʃə'nɒgrəfɪ/ N océanographie *f*

ocelot /'əʊsɪlɒt/ N ocelot *m*

och /ɒx/ EXCL *(Scot)* oh !

ochre, ocher *(US)* /'əʊkəʳ/ N *(= substance)* ocre *f* ; *(= colour)* ocre *m*

ochreous /'əʊkrɪəs/ ADJ ocreux

o'clock /ə'klɒk/ ADV ◆ **it is one ~** il est une heure ◆ **it's 4 ~ in the morning** il est 4 heures du matin ◆ **at 5 ~** à 5 heures ◆ **at exactly 9 ~** à 9 heures précises *or* justes ◆ **at 12 ~** *(= midday)* à midi ; *(= midnight)* à minuit ◆ **the 12 ~ train** *(= midday) (gen)* le train de midi ; *(over loudspeaker)* le train de 12 heures ; *(= midnight) (gen)* le train de minuit ; *(over loudspeaker)* le train de o heure ◆ **the 6 ~ (bus/train** *etc*) le bus/train *etc* de 6 heures ◆ **the Nine O'Clock News** le journal de 21 heures ◆ **aircraft approaching at 5 ~** *(direction)* avion à 5 heures ; → **five**

OCR /ˌəʊˌsiː'ɑːʳ/ N *(Comput)* (abbrev of **optical character reader, optical character recognition**) → **optical**

Oct. abbrev of **October**

octagon /'ɒktəgən/ N octogone *m*

octagonal /ɒk'tægənl/ ADJ octogonal

octahedron /'ɒktə'hiːdrən/ N (pl **octahedrons** *or* **octahedra** /'ɒktə'hiːdrə/) octaèdre *m*

octal /'ɒktəl/ N, ADJ *(Comput)* ◆ **~ (notation)** octal *m*

octane /'ɒkteɪn/ N octane *m* ◆ **high-~ petrol** carburant *m* à indice d'octane élevé

COMP d'octane

octane number, octane rating N indice *m* d'octane

octave /'ɒktɪv/ N *(gen, Mus, Rel, Fencing)* octave *f* ; *(Poetry)* huitain *m*

octavo /ɒk'teɪvəʊ/ N (pl **octavos**) in-octavo *m*

octet /ɒk'tet/ N *(Mus)* octuor *m* ; *(Poetry)* huitain *m*

octillion /ɒk'tɪljən/ N *(Brit)* 10^{48} ; *(US)* 10^{27}

October /ɒk'təʊbəʳ/ N octobre *m* ; *for phrases see* **September** COMP **the October Revolution** N *(Russian Hist)* la Révolution d'octobre

octogenarian /ˌɒktəʊdʒɪ'nɛərɪən/ ADJ, N octogénaire *mf*

octopus /'ɒktəpəs/ (pl **octopuses**) N *(= animal)* pieuvre *f* ; *(Culin)* poulpe *m* ; *(Brit: for luggage etc)* pieuvre *f*, fixe-bagages *m inv* COMP *[organization]* ramifié, à ramifications (multiples)

octosyllabic /'ɒktəʊsɪ'læbɪk/ ADJ octosyllabique N octosyllabe *m*, vers *m* octosyllabique

octosyllable /'ɒktəʊ'sɪləbl/ N *(= line)* octosyllabe *m*, vers *m* octosyllabique ; *(= word)* mot *m* octosyllabique

ocular /'ɒkjʊləʳ/ ADJ, N oculaire *m*

oculist /'ɒkjʊlɪst/ N oculiste *mf*

OD ⁑ /əʊ'diː/ (abbrev of **overdose**) N *(lit)* surdose *f*, overdose *f* VI ① *(lit, gen)* faire une overdose ; *(fatally)* mourir d'une surdose *or* d'une overdose ◆ **to ~ on sth** prendre une surdose de qch ② *(fig, hum)* **to ~ on TV** *etc* faire une overdose de télé *etc* ◆ **to ~ on chocolate** forcer* sur le chocolat

odalisque /'əʊdəlɪsk/ N odalisque *f*

odd /ɒd/ ADJ ① *(= strange)* bizarre, étrange ◆ **(how) ~!** bizarre !, étrange ! ◆ **how ~ that we should meet him** comme c'est étrange que nous l'ayons rencontré ◆ **what an ~ thing for him to do!** c'est bizarre qu'il ait fait cela ! ◆ **they have an ~ way of showing their gratitude** ils ont une drôle de façon de montrer leur reconnaissance ◆ **he says/does some very ~ things** il dit/fait de drôles de choses parfois ◆ **the ~ thing about it is ...** ce qui est bizarre *or* étrange à ce sujet c'est ... ◆ **he's got rather ~ lately** il est bizarre depuis quelque temps

② *(Math) [number]* impair

③ *(= extra, left over)* qui reste(nt) ; *(from pair, set) [shoe, sock]* dépareillé ◆ **I've got it all but the ~ penny** il me manque un penny pour avoir le compte ◆ **£5 and some ~ pennies** 5 livres et quelques pennies ◆ **any ~ piece of wood** un morceau de bois quelconque ◆ **an ~ scrap of paper** un bout de papier ◆ **a few ~ bits of paper** deux ou trois bouts de papier ◆ **this is an ~ size that we don't stock** *(Brit)* c'est une taille peu courante que nous n'avons pas (en stock) ◆ **to be the ~ one over** être en surnombre ◆ **the ~ man out, the ~ one out** l'exception *f* ; see also **comp, odds**

④ *(* = and a few more)* **sixty-~** soixante et quelques ◆ **forty-~ years** une quarantaine d'années, quarante et quelques années ◆ **£20-~** 20 et quelques livres, 20 livres et quelques

[5] *(= occasional, not regular)* **in ~ moments he ...** à ses moments perdus, il ... ◆ **at ~ times** de temps en temps ◆ **in ~ corners all over the house** dans les coins et recoins de la maison ◆ **~ jobs** travaux *mpl* divers, petits travaux *mpl* ; see also **comp** ◆ **I did a lot of ~ jobs before becoming an actor** j'ai fait beaucoup de petits boulots* *or* j'ai touché un peu à tout avant d'être acteur ◆ **to do ~ jobs about the house** *(= housework)* faire des travaux domestiques divers ; *(= do-it-yourself)* bricoler dans la maison ◆ **he does ~ jobs around the garden** il fait des petits travaux de jardinage ◆ **I've got one or two ~ jobs for you (to do)** j'ai deux ou trois choses *or* bricoles* à te faire faire ◆ **he has written the ~ article** il a écrit un ou deux articles ◆ **I get the ~ letter from him** de temps en temps je reçois une lettre de lui ◆ **tomorrow will be mainly sunny with the ~ shower** la journée de demain sera ensoleillée avec quelques averses éparses

COMP **odd-jobber, odd-job man** N homme *m* à tout faire

odd-looking ADJ à l'air bizarre

odd lot N *(on Stock Exchange)* lot *m* fractionné *(au nombre de titres inférieur à 100)*

oddball * /ˈɒdbɔːl/ N excentrique *mf* ADJ loufoque, excentrique ; *[humour]* loufoque

oddbod * /ˈɒdbɒd/ N ◆ **he's a bit of an ~** c'est un drôle d'oiseau*

oddity /ˈɒdɪtɪ/ N [1] *(= strangeness)* ⇒ **oddness** [2] *(= odd person)* personne *f* bizarre, excentrique *mf* ; *(= odd thing)* curiosité *f* ; *(= odd trait)* singularité *f* ◆ **he's a bit of an/a real ~** il est un peu/très spécial ◆ **one of the oddities of the situation** un des aspects insolites de la situation

oddly /ˈɒdlɪ/ ADV curieusement, bizarrement ◆ **they sound ~ like the Beatles** leur style ressemble curieusement à celui des Beatles ◆ **an ~ shaped room** une pièce aux formes bizarres ◆ **~ enough ...** chose curieuse ..., curieusement ... ◆ **it was ~ comforting** curieusement *or* bizarrement, c'était réconfortant ◆ **the group's drummer, the ~ named Foxtrot Tango, ...** le percussionniste du groupe, au nom bizarre de Foxtrot Tango, ... ◆ **the skinhead haircut sits ~ with the tweed suit** la coupe skinhead s'accommode mal du costume en tweed ◆ **his attitude sits ~ with his proclaimed liberalism** son attitude détonne par rapport au libéralisme qu'il affiche

oddment /ˈɒdmənt/ N *(Brit Comm)* fin *f* de série ; *(one of a pair or collection)* article *m* dépareillé ; *[of cloth]* coupon *m*

oddness /ˈɒdnɪs/ N *(NonC)* bizarrerie *f*, étrangeté *f*

odds /ɒdz/ NPL [1] *(Betting)* cote *f* ◆ **he gave him ~ of 5 to 1 (for Jupiter)** il lui a donné une cote de 5 contre 1 (sur Jupiter) ◆ **he gave him ~ of 5 to 1 that he would fail his exams** il lui a parié à 5 contre 1 qu'il échouerait à ses examens ◆ **I got good/short/long ~** on m'a donné une bonne/faible/forte cote ◆ **the ~ on** *or* **against a horse** la cote d'un cheval ◆ **the ~ are 7 to 2 against Lucifer** Lucifer est à 7 contre 2, la cote de Lucifer est de 7 contre 2 ◆ **the ~ are 6 to 4 on** la cote est à 4 contre 6 ◆ **the ~ are 6 to 4 against** la cote est à 6 contre 4 ◆ **what ~ will you give me?** quelle est votre cote ? ◆ **the ~ are 10 to 1 that he'll go** il y a 9 chances sur 10 (pour) qu'il y aille ◆ **I'll lay ~ that he gets it right** *or* **on him getting it right** je suis prêt à parier qu'il y arrivera ◆ **over the ~** *(Brit fig)* plus que nécessaire ◆ **I got £30 over the ~ for it** on me l'a payé 30 livres de plus que je ne demandais (*or* ne m'y attendais *etc*)

[2] *(fig = balance of advantage)* chances *fpl* (*for* pour ; *against* contre) avantage *m* ◆ **all the ~ are against you** vous n'avez pratiquement aucune chance d'y arriver, c'est pratiquement perdu d'avance ◆ **the ~ are against his** *or* **him coming** il est pratiquement certain qu'il ne viendra pas, il y a gros à parier qu'il ne viendra pas ◆ **the ~ against another attack are very high** une nouvelle attaque est hautement improbable ◆ **the ~ are on him coming** *or* **that he will come** il y a gros à parier qu'il viendra, il y a de fortes chances (pour) qu'il vienne ◆ **the ~ are even that he will come** il y a cinquante pour cent de chances qu'il vienne ◆ **by all the ~** *(= unquestionably)* sans aucun doute ; *(= judging from past experience)* à en juger par l'expérience, d'après ce que l'on sait

◆ **against + odds** ◆ **against all ~** contre toute attente ◆ **he won against all ~** contre toute attente, il a gagné ◆ **he managed to succeed against overwhelming ~** *or* **against all the ~** il a réussi alors que tout était contre lui ◆ **to fight against heavy** *or* **great ~** avoir affaire à forte partie ◆ **they are struggling against heavy** *or* **great ~ to survive** ils doivent surmonter les pires obstacles pour survivre ◆ **he had to battle against heavy ~ to set up his own company** il a dû se battre contre vents et marées pour monter son entreprise ; → **stack**

[3] *(= difference)* **it makes no ~** cela n'a pas d'importance, ça ne fait rien* ◆ **it makes no ~ to me** ça m'est complètement égal, ça ne me fait rien ◆ **what's the ~?** * qu'est-ce que ça peut bien faire ?

[4] ◆ **to be at ~ (with sb over sth)** être en désaccord (avec qn sur qch) ◆ **to be at ~ with the world** *(= discontented)* en vouloir au monde entier ◆ **to be at ~ with o.s.** être mal dans sa peau ◆ **his pompous tone was at ~ with the vulgar language he used** son ton pompeux ne cadrait pas avec son langage vulgaire ◆ **to set two people at ~** brouiller deux personnes, semer la discorde entre deux personnes

COMP **odds and ends, odds and sods** * NPL *(gen)* des petites choses *fpl* qui restent ; *[of food]* restes *mpl* ◆ **there were a few ~ and ends lying about the house** quelques objets traînaient çà et là dans la maison ◆ **we still have a few ~ and ends to settle** *(fig)* il nous reste encore quelques points à régler

odds-on ADJ *(Racing)* ◆ **~-on favourite** grand favori *m* ◆ **he's the ~-on favourite for the job** c'est le grand favori pour le poste ◆ **it's ~-on that he'll come** il y a toutes les chances qu'il vienne, il y a gros à parier qu'il viendra

ode /əʊd/ N ode *f* (*to* à ; *on* sur)

odious /ˈəʊdɪəs/ ADJ *[person]* détestable, odieux ; *[behaviour, crime]* odieux

odiously /ˈəʊdɪəslɪ/ ADV odieusement

odiousness /ˈəʊdɪəsnɪs/ N *[of person]* caractère *m* détestable *or* odieux ; *[of crime]* caractère *m* odieux

odium /ˈəʊdɪəm/ N *(NonC)* réprobation *f* générale, anathème *m*

odometer /ɒˈdɒmɪtəʳ/ N *(US)* compteur *m* kilométrique

odontological /ɒ,dɒntəˈlɒdʒɪkəl/ ADJ odontologique

odontologist /,ɒdɒnˈtɒlədʒɪst/ N odontologiste *mf*

odontology /,ɒdɒnˈtɒlədʒɪ/ N odontologie *f*

odor /ˈəʊdəʳ/ N *(US)* ⇒ **odour**

odoriferous /,əʊdəˈrɪfərəs/ ADJ odoriférant, parfumé

odorless /ˈəʊdəlɪs/ ADJ *(US)* ⇒ **odourless**

odorous /ˈəʊdərəs/ ADJ *(liter)* *(gen)* odorant ; *(pleasantly)* parfumé

odour, odor *(US)* /ˈəʊdəʳ/ N odeur *f* ; *(pleasant)* odeur *f* (agréable), parfum *m* ; *(unpleasant)* (mauvaise) odeur *f* ; *(fig)* trace *f*, parfum *m* *(liter)* ◆ **to be in good/bad ~ with sb** *(fig)* être/ne pas être en faveur auprès de qn, être bien/mal vu de qn ◆ **~ of sanctity** odeur *f* de sainteté COMP **odour-free** ADJ inodore

odourless, odorless *(US)* /ˈəʊdəlɪs/ ADJ inodore

Odysseus /əˈdiːsɪəs/ N Ulysse *m*

Odyssey /ˈɒdɪsɪ/ N *(Myth)* Odyssée *f* ◆ **odyssey** *(gen)* odyssée *f*

OE N (abbrev of **Old English**) → **old**

OECD /ˈəʊ,iːsiːˈdiː/ N (abbrev of **Organization for Economic Cooperation and Development**) OCDE *f*

oecumenical /,iːkjʊːˈmenɪkəl/ ADJ ⇒ **ecumenical**

oedema /ɪˈdiːmə/ N (pl **oedemata** /ɪˈdiːmətə/) *(Brit)* œdème *m*

Oedipal /ˈiːdɪpəl/ ADJ œdipien

Oedipus /ˈiːdɪpəs/ N Œdipe *m* COMP **Oedipus complex** N *(Psych)* complexe *m* d'Œdipe

OEIC /ɔɪk/ (pl **OEICs**) N *(Brit)* (abbrev of **open-ended investment company**) société *f* d'investissement à capital variable

oenological /,iːnəˈlɒdʒɪkəl/ ADJ œnologique

oenologist /iːˈnɒlədʒɪst/ N œnologue *mf*

oenology /iːˈnɒlədʒɪ/ N œnologie *f*

o'er /ˈəʊəʳ/ *(liter)* ⇒ **over**

oesophagus /iːˈsɒfəgəs/ N ⇒ **esophagus**

oestrogen /ˈiːstrəʊdʒən/ N œstrogène *m*

oestrone /ˈiːstrəʊn/ N œstrone *f*

oestrous /ˈiːstrəs/ ADJ œstral ◆ **~ cycle** cycle *m* œstral

oestrus /ˈiːstrəs/ N œstrus *m*

œuvre /ˈɜːvrə/ N œuvre *f*

of /ɒv,əv/ PREP

> For expressions such as **free of, rid of, to taste of,** look up the other word.

[1] *(possession)* de ◆ **the wife ~ the doctor** la femme du médecin ◆ **a painting ~ the queen's** un tableau de la reine *or* qui appartient à la reine ◆ **a friend ~ ours** (l')un de nos amis, un ami à nous ◆ **that funny nose ~ hers** son drôle de nez, ce drôle de nez qu'elle a ◆ **the tip ~ it is broken** le bout en est cassé

[2] *(objective genitive)* de, pour ; *(subjective)* de ◆ **his love ~ his father** son amour pour son père, l'amour qu'il porte (*or* portait *etc*) à son père ◆ **love ~ money** amour de l'argent ◆ **a painting ~ the queen** un tableau de la reine *or* qui représente la reine ◆ **a leader ~ men** un meneur d'hommes ◆ **writer ~ legal articles** auteur *m* d'articles de droit

[3] *(partitive)* ◆ **the whole ~ the house** toute la maison ◆ **how much ~ this do you want?** combien *or* quelle quantité en voulez-vous ? ◆ **there were six ~ us** nous étions six ◆ **he asked the six ~ us to lunch** il nous a invités tous les six à déjeuner ◆ **~ the ten only one was absent** sur les dix un seul était absent ◆ **he is not one ~ us** il n'est pas des nôtres ◆ **the 2nd ~ June** le 2 juin ◆ **today ~ all days** ce jour entre tous ◆ **you ~ all people ought to know** vous devriez le savoir mieux que personne ◆ **he is the bravest ~ the brave** *(liter)* c'est un brave entre les braves ◆ **he drank ~ the wine** *(liter)* il but du vin

[4] *(concerning, in respect of)* de ◆ **what do you think ~ him?** que pensez-vous de lui ? ◆ **what ~ it?** et alors ?

[5] *(separation in space or time)* de ◆ **south ~ Paris** au sud de Paris ◆ **within a month/a kilometre ~ ...** à moins d'un mois/d'un kilomètre de ... ◆ **a quarter ~ six** *(US)* six heures moins le quart

[6] *(origin)* de ◆ **~ noble birth** de naissance noble ◆ **~ royal origin** d'origine royale ◆ **a book ~ Dante's** un livre de Dante

7 *(cause)* de ◆ **to die ~ hunger** mourir de faim ◆ **because** ~ à cause de ◆ **for fear** ~ de peur de

8 *(material)* de, en ◆ **dress (made) ~ wool** robe *f* en *or* de laine

9 *(descriptive)* de ◆ **a man ~ courage** un homme courageux ◆ **a girl ~ ten** une petite fille de dix ans ◆ **a question ~ no importance** une question sans importance ◆ **the city ~ Paris** la ville de Paris ◆ **town ~ narrow streets** ville *f* aux rues étroites ◆ **fruit ~ his own growing** fruits *mpl* qu'il a cultivés lui-même ◆ **that idiot ~ a doctor** cet imbécile de docteur ◆ **he has a real palace ~ a house** c'est un véritable palais que sa maison

10 *(agent etc)* de ◆ **beloved ~ all** bien-aimé de tous ◆ **it was nasty ~ him to say so** c'était méchant de sa part de dire cela

11 *(in temporal phrases)* ~ **late** depuis quelque temps ◆ **it was often fine of a morning** *(dial)* il faisait souvent beau le matin

Ofcom /'ɒfkɒm/ **N** *(Brit)* (abbrev of **Office of Communications Regulation**) *organe de régulation des télécommunications*

off /ɒf/

1 PREPOSITION
2 ADVERB
3 ADJECTIVE
4 NOUN
5 INTRANSITIVE VERB
6 TRANSITIVE VERB
7 COMPOUNDS

When **off** is the second element in a phrasal verb, eg **get off**, **keep off**, **take off**, look up the verb. When it is part of a set combination, eg **off duty/work**, **far off**, look up the other word.

1 - PREPOSITION

1 = from de

de + le = du, de + les = des.

◆ **he fell/jumped ~ the wall** il est tombé/a sauté du mur ◆ **the orange fell ~ the table** l'orange est tombée de la table ◆ **he cut a piece ~ the steak and gave it to the dog** il a coupé un morceau du steak et l'a donné au chien ◆ **he was balancing on the wall and fell ~ it** il était en équilibre sur le mur et il est tombé

Note the French prepositions used in the following:

◆ **he took the book ~ the table** il a pris le livre sur la table ◆ **we ate ~ paper plates** nous avons mangé dans des assiettes en carton

2 = missing from ◆ **there are two buttons ~ my coat** il manque deux boutons à mon manteau ◆ **the lid was ~ the tin** le couvercle n'était pas sur la boîte

3 = away from de ◆ **the helicopter was just a few metres ~ the ground** l'hélicoptère n'était qu'à quelques mètres du sol ◆ **he ran towards the car and was 5 yards ~ it when …** il a couru vers la voiture et n'en était plus qu'à 5 mètres lorsque … ◆ **we want a house ~ the main road** nous cherchons une maison en retrait de la route principale

4 = near près de ◆ **a flat just ~ the high street** un appartement près de la rue principale ◆ **it's ~ Baker Street** c'est une rue qui donne dans Baker Street, c'est dans une rue perpendiculaire à Baker Street ◆ **a street (leading) ~ the square** une rue qui part de la place

5 Naut au large de ◆ **~ Portland Bill** au large de Portland Bill ◆ **it's ~ the coast of Brittany** c'est au large de la Bretagne

6 * = not taking, avoiding ◆ **I'm ~ coffee at the moment** je ne bois pas de café en ce moment ◆ **I'm ~ smoking** je ne fume plus ◆ **he's ~ drugs** il ne touche plus à la drogue ; see also **go off**

2 - ADVERB

1 = away ◆ **the house is 5km ~** la maison est à 5 km ◆ **the power station is visible from miles ~** la centrale électrique est visible à des kilomètres à la ronde ◆ **my holiday is a week ~** je suis en vacances dans une semaine

◆ **to be off** * *(= going)* partir ◆ **we're ~ to France today** nous partons pour la France aujourd'hui ◆ **they're ~!** *(Sport)* les voilà partis !, ils sont partis ! ◆ **Dave's not here, he's ~ fishing** Dave n'est pas ici, il est parti pêcher *or* il est allé à la pêche ◆ **I must be ~, it's time I was ~** il faut que je file * *or* me sauve * ◆ **be ~ with you !, ~ you go !** va-t-en !, file ! * ◆ **where are you ~ to ?** où allez-vous ? ◆ **I'm ~ fishing** je vais à la pêche ◆ **he's ~ on his favourite subject** le voilà lancé sur son sujet favori

2 as holiday **to take a day ~** prendre un jour de congé ◆ **I've got this afternoon ~** je ne travaille pas cet après-midi ◆ **he gets two days ~ each week** il a deux jours de congé *or* de repos par semaine ◆ **he gets one week ~ a month** il a une semaine de congé par mois

3 = removed ◆ **he had his coat ~** il avait enlevé son manteau ◆ **the lid was ~** le couvercle n'était pas mis ◆ **the handle is ~** *or* **has come ~** la poignée s'est détachée ◆ **there are two buttons ~** il manque deux boutons ◆ **~ with those socks!** enlève ces chaussettes ! ◆ **~ with his head!** qu'on lui coupe *subj* la tête !

4 as reduction ◆ **10% ~** 10% de remise *or* de réduction ◆ **I'll give you 10% ~** je vais vous faire une remise *or* une réduction de 10%

5 * : referring to time

◆ **off and on** par intermittence ◆ **I'm still working as a waitress ~ and on** je travaille toujours comme serveuse par intermittence *or* de temps à autre ◆ **they lived together ~ and on for six years** ils ont vécu six ans ensemble par intermittence

3 - ADJECTIVE

1 = absent from work ◆ **he's ~ sick** il est malade *or* en congé de maladie ◆ **several teachers were ~ sick** plusieurs enseignants étaient malades ◆ **10% of the workforce were ~ sick** 10% des effectifs *or* du personnel étaient absents pour cause de maladie ◆ **he's been ~ for three weeks** cela fait trois semaines qu'il est absent

2 = off duty ◆ **she's ~ at 4 o'clock today** elle termine à 4 heures aujourd'hui ◆ **he's ~ on Tuesdays** il n'est pas là le mardi, il ne travaille pas le mardi

3 = not functioning, connected, flowing *[brake]* desserré ; *[machine, light]* éteint ; *[engine, gas at main, electricity, water]* coupé ; *[tap]* fermé ◆ **make sure the gas is ~** n'oubliez pas de fermer le gaz ◆ **the light/TV/radio is ~** la lumière/la télé/la radio est éteinte ◆ **the switch was in the ~ position** l'interrupteur était en position "arrêt" *or* n'était pas enclenché

4 = cancelled *[meeting, trip, match]* annulé ◆ **the party is ~** la soirée est annulée ◆ **their engagement is ~** ils ont rompu leurs fiançailles ◆ **the lasagne is ~** *(in restaurant)* il n'y a plus de lasagnes

5 Brit = bad *[fish, meat]* avarié ; *[milk]* tourné ; *[butter]* rance ; *[taste]* mauvais

6 indicating wealth, possession ◆ **they are comfortably ~** ils sont aisés ◆ **they are badly ~ (financially)** ils sont dans la gêne ◆ **how are you ~ for time/money/bread?** tu as assez de temps/d'argent/de pain ?

7 = not right

◆ **a bit off** * ◆ **it was a bit ~, him leaving like that** ce n'était pas très bien de sa part de partir comme ça ◆ **that's a bit ~!** ce n'est pas très sympa ! * ◆ **the timing seems a bit ~, seeing that an election is imminent** le moment est mal choisi étant donné l'imminence des élections

8 Brit Sport ⇒ **offside adj 1**

4 - NOUN

* = start ◆ **they're ready for the ~** ils sont prêts à partir ◆ **from the ~** dès le départ

5 - INTRANSITIVE VERB

esp US ‡ = leave ficher le camp *

6 - TRANSITIVE VERB

US ‡ = kill buter ‡, tuer

7 - COMPOUNDS

off air ADV *(TV, Rad)* hors antenne ◆ **to go ~ air** *[broadcast]* rendre l'antenne ; *[station]* cesser d'émettre ◆ **to take sb ~ air** reprendre l'antenne à qn ◆ **to take sth ~ air** arrêter la diffusion de qch

off-air ADJ *(TV, Rad)* hors antenne

off-balance-sheet reserve N *(Fin)* réserve *f* hors bilan

off-beam * **ADJ** *[statement, person]* à côté de la plaque *

off-Broadway ADJ *(US Theat)* d'avant-garde, off

off-camera ADJ (TV, *Cine*) hors champ

off-campus ADJ *(Univ)* en dehors de l'université *or* du campus

off-centre ADJ *(gen)* désaxé, décentré ; *[construction]* en porte-à-faux ; *(fig) [assessment etc]* pas tout à fait exact

off chance N ◆ **I came on the ~ chance of seeing her** je suis venu avec l'espoir de la voir ◆ **he bought it on the ~ chance that it would come in useful** il l'a acheté pour le cas où cela pourrait servir ◆ **I did it on the ~ chance** * je l'ai fait à tout hasard *or* au cas où *

off-colour ADJ *(Brit)* ◆ **he's ~-colour today** il est mal fichu * *or* il n'est pas dans son assiette * aujourd'hui ◆ **an ~-colour** * **story** une histoire osée *or* scabreuse

off day N *(US) (= holiday)* jour *m* de congé ◆ **he was having an ~ day** *(Brit)* il n'était pas en forme ce jour-là, ce n'était pas son jour

off-key *(Mus)* **ADJ** faux (fausse *f*) **ADV** *[sing]* faux

off-label store N *(US)* magasin *m* de (vêtements) dégriffés

off-licence N *(Brit) (= shop)* magasin *m* de vins et spiritueux ; *(= permit)* licence *f (permettant la vente de boissons alcoolisées à emporter)*

off-limits ADJ *(US Mil)* ◆ **~-limits to troops** interdit au personnel militaire

off-line *(Comput)* **ADJ** autonome **ADV** ◆ **to go ~-line** *[computer]* se mettre en mode autonome ◆ **to put the printer ~-line** mettre l'imprimante en mode manuel

off-load VT *[+ goods]* décharger, débarquer ; *[+ passengers]* débarquer ; *[+ task, responsibilities]* se décharger de *(on or onto sb* sur qn)

off-message ADJ ◆ **he was ~-message** ses propos n'étaient pas dans la ligne

off-off-Broadway ADJ *(US Theat)* résolument expérimental ; → OFF-BROADWAY

off-peak ADJ → **off-peak**

off-piste ADJ, ADV *(Ski)* hors-piste

off-putting ADJ *[task]* rebutant ; *[food]* peu ragoûtant ; *[person, manner]* rébarbatif, peu engageant

off-road ADJ *[driving, racing, cycling]* off-road *inv*

off-roader, off-road vehicle N véhicule *m* tout terrain

off-roading N tout-terrain *m*

off-sales N (Brit) (= sales) vente f de boissons alcoolisées (à emporter) ; (= shop) ≃ marchand m de vins ; (= counter) comptoir m des vins et spiritueux

off screen ADV (Cine, TV) dans le privé, hors écran

off-screen ADJ (Cine, TV) hors écran ◆ **an ~-screen romance** une aventure sentimentale à la ville

off-season ADJ hors saison N morte-saison f ◆ **in the ~-season** en morte-saison

off site ADV à l'extérieur du site

off-site ADJ hors site

off-street parking N place f de parking ◆ **a flat with ~-street parking** un appartement avec une place de parking

off-the-cuff ADJ [remark] impromptu ; [speech] impromptu, au pied levé ; see also **cuff**

off-the-job training N → **job noun 1**

off-the-peg, off-the-rack (US) ADJ de confection ; see also **peg, rack**[1]

off-the-record ADJ (= unofficial) officieux ; (= confidential) confidentiel ; see also **record**

off-the-shelf ADJ [goods, item] disponible dans le commerce ADV ◆ **to buy sth ~-the-shelf** acheter qch dans le commerce ; see also **shelf**

off-the-shoulder ADJ [dress] sans bretelles

off-the-wall* ADJ bizarre, dingue*

off-topic* ADJ hors sujet inv

off-white ADJ blanc cassé inv

off year N (US Pol) année sans élections importantes ; see also **offbeat, offhand, offset, offshore**

OFF-BROADWAY

Dans le monde du théâtre new-yorkais, on qualifie de **off-Broadway** les pièces qui ne sont pas montées dans les grandes salles de Broadway. Le terme a d'abord été utilisé dans les années 1950 pour désigner les productions à petit budget d'auteurs d'avant-garde comme Tennessee Williams ou Edward Albee. Les salles **off-Broadway**, généralement assez petites, proposent des billets à des prix raisonnables. Aujourd'hui, les théâtres les plus à l'avant-garde sont appelés **off-off-Broadway**.

offal /ˈɒfəl/ N (NonC) [1] (Culin) abats mpl (de boucherie) [2] (= refuse, rubbish) ordures fpl ; (= waste or by-product) déchets mpl

offbeat /ˈɒfbiːt/ ADJ [1] (* = unusual) [film, book, comedy, approach] original ; [person, behaviour, clothes] excentrique ◆ **his ~ sense of humour** son sens de l'humour cocasse [2] (Mus) à temps faible N (Mus) temps m faible

offcut /ˈɒfkʌt/ N [of fabric] chute f ; [of wood] copeau m ; [of meat, fish] (for human consumption) parures fpl ; (for animals) déchets mpl

offence, offense (US) /əˈfens/ N [1] (Jur) délit m (against contre), infraction f (against à) ; (Rel = sin) offense f, péché m ◆ **it is an ~ to do that** (Jur) il est contraire à la loi or il est illégal de faire cela ◆ **first ~** premier délit m ◆ **further ~** récidive f ◆ **political ~** délit m or crime m politique ◆ **capital ~** crime m capital ◆ **to commit an ~** commettre un délit, commettre une infraction (à la loi) ◆ **~s against national security** atteintes fpl à la sécurité nationale ◆ **he was charged with four ~s of indecent assault** il a été inculpé de quatre attentats à la pudeur ◆ **~ against God** offense f faite à Dieu ◆ **an ~ against common decency** un outrage aux bonnes mœurs ◆ **it is an ~ to the eye** cela choque or offense la vue ; → **indictable**

[2] (NonC = insult) **to give or cause ~ to sb** froisser or offenser qn ◆ **to take ~ (at)** s'offenser (de), s'offusquer (de) ◆ **no ~ taken!** il n'y a pas de mal ! ◆ **no ~ meant or intended (but ...)!** je ne voulais pas vous offenser or froisser (mais ...) ! ◆ **no ~ to the Welsh, of course!** sans vouloir offenser les Gallois, bien sûr !

[3] (NonC) (Mil: as opposed to defence) attaque f ◆ **the ~** (US Sport) les attaquants mpl ; → **weapon**

offend /əˈfend/ VT [+ person] offenser ; [+ ears, eyes] offusquer, choquer ; [+ reason] choquer, heurter ◆ **to be or become ~ed (at)** s'offenser (de), s'offusquer (de) ◆ **she was ~ed by or at my remark** mon observation l'a offensée or vexée ◆ **you mustn't be ~ed or don't be ~ed if I say ...** sans vouloir vous offenser or vous vexer, je dois dire ... ◆ **it ~s my sense of justice** cela va à l'encontre de or cela choque mon sens de la justice

VI [1] (gen) choquer ◆ **scenes that may ~** des scènes qui peuvent choquer

[2] (Jur) commettre un délit or une infraction ◆ **girls are less likely to ~ than boys** les filles ont moins tendance que les garçons à commettre des délits or infractions

► **offend against** VT FUS [+ law, rule] enfreindre, violer ; [+ good taste] offenser ; [+ common sense] être une insulte or un outrage à ◆ **this bill ~s against good sense** ce projet de loi est une insulte au bon sens

offender /əˈfendəʳ/ N [1] (= lawbreaker) délinquant(e) m(f) ; (against traffic regulations etc) contrevenant(e) m(f) ◆ **first ~** (Jur) délinquant(e) m(f) primaire ◆ **previous ~** récidiviste mf ◆ **persistent or habitual ~** récidiviste mf ◆ **sex ~** délinquant m sexuel ◆ **young ~** jeune délinquant m ◆ **carbon dioxide is one of the main environmental ~s** le dioxyde de carbone est l'un des principaux responsables de la dégradation de l'environnement ◆ **small firms are the worst ~s when it comes to ...** les petites entreprises sont les plus coupables quand il s'agit de ... [2] (= insulter) offenseur m ; (= aggressor) agresseur m

offending /əˈfendɪŋ/ ADJ (hum) ◆ **the ~ word/object** etc le mot/l'objet etc incriminé

offense /əˈfens/ N (US) ⇒ **offence**

offensive /əˈfensɪv/ ADJ [1] (= objectionable, insulting) insultant ; (= shocking) choquant ; (= disgusting) repoussant ; (= rude, unpleasant) déplaisant ◆ **she has said some ~ things about the town** elle a tenu des propos insultants sur la ville ◆ **some people found the play horribly ~** certains ont trouvé la pièce terriblement choquante ◆ **~ language** propos mpl choquants, grossièretés fpl ◆ **these are terms I find deeply ~** ce sont des termes que je trouve absolument odieux ◆ **to be ~ to sb** [person] insulter or injurier qn ; [joke] choquer qn ; [remark] offenser qn ◆ **they found his behaviour very or deeply ~** sa conduite les a profondément indignés ◆ **an ~ smell** une odeur repoussante

[2] (Mil, Sport) [action, tactics] offensif ◆ **to take ~ action** passer à l'offensive

N (Mil, Pol, Sport, Comm) offensive f ◆ **to be on the ~** avoir pris l'offensive ◆ **to go on the ~** passer à l'offensive ◆ **to take the ~** prendre l'offensive ◆ **a sales/an advertising ~** une offensive commerciale/publicitaire ◆ **they mounted an ~ on the government** (Pol) ils ont lancé une offensive contre le gouvernement ◆ **a diplomatic ~** une offensive diplomatique ; → **peace**

COMP **offensive weapon** N (Jur) arme f offensive

offensively /əˈfensɪvlɪ/ ADV [1] (= abusively) [behave] de manière offensante ; [shout] de manière injurieuse ◆ **~ rude** d'une impolitesse outrageante ◆ **~ sexist** d'un sexisme offensant ◆ **an ~ anti-German article** un article injurieux contre les Allemands [2] (= unpleasantly) [loud, bland] désagréablement ◆ **to smell ~** sentir (très) mauvais [3] (Mil, Sport) [use, deploy, play] de manière offensive ◆ **to be good/poor ~** (Sport) être bon/mauvais en attaque

offer /ˈɒfəʳ/ LANGUAGE IN USE 19.5

N (gen, Comm) offre f (of de ; for pour ; to do sth de faire qch) proposition f (of de) ; [of marriage] demande f (en mariage) ◆ **to make a peace ~** faire une proposition or offre de paix ◆ **make me an ~!** faites-moi une proposition or offre ! ◆ **I'm open to ~s** je suis ouvert à toute proposition ◆ **it's my best ~** c'est mon dernier mot ◆ **~s over/around £90,000** offres fpl au-dessus/autour de 90 000 livres ◆ **he's had a good ~ for the house** on lui a fait une offre avantageuse or une proposition intéressante pour la maison ◆ **£50 or near(est) or best ~** (in advertisement) 50 livres à débattre ◆ **he made me an ~ I couldn't refuse** (lit, fig) il m'a fait une offre que je ne pouvais pas refuser ◆ **"this week's special offer"** "promotion de la semaine"

◆ **on + offer** (= available) disponible ◆ **this brand is on (special) ~** cette marque est en promotion ◆ **"on offer this week"** "promotion de la semaine"

◆ **under offer** (Brit) ◆ **these premises are under ~** ces locaux ont fait l'objet d'une offre d'achat

VT [1] [+ job, gift, entertainment, food, friendship etc] offrir (to à) ; [+ help, money] proposer (to à), offrir (to à) ; [+ prayer] faire (to à) ◆ **to ~ to do sth** offrir or proposer de faire qch ◆ **he ~ed me a sweet** il m'a offert un bonbon ◆ **she ~ed me her house for the holidays** elle m'a proposé sa maison pour les vacances ◆ **to ~ o.s. for a mission** être volontaire or se proposer pour exécuter une mission ◆ **to have a lot to ~** avoir beaucoup à offrir ◆ **to ~ (sb) one's hand** tendre la main (à qn) ◆ **he ~ed her his hand in marriage** il lui a proposé le mariage ◆ **to ~ a sacrifice** (Rel) offrir un sacrifice, faire l'offrande d'un sacrifice ◆ **to ~ a prayer to God** prier Dieu ◆ **to ~ one's flank to the enemy** (Mil) présenter le flanc à l'ennemi

[2] [+ apology, difficulty, opportunity, view, advantage] offrir, présenter ; [+ remark] suggérer ; [+ opinion] émettre ; [+ facilities, guarantee, protection] offrir ; → **resistance**

VI [opportunity] s'offrir, se présenter

COMP **offer of cover** N (Fin) promesse f de garantie

offer price N (on Stock Exchange) prix m d'émission

► **offer up** VT SEP (liter) [+ prayers] faire ; [+ sacrifice] offrir, faire l'offrande de

offeree /ɒfəˈriː/ N (Jur, Fin) destinataire m de l'offre

offering /ˈɒfərɪŋ/ N (= act, thing offered) offre f ; (= suggestion) suggestion f ; (Rel) offrande f, sacrifice m ; → **burnt, peace, thank**

offeror /ˈɒfərəʳ/ N (Jur, Fin) auteur m de l'offre, offrant m

offertory /ˈɒfətərɪ/ N (Rel) (= part of service) offertoire m, oblation f ; (= collection) quête f

COMP **offertory box** N tronc m

offhand /ɒfˈhænd/ ADJ (also **offhanded**) [1] (= casual) [person, manner] désinvolte, sans-gêne inv ; [tone] désinvolte [2] (= curt) brusque ADV de but en blanc ◆ **I can't say ~** je ne peux pas vous le dire comme ça* ◆ **do you happen to know ~?** est-ce que vous pouvez me le dire de but en blanc ? ◆ **do you know ~ whether ...?** est-ce que vous pouvez me dire de but en blanc or comme ça* si ... ?

offhanded /ɒfˈhændɪd/ ADJ ⇒ **offhand adj**

offhandedly /ɒfˈhændɪdlɪ/ ADV [1] (= casually) avec désinvolture [2] (= curtly) avec brusquerie

offhandedness /ɒfˈhændɪdnɪs/ N [1] (= casualness) désinvolture f, sans-gêne m [2] (= curtness) brusquerie f

office /ˈɒfɪs/ N [1] (= place, room) bureau m ; (= part of organization) service m ◆ **lawyer's ~**

étude *f* de notaire ◆ **doctor's ~** *(US)* cabinet *m* (médical) ◆ **our London ~** notre siège *or* notre bureau de Londres ◆ **the sales ~** le service des ventes ◆ **he works in an ~** il travaille dans un bureau, il est employé de bureau ◆ **the whole ~ went on strike** tous les gens du bureau ont fait grève, tout le bureau a fait grève ◆ **"usual offices"** *(esp Brit) [of house etc]* "sanitaires" ; → **box office, foreign, head, home, newspaper**

2 *(= function)* fonction *f*, charge *f* ; *(= duty)* fonctions *fpl*, devoir *m* ◆ **it is my ~ to ensure ...** *(frm)* j'ai charge d'assurer ..., il m'incombe d'assurer ... ◆ **he performs the ~ of treasurer** il fait fonction de trésorier ◆ **to be in ~, to hold ~** *[mayor, chairman]* être en fonction, occuper sa charge ; *[government, minister]* détenir *or* avoir un portefeuille ; *[political party]* être au pouvoir *or* au gouvernement ◆ **to take** *or* **come into ~** *[chairman, mayor, government, minister]* entrer en fonction, prendre ses fonctions ; *[political party]* arriver au *or* prendre le pouvoir ◆ **he took ~ as prime minister in January** il est entré dans ses fonctions de premier ministre au mois de janvier ◆ **to be out of ~** *[party, politician]* ne plus être au pouvoir ◆ **to go out of ~** *[mayor, chairman, minister]* quitter ses fonctions ; *[political party, government]* perdre le pouvoir ◆ **to seek ~** se présenter aux élections, se porter candidat ◆ **public ~** fonctions *fpl* officielles ◆ **to be in** *or* **hold public ~** occuper des fonctions officielles, être en fonction ◆ **to be disqualified from (holding) public ~** être révoqué ; → **jack, sweep**

3 ◆ **~s** offices *mpl* ◆ **through his good ~s** par ses bons offices ◆ **through the ~s of ...** par l'entremise de ... ◆ **to offer one's good ~s** *(frm)* offrir ses bons offices

4 *(Rel)* office *m* ◆ **Office for the dead** office *m* funèbre *or* des morts ; → **divine[1]**

COMP *[staff, furniture, work]* de bureau
office automation N bureautique *f*
office bearer N *[of club, society]* membre *m* du bureau *or* comité directeur
office block N *(Brit)* immeuble *m* de bureaux
office boy N garçon *m* de bureau
office building N ⇒ **office block**
office holder N ⇒ **office bearer**
office hours NPL heures *fpl* de bureau ◆ **to work ~ hours** avoir des heures de bureau
office job N ◆ **he's got an ~ job** il travaille dans un bureau
office junior N employé(e) *m(f)* de bureau
office manager N chef *m* de bureau
Office of Fair Trading N ≈ Direction *f* générale de la concurrence, de la consommation et de la répression des fraudes
Office of Management and Budget N *(US) organisme chargé de gérer les ministères et de préparer le budget*
office party N fête *f* au bureau
office politics N *(esp pej)* politique *f* interne
office space N ◆ **"office space to let"** "bureaux à louer" ◆ **100m² of ~ space** 100 m^2 de bureaux
office worker N employé(e) *m(f)* de bureau

officer /ˈɒfɪsəʳ/ N 1 *(in armed forces, on ship, plane)* officier *m* ; → **commission, man, petty**

2 *(= official) [of company, institution, organization, club]* membre *m* du bureau *or* comité directeur ◆ **the Committee shall elect its ~s** *(Admin, Jur)* le comité désigne son bureau ◆ **duly authorized ~** *(Jur)* représentant *m* dûment habilité ; → **local**

3 ◆ **police ~** policier *m* ◆ **~ of the law** fonctionnaire *m* de police ◆ **the ~ in charge of the inquiry** l'inspecteur chargé *or* le fonctionnaire de police chargé de l'enquête ◆ **yes ~** *(to policeman)* oui, monsieur l'agent

VT *(Mil)* *(= command)* commander ; *(= provide with officers)* pourvoir d'officiers *or* de cadres

COMP **officer of the day** N *(Mil)* officier *m or* service *m* de jour
officer of the watch N *(on ship)* officier *m* de quart
officers' mess N mess *m* (des officiers)
Officers' Training Corps N *(Brit)* corps *m* volontaire de formation d'officiers

official /əˈfɪʃəl/ ADJ *(gen)* officiel ; *[uniform]* réglementaire ◆ **it's not yet ~** ce n'est pas encore officiel ◆ **~ biography/biographer** biographie *f*/biographe *mf* officiel(le) ◆ **he learned of her death through ~ channels** il a appris sa mort par des sources officielles ◆ **to apply for sth through ~ channels** faire la demande de qch par les voies officielles ◆ **"for official use only"** "réservé à l'administration"

N *(gen, Sport etc = person in authority)* officiel *m* ; *[of civil service]* fonctionnaire *mf* ; *[of railways, post office etc]* employé(e) *m(f)* ◆ **the ~ in charge of ...** le (*or* la) responsable de ... ◆ **information/personnel ~** responsable *mf* de l'information/du personnel ◆ **town hall ~** employé(e) *m(f)* de mairie ◆ **local government ~** ≈ fonctionnaire *mf* (de l'administration locale) ◆ **government ~** fonctionnaire *mf* (de l'Administration) ◆ **an ~ of the Ministry** un représentant officiel du ministère ; → **elect**

COMP **Official Receiver** N *(Brit Fin)* administrateur *m* judiciaire
the Official Secrets Act N *(Brit) loi relative aux secrets d'État*

officialdom /əˈfɪʃəldəm/ N *(NonC)* administration *f*, bureaucratie *f (also pej)*

officialese /əˌfɪʃəˈliːz/ N *(NonC: pej)* jargon *m* administratif

officially /əˈfɪʃəlɪ/ ADV 1 *(= formally)* officiellement, à titre officiel ◆ **"may be opened officially"** *(Post)* "peut être ouvert d'office" 2 *(= theoretically)* en principe ◆ **~, she shares the flat with another girl** en principe, elle partage l'appartement avec une autre fille

officiate /əˈfɪʃɪeɪt/ VI *(= arbitrate: at competition, sports match etc)* arbitrer ; *(Rel)* officier ◆ **to ~ as** remplir *or* exercer les fonctions de ◆ **to ~ at** assister à titre officiel à ◆ **to ~ at a wedding** célébrer un mariage

officious /əˈfɪʃəs/ ADJ *(pej) [person, behaviour, manner]* trop zélé ◆ **to be ~** être trop empressé, faire du zèle

officiously /əˈfɪʃəslɪ/ ADV *(pej)* avec un zèle excessif

officiousness /əˈfɪʃəsnɪs/ N *(pej)* excès *m* de zèle

offing /ˈɒfɪŋ/ N ◆ **in the ~** *(Naut)* au large ; *(fig)* en perspective

off-peak /ɒfˈpiːk/ *(Brit)* ADJ *[period, time]* creux ; *[train, service, journey, electricity]* en période creuse ; *[telephone call]* à tarif réduit *(aux heures creuses)* ◆ **~ rates** *or* **charges** tarif *m* réduit *(aux heures creuses)* ◆ **~ hours** heures *fpl* creuses ◆ **~ ticket** *(Rail etc)* billet *m* au tarif réduit heures creuses ADV *[travel, cost] (outside of rush hour)* en dehors des heures de pointe ; *(outside of holiday season)* en période creuse

offprint /ˈɒfprɪnt/ N *(Typo)* tirage *m or* tiré *m* à part ◆ **I'll send you an ~ of my article** je vous enverrai une copie de mon article

offset /ˈɒfset/ (vb : pret, ptp **offset**) N 1 *(= counterbalancing factor)* compensation *f* ◆ **as an ~ to sth** pour compenser qch

2 *(Typ)* *(= process)* offset *m* ; *(= smudge etc)* maculage *m*

3 *(Bot)* rejeton *m* ; *(in pipe etc)* coude *m*, courbure *f*

VT 1 *(= counteract, compensate for)* compenser ◆ **loans can be ~ against corporation tax** les emprunts peuvent venir en déduction de l'impôt sur les sociétés ◆ **the increase in pay costs was ~ by higher productivity** l'augmentation des coûts salariaux a été compensée par une amélioration de la productivité ◆ **they'll receive a large shipment of food to help ~ winter shortages** ils recevront une importante cargaison de nourriture pour compenser les pénuries de l'hiver

2 *(= weigh up)* **to ~ one factor against another** mettre en balance deux facteurs

3 *(Typ)* *(= print)* imprimer en offset ; *(= smudge)* maculer

COMP **offset lithography** N ⇒ **offset printing**
offset paper N papier *m* offset
offset press N presse *f* offset
offset printing N offset *m*

offshoot /ˈɒfʃuːt/ N 1 *[of plant, tree]* rejeton *m* 2 *[of organization]* ramification *f*, antenne *f* ; *[of company]* filiale *f* ; *[of scheme, discussion, action]* conséquence *f* ◆ **a firm with many ~s** une société aux nombreuses ramifications ◆ **this group is an ~ of a charitable organization** ce groupe est une émanation d'une organisation caritative

offshore /ɒfˈʃɔːʳ/ ADJ 1 *(= out at sea) [rig, platform]* offshore *inv* ; *[drilling, well]* en mer ◆ **Britain's ~ oil industry** l'industrie pétrolière offshore de la Grande-Bretagne ◆ **~ worker** ouvrier *m* travaillant sur une plateforme offshore 2 *(= near land) [reef, island]* proche du littoral ; *[waters]* côtier, proche du littoral ; *[fishing]* côtier 3 *(= from land) [wind, breeze]* de terre 4 *(Fin) [investment, fund, banking, account]* offshore *inv*, extraterritorial ◆ **~ orders** commandes *fpl* d'outre-mer ADV 1 *(= near coast) [lie, anchor, fish]* au large ; *(nearer)* en vue des côtes ◆ **20 miles ~** à 20 milles de la côte 2 *(= away from coast) [sail]* vers le large 3 *(Fin)* ◆ **to invest ~** faire des investissements offshore *or* extraterritoriaux ◆ **to move one's operations ~** se délocaliser

offside /ˈɒfˈsaɪd/ N 1 *(Sport)* hors-jeu *m inv* 2 *(Driving) (in Brit)* côté *m* droit ; *(in France, US etc)* côté *m* gauche ADJ 1 *(Sport)* **to be ~** être hors jeu ◆ **the ~ rule** la règle du hors-jeu 2 *(Driving) (in Brit)* de droite ; *(in France, US etc)* de gauche

offspring /ˈɒfsprɪŋ/ N *(pl inv)* progéniture *f NonC* ; *(fig)* fruit *m*, résultat *m* ◆ **how are your ~?*** comment va votre progéniture ?*, comment vont vos rejetons ?*

offstage /ˈɒfˈsteɪdʒ/ ADV en coulisse, dans les coulisses ◆ **~, she's a different personality altogether** dans la vie, elle a une personnalité complètement différente ADJ *[voices]* en coulisse, dans les coulisses ◆ **his ~ life** sa vie privée

Ofgas /ˈɒfgæs/ N *(Brit) organisme de contrôle des réseaux de distribution du gaz*

Ofgem /ˈɒfdʒem/ N *(Brit)* (abbrev of **Office of Gas and Electricity Markets**) *organe de régulation des compagnies de gaz et d'électricité*

Oflot /ˈɒflɒt/ N *(Brit) organisme de contrôle de la loterie nationale*

Ofsted /ˈɒfsted/ N *(Brit) organisme de contrôle des établissements scolaires*

OFT /ˌəʊefˈtiː/ N *(Brit)* (abbrev of **Office of Fair Trading**) ≈ DGCCRF *f*

oft /ɒft/ ADV *(liter)* maintes fois, souvent ◆ **many a time and ~** maintes et maintes fois

oft- /ɒft/ PREF ◆ **~repeated** souvent répété ◆ **~quoted** souvent cité ◆ **~times** †† souventes fois †

Oftel /ˈɒftel/ N *(Brit) organisme de contrôle des réseaux de télécommunication*

often /ˈɒfən, ˈɒftən/ ADV souvent ◆ **(all) too ~** trop souvent ◆ **it cannot be said too ~ that ...** on ne dira *or* répétera jamais assez que ... ◆ **once too ~** une fois de trop ◆ **every so ~** *(in time)* de temps en temps, de temps à autre ; *(in spacing, distance)* çà et là ◆ **as ~ as he did it** chaque fois *or* toutes les fois qu'il l'a fait ◆ **as ~ as not, more ~ than not** la plupart du temps ◆ **how ~ have I warned you about him?**

combien de fois t'ai-je dit de te méfier de lui ? ◆ **how ~ do the boats leave?** les bateaux partent tous les combien ? ◆ **how ~ she had asked herself that very question!** combien de fois elle s'était justement posé cette question !

Ofwat /'ɒfwɒt/ N (Brit) *organisme de contrôle des réseaux de distribution d'eau*

ogival /əʊ'dʒaɪvəl/ ADJ ogival, en ogive

ogive /'əʊdʒaɪv/ N ogive *f*

ogle * /'əʊgl/ VT reluquer *, lorgner

ogre /'əʊgə^r/ N ogre *m*

ogress /'əʊgrɪs/ N ogresse *f*

OH abbrev of **Ohio**

oh /əʊ/ EXCL [1] oh !, ah ! ◆ **~ dear!** oh là là !, (oh) mon Dieu ! ◆ **~ what a waste of time!** ah, quelle perte de temps ! ◆ **~ for some fresh air!** si seulement on pouvait avoir un peu d'air frais ! ◆ **~ to be in France!** si seulement je pouvais être en France ! ◆ **~ really?** ce n'est pas vrai ! ◆ **he's going with her – ~ is he!** *(neutral)* il y va avec elle – tiens, tiens *or* ah bon ! ; *(surprise)* il y va avec elle – vraiment ! ; *(disapproval)* il y va avec elle – je vois ! ◆ **~ no you don't! – ~ yes I do!** ah mais non ! – ah mais si *or* oh que si ! ◆ **~, just a minute …** euh, une minute … [2] *(cry of pain)* aïe !

Ohio /əʊ'haɪəʊ/ N Ohio *m* ◆ **in ~** dans l'Ohio

ohm /əʊm/ N ohm *m*

OHMS /əʊeɪtʃem'es/ (Brit) (abbrev of **On His** *or* **Her Majesty's Service**) → **majesty**

OHP N (abbrev of **overhead projector**) → **overhead**

oi ‡ /ɔɪ/ EXCL (Brit) hé !

oi(c)k ‡ /ɔɪk/ N (Brit) péquenaud ‡ *m*

oil /ɔɪl/ N [1] *(NonC: Geol, Ind etc)* pétrole *m* ◆ **to find** *or* **strike ~** *(lit)* trouver du pétrole ; *(fig)* trouver le filon ◆ **to pour ~ on troubled waters** ramener le calme ; → **crude**

[2] *(Aut)* huile *f* ◆ **painted in ~s** peint à l'huile ◆ **to paint in ~s** faire de la peinture à l'huile ◆ **an ~ by Picasso** une huile de Picasso

[3] *(for car engine)* huile *f* ◆ **to check the ~** vérifier le niveau d'huile ◆ **to change the ~** faire la vidange

[4] *(Culin, Pharm etc)* huile *f* ◆ **fried in ~** frit à l'huile ◆ **~ and vinegar dressing** vinaigrette *f* ; → **hair, palm², midnight**

[5] *(Austral)* **the good ~** ‡ la vérité vraie

VT *[+ machine]* graisser, lubrifier ◆ **to ~ the wheels** *or* **works** *(fig)* mettre de l'huile dans les rouages ◆ **to be well ~ed** ‡ *(= drunk)* être beurré ‡ ; see also **oiled**

COMP *[industry, shares]* pétrolier ; *[prices, king, magnate, millionaire]* du pétrole

oil-based paint N peinture *f* glycérophtalique *or* à l'huile

oil-burning ADJ *[lamp]* à pétrole, à huile ; *[stove] (paraffin)* à pétrole ; *(fuel oil)* à mazout ; *[boiler]* à mazout

oil change N vidange *f*

oil colour N peinture *f* à l'huile

oil-cooled ADJ à refroidissement par huile

oil deposits NPL gisements *mpl* pétrolifères *or* de pétrole

oil drill N trépan *m*

oil drum N baril *m* de pétrole

oil filter N filtre *m* à huile

oil find N *(Geol)* découverte *f* de pétrole

oil-fired ADJ *[boiler]* à mazout ; *[central heating]* au mazout

oil gauge N jauge *f* de niveau d'huile

oil industry N industrie *f* pétrolière, secteur *m* pétrolier

oil installation N installation *f* pétrolière

oil lamp N lampe *f* à huile *or* à pétrole

oil level N niveau *m* d'huile

oil men NPL pétroliers *mpl*

oil of cloves N essence *f* de girofle

oil paint N peinture *f* à l'huile ; *(Art)* couleur *f* à l'huile

oil painting N *(= picture, occupation)* peinture *f* à l'huile ◆ **she's no ~ painting** * ce n'est vraiment pas une beauté

oil pipeline N oléoduc *m*, pipeline *m*

oil platform N plateforme *f* pétrolière

oil pollution N pollution *f* due aux hydrocarbures

oil pressure N pression *f* d'huile

oil producers, oil-producing countries NPL pays *mpl* producteurs de pétrole

oil refinery N raffinerie *f* (de pétrole)

oil rig N *(on land)* derrick *m* ; *(at sea)* plateforme *f* pétrolière

oil sheik N émir *m* du pétrole

oil slick N *(at sea)* nappe *f* de pétrole ; *(on beach)* marée *f* noire

oil spill N *(on sea, road)* déversement *m* accidentel de pétrole

oil storage tank N *(industrial)* réservoir *m* de stockage de pétrole ; *(for central heating)* cuve *f* à mazout

oil stove N *(paraffin)* poêle *m* à pétrole ; *(fuel oil)* poêle *m* à mazout

oil tank N *(industrial)* réservoir *m* de pétrole ; *(for central heating)* cuve *f* à mazout

oil tanker N *(= ship)* pétrolier *m*, tanker *m* ; *(= truck)* camion-citerne *m* (à pétrole)

oil terminal N port *m* d'arrivée *or* de départ pour le pétrole

oil well N puits *m* de pétrole

oilcake /'ɔɪlkeɪk/ N tourteau *m (pour bétail)*

oilcan /'ɔɪlkæn/ N *(for lubricating)* burette *f* d'huile *or* de graissage ; *(for storage)* bidon *m* d'huile

oilcloth /'ɔɪlklɒθ/ N toile *f* cirée

oiled /ɔɪld/ ADJ [1] *[cloth, paper]* huilé [2] (‡ *= drunk:* also **well oiled**) beurré ‡

oiler /'ɔɪlə^r/ N *(= ship)* pétrolier *m* ; *(= can)* burette *f* à huile *or* de graissage ; *(= person)* graisseur *m* NPL **oilers** *(US = clothes)* ciré *m*

oilfield /'ɔɪlfiːld/ N gisement *m* pétrolifère *or* de pétrole, champ *m* de pétrole

oiliness /'ɔɪlɪnɪs/ N [1] *[of liquid, consistency, stain]* aspect *m* huileux ; *[of cooking, food]* aspect *m* gras ; *(= greasiness) [of skin, hair]* aspect *m* gras [2] *(pej) [of manners, tone etc]* onctuosité *f*

oilpan /'ɔɪlpæn/ N *(US: in car)* carter *m*

oilpaper /'ɔɪlpeɪpə^r/ N papier *m* huilé

oilskin /'ɔɪlskɪn/ N toile *f* cirée NPL **oilskins** *(Brit = clothes)* ciré *m* ADJ en toile cirée

oilstone /'ɔɪlstəʊn/ N pierre *f* à aiguiser *(lubrifiée avec de l'huile)*

oily /'ɔɪlɪ/ ADJ [1] *(= greasy) [skin, hair, food, cooking]* gras (grasse *f*) ; *[hands]* graisseux, gras (grasse *f*) ; *[rag, clothes]* graisseux ; *[stain]* d'huile ; *[liquid, consistency, substance, flavour]* huileux ; *[road]* couvert d'huile ; *[beach]* mazouté [2] *(pej = smarmy) [person, manner, voice, tone]* onctueux, mielleux COMP **oily fish** N *(Culin)* poisson *m* gras

oink /ɔɪŋk/ VI *[pig]* grogner N grognement *m*

ointment /'ɔɪntmənt/ N onguent *m*, pommade *f*

OJ * /'əʊdʒeɪ/ N (US) (abbrev of **orange juice**) → **orange**

OK¹ abbrev of **Oklahoma**

OK² * /'əʊ'keɪ/ (vb : pret, ptp **OK'd**) EXCL d'accord !, OK * *or* O.K. * ! ◆ **~, ~!** *(= don't fuss)* ça va, ça va ! ◆ **~, the next subject on the agenda is …** bon, le point suivant à l'ordre du jour est …

ADJ [1] *(= agreed)* parfait, très bien ; *(= in order)* en règle ; *(on draft etc: as approval)* (lu et) approuvé ◆ **I'm coming too, ~?** je viens aussi, d'accord *or* OK * ? ◆ **leave me alone, ~?** tu me laisses tranquille, compris * *or* OK * ?

[2] *(= acceptable)* **it's ~ by me** *or* **with me!** (je suis) d'accord !, ça me va !, OK ! * ◆ **is it ~ with you if I come too?** ça ne vous ennuie pas si je vous accompagne ? ◆ **this car is ~ but I prefer the other one** cette voiture n'est pas mal mais je préfère l'autre

[3] *(= no problem)* **everything's ~** tout va bien ◆ **it's ~(, it's not your fault)** ce n'est pas grave, ce n'est pas de ta faute ◆ **can I help? – it's ~, I'm sure I'll manage** je peux vous aider ? – ne vous en faites pas, ça va aller ◆ **thanks! – that's ~** merci ! – de rien

[4] *(= undamaged, in good health)* **are you ~?** *(gen)* tu vas bien ? ; *(after accident)* tu n'as rien ? ◆ **I'm ~** *(gen)* je vais bien, ça va (bien) ; *(after accident)* je n'ai rien ◆ **he's ~, he's only bruised** il n'a rien de grave, seulement quelques bleus ◆ **the car is ~** *(= undamaged)* la voiture est intacte *or* n'a rien ; *(= repaired, functioning)* la voiture marche *or* est en bon état

[5] *(= likeable)* **he's ~, he's an ~ guy** c'est un type bien *

[6] *(= well provided for)* **another drink? – no thanks, I'm ~ (for now)** un autre verre ? – non merci, ça va (pour le moment) ◆ **are you ~ for cash/work** *etc*? question argent/travail *etc*, ça va *or* tu n'as pas de problème ?

ADV *(recovering from illness, operation)* ◆ **she's doing ~** elle va bien ◆ **she's doing ~ (for herself)** *(socially, financially, in career)* elle se débrouille *or* se défend bien ◆ **we managed ~ for the first year** nous nous sommes bien débrouillés la première année

VT *[+ document, plan]* approuver ◆ **his doctor wouldn't ~ the trip** son docteur ne voulait pas donner son accord pour le voyage

N *(gen)* ◆ **to give the** *or* **one's ~** donner son accord *(to* à) ◆ **to give the** *or* **one's ~ to a plan** donner le feu vert à un projet ◆ **I'm free to start work as soon as I get the ~** je suis prêt à commencer à travailler dès que j'aurai reçu le feu vert

okapi /əʊ'kɑːpɪ/ N (pl **okapis** *or* **okapi**) okapi *m*

okay * /'əʊ'keɪ/ ⇒ **OK²**

okey-doke(y) ‡ /'əʊkɪ'dəʊk(ɪ)/ EXCL d'ac ! *, OK * !

Okie /'əʊkiː/ N *(US)* travailleur *m* agricole migrant

Okla. abbrev of **Oklahoma**

Oklahoma /əʊklə'həʊmə/ N Oklahoma *m* ◆ **in ~** dans l'Oklahoma

okra /'əʊkrə/ N gombo *m*

ol' * /əʊl/ ADJ *(esp US)* ⇒ **old**

old /əʊld/ ADJ [1] *(= aged, not young)* vieux (vieille *f*), vieil *m before vowel*, âgé ◆ **an ~ man** un vieil homme, un vieillard ◆ **an ~ lady** une vieille dame ◆ **an ~ woman** une vieille femme ◆ **he's a real ~ woman** il a des manies de petite vieille ◆ **a poor ~ man** un pauvre vieillard, un pauvre vieux ◆ **~ people, ~ folk** *, **~ folks** * les personnes *fpl* âgées ; *(disrespectful)* les vieux *mpl* ◆ **the ~er generation** la génération antérieure *or* précédente ◆ **~er people** les personnes *fpl* d'un certain âge ◆ **it will appeal to ~ and young (alike)** cela plaira aux vieux comme aux jeunes, cela plaira à tous les âges ◆ **to have an ~ head on young shoulders** être mûr pour son âge, faire preuve d'une maturité précoce ◆ **~ for his age** *or* **his years** mûr pour son âge ◆ **to be/grow ~ before one's time** être vieux/vieillir avant l'âge ◆ **to grow** *or* **get ~(er)** vieillir ◆ **he's getting ~** il vieillit ◆ **that dress is too ~ for you** cette robe te vieillit, cette robe fait trop vieux pour toi ◆ **~ Mr Smith** le vieux M. Smith ◆ **~ Smith** *, **~ man Smith** ‡ le vieux Smith, le (vieux) père Smith * ; see also **comp** ; → **fogey, Methuselah, ripe, salt**

[2] (*: *as term of affection*) **~ Paul here** ce bon vieux Paul ◆ **he's a good ~ dog** c'est un brave (vieux) chien ◆ **you ~ scoundrel!** sacré vieux !

◆ **I say, ~ man** *or* **~ fellow** *or* **~ chap** *or* **~ boy** † dites donc, mon vieux* ◆ **my** *or* **the ~ man**‡ *(= husband)* le patron* ; *(= father)* le *or* mon paternel‡, le *or* mon vieux‡ ◆ **my** *or* **the ~ woman**‡ *or* **lady**‡ *(= wife)* la patronne‡, ma bourgeoise* ; *(= mother)* la *or* ma mater‡, la *or* ma vieille‡

3 *(of specified age)* **how ~ are you?** quel âge as-tu ? ◆ **he is ten years ~** il a dix ans ◆ **at ten years ~** à (l'âge de) dix ans ◆ **a six-year-~ boy, a boy (of) six years ~** un garçon (âgé) de six ans ◆ **a three-year-~** *(= child)* un(e) enfant de trois ans ; *(= horse)* un cheval de trois ans ◆ **for 10 to 15-year-~s** *(gen)* destiné aux 10-15 ans ◆ **the firm is 80 years ~** la compagnie a 80 ans ◆ **too ~ for that sort of work** trop vieux *or* âgé pour ce genre de travail ◆ **I didn't know he was as ~ as that** je ne savais pas qu'il avait cet âge-là ◆ **if I live to be as ~ as that** si je vis jusqu'à cet âge-là ◆ **when you're ~er** *(to child)* quand tu seras plus grand ◆ **if I were ~er** si j'étais plus âgé ◆ **if I were ten years ~er** si j'avais dix ans de plus ◆ **he is ~er than you** il est plus âgé que toi ◆ **he's six years ~er than you** il a six ans de plus que toi ◆ **~er brother/son** frère *m*/fils *m* aîné ◆ **his ~est son** son fils aîné ◆ **she's the ~est** elle est *or* c'est elle la plus âgée, elle est l'aînée ◆ **he is ~ enough to dress himself** il est assez grand pour s'habiller tout seul ◆ **they are ~ enough to vote** ils sont en âge de voter ◆ **you're ~ enough to know better!** à ton âge tu devrais avoir plus de bon sens ! ◆ **she's ~ enough to be his mother!** elle a l'âge d'être sa mère !, elle pourrait être sa mère !

4 *(= not new)* vieux (vieille *f*), vieil *m before vowel* ; *(with antique value)* ancien *after n* ; *(= of long standing)* vieux (vieille *f*), vieil *m before vowel* ◆ **an ~ building** un vieil immeuble, un immeuble ancien ◆ **~ wine** vin *m* vieux ◆ **the ~ adage** le vieil adage ◆ **that's an ~ one!** *[story, joke]* elle n'est pas nouvelle !, elle est connue ! ; *[trick etc]* ce n'est pas nouveau ! ◆ **the ~ part of Nice** le vieux Nice ◆ **we're ~ friends** nous sommes de vieux amis *or* des amis de longue date ◆ **an ~ family** une vieille famille, une famille de vieille souche ; see also **comp** ; → **Adam, brigade, hand, hill, lag**[3], **school**[1]

5 *(= former) [school, mayor, home]* ancien *before n* ◆ **~ boy** *(Brit Scol)* ancien élève *m* ; see also **comp** ◆ **~ girl** *(Brit Scol)* ancienne élève *f* ◆ **this is the ~ way of doing it** c'est comme ça que l'on faisait autrefois ◆ **~ campaigner** *(Mil)* vétéran *m* ◆ **in the ~ days** dans le temps, autrefois, jadis ◆ **they chatted about ~ times** ils ont causé du passé ◆ **just like ~ times!** comme au bon vieux temps ! ◆ **in the good ~ days** *or* **times** au bon vieux temps ◆ **those were the good ~ days** c'était le bon vieux temps ; see also **comp** ; → **school**[1], **soldier**

6 *(*: as intensifier)* **any ~ how/where** *etc* n'importe comment/où *etc* ◆ **any ~ thing** n'importe quoi ◆ **we had a great ~ time** on s'est vraiment bien amusé ◆ **it's the same ~ story** c'est toujours la même histoire ◆ **it isn't (just) any ~ painting, it's a Rembrandt** ce n'est pas n'importe quel tableau, c'est un Rembrandt

N ◆ **(in days) of ~** autrefois, (au temps) jadis ◆ **the men of ~** les hommes *mpl* du temps jadis ◆ **I know him of ~** je le connais depuis longtemps

NPL **the old** les personnes *fpl* âgées

COMP **old age** N vieillesse *f* ◆ **in his ~ age** dans sa vieillesse, sur ses vieux jours
old age pension N (pension *f* de) retraite *f (de la sécurité sociale)*
old age pensioner N *(Brit)* retraité(e) *m(f)*
Old Bailey N *(Brit Jur) cour d'assises de Londres*
(the) Old Bill‡ N *(Brit)* les poulets‡ *mpl*, la rousse‡
the old boy network* N *(Brit) le réseau de relations des anciens élèves des écoles privées* ◆ **he heard of it through the ~ boy network** il en a entendu parler par ses relations
the old country N la mère patrie
the Old Dominion N *(US)* la Virginie
Old English N *(= language)* vieil anglais *m*
Old English sheepdog N bobtail *m*
old-established ADJ ancien *after n*, établi (depuis longtemps)
old-fashioned ADJ → **old-fashioned**
old folks' home N ⇒ **old people's home**
Old French N *(= language)* ancien *or* vieux français *m*
Old Glory N *(US)* la bannière étoilée *(drapeau des États-Unis)*
old gold ADJ *(= colour)* vieil or *inv*
old guard N → **guard**
old hat N *(fig)* ◆ **that's ~ hat !*** c'est vieux !, c'est dépassé !
old-line ADJ *(Pol etc)* ultraconservateur (-trice *f*), ultratraditionaliste
old-looking ADJ qui a l'air vieux
old maid N *(pej)* vieille fille *f*
old-maidish ADJ *(pej) [habits]* de vieille fille ◆ **she's very ~-maidish** elle fait très vieille fille
Old Man River N *(US)* le Mississippi
old master N *(Art) (= artist)* grand peintre *m*, grand maître *m* (de la peinture) ; *(= painting)* tableau *m* de maître
old money N 1 *(= fortune)* vieilles fortunes *fpl* 2 *(= currency) ancien système monétaire* ◆ **in old money** *(fig)* selon l'ancien système
old people's home N maison *f* de retraite
old school tie N *(Brit) (lit)* cravate *f* aux couleurs de son ancienne école ; *(fig)* réseau *m* des relations ◆ **it's the ~ school tie** *(fig)* c'est l'art de faire marcher ses relations
the Old South N *(US Hist)* le vieux Sud *(d'avant la guerre de Sécession)*
old stager N vétéran *m*, vieux routier *m*
old-style ADJ à l'ancienne (mode)
Old Testament N Ancien Testament *m*
old-time ADJ du temps jadis ; *(older)* ancien *before n* ◆ **~-time dancing** danses *fpl* d'autrefois
old-timer* N *(US)* vieillard *m*, ancien *m* ; *(as term of address)* le vieux, l'ancien *m*
old wives' tale N conte *m* de bonne femme
old-womanish ADJ *(pej) [behaviour, remark]* de petite vieille ◆ **she's very ~-womanish** on dirait vraiment une petite vieille
the Old World N le Vieux *or* l'Ancien Monde *m*
old-world ADJ → **old-world**

olde †† /ˈəʊldɪ/ ADJ d'antan *(liter)*

olden /ˈəʊldən/ ADJ *(liter)* ◆ **~ days** *or* **times** le temps jadis ◆ **the quaint customs of ~ times** les curieuses coutumes d'antan ◆ **in (the) ~ days** dans le temps jadis ◆ **in ~ times** jadis, autrefois

olde-worlde /ˈəʊldɪˈwɜːldɪ/ ADJ *(hum or pej) (genuinely)* vieillot (-otte *f*) ; *(pseudo)* faussement ancien *after n*

old-fashioned /ˈəʊldˈfæʃnd/ ADJ 1 *(= not modern)* démodé ; *(= traditional)* traditionnel ◆ **to look ~** faire vieux jeu ◆ **a good ~ love story** une bonne vieille histoire d'amour ◆ **she is a good ~ kind of teacher** c'est un professeur de la vieille école ◆ **good ~ discipline** la bonne (vieille) discipline d'autrefois ◆ **good ~ home cooking** la bonne (vieille) cuisine à l'ancienne 2 *(= not progressive) [person, attitude, ideas, values, virtues]* vieux jeu *inv*, dépassé 3 *(Brit = disapproving)* ◆ **to give sb an ~ look** † regarder qn de travers N *(US = cocktail)* old-fashioned *m (cocktail à base de whisky)*

oldie* /ˈəʊldɪ/ N *(= film, song)* vieux succès* *m* ; *(= person)* croulant(e)* *m(f)* ; *(= joke)* bonne vieille blague* *f* ; → **golden**

oldish /ˈəʊldɪʃ/ ADJ assez vieux (vieille *f*), assez vieil *m before vowel*

oldster* /ˈəʊldstəʳ/ N *(US)* ancien *m*, vieillard *m*

old-world /ˈəʊldˈwɜːld/ ADJ 1 *(= traditional) [charm, atmosphere]* suranné, désuet (-ète *f*) ; *[village, cottage]* de l'ancien temps ◆ **an ~ interior** un intérieur de style ancien ◆ **Stratford is very ~** Stratford est une ville au charme suranné 2 *(Geog) [country]* du vieux monde *or* continent

OLE /ˈəʊelˈiː/ N *(Comput)* (abbrev of **object linking and embedding**) liaison *f* OLE

ole* /əʊl/ ADJ *(esp US: often hum)* ⇒ **old**

oleaginous /ˌəʊlɪˈædʒɪnəs/ ADJ oléagineux

oleander /ˌəʊlɪˈændəʳ/ N laurier-rose *m*

olefine /ˈəʊlɪfiːn/ N oléfine *f*

oleo* /ˈəʊlɪəʊ/ N *(US)* abbrev of **oleomargarine**

oleomargarine /ˈəʊlɪəʊˈmɑːdʒəriːn/ N *(US)* margarine *f*

olfactory /ɒlˈfæktərɪ/ ADJ olfactif

oligarchic(al) /ˌɒlɪˈɡɑːkɪk(əl)/ ADJ oligarchique

oligarchy /ˈɒlɪɡɑːkɪ/ N oligarchie *f*

Oligocene /ˈɒlɪɡəʊsiːn/ ADJ, N oligocène *m*

oligopoly /ˌɒlɪˈɡɒpəlɪ/ N oligopole *m*

olive /ˈɒlɪv/ N 1 olive *f* ; (also **olive tree**) olivier *m* ; (also **olive wood**) (bois *m* d')olivier *m* ; → **mount** 2 *(= colour)* (vert *m*) olive *m* ADJ (also **olive-coloured**) *[paint, cloth]* (vert) olive *inv* ; *[complexion, skin]* olivâtre
COMP **olive branch** N *(fig)* ◆ **to hold out the ~ branch to sb** tendre à qn le rameau d'olivier
olive drab *(US)* ADJ gris-vert (olive) *inv* N toile *f* de couleur gris-vert (olive) *(utilisée pour les uniformes de l'armée des USA)*
olive-green ADJ (vert) olive *inv* N (vert *m*) olive *m*
olive grove N olivaie *f or* oliveraie *f*
olive oil N huile *f* d'olive

Olympia /əˈlɪmpɪə/ N 1 *(in Greece)* Olympie 2 *(Brit) nom du palais des expositions de Londres*

Olympiad /əʊˈlɪmpɪæd/ N olympiade *f*

Olympian /əʊˈlɪmpɪən/ ADJ *(Myth, fig)* olympien N *(Myth)* dieu *m* de l'Olympe, Olympien *m* ; *(Sport)* athlète *mf* olympique

Olympic /əʊˈlɪmpɪk/ ADJ olympique NPL **the Olympics** les Jeux *mpl* olympiques
COMP **the Olympic flame** N la flamme olympique
the Olympic Games NPL les Jeux *mpl* olympiques
the Olympic torch N le flambeau olympique

Olympus /əʊˈlɪmpəs/ N *(Geog, Myth:* also **Mount Olympus***)* le mont Olympe, l'Olympe *m*

OM /əʊˈem/ *(Brit)* (abbrev of **Order of Merit**) → **order**

Oman /əʊˈmɑːn/ N ◆ **(the Sultanate of) ~** (le Sultanat d')Oman *m*

Omani /əʊˈmɑːnɪ/ N Omanais(e) *m(f)* ADJ omanais

Omar Khayyám /ˈəʊmɑːkaɪˈɑːm/ N Omar Khayam *m*

OMB /əʊemˈbiː/ N *(US)* (abbrev of **Office of Management and Budget**) *organisme chargé de gérer les ministères et de préparer le budget*

ombudsman /ˈɒmbʊdzmən/ N (pl **-men**) médiateur *m*, ombudsman *m (Admin)*, protecteur *m* du citoyen *(Can)*

omega /ˈəʊmɪɡə/ N oméga *m*

omelet(te) /ˈɒmlɪt/ N omelette *f* ◆ **cheese ~(te)** omelette *f* au fromage ◆ **you can't make an ~(te) without breaking eggs** *(Prov)* on ne fait pas d'omelette sans casser des œufs *(Prov)*

omen /ˈəʊmən/ N présage *m*, augure *m* ◆ **it is a good ~ that ...** il est de bon augure *or* c'est un bon présage que ... + *subj* ◆ **of ill** *or* **bad ~** de mauvais augure *or* présage ; → **bird**

omentum /əʊˈmentəm/ N (pl **omenta** /əʊˈmentə/) épiploon *m* ◆ **lesser/greater ~** petit/grand épiploon *m*

ominous /ˈɒmɪnəs/ ADJ *[sign, development, event]* de mauvais augure ; *[warning, tone, look, clouds]* menaçant ; *[sound]* sinistre, inquiétant ◆ **there was an ~ silence** il y eut un silence qui ne présageait rien de bon ◆ **to look/sound ~** ne rien présager de bon

ominously /ˈɒmɪnəslɪ/ ADV *[say]* d'un ton sinistre ; *[loom, creak]* de façon sinistre *or* inquiétante ◆ **he was ~ quiet** son silence ne présageait rien de bon ◆ **this sounded ~ like a declaration of war** ceci ressemblait de façon inquiétante à une déclaration de guerre ◆ **the deadline was drawing ~ close** l'heure limite s'approchait de façon inquiétante ◆ **more ~, the government is talking of reprisals** fait plus inquiétant, le gouvernement parle de représailles

omission /əʊˈmɪʃən/ N *(= thing omitted)* omission *f*, lacune *f* ; *(Typ) (= words omitted)* bourdon *m* ; *(= act of omitting)* omission *f*, oubli *m* ◆ **it was an ~ on my part** c'est un oubli de ma part ; → **sin**

omit /əʊˈmɪt/ VT *(accidentally)* omettre, oublier *(to do sth* de faire qch*)* ; *(deliberately)* omettre, négliger *(to do sth* de faire qch*)* ◆ **to ~ any reference to sth** passer qch sous silence

omnibus /ˈɒmnɪbəs/ N [1] *(† = bus)* omnibus † *m* [2] ⇒ **omnibus edition** [3] *(= book)* recueil *m*
ADJ *[device]* à usage multiple
COMP **omnibus bill** N *(US Pol)* projet *m* de loi fourre-tout
omnibus edition N *(Publishing)* gros recueil *m* ; *(Brit TV, Rad) récapitulation des épisodes de la semaine ou du mois*

omnidirectional /ˌɒmnɪdɪˈrekʃənl/ ADJ omnidirectionnel

omnipotence /ɒmˈnɪpətəns/ N omnipotence *f*, toute-puissance *f*

omnipotent /ɒmˈnɪpətənt/ ADJ *[God, person, figure]* omnipotent ; *[power]* absolu N ◆ **the Omnipotent** le Tout-Puissant

omnipresence /ˈɒmnɪˈprezəns/ N omniprésence *f*

omnipresent /ˈɒmnɪˈprezənt/ ADJ omniprésent

omniscience /ɒmˈnɪsɪəns/ N omniscience *f*

omniscient /ɒmˈnɪsɪənt/ ADJ omniscient

omnivore /ˈɒmnɪvɔːʳ/ N omnivore *m*

omnivorous /ɒmˈnɪvərəs/ ADJ *[animal, person, diet]* omnivore ; *(fig) [reader]* vorace

on /ɒn/

1 ADVERB	3 ADJECTIVE
2 PREPOSITION	4 COMPOUNDS

1 - ADVERB

When **on** is the second element in a phrasal verb, eg **have on**, **get on**, **go on**, look up the verb. When it is part of a set combination, such as **broadside on**, **farther on**, look up the other word.

[1] = in place ◆ **the lid is ~** le couvercle est mis ◆ **it was not ~ properly** ça avait été mal mis ◆ **~ with your pyjamas!** allez, mets ton pyjama !

[2] in time expressions ◆ **from that time ~** à partir de ce moment-là ◆ **it was well ~ in the night** il était tard dans la nuit ◆ **it was well ~ into September** septembre était déjà bien avancé ◆ **early ~ in the pregnancy** au début de la grossesse ◆ **the vital goal came late ~** le but décisif a été marqué en fin de partie

[3] indicating continuation ◆ **let's drive ~ a bit** continuons un peu *(en voiture)* ◆ **if you read ~, you'll see that ...** si tu continues (à lire), tu verras que ...

[4] set structures

♦ **on and off** par intermittence ◆ **I'm still working as a waitress ~ and off** je travaille toujours comme serveuse, par intermittence *or* de temps à autre ◆ **they lived together ~ and off for six years** ils ont vécu six ans ensemble par intermittence

♦ **on and on** ◆ **they talked ~ and ~ for hours** ils n'ont pas arrêté de parler pendant des heures ◆ **the list goes ~ and ~** la liste n'en finit plus

♦ **to be on about sth** * ◆ **I don't know what you're ~ about** *(= talk)* qu'est-ce que tu racontes ? * ; see also **go on**

♦ **to be on at sb** * ◆ **he is always ~ at me** *(= nag)* il est toujours après moi *

♦ **to be on to sb** * *(= speak to)* parler à qn ◆ **he's been ~ to me about the broken window** il m'a parlé du carreau cassé ◆ **I've been ~ to him on the phone** je lui ai parlé *or* je l'ai eu au téléphone ; see also **get on to**

♦ **to be on to sb/sth** * *(= have found out about)* ◆ **the police are ~ to him** la police est sur sa piste ◆ **I'm ~ to something** je suis sur une piste intéressante ◆ **archeologists knew they were ~ to something big** les archéologues savaient qu'ils allaient faire une découverte importante ◆ **she's ~ to the fact that we met yesterday** elle a découvert *or* elle a su que nous nous étions vus hier ◆ **he's ~ to a good thing** il a trouvé le filon *

2 - PREPOSITION

When **on** occurs in a set combination, eg **on the right**, **on occasion**, **on the dole**, **swear on**, **lecture on**, look up the other word.

[1] indicating place, position sur, à ◆ **the pavement** sur le trottoir ◆ **a house ~ the main road** une maison sur la route principale ◆ **he threw it ~ (to) the table** il l'a jeté sur la table ◆ **I have no money ~ me** je n'ai pas d'argent sur moi ◆ **he climbed (up) ~ (to) the wall** il a grimpé sur le mur ◆ **there was mould ~ the bathroom walls** il y avait de la moisissure sur les murs de la salle de bain ◆ **there were posters ~ the wall** il y avait des posters sur le mur *or* au mur ◆ **he hung his jacket ~ the hook** il a suspendu sa veste à la patère ◆ **what page are we ~?** à quelle page sommes-nous ? ◆ **she had sandals ~ her feet** elle avait des sandales aux pieds ◆ **the ring ~ her finger** la bague qu'elle avait au doigt ◆ **the other side of the road** de l'autre côté de la route

on it and **on them**, (when **them** refers to things), are not translated by preposition + noun:

◆ **you can't wear that shirt, there's a stain ~ it** tu ne peux pas porter cette chemise, il y a une tache dessus ◆ **bottles with no labels ~ them** des bouteilles sans étiquette ◆ **envelopes with no stamps ~ them** des enveloppes non affranchies

[2] with name of place ◆ **~ the continent of Europe** sur le continent européen ◆ **~ an island** dans *or* sur une île ◆ **~ the island of ...** à *or* dans *or* sur l'île de ... ◆ **~ Malta** à Malte

[3] with street names dans ◆ **I live ~ Main Street** j'habite (dans) Main Street ◆ **a house ~ North Street** une maison dans North Street

[4] = on board dans ◆ **there were a lot of people ~ the train/bus/plane** il y avait beaucoup de monde dans le train/le bus/l'avion ◆ **~ the boat** dans *or* sur le bateau

♦ **to go/come on the train/bus** ◆ **I went ~ the train/bus** j'ai pris le train/le bus ◆ **he came ~ the train/bus** il est venu en train/bus

[5] = at the time of

♦ **on** + *noun* ◆ **~ my arrival home** à mon arrivée à la maison ◆ **~ the death of his son** à la mort de son fils ◆ **~ my refusal to go away** devant mon refus de partir

♦ **on** + *-ing* ◆ **~ hearing this** en entendant cela ◆ **~ completing the course, she got a job in an office** à la fin de son stage elle a trouvé un emploi dans un bureau

[6] with day, date ◆ **~ Sunday** dimanche ◆ **~ Sundays** le dimanche ◆ **~ 1 December** le 1er décembre ◆ **~ the evening of 3 December** le 3 décembre au soir ◆ **~ or about the 20th** vers le 20 ◆ **~ or before 9 November** le 9 novembre au plus tard ◆ **~ and after the 20th** à partir *or* à dater du 20 ◆ **~ Easter Day** le jour de Pâques

[7] with number, score avec ; *(phone number)* à ◆ **Smith is second ~ 21, but Jones is top ~ 23** Smith est second avec 21, mais Jones le bat avec 23 points ◆ **you can get me ~ 329 3065** tu peux m'appeler au 329 30 65

[8] Rad, TV à ; *(name of channel)* sur ◆ **~ the radio/TV** à la radio/la télé * ◆ **~ the BBC** à la BBC ◆ **~ Radio 3/Channel 4** sur Radio 3/Channel 4 ◆ **you're ~ air** vous êtes en direct *or* à l'antenne

[9] = earning, getting ◆ **he's ~ $50,000 a year** il gagne 50 000 dollars par an ◆ **how much are you ~?** combien gagnez-vous ? ◆ **a student ~ a grant** un boursier *or* une boursière de l'enseignement supérieur

[10] = taking, using ◆ **I'm back ~ cigarettes** je me suis remis à fumer ◆ **to be ~ drugs** se droguer ◆ **he's ~ heroin** il se drogue à l'héroïne ◆ **to be ~ the pill** prendre la pilule ◆ **what is he ~?** ‡ *(rhetorical question)* à quoi il carbure ? ‡ ◆ **the doctor put her ~ antibiotics/Valium** ® le médecin l'a mise sous antibiotiques/Valium ®

[11] = playing ◆ **with Louis Armstrong ~ trumpet** avec Louis Armstrong à la trompette ◆ **he played it ~ the piano** il l'a joué au piano

[12] = about, concerning sur ◆ **a lecture/book ~ medical ethics** un cours/livre sur l'éthique médicale ◆ **an essay ~ this subject** une dissertation sur ce sujet ◆ **a decision ~ this project** une décision sur ce projet ◆ **we've read Jones ~ Marx** nous avons lu ce que Jones a écrit sur Marx ◆ **have you heard him ~ VAT?** vous l'avez entendu parler de la TVA ? ◆ **while we're ~ the subject** pendant que nous y sommes

[13] = doing ◆ **he's ~ a course** il suit un cours ; *(away from office, home)* il fait un stage ◆ **he was away ~ an errand** il était parti faire une course ◆ **I'm ~ a new project** je travaille à *or* sur un nouveau projet

[14] = at the expense of ◆ **we had a drink ~ the house** nous avons bu un verre aux frais du patron *or* de la maison ◆ **this round's ~ me** c'est ma tournée ◆ **the tickets are ~ me** je paie les billets ◆ **it's ~ me** c'est moi qui paie

[15] indicating membership ◆ **to be ~ the team/committee** faire partie de l'équipe/du comité ◆ **he is ~ the "Evening News"** il travaille à l'"Evening News"

3 - ADJECTIVE

[1] = functioning, operative *[machine, engine]* en marche ; *[radio, TV, electrical apparatus, light]* allumé ; *[handbrake]* mis ; *[electricity]* branché ; *[water tap, gas tap, gas main]* ouvert ◆ **leave the tap ~** laisse le robinet ouvert ◆ **is the water ~?** est-ce que l'arrivée d'eau est ouverte ? ◆ **don't leave the lights ~!** ne laisse pas les lumières allumées ◆ **don't leave the lights ~ in the kitchen** ne laisse pas la lumière allumée dans la cuisine ◆ **the gas is still ~** le gaz est toujours allumé ◆ **are you sure the handbrake is ~?** est-ce que tu as bien mis le frein à main ? ◆ **the "on" switch** l'interrupteur *m* ◆ **the switch is in the "on" position** l'interrupteur est enclenché *or* en position "marche"

2 [= taking place] ◆ **there's a marvellous match ~ at Wimbledon at the moment** il y a un très bon match à Wimbledon en ce moment ◆ **while the meeting was** ~ pendant la réunion ◆ **is the party still** ~? est-ce que la fête a bien *or* toujours lieu ? ◆ **the search for a new Tory leader is ~ again** le Parti conservateur est de nouveau en quête d'un leader

3 [= being performed, shown] ◆ **it's ~ in London** *[play]* ça se joue à Londres ; *[film]* ça passe à Londres ◆ **it's ~ for three nights** *[play]* il y a trois représentations ; *[film]* ça passe trois soirs de suite ◆ **it's still** ~ *[play, film]* ça se joue encore, c'est encore à l'affiche ◆ **what's ~?** *(Theat, Cine)* qu'est-ce qu'on joue ? ; *(Rad, TV)* qu'est-ce qu'il y a à la radio/à la télé ? ◆ **"Eastenders"/Clive James is ~ tonight** *(Rad, TV)* il y a "Eastenders"/Clive James ce soir ◆ **you're ~ now!** *(Rad, TV, Theat)* à vous (maintenant) ! ◆ **you're ~ in five minutes** c'est à vous dans cinq minutes

4 [= on duty] ◆ **I'm ~ every Saturday** je travaille tous les samedis ◆ **which doctor is ~ this morning?** qui est le médecin de garde ce matin ? ◆ **she's not ~ till 6 o'clock** elle n'arrive pas avant 6 heures

5 [= available : in restaurant] ◆ **are the chops still ~ ?** il y a encore des côtelettes ?

6 [indicating agreement] ◆ **you're ~ !*** d'accord ! ◆ **are you ~ for dinner over here tonight?** * est-ce que vous pouvez venir dîner ici ce soir ?

◆ **it's not on*** *(Brit)* *(= not acceptable)* c'est inadmissible ; *(= not feasible)* ce n'est pas concevable

◆ **you're not on !*** *(= no way!)* pas question !

4 - COMPOUNDS

on-campus ADJ *(Univ)* sur le campus, à l'université

on-costs NPL *(Brit Comm)* frais *mpl* généraux

on day N * ◆ **he's having an ~ day today !** * c'est son jour aujourd'hui !, il est dans une forme olympique aujourd'hui !

on-glide N *(Phon)* catastase *f*

on-line N ⇒ **online**

on-message ADJ ◆ **she was ~-message** elle était dans la ligne

on-off ADJ ◆ **~-off switch** interrupteur *m* marche-arrêt ◆ **it's an ~-off affair** * *[relationship, plan etc]* c'est une affaire qui évolue en dents de scie

on screen ADV *(Cine, TV, Comput)* à l'écran

on-screen ADJ *(Cine, TV, Comput)* à l'écran ◆ **their ~-screen romance** leur aventure sentimentale à l'écran

on-side * ADJ ◆ **to keep sb ~-side** garder qn de son côté ; → **onside**

on-site ADJ sur place

on-street parking N stationnement *m* dans la rue

on-the-job ADJ → **job noun 1**

onanism /ˈəʊnənɪzəm/ N onanisme *m*

ONC /ˌəʊenˈsiː/ N *(Brit Educ)* (abbrev of **Ordinary National Certificate**) → **ordinary**

once /wʌns/ ADV 1 *(= on one occasion)* une fois ◆ **he walked away without looking back** ~ il est parti sans regarder une seule fois en arrière ◆ **you ~ said you'd never do that** vous avez dit un jour que vous ne le feriez jamais ◆ **only ~, ~ only** une seule fois ; see also **comp** ◆ **he visited them only** ~ il ne leur a rendu visite qu'une seule fois ◆ **~ or twice** une ou deux fois, une fois ou deux ◆ **more than** ~ plus d'une fois ◆ **never ~, not** ~ pas une seule fois ◆ **~ again, ~ more** encore une fois, une fois de plus ◆ **~ before** une fois déjà ◆ **~ a week** tous les huit jours, une fois par semaine ◆ **~ a month, ~ every month** une fois par mois ◆ **~ every fortnight/two days** une fois tous les quinze jours/tous les deux jours ◆ **~ in a while** *or* **way** (une fois) de temps en temps, de temps à autre ◆ **for** ~ pour une fois ◆ **(just) this** ~ juste pour cette fois-ci, (juste) pour une fois ◆ **~ and for all** une fois pour toutes ◆ **~ a thief, always a thief** qui a volé volera ◆ **~ a smoker, always a smoker** qui a été fumeur le restera toute sa vie

2 *(= ever)* jamais ◆ **if ~ you begin to hesitate** si jamais vous commencez à hésiter

3 *(= formerly)* autrefois ◆ **Texas was ~ ruled by Mexico** le Texas était autrefois gouverné par le Mexique ◆ **a ~ powerful nation** une nation autrefois *or* jadis puissante ◆ **~ upon a time there were three little pigs** *(in children's stories)* il était une fois trois petits cochons ◆ **~ upon a time you could be hanged for stealing a sheep** *(historically)* autrefois *or* jadis, on pouvait être pendu pour avoir volé un mouton

4 *(set structure)*

◆ **at once** *(= immediately)* immédiatement ; *(= simultaneously)* en même temps ◆ **all at ~** *(= simultaneously)* tous (toutes *fpl*) en même temps *or* à la fois ; *(= suddenly)* tout à coup, soudain

CONJ une fois que ◆ **~ she'd seen him she left** l'ayant vu *or* après l'avoir vu *or* une fois qu'elle l'eut vu elle s'en alla ◆ **~ you give him the chance** si jamais on lui en donne l'occasion

COMP **once-only** ADJ ◆ **a ~-only offer** une offre unique

once-over* N *(= quick look)* ◆ **to give sb the ~-over** jauger qn d'un coup d'œil ◆ **to give sth the ~-over** vérifier qch très rapidement, jeter un coup d'œil rapide à qch ◆ **I gave the room a quick ~-over with the duster** *(= quick clean)* j'ai donné *or* passé un coup (de chiffon) dans la pièce

oncologist /ɒŋˈkɒlədʒɪst/ N oncologiste *mf*, oncologue *mf*

oncology /ɒŋˈkɒlədʒɪ/ N oncologie *f*

oncoming /ˈɒnkʌmɪŋ/ ADJ *[traffic, vehicle]* venant en sens inverse ; *[headlights, troops]* qui approche (*or* approchait) ; *[winter, night]* qui arrive (*or* arrivait) ; *[danger]* imminent N *[of winter etc]* approche *f*, arrivée *f*

OND /ˌəʊenˈdiː/ N *(Brit Educ)* (abbrev of **Ordinary National Diploma**) → **ordinary**

one /wʌn/ ADJ 1 *(numerical)* un, une ◆ **~ woman out of** *or* **in two** une femme sur deux ◆ **~ or two people** une ou deux personnes ◆ **~ girl was pretty, the other was ugly** une des filles était jolie, l'autre était laide ◆ **~ hundred and twenty** cent vingt ◆ **God is** ~ Dieu est un ◆ **that's ~ way of doing it** c'est une façon (entre autres) de le faire, on peut aussi le faire comme ça ◆ **she is ~ (year old)** elle a un an ◆ **it's ~ o'clock** il est une heure ◆ **for ~ thing I've got no money** d'abord *or* pour commencer je n'ai pas d'argent ◆ **as ~ man** comme un seul homme ◆ **as ~ woman** toutes ensemble ◆ **with ~ voice** d'une seule voix

2 *(indefinite)* un, une ◆ **~ day** un jour ◆ **~ Sunday morning** un (certain) dimanche matin ◆ **~ hot summer afternoon she went ...** par un chaud après-midi d'été elle partit ... ◆ **~ moment she's laughing, the next she's in tears** elle passe facilement du rire aux larmes

3 *(= sole)* un(e) seul(e), unique ◆ **the ~ man who could do it** le seul qui pourrait *or* puisse le faire ◆ **no ~ man could do it** un homme ne pourrait pas le faire (à lui) seul

◆ **one and only** ◆ **my ~ and only pleasure** mon seul et unique plaisir ◆ **the ~ and only Charlie Chaplin!** le seul, l'unique Charlot ! ◆ **my ~ and only*** *(= partner)* ma moitié* *f*

4 *(= same)* (le/la) même ◆ **they all went in the ~ car** ils sont tous partis dans la même voiture ◆ **they are ~ person** ils sont une seule et même personne ◆ **art and life are ~** l'art et la vie ne font qu'un

◆ **one and the same** ◆ **the two methods are ~ and the same** les deux méthodes sont identiques ◆ **to him, scientific and religious knowledge are ~ and the same thing** selon lui, la connaissance scientifique et religieuse ne font qu'une ◆ **they turned out to be ~ and the same (person)** il s'est avéré qu'ils n'étaient qu'une seule et même personne

N 1 *(= numeral)* un(e) *m(f)* ◆ **~, two, three** un(e), deux, trois ◆ **twenty-~** vingt et un ◆ **there are three ~s in her phone number** il y a trois un dans son numéro de téléphone ◆ **~ of them** *(people)* l'un d'eux, l'une d'elles ; *(things)* (l')un(e) ◆ **any ~ of them** *(people)* n'importe lequel d'entre eux, n'importe laquelle d'entre elles ; *(things)* n'importe lequel, n'importe laquelle ◆ **chapter ~** chapitre *m* un ◆ **price of ~** *(Comm)* prix *m* à la pièce ◆ **these items are sold in ~s** ces articles se vendent à la pièce

2 *(phrases)* **I for ~ don't believe it** pour ma part je ne le crois pas ◆ **who doesn't agree? – I for ~!** qui n'est pas d'accord ? – moi par exemple *or* pour commencer ! ◆ **never (a) ~** pas un (seul) ◆ **~ by ~** un à un, un par un ◆ **by** *or* **in ~s and twos** par petits groupes ◆ **~ after the other** l'un après l'autre ◆ **~ and all** tous tant qu'ils étaient, tous sans exception ◆ **it's all ~** c'est tout un ◆ **it's all ~ to me** cela m'est égal *or* indifférent ◆ **~ and sixpence** †† *(Brit)* un shilling et six pence ◆ **he's president and secretary (all) in ~** il est à la fois président et secrétaire ◆ **it's made all in ~** c'est fait d'une seule pièce *or* tout d'une pièce ◆ **to be** *or* **have/go** *or* **get ~ up (on sb)*** avoir/prendre l'avantage (sur qn) ; see also **comp** ◆ **to go ~ better than sb** faire mieux que qn ◆ **he's had ~ too many*** il a bu un coup de trop* ; → **last¹, number, road**

PRON 1 *(indefinite)* un(e) *m(f)* ◆ **would you like ~?** en voulez-vous (un) ? ◆ **have you got ~?** en avez-vous (un) ? ◆ **the problem is ~ of money** c'est une question d'argent ◆ **~ of these days** un de ces jours ◆ **he's ~ of my best friends** c'est un de mes meilleurs amis ◆ **she's ~ of the family** elle fait partie de la famille ◆ **he's ~ of us** il est des nôtres ◆ **the book is ~ which** *or* **that I've never read** c'est un livre que je n'ai jamais lu ◆ **he's a teacher and I want to be ~ too** il est professeur et je veux l'être aussi ◆ **every ~ of the boys/books** tous les garçons/les livres sans exception ◆ **you can't have ~ without the other** on ne peut avoir l'un sans l'autre ◆ **sit in ~ or other of the chairs** asseyez-vous sur l'une des chaises ; → **anyone, no, someone**

2 *(specific)* **this ~** celui-ci, celle-ci ◆ **these ~s** ceux-ci, celles-ci ◆ **that ~** celui-là, celle-là ◆ **those ~s** ceux-là, celles-là ◆ **which ~?** lequel ?, laquelle ? ◆ **which ~s?** lesquels ?, lesquelles ? ◆ **which is the ~ you want?** lequel voulez-vous ? ◆ **the ~ who** *or* **that** celui qui, celle qui ◆ **the ~ whom** *or* **that** celui que, celle que ◆ **the ~ that** *or* **which is lying on the table** celui *or* celle qui se trouve sur la table ◆ **the ~ on the floor** celui *or* celle qui est par terre ◆ **here's my brother's ~*** voici celui *or* celle de mon frère ◆ **he's the ~ with brown hair** c'est celui qui a les cheveux bruns ◆ **he hit her ~ on the nose*** il lui a flanqué un coup sur le nez* ◆ **I want the red ~/the grey ~s** je veux le rouge/les gris ◆ **this grey ~ will do** ce gris-ci fera l'affaire ◆ **mine's a better ~** le mien *or* la mienne est meilleur(e) ◆ **you've taken the wrong ~** vous n'avez pas pris le bon ◆ **that's a difficult ~!** *(= question)* ça c'est difficile ! ; → **eye, quick**

3 *(= person)* **they thought of the absent ~** ils ont pensé à l'absent ◆ **the little ~s** les petits *mpl* ◆ **my dearest ~** mon chéri, ma chérie ◆ **our dear ~s** ceux qui nous sont chers ◆ **~ John Smith** († *or frm*) un certain *or* un nommé John Smith ◆ **he's a clever ~** c'est un malin ◆ **to sing as ~** chanter en chœur ◆ **for ~ who claims to know the language, he ...** pour quelqu'un qui prétend connaître la langue, il ... ◆ **he looked like ~ who had seen a ghost**

il avait l'air de quelqu'un qui aurait vu un fantôme ◆ **to ~ who can read between the lines ...** à celui qui sait lire entre les lignes ... ◆ **he's never** *or* **not ~ to agree to that sort of thing** il n'est pas de ceux qui acceptent ce genre de choses ◆ **he's a great ~ for chess** c'est un mordu * des échecs ◆ **I'm not ~** *or* **much of a ~ * for sweets** je ne suis pas (grand) amateur de bonbons ◆ **you are a ~!** †* tu en as de bonnes ! * ; → **fine²**

4 ◆ **~ another** ⇒ **each other** ; → **each**

5 *(impersonal, subject)* on ; *(object)* vous ◆ **~ must try to remember** on doit *or* il faut se souvenir ◆ **it tires ~ too much** cela vous fatigue trop ◆ **~ likes to see one's friends happy** on aime voir ses amis heureux, on aime que ses amis soient heureux

COMP **one- ...** ADJ d'un/une (seul(e)) ..., à un/une seul(e) ..., à ... unique

one-acter *, **one-act play** N pièce *f* en un acte

one-arm bandit N ⇒ **one-armed bandit**

one-armed ADJ manchot(-ote *f*)

one-armed bandit * N machine *f* à sous, ≃ jackpot *m*

one-day ADJ *[seminar, course]* d'une journée

one-dimensional ADJ *(Math)* unidimensionnel ; *(fig) [character]* d'une pièce, carré ; *[story]* simpliste

one-eyed ADJ *[person]* borgne ; *[animal etc]* qui n'a qu'un œil

one-handed ADJ *[person]* manchot(-ote *f*), qui a une (seule) main ; *[tool]* utilisable d'une (seule) main ADV d'une (seule) main

one-horse place * N bled * *m*, trou * *m*

one-horse race N *(fig)* ◆ **it's a ~-horse race** c'est couru d'avance

one-horse town * N ⇒ **one-horse place**

one-legged ADJ unijambiste

one-line message N message *m* d'une (seule) ligne

one-liner N *(= joke)* bon mot *m* ; *(* = letter)* note *f*, mot *m*

one-man ADJ → **one-man**

one-night stand N *(Theat)* soirée *f or* représentation *f* unique ; *(sex)* liaison *f* sans lendemain

one-off * ADJ, N *(Brit)* → **one-off**

one-one, one-on-one ADJ, ADV *(US)* ⇒ **one-to-one**

one-owner ADJ qui n'a eu qu'un propriétaire

one-parent family N famille *f* monoparentale

one-party system N *(Pol)* système *m* à parti unique

one-piece *(Dress)* ADJ une pièce *inv*, d'une seule pièce N *(gen)* vêtement *m* une pièce ; *(also* **one-piece swimsuit***)* maillot *m* une pièce

one-reeler N *(US Ciné)* court-métrage *m*, film *m* d'une bobine

one-room(ed) apartment N *(US)* ⇒ **one-room(ed) flat**

one-room(ed) flat N *(Brit)* studio *m*, appartement *m* d'une pièce

one-shot * ADJ, N *(US)* ⇒ **one-off**

one-sided ADJ *[decision]* unilatéral ; *[contest, game]* inégal ; *[judgement, account]* partial ; *[bargain, contract]* inéquitable

one-sidedness N *[of account, presentation]* partialité *f* ; *[of bargain]* caractère *m* inéquitable

one-size ADJ taille unique *inv*

one-stop shop N organe *m* unique (centralisé)

one-stop shopping N *concentration des achats sur un seul point de vente*

one-time ADJ ancien *before n*

one-to-one → **one-to-one**

one-track ADJ *(Rail)* à voie unique ◆ **to have a ~-track mind** n'avoir qu'une idée en tête

one-two N 1 *(Boxing)* gauche-droite *m inv* 2 *(Ftbl)* une-deux *m inv* 3 *(in race) arrivée où le gagnant est suivi d'un coéquipier*

one-up * VT *(US)* ◆ **to ~-up sb** marquer un point sur qn

one-upmanship * N *(hum)* art *m* de faire mieux que les autres

one-way ADJ *[street]* à sens unique ; *[traffic]* en sens unique ; *[transaction]* unilatéral ; *[bottle]* non consigné ; *(fig) [friendship, emotion etc]* non partagé ◆ **~-way mirror** miroir *m* ◆ **~-way trip** (voyage *m*) aller *m* ◆ **a ~-way ticket** un aller simple ◆ **it's a ~-way ticket to disaster** * c'est la catastrophe assurée ◆ **she knew the job was a ~-way ticket to nowhere** * elle savait que ce boulot * ne mènerait à rien

one-woman ADJ *[business, office]* que fait marcher une seule femme ◆ **~-woman show** *(Art)* exposition *f* consacrée à une seule artiste ; *(Rad, Theat, TV)* one woman show *m* ◆ **he's a ~-woman man** c'est l'homme d'une seule femme

one-man /ˈwʌnˈmæn/ ADJ 1 *(= solo) [business, company]* individuel ; *[rule, government]* d'une seule personne 2 *(= designed, suitable for one) [canoe]* monoplace ; *[job]* pour une seule personne 3 *(= monogamous)* ◆ **a ~ woman** la femme d'un seul homme

COMP **one-man band** N *(Mus)* homme-orchestre *m* ◆ **the company is a ~ band** * *(fig)* il *(or* elle) fait marcher l'affaire à lui *(or* elle) tout seul *(or* toute seule)

one-man show N *(Rad, Theat, TV)* one man show *m* ; *(Art)* exposition *f* consacrée à un seul artiste ◆ **this company is a ~ show** * *(fig)* il *(or* elle) fait marcher l'affaire à lui *(or* elle) tout seul *(or* toute seule)

oneness /ˈwʌnnɪs/ N unité *f* ; *(= sameness)* identité *f* ; *(= agreement)* accord *m*, entente *f*

one-off * /ˈwʌnɒf/ *(Brit)* ADJ *[object, building, design, situation, show, concert]* unique ; *[meeting, incident]* qui ne se produit *(or* ne s'est produit) qu'une seule fois, exceptionnel ; *[fee]* forfaitaire ; *[grant, payment]* versé en une seule fois ◆ **it was not a ~ event** ça ne s'est pas produit qu'une seule fois, ça n'était pas exceptionnel N ◆ **it's a ~** c'est le seul *(or* la seule) ; *[event]* ça ne va pas se reproduire, c'est exceptionnel ; *[TV programme]* c'est une émission exceptionnelle

onerous /ˈɒnərəs/ ADJ *(frm) [duty, restrictions]* pénible ; *[task]* pénible, lourd ; *[responsibility]* lourd

> ⚠ **onéreux** usually means 'expensive', not **onerous**.

oneself /wʌnˈself/ PRON *(reflexive)* se, soi-même ; *(after prep)* soi(-même) ; *(emphatic)* soi-même ◆ **to hurt ~** se blesser ◆ **to speak to ~** se parler (à soi-même) ◆ **to be sure of ~** être sûr de soi(-même) ◆ **one must do it ~** il faut le faire soi-même ◆ **to have sth (all) to ~** avoir qch pour soi (tout) seul

◆ **(all) by oneself** (tout) seul

one-to-one /wʌntəˈwʌn/, **one-on-one** *(US)* /wʌnɒnˈwʌn/ ADJ 1 *(= involving two people) [conversation]* en tête-à-tête, seul à seul ; *[talks]* en tête-à-tête ; *[training, therapy, counselling]* individuel ◆ **on a ~ basis** *[discuss etc]* seul à seul, en tête-à-tête ◆ **to teach sb on a ~ basis** donner des leçons particulières à qn ◆ **she has a ~ relationship with her pupils** elle connaît bien chacun de ses élèves ◆ **to have a ~ meeting with sb** voir qn en tête-à-tête *or* seul à seul ◆ **a ~ session** *(gen)* une réunion seul à seul *or* en tête-à-tête ; *(Psych)* un face à face ◆ **~ tuition** leçons *fpl* particulières 2 *(= corresponding exactly) [correspondence]* biunivoque ; *[ratio, rate]* de un pour un ADV 1 *(= person-to-person) [talk, discuss]* seul à seul 2 *(= in exact correspondence) [convert]* au taux de un pour un

ongoing /ˈɒngəʊɪŋ/ ADJ *[debate, process, research]* en cours ; *[crisis, situation]* actuel ◆ **they have an ~ relationship** ils ont des relations suivies

onion /ˈʌnjən/ N oignon *m* ◆ **to know one's ~s** †* *(Brit)* connaître son affaire, s'y connaître ; → **cocktail, spring**

COMP *[soup, pie]* à l'oignon ; *[stew]* aux oignons

onion dome N *(Archit)* bulbe *m*

onion johnny N vendeur *m* d'oignons (ambulant)

onion ring N *(Culin) (raw)* rondelle *f* d'oignon ; *(= fritter)* rondelle *f* d'oignon en beignet

onion-shaped ADJ bulbeux

onion skin N pelure *f* d'oignon

online, on-line /ˈɒnlaɪn/ *(Comput)* ADJ *[business, person]* en ligne ◆ **to go on-line** se mettre en mode interactif ◆ **to put the printer on-line** connecter l'imprimante ADV en ligne

onlooker /ˈɒnlʊkəʳ/ N ◆ **the ~s** *(gen)* les spectateurs *mpl*, l'assistance *f* ; *(after accident)* les badauds *mpl*

only /ˈəʊnlɪ/ ADJ seul, unique ◆ **~ child** enfant *mf* unique ◆ **you're the ~ one to think of that** vous êtes le seul à y avoir pensé, vous seul y avez pensé ◆ **I'm tired! – you're not the ~ one!** * je suis fatigué ! – vous n'êtes pas le seul *or* il n'y a pas que vous ! ◆ **it's the ~ one left** c'est le seul qui reste *subj* ◆ **he is not the ~ one here** il n'est pas le seul ici, il n'y a pas que lui ici ◆ **the ~ book he has** le seul livre qu'il ait ◆ **his ~ friend was his dog** son chien était son seul ami ◆ **his ~ answer was to sigh deeply** pour toute réponse il a poussé un profond soupir ◆ **your ~ hope is to find another one** votre unique espoir est d'en trouver un autre ◆ **the ~ thing is that it's too late** seulement *or* malheureusement il est trop tard ◆ **that's the ~ way to do it** c'est la seule façon de le faire, on ne peut pas le faire autrement ; → **one, pebble**

ADV 1 seulement, ne ... que ◆ **he's ~ ten** il n'a que dix ans ◆ **there are ~ two people who know that** il n'y a que deux personnes qui savent *or* sachent cela ◆ **~ Paul can come** Paul seul peut venir, il n'y a que Paul qui puisse venir ◆ **~ time will tell** c'est l'avenir qui le dira ◆ **I'm ~ the secretary** je ne suis que le secrétaire ◆ **a ticket for one person ~** un billet pour une seule personne ◆ **"ladies only"** "réservé aux dames" ◆ **he can ~ wait** il ne peut qu'attendre ◆ **God ~ knows!** Dieu seul le sait ! ◆ **I can ~ say how sorry I am** tout ce que je peux dire c'est combien je suis désolé ◆ **that ~ makes matters worse** cela ne fait qu'aggraver les choses ◆ **I will ~ say that ...** je me bornerai à dire *or* je dirai simplement que ... ◆ **it will ~ take a minute** ça ne prendra qu'une minute ◆ **I ~ looked at it** je n'ai fait que le regarder ◆ **you ~ have to ask** vous n'avez qu'à demander ◆ **~ think of the situation!** imaginez un peu la situation ! ◆ **~ to think of it** rien que d'y penser ◆ **it's ~ that I thought he might ...** c'est que je pensais qu'il pourrait ...

2 *(phrases)* ◆ **he was ~ too pleased to come** il n'a été que trop content de venir, il ne demandait pas mieux que de venir ◆ **it's ~ too true** ce n'est que trop vrai ◆ **not ~ ... but also ...** non seulement ... mais aussi ... ◆ **not ~ does it look good, it also saves you money** non seulement c'est beau, mais en plus ça vous permet de faire des économies ◆ **~ yesterday** hier encore, pas plus tard qu'hier ◆ **it seems like ~ yesterday** il semble que c'était hier

◆ **only just** ◆ **he has ~ just arrived** il vient tout juste d'arriver ◆ **but I've ~ just bought it!** mais je viens seulement de l'acheter ! ◆ **I caught the train but ~ just** j'ai eu le train mais (c'était) de justesse

CONJ seulement, mais ◆ **I would buy it, ~ it's too dear** je l'achèterais bien, seulement *or* mais il est trop cher ◆ **he would come too, ~ he's ill** il viendrait bien aussi, si ce n'est qu'il est malade *or* seulement il est malade ◆ **if ~** si seulement ◆ **~ if** seulement si

ONO /əʊenˈəʊ/ (abbrev of **or near(est) offer**) à déb., à débattre ; see also **offer**

onomasiology /ˌɒnəʊˌmeɪsɪˈɒlədʒɪ/ N 1 *(Ling)* onomasiologie *f* 2 ⇒ **onomastics**

onomastic /ˌɒnəʊˈmæstɪk/ ADJ onomastique

onomastics /ɒnəˈmæstɪks/ N (NonC) onomastique f

onomatopoeia /ˌɒnəʊmætəʊˈpiːə/ N onomatopée f

onomatopoeic /ˌɒnəʊmætəʊˈpiːɪk/, **onomatopoetic** /ˌɒnəʊmætəʊpəʊˈetɪk/ ADJ onomatopéique

onrush /ˈɒnrʌʃ/ N *[of people]* ruée f ; *[of water]* torrent m

onrushing /ˈɒnˌrʌʃɪŋ/ ADJ *[vehicle]* qui arrive à toute allure ; *[water]* qui arrive à flots

onset /ˈɒnset/ N [1] *(= attack)* attaque f, assaut m [2] *(= beginning)* *[of illness, winter etc]* début m, commencement m ◆ **at the ~** d'emblée

onshore /ˈɒnˈʃɔːʳ/ ADJ [1] *(= towards land)* *[wind, breeze]* de mer, du large [2] *(= on, near land)* *[oilfield, facilities, job, work]* à terre ADV (also **on shore**) [1] *(= towards land)* ◆ **to wash up ~** être rejeté sur le rivage ◆ **the wind was blowing ~** le vent venait du large [2] *(= on land)* *[build, work]* à terre

onside /ɒnˈsaɪd/ ADJ *(Ftbl etc)* ◆ **to be ~** ne pas être hors jeu

onslaught /ˈɒnslɔːt/ N attaque f ◆ **their relentless ~ against the government's plans** leurs attaques implacables contre les projets du gouvernement ◆ **the constant ~ of adverts on TV** le matraquage publicitaire constant à la télé

onstage /ˈɒnsteɪdʒ/ *(Theat)* ADV en scène ADJ ◆ **her ~ presence** sa présence en scène

Ont. abbrev of **Ontario**

Ontario /ɒnˈteərɪəʊ/ N Ontario m ◆ **Lake ~** lac m Ontario

onto /ˈɒntʊ/ PREP ⇒ **on to** ; → **on adv 4**

ontogenesis /ˌɒntəˈdʒenɪsɪs/ N ontogenèse f

ontogeny /ɒnˈtɒdʒənɪ/ N ontogénie f

ontological /ˌɒntəˈlɒdʒɪkəl/ ADJ ontologique

ontology /ɒnˈtɒlədʒɪ/ N ontologie f

onus /ˈəʊnəs/ N (pl **onuses**) *(= responsibility)* responsabilité f ; *(= duty)* charge f ◆ **the ~ of proof rests with him** la charge de la preuve lui incombe ◆ **the ~ is on him to do it** il lui incombe de le faire ◆ **the ~ is on the manufacturers** c'est la responsabilité des fabricants

onward /ˈɒnwəd/ ADJ [1] *(Transport, Comm)* ◆ **~ flight** or **connection** correspondance f ◆ **"British Airways would like to wish you a safe onward journey"** "British Airways vous souhaite de poursuivre agréablement votre voyage" ◆ **a flight to Mykonos, with an ~ boat journey to Paros** un vol jusqu'à Mykonos suivi d'une traversée en bateau jusqu'à Paros ◆ **goods delivered to Staverton for ~ movement by rail** des marchandises livrées à Staverton d'où elles seront transportées par chemin de fer [2] *(= developing)* ◆ **~ progress** avancée f ◆ **the ~ march of sth** la marche en avant de qch ADV *(esp Brit)* ⇒ **onwards**

onwards /ˈɒnwədz/ ADV [1] *(in direction)* ◆ **to continue** (or **walk** or **sail** *etc*) **~** avancer ◆ **to journey ~** poursuivre son voyage ◆ **~!** en avant ! [2] *(in development)* **to move ~** aller de l'avant ◆ **the plot moves breathlessly ~** l'intrigue se déroule à un rythme haletant [3] *(in time)* ◆ **from then ~, from that time ~** depuis, depuis lors ◆ **from now ~** désormais, dorénavant ◆ **from today ~** à partir d'aujourd'hui ◆ **from Saturday/September/1960 ~** à partir de samedi/septembre/1960

onyx /ˈɒnɪks/ N onyx m COMP en onyx, d'onyx

oodles ‡ /ˈuːdlz/ NPL un tas *, des masses * fpl ◆ **~ of** un tas * de, des masses * de

ooh * /uː/ EXCL oh ! VI ◆ **to ~ and aah** pousser des oh ! et des ah !

oohing * /ˈuːɪŋ/ N ◆ **there was a lot of ~ and aahing** on entendait fuser des oh ! et des ah !

oolite /ˈəʊəlaɪt/ N oolithe m

oolitic /ˌəʊəˈlɪtɪk/ ADJ oolithique

oompah /ˈuːmpɑː/ N flonflon m

oomph ‡ /ʊmf/ N *(= energy)* punch * m, dynamisme m ◆ **a pill designed to put the ~ back into your sex life** un médicament conçu pour redonner du tonus à votre vie sexuelle

oophorectomy /ˌəʊəfəˈrektəmɪ/ N ovariectomie f

oophoritis /ˌəʊəfəˈraɪtɪs/ N ovarite f

oops * /ʊps/ EXCL houp ! ◆ **~-a-daisy!** hop-là !

oosphere /ˈəʊəsfɪəʳ/ N oosphère f

oospore /ˈəʊəspɔːʳ/ N oospore f

ooze /uːz/ N vase f, limon m VI *[water, pus, walls etc]* suinter ; *[resin, gum]* exsuder ◆ **she was oozing with confidence** elle débordait d'assurance VT ◆ **his wounds ~d pus** le pus suintait de ses blessures ◆ **she was oozing charm/complacency** *(pej)* le charme/la suffisance lui sortait par tous les pores

► **ooze away** VI *[liquids]* s'en aller, suinter ; *[strength, courage, enthusiasm]* disparaître, se dérober ◆ **his strength** *etc* **was oozing away** ses forces *etc* l'abandonnaient

► **ooze out** VI *[liquids]* sortir, suinter

op[1] * /ɒp/ N *(Med, Mil)* abbrev of **operation noun 2, 3**

op[2] /ɒp/ ADJ *(in compounds)* ◆ **~ art** op art m ◆ **~ artist** artiste mf op art

op. (abbrev of **opus**) op

opacity /əʊˈpæsɪtɪ/ N *[of material]* opacité f ; *[of meaning etc]* obscurité f

opal /ˈəʊpəl/ N opale f COMP *[ring, necklace]* d'opale ; (also **opal-coloured**) opalin

opalescence /ˌəʊpəˈlesns/ N opalescence f

opalescent /ˌəʊpəˈlesnt/ ADJ *(liter)* *[light, sky, glass, colour]* opalescent *(liter)* ; *[eyes]* d'opale

opaque /əʊˈpeɪk/ ADJ *[glass, liquid, darkness, language]* opaque ; *[plan, intention]* obscur ◆ **black tights/stockings** collants mpl/bas mpl noirs opaques COMP **opaque projector** N *(US Opt)* épiscope m

op. cit. /ˈɒpˈsɪt/ (abbrev of **opere citato**) op. cit.

OPEC /ˈəʊpek/ N (abbrev of **Organization of Petroleum-Exporting Countries**) OPEP f

Op-Ed /ˈɒpˈed/ N, ADJ *(US Press)* (abbrev of **opposite editorial**) ◆ **~ (page)** *page contenant les chroniques et commentaires (en face des éditoriaux)*

open /ˈəʊpən/ ADJ [1] *(= not closed)* *[shop, road, door, box, bottle, book, shirt, grave, wound, eye]* ouvert ◆ **the shops are ~** les magasins sont ouverts ◆ **the house is not ~ to visitors** la maison n'est pas ouverte au public ◆ **to welcome sb/sth with ~ arms** accueillir qn/qch à bras ouverts ◆ **the door was slightly ~** la porte était entrouverte or entrebâillée ◆ **the window flew ~** la fenêtre s'ouvrit brusquement ◆ **he is an ~ book** c'est un homme transparent, on lit en lui comme dans un livre ouvert ; see also **comp** ; → **break, cut, eye, mouth, throw**

[2] *[river, water, canal]* ouvert à la navigation ; *[road]* dégagé ; *[pipe]* ouvert ; *[pores]* dilaté ◆ **the way to Paris lay ~** la route de Paris était libre ◆ **the ~ air** le plein air ◆ **in the ~ air** *[eat]* en plein air ; *[live, walk]* au grand air ; *[sleep]* à la belle étoile ; see also **comp** ◆ **the ~ sea** la haute mer, le large ◆ **on the ~ sea(s)** en haute mer, au large ◆ **in ~ country** en rase campagne ; *(outside of town)* à la campagne ◆ **when you reach ~ country** or **~ ground** *(Mil)* quand vous arriverez en rase campagne ◆ **patch of ~ ground** *(between trees)* clairière f ◆ **beyond the woods there were ~ fields** au-delà des bois, il y avait des champs ◆ **the speed permitted on the ~ road** la vitesse autorisée en dehors des agglomérations ◆ **an ~ space for public use** un espace vert à l'usage du public ◆ **the (wide) ~ spaces** les grands espaces mpl ◆ **~ view** or **aspect** vue f dégagée ◆ **have your bowels been ~ this morning?** est-ce que vous êtes allé à la selle ce matin ?

[3] *(= not enclosed)* *[car, carriage]* découvert ; *[boat]* non ponté ; *[drain, sewer]* à ciel ouvert ◆ **~ market** *(in town)* marché m en plein air ; see also **comp**

[4] *(= unrestricted)* *[meeting, trial, discussion]* public (-ique f) ; *[economy, city]* ouvert ◆ **in ~ court** *(Jur)* en audience publique ◆ **to keep ~ house** tenir table ouverte ◆ **we had an ~ invitation (to visit anytime)** on nous avait invités à venir quand nous voulions ◆ **~ tournament** *(Sport)* tournoi m open ◆ **jobs are advertised and filled by ~ competition** le recrutement se fait par voie de presse

[5] *(= exposed)* ouvert ◆ **(wide) ~ to the winds/the elements** ouvert à tous les vents/aux quatre vents

[6] *(fig: to advice, question etc)* ◆ **I'm ~ to advice** je suis ouvert à toutes les suggestions ◆ **it is ~ to doubt whether** ... on peut douter que ... + *subj* ◆ **it is ~ to question or debate if** or **whether** ... (il) reste à savoir si ... ; see also **abuse, attack, correction, criticism, lay**[1]**, offer, persuasion**

[7] *(= available)* *[post, job]* vacant ◆ **this post is still ~** ce poste est encore vacant ◆ **the offer is still ~** cette proposition tient toujours ◆ **the number of jobs ~ to women is limited** le nombre de postes ouverts aux femmes or auxquels les femmes peuvent postuler est limité ◆ **membership is not ~ to women** l'adhésion n'est pas ouverte aux femmes, les femmes ne peuvent pas être membres ◆ **the course is not ~ to men** les hommes ne sont pas acceptés dans ce cours ◆ **it is ~ to you to refuse** libre à vous de refuser ◆ **several methods/choices were ~ to them** plusieurs méthodes/choix s'offraient or se présentaient à eux

[8] *(= frank)* *[person, character, face, manner, hostility]* ouvert ; *(= declared)* *[admiration, envy, attempt]* non dissimulé ◆ **in ~ revolt (against)** en rébellion ouverte (contre) ◆ **I'm going to be completely ~ with you** je vais être tout à fait franc avec vous ◆ **you're not being very ~ with me** tu me caches quelque chose

[9] *(= undecided)* ◆ **they left the matter ~** ils n'ont pas tranché la question, ils ont laissé la question en suspens ◆ **let's leave the date/arrangements ~** attendons avant de fixer une date/avant de prendre ces dispositions ◆ **to keep an ~ mind on sth** réserver son jugement or son opinion sur qch ◆ **I've got an ~ mind about it** je n'ai pas encore formé d'opinion à ce sujet ; see also **comp** ◆ **it's an ~ question whether he will come** (il) reste à voir s'il viendra ◆ **how effective those sanctions are is an ~ question** (il) reste à voir si ces sanctions seront vraiment efficaces ◆ **the legality of these sales is still an ~ question** la légalité de ces ventes n'a pas encore été clairement établie ; → **option**

N [1] *(outside)* ◆ **(out) in the ~** *(= out of doors)* dehors, en plein air ; *(= in the country)* au grand air ; *(= not secretly)* au grand jour ◆ **to sleep (out) in the ~** dormir à la belle étoile ◆ **why can't we do it out in the ~?** *(= not secretly)* pourquoi ne pouvons-nous pas le faire ouvertement ? ◆ **that swindle is now in the ~** cette escroquerie est maintenant sur la place publique ◆ **to come out into the ~** *[fact]* apparaître au grand jour ; *[scandal]* éclater au grand jour ◆ **to come out into the ~ about sth** *[person]* s'exprimer au grand jour sur qch ◆ **he came (out) into the ~ about what had been going on** il s'est exprimé au grand jour sur ce qui s'était passé ◆ **why don't you come into the ~**

about it? pourquoi ne le dites-vous pas ouvertement ? ◆ **to bring a dispute (out) into the ~** révéler des différends au grand jour

2 *(Golf, Tennis)* **the Open** l'open *m*, le tournoi open ◆ **the French Open** (le tournoi de) Roland Garros ◆ **the California Open** l'Open *m* de Californie

VT 1 *(gen)* ouvrir ; *[+ pores]* dilater ; *[+ wound]* (r)ouvrir ; *[+ legs]* écarter ◆ **it ~s the way for new discoveries** cela ouvre la voie à de nouvelles découvertes ◆ **he ~ed his heart to me** il m'a ouvert son cœur ◆ **to ~ sb's mind (to sth)** ouvrir l'esprit de qn (à qch) ◆ **have you ~ed your bowels?** êtes-vous allé à la selle ? ◆ **to ~ wide** ouvrir grand ◆ **~ wide!** *(mouth)* ouvrez grand ! ◆ **to ~ slightly** *(door, window, eyes)* entrouvrir ◆ **to ~ again** rouvrir ; → **eye, mouth**

2 *(= make)* *[+ road]* tracer ; *[+ hole]* percer ; *[+ gulf]* creuser ◆ **this ~ed a gulf between father and son** cela a creusé un fossé entre le père et le fils ◆ **he ~ed his way through the bushes** il s'est frayé un chemin à travers les buissons

3 *(= begin, inaugurate, found)* *[+ meeting, debate, exhibition, trial]* ouvrir ; *[+ account, conversation]* commencer, entamer ; *[+ new building, institution]* inaugurer ; *[+ negotiations]* ouvrir, engager ◆ **he had ~ed the conversation by telling her that ...** il avait commencé par lui dire que ...

4 *(Bridge)* **to ~ (with) two hearts** ouvrir de deux cœurs

VI 1 *[door, book, eyes, flower]* s'ouvrir ; *[shop, museum, bank]* ouvrir ; *[crack]* se former ◆ **the door ~ed** la porte s'est ouverte ◆ **the door ~ed slightly** la porte s'est entrouverte *or* s'est entrebâillée ◆ **to ~ again** *[door]* se rouvrir ; *[shops etc]* rouvrir ◆ **there's a door that ~s onto the garden** il y a une porte qui donne sur le jardin ◆ **the kitchen ~s into the dining room** la cuisine donne sur la salle à manger ◆ **the two rooms ~ into one another** les deux pièces communiquent

2 *(= begin)* commencer ; *(Bridge)* ouvrir ◆ **to ~ with sth** *[debate, meeting, trial]* s'ouvrir sur qch, commencer par qch ; *[class, book, play]* commencer par qch ◆ **the trial ~ed with the testimony of the victim** le procès s'est ouvert sur *or* a commencé par le témoignage de la victime ◆ **he ~ed with a warning about inflation** il a commencé par lancer un avertissement sur l'inflation ◆ **the play/film ~s next week** la première (de la pièce/du film) a lieu la semaine prochaine

COMP **open-air** **ADJ** *[games, activities]* de plein air ; *[swimming pool]* découvert ; *[market, meeting]* en plein air, à ciel ouvert ◆ **~-air theatre** théâtre *m* en plein air

open-and-shut **ADJ** *(fig)* ◆ **it's an ~-and-shut case** la solution est évidente *or* crève les yeux

open-cast **ADJ** *(Brit Min)* à ciel ouvert

open cheque **N** *(Brit)* chèque *m* non barré

open circuit **N** *(Elec)* circuit *m* ouvert

open-cut **ADJ** *(US Min)* ⇒ **open-cast**

open day **N** *(Brit)* journée *f* portes ouvertes

open door *(Econ)* **N** politique *f* d'ouverture **ADJ** *[policy, approach etc]* d'ouverture

open-ended, open-end *(US)* **ADJ** *[tube]* ouvert ; *[discussion, meeting]* sans limite de durée ; *[ticket]* sans réservation de retour ; *[contract]* à durée indéterminée ; *[question]* ouvert ; *[commitment]* inconditionnel ; → **OEIC**

open-eyed **ADJ** *(lit)* les yeux ouverts ◆ **to be ~-eyed about sth** garder les yeux ouverts sur qch

open-faced sandwich **N** *(US)* tartine *f*

open goal **N** *(Ftbl)* but *m* dégarni

open government **N** *(NonC)* politique *f* de transparence *(pratiquée par un gouvernement)*

open-handed **ADJ** ◆ **to be ~-handed** être généreux, avoir le cœur sur la main

open-hearted **ADJ** franc (franche *f*), sincère

open-heart surgery **N** chirurgie *f* à cœur ouvert

open learning **N** *(gen) enseignement universitaire à la carte, notamment par correspondance*, (= *distance learning*) télé-enseignement *m*

open letter **N** lettre *f* ouverte

open market **N** *(Econ)* marché *m* libre

open marriage **N** mariage *m* libre

open-minded **ADJ** à l'esprit ouvert *or* large ◆ **to be very ~-minded** avoir l'esprit très ouvert

open-mindedness **N** ouverture *f* d'esprit

open-mouthed **ADJ, ADV** *(fig)* bouche bée *inv* ◆ **in ~-mouthed disbelief** *or* **amazement** bouche bée ◆ **in ~-mouthed admiration** béat d'admiration

open-necked **ADJ** *(not buttoned up)* à col ouvert ; *(low-cut)* échancré

open pit **N** *(US)* mine *f* à ciel ouvert

open-plan **ADJ** *(Archit)* *[design]* qui élimine les cloisons ; *[house, school]* sans cloison ◆ **~ plan kitchen** cuisine *f* à l'américaine ◆ **~ plan office** bureau *m* paysager

open primary **N** *(US Pol) élection primaire ouverte aux non-inscrits d'un parti*

open prison **N** prison *f* ouverte

open sandwich **N** tartine *f*

open scholarship **N** *(Scol etc) bourse décernée par un concours ouvert à tous*

open season **N** *(Hunting)* saison *f* de la chasse

open secret **N** secret *m* de Polichinelle ◆ **it's an ~ secret that ...** ce n'est un secret pour personne que ...

open shop **N** *(in workplace)* atelier *m* ouvert aux non-syndiqués

open station **N** gare *f* avec libre accès aux quais

open string **N** *(Mus)* corde *f* à vide

open ticket **N** billet *m* open

open-top(ped) **ADJ** *[bus]* à impériale découverte ; *[car]* décourvert

the Open University **N** *(Brit)* ≃ le Centre national d'enseignement par correspondance ◆ **an Open University course** un cours universitaire par correspondance

open verdict **N** verdict *m* constatant un décès sans cause déterminée

open vowel **N** voyelle *f* ouverte

► **open out** **VI** 1 *[view]* ◆ **soon a wonderful view opened out** bientôt une vue magnifique s'offrit à nous ◆ **as he left the town the countryside ~ed out** à la sortie de la ville, la campagne s'offrit à ses yeux

2 *(= widen)* *[passage, tunnel, street]* s'élargir ◆ **to ~ out on to** déboucher sur

3 *[person]* *(= become less shy)* s'ouvrir ; *[team, player etc]* s'affirmer

VT SEP ouvrir ; *[+ map, newspaper]* ouvrir, déplier

► **open up** **VI** 1 *[new shop, business]* s'ouvrir ; *[new career]* commencer ; *[opportunity]* se présenter

2 *(= start shooting)* ouvrir le feu ◆ **they ~ed up with machine guns** ils ont ouvert le feu à la mitrailleuse

3 *[flower]* s'ouvrir

4 *(= confide)* s'ouvrir *(to sb* à qn) ◆ **I couldn't get him to ~ up at all** je ne suis pas arrivé à le faire parler ◆ **he finds it difficult to ~ up** il a de la peine à s'ouvrir *or* à se confier

5 *(Sport)* *[match]* s'animer

6 *(= develop)* *[gulf]* se creuser ; *[split]* se former ◆ **a gulf has ~ed up between the countries involved** un fossé s'est creusé entre les pays concernés

VT SEP 1 *[+ box, building, shop, wound, business, branch]* ouvrir ; *[+ map, newspaper]* ouvrir, déplier ◆ **to ~ up again** rouvrir

2 *[+ oilfield, mine, road, area]* ouvrir ; *[+ possibilities]* offrir ; *[+ virgin country]* défricher ; *[+ blocked road]* dégager ; *[+ blocked pipe]* déboucher ◆ **they ~ed up the way for other women** elles ont ouvert la voie à d'autres femmes ◆ **they ~ed up new paths in transplantation** ils ont ouvert de nouvelles voies en matière de transplantation ◆ **she ~ed up a lead of almost four minutes** elle était en tête avec près de quatre minutes d'avance ◆ **he decided to ~ up China for foreign investors** il décida d'ouvrir la Chine aux investisseurs étrangers

> **OPEN UNIVERSITY**
>
> L'**Open University** est une université ouverte à tous et fonctionnant essentiellement sur le principe du téléenseignement : cours par correspondance et émissions de radio et de télévision diffusées par la BBC. Ces enseignements sont complétés par un suivi pédagogique et par des stages, qui se tiennent généralement en été.

opener /ˈəʊpnəʳ/ **N** 1 *(esp in compounds) personne ou dispositif qui ouvre* ; → **bottle, eye, tin** 2 *(Theat)* (= *artiste*) artiste *mf* en lever de rideau ; (= *act*) lever *m* de rideau 3 *(Bridge)* ouvreur *m* 4 *(fig)* **for ~s** * pour commencer, tout d'abord

opening /ˈəʊpnɪŋ/ **N** 1 ouverture *f* ; *(in wall)* brèche *f* ; *[of door, window]* embrasure *f* ; *(in trees)* trouée *f* ; *(in forest, roof)* percée *f* ; *(in clouds)* éclaircie *f* ; *[of tunnel]* entrée *f*

2 *(= beginning)* *[of meeting, debate, play, speech]* ouverture *f* ; *[of negotiations]* ouverture *f*, amorce *f*

3 *(NonC = act of opening)* *[of door, road, letter]* ouverture *f* ; *[of shooting, war]* déclenchement *m* ; *[of flower]* éclosion *f* ; *(Jur)* exposition *f* des faits ; *(Cards, Chess)* ouverture *f* ; *[of ceremony, exhibition]* inauguration *f* ◆ **the Opening of Parliament** *(Brit)* l'ouverture *f* de la session parlementaire

4 *(= opportunity)* occasion *f* *(to do sth* de faire qch, pour faire qch) ; *(= trade outlet)* débouché *m* (for pour) ◆ **to give one's opponent/the enemy an ~** prêter le flanc à son adversaire/à l'ennemi

5 *(= work: gen)* débouché *m* ; *(= specific job, or work in specific firm)* poste *m* ◆ **there are a lot of ~s in computing** il y a beaucoup de débouchés dans l'informatique ◆ **we have an ~ for an engineer** nous avons un poste (vacant) d'ingénieur ◆ **an ~ with Harper-Collins** un poste vacant chez Harper-Collins

ADJ *[ceremony, speech]* d'inauguration, inaugural ; *[remark]* préliminaire ; *(Stock Exchange)* *[price]* d'ouverture ◆ **~ gambit** *(Chess)* gambit *m* ; *(fig)* manœuvre *f* or ruse *f* (stratégique) ◆ **his favourite ~ gambit is ...** *(in conversation)* sa remarque préférée pour entamer une conversation, c'est ... ◆ **~ hours** heures *fpl* d'ouverture ◆ **~ lines** *[of play]* premières répliques *fpl* ; *[of poem]* premiers vers *mpl* ◆ **~ night** *(Theat)* première *f* ; *[of festival etc]* soirée *f* d'ouverture ◆ **~ shot** *(in battle etc)* premier coup *m* de feu ; *(fig)* *[of campaign etc]* coup *m* d'envoi ◆ **~ time** *(Brit)* l'heure *f* d'ouverture des pubs

openly /ˈəʊpənlɪ/ **ADV** *[admit, acknowledge, talk about]* ouvertement ◆ **to be ~ critical of sb/sth** critiquer qn/qch ouvertement ◆ **she wept ~** elle n'a pas caché ses larmes ◆ **he is ~ gay** il ne cache pas son homosexualité

openness /ˈəʊpnnɪs/ **N** 1 *(= frankness)* franchise *f* ; *(= receptivity)* ouverture *f* d'esprit 2 *(Pol)* ouverture *f* ; *(= glasnost)* transparence *f* ◆ **a new policy of ~** une nouvelle politique d'ouverture ◆ **greater ~ in their financial activities** une plus grande transparence dans leurs opérations financières 3 *[of land, countryside]* aspect *m* découvert *or* exposé

openwork /ˈəʊpənwɜːk/ **N** *(Sewing)* jours *mpl* ; *(Archit)* claire-voie *f*, ajours *mpl* **COMP** *[stockings etc]* ajouré ; *(Archit)* à claire-voie

opera /ˈɒpərə/ **N** 1 opéra *m* ; → **comic, grand, light**² 2 pl of **opus** **COMP** **opera bouffe** **N** opéra *m* bouffe

opera company N troupe *f or* compagnie *f* d'opéra
opera glasses NPL jumelles *fpl* de théâtre
opera-goer N amateur *m* d'opéra
opera hat N (chapeau *m*) claque *m*, gibus *m*
opera house N opéra *m (édifice)*
opera-lover N amateur *m* d'opéra
opera singer N chanteur *m*, -euse *f* d'opéra

operable /ˈɒpərəbl/ ADJ opérable

operand /ˈɒpərænd/ N opérande *m*

operate /ˈɒpəreɪt/ VI 1 *[machine, vehicle]* marcher, fonctionner ; *[system, sb's mind]* fonctionner ; *[law]* jouer ◆ **he believes that a conspiracy is operating to discredit his good name** il pense qu'il se trame un complot visant à le discréditer ◆ **several factors are operating to moderate wage rises** plusieurs facteurs jouent pour freiner les hausses de salaires
2 *[drug, medicine, propaganda]* opérer, faire effet *(on, upon* sur)
3 *[fleet, regiment, thief etc]* opérer ; *(on Stock Exchange)* faire des opérations (de bourse), spéculer ◆ **they can't ~ efficiently on so little money** le manque d'argent les empêche d'opérer *or* de procéder avec efficacité ◆ **this allowed commercial banks to ~ in the country** cela a permis aux banques commerciales d'opérer dans ce pays ◆ **troops were operating from bases along the border** les troupes opéraient *or* menaient leurs opérations à partir de bases le long de la frontière ◆ **I can't ~ under pressure** je ne peux pas travailler sous pression
4 *(Med)* opérer ◆ **he was ~d on for appendicitis** il a été opéré de l'appendicite ◆ **he ~d for appendicitis** *[surgeon]* il l'a opéré de l'appendicite ◆ **to ~ on sb's eyes** opérer qn aux *or* des yeux, opérer les yeux de qn ◆ **he has still not been ~d on** il n'a pas encore été opéré
VT 1 *[person] [+ machine, tool]* utiliser ; *[+ vehicle]* utiliser, conduire ◆ **a machine ~d by electricity** une machine qui marche à l'électricité ◆ **the system that ~s the brakes** le système qui commande *or* actionne les freins
2 *[+ business, factory]* diriger, gérer ; *[+ coalmine, oil well, canal, quarry]* exploiter, faire valoir ◆ **this airline ~s flights to over 30 countries** cette compagnie assure des liaisons avec plus de 30 pays
3 *[+ system]* pratiquer ◆ **the government constantly ~d embargoes against them** le gouvernement les frappait constamment d'embargo

operatic /ˌɒpəˈrætɪk/ ADJ *[aria, role, piece of music]* d'opéra ; *[convention, version]* opératique ◆ **Verdi's Requiem is often criticised for being too ~** on reproche souvent au Requiem de Verdi d'être trop opératique ◆ **an ~ society** une association d'amateurs d'art lyrique N ◆ **(amateur) ~s** opéra *m* d'amateurs

operating /ˈɒpəreɪtɪŋ/ ADJ *[cost, deficit, expenses etc]* d'exploitation
COMP **operating cash** N trésorerie *f* d'exploitation
operating cycle N cycle *m* d'exploitation
operating instructions NPL mode *m or* notice *f* d'emploi
operating manual N manuel *m* d'utilisation
operating profit N bénéfice *m* d'exploitation
operating room N (US) ⇒ **operating theatre**
operating system N *(Comput)* système *m* d'exploitation
operating table N *(Med)* table *f* d'opération
operating theatre N *(Brit)* salle *f* d'opération

operation /ˌɒpəˈreɪʃən/ N 1 *(NonC) [of machine, vehicle]* marche *f*, fonctionnement *m* ; *[of mind, digestion]* fonctionnement *m* ; *[of drug etc]* action *f (on* sur) ; *[of business]* gestion *f* ; *[of mine, oil well, quarry, canal]* exploitation *f* ; *[of system]* application *f* ◆ **to be in ~** *[machine]* être en service ; *[business etc]* fonctionner ; *[mine etc]* être en exploitation ; *[law, system]* être en vigueur ◆ **in full ~** *[machine]* fonctionnant à plein (rendement) ; *[business, factory etc]* en pleine activité ; *[mine etc]* en pleine exploitation ◆ **to come into ~** *[law, system]* entrer en vigueur ; *[machine]* entrer en service ; *[business]* se mettre à fonctionner ◆ **to put into ~** *[machine]* mettre en service ; *[law]* mettre *or* faire entrer en vigueur ; *[plan]* mettre en application
2 *(= enterprise, action)* opération *f* ◆ **that was an expensive ~** l'opération a été coûteuse ◆ **rescue/security ~** opération de sauvetage/de sécurité ◆ **our ~s in Egypt** *(trading company)* nos opérations *or* nos activités en Égypte ; *(oil, mining)* nos exploitations en Égypte ◆ **a multinational ~** *(= company)* une multinationale ◆ **rebuilding ~s began at once** les opérations de reconstruction ont commencé immédiatement ◆ **Operation Overlord** *(Mil)* opération *f* Overlord
3 *(Med)* opération *f*, intervention *f* (chirurgicale) ◆ **to have an ~** se faire opérer *(for de)* ◆ **a lung/heart/kidney ~** une opération des poumons/du cœur/des reins ◆ **to perform an ~ on sb (for sth)** opérer qn (de qch)
COMP **operation code** N *(Comput)* code *m* d'opération
operations research N recherche *f* opérationnelle
operations room N *(Mil, Police)* centre *m* d'opérations

operational /ˌɒpəˈreɪʃənl/ ADJ *[staff, troops, vehicle, plan, system, service]* opérationnel ; *[machine]* en état de marche ; *[cost, expenses, profit]* d'exploitation ; *[problems]* de fonctionnement ◆ **to have ~ control** avoir le contrôle des opérations ◆ **at an ~ level** au niveau opérationnel ◆ **for ~ reasons** pour des raisons opérationnelles ◆ **on ~ duties** *(Police)* en service COMP **operational strategy** N *(Fin, Econ)* stratégie *f* d'intervention

operative /ˈɒpərətɪv/ ADJ 1 *(= functioning) [scheme, plan, system, service]* opérationnel ◆ **the ~ part of the text** *(Jur)* le dispositif 2 ◆ **the ~ word** le mot-clé ◆ **caution has been the ~ word since the killings** prudence est devenu le mot d'ordre depuis la tuerie 3 *(Med) [report]* d'opération ; *[risk]* opératoire N *(= worker)* ouvrier *m*, -ière *f* ; *(= machine operator)* opérateur *m*, -trice *f* ; *(= detective)* détective *m* (privé) ; *(= spy)* espion(ne) *m(f)* ; *(= secret agent)* agent *m* secret ; *(US Pol) (= campaign worker)* membre *m* de l'état-major *(d'un candidat)* ◆ **the steel ~s** la main-d'œuvre des aciéries

operator /ˈɒpəreɪtə^r^/ N 1 *(= person) [of machine, computer etc]* opérateur *m*, -trice *f* ; *(Cine)* opérateur *m*, -trice *f* (de prise de vues) ; *[of telephones]* téléphoniste *mf*, standardiste *mf* ; *[of business, factory]* dirigeant(e) *m(f)*, directeur *m*, -trice *f* ◆ **~s in this section of the industry** ceux qui travaillent dans ce secteur de l'industrie ◆ **he is a shrewd political ~** c'est un politicien habile ◆ **a big-time ~** *(= criminal)* un escroc d'envergure ; → **smooth, tour** 2 *(= company) (telecommunications, television)* opérateur *m* ◆ **cable (TV) ~** câblo-opérateur *m* ◆ **ferry/coach ~** compagnie *f* de ferries/d'autocars 3 *(Math)* opérateur *m*

operetta /ˌɒpəˈretə/ N opérette *f*

ophthalmia /ɒfˈθælmɪə/ N ophtalmie *f*

ophthalmic /ɒfˈθælmɪk/ ADJ *[clinic, hospital, surgery]* ophtalmologique ; *[surgeon]* ophtalmologue ; *[nerve, vein]* ophtalmique COMP **ophthalmic optician** N opticien(ne) *m(f)* optométriste ; *(prescribing)* oculiste *mf* ; *(dispensing)* opticien(ne) *m(f)*

ophthalmologist /ˌɒfθælˈmɒlədʒɪst/ N ophtalmologiste *mf*, ophtalmologue *mf*

ophthalmology /ˌɒfθælˈmɒlədʒɪ/ N ophtalmologie *f*

ophthalmoscope /ɒfˈθælməskəʊp/ N ophtalmoscope *m*

ophthalmoscopy /ˌɒfθælˈmɒskəpɪ/ N ophtalmoscopie *f*

opiate /ˈəʊpɪɪt/ N opiacé *m* ; *(fig)* soporifique *m* ADJ opiacé

opine /əʊˈpaɪn/ VT *(frm) (= think)* être d'avis *(that* que) ; *(= say)* émettre l'avis *(that* que)

opinion /əˈpɪnjən/ LANGUAGE IN USE 1.1, 2.1, 2.2, 6, 26.2
N *(= point of view)* avis *m*, opinion *f* ; *(= belief, judgement)* opinion *f* ; *(= professional advice)* avis *m* ◆ **in my ~** à mon avis, d'après moi ◆ **in the ~ of** d'après, selon ◆ **that's my ~ for what it's worth** c'est mon humble avis ◆ **it's a matter of ~ whether ...** c'est (une) affaire d'opinion pour ce qui est de savoir si ... ◆ **I'm entirely of your ~** je suis tout à fait de votre avis *or* opinion, je partage tout à fait votre opinion ◆ **to be of the ~ that ...** être d'avis que ..., estimer que ... ◆ **political ~s** opinions *fpl* politiques ◆ **she's in a position to influence ~** elle occupe une position d'influence ◆ **what is your ~ of this book?** quel est votre point de vue sur ce livre ? ◆ **her already favourable ~ of him** l'opinion favorable qu'elle avait déjà de lui ◆ **I haven't much of an ~ of him, I've got a low ~ of him** j'ai mauvaise opinion *or* une piètre opinion de lui ◆ **to take counsel's ~** *(Jur)* consulter un avocat ◆ **~ of the court** *(Jur)* jugement *m* rendu par le tribunal ; → **legal, public, second^1^, strong**
COMP **opinion former, opinion maker** N meneur *m*, -euse *f or* leader *m* d'opinion
opinion poll N sondage *m* d'opinion

opinionated /əˈpɪnjəneɪtɪd/ ADJ *(pej)* ◆ **to be ~** avoir des opinions arrêtées

opium /ˈəʊpɪəm/ N opium *m*
COMP **opium addict** N opiomane *m*
opium den N fumerie *f* d'opium

opossum /əˈpɒsəm/ N (pl **opossums** *or* **opossum**) opossum *m*, sarigue *f*

opp. abbrev of **opposite**

opponent /əˈpəʊnənt/ N *(Mil, Sport, in election)* adversaire *mf* ; *(in discussion, debate)* antagoniste *mf* ; *(of government, ideas etc)* adversaire *mf*, opposant(e) *m(f) (of* de) ◆ **he has always been an ~ of nationalization** il a toujours été contre les nationalisations, il s'est toujours opposé aux nationalisations ◆ **~s of the regime** les opposants *mpl* au régime

opportune /ˈɒpətjuːn/ ADJ *[action, remark]* à propos, opportun ◆ **to happen/arrive at an ~ time *or* moment (for sb/sth)** tomber/arriver au moment opportun (pour qn/qch) ◆ **you have come at an ~ moment** vous arrivez à point nommé, vous tombez bien

opportunely /ˈɒpətjuːnlɪ/ ADV opportunément, à propos

opportuneness /ˌɒpəˈtjuːnnɪs/ N opportunité *f*

opportunism /ˌɒpəˈtjuːnɪzəm/ N opportunisme *m*

opportunist /ˌɒpəˈtjuːnɪst/ ADJ, N opportuniste *mf*

opportunistic /ˌɒpətjuːˈnɪstɪk/ ADJ opportuniste

opportunity /ˌɒpəˈtjuːnɪtɪ/ N 1 *(= occasion, chance)* occasion *f* ◆ **a trip to London is a great ~ for shopping** un voyage à Londres est une excellente occasion de faire du shopping ◆ **to have the *or* an ~ to do *or* of doing sth** avoir l'occasion *or* la possibilité de faire qch ◆ **to take the ~ of doing *or* to do sth** profiter de l'occasion pour faire qch ◆ **you really missed your ~ there!** tu as vraiment laissé passer ta chance *or* l'occasion ! ◆ **at the first *or* earliest ~** à la première occasion, dès que l'occasion se présentera ◆ **when the ~ presents itself** *or*

arises à l'occasion ◆ **if the ~ should present itself** *or* **arise** si l'occasion se présente ◆ **if you get the ~** si vous en avez l'occasion

2 *(= possibility for action)* chance *f* ; *(in career etc)* perspective *f* d'avenir ◆ **equality of ~** égalité *f* des chances ◆ **to make the most of one's opportunities** profiter pleinement de ses chances ◆ **this job offers great opportunities** ce poste offre d'excellentes perspectives d'avenir ◆ **I want to see more opportunities for young people** je veux que les jeunes aient davantage de perspectives d'avenir ; → **equal, every**

oppose /ə'pəʊz/ VT 1 *[+ person, argument, opinion, decision, plan]* s'opposer à ; *[+ sb's will, desires, suggestion]* s'opposer à, faire opposition à ; *[+ motion, resolution]* *(Pol)* faire opposition à ; *(in debate)* parler contre ◆ **the government ~s a lifting of the embargo** le gouvernement s'oppose à une levée de l'embargo ◆ **the President ~s sending the refugees back** le président s'oppose au renvoi des réfugiés ◆ **he ~d it** il s'y est opposé 2 *(= set against)* opposer *(sth to sth else* qch à qch d'autre)

opposed /ə'pəʊzd/ LANGUAGE IN USE 8.3, 9.3, 12, 14 ADJ *[aims, attitudes, viewpoints]* opposé ◆ **to be ~ to sth** être opposé à qch ◆ **I'm ~ to your marrying him** je ne veux pas que tu l'épouses *subj* ◆ **as ~ to** par opposition à ◆ **as ~ to that, there is the question of ...** par contre, il y a la question de ...

opposing /ə'pəʊzɪŋ/ ADJ *[factions, forces, views]* opposé ; *(Jur)* adverse ◆ **to be on ~ sides** ne pas être du même bord ◆ **the ~ team** l'équipe *f* adverse ◆ **the ~ votes** les voix *fpl* contre

opposite /'ɒpəzɪt/ ADJ *[house etc]* d'en face ; *[bank, side, end]* opposé, autre ; *[direction, pole]* opposé ; *(fig)* *[attitude, point of view]* opposé, contraire ◆ **"see map on opposite page"** "voir plan ci-contre" ◆ **the ~ sex** l'autre sexe *m* ◆ **we take the ~ view (to his)** nous pensons le contraire (de ce qu'il pense), notre opinion est diamétralement opposée (à la sienne) ◆ **his ~ number** son homologue *mf*

ADV (d')en face ◆ **the house ~** la maison d'en face ◆ **the house is immediately** *or* **directly ~** la maison est directement en face ◆ **~ to** en face de

PREP en face de ◆ **the house is ~ the church** la maison est en face de l'église ◆ **the house and the church are ~ one another** la maison et l'église sont en vis-à-vis ◆ **they sat ~ one another** ils étaient assis face à face *or* en vis-à-vis ◆ **they live ~ us** ils habitent en face de chez nous ◆ **to play ~ sb** *(Cine, Theat etc)* partager la vedette avec qn ◆ **~ Calais** *(Naut)* à la hauteur de Calais

N contraire *m*, inverse *m* ◆ **quite the ~!** bien au contraire ! ◆ **he told me just the ~** *or* **the exact ~** il m'a dit exactement l'inverse *or* le contraire ◆ **he says the ~ of everything I say** il prend le contre-pied de tout ce que je dis, il faut toujours qu'il me contredise ◆ **what's the ~ of white?** quel est le contraire de blanc ? ◆ **~s attract** les contraires s'attirent

Opposition /ˌɒpə'zɪʃən/ *(Brit Pol)* N ◆ **the ~** l'opposition *f* ◆ **the leader of the ~** le chef de l'opposition COMP *[speaker, member, motion, party]* de l'opposition **the Opposition benches** NPL (les bancs *mpl* de) l'opposition *f*

opposition /ˌɒpə'zɪʃən/ N 1 opposition *f* *(also Astron, Pol)* ◆ **his ~ to the scheme** son opposition au projet ◆ **in ~ (to)** en opposition (avec) ◆ **the party in ~** *(Pol)* le parti de l'opposition ◆ **to be in ~** *(Pol)* être dans l'opposition ◆ **the ~** *(in politics)* l'opposition *f* ; *(= opposing team)* l'adversaire *m* ; *(= business competitors)* la concurrence 2 *(Mil etc)* opposition *f*, résistance *f* ◆ **they put up** *or* **offered considerable ~** ils ont opposé une vive résistance ◆ **the army met with little or no ~** l'armée a rencontré peu sinon point de résistance COMP **opposition hold** N *(Climbing)* opposition *f*

oppositionist /ˌɒpə'zɪʃənɪst/ N *(Pol)* opposant(e) *m(f)* (systématique)

oppress /ə'pres/ VT 1 *(Mil, Pol etc)* opprimer ◆ **the ~ed** les opprimés *mpl* 2 *[anxiety, heat etc]* oppresser, accabler

oppression /ə'preʃən/ N *(all senses)* oppression *f*

oppressive /ə'presɪv/ ADJ 1 *(Mil, Pol)* *[system, regime, law]* oppressif 2 *(= uncomfortable)* *[air, heat, silence, mood]* oppressant ; *[weather]* lourd ◆ **the little room was ~** on étouffait dans cette petite pièce

oppressively /ə'presɪvlɪ/ ADV 1 *(Mil, Pol)* *[rule]* de manière oppressive 2 *(= uncomfortably)* ◆ **the room was ~ hot** on étouffait dans cette pièce ◆ **~ humid** d'une humidité oppressante ◆ **it's ~ hot today** il fait très lourd aujourd'hui ◆ **~ drab** *or* **grey** d'un gris sinistre

oppressor /ə'presəʳ/ N oppresseur *m*

opprobrious /ə'prəʊbrɪəs/ ADJ *(frm)* chargé d'opprobre *(liter)*

opprobrium /ə'prəʊbrɪəm/ N opprobre *m*

opt /ɒpt/ VI ◆ **to ~ for sth** opter pour qch ◆ **to ~ to do sth** choisir de faire qch

► **opt in** VI choisir de participer *(to à)*

► **opt out** VI choisir de ne pas participer *(of à)* ; *[hospital, school] choisir l'autonomie par rapport aux autorités locales ; [dentist] choisir de ne plus être conventionné par la Sécurité sociale* ; *(Sociol)* s'évader de *or* rejeter la société (de consommation) ; *(Brit: pension)* choisir une caisse de retraite privée *(par opposition au système de la Sécurité sociale)* ◆ **he ~ed out of going** il a choisi de ne pas y aller ◆ **you can always ~ out** tu peux toujours te retirer *or* te récuser ; see also **opt-out**

optative /'ɒptətɪv/ ADJ, N optatif *m*

optic /'ɒptɪk/ ADJ optique N *(Brit: in bar)* bouchon *m* doseur NPL **optics** optique *f* COMP **optic nerve** N nerf *m* optique

optical /'ɒptɪkəl/ ADJ *[microscope, telescope, system, glass, lens]* optique ; *[instrument]* d'optique, optique

COMP **optical brightener** N agent *m* éclaircissant

optical character reader N lecteur *m* optique de caractères

optical character recognition N reconnaissance *f* optique de caractères

optical computer N ordinateur *m* optique

optical disc, optical disk N disque *m* optique

optical fibre N fibre *f* optique

optical illusion N illusion *f* d'optique

optical scanner N lecteur *m* optique

optical scanning N lecture *f* optique

optician /ɒp'tɪʃən/ N opticien(ne) *m(f)* ; *(prescribing)* oculiste *mf*

optima /'ɒptɪmə/ NPL of **optimum**

optimal /'ɒptɪml/ ADJ optimal

optimism /'ɒptɪmɪzəm/ N optimisme *m*

optimist /'ɒptɪmɪst/ N optimiste *mf*

optimistic /ˌɒptɪ'mɪstɪk/ ADJ optimiste *(about sth* quant à qch) ◆ **she was ~ of success** *or* **that she would succeed** elle avait bon espoir de réussir ◆ **to be cautiously ~** être d'un optimisme prudent

optimistically /ˌɒptɪ'mɪstɪklɪ/ ADV avec optimisme

optimization /ˌɒptɪmaɪ'zeɪʃən/ N optimisation *f*

optimize /'ɒptɪmaɪz/ VT optimiser, optimaliser

optimum /'ɒptɪməm/ ADJ *[level, number, time]* optimum, optimal ◆ **~ conditions** conditions *fpl* optimales ◆ **exercise three times a week for ~ health** faites de l'exercice trois fois par semaine pour être au mieux de votre forme N (pl **optimums** *or* **optima**) optimum *m*

option /'ɒpʃən/ N 1 *(gen)* choix *m*, option *f* ◆ **I have no ~** je n'ai pas le choix ◆ **he had no ~ but to come** il n'a pas pu faire autrement que de venir ◆ **you have the ~ of remaining here** vous pouvez rester ici si vous voulez ◆ **the military ~** l'option *f* militaire ◆ **he left** *or* **kept his ~s open** *(fig)* il n'a pas voulu s'engager (irrévocablement) ◆ **to give sb the ~ of doing sth** donner à qn la possibilité de faire qch ◆ **children are given the ~ of learning French or German** les enfants peuvent choisir entre le français et l'allemand ◆ **borrowing more money is not an ~** emprunter plus n'est pas une option viable ◆ **doing nothing is not an ~** on ne peut pas ne rien faire

2 *(Comm, Fin)* option *f (on* sur) ◆ **to take up the ~** lever l'option ◆ **at the ~ of the purchaser** au gré de l'acheteur ◆ **~ taker** *(Comm, Fin)* optant *m* ◆ **to have the ~ to do sth** avoir l'option de faire qch ◆ **(to have an) ~ to buy/acquire/sell** *(Comm, Fin)* (avoir une) option d'achat/d'acquisition/de vente ◆ **six months with/without the ~ of a fine** *(Jur)* six mois avec/sans substitution d'amende

3 *(Brit Scol = subject/course etc)* (matière *f*/cours *m etc* à) option *f* ◆ **programme offering ~s** programme *m* optionnel

optional /'ɒpʃənl/ ADJ *[course, subject]* *(Scol)* facultatif ; *(Univ)* en option ; *[accessories]* en option ◆ **a medical with ~ eye test** un contrôle médical avec examen de la vue en option ◆ **~ extra** option *f* ◆ **dress ~** tenue *f* de soirée facultative

optometrist /ɒp'tɒmətrɪst/ N optométriste *mf*

optometry /ɒp'tɒmətrɪ/ N optométrie *f*

opt-out /'ɒptaʊt/ ADJ *(Brit)* *[school, hospital] qui a choisi l'autonomie par rapport aux autorités locales* N 1 *(Brit)* *[of school, hospital] choix d'autonomie par rapport aux autorités locales* 2 *(esp Brit:* also **opt-out clause**) *(Jur, Comm)* clause *f* de sortie ; *(from treaty)* clause *f* d'exemption

opulence /'ɒpjʊləns/ N *[of person, lifestyle]* opulence *f* ; *[of palace]* somptuosité *f*, opulence *f* ; *[of room]* somptuosité *f*, richesse *f* ; *[of clothes, furnishings]* somptuosité *f* ; *[of material, voice]* richesse *f* ◆ **a life of ~** une vie opulente ◆ **the ~ of the production** *(Cine, Theat)* la somptuosité de la production

opulent /'ɒpjʊlənt/ ADJ *[person, lifestyle]* opulent ; *[building, room, costume, film, production]* somptueux ◆ **silk curtains give the room an ~ feel** des rideaux de soie rendent la pièce plus somptueuse

opulently /'ɒpjʊləntlɪ/ ADV *[furnish etc]* avec opulence ; *[live]* dans l'opulence

opus /'əʊpəs/ N (pl **opuses** *or* **opera**) opus *m* ; → **magnum**

opuscule /ɒ'pʌskjuːl/ N opuscule *m*

OR abbrev of **Oregon**

or /ɔːʳ/ CONJ ou ; *(with neg)* ni ◆ **red ~ black?** rouge ou noir ? ◆ **~ else** ou bien ◆ **do it ~ else!** * fais-le, sinon (tu vas voir) ! ◆ **without tears ~ sighs** sans larmes ni soupirs ◆ **he could not read ~ write** il ne savait ni lire ni écrire ◆ **an hour ~ so** environ une heure, à peu près une heure ◆ **botany, ~ the science of plants** la botanique, ou la science des plantes *or* autrement dit la science des plantes ; → **either**

oracle /'ɒrəkl/ N *(Hist, fig)* oracle *m* ◆ **the government managed to work the ~ and be re-elected** le gouvernement a réussi l'exploit d'être réélu ◆ **she's the ~ on house buying** c'est une autorité en matière d'immobilier

oracular /ɒ'rækjʊləʳ/ ADJ *(frm)* *(= prophetic)* *[guidance, utterance]* prophétique ; *(= mysterious)* *[person, tone, pronouncement]* sibyllin ◆ **~ shrine** oracle *m*

oral /ˈɔːrəl/ ADJ 1 *[examination, teaching methods]* oral ; *[testimony, message, account]* oral, verbal 2 *(Anat) [cavity]* buccal, oral ; *(Pharm etc) [dose]* par voie orale N oral *m*
COMP **oral examiner** N *(Scol etc)* examinateur *m*, -trice *f* à l'oral
oral history N la tradition orale
oral hygiene N hygiène *f* buccale *or* buccodentaire
oral hygienist N hygiéniste *mf* dentaire
oral sex N *(gen)* rapports *mpl* bucco-génitaux ; *(= fellatio)* fellation *f* ; *(= cunnilingus)* cunnilingus *m*
oral society N société *f* à tradition orale
oral tradition N la tradition orale
oral vowel N voyelle *f* orale

orally /ˈɔːrəlɪ/ ADV 1 *(= verbally) [express, promise, pass down]* oralement ; *[testify, communicate]* oralement, de vive voix 2 *(Med) [take, administer]* par voie orale 3 *(= with mouth)* ◆ **to stimulate sb** ~ stimuler qn avec la bouche *or* par des caresses bucco-génitales

orange /ˈɒrɪndʒ/ N orange *f* ; (also **orange tree**) oranger *m* ; *(= colour)* orange *m*, orangé *m* ◆ **"oranges and lemons"** *chanson et jeu d'enfants* ◆ **Orange** *(Geog)* Orange ; → **blood**
ADJ 1 *(in colour) [dress, shirt, glow]* orange *inv* ◆ **bright** ~ orange vif *inv*
2 *(in taste) [drink, liqueur]* à l'orange ; *[flavour]* d'orange
COMP **orange blossom** N fleur(s) *f(pl)* d'oranger
orange box, orange crate *(US)* N caisse *f* à oranges
Orange Day N *(Ir)* le 12 juillet *(procession annuelle des Orangistes)*
orange flower water N eau *f* de fleur d'oranger
Orange Free State N État *m* libre d'Orange
orange grove N orangeraie *f*
orange juice N jus *m* d'orange
Orange march *or* **parade** N *(Brit)* défilé *m* des Orangistes
orange marmalade N confiture *f* d'oranges
the Orange Order N *(Brit)* l'Ordre *m* d'Orange
orange peel N *(gen)* peau *f or* écorce *f* d'orange ; *(Culin)* zeste *m* d'orange ◆ ~ **peel effect** *(Med)* peau *f* d'orange
orange squash N ≈ orangeade *f*
orange stick N bâtonnet *m (pour manucure etc)*
orange tree N oranger *m*

orangeade /ˈɒrɪndʒˈeɪd/ N soda *m* à l'orange

Orangeman /ˈɒrɪndʒmən/ N (pl **-men**) Orangiste *m*

orangery /ˈɒrɪndʒərɪ/ N orangerie *f*

orangewood /ˈɒrɪndʒwʊd/ N (bois *m* d')oranger *m*

orangey /ˈɒrɪndʒɪ/ ADJ *[colour]* orangé ; *[taste, flavour]* d'orange ◆ **~-red** rouge orangé *inv*

orang-outang /ɔːˌræŋuːˈtæŋ/, **orang-utan** /ɔːˌræŋuːˈtæn/ N orang-outan(g) *m*

orate /ɒˈreɪt/ VI discourir, faire un discours ; *(pej)* pérorer VT déclamer

oration /ɔːˈreɪʃən/ N discours *m* solennel ; → **funeral**

orator /ˈɒrətə^r/ N orateur *m*, -trice *f*

oratorical /ˌɒrəˈtɒrɪkəl/ ADJ oratoire

oratorio /ˌɒrəˈtɔːrɪəʊ/ N (pl **oratorios**) oratorio *m*

oratory¹ /ˈɒrətərɪ/ N *(= art)* art *m* oratoire ; *(= what is said)* éloquence *f*, rhétorique *f* ◆ **brilliant piece of** ~ brillant discours *m*

oratory² /ˈɒrətərɪ/ N *(Rel)* oratoire *m*

orb /ɔːb/ N 1 *(= sphere)* globe *m*, sphère *f* ; *(in regalia)* globe *m* 2 *(liter = eye)* œil *m* 3 *(liter = celestial body)* orbe *m*

orbit /ˈɔːbɪt/ N *(Anat, Astron)* orbite *f* ◆ **to be in/go into/put into ~ (around)** être/entrer/mettre en *or* sur orbite (autour de) ◆ **countries within the communist** ~ pays *mpl* dans l'orbite communiste VT graviter autour de, décrire une *or* des orbite(s) autour de VI orbiter, être *or* rester en *or* sur orbite *(round* autour de)

orbital /ˈɔːbɪtl/ ADJ 1 *(Brit) [road, motorway]* périphérique 2 *(Space)* orbital 3 *(Anat)* orbitaire

orbiter /ˈɔːbɪtə^r/ N *(Space)* orbiteur *m*

Orcadian /ɔːˈkeɪdɪən/ ADJ des (îles) Orcades N habitant(e) *m(f)* des (îles) Orcades

orchard /ˈɔːtʃəd/ N verger *m* ◆ **cherry** ~ champ *m* de cerisiers, cerisaie *f*

orchestra /ˈɔːkɪstrə/ N 1 *(Mus)* orchestre *m* ; → **leader, string** 2 *(US Theat)* (fauteuils *mpl* d')orchestre *m*
COMP **orchestra pit** N fosse *f* d'orchestre
orchestra stalls NPL (fauteuils *mpl* d')orchestre *m*

orchestral /ɔːˈkestrəl/ ADJ *[music]* orchestral, d'orchestre ; *[playing]* de l'orchestre ; *[concert]* d'orchestre ; *[piece, work, arrangement]* pour orchestre ◆ ~ **score** orchestration *f*

orchestrate /ˈɔːkɪstreɪt/ VT orchestrer

orchestration /ˌɔːkɪsˈtreɪʃən/ N orchestration *f*, instrumentation *f*

orchid /ˈɔːkɪd/ N orchidée *f* ◆ **wild** ~ orchis *m*

orchis /ˈɔːkɪs/ N orchis *m*

ordain /ɔːˈdeɪn/ VT 1 *[God, fate]* décréter (*that* que) ; *[law]* décréter (*that* que), prescrire (*that* que + *subj*) ; *[judge]* ordonner (*that* que + *subj*) ◆ **it was ~ed that he should die young** il était destiné à mourir jeune, le sort *or* le destin a voulu qu'il meure jeune 2 *(Rel) [+ priest]* ordonner ◆ **he was ~ed (priest)** il a reçu l'ordination, il a été ordonné prêtre

ordeal /ɔːˈdiːl/ N 1 rude épreuve *f*, supplice *m* ◆ **they suffered terrible ~s** ils sont passés par *or* ils ont subi d'atroces épreuves ◆ **speaking in public was an ~ for him** il était au supplice quand il devait parler en public, parler en public le mettait au supplice ◆ **the painful ~ of the last eight months** l'épreuve pénible qu'ont été ces huit derniers mois ◆ **it was less of an ~ than expected** cela a été moins pénible que prévu 2 *(Hist Jur)* ordalie *f* ◆ ~ **by fire** épreuve *f* du feu

order /ˈɔːdə^r/

LANGUAGE IN USE 20.3, 27.7

1 NOUN	4 COMPOUNDS
2 TRANSITIVE VERB	5 PHRASAL VERBS
3 INTRANSITIVE VERB	

1 - NOUN

1 [= disposition, sequence] ordre *m* ◆ **word** ~ ordre *m* des mots ◆ **what ~ should these documents be in?** dans quel ordre faut-il classer ces documents ? ◆ **to be in** ~ être en ordre ◆ **to put in(to)** ~ mettre en ordre ◆ **the cards were out of** ~ les cartes n'étaient pas en ordre ◆ **the files have got all out of** ~ les dossiers sont sens dessus dessous ◆ **in ~ of merit/precedence** par ordre de mérite/préséance ◆ **"cast in order of appearance:"** *(Theat)* "avec par ordre d'entrée en scène :" ; *(Cine)* "avec par ordre d'apparition :" ◆ **he loves his boat and his family, in that** ~ il aime son bateau et sa famille, dans cet ordre-là

2 [NonC : also **good order**] ordre *m* ◆ **he's got no sense of** ~ il n'a aucun (sens de l')ordre ◆ **in** ~ *[room etc]* en ordre ; *[passport, documents]* en règle ◆ **to put one's room/one's affairs in** ~ mettre de l'ordre dans sa chambre/ses affaires, mettre sa chambre/ses affaires en ordre ◆ **in short** ~ *(US)* sans délai, tout de suite ◆ **to be in running** *or* **working** ~ être en état de marche ◆ **in good** ~ *(= in good condition)* en bon état ◆ **the machine is out of** ~ la machine est en panne *or* détraquée* ◆ **"out of order"** *(on sign)* "hors service" ◆ **the line is out of** ~ *(Telec)* la ligne est en dérangement

3 [expressing purpose]
◆ **in order to** pour, afin de ◆ **I did it in ~ to clarify matters** je l'ai fait pour *or* afin de clarifier la situation
◆ **in order that** afin que + *subj*, pour que + *subj* ◆ **in ~ that there should be no misunderstanding** afin *or* pour qu'il n'y ait pas de malentendu, pour éviter tout malentendu

4 [= correct procedure] *(Parl etc)* ordre *m* ◆ ~, ~! silence ! ◆ **to call sb to** ~ rappeler qn à l'ordre ◆ **he intervened on a point of** ~ il a soulevé un point de procédure ◆ **"(on a) point of order, Mister Chairman ..."** "j'aimerais soulever un point de procédure ..." ◆ **to be in** ~ *(gen) [action, request etc]* être dans les règles ◆ **that's quite in** ~ je n'y vois aucune objection ◆ **is it in ~ to do that?** est-ce que ça se fait ? ◆ **would it be in ~ for me to speak to her?** pourrais-je lui parler ? ◆ **it's quite in ~ for him to do that** rien ne s'oppose à ce qu'il le fasse ◆ **reforms are clearly in** ~ il est évident que des réformes s'imposent ◆ **a drink seems in** ~ un verre s'impose ◆ **congratulations are surely in ~!** recevez toutes nos (*or* mes *etc*) félicitations ! ◆ **it seems a celebration is in ~!** on va devoir fêter ça ! ◆ **out of** ~ * *[remark]* déplacé ◆ **that was well out of ~!*, you're way out of ~!*** ça se fait pas !*

5 [= peace, control] ordre *m* ◆ **to keep** ~ *[police]* faire régner l'ordre, maintenir l'ordre ; *[teacher]* faire régner la discipline ◆ **she can't keep her class in** ~ elle n'arrive pas à tenir sa classe ◆ **keep your dog in ~!** surveillez votre chien !

6 [= category, class] *(Bio)* ordre *m* ; *(= social position)* classe *f* ; *(= kind)* ordre *m* ◆ **the lower/higher ~s** *(= social rank)* les classes *fpl* inférieures/supérieures ◆ **of a high** ~ *(fig)* de premier ordre ◆ ~ **of magnitude** ordre *m* de grandeur ◆ **something in the ~ of 500 euros, something of the ~ of 500 euros** *(Brit)*, **something on the ~ of 500 euros** *(US)* quelque chose de l'ordre de 500 euros ◆ **the present crisis is of a (very) different** ~ la crise actuelle est d'un (tout) autre ordre

7 [= the way things are] ordre *m* ◆ **it is in the ~ of things** c'est dans l'ordre des choses ◆ **the old ~ is changing** le monde change ◆ **a new world** ~ un nouvel ordre mondial ◆ **a new social/political** ~ un nouvel ordre social/politique ◆ **strikes were the ~ of the day** les grèves étaient à l'ordre du jour

8 [Rel] ordre *m* ◆ **the Benedictine Order** l'ordre *m* des bénédictins ◆ **to be in/take (holy) ~s** être/entrer dans les ordres

9 [= command] ordre *m*, consigne *f (Mil)* ◆ **to obey ~s** obéir aux ordres, observer *or* respecter la consigne *(Mil)* ◆ **~s are ~s** les ordres sont les ordres, la consigne c'est la consigne ◆ **that's an ~!** c'est un ordre ! ◆ **on the ~s of ...** sur l'ordre de ... ◆ **by ~ of ...** par ordre de ... ◆ **till further ~s** jusqu'à nouvel ordre ◆ **to give sb ~s to do sth** ordonner à qn de faire qch ◆ **he gave the ~ for it to be done** il a ordonné qu'on le fasse, il a donné l'ordre de le faire ◆ **you can't give me ~s!, I don't take ~s from you!** je ne suis pas à vos ordres !, ce n'est pas à vous de me donner des ordres ! ◆ **I don't take ~s from anyone** je n'ai d'ordres à recevoir de personne ◆ **to be under the ~s of** être sous les ordres de ◆ **to be under ~s to do sth** avoir (reçu l')ordre de faire qch ◆ **sorry, I'm under ~s** désolé, j'ai (reçu) des ordres ◆ **Order in Council** *(Brit Parl)* ordonnance *f* prise en Conseil privé, ≈ décret-loi *m*

10 [Jur] ◆ **judge's** ~ ordonnance *f* ◆ ~ **of bankruptcy** déclaration *f* de faillite ◆ ~ **of the**

Court injonction *f* de la cour ◆ **deportation ~** arrêté *m* d'expulsion

11 [Comm] commande *f* ◆ **made to ~** fait sur commande ◆ **to give an ~ to sb (for sth), to place an ~ with sb (for sth)** passer une commande (de qch) à qn ◆ **we have received your ~ for ...** nous avons bien reçu votre commande de ... ◆ **we have the shelves on ~ for you** vos étagères sont commandées ◆ **to do sth to ~** *(Comm, fig)* faire qch sur commande ◆ **can I take your order?** *(in restaurant)* vous avez choisi ?

12 [= warrant, permit] permis *m* ◆ **~ to view** permis *m* de visiter

13 [Fin] ◆ **pay to the ~ of ...** payer à l'ordre de ... ◆ **pay John Smith or ~** payez John Smith ou à son ordre

14 [= portion] portion *f* ◆ **an ~ of French fries** une portion de frites

15 [Archit] ordre *m*

2 - TRANSITIVE VERB

1 [= command] ordonner à, donner l'ordre à ◆ **to ~ sb to do sth** ordonner à qn de faire qch, donner l'ordre à qn de faire qch ◆ **he ~ed that the army should advance** *(frm)* il a donné l'ordre à l'armée d'avancer ◆ **he was ~ed to be quiet** on lui a ordonné de se taire ◆ **to ~ sb in/out/up** *etc* ordonner à qn d'entrer/de sortir/de monter *etc* ◆ **to ~ a player off** renvoyer un joueur ◆ **to ~ a regiment abroad** envoyer un régiment à l'étranger ◆ **the regiment was ~ed to Berlin** le régiment a reçu l'ordre d'aller à Berlin

2 [= ask for] *[+ goods, meal]* commander ; *[+ taxi]* faire venir ◆ **to ~ more wine** redemander du vin ◆ **I didn't ~ this!** ce n'est pas ce que j'ai commandé !

3 [= put in sequence] classer, ranger ◆ **they are ~ed by date/size** ils sont classés *or* rangés dans l'ordre chronologique/par ordre de grandeur

4 [= put in good order] *[+ one's affairs etc]* régler

3 - INTRANSITIVE VERB

[in restaurant *etc*] passer sa commande ◆ **are you ready to ~?** vous avez choisi ?

4 - COMPOUNDS

order book N *(Comm, Ind)* carnet *m* de commandes ◆ **the company's ~ books were full** les carnets de commandes de l'entreprise étaient pleins
order form N *(Comm)* bulletin *m* or bon *m* de commande
order mark N *(Brit Scol)* avertissement *m*
the Order of Merit N *(Brit)* l'ordre *m* du mérite
Order of Service N *(Rel)* ordre *m* de cérémonie
the Order of the Bath N *(Brit)* l'ordre *m* du Bain
the Order of the Garter N *(Brit)* l'ordre *m* de la Jarretière
order paper N *(Brit Parl)* ordre *m* du jour

5 - PHRASAL VERBS

► **order about, order around** VT SEP commander ◆ **he likes ~ing people about** il aime donner des ordres à tout le monde ◆ **I won't be ~ed about by him!** je ne suis pas à ses ordres !, je n'ai pas d'ordres à recevoir de lui !

ordered /ˈɔːdɪd/ ADJ (also **well ordered**) *[world, society, universe]* ordonné

ordering /ˈɔːdərɪŋ/ N *(Comm)* passation *f* de commandes

orderliness /ˈɔːdəlɪnɪs/ N *(NonC)* (habitudes *fpl* d')ordre *m*

orderly /ˈɔːdəlɪ/ ADJ *[person]* *(= tidy)* ordonné ; *(= methodical)* méthodique ; *(= disciplined)* discipliné ; *[mind, system]* méthodique ; *[life]* rangé, réglé ; *[room, queue]* ordonné ; *[row]* régulier ; *[school]* où règne la discipline ◆ **in an ~ fashion** or **manner** avec ordre N 1 *(Mil)* planton *m*, ordonnance *f* 2 *(Med)* garçon *m* de salle ; → **nursing**
COMP **orderly officer** N *(Mil)* officier *m* de service
orderly room N *(Mil)* salle *f* de rapport

ordinal /ˈɔːdɪnl/ ADJ *[number]* ordinal N (nombre *m*) ordinal *m*

ordinance /ˈɔːdɪnəns/ N ordonnance *f*, arrêté *m*

ordinand /ˈɔːdɪnænd/ N ordinand *m*

ordinarily /ˈɔːdnrɪlɪ/ ADV ◆ **more than ~ polite/honest** d'une politesse/honnêteté qui sort de l'ordinaire ◆ **the car would ~ cost more** cette voiture coûterait normalement plus ◆ **~, I would have disbelieved him** normalement, je ne l'aurais pas cru

ordinary /ˈɔːdnrɪ/ ADJ 1 *(= usual, day-to-day)* ordinaire, normal ◆ **it has 25 calories less than ~ ice cream** elle a 25 calories de moins que les glaces ordinaires ◆ **in ~ use** d'usage *or* d'emploi courant ◆ **my ~ grocer's** mon épicerie habituelle ◆ **the heat made ~ life impossible** la chaleur rendait impossible la routine habituelle ◆ **in the ~ way** † en temps normal, d'ordinaire
2 *(= average, not outstanding)* *[person, day]* ordinaire, comme les autres ; *[intelligence, knowledge, reader etc]* moyen ◆ **a perfectly ~ Monday morning** un lundi matin comme les autres ◆ **mine was a fairly ~ childhood** j'ai eu une enfance normale *or* assez ordinaire ◆ **I'm just an ~ fellow** je suis un homme comme les autres ◆ **~ people** le commun des mortels ◆ **~ Germans** *etc* l'Allemand *m etc* moyen ◆ **it's not what you would call an ~ present** c'est vraiment un cadeau peu ordinaire *or* peu banal ◆ **it was no ~ bar** ce n'était pas un bar ordinaire *or* comme les autres ◆ **she's no ~ woman** ce n'est pas une femme ordinaire *or* comme les autres ◆ **this is no ~ novel, this is a masterpiece** ce n'est pas un roman comme les autres, c'est un chef-d'œuvre
3 *(pej)* *[person, meal etc]* ordinaire, quelconque
N 1 ordinaire *m* ◆ **out of the ~** hors du commun, qui sort de l'ordinaire ◆ **above the ~** au-dessus du commun *or* de l'ordinaire
2 *(Rel)* ◆ **the ~ of the mass** l'ordinaire *m* de la messe
COMP **ordinary degree** N *(Brit Univ)* ≃ licence *f*
Ordinary grade N *(Scot)* ⇒ **Ordinary level**
Ordinary level N *(Brit Educ: formerly)* *examen passé à l'âge de 16 ans dans le cadre des études secondaires*
Ordinary National Certificate N *(Brit Educ)* ≃ brevet *m* de technicien
Ordinary National Diploma N *(Brit Educ)* ≃ brevet *m* de technicien supérieur
ordinary seaman N (pl **ordinary seamen**) *(Brit Navy)* matelot *m* non breveté
ordinary share N *(Stock Exchange)* action *f* ordinaire

ordination /ˌɔːdɪˈneɪʃən/ N *(Rel)* ordination *f*

ordnance /ˈɔːdnəns/ *(Mil)* N *(= guns)* (pièces *fpl* d')artillerie *f* ; *(= unit)* service *m* du matériel et des dépôts
COMP **Ordnance Corps** N Service *m* du matériel
ordnance factory N usine *f* d'artillerie
Ordnance Survey N *(in Brit)* service *m* cartographique de l'État ◆ **Ordnance Survey map** ≃ carte *f* d'état-major

Ordovician /ˌɔːdəʊˈvɪʃɪən/ ADJ ordovicien

ordure /ˈɔːdjʊəʳ/ N ordure *f*

ore /ɔːʳ/ N minerai *m* ◆ **iron ~** minerai *m* de fer

Ore(g). abbrev of **Oregon**

oregano /ˌɒrɪˈɡɑːnəʊ, (US) əˈreɡənəʊ/ N origan *m*

Oregon /ˈɒrɪɡən/ N Oregon *m* ◆ **in ~** dans l'Oregon

Oreo ® /ˈɔːrɪəʊ/ N (US) 1 *(= food)* *gâteau sec au chocolat fourré à la vanille* 2 *(*‡* = person)* Noir(e) *m(f)* qui imite les Blancs

Orestes /ɒˈrestiːz/ N Oreste *m*

organ /ˈɔːɡən/ N 1 *(Mus)* orgue *m*, orgues *fpl* ◆ **grand ~** grandes orgues *fpl* ; → **barrel, mouth**
2 *(Anat)* organe *m* ; *(= penis)* sexe *m* ◆ **vocal ~s, ~s of speech** organes *mpl* vocaux, appareil *m* vocal ◆ **reproductive** *or* **sex(ual) ~s** organes *mpl* génitaux *or* sexuels ◆ **the male ~** le sexe masculin
3 *(fig = instrument)* organe *m* ◆ **the chief ~ of the administration** l'organe principal de l'administration
4 *(Press = mouthpiece)* organe *m*, porte-parole *m inv*
COMP **organ bank** N *(Med)* banque *f* d'organes
organ-builder N facteur *m* d'orgues
organ donor N donneur *m*, -euse *f* d'organe(s)
organ-grinder N joueur *m*, -euse *f* d'orgue de Barbarie ◆ **I want to talk to the ~-grinder, not the (~-grinder's) monkey*** *(pej)* je veux parler au responsable
organ loft N tribune *f* d'orgue
organ pipe N tuyau *m* d'orgue
organ screen N jubé *m*
organ stop N jeu *m* d'orgue
organ transplant N greffe *f or* transplantation *f* d'organe

organdie, organdy (US) /ˈɔːɡəndɪ/ N organdi *m* COMP en organdi, d'organdi

organic /ɔːˈɡænɪk/ ADJ 1 *(Chem)* *[matter, waste, fertilizer, compound]* organique 2 *(Agr, Culin = non-chemical)* *[farm, farming, methods, produce, food]* biologique, bio* *inv* ; *[farmer]* biologique ; *[meat, poultry]* sans hormones ◆ **~ restaurant** restaurant *m* diététique 3 *(frm = integral)* *[society, state, community]* organique ; *[part]* fondamental ◆ **~ whole** tout *m* systématique ◆ **~ law** loi *f* organique 4 *(frm = gradual, natural)* *[growth, development]* organique
COMP **organic chemistry** N chimie *f* organique
organic disease N maladie *f* organique

organically /ɔːˈɡænɪkəlɪ/ ADV 1 *(Agr, Culin = not chemically)* *[farm, grow, produce]* biologiquement, sans engrais chimiques ◆ **~ grown vegetables** légumes *mpl* biologiques ◆ **an ~ rich soil** un sol riche en composés organiques 2 *(= naturally)* *[develop, integrate]* naturellement 3 *(= physically)* *[weak]* physiquement

organism /ˈɔːɡənɪzəm/ N organisme *m (Bio)*

organist /ˈɔːɡənɪst/ N organiste *mf*

organization /ˌɔːɡənaɪˈzeɪʃən/ N 1 *(= association)* organisation *f* ; *(= statutory body)* organisme *m*, organisation *f* ; *(= society)* organisation *f*, association *f* ◆ **youth ~** organisation *f or* organisme *m* de jeunesse ◆ **she belongs to several ~s** elle est membre de plusieurs organisations *or* associations ◆ **a charitable ~** une œuvre *or* une association de bienfaisance ; → **travel**
2 *[of event, activity]* organisation *f* ◆ **his work lacks ~** son travail manque d'organisation ◆ **a project of this size takes a lot of ~** un projet de cette ampleur requiert une bonne organisation
COMP **organization and methods** N *(Comm, Admin)* organisation *f* scientifique du travail, OST *f*
organization chart N organigramme *m*
organization expenses NPL *(Fin)* frais *mpl* d'établissement
organization man N (pl **organization men**) *(pej)* *cadre qui s'identifie complètement à son entreprise*

organizational /ˌɔːɡənaɪˈzeɪʃənl/ ADJ *[skill, ability]* d'organisateur ; *[problems]* d'organisation, organisationnel ; *[support, goals, links, structure]* organisationnel ; *[experience]* de l'organisation ; *[framework]* structurel, organisationnel ◆ **~ change** *(Jur, Comm)* changement *m* structurel, modification *f* structurelle ◆ **at an ~ level** au niveau organisationnel *or* de l'organisation

organize /ˈɔːɡənaɪz/ VT 1 *[+ meeting, scheme, course, visit, elections, strike, campaign, protest]* organiser ◆ **they ~d (it) for me to go to London** ils ont organisé mon départ pour Londres ◆ **I'll ~ something to eat for us*, I'll ~ us something to eat*** *(= buy food)* je vais prévoir quelque chose à manger pour nous ; *(= prepare food)* je vais nous préparer un petit quelque chose ◆ **can you ~ the food for us?** vous pouvez vous occuper de la nourriture ? ◆ **she's always organizing people*** elle veut toujours tout organiser ◆ **to ~ one's thoughts, to get one's thoughts ~d** mettre de l'ordre dans ses idées ◆ **to get (o.s.) ~d** s'organiser ; see also **organized** 2 *(into trade union)* syndiquer ; see also **organized** VI *(= form trade union)* se syndiquer

organized /ˈɔːɡənaɪzd/ ADJ organisé
COMP **organized chaos*** N *(hum)* désordre *m* organisé
organized crime N crime *m* organisé
organized labour N *(Ind)* main-d'œuvre *f* syndiquée
organized religion N religion *f* en tant qu'institution

organizer /ˈɔːɡənaɪzəʳ/ N 1 *[of event, activity]* organisateur *m*, -trice *f* ◆ **the ~s apologize for ...** les organisateurs vous prient de les excuser pour ... 2 ◆ **to be a good/bad ~** être un bon/mauvais organisateur 3 *(= diary)* ◆ **personal ~** Filofax ® *m*, organiseur *m* personnel ◆ **electronic ~** agenda *m* électronique

organizing /ˈɔːɡənaɪzɪŋ/ N *[of event, activity etc]* organisation *f* ◆ **she loves ~** elle adore organiser ADJ *[group, committee]* (qui est) chargé de l'organisation

organophosphate /ɔːˌɡænəʊˈfɒsfeɪt/ N organophosphoré *m*

organza /ɔːˈɡænzə/ N organza *m*

orgasm /ˈɔːɡæzəm/ N orgasme *m* ◆ **to bring sb to ~** amener qn à l'orgasme ◆ **to achieve** *or* **reach ~** atteindre l'orgasme VI avoir un orgasme

orgasmic /ɔːˈɡæzmɪk/ ADJ 1 *[person, state]* orgasmique 2 *(* = enjoyable) [experience, pleasure]* jouissif

orgiastic /ˌɔːdʒɪˈæstɪk/ ADJ orgiaque

orgy /ˈɔːdʒɪ/ N *(lit, fig)* orgie *f* ◆ **an ~ of killing/destruction** une orgie de tueries/destruction ◆ **a spending ~** des dépenses folles

oriel /ˈɔːrɪəl/ N (also **oriel window**) (fenêtre *f* en) oriel *m*

orient /ˈɔːrɪənt/ N *(liter)* orient *m*, levant *m* ◆ **the Orient** l'Orient VT *(lit, fig)* orienter ◆ **to ~ o.s.** s'orienter, se repérer ; see also **oriented**

oriental /ˌɔːrɪˈentəl/ ADJ *[peoples, civilization, design]* oriental ; *[carpet]* d'Orient N ◆ **Oriental** † Oriental(e) *m(f)*

orientalist /ˌɔːrɪˈentəlɪst/ N orientaliste *mf*

orientate /ˈɔːrɪənteɪt/ VT ⇒ **orient vt** ; see also **oriented**

orientated /ˈɔːrɪənteɪtɪd/ ADJ ⇒ **oriented**

orientation /ˌɔːrɪənˈteɪʃən/ N *(gen)* orientation *f* ◆ **the group's political ~** la tendance *or* l'orientation politique du groupe ◆ **~ week** *(US Univ)* semaine *f* d'accueil des étudiants

oriented /ˈɔːrɪəntɪd/ ADJ ◆ **~ to** *or* **towards** *(= giving priority to, influenced by)* axé sur ; *(= specially for needs of)* adapté aux besoins de ◆ **the film is ~ to the British audience** ce film s'adresse en premier lieu au public britannique ◆ **their policies are ~ to(wards) controlling inflation** leurs politiques ont pour objet de *or* visent à juguler l'inflation ◆ **a defence-~ budget** un budget axé sur la défense, un budget qui privilégie la défense ◆ **a strongly export-~ economy** une économie fortement axée sur l'exportation ◆ **industry-~ research** recherche *f* axée sur les besoins de l'industrie ◆ **user-/pupil-** *etc* **~** adapté aux besoins de *or* spécialement conçu pour l'usager/l'élève *etc* ◆ **politically ~** orienté (politiquement) ◆ **he's not very family-~** il n'est pas très famille ◆ **it's still a very male-~ job** cela demeure un emploi essentiellement masculin

orienteering /ˌɔːrɪənˈtɪərɪŋ/ N *(Sport)* course *f* d'orientation

orifice /ˈɒrɪfɪs/ N orifice *m*

origami /ˌɒrɪˈɡɑːmɪ/ N origami *m*

origan /ˈɒrɪɡən/ N origan *m*

origin /ˈɒrɪdʒɪn/ N *(= parentage, source)* origine *f* ; *[of manufactured goods]* origine *f*, provenance *f* ◆ **the ~ of this lies in ...** l'origine en est ... ◆ **to have humble ~s, to be of humble ~** être d'origine modeste, avoir des origines modestes ◆ **his family's ~s are in France** sa famille est d'origine française *or* originaire de France ◆ **country of ~** pays *m* d'origine ◆ **to have its ~s in** *[problem]* provenir de ◆ **the idea has its ~s in medieval Europe** cette idée trouve sa source dans l'Europe du Moyen Âge ◆ **this fruit has its ~s in Asia** ce fruit est originaire d'Asie

original /əˈrɪdʒɪnl/ ADJ 1 *(= first, earliest) [meaning]* originel ; *[inhabitant, member]* premier ; *[purpose, suggestion]* initial, premier ; *[shape, colour]* primitif ; *[edition]* original, princeps *inv* ◆ **~ cost** *(Fin, Comm)* coût *m* d'acquisition ◆ **~ jurisdiction** *(US Jur)* juridiction *f* de première instance ◆ **~ sin** le péché originel 2 *(= not copied etc) [painting, idea, writer]* original ; *[play]* inédit, original 3 *(= unconventional, innovative) [character, person]* original ◆ **he's an ~ thinker, he's got an ~ mind** c'est un esprit original N 1 *[of painting, language, document]* original *m* ◆ **to read Dante in the ~ (Italian)** lire Dante dans le texte 2 *(* = person)* original(e) *m(f)*, phénomène* *m*

originality /əˌrɪdʒɪˈnælɪtɪ/ N originalité *f*

originally /əˈrɪdʒənəlɪ/ ADV 1 *(= initially) [intend, plan]* au départ, à l'origine ◆ **he's ~ from Armenia** il est originaire d'Arménie ◆ **it was ~ a hit for Janis Joplin** au départ, c'était un succès de Janis Joplin 2 *(= unconventionally, innovatively) [dress]* de façon originale ◆ **to think ~** avoir des idées novatrices *or* originales

originate /əˈrɪdʒɪneɪt/ VT *[person]* être l'auteur de, être à l'origine de ; *[event etc]* donner naissance à ◆ **originating bank** banque *f* émettrice VI ◆ **to ~ from** *[person]* être originaire de ; *[goods]* provenir de ◆ **to ~ from sb** *[suggestion, idea]* émaner de qn ◆ **to ~ in** *[stream, custom etc]* prendre naissance *or* sa source dans

origination fee /əˌrɪdʒɪˈneɪʃənˈfiː/ N frais *mpl* de constitution de dossier

originator /əˈrɪdʒɪneɪtəʳ/ N auteur *m*, créateur *m*, -trice *f* ; *[of plan etc]* initiateur *m*, -trice *f*

Orinoco /ˌɒrɪˈnəʊkəʊ/ N Orénoque *m*

oriole /ˈɔːrɪəʊl/ N loriot *m* ; → **golden**

Orion /əˈraɪən/ N *(Astron)* Orion *f* ; *(Myth)* Orion *m*

Orkney /ˈɔːknɪ/ N ◆ **the ~ Islands, the ~s** les Orcades *fpl*

Orlon ® /ˈɔːlɒn/ N orlon ® *m* COMP en orlon ®

ormer /ˈɔːməʳ/ N *(= shellfish)* ormeau *m*

ormolu /ˈɔːməʊluː/ N similor *m*, chrysocale *m* COMP en similor, en chrysocale

ornament /ˈɔːnəmənt/ N 1 *(on building, ceiling, dress etc)* ornement *m* 2 *(= ornamental object)* objet *m* décoratif, bibelot *m* ; *(fig, liter = person, quality)* ornement *m (fig, liter)* ◆ **a row of ~s on the shelf** une rangée de bibelots sur l'étagère 3 *(NonC = ornamentation)* ornement *m* ◆ **rich in ~** richement orné 4 *(Mus)* ornement *m* VT /ˈɔːnəment/ *[+ style]* orner, embellir (*with* de) ; *[+ room, building, ceiling]* décorer, ornementer (*with* de) ; *[+ dress]* agrémenter, orner (*with* de)

ornamental /ˌɔːnəˈmentl/ ADJ 1 *(= decorative) [plant, shrub]* ornemental, décoratif ; *[garden, pond, lake]* d'agrément ; *[design]* décoratif 2 *(*: pej hum) [person, role]* décoratif *(pej)*

ornamentation /ˌɔːnəmenˈteɪʃən/ N *(NonC, gen)* ornementation *f*, décoration *f* ; *(Mus)* ornements *mpl*

ornate /ɔːˈneɪt/ ADJ très orné

ornately /ɔːˈneɪtlɪ/ ADV *[carved, decorated]* richement

ornery* /ˈɔːnərɪ/ ADJ *(US) [person] (= bad-tempered)* désagréable ; *(= nasty)* méchant ; *(= stubborn)* entêté

ornithological /ˌɔːnɪθəˈlɒdʒɪkəl/ ADJ ornithologique

ornithologist /ˌɔːnɪˈθɒlədʒɪst/ N ornithologue *mf*

ornithology /ˌɔːnɪˈθɒlədʒɪ/ N ornithologie *f*

orogeny /ɒˈrɒdʒɪnɪ/ N orogénie *f*, orogenèse *f*

orphan /ˈɔːfən/ N orphelin(e) *m(f)* ADJ orphelin VT ◆ **to be ~ed** devenir orphelin(e) ◆ **the children were ~ed by** *or* **in the accident** les enfants ont perdu leurs parents dans l'accident

orphanage /ˈɔːfənɪdʒ/ N orphelinat *m*

Orpheus /ˈɔːfjuːs/ N Orphée *m* ◆ **~ in the Underworld** *(Mus)* Orphée aux enfers

Orphic /ˈɔːfɪk/ ADJ orphique

orthodontic /ˌɔːθəʊˈdɒntɪk/ ADJ orthodontique

orthodontics /ˌɔːθəʊˈdɒntɪks/ N *(NonC)* orthodontie *f*

orthodontist /ˌɔːθəʊˈdɒntɪst/ N orthodontiste *mf*

orthodox /ˈɔːθədɒks/ ADJ *(gen, Rel) [person, view, method]* orthodoxe ; *(Med) [doctor, practitioner]* exerçant la médecine traditionnelle ; *[medicine]* traditionnel ◆ **~ Jews/Communists** juifs *mpl*/communistes *mpl* orthodoxes COMP **the Orthodox Church** N (also **the Eastern Orthodox Church**) les Églises *fpl* orthodoxes

orthodoxy /ˈɔːθədɒksɪ/ N orthodoxie *f*

orthogonal /ɔːˈθɒɡənl/ ADJ orthogonal

orthographic(al) /ˌɔːθəˈɡræfɪk(əl)/ ADJ orthographique

orthography /ɔːˈθɒɡrəfɪ/ N orthographe *f*

orthopaedic, orthopedic *(US)* /ˌɔːθəʊˈpiːdɪk/ ADJ *[ward, shoes]* orthopédique ; *[patient]* en traitement orthopédique
COMP **orthopaedic bed** N *(specially firm)* lit *m* à sommier anatomique, lit *m* orthopédique
orthopaedic mattress N sommier *m* anatomique
orthopaedic surgeon N chirurgien *m* orthopédiste
orthopaedic surgery N chirurgie *f* orthopédique

orthopaedics, orthopedics *(US)* /ˌɔːθəʊˈpiːdɪks/ N *(NonC)* orthopédie *f*

orthopaedist, orthopedist *(US)* /ˌɔːθəʊˈpiːdɪst/ N orthopédiste *mf*

orthopaedy, orthopedy *(US)* /ˈɔːθəʊpiːdɪ/ N ⇒ **orthopaedics**

ortolan /ˈɔːtələn/ N ortolan *m*

Orwellian /ɔːˈwelɪən/ ADJ *(Literat etc)* d'Orwell, orwellien

oryx /ˈɒrɪks/ N (pl **oryxes** *or* **oryx**) oryx *m*

OS /əʊˈes/ 1 *(Comput)* abbrev of **operating system** 2 *(Brit Navy)* (abbrev of **Ordinary Seaman**)

→ **ordinary** [3] *(Brit)* (abbrev of **Ordnance Survey**) → **ordnance** [4] abbrev of **outsize**

os /ɒs/ N *(Anat)* os *m* COMP **os coxae** N os *m* iliaque *or* coxal

Oscar /ˈɒskəʳ/ N *(Cine)* Oscar *m* ◆ **he won an ~ for best actor/for his last film** il a reçu l'Oscar du meilleur acteur/un Oscar pour son dernier film ◆ **to win an ~ nomination** être nominé aux Oscars, recevoir une nomination aux Oscars ◆ **~-winning** qui a reçu *or* remporté un Oscar (*or* des Oscars) ◆ **~-winner Gary Irons** Gary Irons, qui a reçu *or* remporté l'Oscar du meilleur acteur (*or* réalisateur *etc*) ◆ **his first film, his only ~-winner** son premier film, le seul à avoir reçu un Oscar *or* à avoir été oscarisé

oscillate /ˈɒsɪleɪt/ VI *(gen, Elec, Phys etc)* osciller ; *(fig) [ideas, opinions]* fluctuer, varier ; *[person]* osciller, balancer *(between* entre) VT faire osciller

oscillation /ˌɒsɪˈleɪʃən/ N oscillation *f*

oscillator /ˈɒsɪleɪtəʳ/ N oscillateur *m*

oscillatory /ˌɒsɪˈleɪtərɪ/ ADJ oscillatoire

oscilloscope /ɒˈsɪləskəʊp/ N oscilloscope *m*

osculate /ˈɒskjʊleɪt/ *(hum)* VI s'embrasser VT embrasser

OSHA /ˌəʊeseɪtʃˈeɪ/ N *(US)* (abbrev of **Occupational Safety and Health Administration**) → **occupational**

osier /ˈəʊʒəʳ/ N osier *m* COMP *[branch]* d'osier ; *[basket]* en osier, d'osier

Osiris /əʊˈsaɪrɪs/ N Osiris *m*

Oslo /ˈɒzləʊ/ N Oslo

osmium /ˈɒzmɪəm/ N osmium *m*

osmosis /ɒzˈməʊsɪs/ N *(Phys, fig)* osmose *f* ◆ **by ~** *(lit, fig)* par osmose

osmotic /ɒzˈmɒtɪk/ ADJ osmotique

osprey /ˈɒspreɪ/ N balbuzard *m* (pêcheur)

osseous /ˈɒsɪəs/ ADJ [1] *(Anat, Zool)* osseux [2] ⇒ **ossiferous**

ossicle /ˈɒsɪkl/ N osselet *m*

ossiferous /ɒˈsɪfərəs/ ADJ ossifère

ossification /ˌɒsɪfɪˈkeɪʃən/ N ossification *f*

ossify /ˈɒsɪfaɪ/ *(lit, fig)* VT ossifier VI s'ossifier

ossuary /ˈɒsjʊərɪ/ N ossuaire *m*

Ostend /ɒsˈtend/ N Ostende

ostensible /ɒsˈtensəbl/ ADJ *(frm)* avoué

ostensibly /ɒsˈtensəblɪ/ ADV *(frm) [independent, innocuous etc]* soi-disant ◆ **he was ~ a student** il était soi-disant étudiant ◆ **he went out, ~ to telephone** il est sorti, soi-disant pour téléphoner ◆ **the road is closed, ~ because of landslides** la route est barrée, soi-disant à cause d'éboulements

ostensive /ɒˈstensɪv/ ADJ [1] *(Ling etc)* ostensif [2] ⇒ **ostensible**

ostentation /ˌɒstenˈteɪʃən/ N *(NonC)* ostentation *f*

ostentatious /ˌɒstenˈteɪʃəs/ ADJ [1] *(pej = extravagant) [car, clothes]* tape-à-l'œil *inv* ; *[surroundings]* prétentieux [2] *(pej = flamboyant) [person]* prétentieux ; *[manner]* prétentieux, ostentatoire *(liter)* [3] *(= exaggerated) [gesture, dislike, concern, attempt]* exagéré, ostentatoire *(liter)*

ostentatiously /ˌɒstenˈteɪʃəslɪ/ ADV [1] *(pej = extravagantly) [decorate, live]* avec ostentation ; *[dress]* de façon voyante [2] *(= exaggeratedly) [try, yawn]* avec ostentation ◆ **he looked ~ at his watch** il a regardé sa montre avec ostentation

osteo... /ˈɒstɪəʊ/ PREF ostéo...

osteoarthritis /ˈɒstɪəʊɑːˈθraɪtɪs/ N ostéoarthrite *f*

osteoblast /ˈɒstɪəʊblɑːst/ N ostéoblaste *m*

osteogenesis /ˌɒstɪəʊˈdʒenɪsɪs/ N ostéogenèse *f*, ostéogénie *f*

osteology /ˌɒstɪˈɒlədʒɪ/ N ostéologie *f*

osteomalacia /ˌɒstɪəʊməˈleɪʃɪə/ N ostéomalacie *f*

osteomyelitis /ˌɒstɪəʊmaɪˈlaɪtɪs/ N ostéomyélite *f*

osteopath /ˈɒstɪəpæθ/ N ostéopathe *mf*

osteopathy /ˌɒstɪˈɒpəθɪ/ N ostéopathie *f*

osteophyte /ˈɒstɪəfaɪt/ N ostéophyte *m*

osteoplasty /ˈɒstɪəplæstɪ/ N ostéoplastie *f*

osteoporosis /ˌɒstɪəʊpɔːˈrəʊsɪs/ N ostéoporose *f*

osteotomy /ˈɒstɪˈɒtəmɪ/ N ostéotomie *f*

ostler †† /ˈɒsləʳ/ N *(esp Brit)* valet *m* d'écurie

ostracism /ˈɒstrəsɪzəm/ N ostracisme *m*

ostracize /ˈɒstrəsaɪz/ VT ostraciser

ostrich /ˈɒstrɪtʃ/ N autruche *f*

OT /əʊˈtiː/ [1] *(Bible)* (abbrev of **Old Testament**) → **old** [2] *(Med)* (abbrev of **occupational therapy**) → **occupational**

OTB /ˌəʊtiːˈbiː/ N *(US)* (abbrev of **off-track betting**) ≈ PMU *m*

OTC /ˌəʊtiːˈsiː/ N *(Brit Mil)* (abbrev of **Officers' Training Corps**) → **officer** ADJ abbrev of **over-the-counter**

OTE /ˌəʊtiːˈiː/ N (abbrev of **on-target earnings**) → **target**

other /ˈʌðəʳ/ ADJ autre ◆ **the ~ one** l'autre *mf* ◆ **the ~ five** les cinq autres *mfpl* ◆ **~ people have done it** d'autres l'ont fait ◆ **~ people's property** la propriété d'autrui ◆ **it always happens to ~ people** ça arrive toujours aux autres ◆ **the ~ world** *(fig)* l'au-delà *m*, l'autre monde *m* ; see also **otherworldly** ◆ **the ~ day/week** l'autre jour *m*/semaine *f* ◆ **come back some ~ time** revenez un autre jour ◆ **~ ranks** *(esp Brit: Mil)* ≈ sous-officiers *mpl* et soldats *mpl* ◆ **some writer or ~ said that ...** je ne sais quel écrivain a dit que ..., un écrivain, je ne sais plus lequel, a dit que ... ◆ **some fool or ~** un idiot quelconque ◆ **there must be some ~ way of doing it** on doit pouvoir le faire d'une autre manière ; → **every, hand, time, word**

PRON autre *mf* ◆ **and these five ~s** et ces cinq autres ◆ **there are some ~s** il y en a d'autres ◆ **several ~s have mentioned it** plusieurs autres l'ont mentionné ◆ **one after the ~** l'un après l'autre ◆ **~s have spoken of him** il y en a d'autres qui ont parlé de lui ◆ **he doesn't like hurting ~s** il n'aime pas faire de mal aux autres *or* à autrui ◆ **some like flying, ~s prefer the train** les uns aiment prendre l'avion, les autres préfèrent le train ◆ **some do, ~s don't** il y en a qui le font, d'autres qui ne le font pas ◆ **one or ~ of them will come** il y en aura bien un qui viendra ◆ **somebody or ~ suggested that ...** je ne sais qui a suggéré que ..., quelqu'un, je ne sais qui, a suggéré que ... ◆ **they concentrated on one problem to the exclusion of all ~s** ils se sont concentrés sur un problème, à l'exclusion de tous les autres ◆ **you and no ~** vous et personne d'autre ◆ **no ~ than** nul autre que ; → **each, none**

ADV [1] *(= otherwise)* autrement ◆ **he could not have acted ~ than he did** il n'aurait pas pu agir autrement ◆ **I wouldn't wish him ~ than he is** il est très bien comme il est ◆ **I've never seen her ~ than with her husband** je ne l'ai jamais vue (autrement) qu'avec son mari ◆ **I couldn't do ~ than come, I could do nothing ~ than come** *(frm)* je ne pouvais faire autrement que de venir, je ne pouvais pas ne pas venir

[2] ◆ **~ than ...** *(= apart from)* à part ... ◆ **~ than that, I said nothing** à part ça, je n'ai rien dit, je n'ai rien dit d'autre ◆ **no one ~ than a member of the family** nul autre qu'un membre de la famille ; → **somehow**

COMP **other-directed** ADJ *(US Psych)* conformiste

otherness /ˈʌðənɪs/ N altérité *f*

otherwise /ˈʌðəwaɪz/ ADV [1] *(= in another way)* autrement ◆ **some people think ~** certaines personnes pensent autrement ◆ **I could not do ~** je ne pouvais faire autrement ◆ **it cannot be ~** il ne peut en être autrement ◆ **he was ~ engaged** il était occupé à (faire) autre chose ◆ **Montgomery ~ (known as) Monty** Montgomery alias Monty

◆ **or otherwise** *(= or not)* ◆ **any organization, political or ~** toute organisation, politique ou non ◆ **the success or ~ of the project** la réussite ou l'échec du projet

[2] *(= if this were not the case)* sinon, autrement ◆ **I do lots of sport, ~ I'd go mad** je fais beaucoup de sport, sinon *or* autrement je deviendrais fou

[3] *(in other respects)* par ailleurs ◆ **it was a violent end to an ~ peaceful demonstration** la manifestation, par ailleurs pacifique, s'est terminée dans la violence ◆ **the boat needed repainting, but ~ it was in good condition** le bateau avait besoin d'être repeint, mais sinon *or* autrement il était en bon état

[4] *(= something different)* **they say crime is on the increase, but a recent study suggests ~** ils prétendent que la criminalité augmente, mais une étude récente tend à prouver le contraire ◆ **take 60mg a day, unless ~ advised by a doctor** prendre 60 mg par jour, sauf avis médical contraire ◆ **all the translations are my own, unless ~ stated** toutes les traductions sont de moi, sauf mention contraire ◆ **until proved ~** jusqu'à preuve du contraire

otherworldly /ˌʌðəˈwɜːldlɪ/ ADJ *[attitude]* détaché des contingences ; *[person]* détaché du monde

otiose /ˈəʊʃɪəʊs/ ADJ *(frm)* (= *idle*) oisif ; (= *useless*) oiseux

otitis /əʊˈtaɪtɪs/ N otite *f*

OTT * /ˌəʊtiːˈtiː/ (abbrev of **over the top**) → **top**[1]

Ottawa /ˈɒtəwə/ N (= *city*) Ottawa ; (= *river*) Ottawa *f*, Outaouais *m*

otter /ˈɒtəʳ/ N loutre *f* ; → **sea**

Otto /ˈɒtəʊ/ N *(Hist)* Othon *m* or Otton *m*

Ottoman /ˈɒtəmən/ ADJ ottoman N Ottoman(e) *m(f)*

ottoman /ˈɒtəmən/ N (pl **ottomans**) ottomane *f*

OU /əʊˈjuː/ *(Brit Educ)* [1] (abbrev of **Open University**) → **open** [2] abbrev of **Oxford University**

ouch /aʊtʃ/ EXCL aïe !

ought[1] /ɔːt/ LANGUAGE IN USE 1.1 (pret **ought**) MODAL AUX VB [1] *(indicating obligation, advisability, desirability)* **I ~ to do it** je devrais le faire, il faudrait *or* il faut que je le fasse ◆ **I really ~ to go and see him** je devrais bien aller le voir ◆ **he thought he ~ to tell you** il a pensé qu'il devait vous le dire ◆ **if they behave as they ~** s'ils se conduisent comme ils le doivent, s'ils se conduisent correctement ◆ **this ~ to have been finished long ago** cela aurait dû être terminé il y a longtemps ◆ **oughtn't you to have left by now?** est-ce que vous n'auriez pas dû déjà être parti ?

[2] *(indicating probability)* **they ~ to be arriving soon** ils devraient bientôt arriver ◆ **he ~ to have got there by now I expect** je pense qu'il est arrivé *or* qu'il a dû arriver (à l'heure qu'il est) ◆ **that ~ to do** ça devrait aller ◆ **that ~ to be very enjoyable** cela devrait être très agréable

ought[2] /ɔːt/ N ⇒ **aught**

Ouija ®, **ouija** /ˈwiːdʒə/ N ◆ **~ board** oui-ja *m inv*

ounce /aʊns/ **N** 1 (= *measurement*) once *f* (= 28,35 *grammes*) ; (*fig*) [*of truth, malice, sense, strength etc*] once *f*, gramme *m* 2 (= *animal*) once *f*

our /ˈaʊəʳ/ **POSS ADJ** notre (nos *pl*) ◆ ~ **book** notre livre *m* ◆ ~ **table** notre table *f* ◆ ~ **clothes** nos vêtements *mpl* ◆ **Our Father/Lady** (*Rel*) Notre Père *m*/Dame *f* ◆ **that's OUR car** (*emphatic*) c'est notre voiture à nous

ours /ˈaʊəz/ **POSS PRON** le nôtre, la nôtre, les nôtres ◆ **this car is** ~ cette voiture est à nous *or* nous appartient *or* est la nôtre ◆ **your house is better than** ~ votre maison est mieux que la nôtre ◆ **the house became** ~ la maison est devenue la nôtre ◆ **it is not ~ to decide** (*frm*) ce n'est pas à nous de décider, il ne nous appartient pas de décider ◆ ~ **is a specialized department** nous sommes un service spécialisé

◆ **of ours** ◆ **a friend of** ~ un de nos amis (à nous), un ami à nous* ◆ **I think it's one of** ~ je crois que c'est un des nôtres ◆ **it's no fault of** ~ ce n'est pas de notre faute (à nous) ◆ **that car of** ~ (*pej*) notre fichue* voiture ◆ **that stupid son of** ~ (*pej*) notre idiot de fils ◆ **no advice of ~ could prevent him** aucun conseil de notre part ne pouvait l'empêcher

ourself /ˌaʊəˈself/ **PERS PRON** (*frm, liter: of royal or editorial "we"*) nous-même

ourselves /ˌaʊəˈselvz/ **PERS PRON** (*reflexive: direct and indirect*) nous ; (*emphatic*) nous-mêmes ; (*after prep*) nous ◆ **we enjoyed** ~ nous nous sommes bien amusés ◆ **we said to** ~ nous nous sommes dit, on s'est dit* ◆ **we saw it** ~ nous l'avons vu nous-mêmes ◆ **we've kept three for** ~ nous nous en sommes réservé trois ◆ **people like** ~ des gens comme nous ◆ **we were talking amongst** ~ nous discutions entre nous ◆ **we had the beach to** ~ on avait la plage pour nous

◆ **(all) by ourselves** tout seuls, toutes seules

oust /aʊst/ **VT** évincer (*sb from sth* qn de qch) ◆ **they ~ed him from the chairmanship** ils l'ont évincé de la présidence, ils l'ont forcé à démissionner ◆ **she soon ~ed him as the teenagers' idol** elle eut vite fait de lui prendre sa place d'idole des jeunes

out /aʊt/

1 ADVERB	4 NOUN
2 ADJECTIVE	5 TRANSITIVE VERB
3 PREPOSITION	6 COMPOUNDS

When **out** is the second element in a phrasal verb, eg **get out**, **go out**, **speak out**, look up the verb. When **out** is part of a set combination, eg **day out**, **voyage out**, look up the noun.

1 - ADVERB

1 [= outside] dehors ◆ **it's hot** ~ il fait chaud dehors *or* à l'extérieur ◆ ~ **you go !** sortez !, filez !* ; (*above exit*) ◆ **"out"** "sortie"

2 [person] ◆ **to be** ~ (= *to have gone out*) être sorti ; (= *to go out*) sortir ◆ **Paul is** ~ Paul est sorti *or* n'est pas là ◆ **he's ~ a good deal** il sort beaucoup, il n'est pas souvent chez lui ◆ **he's ~ fishing** il est (parti) à la pêche

out, when followed by a preposition, is not usually translated.

◆ **he's ~ in the garden** il est dans le jardin ◆ **when he was ~ in Iran** lorsqu'il était en Iran ◆ **he's ~ to dinner** il est sorti dîner ◆ **he went ~ to China** il est parti en Chine ; → **out of**

3 [homosexual] ◆ **to be** ~ * assumer publiquement son homosexualité

4 [Tennis] ◆ **(the ball is)** ~ **!** (la balle est) out !

5 [tide] ◆ **when the tide is** ~ à marée basse

6 [expressing distance] ◆ **five days ~ from Liverpool** à cinq jours (de voyage) de Liverpool ◆ **the boat was 10 miles** ~ **(to sea)** le bateau était à 10 milles de la côte ◆ **their house is 10km ~ (of town)** leur maison est à 10 km de la ville ◆ **to be ~ at sea** être en mer

7 [set structures]

◆ **to be out and about** ◆ **you should be ~ and about!** ne restez donc pas enfermé ! ◆ **to be ~ and about again** être de nouveau sur pied

◆ **out here** ici ◆ **come in! – no, I like it ~ here** entrez ! – non, je suis bien ici ◆ **she doesn't know how to get on with the people ~ here** elle a du mal à sympathiser avec les gens d'ici

◆ **out there** (= *in that place*) là ; (*further away*) là-bas ◆ **look ~ there** regardez là-bas

◆ **out with it !** * vas-y, parle !

2 - ADJECTIVE

1 [= extinguished] [*light, fire, gas*] éteint

2 [= available] en vente ◆ **the video is ~ now** la vidéo est maintenant en vente ◆ **a new edition is ~ this month** une nouvelle édition sort ce mois-ci

3 [= unavailable : for lending, renting] ◆ **that book is** ~ ce livre est sorti ◆ **the video I wanted was** ~ la cassette vidéo que je voulais était sortie

4 [= revealed] ◆ **the secret is** ~ le secret n'en est plus un

5 [= unconscious] évanoui, sans connaissance ◆ **he was ~ for 30 seconds** il est resté évanoui *or* sans connaissance pendant 30 secondes

6 [= wrong, incorrect] ◆ **their timing was five minutes** ~ ils s'étaient trompés de cinq minutes ◆ **you were ~ by 20cm, you were 20cm** ~ vous vous êtes trompé *or* vous avez fait une erreur de 20 cm ◆ **you're not far** ~ tu ne te trompes pas de beaucoup, tu n'es pas tombé loin*

7 [= unacceptable] [*idea, suggestion*] ◆ **that's right ~, I'm afraid** il n'en est malheureusement pas question

8 [= defeated] (*in cards, games*) ◆ **you're** ~ tu es éliminé ◆ **the socialists are** ~ (*politically*) les socialistes sont battus

9 [= finished] ◆ **before the month was** ~ avant la fin du mois

10 [= striking] ◆ **the steelworkers are ~ (on strike)** les ouvriers des aciéries sont en grève

11 [= unfashionable] passé de mode, out *inv* ◆ **long skirts are** ~ les jupes longues sont passées de mode *or* out ◆ **romance is making a comeback, reality is** ~ les histoires d'amour font leur come-back, le réalisme est passé de mode *or* out

12 [in society] [*girl*] **is your sister ~?** † est-ce que votre sœur a fait son entrée dans le monde ?

13 [flowers, sun, moon *etc*] ◆ **the roses are** ~ les rosiers sont en fleur(s) ◆ **the trees were** ~ les arbres étaient verts ◆ **the sun was** ~ le soleil brillait ◆ **the moon was** ~ la lune s'était levée, il y avait clair de lune ◆ **the stars were** ~ les étoiles brillaient

14 [set structures]

◆ **to be out to do sth** * (= *seeking to do*) chercher à faire qch ◆ **they're just ~ to make a quick profit** ils ne cherchent qu'à se remplir les poches ◆ **they were ~ to get him** ils voulaient sa peau*

◆ **to be out for sth** * (= *seeking*) ◆ **he's ~ for all he can get** il cherche à profiter au maximum de la situation ◆ **she was just ~ for a good time** elle ne cherchait qu'à s'amuser

3 - PREPOSITION

◆ **out of**

When **out of** is part of a phrasal verb, eg **come out of**, **run out of**, look up the verb. When it is part of a set combination, eg **out of danger**, **out of the way**, **out of bounds**, look up the noun.

1 [= outside] en dehors de, hors de ◆ **he lives ~ of town** il habite en dehors de la ville ◆ **the town was ~ of range of their missiles** la ville était hors d'atteinte de leurs missiles ◆ **the work was done ~ of house** le travail a été fait en externe

◆ **out of it** * (= *escaped from situation*) ◆ **I was glad to be ~ of it** j'étais bien content d'y avoir échappé ◆ **you're well ~ of it** tu n'as rien à regretter ◆ **I felt rather ~ of it at the party** (= *excluded*) je me sentais un peu exclu à cette fête ◆ **he's ~ of it** (= *drunk, drugged*) il est dans les vapes*

2 [expressing distance] ◆ **they were 100km ~ of Paris** ils étaient à 100 km de Paris ◆ **it's 15km ~ of town** c'est à 15 km du centre-ville

3 [= absent from] ◆ **the boss is ~ of town this week** le patron est en déplacement cette semaine ◆ **he's ~ of the office at the moment** il n'est pas au bureau actuellement

4 [= through] par ◆ ~ **of the window** par la fenêtre ◆ **he went ~ of the back door** il est sorti par la porte de derrière

5 [= from] ◆ **only one chapter ~ of the novel** un seul chapitre du roman ◆ **a model made ~ of matchsticks** un modèle réduit construit avec des allumettes ◆ **this is just one chapter ~ of a long novel** ce n'est qu'un chapitre tiré d'un long roman ◆ **he had made the table ~ of a crate** il avait fabriqué la table avec une caisse ◆ **it was like something ~ of a nightmare** c'était cauchemardesque ◆ **he looked like something ~ of "Star Trek"** il semblait sorti tout droit de "Star Trek"

In the following **dans** describes the original position of the thing being moved:

◆ **to take sth ~ of a drawer** prendre qch dans un tiroir ◆ **to drink ~ of a glass** boire dans un verre ◆ **they ate ~ of the same plate** ils mangeaient dans la même assiette ◆ **he copied the poem ~ of a book** il a copié le poème dans un livre

6 [= because of] par ◆ ~ **of curiosity/necessity** par curiosité/nécessité

7 [= from among] sur ◆ **in nine cases ~ of ten** dans neuf cas sur dix ◆ **one ~ of five smokers** un fumeur sur cinq

8 [= without] ◆ **we are ~ of bread/money** nous n'avons plus de pain/d'argent ◆ **we were ~ of petrol** nous n'avions plus d'essence, nous étions en panne d'essence

9 [= sheltered from] à l'abri de ◆ ~ **of the wind** à l'abri du vent

10 [= eliminated from] éliminé de ◆ ~ **of the World Cup** éliminé de la coupe du monde

11 [Racing] ◆ **Lexicon by Hercules ~ of Alphabet** Lexicon issu d'Hercule et d'Alphabet

4 - NOUN

1 [* = means of escape] ◆ **this gives them an ~, a chance to change their minds** cela leur laisse une porte de sortie, une occasion de changer d'avis

◆ **to want out** ◆ **the cat wants** ~ le chat veut sortir ◆ **he wants ~ but he doesn't know what he can do instead** il veut partir mais il ne sait pas trop ce qu'il pourrait faire d'autre ◆ **he wants ~ of his contract** il veut résilier son contrat

2 US ◆ **on the ~s with sb** ‡ brouillé avec qn

5 - TRANSITIVE VERB

= expose as a homosexual révéler l'homosexualité de

6 - COMPOUNDS

out-and-out ADJ *[lie]* pur et simple ; *[liar]* fieffé, fini ; *[cheat, fool, crook]* fini ; *[racist, fascist]* à tout crin ; *[winner]* incontestable ; *[success, victory, defeat]* total

out-and-outer * N *(esp US)* jusqu'au-boutiste *mf*

out-front * ADJ *(US = frank)* ouvert, droit

out-Herod VT ◆ **to ~-Herod Herod** dépasser Hérode en cruauté

out-of-body experience N expérience *f* de sortie de corps

out-of-bounds ADJ *[place]* interdit ; *(US Ftbl) [ball]* sorti

out-of-court ADJ *[settlement, agreement, damages]* à l'amiable

out-of-date ADJ *[passport, ticket]* périmé ; *[custom]* suranné, désuet (-ète *f*) ; *[clothes]* démodé ; *[theory, concept]* périmé, démodé ; *[word]* vieilli

out-of-doors ADV ⇒ **outdoors**

out-of-pocket expenses NPL débours *mpl*, frais *mpl*

out-of-sight ‡ ADJ *(US fig)* formidable, terrible *

out-of-state ADJ *(US) [company, visitor, licence plate]* d'un autre État

out-of-the-body experience N ⇒ **out-of-body experience**

out-of-the-ordinary ADJ *[theory, approach, film, book]* insolite, qui sort de l'ordinaire

out-of-the-way ADJ *(= remote) [spot]* isolé, perdu ; *(= unusual)* ⇒ **out-of-the-ordinary**

out-of-this-world * ADJ *(fig)* sensationnel *, fantastique *

out-of-town ADJ *[shopping centre, cinema]* en périphérie

out-of-towner * N *(US)* étranger *m*, -ère *f* à la ville

out-of-work ADJ au chômage ; *[actor]* sans engagement

out-there * ADJ *(= weird)* bizarre ; *(= daring, experimental)* d'avant-garde

out-tray N corbeille *f* de départ

outa ‡ /'aʊtə/ PREP *(esp US)* (abbrev of **out of**) ◆ **I'm ~ here** *(= I'm going)* moi, je me tire ‡ ◆ **get ~ here!** *(= go away)* fiche le camp ! * ; *(= you're joking)* tu me fais marcher ? * ◆ **that's ~ sight!** *(US) (= amazing)* c'est incroyable ! ; *(= great)* c'est génial ! *

outage /'aʊtɪdʒ/ N 1 *(= break in functioning)* interruption *f* de service ; *(Elec)* coupure *f* de courant 2 *(= amount removed: gen)* quantité *f* enlevée ; *(Cine = cut from film)* film *m (rejeté au montage)* ; *(= amount lost: gen)* quantité *f* perdue ; *(Comm: during transport)* déchet *m* de route *or* de freinte

out-and-out /'aʊtəndaʊt/ ADJ *[lie]* pur et simple ; *[liar]* fieffé, fini ; *[cheat, fool, crook]* fini ; *[racist, fascist]* à tout crin ; *[winner]* incontestable ; *[success, victory, defeat]* total

out-and-outer * /aʊtən'daʊtəʳ/ N *(esp US)* jusqu'au-boutiste *mf*

outasite ‡ /aʊtə'saɪt/ ADJ *(US = out of sight)* formidable, terrible *

outback /'aʊtbæk/ N 1 *(in Australia)* intérieur *m* du pays *(plus ou moins inculte)* 2 *(= back country)* campagne *f* isolée *or* presque déserte, cambrousse * *f*

outbid /aʊt'bɪd/ (pret **outbid** *or* **outbade** /aʊt'bæd/, ptp **outbidden** *or* **outbid**) VT enchérir sur VI surenchérir

outbidding /aʊt'bɪdɪŋ/ N *(Fin)* surenchères *fpl*

outboard /'aʊtbɔːd/ ADJ, N ◆ **~ (motor)** (moteur *m*) hors-bord *m*

outbound /'aʊtbaʊnd/ ADJ *[passengers, train]* en partance

outbox /aʊt'bɒks/ VT boxer mieux que

outbreak /'aʊtbreɪk/ N *[of war, fighting]* début *m*, déclenchement *m* ; *[of violence]* éruption *f* ; *[of emotion]* débordement *m* ; *[of fever, disease]* accès *m* ; *[of spots]* éruption *f*, poussée *f* ; *[of demonstrations]* vague *f* ; *[of revolt]* déclenchement *m* ◆ **at the ~ of the disease** lorsque la maladie se déclara ◆ **at the ~ of war** lorsque la guerre éclata ◆ **the ~ of hostilities** l'ouverture *f* des hostilités ◆ **there has been a renewed** *or* **fresh ~ of fighting** les combats ont repris

outbuilding /'aʊtbɪldɪŋ/ N dépendance *f* ; *(separate)* appentis *m*, remise *f* ◆ **the ~s** les communs *mpl*, les dépendances *fpl*

outburst /'aʊtbɜːst/ N *(gen)* emportement *m* ; *[of anger]* explosion *f*, accès *m* ; *[of violence]* éruption *f* ; *[of energy]* accès *m* ◆ **~ of laughter** grand éclat *m* de rire ◆ **he was ashamed of his ~** *(= anger)* il avait honte de s'être emporté ; *(emotional)* il avait honte d'avoir laissé libre cours à ses émotions ◆ **in an angry ~ she accused him of lying** elle s'est emportée et l'a accusé de mentir

outcast /'aʊtkɑːst/ N exclu(e) *m(f)*, paria *m* ◆ **their government's attitude has made them international ~s** l'attitude de leur gouvernement les a mis au ban de la communauté internationale ◆ **this has made him an ~ from his own family** à cause de cela, il a été rejeté par sa propre famille ◆ **social ~** exclu(e) *m(f)*, paria *m*

outclass /aʊt'klɑːs/ VT *(gen)* surclasser, surpasser ; *(Sport)* surclasser

outcome /'aʊtkʌm/ N *[of election, inquiry]* résultat *m* ; *[of trial, appeal, discussion]* issue *f* ◆ **studies to evaluate the ~ of psychotherapy** des études pour évaluer l'impact de la psychothérapie

outcrop /'aʊtkrɒp/ *(Geol)* N affleurement *m* VI /aʊt'krɒp/ affleurer

outcry /'aʊtkraɪ/ N *(= protest)* tollé *m* (général) ; *(= raised voices)* huées *fpl* ◆ **there was a general ~ against ...** un tollé général s'éleva contre ... ◆ **to raise an ~ about sth** crier haro sur qch, ameuter l'opinion sur qch

outdated /aʊt'deɪtɪd/ ADJ *[technology, equipment]* périmé ; *[clothes]* démodé ; *[method, system, concept, theory, idea, notion, practice]* dépassé, démodé ; *[custom]* suranné, désuet (-ète *f*)

outdid /aʊt'dɪd/ VB pt of **outdo**

outdistance /aʊt'dɪstəns/ VT distancer

outdo /aʊt'duː/ (pret **outdid**, ptp **outdone**) /aʊt'dʌn/ VT l'emporter sur *(sb in sth* qn en qch) ◆ **but he was not to be outdone** mais il refusait de s'avouer vaincu *or* battu ◆ **and I, not to be outdone, said that ...** et moi, pour ne pas être en reste, j'ai dit que ...

outdoor /'aʊtdɔːʳ/ ADJ *[activities, pursuits, sports, games]* de plein air ; *[work, swimming pool, tennis court]* en plein air ; *[toilet]* à l'extérieur ; *[market]* à ciel ouvert ; *[shoes]* de marche ◆ **~ clothing** *(Sport)* vêtements *mpl* sport *inv* ◆ **~ centre** centre *m* aéré ◆ **for ~ use** pour usage extérieur ◆ **to lead an ~ life** vivre au grand air ◆ **he likes the ~ life** il aime la vie au grand air *or* en plein air ◆ **~ living** vie *f* au grand air ◆ **she's the** *or* **an ~ type** elle aime le grand air et la nature

outdoors /'aʊt'dɔːz/ ADV (also **out-of-doors**) *[stay, play, exercise, bathe]* dehors ; *[live]* au grand air ; *[sleep]* dehors, à la belle étoile ◆ **to be ~** être dehors ◆ **to go ~** sortir ◆ **~, there are three heated swimming pools** il y a trois piscines chauffées à l'extérieur N ◆ **the great ~** le grand air ADJ ⇒ **outdoor**

outer /'aʊtəʳ/ ADJ *[layer, surface, skin, shell, wall, edge]* extérieur (-eure *f*) ; *[door]* qui donne sur l'extérieur ◆ **~ garments** vêtements *mpl* de dessus ◆ **~ harbour** avant-port *m* ◆ **the ~ suburbs** la grande banlieue ◆ **the ~ world** le monde extérieur ◆ **the ~ reaches of the solar system** les confins *mpl* du système solaire

COMP **Outer London** N grande banlieue *f* londonienne

Outer Mongolia N Mongolie-Extérieure *f*

outer office N *(= reception area)* réception *f*

outer space N espace *m*

outermost /'aʊtəməʊst/ ADJ *[layer, rim]* extérieur (-eure *f*) ; *[edge]* extrême ◆ **the ~ planet** la planète la plus éloignée ◆ **the ~ suburbs** la grande banlieue ◆ **the ~ limits of ...** les extrémités *fpl* de ...

outerwear /'aʊtəwɛəʳ/ N *(NonC: US)* vêtements *mpl* d'extérieur *(pardessus, manteaux, vestes etc)*

outface /aʊt'feɪs/ VT *(= stare out)* dévisager ; *(fig)* faire perdre contenance à

outfall /'aʊtfɔːl/ N *[of river]* embouchure *f* ; *[of sewer]* déversoir *m*

outfield /'aʊtfiːld/ N *(Baseball, Cricket)* champ *m or* terrain *m* extérieur

outfielder /'aʊtfiːldəʳ/ N *(Baseball, Cricket)* joueur *m*, -euse *f* de champ *or* de terrain extérieur

outfit /'aʊtfɪt/ N 1 *(= set of clothes)* tenue *f* ◆ **did you see the ~ she was wearing?** *(in admiration)* avez-vous remarqué sa toilette ? ; *(pej)* avez-vous remarqué son accoutrement *or* comment elle était accoutrée ? ◆ **she's got a new spring ~** elle s'est achetée une nouvelle tenue pour le printemps ◆ **travelling/skiing ~** tenue *f* de voyage/de ski ◆ **cowboy ~** panoplie *f* de cowboy 2 *(= clothes and equipment)* équipement *m* ; *(= tools)* matériel *m*, outillage *m* ◆ **puncture repair ~** trousse *f* de réparation (de pneus) 3 *(* = company, organization)* boîte * *f* ; *(= pop group)* groupe *m* ; *(= sports team)* équipe *f* ◆ **I wouldn't want to work for that ~** je ne voudrais pas travailler pour cette boîte * VT *(esp US)* équiper

outfitter /'aʊtfɪtəʳ/ N 1 *(Brit)* ◆ **gents' ~** magasin *m* d'habillement *or* de confection pour hommes ◆ **sports ~'s** magasin *m* de sport 2 *(Can) (= shop)* ≃ magasin *m* de sport ; *(= expedition guide)* pourvoyeur *m (Can) (organisateur d'expéditions de chasse et de pêche)*

outflank /aʊt'flæŋk/ VT *(Mil)* déborder ; *(fig)* déjouer les manœuvres de

outflow /'aʊtfləʊ/ N *[of water]* écoulement *m*, débit *m* ; *[of emigrants etc]* exode *m* ; *[of capital]* exode *m*, sortie(s) *f(pl)*

outfox /aʊt'fɒks/ VT se montrer plus futé que

out-front * /aʊt'frʌnt/ ADJ *(US = frank)* ouvert, droit

outgeneral /aʊt'dʒenərəl/ VT *(Mil)* surpasser en tactique

outgoing /'aʊtgəʊɪŋ/ ADJ 1 *(= departing) [president, director, tenant]* sortant ; *[flight, mail]* en partance ; *[tide]* descendant ◆ **"outgoing calls only"** *(Telec)* "appels sortants uniquement" 2 *(= extrovert) [person, personality, nature]* extraverti NPL **outgoings** *(Brit)* dépenses *fpl*, débours *mpl*

outgrow /aʊt'grəʊ/ (pret **outgrew** /aʊt'gruː/) (ptp **outgrown** /aʊt'grəʊn/) VT 1 *[+ clothes]* devenir trop grand pour ◆ **we had ~n our old house** notre ancienne maison était devenue trop petite pour nous 2 *(fig) [hobby, sport, toy]* se désintéresser de (avec le temps) ; *[opinion, way of life]* abandonner (avec le temps) ◆ **we've ~n all that now** nous avons dépassé ce stade, nous n'en sommes plus là ◆ **to ~ one's friends** se détacher de ses amis

outgrowth /'aʊtgrəʊθ/ N *(Geol)* excroissance *f* ; *(fig)* développement *m*, conséquence *f*

outguess /aʊt'ges/ VT (= *outwit*) se montrer plus rapide que

outgun /aʊt'gʌn/ VT 1 (= *surpass in fire power*) avoir une puissance de feu supérieure à 2 (= *surpass in shooting*) tirer mieux que 3 (* = *outperform*) éclipser ◆ **the French team were completely ~ned by the Welsh** l'équipe française a été complètement écrasée par les Gallois

out-Herod /aʊt'herəd/ VT ◆ **to ~ Herod** dépasser Hérode en cruauté

outhouse /'aʊthaʊs/ N 1 appentis *m*, remise *f* ◆ **the ~s** *(gen)* les communs *mpl*, les dépendances *fpl* 2 *(US = outdoor lavatory)* cabinets *mpl* extérieurs

outing /'aʊtɪŋ/ N 1 (= *excursion*) sortie *f*, excursion *f* ◆ **the school ~** la sortie annuelle de l'école ◆ **the annual ~ to Blackpool** l'excursion *f* annuelle à Blackpool ◆ **let's go for an ~ tomorrow** faisons une sortie demain ◆ **to go for an ~ in the car** partir faire une randonnée *or* un tour en voiture ◆ **a birthday ~ to the theatre** une sortie au théâtre pour (fêter) un anniversaire 2 *(NonC: * = exposing as homosexual) [of public figure]* révélation *f* de l'homosexualité

outlandish /aʊt'lændɪʃ/ ADJ *(pej) [clothes]* extravagant ; *[idea, claim]* saugrenu

outlast /aʊt'lɑːst/ VT survivre à

outlaw /'aʊtlɔː/ N hors-la-loi *m* VT *[+ person]* mettre hors la loi ; *[+ activity, organisation]* proscrire, déclarer illégal

outlay /'aʊtleɪ/ N (= *spending*) dépenses *fpl* ; (= *investment*) mise *f* de fonds ◆ **national ~ on education** dépenses *fpl* nationales pour l'éducation

outlet /'aʊtlet/ N 1 *(for water etc)* issue *f*, sortie *f* ; *(US Elec)* prise *f* de courant ; *[of lake]* dégorgeoir *m*, déversoir *m* ; *[of river, stream]* embouchure *f* ; *[of tunnel]* sortie *f* 2 *(fig) (for talents etc)* débouché *m* ; *(for energy, emotions)* exutoire *m* *(for* à) 3 (= *market*) débouché *m* ; (= *store*) point *m* de vente → **retail** COMP *(Tech) [pipe]* d'échappement, d'écoulement ; *[valve]* d'échappement

outlet point N *[of pipe]* point *m* de sortie

outline /'aʊtlaɪn/ N 1 (= *profile, silhouette*) *[of object]* contour *m*, configuration *f* ; *[of building, tree etc]* profil *m*, silhouette *f* ; *[of face]* profil *m* ◆ **he drew the ~ of the house** il traça le contour de la maison ◆ **to draw sth in ~** dessiner qch au trait ◆ **rough ~** *(Art)* premier jet *m*, ébauche *f*

2 (= *plan, summary*) plan *m* ; *(less exact)* esquisse *f*, idée *f* ◆ **~s** (= *main features*) grandes lignes *fpl*, grands traits *mpl* ◆ **rough ~ of an article** canevas *m* d'un article ◆ **to give the broad** *or* **main** *or* **general ~s of sth** décrire qch dans les grandes lignes ◆ **in broad ~ the plan is as follows** dans ses grandes lignes *or* en gros, le plan est le suivant ◆ **I'll give you a quick ~ of what we mean to do** je vous donnerai un aperçu de ce que nous avons l'intention de faire ◆ **"Outlines of Botany"** *(as title)* "Éléments de botanique"

VT 1 (= *emphasize shape of*) tracer le contour de ◆ **she ~d her eyes with a dark pencil** elle a souligné *or* dessiné le contour de ses yeux avec un crayon noir ◆ **the mountain was ~d against the sky** la montagne se profilait *or* se dessinait *or* se découpait sur le ciel

2 (= *summarize*) *[+ theory, plan, idea]* exposer les grandes lignes de ; *[+ book, event]* faire un bref compte rendu de ; *[+ facts, details]* passer brièvement en revue ◆ **to ~ the situation** brosser un tableau *or* donner un aperçu de la situation

COMP **outline agreement** N accord-cadre *m*

outline drawing N dessin *m* au trait

outline map N tracé *m* des contours (d'un pays), carte *f* muette

outline planning permission N *(Brit: for building)* avant-projet *m (valorisant le terrain)*

outline specifications NPL *(Comm)* devis *m* préliminaire

outlive /aʊt'lɪv/ VT (= *survive*) *[+ person, era, war, winter]* survivre à ◆ **he ~d her by ten years** il lui a survécu dix ans ◆ **to have ~d one's usefulness** *[person, object, scheme]* avoir fait son temps

outlook /'aʊtlʊk/ N 1 (= *view*) vue *f (on, over* sur), perspective *f (on, over* de)

2 *(fig)* (= *prospect*) perspective *f* (d'avenir), horizon *m (fig)* ◆ **the ~ for June is wet** on annonce *or* prévoit de la pluie pour juin ◆ **the economic ~** les perspectives *fpl or* les horizons *mpl* économiques ◆ **the ~ for the wheat crop is good** la récolte de blé s'annonce bonne ◆ **the ~ (for us) is rather rosy*** les choses se présentent *or* s'annoncent assez bien (pour nous) ◆ **it's a grim** *or* **bleak ~** l'horizon est sombre *or* bouché, les perspectives sont fort sombres

3 (= *point of view*) attitude *f (on* à l'égard de), point *m* de vue *(on* sur), conception *f (on* de) ◆ **he has a pessimistic ~** il voit les choses en noir ◆ **she has a practical ~** elle est très pragmatique ◆ **they are European in ~** ils sont tournés vers l'Europe

outlying /'aʊtlaɪɪŋ/ ADJ *[area]* écarté ◆ **the ~ villages/islands** les villages *mpl*/îles *fpl* les plus éloigné(e)s ◆ **the ~ suburbs** la grande banlieue

outmanoeuvre, outmaneuver (US) /ˌaʊtmə'nuːvə^r/ VT *(Mil)* dominer en manœuvrant plus habilement ; *(fig)* déjouer les plans de ◆ **domestic car manufacturers are ~d by foreign competitors** les constructeurs automobiles du pays sont surclassés par leurs concurrents étrangers

outmoded /aʊt'məʊdɪd/ ADJ *[attitude, clothes]* démodé ; *[concept, theory, system]* dépassé, démodé ; *[custom]* suranné, désuet (-ète *f*) ; *[equipment]* périmé ; *[industry]* obsolète

outnumber /aʊt'nʌmbə^r/ VT surpasser en nombre, être plus nombreux que ◆ **we were ~ed five to one** ils étaient cinq fois plus nombreux que nous

out-of-town /ˌaʊtəv'taʊn/ ADJ *[shopping centre, cinema]* en périphérie

out-of-towner* /ˌaʊtəv'taʊnə^r/ N (US) étranger *m*, -ère *f* à la ville

outpace /aʊt'peɪs/ VT devancer, distancer

outpatient /'aʊtpeɪʃənt/ N malade *mf* en consultation externe ◆ **~s (department)** service *m* de consultation externe

outperform /ˌaʊtpə'fɔːm/ VT *[person, machine, company]* être plus performant que ; *[product]* donner de meilleurs résultats ; *[shares etc]* réaliser mieux que ◆ **this car ~s its competitors on every score** cette voiture l'emporte sur ses concurrentes sur tous les plans

outplacement /'aʊtˌpleɪsmənt/ N outplacement *m (aide à la réinsertion professionnelle des cadres au chômage)*

outplay /aʊt'pleɪ/ VT *(Sport)* dominer par son jeu

outpoint /aʊt'pɔɪnt/ VT *(gen)* l'emporter sur ; *(in game)* avoir plus de points que

outpost /'aʊtpəʊst/ N *(Mil)* avant-poste *m* ; *[of firm, organization]* antenne *f* ; *(fig)* avant-poste *m*

outpouring /'aʊtpɔːrɪŋ/ N *[of emotion]* épanchement(s) *m(pl)*, effusion(s) *f(pl)* ◆ **this event triggered off an ~ of anger/support** cet événement a provoqué une vague de colère/soutien

output /'aʊtpʊt/ (vb : pret, ptp **output**) N 1 *[of factory, mine, oilfield, writer]* production *f* ; *[of land]* rendement *m*, production *f* ; *[of machine, factory worker]* rendement *m* ◆ **~ fell/rose** le rendement *or* la production a diminué/augmenté ◆ **this factory has an ~ of 600 radios per day** cette usine débite 600 radios par jour ◆ **gross ~** production *f* brute 2 *(Comput)* sortie *f*, restitution *f* ; (also **output data**) données *fpl* de sortie 3 *(Elec)* puissance *f* fournie *or* de sortie VT 1 *(Comput)* sortir ◆ **to ~ sth to a printer** imprimer qch 2 *[factory etc]* sortir, débiter VI *(Comput)* sortir les données *or* les informations ◆ **to ~ to a printer** imprimer

COMP **output device** N *(Comput)* unité *f* périphérique de sortie

outrage /'aʊtreɪdʒ/ N 1 (= *act, event*) atrocité *f* ; *(during riot etc)* acte *m* de violence ; (= *public scandal*) scandale *m* ◆ **the prisoners suffered ~s at the hands of ...** les prisonniers ont été atrocement maltraités par ... ◆ **it's an ~ against humanity** c'est un crime contre l'humanité ◆ **an ~ against justice** un outrage à la justice ◆ **several ~s occurred** *or* **were committed in the course of the night** plusieurs actes de violence ont été commis au cours de la nuit ◆ **bomb ~** attentat *m* au plastic *or* à la bombe ◆ **it's an ~!** c'est un scandale !

2 (= *emotion*) indignation *f* ◆ **sense of ~** sentiment *m* d'indignation ◆ **they expressed ~ at this desecration** ils ont exprimé leur indignation devant cette profanation ◆ **it caused public ~** cela a scandalisé l'opinion publique

VT /aʊt'reɪdʒ/ *[+ morals, sense of decency]* outrager, faire outrage à

outraged /'aʊtreɪdʒd/ ADJ *[person]* outré *(about, at, by sth* de qch), indigné ; *[protest, letter, tone]* indigné ; *[dignity, pride]* offensé

outrageous /aʊt'reɪdʒəs/ ADJ 1 (= *scandalous*) *[behaviour, act, conduct]* scandaleux ; *[prices]* exorbitant ◆ **that's ~!** c'est scandaleux ! ◆ **he's ~!** * il dépasse les bornes ! 2 (= *unconventional, flamboyant*) *[remark]* outrancier ; *[story, claim, clothes, idea]* extravagant ; *[sense of humour]* outré

outrageously /aʊt'reɪdʒəslɪ/ ADV *[expensive, high, funny, exaggerated]* outrageusement ; *[behave]* effrontément ; *[dress]* de manière extravagante ◆ **to flirt/lie ~** flirter/mentir effrontément *or* de façon outrancière

outrank /aʊt'ræŋk/ VT *(Mil)* avoir un grade supérieur à

outré /'uːtreɪ/ ADJ outré, outrancier

outreach /'aʊtriːtʃ/ N *programme destiné à informer les personnes défavorisées de leurs droits et des aides dont elles peuvent bénéficier*, ≈ travail *m* de proximité COMP **outreach worker** N *travailleur social effectuant un travail d'information sur le terrain auprès des groupes défavorisés*, ≈ travailleur *m*, -euse *f* de proximité

outrider /'aʊtˌraɪdə^r/ N *(on motorcycle)* motocycliste *mf*, motard* *m* ; *(on horseback)* cavalier *m* ◆ **there were four ~s** il y avait une escorte de quatre motocyclistes *(or* cavaliers *etc)*

outrigger /'aʊtˌrɪgə^r/ N *(Naut)* outrigger *m*

outright /aʊt'raɪt/ ADV 1 (= *openly*) *[say, tell]* carrément, tout net ; *[laugh]* franchement

2 (= *completely*) *[win]* haut la main ; *[reject, refuse, deny]* catégoriquement ◆ **he won the prize ~** il a gagné le prix haut la main ◆ **to be owned ~ by sb** *(Comm)* appartenir entièrement *or* complètement à qn ◆ **to buy sth ~** (= *buy and pay immediately*) acheter qch au comptant ; (= *buy all of sth*) acheter qch en totalité

3 (= *instantly*) ◆ **to be killed ~** être tué sur le coup

ADJ /'aʊtraɪt/ 1 (= *undisguised*) *[lie, fraud, selfishness, arrogance]* pur ; *[hostility]* franc (franche *f*) ; *[condemnation, denial, refusal, rejection]* catégorique ; *[support, supporter]* inconditionnel

2 (= *absolute*) *[victory]* total, complet (-ète *f*) ; *[independence]* total ; *[majority, ban]* absolu ; *[winner]* incontesté ; *(Comm)* (= *full*) *[owner, own-*

ership] à part entière ; *[grant]* sans conditions ; *[sale, purchase]* (= *paying immediately*) au comptant ; (= *selling all of sth*) en totalité ◆ **to be an ~ opponent of sth** s'opposer catégoriquement à qch

outrival /ˌaʊtˈraɪvəl/ VT surpasser

outrun /aʊtˈrʌn/ (pret, ptp **outrun**) VT 1 *[+ opponent, pursuer]* distancer 2 *(fig)* *[+ resources, abilities]* excéder, dépasser

outsell /ˌaʊtˈsel/ VT *[company]* obtenir de meilleurs résultats que ; *[product]* mieux se vendre que

outset /ˈaʊtset/ N début *m*, commencement *m* ◆ **at the ~** au début ◆ **from the ~** dès le début

outshine /aʊtˈʃaɪn/ (pret, ptp **outshone** /aʊtˈʃɒn/) VT *(fig)* éclipser, surpasser

outside /ˈaʊtˈsaɪd/ ADV 1 *(gen)* à l'extérieur, dehors ◆ **~ in the corridor** dehors dans le couloir ◆ **the car was clean ~ but filthy inside** la voiture était propre à l'extérieur mais dégoûtante à l'intérieur ◆ **the difficulties of life ~ for ex-prisoners** les difficultés de la vie en liberté pour les anciens détenus ◆ **seen from ~** *(lit, fig)* vu du dehors *or* de l'extérieur

2 (= *outdoors*) dehors ◆ **to go ~** sortir (dehors) ◆ **he left the car ~** il a laissé la voiture dans la rue ◆ **the scene was shot ~** *(Cine)* cette scène a été tournée en extérieur

PREP (also **outside of** *) 1 *[+ building]* (= *on the exterior of*) à l'extérieur de, hors de ; (= *in front of*) devant ◆ **store flammable substances ~ the house** conservez les produits inflammables à l'extérieur de *or* hors de la maison ◆ **the noise was coming from ~ the house** le bruit venait de dehors ◆ **a man was standing ~ the house** un homme se tenait devant la maison ◆ **the street ~ his house** la rue devant sa maison ◆ **a crowd had gathered ~ the building** une foule s'était rassemblée à l'extérieur du bâtiment *or* devant le bâtiment ◆ **they chose to live ~ London** ils ont choisi de vivre à l'extérieur de *or* hors de Londres ◆ **they have 45 shops, 38 ~ the UK** ils possèdent 45 magasins dont 38 à l'extérieur du Royaume-Uni *or* hors du Royaume-Uni ◆ **countries ~ Europe** pays *mpl* non européens ◆ **he was waiting ~ the door** il attendait à la porte ◆ **don't go ~ the garden** ne sors pas du jardin ◆ **the ball landed ~ the line** la balle a atterri de l'autre côté de la ligne ◆ **~ the harbour** au large du port ◆ **this fish can live for several hours ~ water** ce poisson peut vivre plusieurs heures hors de l'eau ◆ **women who work ~ the home** les femmes qui travaillent à l'extérieur ◆ **visitors from ~ the area** les visiteurs *mpl* étrangers à la région

2 *(fig = beyond, apart from)* en dehors de, hors de ◆ **investments ~ Europe** investissements *mpl* en dehors de l'Europe *or* hors d'Europe ◆ **their reluctance to get involved militarily ~ NATO** leur réticence à intervenir militairement en dehors du cadre *or* hors du cadre de l'OTAN ◆ **~ the festival proper** en dehors du *or* en marge du festival à proprement parler ◆ **~ office hours** en dehors des heures de bureau ◆ **it's ~ the normal range** ça ne fait pas partie de la gamme habituelle ◆ **that falls ~ the committee's terms of reference** ceci n'est pas du ressort de la commission ◆ **she doesn't see anyone ~ her immediate family** elle ne voit personne en dehors de ses proches parents ◆ **babies born ~ marriage** naissances *fpl* hors mariage, bébés *mpl* nés hors mariage ◆ **sex ~ marriage** relations *fpl* sexuelles hors (du) mariage ◆ **to marry ~ one's religion** se marier avec une personne d'une autre confession ◆ **to marry ~ the Church** (= *with non-Christian*) se marier avec un(e) non-chrétien(ne) ◆ **~ of selling the car, there seemed to be no solution** *(US)* à part vendre la voiture, il ne semblait pas y avoir de solution

N *[of house, car, object]* extérieur *m*, dehors *m* ; (= *appearance*) aspect *m* extérieur, apparence *f* ; *(fig)* *[of prison, convent etc]* (monde *m*) extérieur *m* ◆ **on the ~ of** sur l'extérieur de ; (= *beyond*) à l'extérieur de, hors de, en dehors de ◆ **he opened the door from the ~** il a ouvert la porte du dehors ◆ **there's no window on to the ~** aucune fenêtre ne donne sur l'extérieur ◆ **the box was dirty on the ~** la boîte était sale à l'extérieur ◆ **the ~ of the box was dirty** l'extérieur *or* le dehors de la boîte était sale ◆ **~ in** ⇒ **inside out** ; → **inside** ◆ **to look at sth from the ~** *(lit, fig)* regarder qch de l'extérieur *or* du dehors ◆ **(judging) from the ~** à en juger par les apparences ◆ **he passed the car on the ~** *(in Brit)* il a doublé la voiture sur la droite ; *(in US, Europe etc)* il a doublé la voiture sur la gauche ◆ **at the (very) ~** (= *at most*) (tout) au plus, au maximum ◆ **life on the ~** *[of prison]* la vie en liberté *or* à l'air libre

ADJ 1 (= *outdoor*) *[temperature, aerial, staircase]* extérieur (-eure *f*) ; *[toilet]* à l'extérieur ◆ **~ swimming pool/running track** piscine *f*/piste *f* en plein air

2 (= *outer*) *[wall, edge, measurements]* extérieur (-eure *f*) ◆ **the ~ lane** *(of road, in Brit)* la voie de droite ; *(in US, Europe etc)* la voie de gauche ; *(Sport)* la piste extérieure

3 *(Telec)* ◆ **~ call** appel *m* extérieur ◆ **~ line** ligne *f* extérieure

4 (= *from elsewhere*) *[world, community, influence]* extérieur (-eure *f*) ; *[consultant, investor]* externe ◆ **~ examiner** *(Scol, Univ)* examinateur *m*, -trice *f* externe ◆ **to need ~ help** avoir besoin d'aide extérieure ◆ **without ~ help** sans aide extérieure ◆ **to get an ~ opinion** demander l'avis d'un tiers

5 (= *beyond usual environment*) ◆ **~ commitments** autres responsabilités *fpl* ◆ **~ work** *(in addition to main job)* autre travail *m* ; *(outside the home)* travail *m* à l'extérieur ◆ **~ interests** (= *hobbies*) passe-temps *mpl inv*

6 (= *faint*) ◆ **there is an ~ chance** *or* **possibility that he will come** il y a une petite chance qu'il vienne ◆ **he has an ~ chance of a medal** il a une petite chance de remporter une médaille, il n'est pas impossible qu'il remporte *subj* une médaille

COMP **outside broadcast** N *(Rad, TV)* émission *f* réalisée en extérieur

outside broadcasting unit, outside broadcasting van N *(Rad, TV)* car *m* de reportage

outside-left N *(Ftbl)* ailier *m* gauche

outside-right N *(Ftbl)* ailier *m* droit

outsider /ˈaʊtˈsaɪdəʳ/ N 1 (= *stranger*) étranger *m*, -ère *f* ◆ **we don't want some ~ coming in and telling us what to do** ce n'est pas quelqu'un de l'extérieur qui va nous dire ce qu'il faut faire ◆ **he is an ~** *(pej)* il n'est pas des nôtres 2 (= *horse or person unlikely to win*) outsider *m*

outsize /ˈaʊtsaɪz/ ADJ 1 (also **outsized**) (= *exceptionally large*) *[spectacles, scissors, bed]* énorme ; *[photograph]* géant ; *[ego]* démesuré 2 *(Dress)* *[clothes]* grande taille *inv* ◆ **~ shop** magasin *m* spécialisé dans les grandes tailles 3 *(Transport)* ◆ **~ load** convoi *m* exceptionnel

outskirts /ˈaʊtskɜːts/ NPL *[of town]* périphérie *f*, banlieue *f* ; *[of forest]* orée *f*, lisière *f* ◆ **on the ~ of the city** à la périphérie de la ville

outsmart * /aʊtˈsmɑːt/ VT être *or* se montrer plus malin(-igne *f*) que

outsource /ˈaʊtsɔːs/ VT externaliser, sous-traiter

outsourcing /ˈaʊtsɔːsɪŋ/ N externalisation *f*, sous-traitance *f* ◆ **the ~ of components** l'externalisation de la fabrication de composants

outspend /aʊtˈspend/ (pret, ptp **outspent** /aʊtˈspent/) VT ◆ **to ~ sb** dépenser plus que qn

outspoken /aʊtˈspəʊkən/ ADJ *[person, criticism, comment, answer]* franc (franche *f*) ; *[critic, opponent]* qui ne mâche pas ses mots ; *[attack]* cinglant ; *[views]* tranché ◆ **to be ~** avoir son franc-parler, ne pas mâcher ses mots ◆ **she was ~ in her criticism of the party** elle a critiqué le parti avec véhémence

outspokenly /aʊtˈspəʊkənlɪ/ ADV franchement, carrément

outspokenness /aʊtˈspəʊkənnɪs/ N franc-parler *m*, franchise *f*

outspread /ˈaʊtˈspred/ ADJ *[wings]* déployé ; *[fingers]* écarté ; *[arms]* grand ouvert

outstanding /aʊtˈstændɪŋ/ ADJ 1 (= *exceptional*) *[person, work, service, talent, success, achievement]* remarquable, exceptionnel ; *[example, event]* remarquable ; *[importance]* exceptionnel ; *[feature]* dominant ; *[exception]* notable ◆ **an area of ~ natural beauty** *(in Brit)* une zone naturelle protégée 2 (= *remaining*) *[debt, balance, bill, account]* impayé ; *[loan]* non remboursé ; *[interest]* à échoir ; *[work]* en suspens, en souffrance ; *[issue, problem]* non résolu ◆ **a lot of work is still ~** beaucoup de travail reste à faire ◆ **~ amount** *(Fin, Comm)* montant *m* dû ◆ **~ claims** *(Jur, Fin)* sinistres *mpl* en cours ◆ **~ item** *(Banking)* suspens *m* ◆ **~ share** *(Jur, Fin)* action *f* en circulation N *(Banking)* encours *m*

outstandingly /aʊtˈstændɪŋlɪ/ ADV *[good, beautiful]* exceptionnellement ; *[play]* magnifiquement ◆ **to be ~ successful** réussir remarquablement ◆ **~ well** exceptionnellement bien

outstare /ˌaʊtˈstɛəʳ/ VT ⇒ **stare out**

outstation /ˈaʊtsteɪʃən/ N *(in remote area)* poste *m* éloigné ; *(Comput)* terminal *m*

outstay /aʊtˈsteɪ/ VT *[+ person]* rester plus longtemps que ◆ **I hope I haven't ~ed my welcome** j'espère que je n'ai pas abusé de votre hospitalité ◆ **I know when I've ~ed my welcome** je sais reconnaître quand je deviens indésirable

outstretched /ˈaʊtstretʃt/ ADJ *[arm, hand, leg]* tendu ; *[wings]* déployé

outstrip /aʊtˈstrɪp/ LANGUAGE IN USE 26.3 VT *(Sport, fig)* devancer *(in* en)

outtake /ˈaʊtteɪk/ N *(Cine, TV)* chute *f*

outturn /ˈaʊttɜːn/ N *(US)* *[of factory]* production *f* ; *[of machine, worker]* rendement *m*

outvote /aʊtˈvəʊt/ VT *[+ person]* mettre en minorité, battre ◆ **his project was ~d** son projet a été mis en minorité

outward /ˈaʊtwəd/ ADJ 1 (= *from a place*) *[flight]* à l'aller ; *[ship, freight]* en partance ; *[movement]* vers l'extérieur ◆ **the ~ journey/voyage, the ~ leg of the trip** l'aller *m*, le voyage (d')aller 2 (= *external*) *[appearance, display, sign]* extérieur (-eure *f*) ; *[calm]* apparent ◆ **to make an ~ show of concern** faire mine de s'inquiéter ◆ **to all ~ appearances** selon toute apparence ADV 1 *(esp Brit)* ⇒ **outwards** 2 *(Naut)* ◆ **~ bound (for/from)** en partance (pour/de) COMP **outward-looking** ADJ ouvert sur l'extérieur

outwardly /ˈaʊtwədlɪ/ ADV 1 (= *externally*) *[calm, unattractive]* extérieurement ; *[respectable]* apparemment ◆ **~ he appeared calm and confident** extérieurement, il paraissait calme et confiant ◆ **~ I showed not the faintest sign of anger** extérieurement, je n'ai pas donné le moindre signe de colère 2 *(in direction)* *[point, direct, curve]* vers l'extérieur

outwards /ˈaʊtwədz/ ADV *[move, spread, face, open]* vers l'extérieur ; *[look]* au loin ◆ **the journey/voyage ~** l'aller *m*, le voyage (d')aller

outweigh /aʊtˈweɪ/ VT (= *be more important than*) *(gen)* l'emporter sur ; *[figures, balance etc]* dépasser ; (= *compensate for*) compenser

outwit /aʊtˈwɪt/ VT *(gen)* se montrer plus malin(-igne *f*) *or* spirituel(-le *f*) que ; *[+ pursuer]* dépister, semer *

outwith /ˌaʊtˈwɪθ/ PREP *(Scot)* ⇒ **outside prep 2**

outwork /ˈaʊtwɜːk/ N travail *m* (fait) à domicile

outworker /ˈaʊtwɜːkəʳ/ N travailleur *m*, -euse *f* à domicile, ouvrier *m*, -ière *f* à domicile

outworn /aʊtˈwɔːn/ ADJ *[custom, superstition]* qui n'a plus cours ; *[idea, concept]* périmé

ouzo /ˈuːzəʊ/ N ouzo *m*

ova /ˈəʊvə/ NPL of **ovum**

oval /ˈəʊvəl/ ADJ oval N ovale *m* COMP **the Oval Office** N *(US Pol) (lit)* le bureau ovale *(bureau du président à la Maison-Blanche)* ; *(fig)* la présidence *(des États-Unis)*

ovarian /əʊˈvɛərɪən/ ADJ ovarien

ovariectomy /əʊˌvɛərɪˈektəmɪ/ N ovariectomie *f*

ovariotomy /əʊˌvɛərɪˈɒtəmɪ/ N ovariotomie *f*

ovaritis /əʊvəˈraɪtɪs/ N ovarite *f*

ovary /ˈəʊvərɪ/ N *(Anat, Bot)* ovaire *m*

ovate /ˈəʊveɪt/ ADJ ové

ovation /əʊˈveɪʃən/ N ovation *f*, acclamations *fpl* ◆ **to give sb an ~** ovationner qn, faire une ovation à qn ; → **standing**

oven /ˈʌvn/ N *(Culin)* four *m* ; *(Tech)* four *m*, étuve *f* ◆ **in the ~** *(Culin)* au four ◆ **in a hot ~** à four vif *or* chaud ◆ **in a cool** *or* **slow ~** à four doux ◆ **the room/the town was like an ~** la pièce/la ville était une fournaise *or* une étuve ; → **Dutch, gas**

COMP **oven cleaner** N nettoyant *m* pour four

oven glove N *(Brit)* gant *m* de cuisine, manique *f*

oven-ready ADJ prêt à cuire

ovenproof /ˈʌvnpruːf/ ADJ allant au four

ovenware /ˈʌvnwɛəʳ/ N *(NonC)* plats *mpl* allant au four

over /ˈəʊvəʳ/

1 ADVERB	4 PREFIX
2 ADJECTIVE	5 NOUN
3 PREPOSITION	6 COMPOUNDS

When **over** is the second element in a phrasal verb, eg **come over**, **go over**, **turn over**, look up the verb.

1 - ADVERB

1 [= above] dessus ◆ **this one goes ~ and that one goes under** celui-ci passe dessus et celui-là dessous ◆ **where do you want it, under or ~?** où est-ce que tu veux le mettre, dessus ou dessous ?

2 [= here, there] ◆ **I'll be ~ at 7 o'clock** je serai là à 7 heures ◆ **when you're next ~ this way** la prochaine fois que vous passerez par ici ◆ **they were ~ for the day** ils sont venus passer la journée

◆ **to have sb over** (= *invite*) inviter qn chez soi ◆ **I must have them ~ some time** il faut que je les invite *subj* chez moi un de ces jours ◆ **we had them ~ to dinner last week** ils sont venus dîner chez nous la semaine dernière

3 [with preposition/adverb]

When followed by a preposition or adverb, **over** is not usually translated.

◆ **they're ~ from Canada for the summer** ils sont venus du Canada pour passer ici l'été ◆ **~ here** ici ◆ **they're ~ in France** ils sont en France ◆ **~ there** là-bas ◆ **he drove us ~ to the other side of town** il nous a conduits de l'autre côté de la ville ◆ **and now ~ to our Birmingham studio** *(Rad, TV)* et nous passons maintenant l'antenne à notre studio de Birmingham

◆ **over against** contre ◆ **~ against the wall** contre le mur ◆ **the issue of quality ~ against economy** le problème de l'opposition entre les exigences de la qualité et les contraintes de l'économie

4 [Telec] ◆ **~ (to you) !** à vous ! ◆ **~ and out!** terminé !

5 [= more] plus ◆ **if it is 2 metres or ~, then ...** si ça fait 2 mètres ou plus, alors ... ◆ **those aged 65 and ~** les personnes âgées de 65 ans et plus ◆ **balances of £50,000 and ~** les comptes créditeurs de 50 000 livres et plus ◆ **children of eight and ~** les enfants de huit ans et plus, les enfants à partir de huit ans

6 [= in succession] ◆ **he did it five times ~** il l'a fait cinq fois de suite

◆ **over and over (again)** ◆ **he played the same tune ~ and ~ (again)** il a joué le même air je ne sais combien de fois ◆ **I got bored doing the same thing ~ and ~ again** je m'ennuyais à refaire toujours la même chose ◆ **all directors make the same film ~ and ~ again** tous les réalisateurs ne font qu'un seul film, qu'ils déclinent à l'infini ◆ **they have fallen into this trap ~ and ~ again** ils sont tombés dans ce piège maintes et maintes fois *or* à maintes reprises

7 [= remaining]

Note the impersonal use of **il reste**:

◆ **if there is any meat (left) ~** s'il reste de la viande ◆ **there are three ~** il en reste trois ◆ **four into twenty-nine goes seven and one ~** vingt-neuf divisé par quatre font sept et il reste un BUT **there were two slices each and one ~** il y avait deux tranches pour chacun et une en plus ◆ **when they've paid the bills there's nothing ~ for luxuries** une fois qu'ils ont payé les factures, ils n'ont pas de quoi faire des folies

2 - ADJECTIVE

[= finished] ◆ **after the war was ~** après la guerre ◆ **when this is (all) ~** quand tout cela sera fini ◆ **when the exams/holidays are ~** après les examens/vacances, quand les examens/vacances seront fini(e)s ◆ **our troubles are ~** voilà la fin de nos ennuis

◆ **over and done with** fini et bien fini ◆ **I'll be glad when it's all ~ and done with** je serai content lorsque tout sera fini et bien fini ◆ **as far as we were concerned the incident was ~ and done with** pour nous, l'incident était clos ◆ **to get sth ~ and done with** en finir avec qch

3 - PREPOSITION

When **over** occurs in a set combination, eg **over the phone**, **an advantage over**, look up the noun. When **over** is used with a verb such as **jump**, **trip**, **step**, look up the verb.

1 [= on top of] sur ◆ **she put an apron on ~ her dress** elle a mis un tablier sur sa robe ◆ **I spilled coffee ~ it/them** j'ai renversé du café dessus

2 [= above] au-dessus de ◆ **the water came ~ his knees** l'eau lui arrivait au-dessus du genou ◆ **he's ~ me in the firm** il est au-dessus de moi dans l'entreprise ◆ **a washbasin with a mirror ~ it** un lavabo surmonté d'une glace

3 [= across] de l'autre côté de ◆ **it's just ~ the river** c'est juste de l'autre côté de la rivière ◆ **the noise came from ~ the wall** le bruit venait de l'autre côté du mur ◆ **the bridge ~ the river** le pont qui traverse la rivière ◆ **~ the road** *or* **way** en face ◆ **there is a café ~ the road** il y a un café en face ◆ **the house ~ the way** *or* **the road** la maison d'en face

4 [= during] ◆ **~ the summer** pendant l'été ◆ **~ Christmas** pendant les fêtes de Noël ◆ **a fare which doesn't require a stay ~ Saturday night** un tarif qui n'impose pas de passer sur place la nuit du samedi ◆ **the meetings take place ~ several days** les réunions se déroulent sur plusieurs jours ◆ **~ a period of** sur une période de ◆ **~ the last few years** ces dernières années

5 [= about] ◆ **they fell out ~ money** ils se sont brouillés pour une question d'argent ◆ **the two sides disagreed ~ how much should be spent** les deux côtés n'arrivaient pas à se mettre d'accord sur la somme à dépenser

6 [= more than] plus de ◆ **they stayed for ~ three hours** ils sont restés plus de trois heures ◆ **she is ~ 60** elle a plus de 60 ans ◆ **(the) ~-18s/-21s** les plus de 18/21 ans ◆ **women ~ 21** les femmes de plus de 21 ans ◆ **the boat is ~ 10 metres long** le bateau fait plus de 10 mètres de long ◆ **well ~ 200 people** bien plus de 200 personnes ◆ **all numbers ~ 20** tous les chiffres au-dessus de 20 ◆ **an increase of 5% ~ last year's total** une augmentation de 5% par rapport au total de l'année dernière

◆ **over and above** ◆ **this was ~ and above his normal duties** cela dépassait le cadre de ses fonctions *or* attributions ◆ **spending has gone up by 7% ~ and above inflation** les dépenses ont augmenté de 7%, hors inflation ◆ **~ and above the fact that ...** sans compter que ... ◆ **yes, but ~ and above that, we must ...** oui, mais en plus nous devons ...

7 [= on] ◆ **I spent a lot of time ~ that report** j'ai passé beaucoup de temps sur ce rapport ◆ **he took hours ~ the preparations** il a consacré des heures à ces préparatifs

8 [= while having] ◆ **they talked ~ a cup of coffee** ils ont bavardé autour d'une tasse de café ◆ **we met ~ a meal in the canteen** nous nous sommes vus autour d'un repas à la cantine

9 [= recovered from]

◆ **to be over sth** *[+ illness, bad experience]* s'être remis de qch ◆ **I was heartbroken when she left but I'm ~ it now** j'ai eu le cœur brisé lorsqu'elle est partie mais je m'en suis remis ◆ **hoping you'll soon be ~ your cold** en espérant que tu te remettras vite de ton rhume ◆ **we're ~ the worst now** ça devrait aller mieux maintenant

4 - PREFIX

◆ **overabundant** surabondant ◆ **overabundance** surabondance *f* ; → **overachieve, over-anxious, overmuch** *etc*

5 - NOUN

[Cricket] série *f* de six balles

6 - COMPOUNDS

over-age ADJ trop âgé

over-egg * VT *(Brit fig)* ◆ **to ~-egg the pudding** exagérer

over-the-counter ADJ *[drugs, medicine]* vendu sans ordonnance, *[securities, transactions]* hors cote

over-the-counter market N *(Stock Exchange)* (marché *m*) hors cote *m* ; see also **counter**[1]

overachieve /ˌəʊvərəˈtʃiːv/ VI *[pupil, student]* réussir mieux que prévu ; *[executive]* être un bourreau de travail

overachiever /ˌəʊvərəˈtʃiːvəʳ/ N *(= pupil, student) élève ou étudiant(e) qui réussit mieux que prévu ; (= worker)* bourreau *m* de travail

overact /əʊvərˈækt/ VI *(Theat)* en faire trop *

overactive /əʊvərˈæktɪv/ ADJ trop actif ; *[imagination]* débordant ◆ **to have an ~ thyroid** souffrir d'hyperthyroïdie *f*

overage /ˈəʊvərɪdʒ/ N *(US Comm)* excédent *m (de marchandises etc)*

overall /ˈəʊvərɔːl/ ADJ *[length, width, height, capacity, loss, gain]* total ; *[effect, impression]* d'ensemble ; *[improvement, increase, trend]* global ; *[study, survey]* global, d'ensemble ; *(Sport) [winner, leader, victory]* au classement général ◆ **no party holds ~ control of the council** aucun parti n'a la majorité absolue dans la municipalité ◆ **an ~ majority** une majorité absolue ◆ **a satisfactory ~ performance** une performance globalement satisfaisante ◆ **he has ~ responsibility** il a la responsabilité d'ensemble ◆ **~ measurements** *[of car]* encombrement *m*, dimensions *fpl* hors tout ◆ **~ placings** *(Sport)* le classement général, le combiné ◆ **to be in ~ lead** *(Sport)* être en tête du classement général
ADV /ˌəʊvərˈɔːl/ *[view, survey]* en général ; *[measure]* d'un bout à l'autre, hors tout ; *[cost]* en tout ◆ **he came first ~** *(Sport)* il est arrivé premier au classement général ◆ **~, it was disappointing** dans l'ensemble, ça a été décevant
N /ˈəʊvərɔːl/ *(Brit: shirt-type)* blouse *f*
NPL **overalls** *[of mechanic etc]* bleu *m* (de travail) ; *(= dungarees)* salopette *f*

overanxious /əʊvərˈæŋkʃəs/ ADJ *(= worried)* trop inquiet (-ète *f*), trop anxieux ; *(= zealous)* trop zélé ◆ **~ parents** des parents *mpl* hyperanxieux ◆ **I'm not ~ to go** *(= not keen)* je n'ai pas trop *or* tellement envie d'y aller ; *(= not in a hurry)* je ne suis pas trop pressé d'y aller

overarching /ˈəʊvərˈɑːtʃɪŋ/ ADJ *[structure, framework, principle]* global ; *[question]* primordial

overarm /ˈəʊvərɑːm/ ADV, ADJ *(esp Brit)* par en dessus

overate /əʊvərˈeɪt/ VB pt of **overeat**

overawe /əʊvərˈɔː/ VT *[person]* intimider, impressionner, troubler ; *[sight etc]* impressionner

overbade /əʊvəˈbeɪd/ VB pt of **overbid**

overbalance /ˌəʊvəˈbæləns/ VI *[person]* perdre l'équilibre, basculer ; *[object]* se renverser, basculer VT *[+ object, boat]* (faire) basculer, renverser ; *[+ person]* faire perdre l'équilibre à

overbearing /əʊvəˈbeərɪŋ/ ADJ *(pej)* dominateur (-trice *f*)

overbid /əʊvəˈbɪd/ (pret **overbid** *or* **overbade**, ptp **overbid** *or* **overbidden**) *(at auction)* VT enchérir sur VI surenchérir

overblown /əʊvəˈbləʊn/ ADJ *[flower]* trop ouvert ; *[woman]* plantureux ; *[style]* ampoulé

overboard /ˈəʊvəbɔːd/ ADV *[fall, jump]* par-dessus bord ◆ **man ~!** un homme à la mer ! ◆ **to throw sth ~** *(lit)* jeter qch par-dessus bord ; (* *fig*) ne faire aucun cas de qch ◆ **to go ~** * aller trop loin ◆ **to go ~ about sth** * s'emballer * pour qch ◆ **to go ~ about sb** * s'emballer * pour qn ◆ **don't go ~ with the sugar** * vas-y mollo * *or* doucement avec le sucre ; → **wash**

overbold /əʊvəˈbəʊld/ ADJ *[person, remark]* impudent ; *[action]* trop audacieux

overbook /əʊvəˈbʊk/ VTI *[hotel, airline]* surréserver, surbooker

overbooking /əʊvəˈbʊkɪŋ/ N *[of hotel, flight]* surréservation *f*, surbooking *m*

overburden /əʊvəˈbɜːdn/ VT *(lit)* surcharger ; *(fig)* surcharger, accabler (*with* de)

overburdened /əʊvəˈbɜːdnd/ ADJ *[person] (with work)* surchargé ; *(with problems)* accablé ; *[system]* surchargé ◆ **~ with** *or* **by sth** surchargé *or* accablé de qch

overcame /əʊvəˈkeɪm/ VB pt of **overcome**

overcapacity /ˌəʊvəkəˈpæsɪtɪ/ N surcapacité *f*

overcast /ˈəʊvəˌkɑːst/ (vb : pret, ptp **overcast**) ADJ *[sky]* couvert, sombre ; *[weather, conditions]* couvert ; *[day]* au temps couvert ◆ **it is ~** le temps est couvert ◆ **it/the weather grew ~** ça/le temps s'est couvert N *(Sewing:* also **overcast stitch**) point *m* de surjet VT /ˌəʊvəˈkɑːst/ *(Sewing)* surjeter

overcautious /əʊvəˈkɔːʃəs/ ADJ trop prudent, trop circonspect

overcautiously /əʊvəˈkɔːʃəslɪ/ ADV avec un excès de prudence *or* de circonspection

overcautiousness /əʊvəˈkɔːʃəsnɪs/ N excès *m* de prudence *or* de circonspection

overcharge /ˌəʊvəˈtʃɑːdʒ/ VT 1 ◆ **to ~ sb for sth** faire payer qch trop cher à qn, surfacturer qch à qn 2 *[+ electric circuit]* surcharger VI ◆ **he ~d for it** il le lui a (*or* il me l'a *etc*) fait payer trop cher

overcoat /ˈəʊvəkəʊt/ N pardessus *m* ◆ **wooden ~** * *(hum)* costume *m* en sapin *

overcome /ˌəʊvəˈkʌm/ (pret **overcame**, ptp **overcome**) VT *[+ enemy]* vaincre, triompher de ; *[+ difficulty, obstacle, temptation]* surmonter ; *[+ one's rage, disgust, dislike etc]* maîtriser, dominer ; *[+ opposition]* triompher de ◆ **to be ~ by temptation/remorse/grief** succomber à la tentation/au remords/à la douleur ◆ **sleep overcame him** il a succombé au sommeil ◆ **~ with fear** paralysé par la peur, transi de peur ◆ **~ with cold** transi (de froid) ◆ **she was quite ~** elle fut saisie, elle resta muette de saisissement VI ◆ **we shall ~ !** nous vaincrons !

overcommit /ˌəʊvəkəˈmɪt/ VI trop s'engager VT ◆ **to ~ o.s.** trop s'engager ◆ **to be ~ted** *(financially)* avoir des charges financières excessives ; *(= have too much work)* s'être engagé à faire trop de travail

overcompensate /əʊvəˈkɒmpənseɪt/ VI *(gen)* faire de la surcompensation ; *(Psych)* surcompenser (*for sth* qch)

overcompensation /ˌəʊvəˌkɒmpənˈseɪʃən/ N *(gen, Psych)* surcompensation *f*

overcompress /ˌəʊvəkəmˈpres/ VT surcomprimer

overconfidence /ˌəʊvəˈkɒnfɪdəns/ N *(= assurance)* suffisance *f*, présomption *f* ; *(= trust)* confiance *f* aveugle (*in* en)

overconfident /ˌəʊvəˈkɒnfɪdənt/ ADJ *(= assured)* suffisant, présomptueux ; *(= trusting)* trop confiant (*in* en)

overconsumption /ˌəʊvəkənˈsʌmpʃən/ N *(Comm, Econ)* surconsommation *f*

overcook /ˌəʊvəˈkʊk/ VT trop (faire) cuire

overcritical /ˌəʊvəˈkrɪtɪkəl/ ADJ trop critique

overcrowded /ˌəʊvəˈkraʊdɪd/ ADJ *[city, prison, house]* surpeuplé ; *[classroom]* surchargé ; *[train, bus, office]* bondé ◆ **they live in ~ conditions** ils vivent dans des conditions de surpeuplement

overcrowding /ˌəʊvəˈkraʊdɪŋ/ N *(in housing, prison, town, district)* surpeuplement *m* ; *(in classroom)* effectif(s) *m(pl)* surchargé(s) ; *(in bus etc)* encombrement *m*

overdependence /ˌəʊvədɪˈpendəns/ N dépendance *f* excessive (*on* envers, à l'égard de)

overdependent /ˌəʊvədɪˈpendənt/ ADJ trop dépendant (*on* de)

over-designed /ˌəʊvədɪˈzaɪnd/ ADJ *(pej)* hypersophistiqué

overdevelop /ˌəʊvədɪˈveləp/ VT *(Econ)* surdévelopper

overdeveloped /ˌəʊvədɪˈveləpt/ ADJ *(gen, Phot)* trop développé ; *(Econ)* surdéveloppé

overdevelopment /ˌəʊvədɪˈveləpmənt/ N *(Econ)* surdéveloppement *m*

overdo /ˌəʊvəˈduː/ (pret **overdid** /ˌəʊvəˈdɪd/) (ptp **overdone** /ˌəʊvəˈdʌn/) VT 1 *(= exaggerate) [+ attitude, accent, concern, interest]* exagérer ; *(= eat or drink to excess)* abuser de, forcer sur * ◆ **don't ~ the beer** ne bois pas trop de bière, ne force * pas sur la bière ◆ **she rather overdoes the perfume** elle force * un peu sur le parfum, elle y va un peu fort * avec le parfum ◆ **he rather overdoes the devoted husband bit** * il en rajoute * dans le rôle du mari dévoué ◆ **to ~ it, to ~ things** (– *push o.s. too hard*) s'épuiser ; *(= go too far) (in comments, description etc)* exagérer ◆ **he's overdone it a bit on the sunbed** il y a été un peu fort * avec les UV 2 *(= overcook)* trop cuire

overdone /ˌəʊvəˈdʌn/ VB ptp of **overdo** ADJ 1 *(= exaggerated)* excessif, outré 2 *(= overcooked)* trop cuit

overdose /ˈəʊvədəʊs/ N 1 *(lit)* surdose *f*, overdose *f* ◆ **to take an ~** faire une overdose ◆ **to take an ~ of sth** prendre une surdose de qch ◆ **he died from an ~ (of heroin)** il est mort d'une overdose *or* d'une surdose (d'héroïne) 2 *(fig, hum)* overdose *f* ◆ **I had an ~ of TV last week** j'ai fait une overdose de télé la semaine dernière VI 1 *(lit) (gen)* faire une overdose ; *(fatally)* mourir d'une surdose *or* d'une overdose ◆ **to ~ on sth** prendre une surdose de qch 2 *(fig, hum)* ◆ **to ~ on TV** *etc* faire une overdose de télé *etc* ◆ **to ~ on chocolate** forcer * sur le chocolat

overdraft /ˈəʊvədrɑːft/ *(Banking)* N découvert *m* ◆ **I've got an ~** mon compte est à découvert, j'ai un découvert à la banque
COMP **overdraft facility** N découvert *m* autorisé, autorisation *f* de découvert
overdraft interest N intérêts *mpl* débiteurs, agios *mpl*

overdraw /ˌəʊvəˈdrɔː/ (pret **overdrew**, ptp **overdrawn**) *(Banking)* VI mettre son compte à découvert, dépasser son crédit VT *[+ one's account]* mettre à découvert

overdrawn /ˌəʊvəˈdrɔːn/ VB ptp of **overdraw** ADJ *[person, account]* à découvert ◆ **I'm £500 ~, my account is £500 ~** j'ai un découvert de 500 livres ◆ **I'm ~/my account is ~ by £500** je suis à découvert/mon compte est à découvert de 500 livres

overdress /ˈəʊvədres/ N robe-chasuble *f* VI /ˌəʊvəˈdres/ (also **to be overdressed**) être trop habillé

overdrew /ˌəʊvəˈdruː/ VB pt of **overdraw**

overdrive /ˈəʊvədraɪv/ N *[of car]* (vitesse *f*) surmultipliée *f* ◆ **in ~** en surmultipliée ◆ **to go into ~** * *(fig)* mettre les bouchées doubles

overdue /ˌəʊvəˈdjuː/ ADJ *[train, bus]* en retard ; *[reform]* qui tarde (à être réalisé) ; *[acknowledgement, recognition, apology]* tardif ; *[account]* impayé, en souffrance ◆ **~ payments** arriérés *mpl* ◆ **the plane is 20 minutes ~** l'avion a 20 minutes de retard ◆ **that change is long ~** ce changement se fait attendre depuis longtemps ◆ **she's (a week) ~** *(menstrual period)* elle est en retard (d'une semaine) ; *(baby)* elle a dépassé le terme (d'une semaine), elle aurait déjà dû accoucher (il y a une semaine) ◆ **the baby is (a week) ~** l'enfant aurait déjà dû naître (il y a une semaine) ◆ **my books are (a week) ~** je suis en retard (d'une semaine) pour rendre mes livres

overeager /əʊvərˈiːgə^r/ ADJ trop zélé, trop empressé ◆ **he was not ~ to leave** *(= not keen)* il n'avait pas une envie folle de partir ; *(= not in a hurry)* il n'était pas trop pressé de partir

overeat /əʊvərˈiːt/ (pret **overate**, ptp **overeaten**) VI *(on one occasion)* trop manger ; *(regularly)* trop manger, se suralimenter

overeating /əʊvərˈiːtɪŋ/ N excès *mpl* de table

over-egg * /əʊvərˈeg/ VT *(Brit fig)* ◆ **to ~ the pudding** exagérer

overelaborate /ˌəʊvərɪˈlæbərɪt/ ADJ *[design, plan]* trop compliqué ; *[style, excuse]* contourné ; *[dress]* trop recherché

overemphasis /ˌəʊvərˈemfəsɪs/ N ◆ **to put an ~ on sth** accorder trop d'importance à qch

overemphasize /əʊvərˈemfəsaɪz/ VT accorder trop d'importance à ◆ **the importance of education cannot be ~d** on n'insistera jamais assez sur *or* on ne soulignera jamais assez l'importance de l'éducation

overemphatic /ˌəʊvərɪmˈfætɪk/ ADJ trop catégorique

overemployment /ˌəʊvərɪmˈplɔɪmənt/ N suremploi *m*

over-engineered /ˌəʊvərendʒɪˈnɪəd/ ADJ *(pej)* inutilement compliqué

overenthusiastic /ˌəʊvərɪnˌθuːzɪˈæstɪk/ ADJ trop enthousiaste

overenthusiastically /ˌəʊvərɪnˌθuːzɪˈæstɪkəlɪ/ ADV avec trop d'enthousiasme

overestimate /əʊvərˈestɪmeɪt/ VT *[+ price, costs, importance]* surestimer ; *[+ strength]* trop présumer de ; *[+ danger]* exagérer

overexcite /əʊvərɪkˈsaɪt/ VT surexciter

overexcited /əʊvərɪkˈsaɪtɪd/ ADJ surexcité ◆ **to get ~** se mettre dans un état de surexcitation, devenir surexcité ◆ **don't get ~!** ne vous excitez pas !

overexcitement /əʊvərɪkˈsaɪtmənt/ N surexcitation *f*

overexert /əʊvərɪgˈzɜːt/ VT ◆ **to ~ o.s.** se surmener, s'éreinter

overexertion /əʊvərɪgˈzɜːʃən/ N surmenage *m*

overexpose /əʊvərɪksˈpəʊz/ VT *(Phot)* surexposer

overexposure /əʊvərɪksˈpəʊʒə^r^/ N *(Phot, also fig)* surexposition *f*

overextended /əʊvərɪkˈstendɪd/ ADJ *[person]* qui a trop d'activités ; *[organization]* qui a trop diversifié ses activités

overfamiliar /əʊvəfəˈmɪljə^r^/ ADJ trop familier

overfeed /əʊvəˈfiːd/ VT (pret, ptp **overfed** /əʊvəˈfed/) suralimenter, donner trop à manger à ◆ **to be overfed** *(animal)* être trop nourri ; *(person)* trop manger VI se suralimenter, trop manger

overfeeding /əʊvəˈfiːdɪŋ/ N suralimentation *f*

overfill /əʊvəˈfɪl/ VT trop remplir

overfish /əʊvəˈfɪʃ/ VT surexploiter

overfishing /əʊvəˈfɪʃɪŋ/ N surpêche *f*

overflew /əʊvəˈfluː/ VB pt of **overfly**

overflight /ˈəʊvəflaɪt/ N *(authorized)* survol *m* de l'espace aérien ; *(unauthorized)* violation *f* de l'espace aérien

overflow /ˈəʊvəfləʊ/ N 1 *(= pipe, outlet) [of bath, sink etc]* trop-plein *m* ; *[of canal, reservoir etc]* déversoir *m*, dégorgeoir *m*

2 *(= flooding)* inondation *f* ; *(= excess liquid)* débordement *m*, trop-plein *m*

3 *(= excess) [of people, population]* excédent *m* ; *[of objects]* excédent *m*, surplus *m*

VT /ˌəʊvəˈfləʊ/ *[+ container]* déborder de ◆ **the river has ~ed its banks** la rivière a débordé *or* est sortie de son lit

VI /ˌəʊvəˈfləʊ/ 1 *[liquid, river etc]* déborder ◆ **the river ~ed into the fields** la rivière a inondé les champs

2 *(fig) [people, objects]* déborder ◆ **the crowd ~ed into the next room** la foule a débordé dans la pièce voisine

3 *[container]* déborder *(with* de) ; *[room, vehicle]* regorger *(with* de) ◆ **to be full to ~ing** *[cup, jug]* être plein à ras bords *or* à déborder ; *[room, vehicle]* être plein à craquer ◆ **to fill a cup to ~ing** remplir une tasse à ras bords

4 *(fig = be full of)* déborder, regorger *(with* de), abonder *(with* en) ◆ **the town was ~ing with visitors** la ville regorgeait de visiteurs ◆ **his heart was ~ing with love** son cœur débordait d'amour ◆ **he was ~ing with optimism** il débordait d'optimisme ◆ **he ~ed with suggestions** il abondait en suggestions

COMP /ˈəʊvəˌfləʊ/ *[pipe]* d'écoulement

overfly /əʊvəˈflaɪ/ (pret **overflew**, ptp **overflown** /əʊvəˈfləʊn/) VT survoler

overfond /əʊvəˈfɒnd/ ADJ ◆ **she is not ~ of ...** elle ne raffole pas de ...

overfull /əʊvəˈfʊl/ ADJ trop plein *(of* de)

overgenerous /əʊvəˈdʒenərəs/ ADJ *[person]* prodigue *(with* de) ; *[amount, helping]* excessif

overground /əʊvəˈgraʊnd/ ADJ *(Transport)* à l'air libre

overgrown /ˈəʊvəˈgrəʊn/ ADJ ◆ **the path is ~ (with grass)** le chemin est envahi par l'herbe ◆ **~ with weeds** recouvert de mauvaises herbes ◆ **a wall ~ with ivy/moss** un mur recouvert *or* tapissé de lierre/de mousse ◆ **the garden is very ~** le jardin est une vraie forêt vierge *or* est complètement envahi (par la végétation) ◆ **he's just an ~ schoolboy** c'est un grand gamin

overhand /ˈəʊvəhænd/ *(US)* ADV 1 *(Sport etc) [throw, serve]* par en dessus 2 *(Sewing)* à points de surjet VT *(Sewing)* coudre à points de surjet

overhang /ˌəʊvəˈhæŋ/ (pret, ptp **overhung**) VT *[tree, branch, rocks, balcony]* surplomber ; *[mist, smoke]* planer sur ; *[danger etc]* menacer VI *[tree, branch, cliff, balcony]* être en surplomb N /ˈəʊvəˌhæŋ/ *[of cliff, rock, balcony, building]* surplomb *m*

overhanging /ˌəʊvəˈhæŋɪŋ/ ADJ *[rock, cliff, eaves]* en surplomb, en saillie ; *[tree, branch]* en surplomb

overhastily /ˌəʊvəˈheɪstɪlɪ/ ADV trop hâtivement, de façon trop précipitée

overhasty /ˌəʊvəˈheɪstɪ/ ADJ trop précipité *or* hâtif ◆ **to be ~ in doing sth** faire qch de façon trop précipitée ◆ **he was ~ in his condemnation of ...** il a été trop hâtif en condamnant ...

overhaul /ˈəʊvəhɔːl/ N *[of vehicle, machine]* révision *f* (complète) ; *[of ship]* radoub *m* ; *(fig) [of system, programme]* refonte *f*, remaniement *m* VT /ˌəʊvəˈhɔːl/ 1 *(= check, repair) [+ vehicle, machine]* réviser, remettre en état ; *[+ ship]* radouber ; *(fig) [+ system, programme]* remanier 2 *(= catch up with)* rattraper, gagner de vitesse ; *(= overtake)* dépasser

overhead /ˌəʊvəˈhed/ ADV *(= up above)* au-dessus (de nos *or* vos *etc* têtes) ; *(= in the sky)* dans le ciel ; *(= on the floor above)* (à l'étage) au-dessus, en haut ADJ /ˈəʊvəhed/ 1 *[wires, cables, railway]* aérien 2 *(Comm)* ~ **charges** *or* **costs** *or* **expenses** frais *mpl* généraux N /ˈəʊvəhed/ *(US)* ⇒ **overheads** NPL **overheads** *(Brit)* frais *mpl* généraux

COMP **overhead light** N plafonnier *m*
overhead lighting N éclairage *m* au plafond
overhead projection N rétroprojection *f*
overhead projector N rétroprojecteur *m*
overhead valve N *(in car engine)* soupape *f* en tête

overhear /ˌəʊvəˈhɪə^r^/ (pret, ptp **overheard** /ˌəʊvəˈhɜːd/) VT surprendre, entendre (par hasard) ◆ **he was overheard to say that ...** on lui a entendu dire *or* on l'a surpris à dire que ... ◆ **I overheard your conversation** j'ai entendu ce que vous disiez, j'ai surpris votre conversation

overheat /əʊvəˈhiːt/ VT surchauffer VI *(gen)* devenir surchauffé ; *[engine, brakes]* chauffer

overheated /əʊvəˈhiːtɪd/ ADJ *[room]* surchauffé ; *[brakes, engine, computer]* qui chauffe ; *[economy, market]* en état de surchauffe ◆ **to get ~** *(lit) [person, animal]* avoir trop chaud ; *(fig) [person]* s'emporter

overheating /ˌəʊvəˈhiːtɪŋ/ N *(Econ)* surchauffe *f*

overhung /əʊvəˈhʌŋ/ VB pt, ptp of **overhang**

overimpressed /əʊvərɪmˈprest/ N ◆ **I'm not ~ with him** il ne m'impressionne pas vraiment ◆ **I'm not ~ with his work** je ne suis pas vraiment impressionné par son travail

overindulge /əʊvərɪnˈdʌldʒ/ VI abuser *(in* de) ◆ **I rather ~d last night** j'ai un peu forcé* *or* abusé* hier soir, je me suis laissé aller à des excès hier soir VT *[+ person]* trop gâter, satisfaire tous les caprices de ; *[+ passion, appetite]* céder trop facilement à

overindulgence /əʊvərɪnˈdʌldʒəns/ N indulgence *f* excessive *(of/towards sb* des/envers les caprices de qn), abus *m (in sth* de qch)

overindulgent /əʊvərɪnˈdʌldʒənt/ ADJ trop indulgent *(to, towards* envers)

overinvestment /əʊvərɪnˈvestmənt/ N *(Econ)* surinvestissement *m*

overjoyed /ˌəʊvəˈdʒɔɪd/ ADJ *[person]* ravi, enchanté ◆ **I can't say I'm ~** je ne peux pas dire que je sois enchanté ◆ **~ at** *or* **about** *or* **with sth** ravi *or* enchanté de qch ◆ **to be ~ to see sb** être ravi *or* enchanté de voir qn ◆ **to be ~ that ...** être ravi *or* enchanté que ... + *subj*

overkill /ˈəʊvəkɪl/ N 1 *(Mil)* surarmement *m* 2 *(fig)* **that was a bit of an ~!*** c'était un peu exagéré ! ◆ **such security measures may well be ~** de telles mesures de sécurité sont peut-être exagérées *or* excessives ◆ **her new fitness régime quickly reached ~** elle a vite dépassé la mesure avec son nouveau programme de mise en forme ◆ **every time I switch on the TV, there's football. It's ~** chaque fois que j'allume la télévision, il y a du football : trop, c'est trop ◆ **an ~ in negative propaganda** trop de propagande hostile

overladen /əʊvəˈleɪdn/ ADJ *(gen, also Elec)* surchargé

overlaid /əʊvəˈleɪd/ VB pt, ptp of **overlay**

overland /ˈəʊvəlænd/ ADJ par voie de terre *(to* pour aller à) ◆ **by an ~ route** par voie de terre ADV par voie de terre

overlap /ˈəʊvəlæp/ N empiètement *m*, chevauchement *m* ; *[of tiles]* chevauchement *m* VI /ˌəʊvəˈlæp/ (also **overlap each other**) se recouvrir partiellement ; *[teeth, boards, tiles]* se chevaucher ; *(fig)* se chevaucher ◆ **his work and ours ~** son travail et le nôtre se chevauchent *or* se recoupent ◆ **our holidays ~** nos vacances coïncident en partie *or* (se) chevauchent VT /ˌəʊvəˈlæp/ *[+ tiles, slates]* enchevaucher ; *[+ edges]* chevaucher, déborder de ; *(fig)* recouper ◆ **to ~ each other** → **vi**

overlay /ˌəʊvəˈleɪ/ (pret, ptp **overlaid** /ˌəʊvəˈleɪd/) VT (re)couvrir *(with* de) N /ˈəʊvəˌleɪ/ revêtement *m*

overleaf /ˈəʊvəliːf/ ADV au verso ◆ **see ~** voir au verso

overlie /ˌəʊvəˈlaɪ/ VT recouvrir

overload /ˈəʊvəˌləʊd/ N surcharge *f* VT /ˌəʊvəˈləʊd/ *[+ circuit, truck, animal]* surcharger *(with* de) ; *[+ engine]* surmener

overlook /ˌəʊvəˈlʊk/ VT 1 *(= have a view over) [house, balcony etc]* donner sur, avoir vue sur ; *[window, door]* s'ouvrir sur, donner sur ; *[castle etc]* dominer ◆ **our garden is not ~ed** personne n'a vue sur notre jardin 2 *(= accidentally miss) [+ fact, detail]* oublier, laisser échapper ; *[+ problem, difficulty]* oublier, négliger ◆ **I ~ed that** j'ai oublié cela, cela m'a échappé ◆ **it is easy to ~ the fact that ...** on oublie facilement que ... ◆ **this plant is so small that it is easily ~ed** cette plante est si petite qu'il est facile de ne pas la remarquer 3 *(= deliberately allow to pass, ignore) [+ mistake]* passer sur, fermer les yeux sur ◆ **we'll ~ it this time** nous passerons là-dessus cette fois-ci, nous fermerons les yeux (pour) cette fois 4 *(= supervise)* surveiller

overlord /ˈəʊvəlɔːd/ N *(Hist)* suzerain *m* ; *(= leader)* chef *m* suprême ◆ **the steel/coal** *etc* **~**

(fig) le grand patron de la sidérurgie/des charbonnages *etc*

overly /'əʊvəlɪ/ ADV trop

overmanned /əʊvə'mænd/ ADJ en sureffectif

overmanning /əʊvə'mænɪŋ/ N sureffectif *m*, effectif *m* pléthorique

overmuch /əʊvə'mʌtʃ/ ADV excessivement, à l'excès ◆ **I don't like it** ~ je ne l'aime pas trop ADJ excessif

overnice /əʊvə'naɪs/ ADJ *[person]* trop pointilleux, trop scrupuleux ; *[distinction]* trop subtil

overnight /əʊvə'naɪt/ ADV *(= during the night)* (pendant) la nuit ; *(= until next day)* jusqu'au lendemain ; *(fig = suddenly)* du jour au lendemain ◆ **to stay** ~ **with sb** passer la nuit chez qn ◆ **we drove** ~ nous avons roulé de nuit ◆ **will it keep** ~? est-ce que cela se gardera jusqu'à demain ? ◆ **the town had changed** ~ la ville avait changé du jour au lendemain ADJ /'əʊvə,naɪt/ *[stay]* d'une nuit ; *[journey]* de nuit ◆ **there had been an** ~ **change of plans** *(fig = sudden)* les plans avaient changé du jour au lendemain N nuitée *f* COMP **overnight bag** N nécessaire *m* de voyage

overpaid /əʊvə'peɪd/ VB pt, ptp of **overpay**

overpass /'əʊvəpɑːs/ N *(US) (gen)* pont *m* autoroutier ; *(at flyover)* autopont *m*

overpay /əʊvə'peɪ/ (pret, ptp **overpaid**) VT *[+ person, job]* trop payer, surpayer ◆ **he was overpaid by $50** on lui a payé 50 dollars de trop

overpayment /əʊvə'peɪmənt/ N 1 ◆ ~ **(of wages)** surpaye *f*, rémunération *f* excessive 2 ◆ ~ **(of tax)** trop-perçu *m* ◆ **refund of** ~ remboursement *m* du trop-perçu

overplay /əʊvə'pleɪ/ VT *(fig)* ◆ **to** ~ **one's hand** aller trop loin

overpopulated /əʊvə'pɒpjʊleɪtɪd/ ADJ surpeuplé

overpopulation /əʊvəpɒpjʊ'leɪʃən/ N surpopulation *f (in* dans), surpeuplement *m (of* de)

overpower /,əʊvə'paʊəʳ/ VT *(= defeat)* vaincre, subjuguer ; *(= subdue physically)* dominer, maîtriser ; *(fig) (= overwhelm)* accabler, terrasser

overpowering /,əʊvə'paʊərɪŋ/ ADJ *[desire, urge, need, strength]* irrésistible ; *[feeling]* irrépressible ; *[force]* impérieux ; *[smell, scent, flavour]* envahissant ; *[noise]* assourdissant ; *[heat]* accablant ; *[colour]* tapageur ; *[decoration]* oppressant ; *[person, manner]* dominateur (-trice *f*)

overpraise /əʊvə'preɪz/ VT faire des éloges excessifs de

overprescribe /əʊvəprɪs'kraɪb/ *(Pharm, Med)* VI prescrire trop de médicaments VT prescrire en trop grande quantité

overprice /əʊvə'praɪs/ VT *[+ goods]* vendre trop cher, demander un prix excessif pour

overpriced /əʊvə'praɪst/ ADJ excessivement cher

overprint /əʊvə'prɪnt/ *(Typ)* VT surcharger ◆ **the price had been** ~**ed with the word "sale"** les mots "en solde" avaient été imprimés sur l'ancien prix N /'əʊvəprɪnt/ surcharge *f*

overproduce /əʊvəprə'djuːs/ VT surproduire

overproduction /əʊvəprə'dʌkʃən/ N surproduction *f*

overprotect /əʊvəprə'tekt/ VT *[+ child]* protéger excessivement, surprotéger

overprotective /əʊvəprə'tektɪv/ ADJ protecteur (-trice *f*) à l'excès

overqualified /əʊvə'kwɒlɪfaɪd/ ADJ trop qualifié

overran /əʊvə'ræn/ VB pt of **overrun**

overrate /əʊvə'reɪt/ VT surévaluer, faire trop de cas de

overrated /əʊvə'reɪtɪd/ ADJ surfait, qui ne mérite pas sa réputation

overreach /əʊvə'riːtʃ/ VT ◆ **to** ~ **o.s.** (vouloir) trop entreprendre VI *[person]* tendre le bras trop loin ; *(fig)* aller trop loin

overreact /,əʊvəriː'ækt/ VI *(gen, Psych)* réagir de manière exagérée *or* excessive ◆ **observers considered that the government had** ~**ed** les observateurs ont trouvé excessive la réaction gouvernementale ◆ **she's always** ~**ing** elle exagère toujours, elle dramatise toujours tout

overreaction /,əʊvəriː'ækʃən/ N réaction *f* exagérée *or* excessive *or* disproportionnée

overreliance /,əʊvərɪ'laɪəns/ N *(= dependence)* dépendance *f* excessive *(on* vis-à-vis de) ; *(= trust)* confiance *f* excessive *(on* en)

overrepresented /,əʊvərepri'zentɪd/ ADJ surreprésenté

override /,əʊvə'raɪd/ (pret **overrode**, ptp **overridden** /,əʊvə'rɪdn/) VT *[+ law, duty, sb's rights]* fouler aux pieds ; *[+ order, instructions]* outrepasser ; *[+ decision]* annuler, casser ; *[+ opinion, objection, protests, sb's wishes, claims]* passer outre à, ne pas tenir compte de ; *[+ person]* passer outre aux désirs de ◆ **this fact** ~**s all others** ce fait l'emporte sur tous les autres ◆ **this** ~**s what we decided before** ceci annule ce que nous avions décidé auparavant

overrider /'əʊvəraɪdəʳ/ N *(of car bumper)* tampon *m* (de pare-chocs)

overriding /,əʊvə'raɪdɪŋ/ ADJ *[need, consideration, objective, principle, issue]* primordial ; *[concern, impression, feeling]* premier ; *[factor]* prépondérant ; *(Jur) [act, clause]* dérogatoire ◆ **of** ~ **importance** d'une importance primordiale ◆ **his** ~ **desire was to leave as soon as possible** sa seule envie était de partir le plus vite possible

overripe /,əʊvə'raɪp/ ADJ *[fruit]* trop mûr, blet (blette *f*) ; *[cheese]* trop fait

overrode /,əʊvə'rəʊd/ VB pt of **override**

overrule /,əʊvə'ruːl/ VT *[+ judgement, decision]* annuler, casser ; *[+ claim, objection]* rejeter ◆ **he was** ~**d by the chairman** la décision du président a prévalu contre lui ; → **objection**

overrun /,əʊvə'rʌn/ (pret **overran**, ptp **overrun**) VT 1 *[rats, weeds]* envahir, infester ; *[troops, army]* se rendre maître de, occuper ◆ **the town is** ~ **by** *or* **with tourists** la ville est envahie par les touristes *or* de touristes 2 *[+ line, edge etc]* dépasser, aller au-delà de ◆ **to** ~ **a signal** *(Rail)* brûler un signal ◆ **the train overran the platform** le train s'est arrêté au-delà du quai 3 ◆ **to** ~ **one's time (by ten minutes)** *[speaker]* dépasser le temps alloué (de dix minutes) ; *[programme, concert etc]* dépasser l'heure prévue (de dix minutes) VI ◆ **to** ~ **(by ten minutes)** *[speaker]* dépasser le temps alloué (de dix minutes) ; *[programme, concert etc]* dépasser l'heure prévue (de dix minutes)

oversaw /əʊvə'sɔː/ VB pt of **oversee**

overscrupulous /əʊvə'skruːpjʊləs/ ADJ trop pointilleux, trop scrupuleux

overseas /'əʊvə'siːz/ ADV outre-mer ; *(= abroad)* à l'étranger ◆ **he's back from** ~ il revient de l'étranger ◆ **visitors from** ~ visiteurs *mpl* (venus) d'outre-mer, étrangers *mpl* ADJ *[colony, market]* d'outre-mer ; *[trade]* extérieur (-eure *f*) ; *[visitor]* (venu) d'outre-mer, étranger ; *[aid]* aux pays étrangers ◆ **he got an** ~ **posting** il a été détaché à l'étranger *or* outre-mer ◆ **Minister/Ministry of Overseas Development** *(Brit)* ≃ ministre *m*/ministère *m* de la Coopération COMP **overseas cap** N *(US)* calot *m*, bonnet *m* de police

oversee /əʊvə'siː/ (pret **oversaw**, ptp **overseen**) VT surveiller

overseer /'əʊvəsiːəʳ/ N *(in factory, on roadworks etc)* contremaître *m*, chef *m* d'équipe ; *(in coalmine)* porion *m* ; *[of prisoners, slaves]* surveillant(e) *m(f)*

oversell /əʊvə'sel/ (pret, ptp **oversold**) VT 1 *(lit)* ◆ **the match/show was oversold** on a vendu plus de billets qu'il n'y avait de places pour le match/le spectacle 2 *(fig)* faire trop valoir, mettre trop en avant

oversensitive /əʊvə'sensɪtɪv/ ADJ trop sensible, trop susceptible

oversew /əʊvə'səʊ/ (pret **oversewed**, ptp **oversewed** *or* **oversewn**) VT coudre à points de surjet

oversexed /əʊvə'sekst/ ADJ très porté sur le sexe *or* sur la chose

overshadow /əʊvə'ʃædəʊ/ VT *[leaves etc]* ombrager ; *[clouds]* obscurcir ; *[tree, building]* dominer ; *(fig) (= cloud, spoil) [+ person, period of time]* assombrir ; *(= eclipse) [+ person, sb's achievement]* éclipser ◆ **her childhood was** ~**ed by her mother's death** son enfance a été assombrie par la mort de sa mère

overshoe /'əʊvəʃuː/ N *(gen)* galoche *f* ; *(made of rubber)* caoutchouc *m*

overshoot /,əʊvə'ʃuːt/ (pret, ptp **overshot** /,əʊvə'ʃɒt/) VT dépasser, aller au-delà de ◆ **the plane overshot the runway** l'avion a dépassé la piste d'atterrissage ◆ **to** ~ **the mark** *(lit, fig)* dépasser le but

oversight /'əʊvəsaɪt/ N 1 *(= omission)* omission *f*, oubli *m* ◆ **by** *or* **through an** ~ par mégarde, par inadvertance 2 *(= supervision)* surveillance *f* ◆ **under the** ~ **of** *(frm)* sous la surveillance de

oversimplification /,əʊvə,sɪmplɪfɪ'keɪʃən/ N simplification *f* excessive

oversimplify /əʊvə'sɪmplɪfaɪ/ VT trop simplifier, simplifier à l'extrême

oversize(d) /əʊvə'saɪz(d)/ ADJ 1 *(= too big)* trop grand ; *(Scol) [class]* trop nombreux, pléthorique ; *[family]* trop nombreux 2 *(= huge)* gigantesque, énorme

oversleep /əʊvə'sliːp/ (pret, ptp **overslept** /,əʊvə'slept/) VI *(= wake up too late)* ne pas se réveiller à l'heure ; *(= sleep too long)* dormir trop ◆ **I overslept** *(= woke too late)* je me suis réveillé trop tard

oversold /əʊvə'səʊld/ VB pt, ptp of **oversell**

overspend /əʊvə'spend/ (pret, ptp **overspent**) VT *[+ allowance, resources]* dépenser au-dessus de *or* au-delà de VI trop dépenser ◆ **to** ~ **by $10** dépenser 10 dollars de trop N dépassement *m* de budget

overspending /əʊvə'spendɪŋ/ N *(gen)* dépenses *fpl* excessives ; *(Econ, Admin etc)* dépassements *mpl* de crédits, dépassements *mpl* budgétaires

overspent /əʊvə'spent/ VB pt, ptp of **overspend**

overspill /'əʊvəspɪl/ *(Brit)* N excédent *m* de population ◆ **the London** ~ l'excédent *m* de la population de Londres COMP **overspill town** N ville *f* satellite

overstaffed /əʊvə'stɑːft/ ADJ en sureffectif

overstaffing /əʊvə'stɑːfɪŋ/ N effectif *m* pléthorique, sureffectif *m*

overstate /əʊvə'steɪt/ VT exagérer

overstatement /əʊvə'steɪtmənt/ N exagération *f*

overstay /əʊvə'steɪ/ VT ◆ **to** ~ **one's leave** *(Mil)* excéder la durée fixée de sa permission ; *(gen)* excéder la durée fixée de son congé ◆ **I hope I haven't** ~**ed my welcome** j'espère que je n'ai pas abusé de votre hospitalité ◆ **I know when I've** ~**ed my welcome** je sais reconnaître quand je deviens indésirable

oversteer /,əʊvə'stɪəʳ/ VI trop braquer

overstep /ˌəʊvəˈstep/ VT [+ limits] dépasser, outrepasser ◆ to ~ one's authority abuser de son autorité ; (Pol) outrepasser son mandat ◆ to ~ the line or mark (fig) exagérer (fig), dépasser la mesure or les bornes

overstocked /ˈəʊvəˈstɒkt/ ADJ [pond, river] surchargé de poissons ; [farm] qui a un excès de cheptel ; [shop, market] surapprovisionné

overstrain /ˈəʊvəˈstreɪn/ VT [+ person] surmener ; [+ heart] fatiguer ; [+ strength] abuser de ; [+ horse, metal] forcer ; [+ resources, reserves] surexploiter ◆ to ~ o.s. se surmener

overstretch /ˈəʊvəˈstretʃ/ VT 1 (lit) [+ muscles, legs] trop étirer 2 (fig) [+ budget, finances] grever ; [+ resources] surexploiter ; [+ abilities] trop pousser ◆ to ~ o.s. (= do too much) se surmener ; (financially) dépasser les limites de son budget VI [person, muscles, legs] s'étirer de trop

overstretched /ˈəʊvəˈstretʃt/ ADJ [person] débordé ◆ my budget is ~ mon budget est extrêmement serré

overstrung /ˈəʊvəˈstrʌŋ/ ADJ [piano] à cordes croisées

overstuffed /ˈəʊvəˈstʌft/ ADJ [chair] rembourré

oversubscribed /ˈəʊvəsəbˈskraɪbd/ ADJ (Stock Exchange) sursouscrit ◆ this outing was ~ il y a eu trop d'inscriptions pour cette sortie

overt /əʊˈvɜːt/ ADJ [hostility, interference] manifeste ; [criticism] franc (franche f) ; [discrimination, racism] déclaré ; [sexuality] non réprimé ; [message] évident ◆ ~ and covert operations (Mil, Pol) opérations fpl à découvert et secrètes

overtake /ˌəʊvəˈteɪk/ (pret **overtook**, ptp **overtaken**) VT 1 (= pass) [+ car] (Brit) doubler, dépasser ; [+ competitor, runner] devancer, dépasser

2 (fig = take the lead over) [+ competitor, rival] devancer, dépasser ◆ they have ~n Britain as the world's fifth largest economy ils ont dépassé la Grande-Bretagne et sont devenus la cinquième puissance économique mondiale ◆ lung cancer has ~n breast cancer as the main cause of death for women le cancer des poumons a remplacé le cancer du sein comme principale cause de mortalité chez les femmes

3 (fig = overwhelm) [storm, night] surprendre ◆ the terrible fate that has ~n them le terrible sort qui s'est abattu sur eux or qui les a frappés ◆ ~n by fear frappé d'effroi ◆ to be ~n by events être dépassé par les événements ◆ his fear was quickly ~n by anger sa peur a vite cédé la place à la colère

VI (Brit) doubler, dépasser ◆ "no overtaking" "interdiction de dépasser" ◆ to ~ on the inside dépasser or doubler du mauvais côté

overtax /ˈəʊvəˈtæks/ VT 1 (Fin) surimposer 2 [+ person] surmener ◆ to ~ one's strength abuser de ses forces, se surmener ◆ a singer who has ~ed his voice un chanteur qui a trop poussé sa voix ◆ such a project might ~ the skills of our workforce un tel projet risque de mettre les compétences de notre main-d'œuvre à trop rude épreuve

over-the-counter /ˌəʊvəðəˈkaʊntəʳ/ ADJ 1 [drugs, medicine] vendu sans ordonnance ; see also **counter¹** 2 (Stock Exchange) [securities, transactions] hors cote COMP **over-the-counter market** N (Stock Exchange) marché m hors cote, hors-cote m

overthrow /ˌəʊvəˈθrəʊ/ (pret **overthrew** /ˌəʊvəˈθruː/) (ptp **overthrown** /ˌəʊvəˈθrəʊn/) VT [+ enemy, country, empire] vaincre (définitivement) ; [+ dictator, government, system] renverser N /ˈəʊvəθrəʊ/ [of enemy etc] défaite f ; [of empire, government, system] chute f, renversement m

overtime /ˈəʊvətaɪm/ N 1 (at work) heures fpl supplémentaires ◆ I am on ~, I'm doing or working ~ je fais des heures supplémentaires ◆ £300 per week with ~ 300 livres par semaine heures supplémentaires comprises ◆ to work ~ (lit) faire des heures supplémentaires ; (fig) mettre les bouchées doubles ◆ his imagination was working ~ il s'était laissé emporter par son imagination 2 (US Sport) prolongation f

COMP **overtime pay** N (rémunération f pour) heures fpl supplémentaires
overtime work(ing) N heures fpl supplémentaires

overtired /ˈəʊvəˈtaɪəd/ ADJ (gen) surmené ; [baby, child] énervé ◆ don't get ~ ne te surmène pas, ne te fatigue pas trop

overtly /əʊˈvɜːtlɪ/ ADV [political, sexual] ouvertement

overtone /ˈəʊvətəʊn/ N 1 (Mus) harmonique m or f 2 (fig = hint) note f, accent m ◆ there were ~s or there was an ~ of hostility in his voice on sentait une note or des accents d'hostilité dans sa voix ◆ to have political ~s avoir des connotations or des sous-entendus politiques

overtook /ˌəʊvəˈtʊk/ VB pt of **overtake**

overtrick /ˈəʊvətrɪk/ N (Bridge) levée f de mieux

overtrump /ˈəʊvəˈtrʌmp/ VT (Cards) surcouper

overture /ˈəʊvətjʊəʳ/ N 1 (Mus) ouverture f ◆ the 1812 Overture l'Ouverture f solennelle 2 (fig) ouverture f, avance f ◆ to make ~s to sb faire des ouvertures à qn ◆ peace ~s ouvertures fpl de paix ◆ friendly ~s avances fpl amicales

overturn /ˌəʊvəˈtɜːn/ VT 1 [+ car, chair] renverser ; [+ boat] faire chavirer or capoter 2 [+ government, plans] renverser ; [+ decision, judgement] annuler VI [chair] se renverser ; [car, plane] se retourner, capoter ; [railway coach] se retourner, verser ; [boat] chavirer, capoter

overtype /ˈəʊvəˈtaɪp/ VT taper par-dessus

overuse /ˈəʊvəˈjuːz/ VT [+ object, product] abuser de ◆ the word is ~d c'est un mot galvaudé

overvalue /ˈəʊvəˈvæljuː/ VT (gen) surestimer ; (Econ) [+ currency] surévaluer

overview /ˈəʊvəvjuː/ N 1 (lit) vue f d'ensemble, panorama m 2 (fig) [of situation etc] vue f d'ensemble

overweening /ˌəʊvəˈwiːnɪŋ/ ADJ (frm) [pride, arrogance, ambition, self-confidence, power] démesuré ; [person] outrecuidant (liter) ; [organization, bureaucracy] présomptueux

overweight /ˌəʊvəˈweɪt/ ADJ ◆ to be ~ [person] avoir des kilos en trop ◆ to be 5 kilos ~ peser 5 kilos de trop ◆ to be medically ~ avoir une surcharge pondérale ◆ your luggage is ~ vous avez un excédent de bagages N /ˈəʊvəˌweɪt/ poids m en excès ; [of person] (gen) surpoids m ; (Med) surcharge f pondérale

overwhelm /ˌəʊvəˈwelm/ VT 1 (lit) [flood, waves, sea] [+ land, person, ship] submerger, engloutir ; [earth, lava, avalanche] engloutir, ensevelir ; [+ one's enemy, opponent] écraser

2 (fig) [emotions] accabler, submerger ; [misfortunes] atterrer, accabler ; [shame, praise, kindness] confondre, rendre confus ; [letters, phone calls] submerger, inonder ◆ to ~ sb with questions accabler qn de questions ◆ to ~ sb with favours combler qn de faveurs ◆ I am ~ed by his kindness je suis tout confus de sa gentillesse ◆ to be ~ed with work être débordé or accablé de travail ◆ we have been ~ed with offers of help nous avons été submergés or inondés d'offres d'aide ◆ Venice quite ~ed me Venise m'a bouleversé ◆ to be ~ed with joy être au comble de la joie ◆ to be ~ed with grief être accablé (par la douleur) ◆ to be ~ed with feelings of inadequacy avoir le sentiment accablant de ne pas être à la hauteur

overwhelming /ˌəʊvəˈwelmɪŋ/ ADJ [victory, majority, defeat] écrasant ; [desire, power, pressure] irrésistible ; [success] énorme ; [evidence, misfortune, sorrow, heat] accablant ; [bad news] affligeant, atterrant ; [good news] extrêmement réjouissant ; [welcome, reception] extrêmement chaleureux ; [response] enthousiaste, qui dépasse toute espérance ◆ to give ~ support for sb/sth soutenir qn/qch sans réserves or à fond ◆ one's ~ impression is that ... l'impression dominante est que ... ◆ an ~ vote in favour of the plan une majorité écrasante en faveur du projet ◆ he felt an ~ sense of relief il a ressenti un immense soulagement ◆ they won the competition despite ~ odds ils ont remporté le concours alors que tout était contre eux ◆ the odds against this happening are ~ tout laisse à penser que cela ne se fera pas ◆ the ~ military superiority of the enemy la supériorité militaire écrasante de l'ennemi ◆ for fear of an ~ military response par crainte d'une riposte militaire fulgurante

overwhelmingly /ˌəʊvəˈwelmɪŋlɪ/ ADV 1 (= overpoweringly) [tired, anxious, lucky] extraordinairement 2 (= predominantly) [vote, approve, reject] à une écrasante majorité ; [white, male, positive, negative] en très grande majorité

overwinter /ˌəʊvəˈwɪntəʳ/ VI [person, animal, plant] passer l'hiver VT [+ animal, plant] faire passer l'hiver à

overwork /ˌəʊvəˈwɜːk/ N surmenage m ◆ to be ill from ~ être malade d'avoir trop travaillé or de s'être surmené VT 1 [+ person] surmener, surcharger de travail ; [+ horse] forcer ◆ to ~ o.s. se surmener 2 (= make too elaborate) [+ speech] trop travailler ◆ to ~ one's written style écrire dans un style trop affecté VI trop travailler, se surmener

overwrite /ˌəʊvəˈraɪt/ VT (Comput) écraser

overwrought /ˈəʊvəˈrɔːt/ ADJ 1 (= upset) [person] à bout, sur les nerfs 2 (= overelaborate) [poem, song] tarabiscoté

overzealous /ˈəʊvəˈzeləs/ ADJ trop zélé ◆ to be ~ faire de l'excès de zèle, faire du zèle

Ovid /ˈɒvɪd/ N Ovide m

oviduct /ˈəʊvɪdʌkt/ N oviducte m

oviform /ˈəʊvɪfɔːm/ ADJ ovoïde

ovine /ˈəʊvaɪn/ ADJ ovin

oviparous /əʊˈvɪpərəs/ ADJ ovipare

ovoid /ˈəʊvɔɪd/ ADJ ovoïde N forme f ovoïde

ovulate /ˈɒvjʊleɪt/ VI ovuler

ovulation /ˌɒvjʊˈleɪʃən/ N ovulation f

ovule /ˈɒvjuːl/ N [of plant, animal] ovule m

ovum /ˈəʊvəm/ N (pl **ova**) (Bio) ovule m

ow /aʊ/ EXCL ⇒ **ouch**

owe /əʊ/ VT 1 [+ money etc] devoir (to sb à qn) ◆ he ~s me £5 il me doit 5 livres ◆ I'll ~ it to you je vous le devrai ◆ I still ~ him for the meal je lui dois toujours le (prix du) repas ◆ I ~ you a lunch je vous dois un déjeuner

2 (fig) [+ respect, obedience, one's life] devoir (to sb à qn) ◆ to ~ sb a grudge garder rancune à qn, en vouloir à qn (for de) ◆ I ~ you thanks for your help je tiens à vous remercier de m'avoir aidé or pour votre aide, je ne vous ai pas encore remercié de m'avoir aidé or pour votre aide ◆ I ~ my family my grateful thanks for their understanding je suis profondément reconnaissant à ma famille de sa compréhension ◆ thanks! I ~ you one* merci, je te revaudrai ça ! ◆ you ~ him nothing vous ne lui devez rien ◆ he ~s his talent to his father il tient son talent de son père ◆ he ~s his failure to his own carelessness il doit son échec à sa propre négligence ◆ to what do I ~ the honour of ...? (frm or hum) que me vaut l'honneur de ... ? ◆ they ~ it to you that they succeeded ils vous doivent leur succès or d'avoir réussi ◆ I ~ it to him to do that je lui dois bien de faire cela ◆ you ~ it to yourself to make a success of it vous vous devez de réussir

owing /ˈəʊɪŋ/ LANGUAGE IN USE 17.1 ADJ dû ◆ the amount ~ on the house ce qui reste dû sur le prix de la maison ◆ **a lot of money is ~ to me** on me doit beaucoup d'argent ◆ **the money still ~ to me** la somme qu'on me doit encore, la somme qui m'est redue *(Comm)* PREP ◆ **~ to** en raison de, à cause de

owl /aʊl/ N chouette *f* ; *(with ear tufts)* hibou *m* ◆ **a wise old ~** *(fig = person)* un vieux sage ; → **barn, tawny**

owlet /ˈaʊlɪt/ N chouette *f* ; *(with ear tufts)* jeune hibou *m*

owlish /ˈaʊlɪʃ/ ADJ *[man]* qui a l'air d'un hibou ; *[woman]* qui a l'air d'une chouette ; *(of appearance) [man]* de hibou ; *[woman]* de chouette ◆ **his ~ spectacles** ses lunettes qui lui donnent *(or* donnaient) l'air d'un hibou ◆ **he gave me an ~ stare** il m'a regardé fixement comme un hibou

owlishly /ˈaʊlɪʃlɪ/ ADV *[peer, stare]* avec des yeux de hibou

own /əʊn/ ADJ propre *before n* ◆ **his ~ car** sa (propre) voiture, sa voiture à lui ◆ **it's her ~ company** c'est sa (propre) société ◆ **this is my ~ book** ce livre est à moi, c'est mon livre ◆ **it's my very ~ book** c'est mon livre à moi ◆ **I saw it with my ~ eyes** je l'ai vu de mes propres yeux ◆ **but your ~ brother said so** mais c'est votre frère qui l'a dit ◆ **all my ~ work!** c'est moi qui ai fait tout le travail ! ◆ **it was his ~ idea** c'était son idée à lui ◆ **he's his ~ man** il est son propre maître ◆ **he is his ~ worst enemy** son pire ennemi, c'est lui-même ◆ **he does his ~ cooking** il fait la cuisine lui-même ◆ **the house has its ~ garage** la maison a son garage particulier ◆ **my ~ one** mon chéri, ma chérie ◆ **"own garden"** *(in house-selling)* "jardin privatif" ◆ **~ goal** *(Brit Ftbl)* but *m* contre son camp ◆ **he scored an ~ goal** *(Ftbl)* il a marqué un but contre son camp ; *(fig)* ça s'est retourné contre lui

◆ **to do one's own thing** * faire ce qu'on veut ◆ **the kids can do their ~ thing * while I'm at work** les enfants peuvent faire ce qu'ils veulent quand je suis au travail ◆ **a campaign for Europe to do its ~ thing * in matters of defence** une campagne en faveur de l'indépendance de l'Europe en matière de défense ; → **accord, sake¹, sweet, thing**

PRON ◆ **that's my ~** c'est à moi ◆ **those are his ~** ceux-là sont à lui ◆ **my time is my ~** je suis libre de mon temps, je fais ce que je veux quand il me plaît ◆ **my time's not my ~** je n'ai pas une minute à moi ◆ **I'm so busy I can scarcely call my time my ~** je suis si occupé que je n'ai pas une minute à moi ◆ **I haven't a minute** *or* **a moment to call my ~** je n'ai pas une minute à moi ◆ **it's all my ~** c'est tout à moi ◆ **a style all his ~** un style bien à lui ◆ **it has a charm all (of) its ~** *or* **of its ~** cela possède un charme tout particulier *or* qui lui est propre, cela a un charme bien à soi ◆ **for reasons of his ~** pour des raisons personnelles *or* qui lui sont propres ◆ **a copy of your ~** votre propre exemplaire ◆ **can I have it for my very ~?** puis-je l'avoir pour moi tout seul ? ◆ **it's my very ~** c'est à moi tout seul ◆ **a house of your very ~** une maison bien à vous ◆ **she wants a room of her ~** elle veut sa propre chambre *or* sa chambre à elle ◆ **I have money of my ~** j'ai de l'argent à moi *or* des ressources personnelles ◆ **he gave me one of his ~** il m'a donné un des siens ◆ **Streep made the role her ~** ce rôle est définitivement associé à l'interprétation qu'en a donnée Streep ◆ **he's got nothing to call** *or* **nothing that he can call his ~** il n'a rien à lui ◆ **each to his ~** chacun ses goûts

◆ **on one's own** tout seul ◆ **did you do it (all) on your ~?** est-ce que vous l'avez fait tout seul ? ◆ **if I can get him on his ~** si je réussis à le voir seul à seul ◆ **you're on your ~ now!** à toi de jouer (maintenant) !

◆ **to come into one's own** ◆ **women began to come into their ~ politically** les femmes ont commencé à s'imposer en politique ◆ **I always thought I would come into my ~ in my thirties** j'ai toujours pensé que je m'épanouirais vers la trentaine ◆ **the tulips come into their ~ in May** les tulipes apparaissent dans toute leur splendeur en mai ◆ **the movie really comes into its ~ in the last half hour** le film devient véritablement excellent dans la dernière demi-heure ◆ **in heavy traffic a bicycle really comes into its ~** c'est quand il y a beaucoup de circulation que la bicyclette est vraiment utile

◆ **to get one's own back (on sb for sth)** prendre sa revanche (sur qn de qch) ◆ **he's trying to get his ~ back on me** il essaie de prendre sa revanche sur moi

◆ **to look after one's own** s'occuper des siens

VT 1 *(= possess)* posséder ◆ **who ~s this pen/house/paper?** à qui appartient ce stylo/cette maison/ce journal ? ◆ **he acts as if he ~s the place** * il se comporte comme en pays conquis

2 *(frm = acknowledge)* reconnaître, avouer (que) ◆ **I ~ it** je le reconnais, je l'avoue ◆ **he ~ed his mistake** il a reconnu *or* avoué son erreur ◆ **he ~ed himself defeated** il s'est avoué vaincu ◆ **he ~ed the child as his** il a reconnu l'enfant

VI *(frm)* ◆ **to ~ to a mistake** avouer *or* reconnaître avoir commis une erreur ◆ **he ~ed to debts of £750** il a avoué *or* reconnu avoir 750 livres de dettes ◆ **he ~ed to having done it** il a avoué l'avoir fait *or* qu'il l'avait fait

COMP **own-brand, own-label** ADJ *(Comm) [product]* vendu sous marque distributeur ◆ **their ~-brand** *or* **~-label peas** *etc* leur propre marque *f* de petits pois *etc* ◆ **this supermarket sells ~-brand goods** ce supermarché vend des produits sous sa propre marque N *(= make)* marque *f* (de *or* du) distributeur ◆ **buy supermarket ~ brands wherever possible** achetez, dans la mesure du possible, des produits portant la marque du distributeur

► **own up** VI avouer ◆ **to ~ up to sth** admettre qch ◆ **he ~ed up to having stolen it** il a avoué l'avoir volé *or* qu'il l'avait volé ◆ **come on, ~ up!** allons, avoue !

owner /ˈəʊnəʳ/ N *(gen)* propriétaire *mf* ; *(Jur: in house-building)* maître *m* d'ouvrage ◆ **he is the proud ~ of ...** il est l'heureux propriétaire de ... ◆ **the ~ of car number ...** le propriétaire de la voiture immatriculée ... ◆ **as ~s of this dictionary know, ...** comme les possesseurs de ce dictionnaire le savent, ... ◆ **all dog ~s will agree that ...** tous ceux qui ont un chien conviendront que ... ◆ **who is the ~ of this book?** à qui appartient ce livre ? ◆ **at ~'s risk** *(Comm)* aux risques du client ; → **landowner**

COMP **owner-driver** N conducteur *m* propriétaire

owner-occupied house N maison *f* occupée par son propriétaire

owner-occupier N *(Brit)* propriétaire *m* occupant

ownerless /ˈəʊnəlɪs/ ADJ sans propriétaire

ownership /ˈəʊnəʃɪp/ N possession *f* ◆ **"under new ownership"** *(Comm)* "changement de propriétaire" ◆ **under his ~ business was good** du temps où il était propriétaire, les affaires étaient bonnes ◆ **his ~ of the vehicle was not in dispute** on ne lui contestait pas la propriété du véhicule ◆ **to establish ~ of the estate** faire établir un droit de propriété sur le domaine

◆ **to take ownership of sth** *(= assume responsibility)* assumer la responsabilité de qch ◆ **students need to take ~ of their learning** les étudiants doivent assumer la responsabilité de leurs études

ownsome * /ˈəʊnsəm/, **owny-o** /ˈəʊnɪəʊ/ N *(hum)* ◆ **on one's ~** tout seul

owt /aʊt/ N *(Brit dial)* quelque chose

ox /ɒks/ (pl **oxen**) N bœuf *m* ◆ **as strong as an ~** fort comme un bœuf ◆ **he's a big ~** * *(pej)* c'est un gros balourd

oxalic /ɒkˈsælɪk/ ADJ oxalique

oxblood /ˈɒksblʌd/ ADJ *(in colour)* rouge sang *inv*

oxbow /ˈɒksbəʊ/ N *(in river)* méandre *m* COMP **oxbow lake** N bras *m* mort

Oxbridge /ˈɒksbrɪdʒ/ *(Brit)* N *l'université d'Oxford ou de Cambridge (ou les deux)* COMP *[education]* à l'université d'Oxford ou de Cambridge ; *[accent, attitude]* typique des universitaires *or* des anciens d'Oxford ou de Cambridge

> **OXBRIDGE**
>
> **Oxbridge** désigne collectivement les universités d'Oxford et de Cambridge, notamment lorsque l'on veut souligner le côté élitiste de ces deux prestigieuses institutions britanniques. En effet, beaucoup des étudiants de ces universités se retrouvent ensuite aux postes clés de la politique, de l'industrie et de la diplomatie.

oxcart /ˈɒkskɑːt/ N char *m* à bœufs

oxen /ˈɒksən/ NPL of **ox**

oxeye daisy /ˈɒksaɪˈdeɪzɪ/ N marguerite *f* *(Bot)*

Oxfam /ˈɒksfæm/ N *(Brit)* (abbrev of **Oxford Committee for Famine Relief**) *association caritative d'aide au tiers-monde*

> **OXFAM**
>
> **Oxfam**, acronyme de « Oxford Committee for Famine Relief » est une association caritative d'aide aux pays du tiers-monde ; elle cherche en particulier à y favoriser l'usage des technologies douces et l'utilisation des énergies renouvelables. Les magasins à l'enseigne d'**Oxfam** vendent des vêtements d'occasion et des objets artisanaux fabriqués dans les ateliers et coopératives gérés par l'association dans les pays du tiers-monde.

Oxford /ˈɒksfəd/ N Oxford NPL **Oxfords** *(= shoes)* oxfords *fpl* COMP **the Oxford Movement** N *(Brit Rel)* le Mouvement d'Oxford

oxhide /ˈɒkshaɪd/ N cuir *m* de bœuf

oxidase /ˈɒksɪdeɪs/ N oxydase *f*

oxidation /ˌɒksɪˈdeɪʃən/ N oxydation *f*

oxide /ˈɒksaɪd/ N oxyde *m*

oxidize /ˈɒksɪdaɪz/ VT oxyder VI s'oxyder

Oxon /ˈɒksən/ abbrev of **Oxfordshire**

Oxon. /ˈɒksən/ *(Brit)* (abbrev of **Oxoniensis**) d'Oxford

Oxonian /ɒkˈsəʊnɪən/ ADJ oxonien, oxfordien N Oxonien(ne) *m(f)*, Oxfordien(ne) *m(f)*

oxtail /ˈɒksteɪl/ N queue *f* de bœuf COMP **oxtail soup** N soupe *f* à la queue de bœuf

oxter /ˈɒkstəʳ/ N *(Scot)* aisselle *f*

oxyacetylene /ˈɒksɪəˈsetɪliːn/ ADJ oxyacétylénique

COMP **oxyacetylene burner, oxyacetylene lamp, oxyacetylene torch** N chalumeau *m* oxyacétylénique

oxyacetylene welding N soudure *f* (au chalumeau) oxyacétylénique

oxygen /ˈɒksɪdʒən/ N oxygène *m*

COMP **oxygen bar** N *(US)* bar *m* à oxygène

oxygen bottle, oxygen cylinder N bouteille *f* d'oxygène

oxygen mask N masque *m* à oxygène

oxygen tank N ballon *m* d'oxygène

oxygen tent N tente *f* à oxygène

oxygenate /ˈɒksɪdʒəneɪt/ VT oxygéner

oxygenation /ˌɒksɪdʒəˈneɪʃən/ N oxygénation *f*

oxymoron /ˌɒksɪˈmɔːrɒn/ N (pl **oxymora** /ˌɒksɪˈmɔːrə/) oxymore *m*

oyez /əʊˈjez/ EXCL oyez ! *(cri du crieur public ou d'un huissier)*

oyster /ˈɔɪstəʳ/ N huître *f* ◆ **the world is his ~** le monde est à lui

COMP *[industry]* ostréicole, huîtrier ; *[knife]* à huître

oyster bed N banc *m* d'huîtres, huîtrière *f*

oyster cracker N *(US Culin)* petit biscuit *m* salé

oyster farm N établissement *m* ostréicole

oyster farming N ostréiculture *f*

oyster mushroom N pleurote *f*

oyster shell N coquille *f* d'huître

oyster stew N *(US Culin)* soupe *f* aux huîtres

oystercatcher /ˈɔɪstəkætʃəʳ/ N (= *bird*) huîtrier *m*

Oz * /ɒz/ abbrev of **Australia**

oz abbrev of **ounce(s)**

ozone /ˈəʊzəʊn/ N *(Chem)* ozone *m*

COMP **ozone depletion** N diminution *f* de la couche d'ozone

ozone-friendly ADJ qui préserve la couche d'ozone

ozone hole N trou *m* d'ozone

ozone layer N couche *f* d'ozone

ozone-safe ADJ sans danger pour la couche d'ozone

ozonosphere /əʊˈzəʊnəˌsfɪəʳ/ N ozonosphère *f*

Pp

P¹, p /piː/ **N** 1 *(= letter)* P, p *m* ◆ **to mind** *or* **watch one's Ps and Qs** * se surveiller ◆ **P for Peter** ≈ P comme Pierre

2 (abbrev of **penny** *or* **pence**) penny *m*, pence *mpl* ◆ **10p** 10 pence

3 (abbrev of **page**) p

COMP **P45** **N** *(Brit) attestation de fin de contrat de travail*

p and p **N** (abbrev of **post(age) and packing**) → **post³**

P45

En Grande-Bretagne, le **P45** est l'attestation délivrée à tout employé à la fin de son contrat de travail ; elle indique la rémunération globale versée par l'employeur pendant la période considérée ainsi que les impôts et les cotisations sociales payés par l'employé. Le **P45** doit être présenté à tout nouvel employeur.
L'expression « to get one's **P45** » s'utilise dans le sens propre ou figuré de « être licencié ». Ainsi, on pourra dire du sélectionneur d'une équipe sportive qu'il « risque de recevoir son **P45** » si ses joueurs ne sont pas à la hauteur lors d'un match important.

P² abbrev of **parking**

P. abbrev of **President, Prince**

PA /piːˈeɪ/ 1 (abbrev of **personal assistant**) → **personal** 2 (abbrev of **public-address system**) (also **PA system**) (système *m* de) sonorisation *f*, sono * *f* ◆ **it was announced over the ~ that ...** on a annoncé par haut-parleur que ... 3 (abbrev of **Press Association**) *agence de presse britannique* 4 abbrev of **Pennsylvania**

pa * /pɑː/ **N** papa *m*

Pa. abbrev of **Pennsylvania**

p.a. (abbrev of **per annum**) par an

pabulum /ˈpæbjʊləm/ **N** 1 *(US = nonsense)* niaiseries *fpl* 2 *(rare = food)* aliment *m* semi-liquide

PAC **N** *(US)* (abbrev of **political action committee**) → **political**

pace¹ /peɪs/ **N** 1 *(= measure)* pas *m* ◆ **20 ~s away, at 20 ~s** à 20 pas ◆ **to take two ~s forward** faire deux pas en avant

2 *(= speed) [of movement] (walking)* pas *m* ; *(running)* allure *f* ; *(fig) [of action]* rythme *m* ◆ **to go at a quick** *or* **good ~** *[walker]* aller d'un bon pas ; *[runner, cyclist]* aller à vive allure ◆ **to quicken one's ~** *[walker]* presser *or* hâter le pas ; *[runner, cyclist]* presser *or* accélérer l'allure ◆ **his ~ quickened as he reached his car** il pressa *or* hâta le pas en approchant de sa voiture ◆ **to go at a slow ~** *[walker]* marcher lentement *or* à pas lents ; *[runner, cyclist]* aller à (une) petite allure ◆ **their snail-like ~ in implementing the programme** leur extrême lenteur dans la mise en œuvre du programme ◆ **to force the ~** forcer l'allure *or* le pas ◆ **to do sth at one's own ~** faire qch à son rythme ◆ **he can't stand** *or* **stay the ~** il n'arrive pas à tenir le rythme ◆ **the ~ of life remains slow there** le rythme de vie y reste assez lent ◆ **the ~ of political change** le rythme auquel s'effectuent les réformes ◆ **to speed up the ~ of reform** accélérer le rythme des réformes

◆ **to set the pace** *(Sport)* mener le train, donner l'allure ; *(for meeting etc)* donner le ton

◆ **to gather pace** *(lit)* prendre de la vitesse ; *[campaign etc]* prendre de l'ampleur ; *[economic recovery]* s'accélérer ◆ **the recovery is gathering ~** la reprise s'accélère

◆ **to keep pace with** ◆ **to keep ~ with sb** *(lit)* aller à la même allure que qn ; *(fig)* suivre le rythme de qn ◆ **he can't keep ~ with things** il est dépassé par les événements ◆ **earnings have not kept ~ with inflation** les salaires n'ont pas suivi le rythme de l'inflation

◆ *possessive* + **paces** ◆ **to put a horse through its ~s** faire parader un cheval ◆ **to go through** *or* **show one's ~s** *(fig)* montrer ce dont on est capable ◆ **to put sb through his ~s** *(fig)* mettre qn à l'épreuve, demander à qn de montrer ce dont il est capable

VI marcher à pas mesurés ◆ **to ~ up and down** faire les cent pas, marcher de long en large ◆ **to ~ round a room** faire les cent pas dans une pièce, arpenter une pièce

VT 1 *[+ room, floor, street]* arpenter

2 *(Sport) [+ runner]* régler l'allure de ◆ **to ~ o.s.** *(lit, fig)* se ménager, ménager ses forces

COMP **pace bowler** **N** *(Cricket) lanceur qui envoie des balles très rapides*

▸ **pace out** **VT SEP** *[+ distance]* mesurer en comptant ses pas

pace² /peɪs/ **PREP** *(frm)* n'en déplaise à ◆ **~ your advisers** n'en déplaise à vos conseillers

-paced /peɪst/ **ADJ** *(in compounds)* ◆ **fast-paced** au rythme rapide ◆ **well-paced** au rythme soutenu

pacemaker /ˈpeɪsˌmeɪkəʳ/ **N** 1 *(Med)* stimulateur *m* (cardiaque), pacemaker *m* 2 *(Sport = person)* ◆ **to be (the) ~** mener le train

pacer /ˈpeɪsəʳ/ **N** *(US Sport)* meneur *m*, -euse *f* (de train)

pacesetter /ˈpeɪsˌsetəʳ/ **N** 1 *(Athletics = person)* ◆ **to be (the) ~** mener le train 2 *(= leader)* leader *m* ◆ **Boeing is a ~ in the marketplace** Boeing est l'un des leaders sur le marché ◆ **Manchester United have emerged as the early-season Premiership ~s** Manchester United s'est imposé en tête du championnat en ce début de saison ◆ **Mongolia seemed an unlikely candidate as the ~ for political change in Asia** la Mongolie ne semblait pas être le candidat le plus évident au titre de locomotive du changement politique en Asie

pacey /ˈpeɪsɪ/ **ADJ** *[production, style, book]* au rythme enlevé

pachyderm /ˈpækɪdɜːm/ **N** pachyderme *m*

pacific /pəˈsɪfɪk/ **ADJ** *[intentions, disposition]* pacifique **N** ◆ **Pacific** ⇒ **Pacific Ocean**

COMP **Pacific Daylight Time** **N** *(US)* heure *f* d'été du Pacifique

the Pacific Islands **NPL** les îles *fpl* du Pacifique

the Pacific Ocean **N** le Pacifique, l'océan *m* Pacifique

the Pacific Rim **N** les pays *mpl* riverains du Pacifique

Pacific Standard Time **N** *(US)* heure *f* (normale) du Pacifique

pacifically /pəˈsɪfɪkəlɪ/ **ADV** *[say]* pour calmer les esprits

pacification /ˌpæsɪfɪˈkeɪʃən/ **N** *[of country, territory, population]* pacification *f*

pacifier /ˈpæsɪfaɪəʳ/ **N** 1 *(US = baby's dummy)* tétine *f*, sucette *f* 2 *(= person)* pacificateur *m*, -trice *f*

pacifism /ˈpæsɪfɪzəm/ **N** pacifisme *m*

pacifist /ˈpæsɪfɪst/ **ADJ, N** pacifiste *mf*

pacifistic /ˈpæsɪfɪstɪk/ **ADJ** pacifiste

pacify /ˈpæsɪfaɪ/ **VT** *[+ person, fears]* calmer, apaiser ; *[+ country, creditors]* pacifier

pack /pæk/ **N** 1 *(= packet) [of goods, cereal]* paquet *m* ; *[of cotton, wool]* balle *f* ; *[of pedlar]* ballot *m* ; *[of horse, mule]* charge *f* ; *(Mil)* paquetage *m* ; (also **backpack**) sac *m* à dos ◆ **a ~ of cigarettes** *(= individual packet)* un paquet de cigarettes ; *(= carton)* une cartouche de cigarettes

2 *(= group) [of hounds]* meute *f* ; *[of wolves, thieves]* bande *f* ; *[of brownies, cubs]* meute *f* ; *[of runners, cyclists]* peloton *m* ; *(Comm = set, lot)* pack *m*, lot *m* ◆ **the yoghurt is sold in ~s of four** le yaourt se vend par packs *or* lots de quatre (pots) ◆ **a four-/six-~ (of beer)** un pack de quatre/six bières ◆ **a ~ of lies** un tissu de mensonges ◆ **a ~ of fools** * un tas * *or* une bande * d'imbéciles ◆ **they're behaving like a ~ of kids!** ils se comportent comme de vrais gamins ! ◆ **to stay ahead of the ~** *(fig)* maintenir *or* conserver son avance

3 *(esp Brit) [of cards]* jeu *m*

④ *(Rugby)* (= *forwards*) pack *m* ; (= *scrum*) mêlée *f*
⑤ *(Med)* **cold/wet ~** compresse *f* froide/humide

VT ① (= *parcel up*) *(into box, container)* empaqueter, emballer ; *(into suitcase)* mettre dans une valise, emballer ◆ **to ~ one's things** faire ses bagages ◆ **~ fragile objects in newspaper** emballez les objets fragiles dans du papier journal ◆ **they come ~ed in dozens** ils sont conditionnés en paquets de douze ◆ **have you ~ed your toothbrush?** tu as mis ta brosse à dents dans ta valise ?
② (= *fill tightly*) *[+ trunk, box]* remplir *(with* de) ; *(fig) [+ mind, memory]* bourrer *(with* de) ◆ **to ~ one's case** *or* **suitcase** faire sa valise ◆ **to ~ one's bags** *(lit)* faire ses bagages *or* ses valises ; *(fig)* plier bagage, faire ses paquets *or* son balluchon* ◆ **they ~ed the hall to see him** *(fig)* ils se pressaient *or* se sont entassés dans la salle pour le voir ◆ **to ~ the house** *(Theat) [player, play]* faire salle comble ◆ **the book is ~ed with information and photos** le livre est bourré de renseignements et de photos ; see also **packed**
③ (= *crush together*) *[+ earth, objects] [person]* tasser *(into* dans) ; *[machine]* damer *(into* dans) ; *(Ski) [+ snow]* damer ; *[+ people]* entasser *(into* dans) see also **packed**
④ *(pej)* ◆ **to ~ a jury** composer un jury favorable ◆ **he had ~ed the committee with his own supporters** il avait noyauté le comité en y plaçant ses partisans
⑤ (= *contain*) *[+ power etc]* **he ~s a lot of force in that small frame of his** tout menu qu'il soit, il a énormément de force ◆ **this machine ~s enough power to ...** cette machine a assez de puissance pour ... ◆ **he ~s a good punch, he ~s quite a wallop*** il a un sacré punch* ◆ **a film that still ~s real punch*** un film qui est toujours aussi fort ◆ **to ~ a gun*** *(US)* porter un revolver

VI ① (= *do one's luggage*) faire ses bagages *or* sa valise ; → **send**
② (= *fit*) ◆ **these books ~ easily into that box** ces livres tiennent bien dans cette boîte
③ (= *cram*) **they ~ed into the stadium to hear him** ils se sont entassés dans le stade pour l'écouter ◆ **the crowd ~ed round him** la foule se pressait autour de lui

COMP **pack animal** N bête *f* de somme
pack drill N *(Mil)* marche *f* forcée avec paquetage ◆ **no names, no ~ drill, but ...** *(fig)* je ne veux citer personne, mais ...
pack ice N *(NonC)* banquise *f*, pack *m*
pack trail N sentier *m* muletier

► **pack away** VT SEP ranger

► **pack in*** VI *(fig* = *break down, stop working) [machine, car, watch etc]* tomber en panne, rendre l'âme*
VT SEP *(Brit) [+ person, job]* plaquer* ◆ **to ~ it all in** tout lâcher, tout plaquer* ◆ **~ it in!** *(Brit)* (= *stop doing sth*) laisse tomber !* ; (= *stop talking*) écrase !* ◆ **let's ~ it in for the day** *(Brit)* assez *or* on arrête pour aujourd'hui ◆ **it's ~ing them in** *(fig) [film, play etc]* ça attire les foules

► **pack off*** VT SEP (= *dismiss*) envoyer promener* ◆ **to ~ a child off to bed** expédier *or* envoyer un enfant au lit ◆ **they ~ed John off to London** ils ont expédié* John à Londres

► **pack up** VI ① (= *do one's luggage*) faire sa valise *or* ses bagages ; *(moving house, business etc)* faire ses cartons
② (* = *give up and go*) *(permanently)* plier bagage ◆ **I think I'll ~ up and go home now** *(on one occasion)* bon, je crois que je vais m'arrêter là et rentrer chez moi
③ *(Brit* * = *break down, stop working) [machine, car, watch etc]* tomber en panne, rendre l'âme*

VT SEP ① *[+ object, book]* emballer, empaqueter ◆ **he ~ed up his bits and pieces** il a rassemblé ses affaires ◆ **she ~ed up her few belongings** elle a mis ses quelques affaires dans une valise (or dans un sac *etc*) ; → **bag**
② (* = *give up*) *[+ work, school]* laisser tomber* ◆ **~ it up now!** laisse tomber !*, arrête !

package /ˈpækɪdʒ/ N ① (= *parcel*) paquet *m*, colis *m*
② *(fig: group)* (= *items for sale*) marché *m* global ; (= *contract*) contrat *m* global ; (= *purchase*) achat *m* forfaitaire ; *(Comput)* progiciel *m* ◆ **a ~ of measures** *(Pol)* un train de mesures ◆ **an aid ~** un programme d'aide ◆ **a good financial ~ for those taking voluntary redundancy** une offre financière intéressante en cas de départ volontaire ◆ **payroll/inventory/management ~** *(Comput)* progiciel *m* de paie/de stock *or* inventaire/de gestion ◆ **the president wants his economic plan passed as a ~** le président veut que son plan économique soit accepté en bloc ◆ **the plan will be voted on as a ~** le plan sera soumis au vote en bloc
③ ⇒ **package holiday**

VT *(Comm)* emballer ; *(fig)* présenter ◆ **how are they going to ~ the proposal?** comment vont-ils présenter cette proposition ?

COMP **package deal** N (= *agreement*) accord *m* global ; (= *contract*) contrat *m* global ; (= *purchase*) achat *m* forfaitaire
package holiday N voyage *m* organisé
package policy N *(Insurance)* police *f* multirisque
package store N *(US)* magasin *m* de vins et spiritueux ; → LICENSING LAWS
package tour N voyage *m* organisé

packager /ˈpækɪdʒəʳ/ N *(Publishing)* packager *or* packageur *m*

packaging /ˈpækɪdʒɪŋ/ N *(Comm) [of goods]* conditionnement *m* ; (= *wrapping materials*) emballage *m* ; *(Publishing)* packaging *m*

packed /pækt/ ADJ ① *[room] (with people)* comble, bondé ; *(with furniture etc)* bourré *(with* de) ; *[bus]* bondé ; *(Brit:* also **packed out***) [theatre, hall]* comble ◆ **the bus was ~ (with people)** le bus était bondé ◆ **the book is ~ full of information** le livre est bourré* de renseignements ◆ **the lecture was ~** il y avait foule à la conférence ◆ **to be ~ solid** *or* **tight** *(with people)* être plein à craquer *or* archiplein* ◆ **the car park was ~ solid** le parking était archiplein* ② *(with luggage ready)* **I'm ~ and ready to leave** j'ai fait mes bagages et je suis prêt (à partir) ③ (= *compressed*) *[snow, soil]* tassé ◆ **the snow was ~ hard** la neige était bien tassée COMP **packed lunch** N *(Brit)* panier-repas *m*

-packed /pækt/ ADJ *(in compounds)* ◆ **a fun-packed holiday** des vacances *fpl* pleines de distractions ◆ **a thrill-packed evening** une soirée pleine de *or* riche en péripéties ; → **action**

packer /ˈpækəʳ/ N ① (= *person*) emballeur *m*, -euse *f* ② (= *device*) emballeuse *f*

packet /ˈpækɪt/ N ① (= *parcel*) paquet *m* ; (= *paper bag*) pochette *f* ◆ **to earn a ~*** gagner des sommes folles ◆ **to cost a ~*** coûter une somme folle ◆ **that must have cost a ~!*** *(Brit)* cela a dû coûter les yeux de la tête ! ② *[of sweets]* sachet *m* ; *[of cigarettes, seeds, biscuits, crisps, needles]* paquet *m* ③ *(Naut)* (also **packet boat**) paquebot *m*, malle *f* ◆ **the Dover ~** la malle de Douvres
COMP **packet soup** N soupe *f* en sachet
packet switching N *(Comput, Telec)* commutation *f* par paquets

packhorse /ˈpækhɔːs/ N cheval *m* de bât

packing /ˈpækɪŋ/ N ① *[of parcel, goods etc]* emballage *m*, empaquetage *m* ◆ **to do one's ~** faire sa valise *or* ses bagages ◆ **meat ~** *(Comm)* conserverie *f* de viande *(industrie)* ② (= *act of filling*) *[of space]* remplissage *m* ③ *(Tech) [of piston, joint]* garniture *f* ④ (= *padding*) (fournitures *fpl or* matériaux *mpl* pour) emballage *m* ; *(Tech)* (matière *f* pour) garnitures *fpl*
COMP **packing case** N caisse *f* d'emballage
packing density N *(Comput)* densité *f* d'implantation
packing house N *(US)* entreprise *f* de conditionnement alimentaire

packsaddle /ˈpækˌsædl/ N bât *m*

pact /pækt/ N pacte *m* ◆ **France made a ~ with England** la France conclut *or* signa un pacte avec l'Angleterre ◆ **we made a ~ to share the profits** nous nous sommes mis d'accord pour partager les bénéfices

pacy /ˈpeɪsɪ/ ADJ ⇒ **pacey**

pad /pæd/ N ① *(to prevent friction, damage)* coussinet *m* ; *(to absorb shock)* tampon *m* (amortisseur)
② *(Ftbl)* protège-cheville *m inv* ; *(Hockey etc)* jambière *f* ; *(Fencing)* plastron *m*
③ (= *block of paper*) bloc *m* ; (also **writing pad**) bloc *m* (de papier à lettres) ; (also **notepad**) bloc-notes *m* ; → **blot**
④ *(for inking)* tampon *m* encreur
⑤ *[of rabbit]* patte *f* ; *[of cat, dog]* coussinet *m*, pelote *f* plantaire ; *[of human fingers, toes]* pulpe *f* ◆ **a ~ of fat** un bourrelet de graisse
⑥ *(Space)* (also **launch pad**) rampe *f* (de lancement)
⑦ *[of water lily]* feuille *f* de nénuphar
⑧ (* = *sanitary towel*) serviette *f* hygiénique
⑨ (* = *flat*) piaule* *f*, appart* *m*
⑩ *(US)* **to be on the ~*** *[policeman]* toucher des pots-de-vin, palper*

VI ◆ **to ~ along** *[person, animal]* marcher à pas de loup *or* à pas feutrés ◆ **to ~ about** aller et venir à pas de loup *or* à pas feutrés

VT ① *[+ cushion, shoulders]* rembourrer ; *[+ clothing]* matelasser ; *[+ furniture, door]* matelasser, capitonner ◆ **~ your puppy's bed with something soft** garnissez le panier de votre chiot avec quelque chose de doux ◆ **to ~ with cotton wool** ouater
② *(Fin) [+ expenses]* gonfler

► **pad out** VT SEP ① *[+ clothes, shoulders]* rembourrer
② *(fig) [+ meal]* rendre plus copieux *(with sth* en ajoutant qch) ; *[+ speech, essay]* étoffer ; *(pej)* délayer

padded /ˈpædɪd/ ADJ *[garment]* matelassé, ouatiné ; *[chair]* rembourré ; *[bedhead]* capitonné, matelassé ; *[envelope]* matelassé
COMP **padded bra** N soutien-gorge *m* rembourré
padded cell N cellule *f* capitonnée
padded shoulders NPL épaules *fpl* rembourrées

padding /ˈpædɪŋ/ N ① (= *action*) rembourrage *m* ② (= *material*) bourre *f*, ouate *f* ; *(fig: in book, speech)* délayage *m*, remplissage *m* ◆ **there's too much ~ in this essay** il y a trop de remplissage *or* de délayage dans cette dissertation

paddle /ˈpædl/ N ① *[of canoe]* pagaie *f* ; *[of waterwheel, paddle boat]* aube *f*, palette *f* ; *[of mixer, fan]* pale *f*, palette *f* ② ◆ **to have** *or* **go for a ~** (aller) barboter *or* faire trempette ③ *(US* = *table tennis bat)* raquette *f* de ping-pong VT ① ◆ **to ~ a canoe** faire avancer un canoë à la pagaie ◆ **to ~ one's own canoe** *(fig)* se débrouiller tout seul ② *(US* = *spank)* donner une fessée à VI ① *(in boat, canoe)* **to ~ up/down the river** remonter/descendre la rivière en pagayant *or* à la pagaie ② (= *walk*) *(in water) [person]* barboter, faire trempette ; *[dog, duck]* barboter ; *(in mud)* patauger
COMP **paddle boat, paddle steamer** *(Brit)* N bateau *m* à aubes *or* à roues
paddle wheel N roue *f* à aubes *or* à palettes
paddling pool N *(Brit)* pataugeoire *f*

► **paddle along** VI [1] *(in boat)* pagayer [2] *(= walk in water)* barboter, faire trempette

paddock /'pædək/ N enclos *m (pour chevaux)* ; *(Racing)* paddock *m*

Paddy /'pædɪ/ N [1] dim of **Patrick** [2] (‡ *esp pej*) *surnom des Irlandais*

paddy¹ /'pædɪ/ N paddy *m*, riz *m* non décortiqué COMP **paddy field** N rizière *f*

paddy² * /'pædɪ/ N (= *anger*) rogne * *f* ◆ **to be in a ~** être en rogne *

paddy waggon‡ /'pædɪ,wægən/ N *(US)* panier *m* à salade *

padlock /'pædlɒk/ N *[of door, chain]* cadenas *m* ; *[of cycle]* antivol *m* VT *[+ door]* cadenasser ; *[+ cycle]* mettre un antivol à

padre /'pɑːdrɪ/ N [1] *(Mil, Naut etc)* aumônier *m* [2] (* = *clergyman*) *(Catholic)* curé *m*, prêtre *m* ; *(Protestant)* pasteur *m*

Padua /'pædʒʊə/ N Padoue

paean /'piːən/ N péan *m* ◆ **~s of praise** des éloges *mpl* dithyrambiques ◆ **the film is a ~ to nature** ce film est un hymne à la nature

paederast /'pedəræst/ N ⇒ **pederast**

paediatric /,piːdɪ'ætrɪk/ ADJ *[department]* de pédiatrie ; *[illness, medicine, surgery]* infantile COMP **paediatric nurse** N infirmier *m*, -ière *f* en pédiatrie
paediatric nursing N puériculture *f*

paediatrician /,piːdɪə'trɪʃən/ N pédiatre *mf*

paediatrics /,piːdɪ'ætrɪks/ N *(NonC)* pédiatrie *f*

paedophile /'piːdəʊfaɪl/ N pédophile *m* ◆ **~ ring** réseau *m* pédophile

paedophilia /,piːdəʊ'fɪlɪə/ N pédophilie *f*

paedophiliac /,piːdəʊ'fɪlɪæk/ ADJ pédophile

paella /paɪ'elə/ N paella *f*

pagan /'peɪgən/ ADJ, N *(lit, fig)* païen(ne) *m(f)*

paganism /'peɪgənɪzəm/ N paganisme *m*

page¹ /peɪdʒ/ N *(lit, fig)* page *f* ◆ **on ~ 10** (à la) page 10 ◆ **continued on ~ 20** suite (en) page 20 ◆ **the sports ~s** *(in newspaper)* les pages *fpl* sportives ◆ **a magazine with ~ upon ~ of adverts** un magazine bourré de publicité ◆ **to be on the same ~** *(US = in agreement)* être d'accord
VT *[+ book]* paginer ; *[+ printed sheets]* mettre en pages
COMP **page break** N *(Comput)* saut *m* de page
page proofs NPL *(Typ)* épreuves *fpl* en pages
page three N *(Brit)* la page des pin up
page-turner N livre *m* passionnant ◆ **her novel is a real ~-turner** son roman se lit d'une traite

Page Three

Depuis de nombreuses années, les lecteurs du journal « The Sun » – le quotidien populaire le plus vendu en Grande-Bretagne – découvrent en page trois la photo pleine page d'une jeune femme posant seins nus. Ce genre de pin up est appelée « **page three** girl », et l'expression **page three** s'est étendue aujourd'hui à toutes les photos de modèles aux seins nus publiées dans les tabloïdes.

page² /peɪdʒ/ N [1] (also **pageboy**) *(in hotel)* groom *m*, chasseur *m* ; *(at court)* page *m* [2] *(US: Congress)* jeune huissier *m* [3] *(US)* ⇒ **pageboy 2** VT (= *call for*) *[+ person]* faire appeler ; *[person calling]* appeler *(using pager)* biper ◆ **they're paging Mr Smith** on appelle M. Smith ◆ **paging Mr Smith!** on demande M. Smith !

pageant /'pædʒənt/ N *(historical)* spectacle *m* or reconstitution *f* historique ; *(fig)* spectacle *m* fastueux ◆ **Christmas ~** spectacle *m* de Noël

pageantry /'pædʒəntrɪ/ N apparat *m*, pompe *f*

pageboy /'peɪdʒ,bɔɪ/ N [1] (also **pageboy hairstyle**) (coupe *f* au) carré *m* [2] *(Brit: at wedding)* garçon *m* d'honneur [3] ⇒ **page² noun 1**

pager /'peɪdʒəʳ/ N bip * *m*, Alphapage ® *m*

paginate /'pædʒɪneɪt/ VT paginer

pagination /,pædʒɪ'neɪʃən/ N pagination *f*

paging /'peɪdʒɪŋ/ N [1] *(Comput, also in book)* pagination *f* [2] *(Telec)* radiomessagerie *f*

pagoda /pə'gəʊdə/ N pagode *f*

pah † /pæ/ EXCL pouah !

paid /peɪd/ VB pt, ptp of **pay** ADJ *[staff, employee]* salarié ; *[work]* rémunéré, salarié ; *[holidays]* payé ◆ **to be in ~ employment** avoir un emploi rémunéré or salarié ◆ **highly ~** *[person, job]* très bien payé ◆ **~ gunman** tueur *m* à gages ◆ **a ~ hack** un nègre *(fig)*
COMP **paid-in** ADJ *(Fin) [moneys]* encaissé
paid-up ADJ ◆ **~-up member** membre *m* à jour de sa cotisation ◆ **fully/partly ~-up shares** actions *fpl* entièrement/non entièrement libérées ; see also **pay**

pail /peɪl/ N seau *m* ◆ **a ~** or **~ful of water** un seau d'eau

paillasse /'pælɪæs/ N paillasse *f*

pain /peɪn/ N [1] *(NonC, physical)* douleur *f*, souffrance *f* ; *(mental)* peine *f* ; *(stronger)* douleur *f*, souffrance *f* ◆ **to be in (great) ~** souffrir (beaucoup) ◆ **to cause ~ to** *(physically)* faire mal à, faire souffrir ; *(mentally)* faire de la peine à, peiner ◆ **a cry of ~** un cri de douleur ◆ **no ~, no gain** on n'a rien sans rien
[2] *(localized)* douleur *f* ◆ **I have a ~ in my shoulder** j'ai une douleur à l'épaule ◆ **chest ~** douleurs *fpl* dans la poitrine ◆ **stomach ~s** maux *mpl* d'estomac ◆ **he suffers from back ~** il a mal au dos ◆ **can you tell me where the ~ is?** pouvez-vous me dire où vous avez mal ?
[3] (* = *nuisance*) ◆ **to be a (real) ~** *[person, situation]* être enquiquinant * or embêtant * ◆ **he's a ~ in the neck** il est enquiquinant * or casse-pieds * ◆ **he's a ~ in the arse**‡ *(Brit)* or **the ass**‡ *(esp US)* c'est un emmerdeur‡ fini
[4] ◆ **~s** (= *trouble*) peine *f* ◆ **to take ~s** or **to be at ~s** or **to go to great ~s (not) to do sth** s'employer à (ne pas) faire qch ◆ **to take ~s over sth** se donner beaucoup de mal pour (faire) qch ◆ **to spare no ~s** ne pas ménager ses efforts *(to do sth* pour faire qch) ◆ **for one's ~s** pour sa peine, pour toute récompense
[5] (†† = *punishment*) peine *f*, punition *f* ◆ **on** or **under ~ of death** *(frm)* sous peine de mort
VT faire de la peine à, peiner ; *(stronger)* faire souffrir ◆ **it ~s him that she's unhappy** cela le peine or lui fait de la peine qu'elle soit malheureuse ◆ **it ~s me to think that he's unhappy** cela me fait de la peine de penser qu'il est malheureux
COMP **pain barrier** N *(Sport)* ◆ **to go through the ~ barrier** vaincre la douleur
pain clinic N *service de consultation pour le traitement de la douleur*
pain control N soulagement *m* de la douleur

pained /peɪnd/ ADJ *[smile, expression, voice]* peiné, froissé

painful /'peɪnfʊl/ ADJ [1] (= *causing physical pain*) *[wound etc]* douloureux ◆ **my hand is ~** j'ai mal à la main [2] (= *distressing*) *[sight, duty]* pénible ◆ **it is ~ to see her now** maintenant elle fait peine à voir [3] (= *laborious*) *[climb, task]* pénible, difficile

painfully /'peɪnfəlɪ/ ADV [1] (= *in pain*) *[throb]* douloureusement ; *[move, walk]* péniblement ◆ **~ swollen** enflé et douloureux [2] (= *laboriously*) *[write, climb]* péniblement, à grand-peine [3] (= *agonizingly*) *[learn, realize, understand]* de façon douloureuse ; *[shy, sensitive, thin, slow]* terriblement ◆ **my ignorance was ~ obvious** mon ignorance n'était que trop évidente ◆ **it was ~ clear that ...** il n'était que trop évident que ... ◆ **to be ~ aware of/that ...** être douloureusement conscient de/que ...

painkiller /'peɪn,kɪləʳ/ N calmant *m*, analgésique *m*

painkilling /'peɪn,kɪlɪŋ/ ADJ calmant, analgésique

painless /'peɪnlɪs/ ADJ *[operation]* indolore, sans douleur ; *[experience]* indolore ◆ **a quick and ~ death** une mort rapide et sans souffrance ◆ **a ~ way of paying one's taxes** un moyen indolore de payer ses impôts ◆ **it's a ~ way of learning Chinese** de cette façon, on peut apprendre le chinois sans peine ◆ **the exam was fairly ~** * l'examen n'avait rien de bien méchant *

painlessly /'peɪnlɪslɪ/ ADV *(lit = without pain)* sans douleur ; *(fig = without problems)* sans peine

painstaking /'peɪnz,teɪkɪŋ/ ADJ *[person, work]* minutieux, méticuleux

painstakingly /'peɪnz,teɪkɪŋlɪ/ ADV minutieusement, méticuleusement

paint /peɪnt/ N [1] *(NonC)* peinture *f* ; → **coat, wet**
[2] ◆ **~s** couleurs *fpl* ◆ **a box of ~s** une boîte de couleurs
VT [1] *[+ wall etc]* peindre ◆ **to ~ a wall red** peindre un mur en rouge ◆ **plates ~ed with flowers** des assiettes avec des motifs à fleurs ◆ **to ~ sth again** repeindre qch ◆ **to ~ one's nails** se vernir les ongles ◆ **to ~ one's face** *(gen, pej)* se peinturlurer le visage ◆ **they ~ed the children's faces** ils ont peint le visage des enfants ◆ **to ~ one's lips** se mettre du rouge à lèvres ◆ **to ~ the town red** faire la noce *, faire la bringue * ◆ **to ~ sb into a corner** pousser qn dans ses derniers retranchements ◆ **to ~ o.s. into a corner** se mettre dans une impasse
[2] *(Art) [+ picture, portrait]* peindre ◆ **to ~ the scenery** *(Theat)* brosser les décors ◆ **she ~ed a vivid picture of the moment she escaped** (= *described*) elle a décrit son évasion avec beaucoup de vivacité ◆ **he ~ed the situation in very black colours** il brossa un tableau très sombre de la situation
[3] *(Med) [+ throat, wound]* badigeonner
VI *(Art)* peindre, faire de la peinture ◆ **to ~ in oils** peindre à l'huile, faire de la peinture à l'huile ◆ **to ~ in watercolours** faire de l'aquarelle
COMP **paint gun** N pistolet *m* à peinture
paint remover N décapant *m* (pour peinture)
paint roller N rouleau *m* à peinture
paint spray N pulvérisateur *m* (de peinture) ; *(for car repairs)* bombe *f* de peinture or de laque
paint stripper N (= *chemical*) décapant *m* ; (= *tool*) racloir *m*

► **paint in** VT SEP peindre

► **paint out** VT SEP faire disparaître sous une couche de peinture

► **paint over** VT SEP *[+ slogan, graffiti]* couvrir de peinture

paintballing /'peɪnt,bɔːlɪŋ/ N paintball *m*

paintbox /'peɪntbɒks/ N boîte *f* de couleurs

paintbrush /'peɪntbrʌʃ/ N pinceau *m*

painted /'peɪntɪd/ ADJ *[wall, furniture, room]* peint COMP **painted lady** N (= *butterfly*) belle-dame *f*, vanesse *f* ; *(pej)* (also **painted woman**) femme *f* trop fardée, cocotte * *f (pej)*

painter¹ /'peɪntəʳ/ N [1] *(Art)* peintre *m* ; → **landscape, portrait** [2] (also **housepainter**) peintre *m* (en bâtiments) ◆ **~ and decorator** peintre *m* décorateur

painter² /'peɪntəʳ/ N *(Naut)* amarre *f*

painterly /'peɪntəlɪ/ ADJ *(lit) [talents, skill, eye]* de peintre ; *(fig) [film]* très pictural ; *[account]* pittoresque

painting /ˈpeɪntɪŋ/ N 1 *(NonC: lit, fig)* peinture *f* ◆ **~ in oils** peinture *f* à l'huile ◆ **to study ~** étudier la peinture 2 *(= picture)* tableau *m*, toile *f*

paintpot /ˈpeɪntpɒt/ N pot *m* de peinture *(lit)*

paintwork /ˈpeɪntwɜːk/ N *(NonC)* peinture *f*

pair /pɛəʳ/ N 1 *(= two) [of shoes, socks, scissors, earrings, eyes, spectacles]* paire *f* ◆ **these gloves make** *or* **are a ~** ces gants vont ensemble ◆ **these socks are not a ~** ces chaussettes sont dépareillées ◆ **a ~ of scissors** une paire de ciseaux ◆ **a ~ of pyjamas** un pyjama ◆ **a ~ of tweezers** une pince à épiler ◆ **I've only got one ~ of hands!** je ne peux pas tout faire à la fois ! ◆ **to be** *or* **have a safe ~ of hands** être fiable ◆ **she's got a great ~ of legs*** elle a de belles jambes ◆ **John won with a ~ of aces** John a gagné avec une paire d'as ◆ **the children were shown ~s of words** on a montré aux enfants des mots deux par deux ◆ **in ~s** *(= two together) [work etc]* à deux ; *(= by twos) [enter etc]* par deux
2 *[of animals]* paire *f* ; *(= mated)* couple *m* ; → **carriage**
3 *(= two people)* paire *f* ◆ **you two are a right ~!*** vous faites vraiment la paire tous les deux ! ◆ **~s of identical twins** paires *fpl* de vrais jumeaux
4 *(Brit Parl) un de deux députés de partis opposés qui se sont entendus pour s'absenter lors d'un vote*
VT 1 *[+ socks]* appareiller
2 *[+ animals]* accoupler, apparier ◆ **to be ~ed with/against sb** *(in competition etc)* avoir qn comme partenaire/comme adversaire
VI 1 *[gloves etc]* aller ensemble ◆ **to ~ with** aller avec
2 *[animals]* s'accoupler, s'apparier
COMP **pair bond** N (also **pair-bonding**) union *f* monogame
pairs champions NPL champions *mpl* par couple
pairs championship N championnat *m* en double
pairs skaters NPL patineurs *mpl* par couple
pairs tournament N tournoi *m* en double

► **pair off** VI 1 *[people]* s'arranger deux par deux ◆ **to ~ off with sb** se mettre avec qn
2 *(Brit Parl) s'entendre avec un adversaire pour s'absenter lors d'un vote*
VT SEP mettre par paires ◆ **John was ~ed off with her at the dance** on lui a attribué John comme cavalier

► **pair up** VI *[people]* former un tandem, faire équipe ◆ **he ~ed up with his friend for the race** il a fait équipe avec son ami pour la course

pairing /ˈpɛərɪŋ/ N 1 *(= pair) [of footballers, rugby players, cricketers]* association *f* ; *[of tennis players]* équipe *f* de double ; *[of ice-skaters]* couple *m* ; *[of golfers]* camp *m* ◆ **the ~ of Laurel and Hardy** *(Cine, Theat)* le duo *or* le tandem Laurel et Hardy 2 *(NonC = action)* ◆ **the ~ of Dixon with Winterburn was a success** l'association Dixon-Winterburn a été un succès 3 *[of birds]* appariement *m*

paisley /ˈpeɪzlɪ/ N *(= fabric)* laine *f* à motif cachemire ; *(= design:* also **paisley pattern**) motif *m or* dessin *m* cachemire COMP **paisley shawl** N châle *m* (à motif) cachemire

pajamas /pəˈdʒɑːməz/ NPL *(US)* ⇒ **pyjama**

pak choi /pækˈtʃɔɪ/ N *(Culin)* pak-choi *m*

Paki** /ˈpækɪ/ *(Brit pej)* (abbrev of **Pakistani**) N Pakistanais(e) *m(f)* ADJ pakistanais(e)
COMP **Paki-basher** N *personne qui participe à des attaques racistes contre des immigrés pakistanais*
Paki-bashing N *attaques racistes contre des immigrés pakistanais*

Pakistan /ˌpɑːkɪsˈtɑːn/ N Pakistan *m* ◆ **in ~** au Pakistan

Pakistani /ˌpɑːkɪsˈtɑːnɪ/ ADJ pakistanais N Pakistanais(e) *m(f)*

pakora /pəˈkɔːrə/ N (pl **pakora** *or* **pakoras**) *(Culin)* pakora *m (petit beignet indien)*

PAL /pæl/ N *(TV)* (abbrev of **phase alternation line**) PAL *m*

pal* /pæl/ N copain* *m*, copine* *f* ; *(form of address)* mon vieux* ◆ **they're great ~s** ils sont très copains*, ce sont de grands copains* ◆ **be a ~!** sois sympa !*

► **pal up*** VI devenir copain(s)* *(or* copine(s)*) *(with* avec)

palace /ˈpælɪs/ N palais *m* ◆ **the Palace** *(= the Queen's entourage)* le Palais (de Buckingham) ◆ **bishop's ~** évêché *m*, palais *m* épiscopal ◆ **royal ~** palais *m* royal ◆ **presidential ~** palais *m* présidentiel COMP **palace revolution** N *(fig)* révolution *f* de palais

⚠ In French, **palace** means 'luxury hotel'.

paladin /ˈpælədɪn/ N paladin *m*

palaeo... /ˈpælɪəʊ/ PREF ⇒ **paleo...**

Palaeozoic /ˌpælɪəʊˈzəʊɪk/ ADJ, N *(Geol)* paléozoïque *m*

palais /ˈpæleɪ/ N *(Brit:* also **palais de danse** †) dancing *m*, salle *f* de danse *or* de bal

palatable /ˈpælətəbl/ ADJ *[food]* agréable au goût ; *(fig) [fact etc]* acceptable

palatal /ˈpælətl/ ADJ palatal ◆ **~ l** *(Ling)* l mouillé N palatale *f*

palatalize /ˈpælətəlaɪz/ VT palataliser, mouiller

palate /ˈpælɪt/ N *(Anat)* palais *m* ◆ **to have a discriminating ~** avoir le palais fin ◆ **too sweet for my ~** trop sucré à mon goût ; → **hard, soft**

palatial /pəˈleɪʃəl/ ADJ ◆ **the house is ~** la maison est un véritable palais ◆ **a ~ hotel** un palace ◆ **the ~ splendour of the building** la splendeur palatiale de cet édifice

palatinate /pəˈlætɪnɪt/ N palatinat *m*

palaver /pəˈlɑːvəʳ/ N 1 *(lit = discussion)* palabre *f* 2 *(* = fuss)* palabres *fpl* ◆ **what a ~!** quelle histoire pour si peu ! ◆ **to make a lot of ~ about** *or* **over sth** faire toute une histoire à propos de qch VI palabrer

pale[1] /peɪl/ ADJ *[face, person] (naturally)* pâle ; *(from sickness, fear)* blême ; *[colour]* pâle ; *[dawn, moonlight]* blafard ◆ **~ grey/pink** gris/rose pâle ◆ **to grow ~** *(gen)* pâlir ; *(from sickness, emotion)* blêmir, pâlir ◆ **he looked ~** il était pâle *or* blême ◆ **~ blue eyes** yeux *mpl* bleu pâle VI *[person] (gen, from shock, emotion)* pâlir ; *(from sickness)* blêmir ; *(from fear)* pâlir, blêmir ◆ **to ~ with fear** pâlir *or* blêmir de peur ◆ **it ~s in comparison with ..., it ~s into insignificance beside ...** cela paraît dérisoire par rapport *or* comparé à ... ◆ **her beauty ~d beside her mother's** sa beauté était éclipsée par celle de sa mère
COMP **pale ale** N *(Brit)* pale-ale *f (sorte de bière blonde légère)*
pale-faced ADJ *(= not tanned)* au teint pâle ; *(from sickness, fear etc)* pâle, blême
pale-skinned ADJ à la peau claire

pale[2] /peɪl/ N *(= stake)* pieu *m* ◆ **to be beyond the ~** *[behaviour, ideas, beliefs]* être inadmissible *or* inacceptable ; *[person]* dépasser les bornes

paleface /ˈpeɪlfeɪs/ N Visage pâle *mf*

paleness /ˈpeɪlnɪs/ N pâleur *f*

paleo... /ˈpælɪəʊ/ PREF paléo...

paleographer /ˌpælɪˈɒgrəfəʳ/ N paléographe *mf*

paleography /ˌpælɪˈɒgrəfɪ/ N paléographie *f*

paleolithic /ˌpælɪəʊˈlɪθɪk/ ADJ paléolithique ◆ **the ~ age** le paléolithique

paleontologist /ˌpælɪɒnˈtɒlədʒɪst/ N paléontologue *mf*

paleontology /ˌpælɪɒnˈtɒlədʒɪ/ N paléontologie *f*

Palermo /pəˈlɜːməʊ/ N Palerme

Palestine /ˈpælɪstaɪn/ N Palestine *f*

Palestinian /ˌpæləsˈtɪnɪən/ ADJ palestinien N Palestinien(ne) *m(f)*

palette /ˈpælɪt/ N *(Art, Comput)* palette *f* COMP **palette knife** N (pl **palette knives**) *(Art)* couteau *m* (à palette) ; *(for cakes)* couteau *m* palette ; *(for cooking)* spatule *f*

palfrey /ˈpɔːlfrɪ/ N palefroi *m*

palimony* /ˈpælɪmənɪ/ N pension *f* alimentaire *(versée à un(e) ex-concubin(e))*

palimpsest /ˈpælɪmpsest/ N palimpseste *m*

palindrome /ˈpælɪndrəʊm/ N palindrome *m*

paling /ˈpeɪlɪŋ/ N *(= fence)* palissade *f* ; *(= stake)* palis *m*

palisade /ˌpælɪˈseɪd/ N 1 palissade *f* 2 *(US Geol)* ligne *f* de falaises abruptes

pall[1] /pɔːl/ VI perdre son charme *(on sb* pour qn) ◆ **the job was beginning to ~ for him** il commençait à se lasser de ce poste

pall[2] /pɔːl/ N drap *m* mortuaire ; *(Rel)* pallium *m* ; *(fig) [of smoke]* voile *m* ; *[of snow]* manteau *m* ; *(= depressing atmosphere)* atmosphère *f* lugubre ◆ **to cast a ~ over** *[+ event, celebration]* assombrir

Palladian /pəˈleɪdɪən/ ADJ *(Archit)* palladien

palladium /pəˈleɪdɪəm/ N palladium *m*

pallbearer /ˈpɔːlbɛərəʳ/ N porteur *m* (de cercueil)

pallet /ˈpælɪt/ N 1 *(= mattress)* paillasse *f* ; *(= bed)* grabat *m* 2 *(for handling goods)* palette *f* 3 ⇒ **palette**
COMP **pallet loader** N palettiseur *m*
pallet truck N transpalette *m*

palletization /ˌpælɪtaɪˈzeɪʃən/ N palettisation *f*

palletize /ˈpælɪtaɪz/ VT palettiser

palliasse /ˈpælɪæs/ N ⇒ **paillasse**

palliate /ˈpælɪeɪt/ VT *(Med, fig)* pallier ◆ **palliating drugs** médicaments *mpl* palliatifs

palliative /ˈpælɪətɪv/ ADJ, N palliatif *m*

pallid /ˈpælɪd/ ADJ *[person, complexion]* pâle, blafard ; *[light]* blafard ; *(fig = insipid) [person, entertainment]* insipide

pallidness /ˈpælɪdnɪs/, **pallor** /ˈpæləʳ/ N pâleur *f* ; *[of face]* teint *m* blafard, pâleur *f*

pally* /ˈpælɪ/ ADJ (très) copain* (copine* *f*) *(with* avec)

palm[1] /pɑːm/ N *[of hand]* paume *f* ◆ **she placed the money in his ~** elle lui mit l'argent dans le creux de la main ◆ **to read sb's ~** lire *or* faire les lignes de la main à qn ◆ **to cross sb's ~ with silver** donner la pièce à qn ◆ **to have sb in the ~ of one's hand** faire de qn ce qu'on veut ◆ **he had the audience in the ~ of his hand** il avait le public dans sa poche* ◆ **to grease** *or* **oil sb's ~** graisser la patte* à qn VT *(= conceal)* cacher au creux de la main ; *(= pick up)* subtiliser, escamoter ◆ **to ~ sb sth, to ~ sth to sb** glisser qch *or* faire passer qch à qn

► **palm off** VT SEP *[+ sth worthless]* refiler* *(on, onto* à) ◆ **to ~ sb off** se débarrasser de qn ◆ **they ~ed the children off on me** ils m'ont refilé les enfants*

palm[2] /pɑːm/ N (also **palm tree**) palmier *m* ; *(= branch)* palme *f* ; *(Rel)* rameau *m* ; *(Rel = straw cross)* rameaux *mpl* ◆ **to carry off the ~** remporter la palme
COMP **palm court** ADJ *(Brit) [music, orchestra etc]* ≃ de thé dansant
palm grove N palmeraie *f*
palm oil N huile *f* de palme
Palm Sunday N (dimanche *m* des) Rameaux *mpl*

palmate /ˈpælmeɪt/ ADJ *[leaf, foot]* palmé

palmcorder /ˈpɑːmkɔːdəʳ/ N caméscope m de paume

palmetto /pælˈmetəʊ/ N (pl **palmettos** or **palmettoes**) palmier m nain COMP **the Palmetto State** N (US) la Caroline du Sud

palmist /ˈpɑːmɪst/ N chiromancien(ne) m(f)

palmistry /ˈpɑːmɪstrɪ/ N chiromancie f

palmtop computer /ˈpɑːmtɒpkəmˈpjuːtəʳ/ N ordinateur m de poche

palmy /ˈpɑːmɪ/ ADJ (fig) heureux ; [era] florissant, glorieux

palomino /ˌpæləˈmiːnəʊ/ N (pl **palominos**) alezan m doré à crins blancs

palooka‡ /pəˈluːkə/ N (US pej) pauvre type* m

palpable /ˈpælpəbəl/ ADJ (lit) palpable ; (fig) [tension, fear, unease, frustration, enthusiasm] palpable ; [error] manifeste

palpably /ˈpælpəblɪ/ ADV manifestement, d'une façon évidente

palpate /ˈpælpeɪt/ VT (Med) palper

palpitate /ˈpælpɪteɪt/ VI palpiter

palpitating /ˈpælpɪteɪtɪŋ/ ADJ palpitant

palpitation /ˌpælpɪˈteɪʃən/ N palpitation f ♦ **to have ~s** avoir des palpitations

palsied † /ˈpɔːlzɪd/ ADJ (Med) (= paralyzed) paralysé, paralytique ; (= trembling) (also fig) tremblotant

palsy † /ˈpɔːlzɪ/ N (Med) (= trembling) paralysie f agitante ; (= paralysis) paralysie f

palsy-walsy‡ /ˌpælzɪˈwælzɪ/ ADJ (Brit) ⇒ **pally**

paltry /ˈpɔːltrɪ/ ADJ 1 (= tiny, insignificant) [amount] misérable, dérisoire 2 (= petty) [behaviour] mesquin ; [excuse] piètre

paludism /ˈpæljʊdɪzəm/ N paludisme m

pampas /ˈpæmpəs/ NPL pampa(s) f(pl) COMP **pampas grass** N herbe f des pampas

pamper /ˈpæmpəʳ/ VT [+ person, pet] bichonner, dorloter ♦ **she ~s her husband with small gifts** elle bichonne or dorlote son mari en lui offrant de petits cadeaux ♦ **~ your skin with ...** offrez à votre peau ... ♦ **to ~ o.s.** se faire plaisir ♦ **she ~s herself with luxury beauty products** elle se bichonne avec des produits de beauté de luxe ♦ **go on, ~ yourself!** allez, faites-vous plaisir !

pamphlet /ˈpæmflɪt/ N brochure f ; (Literat) opuscule m ; (= scurrilous tract) pamphlet m

pamphleteer /ˌpæmflɪˈtɪəʳ/ N auteur m de brochures or d'opuscules ; [of tracts] pamphlétaire mf

Pan /pæn/ N Pan m COMP **Pan pipes** NPL flûte f de Pan

pan¹ /pæn/ N 1 (Culin) casserole f ♦ **roasting ~** plat m à rôtir ; → **frying, pot¹** 2 [of scales] plateau m ; [of lavatory] cuvette f ; (Miner) batée f ♦ **to go down the ~**‡ (fig) tomber à l'eau* ; → **brain, flash, salt** 3 (US ‡ = face) binette‡ f, bille f (de clown)‡ ; → **deadpan** VT 1 [+ sand] laver à la batée 2 (* = criticize harshly) [+ film, book] éreinter, démolir ♦ **his work was ~ned by his boss** son patron a descendu en flammes son travail VI ♦ **to ~ for gold** laver le sable aurifère (à la batée)
COMP **pan-fry** VT faire sauter
pan scrubber N tampon m à récurer

► **pan out*** VI (= turn out) tourner, se passer ; (= turn out well) bien tourner, bien se goupiller* ♦ **it all ~ned out in the long run** ça s'est (bien) goupillé* en fin de compte ♦ **things didn't ~ out as he'd planned** les choses ne se sont pas goupillées* comme il l'avait prévu

pan² /pæn/ VI [camera] faire un panoramique, panoramiquer (to sur) ♦ **the camera ~ned across the lawn** la caméra a fait un panoramique or a panoramiqué sur le gazon VT ♦ **to ~ the camera** panoramiquer

pan... /pæn/ PREF pan...

panacea /ˌpænəˈsɪə/ N panacée f

panache /pəˈnæʃ/ N panache m

Pan-African /ˈpænˈæfrɪkən/ ADJ panafricain

Pan-Africanism /ˈpænˈæfrɪkənɪzəm/ N panafricanisme m

Panama /ˈpænəˌmɑː/ N 1 Panama m ♦ **in ~** au Panama 2 (also **Panama hat**) panama m COMP **the Panama Canal** N le canal de Panama

Panamanian /ˌpænəˈmeɪnɪən/ ADJ panaméen N Panaméen(ne) m(f)

Pan-American /ˈpænəˈmerɪkən/ ADJ panaméricain
COMP **Pan-American Highway** N route f panaméricaine
Pan-American Union N Union f panaméricaine

Pan-Americanism /ˈpænəˈmerɪkənɪzəm/ N panaméricanisme m

Pan-Asian /ˈpænˈeɪʃən/ ADJ panasiatique

Pan-Asianism /ˈpænˈeɪʃənɪzəm/ N panasiatisme m

pancake /ˈpænkeɪk/ N 1 (Culin) crêpe f ; → **flat¹** 2 (also **pancake landing**) atterrissage m à plat 3 (= make-up) → **pancake make-up** VI (in plane) se plaquer, atterrir à plat
COMP **pancake coil** N (Elec) galette f
Pancake Day N (Brit) mardi m gras
pancake make-up N (= powder compact) maquillage m compact ; (pej) tartine f de maquillage
pancake roll N (Brit) ≃ rouleau m de printemps
Pancake Tuesday N ⇒ **Pancake Day**

panchromatic /ˈpænkrəʊˈmætɪk/ ADJ panchromatique

pancreas /ˈpæŋkrɪəs/ N pancréas m

pancreatic /ˌpæŋkrɪˈætɪk/ ADJ pancréatique

panda /ˈpændə/ N panda m COMP **panda car** N (Brit) voiture f pie inv (de la police)

pandemic /pænˈdemɪk/ ADJ universel N pandémie f

pandemonium /ˌpændɪˈməʊnɪəm/ N tohu-bohu m, chahut m (monstre) ♦ **it's sheer ~!** c'est un véritable charivari !, quel tohu-bohu ! ♦ **~ broke loose** il y eut un chahut monstre or un véritable tohu-bohu ♦ **scenes of ~** des scènes de désordre indescriptible

pander /ˈpændəʳ/ VI ♦ **to ~ to** [+ person] se prêter aux exigences de ; [+ whims, desires] se plier à ; [+ tastes, weaknesses] flatter

p & h /ˌpiːəndeɪtʃ/ N (US) (abbrev of **postage and handling**) port m et manutention f

P & L (Comm) (abbrev of **profit and loss**) → **profit**

Pandora /pænˈdɔːrə/ N Pandore f COMP **Pandora's box** N boîte f de Pandore

p & p /ˌpiːəndˈpiː/ N (abbrev of **postage and packing**) → **postage**

pandrop /ˈpændrɒp/ N grosse pastille f de menthe

pane /peɪn/ N vitre f, carreau m

panegyric /ˌpænɪˈdʒɪrɪk/ ADJ, N panégyrique m

panel /ˈpænəl/ N 1 (in inquiry) commission f d'enquête ; (= committee) comité m ; [of negotiators etc] table f ronde
2 (Rad, TV etc) (gen) invités mpl ; (for game) jury m ♦ **a ~ of experts** un groupe d'experts, un panel (d'experts)
3 (Jur) (= list) liste f (des jurés) ; (= jury) jury m ♦ **~ of examiners** (Admin, Scol etc) jury m (d'examinateurs)
4 (also **interviewing panel**) jury m d'entretien
5 [of door, wall] panneau m ; [of ceiling] caisson m
6 (also **instrument panel**) tableau m de bord
7 (Brit Med: formerly) **to be on a doctor's ~** être inscrit sur le registre d'un médecin conventionné
8 (Dress) pan m
VT [+ surface] plaquer ; [+ room, wall] recouvrir de panneaux or de boiseries, lambrisser ♦ **~led door** porte f à panneaux ♦ **oak-~led** lambrissé de chêne, garni de boiseries de chêne
COMP **panel-beater** N carrossier m, tôlier m
panel-beating N tôlerie f
panel discussion N (Rad, TV etc) débat m, table f ronde (qui a lieu devant un public)
panel doctor N (Brit: formerly) médecin m conventionné
panel game N (Rad, TV) jeu m radiophonique (or télévisé) (avec des équipes d'invités)
panel patient N (Brit: formerly) malade mf assuré(e) social(e)
panel pin N pointe f, clou m à tête homme
panel truck, panel van N (US) camionnette f

panelling, paneling (US) /ˈpænəlɪŋ/ N (NonC) panneaux mpl, lambris m, boiseries fpl

panellist, panelist (US) /ˈpænəlɪst/ N (Rad, TV) invité(e) m(f) (d'une émission)

Pan-European /ˈpænˌjʊərəˈpiːən/ ADJ paneuropéen

pang /pæŋ/ N serrement m or pincement m de cœur ♦ **a ~ of jealousy/regret** une pointe de jalousie/de regret ♦ **a ~ of conscience** un accès de mauvaise conscience, des remords mpl ♦ **he saw her go without a ~** il l'a vue partir sans regret, cela ne lui a fait ni chaud ni froid* de la voir partir ♦ **hunger ~s, ~s of hunger** tiraillements mpl d'estomac

panhandle /ˈpænhændl/ N 1 (lit) manche m (de casserole) 2 (US = strip of land) bande f de terre ♦ **the Texas ~** la partie septentrionale du Texas VI (US ‡ = beg) faire la manche‡ VT (US ‡ = beg from) mendigoter‡ auprès de COMP **the Panhandle State** N (US) la Virginie occidentale

panhandler‡ /ˈpænhændləʳ/ N (US = beggar) mendiant(e) m(f)

panic /ˈpænɪk/ N (NonC) panique f ♦ **to throw a crowd into a ~** semer la panique dans une foule ♦ **to get into a ~** paniquer* ♦ **to throw sb into a ~** paniquer* qn ♦ **in a ~** complètement affolé or paniqué ♦ **we were in a mad ~** c'était la panique générale ♦ **to do sth in a ~** faire qch en catastrophe ♦ **(there's) no ~*, it can wait** pas de panique* or il n'y a pas le feu*, ça peut attendre
VI être pris de panique, paniquer* ♦ **she's ~king about the future of our relationship** elle est prise de panique or elle panique* quand elle pense à l'avenir de notre relation ♦ **industry is ~king about the recession** l'industrie panique* à cause de la récession ♦ **don't ~!*** pas d'affolement !, pas de panique !
VT [+ crowd] jeter or semer la panique dans ; [+ person] faire paniquer* ♦ **he was ~ked by his wife's strange behaviour** le comportement étrange de sa femme le faisait paniquer* ♦ **they were ~ked by the prospect of ...** ils étaient pris de panique or ils paniquaient* à la perspective de ... ♦ **she was ~ked into burning the letter** dans un moment d'affolement, elle brûla la lettre
COMP [fear] panique ; [decision] pris dans un moment de panique
panic attack N crise f de panique
panic button* N (fig) signal m d'alarme ♦ **to hit or push the ~ button** paniquer*
panic buying N achats mpl de précaution
panic selling N (on Stock Exchange) vente d'actions sous l'effet de la panique

panic stations* NPL ◆ **it was ~ stations** ça a été la panique générale*
panic-stricken ADJ *[person, crowd]* affolé, pris de panique ; *[look]* affolé

panicky /ˈpænɪkɪ/ ADJ *[report, newspaper]* alarmiste ; *[decision, action]* de panique ◆ **to feel ~** être pris de panique

panjandrum /pænˈdʒændrəm/ N grand ponte* *m*, grand manitou* *m*

pannier /ˈpænɪəʳ/ N panier *m*, corbeille *f* ; *[of pack animal]* panier *m* de bât ; *(on cycle, motorcycle:* also **pannier bag***)* sacoche *f*

panoply /ˈpænəplɪ/ N panoplie *f*

panorama /ˌpænəˈrɑːmə/ N panorama *m*

panoramic /ˌpænəˈræmɪk/ ADJ panoramique
COMP **panoramic screen** N écran *m* panoramique
panoramic view N vue *f* panoramique

pansy /ˈpænzɪ/ N 1 (= *plant*) pensée *f* 2 (*‡ pej* = *homosexual*) tante‡ *f*, tapette‡ *f*

pant /pænt/ VI (= *gasp*) *[person]* haleter ; *[animal]* battre du flanc, haleter ◆ **to ~ for breath** chercher (à reprendre) son souffle ◆ **the boy/the dog ~ed along after him** le garçon/le chien le suivait, essoufflé ◆ **he ~ed up the hill** il grimpa la colline en haletant VT (also **pant out**) *[+ words, phrases]* dire d'une voix haletante, dire en haletant N halètement *m*

► **pant for‡** VT FUS ◆ **I'm panting for a drink/a cigarette** je meurs d'envie de boire un coup*/d'en griller une*

pantaloon /ˌpæntəˈluːn/ N 1 ◆ **(a pair of) ~s** une culotte 2 *(Theat)* **Pantaloon** Pantalon *m*

pantechnicon /pænˈteknɪkən/ N *(Brit)* (= *van*) grand camion *m* de déménagement ; (= *warehouse*) entrepôt *m (pour meubles)*

pantheism /ˈpænθɪˌɪzəm/ N panthéisme *m*

pantheist /ˈpænθɪˌɪst/ N panthéiste *mf*

pantheistic /ˌpænθɪˈɪstɪk/ ADJ panthéiste

pantheon /ˈpænθɪən/ N panthéon *m*

panther /ˈpænθəʳ/ N (pl **panthers** or **panther**) panthère *f* ; → **black**

panties* /ˈpæntɪz/ NPL slip *m (de femme)*

pantihose /ˈpæntɪhəʊz/ NPL *(esp US)* ◆ **(a pair of) ~** un collant, des collants *mpl*

pantile /ˈpænˌtaɪl/ N tuile *f* imbriquée

panting /ˈpæntɪŋ/ N halètements *mpl*

panto* /ˈpæntəʊ/ N *(Brit Theat)* abbrev of **pantomime 1**

pantograph /ˈpæntəgrɑːf/ N *(Rail, Tech)* pantographe *m*

pantomime /ˈpæntəmaɪm/ N 1 *(Brit Theat)* (= *show*) *spectacle de Noël pour enfants*
2 (= *mime*) pantomime *f*, mime *m* ◆ **in ~** en mimant
3 *(Brit fig pej* = *fuss)* pantomime *f*, comédie *f* ◆ **the whole thing was a ~** toute cette affaire n'était qu'une pantomime *or* une comédie ◆ **the government should abandon this ~ of secrecy** le gouvernement devrait abandonner cette comédie du secret
COMP **pantomime dame** N *(Brit) rôle travesti de femme dans un spectacle de Noël*

PANTOMIME

La **pantomime** ou **panto** est un spectacle de théâtre pour enfants monté au moment de Noël. Le sujet en est un conte de fées ou une histoire populaire (par ex. Cendrillon ou Aladin), généralement présenté sous la forme d'une comédie bouffonne avec des chansons, des costumes fantaisistes et des décors féeriques. Les acteurs font beaucoup appel à la participation du public. Les principaux rôles masculins et féminins sont souvent interprétés par des acteurs du sexe opposé.

pantry /ˈpæntrɪ/ N *(in hotel, mansion)* office *f* ; *(in house)* garde-manger *m inv*

pants /pænts/ NPL 1 *(Brit* = *underwear)* ◆ **(a pair of) ~** un slip ◆ **that's pure ~‡** c'est complètement nul* 2 *(esp US* * = *trousers)* ◆ **(a pair of) ~** (un) pantalon ◆ **short ~** culottes *fpl* courtes ◆ **long ~** pantalon *m* (long) ◆ **she's the one who wears the ~*** c'est elle qui porte la culotte* ◆ **to be caught with one's ~ down*** être pris au dépourvu ◆ **to bore the ~ off sb*** barber qn*, raser qn* ◆ **to charm the ~ off sb*** séduire qn ◆ **to beat the ~ off sb*** (= *defeat*) mettre une raclée* à qn

pantsuit /ˈpæntsuːt/ N *(esp US)* tailleur-pantalon *m*

panty girdle /ˈpæntɪˌgɜːdl/ N gaine-culotte *f*

pantyhose /ˈpæntɪhəʊz/ NPL ⇒ **pantihose**

panty liner /ˈpæntɪˌlaɪnəʳ/ N protège-slip *m*

panzer /ˈpænzəʳ/ N panzer *m* COMP **panzer division** N division *f* blindée (allemande)

pap¹ /pæp/ N *(Culin)* bouillie *f* ; *(fig pej)* niaiseries *fpl*

pap² †† /pæp/ N (= *nipple*) mamelon *m*

papa /pəˈpɑː/ N père *m*

papacy /ˈpeɪpəsɪ/ N papauté *f*

papadum /ˈpæpədəm/ N poppadum *m*

papal /ˈpeɪpəl/ ADJ *[throne, mass, guards]* pontifical ; *[legate, election, visit]* du Pape
COMP **papal bull** N bulle *f* papale
papal cross N croix *f* papale
papal infallibility N infaillibilité *f* pontificale
papal nuncio N nonce *m* du Pape
Papal States NPL États *mpl* pontificaux *or* de l'Église

Papanicolaou smear /ˌpæpəˈnɪkəluːsmɪəʳ/, **Papanicolaou test** /ˌpæpəˈnɪkəluːtest/ N ⇒ **Pap smear**

paparazzo /ˌpæpəˈrætsəʊ/ N (pl **paparazzi** /ˌpæpəˈrætsiː/) paparazzi *m inv*

papaya /pəˈpaɪə/ N (= *fruit*) papaye *f* ; (= *tree*) papayer *m*

paper /ˈpeɪpəʳ/ N 1 *(NonC)* papier *m* ; *(pej* = *piles of paper)* paperasses *fpl* ◆ **a piece of ~** (= *odd bit*) un bout *or* un morceau de papier ; (= *sheet*) une feuille de papier ◆ **he was asked to put his suggestions down on ~** on lui a demandé de mettre ses suggestions par écrit *or* sur papier ◆ **the project looks impressive enough on ~** sur le papier, le projet semble assez impressionnant ; → **brown, carbon, rice**
2 (also **newspaper**) journal *m* ◆ **to write for the ~s** faire du journalisme ◆ **it was in the ~s yesterday** c'était dans les journaux hier ◆ **I saw it in the ~** je l'ai vu dans le journal ; → **illustrate**
3 *(Scol, Univ)* (= *set of exam questions*) épreuve *f* (écrite) ; (= *student's written answers*) copie *f* ◆ **a geography ~** une épreuve de géographie ◆ **she did a good ~ in French** elle a rendu une bonne copie de français
4 (= *scholarly work*) *(printed)* article *m* ; *(spoken)* communication *f*, intervention *f* ; *(in seminar: by student etc)* exposé *m* ◆ **to write a ~ on** écrire un article sur
5 (= *government publication*) livre *m* ; → **white, green**
6 (also **wallpaper**) papier *m* peint
7 *(Comm)* effet *m* ◆ **commercial ~** effet *m* de commerce
8 *(US* * = *money)* fric* *m*
NPL **papers** (= *documents*) papiers *mpl* ◆ **show me your (identity) ~s** montrez-moi vos papiers (d'identité) ◆ **call-up ~s** *(Mil)* ordre *m* d'appel ◆ **ship's ~s** papiers *mpl* de bord ◆ **voting ~s** bulletin *m* de vote
VT 1 *[+ room, walls]* tapisser ◆ **they ~ed the walls of the cafe with notices about ...** ils ont tapissé *or* complètement recouvert le mur du café d'affiches concernant ...
2 *(US fig* = *fill theatre)* **to ~ the house*** remplir la salle d'invités
COMP *[doll, towel]* en papier, de papier ; *(fig pej) [diploma etc]* sans valeur, bidon‡ *inv* ; *[profits]* sur le papier, théorique
paper bag N sac *m* en papier ; *(small)* poche *f* de papier ◆ **they couldn't fight their way out of a ~ bag*** ils sont complètement nuls*
paper chain N chaîne *f* en papier
paper chase N jeu *m* de piste
paper cup N gobelet *m* en carton
paper currency N billets *mpl* (de banque)
paper dart N avion *m* en papier
paper fastener N attache *f* métallique *(à tête)* ; (= *clip*) trombone *m*
paper handkerchief N mouchoir *m* en papier
paper industry N industrie *f* du papier
paper knife N (pl **paper knives**) coupe-papier *m inv*
paper lantern N lampion *m*
paper loss N *(Fin)* perte *f* comptable
paper mill N (usine *f* de) papeterie *f*
paper money N papier-monnaie *m*, monnaie *f* fiduciaire
paper plate N assiette *f* en carton
paper qualifications NPL diplômes *mpl*
paper round, paper route *(US)* N tournée *f* de distribution des journaux
paper shop N *(Brit)* marchand *m* de journaux
paper-shredder N broyeur *m (pour papiers)*
paper tape N *(Comput)* bande *f* perforée, ruban *m* perforé
paper-thin ADJ *[slice]* extrêmement fin ; *[wall]* fin comme du papier à cigarettes ◆ **to cut sth into ~-thin slices** émincer finement qch
paper tiger N tigre *m* de papier
paper trail N *(esp US)* traces *fpl* écrites

► **paper over** VT FUS *[+ crack in wall etc]* recouvrir de papier ; *(fig) [+ differences, disagreements]* passer sur ◆ **to ~ over the cracks** *(fig)* dissimuler les problèmes *or* les failles

paperback /ˈpeɪpəbæk/ N livre *m* broché ; *(smaller)* livre *m* de poche ◆ **it exists in ~** ça existe en (édition de) poche ADJ ◆ **~(ed) edition** édition *f* brochée ; *(smaller)* édition *f* de poche

paperbound /ˈpeɪpəbaʊnd/ ADJ ⇒ **paperbacked**

paperboy /ˈpeɪpəbɔɪ/ N *(delivering)* livreur *m* de journaux ; *(selling)* vendeur *m or* crieur *m* de journaux

paperclip /ˈpeɪpəklɪp/ N trombone *m* ; (= *bulldog clip*) pince *f*

papergirl /ˈpeɪpəgɜːl/ N *(delivering)* livreuse *f* de journaux ; *(selling)* vendeuse *f* de journaux

paperhanger /ˈpeɪpəˌhæŋəʳ/ N *(Brit* = *decorator)* tapissier-décorateur *m* ; *(US ‡* = *crook)* passeur *m* de faux billets (*or* de chèques falsifiés)

paperless /ˈpeɪpəlɪs/ ADJ ◆ **the ~ office** le bureau informatisé *or* zéro papier

paperweight /ˈpeɪpəweɪt/ N presse-papiers *m inv*

paperwork /ˈpeɪpəwɜːk/ N *(gen)* tâches *fpl* administratives ; *(pej)* paperasserie *f* ◆ **we need**

two more people to deal with the ~ il nous faut deux personnes de plus pour s'occuper des tâches administratives ◆ **he brings home ~ every night** il rapporte du travail à la maison tous les soirs

papery /ˈpeɪpərɪ/ ADJ *(gen)* (fin) comme du papier ; *[skin]* parcheminé

papier-mâché /ˌpæpjeɪˈmæʃeɪ/ N papier *m* mâché

papilla /pəˈpɪlə/ N (pl **papillae** /pəˈpɪliː/) papille *f*

papist /ˈpeɪpɪst/ *(pej)* N papiste *mf (pej)* ADJ de(s) papiste(s) *(pej)*

papistry /ˈpeɪpɪstrɪ/ N *(pej)* papisme *m (pej)*

papoose /pəˈpuːs/ N 1 *(= baby)* bébé *m* amérindien 2 *(= baby sling)* sac *m* kangourou, porte-bébé *m*

pappus /ˈpæpəs/ N aigrette *f (Bot)*

pappy* /ˈpæpɪ/ N *(US dial)* papa *m*

paprika /ˈpæprɪkə/ N paprika *m*

Pap smear /ˈpæpsmɪəʳ/, **Pap test** /ˈpæptest/ N frottis *m* (vaginal)

Papuan /ˈpæpjʊən/ ADJ papou N 1 Papou(e) *m(f)* 2 *(= language)* papou *m*

Papua New Guinea /ˈpæpjʊənjuːˈgɪnɪ/ N Papouasie-Nouvelle-Guinée *f* ADJ papou

Papua-New-Guinean /ˈpæpjʊənjuːˈgɪnɪən/ N Papou(e) *m(f)*

papyrus /pəˈpaɪərəs/ N (pl **papyruses** *or* **papyri** /pəˈpaɪəraɪ/) papyrus *m inv*

par[1] /pɑːʳ/ N 1 *(= equality of value)* égalité *f*, pair *m* ; *(Fin) [of currency]* pair *m* ◆ **to be on a ~ with** être comparable à ◆ **an environmental disaster on a ~ with Chernobyl** une catastrophe écologique comparable à celle de Tchernobyl ◆ **Glasgow is on a ~ with Liverpool for unemployment** Glasgow est comparable à Liverpool pour ce qui est du chômage ◆ **to put sb on a ~ with** *(= compare with)* comparer qn avec ; *(= consider as equal)* considérer qn comme l'égal de ; *(= make level with)* mettre qn sur le même plan que ◆ **above/below ~** *(Fin)* au-dessus/au-dessous du pair ◆ **at ~** *(Fin)* au pair

2 *(= expected standard)* **his work isn't up to ~, his work is below** *or* **under ~** son travail est décevant ◆ **his guitar playing is well below ~** son jeu de guitare est vraiment décevant ◆ **a below ~ effort** une performance décevante ◆ **to feel below** *or* **under ~** *(fig)* ne pas se sentir en forme ◆ **that's ~ for the course** *(fig)* c'est typique, il fallait *(or* faut *etc)* s'y attendre ◆ **his behaviour was ~ for the course** il a eu un comportement typique ◆ **long hours are ~ for the course in that line of work** il faut s'attendre à faire de longues journées dans ce travail

3 *(Golf)* par *m*, normale *f* du parcours ◆ **~ three** par trois ◆ **a ~ three (hole)** un par trois ◆ **four over ~** quatre coups au-dessus du par ◆ **he was five under ~ after the first round** il était cinq coups en dessous du par à la fin de la première partie ◆ **to break ~** être en dessous du par

COMP **par value** N *(Fin)* valeur *f* au pair

par[2]* /pɑːʳ/ N *(Press)* abbrev of **paragraph**

para* /ˈpærə/ N 1 abbrev of **paragraph noun 1** 2 *(Brit Mil)* (abbrev of **paratrooper**) para* *m* ◆ **the ~s** les paras* *mpl* 3 *(Mil)* (abbrev of **parachutist**) **the ~s** les paras* *mpl* ◆ **he's in the ~s** il est para*

para... /ˈpærə/ PREF para...

parable /ˈpærəbl/ N parabole *f* ◆ **to speak in ~s** parler par paraboles

parabola /pəˈræbələ/ N parabole *f (Math)*

parabolic /ˌpærəˈbɒlɪk/ ADJ parabolique

paraboloid /pəˈræbəlɔɪd/ N paraboloïde *m*

Paracelsus /pærəˈselsəs/ N Paracelse *m*

paracetamol /pærəˈsiːtəmɒl/ N paracétamol *m*

parachute /ˈpærəʃuːt/ N parachute *m* VI descendre en parachute ◆ **to ~ behind enemy lines** se faire parachuter derrière les lignes ennemies ◆ **to go parachuting** faire du parachutisme VT *[+ person, supplies]* parachuter ◆ **food supplies were ~d into the mountains** on a parachuté des vivres dans les montagnes

COMP *[cords]* de parachute

parachute drop N parachutage *m*

parachute jump N saut *m* en parachute

parachute regiment N régiment *m* de parachutistes

parachutist /ˈpærəʃuːtɪst/ N parachutiste *mf*

Paraclete /ˈpærəkliːt/ N ◆ **the ~** Le Paraclet

parade /pəˈreɪd/ N 1 *(gen, Mil) (= procession)* défilé *m* ; *(= ceremony)* parade *f*, revue *f* ◆ **to be on ~** *(Mil) (= drilling)* être à l'exercice ; *(for review)* défiler

2 *(fig)* ◆ **~ of** *(= exhibition of) [+ wares, goods]* étalage *m* de ; *(= procession, series of) [+ people]* défilé *m* de ◆ **an endless ~ of advertisements** des publicités à n'en plus finir ◆ **the dockers' ~ of support for their union leader** *(gen)* la manifestation de soutien des dockers à leur leader syndical ; *(pej)* le soutien que les dockers font mine d'apporter au leader de leur syndicat

3 *(esp Brit = road)* boulevard *m (souvent au bord de la mer)*

4 *(Mil:* also **parade ground***)* terrain *m* de manœuvres

VT *[+ troops]* faire défiler ; *(fig = display) [+ one's wealth, possessions]* faire étalage de, afficher ◆ **she never ~d her knowledge** elle ne faisait jamais étalage de ses connaissances ◆ **these reforms were ~d as progress** *(pej)* ces réformes ont été présentées comme un progrès

VI *(Mil)* défiler

▸ **parade about***, **parade around*** VI se balader*, circuler* ◆ **don't ~ about with nothing on!** ne te promène pas *or* ne te balade* pas tout nu !

paradigm /ˈpærədaɪm/ N paradigme *m* COMP **paradigm shift** N révolution *f* conceptuelle

paradigmatic /ˌpærədɪgˈmætɪk/ ADJ paradigmatique

paradisaic /ˌpærədɪˈseɪɪk/, **paradisal** /ˌpærəˈdaɪsəl/ ADJ ⇒ **paradisiacal**

paradise /ˈpærədaɪs/ N paradis *m* ◆ **an earthly ~** un paradis terrestre ◆ **it's a nature-lover's** *etc* **~** c'est un paradis pour les amoureux de la nature *etc* ◆ **to go to ~** *(euph = die)* aller au ciel ; → **fool**[1], **bird**

paradisiacal /ˌpærədɪˈsaɪəkəl/ ADJ paradisiaque

paradox /ˈpærədɒks/ N paradoxe *m*

paradoxical /ˌpærəˈdɒksɪkəl/ ADJ paradoxal

paradoxically /ˌpærəˈdɒksɪkəlɪ/ ADV paradoxalement

paraffin /ˈpærəfɪn/ N *(Chem)* paraffine *f* ; *(Brit = fuel:* also **paraffin oil***)* pétrole *m* (lampant) ◆ **liquid ~** *(Med)* huile *f* de paraffine

COMP **paraffin heater** N poêle *m* à mazout *or* à pétrole

paraffin lamp N lampe *f* à pétrole

paraffin wax N paraffine *f*

paraglide /ˈpærəglaɪd/ VI faire du parapente

paraglider /ˈpærəˌglaɪdəʳ/ N 1 *(= person)* parapentiste *mf* 2 *(= object)* parapente *m*

paragliding /ˈpærəˌglaɪdɪŋ/ N *(NonC)* parapente *m*

paragon /ˈpærəgən/ N modèle *m*, parangon *m* ◆ **a ~ of virtue** un modèle *or* parangon de vertu

paragraph /ˈpærəgrɑːf/ N 1 paragraphe *m* ◆ **"new paragraph"** "à la ligne" ◆ **to begin a new ~** aller à la ligne 2 *(newspaper item)* entrefilet *m* VT diviser en paragraphes COMP **paragraph mark** N *(Typ)* pied *m* de mouche

Paraguay /ˈpærəgwaɪ/ N Paraguay *m* ◆ **in ~** au Paraguay

Paraguayan /ˌpærəˈgwaɪən/ ADJ paraguayen N Paraguayen(ne) *m(f)*

parakeet /ˈpærəkiːt/ N perruche *f* (ondulée)

paralanguage /ˈpærəˌlæŋgwɪdʒ/ N *(Ling)* paralangage *m*

paralegal /ˌpærəˌliːgəl/ N *(esp US)* N *auxiliaire juridique* ADJ *[secretary, assistant]* juridique

paralinguistic /ˌpærəˌlɪŋgwɪstɪk/ ADJ *(Ling)* paralinguistique

parallactic /ˌpærəˈlæktɪk/ ADJ parallactique

parallax /ˈpærəlæks/ N parallaxe *f*

parallel /ˈpærəlel/ ADJ 1 *(Geom, Math etc)* parallèle *(with, to* à*)* ◆ **the road runs ~ to the railway** la route est parallèle à la voie de chemin de fer

2 *(fig) [situation, process, event, operation]* analogue ; *[development]* parallèle *(with, to* à*)* ; *[talks, negotiations]* en parallèle ◆ **a ~ universe** un univers parallèle ◆ **in a ~ step, they ...** de la même manière, ils ...

3 *(Ski)* parallèle

ADV parallèlement *(to* à*)*

N 1 *(Geog)* parallèle *m* ◆ **the 22nd ~** le 22e parallèle

2 *(Math)* (ligne *f*) parallèle *f*

3 *(fig)* parallèle *m*, comparaison *f* ◆ **to draw a ~ between** établir *or* faire un parallèle *or* une comparaison entre ◆ **an event without ~ in the modern era** un événement sans précédent à l'époque moderne ◆ **this wooded landscape is almost without ~ (anywhere else)** ce paysage sylvestre est (pratiquement) unique ◆ **he/she is without ~** il/elle est sans pareil(le) ◆ **to happen** *etc* **in ~ with sth** arriver *etc* parallèlement à *or* en parallèle avec qch

VT *(Math)* être parallèle à ; *(fig) (= find equivalent to)* trouver un équivalent à ; *(= be equal to)* égaler ◆ **a superb performance that no-one (else) could ~** une magnifique performance que personne ne pourrait égaler ◆ **the increase in the number of smokers has been ~ed by an increase in lung cancers** l'augmentation du nombre des fumeurs s'est accompagnée d'une augmentation des cas de cancer du poumon ◆ **his success here has not been ~ed by recognition in his home country** le succès qu'il remporte ici n'a pas trouvé d'équivalent dans son pays d'origine

COMP **parallel bars** NPL barres *fpl* parallèles

parallel-park VI faire un créneau

parallel processing N *(Comput)* traitement *m* en parallèle

parallel turn N virage *m* parallèle

parallelepiped /ˌpærəˌleləˈpaɪped/ N parallélépipède *m*

parallelism /ˈpærəlelɪzəm/ N *(Math, fig)* parallélisme *m*

parallelogram /ˌpærəˈleləʊgræm/ N parallélogramme *m*

Paralympic /ˌpærəˈlɪmpɪk/ ADJ paralympique NPL **Paralympics** ⇒ **Paralympic Games** COMP **Paralympic Games** NPL Jeux *mpl* paralympiques

paralysis /pəˈræləsɪs/ N (pl **paralyses** /pəˈræləsiːz/) 1 *(Med)* paralysie *f* ; → **creeping, infantile** 2 *(fig) [of country, government, trade, talks]* paralysie *f* ; *[of traffic etc]* immobilisation *f* ◆ **political ~** immobilisme *m* politique

paralytic /ˌpærəˈlɪtɪk/ ADJ 1 *(Med)* paralytique 2 *(Brit* ✱ *= drunk)* ivre mort N paralytique *mf*

paralyzation /ˌpærəlaɪˈzeɪʃən/ N immobilisation *f*

paralyze /ˈpærəlaɪz/ **VT** 1 *(Med)* paralyser ◆ **his arm is ~d** il est paralysé du bras ◆ **~d from the waist/neck down** paralysé des membres inférieurs/des quatre membres 2 *(fig) [+ person, traffic, communications]* paralyser ◆ **~d with fear** paralysé *or* transi de peur ◆ **paralyzing cold** froid *m* paralysant ◆ **paralyzing fear/loneliness** peur *f*/solitude *f* pétrifiante ◆ **paralyzing shyness** timidité *f* maladive

paramedic /ˌpærəˈmedɪk/ **N** auxiliaire *mf* médical(e)

paramedical /ˌpærəˈmedɪkəl/ **ADJ** paramédical

parament /ˈpærəmənt/ **N** (pl **paraments** *or* **paramenta** /ˌpærəˈmentə/) parement *m*

parameter /pəˈræmɪtəʳ/ **N** 1 *(Math)* paramètre *m* 2 *(fig = criterion, principle)* critère *m*, paramètre *m* ◆ **to define** *or* **establish** *or* **set the ~s of** *or* **for sth** définir les critères *or* paramètres de qch ◆ **to fall within certain ~s** respecter certains critères ◆ **within the ~s of ...** dans les limites de ... ◆ **the technical ~s of the system** les caractéristiques techniques de ce système ◆ **the ~s of their energy policy** les orientations principales de leur politique énergétique

parametric /ˌpærəˈmetrɪk/ **ADJ** paramétrique

paramilitary /ˌpærəˈmɪlɪtərɪ/ **ADJ** *[organization, group, operation]* paramilitaire **N** *(= member)* membre *m* d'une force paramilitaire ◆ **the paramilitaries** les forces *fpl* paramilitaires **NPL the paramilitary** *(= organizations)* les forces *fpl* paramilitaires

paramnesia /ˌpæræmˈniːzɪə/ **N** paramnésie *f*

paramount /ˈpærəmaʊnt/ **ADJ** primordial ◆ **of ~ importance** d'une importance primordiale, de la plus haute importance ◆ **the interests of the child are ~** les intérêts de l'enfant sont primordiaux *or* passent avant tout

paramour /ˈpærəmʊəʳ/ **N** *(liter)* amant *m*, maîtresse *f*

paranoia /ˌpærəˈnɔɪə/ **N** paranoïa *f*

paranoic /ˌpærəˈnɔɪk/, **paranoiac** /ˌpaærəˈnɔɪæk/ **ADJ, N** paranoïaque *mf*

paranoid /ˈpærənɔɪd/ **ADJ** 1 *(Psych)* paranoïde 2 *(* fig)* parano* **N** paranoïaque *mf*

paranoidal /ˌpærəˈnɔɪdl/ **ADJ** paranoïde

paranormal /ˌpærəˈnɔːməl/ **ADJ** paranormal **N** ◆ **the ~** les phénomènes *mpl* paranormaux

parapet /ˈpærəpɪt/ **N** 1 *[of bridge, roof etc]* parapet *m*, garde-fou *m* ◆ **to put** *or* **stick* one's head above the ~** se mouiller*, prendre un risque ◆ **to keep one's head below the ~** ne pas se mouiller*, ne pas prendre de risques 2 *(Mil)* parapet *m*

paraph /ˈpærəf/ **N** paraphe *m or* parafe *m*

paraphernalia /ˌpærəfəˈneɪlɪə/ **N** (pl *inv*) 1 *(= belongings: also for hobbies, sports etc)* attirail *m* 2 *(* = bits and pieces)* bazar* *m*

paraphrase /ˈpærəfreɪz/ **N** paraphrase *f* **VT** paraphraser

paraphrastic /ˌpærəˈfræstɪk/ **ADJ** paraphrastique

paraplegia /ˌpærəˈpliːdʒə/ **N** paraplégie *f*

paraplegic /ˌpærəˈpliːdʒɪk/ **ADJ** *(gen)* paraplégique ; *[games]* pour les paraplégiques **N** paraplégique *mf*

paraprofessional /ˌpærəprəˈfeʃənl/ **ADJ, N** paraprofessionnel(le) *mf*

parapsychological /ˌpærəsaɪkəˈlɒdʒɪkəl/ **ADJ** parapsychologique, parapsychique

parapsychologist /ˌpærəsaɪˈkɒlədʒɪst/ **N** parapsychologue *mf*

parapsychology /ˌpærəsaɪˈkɒlədʒɪ/ **N** parapsychologie *f*

Paraquat ® /ˈpærəkwɒt/ **N** paraquat ® *m*

parasailing /ˈpærəˌseɪlɪŋ/ **N** *(NonC)* parachutisme *m* ascensionnel

parascending /ˈpærəˌsendɪŋ/ *(Sport)* **N** parachutisme *m* ascensionnel ◆ **to go ~** faire du parachute ascensionnel

parasite /ˈpærəˌsaɪt/ **N** *(lit, fig)* parasite *m*

parasitic(al) /ˌpærəˈsɪtɪk(əl)/ **ADJ** 1 *(lit, fig)* parasite *(on* de) 2 *(Med) [disease]* parasitaire

parasiticidal /ˌpærəˌsɪtɪˈsaɪdl/ **ADJ** parasiticide

parasiticide /ˌpærəˈsɪtɪsaɪd/ **N** parasiticide *m*

parasitism /ˈpærəsɪtɪzəm/ **N** parasitisme *m*

parasitologist /ˌpærəsaɪˈtɒlədʒɪst/ **N** parasitologue *mf*

parasitology /ˌpærəsɪˈtɒlədʒɪ/ **N** parasitologie *f*

parasitosis /ˌpærəsɪˈtəʊsɪs/ **N** parasitose *f*

parasol /ˈpærəˌsɒl/ **N** *(hand-held)* ombrelle *f* ; *(over table etc)* parasol *m*

parasuicide /ˌpærəˈsuɪsaɪd/ **N** faux suicide *m*

parasympathetic /ˌpærəsɪmpəˈθetɪk/ **ADJ** parasympathique **COMP parasympathetic nervous system N** système *m* parasympathique

parataxis /ˌpærəˈtæksɪs/ **N** parataxe *f*

parathyroid /ˌpærəˈθaɪrɔɪd/ **ADJ** parathyroïdien **N** (also **parathyroid gland**) parathyroïde *f*

paratrooper /ˈpærətruːpəʳ/ **N** parachutiste *mf* *(soldat)*

paratroops /ˈpærətruːps/ **NPL** (unités *fpl* de) parachutistes *mpl*

paratyphoid /ˈpærəˈtaɪfɔɪd/ **ADJ** paratyphique ◆ **~ fever** paratyphoïde *f* **N** paratyphoïde *f*

parboil /ˈpɑːbɔɪl/ **VT** *(Culin)* faire bouillir *or* faire cuire à demi

parcel /ˈpɑːsəl/ **N** 1 *(= package)* colis *m*, paquet *m* 2 *(= portion) [of land]* parcelle *f* ; *[of shares]* paquet *m* ; *[of goods]* lot *m* ; → **part** 3 *(esp Brit fig)* **a ~ of lies** un tas* *or* un tissu de mensonges ◆ **it's a ~ of nonsense** c'est des inepties ◆ **a ~ of fools** un tas* *or* une bande* d'idiots **VT** (also **parcel up**) *[+ object, purchases]* emballer, empaqueter

COMP parcel bomb N colis *m* piégé

parcel net N filet *m* à bagages

parcel post N service *m* de colis postaux, service *m* de messageries ◆ **to send sth (by) ~ post** envoyer qch par colis postal

parcel shelf N *(in car)* plage *f* arrière

parcels office N bureau *m* des messageries

► **parcel out VT SEP** *[+ money, jobs, privileges etc]* distribuer ; *[+ inheritance]* partager ; *[+ land]* lotir ; *[+ tasks, duties]* répartir

parch /pɑːtʃ/ **VT** *[+ crops, land]* dessécher, brûler

parched /pɑːtʃt/ **ADJ** *[lips, soil, plants]* desséché ◆ **I'm ~!*** je meurs de soif !*

parchment /ˈpɑːtʃmənt/ **N** parchemin *m* ◆ **~ paper** papier-parchemin *m*

pardner* /ˈpɑːdnəʳ/ **N** *(US)* camarade *m* ◆ **so long, ~!** au revoir, mon pote !*

pardon /ˈpɑːdən/ **N** 1 *(NonC)* pardon *m* ; → **beg**

2 *(Rel)* indulgence *f*

3 *(Jur)* ◆ **(free) ~** grâce *f* ◆ **letter of ~** lettre *f* de grâce ◆ **general ~** amnistie *f* ◆ **royal ~** grâce *f* royale ◆ **to grant sb a posthumous ~** réhabiliter la mémoire de qn

VT 1 *[+ mistake, person] (gen)* pardonner ; *(Rel)* absoudre ◆ **to ~ sb for sth** pardonner qch à qn ◆ **to ~ sb for doing sth** pardonner à qn d'avoir fait qch ◆ **~ me** *(apologizing for sth)* excusez-moi, désolé ; *(disagreeing politely)* excusez-moi ; *(interrupting)* excusez-moi, pardonnez-moi ◆ **~ me?** *(US)* comment ?, pardon ? ◆ **~ me for troubling you** excusez-moi de vous déranger ◆ **~ my asking, but ...** excusez-moi de vous poser cette question, mais ... ◆ **~ me for breathing/speaking/living!*** *(iro)* excuse-moi de respirer/de parler/de vivre ! ◆ **~ my French!*** *(hum: after swearing)* passez-moi *or* pardonnez-moi l'expression ! ◆ **if you'll ~ the expression** si vous me pardonnez l'expression

2 *(Jur) [+ criminal]* gracier ; *(= grant amnesty to)* amnistier ; *(posthumously)* réhabiliter la mémoire de

EXCL *(apologizing)* pardon !, excusez-moi ! ◆ **~?** *(not hearing)* comment ?, pardon ?

pardonable /ˈpɑːdnəbl/ **ADJ** *[mistake]* pardonnable ; *(Jur)* graciable

pardonably /ˈpɑːdnəblɪ/ **ADV** de façon bien excusable *or* bien pardonnable

pare /pɛəʳ/ **VT** 1 *[+ fruit]* peler, éplucher ; *[+ nails]* rogner, couper 2 *(= reduce:* also **pare down**) *[+ expenses]* réduire

parent /ˈpɛərənt/ **N** *(= father)* père *m* ; *(= mother)* mère *f* ◆ **his ~s** ses parents *mpl* ◆ **to be born of Scottish ~s** être né de parents écossais ◆ **the ~ birds/animals** les parents *mpl* de l'oiseau/l'animal

COMP *[interest, involvement etc]* parental, des parents

parent body N organisme *m* de tutelle

parent company N *(Comm, Fin)* maison *f or* société *f* mère

parent power* N *(Scol)* influence *f* des parents d'élèves

parents' evening N *(Scol)* réunion *f* d'information avec les parents (d'élèves)

parent-teacher association N *(Scol)* association *f* de parents d'élèves et de professeurs

parent tree N souche *f*

parentage /ˈpɛərəntɪdʒ/ **N** ◆ **of Scottish ~** *(mother and father)* (né) de parents écossais ◆ **of unknown ~** de parents inconnus ◆ **children of (racially) mixed ~** les enfants issus de couples mixtes ◆ **there was some confusion about his ~** on ne savait pas exactement qui étaient ses parents ◆ **genetic techniques that provide proof of ~** des techniques génétiques qui permettent de prouver les liens de parenté

parental /pəˈrentl/ **ADJ** *[choice]* des parents, parental ; *[involvement, cooperation, responsibility]* parental ; *[rights, attitudes]* des parents ◆ **~ consent** consentement *m* des parents ◆ **~ control** *or* **authority** autorité *f* parentale ◆ **~ responsibility** la responsabilité des parents ◆ **~ rights over a child** *(gen)* les droits *mpl* des parents sur leur enfant ; *(Jur)* la tutelle d'un enfant **COMP parental leave N** congé *m* parental

parenthesis /pəˈrenθɪsɪs/ **N** (pl **parentheses** /pəˈrenθɪsiːz/) parenthèse *f* ◆ **in ~** *or* **in parentheses** entre parenthèses

parenthetic(al) /ˌpærənˈθetɪk(əl)/ **ADJ** entre parenthèses

parenthetically /ˌpærənˈθetɪkəlɪ/ **ADV** entre parenthèses

parenthood /ˈpɛərənthʊd/ **N** condition *f* de parent(s), paternité *f (or* maternité *f)* ◆ **the joys of ~** les joies *fpl* de la maternité *(or* paternité) ◆ **the responsibilities of ~** les responsabilités *fpl* des parents *or* que l'on a quand on a des enfants ◆ **she doesn't feel ready for ~** elle ne se sent pas mûre pour avoir des enfants

parenting /ˈpɛərəntɪŋ/ **N** éducation *f* des enfants ◆ **~ is a full-time occupation** l'éducation d'un enfant *or* élever un enfant est un travail à plein temps ◆ **shared ~** partage *m* de l'éducation des enfants

parer /ˈpɛərəʳ/ **N** épluche-légumes *m inv*

pariah /pəˈraɪə/ **N** paria *m*

parietal /pəˈraɪɪtl/ **ADJ** pariétal **N** *(Anat)* pariétal *m* **NPL parietals** *(US Univ)* heures *fpl* de visite *(du sexe opposé dans les chambres d'étudiants)*

paring /ˈpɛərɪŋ/ **N** 1 ◆ **~s** *[of fruit, vegetable]* épluchures *fpl*, pelures *fpl* ; *[of nails]* bouts *mpl* d'ongles ; *[of metal]* rognures *fpl* (de métal) cisaille *f* ◆ **potato ~s** épluchures *fpl* de pommes de terre 2 action *f* d'éplucher *or* de peler *etc* ◆ **~ knife** couteau *m* à éplucher éplucheur *m* ; → **cheeseparing**

pari passu /ˈpærɪˈpæsuː/ ADV *(frm)* de pair

Paris /ˈpærɪs/ N Paris ◆ **the ~ Basin** *(Geog)* le Bassin parisien ; → **plaster** ADJ *[society, nightlife, metro etc]* parisien ◆ **~ fashions** la mode de Paris, la mode parisienne ◆ **~ people** les Parisiens *mpl*

parish /ˈpærɪʃ/ N *(Rel)* paroisse *f* ; *(Brit: civil)* commune *f* ; *(US: in Louisiana)* ≃ comté *m*
COMP **parish church** N église *f* paroissiale
parish council N ≃ conseil *m* municipal *(d'une petite commune rurale, en Angleterre)*
parish hall N salle *f* paroissiale *or* municipale
parish priest N *(Catholic)* curé *m* ; *(Protestant)* pasteur *m*
parish-pump ADJ *(Brit pej) [subject]* d'intérêt purement local ; *[attitude]* borné ◆ **~-pump mentality/politics/rivalries** esprit *m*/politique *f*/rivalités *fpl* de clocher
parish register N registre *m* paroissial
parish school † N école *f* communale

parishioner /pəˈrɪʃənəʳ/ N paroissien(ne) *m(f)*

Parisian /pəˈrɪzɪən/ ADJ *[district, theatre, street]* parisien, de Paris ; *[habit, personality, society]* parisien ; *[life]* à Paris N Parisien(ne) *m(f)*

parity /ˈpærɪtɪ/ N 1 *[of rights, currencies]* parité *f* ; *(in arms race)* équilibre *m* ◆ **they want ~ with their colleagues in the private sector** ils veulent une parité des salaires et des conditions de travail avec leurs collègues du secteur privé 2 *(Fin)* parité *f* ◆ **at ~ (with)** à parité (avec) ◆ **exchange at ~** change *m* au pair *or* à (la) parité 3 *(US Agr)* taux *m* de parité

park /pɑːk/ N 1 *(= public garden)* jardin *m* public, parc *m* ; *(= garden of country house)* parc *m* ; → **car, national, retail, safari**
2 *(Brit Sport = field)* terrain *m*
VT 1 *[+ car etc]* garer ◆ **to ~ the car** garer la voiture, se garer ◆ **don't ~ the car in the street** ne laisse pas la voiture dans la rue ◆ **a line of ~ed cars** une rangée de voitures en stationnement ◆ **he was ~ed near the theatre** il était stationné *or* garé près du théâtre
2 *(* = leave)* **to ~ a child with sb** laisser un enfant chez qn ◆ **I ~ed granddad in an armchair** j'ai installé pépé dans un fauteuil ◆ **she ~ed herself on the sofa/at our table** elle s'est installée sur le canapé/à notre table
VI stationner, se garer ◆ **I was ~ing when I caught sight of him** j'étais en train de me garer quand je l'aperçus ◆ **do not ~ here** ne stationnez pas ici
COMP **park-and-ride** N *stationnement en périphérie d'agglomération combiné à un système de transport en commun*
park bench N banc *m* de parc
park keeper N *(Brit)* gardien(ne) *m(f)* de parc
park ranger N *(in national park)* gardien(ne) *m(f)* de parc national ; *(in forest)* garde *m* forestier ; *(in game reserve)* garde-chasse *m*
park-ride N ⇒ **park-and-ride**
park warden N ⇒ **park keeper**

parka /ˈpɑːkə/ N parka *f*

parkin /ˈpɑːkɪn/ N gâteau *m* à l'avoine et au gingembre

parking /ˈpɑːkɪŋ/ N stationnement *m* ◆ **"parking"** "parking", "stationnement autorisé" ◆ **"no parking"** "défense de stationner", "stationnement interdit" ◆ **~ is very difficult** il est très difficile de trouver à se garer ◆ **there's plenty of ~ (space)** il y a de la place pour se garer
COMP **parking attendant** N gardien *m* de parking, gardien *m* de parc de stationnement
parking bay N emplacement *m (sur un parking)*
parking brake N *(US)* frein *m* à main
parking garage N *(US)* parking *m* (couvert)
parking lights NPL *(US)* feux *mpl* de position
parking lot N *(US)* parking *m*, parc *m* de stationnement
parking meter N parcmètre *m*
parking place, parking space N place *f* de stationnement ◆ **I couldn't find a ~ place** *or* **space** je n'ai pas pu trouver à me garer
parking ticket N P.-V. * *m*, contravention *f*

parkinsonism /ˈpɑːkɪnsənɪzəm/ N parkinsonisme *m*

Parkinson's (disease) /ˈpɑːkɪnsənz(dɪˌziːz)/ N maladie *f* de Parkinson

Parkinson's law /ˈpɑːkɪnsənzlɔː/ N loi *f* de Parkinson *(principe humoristique selon lequel toute tâche finit par occuper l'intégralité du temps qu'on a alloué à son accomplissement)*

parkland /ˈpɑːklænd/ N espace(s) *m(pl)* vert(s)

parkway /ˈpɑːkweɪ/ N *(US)* route *f* (à plusieurs voies) bordée d'espaces verts

parky* /ˈpɑːkɪ/ ADJ *(Brit)* ◆ **it's a bit ~!** il fait frisquet ! *

parlance /ˈpɑːləns/ N langage *m*, parler *m* ◆ **in common ~** en langage courant ◆ **in medical/legal ~** en langage médical/juridique

parlay /ˈpɑːlɪ/ *(US)* VT *(Betting)* réemployer *(les gains d'un précédent pari et le pari originel)* ; *(fig) [+ talent, inheritance]* faire fructifier VI *(fig)* faire fructifier de l'argent

parley /ˈpɑːlɪ/ N pourparlers *mpl* VI *(also Mil)* parlementer *(with* avec) ; *(more frm)* entrer *or* être en pourparlers *(with* avec)

parliament /ˈpɑːləmənt/ N 1 *(= institution, building)* parlement *m* ◆ **Parliament** *(Brit Hist)* Parlement *m* ◆ **the London** *or* **Westminster Parliament** le Parlement de Londres *or* Westminster ◆ **in Parliament** au Parlement ◆ **to go into** *or* **enter Parliament** entrer au Parlement ◆ **the Queen opened Parliament** la reine a ouvert la session parlementaire ; → **house, member** 2 *(= period between elections)* législature *f* ◆ **during the life of this ~** au cours de cette législature

parliamentarian /ˌpɑːləmenˈtɛərɪən/ N 1 *(Brit Parl = MP)* parlementaire *mf*, membre *m* du Parlement 2 *(Brit Hist)* parlementaire *mf* 3 *(US = expert)* spécialiste *mf* des procédures parlementaires ADJ *(Brit Hist)* parlementaire

parliamentary /ˌpɑːləˈmentərɪ/ ADJ *[debate, session, business, language, majority]* parlementaire ◆ **~ candidate** candidat *m* au Parlement
COMP **parliamentary agent** N agent *m* parlementaire
Parliamentary Commissioner N *(Brit)* médiateur *m*, -trice *f*
parliamentary democracy N démocratie *f* parlementaire
parliamentary election N élections *fpl* législatives
parliamentary government N *(NonC)* gouvernement *m* parlementaire
Parliamentary Labour Party N *(Brit)* députés *mpl* du parti travailliste
parliamentary private secretary N *(Brit) parlementaire attaché à un ministre assurant la liaison avec les autres parlementaires*
parliamentary privilege N *(Brit)* immunité *f* parlementaire
parliamentary secretary N *(Brit)* (parlementaire *mf* faisant fonction de) sous-secrétaire *mf* d'État

parlour, parlor *(US)* /ˈpɑːləʳ/ N († : *in house)* petit salon *m* ; *(in convent)* parloir *m* ; († : *in bar)* arrière-salle *f* ; → **beauty, funeral**
COMP **parlor car** N *(US Rail)* pullman *m*
parlour game N jeu *m* de société

parlourmaid /ˈpɑːləmeɪd/ N servante *f*

parlous /ˈpɑːləs/ ADJ *(frm)* alarmant

Parma /ˈpɑːmə/ N Parme
COMP **Parma ham** N jambon *m* de Parme
Parma violet N violette *f* de Parme

Parmesan /ˌpɑːmɪˈzæn/ N (also **Parmesan cheese**) parmesan *m*

Parnassian /pɑːˈnæsɪən/ ADJ parnassien

Parnassus /pɑːˈnæsəs/ N le Parnasse ◆ **(Mount) ~** le mont Parnasse

parochial /pəˈrəʊkɪəl/ ADJ *(Rel)* paroissial ; *(fig pej) [attitude, outlook]* de repli sur soi ◆ **they're very ~** ils ont vraiment l'esprit de clocher, ils ne sont pas très ouverts sur le monde ◆ **Newcastle seemed ~ after his time in London** Newcastle lui semblait très provincial après son séjour à Londres COMP **parochial school** N *(US)* école *f* catholique

parochialism /pəˈrəʊkɪəlɪzəm/ N esprit *m* de clocher

parodist /ˈpærədɪst/ N parodiste *mf*

parody /ˈpærədɪ/ N *(lit, fig)* parodie *f* VT parodier

parole /pəˈrəʊl/ N 1 *(Jur) (= period of release)* liberté *f* conditionnelle ; *(= act of release)* mise *f* en liberté conditionnelle ◆ **on ~** en liberté conditionnelle ◆ **to release sb on ~** mettre qn en liberté conditionnelle ◆ **to break ~** se rendre coupable d'un délit entraînant la révocation de la libération conditionnelle ◆ **ten years without ~** dix ans de prison sans possibilité de libération conditionnelle 2 *(Mil etc)* parole *f* d'honneur ◆ **on ~** sur parole 3 /pæˈrɒl/ *(Ling)* parole *f* VT *[+ prisoner]* mettre *or* placer en liberté conditionnelle
COMP **parole board** N *(Brit) comité de probation et d'assistance aux prisonniers mis en liberté conditionnelle*
parole officer N *(US)* contrôleur *m* judiciaire *(chargé de surveiller un prisonnier en liberté conditionnelle)*

paroquet /ˈpærəkɪt/ N ⇒ **parakeet**

paroxysm /ˈpærəksɪzəm/ N 1 *(Med)* paroxysme *m* 2 *(fig)* **a ~ of tears/laughter/rage** une crise de larmes/rire/colère ◆ **a ~ of coughing** une violente quinte de toux ◆ **in a ~ of grief/rage** au paroxysme de la douleur/de la colère ◆ **in a ~ of delight** dans un transport de joie ◆ **the news sent her into ~s of delight** la nouvelle l'a transportée de joie

parquet /ˈpɑːkeɪ/ N 1 (also **parquet flooring)** parquet *m* 2 *(US Theat)* parterre *m* VT parqueter

parquetry /ˈpɑːkɪtrɪ/ N parquetage *m*, parqueterie *f*

parricidal /ˈpærɪsaɪdl/ ADJ parricide

parricide /ˈpærɪsaɪd/ N 1 *(= act)* parricide *m* 2 *(= person)* parricide *mf*

parrot /ˈpærət/ N perroquet *m* ◆ **he was sick as a ~** ‡ *(Brit hum)* il en était malade * VT *(= repeat) [+ words, speech]* répéter comme un perroquet ; *(= copy) [+ behaviour, actions]* imiter servilement
COMP **parrot cry** N *(pej)* slogan *m*
parrot disease N psittacose *f*
parrot-fashion ADV comme un perroquet
parrot fever N ⇒ **parrot disease**
parrot fish N (pl **parrot fish** *or* **fishes**) poisson *m* perroquet
parrot phrase N ⇒ **parrot cry**

parry /ˈpærɪ/ VT *[+ blow, attack]* parer ; *[+ question]* éluder ; *[+ difficulty]* tourner, éviter VI parer ◆ **she parried with another insult** elle a riposté avec une autre insulte N *(Fencing)* parade *f*

parse /pɑːz/ VT faire l'analyse grammaticale de

parsec /ˈpɑːsek/ N parsec *m*

Parsee /ˈpɑːsiː/ ADJ, N parsi(e) *m(f)*

parser /ˈpɑːzəʳ/ N *(Comput)* analyseur *m* syntaxique

parsimonious /ˌpɑːsɪˈməʊnɪəs/ ADJ parcimonieux

parsimoniously /ˌpɑːsɪˈməʊnɪəslɪ/ ADV avec parcimonie, parcimonieusement

parsimony /ˈpɑːsɪmənɪ/ N parcimonie *f*

parsing /ˈpɑːzɪŋ/ N (*Ling, Scol*) analyse *f* grammaticale

parsley /ˈpɑːslɪ/ N persil *m*
COMP **parsley butter** N beurre *m* maître d'hôtel
parsley sauce N sauce *f* persillée

parsnip /ˈpɑːsnɪp/ N panais *m*

parson /ˈpɑːsn/ N (= *parish priest*) pasteur *m*
COMP **parson's nose** * N (*Culin*) croupion *m*
Parsons table N (*US*) table *f* (*en plastique*)

parsonage /ˈpɑːsənɪdʒ/ N presbytère *m*

part /pɑːt/ N 1 (= *section, division*) partie *f* ◆ **he spent ~ of his childhood in Wales** il a passé une partie de son enfance au pays de Galles ◆ **he lost ~ of his foot in the accident** il a perdu une partie de son pied lors de l'accident ◆ **~s of the play are good** il y a de bons passages dans la pièce ◆ **the funny ~ of it is that ...** le plus drôle dans l'histoire c'est que ... ◆ **~ of him wanted to call her, ~ of him wanted to forget about her** il était partagé entre le désir de l'appeler et l'envie de l'oublier ◆ **it's all ~ of growing up** c'est normal quand on grandit ◆ **to him, it's just ~ of the job** pour lui, ça fait partie du travail ◆ **respect is an important ~ of any relationship** le respect est un élément important de toute relation ◆ **an important ~ of her work is ...** une part importante de son travail consiste à ... ◆ **his Catholicism was an integral ~ of him** sa foi catholique faisait partie intégrante de lui-même ◆ **she never really felt like ~ of the team** elle n'a jamais vraiment eu l'impression de faire partie de l'équipe ◆ **to be ~ and parcel of sth** faire partie (intégrante) de qch ◆ **a penny is the hundredth ~ of a pound** le penny est le centième de la livre ◆ **a man of (many) ~s** (*liter*) (= *gifted*) un homme très doué ; (= *versatile*) un homme qui a plusieurs cordes à son arc ; → **moving, private**

◆ **for the most part** dans l'ensemble, en général

◆ **in part** en partie, partiellement ◆ **the delay was due in ~ to the postal strike** le retard était dû en partie à une grève de la poste

◆ **in parts** par endroits ◆ **the report was badly written and in ~s inaccurate** le rapport était mal écrit et par endroits inexact ◆ **the road was damaged in ~s** la route était endommagée par endroits ◆ **the film was good in ~s** il y avait de bons passages dans le film

2 (= *episode, instalment*) [*of book, play*] partie *f* ; (*Publishing*) livraison *f*, fascicule *m* ; (*Press, Rad, TV: of serial*) épisode *m* ◆ **a six-~ serial, a serial in six ~s** un feuilleton en six épisodes

3 (*in machine, car*) pièce *f* ◆ **you can't get the ~s for this model** on ne trouve pas de pièces pour ce modèle ◆ **moving ~s** pièces *fpl* mobiles ◆ **spare ~s** pièces *fpl* détachées, pièces *fpl* de rechange

4 (*esp Culin* = *measure*) mesure *f* ◆ **three ~s water to one ~ milk** trois mesures d'eau pour une mesure de lait

5 (*Gram*) **principal ~s** [*of verb*] temps *mpl* principaux ; → **comp**

6 (= *share, involvement*) participation *f*, rôle *m* ; (*Cine, Theat*) rôle *m* ◆ **he was just right for the ~** (*Cine, Theat*) il était parfait pour ce rôle ◆ **we all have our ~ to play** nous avons tous notre rôle à jouer ◆ **he had a large ~ in the organization of ...** il a joué un grand rôle dans l'organisation de ... ◆ **she had some ~ in it** elle y était pour quelque chose ◆ **he had no ~ in it** il n'y était pour rien ◆ **I'll have** *or* **I want no ~ in it, I don't want any ~ of it** je ne veux pas m'en mêler ; → **act, play**

◆ **to take part (in sth)** participer (à qch) ◆ **those taking ~** les participants *mpl*

7 (= *side, behalf*) parti *m*, part *f* ◆ **to take sb's ~** (*in quarrel*) prendre le parti de qn, prendre parti pour qn ◆ **for my ~** pour ma part, quant à moi ◆ **an error on the ~ of his secretary** une erreur de la part de sa secrétaire ◆ **to take sth in good ~** † prendre qch du bon côté

8 (*Mus*) partie *f* ; [*of song, fugue*] voix *f* ; (= *sheet of music*) partition *f* ◆ **the violin ~** la partie de violon ◆ **the alto ~** la partie alto ◆ **two-~ song** chant *m* à deux voix

9 (= *place*) ◆ **in foreign ~s** à l'étranger ◆ **in these ~s, in this ~ of the world** * dans le coin*, par ici ◆ **in my ~ of the world** * dans mon pays, chez moi

10 (*US* = *parting*) (*in hair*) raie *f*

ADV (= *partly*) en partie ◆ **she is ~ French** elle a des origines françaises ◆ **the animal was ~ dog, ~ wolf** cet animal était moitié chien, moitié loup ◆ **this novel is ~ thriller, ~ ghost story** ce roman est à la fois un thriller et une histoire de fantômes ◆ **she was ~ fascinated, ~ horrified by the story** cette histoire provoqua chez elle un mélange de fascination et d'horreur

VT 1 [+ *crowd*] ouvrir un passage dans ; [+ *people, boxers*] séparer ; [+ *curtains*] ouvrir, écarter ; [+ *legs*] écarter ◆ **they were ~ed during the war years** ils sont restés séparés pendant la guerre

2 ◆ **to ~ one's hair** se faire une raie ◆ **he ~s his hair at the side/in the centre, his hair is ~ed at the side/in the centre** il porte *or* a la raie sur le côté/au milieu

3 ◆ **to ~ company with sb** (= *leave*) se séparer de qn, quitter qn ; (= *disagree*) ne plus être d'accord avec qn ◆ **they ~ed company** (*lit*) ils se séparèrent, ils se quittèrent ; (*fig*) ils se trouvèrent en désaccord ◆ **the trailer ~ed company with the car** (*hum*) la remorque a faussé compagnie à la voiture

VI (*gen*) 1 (= *take leave of each other*) se quitter ; (= *break up*) [*couple, boxers*] se séparer ; (= *open up*) [*crowd, lips, clouds, waters*] s'ouvrir ◆ **to ~ from sb** quitter qn ; (*permanently*) se séparer de qn ◆ **to ~ with** [+ *money*] débourser ; [+ *possessions*] se défaire de, renoncer à ; [+ *employee etc*] se séparer de ◆ **they ~ed friends, they ~ed amicably** (*lovers, friends*) ils se sont quittés bons amis ; (*business partners*) ils se sont séparés à l'amiable

2 (= *break*) [*rope*] se rompre

COMP **part exchange** N (*Brit*) reprise *f* (en compte) ◆ **to take a car** *etc* **in ~ exchange** reprendre une voiture *etc* (en compte)
part of speech N partie *f* du discours catégorie *f* grammaticale ◆ **what ~ of speech is "of"?** à quelle catégorie grammaticale est-ce que "of" appartient ?
part owner N copropriétaire *mf*
part payment N (= *exchange*) règlement *m* partiel ; (= *deposit*) arrhes *fpl*
part song N chant *m* à plusieurs voix *or* polyphonique
parts per million NPL parties *fpl* par million
part-time → **part-time**
part-timer N travailleur *m*, -euse *f* *or* employé(e) *m(f)* à temps partiel
part work N (*Brit*) fascicule *m*

partake /pɑːˈteɪk/ (pret **partook**, ptp **partaken**) VI (*frm*) ◆ **to ~ in** prendre part à, participer à ◆ **to ~ of** [+ *meal, refreshment*] prendre ; (*fig*) tenir de, avoir quelque chose de

parthenogenesis /ˈpɑːθɪnəʊˈdʒenɪsɪs/ N parthénogenèse *f*

parthenogenetic /ˌpɑːθɪnəʊdʒɪˈnetɪk/ ADJ parthénogénétique

parthenogenetically /ˌpɑːθɪnəʊdʒɪˈnetɪkəlɪ/ ADV parthénogénétiquement

Parthenon /ˈpɑːθənɒn/ N Parthénon *m*

Parthian /ˈpɑːθɪən/ ADJ ◆ **~ shot** flèche *f* du Parthe

partial /ˈpɑːʃəl/ ADJ 1 (= *in part*) [*success, solution, explanation, withdrawal, eclipse, paralysis*] partiel 2 (= *biased*) [*person, viewpoint*] partial (*to, towards* envers), injuste 3 * ◆ **to be ~ to sth** avoir un faible pour qch, être porté sur qch ◆ **to be ~ to doing sth** aimer bien faire qch ◆ **she is not (too) ~ to being disturbed** elle n'aime pas trop qu'on la dérange

partiality /ˌpɑːʃɪˈælɪtɪ/ N 1 (= *bias*) partialité *f* (*for* pour ; *towards* envers) favoritisme *m* 2 (= *liking*) prédilection *f*, penchant *m*, faible *m* (*for* pour)

partially /ˈpɑːʃəlɪ/ ADV 1 (= *partly*) en partie *after vb* ◆ **~ hidden by the trees** caché en partie par les arbres ◆ **the driver was ~ responsible for the accident** le conducteur était en partie responsable de l'accident ◆ **he was only ~ successful** il n'a eu qu'un succès mitigé ◆ **~ clothed** à moitié nu ◆ **~, they were afraid of reprisals** une des raisons est qu'ils avaient peur des représailles ◆ **~ because he was embarrassed** en partie parce qu'il était gêné 2 (= *with bias*) avec partialité, partialement
COMP **partially-sighted** ADJ ◆ **to be ~-sighted** être malvoyant ; → **disabled**
the partially-sighted NPL les malvoyants *mpl*

participant /pɑːˈtɪsɪpənt/ N participant(e) *m(f)* (*in* à)

participate /pɑːˈtɪsɪpeɪt/ VI participer, prendre part (*in* à)

participation /pɑːˌtɪsɪˈpeɪʃən/ N participation *f* (*in* à)

participative /pɑːˈtɪsɪpətɪv/ ADJ [*management, democracy*] participatif

participatory /pɑːtɪsɪˈpeɪtərɪ/ ADJ [*approach, democracy*] participatif ◆ **fishing is the most popular ~ sport in the UK** la pêche est le sport le plus couramment pratiqué au Royaume-Uni

participial /ˌpɑːtɪˈsɪpɪəl/ ADJ participial

participle /ˈpɑːtɪsɪpl/ N participe *m* ◆ **past/present ~** participe *m* passé/présent

particle /ˈpɑːtɪkl/ N 1 (= *small piece*) (*gen, Phys*) particule *f* ; (*fig*) parcelle *f*, grain *m* ◆ **dust ~s, ~s of dust** grains *mpl* de poussière ◆ **food ~s** quantités *fpl* infimes de nourriture ◆ **subatomic ~** particule *f* subatomique ◆ **a ~ of truth/of sense** une parcelle de vérité/de bon sens ◆ **not a ~ of evidence** pas l'ombre d'une preuve, pas la moindre preuve 2 (*Ling*) particule *f*
COMP **particle accelerator** N (*Phys*) accélérateur *m* de particules
particle board N (*US*) panneau *m* de particules
particle physics N physique *f* des particules élémentaires

parti-coloured, parti-colored (*US*) /ˈpɑːtɪˌkʌləd/ ADJ bariolé

particular /pəˈtɪkjʊləʳ/ ADJ 1 (= *specific, distinct*) particulier ◆ **in this ~ case** dans ce cas particulier *or* précis ◆ **there seemed to be no ~ reason for his outburst** son emportement passager ne semblait pas avoir de raison particulière ◆ **for no ~ reason** sans raison précise *or* bien définie ◆ **that ~ brand** cette marque-là ◆ **his ~ chair** son fauteuil à lui ◆ **her ~ type of humour** son genre particulier d'humour, son humour personnel ◆ **my ~ choice** mon choix personnel ◆ **the report moves from the ~ to the general** (= *specific*) le rapport va du particulier au général

◆ **in particular** en particulier ◆ **anything/anybody in ~** quelque chose/quelqu'un en particulier ◆ **nothing/nobody in ~** rien de/personne en particulier ◆ **are you looking for anything in ~?** (*in shop*) vous cherchez quelque chose en particulier ?

2 *(= special)* particulier, spécial ◆ **nothing ~ happened** il ne s'est rien passé de particulier *or* spécial ◆ **he took ~ care over it** il y a mis un soin (tout) particulier ◆ **to be of ~ interest to sb** intéresser qn (tout) particulièrement ◆ **this is of ~ concern to us** ceci nous préoccupe tout particulièrement ◆ **to pay ~ attention to sth** faire bien *or* particulièrement attention à qch ◆ **a ~ friend of his** un de ses meilleurs amis, un de ses amis intimes ◆ **she didn't say anything** ~ elle n'a rien dit de spécial

3 *(= fussy)* exigeant ◆ **she is ~ about whom she talks to** elle ne parle pas à n'importe qui ◆ **he is ~ about his food** il est exigeant *or* difficile pour la nourriture, il ne mange pas n'importe quoi ◆ **which do you want? – I'm not** ~ lequel voulez-vous ? – cela m'est égal *or* je n'ai pas de préférence

4 *(† = exact, detailed) [account]* détaillé, circonstancié

N *(= detail)* détail *m* ◆ **in every** ~ en tout point ◆ **he is wrong in one** ~ il se trompe sur un point

NPL **particulars** *(= information)* détails *mpl*, renseignements *mpl* ; *(= description)* description *f* ; *[of person] (= description)* signalement *m* ; *(= name, address etc)* nom *m* et adresse *f*, coordonnées *fpl* ; *(for official document etc)* caractéristiques *fpl* signalétiques ◆ **full ~s** tous les détails, tous les renseignements ◆ **for further ~s apply to ...** pour de plus amples renseignements s'adresser à ...

particularity /pəˌtɪkjʊ'lærɪtɪ/ N particularité *f*

particularize /pə'tɪkjʊləraɪz/ VT préciser, individualiser VI préciser

particularly /pə'tɪkjʊləlɪ/ ADV 1 *(= especially) [good, bad, well, badly etc]* particulièrement ; *[specify, insist etc]* (tout) particulièrement ◆ **I ~ told you not to do that** je t'ai bien dit de ne pas faire cela, j'ai bien insisté pour que tu ne fasses pas cela ◆ **it's dangerous for children, ~ young ones** c'est dangereux pour les enfants, surtout *or* en particulier *or* notamment les tout jeunes ◆ **not** ~ pas particulièrement 2 *(= very carefully)* méticuleusement, avec grand soin

particulate /pɑː'tɪkjʊlət/ ADJ ◆ **~ emissions** émissions *fpl* de particules NPL **particulates** particules *fpl* dangereuses

parting /'pɑːtɪŋ/ N 1 séparation *f* ; *[of waters]* partage *m* ◆ **the ~ of the ways** *(lit, fig)* la croisée des chemins 2 *(Brit) [of hair]* raie *f* ; *[of mane]* épi *m* ◆ **to have a side/centre** ~ porter *or* avoir la raie sur le côté/au milieu ADJ *[gift]* d'adieu ◆ **~ words** paroles *fpl* d'adieu ◆ **~ shot** *(fig)* pointe *f*, flèche *f* du Parthe *(liter)* ◆ **he paused to deliver a** *or* **his ~ shot** il s'est arrêté pour lancer une dernière pointe *or* la flèche du Parthe *(liter)*

partisan /ˌpɑːtɪ'zæn/ N *(= supporter, fighter)* partisan *m* ADJ *[politics, debate]* partisan ; *[warfare]* de partisans ◆ **~ spirit** *(Pol etc)* esprit *m* de parti

partisanship /ˌpɑːtɪ'zænʃɪp/ N esprit *m* de parti, partialité *f* ; *(= membership)* appartenance *f* à un parti

partita /pɑː'tiːtə/ N (pl **partitas** *or* **partite** /pɑː'tiːteɪ/) *(Mus)* partita *f*

partition /pɑː'tɪʃən/ N 1 (also **partition wall**) cloison *f* ◆ **a glass** ~ une cloison vitrée 2 *(= dividing) [of property]* division *f* ; *[of country]* partition *f*, partage *m* ; *[of estate]* morcellement *m* VT *[+ property]* diviser, partager ; *[+ country]* partager ; *[+ estate]* morceler ; *[+ room]* cloisonner

► **partition off** VT SEP *[+ room, part of room]* cloisonner

⚠ **partition** is only translated by the French word **partition** when it means the division of a country into parts.

partitive /'pɑːtɪtɪv/ ADJ, N partitif *m*

partly /'pɑːtlɪ/ ADV en partie ◆ **~ blue, ~ green** moitié bleu, moitié vert

partner /'pɑːtnəʳ/ N 1 *(gen)* partenaire *mf* ; *(in business partnership)* associé(e) *m(f)* ◆ **our European ~s** nos partenaires européens ◆ **~s in crime** complices *mpl* ; → **senior, sleeping, trading** 2 *(Sport)* partenaire *mf* ; *(= co-driver)* coéquipier *m*, -ière *f* ; *(Dancing)* cavalier *m*, -ière *f* ◆ **take your ~s for a waltz** choisissez vos partenaires pour la valse 3 *(in relationship)* compagnon *m*, compagne *f* ; *(Admin) (cohabiting)* concubin(e) *m(f)* ◆ **sexual** ~ partenaire *mf* sexuel ◆ **bring your ~ along** venez avec votre conjoint VT *(in business)* être l'associé (de), s'associer à ; *(Motor Racing)* être le coéquipier de ; *(Dancing) (gen)* être le cavalier (*or* la cavalière) de ; *(in competitions)* être le (*or* la) partenaire de

partnership /'pɑːtnəʃɪp/ N *(gen)* association *f* ; *(= business)* ≃ société *f* en nom collectif ◆ **limited** ~ (société *f* en) commandite *f* ◆ **to be in** ~ être en association *(with* avec), être associé ◆ **to enter** *or* **go into** ~ s'associer *(with* à, avec) ◆ **to take sb into** ~ prendre qn comme associé ◆ **a doctors'** ~ un cabinet de groupe *(médical)*, une association de médecins ; → **general, working**

partook /pɑː'tʊk/ VB pret of **partake**

partridge /'pɑːtrɪdʒ/ N (pl **partridges** *or* **partridge**) perdrix *f* ; *(young bird, also Culin)* perdreau *m*

part-time /'pɑː'taɪm/ ADJ 1 *[work, employment]* à temps partiel ; *(= half-time)* à mi-temps ◆ **to do ~ work, to have a ~ job** travailler à temps partiel *or* à mi-temps ◆ **on a ~ basis** à temps partiel 2 *[employee, staff, student]* à temps partiel N ◆ **to be on** ~ * être au chômage partiel ADV *[work, study]* à temps partiel

parturition /ˌpɑːtjʊə'rɪʃən/ N parturition *f*

partway /ˌpɑːt'weɪ/ ADV ◆ **~ along** (*or* **through** *or* **there**) à mi-chemin

party /'pɑːtɪ/ N 1 *(Pol etc)* parti *m* ◆ **political/Conservative/Labour** ~ parti *m* politique/conservateur/travailliste

2 *(= group) [of travellers]* groupe *m*, troupe* *f* ; *[of workmen]* équipe *f*, brigade *f* ; *(Mil)* détachement *m*, escouade *f* ; → **boarding, rescue, working**

3 *(= celebration)* fête *f* ; *(in the evening)* soirée *f* ; *(formal)* réception *f* ◆ **to give** *or* **have** *or* **throw*** **a** ~ organiser une fête, inviter des amis ; *(more formal gathering)* donner une réception *or* une soirée ◆ **birthday** ~ fête *f* d'anniversaire ◆ **farewell** ~ fête *f* d'adieu ◆ **retirement** ~ cocktail *m* *or* pot *m* de départ ◆ **launch** ~ lancement *m* ◆ **children's** ~ goûter *m* d'enfants ◆ **private** ~ réception *f* privée ◆ **what does he bring to the ~?** *(fig)* quelle contribution apporte-t-il ? ; → **bottle, Christmas, dinner, garden, tea**

4 *(Jur etc)* partie *f* ◆ **all parties concerned** toutes les parties concernées, tous les intéressés ◆ **to be ~ to a suit** être en cause ◆ **to become a ~ to a contract** signer un contrat ◆ **injured ~, ~ aggrieved** partie *f* lésée, victime *f* ◆ **innocent** ~ innocent(e) *m(f)* ◆ **I will not be (a) ~ to any dishonesty** je ne me ferai le (*or* la) complice d'aucune malhonnêteté ◆ **to be (a) ~ to a crime/to treachery** être complice d'un crime/d'une trahison ◆ **the government insists it will never become a ~ to this conflict** le gouvernement affirme catégoriquement qu'il ne prendra jamais part à ce conflit ◆ **they refused to be ~ to the negotiations** ils ont refusé de prendre part *or* participer aux négociations ; → **guilty, moving, prevailing, third**

5 *(† ‡ hum = person)* individu *m*

6 *(Telec)* correspondant *m* ◆ **your ~ is on the line** votre correspondant est en ligne

VI * faire la fête ◆ **let's ~!** faisons la fête ! ◆ **I'm not a great one for ~ing*** je ne suis pas fêtard(e)*

COMP *[politics, leader]* de parti, du parti ; *[disputes]* de partis

party animal* N fêtard(e)* *m(f)*

party dress N robe *f* habillée ; *(= evening dress)* robe *f* de soirée

party hat N chapeau *m* de cotillon

party line N *(Pol)* politique *f* *or* ligne *f* du parti ; *(Telec)* ligne *f* commune à plusieurs abonnés ◆ **to follow** *or* **toe the ~ line** *(Pol)* suivre la ligne du parti, être dans la ligne du parti ; see also **toe**

party list N scrutin *m* de liste

party machine N *(Pol)* machine *f* *or* administration *f* du parti

party manners* NPL ◆ **his ~ manners were terrible** sa façon de se tenir en société était abominable ◆ **the children were on their ~ manners** les enfants se sont conduits de façon exemplaire

party piece* N ◆ **to do one's ~ piece** faire son numéro*

party plan N *(= system)* vente *f* par réunions ; *(= party)* réunion *f* de vente à domicile

party political ADJ *(Rad, TV)* ◆ **~ political broadcast** *émission réservée à un parti politique* ◆ **this is not a ~ political question** cette question ne relève pas de la ligne du parti

party politics N politique *f* de parti ; *(pej)* politique *f* politicienne

party pooper* N rabat-joie *m inv*, trouble-fête *mf*

party popper N serpentin *m*

party spirit N *(Pol)* esprit *m* de parti ; *(= gaiety)* entrain *m*

party wall N mur *m* mitoyen

partygoer /'pɑːtɪˌgəʊəʳ/ N *(gen)* habitué(e) *m(f)* des réceptions ; *(on specific occasion)* invité(e) *m(f)*

PASCAL, Pascal /pæs'kæl/ N Pascal *m*

paschal /'pɑːskəl/ ADJ *(Rel)* pascal COMP **the Paschal Lamb** N l'agneau *m* pascal

pasha /'pæʃə/ N pacha *m*

pashmina /pæʃ'miːnə/ N pashmina *m*

pass /pɑːs/ N 1 *(= permit) [of journalist, worker etc]* coupe-file *m*, laissez-passer *m inv* ; *(Rail etc)* carte *f* d'abonnement ; *(Theat)* billet *m* de faveur ; *(to museum etc)* laissez-passer *m* ; *(Naut)* lettre *f* de mer ; *(Mil etc) (= safe conduct)* sauf-conduit *m*

2 *(in mountains)* col *m*, défilé *m* ; → **sell**

3 *(in exam)* moyenne *f*, mention *f* passable ◆ **did you get a ~?** avez-vous eu la moyenne ?, avez-vous été reçu ? ◆ **to get a ~ in history** être reçu en histoire

4 *(* = state)* **things have come to a pretty ~ when ...** il faut que les choses aillent bien mal pour que ... ◆ **things have reached such a ~ that ...** les choses en sont arrivées à un tel point que ...

5 *(Ftbl etc)* passe *f* ; *(Fencing)* botte *f*, attaque *f*

6 *(= sexual advance)* ◆ **to make a ~*** at sb faire des avances* à qn

VI 1 *(= come, go)* passer *(through* par) ; *[procession]* défiler ; *(= overtake)* dépasser, doubler ◆ **to let sb** ~ laisser passer qn ◆ **to ~ behind/in front of** passer derrière/devant ◆ **the procession ~ed down the street** la procession a descendu la rue ◆ **to ~ out of sight** disparaître ◆ **letters ~ed between them** ils ont échangé des lettres ◆ **a knowing look ~ed between them** ils ont échangé un regard complice ◆ **the virus ~es easily from one person to another** le virus se transmet facilement d'une personne à l'autre ◆ **to ~ into history/legend** entrer dans l'histoire/la légende ◆ **the word has ~ed into the language** le mot est entré dans la langue

2 *[time]* (se) passer, s'écouler ◆ **three hours/days/years had ~ed** trois heures/jours/années s'étaient écoulé(e)s ◆ **the afternoon ~ed pleasantly** l'après-midi a passé *or* s'est passé agréablement ◆ **how time ~es!** comme le temps passe ! ◆ **I'm very conscious of time ~ing** j'ai une conscience aiguë du temps qui passe

3 *(esp Chem = change)* se transformer *(into* en)

4 *(esp Jur = transfer)* passer, être transmis ◆ **the estate ~ed to my sister** la propriété est revenue à ma sœur ◆ **the land has now ~ed into private hands** le terrain appartient désormais à un propriétaire privé

5 *(= go away) [pain, crisis]* passer ; *[danger]* disparaître ; *[memory]* s'effacer, disparaître ; *[storm]* cesser ◆ **to let an opportunity ~** laisser passer une occasion ◆ **the deadline ~ed this morning** le délai a expiré ce matin

6 *(in exam)* être reçu *(in* en)

7 *(= take place)* se passer, avoir lieu ◆ **all that ~ed between them** tout ce qui s'est passé entre eux ◆ **to bring sth to ~** *(liter)* accomplir qch, réaliser qch ◆ **it came to ~ that ...** *(liter)* il advint que ...

8 *(= be accepted) [coins]* avoir cours ; *[behaviour]* convenir, être acceptable ; *[project]* passer ◆ **to ~ under the name of ...** être connu sous le nom de ... ◆ **he tried to ~ for a doctor** il a essayé de se faire passer pour (un) médecin ◆ **what ~es for** *or* **as law and order in this country** ce que l'on appelle l'ordre public dans ce pays ◆ **a cup of something that ~ed for coffee** une tasse d'un breuvage auquel ils donnaient le nom de café ◆ **she would ~ for 20** on lui donnerait 20 ans ◆ **will this do? – oh, it'll ~** * est-ce que ceci convient ? – oh, ça peut aller ◆ **let it ~!** * *(of insult)* laisse tomber ! * ◆ **that's not exactly right, but let it ~** ce n'est pas exactement ça, mais passons *or* ça ne fait rien ◆ **he let it ~** il l'a laissé passer, il ne l'a pas relevé ◆ **he couldn't let that ~** il ne pouvait pas laisser passer ça

9 *(Cards)* passer ◆ **(I) ~!** *(in games)* (je) passe ! ; *(fig)* aucune idée ! ◆ **I'll have to ~ on that one** * *(fig = can't answer)* là je donne ma langue au chat ◆ **I'll ~ on that one** * *(= no thanks)* je m'en passerai ; *(in discussion)* je passe mon tour

10 *(Sport)* faire une passe *(to* à) ◆ **to ~ forward/back** faire une passe avant/arrière

VT 1 *(= go past) [+ building, person]* passer devant ; *[+ barrier, frontier, customs]* passer ; *(in car = overtake)* dépasser, doubler ; *(Sport = go beyond)* dépasser ◆ **when you have ~ed the town hall ...** quand vous aurez dépassé la mairie ... ◆ **to ~ the finishing line** *(Sport)* passer la ligne d'arrivée ◆ **they ~ed each other on the way** ils se sont croisés en chemin ◆ **no word ~ed his lips** *(frm)* il ne souffla *or* ne dit pas un mot ◆ **no meat has ~ed my lips for 20 years** *(frm)* il y a 20 ans que je n'ai plus mangé de viande

2 *(= get through) [+ exam]* être reçu à *or* admis à, réussir ◆ **the film ~ed the censors** le film a reçu le visa de la censure ; → **muster**

3 *[+ time]* passer ◆ **just to ~ the time** pour passer le temps ◆ **to ~ the evening reading** passer la soirée à lire ; → **time**

4 *(= hand over)* (faire) passer ◆ **please ~ the salt** faites passer le sel s'il vous plaît ◆ **to ~ a dish round the table** faire passer un plat autour de la table ◆ **~ me the box** passez-moi la boîte ◆ **to ~ sth down the line** faire passer qch (de main en main) ◆ **~ the word that it's time to go** faites passer la consigne que c'est l'heure de partir ◆ **we should ~ this information to the police** nous devrions passer *or* transmettre ces informations à la police ; → **buck**

5 *(on phone)* passer

6 *(= accept, allow) [+ candidate]* recevoir, admettre ; *(Parl) [+ bill]* voter, faire passer ◆ **the censors ~ed the film** le film a reçu le visa de censure ◆ **they didn't ~ him** *(Scol, Univ)* ils l'ont recalé ◆ **the doctor ~ed him fit for work** le docteur l'a déclaré apte à reprendre le travail ◆ **to ~ the proofs (for press)** *(Publishing)* donner le bon à tirer

7 *(= utter)* **to ~ comment (on sth)** faire un commentaire (sur qch) ◆ **to ~ remarks about sb/sth** faire des observations sur qn/qch ; → **judg(e)ment, sentence**

8 *(= move)* passer ◆ **he ~ed his hand over his brow** il s'est passé la main sur le front ◆ **he ~ed his handkerchief over his face** il a passé son mouchoir sur son visage ◆ **to ~ a rope through a ring** passer une corde dans un anneau ◆ **to ~ a cloth over a table** donner *or* passer un coup de chiffon sur une table ◆ **to ~ a knife through sth** enfoncer un couteau dans qch ◆ **to ~ sth through a sieve** *(Culin)* passer qch (au tamis) ◆ **to ~ in review** *(Mil, fig)* passer en revue

9 *(Sport) [+ ball]* passer

10 *[+ forged money]* (faire) passer, écouler ; *[+ stolen goods]* faire passer

11 *(= surpass)* **to ~ comprehension** dépasser l'entendement ◆ **to ~ belief** être incroyable

12 *(Med = excrete)* **to ~ water** uriner ◆ **to ~ blood** avoir du sang dans les urines ◆ **to ~ a stone** évacuer un calcul

COMP **pass degree** N *(Univ)* ≈ licence *f* obtenue sans mention

pass mark N *(Scol, Univ)* moyenne *f* ◆ **to get a ~ mark** avoir la moyenne

pass-the-parcel N ◆ **to play ~-the-parcel** ≈ jouer au furet

pass-through N *(US)* passe-plat *m*

► **pass along** VI passer, circuler, passer son chemin

VT SEP 1 *(lit) [+ object, book etc]* faire passer (de main en main)

2 ⇒ **pass on vt sep**

► **pass away** VI *(euph = die)* s'éteindre *(euph)*, décéder *(frm or euph)*

► **pass back** VT SEP *[+ object]* rendre, retourner ◆ **I will now ~ you back to the studio** *(Rad, TV)* je vais rendre l'antenne au studio

► **pass by** VI passer (à côté) ; *[procession]* défiler ◆ **I saw him ~ing by** je l'ai vu passer ◆ **to ~ by on the other side** *(fig = fail to help)* détourner les yeux

VT SEP ◆ **life has ~ed me by** je n'ai pas vraiment vécu ◆ **the war seemed to ~ them by** la guerre ne semblait pas les toucher ◆ **fashion just ~es him by** la mode le laisse froid

► **pass down** VI *[inheritance etc]* être transmis, revenir *(to* à)

VT SEP transmettre ◆ **to ~ sth down (in a family)** transmettre qch par héritage (dans une famille) ◆ **~ed down from father to son/from mother to daughter** transmis de père en fils/de mère en fille

► **pass in** VT SEP (faire) passer ◆ **she ~ed the parcel in through the window** elle a passé *or* fait passer le colis par la fenêtre

► **pass off** VI 1 *(= subside) [faintness, headache etc]* passer, se dissiper

2 *(= take place) [events]* se passer, se dérouler ◆ **the demonstration ~ed off peacefully/without incident** la manifestation s'est déroulée pacifiquement/sans incident

VT SEP faire passer, faire prendre ◆ **to ~ someone off as someone else** faire passer une personne pour une autre ◆ **to ~ something off as something else** faire passer une chose pour une autre ◆ **to ~ o.s. off as a doctor** se faire passer pour (un) médecin ◆ **to ~ sth off on sb** repasser *or* refiler * qch à qn

► **pass on** VI 1 *(euph = die)* s'éteindre *(euph)*, décéder *(frm or euph)*

2 *(= continue one's way)* passer son chemin, ne pas s'arrêter ◆ **to ~ on to a new subject** passer à un nouveau sujet

VT SEP *(= hand on) [+ object]* (faire) passer *(to* à) ; *[+ news]* faire circuler, faire savoir ; *[+ message]* transmettre ◆ **take it and ~ it on** prends et fais passer ◆ **to ~ on old clothes to sb** repasser de vieux vêtements à qn ◆ **you've ~ed your cold on to me** tu m'as passé ton rhume ◆ **to ~ on a tax to the consumer** répercuter un impôt sur le consommateur

► **pass out** VI 1 *(= faint)* s'évanouir, perdre connaissance, tomber dans les pommes * ; *(from drink)* tomber ivre mort ; *(= fall asleep)* s'endormir comme une masse

2 *(Brit = complete training) (Police)* finir son entraînement *(avec succès)* ; *(Mil)* finir ses classes *(avec succès)*

VT SEP *[+ leaflets etc]* distribuer

► **pass over** VI *(euph) (= die)* ⇒ **pass away**

VT SEP *[+ person, event, matter] (= fail to mention)* ne pas mentionner ; *(= fail to take into consideration)* ne pas prendre en considération ◆ **the good work they have done is ~ed over in this article** le bon travail qu'ils ont fait n'est même pas mentionné dans cet article ◆ **to ~ sth over in silence** passer qch sous silence ◆ **he was ~ed over in favour of his brother** on lui a préféré son frère ◆ **they ~ed over Paul in favour of Robert** ils ont donné la préférence à Robert au détriment de Paul ◆ **she was ~ed over for promotion** on ne lui a pas accordé la promotion qu'elle attendait

VT FUS *(= ignore)* passer sous silence, ne pas relever

► **pass round** VT SEP *[+ bottle]* faire passer ; *[+ sweets, leaflets]* distribuer ◆ **to ~ the hat round** * *(fig)* faire la quête

► **pass through** VI passer ◆ **I can't stop, I'm only ~ing through** je ne peux pas rester, je ne fais que passer

VT FUS *[+ country, area, substance, net]* traverser ; *[+ hardships]* subir, endurer ◆ **this thread is too coarse to ~ through the needle** ce fil est trop gros pour passer dans l'aiguille

► **pass up** VT SEP 1 *(lit)* passer

2 *(* = forego) [+ chance, opportunity]* laisser passer ◆ **she ~ed him up for promotion** elle ne lui a pas accordé la promotion qu'il attendait ◆ **he was ~ed up for the job** on a pris quelqu'un d'autre que lui pour cet emploi ◆ **she ~ed the film up for a rôle in a theatre play** elle a décliné un rôle dans ce film pour jouer dans une pièce de théâtre

⚠ Don't use **passer** in the context 'to pass an exam'.

passable /ˈpɑːsəbl/ ADJ 1 *(= tolerable)* passable, assez bon ◆ **he spoke ~ French** il parlait assez bien (le) français 2 *[road]* praticable, carrossable ; *[river]* franchissable

passably /ˈpɑːsəblɪ/ ADV assez ◆ **he spoke ~ good French** il parlait assez bien (le) français ◆ **she was doing ~ well at school** elle avait d'assez bons résultats à l'école

passage /ˈpæsɪdʒ/ N 1 *(= passing) (lit)* passage *m* ; *[of bill, law]* adoption *f* ; *(fig)* passage *m*, transition *f (from ... to* de ... à) ◆ **with the ~ of time he understood** avec le temps il finit par comprendre ◆ **her ~ through college** le temps qu'elle a passé à l'université ◆ **~ of** *or* **at arms** *(fig, liter)* passe *f* d'armes ; → **bird, rite, safe**

2 *(Naut)* voyage *m*, traversée *f* ◆ **he worked his ~ to Australia** il a travaillé pour se payer la traversée *or* son voyage en Australie

3 *(= way through:* also **passageway)** passage *m* ◆ **to force a ~ through sth** se frayer un passage *or* un chemin à travers qch ◆ **to leave a ~** laisser un passage, laisser le passage libre

4 (also **passageway**) *(indoors)* couloir *m*, corridor *m* ; *(outdoors)* ruelle *f*, passage *m*

5 *(Mus)* passage *m* ; *[of text]* passage *m* ◆ **selected ~s** *(Literat)* morceaux *mpl* choisis

passageway /ˈpæsɪdʒweɪ/ N ⇒ **passage 3, 4**

passbook /ˈpɑːsbʊk/ N (= *bank book*) livret *m* (bancaire)

passé /ˈpæseɪ/ ADJ *[play, book, person]* vieux jeu *inv*, démodé, dépassé* ; *[woman]* défraîchi, fané

passel /ˈpæsəl/ N *(US)* ◆ **a ~ of ...** une ribambelle de ..., un tas* de ...

passenger /ˈpæsndʒəʳ/ N *(in train)* voyageur *m*, -euse *f* ; *(in boat, plane, car)* passager *m*, -ère *f* ◆ **he's just a ~** *(fig pej)* il n'est vraiment qu'un poids mort

COMP **passenger car** N *(US)* ⇒ **passenger coach**

passenger cell N *(in car)* habitacle *m*

passenger coach N *(in train)* voiture *f* or wagon *m* de voyageurs

passenger door N *[of car]* portière *f* avant côté passager

passenger enquiries NPL (also **passenger service enquiries**) renseignements *mpl*

passenger ferry N ferry *m*

passenger jet N avion *m* de ligne

passenger list N liste *f* des passagers

passenger mile N *(on plane)* ≈ kilomètre-passager *m* ; *(on train etc)* ≈ kilomètre-voyageur *m*

passenger seat N *[of car] (in front)* siège *m* du passager ; *(in back)* siège *m* arrière

passenger ship N navire *m* à passagers

passenger station N *(Rail)* gare *f* de voyageurs

passenger train N train *m* de voyageurs

passe-partout /ˈpæspɑːtuː/ N 1 (= *master key*) passe-partout *m inv (clé)*, passe *m* 2 *(Art)* ~ **(frame)** (encadrement *m* en) sous-verre *m*

passer-by /ˈpɑːsəˈbaɪ/ N (pl **passers-by**) passant(e) *m(f)*

passim /ˈpæsɪm/ ADV passim

passing /ˈpɑːsɪŋ/ ADJ 1 (= *moving by*) *[person, car]* qui passe (or passait etc)

2 (= *brief*) éphémère, passager ◆ **a ~ desire** un désir fugitif ◆ **a ~ interest in sth/sb** un intérêt éphémère pour qch/qn, un intérêt passager pour qch/qn ◆ **a ~ acquaintance** une vague connaissance ◆ **to have a ~ acquaintance with sb/sth** connaître vaguement qn/qch ◆ **a ~ remark** une remarque en passant ◆ **to bear only a ~ resemblance to sb/sth** ne ressembler que vaguement à qn/qch ◆ **to bear more than a ~ resemblance to sb/sth** ressembler beaucoup à qn/qch ◆ **with each** or **every ~ day** de jour en jour ◆ **with each** or **every ~ year** d'année en année, année après année

ADV († or *liter*) extrêmement ◆ **~ fair** de toute beauté

N 1 ◆ **with the ~ of time** avec le temps ◆ **in ~** en passant

2 *[of train, car]* passage *m* ; *(in car = overtaking)* dépassement *m*

3 *(euph = death)* mort *f*, trépas *m (liter)*

COMP **passing bell** N glas *m*

passing note N *(Mus)* note *f* de passage

passing-out parade N *(Mil)* défilé *m* de promotion

passing place N *(in road)* aire *f* de croisement

passing shot N *(Tennis)* passing-shot *m*, tir *m* passant

passion /ˈpæʃən/ N 1 (= *love*) passion *f (for de)* ◆ **to have a ~ for music** être passionné de musique, adorer la musique ◆ **I have a ~ for strong colours** j'adore les couleurs vives 2 (= *burst of anger*) colère *f* ; *(stronger)* rage *f* ◆ **fit of ~** accès *m* de rage ◆ **to be in a ~** être furieux ; → **fly³** 3 (= *strong emotion*) passion *f*, émotion *f* violente 4 *(Rel, Mus)* **Passion** Passion *f* ◆ **the St John/St Matthew Passion** la Passion selon saint Jean/saint Matthieu

COMP **passion fruit** N fruit *m* de la passion, maracuja *m*

Passion play N *(Rel)* mystère *m* de la Passion *(représentation théâtrale)*

Passion Sunday N *(Rel)* dimanche *m* de la Passion

Passion Week N *(Rel)* semaine *f* de la Passion

passionate /ˈpæʃənɪt/ ADJ *[person, plea, love, embrace]* passionné ; *[speech]* véhément

passionately /ˈpæʃənɪtlɪ/ ADV *[argue, kiss, make love]* avec passion ; *[believe]* passionnément ; *[convinced, concerned]* passionnément ; *[opposed]* farouchement ◆ **to be ~ fond of sth** adorer qch ◆ **to be ~ in love with sb** aimer passionnément qn ◆ **a ~-held opinion** une opinion défendue or soutenue avec passion

passionflower /ˈpæʃən,flaʊəʳ/ N passiflore *f*, fleur *f* de la Passion

passionless /ˈpæʃənlɪs/ ADJ sans passion

passive /ˈpæsɪv/ ADJ 1 *[person]* (= *motionless*) passif, inerte ; (= *unresponsive*) passif, soumis ; *[role, attitude]* passif ◆ **his response was ~** il n'a pas vraiment réagi 2 *(Ling) [vocabulary, understanding]* passif 3 *(Gram) [tense, voice etc]* passif ; *[verb]* au passif N *(Gram)* passif *m* ◆ **in the ~** au passif

COMP **passive balance of trade** N balance *f* commerciale déficitaire

passive disobedience N *(Pol)* désobéissance *f* passive

passive resistance N *(Pol)* résistance *f* passive

passive restraint N *(in car)* dispositif *m* de sécurité passive

passive smoker N non-fumeur *m*, -euse *f* affecté(e) par le tabagisme passif

passive smoking N tabagisme *m* passif

passively /ˈpæsɪvlɪ/ ADV passivement ; *(Gram)* au passif

passiveness /ˈpæsɪvnɪs/, **passivity** /pæˈsɪvɪtɪ/ N passivité *f*

passkey /ˈpɑːskiː/ N passe-partout *m inv*, passe* *m*

Passover /ˈpɑːsəʊvəʳ/ N pâque *f* (juive)

passport /ˈpɑːspɔːt/ N passeport *m* ◆ **a British/American/French** *etc* **~** un passeport britannique/américain/français *etc* ◆ **visitor's ~** *(Brit)* passeport *m* temporaire ◆ **~ to success** clé *f* de la réussite ◆ **the lottery could be your ~ to riches** la loterie pourrait vous ouvrir les portes de la fortune

COMP **passport control** N contrôle *m* des passeports

passport holder N titulaire *mf* de passeport ◆ **are you a British ~ holder?** avez-vous un passeport britannique ?

passport office N (= *building*) bureau *m* du contrôle des passeports ; (= *organization*) service *m* du contrôle des passeports

password /ˈpɑːswɜːd/ N mot *m* de passe

past /pɑːst/ N 1 passé *m* ◆ **in the ~** *(gen)* dans le passé ; *(longer ago)* autrefois ◆ **several times in the ~** plusieurs fois dans le passé ◆ **in the ~, many of these babies would have died** autrefois, beaucoup de ces bébés seraient morts ◆ **all the happy times in the ~** tous les moments heureux du passé ◆ **events in the recent ~ have demonstrated that ...** certains événements récents ont montré que ... ◆ **as in the ~** comme par le passé ◆ **she lives in the ~** elle vit dans le passé ◆ **it's a thing of the ~** cela appartient au passé ◆ **new vaccines could make these illnesses a thing of the ~** de nouveaux vaccins pourraient faire disparaître ces maladies ◆ **I thought you'd quarrelled? – that's a thing of the ~** or **that's all in the ~** je croyais que vous vous étiez disputés ? – c'est de l'histoire ancienne ◆ **we have to learn the lessons of the ~** il nous faut tirer les leçons du passé ◆ **do you know about his ~?** vous connaissez son passé ? ◆ **a woman with a ~** une femme au passé chargé

2 *(Gram)* passé *m* ◆ **in the ~** au passé

ADJ 1 *(gen)* passé ◆ **for some time ~** depuis quelque temps ◆ **in times ~** autrefois, (au temps) jadis ◆ **in ~ centuries** pendant les siècles passés ◆ **the ~ week** la semaine dernière or passée ◆ **the ~ few days/years** ces derniers jours/dernières années ◆ **she's been out of work for the ~ three years** elle est au chômage depuis trois ans ◆ **all that is now ~** tout cela c'est du passé ◆ **the time for recriminations is ~** le temps des récriminations est révolu ◆ **~ president** ancien président *m*

2 *(Gram: gen)* passé ; *[verb]* au passé ; *[form, ending]* du passé

PREP 1 *(beyond in time)* plus de ◆ **it is ~ 11 o'clock** il est plus de 11 heures, il est 11 heures passées ◆ **half ~ three** *(Brit)* trois heures et demie ◆ **(a) quarter ~ three** *(Brit)* trois heures et quart ◆ **at 20 ~ three** *(Brit)* à 3 heures 20 ◆ **the train goes at five ~** * *(Brit)* le train part à cinq* ◆ **she is ~ 60** elle a plus de 60 ans, elle a 60 ans passés

2 (= *beyond in space*) au delà de, plus loin que ◆ **~ it** au delà, plus loin ◆ **just ~ the post office** un peu plus loin que la poste, juste après la poste ◆ **I think we've gone ~ it** (= *missed it*) je pense que nous l'avons dépassé ◆ **he stared straight ~ me** il a fait comme s'il ne me voyait pas

3 (= *in front of*) devant ◆ **he goes ~ the house every day** tous les jours il passe devant la maison ◆ **he rushed ~ me** il est passé devant moi à toute allure ; (= *overtook me*) il m'a dépassé à toute allure

4 (= *beyond limits of*) au delà de ◆ **~ endurance** insupportable ◆ **it is ~ all understanding** cela dépasse l'entendement ◆ **I'm ~ caring** je ne m'en fais plus, j'ai cessé de m'en faire ◆ **he's ~ work** il n'est plus en état de travailler ◆ **I'm long ~ being surprised at anything he does** il y a longtemps que je ne m'étonne plus de ce qu'il peut (encore) inventer ◆ **he's a bit ~ it (now)*** il n'est plus dans la course* ◆ **that cake is ~ its best** ce gâteau n'est plus très frais ◆ **I wouldn't put it ~ her* to have done it** je la crois capable d'avoir fait ça ◆ **I wouldn't put it ~ him** cela ne m'étonnerait pas de lui

ADV

> When **past** is an element in a phrasal verb, eg **let past**, **run past**, **squeeze past**, look up the verb.

auprès, devant ◆ **to go** or **walk ~** passer ; → **march**

COMP **past anterior** N passé *m* antérieur

past definite N ⇒ **past historic**

past historic N passé *m* simple

past master N *(fig)* ◆ **to be a ~ master at** or **of sth** être expert en qch ◆ **to be a ~ master at doing sth** avoir l'art de faire qch

past participle N participe *m* passé

past perfect N plus-que-parfait *m*

past tense N passé *m*, forme *f* passée ◆ **in the ~ tense** au passé

pasta /ˈpæstə/ N *(NonC)* pâtes *fpl*

paste /peɪst/ N 1 *(Culin = spread etc) (meat)* pâté *m* ; *(fish)* beurre *m*, mousse *f* ; *(vegetable, fruit)* purée *f* ◆ **mix the butter and flour into a ~** travaillez le beurre et la farine pour en faire une pâte ◆ **liver ~** pâté *m* or crème *f* de foie ◆ **tomato ~** concentré *m* or purée *f* de tomate ◆ **garlic ~** purée *f* d'ail ◆ **almond ~** pâte *f* d'amandes

2 (= *glue*) colle *f* ◆ **wallpaper ~** colle *f* pour papier peint

3 *(jewellery)* strass *m*

VT 1 coller ; *[+ wallpaper]* enduire de colle ◆ **to ~ photos into an album** coller des photos dans un album

2 (*Comput*) coller, insérer ◆ **to ~ text into a document** insérer du texte dans un document 3 ⁑ (*= thrash*) flanquer une raclée à * ; (*= defeat*) flanquer une déculottée à * ; (*= criticize*) descendre en flammes *

COMP [*jewellery*] en strass

paste-up N (*Comput*) collage *m* ; (*Typ*) montage *m*

► **paste up** VT SEP [*+ notice, list*] afficher ; [*+ photos etc*] coller ; (*Typ*) monter

N ◆ **paste-up** → **paste**

pasteboard /ˈpeɪstbɔːd/ N 1 (*= card*) carton *m* 2 (*US:* also **pastry board**) planche *f* à pâtisserie

pastel /ˈpæstəl/ N 1 (*= pencil*) (crayon *m*) pastel *m* 2 (*= drawing*) (dessin *m* au) pastel *m* 3 (also **pastel colour**) ton *m* pastel *inv*

pastern /ˈpæstən/ N paturon *m*

pasteurization /ˌpæstəraɪˈzeɪʃən/ N pasteurisation *f*

pasteurize /ˈpæstəraɪz/ VT pasteuriser

pasteurized /ˈpæstəraɪzd/ ADJ pasteurisé

pastiche /pæsˈtiːʃ/ N pastiche *m*

pastille /ˈpæstɪl/ N pastille *f*

pastime /ˈpɑːstaɪm/ N passe-temps *m inv*, divertissement *m*, distraction *f*

pasting ⁑ /ˈpeɪstɪŋ/ N (*= thrashing*) raclée * *f* ; (*= defeat*) déculottée * *f* ◆ **to give sb a ~** (*physically*) flanquer une raclée à qn * ; (*= defeat*) flanquer une déculottée à qn * ; (*= criticize*) descendre qn en flammes *

pastor /ˈpɑːstəʳ/ N pasteur *m*

pastoral /ˈpɑːstərəl/ ADJ 1 (*= rural*) pastoral, champêtre ; (*Agr*) de pâture ; (*Literat*) pastoral ; (*fig, liter*) bucolique, champêtre ◆ **~ land** pâturages *mpl* 2 (*Rel*) pastoral ◆ **~ letter** lettre *f* pastorale 3 (*Educ etc*) [*role, duties*] de conseiller ◆ **in a ~ capacity** dans un rôle de conseiller N (*Literat, Rel*) pastorale *f* COMP **pastoral care** N (*Educ*) tutorat *m*

pastrami /pəˈstrɑːmɪ/ N *bœuf fumé très épicé*

pastry /ˈpeɪstrɪ/ N 1 (*NonC*) pâte *f* ; → **puff, short** 2 (*= cake*) pâtisserie *f*

COMP **pastry board** N planche *f* à pâtisserie

pastry brush N pinceau *m* à pâtisserie

pastry case N croûte *f* ◆ **in a ~ case** en croûte

pastry chef, pastry cook N pâtissier *m*, -ière *f*

pastry cutter N (*for cutting*) coupe-pâte *m inv* ; (*for shapes*) emporte-pièce *m*

pasturage /ˈpɑːstjʊrɪdʒ/ N pâturage *m*

pasture /ˈpɑːstʃəʳ/ N (*Agr*) pré *m*, pâturage *m* ◆ **to put out to ~** (*lit*) mettre au pré *or* au pâturage ; (*fig*) mettre à la retraite ◆ **to move on to ~s new** changer d'horizon *or* d'air ◆ **to seek ~s new** chercher de nouveaux horizons, chercher à changer d'air *or* d'horizon ◆ **greener ~s** cieux *mpl* plus cléments VI paître VT faire paître, pacager COMP **pasture land** N herbage *m*, pâturage(s) *m(pl)*

pasty[1] /ˈpeɪstɪ/ ADJ pâteux ; (*pej*) [*face, complexion*] terreux ◆ **~-faced** (*pej*) au teint terreux ◆ **you look a bit ~** vous avez une mine de papier mâché

pasty[2] /ˈpæstɪ/ N (*Brit Culin*) ≈ petit pâté *m* en croûte (*contenant généralement de la viande, des oignons et des pommes de terre*)

Pat /pæt/ N 1 dim of **Patrick, Patricia** 2 *surnom des Irlandais*

pat[1] /pæt/ VT [*+ object*] tapoter, donner une tape à ; [*+ animal*] flatter ◆ **he ~ted my hand** il me tapota la main ◆ **to ~ one's stomach** se frotter le ventre ◆ **to ~ sb on the back** (*lit*) tapoter qn dans le dos ; (*fig*) complimenter qn, congratuler qn ◆ **to ~ o.s. on the back** s'envoyer des fleurs, s'applaudir N 1 (*= tap*) coup *m* léger, petite tape *f* ; (*on animal*) petite tape *f* ◆ **to give sb a ~ on the back** (*lit*) tapoter qn dans le dos ; (*fig*) complimenter qn, congratuler qn ◆ **give yourselves** *or* **you deserve a ~ on the back** vous pouvez être contents de vous *or* fiers ◆ **to give o.s. a ~ on the back** s'envoyer des fleurs, s'applaudir 2 (also **pat of butter**) (*individual*) plaquette *f* (individuelle) de beurre ; (*larger*) plaque *f* de beurre

► **pat down** VT SEP (*= search*) fouiller

pat[2] /pæt/ ADV 1 (*= exactly suitable*) à propos, à point ◆ **to answer ~** (*= immediately*) répondre sur-le-champ ; (*= with repartee*) répondre du tac au tac ◆ **he had his explanation ~** il avait son explication toute prête 2 (*= perfectly*) [*learn*] par cœur ◆ **to know sth off ~** savoir qch sur le bout du doigt ◆ **she had all the answers off ~** elle a pu répondre du tac au tac 3 (*= firm, unmoving*) [*remain*] inflexible ◆ **to stand ~** * (*US*) ne rien faire, refuser de bouger ADJ [*example, answer, remark*] tout prêt

Patagonia /ˌpætəˈgəʊnɪə/ N Patagonie *f*

Patagonian /ˌpætəˈgəʊnɪən/ ADJ patagonien N Patagonien(ne) *m(f)*

patch /pætʃ/ N 1 (*for clothes*) pièce *f* ; (*for inner tube, airbed*) rustine ® *f* ; (*over eye*) cache *m* ; (*cosmetic: on face*) mouche *f* ; (*Med*) (*nicotine, HRT etc*) patch *m*, timbre *m*

2 (*= small area*) [*of colour*] tache *f* ; [*of sky*] pan *m*, coin *m* ; [*of land*] parcelle *f* ; [*of vegetables*] carré *m* ; [*of ice*] plaque *f* ; [*of mist*] nappe *f* ; [*of water*] flaque *f* ; (*on dog's back etc*) tache *f* ◆ **a damp ~ on the wall/sheet** une tache d'humidité sur le mur/drap ◆ **he's got a bald ~** il a le crâne un peu dégarni ◆ **a man with a bald ~** un homme à la calvitie naissante *or* au crâne un peu dégarni

3 (*fig*) ◆ **a bad** *or* **rough** *or* **sticky** * **~** un moment difficile, une mauvaise passe ◆ **to hit** *or* **strike a bad ~** entrer dans une mauvaise passe ◆ **to go through a rough ~** traverser une mauvaise passe ◆ **good in ~es** bon par moments ◆ **it isn't a ~ on ...** ça ne soutient pas la comparaison avec ... ◆ **he's not a ~ on our old boss** * il est loin de valoir notre ancien patron ; (*stronger*) il n'arrive pas à la cheville de notre ancien patron *

4 (*Comput*) correction *f* (de programme)

5 (*Brit* *) [*of policeman, social worker etc*] secteur *m* ◆ **they're off my ~ now** ils ont quitté mon secteur

VT [*+ clothes*] rapiécer ; [*+ tyre*] réparer, poser une rustine ® à

COMP **patch pocket** N poche *f* appliquée *or* plaquée

patch test N (*Med*) test *m* cutané

► **patch together** VT SEP [*+ garment*] rapiécer ; (*hum*) [*+ old car etc*] retaper * ◆ **a new government was hastily ~ed together** un gouvernement de fortune a été mis sur pied à la hâte

► **patch up** VT SEP [*+ clothes*] rapiécer ; [*+ machine*] rafistoler * ; * [*+ injured person*] rafistoler * ◆ **to ~ up a quarrel** se rabibocher *, se raccommoder * ◆ **they soon ~ed up their differences** ils se sont vite rabibochés * *or* raccommodés *

patchwork /ˈpætʃwɜːk/ N (*lit, fig*) patchwork *m* COMP [*quilt*] en patchwork ; [*landscape*] bigarré ; (*pej = lacking in unity*) fait de pièces et de morceaux, fait de bric et de broc

patchy /ˈpætʃɪ/ (*pej*) ADJ 1 (*lit*) ◆ **~ fog made driving conditions hazardous** des nappes de brouillard rendaient la conduite difficile ◆ **bottle tans can make your skin look a ~ orange colour** les autobronzants peuvent parfois produire des taches orange sur la peau ◆ **brown, ~ grass** des touffes d'herbe brunes et clairsemées 2 (*fig*) inégal ◆ **the acting in this film is ~** l'interprétation dans ce film est inégale ◆ **the evidence is ~** les preuves sont fragmentaires *or* incomplètes ◆ **transport is difficult, communications are ~** les déplacements sont malaisés, les communications mauvaises

pate /peɪt/ N tête *f* ◆ **a bald ~** un crâne chauve

pâté /ˈpæteɪ/ N (*NonC: Culin*) pâté *m*

patella /pəˈtelə/ N (pl **patellae** /pəˈteliː/) rotule *f*

paten /ˈpætən/ N patène *f*

patent /ˈpætənt/ ADJ 1 (*frm = obvious*) [*fact, dishonesty*] patent, manifeste ◆ **it was a ~ impossibility** c'était manifestement impossible 2 [*invention*] breveté ◆ **~ medicine** spécialité *f* pharmaceutique

3 (also **patent leather**) cuir *m* verni ◆ **~ (leather) shoes** chaussures *fpl* vernies *or* en cuir verni

N (*= licence*) brevet *m* d'invention ; (*= invention*) invention *f* brevetée ◆ **to take out a ~ (on sth)** déposer un brevet (pour qch) ◆ **"patent(s) applied for"** "demande de brevet déposée" ◆ **"patent pending"** "brevet en cours d'homologation" ◆ **to come out of** *or* (*US*) **come off ~** tomber dans le domaine public

VT faire breveter

COMP **patent agent** N (*Jur*) conseil *m* en propriété industrielle

Patent and Trademark Office N (*US*) ⇒ **Patent Office**

patent attorney N (*US*) ⇒ **patent agent**

patent engineer N conseil *m* en brevets d'invention

patent holder N détenteur *m*, -trice *f* *or* titulaire *mf* d'un brevet d'invention

patent leather N → **adj 3**

Patent Office N (*Brit*) ≃ Institut *m* national de la propriété industrielle

patent right N propriété *f* industrielle

Patent Rolls NPL (*Brit*) registre *m* des brevets d'invention

patent still N *alambic dans lequel la distillation est ininterrompue*

patentable /ˈpeɪtəntəbl/ ADJ (*Jur etc*) brevetable

patentee /ˌpeɪtənˈtiː/ N breveté(e) *m(f)*

patently /ˈpeɪtəntlɪ/ ADV (*frm*) manifestement, de toute évidence ◆ **~ obvious** tout à fait évident, absolument évident

patentor /ˈpeɪtəntəʳ/ N (*Jur etc*) breveteur *m*, -euse *f*

pater †⁑ /ˈpeɪtəʳ/ N (*esp Brit*) pater⁑ *m*, paternel⁑ *m*

paterfamilias /ˌpeɪtəfəˈmɪlɪæs/ N (pl **patresfamilias** /ˌpɑːtreɪzfəˈmɪlɪæs/) pater familias *m*

paternal /pəˈtɜːnl/ ADJ paternel

paternalism /pəˈtɜːnəlɪzəm/ N paternalisme *m*

paternalist /pəˈtɜːnəlɪst/ ADJ paternaliste

paternalistic /pəˌtɜːnəˈlɪstɪk/ ADJ (*pej*) (trop) paternaliste

paternalistically /pəˌtɜːnəˈlɪstɪklɪ/ ADV (*pej*) de façon (trop) paternaliste

paternally /pəˈtɜːnəlɪ/ ADV paternellement

paternity /pəˈtɜːnɪtɪ/ N (*lit, fig*) paternité *f*

COMP **paternity leave** N congé *m* de paternité

paternity order N (*Jur*) (ordonnance *f* de) reconnaissance *f* de paternité

paternity suit N (*Jur*) action *f* en recherche de paternité

paternity test N test *m* de paternité

paternoster /ˌpætəˈnɒstəʳ/ N 1 (*Rel*) Pater *m* ◆ **the Paternoster** le Pater, le Notre Père 2 (*= elevator*) pater noster *m*

path[1] /pɑːθ/ N 1 (also **pathway**) (*in woods etc*) sentier *m*, chemin *m* ; (*in garden*) allée *f* ; (also **footpath : beside road**) sentier *m* (pour les piétons) ◆ **to clear a ~ through the woods** ouvrir un sentier *or* un chemin dans les bois ◆ **to beat a ~ to sb's door** accourir en foule chez qn ; → **primrose**

2 (*= trajectory, route*) [*of river*] cours *m* ; [*of sun*] route *f* ; [*of bullet, missile, spacecraft, planet, hurri-*

cane] trajectoire *f* ; *[of advancing person]* chemin *m* ◆ **to cross sb's** ~ se trouver sur le chemin de qn ◆ **our ~s have often crossed** nos chemins se sont souvent croisés ◆ **to destroy everything in one's** ~ *[person, storm etc]* tout détruire sur son chemin *or* son passage ◆ **he found his ~ barred** il trouva le chemin *or* le passage barré ◆ **he stepped off the kerb into the ~ of a car** il est descendu du trottoir au moment où une voiture arrivait

3 *(fig = way)* voie *f* ◆ **she criticized the ~ the government was taking** elle a critiqué la voie suivie par le gouvernement ◆ **the ~ to success** la voie *or* le chemin du succès ◆ **the ~ towards peace/independence** la voie menant à la paix/l'indépendance ◆ **to break a new ~** *(esp US)* montrer une voie nouvelle

COMP **path-breaking** ADJ *(esp US)* révolutionnaire

path name N *(Comput)* nom *m* d'accès

path² * /pɑːθ/ N abbrev of **pathology** COMP

path lab N laboratoire *m or* labo * *m* d'analyses

Pathan /pəˈtɑːn/ ADJ pathan N Pathan(e) *m(f)*

pathetic /pəˈθetɪk/ ADJ 1 *(= very sad) [sight, grief]* pitoyable, navrant ◆ **a ~ attempt** une tentative désespérée ◆ **it was ~ to see it** cela faisait peine à voir, c'était un spectacle navrant 2 *(* = feeble) [person, piece of work, performance]* pitoyable, minable 3 *(Literat)* **(the) ~ fallacy** l'anthropomorphisme *m*

pathetically /pəˈθetɪkəlɪ/ ADV 1 *(= pitifully) [behave, moan, weep]* d'une façon pitoyable, pitoyablement ◆ **~ thin/shy** d'une maigreur/timidité pitoyable ◆ **she was ~ glad to see him** elle était terriblement heureuse de le voir 2 *(pej = feebly)* lamentablement ◆ **I wimped out, ~** je me suis lamentablement dégonflé *

pathfinder /ˈpɑːθ,faɪndəʳ/ N *(gen)* pionnier *m*, -ière *f* ; *(= plane)* avion *m* éclaireur

pathogen /ˈpæθədʒən/ N *(Med)* agent *m* pathogène

pathogenic /,pæθəˈdʒenɪk/ ADJ pathogène

pathological /,pæθəˈlɒdʒɪkəl/ ADJ pathologique

pathologically /,pæθəˈlɒdʒɪkəlɪ/ ADV *[jealous, violent]* pathologiquement

pathologist /pəˈθɒlədʒɪst/ N pathologiste *mf*

pathology /pəˈθɒlədʒɪ/ N pathologie *f*

pathos /ˈpeɪθɒs/ N pathétique *m* ◆ **the ~ of the situation** ce que la situation a *(or* avait *etc)* de pathétique, le pathétique de la situation ◆ **told with great ~** raconté d'une façon très émouvante *or* très pathétique ◆ **a film full of ~** un film très triste et émouvant

pathway /ˈpɑːθweɪ/ N 1 *(in woods etc)* sentier *m*, chemin *m* ; *(in garden)* allée *f* 2 *(fig)* voie *f* ◆ **diplomacy will smooth your ~ to success** un peu de diplomatie vous rendra les choses plus faciles sur la voie du succès ◆ **walking can be a good ~ to fitness** la marche peut être un bon moyen de garder la forme

patience /ˈpeɪʃəns/ N 1 patience *f* ◆ **to have ~** prendre patience, savoir patienter ◆ **she doesn't have much ~ with children** elle n'est pas très patiente *or* elle n'a pas beaucoup de patience avec les enfants ◆ **I have no ~ with these people** ces gens m'exaspèrent ◆ **to lose (one's) ~** perdre patience *(with sb/sth* avec qn/qch), s'impatienter *(with sb/sth* contre qn/qch) ◆ **my ~ is wearing thin** ma patience a des limites ◆ **I am out of ~, my ~ is exhausted** ma patience est à bout, je suis à bout de patience ◆ **the ~ of Job** une patience d'ange ; → **possess, tax, try** 2 *(Brit Cards)* réussite *f* ◆ **to play ~** faire des réussites

patient /ˈpeɪʃənt/ ADJ patient *(with* avec) ◆ **(you must) be ~!** patientez !, (un peu de) patience ! * ◆ **I've been ~ long enough!** j'ai assez patienté *or* attendu !, ma patience a des limites ! N *(gen)* patient(e) *m(f)* ; *(post-operative)* opéré(e) *m(f)* ◆ **a doctor's ~s** *(undergoing treatment)* les patients *or* les malades d'un médecin ; *(on his/her list)* les clients *mpl* d'un médecin ◆ **psychiatric ~** malade *mf* psychiatrique ◆ **cancer ~** cancéreux *m*, -euse *f* ◆ **heart ~** cardiaque *mf* ; → **in, outpatient**

patiently /ˈpeɪʃəntlɪ/ ADV patiemment, avec patience

patina /ˈpætɪnə/ N 1 *(on surface)* patine *f* 2 *(= small amount)* vernis *m*, aura *f*

patio /ˈpætɪəʊ/ N patio *m* COMP **patio doors** NPL *(esp Brit)* portes-fenêtres *fpl (donnant sur un patio)*

Patna /ˈpætnə/ N Patna COMP **Patna rice** N *riz à grain long*

patois /ˈpætwɑː/ N (pl **patois**) patois *m*

pat. pend. (abbrev of **patent pending**) → **patent**

patriarch /ˈpeɪtrɪɑːk/ N patriarche *m*

patriarchal /,peɪtrɪˈɑːkəl/ ADJ patriarcal

patriarchy /,peɪtrɪˈɑːkɪ/ N patriarcat *m*, gouvernement *m* patriarcal

patrician /pəˈtrɪʃən/ ADJ, N patricien(ne) *m(f)*

patricide /ˈpeɪtrɪsaɪd/ N *(= crime)* parricide *m* ; *(= person)* parricide *mf*

patrimony /ˈpætrɪmənɪ/ N 1 patrimoine *m*, héritage *m* 2 *(Rel)* biens-fonds *mpl (d'une église)*

patriot /ˈpeɪtrɪət/ N patriote *mf*

patriotic /,pætrɪˈɒtɪk/ ADJ *[deed, speech]* patriotique ; *[person]* patriote COMP **the Patriotic Front** N *(Pol)* le Front patriote

patriotically /,pætrɪˈɒtɪkəlɪ/ ADV patriotiquement, en patriote

patriotism /ˈpætrɪətɪzəm/ N patriotisme *m*

patrol /pəˈtrəʊl/ N 1 *(NonC)* patrouille *f* ◆ **to go on ~** aller en patrouille, faire une ronde ◆ **to be on ~** être de patrouille 2 *[of troops, police, scouts, guides etc]* patrouille *f* ; *(= ship, aircraft on patrol)* patrouilleur *m* ; *(= police officer)* agent *m* de police ; → **border, immigration, customs** VT *[police, troops etc] [+ district, town, streets]* patrouiller dans, faire une patrouille dans VI *[troops, police]* patrouiller, faire une patrouille ◆ **to ~ up and down** *(fig = walk about)* faire les cent pas

COMP *[helicopter, vehicle]* de patrouille

patrol car N *(Police)* voiture *f* de police

patrol leader N *(Mil, scouts, guides)* chef *mf* de patrouille

patrol wagon N *(US)* voiture *f or* fourgon *m* cellulaire

patrolboat /pəˈtrəʊlbəʊt/ N *(Naut)* patrouilleur *m*

patrolman /pəˈtrəʊlmən/ N (pl **-men**) 1 *(US)* agent *m* de police ◆ **Patrolman Jim Sheppe** l'agent *m* Jim Sheppe 2 *(on motorway)* agent *m (d'une société de dépannage)*

patrolwoman /pəˈtrəʊl,wʊmən/ N (pl **-women**) *(US)* femme *f* agent de police ◆ **Patrolwoman Jill Brown** l'agent *m* Jill Brown

patron /ˈpeɪtrən/ N 1 *[of artist]* protecteur *m*, -trice *f* ; *[of a charity]* parrain *m*, marraine *f* 2 *(= customer) [of hotel, shop]* client(e) *m(f)* ◆ **our ~s** *(Comm)* notre clientèle *f* ; *(Theat)* notre public *m* ◆ **"parking for patrons only"** "stationnement réservé à la clientèle" ◆ **"patrons are reminded that ..."** "nous rappelons à notre aimable clientèle que ..." 3 ⇒ **patron saint**

COMP **patron of the arts** N protecteur *m*, -trice *f* des arts, mécène *m*

patron saint N saint(e) patron(ne) *m(f)*

> ⚠ **patron** is only translated by the French word **patron** in the expression 'patron saint'.

patronage /ˈpætrənɪdʒ/ N 1 *(gen) (= support) [of artist etc]* patronage *m* ; *(= financial backing)* parrainage *m*, sponsoring *m* ◆ **under the ~ of ...** sous le patronage de ..., sous les auspices de ... ◆ **~ of the arts** mécénat *m*, protection *f* des arts 2 *(Rel)* droit *m* de disposer d'un bénéfice ; *(Pol)* droit *m* de présentation 3 *(Pol pej)* népotisme *m* ◆ **to give out ~ jobs** *(US)* nommer ses amis politiques à des postes de responsabilité, attribuer des postes aux petits copains *

patroness † /ˈpætrənes/ N *[of artist]* protectrice *f*

patronize /ˈpætrənaɪz/ VT 1 *(pej)* traiter avec condescendance 2 *(Comm) [+ shop, firm]* donner *or* accorder sa clientèle à ; *[+ bar, cinema, club]* fréquenter

patronizing /ˈpætrənaɪzɪŋ/ ADJ *[person]* condescendant ; *[look, tone, smile, manner]* condescendant, de condescendance

patronizingly /ˈpætrənaɪzɪŋlɪ/ ADV *[speak]* d'un ton condescendant, avec condescendance ; *[behave, bow, pat, laugh]* de façon condescendante ; *[smile]* d'un air condescendant

patronymic /,pætrəˈnɪmɪk/ N patronyme *m*, nom *m* patronymique ADJ patronymique

patsy‡ /ˈpætsɪ/ N *(US)* pigeon * *m*, gogo * *m*, victime *f*

patter¹ /ˈpætəʳ/ N *[of comedian, conjurer]* bavardage *m*, baratin * *m* ; *[of salesman etc]* boniment *m*, baratin * *m* VI (also **patter away, patter on**) jacasser, baratiner *

patter² /ˈpætəʳ/ N *[of rain, hail]* crépitement *m*, bruit *m* ◆ **a ~ of footsteps** un petit bruit de pas pressés ◆ **we'll soon be hearing the ~ of tiny feet** *(hum)* on attend un heureux événement VI *[footsteps]* trottiner ; *[rain]* tambouriner *(on* contre) ; *[hail]* crépiter COMP **patter song** N *(Mus)* ≈ ritournelle *f*

► **patter about, patter around** VI trottiner çà et là

pattern /ˈpætən/ N 1 *(= design: on material, wallpaper etc)* dessin(s) *m(pl)*, motif *m* ◆ **a floral ~** un motif floral *or* à fleurs ◆ **a ~ of small dots on the page** un motif de petits points sur la page ◆ **the torches made ~s of light on the walls** la lumière des torches dessinait des formes sur les murs ◆ **the ~ on a tyre** les sculptures *fpl* d'un pneu

2 *(= style)* style *m* ◆ **various ~s of cutlery** différents modèles de couverts ◆ **dresses of different ~s** des robes de styles différents

3 *(Sewing:* also **paper pattern**) patron *m* ; (also **knitting pattern**) modèle *m*

4 *(fig = model)* exemple *m*, modèle *m* ◆ **~ of living** *(fig)* mode *m* de vie ◆ **on the ~ of ...** sur le modèle de ... ◆ **this set a** *or* **the ~ for future meetings** cela a institué un modèle pour les réunions suivantes

5 *(= standard, coherent behaviour etc)* **eating ~s** habitudes *fpl* alimentaires ◆ **behaviour ~s of teenagers** les types *mpl* de comportement chez les adolescents ◆ **my sleep(ing) ~s became very disturbed** mes habitudes de sommeil se sont trouvées très perturbées ◆ **his sleep(ing) ~s have returned to normal** il s'est remis à dormir comme avant ◆ **the earth's weather ~s** les tendances *fpl* climatiques de la terre ◆ **I began to notice a ~ in their behaviour/reactions** *etc* j'ai commencé à remarquer certaines constantes dans leur conduite/leurs réactions *etc* ◆ **to be part of a ~** faire partie d'un tout ◆ **it followed the usual ~** *[meeting, interview, crime, epidemic, drought, storm]* cela s'est passé selon le scénario habituel ; *[timetable, schedule]* cela suivait le schéma habituel ◆ **a clear ~ emerges from these statistics** un schéma très net ressort *or* se dégage de ces statistiques ◆ **the disease followed the same ~ everywhere** la maladie a présenté partout les mêmes caractéristiques ◆ **this week's vio-**

lence follows a sadly familiar ~ les actes de violence de cette semaine suivent un scénario trop familier ◆ **these strikes/attacks all followed the same** ~ ces grèves/attaques se sont toutes déroulées de la même manière ◆ **the ~ of trade** *(Econ)* la structure *or* la physionomie des échanges

6 *(= sample) [of material etc]* échantillon *m*

7 *(Ling)* modèle *m* ; *[of sentence]* structure *f* ◆ **on the ~ of ...** sur le modèle de ...

VT 1 *(= model)* modeler *(on* sur) ◆ **to ~ o.s. on sb** prendre modèle sur qn

2 *(= decorate)* orner de motifs

COMP pattern book N *(material, wallpaper etc)* album *m* d'échantillons ; *(Sewing)* catalogue *m or* album *m* de patrons

pattern maker N *(Metal)* modeleur *m*

patterned /ˈpætənd/ **ADJ** *[material, fabric, china]* à motifs

patterning /ˈpætənɪŋ/ **N** *(NonC)* 1 *(= markings) [of creature]* (motifs *mpl* de la) livrée *f* ◆ **the ~ of the bird's winter/summer plumage** la livrée de cet oiseau pendant l'hiver/l'été 2 *(Psych = conditioning)* conditionnement *m*

patty /ˈpætɪ/ **N** rondelle *f* (de viande hachée)

COMP patty pan N petit moule *m*

patty shell N croûte *f* feuilletée

paucity /ˈpɔːsɪtɪ/ **N** *[of crops, coal, oil]* pénurie *f* ; *[of money]* manque *m* ; *[of news, supplies, water]* disette *f* ; *[of ideas]* indigence *f*, disette *f*

Pauline /ˈpɔːlaɪn/ **ADJ** *(Rel = relating to St Paul)* paulinien

paulownia /pɔːˈləʊnɪə/ **N** paulownia *m*

paunch /pɔːntʃ/ **N** *[of person]* ventre *m*, panse *f*, bedaine * *f* ; *[of ruminants]* panse *f*

paunchy /ˈpɔːntʃɪ/ **ADJ** ventripotent

pauper /ˈpɔːpəʳ/ **N** indigent(e) *m(f)*, pauvre(sse) *m(f)* ◆ **~'s grave** fosse *f* commune

pauperism /ˈpɔːpərɪzəm/ **N** paupérisme *m*

pause /pɔːz/ **N** pause *f* ; *(Mus)* point *m* d'orgue ; *(Poetry)* césure *f* ◆ **to give sb ~ for thought, to give ~ to sb** *(frm)* faire hésiter qn, donner à réfléchir à qn ◆ **a ~ in the conversation** un petit *or* bref silence (dans la conversation) ◆ **after a ~, he added ...** il marqua une pause et ajouta ... ◆ **he continued speaking without a ~** il continua sur sa lancée *or* dans la foulée ◆ **there was a ~ for discussion/for refreshments** on s'arrêta pour discuter/pour prendre des rafraîchissements

VI 1 *(in work, activity)* marquer un temps d'arrêt ; *(for a rest)* faire une pause ◆ **to ~ for breath** s'arrêter pour reprendre haleine ◆ **they ~d for lunch** il ont fait une pause pour le déjeuner *or* une pause-déjeuner

2 *(in speaking)* marquer une pause, marquer un temps d'arrêt ◆ **to ~ for thought** prendre le temps de réfléchir ◆ **without pausing to consider the consequences** sans prendre le temps de réfléchir aux conséquences

3 *(= linger over)* s'arrêter *(on* sur)

VT ◆ **to ~ a video/tape** appuyer sur la touche "pause" d'un magnétoscope/magnétophone ◆ **can you ~ it there?** pouvez-vous appuyer sur la touche "pause" ?

pavane /pəˈvɑːn/ **N** pavane *f*

pave /peɪv/ **VT** *[+ street]* paver ; *[+ yard]* carreler, paver ◆ **~d with gold** pavé d'or ◆ **to ~ the way (for)** ouvrir la voie (à)

pavement /ˈpeɪvmənt/ **N** 1 *(Brit)* trottoir *m* 2 *(= road surface) (of stone, wood)* pavé *m*, pavage *m* ; *(stone slabs)* dallage *m* ; *(ornate)* pavement *m* 3 *(US = roadway)* chaussée *f*

COMP pavement artist N *(Brit)* artiste *mf* de rue

pavement café N *(Brit)* café *m* avec terrasse *(sur le trottoir)*

pavilion /pəˈvɪlɪən/ **N** 1 *(= tent, building)* pavillon *m (tente, construction)* 2 *(Brit Sport)* pavillon *m* des vestiaires

paving /ˈpeɪvɪŋ/ **N** 1 *(material) (= stone)* pavé *m* ; *(= flagstones)* dalles *fpl* ; *(= tiles)* carreaux *mpl* 2 *(= paved ground)* pavage *m*, dallage *m*, carrelage *m* ; → **crazy COMP paving stone N** pavé *m*

Pavlovian /pævˈləʊvɪən/ **ADJ** pavlovien

paw /pɔː/ **N** 1 *[of animal]* patte *f* 2 (* = *hand*) patte * *f* ◆ **keep your ~s off!** bas les pattes ! * **VT** 1 (also **paw at**) *[animal]* donner un coup de patte à ◆ **to ~ the ground** *[horse]* piaffer 2 (* *pej*) *[person]* tripoter * ; *(amorously)* tripoter *, peloter *

pawky /ˈpɔːkɪ/ **ADJ** *(Scot)* narquois

pawl /pɔːl/ **N** cliquet *m*

pawn¹ /pɔːn/ **N** 1 *(Chess)* pion *m* 2 *(fig)* **to be sb's ~** être le jouet de qn, se laisser manœuvrer par qn ◆ **he is a mere ~ (in the game)** il n'est qu'un pion sur l'échiquier

pawn² /pɔːn/ **VT** *[+ one's watch etc]* mettre en gage *or* au mont-de-piété **N** 1 *(= thing pledged)* gage *m*, nantissement *m* 2 *(NonC)* **in ~** en gage, au mont-de-piété ◆ **to get sth out of ~** dégager qch du mont-de-piété **COMP pawn ticket N** reconnaissance *f* du mont-de-piété

pawnbroker /ˈpɔːnˌbrəʊkəʳ/ **N** prêteur *m*, -euse *f* sur gages ◆ **~'s** ⇒ **pawnshop**

pawnshop /ˈpɔːnʃɒp/ **N** bureau *m* de prêteur sur gages, mont-de-piété *m*

pawpaw /ˈpɔːpɔː/ **N** papaye *f*

pax /pæks/ **EXCL** *(Brit* † *: *during game)* pouce ! **N** *(Rel)* paix *f* ◆ **Pax Romana** *(Hist)* pax *f* romana ◆ **Pax Americana/Britannica** *(Pol)* pax *f* americana/britannica

pay /peɪ/ (vb : pret, ptp **paid**) **N** *(gen)* salaire *m* ; *(esp of manual worker)* paie *or* paye *f* ; *[of sailor, soldier]* solde *f*, paie *f* ◆ **three weeks' ~** trois semaines de salaire *or* paie ◆ **to be on half/full ~** toucher la moitié/l'intégralité de son salaire *or* de sa paie ◆ **the ~'s not very good** ce n'est pas très bien payé ◆ **holidays with ~** congés *mpl* payés ◆ **time off without ~** congé *m* sans solde

◆ **in the pay of** *(pej)* à la solde de ◆ **he was killed by gunmen in the ~ of drug traffickers** il a été assassiné par des tueurs à la solde des trafiquants de drogue ; → **equal, half, holiday, take**

VT 1 *[+ person]* payer *(to do sth* à faire qch ; *for doing sth* pour faire qch) ; *[+ tradesman, bill, fee]* payer, régler ◆ **to ~ sb $20** payer qn 20 dollars ◆ **he paid them for the book/the ticket** il les a payés pour le livre/le billet ◆ **he paid them $20 for the book/the ticket** il leur a acheté le livre/le billet pour 20 dollars ◆ **he paid them $20 for the work** il les a payés 20 dollars pour ce travail ◆ **he paid me for my trouble** il m'a dédommagé de mes peines ◆ **I don't ~ you to ask questions** je ne vous paie pas pour poser des questions ◆ **we're not paid for that** on n'est pas payé pour cela, on n'est pas payé pour * ◆ **that's what you're paid for** c'est pour cela qu'on vous paie ◆ **I get paid on Fridays** je touche ma paie *or* mon salaire le vendredi ◆ **I am paid on a monthly basis** *or* **by the month** je suis payé au mois

2 *[+ instalments, money]* payer ; *[+ deposit]* verser ; *[+ debt]* payer, rembourser ; *[+ loan]* rembourser ◆ **he paid $20 for the ticket** il a payé le billet 20 dollars ◆ **the company paid a high premium for Mr Peter's services** la société a payé cher pour obtenir les services de M. Peter ◆ **he paid a lot for his suit** son costume lui a coûté cher, il a payé son costume très cher ◆ **they ~ good wages** ils paient bien ◆ **to ~ cash (down)** payer comptant ◆ **to ~ money into an account** verser de l'argent sur un compte

3 *(Fin) [+ interest]* rapporter ; *[+ dividend]* distribuer ◆ **shares that ~ 5%** des actions qui rapportent 5% ◆ **his generosity paid dividends** *(fig)* sa générosité a porté ses fruits ◆ **... but it paid him in the long run** ... mais il y a gagné en fin de compte ◆ **it would ~ you to be nice to him** vous gagneriez à être aimable avec lui ◆ **it won't ~ him to tell the truth** il ne gagnera rien à dire la vérité

4 *(fig)* ◆ **he's paid his dues** *(for achievement)* il en a bavé * ; *(for crime, error)* il a payé sa dette *(fig)* ◆ **he's paid his debt to society** il a payé sa dette envers la société ◆ **the business is ~ing its way now** l'affaire couvre ses frais maintenant ◆ **he likes to ~ his (own) way** il préfère payer sa part *or* son écot ◆ **he who ~s the piper calls the tune** *(Prov)* celui qui paie a le droit de décider comment sera dépensé son argent

◆ **pay + price** ◆ **to ~ the price (for sth)** subir *or* payer les conséquences (de qch) ◆ **to ~ the price of fame/success** payer le prix de la célébrité/du succès ◆ **the city is still ~ing the price of war** la ville souffre encore des conséquences de la guerre ◆ **he has paid a high price to stay in power** il a payé très cher sa place au pouvoir

◆ **to put paid to** ◆ **the war put paid to her hopes of a musical career** avec la guerre, elle a dû abandonner tout espoir de faire carrière dans la musique ◆ **your findings have put paid to this theory** vos conclusions ont démenti cette théorie ◆ **I had my own business, but the recession put paid to that** j'avais ma propre entreprise, mais la récession s'est chargée de détruire tout cela ; see also **vi 2**

5 ◆ **to ~ sb a visit** rendre visite à qn ◆ **we paid a visit to Paris on our way south** nous avons fait un petit tour à Paris en descendant vers le sud ◆ **to ~ a visit** * *or* **a call** * *(= go to the toilet)* aller au petit coin * ◆ **to ~ one's last respects to sb** rendre un dernier hommage à qn

VI 1 payer ◆ **his job ~s well** son travail paie bien ◆ **they ~ very poorly** ils paient très mal ◆ **"pay on entry"** *(on bus)* "paiement à l'entrée"

◆ **to pay for** *[+ person]* payer pour ; *[+ thing]* payer ◆ **I offered to ~ for my mother** j'ai proposé de payer pour ma mère ◆ **to ~ for the meal** payer le repas ◆ **you'll ~ for this!** *(fig)* vous (me) le payerez ! ◆ **I'll make him ~ for that** *(fig)* je lui ferai payer ça ◆ **he's had to ~ for it** *(fig) (for achievement)* il en a bavé * ◆ **he made a mistake and he's had to ~ for it** il a fait une erreur et il l'a payée cher ◆ **he paid dearly for it** *(fig)* il l'a payé cher ◆ **to ~ through the nose for sth** * payer le prix fort pour qch ◆ **we'll have to ~ through the nose for it** * ça va nous coûter les yeux de la tête * ; → **cash, instalment, nail**

2 *(= be profitable) [business, deal]* rapporter, être rentable ◆ **does it ~?** est-ce que ça rapporte ?, c'est rentable ? ◆ **we need to sell 600 copies to make it ~** nous devons vendre 600 exemplaires pour rentrer dans nos frais *or* pour que ce soit rentable ◆ **crime doesn't ~** le crime ne paie pas ◆ **it ~s to advertise** la publicité rapporte ◆ **it always ~s to ask an expert's opinion** on a toujours intérêt à demander l'avis d'un expert ◆ **it doesn't ~ to be polite these days** on ne gagne rien à être *or* cela ne paie pas d'être poli de nos jours ◆ **it doesn't ~ to tell lies** cela ne sert à rien de mentir, on ne gagne rien à mentir

◆ **to pay for itself/themselves** être amorti *or* rentabilisé ◆ **insulation soon ~s for itself** l'isolation est vite rentabilisée *or* amortie

COMP *[dispute, negotiation]* salarial

pay-and-display ADJ *(Brit) [car park]* à horodateur

pay as you earn N retenue *f* à la source de l'impôt sur le revenu

pay-as-you-go ADJ *[mobile phone]* à carte rechargeable **N** *(US Tax)* → **pay as you earn**

pay award N augmentation *f* de salaire collective

pay bargaining N *(NonC)* négociations *fpl* salariales
pay bed N *(Brit)* lit *m* (d'hôpital) payant *(par opposition aux soins gratuits du système de Sécurité sociale britannique)*
Pay Board N Commission *f* des salaires
pay-cable channel N *(TV)* chaîne *f* câblée payante
pay check N *(US)* ⇒ **pay cheque**
pay cheque N *(Brit)* salaire *m*, paie *or* paye *f*
pay claim N revendication *f* salariale
pay day N jour *m* de paie ◆ **to have a big ~ day** *(Sport)* décrocher le gros lot
pay desk N caisse *f* ; *(Theat)* caisse *f*, guichet *m*
pay dirt‡ N *(Min)* filon *m* ◆ **to hit** *or* **strike ~ dirt** *(lit)* découvrir un filon ; *(fig)* trouver le filon
pay envelope N *(US)* enveloppe *f* de paie
pay increase N ⇒ **pay rise**
pay packet N *(Brit)* enveloppe *f* de paie ; *(fig)* paie *f*, salaire *m*
pay-per-view N pay per view *m*, télévision *f* à la carte ADJ ◆ **~-per-view television** le pay per view, la télévision à la carte ◆ **~-per-view channel** (chaîne *f* de) télévision *f* en pay per view *or* à la carte ◆ **~-per-view programme** émission *f* en pay per view *or* à la carte ◆ **on a ~-per-view basis** en pay per view, à la carte
pay phone N téléphone *m* public
pay raise N *(US)* ⇒ **pay rise**
pay rise N *(Brit)* augmentation *f* de salaire
pay station N *(US)* téléphone *m* public
pay structure N *(Ind)* barème *m* des salaires
pay-TV N télévision *f* payante

▸ **pay back** VT SEP 1 *[+ stolen money]* rendre, restituer ; *[+ loan]* rembourser ; *[+ person]* rembourser ◆ **I paid my brother back the £10 I owed him** j'ai remboursé à mon frère les 10 livres que je lui devais
2 *(fig = get even with)* **to ~ sb back for doing sth** faire payer à qn qch qu'il a fait ◆ **I'll ~ you back for that!** je vous le revaudrai !
N ◆ **payback** → **payback**

▸ **pay down** VT SEP ◆ **he paid £10 down** *(as deposit)* il a versé un acompte de 10 livres ; *(whole amount in cash)* il a payé 10 livres comptant

▸ **pay in** VT SEP verser *(to à)* ◆ **to ~ in money at the bank** verser de l'argent sur son compte, créditer son compte (bancaire) ◆ **to ~ a sum in to an account** verser une somme sur un compte ◆ **to ~ in a cheque** déposer un chèque

▸ **pay off** VI *[risk, trick, scheme, work]* être payant ; *[decision]* être valable *or* payant ; *[perseverance, patience]* être récompensé ◆ **his patience paid off in the long run** finalement il a été récompensé de sa patience *or* sa patience a été récompensée
VT SEP 1 *[+ debts]* s'acquitter de, régler ; *[+ bill]* régler ; *[+ creditor, loan]* rembourser ◆ **to ~ sb off** *(= bribe)* donner des pots-de-vin à qn, acheter qn ◆ **to ~ off an old score** *(fig)* régler un vieux compte ◆ **to ~ off a grudge** *(fig)* satisfaire un désir de vengeance
2 *(= discharge) [+ worker, staff]* licencier ; *[+ servant]* donner son compte à, congédier ; *(Naut) [+ crew]* débarquer
N ◆ **payoff** → **payoff**

▸ **pay out** VI *[fruit machine etc, insurance policy]* rembourser
VT SEP 1 *[+ rope]* laisser filer
2 *[+ money] (= spend)* débourser, dépenser ◆ **they paid out a large sum of money on new equipment** ils ont dépensé beaucoup d'argent pour acheter de nouveaux équipements

▸ **pay up** VI payer ◆ **~ up!** payez !
VT FUS *[+ amount]* payer, verser ◆ **~ up what you owe me!** payez-moi *or* remboursez-moi ce que vous me devez ! ; → **paid**

payable /ˈpeɪəbəl/ ADJ *(= due, owed)* payable ◆ **~ in/over three months** payable dans/en trois mois ◆ **~ when due** payable à l'échéance ◆ **~ to bearer/on demand/at sight** payable au porteur/sur présentation/à vue ◆ **to make a cheque ~ to sb** faire un chèque à l'ordre de qn ◆ **please make cheques ~ to ..., cheques should be made ~ to ...** les chèques doivent être libellés à l'ordre de ... ◆ **the interest ~ on the loan** les intérêts à payer sur le prêt

payback /ˈpeɪ,bæk/ N 1 *[of investment]* retour *m*, bénéfice *m* ; *[of debt]* remboursement *m* ; *(fig) (= benefit)* avantage *m* 2 *(= revenge)* revanche *f*

PAYE /,piːerwaɪˈiː/ *(Brit)* (abbrev of **pay as you earn**) → **pay**

payee /peɪˈiː/ N *[of cheque]* bénéficiaire *mf* ; *[of postal order]* destinataire *mf*, bénéficiaire *mf*

payer /ˈpeɪəʳ/ N payeur *m*, -euse *f* ; *[of cheque]* tireur *m*, -euse *f* ◆ **to be a bad ~** être un mauvais payeur ◆ **late ~s** personnes *fpl* qui paient avec du retard

paying /ˈpeɪɪŋ/ ADJ 1 *(= who pays)* payant ◆ **~ guest** pensionnaire *mf*, hôte *m* payant 2 *(= profitable) [business]* rémunérateur (-trice *f*), qui rapporte, rentable ; *[scheme, proposition]* rentable N *[of debt]* règlement *m*, acquittement *m* ; *[of creditor]* remboursement *m* ; *[of money]* paiement *m*, versement *m*
COMP **paying-in book** N *(Banking)* carnet *m* de bordereaux de versement
paying-in slip N *(Banking)* bordereau *m* de versement

payload /ˈpeɪləʊd/ N *(= cargo)* charge *f* ; *[of vehicle, boat, spacecraft]* charge *f* utile ; *(= explosive energy) [of warhead, bomb load]* puissance *f*

paymaster /ˈpeɪ,mɑːstəʳ/ N *(gen)* intendant *m*, caissier *m*, payeur *m* ; *(Naut)* commissaire *m* ; *(Mil)* trésorier *m* COMP **Paymaster General** N *(Brit) trésorier-payeur de l'Échiquier*

payment /ˈpeɪmənt/ LANGUAGE IN USE 20.6
N 1 *(= money) (gen)* paiement *m* ; *(to creditor)* remboursement *m* ; *(into account)* versement *m* ; *(= monthly repayment)* mensualité *f* ◆ **to make (a) ~** faire *or* effectuer un paiement ◆ **method of ~** mode *m* de paiement ◆ **$150, in monthly ~s of $10** 150 dollars, payables en mensualités de 10 dollars ◆ **prompt/late ~** paiement *m* rapide/en retard ◆ **without ~** à titre gracieux ◆ **we demand ~ in full** nous exigeons le paiement intégral ◆ **~ by instalments** paiement *m* par traites *or* à tempérament ◆ **~ by results** prime *f* au rendement ◆ **on ~ of a supplement/a deposit/$50** moyennant un supplément/une caution/la somme de 50 dollars ◆ **the car will be yours on ~ of the balance** la voiture vous appartiendra une fois que vous aurez réglé le solde ◆ **as** *or* **in ~ for ...** en règlement *or* paiement de ... ◆ **as** *or* **in ~ for a debt** en règlement d'une dette ◆ **most major credit cards are accepted in ~** les principales cartes de crédit sont acceptées comme moyen de paiement ◆ **as** *or* **in ~ for your help** pour vous remercier de votre aide ; → **balance, down[1], easy, ex gratia, interest, kind, miss[1], mortgage, nonpayment, part, redundancy, stop**
2 *(fig: for favour)* récompense *f* ◆ **those who fought alongside the conquistadors were granted land in ~** ceux qui combattaient aux côtés des conquistadors recevaient une terre en récompense ◆ **travelling minstrels provided entertainment and were given food and lodging in ~** les ménestrels offraient un spectacle et recevaient le gîte et le couvert en échange
COMP **payment card** N carte *f* de paiement
payment date N date *f* de paiement ◆ **your first ~ date will be ...** la date de votre premier remboursement est le ...
payment system N système *m* de paiement *or* de règlement
payment terms NPL modalités *fpl* de paiement

payoff /ˈpeɪɒf/ N 1 *[of person]* remboursement *m* (total) ; *[of debt etc]* règlement *m* (total) ; *(* = reward)* récompense *f* ; *(* = bribe)* pot-de-vin *m* 2 *(* = outcome)* résultat *m* final ; *(= climax)* comble *m*, bouquet* *m* 3 *(= punch line)* chute *f*

payola* /peɪˈəʊlə/ N *(NonC: US)* pots-de-vin *mpl*

payout /ˈpeɪaʊt/ N *(in competition)* prix *m* ; *(from insurance)* dédommagement *m*

payroll /ˈpeɪrəʊl/ N *(= list)* registre *m* du personnel ; *(= money)* masse *f* salariale ; *(= all the employees)* personnel *m*, effectifs *mpl* ◆ **the factory has 60 people on the ~** *or* **a ~ of 60** l'usine compte 60 employés *or* salariés ◆ **to be on a firm's ~** être employé par une société
COMP **payroll tax** N taxe *f* sur les traitements et salaires

payslip /ˈpeɪslɪp/ N bulletin *m* de salaire

PB N *(Sport)* (abbrev of **personal best**) → **personal**

PBS /,piːbiːˈes/ N *(US)* abbrev of **Public Broadcasting Service**

PBX /,piːbiːˈeks/ N *(Brit Telec)* (abbrev of **private branch exchange**) PBX *m*, commutateur *m* privé

PC /piːˈsiː/ N 1 (abbrev of **personal computer**) PC *m* 2 (abbrev of **Police Constable**) → **police** ; see also **plod** 3 (abbrev of **Privy Councillor**) → **privy** ADJ (* abbrev of **politically correct**) → **politically**

pc /piːˈsiː/ N abbrev of **postcard**

p.c. (abbrev of **per cent**) → **per**

p/c N 1 (abbrev of **prices current**) prix *mpl* courants 2 (abbrev of **petty cash**) → **petty**

PCB /,piːsiːˈbiː/ N 1 (abbrev of **polychlorinated biphenyl**) PCB *m* 2 (abbrev of **printed circuit board**) → **printed**

PCI /,piːsiːˈaɪ/ N *(Comput)* (abbrev of **Peripheral Component Interconnect**) pci *m*

pcm ADV (abbrev of **per calendar month**) par mois ◆ **€500 ~** 500 €/m, 500 € par mois

PCP /,piːsiːˈpiː/ N 1® *(Drugs)* (abbrev of **phencyclidine**) PCP ® *f*, phencyclidine *f* 2 *(Med)* abbrev of **pneumocystis carinii pneumonia**

PD /piːˈdiː/ N *(US)* (abbrev of **police department**) → **police**

pd (abbrev of **paid**) payé

PDA /piːdiːˈeɪ/ N (abbrev of **personal digital assistant**) PDA *m*, assistant *m* personnel (numérique)

PDF, pdf /,piːdiːˈef/ N *(Comput)* (abbrev of **Portable Document Format**) pdf *m*

pdq‡ /,piːdiːˈkjuː/ ADV (abbrev of **pretty damn quick**) en vitesse*

PDSA /,piːdiːesˈeɪ/ N *(Brit)* (abbrev of **People's Dispensary for Sick Animals**) → **people**

PDT /,piːdiːˈtiː/ *(US)* (abbrev of **Pacific Daylight Time**) → **pacific**

PE /piːˈiː/ N *(Scol)* (abbrev of **physical education**) → **physical**

pea /piː/ N pois *m* ◆ **garden** *or* **green ~s** petits pois *mpl* ◆ **they are as like as two ~s (in a pod)** ils se ressemblent comme deux gouttes d'eau ; → **process[1], shell, split, sweet**
COMP **pea green** N vert *m inv* pomme
pea-green ADJ vert pomme *inv*
pea jacket N *(Naut)* caban *m*
pea soup N soupe *f* aux pois ; *(from split peas)* soupe *f* aux pois cassés

peace /piːs/ N 1 *(NonC) (= not war)* paix *f* ; *(= treaty)* (traité *m* de) paix *f* ◆ **a lasting ~** une paix durable ◆ **after a long (period of) ~ war broke out** après une longue période de paix la guerre éclata ◆ **to be at ~** être en paix ◆ **to come in ~** venir en ami(s) ◆ **to live in** *or* **at ~ with ...** vivre en paix avec ... ◆ **to make ~** faire la paix ◆ **to make ~ with ...** signer *or* conclure la paix avec ... ◆ **to make (one's) ~ with sb** se réconcilier avec qn

2 *(= calm)* paix *f*, tranquillité *f* ◆ **to be at ~ with oneself** avoir la conscience tranquille *or* en paix ◆ **to live at ~ with the world** avoir une vie paisible ◆ **to be at ~ with the world** ne pas avoir le moindre souci ◆ **~ of mind** tranquillité *f* d'esprit ◆ **to disturb sb's ~ of mind** troubler l'esprit de qn ◆ **leave him in ~** laisse-le tranquille, fiche-lui la paix* ◆ **to sleep in ~** dormir tranquille ◆ **he gives them no ~** il ne les laisse pas en paix ◆ **anything for the sake of ~ and quiet** n'importe quoi pour avoir la paix ◆ **I need a bit of ~ and quiet** j'ai besoin d'un peu de calme ◆ **to hold** *or* **keep one's ~** † garder le silence, se taire ; → **rest**

3 *(Jur etc = civil order)* paix *f*, ordre *m* public ◆ **to disturb** *or* **break the ~** troubler l'ordre public ◆ **to keep the ~** *[citizen]* ne pas troubler l'ordre public ; *[police]* veiller à l'ordre public ; *(fig)* *(= stop disagreement)* maintenir le calme *or* la paix ; → **breach, justice**

COMP *(Pol)* *[poster, march, meeting, demonstration]* pour la paix

peace campaign N campagne *f* pour la paix ; *(for nuclear disarmament)* campagne *f* pour le désarmement nucléaire

peace campaigner N militant(e) *m(f)* pour la paix ; *(for nuclear disarmament)* militant(e) *m(f)* pour le désarmement nucléaire

peace conference N conférence *f* de paix

Peace Corps N *(US) organisation américaine de coopération et d'aide aux pays en développement*

peace dividend N dividende *m* de la paix

peace initiative N initiative *f* de paix

peace lobby N lobby *m* pour la paix ; *(for nuclear disarmament)* lobby *m* pour le désarmement nucléaire

peace-loving ADJ pacifique

Peace Movement N Mouvement *m* pour la paix ; *(for nuclear disarmament)* Mouvement *m* pour le désarmement nucléaire

peace offensive N offensive *f* de paix

peace offering N *(Rel = sacrifice)* offrande *f* propitiatoire ; *(fig)* cadeau *m* *or* gage *m* de réconciliation

peace pipe N calumet *m* de la paix

the peace process N le processus de paix

peace studies NPL *(Educ)* études *fpl* sur la paix

peace talks NPL pourparlers *mpl* de paix

peace treaty N (traité *m* de) paix *f*

peaceable /ˈpiːsəbl/ ADJ *[people, folk]* pacifique ; *[person]* paisible ◆ **he proclaims himself to be a ~ family man** il se décrit comme un paisible père de famille

peaceably /ˈpiːsəblɪ/ ADV *[say, speak, agree]* pacifiquement ; *[gather, assemble, behave]* de manière pacifique

peaceful /ˈpiːsfʊl/ ADJ 1 *(= quiet)* *[, countryside, atmosphere, reign, period]* paisible ; *[life, place, sleep]* paisible, tranquille ; *[meeting]* calme 2 *(= not quarrelsome)* *[person, disposition, nation]* pacifique, paisible ; *(= non-violent)* *[demonstration]* non violent ; *[solution]* pacifique ◆ **~ coexistence** coexistence *f* pacifique ◆ **to do sth by** *or* **through ~ means** faire qch en utilisant des moyens pacifiques ◆ **the ~ uses of atomic energy** l'utilisation pacifique de l'énergie nucléaire ◆ **for ~ purposes** à des fins pacifiques

peacefully /ˈpiːsfəlɪ/ ADV *[demonstrate, disperse]* paisiblement, dans le calme ; *[live, sleep, lie]* paisiblement, tranquillement ; *[die]* paisiblement ◆ **the demonstration passed off ~** la manifestation s'est déroulée dans le calme *or* paisiblement

peacefulness /ˈpiːsfʊlnɪs/ N paix *f*, tranquillité *f*, calme *m*

peacekeeper /ˈpiːs,kiːpəʳ/ N *(= soldier)* soldat *m* de la paix

peacekeeping /ˈpiːs,kiːpɪŋ/ N maintien *m* de la paix

COMP *[operation, policy]* de maintien de la paix

peacekeeping force N force *f* de maintien de la paix

peacemaker /ˈpiːs,meɪkəʳ/ N pacificateur *m*, -trice *f*, conciliateur *m*, -trice *f* ; *(esp international politics)* artisan *m* de la paix

peacemaking /ˈpiːs,meɪkɪŋ/ N *(NonC)* négociations *fpl* de paix ADJ *[efforts]* de conciliation ; *[role]* de conciliateur ◆ **the ~ process** le processus de paix

peacenik * /ˈpiːsnɪk/ N *(pej)* pacifiste *mf*

peacetime /ˈpiːstaɪm/ N ◆ **in** *or* **during ~** en temps de paix ADJ en temps de paix

peach¹ /piːtʃ/ N 1 pêche *f* ; (also **peach tree**) pêcher *m* 2 *(* = beauty)* ◆ **she's a ~!** elle est jolie comme un cœur !* ◆ **that was a ~ of a shot!** *(Sport)* quel beau coup ! ◆ **what a ~ of a dress!** quel amour* de robe ! ADJ (couleur) pêche *inv*

COMP **peach blossom** N fleur *f* de pêcher

peaches-and-cream complexion N teint *m* de pêche

peach melba N pêche *f* Melba

the Peach State N *(US)* la Géorgie

peach stone N noyau *m* de pêche

peach² * /piːtʃ/ VTI *(Prison)* ◆ **to ~ (on) sb** moucharder qn*

peachy /ˈpiːtʃɪ/ ADJ 1 *(in colour)* *[complexion]* de pêche 2 *(esp US: * = excellent)* super* ◆ **how's it going? – just ~!** ça va ? – ça roule !

peacock /ˈpiːkɒk/ N paon *m*

COMP **peacock blue** N bleu *m* paon

peacock-blue ADJ bleu paon *inv*

peacock butterfly N paon *m* de jour ; → **proud**

peahen /ˈpiːhen/ N paonne *f*

peak /piːk/ N 1 *(= high point)* *[of career]* sommet *m*, apogée *m* ; *(on graph)* sommet *m* ◆ **the ~ of perfection** la perfection absolue ◆ **the economy has ~s and troughs** l'économie peut avoir des hauts et des bas ◆ **membership has fallen from a ~ of fifty thousand** le nombre d'adhérents est retombé après avoir atteint un niveau record de cinquante mille ◆ **at the ~ of his fame** à l'apogée *or* au sommet de sa gloire ◆ **discontent reached its ~** le mécontentement était à son comble ◆ **traffic reaches its ~ about 5 o'clock** l'heure de pointe (de la circulation) est vers 17 heures ◆ **at** *or* **in the ~ of condition** *or* **physical fitness** au meilleur *or* au mieux de sa forme

◆ **to be at + peak** ◆ **when the Empire was at its ~** quand l'Empire était à son apogée ◆ **when demand was at its ~** quand la demande était à son maximum ◆ **to be at the ~ of one's popularity** être au faîte de sa popularité

2 *(= summit)* *[of mountain]* cime *f*, sommet *m* ; *(= mountain itself)* pic *m*

3 *[of cap]* visière *f* ; → **off-peak, widow**

VI *[sales, demand etc]* atteindre son plus haut niveau ◆ **to ~ at 45%** atteindre 45% à son plus haut niveau

COMP **peak demand** N *(Comm)* demande *f* maximum *or* record *inv* ; *(Elec)* heures *fpl* de pointe *(de la consommation d'électricité)*

peak experience N *(fig)* expérience *f* ineffable

peak hours NPL *(for shops)* heures *fpl* d'affluence ; *(for traffic)* heures *fpl* d'affluence *or* de pointe

peak listening time N *(Rad)* heures *fpl* de grande écoute

peak load N *(Elec etc)* charge *f* maximum

peak period N *(for shops, business)* période *f* de pointe ; *(for traffic)* période *f* d'affluence *or* de pointe

peak production N production *f* maximum

peak rate N plein tarif *m*

peak season N pleine saison *f*

peak time N *(Brit)* *(TV)* prime time *m* ; *(Rad)* heure *f* de plus forte écoute ; *(Elec)* périodes *fpl* de pointe ; *(for traffic, train services)* heures *fpl* de pointe

peak-time ADJ *(Brit)* *[programme]* *(TV)* de prime time ; *(Rad)* des heures de plus forte écoute ; *[electricity consumption, traffic, train services]* des périodes de pointe

peak traffic N circulation *f* aux heures d'affluence *or* de pointe

peak viewing (time) N *(TV)* heures *fpl* de grande écoute

peak year N année *f* record *inv*

peaked /piːkt/ ADJ *[cap]* à visière ; *[roof]* pointu

peaky* /ˈpiːkɪ/ ADJ fatigué ◆ **to look ~** avoir mauvaise mine, avoir l'air mal fichu* ◆ **to feel ~** ne pas se sentir très en forme, se sentir mal fichu*

peal /piːl/ N ◆ **~ of bells** *(= sound)* sonnerie *f* de cloches, carillon *m* ; *(set)* carillon *m* ◆ **a ~ of thunder** un coup de tonnerre ◆ **the ~s of the organ** le ronflement de l'orgue ◆ **a ~ of laughter** un éclat de rire ◆ **to go (off) into ~s of laughter** rire aux éclats *or* à gorge déployée VI (also **peal out**) *[bells]* carillonner ; *[thunder]* gronder ; *[organ]* ronfler ; *[laughter]* éclater VT *[+ bells]* sonner (à toute volée)

peanut /ˈpiːnʌt/ N *(= nut)* cacahuète *f* ; *(= plant)* arachide *f* ◆ **to work for ~s*** travailler pour trois fois rien *or* des clopinettes ◆ **$300 is ~s for him*** pour lui 300 dollars représentent une bagatelle ◆ **if you pay ~s, you get monkeys** *(Prov)* * qui ne paie rien n'a que des bons à rien

COMP **peanut butter** N beurre *m* de cacahuètes

peanut gallery* N *(US)* poulailler* *m* *(dans un théâtre)*

peanut oil N huile *f* d'arachide

peapod /ˈpiːpɒd/ N cosse *f* de pois

pear /peəʳ/ N poire *f* ; (also **pear tree**) poirier *m* ; → **prickly** COMP **pear-shaped** ADJ en forme de poire, piriforme ◆ **to be ~-shaped*** *[woman]* avoir de fortes hanches ◆ **things started to go ~-shaped*** les choses ont commencé à mal tourner

pearl /pɜːl/ N perle *f* ◆ **real/cultured ~s** perles *fpl* fines/de culture ◆ **~s of wisdom** *(liter or hum)* trésors *mpl* de sagesse ◆ **a ~ among women** *(liter)* la perle des femmes ◆ **to cast ~s before swine** *(liter)* jeter des perles aux pourceaux, donner de la confiture aux cochons* ◆ **it's (just) ~s before swine*** c'est (donner) de la confiture à des cochons* ; → **seed, string**

VI 1 *[water]* perler, former des gouttelettes

2 *(= dive for pearls)* pêcher les perles

COMP **pearl barley** N orge *m* perlé

pearl button N bouton *m* de nacre

pearl diver N pêcheur *m*, -euse *f* de perles

pearl diving N pêche *f* des perles

pearl grey N gris *m* perle *inv*

pearl-grey ADJ gris perle *inv*

pearl-handled ADJ *[knife]* à manche de nacre ; *[revolver]* à crosse de nacre

pearl necklace N collier *m* de perles

pearl oyster N huître *f* perlière

pearly /ˈpɜːlɪ/ ADJ *(= made of pearl)* en *or* de nacre ; *(in colour)* nacré ◆ **~ teeth** dents *fpl* nacrées *or* de perle

COMP **the Pearly Gates** NPL *(hum)* les portes *fpl* du Paradis

pearly king, pearly queen N *(Brit)* *marchand(e) des quatre saisons de Londres qui porte des vêtements couverts de boutons de nacre*

pearly white ADJ *(liter or hum)* *[teeth, skin]* d'un blanc éclatant

peasant /ˈpezənt/ N paysan(ne) *m(f)* ; *(pej)* paysan(ne) *m(f)*, péquenaud(e)* *m(f)*, rustre *m* ◆ **the ~s** *(Hist, Sociol)* la paysannerie, les paysans *mpl* ; *(Econ)* *(= small farmers)* les agriculteurs *mpl*, les ruraux *mpl* ADJ *[crafts, life]* rural, paysan ◆ **~ farmer** petit(e) exploitant(e) *m(f)* agricole ◆ **~ farming** petite exploitation *f* agricole

peasantry /ˈpezəntrɪ/ **N** ◆ **the** ~ la paysannerie, les paysans *mpl* ; (= *countryfolk*) les campagnards *mpl*

pease pudding /ˌpiːzˈpʊdɪŋ/ **N** purée *f* de pois cassés

peashooter /ˈpiːʃuːtəʳ/ **N** (*lit, fig*) sarbacane *f*

peasouper * /ˌpiːˈsuːpəʳ/ **N** brouillard *m* à couper au couteau *, purée *f* de pois

peat /piːt/ **N** (*NonC*) tourbe *f* ; (*one piece*) motte *f* de tourbe ◆ **to dig** *or* **cut** ~ extraire de la tourbe
COMP **peat bog N** tourbière *f*
peat pot N pot *m or* godet *m* de tourbe

peaty /ˈpiːtɪ/ **ADJ** [*soil*] tourbeux ; [*smell, taste*] de tourbe

pebble /ˈpebl/ **N** 1 (= *stone*) caillou *m* ; (*on beach*) galet *m* ◆ **he's not the only** ~ **on the beach** il n'est pas unique au monde, il n'y a pas que lui 2 (*Opt*) lentille *f* en cristal de roche
COMP **pebble glasses** * **NPL** gros carreaux * *mpl* de myope

pebbledash /ˈpebldæʃ/ **N** crépi *m* granité **VT** recouvrir d'un crépi granité, graniter (*SPEC*)

pebbledashed /ˈpebldæʃt/ **ADJ** [*wall, house*] recouvert d'un crépi granité

pebbleweave (cloth) /ˈpeblwiːv(ˌklɒθ)/ **N** granité *m*

pebbly /ˈpeblɪ/ **ADJ** [*surface, road*] caillouteux ◆ **a** ~ **beach** une plage de galets

pecan /pɪˈkæn/ **N** (= *nut*) (noix *f*) pacane *f* ; (= *tree*) pacanier *m*

peccadillo /ˌpekəˈdɪləʊ/ **N** (pl **peccadillos** *or* **peccadilloes**) peccadille *f*, vétille *f*

peccary /ˈpekərɪ/ **N** (pl **peccary** *or* **peccaries**) pécari *m*

peck¹ /pek/ **N** 1 [*of bird*] coup *m* de bec 2 (= *hasty kiss*) bise *f* ◆ **to give sb a** ~ **on the cheek** donner à qn une bise sur la joue **VT** [*bird*] [+ *object, ground*] becqueter, picoter ; [+ *food*] picorer ; [+ *person, attacker*] donner un coup de bec à ◆ **to** ~ **a hole in sth** faire un trou dans qch à (force de) coups de bec ◆ **the bird nearly** ~**ed his eyes out** l'oiseau a failli lui crever les yeux à coups de bec **VI** ◆ **to** ~ **at** [*bird*] [+ *object, ground*] becqueter, picoter ; [+ *food*] picorer ; [+ *person, attacker*] donner un coup de bec à ◆ **to** ~ **at one's food** [*person*] manger du bout des dents, chipoter *
COMP **pecking order, peck order** (*US*) **N** [*of birds*] ordre *m* hiérarchique ; (*fig*) hiérarchie *f*, ordre *m* des préséances

peck² /pek/ **N** (*Measure*) picotin *m* ◆ **a** ~ **of troubles** bien des ennuis

pecker /ˈpekəʳ/ **N** 1 (*Brit*) **to keep one's** ~ **up** * garder le moral 2 (*US* ** = *penis*) quéquette * *f*

peckish * /ˈpekɪʃ/ **ADJ** ◆ **to be** *or* **feel** ~ avoir un petit creux

pecs * /peks/ **NPL** pectoraux *mpl*

pectin /ˈpektɪn/ **N** pectine *f*

pectoral /ˈpektərəl/ **ADJ** pectoral **N** 1 ◆ ~**s** (= *muscles*) pectoraux *mpl* 2 pectoral *m* (*ornement*)

peculate /ˈpekjʊleɪt/ **VI** détourner des fonds (publics)

peculation /ˌpekjʊˈleɪʃən/ **N** détournement *m* de fonds (publics), péculat *m*

peculiar /pɪˈkjuːlɪəʳ/ **ADJ** 1 (= *odd*) bizarre ◆ **to feel** ~ se sentir bizarre
2 (*frm* = *especial*) particulier, spécial ◆ **a matter of** ~ **importance** une question d'une importance particulière
3 (*frm* = *particular*) particulier ◆ **the** ~ **properties of this drug** les propriétés particulières de ce médicament ◆ **the region has its** ~ **dialect** cette région a son dialecte particulier *or* son propre dialecte
♦ **peculiar to** particulier à, propre à ◆ **a phrase** ~ **to him** une expression qui lui est particulière *or* propre ◆ **an animal** ~ **to Africa** un animal qui n'existe qu'en Afrique ◆ **this problem is not** ~ **to the UK** ce problème n'est pas propre au Royaume-Uni

peculiarity /pɪˌkjʊlɪˈærɪtɪ/ **N** 1 (= *distinctive feature*) particularité *f*, trait *m* distinctif ◆ **it has the** ~ **of being ...** cela a *or* présente la particularité d'être ... 2 (= *oddity*) bizarrerie *f*, singularité *f* (*liter*) ◆ **she's got her little peculiarities** elle a ses petites manies

peculiarly /pɪˈkjuːlɪəlɪ/ **ADV** 1 (= *oddly*) étrangement, singulièrement 2 (*frm* = *uniquely*) particulièrement ◆ **a** ~ **British characteristic** une caractéristique propre aux Britanniques *or* typiquement britannique

pecuniary /pɪˈkjuːnɪərɪ/ **ADJ** (*frm*) pécuniaire, financier ◆ ~ **difficulties** ennuis *mpl* d'argent, embarras *mpl* pécuniaires

pedagogic(al) /ˌpedəˈgɒdʒɪk(əl)/ **ADJ** pédagogique

pedagogically /ˌpedəˈgɒdʒɪkəlɪ/ **ADV** (*frm*) d'un point de vue pédagogique

pedagogue /ˈpedəgɒg/ **N** (*Hist, fig*) pédagogue *mf*

pedagogy /ˈpedəgɒgɪ/ **N** pédagogie *f*

pedal /ˈpedl/ **N** 1 (= *lever*) [*of car, bicycle, piano etc*] pédale *f* ◆ **to put the** ~ **to the floor** *or* **boards** *or* **metal** * (= *accelerate fast*) mettre le pied au plancher * ; (*fig*) foncer dans le brouillard * ; → **clutch** 2 (*Mus*) basse *f* continue **VI** [*cyclist*] pédaler ◆ **he** ~**led through the town** il a traversé la ville à bicyclette *or* à vélo ; → **soft VT** [+ *machine, cycle*] appuyer sur la *or* les pédale(s) de ◆ **Gavin** ~**led the three miles to the restaurant** Gavin a fait les trois miles jusqu'au restaurant à bicyclette *or* à vélo
COMP **pedal bin N** poubelle *f* à pédale
pedal cycle N bicyclette *f* à pédales
pedal cyclist N cycliste *mf*
pedal pushers NPL (pantalon *m*) corsaire *m*

pedalboat /ˈpedlbəʊt/ **N** pédalo ® *m*

pedalcar /ˈpedlkɑːʳ/ **N** voiture *f* à pédales

pedalo /ˈpedələʊ/ **N** (pl **pedalos** *or* **pedaloes**) pédalo ® *m*

pedant /ˈpedənt/ **N** (*parading knowledge*) pédant(e) *m(f)* ; (*obsessed with detail*) ◆ **he's a** ~ il est trop pointilleux

pedantic /pɪˈdæntɪk/ **ADJ** [*person, approach*] pointilleux (-euse *f*) ◆ **my aunt in her** ~ **way worked out the exact cost** ma tante, pointilleuse comme toujours, calcula le coût exact ◆ **a** ~ **lecture** un exposé aride ◆ **don't be so** ~**!** arrête de pinailler !

> ⚠ The French word **pédant** refers not to a person obsessed with detail but to someone who shows off their knowledge.

pedantically /pɪˈdæntɪkəlɪ/ **ADV** ◆ **Guy** ~ **raised points of grammar** Guy, pointilleux, soulevait des points de grammaire

pedantry /ˈpedəntrɪ/ **N** ◆ **he rises above narrow academic** ~ son approche se situe au-delà de celle, pointilleuse et bornée, des universitaires

peddle /ˈpedl/ **VI** faire du colportage **VT** [+ *goods*] colporter ; (*fig pej*) [+ *gossip*] colporter, répandre ; [+ *ideas*] propager ; [+ *drugs*] faire le trafic de

peddler /ˈpedləʳ/ **N** 1 (*esp US*) ⇒ **pedlar** 2 [*of drugs*] revendeur *m*, -euse *f*

pederast /ˈpedəræst/ **N** pédéraste *m*

pederasty /ˈpedəræstɪ/ **N** pédérastie *f*

pedestal /ˈpedɪstl/ **N** piédestal *m*, socle *m* ; (*fig*) piédestal *m* ◆ **to put** *or* **set sb on a** ~ mettre qn sur un piédestal ◆ **to knock sb off their** ~ faire descendre *or* faire tomber qn de son piédestal
COMP **pedestal basin N** lavabo *m* sur colonne
pedestal desk N bureau *m* ministre *inv*
pedestal table N guéridon *m*

pedestrian /pɪˈdestrɪən/ **N** piéton *m* **ADJ** (*fig* = *prosaic*) dépourvu d'imagination ◆ **his more** ~ **colleagues** ses collègues, qui avaient moins d'imagination
COMP **pedestrian crossing N** (*Brit*) passage *m* pour piétons, passage *m* clouté
pedestrian mall, pedestrian precinct N (*Brit*) zone *f* piétonne
pedestrian traffic N piétons *mpl* ◆ ~ **traffic is increasing here** les piétons deviennent de plus en plus nombreux ici ◆ **"pedestrian traffic only"** "réservé aux piétons"
pedestrian zone N (*US*) ⇒ **pedestrian precinct**

pedestrianization /pɪˌdestrɪənaɪˈzeɪʃən/ **N** transformation *f* en zone piétonne *or* piétonnière, création *f* de zone(s) piétonne(s) *or* piétonnière(s)

pedestrianize /pɪˈdestrɪəˌnaɪz/ **VT** [+ *area*] transformer en zone piétonne *or* piétonnière

pediatric /ˌpiːdɪˈætrɪk/ **ADJ** ⇒ **paediatric**

pedicab /ˈpedɪkæb/ **N** cyclopousse *m* (à deux places)

pedicure /ˈpedɪkjʊəʳ/ **N** pédicurie *f* ◆ **to have a** ~ se faire soigner les pieds (*par un pédicure*)

pedigree /ˈpedɪgriː/ **N** 1 (= *lineage*) [*of animal*] pedigree *m* ; [*of person*] ascendance *f*, lignée *f* 2 (= *genealogy*) [*of person, animal*] arbre *m* généalogique 3 (= *document*) [*of dogs, horses etc*] pedigree *m* ; [*of person*] pièce *f or* document *m* généalogique **COMP** [*dog, cattle etc*] de (pure) race

pediment /ˈpedɪmənt/ **N** fronton *m*

pedlar /ˈpedləʳ/ **N** (*door to door*) colporteur *m* ; (*in street*) camelot *m*

pedological /ˌpiːdəˈlɒdʒɪkl/ **ADJ** pédologique

pedologist /pɪˈdɒlədʒɪst/ **N** pédologue *mf*

pedology /pɪˈdɒlədʒɪ/ **N** pédologie *f*

pedometer /pɪˈdɒmɪtəʳ/ **N** podomètre *m*

pedophile /ˈpiːdəʊfaɪl/ **N** ⇒ **paedophile**

pee ** /piː/ **VI** pisser **, faire pipi * **N** pisse ** *f*, pipi * *m*

peek /piːk/ **N** coup *m* d'œil (furtif) ◆ **to take a** ~ **at sb/sth** jeter un coup d'œil (furtif) à *or* sur qn/qch **VI** jeter un coup d'œil (furtif) (*at* sur, à) ◆ **no** ~**ing!** on ne regarde pas !
COMP **peek-a-boo** * **EXCL** coucou !
peek-a-boo blouse * **N** (*US*) corsage *m* semi-transparent

peel /piːl/ **N** [*of apple, potato*] pelure *f*, épluchure *f* ; [*of orange*] écorce *f*, peau *f* ; (*Culin*) zeste *m*
VT [+ *fruit*] peler, éplucher ; [+ *potato*] éplucher ; [+ *stick*] écorcer ; [+ *shrimps*] décortiquer, éplucher ◆ **to keep one's eyes** ~**ed** * faire attention, ouvrir l'œil * ◆ **keep your eyes** ~**ed** * **for a signpost!** ouvre l'œil ** et tâche d'apercevoir un panneau !
VI [*fruit*] se peler ; [*paint*] s'écailler ; [*skin, part of body*] peler

► **peel away VI** [*skin*] peler ; (*Med*) se desquamer ; [*paint*] s'écailler ; [*wallpaper*] se décoller
VT SEP [+ *rind, skin*] peler ; [+ *film, covering*] détacher, décoller

► **peel back VT SEP** [+ *film, covering*] détacher, décoller

► **peel off VI** 1 ⇒ **peel away vi**
2 (= *leave formation, group etc*) [*plane*] se détacher de la formation ; [*motorcyclists etc*] se détacher du groupe (*or du cortège etc*) en virant ◆ **to** ~ **off from** s'écarter de, se détacher en virant de
VT SEP 1 ⇒ **peel away vt sep**
2 (* *fig*) [+ *garment*] enlever, ôter ◆ **to** ~ **off one's clothes** enlever ses vêtements, se déshabiller

peeler /ˈpiːləʳ/ **N** 1 (= gadget) (couteau-)éplucheur *m* ; *(electric)* éplucheur *m* électrique 2 *(Brit †† = policeman)* sergent *m* de ville

peelie-wally * /ˈpiːlɪˈwælɪ/ **ADJ** *(Scot)* chétif, souffreteux

peeling /ˈpiːlɪŋ/ **N** ◆ **~s** *[of fruit, vegetables]* pelures *fpl*, épluchures *fpl* ◆ **potato ~s** épluchures *fpl* de pommes de terre **ADJ** *[skin]* qui pèle ; *[wallpaper]* qui se décolle ; *[paint]* qui s'écaille

peep¹ /piːp/ **N** 1 (= *peek*) coup *m* d'œil, regard *m* furtif ◆ **have a ~!** jette un coup d'œil ! ◆ **to have** *or* **take a ~ at sth** jeter un coup d'œil à *or* sur qch, regarder qch furtivement *or* à la dérobée ◆ **she had a ~ at her present** elle a jeté un (petit) coup d'œil à son cadeau ◆ **to get** *or* **have a ~ at the exam papers** jeter un (petit) coup d'œil discret sur les sujets d'examen

2 *[of gas]* veilleuse *f*, (toute) petite flamme *f* ◆ **a ~ of light showed through the curtains** un rayon de lumière filtrait entre les rideaux

VI jeter un coup d'œil, regarder furtivement ◆ **to ~ at sth** jeter un coup d'œil à qch, regarder qch furtivement ◆ **she ~ed into the box** elle a jeté un coup d'œil *or* elle a regardé furtivement à l'intérieur de la boîte ◆ **he was ~ing at us from behind a tree** il nous regardait furtivement *or* à la dérobée de derrière un arbre ◆ **to ~ over a wall** regarder furtivement par-dessus un mur, passer la tête par-dessus un mur ◆ **to ~ through a window** regarder furtivement *or* jeter un coup d'œil par la fenêtre

COMP **peep-bo** * **EXCL** coucou !
Peeping Tom **N** voyeur *m*
peep show **N** (= *box*) visionneuse *f* ; (= *pictures*) vues *fpl* stéréoscopiques ; (= *event*) peep-show *m*

► **peep out** **VI** 1 (= *peek*) ◆ **she was peeping out from behind the curtains** elle passait le nez de derrière les rideaux ◆ **the sun ~ed out from behind the clouds** le soleil s'est montré entre les nuages
2 (= *appear*) *[gun, petticoat etc]* dépasser (*from* de)
VT ◆ **she peeped her head out** elle a passé la tête

peep² /piːp/ **N** *[of bird]* pépiement *m*, piaulement *m* ; *[of mouse]* petit cri *m* aigu ◆ **one ~ out of you and I'll send you to bed!** * si tu ouvres la bouche je t'envoie te coucher ! ◆ **there wasn't a ~ of protest about this** il n'y a pas eu la moindre protestation à ce sujet **VI** *[bird]* pépier, piauler ; *[mouse]* pousser de petits cris aigus

peepers ‡ /ˈpiːpəz/ **NPL** quinquets ‡ *mpl*

peephole /ˈpiːphəʊl/ **N** *(gen)* trou *m* (pour épier) ; *(in front door etc)* judas *m*

peeptoe /ˈpiːptəʊ/ **ADJ** ◆ **~ sandal/shoe** sandale *f*/chaussure *f* à bout découpé

peer¹ /pɪəʳ/ **VI** (= *look*) ◆ **to ~ at sb** regarder qn ; *(inquiringly/doubtfully/anxiously)* regarder qn d'un air interrogateur/dubitatif/inquiet ; *(short-sightedly)* regarder qn avec des yeux de myope ◆ **to ~ at a book/photograph** scruter (du regard) un livre/une photographie ◆ **she ~ed into the room** elle regarda dans la pièce d'un air interrogateur *or* dubitatif *etc* ◆ **to ~ out of the window/over the wall** regarder par la fenêtre/par-dessus le mur d'un air interrogateur *etc* ◆ **to ~ into sb's face** regarder qn d'un air interrogateur *etc*, dévisager qn ◆ **she ~ed around over her spectacles** elle regarda autour d'elle par-dessus ses lunettes

peer² /pɪəʳ/ **N** 1 (= *social equal*) pair *m* ◆ **accepted by his ~s** accepté par ses pairs 2 *(liter: in achievement etc)* égal(e) *m(f)* ◆ **as a musician he has no ~** comme musicien il est hors pair *or* il n'a pas son pareil 3 (= *noble*: also **peer of the realm**) pair *m* (du royaume) ; → **hereditary, life**

COMP **peer group** **N** *(Sociol)* pairs *mpl*
peer pressure **N** pressions *fpl* exercées par l'entourage

peerage /ˈpɪərɪdʒ/ **N** (= *rank*) pairie *f* ; *(collective = the peers)* pairs *mpl*, noblesse *f* ; (= *list of peers*) nobiliaire *m* ◆ **to inherit a ~** hériter d'une pairie ◆ **to be given a ~** être anobli ; → **life**

peeress /ˈpɪərɪs/ **N** pairesse *f*

peerless /ˈpɪəlɪs/ **ADJ** hors pair, sans pareil

peeve * /piːv/ **VT** mettre en rogne * **N** ◆ **pet ~** bête *f* noire *(fig)*

peeved * /piːvd/ **ADJ** irrité, en rogne *

peevish /ˈpiːvɪʃ/ **ADJ** grincheux, maussade ; *[child]* grognon, de mauvaise humeur

peevishly /ˈpiːvɪʃlɪ/ **ADV** d'un air maussade, avec (mauvaise) humeur

peevishness /ˈpiːvɪʃnɪs/ **N** maussaderie *f*, mauvaise humeur *f*

peewee * /ˈpiːwiː/ *(US)* **ADJ** minuscule **N** (= *child*) petit bout *m* de chou *

peewit /ˈpiːwɪt/ **N** vanneau *m*

peg /peg/ **N** 1 *(wooden)* cheville *f* ; *(metal)* fiche *f* ; *(for coat, hat)* patère *f* ; (= *tent peg*) piquet *m* ; *(Climbing)* piton *m* ; *[of violin]* cheville *f* ; *[of cask]* fausset *m* ; *(Croquet)* piquet *m* ; *(Brit = clothes peg)* pince *f* à linge ◆ **to buy a dress off the ~** *(Brit)* acheter une robe de prêt-à-porter *or* de confection ◆ **I bought this off the ~** c'est du prêt-à-porter, j'ai acheté ça tout fait ; see also **off** ◆ **to take sb down a ~ or two** remettre qn à sa place, rabattre le caquet à qn ◆ **a ~ to hang a complaint on** *(fig)* un prétexte de plainte, un prétexte *or* une excuse pour se plaindre ; → **level, square**

2 *(Brit)* **a ~ of whisky** un whisky-soda

VT 1 *(gen)* fixer à l'aide de fiches (*or* de piquets *etc*) ; *(Tech)* cheviller ◆ **to ~ a tent down** fixer une tente avec des piquets ◆ **to ~ clothes (out) on the line** étendre du linge sur la corde
2 *(Econ) [+ prices, wages]* stabiliser, bloquer ◆ **to ~ prices to sth** lier les prix à qch ◆ **they ~ged their currencies to the dollar** ils ont fixé le cours de leurs monnaies par rapport au dollar
3 *(US * = categorize)* ◆ **to have sb ~ged as an extremist/a delinquent** cataloguer qn comme extrémiste/délinquant
4 *(Climbing)* pitonner

COMP **peg pants** **NPL** *(US)* ≃ pantalon *m* fuseau

► **peg away** * **VI** bosser *, bûcher * ◆ **he's ~ging away at his maths** il bosse * *or* bûche * ses maths

► **peg out** **VI** (‡ = *die*) casser sa pipe ‡, clamser ‡
VT SEP *[+ piece of land]* piqueter, délimiter ; see also **peg vt 1**

Pegasus /ˈpegəsəs/ **N** Pégase *m*

pegboard /ˈpegbɔːd/ **N** *(Games)* plateau *m* perforé *(utilisé dans certains jeux)*

pegleg ‡ /ˈpegleg/ **N** jambe *f* de bois

pejoration /ˌpiːdʒəˈreɪʃən/ **N** péjoration *f*

pejorative /pɪˈdʒɒrətɪv/ **ADJ** péjoratif

peke * /piːk/ **N** abbrev of **pekin(g)ese**

Pekin /piːˈkɪn/, **Peking** /piːˈkɪŋ/ **N** Pékin **COMP** **Peking duck** **N** canard *m* laqué

Pekin(g)ese /ˌpiːkɪˈniːz/ **N** *(pl inv = dog)* pékinois *m*

Pekinologist /ˌpiːkəˈnɒlədʒɪst/ **N** *(Pol)* sinologue *mf*

pekoe /ˈpiːkəʊ/ **N** (thé *m*) pekoe *m*

pelagic /pɪˈlædʒɪk/ **ADJ** pélagique

pelargonium /ˌpeləˈgəʊnɪəm/ **N** pélargonium *m*

pelf /pelf/ **N** *(pej)* lucre *m* *(pej)*, richesses *fpl*

pelican /ˈpelɪkən/ **N** pélican *m* **COMP** **pelican crossing** **N** *(Brit)* passage *m* pour piétons *(avec feux de circulation)*

pellagra /pəˈleɪgrə/ **N** pellagre *f*

pellet /ˈpelɪt/ **N** *[of paper, bread]* boulette *f* ; *(for gun)* (grain *m* de) plomb *m* ; *(Med)* pilule *f* ; *[of owl etc]* boulette *f* (de résidus regorgés) ; *[of chemicals]* pastille *f*

pell-mell /ˈpelˈmel/ **ADV** 1 (= *in a jumble*) *[throw, heap]* pêle-mêle ◆ **the puppies tumbled ~ into their basket** les chiots se sont précipités pêle-mêle dans leur panier 2 (= *full tilt*) *[run, dash, drive]* comme un fou ◆ **she ran ~ to the hospital** elle a couru comme une folle à l'hôpital

pellucid /peˈluːsɪd/ **ADJ** pellucide *(liter)*, transparent ; *(fig) [style]* clair, limpide ; *[mind]* lucide, clair

pelmet /ˈpelmɪt/ **N** *(esp Brit) (wooden)* lambrequin *m* ; *(cloth)* cantonnière *f*

Peloponnese /ˌpeləpəˈniːs/ **N** ◆ **the ~** le Péloponnèse

Peloponnesian /ˌpeləpəˈniːʃən/ **ADJ** péloponnésien ◆ **the ~ War** la guerre du Péloponnèse

pelota /pɪˈləʊtə/ **N** pelote *f* basque

pelt¹ /pelt/ **VT** bombarder (*with* de) ◆ **they were ~ed with stones/tomatoes** on les a bombardés de pierres/de tomates **VI** 1 **the rain is** *or* **it's ~ing down *, it's ~ing with rain** * il tombe des cordes *, il pleut à torrents *or* à seaux ◆ **~ing rain** pluie *f* battante 2 (= *run*) ◆ **to ~ down the street** descendre la rue à toutes jambes ◆ **she ~ed out of the house** elle est sortie de la maison en trombe *or* comme une flèche **N** ◆ **(at) full ~** à toute vitesse, à fond de train

pelt² /pelt/ **N** (= *skin*) peau *f* ; (= *fur*) fourrure *f*

pelves /ˈpelviːz/ **NPL** of **pelvis**

pelvic /ˈpelvɪk/ **ADJ** pelvien
COMP **pelvic floor** **N** plancher *m* pelvien
pelvic girdle **N** ceinture *f* pelvienne
pelvic inflammatory disease **N** salpingite *f* aiguë, pelvipéritonite *f*

pelvis /ˈpelvɪs/ **N** (pl **pelvises** *or* **pelves**) bassin *m*, pelvis *m*

pem(m)ican /ˈpemɪkən/ **N** pemmican *m*

pen¹ /pen/ **N** stylo *m* ; (= *ball-point*) stylo *m* à bille ; (= *felt-tip*) (crayon *m*) feutre *m* ; (= *fountain-pen*) stylo *m* à plume ◆ **to put ~ to paper** prendre la plume, écrire ◆ **a new novel from the ~ of ...** un nouveau roman de ... ◆ **to live by one's ~** vivre de sa plume ; → **quill** **VT** *[+ letter]* écrire ; *[+ article]* rédiger
COMP **pen-and-ink drawing** **N** dessin *m* à la plume
pen friend **N** *(Brit)* correspondant(e) *m(f)*
pen name **N** pseudonyme *m*, nom *m* de plume
pen nib **N** plume *f* *(de stylo)*
pen pal * **N** ⇒ **pen friend**

pen² /pen/ (vb : pret **penned**, ptp **penned** *or* **pent**) **N** *[of animals]* parc *m*, enclos *m* ; (also **playpen**) parc *m* (d'enfant) ; (also **submarine pen**) abri *m* de sous-marins **VT** (also **pen in, pen up**) *[+ animals]* parquer ; *[+ people]* enfermer, parquer *(pej)*

pen³ /pen/ **N** (= *swan*) cygne *m* femelle

pen⁴ ‡ /pen/ **N** *(US)* (abbrev of **penitentiary**) taule ‡ *f or* tôle ‡ *f*, trou ‡ *m*

penal /ˈpiːnl/ **ADJ** 1 *[law, clause, policy]* pénal ; *[offence]* punissable ◆ **~ reform** réforme *f* du système pénal 2 (= *harsh*) *[taxation]* très lourd ; *[rate of interest]* exorbitant
COMP **penal code** **N** code *m* pénal
penal colony **N** colonie *f* pénitentiaire
penal servitude **N** *(Jur)* ◆ **~ servitude (for life)** travaux *mpl* forcés (à perpétuité)
penal settlement **N** ⇒ **penal colony**

penalization /ˌpiːnəlaɪˈzeɪʃən/ **N** pénalisation *f*

penalize /ˈpiːnəlaɪz/ VT 1 (= *punish*) [+ *person*] pénaliser ; [+ *action, mistake*] réprimer ◆ **he was ~d for refusing (to ...)** il a été pénalisé pour avoir refusé (de ...) ◆ **to be ~d for a foul** (*Sport*) être pénalisé pour une faute 2 (= *work against*) pénaliser, défavoriser ◆ **a law that ~s single mothers** une loi qui pénalise *or* défavorise les mères célibataires ◆ **the rail strike ~s those who haven't got a car** la grève des chemins de fer pénalise ceux qui n'ont pas de voiture

penalty /ˈpenəltɪ/ N (= *punishment*) peine *f* ; (= *fine*) pénalité *f*, amende *f* ; (*Sport*) pénalisation *f* ; (*Ftbl etc*) penalty *m* ◆ **the ~ for murder is death** le meurtre est passible de la peine de mort ◆ **"no smoking: maximum penalty £500"** "interdiction de fumer : jusqu'à 500 livres d'amende en cas d'infraction" ◆ **a five-point ~ for a wrong answer** (*in games*) cinq points de pénalité pour chaque erreur ◆ **on ~ of** sous peine de ◆ **under ~ of death** sous peine de mort ◆ **he has paid the ~ for neglecting his responsibilities** il n'a pas assumé ses responsabilités et en a subi les conséquences ◆ **he has paid the ~ for (his) success** il a payé la rançon du succès

COMP **penalty area, penalty box** N (*Ftbl*) surface *f* de réparation
penalty clause N (*Jur*) clause *f* pénale
penalty corner N (*Hockey*) corner *m*
penalty goal N (*Rugby etc*) but *m* sur pénalité
penalty kick N (*Ftbl*) penalty *m* ; (*Rugby*) coup *m* de pied de pénalité
penalty point N (*Aut, Jur, Sport*) point *m* de pénalité
penalty shoot-out N (*Ftbl*) (épreuve *f* des) tirs *mpl* au but
penalty spot N (*Ftbl*) point *m* de penalty *or* de réparation

penance /ˈpenəns/ N (*Rel, fig*) pénitence *f* (*for* de, pour) ◆ **to give (sb) ~** (*Rel*) [*priest*] donner une pénitence (à qn) ◆ **to do ~ for sth** faire pénitence pour qch

pence /pens/ NPL of **penny**

penchant /ˈpɑːʃɑːŋ/ N penchant *m* (*for* pour), inclination *f* (*for* pour)

pencil /ˈpensl/ N 1 crayon *m* ◆ **to write/draw in ~** écrire/dessiner au crayon ◆ **a coloured ~** un crayon de couleur ; → **lead², propel**
2 (= *thin beam*) ◆ **a ~ of light shone from his torch** sa lampe de poche projetait un pinceau lumineux
VT [+ *note*] crayonner, écrire au crayon
COMP [*note, line, mark*] au crayon
pencil box N plumier *m*
pencil case N trousse *f* (d'écolier)
pencil drawing N dessin *m* au crayon, crayonnage *m*
pencil pusher* N (*US pej*) gratte-papier* *m*, rond-de-cuir* *m*
pencil rubber N gomme *f* (à crayon)
pencil sharpener N taille-crayon *m*

► **pencil in** VT SEP 1 (*lit*) [+ *note*] crayonner, écrire au crayon ◆ **to ~ in one's eyebrows** se faire les sourcils au crayon
2 (*fig*) [+ *date, meeting*] fixer provisoirement ◆ **we had three dates pencilled in** nous avions fixé trois dates possibles, nous avions retenu provisoirement trois dates ◆ **I've pencilled you in for Thursday** j'ai marqué votre nom provisoirement pour jeudi

pendant /ˈpendənt/ N (*on necklace*) pendentif *m* ; (= *earring*) pendant *m* (d'oreille) ; (= *ceiling lamp*) lustre *m* ; (*on chandelier etc*) pendeloque *f*

pendency /ˈpendənsɪ/ N (*Jur*) ◆ **during the ~ of the action** en cours d'instance

pending /ˈpendɪŋ/ ADJ [*case, action*] pendant, en instance ; [*business, question*] en suspens, en souffrance ◆ **the ~ tray** le casier des affaires en souffrance ◆ **other matters ~ will be dealt with next week** les affaires en suspens seront réglées la semaine prochaine PREP dans l'attente de

pendulous /ˈpendjʊləs/ ADJ 1 (= *hanging*) [*lips, cheeks, nest*] pendant ; [*flowers*] pendant, qui retombe 2 (= *swinging*) [*movement*] de balancement, oscillant

pendulum /ˈpendjʊləm/ N 1 (*gen*) pendule *m* ; [*of clock*] balancier *m* ; see also **swing** 2 (*Climbing*) pendule *m*

Penelope /pəˈneləpɪ/ N Pénélope *f*

peneplain, peneplane /ˈpiːnɪpleɪn/ N pénéplaine *f*

penes /ˈpiːniːz/ NPL of **penis**

penetrable /ˈpenɪtrəbl/ ADJ pénétrable

penetrate /ˈpenɪtreɪt/ VT 1 [+ *area, region, territory*] pénétrer dans ◆ **rescue workers are penetrating this remote region** les sauveteurs pénètrent dans cette région isolée ◆ **to ~ enemy territory** pénétrer en *or* entrer en territoire ennemi ◆ **to ~ the enemy's defences/lines** pénétrer *or* percer les défenses ennemies/le front ennemi ◆ **the bullet ~d his heart** la balle lui a perforé le cœur ◆ **the knife ~d his heart** le couteau lui est entré dans le cœur ◆ **the car's lights ~d the darkness** les phares de la voiture perçaient l'obscurité ◆ **sunlight cannot ~ the thick foliage** la lumière du soleil ne peut pas passer à travers cette épaisse végétation ◆ **to ~ a mystery/sb's mind** pénétrer *or* comprendre un mystère/les pensées de qn ◆ **to ~ sb's disguise** percer le déguisement de qn ◆ **subversive elements have ~d the party** (*Pol*) des éléments subversifs se sont infiltrés dans le parti ◆ **they managed to ~ the foreign market** (*Comm*) ils ont réussi à pénétrer le marché étranger
2 (*during sex*) pénétrer
VI ◆ **to ~ into** [+ *area, region, territory*] pénétrer dans ; [*light, water*] pénétrer (dans), filtrer dans ◆ **to ~ through** traverser ◆ **the noise ~d into the lobby** le bruit est parvenu *or* est arrivé jusque dans le hall

penetrating /ˈpenɪtreɪtɪŋ/ ADJ 1 [*wind, rain*] pénétrant ; [*cold*] pénétrant, mordant ; [*sound, voice, look*] pénétrant, perçant 2 (= *acute, discerning*) [*mind, remark*] pénétrant, perspicace ; [*person, assessment*] clairvoyant, perspicace

penetratingly /ˈpenɪtreɪtɪŋlɪ/ ADV 1 (= *piercingly*) [*speak, shriek*] d'une voix perçante 2 (= *acutely, discerningly*) [*assess, observe*] avec pénétration, avec perspicacité

penetration /ˌpenɪˈtreɪʃən/ N (*NonC*) pénétration *f*

penetrative /ˈpenɪtrətɪv/ ADJ pénétrant ◆ **~ sex** (relations *fpl* sexuelles avec) pénétration *f*

penguin /ˈpeŋgwɪn/ N (= *bird*) manchot *m*

penholder /ˈpenˌhəʊldəʳ/ N porte-plume *m*

penicillin /ˌpenɪˈsɪlɪn/ N pénicilline *f*

penile /ˈpiːnaɪl/ ADJ pénien

peninsula /pɪˈnɪnsjʊlə/ N péninsule *f*

peninsular /pɪˈnɪnsjʊləʳ/ ADJ péninsulaire
COMP **the Peninsular War** N la guerre d'Espagne (*napoléonienne*)

penis /ˈpiːnɪs/ N (pl **penises** *or* **penes**) pénis *m*
COMP **penis envy** N (*Psych*) envie *f* du pénis

penitence /ˈpenɪtəns/ N repentir *m*

penitent /ˈpenɪtənt/ ADJ repentant(e) *m(f)* N personne *f* repentante

penitential /ˌpenɪˈtenʃəl/ ADJ contrit ◆ **~ psalm** (*Rel*) psaume *m* de la pénitence *or* pénitentiel N [*code*] pénitentiel *m*

penitentiary /ˌpenɪˈtenʃərɪ/ N 1 (*US* = *prison*: also **state penitentiary**) prison *f*, (maison *f*) centrale *f* 2 (*Rel*) (= *cleric*) pénitencier *m* ; (= *tribunal*) pénitencerie *f*

penitently /ˈpenɪtəntlɪ/ ADV d'un air *or* d'un ton contrit

penknife /ˈpennaɪf/ N (pl **-knives**) canif *m*

penmanship /ˈpenmənʃɪp/ N calligraphie *f*

Penn., Penna. (*US*) abbrev of **Pennsylvania**

pennant /ˈpenənt/ N (*Sport etc, also on car, bicycle*) fanion *m* ; (*Naut*) flamme *f*

penniless /ˈpenɪlɪs/ ADJ sans le sou, sans ressources ◆ **he's quite ~** il n'a pas le sou, il est sans le sou *or* sans ressources

Pennine /ˈpenaɪn/ N ◆ **the ~s, the ~ Range** les Pennines *fpl*, la chaîne Pennine

pennon /ˈpenən/ N flamme *f*, banderole *f* ; (*Naut*) flamme *f*

penn'orth † /ˈpenəθ/ N (*Brit*) ⇒ **pennyworth**

Pennsylvania /ˌpensɪlˈveɪnɪə/ N Pennsylvanie *f* ◆ **in ~** en Pennsylvanie COMP **Pennsylvania Dutch** NPL (= *people*) Allemands *mpl* de Pennsylvanie N (= *language*) *dialecte des Allemands de Pennsylvanie*

penny /ˈpenɪ/ N (*value*) (pl **pence**) (*coins*) (pl **pennies**) penny *m* ◆ **one old/new ~** un ancien/un nouveau penny ◆ **it costs 50 pence** cela coûte 50 pence ◆ **I have five pennies** j'ai cinq pennies, j'ai cinq pièces de un penny ◆ **one ~ in the pound** ≈ un centime l'euro ◆ **they're two** *or* **ten a ~** (*fig*) on en trouve partout ◆ **he hasn't a ~ to his name, he hasn't got two pennies to rub together** il est sans le sou, il n'a pas un sou vaillant ◆ **he didn't get a ~ (out of it)** il n'en a pas tiré un sou ◆ **I'll pay you back every ~** je te rembourserai ce que je te dois jusqu'au dernier sou ◆ **(a) ~ for your thoughts!*** à quoi penses-tu ? ◆ **the ~ dropped*** ça a fait tilt !* ◆ **to count** *or* **watch the pennies** regarder à la dépense ◆ **he keeps turning up like a bad ~** pas moyen de se débarrasser de lui ◆ **a ~ saved is a ~ gained** (*Prov*) un sou est un sou ◆ **in for a ~ in for a pound** (*Prov*) (au point où on en est) autant faire les choses jusqu'au bout ◆ **look after the pennies and the pounds will look after themselves** (*Prov*) les petits ruisseaux font les grandes rivières (*Prov*) il n'y a pas de petites économies ; → **honest, pretty, spend, worth**
COMP [*book, pencil*] de quatre sous
penny-a-liner* N pigiste *mf*, journaliste *mf* à la pige *or* à deux sous la ligne
penny arcade N (*US*) salle *f* de jeux (*avec machines à sous*)
Penny Black N (= *stamp*) penny *m* noir (*premier timbre-poste britannique*)
penny dreadful †* N (*Brit*) (pl **penny dreadfuls**) roman *m* à quatre sous, roman *m* à sensation
penny-farthing N (*Brit*) vélocipède *m*
penny-in-the-slot machine N (*for amusements*) machine *f* à sous ; (*for selling*) distributeur *m* automatique
penny loafer N (*US*) mocassin *m*
penny-pincher N pingre *mf*, radin(e)* *m(f)*
penny-pinching N économies *fpl* de bouts de chandelle ADJ [*person*] pingre, radin*
penny whistle N flûteau *m*
penny-wise ADJ ◆ **to be ~-wise and pound-foolish** économiser un franc et en prodiguer mille

pennyweight /ˈpenɪweɪt/ N gramme *m* et demi

pennyworth /ˈpenəθ/ N ◆ **I want a ~ of sweets** je voudrais pour un penny de bonbons

penologist /piːˈnɒlədʒɪst/ N pénologue *mf*

penology /piːˈnɒlədʒɪ/ N pénologie *f*

penpusher /ˈpenˌpʊʃəʳ/ N (*esp Brit pej*) gratte-papier* *m*, rond-de-cuir* *m*

penpushing /ˈpenˌpʊʃɪŋ/ N (*esp Brit pej*) travail *m* de gratte-papier*

pension /ˈpenʃən/ N [1] *(= state payment)* pension *f* ◆ **(old age)** ~ pension *f* de retraite ◆ **retirement** ~ (pension *f* de) retraite *f* ◆ **war/widow's/disability** ~ pension *f* de guerre/de veuve/d'invalidité ; → **eligible** [2] *(from company etc)* retraite *f* ◆ **to get a** ~ toucher une retraite *or* une pension (de retraite) ◆ **it is possible to retire on a** ~ **at 55** il est possible de toucher une retraite à partir de 55 ans [3] *(= allowance: to artist, former servant etc)* pension *f*
COMP **pension book** N ≈ titre *m* de pension
pension fund N caisse *f or* fonds *m* de retraite, assurance *f* vieillesse
pension plan N plan *m* de retraite
pension scheme N régime *m* de retraite
▸ **pension off** VT SEP mettre à la retraite

pensionable /ˈpenʃnəbl/ ADJ ◆ **to be of** ~ **age** avoir atteint l'âge de la retraite ◆ **this is a** ~ **job** c'est un emploi qui donne droit à une retraite

pensioner /ˈpenʃənəʳ/ N (also **old age pensioner**) retraité(e) *m(f)* ; *(any kind of pension)* pensionné(e) *m(f)* ; (also **war pensioner**) militaire *m* retraité ; *(disabled)* invalide *m* de guerre

> ⚠ **pensioner** is not translated by **pensionnaire**, which means 'boarder'.

pensive /ˈpensɪv/ ADJ pensif, songeur

pensively /ˈpensɪvlɪ/ ADV pensivement, d'un air pensif

pent /pent/ VB ptp of **pen²** ADJ *(liter)* emprisonné COMP **pent-up** ADJ *[emotions, rage]* refoulé, réprimé ; *[energy]* refoulé, contenu ◆ **she was very ~-up** elle était sur les nerfs *or* très tendue

pentacle /ˈpentəkl/ N pentacle *m*

Pentagon /ˈpentəgən/ N *(US)* ◆ **the** ~ le Pentagone

pentagon /ˈpentəgən/ N pentagone *m*

pentagonal /penˈtægənl/ ADJ pentagonal

pentagram /ˈpentəgræm/ N pentagramme *m*

pentahedron /ˌpentəˈhiːdrən/ N (pl **pentahedrons** *or* **pentahedra** /ˌpentəˈhiːdrə/) pentaèdre *m*

pentameter /penˈtæmɪtəʳ/ N pentamètre *m* ; → **iambic**

Pentateuch /ˈpentətjuːk/ N Pentateuque *m*

pentathlete /penˈtæθliːt/ N pentathlonien(ne) *m(f)*

pentathlon /penˈtæθlən/ N (also **modern pentathlon**) pentathlon *m*

pentatonic /ˌpentəˈtɒnɪk/ ADJ pentatonique

Pentecost /ˈpentɪkɒst/ N Pentecôte *f*

Pentecostal /ˌpentɪˈkɒstl/ ADJ de (la) Pentecôte ; *[church, beliefs]* pentecôtiste

Pentecostalism /ˌpentɪˈkɒstlɪzəm/ N pentecôtisme *m*

Pentecostalist /ˌpentɪˈkɒstlɪst/ ADJ, N pentecôtiste *mf*

penthouse /ˈpenthaʊs/ N [1] (also **penthouse flat or apartment**) appartement *m* de grand standing *(construit sur le toit d'un immeuble)* [2] *(Archit = lean-to)* auvent *m*, abri *m* extérieur ◆ ~ **roof** appentis *m*, toit *m* en auvent

penultimate /pɪˈnʌltɪmɪt/ ADJ avant-dernier, pénultième N *(Ling)* pénultième *f*, avant-dernière syllabe *f*

penumbra /pɪˈnʌmbrə/ N (pl **penumbras** *or* **penumbrae** /pɪˈnʌmbriː/) *(Astron)* pénombre *f*

penurious /pɪˈnjʊərɪəs/ ADJ *(frm)* [1] *(= poor)* indigent, misérable [2] *(= mean)* parcimonieux, ladre

penury /ˈpenjʊrɪ/ N misère *f*, indigence *f* ◆ **in** ~ dans la misère *or* l'indigence

penwiper /ˈpenˌwaɪpəʳ/ N essuie-plume *m inv*

peon /ˈpiːən/ N péon *m*

peony (rose) /ˈpɪənɪ(ˌrəʊz)/ N pivoine *f*

people /ˈpiːpl/ NPL [1] *(= persons)* gens *pl preceding adj gen fem*, personnes *fpl* ◆ **clever** ~ les gens *mpl* intelligents ◆ **all these good** ~ toutes ces bonnes gens, tous ces braves gens ◆ **old** ~ les personnes *fpl* âgées ; *(less respectful)* les vieux *mpl* ◆ **young** ~ les jeunes *mpl* ◆ ~ **are more important than animals** les gens *or* les êtres humains sont plus importants que les animaux ◆ **a lot of** ~ beaucoup de gens *or* de monde ◆ **what a lot of** ~**!** que de monde ! ◆ **the place was full of** ~ il y avait beaucoup de monde, il y avait un monde fou* ◆ **she doesn't know many** ~ elle ne connaît pas grand monde ◆ **several** ~ **said ...** plusieurs personnes ont dit ... ◆ **some** ~ **might prefer to wait** il y a peut-être des gens qui préféreraient attendre, certains préféreraient peut-être attendre ◆ **how many** ~**?** combien de personnes ? ◆ **there were 120** ~ **at the lecture** il y avait 120 personnes à la conférence ◆ **they're strange** ~ ce sont de drôles de gens ◆ **why ask me of all** ~**?** pourquoi me le demander à moi ? ◆ **you of all** ~ **should know that** s'il y a quelqu'un qui devrait le savoir, c'est bien toi ◆ **what do you** ~* **think?** qu'est-ce que vous en pensez, vous (tous) *or* vous autres ? ; → **little¹, other**
[2] *(in general)* **what will** ~ **think?** que vont penser les gens ?, que va-t-on penser ? ◆ ~ **say ...** on dit ... ◆ **don't tell** ~ **about that!** n'allez pas raconter ça (aux gens) ! ◆ ~ **get worried when they see that** on s'inquiète quand on voit cela, les gens s'inquiètent quand ils voient cela
[3] *(= inhabitants, natives) [of a country]* population *f* ; *[of district, town]* habitants *mpl*, population *f* ◆ **country** ~ les gens *mpl* de la campagne ◆ **town** ~ les habitants *mpl* des villes, les citadins *mpl* ◆ **Liverpool** ~ **are friendly** à Liverpool les gens sont gentils, les habitants de Liverpool sont gentils ◆ **the** ~ **of France** les Français *mpl* ◆ **the American** ~ le peuple américain ◆ **English/French** ~ les Anglais *mpl*/Français *mpl*
[4] *(Pol)* **the** ~ le peuple ◆ **government by the** ~ gouvernement *m* par le peuple ◆ **the will of the** ~ la volonté du peuple *or* populaire ◆ **the** ~**'s princess** la princesse du peuple ◆ ~ **of the Republic!** citoyens ! ◆ **the** ~ **at large** le grand public ◆ **the minister must tell the** ~ **the truth** le ministre doit dire la vérité au pays ◆ **a man of the** ~ un homme du peuple ◆ **the** ~**'s army** l'armée *f* populaire ◆ ~**'s democracy** démocratie *f* populaire ◆ **People's Democratic Republic (of ...)** *(in country's name)* République *f* populaire (de ...) ◆ **the** ~**'s war** la guerre du peuple ◆ ~**'s park** *(US)* jardin *m* public ; → **common**
[5] *(* = family)* famille *f*, parents *mpl* ◆ **how are your** ~**?** comment va votre famille ?, comment ça va chez vous ?*
[6] *(* = employees, workers)* **the marketing** ~ les gens *mpl* du marketing ◆ **the TV** ~ les gens *mpl* de la télé ◆ **I'll get my** ~ **to look into it** je vais demander à mon personnel d'examiner cela
N *(sg = nation, race etc)* peuple *m*, nation *f*, race *f* ◆ **the Jewish** ~ le peuple juif ◆ **the** ~**s of the East** les nations de l'Orient
VT peupler (with de)
COMP **people-carrier** N *(Brit = car)* monospace *m*
People's Dispensary for Sick Animals N *(Brit) association qui dispense des soins vétérinaires gratuits*
people mover N
[1] *(= car)* monospace *m* [2] *(= escalator)* escalator *m* ; *(= moving pavement)* trottoir *m* roulant
people power N action *f* citoyenne

PEP /pep/ N *(Brit Fin)* (abbrev of **personal equity plan**) ≈ CEA *m*

pep* /pep/ N *(NonC)* entrain *m*, punch* *m* ◆ **to be full of** ~ avoir la pêche* *or* la frite*
COMP **pep pill*** N excitant *m*, stimulant *m*
pep rally N *(US Scol) réunion des élèves (ou des étudiants) avant un match interscolaire, pour encourager leur équipe*
pep talk* N discours *m or* paroles *fpl* d'encouragement
▸ **pep up*** VI *[person]* s'animer, être ragaillardi ; *[business, trade]* reprendre, remonter VT SEP *[+ person]* remonter le moral à, ragaillardir ; *[+ one's social life, love life]* redonner du piment à ; *[+ party, conversation]* animer ; *[+ drink, plot]* corser

> **PEP RALLY**
>
> Aux États-Unis, un **pep rally** est une réunion de lycéens ou d'étudiants qui souhaitent stimuler le moral de leur équipe sportive avant un match. La manifestation comprend des discours d'encouragement mais aussi un défilé de l'orchestre de l'école (ou de l'université) avec ses majorettes. Le terme est parfois utilisé pour les meetings politiques ou les séminaires d'entreprise ayant pour but de motiver les militants ou les employés.

peplos, peplus /ˈpepləs/ N (pl **peploses**) péplum *m*

pepper /ˈpepəʳ/ N [1] *(= spice)* poivre *m* ◆ **white/black** ~ poivre *m* blanc/gris *or* noir [2] *(= vegetable)* poivron *m* ◆ **red/green** ~ poivron *m* rouge/vert VT [1] *(Culin)* poivrer [2] *(fig)* **to** ~ **sb with shot** cribler qn de plombs ◆ **to** ~ **a speech with quotations** émailler *or* truffer un discours de citations ◆ **the minister was ~ed with questions** le ministre a été assailli *or* bombardé de questions
COMP **pepper-and-salt** ADJ *[cloth]* chiné noir *inv* et blanc *inv* ; *[beard, hair]* poivre et sel *inv*
pepper gas N gaz *m* poivre
pepper mill N moulin *m* à poivre
pepper shaker N ⇒ **pepperpot**

peppercorn /ˈpepəkɔːn/ N grain *m* de poivre
COMP **peppercorn rent** N *(Brit)* loyer *m* très modique

peppermint /ˈpepəmɪnt/ N [1] *(= sweet)* pastille *f* de menthe [2] *(= plant)* menthe *f* poivrée ADJ (also **peppermint-flavoured**) à la menthe

pepperoni /ˌpepəˈrəʊnɪ/ N *saucisson sec de porc et de bœuf très poivré*

pepperpot /ˈpepəpɒt/ N poivrier *m*, poivrière *f*

peppery /ˈpepərɪ/ ADJ *[food, taste]* poivré ; *(fig) [person]* irascible, emporté ; *[speech]* irrité

peppy* /ˈpepɪ/ ADJ *(US) [person] (= energetic)* énergique ; *(= lively)* plein d'entrain ; *[car]* nerveux

pepsin /ˈpepsɪn/ N pepsine *f*

peptic /ˈpeptɪk/ ADJ digestif COMP **peptic ulcer** N *(Med)* ulcère *m* de l'estomac ◆ **he has a** ~ **ulcer** il a un ulcère à l'estomac

peptide /ˈpeptaɪd/ N peptide *m*
COMP **peptide bond** N liaison *f* peptidique
peptide chain N chaîne *f* peptidique

peptone /ˈpeptəʊn/ N peptone *f*

per /pɜːʳ/ PREP [1] par ◆ ~ **head** par tête, par personne ◆ ~ **head of population** par habitant ◆ **30 miles** ~ **gallon** ≈ 8 litres aux cent (km) ◆ **to drive at 100km** ~ **hour** rouler à 100 (km) à l'heure ◆ **she is paid 13 euros** ~ **hour** elle est payée 13 euros (de) l'heure ◆ **5 euros** ~ **kilo** 5 euros le kilo [2] *(Comm)* ~ **post** par la poste ◆ **as** ~ **invoice** suivant facture ◆ **as** ~ **normal*** *or* **usual*** comme d'habitude ◆ ~ **pro** *(Jur)* (abbrev of **per procurationem**) *(= by proxy)* p.p.
COMP **per annum** ADV par an
per capita ADV par personne

per capita income N *(Econ)* revenu *m* par habitant

per cent ADV pour cent ◆ **a ten ~ cent discount/increase** un rabais/une augmentation de dix pour cent

per day, per diem ADV par jour ◆ **a ~ diem of 100 dollars** *(US)* une indemnité journalière de 100 dollars

per se ADV en soi

peradventure /ˌperəd'ventʃəʳ/ ADV *(liter)* par hasard, d'aventure *(liter)*

perambulate /pə'ræmbjʊleɪt/ *(frm)* VT parcourir *(un terrain, surtout en vue de l'inspecter)* VI marcher, faire les cent pas

perambulation /pəˌræmbjʊ'leɪʃən/ N *(frm)* marche *f*, promenade(s) *f(pl)*, déambulation *f*

perambulator † /'præmbjʊleɪtəʳ/ N *(Brit)* voiture *f* d'enfant, landau *m*

perborate /pə'bɔːreɪt/ N perborate *m*

perceive /pə'siːv/ VT [1] *(= see, hear)* [*+ sound, light*] percevoir [2] *(= notice)* remarquer, apercevoir ; *(= realize)* s'apercevoir de ◆ **he ~d that ...** il a remarqué *or* s'est aperçu que ... [3] *(= view, regard)* [*+ person, situation*] percevoir ◆ **she was ~d as a threat** elle était perçue comme une menace ◆ **the things children ~ as being important** les choses que les enfants perçoivent comme étant importantes ◆ **they ~ themselves as rebels** ils se considèrent comme des rebelles [4] *(= understand)* [*+ implication, meaning*] percevoir, saisir

perceived /pə'siːvd/ ADJ ◆ **~ problems** ce que certains considèrent comme des problèmes ◆ **how would they tackle ~ problems of staff morale?** comment aborderaient-ils ce que certains considèrent comme des problèmes de motivation au sein du personnel ? ◆ **there are a lot of ~ problems as opposed to actual problems** il y a beaucoup de problèmes imaginaires par opposition aux problèmes réels ◆ **the ~ threat of nuclear weapons** la menace que constituent les armes nucléaires aux yeux des gens ◆ **the president's ~ failure to deal with these problems** le fait qu'aux yeux du public le président n'ait pas réussi à régler ces problèmes

percent /pə'sent/ ADV → **per**

percentage /pə'sentɪdʒ/ N [1] *(= proportion)* proportion *f* ; *(Math)* pourcentage *m* ◆ **the figure is expressed as a ~** le chiffre est exprimé *or* donné en pourcentage ◆ **a high ~ were girls** les filles représentaient un fort pourcentage, il y avait une forte proportion de filles ◆ **few foods have such a high ~ of protein** peu d'aliments contiennent autant de protéines [2] *(* = share, profit)* ◆ **to get a ~ on sth** recevoir *or* toucher un pourcentage sur qch ◆ **there's no ~ in getting angry with him** *(fig)* ça ne sert à rien de se mettre en colère contre lui

COMP **percentage distribution** N *(Econ)* ventilation *f* en pourcentage

percentage point N point *m* ◆ **ten ~ points** dix pour cent, dix points

percentile /pə'sentaɪl/ N centile *m* ◆ **she is in the top earning ~** elle est dans la catégorie des hauts salaires ◆ **he's in the lowest 10th ~ for reading and writing** il est dans la tranche des 10% les moins bons en lecture et en écriture

COMP **percentile ranking** N classement *m* par pourcentage

perceptible /pə'septəbl/ ADJ [*sound, movement*] perceptible ; [*difference, increase*] perceptible

perceptibly /pə'septɪblɪ/ ADV *(gen)* sensiblement ; *(= visibly)* visiblement ◆ **to improve ~** s'améliorer sensiblement ◆ **the weather was ~ warmer** il faisait sensiblement plus chaud ◆ **he brightened ~** il s'égaya visiblement

perception /pə'sepʃən/ N [1] *(= impression, opinion)* **their ~ of foreigners** la façon dont ils voient les étrangers, l'image qu'ils ont des étrangers ◆ **the public's ~ of the police/the Conservative party** l'image *f* de la police/du parti conservateur ◆ **our ~ of the situation is that these problems are due to ...** d'après notre analyse de la situation, ces problèmes sont dus à ... ◆ **the President has been giving his ~ of the situation** le président a donné son analyse de la situation ◆ **consumers have a rather different ~ of the situation** les consommateurs se font une idée assez différente de la situation, les consommateurs voient la situation de façon assez différente ◆ **there is a popular ~ that she ...** beaucoup de gens croient qu'elle ...

[2] *(= insight)* perspicacité *f* ◆ **a person of extraordinary ~** une personne d'une extraordinaire perspicacité ◆ **his powers of ~** sa grande perspicacité

[3] [*of sound, sight etc*] *(also Psych)* perception *f* ◆ **visual ~** la perception visuelle ◆ **one's powers of ~ decrease with age** la faculté de perception diminue avec l'âge

[4] *(Jur)* [*of rents, taxes, profits*] perception *f*

> ⚠ When it means 'impression' or 'insight' **perception** is not translated by the French word **perception.**

perceptive /pə'septɪv/ ADJ [1] *(= perspicacious)* [*analysis, assessment*] pénétrant ; [*person*] perspicace ◆ **how very ~ of you!** vous êtes très perspicace ! [2] [*faculty*] percepteur (-trice *f*), de (la) perception

perceptively /pə'septɪvlɪ/ ADV avec perspicacité

perceptiveness /pə'septɪvnɪs/ N ⇒ **perception 2**

perceptual /pə'septjʊəl/ ADJ [*capacity, system, process, error*] de perception ◆ **~ distortion** *(Med, Psych)* troubles *mpl* de la perception

perch[1] /pɜːtʃ/ N (pl **perch** *or* **perches**) (= *fish*) perche *f*

perch[2] /pɜːtʃ/ N [1] [*of bird*] perchoir *m*, juchoir *m* ◆ **to knock sb off his ~** * faire dégringoler qn de son perchoir * ◆ **to fall** *or* **drop** *or* **topple off one's ~** * *(Brit hum = die)* casser sa pipe * [2] *(= measure)* perche *f* VI [*bird*] (se) percher ; [*person*] se percher, se jucher ◆ **she ~ed on the arm of my chair** elle se percha *or* se jucha sur le bras de mon fauteuil ◆ **the tower ~es on the edge of the cliff** la tour est perchée *or* juchée au bord de la falaise VT [*+ object, child, building etc*] percher, jucher

perchance /pə'tʃɑːns/ ADV (†† *or hum*) peut-être

percipient /pə'sɪpɪənt/ ADJ [*faculty*] percepteur (-trice *f*) ; [*person*] fin, perspicace ; [*choice*] éclairé N personne *f* qui perçoit

percolate /'pɜːkəleɪt/ VT ◆ **to ~ the coffee** passer le café ◆ **~d coffee** café *m* fait dans une cafetière à pression VI [*coffee, water*] passer *(through* par) ◆ **the news ~d through from the front** la nouvelle a filtré du front ◆ **new fashions took a long time to ~ down** les modes mettaient longtemps à se propager

percolation /ˌpɜːkə'leɪʃən/ N percolation *f*

percolator /'pɜːkəleɪtəʳ/ N cafetière *f* à pression ; *(in café)* percolateur *m* ◆ **electric ~** cafetière *f* électrique

percussion /pə'kʌʃən/ N [1] *(= impact, noise)* percussion *f*, choc *m* [2] *(Mus)* percussion *f* ◆ **the ~ (section)** les percussions *fpl*

COMP **percussion bullet** N balle *f* explosive

percussion cap N capsule *f* fulminante

percussion drill N perceuse *f* à percussion

percussion instrument N *(Mus)* instrument *m* à percussion

percussion player N percussionniste *mf*

percussionist /pə'kʌʃənɪst/ N percussionniste *mf*

percussive /pə'kʌsɪv/ ADJ percutant

perdition /pə'dɪʃən/ N perdition *f*, ruine *f*, perte *f* ; *(Rel)* perdition *f*, damnation *f*

peregrination † /ˌperɪgrɪ'neɪʃən/ N *(frm)* pérégrination *f* ◆ **~s** voyage *m*, pérégrinations *fpl*

peregrine falcon /ˌperɪgrɪn'fɔːlkən/ N faucon *m* pèlerin

peremptorily /pə'remptərɪlɪ/ ADV [*speak*] d'un ton péremptoire ; [*behave, gesture*] de manière péremptoire, péremptoirement

peremptory /pə'remptərɪ/ ADJ [*instruction, order*] péremptoire, formel ; [*argument*] décisif, sans réplique ; [*tone*] tranchant, péremptoire

perennial /pə'renɪəl/ ADJ [1] *(= long-lasting, enduring)* perpétuel, éternel ; [*problem*] éternel, chronique ◆ **a ~ shortage of teachers** un manque chronique d'enseignants ◆ **the piece has been a ~ favourite in orchestral repertoires** cette œuvre est l'une de celles qui reviennent le plus souvent dans le répertoire orchestral [2] [*plant*] vivace, pluriannuel N *(= plant)* (plante *f*) vivace *f*, plante *f* pluriannuelle ; → **hardy**

perennially /pə'renɪəlɪ/ ADV *(= always)* perpétuellement, constamment ◆ **~ popular** éternellement populaire

perestroika /perə'strɔɪkə/ N perestroïka *f*

perfect /'pɜːfɪkt/ ADJ [1] *(= ideal)* parfait ◆ **no one is ~** personne n'est parfait, la perfection n'est pas de ce monde ◆ **she is ~ for the job** c'est la personne idéale pour le poste ◆ **in a ~ world** dans un monde parfait ◆ **she speaks ~ English** son anglais est parfait *or* impeccable ◆ **his Spanish is far from ~** son espagnol est loin d'être parfait ◆ **it was the ~ moment to speak to him about it** c'était le moment idéal pour lui en parler ◆ **I've got the ~ solution!** j'ai trouvé la solution idéale ! ; → **word**

[2] *(emphatic = complete)* véritable, parfait ◆ **he's a** *or* **the ~ gentleman** c'est le parfait gentleman ◆ **he's a ~ stranger** personne ne le connaît ◆ **he's a ~ stranger to me** il m'est complètement inconnu ◆ **I am a ~ stranger in this town** je ne connais absolument rien de cette ville ◆ **a ~ pest** un véritable fléau ◆ **a ~ fool** un parfait imbécile, un imbécile fini ◆ **I have a ~ right to be here** j'ai tout à fait le droit d'être ici ◆ **it makes ~ sense to me** cela me paraît tout à fait évident

N *(Gram)* parfait *m* ◆ **in the ~** au parfait

VT /pə'fekt/ [*+ technique, skill, work of art*] parfaire ; [*+ methods*] mettre au point, perfectionner ; [*+ plan*] mettre au point ; [*+ product, design*] perfectionner ◆ **to ~ one's French** se perfectionner en français

COMP **perfect pitch** N *(Mus)* ◆ **to have ~ pitch** avoir l'oreille absolue

perfect tense N *(Gram)* parfait *m*

perfectibility /pəˌfektɪ'bɪlɪtɪ/ N perfectibilité *f*

perfectible /pə'fektɪbl/ ADJ perfectible

perfection /pə'fekʃən/ N [1] *(= faultlessness)* perfection *f* ◆ **physical ~** perfection *f* physique ◆ **to ~** à la perfection [2] *(NonC = process of perfecting)* perfectionnement *m* ◆ **the ~ of production methods** le perfectionnement des méthodes de production

perfectionism /pə'fekʃənɪzəm/ N perfectionnisme *m*

perfectionist /pə'fekʃənɪst/ ADJ, N perfectionniste *mf*

perfective /pə'fektɪv/ *(Gram)* ADJ perfectif N [1] *(= aspect)* aspect *m* perfectif [2] *(= verb)* verbe *m* perfectif

perfectly /'pɜːfɪktlɪ/ ADV [1] *(= to perfection)* parfaitement [2] *(= completely)* parfaitement, tout à fait ◆ **but it's a ~ good car!** mais il n'y a aucun problème avec cette voiture !, mais cette voiture marche parfaitement ! ◆ **you know ~ well!** tu le sais parfaitement bien !

◆ **to be ~ honest, I hate classical music** pour être parfaitement *or* tout à fait honnête, je déteste la musique classique ◆ **it was ~ horrible** † c'était parfaitement horrible

perfidious /pɜːˈfɪdɪəs/ ADJ *(liter)* perfide, traître (traîtresse *f*) ◆ **~ Albion** la perfide Albion

perfidiously /pɜːˈfɪdɪəslɪ/ ADV *(liter)* perfidement, traîtreusement ; *[act]* en traître, perfidement

perfidy /ˈpɜːfɪdɪ/ N *(liter)* perfidie *f*

perforate /ˈpɜːfəreɪt/ VT *[+ paper, metal]* perforer, percer ; *[+ ticket]* perforer, poinçonner ◆ **~d tape** *(Comput)* bande *f* perforée ◆ **"tear along the perforated line"** "détachez suivant le pointillé"

perforation /ˌpɜːfəˈreɪʃən/ N perforation *f*

perforce † /pəˈfɔːs/ ADV *(frm)* nécessairement, forcément

perform /pəˈfɔːm/ VT 1 *[+ task]* exécuter, accomplir ; *[+ duty]* accomplir, s'acquitter de ; *[+ function]* remplir ; *[+ miracle]* accomplir ; *[+ rite, ceremony]* célébrer ; *[+ cunnilingus, fellatio]* pratiquer ; *(Jur) [+ contract]* exécuter ◆ **to ~ an operation** *(gen)* accomplir *or* exécuter une opération ; *(Med)* pratiquer une opération, opérer ◆ **to ~ an abortion** pratiquer un avortement

2 *(Mus, Theat etc) [+ play, ballet, opera, symphony etc]* interpréter ◆ **to ~ a part** interpréter un rôle

VI 1 *[person]* se produire ; *[actor, musician]* jouer ; *[singer]* chanter ; *[dancer]* danser ; *[clown, acrobat, trained animal]* exécuter un *or* des numéro(s) ◆ **he's ~ing at the Vic tonight** *[actor]* il joue ce soir au Vic ◆ **to ~ on the violin** jouer du violon, exécuter un morceau au violon ◆ **he ~ed brilliantly as Hamlet** il a brillamment interprété Hamlet ◆ **when we ~ed in Edinburgh** *(Theat)* quand nous avons donné une *or* des représentation(s) à Édimbourg, quand nous avons joué à Édimbourg ◆ **the clowns ~ed well** les clowns ont bien exécuté leur numéro ; see also **performing**

2 *[machine, vehicle]* marcher, fonctionner ◆ **the car is not ~ing properly** la voiture ne marche pas bien

3 *(Econ)* **to ~ well/badly** *[economy, industry, factory]* avoir de bons/mauvais résultats ◆ **their shares are ~ing strongly** leurs actions se comportent très bien

performance /pəˈfɔːməns/ N 1 *(= session, show) (gen)* spectacle *m* ; *(Theat, Mus)* représentation *f* ; *(at circus, variety show)* séance *f* ◆ **"no performance tonight"** "ce soir relâche" ◆ **what a ~!** * *(= rigmarole)* quelle affaire !, quelle histoire ! * ; *(= fuss about nothing)* quel cinéma ! *

2 *(= rendering) [of composition]* interprétation *f* ; *[of one's act]* numéro *m* ◆ **her ~ as** *or* **of Desdemona** son interprétation de Desdémone, son jeu dans le rôle de Desdémone ◆ **the pianist gave a splendid ~** le pianiste a joué de façon magnifique ◆ **Kingsley gives an Oscar-winning ~ as Gandhi** l'interprétation de Kingsley dans le rôle de Gandhi lui a valu un oscar

3 *(= record, success) [of racehorse, athlete, team]* performance *f* ; *[of economy, business, factory]* résultats *mpl* ; *[of currency]* tenue *f* ; *(Comm) [of product]* comportement *m* ; *(Fin) [of investment]* rentabilité *f*, rendement *m* ◆ **their ~ in the election/in the exam/in maths** leurs résultats aux élections/à l'examen/en maths ◆ **his ~ in the debate** sa prestation lors du débat ◆ **economic/financial/academic ~** résultats *mpl* économiques/financiers/universitaires ◆ **drinking too much can affect your sexual ~** l'excès d'alcool peut affecter vos performances sexuelles ◆ **on past ~, an England victory seems unlikely** si l'on se réfère au passé *or* d'après ses résultats passés, l'Angleterre semble avoir peu de chances de gagner

4 *[of engine, vehicle]* performance *f* ; → **high**

5 *(NonC = carrying out) [of task, duty]* exécution *f* ; *[of miracle]* accomplissement *m* ; *[of ritual]* célébration *f (of de)* ◆ **in the ~ of my/his duties** dans l'exercice de mes/ses fonctions

6 *(Ling)* performance *f*

COMP **performance anxiety** N trac *m*

performance art N art *m* performance

performance artist N performer *m (artiste pratiquant l'art performance)*

performance bond N garantie *f* de bonne fin *or* de bonne exécution

performance bonus N prime *f* de rendement

performance car N voiture *f* à hautes performances

performanceenhancing drug N dopant *m*

performance indicator N indicateur *m* de performance

performance-related pay N salaire *m* au rendement

performative /pəˈfɔːmətɪv/ *(Ling)* ADJ, N ◆ **~ (verb)** (verbe *m*) performatif *m*

performer /pəˈfɔːməʳ/ N 1 *(= musician, actor etc)* artiste *mf*, interprète *mf* 2 ◆ **to be a high ~** *[company]* afficher de très bonnes performances ; *[employee]* être très performant

performing /pəˈfɔːmɪŋ/ ADJ ◆ **the ~ arts** les arts *mpl* du spectacle ◆ **~ artists** les gens *mpl* du spectacle ◆ **~ dogs** chiens *mpl* savants ◆ **~ flea/seal** puce *f*/otarie *f* savante

perfume /ˈpɜːfjuːm/ N parfum *m* VT /pəˈfjuːm/ parfumer

perfumery /pəˈfjuːmərɪ/ N parfumerie *f*

perfunctorily /pəˈfʌŋktərɪlɪ/ ADV *[smile]* d'un air indifférent ; *[kiss, thank]* sans conviction, sans enthousiasme ; *[answer, examine, check, deal with]* de façon superficielle ◆ **to glance at sth ~** jeter un coup d'œil indifférent à qch

perfunctory /pəˈfʌŋktərɪ/ ADJ *[nod, kiss, greeting]* indifférent ; *[effort, search]* superficiel ◆ **the medics made a ~ effort at resuscitation** les secouristes ont fait une tentative de réanimation pour la forme

pergola /ˈpɜːgələ/ N pergola *f*

perhaps /pəˈhæps, præps/ LANGUAGE IN USE 1, 2.2, 3.2, 15.3, 26.3 ADV peut-être ◆ **~ he is right** il a peut-être raison, peut-être qu'il a raison, peut-être a-t-il raison *(frm)* ◆ **coincidence? ~ (so)** coïncidence ? peut-être (que oui) ◆ **should he have resigned? ~ he should** aurait-il dû démissionner ? peut-être (que oui) ◆ **the worst prime minister of the century? ~ not, but ...** le pire Premier ministre du siècle ? peut-être pas *or* peut-être que non, mais ... ◆ **is there no hope left? ~ there is** n'y a-t-il plus d'espoir ? peut-être que si

perianth /ˈperɪænθ/ N périanthe *m*

pericardium /ˌperɪˈkɑːdɪəm/ N (pl **pericardia** /ˌperɪˈkɑːdɪə/) péricarde *m*

pericarp /ˈperɪkɑːp/ N péricarpe *m*

peridot /ˈperɪdɒt/ N péridot *m*

perigee /ˈperɪdʒiː/ N périgée *m*

periglacial /ˌperɪˈgleɪʃəl/ ADJ périglaciaire

peril /ˈperɪl/ N *(esp liter)* péril *m*, danger *m* ◆ **he is in great ~** il court un grand péril ◆ **to be in ~ of annihilation** risquer d'être anéanti ◆ **he's in ~ of his life** sa vie est en danger ◆ **the cliff is in ~ of collapsing** la falaise risque de s'effondrer ◆ **at the ~ of** au péril de ◆ **at your ~** à vos risques et périls ◆ **insured ~** *(Insurance)* risque *m* assuré

perilous /ˈperɪləs/ ADJ périlleux

perilously /ˈperɪləslɪ/ ADV périlleusement ◆ **~ close** terriblement proche ◆ **to be/come ~ close to disaster/death** *etc* frôler *or* friser la catastrophe/la mort *etc* ◆ **I came ~ close to telling her everything** il s'en est fallu d'un cheveu que je ne lui dise tout

perimeter /pəˈrɪmɪtəʳ/ N périmètre *m* COMP **perimeter fence** N périmètre *m* enclos, clôture *f* d'enceinte

perinatal /ˌperɪˈneɪtl/ ADJ périnatal

perinea /ˌperɪˈniːə/ NPL of **perineum**

perineal /ˌperɪˈniːəl/ ADJ périnéal

perineum /ˌperɪˈniːəm/ N (pl **perinea**) périnée *m*

period /ˈpɪərɪəd/ N 1 *(= epoch)* période *f*, époque *f* ; *(Geol)* période *f* ; *(= stage: in career, development etc)* époque *f*, moment *m* ; *(= length of time)* période *f* ◆ **the classical ~** la période classique ◆ **costumes/furniture of the ~** costumes *mpl*/meubles *mpl* de l'époque ◆ **Picasso's blue ~** la période bleue de Picasso ◆ **the ~ from 1600 to 1750** la période entre 1600 et 1750 ◆ **the post-war ~** (la période de) l'après-guerre *m* ◆ **during the whole ~ of the negotiations** pendant toute la période *or* durée des négociations ◆ **at a later ~** à une époque ultérieure, plus tard ◆ **at that ~ in** *or* **of his life** à cette époque *or* à ce moment de sa vie ◆ **a ~ of social upheaval** une période *or* une époque de bouleversements sociaux ◆ **the magazine was forced to close down for a ~** le magazine a dû interrompre sa publication pendant quelque temps *or* un certain temps ◆ **the factory will be closed for an indefinite ~** l'usine sera fermée pour une durée indéterminée ◆ **after a short ~ in hospital** après un court séjour à l'hôpital ◆ **he had several ~s of illness** il a été malade à plusieurs reprises ◆ **the holiday ~** la période des vacances ◆ **bright/rainy ~s** périodes *fpl* ensoleillées/de pluie ◆ **in the ~ of a year** en l'espace d'une année ◆ **it must be done within a three-month ~** il faut le faire dans un délai de trois mois ; → **safe**

2 *(Scol = lesson)* ≈ heure *f* ◆ **first ~** la première heure ◆ **a double ~ of French** ≈ deux heures de français

3 *(US = full stop)* point *m* ◆ **I won't do it, ~** je ne veux pas le faire *or* je ne le ferai pas, un point c'est tout

4 *(= menstruation)* règles *fpl*

5 *(Phys, Math = reciprocal of frequency)* période *f*

COMP **period costume, period dress** N costume *m* d'époque

period furniture N *(genuine)* meuble *m* d'époque ; *(copy)* meuble *m* de style ancien

period of revolution *or* **rotation** N *(Astron)* période *f* de rotation

period pain(s) NPL *(Med)* règles *fpl* douloureuses

period piece N *(fig)* curiosité *f*

periodic /ˌpɪərɪˈɒdɪk/ ADJ périodique COMP **periodic table** N classification *f* périodique des éléments

periodical /ˌpɪərɪˈɒdɪkəl/ ADJ périodique N (journal *m*) périodique *m*, publication *f* périodique

periodically /ˌpɪərɪˈɒdɪkəlɪ/ ADV périodiquement

periodicity /ˌpɪərɪəˈdɪsɪtɪ/ N périodicité *f*

periodontal /perɪˈdɒntl/ ADJ parodontal

periosteum /ˌperɪˈɒstɪəm/ N (pl **periostea** /ˌperɪˈɒstɪə/) périoste *m*

peripatetic /ˌperɪpəˈtetɪk/ ADJ *(= itinerant)* ambulant ; *(Brit) [teacher]* qui exerce sur plusieurs établissements ; *(Philos)* péripatétique

peripheral /pəˈrɪfərəl/ ADJ *[activity, interest]* accessoire ; *[area]* périphérique ◆ **to be ~ to sth** *(= of minor importance to)* être accessoire par rapport à ◆ **science is ~ to that debate** l'aspect scientifique n'entre pas dans ce débat N *(Comput)* périphérique *m*

periphery /pəˈrɪfərɪ/ N périphérie *f* ◆ **on the ~** *[of subject]* en marge ; *[of area, place]* à la périphérie

periphrasis /pəˈrɪfrəsɪs/ N (pl **periphrases** /pəˈrɪfrəsiːz/) périphrase *f*, circonlocution *f*

periscope /ˈperɪskəʊp/ N périscope *m*

perish /ˈperɪʃ/ VI 1 (*liter* = *die*) périr, mourir (*from* de) ◆ **they ~ed in the attempt** ils y ont laissé la vie ◆ **~ the thought!** jamais de la vie !, loin de moi cette pensée ! ◆ **if, ~ the thought, you should die suddenly** si par malheur *or* si, Dieu nous en préserve, vous veniez à mourir subitement 2 [*rubber, material, leather*] se détériorer, s'abîmer ; [*food*] se détériorer, s'abîmer VT [+ *rubber, food*] abîmer, détériorer

perishable /ˈperɪʃəbl/ ADJ périssable NPL **perishables** denrées *fpl* périssables

perished /ˈperɪʃt/ ADJ 1 [*rubber*] détérioré, abîmé 2 (*esp Brit* = *cold*) ◆ **to be ~** †* être frigorifié*, crever* de froid

perisher‡ /ˈperɪʃəʳ/ N (*Brit*) enquiquineur* *m*, -euse* *f* ◆ **you little ~!** petite peste !

perishing /ˈperɪʃɪŋ/ ADJ 1 (= *very cold*) très froid ◆ **outside in the ~ cold** dehors dans le froid glacial *or* intense ◆ **it was ~* (cold)** il faisait un froid de loup *or* de canard* ◆ **to be ~** * [*person*] être frigorifié*, crever* de froid ; → **perish** 2 (*Brit* † ‡) sacré* *before n*, damné* *before n* ◆ **it's a ~ nuisance!** c'est vraiment enquiquinant !*

peristalsis /ˌperɪˈstælsɪs/ N (pl **peristalses** /ˌperɪˈstælsiːz/) péristaltisme *m*

peristyle /ˈperɪstaɪl/ N péristyle *m*

peritoneum /ˌperɪtəˈniːəm/ N (pl **peritoneums** *or* **peritonea** /ˌperɪtəˈniːə/) péritoine *m*

peritonitis /ˌperɪtəˈnaɪtɪs/ N péritonite *f*

periwig /ˈperɪwɪg/ N (*Hist*) perruque *f*

periwinkle /ˈperɪˌwɪŋkl/ N (= *plant*) pervenche *f* ; (= *shellfish*) bigorneau *m*

perjure /ˈpɜːdʒəʳ/ VT ◆ **to ~ o.s.** se parjurer ; (*Jur*) faire un faux serment ◆ **~d evidence** (*Jur*) faux serment *m*, faux témoignage *m* (volontaire)

perjurer /ˈpɜːdʒərəʳ/ N parjure *mf*

perjury /ˈpɜːdʒərɪ/ N (*Jur*) faux serment *m* ◆ **to commit ~** se parjurer ; (*Jur*) faire un faux serment

perk¹ /pɜːk/ VI ◆ **to ~ up** (= *cheer up*) se ragaillardir ; (*after illness*) se remonter, se retaper* ; (= *show interest*) s'animer, dresser l'oreille ◆ **his ears ~ed up** (*lit, fig*) il a dressé l'oreille VT ◆ **to ~ sb up** ragaillardir qn, retaper qn* ◆ **she ~ed up her outfit with a bright scarf** elle a égayé sa tenue avec une écharpe de couleur vive

perk²* /pɜːk/ N (abbrev of **perquisite**) (= *benefit*) à-côté *m*, avantage *m* annexe ◆ **it's one of the ~s of the job** c'est l'un des avantages *or* des à-côtés du métier ◆ **one of the ~s of being a student is ...** l'un des avantages à être étudiant est ...

perk³* /pɜːk/ VI (abbrev of **percolate**) [*coffee*] passer

perkily /ˈpɜːkɪlɪ/ ADV [*speak*] d'un ton guilleret ; [*move*] vivement, avec vivacité ◆ **a bow pinned ~ to her cap** un nœud coquin attaché à son chapeau

perkiness* /ˈpɜːkɪnɪs/ N entrain *m*

perky* /ˈpɜːkɪ/ ADJ (= *cheerful*) guilleret, gai ; (= *lively*) plein d'entrain

perm¹ /pɜːm/ N (*esp Brit*) (abbrev of **permanent**) permanente *f* ◆ **to have a ~** se faire faire une permanente VT ◆ **to ~ sb's hair** faire une permanente à qn ◆ **to have one's hair ~ed** se faire faire une permanente

perm²* /pɜːm/ N abbrev of **permutation** VTI abbrev of **permutate**

permafrost /ˈpɜːməfrɒst/ N permafrost *m*, pergélisol *m*

permanence /ˈpɜːmənəns/ N permanence *f*

permanency /ˈpɜːmənənsɪ/ N 1 → **permanence** 2 (*job*) emploi *m* permanent, poste *m* fixe

permanent /ˈpɜːmənənt/ ADJ permanent ◆ **the five ~ members of the UN Security Council** les cinq membres permanents du Conseil de sécurité de l'ONU ◆ **the ban is intended to be ~** l'interdiction est censée être définitive ◆ **we cannot make any ~ arrangements** nous ne pouvons pas prendre de dispositions définitives ◆ **I'm not ~ here** je ne suis pas ici à titre définitif ◆ **~ address** résidence *f or* adresse *f* fixe ◆ **appointment to the ~ staff** nomination *f* à titre définitif ◆ **a ~ fixture** (= *feature, object*) une constante ◆ **a ~ fixture of government** une constante dans le gouvernement ◆ **he's a ~ fixture*** il fait partie des meubles* ◆ **he's no longer a ~ fixture* on the political scene** il n'est plus le personnage omniprésent *or* incontournable qu'il a été sur la scène politique

N (*US* †: *for hair*) permanente *f*

COMP **permanent-press** ADJ [*trousers*] à pli permanent ; [*skirt*] indéplissable

Permanent Secretary N (*Brit Admin*) secrétaire *m* général (de ministère)

permanent wave † N permanente *f*

permanent way N (*Brit Rail*) voie *f* ferrée

permanently /ˈpɜːmənəntlɪ/ ADV 1 [*change, live*] définitivement ; [*damage*] de façon permanente 2 [*open, closed*] en permanence ; [*tired, angry, unhappy etc*] éternellement, constamment

permanganate /pɜːˈmæŋgənɪt/ N permanganate *m*

permeability /ˌpɜːmɪəˈbɪlɪtɪ/ N perméabilité *f*

permeable /ˈpɜːmɪəbl/ ADJ perméable, pénétrable

permeate /ˈpɜːmɪeɪt/ VT 1 (= *be prevalent in*) être omniprésent dans ◆ **bias against women ~s the legal system** la misogynie est omniprésente dans le système judiciaire ◆ **the melancholy which ~d all his work** la mélancolie omniprésente dans son œuvre

2 (= *fill*) [*feeling, smell*] pénétrer dans *or* parmi, se répandre dans *or* parmi ; [*liquid*] pénétrer, filtrer à travers ◆ **to be ~d with** *or* **by** être empreint de ◆ **a feeling akin to euphoria began to ~ her being** un sentiment proche de l'euphorie commença à gagner tout son être

VI (= *spread*) se répandre, pénétrer ◆ **this shows how far drugs have ~d into our culture** ceci montre à quel point la drogue s'est répandue dans notre culture ◆ **the message has not ~d to the North Bridge offices** le message n'a pas gagné les bureaux de North Bridge ◆ **to ~ through** [+ *society, system*] se diffuser *or* se répandre dans ◆ **water will ~ through the concrete** l'eau s'infiltrera à travers le béton

Permian /ˈpɜːmɪən/ N, ADJ (*Geol*) permien *m*

permissible /pəˈmɪsɪbl/ LANGUAGE IN USE 9.4 ADJ [*action etc*] permis ; [*behaviour, attitude, level, limit*] acceptable ◆ **it is ~ to refuse** il est permis de refuser ◆ **would it be ~ to say that ...?** serait-il acceptable de dire que ... ? ◆ **the degree of ~ error is 2%** la marge d'erreur acceptable *or* tolérable est de 2%

permission /pəˈmɪʃən/ LANGUAGE IN USE 9.2 N permission *f* ; (*official*) autorisation *f* ◆ **without ~** sans permission, sans autorisation ◆ **with your ~** avec votre permission ◆ **"by kind permission of ..."** "avec l'aimable autorisation de ..." ◆ **no ~ is needed** il n'est pas nécessaire d'avoir une autorisation ◆ **he gave ~ for the body to be exhumed** il a autorisé l'exhumation du corps ◆ **she gave ~ for her daughter's marriage** elle a consenti au mariage de sa fille ◆ **she gave her daughter ~ to marry** elle a autorisé sa fille à se marier ◆ **~ is required in writing from the committee** il est nécessaire d'obtenir l'autorisation écrite du comité ◆ **who gave you ~ to do that?** qui vous a autorisé à *or* qui vous a permis de faire cela ? ◆ **you have my ~ to do that** je vous permets de *or* vous autorise à faire cela, je vous accorde la permission *or* l'autorisation de faire cela ◆ **you have my ~ to leave** je vous autorise à partir ◆ **to ask (sb's) ~ to do sth** demander (à qn) la permission *or* l'autorisation de faire qch ◆ **to ask ~ for sb to do sth** demander que qn ait la permission de faire qch

permissive /pəˈmɪsɪv/ ADJ (= *tolerant*) [*person, parent*] permissif ◆ **the ~ society** la société permissive

permissively /pəˈmɪsɪvlɪ/ ADV de façon permissive

permissiveness /pəˈmɪsɪvnɪs/ N permissivité *f*

permit /ˈpɜːmɪt/ N autorisation *f* écrite ; (*for specific activity*) permis *m* ; (*for entry*) laissez-passer *m inv* ; (*for goods at Customs*) passavant *m* ◆ **fishing ~** permis *m* de pêche ◆ **building ~** permis *m* de construire ◆ **you need a ~ to go into the laboratory** pour entrer dans le laboratoire il vous faut une autorisation écrite *or* un laissez-passer ; → **entry**

VT /pəˈmɪt/ (*gen*) permettre (*sb to do sth* à qn de faire qch), autoriser (*sb to do sth* qn à faire qch) ◆ **he was ~ted to leave** on lui a permis de partir, on l'a autorisé à partir ◆ **camping is ~ted here** il est permis de camper ici ◆ **is it ~ted to smoke?** est-il permis de fumer ? ◆ **it is not ~ted to smoke** il n'est pas permis *or* il est interdit de fumer ◆ **we could never ~ that to happen** nous ne pourrions jamais permettre que cela se produise, nous ne pourrions jamais laisser cela se produire ◆ **I won't ~ it** je ne le permettrai pas ◆ **her mother will never ~ the sale of the house** sa mère n'autorisera jamais la vente de la maison ◆ **her mother will not ~ her to sell the house** sa mère ne lui permet pas de *or* ne l'autorise pas à vendre la maison ◆ **the law ~s the sale of this substance** la loi autorise la vente de cette substance ◆ **the vent ~s the escape of gas** l'orifice permet l'échappement du gaz ◆ **~ me to help you** (*frm*) permettez-moi de vous aider ◆ **to ~ o.s. sth** (*frm*) se permettre qch

VI /pəˈmɪt/ permettre ◆ **weather ~ting, if the weather ~s** si le temps le permet ◆ **if time ~s** si j'ai (*or* nous avons *etc*) le temps ◆ **to ~ of sth** (*frm*) permettre qch ◆ **it does not ~ of doubt** (*frm*) cela ne permet pas le moindre doute

permutate /ˈpɜːmjʊˌteɪt/ VTI permuter

permutation /ˌpɜːmjʊˈteɪʃən/ N permutation *f*

permute /pəˈmjuːt/ VT permuter

pernicious /pɜːˈnɪʃəs/ ADJ (*gen, also Med*) pernicieux COMP **pernicious anaemia** N anémie *f* pernicieuse

perniciously /pɜːˈnɪʃəslɪ/ ADV pernicieusement

pernickety* /pəˈnɪkɪtɪ/ ADJ (= *fussy about*) pointilleux, formaliste ; (= *hard to please*) difficile ; [*job*] délicat, minutieux ◆ **he's very ~** il est très pointilleux, il cherche toujours la petite bête ◆ **he's very ~ about what he wears/about his food** il est très difficile pour ses vêtements/pour sa nourriture

peroration /ˌperəˈreɪʃən/ N péroraison *f*

peroxide /pəˈrɒksaɪd/ N (*Chem*) peroxyde *m* ; (*for hair*) eau *f* oxygénée ◆ **~ blonde** * blonde *f* décolorée *or* oxygénée* ; → **hydrogen**

perpendicular /ˌpɜːpənˈdɪkjʊləʳ/ ADJ (*also Archit, Math*) perpendiculaire (*to* à) ; [*cliff, slope*] à pic N perpendiculaire *f* ◆ **to be out of ~** être hors d'aplomb, sortir de la perpendiculaire COMP **perpendicular Gothic** ADJ (*Archit*) gothique *m* perpendiculaire anglais

perpendicularly /ˌpɜːpənˈdɪkjʊləlɪ/ ADV perpendiculairement

perpetrate /ˈpɜːpɪtreɪt/ VT *[+ crime]* perpétrer, commettre ; *[+ blunder, hoax]* faire

perpetration /ˌpɜːpɪˈtreɪʃən/ N perpétration *f*

perpetrator /ˈpɜːpɪtreɪtəʳ/ N auteur *m* ◆ **~ of a crime** auteur *m* d'un crime

perpetual /pəˈpetjʊəl/ ADJ *[movement, calendar, rain, sunshine, flower]* perpétuel ; *[nuisance, worry]* perpétuel, constant ; *[noise, questions, complaints]* perpétuel, continuel ; *[snows]* éternel ◆ **he's a ~ nuisance** il ne cesse d'embêter le monde

perpetually /pəˈpetjʊəlɪ/ ADV *[live]* perpétuellement ; *[complain]* continuellement, sans cesse ◆ **we were ~ at war with the other members** nous étions perpétuellement en guerre avec les autres membres

perpetuate /pəˈpetjʊeɪt/ VT perpétuer

perpetuation /pəˌpetjʊˈeɪʃən/ N perpétuation *f*

perpetuity /ˌpɜːpɪˈtjuːɪtɪ/ N perpétuité *f* ◆ **in** *or* **for ~** à perpétuité

perplex /pəˈpleks/ VT *(= puzzle)* plonger dans la perplexité, rendre perplexe

perplexed /pəˈplekst/ ADJ *[person]* embarrassé, perplexe ; *[tone, glance]* perplexe ◆ **to look ~** avoir l'air perplexe *or* embarrassé

perplexedly /pəˈpleksɪdlɪ/ ADV avec perplexité

perplexing /pəˈpleksɪŋ/ ADJ *[matter, question]* embarrassant, compliqué ; *[situation]* embarrassant, confus

perplexity /pəˈpleksɪtɪ/ N *(= puzzlement)* perplexité *f*

perquisite /ˈpɜːkwɪzɪt/ N *(frm)* avantage *m* annexe ; *(in money)* à-côté *m*, gratification *f*

perry /ˈperɪ/ N poiré *m*

persecute /ˈpɜːsɪkjuːt/ VT *(= harass, oppress)* *[+ minorities etc]* persécuter ; *(= annoy)* harceler *(with* de*)*, tourmenter, persécuter

persecution /ˌpɜːsɪˈkjuːʃən/ N persécution *f* ◆ **to have a ~ complex** avoir la manie *or* le délire de la persécution

persecutor /ˈpɜːsɪkjuːtəʳ/ N persécuteur *m*, -trice *f*

Persephone /pəˈsefənɪ/ N Perséphone *f*

Perseus /ˈpɜːsjuːs/ N Persée *m*

perseverance /ˌpɜːsɪˈvɪərəns/ N persévérance *f*

persevere /ˌpɜːsɪˈvɪəʳ/ VI persévérer *(in sth* dans qch ; *at doing sth* à faire qch*)*

persevering /ˌpɜːsɪˈvɪərɪŋ/ ADJ persévérant

perseveringly /ˌpɜːsɪˈvɪərɪŋlɪ/ ADV avec persévérance

Persia /ˈpɜːʃə/ N Perse *f*

Persian /ˈpɜːʃən/ ADJ *(in antiquity)* perse ; *(from 7th century onward)* persan N 1 *(= person)* Persan(e) *m(f)* ; *(in antiquity)* Perse *mf* 2 *(= language)* persan *m*

COMP **Persian blinds** NPL persiennes *fpl*
Persian carpet N tapis *m* de Perse
Persian cat N chat *m* persan
Persian Gulf N golfe *m* Persique
Persian lamb N astrakan *m*, agneau *m* rasé

persiflage /ˌpɜːsɪˈflɑːʒ/ N persiflage *m*, ironie *f*, raillerie *f*

persimmon /pɜːˈsɪmən/ N *(= tree)* plaqueminier *m* de Virginie *or* du Japon, kaki *m* ; *(= fruit)* kaki *m*

persist /pəˈsɪst/ VI *[person]* persister, s'obstiner *(in sth* dans qch ; *in doing sth* à faire qch*)* ; *[pain, opinion]* persister

persistence /pəˈsɪstəns/, **persistency** /pəˈsɪstənsɪ/ N (NonC) *[of person]* *(= perseverance)* persévérance *f* ; *(= obstinacy)* obstination *f* ; *[of pain]* persistance *f* ◆ **as a reward for her ~** pour la récompenser de sa persévérance ◆ **his ~ in seeking out the truth** son obstination à rechercher la vérité

persistent /pəˈsɪstənt/ ADJ 1 *[person]* *(= persevering)* persévérant ; *(= obstinate)* obstiné 2 *(= continual)* *[smell, chemical substance]* persistant ; *[warnings, complaints, interruptions]* continuel, répété ; *[noise, nuisance]* continuel, incessant ; *[pain, fever, cough]* persistant, tenace ; *[fears, doubts]* continuel, tenace

COMP **persistent offender** N *(Jur)* multirécidiviste *mf*
persistent organic pollutant N polluant *m* organique persistant
persistent vegetative state N état *m* végétatif persistant *or* permanent

persistently /pəˈsɪstəntlɪ/ ADV 1 *(= determinedly, obstinately)* obstinément ◆ **those who ~ break the law** ceux qui persistent à enfreindre la loi 2 *(= constantly)* constamment ◆ **~ high unemployment** un taux de chômage qui demeure élevé

persnickety * /pəˈsnɪkɪtɪ/ ADJ *(US)* ⇒ **pernickety**

person /ˈpɜːsn/ N 1 personne *f*, individu *m* *(often pej)* ; *(Jur)* personne *f* ◆ **I know no such ~** *(= no one of that name)* je ne connais personne de ce nom ; *(= no one like that)* je ne connais personne de ce genre ◆ **I like him as a ~, but not as a politician** je l'aime bien en tant que personne mais pas comme homme politique ◆ **in ~** *[go, meet, appear, speak etc]* en personne ◆ **give it to him in ~** remettez-le-lui en mains propres ◆ **in the ~ of** dans *or* en la personne de ◆ **I'm not the kind of ~ to ...** je ne suis pas du genre à ... ◆ **I'm not much of a city ~** je n'aime pas beaucoup la ville ◆ **she likes dogs, but I'm more of a cat ~** elle aime les chiens mais personnellement je préfère les chats ◆ **a ~ to ~ call** *(Telec)* une communication (téléphonique) avec préavis ◆ **he had a knife concealed on** *or* **about his ~** *(Jur)* il avait un couteau caché sur lui ◆ **acting with ~ or ~s unknown** *(Jur)* (agissant) de concert *or* en complicité avec un ou des tiers non identifiés ; → **displace, private**

2 *(Gram)* personne *f* ◆ **in the first ~ singular** à la première personne du singulier

persona /pɜːˈsəʊnə/ N (pl **personae**) 1 *(Literat, Psych etc)* personnage *m*, image *f* (publique) ◆ **James had adopted a new ~** James s'est créé un nouveau personnage *or* une nouvelle image ◆ **I'm able to project an extrovert, energetic ~** je peux donner l'image de quelqu'un d'extraverti et d'énergique 2 ◆ **~ grata/non grata** persona grata/non grata

personable /ˈpɜːsnəbl/ ADJ bien de sa personne

personae /pɜːˈsəʊniː/ NPL of **persona**

personage /ˈpɜːsnɪdʒ/ N *(Theat, gen)* personnage *m*

personal /ˈpɜːsnl/ ADJ *(= private)* *[opinion, matter]* personnel ; *(= individual)* *[style]* personnel, particulier ; *[liberty]* personnel, individuel ; *(= for one's own use)* *[luggage, belongings]* personnel ; *(= to do with the body)* *[habits]* intime ; *(= in person)* *[call, visit]* personnel ; *[application]* (fait) en personne ; *(Gram)* personnel ; *(= indiscreet)* *[remark, question]* indiscret (-ète *f*) ◆ **my ~ belief is ...** personnellement *or* pour ma part je crois ... ◆ **I have no ~ knowledge of this** personnellement je ne sais rien à ce sujet ◆ **a letter marked "personal"** une lettre marquée "personnel" ◆ **his ~ interests were at stake** ses intérêts personnels étaient en jeu ◆ **his ~ appearance leaves much to be desired** son apparence (personnelle) *or* sa tenue laisse beaucoup à désirer ◆ **to make a ~ appearance** apparaître en personne ◆ **I will give the matter my ~ attention** je m'occuperai personnellement de cette affaire ◆ **these children need the ~ attention of trained carers** ces enfants ont besoin d'éducateurs spécialisés qui s'occupent individuellement de chacun ◆ **the conversation/argument grew ~** la conversation/la discussion prit un ton *or* un tour personnel ◆ **don't be ~!** * ne sois pas si blessant ! ◆ **don't let's get ~!** * abstenons-nous d'allusions personnelles ! ◆ **his ~ life** sa vie privée ◆ **for ~ reasons** pour des raisons personnelles ◆ **the president believes his ~ safety is at risk** le président craint pour sa sécurité personnelle ◆ **to give sth the ~ touch** ajouter une note personnelle à qch

N *(US Press)* *(= article)* entrefilet *m* mondain ; *(= ad)* petite annonce *f* personnelle

COMP **personal accident insurance** N assurance *f* individuelle contre les accidents
personal ad * N petite annonce *f* personnelle
personal allowance N *(Tax)* abattement *m* personnel
personal assistant N secrétaire *mf* particulier (-ière)
personal best N *(Sport)* record *m* personnel
personal call N *(Brit Telec)* *(= person to person)* communication *f* (téléphonique) avec préavis ; *(= private)* appel *m* personnel
personal chair N *(Brit Univ)* ◆ **to have a ~ chair** être professeur à titre personnel
personal cleanliness N hygiène *f* intime
personal column N *(Press)* annonces *fpl* personnelles
personal computer N ordinateur *m* individuel *or* personnel
personal details NPL *(= name, address etc)* coordonnées * *fpl*
personal effects NPL effets *mpl* personnels
personal estate N *(Jur)* biens *mpl* personnels
personal friend N ami(e) *m(f)* intime
personal growth N *(Psych)* développement *m* personnel
personal hygiene N ⇒ **personal cleanliness**
personal identification number N code *m* personnel
personal insurance N assurance *f* personnelle
personal loan N *(Banking)* prêt *m* personnel
personal organizer N *(= Filofax)* agenda *m* (personnel), Filofax ® *m* ; *(electronic)* agenda *m* électronique
personal pension plan N plan *m* d'épargne retraite
personal pronoun N *(Gram)* pronom *m* personnel
personal property N ⇒ **personal estate**
personal space N espace *m* vital
personal stationery N papier *m* à lettres à en-tête personnel
personal stereo N baladeur *m*, Walkman ® *m*
personal trainer N entraîneur *m* personnel
personal tuition N cours *mpl* particuliers (in de)

personality /ˌpɜːsəˈnælɪtɪ/ N 1 (NonC: *also Psych*) personnalité *f* ◆ **you must allow him to express his ~** il faut lui permettre d'exprimer sa personnalité ◆ **she has a pleasant/strong ~** elle a une personnalité sympathique/forte ◆ **he has a lot of ~** il a beaucoup de personnalité ◆ **cats all have their own personalities** les chats ont tous leur personnalité propre ◆ **the house seemed to have a ~ of its own** la maison semblait avoir une personnalité propre ; → **dual, split**

2 *(= celebrity)* personnalité *f*, personnage *m* connu ◆ **a well-known television ~** une vedette de la télévision *or* du petit écran ◆ **it was more about personalities than about politics** *(election etc)* c'était plus une confrontation de personnalités que d'idées politiques

COMP *(gen, Psych)* *[problems]* de personnalité
personality cult N culte *m* de la personnalité
personality disorder N troubles *mpl* de la personnalité
personality test N test *m* de personnalité, test *m* projectif *(SPEC)*

personalize /ˈpɜːsənəˌlaɪz/ VT personnaliser

personalized /ˈpɜːsənəˌlaɪzd/ ADJ personnalisé COMP **personalized number plate** N (Brit) plaque f d'immatriculation personnalisée ; → VANITY PLATE

personally /ˈpɜːsnəlɪ/ LANGUAGE IN USE 1.1, 6.2, 26.2 ADV personnellement ◆ ~ **I disapprove of gambling** personnellement je désapprouve les jeux d'argent ◆ **I like him ~ but not as an employer** je l'apprécie en tant que personne, mais pas comme patron ◆ **that's something you would have to raise with the director** ~ il faudrait en parler au directeur en personne ◆ **I spoke to him** ~ je lui ai parlé en personne ◆ **to be ~ responsible** or **liable (for sth)** être personnellement responsable (de qch) ◆ **I hold you ~ responsible (for this)** je vous en tiens personnellement responsable ◆ **I'm sorry, I didn't mean it** ~ excusez-moi, je ne vous visais pas personnellement ◆ **don't take it ~!** ne le prenez pas pour vous !

personalty /ˈpɜːsnltɪ/ N (Jur) biens mpl personnels

personate /ˈpɜːsəneɪt/ VT 1 (Theat) incarner (le rôle de) 2 (= personify) personnifier 3 (Jur = impersonate) se faire passer pour

personification /pɜːˌsɒnɪfɪˈkeɪʃən/ N (all senses) personnification f ◆ **she's the ~ of good taste** elle est la personnification or l'incarnation f du bon goût

personify /pɜːˈsɒnɪfaɪ/ VT personnifier ◆ **she's kindness personified** c'est la bonté personnifiée or en personne ◆ **he's fascism personified** il est le fascisme personnifié

personnel /ˌpɜːsəˈnel/ N personnel m COMP **personnel agency** N agence f pour l'emploi, bureau m de placement
personnel carrier N (Mil) véhicule m de transport de troupes
personnel department N service m du personnel
personnel management N gestion f or direction f du personnel
personnel manager N chef mf du (service du) personnel
personnel officer N responsable mf (de la gestion) du personnel

perspective /pəˈspektɪv/ N 1 (Archit, Art, Surv, gen) perspective f ◆ **in/out of** ~ en perspective/qui ne respecte pas la perspective
2 (fig = viewpoint) point m de vue, perspective f ◆ **in a historical** ~ dans une perspective or une optique historique ◆ **the reconstruction of history from a feminist** ~ la reconstitution de l'histoire d'un point de vue féministe ◆ **the book is written from the ~ of a parent** le livre est écrit du point de vue d'un parent ◆ **to see things from a different** ~ voir les choses d'un point de vue différent or sous un angle différent or sous un jour différent ◆ **you see things from a different ~ if you're the bride** on voit les choses différemment quand on est la mariée ◆ **a child's ~ of the world** l'image f que se fait un enfant du monde ◆ **let me put this case in (its proper)** ~ je vais replacer cette affaire dans son contexte ◆ **let's keep this in** ~ ne perdons pas or gardons le sens des proportions

Perspex ® /ˈpɜːspeks/ N (esp Brit) plexiglas ® m

perspicacious /ˌpɜːspɪˈkeɪʃəs/ ADJ [person] perspicace ; [analysis] pénétrant

perspicacity /ˌpɜːspɪˈkæsɪtɪ/ N perspicacité f, clairvoyance f

perspicuity /ˌpɜːspɪˈkjuːɪtɪ/ N 1 ⇒ **perspicacity** 2 [of explanation, statement] clarté f, netteté f

perspicuous /pəˈspɪkjʊəs/ ADJ clair, net

perspiration /ˌpɜːspəˈreɪʃən/ N transpiration f ◆ **bathed in** or **dripping with** ~ en nage

perspire /pəsˈpaɪəʳ/ VI transpirer

persuadable * /pəˈsweɪdəbl/ ADJ qui peut être persuadé

persuade /pəˈsweɪd/ VT (= urge) persuader (sb of sth qn de qch ; sb that qn que) ; (= convince) convaincre (sb of sth qn de qch) ◆ **it doesn't take much to ~ him** il n'en faut pas beaucoup pour le persuader or le convaincre ◆ **I am (quite) ~d that he is wrong** (frm) je suis (tout à fait) persuadé qu'il a tort ◆ **I'm not ~d of the benefits of your approach** je ne suis pas convaincu des avantages de votre approche ◆ **to ~ sb to do sth** persuader qn de faire qch ◆ **to ~ sb not to do sth** persuader qn de ne pas faire qch, dissuader qn de faire qch ◆ **I wanted to help but they ~d me not to** je voulais aider mais on m'en a dissuadé ◆ **to ~ sb into doing sth** * persuader qn de faire qch ◆ **they ~d me that I ought to see him** ils m'ont persuadé que je devais le voir ◆ **to ~ o.s. that ...** se persuader que ... ◆ **to ~ sb of the need for sth** persuader qn de la nécessité de qch ◆ **she is easily ~d** elle se laisse facilement persuader or convaincre

persuasion /pəˈsweɪʒən/ N 1 (NonC) persuasion f ◆ **he needed a lot of** ~ il a fallu beaucoup de persuasion pour le convaincre ◆ **I don't need much ~ to stop working** il n'en faut pas beaucoup pour me persuader de m'arrêter de travailler ◆ **he is open to** ~ il est prêt à se laisser convaincre 2 (= belief, conviction) (gen) croyance f ; (religious) confession f ; (political) conviction f politique ◆ **people of all religious ~s** des gens de toutes les religions or confessions ◆ **people of all political ~s** des gens de tous horizons or de toutes tendances politiques ◆ **I am not of that ~ myself** personnellement je ne partage pas cette croyance

persuasive /pəˈsweɪsɪv/ ADJ [person, voice] persuasif ; [evidence, argument] convaincant

persuasively /pəˈsweɪsɪvlɪ/ ADV 1 (= convincingly) [argue, write, speak] de façon persuasive 2 (= attempting to persuade) ◆ **he smiled** ~ il eut un sourire qui cherchait à convaincre ◆ **"oh go on, you know you want to", he said** ~ "allons, tu sais que tu en as envie" dit-il en cherchant à le (or la) convaincre

persuasiveness /pəˈsweɪsɪvnɪs/ N pouvoir m or force f de persuasion

pert /pɜːt/ ADJ 1 (= coquettish) [person] coquin ◆ **a ~ little hat** un petit chapeau coquin 2 (= neat, firm) [bottom, buttocks, breasts] ferme ; [nose] mutin

pertain /pɜːˈteɪn/ VI 1 (frm = relate) **to ~ to** se rapporter à, se rattacher à ◆ **documents ~ing to the case** documents se rapportant à or relatifs à l'affaire 2 (Jur etc) [land] appartenir (to à)

pertinacious /ˌpɜːtɪˈneɪʃəs/ ADJ (frm) (= stubborn) entêté, obstiné ; (in opinions etc) opiniâtre

pertinaciously /ˌpɜːtɪˈneɪʃəslɪ/ ADV (frm) [maintain position] obstinément ; [argue] avec persistance

pertinacity /ˌpɜːtɪˈnæsɪtɪ/ N (frm) opiniâtreté f

pertinence /ˈpɜːtɪnəns/ N justesse f, à-propos m, pertinence f ; (Ling) pertinence f

pertinent /ˈpɜːtɪnənt/ ADJ pertinent ◆ **to be ~ to sth** se rapporter à qch

pertinently /ˈpɜːtɪnəntlɪ/ ADV [say, add] fort pertinemment, fort à propos ◆ **more ~ ...** ce qui est plus important, c'est que ...

pertly /ˈpɜːtlɪ/ ADV (= cheekily) avec effronterie, avec impertinence

pertness /ˈpɜːtnɪs/ N (= cheek) effronterie f, impertinence f

perturb /pəˈtɜːb/ VT perturber, inquiéter

perturbation /ˌpɜːtɜːˈbeɪʃən/ N (frm) perturbation f, agitation f

perturbed /pəˈtɜːbd/ ADJ perturbé, inquiet (-ète f) ◆ **I was ~ to hear that ...** j'ai appris avec inquiétude que ...

perturbing /pəˈtɜːbɪŋ/ ADJ troublant, inquiétant

pertussis /pəˈtʌsɪs/ N coqueluche f

Peru /pəˈruː/ N Pérou m ◆ **in** ~ au Pérou

Perugia /pəˈruːdʒə/ N Pérouse

perusal /pəˈruːzəl/ N (frm) lecture f ; (thorough) lecture f attentive

peruse /pəˈruːz/ VT lire ; (thoroughly) lire attentivement

Peruvian /pəˈruːvɪən/ ADJ péruvien N Péruvien(ne) m(f)

perv ‡ /pɜːv/ N abbrev of **pervert**

pervade /pɜːˈveɪd/ VT [smell] se répandre dans ; [influence] s'étendre dans ; [ideas] s'insinuer dans, pénétrer dans ; [gloom] envahir ; [problem] sévir dans ◆ **this atmosphere ~s the whole book** tout le livre baigne dans cette atmosphère

pervading /pɜːˈveɪdɪŋ/ ADJ [uncertainty, influence] sous-jacent(e) ◆ **there is a ~ atmosphere of doom and gloom in the film** tout le film baigne dans une atmosphère sinistre ◆ **throughout the book there is a ~ sense of menace** tout au long du roman on ressent comme une menace sourde ◆ **the ~ feeling is that economic recovery is near** le sentiment général est que la reprise (économique) est proche ; see also **all**

pervasive /pɜːˈveɪsɪv/ ADJ [smell, ideas] pénétrant ; [gloom] envahissant ; [influence] omniprésent

perverse /pəˈvɜːs/ ADJ 1 (= twisted) [pleasure, desire, humour] pervers 2 (= stubborn) têtu, entêté ; (= contrary) contrariant ◆ **how ~ of him!** qu'il est contrariant ! ◆ **what ~ behaviour!** quel esprit de contradiction ! ◆ **it would be ~ to refuse** ce serait faire preuve d'esprit de contradiction que de refuser

perversely /pəˈvɜːslɪ/ ADV 1 (= determinedly) obstinément ; (= in order to annoy) par esprit de contradiction 2 (= paradoxically) paradoxalement ◆ **~ enjoyable/engaging/appropriate** paradoxalement agréable/engageant/approprié

perverseness /pəˈvɜːsnɪs/ N ⇒ **perversity**

perversion /pəˈvɜːʃən/ N (also Psych) perversion f ; [of facts] déformation f, travestissement m ◆ **sexual ~s** perversions fpl sexuelles ◆ **~ of a function** (Med) perversion f or altération f d'une fonction ◆ **a ~ of justice** (gen) un travestissement de la justice ; (Jur) un déni de justice ◆ **a ~ of the truth** un travestissement de la vérité

perversity /pəˈvɜːsɪtɪ/ N 1 (= wickedness) perversité f, méchanceté f 2 (= stubbornness) obstination f, entêtement m ; (= contrariness) caractère m contrariant, esprit m de contradiction

pervert /pəˈvɜːt/ VT [+ person] pervertir, dépraver ; (Psych) pervertir ; (Rel) détourner de ses croyances ; [+ habits etc] dénaturer, dépraver ; [+ fact] fausser, travestir ; [+ sb's words] dénaturer, déformer ; [+ justice, truth] travestir ◆ **to ~ the course of justice** entraver le cours de la justice N /ˈpɜːvɜːt/ (Psych: also **sexual pervert**) pervers m sexuel, pervertie f sexuelle

perverted /pəˈvɜːtɪd/ ADJ (frm) pervers

pervious /ˈpɜːvɪəs/ ADJ perméable, pénétrable ; (fig) accessible (to à)

pervy /ˈpɜːvɪ/ ‡ ADJ (Brit) pervers

peseta /pəˈsetə/ N peseta f

pesky * /ˈpeskɪ/ ADJ (esp US) sale * before n ◆ **those ~ kids** * ces sales mômes *

peso /ˈpeɪsəʊ/ N peso m

pessary /'pesərɪ/ N pessaire *m*

pessimism /'pesɪmɪzəm/ N pessimisme *m*

pessimist /'pesɪmɪst/ N pessimiste *mf*

pessimistic /,pesɪ'mɪstɪk/ ADJ pessimiste *(about* au sujet de, sur) ◆ **I'm very ~ about it** je suis très pessimiste à ce sujet *or* là-dessus ◆ **they are ~ about making a profit** ils n'ont pas grand espoir de faire des bénéfices

pessimistically /,pesɪ'mɪstɪkəlɪ/ ADV avec pessimisme

pest /pest/ N 1 *(= insect)* insecte *m* nuisible ; *(= animal)* animal *m* nuisible ; *(agricultural)* ennemi *m* des cultures ◆ **rabbits are classed as a ~ in Australia** en Australie le lapin est considéré comme un (animal) nuisible 2 *(* = person)* casse-pieds* *mf inv*, enquiquineur* *m*, -euse* *f* ◆ **you little ~!** que tu es enquiquinant !* ; *(to girl)* espèce de petite peste ! ◆ **a sex ~** un vicieux *or* une vicieuse *(qui harcèle qn sexuellement)* COMP **pest control** N *[of insects]* désinsectisation *f*, lutte *f* contre les insectes ; *[of rats]* dératisation *f* ◆ **~ control officer** *(Admin)* préposé(e) *m(f)* à la lutte antiparasitaire

pester /'pestəʳ/ VT harceler ◆ **to ~ sb with questions** harceler qn de questions ◆ **she has been ~ing me for an answer** elle n'arrête pas de me réclamer une réponse ◆ **he ~ed me to go to the cinema with him** il n'a pas arrêté d'insister *or* il m'a cassé les pieds* pour que j'aille au cinéma avec lui ◆ **he ~ed me into going to the cinema with him** il n'a pas arrêté d'insister *or* il m'a cassé les pieds* pour que j'aille au cinéma avec lui, et j'ai fini par l'accompagner ◆ **he ~ed his father into lending him the car** à force d'insister auprès de son père, il a fini par se faire prêter la voiture ◆ **he ~s the life out of me*** il me casse les pieds* ◆ **stop ~ing me!** laisse-moi tranquille !, fiche-moi la paix !* ◆ **stop ~ing me about your bike** fiche-moi la paix* avec ton vélo ◆ **is this man ~ing you?** est-ce que cet homme vous importune ?

COMP **pester power** N pouvoir *m* de harcèlement *(des enfants en matière de consommation)*

pesticidal /,pestɪ'saɪdl/ ADJ pesticide

pesticide /'pestɪsaɪd/ N *(gen)* pesticide *m*

pestiferous /pes'tɪfərəs/ ADJ ⇒ **pestilent**

pestilence /'pestɪləns/ N peste *f*

pestilent /'pestɪlənt/, **pestilential** /,pestɪ'lenʃəl/ ADJ 1 *(= causing disease)* pestilentiel ; *(= pernicious)* nuisible 2 *(* = annoying)* fichu* *before n*, sacré‡ *before n*

pestle /'pesl/ N pilon *m*

pesto /'pestəʊ/ N pesto *m*

pet[1] /pet/ N 1 *(= animal)* animal *m* domestique *or* de compagnie ◆ **do you have any ~s?** avez-vous des animaux domestiques ? ; *(said by or to child)* as-tu des animaux chez toi *or* à la maison ? ◆ **she keeps a goldfish as a ~** en fait d'animal elle a un poisson rouge ◆ **"no pets (allowed)"** "les animaux sont interdits"

2 *(* = favourite)* chouchou(te)* *m(f)* ◆ **the teacher's ~** le chouchou* du professeur ◆ **to make a ~ of sb** chouchouter qn*

3 *(*: term of affection)* **be a ~ and fetch my slippers** sois un chou* *or* sois gentil, va chercher mes chaussons ◆ **he's a real ~** c'est un chou*, il est adorable ◆ **come here ~** viens ici mon chou* *or* mon lapin*

ADJ 1 *[lion, snake]* apprivoisé ◆ **he's got a ~ rabbit/dog** il a un lapin/chien ◆ **Jean-François has a ~ alligator** Jean-François a un alligator comme animal de compagnie *or* un alligator apprivoisé

2 *(* = favourite) [theory, project, charity, theme]* favori(te) *m(f)* ◆ **~ aversion** *or* **hate** bête *f* noire ◆ **it's his ~ subject** c'est sa marotte, c'est son dada* ◆ **once he gets onto his ~ subject ...** quand il enfourche son cheval de bataille *or* son dada* ...

VT *(= indulge)* chouchouter* ; *(= fondle)* câliner ; *(*: sexually)* caresser, peloter‡

VI *(*: sexually)* se caresser, se peloter‡

COMP **pet food** N aliments *mpl* pour animaux

pet name N petit nom *m* (d'amitié)

pet passport N passeport *m* pour animal domestique

pet shop N boutique *f* d'animaux

pet[2]* /pet/ N ◆ **to be in a ~** être de mauvais poil*

petal /'petl/ N pétale *m* ◆ **~-shaped** en forme de pétale

petard /pɪ'tɑːd/ N pétard *m* ; → **hoist**

Pete /piːt/ N 1 dim of **Peter** 2 ◆ **for ~'s sake !*** mais enfin !, bon sang !*

Peter /'piːtəʳ/ N Pierre *m* COMP **Peter's pence** N *(Rel)* denier *m* de saint Pierre ; → **blue, rob**

peter[1] /'piːtəʳ/ VI ◆ **to ~ out** *[supplies]* s'épuiser ; *[stream, conversation]* tarir ; *[plans]* tomber à l'eau ; *[story, plot, play, book]* tourner court ; *[fire, flame]* mourir ; *[road]* se perdre

peter[2]*‡ /'piːtəʳ/ N *(US = penis)* bite*‡ *f*

pethidine /'peθɪdiːn/ N *(Med)* péthédine *f*, mépéridine *f*

petite /pə'tiːt/ ADJ *[woman]* menue

petit-four /'petɪ'fɔːʳ/ N (pl **petits-fours**) petit-four *m*

petition /pə'tɪʃən/ N 1 *(= list of signatures)* pétition *f* ◆ **to get up a ~ against/for sth** organiser une pétition contre/en faveur de qch

2 *(= prayer)* prière *f* ; *(= request)* requête *f*, supplique *f*

3 *(Jur)* requête *f*, pétition *f* ◆ **a ~ for divorce** une demande de divorce ◆ **a ~ for** *or* **in bankruptcy** une demande de mise en liquidation judiciaire ◆ **right of ~** droit *m* de pétition ; → **file**[2]

VT 1 *(= address petition to)* adresser une pétition à, pétitionner ◆ **they ~ed the king for the release of the prisoner** ils ont adressé une pétition au roi pour demander la libération du prisonnier

2 *(frm = request)* implorer, prier *(sb to do sth* qn de faire qch)

3 *(Jur)* **to ~ the court** adresser *or* présenter une pétition en justice

VI adresser une pétition, pétitionner ◆ **to ~ for divorce** *(Jur)* faire une demande de divorce ◆ **to ~ for bankruptcy** faire une demande de mise en liquidation judiciaire

petitioner /pə'tɪʃnəʳ/ N pétitionnaire *mf* ; *(Jur)* requérant(e) *m(f)*, pétitionnaire *mf* ; *(in divorce)* demandeur *m*, -deresse *f* (en divorce)

petit jury /,petɪ'dʒʊərɪ/ N *(US)* jury *m* (de jugement)

petit mal /pətiː'mæl/ N *(NonC: Med)* petit mal *m*

petits pois /pətiː'pwɑː/ NPL petits-pois *mpl*

petnapping* /'petnæpɪŋ/ N *(US)* vol *m* d'animaux familiers *(pour les revendre aux laboratoires)*

Petrarch /'petrɑːk/ N Pétrarque *m*

petrel /'petrəl/ N pétrel *m* ; → **stormy**

Petri dish /'piːtrɪdɪʃ/ N boîte *f* de Petri

petrifaction /,petrɪ'fækʃən/ N *(lit, fig)* pétrification *f*

petrified /'petrɪfaɪd/ ADJ 1 *(lit = turned to stone)* pétrifié 2 *(fig = terrified)* pétrifié *or* paralysé de peur ◆ **I was absolutely ~!** j'étais terrifié !, j'étais pétrifié de peur !

petrify /'petrɪfaɪ/ VT 1 *(lit = turn to stone)* pétrifier 2 *(fig = terrify)* terrifier VI se pétrifier *(lit)*

petro... /'petrəʊ/ PREF pétro...

petrochemical /,petrəʊ'kemɪkəl/ N produit *m* pétrochimique ADJ pétrochimique

petrocurrency /'petrəʊ,kʌrənsɪ/ N pétrodevise *f*

petrodollar /'petrəʊ,dɒləʳ/ N pétrodollar *m*

petrographic(al) /,petrə'græfɪk(əl)/ ADJ pétrographique

petrography /pe'trɒgrəfɪ/ N pétrographie *f*

petrol /'petrəl/ *(Brit)* N essence *f* ◆ **my car's very heavy on ~** ma voiture consomme beaucoup (d'essence) ◆ **this car runs on ~** cette voiture roule à l'essence ; → **star**

COMP **petrol bomb** N cocktail *m* Molotov

petrol can N bidon *m* à essence

petrol cap N ⇒ **petrol filler cap**

petrol-driven ADJ à essence

petrol engine N moteur *m* à essence

petrol filler cap N bouchon *m* de réservoir d'essence

petrol gauge N jauge *f* d'essence

petrol pump N *(on forecourt, in engine)* pompe *f* à essence

petrol rationing N rationnement *m* de l'essence

petrol station N station-service *f*, poste *m* d'essence

petrol tank N réservoir *m* (d'essence)

petrol tanker N *(= ship)* pétrolier *m*, tanker *m* ; *(= truck)* camion-citerne *m (transportant de l'essence)*

> ⚠ The French word **pétrole** means 'oil', not **petrol**.

petroleum /pɪ'trəʊlɪəm/ N pétrole *m* ◆ **~ industry** industrie *f* pétrolière COMP **petroleum jelly** N Vaseline ® *f*

petroliferous /,petrə'lɪfərəs/ ADJ pétrolifère

petrology /pe'trɒlədʒɪ/ N pétrologie *f*

petticoat /'petɪkəʊt/ N *(= underskirt)* jupon *m* ; *(= slip)* combinaison *f*

pettifogging /'petɪfɒgɪŋ/ ADJ *(= trifling) [details]* insignifiant ; *[objections]* chicanier

pettily /'petɪlɪ/ ADV avec mesquinerie, de façon mesquine

pettiness /'petɪnɪs/ N *(NonC)* 1 *(= small-mindedness) [of person, behaviour]* mesquinerie *f* 2 *(= triviality) [of detail, complaint]* insignifiance *f*

petting* /'petɪŋ/ N *(NonC)* caresses *fpl* ◆ **heavy ~** pelotage* *m* ◆ **to indulge in heavy ~** se peloter* COMP **petting zoo** N *(esp US)* zoo *ou partie d'un zoo où sont réunis des animaux, souvent jeunes, que les enfants peuvent caresser*

pettish /'petɪʃ/ ADJ *[person]* de mauvaise humeur, irritable ; *[remark]* maussade ; *[child]* grognon

pettishly /'petɪʃlɪ/ ADV avec mauvaise humeur, d'un air *or* d'un ton maussade

petty /'petɪ/ ADJ 1 *(= small-minded) [person, behaviour]* mesquin 2 *(= trivial) [detail, complaint]* insignifiant, sans importance ◆ **~ annoyances** désagréments *mpl* mineurs, tracasseries *fpl* ◆ **~ regulations** règlement *m* tracassier 3 *(Naut)* **~ officer** ≈ maître *m* ◆ **~ officer third class** *(US Navy)* quartier-maître *m* de première classe

COMP **petty cash** N petite caisse *f*, caisse *f* de dépenses courantes

petty crime N 1 *(NonC = illegal activities)* petite délinquance *f* 2 *(= illegal act)* délit *m* mineur

petty criminal N petit malfaiteur *m*, malfaiteur *m* à la petite semaine

petty expenses NPL menues dépenses *fpl*

petty larceny N *(Jur)* larcin *m*

petty official N fonctionnaire *mf* subalterne, petit fonctionnaire *m*

Petty Sessions NPL *(Brit Jur)* sessions *fpl* des juges de paix

petulance /'petjʊləns/ N mauvaise humeur *f*

petulant /ˈpetjʊlənt/ ADJ *(by nature)* irritable, irascible ; *(on one occasion)* irrité ; *[expression, gesture]* irrité ◆ **in a ~ mood** de mauvaise humeur ◆ **a ~ behaviour** irritabilité *f*, irascibilité *f* ; *(on one occasion)* mauvaise humeur *f*

petulantly /ˈpetjʊləntlɪ/ ADV avec humeur

petunia /pɪˈtjuːnɪə/ N pétunia *m*

pew /pjuː/ N *(Rel)* banc *m* (d'église) ◆ **take a ~*** *(hum)* prenez donc un siège

pewter /ˈpjuːtəʳ/ N étain *m* ◆ **to collect ~** collectionner les étains COMP *[pot etc]* en étain, d'étain

peyote /peɪˈəʊtɪ/ N peyotl *m*

PFC /ˌpiːefˈsiː/ N *(US Mil)* (abbrev of **Private First Class**) → **private**

pfennig /ˈfenɪg/ N pfennig *m*

PFI /ˌpiːefˈaɪ/ N (pl **PFIs**) *(Brit Pol)* (abbrev of **private finance initiative**) PFI *f*

PFLP /ˌpiːefelˈpiː/ N (abbrev of **Popular Front for the Liberation of Palestine**) FPLP *m*

PG /piːˈdʒiː/ ABBR *(Cine: film censor's rating)* (abbrev of **Parental Guidance**) *certaines scènes peuvent heurter la sensibilité des jeunes enfants* N (abbrev of **paying guest**) → **paying**

PG 13 /ˌpiːdʒiːθɜːˈtiːn/ *(US Cine)* (abbrev of **Parental Guidance 13**) *interdit aux moins de 13 ans sans autorisation parentale*

PGA /ˌpiːdʒiːˈeɪ/ N (abbrev of **Professional Golfers' Association**) PGA *f*

PGCE /ˌpiːdʒiːsiːˈiː/ N *(Brit)* (abbrev of **Postgraduate Certificate in Education**) *diplôme d'aptitude à l'enseignement*

PH /piːˈeɪtʃ/ *(US Mil)* (abbrev of **Purple Heart**) → **purple**

pH /piːˈeɪtʃ/ N pH *m*

Phaedra /ˈfiːdrə/ N Phèdre *f*

phaeton /ˈfeɪtən/ N phaéton *m*

phagocyte /ˈfægəˌsaɪt/ N phagocyte *m*

phagocytosis /ˌfægəsaɪˈtəʊsɪs/ N phagocytose *f*

phalangeal /fəˈlændʒɪəl/ ADJ phalangien

phalanx /ˈfælæŋks/ N (pl **phalanges** /fæˈlændʒiːz/) *(gen, Mil, Hist, Anat)* phalange *f*

phalarope /ˈfæləˌrəʊp/ N phalarope *m*

phalli /ˈfælaɪ/ NPL of **phallus**

phallic /ˈfælɪk/ ADJ phallique COMP **phallic symbol** N symbole *m* phallique

phallocentric /ˌfæləˈsentrɪk/ ADJ phallocentrique

phallus /ˈfæləs/ N (pl **phalluses** or **phalli**) phallus *m*

phantasm /ˈfæntæzəm/ N fantasme *m*

phantasmagoria /ˌfæntæzməˈgɔːrɪə/ N fantasmagorie *f*

phantasmagoric(al) /ˌfæntæzməˈgɒrɪk(əl)/ ADJ fantasmagorique

phantasmal /fænˈtæzməl/ ADJ fantomatique

phantasy /ˈfæntəzɪ/ N ⇒ **fantasy**

phantom /ˈfæntəm/ N *(= ghost)* fantôme *m* ; *(= vision)* fantasme *m* ◆ **the ~ pencil thief strikes again!** *(hum)* le voleur de crayons masqué a encore frappé ! COMP **phantom pregnancy** N grossesse *f* nerveuse

Pharaoh /ˈfeərəʊ/ N pharaon *m* ; *(as name)* Pharaon *m*

Pharisaic(al) /ˌfærɪˈseɪk(əl)/ ADJ pharisaïque

Pharisee /ˈfærɪsiː/ N pharisien(ne) *m(f)*

pharmaceutical /ˌfɑːməˈsjuːtɪkəl/ ADJ pharmaceutique NPL **pharmaceuticals** médicaments *mpl*, produits *mpl* pharmaceutiques

pharmacist /ˈfɑːməsɪst/ N *(= person)* pharmacien(ne) *m(f)* ; *(Brit)* (also **pharmacist's**) pharmacie *f*

pharmacological /ˌfɑːməkəˈlɒdʒɪkəl/ ADJ pharmacologique

pharmacologist /ˌfɑːməˈkɒlədʒɪst/ N pharmacologue *mf*

pharmacology /ˌfɑːməˈkɒlədʒɪ/ N pharmacologie *f*

pharmacopoeia /ˌfɑːməkəˈpiːə/ N pharmacopée *f*

pharmacy /ˈfɑːməsɪ/ N pharmacie *f*

pharynges /fæˈrɪndʒiːz/ NPL of **pharynx**

pharyngitis /ˌfærɪnˈdʒaɪtɪs/ N pharyngite *f*, angine *f* ◆ **to have ~** avoir une pharyngite

pharynx /ˈfærɪŋks/ N (pl **pharynxes** or **pharynges**) pharynx *m*

phase /feɪz/ N 1 *(= stage in process)* phase *f*, période *f* ◆ **a critical ~ in the negotiations** une phase *or* un stade critique des négociations ◆ **the first ~ of the work** la première tranche des travaux ◆ **the ~s of a disease** les phases *fpl* d'une maladie ◆ **the ~s of the moon** les phases *fpl* de la lune ◆ **every child goes through a difficult ~** tout enfant passe par une phase *or* une période difficile ◆ **a passing ~** *(gen)* un état passager ; *(= fad)* une passade ◆ **it's just a ~ he's going through** ça lui passera

2 *(Astron, Chem, Elec, Phys etc)* phase *f* ◆ **in ~** *(Elec, fig)* en phase ◆ **out of ~** *(Elec, fig)* déphasé

VT *[+ innovations, developments]* introduire graduellement ; *[+ execution of plan]* procéder par étapes à ◆ **the modernization of the factory was ~d over three years** la modernisation de l'usine s'est effectuée en trois ans par étapes ◆ **the changes were ~d carefully so as to avoid unemployment** on a pris soin d'introduire les changements graduellement afin d'éviter le chômage ◆ **we must ~ the various processes so as to lose as little time as possible** nous devons arranger *or* organiser les diverses opérations de façon à perdre le moins de temps possible ◆ **~d changes** changements *mpl* organisés de façon progressive ◆ **a ~d withdrawal of troops** un retrait progressif des troupes

COMP **phase-out** N suppression *f* progressive

► **phase in** VT SEP *[+ new machinery, measures etc]* introduire progressivement *or* graduellement

► **phase out** VT SEP *[+ machinery]* retirer progressivement ; *[+ jobs]* supprimer graduellement ; *[+ techniques, differences]* éliminer progressivement

phatic /ˈfætɪk/ ADJ phatique

PhD /ˌpiːeɪtʃˈdiː/ N *(Univ)* (abbrev of **Doctor of Philosophy**) *(= qualification)* doctorat *m* ; *(= person)* ≈ titulaire *mf* d'un doctorat ◆ **to have a ~ in ...** avoir un doctorat de ...

pheasant /ˈfeznt/ N faisan *m* ◆ **cock ~** faisan *m* ◆ **hen ~** poule *f* faisane

phencyclidine /fenˈsɪklɪˌdiːn/ N phencyclidine *f*

phenix /ˈfiːnɪks/ N *(US)* ⇒ **phoenix**

phenobarbitone /ˈfiːnəʊˈbɑːbɪtəʊn/ N phénobarbital *m*

phenol /ˈfiːnɒl/ N phénol *m*

phenomena /fɪˈnɒmɪnə/ NPL of **phenomenon**

phenomenal /fɪˈnɒmɪnl/ ADJ *(lit, fig)* phénoménal

phenomenally /fɪˈnɒmɪnəlɪ/ ADV *[good, popular, well, quick etc]* phénoménalement ; *[rise, increase]* de façon phénoménale ◆ **she has been ~ successful** elle a eu un succès phénoménal

phenomenological /fənɒmənəˈlɒdʒɪkəl/ ADJ phénoménologique

phenomenologist /fənɒməˈnɒlədʒɪst/ N phénoménologue *mf*

phenomenology /fənɒməˈnɒlədʒɪ/ N phénoménologie *f*

phenomenon /fɪˈnɒmɪnən/ N (pl **phenomenons** or **phenomena**) *(lit, fig)* phénomène *m*

pheromone /ˈferəˌməʊn/ N phéromone *f*

phew /fjuː/ EXCL *(relief)* ouf ! ; *(heat)* pfff ! ; *(disgust)* pouah ! ; *(surprise)* oh !

phial /ˈfaɪəl/ N fiole *f*

Phi Beta Kappa /ˈfaɪˈbeɪtəˈkæpə/ N *(US Univ)* *association élitiste d'anciens étudiants très brillants, ou membre de cette association*

PHI BETA KAPPA

Le **Phi Beta Kappa** est le club estudiantin le plus ancien et le plus prestigieux des États-Unis. Fondé en 1776, il est réservé aux étudiants les plus brillants et l'adhésion se fait par élection des membres au cours de la troisième ou de la quatrième année d'études universitaires. Le nom du club vient de l'expression grecque « philosophia biou kybernetes » (la philosophie est le timonier de la vie), qui lui sert de devise. Un membre du club est un **phi beta kappa**.

Phil abbrev of **Philadelphia**

Philadelphia /ˌfɪləˈdelfɪə/ N Philadelphie

philander /fɪˈlændəʳ/ VI courir après les femmes, faire la cour aux femmes

philanderer /fɪˈlændərəʳ/ N coureur *m* (de jupons), don Juan *m*

philandering /fɪˈlændərɪŋ/ N *(NonC)* flirts *mpl*, liaisons *fpl*

philanthropic /ˌfɪlənˈθrɒpɪk/ ADJ philanthropique

philanthropist /fɪˈlænθrəpɪst/ N philanthrope *mf*

philanthropy /fɪˈlænθrəpɪ/ N philanthropie *f*

philatelic /ˌfɪləˈtelɪk/ ADJ philatélique

philatelist /fɪˈlætəlɪst/ N philatéliste *mf*

philately /fɪˈlætəlɪ/ N philatélie *f*

...phile /faɪl/ SUF ...phile ◆ **francophile** ADJ, N francophile *mf*

Philemon /faɪˈliːmɒn/ N Philémon *m*

philharmonic /ˌfɪlɑːˈmɒnɪk/ ADJ philharmonique

philhellene /fɪlˈheliːn/ N, ADJ philhellène *mf*

philhellenic /ˌfɪlheˈliːnɪk/ ADJ philhellène

philhellenism /fɪlˈhelɪnɪzəm/ N philhellénisme *m*

...philia /ˈfɪlɪə/ SUF ...philie *f* ◆ **francophilia** francophilie *f*

Philippi /ˈfɪlɪpaɪ/ N Philippes

Philippians /fɪˈlɪpɪəns/ NPL Philippiens *mpl*

philippic /fɪˈlɪpɪk/ N *(liter)* philippique *f*

Philippine /ˈfɪlɪpiːn/ NPL **Philippines** ⇒ **the Philippine Islands** COMP **the Philippine Islands** NPL Philippines *fpl*

philistine /ˈfɪlɪstaɪn/ ADJ 1 *(fig)* béotien 2 ◆ **Philistine** philistin N 1 *(Bible)* ◆ **Philistine** Philistin *m* 2 *(fig)* philistin *m*, béotien(ne) *m(f)*

philistinism /ˈfɪlɪstɪˌnɪzəm/ N philistinisme *m*

Phillips ® /ˈfɪlɪps/ *(in compounds)* ◆ **~ screw** vis *f* cruciforme ◆ **~ screwdriver** tournevis *m* cruciforme

philodendron /ˌfɪləˈdendrən/ N (pl **philodendrons** or **philodendra** /ˌfɪləˈdendrə/) philodendron *m*

philological /ˌfɪləˈlɒdʒɪkəl/ ADJ philologique

philologist /fɪˈlɒlədʒɪst/ N philologue *mf*

philology /fɪˈlɒlədʒɪ/ N philologie *f*

philosopher /fɪˈlɒsəfəʳ/ N philosophe *mf* ◆ **he is something of a ~** *(fig)* il est du genre philosophe COMP **philosopher's stone** N pierre *f* philosophale

philosophic(al) /ˌfɪləˈsɒfɪk(əl)/ ADJ 1 *(= relating to philosophy) [subject, debate, discussion, tradition]* philosophique 2 *(= calm, resigned)* philosophe ◆ **in a ~(al) tone** d'un ton philosophe ◆ **to be ~(al) about sth** prendre qch avec philosophie

philosophically /ˌfɪləˈsɒfɪkəlɪ/ ADV 1 *(= with resignation)* avec philosophie 2 **~ important/disputable** *etc* philosophiquement important/discutable *etc*, important/discutable *etc* sur le plan philosophique ◆ **to be ~ inclined** *or* **minded** avoir l'esprit philosophique ◆ **he's ~ opposed to war** il est, par philosophie, opposé à la guerre

philosophize /fɪˈlɒsəfaɪz/ VI philosopher *(about, on* sur)

philosophy /fɪˈlɒsəfɪ/ N philosophie *f* ◆ **his ~ of life** sa philosophie, sa conception de la vie ◆ **our management ~** notre conception de la gestion ◆ **the best ~ is to change your food habits to a low-sugar diet** la meilleure solution est d'adopter un régime à faible teneur en sucres ◆ **he developed a ~ of health and safety ...** il a mis en place une politique centrée sur la sécurité des conditions de travail ... ; → **moral, natural**

philtre, philter *(US)* /ˈfɪltəʳ/ N philtre *m*

phishing /ˈfɪʃɪŋ/ N phising *m*

phiz‡ /fɪz/, **phizog**‡ /fɪˈzɒg/ N (abbrev of **physiognomy**) binette‡ *f*, bouille‡ *f*

phlebitis /flɪˈbaɪtɪs/ N phlébite *f*

phlebology /flɪˈbɒlədʒɪ/ N phlébologie *f*

phlebotomist /flɪˈbɒtəmɪst/ N phlébotomiste *mf*

phlebotomy /flɪˈbɒtəmɪ/ N phlébotomie *f*

phlegm /flem/ N 1 *(= mucus)* mucosité *f* 2 *(= equanimity)* flegme *m*

phlegmatic /flegˈmætɪk/ ADJ flegmatique

phlegmatically /flegˈmætɪkəlɪ/ ADV flegmatiquement, avec flegme

phlox /flɒks/ N (pl **phlox** *or* **phloxes**) phlox *m inv*

Phnom-Penh /ˈnɒmˈpen/ N Phnom-Penh

...phobe /fəʊb/ SUF ...phobe ◆ **francophobe** ADJ, N francophobe *mf*

phobia /ˈfəʊbɪə/ N phobie *f* ◆ **I've got a ~ about ...** j'ai la phobie de ...

...phobia /ˈfəʊbɪə/ SUF ...phobie *f* ◆ **anglophobia** anglophobie *f*

phobic /ˈfəʊbɪk/ ADJ, N phobique *mf*

phoenix, phenix *(US)* /ˈfiːnɪks/ N phénix *m* ◆ **like a ~ from the ashes** comme le phénix qui renaît de ses cendres

phonatory /ˈfəʊnətərɪ/ ADJ phonateur (-trice *f*), phonatoire

phone¹ /fəʊn/ LANGUAGE IN USE 27 (abbrev of **telephone**)

N 1 *(= telephone)* téléphone *m* ◆ **on** *or* **over the ~** *(gen)* au téléphone ◆ **by ~** par téléphone ◆ **to be on the ~** *(Brit) (= be a subscriber)* avoir le téléphone ; *(= be speaking)* être au téléphone ◆ **I've got Jill on the ~** j'ai Jill au téléphone *or* au bout du fil*

2 *(Brit)* **to give sb a ~*** *(= phone call)* passer un coup de fil* à qn

VT (also **phone up**) téléphoner à, appeler, passer un coup de fil à*

VI téléphoner

COMP **phone bill** N facture *f* de téléphone

phone book N annuaire *m* (de téléphone)

phone booth N 1 *(in station, hotel etc)* téléphone *m* public 2 *(US: in street)* cabine *f* téléphonique

phone box N *(Brit)* cabine *f* téléphonique

phone call N coup *m* de téléphone *or* de fil*, appel *m* téléphonique ◆ **to make a ~ call** passer un coup de téléphone *or* de fil*, téléphoner

phone-in (programme) N *(Brit) émission où les auditeurs ou téléspectateurs sont invités à intervenir par téléphone pour donner leur avis ou pour parler de leurs problèmes*

phone number N numéro *m* de téléphone

phone tapping N mise *f* sur écoutes téléphoniques

► **phone back** VT SEP *(returning call)* rappeler ; *(calling again)* rappeler, retéléphoner à VI *(= return call)* rappeler ; *(= call again)* rappeler, retéléphoner

► **phone in** VI téléphoner ◆ **to ~ in sick** appeler pour dire qu'on est malade VT SEP *[+ order]* passer par téléphone ; *[+ article]* dicter au téléphone

phone² /fəʊn/ N *(Ling)* phone *m*

phonecam /ˈfəʊnkæm/ N (téléphone *m*) portable *m* appareil photo

phonecard /ˈfəʊnkɑːd/ N *(Brit Telec)* télécarte ® *f*

phoneme /ˈfəʊniːm/ N phonème *m*

phonemic /fəʊˈniːmɪk/ ADJ phonémique

phonemics /fəʊˈniːmɪks/ N *(NonC)* phonémique *f*, phonématique *f*

phonetic /fəʊˈnetɪk/ ADJ phonétique

COMP **phonetic alphabet** N alphabet *m* phonétique

phonetic law N loi *f* phonétique

phonetically /fəʊˈnetɪkəlɪ/ ADV *[spell, learn]* phonétiquement ◆ **~ speaking** phonétiquement parlant

phonetician /ˌfəʊnɪˈtɪʃən/ N phonéticien(ne) *m(f)*

phonetics /fəʊˈnetɪks/ N *(NonC = subject, study)* phonétique *f* ◆ **articulatory/acoustic/auditory ~** phonétique *f* articulatoire/acoustique/auditoire NPL *(= symbols)* transcription *f* phonétique ◆ **the ~ are wrong** la transcription phonétique est fausse COMP *[teacher, student, exam, degree, textbook, laboratory]* de phonétique

phoney* /ˈfəʊnɪ/ *(esp US)* ADJ *[name]* faux (fausse *f*) ; *[jewels]* faux (fausse *f*), en toc ; *[emotion]* factice, simulé ; *[excuse, story, report]* bidon* *inv*, à la noix* ; *[person]* pas franc (franche *f*), poseur ◆ **this diamond is ~** ce diamant est faux ◆ **apparently he was a ~ doctor** il paraît que c'était un charlatan *or* un médecin marron ◆ **a ~ company** une société bidon* ◆ **it sounds ~** cela a l'air d'être de la frime* *or* de la blague* N (pl **phoneys**) *(= person)* charlatan *m*, poseur *m*, faux jeton* *m* ◆ **that diamond is a ~** ce diamant est faux COMP **the phoney war*** N *(Brit Hist: in 1939)* la drôle de guerre

phonic /ˈfɒnɪk/ ADJ phonique

phono... /ˈfəʊnəʊ/ PREF phono...

phonograph † /ˈfəʊnəgrɑːf/ N électrophone *m*, phonographe † *m*

phonological /ˌfəʊnəˈlɒdʒɪkəl/ ADJ phonologique

phonologically /ˌfəʊnəˈlɒdʒɪklɪ/ ADV phonologiquement

phonologist /fəˈnɒlədʒɪst/ N phonologue *mf*

phonology /fəʊˈnɒlədʒɪ/ N phonologie *f*

phony* /ˈfəʊnɪ/ ADJ, N ⇒ **phoney**

phooey* /ˈfuːɪ/ EXCL *(scorn)* peuh !, pfft !

phosgene /ˈfɒzdʒiːn/ N phosgène *m*

phosphate /ˈfɒsfeɪt/ N *(Chem)* phosphate *m* ◆ **~s** *(Agr)* phosphates *mpl*, engrais *mpl* phosphatés

phosphene /ˈfɒsfiːn/ N phosphène *m*

phosphide /ˈfɒsfaɪd/ N phosphure *m*

phosphine /ˈfɒsfiːn/ N phosphine *f*

phosphoresce /ˌfɒsfəˈres/ VI être phosphorescent

phosphorescence /ˌfɒsfəˈresns/ N phosphorescence *f*

phosphorescent /ˌfɒsfəˈresnt/ ADJ phosphorescent

phosphoric /fɒsˈfɒrɪk/ ADJ phosphorique

phosphorous /ˈfɒsfərəs/ ADJ phosphoreux

phosphorus /ˈfɒsfərəs/ N phosphore *m*

photo /ˈfəʊtəʊ/ N (pl **photos**) (abbrev of **photograph**) photo *f* ; see also **photograph**

COMP **photo album** N album *m* de photos

photo booth N photomaton ® *m*

photo finish N *(Sport)* photo-finish *m*

photo-offset N *(Typ)* offset *m (processus)*

photo opportunity N séance *f* photo *or* de photos *(pour la presse)* ◆ **it is a great ~ opportunity** il y a de bonnes photos à prendre

photo session N séance *f* photo *or* de photos

photo... /ˈfəʊtəʊ/ PREF photo...

photocall /ˈfəʊtəʊˌkɒl/ N *(Brit Press)* séance *f* de photos pour la presse

photocell /ˈfəʊtəʊˌsel/ N photocellule *f*

photochemical /ˌfəʊtəʊˈkemɪkəl/ ADJ photochimique

photochemistry /ˌfəʊtəʊˈkemɪstrɪ/ N photochimie *f*

photocompose /ˌfəʊtəʊkəmˈpəʊz/ VT photocomposer

photocomposer /ˌfəʊtəʊkəmˈpəʊzəʳ/ N photocomposeuse *f*

photocomposition /ˌfəʊtəʊkɒmpəˈzɪʃən/ N photocomposition *f*

photocopier /ˈfəʊtəʊˌkɒpɪəʳ/ N photocopieur *m*, photocopieuse *f*

photocopy /ˈfəʊtəʊˌkɒpɪ/ N photocopie *f* VT photocopier

photodisintegration /ˌfəʊtəʊdɪˌsɪntɪˈgreɪʃən/ N photodissociation *f*

photodisk /ˈfəʊtəʊˌdɪsk/ N *(Comput)* photodisque *m*

photoelectric(al) /ˌfəʊtəʊɪˈlektrɪk(əl)/ ADJ photo-électrique ◆ **~(al) cell** cellule *f* photo-électrique

photoelectricity /ˌfəʊtəʊɪlekˈtrɪsɪtɪ/ N photoélectricité *f*

photoelectron /ˌfəʊtəʊɪˈlektrɒn/ N photoélectron *m*

photoengrave /ˌfəʊtəʊɪnˈgreɪv/ VT photograver

photoengraving /ˌfəʊtəʊɪnˈgreɪvɪŋ/ N photogravure *f*

Photofit ® /ˈfəʊtəʊˌfɪt/ N *(Brit:* also **Photofit picture**) portrait-robot *m*

photoflash /ˈfəʊtəʊˌflæʃ/ N flash *m*

photoflood /ˈfəʊtəʊˌflʌd/ N projecteur *m*

photogenic /ˌfəʊtəˈdʒenɪk/ ADJ photogénique

photogeology /ˌfəʊtəʊdʒɪˈɒlədʒɪ/ N photogéologie *f*

photograph /ˈfəʊtəgræf/ N photo *f*, photographie † *f* ◆ **to take a ~ of sb/sth** prendre une photo de qn/qch, prendre qn/qch en photo ◆ **he takes good ~s** il fait de bonnes photos ◆ **he takes a good ~*** *(= is photogenic)* il est photogénique, il est bien en photo* ◆ **in** *or* **on the ~** sur la photo ; → **aerial, colour** VT photographier, prendre en photo VI ◆ **to ~ well** être photogénique, être bien en photo* COMP **photograph album** N album *m* de photos *or* de photographies †

⚠ In French, the word **photographe** means 'photographer', not **photograph**.

photographer /fəˈtɒɡrəfəʳ/ N (also Press etc) photographe mf ◆ **press** ~ photographe mf de la presse, reporter m photographe ◆ **street** ~ photostoppeur m ◆ **he's a keen** ~ il est passionné de photo

photographic /ˌfəʊtəˈɡræfɪk/ ADJ photographique ◆ ~ **library** photothèque f COMP **photographic memory** N mémoire f photographique

photographically /ˌfəʊtəˈɡræfɪkəlɪ/ ADV photographiquement

photography /fəˈtɒɡrəfɪ/ N (NonC) photographie f NonC ; → **colour, trick**

photogravure /ˌfəʊtəʊɡrəˈvjʊəʳ/ N photogravure f, héliogravure f

photojournalism /ˌfəʊtəʊˈdʒɜːnəlɪzəm/ N photojournalisme m, photoreportage m

photojournalist /ˌfəʊtəʊˈdʒɜːnəlɪst/ N photojournaliste mf, journaliste mf photographe

photokinesis /ˌfəʊtəʊkɪˈniːsɪs/ N photokinésie f

photokinetic /ˌfəʊtəʊkɪˈnetɪk/ ADJ photokinétique

photolitho /ˌfəʊtəʊˈlaɪθəʊ/ N abbrev of **photolithography**

photolithograph /ˌfəʊtəʊˈlɪθəˌɡrɑːf/ N gravure f photolithographique

photolithography /ˌfəʊtəʊlɪˈθɒɡrəfɪ/ N photolithographie f

photolysis /fəʊˈtɒlɪsɪs/ N photolyse f

photomachine /ˌfəʊtəʊməˈʃiːn/ N photomaton ® m

photomap /ˈfəʊtəʊˌmæp/ N photoplan m

photomechanical /ˌfəʊtəʊmɪˈkænɪkl/ ADJ photomécanique

photometer /fəʊˈtɒmɪtəʳ/ N photomètre m

photometric /ˌfəʊtəˈmetrɪk/ ADJ photométrique

photometry /fəʊˈtɒmɪtrɪ/ N photométrie f

photomontage /ˌfəʊtəʊmɒnˈtɑːʒ/ N photomontage m

photomultiplier /ˌfəʊtəʊˈmʌltɪˌplaɪəʳ/ N photomultiplicateur m

photon /ˈfəʊtɒn/ N photon m

photoperiodic /ˌfəʊtəʊˌpɪərɪˈɒdɪk/ ADJ photopériodique

photoperiodism /ˌfəʊtəʊˈpɪərɪədɪzəm/ N photopériodisme m

photophobia /ˌfəʊtəʊˈfəʊbɪə/ N photophobie f

photorealism /ˌfəʊtəʊˈrɪəˌlɪzəm/ N photoréalisme m

photoreconnaissance /ˌfəʊtəʊrɪˈkɒnɪsəns/ N reconnaissance f photographique

photosensitive /ˌfəʊtəʊˈsensɪtɪv/ ADJ photosensible

photosensitivity /ˌfəʊtəʊsensɪˈtɪvɪtɪ/ N photosensibilité f

photosensitize /ˌfəʊtəʊˈsensɪˌtaɪz/ VT photosensibiliser

photosensor /ˈfəʊtəʊˌsensəʳ/ N dispositif m photosensible

photoset /ˈfəʊtəʊˌset/ VT photocomposer

Photostat ® /ˈfəʊtəʊˌstæt/ N photostat m VT photocopier

photosynthesis /ˌfəʊtəʊˈsɪnθɪsɪs/ N photosynthèse f

photosynthesize /ˌfəʊtəʊˈsɪnθɪˌsaɪz/ VT photosynthétiser

photosynthetic /ˌfəʊtəʊsɪnˈθetɪk/ ADJ photosynthétique

phototelegram /ˌfəʊtəʊˈteleˌɡræm/ N phototélégramme m

phototelegraphy /ˌfəʊtəʊtɪˈleɡrəfɪ/ N phototélégraphie f

phototropic /ˌfəʊtəʊˈtrɒpɪk/ ADJ phototropique

phototropism /ˌfəʊtəʊˈtrɒpɪzəm/ N phototropisme m

phototype /ˈfəʊtəʊˌtaɪp/ N (= process) phototypie f

phototypesetting /ˌfəʊtəʊˈtaɪpˌsetɪŋ/ N (US Typ) photocomposition f

phototypography /ˌfəʊtəʊtaɪˈpɒɡrəfɪ/ N phototypographie f

phrasal /ˈfreɪzəl/ ADJ syntagmatique COMP **phrasal verb** N verbe m à particule

phrase /freɪz/ N 1 (= saying) expression f ◆ **as the** ~ **is** or **goes** comme on dit, selon l'expression consacrée ◆ **to use Mrs Thatcher's** ~ ... comme dirait Mme Thatcher ... ◆ **in Marx's famous** ~ ... pour reprendre la célèbre formule de Marx ... ◆ **that's exactly the** ~ **I'm looking for** voilà exactement l'expression que je cherche ; → **set, turn**

2 (Ling: gen) locution f ; (Gram) syntagme m ◆ **noun/verb** ~ syntagme m nominal/verbal

3 (Mus) phrase f

VT 1 [+ thought] exprimer ; [+ letter] rédiger ◆ **a neatly ~d letter** une lettre bien tournée ◆ **can we ~ it differently?** peut-on exprimer or tourner cela différemment ? ◆ **she ~d her question carefully** elle a très soigneusement formulé sa question

2 (Mus) phraser

COMP **phrase marker** N (Ling) marqueur m syntagmatique

phrase structure N (Ling) structure f syntagmatique ADJ [rule, grammar] syntagmatique

phrasebook /ˈfreɪzbʊk/ N guide m de conversation

phraseology /ˌfreɪzɪˈɒlədʒɪ/ N phraséologie f

phrasing /ˈfreɪzɪŋ/ N 1 [of ideas] expression f ; [of text] formulation f, choix m des mots ◆ **the** ~ **is unfortunate** les termes sont mal choisis 2 (Mus) phrasé m

phrenetic /frɪˈnetɪk/ ADJ ⇒ **frenetic**

phrenic /ˈfrenɪk/ ADJ (Anat) phrénique

phrenologist /frɪˈnɒlədʒɪst/ N phrénologue mf, phrénologiste mf

phrenology /frɪˈnɒlədʒɪ/ N phrénologie f

phthisis /ˈθaɪsɪs/ N phtisie f

phut ‡ /fʌt/ ADV ◆ **to go** ~ [machine, object] péter‡, rendre l'âme * ; [scheme, plan] tomber à l'eau

phwoar ‡ /fwɔːʳ/ EXCL (Brit) mazette * !, wow * !

phycology /faɪˈkɒlədʒɪ/ N phycologie f

phyla /ˈfaɪlə/ NPL of **phylum**

phylactery /fɪˈlæktərɪ/ N phylactère m

phylactic /fɪˈlæktɪk/ ADJ phylactique

phyletic /faɪˈletɪk/ ADJ phylogénique

phylloxera /ˌfɪlɒkˈsɪərə/ N phylloxéra m

phylogenesis /ˌfaɪləʊˈdʒenɪsɪs/ N phylogenèse f

phylogenetic /ˌfaɪləʊdʒɪˈnetɪk/ ADJ phylogénique

phylum /ˈfaɪləm/ N (pl **phyla**) embranchement m, phylum m (SPÉC)

physic †† /ˈfɪzɪk/ N médicament m

physical /ˈfɪzɪkəl/ ADJ 1 (= of the body) physique ◆ ~ **contact** contact m physique ◆ ~ **abuse** mauvais traitements mpl ◆ **he appeared to be in good** ~ **condition** il semblait être en bonne forme physique ◆ ~ **strength** force f (physique) ◆ ~ **violence** violences fpl ◆ ~ **symptoms** symptômes mpl physiques ◆ ~ **exertion** effort m physique ◆ ~ **deformity** difformité f ◆ ~ **disabilities** handicaps mpl physiques ◆ ~ **frailty** constitution f frêle ◆ ~ **closeness** contact m physique ◆ ~ **cruelty** brutalité f, sévices mpl ◆ **it's a** ~ **impossibility for him to get there on time** il lui est physiquement or matériellement impossible d'arriver là-bas à l'heure

2 (= sexual) [love, relationship] physique ◆ ~ **attraction** attirance f physique ◆ **the attraction between them is** ~ l'attirance qu'ils ont l'un pour l'autre est physique

3 [geography, properties] physique ; [world, universe, object] matériel

4 (* = tactile) [person] qui aime les contacts physiques

5 (= real) physique ◆ ~ **and ideological barriers** des barrières physiques et idéologiques ◆ **do you have any** ~ **evidence to support your story?** avez-vous des preuves matérielles de ce que vous avancez ?

N (Med *) examen m médical, bilan m de santé, check-up * m inv ◆ **to go for a** ~ aller passer une visite médicale ◆ **she failed her** ~ les résultats de sa visite médicale n'étaient pas assez bons

COMP **physical activity** N activité f physique

physical education N (Scol) éducation f physique

physical examination N examen m médical, bilan m de santé

physical exercise N exercice m physique

physical fitness N forme f physique

physical handicap N handicap m physique

physical jerks † * NPL (Brit Scol) exercices mpl d'assouplissement, gymnastique f

physical sciences N sciences fpl physiques

physical therapist N (US Med) physiothérapeute mf, kinésithérapeute mf

physical therapy N (US Med) physiothérapie f, kinésithérapie f ◆ **to have** ~ **therapy** faire de la rééducation

physical training † N (Scol) éducation f physique

physicality /fɪzɪˈkælɪtɪ/ N présence f physique

physically /ˈfɪzɪkəlɪ/ ADV [restrain] de force ; [violent, attractive, demanding, separate] physiquement ; [possible, impossible] matériellement ◆ **to be** ~ **fit** être en bonne forme physique ◆ **to be** ~ **capable/incapable of (doing) sth** être physiquement capable/incapable de faire qch ◆ **to be** ~ **sick** vomir ◆ **to feel** ~ **sick** avoir envie de vomir ◆ **he is** ~ **handicapped** or **disabled** or **challenged** c'est un handicapé physique, il a un handicap physique ◆ **to abuse sb** ~ [+ partner] battre qn ; [+ child] maltraiter qn ◆ **she was abused** ~ **but not sexually** elle a été brutalisée mais pas violée

physician /fɪˈzɪʃən/ N médecin m

⚠ The French word **physicien** means 'physicist'.

physicist /ˈfɪzɪsɪst/ N physicien(ne) m(f) ◆ **experimental/theoretical** ~ physicien(ne) m(f) de physique expérimentale/théorique ; → **atomic**

physics /ˈfɪzɪks/ N (NonC) physique f ◆ **experimental/theoretical** ~ physique f expérimentale/théorique ; → **atomic, nuclear**

physio * /ˈfɪzɪəʊ/ N (Brit) 1 abbrev of **physiotherapy** 2 abbrev of **physiotherapist**

physiognomy /ˌfɪzɪˈɒnəmɪ/ N (gen) physionomie f ; (* hum = face) bobine‡ f, bouille‡ f

physiological /ˌfɪzɪəˈlɒdʒɪkəl/ ADJ physiologique

physiologically /ˌfɪzɪəˈlɒdʒɪkəlɪ/ ADV physiologiquement

physiologist /ˌfɪzɪˈɒlədʒɪst/ N physiologiste mf

physiology /ˌfɪzɪˈɒlədʒɪ/ N physiologie f

physiotherapist /ˌfɪzɪəˈθerəpɪst/ **N** physiothérapeute *mf*, ≃ kinésithérapeute *mf*

physiotherapy /ˌfɪzɪəˈθerəpɪ/ **N** physiothérapie *f*, ≃ kinésithérapie *f*

physique /fɪˈziːk/ **N** physique *m* ◆ **he has the ~ of a footballer** il est bâti comme un footballeur ◆ **he has a fine/poor ~** il est bien/mal bâti

phytogeography /ˌfaɪtəʊdʒɪˈɒgrəfɪ/ **N** phytogéographie *f*

phytology /faɪˈtɒlədʒɪ/ **N** phytobiologie *f*

phytopathology /ˌfaɪtəʊpəˈθɒlədʒɪ/ **N** phytopathologie *f*

phytoplankton /ˌfaɪtəˈplæŋktən/ **N** phytoplancton *m*

PI /piːˈaɪ/ **N** (abbrev of **private investigator**) → **private**

pi¹ * /paɪ/ **ADJ** *(Brit pej)* (abbrev of **pious**) *[person]* satisfait de soi, suffisant ; *[expression]* suffisant, béat ; *(= sanctimonious)* bigot

pi² /paɪ/ **N** (pl **pis**) *(Math)* pi *m*

pianissimo /pɪəˈnɪsɪˌməʊ/ **ADJ, ADV** pianissimo

pianist /ˈpɪənɪst/ **N** pianiste *mf*

piano /ˈpjɑːnəʊ/ **N** (pl **pianos**) piano *m* ; → **baby, grand, upright** **ADV** *(Mus)* piano

COMP **piano-accordion** **N** accordéon *m* à clavier

piano concerto **N** concerto *m* pour piano

piano duet **N** morceau *m* pour quatre mains

piano lesson **N** leçon *f* de piano

piano music **N** ◆ **I'd like some ~ music** je voudrais de la musique pour piano ◆ **I love ~ music** j'adore écouter de la musique pour piano, j'adore le piano

piano organ **N** piano *m* mécanique

piano piece **N** morceau *m* pour piano

piano stool **N** tabouret *m* de piano

piano teacher **N** professeur *m* de piano

piano tuner **N** accordeur *m* (de piano)

pianoforte /ˌpjɑːnəʊˈfɔːtɪ/ **N** *(frm)* ⇒ **piano noun**

Pianola ® /pɪəˈnəʊlə/ **N** piano *m* mécanique, Pianola ® *m*

piazza /pɪˈætsə/ **N** 1 *(= square)* place *f*, piazza *f* 2 *(US)* véranda *f*

pibroch /ˈpiːbrɒx/ **N** pibroch *m*

pic /pɪk/ (abbrev of **picture**) 1 *(= photo)* photo *f* 2 *(= film)* film *m*

pica /ˈpaɪkə/ **N** *(Typ)* douze *m*, cicéro *m*

picador /ˈpɪkədɔːʳ/ **N** picador *m*

Picardy /ˈpɪkədɪ/ **N** Picardie *f*

picaresque /ˌpɪkəˈresk/ **ADJ** picaresque

picayune * /ˌpɪkəˈjuːn/ **ADJ** *(US)* insignifiant, mesquin

piccalilli /ˈpɪkəˌlɪlɪ/ **N** *condiment à base de légumes conservés dans une sauce moutardée*

piccaninny /ˈpɪkəˌnɪnɪ/ **N** négrillon(ne) *m(f)*

piccolo /ˈpɪkələʊ/ **N** (pl **piccolos**) piccolo *m*

pick /pɪk/ **N** 1 *(= tool)* pioche *f*, pic *m* ; *(Climbing:* also **ice pick**) piolet *m* ; *[of mason]* smille *f* ; *[of miner]* pic *m* ; → **ice, toothpick**

2 *(= choice)* choix *m* ◆ **to have one's ~ of sth** avoir le choix de qch ◆ **she could have had her ~ of any man in the room** aucun des hommes de l'assistance n'aurait pu lui résister, elle aurait pu jeter son dévolu sur n'importe quel homme dans l'assistance ◆ **children living closest to the school get first ~** * les enfants qui vivent le plus près de l'école sont prioritaires ◆ **squatters get first ~ * of all these empty flats** les squatters ont la priorité pour choisir parmi tous ces appartements vides ◆ **to take one's ~** faire son choix ◆ **take your ~** choisissez, vous avez le choix

3 *(= best)* meilleur ◆ **the ~ of the bunch** * *or* **the crop** le meilleur de tous

VT 1 *(= choose)* choisir ◆ **to ~ sb to do sth** choisir qn pour faire qch ◆ **~ a card, any card** choisissez une carte ◆ **to ~ (the) sides** *(Sport)* former *or* sélectionner les équipes ◆ **she was ~ed for England** *(Sport)* elle a été sélectionnée pour être dans l'équipe d'Angleterre ◆ **he ~ed the winner** *(Racing)* il a pronostiqué le (cheval) gagnant ◆ **I'm not very good at ~ing the winner** *(Racing)* je ne suis pas très doué pour choisir le gagnant ◆ **they certainly ~ed a winner in Colin Smith** *(fig)* avec Colin Smith ils ont vraiment tiré le bon numéro

2 ◆ **to ~ one's way through/among** avancer avec précaution à travers/parmi ◆ **to ~ a fight** *(physical)* chercher la bagarre * ◆ **to ~ a fight** *or* **a quarrel with sb** chercher noise *or* querelle à qn

3 *(= pluck) [+ fruit, flower]* cueillir ; *[+ mushrooms]* ramasser ◆ **"pick your own"** *(at fruit farm)* "cueillette à la ferme"

4 *(= pick at, fiddle with) [+ spot, scab]* gratter, écorcher ◆ **to ~ one's nose** se mettre les doigts dans le nez, se curer le nez ◆ **to ~ a splinter from one's hand** s'enlever une écharde de la main ◆ **to ~ a bone** *(with teeth)* ronger un os ; *[bird]* nettoyer un os ; see also **bone** ◆ **to ~ one's teeth** se curer les dents ◆ **you've ~ed a hole in your jersey** à force de tirer sur un fil tu as fait un trou à ton pull ◆ **to ~ holes in an argument** relever les défauts *or* les failles d'un raisonnement ◆ **their lawyers ~ed holes in the evidence** leurs avocats ont relevé des failles dans le témoignage ◆ **to ~ sb's brains** * faire appel aux lumières de qn ◆ **I need to ~ your brains about something** * j'ai besoin de vos lumières à propos de quelque chose ◆ **to ~ a lock** crocheter une serrure ◆ **to ~ pockets** pratiquer le vol à la tire ◆ **I've had my pocket ~ed** on m'a fait les poches

VI 1 *(= choose)* choisir ; *(= be fussy)* faire la fine bouche ◆ **to ~ and choose** faire le (*or* la) difficile ◆ **I haven't got time to ~ and choose** je n'ai pas le temps de faire la fine bouche ◆ **you can afford to ~ and choose** tu peux te permettre de faire la fine bouche *or* de faire le difficile ◆ **you can ~ and choose from the menu** vous pouvez choisir ce que vous voulez dans le menu ◆ **consumers can ~ and choose from among the many telephone companies** les consommateurs peuvent choisir *or* ont le choix entre les nombreuses compagnies de téléphone

2 *(= poke, fiddle)* ◆ **to ~ at one's food** manger du bout des dents, chipoter * ◆ **the bird ~ed at the bread** l'oiseau picorait le pain ◆ **don't ~!** *(at food)* ne chipote pas ! ; *(at spot, scab)* ne gratte pas ! ◆ **don't ~ at your spots!** ne gratte pas tes boutons !

COMP **pick-and-mix** ⇒ **pick 'n' mix**

pick-me-up * **N** remontant *m*

pick 'n' mix * **ADJ** *[approach, selection, collection]* hétéroclite ; *[morality, politics] qui réunit sélectivement des éléments hétéroclites* **VT** choisir **VI** faire son choix

► **pick at** * **VT FUS** *(US)* ⇒ **pick on 1**

► **pick off** **VT SEP** 1 *[+ paint]* gratter, enlever ; *[+ flower, leaf]* cueillir, enlever

2 *(= kill)* ◆ **he picked off the sentry** il a visé soigneusement et a abattu la sentinelle ◆ **he ~ed off the three sentries** il a abattu les trois sentinelles l'une après l'autre ◆ **the lions ~ off any stragglers** les lions éliminent les traînards

► **pick on** **VT FUS** 1 *(* = nag, harass)* harceler, s'en prendre à * ◆ **he's always ~ing on Robert** il s'en prend toujours à Robert *, c'est toujours après Robert qu'il en a * ◆ **~ on someone your own size!** ne t'en prends pas à un plus petit que toi !

2 *(= choose)* choisir ; *(= single out)* choisir, désigner ◆ **why did they ~ on Venice for their holiday?** pourquoi ont-ils choisi Venise comme destination de vacances ? ◆ **the teacher ~ed on him to collect the books** le professeur le choisit *or* le désigna pour ramasser les livres ◆ **why ~ on me? All the rest did the same** pourquoi t'en (*or* s'en) prendre à moi ? Les autres ont fait la même chose

► **pick out** **VT SEP** 1 *(= choose)* choisir ◆ **~ out two or three you would like to keep** choisissez-en deux ou trois que vous aimeriez garder ◆ **she ~ed two apples out of the basket** elle choisit deux pommes dans le panier ◆ **he had already ~ed out his successor** il avait déjà choisi son successeur

2 *(= distinguish)* repérer, distinguer ; *(in identification parade)* identifier ◆ **I couldn't ~ out anyone I knew in the crowd** je ne pouvais repérer *or* distinguer personne de ma connaissance dans la foule ◆ **can you ~ out the melody in this passage?** pouvez-vous repérer *or* distinguer la mélodie dans ce passage ? ◆ **can you ~ me out in this photo?** pouvez-vous me reconnaître sur cette photo ? ◆ **to ~ out a tune on the piano** *(= play)* retrouver un air au piano

3 *(= highlight)* **to ~ out a colour** rehausser *or* mettre en valeur une couleur ◆ **letters ~ed out in gold on a black background** caractères rehaussés d'or sur fond noir ◆ **the bright light ~ed out all her grey hairs** la lumière crue faisait ressortir tous ses cheveux gris

► **pick over** **VT SEP** *(= examine, sort through) [+ fruit, lentils, rice]* trier ; *[+ events, details, evidence]* décortiquer ◆ **she was ~ing over the shirts in the sale** elle examinait les chemises en solde les unes après les autres ◆ **it's no good ~ing over the past** cela ne sert à rien de ressasser le passé

► **pick through** **VT FUS** ⇒ **pick over**

► **pick up** **VI** 1 *(= improve) [conditions, programme, weather]* s'améliorer ; *[prices, wages]* remonter ; *[trade, business]* reprendre ; *[invalid]* se rétablir, se remettre ◆ **business has ~ed up recently** les affaires ont repris récemment ◆ **his support has ~ed up recently** sa cote de popularité a remonté récemment ◆ **the market will ~ up soon** *(Comm, Fin)* le marché va bientôt remonter ◆ **things are ~ing up a bit** * ça commence à aller mieux

2 *(= resume)* continuer, reprendre ◆ **to ~ up (from) where one had left off** reprendre là où on s'était arrêté ◆ **so, to ~ up where I left off, ...** alors je reprends là où je m'étais arrêté ...

◆ **to pick up on** ◆ **to ~ up on a point** *(= develop)* revenir sur un point ◆ **to ~ sb up on sth** *(= correct)* reprendre qn sur qch

VT SEP 1 *(= lift) [+ sth dropped, book, clothes etc]* ramasser ◆ **to ~ o.s. up** *(after fall)* se relever, se remettre debout ◆ **he ~ed up the child** *(gen)* il a pris l'enfant dans ses bras ; *(after fall)* il a relevé l'enfant ◆ **he ~ed up the phone and dialled a number** il a décroché (le téléphone) et a composé un numéro ◆ **~ up all your clothes before you go out!** ramasse tous tes vêtements avant de sortir ! ◆ **to ~ up the pieces** *(lit)* ramasser les morceaux ; *(fig)* recoller les morceaux ◆ **she's trying to ~ up the pieces of her career/her marriage** elle essaie de recoller les morceaux de sa carrière/de son couple ◆ **to ~ up the threads of one's life** se reprendre en main

2 *(= collect)* (passer) prendre ◆ **can you ~ up my coat from the cleaners?** pourrais-tu (passer) prendre mon manteau chez le teinturier ? ◆ **I'll ~ up the books next week** je passerai prendre les livres la semaine prochaine

3 *[+ passenger, hitch-hiker] (in bus, car etc)* prendre ; *(in taxi)* charger ◆ **I'll ~ you up at 6 o'clock** je passerai vous prendre à 6 heures, je viendrai vous chercher à 6 heures

④ *[+ girl, boy]* ramasser*, lever* ◆ **he ~ed up a girl at the cinema** il a ramassé une fille au cinéma

⑤ *(= buy, obtain)* dénicher ◆ **she ~ed up a secondhand car for just $800** elle a déniché une voiture d'occasion pour seulement 800 dollars ◆ **it's a book you can ~ up anywhere** c'est un livre que l'on peut trouver partout ◆ **to ~ up a bargain in the sales** trouver une bonne affaire dans les soldes

⑥ *(= acquire, learn) [+ language, skill]* apprendre ; *[+ habit]* prendre ◆ **he ~ed up French very quickly** il n'a pas mis longtemps à apprendre le français ◆ **I've ~ed up a bit of German** j'ai appris quelques mots d'allemand ◆ **you'll soon ~ it up** tu t'y mettras rapidement, ça viendra vite ◆ **you'll soon ~ it up again** tu t'y remettras rapidement, ça reviendra vite ◆ **to ~ up an accent** prendre un accent ◆ **to ~ up bad habits** prendre de mauvaises habitudes ◆ **I ~ed up a bit of news about him today** j'ai appris quelque chose sur lui aujourd'hui ◆ **see what you can ~ up about their export scheme** essayez d'avoir des renseignements *or* des tuyaux* sur leur plan d'exportations ◆ **our agents have ~ed up something about it** nos agents ont appris *or* découvert quelque chose là-dessus ◆ **the papers ~ed up the story** les journaux se sont emparés de l'affaire

⑦ *(= detect) [security camera etc] [+ person, object, sound]* détecter ; *(Rad, Telec) [+ station, signal, programme, message]* capter ◆ **the dogs immediately ~ed up the scent** les chiens ont tout de suite détecté l'odeur ◆ **the cameras ~ed him up as he left the hall** en sortant du hall il est entré dans le champ des caméras

⑧ *(= rescue)* recueillir ; *(from sea)* recueillir, repêcher ◆ **the helicopter/lifeboat ~ed up ten survivors** l'hélicoptère/le canot de sauvetage a recueilli dix survivants

⑨ *(* = take in) [+ suspect]* interpeller, cueillir* ◆ **they ~ed him up for questioning** on l'a interpellé pour l'interroger

⑩ *(= notice) [+ sb's error etc]* relever, ne pas laisser passer ◆ **he ~ed up ten misprints** il a relevé *or* repéré dix fautes d'impression ◆ **he ~ed up every mistake** il n'a pas laissé passer une seule erreur

⑪ *(= reprimand)* faire une remarque à, reprendre ◆ **she ~ed me up for this mistake** elle m'a repris sur cette erreur

⑫ *(= gain)* **to ~ up speed** *[car, boat]* prendre de la vitesse ◆ **he managed to ~ up a few points in the later events** *(Sport)* il a réussi à gagner *or* rattraper quelques points dans les épreuves suivantes ◆ **he ~ed up a reputation as a womanizer** il s'est fait une réputation de coureur de jupons

VT FUS * *(= earn)* gagner, toucher* ◆ **to ~ up the bill** *or* **tab** *(= pay)* payer la note *or* l'addition

N ◆ **pickup** ⇒ **pickup**

N ◆ **pick-me-up** * → **pick**

pickaback /ˈpɪkəbæk/ ⇒ **piggyback adv, adj, noun 1**

pickaninny /ˈpɪkə,nɪnɪ/ **N** ⇒ **piccaninny**

pickaxe, pickax *(US)* /ˈpɪkæks/ **N** pic *m*, pioche *f*

picker /ˈpɪkəʳ/ **N** *(gen in compounds)* cueilleur *m*, -euse *f* ◆ **apple-~** cueilleur *m*, -euse *f* de pommes ; → **cherry**

picket /ˈpɪkɪt/ **N** ① *(during strike)* piquet *m* de grève ; *(at civil demonstrations)* piquet *m* (de manifestants) ② *(= group of soldiers)* détachement *m* (de soldats) ; *(= sentry)* factionnaire *m* ◆ **fire ~** piquet *m* d'incendie ③ *(= stake)* pieu *m*, piquet *m* **VT** ① **to ~ a factory** mettre un piquet de grève aux portes d'une usine ◆ **the demonstrators ~ed the embassy** les manifestants ont formé un cordon devant l'ambassade ② *[+ field]* clôturer **VI** *[strikers]* organiser un piquet de grève

COMP picket duty N ◆ **to be on ~ duty** faire partie d'un piquet de grève

picket fence N palissade *f*

picket line N piquet *m* de grève ◆ **to cross a ~ line** traverser un piquet de grève

picketing /ˈpɪkɪtɪŋ/ **N** *(NonC)* piquets *mpl* de grève ◆ **there was no ~** il n'y a pas eu de piquet de grève ; → **secondary**

picking /ˈpɪkɪŋ/ **N** *[of object from group]* choix *m* ; *[of candidate, leader]* choix *m*, sélection *f* ; *[of fruit, vegetables]* cueillette *f* ; *[of lock]* crochetage *m* ; *(= careful choosing)* triage *m* **NPL pickings** ① *(of food)* restes *mpl* ② *(fig = profits etc)* **there are rich ~s to be had** ça pourrait rapporter gros ◆ **easy ~s for thieves** butin *m* facile pour des voleurs

pickle /ˈpɪkl/ **N** ① *(NonC: Culin) (= brine)* saumure *f* ; *(= wine, spices)* marinade *f* ; *(= vinegar)* vinaigre *m* ② **~(s)** pickles *mpl (petits légumes macérés dans du vinaigre)* ③ *(* = awkward situation)* ◆ **to be in a (pretty** *or* **fine) ~** être dans de beaux draps, être dans le pétrin ◆ **I'm in rather a ~** je suis plutôt dans le pétrin **VT** *(in brine)* conserver dans de la saumure ; *(in vinegar)* conserver dans du vinaigre **COMP pickling onions NPL** petits oignons *mpl*

pickled /ˈpɪkld/ **ADJ** ① *[cucumber, herring, cabbage]* conservé *or* macéré dans du vinaigre ② *(*‡ = drunk)* bourré*‡, ivre

picklock /ˈpɪklɒk/ **N** ① *(= key)* crochet *m*, rossignol *m* ② *(= thief)* crocheteur *m*

pickpocket /ˈpɪk,pɒkɪt/ **N** pickpocket *m*, voleur *m*, -euse *f* à la tire

pickup /ˈpɪkʌp/ **N** ① *[of record-player]* pick-up *m inv*, lecteur *m* ② *(Aut = passenger)* passager *m*, -ère *f* ramassé(e) en route ◆ **the bus made three ~s** l'autobus s'est arrêté trois fois pour prendre des passagers ③ *(* = casual lover)* partenaire *mf* de rencontre ④ *(= collection)* **to make a ~** *[truck driver]* s'arrêter pour charger (des marchandises) ; *[drug runner, spy]* aller chercher de la marchandise ◆ **~ point** *(for people)* point *m* de rendez-vous ; *(for goods)* point de collecte ⑤ *(NonC: Aut = acceleration)* reprise(s) *f(pl)* ⑥ *(= recovery) (Med)* rétablissement *m* ; *(in trade etc)* reprise *f* (d'activité) ⑦ (*: also **pick-me-up**) remontant *m* ⑧ ⇒ **pickup truck ADJ** *(Sport) [game]* impromptu, improvisé ◆ **~ side** équipe *f* de fortune **COMP pickup truck, pickup van N** *(Brit)* camionnette *f* (découverte), pick-up *m*

picky * /ˈpɪkɪ/ **ADJ** difficile (à satisfaire)

picnic /ˈpɪknɪk/ (vb : pret, ptp **picnicked**) **N** pique-nique *m* ◆ **let's go on a ~** allons piqueniquer ◆ **it's no ~** * ce n'est pas une partie de plaisir, c'est pas de la tarte* ◆ **it's no ~* bringing up children on your own** ce n'est pas une partie de plaisir d'élever seul des enfants **VI** pique-niquer, faire un pique-nique

COMP picnic basket N panier *m* à pique-nique

picnic ham N *(US)* ≃ jambonneau *m*

picnic hamper N ⇒ **picnic basket**

picnicker /ˈpɪknɪkəʳ/ **N** pique-niqueur *m*, -euse *f*

Pict /pɪkt/ **N** Picte *mf*

Pictish /ˈpɪktɪʃ/ **ADJ** picte

pictogram /ˈpɪktə,græm/ **N** pictogramme *m*

pictograph /ˈpɪktəgrɑːf/ **N** ① *(= record, chart etc)* pictogramme *m* ② *(Ling) (= symbol)* idéogramme *m* ; *(= writing)* idéographie *f*

pictorial /pɪkˈtɔːrɪəl/ **ADJ** *[magazine, calendar]* illustré ; *[record]* en images ; *[work]* pictural ; *[masterpiece]* pictural, de peinture **N** illustré *m*

pictorially /pɪkˈtɔːrɪəlɪ/ **ADV** en images, au moyen d'images, à l'aide d'images

picture /ˈpɪktʃəʳ/ **N** ① *(gen)* image *f* ; *(= illustration)* image *f*, illustration *f* ; *(= photograph)* photo *f* ; *(TV)* image *f* ; *(= painting)* tableau *m*, peinture *f* ; *(= portrait)* portrait *m* ; *(= engraving)* gravure *f* ; *(= reproduction)* reproduction *f* ; *(= drawing)* dessin *m* ◆ **a ~ by David Hockney** un tableau de David Hockney ◆ **a ~ of David Hockney** un tableau de *or* représentant David Hockney, un portrait de David Hockney ◆ **a ~ of David Hockney's** *(= owned by him)* un tableau appartenant à David Hockney ◆ **~s made by reflections in the water** images *fpl* produites par les reflets sur l'eau ◆ **we have the sound but no ~** *(TV)* nous avons le son mais pas l'image ◆ **to paint/draw a ~** faire un tableau/un dessin ◆ **to paint/draw a ~ of sth** peindre/dessiner qch ◆ **every ~ tells a story** *(Prov)* chaque image raconte une histoire ◆ **a ~ is worth a thousand words** *(Prov)* une image en dit plus que de longs discours *(Prov)* → **pretty**

② *(fig = description) (spoken)* tableau *m* ; *(= mental image)* image *f*, représentation *f* ◆ **he gave us a ~ of the scenes at the front line** il nous brossa *or* nous fit un tableau de la situation au front ◆ **to paint a gloomy/optimistic ~ of sth** brosser un sombre tableau/un tableau optimiste de qch ◆ **eye witness accounts painted a ~ of anarchy** les récits des témoins oculaires (nous) ont donné l'image d'une situation anarchique ◆ **to form a ~ of sth** se faire une idée de qch ◆ **I have a clear ~ of him as he was when I saw him last** je le revois clairement *or* je me souviens très bien de lui tel qu'il était la dernière fois que je l'ai vu ◆ **I have no very clear ~ of the room** je ne me représente pas très bien la pièce ◆ **these figures give the general ~** ces chiffres donnent un tableau général de la situation ◆ **(do you) get the ~?*** tu vois le tableau ?*, tu piges ?* ◆ **OK, I get the ~** * ça va, j'ai compris *or* pigé* ◆ **to be/put sb/keep sb in the ~** être/mettre qn/tenir qn au courant ◆ **to be left out of the ~** être mis sur la touche *or* éliminé de la scène

③ *(fig phrases)* **she was a ~ in her new dress** elle était ravissante dans sa nouvelle robe ◆ **the garden is (like) a ~ in June** le jardin est magnifique en juin ◆ **he is the** *or* **a ~ of health/happiness** il respire la santé/le bonheur ◆ **he is** *or* **looks the ~ of misery** c'est la tristesse incarnée ◆ **the other side of the ~** le revers de la médaille ◆ **his face was a ~!*** son expression en disait long !, si vous aviez vu sa tête !* ◆ **we should look at the big ~** il faudrait que nous regardions la situation dans son ensemble

④ *(Cine)* film *m* ◆ **they made a ~ about it** on en a fait *or* tiré un film ◆ **to go to the ~s** † *(esp Brit)* aller au cinéma, aller voir un film ◆ **what's on at the ~s?** † *(esp Brit)* qu'est-ce qui passe *or* qu'est-ce qu'on donne au cinéma ? ; → **motion**

VT ① *(= imagine)* s'imaginer, se représenter ◆ **I can just ~ the consequences** je m'imagine très bien les conséquences ◆ **can you ~ him as a father?** tu l'imagines père ? ◆ **I can't quite ~ it somehow** j'ai du mal à imaginer ça ◆ **~ yourself as a father/lying on the beach** imaginez-vous dans le rôle de père/étendu sur la plage

② *(= describe)* dépeindre, décrire

③ *(by drawing etc)* représenter ◆ **the photo ~d her crossing the finishing line** la photo la représentait en train de franchir la ligne d'arrivée

COMP picture book N livre *m* d'images

picture card N *(Cards)* figure *f*

picture desk N *(Brit Press)* service *m* photo *(d'un journal)*

picture editor N *(Press)* directeur *m*, -trice *f* du service photo *(d'un journal)*

picture frame N cadre *m*

picture-framer N encadreur *m*, -euse *f*

picture-framing N encadrement *m*

picture gallery N *(public)* musée *m* (de peinture) ; *(private)* galerie *f* (de peinture)

picture hat N capeline *f*
picture house † N cinéma *m*
picture-in-picture N *(NonC: TV, Comput)* insertion *f* d'image
picture library N photothèque *f*
picture messaging N envoi *m* de photos par MMS
picture postcard N carte *f* postale (illustrée)
picture rail N cimaise *f*
picture show N *(US †) (= cinema)* cinéma *m* ; *(= film)* film *m*
picture tube N *(TV)* tube *m* cathodique
picture window N fenêtre *f* panoramique
picture writing N écriture *f* pictographique

picturegoer /ˈpɪktʃəˌɡəʊəʳ/ N cinéphile *mf*, amateur *m* de cinéma

picturesque /ˌpɪktʃəˈresk/ ADJ pittoresque

picturesquely /ˌpɪktʃəˈresklɪ/ ADV pittoresquement ◆ **a cliff ~ known as the Black Ladders** une falaise surnommée de façon pittoresque les Échelles Noires

picturesqueness /ˌpɪktʃəˈresknɪs/ N pittoresque *m*

PID /ˌpiːaɪˈdiː/ N (abbrev of **pelvic inflammatory disease**) → **pelvic**

piddle * /ˈpɪdl/ VI faire pipi * N ◆ **to do a ~** faire un petit pipi *

piddling * /ˈpɪdlɪŋ/ ADJ *(= insignificant)* insignifiant, futile ; *(= small)* négligeable, de rien

pidgin /ˈpɪdʒɪn/ N 1 *(NonC)* (also **pidgin English**) pidgin-english *m* 2 *(Ling * = improvised language)* sabir *m* 3 *(fig pej = illiterate language)* charabia *m*, jargon *m* ◆ **~ English/French** mauvais anglais *m*/français *m* 4 * ⇒ **pigeon noun 2**

pie /paɪ/ N *[of fruit, fish, meat with gravy etc]* tourte *f* ; *(with compact filling)* pâté *m* en croûte ◆ **apple ~** tourte *f* aux pommes ◆ **rabbit/chicken ~** tourte *f* au lapin/au poulet ◆ **pork ~** pâté *m* en croûte ◆ **it's (all) ~ in the sky** * ce sont des promesses en l'air *or* de belles promesses *(iro)* ◆ **they want a piece of the ~** *(fig)* ils veulent leur part du gâteau ◆ **Robert has a finger in the** *or* **that ~** *(gen)* il y a du Robert là-dessous, Robert y est pour quelque chose ; *(financially)* Robert a des intérêts là-dedans *or* dans cette affaire ◆ **he's got a finger in every ~** il se mêle de tout, il est mêlé à tout ◆ **that's ~ to him** * *(US)* pour lui, c'est du gâteau * ; → **humble, mud**

COMP **pie chart** N *(Math)* graphique *m* circulaire, camembert * *m*
pie dish N plat *m* allant au four, terrine *f*
pie-eyed * ADJ beurré *, rond *
pie plate N moule *m* à tarte, tourtière *f*

piebald /ˈpaɪbɔːld/ ADJ *[horse]* pie *inv* N cheval *m* *or* jument *f* pie

piece /piːs/

1 NOUN
2 COMPOUNDS
3 PHRASAL VERB

1 - NOUN

1 = bit, portion morceau *m* ; *[of cloth, chocolate, glass, paper]* morceau *m*, bout *m* ; *[of bread, cake]* morceau *m*, tranche *f* ; *[of wood]* bout *m*, morceau *m* ; *(large)* pièce *f* ; *[of ribbon, string]* bout *m* ; *(= broken or detached part)* morceau *m*, fragment *m* ; *(Comm, Ind = part)* pièce *f* ; *(= item, section, also Chess)* pièce *f* ; *(Draughts)* pion *m* ◆ **a ~ of silk/paper** *etc* un morceau de soie/de papier *etc* ◆ **a ~ of land** *(for agriculture)* une pièce *or* parcelle de terre ; *(for building)* un lotissement ◆ **a ~ of meat** un morceau *or* une pièce de viande ; *(left over)* un morceau *or* un bout de viande ◆ **I bought a nice ~ of beef** j'ai acheté un beau morceau de bœuf ◆ **a sizeable ~ of beef** une belle pièce de bœuf ◆ **I've got a ~ of grit in my eye** j'ai une poussière *or* une escarbille dans l'œil ◆ **a ~ of clothing** un vêtement ◆ **a ~ of fabric** un morceau de tissu ◆ **a ~ of fruit** *(= whole fruit)* un fruit ; *(= segment: of orange, grapefruit etc)* un quartier de fruit ◆ **a ~ of furniture** un meuble ◆ **a ~ of software** un logiciel ◆ **a 30-~ tea set** un service à thé de 30 pièces ◆ **three ~s of luggage** trois bagages ◆ **how many ~s of luggage have you got?** qu'est-ce que vous avez comme bagages ? ◆ **~ by ~** morceau par morceau ◆ **there's a ~ missing** *(of jigsaw, game)* il y a une pièce qui manque ◆ **to put** *or* **fit together the ~s of a mystery** résoudre un mystère en rassemblant les éléments

♦ **in one piece** ◆ **the vase is still in one ~** le vase ne s'est pas cassé *or* est intact ◆ **he had a nasty fall but he's still in one ~** * il a fait une mauvaise chute mais il est entier * *or* indemne ◆ **we got back in one ~** * nous sommes rentrés sains et saufs

♦ **(all) of a piece** ◆ **the back is (all) of a ~ with the seat** le dossier et le siège sont d'un seul tenant ◆ **this latest volume is all of a ~ with her earlier poetry** ce dernier volume est dans l'esprit de ses poèmes précédents

♦ **by the piece** ◆ **sold by the ~** vendu à la pièce *or* au détail ◆ **paid by the ~** payé à la pièce

♦ **in pieces** *(= broken)* en pièces, en morceaux ; *(= not yet assembled: furniture etc)* en pièces détachées

♦ **to come/fall/go** *etc* **to pieces** ◆ **it comes** *or* **takes to ~s** c'est démontable ◆ **it just came to ~s** c'est parti en morceaux *or* en pièces détachées *(hum)* ◆ **the chair comes to ~s if you unscrew the screws** la chaise se démonte si on desserre les vis ◆ **to cut sth to ~s** couper qch en morceaux ◆ **it fell to ~s** c'est tombé en morceaux ◆ **to take sth to ~s** démonter qch, désassembler qch ◆ **to smash sth to ~s** briser qch en mille morceaux, mettre qch en miettes ◆ **the boat was smashed to ~s** le bateau vola en éclats ◆ **to go to ~s** * *[person] (= collapse)* s'effondrer ; *(emotionally)* craquer * ; *[team etc]* se désintégrer ◆ **his confidence is shot to ~s** * il a perdu toute confiance en lui ◆ **the economy is shot to ~s** * l'économie est ruinée ; → **pull, tear¹**

2 with abstract nouns ◆ **a ~ of information** un renseignement ◆ **a ~ of advice** un conseil ◆ **a ~ of news** une nouvelle ◆ **a ~ of research** une recherche ◆ **a good ~ of work** du bon travail ◆ **he's a nasty ~ of work** * c'est un sale type * ◆ **it's a ~ of folly** c'est de la folie ◆ **a ~ of nonsense** une absurdité, une bêtise ◆ **what a ~ of nonsense!** quelle absurdité !, quelle bêtise ! ◆ **that was a ~ of luck!** c'était un coup de chance ! ◆ **to give sb a ~ of one's mind** * dire ses quatre vérités à qn, dire son fait à qn

3 = musical passage morceau *m* ◆ **a piano ~, a ~ of piano music** un morceau pour piano ◆ **a ~ by Grieg** un morceau de Grieg ◆ **ten-~ band** *(= instrument, player)* orchestre *m* de dix exécutants

4 = artwork, antique pièce *f*, objet *m* ◆ **this is an interesting ~** c'est un objet intéressant *or* une pièce intéressante ◆ **her latest ~ is a multimedia installation** son œuvre la plus récente est une installation multimédia

5 = poem poème *m*, (pièce *f* de) vers *mpl* ; *(= passage, excerpt)* passage *m* ; *(= article)* article *m* ◆ **a ~ of poetry** un poème, une poésie, une pièce de vers *(liter)* ◆ **a good ~ of writing** un bon texte ◆ **read me a ~ out of "Ivanhoe"** lisez-moi un passage *or* un extrait d'"Ivanhoé" ◆ **there's a ~ in the newspaper about ...** il y a un article dans le journal sur ...

6 Mil (also **piece of artillery**) pièce *f* (d'artillerie)

7 * = handgun calibre * *m*, flingue * *m* ◆ **he was packing a ~** il avait un calibre * *or* flingue *

8 = coin pièce *f* ◆ **a 2-euro ~** une pièce de 2 euros ◆ **~ of eight** dollar *m* espagnol

9 = girl ◆ **she's a nice ~** * c'est un beau brin de fille

2 - COMPOUNDS

piece rate N *(Ind)* tarif *m* à la pièce
piece to camera N *(TV, Cine)* ◆ **to do a ~ to camera** faire face à la caméra *(pour s'adresser directement au public)*

3 - PHRASAL VERB

► **piece together** VT SEP *[+ broken object]* rassembler ; *[+ jigsaw]* assembler ; *(fig) [+ story]* reconstituer ; *[+ facts]* rassembler, faire concorder ◆ **I managed to ~ together what had happened from what he said** à partir de ce qu'il a dit, j'ai réussi à reconstituer les événements

⚠ Check what kind of piece it is before translating **piece** by the French word **pièce**.

piecemeal /ˈpiːsmiːl/ ADV *(= bit by bit) [construct]* petit à petit, par morceaux ; *(= haphazardly)* sans (véritable) plan d'ensemble, au coup par coup ; *[tell, explain, recount]* par bribes ◆ **the railway system developed ~** le système ferroviaire s'est développé sans plan d'ensemble *or* au coup par coup ◆ **he tossed the books ~ into the box** il jeta les livres en vrac dans la caisse
ADJ *(= bit by bit)* en plusieurs étapes ; *(= haphazard)* au coup par coup ; *(= unstructured)* décousu ◆ **technology developed in a rapid and ~ fashion** la technologie s'est développée rapidement et au coup par coup ◆ **the castle was built in ~ fashion** le château a été construit en plusieurs étapes, le château date de plusieurs époques ◆ **the structure of the company has evolved in a ~ way** la structure de la société a évolué par étapes ◆ **he gave me a ~ description of it** il m'en a fait une description fragmentaire *or* décousue ◆ **a ~ argument** une argumentation décousue

piecework /ˈpiːswɜːk/ N travail *m* à la pièce ◆ **to be on ~, to do ~** travailler à la pièce

pieceworker /ˈpiːsˌwɜːkəʳ/ N ouvrier *m*, -ière *f* payé(e) à la pièce

piecrust /ˈpaɪkrʌst/ N croûte *f* de *or* pour pâté

pied /paɪd/ ADJ bariolé, bigarré ; *[animal]* pie *inv*
COMP **the Pied Piper** N le joueur de flûte d'Hameln

pied-à-terre /ˌpjeɪdɑːˈtɛəʳ/ N (pl **pieds-à-terre** /ˌpjeɪdɑːˈtɛəʳ/) pied-à-terre *m inv*

Piedmont /ˈpiːdmɒnt/ N 1 *(Geog)* Piémont *m* 2 *(Geol)* **piedmont** piémont *m* ◆ **piedmont glacier** glacier *m* de piémont

Piedmontese /ˌpiːdmɒnˈtiːz/ ADJ *(Geog)* piémontais N 1 *(= person)* Piémontais(e) *m(f)* 2 *(= dialect)* piémontais *m*

pier /pɪəʳ/ N 1 *(with amusements etc)* jetée *f* *(promenade)* ; *(= landing stage)* appontement *m*, embarcadère *m* ; *(= breakwater)* brise-lames *m* ; *(in airport)* jetée *f* d'embarquement (*or* de débarquement) 2 *(Archit) (= column)* pilier *m*, colonne *f* ; *[of bridge]* pile *f* ; *(= brickwork)* pied-droit *or* piédroit *m*
COMP **pier glass** N (glace *f* de) trumeau *m*

pierce /pɪəs/ VT 1 *(= make hole in, go through)* percer, transpercer ◆ **the arrow ~d his armour** la flèche perça son armure ◆ **the bullet ~d his arm** la balle lui transperça le bras ◆ **to have** *or* **get one's ears/nose** *etc* **~d** se faire percer les oreilles/le nez *etc* ◆ **to have ~d ears** avoir les oreilles percées ◆ **~d earrings** *, **earrings for ~d ears** boucles *fpl* d'oreilles pour oreilles percées 2 *[sound, light]* percer ; *[cold, wind]* transpercer ◆ **the words ~d his heart** *(liter)* ces paroles lui percèrent le cœur

piercing /ˈpɪəsɪŋ/ ADJ *[sound, voice]* aigu (-guë *f*), perçant ; *[look]* perçant ; *[cold, wind]* glacial, pénétrant ◆ **~ blue eyes** yeux *mpl* bleus perçants
N (also **body piercing**) piercing *m* ◆ **to get a ~ (done)** se faire faire un piercing

piercingly /ˈpɪəsɪŋlɪ/ ADV *[scream]* d'une voix perçante ; *[look]* d'un œil perçant ◆ **~ blue eyes** yeux *mpl* bleus perçants

pierhead /ˈpɪəhed/ N musoir *m*

pierrot /ˈpɪərəʊ/ N pierrot *m*

pietism /ˈpaɪɪˌtɪzəm/ N piétisme *m*

pietist /ˈpaɪɪtɪst/ ADJ, N piétiste *mf*

piety /ˈpaɪətɪ/ N piété *f* NPL **pieties** *(gen pej)* sermons *mpl* moralisateurs

piezoelectric /paɪˌiːzəʊɪˈlektrɪk/ ADJ piézoélectrique

piezoelectricity /paɪˌiːzəʊɪlekˈtrɪsɪtɪ/ N piézoélectricité *f*

piezometer /ˌpaɪɪˈzɒmɪtəʳ/ N piézomètre *m*

piffle †* /ˈpɪfl/ N balivernes *fpl*, fadaises *fpl*

piffling /ˈpɪflɪŋ/ ADJ *(= trivial)* futile, frivole ; *(= worthless)* insignifiant

pig /pɪg/ N 1 cochon *m*, porc *m* ◆ **they were living like ~s** ils vivaient comme des porcs *or* dans une (vraie) porcherie ◆ **it was a ~*** **to do** c'était vachement* difficile à faire ◆ **to buy a ~ in a poke** acheter chat en poche ◆ **~s might fly!*** ce n'est pas demain la veille !*, quand les poules auront des dents ! ◆ **to be as happy as a ~ in muck*** *or* **shit** *(Brit)**‡ être dans son élément ◆ **he was as sick as a ~*** *(Brit)* il en était malade* ◆ **to make a ~'s ear* of sth** *(Brit)* cochonner qch* ◆ **in a ~'s eye!**‡ *(US)* jamais de la vie !, mon œil !* ; → **Guinea, suckling pig**
2 *(* pej = person) (mean)* vache‡ *f* ; *(dirty)* cochon(ne)* *m(f)* ; *(greedy)* goinfre *m* ◆ **to make a ~ of o.s.** manger comme un goinfre, se goinfrer*
3 *(‡ pej = policeman)* flicard* *m*, poulet* *m* ◆ **the ~s** la flicaille‡
VI *[sow]* mettre bas, cochonner
VT ◆ **to ~ o.s.*** se goinfrer *(on de)* ; ◆ **to ~ it**‡ vivre comme un cochon* *(or des cochons)*
COMP **pig breeding** N élevage *m* porcin
pig farmer N éleveur *m*, -euse *f* de porcs
pig-ignorant‡ ADJ d'une ignorance crasse
pig industry N industrie *f* porcine
pig in the middle N *(= game)* jeu où deux enfants se lancent un ballon tandis qu'un troisième, placé au milieu, essaie de l'intercepter ◆ **he's the ~ in the middle** *(fig)* il est impliqué dans des disputes qui ne le concernent pas
pig iron N saumon *m* de fonte
Pig Latin N ≈ javanais* *m*
pig meat N charcuterie *f*
pig-swill N pâtée *f* pour les porcs

► **pig out*** VI s'empiffrer* *(on de)*

pigeon /ˈpɪdʒən/ N 1 *(also Culin)* pigeon *m* ; → **carrier, clay, homing, woodpigeon** 2 * affaire *f* ◆ **that's not my ~** ça n'est pas mes oignons*
COMP **pigeon-chested** ADJ à la poitrine bombée
pigeon fancier N colombophile *mf*
pigeon house, pigeon loft N pigeonnier *m*
pigeon post N ◆ **by ~ post** par pigeon voyageur
pigeon shooting N tir *m* aux pigeons
pigeon-toed ADJ ◆ **to be ~-toed** avoir *or* marcher les pieds tournés en dedans

pigeonhole /ˈpɪdʒɪnˌhəʊl/ N *(in desk)* case *f*, casier *m* ; *(on wall etc)* casier *m* VT 1 *(= store away) [+ papers]* classer, ranger 2 *(= shelve) [+ project, problem]* enterrer provisoirement ◆ **to ~ a bill** *(US Pol)* enterrer un projet de loi 3 *(= classify) [+ person]* étiqueter, cataloguer *(as comme)*

piggery /ˈpɪgərɪ/ N porcherie *f*

piggish* /ˈpɪgɪʃ/ ADJ *(pej) (in manners)* sale, grossier ; *(= greedy)* goinfre ; *(= stubborn)* têtu

piggy /ˈpɪgɪ/ N *(baby talk)* cochon *m* ADJ *[eyes]* porcin, comme un cochon COMP **piggy in the middle** N ⇒ **pig in the middle** ; → **pig**

piggyback /ˈpɪgɪˌbæk/ ADV *[ride, be carried]* sur le dos ◆ **the space shuttle rides ~ on the rocket** la navette spatiale est transportée sur le dos de la fusée ADJ *[ride etc]* sur le dos N 1 ◆ **to give sb a ~** porter qn sur son dos ◆ **give me a ~, Daddy!** fais-moi faire un tour (à dada) sur ton dos, Papa ! 2 *(US Rail)* ferroutage *m* VT 1 *(= carry on one's back)* porter sur son dos 2 *(US Rail)* ferrouter 3 *(fig) [+ plan etc]* englober, couvrir VI *[plan, expenditure etc]* être couvert, être pris en charge

piggybank /ˈpɪgɪbæŋk/ N tirelire *f (surtout en forme de cochon)*

pigheaded /ˌpɪgˈhedɪd/ ADJ *(pej)* entêté, obstiné

pigheadedly /ˌpɪgˈhedɪdlɪ/ ADV *(pej)* obstinément, avec entêtement

pigheadedness /ˌpɪgˈhedɪdnɪs/ N *(pej)* entêtement *m*, obstination *f*

piglet /ˈpɪglɪt/ N porcelet *m*, petit cochon *m*

pigman /ˈpɪgmən/ N (pl **-men**) porcher *m*

pigment /ˈpɪgmənt/ N pigment *m*

pigmentation /ˌpɪgmənˈteɪʃən/ N pigmentation *f*

pigmented /pɪgˈmentɪd/ ADJ pigmenté

pigmy /ˈpɪgmɪ/ N, ADJ ⇒ **pygmy**

pigpen /ˈpɪgpen/ N *(US)* porcherie *f*

pigskin /ˈpɪgskɪn/ N 1 *(= leather)* peau *f* de porc 2 *(US Ftbl)* ballon *m (de football américain)* COMP *[briefcase, gloves, book-binding etc]* en (peau de) porc

pigsty /ˈpɪgstaɪ/ N *(lit, fig)* porcherie *f* ◆ **your room is like a ~!** ta chambre est une vraie porcherie !

pigtail /ˈpɪgteɪl/ N *[of hair]* natte *f* ◆ **to have** *or* **wear one's hair in ~s** porter des nattes

pike¹ /paɪk/ N *(= weapon)* pique *f*

pike² /paɪk/ N (pl **pike** *or* **pikes**) *(= fish)* brochet *m*

pike³ /paɪk/ N 1 ⇒ **turnpike** 2 *(US)* ◆ **to come down the ~** faire son apparition

pikeman /ˈpaɪkmən/ N (pl **-men**) *(Hist)* piquier *m*

pikeperch /ˈpaɪkpɜːtʃ/ N (pl **pikeperch** *or* **pikeperches**) sandre *m*

piker‡ /ˈpaɪkəʳ/ N *(US) (= small gambler)* thunard‡ *m* ; *(= small speculator)* boursicoteur *m*, -euse *f* ; *(= stingy person)* pingre *mf* ; *(= contemptible person)* minable *mf*

pikestaff /ˈpaɪkstɑːf/ N → **plain**

pilaf(f) /ˈpɪlæf/ N pilaf *m*

pilaster /pɪˈlæstəʳ/ N pilastre *m*

Pilate /ˈpaɪlət/ N Pilate *m*

Pilates /pɪˈlɑːtiːz/ N Pilates *m*

pilau /pɪˈlaʊ/ N pilaf *m* COMP **pilau rice** N riz *m* pilaf

pilchard /ˈpɪltʃəd/ N pilchard *m*, sardine *f*

pile¹ /paɪl/ N 1 *(Constr etc)* pieu *m* de fondation ; *(in water)* pilotis *m* ; *[of bridge]* pile *f* 2 *(= pointed stake)* pieu *m* VT *[+ land]* enfoncer des pieux *or* des pilotis dans
COMP **pile driver** N *(Constr)* sonnette *f*, hie *f*, mouton *m*
pile dwelling N *(Hist)* maison *f* sur pilotis

pile² /paɪl/ N 1 *(= neat stack)* pile *f* ; *(= heap)* tas *m* ◆ **the linen was in a neat ~** le linge était rangé en une pile bien nette ◆ **his clothes lay in a ~** ses vêtements étaient en tas ◆ **the magazines were in an untidy ~** les magazines étaient entassés pêle-mêle ◆ **to make a ~ of books, to put books in a ~** empiler des livres, mettre des livres en tas *or* en pile ◆ **to be at the top/bottom of the ~** *(fig)* être en haut/en bas de l'échelle ◆ **companies at the bottom of the financial ~** *(fig)* des entreprises ayant très peu de poids d'un point de vue financier
2 *(* = fortune)* fortune *f* ◆ **to make one's ~** faire son beurre*, faire fortune ◆ **he made a ~ on this deal** il a ramassé un joli paquet* avec cette affaire ◆ **~s of** *[+ butter, honey]* beaucoup de, des masses de* ; *[+ cars, flowers]* beaucoup de, un tas de* ◆ **to have/make a ~ of** *or* **~s of money** avoir/faire beaucoup d'argent *or* un argent fou
3 *(Phys)* pile *f* ; → **atomic**
4 *(liter or hum = imposing building)* édifice *m*
NPL **piles** *(Med)* hémorroïdes *fpl*
VT 1 *(= stack up)* empiler ◆ **he ~d the plates onto the tray** il a empilé les assiettes sur le plateau ◆ **he ~d the books (up) one on top of the other** il a empilé les livres les uns sur les autres ◆ **a table ~d up** *or* **high with books** une table couverte de piles de livres
2 *(= pack in)* ◆ **he ~d the books into the box** il a empilé *or* entassé les livres dans la caisse ◆ **I ~d the children into the car*** j'ai entassé les enfants dans la voiture ◆ **to ~ coal on the fire, to ~ the fire up with coal** rajouter du charbon dans le feu
VI * ◆ **we all ~d into the car** nous nous sommes tous entassés *or* empilés* dans la voiture ◆ **we ~d off the train** nous sommes descendus du train en nous bousculant ◆ **they ~d through the door** ils sont entrés *or* sortis en se bousculant

► **pile in*** VI *[people]* s'entasser ◆ **the taxi arrived and we all ~d in** le taxi est arrivé et nous nous sommes tous entassés dedans* ◆ **~ in!** entassez-vous* là-dedans !

► **pile off*** VI *[people]* descendre en désordre

► **pile on*** VT SEP ◆ **to pile it on** exagérer, en rajouter* ◆ **he does tend to ~ it on** il faut toujours qu'il en rajoute *subj* ◆ **to ~ on the pressure** mettre toute la gomme* ◆ **to ~ on weight** *or* **the pounds** prendre kilo sur kilo, grossir
VI ◆ **the bus/train arrived and we all piled on** l'autobus/le train est arrivé et nous nous sommes tous entassés *or* empilés* dedans

► **pile out*** VI sortir en désordre *or* en se bousculant

► **pile up** VI 1 *(= accumulate) [snow, leaves]* s'amonceler ; *[work, bills, debts, problems, reasons]* s'accumuler ; *[letters, papers, rubbish]* s'entasser, s'accumuler ◆ **the evidence ~d up against him** les preuves s'amoncelaient *or* s'accumulaient contre lui
2 *(* = crash)* **ten cars ~d up on the motorway** dix voitures se sont carambolées sur l'autoroute ◆ **the ship ~d up on the rocks** le bateau s'est fracassé sur les rochers
VT SEP 1 *(lit)* → **pile² vt 1**
2 *[+ evidence, reasons, debts, losses]* accumuler
3 *(* = crash)* **he ~d up the car/the motorbike last night** hier soir il a bousillé* la voiture/la moto

pile³ /paɪl/ N *[of fabric]* poils *mpl* ◆ **the ~ of a carpet** les poils *mpl* d'un tapis ◆ **a carpet with a deep ~** un tapis de haute laine

pileup /ˈpaɪlʌp/ N carambolage *m* ◆ **there was a ten-car ~ on the motorway** dix voitures se sont carambolées sur l'autoroute

pilfer /ˈpɪlfəʳ/ VT chaparder* VI se livrer au chapardage*

pilferage /ˈpɪlfərɪdʒ/ N chapardage* *m*, coulage *m*

pilferer /ˈpɪlfərəʳ/ N chapardeur* *m*, -euse* *f*

pilfering /ˈpɪlfərɪŋ/ N chapardage* *m*

pilgrim /ˈpɪlgrɪm/ N pèlerin *m* ◆ **the ~s to Lourdes** les pèlerins de Lourdes ◆ **"Pilgrim's Progress"** "Le Voyage du Pèlerin" COMP **the**

Pilgrim Fathers NPL *(Hist)* les (Pères *mpl*) pèlerins *mpl*

> **PILGRIM FATHERS**
>
> Les « Pères pèlerins » sont un groupe de puritains qui quittèrent l'Angleterre en 1620 pour fuir les persécutions religieuses. Ayant traversé l'Atlantique à bord du « Mayflower », ils fondèrent New Plymouth en Nouvelle-Angleterre, dans ce qui est aujourd'hui le Massachusetts, et inaugurèrent ainsi le processus de colonisation anglaise de l'Amérique. Ces Pères pèlerins sont considérés comme les fondateurs des États-Unis, et l'on commémore chaque année, le jour de « Thanksgiving », la réussite de leur première récolte. → THANKSGIVING

pilgrimage /ˈpɪlgrɪmɪdʒ/ N pèlerinage *m* ◆ **to make** *or* **go on a ~** faire un pèlerinage

piling /ˈpaɪlɪŋ/ N *(NonC)*, **pilings** /ˈpaɪlɪŋz/ NPL *(for bridge)* piles *fpl* ; *(for building)* pilotis *m*

pill /pɪl/ N 1 *(Med, fig)* pilule *f* ◆ **to coat** *or* **sugar** *or* **sweeten the ~** *(fig)* dorer la pilule *(for sb* à qn) → **bitter** 2 (also **Pill, contraceptive pill**) pilule *f* ◆ **to be on the ~** prendre la pilule ◆ **to come off the ~** arrêter (de prendre) la pilule COMP **pill popper*** N *personne qui se gave de pilules*

pillage /ˈpɪlɪdʒ/ N pillage *m*, saccage *m* VT piller, saccager, mettre à sac VI se livrer au pillage *or* au saccage

pillar /ˈpɪləʳ/ N 1 *(Archit)* pilier *m*, colonne *f* ; *(Min, also Climbing)* pilier *m* ◆ **the Pillars of Hercules** *(Geog)* les Colonnes *fpl* d'Hercule ◆ **a ~ of salt** *(Bible)* une statue de sel ◆ **a ~ of smoke** une colonne de fumée ◆ **a ~ of water** une trombe d'eau ◆ **he was sent from ~ to post** on se le renvoyait de l'un à l'autre ◆ **after giving up his job he went from ~ to post until ...** après avoir quitté son emploi il a erré à droite et à gauche jusqu'au jour où ... 2 *(fig = mainstay)* pilier *m* ◆ **he was a ~ of the Church/the community** c'était un pilier de l'Église/de la communauté ◆ **he was a ~ of strength** il a vraiment été d'un grand soutien COMP **pillar-box** N *(Brit)* boîte *f* aux *or* à lettres *(publique)* ◆ **~-box red** rouge vif *m inv*

pillbox /ˈpɪlbɒks/ N *(Med)* boîte *f* à pilules ; *(Mil)* casemate *f*, blockhaus *m inv* ; *(= hat)* toque *f*

pillion /ˈpɪljən/ N *[of motorcycle]* siège *m* arrière, tansad *m* ; *[of horse]* selle *f* de derrière ◆ **~ passenger** passager *m*, -ère *f* de derrière ADV ◆ **to ride ~** *(on horse)* monter en croupe ; *(on motorcycle)* monter derrière

pillock‡ /ˈpɪlək/ N *(Brit)* con‡ *m*

pillory /ˈpɪlərɪ/ N pilori *m* VT *(Hist, fig)* mettre au pilori

pillow /ˈpɪləʊ/ N 1 oreiller *m* ◆ **a ~ of moss** un coussin de mousse 2 *(Tech:* also **lace pillow***)* carreau *m* (de dentellière) VT *[+ head]* reposer ◆ **she ~ed her head in her arms** elle a reposé sa tête sur ses bras
COMP **pillow fight** N bataille *f* d'oreillers *or* de polochons*
pillow lace N guipure *f*
pillow slip N ⇒ **pillowcase**

pillowcase /ˈpɪləʊkeɪs/ N taie *f* d'oreiller

pillowtalk /ˈpɪləʊtɔːk/ N confidences *fpl* sur l'oreiller

pilot /ˈpaɪlət/ N 1 *(= person)* pilote *m* ◆ **airline/fighter ~** pilote *m* de ligne/de chasse ; → **automatic**
2 *(Rad, TV)* (also **pilot episode**) pilote *m*
VT 1 *[+ ship, plane]* piloter ◆ **she ~ed the country through the difficult postwar period** elle a guidé *or* dirigé le pays à travers les difficultés de l'après-guerre ◆ **to ~ a bill through the House** *(Parl)* assurer le passage d'un projet de loi
2 *(= test) [programme, scheme]* tester
COMP **pilot boat** N bateau-pilote *m*
pilot film N *(TV)* film-pilote *m*
pilot fish N (pl **pilot fish** *or* **fishes**) poisson *m* pilote
pilot house N poste *m* de pilotage
pilot jacket N blouson *m* d'aviateur
pilot light N veilleuse *f (de cuisinière, de chauffe-eau etc)*
pilot officer N sous-lieutenant *m* (de l'armée de l'air)
pilot production N *(in manufacturing)* présérie *f*
pilot scheme N projet *m* pilote, projet *m* expérimental
pilot study N étude *f* pilote

Pils /pɪls, pɪlz/ N bière *f* Pils

pimento /pɪˈmentəʊ/ N (pl **pimentos**) piment *m*

pimp /pɪmp/ N souteneur *m*, maquereau‡ *m*, marlou‡ *m* VI être souteneur, faire le maquereau‡

pimpernel /ˈpɪmpənel/ N mouron *m* ; → **scarlet**

pimple /ˈpɪmpl/ N bouton *m (Med)* ◆ **to come out in ~s** avoir une poussée de boutons

pimply /ˈpɪmplɪ/ ADJ *[face, person]* boutonneux

PIN /pɪn/ N (abbrev of **personal identification number**) ◆ **~ (number)** code *m* confidentiel *or* personnel

pin /pɪn/ N 1 *(Sewing: also for paper, hair, tie etc)* épingle *f* ; *(Brit:* also **drawing pin***)* punaise *f* ; *(= badge)* badge *m* ; *(= lapel badge)* pin *m* ; (also **hatpin**) épingle *f* à chapeau ◆ **(as) clean as a new ~** propre comme un sou neuf ◆ **the room was as neat as a new ~** la pièce était impeccable ◆ **you could have heard a ~ drop** on aurait entendu voler une mouche ◆ **I've got ~s and needles (in my foot)** j'ai des fourmis (au pied) ◆ **to be (sitting) on ~s and needles** *(US)* être sur des charbons ardents ◆ **for two ~s* I'd hand in my resignation** je suis à deux doigts de démissionner, il s'en faudrait d'un rien pour que je démissionne *subj* ; → **rolling, safety**
2 *(Tech)* goupille *f*, goujon *m* ; *[of hand grenade]* goupille *f* ; *[of pulley]* essieu *m* ; *(Elec)* fiche *f or* broche *f* (de prise de courant) ; *(Med: in limb)* broche *f* ◆ **three-~ plug** *(Elec)* prise *f* à trois fiches *or* broches
3 *(Bowling)* quille *f* ; *(Golf)* drapeau *m* de trou
NPL **pins**‡ *(= legs)* guibol(l)es* *fpl*, quilles* *fpl* ◆ **he's not very steady on his ~s** il ne tient pas sur ses guibolles*
VT 1 *(= put pin in) [+ dress]* épingler ; *[+ papers] (together)* attacher avec une épingle ; *(to wall etc)* fixer avec une punaise ◆ **he ~ned the medal to his uniform** il a épinglé la médaille sur son uniforme ◆ **he ~ned the calendar on** *or* **to the wall** il a fixé le calendrier au mur (avec une punaise)
2 *(= trap)* clouer ◆ **to ~ sb against a wall/tree** clouer qn contre un mur/arbre ◆ **to ~ sb to the floor/ground** clouer qn au plancher/sol ◆ **his arms were ~ned to his sides** il avait les bras collés au corps
3 *(fig = attach)* **to ~ (all) one's hopes on sth/sb** mettre tous ses espoirs dans qch/en qn ◆ **you can't ~ it** *or* **the blame on me*** tu ne peux pas me mettre ça sur le dos ◆ **they tried to ~ the crime on him*** ils ont essayé de lui mettre le crime sur le dos *or* de lui faire endosser le crime
4 *(Tech)* cheviller, goupiller
5 *(US)* **to ~ a girl*** *(as sign of love) offrir à une jeune fille son insigne de confrérie en gage d'affection*
COMP **pin money*** N argent *m* de poche
pin table N ⇒ **pinball machine** ; → **pinball**
► **pin back** VT SEP retenir (avec une épingle) ◆ **~ back your ears!*** ouvre grand les oreilles ! ◆ **she had her ears ~ned back* listening for the baby's crying** elle ouvrait grand les oreilles pour entendre le bébé pleurer ◆ **to ~ sb's ears back*** *(US) (= scold)* passer un savon* à qn ; *(= beat up)* ficher une raclée à qn
► **pin down** VT SEP 1 *(= secure)* attacher *or* fixer avec une épingle *or* une punaise
2 *(= trap)* immobiliser, coincer ◆ **to be ~ned down by a fallen tree** être immobilisé par *or* coincé sous un arbre tombé ◆ **the battalion had been ~ned down by guerillas** le bataillon avait été bloqué par des guérilleros
3 *(fig)* ◆ **to pin sb down to a promise** obliger qn à tenir sa promesse ◆ **I couldn't ~ her down to a date** je n'ai pas réussi à lui faire fixer une date ◆ **see if you can ~ him down to naming a price** essaie de lui faire dire un prix
4 *(= define) [+ problem]* définir précisément, mettre le doigt sur ; *[+ feeling, meaning, quality]* définir précisément ; *[+ facts]* déterminer exactement
► **pin on** VT SEP attacher avec une punaise *or* une épingle, épingler
► **pin together** VT SEP épingler
► **pin up** VT SEP *[+ notice]* fixer (au mur) avec une punaise, punaiser, afficher ; *[+ hem]* épingler ; *[+ hair]* épingler, relever avec des épingles
N ◆ **pinup** ADJ → **pinup**

piña colada /ˌpiːnəkəˈlɑːdə/ N pinacolada *f*

pinafore /ˈpɪnəfɔːʳ/ N *(= apron)* tablier *m* ; *(= overall)* blouse *f (de travail)* ◆ **~ dress** robe *f* chasuble

pinball /ˈpɪnbɔːl/ N *(= game)* flipper *m* ◆ **~ machine** flipper *m*, billard *m* électrique

pinboard /ˈpɪnbɔːd/ N panneau *m* d'affichage

pince-nez /ˌpænsˈneɪ/ N *(pl inv)* pince-nez *m inv*

pincer /ˈpɪnsəʳ/ N 1 *[of crab]* pince *f* 2 *(= tool)* **~s** tenailles *fpl* COMP **pincer movement** N *(fig, Mil)* mouvement *m* de tenailles

pinch /pɪntʃ/ N 1 *(= action)* pincement *m* ; *(= mark)* pinçon *m* ◆ **to give sb a ~ (on the arm)** pincer qn (au bras) ◆ **we're feeling the ~* (of the latest tax increases)** (à cause des dernières augmentations d'impôts) nous sommes juste *or* (financièrement) très serrés ◆ **if it comes to the ~ ...** si la situation devient critique ...
◆ **at a pinch, in a pinch** *(US)* à la limite, à la rigueur ◆ **it'll do at a ~** cela fera l'affaire à la rigueur *or* faute de mieux
2 *(= small amount) [of salt]* pincée *f* ; *[of snuff]* prise *f* ◆ **you have to take his remarks with a ~ of salt** il ne faut pas prendre ses remarques pour argent comptant *or* au pied de la lettre
VT 1 *(= squeeze)* pincer ; *[shoes]* serrer ◆ **she ~ed me on the arm, she ~ed my arm** elle m'a pincé le bras *or* au bras
2 *(* = steal)* piquer*, faucher* ◆ **I had my car ~ed** on m'a fauché* *or* piqué* ma voiture ◆ **he ~ed that idea from Shaw** il a chipé* *or* piqué* cette idée à Shaw ◆ **Robert ~ed John's girlfriend** Robert a piqué* sa petite amie à John
3 *(‡ = arrest)* pincer* ◆ **to get ~ed** se faire pincer* ◆ **he got ~ed for speeding** il s'est fait pincer* pour excès de vitesse
VI 1 *[shoe]* être étroit, serrer
2 ◆ **to ~ and scrape** rogner sur tout, se serrer la ceinture*
COMP **pinch-hit** VI → **pinch-hit**
► **pinch back, pinch off** VT SEP *[+ bud]* épincer, pincer

pinchbeck /ˈpɪntʃbek/ N 1 *(= metal)* chrysocale *m*, similor *m* 2 *(= sth sham)* toc *m* ADJ 1 *(lit)* en chrysocale, en similor 2 *(= sham)* en toc, de pacotille

pinched /ˈpɪntʃt/ ADJ 1 *(= drawn)* **to look ~** avoir les traits tirés ◆ **to look ~ with cold/with hunger** avoir l'air transi de froid/tenaillé par la faim 2 ◆ **~ for money/time** à court d'argent/de temps ◆ **~ for space** à l'étroit

pinch-hit /ˈpɪntʃhɪt/ VI (*US Baseball*) jouer en remplaçant ◆ **to ~ for sb** (*US fig*) assurer le remplacement de qn au pied levé

pinch-hitter /ˈpɪntʃˌhɪtəʳ/ N remplaçant *m*, substitut *m*

pinchpenny /ˈpɪntʃˌpenɪ/ ADJ grippe-sou

pincushion /ˈpɪnˌkʊʃən/ N pelote *f* à épingles

Pindar /ˈpɪndəʳ/ N Pindare *m*

Pindaric /pɪnˈdærɪk/ ADJ pindarique

pindling * /ˈpɪndlɪŋ/ ADJ (*US*) chétif, malingre

pine[1] /paɪn/ N (also **pine tree**) pin *m*
COMP **pine cone** N pomme *f* de pin
pine grove N pinède *f*
pine kernel N pignon *m* (de pin)
pine marten N martre *f*
pine needle N aiguille *f* de pin
pine nut N ⇒ **pine kernel**
the Pine Tree State N (*US*) le Maine

pine[2] /paɪn/ VI se languir (*for* de) ◆ **he's pining (for his girlfriend)** il se languit (de sa petite amie) ◆ **an exile pining for home** un exilé qui se languit de son pays *or* qui se languit, loin de son pays ◆ **after six months in London she began to ~ for home** après six mois passés à Londres elle commençait à avoir le mal du pays
► **pine away** VI languir, dépérir

pineal body /ˈpɪnɪəlˌbɒdɪ/, **pineal gland** /ˈpɪnɪəlɡlænd/ N glande *f* pinéale, épiphyse *f*

pineapple /ˈpaɪnˌæpl/ N ananas *m*
COMP [*flavour, ice cream*] à l'ananas
pineapple juice N jus *m* d'ananas

pinewood /ˈpaɪnwʊd/ N 1 (= *grove*) bois *m* de pins, pinède *f* 2 (*NonC* = *material*) pin *m*

ping /pɪŋ/ N bruit *m* métallique ; [*of bell, clock*] tintement *m* ; (*US: of car engine*) cliquettement *m* VI faire un bruit métallique ; [*bell, clock*] tinter ; (*US: car engine*) cliqueter COMP **Ping-Pong** ® N ping-pong *m* ◆ **~-pong ball** balle *f* de ping-pong ◆ **~-pong player** pongiste *mf* joueur *m*, -euse *f* de ping-pong

pinging /ˈpɪŋɪŋ/ N (*US: of car engine*) cliquettement *m*

pinhead /ˈpɪnhed/ N 1 (*lit*) tête *f* d'épingle 2 (*‡ pej* = *idiot*) imbécile *mf*, andouille‡ *f*

pinhole /ˈpɪnhəʊl/ N trou *m* d'épingle ; (*Phot*) sténopé *m*

pinion[1] /ˈpɪnjən/ N [*of bird*] aileron *m* VT 1 [+ *person*] lier ◆ **to ~ sb's arms** (= *hold*) tenir les bras de qn ; (= *tie up*) lier les bras à qn ◆ **she ~ed his arms behind his back** (= *hold*) elle lui a tenu les bras derrière le dos ; (= *tie up*) elle lui a lié les bras derrière le dos ◆ **he was ~ed against the wall** (*by person*) il était plaqué contre le mur ; (*by object*) il était coincé contre le mur 2 [+ *bird*] rogner les ailes à

pinion[2] /ˈpɪnjən/ N (= *cogwheel*) pignon *m* ; → **rack**[1] COMP **pinion wheel** N roue *f* à pignon

pink[1] /pɪŋk/ N 1 (= *colour*) rose *m* ; → **hunting, salmon**
2 * ◆ **to be in the ~** se porter comme un charme ◆ **in the ~ of condition** en excellente *or* pleine forme
3 (= *plant*) œillet *m*, mignardise *f*
ADJ 1 [*cheek, clothes, paper*] rose ◆ **the petals turn ~** les pétales rosissent ◆ **he turned ~ with embarrassment** il rougit de confusion ◆ **to be seeing ~ elephants** * voir des éléphants roses ; (**: = homosexual*) gay *, homo * ; → **strike, tickle**
2 (*Pol*) gauchisant
COMP **pink eye** N (*Med*) conjonctivite *f* aiguë contagieuse
pink gin N cocktail *m* de gin et d'angustura
pink lady N (= *cocktail*) *cocktail à base de gin, cognac, jus de citron et grenadine*
the pink pound * N *le pouvoir d'achat de la communauté gay*
pink slip * N (*US: terminating employment*) avis *m* de licenciement
pink-slip * VT (*US* = *dismiss*) licencier
pink-slipped * ADJ (*US* = *dismissed*) [*worker*] licencié

> **PINK SLIP**
>
> Aux États-Unis, la « feuille rose » (**pink slip**) désigne familièrement l'avis de licenciement. Cette expression est en usage depuis les années 1920, où l'on glissait dans l'enveloppe de paie d'un employé licencié la copie carbone de couleur rose qui lui notifiait son renvoi. Elle s'utilise aussi comme verbe ou adjectif : ainsi, on dira « they **pink-slipped** him » (ils l'ont licencié), ou « a **pink-slipped** worker » (un ouvrier licencié).

pink[2] /pɪŋk/ VT 1 (*Sewing*) denteler 2 (= *put holes in*) perforer 3 (= *pierce*) percer COMP **pinking scissors, pinking shears** NPL ciseaux *mpl* à denteler

pink[3] /pɪŋk/ VI (*Brit*) [*car engine etc*] cliqueter

pinkie /ˈpɪŋkɪ/ N petit doigt *m*, auriculaire *m*

pinking /ˈpɪŋkɪŋ/ N (*Brit: of car engine*) cliquettement *m*

pinkish /ˈpɪŋkɪʃ/ ADJ 1 rosé, rosâtre ◆ **~ red/orange/grey** *etc* rouge/orange/gris *etc* tirant sur le rose ◆ **~ brown** brun rosâtre 2 (*Pol*) gauchisant

pinko * /ˈpɪŋkəʊ/ ADJ, N (pl **pinkos** *or* **pinkoes**) (*esp US Pol pej*) gauchisant(e) *m(f)*

pinnace /ˈpɪnɪs/ N chaloupe *f*

pinnacle /ˈpɪnəkl/ N (*Archit*) pinacle *m* ; (= *mountain peak*) pic *m*, cime *f* ; (*Climbing*) gendarme *m* ; (*fig*) apogée *m*, sommet *m*, pinacle *m* ◆ **the ~ of her career** l'apogée *or* le sommet de sa carrière

pinny * /ˈpɪnɪ/ N (*Brit*) (abbrev of **pinafore**) tablier *m*

Pinocchio /pɪˈnəʊkjəʊ/ N Pinocchio *m*

pinochle /ˈpiːnʌkəl/ N (*US*) (sorte *f* de) belote *f*

pinpoint /ˈpɪnpɔɪnt/ N (*lit*) pointe *f* d'épingle VT [+ *place*] localiser avec précision ; [+ *problem*] mettre le doigt sur

pinprick /ˈpɪnprɪk/ N piqûre *f* d'épingle ◆ **a ~ of light** un rai de lumière

pinstripe /ˈpɪnstraɪp/ N rayure *f* très fine ◆ **black material with a white ~** tissu *m* noir finement rayé de blanc ◆ **~ suit** costume *m* rayé

pinstriped /ˈpɪnstraɪpt/ ADJ à fines rayures

pint /paɪnt/ N 1 pinte *f*, ≃ demi-litre *m* (*Brit* = *0,57 litre, US* = *0,47 litre*) ; → **IMPERIAL SYSTEM** 2 (*Brit* * = *beer*) pinte *f* (de bière) ◆ **let's go for a ~** allons prendre un pot * ◆ **she had a few ~s** ≃ elle a bu quelques bières ◆ **he likes his ~** il aime son verre de bière COMP **pint-size(d)** * ADJ minuscule

pinta * /ˈpaɪntə/ N (*Brit*) (abbrev of **pint of milk**) ≃ demi-litre *m* de lait

pinto /ˈpɪntəʊ/ ADJ [*horse*] pie *inv* N cheval *m or* jument *f* pie COMP **pinto bean** N haricot *m* bicolore (*du sud-ouest des États-Unis*)

pinup * /ˈpɪnʌp/ N (= *girl*) pin up * *f* ; (= *photo*) photo *f* de pin up *

pioneer /ˌpaɪəˈnɪəʳ/ N (*gen*) pionnier *m*, -ière *f* ; (= *early settler*) pionnier *m*, -ière *f*, colon *m* ; (*Mil*) pionnier *m*, sapeur *m* ; (= *explorer*) explorateur *m*, -trice *f* ; [*of scheme, science, method*] pionnier *m*, -ière *f*, précurseur *m* ◆ **she was one of the ~s in this field** elle a été l'une des pionnières *or* l'un des précurseurs dans ce domaine ◆ **one of the ~s of aviation/scientific research** l'un des pionniers de l'aviation/de la recherche scientifique ◆ **a medical ~** un pionnier dans le domaine médical
VT ◆ **to ~ the study of sth** être l'un des premiers (*or* l'une des premières) à étudier qch ◆ **she ~ed research in this field** elle a été à l'avant-garde de la recherche *or* une pionnière de la recherche dans ce domaine ◆ **he ~ed the use of this drug** il a lancé l'usage de ce médicament ◆ **innovations being ~ed by the new universities** des innovations mises au point par les nouvelles universités ◆ **this battle strategy was ~ed by the Russians** cette stratégie militaire a été utilisée pour la première fois par les Russes ; see also **pioneering**
COMP [*research, study*] complètement nouveau (nouvelle *f*)
pioneer work N (*NonC*) ◆ **he did ~ work in the development of …** il a été le premier à développer …

pioneering /ˌpaɪəˈnɪərɪŋ/ ADJ [*work*] novateur ; [*spirit*] pionnier ; [*approach*] original, novateur ◆ **America has always retained her ~ spirit** l'Amérique a toujours gardé son esprit pionnier ◆ **his ~ approach to architecture** son approche originale *or* novatrice de l'architecture ◆ **his life was saved by ~ brain surgery** il a été sauvé par une technique neurochirurgicale entièrement nouvelle ◆ **she was given part of a pig's heart, in a ~ operation** elle a reçu une partie d'un cœur de cochon lors d'une opération sans précédent

pious /ˈpaɪəs/ ADJ 1 (= *religious*) pieux 2 (*pej* = *sanctimonious*) hypocrite ◆ **a ~ hope** un vœu pieux ◆ **not ~ intentions, but real actions** pas de bonnes intentions, mais des actes

piously /ˈpaɪəslɪ/ ADV 1 (= *with piety*) avec piété, pieusement 2 (= *sanctimoniously*) d'un air sentencieux, avec componction

pip[1] /pɪp/ N 1 [*of fruit*] pépin *m* 2 [*of card, dice*] point *m* 3 (*Brit Mil: on uniform*) ≃ galon *m* 4 (*Telec*) top *m* ◆ **the ~s** * le bip-bip * ◆ **put more money in when you hear the ~s** * introduisez des pièces supplémentaires quand vous entendrez le bip-bip ◆ **at the third ~ it will be 6.49 and 20 seconds** au troisième top il sera exactement 6 heures 49 minutes 20 secondes 5 (*on radar*) spot *m*

pip[2] /pɪp/ N (= *disease of chickens*) pépie *f* ◆ **he gives me the ~** † * (*Brit*) il me hérisse le poil *

pip[3] * /pɪp/ VT 1 (= *hit*) atteindre d'une balle 2 (*Brit*) **to be ~ped at** *or* **to the post** se faire coiffer au poteau ◆ **a woman ~ped him for the job/for second place** c'est une femme qui lui a soufflé * le poste/la seconde place, il s'est vu souffler * le poste/la seconde place par une femme

pipe /paɪp/ N 1 (*for water*) tuyau *m*, conduite *f* ; (*smaller*) tube *m* ; (*for gas*) tuyau *m* ◆ **to lay water ~s** poser des conduites d'eau *or* une canalisation d'eau ◆ **sewage ~** égout *m* ; → **drainpipe, windpipe**
2 (*for smoking*) pipe *f* ◆ **he smokes a ~** il fume la pipe ◆ **he smoked a ~ before he left** il fuma une pipe avant de partir ◆ **to fill a ~** bourrer une pipe ◆ **a ~(ful) of tobacco** une pipe de tabac ◆ **put that in your ~ and smoke it!** * si ça ne te plaît pas, c'est le même prix ! *, mets ça dans ta poche et ton mouchoir par-dessus ! ; → **peace**
3 (*Mus*) pipeau *m*, chalumeau *m* ; [*of organ*] tuyau *m* ; (*boatswain's*) sifflet *m* ; (also **bagpipes**) ◆ **~s** cornemuse *f* ; → **Pan**
VT 1 (*Agr, Comm etc*) [+ *liquid*] amener par tuyau *or* conduite *or* canalisation *etc* ◆ **water is ~d to the farm** l'eau est amenée jusqu'à la ferme par une canalisation ◆ **hot water is ~d to all the rooms** l'eau chaude est amenée par conduites dans toutes les pièces ◆ **to ~ oil across the desert** transporter du pétrole à travers le désert par pipeline *or* oléoduc ◆ **to ~ oil into a tank** verser *or* faire passer du pétrole

dans un réservoir à l'aide d'un tuyau ◆ **to ~ music into a room** * *(hum)* passer de la musique dans une pièce

[2] *(Mus)* *[+ tune]* jouer (sur un pipeau *etc*) ; *(Naut)* *[+ order]* siffler ◆ **to ~ all hands on deck** rassembler l'équipage sur le pont (au son du sifflet) ◆ **to ~ sb in/out** saluer l'arrivée/le départ de qn (au son du sifflet) ◆ **the commander was ~d aboard** le commandant a reçu les honneurs du sifflet en montant à bord

[3] *(Sewing)* passepoiler, garnir d'un passepoil ◆ **~d with blue** passepoilé de bleu, garni d'un passepoil bleu

[4] *(Culin)* **to ~ cream onto a cake** décorer un gâteau avec de la crème chantilly (à l'aide d'une douille)

[5] *(= say)* dire d'une voix flûtée ; *(= sing)* chanter d'une voix flûtée ◆ **"it's for you", he ~d** "c'est pour toi" dit-il d'une voix flûtée

VI [1] *(Mus)* *(flute)* jouer du pipeau (*or* du chalumeau) ; *(bagpipes)* jouer de la cornemuse

[2] *(Naut)* donner un coup de sifflet

COMP **pipe bomb** N bombe *f* artisanale *(fabriquée à partir d'un morceau de tuyau)*

pipe cleaner N cure-pipe *m*

piped music N musique *f* d'ambiance enregistrée

pipe dream N projet *m* chimérique

pipe organ N grandes orgues *fpl*

pipe rack N râtelier *m* à pipes

pipe smoker N fumeur *m* de pipe

pipe tobacco N tabac *m* à pipe

► **pipe down** * VI se taire ◆ **~ down!** mets-la en sourdine ! *

► **pipe up** * VI se faire entendre

pipeclay /ˈpaɪpkleɪ/ N terre *f* de pipe

pipefitter /ˈpaɪpˌfɪtəʳ/ N tuyauteur *m*

pipeline /ˈpaɪplaɪn/ N pipeline *m* ; *(for oil)* oléoduc *m* ; *(for natural gas)* gazoduc *m* ; *(for milk)* lactoduc *m*

◆ **in the pipeline** *(= planned or about to happen)* prévu ; *(= begun or about to be completed)* en cours de réalisation ◆ **there are redundancies in the ~** des licenciements sont prévus ◆ **they've got a pay increase in the ~** il est prévu qu'ils reçoivent *or* ils doivent recevoir une augmentation de salaire ◆ **there's a new model in the ~** un nouveau modèle est en cours de réalisation, on est en train de développer un nouveau modèle

piper /ˈpaɪpəʳ/ N [1] *(= flautist)* joueur *m*, -euse *f* de pipeau (*or* de chalumeau) [2] (also **bagpiper**) joueur *m*, -euse *f* de cornemuse ; → **pay**

pipette /pɪˈpet/ N pipette *f*

pipework /ˈpaɪpwɜːk/ N *(NonC)* tuyauterie *f*

piping /ˈpaɪpɪŋ/ N *(NonC)* [1] *(in house)* tuyauterie *f*, canalisation *f* [2] *(Mus)* *(of flute)* son *m* du pipeau *or* du chalumeau ; *(of bagpipes)* son *m* de la cornemuse [3] *(Sewing)* passepoil *m* [4] *(on cake)* décorations *fpl* (appliquées) à la douille ADJ *[voice, tone]* flûté ADV ◆ **~ hot** tout chaud, tout bouillant COMP **piping cord** N ganse *f*

pipit /ˈpɪpɪt/ N *(Orn)* pipit *m*

pipkin /ˈpɪpkɪn/ N poêlon *m* (en terre)

pippin /ˈpɪpɪn/ N (pomme *f*) reinette *f*

pipsqueak † /ˈpɪpskwiːk/ N foutriquet † *m*

piquancy /ˈpiːkənsɪ/ N *(flavour)* goût *m* piquant ; *[of story]* sel *m*, piquant *m*

piquant /ˈpiːkənt/ ADJ *[flavour, story]* piquant

piquantly /ˈpiːkəntlɪ/ ADV d'une manière piquante

pique /piːk/ VT [1] *[+ person]* froisser ; *(stronger)* piquer au vif [2] *[+ sb's curiosity, interest]* piquer, exciter N ressentiment *m*, dépit *m* ◆ **in a fit of ~** dans un accès de dépit ◆ **to do sth out of ~** faire qch par dépit

piquet /pɪˈket/ N piquet *m (jeu de cartes)*

piracy /ˈpaɪərəsɪ/ N *(NonC)* [1] piraterie *f* ◆ **a tale of ~** une histoire de pirates [2] *(fig)* *[of book, film, tape, video]* piratage *m* ; *[of idea]* pillage *m*, vol *m* ; *(Comm)* contrefaçon *f* ◆ **video/computer/software ~** piratage *m* vidéo/informatique/de logiciels

piranha /pɪˈrɑːnjə/ N piranha *m*

pirate /ˈpaɪərɪt/ N [1] *(Hist)* pirate *m*, corsaire *m*, flibustier *m* [2] *(Comm: gen)* contrefacteur *m* ; *[of book, tape, film, video]* pirate *m* ; *[of ideas]* voleur *m*, -euse *f* VT *[+ book, tape, film, video, software, product, invention, idea]* pirater

COMP *[flag, ship]* de pirates

pirate copy N copie *f* pirate

pirate radio N radio *f* pirate

pirated /ˈpaɪərɪtɪd/ ADJ *[book, tape, film, video]* pirate ◆ **~ edition** édition *f* pirate

piratical /paɪˈrætɪkəl/ ADJ *[band, family]* de pirates ; *[appearance]* de pirate

pirating /ˈpaɪərɪtɪŋ/ N piratage *m*

pirouette /ˌpɪrʊˈet/ N pirouette *f* VI faire la pirouette, pirouetter

Pisa /ˈpiːzə/ N Pise

Piscean /ˈpaɪsɪən/ N ◆ **to be a ~** être Poisson(s)

Pisces /ˈpaɪsiːz/ N *(Astron)* Poissons *mpl* ◆ **I'm (a) ~** *(Astrol)* je suis Poisson(s)

piss⁑ /pɪs/ N pisse⁑ *f* ◆ **it's ~ easy** *or* **a piece of ~** *(Brit)* c'est fastoche⁑ ◆ **to go for** *or* **have** *or* **take a ~** pisser un coup⁑ ◆ **to take the ~** charrier ◆ **to take the ~ out of sb** *(Brit)* se foutre de la gueule de qn*⁑ ◆ **he took the ~ out of my accent** *(Brit)* il s'est foutu⁑ de moi à cause de mon accent ◆ **to go out on the ~** *(Brit = go drinking)* aller se soûler la gueule⁑ dans les bars

VI pisser⁑ ◆ **it's ~ing down** *or* **~ing with rain** *(Brit)* il pleut comme vache qui pisse *

VT ◆ **to ~ one's pants** *or* **o.s.** *(= urinate)* pisser⁑ dans sa culotte ◆ **to ~ o.s. (laughing)** *(Brit)* pisser de rire⁑

COMP **piss artist**⁑ N *(Brit)* soûlographe * *mf*, poivrot(e) * *m(f)*

piss easy⁑ ADJ *(Brit)* → **noun**

piss-poor⁑ ADJ nullard *, minable *

piss-take⁑ N mise *f* en boîte *

piss-up⁑ N *(Brit)* soûlerie *f*, beuverie * *f* ◆ **he couldn't organize a ~-up in a brewery** *(Brit)* il est complètement nul *, c'est un vrai nullard *

► **piss about, piss around**⁑ VI *(Brit = waste time)* glandouiller⁑ ◆ **to ~ about with sth** déconner⁑ avec qch ◆ **to ~ about with sb** se foutre de la gueule de qn*⁑

VT *(Brit)* *[+ person]* se foutre de la gueule de*⁑

► **piss off**⁑ VI foutre le camp⁑ ◆ **~ off!** fous(-moi) le camp !⁑

VT *[person, situation]* *[+ person]* faire chier⁑ ◆ **she ~es me off sometimes** il y a des moments où elle me fait chier⁑ ◆ **I'm ~ed off** j'en ai ras le bol * *or* le cul*⁑

pissed⁑ /pɪst/ ADJ [1] *(Brit = drunk)* bituré⁑, bourré⁑ ◆ **to get ~** se soûler la gueule⁑ ◆ **~ as a newt** *or* **a fart, ~ out of one's mind** complètement bituré⁑ *or* bourré⁑ [2] *(US)* ⇒ **pissed off** ; → **piss off vt**

pisser*⁑ /ˈpɪsəʳ/ N emmerdement⁑ *m*, merde*⁑ *f*

pisshead⁑ /ˈpɪshed/ N *(Brit)* poivrot(e) * *m(f)*, soûlard(e) * *m(f)*

pistachio /pɪsˈtɑːʃɪəʊ/ N (pl **pistachios**) [1] *(= nut)* pistache *f* ; *(= tree)* pistachier *m* [2] *(= colour)* (vert *m*) pistache *inv* COMP **pistachio ice cream** N glace *f* à la pistache

piste /piːst/ N *(Ski)* piste *f* ◆ **off ~** hors piste

pisted /ˈpiːstɪd/ ADJ *(Ski)* ◆ **it's well ~ down** c'est bien damé

pistil /ˈpɪstɪl/ N pistil *m*

pistol /ˈpɪstl/ N pistolet *m* ; *(Sport:* also **starter's pistol**) pistolet *m* (de starter)

COMP **pistol point** N ◆ **at ~ point** sous la menace du pistolet

pistol shot N coup *m* de pistolet

pistol-whip VT frapper avec un pistolet

piston /ˈpɪstən/ N piston *m*

COMP **piston engine** N moteur *m* à pistons

piston-engined ADJ à moteur à pistons

piston pin N *(US)* goupille *f*

piston ring N segment *m* (de pistons)

piston rod N tige *f* de piston

pit[1] /pɪt/ N [1] *(= large hole)* fosse *f*, trou *m* ; *(on moon's surface etc)* cratère *m*, dépression *f* ; (also **coalpit**) mine *f*, puits *m* de mine ; *(as game trap etc)* trappe *f*, fosse *f* ; *(= quarry)* carrière *f* ; *(in garage)* fosse *f* ◆ **chalkpit** carrière *f* à chaux ◆ **to go down the ~** *(= mine)* *(gen)* descendre au fond de la mine ; *(= start work there)* aller travailler à la mine ◆ **he works in the ~s** il travaille à la mine, il est mineur (de fond)

[2] *(liter = hell)* ◆ **the ~** l'enfer *m*

[3] *(= small depression)* *(in metal, glass)* petit trou *m* ; *(on face)* (petite) marque *f or* cicatrice *f*

[4] *[of stomach]* creux *m* ◆ **he felt sick to the ~ of his stomach** il en était malade * ; → **armpit**

[5] *(Brit Theat)* (fauteuils *mpl* d')orchestre *m* ; *(for cock fighting)* arène *f* ; *(US Stock Exchange)* parquet *m* de la Bourse ◆ **the wheat ~** *(US Stock Exchange)* la Bourse du blé

[6] *(Motor Racing)* **the ~s** le stand de ravitaillement ◆ **it's the ~s!**⁑ c'est merdique !⁑

VT [1] **to ~ sb against** *(= make opponent of)* opposer qn à ; *(= make enemy of)* dresser qn contre ◆ **to ~ o.s. against sb** se mesurer à qn ◆ **to ~ one's strength against sb** se mesurer à qn ◆ **to be ~ted against sb** avoir qn comme *or* pour adversaire ◆ **a debate which has seen Tory ~ted against Tory** un débat qui a divisé les conservateurs ◆ **one man ~ted against the universe** un homme seul contre l'univers ◆ **to ~ one's wits against** jouer au plus fin avec, se mesurer avec

[2] *[+ metal]* trouer, piqueter ; *[+ face, skin]* *(smallpox)* grêler ; *(acne)* marquer ◆ **a car ~ted with rust** une voiture piquée de rouille ◆ **his face was ~ted with smallpox/acne scars** son visage était grêlé (par la variole)/par l'acné ◆ **the ~ted surface of the glass** la surface piquetée du verre ◆ **a ~ted road surface** une route pleine de nids-de-poule

COMP **pit bull terrier** N pit-bull *m*

pit pony N cheval *m* de mine

pit prop N poteau *m or* étai *m* de mine

pit stop N *(Motor Racing)* arrêt *m* au stand

pit worker N mineur *m* de fond

pit[2] /pɪt/ N *(= fruit-stone)* noyau *m* VT dénoyauter ◆ **~ted prunes/cherries** pruneaux *mpl*/cerises *fpl* dénoyauté(e)s

pita /ˈpɪtə/, **pita bread** N *(US)* ⇒ **pitta**

pitapat /ˈpɪtəˈpæt/ ADV ◆ **to go ~** *[feet]* trottiner ; *[heart]* palpiter, battre ; *[rain]* crépiter

pitch[1] /pɪtʃ/ N [1] *(= throw)* acte *m* de lancer, lancement *m* ◆ **the ball went full ~ over the fence** le ballon a volé par-dessus la barrière

[2] *(= degree)* degré *m* ◆ **he had worked himself up to such a ~ of indignation that ...** il était parvenu à un tel degré d'indignation que ... ◆ **things have reached such a ~ that ...** les choses en sont arrivées à un point tel que ... ◆ **excitement was at fever ~** l'excitation était à son comble

[3] *(Mus)* *[of instrument, voice]* ton *m* ; *[of note, sound]* hauteur *f* ; *(Phon)* hauteur *f* ; → **concert, perfect**

[4] *(Brit Sport = ground)* terrain *m* ◆ **football/cricket** *etc* **~** terrain *m* de football/de cricket *etc*

[5] *(Brit)* *[of trader]* place *f* (habituelle) ; → **queer**

[6] *(= sales talk)* baratin * *m*, boniment *m* ◆ **to make a ~ for sth** *(= support)* *[+ plan, suggestion, sb's point of view]* préconiser qch ; → **sale**

[7] *[of roof]* degré *m* de pente

8 *(= movement of boat)* tangage *m*

9 *[of propeller]* pas *m* ◆ **variable ~ propeller** hélice *f* à pas variable

10 *(Climbing)* longueur *f* (de corde)

VT 1 *(= throw) [+ ball] (also Baseball)* lancer ; *[+ object]* jeter, lancer ; *(Agr) [+ hay]* lancer avec une fourche ; *(= discard)* jeter ◆ **~ it over here!** * jette-le *or* lance-le par ici ! ◆ **to ~ sth over/through/under** *etc* lancer *or* jeter qch par-dessus/à travers/par-dessous *etc* ◆ **the horse ~ed him off** le cheval l'a jeté à bas *or* à terre ◆ **~ it!** * *(US)* balance-le ! * ◆ **the incident ~ed him into the political arena** cet incident l'a propulsé dans l'arène politique ◆ **this could ~ the government into confrontation with the unions** cela pourrait précipiter le gouvernement dans un conflit avec les syndicats

2 *(Mus) [+ note]* donner ; *[+ melody]* donner le ton de *or* à ◆ **she can't ~ a note properly** elle ne sait pas trouver la note juste *(lit)* ◆ **I'll ~ you a note** je vous donne une note pour commencer ◆ **to ~ the voice higher/lower** hausser/baisser le ton de la voix ◆ **this song is ~ed too low** cette chanson est dans un ton trop bas ◆ **the prices of these cars are ~ed extremely competitively** le prix de ces voitures est très compétitif ◆ **to ~ one's aspirations too high** aspirer *or* viser trop haut, placer ses aspirations trop haut ◆ **it is ~ed in rather high-flown terms** c'est exprimé en des termes assez ronflants ◆ **the speech must be ~ed at the right level for the audience** le ton du discours doit être adapté au public ◆ **you're ~ing it a bit high!** *or* **strong!** tu exagères un peu !, tu y vas un peu fort ! ◆ **he ~ed me a story about having lost his wallet** * il m'a débité *or* m'a sorti * une histoire comme quoi il avait perdu son portefeuille

3 *(= set up)* **to ~ a tent** dresser une tente ◆ **to ~ camp** établir un camp

4 *(Comm etc: * = promote, propose) [+ product]* promouvoir, faire du battage pour ; *[+ plan, idea]* présenter ◆ **she ~ed the plan to business leaders** elle a présenté le plan à des chefs d'entreprise

VI 1 *(= fall)* tomber ; *(= be jerked)* être projeté ; *[ball]* rebondir, tomber ◆ **she slipped and ~ed forward** elle a glissé et est tombée le nez en avant *or* et a piqué du nez ◆ **he ~ed forward as the bus stopped** il a été projeté en avant quand l'autobus s'est arrêté ◆ **he ~ed head first into the lake** il est tombé la tête la première dans le lac ◆ **to ~ off a horse** tomber de cheval ◆ **the aircraft ~ed into the sea** l'avion a plongé dans la mer ◆ **he ~ed over (backwards)** il est tombé (à la renverse)

2 *(Naut)* tanguer ◆ **the ship ~ed and tossed** le navire tanguait

3 *(Baseball)* lancer la balle ◆ **he's in there ~ing** * *(US)* il est solide au poste

COMP **pitch-and-putt** N *(Golf)* pitch-and-putt *m (jeu de golf limité à deux clubs)*

pitch-and-toss N *sorte de jeu de pile ou face*

pitch invasion N *(Brit Sport)* invasion *f* du terrain ◆ **there was a ~ invasion** les spectateurs ont envahi le terrain

pitch pipe N *(Mus)* diapason *m (en forme de sifflet)*

► **pitch in** * VI s'atteler *or* s'attaquer au boulot *, s'y coller * ◆ **they all ~ed in to help him** ils s'y sont tous mis *or* collés * pour l'aider ◆ **come on, ~ in all of you!** allez, mettez-vous-y *or* collez-vous-y * tous !

► **pitch into** * VT FUS 1 *(= attack)* tomber sur ; *(fig) (= criticize) [reviewer, critic, journalist] [+ author, work]* éreinter ◆ **the boss ~ed into me** le patron s'en est pris à moi *or* m'est tombé dessus *

2 s'attaquer à ◆ **they ~ed into the work** ils se sont attaqués *or* collés * au travail ◆ **they ~ed into the meal** ils se sont attaqués au repas, ils y sont allés d'un bon coup de fourchette

► **pitch on** VT FUS arrêter son choix sur

► **pitch out** VT SEP *(= get rid of) [+ person]* expulser, éjecter *, vider * ; *[+ thing]* jeter, bazarder * ◆ **the car overturned and the driver was ~ed out** la voiture a fait un tonneau et le conducteur a été éjecté

► **pitch upon** VT FUS ⇒ **pitch on**

pitch² /pɪtʃ/ N *(= tar)* poix *f*, brai *m* ◆ **mineral ~** asphalte *m* minéral, bitume *m* ◆ **as black as ~** ⇒ **pitch-black** VT brayer, enduire de poix *or* de brai

COMP **pitch-black** ADJ *(gen)* noir comme du charbon *or* comme de la suie ◆ **it's ~-black outside** il fait noir comme dans un four dehors

pitch blackness N noir *m* absolu *or* complet

pitch-dark ADJ ◆ **it's ~-dark** il fait noir comme dans un four ◆ **it's a ~-dark night** il fait nuit noire

pitch darkness N ⇒ **pitch blackness**

pitch pine N *(= wood)* pitchpin *m*

pitchblende /ˈpɪtʃblend/ N pechblende *f*

pitched /pɪtʃt/ ADJ ◆ **~ battle** *(Mil)* bataille *f* rangée ; *(fig)* véritable bataille *f* COMP **pitched roof** N toit *m* en pente

pitcher¹ /ˈpɪtʃəʳ/ N *(esp US)* cruche *f* ; *(bigger)* broc *m* COMP **pitcher plant** N sarracéniale *f*

pitcher² /ˈpɪtʃəʳ/ N *(Baseball)* lanceur *m*

pitchfork /ˈpɪtʃfɔːk/ N fourche *f* (à foin) VT 1 *(Agr)* fourcher, lancer avec une fourche 2 * **I was ~ed into this** j'ai dû faire cela du jour au lendemain ◆ **he was ~ed into the job** il a été parachuté * à ce poste

pitchman * /ˈpɪtʃmən/ N (pl **-men**) *(US) (= street seller)* camelot *m* ; *(TV)* présentateur *m* de produits

piteous /ˈpɪtɪəs/ ADJ *(esp liter)* pitoyable ◆ **a ~ sight** un spectacle pitoyable *or* à faire pitié

piteously /ˈpɪtɪəslɪ/ ADV *[say, complain]* d'un ton pitoyable, pitoyablement ; *[look at, weep]* d'un air pitoyable, pitoyablement ; *[howl, whine, meow]* d'une manière pitoyable, pitoyablement

pitfall /ˈpɪtfɔːl/ N 1 *(lit)* trappe *f*, piège *m* 2 *(fig)* piège *m*, embûche *f* ◆ **the ~s of English** les pièges de l'anglais ◆ **there are many ~s ahead** de nombreuses embûches nous (*or* les *etc*) guettent

pith /pɪθ/ N 1 *[of bone, plant]* moelle *f* ; *[of orange, grapefruit etc]* peau *f* blanche 2 *(fig) (= essence)* essence *f*, moelle *f (fig) (= force)* force *f*, vigueur *f* COMP **pith helmet** N casque *m* colonial

pithead /ˈpɪthed/ N *(Min)* carreau *m* de mine

pithecanthropine /ˌpɪθɪˈkænθrəʊˌpaɪn/ ADJ pithécanthropien N pithécanthrope *m*

pithecanthropus /ˌpɪθɪkænˈθrəʊpəs/ N (pl **pithecanthropi** /ˌpɪθɪkænˈθrəʊˌpaɪ/) pithécanthrope *m*

pithiness /ˈpɪθɪnɪs/ N *[of style]* vigueur *f*, concision *f*

pithy /ˈpɪθɪ/ ADJ *(= forceful)* nerveux, vigoureux ; *(= terse)* concis ; *(= pointed)* savoureux, piquant ◆ **a ~ saying** une remarque piquante

pitiable /ˈpɪtɪəbl/ ADJ *[hovel]* pitoyable ; *[income]* misérable, de misère ; *[appearance]* piteux, minable ; *[attempt]* piteux ◆ **a ~ situation** une situation pitoyable *or* navrante

pitiably /ˈpɪtɪəblɪ/ ADV ⇒ **pitifully**

pitiful /ˈpɪtɪfʊl/ ADJ 1 *(= touching) [appearance, sight, person]* pitoyable 2 *(= deplorable) [cowardice]* lamentable, déplorable ◆ **his ~ efforts to speak French** ses lamentables efforts pour parler français

pitifully /ˈpɪtɪfəlɪ/ ADV *[say, complain, weep]* d'un ton pitoyable, pitoyablement ; *[look at]* d'un air pitoyable, pitoyablement ; *[howl, whine, meow]* d'une manière pitoyable, pitoyablement ◆ **~ thin/poor/inadequate** d'une maigreur/pauvreté/insuffisance affligeante ◆ **a ~ bad play** une pièce lamentable ◆ **a ~ small army** une armée si petite qu'elle fait (*or* faisait *etc*) pitié

pitiless /ˈpɪtɪlɪs/ ADJ sans pitié, impitoyable

pitilessly /ˈpɪtɪlɪslɪ/ ADV impitoyablement, sans pitié

pitman /ˈpɪtmən/ N (pl **-men**) *(Brit)* mineur *m*

piton /ˈpiːtɒn/ N *(Climbing)* piton *m*

pitta /ˈpɪtə/, **pitta bread** N pain *m* pitta

pittance /ˈpɪtəns/ N *(pej) (= sum)* somme *f* dérisoire ; *(= income)* maigre revenu *m* ; *(= wage)* salaire *m* de misère ◆ **she's living on a ~** elle n'a presque rien pour vivre ◆ **they're offering a mere ~** ils offrent un salaire de misère

pitter-pat /ˈpɪtəˈpæt/ ADV ⇒ **pitapat**

pitter-patter /ˈpɪtəˈpætəʳ/ ADV ⇒ **pitapat** N ⇒ **patter¹**

pituitary /pɪˈtjuːɪtərɪ/ ADJ pituitaire COMP **pituitary gland** N glande *f* pituitaire, hypophyse *f*

pity /ˈpɪtɪ/ LANGUAGE IN USE 14, 26.3

N 1 *(= mercy, compassion)* pitié *f* ◆ **for ~'s sake** par pitié, de grâce ◆ **to have ~ on sb** avoir pitié de qn ◆ **have ~ on him!** ayez pitié de lui ! ◆ **to take ~ on sb** avoir pitié de qn, prendre qn en pitié ◆ **to feel ~ for sb** avoir pitié de qn, s'apitoyer sur qn ◆ **to move sb to ~** exciter la compassion de qn, apitoyer qn ◆ **out of ~ (for him)** par pitié (pour lui)

2 *(= misfortune)* dommage *m* ◆ **it is a (great) ~** c'est (bien) dommage ◆ **it's a ~ about the job** c'est dommage pour le travail ◆ **it would be a ~ if he lost** *or* **were to lose this job** cela serait dommage qu'il perde *or* s'il perdait ce travail ◆ **it is a thousand pities that ...** *(liter)* il est mille fois *or* extrêmement dommage que ... + *subj* ◆ **it's a ~ (that) you can't come** il est *or* quel dommage que vous ne puissiez (pas) venir ◆ **it would be a ~ to waste the opportunity** cela serait dommage de rater cette occasion ◆ **what a ~!** quel dommage ! ◆ **more's the ~!** c'est bien dommage ! ◆ **the ~ of it is that ...** le plus malheureux c'est que ...

VT *[+ person]* plaindre ; *[+ sb's fate, sb's situation]* s'apitoyer sur ◆ **you don't deserve to be pitied!** tu ne mérites pas que l'on te plaigne !

pitying /ˈpɪtɪɪŋ/ ADJ 1 *(= compassionate)* compatissant, plein de pitié 2 *(= contemptuous)* méprisant

pityingly /ˈpɪtɪɪŋlɪ/ ADV avec pitié

Pius /ˈpaɪəs/ N Pie *m*

pivot /ˈpɪvət/ N *(Mil, Tech)* pivot *m* ; *(fig)* centre *m* ◆ **their daughter was the ~ of their lives** leur vie tournait autour de leur fille ◆ **the ~ of his argument is that ...** son argument repose sur l'idée que ... VT *(= turn)* faire pivoter ; *(= mount on pivot)* monter sur pivot VI pivoter, tourner ◆ **she ~ed round and round** elle tournoyait sans s'arrêter ◆ **he ~ed on his heel** il a tourné sur ses talons ◆ **his argument ~s on** *or* **around the fact that ...** son argument repose sur le fait que ... COMP **pivot joint** N diarthrose *f* rotatoire

pivotal /ˈpɪvətl/ ADJ essentiel, central NPL **pivotals** *(Stock Exchange)* valeurs *fpl* essentielles *or* clés

pix * /pɪks/ NPL (abbrev of **pictures**) *(= films)* ciné * *m* ; *(= photos)* photos *fpl*

pixel /ˈpɪksəl/ N pixel *m*

pixelate /ˈpɪksəleɪt/ VT *(TV etc)* pixéliser

pixie /ˈpɪksɪ/ N lutin *m*, fée *f* COMP **pixie hat, pixie hood** N bonnet *m* pointu

pixil(l)ated * /ˈpɪksɪleɪtɪd/ ADJ farfelu

pizza /ˈpiːtsə/ N pizza *f*

COMP **pizza base** N pizza *f* à garnir

pizza delivery service N service *m* de livraison de pizzas (à domicile)
pizza oven N four *m* à pizzas
pizza parlour N pizzeria *or* pizzéria *f*

piz(z)azz * /pɪ'zæz/ N (*gen*) énergie *f*, vigueur *f* ; (*US: in car*) allure *f* ; (*pej*) (*= garishness*) tape-à-l'œil *m*

pizzeria /ˌpiːtsə'riːə/ N pizzeria *or* pizzéria *f*

pizzicato /ˌpɪtsɪ'kɑːtəʊ/ ADJ, ADV pizzicato

PJs * /piː'dʒeɪz/ NPL abbrev of **pyjamas**

pkt (abbrev of **packet**) paquet *m*

Pl. abbrev of **Place**

placard /'plækɑːd/ N (*gen*) affiche *f*, placard *m* ; (*at demo etc*) pancarte *f* VT [*+ wall*] placarder ; [*+ announcement*] afficher

placate /plə'keɪt/ VT calmer, apaiser

placating /plə'keɪtɪŋ/, **placatory** /plə'keɪtərɪ/ ADJ apaisant

place /pleɪs/

1 NOUN	3 INTRANSITIVE VERB
2 TRANSITIVE VERB	4 COMPOUNDS

1 - NOUN

1 [gen] endroit *m* ◆ **we came to a ~ where …** nous sommes arrivés à un endroit où … ◆ **this is no ~ for children** ce n'est pas un endroit pour les enfants ◆ **can't you put it a safer ~?** tu ne peux pas le mettre dans un endroit plus sûr ? ◆ **can you find a ~ for this bag?** pouvez-vous trouver un endroit où mettre ce sac ? ◆ **this isn't a very nice ~ for a picnic** ce n'est pas l'endroit idéal pour pique-niquer ◆ **from ~ to ~** d'un endroit à l'autre ◆ **the time and ~ of the crime** l'heure et le lieu du crime ◆ **I can't be in two ~s at once !*** je ne peux pas être partout à la fois !, je n'ai pas le don d'ubiquité ! ◆ **this is the ~** c'est ici ◆ **any ~ will do** n'importe où fera l'affaire ◆ **to find/lose one's ~ in a book** trouver/perdre sa page dans un livre

◆ **to take place** avoir lieu

◆ **any/some/no place** * (*US*) ◆ **I couldn't find it any ~** je ne l'ai trouvé nulle part ◆ **some ~** quelque part ◆ **it must be some ~ in the house** ça doit être quelque part dans la maison ◆ **some ~ else** quelque part ailleurs ◆ **the kids* have no ~ to go** les gosses* n'ont pas d'endroit *or* n'ont nulle part où aller

◆ **place of** + *noun* (*frm*) ◆ **~ of birth/residence/work** lieu *m* de naissance/de résidence/de travail ◆ **~ of refuge** refuge *m* ◆ **he is at his ~ of business** il est sur son lieu de travail ◆ **~ of worship** lieu *m* de culte ◆ **~ of articulation** (*Phon*) lieu *m or* point *m* d'articulation

2 [= geographical location] endroit *m* ◆ **the train doesn't stop at that ~ any more** le train ne s'arrête plus à cet endroit *or* ne s'y arrête plus ◆ **the train doesn't stop at many ~s** le train ne fait pas beaucoup d'arrêts

A more specific word is often used to translate **place**:

◆ **it's a small ~** (*= village*) c'est un village ◆ **it's just a little country ~** ce n'est qu'un petit village de campagne ◆ **Venice is a lovely ~** Venise est une très belle ville *or* un endroit charmant ◆ **Brighton is a good ~ to live** Brighton est une ville où il fait bon vivre ◆ **we found some excellent ~s to eat** nous avons trouvé d'excellents restaurants

Note adjective + **place** translated by adjective alone:

◆ **the Atlantic coast is a fine ~ for yachting** la côte atlantique est parfaite pour la voile ◆ **the museum is a huge ~** le musée est immense ◆ **it's a small ~** c'est tout petit

◆ **to go places** * (*US = travel*) voyager, voir du pays ◆ **we like to go ~s at weekends** le week-end, nous aimons faire un tour *or* bouger* ◆ **he'll go ~s all right!** (*fig = make good*) il ira loin ! ◆ **he's going ~s** il fait son chemin ◆ **we're going ~s at last** (*= make progress*) nous avançons enfin

3 [* = house] ◆ **we were at Anne's ~** nous étions chez Anne ◆ **come over to our ~** passez à la maison ◆ **your ~ or mine?** on va chez moi ou chez toi ? ◆ **he has a ~ in the country** il a une maison de campagne ◆ **his family is growing, he needs a bigger ~** sa famille s'agrandit, il lui faut quelque chose de plus grand ◆ **the house is a vast great ~** la maison est immense ◆ **his business is growing, he needs a bigger ~** son affaire s'agrandit, il lui faut quelque chose de plus grand *or* des locaux plus grands

4 [= seat, space] place *f* ; (*laid at table*) couvert *m* ◆ **a car park with 200 ~s** un parking de 200 places ◆ **keep a ~ for me** gardez-moi une place ◆ **go back to your ~s** (*Scol*) retournez à *or* reprenez vos places ◆ **to lay** *or* **set an extra ~ (at table)** mettre un couvert supplémentaire

5 [= position] place *f* ; [*of star, planet*] position *f* ◆ **put the book back in its ~** remets le livre à sa place ◆ **the key wasn't in its ~** la clé n'était pas à sa place ◆ **a ~ for everything and everything in its ~** une place pour chaque chose et chaque chose à sa place ◆ **(if I were) in your ~ …** (si j'étais) à votre place … ◆ **to keep/lose one's ~ in the queue** garder/perdre sa place dans la queue ◆ **to give ~ to …** céder la place à … ◆ **to go back** *or* **fall back into ~** se remettre en place ◆ **to take the ~ of sb/sth** prendre la place de qn/qch, remplacer qn/qch ◆ **to take** *or* **fill sb's ~** remplacer qn ; (*fig*) ◆ **to fall** *or* **fit** *or* **click into ~** (*= become clear*) devenir clair ◆ **the moment I changed jobs everything fell into ~** (*= turned out well*) il a suffit que je change de travail pour que tout s'arrange

6 [in competition, hierarchy] ◆ **Paul won the race with Robert in second ~** Paul a gagné la course et Robert est arrivé deuxième ◆ **to back a horse for a ~** (*Racing*) jouer un cheval placé ◆ **Sweden took second ~ in the championships** la Suède s'est classée deuxième aux championnats ◆ **he took second ~ in history/in the history exam** il a été deuxième en histoire/à l'examen d'histoire ◆ **my personal life has had to take second ~ to my career** ma vie privée a dû passer après ma carrière ◆ **the team was in third ~** l'équipe était en troisième position ◆ **he has risen to second ~ in the opinion polls** il occupe maintenant la deuxième place dans les sondages ◆ **I know my ~** je sais rester à ma place ◆ **people in high ~s** les gens haut placés ◆ **to put sb in his ~** remettre qn à sa place

7 [= job] poste *m*, place *f* ◆ **~s for 500 workers** des places *fpl or* des emplois *mpl* pour 500 ouvriers ◆ **we have a ~ for a receptionist** nous avons un poste de réceptionniste ◆ **we will try to find a ~ for him** on va essayer de lui trouver une place *or* un poste

8 [in school] place *f* ◆ **a few private schools give free ~s** quelques écoles privées offrent des places gratuites ◆ **I've got a ~ to do sociology** (*Univ*) j'ai réussi à m'inscrire en sociologie ◆ **he's got a ~ in the first team** (*in team*) il a été admis dans l'équipe première

9 [= role] ◆ **it's not your ~ to criticize** ce n'est pas à vous de critiquer, ce n'est pas votre rôle de critiquer

10 [= room, scope] ◆ **there is no ~ for racism in the Party** le parti ne peut tolérer le racisme ◆ **there is a ~ for this sort of counselling** ce genre d'assistance aurait son utilité

11 [set structures]

◆ **all over the place** * (*= everywhere*) partout ◆ **I've looked for him all over the ~** je l'ai cherché partout ◆ **his clothes were all over the ~** ses vêtements traînaient partout *or* étaient éparpillés un peu partout ◆ **he was careful and diligent, I was all over the ~** (*= confused*) il était soigneux et appliqué, moi j'étais complètement désorganisé

◆ **to be in place** [*object*] être à sa place ; [*measure, policy, elements*] être en place ; [*conditions*] être rassemblé ; [*law, legislation*] être en vigueur

◆ **in places** (*= here and there*) par endroits ◆ **the snow is very deep in ~s** la neige est très profonde par endroits

◆ **in place of** à la place de, au lieu de ◆ **Lewis came onto the field in ~ of Jenkins** Lewis est entré sur le terrain à la place de Jenkins

◆ **in the first place** (*= firstly*) tout d'abord, premièrement ◆ **in the first ~, it will be much cheaper** d'abord *or* premièrement, ça sera beaucoup moins cher ◆ **he shouldn't have been there in the first ~** (*= to start with*) et d'abord il n'aurait pas dû être là, il n'aurait même pas dû être là ◆ **the Latvians never agreed to join the Soviet Union in the first ~** d'ailleurs, les Lettons n'ont jamais voulu être rattachés à l'Union soviétique ◆ **we need to consider why so many people are in prison in the first ~** nous devons commencer par chercher à comprendre pourquoi tant de gens sont en prison ◆ **what brought you here in the first ~?** qu'est-ce qui vous a amené ici ?

◆ **in the second place** deuxièmement, ensuite ◆ **in the second ~, it's not worth the money** ensuite *or* deuxièmement, c'est trop cher

◆ **out of place** [*object, remark*] déplacé ◆ **such remarks were out of ~ at a funeral** de telles remarques étaient déplacées lors d'un enterrement ◆ **dahlias look out of ~ in a formal garden** les dahlias détonnent *or* ne vont pas bien dans un jardin à la française ◆ **I feel rather out of ~ here** je ne me sens pas à ma place ici

2 - TRANSITIVE VERB

1 [= put] mettre ◆ **she ~d a roll on each plate** elle a mis *or* posé un petit pain sur chaque assiette ◆ **to ~ an advertisement in the paper** mettre *or* passer une annonce dans le journal ◆ **events have ~d the president in a difficult position** les événements ont mis le président en mauvaise posture ◆ **to ~ confidence in sb/sth** placer sa confiance en qn/qch ◆ **to ~ a book with a publisher** faire accepter un livre par un éditeur

◆ **to be + placed** ◆ **the picture is ~d rather high up** le tableau est un peu trop haut ◆ **the house is well ~d** la maison est bien située ◆ **the shop is awkwardly ~d** le magasin est mal situé *or* mal placé ◆ **we are now well ~d to …** nous sommes maintenant bien placés pour … ◆ **we are better ~d than we were a month ago** notre situation est meilleure qu'il y a un mois ◆ **I am rather awkwardly ~d at the moment** je suis dans une position délicate en ce moment

2 [= rank] (*in exam*) placer, classer ; (*in race*) placer ◆ **he wasn't ~d in the race** il n'a pas été placé dans la course ◆ **my horse wasn't ~d** mon cheval n'a pas été placé ◆ **to be ~d first/second** se classer *or* se placer premier/second ◆ **he ~s good health among his greatest assets** il considère sa (bonne) santé comme l'un de ses meilleurs atouts ◆ **our team is well ~d in the league** notre équipe est en bonne position *or* est bien classée ◆ **to ~ local interests above** *or* **before** *or* **over those of central**

government faire passer les intérêts locaux avant ceux du pouvoir central

3 = classify classer ◆ **the authorities have ~d the drug in Class A** les autorités ont classé cette drogue dans la catégorie A

4 = make *[+ order, contract]* passer ; *[+ bet]* engager ◆ **thousands of people ~d bets with Ladbrokes** des milliers de personnes ont engagé des paris chez Ladbrokes ◆ **I'd like to ~ an overseas call** je voudrais téléphoner à l'étranger

5 = invest *[+ money]* placer, investir

6 = find job for trouver une place *or* un emploi pour ◆ **we have so far ~d 28 people in permanent jobs** jusqu'à présent nous avons réussi à trouver des emplois permanents à 28 personnes ◆ **the agency is trying to ~ him with a building firm** l'agence essaie de lui trouver une place *or* de le placer dans une entreprise de construction

7 = find home for placer ◆ **older children are difficult to ~** il est difficile de placer les enfants plus âgés

8 = identify situer ◆ **he looked familiar, but I couldn't immediately ~ him** sa tête me disait quelque chose mais je n'arrivais pas à le situer

3 - INTRANSITIVE VERB

US Racing être placé

4 - COMPOUNDS

place card N *carte placée sur la table pour marquer la place des convives*
place kick N *(Rugby)* coup *m* de pied placé
place mat N set *m* (de table)
place-name N nom *m* de lieu ◆ **~-names** *(as study, as group)* toponymie *f*
place setting N couvert *m*

> ⚠ Check what kind of place it is before translating **place** by the French word **place**.

placebo /plə'siːbəʊ/ N (pl **placebos** or **placeboes**) *(Med, fig)* placebo *m* COMP **placebo effect** N *(Med, fig)* effet *m* placebo

placeman /'pleɪsmən/ N (pl **-men**) *(Brit: pej) fonctionnaire qui doit son poste à ses obédiences politiques et en tire profit*

placement /'pleɪsmənt/ N *(Fin)* placement *m*, investissement *m* ; *(Univ etc: during studies)* stage *m*
COMP **placement office** N *(US Univ) (for career guidance)* centre *m* d'orientation ; *(for jobs)* bureau *m* de placement pour étudiants
placement test N *(US Scol etc)* test *m* de niveau

placenta /plə'sentə/ N (pl **placentas** or **placentae** /plə'sentiː/) placenta *m*

placer /'pleɪsəʳ/ N *(US Geol)* sable *m or* gravier *m* aurifère

placid /'plæsɪd/ ADJ *[person, smile]* placide, calme, serein ; *[waters]* tranquille, calme

placidity /plə'sɪdɪtɪ/ N placidité *f*, calme *m*, tranquillité *f*

placidly /'plæsɪdlɪ/ ADV avec placidité, placidement

placing /'pleɪsɪŋ/ N *[of money, funds]* placement *m*, investissement *m* ; *[of ball, players]* position *f*

placings /'pleɪsɪŋz/ NPL *(in competition)* classement *m*

placket /'plækɪt/ N double patte *f*

plagal /'pleɪgəl/ ADJ *(Mus)* plagal

plagiarism /'pleɪdʒjərɪzəm/ N plagiat *m*, démarquage *m*

plagiarist /'pleɪdʒjərɪst/ N plagiaire *mf*, démarqueur *m*, -euse *f*

plagiarize /'pleɪdʒjəraɪz/ VT plagier, démarquer

plague /pleɪg/ N 1 *(Med)* peste *f* ◆ **to avoid sb/sth like the ~** fuir qn/qch comme la peste ; → **bubonic**
2 *(= epidemic)* épidémie *f*
3 *(= scourge)* fléau *m* ; *(= annoying person)* plaie *f* ◆ **a ~ of rats/locusts/ants** une invasion de rats/de sauterelles/de fourmis ◆ **we're suffering from a ~ of car thefts at the moment** nous avons affaire à une vague de vols de voitures en ce moment ◆ **he's the ~ of my life!** il m'empoisonne la vie !
VT *[person, fear etc]* harceler ; *(stronger)* tourmenter ◆ **to ~ sb with questions** harceler qn de questions ◆ **they ~d me to tell them** ... ils m'ont cassé les pieds* pour que je leur dise ... ◆ **my illness has ~d me for 12 years** cette maladie m'a empoisonné la vie *or* m'a tourmenté pendant 12 ans ◆ **to be ~d by injury/kidney trouble** souffrir de blessures à répétition/de problèmes de reins chroniques ◆ **to be ~d by bad luck** jouer de malchance ◆ **~d by** *or* **with** *[+ doubts, fears, remorse]* rongé par ; *[+ nightmares]* hanté par ; *[+ mosquitoes]* tourmenté par
COMP **plague-ridden, plague-stricken** ADJ *[region, household]* frappé par la peste ; *[person]* pestiféré

plaguey († : *) /'pleɪgɪ/ ADJ fâcheux, assommant

plaice /pleɪs/ N (pl **plaice** or **plaices**) carrelet *m*, plie *f*

plaid /plæd/ N 1 *(NonC: esp US = cloth, pattern)* tissu *m* écossais 2 *(over shoulder)* plaid *m* ADJ (en tissu) écossais

plain /pleɪn/ ADJ 1 *(= obvious)* clair, évident ◆ **the path is quite ~** la voie est clairement tracée ◆ **in ~ view** à la vue de tous ◆ **the tower was in ~ view** on voyait parfaitement la tour ◆ **it must be ~ to everyone that** ... il doit être clair pour tout le monde que ..., il ne doit échapper à personne que ... ◆ **the facts are quite ~** les faits parlent d'eux-mêmes ◆ **it's as ~ as a pikestaff** *or* **as the nose on your face*** c'est clair comme le jour *or* comme de l'eau de roche ◆ **it is ~ from his comments that** ... ses remarques montrent clairement que ... ◆ **the reason for their success is ~ to see** la raison de leur succès est évidente ◆ **a ~ case of jealousy** un cas manifeste *or* évident de jalousie ◆ **I must make it ~ that** ... vous devez bien comprendre que ... ◆ **he made his feelings ~** il ne cacha pas ce qu'il ressentait *or* pensait ◆ **he made it quite ~ that he would never agree** il a bien fait comprendre qu'il n'accepterait jamais ◆ **to make sth ~ to sb** faire comprendre qch à qn
2 *(= unambiguous)* clair, franc (franche *f*) ; *[statement, assessment]* clair ◆ **~ talk, ~ speaking** *(gen)* propos *mpl* sans équivoque ◆ **I like ~ speaking** j'aime le franc-parler *or* la franchise ◆ **to be a ~ speaker** avoir son franc-parler ◆ **it's a ~ statement of fact** ce sont les faits, ni plus ni moins ◆ **to use ~ language** parler sans ambages ◆ **in ~ words** *or* **in ~ English, I think you made a mistake** je vous le dis *or* pour vous le dire carrément, je pense que vous vous êtes trompé ◆ **I explained it all in ~ words** *or* **in ~ English** j'ai tout expliqué très clairement ◆ **I gave him a ~ answer** je lui ai répondu carrément *or* sans détours *or* sans ambages ◆ **the ~ truth of the matter is (that)** ... à dire vrai ..., à la vérité ... ◆ **let me be quite ~ with you** je serai franc avec vous ◆ **do I make myself ~?** est-ce que je me fais bien comprendre ?
3 *(= sheer, utter)* pur (et simple) ◆ **it's ~ folly** c'est de la pure folie
4 *(= simple, unadorned) [dress, style, diet, food]* simple ; *(= in one colour) [fabric, suit, background, paper]* uni ; *[envelope]* ordinaire ◆ **~ white walls** murs *mpl* blancs unis ◆ **~ living** mode *m* de vie tout simple *or* sans luxe ◆ **I like good ~ cooking** j'aime la cuisine simple ◆ **don't worry about "Mr Furness-Gibbon", just call me "Simon"** ne vous embêtez pas avec "Monsieur Furness-Gibbon", appelez-moi "Simon" tout court ◆ **~ stitch** *(Knitting) (= one stitch)* maille *f* à l'endroit ; *(= technique)* point *m* mousse ◆ **one ~, one purl** *(Knitting)* une maille à l'endroit, une maille à l'envers ◆ **a row of ~, a ~ row** un rang à l'endroit ◆ **to send sth under ~ cover** envoyer qch sous pli discret ◆ **~ flour** farine *f (sans levure)* ◆ **~ yoghurt** yaourt *m* nature ◆ **~ chocolate** chocolat *m* à croquer ◆ **it's ~ sailing from now on** maintenant tout va marcher comme sur des roulettes
5 *(= not pretty)* quelconque, ordinaire *(pej)* ◆ **she's very ~** elle n'a rien d'une beauté, elle est tout à fait quelconque ◆ **she's rather a ~ Jane*** ce n'est pas une beauté
ADV 1 *(= clearly)* ◆ **I can't put it ~er than this** je ne peux pas m'exprimer plus clairement que cela *or* en termes plus explicites
2 *(* = simply)* tout bonnement ◆ **she's just ~ shy** elle est tout bonnement timide ◆ **it's (just) ~ wrong** c'est tout simplement faux ◆ **(just) ~ stupid** tout simplement idiot
N plaine *f* ◆ **the (Great) Plains** *(US)* les Prairies *fpl*, la Grande Prairie
COMP **plain clothes** NPL ◆ **in ~ clothes** en civil
plain-clothes ADJ ◆ **a ~-clothes policeman** un policier en civil ◆ **~-clothes officers** *(Police)* personnel *m* en civil
plain-spoken ADJ qui a son franc-parler, qui appelle les choses par leur nom

plainchant /'pleɪntʃɑːnt/ N plain-chant *m*

plainly /'pleɪnlɪ/ ADV 1 *(= obviously)* manifestement ◆ **there has ~ been a mistake** il y a manifestement erreur, il est clair qu'il y a erreur ◆ **~, these new techniques are a great improvement** à l'évidence, ces nouvelles techniques représentent un grand progrès 2 *(= unambiguously, distinctly) [speak, explain]* clairement ; *[see, hear]* distinctement ◆ **~ visible** bien visible 3 *(= simply) [dressed, furnished]* simplement, sans recherche

plainness /'pleɪnnɪs/ N 1 *(= simplicity) [of food, décor, dress, language]* simplicité *f*, sobriété *f* 2 *(= lack of beauty)* manque *m* de beauté

plainsman /'pleɪnzmən/ N (pl **-men**) habitant *m* de la plaine

plainsong /'pleɪnsɒŋ/ N ⇒ **plainchant**

plaint /pleɪnt/ N *(liter)* plainte *f*

plaintiff /'pleɪntɪf/ N *(Jur)* demandeur *m*, -deresse *f*, plaignant(e) *m(f)*

plaintive /'pleɪntɪv/ ADJ *[voice, cry, question, expression]* plaintif

plaintively /'pleɪntɪvlɪ/ ADV *[ask, say]* plaintivement, d'un ton plaintif ; *[howl, whine, meow]* plaintivement

plait /plæt/ N *(esp Brit) [of hair]* natte *f*, tresse *f* ◆ **she wears her hair in ~s** elle porte des tresses VT *(esp Brit) [+ hair, string]* natter, tresser ; *[+ basket, wicker]* tresser ; *[+ straw]* ourdir

plan /plæn/ LANGUAGE IN USE 8
N 1 *(= drawing, map) [of building, estate, district etc]* plan *m* ; → **seating**
2 *(= project, intention)* plan *m*, projet *m* ◆ **her ~ for union reform** son plan *or* projet de réforme syndicale ◆ **~ of action** plan *m* d'action ◆ **~ of campaign** plan *m* de campagne ◆ **development ~** plan *m or* projet *m* de développement ◆ **to draw up a ~** dresser un plan ◆ **everything is going according to ~** tout se passe selon les prévisions *or* comme prévu ◆ **to make ~s** faire des projets ◆ **to upset** *or* **spoil sb's ~s** déranger les projets de qn ◆ **to change one's ~s** changer d'idée, prendre d'autres dispositions ◆ **the best ~ would be to leave tomorrow** le mieux serait de partir demain ◆ **the ~ is to come back here after the show** notre idée est *or* nous prévoyons de revenir ici après le

spectacle ◆ **what ~s do you have for the holidays/for your retirement?** quels sont vos projets pour les vacances/pour votre retraite ? ◆ **I haven't any particular ~s** je n'ai aucun projet précis ◆ **have you got any ~s for tonight?** est-ce que vous avez prévu quelque chose pour ce soir ? ◆ **there are ~s to modernize the building** on projette de moderniser l'immeuble ◆ **the government said they had no ~s to increase taxes** le gouvernement a dit qu'il n'avait pas l'intention d'augmenter les impôts

VT 1 *[+ research, project, enterprise] (= devise and work out)* élaborer, préparer ; *(= devise and schedule)* planifier ◆ **to ~ the future of an industry** planifier l'avenir d'une industrie ; see also **planned** ; → **obsolescence**

2 *(= make plans for) [+ house, estate, garden etc]* concevoir, dresser les plans de ; *[+ programme, holiday, journey, crime]* préparer à l'avance, organiser ; *[+ essay]* faire le plan de ; *(Mil) [+ campaign, attack]* organiser ◆ **who ~ned the house/garden?** qui a dressé les plans de la maison/du jardin ? ◆ **a well-~ned house** une maison bien conçue ◆ **to ~ one's day** organiser sa journée ◆ **they ~ned the attack together** ils ont concerté l'attaque ◆ **he has got it all ~ned** il a tout prévu, il a pensé à tout ◆ **that wasn't ~ned** cela n'était pas prévu ◆ **we shall go on as ~ned** nous continuerons comme prévu ◆ **couples can now ~ their families** les couples peuvent maintenant choisir quand avoir des enfants ; see also **planned**

3 *(= intend) [+ visit, holiday]* projeter ◆ **to ~ to do sth, to ~ on doing sth** projeter de *or* avoir l'intention de faire qch ◆ **how long do you ~ to be away (for)?** combien de temps avez-vous l'intention de vous absenter *or* pensez-vous être absent ? ◆ **will you stay for a while? – I wasn't ~ning to** resterez-vous un peu ? – ce n'était pas dans mes intentions ◆ **she's ~ning a career in law** elle envisage une carrière de juriste

VI faire des projets ◆ **one has to ~ months ahead** il faut s'y prendre des mois à l'avance ◆ **we are ~ning for the future/the holidays** *etc* nous faisons des projets *or* nous prenons nos dispositions pour l'avenir/les vacances *etc* ◆ **we didn't ~ for** *or* **on such a large number of visitors** nous n'avions pas prévu un si grand nombre de visiteurs

► **plan on VT FUS** 1 *(= intend)* ◆ **to plan on (taking) a trip** avoir l'intention de partir en voyage ◆ **I'm ~ning on a hot bath and an early night** j'ai l'intention de prendre un bain bien chaud et d'aller me coucher tôt ◆ **to ~ on doing sth** avoir l'intention de faire qch, compter faire qch ◆ **she ~s on staying in London** elle a l'intention de *or* elle compte rester à Londres

2 *(= foresee, reckon with)* prévoir ◆ **he hadn't ~ned on the bad weather** il n'avait pas prévu qu'il ferait mauvais temps ◆ **I hadn't ~ned on being paid for my help** je n'avais pas prévu d'être dédommagé, je n'escomptais pas être dédommagé

► **plan out VT SEP** préparer *or* organiser dans tous les détails

planchette /plɑːnˈʃet/ **N** planchette *f (spiritisme)*

plane[1] /pleɪn/ **N** (abbrev of **aeroplane** *or* **airplane**) avion *m* ◆ **by ~** par avion

COMP **plane crash** **N** accident *m* d'avion
plane journey **N** voyage *m* en avion
plane ticket **N** billet *m* d'avion

plane[2] /pleɪn/ *(Carpentry)* **N** rabot *m* **VT** (also **plane down**) raboter

plane[3] /pleɪn/ **N** (also **plane tree**) platane *m*

plane[4] /pleɪn/ **N** *(Archit, Art, Math, fig)* plan *m* ◆ **horizontal ~** plan *m* horizontal ◆ **the physical/spiritual ~** le plan physique/spirituel ◆ **a higher ~ of consciousness** un niveau de conscience supérieur ◆ **he seems to exist on another ~ altogether** il semble vivre dans un autre monde *or* univers **ADJ** *(gen, Math)* plan ◆ **~ geometry** géométrie *f* plane

plane[5] /pleɪn/ **VI** *[bird, glider, boat]* planer ; *[car]* faire de l'aquaplanage

► **plane down VI** *[bird, glider]* descendre en vol plané

planeload /ˈpleɪnləʊd/ **N** ◆ **~s of tourists, tourists by the ~** des cargaisons *fpl* de touristes

planet /ˈplænɪt/ **N** planète *f* ◆ **the ~ Mars/Venus** la planète Mars/Vénus ◆ **what ~ is he/she on?** * sur quelle planète est-il/elle ?

planetarium /ˌplænɪˈtɛərɪəm/ **N** (pl **planetariums** *or* **planetaria** /ˌplænɪˈtɛərɪə/) planétarium *m*

planetary /ˈplænɪtərɪ/ **ADJ** planétaire

planetology /ˌplænɪˈtɒlədʒɪ/ **N** planétologie *f*

plangent /ˈplændʒənt/ **ADJ** *(liter)* retentissant

planisphere /ˈplænɪsfɪəʳ/ **N** *[of world]* planisphère *m* ; *[of stars]* planisphère *m* céleste

plank /plæŋk/ **N** planche *f* ; *(fig: of policy, argument)* article *m*, point *m* ◆ **to walk the ~** subir le supplice de la planche *(sur un bateau de pirates)* **VT** (*: also **plank down**) déposer brusquement, planter

planking /ˈplæŋkɪŋ/ **N** *(NonC)* planchéiage *m* ; *(Naut)* planches *fpl*, bordages *mpl*, revêtement *m*

plankton /ˈplæŋktən/ **N** *(NonC)* plancton *m*

planned /plænd/ **ADJ** 1 *(Econ, Pol, Ind, Comm = organized)* planifié ◆ **~ economy** économie *f* planifiée ◆ **~ parenthood** planning *m* familial, contrôle *m or* régulation *f* des naissances ◆ **~ pregnancies** grossesses *fpl* programmées 2 *(= premeditated) [crime etc]* prémédité 3 *(= proposed, intended)* prévu

planner /ˈplænəʳ/ **N** 1 (also **town planner**) urbaniste *mf* 2 *(Econ)* planificateur *m*, -trice *f*

planning /ˈplænɪŋ/ **N** 1 *(= organizing)* planification *f* ◆ **forward ~** planification *f* à long terme ◆ **we must do some ~ for the holidays** on va devoir organiser nos vacances ◆ **financial ~** *(in company, administration)* gestion *f* prévisionnelle des dépenses 2 (also **town** *or* **urban planning**) urbanisme *m* ; → **family, town**

COMP **planning board, planning committee** **N** service *m or* bureau *m* de planification ; *(in local government)* ≃ service *m* de l'urbanisme
planning department **N** service *m* de l'urbanisme
planning permission **N** permis *m* de construire
planning stage **N** ◆ **it's still at the ~ stage** c'est encore à l'état d'ébauche

plant /plɑːnt/ **N** 1 *(Bot)* plante *f*

2 *(NonC) (= machinery, equipment)* matériel *m*, biens *mpl* d'équipement ; *(fixed)* installation *f* ; *(= equipment and buildings)* bâtiments *mpl* et matériel ◆ **the heating ~** l'installation *f* de chauffage ◆ **he had to hire the ~ to do it** il a dû louer le matériel *or* l'équipement pour le faire ◆ **heavy ~** engins *mpl* ◆ **"heavy plant crossing"** "sortie d'engins"

3 *(= factory)* usine *f*, fabrique *f* ◆ **a steel ~** une aciérie ; → **nuclear**

4 *(Theat * = stooge)* acolyte *m*, complice *mf* ; *(* = infiltrator, mole)* taupe * *f*, agent *m* infiltré

VT 1 *[+ seeds, plants, bulbs]* planter ; *[+ field etc]* planter *(with en)* ◆ **a field ~ed with wheat** un champ planté de *or* en blé

2 *(= place) [+ flag, stick etc]* planter, enfoncer ; *[+ bomb]* poser ; *[+ spy, informer]* introduire ◆ **he ~ed his chair next to hers** il a planté sa chaise à côté de la sienne ◆ **to ~ a kiss on sb's cheek** planter un baiser sur la joue de qn ◆ **he ~ed his fist in my guts** il m'a planté son poing dans le ventre ◆ **to ~ o.s. in front of sb/sth** se planter devant qn/qch ◆ **to ~ an idea in sb's mind** mettre une idée dans la tête de qn ◆ **to ~ doubts in sb's mind** semer le doute dans l'esprit de qn ◆ **to ~ drugs/evidence on sb** dissimuler de la drogue/des preuves sur qn (pour l'incriminer) ◆ **the drugs were ~ed!** quelqu'un a dissimulé la drogue dans mes *(or* ses *etc)* affaires !

COMP **plant breeder** **N** phytogénéticien(ne) *m(f)*
plant food **N** engrais *m*
plant-hire firm **N** *(hiring equipment)* entreprise *f* de location de matériel industriel
the plant kingdom **N** le règne végétal
plant life **N** flore *f*
plant louse **N** puceron *m*
plant pot **N** pot *m* de fleurs

► **plant down VT SEP** planter, camper

► **plant out VT SEP** *[+ seedlings]* repiquer

Plantagenet /plænˈtædʒɪnɪt/ **N** Plantagenêt

plantain /ˈplæntɪn/ **N** 1 *(= plant)* plantain *m* 2 *(= fruit)* banane *f* plantain

plantar /ˈplæntəʳ/ **ADJ** plantaire

plantation /plænˈteɪʃən/ **N** *(all senses)* plantation *f* ◆ **coffee/rubber ~** plantation *f* de café/de caoutchouc

planter /ˈplɑːntəʳ/ **N** *(= person)* planteur *m* ; *(= machine)* planteuse *f* ; *(= plant pot)* pot *m* ; *(bigger, decorative)* jardinière *f* ◆ **coffee/rubber ~** planteur *m* de café/de caoutchouc

planting /ˈplɑːntɪŋ/ **N** plantations *fpl* ◆ **autumn ~** les plantations d'automne

plaque /plæk/ **N** 1 *(= plate)* plaque *f* 2 *(NonC: on teeth)* plaque *f* dentaire

plash /plæʃ/ **N** *[of waves]* clapotis *m*, clapotement *m* ; *[of object falling into water]* floc *m* **VI** clapoter, faire floc *or* flac

plasm /ˈplæzəm/ **N** protoplasme *m*

plasma /ˈplæzmə/ **N** plasma *m* ; → **blood**

COMP **plasma screen** écran *m* plasma
plasma TV **N** téléviseur *m* plasma

plaster /ˈplɑːstəʳ/ **N** 1 *(Constr)* plâtre *m*

2 *(Med: for broken bones)* plâtre *m* ◆ **he had his leg in ~** il avait la jambe dans le plâtre *or* la jambe plâtrée

3 *(Brit Med:* also **adhesive** *or* **sticking plaster***)* sparadrap *m* ◆ **a (piece of) ~** un pansement adhésif ; → **mustard**

VT 1 *(Constr, Med)* plâtrer

2 *(fig = cover, stick)* couvrir *(with de)* ◆ **~ed with** couvert de ◆ **to ~ a wall with posters, to ~ posters over a wall** couvrir *or* tapisser un mur d'affiches ◆ **the story was ~ed * all over the front page/all over the newspapers** l'histoire s'étalait sur toute la première page/à la une de tous les journaux ◆ **his fringe was ~ed to his forehead** sa frange était plaquée sur son front ◆ **to ~ one's face with make-up** se maquiller outrageusement

3 *(* = bash up)* tabasser *, battre comme plâtre *

COMP *[model, figure, moulding]* de *or* en plâtre
plaster cast **N** *(Med)* plâtre *m* ; *(Sculp)* moule *m* (en plâtre)
plaster of Paris **N** plâtre *m* à mouler
plaster work **N** *(NonC: Constr)* plâtre(s) *m(pl)*

► **plaster down VT** ◆ **to plaster one's hair down** se plaquer les cheveux

► **plaster on** * **VT SEP** *[+ butter, hair cream, make-up etc]* étaler *or* mettre une couche épaisse de

► **plaster over, plaster up VT SEP** *[+ crack, hole]* boucher

plasterboard /ˈplɑːstəbɔːd/ **N** *(NonC)* Placoplâtre ® *m*

plastered /ˈplɑːstəd/ ADJ (✻ = drunk) beurré✻, bourré✻ ◆ **to get** ~ se soûler (la gueule✻)

plasterer /ˈplɑːstərəʳ/ N plâtrier *m*

plastering /ˈplɑːstərɪŋ/ N *(Constr)* plâtrage *m*

plastic /ˈplæstɪk/ N 1 *(= substance)* plastique *m*, matière *f* plastique ◆ **~s** matières *fpl* plastiques

2 *(NonC: * = credit cards)* cartes *fpl* de crédit

ADJ 1 *(= made of plastic) [toy, box, dish]* en (matière) plastique ; see also **comp**

2 *(* : fig, pej) [food, coffee etc]* synthétique ◆ **actresses with ~ smiles** des actrices *fpl* aux sourires artificiels

3 *(Art)* plastique ; *(= flexible)* plastique, malléable

COMP **plastic bag** N sac *m* en plastique
plastic bomb N bombe *f* au plastic ◆ **~ bomb attack** attentat *m* au plastic, plasticage *m*
plastic bullet N balle *f* de plastique
plastic explosive N plastic *m*
plastic foam N mousse *f* de plastique
plastic money N carte(s) *f(pl)* de crédit
plastics industry N industrie *f* (des) plastique(s)
plastic surgeon N spécialiste *mf* de chirurgie esthétique
plastic surgery N chirurgie *f* esthétique
plastic wrap N *(US)* film *m* alimentaire

plasticated /ˈplæstɪˌkeɪtɪd/ ADJ *(lit)* plastifié ; *(fig)* synthétique, artificiel

Plasticine ® /ˈplæstɪsiːn/ N *(NonC)* pâte *f* à modeler

plasticity /plæsˈtɪsɪtɪ/ N plasticité *f*

Plate /pleɪt/ N ◆ **the River** ~ le Rio de la Plata

plate /pleɪt/ N 1 *(Culin)* assiette *f* ; *(= platter)* plat *m* ; *(in church)* plateau *m* de quête ◆ **a ~ of soup/sandwiches** une assiette de soupe/de sandwichs ◆ **to clean** *or* **to clear one's ~** nettoyer son assiette ◆ **to hand** *or* **give sth to sb on a ~*** *(fig)* apporter qch à qn sur un plateau ◆ **to have a lot** *or* **enough on one's ~*** *(things to do)* avoir déjà beaucoup à faire ; *(problems)* avoir déjà beaucoup de problèmes ◆ **he's got too much on his ~ already*** *(fig)* il ne sait déjà plus où donner de la tête ; → **dinner, soup, tea**

2 *(NonC, gold dishes)* orfèvrerie *f*, vaisselle *f* d'or ; *(silver dishes)* argenterie *f*, vaisselle *f* d'argent

3 *(= flat metal)* plaque *f* ; *(= metal coating)* placage *m* ; *(= coated metal)* plaqué *m* ◆ **it's not silver, it's only ~** ce n'est pas de l'argent massif, ce n'est que du plaqué

4 *(on wall, door, in battery, armour)* plaque *f* ; *(in car:* also **pressure plate**) plateau *m* d'embrayage ; *(on car:* also **number plate**) plaque *f* d'immatriculation, plaque *f* minéralogique ; → **clutch, hotplate, number**

5 *(Geol)* (also **tectonic plate**) plaque *f*

6 *(Phot)* plaque *f* ; *(Typ)* cliché *m* ; *(for engraving)* planche *f* ; *(= illustration: in book)* planche *f* ◆ **full-page ~** *(in book)* gravure *f* hors-texte, planche *f* ; → **fashion**

7 *(Dentistry:* also **dental plate**) dentier *m* ; *(Med: repairing fracture etc)* broche *f*

8 *(Racing = prize, race)* coupe *f*

9 *(for microscope)* lamelle *f*

VT 1 *(gen: with metal)* plaquer ; *(with gold)* dorer ; *(with silver)* argenter ; *(with nickel)* nickeler ; → **armour**

2 *[+ ship etc]* blinder

COMP **plate armour** N *(NonC)* blindage *m*
plate glass N *(NonC)* verre *m* à vitre
plate-glass window N baie *f* vitrée
plate rack N *(for drying)* égouttoir *m* ; *(for storing)* range-assiettes *m inv*
plate tectonics N *(NonC: Geol)* tectonique *f* des plaques
plate warmer N chauffe-assiette(s) *m*

plateau /ˈplætəʊ/ N (pl **plateaus** *or* **plateaux** /ˈplætəʊz/) *(Geog)* plateau *m* ; *(fig)* palier *m* VI atteindre un palier, se stabiliser

plateful /ˈpleɪtfʊl/ N assiettée *f*, assiette *f*

platelayer /ˈpleɪtˌleɪəʳ/ N *(Brit Rail)* poseur *m* de rails

platelet /ˈpleɪtlɪt/ N plaquette *f*

platen /ˈplætən/ N *[of printing press]* platine *f* ; *[of typewriter]* rouleau *m*

platform /ˈplætfɔːm/ N 1 *(on oil rig, bus, scales, in scaffolding etc)* plateforme *f* ; *(for band, in hall)* estrade *f* ; *(at meeting etc)* tribune *f* ; *(Rail)* quai *m* ◆ **~ (number) six** *(Rail)* quai *m* (numéro) six ◆ **he was on the ~ at the last meeting** il était sur l'estrade *or* il était à la tribune (d'honneur) lors de la dernière réunion ◆ **he campaigned on a socialist ~** il a adopté une plateforme socialiste pour sa campagne électorale ◆ **they campaigned on a ~ of national sovereignty** ils ont fait campagne sur le thème de la souveraineté de l'État ◆ **this gave him a ~ for his views** cela lui a fourni une tribune pour exprimer ses opinions ; → **diving**

2 **~s*** *(= shoes)* ⇒ **platform shoes**

COMP **the platform party** N *(at meeting)* la tribune
platform scales NPL (balance *f* à) bascule *f*
platform shoes, platform soles* NPL chaussures *fpl* à semelles compensées
platform ticket N *(Brit Rail)* billet *m* de quai

plating /ˈpleɪtɪŋ/ N 1 *(Metal)* placage *m* ◆ **tin-/copper-~** *etc* placage *m* (à l')étain/(au) cuivre *etc* ; → **chromium, silver** 2 *(Naut, Mil) [of ship]* bordé *m* ; *[of armoured vehicle]* blindage *m* ◆ **hull ~** bordé *m* ; → **armour**

platinum /ˈplætɪnəm/ N *(NonC)* platine *m*
COMP *[jewellery]* en *or* de platine
platinum-blond ADJ *[hair]* blond platiné *or* platine ; *[person]* (aux cheveux) blond platiné *or* platine
platinum blond(e) N blond(e) *m(f)* platiné(e) *or* platine
platinum disc N *(= award)* disque *m* de platine

platitude /ˈplætɪtjuːd/ N platitude *f*, lieu *m* commun

platitudinize /ˌplætɪˈtjuːdɪnaɪz/ VI débiter des platitudes *or* des lieux communs

platitudinous /ˌplætɪˈtjuːdɪnəs/ ADJ banal, d'une grande platitude, rebattu

Plato /ˈpleɪtəʊ/ N Platon *m*

Platonic /pləˈtɒnɪk/ ADJ 1 *[philosophy]* platonicien 2 ◆ **platonic** *[relationship, love]* platonique

Platonism /ˈpleɪtənɪzəm/ N platonisme *m*

Platonist /ˈpleɪtənɪst/ ADJ, N platonicien(ne) *m(f)*

platoon /pləˈtuːn/ N *(Mil)* section *f* ; *[of policemen, firemen etc]* peloton *m* COMP **platoon sergeant** N *(US Mil)* adjudant *m*

platter /ˈplætəʳ/ N 1 *(esp US = large dish)* plat *m* ◆ **on a (silver) ~** *(fig)* sur un plateau (d'argent) ◆ **she was handed it on a ~** *(fig)* on le lui a offert *or* apporté sur un plateau 2 *(= meal, course)* assiette *f* ◆ **seafood ~** assiette *f* de fruits de mer 3 *(US ✻ = record)* disque *m*

platypus /ˈplætɪpəs/ N ornithorynque *m*

plaudits /ˈplɔːdɪts/ NPL applaudissements *mpl*, acclamations *fpl*, ovations *fpl*

plausibility /ˌplɔːzəˈbɪlɪtɪ/ N *[of argument, excuse]* plausibilité *f* ; *[of person]* crédibilité *f* ◆ **her ~ as party leader** sa crédibilité en tant que chef du parti

plausible /ˈplɔːzəbl/ ADJ *[argument, excuse]* plausible, vraisemblable ; *[person]* convaincant

plausibly /ˈplɔːzəblɪ/ ADV de façon plausible

play /pleɪ/

1 NOUN
2 TRANSITIVE VERB
3 INTRANSITIVE VERB
4 COMPOUNDS
5 PHRASAL VERBS

1 - NOUN

1 gen, Sport, fig jeu *m* ◆ **there was some good ~ in the second half** on a assisté à du beau jeu pendant la deuxième mi-temps ◆ **that was a clever piece of ~** c'était finement *or* astucieusement joué ◆ **~ starts at 11 o'clock** le match commence à 11 heures ◆ **ball in ~** ballon *m or* balle *f* en jeu ◆ **ball out of ~** ballon *m or* balle *f* hors jeu ◆ **children learn through ~** les enfants apprennent par le jeu *or* en jouant ◆ **to say sth in ~** dire qch en plaisantant ◆ **the ~ of light on water** le jeu de la lumière sur l'eau

◆ **at play** *(children, animals)* en train de jouer ◆ **the different factors at ~** les divers facteurs qui entrent en jeu

◆ **to bring sth into play** mettre qch en œuvre

◆ **to call sth into play** faire entrer qch en jeu

◆ **to come into play** entrer en jeu

◆ **to make a play for sb** faire des avances à qn

◆ **to make a play for sth** s'efforcer d'obtenir qch

2 Tech, fig = movement jeu *m* ◆ **there's too much ~ in the clutch** il y a trop de jeu dans l'embrayage ◆ **to give full** *or* **free ~ to one's imagination/emotions** donner libre cours à son imagination/à ses sentiments ◆ **the ~ of different forces** le jeu des différentes forces ◆ **the free ~ of market forces** le libre jeu du marché ◆ **the ~ of ideas in the film is fascinating** l'interaction *f* des idées dans ce film est fascinante

3 Theat pièce *f* (de théâtre) ◆ **the ~s of Molière** les pièces *fpl or* le théâtre de Molière ◆ **radio ~** pièce *f* radiophonique ◆ **television ~** dramatique *f* ◆ **the ~ ends at 10.30** la pièce se termine à 22 h 30 ◆ **a ~ by Pinter, a Pinter ~** une pièce de Pinter ◆ **to be in a ~** *[actor]* jouer dans une pièce ◆ **the customs officers made (a) great ~ of examining our papers** *(Brit fig)* les douaniers ont examiné nos papiers en prenant un air important

2 - TRANSITIVE VERB

1 + game, sport jouer à ◆ **to ~ chess/bridge** jouer aux échecs/au bridge ◆ **to ~ football** jouer au football ◆ **will you ~ tennis with me?** voulez-vous faire une partie de tennis avec moi ? ◆ **to ~ a match against sb** disputer un match avec qn ◆ **the match will be ~ed on Saturday** le match aura lieu samedi ◆ **what position does she ~?** *(in hockey, football etc)* à quelle place joue-t-elle ? ◆ **to ~ centre-forward** *etc* jouer avant-centre *etc* ◆ **the boys were ~ing soldiers** les garçons jouaient aux soldats ◆ **the children were ~ing a game in the garden** les enfants jouaient dans le jardin ◆ **to ~ a game** *(board game etc)* jouer à un jeu ; *(of tennis etc)* faire une partie ; *(fig: trickery)* jouer *(fig)* ◆ **to ~ the ball** *(Ftbl)* jouer le ballon ◆ **to ~ ball with sb** *(fig)* coopérer avec qn ◆ **he won't ~ ball** *(fig)* il refuse de jouer le jeu ◆ **England will be ~ing Smith (in the team)** *(fig)* l'Angleterre a sélectionné Smith (pour jouer dans l'équipe)

◆ **to play the game** *(fig = play fair) (gen)* jouer le jeu ; *(in sports match, race etc)* jouer selon les règles

◆ **to play + games** *(fig)* se moquer du monde ◆ **don't ~ games with me!** ne vous moquez pas de moi ! ◆ **he accused me of ~ing games** il m'a accusé de me moquer du monde ◆ **he's just ~ing silly games** il n'est pas sérieux

♦ **to play the field** * papillonner ♦ **he gave up ~ing the field and married a year ago** il a cessé de papillonner et s'est marié il y a un an

2 [+ opponent, opposing team] jouer contre ♦ **England are ~ing Scotland on Saturday** l'Angleterre joue contre *or* rencontre l'Écosse samedi ♦ **I'll ~ you for the drinks** jouons la tournée

3 [= move] *[+ chess piece]* jouer ♦ **he ~ed the ball into the net** *(Tennis)* il a mis *or* envoyé la balle dans le filet

4 [Cards] ♦ **to ~ cards** jouer aux cartes ♦ **to ~ a card** jouer une carte ♦ **to ~ hearts/trumps** jouer cœur/atout ♦ **he ~ed a heart** il a joué (un) cœur ♦ **to ~ one's best/last card** *(fig)* jouer sa meilleure/dernière carte ♦ **to ~ one's cards well** *or* **right** bien jouer ♦ **he ~ed his ace** *(lit)* il a joué son as ; *(fig)* il a joué sa carte maîtresse

5 [Stock Exchange] ♦ **to ~ the market** jouer à la Bourse

6 [Theat *etc*] *[+ part]* jouer, interpréter ; *[+ play] [actors]* jouer ; *[director, producer, theatre]* présenter, donner ♦ **they ~ed it as a comedy** ils en ont donné une interprétation comique, ils l'ont joué comme une comédie ♦ **let's ~ it for laughs** * jouons-le en farce ♦ **we ~ed Brighton last week** nous avons joué à Brighton la semaine dernière ♦ **he ~ed (the part of) Macbeth** il a joué (le rôle de) Macbeth ♦ **what (part) did you ~ in "Macbeth"?** quel rôle jouiez-vous *or* interprétiez-vous dans "Macbeth" ? ♦ **he ~ed Macbeth as a well-meaning fool** il a fait de Macbeth un sot bien intentionné ♦ **to ~ one's part well** *(lit, fig)* bien jouer ♦ **he was only ~ing a part** il jouait la comédie ♦ **to ~ a part in sth** *[person]* prendre part à qch, contribuer à qch ; *[quality, object]* contribuer à qch ♦ **he ~ed no part in it** il n'y était pour rien ♦ **to ~ the peacemaker/the devoted husband** jouer les conciliateurs/les maris dévoués ♦ **to ~ it cautious** ne prendre aucun risque ♦ **to ~ it cool** * garder son sang-froid, ne pas s'énerver ♦ **to ~ (it) safe** ne prendre aucun risque ♦ **we could have ~ed it differently** nous aurions pu agir différemment

7 [Mus] *[+ instrument]* jouer de ; *[+ note, tune, concerto]* jouer ; *[+ record, CD]* passer, jouer * ♦ **to ~ the piano/the clarinet** jouer du piano/de la clarinette ♦ **they were ~ing Beethoven** ils jouaient du Beethoven

8 [= direct] *[+ hose, searchlight]* diriger *(on, onto* sur*)* ♦ **they ~ed the searchlights over the front of the building** ils ont promené les projecteurs sur la façade du bâtiment

3 - INTRANSITIVE VERB

1 [gen, Cards, Sport *etc*] jouer ; *[lambs, puppies, kittens]* s'ébattre, folâtrer ♦ **it's you** *or* **your turn to ~** c'est votre tour (de jouer) ♦ **is Paul coming out to ~?** est-ce que Paul vient jouer ? ♦ **what are you doing? – just ~ing** que faites-vous ? – rien, on joue *or* s'amuse ♦ **to ~ fair** *(Sport etc)* jouer franc jeu, jouer selon les règles ; *(fig)* jouer le jeu, être loyal ; → **fast¹, hard, dirty**

♦ **play** + *preposition* ♦ **England is ~ing against Scotland (in the semi-final)** l'Angleterre joue contre l'Écosse (en demi-finale) ♦ **to ~ at soldiers/chess/bridge** jouer aux soldats/aux échecs/au bridge ♦ **the little girl was ~ing at being a lady** la petite fille jouait à la dame ♦ **he just ~s at being a soldier** *(fig)* il ne prend pas au sérieux son métier de soldat ♦ **they're ~ing at happy families for the sake of the children** *(iro)* ils jouent les familles unies pour les enfants ♦ **what's he ~ing at?** * à quoi il joue ? ♦ **what do you think you're ~ing at!** * qu'est-ce que tu fabriques * ? ♦ **to ~ for money/matches** jouer de l'argent/des allumettes ♦ **he ~s for Manchester** il joue dans l'équipe de Manchester ♦ **to ~ for high stakes** *(lit, fig)* jouer gros (jeu) ♦ **to ~ for time** *(lit, fig)* essayer de gagner du temps ♦ **to ~ in defence/in goal** *(Sport)* jouer en défense/dans les buts ♦ **he ~ed into the trees** *(Golf = hit, shoot)* il a envoyé sa balle dans les arbres ♦ **she ~ed into the back of the net** *(Ftbl)* elle a envoyé le ballon au fond des filets ♦ **to ~ into sb's hands** *(fig)* faire le jeu de qn ♦ **to ~ to one's strengths** exploiter ses points forts ♦ **to ~ with** *[+ object, pencil, toy]* jouer avec ♦ **to ~ with o.s.** * *(euph)* se masturber ♦ **to ~ with fire/words** jouer avec le feu/les mots ♦ **how much time/money do we have to ~ with?** * combien de temps/d'argent avons-nous ? ♦ **it's not a question to be ~ed with** ce n'est pas une question qui se traite à la légère ♦ **he's not a man to be ~ed with** ce n'est pas un homme avec qui on plaisante ♦ **he's just ~ing with you** il te fait marcher ♦ **to ~ with an idea** caresser une idée

2 [light, fountain] jouer *(on* sur*)* ♦ **a smile ~ed on** *or* **over his lips** un sourire s'ébauchait sur ses lèvres

3 [Mus] *[person, organ, orchestra]* jouer ♦ **to ~ on the piano** jouer du piano ♦ **will you ~ for us?** *(= perform)* voulez-vous nous jouer quelque chose ? ; *(= accompany)* voulez-vous nous accompagner ? ♦ **there was music ~ing** il y avait de la musique ♦ **a record was ~ing in the background** *(as background music)* un disque passait en fond sonore

4 [Theat, Cine = act] jouer ♦ **he ~ed in a film with Greta Garbo** il a joué dans un film avec Greta Garbo ♦ **we have ~ed all over the South** nous avons joué partout dans le Sud ♦ **the film now ~ing at the Odeon** le film qui passe actuellement à l'Odéon ♦ **to ~ dead** *(fig)* faire le mort

5 [= be received] être accueilli ♦ **how will these policies ~?** comment cette politique sera-t-elle accueillie ?

4 - COMPOUNDS

play box N coffre *m* à jouets
play-by-play ADJ *[account etc] (Sport)* suivi ; *(fig)* circonstancié
play clothes NPL vêtements *mpl* qui ne craignent rien *(pour jouer)*
Play-Doh ® N pâte *f* à modeler, Play-Doh ®
play-off N *(Sport) (after a tie)* ≈ match *m* de barrage *(départageant des concurrents à égalité)* ; *(US) (for championship)* match *m* de qualification (de coupe *or* de championnat)
play on words N jeu *m* de mots, calembour *m*
play park N terrain *m* de jeu
play reading N lecture *f* d'une pièce de théâtre

5 - PHRASAL VERBS

► **play about** VI 1 *[children etc]* jouer, s'amuser
2 *(= toy, fiddle)* jouer, s'amuser *(with* avec*)* ♦ **he was ~ing about with the gun when it went off** il s'amusait *or* jouait avec le fusil quand le coup est parti ♦ **stop ~ing about with that watch** arrête de tripoter cette montre, laisse cette montre tranquille ♦ **he's just ~ing about with you** * il te fait marcher, il se moque de toi

► **play along** VI *(fig)* ♦ **to play along with sb** entrer dans le jeu de qn
VT SEP *(fig)* ♦ **to ~ sb along** tenir qn en haleine

► **play around** VI 1 ♦ **to play around with an idea** retourner une idée dans sa tête
2 *(* = sleep around)* coucher à droite et à gauche
3 ⇒ **play about**

► **play back** VT SEP *[+ tape]* réécouter, repasser

► **play down** VT SEP *(= minimize importance of) [+ decision, effect]* minimiser ; *[+ situation, attitude]* dédramatiser ; *[+ opinion, dissent]* mettre une sourdine à ; *[+ language]* atténuer ; *[+ policy]* mettre en sourdine

► **play in** VT SEP 1 ♦ **to play o.s. in** *(esp Cricket)* s'habituer aux conditions de jeu ; *(fig)* s'acclimater
2 ♦ **the band played the procession in** le défilé entra au son de la fanfare

► **play off** VT SEP 1 *[+ person]* ♦ **to play off A against B** jouer A contre B (pour en tirer profit)
2 *(Sport)* **to ~ a match off** jouer la belle

► **play on** VT FUS *[+ sb's emotions, credulity, good nature]* jouer sur, miser sur ♦ **to ~ on words** jouer sur les mots ♦ **the noise began to ~ on her nerves** le bruit commençait à l'agacer *or* à lui taper sur les nerfs *

► **play out** VT SEP 1 ♦ **the band played the procession out** le cortège sortit au son de la fanfare
2 ♦ **to be played out** * *[person]* être éreinté * *or* vanné * ; *[argument]* être périmé, avoir fait son temps
3 *[+ fantasies, roles, scenes]* jouer

► **play over, play through** VT SEP *[+ piece of music]* jouer

► **play up** VI 1 *(Sport)* bien jouer ♦ **~ up!** † allez-y !
2 *(esp Brit * = give trouble)* **the engine is ~ing up** le moteur fait des siennes *or* ne tourne pas rond ♦ **his rheumatism/his leg is ~ing up** ses rhumatismes/sa jambe le tracasse(nt) ♦ **the children have been ~ing up all day** les enfants ont été insupportables *or* ont fait des leurs toute la journée
3 *(= curry favour)* **to ~ up to sb** * chercher à se faire bien voir de qn, faire de la lèche à qn *
VT SEP 1 *(esp Brit: * = give trouble to)* ♦ **his rheumatism/his leg is playing him up** ses rhumatismes/sa jambe le tracasse(nt) ♦ **that boy ~s his father up** ce garçon en fait voir à son père
2 *(= magnify importance of)* insister sur (l'importance de)

► **play upon** VT FUS ⇒ **play on**

playact /ˈpleɪækt/ VI *(lit)* jouer la comédie, faire du théâtre ; *(fig)* jouer la comédie, faire du cinéma *

playacting /ˈpleɪ,æktɪŋ/ N *(fig)* ♦ **it's only ~** c'est de la comédie *or* du cinéma *

playactor /ˈpleɪ,æktəʳ/ N *(fig)* ♦ **he's a ~** c'est un vrai comédien, il joue continuellement la comédie

playback /ˈpleɪbæk/ N *(Recording)* enregistrement *m* ; *(function)* (touche *f* de *or* position *f*) lecture *f*

playbill /ˈpleɪbɪl/ N affiche *f* (de théâtre) ♦ **Playbill** ® *(US Theat)* programme *m*

playboy /ˈpleɪbɔɪ/ N playboy *m*

player /ˈpleɪəʳ/ N 1 *(Sport)* joueur *m*, -euse *f* ♦ **football ~** joueur *m*, -euse *f* de football ♦ **he's a very good ~** il joue très bien, c'est un excellent joueur 2 *(Theat)* acteur *m*, -trice *f* 3 *(Mus)* musicien(ne) *m(f)*, exécutant(e) *m(f)* ♦ **flute ~** joueur *m*, -euse *f* de flûte, flûtiste *mf* ♦ **he's a good ~** c'est un bon musicien, il joue bien 4 *(esp Comm = party involved)* protagoniste *mf* ♦ **one of the main** *or* **major ~s in ...** un des principaux protagonistes de ... COMP **player piano** N piano *m* mécanique

playfellow † /ˈpleɪ,feləʊ/ N ⇒ **playmate**

playful /ˈpleɪfʊl/ ADJ *[mood, tone, remark]* badin, enjoué ; *[person]* enjoué, taquin ; *[child, puppy, etc]* espiègle ♦ **he's only being ~** il fait ça pour s'amuser, c'est de l'espièglerie

playfully /ˈpleɪfəlɪ/ ADV *[nudge, tickle]* par jeu ; *[remark, say]* en plaisantant ; *[joke]* d'un ton taquin

playfulness /ˈpleɪfʊlnɪs/ N *(gen)* caractère *m* badin *or* enjoué ; *[of person]* enjouement *m* ; *[of child, puppy etc]* espièglerie *f*

playgoer /ˈpleɪˌgəʊəʳ/ N amateur *m* de théâtre ♦ **he is a regular ~** il va régulièrement au théâtre

playground /ˈpleɪgraʊnd/ N cour *f* de récréation ♦ **a millionaires' ~** un terrain de jeu pour milliardaires

playgroup /ˈpleɪgruːp/ N ≈ garderie *f*

playhouse /ˈpleɪhaʊs/ N 1 *(Theat)* théâtre *m* 2 *(for children)* maison *f* (pliante)

playing /ˈpleɪɪŋ/ N *(NonC)* 1 *(Sport)* jeu *m* ♦ **there was some good ~ in the second half** il y a eu du beau jeu à la deuxième mi-temps 2 *(Mus)* interprétation *f* ♦ **the orchestra's ~ of the symphony was uninspired** l'orchestre manquait d'inspiration dans l'interprétation de la symphonie ♦ **there was some fine ~ in the violin concerto** il y a eu des passages bien joués dans le concerto pour violon
COMP **playing card** N carte *f* à jouer
playing field N terrain *m* de jeu *or* de sport

playlet /ˈpleɪlət/ N courte pièce *f* (de théâtre)

playlist /ˈpleɪlɪst/ N *(Rad, Mus)* playlist *f*

playmaker /ˈpleɪˌmeɪkəʳ/ N *(Ftbl)* meneur *m*, -euse *f* de jeu

playmate /ˈpleɪmeɪt/ N camarade *mf* de jeu, (petit) copain *m*, (petite) copine *f*

playpen /ˈpleɪpen/ N parc *m (pour bébés)*

playroom /ˈpleɪrʊm/ N salle *f* de jeux

playschool /ˈpleɪskuːl/ N ⇒ **playgroup**

playsuit /ˈpleɪsuːt/ N ensemble *m* short

plaything /ˈpleɪθɪŋ/ N *(lit, fig)* jouet *m*

playtime /ˈpleɪtaɪm/ N *(Scol)* récréation *f*

playwright /ˈpleɪraɪt/ N dramaturge *m*, auteur *m* dramatique

plaza /ˈplɑːzə/ N 1 *(= public square)* place *f*, grand-place *f* 2 *(US)* *(= motorway services)* aire *f* de service *(sur une autoroute)* ; *(= toll)* péage *m* (d'autoroute) 3 *(US: for parking etc)* aire *f* de stationnement

PLC, plc /piːelˈsiː/ N *(Brit)* (abbrev of **public limited company**) SARL *f* ♦ **Smith & Co. ~** Smith et Cie SARL

plea /pliː/ N 1 *(= entreaty)* appel *m* (*for* à), supplication *f* ♦ **to make a ~ for mercy** implorer la clémence
2 *(Jur)* *(= allegation)* argument *m* (*that* selon lequel) ; *(= answer, defence)* défense *f* (*that* selon laquelle) ♦ **to put forward** *or* **make a ~ of self-defence** plaider la légitime défense ♦ **to enter a ~ of guilty/not guilty** plaider coupable/non coupable
3 *(= excuse)* excuse *f* ♦ **on the ~ of ...** en alléguant ..., en invoquant ... ♦ **on the ~ that ...** en alléguant *or* en invoquant que ...
COMP **plea agreement, plea bargain** N *(Jur) accord entre le procureur et l'avocat de la défense pour revoir à la baisse les chefs d'inculpation*
plea-bargain VI *(Jur) négocier pour parvenir à un accord en vue de revoir à la baisse les chefs d'inculpation*
plea bargaining N *(Jur) négociations entre le procureur et l'avocat de la défense visant à revoir à la baisse les chefs d'inculpation*

pleached /ˈpliːtʃd/ ADJ *[tree]* taillé

plead /pliːd/ (pret, ptp **pleaded** *or* *(esp US and Scot)* **pled**) VI 1 ♦ **to ~ with sb to do sth** supplier *or* implorer qn de faire qch ♦ **he ~ed for help** il a imploré *or* supplié qu'on l'aide *subj* ♦ **he ~ed with them for help** il a imploré leur aide ♦ **to ~ for mercy** implorer la clémence ♦ **he ~ed for mercy for his brother** il a imploré la clémence pour son frère ♦ **to ~ for a scheme/programme** *etc* plaider pour un projet/un programme *etc*
2 *(Jur)* plaider (*for* pour, en faveur de ; *against* contre) ♦ **to ~ guilty/not guilty** plaider coupable/non coupable ♦ **how do you ~?** plaidez-vous coupable ou non coupable ?
VT 1 *(Jur etc = argue)* plaider ♦ **to ~ sb's case, to ~ sb's cause** *(Jur, fig)* plaider la cause de qn *(Jur, fig)*
2 *(= give as excuse)* alléguer, invoquer ; *(Jur)* plaider ♦ **to ~ ignorance** alléguer *or* invoquer son ignorance ♦ **he ~ed poverty as a reason for ...** il a invoqué la pauvreté pour expliquer ... ♦ **to ~ insanity** *(Jur)* plaider la démence ; → **fifth**

pleading /ˈpliːdɪŋ/ N 1 *(NonC)* prières *fpl* (*for sb* en faveur de qn), intercession *f* *(liter)* 2 *(Jur)* plaidoirie *f*, plaidoyer *m* ♦ **~s** conclusions *fpl* *(des parties)* ADJ implorant, suppliant

pleadingly /ˈpliːdɪŋlɪ/ ADV *[say]* d'un ton suppliant ; *[look at]* d'un air suppliant

pleasant /ˈpleznt/ LANGUAGE IN USE 7.3 ADJ 1 *(= pleasing)* *[house, town, surroundings, voice]* agréable ; *[smell, taste]* agréable, bon ; *[weather, summer]* agréable, beau (belle *f*) ; *[surprise]* agréable, bon ♦ **they had a ~ time** ils se sont bien amusés ♦ **they spent a ~ afternoon** ils ont passé un après-midi très agréable ♦ **it's very ~ here** on est bien ici ♦ **Barcombe is a ~ place** Barcombe est un endroit agréable ♦ **~ dreams!** fais de beaux rêves ! 2 *(= polite, genial)* aimable ♦ **try and be a bit more ~ to your sister** essaie d'être un peu plus aimable avec ta sœur ♦ **he was very ~ to** *or* **with us** il s'est montré très aimable avec nous ♦ **he has a ~ manner** il est (d'un abord) charmant

pleasantly /ˈplezntlɪ/ ADV *[behave, smile, answer]* aimablement ♦ **to be ~ surprised** être agréablement surpris ♦ **the weather was ~ warm/cool** il faisait une chaleur/fraîcheur agréable

pleasantness /ˈplezntnɪs/ N *[of person, manner, welcome]* amabilité *f* ; *[of place, house]* agrément *m*, attrait *m*, charme *m*

pleasantry /ˈplezntrɪ/ N 1 *(= joke)* plaisanterie *f* 2 ♦ **pleasantries** *(= polite remarks)* civilités *fpl*, propos *mpl* aimables ♦ **to exchange pleasantries** échanger des civilités

please /pliːz/ LANGUAGE IN USE 4, 21.1
ADV s'il vous (*or* te) plaît ♦ **yes ~** oui, merci ♦ **would you like some cheese? – yes ~** voulez-vous du fromage ? – volontiers *or* oui, merci ♦ **~ come in, come in ~** entrez, je vous prie ♦ **~ be seated** *(frm)* veuillez vous asseoir *(frm)* ♦ **~ do not smoke** *(on notice)* prière de ne pas fumer ; *(spoken)* ne fumez pas s'il vous plaît, je vous prie de ne pas fumer ♦ **~ let me know if I can help you** ne manquez pas de me faire savoir si je peux vous aider ♦ **may I suggest something? – ~ do!** puis-je faire une suggestion ? – je vous en prie ! ♦ **shall I tell him? – ~ do!** je le lui dis ? – mais oui bien sûr *or* mais oui allez-y ! * ♦ **~!** *(entreating)* s'il vous plaît ! ; *(protesting)* (ah non !) je vous en prie *or* s'il vous plaît ! ♦ **~ don't!** ne faites pas ça s'il vous plaît ! ♦ **~ let him be all right** *(in prayer)* mon Dieu, faites qu'il ne lui soit rien arrivé
VI 1 *(frm = think fit)* **I shall do as I ~** je ferai comme il me plaira *or* comme je veux ♦ **do as you ~!** faites comme vous voulez *or* comme bon vous semble ! ♦ **as you ~!** comme vous voulez !, à votre guise ! ♦ **you may take as many as you ~** vous pouvez en prendre autant qu'il vous plaira ♦ **if you ~** *(= please)* s'il vous plaît ♦ **he wanted £50 if you ~!** *(iro)* il voulait 50 livres, rien que ça *or* s'il vous plaît !
2 *(= satisfy, give pleasure)* plaire, faire plaisir ♦ **our aim is to ~** *(esp Comm)* nous ne cherchons qu'à satisfaire ♦ **he is very anxious to ~** il est très désireux de plaire ♦ **a gift that is sure to ~** un cadeau qui ne peut que faire plaisir *or* que plaire
VT 1 *(= give pleasure to)* plaire à, faire plaisir à ; *(= satisfy)* satisfaire, contenter ♦ **the gift ~d him** le cadeau lui a plu *or* lui a fait plaisir ♦ **I did it just to ~ you** je ne l'ai fait que pour te faire plaisir ♦ **that will ~ him** ça va lui faire plaisir, il va être content ♦ **he is easily ~d/hard to ~** il est facile/difficile à contenter *or* à satisfaire ♦ **there's no pleasing him** * il n'y a jamais moyen de le contenter *or* de le satisfaire ♦ **you can't ~ all (of) the people all (of) the time** on ne saurait contenter tout le monde ♦ **music that ~s the ear** musique *f* plaisante à l'oreille *or* qui flatte l'oreille ♦ **it ~d him to** *or* **he was ~d to refuse permission** *(frm)* il a trouvé bon de ne pas consentir
2 ♦ **to ~ oneself** faire comme on veut ♦ **~ yourself!** comme vous voulez !, à votre guise ! ♦ **you must ~ yourself whether you do it or not** c'est à vous de décider si vous voulez le faire ou non ♦ **~ God he comes!** *(liter)* plaise à Dieu qu'il vienne !

pleased /pliːzd/ ADJ content, heureux (*with* de) ♦ **as ~ as Punch** * heureux comme un roi, aux anges ♦ **he looked very ~ at the news** la nouvelle a eu l'air de lui faire grand plaisir ♦ **he was ~ to hear that ...** il a été heureux *or* content d'apprendre que ... ♦ **~ to meet you!** * enchanté ! ♦ **I am ~ that you can come** je suis heureux *or* content que vous puissiez venir ♦ **we are ~ to inform you that ...** *(frm)* nous avons le plaisir de *or* l'honneur de vous faire savoir que ... ♦ **to be ~ with o.s./sb/sth** *(more frm)* être content de soi/qn/qch ♦ **they were anything but ~ with the decision** la décision était loin de leur faire plaisir ; → **graciously**

pleasing /ˈpliːzɪŋ/ ADJ *[personality, climate]* agréable ♦ **he creates a ~ effect with this border of pot plants** il crée un joli effet avec cette bordure de pots de fleurs ♦ **it's ~ to see some people have a conscience** ça fait plaisir de voir qu'il y a des gens qui ont une conscience ♦ **she has made ~ progress this term** elle a fait des progrès satisfaisants ce trimestre ♦ **it was very ~ to him** cela lui a fait grand plaisir

pleasingly /ˈpliːzɪŋlɪ/ ADV agréablement ♦ **the interior design is ~ simple** la décoration (intérieure) est d'une simplicité agréable ♦ **~ furnished with natural materials** décoré avec bonheur de matériaux naturels

pleasurable /ˈpleʒərəbl/ ADJ (très) agréable

pleasurably /ˈpleʒərəblɪ/ ADV *(with vb)* avec plaisir ; *(with adj)* agréablement

pleasure /ˈpleʒəʳ/ LANGUAGE IN USE 3.2, 7.2, 11.3, 20.2, 25.1
N 1 *(NonC = enjoyment, satisfaction)* plaisir *m* ♦ **to do sth for ~** faire qch pour le plaisir ♦ **sexual ~** plaisir *m* (sexuel) ♦ **toys which can give children hours of ~** des jouets avec lesquels les enfants peuvent s'amuser pendant des heures ♦ **has he gone to Paris on business or for ~?** est-il allé à Paris pour affaires ou pour son plaisir ? ♦ **to get ~ from** *or* **out of doing sth** prendre plaisir à faire qch ♦ **he gets a lot of ~ out of his hobby** son passe-temps lui apporte beaucoup de plaisir ♦ **I no longer get much ~ from my work** mon travail ne me plaît plus vraiment ♦ **if it gives you any ~** si ça peut vous faire plaisir ♦ **it gave me much ~ to hear that ...** *(frm)* cela m'a fait grand plaisir d'apprendre que ... ♦ **to take great ~ in doing sth** prendre beaucoup de plaisir à faire qch ♦ **he finds** *or* **takes great ~ in reading/music** il prend beaucoup de plaisir à lire/écouter de la musique ♦ **she takes ~ in the simple things in life** elle apprécie les choses simples ♦ **they took great ~ in his success** ils se sont réjouis de son succès ♦ **it takes all the ~ out of it** ça vous gâche le plaisir ♦ **to listen/read/remember** *etc* **with ~** écouter/lire/se rappeler *etc* avec plaisir
2 *(= source of enjoyment)* plaisir *m* ♦ **one of my greatest ~s** un de mes plus grands plaisirs, une de mes plus grandes joies ♦ **she has very few ~s in life** elle a très peu de plaisirs dans la vie ♦ **it's her only real ~ in life** c'est son seul

véritable plaisir dans la vie ◆ **the film was a ~ to watch** j'ai eu beaucoup de plaisir à regarder ce film ◆ **the book was a ~ to read** c'était un plaisir que de lire ce livre ◆ **the children's singing was a ~ to hear** c'était un plaisir que d'écouter les enfants chanter ◆ **it's always a ~ talking to her** *or* **to talk to her, she's always a ~ to talk to** c'est toujours un plaisir (que) de parler avec elle ◆ **it's a ~ to work with him, he's a ~ to work with** c'est un plaisir (que) de travailler avec lui

3 *(in polite phrases)* **it's a ~!, my ~!*, the ~ is mine!** je vous en prie ! ◆ **it's a ~ to see you again!** quel plaisir de vous revoir ! ◆ **it has been a ~ meeting you** *or* **to meet you** j'ai été enchanté de vous rencontrer ◆ **with ~** *(= willingly) [do, agree, help]* avec plaisir, volontiers ◆ **would you care to join us? – with ~!** voudriez-vous vous joindre à nous ? – avec plaisir *or* volontiers ! ◆ **would you mind helping me with this? – with ~!** pourriez-vous m'aider ? – avec plaisir *or* volontiers ! ◆ **may I have the ~?** *(frm: at dance)* voulez-vous m'accorder cette danse ? ◆ **may we have the ~ of your company at dinner?** *(frm)* voulez-vous nous faire le plaisir de dîner avec nous ? ◆ **I don't think I've had the ~** *(frm)* je ne crois pas que nous nous soyions déjà rencontrés ◆ **I have ~ in accepting ...** *(frm)* j'ai l'honneur d'accepter ... ◆ **it is my very great ~ to introduce to you ...** *(frm)* j'ai l'honneur de vous présenter ... ◆ **Mrs Torrance requests the ~ of Mr Simmonds's company at dinner** *(frm)* Mme Torrance prie M. Simmonds de lui faire l'honneur de venir dîner ◆ **Mr and Mrs Brewis request the ~ of your company at the marriage of their daughter Katherine** *(frm)* M. et Mme Brewis sont heureux de vous faire part du mariage de leur fille Katherine et vous prient d'assister à la bénédiction nuptiale

4 *(NonC = will, desire)* bon plaisir *m*, volonté *f* ◆ **at ~** à volonté ◆ **at your ~** à votre gré ◆ **at** *or* **during His** *or* **Her Majesty's ~** *(Jur)* aussi longtemps qu'il plaira à Sa Majesté ◆ **we await your ~** *(Comm)* nous sommes à votre entière disposition

VT *[give sexual pleasure to]* faire jouir ◆ **to ~ o.s.** se masturber

COMP **pleasure boat** N bateau *m* de plaisance
pleasure craft NPL bateaux *mpl* de plaisance
pleasure cruise N croisière *f* ; *(short)* promenade *f* en mer *or* en bateau
pleasure-loving ADJ qui aime le(s) plaisir(s)
the pleasure principle N *(Psych)* le principe de plaisir
pleasure-seeker N hédoniste *mf*
pleasure-seeking ADJ hédoniste
pleasure steamer N vapeur *m* de plaisance
pleasure trip N excursion *f*

pleat /pliːt/ N pli *m* VT plisser

pleb* /pleb/ N *(Brit pej)* prolo *mf** ◆ **the ~s** le peuple

plebe* /pliːb/ N *(US)* élève *mf* de première année *(d'une école militaire ou navale)*

plebeian /plɪ'biːən/ ADJ, N plébéien(ne) *m(f)*

plebiscite /'plebɪsɪt/ N plébiscite *m* ◆ **to hold a ~** faire un plébiscite

plectron /'plektrən/, **plectrum** /'plektrəm/ N (pl **plectrons** *or* **plectra** /'plektrə/) plectre *m*

pled* /pled/ VB *(esp US and Scot)* pt, ptp of **plead**

pledge /pledʒ/ N 1 *(= security, token: also in pawnshop)* gage *m* ◆ **as a ~ of his love** en gage *or* témoignage de son amour

2 *(= promise)* promesse *f*, engagement *m* ; *(= agreement)* pacte *m* ◆ **I give you this ~** je vous fais cette promesse ◆ **he made a ~ of secrecy** il a promis de *or* il s'est engagé à garder le secret ◆ **to be under a ~ of secrecy** avoir promis de ne rien dire ◆ **it was told me under a ~ of secrecy** on me l'a raconté contre la promesse de ne rien en dire ◆ **the government did not honour its ~ to cut taxes** le gouvernement n'a pas honoré son engagement *or* n'a pas tenu sa promesse de réduire les impôts ◆ **an election ~** une promesse électorale ◆ **a ~ on pay rises** un engagement concernant les augmentations de salaires ◆ **the countries signed a ~ to help each other** les pays ont signé un pacte d'aide mutuelle ◆ **to sign** *or* **take the ~** faire vœu de tempérance

3 *(US Univ) (= promise) promesse d'entrer dans une confrérie ; (= student) étudiant(e) qui accomplit une période d'essai avant d'entrer dans une confrérie*

4 *(= toast)* toast *m (to* à)

COMP **Pledge of Allegiance** N *(US)* Serment *m* d'allégeance

VT 1 *(= pawn)* engager, mettre en gage

2 *(= promise) [+ one's help, support, allegiance]* promettre ◆ **to ~ (o.s.) to do sth** *(gen)* promettre de faire qch, s'engager à faire qch ; *(solemnly)* faire vœu de faire qch ◆ **to ~ sb to secrecy** faire promettre le secret à qn ◆ **he is ~d to secrecy** il a promis de garder le secret ◆ **to ~ one's word (that ...)** donner sa parole (que ...) ◆ **they ~d that there would be no tax increases** ils ont promis qu'il n'y aurait pas d'augmentation des impôts

3 *(US Univ: into fraternity)* coopter ◆ **to be ~d to a fraternity** *accomplir une période d'essai avant d'entrer dans une confrérie*

4 *(= toast)* boire à la santé de

PLEDGE OF ALLEGIANCE

Le Serment d'allégeance (**Pledge of Allegiance**) date de 1892 ; il est prononcé chaque jour par les élèves des écoles primaires américaines, qui, debout devant le drapeau des États-Unis, la main sur le cœur, proclament : « Je jure allégeance au drapeau des États-Unis d'Amérique et à la république qu'il représente, une nation placée sous la protection de Dieu, indivisible et garantissant liberté et justice pour tous ».

Pleiades /'plaɪədiːz/ NPL Pléiades *fpl*

Pleistocene /'plaɪstəsiːn/ ADJ, N pléistocène *m*

plena /'pleːnə/ NPL of **plenum**

plenary /'pliːnərɪ/ ADJ *[power]* absolu ; *[assembly]* plénier ; *(Rel)* plénier ◆ **(in) ~ session** (en) séance plénière ◆ **~ meeting** réunion *f* plénière, plenum *m* N (also **plenary session**) séance *f* plénière, plenum *m*

plenipotentiary /ˌplenɪpə'tenʃərɪ/ ADJ, N plénipotentiaire *mf* ◆ **ambassador ~** ambassadeur *m* plénipotentiaire

plenitude /'plenɪtjuːd/ N *(liter)* plénitude *f*

plenteous /'plentɪəs/, **plentiful** /'plentɪfʊl/ ADJ *[harvest, food]* abondant ; *[meal, amount]* copieux ◆ **construction jobs are ~** les emplois ne manquent pas dans le secteur du bâtiment ◆ **a ~ supply of** une abondance *or* une profusion de

plentifully /'plentɪfəlɪ/ ADV abondamment

plenty /'plentɪ/ N 1 *(NonC = abundance)* abondance *f* ◆ **it grows here in ~** cela pousse en abondance *or* à foison ici ◆ **he had friends in ~** il ne manquait pas d'amis ◆ **to live in ~** vivre dans l'abondance ◆ **land of ~** pays *m* de cocagne ; → **horn**

2 ◆ **I've got ~** j'en ai bien assez ◆ **I've got ~ to do** j'ai largement de quoi m'occuper ◆ **~ of** (bien) assez de ◆ **he's got ~ of friends** il ne manque pas d'amis ◆ **he's got ~ of money** il n'est pas pauvre ◆ **ten is ~** dix suffisent (largement *or* amplement) ◆ **that's ~** ça suffit (amplement) ◆ **there's ~ to go on** *(clues etc)* nous avons toutes les données nécessaires pour le moment

ADJ *(‡ or dial)* ⇒ **plenty of** → **noun 2**

ADV * assez ◆ **it's ~ big enough!** c'est bien assez grand ! ◆ **it sure rained ~!** *(US)* qu'est-ce qu'il est tombé !*

plenum /'pliːnəm/ N (pl **plenums** *or* **plena**) plenum *m*, réunion *f* plénière

pleonasm /'pliːənæzəm/ N pléonasme *m*

pleonastic /pliːə'næstɪk/ ADJ pléonastique

plethora /'pleθərə/ N pléthore *f*, surabondance *f (of* de) ; *(Med)* pléthore *f*

plethoric /ple'θɒrɪk/ ADJ pléthorique

pleura /'plʊərə/ N (pl **pleurae** /'plʊəriː/) plèvre *f*

pleurisy /'plʊərɪsɪ/ N *(NonC)* pleurésie *f* ◆ **to have ~** avoir une pleurésie

pleuritic /plʊə'rɪtɪk/ ADJ pleurétique

Plexiglas ® /'pleksɪglɑːs/ N *(US)* plexiglas ® *m*

plexus /'pleksəs/ N (pl **plexuses** *or* **plexus**) plexus *m* ; → **solar**

pliability /ˌplaɪə'bɪlɪtɪ/ N 1 *[of material]* flexibilité *f* 2 *[of character, person]* malléabilité *f*

pliable /'plaɪəbl/, **pliant** /'plaɪənt/ ADJ *[material]* flexible ; *[character, person]* malléable

pliers /'plaɪəz/ NPL (also **pair of pliers**) pince(s) *f(pl)*, tenaille(s) *f(pl)*

plight¹ /plaɪt/ N situation *f* critique, état *m* critique ◆ **the country's economic ~** la crise *or* les difficultés *fpl* économique(s) du pays ◆ **in a sad** *or* **sorry ~** dans un triste état ◆ **what a dreadful ~ (to be in)!** quelles circonstances désespérées !, quelle situation lamentable !

plight² †† /plaɪt/ VT *(liter)* ◆ **to ~ one's word** engager sa parole ◆ **to ~ one's troth** *(also hum)* engager sa foi †, se fiancer

plimsoll /'plɪmsəl/ N *(Brit)* chausson *m* de gym(nastique) COMP **Plimsoll line, Plimsoll mark** N *(Naut)* ligne *f* de flottaison en charge

plink /plɪŋk/ *(US)* VI 1 *(= sound)* tinter 2 *(= shoot)* canarder* VT 1 *(= sound)* faire tinter 2 *(= shoot at)* canarder*

plinth /plɪnθ/ N *[of column, pedestal]* plinthe *f* ; *[of statue, record player]* socle *m*

Pliny /'plɪnɪ/ N Pline *m*

Pliocene /'plaɪəʊsiːn/ ADJ, N pliocène *m*

PLO /piːel'əʊ/ N (abbrev of **Palestine Liberation Organization**) OLP *f*

plod /plɒd/ VI 1 *(= trudge)* (also **plod along**) avancer d'un pas lourd *or* pesant ◆ **to ~ in/out** *etc* entrer/sortir *etc* d'un pas lourd *or* pesant

2 * **he was ~ding through his maths** il bûchait* ses maths ◆ **I'm ~ding through his book** je lis son livre mais c'est laborieux ◆ **I've already ~ded through 900 pages of this!** je me suis déjà tapé* 900 pages de ce pavé !

VT ◆ **we ~ded the streets for another hour** nous avons continué à errer dans la rue pendant une heure

N 1 *(= trudge)* ◆ **they went at a steady ~** ils marchaient pesamment, d'un pas égal ◆ **I heard the ~ of his footsteps behind me** j'entendais son pas lourd derrière moi

2 *(‡ = policeman)* poulet* *m* ◆ **PC Plod, Policeman Plod** *agent de police*

► **plod along** VI → **plod vi 1**

► **plod on** VI *(lit)* continuer *or* poursuivre son chemin ; *(fig)* persévérer *or* perséverer (laborieusement)

plodder /'plɒdəʳ/ N travailleur *m*, -euse *f* assidu(e), bûcheur* *m*, -euse* *f*

plodding /'plɒdɪŋ/ ADJ *[step]* lourd, pesant ; *[student, worker]* bûcheur

plonk /plɒŋk/ N *(esp Brit)* 1 *(= sound)* plouf *m*, floc *m* 2 *(* = cheap wine)* vin *m* ordinaire, pinard‡ *m* ADV *(esp Brit)* ◆ **it fell ~ in the middle of the table** * c'est tombé au beau milieu de la table VT *(esp Brit *: also* **plonk down**) poser (bruyamment) ◆ **he ~ed the book (down) on**

to the table il a posé (bruyamment) *or* a flanqué* le livre sur la table ◆ **he ~ed himself (down) into the chair** il s'est laissé tomber dans le fauteuil

plonker⁎ /ˈplɒŋkəʳ/ **N** *(Brit)* imbécile* *mf*, con⁎ *m*

plop /plɒp/ **N** ploc *m*, floc *m* **ADV** ◆ **it went ~ into the water** * c'est tombé dans l'eau (en faisant ploc *or* floc) **VI** *[stone]* faire ploc *or* floc ; *[single drop]* faire floc ; *[raindrops]* faire flic flac ◆ **to ~ down*** *[person]* s'asseoir lourdement, s'affaler **VT** ◆ **to ~ o.s. down*** *[person]* s'asseoir lourdement, s'affaler

plosive /ˈpləʊsɪv/ *(Ling)* **ADJ** occlusif **N** consonne *f* occlusive

plot /plɒt/ **N** 1 *[of ground]* (lot *m* de) terrain *m*, lotissement *m* ◆ **~ of grass** gazon *m* ◆ **building ~** terrain *m* à bâtir ◆ **the vegetable ~** le coin des légumes 2 *(= plan, conspiracy)* complot *m*, conspiration *f* *(against* contre ; *to do sth* pour faire qch) 3 *(Literat, Theat)* intrigue *f*, action *f* ◆ **the ~ thickens** *(fig)* l'affaire *or* ça se corse ! ◆ **to lose the ~*** perdre l'objectif de vue **VT** 1 *(= mark out:* also **plot out**) *[+ course, route]* déterminer ; *[+ graph, curve, diagram]* tracer point par point ; *[+ progress, development]* faire le graphique de ; *[+ boundary, piece of land]* relever ◆ **to ~ one's position on the map** *(Naut)* pointer la carte 2 *[+ sb's death, ruin etc]* comploter ◆ **to ~ to do sth** comploter de faire qch **VI** *(= conspire)* comploter, conspirer *(against* contre)

plotless /ˈplɒtlɪs/ **ADJ** *(pej)* *[play, film etc]* sans intrigue

plotter¹ /ˈplɒtəʳ/ **N** *(= conspirator)* conspirateur *m*, -trice *f* ; *(against the government)* conjuré(e) *m(f)*

plotter² /ˈplɒtəʳ/ **N** *(Comput etc)* traceur *m* (de courbes)

plotting /ˈplɒtɪŋ/ **N** *(NonC)* complots *mpl*, conspirations *fpl* **COMP** **plotting board, plotting table** **N** *(Comput etc)* table *f* traçante

plotzed⁎ /plɒtst/ **ADJ** *(US = drunk)* bourré⁎, ivre

plough, plow *(US)* /plaʊ/ **N** *(Agr)* charrue *f* ◆ **the Plough** *(Astron)* la Grande Ourse, le Grand Chariot ; → **snowplough**

VT *(Agr) [+ field]* labourer ; *[+ furrow]* creuser, tracer ◆ **to ~ a lonely furrow** *(fig)* travailler dans son coin ◆ **she didn't want to ~ the same furrow as her brother** elle ne voulait pas suivre la même voie que son frère ◆ **to ~ money into sth** investir gros dans qch ◆ **we've ~ed millions into this project** nous avons investi des millions dans ce projet ◆ **to ~ one's way** → **vi 2**

VI 1 *(Agr)* labourer

2 *(fig:* also **plough one's** *or* **its way**) **to ~ through the mud/snow** avancer péniblement dans la boue/la neige ◆ **the ship ~ed through the waves** le bateau fendait les flots ◆ **the lorry ~ed into the wall** le camion est allé se jeter contre le mur ◆ **the car ~ed through the fence** la voiture a défoncé la barrière ◆ **to ~ through a book** lire laborieusement un livre ◆ **he was ~ing through his maths** il bûchait* ses maths

3 *(Brit* † * *= fail an exam) [candidate]* se faire recaler*, être recalé*

COMP **plough horse** **N** cheval *m* de labour *or* de trait

▸ **plough back** **VT SEP** *[+ profits]* réinvestir, reverser *(into* dans)

N ◆ **ploughing back** → **ploughing**

▸ **plough in** **VT SEP** 1 (also **plough under**) *[+ crops, grass]* recouvrir *or* enterrer en labourant

2 *[+ fertilizer]* enfouir en labourant

▸ **plough up** **VT SEP** 1 *[+ field, bushes, path, right of way]* labourer

2 *(fig = churn up)* **the tanks ~ed up the field** les tanks ont labouré *or* défoncé le champ

ploughing /ˈplaʊɪŋ/ **N** *(NonC)* labour *m* ; *[of field etc]* labourage *m* ◆ **the ~ back of profits** le réinvestissement des bénéfices

ploughland /ˈplaʊlænd/ **N** terre *f* de labour, terre *f* arable

ploughman /ˈplaʊmən/ **N** (pl **-men**) laboureur *m* **COMP** **ploughman's lunch** **N** *(Brit Culin)* assiette de fromage et de pickles

ploughshare /ˈplaʊʃɛəʳ/ **N** soc *m* (de charrue) ; → **sword**

plover /ˈplʌvəʳ/ **N** pluvier *m*

plow /plaʊ/ *(US)* ⇒ **plough**

ploy* /plɔɪ/ **N** stratagème *m*, truc* *m* *(to do sth* pour faire qch)

PLP /ˌpiːelˈpiː/ **N** *(Brit)* (abbrev of **Parliamentary Labour Party**) → **parliamentary**

PLR /ˌpiːelˈɑːʳ/ **N** *(Brit Admin)* (abbrev of **public lending right**) → **public**

pls (abbrev of **please**) SVP

pluck /plʌk/ **VT** *[+ fruit, flower]* cueillir ; *(Mus) [+ strings]* pincer ; *[+ guitar]* pincer les cordes de ; *(Culin) [+ bird]* plumer ◆ **to ~ one's eyebrows** s'épiler les sourcils ◆ **it's an idea/example I ~ed out of the air** c'est une idée/un exemple qui m'est venu(e) comme ça **N** 1 *(NonC:* * *= courage)* courage *m*, cran* *m* 2 *(NonC: Culin)* fressure *f* 3 *(= tug)* petit coup *m*

▸ **pluck at** **VT FUS** ◆ **to pluck at sb's sleeve** tirer qn doucement par la manche

▸ **pluck off** **VT SEP** *[+ feathers]* arracher ; *[+ fluff etc]* détacher, enlever

▸ **pluck out** **VT SEP** *(esp liter)* arracher

▸ **pluck up** **VT SEP** 1 *[+ weed]* arracher, extirper 2 *(= summon up)* ◆ **to pluck up courage** prendre son courage à deux mains ◆ **he ~ed up (the) courage to tell her** il a (enfin) trouvé le courage de *or* il s'est (enfin) décidé à le lui dire

pluckily* /ˈplʌkɪlɪ/ **ADV** courageusement, avec cran*

pluckiness* /ˈplʌkɪnɪs/ **N** *(NonC)* courage *m*, cran* *m*

plucky* /ˈplʌkɪ/ **ADJ** courageux, qui a du cran*

plug /plʌg/ **N** 1 *(for draining) [of bath, basin]* bonde *f*, vidange *f* ; *[of barrel]* bonde *f* ; *(to stop a leak)* tampon *m* ; *(= stopper)* bouchon *m* ; *(for fixing)* cheville *f* ; *(Geol: in volcano)* culot *m* ◆ **a ~ of cotton wool** un tampon de coton ◆ **to put in/pull out the ~** mettre/enlever *or* ôter la bonde ◆ **to pull the ~** *(in lavatory)* * tirer la chasse d'eau ◆ **to pull the ~ on**⁎ *(fig) [+ patient]* débrancher ; *[+ accomplice, wrongdoer]* exposer ; *[+ project etc]* laisser tomber* ; → **earplugs**

2 *(Elec) (on flex, apparatus)* prise *f* (de courant) *(mâle)* ; (* *= socket:* also **wall plug**) prise *f* (de courant) *(femelle)* ; *[of switchboard]* fiche *f* ; → **amp, fused, pin**

3 *(Aut:* also **sparking plug**) bougie *f*

4 *(US:* also **fire plug**) bouche *f* d'incendie

5 (* *= publicity)* publicité *f* ◆ **to give sth/sb a ~, to put in a ~ for sth/sb** donner un coup de pouce (publicitaire) à qch/qn, faire de la publicité pour qch/qn

6 *(of tobacco, for smoking)* carotte *f* ; *(for chewing)* chique *f*

VT 1 (also **plug up**) *[+ hole, crack]* boucher, obturer ; *[+ barrel, jar]* boucher ; *[+ leak]* colmater ; *(on boat)* aveugler ; *[+ tooth]* obturer *(with* avec) ◆ **to ~ the gap in the tax laws** mettre fin aux échappatoires en matière de fiscalité ◆ **to ~ the drain on gold reserves** arrêter l'hémorragie *or* la fuite des réserves d'or

2 ◆ **to ~ sth into a hole** enfoncer qch dans un trou ◆ **~ the TV into the wall** branchez le téléviseur (sur le secteur)

3 (* *= publicize) (on one occasion)* faire de la réclame *or* de la publicité pour ; *(repeatedly)* matraquer*

4 ⁎ *(= shoot)* flinguer⁎, ficher* *or* flanquer* une balle dans la peau à ; *(= punch)* ficher* *or* flanquer* un coup de poing à

COMP **plug-and-play** **ADJ** *(Comput)* prêt à l'emploi

plug hat **N** *(US)* (chapeau *m* en) tuyau *m* de poêle

plug-in **ADJ** *(Elec)* qui se branche sur le secteur

plug-ugly* **N** dur *m*, brute *f*

▸ **plug away*** **VI** bosser⁎, travailler dur *(at doing sth* pour faire qch) ◆ **he was ~ging away at his maths** il bûchait* ses maths

▸ **plug in** **VT SEP** *[+ lead, apparatus]* brancher **VI** se brancher ◆ **the TV ~s in over there** la télé se branche là-bas ◆ **does your radio ~ in?** est-ce que votre radio peut se brancher sur le secteur ?

ADJ ◆ **plug-in** → **plug**

▸ **plug into*** **VT FUS** *[+ ideas etc]* se brancher à l'écoute de*

▸ **plug up** **VT SEP** ⇒ **plug vt 1**

plughole /ˈplʌghəʊl/ **N** trou *m* (d'écoulement *or* de vidange), bonde *f*, vidange *f* ◆ **it went down the ~** *(lit)* c'est tombé dans le trou (du lavabo *or* de l'évier etc) ; *(fig) [idea, project]* c'est tombé à l'eau

plum /plʌm/ **N** 1 *(= fruit)* prune *f* ; (also **plum tree**) prunier *m* ◆ **to speak with** *or* **have a ~ in one's mouth** * *(Brit hum)* parler avec un accent snob 2 (* fig) *(= choice thing)* meilleur morceau *m* *(fig)*, meilleure part *f* *(fig)* *(= good job)* boulot* *m* en or **ADJ** 1 (also **plum-coloured**) prune *inv*, lie-de-vin *inv* 2 (* *= best, choice)* de choix, le plus chouette* ◆ **he got the ~ job** c'est lui qui a décroché le meilleur travail *or* le travail le plus chouette* ◆ **he has a ~ job** il a un boulot* en or

COMP **plum duff, plum pudding** **N** (plum-)pudding *m*

plum tomato **N** *(Culin)* olivette *f*

plumage /ˈpluːmɪdʒ/ **N** plumage *m*

plumb /plʌm/ **N** plomb *m* ◆ **out of ~** hors d'aplomb

ADJ vertical

ADV 1 en plein, exactement ◆ **~ in the middle of** en plein milieu de, au beau milieu de

2 *(esp US* *) complètement

VT 1 *(= descend to)* sonder ◆ **to ~ the depths** *(lit)* sonder les profondeurs ; *(fig)* toucher le fond ◆ **to ~ the depths of desperation/loneliness** toucher le fond du désespoir/de la solitude ◆ **to ~ the depths of stupidity/tastelessness/mediocrity** atteindre le comble de la stupidité/du mauvais goût/de la médiocrité ◆ **the film ~s the depths of sexism and racism** ce film est d'un sexisme et d'un racisme inimaginables ◆ **these terrorists have ~ed new depths** ces terroristes sont allés encore plus loin dans l'horreur ◆ **the pound ~ed new depths yesterday** la livre a atteint son niveau le plus bas hier

2 *(= connect plumbing in) [+ sink, washing machine]* installer la plomberie de

▸ **plumb in** **VT SEP** *[+ sink, washing machine etc]* faire le raccordement de ; *[+ gas fire]* brancher

plumbago /plʌmˈbeɪgəʊ/ **N** (pl **plumbagos**) 1 *(= graphite)* plombagine *f* 2 *(= plant)* plumbago *m*

plumber /ˈplʌməʳ/ **N** 1 plombier *m* 2 *(US* *) agent *m* de surveillance gouvernementale, plombier* *m*

COMP **plumber's mate** **N** aide-plombier *m*

plumber's merchant **N** grossiste *m* en plomberie

plumbic /ˈplʌmbɪk/ **ADJ** plombifère

plumbing /ˈplʌmɪŋ/ N (= trade) (travail m de) plomberie f ; (= system) plomberie f, tuyauterie f

plumbline /ˈplʌmlaɪn/ N (Constr etc) fil m à plomb ; (Naut) sonde f

plumcake /ˈplʌmkeɪk/ N (plum-)cake m

plume /pluːm/ N 1 (= large feather) (grande) plume f ; (= cluster of feathers) (on bird) plumes fpl, aigrette f ; (on hat, helmet) plumet m, aigrette f ; (larger) panache m ◆ **in borrowed ~s** portant des vêtements empruntés 2 (fig) [of smoke, dust] panache m ◆ **a ~ of water** un jet d'eau VT [bird] [+ wing, feather] lisser ◆ **the bird was pluming itself** l'oiseau se lissait les plumes ◆ **to ~ o.s. on sth** (fig) enorgueillir de qch

plumed /pluːmd/ ADJ [bird] à aigrette ; [helmet] à plumet

plummet /ˈplʌmɪt/ VI [price, sales, popularity] dégringoler, s'effondrer ; [amount, weight, numbers] baisser brusquement ; [temperature] baisser or descendre brusquement ; [spirits, morale] tomber à zéro ; [aircraft, bird] plonger N plomb m

plummy * /ˈplʌmɪ/ ADJ 1 (Brit) [accent, voice] snob 2 (= colour) prune inv, lie-de-vin inv

plump¹ /plʌmp/ ADJ [person] grassouillet, empâté ; [baby, child, hand] potelé ; [cheek, face] rebondi, plein ; [lips] charnu ; [arm, leg, chicken] dodu ; [cushion] rebondi, bien rembourré VT (also **plump up**) [+ pillow] tapoter

► **plump out** VI devenir rondelet, grossir

plump² /plʌmp/ VT (= drop) laisser tomber lourdement, flanquer * VI tomber lourdement ADV 1 en plein, exactement ◆ **~ in the middle of** en plein milieu de, au beau milieu de 2 (= in plain words) carrément, sans mâcher ses mots

► **plump down** VI s'affaler VT SEP laisser tomber lourdement ◆ **to ~ o.s. down on the sofa** s'affaler sur le sofa

► **plump for** * VT FUS fixer son choix sur, se décider pour

plumpness /ˈplʌmpnɪs/ N [of person] rondeur f, embonpoint m

plunder /ˈplʌndəʳ/ N (NonC) (= act) pillage m ; (= loot) butin m VT piller

plunderer /ˈplʌndərəʳ/ N pillard m

plundering /ˈplʌndərɪŋ/ N (NonC = act) pillage m ADJ pillard

plunge /plʌndʒ/ N [of bird, diver] plongeon m ; (= steep fall) chute f ; (fig = fall) chute f, dégringolade * f ; (= rash investment) spéculation f hasardeuse (on sur) ◆ **to take a ~** [diver etc] plonger ; [bather] faire un (petit) plongeon ; [shares, prices etc] chuter, dégringoler ◆ **his popularity has taken a ~** sa popularité a chuté ◆ **prices started a downward ~** les prix ont commencé à chuter or dégringoler ◆ **a ~ in the value of the pound** une chute de la valeur de la livre ◆ **to take the ~** (fig) se jeter à l'eau, sauter le pas

VT [+ hand, knife, dagger] (gen) plonger, enfoncer (into dans) ; (into water) plonger (into dans) ; (fig) plonger ◆ **they were ~d into war/darkness/despair** etc ils ont été plongés dans la guerre/l'obscurité/le désespoir etc

VI 1 (= dive) [diver, goalkeeper, penguin, submarine] plonger (into dans ; from de) ; [ship] piquer de l'avant or du nez

2 [road, cliff] plonger (into dans) ◆ **the stream/road ~d down the mountainside** le ruisseau/la route dévalait le flanc de la colline

3 (= fall) [person] tomber, faire une chute (from de) ; [vehicle] tomber (from de) ; [prices etc] chuter, dégringoler ◆ **he ~d to his death** il a fait une chute mortelle ◆ **he ~d over the cliff to his death** il s'est tué en tombant du haut de la falaise ◆ **the plane ~d to the ground/into the sea** l'avion s'est écrasé au sol/est tombé dans la mer ◆ **the car ~d over the cliff** la voiture est tombée de or a plongé par-dessus la falaise

4 (= rush, lurch) ◆ **to ~ in/out/across** etc entrer/sortir/traverser etc précipitamment or à toute allure ◆ **he ~d into the crowd** il s'est jeté dans la foule ◆ **he ~d through the crowd** il s'est frayé un chemin à travers la foule ◆ **he ~d through the hedge** il a piqué brusquement or s'est jeté au travers de la haie ◆ **the truck ~d across the road** le camion a fait une embardée en travers de la route

5 (fig) **to ~ into** [+ debt, recession, turmoil] sombrer dans ◆ **he ~d into the argument** il s'est lancé dans la discussion

6 (= plummet) [sales, prices, profits, currency] chuter, dégringoler ; [temperature] tomber brusquement ◆ **sales have ~d by 24%** les ventes ont chuté de 24%

7 * (= gamble) jouer gros jeu, flamber ; (= speculate rashly) spéculer imprudemment

COMP **plunge pool** N (in sauna etc) bassin m

► **plunge in** VI [diver etc] plonger ; (fig: into work etc) s'y mettre de grand cœur

VT SEP (y) plonger

plunger /ˈplʌndʒəʳ/ N 1 (= piston) piston m ; (also **sink plunger**) (for blocked pipe) débouchoir m à ventouse f 2 (= gambler) flambeur m ; (= rash speculator) (spéculateur m) risque-tout m inv

plunging /ˈplʌndʒɪŋ/ N (NonC = action) plongement m ; [of diver etc] plongées fpl ; [of boat] tangage m ADJ ◆ **~ neckline** décolleté m plongeant

plunk /plʌŋk/ (US) ⇒ **plonk**

pluperfect /ˈpluːˈpɜːfɪkt/ N plus-que-parfait m

plural /ˈplʊərəl/ ADJ 1 (Gram) [form, number, ending, person] pluriel, du pluriel ; [verb, noun] au pluriel 2 [vote] plural 3 [society] pluriel, diversifié N (Gram) pluriel m ◆ **in the ~** au pluriel

pluralism /ˈplʊərəlɪzəm/ N (Philos) pluralisme m ; (Rel) cumul m

pluralist /ˈplʊərəlɪst/ ADJ, N pluraliste mf

pluralistic /ˌplʊərəˈlɪstɪk/ ADJ pluraliste

plurality /plʊəˈrælɪtɪ/ N 1 (= multitude, diversity) pluralité f ; [of benefices etc] cumul m 2 (US Pol) majorité f relative ◆ **a ~ of 5,000 votes** une majorité de 5 000 voix

plus /plʌs/ PREP plus ◆ **three ~ four** trois plus or et quatre ◆ **... ~ what I've done already** ... plus ce que j'ai déjà fait ◆ **we are ~ five** (Bridge etc) nous menons par cinq points

CONJ * en plus, d'ailleurs ◆ **... ~ I don't like nightclubs** ... en plus or d'ailleurs, je n'aime pas les boîtes de nuit

ADJ 1 (Elec, Math) positif ◆ **on the ~ side (of the account)** (lit) à l'actif du compte ◆ **on the ~ side (of the account) we have his support** (fig) l'aspect positif, c'est que nous bénéficions de son soutien ◆ **a ~ factor** (fig) un atout

2 ◆ **ten-~ hours a week** * un minimum de dix heures or plus de dix heures par semaine ◆ **A/B** etc **~** (Scol) A/B etc plus ◆ **we've sold 100 ~** * nous en avons vendu 100 et quelques or plus de 100

N 1 (Math = sign) (signe m) plus m

2 (= bonus, advantage) avantage m additionnel, atout m ◆ **the ~es** (of situation etc) les côtés mpl positifs

COMP **plus fours** NPL culotte f de golf

plus sign N (Math) signe m plus

plush /plʌʃ/ N (= fabric) peluche f ADJ 1 (= made of plush) de or en peluche ; (= plush-like) pelucheux 2 (* = sumptuous) rupin ‡, somptueux

plushly /ˈplʌʃlɪ/ ADV somptueusement

plushy * /ˈplʌʃɪ/ ADJ rupin *, somptueux

Plutarch /ˈpluːtɑːk/ N Plutarque m

Pluto /ˈpluːtəʊ/ N (Astron) Pluton f ; (Myth) Pluton m

plutocracy /pluːˈtɒkrəsɪ/ N ploutocratie f

plutocrat /ˈpluːtəʊkræt/ N ploutocrate m

plutocratic /ˌpluːtəʊˈkrætɪk/ ADJ ploutocratique

plutonium /pluːˈtəʊnɪəm/ N plutonium m

pluviometer /ˌpluːvɪˈɒmɪtəʳ/ N pluviomètre m

ply¹ /plaɪ/ N 1 [of wood] feuille f, épaisseur f ; [of wool] fil m, brin m ; [of rope] toron m, brin m 2 (compound ending) **four-~ rope** corde f quatre fils ◆ **four-~ wood** contreplaqué m quatre épaisseurs ◆ **three-~ (wool)** laine f trois fils ◆ **two-~ tissues/napkins** mouchoirs mpl/serviettes fpl (en papier) double épaisseur

ply² /plaɪ/ VT 1 [+ needle, tool] manier, jouer (habilement) de ; [+ oar] manier ; [ship] [+ river, sea] naviguer sur, voguer sur (liter) ◆ **they plied their oars with a will** ils faisaient force de rames ◆ **to ~ one's trade (as)** exercer son métier (de) 2 [+ person] ◆ **to ~ sb with questions** presser qn de questions ◆ **to ~ sb for information** demander continuellement des renseignements à qn ◆ **he plied them with drink** il ne cessait de remplir leur verre VI ◆ **to ~ between** [ship, coach etc] faire la navette entre ◆ **to ~ for hire** (Jur) [taxi] faire un service de taxi

plywood /ˈplaɪwʊd/ N contreplaqué m

PM /piːˈem/ N (Brit) (abbrev of **Prime Minister**) → **prime**

pm /piːˈem/ (abbrev of **post meridiem**) de l'après-midi ◆ **3pm** 3 heures de l'après-midi, 15 heures ◆ **10pm** 10 heures du soir, 22 heures

PMG /ˌpiːemˈdʒiː/ N 1 (Brit) (abbrev of **Paymaster General**) → **paymaster** 2 (abbrev of **Postmaster General**) → **postmaster**

PMS /ˌpiːemˈes/ N (abbrev of **premenstrual syndrome**) SPM m, syndrome m prémenstruel

PMT /ˌpiːemˈtiː/ N (abbrev of **premenstrual tension**) SPM m, syndrome m prémenstruel

pneumatic /njuːˈmætɪk/ ADJ pneumatique

COMP **pneumatic drill** N marteau-piqueur m

pneumatic tyre N pneu m

pneumatically /njuːˈmætɪkəlɪ/ ADV [controlled, operated etc] pneumatiquement

pneumoconiosis /ˌnjuːməʊˌkəʊnɪˈəʊsɪs/ N (Med) pneumoconiose f

pneumocystis carinii pneumonia /ˌnjuːməʊˈsɪstɪskəˈraɪnɪaɪnjuːˈməʊnɪə/ N pneumocystose f

pneumonia /njuːˈməʊnɪə/ N (NonC) pneumonie f

pneumonologist /ˌnjuːməˈnɒlədʒɪst/ N pneumologue mf

pneumonology /ˌnjuːməˈnɒlədʒɪ/ N pneumologie f

PO /piːˈəʊ/ N 1 (abbrev of **post office**) ◆ **Box 24** BP f 24 2 (abbrev of **Petty Officer**) → **petty** 3 (abbrev of **Pilot Officer**) → **pilot**

Po /pəʊ/ N (= river) Pô m

po ‡ /pəʊ/ (Brit) N († = potty) pot m (de chambre)

COMP **po-faced** ‡ ADJ à l'air pincé

p.o. /piːˈəʊ/ (Brit) (abbrev of **postal order**) → **postal**

POA /ˌpiːəʊˈeɪ/ N (Brit) (abbrev of **Prison Officers' Association**) syndicat

poach¹ /pəʊtʃ/ VT (Culin) pocher COMP **poached egg** N œuf m poché

poach² /pəʊtʃ/ VT [+ game] braconner, chasser illégalement ; [+ fish] braconner, pêcher illégalement ; (fig) [+ employee] débaucher VI braconner ◆ **to ~ for salmon** etc braconner du saumon etc ◆ **to ~ on sb's preserves** or **territory** (lit, fig) braconner sur les terres de qn

◆ **stop ~ing!** * *(fig) (in tennis)* arrête de me chiper la balle ! * ; *(in work)* arrête de marcher sur mes plates-bandes ! *

poacher[1] /ˈpəʊtʃəʳ/ N *(for eggs)* pocheuse *f*

poacher[2] /ˈpəʊtʃəʳ/ N *(of game etc)* braconnier *m*

poaching /ˈpəʊtʃɪŋ/ N braconnage *m*

pock /pɒk/ N *(Med)* pustule *f* de petite vérole

pocket /ˈpɒkɪt/ N 1 *(in garment, suitcase, file, wallet etc)* poche *f* ◆ **with his hands in his ~s** les mains dans les poches ◆ **with (one's) ~s full of ...** les poches pleines de ... ◆ **in his trouser/jacket ~** dans la poche de son pantalon/sa veste ; → **back, breast, hip**[1] ◆ **to go through sb's ~s** faire les poches à qn ◆ **to be in sb's ~** *(fig)* être à la solde de qn ◆ **to have sb in one's ~** avoir qn dans sa manche *or* dans sa poche ◆ **to live in each other's** *or* **one another's ~s** vivre les uns sur les autres ◆ **he has the game in his ~** il a le jeu dans sa poche

2 *(fig = budget, finances)* **it's a drain on his ~** ça grève son budget ◆ **the deal put $500 in his ~** l'affaire lui a rapporté 500 dollars ◆ **that will hurt his ~** ça fera mal à son porte-monnaie ◆ **to line one's ~s** se remplir les poches ◆ **he is always putting his hand in his ~** il n'arrête pas de débourser ◆ **to pay for sth out of one's own ~** payer qch de sa poche ◆ **to have deep ~s** avoir de gros moyens ◆ **investors with deep ~s** les investisseurs *mpl* disposant de gros moyens

◆ **to be in pocket** avoir une marge de bénéfice

◆ **out of pocket** ◆ **to be out of ~** en être de sa poche ◆ **I could end up well out of ~** je pourrais en être sérieusement de ma poche ◆ **I was £50 out of ~** ça m'avait coûté 50 livres ◆ **it left me £50 out of ~** ça m'a coûté 50 livres ◆ **out-of-~** → **out**

3 *(= small area) [of gas, fog]* poche *f* ; *[of land]* parcelle *f* ; *(Flying:* also **air pocket**) trou *m* d'air ; *(Billiards etc)* blouse *f* ◆ **~ of infection** foyer *m* de contagion ◆ **~s of resistance** poches *fpl* de résistance ◆ **there are still some ~s of unemployment** il reste quelques petites zones de chômage

VT 1 *(lit, fig) [+ object, money, prize]* empocher

2 *(* = steal)* empocher, barboter *

COMP *[flask, torch, dictionary, edition etc]* de poche

pocket battleship N cuirassé *m* de poche

pocket billiards NPL *(US)* billard *m* américain

pocket calculator N calculatrice *f* de poche, calculette *f*

pocket-handkerchief N mouchoir *m* de poche ADJ *(fig)* grand comme un mouchoir de poche

pocket-money N argent *m* de poche

pocket-size(d) ADJ *(lit)* de poche ; *(fig) [house, garden etc]* tout petit

pocket veto N *(US Pol) veto implicite du Président qui ne signe pas un projet de loi dans les délais impartis*

pocketbook /ˈpɒkɪtbʊk/ N 1 *(US)* (= *wallet*) portefeuille *m* ; (= *handbag*) sac *m* à main 2 (= *notebook*) calepin *m*, carnet *m*

pocketful /ˈpɒkɪtfʊl/ N (pl **pocketfuls**) poche *f* pleine ◆ **with ~s of ...** les poches pleines de ...

pocketknife /ˈpɒkɪtnaɪf/ N (pl **-knives**) couteau *m* de poche, canif *m*

pockmark /ˈpɒkmɑːk/ N cicatrice *f* de variole

pockmarked /ˈpɒkmɑːkt/ ADJ *[face]* grêlé ; *[surface]* criblé de trous

pod /pɒd/ N *[of bean, pea etc]* cosse *f* ; *(Space)* nacelle *f* ◆ **in ~** ‡ *(hum = pregnant)* en cloque ‡

podcasting /ˈpɒdkɑːstɪŋ/ N podcasting *m*

podgy * /ˈpɒdʒɪ/ ADJ *(esp Brit)* grassouillet

podia /ˈpəʊdɪə/ NPL of **podium**

podiatrist /pɒˈdiːətrɪst/ N *(US)* pédicure *mf*, podologue *mf*

podiatry /pɒˈdiːətrɪ/ N *(US)* (= *science*) podologie *f* ; (= *treatment*) soins *mpl* du pied, traitement *m* des maladies du pied

podium /ˈpəʊdɪəm/ N (pl **podia**) podium *m*

Podunk /ˈpəʊdʌŋk/ N *(US)* petit village *m* perdu, ≃ Trifouilly-les-Oies

POE (abbrev of **port of embarkation**) → **port**[1]

poem /ˈpəʊɪm/ N poème *m* ◆ **the ~s of Keats** les poèmes *mpl* de Keats

poet /ˈpəʊɪt/ N poète *m* COMP **poet laureate** N (pl **poets laureate**) poète *m* lauréat

poetaster /ˌpəʊɪˈtæstəʳ/ N mauvais poète *m*, rimailleur *m*

poetess /ˈpəʊɪtes/ N poétesse *f*

poetic /pəʊˈetɪk/ ADJ poétique ◆ **~ licence** licence *f* poétique ◆ **it's ~ justice** il y a une justice immanente

poetical /pəʊˈetɪkəl/ ADJ poétique

poetically /pəʊˈetɪkəlɪ/ ADV poétiquement

poeticize /pəʊˈetɪsaɪz/ VT poétiser

poetics /pəʊˈetɪks/ NPL poétique *f*

poetry /ˈpəʊɪtrɪ/ N *(NonC: lit, fig)* poésie *f* ◆ **the ~ of Keats** la poésie de Keats ◆ **he writes ~** il écrit des poèmes, il est poète COMP **poetry reading** N lecture *f* de poèmes

pogo /ˈpəʊgəʊ/ N pogo *m* VI *(Brit = dance)* pogoter, danser le pogo COMP **pogo stick** N échasse *f* sauteuse

pogrom /ˈpɒgrəm/ N pogrom *m* VT massacrer (au cours d'un pogrom)

poignancy /ˈpɔɪnjənsɪ/ N ◆ **the ~ of the lyrics** le caractère poignant des paroles ◆ **it was a moment of extraordinary ~** c'était un moment très poignant

poignant /ˈpɔɪnjənt/ ADJ (= *touching*) émouvant ◆ **a ~ love story** une histoire d'amour émouvante ◆ **he found the sight of her inexpressibly ~** le fait de la voir éveillait en lui une émotion indicible

> ⚠ **poignant** is rarely translated by the French word **poignant**, which means 'harrowing'.

poignantly /ˈpɔɪnjəntlɪ/ ADV *[describe, express, evoke]* d'une manière émouvante ◆ **I am reminded very ~ of this** je me souviens de ceci avec beaucoup d'émotion

poinsettia /pɔɪnˈsetɪə/ N poinsettia *m*

point /pɔɪnt/

LANGUAGE IN USE 11.1, 26.1, 26.2, 26.3

1 NOUN	4 INTRANSITIVE VERB
2 PLURAL NOUN	5 COMPOUNDS
3 TRANSITIVE VERB	6 PHRASAL VERBS

1 - NOUN

1 [= sharp end] *[of pencil, needle, knife, jaw]* pointe *f* ◆ **a knife with a sharp ~** un couteau très pointu ◆ **a star with five ~s** une étoile à cinq branches ◆ **a stag with ten ~s** un cerf (de) dix cors ◆ **to be** *or* **dance on ~s** *(Ballet)* faire les pointes ◆ **at the ~ of a gun** sous la menace d'un revolver ◆ **not to put too fine a ~ on it** (= *frankly*) pour être franc

2 [= dot] *(Geom, Typ)* point *m* ; *(Math:* also **decimal point**) virgule *f* (décimale) ◆ **three ~ six** *(3.6)* trois virgule six *(3,6)* ◆ **eight-~ type** caractères *mpl* en corps huit ◆ **~ A** *(Geom)* le point A

3 [on scale, in space, in time] point *m* ◆ **the highest ~ in the district** le point culminant de la région ◆ **at that ~ in the road** à cet endroit de la route ◆ **at the ~ where the road forks** là où la route bifurque ◆ **he had reached a ~ where he began to doubt whether ...** il en était arrivé à se demander si ... ◆ **to reach a low ~** *[morale]* être au plus bas ; *[production, reputation]* toucher le fond ◆ **this was the low ~ (of his career)** c'est à ce moment-là qu'il a touché le fond (dans sa carrière) ◆ **from that ~ onwards** à partir de ce moment ◆ **at this** *or* **that ~** *(in space)* là, à cet endroit ; *(in time)* à ce moment-là ◆ **at this ~ in time** à ce stade ◆ **the train stops at Slough, and all ~s west** le train s'arrête à Slough et dans toutes les gares à l'ouest de Slough ◆ **the (thirty-two) ~s of the compass** les points *mpl* de la boussole ◆ **from all ~s (of the compass)** de toutes parts, de tous côtés

◆ **point of** + *noun* ◆ **there was no ~ of contact between them** ils n'avaient aucun point commun ◆ **he was strict to the ~ of cruelty** il était sévère au point d'être cruel ◆ **on** *or* **at the ~ of death** à l'article de la mort ◆ **~ of departure** point *m* de départ ◆ **~ of entry (into a country)** point *m* d'arrivée (dans un pays) ◆ **he had reached the ~ of no return** il avait atteint le point de non-retour

◆ **the point of** + *-ing* ◆ **to be on the ~ of doing sth** être sur le point de faire qch ◆ **when it came to the ~ of paying, ...** quand il s'est agi de payer, ... ◆ **he had reached the ~ of resigning** il en était arrivé au point de donner sa démission

◆ **up to a point** jusqu'à un certain point, dans une certaine mesure

4 [= unit] *(in score, on scale)* point *m* ; *(on thermometer)* degré *m* ◆ **on ~s** *(Boxing)* aux points ◆ **the cost-of-living index went up two ~s** l'indice du coût de la vie a augmenté de deux points ◆ **to rise** *or* **gain three ~s** *(on Stock Exchange)* augmenter de *or* gagner trois points

5 [= idea, question] point *m* ◆ **on this ~ we are agreed** sur ce point *or* là-dessus nous sommes d'accord ◆ **on all ~s** en tous points ◆ **12-~ plan** plan *m* en 12 points ◆ **the main ~s to remember** les principaux points à retenir ◆ **~ by ~** point par point ; see also **compounds** ◆ **you have a ~ there!** c'est juste !, il y a du vrai dans ce que vous dites ! ◆ **to carry** *or* **gain** *or* **win one's ~** avoir gain de cause ◆ **he made the ~ that ...** il fit remarquer que ... ◆ **he made a good ~ when he said that ...** il a mis le doigt dessus lorsqu'il a dit que ... ◆ **I'd like to make a ~ if I may** j'aurais une remarque à faire si vous le permettez ◆ **you've made your ~!** (= *had your say*) vous avez dit ce que vous aviez à dire ! ; (= *convinced me*) vous m'avez convaincu ! ◆ **I take your ~** je vois ce que vous voulez dire ◆ **~ taken!** * d'accord(, je te le concède) !

◆ **point of** + *noun* ◆ **it's a ~ of detail** c'est un point de détail ◆ **it was a ~ of honour with him never to refuse** il se faisait un point d'honneur de ne jamais refuser, il mettait son point d'honneur à ne jamais refuser ◆ **~ of interest/of no importance** point *m* intéressant/sans importance ◆ **a ~ of law** un point de droit ◆ **on a ~ of principle** sur une question de principe ; → **order**

6 [= important part, main idea] *[of argument etc]* objet *m* ; *[of joke]* astuce *f* ◆ **that's not the ~** il ne s'agit pas de ça, là n'est pas la question ◆ **that is hardly the ~, that is beside the ~** cela n'a rien à voir ◆ **the whole ~ was to do it today** tout l'intérêt était justement de le faire aujourd'hui ◆ **that's the (whole) ~!, that's just the ~!** justement ! ◆ **the ~ is that you had promised it for today!** le fait est que vous l'aviez promis pour aujourd'hui ! ◆ **to come to the ~** *[person]* en venir au fait ◆ **when it comes to the ~, they don't value education** au fond, ils n'accordent pas beaucoup d'importance à l'éducation ◆ **we're getting off the ~** nous nous éloignons du sujet ◆ **get** *or* **come to the ~!** venez-en à l'essentiel !, cessez de tourner autour du pot ! * ◆ **let's get back to the ~**

revenons à nos moutons* ◆ **to keep** *or* **stick to the ~** ne pas s'éloigner du sujet

7 [= meaning, purpose] ◆ **what was the ~ of his visit ?** quel était le but *or* l'objet de sa visite ? ◆ **there's some** *or* **a ~ in it** ça a une utilité ◆ **a long story that seemed to have no ~ at all** une longue histoire sans rime ni raison ◆ **the ~ of this story is that ...** la morale de l'histoire, c'est que ... ◆ **(very much) to the ~** (très) pertinent ◆ **his remarks lack ~** ses remarques ne sont pas très pertinentes ◆ **the news gave ~ to his arguments** cette nouvelle a souligné la pertinence de ses arguments ◆ **to get** *or* **see the ~** comprendre ◆ **you get the ~?** vous saisissez ?* ◆ **to make a ~ of doing sth, to make it a ~ to do sth** ne pas manquer de faire qch

8 [= use] ◆ **what's the ~ ?** à quoi bon ? ◆ **what's the ~ of** *or* **in waiting?** à quoi bon attendre ? ◆ **there's no ~ in waiting** ça ne sert à rien d'attendre ◆ **there's little ~ in saying ...** ça ne sert pas à grand-chose de dire ... ◆ **I don't see any ~ in doing that** je ne vois aucun intérêt à faire cela

9 [= characteristic] caractéristique *f* ◆ **good ~s** qualités *fpl* ◆ **bad ~s** défauts *mpl* ◆ **it is not his strong ~** ce n'est pas son fort ◆ **he has his ~s** il a ses bons côtés ◆ **the ~s to look (out) for when buying a car** les choses *fpl* auxquelles il faut faire attention lorsqu'on achète une voiture

10 [= geographical feature] pointe *f*

11 [in car engine] vis *f* platinée

12 [Brit Elec : also **power point**] prise *f* (de courant) *(femelle)*

2 - PLURAL NOUN

points *(Brit Rail)* aiguillage *m*, aiguilles *fpl*

3 - TRANSITIVE VERB

1 [= aim, direct] *[+ telescope, hosepipe]* pointer, diriger (*at* sur) ◆ **to ~ a gun at sb** braquer un revolver sur qn ◆ **he ~ed his stick towards the house** il a indiqué la maison avec sa canne ◆ **~ your browser at ...** pointez votre navigateur sur ... ◆ **to ~ sb in the direction of** diriger qn vers ◆ **she ~ed him in the right direction** * elle lui a montré le chemin ◆ **he ~ed the boat towards the harbour** il a mis le cap sur le port ◆ **he ~ed the car towards Paris** il a tourné en direction de Paris ◆ **he ~ed his finger at me** il a pointé le doigt sur *or* vers moi

2 [= mark, show]

♦ **to point the way** ◆ **the signs ~ the way to London** les panneaux indiquent la direction de Londres ◆ **it ~s the way to closer cooperation** cela montre la voie d'une plus grande coopération

3 [Constr] *[+ wall]* jointoyer (*with* de)

4 [= punctuate] ponctuer ; *[+ Hebrew, Arabic etc]* mettre les points-voyelles à ; *[+ psalm]* marquer de points

5 [+ toes] pointer

4 - INTRANSITIVE VERB

1 [person] montrer *or* indiquer du doigt ◆ **it's rude to ~** ce n'est pas poli de montrer du doigt ◆ **to ~ at** *or* **towards sth/sb** indiquer *or* désigner qch/qn du doigt ◆ **he ~ed at the house with his stick** il montra *or* indiqua la maison avec sa canne ◆ **I want to ~ to one or two facts** je veux attirer votre attention sur un ou deux faits ◆ **all the evidence ~s to him** *or* **to his guilt** tous les faits l'accusent ◆ **everything ~s to a brilliant career for him** tout indique qu'il aura une brillante carrière ◆ **it all ~s to the fact that ...** tout laisse à penser que ... ◆ **everything ~s to murder/suicide** tout laisse à penser qu'il s'agit d'un meurtre/d'un suicide ◆ **everything ~s that way** tout nous amène à cette conclusion

2 [signpost] indiquer la direction (*towards* de) ; *[gun]* être braqué (*at* sur) ; *[vehicle etc]* être dirigé, être tourné (*towards* vers) ◆ **the needle is ~ing north** l'aiguille indique le nord ◆ **the little hand is ~ing to four** la petite aiguille indique quatre heures ◆ **the car isn't ~ing in the right direction** la voiture n'est pas tournée dans la bonne direction *or* dans le bon sens

3 [dancer] faire des pointes

4 [dog] tomber en arrêt

5 - COMPOUNDS

point-and-click ADJ *[browser, interface]* pointer-cliquer *inv*

point-blank ADJ → **point-blank**

point-by-point ADJ méthodique

point duty N *(Brit Police etc)* ◆ **to be on ~ duty** diriger la circulation

point of reference N point *m* de référence

point of sale N point *m* de vente

point-of-sale ADJ ◆ **~-of-sale advertising** publicité *f* sur le lieu de vente, PLV *f* ◆ **~-of-sale material** matériel *m* PLV ◆ **~-of-sale terminal** terminal *m* point de vente

point of view N point *m* de vue ◆ **from that/my ~ of view** de ce/mon point de vue ◆ **from the social ~ of view** du point de vue social

points decision N *(Boxing)* décision *f* aux points

points failure N panne *f* d'aiguillage

points system N *(gen)* système *m* par points ; *[of driving licence]* permis *m* à points

points win N victoire *f* aux points

point-to-point (race) N *(Racing)* *steeple-chase champêtre réservé à des cavaliers amateurs*

6 - PHRASAL VERBS

► **point out** VT SEP 1 (= *show*) *[+ person, object, place]* montrer, indiquer

2 (= *mention*) faire remarquer (*that que*) ◆ **to ~ sth out to sb** faire remarquer qch à qn, attirer l'attention de qn sur qch ◆ **he ~ed out to me that I was wrong** il m'a fait remarquer que j'avais tort ◆ **I should ~ out that ...** je dois vous dire *or* signaler que ...

► **point up** VT SEP mettre en évidence, souligner

---

point-blank /ˈpɔɪntˈblæŋk/ ADJ *[shot]* à bout portant ; *(fig) [refusal]* net, catégorique ; *[request]* de but en blanc, à brûle-pourpoint ◆ **at** *or* **from ~ range** à bout portant ADV *[fire, shoot]* à bout portant ; *(fig) [refuse]* tout net, catégoriquement ; *[request, demand]* de but en blanc, à brûle-pourpoint

pointed /ˈpɔɪntɪd/ ADJ 1 *[knife, stick, pencil, roof, chin, nose, shoes]* pointu ; *[beard]* en pointe, pointu ; *(Archit) [window, arch]* en ogive ◆ **the ~ end** le bout pointu 2 *(fig) [remark, question, look]* lourd de sous-entendus

pointedly /ˈpɔɪntɪdlɪ/ ADV *[say]* d'un ton plein de sous-entendus ; *[behave, smile, ignore]* ostensiblement ◆ **she looked ~ at me** elle m'a lancé un regard qui en disait long

pointer /ˈpɔɪntəʳ/ N 1 (= *piece of advice*) conseil *m* ◆ **he gave me some ~s on what to do** il m'a donné quelques conseils (pratiques) sur la marche à suivre

2 (= *clue, indication*) indice *m* ◆ **this is a sure ~ that something's amiss** ceci indique clairement que quelque chose ne va pas

♦ **to be a pointer to sth** annoncer qch ◆ **an incident which was a ~ to troubles to come** un incident qui annonçait des problèmes à venir ◆ **there is at present no ~ to the outcome** rien ne permet de prévoir l'issue pour le moment ◆ **the elections should be a ~ to the public mood** les élections devraient permettre de prendre le pouls de l'opinion

3 (= *stick*) baguette *f* ; (*on scale*) (= *indicator*) index *m* ; (= *needle*) aiguille *f* ; (*on screen* = *arrow*) flèche *f* lumineuse

4 (= *dog*) chien *m* d'arrêt

pointillism /ˈpwæntɪlɪzəm/ N pointillisme *m*

pointing /ˈpɔɪntɪŋ/ N *(Constr)* (= *work*) jointoiement *m* ; (= *cement*) joints *mpl*

pointless /ˈpɔɪntlɪs/ ADJ *[attempt, task, suffering]* inutile, vain ; *[murder, violence]* gratuit ; *[explanation, joke, story]* sans rime ni raison, qui ne rime à rien ◆ **it is ~ to complain** il ne sert à rien *or* il est inutile de se plaindre ◆ **it is ~ for him to leave, it is ~ him leaving** ça ne servirait à rien *or* il est inutile qu'il parte ◆ **life seemed ~ to her** la vie lui paraissait dénuée de sens ◆ **a ~ exercise** * une perte de temps

pointlessly /ˈpɔɪntlɪslɪ/ ADV *[try, work, suffer]* inutilement, en vain ; *[say, protest]* sans raison ; *[kill]* gratuitement, sans raison ; *[die]* pour rien ◆ **the film is ~ violent/obscure** la violence/complexité de ce film n'est pas justifiée

pointlessness /ˈpɔɪntlɪsnɪs/ N *[of activity, organization, sb's death]* absurdité *f* ; *[of existence]* futilité *f* ◆ **she stressed the ~ of protesting** elle a souligné à quel point il était inutile de protester

pointsman /ˈpɔɪntsmən/ N (pl **-men**) *(Rail)* aiguilleur *m*

pointy * /ˈpɔɪntɪ/ ADJ *[ears, hat, shoes]* pointu ; *[beard]* en pointe, pointu COMP

pointy-headed ⁑ ADJ *(US fig pej)* ◆ **a ~-headed intellectual** un intello* à lunettes ◆ **that ~-headed professor** ce professeur Tournesol

poise /pɔɪz/ N (= *balance*) équilibre *m* ; (= *carriage*) maintien *m* ; *[of head, body etc]* port *m* ; *(fig)* (= *composure etc*) calme *m*, sang-froid *m* ; (= *self-confidence*) (calme) assurance *f* ; (= *grace*) grâce *f* ◆ **a woman of great ~** une femme pleine de grâce *or* empreinte d'une tranquille assurance ◆ **he is young and lacks ~** il est jeune et manque d'assurance ◆ **to recover** *or* **regain one's ~** *(lit, fig)* retrouver son calme *or* son sang-froid VT (= *balance*) mettre en équilibre ; (= *hold balanced*) tenir en équilibre, maintenir en équilibre

poised /pɔɪzd/ ADJ 1 (= *balanced*) en équilibre ; (= *held, hanging*) suspendu immobile ; (= *hovering*) immobile *or* suspendu (en l'air) ◆ **the swimmers stood** *or* **were ~ at the edge of the pool** les nageurs étaient en position sur les plots de départ ◆ **~ on the brink of success/ruin** au bord de la réussite/la ruine ◆ **to be ~ between life and death** être entre la vie et la mort ◆ **the world was ~ between peace and war** le monde oscillait entre la paix et la guerre

2 (= *ready*) prêt ◆ **the tiger was ~ (ready) to spring** le tigre se tenait prêt à bondir ◆ **powerful military forces, ~ for invasion** des forces armées puissantes, prêtes pour l'invasion ◆ **he was ~ to become champion** il allait devenir champion ◆ **a waitress approached, pencil and pad ~** une serveuse s'est approchée, armée de son bloc et de son crayon

3 (= *self-possessed*) posé ◆ **she appeared ~ and calm** elle semblait calme et posée

poison /ˈpɔɪzn/ N *(lit, fig)* poison *m* ; *[of snake]* venin *m* ◆ **to take ~** s'empoisonner ◆ **to die of ~** mourir empoisonné ◆ **she's absolute ~** † c'est une vraie poison † ◆ **what's your ~?*** *(hum: offering drink)* à quoi tu carbures* ? ; → **hate, rat**

VT *[person]* *[+ person, food, well, arrow]* empoisonner ; *[chemicals]* *[+ air, water, land]* contaminer ◆ **to ~ o.s.** s'empoisonner ◆ **a ~ed foot/finger** *etc* un pied/doigt *etc* infecté ◆ **the drugs are ~ing his system** les drogues l'intoxiquent ◆ **eggs ~ed with salmonella** des œufs contaminés par la salmonelle ◆ **it is ~ing their** friendship cela empoisonne leur amitié ◆ **an atmosphere ~ed by cruelty** une atmosphère empoisonnée par la cruauté ◆ **a ~ed chalice** *(esp Brit fig)* un cadeau empoisonné ◆ **to ~ sb's mind** *(= corrupt)* corrompre qn ; *(= instil doubts)* faire douter qn ◆ **he ~ed her mind against her husband** il l'a montée contre son mari

COMP **poison fang** N crochet *m* venimeux *(d'un serpent)*

poison gas N gaz *m* toxique *or* asphyxiant

poison gland N glande *f* à venin

poison ivy N sumac *m* vénéneux

poison oak N *(NonC)* sumac *m* vénéneux

poison-pen letter N lettre *f* anonyme (de menace *or* d'insulte)

poison pill N *(Fin)* pilule *f* empoisonnée *(prix prohibitif visant à empêcher une société extérieure de lancer une OPA)*

poisoner /ˈpɔɪznəʳ/ N empoisonneur *m*, -euse *f* *(lit)*

poisoning /ˈpɔɪznɪŋ/ N *(gen)* empoisonnement *m* ; *(accidental)* intoxication *f* ◆ **the cause of his death was ~** il est mort empoisonné ◆ **alcohol(ic) ~** empoisonnement *m* par l'alcool éthylisme *m* ◆ **arsenic(al) ~** empoisonnement *m* à l'arsenic ◆ **mercury ~** intoxication *f* par le mercure, hydrargyrisme *m* ; → **blood, food, lead[2], salmonella, self**

poisonous /ˈpɔɪznəs/ ADJ *[snake]* venimeux ; *[plant]* vénéneux ; *[gas, fumes, substance, algae]* toxique ; *(fig) [remark, allegation, comment, dispute]* pernicieux

poke[1] /pəʊk/ N (†† *or dial*) sac *m* ; → **pig**

poke[2] /pəʊk/ N [1] *(= push)* poussée *f* ; *(= jab)* (petit) coup *m (de canne, avec le doigt etc)* ; *(* = punch)* coup *m* de poing ◆ **she gave him a little ~** elle lui a donné un petit coup ◆ **to give the fire a ~** tisonner le feu ◆ **to give sb a ~ in the ribs** enfoncer son doigt dans les côtes de qn ◆ **he gave the ground a ~ with his stick** il a tapoté le sol de sa canne ◆ **it's better than a ~ in the eye (with a sharp stick)** * c'est mieux que rien ◆ **to have a ~ around** * *(= rummage)* farfouiller* ◆ **to take a ~ at sb** * *(lit = punch)* donner un coup de poing à qn ; *(fig)* s'en prendre à qn ◆ **a ~ at sth** *(fig)* une pique contre qch

[2] ***baise *f*** ◆ **he'd like to give her a good ~** il aimerait bien la baiser**

VT [1] *(= jab with finger, stick etc)* pousser, donner un coup (de canne *or* avec le doigt) à ; *(* = punch)* donner un coup de poing à ; *(= thrust) [+ stick, finger etc]* enfoncer *(into* dans ; *through* à travers) ; *[+ rag etc]* fourrer *(into* dans) ◆ **to ~ the fire** tisonner le feu ◆ **he ~d me with his umbrella** il m'a donné un petit coup avec la pointe de son parapluie ◆ **he ~d his finger in her eye** il lui a mis le doigt dans l'œil ◆ **to ~ a finger into sth** enfoncer le doigt dans qch ◆ **he ~d the ground with his stick** il a tapoté le sol de sa canne ◆ **he ~d me in the ribs** il m'a enfoncé son doigt dans les côtes ◆ **he ~d me one in the stomach** * *(US)* il m'a envoyé son poing dans l'estomac ◆ **he ~d his finger up his nose** il s'est fourré le doigt dans le nez ◆ **to ~ one's head out of the window** passer la tête hors de *or* par la fenêtre ◆ **to ~ a hole in sth (with one's finger/stick** *etc***)** faire un trou dans qch *or* percer qch (avec le doigt/sa canne *etc*) ◆ **to ~ holes in an argument** trouver des failles dans une argumentation ; → **fun, nose**

[2] *(Brit ** = have sex with)* baiser**, tringler**

VI [1] (also **poke out**) *[elbows, stomach, stick]* sortir, dépasser *(from, through* de)

[2] (also **poke up**) dépasser

[3] (also **poke through**) dépasser

[4] ◆ **he ~d at me with his finger** il m'a touché du bout du doigt ◆ **he ~d at the suitcase with his stick** il poussa la valise avec sa canne ◆ **she ~d at her food with a fork** elle jouait avec sa nourriture du bout de sa fourchette ◆ **to ~ into sth** * *(fig)* fourrer son nez dans qch

▸ **poke about*, poke around*** VI farfouiller* ; *(pej)* fouiner ◆ **to ~ about in a drawer** farfouiller* *or* fourrager dans un tiroir ◆ **I spent the morning poking about in antique shops** j'ai passé la matinée à farfouiller* dans les magasins d'antiquités ◆ **I found him poking about among your cupboards** je l'ai pris à fouiner dans vos placards

▸ **poke in** VT SEP *[+ head]* passer (à l'intérieur) ; *[+ stick etc]* enfoncer ; *[+ rag]* fourrer ◆ **to ~ one's nose in** * *(fig)* fourrer son nez dans les affaires des autres, se mêler de ce qui ne vous regarde pas

▸ **poke out** VI [1] ⇒ **poke[2] vi 1**

[2] *(= bulge) [stomach, chest, bottom]* être protubérant *or* proéminent

VT SEP [1] *(= stick out)* sortir ◆ **the tortoise ~d its head out** la tortue a sorti la tête

[2] *(= remove, dislodge)* faire partir, déloger ◆ **he ~d the ants out with a stick** il a délogé les fourmis avec un bâton ◆ **to ~ sb's eyes out** crever les yeux à qn

poker[1] /ˈpəʊkəʳ/ N *(for fire etc)* tisonnier *m* ; → **stiff** COMP **poker work** N *(NonC) (= craft)* pyrogravure *f* ; *(= objects)* pyrogravures *fpl*

poker[2] /ˈpəʊkəʳ/ N *(Cards)* poker *m*

COMP **poker dice** N [1] *(= single dice)* dé *m* de poker d'as [2] *(NonC = game)* poker *m* d'as

poker face N visage *m* impassible

poker-faced ADJ au visage impassible

pokey /ˈpəʊkɪ/ N *(US ‡ = jail)* trou* *m*, taule‡ *f*

ADJ ⇒ **poky**

poky /ˈpəʊkɪ/ ADJ *(pej) [house, room]* exigu (-guë *f*) et sombre

pol* /pɒl/ N *(US)* abbrev of **politician**

Polack** /ˈpəʊlæk/ N *(pej)* Polaque *mf (pej)*, Polonais(e) *m(f)*

Poland /ˈpəʊlənd/ N Pologne *f*

polar /ˈpəʊləʳ/ ADJ *(Elec, Geog)* polaire ◆ **~ explorers** explorateurs *mpl* polaires ◆ **they are ~ opposites** ils sont aux antipodes l'un de l'autre

COMP **polar bear** N ours *m* blanc

Polar Circle N cercle *m* polaire

polar distance N distance *f* polaire

polar front N front *m* polaire

polar lights NPL aurore *f* polaire *or* boréale

polarimeter /ˌpəʊləˈrɪmɪtəʳ/ N polarimètre *m*

polariscope /pəʊˈlærɪskəʊp/ N polariscope *m*

polarity /pəʊˈlærɪtɪ/ N polarité *f*

polarization /ˌpəʊləraɪˈzeɪʃən/ N *(lit, fig)* polarisation *f*

polarize /ˈpəʊləraɪz/ VT *(lit, fig)* polariser

Polaroid ® /ˈpəʊlərɔɪd/ ADJ Polaroïd ® *inv* N (also **Polaroid camera**) (appareil *m*) Polaroïd ® *m* ; (also **Polaroid print**) photo *f* Polaroïd ®, Polaroïd ® *m* ◆ **~s** *(= sunglasses)* lunettes *fpl* de soleil (en) Polaroïd ®

Pole /pəʊl/ N Polonais(e) *m(f)*

pole[1] /pəʊl/ N [1] *(= rod)* perche *f* ; *(fixed)* poteau *m*, mât *m* ; (also **flagpole, tent pole**) mât *m* ; (also **telegraph pole**) poteau *m* télégraphique ; (also **curtain pole**) tringle *f* ; (also **barber's pole**) enseigne *f* de coiffeur ; *(in fire station)* perche *f* ; *(for vaulting, punting)* perche *f* ◆ **to be up the ~** * *(= mistaken)* se gourer‡, se planter* ; *(= mad)* dérailler* *(fig)* ◆ **to send** *or* **drive sb up the ~** * *(= mad)* rendre qn dingue* ; → **greasy, ski**

[2] *(Ski) (= ski stick)* bâton *m* ; *(marking run)* piquet *m*

VT *[+ punt etc]* faire avancer (à l'aide d'une perche)

COMP **pole dancer** N danseuse *f* de pole dancing

pole dancing N pole dancing *m (danse érotique autour d'une barre de strip-tease)*

pole jump N *(Sport)* saut *m* à la perche

pole jumper N sauteur *m*, -euse *f* à la perche, perchiste *mf*

pole jumping N *(NonC)* saut *m* à la perche

pole position N *(Motor Racing)* pole position *f* ; *(fig)* pole position *f*, meilleure place *f* ◆ **in ~ position** *(Motor Racing)* en pole position ; *(fig)* en pole position, à la meilleure place

pole vault N ⇒ **pole jump**

pole-vault VI sauter à la perche

pole-vaulter N ⇒ **pole jumper**

pole-vaulting N ⇒ **pole jumping**

pole[2] /pəʊl/ N *(Elec, Geog)* pôle *m* ◆ **North/South Pole** pôle *m* Nord/Sud ◆ **from ~ to ~** d'un pôle à l'autre ◆ **negative/positive ~** pôle *m* négatif/positif ◆ **they are ~s apart** ils sont aux antipodes l'un de l'autre ◆ **at opposite ~s of sth** aux deux pôles de qch COMP **the Pole Star** N l'étoile *f* Polaire

poleaxe, poleax (US) /ˈpəʊlæks/ N *(= weapon)* hache *f* d'armes ; *[of butcher etc]* merlin *m* VT *[+ cattle etc]* abattre, assommer ; *(fig) [+ person]* terrasser

polecat /ˈpəʊlkæt/ N (pl **polecats** or **polecat**) putois *m* ◆ **lazy as a ~** fainéant

pol. econ. (abbrev of **political economy**) → **political**

polemic /pɒˈlemɪk/ ADJ polémique N *(= argument)* ◆ **a ~ against sth** un réquisitoire contre qch ◆ **a ~ for sth** un plaidoyer pour qch

polemical /pɒˈlemɪkəl/ ADJ polémique

polemicist /pɒˈlemɪsɪst/ N polémiste *mf*

polemics /pɒˈlemɪks/ N *(NonC)* arguments *mpl*

polenta /pəʊˈlentə/ N polenta *f*

police /pəˈliːs/ N *(NonC)* [1] *(= organization)* ≈ police *f*, gendarmerie *f* ◆ **the ~** *(collective)* la police, les gendarmes *mpl* ◆ **to join the ~** entrer dans la police, se faire policier *or* gendarme ◆ **he is in the ~** il est dans *or* de la police ◆ **one hundred ~** cent policiers *mpl or* gendarmes *mpl* ◆ **extra ~ were called in** on a fait venir des renforts de police ◆ **the ~ are looking for his car** la police recherche sa voiture ◆ **river/railway ~** police *f* fluviale/des chemins de fer ; → **mounted, transport**

[2] *(US Mil)* corvée *f* (militaire) de rangement et de nettoyage

VT [1] *(lit: with policemen) [+ place]* maintenir l'ordre dans ◆ **the demonstration was heavily ~d** d'importantes forces de police étaient présentes lors de la manifestation

[2] *[vigilantes, volunteers] [+ district, road]* faire la police dans ; *(Mil) [+ frontier, territory]* contrôler ; *(fig) [+ agreements, controls, cease-fires]* veiller à l'application de ; *[+ prices etc]* contrôler ◆ **the border is ~d by UN patrols** la frontière est sous la surveillance des patrouilles de l'ONU

[3] *(US = keep clean)* nettoyer

COMP *(gen)* de la police ; *[leave, vehicle, members]* de la police *or* de la gendarmerie ; *[campaign, control, inquiry]* policier, de la police *or* de la gendarmerie ; *[sergeant, inspector etc]* de police ; *[harassment]* par la police

police academy N école *f* de police

police car N voiture *f* de police

police chief N *(Brit)* ≈ préfet *m* (de police) ; *(US)* ≈ (commissaire *m*) divisionnaire *m*

Police Complaints Board N ≈ Inspection *f* générale des services

police constable N → **constable**

police court N tribunal *m* de police

police custody N → **custody**

police department N *(US)* service *m* de police

police dog N *(Police)* chien *m* policier ; *(US) (= Alsatian)* berger *m* allemand

police escort N escorte *f* policière

the police force N la police, les gendarmes *mpl*, les forces *fpl* de l'ordre ◆ **member of the ~ force** policier *m* ◆ **to join the ~ force** entrer dans la police

police headquarters NPL quartier *m* général de la police, siège *m* central
police intervention N intervention *f* de la police
police marksman N tireur *m* d'élite (de la police)
police office N gendarmerie *f* *(bureaux)*
police officer N policier *m*, fonctionnaire *mf* de la police ◆ **to become a ~ officer** entrer dans la police
police presence N présence *f* policière
police protection N protection *f* de la police
police record N ◆ **to have a ~ record** avoir un casier judiciaire ◆ **he hasn't got a ~ record** il n'a pas de casier judiciaire, il a un casier judiciaire vierge
the police service N la police
police state N état *m* policier
police station N poste *m* *or* commissariat *m* de police, gendarmerie *f*
police wagon N (US) voiture *f* *or* fourgon *m* cellulaire
police work N le métier de policier

policeman /pəˈliːsmən/ N (pl **-men**) *(in town)* agent *m* de police, gardien *m* de la paix ; *(in country)* gendarme *m* ◆ **to become a ~** entrer dans la police ◆ **I knew he was a ~** je savais qu'il était dans la police

policewoman /pəˈliːsˌwʊmən/ N (pl **-women**) femme *f* policier, femme *f* agent (de police)

policing /pəˈliːsɪŋ/ N *(by police)* maintien *m* de l'ordre ; *(by regulator)* contrôle *m*, réglementation *f* ◆ **the ~ of public places** la surveillance policière dans les endroits publics ◆ **he wants more ~ of pornography** il veut que la pornographie soit mieux contrôlée *or* réglementée

policy¹ /ˈpɒlɪsɪ/ N 1 *(= aims, principles etc)* *(Pol)* politique *f* ; *[of newspaper, company, organization]* politique *f* ; *(= course of action)* conduite *f* ◆ **it's company ~** c'est la politique de l'entreprise *or* de la société ◆ **economic/foreign/social ~** politique *f* étrangère/économique/sociale ◆ **to follow a ~ of doing sth** avoir pour règle de faire qch ◆ **it is good/bad ~ to ...** c'est une bonne/mauvaise politique que de ... ◆ **the government's policies** la politique du gouvernement ◆ **official ~** politique *f* officielle ◆ **it has always been our ~ to deliver goods free** nous avons toujours eu pour règle de livrer les marchandises franco de port ◆ **it is our ~ to use recycled paper** nous avons pour principe d'utiliser du papier recyclé ◆ **my ~ has always been to wait and see** j'ai toujours eu pour principe de voir venir
◆ **as a matter of policy** par principe ◆ **as a matter of ~ we do not discuss individual cases** par principe, nous ne commentons pas les cas individuels, nous ne commentons pas les cas individuels, c'est une affaire de principe
◆ **the best policy** ◆ **complete frankness is the best ~** la franchise totale est la meilleure conduite à suivre *or* attitude à adopter ◆ **caution was the best ~** la prudence était la meilleure attitude à adopter ; → **honesty**
2 *(NonC: † = prudence)* (bonne) politique *f* ◆ **it would not be ~ to refuse** il ne serait pas politique de refuser
COMP *(gen)* *[discussions etc]* de politique générale
policy committee N comité *m* directeur
policy decision N décision *f* de principe
policy document N document *m* de politique générale
policy maker N *(within organization, firm etc)* décideur *m* ; *(for political party etc)* responsable *mf* politique
policy-making N prise *f* de décisions ADJ *[process]* de décision ; *[body, role]* décisionnaire
policy matter N question *f* de politique générale *or* de principe
policy paper N ⇒ **policy document**
policy statement N déclaration *f* de principe ◆ **to make a ~ statement** faire une déclaration de principe
policy unit N *(Brit Pol)* conseillers *mpl* politiques
policy wonk* N *(esp US Pol)* conseiller *m*, -ère *f* politique

> ⚠ The French word **police** can mean **policy**, but only in the sense 'insurance policy'.

policy² /ˈpɒlɪsɪ/ N *(Insurance)* police *f* (d'assurance) ◆ **to take out a ~** souscrire une (police d')assurance

policyholder /ˈpɒlɪsɪˌhəʊldəʳ/ N assuré(e) *m(f)*

polio /ˈpəʊlɪəʊ/ N (abbrev of **poliomyelitis**) polio *f*

poliomyelitis /ˈpəʊlɪəʊmaɪəˈlaɪtɪs/ N poliomyélite *f*

Polish /ˈpəʊlɪʃ/ ADJ *(gen)* polonais ; *[ambassador, embassy]* de Pologne ; *[teacher, dictionary]* de polonais N *(= language)* polonais *m*

polish /ˈpɒlɪʃ/ N 1 *(= substance)* *(for shoes)* cirage *m*, crème *f* (pour chaussures) ; *(for floor, furniture)* encaustique *f*, cire *f* ; *(for nails)* vernis *m* (à ongles) ◆ **metal ~** produit *m* d'entretien pour les métaux
2 *(= act)* **to give sth a ~** faire briller qch ◆ **my shoes need a ~** mes chaussures ont besoin d'être cirées
3 *(= shine)* poli *m* ◆ **high ~** lustre *m* ◆ **to put a ~ on sth** faire briller qch ◆ **the candlesticks were losing their ~** les chandeliers perdaient de leur éclat
4 *(fig = refinement)* *[of person]* raffinement *m* ; *[of style, work, performance]* perfection *f*, élégance *f*
VT (also **polish up**) *[+ stones, glass]* polir ; *[+ shoes]* cirer ; *[+ floor, furniture]* cirer, astiquer ; *[+ car]* astiquer, briquer ; *[+ metal]* fourbir, astiquer ; *[+ leather]* lustrer ; *(fig)* *[+ person]* parfaire l'éducation de ; *[+ manners]* affiner ; *[+ style, language]* polir, châtier ◆ **to ~ (up) one's French** perfectionner *or* travailler son français ◆ **the style needs ~ing** le style aurait besoin d'être plus soigné ; see also **polished**

▸ **polish off*** VT SEP *[+ food, drink]* finir ; *[+ work, correspondence]* expédier ; *[+ competitor, enemy]* régler son compte à, en finir avec ◆ **he ~ed off the meal** il a tout mangé jusqu'à la dernière miette ◆ **he ~ed off his scotch** il a avalé son whisky d'un trait ◆ **he ~ed off all the scotch** il a sifflé* tout le whisky ◆ **she ~ed off the cheese** elle a englouti* tout le fromage

▸ **polish up** VT SEP ⇒ **polish vt**

polished /ˈpɒlɪʃt/ ADJ 1 *(= shiny)* *[surface]* poli, brillant ; *[floor, shoes]* ciré, brillant ; *[leather]* lustré ; *[silver, ornaments]* astiqué ; *[stone, glass]* poli 2 *(fig = refined)* *[person]* qui a de l'éducation *or* du savoir-vivre ; *[manners]* raffiné ; *[style]* poli, châtié ; *[performer]* accompli ; *[performance]* impeccable

polisher /ˈpɒlɪʃəʳ/ N *(= person)* polisseur *m*, -euse *f* ; *(= machine)* *(gen)* polissoir *m* ; *(for floors)* cireuse *f* ; *(for pebbles etc)* polisseuse *f*

Politburo /ˈpɒlɪtbjʊərəʊ/ N Politburo *m*

polite /pəˈlaɪt/ ADJ *[person, smile, request, refusal, applause]* poli ◆ **to be ~ to sb** être poli avec qn ◆ **when I said it was not his best work I was being ~** en disant que ce n'est pas sa meilleure œuvre j'ai été poli ◆ **be ~ about his car!** ne dis pas de mal de sa voiture ! ◆ **in ~ society** dans la bonne société ◆ **it is ~ to ask permission** il est poli de demander la permission ◆ **to make ~ conversation** échanger des politesses

politely /pəˈlaɪtlɪ/ ADV poliment ◆ **what he ~ called an "inaccuracy"** ce qu'il a appelé poliment une "inexactitude"

politeness /pəˈlaɪtnɪs/ N politesse *f* ◆ **to do sth out of ~** faire qch par politesse

politic /ˈpɒlɪtɪk/ ADJ *(frm)* politique *(liter)* ◆ **he thought** *or* **deemed it ~ to refuse** il a jugé politique de refuser ◆ **it would be ~ to tell him before someone else does** il serait diplomatique de le lui dire avant que quelqu'un d'autre ne le fasse ; → **body**

political /pəˈlɪtɪkəl/ ADJ 1 *(Pol)* politique ◆ **~ analyst** *or* **commentator** politologue *mf* ; → **party**
2 *(fig = politicized)* **he was always very ~** il a toujours été très politisé ◆ **he's a ~ animal** il a la politique dans le sang
3 *(= expedient, tactical)* **it was a ~ decision** c'était une décision tactique
COMP **political action committee** N (US) comité *m* de soutien *(d'un candidat)*
political asylum N ◆ **to ask for ~ asylum** demander le droit d'asile (politique)
political convention N (US) convention *f* politique
political correctness N *(esp pej)* ◆ **our society's obsession with ~ correctness** l'obsession de notre société pour ce qui est politiquement correct ◆ **in this age of ~ correctness*** *(pej)* à l'heure de la pensée politiquement correcte, à l'heure du politiquement correct ; → POLITICALLY CORRECT
political economy N économie *f* politique
political football* N *(pej)* ◆ **the drug issue will continue to be a ~ football** la question de la drogue continuera à être une sorte de balle que tout le monde se renvoie dans le monde politique ◆ **he/this charter is being used as a ~ football** il/cette charte est le prétexte à des débats de politique politicienne
political geography N géographie *f* politique
political prisoner N prisonnier *m* politique
political science N sciences *fpl* politiques
political scientist N spécialiste *mf* des sciences politiques

politically /pəˈlɪtɪkəlɪ/ ADV d'un point de vue politique, politiquement ◆ **~ acceptable/expedient/sensitive** acceptable/opportun/délicat d'un point de vue politique, politiquement acceptable/opportun/délicat ◆ **~ stable** politiquement stable, stable d'un point de vue politique ◆ **~ motivated** ayant une motivation politique ◆ **~ aware** politisé ◆ **~ speaking** politiquement parlant
COMP **politically correct** ADJ politiquement correct
politically incorrect ADJ qui n'est pas politiquement correct ◆ **his jokes are ~ incorrect but very funny** ses plaisanteries ne sont pas politiquement correctes mais elles sont très drôles
politically-minded, politically-orientated ADJ politisé

> **POLITICALLY CORRECT**
>
> Une personne politiquement correcte (**politically correct**, ou **PC**) évite d'employer certains termes, jugés dégradants ou insultants, pour désigner les membres de minorités ou de groupes défavorisés tels que les minorités ethniques, les femmes, les handicapés ou les homosexuels. Ainsi est-on passé successivement de « Negroes » (terme qu'utilisait Martin Luther King) à « coloured people », puis à « Black people » ; de même dira-t-on d'un aveugle qu'il est malvoyant (« he's visually impaired »). Les adeptes de ce mouvement d'origine américaine estiment ainsi remettre en question les présupposés idéologiques de la civilisation occidentale. Aujourd'hui, cependant, l'expression **politically correct** est souvent utilisée de façon péjorative par les opposants à ces idées libérales.

politician /ˌpɒlɪˈtɪʃən/ N homme *m* politique, femme *f* politique

politicization /pəlɪtɪsaɪˈzeɪʃən/ N politisation *f*

politicize /pəˈlɪtɪsaɪz/ VT politiser

politicking /ˈpɒlɪtɪkɪŋ/ N *(pej)* politique *f* politicienne

politico* /pəˈlɪtɪkəʊ/ N (pl **politicos**) *(pej) (= politician)* politicard *m* ◆ **he's a real** ~ *(= political person)* il est très politisé

politico... /pəˈlɪtɪkəʊ/ PREF politico...

politics /ˈpɒlɪtɪks/ N *(Pol)* politique *f* ◆ **to go into** ~ se lancer dans la *or* entrer en politique ◆ **to be in** ~ faire de la politique ◆ **to study** ~ étudier les sciences politiques ◆ **to talk** ~ parler politique ◆ **foreign** ~ la politique étrangère ◆ **to play** ~ **(with education/the economy)** *(pej)* faire de la politique politicienne *(pej)* (en matière d'éducation/d'économie) ◆ **what they are doing is playing** ~ **with people's lives** ils jouent avec la vie des gens à des fins politiques ; → **office, party, sexual** NPL *(= political ideas)* opinions *fpl* politiques ◆ **what are your/his** ~? quelles sont vos/ses opinions politiques ? ◆ **the influence of socialist ideas on his** ~ l'influence des idées socialistes sur ses opinions politiques

polity /ˈpɒlɪtɪ/ N *(= system of government)* régime *m*, administration *f* politique ; *(= government organization)* constitution *f* politique ; *(= the State)* État *m*

polka /ˈpɒlkə/ N (pl **polkas**) polka *f*
COMP **polka dot** N pois *m*
polka-dot ADJ ◆ **a** ~**-dot blouse** un chemisier à pois

poll /pəʊl/ N 1 *(= vote in general: gen pl)* vote *m* ; *(= voting at election)* scrutin *m* ; *(= election)* élection(s) *f(pl)* ; *(= list of voters)* liste *f* électorale ; *(= voting place)* bureau *m* de vote ; *(= votes cast)* voix *fpl*, suffrages *mpl* ◆ **the result of the** ~**s** le résultat de l'élection *or* du scrutin ◆ **on the eve of the** ~**s** à la veille de l'élection *or* du scrutin ◆ **to go to the** ~**s** aller aux urnes, aller voter ◆ **a crushing defeat at the** ~**s** une écrasante défaite aux élections ◆ **there was a 64% turnout at the** ~**s** 64% des inscrits ont voté, la participation électorale a été de (l'ordre de) 64% ◆ **the conservatives' highest** ~ **for ten years** le meilleur score des conservateurs en dix ans ◆ **he got 20% of the** ~ il a obtenu 20% des suffrages exprimés ◆ **he achieved a** ~ **of 5,000 votes** il a obtenu 5 000 voix ; → **standing**
2 *(= opinion survey)* sondage *m* ◆ **(public) opinion** ~ sondage *m* d'opinion ◆ **to take** *or* **conduct a** ~ effectuer un sondage *(of* auprès de) ◆ **to take a** ~ **of 3,000 people** effectuer un sondage auprès de 3 000 personnes ◆ **a telephone** ~ un sondage téléphonique ◆ **a** ~ **of** ~**s** une analyse de sondages ; → **Gallup**
3 *(†† = head)* chef † *m*
VT 1 *[+ votes]* obtenir ; *[+ people]* sonder l'opinion de, interroger ◆ **they** ~**ed the students to find out whether** ... ils ont sondé l'opinion des étudiants pour savoir si ... ◆ **40% of those** ~**ed supported the government** 40% des personnes interrogées étaient favorables au gouvernement
2 *[+ cattle]* décorner ; *[+ tree]* étêter, écimer
VI ◆ **the nationalists** ~**ed well** les nationalistes ont obtenu un bon score
COMP **poll taker** N *(US)* sondeur *m*
poll tax N *(gen)* capitation *f* ; *(Brit) (formerly)* ≃ impôts *mpl* locaux

pollack /ˈpɒlək/ N (pl **pollacks** *or* **pollack**) lieu *m* jaune

pollard /ˈpɒləd/ N *(= animal)* animal *m* sans cornes ; *(= tree)* têtard *m*, arbre *m* étêté *or* écimé VT *[+ animal]* décorner ; *[+ tree]* étêter, écimer

pollen /ˈpɒlən/ N pollen *m* COMP **pollen count** N taux *m* de pollen

pollinate /ˈpɒlɪneɪt/ VT féconder (avec du pollen)

pollination /ˌpɒlɪˈneɪʃən/ N pollinisation *f*, fécondation *f*

pollinator /ˈpɒlɪneɪtəʳ/ N pollinisateur *m*, -trice *f*

polling /ˈpəʊlɪŋ/ N élections *fpl* ◆ ~ **is on Thursday** les élections ont lieu jeudi, on vote jeudi ◆ **the** ~ **was extremely low** le taux de participation était extrêmement faible
COMP **polling booth** N isoloir *m*
polling day N jour *m* des élections
polling place N *(US)* ⇒ **polling station**
polling station N *(Brit)* bureau *m* de vote

polliwog /ˈpɒlɪwɒg/ N *(US = tadpole)* têtard *m*

pollock /ˈpɒlək/ N ⇒ **pollack**

pollster /ˈpəʊlstəʳ/ N sondeur *m*, enquêteur *m*, -euse *f*

pollutant /pəˈluːtənt/ N polluant *m*

pollute /pəˈluːt/ VT polluer ; *(fig)* contaminer ; *(= corrupt)* corrompre ; *(= desecrate)* profaner, polluer *(liter)* ◆ **the river was** ~**d with chemicals** la rivière était polluée par des produits chimiques

polluter /pəˈluːtəʳ/ N pollueur *m*, -euse *f* ◆ **the** ~ **pays** les pollueurs sont les payeurs

pollution /pəˈluːʃən/ N 1 *(lit, Chem etc)* pollution *f* ◆ **air/atmospheric/marine** ~ pollution *f* de l'air/atmosphérique/marine 2 *(fig = impurity, corruption)* souillure *f (liter)* ◆ **spiritual** ~ souillure *f (liter)* de l'esprit ; → **light¹, noise**

Pollyanna /pɒlɪˈænə/ N optimiste *m(f)* béat(e)

pollywog /ˈpɒlɪwɒg/ N ⇒ **polliwog**

polo /ˈpəʊləʊ/ N polo *m* ; → **water**
COMP **polo-neck** N col *m* roulé ADJ (also **polo-necked**) à col roulé
polo shirt N polo *m*, chemise *f* polo
polo stick N maillet *m* (de polo)

polonaise /ˌpɒləˈneɪz/ N *(Mus, Dancing)* polonaise *f*

polonium /pəˈləʊnɪəm/ N polonium *m*

poltergeist /ˈpɔːltəgaɪst/ N esprit *m* frappeur

poltroon † /pɒlˈtruːn/ N poltron *m*

poly* /ˈpɒlɪ/ N *(Brit Hist)* (abbrev of **polytechnic**) ≃ IUT *m* ADJ *(* Brit)* (abbrev of **polythene**) en polyéthylène COMP **poly bag** N *(= polythene bag)* sac *m* en plastique

poly... /ˈpɒlɪ/ PREF poly...

polyandrous /ˌpɒlɪˈændrəs/ ADJ polyandre

polyandry /ˈpɒlɪændrɪ/ N polyandrie *f*

polyanthus /ˌpɒlɪˈænθəs/ N primevère *f* (multiflore)

polyarchy /ˈpɒlɪˌɑːkɪ/ N polyarchie *f*

polychlorinated biphenyl /ˌpɒlɪˈklɔːrɪneɪtɪdbaɪˈfenəl/ N polychlorobiphényle *m*

polychromatic /ˌpɒlɪkrəʊˈmætɪk/ ADJ polychrome

polychrome /ˈpɒlɪkrəʊm/ ADJ polychrome N *(= statue)* statue *f* polychrome ; *(= picture)* tableau *m* polychrome

polyclinic /ˈpɒlɪklɪnɪk/ N polyclinique *f*

polycotton /ˌpɒlɪˈkɒtən/ N polyester *m* et coton *m*

polyester /ˌpɒlɪˈestəʳ/ N polyester *m* COMP de *or* en polyester

polyethylene /ˌpɒlɪˈeθəliːn/ N polyéthylène *m*, polythène *m*

polygamist /pɒˈlɪgəmɪst/ N polygame *mf*

polygamous /pɒˈlɪgəməs/ ADJ polygame

polygamy /pɒˈlɪgəmɪ/ N polygamie *f*

polygenesis /ˌpɒlɪˈdʒenɪsɪs/ N polygénisme *m*

polygenetic /ˌpɒlɪdʒɪˈnetɪk/ ADJ polygénétique

polyglot /ˈpɒlɪglɒt/ ADJ, N polyglotte *mf*

polygon /ˈpɒlɪgən/ N polygone *m*

polygonal /pɒˈlɪgənl/ ADJ polygonal

polygraph /ˈpɒlɪgrɑːf/ N détecteur *m* de mensonges

polyhedra /ˌpɒlɪˈhiːdrə/ NPL of **polyhedron**

polyhedral /ˌpɒlɪˈhiːdrəl/ ADJ polyédrique

polyhedron /ˌpɒlɪˈhiːdrən/ N (pl **polyhedrons** *or* **polyhedra**) polyèdre *m*

polymath /ˈpɒlɪmæθ/ N esprit *m* universel

polymer /ˈpɒlɪməʳ/ N polymère *m*

polymerization /ˈpɒlɪməraɪˈzeɪʃən/ N polymérisation *f*

polymorphism /ˌpɒlɪˈmɔːfɪzəm/ N polymorphisme *m*, polymorphie *f*

polymorphous /ˌpɒlɪˈmɔːfəs/ ADJ polymorphe

Polynesia /ˌpɒlɪˈniːzɪə/ N Polynésie *f*

Polynesian /ˌpɒlɪˈniːzɪən/ ADJ polynésien N 1 *(= person)* Polynésien(ne) *m(f)* 2 *(= language)* polynésien *m*

polynomial /ˌpɒlɪˈnəʊmɪəl/ ADJ, N polynôme *m*

polyp /ˈpɒlɪp/ N *(= marine animal, tumour)* polype *m*

polyphase /ˈpɒlɪfeɪz/ ADJ polyphasé

polyphonic /ˌpɒlɪˈfɒnɪk/ ADJ polyphonique

polyphony /pəˈlɪfənɪ/ N polyphonie *f*

polypi /ˈpɒlɪpaɪ/ NPL of **polypus**

polypropylene /ˌpɒlɪˈprɒpɪliːn/ N polypropylène *m*

polypus /ˈpɒlɪpəs/ N (pl **polypi**) *(Med)* polype *m*

polysemic /ˌpɒlɪˈsiːmɪk/ ADJ polysémique

polysemous /pɒˈlɪsəməs/ ADJ polysémique

polysemy /pɒˈlɪsəmɪ/ N polysémie *f*

polystyrene /ˌpɒlɪˈstaɪriːn/ N *(esp Brit)* polystyrène *m* ◆ **expanded** ~ polystyrène *m* expansé
COMP **polystyrene cement** N colle *f* polystyrène
polystyrene chips NPL billes *fpl* (de) polystyrène

polysyllabic /ˈpɒlɪsɪˈlæbɪk/ ADJ polysyllabe, polysyllabique

polysyllable /ˈpɒlɪˌsɪləbl/ N polysyllabe *m*, mot *m* polysyllabique

polytechnic /ˌpɒlɪˈteknɪk/ N *(in Brit until 1992)* ≃ IUT *m*, Institut *m* universitaire de technologie

polytheism /ˈpɒlɪθiːɪzəm/ N polythéisme *m*

polytheistic /ˌpɒlɪθiːˈɪstɪk/ ADJ polythéiste

polythene /ˈpɒlɪθiːn/ *(Brit)* N polyéthylène *m*, polythène *m* COMP **polythene bag** N sachet *m* en plastique

polyunsaturate /ˌpɒlɪʌnˈsætʃʊrɪt/ N (acide *m* gras) polyinsaturé *m*

polyunsaturated /ˌpɒlɪʌnˈsætʃʊˌreɪtɪd/ ADJ polyinsaturé

polyurethane /ˌpɒlɪˈjʊərɪθeɪn/ N polyuréthane *m*

polyvalent /pəˈlɪvələnt/ ADJ polyvalent

polyvinyl /ˈpɒlɪvaɪnl/ N polyvinyle *m*

pom /pɒm/ N, ADJ ⇒ **pommy**

pomade /pəˈmɑːd/ N pommade *f* VT pommader

pomander /pəʊˈmændəʳ/ N *(china)* diffuseur *m* de parfum

pomegranate /ˈpɒməˌgrænɪt/ N *(= fruit)* grenade *f* ; *(= tree)* grenadier *m*

pomelo /ˈpɒmɪləʊ/ N (pl **pomelos**) pomélo *m*

Pomeranian /ˌpɒməˈreɪnɪən/ N *(= dog)* loulou *m* (de Poméranie)

pommel /ˈpʌml/ N pommeau *m* VT ⇒ **pummel**
COMP **pommel horse** N cheval *m* d'arçons

pommy ⁑ /ˈpɒmɪ/ *(Austral pej)* N Anglais(e) *m(f)*, rosbif *m (pej)* ADJ anglais

pomp /pɒmp/ N pompe *f*, faste *m*, apparat *m* ◆ **~ and circumstance** grand apparat *m*, pompes *fpl (liter)* ◆ **with great ~** en grande pompe

Pompadour /ˈpɒmpəˌdʊəʳ/ N *(US = hairstyle)* banane *f (coiffure)*

Pompeii /pɒmˈpeɪ/ N Pompéi

Pompey /ˈpɒmpɪ/ N Pompée *m*

pompom /ˈpɒmpɒm/ N [1] *(= bobble)* pompon *m* [2] *(Mil)* canon-mitrailleuse *m* (de DCA)

pompon /ˈpɒmpɒn/ N *(= bobble)* pompon *m*
COMP **pompon dahlia** N dahlia *m* pompon
pompon rose N rose *f* pompon

pomposity /pɒmˈpɒsɪtɪ/ N *(pej)* manières *fpl* pompeuses, air *m or* ton *m* pompeux, solennité *f*

pompous /ˈpɒmpəs/ ADJ *[person]* pontifiant ; *[remark, speech, tone]* pompeux, pontifiant ; *[style]* pompeux, ampoulé

pompously /ˈpɒmpəslɪ/ ADV *[speak]* sur un ton pompeux ; *[write]* dans un style pompeux ; *[behave]* pompeusement

ponce ⁑ /pɒns/ *(Brit)* N [1] *(= pimp)* maquereau⁑ *m*, souteneur *m* [2] *(pej = homosexual)* pédé⁑ *m* VI faire le maquereau⁑, être souteneur

► **ponce about** ⁑, **ponce around** ⁑ VI *(pej)* se pavaner

poncey * /ˈpɒnsɪ/ ADJ *(Brit pej) [person]* affecté ; *[restaurant, school]* snob ; *[clothes]* de poseur

poncho /ˈpɒntʃəʊ/ N (pl **ponchos**) poncho *m*

poncy * /ˈpɒnsɪ/ ADJ → **poncey**

pond /pɒnd/ N étang *m* ; *(stagnant)* mare *f* ; *(artificial)* bassin *m* ◆ **the ~*** *(= the Atlantic Ocean)* l'océan *m* atlantique ◆ **across the ~** outre-atlantique ; → **big, millpond**
COMP **pond life** N *(lit)* faune *f* et flore *f* des étangs ; *(fig)* * *(= person)* zéro *m* ; *(= group)* individus *mpl*

ponder /ˈpɒndəʳ/ VT réfléchir à *or* sur ◆ **I constantly ~ed this question** je réfléchissais constamment à cette question ◆ **I'm always ~ing how to improve it** je me demande tout le temps comment l'améliorer VI méditer *(over, on* sur*)*, réfléchir *(over, on* à, sur*)*

ponderable /ˈpɒndərəbl/ ADJ pondérable

ponderous /ˈpɒndərəs/ ADJ *[movement, object]* lourd, pesant ; *[style, joke]* lourd ; *[speech, tone, voice]* pesant et solennel

ponderously /ˈpɒndərəslɪ/ ADV *[move]* pesamment, lourdement ; *[write]* avec lourdeur ; *[say, speak]* d'un ton solennel et pesant

pondweed /ˈpɒndwiːd/ N épi *m* d'eau, potamot *m*

pone /pəʊn/ N *(US)* pain *m* de maïs

pong * /pɒŋ/ *(Brit)* N mauvaise odeur *f* ; *(stronger)* puanteur *f* ◆ **what a ~ in here!** ça (s)chlingue* ici ! VI (s)chlinguer* ◆ **it ~s!*** pouah !, ça (s)chlingue !*

pons Varolii /pɒnzvəˈrəʊlɪaɪ/ N pont *m* de Varole, protubérance *f* annulaire

pontiff /ˈpɒntɪf/ N *(Rel) (= dignitary)* pontife *m* ; *(= pope)* souverain *m* pontife, pontife *m* romain

pontifical /pɒnˈtɪfɪkəl/ ADJ *(Rel)* pontifical ; *(fig)* pontifiant

pontificate /pɒnˈtɪfɪkɪt/ N *(Rel)* pontificat *m* VI /pɒnˈtɪfɪkeɪt/ *(fig)* pontifier *(about* au sujet de, sur*)*

Pontius Pilate /ˈpɒnʃəsˈpaɪlət/ N Ponce Pilate *m*

pontoon /pɒnˈtuːn/ N [1] *(gen)* ponton *m* ; *(on aircraft)* flotteur *m* [2] *(Brit Cards)* vingt-et-un *m*
COMP **pontoon bridge** N pont *m* flottant

pony /ˈpəʊnɪ/ N poney *m* ; *(Brit* ⁑ *= £25)* 25 livres ; *(US Scol* ⁑ *= crib)* traduc* *f*, corrigé *m (utilisé illicitement)*
COMP **pony express** N *(US Hist)* messageries *fpl* rapides par relais de cavaliers
pony trekking N randonnée *f* équestre *or* à cheval

ponytail /ˈpəʊnɪteɪl/ N queue *f* de cheval ◆ **to have** *or* **wear one's hair in a ~** avoir une queue de cheval

poo * /puː/ *(Brit) (baby talk)* N caca* *m (baby talk)* ◆ **to do a ~** faire caca* *(baby talk)* VI faire caca* *(baby talk)*

pooch ⁑ /puːtʃ/ N cabot* *m*, clebs⁑ *m*

poodle /ˈpuːdl/ N caniche *m* ; *(fig = servile person)* chien *m*

poof /pʊf/ N *(Brit* ⁑ *pej)* tante⁑ *f*, tapette⁑ *f* EXCL hop !

poofter ⁑ /ˈpʊftəʳ/ N *(Brit pej)* ⇒ **poof**

poofy ⁑ /ˈpʊfɪ/ ADJ *(Brit pej)* efféminé, du genre tapette⁑ ◆ **it's ~** ça fait fille

pooh /puː/ EXCL bah !, peuh ! N ⇒ **poo** VI ⇒ **poo**
COMP **pooh-pooh** VT ◆ **to pooh-pooh sth** faire fi de qch, dédaigner qch

pool¹ /puːl/ N [1] *(= puddle) [of water, rain]* flaque *f* (d'eau) ; *[of spilt liquid]* flaque *f* ; *(larger)* mare *f* ; *(fig) [of light from lamp, spot, flood]* rond *m* ; *[of sunlight]* flaque *f* ; *[of shadow]* zone *f* ◆ **lying in a ~ of blood** étendu dans une mare de sang ◆ **in a ~ of light** dans une flaque *or* un rond de lumière [2] *(= pond) (natural)* étang *m* ; *(artificial)* bassin *m*, pièce *f* d'eau ; *(in river)* plan *m* d'eau ; *(= water hole)* point *m* d'eau ; (also **swimming pool**) piscine *f* ; → **paddle**
COMP **pool attendant** N surveillant(e) *m(f)* de baignade, maître *m* nageur

pool² /puːl/ N [1] *(Cards etc = stake)* poule *f*, cagnotte *f* ; *(gen = common fund)* cagnotte *f*
[2] *(fig) (of things owned in common)* fonds *m* commun ; *(= reserve, source) [of ideas, experience, ability]* réservoir *m* ; *[of advisers, experts]* équipe *f* ◆ **a ~ of vehicles** un parc de voitures ◆ **typing ~** pool *m* de dactylos ◆ **~ of reporters** pool *m* de presse ◆ **a very good ~ of players/talent** *etc* un très bon réservoir de joueurs/talents *etc* ◆ **genetic ~** pool *m* génétique
[3] *(Econ = consortium)* pool *m* ; *(US = monopoly trust)* trust *m* ◆ **the coal and steel ~** le pool charbon acier
[4] *(= billiards)* billard *m* américain ◆ **to shoot** *or* **play ~** jouer au billard américain
NPL **the pools** * *(Brit)* ⇒ **the football pools** ; → **football**
VT *[+ money, resources, objects, knowledge, ideas]* mettre en commun ; *[+ efforts]* unir ; *[+ workers]* rassembler
COMP **pool table** N billard *m (table)*

poolroom /ˈpuːlrʊm/ N *(Billiards)* (salle *f* de) billard *m*

poop¹ /puːp/ *(Naut)* N poupe *f*
COMP **poop deck** N dunette *f*

poop² ⁑ /puːp/ N *(esp US = excrement)* crotte *f*
COMP **poop scoop** N ramasse-crottes *m inv*

poop³ * /puːp/ N *(US = information)* tuyau* *m*, bon renseignement *m*

pooped ⁑ /puːpt/ ADJ *(esp US = exhausted)* pompé⁑, crevé*, à plat*

pooper-scooper * /ˈpuːpəˈskuːpəʳ/ N ramasse-crottes *m inv*

poor /pʊəʳ/ ADJ [1] *(= not rich) [person, family, nation]* pauvre ◆ **as ~ as a church-mouse** pauvre comme Job ◆ **to become ~er** s'appauvrir ◆ **he was a thousand pounds (the) ~er** il avait perdu mille livres ◆ **in ~ circumstances** dans le besoin, dans la gêne ◆ **soil that is ~ in zinc** *(fig = lacking)* un sol pauvre en zinc ; see also **comp**
[2] *(= inferior) [amount, sales, harvest, output]* maigre, médiocre ; *[work, worker, soldier, film, result, performance, food, summer]* médiocre, piètre *before n* ; *[pay]* maigre, faible ; *[effort, ventilation]* insuffisant ; *[light]* faible ; *[sight]* faible, mauvais ; *[soil]* pauvre, peu productif ; *[quality]* médiocre ; *[housing]* insalubre ; *[hygiene, sanitation, visibility, conditions, management]* mauvais ◆ **"poor"** *(Scol etc: as mark)* "faible", "médiocre" ◆ **to be ~ at (doing) sth** ne pas être doué pour (faire) qch ◆ **clients who have had ~ service** les clients qui ont eu à se plaindre de l'insuffisance du service ◆ **he had a very ~ attendance record** il avait souvent été absent ◆ **he has a ~ chance of survival** il a peu de chances de survivre ◆ **to be in ~ health** ne pas être en bonne santé, être en mauvaise santé ◆ **to have ~ hearing** être dur d'oreille ◆ **he has a ~ memory** il a mauvaise mémoire ◆ **people with ~ circulation** les gens qui ont une mauvaise circulation ◆ **she had a ~ grasp of German** son allemand n'était pas très bon ◆ **he showed a ~ grasp of the facts** il a manifesté un manque de compréhension des faits ◆ **to have a ~ opinion of o.s.** avoir une mauvaise opinion de soi-même ◆ **a ~ substitute (for sth)** un piètre substitut (de qch) ◆ **a ~ imitation of sth** une pâle imitation de qch ◆ **this sparkling wine is just a ~ relation of champagne** ce vin pétillant n'est qu'une pâle imitation de champagne ◆ **I'm a ~ sailor** je n'ai pas le pied marin ◆ **he is a ~ traveller** il supporte mal les voyages ◆ **he's a ~ loser** il est mauvais perdant ; → **second¹, show**
[3] *(= pitiable)* pauvre ◆ **~ little thing!** pauvre petit(e) ! ◆ **she's all alone, ~ woman** elle est toute seule, la pauvre ◆ **~ chap, he was killed in an air crash** le pauvre, il est mort dans un accident d'avion ◆ **~ things*, they look cold** les pauvres, ils ont l'air d'avoir froid ◆ **you ~ old thing!*** mon pauvre vieux !, ma pauvre vieille ! ◆ **~ little rich girl** *(iro)* pauvre petite fille *f* riche
NPL **the poor** les pauvres *mpl*
COMP **poor boy** N *(US Culin)* grand sandwich *m* mixte
poor law N *(Hist)* ◆ **the ~ laws** les lois *fpl* sur l'assistance publique
poor-mouth * VT *(US)* ◆ **to ~-mouth sb/sth** parler en termes désobligeants de qn/qch
poor-spirited ADJ timoré, pusillanime
poor White N *(esp pej)* petit Blanc *m*

poorbox /ˈpʊəbɒks/ N *(Rel)* tronc *m* des pauvres

poorhouse /ˈpʊəhaʊs/ N *(Hist)* hospice *m* (des pauvres)

poorly /ˈpʊəlɪ/ ADJ *(esp Brit:* *) souffrant, malade ◆ **the hospital described his condition as ~** les médecins ont déclaré que son état était préoccupant ADV *[live, dress]* pauvrement ; *[perform, eat, sell]* mal ◆ **~ lit/paid/designed** *etc* mal éclairé/payé/conçu *etc* ◆ **to be ~ off** être pauvre

poorness /ˈpʊənɪs/ N [1] *(= poverty)* pauvreté *f* [2] *(= poor quality)* mauvaise qualité *f*, médiocrité *f*

POP /ˌpiːəʊˈpiː/ N [1] *(Comput)* (abbrev of **point of presence**) POP *m* [2] (abbrev of **persistent organic pollutant**) POP *m*

pop¹ /pɒp/ N [1] *(= sound) [of cork etc]* pan *m* ; *[of press stud etc]* bruit *m* sec ◆ **to go ~** *[cork]* sauter ; *[balloon]* éclater ; *[bulb, stud]* faire un (petit) bruit sec
[2] *(NonC * = drink)* boisson *f* gazeuse ◆ **orange ~** orangeade *f*
[3] *(= try)* ◆ **to have** *or* **take a ~ at (doing) sth** * s'essayer à (faire) qch
[4] *(= criticize)* ◆ **to have** *or* **take a ~ at sb/sth** * s'en prendre à qn/qch
[5] *(US)* ◆ **the drinks go for a dollar a ~** * les boissons sont à un dollar chaque *or* chacune

VT 1 *[+ balloon]* crever ; *[+ cork]* faire sauter ; *[+ corn]* faire éclater ; *[+ press stud]* fermer ◆ **to ~ one's cork** prendre son pied* ◆ **to ~ one's clogs** *(Brit hum)* casser sa pipe*

2 *(* = put)* mettre ◆ **to ~ one's head round the door/out of the window** passer brusquement la tête par la porte/par la fenêtre ◆ **to ~ one's head in** passer la tête par la porte *(or* par la fenêtre *etc)* ◆ **to ~ sth into the oven** passer *or* mettre qch au four ◆ **he ~ped it into his mouth** il l'a fourré *or* l'a mis dans sa bouche ◆ **to ~ pills** se bourrer de médicaments ◆ **could you ~ this letter into the postbox?** tu peux mettre cette lettre à la boîte ? ◆ **to ~ the question** *(= propose)* faire sa demande (en mariage)

3 *(† ‡ = pawn)* mettre au clou*

VI 1 *[balloon]* éclater ; *[cork, stud, buttons]* sauter ◆ **my ears ~ped** mes oreilles se sont débouchées ◆ **his eyes ~ped** il a écarquillé les yeux, il a ouvert des yeux ronds *or* de grands yeux ◆ **his eyes were ~ping out of his head** les yeux lui sortaient de la tête, il avait les yeux exorbités ◆ **her eyes were ~ping with amazement** elle écarquillait les yeux (sous l'effet de la surprise), elle ouvrait des yeux comme des soucoupes

2 *(* = go)* **I ~ped over** (or **round** *or* **across** *or* **out) to the grocer's** j'ai fait un saut à l'épicerie ◆ **he ~ped into a café** il est entré dans un café en vitesse ◆ **a letter ~ped through his letterbox** une lettre est tombée dans sa boîte aux lettres

COMP **pop quiz** N *(US Scol)* interrogation *f* (écrite) surprise

pop socks NPL *(Brit)* mi-bas *mpl* (fins)

pop-up N *(Comput)* pop-up *m*, fenêtre *f* pop-up

pop-up advertisement N pop-up *m* publicitaire

pop-up book N livre *m* animé

pop-up menu N *(Comput)* menu *m* *(qui s'affiche à l'écran sur commande)*

pop-up toaster N grille-pain *m inv* (à éjection automatique)

► **pop back*** VI revenir, retourner (en vitesse *or* pour un instant)

► **pop in*** VI entrer en passant, ne faire que passer ◆ **I ~ped in to say hullo to them** je suis entré (en passant) leur dire bonjour ◆ **she kept ~ping in and out** elle n'a pas cessé d'entrer et de sortir

► **pop off** VI 1 *(* = leave)* partir ◆ **they ~ped off to Spain for a few days** ils sont partis passer quelques jours en Espagne, ils ont filé* pour quelques jours en Espagne

2 *(‡ = die)* mourir (subitement), claquer*

3 *(US ‡ = shout)* donner de la gueule‡

► **pop on*** VT SEP 1 *(= switch on)* allumer, mettre en marche ◆ **to ~ the kettle on** mettre de l'eau à chauffer

2 *[+ clothes, shirt etc]* enfiler

► **pop out** VI *[person]* sortir ; *[head]* émerger ; *[cork]* sauter

► **pop round*** VI passer, faire un saut ◆ **~ round anytime** passe n'importe quand ; see also **pop vi 2**

► **pop up** VI *(from water, above wall etc)* surgir ◆ **he ~ped up unexpectedly in Tangier** * il a réapparu inopinément à Tanger

pop² /pɒp/ (abbrev of **popular**) **N** (musique *f*) pop *m* ◆ **to be top of the ~s** ≈ être en tête du Top 50

COMP *[music, song, singer, concert, group]* pop *inv*

pop art N pop art *m*

pop psychology N psychologie *f* de bazar

pop star N pop star *f*

pop³* /pɒp/ N *(esp US)* papa *m* ◆ **yes ~(s)** *(to old man)* oui grand-père*, oui pépé*

popcorn /ˈpɒpkɔːn/ N pop-corn *m inv*

pope /pəʊp/ N pape *m* ◆ **Pope John Paul II** le pape Jean-Paul II ◆ **~ Joan** *(Cards)* le nain jaune

popemobile* /ˈpəʊpməbiːl/ N papamobile* *f*

popery /ˈpəʊpərɪ/ N *(pej)* papisme *m (pej)*

popeyed /ˌpɒpˈaɪd/ ADJ aux yeux exorbités

popgun /ˈpɒpgʌn/ N pistolet *m* à bouchon

popinjay † /ˈpɒpɪndʒeɪ/ N fat *m*, freluquet *m*

popish /ˈpəʊpɪʃ/ ADJ *(pej)* papiste *(pej)*

poplar /ˈpɒpləʳ/ N peuplier *m*

poplin /ˈpɒplɪn/ **N** popeline *f* **COMP** de *or* en popeline

popover /ˈpɒpˌəʊvəʳ/ N *(US Culin)* ≈ chausson *m*

poppa* /ˈpɒpə/ N *(US)* papa *m*

poppadum /ˈpɒpədəm/ N poppadum *m*

popper /ˈpɒpəʳ/ N 1 *(Brit * = press stud)* pression *f*, bouton-pression *m* 2 *(Drugs *)* popper *m*

poppet* /ˈpɒpɪt/ N *(Brit)* ◆ **yes, (my) ~** oui, mon petit chou* ◆ **she's a (little) ~** elle est à croquer, c'est un amour

poppy /ˈpɒpɪ/ **N** 1 *(= flower)* pavot *m* ; *(growing wild)* coquelicot *m* 2 *(Brit: commemorative buttonhole)* coquelicot *m* en papier *(vendu le jour de l'Armistice)* **ADJ** *(= colour)* ponceau *inv*

COMP **Poppy Day** *(Brit)* N ≈ l'Armistice *m*

poppy seed N graine *f* de pavot

> **Poppy Day**
>
> **Poppy Day**, littéralement « la journée du coquelicot », désigne familièrement « Remembrance Day », c'est-à-dire la commémoration des armistices des deux Guerres mondiales, fixée en Grande-Bretagne au deuxième dimanche de novembre. Dans les jours qui précèdent, des coquelicots de papier sont vendus dans la rue au profit des associations caritatives d'aide aux anciens combattants et à leurs familles. → **Legion**

poppycock †* /ˈpɒpɪkɒk/ N *(NonC)* balivernes *fpl*

Popsicle ® /ˈpɒpsɪkl/ N *(US)* glace *f* à l'eau *(à deux bâtonnets)*

popsy †‡ /ˈpɒpsɪ/ N *(Brit)* souris‡ *f*, fille *f*

populace /ˈpɒpjʊlɪs/ N population *f*, populace *f (pej)*

popular /ˈpɒpjʊləʳ/ **ADJ** 1 *(= well-liked) [person, decision, book, sport]* populaire ; *(= fashionable) [style, model, place]* prisé *(with* de), en vogue ; *[name]* en vogue ; *[habit, practice]* populaire, courant ◆ **these cameras are ~ among professionals** les professionnels utilisent beaucoup ces appareils photo ◆ **this is a very ~ colour** cette couleur se vend beaucoup ◆ **it is ~ to be patriotic** le patriotisme est à la mode *or* en vogue ◆ **it is never ~ to raise taxes** les augmentations d'impôts ne sont jamais populaires

◆ **to be popular with** être très apprécié de, avoir beaucoup de succès auprès de ◆ **a part of the capital ~ with tourists** un quartier de la capitale très apprécié des touristes ◆ **he remains very ~ with the American people** il reste très aimé des Américains, il jouit toujours d'une grande popularité auprès des Américains ◆ **he's ~ with his colleagues** ses collègues l'aiment beaucoup, il jouit d'une grande popularité auprès de ses collègues ◆ **he's ~ with the girls** il a du succès *or* il a la cote* auprès des filles ◆ **I'm not very ~ with the boss just now*** je ne suis pas très bien vu du patron *or* je n'ai pas la cote* auprès du patron en ce moment

2 *(= of, for, by the people) [music, concert, myth, newspaper, art, appeal]* populaire ; *[lecture, journal]* de vulgarisation, grand public ; *[government, discontent]* populaire, du peuple ◆ **at ~ prices** à la portée de toutes les bourses ◆ **by ~ demand** *or* **request** à la demande générale ◆ **contrary to ~ belief** *or* **opinion** contraire ment aux idées reçues ◆ **this decision does not reflect ~ opinion** cette décision ne reflète pas l'opinion publique ◆ **to win ~ support** obtenir le soutien de la population

COMP **popular culture** N culture *f* populaire

popular front N *(Pol)* front *m* populaire

popular vote N ◆ **Jackson won the ~ vote** Jackson a remporté l'élection au suffrage universel ◆ **fifty per cent of the ~ vote** cinquante pour cent des voix ◆ **he was elected with a huge ~ vote to the Congress** il a été élu au Congrès à une énorme majorité

popularist /ˈpɒpjʊlərɪst/ ADJ populaire, qui s'adresse au peuple

popularity /ˌpɒpjʊˈlærɪtɪ/ N popularité *f (with* auprès de ; *among* parmi) ◆ **to gain (in)** *or* **grow in ~** être de plus en plus populaire, acquérir une popularité de plus en plus grande ◆ **to decline in ~** être de moins en moins populaire, perdre de sa popularité ◆ **it enjoyed a certain ~** cela a joui d'une certaine popularité *or* faveur

popularization /ˈpɒpjʊləraɪˈzeɪʃən/ N 1 *(NonC) (= making prevalent)* popularisation *f* ; *(= making accessible)* vulgarisation *f* 2 *(= popularized work)* ouvrage *m* de vulgarisation

popularize /ˈpɒpjʊləraɪz/ VT *(= make prevalent) [+ sport, music, fashion, product]* populariser, rendre populaire ; *(= make accessible) [+ science, ideas]* vulgariser

popularizer /ˈpɒpjʊləraɪzəʳ/ N 1 *[of sport, fashion]* promoteur *m*, -trice *f* ◆ **Bruce Lee was a ~ of martial arts** Bruce Lee a popularisé les arts martiaux 2 *[of science, ideas]* vulgarisateur *m*, -trice *f*

popularly /ˈpɒpjʊləlɪ/ ADV ◆ **~ known as ...** communément connu *or* connu de tous sous le nom de ... ◆ **it is ~ supposed that ...** il est communément *or* généralement présumé que ..., on croit généralement que ... ◆ **he is ~ believed to be rich** il passe communément *or* généralement pour être riche ◆ **it's far more common than is ~ imagined** c'est bien plus fréquent qu'on ne l'imagine généralement ◆ **~ elected** démocratiquement élu

populate /ˈpɒpjʊleɪt/ VT peupler ◆ **densely/sparsely ~d** très/peu peuplé, à forte/faible densité de population ◆ **to be ~d with** être peuplé de

population /ˌpɒpjʊˈleɪʃən/ **N** population *f* ◆ **a fall/rise in (the) ~** une diminution/un accroissement de la population ◆ **the ~ of the town is 15,000** la population de la ville est de *or* la ville a une population de 15 000 habitants ◆ **the civilian ~** la population civile ◆ **the working ~** la population active

COMP *[increase]* de la population, démographique

population explosion N explosion *f* démographique

population figures NPL (chiffres *mpl* de la) démographie *f*

population planning N planification *f* démographique

populism /ˈpɒpjʊlɪzəm/ N populisme *m*

populist /ˈpɒpjʊlɪst/ ADJ, N populiste *mf*

populous /ˈpɒpjʊləs/ ADJ populeux, très peuplé

porcelain /ˈpɔːsəlɪn/ **N** *(NonC = substance, objects)* porcelaine *f* ◆ **a piece of ~** une porcelaine

COMP *[dish]* de *or* en porcelaine ; *[clay, glaze]* à porcelaine

porcelain ware N *(NonC)* vaisselle *f* en *or* de porcelaine

porch /pɔːtʃ/ N *[of house, church]* porche *m* ; *[of hotel]* marquise *f* ; *(US)* (also **sun porch**) véranda *f*

porcine /ˈpɔːsaɪn/ ADJ *(frm)* porcin, de porc

porcupine /ˈpɔːkjʊpaɪn/ **N** porc-épic *m* ; → **prickly** **COMP** **porcupine fish** N (pl **porcupine fish** *or* **fishes**) poisson-globe *m*

pore¹ /pɔːʳ/ N (*in skin*) pore *m* ◆ **she oozes sexuality from every ~** la sensualité se dégage de toute sa personne

pore² /pɔːʳ/ VI ◆ **to ~ over** *[+ book]* être absorbé dans ; *[+ letter, map]* étudier de près ; *[+ problem]* méditer longuement ◆ **he was poring over the book** il était plongé dans *or* absorbé par le livre

pork /pɔːk/ (*Culin*) N porc *m*
COMP *[chop etc]* de porc
pork barrel * (*US Pol*) N électoralisme *m* (*travaux publics ou programme de recherche etc entrepris à des fins électorales*) ADJ *[project etc]* électoraliste
pork butcher N ≈ charcutier *m*, -ière *f*
pork pie N
1 pâté *m* en croûte 2 ‡ ⇒ **porky noun**
pork-pie hat N (chapeau *m* en) feutre *m* rond
pork sausage N saucisse *f* (de porc)
pork scratchings NPL *amuse-gueules de couennes de porc frites*

porker /ˈpɔːkəʳ/ N porc *m* à l'engrais, goret *m*

porky /ˈpɔːkɪ/ ADJ (*: *pej*) gras (grasse *f*) comme un porc, bouffi N (‡ = *lie*: also **porky pie**) bobard* *m* ◆ **to tell porkies** raconter des bobards*

porn * /pɔːn/ N (*NonC*) (abbrev of **pornography**) porno* *m* ADJ *[magazine, video]* porno* ; *[actor]* de porno* ◆ **~ shop** sex shop *m* ; → **hard, soft**

porno * /ˈpɔːnəʊ/ ADJ *[magazine, video]* porno* ; *[actor]* de porno*

pornographer /pɔːˈnɒɡrəfəʳ/ N pornographe *m*

pornographic /ˌpɔːnəˈɡræfɪk/ ADJ pornographique

pornography /pɔːˈnɒɡrəfɪ/ N pornographie *f*

porosity /pɔːˈrɒsɪtɪ/ N porosité *f*

porous /ˈpɔːrəs/ ADJ poreux, perméable

porousness /ˈpɔːrəsnɪs/ N porosité *f*

porphyry /ˈpɔːfɪrɪ/ N porphyre *m*

porpoise /ˈpɔːpəs/ N (pl **porpoise** *or* **porpoises**) marsouin *m*

porridge /ˈpɒrɪdʒ/ N 1 porridge *m*, bouillie *f* de flocons d'avoine ◆ **~ oats** flocons *mpl* d'avoine 2 (*Brit* ‡) taule‡ *f* ◆ **to do ~** faire de la taule‡

porringer † /ˈpɒrɪndʒəʳ/ N bol *m*, écuelle *f*

port¹ /pɔːt/ N (= *harbour, town*) port *m* ◆ **~ of call** (*Naut*) (port *m* d')escale *f* ◆ **I've only one more ~ of call** (*fig*) il ne me reste plus qu'une course à faire ◆ **~ of dispatch** *or* (*US*) **shipment** port *m* d'expédition ◆ **~ of embarkation** port *m* d'embarquement ◆ **~ of entry** port *m* de débarquement *or* d'arrivée ◆ **naval/fishing ~** port *m* militaire/de pêche ◆ **to come into ~** entrer dans le port ◆ **they put into ~ at Dieppe** ils ont relâché dans le port de Dieppe ◆ **to make ~** (*Naut*) arriver au port ◆ **to run into ~** entrer au port ◆ **to leave ~** appareiller, lever l'ancre ◆ **a ~ in a storm** (*fig*) (= *person offering help*) une main secourable ; (= *refuge*) un havre de paix ◆ **the yen is the safest ~ in the current economic storm** le yen est la monnaie la plus sûre dans la crise économique actuelle ◆ **any ~ in a storm** nécessité fait loi (*Prov*) → **seaport, trading**
COMP *[facilities, security]* portuaire, du port
port authorities NPL autorités *fpl* portuaires
port dues NPL droits *mpl* de port

port² /pɔːt/ N 1 ⇒ **porthole** 2 (*Comput*) port *m*, porte *f* (d'accès), point *m* d'accès

port³ /pɔːt/ (*Naut*) N (also **port side**) bâbord *m* ◆ **to ~** à bâbord ◆ **land to ~!** terre par bâbord ! ◆ **to put the rudder to ~** mettre la barre à bâbord ADJ *[guns, lights]* de bâbord VT ◆ **to ~ the helm** mettre la barre à bâbord

port⁴ /pɔːt/ N (= *wine*) porto *m*

portability /pɔːtəˈbɪlɪtɪ/ N (*esp Comput*) portabilité *f* ; (*of software*) transférabilité *f*

portable /ˈpɔːtəbl/ ADJ (*gen*) portatif ; *[computer, telephone, television, software]* portable ◆ **a ~ language** (*Comput*) un langage de programmation portable ◆ **~ pension** pension *f* transférable N (= *computer*) portable *m* ; (= *tape recorder*) petit magnétophone *m* ; (= *television*) téléviseur *m* portable

portage /ˈpɔːtɪdʒ/ N (= *action, route*) portage *m* ; (= *cost*) frais *mpl* de portage

Portakabin ® /ˈpɔːtəkæbɪn/ N (*gen*) bâtiment *m* préfabriqué ; (= *extension to office etc*) petite annexe *f* préfabriquée ; (= *works office etc*) baraque *f* de chantier

portal /ˈpɔːtl/ N (*also Comput*) portail *m*

Portaloo ® /ˈpɔːtəluː/ N (*Brit*) toilettes *fpl* publiques provisoires

portcullis /pɔːtˈkʌlɪs/ N herse *f* (*de château fort*)

portend /pɔːˈtend/ VT (*liter*) présager, annoncer

portent /ˈpɔːtent/ N (*liter*) 1 (= *omen*) prodige *m*, présage *m* ◆ **of evil ~** de mauvais présage 2 (= *significance*) grande importance *f* ◆ **it's a day of ~** c'est un jour très important

portentous /pɔːˈtentəs/ ADJ (*liter*) (= *ominous*) de mauvais augure ; (= *marvellous*) prodigieux ; (= *grave*) solennel ; (*pej*) (= *pompous*) pompeux, pontifiant

portentously /pɔːˈtentəslɪ/ ADV (*liter*) *[say, announce]* (*pej* = *pompously*) pompeusement ; (*pej* = *ominously*) solennellement ◆ **the sky was ~ dark** le ciel noir ne présageait rien de bon

porter /ˈpɔːtəʳ/ N 1 (*for luggage: in station, hotel etc, on climb or expedition*) porteur *m* 2 (*US Rail* = *attendant*) employé(e) *m(f)* des wagons-lits 3 (*Brit* = *doorkeeper*) *[of private housing]* concierge *mf* ; *[of public building]* portier *m*, gardien(ne) *m(f)* ; (*Univ*) appariteur *m* 4 *[of hospital]* brancardier *m*, -ière *f* 5 (= *beer*) porter *m*, bière *f* brune COMP **porter's lodge** N loge *f* du portier

porterage /ˈpɔːtərɪdʒ/ N (= *act*) portage *m* ; (= *cost*) frais *mpl* de portage

porterhouse /ˈpɔːtəhaʊs/ N (also **porterhouse steak**) chateaubriand *m*

portfolio /pɔːtˈfəʊlɪəʊ/ N (pl **portfolios**) 1 (*Pol* = *object, post*) portefeuille *m* ◆ **minister without ~** ministre *m* sans portefeuille 2 *[of shares]* portefeuille *m* 3 *[of artist]* portfolio *m* ; *[of model]* book *m* 4 (*Comm* = *range*) gamme *f* COMP **portfolio manager** N portefeuilliste *mf*

porthole /ˈpɔːthəʊl/ N *[of plane, ship]* hublot *m* ; (*for ship's guns, cargo*) sabord *m*

portico /ˈpɔːtɪkəʊ/ N (pl **porticoes** *or* **porticos**) portique *m*

portion /ˈpɔːʃən/ N (= *part, percentage*) portion *f*, partie *f* ; *[of train, ticket etc]* partie *f* ; (= *share*) portion *f*, (quote-)part *f* ; *[of estate, inheritance etc]* portion *f*, part *f* ; (*of food* = *helping*) portion *f* ; († : also **marriage portion**) dot *f* ; (*liter*) (= *fate*) sort *m*, destin *m* VT (also **portion out**) répartir (*among, between* entre)

portliness /ˈpɔːtlɪnɪs/ N embonpoint *m*, corpulence *f*

portly /ˈpɔːtlɪ/ ADJ corpulent

portmanteau /pɔːtˈmæntəʊ/ N (pl **portmanteaus** *or* **portmanteaux** /pɔːtˈmæntəʊz/) grosse valise *f* (*de cuir*) COMP **portmanteau word** N (*Ling*) mot-valise *m*

portrait /ˈpɔːtrɪt/ N (*gen, Art*) portrait *m* ◆ **to paint sb's ~** peindre (le portrait de) qn
COMP **portrait gallery** N galerie *f* de portraits
portrait lens N (*gen*) objectif *m* à portrait ; (= *extension lens*) bonnette *f*
portrait mode N (*Comput*) ◆ **to output sth in ~ mode** imprimer qch à la française *or* au format portrait
portrait painter N portraitiste *mf*
portrait photographer N photographe *mf* spécialisé(e) dans les portraits, portraitiste *mf*
portrait photography N art *m* du portrait photographique ◆ **to do ~ photography** faire des portraits photographiques

portraitist /ˈpɔːtrɪtɪst/ N portraitiste *mf*

portraiture /ˈpɔːtrɪtʃəʳ/ N (*NonC*) (= *art*) art *m* du portrait ; (= *portrait*) portrait *m* ; (*NonC, collectively*) portraits *mpl*

portray /pɔːˈtreɪ/ VT *[painter]* peindre, faire le portrait de ; *[painting]* représenter ◆ **he ~ed him as an embittered man** *[painter]* il l'a peint sous les traits d'un homme aigri ; *[writer, speaker, actor]* il en a fait un homme aigri ◆ **the film ~ed him as a saint** le film le présentait comme un saint

portrayal /pɔːˈtreɪəl/ N (*in play, film, book*) évocation *f* ; (*by actor*) *[of character]* interprétation *f* ◆ **the novel is a hilarious ~ of Jewish life in the 1920s** ce roman dépeint *or* évoque d'une façon hilarante le monde juif des années 20

Portugal /ˈpɔːtjʊɡəl/ N Portugal *m* ◆ **in ~** au Portugal

Portuguese /ˌpɔːtjʊˈɡiːz/ ADJ (*gen*) portugais ; *[ambassador, embassy]* du Portugal ; *[teacher]* de portugais N 1 (*pl inv*) Portugais(e) *m(f)* 2 (= *language*) portugais *m* NPL **the Portuguese** les Portugais *mpl* COMP **Portuguese man-of-war** N (pl **Portuguese men-of-war**) (= *jellyfish*) galère *f*

POS /ˌpiːəʊˈes/ N (abbrev of **point of sale**) PLV *m*

pose /pəʊz/ N (= *body position*) (*gen, pej*) pose *f*, attitude *f* ; (*Art*) pose *f* ; (*fig*) pose *f* ◆ **to strike a ~** (*lit*) poser (pour la galerie) ; (*fig*) se composer une attitude ◆ **it's probably just a ~** ce n'est sans doute qu'une attitude VI (*Art, Phot*) poser (*for* pour ; *as* en) ; (*pej*) (= *attitudinize*) poser pour la galerie ◆ **to ~ as a doctor** se faire passer pour un docteur ◆ **to ~ nude** poser nu VT 1 (= *present*) *[+ problem, question]* poser ; *[+ difficulties]* poser, comporter ; *[+ threat, challenge]* constituer, représenter ; (*frm*) (= *state*) *[+ argument, claim, question]* formuler ; *[+ solution]* présenter ◆ **the danger ~d by nuclear weapons** le danger que constituent *or* représentent les armes nucléaires 2 *[+ artist's model]* faire prendre une pose à ; *[+ person]* faire poser COMP **posing pouch** N cache-sexe *m* (*pour homme*)

Poseidon /pɒˈsaɪdən/ N Poséidon *m*

poser /ˈpəʊzəʳ/ N 1 (*pej*) (= *person*) poseur *m*, -euse *f* (*pej*) 2 (= *problem, question*) question *f* difficile ◆ **that's a bit of a ~!** c'est un véritable casse-tête *or* une sacrée colle !* ◆ **how he did it remains a ~** nul ne sait comment il y est arrivé

poseur /pəʊˈzɜːʳ/ N (*pej*) poseur *m*, -euse *f* (*pej*)

posh * /pɒʃ/ ADJ 1 (= *distinguished*) *[house, neighbourhood, hotel, car, clothes]* chic ; *[occasion]* select *inv or* sélect ◆ **a ~ London restaurant** un restaurant londonien très chic ◆ **he was looking very ~** il faisait très chic, il s'était mis sur son trente et un 2 (*pej*) *[person, accent]* snob *f inv* ; *[house, neighbourhood, school, car]* huppé ◆ **~ people** les snob(s) *mpl*, les gens *mpl* de la haute* ◆ **my ~ aunt** ma tante qui est très snob ◆ **a ~ wedding** un mariage chic *or* en grand tralala* ADV (*pej*) ◆ **to talk ~** ‡ parler comme les gens de la haute*

► **posh up** ‡ VT SEP *[+ house, room]* redonner un coup de jeune à* ◆ **to ~ o.s. up** se pomponner, se bichonner ◆ **he was all ~ed up** il était sur son trente et un, il était bien pomponné

posidrive /ˈpɒzɪˌdraɪv/ ADJ ◆ **~ screw/screwdriver** vis *f*/tournevis *m* cruciforme

posit /ˈpɒzɪt/ VT postuler, poser comme postulat

position /pəˈzɪʃən/ LANGUAGE IN USE 6.3, 12.3, 15.4, 19
N 1 (*physical*) *[of person, object]* position *f* (*also Geog, Math, Mil, Mus, Naut, Phys etc*), place *f* ; *[of house, shop, town]* emplacement *m*, situation *f* ;

[of gun] emplacement *m* ◆ **to change the ~ of sth** changer qch de place ◆ **to change (one's) ~** changer de position ◆ **to take up (one's) ~** prendre position *or* place ◆ **to be in a good ~** *[house]* être bien placé ; see also **noun 4** ◆ **the enemy ~s** *(Mil etc)* les positions *fpl* de l'ennemi ◆ **what ~ do you play (in)?** *(Sport)* à quelle place jouez-vous ? ◆ **to jockey** *or* **jostle** *or* **manoeuvre for ~** *(lit, fig)* manœuvrer pour se placer avantageusement ◆ **"position closed"** *(in post office, bank)* "guichet fermé"

◆ **in position** en position

◆ **into position** en place, en position ◆ **troops are moving into ~** les troupes se mettent en place *or* en position ◆ **to push/slide sth into ~** mettre qch en place en le poussant/le faisant glisser ◆ **to get o.s. into ~** se placer ◆ **to lock into ~** verrouiller

◆ **in a ... position** *(physically)* ◆ **in a horizontal ~** en position horizontale ◆ **in an uncomfortable ~** dans une position incommode ◆ **in a sitting ~** en position assise

2 *(in class, league)* position *f*, place *f* ; *(socially)* position *f*, condition *f* ◆ **he finished in third ~** il est arrivé en troisième position *or* à la troisième place ◆ **his ~ in society** sa position dans la société ◆ **a man in his ~ should not ...** un homme dans sa position *or* de sa condition ne devrait pas ... ; see also **noun 4** ◆ **the priest she looked upon as a father figure abused his ~ of trust** le prêtre qu'elle considérait comme son père a abusé de sa confiance

3 *(= job)* poste *m*, emploi *m* ◆ **top management ~s** les postes *mpl* de cadre supérieur ◆ **his ~ in (the) government** son poste *or* sa fonction dans le gouvernement ◆ **a high ~ in the Cabinet** une haute fonction au ministère ◆ **he's in a ~ of power** il occupe un poste d'influence ◆ **he is using his ~ of power for personal gain** il utilise son pouvoir à des fins personnelles

4 *(= situation, circumstances)* situation *f*, place *f* ◆ **what would you do in my ~?** que feriez-vous à ma place ? ◆ **our ~ is desperate** notre situation est désespérée ◆ **the economic ~** la situation économique ◆ **to be in a good/bad ~** être dans une bonne/mauvaise situation ◆ **we were in an awkward ~** nous étions dans une situation délicate ◆ **put yourself in my ~** mettez-vous à ma place ◆ **a man in his ~ cannot expect mercy** un homme dans sa situation ne peut s'attendre à la clémence ; see also **noun 2** ◆ **what's the ~ on deliveries/sales?** où en sont les livraisons/ventes ?

◆ **to be in a position to do sth** être en mesure de faire qch ◆ **the UN will be in a ~ to support relief efforts** les Nations unies seront en mesure de soutenir les opérations de secours ◆ **I was glad I'd been in a ~ to help** j'étais content d'avoir pu être utile ◆ **he's in a good/bad ~ to judge** il est bien/mal placé pour juger

◆ **to be in no position to do sth** ne pas être en mesure de faire qch ◆ **he's in no ~ to decide** il n'est pas en position *or* en mesure de décider ◆ **she's in no ~ to criticize** elle est mal placée pour critiquer

5 *(= point of view, opinion)* position *f*, opinion *f* ◆ **you must make your ~ clear** vous devez dire franchement quelle est votre position ◆ **the Church's ~ on homosexuality** la position de l'Église face à *or* sur l'homosexualité ◆ **to take up a ~ on sth** prendre position sur qch ◆ **he took up the ~ that ...** il a adopté le point de vue selon lequel ... ◆ **he took a moderate ~ on most issues** il avait une position modérée sur la plupart des sujets ◆ **they were reluctant to state a clear ~ on the crisis** ils hésitaient à exposer clairement leur position sur la crise

VT 1 *(= adjust angle of)* *[+ light, microscope, camera]* positionner

2 *(= put in place)* *[+ gun, chair, camera]* mettre en place, placer ; *[+ house, school]* situer, placer ; *[+ guards, policemen]* placer, poster ; *[+ army, ship]* mettre en position ; *(Marketing)* *[+ product]* positionner ◆ **he ~ed each item with great care** il a très soigneusement disposé chaque article ◆ **to ~ o.s.** se mettre, se placer ◆ **the company is well ~ed to sell a million cars this year** la société est bien placée pour vendre un million de voitures cette année ◆ **he ~ed his party as the defender of the constitution** il a présenté son parti comme le défenseur de la constitution

3 *(= find position of)* déterminer la position de

COMP **position paper** **N** document *m* d'orientation

positioning /pəˈzɪʃənɪŋ/ **N** *(Comm)* positionnement *m*

positive /ˈpɒzɪtɪv/ **ADJ** 1 *(= not negative: gen, Elec, Gram, Math, Phot, Typ)* positif ; *[test, result, reaction]* positif ; *(= affirmative: Ling etc)* affirmatif ; *(= constructive)* *[suggestion]* positif, concret (-ète *f*) ; *[attitude, criticism]* positif ; *[response]* favorable, positif ◆ **to take ~ action** prendre des mesures concrètes ◆ **we need some ~ thinking** soyons positifs ◆ **he's very ~ about it** il a une attitude très positive à ce sujet ◆ **she is a very ~ person** c'est quelqu'un de très positif

2 *(= definite, indisputable)* *[order, rule, instruction]* catégorique, formel ; *[fact]* indéniable, irréfutable ; *[change, increase, improvement]* réel, tangible ◆ **~ proof, proof ~** preuve *f* formelle ◆ **there is ~ evidence that ...** il y a des preuves indéniables selon lesquelles ... ◆ **to make a ~ identification** *or* **ID on a body** formellement identifier un corps ◆ **~ progress has been made** un réel progrès *or* un progrès tangible a été fait ◆ **he has made a ~ contribution to the scheme** il a apporté une contribution effective au projet, il a contribué de manière effective au projet ◆ **it'll be a ~ pleasure to get rid of him!** ce sera un vrai *or* un véritable plaisir (que) de se débarrasser de lui ! ◆ **your room is a ~ disgrace** ta chambre est une véritable porcherie

3 *(= sure, certain)* *[person]* sûr, certain *(about, on, of* de*)* ◆ **are you quite ~?** en êtes-vous bien sûr *or* certain ? ◆ **I'm absolutely ~ I put it back** je suis absolument sûr de l'avoir remis à sa place ◆ **... he said in a ~ tone of voice** ... dit-il d'un ton très assuré ◆ **I am ~ that I can mend it** je suis sûr de pouvoir le réparer

N *(Elec)* pôle *m* positif ; *(Gram)* affirmatif *m* ; *(Math)* nombre *m* positif, quantité *f* positive ; *(Phot)* épreuve *f* positive, positif *m* ◆ **in the ~** *(Ling)* à l'affirmatif ◆ **he replied in the ~** il a répondu par l'affirmative ◆ **the ~s far outweigh the negatives** les points positifs compensent largement les points négatifs

ADV *(Drugs, Sport)* ◆ **to test ~** subir un contrôle positif, être positif ◆ **he tested ~ for HIV** son test du sida était positif ◆ **to show ~** *[test]* se révéler positif ; *[person]* être positif ◆ **to think ~** être positif ◆ **think ~!** soyez positif !

COMP **positive discrimination** **N** *(Brit)* discrimination *f* positive

positive feedback **N** *(Elec)* réaction *f* positive ; *(= praise)* réactions *fpl* positives ◆ **to give sb/get ~ feedback (about sb/sth)** faire part à qn/recevoir des réactions positives (sur qn/qch)

positive vetting **N** enquête *f* de sécurité *(of sb* sur qn*)* ◆ **a policy of ~ vetting** une politique d'enquêtes de sécurité

positively /ˈpɒzɪtɪvlɪ/ **ADV** 1 *(= constructively, favourably)* *[act, contribute]* de façon positive, positivement ◆ **to think ~** être positif ◆ **to respond ~** *(in negotiations, to event etc)* réagir favorablement ◆ **to respond ~ to treatment/medication** *[patient]* bien réagir à un traitement/un médicament ◆ **to be ~ disposed to sb/sth** être bien disposé envers qn/qch

2 *(= actively)* ◆ **I didn't object, in fact I ~ approved** je ne m'y suis pas opposé, j'étais même carrément d'accord ◆ **she never refused his advances, but she never ~ invited them either** elle n'a jamais repoussé ses avances mais elle ne les a jamais encouragées non plus ◆ **she doesn't mind being photographed, in fact she ~ loves it** cela ne la dérange pas qu'on la photographie, en fait, elle adore ça

3 *(= absolutely, literally)* carrément ◆ **she's ~ obsessed** c'est carrément une obsession chez elle ◆ **this is ~ the worst thing that could happen** c'est vraiment la pire des choses qui pouvaient arriver ◆ **he was ~ rude to me** il a été carrément grossier avec moi ◆ **this is ~ the last time** cette fois, c'est vraiment la dernière ◆ **I ~ forbid it!** je l'interdis formellement ! ◆ **she ~ glowed with happiness** elle rayonnait littéralement de bonheur

4 *(= definitely)* *[identify]* formellement ◆ **cholesterol has been ~ associated with heart disease** le cholestérol a été formellement associé aux maladies cardiovasculaires

5 **he tested ~ for drugs/HIV, he was ~ tested for drugs/HIV** son test antidopage/du sida était positif

6 *(Elec, Phys)* ◆ **~ charged** chargé positivement, à charge positive

positivism /ˈpɒzɪtɪvɪzəm/ **N** positivisme *m*

positivist /ˈpɒzɪtɪvɪst/ **ADJ, N** positiviste *mf*

positron /ˈpɒzɪtrɒn/ **N** positon *m*, positron *m*

poss* /pɒs/ **ADJ** (abbrev of **possible**) possible ◆ **as soon as ~** dès que possible

posse /ˈpɒsɪ/ **N** *(gen, fig hum)* petite troupe *f*, détachement *m*

possess /pəˈzes/ **VT** 1 *(= own, have)* *[+ property, qualities]* posséder, avoir ; *[+ documents, money, proof]* posséder, être en possession de ◆ **all I ~** tout ce que je possède ◆ **she was accused of ~ing a firearm/drugs** *(illegally)* elle a été accusée de port d'armes prohibé/de détention illégale de stupéfiants ◆ **it ~es several advantages** cela présente plusieurs avantages ◆ **to ~ o.s. of sth** s'emparer de qch ◆ **to be ~ed of** *(frm)* posséder ◆ **to ~ one's soul in patience** *(liter)* s'armer de patience

2 *[demon, rage]* posséder ; *(fig = obsess)* posséder, obséder ◆ **he was ~ed by the devil** il était possédé du démon ◆ **~ed with** *or* **by jealousy** obsédé *or* dévoré par la jalousie, en proie à la jalousie ◆ **I was ~ed by an irrational fear** j'étais en proie à une peur irraisonnée ◆ **like one ~ed** comme un(e) possédé(e) ◆ **like a man/woman ~ed** comme un(e) possédé(e) ◆ **what can have ~ed him to say that?** qu'est-ce qui lui a pris de dire ça ?*

possession /pəˈzeʃən/ **N** 1 *(NonC = act, state)* possession *f* ; *(Jur = occupancy)* jouissance *f* ; *(illegal) [of drugs]* détention *f* illégale ◆ **illegal ~ of a firearm** port *m* d'arme prohibé ◆ **in ~ of** en possession de ◆ **to have ~ of** *(gen)* posséder ; *(Jur)* avoir la jouissance de ◆ **to have sth in one's ~** avoir qch en sa possession ◆ **to get ~ of sth** obtenir qch ; *(by force)* s'emparer de qch ; *(improperly)* s'approprier qch ◆ **to get ~ of the ball** *(Rugby)* s'emparer du ballon ◆ **to come into ~ of** entrer en possession de ◆ **to come into sb's ~** tomber en la possession de qn ◆ **he was in full ~ of all his faculties** il était en pleine possession de ses facultés, il avait le plein usage de ses facultés ◆ **according to the information in my ~** selon les renseignements dont je dispose ◆ **to take ~ of sth** prendre possession de qch ; *(improperly)* s'approprier qch ; *(= confiscate)* confisquer qch ◆ **to take ~** *(Jur)* prendre possession ◆ **to be in ~** *(Jur)* occuper les lieux ◆ **a house with vacant ~** *(Jur etc)* une maison avec jouissance immédiate ◆ **~ is nine points** *or* **tenths of the law** *(Prov)* ≈ (en fait de meubles) la possession vaut titre

2 *(= object)* possession *f*, bien *m* ; *(= territory)* possession *f* ◆ **all his ~s** tous ses biens, tout ce

qu'il possède ◆ **he had few ~s** il possédait très peu de choses

COMP **possession order** N (Brit Jur) *injonction autorisant le propriétaire d'un logement à en reprendre possession en expulsant les occupants*

possessive /pəˈzesɪv/ ADJ 1 *[person, nature, attitude, love]* possessif ◆ **to be ~ about sth** ne pas vouloir partager qch ◆ **to be ~ towards** or **with sb** être possessif avec *or* à l'égard de qn ◆ **his mother is terribly ~** sa mère est très possessive, il a une mère abusive 2 *(Gram)* possessif N *(Gram)* ◆ **the ~** le possessif ◆ **in the ~** au possessif

COMP **possessive adjective** N adjectif *m* possessif

possessive pronoun N pronom *m* possessif

possessively /pəˈzesɪvlɪ/ ADV d'une façon possessive

possessiveness /pəˈzesɪvnɪs/ N *(NonC)* possessivité *f*

possessor /pəˈzesəʳ/ N possesseur *m* ; (= *owner*) propriétaire *mf* ◆ **to be the ~ of** être possesseur de, posséder ◆ **he was the proud ~ of ...** il était l'heureux propriétaire de ...

possibility /ˌpɒsəˈbɪlɪtɪ/ LANGUAGE IN USE 19.1, 26.3 N 1 *(NonC)* possibilité *f* ◆ **within the bounds of ~** dans la limite du possible ◆ **not beyond the realms** *or* **bounds of ~** pas impossible ◆ **if by any ~ ...** si par impossible ..., si par hasard ... ◆ **there is some ~/not much ~ of success** il y a quelques chances/peu de chances que ça marche ◆ **there is no ~ of my leaving** il n'est pas possible que je parte

2 *(= possible event)* possibilité *f*, éventualité *f* ◆ **to foresee all (the) possibilities** envisager toutes les possibilités *or* éventualités ◆ **there's a ~ that we might be wrong** il se peut *or* il est possible que nous nous trompions ◆ **it's a distinct ~** c'est bien possible ◆ **we must allow for the ~ that he may refuse** nous devons nous préparer à *or* nous devons envisager l'éventualité de son refus ◆ **he is a ~ for the job** c'est un candidat possible

3 *(= promise, potential)* perspectives *fpl*, potentiel *m* ◆ **the firm saw good possibilities for expansion** la compagnie entrevoyait de bonnes perspectives d'expansion ◆ **the scheme/ the job has real possibilities** c'est un projet/un emploi qui ouvre toutes sortes de perspectives ◆ **she agreed that the project had possibilities** elle a admis que le projet avait un certain potentiel

possible /ˈpɒsəbl/ LANGUAGE IN USE 12.2, 15.2, 15.3, 16.3, 26.3

ADJ 1 possible ; *[event, reaction, victory, loss]* possible, éventuel ◆ **it's just ~** ce n'est pas impossible ◆ **it's not ~!** ce n'est pas possible !, pas possible ! * ◆ **it is ~ that ...** il se peut que ... + *subj*, il est possible que ... + *subj* ◆ **it's just ~ that ...** il n'est pas impossible que ... + *subj*, il y a une chance que ... + *subj* ◆ **it's ~ to do so** il est possible de le faire, c'est faisable ◆ **it is ~ for us to measure his progress** il nous est possible de mesurer ses progrès ◆ **to make sth ~** rendre qch possible ◆ **he made it ~ for me to go to Spain** il a rendu possible mon voyage en Espagne ◆ **if (at all) ~** si possible ◆ **he visits her whenever ~** il va la voir aussi souvent que possible *or* chaque fois qu'il le peut ◆ **whenever** *or* **wherever ~, we try to find ...** dans la mesure du possible, nous essayons de trouver ... ◆ **at the worst ~ time** au pire moment ◆ **he chose the worst ~ job for a man with a heart condition** il a choisi le pire des emplois pour un cardiaque ◆ **the best ~ result** le meilleur résultat possible ◆ **one ~ result** un résultat possible *or* éventuel ◆ **what ~ interest can you have in it?** qu'est-ce qui peut bien vous intéresser là-dedans ? ◆ **what ~ motive could she have?** quels pouvaient bien être ses motifs ? ◆ **there is no ~ excuse for his behaviour** sa conduite n'a aucune excuse *or* est tout à fait inexcusable

◆ **as ... as possible** ◆ **as far as ~** dans la mesure du possible ◆ **as much as ~** autant que possible ◆ **he did as much as ~** il a fait tout ce qu'il pouvait ◆ **as soon as ~** dès que possible, aussitôt que possible ◆ **as quickly as ~** le plus vite possible

2 *(= perhaps acceptable) [candidate, successor]* possible, acceptable ◆ **a ~ solution** une solution possible *or* à envisager ◆ **it is a ~ solution to the problem** ce pourrait être une manière de résoudre le problème

N 1 ◆ **the art of the ~** l'art *m* du possible

2 * **a list of ~s for the job** une liste de personnes susceptibles d'être retenues pour ce poste ◆ **he's a ~ for the match on Saturday** c'est un joueur éventuel pour le match de samedi ◆ **the Possibles versus the Probables** *(Sport)* la sélection B contre la sélection A

possibly /ˈpɒsəblɪ/ LANGUAGE IN USE 4 ADV 1 *(with "can" etc)* **he did all he ~ could (to help them)** il a fait tout son possible (pour les aider) ◆ **I'll come if I ~ can** je ferai mon possible pour venir ◆ **I go as often as I ~ can** j'y vais aussi souvent que possible ◆ **I cannot ~ come** il m'est absolument impossible de venir ◆ **you can't ~ do that!** tu ne vas pas faire ça quand même ! ◆ **it can't ~ be true!** ce n'est pas possible !

2 *(= perhaps)* peut-être ◆ **Belgian beer is ~ the finest in the world** la bière belge est peut-être la meilleure du monde ◆ **~ they've left already** ils sont peut-être déjà partis, il se peut qu'ils soient déjà partis ◆ **was he lying? (very** *or* **quite) ~** est-ce qu'il mentait ? c'est (tout à fait *or* très) possible ◆ **~ not** peut-être pas, peut-être que non

possum * /ˈpɒsəm/ N *(US)* (abbrev of **opossum**) opossum *m* ◆ **to play ~** * faire le mort

POST N (abbrev of **point-of-sale terminal**) → **point**

post¹ /pəʊst/ N *(of wood, metal)* poteau *m* ; (= *stake*) pieu *m* ; *(for door etc: upright)* montant *m* ; (also **goal post**) poteau *m* (de but) ◆ **starting/finishing** *or* **winning ~** *(Sport)* poteau *m* de départ/d'arrivée ◆ **to be left at the ~** manquer le départ, rester sur la touche ◆ **to be beaten at the ~** *(Sport, fig)* être battu *or* coiffé sur le poteau ; → **deaf, gatepost, lamppost, pip³** VT 1 (also **post up**) *[+ notice, list]* afficher 2 *(= announce) [+ results]* annoncer ◆ **to be ~ed (as) missing** être porté disparu 3 ◆ **to ~ a wall with advertisements** poser *or* coller des affiches publicitaires sur un mur

post² /pəʊst/ LANGUAGE IN USE 19

N 1 *(Mil, gen)* poste *m* ◆ **at one's ~** à son poste ; → **forward, last¹**

2 *(esp Can, US:* also **trading post***)* comptoir *m*

3 *(= situation, job)* poste *m*, situation *f* ; *(in civil service, government etc)* poste *m* ◆ **a ~ as a manager** un poste *or* une situation de directeur ◆ **his ~ as head of the ruling party** son poste de dirigeant du parti au pouvoir ◆ **to be in ~** être en fonctions, occuper un poste ◆ **to hold a ~** occuper un poste

VT 1 *(Mil = position) [+ sentry, guard]* poster ◆ **they ~ed a man by the stairs** ils ont posté un homme près de l'escalier

2 *(esp Brit = send, assign) (Mil)* poster (*to* à) ; *(Admin, Comm)* affecter, nommer (*to* à) ◆ **to ~ sb abroad/to Paris** envoyer qn à l'étranger/à Paris

3 *(US Jur)* **to ~ bail** déposer une caution ◆ **to ~ the collateral required** fournir les garanties

COMP **post exchange** N *(US Mil)* magasin *m* de l'armée

post-holder N détenteur *m*, -trice *f* du poste

post³ /pəʊst/ *(esp Brit)* N 1 *(NonC)* poste *f* ; (= *letters*) courrier *m* ◆ **by ~** par la poste ◆ **by return (of) ~** par retour du courrier ◆ **by first-/second-class ~** ≈ tarif accéléré/normal ◆ **winners will be notified by ~** les gagnants seront avisés (personnellement) par courrier ◆ **your receipt is in the ~** votre reçu est déjà posté ◆ **I'll put it in the ~ today** je le posterai aujourd'hui ◆ **it went first ~ this morning** c'est parti ce matin par le premier courrier ◆ **to catch/miss the ~** avoir/manquer la levée ◆ **drop it in the ~ on your way** mettez-le à la boîte en route ◆ **the ~ was lifted** *or* **collected at 8 o'clock** la levée a eu lieu à 8 heures ◆ **has the ~ been** *or* **come yet?** le courrier est-il arrivé ?, le facteur est-il passé ? ◆ **the ~ is late** le courrier a du retard ◆ **is there any ~ for me?** est-ce que j'ai du courrier ?, y a-t-il une lettre pour moi ? ◆ **you'll get these through the ~** vous les recevrez par la poste ◆ **Minister/Ministry of Posts and Telecommunications** *(Brit)* ministre *m*/ministère *m* des Postes et (des) Télécommunications ; → **registered**

2 *(Hist = riders etc)* poste *f* ; → **general**

VT 1 *(= send)* envoyer ; *(Brit) (= put in mailbox)* poster, mettre à la poste ; *(Comput)* envoyer (par voie électronique)

2 *(Accounting:* also **post up***) [+ transaction]* inscrire ◆ **to ~ an entry to the ledger** passer une écriture dans le registre ◆ **to ~ (up) a ledger** tenir un registre à jour ◆ **to keep sb ~ed** tenir qn au courant

VI *(Hist = travel by stages)* voyager par la poste, prendre le courrier ; (†† *= hasten)* courir la poste ††, faire diligence †

COMP **post and packing** N (= *cost*) frais *mpl* de port et d'emballage

post chaise N *(Hist)* chaise *f* de poste

post-free ADJ (en) port payé

post horn N *(Mus)* cornet *m* de poste *or* de postillon

post house N *(Hist)* relais *m* de poste

Post-it ®, Post-it note ® N Post-it ® *m inv*

post office N → **post office**

post-paid ADJ port payé

► **post on** VT SEP *[+ letter, parcel]* faire suivre

► **post up** VT SEP ⇒ **post³ vt 2**

post... /pəʊst/ PREF post... ◆ **postglacial** postglaciaire ◆ **post-1950** ADJ postérieur (-eure *f*) à (l'année) 1950, d'après 1950 ADV après 1950 ; → **postdate, postimpressionism** *etc*

postage /ˈpəʊstɪdʒ/ N *(NonC)* tarifs *mpl* postaux *or* d'affranchissement ◆ **~: £2** *(in account etc)* frais *mpl* de port : 2 livres ◆ **~ due 20p** surtaxe 20 pence

COMP **postage and packing** N *(Comm)* frais *mpl* de port et d'emballage

postage meter N *(US)* machine *f* à affranchir (les lettres)

postage paid ADJ port payé *inv*

postage rates NPL tarifs *mpl* postaux

postage stamp N timbre-poste *m* ◆ **what she knows about children would fit on the back of a ~ stamp** les enfants, elle n'y connaît rien

postal /ˈpəʊstəl/ ADJ 1 *[code, zone]* postal ; *[application]* par la poste ◆ **~ charges, ~ rates** tarifs *mpl* postaux ◆ **~ dispute** conflit *m* (des employés) des postes ◆ **~ district** district *m* postal ◆ **the ~ services** les services *mpl* postaux ◆ **two-tier ~ service** courrier *m* à deux vitesses ◆ **~ strike** grève *f* des employés des postes ◆ **~ worker** employé(e) *m(f)* des postes, postier *m*, -ière *f* 2 * *(US)* (= *crazy*) **to go ~** péter les plombs *

COMP **postal card** N *(US)* carte *f* postale

postal order N *(Brit)* mandat *m* (postal) ◆ **a ~ order for €50** un mandat de 100 €

postal vote N (= *paper*) bulletin *m* de vote par correspondance ; (= *system*) vote *m* par correspondance

postbag /ˈpəʊstbæɡ/ N (Brit) sac *m* postal ◆ **we've had a good ~*** **on this** nous avons reçu beaucoup de courrier à ce sujet

postbox /ˈpəʊstbɒks/ N (esp Brit) boîte *f* à *or* aux lettres

postcard /ˈpəʊstkɑːd/ N carte *f* postale

postcode /ˈpəʊstkəʊd/ N (Brit) code *m* postal COMP **postcode prescribing** N *inégalité dans la disponibilité de certains médicaments selon le lieu où l'on habite*

postcoital /ˈpəʊstˈkɔɪtəl/ ADJ (d')après l'amour

postdate /ˌpəʊstˈdeɪt/ VT postdater

postdoctoral /pəʊstˈdɒktərəl/ ADJ (Univ) *[research, studies]* post-doctoral ◆ **~ fellow** chercheur *m* qui a son doctorat ◆ **~ fellowship** poste *m* de chercheur (qui a son doctorat)

poster /ˈpəʊstəʳ/ N affiche *f* ; *(decorative)* poster *m*
COMP **poster boy***, **poster child***, **poster girl*** N (US) incarnation *f*
poster paint N gouache *f*

poste restante /ˌpəʊstˈrestɑ̃ːnt/ N, ADV (esp Brit) poste *f* restante

posterior /pɒsˈtɪərɪəʳ/ ADJ (frm) postérieur (-eure *f*) (to à) N (* hum) derrière *m*, postérieur* *m*

posterity /pɒsˈterɪtɪ/ N postérité *f* ◆ **to go down to** *or* **in ~ as sth/for sth** entrer dans la postérité en tant que qch/pour qch ◆ **for ~** pour la postérité

postern /ˈpɒstən/ N poterne *f*

postfeminist /ˌpəʊstˈfemɪnɪst/ ADJ, N postféministe *mf*

postgrad* /ˈpəʊstˈɡræd/ N, ADJ abbrev of **postgraduate**

postgraduate /ˈpəʊstˈɡrædjʊɪt/ ADJ *[studies, course, grant, diploma]* ≃ de troisième cycle (universitaire) N (also **postgraduate student**) étudiant(e) *m(f)* de troisième cycle

posthaste /ˌpəʊstˈheɪst/ ADV à toute allure

posthumous /ˈpɒstjʊməs/ ADJ posthume

posthumously /ˈpɒstjʊməslɪ/ ADV à titre posthume

postiche /pɒsˈtiːʃ/ N, ADJ postiche *m*

postie* /ˈpəʊstɪ/ N (Austral, Brit dial) facteur *m*, -trice *f*

postil(l)ion /pəsˈtɪlɪən/ N postillon *m*

postimpressionism /ˈpəʊstɪmˈpreʃənɪzəm/ N postimpressionnisme *m*

postimpressionist /ˈpəʊstɪmˈpreʃənɪst/ ADJ, N postimpressionniste *mf*

postindustrial /ˌpəʊstɪnˈdʌstrɪəl/ ADJ postindustriel

posting /ˈpəʊstɪŋ/ N 1 (NonC = *sending by post*) expédition *f or* envoi *m* par la poste 2 (Brit) (= *assignment*) mutation *f* ; *(Mil)* affectation *f* ◆ **I've been given an overseas ~ to Japan** j'ai été muté *or* affecté au Japon 3 *(Accounts = entry)* passation *f* COMP **posting error** N *(Accounting)* erreur *f* d'écriture

postman /ˈpəʊstmən/ N (pl **-men**) facteur *m*, préposé *m* (Admin) COMP **postman's knock** N (= *game*) ≃ le mariage chinois

postmark /ˈpəʊstmɑːk/ N oblitération *f*, cachet *m* de la poste ◆ **date as ~** le cachet de la poste faisant foi ; *(on letter)* pour la date, se référer au cachet de la poste ◆ **letter with a French ~** lettre *f* oblitérée en France ◆ **it is ~ed Paris** ça porte le cachet de Paris VT tamponner, timbrer

postmaster /ˈpəʊstˌmɑːstəʳ/ N receveur *m* des postes COMP **Postmaster General** N (pl **Postmasters General**) (Brit) ministre *m* des Postes et Télécommunications

postmistress /ˈpəʊstˌmɪstrɪs/ N receveuse *f* des postes

postmodern /ˌpəʊstˈmɒdən/ ADJ postmoderne

postmodernism /ˌpəʊstˈmɒdənɪzəm/ N postmodernisme *m*

postmodernist /ˌpəʊstˈmɒdənɪst/ ADJ, N postmoderniste *mf*

post-mortem /ˈpəʊstˈmɔːtəm/ ADJ ◆ **~ examination** autopsie *f* N (Med, also fig) autopsie *f* ◆ **to hold a ~** faire une autopsie ◆ **to hold** *or* **carry out a ~ on** (lit) faire l'autopsie de, autopsier ; *(fig)* disséquer, faire l'autopsie de

postnatal /ˈpəʊstˈneɪtl/ ADJ postnatal COMP **postnatal depression** N dépression *f* post-partum, bébé blues* *m*
postnatal ward N (service *m*) maternité *f*

post office /ˈpəʊstˌɒfɪs/ N (= *place*) (bureau *m* de) poste *f* ; (= *organization*) administration *f* des postes, service *m* des postes ◆ **he works in the ~** il travaille à la poste ◆ **the main ~** la grande poste ◆ **Post Office Box No. 24** boîte postale n° 24 ◆ **Post Office Department** (US) ministère *m* des Postes et Télécommunications ◆ **he has £100 in ~ savings** *or* **in the Post Office Savings Bank** ≃ il a 100 livres sur son livret de caisse d'épargne (de la poste), il a 100 livres à la caisse d'épargne (de la poste) ◆ **~ worker** employé(e) *m(f)* des postes, postier *m*, -ière *f* ; → **general**

post-op* /ˈpəʊstɒp/ ADJ abbrev of **postoperative**

postoperative /ˌpəʊstˈɒpərətɪv/ ADJ postopératoire

postpartum /ˌpəʊstˈpɑːtəm/ (frm) ADJ postnatal COMP **postpartum depression** N dépression *f* post-partum

postpone /pəʊstˈpəʊn/ VT remettre à plus tard, reporter (for de ; until à)

postponement /pəʊstˈpəʊnmənt/ N report *m*

postposition /ˈpəʊstpəˈzɪʃən/ N postposition *f*

postpositive /ˈpəʊstˈpɒzɪtɪv/ ADJ postpositif N postposition *f*

postprandial /ˈpəʊstˈprændɪəl/ ADJ (liter or hum) (d')après le repas

postproduction /ˌpəʊstprəˈdʌkʃən/ N travail *m* postérieur à la production COMP *[cost etc]* qui suit la production

postscript /ˈpəʊsskrɪpt/ N (to letter: abbr PS) post-scriptum *m inv* ; *(to book)* postface *f* ◆ **to add sth as a ~** ajouter qch en post-scriptum ◆ **I'd like to add a ~ to what you have said** je voudrais ajouter un mot à ce que vous avez dit

poststructuralism /ˌpəʊstˈstrʌktʃərəlɪzəm/ N poststructuralisme *m*

poststructuralist /ˌpəʊstˈstrʌktʃərəlɪst/ ADJ, N poststructuraliste *mf*

postsynchronization /pəʊstˌsɪŋkrənaɪˈzeɪʃən/ N postsynchronisation *f*

postsynchronize /pəʊstˈsɪŋkrəˌnaɪz/ VT postsynchroniser

post-Tertiary /ˌpəʊstˈtɜːʃərɪ/ ADJ (Geol) ◆ **~ period** ère *f* posttertiaire

post-traumatic stress disorder /ˌpəʊsttrɔːˈmætɪkˈstresdɪsˈɔːdəʳ/ N névrose *f* (post-)traumatique

postulant /ˈpɒstjʊlənt/ N (Rel) postulant(e) *m(f)*

postulate /ˈpɒstjʊlɪt/ N postulat *m* VT /ˈpɒstjʊleɪt/ poser comme principe ; *(Philos)* postuler

postural /ˈpɒstjərəl/ ADJ postural

posture /ˈpɒstʃəʳ/ N posture *f*, position *f* ; *(fig)* attitude *f*, position *f* ◆ **his ~ is very poor** *or* **bad, he has poor ~** il se tient très mal ◆ **in the ~ of** à la manière de VI (pej) poser, prendre des poses

posturing /ˈpɒstjərɪŋ/ N pose *f*, affectation *f*

postviral (fatigue) syndrome /ˌpəʊstˈvaɪərəlfəˈtiːɡˈsɪndrəʊm/ N séquelles *fpl* d'une infection virale

postvocalic /pəʊstvəʊˈkælɪk/ ADJ (Phon) postvocalique

postwar /ˈpəʊstˈwɔːʳ/ ADJ *[event]* de l'après-guerre ; *[government, structure]* d'après-guerre ◆ **~ credits** (Brit Fin) *crédits gouvernementaux résultant d'une réduction dans l'abattement fiscal pendant la seconde guerre mondiale* ◆ **the ~ period, the ~ years** l'après-guerre *m*

postwoman /ˈpəʊstˌwʊmən/ N (pl **-women**) factrice *f*, préposée *f* (Admin)

posy /ˈpəʊzɪ/ N petit bouquet *m* (de fleurs)

pot¹ /pɒt/ N 1 (for flowers, jam, dry goods etc) pot *m* ; († : for beer) chope *f* ; (= *piece of pottery*) poterie *f* ; *(for cooking)* marmite *f*, pot † *m* ; (= *saucepan*) casserole *f* ; (also **teapot**) théière *f* ; (also **coffeepot**) cafetière *f* ; (= *potful*) *[of stew]* marmite *f* ; *[of cream]* pot ; (also **chamberpot**) pot *m* (de chambre), vase *m* de nuit ◆ **jam ~** pot *m* à confiture ◆ **~ of jam** pot *m* de confiture ◆ **~s and pans** casseroles *fpl*, batterie *f* de cuisine ◆ **to wash the ~s** faire la vaisselle ◆ **... and one for the ~** *(making tea)* ... et une cuillerée pour la théière ◆ **it's the ~ calling the kettle black** (Prov) c'est la paille et la poutre ◆ **he can just keep the ~ boiling** *(fig)* il arrive tout juste à faire bouillir la marmite, il arrive à peine à joindre les deux bouts ◆ **keep the ~ boiling!** *(in game etc)* allez-y !, à votre tour ! ; → **flowerpot**
2 (* fig) (= *prize*) coupe *f* ; (= *large stomach*) brioche* *f*, bedaine* *f* ; *(esp US = kitty)* cagnotte *f* ◆ **to have ~s of money*** avoir un argent fou, rouler sur l'or ◆ **to go/be to ~*** aller/être à vau-l'eau
3 (Billiards, Snooker) **what a ~!** quel coup ! ◆ **if he sinks this ~ he's won** s'il met cette boule, il a gagné ◆ **to take a ~ at sb*** *(fig = criticize)* chercher des crosses à qn* ◆ **to take a ~ at goal*** (Ftbl) tirer au but
VT 1 *[+ plant, jam etc]* mettre en pot ; see also **potted**
2 (Billiards, Snooker) mettre
3 (* = *shoot*) *[+ duck, pheasant]* abattre, descendre*
VI 1 (= *make pottery*) faire de la poterie
2 (= *shoot*) **to ~ at sth*** tirer qch, canarder qch
COMP **pot-bound** ADJ ◆ **this plant is ~-bound** cette plante est (trop) à l'étroit dans son pot
pot cheese N (US) ≃ fromage *m* blanc (égoutté *or* maigre)
pot luck N *(fig)* ◆ **to take ~ luck** *(gen)* s'en remettre au hasard ; *(at meal)* manger à la fortune du pot
pot plant N (Brit) ⇒ **potted plant** ; → **potted**
pot roast (Culin) N rôti *m* braisé, rôti *m* à la cocotte
pot-roast VT faire braiser, faire cuire à la cocotte
pot scourer, pot scrubber N tampon *m* à récurer
potting compost N terreau *m*
potting shed N abri *m* de jardin
pot-trained ADJ *[child]* propre

pot²* /pɒt/ N (= *cannabis*) marijuana *f*, herbe *f* ; (= *hashish*) hasch* *m*

potable /ˈpəʊtəbl/ ADJ potable (lit)

potash /ˈpɒtæʃ/ N (carbonate *m* de) potasse *f*

potassium /pəˈtæsɪəm/ N potassium *m* COMP de potassium

potation /pəʊˈteɪʃən/ N (gen pl: frm) libation *f*

potato /pəˈteɪtəʊ/ (pl **potatoes**) N pomme *f* de terre ◆ **is there any ~ left?** est-ce qu'il reste des pommes de terre ? ◆ **it's small ~es*** (esp US) c'est de la petite bière* ; → **fry², hot, mash, sweet**
COMP *[field, salad, soup]* de pommes de terre
potato beetle N doryphore *m*

potato blight N maladie *f* des pommes de terre
potato bug N ⇒ **potato beetle**
potato cake N croquette *f* de pommes de terre
potato chips NPL *(US)* ⇒ **potato crisps**
potato crisps NPL *(Brit)* chips *fpl*
potato-masher N presse-purée *m inv*
potato omelette N omelette *f* aux pommes de terre *or* Parmentier
potato-peeler N économe *m*, épluche-légumes *m inv*
potato topping N ◆ **with a ~ topping** recouvert de pommes de terre au gratin

potbellied /ˌpɒtˈbelɪd/ ADJ *(from overeating)* ventru, bedonnant* ; *(from malnutrition)* au ventre ballonné ; *[vase, stove]* ventru, renflé

potbelly /ˌpɒtˈbelɪ/ N *(from overeating)* gros ventre *m*, bedaine* *f* ; *(from malnutrition)* ventre *m* ballonné

potboiler /ˈpɒtˌbɔɪləʳ/ N *(fig pej)* œuvre *f* alimentaire

poteen /pɒˈtiːn, pɒˈtʃiːn/ N whisky *m* (illicite)

potency /ˈpəʊtənsɪ/ N (pl **potencies** *or* **potences** /ˈpəʊtənsɪz/) 1 *[of remedy, drug, charm, argument]* puissance *f*, force *f* ; *[of drink]* forte teneur *f* en alcool 2 *[of male]* virilité *f*

potent /ˈpəʊtənt/ ADJ 1 *[remedy, drug, charm]* puissant ; *[drink]* fort ; *[argument, reason]* convaincant 2 *[male]* viril

potentate /ˈpəʊtənteɪt/ N potentat *m*

potential /pəʊˈtenʃəl/ ADJ potentiel ; *[leader, minister]* en puissance, potentiel ◆ **a ~ problem** un problème potentiel ◆ **a ~ rapist** un violeur potentiel *or* en puissance ◆ **he's a ~ Prime Minister** c'est un premier ministrable, c'est un Premier ministre potentiel
N *(NonC)* 1 *(Elec, Gram, Math, Phys etc)* potentiel *m* ◆ **military ~** potentiel *m* militaire ◆ **the destructive ~ of conventional weapons** le potentiel de destruction des armes conventionnelles
2 *(= promise, possibilities)* potentiel *m*, possibilités *fpl* ◆ **they have recognized the ~ of wind power** ils ont reconnu le potentiel de l'énergie éolienne ◆ **he hasn't yet realized his full ~** il n'a pas encore donné toute sa mesure *or* réalisé tout son potentiel ◆ **our ~ for increasing production** nos possibilités d'augmenter la production, notre potentiel d'augmentation de la production ◆ **I was shocked by his ~ for violence** j'ai été choqué de voir la violence dont il était capable
♦ **to have potential** avoir du potentiel ◆ **to have great ~** avoir beaucoup de potentiel ◆ **he's got ~ as a footballer** il a toutes les qualités requises pour devenir un bon footballeur, il a du potentiel en tant que footballeur ◆ **he's got ~ in maths** il a des aptitudes en maths ◆ **to have management ~** avoir les aptitudes requises pour devenir cadre supérieur
♦ **to have no potential for sth** *[person]* ne pas avoir les aptitudes requises pour qch ◆ **his book had no ~ for motion picture adaptation** son livre ne se prêtait pas à l'adaptation cinématographique
♦ **to have the potential to do sth** *[person]* être tout à fait capable de faire qch ◆ **the situation has the ~ to get out of hand** la situation pourrait facilement échapper à tout contrôle
♦ **the potential for** *[+ expansion, growth]* le potentiel de ; *[+ violence, disorder, unrest]* les possibilités *fpl* de ◆ **they believe this increases the ~ for miscalculation** ils pensent que cela augmente les possibilités d'erreur ◆ **the ~ for conflict is great** un conflit pourrait facilement éclater

potentiality /pəʊˌtenʃɪˈælɪtɪ/ N potentialité *f* ◆ **potentialities** ⇒ **potential noun 2**

potentially /pəʊˈtenʃəlɪ/ ADV *[dangerous, lethal, carcinogenic, serious]* potentiellement ◆ **~ important/useful/lucrative** qui peut être *or* s'avérer important/utile/rentable ◆ **the sea level is rising, with ~ disastrous consequences** le niveau de la mer monte, ce qui pourrait avoir des conséquences désastreuses ◆ **it was a ~ violent confrontation** il s'agissait d'une confrontation qui pouvait prendre un tour violent *or* devenir violente ◆ **it's ~ a rich country** c'est un pays qui pourrait devenir riche ◆ **~, these problems are very serious** ces problèmes pourraient devenir très sérieux

potful /ˈpɒtfʊl/ N *[of rice, stew]* casserole *f* ; *[of jam]* pot *m*

pothead †‡ /ˈpɒthed/ N drogué(e) *m(f)* à la marijuana (*or* au hasch*)

pother * /ˈpɒðəʳ/ N *(NonC)* *(= fuss)* agitation *f* ; *(= noise)* vacarme *m*, tapage *m*

potherbs /ˈpɒthɜːbz/ NPL herbes *fpl* potagères

pothole /ˈpɒthəʊl/ N 1 *(in road)* nid-de-poule *m* 2 *(under ground)* caverne *f* ; *(larger)* grotte *f*

potholed /ˈpɒthəʊld/ ADJ plein de nids-de-poule

potholer /ˈpɒtˌhəʊləʳ/ N *(Brit)* spéléologue *mf*

potholing /ˈpɒtˌhəʊlɪŋ/ N *(Brit)* spéléologie *f*, spéléo* *f* ◆ **to go ~** faire de la spéléologie

pothook /ˈpɒthʊk/ N *(lit)* crémaillère *f* ; *(in handwriting)* boucle *f*

pothunter * /ˈpɒtˌhʌntəʳ/ N chasseur *m* acharné de trophées

potion /ˈpəʊʃən/ N *(= medicine)* potion *f* ; *(= magic drink)* philtre *m*, breuvage *m* magique ◆ **love ~** philtre *m* (d'amour)

potlatch /ˈpɒtˌlætʃ/ N *(US)* fête *f* où l'on échange des cadeaux

potpie /ˈpɒtpaɪ/ N *(US)* tourte *f* à la viande

potpourri /pəʊˈpʊrɪ/ N *[of flowers]* pot *m* pourri ; *(fig, Literat, Mus)* pot-pourri *m*

potsherd /ˈpɒtʃɜːd/ N *(Archeol)* tesson *m* (de poterie)

potshot * /ˈpɒtʃɒt/ N *(with gun, missile)* tir *m* au jugé ; *(fig)* *(= criticism)* attaque *f*, critique *f* ◆ **to take a ~ at sth** tirer sur qch au jugé

potted /ˈpɒtɪd/ ADJ 1 *(Culin)* ◆ **~ meat** *rillettes de viande* ◆ **~ shrimps** *crevettes conservées dans du beurre fondu* ◆ **~ plant** plante *f* verte, plante *f* d'appartement 2 * *(fig)* ◆ **a ~ version of "Ivanhoe"** un abrégé *or* une version abrégée d'"Ivanhoé" ◆ **he gave me a ~ lesson in car maintenance** il m'a donné un cours rapide sur l'entretien des voitures

potter¹ /ˈpɒtə/ VI *(esp Brit)* mener sa petite vie tranquille, bricoler* ◆ **to ~ round the house** suivre son petit train-train* *or* faire des petits travaux dans la maison ◆ **to ~ round the shops** faire les magasins sans se presser
► **potter about** VI suivre son petit train-train*, bricoler*
► **potter along** VI aller son petit bonhomme de chemin, poursuivre sa route sans se presser ◆ **we ~ along** nous continuons notre train-train*
► **potter around** VI ⇒ **potter about**

potter² /ˈpɒtə/ N potier *m*, -ière *f*
COMP **potter's clay, potter's earth** N argile *f* *or* terre *f* à *or* de potier
potter's field N *(US = cemetery)* cimetière *m* des pauvres
potter's wheel N tour *m* de potier

pottery /ˈpɒtərɪ/ N 1 *(NonC)* *(= craft, occupation)* poterie *f* ; *(= objects)* poteries *fpl* ; *(glazed)* faïencerie *f NonC* ; *(= ceramics)* céramiques *fpl* ◆ **a piece of ~** une poterie ◆ **Etruscan ~** poterie(s) *f(pl)* étrusque(s) 2 *(= place)* poterie *f* ◆ **the Potteries** *(Brit Geog)* la région des Poteries *(dans le Staffordshire)* COMP *[jug, dish]* de *or* en terre ; *(ceramic)* de *or* en céramique ; *(glazed)* de *or* en faïence

potty¹ * /ˈpɒtɪ/ N pot *m* (de bébé)
COMP **potty-train** VT apprendre la propreté
potty-trained ADJ propre
potty-training N apprentissage *m* de la propreté

potty² * /ˈpɒtɪ/ ADJ *(Brit)* 1 *[person]* toqué*, dingue* ; *[idea]* farfelu ◆ **to be ~ about sb/sth** être toqué* de qn/qch ◆ **to go ~*** perdre la boule* 2 *(slightly pej)* **a ~ little house** une maison de rien du tout

pouch /paʊtʃ/ N petit sac *m* ; *(for money)* bourse *f* ; *(for ammunition)* étui *m* ; *(for cartridges)* giberne *f* ; *(for tobacco)* blague *f* ; *(US Diplomacy)* valise *f* (diplomatique) ; *[of kangaroo etc]* poche *f* (ventrale) ; *(under eye)* poche *f*

pouf(fe) /puːf/ N 1 *(= stool)* pouf *m* 2 *(Brit* ‡*)* ⇒ **poof**

poulterer /ˈpəʊltərəʳ/ N marchand(e) *m(f)* de volailles, volailler *m*, -ère *f*

poultice /ˈpəʊltɪs/ N cataplasme *m* VT mettre un cataplasme à

poultry /ˈpəʊltrɪ/ N *(NonC)* volaille *f NonC*, volailles *fpl*
COMP **poultry dealer** N volailler *m*
poultry farm N élevage *m* de volaille(s)
poultry farmer N volailleur *m*, -euse *f*, aviculteur *m*, -trice *f*
poultry farming N *(NonC)* élevage *m* de volaille(s), aviculture *f*

pounce /paʊns/ N bond *m*, attaque *f* subite VI bondir, sauter ◆ **to ~ on** *(also fig)* *[+ prey etc]* bondir sur, sauter sur ; *[+ book, small object]* se précipiter sur ; *(fig)* *[+ idea, suggestion]* sauter sur

pound¹ /paʊnd/ N 1 *(= weight)* livre *f* (= 453,6 grammes) ◆ **sold by the ~** vendu à la livre ◆ **$3 a ~** 3 dollars la livre ◆ **to demand one's ~ of flesh** exiger son dû impitoyablement ; → IMPERIAL SYSTEM 2 *(= money)* livre *f* ◆ **~ sterling** livre *f* sterling ◆ **ten ~s sterling** dix livres *fpl* sterling ; → **penny**
COMP **pound cake** N quatre-quarts *m inv*
pound coin N pièce *f* d'une livre
pound note N billet *m* d'une livre
pound sign N 1 *(for sterling)* symbole *m* de la livre sterling 2 *(US = hash symbol)* dièse *f*

pound² /paʊnd/ VT *[+ drugs, spices, nuts, rice etc]* piler ; *[+ meat]* attendrir ; *[+ dough]* pétrir vigoureusement ; *[+ rocks]* concasser ; *[+ earth, paving slabs]* pilonner ; *[guns, bombs, shells]* pilonner ◆ **to ~ sth to a pulp** réduire *or* mettre qch en bouillie ◆ **to ~ sth to a powder** réduire qch en poudre ◆ **the ship was ~ed by huge waves** d'énormes vagues battaient contre le navire ◆ **to ~ sth with one's fists** marteler qch à coups de poing ◆ **he was ~ing the piano/typewriter** il tapait comme un sourd sur son piano/sa machine à écrire ◆ **to ~ the beat** *[policeman]* faire sa ronde ; *(fig = be ordinary policeman)* être simple agent
VI 1 *[heart]* battre fort ; *(with fear, excitement)* battre la chamade ; *[sea, waves]* battre (*on, against* contre) ◆ **he ~ed at** *or* **on the door** il martela la porte (à coups de poing), il frappa de grands coups à la porte ◆ **he ~ed on the table** il donna de grands coups sur la table, il frappa du poing sur la table ◆ **the drums were ~ing** les tambours battaient, on entendait battre le tambour
2 *(= move heavily)* **to ~ in/out** *etc (heavily)* entrer/sortir *etc* à pas lourds ; *(at a run)* entrer/sortir *etc* en courant bruyamment ◆ **he was ~ing up and down his room** il arpentait sa chambre à pas lourds
► **pound away** VI ◆ **he was pounding away at the piano/at** *or* **on the typewriter** il a tapé comme un sourd sur son piano/sa machine à écrire

► **pound down** VT SEP *[+ drugs, spices, nuts]* piler ; *[+ rocks]* concasser ; *[+ earth, paving slabs]* pilonner ◆ **to ~ sth down to a pulp** réduire *or* mettre qch en bouillie

► **pound out** VT SEP ◆ **to pound out a tune on the piano** marteler un air au piano ◆ **to ~ out a letter on the typewriter** taper comme un sourd sur sa machine à écrire pour écrire une lettre

► **pound up** VT SEP *[+ drugs, spices, nuts]* piler ; *[+ rocks]* concasser ; *[+ earth, paving slabs]* pilonner

pound[3] /paʊnd/ N *(for dogs, cars)* fourrière *f*

poundage /'paʊndɪdʒ/ N ① *(= tax/commission)* impôt *m*/commission *f* de tant par livre *(sterling ou de poids)* ② *(= weight)* poids *m* (en livres)

-pounder /'paʊndəʳ/ N *(in compounds)* ◆ **thirty-pounder** *(= gun)* pièce *f* or canon *m* de trente ◆ **seven-pounder** *(= baby/fish)* bébé *m*/poisson *m* de 3,2 kg

pounding /'paʊndɪŋ/ ADJ *[heart] (gen)* battant à tout rompre ; *(with fear, excitement)* battant la chamade ; *[waves, surf]* d'une violence inouïe ◆ **he could hear the sound of ~ hooves/feet/drums/artillery** il entendait le martèlement des sabots/des talons/des tambours/de l'artillerie ◆ **with ~ heart** le cœur battant à tout rompre ◆ **a ~ headache** un violent mal de tête

N ① *[of heart, waves, surf]* battement *m* ; *[of feet, hooves, drums]* martèlement *m* ; *[of guns]* pilonnage *m*, martèlement *m*

② *(esp Brit *)* ◆ **to take a ~** *[person]* en prendre pour son grade ◆ **the city took a real ~ in the war/in the storm** la guerre/la tempête a fait des ravages dans cette ville ◆ **the forwards often take a ~ in the scrum** les avants prennent souvent des coups dans la mêlée ◆ **Manchester United took a real ~ from Liverpool** Manchester United s'est fait battre à plate couture par Liverpool *or* a pris une déculottée* contre Liverpool ◆ **the Socialists took a terrible ~ in the last election** les socialistes se sont fait battre à plate couture lors des dernières élections ◆ **the Conservatives have been taking a ~ from the press** les conservateurs se sont fait éreinter par la presse

pour /pɔːʳ/ VT *[+ liquid]* verser ◆ **she ~ed him a cup of tea** elle lui a versé *or* servi une tasse de thé ◆ **~ yourself some tea** servez-vous *or* versez-vous du thé ◆ **shall I ~ the tea?** je sers le thé ? ◆ **he ~ed me a drink** il m'a versé *or* servi à boire ◆ **she ~ed the salt into the salt cellar** elle a versé le sel dans la salière ◆ **she ~ed the water off the carrots** elle a vidé l'eau des carottes ◆ **to ~ metal/wax into a mould** couler du métal/de la cire ◆ **to ~ money into a scheme** investir énormément d'argent dans un projet ◆ **to ~ scorn on sb/sth** dénigrer qn/qch ◆ **she looked as if she had been ~ed into her dress*** elle semblait moulée dans sa robe ◆ **to ~ it on*** *(US fig)* y mettre le paquet*, foncer* ; → **oil**

VI ① *[water, blood etc]* couler à flots *(from* de) ◆ **water came ~ing into the room** l'eau entra à flots dans la pièce ◆ **water was ~ing down the walls** l'eau ruisselait le long des murs ◆ **smoke was ~ing from the window** des nuages de fumée sortaient par la fenêtre ◆ **sunshine ~ed into the room** le soleil entrait à flots dans la pièce ◆ **the sweat ~ed off him** il ruisselait de sueur ◆ **goods are ~ing out of the factories** les usines déversent des quantités de marchandises

② ◆ **it is ~ing (with rain)*** il pleut à verse ◆ **it ~ed for four days** il n'a pas arrêté de pleuvoir à torrents pendant quatre jours ; → **rain**

③ *[people, cars, animals]* affluer ◆ **to ~ in/out** entrer/sortir en grand nombre *or* en masse ◆ **refugees ~ed into the country** les réfugiés affluaient dans le pays ◆ **cars ~ed off the ferry** un flot de voitures sortait du ferry ◆ **complaints came ~ing in from all over the country** des plaintes affluaient de tout le pays

④ *[jug, teapot]* verser ◆ **this teapot doesn't ~ very well** cette théière ne verse pas très bien

⑤ *[person]* servir ◆ **shall I ~?** je vous sers ?

⑥ *(US = act as hostess)* jouer le rôle de maîtresse de maison

► **pour away** VT SEP *[+ dregs etc]* vider

► **pour down** VI ◆ **the rain** *or* **it was pouring down** il pleuvait à verse *or* à torrents

► **pour forth** VT SEP ⇒ **pour out vt sep 2**

► **pour in** VI *[water, sunshine, rain]* entrer (à flots) ; *[people]* affluer ; *[cars, animals]* arriver de toutes parts *or* en masse ◆ **complaints/letters ~ed in** il y a eu un déluge *or* une avalanche de réclamations/de lettres

VT SEP *[+ liquid]* verser ◆ **they ~ed in capital** ils y ont investi d'énormes capitaux

► **pour off** VT SEP *[+ liquid]* vider

► **pour out** VI *[water]* sortir à flots ; *[people, cars, animals]* sortir en masse ◆ **the words came ~ing out** ce fut une cascade *or* un flot de paroles

VT SEP ① *[+ tea, coffee, drinks]* verser, servir *(for sb* à qn) ; *[+ dregs, unwanted liquid]* vider ◆ **the factory ~s out hundreds of cars a day** l'usine sort des centaines de voitures chaque jour

② *(fig) [+ anger, emotion]* donner libre cours à ; *[+ troubles]* épancher ; *[+ complaint]* déverser ◆ **to ~ out one's heart to sb** s'épancher avec *or* auprès de qn ◆ **he ~ed out his story to me** il m'a raconté *or* sorti* toute son histoire

pouring /'pɔːrɪŋ/ ADJ ① (also **of pouring consistency**) *(sauce etc)* liquide ② ◆ **(in) the ~ rain** (sous) la pluie torrentielle *or* battante

pout /paʊt/ N moue *f* ◆ **... she said with a ~** ... dit-elle en faisant la moue VI faire la moue VT ◆ **to ~ one's lips** faire la moue ◆ **"no" she ~ed** "non" dit-elle en faisant la moue

poverty /'pɒvətɪ/ N ① *(lit)* pauvreté *f* ◆ **to live in ~** vivre dans le besoin *or* dans la gêne ◆ **to live in extreme ~** vivre dans une misère extrême ② *(fig) [of ideas, information]* déficit *m* ◆ **~ of resources** insuffisance *f* de ressources

COMP **poverty level, poverty line** N ◆ **below/above ~ level** *or* **the ~ line** au-dessous *or* en dessous du/au-dessus du seuil de pauvreté

poverty-stricken ADJ *(lit) [person, family]* dans le dénuement ; *[district]* miséreux, misérable ; *[conditions]* misérable ◆ **I'm ~-stricken** *(= hard up)* je suis fauché* (comme les blés), je suis sans le sou

the poverty trap N *(Brit)* cercle vicieux *auquel sont confrontés les bénéficiaires d'allocations de chômage ou d'insertion qui ne peuvent travailler, même de manière temporaire, sans perdre leurs droits*

POW /,piːəʊ'dʌbljʊ/ N *(Mil)* (abbrev of **prisoner of war**) → **prisoner**

pow* /paʊ/ EXCL bang*

powder /'paʊdəʳ/ N ① *(= particles)* poudre *f* ◆ **milk ~** *(Culin)* lait *m* en poudre ◆ **in the form of a ~, in ~ form** en poudre ◆ **to reduce sth to a ~** pulvériser qch, réduire qch en poudre ◆ **to keep one's ~ dry** *(fig)* être paré ◆ **to take a ~*** *(US)* prendre la poudre d'escampette*, décamper* ; → **baking, face, talc**

② *(= fine snow)* poudreuse *f*

VT ① *[+ chalk, rocks]* réduire en poudre, pulvériser ; *[+ milk, eggs]* réduire en poudre ◆ **~ed milk** lait *m* en poudre

② *[+ face, body]* poudrer ; *(Culin) [+ cake etc]* saupoudrer *(with* de) ◆ **to ~ one's nose** *(lit)* se mettre de la poudre ; *(* euph)* (aller) se refaire une beauté *(euph)* ◆ **trees ~ed with snow** arbres *mpl* saupoudrés de neige

COMP **powder blue** N bleu *m* pastel *inv*

powder-blue ADJ bleu pastel *inv* ◆ **~-blue dress** robe *f* bleu pastel

powder burn N brûlure *f* (superficielle) causée par la poudre

powder compact N poudrier *m*

powdered sugar N *(US)* sucre *m* glace

powder keg N *(lit)* baril *m* de poudre ; *(fig)* poudrière *f* ◆ **the Prime Minister is sitting on a ~ keg** le Premier ministre est sur une poudrière

powder magazine N poudrière *f*

powder puff N houppette *f* ; *(big, fluffy)* houppe *f*

powder room N *(euph)* toilettes *fpl* (pour dames)

powdering /'paʊdərɪŋ/ N ◆ **a ~ of snow** une mince pellicule de neige ◆ **a ~ of sugar** un saupoudrage de sucre

powdery /'paʊdərɪ/ ADJ ① *(in consistency) [substance, snow]* poudreux ; *[stone]* friable ② *(= covered with powder) [surface]* couvert de poudre

power /'paʊəʳ/ N ① *(= ability, capacity)* pouvoir *m*, capacité *f* ; *(= faculty)* faculté *f* ◆ **it is not (with)in my ~ to help you** il n'est pas en mon pouvoir de vous aider ◆ **he did everything** *or* **all in his ~ to help us** il a fait tout son possible *or* tout ce qui était en son pouvoir pour nous aider ◆ **it is quite beyond her ~ to save him** il n'est pas en son pouvoir de le sauver, elle est tout à fait impuissante à le sauver ◆ **the ~ of hearing/movement** la faculté d'entendre/de se mouvoir ◆ **he lost the ~ of speech** il a perdu (l'usage de) la parole ◆ **mental ~s** facultés *fpl* mentales ◆ **the body's recuperative ~** la puissance de récupération de l'organisme, la capacité régénératrice du corps ◆ **his ~s of resistance** sa capacité de résistance ◆ **his ~s of persuasion** son pouvoir *or* sa force de persuasion ◆ **his ~s of imagination/concentration** sa faculté d'imagination/de concentration ◆ **earning ~** (niveau *m* de) rémunération *f* ◆ **purchasing** *or* **spending ~** pouvoir *m* d'achat ; see also **noun 3** ; → **height**

♦ **a power of*** ◆ **it did me a ~ of good** ça m'a fait un bien immense, ça m'a rudement* fait du bien ◆ **he made a ~ of money** il a gagné un argent fou

② *(= force) [of person, blow, sun, explosion]* puissance *f*, force *f* ; *(Ling: of grammar)* puissance *f* ◆ **the ~ of love/thought** la force de l'amour/de la pensée ◆ **sea/air ~** puissance *f* navale/aérienne ◆ **more ~ to your elbow!** tous mes vœux de réussite !

③ *(= authority)* pouvoir *m (also Pol)*, autorité *f* ◆ **the ~ of the President/the police/the army** l'autorité *f or* le pouvoir du Président/de la police/de l'armée ◆ **student/pupil** *etc* **~** le pouvoir des étudiants/lycéens *etc* ◆ **he has the ~ to act** il a le pouvoir d'agir ◆ **they have no ~ in economic matters** ils n'ont aucune autorité en matière économique ◆ **that does not fall within my ~(s), that is beyond** *or* **outside my ~(s)** ceci n'est pas *or* ne relève pas de ma compétence ◆ **he exceeded his ~s** il a outrepassé *or* excédé ses pouvoirs ◆ **at the height of his ~** à l'apogée de son pouvoir ◆ **to have the ~ of life and death over sb** avoir droit de vie et de mort sur qn ◆ **to have ~ over sb** avoir autorité sur qn ◆ **to have sb in one's ~** avoir qn en son pouvoir ◆ **to fall into sb's ~** tomber sous l'emprise de qn, tomber sous la coupe de qn ◆ **in ~** *(Pol)* au pouvoir ◆ **Labour was in ~ at the time** le parti travailliste était alors au pouvoir ◆ **to come to ~** accéder au pouvoir ; → **absolute, attorney, veto**

④ *(fig)* ◆ **they are the real ~ in the government** ce sont eux qui détiennent le pouvoir réel dans le gouvernement ◆ **he is a ~ in the university** il est très influent à l'université ◆ **he is a ~ in the land** c'est un homme très puissant *or* très influent ◆ **the ~ behind the throne** l'éminence *f* grise, celui (*or* celle) qui tire les ficelles ◆ **the Church is no longer the ~ it was** l'Église n'est plus la puissance qu'elle était ◆ **the ~s that be** les autorités *fpl* constituées ; → **above, darkness, evil**

5 *(= nation)* puissance *f* ◆ **the nuclear/world ~s** les puissances *fpl* nucléaires/mondiales ◆ **one of the great naval ~s** une des grandes puissances navales

6 *[of engine, telescope etc]* puissance *f* ; *(Elec, Phys, Tech etc)* puissance *f*, force *f* ; *(= energy)* énergie *f* ; *(= output)* rendement *m* ; *(= electricity)* électricité *f*, courant *m* ◆ **nuclear ~** l'énergie *f* nucléaire ◆ **they cut off the ~** *(Elec)* ils ont coupé le courant ◆ **our consumption of ~ has risen** *(Elec)* notre consommation d'électricité a augmenté ◆ **a cheap source of ~** une source d'énergie bon marché ◆ **a low-~ microscope** un microscope de faible puissance ◆ **magnifying ~** grossissement *m* ◆ **engines at half ~** moteurs *mpl* à mi-régime ◆ **the ship returned to port under her own ~** le navire est rentré au port par ses propres moyens ◆ **microwave on full ~ for a minute** faites chauffer au micro-ondes à puissance maximale pendant une minute ; → **horsepower, wind[1]**

7 *(Math)* puissance *f* ◆ **five to the ~ of three** cinq puissance trois ◆ **to the nth ~** (à la) puissance n

VT faire marcher, faire fonctionner ◆ **~ed by nuclear energy** qui marche *or* fonctionne à l'énergie nucléaire ◆ **~ed by jet engines** propulsé par des moteurs à réaction

COMP *[saw, loom, lathe]* mécanique ; *[brakes]* assisté ; *[strike, dispute]* des travailleurs des centrales électriques

power-assisted ADJ *[stearing etc]* assisté
power base N *(Pol)* réseau *m* d'influence, support *m* politique
power broker N *(Pol)* éminence *f* grise
power cable N *(Elec)* câble *m* électrique
power cut N *(Brit)* coupure *f* de courant
power dive N *(in plane)* descente *f* en piqué
power dressing N *tenue élégante, sobre et sévère adoptée par certaines femmes cadres*
power-driven ADJ à moteur ; *(Elec)* électrique
power elite N élite *f* au pouvoir
power failure N panne *f* de courant
power game N *(Brit)* lutte *f* pour le pouvoir, jeu *m* de pouvoir
power lifting N *(Sport)* power-lifting *m*
power line N *(Elec)* ligne *f* à haute tension
power lunch N déjeuner *m* d'affaires
power pack N *(Elec)* bloc *m* d'alimentation
power plant N *(= building)* centrale *f* (électrique) ; *(in vehicle etc)* groupe *m* moteur
power play N *(Ice Hockey)* attaque *f* en force ; *(fig) (= attack)* attaque *f* en force ; *(= struggle)* épreuve *f* de force
power point N *(Brit Elec)* prise *f* de courant
power politics N politique *f* de coercition
power sharing N *(Pol)* le partage du pouvoir
power station N *(Elec)* centrale *f* (électrique)
power steering N direction *f* assistée
power structure N *(Pol) (= way power is held)* répartition *f* des pouvoirs ; *(= those with power)* détenteurs *mpl* du pouvoir
power struggle N lutte *f* pour le pouvoir
power supply N *(Elec)* alimentation *f* électrique
power surge N *(Elec)* surtension *f*, survoltage *m*
power tool N outil *m* électrique
power walking N marche *f* sportive
power workers NPL *(in power plants)* travailleurs *mpl* des centrales électriques

► **power down** VT SEP *[+ computer]* éteindre

► **power up** VT SEP *[+ computer]* allumer

powerboat /ˈpaʊəbəʊt/ **N** hors-bord *m inv*, (bateau *m*) offshore *m* **COMP** **powerboat racing** N (course *f*) offshore *m*

-powered /ˈpaʊəd/ ADJ *(in compounds)* ◆ **nuclear-powered** qui marche *or* fonctionne à l'énergie nucléaire ; → **high**

powerful /ˈpaʊəfʊl/ ADJ *[engine, machine, computer]* puissant ; *[kick, blow]* fort, violent ; *[person, build, smell]* fort ; *[influence, effect]* profond ; *[description, portrayal, performance]* (très) fort ; *[argument]* convaincant ◆ **I find his argument very ~** je trouve son argument très convaincant ◆ **he gave a ~ performance as Hamlet** il a donné une interprétation très forte de Hamlet ◆ **a ~ earthquake** un violent tremblement de terre ◆ **a ~ lot of** * un tas de *, beaucoup de

powerfully /ˈpaʊəfəlɪ/ ADV *[hit, strike]* avec force ; *[affect]* fortement ; *[influence]* profondément ; *[erotic, evocative]* profondément ◆ **the room smelt ~ of cats** une forte odeur de chat régnait dans la pièce ◆ **to write ~** écrire dans un style puissant *or* incisif ◆ **to argue ~ (for new legislation)** avancer des arguments percutants (en faveur d'une nouvelle législation) ◆ **~ built** solidement charpenté, qui a une forte carrure ◆ **~ addictive** à fort effet d'accoutumance

powerhouse /ˈpaʊəhaʊs/ N 1 *(lit)* centrale *f* électrique 2 *(fig)* personne *f* (*or* groupe *m*) très dynamique ◆ **a ~ of new ideas** une mine d'idées nouvelles

powerless /ˈpaʊəlɪs/ ADJ impuissant *(against* contre) ◆ **the government is ~ in the face of recession** le gouvernement est impuissant face à la récession ◆ **he is ~ to help you** il ne peut rien faire pour vous aider, il est impuissant à vous aider

powerlessly /ˈpaʊəlɪslɪ/ ADV ◆ **I looked on ~** j'ai assisté au spectacle, impuissant *or* sans pouvoir rien faire

powerlessness /ˈpaʊəlɪsnɪs/ N impuissance *f*

powwow /ˈpaʊwaʊ/ **N** assemblée *f (des Indiens d'Amérique)* ; (* *fig)* tête-à-tête *m inv* **VI** (* *fig)* s'entretenir, palabrer *(pej)*

pox /pɒks/ N († : *gen)* variole *f*, petite vérole *f* ◆ **the ~** * *(= syphilis)* la vérole * ◆ **a ~ on ...!** † maudit soit ... ! ; → **chickenpox, cowpox**

poxy ‡ /ˈpɒksɪ/ ADJ *(Brit)* merdique ‡

pp[1] /piːˈpiː/ (abbrev of **per procurationem**) *(= by proxy)* **PREP** p.p. **VT** ◆ **to pp a letter (for sb)** signer une lettre pour qn

pp[2] 1 (abbrev of **parcel post**) → **parcel** 2 (abbrev of **post-paid**) → **post[3]**

PPE /ˈpiːˌpiːˈiː/ N *(Univ)* (abbrev of **philosophy, politics and economics**) philosophie, sciences politiques et économie *fpl*

ppm (abbrev of **parts per million**) → **part**

PPS /ˈpiːˌpiːˈes/ N 1 *(Brit Parl)* (abbrev of **Parliamentary Private Secretary**) → **parliamentary** 2 (abbrev of **post postscriptum**) PPS *m*

PPV /ˌpiːpiːˈviː/ N (abbrev of **pay-per-view**) PPV *m*

PQ *(Can Post)* abbrev of **Province of Quebec**

PR[1] /piːˈɑːʳ/ N (abbrev of **public relations**) → **public**

PR[2] abbrev of **Puerto Rico**

PR[3] /piːˈɑːʳ/ N (abbrev of **proportional representation**) RP *f*

Pr. abbrev of **Prince**

practicability /ˌpræktɪkəˈbɪlɪtɪ/ N *[of scheme, plan]* faisabilité *f* ; *[of suggestion, idea]* possibilité *f* d'être mis en pratique

practicable /ˈpræktɪkəbl/ ADJ *[task, plan]* faisable, réalisable ; *[idea]* qui peut être mis en pratique

practical /ˈpræktɪkəl/ **ADJ** 1 *(= concrete, not theoretical) [suggestion]* concret (-ète *f*) ◆ **a ~ way of ...** un moyen concret de ... ◆ **to be of no ~ use** n'avoir aucun intérêt pratique ◆ **for (all) ~ purposes** en pratique ◆ **to become ~** *[scheme, idea etc]* devenir réalisable 2 *(= down-to-earth) [person]* pratique, pragmatique ◆ **to be ~** avoir le sens pratique *or* le sens des réalités 3 *(= functional, appropriate) [clothes, shoes, gadget]* pratique 4 *(= near)* ◆ **it's a ~ certainty** c'est une quasi-certitude **N** *(= exam)* épreuve *f* pratique ; *(= lesson)* travaux *mpl* pratiques

COMP **practical joke** N farce *f*
practical joker N farceur *m*, -euse *f*
practical nurse N *(US)* infirmier *m*, -ière *f* auxiliaire aide-soignant(e) *m(f)*

practicality /ˌpræktɪˈkælɪtɪ/ **N** *(NonC) [of person]* sens *m or* esprit *m* pratique ; *[of suggestion]* aspect *m* pratique ◆ **I doubt the ~ of this scheme** je doute de la faisabilité de ce projet, je doute que ce projet soit réalisable (d'un point de vue pratique) ◆ **they are worried about the ~ of building the system** ils craignent que ce système ne soit pas réalisable sur le plan pratique **NPL** **practicalities** détails *mpl* pratiques

practically /ˈpræktɪklɪ/ ADV 1 *(= almost)* pratiquement 2 *(= from a practical point of view)* pratiquement, d'un point de vue pratique ◆ **~ speaking** *(= in practice)* pour parler concrètement, en pratique 3 *(= in a practical way) [say, ask, suggest]* avec pragmatisme ; *[help]* sur le plan *or* d'un point de vue pratique ◆ **let's think ~** soyons pratiques, faisons preuve de sens pratique ◆ **he's very ~ minded, he thinks very ~** il a vraiment l'esprit *or* le sens pratique

practicalness /ˈpræktɪkəlnɪs/ N ⇒ **practicality noun**

practice /ˈpræktɪs/ **N** 1 *(= way of behaving)* pratique *f* ◆ **such ~s as arbitrary arrest and torture** des pratiques telles que les arrestations arbitraires et la torture ◆ **this ~ is illegal in other countries** cette pratique est illégale dans d'autres pays ◆ **to make a ~ of doing sth, to make it a ~ to do sth** avoir l'habitude *or* se faire une habitude de faire qch ◆ **it is not my ~ to do so** il n'est pas dans mes habitudes de faire ainsi ◆ **it's normal** *or* **standard** *or* **common ~ to ...** il est d'usage de ... ◆ **that's common ~** c'est courant ◆ **as is common ~, as is the ~** comme il est d'usage ◆ **best ~** meilleures pratiques *fpl* ; → **restrictive, sharp**

2 *(= exercises)* exercices *mpl* ; *(= training)* entraînement *m* ; *(= experience)* expérience *f* ; *(= rehearsal)* répétition *f* ◆ **I need more ~** je manque d'entraînement, je ne me suis pas assez exercé ◆ **he does six hours' piano ~ a day** il s'exerce au piano six heures par jour, il fait six heures de piano par jour ◆ **she's had lots of ~** elle a de l'expérience ◆ **it takes years of ~** il faut de longues années d'expérience ◆ **with ~** avec de l'entraînement ◆ **~ makes perfect** *(Prov)* c'est en forgeant qu'on devient forgeron *(Prov)* → **target**

◆ **out of practice** rouillé *(fig)*

3 *(NonC: as opposed to theory)* pratique *f* ◆ **a gap between theory and ~** un fossé entre la théorie et la pratique

◆ **in practice** dans la pratique

◆ **to put sth into practice** mettre qch en pratique ◆ **he then had an opportunity to put his ideas into ~** il eut alors l'occasion de mettre ses idées en pratique

4 *(= profession: of law, medicine etc)* exercice *m* ; *(= business, clients)* clientèle *f*, cabinet *m* ◆ **to go into ~** *or* **to set up in ~ as a doctor/lawyer** s'installer *or* s'établir docteur/avocat ◆ **he is in ~ in Valence** il exerce à Valence ◆ **he has a large ~** il a une nombreuse clientèle, il a un cabinet important ; → **general**

VTI *(US)* ⇒ **practise**

COMP *[flight, run]* d'entraînement
practice exam N examen *m* blanc
practice teacher N *(US Scol)* professeur *m* stagiaire ; *(in primary school)* instituteur *m*, -trice *f* stagiaire
practice test N ⇒ **practice exam**

⚠ Check what kind of practice it is before translating **practice** by **pratique**.

practise, practice *(US)* /ˈpræktɪs/ VT 1 *(= put into practice) [+ restraint, kindness, charity, technique, meditation, one's religion]* pratiquer ; *[+ method]* employer, appliquer ◆ **to ~ torture on sb** faire subir *or* infliger des tortures à qn ◆ **to ~ cruelty on sb** faire preuve de cruauté envers *or* à l'égard de qn ◆ **to ~ what one preaches** prêcher par l'exemple *or* d'exemple ◆ **to ~ medicine/law** exercer la médecine *or* la profession de médecin/la profession d'avocat
2 *(= exercise in) [+ sport]* s'entraîner à ; *[+ violin etc]* s'exercer à, travailler ; *[+ song, chorus, recitation]* travailler ◆ **she was practising her scales** elle faisait ses gammes ◆ **I need to ~ my backhand** j'ai besoin de travailler mon revers ◆ **to ~ doing sth** s'entraîner *or* s'exercer à faire qch ◆ **I'm going to ~ my German on him** je vais m'exercer à parler allemand avec lui ; see also **practised**
VI 1 *(Mus)* s'exercer ; *(Sport)* s'entraîner ; *[beginner]* faire des exercices ◆ **to ~ on the piano** s'exercer au piano, travailler le piano ◆ **he ~s for two hours every day** il fait deux heures d'entraînement *or* d'exercices par jour
2 *[doctor, lawyer]* exercer ◆ **to ~ as a doctor/lawyer** exercer la médecine *or* la profession de médecin/la profession d'avocat

practised, practiced *(US)* /ˈpræktɪst/ ADJ *[teacher, nurse, soldier]* expérimenté, chevronné ; *[eye, ear]* exercé ; *[movement]* expert ; *[performance]* accompli

practising, practicing *(US)* /ˈpræktɪsɪŋ/ ADJ *[doctor]* exerçant ; *[lawyer]* en exercice ; *[architect]* en activité ; *[Catholic, Buddhist]* pratiquant ◆ **a ~ Christian** un (chrétien) pratiquant ◆ **he's a ~ homosexual** c'est un homosexuel actif

practitioner /prækˈtɪʃənəʳ/ N *(of an art)* praticien(ne) *m(f)* ; *(Med:* also **medical practitioner**) médecin *m* ; → **general**

praesidium /prɪˈsɪdɪəm/ N présidium *m*

praetorian, pretorian *(US)* /prɪˈtɔːrɪən/ ADJ prétorien COMP **praetorian guard** N *(Hist, fig)* garde *f* prétorienne

pragmatic /prægˈmætɪk/ ADJ *(gen, Philos)* pragmatique

pragmatical /prægˈmætɪkl/ ADJ pragmatique

pragmatically /prægˈmætɪklɪ/ ADV avec pragmatisme, d'une manière pragmatique

pragmatics /prægˈmætɪks/ N *(NonC)* pragmatique *f*

pragmatism /ˈprægmətɪzəm/ N pragmatisme *m*

pragmatist /ˈprægmətɪst/ ADJ, N pragmatiste *mf*

Prague /prɑːg/ N Prague

prairie /ˈprɛərɪ/ N plaine *f* (herbeuse) ◆ **the ~(s)** *(US)* la Grande Prairie, les Prairies *fpl*
COMP **prairie chicken** N *(US Zool)* cupidon *m* (des prairies), tétras cupidon *m*
prairie cocktail N *(US)* ⇒ **prairie oyster**
prairie dog N chien *m* de prairie
prairie oyster N *(US)* œuf *m* cru assaisonné et bu dans de l'alcool *(remède contre la gueule de bois)*
Prairie Provinces NPL *(Can)* Provinces *fpl* des Prairies
prairie schooner N *(US)* grand chariot *m* bâché (des pionniers américains)
the Prairie State N *(US)* l'Illinois *m*
prairie wolf N *(US)* coyote *m*

praise /preɪz/ N 1 éloge(s) *m(pl)*, louange(s) *f(pl)* ◆ **in ~ of** à la louange de ◆ **to speak** (*or* **write** *etc*) **in ~ of sb/sth** faire l'éloge de qn/qch ◆ **it is beyond ~** c'est au-dessus de tout éloge ◆ **to be full of ~ for sb/sth** ne pas tarir d'éloges sur qn/qch ◆ **to give ~** être élogieux ◆ **I have nothing but ~ for what he has done** je ne peux que le louer de ce qu'il a fait ◆ **I have nothing but ~ for him** je n'ai qu'à me louer *or* me féliciter de lui ◆ **all ~ to him for speaking out!** il a dit ce qu'il pensait et je lui tire mon chapeau ! ◆ **he was loud** *or* **warm in his ~(s) of ...** il n'a pas tari d'éloges sur ..., il a chanté les louanges de ... ; → **sing**
2 *(Rel)* **a hymn of ~** un cantique ◆ **~ be to God!** Dieu soit loué ! ◆ **~ be!** * Dieu merci !
VT 1 *[+ person, action, sb's courage etc]* faire l'éloge de, louer ◆ **to ~ sb for sth/for doing sth** louer qn pour qch/d'avoir fait qch ◆ **to ~ sb to the skies** porter qn aux nues ◆ **to ~ the virtues of sb/sth** vanter les mérites de qn/qch
2 *(Rel)* louer, glorifier ◆ **~ God!** Dieu soit loué !

praiseworthiness /ˈpreɪzˌwɜːðɪnɪs/ N mérite *m*

praiseworthy /ˈpreɪzˌwɜːðɪ/ ADJ *[person]* digne d'éloges ; *[effort, attempt]* digne d'éloges, louable

praline /ˈprɑːliːn/ N *(nutty)* praline *f* ; *(= almond)* dragée *f*

pram /præm/ N *(Brit)* voiture *f* d'enfant, landau *m* ◆ **~ park** emplacement *m* réservé aux voitures d'enfants

prance /prɑːns/ VI *[horse, child]* caracoler ; *[dancer]* cabrioler ◆ **the horse was prancing about** le cheval caracolait ◆ **she was prancing* around** *or* **about with nothing on** elle se baladait* toute nue ◆ **to ~ in/out** *etc [horse]* entrer/sortir *etc* en caracolant ; *[person] (gaily)* entrer/sortir *etc* allégrement ; *(arrogantly)* entrer/sortir *etc* en se pavanant

prang †* /præŋ/ VT *(Brit) (= crash) [+ plane, car]* bousiller* ; *[+ bomb]* pilonner

prank /præŋk/ N *(= joke)* farce *f*, niche † *f* ◆ **a childish ~** une gaminerie ◆ **schoolboy ~** farce *f* d'écolier ◆ **to play a ~ on sb** faire une farce *or* une niche † à qn

prankster † /ˈpræŋkstəʳ/ N farceur *m*, -euse *f*

praseodymium /ˌpreɪzɪəʊˈdɪmɪəm/ N praséodyme *m*

prat** /præt/ N *(Brit)* con** *m*, conne** *f*

prate /preɪt/ VI jaser, babiller *(pej)* ◆ **to ~ on about sth** parler à n'en plus finir de qch

pratfall* /ˈprætˌfɔːl/ N *(US)* chute *f* sur le derrière

prattle /ˈprætl/ VI *[one person]* jaser, babiller *(pej)* ; *[several people]* papoter, jacasser ; *[child]* babiller, gazouiller ◆ **to ~ on about sth** parler à n'en plus finir de qch ◆ **he ~s on and on** c'est un vrai moulin à paroles N *[of one person]* bavardage *m*, babillage *m (pej)* ; *[of several people]* jacasserie *f*, papotage *m* ; *[of child]* babil *m*, babillage *m*

prawn /prɔːn/ N *(esp Brit)* crevette *f* rose, bouquet *m* ; → **Dublin**
COMP **prawn cocktail** N cocktail *m* de crevettes
prawn cracker N beignet *m* de crevettes

pray /preɪ/ VI prier ◆ **they ~ed to God to help them** ils prièrent Dieu de les secourir ◆ **he ~ed to be released from his suffering** il pria le ciel de mettre fin à ses souffrances ◆ **to ~ for sb/sb's soul** prier pour qn/l'âme de qn ◆ **he ~ed for forgiveness** il pria Dieu de lui pardonner ◆ **to ~ for rain** prier pour qu'il pleuve ◆ **to ~ for guidance** demander conseil à Dieu ◆ **we're ~ing for fine weather** nous prions pour qu'il fasse beau
VT 1 *(†, liter = request)* prier *(sb to do sth* qn de faire qch)
2 *(Rel)* prier *(that* pour que *+ subj)* ◆ **they ~ed God to help him** ils prièrent Dieu de lui venir en aide ◆ **~ God he'll recover** prions Dieu qu'il guérisse
ADV †† ◆ **~ be seated** veuillez vous asseoir, asseyez-vous je vous prie ◆ **what good is that, ~?** *(iro)* à quoi cela peut-il bien servir, je vous le demande ?

prayer /prɛəʳ/ N 1 *(Rel)* prière *f* ◆ **to be at ~** *or* **at one's ~s** être en prière ◆ **family ~s** prières *fpl* en famille ◆ **he was kneeling in ~** il priait à genoux ◆ **to say one's ~s** faire sa prière ◆ **they said a ~ for him** ils ont dit une prière pour lui, ils ont prié pour lui ◆ **~s** *(as service)* office *m* ◆ **he will lead us in ~, he will lead our ~s** il va diriger nos prières ◆ **he didn't have a ~** * il n'avait pas la moindre chance ; → **common, evening, lord**
2 *(= desire, wish)* vœu *m*, souhait *m*
COMP **prayer beads** NPL chapelet *m*
prayer book N livre *m* de prières ◆ **the Prayer Book** le rituel de l'Église anglicane
prayer mat N tapis *m* de prière
prayer meeting N réunion *f* de prière
prayer rug N tapis *m* de prière
prayer shawl N *(in Judaism)* taleth *m*
prayer wheel N moulin *m* à prières

praying /ˈpreɪɪŋ/ N *(NonC)* prière(s) *f(pl)* ADJ en prière COMP **praying mantis** N mante *f* religieuse

pre... /priː/ PREF pré... ◆ **preglacial** préglaciaire ◆ **pre-1950** ADJ antérieur (-eure *f*) à (l'année) 1950, d'avant 1950 ADV avant 1950 ; → **predate, pre-record**

preach /priːtʃ/ VI *(Rel)* prêcher *(also fig pej)* évangéliser ; *(in church)* prêcher ◆ **to ~ to sb** prêcher qn ◆ **to ~ to** *or* **at sb** *(fig pej)* prêcher *or* sermonner qn ◆ **don't ~!** pas de morale, s'il te plaît ! ◆ **you're ~ing to the converted** vous prêchez un converti ; → **practise** VT *[+ religion, the Gospel, crusade, doctrine]* prêcher ; *(fig) [+ patience]* préconiser, prôner ; *[+ advantage]* prôner ◆ **to ~ a sermon** prêcher, faire un sermon ◆ **to ~ that ...** proclamer que ...

preacher /ˈpriːtʃəʳ/ N prédicateur *m* ; *(US = clergyman)* pasteur *m*

preachify* /ˈpriːtʃɪfaɪ/ VI *(pej)* prêcher, faire la morale

preaching /ˈpriːtʃɪŋ/ N *(NonC)* prédication *f*, sermon *m* ; *(fig pej)* prêchi-prêcha* *m inv (pej)*

preachy* /ˈpriːtʃɪ/ ADJ *(pej)* prêcheur, sermonneur

preamble /priːˈæmbl/ N préambule *m* ; *(in book)* préface *f*

preamplifier /ˌpriːˈæmplɪfaɪəʳ/ N préamplificateur *m*, préampli* *m*

prearrange /ˈpriːəˈreɪndʒ/ VT arranger *or* organiser à l'avance

prebend /ˈprebənd/ N prébende *f*

prebendary /ˈprebəndərɪ/ N prébendier *m*

precancerous /ˈpriːˈkænsərəs/ ADJ précancéreux

precarious /prɪˈkɛərɪəs/ ADJ *(= uncertain) [situation, position]* précaire ; *(= unsteady) [ladder etc]* mal assuré, en équilibre instable ◆ **that stepladder looks a bit ~** cet escabeau n'a pas l'air très stable

precariously /prɪˈkɛərɪəslɪ/ ADV *[cling, hang, lean]* d'une manière précaire *or* instable ◆ **~ perched** *or* **balanced** en équilibre précaire ◆ **to cling ~ to life** s'accrocher désespérément à la vie ◆ **to live ~** *(= in danger of poverty)* vivre dans la précarité ; *(= live for the moment)* vivre au jour le jour

precast /ˈpriːˈkɑːst/ ADJ *(Theat, Cine) [play, film]* dont les rôles sont distribués d'avance COMP **precast concrete** N béton *m* précontraint

precaution /prɪˈkɔːʃən/ N précaution *f (against* contre) ◆ **as a ~** par précaution ◆ **to take ~s** *(also euph)* prendre ses précautions ◆ **to take the ~ of doing sth** prendre la précaution de faire qch ◆ **fire ~s** mesures *fpl* de sécurité contre les incendies ◆ **safety** *or* **security ~s** mesures *fpl* de sécurité

precautionary /prɪˈkɔːʃənərɪ/ ADJ de précaution, préventif ◆ **as a ~ measure** par mesure de précaution ◆ **to take ~ measures** prendre des mesures de précaution

precede /prɪˈsiːd/ VT *(in space, time)* précéder ; *(in rank)* avoir la préséance sur ◆ **the week preceding his death** la semaine qui a précédé sa mort, la semaine avant sa mort

precedence /ˈpresɪdəns/ N *(in rank)* préséance *f* ; *(in importance)* priorité *f* ◆ **to have** *or* **take ~ over sb** avoir la préséance *or* le pas sur qn ◆ **this question must take ~ over all others** ce problème doit passer avant tous les autres *or* doit avoir la priorité sur tous les autres ◆ **to give ~ to sth** donner *or* accorder la priorité à qch

precedent /ˈpresɪdənt/ N précédent *m* ◆ **without ~** sans précédent ◆ **to act as** *or* **form a ~** constituer un précédent ◆ **to set** *or* **establish** *or* **create a ~** créer un précédent ◆ **to break with ~** rompre avec la tradition

preceding /prɪˈsiːdɪŋ/ ADJ précédent ◆ **the ~ day** le jour précédent, la veille

precentor /prɪˈsentəʳ/ N premier chantre *m*, maître *m* de chapelle

precept /ˈpriːsept/ N précepte *m*

preceptor /prɪˈseptəʳ/ N précepteur *m*, -trice *f*

precession /prɪˈseʃən/ N précession *f* COMP **precession of the equinoxes** N *(Astron)* précession *f* des équinoxes

pre-Christian /priːˈkrɪstʃən/ ADJ préchrétien

precinct /ˈpriːsɪŋkt/ N ① *(round cathedral)* enceinte *f* ; *(= boundary)* pourtour *m* ◆ **within the ~s of ...** *(fig)* dans les limites de ... ◆ **the ~s** *(= neighbourhood)* les alentours *mpl*, les environs *mpl* ; → **pedestrian, shopping** ② *(US Police)* circonscription *f* administrative ; *(US Pol)* circonscription *f* électorale, arrondissement *m*
COMP **precinct captain** N *(US)* *(Pol)* responsable *mf* politique de quartier ; *(Police)* commissaire *m* (de police) de quartier
precinct cop * N *(US)* flic * *m* de quartier
precinct police N *(US)* police *f* de quartier
precinct station N *(US Police)* poste *m* de police de quartier, commissariat *m* de quartier
precinct worker N *(US Pol)* *militant(e) politique à l'échelon du quartier*

preciosity /ˌpresɪˈɒsɪtɪ/ N préciosité *f*

precious /ˈpreʃəs/ ADJ ① *[person, moment]* précieux ; *[object, book, possession]* précieux, de valeur ; *(* iro)* chéri, cher ◆ **don't waste ~ time arguing** ne perds pas un temps précieux à discuter ◆ **this book is very ~ to me** ce livre a une très grande valeur pour moi, je tiens énormément à ce livre ◆ **the child is very ~ to him** il tient énormément à cet enfant ◆ **your ~ son** * *(iro)* ton fils chéri, ton cher fils ◆ **your ~ car** *(iro)* ta voiture chérie, ta chère voiture ◆ **your ~ career** *(iro)* ta chère carrière ② *[style, language]* précieux, affecté ADV * ◆ **~ few, ~ little** fort *or* bien peu N ◆ **(my) ~ !** † mon trésor !
COMP **precious metal** N métal *m* précieux
precious stone N pierre *f* précieuse

precipice /ˈpresɪpɪs/ N *(gen)* à-pic *m inv* ◆ **to fall over a ~** tomber dans un précipice

precipitance /prɪˈsɪpɪtəns/, **precipitancy** /prɪˈsɪpɪtənsɪ/ N précipitation *f*

precipitant /prɪˈsɪpɪtənt/ ADJ *(frm)* ⇒ **precipitate adj** N *(Chem)* précipitant *m*

precipitate /prɪˈsɪpɪteɪt/ VT ① *(frm)* *(= hasten)* *[+ event, crisis]* hâter, précipiter ; *(= hurl)* *[+ person]* précipiter (*into* dans) ② *(Chem)* précipiter ; *[+ moisture]* condenser VI *(Chem)* (se) précipiter ; *[moisture]* se condenser N *(Chem)* précipité *m* ADJ /prɪˈsɪpɪt/ *(frm)* irréfléchi, hâtif

precipitately /prɪˈsɪpɪtɪtlɪ/ ADV *(frm)* précipitamment

precipitation /prɪˌsɪpɪˈteɪʃən/ N précipitation *f* *(also Chem, Met)*

precipitous /prɪˈsɪpɪtəs/ ADJ *(frm)* ① escarpé, abrupt ② ⇒ **precipitate adj**

precipitously /prɪˈsɪpɪtəslɪ/ ADV *(frm)* à pic, abruptement

précis /ˈpreɪsiː/ N (pl inv /ˈpreɪsiːz/) résumé *m*, précis *m* VT faire un résumé *or* précis de

precise /prɪˈsaɪs/ ADJ ① *[details, instructions, description]* précis ; *[measurement, meaning, account, nature, location]* précis, exact ◆ **be (more) ~!** soyez (plus) précis ! ◆ **the ~ amount of energy they need** la quantité exacte d'énergie dont ils ont besoin ◆ **at that ~ moment** à ce moment précis *or* même
◆ **to be precise** pour être exact *or* précis ◆ **there were eight to be ~** il y en avait huit pour être exact *or* précis ◆ **I have to be up early, 4am to be ~** il faut que je me lève tôt, à 4 heures du matin pour être exact *or* précis
② *(= meticulous)* *[movement]* précis ; *[person, manner]* méticuleux, minutieux ; *(pej = overprecise)* pointilleux, maniaque ◆ **in that ~ voice of hers** de son ton si net ◆ **she speaks very ~ English** elle parle un anglais très correct

precisely /prɪˈsaɪslɪ/ LANGUAGE IN USE 26.3 ADV *[explain, describe]* de façon précise ; *[measure, define]* avec précision ; *[speak, enunciate]* d'une voix très nette ◆ **10 o'clock ~, ~ 10 o'clock** 10 heures précises *or* sonnantes ◆ **~ nine minutes** exactement *or* très précisément neuf minutes ◆ **hormones, or more ~, progesterone** des hormones, ou plus précisément *or* exactement de la progestérone ◆ **~ what does that mean?** qu'est-ce que cela veut dire exactement *or* au juste ? ◆ **he said ~ nothing** il n'a absolument rien dit ◆ **~!** précisément ! ◆ **I didn't feel the pain, ~ because I was so cold** justement, c'est parce que j'avais si froid que je ne sentais pas la douleur ◆ **that is ~ the problem** c'est bien là le problème

preciseness /prɪˈsaɪsnɪs/ N ⇒ **precision noun**

precision /prɪˈsɪʒən/ N précision *f* ◆ **with deadly/military/clinical ~** avec une précision implacable/militaire/chirurgicale
COMP *[tool]* de précision
precision bombing N bombardement *m* de précision
precision engineering N mécanique *f* de précision
precision instrument N instrument *m* de précision
precision-made ADJ de haute précision

preclude /prɪˈkluːd/ VT *[+ doubt]* écarter, dissiper ; *[+ misunderstanding]* prévenir ; *[+ possibility]* exclure ◆ **to be ~d from doing sth** être empêché de faire qch ◆ **to ~ sth happening** empêcher que qch n'arrive *subj* ◆ **that ~s his leaving** cela l'empêche de partir

precocious /prɪˈkəʊʃəs/ ADJ *(gen, pej)* précoce ◆ **a ~ brat** * un petit prodige ◆ **at a ~ age** à un âge précoce

precociously /prɪˈkəʊʃəslɪ/ ADV ◆ **~ mature** d'une maturité précoce ◆ **a ~ talented/brilliant player** un joueur au talent/génie précoce ◆ **"mummy, it's frankly horrifying", he said ~** "franchement maman, c'est l'horreur" dit-il avec une précocité étonnante

precociousness /prɪˈkəʊʃəsnɪs/, **precocity** /prəˈkɒsɪtɪ/ N précocité *f*

precognition /ˌpriːkɒgˈnɪʃən/ N préconnaissance *f*

precombustion /ˈpriːkəmˈbʌstʃən/ N précombustion *f*

preconceived /ˈpriːkənˈsiːvd/ ADJ ◆ **~ notion** *or* **idea** idée *f* préconçue

preconception /ˈpriːkənˈsepʃən/ N idée *f* préconçue

preconcerted /ˈpriːkənˈsɜːtɪd/ ADJ concerté d'avance

precondition /ˌpriːkənˈdɪʃən/ N condition *f* préalable VT ◆ **to ~ sb to do sth** conditionner qn pour qu'il fasse qch

precook /priːˈkʊk/ VT faire cuire à l'avance

precooked /priːˈkʊkt/ ADJ précuit

precool /priːˈkuːl/ VT refroidir d'avance

precursor /priːˈkɜːsəʳ/ N *(= person, thing)* précurseur *m* ; *(= event)* annonce *f*, signe *m* avant-coureur

precursory /priːˈkɜːsərɪ/ ADJ *[remark]* préliminaire ; *[taste, glimpse]* annonciateur (-trice *f*)

predaceous, predacious /prɪˈdeɪʃəs/ ADJ ⇒ **predatory**

predate /priːˈdeɪt/ VT ① *(= put earlier date on)* *[+ cheque, document]* antidater ② *(= come before in time)* *[+ event]* précéder, avoir lieu avant ; *[+ document]* être antérieur à, précéder

predator /ˈpredətəʳ/ N prédateur *m*, rapace *m*

predatory /ˈpredətərɪ/ ADJ *[animal, bird, insect]* de proie, prédateur (-trice *f*), rapace ; *[habits]* de prédateur(s) ; *[person]* rapace ; *[armies]* pillard ; *[look]* vorace, avide ◆ **~ pricing** *(Comm)* politique *f* de prix déloyale

predecease /ˈpriːdɪˈsiːs/ VT prédécéder

predecessor /ˈpriːdɪsesəʳ/ N prédécesseur *m*

predestination /priːˌdestɪˈneɪʃən/ N prédestination *f*

predestine /priːˈdestɪn/ VT *(also Rel)* prédestiner (*to* à ; *to do sth* à faire qch)

predetermination /ˈpriːdɪˌtɜːmɪˈneɪʃən/ N détermination *f* antérieure ; *(Philos, Rel)* prédétermination *f*

predetermine /ˈpriːdɪˈtɜːmɪn/ VT déterminer d'avance ; *(Philos, Rel)* prédéterminer ◆ **soon it will be possible to ~ the sex of your children** il sera bientôt possible de déterminer d'avance le sexe de vos enfants

predeterminer /ˌpriːdɪˈtɜːmɪnəʳ/ N *(Gram)* prédéterminant *m*, préarticle *m*

predicable /ˈpredɪkəbl/ ADJ, N *(Philos)* prédicable *m*

predicament /prɪˈdɪkəmənt/ N situation *f* difficile *or* fâcheuse ◆ **I'm in a real ~!** je suis dans une situation très difficile

predicate /ˈpredɪkeɪt/ VT ① *(= affirm: gen, Philos)* affirmer (*that* que) ② *(= imply)* *[+ existence of sth etc]* impliquer, supposer ③ *(= base)* *[+ statement, belief, argument]* baser, fonder (*on, upon* sur) ◆ **this is ~d on the fact that ...** ceci est fondé *or* basé sur le fait que ... N /ˈpredɪkɪt/ *(Gram)* prédicat *m* ; *(Philos)* prédicat *m*, attribut *m* ADJ /ˈpredɪkɪt/ *(Gram)* prédicatif ; *(Philos)* attributif

predicative /prɪˈdɪkətɪv/ ADJ *(Gram)* prédicatif

predicatively /prɪˈdɪkətɪvlɪ/ ADV *(Gram)* en tant que prédicat

predict /prɪˈdɪkt/ VT prédire

predictability /prɪdɪktəˈbɪlɪtɪ/ N prévisibilité *f*

predictable /prɪˈdɪktəbl/ ADJ *[behaviour]* prévisible ; *[person, book]* sans surprise ◆ **his reaction was ~** sa réaction était prévisible

predictably /prɪˈdɪktəblɪ/ ADV *[behave, say, react]* d'une manière prévisible ◆ **his father was furious, ~, his father was furious** comme on pouvait s'y attendre *or* comme on pouvait le prévoir, son père était furieux

prediction /prɪˈdɪkʃən/ N *(= forecast)* prévision *f* ; *[of soothsayer]* prédiction *f*

predictive /prɪˈdɪktɪv/ ADJ prophétique

predictor /prɪˈdɪktəʳ/ N indice *m*

predigested /ˌpriːdaɪˈdʒestɪd/ ADJ prédigéré

predilection /ˌpriːdɪˈlekʃən/ N prédilection *f*

predispose /ˈpriːdɪsˈpəʊz/ VT prédisposer (*to or towards sth* à qch ; *to do(ing) sth* à faire qch)

predisposition /ˌpriːˌdɪspəˈzɪʃən/ **N** prédisposition *f* (*to* à)

predominance /prɪˈdɒmɪnəns/ **N** prédominance *f*

predominant /prɪˈdɒmɪnənt/ **ADJ** prédominant

predominantly /prɪˈdɒmɪnəntlɪ/ **ADV** principalement, essentiellement ◆ **they are ~ French** ce sont principalement *or* essentiellement des Français ◆ **acne is ~ a teenage problem** l'acné est principalement *or* essentiellement un problème d'adolescent

predominate /prɪˈdɒmɪneɪt/ **VI** prédominer (*over* sur), prévaloir

predominately /prɪˈdɒmɪneɪtlɪ/ **ADV** ⇒ **predominantly**

preemie‡ /ˈpriːmɪ/ **N** (*US Med*) prématuré(e) *m(f)*

pre-eminence /priːˈemɪnəns/ **N** prééminence *f*

pre-eminent /priːˈemɪnənt/ **ADJ** prééminent

pre-eminently /priːˈemɪnəntlɪ/ **ADV** avant tout, essentiellement

pre-empt /priːˈempt/ **VT** 1 (= *anticipate*) *[+ sb's decision, action]* anticiper, devancer 2 (= *prevent*) prévenir ◆ **you can ~ pain by taking a painkiller** vous pouvez prévenir la douleur en prenant un calmant ◆ **the government ~ed a threatened strike** le gouvernement a pris les devants pour empêcher la grève annoncée 3 *[+ painting, land]* acquérir par (droit de) préemption

pre-emption /priːˈempʃən/ **N** (*Fin*) (droit *m* de) préemption *f* ; (*Mil*) opérations *fpl* préventives

pre-emptive /priːˈemptɪv/ **ADJ** *[right]* de préemption ; *[attack, strike]* préventif ◆ **~ bid** (*Bridge*) (demande *f* de) barrage *m*

preen /priːn/ **VT** *[+ feathers, tail]* lisser ◆ **the bird was ~ing itself** l'oiseau se lissait les plumes ◆ **she was ~ing herself in front of the mirror** elle se pomponnait complaisamment devant la glace ◆ **to ~ o.s. on sth/on doing sth** (*liter*) s'enorgueillir de qch/de faire qch **VI** *[bird]* se lisser les plumes ; *[person]* se pomponner

pre-establish /ˈpriːɪsˈtæblɪʃ/ **VT** préétablir

pre-exist /ˈpriːɪgˈzɪst/ **VI** préexister **VT** préexister à

pre-existence /ˈpriːɪgˈzɪstəns/ **N** préexistence *f*

pre-existent /ˈpriːɪgˈzɪstənt/, **pre-existing** /ˈpriːɪgˈzɪstɪŋ/ **ADJ** préexistant

prefab* /ˈpriːfæb/ **N** (abbrev of **prefabricated building**) préfabriqué *m*

prefabricate /ˌpriːˈfæbrɪkeɪt/ **VT** préfabriquer

preface /ˈprefɪs/ **N** (*to book*) préface *f*, avant-propos *m inv* ; (*to speech*) introduction *f*, préambule *m* **VT** *[+ book]* faire précéder (*by* de) ◆ **he ~d this by saying ...** en avant-propos il a dit ..., il a commencé par dire ... ◆ **he ~d his speech by saying ...** en guise d'introduction à son discours, il a dit ... ◆ **he had the irritating habit of prefacing his sentences with ...** il avait la manie agaçante de commencer toutes ses phrases par ...

prefaded /ˌpriːˈfeɪdɪd/ **ADJ** *[jeans etc]* délavé

prefatory /ˈprefətərɪ/ **ADJ** *[remarks]* préliminaire ; *[page]* liminaire

prefect /ˈpriːfekt/ **N** (*French Admin*) préfet *m* ; (*Brit Scol*) *élève des grandes classes chargé(e) de la discipline*

prefecture /ˈpriːfektjʊəʳ/ **N** préfecture *f*

prefer /prɪˈfɜːʳ/ **LANGUAGE IN USE 5.2, 7.4** **VT** 1 préférer ◆ **to ~ A to B** préférer A à B, aimer mieux A que B ◆ **I ~ bridge to chess** je préfère le bridge aux échecs ◆ **to ~ doing sth** *or* **to do sth** aimer mieux *or* préférer faire qch ◆ **children ~ watching television to reading books** les enfants préfèrent la télévision à la lecture *or* aiment mieux regarder la télévision que lire ◆ **would you ~ me to drive?** préférerais-tu que je prenne le volant ? ◆ **I'd ~ that you didn't come to New York with me** je préférerais que tu ne viennes pas à New York avec moi, j'aimerais mieux que tu ne viennes pas à New York avec moi ◆ **I would ~ not to (do it)** je préférerais *or* j'aimerais mieux ne pas le faire ◆ **she ~red not to give her name** elle a préféré ne pas donner son nom ◆ **I much ~ Scotland** je préfère de beaucoup l'Écosse, j'aime beaucoup mieux l'Écosse ◆ **~red stock** (*US Fin*) ⇒ **preference shares** ; → **preference**

2 (*Jur*) *[+ charge]* porter ; *[+ action]* intenter ; *[+ request]* formuler ; *[+ petition]* adresser ; *[+ argument, reason]* présenter ◆ **to ~ a complaint against sb** déposer une plainte *or* porter plainte contre qn

3 (*esp Rel* = *promote*) élever (*to* à)

preferable /ˈprefərəbl/ **LANGUAGE IN USE 1.1** **ADJ** préférable (*to sth* à qch) ◆ **it is ~ to use vegetable oil for cooking** il est préférable de cuisiner à l'huile végétale ◆ **any death is ~ to being drowned** il n'y a pas pire mort que la noyade

preferably /ˈprefərəblɪ/ **ADV** de préférence

preference /ˈprefərəns/ **LANGUAGE IN USE 7.5** **N** (= *liking*) préférence *f* (*for* pour) ; (= *priority: also Econ*) priorité *f* (*over* sur), préférence *f* ◆ **what is your ~?** que préférez-vous ? ◆ **in ~ to sth** de préférence à qch, plutôt que qch ◆ **in ~ to doing sth** plutôt que de faire qch ◆ **to give A ~ (over B)** accorder *or* donner la préférence à A (plutôt qu'à B) ◆ **I have no strong ~** je n'ai pas vraiment de préférence ◆ **by ~** de préférence

COMP **preference shares** **NPL** (*Brit Fin*) actions *fpl* privilégiées *or* de priorité

preference stock **N** ⇒ **preference shares**

preferential /ˌprefəˈrenʃəl/ **ADJ** *[tariff, terms]* préférentiel ; *[treatment]* de faveur ; *[trade, ballot, voting]* préférentiel

preferentially /ˌprefəˈrenʃəlɪ/ **ADV** (= *by preference*) de préférence ◆ **no-one should be treated ~** personne ne devrait bénéficier d'un traitement préférentiel *or* de faveur

preferment /prɪˈfɜːmənt/ **N** (*esp Rel*) avancement *m*, élévation *f* (*to* à)

prefiguration /ˌpriːfɪgəˈreɪʃən/ **N** préfiguration *f*

prefigure /priːˈfɪgəʳ/ **VT** (= *foreshadow*) préfigurer ; (= *imagine*) se figurer d'avance

prefix /ˈpriːfɪks/ **N** *[of word]* préfixe *m* ; *[of phone number]* indicatif *m* **VT** préfixer

preflight /ˈpriːˈflaɪt/ **ADJ** d'avant le décollage

preform /ˈpriːˈfɔːm/ **VT** préformer

preformation /ˈpriːfɔːˈmeɪʃən/ **N** préformation *f*

prefrontal /ˌpriːˈfrʌntl/ **ADJ** préfrontal

preggers †‡ /ˈpregəz/ **ADJ** (*Brit*) ◆ **to be ~** (= *pregnant*) attendre un gosse*

pregnancy /ˈpregnənsɪ/ **N** *[of woman]* grossesse *f* ; *[of animal]* gestation *f* ; see also **phantom, unwanted** **COMP** **pregnancy test** **N** test *m* de grossesse

pregnant /ˈpregnənt/ **ADJ** *[woman]* enceinte ; *[animal]* pleine ; (*fig*) *[pause, silence]* lourd de sens ; *[idea]* fécond ◆ **to fall ~** tomber enceinte ◆ **three months ~** enceinte de trois mois ◆ **to be ~ by sb** être enceinte de qn ◆ **while she was ~ with Marie** alors qu'elle était enceinte de sa fille Marie ◆ **you can't be half ~** (*hum*) il y a des choses que l'on ne peut pas faire à moitié ◆ **~ with meaning** lourd de sens

preheat /ˈpriːˈhiːt/ **VT** préchauffer ◆ **~ed oven** four *m* préchauffé ◆ **~ the oven to ...** préchauffer le four à ...

prehensile /prɪˈhensaɪl/ **ADJ** préhensile

prehistoric /ˈpriːhɪsˈtɒrɪk/ **ADJ** préhistorique

prehistory /ˈpriːˈhɪstərɪ/ **N** préhistoire *f*

pre-ignition /ˈpriːɪgˈnɪʃən/ **N** autoallumage *m*

pre-industrial /ˈpriːɪnˈdʌstrɪəl/ **ADJ** préindustriel

prejudge /ˈpriːˈdʒʌdʒ/ **VT** *[+ question]* préjuger de ; *[+ person]* juger d'avance

prejudice /ˈpredʒʊdɪs/ **N** 1 préjugé *m* ; (*NonC*) préjugés *mpl* ◆ **racial ~** préjugés *mpl* raciaux ◆ **to have a ~ against/in favour of sb/sth** avoir un préjugé contre/en faveur de qn/qch ◆ **he is quite without ~ in this matter** il est sans parti pris dans cette affaire 2 (*esp Jur* = *detriment*) préjudice *m* ◆ **to the ~ of** au préjudice de ◆ **without ~ (to)** sans préjudice (de) **VT** 1 *[+ person]* influencer (*against* contre ; *in favour of* en faveur de) see also **prejudiced** 2 (*also Jur*) *[+ claim, chance]* porter préjudice à

> ⚠ **prejudice** is only translated by the French word **préjudice** when it means 'detriment'.

prejudiced /ˈpredʒʊdɪst/ **ADJ** *[person]* plein de préjugés ; *[idea, opinion]* préconçu, partial ◆ **he was even more ~ than Harold** il avait encore plus de préjugés qu'Harold ◆ **to be ~ against sb/sth** avoir des préjugés contre qn/qch ◆ **to be racially ~** avoir des préjugés raciaux

prejudicial /ˌpredʒʊˈdɪʃəl/ **ADJ** préjudiciable, nuisible (*to* à) ◆ **to be ~ to** nuire à

prelacy /ˈpreləsɪ/ **N** (= *office*) prélature *f* ; (= *prelates collectively*) prélats *mpl*

prelate /ˈprelɪt/ **N** prélat *m*

pre-law /ˌpriːˈlɔː/ **N** (*US Univ: also* **pre-law program**) enseignement *m* préparatoire aux études de droit

prelim* /ˈpriːlɪm/ **N** (abbrev of **preliminary**) (*Univ*) examen *m* préliminaire ; (*Sport*) (épreuve *f*) éliminatoire *f*

preliminary /prɪˈlɪmɪnərɪ/ **ADJ** *[exam, inquiry, report, remark]* préliminaire ; *[stage]* premier, initial ◆ **~ estimate** (*Constr etc*) devis *m* estimatif ◆ **~ hearing** (*Brit Jur*) audience *f* préliminaire **N** préliminaire *m* ◆ **the preliminaries** les préliminaires *mpl* ◆ **as a ~** en guise de préliminaire, au préalable **COMP** **Preliminary Scholastic Aptitude Test** **N** (*US Scol, Univ*) *test déterminant l'aptitude d'un candidat à présenter l'examen d'entrée à l'université*

prelude /ˈpreljuːd/ **N** (*gen, Mus*) prélude *m* (*to* de) **VT** préluder à

premarital /ˈpriːˈmærɪtl/ **ADJ** avant le mariage ◆ **~ contract** contrat *m* de mariage

premature /ˈpremətʃʊəʳ/ **ADJ** *[decision etc]* prématuré ; *[birth]* prématuré, avant terme ; *[senility, menopause, labour]* précoce ◆ **~ baby** (enfant *mf*) prématuré(e) *m(f)*, enfant *mf* né(e) avant terme ◆ **you are a little ~** (*fig*) vous anticipez un peu

prematurely /ˈprematʃʊəlɪ/ **ADV** (*gen*) prématurément ; *[be born, give birth]* avant terme ◆ **his career was ~ ended by an arm injury** une blessure au bras a prématurément mis fin à sa carrière ◆ **~ bald/menopausal** atteint(e) de calvitie/ménopause précoce ◆ **~ old** *or* **aged** prématurément vieilli ◆ **he's ~ middle-aged** il a vieilli avant l'âge

pre-med* /ˈpriːˈmed/ **N** 1 (*Brit*) abbrev of **premedication** 2 (*US*) ⇒ **pre-med program** **ADJ** (*US*) (abbrev of **premedical**) ◆ **~ program** enseignement *m* préparatoire aux études de médecine ◆ **~ student** étudiant(e) *m(f)* en année préparatoire de médecine

premedication /ˌpriːmedɪˈkeɪʃən/ **N** prémédication *f*

premeditate /priːˈmedɪteɪt/ **VT** préméditer

premeditation /priːˌmedɪˈteɪʃən/ **N** préméditation *f*

premenstrual /priːˈmenstrʊəl/ ADJ prémenstruel COMP **premenstrual syndrome, premenstrual tension** N syndrome *m* prémenstruel

premier /ˈpremɪəʳ/ ADJ premier N *(Pol) (= Prime Minister)* Premier ministre *m* ; *(= President)* chef *m* de l'État
COMP **Premier Division** N *(Ftbl: in Scot)* première division *f* d'Écosse
Premier League N *(Ftbl: in England and Wales)* première division *f* d'Angleterre et du pays de Galles

premiere /ˈpremɪεəʳ/ *(Cine, Theat)* N première *f* ♦ **the film has just received its London ~** la première londonienne du film vient d'avoir lieu VT donner la première de ♦ **the film was ~d in Paris** la première du film a eu lieu à Paris VI ♦ **the movie ~d in May 1998** la première du film a eu lieu en mai 1998

premiership /ˈpremɪəʃɪp/ N *(Pol) [of Prime Minister]* fonction *f* de Premier ministre ; *[of President]* fonction *f* de chef d'État ; *(Ftbl, Rugby)* championnat *m* de première division ♦ **during his ~** *(of Prime Minister)* sous son ministère, pendant qu'il était Premier ministre ; *(of President)* pendant qu'il était chef de l'État ♦ **he staked his claim for the ~** il revendiquait le poste de Premier ministre *or* de chef d'État

premise /ˈpremɪs/ N *(gen, Philos = hypothesis)* prémisse *f* ♦ **on the ~ that ...** en partant du principe que ..., si l'on pose en principe que ...
NPL **premises** *(= property)* locaux *mpl*, lieux *mpl* ♦ **business ~s** locaux *mpl* commerciaux ♦ **on the ~s** sur les lieux, sur place ♦ **off the ~s** à l'extérieur, hors des lieux ♦ **to escort sb off the ~s** escorter *or* accompagner qn dehors ♦ **get off the ~s** videz *or* évacuez les lieux VT *(frm)* ♦ **to be ~d on ...** être fondé *or* basé sur ...

premiss /ˈpremɪs/ N ⇒ **premise noun 1**

premium /ˈpriːmɪəm/ N 1 *(gen, Comm, Fin, Insurance)* prime *f* ; *(Jur: paid on lease)* reprise *f* ♦ **to be sold at a ~** *(on Stock Exchange)* être vendu à prime ♦ **to set** *or* **put** *or* **place a (high) ~ on** *[+ person]* faire grand cas de ; *[+ situation, event]* donner beaucoup d'importance à
♦ **to be at a premium** *(= scarce) [time, space]* être limité ♦ **if space is at a ~, choose adaptable furniture** si l'espace est limité, choisissez des meubles modulables
2 *(US = gasoline)* super(carburant) *m*
ADJ *[goods, brand]* de qualité supérieure
COMP **premium bond** N *(Brit)* obligation *f* à prime, bon *m* à lots
premium fuel N *(Brit)* super(carburant) *m*
premium gasoline N *(US)* → **premium fuel**
premium price N prix *m* fort
premium-rate ADJ *(Brit Telec)* facturé au tarif fort *(pour renseignements, téléphone rose, etc)*

premolar /priːˈməʊləʳ/ N prémolaire *f*

premonition /ˌpreməˈnɪʃən/ N prémonition *f*, pressentiment *m* ♦ **to have a ~ that ...** avoir le pressentiment que ..., pressentir que ...

premonitory /prɪˈmɒnɪtərɪ/ ADJ prémonitoire, précurseur

prenatal /priːˈneɪtl/ ADJ prénatal

prenuptial /ˌpriːˈnʌpʃəl/ ADJ prénuptial COMP **prenuptial agreement** N contrat *m* de mariage

preoccupation /priːˌɒkjʊˈpeɪʃən/ N préoccupation *f* ♦ **keeping warm was his main ~** sa grande préoccupation *or* son souci majeur était de se protéger du froid ♦ **his ~ with money/with winning** son obsession *f* de l'argent/de gagner

preoccupy /priːˈɒkjʊpaɪ/ VT *[+ person, mind]* préoccuper ♦ **to be preoccupied** être préoccupé *(by, with* de)

pre-op * /ˈpriːˈɒp/ N prémédication *f*, médication *f* préopératoire

preordain /ˌpriːɔːˈdeɪn/ VT ordonner *or* régler d'avance ; *(Philos, Rel)* préordonner

preordained /ˌpriːɔˈdeɪnd/ ADJ prédestiné

pre-owned /ˈpriːˈəʊnd/ ADJ d'occasion

prep * /prep/ N (abbrev of **preparation**) 1 *(Scol) (= work)* devoirs *mpl*, préparation *f* ; *(= period)* étude *f* (surveillée) 2 *(US Med)* préparation *f* *(d'un(e) malade)* VI *(US)* 1 ♦ **to ~ for sth** se préparer pour qch 2 *(US Scol)* entrer en classe préparatoire (pour l'université) VT *(US)* ♦ **to ~ o.s.** se préparer COMP **prep school** N *(Brit)* ⇒ **preparatory school** ; → **preparatory**

prepack /ˈpriːˈpæk/, **prepackage** /ˈpriːˈpækɪdʒ/ VT *(Comm)* préconditionner

prepaid /ˈpriːˈpeɪd/ VB pt, ptp of **prepay** ADJ *(gen)* payé (d'avance) ♦ **a ~ phone** un téléphone à communications préchargées ♦ **carriage ~** *(Comm)* port payé ♦ **reply ~** réponse payée ♦ **~ expenses** *(Fin etc)* compte *m* de régularisation de l'actif ♦ **~ health care** *(in US)* médecine *f* prépayée

preparation /ˌprepəˈreɪʃən/ N 1 *(= act of preparing)* préparation *f* ; *(Culin, Pharm etc = thing prepared)* préparation *f*
♦ **to be in preparation** *[book, film etc]* être en préparation ♦ **Latin is a good ~ for Greek** le latin prépare bien au grec, le latin est une bonne formation pour le grec
♦ **in preparation for** en vue de, en prévision de
♦ **preparations** *(= getting ready)* préparatifs *mpl* ♦ **the country's ~s for war** les préparatifs *mpl* de guerre du pays ♦ **to make ~s for sth** prendre ses dispositions pour qch, faire les préparatifs de qch ♦ **~s for the party are under way** les préparatifs de la soirée sont en cours
2 *(NonC: Scol) (= work)* devoirs *mpl*, préparation *f* ; *(= period)* étude *f*

preparatory /prɪˈpærətərɪ/ ADJ *[work]* préparatoire ; *[measure, step]* préliminaire, préalable ♦ **~ to sth** préalablement à qch, en vue de qch ♦ **~ to doing sth** en vue de faire qch ♦ **he cleared his throat, ~ to speaking** il s'est éclairci la voix avant de parler
COMP **preparatory school** N *(Brit)* école *f* primaire privée ; *(US)* école *f* secondaire privée

PREPARATORY SCHOOL

En Grande-Bretagne, une **preparatory school**, ou **prep school**, est une école primaire, généralement non mixte, qui prépare les élèves à entrer dans un établissement secondaire privé. L'uniforme y est obligatoire et la discipline relativement stricte.
Aux États-Unis, le terme désigne une école secondaire privée préparant les élèves aux études supérieures. Dans les deux cas, la clientèle de ces écoles est issue de milieux privilégiés. Le mot « preppy », utilisé comme substantif ou comme adjectif, désigne les élèves des **prep schools** américaines, ou leur style vestimentaire BCBG.

prepare /prɪˈpεəʳ/ VT *[+ plan, speech, lesson, work, medicine, sauce]* préparer ; *[+ meal, dish]* préparer, apprêter ; *[+ surprise]* préparer, ménager *(for sb* à qn) ; *[+ room, equipment]* préparer *(for* pour) ♦ **to ~ sb for an exam/an operation** préparer qn à un examen/pour une opération ♦ **to ~ sb for a shock/for bad news** préparer qn à un choc/à une mauvaise nouvelle ♦ **~ yourself for a shock!** prépare-toi à (recevoir) un choc !, tiens-toi bien ! ♦ **to ~ o.s. for** ⇒ **to prepare for** → vi ♦ **to ~ the way/ground for sth** préparer la voie/le terrain pour qch ; see also **prepared**
VI ♦ **to ~ for** *(= make arrangements) [+ journey, sb's arrival, event]* faire des préparatifs pour, prendre ses dispositions pour ; *(= prepare o.s. for) [+ storm, flood, meeting, discussion]* se préparer pour ; *[+ war]* se préparer à ; *[+ examination]* préparer ♦ **to ~ to do sth** s'apprêter *or* se préparer à faire qch

prepared /prɪˈpεəd/ LANGUAGE IN USE 3.1, 11.3 ADJ *[person, army, country]* prêt ; *[statement, answer]* préparé à l'avance ; *(Culin) [sauce, soup]* tout prêt ♦ **be ~!** soyez sur le qui-vive ! ♦ **be ~ for bad news** préparez-vous à une mauvaise nouvelle ♦ **I am ~ for anything** *(= can cope with anything)* j'ai tout prévu, je suis paré ; *(= won't be surprised at anything)* je m'attends à tout ♦ **to be ~ to do sth** être prêt *or* disposé à faire qch

preparedness /prɪˈpεərɪdnɪs/ N 1 *(Mil)* capacité *f* de réaction ♦ **the city's ~ for war** la capacité de réaction de la ville en cas de guerre ♦ **I want Britain's disaster ~ to be very much better** je veux que la Grande-Bretagne soit beaucoup mieux préparée en cas de catastrophe 2 *(= willingness)* disposition *f* ♦ **their ~ to help countries affected by the famine** leur disposition à aider les pays touchés par la famine

prepay /ˈpriːˈpeɪ/ (pret, ptp **prepaid**) VT payer d'avance ; see also **prepaid**

prepayment /ˈpriːˈpeɪmənt/ N paiement *m* d'avance

preponderance /prɪˈpɒndərəns/ N *(in numbers)* supériorité *f* numérique ; *(in influence)* prépondérance *f* *(over* sur)

preponderant /prɪˈpɒndərənt/ ADJ *(in numbers)* numériquement supérieur ; *(in influence)* prépondérant

preponderantly /prɪˈpɒndərəntlɪ/ ADV principalement, essentiellement

preponderate /prɪˈpɒndəreɪt/ VI *(in numbers)* être en supériorité numérique *(over* par rapport à) ; *(in influence)* l'emporter *(over* sur)

preposition /ˌprepəˈzɪʃən/ N préposition *f*

prepositional /ˌprepəˈzɪʃənl/ ADJ *[phrase]* prépositif, prépositionnel ; *[use]* prépositionnel

prepositionally /ˌprepəˈzɪʃənəlɪ/ ADV prépositivement

prepossess /ˌpriːpəˈzes/ VT *(= preoccupy)* préoccuper ; *(= bias)* prévenir, influencer ; *(= impress favourably)* impressionner favorablement

prepossessing /ˌpriːpəˈzesɪŋ/ ADJ *[person, appearance]* avenant

preposterous /prɪˈpɒstərəs/ ADJ ridicule, grotesque

preposterously /prɪˈpɒstərəslɪ/ ADV ridiculement

preposterousness /prɪˈpɒstərəsnɪs/ N (NonC) ridicule *m*, grotesque *m*

preppie *, **preppy** * /ˈprepɪ/ *(US)* ADJ bon chic bon genre *, BCBG * N élève *mf* d'une boîte * privée ; → PREPARATORY SCHOOL

preprandial /ˌpriːˈprændɪəl/ ADJ *(frm or hum) [drink]* avant le repas

preprepared /ˌpriːprɪˈpεəd/ ADJ tout prêt

preproduction /ˌpriːprəˈdʌkʃən/ N travail *m* antérieur à la production
COMP **preproduction model** N prototype *m*
preproduction trial N mise *f* à l'essai du prototype

preprogrammed /ˈpriːˈprəʊgræmd/ ADJ programmé à l'avance

prepubescent /ˌpriːpjuːˈbesənt/ ADJ prépubère

prepuce /ˈpriːpjuːs/ N prépuce *m*

prequel /ˈpriːkwəl/ N *film ou roman ayant pour thème des événements antérieurs à ceux d'un film ou d'un roman déjà sorti, la jeunesse ou l'enfance d'un héros célèbre par exemple*

Pre-Raphaelite /ˈpriːˈræfəlaɪt/ ADJ, N préraphaélite *mf*

pre-record /ˌpriːrɪˈkɔːd/ VT [+ song, programme] enregistrer à l'avance ◆ **~ed broadcast** émission f en différé ◆ **~ed cassette** cassette f préenregistrée

prerelease showing /ˌpriːrɪˈliːsˈʃəʊɪŋ/ N (Cine) avant-première f

prerequisite /ˈpriːˈrekwɪzɪt/ N 1 (gen) condition f préalable 2 (US Univ) *unité de valeur dont l'obtention est obligatoire pour pouvoir s'inscrire dans l'unité de valeur supérieure* ADJ nécessaire

prerogative /prɪˈrɒgətɪv/ N prérogative f ◆ **to exercise the Royal Prerogative** (Brit) faire acte de souverain

Pres. (abbrev of **president**) Pdt

presage /ˈpresɪdʒ/ (frm) N (= omen) présage m ; (= foreboding) pressentiment m VT présager, annoncer

presbyopia /ˌprezbɪˈəʊpɪə/ N presbytie f

Presbyterian /ˌprezbɪˈtɪərɪən/ ADJ, N presbytérien(ne) m(f)

Presbyterianism /ˌprezbɪˈtɪərɪənɪzəm/ N presbytérianisme m

presbytery /ˈprezbɪtərɪ/ N (= part of church) chœur m ; (= residence) presbytère m ; (= court) consistoire m

pre-school /ˌpriːˈskuːl/ ADJ [years, age] préscolaire ; [child] d'âge préscolaire ◆ **~ education** enseignement m préscolaire ◆ **~ playgroup** ≃ garderie f

preschooler /ˈpriːskuːləʳ/ N (US) enfant mf d'âge préscolaire

prescience /ˈpresɪəns/ N prescience f

prescient /ˈpresɪənt/ ADJ prescient

prescribe /prɪsˈkraɪb/ VT (gen, Admin, Jur, Med) prescrire (sth for sb qch à qn) ◆ **the ~d dose/form/punishment** la dose/le formulaire/la punition prescrit(e) ◆ **~d books** œuvres fpl (inscrites) au programme ◆ **this diet is ~d in some cases** ce régime se prescrit dans certains cas ◆ **he ~d complete rest** il a prescrit *or* ordonné le repos absolu ◆ **what do you ~?** (fig) que me conseillez-vous ?, que me recommandez-vous ?

prescription /prɪsˈkrɪpʃən/ N 1 (Med) ordonnance f, prescription f médicale ◆ **to make out** *or* **write out a ~ for sb** faire une ordonnance pour qn ◆ **to make up** *or* (US) **fill a ~** exécuter une ordonnance ◆ **on ~** sur ordonnance ◆ **he gets free ~s** les médicaments qu'on lui prescrit sont intégralement pris en charge ◆ **without ~** sans ordonnance

2 (fig = proposal) proposition f ◆ **this is not necessarily a ~ for a happy family life** cela ne garantit pas nécessairement une vie de famille heureuse

COMP [medicine] (= made according to prescription) prescrit ; (= available only on prescription) vendu sur ordonnance seulement

prescription charge N (Brit) *montant forfaitaire payé sur les médicaments*, ≃ ticket m modérateur

prescription glasses, prescription spectacles NPL lunettes fpl de vue

PRESCRIPTION CHARGE

En Grande-Bretagne, les patients paient, à la façon du ticket modérateur en France, un montant forfaitaire sur tous les médicaments prescrits par un médecin : c'est la **prescription charge**, dont sont néanmoins exemptées certaines catégories de personnes : enfants, femmes enceintes, personnes âgées ou bénéficiaires de prestations sociales. → **NHS**

prescriptive /prɪsˈkrɪptɪv/ ADJ (= giving precepts) (gen, Gram) normatif ; (= legalized by custom) [rights etc] consacré par l'usage

prescriptivism /prɪˈskrɪptɪˌvɪzəm/ N (Ling) normativisme m

pre-select /ˌpriːsɪˈlekt/ VT présélectionner

presell /ˌpriːˈsel/ VT vendre à l'avance

pre-seminal /ˈpriːˈsemɪnəl/ ADJ (Med) pré-éjaculatoire ◆ **~ fluid** liquide m pré-éjaculatoire

presence /ˈprezns/ N 1 présence f ◆ **I felt comfortable in her ~** je me sentais à l'aise en sa présence ◆ **in the ~ of** en présence de ; (Jur) par-devant ◆ **your ~ is requested at ...** vous êtes prié d'assister à ... ◆ **they were admitted to the royal ~** (liter, frm) ils furent admis en présence du roi (or de la reine) ◆ **he certainly made his ~ felt** * sa présence n'est vraiment pas passée inaperçue ◆ **a ghostly ~** une présence surnaturelle ◆ **this country will maintain a ~ in North Africa** ce pays maintiendra une présence en Afrique du Nord ◆ **police ~** présence f policière ◆ **there was a heavy police ~ at the match** il y avait une forte présence policière au match

2 (= bearing etc) présence f ◆ **to lack ~** manquer de présence ◆ **he has a good stage ~** il a de la présence (sur scène) ◆ **a man of noble ~** (liter) un homme de belle prestance *or* de belle allure

COMP **presence of mind** N présence f d'esprit

present /ˈpreznt/ ADJ 1 (= in attendance, in existence) présent ◆ **~ at** présent à ◆ **to be ~ at sth** être présent à qch, assister à qch ◆ **my husband was ~ at the birth** mon mari a assisté à l'accouchement ◆ **~ in** présent dans ◆ **who was ~?** qui était là ? ◆ **is there a doctor ~?** y a-t-il un docteur ici *or* dans l'assistance ? ◆ **those ~** les personnes fpl présentes, l'assistance f ◆ **~ company excepted** les personnes ici présentes exceptées, à l'exception des personnes ici présentes ◆ **all ~ and correct!** tous présents à l'appel !

2 (= existing now) [state, epoch, year, circumstances, techniques, residence, job] présent *after n*, actuel ; (= in question) présent *before n*, en question ; (Gram) présent *after n* ◆ **her ~ husband** son mari actuel ◆ **the ~ writer believes that ...** l'auteur croit que ... ◆ **the ~ government** le gouvernement actuel ◆ **in the ~ day** aujourd'hui ; see also **comp** ◆ **at the ~ moment** *or* **time** actuellement, à présent ; (more precisely) en ce moment même ◆ **the ~ month** le mois courant, ce mois-ci ◆ **in the ~ case** dans le cas présent

N 1 (also Gram) présent m ◆ **the ~ simple** le présent simple ◆ **the ~ continuous** le présent continu *or* progressif ◆ **(there's) no time like the ~!** il ne faut jamais remettre au lendemain ce que l'on peut faire le jour même ! ◆ **up to the ~** jusqu'à présent

◆ **at present** (= right now) actuellement, en ce moment ; (= for the time being) pour le moment ◆ **at ~ children under 14 are not admitted** actuellement, les enfants de moins de 14 ans ne sont pas admis ◆ **that's all we know at ~** c'est tout ce que nous savons pour le moment *or* pour l'instant ◆ **as things are at ~** dans l'état actuel des choses

◆ **for the present** (= at the moment) pour le moment

◆ **in the present** (gen) dans le présent ; (Gram) au présent ◆ **to live in the ~** (= not be hidebound) vivre dans le présent ; (= live from day to day) vivre au jour le jour

2 (= gift) cadeau m ◆ **it's for a ~** c'est pour offrir ◆ **she gave me the book as a ~** elle m'a offert le livre (en cadeau) ◆ **to make sb a ~ of sth** (lit, fig) faire cadeau *or* don de qch à qn ; → **birthday, Christmas**

3 (Jur) **by these ~s** par les présentes

VT /prɪˈzent/ 1 ◆ **to ~ sb with sth, to ~ sth to sb** (= give as gift) offrir qch à qn, faire cadeau de qch à qn ; (= hand over) [+ prize, medal] remettre qch à qn ◆ **she ~ed him with a son** elle lui a donné un fils ◆ **we were ~ed with a fait accompli** nous nous sommes trouvés devant un fait accompli ◆ **to ~ arms** (Mil) présenter les armes ◆ **~ arms!** présentez armes !

2 [+ tickets, documents, credentials, one's compliments, apologies] présenter (to à) ; [+ plan, account, proposal, report, petition, information] présenter, soumettre (to à) ; [+ complaint] déposer ; [+ proof, evidence] apporter, fournir ; (Parl) [+ bill] introduire, présenter ; (Jur etc) [+ case] exposer ◆ **to ~ o.s. at the desk/for an interview** se présenter au bureau/à un entretien ◆ **to ~ a cheque (for payment)** encaisser *or* présenter un chèque ◆ **how is the data ~ed?** comment les données sont-elles présentées ? ◆ **his report ~s the matter in another light** son rapport présente la question sous un autre jour, son rapport jette une lumière différente sur la question ◆ **to ~ o.s.** se présenter ◆ **how you ~ yourself is very important** la manière dont vous vous présentez est très importante

3 (= constitute, offer) [+ problem] présenter, poser ; [+ difficulties, features] présenter ; [+ opportunity] donner ; [+ challenge] constituer ◆ **the bay ~s a magnificent sight** la baie présente un spectacle splendide ◆ **the opportunity ~ed itself** l'occasion s'est présentée ◆ **to ~ the appearance of sth** avoir *or* donner (toute) l'apparence de qch ◆ **the patrol ~ed an easy target** la patrouille offrait *or* constituait une cible facile ◆ **the Committee ~ed an easy target for criticism** le comité était une cible facile pour les critiques

4 [+ play, concert] donner ; [+ film, play, programme] donner, passer ; (= act as presenter of) présenter ◆ **we are proud to ~ ...** (Theat) nous sommes heureux de vous présenter ... ◆ **"presenting Glenda Jackson as Lady Macbeth"** "avec Glenda Jackson dans le rôle de Lady Macbeth"

5 (frm = introduce) présenter (sb to sb qn à qn) ◆ **may I ~ Miss Smith?** permettez-moi de vous présenter Mademoiselle Smith ◆ **to be ~ed (at Court)** (Brit) être présenté à la Cour

VI (Med) ◆ **he ~ed last month (here at the clinic)** [patient] il est venu nous consulter *or* il s'est présenté le mois passé (à la clinique) ◆ **she initially ~ed with headaches and insomnia** lorsqu'elle s'est présentée pour la première fois elle souffrait de maux de tête et d'insomnie ◆ **the patient ~s with lesions to the abdomen** ce patient présente des lésions à l'abdomen ◆ **he ~s as a chronic alcoholic** il présente tous les symptômes de l'alcoolisme chronique

COMP **present-day** ADJ d'aujourd'hui, contemporain

present perfect N (Gram) passé m composé

presentable /prɪˈzentəbl/ ADJ [person, appearance, room] présentable ; [clothes] présentable, mettable ◆ **go and make yourself (look) ~** va t'arranger un peu ◆ **I'm not very ~** je ne suis guère présentable, je ne peux guère me montrer

presentably /prɪˈzentəblɪ/ ADV de manière présentable

presentation /ˌprezənˈteɪʃən/ N 1 (NonC = act or fact of presenting) [of plan, account, proposal, report, petition, evidence] présentation f, soumission f ; [of complaint] déposition f ; [of parliamentary bill] présentation f, introduction f ; [of cheque] encaissement m ; [of case] exposition f ◆ **on ~ of this ticket** sur présentation de ce billet

2 (= packaging, way of presenting) présentation f ◆ **the subject matter is good but the ~ is poor** le fond est bon mais la présentation laisse à désirer ◆ **it's just a problem of ~** c'est une question de présentation ◆ **his ~ of the play** (= the way he did it) sa mise en scène de la pièce ◆ **a theatrical ~ of "Danton's Death"** une représentation théâtrale de "La mort de Danton"

3 *(= introduction)* présentation *f (to* à)

4 *(= ceremony)* remise *f* du cadeau *(or* de la médaille *etc)* ◆ **who made the ~?** qui a remis le cadeau *(or* la médaille *etc)* ? ◆ **to make a ~ of sth to sb** remettre qch à qn

5 *(Univ, Comm etc = lecture, talk)* exposé *m* oral ◆ **a business ~** une présentation commerciale

COMP **presentation box, presentation case** N coffret *m* **presentation copy** N *[of book] (for inspection, review)* spécimen *m* (gratuit), exemplaire *m* envoyé à titre gracieux ; *(from author)* exemplaire *m* offert en hommage

presentational /ˌprezənˈteɪʃənl/ ADJ ◆ **for ~ reasons** pour des raisons de présentation

presenter /prɪˈzentəʳ/ N *(Brit Rad, TV)* présentateur *m*, -trice *f*, speaker(ine) *m(f)*

presentiment /prɪˈzentɪmənt/ N pressentiment *m*

presently /ˈprezntlɪ/ ADV 1 *(Brit) (= in a moment)* tout à l'heure ; *(= some time later)* peu de temps après, un peu plus tard 2 *(= currently)* actuellement, à présent

presentment /prɪˈzentmənt/ N *[of note, bill of exchange etc]* présentation *f* ; *(Jur)* déclaration *f* émanant du jury

preservation /ˌprezəˈveɪʃən/ N *(= protection, safeguarding)* sauvegarde *f*, préservation *f* ; *(= continuance, maintenance)* maintien *m* ◆ **in a good state of ~** bien préservé, en bon état de conservation ◆ **the ~ of the monument is our first priority** notre priorité est de sauvegarder le monument ◆ **the ~ of peace in the Middle East** le maintien de la paix au Proche-Orient

COMP **preservation order** N *(Brit Admin)* ◆ **to put a ~ order on a building** classer un édifice (monument historique)

preservation society N *(Archit)* association *f* pour la sauvegarde et la conservation des sites et monuments

preservationist /ˌprezəˈveɪʃənɪst/ N *(esp US) [of historic buildings]* défenseur *m* du patrimoine historique ; *(environmental)* défenseur *m* de l'environnement

preservative /prɪˈzɜːvətɪv/ N *(Culin)* agent *m* de conservation, conservateur *m*

> ⚠ Caution! **préservatif** means 'condom', not **preservative**.

preserve /prɪˈzɜːv/ VT 1 *(= keep, maintain) [+ building, traditions, manuscript, eyesight, position]* conserver ; *[+ leather, wood]* entretenir ; *[+ memory]* conserver, garder ; *[+ dignity, sense of humour, reputation]* garder ; *[+ peace]* maintenir ; *[+ silence]* observer, garder ◆ **well-/badly-~d** en bon/mauvais état de conservation ◆ **she is very well-~d** *(hum)* elle est bien conservée ◆ **to ~ one's looks** conserver sa beauté ◆ **have you ~d the original?** avez-vous gardé *or* conservé l'original ?

2 *(from harm etc)* préserver, garantir *(from* de), protéger *(from* contre) ◆ **may God ~ you!** † Dieu vous garde !, que Dieu vous protège ! ◆ **(heaven** *or* **the saints) ~ me from that!** † le ciel m'en préserve !

3 *(Culin) [+ fruit etc]* conserver, mettre en conserve ◆ **~d** en conserve ◆ **~d food** *(in bottles, cans)* conserves *fpl* ; *(frozen)* produits *mpl* surgelés

N 1 *(Brit Culin) (= jam)* confiture *f* ; *(= chutney)* condiment *m* à base de fruits

2 *(= bottled fruit/vegetables)* fruits *mpl*/légumes *mpl* en conserve

3 *(Hunting)* réserve *f* ◆ **game ~** chasse *f* gardée *or* interdite

4 *(fig = prerogative)* chasse *f* gardée ◆ **that's his ~** c'est sa chasse gardée, c'est son domaine particulier

COMP **preserving pan** N bassine *f* à confiture

preserver /prɪˈzɜːvəʳ/ N *(= person)* sauveur *m* ; → **life**

preset /ˈpriːˈset/ VT (pret, ptp **preset**) programmer

preshrunk /ˈpriːˈʃrʌŋk/ ADJ irrétrécissable

preside /prɪˈzaɪd/ VI présider ◆ **to ~ at** *or* **over a meeting** présider une réunion COMP **presiding officer** N *(Parl)* président(e) *m(f)* du parlement *(en Écosse, au pays de Galles et en Irlande du Nord)* ; *(at polling station)* président(e) *m(f)* du bureau de vote

presidency /ˈprezɪdənsɪ/ N présidence *f*

president /ˈprezɪdənt/ N *(Pol etc)* président *m* ; *(US Comm)* président-directeur *m* général, PDG *m* ; *(US Univ)* président *m* (d'université) *m*

COMP **president-elect** N *titre que porte le président des États-Unis nouvellement élu (en novembre) jusqu'à son investiture (en janvier de l'année suivante)*

President of the Board of Trade N *(Brit Parl)* ≈ ministre *m* du Commerce

Presidents' Day N *(US) jour férié le troisième lundi de février, en souvenir des présidents Lincoln et Washington*

presidential /ˌprezɪˈdenʃəl/ ADJ 1 *(gen) [decision, suite etc]* présidentiel, du président ◆ **~ elections** élection *f* présidentielle ◆ **his ~ hopes** l'espoir qu'il a de devenir président 2 *(= of one specific President) [staff, envoy, representative]* du Président ◆ **~ adviser** *(US Pol)* conseiller *m* personnel du Président 3 *(= reminiscent of a president) [style, regime, politician]* présidentiel ◆ **the new Prime Minister is more ~ (in style) than his predecessors** le nouveau Premier ministre a un style plus présidentiel que ses prédécesseurs ◆ **a ~-style campaign** une campagne à l'américaine

presidentially /ˌprezɪˈdenʃəlɪ/ ADV en tant que président

presidium /prɪˈsɪdɪəm/ N ⇒ **praesidium**

pre-soak /ˈpriːˈsəʊk/ VT faire tremper

press /pres/ N 1 *(= apparatus) (for wine, olives, cheese etc)* pressoir *m* ; *(for gluing, moulding etc)* presse *f* ◆ **cider ~** pressoir *m* à cidre ◆ **hydraulic ~** presse *f* hydraulique ◆ **racket ~** presse-raquette *m inv* ◆ **trouser ~** presse *f* à pantalon

2 *(Printing) (= machine: also* **printing press***)* presse *f* (typographique) ; *(= place, publishing firm)* imprimerie *f* ◆ **rotary ~** presse *f* rotative ◆ **to set the ~es rolling** mettre les presses en marche ◆ **to pass sth for ~** *(Publishing)* donner le bon à tirer de qch ◆ **to go to ~** *[book etc]* être mis sous presse ; *[newspaper]* aller à l'impression ◆ **correct at time of going to ~** *(Publishing)* correct au moment de mettre sous presse

3 *(= reporting, journalists collectively)* presse *f* ◆ **a free ~** une presse libre ◆ **to get a good/bad ~** avoir bonne/mauvaise presse ◆ **I saw it in the ~** je l'ai lu dans la presse *or* dans les journaux ◆ **to advertise in the ~** *(Comm)* faire de la publicité dans la presse *or* dans les journaux ; *(privately)* mettre une annonce dans les journaux ◆ **a member of the ~** un(e) journaliste ◆ **the national ~** la presse nationale ◆ **is (anyone from) the ~ present?** la presse est-elle représentée ? ◆ **the ~ reported that ...** la presse a relaté que ..., on a rapporté dans la presse que ...

4 *(= pressure: with hand, instrument)* pression *f* ◆ **he gave his trousers a ~** il a donné un coup de fer à son pantalon ; → **permanent**

5 *(Weight Lifting)* développé *m*

6 *(Ir, Scot = cupboard)* armoire *f*, placard *m*

7 *(= pressure of people)* foule *f*, presse *f (liter)* ◆ **he lost his hat in the ~ to get out** il a perdu son chapeau dans la bousculade à la sortie

VT 1 *(= push) [+ button, switch, accelerator]* appuyer sur ; *(= squeeze) [+ sb's hand etc]* serrer, presser ◆ **he ~ed his fingertips together** il a pressé les extrémités de ses doigts les unes contre les autres ◆ **he ~ed his nose against the window** il a collé son nez à la fenêtre ◆ **to ~ the flesh*** *(US)* serrer une multitude de mains, prendre un bain de foule ◆ **he ~ed her to him** il la serra *or* pressa contre lui ◆ **as the crowd moved back he found himself ~ed (up) against a wall** au moment où la foule a reculé il s'est trouvé acculé *or* pressé contre un mur

2 *(= crush) [+ grapes, olives, lemons, flowers]* presser

3 *(= iron) [+ clothes etc]* repasser, donner un coup de fer à

4 *(= make by pressing) [+ object, machine part]* mouler ; *[+ record, disk]* presser

5 *(= pressure) (in battle, game)* presser, attaquer constamment ; *[pursuer]* talonner, serrer de près ; *[creditor]* poursuivre, harceler ◆ **to ~ sb to do sth** insister pour que qn fasse qch ◆ **I am really ~ed today** je suis débordé (de travail) aujourd'hui ◆ **to ~ sb for payment/an answer** presser qn de payer/de répondre ◆ **to be ~ed for time** être pressé ◆ **to be ~ed for money** être à court d'argent, manquer d'argent ◆ **he didn't need much ~ing** il ne s'est guère fait prier ◆ **to ~ a gift/money on sb** presser qn d'accepter *or* insister pour que qn accepte *subj* un cadeau/de l'argent, offrir avec insistance un cadeau/de l'argent à qn ◆ **to ~ one's suit** († *or hum*) faire sa demande (en mariage) ; → **hard**

6 *(= press-gang: lit, Hist)* enrôler de force ◆ **to ~ sb into doing sth** forcer qn à faire qch ◆ **we were all ~ed into service** nous avons tous été mis à contribution ◆ **the church hall was ~ed into service as a school** la salle paroissiale a été réquisitionnée pour servir d'école ◆ **buildings that were ~ed into service to house the victims** des bâtiments qui ont été réquisitionnés pour accueillir les victimes

7 *(= pursue, press home) [+ attack]* poursuivre ; *[+ advantage]* pousser ; *[+ claim, demand]* renouveler, insister sur ◆ **to ~ charges (against sb)** *(Jur)* porter plainte (contre qn) ◆ **I shan't ~ the point** je n'insisterai pas

8 *(Weight Lifting)* soulever

VI 1 *(= exert pressure: with hand etc)* appuyer *(on* sur) ; *[weight, burden]* faire pression, peser *(on* sur) ; *[debts, troubles]* peser *(on sb* à qn) ◆ **time ~es!** le temps presse !, l'heure tourne ! ◆ **to ~ for sth** faire pression pour obtenir qch, demander instamment qch ◆ **they are ~ing to have the road diverted** ils font pression pour (obtenir) que la route soit déviée

2 ◆ **he ~ed through the crowd** il s'est frayé un chemin dans la foule ◆ **he ~ed in/out** *etc* il est entré/sorti *etc* en jouant des coudes ◆ **they ~ed in/out** *etc* ils sont entrés/sortis *etc* en masse ◆ **crowds ~ed round him** une foule se pressait autour de lui

COMP *[campaign, card etc]* de presse

press agency N agence *f* de presse

press agent N agent *m* de publicité

the Press Association N *agence de presse britannique*

press attaché N attaché(e) *m(f)* de presse

press baron N magnat *m* de la presse

press box N tribune *f* de la presse

press button N bouton(-poussoir) *m*

press clipping N ⇒ **press cutting**

Press Complaints Commission N *(in Brit) commission des plaintes contre la presse*

press conference N conférence *f* de presse

press corps N *(esp US)* la presse *(travaillant à un endroit donné)*

press cutting N coupure *f* de presse *or* de journal ◆ **~ cutting agency** argus *m* de la presse

press gallery N *(esp Parl)* tribune *f* de la presse

press-gang N *(Hist)* racoleurs *mpl* VT *(fig)* ◆ **to ~-gang sb into doing sth** faire pression sur qn *or* forcer la main à qn pour qu'il fasse qch

press hold N *(Climbing)* appui *m*

press kit N dossier *m* de presse

press lord N ⇒ **press baron**

press office N service *m* de presse
press officer N attaché(e) *m(f)* de presse
press pack N presse *f* à scandale ; *(at event)* meute *f* de journalistes
press photographer N photographe *mf* de (la) presse, reporter *m* photographe
press release N communiqué *m* de presse
press report N reportage *m*
press room N salle *f* de presse
press run N *(US)* tirage *m* (d'une revue *etc*)
press secretary N *(US)* ◆ **the White House** *etc* **~ secretary** le porte-parole de la Maison-Blanche *etc*
press stud N *(Brit)* bouton-pression *m*, pression *f*
press-up N *(Brit Gym)* traction *f* ◆ **to do ~-ups** faire des pompes *
press view N *(Cine)* avant-première *f*

► **press ahead** VI ⇒ **press on**

► **press back** VI SEP *[+ crowd, enemy]* refouler

► **press down** VI appuyer (on sur)
VT SEP *[+ knob, button, switch]* appuyer sur

► **press in** VT SEP *[+ panel etc]* enfoncer

► **press on** VI *(in work, journey etc)* continuer ◆ **~ on!** *(= don't give up)* persévérez !, n'abandonnez pas ! ◆ **(let's) ~ on regardless!** * continuons quand même ! ◆ **to ~ on with sth** continuer résolument (à faire) qch ◆ **they are ~ing on with the nuclear agreement** ils continuent à tout faire pour que l'accord nucléaire se réalise

► **press out** VT SEP *[+ juice, liquid]* exprimer

pressing /ˈpresɪŋ/ ADJ *(= urgent) [business, problem]* urgent ; *[danger, invitation]* pressant N *[of clothes]* repassage *m* ◆ **to send sth for ~** faire repasser qch

pressman /ˈpresmən/ N (pl **-men**) *(Brit)* journaliste *m*

pressmark /ˈpresmɑːk/ N *(Brit)* cote *f* *(d'un livre de bibliothèque)*

pressure /ˈpreʃəʳ/ N 1 *(gen, Met, Phys, Tech)* pression *f* ◆ **the boilers were running at full ~** la pression dans les chaudières était à son maximum ◆ **at high ~** à haute pression ◆ **to exert** *or* **put ~ on sth** exercer une pression sur qch, appuyer sur qch ◆ **a ~ of 2kg to the square cm** une pression de 2 kg par cm² ◆ **atmospheric ~** pression *f* atmosphérique ◆ **oil ~** pression *f* d'huile ; (also **tyre pressure**) pression *f* (de gonflage) ◆ **water ~** pression *f* de l'eau ; → **blood pressure**

2 *(fig)* pression *f* ◆ **parental ~** la pression des parents ◆ **to put ~ on sb (to do sth), to bring ~ to bear on sb (to do sth)** faire pression *or* exercer une pression sur qn (pour qu'il fasse qch) ◆ **they're putting the ~ on now** ils commencent à mettre la pression ◆ **to use ~ to obtain a confession** user de contrainte pour obtenir une confession ◆ **the ~(s) of these events/of life today** la tension créée par ces événements/par la vie d'aujourd'hui ◆ **~ of work prevented him from going** le travail l'a empêché d'y aller, il n'a pas pu y aller parce qu'il avait trop de travail ◆ **the ~(s) of meeting deadlines** la contrainte des délais à respecter

◆ **under pressure** ◆ **he was acting under ~ when he said ...** il agissait sous la contrainte *or* il n'agissait pas de son plein gré quand il a dit ... ◆ **under ~ from his staff** sous la pression de son personnel ◆ **he has been under a lot of ~ recently** il a été sous pression * ces derniers temps ◆ **I work badly under ~** je travaille mal quand je suis sous pression * ◆ **I can't work well under such ~** je n'arrive pas à bien travailler quand je suis sous pression * à ce point

◆ **to come under pressure** subir des pressions ◆ **he's clearly come under ~ from hardliners** il est clair qu'il a subi des pressions de la part des tenants de la ligne dure ◆ **the Prime Minister came under ~ to resign** on a fait pression sur le Premier ministre pour qu'il démissionne

VT ◆ **don't ~ me!** * ne me bouscule pas ! ◆ **to ~ sb to do sth** faire pression sur qn pour qu'il fasse qch ◆ **to ~ sb into doing sth** forcer qn à *or* contraindre qn à faire qch ◆ **to feel ~d into sth** *or* **to do sth** se sentir forcé de faire qch ◆ **do you feel ~d by your family to have a baby?** avez-vous le sentiment que votre famille fait pression sur vous pour que vous fassiez un enfant ? ◆ **don't feel ~d!** * ne te sens pas obligé !

COMP **pressure cabin** N *(in plane)* cabine *f* pressurisée *or* sous pression
pressure-cook VT cuire à la cocotte-minute ®
pressure cooker N autocuiseur *m*, cocotte-minute ® *f*
pressure-feed N alimentation *f* par pression
pressure gauge N manomètre *m*, jauge *f* de pression
pressure group N *(Pol etc)* groupe *m* de pression
pressure point N *(Anat)* point *m* de compression digitale d'une artère
pressure suit N *(Space etc)* scaphandre *m* pressurisé

pressurization /ˌpreʃəraɪˈzeɪʃən/ N pressurisation *f*, mise *f* en pression

pressurize /ˈpreʃəraɪz/ VT 1 *[+ cabin, spacesuit]* pressuriser 2 * *(fig)* ⇒ **pressure vt**
COMP **pressurized cabin** N cabine *f* pressurisée *or* sous pression
pressurized water reactor N réacteur *m* à eau sous pression

pressy *, **pressie** * /ˈprezɪ/ N *(Brit)* cadeau *m*

Prestel ® /ˈpresˌtel/ N ≈ Télétel ® *m*

prestidigitation /ˈprestɪˌdɪdʒɪˈteɪʃən/ N *(frm)* prestidigitation *f*

prestige /presˈtiːʒ/ N prestige *m* ADJ *[car, production, politics etc]* de prestige

prestigious /presˈtɪdʒəs/ ADJ prestigieux

presto /ˈprestəʊ/ ADV *(Mus, gen)* presto ◆ **hey ~!** le tour est joué ! ◆ **and hey ~! there he was** et abracadabra ! il était là

prestressed /ˈpriːˈstrest/ ADJ précontraint ◆ **~ concrete** (béton *m* armé) précontraint *m*

presumable /prɪˈzjuːməbl/ ADJ présumable

presumably /prɪˈzjuːməblɪ/ ADV *(= probably)* sans doute, vraisemblablement ◆ **~ the front door was locked?** je suppose que la porte d'entrée était fermée à clé ?

presume /prɪˈzjuːm/ VT 1 *(= suppose)* présumer *(also Jur)*, supposer *(that* que) ; *[+ sb's death]* présumer ◆ **to be ~d dead** être présumé mort ◆ **every man is ~d (to be) innocent** tout homme est présumé (être) innocent ◆ **he is ~d to be living in Spain** on présume *or* suppose qu'il vit en Espagne ◆ **it may be ~d that ...** on peut présumer que ... ◆ **I ~ so** je (le) présume, je (le) suppose ◆ **I ~ not** je suppose que non ◆ **you are presuming rather a lot** vous faites pas mal de suppositions, vous présumez pas mal de choses

2 *(= take liberty)* ◆ **to ~ to do sth** se permettre de faire qch

VI *(frm)* ◆ **you ~ too much!** vous êtes bien présomptueux ! ◆ **I hope I'm not presuming** je ne voudrais pas être impertinent ; *(when asking a favour)* je ne voudrais pas abuser de votre gentillesse ◆ **to ~ (up)on** abuser de

presumption /prɪˈzʌmpʃən/ N 1 *(= supposition)* présomption *f*, supposition *f* ◆ **the ~ is that ...** on présume que ..., on suppose que ... ◆ **there is a strong ~ that ...** tout porte à croire que ... 2 *(NonC: frm)* présomption *f* ◆ **if you'll excuse my ~** si vous me le permettez, si vous voulez bien pardonner mon audace

presumptive /prɪˈzʌmptɪv/ ADJ *[heir]* présomptif ; *(Jur) [evidence]* par présomption

presumptuous /prɪˈzʌmptjʊəs/ ADJ *[person, letter, question]* présomptueux, impertinent

presumptuously /prɪˈzʌmptjʊəslɪ/ ADV présomptueusement, avec présomption

presumptuousness /prɪˈzʌmptjʊəsnɪs/ N *(NonC)* ⇒ **presumption 2**

presuppose /ˌpriːsəˈpəʊz/ VT présupposer *(that* que)

presupposition /ˌpriːsʌpəˈzɪʃən/ N présupposition *f*

pre-tax /ˌpriːˈtæks/ ADJ, ADV avant impôts

pre-teen /ˌpriːˈtiːn/ ADJ préadolescent N ◆ **the ~s** les 10 à 12 ans

pretence, pretense *(US)* /prɪˈtens/ N 1 *(= pretext)* prétexte *m*, excuse *f* ; *(= claim)* prétention *f* ; *(NonC) (= affectation)* prétention *f* ◆ **he makes no ~ to learning** il n'a pas la prétention d'être savant ◆ **under** *or* **on the ~ of (doing) sth** sous prétexte *or* sous couleur de (faire) qch ; → **false** 2 *(= make-believe)* **to make a ~ of doing sth** faire semblant *or* feindre de faire qch ◆ **he made a ~ of friendship** il a feint l'amitié ◆ **it's all (a) ~** tout cela est pure comédie *or* une feinte ◆ **I'm tired of their ~ that all is well** je suis las de les voir faire comme si tout allait bien ◆ **his ~ of sympathy did not impress me** sa feinte sympathie m'a laissé froid

pretend /prɪˈtend/ VT 1 *(= feign) [+ ignorance, concern, illness]* feindre, simuler ◆ **to ~ to do sth** faire semblant *or* faire mine de faire qch ◆ **he ~ed to be ill** il a fait semblant *or* mine d'être malade ◆ **they ~ed to be soldiers** *(as subterfuge)* ils se sont fait passer pour des soldats ◆ **let's ~ we're soldiers** *(as game)* jouons aux soldats ◆ **he ~ed he/she was out** il a essayé de faire croire qu'il/qu'elle était sorti(e)

2 *(frm = claim)* prétendre *(that* que) ◆ **I don't ~ to know everything about it** je ne prétends pas tout savoir là-dessus, je n'ai pas la prétention de tout savoir là-dessus

VI 1 *(= feign)* faire semblant ◆ **the children were playing at "let's pretend"** les enfants jouaient à faire semblant ◆ **he's not really ill, he's just ~ing** il n'est pas malade, il fait semblant ◆ **I was only ~ing!** *(for fun)* c'était pour rire !, je plaisantais ! ◆ **let's stop ~ing!** assez joué la comédie ! ◆ **let's not ~ to each other** ne nous jouons pas la comédie, soyons francs l'un avec l'autre

2 *(frm = claim)* **to ~ to learning/infallibility** avoir la prétention d'être *or* prétendre être érudit/infaillible

ADJ * *[money, house etc]* pour (de) rire * ◆ **it's only ~!** c'est pour rire ! *

> ⚠ **prétendre** is the equivalent of **to pretend** only when it means 'to claim'.

pretended /prɪˈtendɪd/ ADJ *(frm)* prétendu, soi-disant *inv*

pretender /prɪˈtendəʳ/ N prétendant(e) *m(f)* ◆ **a ~ to the throne (of ...)** un prétendant au trône (de ...) ◆ **the Old Pretender** *(Brit Hist)* le Prétendant *(Jacques Francis Édouard Stuart)* ◆ **the Young Pretender** le (Jeune) Prétendant *(Charles Édouard Stuart)*

pretense /prɪˈtens/ N *(US)* ⇒ **pretence**

pretension /prɪˈtenʃən/ N 1 *(= claim: also pej)* prétention *f (to sth* à qch) ◆ **this work has serious literary ~s** cette œuvre peut à juste titre prétendre à *or* cette œuvre a droit à la reconnaissance littéraire ◆ **he has social ~s** *(pej)* il a des prétentions sociales 2 *(NonC = pretentiousness)* prétention *f*

pretentious /prɪˈtenʃəs/ ADJ prétentieux

pretentiously /prɪˈtenʃəslɪ/ ADV prétentieusement

pretentiousness /prɪˈtenʃəsnɪs/ N (NonC) prétention *f*

preterite /ˈpretərɪt/ N prétérit *m*, passé *m* simple

pre-term /ˌpriːˈtɜːm/ ADJ *[baby]* prématuré ADV prématurément, avant terme

preternatural /ˌpriːtəˈnætʃrəl/ ADJ surnaturel

preternaturally /ˌpriːtəˈnætʃrəlɪ/ ADV *(frm)* surnaturellement

pretext /ˈpriːtekst/ N prétexte *m* ◆ **under** *or* **on the ~ of (doing) sth** sous prétexte de (faire) qch

pretorian /prɪˈtɔːrɪən/ ADJ *(US)* ⇒ **praetorian**

pre-trial /ˌpriːˈtreɪəl/ ADJ *(Jur)* avant procès

prettify /ˈprɪtɪfaɪ/ VT *[+ dress]* enjoliver ; *[+ house, garden]* essayer d'embellir

prettily /ˈprɪtɪlɪ/ ADV *[arrange, decorate]* joliment ; *[smile, blush]* de façon charmante

prettiness /ˈprɪtɪnɪs/ N *[of person, place]* charme *m*

pretty /ˈprɪtɪ/ ADJ 1 *(= attractive) [child, flower, music etc]* joli *before n* ◆ **as ~ as a picture** *[person]* joli comme un cœur, joli à croquer ; *[garden etc]* ravissant ◆ **she's not just a ~ face*** elle n'a pas seulement un joli minois, elle a d'autres atouts que son joli visage ◆ **it wasn't a ~ sight** ce n'était pas beau à voir ◆ **~ Polly!** *(to parrot)* bonjour Jacquot !

2 *(iro = fine)* joli, beau (belle *f*) ◆ **that's a ~ state of affairs!** c'est du joli ! ◆ **you've made a ~ mess of it!** vous avez fait là de la jolie besogne !

3 *(* = considerable) [sum, price]* joli, coquet ◆ **it will cost a ~ penny** cela coûtera une jolie somme

ADV *(* = fairly)* assez ◆ **it's ~ cold** il fait assez froid, il ne fait pas chaud ◆ **how's it going? – ~ well!** ça va bien ? – pas mal ! ◆ **we've ~ well finished** nous avons presque *or* pratiquement fini ◆ **it's ~ much the same thing** c'est à peu près *or* pratiquement la même chose ◆ **~ damn quick**** illico (presto)* ◆ **you'd have to be ~ damn good**** **to get a job like that** il faut être drôlement* *or* sacrément* bon pour trouver un travail comme celui-là ◆ **he's ~ nearly better** il est presque *or* pratiquement guéri ◆ **to have a ~ good** *or* **fair idea of sth** avoir sa petite idée sur qch ; → **sit**

COMP **pretty-pretty*** ADJ un peu trop joli

► **pretty up*** VT SEP ⇒ **prettify**

pretzel /ˈpretsl/ N bretzel *m*

prevail /prɪˈveɪl/ VI 1 *(= triumph)* l'emporter *(over* sur) ◆ **let us hope that commonsense will ~** espérons que le bon sens finira par l'emporter *or* s'imposer ◆ **fortunately justice ~ed** heureusement, la justice l'a emporté

2 *(= exist) [situation, chaos]* régner ◆ **a similar situation ~s in America** une situation semblable règne en Amérique ◆ **the situation which now ~s** la situation actuelle ◆ **the hostile atmosphere that ~ed in relations between young blacks and the police** l'hostilité qui présidait aux relations entre les jeunes Noirs et la police ◆ **he found a different attitude ~ed** il s'aperçut que les attitudes étaient différentes ◆ **state control of industry which had ~ed since the 1930s** le contrôle de l'industrie par l'État, en vigueur depuis les années 1930

3 *(= gain victory)* l'emporter ◆ **I hope he will ~ over the rebels** j'espère qu'il l'emportera sur les rebelles ◆ **he appears to have the votes he needs to ~** il semble avoir les voix nécessaires pour l'emporter

4 *(frm)* ◆ **to ~ (up)on sb to do sth** réussir à persuader qn de faire qch ◆ **they ~ed on him to honour his contract** ils ont réussi à le persuader d'honorer son contrat ◆ **can I ~ on you to delay your departure?** comment puis-je vous persuader de retarder votre départ ?

prevailing /prɪˈveɪlɪŋ/ ADJ 1 *[wind]* dominant 2 *(= widespread) [belief, opinion, attitude]* courant, répandu 3 *(= current) [conditions, situation, customs] (today)* actuel ; *(at that time)* à l'époque ; *[style, taste, prices] (today)* actuel, du jour ; *(at that time)* de l'époque, du jour ◆ **~ market rate** *(Econ)* cours *m* du marché 4 *(Jur)* **the ~ party** la partie gagnante

prevalence /ˈprevələns/ N *(= predominance, currency) [of illness]* fréquence *f* ; *[of belief, opinion, attitude]* prédominance *f*, fréquence *f* ; *[of conditions, situation, customs]* caractère *m* généralisé ; *[of fashion, style]* popularité *f*, vogue *f* ◆ **I'm surprised by the ~ of that idea** je suis surpris que cette idée soit si répandue

prevalent /ˈprevələnt/ ADJ 1 *(= widespread) [belief, opinion, attitude]* courant, répandu ; *[illness]* répandu ◆ **smoking became increasingly ~** il devenait de plus en plus courant de fumer 2 *(= current) [conditions, customs] (today)* actuel ; *(at that time)* à l'époque ; *[style, taste] (today)* actuel, du jour ; *(at that time)* de l'époque, du jour

prevaricate /prɪˈværɪkeɪt/ VI tergiverser

prevarication /prɪˌværɪˈkeɪʃən/ N faux-fuyant(s) *m(pl)*

prevent /prɪˈvent/ VT empêcher *(sb from doing sth, sb's doing sth* qn de faire qch) ; *[+ event, action]* empêcher ; *[+ illness]* prévenir ; *[+ accident, fire, war]* empêcher, éviter ◆ **nothing could ~ him (from doing it)** rien ne pouvait l'en empêcher ◆ **she couldn't ~ his death** elle n'a pu empêcher qu'il ne meure *or* l'empêcher de mourir ◆ **I couldn't ~ the door from closing** je n'ai pas pu empêcher la porte de se fermer *or* éviter que la porte ne se ferme *subj*

preventable /prɪˈventəbl/ ADJ évitable

preventative /prɪˈventətɪv/ ADJ préventif

prevention /prɪˈvenʃən/ N (NonC) prévention *f* ◆ **~ is better than cure** *(Prov)* mieux vaut prévenir que guérir ◆ **Society for the Prevention of Cruelty to Animals** Société *f* protectrice des animaux ; → **accident, fire**

preventive /prɪˈventɪv/ ADJ *[medicine, measures]* préventif ◆ **~ detention** *(Jur)* (forte) peine *f* de prison N *(= measure)* mesure *f* préventive *(against* contre) ; *(= medicine)* médicament *m* préventif *(against* contre)

preverbal /ˌpriːˈvɜːbəl/ ADJ préverbal

preview /ˈpriːvjuː/ N *[of film, exhibition]* avant-première *f* ; *(= art exhibition)* vernissage *m* ◆ **to give sb a ~ of sth** *(fig)* donner à qn un aperçu de qch ◆ **for a ~ of today's main events over now to Jack Smith** *(Rad, TV)* et maintenant pour un tour d'horizon des principaux événements de la journée je passe l'antenne à Jack Smith

previous /ˈpriːvɪəs/ ADJ 1 *(gen) (= immediately before)* précédent ; *(= sometime before)* antérieur (-eure *f*) ◆ **have you made any ~ applications?** avez-vous déjà fait des demandes ? ◆ **the car has had two ~ owners** la voiture a déjà eu deux propriétaires, c'est une voiture de troisième main ◆ **the ~ letter** la précédente lettre, la lettre précédente ◆ **a ~ letter** une lettre précédente *or* antérieure ◆ **the ~ week** la semaine précédente ◆ **the ~ year** l'année *f* précédente ◆ **the ~ day** la veille ◆ **the ~ evening** la veille au soir ◆ **in a ~ life** dans une vie antérieure ◆ **on ~ occasions** précédemment, auparavant ◆ **I have a ~ engagement** je suis déjà pris ◆ **to have no ~ convictions** *(Jur)* avoir un casier judiciaire vierge ◆ **he has three ~ convictions** *(Jur)* il a déjà eu trois condamnations ◆ **"no previous experience necessary"** *(Comm)* "débutants acceptés", "aucune expérience (préalable) exigée" ◆ **~ to** antérieur à

2 *(frm = hasty)* prématuré ◆ **this seems somewhat ~** ceci semble quelque peu prématuré ◆ **you have been rather ~ in inviting him** vous avez été bien pressé de l'inviter

ADV 1 *(= previously)* ◆ **three months ~*** trois mois auparavant *or* plus tôt

2 *(frm)* ◆ **~ to ~ to (his) leaving he ...** avant de partir *or* avant son départ il ... ◆ **~ to his leaving we ...** avant son départ *or* avant qu'il ne parte nous ...

previously /ˈpriːvɪəslɪ/ ADV auparavant ◆ **three months ~** trois mois auparavant *or* plus tôt ◆ **~ unknown** jusque-là inconnu ◆ **~ unreleased** *or* **unpublished** jusque-là inédit

prewar /ˈpriːˈwɔːʳ/ ADJ d'avant-guerre ADV avant-guerre

prewash /ˈpriːwɒʃ/ N prélavage *m*

prex* /preks/, **prexie***, **prexy*** /ˈpreksɪ/ N *(US Univ)* président *m* (d'université)

prey /preɪ/ N *(lit, fig)* proie *f* ◆ **bird of ~** oiseau *m* de proie, rapace *m* ◆ **to be a ~ to** *[+ nightmares, illnesses]* être en proie à ◆ **to fall (a) ~ to** devenir la proie de VI ◆ **to ~ on** *[animal etc]* faire sa proie/sa victime de ; *[person]* s'attaquer continuellement à ; *[fear, anxiety]* ronger, miner ◆ **something is ~ing on her mind** il y a quelque chose qui la tourmente *or* la travaille*

prezzie** /ˈprezɪ/ N *(= present)* cadeau *m*

Priam /ˈpraɪəm/ N Priam *m*

price /praɪs/ N 1 *(= cost)* prix *m (also fig) (= estimate)* devis *m* ; *(on Stock Exchange)* cours *m* ◆ **he got a good ~ (for it)** il (en) a obtenu un bon prix ◆ **he gave me a good ~ (on it)** il m'a fait un prix ◆ **a special ~ of $100 per night** un tarif spécial de 100 dollars la nuit ◆ **book your tickets in advance at the special ~ of £4** achetez vos billets à l'avance au tarif préférentiel de 4 livres ◆ **order any three videos for a special ~ of only £29.99** commandez trois cassettes vidéo au choix pour le prix promotionnel de 29,99 livres ◆ **we pay top ~s for gold and silver** nous achetons l'or et l'argent au prix fort ◆ **ask him for a ~ for putting in a new window** demandez-lui un devis pour poser *or* combien ça coûterait de poser une nouvelle fenêtre ◆ **that's my ~, take it or leave it** c'est mon dernier prix, c'est à prendre ou à laisser ◆ **he'll do it for a ~** il le fera si on y met le prix ◆ **to put a ~ on sth** fixer le prix de qch ; see also **noun 4** ◆ **the ~ is right** *(fair price)* c'est un prix correct ; *(= right for me)* le prix me convient ◆ **to go up** *or* **rise in ~** augmenter ◆ **to drop** *or* **fall in ~** baisser ◆ **their products range in ~ from $12 to $48** le prix de leurs articles va de 12 à 48 dollars ◆ **the ~ in dollars/sterling, the dollar/sterling ~** le prix en dollars/livres sterling ◆ **to make a ~** *(Stock Exchange)* fixer un cours ◆ **market ~** *(Stock Exchange)* cours *m* du marché

2 *(fig)* **every man has his ~** tout homme peut être acheté ◆ **there's a ~ on his head, he has got a ~ on his head** sa tête a été mise à prix ◆ **to put a ~ on sb's head** mettre à prix la tête de qn ◆ **he paid a high** *or* **big ~ for his success** il a payé cher *or* chèrement son succès ◆ **it's a high** *or* **big ~ to pay for it** c'est un bien grand prix à payer ◆ **it's a small ~ to pay for it** c'est un bien faible prix à payer ; → **cheap, closing, reduced**

3 ◆ **at any ~ I wouldn't buy it at any ~** je ne l'achèterais à aucun prix ◆ **I wouldn't help him at any ~!** je ne l'aiderais à aucun prix ! ◆ **they want peace at any ~** ils veulent la paix coûte que coûte *or* à tout prix ◆ **will you do it? – not at any ~!** vous allez le faire ? – pour rien au monde *or* pas question ! ◆ **you can get it but at a ~!** vous pouvez l'avoir mais cela vous coûtera cher ! ◆ **he's famous now but at what a ~!** il est célèbre maintenant mais à quel prix !

4 *(= value)* prix *m*, valeur *f* ◆ **to put a ~ on a jewel/picture** évaluer un bijou/un tableau

◆ **you can't put a ~ on friendship/honesty** l'honnêteté/l'amitié n'a pas de prix ◆ **I cannot put a ~ on his friendship** son amitié n'a pas de prix (pour moi), je ne saurais dire combien j'apprécie son amitié ◆ **he sets** *or* **puts a high ~ on loyalty** il attache beaucoup de valeur *or* un grand prix à la loyauté ◆ **what ~ * all his promises now?** *(fig)* que valent toutes ses promesses maintenant ? ◆ **beyond ~, without ~** *(liter)* qui n'a pas de prix, sans prix

5 *(Betting = odds)* cote *f* ◆ **what ~ are they giving on Black Beauty?** quelle est la cote de Black Beauty ? ◆ **what ~ he'll change his mind?** * vous pariez combien qu'il va changer d'avis ?

VT *(= fix price of)* fixer le prix de ; *(= mark price on)* marquer le prix de ; *(= ask price of)* demander le prix de, s'informer du prix de ; *(fig = estimate value of)* évaluer ◆ **it is ~d at £10** ça coûte 10 livres, ça se vend 10 livres ◆ **shares were ~d at 50 pence** les actions étaient cotées 50 pence ◆ **tickets ~d (at) £20** billets *mpl* vendus 20 livres ◆ **Japanese gas is ~d high** *(St Ex)* le gaz japonais est coté très cher

COMP *[control, index]* des prix ; *[reduction, rise]* de(s) prix

price bracket N ⇒ **price range**

Price Commission † N *(Brit)* ≃ Direction *f* générale de la concurrence et de la consommation

price competitiveness N compétitivité-prix *f*

price cut N réduction *f*, rabais *m*

price cutting N réduction(s) *f(pl)* de prix

price-earnings ratio N *(St Ex)* rapport *m* cours-bénéfices, taux *m or* coefficient *m* de capitalisation (des résultats)

price escalation N flambée *f* des prix ◆ **~ escalation clause** *(Jur)* clause *f* de révision des prix

price-fixing N *(by government)* contrôle *m* des prix ; *(pej: by firms)* entente *f* (illicite) sur les prix

price freeze N blocage *m* des prix

price inflation N inflation *f* des coûts

price limit N ◆ **to put a ~ limit on sth** fixer le prix maximum de qch ◆ **my ~ limit is $400** je ne vais pas au-dessus de 400 dollars

price list N tarif *m*, prix *m* courant

price maintenance N *(gen)* vente *f* à prix imposé ; *[of manufacturer]* fixation *f* des prix

price range N éventail *m or* gamme *f* de prix ◆ **within my ~ range** dans mes prix ◆ **in the medium ~ range** d'un prix modéré, dans les prix moyens

price-rigging N *(pej: by firms)* entente *f* (illicite) sur les prix

price ring N cartel *m* des prix

prices and incomes policy N politique *f* des prix et des revenus

prices index N *(Brit)* indice *m* des prix

price support N *(US Econ)* (politique *f* de) soutien *m* des prix

price tag N *(lit)* étiquette *f* ; *(fig = cost)* prix *m*, coût *m* ◆ **it's got a heavy ~ tag** le prix est très élevé, ça coûte cher ◆ **what's the ~ tag on that house?** quel prix demandent-ils pour cette maison ?

price ticket N étiquette *f*

price variation clause N *(Jur)* clause *f* de révision des prix

price war N guerre *f* des prix

► **price down** VT SEP *(Comm) (= reduce price of)* réduire le prix de, solder ; *(= mark lower price on)* inscrire un prix réduit sur

► **price out** VT SEP ◆ **to price one's goods out of the market** perdre un marché en voulant demander des prix trop élevés ◆ **Japanese products have ~d ours out of the market** nos produits ne peuvent plus soutenir la concurrence des prix japonais ◆ **the French have ~d us out of that market** les bas prix pratiqués par les Français nous ont chassés de ce marché ◆ **the workers are in danger of pricing themselves out of the market** les ouvriers risquent de devenir trop chers sur le marché de l'emploi

► **price up** VT SEP *(Comm) (= raise price of)* augmenter ; *(= mark higher price on)* inscrire un prix plus élevé sur

-priced /praɪst/ ADJ *(in compounds)* ◆ **high-priced** coûteux, cher ; → **low¹**

priceless /ˈpraɪslɪs/ ADJ 1 *[picture, jewel]* qui n'a pas de prix, inestimable ; *[friendship, contribution, gift]* inestimable, très précieux 2 (* *= amusing)* impayable *

pricey * /ˈpraɪsɪ/ ADJ cher, chérot * *m only*

pricing /ˈpraɪsɪŋ/ N *(= setting price)* détermination *f or* fixation *f* des prix ; *(for service)* tarification *f* ; *[of stock]* évaluation *f* ◆ **~ policy** *or* **strategy** politique *f* des prix

prick /prɪk/ N 1 *(= act, sensation, mark)* piqûre *f* ◆ **to give sth a ~** piquer qch ◆ **the ~s of conscience** les aiguillons *mpl* de la conscience, le remords ; → **kick**

2 (****** *= penis)* bite ****** *or* bitte ****** *f*

3 (****** *= person)* con ****** *m*

VT 1 *[person, thorn, pin, hypodermic]* piquer ; *[+ balloon, blister]* crever ; *[+ name on list etc]* piquer, pointer ◆ **she ~ed her finger with a pin** elle s'est piqué le doigt avec une épingle ◆ **she ~ed herself on the thorns** elle s'est piquée avec les épines ◆ **to ~ a hole in sth** faire un trou d'épingle (*or* d'aiguille *etc*) dans qch ◆ **his conscience was ~ing him** il avait mauvaise conscience, il n'avait pas la conscience tranquille

2 ◆ **to ~ (up) one's ears** *[animal]* dresser les oreilles ; *[person] (fig)* dresser *or* tendre l'oreille

VI 1 *[thorn etc]* piquer ◆ **his conscience was ~ing** il avait mauvaise conscience

2 *(= tingle)* ◆ **my eyes are ~ing** les yeux me cuisent

COMP **prick-tease** ****** N *(pej = woman)* allumeuse * *f* VI *[woman]* faire l'allumeuse * VT allumer *

► **prick out** VT SEP 1 *(= plant) [+ seedlings]* repiquer

2 *(with pin etc) [+ outline, design]* piquer, tracer en piquant

► **prick up** VI *(lit)* ◆ **the dog's ears ~ed up** le chien a dressé l'oreille ◆ **his ears ~ed up** *(fig)* il a dressé l'oreille

VT SEP ⇒ **prick vt 2**

pricking /ˈprɪkɪŋ/ N picotement *m*, sensation *f* cuisante ◆ **~s of conscience** remords *m(pl)*

prickle /ˈprɪkl/ N 1 *(= spine) [of plant]* épine *f*, piquant *m* ; *[of hedgehog etc]* piquant *m* 2 *(= pricking sensation: on skin etc)* picotement *m*, sensation *f* cuisante VT piquer VI *[skin, fingers etc]* fourmiller, picoter

prickly /ˈprɪklɪ/ ADJ 1 *(= spiky) [plant]* épineux ; *[animal]* armé de piquants ◆ **his beard was ~** sa barbe piquait ◆ **my arm feels ~** j'ai des fourmis *or* des fourmillements dans le bras 2 *(fig) (= irritable) [person]* ombrageux, irritable ; *(= delicate) [subject]* épineux, délicat ◆ **he is as ~ as a porcupine** c'est un vrai hérisson

COMP **prickly heat** N fièvre *f* miliaire

prickly pear N *(= fruit)* figue *f* de Barbarie ; *(= plant)* figuier *m* de Barbarie

pride /praɪd/ N 1 *(NonC) (= self-respect)* fierté *f*, amour-propre *m* ; *(= satisfaction)* fierté *f* ; *(pej = arrogance)* orgueil *m* ◆ **his ~ was hurt** il était blessé dans son orgueil *or* dans son amour-propre ◆ **he has too much ~ to ask for help** il est trop fier pour demander de l'aide ◆ **she has no ~** elle n'a pas d'amour-propre ◆ **the sin of ~** le péché d'orgueil ◆ **false ~** vanité *f* ◆ **~ comes** *or* **goes before a fall** *(Prov)* l'orgueil précède la chute ◆ **her son's success is a great source of ~ to her** elle s'enorgueillit *or* elle est très fière du succès de son fils ◆ **her ~ in her family** la fierté qu'elle tire de sa famille ◆ **he spoke of them with ~** il parla d'eux avec fierté ◆ **to take** *or* **have (a) ~ in** *[+ children, achievements]* être très fier de ; *[+ house, car etc]* prendre (grand) soin de ◆ **she takes (a) ~ in her appearance** elle prend soin de sa personne ◆ **to take (a) ~ in doing sth** mettre sa fierté à faire qch ◆ **to take** *or* **have ~ of place** avoir la place d'honneur

2 *(= object of pride)* fierté *f* ◆ **she is her father's ~ and joy** elle est la fierté de son père

3 *[of lions]* troupe *f*

VT ◆ **to ~ o.s. (up)on (doing) sth** être fier *or* s'enorgueillir de (faire) qch

priest /priːst/ N *(Christian, pagan)* prêtre *m* ; *(= parish priest)* curé *m* ; → **assistant, high** COMP **priest-ridden** ADJ *(pej)* dominé par le clergé, sous la tutelle des curés *(pej)*

priestess /ˈpriːstɪs/ N prêtresse *f*

priesthood /ˈpriːsthʊd/ N *(= function)* prêtrise *f*, sacerdoce *m* ; *(= priests collectively)* clergé *m* ◆ **to enter the ~** se faire prêtre, entrer dans les ordres

priestly /ˈpriːstlɪ/ ADJ sacerdotal, de prêtre

prig /prɪg/ N donneur *m*, -euse *f* de leçons ◆ **what a ~ she is!** ce qu'elle est donneuse de leçons ! ◆ **don't be such a ~!** ne fais pas le petit saint (*or* la petite sainte) !

priggish /ˈprɪgɪʃ/ ADJ moralisateur (-trice *f*)

priggishness /ˈprɪgɪʃnɪs/ N *(NonC)* attitude *f* moralisatrice

prim /prɪm/ ADJ 1 *(pej) [person] (= prudish:* also **prim and proper)** collet monté *inv*, guindé ; *[manner, smile, look, expression]* guindé ; *[dress, hat]* très correct, très convenable ; *[house, garden]* trop coquet *or* net *or* impeccable 2 *(= demure)* très convenable, comme il faut

prima ballerina /ˌpriːməˌbæləˈriːnə/ N (pl **prima ballerina** *or* **prima ballerinas**) danseuse *f* étoile

primacy /ˈpraɪməsɪ/ N *(= supremacy)* primauté *f* ; *(Rel)* primatie *f*

prima donna /ˌpriːməˈdɒnə/ N (pl **prima donna** *or* **prima donnas**) *(lit)* prima donna *f inv* ◆ **she's a real ~** *(fig)* elle est capricieuse, elle joue les divas

primaeval /praɪˈmiːvəl/ ADJ *(Brit)* ⇒ **primeval**

prima facie /ˈpraɪməˈfeɪʃɪ/ *(frm)* ADV à première vue, de prime abord ADJ *(Jur)* recevable, bien fondé ; *(gen)* légitime (à première vue) ◆ **to have a ~ case** *(Jur)* avoir une affaire recevable ; *(gen)* avoir raison à première vue ◆ **~ evidence** *(Jur)* commencement *m* de preuve ◆ **there are ~ reasons why ...** on peut a priori raisonnablement expliquer pourquoi ...

primal /ˈpraɪməl/ ADJ 1 *(= first in time, primeval)* primitif, des premiers âges ◆ **~ scream** *(Psych)* cri *m* primal 2 *(= first in importance, primordial)* principal, primordial

primarily /ˈpraɪmərɪlɪ/ ADV *(= chiefly)* essentiellement, surtout

primary /ˈpraɪmərɪ/ ADJ 1 *(= first: Astron, Chem, Econ, Elec, Geol, Med etc)* primaire

2 *(= basic) [reason, cause]* principal ; *[concern, aim]* principal, premier *before n* ◆ **of ~ importance** d'une importance primordiale, de la plus haute importance ◆ **the ~ meaning of a word** le sens premier d'un mot

N *(= school)* école *f* primaire ; *(= colour)* couleur *f* fondamentale ; *(= feather)* rémige *f* ; *(Elec)* enroulement *m* primaire ; *(US Pol)* primaire *f*

COMP **primary cause** N *(Philos)* cause *f* première

primary colour N couleur *f* fondamentale *or* primaire

primary education N enseignement *m* primaire

primary election N *(US Pol)* élection *f* primaire
primary feather N rémige *f*
primary health care N soins *mpl* de santé primaires
primary industries NPL *(Econ)* le secteur primaire
primary producer N *(Econ)* producteur *m* du secteur primaire
primary producing country N *(Econ)* pays *m* de production primaire
primary product N *(Econ)* produit *m* primaire *or* de base
primary school N *(esp Brit)* école *f* primaire
primary schoolteacher N *(esp Brit)* instituteur *m*, -trice *f*
primary stress N *(Phon)* accent *m* principal
primary teacher N ⇒ **primary schoolteacher**
primary tense N *(Gram)* temps *m* primitif
primary winding N *(Elec)* enroulement *m* primaire

primate /ˈpraɪmɪt/ N ① *(Rel)* primat *m* ② /ˈpraɪmeɪt/ *(= animal)* primate *m*

prime /praɪm/ ADJ ① *(= principal)* *[reason etc]* primordial, principal ; *[concern, aim]* principal, premier *before n* ◆ **a ~ factor in ...** un facteur primordial *or* fondamental dans ... ; see also **comp** ◆ **of ~ importance** d'une importance primordiale, de la plus haute importance

② *(= excellent, superior)* *[advantage]* de premier ordre ; *[site]* exceptionnel ; *(= best)* *[meat]* de premier choix ◆ **in ~ condition** *[animal, athlete]* en parfaite condition ◆ **~ cut** *(Culin)* morceau *m* de premier choix ◆ **a ~ example of what to avoid** un excellent exemple de ce qu'il faut éviter ◆ **of ~ quality** de première qualité ◆ **~ ribs** côtes *fpl* premières

③ *(Math)* ◆ **7 is ~** 7 est un nombre premier

N ① *(= peak)* ◆ **when the Renaissance was in its ~** quand la Renaissance était à son apogée, aux plus beaux jours de la Renaissance ◆ **in the ~ of life, in one's ~** dans *or* à la fleur de l'âge ◆ **he is past his ~** il est sur le retour ◆ **this grapefruit is past its ~** * *(hum)* ce pamplemousse n'est plus de la première fraîcheur, ce pamplemousse a vu des jours meilleurs *(hum)*

② *(Math)* (also **prime number**) nombre *m* premier

③ *(Rel)* prime *f*

VT ① *[+ gun, pump]* amorcer ◆ **to ~ the pump** *(fig)* renflouer une entreprise *or* une affaire ◆ **to ~ sb with drink** faire boire qn (tant et plus) ◆ **he was well ~d (with drink)** il avait bu plus que de raison

② *[+ surface for painting]* apprêter

③ *(fig)* *[+ person]* mettre au fait, mettre au courant ◆ **they ~d him about what he should say** ils lui ont bien fait répéter ce qu'il avait à dire ◆ **he was ~d to say that** ils lui ont fait la leçon pour qu'il dise cela ◆ **she came well ~d for the interview** elle est arrivée à l'entrevue tout à fait préparée

COMP **prime bill** N *(Econ, Fin)* effet *m* de premier ordre
prime cost N *(Comm, Econ)* prix *m* de revient, prix *m* coûtant
prime factor N *(Math)* facteur *m* premier, diviseur *m* premier
prime meridian N *(Geog)* premier méridien *m*
prime minister N Premier ministre *m*
prime ministerial ADJ du Premier ministre
prime ministership, prime ministry N ministère *m*, fonctions *fpl* de Premier ministre
prime mover N *(Phys, Tech)* force *f* motrice ; *(Philos)* premier moteur *m*, cause *f* première ; *(fig = person)* instigateur *m*, -trice *f*
prime number N nombre *m* premier
prime rate N *(Econ, Fin)* taux *m* préférentiel *or* de base
prime time N *(Rad, TV)* prime time *m*, heure(s) *f(pl)* de grande écoute ADJ *[programme, audience etc]* aux heures de grande écoute

primer /ˈpraɪməʳ/ N ① *(= textbook)* premier livre *m*, livre *m* élémentaire ② *(= reading book)* abécédaire *m* ③ *(= paint)* apprêt *m*

primeval, primaeval *(Brit)* /praɪˈmiːvəl/ ADJ primitif ◆ **~ forest** forêt *f* primitive

priming /ˈpraɪmɪŋ/ N ① *[of pump]* amorçage *m* ; *[of gun]* amorce *f* ② *(Painting)* *(= substance)* couche *f* d'apprêt ; *(= action)* apprêt *m*

primitive /ˈprɪmɪtɪv/ ADJ, N *(all senses)* primitif *m*

primitivism /ˈprɪmɪtɪˌvɪzəm/ N primitivisme *m*

primly /ˈprɪmlɪ/ ADV ① *(= demurely)* bien sagement ◆ **to be ~ dressed** être habillé très comme il faut, être tiré à quatre épingles ② *(pej = priggishly)* *[say]* d'un ton guindé, d'un air bégueule ; *[behave]* d'une manière guindée

primness /ˈprɪmnɪs/ N ① *(= demureness)* *[of person]* façons *fpl* très correctes *or* très convenables ; *[of appearance, attire]* aspect *m* très comme il faut *or* très convenable ② *(= prudishness)* *[of person]* façons *fpl* guindées *or* compassées, air *m* collet monté

primogeniture /ˌpraɪməʊˈdʒenɪtʃəʳ/ N *(Jur etc)* primogéniture *f*

primordial /praɪˈmɔːdɪəl/ ADJ primordial

primp /prɪmp/ VI se pomponner, se bichonner VT pomponner, bichonner

primrose /ˈprɪmrəʊz/ N primevère *f* (jaune) ◆ **the ~ path** le chemin *or* la voie de la facilité ADJ (also **primrose yellow**) jaune pâle *inv*, jaune primevère *inv*

primula /ˈprɪmjʊlə/ N primevère *f* (espèce)

Primus ® /ˈpraɪməs/ N *(esp Brit)* (also **Primus stove**) réchaud *m* de camping (à pétrole), Primus ® *m*

prince /prɪns/ N ① prince *m* (also *fig*) ◆ **Prince Charles** le prince Charles ◆ **the Prince of Wales** le prince de Galles ◆ **~ consort** prince *m* consort ◆ **~ regent** prince *m* régent ◆ **Prince Charming** le prince charmant ◆ **the Prince of Darkness** le prince des ténèbres *or* des démons ◆ **the ~s of this world** les princes *mpl* de la terre, les grands *mpl* de ce monde ② *(US fig = fine man)* chic type * *m* COMP **Prince Edward Island** N l'île *f* du Prince-Édouard

princeling /ˈprɪnslɪŋ/ N principicule *m*

princely /ˈprɪnslɪ/ ADJ *(lit, fig)* princier ◆ **the ~ sum of ...** la somme rondelette de ..., la coquette somme de

princess /prɪnˈses/ N princesse *f* ◆ **Princess Anne** la princesse Anne ◆ **Princess Royal** Princesse Royale *(titre donné parfois à la fille aînée du monarque)*

principal /ˈprɪnsɪpəl/ ADJ principal ◆ **~ boy** *(Brit Theat)* jeune héros *m (rôle tenu par une actrice dans les spectacles de Noël)* ◆ **~ clause** *(Gram)* (proposition *f*) principale *f* ◆ **~ parts of a verb** *(Gram)* temps *mpl* primitifs d'un verbe ◆ **~ horn/violin** *(Mus)* premier cor *m*/violon *m* ◆ **~ nursing officer** *(Brit)* ≃ surveillant(e) *m(f)* général(e) *(dans un hôpital)*

N ① *(Scol etc: gen)* chef *m* d'établissement ; *[of lycée]* proviseur *m* ; *[of college]* principal(e) *m(f)*
② *(in orchestra)* chef *m* de pupitre ; *(Theat)* vedette *f*
③ *(Fin, Jur = person employing agent, lawyer etc)* mandant *m*, commettant *m* ; *(Jur = chief perpetrator of a crime)* auteur *m* (d'un crime), principal *m* responsable ◆ **~ and agent** *(Jur, Fin)* commettant *m* et agent *m*
④ *(Fin = capital sum)* principal *m*, capital *m* ◆ **~ and interest** principal *m or* capital *m* et intérêts *mpl*

principality /ˌprɪnsɪˈpælɪtɪ/ N principauté *f* ◆ **the Principality** (= Wales) le pays de Galles

principally /ˈprɪnsɪpəlɪ/ ADV principalement

principle /ˈprɪnsəpl/ N *(all senses)* principe *m* ◆ **to go back to first ~s** repartir sur de bonnes bases ◆ **in ~** en principe ◆ **on ~, as a matter of ~** par principe ◆ **I make it a ~ never to lend money, it's against my ~s to lend money** j'ai pour principe de ne jamais prêter d'argent ◆ **that would be totally against my ~s** cela irait à l'encontre de tous mes principes ◆ **for the ~ of the thing** * pour le principe ◆ **he is a man of ~(s), he has high ~s** c'est un homme qui a des principes ◆ **all these machines work on the same ~** toutes ces machines marchent sur *or* selon le même principe

principled /ˈprɪnsəpld/ ADJ *[person]* qui a des principes ; *[behaviour]* réglé par des principes

-principled /ˈprɪnsəpld/ ADJ *(in compounds)* → **high, low¹**

prink /prɪŋk/ VI, VT ⇒ **primp**

print /prɪnt/ N ① *(= mark)* *[of hand, foot, tyre etc]* empreinte *f* ; *(= finger print)* empreinte *f* (digitale) ◆ **a thumb/paw** *etc* **~** l'empreinte *f* d'un pouce/d'une patte *etc* ◆ **to take sb's ~s** *(Police etc)* prendre les empreintes de qn ; → **fingerprint, footprint**

② *(NonC: Typ)* *(= actual letters)* caractères *mpl* ; *(= printed material)* texte *m* imprimé ◆ **in small/large ~** en petits/gros caractères ◆ **read the small** *or* **fine ~ before you sign** lisez toutes les clauses avant de signer ◆ **the ~ is poor** les caractères ne sont pas nets ◆ **it was there in cold ~!** c'était là noir sur blanc ! ◆ **out of ~** *[book]* épuisé ◆ **in ~** disponible (en librairie) ◆ **"books in print"** "livres en librairie", "catalogue courant" ◆ **he wants to see himself in ~** il veut être publié ◆ **to rush into ~** se hâter *or* s'empresser de publier ◆ **don't let that get into ~** n'allez pas imprimer *or* publier cela

③ *(= etching, woodcut etc)* estampe *f*, gravure *f* ; *(= reproduction)* tirage *m* ; *(Phot)* tirage *m*, épreuve *f* ; *[of cinema film]* copie *f* ; *(Tex)* *(= material, design)* imprimé *m* ; *(= printed dress)* robe *f* imprimée ◆ **to make a ~ from a negative** *(Phot)* faire un tirage à partir d'un négatif, tirer une épreuve d'un cliché ◆ **a cotton ~** une cotonnade imprimée ; → **blueprint**

ADJ *[dress etc]* en (tissu) imprimé

VT ① *(Typ, Comput)* imprimer ; *(= publish)* imprimer, publier ◆ **~ed in England** imprimé en Angleterre ◆ **the book is being ~ed just now** le livre est sous presse *or* à l'impression en ce moment ◆ **100 copies were ~ed** il a été tiré *or* imprimé à 100 exemplaires ◆ **they didn't dare ~ it** ils n'ont pas osé l'imprimer *or* le publier ◆ **to ~ money** *(lit)* imprimer des billets ◆ **it's a licence to ~ money** *(fig)* c'est une affaire extrêmement rentable *or* qui rapporte gros * ◆ **the memory of that day is indelibly ~ed on his memory** le souvenir de ce jour est imprimé à jamais dans sa mémoire ; see also **printed**

② *[+ fabric]* imprimer ; *[+ photo]* tirer

③ *(= write in block letters)* écrire en capitales *or* en caractères d'imprimerie ◆ **~ it in block capitals** écrivez-le en lettres majuscules

VI ① *[machine]* imprimer ; *[document]* être imprimé ◆ **the book is ~ing now** le livre est à l'impression *or* sous presse en ce moment ◆ **"your document is printing"** *(Comput)* "l'impression de votre document est en cours" ◆ **"printing"** "impression en cours"

② *(on form)* **"please print"** "écrivez en capitales"

COMP **print journalism** N journalisme *m* de presse écrite
print media N presse *f* écrite
print reporter N *(US)* journaliste *mf* de la presse écrite
print run N *(Publishing)* tirage *m*

print shop N (Typ) imprimerie f ; (= art shop) boutique f d'art (spécialisée dans la vente de reproductions, affiches etc)

print unions NPL syndicats mpl des typographes

► **print off** VT SEP (Comput, Typ) tirer, imprimer ; (Phot) tirer

► **print out** (Comput) VT SEP imprimer

printable /'prɪntəbl/ ADJ (lit) imprimable ; (= publishable) publiable ◆ **what he said is just not ~** * (hum) ce qu'il a dit est franchement impubliable, il ne serait pas convenable de répéter ce qu'il a dit

printed /'prɪntɪd/ ADJ imprimé ◆ **~ matter, ~ papers** imprimés mpl ◆ **the ~ word** tout ce qui est imprimé, la chose imprimée ◆ **~ circuit (board)** (Elec) circuit m imprimé

printer /'prɪntə^r/ N 1 imprimeur m ; (= typographer) typographe mf, imprimeur m ◆ **the text has gone to the ~** le texte est chez l'imprimeur 2 (Comput) imprimante f 3 (Phot) tireuse f

COMP **printer's devil** N apprenti m imprimeur

printer's error N faute f d'impression, coquille f

printer's ink N encre f d'imprimerie

printer's mark N marque f de l'imprimeur

printer's reader N correcteur m, -trice f (d'épreuves)

printing /'prɪntɪŋ/ N impression f ; [of photo] tirage m ; (= block writing) écriture f en caractères d'imprimerie

COMP **printing frame** N (Phot) châssis-presse m

printing house N imprimerie f

printing ink N encre f d'imprimerie

printing office N imprimerie f

printing press N presse f typographique

printing works N imprimerie f (atelier)

printmaker /'prɪnt,meɪkə^r/ N graveur m

printmaking /'prɪnt,meɪkɪŋ/ N (NonC) gravure f (de planches de reproduction)

printout /'prɪntaʊt/ N sortie f sur imprimante, sortie f papier ◆ **to do a ~ of sth** imprimer qch

prion /'praɪəʊn/ N prion m

prior /'praɪə^r/ ADJ précédent, antérieur (-eure f) ; [consent] préalable ◆ **~ to** antérieur à ◆ **without ~ notice** sans préavis, sans avertissement préalable ◆ **to have a ~ claim to sth** avoir droit à qch par priorité ◆ **~ restraint** (US Jur) interdiction f judiciaire ADV ◆ **~ to** antérieurement à, préalablement à, avant ◆ **~ to (his) leaving he ...** avant de partir or avant son départ, il ... ◆ **~ to his leaving we ...** avant son départ or avant qu'il ne parte, nous ... N (Rel) prieur m

prioress /'praɪərɪs/ N prieure f

prioritize /praɪ'ɒrɪtaɪz/ VT (= give priority to) donner la priorité à VI (= establish priorities) établir la liste des priorités, identifier ses priorités

priority /praɪ'ɒrɪtɪ/ N priorité f ◆ **to have or take ~ (over)** avoir la priorité (sur) ◆ **housing must be given first or top ~** on doit donner la priorité absolue au logement ◆ **schools were low on the list of priorities or the ~ list** les écoles venaient loin sur la liste des priorités or étaient loin de venir en priorité ◆ **you must get your priorities right** vous devez décider de ce qui compte le plus pour vous ◆ **to give sb (a) high/low ~** donner/ne pas donner la priorité à qn ◆ **it is a high/low ~** c'est/ce n'est pas une priorité

COMP **priority case** N affaire f prioritaire

priority share N (Stock Exchange) action f prioritaire

priory /'praɪərɪ/ N prieuré m

prise /praɪz/ VT (Brit) ◆ **to ~ open a box** ouvrir une boîte en faisant levier, forcer une boîte ◆ **to ~ the lid off a box** forcer le couvercle d'une boîte ◆ **I ~d him out of his chair** je l'ai enfin fait décoller* de sa chaise ◆ **to ~ a secret out of sb** arracher un secret à qn

► **prise off** VT SEP enlever en faisant levier

► **prise up** VT SEP soulever en faisant levier

prism /'prɪzəm/ N prisme m ◆ **through the ~ of time/memory** à travers le prisme du temps/de la mémoire ; → **prune¹**

prismatic /prɪz'mætɪk/ ADJ [surface, shape, colour] prismatique (also fig) ◆ **~ compass** boussole f topographique à prismes

prison /'prɪzn/ N (= place) prison f ; (= imprisonment) prison f, réclusion f ◆ **he is in ~** il est en prison, il fait de la prison ◆ **to put sb in ~** mettre qn en prison, emprisonner qn ◆ **to send sb to ~** condamner qn à la prison ◆ **to send sb to ~ for five years** condamner qn à cinq ans de prison ◆ **he was in ~ for five years** il a fait cinq ans de prison

COMP [food, life, conditions] dans la (or les) prison(s) ; [system] carcéral, pénitentiaire ; [organization, colony] pénitentiaire

prison authorities NPL administration f pénitentiaire

prison camp N camp m de prisonniers

prison farm N ferme dépendant d'une maison d'arrêt

prison governor N directeur m, -trice f de prison

prison guard N (US) gardien(ne) m(f) or surveillant(e) m(f) (de prison)

prison officer N gardien(ne) m(f) or surveillant(e) m(f) (de prison)

prison population N population f carcérale

prison riot N mutinerie f (dans une prison)

prison van N voiture f cellulaire

prison visitor N visiteur m, -euse f de prison

prison yard N cour f or préau m de prison

prisoner /'prɪznə^r/ N (gen) prisonnier m, -ière f ; (in jail) détenu(e) m(f), prisonnier m, -ière f ◆ **~ of conscience** détenu(e) m(f) or prisonnier m, -ière f politique ◆ **~ of war** prisonnier m, -ière f de guerre ◆ **~ at the bar** (Jur) accusé(e) m(f), inculpé(e) m(f) ◆ **he was taken ~ (by the enemy)** il a été fait prisonnier (par l'ennemi) ◆ **to hold sb ~** détenir qn, garder qn en captivité ◆ **to take no ~s** (fig) ne pas faire de quartier

prissy * /'prɪsɪ/ ADJ (= prudish) bégueule ; (= effeminate) efféminé ; (= fussy) pointilleux

pristine /'prɪstaɪn/ ADJ 1 (= unspoiled) parfait, virginal ◆ **in ~ condition** en parfait état 2 (= original) original, d'origine

prithee †† /'prɪðiː/ EXCL je vous prie

privacy /'prɪvəsɪ/ N intimité f ◆ **in ~** en toute intimité ◆ **in the ~ of your own home** dans l'intimité de votre foyer, tranquillement chez vous ◆ **his desire for ~** son désir d'être seul, son désir de solitude ; [of public figure etc] son désir de préserver sa vie privée ◆ **lack of ~** promiscuité f, impossibilité f de s'isoler ◆ **there is no ~ in these flats** impossible de s'isoler or on ne peut avoir aucune vie privée dans ces appartements ◆ **everyone needs some ~** tout le monde a besoin de pouvoir s'isoler de temps en temps ; → **invasion** COMP **Privacy Act** N (Jur) loi f sur la protection de la vie privée

private /'praɪvɪt/ ADJ 1 (= not open to public) [conversation, meeting, interview, party, land, property, road] privé ; [gardens] privatif ; [letter] personnel ◆ **~ agreement** (Jur) accord m à l'amiable ◆ **they have a ~ agreement to help each other** ils ont convenu (entre eux) de s'aider mutuellement, ils se sont entendus or se sont mis d'accord pour s'aider mutuellement ◆ **"private fishing"** "pêche réservée or gardée" ◆ **~ performance** (Theat etc) représentation f à guichets or bureaux fermés ◆ **~ room** (in hotel etc) salon m réservé ; see also **adj 2** ◆ **~ showing** [of film] séance f privée ◆ **a ~ wedding** un mariage célébré dans l'intimité ◆ **this matter is strictly ~** cette affaire est strictement confidentielle ◆ **I have ~ information that ...** je sais de source privée que ... ◆ **a ~ place** un coin retiré, un petit coin tranquille ◆ **it's not very ~ here** ce n'est pas très tranquille ici ◆ **let's go somewhere more ~** allons dans un endroit plus tranquille ◆ **he's a very ~ person** (gen) c'est un homme très secret or qui ne se confie pas ; (public figure etc) il tient à préserver sa vie privée ◆ **"private"** (on door etc) "privé", "interdit au public" ; (on envelope) "personnel"

◆ **in private** ⇒ **privately 1, 2**

2 (= personal, domestic) [house, lesson, room] particulier ; (= personal) [car, bank account] personnel ; [plane, army] privé ◆ **a ~ house** une maison particulière ◆ **a room with ~ bath(room)** une chambre avec salle de bain particulière ◆ **he has a ~ income, he has ~ means** il a une fortune personnelle ◆ **a ~ citizen** un simple citoyen ◆ **in his ~ capacity** à titre personnel ◆ **for (his) ~ use** pour son usage personnel ◆ **in (his) ~ life** dans sa vie privée, dans le privé ◆ **the ~ life of Henry VIII** la vie privée d'Henri VIII ◆ **it's a ~ matter or affair** c'est une affaire privée ◆ **it is my ~ opinion that ...** pour ma part je pense que ... ◆ **for ~ reasons** pour des raisons personnelles ◆ **in his ~ thoughts** dans ses pensées secrètes or intimes ◆ **~ pupil** élève mf en leçons particulières ◆ **~ tutor** (for full education) précepteur m, -trice f ; (for one subject) répétiteur m, -trice f ◆ **he's got a ~ teacher or tutor for maths** il prend des leçons particulières en maths, il a un répétiteur en maths ◆ **~ tuition** leçons fpl particulières

3 (= outside public sector) [company, institution] privé ; [clinic, hospital, nursing home] privé, non conventionné ◆ **~ pension (scheme)** (plan m de) retraite f complémentaire ◆ **~ health insurance** assurance f maladie privée ◆ **~ patient** (Brit) patient(e) m(f) consultant en clientèle privée ◆ **his ~ patients** (Brit) sa clientèle privée ◆ **~ treatment** ≈ traitement m non remboursé ◆ **to be in ~ practice** ≈ être médecin non conventionné

4 (Mil) **~ soldier** simple soldat m, soldat m de deuxième classe

N (Mil) (simple) soldat m, soldat m de deuxième classe ◆ **Private Martin** le soldat Martin ◆ **Private Martin!** soldat Martin ! ◆ **~ first class** (US) ≈ caporal m

NPL **privates** (*, euph) parties fpl intimes

COMP **private branch exchange** N (Brit Telec) commutateur m privé

private detective N détective m privé

private dick* N ⇒ **private eye**

private enterprise N (Econ) entreprise f privée

private eye* N privé* m

private finance initiative N (Brit) initiative f de financement privé

private hearing N (Admin, Jur) audience f à huis clos

private hotel N pension f de famille

private investigator N ⇒ **private detective**

private joke N plaisanterie f pour initiés

private member N (Parl) simple député m

private member's bill N (Parl) proposition f de loi (émanant d'un simple député)

private parts* NPL (euph) parties fpl intimes

private property N propriété f privée

private prosecution N (Jur) poursuites pénales engagées par la partie civile

private school N école f privée, ≈ école f libre

private secretary N secrétaire m particulier, secrétaire f particulière

the private sector N le secteur privé

private study N (Brit Scol) étude f

private view, private viewing N (Art etc) vernissage m

privateer /,praɪvə'tɪə^r/ N (= man, ship) corsaire m

privately /'praɪvɪtlɪ/ ADV 1 (= in private) en privé ◆ **may I speak to you ~?** puis-je vous parler en privé *or* vous dire un mot seul à seul ? ◆ **he told me ~ that ...** il m'a dit en privé que ... ◆ **the committee sat ~** le comité s'est réuni en séance privée *or* à huis clos

2 *(= secretly, internally)* en *or* dans son (*or* mon *etc*) for intérieur, intérieurement ◆ **~, he was against the scheme** dans son for intérieur *or* intérieurement, il était opposé au projet

3 *(= as private individual)* *[write, apply, object]* à titre personnel *or* privé ◆ **I bought/sold my car ~, not through a garage** j'ai acheté/vendu ma voiture à un particulier, pas à un garage

4 *(= not through the state)* ◆ **~ owned** privé ◆ **~ controlled** sous contrôle privé ◆ **she is having the operation ~** *(private hospital)* elle se fait opérer dans un hôpital privé ; *(private surgeon)* elle se fait opérer par un chirurgien non conventionné ◆ **to be ~ educated** faire (*or* avoir fait) ses études dans une école privée (*or* des écoles privées)

privation /praɪˈveɪʃən/ N privation *f*

privative /ˈprɪvətɪv/ ADJ, N *(also Ling)* privatif *m*

privatization /ˌpraɪvətaɪˈzeɪʃən/ N privatisation *f*

privatize /ˈpraɪvəˌtaɪz/ VT privatiser

privet /ˈprɪvɪt/ N troène *m* COMP **privet hedge** N haie *f* de troènes

privilege /ˈprɪvɪlɪdʒ/ N privilège *m* ; *(NonC: Parl etc)* prérogative *f*, immunité *f* ◆ **to have the ~ of doing sth** avoir le privilège *or* jouir du privilège de faire qch ◆ **I hate ~** je déteste les privilèges VT 1 *(= favour)* privilégier 2 ◆ **to be ~d to do sth** avoir le privilège de faire qch ◆ **I was ~d to meet him once** j'ai eu le privilège de le rencontrer une fois

privileged /ˈprɪvɪlɪdʒd/ ADJ *[person, group, situation, position]* privilégié ◆ **a ~ few** quelques privilégiés *mpl* ◆ **the ~ few** les privilégiés *mpl* ◆ **~ information** renseignements *mpl* confidentiels *(obtenus dans l'exercice de ses fonctions)* ; → **underprivileged**

privily †† /ˈprɪvɪlɪ/ ADV en secret

privy /ˈprɪvɪ/ ADJ († *or Jur*) privé, secret (-ète *f*) ◆ **~ to** au courant de, dans le secret de N † cabinets *mpl*, W.-C. *mpl*

COMP **Privy Council** N *(Brit) conseil privé du souverain britannique*

Privy Councillor N *(Brit) membre du conseil privé du souverain britannique*

Privy Purse N cassette *f* royale

Privy Seal N Petit Sceau *m*

prize¹ /praɪz/ N 1 *(gen, Scol, fig)* prix *m* ; *(in lottery)* lot *m* ◆ **to win first ~** *(Scol etc)* remporter le premier prix *(in* de) ; *(in lottery)* gagner le gros lot ◆ **there's a ~ for the best costume** il y a un prix pour le meilleur costume ◆ **no ~s for guessing ...** * vous n'aurez aucun mal à deviner ..., il n'est pas difficile de deviner ... ◆ **the Nobel Prize** le prix Nobel ; → **cash**

2 *(Naut)* prise *f* de navire (*or* de cargaison)

ADJ 1 *(= prize-winning)* primé, qui a remporté un prix ◆ **a ~ sheep** un mouton primé ◆ **he grows ~ onions** il cultive des oignons pour les concours agricoles

2 *(fig) (= outstanding)* ◆ **a ~ example of official stupidity** un parfait exemple de la bêtise des milieux officiels ◆ **what a ~ fool he'd been** * il s'était conduit comme un parfait imbécile

VT attacher beaucoup de prix à, tenir beaucoup à ◆ **to ~ sth very highly** attacher énormément de prix à qch ◆ **his most ~d possession was his car** la chose à laquelle il attachait le plus de prix *or* il tenait le plus était sa voiture ◆ **gold is ~d for its beauty/its electrical conductivity** l'or est recherché *or* (très) apprécié pour sa beauté/sa conductivité ◆ **lead soldiers are (greatly) ~d by collectors** les soldats de plomb sont très appréciés des collectionneurs *or* très prisés par les collectionneurs

COMP **prize day** N *(Scol)* (jour *m* de la) distribution *f* des prix

prize draw N tombola *f*

prize fight N *(Boxing)* combat *m* professionnel

prize fighter N boxeur *m* professionnel

prize fighting N boxe *f* professionnelle

prize-giving N *(Scol etc)* distribution *f* des prix

prize list N palmarès *m*, liste *f* des lauréats *or* des gagnants

prize money N *(NonC, gen, Sport)* prix *m* (en argent) ; *(Naut)* part *f* de prise

prize ring N *(Boxing)* ring *m (pour la boxe professionnelle)*

prize² /praɪz/ ⇒ **prise**

prizewinner /ˈpraɪzˌwɪnəʳ/ N *(Scol, gen)* lauréat(e) *m(f)* ; *(in lottery)* gagnant(e) *m(f)*

prizewinning /ˈpraɪzˌwɪnɪŋ/ ADJ *[essay, novel, entry etc]* primé, lauréat ; *[ticket]* gagnant

PRO N (abbrev of **public relations officer**) → **public**

pro¹ /prəʊ/ PREP * pour ◆ **are you ~ (or anti) the idea?** êtes-vous pour (ou contre) l'idée ? ADJ * pour ◆ **he's very ~** il est tout à fait pour N 1 *(= advantage)* ◆ **the ~s and the cons** le pour et le contre 2 *(= supporter)* **the ~s and the antis** les pour et les contre

pro² * /prəʊ/ N 1 (abbrev of **professional**) *(Sport etc)* pro *mf* ◆ **you can see he's a ~** *(fig)* on voit bien qu'on a affaire à un professionnel, on dirait qu'il a fait ça toute sa vie 2 *(= prostitute)* professionnelle *f*

COMP **pro-am** ADJ *(Golf)* (abbrev of **professional-amateur**) pro-am ◆ **~-am tournament** tournoi *m* pro-am

pro-celeb * ADJ ⇒ **pro-celebrity**

pro-celebrity ADJ ◆ **~-celebrity tournament** *tournoi opposant des célébrités à des joueurs professionnels*

pro- /prəʊ/ PREF 1 *(= in favour of)* pro ... ◆ **~French/European** profrançais/proeuropéen ◆ **~Europe** proeuropéen ◆ **he was ~Hitler** il était partisan d'Hitler ◆ **they were ~Moscow** ils étaient prosoviétiques 2 *(= acting for)* **pro ...** pro-, vice- ; → **proconsul**

pro-abortion /ˌprəʊəˈbɔːʃən/ ADJ en faveur de l'avortement

pro-abortionist /ˌprəʊəˈbɔːʃənɪst/ N partisan(e) *m(f)* de l'avortement

proactive /ˌprəʊˈæktɪv/ ADJ ◆ **to be ~** faire preuve d'initiative

probabilistic /ˌprɒbəbəˈlɪstɪk/ ADJ probabiliste

probability /ˌprɒbəˈbɪlɪtɪ/ N probabilité *f* ◆ **the ~ of sth** *(of an undesirable event)* les risques *mpl* de qch ; *(of a desirable event)* les chances *fpl* de qch ◆ **the ~ of sth happening** la probabilité que qch arrive ; *(desirable event)* les chances *fpl* que qch arrive ◆ **in all ~** selon toute probabilité ◆ **the ~ is that ...** il est très probable que ... + *indic*, il y a de grandes chances pour que ... + *subj* ◆ **there is little ~ that ...** il est peu probable que ... + *subj*

probable /ˈprɒbəbl/ ADJ 1 *(= likely)* *[reason, success, event, election]* probable ◆ **it is ~ that he will succeed** il est probable qu'il réussira ◆ **it is not/hardly ~ that ...** il est improbable/peu probable que ... + *subj* 2 *(= credible)* vraisemblable ◆ **his explanation did not sound very ~** son explication ne m'a pas paru très vraisemblable N ◆ **he is a ~** * for the match il y a de fortes chances qu'il fasse partie des joueurs sélectionnés pour le match ; → **possible**

probably /ˈprɒbəblɪ/ LANGUAGE IN USE 15.2, 16.2, 26.3 ADV probablement ◆ **most ~** très probablement ◆ **~ not** probablement pas

probate /ˈprəʊbɪt/ *(Jur)* N homologation *f (d'un testament)* ◆ **to value sth for ~** évaluer *or* expertiser qch pour l'homologation d'un testament ◆ **to grant/take out ~ of a will** homologuer/faire homologuer un testament VT *(US) [+ will]* homologuer COMP **probate court** N tribunal *m* des successions

probation /prəˈbeɪʃən/ N 1 *(Jur)* ≈ mise *f* à l'épreuve ; *(for minors)* mise *f* en liberté surveillée ◆ **to be on ~** ≈ être en sursis avec mise à l'épreuve *or* en liberté surveillée ◆ **to put sb on ~** mettre qn en sursis avec mise à l'épreuve *or* en liberté surveillée 2 *(= trial period)* ◆ **he is on ~** *[employee]* il a été engagé à l'essai ; *(Rel)* il est novice ; *(US Educ)* il a été pris (*or* repris) à l'essai ◆ **a semester on ~** *(US Educ)* un semestre à l'essai, un semestre probatoire COMP **probation officer** N *(Jur)* contrôleur *m* judiciaire

probationary /prəˈbeɪʃnərɪ/ ADJ *(gen)* d'essai ; *(Jur)* de sursis, avec mise à l'épreuve ; *(Rel)* de probation, de noviciat ◆ **~ year** année *f* probatoire ◆ **for a ~ period** pendant une période d'essai ◆ **a ~ period of three months** une période probatoire de trois mois

probationer /prəˈbeɪʃnəʳ/ N *(in business, factory etc)* employé(e) *m(f)* engagé(e) à l'essai ; *(Brit Police)* stagiaire *mf* ; *(Rel)* novice *mf* ; *(Jur)* ≈ condamné(e) *m(f)* sursitaire avec mise à l'épreuve ; *(= minor)* ≈ délinquant(e) *m(f)* en liberté surveillée

probe /prəʊb/ N 1 *(gen, Med, Dentistry, Space)* sonde *f* ; *[of insect]* trompe *f* ◆ **Venus ~** *(Space)* sonde *f* spatiale à destination de Vénus

2 *(fig = investigation)* enquête *f (into* sur), investigation *f (into* de)

VT 1 *(lit) (= explore)* *[+ hole, crack]* explorer, examiner ; *(Med)* sonder ; *(Space)* explorer ◆ **he ~d the ground with his stick** il fouilla la terre de sa canne

2 *(fig = inquire into)* *[+ sb's subconscious]* sonder ; *[+ past]* explorer ; *[+ private life]* chercher à découvrir ; *[+ causes, sb's death]* chercher à éclaircir ; *[+ mystery]* approfondir ; *[+ sb's activities]* enquêter sur

3 *(= inquire)* ◆ **"why did you say that ?" ~d Dennis** "pourquoi avez-vous dit cela ?" s'enquit Dennis

VI *(gen, Med etc)* faire un examen avec une sonde, faire un sondage ; *(fig = inquire)* faire des recherches ◆ **to ~ for sth** *(gen, Med)* chercher à localiser *or* à découvrir qch ; *(fig: by investigation)* rechercher qch ◆ **the police should have ~d more deeply** la police aurait dû pousser plus loin ses investigations ◆ **to ~ into sth** ⇒ **to probe sth** → **vt 2**

probing /ˈprəʊbɪŋ/ ADJ 1 *[instrument]* pour sonder 2 *(fig)* *[question, study]* pénétrant ; *[interrogation]* serré ; *[look]* inquisiteur (-trice *f*) N *(NonC, gen, Med)* sondage *m* ; *(fig = investigations)* investigations *fpl (into* de)

probity /ˈprəʊbɪtɪ/ N probité *f*

problem /ˈprɒbləm/ LANGUAGE IN USE 26.1

N 1 *(= difficulty)* problème *m* ◆ **the housing ~** le problème *or* la crise du logement ◆ **he is a great ~ to his mother** il pose de gros problèmes à sa mère ◆ **we've got ~s with the car** nous avons des ennuis avec la voiture ◆ **he's got a drink ~** il boit, il est porté sur la boisson ◆ **it's not my ~** ça ne me concerne pas ◆ **that's YOUR ~!** ça c'est ton problème ! ◆ **that's no ~ (to him)** ça ne (lui) pose pas de problème ◆ **no ~!** * pas de problème ! * ◆ **~ solved!** * (ça y est,) c'est réglé ! ◆ **what's the ~?** qu'est-ce qui ne va pas ?, quel est le problème ? ◆ **hey, what's your ~?** * t'as un problème ou quoi ? * ◆ **I had no ~ in getting the money, it was no ~ to get the money** je n'ai eu aucun mal à obtenir l'argent

2 *(* = objection)* **I have no ~ with that** j'y vois pas de problème * ◆ **my ~ (with that) is that ...** ce qui me chiffonne *or* me gêne, c'est que ... ◆ **do you have a ~ (with that)?** il y a quelque chose qui te gêne ?

3 *(Math etc = exercise)* problème *m*

ADJ 1 (= causing problems) [situation] difficile ; [family, group] qui pose des problèmes ; [child] caractériel, difficile ◆ ~ **cases** (Sociol) des cas mpl sociaux

2 (Literat etc) [novel, play] à thèse

COMP **problem-free** ADJ sans problème

problem page N (Press) courrier m du cœur

problem-solving N résolution f de problèmes ADJ [technique, abilities] de résolution de problèmes

problematic(al) /ˌprɒblɪˈmætɪk(l)/ ADJ problématique

pro bono /prəʊˈbəʊnəʊ/ (US Jur) ADJ bénévole ADV bénévolement

proboscis /prəʊˈbɒsɪs/ N (pl **proboscises** or **probocides** /prəʊˈbɒsɪˌdiːz/) [of animal, insect] trompe f ; (hum) (= nose) appendice m (hum)

procedural /prəˈsiːdjʊrəl/ ADJ (Admin, Insurance, Jur etc) de procédure N (also **police procedural**) (= novel) (roman m) policier m ; (= film) film m policier

procedure /prəˈsiːdʒəʳ/ N procédure f ◆ **what is the ~?** quelle est la procédure à suivre ?, comment doit-on procéder ? ◆ **the correct** or **normal ~ is to apply to ...** pour suivre la procédure normale il faut s'adresser à ... ◆ **order of ~** (Admin, Jur etc) règles fpl de procédure

proceed /prəˈsiːd/ VI 1 (frm, lit = move along) avancer ◆ **he was ~ing along the road** il avançait sur la route ◆ **"proceed with caution"** (on foot) "avancer avec prudence" ; (in vehicle) "rouler au pas"

2 (frm = go on) continuer ◆ **please ~!** veuillez continuer or poursuivre ◆ **to ~ on one's way** poursuivre son chemin or sa route ◆ **they then ~ed to London** ils se sont ensuite rendus à Londres ◆ **let us ~ to the next item** passons à la question suivante ◆ **before we ~ any further** avant d'aller plus loin

◆ **to proceed to do sth** se mettre à faire qch, entreprendre de faire qch ◆ **the police stopped the car and (then) ~ed to search it** les policiers arrêtèrent la voiture et entreprirent ensuite de la fouiller

◆ **to proceed with sth** ◆ **~ with your work** continuez or poursuivez votre travail ◆ **they ~ed with their plan** ils ont donné suite à leur projet ◆ **they did not ~ with the charges against him** (Jur) ils ont abandonné les poursuites (engagées) contre lui

3 (fig = act, operate) procéder, agir ◆ **you must ~ cautiously** il faut procéder or agir avec prudence ◆ **I am not sure how to ~** je ne sais pas très bien comment procéder or m'y prendre ◆ **it is all ~ing according to plan** tout se passe comme prévu ◆ **the discussions are ~ing normally** les discussions se poursuivent normalement ◆ **everything is ~ing well** les choses suivent leur cours de manière satisfaisante ◆ **to ~ from the assumption** or **premise that ...** [person, idea] partir du principe que ...

4 (= originate) ◆ **to ~ from** venir de, provenir de ; (fig) relever de

5 (Jur) ◆ **to ~ against sb** engager des poursuites contre qn

VT continuer ◆ **"well" she ~ed** "eh bien" continua-t-elle

N → **proceeds**

proceeding /prəˈsiːdɪŋ/ N (= course of action) façon f or manière f d'agir or de procéder

NPL **proceedings** 1 (= manoeuvres) opérations fpl ; (= ceremony) cérémonie f ; (= meeting) séance f, réunion f ; (= discussions) débats mpl ◆ **the ~s begin at 7 o'clock** la réunion or la séance commencera à 19 heures ◆ **the secretary recorded the ~s** le secrétaire a enregistré les débats ◆ **the ~s of parliament** la séance du Parlement ◆ **the main business of the ~s was to elect a new chairman** l'objectif principal de la séance or réunion était d'élire un nouveau président

2 (esp Jur = measures) mesures fpl ◆ **legal ~s** procès m ◆ **to take ~s** prendre des mesures (in order to do sth pour faire qch ; against sb contre qn) ◆ **to take (legal) ~s against sb** (Jur) engager des poursuites contre qn, intenter un procès à qn ◆ **disciplinary ~s are to be taken against two senior police officers** des mesures disciplinaires vont être prises à l'encontre de deux officiers de police supérieurs ◆ **criminal ~s against the former Prime Minister** des poursuites judiciaires contre l'ancien Premier ministre ◆ **the company has entered bankruptcy ~s** la société a entrepris une procédure de faillite ◆ **to start extradition ~s against sb** entreprendre une procédure d'extradition à l'encontre de qn ; → **commence, divorce, institute**

3 (= records) compte m rendu, rapport m ◆ **it was published in the Society's ~s** cela a été publié dans les actes de la Société ◆ **Proceedings of the Historical Society** (as title) Actes mpl de la Société d'histoire

proceeds /ˈprəʊsiːdz/ NPL montant m des recettes ◆ **~ of insurance** (Jur, Fin) indemnité f versée par la compagnie ◆ **the ~ of the arms sales** le produit de la vente d'armes

process[1] /ˈprəʊses/ N 1 (Chem, Bio, Ling, Sociol etc) processus m ; (fig, Admin, Jur) procédure f ◆ **the ~ of digestion/growing up** etc le processus de la digestion/de la croissance etc ◆ **a natural/chemical ~** un processus naturel/chimique ◆ **the thawing/preserving** etc **~** le processus de décongélation/de conservation etc ◆ **the building ~** la construction ◆ **the best way to proceed is by a ~ of elimination** la meilleure solution est de procéder par élimination ◆ **the ageing ~** le (processus de) vieillissement ◆ **the legal/administrative ~ takes a year** la procédure juridique/administrative prend un an ◆ **the ~es of the law** le processus de la justice ◆ **it's a slow** or **long ~** (Chem etc) c'est un processus lent ; (fig) ça prend du temps ◆ **he supervised the whole ~** il a supervisé l'opération du début à la fin

◆ **in the process** ◆ **to be in the ~ of modernization/negotiation/construction** être en cours de modernisation/négociation/construction ◆ **to be in the ~ of moving/changing** être en train de déménager/changer ◆ **in the ~ of cleaning the picture, they discovered ...** au cours du nettoyage du tableau or pendant qu'ils nettoyaient le tableau ils ont découvert ... ◆ **she tried to help, and ruined everything in the ~** elle a essayé d'aider mais, ce faisant or du coup*, elle a tout gâché ◆ **he saved the girl, but injured himself in the ~** il a sauvé la petite fille mais, ce faisant or du coup*, il s'est blessé

2 (= specific method) procédé m, méthode f ◆ **the Bessemer ~** le procédé Bessemer ◆ **he has devised a ~ for controlling weeds** il a mis au point un procédé or une méthode pour venir à bout des mauvaises herbes ◆ **to work sth out by ~ of elimination** résoudre qch en procédant par élimination ; see also **elimination**

3 (Jur) (= action) procès m ; (= summons) citation f à comparaître ◆ **to bring a ~ against sb** intenter un procès à qn ◆ **to serve a ~ on sb** signifier une citation à qn ; → **serve**

4 (= outgrowth) excroissance f, protubérance f

VT [+ raw materials, food] traiter, transformer ; [+ seeds, waste] traiter ; [+ film] développer ; [+ information, data] traiter ; [+ computer tape] faire passer en machine ; [+ an application, papers, records] s'occuper de ◆ **the material will be ~ed into plastic pellets** le matériau sera transformé en pastilles de plastique ◆ **your application will take six weeks to ~** l'examen de votre candidature prendra six semaines ◆ **they ~ 10,000 forms per day** 10 000 formulaires passent chaque jour entre leurs mains ◆ **in order to ~ your order** (Comm) afin de donner suite à votre commande

COMP **process control** N (in industry) régulation f des processus industriels

process industry N industrie f de transformation

process printing N quadrichromie f

process-server N (Jur) ≈ huissier m de justice

process[2] /prəˈses/ VI (Brit = go in procession) défiler, avancer en cortège ; (Rel) aller en procession

processed /ˈprəʊsest/ ADJ [food] traité

COMP **processed cheese** N (for spreading) fromage m fondu ; (in slices) fromage reconstitué en tranches

processed peas NPL petits pois mpl en boîte

processing /ˈprəʊsesɪŋ/ N (NonC) [of food, radioactive waste, application, papers, records] traitement m ; [of raw materials] traitement m, transformation f ; (Phot) [of film etc] développement m ◆ **advances in information ~** les progrès réalisés dans le traitement de l'information ◆ **America sent cotton to England for ~** l'Amérique envoyait du coton en Angleterre pour le faire traiter ; → **data, food, word** COMP

processing unit N (Comput) unité f de traitement

procession /prəˈseʃən/ N [of people, cars] cortège m, défilé m ; (Rel) procession f ◆ **to walk in (a) ~** défiler, aller en cortège or en procession ; → **funeral**

processional /prəˈseʃənl/ (Rel) ADJ processionnel N hymne m processionnel

processor /ˈprəʊsesəʳ/ N 1 (Comput) processeur m ; → **data, word** 2 ⇒ **food processor** ; → **food**

pro-choice /ˌprəʊˈtʃɔɪs/ ADJ en faveur de l'avortement

pro-choicer* /ˌprəʊˈtʃɔɪsəʳ/ N partisan(e) m(f) de l'avortement

proclaim /prəˈkleɪm/ VT 1 (= announce) proclamer, déclarer (that que) ; [+ holiday] instituer ; [+ one's independence, innocence] proclamer ; [+ war, one's love] déclarer ; [+ edict] promulguer ◆ **to ~ sb king** proclamer qn roi ◆ **to ~ a state of emergency** décréter l'état d'urgence, proclamer l'état d'urgence ◆ **to ~ peace** annoncer le rétablissement de la paix 2 (= reveal, demonstrate) démontrer, révéler ◆ **his tone ~ed his confidence** le ton de sa voix démontrait or révélait sa confiance ◆ **their expressions ~ed their guilt** la culpabilité se lisait sur leurs visages

proclamation /ˌprɒkləˈmeɪʃən/ N proclamation f

proclivity /prəˈklɪvɪtɪ/ N (frm) propension f, inclination f (to sth à qch ; to do sth à faire qch)

proconsul /ˈprəʊˈkɒnsəl/ N proconsul m

procrastinate /prəʊˈkræstɪneɪt/ VI atermoyer, tergiverser

procrastination /prəʊˌkræstɪˈneɪʃən/ N (NonC) atermoiements mpl, tergiversations fpl

procrastinator /prəʊˌkræstɪˈneɪtəʳ/ N personne f qui remet tout au lendemain

procreate /ˈprəʊkrɪeɪt/ VI se reproduire VT procréer, engendrer

procreation /ˌprəʊkrɪˈeɪʃən/ N procréation f

Procrustean /prəʊˈkrʌstɪən/ ADJ de Procuste

proctor /ˈprɒktəʳ/ N 1 (Jur etc) fondé m de pouvoir 2 (Univ) (Oxford, Cambridge) responsable mf de la discipline ; (US) (= invigilator) surveillant(e) m(f) (à un examen)

procurable /prəˈkjʊərəbl/ ADJ que l'on peut se procurer ◆ **it is easily ~** on peut se le procurer facilement

procuration /ˌprɒkjʊˈreɪʃən/ N 1 (= *act of procuring*) obtention f, acquisition f 2 (*Jur* = *authority*) procuration f 3 (= *crime*) proxénétisme m

procurator /ˈprɒkjʊreɪtəʳ/ N (*Jur*) fondé m de pouvoir COMP **Procurator Fiscal** N (*Scot Jur*) ≈ procureur m (de la République)

procure /prəˈkjʊəʳ/ VT 1 (= *obtain for o.s.*) se procurer, obtenir ; [+ *sb's release etc*] obtenir ◆ **to ~ sth for sb, to ~ sb sth** procurer qch à qn, faire obtenir qch à qn ◆ **to ~ sb's death** † faire assassiner qn 2 (*Jur*) [+ *prostitute etc*] offrir les services de, procurer VI (*Jur*) faire du proxénétisme

procurement /prəˈkjʊəmənt/ N (*gen*) obtention f ; (= *buying supplies*) approvisionnement m ; (*Mil*) acquisition f de matériel militaire COMP **procurement department** N service m des achats *or* de l'approvisionnement

procurer /prəˈkjʊərəʳ/ N (*Jur*) entremetteur m, proxénète m

procuress /prəˈkjʊərɪs/ N (*Jur*) entremetteuse f, proxénète f

procuring /prəˈkjʊərɪŋ/ N 1 [*of goods, objects*] obtention f 2 (*Jur*) proxénétisme m

Prod * /prɒd/, **Proddie** * /ˈprɒdɪ/ N (*Brit pej*) protestant(e) m(f), parpaillot(e) * m(f)

prod /prɒd/ N (= *push*) poussée f ; (= *jab*) (petit) coup m (*de canne, avec le doigt etc*) ◆ **to give sb a ~** pousser qn doucement (du doigt *or* du pied *or* avec la pointe d'un bâton *etc*) ; (*fig*) pousser qn ◆ **he needs a ~ from time to time** (*fig*) il a besoin d'être poussé *or* qu'on le secoue * *subj* un peu de temps en temps VT pousser doucement ◆ **to ~ sb** pousser qn doucement (du doigt *or* du pied *or* avec la pointe d'un bâton *etc*) ; (*fig*) pousser qn ◆ **she ~ded the jellyfish with a stick** elle a poussé la méduse avec la pointe d'un bâton ◆ **to ~ sb to do sth** *or* **into doing sth** pousser *or* inciter qn à faire qch ◆ **he needs ~ding** il a besoin d'être poussé *or* qu'on le secoue * *subj* VI ◆ **to ~ at sb/sth** ⇒ **to prod sb/sth** → vt

prodigal /ˈprɒdɪɡəl/ ADJ prodigue (*of* de) ◆ **the ~ (son)** (*Bible*) le fils prodigue ; (*fig*) l'enfant m prodigue

prodigality /ˌprɒdɪˈɡælɪtɪ/ N prodigalité f

prodigally /ˈprɒdɪɡəlɪ/ ADV avec prodigalité

prodigious /prəˈdɪdʒəs/ ADJ (*frm*) prodigieux, extraordinaire

prodigiously /prəˈdɪdʒəslɪ/ ADV (*frm*) prodigieusement

prodigy /ˈprɒdɪdʒɪ/ N prodige m, merveille f ◆ **child ~, infant ~** enfant mf prodige ◆ **a ~ of learning** un puits de science

produce /prəˈdjuːs/ VT 1 (= *make, yield, manufacture*) [+ *milk, oil, coal, ore, crops*] produire ; [+ *cars, radios*] produire, fabriquer ; [*writer, artist, musician etc*] produire ; (*Fin*) [+ *interest, profit*] rapporter ; [+ *offspring*] [*animal*] produire, donner naissance à ; [*woman*] donner naissance à ◆ **his shares ~ a yield of 7%** (*Fin*) ses actions rapportent 7% ◆ **that investment ~s no return** cet investissement ne rapporte rien ◆ **Scotland ~s whisky** l'Écosse produit du whisky *or* est un pays producteur de whisky ◆ **coal ~s electricity** le charbon produit *or* donne de l'électricité ◆ **these magazines are ~d by the same firm** ces revues sont éditées par la même maison ◆ **he ~d a masterpiece** il a produit un chef-d'œuvre ◆ **well-~d** [+ *book*] bien présenté ; [+ *goods*] bien fait ; see also **vt 4** ◆ **he has ~d a new single** il a sorti un nouveau single

2 (= *bring out, show*) [+ *gift, handkerchief, gun*] sortir (*from* de) ; [+ *ticket, documents etc*] présenter ; [+ *witness*] produire ; [+ *proof*] fournir, apporter ◆ **he suddenly ~d a large parcel** il a soudain sorti un gros paquet ◆ **I can't ~ $100 just like that!** je ne peux pas trouver 100 dollars comme ça ! ◆ **he ~d a sudden burst of energy** il a eu un sursaut d'énergie

3 (= *cause*) [+ *famine, deaths*] causer, provoquer ; [+ *dispute, bitterness*] provoquer, causer ; [+ *results*] produire, donner ; [+ *impression*] faire, donner ; [+ *pleasure, interest*] susciter ; (*Elec*) [+ *current*] engendrer ; [+ *spark*] faire jaillir ◆ **it ~d a burning sensation in my finger** cela a provoqué une sensation de brûlure dans mon doigt

4 (*Theat*) mettre en scène ; (*Cine*) produire ; (*Rad*) [+ *play*] mettre en ondes ; [+ *programme*] réaliser ; (*TV*) [+ *play, film*] mettre en scène ; [+ *programme*] réaliser ◆ **well ~d** bien monté

5 (*Geom*) [+ *line, plane*] (= *extend*) prolonger, continuer

VI 1 [*mine, oil well, factory*] produire ; [*land, trees, cows*] produire, rendre

2 (*Theat*) assurer la mise en scène ; (*Cine*) assurer la production (*d'un film*) ; (*Rad, TV*) assurer la réalisation d'une émission

N /ˈprɒdjuːs/ (*NonC* = *food*) produits mpl (*d'alimentation*) ◆ **agricultural/garden/foreign ~** produits mpl agricoles/maraîchers/étrangers ◆ **"produce of France"** "produit français", "produit de France" ◆ **"produce of more than one country"** "produit de différents pays" ◆ **we eat mostly our own ~** nous mangeons surtout nos propres produits *or* ce que nous produisons nous-mêmes

producer /prəˈdjuːsəʳ/ N 1 (= *maker, grower*) producteur m, -trice f 2 (*Theat, Cine, Mus*) producteur m, -trice f ; (*Rad, TV*) réalisateur m, -trice f, metteur m en ondes

COMP **producer gas** N gaz m fourni par gazogène

producer goods NPL (*Econ*) biens mpl de production

-producing /prəˈdjuːsɪŋ/ ADJ (*in compounds*) producteur (-trice f) de ... ◆ **oil-producing** producteur (-trice f) de pétrole ◆ **one of the coal-producing countries** un des pays producteurs de charbon

product /ˈprɒdʌkt/ N (*gen, Math*) produit m ◆ **food ~s** produits mpl alimentaires, denrées fpl (alimentaires) ◆ **it is the ~ of his imagination** c'est le fruit de son imagination ◆ **she is the ~ of a broken home** elle est le résultat d'un foyer désuni ◆ **a public-school ~** un (pur) produit des public schools ; → **finished, gross, waste**

COMP **product acceptance** N mesure f du succès d'un produit auprès des consommateurs

product liability N responsabilité f du fabricant

product line N ⇒ **product range**

product manager N chef m de produit

product placement N (*Cine, Comm*) placement m de produit(s)

product range N gamme f *or* ligne f de produits

production /prəˈdʌkʃən/ N 1 (*NonC* = *manufacturing*) production f ◆ **to put sth into ~** entreprendre la production de qch ◆ **to take sth out of ~** retirer qch de la production ◆ **the factory is in full ~** l'usine tourne à plein rendement ◆ **car/oil** *etc* **~ has risen recently** la production automobile/pétrolière *etc* a récemment augmenté ◆ **industrial/agricultural ~ fell by 1.7% last month** la production industrielle/agricole a baissé de 1,7% le mois dernier ◆ **we hope to go into ~ soon** nous espérons commencer la production bientôt ◆ **the new model goes into ~ soon** on commencera bientôt la fabrication du nouveau modèle

2 (*NonC* = *act of showing*) présentation f ◆ **on ~ of this ticket** sur présentation de ce billet

3 (*NonC* = *activity*) (*Theat*) mise f en scène ; (*Cine, Mus, Rad, TV*) production f ◆ **film ~** la production cinématographique ◆ **TV ~** la production *or* création télévisuelle ◆ **he was writing plays for ~ at the Blackfriars Theatre** il écrivait des pièces pour les monter au "Blackfriars Theatre"

4 (= *work produced*) (*Theat, Mus*) représentation f, mise f en scène ; (*Cine, Rad, TV*) production f ◆ **a theatrical** *or* **stage ~** une pièce de théâtre ◆ **a new ~ of "Macbeth"** une nouvelle mise en scène de "Macbeth" ◆ **"Macbeth": a new ~ by ...** "Macbeth" : une nouvelle mise en scène de ... ◆ **the Theatre Royal's ~ of "Cats" ran for three years** "Cats" s'est joué pendant trois ans au "Theatre Royal"

COMP **production company** N société f de production

production costs NPL coûts mpl de production

production department N (*Publishing*) service m fabrication

production line N chaîne f de fabrication ◆ **he works on the ~ line** il travaille à la chaîne ◆ **~ line work** travail m à la chaîne

production manager N directeur m de (la) production

production number N (*Theat, Cine*) numéro m de production

production run N série f

production values NPL (*Cine*) ◆ **a film with high ~ values** un film à gros budget

productive /prəˈdʌktɪv/ ADJ [*land, imagination*] fertile, fécond ; [*meeting, discussion, work*] fructueux, productif ; (*Econ*) [*employment, labour*] productif ; (*Ling*) productif ◆ **to be ~ of sth** produire qch, engendrer qch, être générateur de qch ◆ **I've had a very ~ day** j'ai eu une journée très fructueuse, j'ai bien travaillé aujourd'hui ◆ **~ life of an asset** (*Fin*) vie f utile d'un bien

productively /prəˈdʌktɪvlɪ/ ADV de manière fructueuse *or* productive

productivity /ˌprɒdʌkˈtɪvɪtɪ/ N (*NonC*) productivité f

COMP [*fall, increase*] de (la) productivité

productivity agreement N (*Brit*) accord m de productivité

productivity bonus N prime f à la productivité

prof. /prɒf/ N (*Univ*) (abbrev of **professor**) professeur m ◆ **Prof. C. Smith** (*on envelope*) Monsieur C. Smith ADJ abbrev of **professional**

profanation /ˌprɒfəˈneɪʃən/ N profanation f

profane /prəˈfeɪn/ ADJ 1 (= *secular, lay*) [*music etc*] profane 2 (*pej* = *blasphemous*) [*language etc*] impie, sacrilège ; → **sacred** VT profaner

profanity /prəˈfænɪtɪ/ N 1 (= *oath*) juron m, blasphème m ◆ **he uttered a torrent of profanities** il a proféré un torrent d'injures 2 (*NonC*) [*of language etc*] caractère m profane

profess /prəˈfes/ VT 1 (= *claim*) prétendre (*that* que) ◆ **to ~ ignorance of sth** prétendre ne rien savoir sur qch ◆ **to ~ knowledge of sth** prétendre connaître qch ◆ **he ~es to know all about it** il prétend tout savoir sur ce sujet ◆ **I don't ~ to be an expert** je ne prétends pas être expert en la matière ◆ **why do organisations ~ that they care?** pourquoi les sociétés prétendent-elles se sentir concernées ? ◆ **"I don't know," he replied, ~ing innocence** "Je ne sais pas," dit-il, feignant l'innocence ◆ **their ~ed support for traditional family values** leur prétendu attachement aux valeurs familiales traditionnelles

2 (= *declare*) déclarer (*that* que) ; [+ *faith, religion*] professer ; (*publicly*) professer, faire profession de ; [+ *an opinion, respect, hatred*] professer ◆ **to ~ concern at sth** exprimer son inquiétude devant qch, se déclarer inquiet de qch ◆ **he ~ed himself satisfied** il s'est déclaré satisfait ◆ **he ~ed to be content with the arrangement** il s'est déclaré satisfait de cet arrangement

3 *(frm = have as one's profession)* **to ~ law/medicine** exercer la profession d'avocat/de médecin

professed /prəˈfest/ ADJ *[atheist, communist etc]* déclaré ; *(Rel) [monk, nun]* profès (-esse *f*) ◆ **a ~ indifference to any form of Christianity** une indifférence affichée à toute forme de christianisme

professedly /prəˈfesɪdlɪ/ ADV de son *(or leur etc)* propre aveu, d'après lui *(or eux etc)* ; *(= allegedly)* soi-disant, prétendument

profession /prəˈfeʃən/ N 1 *(= calling)* profession *f* ; *(= body of people)* (membres *mpl* d'une) profession *f* ◆ **by ~** de son *(or mon etc)* métier *or* état ◆ **the medical ~** *(= calling)* la profession de médecin, la médecine ; *(= doctors collectively)* le corps médical, les médecins *mpl* ◆ **the ~s** les professions *fpl* libérales ◆ **the oldest ~** *(euph)* le plus vieux métier du monde ; → **learned** 2 *(= declaration)* profession *f*, déclaration *f* ◆ **~ of faith** profession *f* de foi ◆ **to make one's ~** *[monk, nun]* faire sa profession, prononcer ses vœux

professional /prəˈfeʃənl/ ADJ 1 *[skill, organization, training, etiquette]* professionnel ◆ **to be a ~ person** *[doctor, lawyer etc]* exercer une profession libérale ; *[other white-collar worker]* avoir une situation ◆ **the ~ classes** les (membres *mpl* des) professions *fpl* libérales ◆ **to take ~ advice** *(medical/legal)* consulter un médecin/un avocat ; *(on practical problem)* consulter un professionnel *or* un homme de métier ◆ **it is not ~ practice to do so** faire cela est contraire à l'usage professionnel

2 *(= by profession) [writer, politician]* professionnel, de profession ; *[footballer, tennis player]* professionnel ; *[diplomat, soldier]* de carrière ; *(fig = of high standard) [play, piece of work]* de haute qualité, excellent ◆ **~ football/tennis** *etc* football *m*/tennis *m etc* professionnel ◆ **to turn** *or* **go ~** *(Sport)* passer professionnel ◆ **to have a very ~ attitude to one's work** prendre son travail très au sérieux ◆ **it is well up to ~ standards** c'est d'un niveau de professionnel

N *(all senses)* professionnel *m*, -elle *f* ◆ **a health ~** un professionnel de la santé ◆ **£40,000 is not excessive for a highly-skilled ~** 40 000 livres n'ont rien d'excessif pour un cadre hautement qualifié

COMP **professional army** N armée *f* de métier
professional foul N *(Ftbl)* faute *f* délibérée
Professional Golfers' Association N PGA *f* *(association de golfeurs professionnels)*
professional school N *(US) (Univ = faculty)* faculté *f* de droit *or* de médecine ; *(= business school)* grande école *f* commerciale

professionalism /prəˈfeʃnəlɪzəm/ N *[of writer, actor etc]* professionnalisme *m* ; *(Sport)* professionnalisme *m* ; *[of play, piece of work]* excellence *f*, haute qualité *f*

professionalization /prəˌfeʃnəlaɪˈzeɪʃən/ N professionnalisation *f*

professionalize /prəˈfeʃnəlaɪz/ VT professionnaliser

professionally /prəˈfeʃnəlɪ/ ADV 1 *(= vocationally)* professionnellement ◆ **he sings/dances** *etc* ~ il est chanteur/danseur *etc* professionnel ◆ **to be ~ qualified** avoir une qualification professionnelle ◆ **I know him only ~** je n'ai que des rapports de travail avec lui ◆ **she is known ~ as Julia Wills** dans la profession *or* le métier, elle est connue sous le nom de Julia Wills ◆ **speaking ~, I have to tell you that ...** d'un point de vue professionnel, je dois vous dire que ... ◆ **it was a difficult time both personally and ~** ce fut une période difficile sur le plan aussi bien personnel que professionnel ◆ **the boat was ~ built** le bateau a été construit par des professionnels ◆ **the play was ~ produced** la mise en scène (de la pièce) était l'œuvre d'un professionnel

2 *(= expertly)* de manière professionnelle

3 *(= according to professional standards)* en professionnel(le), de manière professionnelle ◆ **he claims he acted ~ and responsibly throughout** il affirme qu'il s'est toujours comporté de manière professionnelle et responsable

professor /prəˈfesəʳ/ N 1 *(Univ)* professeur *m* (titulaire d'une chaire) ◆ **~ of French, French ~** professeur *m* (titulaire de la chaire) de français ◆ **good morning, Professor Smith** bonjour Monsieur Smith, bonjour Monsieur (le professeur) ◆ **Dear Professor Smith** *(in letters)* monsieur, Cher Monsieur *(less frm)* ; *(if known to writer)* Cher Professeur ◆ **Professor C. Smith** *(on envelope)* Monsieur C. Smith ; → **assistant** 2 *(US ⁑: iro)* maestro *m*, maître *m*

professorial /ˌprɒfəˈsɔːrɪəl/ ADJ professoral

professorship /prəˈfesəʃɪp/ N chaire *f* (of de) ◆ **he has a ~** il est titulaire d'une chaire

proffer /ˈprɒfəʳ/ VT *[+ object, arm]* offrir, tendre ; *[+ a remark, suggestion]* faire ; *[+ one's thanks, apologies]* offrir, présenter ◆ **to ~ one's hand to sb** tendre la main à qn

proficiency /prəˈfɪʃənsɪ/ N (grande) compétence *f* (in en) ◆ **Cambridge Certificate of Proficiency** *diplôme d'anglais langue étrangère*

proficient /prəˈfɪʃənt/ ADJ (très) compétent (in en)

profile /ˈprəʊfaɪl/ N 1 *[of head, building, hill etc]* profil *m (also Archit)* ; *(fig = description) [of person]* portrait *m* ; *[of situation etc]* profil *m*, esquisse *f* ◆ **in ~** de profil ◆ **genetic ~** profil *m* génétique ◆ **psychological ~** profil *m* psychologique ◆ **he has the right ~ for the job** il a le profil qui convient pour ce poste

◆ **high profile** ◆ **to maintain a high ~** *(in media etc)* garder la vedette ; *(= be seen on streets etc)* être très en évidence ◆ **troops have been maintaining a high ~ in the capital** les troupes sont très en évidence dans la capitale ◆ **the foundation already has a high ~** la fondation est déjà très en vue ◆ **Egypt will be given a much higher ~ in the upcoming peace talks** l'Égypte prendra une place bien plus importante dans les négociations de paix prochaines ◆ **football is a high ~ business** le foot est un domaine très médiatisé

◆ **low profile** ◆ **to keep** *or* **take a low ~** essayer de ne pas (trop) se faire remarquer, adopter une attitude discrète ◆ **the party had a low ~ in this constituency** le parti n'était pas très représenté dans cette circonscription

◆ **to raise + profile** ◆ **to raise one's profile** améliorer son image ◆ **his main task will be to raise the ~ of the party** sa principale tâche sera d'améliorer l'image du parti

2 *(= graph or table)* profil *m*

VT 1 *(= show in profile)* profiler *(also Archit)*

2 *(gen) (= describe) [+ person]* brosser *or* dresser le portrait de ; *[+ situation]* établir le profil de, tracer une esquisse de ; *(Police) [+ suspect]* établir le profil psychologique de

profit /ˈprɒfɪt/ N *(Comm)* profit *m*, bénéfice *m* ; *(fig)* profit *m*, avantage *m* ◆ **~ and loss** profits *mpl* et pertes *fpl* ; see also **comp** ◆ **gross/net ~** bénéfice *m* brut/net ◆ **to make** *or* **turn a ~** faire un bénéfice *or* des bénéfices ◆ **to make a ~ of $100** faire un bénéfice de 100 dollars (*on sth* sur qch) ◆ **to sell sth at a ~** vendre qch à profit ◆ **to show** *or* **yield a ~** rapporter (un bénéfice) ◆ **there's not much ~ in doing that** *(lit, fig)* on ne gagne pas grand-chose à faire cela ◆ **with ~s policy** *(Insurance)* police *f* (d'assurance) avec participation aux bénéfices ◆ **with ~** *(fig)* avec profit, avec fruit ◆ **to turn sth to ~** *(fig)* mettre à profit qch, tirer parti de qch

VI *(fig)* tirer un profit *or* un avantage ◆ **to ~ by** *or* **from sth** tirer avantage *or* profit de qch, bien profiter de qch ◆ **I can't see how he hopes to ~ (by it)** je ne vois pas ce qu'il espère en retirer *or* y gagner

VT *(†† or liter)* profiter à ◆ **it will ~ him nothing** cela ne lui profitera en rien

COMP **profit and loss account** N *(Accounts)* compte *m* de profits et pertes, compte *m* de résultat
profit-making ADJ rentable ◆ **a ~-making/non-~-making organization** une organisation à but lucratif/non lucratif
profit margin N marge *f* bénéficiaire
profit motive N recherche *f* du profit
profit-seeking ADJ à but lucratif
profit sharing N participation *f or* intéressement *m* aux bénéfices
profit-sharing scheme N système *m* de participation *or* d'intéressement aux bénéfices
profit squeeze N compression *f* des bénéfices
profit taking N *(Stock Exchange)* prise *f* de bénéfices
profit warning N profit warning *m*, *annonce d'une baisse des prévisions par rapport aux résultats escomptés*

profitability /ˌprɒfɪtəˈbɪlɪtɪ/ N *(lit, fig)* rentabilité *f* COMP **profitability study** N étude *f* de rentabilité

profitable /ˈprɒfɪtəbl/ ADJ *[deal, sale, investment]* rentable, lucratif ; *[company]* bénéficiaire, rentable ; *(fig) [scheme, agreement, contract]* rentable ; *[meeting, discussion, visit]* fructueux, payant *(fig)*, profitable, fructueux ◆ **we don't stock them any more as they were not ~** nous ne les stockons plus parce qu'ils n'étaient pas rentables ◆ **it was a very ~ half-hour** cela a été une demi-heure très fructueuse *or* profitable ◆ **you would find it ~ to read this** vous trouveriez la lecture de ceci utile *or* profitable

profitably /ˈprɒfɪtəblɪ/ ADV 1 *(lit) [sell]* à profit ◆ **the company is now trading ~** cette société enregistre à présent des bénéfices, cette société est à présent bénéficiaire 2 *(fig = usefully)* utilement, de manière utile ◆ **the same technology could be ~ employed finding alternative sources of energy** on pourrait employer utilement cette même technologie pour trouver d'autres sources d'énergie ◆ **there was little I could ~ do** je ne pouvais pas faire grand-chose d'utile

profiteer /ˌprɒfɪˈtɪəʳ/ N profiteur *m*, mercanti *m* VI faire des bénéfices excessifs

profiteering /ˌprɒfɪˈtɪərɪŋ/ N *(pej)* réalisation *f* de bénéfices excessifs

profitless /ˈprɒfɪtlɪs/ ADJ *(lit) [company, factory]* qui n'est pas rentable ; *[shares]* qui ne rapporte rien ; *[year]* improductif ; *(fig)* infructueux

profitlessly /ˈprɒfɪtlɪslɪ/ ADV *(lit)* sans dégager de bénéfices ; *(fig)* d'une manière infructueuse

profligacy /ˈprɒflɪgəsɪ/ N *(frm) (= debauchery)* débauche *f*, libertinage *m* ; *(= extravagance)* extrême prodigalité *f*

profligate /ˈprɒflɪgɪt/ *(frm)* ADJ *(= debauched) [person, behaviour]* débauché, libertin, dissolu ; *[life]* de débauche, de libertinage ; *(= extravagant)* extrêmement prodigue N débauché(e) *m(f)*, libertin(e) *m(f)*

pro-form /ˈprəʊˌfɔːm/ N *(Ling)* proforme *f*

pro forma /ˈprəʊˈfɔːmə/ ADJ pro forma *inv* N (also **pro forma invoice**) facture *f* pro forma ; (also **pro forma letter**) (formule *f* de) lettre *f* toute faite ADV selon les règles

profound /prəˈfaʊnd/ ADJ *(all senses)* profond

profoundly /prəˈfaʊndlɪ/ ADV *[different, moving, undemocratic etc]* profondément ; *[deaf]* totalement, complètement

profundity /prəˈfʌndɪtɪ/ **N** 1 (*NonC*) profondeur *f* 2 (*= profound remark*) remarque *f* profonde

profuse /prəˈfjuːs/ **ADJ** *[vegetation, bleeding]* abondant ; *[thanks, praise, apologies]* profus, multiple ◆ **~ in ...** prodigue de ... ◆ **to be ~ in one's thanks/excuses** se confondre en remerciements/excuses

profusely /prəˈfjuːslɪ/ **ADV** *[bleed, sweat]* abondamment ; *[grow]* à profusion, en abondance ◆ **to apologize ~** se confondre *or* se répandre en excuses ◆ **to thank sb ~** remercier qn avec effusion

profusion /prəˈfjuːʒən/ **N** profusion *f*, abondance *f* (*of* de) ◆ **in ~** à profusion, à foison

prog. * /prɒg/ **N** (*Brit TV etc*) (abbrev of **programme**) émission *f*, programme *m*

progenitor /prəʊˈdʒenɪtəʳ/ **N** (*lit*) ancêtre *m* ; (*fig*) auteur *m*

progeny /ˈprɒdʒɪnɪ/ **N** (*= offspring*) progéniture *f* ; (*= descendants*) lignée *f*, descendants *mpl*

progesterone /prəʊˈdʒestəˌrəʊn/ **N** progestérone *f*

prognathous /prɒgˈneɪθəs/ **ADJ** prognathe

prognosis /prɒgˈnəʊsɪs/ **N** (pl **prognoses** /prɒgˈnəʊsiːz/) pronostic *m*

prognostic /prɒgˈnɒstɪk/ **N** (*frm*) présage *m*, signe *m* avant-coureur

prognosticate /prɒgˈnɒstɪkeɪt/ **VT** pronostiquer **VI** faire des pronostics

prognostication /prɒgˌnɒstɪˈkeɪʃən/ **N** pronostic *m*

program /ˈprəʊgræm/ **N** 1 (*Comput*) programme *m* 2 (*US*) ⇒ **programme noun 1** **VI** (*Comput*) établir un (*or* des) programme(s) **VT** 1 (*Comput*) programmer ◆ **to ~ sth to do sth** programmer qch de façon à faire qch 2 (*US*) ⇒ **programme vt 1** **COMP** (*Comput*) *[specification, costs]* du *or* d'un programme

programmable, programable (*US*) /ˈprəʊgræməbl/ **ADJ** (*Comput*) programmable

programmatic /ˌprəʊgrəˈmætɪk/ **ADJ** programmatique

programme (*Brit*), **program** (*esp US*) /ˈprəʊgræm/ **N** 1 (*most senses*) programme *m* ; (*Rad, TV = broadcast*) émission *f* (*on* sur ; *about* au sujet de) ; *[of course]* emploi *m* du temps ; (*= station*) (*Rad*) poste *m* ; (*TV*) chaîne *f* ◆ **what's the ~ for today?** (*during course etc*) quel est l'emploi du temps aujourd'hui ? ; (*fig*) qu'est-ce qu'on fait aujourd'hui ? ◆ **in the ~ for the day** au programme de la journée ◆ **what's on the ~?** qu'est-ce qu'il y a au programme ? ◆ **details of the morning's ~s** (*Rad, TV*) le programme de la matinée ; → **detoxi(fi)cation, request**

2 (*Comput*) ⇒ **program**

VT 1 *[+ washing machine, video etc]* programmer (*to do sth* pour faire qch) ; (*fig*) *[+ person]* conditionner ◆ **our bodies are ~d to fight disease** notre corps est programmé pour combattre la maladie ◆ **we are genetically ~d for motherhood** nous sommes génétiquement programmées pour être mères ◆ **~d learning** enseignement *m* programmé

2 (*Comput*) ⇒ **program**

COMP **programme editor** **N** (*Rad, TV*) éditorialiste *mf*

programme-maker **N** (*TV, Rad*) réalisateur *m*, -trice *f*

programme music **N** (*NonC*) musique *f* à programme

programme notes **NPL** (*Mus, Theat*) commentaires *mpl* sur le programme

programme seller **N** (*Theat*) vendeur *m*, -euse *f* de programmes

programmer, programer (*US*) /ˈprəʊgræməʳ/ **N** (*= person:* also **computer programmer**) programmeur *m*, -euse *f* ; (*= device*) programmateur *m*

programming /ˈprəʊgræmɪŋ/ **N** 1 (also **computer programming**) programmation *f* 2 (*TV, Rad*) programmation *f* **COMP** *[error, language etc]* de programmation

progress /ˈprəʊgres/ **N** 1 (*NonC: lit, fig*) progrès *m(pl)* ◆ **in the name of ~** au nom du progrès ◆ **you can't stop ~** on n'arrête pas le progrès ◆ **~ was slow** les choses n'avançaient pas vite ◆ **she kept me abreast of the ~ by phone** elle m'a tenu au courant de la progression par téléphone ◆ **the ~ of events** le cours des événements

♦ **to make + progress** ◆ **we made slow ~ through the mud** nous avons avancé lentement dans la boue ◆ **we are making good ~ in our search for a solution** nos travaux pour trouver une solution progressent de manière satisfaisante ◆ **medical research continues to make ~ in the fight against cancer** la recherche médicale continue de progresser *or* d'avancer dans la lutte contre le cancer ◆ **we have made little/no ~** nous n'avons guère fait de progrès/fait aucun progrès ◆ **they made little ~ towards agreement** ils n'ont pas beaucoup progressé *or* avancé dans leur recherche d'un terrain d'entente ◆ **he is making ~** *[student etc]* il fait des progrès, il est en progrès ; *[patient]* son état (de santé) s'améliore

♦ **in progress** ◆ **the meeting is in ~** la réunion est en cours *or* a déjà commencé ◆ **while the meeting was in ~** pendant la réunion ◆ **the work in ~** les travaux en cours ◆ **"silence: exam in progress"** "silence : examen" ◆ **to be in full ~** battre son plein

2 (*†† = journey*) voyage *m* ; → **pilgrim**

VI /prəˈgres/ (*lit, fig*) aller, avancer (*towards* vers) ; *[student etc]* faire des progrès, progresser ; *[patient]* aller mieux ; *[search, investigations, researches, studies etc]* progresser, avancer ◆ **he started off sketching and then ~ed to painting** il a commencé par des croquis puis il a évolué vers la peinture ◆ **she ~ed to a senior position** elle a accédé à un poste à responsabilités ◆ **matters are ~ing slowly** les choses progressent lentement ◆ **as the game ~ed** à mesure que la partie se déroulait ◆ **while the discussions were ~ing** pendant que les discussions se déroulaient ◆ **he checked how his new staff were ~ing** il a regardé comment s'en sortaient les nouvelles recrues ◆ **his disease ~ed quickly** sa maladie faisait de rapides progrès, sa maladie progressait rapidement ◆ **as the evening ~ed ...** à mesure que la soirée avançait ..., au fil de la soirée ... ◆ **life became harder as the war ~ed** la vie devenait de plus en plus difficile à mesure que l'on s'enfonçait dans la guerre

VT (*= advance*) faire progresser

COMP **progress board** **N** tableau *m* de planning

progress chaser **N** responsable *mf* du suivi (d'un projet)

progress chasing **N** suivi *m* (d'un projet)

progress payment **N** (*Fin*) acompte *m* (*versé au prorata de l'avancement des travaux*)

progress report **N** (*gen*) compte *m* rendu (*on* de) ; (*Med*) bulletin *m* de santé ; (*Scol*) bulletin *m* scolaire ; (*Admin*) état *m* périodique, rapport *m* sur l'avancement des travaux ◆ **to make a ~ report on** (*gen*) rendre compte de l'évolution de ; (*Scol: on pupil*) rendre compte des progrès de ; (*Med: on patient*) rendre compte de l'évolution de l'état de santé de ; (*Admin*) dresser un état périodique de

progression /prəˈgreʃən/ **N** (*gen, Math*) progression *f* ◆ **by arithmetical/geometrical ~** selon une progression arithmétique/géométrique ◆ **it's a logical ~** c'est une suite logique

progressive /prəˈgresɪv/ **ADJ** 1 *[movement, taxation, disease, improvement]* progressif ; *[idea, party, person, outlook]* progressiste (*also Pol*) ; *[age]* de *or* du progrès ◆ **in ~ stages** par degrés, par étapes 2 (*Gram, Phon*) progressif **N** 1 (*Pol etc*) progressiste *mf* 2 (*Gram*) temps *m* progressif **COMP** **progressive education** **N** éducation *f* nouvelle

progressively /prəˈgresɪvlɪ/ **ADV** progressivement ◆ **to get** *or* **grow** *or* **become ~ harder/easier** devenir de plus en plus difficile/facile ◆ **the weather was getting ~ worse** le temps allait en empirant ◆ **his health is getting ~ better** sa santé s'améliore de jour en jour

progressiveness /prəˈgresɪvnɪs/ **N** progressivité *f*

progressivity /ˌprəʊgreˈsɪvɪtɪ/ **N** progressivité *f*

prohibit /prəˈhɪbɪt/ **VT** 1 (*= forbid*) interdire, défendre (*sb from doing sth* à qn de faire qch) ; (*Admin, Jur etc*) *[+ weapons, drugs, swearing]* prohiber ◆ **smoking ~ed** défense de fumer ◆ **feeding the animals is ~ed** il est interdit *or* défendu de donner à manger aux animaux ◆ **pedestrians are ~ed from using this bridge** il est interdit aux piétons d'utiliser ce pont, l'usage de ce pont est interdit aux piétons 2 (*= prevent*) empêcher (*sb from doing sth* qn de faire qch) ◆ **my health ~s me from swimming** mon état de santé m'interdit de nager, la natation m'est interdite pour des raisons de santé **COMP** **prohibited substance** **N** substance *f* prohibée

prohibition /ˌprəʊɪˈbɪʃən/ **N** 1 *[of weapons, drugs, swearing etc]* interdiction *f*, prohibition *f* ◆ **there was a strict ~ on speaking Welsh** il était strictement interdit de parler gallois 2 (*US Hist*) ◆ **Prohibition** la prohibition ◆ **during Prohibition** pendant la prohibition **COMP** (*US Hist:* also **Prohibition**) *[laws, party]* prohibitionniste

prohibitionism /ˌprəʊɪˈbɪʃənɪzəm/ **N** prohibitionnisme *m*

prohibitionist /ˌprəʊɪˈbɪʃənɪst/ **ADJ, N** prohibitionniste *mf*

prohibitive /prəˈhɪbɪtɪv/ **ADJ** *[price, tax, laws]* prohibitif

prohibitively /prəˈhɪbɪtɪvlɪ/ **ADV** ◆ **~ expensive** à un prix prohibitif ◆ **internal flights are ~ expensive** le prix des vols intérieurs est prohibitif

prohibitory /prəˈhɪbɪtərɪ/ **ADJ** prohibitif

project /ˈprɒdʒekt/ **N** 1 (*= plan, scheme*) projet *m* (*to do sth, for doing sth* pour faire qch) ; (*= undertaking*) opération *f*, entreprise *f* ; (*Constr*) grands travaux *mpl* ◆ **they are studying the ~ for the new road** ils étudient le projet de construction de la nouvelle route ◆ **the whole ~ will cost 20 million** l'opération *or* le projet coûtera 20 millions en tout

2 (*= study*) étude *f* (*on* de) ; (*Scol*) dossier *m* (*on* sur) ; (*Univ*) mémoire *m* (*on* sur)

3 (*US:* also **housing project**) cité *f*, lotissement *m* ◆ **they live in the ~s** ils habitent dans une cité

VT /prəˈdʒekt/ 1 (*gen, Psych, Math*) projeter ◆ **to ~ o.s.** (*Psych*) se projeter ◆ **he ~ed his feelings of guilt on his wife** il projetait son sentiment de culpabilité sur sa femme ◆ **she ~ed an image of innocence** elle projetait *or* présentait l'image de l'innocence même ◆ **in view of the ~ed contract** étant donné le projet de contrat ◆ **to ~ quantities/costs** *etc* **from sth** prévoir la quantité/le coût *etc* à partir de qch

2 (*= propel*) *[+ object]* propulser ◆ **to ~ one's voice** projeter sa voix

3 (*= cause to jut out*) *[+ part of building etc]* projeter en avant

VI /prəˈdʒekt/ 1 (*= jut out*) faire saillie, saillir ◆ **to ~ over sth** surplomber qch ◆ **to ~ into sth** s'avancer (en saillie) dans qch

[2] *(= show personality)* **how does he ~?** quelle image de lui-même présente-t-il *or* projette-t-il ?

[3] *[actor, singer, speaker]* projeter sa (*or* leur *etc*) voix ◆ **his voice ~s very well** sa voix porte vraiment bien

COMP *[budget]* de l'opération ; *[staff]* travaillant sur le projet

project leader, project manager N *(gen)* chef *m* de projet ; *(Constr)* maître *m* d'œuvre

⚠ **project** is not translated by **projet** when it means schoolwork, or a housing project.

projectile /prəˈdʒektaɪl/ N projectile *m*

projecting /prəˈdʒektɪŋ/ ADJ *[construction]* saillant, en saillie ; *[tooth]* qui avance

projection /prəˈdʒekʃən/ N [1] *(gen)* projection *f* ; *[of rocket]* propulsion *f* ; *(from opinion polls, sample votes etc)* prévisions *fpl* par extrapolation, projections *fpl* [2] *(= overhang)* saillie *f*, ressaut *m* COMP **projection booth, projection room** N *(Cine)* cabine *f* de projection

projectionist /prəˈdʒekʃənɪst/ N projectionniste *mf*

projective /prəˈdʒektɪv/ ADJ projectif

projector /prəˈdʒektəʳ/ N *(Cine etc)* projecteur *m*

prolactin /prəʊˈlæktɪn/ N prolactine *f*

prolapse /ˈprəʊlæps/ *(Med)* N *(gen)* descente *f* d'organe, ptose *f*, prolapsus *m* ; *[of womb]* descente *f* de matrice *or* de l'utérus VI descendre ◆ **a ~d uterus** un utérus prolabé, un prolapsus (de l'utérus)

prole* /prəʊl/ ADJ, N *(esp Brit: pej)* (abbrev of **proletarian**) prolo* *m*

proletarian /ˌprəʊləˈteərɪən/ N prolétaire *mf* ADJ *[class, party]* prolétarien ; *[life, ways, mentality]* de prolétaire

proletarianize /ˌprəʊləˈteərɪənaɪz/ VT prolétariser

proletariat /ˌprəʊləˈteərɪət/ N prolétariat *m*

pro-life /ˌprəʊˈlaɪf/ ADJ contre l'avortement ◆ **the ~ lobby** les adversaires *mpl* de l'avortement

pro-lifer* /ˌprəʊˈlaɪfəʳ/ N adversaire *mf* de l'avortement

proliferate /prəˈlɪfəreɪt/ VI proliférer

proliferation /prəˌlɪfəˈreɪʃən/ N *(gen, Mil)* prolifération *f*

proliferous /prəˈlɪfərəs/ ADJ prolifère

prolific /prəˈlɪfɪk/ ADJ prolifique

prolix /ˈprəʊlɪks/ ADJ *(frm)* prolixe

prolixity /prəʊˈlɪksɪtɪ/ N *(frm)* prolixité *f*

prologue /ˈprəʊlɒg/ N *(Literat etc)* prologue *m* (to de) ; *(fig)* prologue *m* (to à)

prolong /prəˈlɒŋ/ VT prolonger ◆ **I won't ~ the agony** *(fig)* je vais abréger tes souffrances

prolongation /ˌprəʊlɒŋˈgeɪʃən/ N *(in space)* prolongement *m* ; *(in time)* prolongation *f*

prolonged /prəˈlɒŋd/ ADJ prolongé ; *[period]* long (longue *f*) ◆ **~ leave of absence** congé *m* prolongé *or* de longue durée ◆ **~ sick leave** congé *m* de longue maladie ◆ **after a ~ absence** après une longue absence *or* une absence prolongée

PROM N *(Comput)* (abbrev of **Programmable Read Only Memory**) PROM *f*, mémoire *f* morte programmable

prom* /prɒm/ N (abbrev of **promenade**) [1] *(Brit: by sea)* promenade *f*, front *m* de mer

[2] *(Brit)* **~s** *série de concerts de musique classique*

[3] *(US)* bal *m* d'étudiants (*or* de lycéens)

PROM

En Grande-Bretagne, les **proms** (pour « promenade concerts ») sont des concerts de musique classique où une grande partie du public est debout. Les **proms** les plus célèbres sont ceux organisés chaque été au Royal Albert Hall à Londres. Le dernier concert de la saison, appelé « Last Night of the **Proms** », est une grande manifestation mondaine, au cours de laquelle sont interprétés notamment des chants patriotiques. Aux États-Unis, le **prom** est un grand bal organisé dans un lycée ou une université. Le « senior **prom** » des classes de terminale est une soirée particulièrement importante, à laquelle les élèves se rendent en tenue de soirée accompagnés de leur cavalier ou cavalière.

promenade /ˌprɒmɪˈnɑːd/ N [1] *(= walk)* promenade *f* [2] *(= place) (by sea)* promenade *f*, front *m* de mer ; *(in park etc)* avenue *f* ; *(in theatre, hall etc)* promenoir *m* [3] *(US)* → **prom 3** VI *(frm = walk)* se promener VT *(frm) [person]* promener ; *[+ avenue]* se promener le long de COMP **Promenade Concerts** NPL → **prom 2** **promenade deck** N *(Naut)* pont *m* promenade

promenader* /ˌprɒmɪˈnɑːdəʳ/ N *(Brit Mus)* auditeur *m*, -trice *f* d'un "promenade concert" ; → **promenade**

Promethean /prəˈmiːθɪən/ ADJ prométhéen

Prometheus /prəˈmiːθjuːs/ N Prométhée *m*

promethium /prəˈmiːθɪəm/ N prométhéum *m*

prominence /ˈprɒmɪnəns/ N [1] *(lit) [of ridge, structure, nose, feature]* caractère *m* proéminent, proéminence *f (frm)* ; *[of cheekbones]* aspect *m* saillant ; *[of pattern, markings]* aspect *m* frappant ◆ **the ~ of his teeth** ses dents en avant

[2] *(fig)* importance *f* ◆ **to give ~ to sth** accorder de l'importance à qch ◆ **to come** *or* **rise (in)to ~** *[person]* venir occuper le devant de la scène ; *[phenomenon]* prendre de l'importance ◆ **Gough shot to ~ last year** Gough a été propulsé sur le devant de la scène l'année dernière ◆ **to achieve national/international ~** venir occuper le devant de la scène nationale/internationale ◆ **his sudden rise to ~** sa célébrité soudaine ◆ **since the rise to ~ of the environmental movement** depuis que le mouvement écologique a pris de l'importance ◆ **to bring sb (in)to ~** placer qn sur le devant de la scène ◆ **to bring sth (in)to ~** attirer l'attention sur qch ◆ **to be in a position of ~** *(= clearly visible)* être bien en évidence ; *(= important)* occuper une place importante ◆ **a position of ~** *(= important role)* un poste important

[3] *(frm = protuberance)* proéminence *f*, relief *m* ; *(Anat)* protubérance *f*

prominent /ˈprɒmɪnənt/ ADJ *[ridge, structure, nose]* proéminent ; *[cheekbones]* saillant ; *[tooth]* qui avance ; *(fig = striking) [pattern, markings]* frappant ; *[feature]* marquant ; *(fig = outstanding) [person]* important, éminent *before n* ◆ **he is a ~ member of ...** c'est un membre important de ..., c'est un éminent membre de ... ◆ **she is ~ in London literary circles** elle est très en vue dans les cercles littéraires londoniens ◆ **he was very ~ in ..., he played a ~ part in ...** il a joué un rôle important dans ... ◆ **to put sth in a ~ position** mettre qch bien en vue *or* en valeur ◆ **he occupies a ~ position in ...** *(fig)* il occupe une position importante *or* en vue dans ...

prominently /ˈprɒmɪnəntlɪ/ ADV *[displayed, placed, set]* bien en évidence, bien en vue ◆ **the murder was ~ reported in the press** ce meurtre a fait l'objet de nombreux articles dans la presse ◆ **to figure** *or* **feature ~ (in sth)** occuper une place importante (dans qch) ◆ **his name figured** *or* **feature ~ in the case** on a beaucoup entendu parler de lui dans cette affaire, son nom revenait souvent dans cette affaire

promiscuity /ˌprɒmɪsˈkjuːɪtɪ/ N [1] *(pej: sexual)* promiscuité *f* sexuelle [2] *(gen)* promiscuité *f*

promiscuous /prəˈmɪskjʊəs/ ADJ [1] *(pej: in sexual matters) [person]* de mœurs faciles *or* légères ; *[conduct]* immoral, très libre ◆ **he/she is very ~** il/elle change sans arrêt de partenaire, il/elle couche avec n'importe qui [2] *(= disorderly, mixed) [collection, heap]* confus

promiscuously /prəˈmɪskjʊəslɪ/ ADV [1] *(pej) [behave]* immoralement [2] *[heap, collect]* confusément

promiscuousness /prəˈmɪskjʊəsnɪs/ N ⇒ **promiscuity**

promise /ˈprɒmɪs/ N [1] *(= undertaking)* promesse *f* ◆ **of marriage** promesse *f* de mariage ◆ **under (a** *or* **the) ~ of** sous promesse de ◆ **to make sb a ~** faire une promesse à qn *(to do sth* de faire qch) ◆ **is that a ~?** c'est promis ? ◆ **to keep one's ~** tenir sa promesse ◆ **to hold sb to his ~** faire tenir sa promesse à qn, obliger qn à tenir sa promesse ◆ **~s, ~s!** *(dismissively)* oh, on dit ça, on dit ça ! ◆ **to be on a ~*** être sur un coup*

[2] *(= hope, prospect)* promesse(s) *f(pl)*, espérance(s) *f(pl)* ◆ **a young man of great ~** un jeune homme très prometteur, un jeune homme qui promet ◆ **he shows great ~** c'est quelqu'un qui promet, c'est quelqu'un de très prometteur ◆ **it holds out a ~ of peace** cela promet *or* fait espérer la paix

VT [1] promettre *(sth to sb* qch à qn ; *sb to do sth* à qn de faire qch ; *that* que) ◆ **I ~ you!** je vous le promets ! ◆ **"I will help you" she ~d** "je vous aiderai" promit-elle ◆ **I can't ~ anything** je ne peux rien (vous) promettre ◆ **to ~ sb the earth** *or* **the moon** promettre monts et merveilles à qn, promettre la lune à qn ◆ **to ~ o.s. (to do) sth** se promettre (de faire) qch

[2] *(= give outlook of)* promettre, annoncer ◆ **they've ~d us rain for tomorrow** on nous a promis *or* annoncé de la pluie pour demain ◆ **it ~d to be another scorching day** une nouvelle journée très chaude s'annonçait, la journée promettait encore d'être très chaude ◆ **this ~s to be difficult** ça promet d'être *or* ça s'annonce difficile

[3] *(= assure)* assurer ◆ **he did say so, I ~ you** il l'a vraiment dit, je vous assure

VI [1] *(= pledge)* promettre ◆ **I ~!** je vous le promets ! ◆ **(will you) ~?** (c'est) promis ?, juré ? ◆ **I can't ~ but I'll do my best** je ne (vous) promets rien mais je ferai de mon mieux

[2] *(in outlook)* **to ~ well** *[situation, event]* être plein de promesses, être prometteur ; *[crop, business]* s'annoncer bien ; *[first book]* promettre, être prometteur ◆ **this doesn't ~ well** ce n'est guère prometteur, ça ne s'annonce pas bien

promised /ˈprɒmɪst/ ADJ promis ◆ **the Promised Land** la Terre Promise

promising /ˈprɒmɪsɪŋ/ ADJ [1] *(= encouraging) [situation, sign]* prometteur ; *(Comm) [market]* porteur ◆ **the future is ~** l'avenir s'annonce bien ◆ **that's ~** c'est prometteur ; *(iro)* ça promet ! *(iro)* ◆ **it doesn't look very ~** ça ne semble guère prometteur, ça ne se présente *or* s'annonce pas bien [2] *(= full of promise) [person]* prometteur ◆ **we have two ~ candidates** nous avons deux candidats prometteurs ◆ **he is a ~ pianist** c'est un pianiste d'avenir

promisingly /ˈprɒmɪsɪŋlɪ/ ADV d'une façon prometteuse ◆ **it began quite ~** tout s'annonçait bien, c'était bien parti ◆ **it's going quite ~** c'est prometteur, ça marche bien

promissory note /ˈprɒmɪsərɪˌnəʊt/ N billet *m* à ordre

promo* /ˈprəʊməʊ/ **N** (pl **promos**) [1] *(Comm = promotional material)* matériel *m* promotionnel [2] *(US Comm)* (abbrev of **promotion**) promotion *f*

promontory /ˈprɒməntrɪ/ **N** promontoire *m*

promote /prəˈməʊt/ **VT** [1] *[+ person]* promouvoir *(to à)* ◆ **to be ~d** être promu, monter en grade ◆ **he was ~d (to) colonel** *or* **to the rank of colonel** il a été promu (au grade de) colonel ◆ **they've been ~d to the first division** *(Ftbl etc)* ils sont montés en première division

[2] *(= encourage, publicize) [+ plan, product, firm, campaign, cooperation]* promouvoir ; *[+ trade]* promouvoir, encourager ; *[+ cause, idea, language]* défendre ; *(Parl) [+ bill]* présenter ◆ **the government's efforts to ~ economic cooperation** les efforts du gouvernement pour promouvoir la coopération économique ◆ **you don't have to sacrifice the environment to ~ economic growth** il n'est pas nécessaire de sacrifier l'environnement pour encourager *or* favoriser la croissance économique ◆ **our society actively ~s alcoholism** notre société encourage l'alcoolisme

promoter /prəˈməʊtəʳ/ **N** *[of sport]* organisateur *m*, -trice *f* ; *(Comm) [of product]* promoteur *m* de vente ; *[of business, company]* fondateur *m*, -trice *f* ; *(Mus)* agent *m*, impresario *m* ◆ **he was a great ~ of American music** *(= popularizer)* il a beaucoup contribué à faire connaître la musique américaine ◆ **Germany sees itself as a ~ of peace** l'Allemagne se considère comme le défenseur de la paix

promotion /prəˈməʊʃən/ **N** [1] *(in job etc)* promotion *f*, avancement *m* ◆ **to get ~** être promu, avoir une promotion

[2] *(Sport: to higher division)* accession *f*, passage *m* ◆ **the ~ of Westerhill Wanderers to the first division** l'accession *or* le passage de l'équipe des Westerhill Wanderers en première division

[3] *(Comm)* promotion *f*

[4] *(US Scol)* passage *m* de classe

[5] *(NonC = encouragement, publicity) [of plan, product, firm, campaign]* promotion *f* ; *[of cause, idea]* défense *f* ; *(Parl) [of bill]* présentation *f* ◆ **their priority is the ~ of healthy eating habits/economic cooperation** ils ont pour priorité d'encourager les gens à se nourrir sainement/de promouvoir la coopération économique ◆ **she devoted her life to the ~ of the Breton language** elle a consacré sa vie à la défense de la langue bretonne

COMP **promotion board** **N** comité *m* de promotion

promotion campaign **N** campagne *f* publicitaire

promotion prospects **NPL** possibilités *fpl* de promotion *or* d'avancement

promotions director, promotions manager **N** directeur *m*, -trice *f* des promotions

promotional /prəˈməʊʃənl/ **ADJ** *(Comm)* promotionnel, publicitaire

prompt /prɒmpt/ **ADJ** [1] *(= speedy) [action]* rapide, prompt ; *[delivery, reply, service]* rapide ◆ **~ payment** paiement *m* rapide ; *(Comm)* paiement *m* dans les délais ◆ **they were ~ to offer their services** ils ont été prompts à offrir leurs services, ils ont offert leurs services sans tarder

[2] *(= punctual)* ponctuel, à l'heure

ADV ponctuellement ◆ **at 6 o'clock ~** à 6 heures pile *or* tapantes *or* sonnantes ◆ **I want it on 6 May ~** je le veux le 6 mai sans faute *or* au plus tard

VT [1] *[+ person]* pousser, inciter *(to do sth* à faire qch) ; *[+ protest, reaction]* provoquer, susciter ◆ **I felt ~ed to protest** cela m'a incité à protester, je me suis senti obligé de protester ◆ **he was ~ed by a desire to see justice done** il était animé *or* poussé par un désir de voir la justice triompher ◆ **it ~s the thought that ...** cela incite à penser que ..., cela vous fait penser que ... ◆ **to ~ a great deal of interest** susciter beaucoup d'intérêt ◆ **a feeling of regret ~ed by the sight of ...** un sentiment de regret provoqué *or* suscité par la vue de ...

[2] *(Theat)* souffler à

N [1] *(Theat)* **to give sb a ~** souffler une réplique à qn

[2] *(Comput)* (message *m* de) guidage *m* ◆ **at the ~** à l'apparition du message de guidage

COMP **prompt box** **N** *(Theat)* trou *m* du souffleur

prompt side **N** *(Theat) (Brit)* côté *m* cour ; *(US)* côté *m* jardin ◆ **off ~ side** *(Brit)* côté jardin ; *(US)* côté cour

prompter /ˈprɒmptəʳ/ **N** *(Theat)* souffleur *m*, -euse *f*

prompting /ˈprɒmptɪŋ/ **N** incitation *f* ◆ **he did it at my ~** il l'a fait à mon instigation ◆ **he did it without (any) ~** il l'a fait de son propre chef

promptitude /ˈprɒmptɪtjuːd/ **N** *(frm)* [1] *(= speed)* promptitude *f*, empressement *m* *(in doing sth* à faire qch) [2] *(= punctuality)* ponctualité *f*

promptly /ˈprɒmptlɪ/ **ADV** [1] *(= without delay)* rapidement ◆ **to pay ~** payer dans les délais [2] *(= punctually)* à l'heure ◆ **he arrived ~ at three** il est arrivé à trois heures précises [3] *(= thereupon)* aussitôt, aussi sec* ◆ **she sat down and ~ fell asleep** elle s'est assise et s'est aussitôt endormie

promptness /ˈprɒmptnɪs/ **N** ⇒ **promptitude**

promulgate /ˈprɒməlgeɪt/ **VT** *(frm) [+ law, decree, constitution]* promulguer ; *[+ idea, doctrine, creed]* répandre, disséminer

promulgation /ˌprɒməlˈgeɪʃən/ **N** *(frm) [of law, decree, constitution]* promulgation *f* ; *[of idea, doctrine, creed]* diffusion *f*, dissémination *f*

prone /prəʊn/ **ADJ** [1] *(= liable)* enclin, sujet *(to sth* à qch ; *to do sth* à faire qch) ; ◆ **to be injury/accident ~** avoir tendance à se blesser/à avoir des accidents [2] *(= face down)* (couché) sur le ventre, étendu face contre terre

proneness /ˈprəʊnnɪs/ **N** tendance *f*, prédisposition *f* *(to sth* à qch ; *to do sth* à faire qch)

prong /prɒŋ/ **N** [1] *[of fork]* dent *f* ; *[of antler]* pointe *f* [2] *[of policy, strategy]* front *m*

pronged /prɒŋd/ **ADJ** à dents

-pronged /prɒŋd/ **ADJ** *(in compounds)* ◆ **three-pronged** *[fork]* à trois dents ; *(Mil etc) [attack, advance]* sur trois fronts, triple

pronominal /prəʊˈnɒmɪnl/ **ADJ** pronominal

pronoun /ˈprəʊnaʊn/ **N** pronom *m*

pronounce /prəˈnaʊns/ **VT** [1] *[+ letter, word]* prononcer ◆ **how is it ~d?** comment ça se prononce ? ◆ **the "k" in "knee" is not ~d** on ne prononce pas le "k" dans "knee", le "k" dans "knee" est muet

[2] *(= declare)* déclarer, prononcer *(that que)* ◆ **to ~ sentence** *(Jur)* prononcer la sentence ◆ **they ~d him unfit to drive** ils l'ont déclaré inapte à conduire ◆ **he was ~d dead** ils l'ont déclaré mort ◆ **he ~d himself in favour of the suggestion** il s'est prononcé *or* il s'est déclaré en faveur de la suggestion ◆ **"I'm not going!" she ~d (to them)** "je n'y vais pas !" (leur) déclara-t-elle ◆ **"I now pronounce you man and wife"** "je vous déclare unis par les liens du mariage"

VI se prononcer *(on* sur ; *for* en faveur de ; *against* contre) ; *(Jur)* prononcer *(for* en faveur de ; *against* contre) rendre un arrêt

pronounceable /prəˈnaʊnsəbl/ **ADJ** prononçable

pronounced /prəˈnaʊnst/ **ADJ** prononcé, marqué

pronouncement /prəˈnaʊnsmənt/ **N** déclaration *f*

pronto* /ˈprɒntəʊ/ **ADV** illico*

pronunciation /prəˌnʌnsɪˈeɪʃən/ **N** prononciation *f*

proof /pruːf/ **N** [1] *(= evidence: gen, Jur, Math etc)* preuve *f* ◆ **by way of ~** en guise de preuve, pour preuve ◆ **as (a) ~ of, in ~ of** pour preuve de ◆ **I've got ~ that he did it** j'ai la preuve *or* je peux prouver qu'il l'a fait ◆ **it is ~ that he is honest** c'est la preuve qu'il est honnête ◆ **he showed** *or* **gave ~ of great courage** il a fait preuve *or* il a témoigné de beaucoup de courage ◆ **to be living ~ of sth** être la preuve vivante de qch ◆ **to be living ~ that ...** être la preuve vivante que ... ◆ **the burden of ~ lies with the prosecution** *(Jur)* la charge de la preuve incombe au ministère public ; → **positive**

[2] *(= test)* épreuve *f* ◆ **to put sth/sb to the ~** mettre qch/qn à l'épreuve, éprouver qch/qn ◆ **the ~ of the pudding is in the eating** *(Prov)* c'est à l'usage que l'on peut juger de la qualité d'une chose

[3] *[of book, pamphlet, engraving, photograph]* épreuve *f* ◆ **to read** *or* **correct the ~s** corriger les épreuves ◆ **to pass the ~s** donner le bon à tirer ; → **galley, page¹**

[4] *(of alcohol)* teneur *f* en alcool ◆ **this whisky is 70° ~** ≈ ce whisky titre 40° d'alcool ◆ **under/over ~** moins de/plus de la teneur normale *or* exigée en alcool

ADJ ◆ **~ against** *[bullets, time, wear, erosion]* à l'épreuve de ; *[temptation, suggestion]* insensible à

VT [1] *[+ fabric, anorak, tent]* imperméabiliser

[2] *(Typ etc)* corriger les épreuves de

COMP **proof of identity** **N** *(NonC)* papiers *mpl* or pièce(s) *f(pl)* d'identité

proof of postage **N** justificatif *m* d'expédition

proof of purchase **N** justificatif *m* d'achat

proof sheets **NPL** épreuves *fpl*

proof spirit **N** *(Brit)* alcool *m* à 57° ; *(US)* alcool *m* à 60°

proof stage **N** ◆ **at ~ stage** au stade des épreuves

...proof /pruːf/ **ADJ** *(in compounds)* à l'épreuve de ; → **bulletproof, foolproof**

proofread /ˈpruːfriːd/ **VT** corriger les épreuves de

proofreader /ˈpruːfˌriːdəʳ/ **N** correcteur *m*, -trice *f* d'épreuves *or* d'imprimerie

proofreading /ˈpruːfˌriːdɪŋ/ **N** correction *f* des épreuves

prop¹ /prɒp/ **N** [1] support *m* ; *(for wall, in mine, tunnel etc)* étai *m* ; *(for clothes-line)* perche *f* ; *(for vines, hops etc)* échalas *m* ; *(for beans, peas)* rame *f* ; *(for seedlings)* tuteur *m* ; *(fig)* soutien *m*, appui *m* *(to, for de)* ◆ **his presence was a great ~ to her morale** elle trouvait beaucoup de réconfort dans sa présence, sa présence lui était d'un grand réconfort (moral) ◆ **do you ever use alcohol as a ~?** vous arrive-t-il de boire (de l'alcool) pour vous donner du courage ?

[2] *(Rugby)* **~ (forward)** pilier *m*

VT [1] (also **prop up**) *(= lean) [+ ladder, cycle]* appuyer *(against* contre) ; *(= support, shore up) [+ tunnel, wall, building]* étayer ; *[+ clothes-line, lid]* caler ; *[+ vine, hops]* échalasser ; *[+ beans, peas]* mettre une rame à ; *[+ seedlings]* mettre un tuteur à ; *(fig) [+ régime]* maintenir ; *[+ business, company]* soutenir, renflouer ; *[+ organization]* soutenir, patronner ; *(Fin) [+ the pound]* venir au secours de ◆ **to ~ o.s. (up) against** se caler contre, s'adosser à

[2] ◆ **he ~ped the door open with a book** il a maintenu la porte ouverte avec un livre

prop² /prɒp/ **N** *(Theat)* (abbrev of **property**) accessoire *m*

prop³* /prɒp/ N (Aviat) ⇒ **propeller** COMP **prop shaft*** N ⇒ **propeller shaft** ; → **propeller**

prop. (Comm) abbrev of **proprietor**

propaganda /ˌprɒpəˈgændə/ N propagande *f* COMP *[leaflet, campaign]* de propagande

propagandist /ˌprɒpəˈgændɪst/ ADJ, N propagandiste *mf*

propagandize /ˌprɒpəˈgændaɪz/ VI faire de la propagande VT *[+ doctrine]* faire de la propagande pour ; *[+ person]* soumettre à la propagande, faire de la propagande à

propagate /ˈprɒpəgeɪt/ (lit, fig) VT propager VI se propager

propagation /ˌprɒpəˈgeɪʃən/ N propagation *f*

propagator /ˈprɒpəgeɪtəʳ/ N (for plants) germoir *m*

propane /ˈprəʊpeɪn/ N propane *m*

propel /prəˈpel/ VT 1 *[+ vehicle, boat, machine]* propulser, faire avancer 2 (= push) pousser ◆ **to ~ sth/sb along** faire avancer qch/qn (en le poussant) ◆ **they ~led him into the room** ils l'ont poussé dans la pièce ; *(more violently)* ils l'ont propulsé dans la pièce COMP **propelling pencil** N (Brit) portemine *m*

propellant /prəˈpelənt/ N *[of rocket]* propergol *m*, combustible *m* (pour fusée) ; *[of aerosol]* propulseur *m*

propellent /prəˈpelənt/ ADJ propulseur, propulsif N ⇒ **propellant**

propeller /prəˈpeləʳ/ N *[of plane, ship]* hélice *f* COMP **propeller shaft** N *[of car]* arbre *m* de transmission ; *[of boat, plane]* arbre *m* d'hélice

propensity /prəˈpensɪtɪ/ N propension *f*, tendance *f* (naturelle) *(to, towards, for* à ; *to do sth, for doing sth* à faire qch)

proper /ˈprɒpəʳ/ ADJ 1 (= suitable) convenable, adéquat ; (= correct) correct ; (= appropriate) approprié ◆ **you'll have to put the lid on the ~ way** il faut que vous mettiez *subj* le couvercle comme il faut ◆ **you'll have to apply for it in the ~ way** il faudra faire votre demande dans les règles ◆ **the ~ dress for the occasion** la tenue de rigueur pour l'occasion ◆ **the ~ spelling** l'orthographe *f* correcte ◆ **in the ~ sense of the word** au sens propre du mot ◆ **if you had come at the ~ time** si vous étiez venu à la bonne heure *or* à l'heure dite ◆ **the staff were not given ~ training** le personnel n'a pas reçu une formation appropriée *or* adéquate ◆ **I regret not having had a ~ education** je regrette de ne pas avoir eu une véritable éducation *or* suivi de véritables études ◆ **you must go through the ~ channels** (Admin etc) vous devez passer par la filière officielle ◆ **the ~ reply would have been "no"** la réponse qui aurait convenu c'est "non" ◆ **to make a ~ job of sth** bien réussir qch *(also iro)* ◆ **to do the ~ thing by sb** bien agir *or* agir honorablement envers qn ◆ **do as you think ~** faites ce qui vous semble bon, faites comme bon vous semblera ◆ **if you think it ~ to do so** si vous jugez convenable d'agir ainsi ◆ **in a manner ~ to his position** ainsi que l'exigeait sa position ◆ **the qualities which are ~ to this substance** les qualités propres à *or* typiques de cette substance ; → **right**

2 (= authentic) véritable ; (after n) (= strictly speaking) proprement dit, même ◆ **he's not a ~ electrician** ce n'est pas un véritable électricien ◆ **I've never had a ~ job** je n'ai jamais eu un vrai *or* véritable travail ◆ **I'm not a ~ Londoner** *or* **a Londoner ~** je ne suis pas à proprement parler londonien ◆ **outside Paris ~** en dehors de Paris même *or* de Paris proprement dit

3 (= seemly) *[person]* comme il faut*, convenable ; *[book, behaviour]* convenable, correct ◆ **it isn't ~ to do that** cela ne se fait pas ◆ **I don't think it would be ~ for me to comment** je ne pense pas qu'il serait convenable que je fasse des commentaires ; → **prim**

4 (* † = real, total) **he's a ~ fool** c'est un imbécile fini ◆ **I felt a ~ idiot** je me suis senti vraiment idiot ◆ **he's a ~ gentleman** c'est un monsieur très comme il faut*, c'est un vrai gentleman ◆ **he made a ~ mess of it** il (en) a fait un beau gâchis ◆ **it's a ~ mess in there!** c'est la pagaille complète* là-dedans !

ADV 1 ‡ *[behave, talk]* comme il faut

2 (dial) vraiment, très ◆ **he did it ~ quick** il l'a fait vraiment très vite ◆ **it's ~ cruel!** qu'est-ce que c'est cruel ! * ◆ **he's ~ poorly** il n'est vraiment pas bien, il est vraiment malade

N (Rel) (also **Proper**) propre *m*

COMP **proper fraction** N (Math) fraction *f* inférieure à l'unité

proper name, proper noun N (Gram) nom *m* propre

proper psalm N (Rel) psaume *m* du jour

properly /ˈprɒpəlɪ/ LANGUAGE IN USE 26.3 ADV 1 (= correctly) *[eat, behave, dress]* correctement ; (= in a seemly way) convenablement, comme il faut ◆ **he didn't do it ~** il ne l'a pas fait comme il le fallait ◆ **~ speaking** à proprement parler ◆ **he very ~ refused** il a refusé à juste titre 2 (* = completely) vraiment, drôlement* ◆ **to be ~ ashamed** avoir vraiment *or* drôlement* honte ◆ **we were ~ beaten** nous avons été battus à plate(s) couture(s)

propertied /ˈprɒpətɪd/ ADJ possédant

property /ˈprɒpətɪ/ N 1 (NonC = possessions) objets *mpl*, biens *mpl* ◆ **is this your ~?** est-ce que cela vous appartient ?, est-ce à vous ? ◆ **it is the ~ of ...** cela appartient à ..., c'est la propriété de ... ◆ **personal ~ must not be left in the cloakroom** il ne faut pas laisser d'effets personnels dans le vestiaire ◆ **personal ~** (Jur) biens *mpl* personnels *or* mobiliers ◆ **government/company ~** propriété *f* du gouvernement/de l'entreprise ◆ **it is common ~** (lit) c'est la propriété de tous, ce sont des biens communs ◆ **it is common ~ that ...** (fig) chacun sait que ..., il est de notoriété publique que ... ◆ **a man/woman of ~** un homme/une femme qui a du bien *or* des biens ; → **lost, real**

2 (NonC = estate) propriété *f* ; (= lands) terres *fpl* ; (= buildings) biens *mpl* immobiliers ◆ **he has** *or* **owns ~ in Ireland** il a des terres (*or* des biens immobiliers) en Irlande, il est propriétaire en Irlande ◆ **get off my ~** décampez de ma propriété *or* de mes terres

3 (= house etc) propriété *f* ◆ **a fine ~ with views over the lake** une belle propriété avec vue sur le lac

4 (Chem, Phys etc = quality) propriété *f* ◆ **this plant has healing properties** cette plante a des propriétés *or* des vertus thérapeutiques

5 (Theat) accessoire *m*

COMP **property centre** N (Brit) ≃ agence *f* immobilière

property developer N promoteur *m* immobilier

property insurance N assurance *f* sur le capital immobilier

property law N droit *m* immobilier

property man N (pl **property men**) (Theat) accessoiriste *m*

property market, property mart N marché *m* immobilier

property mistress N (Theat) accessoiriste *f*

property owner N propriétaire *m* foncier

property settlement N (US Jur) répartition *f* des biens (en cas de divorce)

property speculation N spéculation *f* immobilière

property speculator N spéculateur *m* immobilier

property tax N impôt *m* foncier

prophecy /ˈprɒfɪsɪ/ N prophétie *f*

prophesy /ˈprɒfɪsaɪ/ VT prédire *(that* que) ; *[+ event]* prédire, prophétiser VI prophétiser, faire des prophéties

prophet /ˈprɒfɪt/ N prophète *m* ◆ **the Prophet Samuel** *etc* le prophète Samuel *etc* ◆ **The Prophets** (Bible) les (livres des) Prophètes ◆ **a ~ of doom** (fig) un prophète de malheur

prophetess /ˈprɒfɪtɪs/ N prophétesse *f*

prophetic(al) /prəˈfetɪk(əl)/ ADJ prophétique

prophetically /prəˈfetɪkəlɪ/ ADV *[say, write]* prophétiquement ◆ **"sooner than you think", he commented ~** "plus tôt que tu ne le penses", dit-il prophétiquement

prophylactic /ˌprɒfɪˈlæktɪk/ ADJ prophylactique N prophylactique *m* ; (= contraceptive) préservatif *m*

prophylaxis /ˌprɒfɪˈlæksɪs/ N prophylaxie *f*

propinquity /prəˈpɪŋkwɪtɪ/ N (frm) (in time, space) proximité *f* ; (in relationship) parenté *f* proche, consanguinité *f* ; *[of ideas etc]* ressemblance *f*, affinité *f*

propitiate /prəˈpɪʃɪeɪt/ VT *[+ person, the gods]* se concilier

propitiation /prəˌpɪʃɪˈeɪʃən/ N propitiation *f*

propitiatory /prəˈpɪʃɪətərɪ/ ADJ propitiatoire

propitious /prəˈpɪʃəs/ ADJ propice, favorable (to à)

propitiously /prəˈpɪʃəslɪ/ ADV d'une manière propice, favorablement

proponent /prəˈpəʊnənt/ N partisan(e) *m(f)*, adepte *mf* (of de)

proportion /prəˈpɔːʃən/ N 1 proportion *f* ◆ **the ~ of men to women** la proportion *or* le pourcentage d'hommes par rapport aux femmes ◆ **he has no sense of ~** il n'a pas le sens des proportions

◆ **in + proportion** ◆ **add milk in ~ to the weight of flour** ajoutez du lait proportionnellement au poids de la farine ◆ **her weight is not in ~ to her height** son poids n'est pas proportionné à sa taille ◆ **contributions in ~ to one's earnings** contributions au prorata de *or* en proportion de ses revenus ◆ **in ~ to what she earns, what she gives is enormous** en proportion de ce qu'elle gagne, ce qu'elle donne est énorme ◆ **in due ~** selon une proportion équitable *or* une juste proportion ◆ **to be in direct/inverse ~ to sth** être directement/inversement proportionnel à qch ◆ **to see sth in ~** (fig) relativiser qch ◆ **let's get things in ~** ne dramatisons pas ◆ **in ~ as ...** à mesure que ... ◆ **in ~ with ...** proportionnellement à ...

◆ **out of (all) proportion** hors de (toute) proportion ◆ **out of ~ to** hors de proportion avec, disproportionné à *or* avec ◆ **he's got it out of ~** *[artist]* il n'a pas respecté les proportions, c'est mal proportionné ; *(fig)* il a exagéré, c'est hors de proportion

2 (= part) part *f*, partie *f* ◆ **in equal ~s** à parts égales ◆ **a certain ~ of the staff** une certaine partie *or* un certain pourcentage du personnel ◆ **what ~ is rented?** quel est le pourcentage de ce qui est loué ? ◆ **a high ~ of women** une proportion élevée de femmes

NPL **proportions** (= size) proportions *fpl*, dimensions *fpl*

VT proportionner (to à) ◆ **well-~ed** bien proportionné

proportional /prəˈpɔːʃənl/ ADJ proportionnel, proportionné (to à) COMP **proportional representation** N (Pol) représentation *f* proportionnelle

proportionality /prəˌpɔːʃəˈnælɪtɪ/ N (frm) proportionnalité *f* ◆ **there is a need for ~ in sentencing** il faut que la peine soit proportionnée à la gravité du crime

proportionally /prəˈpɔːʃnəlɪ/ ADV proportionnellement ◆ **men have ~ larger feet than women** proportionnellement, les hommes ont les pieds plus grands que les femmes

proportionate ADJ /prəˈpɔːʃənɪt/ ⇒ **proportional adj** VT /prəˈpɔːʃəˌneɪt/ ⇒ **proportion vt**

proportionately /prəˈpɔːʃnɪtlɪ/ ADV ⇒ **proportionally**

proposal /prəˈpəʊzl/ N 1 *(= offer)* proposition *f*, offre *f* ; *[of marriage]* demande *f* en mariage, offre *f* de mariage 2 *(= plan)* projet *m*, plan *m* *(for sth de or pour qch ; to do sth pour faire qch)* ; *(= suggestion)* proposition *f*, suggestion *f (to do sth de faire qch)* ◆ **~s for the amendment of this treaty** *(Jur)* projet *m* tendant à la révision du présent traité

propose /prəˈpəʊz/ VT 1 *(= suggest)* proposer, suggérer *(sth to sb* qch à qn ; *doing sth* de faire qch ; *that* que + *subj)* ; *[+ measures, plan, motion, course, candidate]* proposer ; *[+ toast]* porter ; *[+ candidate]* proposer ◆ **to ~ sb's health** porter un toast à la santé de qn ◆ **to ~ marriage to sb** faire sa demande à qn, demander qn en mariage ◆ **he ~d Smith as** *or* **for chairman** il a proposé Smith pour la présidence 2 *(= have in mind)* **to ~ to do sth** *or* **doing sth** se proposer *or* avoir l'intention de faire qch, penser *or* compter faire qch VI *(= offer marriage)* faire une demande en mariage *(to sb* à qn)

proposed /prəˈpəʊzd/ ADJ proposé ◆ **your ~ solution** la solution que vous avez proposée ◆ **a ~ nature reserve/housing scheme** un projet de réserve naturelle/de cité

proposer /prəˈpəʊzəʳ/ N *(Admin, Parl etc)* auteur *m* de la proposition ; *(for club membership etc)* parrain *m*, marraine *f*

proposition /ˌprɒpəˈzɪʃən/ N 1 *(gen = statement, offer)* proposition *f* 2 *(= affair, enterprise)* **that's quite another ~** *or* **a different ~** ça c'est une tout autre affaire ◆ **the journey alone is quite a ~** *or* **is a big ~** le voyage n'est déjà pas une mince affaire *or* une partie de plaisir ◆ **it's a tough ~** c'est ardu, ça présente de grandes difficultés ◆ **he's a tough ~** * il est coriace, il n'est pas commode ; → **economic, paying** 3 *(pej: immoral)* proposition *f* malhonnête VT faire des propositions (malhonnêtes) à

propound /prəˈpaʊnd/ VT *(= put up) [+ theory, idea]* avancer, proposer ; *[+ problem, question]* poser ; *(= explain, develop) [+ programme]* exposer

proprietary /prəˈpraɪətərɪ/ ADJ 1 *(Comm) [article]* de marque déposée 2 *[duties etc]* de propriétaire 3 *(= possessive, protective) [behaviour, attitude]* possessif

COMP **proprietary brand** N (produit *m* de) marque *f* déposée

proprietary colony N *(US Hist) colonie accordée par la Couronne à une personne en pleine propriété*

proprietary medicine N spécialité *f* pharmaceutique

proprietary name N marque *f* déposée

proprietary rights NPL droit *m* de propriété

proprietor /prəˈpraɪətəʳ/ N propriétaire *m*

proprietorial /prəˌpraɪəˈtɔːrɪəl/ ADJ *[rights, duties]* de propriétaire ; *[behaviour, attitude]* possessif

proprietorship /prəˈpraɪətəʃɪp/ N *(= right)* droit *m* de propriété ◆ **under his ~** quand il en était (*or* sera) le propriétaire, lui (étant) propriétaire

proprietress /prəˈpraɪətrɪs/, **proprietrix** /prəˈpraɪətrɪks/ N propriétaire *f*

propriety /prəˈpraɪətɪ/ N 1 *(= decency)* **proprieties** bienséances *fpl*, convenances *fpl* ◆ **to observe the proprieties** respecter *or* observer les bienséances *or* les convenances 2 *(NonC = appropriateness, correctness etc) [of phrase, expression]* justesse *f*, correction *f* ◆ **~ of behaviour** *or* **conduct** comportement *m* bienséant

propulsion /prəˈpʌlʃən/ N propulsion *f*

propulsive /prəˈpʌlsɪv/ ADJ *[energy]* propulsif ; *[music, rhythm]* entraînant

pro rata /ˈprəʊˈrɑːtə/ ADV au prorata ◆ **salary £20,000 ~** salaire au prorata du temps de travail (20 000 livres pour un plein temps) ADJ proportionnel

prorate /ˈprəʊreɪt/ VT *(US)* distribuer au prorata

prorogation /ˌprəʊrəˈgeɪʃən/ N prorogation *f*

prorogue /prəˈrəʊg/ VT *(esp Parl)* proroger

prosaic /prəʊˈzeɪɪk/ ADJ *(= banal)* prosaïque *(liter)*, commun

prosaically /prəʊˈzeɪɪkəlɪ/ ADV prosaïquement *(liter)*, communément ◆ **more ~ known as ...** plus communément connu sous le nom de ...

proscenium /prəʊˈsiːnɪəm/ N (pl **prosceniums** *or* **proscenia** /prəʊˈsiːnɪə/) proscenium *m*, avant-scène *f* COMP **proscenium arch** N *(Theat)* arc *m* de scène ; *(imitating curtains)* manteau *m* d'Arlequin

proscribe /prəʊˈskraɪb/ VT proscrire

proscription /prəʊˈskrɪpʃən/ N proscription *f*

prose /prəʊz/ N 1 *(NonC: Literat)* prose *f* ◆ **in ~** en prose 2 *(Scol, Univ:* also **prose translation**) thème *m*

COMP *[poem, comedy]* en prose

prose writer N prosateur *m*

prosecute /ˈprɒsɪkjuːt/ VT 1 *(Jur)* poursuivre (en justice), engager des poursuites (judiciaires) contre ◆ **he was ~d for speeding** il a été poursuivi pour excès de vitesse ; → **trespasser** 2 *(frm = carry on) [+ enquiry, research, war]* poursuivre VI 1 *(= take legal action)* engager des poursuites judiciaires ◆ **"we always prosecute"** "tout délit donnera lieu à des poursuites" 2 *[lawyer]* **Mr Paul Lambotte, prosecuting, pointed out that ...** Me Paul Lambotte, représentant la partie plaignante, a fait remarquer que ... ; *(in higher court)* Me Paul Lambotte, représentant le ministère public *or* l'accusation, a fait remarquer que ... ; see also **prosecuting**

prosecuting /ˈprɒsɪkjuːtɪŋ/ ADJ *(Jur)* ◆ **to appear as ~ counsel** représenter le ministère public COMP **prosecuting attorney** N avocat *m* général

prosecution /ˌprɒsɪˈkjuːʃən/ N 1 *(Jur = act of prosecuting)* poursuites *fpl* (judiciaires) ◆ **to bring a ~ against sb** engager des poursuites (judiciaires) contre qn ◆ **to take out a private ~ (against sb)** engager des poursuites (contre qn) à titre privé ◆ **there have been seven ~s in the last three years** il y a eu sept actions en justice au cours des trois dernières années ; → **crown, director**

2 *(Jur = side)* ◆ **the ~** *(in civil case)* la partie plaignante ; *(in criminal case)* l'accusation *f* ◆ **witness for the ~** témoin *m* à charge ◆ **to give evidence for the ~** être témoin à charge ◆ **to appear as counsel for the ~** *(in civil case)* représenter la partie plaignante ; *(in criminal case)* représenter le ministère public *or* l'accusation ◆ **Giles Harrison, for the ~, told the jury that ...** *(in civil case)* Giles Harrison, représentant la partie plaignante, a déclaré au jury que ... ; *(in criminal case)* Giles Harrison, représentant le ministère public *or* l'accusation, a déclaré au jury que ...

3 *(frm = furtherance) [of enquiry, research, war]* poursuite *f* ◆ **in the ~ of my duties** dans l'exercice de mes fonctions

prosecutor /ˈprɒsɪkjuːtəʳ/ N plaignant *m* ; (also **public prosecutor**) procureur *m* (de la République), ministère *m* public

proselyte /ˈprɒsɪlaɪt/ N prosélyte *mf* VTI *(US)* ⇒ **proselytize**

proselytism /ˈprɒsɪlɪtɪzəm/ N prosélytisme *m*

proselytize /ˈprɒsɪlɪtaɪz/ VI faire du prosélytisme VT *[+ person]* convertir, faire un(e) prosélyte de

prosodic /prəˈsɒdɪk/ ADJ prosodique ◆ **~ feature** *(Phon)* trait *m* prosodique

prosody /ˈprɒsədɪ/ N prosodie *f*

prospect /ˈprɒspekt/ N 1 *(= view)* vue *f*, perspective *f (of, from* de) ; *(fig) (= outlook)* perspective *f* ; *(= future)* (perspectives *fpl* d')avenir *m* ; *(= hope)* espoir *m* ◆ **this ~ cheered him up** cette perspective l'a réjoui ◆ **what are his ~s?** quelles sont ses perspectives d'avenir ? ◆ **he has good ~s** il a de l'avenir ◆ **he has no ~s** il n'a aucun avenir ◆ **the job has no ~s** c'est un emploi sans avenir ◆ **to improve one's career ~s** améliorer ses chances de promotion *or* d'avancement

◆ **in prospect** ◆ **to have sth in ~** avoir qch en perspective *or* en vue ◆ **the events in ~** les événements *mpl* en perspective

◆ **prospects for** ◆ **the ~s for the harvest are good/poor** la récolte s'annonce bien/mal ◆ **future ~s for the steel industry** les perspectives d'avenir de la sidérurgie

◆ **prospect of** ◆ **there is little ~ of his coming** il y a peu de chances *or* d'espoir (pour) qu'il vienne ◆ **he has little ~ of succeeding** il a peu de chances de réussir, il y a peu de chances qu'il réussisse ◆ **there is no ~ of that** rien ne laisse prévoir cela ◆ **there is every ~ of success/of succeeding** tout laisse prévoir le succès/qu'on réussira ◆ **to face the ~ of** faire face à la perspective de ◆ **"good prospects of promotion"** "réelles perspectives d'évolution" ◆ **the job offered the ~ of foreign travel** l'emploi offrait la possibilité de voyager à l'étranger

2 *(= likely person, thing: for marriage)* parti *m* ◆ **he is a good ~ for the England team** c'est un bon espoir pour l'équipe anglaise ◆ **he seems quite a good ~** il semble prometteur ◆ **this product is an exciting ~ for the European market** ce produit ouvre des perspectives passionnantes en ce qui concerne le marché européen ◆ **their offer/the deal seemed quite a good ~** leur proposition/l'affaire semblait prometteuse

VI /prəˈspekt/ prospecter ◆ **to ~ for gold** *etc* prospecter pour trouver de l'or *etc*, chercher de l'or *etc*

VT /prəˈspekt/ *[+ land, district]* prospecter

prospecting /prəˈspektɪŋ/ N *(Min etc)* prospection *f*

prospective /prəˈspektɪv/ ADJ *[son-in-law, home, legislation]* futur *before n* ; *[journey]* en perspective ; *[customer]* éventuel, potentiel ◆ **a ~ employee** un candidat à un emploi ◆ **his ~ employers** ceux qui devaient l'employer

prospector /prəˈspektəʳ/ N prospecteur *m*, -trice *f* ◆ **gold ~** chercheur *m* d'or

prospectus /prəˈspektəs/ N brochure *f*, prospectus *m*

prosper /ˈprɒspəʳ/ VI *[person]* prospérer ; *[company, enterprise]* prospérer, réussir VT (†, *liter*) favoriser, faire prospérer

prosperity /prɒsˈperɪtɪ/ N *(NonC)* prospérité *f*

prosperous /ˈprɒspərəs/ ADJ *[person, city, business]* prospère, florissant ; *[period, years]* prospère ; *[undertaking]* prospère, qui réussit ; *[look, appearance]* prospère, de prospérité ; *(liter) [wind]* favorable

prosperously /ˈprɒspərəslɪ/ ADV de manière prospère *or* florissante

prostaglandin /ˌprɒstəˈglændɪn/ N prostaglandine *f*

prostate /ˈprɒsteɪt/ N (also **prostate gland**) prostate *f* ◆ **to have a ~ operation** se faire opérer de la prostate

prosthesis /prɒs'θiːsɪs/ N (pl **prostheses** /prɒs'θiːsiːz/) prosthèse *or* prothèse *f*

prosthetic /prɒs'θetɪk/ ADJ prosthétique *or* prothétique

prosthodontics /ˌprɒsθə'dɒntɪks/ N prothèse *f* dentaire

prosthodontist /'prɒsθə'dɒntɪst/ N prothésiste *mf* dentaire

prostitute /'prɒstɪtjuːt/ N prostituée *f* ◆ **male ~** prostitué *m* VT (*lit, fig*) prostituer ◆ **to ~ o.s.** se prostituer

prostitution /ˌprɒstɪ'tjuːʃən/ N (*NonC*) (*lit*) prostitution *f* ; (*fig*) perversion *f*

prostrate /'prɒstreɪt/ ADJ (*lit*) à plat ventre ; (*in respect, submission*) prosterné ; (*in exhaustion*) prostré ; (*fig: nervously, mentally*) prostré, accablé VT /prɒs'treɪt/ 1 ◆ **to ~ o.s.** se prosterner 2 (*fig*) accabler ◆ **the news ~d him** la nouvelle l'a accablé *or* abattu ◆ **~d with grief/by the heat** accablé de chagrin/par la chaleur

prostration /prɒs'treɪʃən/ N (= *act*) prosternation *f*, prosternement *m* ; (*Rel*) prostration *f* ; (*fig* = *nervous exhaustion*) prostration *f* ◆ **in a state of ~** prostré

prosy /'prəʊzɪ/ ADJ ennuyeux, insipide

prot * /prɒt/ N (*pej*) abbrev of **Protestant**

protactinium /ˌprəʊtæk'tɪnɪəm/ N protactinium *m*

protagonist /prəʊ'tægənɪst/ N protagoniste *mf*

Protagoras /prəʊ'tægəræs/ N Protagoras *m*

protean /'prəʊtɪən/ ADJ changeant, inconstant

protect /prə'tekt/ VT [+ *person, property, country, plants*] protéger (*from* de ; *against* contre) ; [+ *interests, rights*] sauvegarder ; (*Econ*) [+ *industry*] protéger ◆ **the tigress fought to ~ her cubs** la tigresse s'est battue pour défendre ses petits ◆ **don't lie to ~ your brother** ne cherche pas à protéger ton frère en mentant COMP **protected species** N espèce *f* protégée

protection /prə'tekʃən/ N 1 [*of person, property, country, plants*] protection *f* (*from or against sth* contre qch) ; [*of interests, rights*] sauvegarde *f* ◆ **he wore a helmet for ~ against rock falls** il portait un casque pour se protéger des *or* contre les chutes de pierres ◆ **the grease offers** *or* **affords some ~ against the cold** la graisse offre une certaine protection contre le froid

2 (*Insurance*) garantie *f* (*against sth* contre qch), couverture *f* (*against sth* en cas de qch)

3 (*gen pl* = *safeguard*) mesure *f* de protection ◆ **benefits and ~s for employees** avantages *mpl* et garanties *fpl or* mesures *fpl* de protection pour les employés

4 (*in protection racket*) protection *f* ◆ **he pays 200 dollars a week (for** *or* **as) ~** il achète sa tranquillité 200 dollars par semaine ; see also **police**

5 (= *barrier contraception*) protection *f* ◆ **they didn't use any ~** ils n'ont pas utilisé de protection

COMP **protection factor** N [*of sun cream*] indice *m* de protection

protection money N ◆ **he pays 200 dollars a week ~ money** il achète sa tranquillité 200 dollars par semaine ◆ **he pays ~ money to Big Joe** il verse de l'argent à Big Joe pour qu'on le laisse *subj* en paix

protection order N (*to protect child*) ordonnance *f* de placement provisoire ; (*to protect partner, spouse*) ordonnance *f* de protection

protection racket N racket *m* ◆ **he's running a ~ racket** il est à la tête d'un racket, il extorque de l'argent par intimidation

protectionism /prə'tekʃənɪzəm/ N 1 (*Econ*) protectionnisme *m* 2 (*US*) [*of wildlife*] protection *f* de l'environnement

protectionist /prə'tekʃənɪst/ ADJ 1 (*Econ*) protectionniste 2 (*US: of wildlife*) [*measure etc*] pour la défense de l'environnement N 1 (*Econ*) protectionniste *mf* 2 (*US: of wildlife*) défenseur *m* de l'environnement

protective /prə'tektɪv/ ADJ [*layer, attitude, gesture*] protecteur (-trice *f*), de protection ; [*clothing, covering*] de protection ; (*Econ*) [*tariff, duty, system*] protecteur (-trice *f*) ◆ **~ colouring** *or* **coloration** (*in animals*) mimétisme *m*, homochromie *f* COMP **protective custody** N (*Jur*) détention *f* provisoire (*comme mesure de protection*)

protectively /prə'tektɪvlɪ/ ADV ◆ **he put his arm ~ around Julie's shoulders** il a passé un bras protecteur autour des épaules de Julie ◆ **she stepped ~ in front of him** elle se mit devant lui pour le protéger ◆ **he crossed his forearms ~ over his face** il croisa les avant-bras sur son visage pour se protéger

protectiveness /prə'tektɪvnɪs/ N attitude *f* protectrice

protector /prə'tektə^r^/ N (= *person*) protecteur *m* ; (= *object, device*) dispositif *m* de protection ◆ **the (Lord) Protector** (*Brit Hist*) le Protecteur

protectorate /prə'tektərɪt/ N protectorat *m* (*also Brit Hist*)

protectress /prə'tektrɪs/ N protectrice *f*

protégé /'prəʊtɪʒeɪ, 'prɒtɪʒeɪ/ N protégé *m*

protégée /'prəʊtɪʒeɪ, 'prɒtɪʒeɪ/ N protégée *f*

protein /'prəʊtiːn/ N protéine *f*

COMP [*intake, deficiency*] de protéines ; [*foods, diet*] riche en protéines

protein content N teneur *f* en protéines

pro tem /'prəʊ'tem/, **pro tempore** † /'prəʊ'tempərɪ/ ADV temporairement ; (*in jobs*) par intérim ◆ **he's replacing the chairman ~** il remplace le président à titre temporaire ADJ temporaire ◆ **on a ~ basis** temporairement ◆ **the ~ chairman** le président par intérim, le président intérimaire

protest /'prəʊtest/ LANGUAGE IN USE 14, 26.3

N 1 (*gen*) protestation *f* (*against* contre ; *about* à propos de) ; (= *demonstration*) manifestation *f* ◆ **to do sth under ~** faire qch en protestant *or* contre son gré ◆ **to make a ~** protester, élever une protestation (*against* contre) ◆ **in ~** en signe de protestation (*against* contre) ◆ **without ~** sans protester ◆ **to stage a ~** organiser une manifestation

2 (*Fin, Jur: in case of dishonour of a bill*) protêt *m*

VT /prə'test/ 1 (= *declare, affirm*) protester (*that* que) ; [+ *loyalty*] protester de ◆ **"I didn't do it" he ~ed** "ce n'est pas moi" protesta-t-il ; see also **innocence**

2 (*US*) protester contre

VI /prə'test/ protester, élever une *or* des protestation(s) (*against* contre ; *about* à propos de ; *to sb* auprès de qn)

COMP (*Pol etc*) [*meeting*] de protestation

protest demonstration, protest march N manifestation *f*

protest vote N vote *m* de protestation

Protestant /'prɒtɪstənt/ ADJ, N protestant(e) *m(f)* ◆ **~ ethic** morale *f* protestante

Protestantism /'prɒtɪstəntɪzəm/ N protestantisme *m*

protestation /ˌprɒtes'teɪʃən/ N protestation *f*

protester /prə'testə^r^/ N protestataire *mf* ; (*on march, in demonstration*) manifestant(e) *m(f)*

proto... /'prəʊtəʊ/ PREF proto...

protocol /'prəʊtəkɒl/ N (*also Comput*) protocole *m*

proton /'prəʊtɒn/ N proton *m*

protoplasm /'prəʊtəʊplæzəm/ N protoplasme *m*, protoplasma *m*

prototype /'prəʊtəʊtaɪp/ N prototype *m* ◆ **a ~ aircraft** le prototype d'un avion

prototypical /ˌprəʊtəʊ'tɪpɪkəl/ ADJ par excellence ◆ **he's a ~ socialist** c'est l'archétype du socialiste

protozoan, protozoon /ˌprəʊtə'zəʊən/ N (pl **protozoa** /ˌprəʊtə'zəʊə/) (*Bio*) protozoaire *m*

protract /prə'trækt/ VT prolonger, faire durer

protracted /prə'træktɪd/ ADJ prolongé, très long (longue *f*) ◆ **the struggle would be bitter and ~** la lutte serait longue et féroce

protraction /prə'trækʃən/ N prolongation *f*

protractor /prə'træktə^r^/ N (*Geom*) rapporteur *m*

protrude /prə'truːd/ VI [*stick, gutter, rock, shelf*] dépasser, faire saillie ; [*teeth*] avancer ; [*eyes*] être globuleux VT faire dépasser

protruding /prə'truːdɪŋ/ ADJ [*teeth*] qui avance ; [*eyes*] globuleux ; [*chin*] saillant ; [*shelf, rock*] en saillie

protrusion /prə'truːʒən/ N saillie *f*, avancée *f*

protrusive /prə'truːsɪv/ ADJ (*frm*) ⇒ **protruding**

protuberance /prə'tjuːbərəns/ N (*frm*) protubérance *f*

protuberant /prə'tjuːbərənt/ ADJ (*frm*) protubérant

proud /praʊd/ ADJ 1 [*person*] fier (*of sb/sth* de qn/qch ; *that* que + *subj* ; *to do sth* de faire qch) ; (= *arrogant*) arrogant, orgueilleux ◆ **the ~ father/owner** l'heureux père *m*/propriétaire *m* ◆ **that's nothing to be ~ of!** il n'y a pas de quoi être fier ! ◆ **I'm not very ~ of myself** je ne suis pas très fier de moi ◆ **as ~ as a peacock** fier comme Artaban ; (*pej*) fier comme un paon ◆ **it was a ~ day for us when ...** nous avons été remplis de fierté *or* très fiers le jour où ... ; → **possessor**

2 ◆ **my ~est possession** ce dont je suis le plus fier ◆ **to do o.s. ~** * ne se priver de rien ◆ **to do sb ~** * (= *entertain etc*) se mettre en frais pour qn, recevoir qn comme un roi (*or* une reine) ; (= *honour*) faire beaucoup d'honneur à qn

3 (*frm* = *splendid*) [*building, ship*] imposant, majestueux ; [*stallion*] fier

4 (*Brit*) **to stand ~ of sth** † faire saillie sur qch

proudly /'praʊdlɪ/ ADV fièrement

provable /'pruːvəbl/ ADJ démontrable, prouvable

prove /pruːv/ LANGUAGE IN USE 26.1

VT 1 (= *give proof of*) prouver (*also Jur*) ; (= *show*) prouver, démontrer ◆ **that ~s his innocence** *or* **him innocent** *or* **that he is innocent** cela prouve son innocence *or* qu'il est innocent ◆ **you can't ~ anything against me** vous n'avez aucune preuve contre moi ◆ **that ~d that she did it** cela prouvait bien *or* c'était bien la preuve qu'elle l'avait fait ◆ **he ~d that she did it** il a prouvé *or* démontré qu'elle l'avait (bien) fait ◆ **he managed to ~ it against her** il a réussi à prouver qu'elle l'avait fait *or* qu'elle était coupable ◆ **he couldn't ~ anything against her** il n'a rien pu prouver contre elle ◆ **the theory remains to be ~d** il reste à prouver *or* démontrer cette théorie, cette théorie n'est pas encore prouvée ◆ **whether he was right remains to be ~d** reste à prouver *or* encore faut-il prouver qu'il avait raison ◆ **he was ~d right** il s'est avéré qu'il avait raison, les faits lui ont donné raison ◆ **it all goes to ~ that ...** tout cela montre bien *or* prouve que ... ◆ **to ~ one's point** prouver ce que l'on avance (*or* a avancé *etc*) ◆ **to ~ a point** (= *show one is right*) montrer que l'on a raison ; (= *show one is capable*) montrer qu'on en est capable ◆ **can you ~ it?** pouvez-vous le prouver ? ◆ **that ~s it!** c'est la preuve ! ◆ **he ~d himself innocent** il a prouvé son innocence ◆ **he ~d himself useful** il s'est révélé *or* montré utile ; see also **proven**

2 *(= test)* mettre à l'épreuve ; *[+ will]* homologuer ◆ **to ~ o.s.** faire ses preuves
3 *(Culin) [+ dough]* laisser lever
4 *(Jur, Fin)* **to ~ a debt** produire une dette (à la faillite)
VI 1 *[person]* se révéler ; *[fact, object]* s'avérer, se révéler ◆ **he ~d (to be) incapable of helping us** il s'est montré *or* révélé incapable de nous aider ◆ **the information ~d (to be) correct** les renseignements se sont avérés *or* révélés justes ◆ **the mistake ~d (to be) costly** l'erreur s'est avérée *or* révélée coûteuse ◆ **it ~d very useful** cela a été *or (more frm)* s'est révélé très utile ◆ **the exhibition ~d (to be) a success** l'exposition a été une réussite ◆ **if it ~s otherwise** s'il en est autrement *or* différemment
2 *(Culin) [dough]* lever
COMP **proving ground** N terrain *m* d'essai, lieu *m* d'expérimentation

proven /ˈpruːvən, ˈprəʊvən/ **VB** ptp of **prove** **ADJ** *[formula, method]* qui a fait ses preuves ; *[abilities]* indubitable ◆ **a ~ track record** une expérience confirmée ◆ **verdict of not ~** *(Scot Jur)* (ordonnance *f* de) non-lieu *m (en l'absence de charges suffisantes)* ◆ **the case was not ~** il y a eu ordonnance de non-lieu

provenance /ˈprɒvɪnəns/ N provenance *f*

Provençal /ˌprɒvɑːnˈsɑːl/ **ADJ** provençal **N** 1 Provençal(e) *m(f)* 2 *(= language)* provençal *m*

Provence /prɒˈvɑːns/ N Provence *f* ◆ **in ~** en Provence

provender † /ˈprɒvɪndəʳ/ N fourrage *m*, provende *f*

proverb /ˈprɒvɜːb/ N proverbe *m* ◆ **(the Book of) Proverbs** *(Bible)* le livre des Proverbes

proverbial /prəˈvɜːbɪəl/ ADJ proverbial ◆ **it's like the ~ needle in a haystack** comme on dit, c'est chercher une aiguille dans une botte de foin

proverbially /prəˈvɜːbɪəlɪ/ ADV *[say]* proverbialement ◆ **prevention is ~ better than cure** comme le dit le proverbe, mieux vaut prévenir que guérir ◆ **British food is ~ bad** * la mauvaise qualité de la nourriture en Grande-Bretagne est proverbiale *or* bien connue

provide /prəˈvaɪd/ **VT** 1 *(= supply)* fournir *(sb with sth, sth for sb* qch à qn) ; *(= equip)* munir, pourvoir *(sb with sth* qn de qch) ◆ **to ~ o.s. with sth** se procurer qch ◆ **I will ~ food for everyone** c'est moi qui fournirai la nourriture pour tout le monde ◆ **he ~d the school with a new library** il a pourvu l'école d'une nouvelle bibliothèque ◆ **candidates must ~ their own pencils** les candidats doivent apporter leurs crayons ◆ **can you ~ a substitute?** pouvez-vous trouver un remplaçant ? ◆ **it ~s accommodation for five families** on peut loger cinq familles ◆ **the field ~s plenty of space for a car park** le champ offre suffisamment d'espace pour le stationnement des voitures ◆ **I am already ~d with all I need** je suis déjà bien pourvu, j'ai déjà tout ce qu'il me faut ◆ **the car is ~d with a radio** la voiture est équipée d'une radio
2 *[legislation, treaty etc]* stipuler, prévoir *(that que)* ◆ **unless otherwise ~d** sauf dispositions contraires
VI 1 *(esp financially)* **to ~ for** *(gen)* pourvoir *or* subvenir aux besoins de ; *(family)* entretenir ; *(in the future)* assurer l'avenir de ◆ **I'll see you well ~d for** je ferai le nécessaire pour que vous ne manquiez *subj* de rien ◆ **the Lord will ~** Dieu y pourvoira
2 *(= make arrangements)* **to ~ for sth** prévoir qch ; *[treaty, legislation]* prévoir *or* stipuler qch ◆ **they hadn't ~d for such a lot of spectators** le nombre de spectateurs les a pris au dépourvu ◆ **he had ~d for any eventuality** il avait paré à toute éventualité ◆ **to ~ against** se prémunir contre, prendre ses précautions contre

provided /prəˈvaɪdɪd/ CONJ ◆ **~ (that)** à condition que + *subj*, à condition de + *infin* ◆ **you can go ~ it doesn't rain** tu peux y aller à condition qu'il ne pleuve pas ◆ **you can go ~ you pass your exam** tu peux y aller à condition de réussir ton examen ◆ **~ you always keep it closed** à condition de le garder toujours bien fermé ◆ **~ always that …** *(Admin, Jur)* sous réserve que … + *subj*

providence /ˈprɒvɪdəns/ N 1 *(Rel etc)* providence *f* ◆ **Providence** la Providence 2 († *= foresight*) prévoyance *f*, prudence *f*

provident /ˈprɒvɪdənt/ ADJ *[person]* prévoyant, prudent ; *(Brit) [fund, society]* de prévoyance

providential /ˌprɒvɪˈdenʃəl/ ADJ *(frm)* providentiel

providentially /ˌprɒvɪˈdenʃəlɪ/ ADV *(frm)* providentiellement ◆ **~, he had brought a torch with him** par un heureux hasard, il avait apporté une lampe de poche

providently /ˈprɒvɪdəntlɪ/ ADV *(frm)* avec prévoyance, prudemment

provider /prəˈvaɪdəʳ/ N pourvoyeur *m*, -euse *f* ; *(Comm)* fournisseur *m*, -euse *f* ◆ **~s of care** *(Social Work)* dispensateurs *mpl* de soins ◆ **she is the family's sole ~** elle est seule à subvenir aux besoins de la famille

providing /prəˈvaɪdɪŋ/ CONJ ⇒ **provided**

province /ˈprɒvɪns/ **N** 1 province *f* 2 *(fig)* domaine *m*, compétence *f (esp Admin)* ◆ **that is not my ~, it is not within my ~** cela n'est pas de mon ressort *or* ne relève pas de ma compétence ◆ **his particular ~ is housing** le logement est son domaine *or* sa spécialité 3 *(Rel)* archevêché *m* **NPL** **the provinces** la province ◆ **in the ~s** en province

provincial /prəˈvɪnʃəl/ **ADJ** *(gen, also pej)* provincial, de province ◆ **~ branch** *(Comm)* branche *f or* agence *f* régionale **N** provincial(e) *m(f)*

provincialism /prəˈvɪnʃəlɪzəm/ N *(pej)* provincialisme *m*

provirus /ˈprəʊˌvaɪrəs/ N provirus *m*

provision /prəˈvɪʒən/ **N** 1 *(= supply)* provision *f* ◆ **to lay in** *or* **get in a ~ of coal** faire provision de charbon
2 *(NonC = supplying) [of food]* fourniture *f*, approvisionnement *m* ; *[of equipment]* fourniture *f* ; *[of housing, education]* offre *f* ◆ **~ of food to the soldiers** approvisionnement *m* des soldats en nourriture ◆ **~ of capital** *(Fin)* apport *m or* fourniture *f* de capitaux ◆ **~ of services** prestation *f* de services ◆ **to make ~ for** *[+ one's family, dependents etc]* pourvoir aux besoins de, assurer l'avenir de ; *[+ journey, siege, famine]* prendre des dispositions *or* des précautions pour
3 *(Admin) (= funding)* financement *m (of, for* de) ; *(= funds)* fonds *mpl*
4 *(Admin, Jur etc = stipulation)* disposition *f*, clause *f* ◆ **according to the ~s of the treaty** selon les dispositions du traité ◆ **it falls within the ~s of this law** cela tombe sous le coup de cette loi, c'est un cas prévu par cette loi ◆ **~ to the contrary** clause *f* contraire ◆ **there is no ~ for this in the rules, the rules make no ~ for this** le règlement ne prévoit pas cela
NPL **provisions** *(= food etc)* provisions *fpl* ◆ **to get ~s in** faire des provisions
VT approvisionner, ravitailler *(with* en)
COMP **provision merchant** N marchand *m* de comestibles

provisional /prəˈvɪʒənl/ **ADJ** *[government]* provisoire ; *[arrangement, agreement, acceptance]* à titre conditionnel ; *(Admin) [appointment]* à titre provisoire ; *(Jur)* provisionnel **N** *(Pol: in Ireland)* ◆ **the Provisionals** (les membres *mpl* de) l'IRA *f* provisoire
COMP **provisional driving licence** N *(Brit)* permis *m* de conduire provisoire *(obligatoire pour l'élève conducteur)* ; → DRIVING LICENCE
the Provisional IRA N l'IRA *f* provisoire

provisionally /prəˈvɪʒnəlɪ/ ADV provisoirement

proviso /prəˈvaɪzəʊ/ N (pl **provisos** *or* **provisoes**) stipulation *f*, condition *f* ; *(Jur)* clause *f* restrictive, condition *f* formelle ◆ **with the ~ that …** à condition que … + *subj*

provisory /prəˈvaɪzərɪ/ ADJ ⇒ **provisional adj**

Provo * /ˈprɒvəʊ/ N *(Pol: in Ireland)* ◆ **the ~s** (les membres *mpl* de) l'IRA *f* provisoire

provocateur /prəvɒkəˈtɜːʳ/ N poil *m* à gratter

provocation /ˌprɒvəˈkeɪʃən/ N provocation *f* ◆ **under ~** *(Chem, Bio)* en réponse à une provocation

provocative /prəˈvɒkətɪv/ ADJ 1 *(= aggressive) [gesture, remark]* provocant, provocateur (-trice *f*) ◆ **now you're trying to be ~** là vous essayez de me *(or* le *or* lui *etc)* provoquer, là vous me *(or* lui *etc)* cherchez querelle 2 *(= thought-provoking) [book, title, talk]* qui force à réagir, qui ne laisse pas indifférent 3 *(= seductive) [woman, movement, smile]* provocant

provocatively /prəˈvɒkətɪvlɪ/ ADV *(= challengingly, suggestively) [say, ask, look, behave]* de manière provocante ◆ **~ entitled …** portant le titre provocateur de … ◆ **~ dressed** habillé de manière provocante

provoke /prəˈvəʊk/ VT 1 *(= rouse) [+ person]* provoquer ; *[+ war, dispute, revolt]* provoquer, faire naître ; *[+ reply]* provoquer, susciter ◆ **to ~ sb to do sth** *or* **into doing sth** inciter qn à faire qch ◆ **it ~d them to action** cela les a incités à agir 2 ◆ **to ~ sb (to anger), to ~ sb's anger** provoquer qn

provoking /prəˈvəʊkɪŋ/ ADJ *(= annoying)* contrariant, agaçant ; *(= thought-provoking)* provocateur (-trice *f*) ; → **thought**

provost /ˈprɒvəst/ **N** *(Brit Univ)* président *m* ; *(US Univ)* ≃ doyen *m* ; *(Scot)* maire *m* ; *(Rel)* doyen *m* ; → **lord**
COMP **provost court** N *(Mil)* tribunal *m* prévôtal
provost guard N prévôté *f*
provost marshal N prévôt *m*

prow /praʊ/ N proue *f*

prowess /ˈpraʊɪs/ N prouesse *f*

prowl /praʊl/ **VI** (also **prowl about, prowl around**) rôder **VT** *[+ streets etc]* arpenter **N** ◆ **to be on the ~** rôder **COMP** **prowl car** N *(US Police)* voiture *f* de police

prowler /ˈpraʊləʳ/ N rôdeur *m*, -euse *f*

prowling /ˈpraʊlɪŋ/ ADJ rôdeur ; *[taxi]* en maraude

proximity /prɒkˈsɪmɪtɪ/ **N** proximité *f* ◆ **in ~ to, in the ~ of** à proximité de ◆ **the shops are in close ~** les magasins sont à deux pas
COMP **proximity fuse** N fusée *f* de proximité
proximity talks NPL pourparlers *mpl* de proximité

proximo /ˈprɒksɪməʊ/ ADV *(Comm)* (du mois) prochain

proxy /ˈprɒksɪ/ **N** *(= power)* procuration *f* ; *(= person)* fondé(e) *m(f)* de pouvoir, mandataire *mf* ◆ **by ~** par procuration
COMP **proxy conflict** N *(Mil euph)* conflit *m* par personnes interposées
proxy vote N vote *m* par procuration

Prozac ® /ˈprəʊzæk/ N Prozac ® *m*

PRP /ˌpiːɑːˈpiː/ N (abbrev of **performance-related pay**) → **performance**

PRS /ˌpiːɑːrˈes/ N (abbrev of **Performing Rights Society**) ≃ SACEM *f*

prude /pruːd/ N prude *f*, bégueule *f* ◆ **he's a ~** il est pudibond

prudence /ˈpruːdəns/ N prudence *f*, circonspection *f*

prudent /ˈpruːdənt/ ADJ prudent, circonspect ◆ **it would be ~ to leave** il serait prudent de partir

prudential /pru(ː)ˈdenʃəl/ ADJ prudent

prudently /ˈpruːdəntlɪ/ ADV prudemment, avec prudence

prudery /ˈpruːdərɪ/ N pruderie *f*, pudibonderie *f*

prudish /ˈpruːdɪʃ/ ADJ pudibond, bégueule*

prudishness /ˈpruːdɪʃnɪs/ N ⇒ **prudery**

prune¹ /pruːn/ N (= *fruit*) pruneau *m* ; (*pej* = *person*) repoussoir *m* ◆ **~s and prisms** (*fig*) afféterie *f*, préciosité *f*

⚠ In French, **prune** means 'plum', not **prune**.

prune² /pruːn/ VT (*to promote growth*) [+ *tree, bush*] tailler ; (= *thin out*) élaguer, émonder ; (*fig*: also **prune down**) [+ *article, essay*] élaguer, faire des coupures dans

► **prune away** VT SEP [+ *branches*] élaguer ; (*fig*) [+ *paragraph, words*] élaguer

pruning /ˈpruːnɪŋ/ N 1 (*lit*) [*of tree, bush*] (*to promote growth*) taille *f* ; (*to remove unwanted branches, dead wood etc*) élagage *m*, émondage *m* 2 (*fig*) [*of article, essay*] élagage *m*
COMP **pruning hook** N émondoir *m*, ébranchoir *m*
pruning knife N (pl **pruning knives**) serpette *f*
pruning shears NPL (= *secateurs*) cisailles *fpl*, coupe-branches *m* ; (= *hedge shears*) taille-haies *m*, cisailles *fpl* à haies

prurience /ˈprʊərɪəns/ N (*frm*) lascivité *f*, luxure *f*

prurient /ˈprʊərɪənt/ ADJ (*frm*) lascif

Prussia /ˈprʌʃə/ N Prusse *f*

Prussian /ˈprʌʃən/ ADJ prussien ◆ **~ blue** bleu *m* de Prusse N Prussien(ne) *m(f)*

prussic acid /ˌprʌsɪkˈæsɪd/ N acide *m* prussique

pry¹ /praɪ/ VI mettre son nez dans les affaires des autres, s'occuper de ce qui ne vous regarde pas ◆ **I don't want to ~ but ...** je ne veux pas être indiscret (-ète *f*) mais ... ◆ **stop ~ing!** occupez-vous de ce qui vous regarde ! ◆ **to ~ into sb's secrets** chercher à découvrir les secrets de qn

pry² /praɪ/ VT (*US*) ⇒ **prise**

prying /ˈpraɪɪŋ/ ADJ fureteur, indiscret (-ète *f*) ◆ **to keep sth safe from ~ eyes** mettre qch à l'abri des regards indiscrets

PS /piːˈes/ N 1 (abbrev of **postscript**) P.-S. *or* PS *m* 2 (abbrev of **private secretary**) → **private**

psalm /sɑːm/ N psaume *m* ◆ **(the Book of) Psalms** (*Bible*) le livre des Psaumes

psalmist /ˈsɑːmɪst/ N psalmiste *m*

psalmody /ˈsælmədɪ/ N psalmodie *f*

psalter /ˈsɔːltəʳ/ N psautier *m*

PSAT /ˌpiːeseɪˈtiː/ N (*US Scol, Univ*) (abbrev of **Preliminary Scholastic Aptitude Test**) → **preliminary**

PSBR /ˌpiːesbiːˈɑːʳ/ N (*Econ*) (abbrev of **public sector borrowing requirement**) → **public**

psephologist /seˈfɒlədʒɪst/ N spécialiste *mf* des élections

psephology /səˈfɒlədʒɪ/ N étude *f* des élections

pseud* /sjuːd/ (*Brit*) N bêcheur* *m*, -euse* *f* ADJ qui manque de sincérité, artificiel

pseudo* /ˈsjuːdəʊ/ ADJ insincère, faux (fausse *f*)

pseudo- /ˈsjuːdəʊ/ PREF pseudo- ◆ **~antique** pseudoantique ◆ **~autobiography** pseudoautobiographie *f* ◆ **~apologetically** sous couleur de s'excuser

pseudonym /ˈsjuːdənɪm/ N pseudonyme *m*

pseudonymous /sjuːˈdɒnɪməs/ ADJ pseudonyme

pshaw /pʃɔː/ EXCL peuh !

psi¹ /piːesˈaɪ/ N (abbrev of **pounds per square inch**) ≈ kg/cm³

psi² /piːesˈaɪ/ N (*NonC* = *psychic phenomena*) phénomènes *mpl* parapsychiques *or* paranormaux

psittacosis /ˌpsɪtəˈkəʊsɪs/ N psittacose *f*

psoriasis /sɒˈraɪəsɪs/ N psoriasis *m*

psst /pst/ EXCL psitt, pst, hep

PST /ˌpiːesˈtiː/ (*US*) (abbrev of **Pacific Standard Time**) → **pacific**

PSV /ˌpiesˈviː/ N (abbrev of **public service vehicle**) → **public**

psych* /saɪk/ VT (abbrev of **psychoanalyse**) 1 (= *guess, anticipate*) [+ *sb's reactions etc*] deviner, prévoir
2 (= *make uneasy*: also **psych out**) intimider, déconcerter (volontairement) ◆ **that doesn't ~ me (out)** ça ne me panique* pas
3 (= *prepare psychologically*: also **psych up**) préparer (mentalement) (*for sth* à *or* pour qch ; *to do sth* pour faire qch) ◆ **to get o.s. ~ed up for sth** se préparer (mentalement) à qch ◆ **he was all ~ed up to start, when ...** il était gonflé à bloc*, tout prêt à commencer, quand ...
N (*US*) 1 (abbrev of **psychology**) psycho* *f*
2 abbrev of **psychiatry**

► **psych out*** VI (= *break down*) craquer*
VT SEP 1 (= *cause to break down*) faire craquer*
2 → **psych 2**
3 (*US* = *analyse, work out*) piger*, comprendre (*that* que) ; [+ *situation etc*] analyser, comprendre ◆ **to ~ sb out** voir clair dans le jeu de qn ◆ **I ~ed it all out for myself** je m'y suis retrouvé tout seul

► **psych up*** VT SEP → **psych 3**

psyche /ˈsaɪkɪ/ N psychisme *m*, psyché *f*

psychedelia /ˌsaɪkəˈdelɪə/ N (*NonC*) (= *objects*) objets *mpl* psychédéliques ; (= *atmosphere*) univers *m* psychédélique

psychedelic /ˌsaɪkəˈdelɪk/ ADJ psychédélique

psychiatric /ˌsaɪkɪˈætrɪk/ ADJ [*hospital, treatment, medicine*] psychiatrique ; [*disease*] mental

psychiatrist /saɪˈkaɪətrɪst/ N psychiatre *mf*

psychiatry /saɪˈkaɪətrɪ/ N psychiatrie *f*

psychic /ˈsaɪkɪk/ ADJ 1 (= *supernatural*) [*phenomenon, powers etc*] parapsychologique ; [*person*] télépathe ◆ **~ research** recherches *fpl* parapsychologiques ◆ **the ~ world** le monde du paranormal ◆ **I'm not ~!*** je ne suis pas devin ! 2 (*Psych*) psychique N médium *m*

psychical /ˈsaɪkɪkəl/ ADJ ⇒ **psychic adj**

psycho* /ˈsaɪkəʊ/ abbrev of **psychopath, psychopathic, psychotic**

psycho... /ˈsaɪkəʊ/ PREF psych(o)...

psychoactive /ˌsaɪkəʊˈæktɪv/ ADJ (*Med*) psychotrope

psychoanalysis /ˌsaɪkəʊəˈnælɪsɪs/ N psychanalyse *f*

psychoanalyst /ˌsaɪkəʊˈænəlɪst/ N psychanalyste *mf*

psychoanalytic(al) /ˈsaɪkəʊˌænəˈlɪtɪk(əl)/ ADJ psychanalytique

psychoanalyze /ˌsaɪkəʊˈænəlaɪz/ VT psychanalyser

psychobabble* /ˈsaɪkəʊˌbæbəl/ N (*NonC*) jargon *m* de psy*

psychodrama /ˈsaɪkəʊdrɑːmə/ N psychodrame *m*

psychodynamic /ˌsaɪkəʊdaɪˈnæmɪk/ ADJ psychodynamique N (*NonC*) ◆ **~s** psychodynamisme *m*

psychokinesis /ˌsaɪkəʊkɪˈniːsɪs/ N psychocinèse *f*, psychokinésie *f*

psychokinetic /ˌsaɪkəʊkɪˈnetɪk/ ADJ psychocinétique

psycholinguistic /ˈsaɪkəʊlɪŋˈgwɪstɪk/ ADJ psycholinguistique N (*NonC*) ◆ **~s** psycholinguistique *f*

psychological /ˌsaɪkəˈlɒdʒɪkəl/ ADJ [*method, study, state, moment, warfare*] psychologique ◆ **it's only ~*** c'est psychologique

psychologically /ˌsaɪkəˈlɒdʒɪkəlɪ/ ADV [*important, damaging, disturbed etc*] psychologiquement ◆ **~, he's very strong** psychologiquement, il est très fort ◆ **to be ~ prepared for sth** être psychologiquement prêt pour qch ◆ **~ speaking** d'un point de vue psychologique

psychologist /saɪˈkɒlədʒɪst/ N psychologue *mf* ; → **child, industrial**

psychology /saɪˈkɒlədʒɪ/ N psychologie *f* ◆ **the ~ of his opponent** la psychologie de son adversaire ; → **child**

psychometric /ˌsaɪkəʊˈmetrɪk/ ADJ psychométrique

psychometrics /ˌsaɪkəʊˈmetrɪks/ N (*NonC*) psychométrie *f*

psychometry /saɪˈkɒmɪtrɪ/ N psychométrie *f*

psychomotor /ˈsaɪkəʊˈməʊtəʳ/ ADJ psychomoteur (-trice *f*)

psychoneurosis /ˈsaɪkəʊnjʊəˈrəʊsɪs/ N (pl **psychoneuroses** /ˈsaɪkəʊnjʊəˈrəʊsiːz/) psychonévrose *f*

psychoneurotic /ˈsaɪkəʊnjʊəˈrɒtɪk/ ADJ psychonévrotique

psychopath /ˈsaɪkəʊpæθ/ N psychopathe *mf*

psychopathic /ˌsaɪkəʊˈpæθɪk/ ADJ [*person*] psychopathe ; [*condition*] psychopathique

psychopathology /ˈsaɪkəʊpəˈθɒlədʒɪ/ N psychopathologie *f*

psychopharmacological /ˈsaɪkəʊfɑːməkəˈlɒdʒɪkəl/ ADJ psychopharmacologique

psychopharmacology /ˈsaɪkəʊfɑːməˈkɒlədʒɪ/ N psychopharmacologie *f*

psychophysical /ˈsaɪkəʊˈfɪzɪkəl/ ADJ psychophysique

psychophysics /ˈsaɪkəʊˈfɪzɪks/ N (*NonC*) psychophysique *f*

psychophysiological /ˈsaɪkəʊˌfɪzɪəˈlɒdʒɪkəl/ ADJ psychophysiologique

psychophysiology /ˈsaɪkəʊfɪzɪˈɒlədʒɪ/ N psychophysiologie *f*

psychoses /saɪˈkəʊsiːz/ NPL of **psychosis**

psychosexual /ˌsaɪkəʊˈseksjʊəl/ ADJ psychosexuel

psychosis /saɪˈkəʊsɪs/ N (pl **psychoses**) psychose *f*

psychosocial /ˈsaɪkəʊˈsəʊʃəl/ ADJ psychosocial

psychosomatic /ˈsaɪkəʊsəʊˈmætɪk/ ADJ psychosomatique

psychosurgery /ˈsaɪkəʊˈsɜːdʒərɪ/ N psychochirurgie *f*

psychotherapist /ˈsaɪkəʊˈθerəpɪst/ N psychothérapeute *mf*

psychotherapy /ˈsaɪkəʊˈθerəpɪ/ N psychothérapie *f*

psychotic /saɪˈkɒtɪk/ ADJ, N psychotique *mf*

psychotropic /ˌsaɪkəʊˈtrɒpɪk/ ADJ [*drug*] psychotrope

PT † /piːˈtiː/ N (*Scol*) (abbrev of **physical training**) → **physical**

pt abbrev of **part(s), pint(s), point(s)**

PTA /ˌpiːtiːˈeɪ/ N 1 (*Scol*) (abbrev of **Parent-Teacher Association**) → **parent** 2 (*Brit*) (abbrev of **Prevention of Terrorism Act**) *loi antiterroriste*

ptarmigan /ˈtɑːmɪgən/ **N** (pl **ptarmigans** *or* **ptarmigan**) lagopède *m* des Alpes

Pte *(Mil)* (abbrev of **Private**) ~ **J. Smith** *(on envelope)* le soldat J. Smith

pterodactyl /ˌterəʊˈdæktɪl/ **N** ptérodactyle *m*

PTO (abbrev of **please turn over**) TSVP

Ptolemaic /ˌtɒləˈmeɪɪk/ **ADJ** ptolémaïque

Ptolemy /ˈtɒləmɪ/ **N** Ptolémée *m*

ptomaine /ˈtəʊmeɪn/ **N** ptomaïne *f* ◆ ~ **poisoning** intoxication *f* alimentaire

ptosis /ˈtəʊsɪs/ **N** (pl **ptoses** /ˈtəʊsiːz/) ptose *f*

PTSD /ˌpiːtiːesˈdiː/ **N** abbrev of **post-traumatic stress disorder**

ptyalin /ˈtaɪəlɪn/ **N** ptyaline *f*

pub /pʌb/ *(Brit)* (abbrev of **public house**) **N** ≈ café *m* ; *(in British or Irish context)* pub *m*

COMP **pub-crawl** * **N, VI** ◆ **to go on a ~-crawl, to go ~-crawling** faire la tournée des bars *or* des bistrots * *or* des pubs

pub food, pub grub * **N** cuisine *f or* nourriture *f* de bistrot *

pub lunch **N** repas *m* de bistrot * ◆ **to go for a ~ lunch** aller manger au bistrot *

Pub

Les **pubs** jouent un rôle essentiel dans la vie sociale britannique. Traditionnellement, l'accès au **pub** est interdit aux moins de 18 ans, mais certains établissements ont un espace réservé (ou une terrasse en jardin) pour les familles. En Angleterre et au pays de Galles, les **pubs** sont généralement ouverts de 11 heures à 23 heures alors qu'en Écosse et en Irlande, les horaires d'ouverture sont plus flexibles. Certains **pubs** appartiennent à des brasseries et ne vendent que leurs propres marques de bière ; d'autres, les « free houses », appartiennent à des propriétaires privés et offrent, de ce fait, un plus grand choix de bières.

pub. (abbrev of **published**) publié

pubertal /ˈpjuːbətəl/ **ADJ** pubère

puberty /ˈpjuːbətɪ/ **N** puberté *f*

pubes[1] /ˈpjuːbiːz/ **NPL** of **pubis**

pubes[2] * /pjuːbz/ **NPL** *(= pubic hair)* poils *mpl* du pubis, toison *f*

pubescence /pjuːˈbesəns/ **N** pubescence *f*

pubescent /pjuːˈbesənt/ **ADJ** pubescent

pubic /ˈpjuːbɪk/ **ADJ** *[region etc]* pubien

COMP **pubic hair** **N** poils *mpl* pubiens *or* du pubis

pubic lice **NPL** morpions *mpl*

pubis /ˈpjuːbɪs/ **N** (pl **pubes**) pubis *m*

public /ˈpʌblɪk/ **ADJ** 1 *(gen: Admin, Econ, Fin etc)* public (-ique *f*) ; *(= owned by the nation) [enterprise etc]* nationalisé, étatisé ◆ **in the ~ domain** *(copyright)* dans le domaine public ◆ **to go ~** *[company]* s'introduire en Bourse ; see also **comp**

2 *(= of, for, by everyone) [meeting, park, indignation]* public (-ique *f*) ◆ **"this is a public announcement: would passengers …"** "votre attention s'il vous plaît : les passagers sont priés de …" ◆ **to be in the ~ eye** être très en vue ◆ **to disappear from the ~ eye** disparaître des feux de l'actualité ◆ **he's a ~ figure** c'est quelqu'un qui est très en vue, c'est une personnalité très connue ◆ **it is a matter of ~ interest** c'est une question d'intérêt public *or* général ◆ **he has the ~ interest at heart** il a à cœur l'intérêt *or* le bien public ◆ **a man in ~ life** un homme public ◆ **to go into ~ life** se consacrer aux affaires publiques ◆ **to be active in ~ life** prendre une part active aux affaires publiques ◆ **he's really a ~ nuisance** * c'est une calamité publique *, il empoisonne le monde * ◆ **there was a ~ protest against …** il y a eu de nombreux mouvements de protestation contre … ; see also **adj 3** ◆ **the house has two ~ rooms and three bedrooms** *(Scot)* la maison a cinq pièces dont trois chambres ◆ **she is a good ~ speaker** elle parle bien en public ◆ **~ speakers know that …** les personnes amenées à parler fréquemment en public savent que … ; → **image**

3 *(= open to everyone, not secret)* public (-ique *f*) ◆ **to make sth ~** rendre qch public, publier qch, porter qch à la connaissance du public ◆ **it was all quite ~** cela n'avait rien de secret, c'était tout à fait officiel ◆ **he made a ~ protest** il a protesté publiquement ◆ **his ~ support of the strikers** son appui déclaré *or* ouvert aux grévistes ◆ **let's go over there, it's too ~ here** allons là-bas, il y a trop de monde ici

N public *m* ◆ **the ~'s confidence in the government** la confiance des gens dans le gouvernement ◆ **the reading/sporting ~** les amateurs *mpl* de lecture/de sport ◆ **the French/English ~** les Français *mpl*/Anglais *mpl* ◆ **the American voting ~** les électeurs *mpl* américains ◆ **the great British ~** *(hum)* les sujets *mpl* de Sa (Gracieuse) Majesté ◆ **the house is open to the ~** la maison est ouverte au public ◆ **he couldn't disappoint his ~** *(= audience)* il ne pouvait pas décevoir son public ; → **general**

◆ **in public** en public

COMP **public access television** **N** *(US TV)* chaînes *fpl* câblées non commerciales

public-address system **N** (système *m* de) sonorisation *f*

public affairs **NPL** affaires *fpl* publiques

public analyst **N** analyste *mf* d'État *or* officiel(le)

public assistance † **N** *(NonC)* assistance *f* publique

public bar **N** *(Brit)* bar *m*

public building **N** édifice *m* public

public company **N** société *f* anonyme par actions

public convenience **N** *(Brit Admin)* toilettes *fpl* publiques

public corporation **N** *(Brit)* entreprise *f* nationale

the public debt **N** *(Econ)* la dette publique

public defender **N** *(US Jur)* avocat *m* de l'assistance judiciaire

public enemy **N** ennemi *m* public ◆ **~ enemy number one** * *(fig)* ennemi *m* public numéro un

public examination **N** *(Scol etc)* examen *m* national

public footpath **N** *(Brit Admin)* passage *m* public pour piétons, sentier *m* public

public gallery **N** *(in parliament, courtroom)* tribune *f* réservée au public

public health **N** santé *f or* hygiène *f* publique

Public Health Service **N** *(US)* ≃ Direction *f* des affaires sanitaires et sociales

public holiday **N** jour *m* férié, fête *f* légale

public house **N** *(Brit)* pub *m*

public housing **N** *(US)* logements *mpl* sociaux, ≃ HLM *fpl*

public housing project **N** *(US)* cité *f* HLM

public lavatory **N** toilettes *fpl* publiques

public law **N** droit *m* public

public lending right **N** *(Brit Admin) droits dédommageant un auteur pour le prêt de ses ouvrages en bibliothèque*

public library **N** bibliothèque *f* municipale

public limited company **N** *(Brit)* ≃ société *f* à responsabilité limitée

public medicine **N** *(US)* ⇒ **public health**

public money **N** *(Econ)* deniers *mpl* publics

public opinion **N** opinion *f* publique

public opinion poll **N** sondage *m* d'opinion publique

public ownership **N** *(Econ)* ◆ **under ~ ownership** nationalisé, étatisé ◆ **to take sth into ~ ownership** nationaliser qch, étatiser qch

public property **N** *(NonC = land etc)* biens *mpl* publics, propriété *f* publique ◆ **to treat sb as ~ property** ne pas avoir d'égards pour la vie privée de qn

Public Prosecutor **N** *(Jur)* ≈ procureur *m* (de la République), ministère *m* public

Public Prosecutor's Office **N** *(Jur)* parquet *m*

the public purse **N** *(Econ)* le trésor public

Public Record Office **N** *(Brit)* ≃ Archives *fpl* nationales

public relations **NPL** relations *fpl* publiques ◆ **~ relations officer** responsable *mf* de relations publiques ◆ **it's just a ~ relations exercise** il *etc* a fait ça uniquement dans le but de se faire bien voir

public school **N** *(Brit = private school)* public school *f*, collège *m* secondaire privé ; *(US) (= state school)* école *f* secondaire publique

public schoolboy, public schoolgirl **N** *(Brit)* élève *mf* d'une public school

the public sector **N** *(Econ)* le secteur public

public sector borrowing **N** emprunts *mpl* d'État

public sector borrowing requirement **N** besoins *mpl* de financement du secteur public

public servant **N** fonctionnaire *mf*

public service **N** service *m* public

public service corporation **N** *(US)* service *m* public non nationalisé

public service vehicle **N** *(Brit Admin)* véhicule *m* de transport en commun

public speaking **N** art *m* oratoire

public spending **N** *(NonC)* dépenses *fpl* publiques

public spirit **N** civisme *m*, sens *m* civique

public-spirited **ADJ** ◆ **to be ~-spirited** faire preuve de civisme

public television **N** *(US)* télévision *f* éducative (non commerciale)

public transport **N** *(NonC)* transports *mpl* en commun, transports *mpl* publics

public utility **N** *(= company)* entreprise *f* de service public ; *(= service)* service *m* public

public welfare **N** assistance *f* publique

public works **NPL** travaux *mpl* publics

Public Access Television

Aux États-Unis, **public access television** désigne les chaînes câblées non commerciales produites par des associations locales et autres institutions à but non lucratif. Le principe est de permettre aux communautés locales de s'exprimer et d'éviter que les chaînes câblées ne deviennent des monopoles. Selon la loi de 1984 sur la télévision câblée (Cable Act), une communauté locale peut exiger du propriétaire d'une chaîne câblée qu'il lui réserve une **public access television** et mette à sa disposition le studio, le matériel d'enregistrement et le personnel technique nécessaires.

publican /ˈpʌblɪkən/ **N** 1 *(Brit = pub manager)* patron(ne) *m(f)* de bistrot 2 *(Bible = taxman)* publicain *m*

publication /ˌpʌblɪˈkeɪʃən/ **N** 1 *(NonC = act of publishing) [of book etc]* publication *f* ; *(Jur) [of banns]* publication *f* ; *[of decree]* promulgation *f*, publication *f* ◆ **after the ~ of the book** après la publication *or* la parution du livre ◆ **this is not for ~** ceci doit rester entre nous 2 *(= published work)* publication *f* **COMP** **publication date** **N** date *f* de parution *or* de publication

publicist /ˈpʌblɪsɪst/ **N** *(Jur)* spécialiste *mf* de droit public international ; *(Press)* journaliste *mf* ; *(Advertising)* (agent *m*) publicitaire *m*, agent *m* de publicité

publicity /pʌbˈlɪsɪtɪ/ **N** *(NonC)* publicité *f* *(for* pour) ◆ **can you give us some ~ for the concert?** pouvez-vous nous faire de la publicité pour le concert ? ◆ **adverse ~** contre-publicité *f* ◆ **I keep getting ~ about the society's**

meetings je reçois tout le temps des circulaires concernant les réunions de la société ◆ **I've seen some of their** ~ j'ai vu des exemples de leur publicité

COMP **publicity agency** N agence *f* publicitaire *or* de publicité

publicity agent N (agent *m*) publicitaire *m*, agent *m* de publicité

publicity campaign N campagne *f* d'information ; *(= advertising)* campagne *f* de publicité

publicity stunt * N coup *m* de pub *

publicize /ˈpʌblɪsaɪz/ VT 1 *(= make public)* rendre public, publier ◆ **I don't ~ the fact, but …** je ne le crie pas sur les toits, mais … ◆ **well-~d** dont on parle beaucoup (*or* dont on a beaucoup parlé *etc*) ; see also **2** 2 *(= advertise)* faire de la publicité pour ◆ **well-~d** annoncé à grand renfort de publicité

publicly /ˈpʌblɪklɪ/ ADV 1 *(= in public)* publiquement, en public ◆ **to be ~ accountable** devoir répondre de ses actes devant l'opinion 2 *(Econ)* **~-owned** d'État, du secteur public ◆ **~ funded** financé par l'État COMP **publicly-quoted company** N société *f* anonyme cotée en Bourse

publish /ˈpʌblɪʃ/ VT 1 *[+ news]* publier, faire connaître ◆ **to ~ the banns** *(Jur, Rel)* publier les bans 2 *[+ book]* publier ; *[+ periodical]* faire paraître ; *[+ author]* éditer ◆ **to be ~ed** *[book, author]* être publié ◆ **"to be published"** "à paraître" ◆ **"just published"** "vient de paraître" ◆ **"published monthly"** "paraît tous les mois" VI publier

publisher /ˈpʌblɪʃəʳ/ N éditeur *m*, -trice *f*

publishing /ˈpʌblɪʃɪŋ/ N *[of book etc]* publication *f* ◆ **he's** *or* **he works in ~** il travaille dans l'édition COMP **publishing house** N maison *f* d'édition

puce /pjuːs/ ADJ puce *inv*

puck¹ /pʌk/ N *(= elf)* lutin *m*, farfadet *m*

puck² /pʌk/ N *(Ice Hockey)* palet *m*

pucker /ˈpʌkəʳ/ VI (also **pucker up**) *[face, feature, forehead]* se plisser ; *(Sewing)* goder ◆ **she ~ed up, waiting for his kiss** elle avança les lèvres, attendant son baiser VT 1 *(Sewing)* froncer 2 (also **pucker up**) *[+ lips]* avancer ◆ **to ~ (up) one's brow** *or* **forehead** plisser son front N *(Sewing)* faux pli *m*

puckish /ˈpʌkɪʃ/ ADJ *(liter)* de lutin, malicieux

pud ‡ /pʊd/ N *(Brit)* abbrev of **pudding**

pudding /ˈpʊdɪŋ/ N 1 *(= cooked dessert)* **steamed ~** pudding *m* ◆ **apple ~** dessert *m* aux pommes ◆ **rice ~** riz *m* au lait ; → **milk, proof** 2 *(Brit = dessert course in meal)* dessert *m* ◆ **what's for ~?** qu'y a-t-il comme dessert ? 3 *(= cooked meat etc dish)* ◆ **steak-and-kidney ~** pain *m* de viande et de rognons à la vapeur 4 *(= cooked sausage)* **black/white ~** boudin *m* noir/blanc 5 *(* pej = fat person)* patapouf * *mf* COMP **pudding basin** N *(Brit)* jatte *f (dans laquelle on fait cuire le pudding)*

pudding-face ‡ N *(fig pej)* (face *f* de) lune * *f*

pudding-head ‡ N *(fig pej)* empoté(e) * *m(f)*, andouille * *f*

pudding rice N *(Culin)* riz *m* à grains ronds

puddingstone /ˈpʊdɪŋstəʊn/ N *(Geol)* poudingue *m*, conglomérat *m*

puddle /ˈpʌdl/ N flaque *f* VI former une flaque

pudenda /puːˈdendə/ NPL parties *fpl* génitales

pudgy /ˈpʌdʒɪ/ ADJ ⇒ **podgy**

pueblo /ˈpwebləʊ/ N (pl **pueblos**) *(in US) village indien du sud-ouest des États-Unis* COMP **the Pueblo Indians** NPL les (Indiens *mpl*) Pueblos *mpl*

puerile /ˈpjʊəraɪl/ ADJ puéril (puérile *f*)

puerility /pjʊəˈrɪlɪtɪ/ N puérilité *f*

puerperal /pju(ː)ˈɜːpərəl/ ADJ puerpéral ◆ **~ fever** fièvre *f* puerpérale

Puerto Rican /ˈpwɜːtəʊˈriːkən/ ADJ portoricain N Portoricain(e) *m(f)*

Puerto Rico /ˈpwɜːtəʊˈriːkəʊ/ N Porto Rico

puff /pʌf/ N 1 *[of air]* bouffée *f*, souffle *m* ; *(from mouth)* souffle *m* ; *[of wind, smoke]* bouffée *f* ; *(sound of engine)* teuf-teuf *m* ◆ **he blew out the candles with one ~** il a éteint les bougies d'un seul souffle ◆ **our hopes vanished in a ~ of smoke** nos espoirs se sont évanouis *or* s'en sont allés en fumée ◆ **to be out of ~** * être à bout de souffle, être essoufflé ◆ **to get one's ~ * back** reprendre son souffle, reprendre haleine ◆ **he took a ~ at his pipe/cigarette** il a tiré une bouffée de sa pipe/cigarette ◆ **just time for a quick ~!** * juste le temps de griller une clope * *or* d'en griller une * !

2 (also **powder puff**) houppe *f* ; *(small)* houppette *f* ; *(in dress)* bouillon *m* ; *(= pastry)* feuilleté *m* ◆ **jam ~** feuilleté *m* à la confiture

3 *(Press, Rad, TV * = advertisement)* réclame *f NonC*, boniment *m NonC* ; *(= written article)* papier *m* ◆ **a ~ about his new book** un papier sur son nouveau livre

VI *(= blow)* souffler ; *(= pant)* haleter ; *[wind]* souffler ◆ **smoke was ~ing from the ship's funnel** des bouffées de fumée sortaient de la cheminée du navire ◆ **he was ~ing hard** *or* **~ing and panting** il soufflait comme un phoque *or* un bœuf ◆ **to ~ (away) at** *or* **on one's pipe/cigarette** tirer des bouffées de sa pipe/cigarette ◆ **the doctor came ~ing in** le docteur entra en haletant ◆ **to ~ in/out** *etc [train]* entrer/sortir *etc* en envoyant des bouffées de fumée ; see also **puffed**

VT 1 **to ~ (out) smoke** *[person, chimney, engine, boat]* envoyer des bouffées de fumée ◆ **stop ~ing smoke into my face** arrête de m'envoyer ta fumée dans la figure ◆ **he ~ed his pipe** il tirait des bouffées de sa pipe

2 (also **puff out**) *[+ sails etc]* gonfler ◆ **to ~ (out) one's cheeks** gonfler ses joues ◆ **to ~ out one's chest** gonfler *or* bomber sa poitrine ◆ **the bird ~ed out** *or* **up its feathers** l'oiseau a hérissé ses plumes ◆ **his eyes are ~ed (up)** il a les yeux gonflés *or* bouffis

3 *(* = praise:* also **puff up**) faire mousser *, faire du battage autour de

COMP **puff adder** N vipère *f* heurtante

puffed rice N riz *m* soufflé

puffed sleeves NPL ⇒ **puff sleeves** ; → **puff**

puff paste N *(US)* ⇒ **puff pastry**

puff pastry N pâte *f* feuilletée

puff-puff * N *(baby talk = train)* teuf-teuf * *m (baby talk)*

puff sleeves NPL manches *fpl* bouffantes

▸ **puff along** VI *[person]* se déplacer en haletant ; *[steam train, ship]* avancer en haletant

▸ **puff away** VI → **puff vi**

▸ **puff out** VI *[sails etc]* se gonfler ; see also **puff vi**

VT SEP → **puff vt**

▸ **puff up** VI *[sails etc]* se gonfler ; *[eye, face]* enfler

VT SEP *(= inflate)* gonfler ◆ **to be ~ed up (with pride)** *(fig)* être bouffi d'orgueil ; see also **puff vt**

puffball /ˈpʌfbɔːl/ N vesse-de-loup *f*

puffed * /pʌft/ ADJ *(= breathless:* also **puffed out**) à bout de souffle

puffer /ˈpʌfəʳ/ N 1 (also **puffer fish**) poisson-globe *m* 2 *(* = train)* train *m* à vapeur 3 *(Med * = inhaler)* inhalateur *m* 4 *(* = smoker)* fumeur *m*, -euse *f*

puffery /ˈpʌfərɪ/ N *(pej)* battage *m* (publicitaire)

puffin /ˈpʌfɪn/ N macareux *m*, perroquet *m* de mer

puffiness /ˈpʌfɪnɪs/ N *[of eye, face]* gonflement *m*, bouffissure *f*

puffy /ˈpʌfɪ/ ADJ *[eye, face]* gonflé, bouffi ; *[cloud]* cotonneux

pug /pʌg/ N *(= dog)* carlin *m*

COMP **pug nose** N nez *m* retroussé

pug-nosed ADJ au nez retroussé

pugilism /ˈpjuːdʒɪlɪzəm/ N boxe *f*

pugilist † /ˈpjuːdʒɪlɪst/ N pugiliste *m*, boxeur *m*

pugnacious /pʌgˈneɪʃəs/ ADJ pugnace, querelleur

pugnaciously /pʌgˈneɪʃəslɪ/ ADV avec pugnacité, d'un ton querelleur

pugnacity /pʌgˈnæsɪtɪ/ N pugnacité *f*

puke ‡ /pjuːk/ VI (also **puke up**) dégueuler ‡, dégobiller ‡ ◆ **it makes you ~** *(fig)* c'est à faire vomir, c'est dégueulasse ‡ VT (also **puke up**) dégueuler ‡ N 1 *(= vomit)* dégueulis ‡ *m* 2 *(US pej = person)* salaud ‡ *m*

▸ **puke up** ‡ ⇒ **puke vi, vt**

pukka * /ˈpʌkə/ ADJ *(Brit)* 1 *(= genuine)* vrai, véritable ; *(= excellent)* de premier ordre 2 *(= socially superior)* snob *inv*

pulchritude /ˈpʌlkrɪtjuːd/ N *(liter or hum)* vénusté *f (liter)*

pulchritudinous /ˌpʌlkrɪˈtjuːdɪnəs/ ADJ *(liter or hum)* bien tourné †, beau (belle *f*)

Pulitzer prize /ˈpʊlɪtsəˌpraɪz/ N *(US)* prix *m* Pulitzer

> **PULITZER PRIZE**
>
> Aux États-Unis, les prix Pulitzer sont des récompenses prestigieuses décernées chaque année aux personnes jugées les plus méritantes dans les domaines du journalisme, de la littérature ou de la musique. Il existe treize catégories en journalisme (enquête, articles de fond, etc) et six en littérature. Ces prix ont été créés et financés par le journaliste et propriétaire de journaux Joseph Pulitzer (1847-1911).

pull /pʊl/ N 1 *(= act, effect)* traction *f* ; *[of moon]* attraction *f* ; *(= attraction: magnetic, fig)* (force *f* d')attraction *f*, magnétisme *m* ◆ **one more ~ and we'll have it up** encore un coup et on l'aura ◆ **I felt a ~ at my sleeve** j'ai senti quelqu'un qui tirait ma manche ◆ **to give sth a ~, to give a ~ on** *or* **at sth** tirer (sur) qch ◆ **he's got ~ *** *(fig)* il a le bras long ◆ **the ~ of the current** la force du courant ◆ **the ~ of family ties** *(fig)* la force des liens familiaux ◆ **the ~ of the South/the sea** *etc (fig)* l'attraction *f or* l'appel *m* du Sud/de la mer *etc* ◆ **to be on the ~ ‡** *(fig)* draguer * ◆ **to have a ~ over sb** *(fig = have a hold over)* avoir barre sur qn ◆ **it was a long ~ to the shore** *(Rowing)* il a fallu ramer longtemps pour arriver jusqu'au rivage ◆ **it was a long (hard) ~ up the hill** la montée était longue (et raide) pour arriver en haut de la colline ◆ **to have (some) ~ with sb** *(= influence)* avoir de l'influence auprès de qn ; → **leg**

2 *(= swig, puff: at bottle, glass, drink)* gorgée *f* ◆ **he took a ~ at the bottle** il a bu une gorgée à même la bouteille ◆ **he took a ~ at his beer** il a bu une gorgée de bière ◆ **he took a long ~ at his cigarette/pipe** il a tiré longuement sur sa cigarette/pipe

3 *(= handle)* poignée *f* ; *(= cord)* cordon *m* ; → **bell¹**

4 *(Typ)* épreuve *f*

5 *(Golf)* coup *m* hooké

VT 1 *(= draw) [+ cart, carriage, coach, caravan, curtains]* tirer ◆ **she ~ed her jacket around her shoulders** elle ramena sa veste autour de ses épaules ◆ **to ~ a door open** ouvrir une porte (en la tirant) ◆ **he ~ed the box over to the window** il a traîné la caisse jusqu'à la fenêtre ◆ **to ~ a door shut** tirer une porte derrière soi ◆ **~ your chair closer to the table** approchez votre chaise de la table ◆ **he ~ed her towards him** il l'attira vers lui ◆ **to ~ sb clear of** *[+ wreckage, rubble]* dégager qn de ; *[+ water, mud]* retirer qn de

2 *(= tug) [+ bell, rope, thread]* tirer ; *[+ trigger]* presser ; *[+ oars]* manier ◆ **to ~ to pieces** *or* **to bits** *(lit) [+ toy, box etc]* mettre en pièces *or* en morceaux, démolir ; *[+ daisy]* effeuiller ; (* *fig*) *[+ argument, scheme, play, film]* démolir* ; * *[+ person]* éreinter ◆ **to ~ sb's hair** tirer les cheveux à qn ◆ ~ **the other one (it's got bells on)!**⁑ à d'autres !, mon œil !* ◆ **to ~ a horse** *(Racing)* retenir un cheval ◆ **to ~ one's punches** *(Boxing, also fig)* ménager son adversaire ◆ **he didn't ~ any punches** il n'y est pas allé de main morte, il n'a pas pris de gants ◆ **to ~ one's weight** *(fig)* faire sa part du travail, fournir sa part d'effort ; → **leg, string, wire**

3 *(= draw out) [+ tooth]* arracher, extraire ; *[+ cork, stopper]* ôter, retirer ; *[+ gun, knife]* sortir ; *[+ flowers]* cueillir ; *[+ weeds]* arracher, extirper ; *[+ beer]* tirer ; *(Culin) [+ chicken]* vider ◆ **he ~ed a gun on me** il a sorti un revolver et l'a braqué sur moi ◆ **he's ~ing pints* somewhere in London** il est barman quelque part à Londres ◆ **to ~ trumps*** *(Cards)* faire tomber les atouts ◆ **to ~ rank on sb** *(fig)* en imposer hiérarchiquement à qn

4 *(= strain, tear) [+ muscle, tendon, ligament]* se déchirer

5 *(Typ)* tirer

6 *(Golf etc) [+ ball]* hooker ◆ **to ~ a shot** hooker

7 (* *= cancel) [+ TV programme]* annuler

8 (* *= make, do)* faire, commettre ◆ **the gang ~ed several bank raids/several burglaries last month** le gang a fait *or* commis plusieurs hold-up de banques/plusieurs cambriolages le mois dernier ◆ **to ~ a trick on sb** jouer un mauvais tour à qn ; → **face, fast¹, long¹**

9 (* *fig = attract) [+ public]* attirer ; *[+ votes]* ramasser

10 *(Brit* ⁑ *= get off with)* lever⁑

VI 1 *(= tug)* tirer *(at, on sur)* ◆ **stop ~ing!** arrêtez de tirer ! ◆ **he ~ed at her sleeve** il lui tira la manche, il la tira par la manche ◆ **the car/the steering is ~ing to the left** la voiture/la direction porte à gauche ◆ **the brakes ~ to the left** quand on freine la voiture porte à gauche *or* est déportée sur la gauche ◆ **to ~ for sb*** *(fig)* appuyer qn ; see also **vi 2**

2 *(= move)* **the train ~ed into/out of the station** le train est entré en gare/est sorti de la gare ◆ **he soon ~ed clear of the traffic** il eut vite fait de laisser le gros de la circulation derrière lui ◆ **to ~ sharply to the left** *[car, driver]* virer brusquement à gauche ; see also **vi 1** ◆ **the car isn't ~ing very well** la voiture manque de reprises

3 *(= swig, puff)* ◆ **he ~ed at his beer** il a bu une gorgée de bière ◆ **to ~ at a cigarette/pipe** *etc* tirer sur une cigarette/pipe *etc*

4 *(= row)* ramer *(for vers)*

5 *(⁑ Brit) (= get off with sb)* emballer*

COMP **pull-back** N *(Mil)* repli *m*

pull-down ADJ *[bed]* rabattable, escamotable ◆ **~-down seat** strapontin *m*

pull-down menu N *(Comput)* menu *m* déroulant

pull-in N *(Brit) (= lay-by)* parking *m* ; *(= café)* café *m* de bord de route, routier *m*

pull-off N *(US)* parking *m*

pull-out N, ADJ → **pull-out**

pull-ring, pull-tab N *(on can)* anneau *m*, bague *f*

pull-up N *(Brit: by roadside)* ⇒ **pull-in** *(Gym)* traction *f (sur barre etc)*

► **pull about** VT SEP 1 *[+ wheeled object etc]* tirer derrière soi

2 *(= handle roughly) [+ object]* tirailler ; *[+ person]* malmener

► **pull ahead** VI *(in race, election etc)* prendre la tête ◆ **he began to ~ ahead of his pursuers** il a commencé à prendre de l'avance sur *or* à distancer ses poursuivants

► **pull along** VT SEP *[+ wheeled object etc]* tirer derrière *or* après soi ◆ **to ~ o.s. along** se traîner

► **pull apart** VI ◆ **this box pulls apart** cette boîte est démontable *or* se démonte

VT SEP 1 *(= pull to pieces)* démonter ; *(= break)* mettre en pièces *or* en morceaux ◆ **the police ~ed the whole house apart looking for drugs** * la police a mis la maison sens dessus dessous en cherchant de la drogue ◆ **his parents' rows were ~ing him apart** les disputes de ses parents le déchiraient ◆ **nationalism was threatening to ~ the country apart** le nationalisme menaçait de déchirer le pays

2 *(= separate) [+ dogs, adversaries]* séparer ; *[+ sheets of paper etc]* détacher, séparer

3 *(fig = criticize) [+ play, performance]* éreinter ; *[+ argument, suggestion]* démolir

► **pull around** VT SEP ⇒ **pull about**

► **pull away** VI *[vehicle, ship]* démarrer ; *[train]* démarrer, s'ébranler ◆ **he ~ed away from the kerb** il s'est éloigné du trottoir ◆ **he began to ~ away from his pursuers** il a commencé à prendre de l'avance sur *or* à distancer ses poursuivants ◆ **she suddenly ~ed away from him** elle se dégagea soudain de son étreinte

VT SEP *(= withdraw)* retirer brusquement *(from sb* à qn) ; *(= snatch)* ôter, arracher *(from sb* à qn, des mains de qn) ◆ **he ~ed the child away from the fire** il a éloigné *or* écarté l'enfant du feu

► **pull back** VI *(Mil, gen, fig = withdraw)* se retirer

VT SEP 1 *(= withdraw) [+ object]* retirer *(from* de) ; *[+ person]* tirer en arrière *(from* loin de) ; *(Mil)* retirer, ramener à *or* vers l'arrière ◆ **to ~ back the curtains** ouvrir les rideaux

2 *[+ lever]* tirer *(sur)*

► **pull down** VT SEP 1 *[+ blind]* baisser, descendre ◆ **he ~ed his opponent down (to the ground)** il a mis à terre son adversaire ◆ **he ~ed his hat down over his eyes** il ramena *or* rabattit son chapeau sur ses yeux ◆ **~ your skirt down over your knees** ramène *or* tire ta jupe sur tes genoux ◆ **she slipped and ~ed everything down off the shelf with her** elle a glissé et entraîné dans sa chute tout ce qui était sur l'étagère

2 *(= demolish) [+ building]* démolir, abattre ; *[+ tree]* abattre ◆ **the whole street has been ~ed down** la rue a été complètement démolie ◆ **to ~ down the government** renverser le gouvernement

3 *(= weaken, reduce)* affaiblir, abattre ◆ **that bout of flu ~ed him down quite a lot** cette grippe l'a considérablement affaibli ◆ **his geography marks ~ed him down** ses notes de géographie ont fait baisser sa moyenne

► **pull in** VI *(Aut etc) (= arrive)* arriver ; *(= enter)* entrer ; *(= stop)* s'arrêter ◆ **when the train ~ed in (at the station)** quand le train est entré en gare

VT SEP 1 *[+ rope, fishing line]* ramener ◆ **to ~ sb in** *(into room, car)* faire entrer qn, tirer qn à l'intérieur ; *(into pool etc)* faire piquer une tête dans l'eau à qn ◆ **~ your chair in (to the table)** rentre ta chaise (sous la table) ◆ **~ your stomach in!** rentre le ventre ! ◆ **the film is certainly ~ing people in** il est certain que ce film attire les foules ; → **belt, horn**

2 (* *= pick up)* **the police ~ed him in for questioning** la police l'a appréhendé pour l'interroger

3 *(= restrain) [+ horse]* retenir

4 (* *= earn) [person]* gagner ; *[business, shop etc]* rapporter

N ◆ **pull-in** → **pull**

► **pull off** VT SEP 1 *(= remove) [+ handle, lid, cloth]* enlever, ôter ; *[+ gloves, shoes, coat, hat]* enlever, ôter

2 *(Driving)* ◆ **he pulled the car off the road** *or* **onto the verge** il a arrêté la voiture sur le bord de la route

3 *(fig) [+ plan, aim]* réaliser ; *[+ deal]* mener à bien, conclure ; *[+ attack, hoax]* réussir ◆ **he didn't manage to ~ it off** il n'a pas réussi son coup

VI 1 *(= start) [car, bus etc]* démarrer, partir

2 ◆ **to pull off the road** *[vehicle, driver]* quitter la route

N ◆ **pull-off** → **pull**

► **pull on** VI ◆ **the cover pulls on** la housse s'enfile

VT SEP *[+ gloves, coat, cover]* mettre, enfiler ; *[+ shoes, hat]* mettre

► **pull out** VI 1 *(= leave) [train]* s'ébranler, démarrer ; *[car, bus, ship]* démarrer, partir

2 *(= withdraw) (lit, fig)* se retirer *(of* de) ◆ **to ~ out of a dive** *[pilot]* se redresser ◆ **he ~ed out of the deal at the last minute** il a tiré son épingle du jeu *or* il s'est retiré à la dernière minute

3 *(Driving)* déboîter, sortir de la file ◆ **he ~ed out to overtake the truck** il a déboîté pour doubler le camion

4 ◆ **the drawers pull out easily** les tiroirs coulissent bien ◆ **the table ~s out to seat eight** avec la rallonge huit personnes peuvent s'asseoir à la table ◆ **the centre pages ~ out** les pages du milieu sont détachables *or* se détachent

VT SEP 1 *(= extract, remove) [+ nail, hair, page]* arracher ; *[+ splinter]* enlever ; *[+ cork, stopper]* ôter, retirer ; *[+ tooth]* arracher, extraire ; *[+ weeds]* arracher, extirper ; *[+ gun, knife, cigarette lighter]* sortir ◆ **he ~ed a rabbit out of his hat** il a sorti *or* tiré un lapin de son chapeau ◆ **to ~ sb out of a room** faire sortir qn d'une pièce ◆ **they ~ed him out of the wreckage alive** ils l'ont tiré *or* sorti vivant des débris ; → **finger, stop**

2 *(= withdraw) [+ troops, police etc]* retirer *(of* de) ◆ **the union has ~ed all the workers out on strike** tous les ouvriers ont répondu à la consigne de grève donnée par le syndicat

3 (* *fig = produce) [+ reason, argument]* sortir* ◆ **he ~ed out one last trick** *(fig)* il a usé d'un dernier stratagème

► **pull over** VI *(in car)* ◆ **he ~ed over (to one side) to let the ambulance past** il s'est rangé *or* garé sur le côté pour laisser passer l'ambulance

VT SEP 1 ◆ **he pulled the box over to the window** il a traîné la caisse jusqu'à la fenêtre ◆ **she ~ed the chair over and stood on it** elle a tiré la chaise à elle pour grimper dessus ◆ **they ~ed him over to the door** ils l'ont entraîné jusqu'à la porte

2 (* *= stop) [+ motorist, car]* contraindre à s'arrêter

3 ◆ **they climbed the wall and pulled him over** ils ont grimpé sur le mur et l'ont hissé de l'autre côté

4 *(= topple)* **the vandals ~ed the gatepost over** les vandales ont renversé *or* fait tomber le montant du portail ◆ **he ~ed the bookcase over on top of himself** il a entraîné la bibliothèque dans sa chute

► **pull round** VI *[unconscious person]* revenir à soi, reprendre conscience ; *[sick person]* s'en sortir

VT SEP 1 *[+ chair etc]* faire pivoter, tourner ◆ **he ~ed me round to face him** il m'a fait me retourner pour me forcer à lui faire face

2 *[+ unconscious person]* ramener à la conscience

► **pull through** VI *(from illness)* s'en tirer, s'en sortir ; *(from difficulties)* s'en sortir, s'en tirer

VT SEP *[+ rope etc] (gen)* faire passer ; *(Climbing)* rappeler

VT FUS *[+ illness]* réchapper à ; *[+ difficulties, crisis]* se sortir de

► **pull together** VI 1 *(on rope etc)* tirer ensemble *or* simultanément ; *(on oars)* ramer simultanément *or* à l'unisson

2 *(fig = cooperate)* (s'entendre pour) faire un effort

VT SEP 1 *(= join) [+ rope ends etc]* joindre ◆ **let me now ~ together the threads of my argument** je vais maintenant faire la synthèse de mes arguments ◆ **data exists but it needs ~ing together** les données existent mais il faut les rassembler

2 * **to ~ o.s. together** se reprendre, se ressaisir ◆ **~ yourself together!** ressaisis-toi !, reprends-toi !

► **pull up** VI 1 *(= stop) [vehicle]* s'arrêter, stopper ; *[athlete, horse]* s'arrêter (net)

2 *(= draw level with)* **he ~ed up with the leaders** il a rattrapé *or* rejoint ceux qui menaient

VT SEP 1 *(= raise) [+ object]* remonter ; *(= haul up)* hisser ; *[+ stockings]* remonter, tirer ; *[+ chair]* approcher ◆ **when the bucket was full he ~ed it up** une fois le seau plein il l'a remonté ◆ **he leaned down from the wall and ~ed the child up** il s'est penché du haut du mur et a hissé l'enfant jusqu'à lui ◆ **he ~ed me up out of the armchair** il m'a tiré *or* fait sortir du fauteuil ◆ **your geography mark has ~ed you up** votre note de géographie vous a remonté* ; → **sock¹**

2 *(= bring close)* **~ up a chair!** prends une chaise !

3 *[+ tree etc]* arracher, déraciner ; *[+ weed]* arracher, extirper ◆ **to ~ up one's roots** se déraciner

4 *(= halt) [+ vehicle]* arrêter, stopper ; *[+ horse]* arrêter ◆ **the chairman ~ed the speaker up (short)** le président a coupé la parole à *or* a interrompu l'orateur ◆ **he ~ed himself up (short)** il s'arrêta net *or* pile ◆ **the police ~ed him up for speeding** la police l'a arrêté pour excès de vitesse ◆ **the headmaster ~ed him up for using bad language** il a été repris *or* réprimandé par le directeur pour avoir été grossier

N ◆ **pull-up** → **pull**

pullet /ˈpʊlɪt/ N jeune poule *f*, poulette *f*

pulley /ˈpʊlɪ/ N 1 *(= block)* poulie *f* 2 *(Scot: for clothes-drying)* séchoir *m* à linge (suspendu)

Pullman ® /ˈpʊlmən/ N (pl **Pullmans**) *(Brit Rail:* also **Pullman carriage**) pullman *m*, voiture-salon *f*, wagon-salon *m* ; *(US = sleeper:* also **Pullman car**) voiture-lit *f*, wagon-lit *m* ; *(= train)* (also **Pullman train**) train *m* Pullman

pull-out /ˈpʊlaʊt/ N 1 *(in magazine etc)* supplément *m* détachable 2 *[of troops]* retrait *m* ADJ *[magazine section]* détachable ; *[table leaf, shelf]* rétractable ◆ **~ bed** meuble-lit *m*

pullover /ˈpʊlˌəʊvəʳ/ N *(esp Brit)* pull *m*, pullover *m*

pullulate /ˈpʌljʊleɪt/ VI *(frm)* pulluler

pully * /ˈpʊlɪ/ N *(Brit)* (abbrev of **pullover**) pull *m*

pulmonary /ˈpʌlmənərɪ/ ADJ pulmonaire

pulp /pʌlp/ N 1 *(= paste)* pulpe *f* ; *(= part of fruit)* pulpe *f*, chair *f* ; *(for paper)* pâte *f* à papier, pulpe *f* (à papier) ◆ **to reduce** *or* **crush to a ~** *[+ wood]* réduire en pâte *or* en pulpe ; *[+ fruit]* réduire en purée ◆ **his arm was crushed to a ~** il a eu le bras complètement écrasé ◆ **to beat sb to a ~** passer qn à tabac*, tabasser* qn ; → **pound²** 2 *(pej = literature)* littérature *f* de gare ◆ **~ fiction/novel** romans *mpl*/roman *m* de gare ◆ **~ magazine** magazine *m* à sensation, torchon* *m* VT *[+ wood, linen]* réduire en pâte *or* en pulpe ; *[+ fruit]* réduire en purée ; *[+ book]* mettre au pilon, pilonner ; *[+ money, documents]* détruire *(par broyage)* COMP **pulp cavity** N *(in tooth)* cavité *f* pulpaire

pulpit /ˈpʊlpɪt/ N chaire *f* *(Rel)*

pulpy /ˈpʌlpɪ/ ADJ 1 *(= soft) [fruit]* charnu, pulpeux ; *[consistency]* pâteux ; *(Bio) [tissue]* pulpeux 2 *(* = trashy) [novel, literature]* de gare *(pej)*

pulsar /ˈpʌlsɑːʳ/ N pulsar *m*

pulsate /pʌlˈseɪt/ VI *[heart, vein]* palpiter ; *[blood]* battre ; *[music]* vibrer ◆ **the pulsating rhythm of the drums** le battement rythmique des tambours

pulsating /pʌlˈseɪtɪŋ/ ADJ *[heart, vein]* palpitant ; *[music]* vibrant ; *(fig = exciting)* palpitant

pulsation /pʌlˈseɪʃən/ N *[of heart]* battement *m*, pulsation *f* ; *(Elec, Phys)* pulsation *f*

pulse¹ /pʌls/ N *(Med)* pouls *m* ; *(Elec, Phys, Rad)* vibration *f* ; *[of radar]* impulsion *f* ; *(fig) [of drums etc]* battement *m* rythmique ; *[of emotion]* frémissement *m*, palpitation *f* ◆ **to take sb's ~** *(also fig)* prendre le pouls de qn ◆ **to have** *or* **keep one's finger on the ~** être à l'écoute de ce qui se passe VI *[heart]* battre fort ; *[blood]* battre ; *[sound]* vibrer ◆ **it sent the blood pulsing through his veins** cela lui fouetta le sang ◆ **the life pulsing in a great city** la vie qui palpite au cœur d'une grande ville COMP **pulse rate** N *(Med)* pouls *m*

pulse² /pʌls/ N *(Bot)* légume *m* à gousse ; *(Culin) (dried)* légume *m* sec

pulsebeat /ˈpʌlsbiːt/ N *(Med, Mus)* pulsation *f*

pulverization /ˌpʌlvəraɪˈzeɪʃən/ N pulvérisation *f*

pulverize /ˈpʌlvəraɪz/ VT *(lit, fig)* pulvériser

puma /ˈpjuːmə/ N puma *m*

pumice /ˈpʌmɪs/ N (also **pumice stone**) pierre *f* ponce

pummel /ˈpʌml/ VT *(in fight)* bourrer *or* rouer de coups ; *(in massage)* pétrir

pummelling /ˈpʌməlɪŋ/ N *(in fight)* volée *f* de coups ; *(in massage)* pétrissage *m* ◆ **to take a ~** *(lit)* se faire rouer de coups ; *(Sport = be beaten)* se faire battre à plate(s) couture(s) ; *(= be criticized/attacked)* se faire violemment critiquer/attaquer

pump¹ /pʌmp/ N *(all senses)* pompe *f* ; → **parish, petrol, prime**

VT 1 **to ~ water into sth** pomper de l'eau dans qch ◆ **to ~ water out of sth** pomper l'eau de qch ◆ **they ~ed the remaining oil out of the ship** ils ont pompé le pétrole qui restait dans le navire ◆ **they ~ed the tank dry** ils ont vidé *or* asséché le réservoir (à la pompe) ◆ **to ~ air into sth** gonfler qch ◆ **the water is ~ed up to the house** l'eau est amenée jusqu'à la maison au moyen d'une pompe ◆ **the heart ~s the blood round the body** le cœur fait circuler le sang dans le corps ◆ **to ~ oil through a pipe** faire passer *or* faire couler du pétrole dans un pipeline (à l'aide d'une pompe) ◆ **to ~ sb's stomach** *(Med)* faire un lavage d'estomac à qn ◆ **to ~ iron** * *(Sport)* faire de l'haltérophilie ◆ **to ~ sb full of drugs** * bourrer qn de calmants* ◆ **to ~ bullets into sb** * cribler qn de balles ; → **lead²** ◆ **they ~ed money into the project** * ils ont injecté de l'argent dans le projet ◆ **he ~ed facts into their heads** il leur bourrait* la tête de faits précis

2 *(* = question)* **to ~ sb for sth** essayer de soutirer qch à qn ◆ **they'll try to ~ you (for information)** ils essayeront de vous faire parler *or* de vous tirer les vers* du nez

3 *[+ accelerator, brake]* appuyer plusieurs fois sur ; *[+ handle etc]* lever et abaisser

VI *[pump, machine, person]* pomper ; *[heart]* battre fort ◆ **blood ~ed from the artery** le sang coulait à flots de l'artère ◆ **the oil was ~ing along the pipeline** le pétrole coulait dans le pipeline ◆ **the piston was ~ing up and down** le piston montait et descendait régulièrement

COMP **pump-action** ADJ *[shotgun]* à pompe

pump attendant N *(Brit)* pompiste *mf*

pump house, pumping station N station *f* d'épuisement *or* de pompage

pump prices NPL ◆ **a rise in ~ prices** *[of petrol]* une hausse (des prix) à la pompe

pump priming N *(Econ)* mesures *fpl* de relance de l'économie

pump room N buvette *f (où l'on prend les eaux dans une station thermale)*

pump-water N eau *f* de la pompe

► **pump away** VI *[heart]* battre la chamade ◆ **he was ~ing away on the lever** il faisait fonctionner *or* actionnait le levier

► **pump in** VT SEP *[+ water, oil, gas etc]* refouler (à l'aide d'une pompe) ◆ **~ some more air in** donnez plus d'air

► **pump out** VI *[blood, oil]* couler à flots *(of de)*

VT SEP 1 *[+ water, oil, gas etc]* pomper, aspirer (à l'aide d'une pompe)

2 *(* = produce)* pondre en masse* ◆ **this station ~s out pop music 24 hours a day** *(TV, Rad)* cette station balance* de la musique pop 24 heures par jour

► **pump up** VT SEP *[+ tyre, airbed]* gonfler ; see also **pump vt 1**

pump² /pʌmp/ N *(esp Brit = sports shoe)* chausson *m* de gym(nastique) ; *(US = court shoe)* escarpin *m*

pumpernickel /ˈpʌmpənɪkl/ N pumpernickel *m*, pain *m* de seigle noir

pumpkin /ˈpʌmpkɪn/ N citrouille *f* ; *(bigger)* potiron *m* ; *[of Cinderella]* citrouille *f* ◆ **~ pie** tarte *f* à la citrouille

pun /pʌn/ N calembour *m*, jeu *m* de mots VI faire un *or* des calembour(s), faire un *or* des jeu(x) de mots ◆ **"foot and mouth is a big problem, in fact it's a pig* of a problem" he ~ned** "la fièvre aphteuse est un problème très sérieux, c'est même vachement* sérieux" dit-il en voulant faire un jeu de mots

Punch /pʌntʃ/ N Polichinelle *m* ◆ **~ and Judy show** (théâtre *m* de) guignol *m* ; → **pleased**

punch¹ /pʌntʃ/ N 1 *(= blow)* coup *m* de poing ◆ **to give sb a ~ (on the nose)** donner un coup de poing (sur le nez) à qn ◆ **he's got a good ~** *(Boxing)* il a du punch ◆ **to ride with the ~es** *(esp US)* encaisser* ; → **pack, pull, rabbit**

2 *(NonC = punchiness)* punch* *m* ◆ **a phrase with more ~** une expression plus frappante *or* plus incisive ◆ **we need a presentation with some ~ to it** il nous faut une présentation énergique *or* vigoureuse ◆ **a film with no ~ to it** un film qui manque de punch*

3 *(= tool) (for tickets)* poinçonneuse *f* ; *(for holes in paper)* perforateur *m* ; *(for metal-working)* poinçonneuse *f*, emporte-pièce *m inv* ; *(for stamping design)* étampe *f* ; *(smaller)* poinçon *m* ; *(for driving in nails)* chasse-clou *m*

VT 1 *(with fist) [+ person]* donner un coup de poing à ; *[+ ball, door]* frapper d'un coup de poing ◆ **to ~ sb's nose/face, to ~ sb in the nose/face** donner un coup de poing sur le nez/dans la figure de qn ◆ **to ~ sb in the stomach/in the kidneys/on the jaw** donner un coup de poing dans le ventre/les reins/la mâchoire à qn ◆ **to ~ the air** lever le poing en signe de victoire ◆ **he ~ed his fist through the glass** il a passé son poing à travers la vitre, il a brisé la vitre d'un coup de poing ◆ **the goalkeeper ~ed the ball over the bar** d'un coup de poing le gardien de but a envoyé le ballon par-dessus la barre ◆ **he ~ed his way through** il s'est ouvert un chemin à (force de) coups de poing *or* en frappant à droite et à gauche

2 *(US)* **to ~ cattle** conduire le bétail (à l'aiguillon)

3 *(with tool) [+ paper]* poinçonner, perforer ; *[+ ticket] (by hand)* poinçonner ; *(automatically)* composter ; *[+ computer cards]* perforer ; *[+ metal]* poinçonner, découper à l'emporte-pièce ; *[+ design]* estamper ; *[+ nails]* enfoncer profondément (au chasse-clou) ◆ **to ~ a hole in sth** faire un trou dans qch ◆ **to ~ the time clock, to ~ one's card** † pointer
4 *(with finger) [+ button]* taper sur
VI frapper (dur), cogner ◆ **he ~es well** *(Boxing)* il sait frapper ◆ **to ~ above one's weight** *(fig)* jouer dans la cour des grands
COMP **punch bag** N *(Brit) (Sport)* sac *m* de sable ; *(fig)* souffre-douleur *m inv* ◆ **to use sb as a ~ bag** faire de qn son souffre-douleur, se servir de qn comme d'un punching-ball
punch card N carte *f* perforée ◆ **~ card system** système *m* à cartes perforées
punch-drunk ADJ *(Boxing)* groggy, sonné* ; *(fig)* abruti
punching bag N *(US)* ⇒ **punch bag**
punching ball N ⇒ **punchball**
punch line N *[of joke etc]* chute *f*, conclusion *f* (comique) ; *[of speech etc]* mot *m* de la fin
punch operator N *(Comput)* mécanographe *mf*
punch tape N *(Comput)* bande *f* perforée
punch-up* N bagarre *f* ◆ **to have a ~-up** *(Brit)* se bagarrer*
► **punch in** VI † *(on time clock)* pointer (en arrivant)
VT SEP 1 *[+ door, lid etc]* ouvrir d'un coup de poing ◆ **to ~ sb's face** *or* **head in**‡ casser la gueule à qn‡
2 *(= key in) [+ code number etc]* taper
► **punch out** VI † *(on time clock)* pointer (en partant)
VT SEP *[+ hole]* faire au poinçon *or* à la poinçonneuse ; *[+ machine parts]* découper à l'emporte-pièce ; *[+ design]* estamper

punch² /pʌntʃ/ N *(= drink)* punch *m* COMP **punch bowl** N bol *m* à punch

punchball /ˈpʌntʃbɔːl/ N 1 *(Brit)* punching-ball *m* 2 *(US) variante simplifiée du baseball, qui se joue sans batte*

punchy* /ˈpʌntʃɪ/ ADJ 1 *(= forceful) [person]* qui a du punch*, dynamique ; *[remark, reply]* incisif, mordant 2 ⇒ **punch-drunk** ; → **punch¹**

punctilio /pʌŋkˈtɪlɪəʊ/ N (pl **punctilios**) *(NonC: frm) (= formality)* formalisme *m* ; *(= point of etiquette)* point *m* or détail *m* d'étiquette

punctilious /pʌŋkˈtɪlɪəs/ ADJ scrupuleux

punctiliously /pʌŋkˈtɪlɪəslɪ/ ADV scrupuleusement

punctual /ˈpʌŋktjʊəl/ ADJ *[person, train]* à l'heure ; *[payment]* ponctuel ◆ **he is always ~** il est très ponctuel, il est toujours à l'heure ◆ **be ~** soyez *or* arrivez à l'heure

punctuality /ˌpʌŋktjʊˈælɪtɪ/ N *[of person]* ponctualité *f*, exactitude *f* ; *[of train]* ponctualité *f*

punctually /ˈpʌŋktjʊəlɪ/ ADV ponctuellement

punctuate /ˈpʌŋktjʊeɪt/ VT *(lit, fig)* ponctuer (with de)

punctuation /ˌpʌŋktjʊˈeɪʃən/ N ponctuation *f* ◆ **~ mark** signe *m* de ponctuation

puncture /ˈpʌŋktʃəʳ/ N *(in tyre)* crevaison *f* ; *(in skin, paper, leather)* piqûre *f* ; *(Med)* ponction *f* ◆ **I've got a ~** j'ai (un pneu) crevé ◆ **they had a ~ outside Limoges** ils ont crevé près de Limoges VT *[+ tyre, balloon]* crever ; *[+ skin, leather, paper]* piquer ; *(Med) [+ abscess]* percer, ouvrir ◆ **the bullet ~d his skull** la balle lui a transpercé le crâne ◆ **his pride had been ~d** sa fierté en avait pris un coup VI *[tyre etc]* crever
COMP **puncture repair kit** N trousse *f* à outils pour crevaisons
puncture wound N perforation *f*

pundit /ˈpʌndɪt/ N expert *m*, pontife *m*

pungency /ˈpʌndʒənsɪ/ N *[of smell, taste]* âcreté *f* ; *[of sauce]* goût *m* piquant *or* relevé ; *[of remark, criticism]* mordant *m*, causticité *f*

pungent /ˈpʌndʒənt/ ADJ *[fumes, smoke]* âcre ; *[smell, taste]* âcre, piquant ; *[sauce]* piquant, relevé ; *[remark, criticism, satire]* mordant, caustique

pungently /ˈpʌndʒəntlɪ/ ADV *[remark]* d'un ton mordant *or* caustique ; *[criticize]* de façon mordante *or* caustique ◆ **~ flavoured** (au goût) relevé

Punic /ˈpjuːnɪk/ ADJ punique ◆ **the ~ Wars** *(Hist)* les guerres puniques

punish /ˈpʌnɪʃ/ VT 1 *[+ person]* punir *(for sth* de qch ; *for doing sth* pour avoir fait qch) ; *[+ theft, fault]* punir ◆ **he was ~ed by having to clean it all up** pour le punir on lui a fait tout nettoyer, pour sa punition il a dû tout nettoyer 2 *(fig) [+ opponent in fight, boxer, opposing team]* malmener ; *[+ engine]* fatiguer ◆ **the jockey really ~ed his horse** le jockey a vraiment forcé *or* fatigué son cheval

punishable /ˈpʌnɪʃəbl/ ADJ *[offence]* punissable ◆ **~ by death/imprisonment** passible de la peine de mort/d'une peine de prison

punishing /ˈpʌnɪʃɪŋ/ N *(= act)* punition *f* ◆ **to take a ~** *(fig) [boxer, opponent, opposing team]* se faire malmener ADJ *[speed, heat, game, work]* épuisant, exténuant

punishment /ˈpʌnɪʃmənt/ N *(gen)* punition *f* ; *(solemn)* châtiment *m* ; *(formal: against employee, student etc)* sanctions *fpl* ◆ **as a ~ (for)** en punition (de) ◆ **he took his ~ bravely** *or* **like a man** il a subi sa punition sans se plaindre ◆ **to make the ~ fit the crime** adapter le châtiment au crime, proportionner la peine au délit ◆ **to take a lot of ~** *(fig) [boxer, opponent in fight]* encaisser* ; *[opposing team]* se faire malmener ; → **capital, corporal²** COMP **punishment beating** N action *f* punitive

punitive /ˈpjuːnɪtɪv/ ADJ *[expedition, measure]* punitif ◆ **a ~ bombing raid** un raid aérien de représailles
COMP **punitive damages** NPL *(Jur)* dommages-intérêts *mpl* dissuasifs *(très élevés)*
punitive taxation N *(NonC)* fiscalité *f* dissuasive

Punjab /pʌnˈdʒɑːb/ N Pendjab *m*

Punjabi /pʌnˈdʒɑːbɪ/ ADJ pendjabi N 1 *(= person)* Pendjabi *mf* 2 *(= language)* pendjabi *m*

punk /pʌŋk/ N 1 *(= music)* punk *m* 2 *(= musician, fan)* punk *mf* 3 *(US* ‡ *= ruffian)* voyou* *m* ADJ 1 *[band, music, style]* punk *inv* ◆ **~ rock** punk rock *m* ◆ **~ rocker** punk *mf* 2 *(US* ‡ *= ill)* mal foutu‡

punnet /ˈpʌnɪt/ N *(Brit)* barquette *f*

punster /ˈpʌnstəʳ/ N personne *f* qui fait des calembours

punt¹ /pʌnt/ N *(= boat)* barque *f* à fond plat VT *[+ boat]* faire avancer à la perche ; *[+ goods]* transporter en bachot VI ◆ **to go ~ing** faire un tour de rivière, aller se promener en bachot

punt² /pʌnt/ *(Ftbl, Rugby)* VT *[+ ball]* envoyer d'un coup de volée N coup *m* de volée

punt³ /pʌnt/ VI *(Brit = bet)* parier

punt⁴ /pʌnt/ N livre *f* irlandaise

punter /ˈpʌntəʳ/ N 1 *(Brit) (Racing)* turfiste *mf*, parieur *m*, -euse *f* ; *(in casino)* joueur *m*, -euse *f* 2 *(* = customer)* client(e) *m(f)* ; *[of prostitute]* micheton* *m* ; *(on Stock Exchange)* boursicoteur *m*, -euse *f* ◆ **the ~(s)** *(Brit = customer, member of public)* le public, la clientèle ◆ **your average ~** Monsieur Tout-le-monde

puny /ˈpjuːnɪ/ ADJ *[person, animal]* chétif, malingre ; *[effort]* faible, piteux

pup /pʌp/ N 1 *(= dog)* chiot *m*, jeune chien(ne) *m(f)* ; *(= seal)* bébé *m* phoque, jeune phoque *m* ◆ **to sell sb a ~*** rouler* qn ◆ **to be sold a ~*** se faire rouler *or* avoir* 2 *(† * pej) (= frivolous youth)* freluquet † *m* ; *(= inexperienced youth)* blanc-bec *m* VI mettre bas COMP **pup tent** N tente *f* à deux places

pupa /ˈpjuːpə/ N (pl **pupae** /ˈpjuːpiː/) chrysalide *f*, pupe *f*

pupate /ˈpjuːpeɪt/ VI devenir chrysalide *or* pupe

pupil¹ /ˈpjuːpl/ N *(Scol etc)* élève *mf*
COMP **pupil nurse** N *(Brit)* élève *mf* infirmier (-ière) *(qui suit une formation courte)*
pupil power N pouvoir *m* des élèves
pupil teacher N professeur *m* stagiaire

pupil² /ˈpjuːpl/ N *[of eye]* pupille *f*

puppet /ˈpʌpɪt/ N 1 *(lit)* marionnette *f* ; *(= flat cutout)* pantin *m* 2 *(fig = pawn)* pantin *m* ◆ **he was like a ~ on a string** ce n'était qu'un pantin ; → **glove**
COMP *[theatre, play]* de marionnettes ; *(fig, esp Pol) [state, leader, cabinet]* fantoche
puppet show N (spectacle *m* de) marionnettes *fpl*

puppeteer /ˌpʌpɪˈtɪəʳ/ N montreur *m*, -euse *f* de marionnettes, marionnettiste *mf*

puppetry /ˈpʌpɪtrɪ/ N art *m* des marionnettes

puppy /ˈpʌpɪ/ N ⇒ **pup noun** COMP **puppy farm** N centre *m* d'élevage de chiots de race
puppy fat* N rondeurs *fpl* d'adolescent(e)
puppy love* N premier amour *m* (d'adolescent)

purblind /ˈpɜːblaɪnd/ ADJ *(liter)* 1 *(= blind)* aveugle ; *(= poorly sighted)* qui voit très mal, qui a une vue très faible 2 *(fig = stupid)* aveugle

purchase /ˈpɜːtʃɪs/ N 1 *(Comm etc)* achat *m* ◆ **to make a ~** faire un achat 2 *(= grip, hold)* prise *f* ◆ **the wheels can't get enough ~ on this surface** les roues n'ont pas assez de prise sur cette surface ◆ **I can't get enough ~ on this rock** je n'arrive pas à trouver assez de prise sur ce rocher VT acheter *(sth from sb* qch à qn ; *sth for sb* qch pour *or* à qn)
COMP **purchase ledger** N grand livre *m* des achats
purchase money, purchase price N prix *m* d'achat
purchase tax N *(Brit)* taxe *f* à l'achat

purchaser /ˈpɜːtʃɪsəʳ/ N acheteur *m*, -euse *f*

purchasing /ˈpɜːtʃɪsɪŋ/ N achat *m*
COMP **purchasing department** N service *m* (des) achats
purchasing officer N responsable *mf* des achats
purchasing power N pouvoir *m* d'achat

purdah /ˈpɜːdə/ N *(Rel)* purdah *m* ◆ **to live in ~** vivre cloîtré ◆ **the President is in ~** le Président garde un profil bas

pure /pjʊəʳ/ ADJ *(gen)* pur ◆ **as ~ as the driven snow** innocent comme l'enfant qui vient de naître ◆ **~ in heart** *(Bible)* au cœur pur ◆ **~ science** science *f* pure ◆ **~ line** *(Genetics)* hérédité *f* pure ◆ **~ alcohol** alcool *m* absolu ◆ **a ~ wool suit** un complet pure laine ◆ **~ and simple** pur et simple ◆ **it was ~ hypocrisy** c'était de la pure hypocrisie *or* de l'hypocrisie pure
COMP **pure-hearted** ADJ (au cœur) pur
pure-minded ADJ pur (d'esprit)
pure new wool N laine *f* vierge
pure vowel N *(Phon)* voyelle *f* pure

purebred /ˈpjʊəbred/ ADJ de race N animal *m* de race ; *(= horse)* pur-sang *m inv*

purée /ˈpjʊəreɪ/ N purée *f* ◆ **tomato ~** purée *f* de tomates VT réduire en purée

purely /ˈpjʊəlɪ/ ADV *(with adj)* purement ◆ **~ and simply** purement et simplement

pureness /ˈpjʊənɪs/ N *(NonC)* pureté *f*

purgation /pɜːˈgeɪʃən/ N *(Rel)* purgation *f*, purification *f* ; *(Pol)* purge *f*, épuration *f* ; *(Med)* purge *f*

purgative /ˈpɜːgətɪv/ ADJ, N purgatif *m*

purgatory /ˈpɜːɡətərɪ/ N *(lit, fig)* purgatoire *m* ◆ **it was** ~ *(fig)* c'était un vrai purgatoire *or* supplice ◆ **it was ~ for me** j'étais au supplice

purge /pɜːdʒ/ N *(= act) (gen, Med)* purge *f* ; *(Pol)* purge *f*, épuration *f* ; *(= medicament)* purge *f*, purgatif *m* ◆ **the (political) ~s which followed the revolution** les purges politiques qui ont *or* l'épuration politique qui a suivi la révolution ◆ **a ~ of the dissidents** une purge des dissidents VT [1] *(gen)* purger *(of* de) ; *(Med) [+ person, body]* purger ; *(Pol) [+ state, nation, party]* purger *(of* de) ; *[+ traitors, bad elements]* éliminer ; *[+ sins]* purger, expier [2] *(Jur) [+ person]* disculper *(of* de) ; *[+ accusation]* se disculper de ◆ **to ~ an offence** purger une peine ◆ **to ~ one's contempt (of Congress)** *(US)* purger sa contumace

purification /ˌpjʊərɪfɪˈkeɪʃən/ N [1] *[of air, water, metal etc]* épuration *f*, *[of drinking water]* filtrage *m* [2] *(Rel etc) [of person]* purification *f*

purifier /ˈpjʊərɪfaɪəʳ/ N épurateur *m*, purificateur *m* ◆ **air** ~ purificateur *m* d'air ; → **water**

purify /ˈpjʊərɪfaɪ/ VT *[+ substance]* épurer, purifier ; *[+ person]* purifier

Purim /ˈpʊərɪm/ N *(Rel)* Pourim *m*

purism /ˈpjʊərɪzəm/ N purisme *m*

purist /ˈpjʊərɪst/ ADJ, N puriste *mf*

puritan /ˈpjʊərɪtən/ ADJ, N puritain(e) *m(f)*

puritanical /ˌpjʊərɪˈtænɪkəl/ ADJ puritain, de puritain

puritanism /ˈpjʊərɪtənɪzəm/ N puritanisme *m*

purity /ˈpjʊərɪtɪ/ N pureté *f*

purl /pɜːl/ *(Knitting)* N (also **purl stitch**) *(= one stitch)* maille *f* à l'envers ◆ **a row of** ~ un rang à l'envers ; → **plain** ADJ à l'envers VT tricoter à l'envers ; → **knit**

purlieus /ˈpɜːljuːz/ NPL *(frm)* alentours *mpl*, abords *mpl*, environs *mpl*

purloin /pɜːˈlɔɪn/ VT dérober

purple /ˈpɜːpl/ ADJ *(bluish)* violet ; *(reddish)* pourpre ; *(lighter)* mauve ◆ **to go ~ (in the face)** devenir cramoisi *or* pourpre ◆ ~ **passage** *or* **patch** *(Literat)* morceau *m* de bravoure N *(= colour) (bluish)* violet *m* ; *(reddish)* pourpre *m* ◆ **the** ~ *(Rel)* la pourpre

COMP **Purple Heart** N *(US Mil) décoration attribuée aux blessés de guerre*

purple heart * N *(Drugs)* pilule *f* du bonheur ⁑

purplish /ˈpɜːplɪʃ/ ADJ violacé, qui tire sur le violet

purport /ˈpɜːpət/ *(frm)* N *(= meaning)* signification *f* VT /pɜːˈpɔːt/ ◆ **to ~ to be sth/sb** *[person]* se présenter comme étant qch/qn ◆ **to ~ to be objective** *[book, film, statement etc]* se vouloir objectif ◆ **he ~s to represent the views of the people** il prétend représenter l'opinion du (grand) public ◆ **a man ~ing to come from the Ministry** un homme qui se prétend (*or* prétendait) envoyé par le ministère ◆ **a document ~ing to come** *or* **be from the French embassy** un document censé émaner de l'ambassade de France ◆ **a book ~ing to be written for children** un livre censé s'adresser aux enfants

purportedly /pɜːˈpɔːtədlɪ/ ADV *(frm)* soi-disant ◆ **~ written by ...** censé avoir été écrit par ..., qui aurait été écrit par ...

purpose /ˈpɜːpəs/ LANGUAGE IN USE 18.4

N *(= aim, intention)* but *m*, objet *m* ◆ **what was the ~ of the meeting?** quel était le but *or* l'objet de cette réunion ? ◆ **a man with a ~ (in life)** un homme qui a un but *or* un objectif (dans la vie) ◆ **an interview is a conversation with a** ~ une interview est une conversation qui a un but *or* un objectif ◆ **my ~ in doing this is ...** la raison pour laquelle je fais ceci est ... ◆ **to achieve one's** ~ parvenir à ses fins ◆ **with the ~ of ...** dans le but *or* l'intention de ... ◆ **his activities seem to lack** ~ il semble agir sans but précis ◆ **to have a sense of** ~ être motivé *or* déterminé ◆ **he has no sense of** ~ il n'a pas de but dans la vie ◆ **regular attendance at classes can help provide you with a sense of** ~ l'assiduité aux cours peut contribuer à vous motiver *or* à vous donner une motivation ; → **infirm, strength**

◆ **for + purposes** ◆ **it is adequate for the** ~ cela fait l'affaire ◆ **for the ~ of doing sth** dans le but *or* l'intention de faire qch ◆ **the flat is perfect for my ~s** l'appartement est parfait pour ce que je veux faire ◆ **for my ~s, these terms are merely convenient labels** en ce qui me concerne, ces termes ne sont que des étiquettes bien pratiques ◆ **for the ~s of the meeting** pour (les besoins de) cette réunion ◆ **for the ~s of this Act** *(Jur)* aux fins de la présente loi ◆ **for this** ~ à cet effet, à cette fin

◆ **to + purpose** ◆ **to good** ~ utilement ◆ **the money will be used to good** ~ l'argent sera bien *or* utilement employé ◆ **to no (good)** ~ en vain, inutilement ◆ **he was wearing himself out to no** ~ il s'épuisait en vain *or* inutilement ◆ **taxes have remained high to no good** ~ les impôts sont restés élevés mais cela n'a servi à rien ◆ **to no ~ at all** en pure perte ◆ **to the** ~ *(= relevant)* à propos, pertinent ◆ **more to the ~ is his next point** son argument suivant est plus à propos *or* plus pertinent ◆ **not to the** ~ hors de propos ◆ **these questions were not to the** ~ ces questions étaient hors de propos

◆ **on purpose** exprès, délibérément ◆ **he did it on** ~ il l'a fait exprès *or* délibérément ◆ **he did it on ~ to annoy me** il l'a fait exprès pour me contrarier

VT *(frm)* ◆ **to ~ to do sth** se proposer de faire qch

COMP **purpose-built** ADJ spécialement construit *or* conçu

purposeful /ˈpɜːpəsfʊl/ ADJ *(= determined) [person]* résolu, déterminé ; *[gesture, look]* résolu, décidé, déterminé ; *(= intentional) [act]* intentionnel

purposefully /ˈpɜːpəsfəlɪ/ ADV ◆ **he strode ~ across the paddock to his car** il traversa l'enclos d'un pas décidé en direction de sa voiture ◆ **she rose ~ from her chair** elle se leva d'un air décidé

purposefulness /ˈpɜːpəsfʊlnɪs/ N détermination *f* ◆ **there was an atmosphere of** ~ il y avait une certaine détermination dans l'air ◆ **there's a ~ to her life now** elle a désormais un but dans la vie

purposeless /ˈpɜːpəslɪs/ ADJ *[character]* indécis, irrésolu ; *[act]* sans but *or* objet (précis) ◆ **I felt** ~ je ne savais pas quoi faire

purposely /ˈpɜːpəslɪ/ ADV exprès, à dessein *(frm)*, de propos délibéré *(frm)* ◆ **he made a ~ vague statement** il a fait exprès de faire une déclaration peu précise ◆ **the government's statement was ~ vague** la déclaration du gouvernement a été délibérément vague *or* a été vague à dessein

purposive /ˈpɜːpəsɪv/ ADJ *(frm)* calculé

purr /pɜːʳ/ VI *[cat]* ronronner, faire ronron ; *[person, engine, car]* ronronner VT roucouler ◆ **"sit down, darling", she ~ed** "assieds-toi, chéri", roucoula-t-elle N *[of cat]* ronronnement *m*, ronron *m* ; *[of engine, car]* ronronnement *m*

purring /ˈpɜːrɪŋ/ N ⇒ **purr noun**

purse /pɜːs/ N [1] *(Brit) (for coins)* porte-monnaie *m inv*, bourse *f* ; *(= wallet)* portefeuille *m* ◆ **it's beyond my** ~ c'est trop cher pour moi, c'est au-dessus de mes moyens ; → **public** [2] *(US = handbag)* sac *m* à main [3] *(= prize: esp Sport)* prix *m*, récompense *f* VT ◆ **to ~ (up) one's lips** faire la moue, pincer les lèvres

COMP **purse-proud** ADJ fier de sa fortune

purse snatcher * N *(US)* voleur *m*, -euse *f* à la tire

purse strings NPL *(fig)* ◆ **to hold/tighten the ~ strings** tenir/serrer les cordons de la bourse

purser /ˈpɜːsəʳ/ N *(Naut)* commissaire *m* (du bord)

pursuance /pəˈsjuːəns/ N *(frm)* exécution *f* ◆ **in ~ of** dans l'exécution de

pursuant /pəˈsjuːənt/ ADJ *(frm)* ◆ **~ to** *(= following on)* suivant ; *(= in accordance with)* conformément à

pursue /pəˈsjuː/ VT [1] *(= carry on) [+ studies, career, plan, theme, inquiry]* poursuivre ; *[+ profession]* exercer ; *[+ course of action]* suivre ; *[+ policy]* mener ◆ **to ~ one's own interests** faire ce à quoi on s'intéresse ◆ **to ~ one's interest in art** s'adonner à sa passion pour l'art [2] *(= search for) [+ happiness]* rechercher ; *[+ success, fame, objective]* poursuivre [3] *[+ matter]* suivre, approfondir ◆ **to ~ the matter** approfondir la question ◆ **to ~ a case** *(Jur)* poursuivre une affaire [4] *(= chase after) [+ person, animal]* poursuivre, pourchasser ; *[+ vehicle]* poursuivre ◆ **his eyes ~d me round the room** il me suivait du regard à travers la pièce ◆ **he is ~d by misfortune** *(liter)* la malchance le poursuit ◆ **he won't stop pursuing her** il n'arrête pas de la poursuivre de ses assiduités

pursuer /pəˈsjuːəʳ/ N poursuivant(e) *m(f)*

pursuit /pəˈsjuːt/ N [1] *(= search) [of pleasure, happiness]* recherche *f*, poursuite *f* ; *[of excellence, wealth]* poursuite *f* ; *[of truth, peace, power]* recherche *f* ◆ **in ~ of** à la recherche de [2] *(= chase: also Cycling, Skating)* poursuite *f* ◆ **(to go) in ~ of sb/sth** (se mettre) à la poursuite de qn/qch ◆ **he escaped with two policemen in hot** ~ il s'est enfui avec deux agents à ses trousses [3] *(= occupation)* activité *f* ; *(= pastime)* passe-temps *m inv* ◆ **scientific ~s** travaux *mpl* *or* recherches *fpl* scientifiques COMP **pursuit plane** N chasseur *m*, avion *m* de chasse

purulence /ˈpjʊərʊləns/ N purulence *f*

purulent /ˈpjʊərʊlənt/ ADJ purulent

purvey /pəˈveɪ/ VT *(Comm etc)* fournir *(sth to sb* qch à qn), approvisionner *(sth to sb* qn en qch)

purveyance /pəˈveɪəns/ N *(Comm etc)* approvisionnement *m*, fourniture *f* de provisions

purveyor /pəˈveɪəʳ/ N *(Comm etc)* fournisseur *m*, -euse *f*, approvisionneur *m*, -euse *f* *(of sth* en qch ; *to sb* de qn)

purview /ˈpɜːvjuː/ N *(frm) [of act, bill]* articles *mpl* ; *[of the law]* domaine *m*, limites *fpl* ; *[of inquiry]* champ *m*, limites *fpl* ; *[of committee]* capacité *f*, compétence *f* ; *[of book, film]* limites *fpl*, portée *f*

pus /pʌs/ N pus *m*

push /pʊʃ/

1 NOUN	4 COMPOUNDS
2 TRANSITIVE VERB	5 PHRASAL VERBS
3 INTRANSITIVE VERB	

1 - NOUN

[1] [= shove] poussée *f* ◆ **to give sb/sth a** ~ pousser qn/qch ◆ **the car needs a** ~ il faut pousser la voiture ◆ **with one** ~ en poussant une seule fois ◆ **there was a great ~ as the crowd emerged** quand la foule est sortie, il y a eu une grande bousculade

[2] [Brit * = dismissal] ◆ **to give sb the** ~ *[employer]* virer qn * ; *[boyfriend, girlfriend]* plaquer qn ⁑ ◆ **he got the** ~ *(from employer)* il s'est fait virer * ; *(from girlfriend)* il s'est fait plaquer ⁑

[3] [Mil, Pol = advance] poussée *f*, avance *f* ◆ **they made a ~ to the coast** ils ont fait une poussée *or* ils ont avancé jusqu'à la côte

[4] [fig] *(= effort)* gros effort *m*, coup *m* de collier ; *(= campaign)* campagne *f* ◆ **they made a ~ to**

get everything finished in time ils ont fait un gros effort *or* ils ont donné un coup de collier pour tout terminer à temps ◆ **they were having a ~ on sales** *or* **a sales ~** ils avaient organisé une campagne de promotion des ventes ◆ **we're having a ~ for more teachers** nous menons une campagne pour une augmentation du nombre d'enseignants ◆ **when it comes to the ~*** au moment critique *or* crucial ◆ **when ~ comes to shove*** le moment venu

♦ **at a push*** ◆ **the table seats three at a ~** il y a de la place pour trois maximum autour de la table ◆ **at a ~, he will concede that he's a bit bored by it all** si on insiste, il admet que tout cela l'ennuie un peu

2 - TRANSITIVE VERB

1 lit *[+ car, pram, barrow, door, person]* pousser ; *[+ knob, button]* appuyer sur ; *[+ stick, finger etc]* enfoncer (*into* dans ; *between* entre) ; *[+ rag etc]* fourrer (*into* dans) ◆ **don't ~ me!** ne (me) poussez pas !

♦ **to push** *+ preposition/adverb* ◆ **to ~ sb in/out/up** *etc* faire entrer/sortir/monter *etc* qn en le poussant ◆ **to ~ sb against a wall** pousser qn contre un mur ◆ **bulldozers ~ed the snow aside** des bulldozers déblayaient la neige ◆ **he ~ed him down the stairs** il l'a poussé et l'a fait tomber dans l'escalier ◆ **to ~ sb into a room** pousser qn dans une pièce ◆ **he ~ed the book into my hand** il m'a fourré* le livre dans la main ◆ **they ~ed me off the pavement** ils m'ont poussé et m'ont forcé à descendre du trottoir ◆ **he ~ed the cat off the table** il a poussé le chat et l'a forcé à descendre de la table ◆ **she ~ed the books off the table** elle a poussé les livres et les a fait tomber de la table ◆ **they ~ed the car off the cliff** ils ont poussé la voiture dans le précipice, ils ont poussé la voiture et l'ont fait tomber de la falaise ◆ **they ~ed the car off the road** ils ont poussé la voiture sur le bas-côté ◆ **to ~ a door open** ouvrir une porte en la poussant, pousser une porte (pour l'ouvrir) ◆ **they ~ed him out of the car** ils l'ont poussé hors de la voiture ◆ **to ~ sb/sth out of the way** écarter qn/qch en le poussant ◆ **it ~ed the matter right out of my mind** cela m'a fait complètement oublier cette affaire ◆ **to ~ a door shut** fermer une porte en la poussant, pousser une porte (pour la fermer) ◆ **he ~ed his head through the window** il a passé la tête par la fenêtre ◆ **to ~ one's way through a crowd** se frayer *or* s'ouvrir un chemin dans la foule ◆ **he ~ed the bill through Parliament** il a réussi à faire voter le projet de loi ◆ **he ~ed the thought to the back of his mind** il a repoussé *or* écarté cette pensée ◆ **he ~ed the box under the table** il a poussé la boîte sous la table

♦ **to be pushing** *+ age** ◆ **he must be ~ing* 60** il ne doit pas avoir loin de 60 ans, il doit friser la soixantaine

2 fig = press, advance *[+ one's views]* mettre en avant ; *[+ claim]* présenter avec insistance ; *[+ plan, method, solution]* essayer d'imposer ; *[+ product]* pousser la vente de ; *[+ candidate etc]* essayer de placer ; *[+ business]* développer en priorité

3 fig = go too far with ◆ **that's ~ing it a bit !*** *(indignantly)* c'est un peu fort ! ; *(not much time etc)* c'est un peu juste !

4 fig *(= put pressure on)* pousser ; *(= harass)* importuner, harceler ◆ **don't ~ him too hard** *or* **too far** n'insistez pas trop, ne le poussez pas à bout ◆ **they ~ed him to the limits of his endurance** on l'a poussé jusqu'à la limite de ses forces ◆ **to ~ sb to do sth** pousser qn à faire qch, insister pour que qn fasse qch ◆ **to ~ sb for payment/for an answer** presser qn de payer/de répondre ◆ **to ~ sb into doing sth** forcer *or* obliger qn à faire qch ◆ **I was ~ed into it** on m'y a poussé *or* forcé ◆ **he was ~ed into teaching** on l'a poussé à devenir professeur *or* à faire de l'enseignement ◆ **to ~ o.s. hard** exiger beaucoup de soi-même ◆ **he ~es himself too hard** il se surmène

5 US Golf **to ~ the ball** couper *or* faire dévier la balle

3 - INTRANSITIVE VERB

1 = press pousser ; *(on bell)* appuyer *(on* sur) ◆ **you ~ and I'll pull** poussez et moi je vais tirer ◆ **"push"** *(on door)* "poussez" ; *(on bell)* "appuyez", "sonnez" ◆ **to ~ for better conditions/higher wages** *etc (fig)* faire pression pour obtenir de meilleures conditions/une augmentation de salaire *etc*

2 = move **they ~ed into/out of the room** ils sont entrés dans la pièce/sortis de la pièce en se frayant un passage ◆ **he ~ed past me** il m'a dépassé en me bousculant ◆ **she ~ed through the crowd** elle s'est frayé *or* ouvert un chemin dans la foule

3 Mil **to ~ into enemy territory** *(= advance)* avancer en territoire ennemi

4 - COMPOUNDS

push-bike* N *(Brit)* vélo *m*
push-button N, ADJ ⇒ **push-button**
push-pull circuit N *(Elec)* push-pull *m inv*
push rod N *(in engine)* tige *f* de culbuteur
push-start N, VT ◆ **to give a car a ~-start, to ~-start a car** faire démarrer une voiture en la poussant, pousser une voiture pour la faire démarrer
push-up N *(US Gym)* traction *f*, pompe* *f* ◆ **to do ~-ups** faire des tractions *or* des pompes*

5 - PHRASAL VERBS

► **push about** VT SEP ⇒ **push around**

► **push ahead** VI *(= make progress)* avancer à grands pas ◆ **the government intends to ~ ahead with its reform programme** le gouvernement a l'intention d'avancer dans son programme de réformes

► **push along** VI 1 *(* = leave)* filer*, se sauver*
2 *(= move quickly)* aller bon train
VT SEP *[+ person, cart, chair]* pousser ; *(fig = hasten) [+ work]* activer, accélérer

► **push around** VT SEP 1 *[+ cart, toy]* pousser de-ci de-là, pousser à droite et à gauche
2 *(* fig = bully)* bousculer*

► **push aside** VT SEP *[+ person, chair]* écarter (brusquement) ; *(fig) [+ objection, suggestion]* écarter, rejeter

► **push away** VT SEP *[+ person, chair, one's plate, sb's hand]* repousser ; *[+ gift]* repousser, rejeter

► **push back** VT SEP *[+ cover, blankets, lock of hair]* rejeter *or* repousser (en arrière) ; *[+ curtains]* repousser ; *[+ person, crowd, enemy]* repousser, faire reculer ; *(fig) [+ desire, impulse]* réprimer

► **push down** VI appuyer *(on* sur)
VT SEP 1 *[+ switch, lever]* abaisser ; *[+ knob, button]* appuyer sur ; *[+ pin, stick]* enfoncer ; *(= knock over) [+ fence, barrier, person]* renverser ◆ **he ~ed the tile down off the roof** il a poussé la tuile et l'a fait tomber du toit, il a fait tomber la tuile du toit en la poussant ◆ **he ~ed his clothes down into the suitcase** il a fourré ses vêtements dans la valise
2 *(fig = reduce) [+ prices, inflation, value]* faire baisser

► **push forward** VI avancer
♦ **to push forward with sth** avancer dans qch ◆ **they are eager to ~ forward with reform** ils tiennent à avancer dans les réformes
VT SEP *[+ person, box etc]* pousser en avant, faire avancer ◆ **to ~ one's way forward** se frayer *or* s'ouvrir un chemin ◆ **he ~ed himself forward** il s'est frayé *or* ouvert un chemin ; *(fig)* il s'est mis en avant, il s'est fait valoir

► **push in** VI s'introduire de force ; *(fig = interfere)* intervenir ◆ **he's always ~ing in where he's not wanted** il se mêle toujours de *or* il intervient toujours dans ce qui ne le regarde pas
VT SEP 1 *[+ stick, pin, finger]* enfoncer ; *[+ rag]* fourrer dedans ; *[+ person]* pousser dedans ; *[+ knob, button]* appuyer sur ◆ **they opened the door and ~ed him in** ils ouvrirent la porte et le poussèrent à l'intérieur ◆ **they took him to the pond and ~ed him in** ils l'ont amené à l'étang et l'ont poussé dedans
2 *(= break) [+ window, door, sides of box]* enfoncer
3 ◆ **to push one's way in** s'introduire de force

► **push off** VI 1 *(Naut)* pousser au large
2 *(* = leave)* filer*, se sauver* ◆ **I must ~ off now** il faut que je file* *subj or* que je me sauve* *subj* ◆ **~ off!** fichez le camp !*, filez !*
3 ◆ **the top just pushes off** il suffit de pousser le haut pour l'enlever
VT SEP → **push vt 1**

► **push on** VI *(in journey)* pousser *(to* jusqu'à), continuer son chemin ; *(in work)* continuer, persévérer ◆ **to ~ on with sth** continuer (à faire) qch
VT SEP 1 *[+ lid, cover]* placer (en appuyant)
2 *(fig = incite)* pousser, inciter *(to do sth* à faire qch)

► **push out** VI *[roots, branches]* pousser ; *[shoots]* pointer, sortir
VT SEP 1 *[+ person, object]* pousser dehors ; *[+ stopper]* faire sortir (en poussant) ; *(fig) [+ employee, office holder]* évincer, se débarrasser de ◆ **to ~ the boat out** *(lit)* pousser au large ; *(fig)* faire la fête
2 *[+ roots, shoots]* produire
3 *(* = produce) [+ information, products etc]* débiter
4 ◆ **to push one's way out** se frayer *or* s'ouvrir un chemin (à travers la foule)

► **push over** VT SEP 1 *(= pass) [+ object]* pousser *(to sb* vers qn)
2 *(= cause to fall off: over cliff, bridge etc)* pousser, faire tomber
3 *(= cause to topple) [+ chair, vase, person]* renverser, faire tomber
4 ◆ **to push one's way over to sb** se frayer *or* s'ouvrir un chemin vers qn

► **push through** VI se frayer *or* s'ouvrir un chemin
VT SEP 1 *[+ stick, hand etc]* enfoncer, (faire) passer
2 *(fig) [+ deal, business]* conclure à la hâte ; *[+ decision]* faire accepter à la hâte ; *(Parl) [+ bill]* réussir à faire voter
3 ◆ **push one's way through** se frayer *or* s'ouvrir un chemin

► **push to** VT SEP *[+ door]* fermer (en poussant), pousser pour fermer

► **push up** VT SEP 1 *[+ stick, hand, lever, switch]* (re)lever ; *[+ spectacles]* relever ◆ **he's ~ing up (the) daisies*** *(hum = dead)* il mange les pissenlits par la racine*
2 *(fig = increase) [+ numbers, taxes, sales, speed]* augmenter ; *[+ prices, demand, sb's temperature, blood pressure]* faire monter ◆ **that ~es up the total to over 100** cela fait monter le total à plus de 100

---

push-button /ˈpʊʃ,bʌtn/ N bouton *m*, poussoir *m* ADJ *[machine etc]* à commande automatique ; *[telephone]* à touches ◆ **~ controls** commande *f* automatique ◆ **~ warfare** guerre *f* presse-bouton

pushcart /ˈpʊʃkɑːt/ N charrette *f* à bras

pushchair /ˈpʊʃtʃeəʳ/ N *(Brit)* poussette *f*

pushed /pʊʃt/ ADJ * ◆ **to be ~ for money** être à court d'argent, être fauché* ◆ **I'm ~ for time** je n'ai pas le temps

pusher /ˈpʊʃəʳ/ N [1] (*: also **drug-pusher**) revendeur *m*, -euse *f* (de drogue), dealer* *m* [2] *(pej)* arriviste *mf* ; → **penpusher**

pushfulness * /ˈpʊʃfʊlnɪs/, **pushiness** * /ˈpʊʃɪnɪs/ N *(pej)* arrivisme *m*, excès *m* d'ambition ; *[of manner]* arrogance *f*

pushing /ˈpʊʃɪŋ/ N [1] *(lit)* cohue *f* ◆ **~ and shoving** bousculade *f* [2] *(fig = persuasion)* persuasion *f* ◆ **he agreed to do it, after a lot of ~** il a accepté (de le faire) après s'être fait beaucoup prier

Pushkin /ˈpʊʃkɪn/ N Pouchkine *m*

pushover * /ˈpʊʃəʊvəʳ/ N ◆ **it was a ~** c'était la facilité même, c'était un jeu d'enfant ◆ **he's a ~** il se laisse facilement faire ◆ **he's a ~ for blondes** il craque * dès qu'il voit une blonde

pushpin /ˈpʊʃpɪn/ N épingle *f* (à tête de couleur)

pushy * /ˈpʊʃɪ/ ADJ *(pej)* *[person]* arriviste, qui se fait valoir, qui se met trop en avant ; *[manner]* arrogant

pusillanimity /ˌpjuːsɪləˈnɪmɪtɪ/ N pusillanimité *f*

pusillanimous /ˌpjuːsɪˈlænɪməs/ ADJ pusillanime

puss * /pʊs/ N (= *cat*) minet(te) *m(f)*, minou *m* ◆ **~, ~!** *(to cat)* minet, minet !, minou, minou ! ◆ **Puss in Boots** le Chat Botté

pussy /ˈpʊsɪ/ N [1] (* = *cat*) minet(te) *m(f)*, minou *m*, chat(te) *m(f)* [2] (*** = *female genitals*) chatte*** *f* [3] *(NonC:* *** = *intercourse)* baise*** *f* COMP **pussy willow** N saule *m* (blanc)

pussycat * /ˈpʊsɪkæt/ N (= *cat*) minet(te) *m(f)*, minou *m* ◆ **hi, ~!** *(US = sweetheart)* bonjour, mon chou* *or* mon ange ! ◆ **he's a real ~** (= *harmless*) il ne ferait pas de mal à une mouche*

pussyfoot * /ˈpʊsɪfʊt/ VI marcher à pas de loup ; *(fig)* ne pas se mouiller*, ménager la chèvre et le chou

pussyfooting * /ˈpʊsɪˌfʊtɪŋ/ ADJ *(fig)* *[person]* qui a peur de se mouiller* ; *[attitude]* timoré N (also **pussyfooting about** *or* **around**) tergiversations *fpl*

pustule /ˈpʌstjuːl/ N pustule *f*

put /pʊt/

vb : pret, ptp **put**

LANGUAGE IN USE 26.2

1 TRANSITIVE VERB
2 INTRANSITIVE VERB
3 NOUN
4 COMPOUNDS
5 PHRASAL VERBS

1 - TRANSITIVE VERB

For set combinations consisting of **put** + noun, eg **put to use**, **put in danger/out of business/an end to**, look up the noun. For **put** + preposition/adverb combinations, see also phrasal verbs.

[1] [= place] mettre ◆ **~ it in the drawer** mettez-le dans le tiroir ◆ **to ~ sth in one's pocket** mettre qch dans sa poche ◆ **he ~ her into a taxi** il l'a mise dans un taxi ◆ **~ yourself in my place** mets-toi à ma place ◆ **I didn't know where to ~ myself!** * je ne savais plus où me mettre ! ◆ **to ~ an advertisement in the paper** mettre *or* passer une annonce dans le journal ◆ **he ~ the shell to her ear** il a mis le coquillage contre son oreille, il a porté le coquillage à son oreille ◆ **rather than ~ him in hospital he cared for him at home** il a préféré s'occuper de lui à la maison plutôt que de le mettre à l'hôpital ◆ **~ the book in its proper place** remets le livre à sa place ◆ **to ~ a bullet into sb** tirer sur qn, coller une balle dans la peau de qn* ; *(= give me your hand)* ◆ **~ it there!** * tope là !, affaire conclue !

◆ **to put + on** ◆ **to ~ a button on a shirt** mettre *or* coudre un bouton à une chemise ◆ **to ~ sb on a diet** mettre qn au régime ◆ **he ~ some more coal on the fire** il a remis *or* rajouté du charbon sur le feu ◆ **he ~ me on the train** il m'a accompagné au train ◆ **to ~ one's signature on sth** apposer sa signature sur qch, signer qch ◆ **to ~ sb on a committee** nommer qn à un comité ; see also **put on**

◆ **to put + over** ◆ **he ~ his hand over his mouth** il a mis sa main devant la bouche ◆ **he ~ his hand over her mouth** il a plaqué sa main sur sa bouche ◆ **he ~ his rucksack over the fence** il a passé son sac à dos par-dessus la barrière ◆ **someone has been ~ over him at the office** il a maintenant un chef au bureau ; see also **put over**

◆ **to put one over on** *or* **across sb** * (= *deceive*) pigeonner* qn embobiner* qn ◆ **he tried to ~ one over on** *or* **across me** il a essayé de me pigeonner* *or* de m'embobiner* ◆ **you'll never ~ one over on him** on ne la lui fait pas*

◆ **to put + round** ◆ **to ~ one's arms round sb** enlacer qn, prendre qn dans ses bras ◆ **he ~ his head round the door** il a passé la tête par la porte ; see also **put round**

◆ **to put + through** ◆ **he ~ his head through the window** il a mis son nez à la fenêtre ◆ **to ~ one's fist through a window** passer le poing à travers une vitre ◆ **to ~ one's pen through a word** rayer *or* barrer un mot ◆ **she ~ a bullet through his head** elle lui a tiré une balle dans la tête ; see also **put through**

[2] [= set] *[+ clock, watch]* mettre ◆ **to ~ a watch to the right time** mettre une montre à l'heure ◆ **I ~ him to work at once** je l'ai aussitôt mis au travail ◆ **they had to ~ four men on to this job** ils ont dû employer quatre hommes à ce travail *or* pour faire ce travail ◆ **she ~ my brother against me** elle a monté mon frère contre moi

[3] [= rank] placer ◆ **I ~ Joyce above Lawrence** je place Joyce au-dessus de Lawrence ◆ **I wouldn't ~ him among the greatest poets** je ne le placerais *or* classerais pas parmi les plus grands poètes ◆ **we should ~ happiness before** *or* **above money** on devrait faire passer le bonheur avant l'argent ◆ **he ~s good health among his greatest blessings** il estime que sa santé est l'un de ses meilleurs atouts

[4] [= express] dire ◆ **how shall I ~ it?** comment dire ?, comment dirais-je ? ◆ **I don't quite know how to ~ it** je ne sais pas trop comment le dire ◆ **try ~ting it another way** essayez de le dire d'une autre façon ◆ **let me ~ it this way: she's not exactly diplomatic** disons qu'elle n'a pas beaucoup de tact ◆ **how will you ~ it to him?** comment vas-tu le lui présenter la chose ?, comment vas-tu le lui dire ? ◆ **as Shakespeare ~s it** comme le dit Shakespeare ◆ **as the president memorably ~ it** selon la célèbre formule du président ◆ **to ~ it bluntly** pour parler franc ◆ **as he would ~ it** pour employer sa formule *or* son expression ◆ **~ it so as not to offend her** présente la chose de façon à ne pas la blesser ◆ **some expressions are impossible to ~ into French** certaines expressions sont impossibles à traduire en français ◆ **to ~ into verse** mettre en vers

[5] [= suggest] ◆ **I ~ it to you that ...** n'est-il pas vrai que ... ? ◆ **it was ~ to me in no uncertain terms that I should resign** on m'a déclaré en termes très clairs que je devrais donner ma démission

[6] [= submit, expound] *[+ case, problem]* exposer, présenter ; *[+ opinion, suggestion]* présenter ; *[+ proposal]* soumettre ; *[+ question]* poser ◆ **he ~ the arguments for and against the project** il a présenté les arguments pour et contre le projet ◆ **he ~ his views very clearly** il a présenté *or* exposé très clairement sa position

[7] [= cause to be] mettre ◆ **to ~ sb in a good/bad mood** mettre qn de bonne/mauvaise humeur

[8] [= invest]

◆ **to put + into** ◆ **to ~ money into a company** placer *or* investir de l'argent dans une société ◆ **he ~ all his savings into the project** il a placé *or* mis toutes ses économies dans ce projet ◆ **he has ~ a lot into his marriage** il a fait beaucoup d'efforts pour que leur couple marche ◆ **I've ~ a lot of time and trouble into it** j'y ai consacré beaucoup de temps et d'efforts

[9] [= estimate]

◆ **to put + at** estimer, évaluer ◆ **they ~ the loss at $10,000** ils estiment *or* évaluent à 10 000 dollars la perte subie ◆ **the population was ~ at 50,000** on a évalué *or* estimé le nombre d'habitants à 50 000 ◆ **what would you ~ it at?** à combien l'estimez-vous *or* l'évaluez-vous ? BUT **I'd ~ her** *or* **her age at 50** je lui donnerais 50 ans

[10] Sport ◆ **to ~ the shot** *or* **the weight** lancer le poids

[11] Stock Exchange = offer to sell *[+ stock, security]* se déclarer vendeur de

2 - INTRANSITIVE VERB

Naut ◆ **to ~ into port** mouiller, jeter l'ancre ◆ **the ship ~ into Southampton** le navire a mouillé *or* jeté l'ancre dans le port de Southampton ◆ **to ~ to sea** appareiller

3 - NOUN

Stock Exchange = premium prime *f* pour livrer ◆ **~ (option)** option *f* de vente, put *m*

4 - COMPOUNDS

put-down * N humiliation *f*, remarque *f* humiliante

put-in N *(Rugby)* introduction *f*

put-on * N (= *pretence*) comédie *f* ; (= *hoax*) mystification *f*, farce *f* ADJ (= *feigned*) affecté, feint

put option N → **noun**

put-up job * N coup *m* monté

put-upon * ADJ ◆ **I feel ~-upon** je trouve qu'on profite de moi, je me sens exploité ◆ **she is ~-upon** on abuse de sa gentillesse ◆ **I won't be ~-upon any more!** je ne vais plus me laisser faire ! *or* me laisser marcher sur les pieds !

put-you-up N *(Brit)* canapé-lit *m*, divan *m*

5 - PHRASAL VERBS

► **put about**

VI *(Naut)* virer de bord

VT SEP [1] *(esp Brit)* *[+ rumour]* faire courir, faire circuler ◆ **he ~ it about that ...** il a fait courir *or* circuler le bruit que ...

[2] *(Naut)* **to ~ the ship about** virer de bord

[3] ◆ **to put o.s. about** * *[ambitious person]* se faire mousser*

► **put across** VT SEP (= *communicate*) *[+ ideas, intentions, desires]* faire comprendre, communiquer *(to sb* à qn) ◆ **to ~ sth across to sb** faire comprendre qch à qn ◆ **the play ~s the message across very well** la pièce arrive très bien à faire passer le message ◆ **he knows his stuff but he can't ~ it across** il connaît son sujet à fond mais il n'arrive pas à le faire comprendre aux autres ◆ **it all depends on how you ~ yourself across** tout dépend de la façon dont on se présente ◆ **she ~ the song across beautifully** elle a donné une très belle interprétation de cette chanson

► **put around** VT SEP ⇒ **put about vt sep 1**

► **put aside** VT SEP 1 *[+ object]* mettre de côté ; *(= keep, save) [+ food, money]* mettre de côté, garder en réserve ◆ **he ~ aside the document to read later** il a mis le document de côté pour le lire plus tard ◆ **she ~ her book aside when I came in** elle a posé son livre quand je suis entré ◆ **I'll ~ one aside for you** *(Comm)* je vous en mettrai un de côté

2 *[+ differences, disagreement, feeling]* mettre de côté

► **put away** VT SEP 1 ⇒ **put aside 1**

2 ⇒ **put aside 2**

3 *(= put in proper place) [+ clothes, toys, books]* ranger ◆ **to ~ the car away** rentrer la voiture, mettre la voiture au garage ◆ **~ that knife away!** *(to person with weapon)* pose *or* jette ce couteau !

4 *(Sport) [+ ball]* mettre au fond des filets

5 *(* = confine) (in prison)* enfermer, coffrer* ; *(in mental hospital)* enfermer

6 *(* = consume) [+ food]* avaler ; *[+ drink]* siffler*

7 *(US = beat)* battre

8 ⇒ **put down VT SEP 9**

► **put back**

VI *(Naut)* ◆ **to put back to port** rentrer au port ◆ **they ~ back to Dieppe** ils sont rentrés *or* retournés à Dieppe

VT SEP 1 *(= replace)* remettre (à sa place *or* en place) ◆ **~ it back!** remets-le à sa place ! ◆ **~ it back on the shelf** remettez-le sur l'étagère

2 *(= retard) [+ development, progress]* retarder, freiner ; *[+ clock]* retarder ◆ **the disaster ~ the project back (by) ten years** ce désastre a retardé de dix ans la réalisation du projet ◆ **this will ~ us back ten years** cela nous fera perdre dix ans ; see also **clock**

3 *(= postpone)* remettre *(to* à)

► **put by** VT SEP ⇒ **put aside 1**

► **put down**

VI *[aircraft, pilot]* se poser, atterrir ; *(on carrier)* apponter

VT SEP 1 *[+ parcel, book, child]* poser ; *[+ passenger]* déposer, laisser ◆ **he ~ down a simple catch** *(Cricket)* il a relâché une balle pourtant facile ◆ **~ it down!** pose ça ! ◆ **she ~ her book down and stood up** elle posa son livre et se leva ◆ **I simply couldn't ~ that book down** j'ai dévoré ce livre ; → **foot, root**

2 *[+ aircraft]* poser

3 *[+ umbrella]* fermer

4 *(= pay) [+ deposit]* verser *(on* pour) ◆ **he ~ down £500 on the car** il a versé 500 livres d'arrhes pour la voiture

5 *[+ wine]* mettre en cave

6 *(= suppress) [+ revolt, movement]* réprimer, juguler

7 * *[+ person] (= criticize)* critiquer ; *(= denigrate)* dénigrer ◆ **my boyfriend keeps ~ting me down** mon copain n'arrête pas de me critiquer ◆ **it's a way of ~ting down minorities** c'est un moyen de dénigrer les minorités ◆ **you must stop ~ting yourself down** arrête donc de te déprécier

8 *(= record)* noter ◆ **to ~ sth down in writing** *or* **on paper** mettre qch par écrit ◆ **~ it down on my account** *(Comm)* mettez-le sur mon compte ◆ **I've ~ you down as unemployed** j'ai mis que vous étiez chômeur ◆ **~ me down for £10** je donnerai 10 livres ◆ **I'll ~ you down for the next vacancy** je vais inscrire votre nom pour la prochaine place disponible ; → **name**

9 *(Brit euph = have destroyed) [+ dog, cat]* faire piquer ; *[+ horse]* faire abattre

► **put down as** VT SEP *(= consider, assess)* considérer comme ◆ **he'll be ~ down as one of our best Prime Ministers** il passera à la postérité comme l'un de nos meilleurs premiers ministres ◆ **I had ~ him down as a complete fool** je l'avais catalogué comme un parfait imbécile, j'étais convaincu qu'il était complètement stupide ◆ **I would ~ her down as about forty** je lui donnerais la quarantaine

► **put down to** VT SEP *(= attribute)* mettre sur le compte ◆ **I ~ it down to his inexperience** je mets ça sur le compte de son manque d'expérience ◆ **the accident must be ~ down to negligence** l'accident doit être imputé à la négligence

► **put forth** VT SEP *(liter) [+ leaves, roots, shoots]* produire ; *[+ idea, suggestion, theory, proposal]* émettre ; *[+ programme, plan]* proposer ; *[+ effort]* fournir, déployer

► **put forward** VT SEP 1 *(= propose) [+ idea, suggestion, theory, proposal]* émettre ; *[+ argument]* avancer, présenter ; *[+ reason]* donner ; *[+ opinion]* exprimer, émettre ; *[+ plan]* proposer ◆ **he ~ his name forward as a candidate** il s'est porté candidat ◆ **he ~ himself forward for the job** il s'est porté candidat au poste, il a posé sa candidature au poste ◆ **he ~ forward (the name of) Harry Green for the job** il a proposé Harry Green pour ce poste

2 *(= advance) [+ meeting, starting time, clock, schedule, programme]* avancer *(by* de ; *to, until* à)

► **put in**

VI *(Naut)* mouiller *(at* dans le port de)

VT SEP 1 *(into box, drawer, room)* mettre dans ; *[+ seeds]* semer ; *[+ plant]* planter ◆ **he ~ his head in at the window** il a passé la tête par la fenêtre ◆ **I've ~ the car in for repairs** j'ai donné la voiture à réparer ◆ **have you ~ in the camera?** *(= pack)* est-ce que tu as pris l'appareil photo ?

2 *(= insert) [+ word, paragraph]* ajouter ; *[+ remark]* ajouter, glisser ; *(= include) [+ information]* inclure ◆ **have you ~ in why you are not going?** est-ce que vous avez expliqué pourquoi vous n'y allez pas ? ◆ **"but it's cold" he ~ in** "mais il fait froid" fit-il remarquer

3 *(= submit)* ◆ **to put in a request for sth** faire une demande de qch ◆ **to ~ in a claim for damages** faire une demande d'indemnité ◆ **to ~ in a plea** *(Jur)* plaider ◆ **to ~ sb in for an exam** présenter qn à un examen ◆ **to ~ sb in for a scholarship** recommander qn pour une bourse ; → **put in for**

4 *(= install) [+ political party]* élire ; *[+ person]* nommer ; *[+ central heating, double glazing]* faire installer

5 *(= spend) [+ time]* passer ◆ **I've ~ in a lot of time on it** j'y ai passé *or* consacré beaucoup de temps ◆ **she ~s in an hour a day at the piano** elle fait une heure de piano par jour

6 *(= work)* travailler ◆ **they ~ in at least 40 hours a week** ils travaillent plus de 40 heures par semaines ◆ **can you ~ in a few hours at the weekend?** pourrais-tu travailler quelques heures ce week-end ?

► **put in for** VT FUS *[+ job]* poser sa candidature à ; *[+ promotion, transfer, divorce]* faire une demande de, demander ; *[+ rise]* demander

► **put off**

VI *(Naut)* appareiller *(from* de)

VT SEP 1 *(= postpone) [+ departure, appointment, meeting]* retarder, repousser ; *[+ decision]* remettre à plus tard, différer ; *[+ visitor]* décommander ◆ **to ~ sth off for ten days/until January** remettre qch de dix jours/jusqu'à janvier ◆ **he is ~ting off the evil day** *or* **hour when he'll finally give up smoking** *(Brit)* il repousse indéfiniment le moment où il devra s'arrêter de fumer ◆ **I'm sorry to have to ~ you off** je suis désolé d'avoir à vous décommander ◆ **he ~ off writing the letter** il a décidé d'écrire cette lettre plus tard

2 *(= discourage)* dissuader ; *(= repel)* dégoûter ◆ **the failure may ~ them off trying again** il est possible que cet échec les dissuade d'essayer à nouveau ◆ **his eccentricities ~ them off** ses petites manies les ont dégoûtés ◆ **the divorce figures don't seem to ~ people off marriage** les statistiques de divorce ne semblent pas dégoûter les gens du mariage ◆ **the country's reputation may ~ off tourists** la réputation du pays pourrait dissuader les touristes de s'y rendre ◆ **it certainly ~ me off going to Greece** cela m'a certainement ôté l'envie d'aller en Grèce

3 *(= remove desire for)* ◆ **his remarks put me off my food** ses remarques m'ont coupé l'appétit

4 *(= distract)* ◆ **talking in the audience ~ him off** les bavardages de l'auditoire le déconcentraient ◆ **it ~ her off revising for her exams** cela l'a distraite de son travail de révision pour ses examens ; → **scent, stroke**

5 *(= fob off)* ◆ **he ~ her off with vague promises** il la faisait patienter avec de vagues promesses ◆ **you're not going to ~ me off with flattery** tu n'arriveras pas à m'amadouer en me flattant

6 *[+ passenger]* déposer, débarquer

7 *(= switch off) [+ light, gas, radio, TV, heater]* éteindre ◆ **he ~ off the lights one by one** il a éteint les lumières une à une

► **put on** VT SEP 1 *[+ clothes, hat, glasses, lotion]* mettre ; *[+ jumper, trousers, gloves, socks]* mettre, enfiler ◆ **to ~ on one's make-up** se maquiller

2 *(= increase) [+ speed]* augmenter ◆ **to ~ on weight** prendre du poids, grossir ◆ **he ~ on 3 kilos** il a pris 3 kilos, il a grossi de 3 kilos ◆ **they ~ on another goal in the second half** ils ont marqué un autre but en deuxième mi-temps ◆ **the proposal could ~ 5p on a litre of petrol** cette proposition augmenterait le prix du litre d'essence de 5 pence

3 *(= assume) [+ air]* prendre, se donner ; *[+ accent]* prendre ◆ **to ~ on an act, to ~ it on** *(= pretend)* faire semblant ◆ **she ~ on a show of enthusiasm** elle faisait semblant d'être enthousiaste ◆ **he's just ~ting it on** il fait semblant, c'est tout

4 *(= deceive) [+ person]* faire marcher* ◆ **you're ~ting me on!** * tu me fais marcher ! *

5 *(= organize) [+ concert, play, show]* organiser ; *[+ film]* projeter ; *[+ extra train, bus]* mettre en service ◆ **the party ~ on a convincing display of unity** le parti a donné une image d'unité assez convaincante

6 *(Telec)* ◆ **~ me on to Mr Brown** passez-moi M. Brown ◆ **would you ~ on Mrs Smith?** pouvez-vous me passer Mme Smith ?

7 *(= start functioning) [+ light, gas, radio, TV, heater]* allumer ; *[+ tape, CD, music]* mettre ◆ **to ~ the brakes on** freiner

8 *(= begin to cook, heat)* ◆ **~ the kettle on** mets de l'eau à chauffer ◆ **I'll just ~ the potatoes on** je vais juste mettre les pommes de terre à cuire

9 *(= advance) [+ clock]* avancer *(by* de)

10 *[+ money, bet]* parier sur, miser sur ◆ **he ~ £10 on Black Beauty** il a parié *or* misé 10 livres sur Black Beauty ◆ **I wouldn't ~ money on it!** je n'en mettrais pas ma main au feu !

► **put onto, put on to** VT SEP ◆ **to ~ sb onto** *or* **on to sth** parler de qch à qn ◆ **Alice ~ us onto him** Alice nous a parlé de lui ◆ **a fellow journalist ~ me onto the story** c'est un collègue journaliste qui m'a mis sur l'affaire* ◆ **they ~ the police onto him** ils l'ont signalé à la police ◆ **can you ~ me onto a good dentist?** pourriez-vous m'indiquer un bon dentiste ? ◆ **Paul ~ us onto you** c'est Paul qui nous a dit de nous adresser à vous ◆ **what ~ you onto it?** qu'est-ce qui vous en a donné l'idée ?

► **put out**

VI *(Naut)* prendre le large ◆ **to ~ out to sea** prendre le large, quitter le port ◆ **to ~ out from Dieppe** quitter le port de Dieppe

VT SEP 1 *(= put outside) [+ rubbish]* sortir, mettre dehors ; *(= expel) [+ person]* expulser *(of* de) ; *[+ country, organization]* exclure *(of* de) ◆ **he ~ the rug out to dry** il a mis le tapis à sécher dehors

♦ **he ~ the cat out for the night** il a fait sortir le chat *or* il a mis le chat dehors pour la nuit ♦ **to ~ sb's eyes out** crever les yeux à qn ♦ **to ~ sth out of one's head** *or* **mind** ne plus penser à qch

2 *(Naut) [+ boat]* mettre à l'eau *or* à la mer

3 *(= stretch out, extend) [+ arm, leg]* allonger, étendre ; *[+ foot]* avancer ; *[+ tongue]* tirer *(at sb* à qn) ; *[+ leaves, shoots, roots]* produire ♦ **to ~ out one's hand** tendre la main ; *[traffic policeman]* tendre le bras ♦ **to ~ one's head out of the window** passer la tête par la fenêtre ♦ **the snail ~ out its horns** l'escargot a sorti ses cornes

4 *(= lay out in order) [+ cards, clothes]* étaler ; *[+ chessmen]* disposer ; *[+ best china]* sortir

5 *(= extinguish) [+ light, flames, gas, cigarette]* éteindre ♦ **to ~ out fires** *(fig)* limiter les dégâts

6 *(= make unconscious)* endormir

7 *(= annoy)* contrarier *(about* par) ♦ **she looked very ~ out** elle avait l'air très contrariée ♦ **he was very ~ out at finding her there** il était très contrarié de la trouver là

8 *(= disconcert)* déconcerter, dérouter *(by* par)

9 *(= inconvenience)* déranger, gêner ♦ **I don't want to ~ you out** je ne voudrais pas vous déranger ♦ **don't ~ yourself out** ne vous dérangez pas ; *(iro)* surtout ne vous gênez pas ! ♦ **she really ~ herself out for us** elle s'est donné beaucoup de mal pour nous, elle s'est mise en quatre pour nous

10 *(= issue) [+ announcement, statement, report]* publier ; *[+ news]* annoncer ; *[+ appeal, warning]* lancer ; *[+ propaganda]* faire ; *[+ book, leaflet, edition]* sortir, publier ; *[+ album]* sortir ♦ **the government will ~ out a statement about it** le gouvernement va faire une déclaration *or* va publier un communiqué à ce sujet

11 *(= broadcast) [+ programme]* passer ; *(= give out) [+ signal]* émettre

12 *(= spend)* dépenser

13 ♦ **to ~ out to tender** *[+ contract, service]* mettre en adjudication

14 *(= exert)* déployer, user de

15 *(= dislocate) [+ shoulder]* se déboîter, se démettre ; *[+ ankle, knee, back]* se démettre

16 *(Sport = eliminate) [+ team, contestant]* éliminer *(of* de) ; *(Baseball) [+ ball]* mettre hors jeu ♦ **a knee injury ~ him out of the first two games** une blessure au genou l'a empêché de jouer les deux premiers matchs

► **put over** VT SEP ⇒ **put across**

► **put round** VT SEP *[+ rumour]* faire courir, faire circuler

► **put through** VT SEP 1 *(= make, complete) [+ reform, change]* instituer, instaurer ; *[+ deal]* conclure ; *[+ plan]* mener à bien ; *[+ motion, amendment]* voter ; → **pace¹**

2 *(Telec = connect) [+ call]* passer ; *[+ caller]* brancher, mettre en communication ♦ **I'm ~ting you through now** vous êtes en ligne, je vous mets en communication ♦ **~ me through to Mr Smith** passez-moi M. Smith

3 *(US)* ♦ **to ~ sb through college** payer les études de qn

4 *(= make suffer)* ♦ **to ~ sb through hell** mener la vie dure à qn ♦ **they really ~ him through it*** ils lui en ont fait voir de dures*, ils lui ont fait passer un mauvais quart d'heure ; → **put transitive verb 1**

► **put together** VT SEP 1 *(lit)* mettre ensemble ♦ **don't ~ two hamsters together** ne mettez pas deux hamsters ensemble ♦ **don't ~ two hamsters together in one cage** ne mettez pas deux hamsters dans la même cage ♦ **he's worth more than the rest of the family ~ together** à lui tout seul il vaut plus que toute la famille réunie ♦ **it's more important than all the other factors ~ together** c'est plus important que tous les autres facteurs mis ensemble

2 *(= assemble) [+ table, bookcase]* assembler, monter ; *[+ book, story, account]* composer ; *[+ facts, what happened]* reconstituer ; *[+ team]* monter, constituer ♦ **she ~ together an excellent meal** elle a improvisé un délicieux repas

3 *(= design, draw up) [+ agreement, plan, package]* mettre au point

► **put up**

VI 1 *(= stay)* descendre *(at* dans) ♦ **to ~ up for the night at a hotel** passer la nuit dans un hôtel

2 *(Pol = offer o.s.)* se porter candidat(e) *(for* à), se présenter comme candidat(e) *(for* à) ♦ **to ~ up for a constituency** *(Parl)* chercher à avoir l'investiture de son parti dans une circonscription électorale

VT SEP 1 *(= raise) [+ hand]* lever ; *[+ flag, sail]* hisser ; *[+ tent]* monter ; *[+ collar, car window]* remonter ; *[+ umbrella]* ouvrir ; *[+ notice]* mettre, afficher *(on* sur) ; *[+ picture]* mettre, accrocher *(on* sur) ; *[+ building]* construire, ériger ; *[+ fence, barrier]* ériger, dresser ♦ **to ~ a ladder up against a wall** poser une échelle contre un mur ; see also **back, foot**

2 *(= increase) [+ numbers, taxes, sales]* augmenter ; *[+ prices]* faire monter ; *[+ demand]* accroître ; *[+ sb's temperature, blood pressure]* faire monter ♦ **that ~s up the total to over 1,000** cela fait monter le total à plus de 1 000

3 *(= offer) [+ proposal, case]* présenter, soumettre ; *[+ prayer]* faire ; *[+ resistance]* opposer ♦ **to ~ sb up as a candidate for** proposer qn comme candidat à ♦ **to ~ up a struggle** *or* **a fight** se battre ♦ **he ~ up a real fight to keep you in your job** il s'est vraiment battu pour que tu conserves *subj* ton poste ♦ **the matter was ~ up to the board for a decision** l'affaire a été soumise au conseil d'administration qui prendra une décision ♦ **to ~ sth up for sale/auction** mettre qch en vente/aux enchères ♦ **to ~ a child up for adoption** faire adopter un enfant ♦ **he was ~ up by his local branch** il a été présenté comme candidat par sa section locale ♦ **they ~ him up for the chairmanship** on l'a présenté *or* proposé comme candidat à la présidence ♦ **I'll ~ you up for the club** je vous proposerai comme membre du club

4 *(= provide) [+ money, funds]* fournir *(for* pour) ; *[+ reward]* offrir ♦ **to ~ up money for a project** financer un projet, fournir les fonds pour un projet ♦ **how much can you ~ up?** combien pouvez-vous mettre ?

5 *(= preserve) [+ fruit]* mettre en bocaux

6 *(= lodge)* loger, héberger

► **put up to** VT SEP 1 *(= incite)* ♦ **to ~ sb up to doing sth** pousser *or* inciter qn à faire qch ♦ **someone must have ~ him up to it** quelqu'un a dû le pousser *or* l'inciter à le faire

2 *(= give information about)* ♦ **to ~ sb up to sth** renseigner qn sur qch ♦ **he ~ her up to all the ways of avoiding tax** il l'a renseignée sur *or* lui a montré tous les moyens d'éviter de payer des impôts ♦ **a friend of mine ~ me up to it** c'est un ami qui m'en a donné l'idée

► **put up with** VT FUS tolérer, supporter ♦ **he has a lot to ~ up with** il a beaucoup de problèmes, il n'a pas la vie facile ♦ **it is difficult to ~ up with** c'est difficile à supporter, c'est difficilement supportable

putative /ˈpjuːtətɪv/ ADJ *(frm)* putatif

putrefaction /ˌpjuːtrɪˈfækʃən/ N putréfaction *f*

putrefy /ˈpjuːtrɪfaɪ/ VT putréfier VI se putréfier

putrescence /pjuːˈtresns/ N putrescence *f*

putrescent /pjuːˈtresnt/ ADJ putrescent, en voie de putréfaction

putrid /ˈpjuːtrɪd/ ADJ 1 *(= rotting)* putride, pourrissant 2 (*‡* = *awful)* dégoûtant, dégueulasse‡

putsch /pʊtʃ/ N putsch *m*, coup *m* d'État

putt /pʌt/ *(Golf)* N putt *m*, coup *m* roulé VTI putter

puttee /ˈpʌtiː/ N (pl **puttees** /ˈpʌtiːz/) bande *f* molletière

putter¹ /ˈpʌtəʳ/ N *(Golf)* putter *m*

putter² /ˈpʌtəʳ/ VI *(US)* ⇒ **potter¹**

putter³ /ˈpʌtəʳ/ VI *[engine, car, boat etc]* brouter

putting /ˈpʌtɪŋ/ N putting *m* COMP **putting green** N *(= part of golf course)* green *m*

putty /ˈpʌtɪ/ N mastic *m (ciment)* ♦ **she's (like) ~ in my hands** j'en fais ce que je veux VT mastiquer COMP **putty knife** N (pl **putty knives**) couteau *m* de vitrier

putz /pʌts/ N *(US)* 1 (* *= person)* couillon(ne)‡ *m(f)* 2 (**** *= penis)* bitte** *f*

puzzle /ˈpʌzl/ N 1 *(= mystery)* énigme *f*, mystère *m* ♦ **he's a real ~ to me** c'est une énigme vivante pour moi ♦ **it's a ~ to me how** *or* **that he got the job** je trouve curieux qu'il ait pu obtenir ce poste

2 *(= game)* casse-tête *m inv* ; *(= word game)* rébus *m* ; *(= crossword)* mots *mpl* croisés ; *(= jigsaw)* puzzle *m* ; *(= riddle)* devinette *f*

VT rendre *or* laisser perplexe ♦ **that really ~d him** ça l'a vraiment rendu *or* laissé perplexe ♦ **it ~s me that ...** je trouve curieux que ... ♦ **to ~ one's head about sth** se creuser la tête au sujet de qch ; see also **puzzled**

VI ♦ **to ~ over** *or* **about** essayer de comprendre ♦ **I'm still puzzling over where he might have hidden it** j'en suis encore à me demander où il a bien pu le cacher

COMP **puzzle book** N livre *m* de jeux

► **puzzle out** VT SEP *[+ problem]* résoudre ; *[+ mystery]* éclaircir, élucider ; *[+ writing]* déchiffrer ; *[+ answer, solution]* trouver, découvrir ; *[+ sb's actions, attitude]* comprendre ♦ **I'm trying to ~ out why he did it** j'essaie de comprendre *or* découvrir pourquoi il l'a fait

puzzled /ˈpʌzld/ ADJ perplexe ♦ **they were ~ to find/see ...** ils n'en revenaient pas de trouver/voir ... ♦ **to be ~ that ...** ne pas arriver à comprendre pourquoi ... ♦ **I am ~ (to know) why** je n'arrive pas à comprendre pourquoi ♦ **he was ~ about what to say** il ne savait pas trop quoi dire ; see also **puzzle**

puzzlement /ˈpʌzlmənt/ N *(NonC)* perplexité *f*

puzzler /ˈpʌzləʳ/ N *(gen)* énigme *f* ; *(= problem)* question *f* difficile, casse-tête *m inv*

puzzling /ˈpʌzlɪŋ/ ADJ curieux

PVC /ˌpiːviːˈsiː/ N *(Tex)* (abbrev of **polyvinyl chloride**) PVC *m*

PVS /ˌpiːviːˈes/ N 1 abbrev of **postviral syndrome** 2 (abbrev of **persistent vegetative state**) → **persistent**

Pvt. *(Mil)* abbrev of **Private noun 1**

PW /piːˈdʌbljuː/ N 1 *(US Mil)* (abbrev of **prisoner of war**) → **prisoner** 2 *(Brit)* abbrev of **policewoman**

p.w. (abbrev of **per week**) par semaine

PWR /piːˌdʌbljuːˈɑːʳ/ N (abbrev of **pressurized water reactor**) → **pressurize**

PX /piːˈeks/ N *(US Mil)* (abbrev of **post exchange**) → **post²**

pygmy /ˈpɪgmɪ/ N Pygmée *mf* ; *(fig)* pygmée *m* ADJ pygmée *f inv* ; *[animal]* nain

pyjama /pɪˈdʒɑːmə/ *(Brit)* NPL **pyjamas** pyjama *m* ♦ **a pair of ~s** un pyjama ♦ **in (one's) ~s** en pyjama COMP *[jacket, trousers]* de pyjama

pylon /ˈpaɪlən/ N pylône *m*

pylori /paɪˈlɔːraɪ/ NPL of **pylorus**

pyloric /paɪˈlɔːrɪk/ ADJ pylorique

pylorus /paɪˈlɔːrəs/ N (pl **pylori**) pylore *m*

pyorrhea /paɪəˈrɪə/ N pyorrhée f alvéolaire

pyramid /ˈpɪrəmɪd/ N pyramide f VT (US Fin) ◆ to ~ winnings spéculer en réinvestissant les bénéfices réalisés COMP **pyramid selling** N vente f pyramidale

pyramidal /pɪˈræmɪdl/ ADJ pyramidal

Pyramus /ˈpɪrəməs/ N ◆ ~ **and Thisbe** Pyrame m et Thisbé f

pyre /paɪəʳ/ N bûcher m funéraire

Pyrenean /pɪrəˈniːən/ ADJ pyrénéen, des Pyrénées

Pyrenees /pɪrəˈniːz/ NPL Pyrénées fpl

pyrethrum /paɪˈriːθrəm/ N pyrèthre m

pyretic /paɪˈretɪk/ ADJ pyrétique

Pyrex ® /ˈpaɪreks/ N pyrex ® m COMP [dish] en pyrex ®

pyrexia /paɪˈreksɪə/ N pyrexie f

pyrexic /paɪˈreksɪk/ ADJ pyrexique

pyrites /paɪˈraɪtiːz/ N (pl **pyrites**) pyrite f ◆ **iron** ~ sulfure m de fer, fer m sulfuré

pyritic /paɪˈrɪtɪk/ ADJ pyriteux

pyro... /ˈpaɪərəʊ/ PREF pyro...

pyromania /ˌpaɪərəʊˈmeɪnɪə/ N pyromanie f

pyromaniac /ˌpaɪərəʊˈmeɪnɪæk/ N pyromane mf, incendiaire mf

pyrotechnic /ˌpaɪərəʊˈteknɪk/ ADJ pyrotechnique ◆ ~ **display** feu(x) m(pl) d'artifice N (NonC: Phys) ◆ ~**s** pyrotechnie f ; (pl: fig hum) feux mpl d'artifice

Pyrrhic /ˈpɪrɪk/ ADJ ◆ ~ **victory** victoire f à la Pyrrhus

Pyrrhus /ˈpɪrəs/ N Pyrrhus m

Pythagoras /paɪˈθægərəs/ N Pythagore m

Pythagorean /paɪˌθægəˈrɪən/ ADJ (gen) pythagoricien ; [number, letter] pythagorique

python /ˈpaɪθən/ N python m

pyx /pɪks/ N (in church) ciboire m ; (for sick communions) pyxide f

pzazz * /pəˈzæz/ N (US) ⇒ **piz(z)azz**

Q, q /kjuː/ N (= *letter*) Q, q *m* ◆ **Q for Queen** ≃ Q comme Québec

Q and A /ˈkjuːəndˈeɪ/ N (abbrev of **questions and answers**) questions-réponses *fpl*

qat /kæt/ N ⇒ **khat**

Qatar /kæˈtɑːʳ/ [N] [1] (= *country*) Qatar *m* ◆ **in ~** au Qatar [2] (= *inhabitant*) Qatari(e) *m(f)* [ADJ] qatari

QC /ˌkjuːˈsiː/ N (*Brit Jur*) (abbrev of **Queen's Counsel**) → **counsel**

QE2 /ˌkjuːiːˈtuː/ N (*Brit Naut*) (abbrev of **Queen Elizabeth II**) *paquebot*

QED /ˌkjuːiːˈdiː/ (*Math*) (abbrev of **quod erat demonstrandum**) CQFD

qt N abbrev of **quart(s)**

q.t. /ˈkjuːˈtiː/ N (abbrev of **quiet**) ◆ **on the ~*** en douce*, en cachette

Q-tip ® /ˈkjuːtɪp/ N Coton-tige ® *m*

qty N abbrev of **quantity**

qua /kweɪ/ ADV ◆ **the actor ~ actor** l'acteur en tant que tel ◆ **religion ~ religion** la religion en tant que telle

quack¹ /kwæk/ [N] coin-coin *m inv* (*cri du canard*) [VI] faire coin-coin [COMP] **quack-quack** N (*baby talk*) coin-coin *m inv*

quack²* /kwæk/ N (= *imposter, bogus doctor*) charlatan *m* ; (*hum*) (= *doctor*) toubib* *m*

quackery /ˈkwækərɪ/ N (*NonC*) charlatanisme *m*

quad¹ /kwɒd/ [N] abbrev of **quadruplet, quadrangle** [NPL] **quads** * (= *muscles*) abbrev of **quadriceps** [COMP] **quad bike** N moto *f* à quatre roues motrices

quad²* /kwɒd/ N ⇒ **quod**

quadr... PREF ⇒ **quadri...**

Quadragesima /kwɒdrəˈdʒesɪmə/ N Quadragésime *f*

quadrangle /ˈkwɒdræŋgl/ N [1] (*Math*) quadrilatère *m* [2] (= *courtyard*) cour *f*

quadrangular /kwɒˈdræŋgjʊləʳ/ ADJ quadrangulaire

quadrant /ˈkwɒdrənt/ N [*of circle*] quadrant *m*, quart *m* de cercle

quadraphonic /ˌkwɒdrəˈfɒnɪk/ ADJ quadriphonique, tétraphonique ◆ **in ~ (sound)** en quadriphonie, en tétraphonie

quadraphonics /ˌkwɒdrəˈfɒnɪks/ N (*NonC*) quadriphonie *f*, tétraphonie *f*

quadraphony /kwɒdˈrɒfənɪ/ N ⇒ **quadraphonics**

quadraplegic /ˌkwɒdrəˈpliːdʒɪk/ N, ADJ tétraplégique *mf*

quadrasonic /ˌkwɒdrəˈsɒnɪk/ ADJ quadriphonique, tétraphonique

quadrasonics /ˌkwɒdrəˈsɒnɪks/ N (*NonC*) quadriphonie *f*, tétraphonie *f*

quadrat /ˈkwɒdrət/ N (*Typo*) cadrat *m*

quadratic /kwɒˈdrætɪk/ (*Math*) [ADJ] quadratique [COMP] **quadratic equation** N équation *f* quadratique *or* du second degré

quadrature /ˈkwɒdrətʃəʳ/ N quadrature *f*

quadrennial /kwɒˈdrenɪəl/ ADJ quadriennal

quadri... /ˈkwɒdrɪ/ PREF quadri..., quadru...

quadriceps /ˈkwɒdrɪseps/ N (pl **quadricepses** *or* **quadriceps**) quadriceps *m*

quadrilateral /ˌkwɒdrɪˈlætərəl/ (*Math*) [ADJ] quadrilatère, quadrilatéral [N] quadrilatère *m*

quadrilingual /ˌkwɒdrɪˈlɪŋgwəl/ ADJ quadrilingue

quadrille /kwəˈdrɪl/ N (*Dancing*) quadrille *m*

quadrillion /kwɒˈdrɪljən/ N (*Brit*) quatrillion *m* ; (*US*) ancien quatrillion *m* (10^{15})

quadripartite /ˌkwɒdrɪˈpɑːtaɪt/ ADJ quadriparti (-tie *or* -tite *f*)

quadriplegia /ˌkwɒdrɪˈpliːdʒɪə/ N tétraplégie *f*, quadriplégie *f*

quadriplegic /ˌkwɒdrɪˈpliːdʒɪk/ ADJ, N tétraplégique *mf*, quadriplégique *mf*

quadroon /kwɒˈdruːn/ N quarteron(ne) *m(f)*

quadrophonic /ˌkwɒdrəˈfɒnɪk/ ADJ ⇒ **quadraphonic**

quadruped /ˈkwɒdrʊped/ ADJ, N quadrupède *m*

quadruple /ˈkwɒdrʊpl/ [ADJ, N] quadruple *m* [VTI] /kwɒˈdruːpl/ quadrupler

quadruplet /kwɒˈdruːplɪt/ N quadruplé(e) *m(f)*

quadruplicate /kwɒˈdruːplɪkɪt/ [ADJ] quadruple [N] ◆ **in ~** en quatre exemplaires

quads /kwɒdz/ NPL (= *quadriceps*) quadriceps *mpl* ; (= *quadruplets*) quadruplés *mpl*

quaff /kwɒf/ VT (†† *or hum*) (= *drink*) avaler

quaffable /ˈkwɒfəbl/ ADJ ◆ **a ~ wine** un vin qui se laisse boire

quag /kwæg/ N ⇒ **quagmire**

quagga /ˈkwægə/ N (pl **quaggas** *or* **quagga**) couagga *m*

quagmire /ˈkwægmaɪəʳ/ N (*lit, fig*) bourbier *m*

quahaug, quahog /ˈkwɑːhɒg/ N (*US*) clam *m*

quail¹ /kweɪl/ VI [*person*] trembler (*before* devant) ◆ **I ~ed at the thought of having to organize everything** je tremblais à l'idée de devoir tout organiser ◆ **his heart ~ed** son courage vacilla

quail² /kweɪl/ N (pl **quail** *or* **quails**) (= *bird*) caille *f*

quaint /kweɪnt/ ADJ [1] (= *picturesque*) [*place*] pittoresque ; [*person*] original ◆ **a ~ little village** un petit village pittoresque *or* qui a du cachet [2] (= *old-fashioned*) [*custom, tradition, word, notion*] désuet (-ète *f*) ; (*pej*) vieillot ◆ **how ~!** comme c'est curieux !

quaintly /ˈkweɪntlɪ/ ADV (= *strangely*) curieusement ◆ **~ old-fashioned** d'un charme désuet ◆ **a pub ~ called** *or* **named "The Dew Drop"** un pub qui porte le nom désuet de "La Goutte de Rosée"

quaintness /ˈkweɪntnɪs/ N [1] [*of place, object*] (= *picturesqueness*) pittoresque *m* ; (= *old-fashionedness*) charme *m* désuet, charme *m* vieillot [2] (= *peculiarity*) [*of custom, word, idea, question*] côté *m or* aspect *m* curieux

quake /kweɪk/ [VI] [*earth, person*] trembler ◆ **I was quaking (in my boots*)** je tremblais comme une feuille ◆ **to ~ with fear** trembler de peur [N] (abbrev of **earthquake**) tremblement *m* de terre, séisme *m*

Quaker /ˈkweɪkəʳ/ [N] quaker(esse) *m(f)* [COMP] [*community, school*] de quakers ; [*person, family*] quaker *f inv* ; [*beliefs*] des quakers **Quaker meeting** N réunion *f* de quakers **Quaker meeting house** N église *f* de quakers

Quakerism /ˈkweɪkərɪzəm/ N quakerisme *m*

qualification /ˌkwɒlɪfɪˈkeɪʃən/ N [1] (= *ability*) compétence *f* (*for* en ; *to do sth* pour faire qch) aptitude *f* (*for* à), capacité *f* (*to do sth* pour faire qch) ◆ **I doubt his ~ to teach English** je doute qu'il ait les compétences *or* les capacités requises pour enseigner l'anglais ◆ **we have never questioned his ~ for the job** nous n'avons jamais mis en doute son aptitude à occuper ce poste

[2] (= *degree, diploma*) diplôme *m*, titre *m* (*in* de) ◆ **his only ~ for the job was his experience in similar work** seule son expérience dans des domaines similaires le qualifiait pour ce travail ◆ **what are your ~s?** (= *skill, degrees, experience*) quelle est votre formation ? ; (also **paper qualifications**) qu'est-ce que vous avez comme diplômes *or* qualifications professionnelles ? ◆ **he has a lot of experience but no paper ~s** *or* **formal ~s** il a beaucoup d'expérience mais il n'a aucun diplôme *or* il n'a aucun titre *or* il n'a pas de qualifications professionnelles ◆ **I have no teaching ~(s)** je n'ai pas le(s) diplôme(s) requis pour enseigner

[3] *(= limitation)* réserve *f*, restriction *f* ◆ **to accept a plan with ~(s)** accepter un projet avec des réserves *or* avec des restrictions ◆ **without ~(s)** sans réserves *or* restrictions
[4] *(= graduation)* ◆ **my first job after ~ (as a vet)** mon premier emploi après que j'ai obtenu mon diplôme (de vétérinaire)
[5] *(gen, Gram: qualifying)* qualification *f*

qualified /ˈkwɒlɪfaɪd/ ADJ [1] *(= trained, suitable)* *[person, staff, craftsman, player, pilot]* qualifié ; *[engineer, doctor, nurse, teacher, accountant]* diplômé ◆ **suitably ~ candidates** les candidats ayant les qualifications requises ◆ **~ for a job** qualifié pour un poste *or* un travail ◆ **he was well ~ for the post of president** il avait les qualités requises pour être président ◆ **~ to do sth** qualifié pour faire qch, habilité à faire qch *(frm)* ◆ **he is ~ to teach** il a les qualifications requises pour enseigner ◆ **they are not ~ to vote** ils ne sont pas habilités à voter ◆ **he is well ~ to captain the team** il est tout à fait qualifié pour être le capitaine de l'équipe ◆ **I'm not ~ to speak for her** je ne suis pas habilité à parler en son nom ◆ **I don't feel ~ to judge** je ne me sens pas en mesure d'en juger
[2] *(= limited)* *[praise, support, approval]* mitigé ; *[acceptance]* conditionnel ◆ **a ~ success** une demi-réussite ◆ **a ~ yes** un oui mitigé, un oui mais ◆ **a ~ majority** une majorité qualifiée

qualifier /ˈkwɒlɪfaɪəʳ/ N *(Gram)* qualificatif *m*, qualificateur *m* ; *(Sport) (= team)* équipe *f* qualifiée ; *(= person)* athlète *mf* qualifié(e)

qualify /ˈkwɒlɪfaɪ/ LANGUAGE IN USE 26.3
VT [1] *(= make competent)* **to ~ sb to do sth/for sth** *(gen)* qualifier qn pour faire qch/pour qch ; *[experience]* donner à qn les compétences *or* qualités requises pour faire/pour qch ; *[degree, diploma]* donner à qn les diplômes *or* titres requis pour faire/pour qch ; *[trade diploma, certificates]* donner à qn les qualifications professionnelles nécessaires pour faire/pour qch ◆ **to ~ sb to do sth** *(Jur)* habiliter qn à faire qch ◆ **that doesn't ~ him to speak on it** cela ne lui donne pas qualité pour en parler
[2] *(= modify)* *[+ approval, support, praise]* mettre des réserves à ; *[+ statement, opinion]* nuancer ◆ **to ~ one's acceptance of sth** accepter qch sous réserve *or* sous condition ◆ **I think you should ~ that remark** je pense que vous devriez nuancer cette remarque
[3] *(= describe)* qualifier *(as* de) ; *(Gram)* qualifier
VI [1] *(= obtain qualifications)* obtenir son diplôme *(or* son brevet *etc)* *(in* en) ◆ **to ~ as a doctor/a nurse/an engineer** obtenir son diplôme de médecin/d'infirmière/d'ingénieur ◆ **he has qualified as a teacher** il a obtenu son diplôme de professeur ◆ **while he was ~ing as an architect** pendant qu'il faisait des études d'architecture ◆ **to ~ for the final** *(Sport)* se qualifier pour la finale
[2] *(= fulfil requirements)* **to ~ for a job** avoir les compétences requises pour un poste ◆ **does he ~?** est-ce qu'il remplit les conditions requises ? ◆ **to ~ as a refugee** avoir droit au statut de réfugié ◆ **to ~ as a member** remplir les conditions d'adhésion ◆ **does this country still ~ as a superpower?** peut-on encore considérer ce pays comme une superpuissance ? ◆ **it doesn't ~ as art** cela ne mérite pas le nom d'art

qualifying /ˈkwɒlɪfaɪɪŋ/ ADJ [1] *[mark]* de passage, qui permet de passer ; *[examination]* d'entrée ; *[score]* qui permet de se qualifier ◆ **~ period** *(gen)* période *f* d'attente ; *(Jur)* période *f* probatoire ◆ **~ heat** *(Sport)* éliminatoire *f* ◆ **~ round** série *f* éliminatoire ◆ **~ shares** *(Stock Exchange)* actions *fpl* de garantie [2] *(Gram)* qualificatif

qualitative /ˈkwɒlɪtətɪv/ ADJ qualitatif

qualitatively /ˈkwɒlɪtətɪvlɪ/ ADV qualitativement

quality /ˈkwɒlɪtɪ/ N [1] *(= nature, kind)* qualité *f* ◆ **of the best ~** de première qualité, de premier ordre *or* choix ◆ **of good** *or* **high ~** de bonne qualité, de qualité supérieure ◆ **of poor** *or* **bad** *or* **low ~** de mauvaise qualité, de qualité inférieure ◆ **the ~ of life** la qualité de la vie
[2] *(NonC = goodness)* qualité *f* ◆ **guarantee of ~** garantie *f* de qualité ◆ **it's ~ rather than quantity that counts** c'est la qualité qui compte plus que la quantité ◆ **this wine has ~** ce vin a de la qualité *or* est de qualité ◆ **he has real ~** il a de la classe
[3] *(= attribute)* qualité *f* ◆ **natural qualities** qualités *fpl* naturelles ◆ **one of his (good) qualities** une de ses qualités ◆ **one of his bad qualities** un de ses défauts ◆ **he has many artistic qualities** il a beaucoup de qualités *or* de dons *mpl* artistiques
[4] *[of voice, sound]* qualité *f*, timbre *m*
[5] *(† or hum = high rank)* qualité † *f*
COMP *[car, film, product]* de qualité
quality control N contrôle *m* de qualité
quality controller N contrôleur *m*, -euse *f* de la qualité
quality papers NPL *(Press)* presse *f* de qualité
quality time N moments *mpl* de qualité ◆ **I don't work on Fridays, which means I get more ~ time with my son** je ne travaille pas le vendredi, ce qui me permet de passer plus de bons moments avec mon fils

qualm /kwɑːm/ N [1] *(= scruple)* doute *m*, scrupule *m* ; *(= misgiving)* appréhension *f*, inquiétude *f* ◆ **~s of conscience** scrupules *mpl* de conscience ◆ **he did it without a ~** il l'a fait sans le moindre scrupule ◆ **I would feel no ~s about doing that** je n'aurais pas le moindre scrupule à faire cela ◆ **I had some ~s about his future** j'avais quelques inquiétudes sur *or* pour son avenir [2] *(= nausea)* nausée *f*

quandary /ˈkwɒndərɪ/ N dilemme *m* ◆ **to be in a ~** être pris dans un dilemme ◆ **he was in a ~ about** *or* **as to** *or* **over what to do** il était pris dans un dilemme et ne savait pas quoi faire ◆ **that got him out of a ~** ça l'a sorti d'un dilemme

quango /ˈkwæŋɡəʊ/ N *(Brit)* (abbrev of **quasi-autonomous nongovernmental organization**) organisation *f* non gouvernementale quasi autonome

> **QUANGO**
>
> Cet acronyme de « quasi-autonomous non-governmental organization » désigne des organismes mis en place par le gouvernement britannique dans les années 70 mais qui ne relèvent d'aucun ministère : c'est le cas par exemple de la Commission pour l'égalité des chances (Equal Opportunities Commission) ou de la Commission pour les relations interraciales (Commission for Racial Equality). Certaines de ces organisations disposent d'un pouvoir de décision, d'autres ont un rôle purement consultatif.
> → **EOC, EEOC**

quanta /ˈkwɒntə/ NPL of **quantum**

quantifiable /ˌkwɒntɪˈfaɪəbl/ ADJ quantifiable

quantifier /ˈkwɒntɪfaɪəʳ/ N *(Ling, Philos, Math)* quantificateur *m*

quantify /ˈkwɒntɪfaɪ/ VT quantifier

quantitative /ˈkwɒntɪtətɪv/ ADJ *(gen)* quantitatif ; *(Ling, Poetry)* de quantité

quantitatively /ˈkwɒntɪtətɪvlɪ/ ADV quantitativement

quantity /ˈkwɒntɪtɪ/ N quantité *f* ◆ **a small ~ of rice** une petite quantité de riz ◆ **what ~ do you want?** quelle quantité (en) voulez-vous ? ◆ **in ~** en (grande) quantité ◆ **in large quantities** en grandes quantités ◆ **a ~ of, any ~ of, quantities of** une quantité de, (des) quantités de, un grand nombre de ; → **quality, unknown**
COMP *(Comm) [production]* sur une grande échelle, en série
quantity mark N *(Ling, Poetry)* signe *m* de quantité
quantity surveying N *(NonC: Brit)* métrage *m*
quantity surveyor N *(Brit)* métreur *m* (vérificateur)

quantum /ˈkwɒntəm/ (pl **quanta**) N quantum *m*
COMP **quantum leap** N *(fig)* bond *m* prodigieux ; *(forwards)* bond *m* en avant ◆ **to take** *or* **make a ~ leap** faire un bond (en avant) prodigieux
quantum mechanics N *(NonC)* mécanique *f* quantique
quantum number N nombre *m* quantique
quantum theory N théorie *f* quantique *or* des quanta

quarantine /ˈkwɒrəntiːn/ N quarantaine *f* *(pour raisons sanitaires)* ◆ **in ~** en quarantaine VT mettre en quarantaine COMP *[regulations, period]* de quarantaine

quark /kwɑːk/ N [1] *(Phys)* quark *m* [2] *(Culin)* fromage *m* blanc

quarrel /ˈkwɒrəl/ N [1] *(= dispute)* querelle *f*, dispute *f* ; *(more intellectual)* différend *m* ; *(= breach)* brouille *f* ◆ **I had a ~ with him yesterday** je me suis disputé *or* querellé avec lui hier ◆ **they've had a ~** *(= argued)* ils se sont disputés *or* querellés ; *(= fallen out)* ils se sont brouillés ◆ **the ~ between the professor and his assistant** la querelle entre le professeur et son assistant ; *(longer: more frm)* la querelle qui oppose *(or* opposait *etc)* le professeur à son assistant ◆ **to start a ~** provoquer *or* susciter une querelle *or* dispute ◆ **to pick a ~ with sb, to try to start a ~ with sb** chercher querelle à qn ◆ **I have no ~ with you** je n'ai rien contre vous ◆ **he had no ~ with what we had done** il n'avait rien à redire à ce que nous avions fait
VI *(= have a dispute)* se quereller, se disputer *(with sb* avec qn ; *about, over* à propos de) ; *(= break off friendship)* se brouiller *(with sb* avec qn) ◆ **I cannot ~ with that** je n'ai rien à redire à cela ◆ **what he ~s with is ...** ce contre quoi il s'insurge c'est ...

quarrelling, quarreling *(US)* /ˈkwɒrəlɪŋ/ N *(NonC)* disputes *fpl*, querelles *fpl* ; *(petty)* chamailleries * *fpl* ADJ qui se disputent

quarrelsome /ˈkwɒrəlsəm/ ADJ querelleur

quarrier /ˈkwɒrɪəʳ/ N (ouvrier *m*) carrier *m*

quarry¹ /ˈkwɒrɪ/ N carrière *f* ; → **marble** VT [1] *[+ stone]* extraire [2] *[+ hillside]* exploiter *(en carrière)* VI exploiter une carrière ◆ **they are ~ing for marble** ils exploitent une carrière de marbre
COMP **quarry tile** N carreau *m*
quarry-tiled floor N sol *m* carrelé
► **quarry out** VT SEP *[+ block, stone]* extraire

quarry² /ˈkwɒrɪ/ N *[of animal, bird]* proie *f* ; *(Hunting = game)* gibier *m* ◆ **the detectives lost their ~** les policiers ont perdu la trace de celui qu'ils pourchassaient

quarryman /ˈkwɒrɪmən/ N (pl **-men**) (ouvrier *m*) carrier *m*

quart /kwɔːt/ N *(= measure)* ≈ litre *m* *(Brit* = 1,136 litre, *US* = 0,946 litre) ◆ **it's like trying to put a ~ into a pint pot** autant essayer de vider la mer avec une petite cuiller

quarter /ˈkwɔːtəʳ/ N [1] *(= fourth part)* quart *m* ◆ **to divide sth into ~s** diviser qch en quatre (parties égales) *or* en (quatre) quartiers ◆ **a ~ (of a pound) of tea** un quart (de livre) de thé ◆ **a ~ full/empty** au quart plein/vide ◆ **it's a ~ gone already** il y en a déjà un quart de parti ◆ **a ~ as big as** quatre fois moins grand que ◆ **I bought it for a ~ of the price** *or* **for ~ the price** je l'ai acheté au quart du prix *or* pour le quart de son prix

2 *(in expressions of time)* quart *m* (d'heure) ◆ **a ~ of an hour** un quart d'heure ◆ **a ~ to seven, a ~ of seven** *(US)* sept heures moins le quart *or* moins un quart ◆ **a ~ past six, a ~ after six** *(US)* six heures un quart *or* et quart ◆ **to drive with one's hands at a ~ to three** *(on steering wheel)* conduire avec les mains à neuf heures et quart ◆ **it wasn't the ~ yet** il n'était pas encore le quart ◆ **the clock strikes the ~s** l'horloge sonne les quarts

3 *(= specific fourth parts) [of year]* trimestre *m* ; *(US and Can money)* quart *m* de dollar, vingt-cinq cents *mpl* ; *(Brit weight)* = 28 livres (= 12,7 kg) ; *(US weight)* = 25 livres (= 11,34 kg) ; *(Her)* quartier *m* ; *[of beef, apple]* quartier *m* ; *[of moon]* quartier *m* ◆ **to pay by the ~** payer tous les trois mois *or* par trimestre ◆ **a ~'s rent** un terme (de loyer) ; → **forequarters, hindquarters**

4 *(= compass point)* point *m* cardinal ◆ **on the port/starboard ~** *(Naut)* par la hanche de bâbord/tribord ◆ **from all ~s** de toutes parts, de tous côtés ◆ **you must report that to the proper ~** *(frm)* vous devez signaler cela à qui de droit ◆ **in responsible ~s** dans les milieux autorisés

5 *(= part of town)* quartier *m* ◆ **the Latin ~** le quartier latin

6 *(NonC: liter = mercy)* quartier *m* *(liter)*, grâce *f* ◆ **to give/cry ~** faire/demander quartier ◆ **to give no ~** ne pas faire de quartier

NPL **quarters** (= *lodgings*) résidence *f*, domicile *m* ; *(Mil)* quartiers *mpl* ; *(temporary)* cantonnement *m* ◆ **they are living in very cramped ~s** ils sont logés très à l'étroit ; → **married**

VT 1 *(= divide into four)* diviser en quatre (parts égales), diviser en (quatre) quartiers ; *[+ traitor's body]* écarteler ; *(Her)* écarteler ; → **hang**

2 *(= lodge) (Mil) [+ troops]* caserner ; *(temporarily)* cantonner ; *(gen)* loger (on chez)

3 **to ~ the ground** *[dogs]* quêter ◆ **to ~ a town in search of sb** *[police]* quadriller une ville à la recherche de qn

ADJ quart de ◆ **the ~ part of** le quart de ◆ **a ~ share in sth** (une part d')un quart de qch ; see also **comp**

COMP **quarter day** N *(Fin, Jur)* (jour *m* du) terme *m*

quarter-deck N *(Naut)* plage *f* arrière ; *[of sailing ship]* gaillard *m* d'arrière

quarter final N quart *m* de finale

quarter-finalist N quart de finaliste *mf*

quarter-hour N *(period of time)* quart *m* d'heure ◆ **on the ~-hour** *(division of clock face)* tous les quarts d'heure

quarter light N *(Brit: in car)* déflecteur *m*

quarter mile N *(Sport)* (course *f* d')un quart *m* de mille

quarter note N *(US Mus)* noire *f*

quarter pound N quart *m* de livre

quarter-pound ADJ d'un quart de livre

quarter-pounder N *(Culin)* *hamburger contenant un steak haché d'environ 100 grammes*

quarter sessions NPL *(Jur)* *(= sessions)* ≈ assises *fpl* trimestrielles (de tribunal de grande instance) ; *(= court)* ≈ tribunal *m* de grande instance *(jusqu'en 1972)*

quarter turn N quart *m* de tour

quarter window N *(US: in car)* déflecteur *m*

quarterback /ˈkwɔːtəbæk/ *(US)* N *(Ftbl)* stratège *m* *(souvent en position d'arrière)*, quarterback *m*, quart-arrière *m* *(Can)* VT 1 *(Ftbl)* jouer quarter-back *or* quart-arrière *(Can)* dans 2 *(fig)* déterminer la stratégie de VI *(Ftbl)* jouer quarter-back *or* quart-arrière *(Can)*

quartering /ˈkwɔːtərɪŋ/ N *(NonC)* 1 *(= splitting into quarters)* division *f* en quatre ; *(Her)* écartelure *f* 2 *(Mil = lodging)* cantonnement *m*

quarterly /ˈkwɔːtəlɪ/ ADJ trimestriel N *(= periodical)* publication *f* trimestrielle ADV tous les trois mois

quartermaster /ˈkwɔːtəˌmɑːstəʳ/ N 1 *(Mil)* intendant *m* militaire de troisième classe 2 *(Naut)* maître *m* de manœuvre

COMP **quartermaster general** N *(Mil)* intendant *m* général d'armée de première classe

quartermaster sergeant N *(Mil)* intendant *m* militaire adjoint

quartet(te) /kwɔːˈtet/ N *[of classical music players]* quatuor *m* ; *[of jazz players]* quartette *m* ; *(hum = four people)* quatuor * *m*

quarto /ˈkwɔːtəʊ/ N in-quarto *m* ADJ *[paper]* in-quarto *inv*

quartz /ˈkwɔːts/ N quartz *m*

COMP de *or* en quartz

quartz clock N pendule *f* à quartz

quartz crystal N cristal *m* de quartz

quartz(-iodine) lamp N lampe *f* à iode

quartz watch N montre *f* à quartz

quartzite /ˈkwɔːtsaɪt/ N quartzite *m*

quasar /ˈkweɪzɑːʳ/ N quasar *m*

quash /kwɒʃ/ VT *[+ decision, verdict, judgement]* casser, annuler ; *[+ rebellion]* réprimer, étouffer ; *[+ proposal, suggestion]* rejeter

quasi- /ˈkweɪzaɪ/ PREF *(+ n)* quasi- ; *(+ adj)* quasi, presque ◆ **~marriage** quasi-mariage *m* ◆ **~religious** quasi *or* presque religieux

quatercentenary /ˌkwætəsenˈtiːnərɪ/ N quatre-centième anniversaire *m*

quaternary /kwəˈtɜːnərɪ/ ADJ *(Chem, Geol, Math)* quaternaire N *(= set of four)* ensemble *m* de quatre ; *(= number four)* quatre *m* ◆ **the Quaternary** *(Geol)* le quaternaire

quatrain /ˈkwɒtreɪn/ N quatrain *m*

quaver /ˈkweɪvəʳ/ N 1 *(esp Brit Mus = note)* croche *f* 2 *(= voice tremor)* tremblement *m*, chevrotement *m* VI *[voice]* chevroter, trembloter ; *[person]* chevroter, parler d'une voix chevrotante *or* tremblotante VT (also **quaver out**) chevroter COMP **quaver rest** N *(esp Brit Mus)* demi-soupir *m*

quavering /ˈkweɪvərɪŋ/ ADJ chevrotant, tremblotant N tremblotement *m*

quaveringly /ˈkweɪvərɪŋlɪ/ ADV d'une voix chevrotante *or* tremblotante, avec des tremblements dans la voix

quavery /ˈkweɪvərɪ/ ADJ ⇒ **quavering adj**

quay /kiː/ N *(Naut etc)* quai *m* ◆ **on the ~** sur le quai ◆ **along the ~** le long du quai

quayside /ˈkiːsaɪd/ N quai *m* ; *(= whole area)* quais *mpl* ◆ **the ship drew up along the ~** le navire est arrivé à quai

queasiness /ˈkwiːzɪnɪs/ N *(NonC)* nausée *f*, malaise *m*

queasy /ˈkwiːzɪ/ ADJ 1 *(= nauseous)* ◆ **he was ~, he felt ~** il avait mal au cœur, il avait la nausée ◆ **it makes me (feel) ~** ça me donne mal au cœur, ça me donne la nausée ◆ **his stomach was ~** il avait l'estomac barbouillé 2 *(= uncomfortable)* mal à l'aise ◆ **I had a ~ feeling about the whole thing** tout ça me mettait mal à l'aise ◆ **to feel ~ (about sth)** se sentir mal à l'aise (à propos de qch)

Quebec /kwɪˈbek/ N 1 *(= city)* Québec 2 *(= province)* Québec *m* ◆ **in ~** au Québec ADJ québécois ◆ **~ French** québécois *m*

Quebec(k)er /kwɪˈbekəʳ/ N Québécois(e) *m(f)*

Quebecois /kebeˈkwɑː/ N *(pl inv = person)* Québécois(e) *m(f)*

queen /kwiːn/ N 1 *(also fig)* reine *f* ◆ **Queen Elizabeth** la reine Élisabeth ◆ **she was ~ to George III** elle était l'épouse de Georges III ◆ **Queen Anne's dead!** * *(iro)* ce n'est pas une nouvelle !, tu ne nous apprends rien ! ; see also **comp** ◆ **~ of the ball** reine *f* du bal ; → **beauty, Mary, May**

2 *(= ant, bee, wasp)* reine *f*

3 *(Chess)* dame *f*, reine *f*

4 *(Cards)* dame *f*

5 (‡ *pej* = *homosexual)* folle‡ *f*, tante‡ *f*

VT 1 * **to ~ it** faire la grande dame ◆ **to ~ it over sb** prendre des airs d'impératrice avec qn

2 *(Chess) [+ pawn]* damer

COMP **Queen Anne** ADJ *[furniture]* de l'époque de la reine Anne *(début 18e)*

queen bee N reine *f* des abeilles ◆ **she's the ~ bee** * c'est elle qui commande

queen consort N reine *f* *(épouse du roi)*

queen dowager N reine *f* douairière

Queen Mother N reine *f* mère

Queen's Bench N *(Brit Jur)* cour *f* supérieure de justice

Queen's Counsel N *(Jur)* avocat *m* de la Couronne

Queen's evidence N *(Jur)* ◆ **to turn Queen's evidence** témoigner contre ses complices

the Queen's highway N la voie publique

queen-size bed N *grand lit double*

Queen's Messenger N courrier *m* diplomatique

Queen's speech N *(Brit)* discours *m* de la reine

QUEEN'S SPEECH, KING'S SPEECH

Chaque année, au moment de la rentrée parlementaire, le monarque britannique prononce une allocution devant les deux chambres du Parlement : c'est le discours de la reine (**Queen's speech**) ou du roi (**King's speech**), qui est diffusé à la télévision et à la radio. Ce discours est rédigé par le gouvernement, qui y expose son programme pour l'année à venir ainsi que les lois qu'il désire proposer. Conformément à la tradition, le souverain utilise l'expression « mon gouvernement ».

queencake /ˈkwiːnkeɪk/ N *petit gâteau aux raisins secs*

queenly /ˈkwiːnlɪ/ ADJ *[woman]* au port de reine ; *[behaviour]* de reine

Queensland /ˈkwiːnzlənd/ N Queensland *m* ◆ **in ~** dans le Queensland

queer /kwɪəʳ/ ADJ 1 *(= strange)* étrange, bizarre ; *(= suspicious)* louche, suspect ◆ **there's something ~ going on** il se passe quelque chose de louche ◆ **there's something ~ about the way he always has money** c'est louche qu'il ait toujours de l'argent ◆ **a ~ fellow** *or* **fish** * un curieux personnage *or* bonhomme ◆ **a ~ customer** * un drôle d'individu *or* de type * ◆ **~ in the head** * *(pej)* toqué * ◆ **to be in Queer Street** * *(Brit)* être dans une mauvaise passe

2 († ‡ = *homosexual) (gen pej) [man]* pédé‡ *(pej)* ; *(used by some homosexuals) [culture, politics, cinema]* gay *inv* ◆ **he's/she's ~** *(pej)* c'est un pédé‡/une gouine‡ *(pej)*

3 *(Brit* † = *unwell)* ◆ **to feel ~** se sentir tout chose ◆ **to come over ~** avoir un malaise

4 *(US)* ◆ **to be ~ for sth** * être dingue * de qch

N († ‡ *pej* = *homosexual, male)* pédé‡ *m*, pédale‡ *f* ; *(= female)* gouine‡ *f*

VT gâter, abîmer ◆ **to ~ sb's pitch** *(Brit)* couper l'herbe sous les pieds à *or* de qn

COMP **queer-bashing**‡ N chasse *f* aux pédés‡, agressions *fpl* contre les homosexuels

queer-looking ADJ ◆ **he was a ~-looking man** il avait une drôle d'allure

queer-sounding ADJ ◆ **it was a ~-sounding name** c'était un nom bizarre

queerly /ˈkwɪəlɪ/ ADV bizarrement

queerness /ˈkwɪənɪs/ N 1 *(= strangeness)* étrangeté *f*, bizarrerie *f* 2 *(= homosexuality)* homosexualité *f*

quell /kwel/ VT *[+ rebellion, rage, anxieties]* réprimer, étouffer ◆ **she ~ed him with a glance** elle l'a fait rentrer sous terre d'un regard, elle l'a foudroyé du regard

quench /kwentʃ/ **VT** *[+ flames, fire]* éteindre ; *[+ steel]* tremper ; *[+ hope, desire]* réprimer, étouffer ; *[+ enthusiasm]* refroidir ◆ **to ~ one's thirst** se désaltérer

quenchless /ˈkwentʃlɪs/ **ADJ** *(liter)* inextinguible

quern /kwɜːn/ **N** moulin *m* à bras *(pour le grain)*

querulous /ˈkwerʊləs/ **ADJ** grincheux

querulously /ˈkwerʊləslɪ/ **ADV** d'un ton grincheux

query /ˈkwɪərɪ/ **N** 1 *(= question)* question *f* ; *(= doubt)* doute *m* ◆ **readers' queries** questions *fpl* des lecteurs ◆ **this raises a ~ about the viability of the scheme** cela met en question la viabilité de ce projet 2 *(Gram = question mark)* point *m* d'interrogation 3 *(Comput)* interrogation *f* **VT** 1 *[+ statement, motive, evidence]* mettre en doute *or* en question ◆ **I ~ that!** je me permets d'en douter ! ◆ **to ~ whether ...** demander si ..., chercher à savoir si ... 2 *(= write "?" against) [+ part of text]* marquer d'un point d'interrogation **COMP** **query language N** *(Comput)* langage *m* d'interrogation

quest /kwest/ *(liter)* **N** quête *f (liter) (for de)* ◆ **in ~ of** en quête de ◆ **his ~ for peace** sa quête de la paix **VI** ◆ **to ~ for sth** être en quête de qch

questing /ˈkwestɪŋ/ **ADJ** *[hand]* chercheur ; *[look, voice]* interrogateur (-trice *f*)

question /ˈkwestʃən/ LANGUAGE IN USE 8.3, 9.3, 12, 16.1, 16.3, 26

N 1 *(= thing asked)* question *f* ◆ **to ask sb a ~, to put a ~ to sb, to put down a ~ for sb** *(Parl)* poser une question à qn ◆ **what a ~ to ask!** quelle question !, belle question ! *(iro)* ◆ **(that's a) good ~!** (c'est une) bonne question ! ◆ **indirect** *or* **oblique ~** *(Gram)* interrogation *f* indirecte ◆ **to put sth to the ~** soumettre qch au vote ; → **leading¹, pop¹, sixty**

2 *(NonC = doubt)* doute *m* ◆ **there is no ~ about it** cela ne fait aucun doute ◆ **there's no ~ that this is better** une chose est sûre, ceci est mieux ◆ **there's some ~ as to whether this is true** il n'est pas certain que ce soit vrai ◆ **to accept/obey without ~** accepter/obéir sans poser de questions ◆ **her loyalty is beyond ~** sa loyauté ne fait pas l'ombre d'un doute ◆ **she is without ~ one of the greatest writers of her generation** elle est sans conteste l'un des plus grands écrivains de sa génération ; → **bring**

3 *(= matter, subject)* question *f* ◆ **that's the ~!** là est la question !, c'est là (toute) la question ! ◆ **that's not the ~** là n'est pas la question, il ne s'agit pas de cela ◆ **that's another ~ altogether** ça c'est une tout autre affaire ◆ **there's some/no ~ of closing the shop** il est/il n'est pas question de fermer *or* qu'on ferme *subj* le magasin ◆ **there's no ~ of that** il n'en est pas question, c'est hors de question ◆ **the ~ is how many** la question c'est de savoir combien, il s'agit de savoir combien ; *(in concluding)* reste à savoir combien ◆ **the ~ is to decide ...** il s'agit de décider ... ; *(in concluding)* reste à décider ... ◆ **the German ~** la question allemande, le problème allemand ◆ **it is a ~ of sincerity** c'est une question de sincérité ◆ **it's (all) a ~ of what you want to do eventually** tout dépend de ce que tu veux faire en fin de compte ◆ **it's an open ~** la question reste posée *or* ouverte ◆ **it's an open ~ whether ...** il reste à savoir si ..., personne ne sait si ... ◆ **success is merely a ~ of time** le succès n'est qu'une affaire *or* qu'une question de temps ; → **burning, time**

◆ **in question** en question ◆ **the person in ~** la personne en question *or* dont il s'agit

◆ **out of the question** hors de question ◆ **that is out of the ~** il n'en est pas question, c'est hors de question

◆ **to call sth into question** remettre qch en question

VT 1 interroger, questionner *(on* sur ; *about* au sujet de, à propos de) ; *(Police)* interroger ◆ **we ~ed him closely to find out whether ...** nous l'avons soumis à un interrogatoire pour savoir si ... ◆ **I will not be ~ed about it** je refuse d'être l'objet de questions à ce sujet

2 *[+ motive, account, sb's honesty]* mettre en doute *or* en question ; *[+ claim]* contester ◆ **to ~ whether ...** douter que ... + *subj*

COMP **question mark N** point *m* d'interrogation ◆ **there is a ~ mark over whether he meant to do it** on ne sait pas au juste s'il avait l'intention de le faire ◆ **a big ~ mark hangs over his future** l'incertitude plane sur son avenir

question tag N fin *f* de phrase interrogative

question time N *(Brit Parl)* questions *fpl* écrites ou orales *(adressées par des parlementaires au gouvernement)*

questionable /ˈkwestʃənəbl/ **ADJ** *[quality, taste]* douteux ; *[value]* douteux, discutable ; *[statement, figures]* discutable ; *[motive, behaviour, practice, deal]* suspect ◆ **it is ~ whether ...** il est douteux que ... + *subj*

questioner /ˈkwestʃənəʳ/ **N** personne *f* qui interroge ◆ **she looked at her ~** elle regarda la personne qui l'interrogeait

questioning /ˈkwestʃənɪŋ/ **N** interrogation *f* **ADJ** 1 *(= curious) [nature]* curieux ◆ **to have a ~ mind** être curieux de nature 2 *(= querying) [look, expression]* interrogateur (-trice *f*)

questioningly /ˈkwestʃənɪŋlɪ/ **ADV** d'un air interrogateur

questionmaster /ˈkwestʃən,mɑːstəʳ/ **N** meneur *m*, -euse *f* de jeu ; *(Rad, TV)* animateur *m*, -trice *f*

questionnaire /,kwestʃəˈnɛəʳ/ **N** questionnaire *m*

queue /kjuː/ **N** 1 *(Brit) [of people]* queue *f*, file *f* (d'attente) ; *[of cars]* file *f* ◆ **to stand in a ~, to form a ~** faire la queue ◆ **go to the end of the ~!** prenez la queue ! ◆ **he joined the theatre ~** il s'est joint aux personnes qui faisaient la queue au théâtre ◆ **ticket ~** queue *f* devant les guichets ; → **jump** 2 *(Comput)* file *f* d'attente **VI** *(Brit:* also **queue up**) *[people, cars]* faire la queue *(for* pour) ◆ **we ~d (up) for an hour** nous avons fait une heure de queue ◆ **people are queuing up to ...** *(Brit fig)* les gens se battent pour ...

COMP **queue-jump VI** *(Brit)* passer avant son tour, ne pas attendre son tour

queue-jumper N *(Brit)* resquilleur *m*, -euse *f* *(qui passe avant son tour)*

queue-jumping N *(Brit)* resquille *f (pour passer avant son tour)*

quibble /ˈkwɪbl/ **N** chicane *f*, argutie *f* ◆ **that's just a ~** c'est couper les cheveux en quatre* **VI** chicaner, ergoter *(over* sur)

quibbler /ˈkwɪbləʳ/ **N** chicaneur *m*, -euse *f*, chicanier *m*, -ière *f*, ergoteur *m*, -euse *f*

quibbling /ˈkwɪblɪŋ/ **ADJ** *[person]* ergoteur, chicaneur, chicanier ; *[argument]* captieux, spécieux ; *[objection]* spécieux **N** *(NonC)* chicanerie *f*

quiche /kiːʃ/ **N** quiche *f*

quick /kwɪk/ **ADJ** 1 *(= rapid) [pulse, train, movement, route, decision, method]* rapide ; *[recovery, answer]* prompt ◆ **be ~!** dépêche-toi ! ◆ **try to be ~er next time** essaie de faire plus vite la prochaine fois ◆ **at a ~ pace** d'un pas vif *or* rapide, d'un bon pas ◆ **~ march!** *(Mil)* en avant, marche ! ◆ **I had a ~ chat with her** *or* **a few ~ words with her** j'ai échangé quelques mots (rapides) avec elle ◆ **going cheap for a ~ sale** sacrifié pour vente rapide ◆ **we had a ~ meal** nous avons mangé en vitesse *or* sur le pouce* ◆ **to have a ~ one** (* *= drink)* prendre un pot* en vitesse ; (*‡ = sex)* tirer un coup en vitesse‡ ◆ **it's ~er by train** c'est plus rapide *or* ça va plus vite par le train ◆ **he's a ~ worker** il travaille vite ; (* *iro)* il ne perd pas de temps *(iro)*, il va vite en besogne *(iro)* ; → **double, draw**

2 *(= lively) [mind]* vif ; *[child]* vif, éveillé ◆ **he's too ~ for me** il est trop rapide pour moi, il va trop vite pour moi ◆ **he has a ~ eye for mistakes** il repère vite les fautes ◆ **to have a ~ ear** avoir l'oreille fine ◆ **to have a ~ wit** avoir la repartie facile *or* de la repartie ; see also **comp** ◆ **he was ~ to see that ...** il a tout de suite vu *or* remarqué que ... ◆ **she was ~ to point out that ...** elle n'a pas manqué de faire remarquer que ... ◆ **to be ~ to take offence** être prompt à s'offenser, s'offenser pour un rien ◆ **to have a ~ temper** s'emporter facilement, être soupe au lait* ; see also **comp** ◆ **to be ~ to anger** *(liter)* avoir la tête chaude, être prompt à s'emporter ◆ **he is ~ at figures** il calcule vite

N 1 *(Anat)* vif *m* ◆ **to bite one's nails to the ~** se ronger les ongles jusqu'au sang ◆ **to cut** *or* **sting sb to the ~** piquer *or* blesser qn au vif

2 (††, *liter)* **the ~ and the dead** les vivants *mpl* et les morts *mpl*

ADV *(= quickly)* ◆ **~, over here!** vite, par ici ! ◆ **as ~ as lightning** *or* **as a flash** avec la rapidité de l'éclair ; *for other phrases see* **quickly**

COMP **quick-acting ADJ** *[drug etc]* qui agit rapidement

quick-assembly furniture N *(NonC)* meubles *mpl* en kit

quick assets NPL *(Fin)* actif *m* disponible à court terme

quick-change artist N *(Theat)* spécialiste *mf* des transformations rapides

quick-drying ADJ *[paint, concrete]* qui sèche rapidement

quick-fire ADJ ◆ **a series of ~-fire questions** un feu roulant de questions ◆ **to shoot ~-fire questions at sb** mitrailler qn de questions

quick-firing ADJ *(Mil)* à tir rapide

quick fix N *(pej)* solution *f* de fortune ◆ **there is no ~ fix to the country's economic problems** il n'y a pas de solution miracle aux problèmes économiques du pays

quick-freeze VT surgeler

quick money N *(NonC: Fin)* capital *m* investi réalisable sur demande

quick-setting ADJ *[cement]* à prise rapide ; *[jelly]* qui prend facilement

quick-tempered ADJ ◆ **to be ~-tempered** s'emporter facilement, être soupe au lait* *inv*

quick time N *(US Mil)* marche *f* normale *(120 pas/minute)*

quick-witted ADJ à l'esprit vif *or* délié ; *(in answering)* qui a la repartie facile *or* de la repartie

quicken /ˈkwɪkən/ **VT** 1 *(lit)* accélérer, presser ◆ **to ~ the tempo** *(Mus)* presser l'allure *or* la cadence ; → **pace¹** 2 *(fig) [+ feelings, imagination]* exciter, stimuler ; *[+ appetite]* stimuler, aiguiser **VI** 1 *[pace, movement]* s'accélérer, devenir *or* se faire plus rapide 2 *[hope]* se ranimer 3 *[foetus]* remuer

quickie* /ˈkwɪkɪ/ **N** chose *f* faite en vitesse *or* à la hâte ; *(= question)* question *f* rapide ; (*‡ = sex)* coup *m* rapide* ; *(Cine)* court-métrage *m* vite fait ◆ **have you got time for a ~?** *(= drink)* tu as le temps de prendre un verre vite fait ?* **COMP** **quickie divorce N** divorce *m* rapide

quicklime /ˈkwɪklaɪm/ **N** chaux *f* vive

quickly /ˈkwɪklɪ/ **ADV** 1 *(= with great speed) [speak, work]* vite ◆ **~!** vite !, dépêchez-vous ! ◆ **as ~ as possible** aussi vite que possible, au plus vite ◆ **as ~ as I can** aussi vite que je peux 2 *(= in short time) [die, embrace]* rapidement ; *(= without delay) [arrive, answer, react]* sans tarder ◆ **the police were ~ on the scene** la police est arrivée rapidement *or* sans tarder sur les lieux

quickness /'kwɪknɪs/ N vitesse f, rapidité f ; *[of intelligence, sight, gesture]* vivacité f ; *[of mind]* promptitude f, vivacité f ; *[of pulse]* rapidité f ; *[of hearing]* finesse f ◆ ~ **of temper** promptitude f à s'emporter ◆ ~ **of wit** vivacité f d'esprit

quicksand(s) /'kwɪksænd(z)/ N(PL) sables mpl mouvants ◆ **to get stuck in ~(s)** s'enliser

quickset hedge /'kwɪkset'hedʒ/ N haie f vive ; *(= hawthorn)* haie f d'aubépine

quicksilver /'kwɪksɪlvər/ N vif-argent m, mercure m ADJ *[movements, changes]* brusque, subit

quickstep /'kwɪkstep/ N *(Dancing)* fox-trot m

quickthorn /'kwɪkθɔːn/ N aubépine f

quid¹ * /kwɪd/ N *(pl inv: Brit = pound)* livre f *(sterling)* ◆ **to be ~s in** *(= to have money)* être en fonds

quid² /kwɪd/ N *[of tobacco]* chique f

quiddity /'kwɪdɪtɪ/ N *(Philos)* quiddité f

quid pro quo /'kwɪdprəʊ'kwəʊ/ N (pl **quid pro quos**) contrepartie f ◆ **there must be a ~** il faut qu'il y ait une contrepartie ◆ **it's a ~ (for)** c'est en contrepartie (de), c'est à titre de réciprocité (pour)

quiescence /kwaɪ'esns/ N *(frm)* *[of person]* inactivité f ; *[of plant]* dormance f ; *[of volcano]* sommeil m

quiescent /kwɪ'esnt/ ADJ *(frm)* *[person]* *(= passive)* passif ; *(= quiet)* tranquille ; *[symptoms, disease, problem]* latent ; *[volcano]* endormi ◆ **in a ~ state** à l'état latent

quiet /'kwaɪət/ ADJ 1 *(= not loud)* *[voice]* bas (basse f) ; *[music]* doux (douce f) ; *[sound]* léger ◆ **she spoke in ~ tones** elle parlait doucement ◆ **... she said with a ~ laugh** ... dit-elle avec un petit rire ; see also **adj 5**

2 *(= not noisy, not busy)* *[street, room, village, neighbour]* tranquille ◆ **isn't it ~!** quel calme ! ◆ **try to be a little ~er** essayez de ne pas faire autant de bruit ◆ **this town is too ~ for me** cette ville est trop endormie pour moi ◆ **business is ~** les affaires sont calmes ◆ **the market was ~** *(St Ex)* la Bourse était calme

3 *(= silent)* ◆ **to be ~** *[person]* être silencieux ◆ **you're very ~ today** tu ne dis rien *or* pas grand-chose aujourd'hui ◆ **be ~!, keep ~!** taisez-vous !, silence ! ◆ **to keep** *or* **stay ~** garder le silence, ne pas piper mot ◆ **that book should keep him ~ for a while** avec ce livre, il devrait se tenir tranquille un moment ◆ **it was ~ as the grave** il y avait un silence de mort ◆ **to be ~ as a mouse** ne faire aucun bruit

4 *(= placid)* *[person]* calme ; *[child]* calme, doux (douce f) ; *[dog, horse]* docile ◆ **my daughter is a very ~ girl** ma fille est d'un tempérament très calme ◆ **~ as a lamb** très calme

5 *(= discreet)* *[dinner]* intime ; *[funeral, ceremony]* dans l'intimité ; *[despair]* silencieux ; *[irony]* voilé, discret (-ète f) ; *[optimism, diplomacy]* discret (-ète f) ◆ **the wedding was very ~** le mariage a été célébré dans l'intimité ◆ **they had a ~ laugh over it** ils en ont ri sous cape ◆ **... he said with a ~ smile** ... dit-il avec un petit sourire ◆ **with ~ humour** avec une pointe d'humour ◆ **he had a ~ dig at his brother** il a lancé une petite pique à son frère ◆ **to have a ~ word with sb** parler en particulier avec qn ◆ **to keep ~ about sth, to keep sth ~** ne pas ébruiter qch ◆ **keep it ~** gardez-le pour vous

6 *(= untroubled)* *[night]* paisible ; *[life]* paisible, tranquille ◆ **we had a ~ time on holiday** on a passé des vacances tranquilles *or* relax * ◆ **he went to sleep with a ~ mind** il s'endormit l'esprit tranquille ◆ **all ~** *(Mil or hum)* rien à signaler, RAS * ◆ **all ~ on the western front** à l'ouest rien de nouveau

7 *(= muted)* *[colours, clothes]* sobre, discret (-ète f) ; *[decoration, style]* sobre

N *(NonC)* 1 *(= silence)* silence m, tranquillité f ◆ **in the ~ of the night** dans le silence de la nuit ◆ **let's have complete ~ for a few minutes** faisons silence complet pendant quelques minutes

◆ **on the quiet** * en cachette, en douce * ◆ **to do sth on the ~** faire qch en cachette *or* en dessous ◆ **she had a drink on the ~** elle a pris un verre en douce * *or* en suisse ◆ **he told me on the ~** il me l'a dit en confidence

2 *(= peace)* calme m ◆ **there was a period of ~ after the fighting** il y a eu une accalmie après les combats ; → **peace**

VT *(US)* ⇒ **quieten**

► **quiet down** VI, VT SEP ⇒ **quieten down**

quieten /'kwaɪətn/ VT *(esp Brit)* *[+ person, crowd, horse, suspicion]* calmer, apaiser ; *[+ fear]* calmer, dissiper ; *[+ pain]* calmer ; *[+ conscience]* tranquilliser, apaiser

► **quieten down** VI *(= make less noise)* se calmer ; *(fig)* *(after unruly youth)* se ranger ◆ **their children have ~ed down a lot** leurs enfants se sont beaucoup assagis *or* calmés

VT SEP *[+ person, dog, horse]* calmer, apaiser

quietism /'kwaɪɪtɪzəm/ N quiétisme m

quietist /'kwaɪɪtɪst/ ADJ, N quiétiste mf

quietly /'kwaɪətlɪ/ ADV 1 *(= not loudly)* *[say, speak, sing]* doucement 2 *(= silently)* sans bruit 3 *(= discreetly)* discrètement ◆ **~ dressed** habillé simplement *or* discrètement ◆ **I'm ~ confident about the future** je suis confiant en *or* dans l'avenir 4 *(= without fuss)* *[get married, be buried]* en toute simplicité ; *[read, sit]* tranquillement ◆ **she lives ~ in a cottage in Suffolk** elle mène une vie tranquille *or* paisible dans un cottage du Suffolk ◆ **he was made to resign ~** on l'a forcé à démissionner sans faire de vagues 5 *(Police = voluntarily)* *[go]* de son plein gré ◆ **are you going to come ~?** allez-vous nous suivre de votre plein gré ?

quietness /'kwaɪətnɪs/ N *(= silence)* silence m ; *(= stillness, peacefulness)* calme m, tranquillité f ; *(= gentleness)* douceur f

quietude /'kwaɪətjuːd/ N quiétude f

quietus /kwaɪ'iːtəs/ N (pl **quietuses**) *(Jur)* quittance f ; *(fig)* *(= release)* coup m de grâce *(lit, fig)* *(= death)* mort f

quiff /kwɪf/ N *(Brit: also **quiff of hair**)* *(on forehead)* mèche f ; *(on top of head)* épi m ; *(on baby's head)* coque f

quill /kwɪl/ N *(= feather)* penne f ; *(= part of feather)* tuyau m de plume ; (also **quill-pen**) plume f d'oie ; *[of porcupine]* piquant m

quilt /kwɪlt/ N *(= bed cover)* édredon m (piqué), courtepointe f ; *(= duvet)* (also **continental quilt**) couette f VT *[+ eiderdown, cover]* matelasser, ouater et piquer ; *[+ dressing gown]* matelasser, ouatiner ; *[+ furniture, bedhead]* capitonner

quilted /'kwɪltɪd/ ADJ *[jacket, dressing gown]* matelassé, ouatiné ; *[bedspread]* matelassé ; *[bedhead]* capitonné

quilting /'kwɪltɪŋ/ N *(NonC)* *(= process)* ouatage m, capitonnage m ; *(= material)* ouate f, matelassé m, ouatine f, capitonnage m

quim ** /kwɪm/ N *(Brit)* chatte ** f

quin /kwɪn/ N *(Brit)* abbrev of **quintuplet**

quince /kwɪns/ N *(= fruit)* coing m ; *(= tree)* cognassier m COMP *[jam]* de coings

quincentenary /,kwɪnsen'tiːnərɪ/ N cinq-centième anniversaire m

quinine /kwɪ'niːn/ N quinine f

Quinquagesima /,kwɪŋkwə'dʒesɪmə/ N Quinquagésime f

quinquennial /kwɪŋ'kwenɪəl/ ADJ quinquennal

quinsy /'kwɪnzɪ/ N *(Med ††)* amygdalite f purulente

quintessence /kwɪn'tesns/ N quintessence f

quintessential /,kwɪntɪ'senʃəl/ ADJ par excellence ◆ **he is the ~ English composer** c'est le compositeur anglais par excellence ◆ **a ~ example of sth** un parfait exemple de qch

quintet(te) /kwɪn'tet/ N quintette m

quintillion /kwɪn'tɪljən/ N (pl **quintillions** *or* **quintillion**) *(Brit)* quintillion m ; *(US, Can)* 10^{18}

quintuple /'kwɪntjʊpl/ ADJ, N quintuple m VTI /kwɪn'tjuːpl/ quintupler

quintuplet /kwɪn'tjuːplɪt/ N quintuplé(e) m(f)

quip /kwɪp/ N quolibet m VI railler, lancer des pointes VT ◆ **"never on a Sunday" she ~ped** "jamais le dimanche" dit-elle avec esprit

quire /'kwaɪər/ N 1 *(Bookbinding = part of book)* cahier m (d'un livre) *(quatre feuilles)* ◆ **book in ~s** livre m en feuilles (détachées) *or* en cahiers 2 *[of paper]* ≈ main f *(de papier)*

quirk /kwɜːk/ N 1 bizarrerie f, excentricité f ◆ **it's just one of his ~s** c'est encore une de ses excentricités ◆ **by a ~ of fate** par un caprice du destin ◆ **by some ~ of nature/of circumstance** par une bizarrerie de la nature/de(s) circonstance(s) 2 *(= flourish)* *(Art, Mus)* arabesque f ; *(in signature)* paraphe *or* parafe m ; *(in handwriting)* fioriture f

quirky /'kwɜːkɪ/ ADJ *[humour, behaviour, style]* original, décalé ; *[person]* excentrique

quirt /kwɜːt/ *(US)* N cravache f (tressée) VT cravacher

quisling /'kwɪzlɪŋ/ N collaborateur m, -trice f *(pej)*, collabo * mf

quit /kwɪt/ (pret, ptp **quit** *or* **quitted**) VT 1 *(= leave)* *[+ place, premises]* quitter, s'en aller de ; *[+ person]* quitter, laisser ◆ **to ~ school** *(esp US)* quitter l'école ◆ **to ~ one's job** *(esp US)* quitter son emploi 2 *(esp US = stop)* **to ~ doing sth** arrêter de faire qch ◆ **to ~ hold** lâcher prise ◆ **to ~ hold of sth** lâcher qch ◆ **to ~ work** cesser le travail ◆ **~ fooling!** arrête de faire l'idiot ! 3 *(Comput)* *[+ file window]* quitter VI 1 *(esp US)* *(= give up: in game)* se rendre ; *(= accept defeat)* abandonner la partie, renoncer ; *(= resign)* démissionner ◆ **I ~!** j'arrête !, j'abandonne ! ◆ **he ~s too easily** il se laisse décourager *or* il abandonne la partie trop facilement 2 *(= leave)* ◆ **to give a tenant notice to ~** donner congé à un locataire 3 *(Comput)* sortir, quitter ADJ ◆ **~ of** débarrassé de

quite /kwaɪt/ ADV 1 *(= to some degree, moderately)* plutôt, assez ◆ **they're ~ friendly** ils sont assez *or* plutôt sympathiques ◆ **it was ~ dark for 6 o'clock** il faisait plutôt sombre pour 6 heures ◆ **your essay was ~ good** votre dissertation n'était pas mal *inv or* pas mauvaise du tout ◆ **I ~ like this painting** j'aime assez ce tableau ◆ **we waited ~ a time** *or* **~ some time** on a attendu un bon bout de temps *

◆ **quite a +** *adjective* ◆ **we waited ~ a long time** on a attendu un bon bout de temps * ◆ **he is ~ a good singer** c'est un assez bon chanteur ◆ **they've got ~ a big flat** ils ont un appartement assez grand

◆ **quite a few/a lot** ◆ **~ a few people** un bon *or* assez grand nombre de gens, pas mal de gens * ◆ **~ a lot of paper** une assez grande quantité de papier, pas mal de papier * ◆ **he cried ~ a lot** il a pas mal pleuré * ◆ **there's ~ a lot left** il en reste une certaine quantité (*or* un certain nombre), il en reste pas mal *

2 *(= entirely)* tout à fait ◆ **he was ~ right** il avait bien raison *or* tout à fait raison ◆ **~ new** tout (à fait) neuf ◆ **he was ~ alone** il était tout seul ◆ **he's ~ mad** il est complètement fou ◆ **it is ~ lovely** c'est vraiment magnifique ◆ **~ (so)!** exactement ! ◆ **Pete is ~ the artist/gentleman** Pete est un vrai artiste/gentleman ◆ **I ~**

agree with you je suis entièrement *or* tout à fait de votre avis ◆ **he ~ realizes that he must go** il se rend parfaitement compte qu'il doit partir ◆ **I ~ understand** je comprends tout à fait *or* très bien ◆ **I can ~ believe it** je le crois volontiers *or* sans difficulté, je n'ai aucun mal à le croire ◆ **that's ~ enough!** ça suffit comme ça ! ◆ **that's ~ enough for me** j'en ai vraiment assez ◆ **it was ~ something*** c'était vraiment quelque chose* ◆ **that's ~ another matter** c'est une tout autre affaire ◆ **it's difficult to know ~ how much to spend** il est difficile de savoir exactement ce qu'on doit dépenser ; → **contrary, opposite, reverse**

♦ **quite a ...** *(expressing admiration)* ◆ **he's ~ a guy*** c'est quelqu'un de vraiment bien* *or* c'est un type vraiment bien* ◆ **she's ~ a character** c'est un vrai personnage ◆ **that's ~ a car!** ça, c'est de la voiture ! * ◆ **she was ~ a beauty** c'était une véritable beauté

♦ **not quite** pas tout à fait ◆ **nearly, but not ~** presque, mais pas tout à fait ◆ **it wasn't ~ what I wanted** ce n'était pas exactement *or* tout à fait ce que je voulais ◆ **not ~ as many as last week** pas tout à fait autant que la semaine dernière ◆ **I don't ~ know** je ne sais pas bien *or* trop ◆ **I don't ~ see what he means** je ne vois pas tout à fait *or* pas trop ce qu'il veut dire

quits* /kwɪts/ **ADJ** ◆ **to be ~ (with sb)** être quitte (envers qn) ◆ **to call it ~** s'en tenir là

quittance /ˈkwɪtəns/ **N** *(Fin etc)* quittance *f*

quitter* /ˈkwɪtəʳ/ **N** *(pej)* velléitaire *mf* ◆ **he's no ~** il n'est pas du genre à baisser les bras

quiver[1] /ˈkwɪvəʳ/ **VI** *[person]* frémir, frissonner *(with* de) ; *[voice]* trembler, trembloter ; *[leaves]* frémir, frissonner ; *[flame]* vaciller ; *[wings]* battre, palpiter ; *[lips]* trembler, frémir ; *[eyelids]* battre ; *[flesh, heart]* frémir, palpiter ; *[violin]* frémir **N** *[of lips, voice, hand]* tremblement *m* ◆ **a ~ of fear** un frisson de terreur

quiver[2] /ˈkwɪvəʳ/ **N** *(for arrows)* carquois *m*

qui vive /kiːˈviːv/ **N** ◆ **on the ~** sur le qui-vive

Quixote /ˈkwɪksət/ **N** ◆ **Don ~** don Quichotte *m*

quixotic /kwɪkˈsɒtɪk/ **ADJ** *[person, mission, quest, venture]* chimérique

quixotically /kwɪkˈsɒtɪkəlɪ/ **ADV** ◆ **to behave ~** jouer les don Quichotte ◆ **he volunteered ~ to go himself** chevaleresque, il offrit d'y aller lui-même

quixotism /ˈkwɪksətɪzəm/, **quixotry** /ˈkwɪksətrɪ/ **N** donquichottisme *m*

quiz /kwɪz/ **N** (pl **quizzes**) 1 *(Rad, TV)* quiz(z) *m*, jeu-concours *m* (radiophonique *or* télévisé) ; *(in magazine etc)* série *f* de questions ; *(= puzzle)* devinette *f* 2 *(US Scol)* interrogation *f* rapide *(orale ou écrite)* **VT** 1 *(gen)* interroger, presser de questions *(about* au sujet de) 2 *(US Scol)* interroger rapidement

COMP **quiz kid*** **N** *(US)* enfant *mf* prodige

quiz programme **N** jeu *m* (radiophonique *or* télévisé), quiz *m*

quizmaster /ˈkwɪzmɑːstəʳ/ **N** meneur *m*, -euse *f* de jeu ; *(Rad, TV)* animateur *m*, -trice *f*

quizzical /ˈkwɪzɪkəl/ **ADJ** *[smile, expression, look]* interrogateur (-trice *f*), interrogatif ◆ **she raised a ~ eyebrow** elle a levé un sourcil interrogateur

quizzically /ˈkwɪzɪkəlɪ/ **ADV** *[look at]* d'un air interrogateur *or* interrogatif

quod‡ /kwɒd/ **N** *(Brit)* taule‡ *f* ◆ **to be in ~** être en taule‡

quoin /kwɔɪn/ **N** *(= angle)* coin *m or* angle *m* d'un mur ; *(= stone)* pierre *f* d'angle

quoit /kɔɪt/ **N** palet *m* ◆ **~s** *(= game)* jeu *m* du palet ◆ **to play ~s** jouer au palet

quondam /ˈkwɒndæm/ **ADJ** *(liter)* ancien *before n*, d'autrefois

Quonset hut ® /ˈkwɒnsɪtˈhʌt/ **N** *(US)* baraque *f or* hutte *f* préfabriquée *(en tôle, cylindrique)*

quorate /ˈkwɔːreɪt/ **ADJ** *(Brit Admin)* qui a le quorum, où le quorum est atteint

Quorn ® /kwɔːn/ **N** *substitut de viande à base de protéines végétales*

quorum /ˈkwɔːrəm/ **N** quorum *m* ◆ **to make a ~** atteindre le quorum ◆ **we have not got a ~** nous n'avons pas de quorum, le quorum n'est pas atteint

quota /ˈkwəʊtə/ **N** 1 *(= share)* quote-part *f*, part *f* 2 *(= permitted amount) [of imports, immigrants]* quota *m*, contingent *m* **COMP** **quota system** **N** système *m* de quotas

quotable /ˈkwəʊtəbl/ **ADJ** 1 *(= which one may quote)* que l'on peut (*or* puisse) citer ; *(= worth quoting)* digne d'être cité, bon à citer 2 *(Stock Exchange) [securities]* cotable

quotation /kwəʊˈteɪʃən/ **N** 1 *(= passage cited)* citation *f (from* de) 2 *(St Ex)* cours *m*, cote *f* ; *(Comm = estimate)* devis *m* (estimatif) **COMP** **quotation marks** **NPL** guillemets *mpl* ◆ **in ~ marks** entre guillemets ◆ **to open/close the ~ marks** ouvrir/fermer les guillemets

quote /kwəʊt/ **VT** 1 *[+ author, poem, fact, text]* citer ; *[+ words]* rapporter, citer ; *[+ reference number etc]* rappeler ◆ **to ~ Shelley** citer Shelley ◆ **to ~ sb as an example** citer *or* donner qn en exemple ◆ **you can ~ me on that** vous pouvez rapporter mes paroles ◆ **don't ~ me on that** ne me citez pas ◆ **he was ~d as saying that ...** il aurait dit que ... ◆ **she said the text was, and I ~, "full of mistakes", she said the text was, ~, unquote, "full of mistakes"** elle m'a dit que le texte était, je cite, "plein de fautes" ◆ **can you ~ (me) a recent instance of this?** pouvez-vous (m')en citer un exemple récent ? ◆ **when ordering please ~ this number** pour toute commande prière de rappeler ce numéro

2 *[+ price]* indiquer ; *(Stock Exchange)* coter *(at* à) ◆ **this was the best price he could ~ us** c'est le meilleur prix qu'il a pu nous faire *or* proposer ◆ **she ~d me £500 for the job** elle m'a fait un devis de 500 livres pour ces travaux ◆ **~d company** *(Stock Exchange)* société *f* cotée en Bourse

VI 1 *(Literat etc)* faire des citations ◆ **to ~ from the Bible** citer la Bible

2 *(Comm)* **to ~ for a job** établir *or* faire un devis pour un travail

N 1 *(= quotation)* citation *f (from* de)

2 *(= short statement: to journalist etc)* déclaration *f*, commentaire *m*

3 *(* = estimate)* devis *m*

NPL **quotes** * *(= quotation marks)* guillemets *mpl* ◆ **in ~s** entre guillemets

quoth /kwəʊθ/ **DEFECTIVE VB** *(†† or hum)* ◆ **... ~ he** ... fit-il, ... dit-il

quotidian /kwəʊˈtɪdɪən/ **ADJ** *(frm)* quotidien

quotient /ˈkwəʊʃənt/ **N** *(esp Math)* quotient *m* ; → **intelligence**

qv (abbrev of **quod vide**) q.v., voir ce mot

QWERTY, qwerty /ˈkwɜːtɪ/ **ADJ** ◆ **~ keyboard** clavier *m* QWERTY

Rr

R, r /ɑːʳ/ N 1 *(= letter)* R, r *m* ◆ **the three R's** * *la lecture, l'écriture et l'arithmétique* ◆ **R for Robert, R for Roger** *(US)* ≈ R comme Robert 2 *(US Cine)* (abbrev of **Restricted**) interdit aux moins de 17 ans 3 (abbrev of **right**) droite *f* 4 *(Geog)* abbrev of **river** 5 (abbrev of **Réaumur**) R 6 *(Brit)* (abbrev of **Rex, Regina**) **George R** le roi Georges ◆ **Elizabeth R** la reine Élisabeth 7 *(US)* (abbrev of **Republican**) républicain

® (abbrev of **registered trademark**) ®

RA /ɑːˈreɪ/ N *(Brit)* (abbrev of **Royal Academy**) *membre de l'Académie royale*

RAAF /ˌɑːreɪeɪˈef/ N abbrev of **Royal Australian Air Force**

Rabat /rəˈbɑːt/ N Rabat

rabbet /ˈræbɪt/ N feuillure *f*, rainure *f*

rabbi /ˈræbaɪ/ N rabbin *m* ◆ **Rabbi Schulman** le rabbin Schulman ; → **chief**

Rabbinic /rəˈbɪnɪk/ N *(= medieval Hebrew)* hébreu *m* rabbinique

rabbinic(al) /rəˈbɪnɪk(əl)/ ADJ rabbinique

rabbit /ˈræbɪt/ N lapin *m* ◆ **doe ~** lapine *f* ◆ **wild ~** lapin *m* de garenne ◆ **~ food** * herbe *f* à lapins * ◆ **like a ~ caught in the headlights** tétanisé ◆ **to pull a ~ out of the** *or* **one's hat** *(fig)* sortir un lapin de son chapeau ; → **Welsh**

VI 1 *(= shoot rabbits)* **to go ~ing** chasser le lapin 2 *(Brit* *: also **rabbit on, go rabbiting on**) ne pas cesser de parler ◆ **to ~ on about sth** ne pas cesser de parler de qch, s'étendre à n'en plus finir sur qch

COMP **rabbit burrow, rabbit hole** N terrier *m* (de lapin)

rabbit hutch N clapier *m*, cabane *f* or cage *f* à lapins

rabbit punch N *(Boxing etc)* coup *m* du lapin

rabbit warren N *(lit)* garenne *f* ; *(fig) (= streets, corridors)* labyrinthe *m*

rabble /ˈræbl/ N *(= disorderly crowd)* cohue *f* ; *(pej = lower classes)* ◆ **the ~** la populace *(pej)*

COMP **rabble-rouser** N *(pej)* fomentateur *m*, -trice *f* de troubles, agitateur *m*, -trice *f*

rabble-rousing *(pej)* N incitation *f* à la révolte *or* à la violence ADJ qui incite à la révolte *or* à la violence, qui cherche à soulever les masses

Rabelaisian /ˌræbəˈleɪzɪən/ ADJ *(Literat)* rabelaisien

rabid /ˈræbɪd/ ADJ 1 *(Med) [animal]* qui a la rage, enragé ; *[person]* atteint de la rage 2 *(pej = fanatical) [nationalist, extremism, hysteria]* fanatique ; *[hatred]* farouche, féroce

rabidly /ˈræbɪdlɪ/ ADV farouchement, fanatiquement

rabies /ˈreɪbiːz/ N rage *f (Med)* COMP *[virus]* rabique, de la rage ; *[injection, precautions, laws]* contre la rage, antirabique

RAC /ˌɑːreɪˈsiː/ N *(Brit)* (abbrev of **Royal Automobile Club**) *société de dépannage*

raccoon /rəˈkuːn/ N raton *m* laveur COMP en (fourrure de) raton (laveur)

race[1] /reɪs/ N 1 *(Sport, fig)* course *f* ◆ **the 100 metres ~** le 100 mètres, la course de 100 mètres ◆ **horse ~** course *f* de chevaux ◆ **cycle ~** course *f* cycliste ◆ **the ~s** *(Racing)* les courses *fpl* (de chevaux) ◆ **to ride a ~** *[jockey]* monter dans une course ◆ **~ against time** *or* **the clock** *(lit, fig)* course *f* contre la montre ◆ **the ~ for** *or* **to the White House** la course à la Maison-Blanche ◆ **the ~ to find a cure for cancer** la course pour trouver un traitement contre le cancer ◆ **the ~ is on to build a prototype** c'est la course pour construire un prototype ; → **arm[2], long[1], relay**

2 *(= swift current) (in sea)* raz *m* ; *(in stream)* courant *m* fort ; → **mill**

3 *(liter) [of sun, moon]* cours *m*

VT 1 *[+ person]* faire la course avec ◆ **I'll ~ you to school!** le premier à l'école a gagné ! ◆ **he ~d the train in his car** il faisait la course avec le train dans sa voiture

2 *(= cause to speed) [+ car]* lancer (à fond) ◆ **to ~ the engine** emballer le moteur

3 *(Sport) [+ horse, dog]* faire courir ◆ **to ~ pigeons** faire des courses de pigeon ◆ **Schumacher ~s Ferraris** Schumacher court sur Ferrari

VI 1 *(= compete) [racing driver, athlete, jockey etc]* courir, faire la course ◆ **to ~ against sb** faire la course avec qn ◆ **we'll have to ~ against time** *or* **the clock** ça va être une course contre la montre ◆ **he ~s at Cheltenham every week** *[horse owner]* il fait courir un cheval (*or* des chevaux) à Cheltenham toutes les semaines

2 *(= rush) [person]* aller *or* courir à toute allure *or* à toute vitesse ◆ **to ~ in/out/across** *etc* entrer/sortir/traverser *etc* à toute allure ◆ **to ~ after sb** courir après qn, essayer de rattraper qn ◆ **to ~ for a taxi** courir pour avoir un taxi ◆ **to ~ for the door** se précipiter vers la porte ◆ **to ~ to the station** courir à la gare, foncer jusqu'à la gare ◆ **to ~ to the telephone** se précipiter vers le téléphone ◆ **to ~ along** filer (à toute allure) ◆ **he ~d down the street** il a descendu la rue à toute vitesse ◆ **he ~d through his work** il a fait son travail à toute vitesse ◆ **we are racing towards complete economic collapse** nous nous précipitons vers un effondrement total de l'économie

3 *[engine]* s'emballer ; *[pulse]* être très rapide ◆ **memories of the past ~d through her mind** les souvenirs du passé se sont mis à défiler dans son esprit ◆ **thoughts ~d around in her head** les pensées se bousculaient dans sa tête ◆ **her mind was racing** elle réfléchissait à toute vitesse ◆ **my heart began to ~ with fear** mon cœur s'est mis à battre la chamade

COMP **race card** N programme *m* (des courses)

race meeting N *(Brit)* courses *fpl*

race[2] /reɪs/ N *(= species: lit, fig)* race *f* ◆ **the human ~** le genre humain

COMP *[hatred, prejudice]* racial

race hate N haine *f* raciale

race-hate ADJ *[attack, crime]* racial ◆ **~-hate campaign** campagne *f* d'incitation à la haine raciale **race relations** NPL relations *fpl* interraciales ; *(Brit)* ◆ **the Race Relations Board** *commission pour les relations interraciales* ; → QUANGO

race riot N émeute(s) *f(pl)* raciale(s)

racecourse /ˈreɪskɔːs/ N *(esp Brit)* champ *m* de courses, hippodrome *m*

racegoer /ˈreɪsgəʊəʳ/ N *(Brit)* turfiste *mf*

racehorse /ˈreɪshɔːs/ N cheval *m* de course

raceme /ˈræsiːm/ N racème *m (rare)*, grappe *f*

racer /ˈreɪsəʳ/ N *(= person)* coureur *m*, -euse *f* ; *(= car, yacht)* racer *m* ; *(= horse)* cheval *m* de course ; *(= cycle)* vélo *m* de course

racetrack /ˈreɪstræk/ N *(US)* champ *m* de courses ; *(Brit)* piste *f*

raceway /ˈreɪsweɪ/ N *(US: for horses, cars)* piste *f*

rachitic /ræˈkɪtɪk/ ADJ rachitique

rachitis /rəˈkaɪtɪs/ N *(Med)* rachitisme *m*

Rachmanism /ˈrækməˌnɪzəm/ N *(Brit) intimidation de locataires par des propriétaires sans scrupule*

racial /ˈreɪʃəl/ ADJ *[harmony, identity, purity]* racial ; *[attack, prejudice, stereotype, violence]* racial, raciste ; *[inequality]* entre les races ◆ **to vote along ~ lines** voter selon des critères raciaux

COMP **racial discrimination** N discrimination *f* raciale

racial harassment N harcèlement *m* raciste

racial minority N minorité *f* raciale

racial segregation N ségrégation *f* raciale

racialism † /ˈreɪʃəlɪzəm/ N *(esp Brit)* racisme *m*

racialist † /ˈreɪʃəlɪst/ ADJ, N *(esp Brit)* raciste *mf*

racially /ˈreɪʃəlɪ/ ADV *[sensitive, diverse, divided, pure, superior]* d'un point de vue racial ◆ **~ mixed marriages** les mariages mixtes *or* interraciaux ◆ **a ~ motivated attack** une agression raciste ◆ **to be ~ prejudiced** avoir des préjugés raciaux ◆ **to be ~ abused** être victime d'insultes racistes ◆ **the schools are ~ segre-**

gated les écoles pratiquent la ségrégation raciale ◆ **the schools were ~ integrated** les écoles pratiquaient l'intégration raciale

racily /ˈreɪsɪlɪ/ **ADV** *[write] (= in risqué style)* lestement ; *(= in lively style)* avec verve

raciness /ˈreɪsɪnɪs/ **N** *[of story, style]* caractère *m* leste ; *[of joke]* grivoiserie *f*

racing /ˈreɪsɪŋ/ **N** courses *fpl* ; (also **horse-racing**) courses *fpl* de chevaux, hippisme *m* ◆ **motor ~** course *f* automobile ◆ **I'm not a ~ man** je ne suis pas amateur de courses ◆ **the ~ world** le monde des courses
COMP *[calendar, stables]* de(s) courses
racing bicycle N bicyclette *f* de course
racing bike N vélo *m* de course
racing car N voiture *f* de course
racing certainty N *(Brit fig)* certitude *f* absolue
racing colours NPL couleurs *fpl* d'une écurie *(portées par le jockey)*
racing cyclist N coureur *m*, -euse *f* cycliste
racing driver N coureur *m*, -euse *f* automobile, pilote *m* de courses
racing pigeon N pigeon *m* voyageur de compétition
racing yacht N racer *m*, yacht *m* de course

racism /ˈreɪsɪzəm/ **N** racisme *m*

racist /ˈreɪsɪst/ **ADJ, N** raciste *mf*

rack¹ /ræk/ **N** 1 *(for bottles, documents)* casier *m* ; *(for luggage)* porte-bagages *m inv* ; *(for dishes)* égouttoir *m* ; *(for hanging tools/ties etc)* porte-outils/-cravates *etc m* ; *(for vegetables)* bac(s) *m(pl)* à légumes ; *(for fodder, rifles, pipes)* râtelier *m* ◆ **off the ~** *(US)* en confection, en prêt-à-porter ; → **bicycle, hatrack, luggage, toast**
2 *(Hist) (torture)* chevalet *m* ◆ **to put sb on the ~** *(lit)* infliger *or* faire subir à qn le supplice du chevalet ; *(fig)* mettre qn au supplice ◆ **we had the opposition on the ~** nous tenions l'opposition à la gorge
VT *(Hist) (torture)* faire subir le supplice du chevalet à ; *(fig) [pain]* torturer, tourmenter ◆ **~ed by remorse** tenaillé par le remords ◆ **~ed by doubt** assailli de doutes ◆ **to ~ one's brains** se creuser la tête *or* la cervelle *
COMP rack and pinion N crémaillère *f*
rack (and pinion) railway N chemin *m* de fer à crémaillère
rack rent N loyer *m* exorbitant

► **rack up VT FUS** *[+ profits, losses, sales, wins]* accumuler ◆ **to ~ up an impressive score** réaliser un score impressionnant

rack² /ræk/ **N** ◆ **to go to ~ and ruin** *[building]* tomber en ruine ; *[business, economy]* aller à vau-l'eau ; *[person, country]* aller à la ruine

racket¹ /ˈrækɪt/ **N** *(Sport)* raquette *f* **NPL rackets** *(= game)* (jeu *m* de) paume *f*
COMP racket press N presse-raquette *m inv*, presse *f*

racket² /ˈrækɪt/ **N** 1 *(= noise) [of people]* tapage *m*, boucan * *m* ; *[of machine]* vacarme *m* ◆ **to make a ~** *[people]* faire du tapage *or* du boucan * ; *[machine]* faire du vacarme 2 *(= organized crime)* trafic *m* ; *(= dishonest scheme)* escroquerie *f* ◆ **an extortion ~** un racket ◆ **the drugs/stolen car ~** le trafic de drogue/des voitures volées ◆ **he's in on the ~** * *(fig)* il est dans le coup * ◆ **what's your ~?** * *(fig = job etc)* qu'est-ce que vous faites dans la vie ? ◆ **teaching isn't really my ~** * l'enseignement n'est pas vraiment mon truc * **VI** † *(= make a noise)* faire du tapage *or* du boucan * ; (also **racket about, racket around**) *(= lead a hectic social life)* faire la bombe * *or* la bringue ‡

racketeer /ˌrækɪˈtɪəʳ/ **N** racketter *m*, racketteur *m* ◆ **drugs ~** trafiquant *m* de drogue

racketeering /ˌrækɪˈtɪərɪŋ/ **N** *(NonC)* racket *m* ◆ **drugs ~** trafic *m* de drogue

racking /ˈrækɪŋ/ **ADJ** *[pain, sobs]* déchirant ; *[cough]* convulsif

raconteur /ˌrækɒnˈtɜːʳ/ **N** conteur *m*, -euse *f*

racoon /rəˈkuːn/ **N** ⇒ **raccoon**

racquet /ˈrækɪt/ **N** ⇒ **racket¹**

racquetball /ˈrækɪtˌbɔːl/ **N** *(NonC)* racket-ball *m*

racy /ˈreɪsɪ/ **ADJ** 1 *(= risqué) [story, book, film, language]* leste 2 *(= lively) [style of writing, speaking]* plein de verve

RADA /ˈrɑːdə/ **N** *(in Brit)* (abbrev of **Royal Academy of Dramatic Art**) ≈ Conservatoire *m* d'art dramatique

radar /ˈreɪdɑːʳ/ **N** radar *m* ◆ **by ~** au radar
COMP *[antenna, echo, screen, station]* radar *inv*
radar astronomy N radarastronomie *f*
radar beacon N radiophare *m* pour radar
radar operator N radariste *mf*
radar scanner N *(= antenna)* antenne *f* radar *inv*
radar screen N écran *m* radar ◆ **to vanish from ~ screens** *(lit: aircraft)* disparaître des écrans radar ; *(fig: person)* disparaître de la circulation
radar sensor N détecteur *m* (radar *inv*)
radar trap N *(on road)* contrôle *m* radar *inv* ◆ **to get caught in a ~ trap** se faire piéger par un radar

raddle /ˈrædl/ **N** ocre *f* rouge **VT** *[+ sheep]* marquer (à l'ocre)

raddled /ˈrædld/ **ADJ** *[face]* marqué, aux traits accusés, fripé ; *[person]* au visage marqué, aux traits accusés

radial /ˈreɪdɪəl/ **ADJ** *[streets]* (also *Med*) radial ; *[pattern]* en étoile **N** (also **radial tyre**) pneu *m* à carcasse radiale
COMP radial engine N moteur *m* en étoile
radial road N radiale *f*
radial tyre N pneu *m* à carcasse radiale

radially /ˈreɪdɪəlɪ/ **ADV** *[arrange, extend]* en étoile

radiance /ˈreɪdɪəns/, **radiancy** /ˈreɪdɪənsɪ/ **N** *[of sun, lights etc]* éclat *m* ; *[of face, personality, beauty]* éclat *m*, rayonnement *m*

radiant /ˈreɪdɪənt/ **ADJ** *[person, smile, beauty, sunshine]* radieux ; *[optimism]* rayonnant ; *[complexion, colour]* éclatant ◆ **~ with joy/health** rayonnant de joie/de santé ◆ **to look ~** être radieux **N** *(Phys)* point *m* radiant ; *(Math)* radian *m* ; *(Astron)* (point *m*) radiant *m*
COMP radiant energy N *(Phys)* énergie *f* rayonnante
radiant heat N *(Phys)* chaleur *f* radiante *or* rayonnante
radiant heater N radiateur *m* à foyer rayonnant
radiant heating N chauffage *m* par rayonnement

radiantly /ˈreɪdɪəntlɪ/ **ADV** *[smile, say]* d'un air radieux ; *[shine]* d'un vif éclat ◆ **to be ~ happy** être rayonnant de bonheur ◆ **~ beautiful** à la beauté radieuse

radiate /ˈreɪdɪeɪt/ **VI** *(= emit rays)* irradier, rayonner *(liter)* ; *(= emit heat)* rayonner ; *(Phys)* irradier ; *(fig) [lines, roads]* rayonner *(from* de), partir du même centre **VT** *[+ heat] (Tech)* émettre ; *(gen)* répandre ◆ **to ~ happiness** être rayonnant *or* rayonner de bonheur ◆ **he ~s enthusiasm** il respire l'enthousiasme

radiation /ˌreɪdɪˈeɪʃən/ **N** *[of light]* rayonnement *m*, rayons *mpl* ; *[of heat]* rayonnement *m* ; *(= radioactivity)* radiations *fpl* ◆ **the ozone layer protects us from ultra violet ~ from the sun** la couche d'ozone nous protège du rayonnement ultraviolet *or* des rayons ultraviolets du soleil
COMP radiation exposure N irradiation *f*
radiation levels NPL niveaux *mpl* de radiation
radiation sickness N mal *m* des rayons
radiation treatment N *(Med)* radiothérapie *f*

radiator /ˈreɪdɪeɪtəʳ/ **N** radiateur *m*
COMP radiator cap N *(on car radiator)* bouchon *m* de radiateur
radiator grill(e) N *(on car)* calandre *f*

radical /ˈrædɪkəl/ **ADJ, N** *(gen, Pol, Ling, Bot, Math)* radical *m*

radicalism /ˈrædɪkəlɪzəm/ **N** radicalisme *m*

radicalization /ˌrædɪkəlaɪˈzeɪʃən/ **N** radicalisation *f*

radicalize /ˈrædɪkəlaɪz/ **VT** radicaliser

radically /ˈrædɪkəlɪ/ **ADV** *[differ, change, affect, improve, reduce]* radicalement, de façon radicale ◆ **~ different** radicalement différent ◆ **there's something ~ wrong with this approach** il y a quelque chose qui ne va pas du tout avec cette méthode

radicchio /ræˈdiːkɪəʊ/ **N** (pl **radicchios**) trévise *f*

radices /ˈreɪdɪsiːz/ **NPL** of **radix**

radicle /ˈrædɪkl/ **N** *(Bot)* radicule *f*, radicelle *f* ; *(Chem)* radical *m*

radii /ˈreɪdɪaɪ/ **NPL** of **radius**

radio /ˈreɪdɪəʊ/ **N** 1 (also **radio set**) radio *f* ◆ **on the ~** à la radio ◆ **he has got a ~** il a un poste de radio, il a la radio ◆ **to put the ~ on/off** allumer/éteindre la radio *or* le poste ; → **transistor**
2 *(NonC: Telec)* radio *m* ◆ **to send a message by ~** envoyer un (message) radio ◆ **they communicated by ~** ils communiquaient par radio
VT *[+ person]* appeler *or* joindre par radio ; *[+ information]* communiquer par radio ◆ **to ~ a message** envoyer un (message) radio
VI ◆ **to ~ for help** appeler au secours par radio
COMP *[talk, programme]* de radio
radio alarm (clock) N radio-réveil *m*
radio amateur N radioamateur *m*
radio announcer N speaker(ine) *m(f)*
radio astronomy N radioastronomie *f*
radio beacon N radiophare *m*, radiobalise *f*
radio beam N faisceau *m* radio *inv*
radio broadcast N émission *f* de radio *or* radiophonique
radio buoy N ⇒ **radio sono-buoy**
radio cab N radio-taxi *m*
radio car N voiture *f* radio *inv*
radio cassette (recorder) N *(esp Brit)* radiocassette *m*
radio compass N radiocompas *m*
radio contact N radiocommunication *f*
radio control N radiocommande *f*
radio-controlled ADJ radiocommandé
radio direction finding N radiogoniométrie *f*
radio engineer N ingénieur *m* radio *inv*
radio frequency N radiofréquence *f*
radio galaxy N radiogalaxie *f*
radio ham * N radioamateur *m*
radio link N liaison *f* radio *inv*
radio mast N mât *m* d'antenne, pylône *m*
radio operator N opérateur *m* (radio *inv*), radio *m*
radio play N pièce *f* radiophonique, audiodrame *m*
radio programme N émission *f* de radio *or* radiophonique
radio receiver N récepteur *m* de radio
radio set N poste *m* (de radio), radio *f*
radio silence N silence *m* radio *inv* ◆ **to maintain ~ silence** garder le silence radio
radio sono-buoy N bouée *f* sonore
radio source, radio star N radiosource *f*
radio station N *(= broadcasting organization)* station *f* de radio ; *(= installation)* poste *m* émetteur
radio taxi N radio-taxi *m*
radio telescope N radiotélescope *m*
radio valve N valve *f*, tube *m* à vide
radio van N *(Rad, TV)* studio *m* mobile (de radiodiffusion *or* d'enregistrement)
radio wave N onde *f* hertzienne

radioactive /ˌreɪdɪəʊˈæktɪv/ ADJ radioactif ◆ **~ waste** déchets *mpl* radioactifs

radioactivity /ˌreɪdɪəʊækˈtɪvɪtɪ/ N radioactivité *f*

radiobiology /ˌreɪdɪəʊbaɪˈɒlədʒɪ/ N radiobiologie *f*

radiocarbon /ˌreɪdɪəʊˈkɑːbən/ N radiocarbone *m*, carbone *m* COMP **radiocarbon dating** N datation *f* au carbone 14

radiochemistry /ˌreɪdɪəʊˈkemɪstrɪ/ N radiochimie *f*

radiocommunication /ˌreɪdɪəʊkəˈmjuːnɪˈkeɪʃən/ N contact(s) *m(pl)* radio *inv*

radioelement /ˌreɪdɪəʊˈelɪmənt/ N radioélément *m*

radiogram /ˈreɪdɪəʊɡræm/ N 1 († = *message*) radiogramme *m*, radio *m* 2 (*Brit* = *apparatus*) combiné *m* (*avec radio et pick-up*)

radiograph /ˈreɪdɪəʊɡrɑːf/ N radio *f*, radiographie *f*

radiographer /ˌreɪdɪˈɒɡrəfəʳ/ N radiologue *mf* (*technicien*)

radiography /ˌreɪdɪˈɒɡrəfɪ/ N radiographie *f*, radio *f*

radioisotope /ˌreɪdɪəʊˈaɪsətəʊp/ N radio-isotope *m*

radiological /ˌreɪdɪəˈlɒdʒɪkəl/ ADJ radiologique

radiologist /ˌreɪdɪˈɒlədʒɪst/ N radiologue *mf* (*médecin*)

radiology /ˌreɪdɪˈɒlədʒɪ/ N radiologie *f*

radiolysis /ˌreɪdɪˈɒlɪsɪs/ N radiolyse *f*

radiometer /ˌreɪdɪˈɒmɪtəʳ/ N radiomètre *m*

radiopager /ˌreɪdɪəʊˈpeɪdʒəʳ/ N bip* *m*, pager *m*

radiopaging /ˌreɪdɪəʊˈpeɪdʒɪŋ/ N (service *m* de) radiomessagerie *f*

radioscopy /ˌreɪdɪˈɒskəpɪ/ N radioscopie *f*

radiotelegraph /ˌreɪdɪəʊˈtelɪɡrɑːf/ N radiotélégramme *m*, radiogramme *m*

radiotelegraphy /ˌreɪdɪəʊtɪˈleɡrəfɪ/ N radiotélégraphie *f*

radiotelephone /ˌreɪdɪəʊˈtelɪfəʊn/ N radiotéléphone *m*

radiotelephony /ˌreɪdɪəʊtɪˈlefənɪ/ N radiotéléphonie *f*

radiotherapist /ˌreɪdɪəʊˈθerəpɪst/ N radiothérapeute *mf*

radiotherapy /ˌreɪdɪəʊˈθerəpɪ/ N radiothérapie *f* ◆ **to have ~ (treatment)** subir une radiothérapie

radish /ˈrædɪʃ/ N radis *m*

radium /ˈreɪdɪəm/ N radium *m* COMP **radium therapy, radium treatment** N (*Med*) radiumthérapie *f*, curiethérapie *f*

radius /ˈreɪdɪəs/ N (pl **radiuses** *or* **radii**) (*Math, fig*) rayon *m* ; (*Anat*) radius *m* ◆ **within a 6km ~ of Paris** dans un rayon de 6 km autour de Paris

radix /ˈreɪdɪks/ N (pl **radixes** *or* **radices**) (*Math*) base *f* ; (*Ling*) radical *m*

radon /ˈreɪdɒn/ N (also **radon gas**) radon *m*

RAF /ˌɑːreɪˈef/ N (*Brit*) (abbrev of **Royal Air Force**) RAF *f*

raffia /ˈræfɪə/ N raphia *m* COMP en raphia

raffish /ˈræfɪʃ/ ADJ [*charm, appearance, air, behaviour*] canaille ; [*person*] à l'air canaille ; [*place*] louche ◆ **to cut a ~ figure** avoir l'air canaille

raffle /ˈræfl/ N tombola *f* VT mettre en tombola COMP **raffle ticket** N billet *m* de tombola

raft /rɑːft/ N 1 (*flat structure*) radeau *m* ; (*logs*) train *m* de flottage ; → **life** 2 (*fig*) **a ~ of ...** un tas de ...

rafter /ˈrɑːftəʳ/ N (*Archit*) chevron *m*

rafting /ˈrɑːftɪŋ/ N rafting *m* ◆ **to go ~** faire du rafting

rag[1] /ræɡ/ N 1 lambeau *m*, loque *f* ; (*for wiping etc*) chiffon *m* ◆ **to feel like a wet ~** * (*emotionally*) se sentir vidé *or* mou comme une chiffe ; (*physically*) se sentir ramollo* *inv* ◆ **~s** (*for papermaking*) chiffons *mpl*, peilles *fpl* ; (= *old clothes*) guenilles *fpl*, haillons *mpl* ◆ **his clothes were in ~s** ses vêtements étaient en lambeaux *or* tombaient en loques ◆ **to be (dressed) in ~s** être vêtu de guenilles *or* de haillons, être déguenillé ◆ **in ~s and tatters** tout en loques ◆ **to go from ~s to riches** passer de la misère à la richesse ◆ **to lose one's ~**‡ se mettre en rogne*, se foutre en rogne‡ ; → **glad, red**

2 (* *pej* = *newspaper*) torchon* *m*, feuille *f* de chou*

3 (‡ = *sanitary towel*) serviette *f* hygiénique ◆ **to be on the ~** avoir ses ragnagnas*

4 (*Mus*) ragtime *m*

COMP **rag-and-bone man** N (pl **rag-and-bone men**) (*Brit*) chiffonnier *m*

rag doll N poupée *f* de chiffon

rag rug N carpette *f* faite de chutes de tissu

the rag trade * N la confection

rag[2] * /ræɡ/ (*Brit*) N (= *joke*) farce *f*, blague* *f* ◆ **for a ~** par plaisanterie, pour s'amuser, pour blaguer* VT † (= *tease*) taquiner, mettre en boîte* ; (= *play trick on*) faire une blague* à ; (*Scol*) [+ *teacher*] chahuter COMP **rag week** N (*Univ*) *semaine où les étudiants organisent des attractions au profit d'œuvres de bienfaisance*

raga /ˈrɑːɡə/ N raga *m inv*

ragamuffin /ˈræɡəˌmʌfɪn/ N (= *urchin*) galopin* *m* ; (= *ragged fellow*) va-nu-pieds *mf inv*

ragbag /ˈræɡbæɡ/ N 1 (*lit*) sac *m* à chiffons 2 (*Brit fig*) **a ~ of ...** un groupe hétéroclite de ...

rage /reɪdʒ/ N rage *f*, fureur *f* ; [*of sea*] furie *f* ◆ **he was shaking with ~** il tremblait de rage ◆ **to be in a ~** être furieux *or* en fureur *or* en rage ◆ **to put sb into a ~** mettre qn en rage *or* en fureur ◆ **to fly into a ~** entrer en fureur, se mettre en rage, sortir de ses gonds ◆ **he shot her in a fit of ~** il lui a tiré dessus dans un accès de fureur *or* rage ◆ **golf/trolley ~** comportement *m* agressif sur un parcours de golf/dans un supermarché ◆ **computer ~** *comportement d'une personne excédée par son ordinateur* ◆ **to be (all) the ~** faire fureur ; → **air**

VI [*person*] être furieux (*against* contre), rager* ; [*battle, fire*] faire rage ; [*sea*] être démonté, être en furie ; [*storm*] se déchaîner, faire rage ; [*wind*] être déchaîné ◆ **"you shouldn't have done that" she ~d** "tu n'aurais pas dû faire ça", dit-elle, furieuse ◆ **the fire ~d through the city** l'incendie s'est propagé dans la ville avec une violence inouïe ◆ **she ~d at her fate** elle était furieuse de ce qui lui arrivait ◆ **he ~d about the unfairness of this rule** l'injustice de cette règle le révoltait ◆ **the fierce arguments raging over the future of the hospital** les féroces controverses sur l'avenir de l'hôpital

ragga /ˈræɡə/ N (*Mus*) raga(muffin) *m*

ragged /ˈræɡɪd/ ADJ 1 (= *in tatters*) [*person*] déguenillé, en haillons ; [*clothes*] en lambeaux, en loques ; [*cuff*] effiloché 2 (= *uneven*) [*edge, rock*] déchiqueté ; [*hole*] aux bords déchiquetés *or* irréguliers ; [*line, beard*] irrégulier ; [*cloud*] effiloché ◆ **on the ~ edge** * (*US* = *anxious*) au bord de la crise de nerfs ◆ **to run sb ~** * éreinter *or* épuiser qn ◆ **to run o.s. ~** * s'épuiser 3 (= *disorganized*) [*performance*] inégal ◆ **the orchestra sounded rather ~ in places** l'orchestre a donné une prestation assez inégale COMP **ragged robin** N (= *plant*) fleur *f* de coucou

raggedly /ˈræɡɪdlɪ/ ADV 1 (= *in rags*) ◆ **~ dressed** déguenillé, en haillons 2 (= *unevenly*) ◆ **they marched ~ up and down** ils ont défilé en désordre ◆ **the orchestra played ~** la prestation de l'orchestre a été assez inégale

raggle-taggle /ˌræɡlˈtæɡl/ ADJ [*gipsy*] dépenaillé ; [*army, group*] disparate

raging /ˈreɪdʒɪŋ/ ADJ [*pain*] atroce ; [*storm, wind, torrent*] déchaîné ; [*sea*] déchaîné, démonté ; [*fire*] violent ; [*inflation*] galopant ; [*debate*] houleux ; [*feminist, nationalist, nationalism*] fanatique ◆ **a ~ inferno** un immense brasier ◆ **to be in a ~ temper, to be ~ mad** * être dans une colère noire ◆ **~ temperature** *or* **fever** fièvre *f* de cheval ◆ **he had a ~ thirst** il mourait de soif ◆ **~ toothache** rage *f* de dents ◆ **a ~ success** un succès prodigieux N [*of person*] rage *f*, fureur *f* ; [*of elements*] déchaînement *m* ◆ **the ~ of the sea** la mer en furie

raglan /ˈræɡlən/ ADJ, N raglan *m inv*

ragman /ˈræɡmæn/ N (pl **men**) chiffonnier *m*

ragout /ˈræɡuː/ N ragoût *m*

ragtag /ˈræɡˌtæɡ/ N ◆ **~ and bobtail** racaille *f*, populace *f*

ragtime /ˈræɡtaɪm/ N ragtime *m*

ragtop‡ /ˈræɡtɒp/ N (*US* = *car*) décapotable *f*

ragweed /ˈræɡwiːd/ N ambroisie *f*

ragwort /ˈræɡwɜːt/ N jacobée *f*

rah * /rɑː/ (*US*) EXCL hourra !, bravo ! COMP **rah-rah** * ADJ enthousiaste, exubérant

raid /reɪd/ N (*Mil*) raid *m*, incursion *f* ; (*by police*) descente *f* (de police) ; (*with arrests*) rafle *f* ; (*by bandits*) razzia *f* ; (*Brit: by thieves*) hold-up *m inv* ; (*Fin*) raid *m*, tentative *f* de prise de contrôle ◆ **air ~** raid *m* (aérien), bombardement *m* aérien ◆ **bank ~** (*Brit*) hold-up *m inv or* braquage* *m* d'une banque VT 1 (*Mil*) faire une incursion *or* un raid dans ; (= *bomb from plane*) bombarder, faire un raid sur ; [*police*] faire une descente *or* une rafle dans ; [*bandits*] razzier ; (*Brit*) [*thieves*] faire un hold-up à, braquer* 2 (*fig*) [+ *orchard*] marauder dans ; (*hum*) [+ *cashbox, piggybank*] puiser dans ; (*hum*) [+ *larder, fridge*] dévaliser, faire une descente dans* ; (*Fin*) lancer une tentative de prise de contrôle de

raider /ˈreɪdəʳ/ N (= *thief*) braqueur* *m* ; (= *ship*) navire *m* qui accomplit un raid, raider *m* ; (= *plane*) bombardier *m* ; (*Fin*) raider *m*

raiding /ˈreɪdɪŋ/ N (*Mil*) raids *mpl* ; [*of police*] raids *mpl*, descentes *fpl* COMP **raiding party** N groupe *m* d'attaque

rail[1] /reɪl/ N 1 (= *bar*) [*of bridge, quay*] garde-fou *m* ; [*of boat*] bastingage *m*, rambarde *f* ; [*of balcony, terrace*] balustrade *f* ; (= *handrail: on wall*) main *f* courante ; (= *banister*) rampe *f* ; (*for carpet, curtains, spotlights etc*) tringle *f* ◆ **the horse was close to the ~s** (*Racing*) le cheval tenait la corde ◆ **~s** (= *fence*) grille *f*, barrière *f* ; → **altar, towel**

2 (*for train, tram*) rail *m* ◆ **to travel by ~** voyager en train ◆ **to send by ~** envoyer par (le) train *or* par chemin de fer ◆ **to go off the ~s** (*lit*) [*train etc*] dérailler ; (*fig*) [*person*] (= *err*) s'écarter du droit chemin ; (= *be confused*) être déboussolé* ◆ **to keep sb on the ~s** maintenir qn sur le droit chemin ; → **live**[2]

COMP [*ticket*] de train, de chemin de fer ; [*journey*] en train, en chemin de fer ; [*dispute*] des employés des chemins de fer

rail strike N grève *f* des employés des chemins de fer

rail traffic N trafic *m* ferroviaire

rail transport N transport *m* ferroviaire

► **rail in** VT SEP clôturer, entourer d'une clôture *or* d'une barrière

► **rail off** VT SEP fermer au moyen d'une clôture *or* d'une barrière

rail[2] /reɪl/ VI (*frm*) ◆ **to ~ at** *or* **against sb** se répandre en injures contre qn

railcar /ˈreɪlkɑːʳ/ N autorail *m*

railcard /ˈreɪlkɑːd/ N carte *f* de chemin de fer ◆ **family** ~ ≃ carte *f* couple-famille ◆ **Senior Citizen** ~ carte *f* vermeil ◆ **student** ~ carte *f* de train tarif étudiant ◆ **young person's** ~ carte *f* de train tarif jeune

railhead /ˈreɪlhed/ N tête *f* de ligne

railing /ˈreɪlɪŋ/ N 1 *(= rail) [of bridge, quay]* garde-fou *m* ; *[of balcony, terrace]* balustrade *f* ; *(on stairs)* rampe *f* ; *(on wall)* main *f* courante 2 *(= part of fence)* barreau *m* ; *(= fence:* also **railings***)* grille *f*

raillery /ˈreɪlərɪ/ N taquinerie *f*, badinage *m*

railroad /ˈreɪlrəʊd/ N *(US)* ⇒ **railway** VT 1 *(US)* expédier par chemin de fer *or* par rail 2 *(* = force)* **to ~ a bill** faire voter un projet de loi (après un débat sommaire) ◆ **to ~ sb into doing sth** forcer qn à faire qch sans qu'il ait le temps de réfléchir *or* de faire ouf *

railway /ˈreɪlweɪ/ N 1 *(Brit) (= system)* chemin *m* de fer ; *(= track)* voie *f* ferrée ; → **aerial, elevated, scenic, underground** 2 *(US: for trams etc)* rails *mpl*

COMP *[bridge, ticket]* de chemin de fer
railway carriage N voiture *f*, wagon *m*
railway engine N locomotive *f*
railway guide N indicateur *m* des chemins de fer
railway journey N voyage *m* en train *or* en chemin de fer
railway line N ligne *f* de chemin de fer ; *(= track)* voie *f* ferrée
railway network N réseau *m* ferroviaire
railway porter N porteur *m*
railway station N gare *f* ; *(small)* station *f* de chemin de fer
railway timetable N horaire *m* des chemins de fer
railway workers NPL employés *mpl* des chemins de fer, cheminots *mpl*
railway yard N dépôt *m* (d'une gare)

railwayman /ˈreɪlweɪmən/ N (pl **-men**) *(Brit)* cheminot *m*

railworkers /ˈreɪlwɜːkəz/ NPL employés *mpl* des chemins de fer, cheminots *mpl*

raiment /ˈreɪmənt/ N *(liter)* vêtements *mpl*

rain /reɪn/ N 1 *(lit)* pluie *f* ◆ **it looks like** ~ le temps est à la pluie ◆ **in the** ~ sous la pluie ◆ **heavy/light** ~ pluie *f* battante/fine ◆ **the ~'s on** * *(Scot)* ça pleut * ◆ **(come) ~ (hail) or shine** *(lit)* par tous les temps, qu'il pleuve ou qu'il vente ; *(fig)* quoi qu'il arrive ◆ **the ~s** la saison des pluies ; → **right**

2 *(fig) [of arrows, blows, bullets]* pluie *f*

VT *[+ blows]* faire pleuvoir

VI pleuvoir ◆ **it is ~ing** il pleut ◆ **it is ~ing heavily** il pleut à verse ◆ **it's ~ing cats and dogs** *, **it's ~ing buckets** * il pleut des cordes * ◆ **to ~ on sb's parade** * mettre des bâtons dans les roues de qn ◆ **it never ~s but it pours** *(Prov)* un malheur n'arrive jamais seul *(Prov)*

COMP **rain belt** N zone *f* des pluies
rain check * N *(US)* billet *m* pour un autre match *(or* pour un autre spectacle*)* ◆ **to give sb a ~ check** *(US fig)* inviter qn une autre fois (à la place) ◆ **I'll take a ~ check (on that)** *(esp US fig)* ça sera pour une autre fois
rain cloud N nuage *m* chargé de pluie
rain dance N danse *f* de la pluie
rain gauge N pluviomètre *m*
rain hood N capuche *f* en plastique

► **rain down** VI *[bullets, stones etc]* pleuvoir

► **rain off, rain out** *(US)* VT SEP ◆ **the match was rained off** *or* **out** le match a été annulé (*or* abandonné) à cause de la pluie

rainbow /ˈreɪnbəʊ/ N arc-en-ciel *m* ◆ **of all colours of the** ~ de toutes les couleurs de l'arc-en-ciel ◆ **to look for the pot** *or* **crock of gold at the end of the** ~ poursuivre un rêve impossible NPL **Rainbows** *(Brit = Brownies)* *fillettes scoutes*

COMP **rainbow coalition** N *(Pol)* coalition *f* hétéroclite
rainbow trout N truite *f* arc-en-ciel
rainbow wrasse N girelle *f*

raincoat /ˈreɪnkəʊt/ N imperméable *m*, imper * *m*

raindrop /ˈreɪndrɒp/ N goutte *f* de pluie

rainfall /ˈreɪnfɔːl/ N *(= shower)* chute *f* de pluie ; *(= amount)* pluviosité *f*, pluviométrie *f*

rainforest /ˈreɪnfɒrɪst/ N (also **tropical rainforest**) forêt *f* pluviale COMP *[plant, species, conservation, destruction]* de la forêt tropicale (humide)

rainless /ˈreɪnlɪs/ ADJ sec (sèche *f*), sans pluie

rainmaker /ˈreɪnmeɪkəʳ/ N faiseur *m*, -euse *f* de pluie ; *(fig) employé très performant qui crée de nouveaux marchés et génère le plus de revenus pour l'entreprise*

rainmaking /ˈreɪnmeɪkɪŋ/ ADJ *[ceremony etc]* destiné à faire venir la pluie

rainout /ˈreɪnaʊt/ N *(US Sport) match annulé pour cause de pluie*

rainproof /ˈreɪnpruːf/ ADJ imperméable VT imperméabiliser

rainstick /ˈreɪnstɪk/ N bâton *m* de pluie

rainstorm /ˈreɪnstɔːm/ N pluie *f* torrentielle, trombes *fpl* d'eau

rainswept /ˈreɪnswept/ ADJ *[place]* balayé par la pluie

rainwater /ˈreɪnwɔːtəʳ/ N eau *f* de pluie

rainwear /ˈreɪnwɛəʳ/ N *(NonC: Comm)* vêtements *mpl* de pluie

rainy /ˈreɪnɪ/ ADJ *[place]* pluvieux ◆ **the ~ season** la saison des pluies ◆ **a ~ day** une journée pluvieuse *or* de pluie ◆ **to put something away** *or* **save something for a ~ day** garder une poire pour la soif

raise /reɪz/ LANGUAGE IN USE 26.1

VT 1 *(= lift, cause to rise) [+ arm, leg, eyes]* lever ; *[+ object, weight]* lever, soulever ; *[+ dust]* soulever ◆ **to ~ a blind** (re)lever un store ◆ **to ~ the curtain** *(Theat)* lever le rideau ◆ **to ~ one's eyebrows** *(lit)* hausser les sourcils ◆ **they ~d their eyebrows when they heard ...** *(in surprise)* ils ont eu une expression perplexe *or* l'étonnement s'est lu sur leur visage quand ils ont entendu ... ◆ **that will make him ~ his eyebrows** *(fig)* cela le fera tiquer ◆ **he didn't ~ an eyebrow** il n'a pas sourcillé *or* tiqué ◆ **she ~d a few eyebrows with her saucy jokes** elle a provoqué quelques froncements de sourcils avec ses plaisanteries grivoises ◆ **to ~ one's hat to sb** donner un coup de chapeau à qn ; *(fig)* tirer son chapeau à qn * ◆ **to ~ one's glass to sb** lever son verre à qn, boire à la santé de qn ◆ **to ~ one's hand to sb** lever la main sur qn ◆ **to ~ one's fist to sb** menacer qn du poing ◆ **to ~ sb from the dead** ressusciter qn (d'entre les morts) ◆ **to ~ one's voice** *(= speak louder)* hausser la voix ; *(= get angry)* élever la voix, hausser le ton ◆ **don't ~ your voice to me!** ne hausse pas le ton quand tu me parles ! ◆ **not a voice was ~d in protest** personne n'a élevé la voix pour protester ◆ **to ~ sb's spirits** remonter le moral de qn ◆ **to ~ sb's hopes** donner à espérer à qn ◆ **he ~d the people to revolt** il souleva le peuple ◆ **to ~ the roof** * *(fig)* faire un boucan monstre ⁑ ; *(in protest)* rouspéter ferme * ◆ **to ~ the level of the ground** rehausser le niveau du sol ◆ **to ~ a sunken ship** *(Naut)* renflouer un navire coulé ; → **tone**

2 *(= increase) [+ salary]* augmenter, relever *(Admin)* ; *[+ price]* majorer, augmenter ; *[+ standard, level]* élever ; *[+ age limit]* reculer ; *[+ temperature]* faire monter ◆ **to ~ the school-leaving age** prolonger la scolarité obligatoire

3 *(= build, erect) [+ monument]* élever, ériger ; *[+ building]* édifier, bâtir

4 *(= produce) [+ spirit]* évoquer ; *[+ ghosts]* faire apparaître ; *[+ problems, difficulties]* soulever, provoquer ; *[+ doubts]* faire naître ◆ **to ~ a blister** provoquer une ampoule ◆ **to ~ a laugh** provoquer le rire, faire rire ◆ **to ~ a cheer** *(oneself)* crier "hourra" ; *(in others)* faire jaillir des hourras ◆ **to ~ difficulties** soulever *or* faire des difficultés ◆ **to ~ a smile** *(oneself)* ébaucher un sourire ; *(in others)* faire sourire, donner à sourire ◆ **to ~ suspicion in sb's mind** faire naître des soupçons dans l'esprit de qn ◆ **to ~ Cain** * *or* **hell** ⁑ *(= make a noise)* faire un éclat *or* du boucan * ; *(= make a fuss)* faire une scène de tous les diables *

5 *(= bring to notice) [+ question, issue]* soulever ; *[+ objection, protest]* élever

6 *(= grow, breed) [+ animals, children, family]* élever ; *[+ corn, wheat]* cultiver, faire pousser

7 *(= get together) [+ army, taxes]* lever ; *[+ money]* se procurer ◆ **to ~ funds for sth** *(gen)* réunir *or* rassembler *or* se procurer les fonds pour qch ; *[professional fundraiser]* collecter des fonds pour qch ; *(Fin, Econ)* mobiliser des fonds pour qch ◆ **to ~ a loan** *[government etc]* lancer *or* émettre un emprunt ; *[person]* emprunter ◆ **to ~ money on sth** emprunter de l'argent sur qch ◆ **I can't ~ the $500 I need** je n'arrive pas à me procurer les 500 dollars dont j'ai besoin ; → **mortgage**

8 *(= end) [+ siege, embargo]* lever

9 *(Cards)* faire une mise supérieure à ; *(Bridge)* faire une annonce supérieure à ◆ **I'll ~ you six/$10** je fais une relance *or* je relance de six/10 dollars ; → **bid**

10 *(= contact: on radio etc)* contacter

N 1 *(US, also Brit * = pay rise)* augmentation *f* (de salaire)

2 *(Cards)* relance *f*, mise *f* supérieure ; *(Bridge)* annonce *f* supérieure, enchère *f*

COMP **raising agent** N *(Culin)* poudre *f* à lever

► **raise up** VT SEP lever, soulever ◆ **he ~d himself up on his elbow** il s'est soulevé sur son coude

raiser /ˈreɪzəʳ/ N 1 *(Agr)* éleveur *m* ◆ **cattle-/sheep-~** éleveur *m* de bétail/de moutons 2 *(in compounds)* → **fire, fund**

raisin /ˈreɪzən/ N raisin *m* sec COMP **raisin bread** N pain *m* aux raisins secs

raj /rɑːdʒ/ N ◆ **the (British) Raj** l'empire *m* britannique des Indes

rajah /ˈrɑːdʒə/ N raja(h) *or* radja(h) *m*

rake[1] /reɪk/ N *(for gardener, croupier)* râteau *m* ; *(for grate)* râble *m*, ringard *m*

VT 1 *[+ garden, leaves]* ratisser ; *[+ hay]* râteler ◆ **to ~ a fire** tisonner un feu ◆ **to ~ the stones off the lawn** enlever les cailloux de la pelouse (à l'aide d'un râteau) ◆ **to ~ dead leaves into a pile** ratisser les feuilles mortes et en faire un tas ◆ **to ~ through one's memory** fouiller dans sa mémoire *or* dans ses souvenirs

2 *(= sweep)* **his glance ~d the crowd** il a parcouru la foule du regard ◆ **enemy searchlights ~d the sea** les projecteurs ennemis balayaient la mer ◆ **the car was ~d with bullets** la voiture a été criblée de balles

VI *(fig = search)* ◆ **to ~ among** *or* **through** fouiller dans ◆ **to ~ through dustbins** faire les poubelles

COMP **rake-off** * N *(pej)* pourcentage *m* ◆ **he gets a ~-off on each sale** il prélève son pourcentage sur chaque vente

► **rake in** * VT SEP *[+ money]* amasser ◆ **he's just raking it in!** il remue le fric à la pelle ! ⁑

► **rake out** VT SEP ◆ **to rake out a fire** éteindre un feu en faisant tomber la braise

► **rake over** VT SEP *[+ flower bed]* ratisser ; *(fig) [+ memories, past]* remuer ◆ **to ~ over the coals** *or* **ashes** *(esp Brit fig)* remuer le passé

► **rake up** VT SEP *[+ fire]* attiser ; *[+ leaves]* ramasser avec un râteau, ratisser ; *(fig) [+ grievance]* rappeler ◆ **to ~ up the past** remuer le passé ◆ **to ~ up sb's past** fouiller dans le passé de qn

rake[2] † /reɪk/ N *(= person)* roué † *m*, débauché *m*, coureur *m*

rake³ /reɪk/ **N** (= slope) (Naut) [of mast] quête f ; [of stage] pente f ; [of car seat] inclinaison f **VI** [mast] être incliné ; [stage] être en pente

raked /reɪkt/ **ADJ** [stage] en pente

rakish¹ /ˈreɪkɪʃ/ **ADJ** 1 († = dissolute) [person, appearance, moustache] canaille ♦ **to look** ~ avoir l'air canaille 2 (= jaunty) ♦ **worn at a ~ angle** porté de travers pour se donner un air désinvolte

rakish² /ˈreɪkɪʃ/ **ADJ** (Naut) élancé, à la ligne élancée

rakishly /ˈreɪkɪʃlɪ/ **ADV** 1 († = dissolutely) [behave] en débauché 2 (= jauntily) ♦ **a hat cocked ~ over one eye** un chapeau porté de travers pour se donner un air désinvolte ♦ **he wore a ~-knotted cravat** sa façon de nouer son foulard lui donnait un air désinvolte

rally¹ /ˈrælɪ/ **N** 1 [of troops] rassemblement m, ralliement m ; [of people] rassemblement m ; (Pol) rassemblement m, meeting m ; (= car rally) rallye m ; (Tennis) échange m ♦ **youth/peace ~** rassemblement m de la jeunesse/en faveur de la paix ♦ **electoral ~** meeting m de campagne électorale

2 (in health) amélioration f, mieux m ; (St Ex) reprise f

VT [+ troops] rassembler, rallier ; [+ supporters] rallier ; [+ one's strength] retrouver, reprendre ♦ **hoping to ~ opinion within the party** en espérant rallier à sa cause des membres du parti

VI [troops, people] se rallier ; [sick person] aller mieux, reprendre des forces or le dessus ♦ **to ~ to a movement/to the support of sb** se rallier à un mouvement/à la cause de qn ♦ **to go ~ing** (= car rally) faire un or des rallye(s) ♦ **the market rallied** (St Ex) les cours ont repris

COMP **rally car** N voiture f de rallye
rally driver N pilote m de rallye
rally driving N rallye m
rallying call, rallying cry N cri m de ralliement
rallying point N point m de ralliement

► **rally round** **VI** venir en aide
VT FUS ♦ **during her husband's illness everyone rallied round her** pendant la maladie de son mari tout le monde est venu lui apporter son soutien

rally² /ˈrælɪ/ **VT** (= tease) taquiner, se moquer (gentiment) de

rallycross /ˈrælɪkrɒs/ **N** (NonC) rallye-cross m

RAM /ræm/ **N** (Comput) (abbrev of **random access memory**) RAM f inv **COMP** **RAM chip** N barrette f mémoire

ram /ræm/ **N** bélier m (also Astron) ; (Tech) hie f, dame f ; [of pile driver] mouton m ; (for water) bélier m hydraulique ; → **battering**

VT 1 (= push down) enfoncer (avec force) ; (= pack down) tasser (into dans) ♦ **he ~med a newspaper into the pipe** il a enfoncé un journal dans le tuyau ♦ **he ~med the clothes into the case** il a entassé les vêtements dans la valise ♦ **to ~ a charge home** (Mil, Min) refouler une charge ♦ **to ~ home an argument** enfoncer le clou ♦ **it is up to parents to ~ home the dangers to their children** c'est aux parents d'inculquer cette notion de danger à leurs enfants ♦ **to ~ sth down sb's throat** rebattre les oreilles à qn de qch ♦ **to ~ sth into sb's head** enfoncer qch dans la tête or dans le crâne de qn

2 (= crash into) [+ another ship] heurter (de l'avant or par l'étrave) ; (in battle) éperonner ; [+ another vehicle] emboutir ; [+ post, tree] percuter (contre)

COMP **ram raid** N casse-bélier* m (cambriolage éclair réalisé à l'aide d'une voiture lancée dans une vitrine)
ram raider N auteur m d'un casse-bélier*
ram raiding N pillage de magasins avec une voiture-bélier

► **ram down** **VT SEP** [+ earth] tasser ; (Tech) damer ; [+ piles] enfoncer ♦ **his hat ~med down over his ears** le chapeau enfoncé jusqu'aux oreilles

► **ram in** **VT SEP** enfoncer

Ramadan /ˌræməˈdɑːn/ **N** ramadan m ♦ **in** or **at ~** pendant le ramadan ♦ **to observe ~** faire le ramadan

ramble /ˈræmbl/ **N** randonnée f (pédestre) ♦ **to go for a ~** faire une randonnée ♦ **to go on a ~** partir en randonnée **VI** 1 (= wander about) se promener au hasard ; (also **go rambling**) (= go on hike) partir en randonnée f (pédestre) 2 (pej: in speech: also **ramble on**) parler pour ne rien dire ; [old person] radoter ♦ **he ~d on for half an hour** il a discouru or n'a cessé de discourir pendant une demi-heure

rambler /ˈræmbləʳ/ **N** 1 (Brit = hiker) randonneur m, -euse f, promeneur m, -euse f 2 (also **rambler rose**) rosier m grimpant

rambling /ˈræmblɪŋ/ **ADJ** 1 (= extensive) [building] construit de manière anarchique ; [garden] vaste et chaotique ; [plant] qui pousse en tous sens 2 (pej = confused) [conversation, story, speech, letter] sans queue ni tête ; [person] qui divague **N** 1 (= incoherent speech) divagations fpl, radotages mpl 2 (= walking in country) randonnée f (pédestre) ♦ **to go ~** partir en randonnée
COMP **rambling club** N club m de randonnée
rambling rose N rosier m grimpant

Ramboesque* /ˌræmbəʊˈesk/ **ADJ** digne de Rambo

rambunctious /ræmˈbʌŋkʃəs/ **ADJ** (US) ⇒ **rumbustious**

RAMC /ˌɑːreɪemˈsiː/ **N** (Brit) (abbrev of **Royal Army Medical Corps**) service de santé de l'armée britannique

ramekin /ˈræmɪkɪn/ **N** ramequin m

ramification /ˌræmɪfɪˈkeɪʃən/ **N** (= complexities, consequences) ramification f

ramify /ˈræmɪfaɪ/ **VT** ramifier **VI** se ramifier

ramjet /ˈræmdʒet/ **N** [of plane] statoréacteur m

rammer /ˈræməʳ/ **N** (Tech) dame f, hie f ; [of cannon] refouloir m

ramp /ræmp/ **N** rampe f ; (in road: for speed control) ralentisseur m ; (in garage etc) pont m de graissage ♦ **(approach** or **boarding) ~** (to plane) passerelle f ♦ **hydraulic ~** (in garage) pont m élévateur ♦ **"ramp"** (sign on road) (= speed bump) "ralentisseur" ; (= uneven road surface) "chaussée déformée"

rampage /ˈræmpeɪdʒ/ **N** ♦ **to be** or **go on the ~** se déchaîner ; (= looting etc) tout saccager **VI** /ræmˈpeɪdʒ/ (also **rampage about, rampage around**) se déchaîner

rampancy /ˈræmpənsɪ/ **N** [of plants] exubérance f ; (fig) [of evil etc] déchaînement m

rampant /ˈræmpənt/ **ADJ** 1 [vegetation] luxuriant ; [inflation] galopant ; [crime, disease, corruption] endémique ♦ **to be** or **run ~** (gen) sévir ; [person] avoir la bride sur le cou 2 (Her) **a lion ~** un lion rampant

> ⚠ **rampant** only corresponds to the French word **rampant** in the heraldic sense.

rampart /ˈræmpɑːt/ **N** (lit, fig) rempart m

rampike /ˈræmpaɪk/ **N** (US) arbre m mort (debout)

ramrod /ˈræmrɒd/ **N** [of gun] baguette f ; [of cannon] refouloir m **COMP** **ramrod straight** ADJ raide or droit comme un piquet

ramshackle /ˈræmˌʃækl/ **ADJ** [building] délabré, branlant ; [table] branlant ; [machine] (tout) déglingué* ; [system] délabré ; [alliance, coalition, collection] fragile, précaire ♦ **a ~ old car** une vieille guimbarde

RAN /ˌɑːreɪˈen/ **N** abbrev of **Royal Australian Navy**

ran /ræn/ **VB** pt of **run**

ranch /rɑːntʃ/ **N** ranch m
COMP **ranch hand** N ouvrier m agricole
ranch house, ranch-type house N maison f style ranch ; → HOUSE

rancher /ˈrɑːntʃəʳ/ **N** (US) (= owner) propriétaire mf de ranch ; (= employee) cow-boy m

ranching /ˈrɑːntʃɪŋ/ **N** (US) élevage m en ranch

rancid /ˈrænsɪd/ **ADJ** rance ♦ **to go ~** rancir, devenir rance ♦ **to taste ~** avoir un goût de rance

rancidity /rænˈsɪdɪtɪ/, **rancidness** /ˈrænsɪdnɪs/ **N** rance m

rancor /ˈræŋkəʳ/ **N** (US) ⇒ **rancour**

rancorous /ˈræŋkərəs/ **ADJ** (frm) [person] rancunier ; [argument] plein de rancœur

rancour, rancor (US) /ˈræŋkəʳ/ **N** rancœur f, rancune f

rand /rænd/ **N** (pl inv = monetary unit) rand m

R & B /ˌɑːrənˈbiː/ **N** (abbrev of **rhythm and blues**) → **rhythm**

R & D /ˌɑːrənˈdiː/ **N** (abbrev of **research and development**) R&D f

random /ˈrændəm/ **ADJ** [selection, sampling] aléatoire ; [attack, killings] aveugle ♦ **~ bullet** balle f perdue ♦ **~ sample** échantillon m pris au hasard
♦ **at random** au hasard, à l'aveuglette (pej) ♦ **chosen at ~** choisi au hasard ♦ **to walk about at ~** se promener à l'aventure ♦ **to hit out at ~** lancer des coups à l'aveuglette
COMP **random access** N (Comput) accès m sélectif or aléatoire
random access memory N (Comput) mémoire f vive
random number N nombre m aléatoire

randomization /ˈrændəmaɪˌzeɪʃən/ **N** (Stat) randomisation f, hasardisation f

randomize /ˈrændəmaɪz/ **VT** (Stat) randomiser

randomly /ˈrændəmlɪ/ **ADV** au hasard, à l'aveuglette (pej)

R & R /ˌɑːrəndˈɑːʳ/ **N** (US Mil) (abbrev of **rest and recreation**) permission f ♦ **for a bit of ~*** pour se la couler douce*, pour se détendre

randy* /ˈrændɪ/ **ADJ** (Brit) (= aroused) excité ; (by nature) porté sur la chose ♦ **to make sb ~** exciter qn ♦ **to feel ~** être tout excité ♦ **he's a ~ sod** ‡ c'est un chaud lapin* ♦ **he's a ~ old devil** c'est un vieux cochon*

ranee /ˈrɑːniː/ **N** ⇒ **rani**

rang /ræŋ/ **VB** pt of **ring²**

range /reɪndʒ/ **N** 1 (= extent between limits) [of temperature] écarts mpl, variations fpl ; [of prices] fourchette f ; [of salaries] échelle f ; [of musical instrument, voice] étendue f, registre m

2 (= selection) [of colours, feelings, speeds, goods, patterns] gamme f ♦ **available in a wide ~ of colours and patterns** disponible dans une vaste gamme de coloris et de motifs ♦ **there will be a wide ~ of subjects** il y aura un grand choix de sujets ♦ **they discussed a ~ of issues** ils ont parlé de sujets divers ♦ **a car/house at the lower end of the ~** (Comm) une voiture/maison bas de gamme ♦ **the ~ includes chests of drawers, tables and wardrobes** la gamme comporte des commodes, des tables et des armoires

3 (= scope, distance covered) [of telescope, gun, missile] portée f ; [of plane, ship, mooncraft] rayon m d'action, autonomie f ♦ **at a ~ of ...** à une distance de ... ♦ **at long ~** à longue portée ♦ **to find the ~** (Mil) régler son tir ♦ **to be out of ~** (lit, fig) être hors de portée ♦ **within (firing) ~** à portée de tir ♦ **within my ~** (fig) à ma portée ♦ ~

of vision champ *m* visuel ; → **free, long¹, shooting**

4 *(= domain, sphere) [of activity]* champ *m*, rayon *m* ; *[of influence]* sphère *f* ; *[of knowledge]* étendue *f* ◆ **the ~ of his ideas is limited** le cercle de ses idées est restreint

5 *[of mountains]* chaîne *f* ; *(= row)* rangée *f*, rang *m*

6 *[of animal, plant]* habitat *m*, région *f*

7 (also **shooting range**) *(Mil)* champ *m* de tir ; *(at fair)* stand *m* (de tir) ; → **rifle²**

8 *(Surv)* direction *f*, alignement *m* ◆ **in ~ with** dans l'alignement *or* le prolongement de

9 (also **kitchen range**) cuisinière *f (à l'ancienne)*

10 *(US = grazing land)* prairie *f*, (grand) pâturage *m*

VT 1 *(= place in a row) [+ objects]* ranger ; *[+ troops]* aligner ◆ **books had been ~d on shelves on the walls** on avait rangé des livres sur des étagères, contre le mur ◆ **to ~ o.s. on the side of ...** *(fig)* se ranger du côté de ... ◆ **the prisoners were ~d along one wall of the cave** les prisonniers étaient alignés contre une paroi de la grotte ◆ **they ~d themselves along the pavement to see the procession** ils se sont postés le long du trottoir pour regarder le défilé ◆ **the boys ~d themselves in rows** les garçons se sont mis en rangs

2 *(= classify)* ranger, classer *(among* parmi)

3 *(= roam over)* parcourir ◆ **he ~d the whole country looking for ...** il a parcouru le pays à la recherche de ... ◆ **to ~ the seas** parcourir *or* sillonner les mers

4 *(= direct) [+ gun, telescope]* braquer *(on* sur)

VI 1 *(= extend) [discussion, quest]* s'étendre *(from ... to* de ... à ; *over* sur) ; *[results, opinions]* aller *(from ... to* de ... à), varier *(from ... to* entre ... et) ◆ **the search ~d over the whole country** les recherches se sont étendues sur tout le pays ◆ **the numbers ~ from 10 to 20** les numéros vont de 10 à 20 ◆ **the temperature ~s from 18° to 24°** *or* **between 18° and 24°** la température varie entre 18° et 24° ◆ **researches ranging over a wide field** *(fig)* recherches qui embrassent un large domaine

2 *(= roam)* errer, vagabonder ◆ **to ~ over the area** parcourir la région ◆ **animals ranging across the savannah** des animaux qui parcourent la savane

3 ◆ **to ~ over** *[guns, missiles, shells]* avoir une portée de, porter à

rangefinder /ˈreɪndʒfaɪndəʳ/ **N** *(Mil, Naut, Phot)* télémètre *m* ◆ **~ camera** appareil *m* à visée télémétrique

rangeland /ˈreɪndʒlænd/ **N** *(US)* prairie *f*

ranger /ˈreɪndʒəʳ/ **N** 1 (also **forest ranger**) garde *m* forestier ; → **park** 2 *(US = mounted patrolman)* gendarme *m* à cheval ◆ **~s** *(US)* gendarmerie *f* à cheval **COMP Ranger (Guide)** **N** guide *f* aînée

Rangoon /ræŋˈguːn/ **N** Rangoon

rangy /ˈreɪndʒɪ/ **ADJ** grand et élancé, sans une once de graisse

rani /ˈrɑːniː/ **N** rani *f*

rank¹ /ræŋk/ **N** 1 *(= row)* rang *m* ; *(Brit:* also **taxi rank**) station *f* de taxis ◆ **the taxi at the head of the ~** le taxi en tête de file ◆ **to break ~s** *[soldiers]* rompre les rangs ; *(fig) [splinter group]* faire bande à part ◆ **to serve in the ~s** servir dans les rangs ◆ **other ~s** *(Brit Mil)* les sous-officiers *mpl* et hommes *mpl* de troupe ◆ **the ~ and file** *(Mil)* les hommes de troupe ; *(fig)* la masse, le peuple ◆ **the ~ and file of the party** *(Pol)* la base du parti ◆ **the ~ and file workers** la base, les ouvriers *mpl* ◆ **to rise from the ~s** sortir du rang ◆ **they were drawn from the ~s of the unemployed** on les avait tirés des rangs des chômeurs ; → **close², reduce**

2 *(Mil = grade)* grade *m*, rang *m* ◆ **to reach the ~ of general** atteindre le grade de général ; → **pull**

3 *(= class, position)* rang *m* (social) ◆ **people of all ~s** gens *mpl* de toutes conditions ◆ **a person of ~** une personne de haut rang ◆ **a singer of the first ~** un chanteur de (tout) premier ordre ◆ **a second-~ painter** un peintre de seconde zone *or* de deuxième ordre

4 *(Gram)* rang *m*

5 *[of organ]* rang *m*

VT 1 *(= place)* classer ◆ **I ~ it as one of the best red wines** je le classe parmi les meilleurs vins rouges ◆ **I ~ Beethoven among the great** je compte Beethoven parmi les grands ◆ **to be ~ed high/low in class** *(US Scol)* avoir un bon/mauvais classement

2 *(US Mil)* ⇒ **outrank**

VI compter ◆ **he ~s among my friends** il compte parmi mes amis ◆ **to ~ above/below sb** être supérieur (-eure *f*)/inférieur (-eure *f*) à qn ◆ **to ~ high among ...** occuper un rang élevé parmi ... ◆ **the British team only ~ed tenth on the medals table** l'équipe britannique n'était que dixième au tableau des médaillés ◆ **the country ~s as one of the poorest in the world** ce pays compte parmi les plus pauvres du monde ◆ **it ~s with the best films of the decade** il se classe parmi les meilleurs films de la décennie ; see also **ranking**

rank² /ræŋk/ **ADJ** 1 *(= absolute) [outsider, amateur]* parfait *before n* ; *[prejudice, treachery]* pur *before n* ; *[beginner]* pur, parfait ; *[injustice]* criant, flagrant ; *[insolence]* caractérisé 2 *(pej = pungent) [smell, breath, dustbin, drains]* fétide ; *[room]* nauséabond 3 *(= luxuriant) [vegetation, plants]* luxuriant ; *[weeds, grass]* touffu ◆ **the lawns were ~ with weeds** les pelouses étaient envahies par les mauvaises herbes

ranker /ˈræŋkəʳ/ **N** *(Mil)* *(= soldier)* simple soldat *m* ; *(= officer)* officier *m* sorti du rang

ranking /ˈræŋkɪŋ/ **N** classement *m* ◆ **he currently holds the number two ~ in world golf** il occupe actuellement la deuxième place au classement mondial de golf **NPL rankings** *(Sport)* classement *m* officiel **ADJ** 1 *(in hierarchy) (Mil, Admin)* ◆ **high-~** de haut rang *or* grade ◆ **low-~** de rang *or* grade inférieur ◆ **middle-~** de rang *or* grade intermédiaire ◆ **the ~ officer** *(Mil)* l'officier *m* responsable *or* le plus haut en grade 2 *(esp US = prominent)* le plus haut placé ◆ **the ~ member of the committee** le membre le plus haut placé du comité ◆ **the ~ American diplomat in Baghdad** le plus haut diplomate américain de Baghdad

rankle /ˈræŋkl/ **VI** rester sur le cœur *(with* à) ◆ **it ~d with him** il l'avait sur le cœur, ça lui était resté sur le cœur

rankness /ˈræŋknɪs/ **N** 1 *(= smell)* odeur *f* fétide ; *(= taste)* goût *m* rance 2 *[of plants etc]* exubérance *f*, luxuriance *f*

rankshifted /ˈræŋkʃɪftɪd/ **ADJ** *(Gram)* déplacé d'une catégorie à une autre

ransack /ˈrænsæk/ **VT** *(= pillage) [+ house, shop]* saccager, piller ; *[+ town, region]* mettre à sac ; *(= search) [+ room, luggage, drawer]* fouiller (à fond), mettre tout sens dessus dessous dans ; *[+ files, one's memory]* fouiller dans *(for* pour trouver)

ransom /ˈrænsəm/ **N** *(lit, fig)* rançon *f* ◆ **to hold sb to ~** mettre qn à rançon ; *(fig)* exercer un chantage sur qn ◆ **they are being held to ~** *(fig)* ils ont le couteau sur la gorge ; → **king VT** racheter

rant /rænt/ **VI** 1 *(pej) [orator etc]* déclamer (de façon exagérée) 2 (also **rant on**) divaguer ◆ **to ~ and rave** tempêter ◆ **to ~ (and rave) at sb** tempêter *or* fulminer contre qn **N** * *(= polemic)* diatribe *f* ◆ **she went into a long ~ about her job** elle s'est lancée dans une longue diatribe sur son travail

ranting /ˈræntɪŋ/ **N** tirade(s) *f(pl)* **ADJ** *[person]* qui vocifère ; *[style]* déclamatoire

ranunculus /rəˈnʌŋkjʊləs/ **N** (pl **ranunculuses** *or* **ranunculi** /rəˈnʌŋkjʊˌlaɪ/) renoncule *f*

rap /ræp/ **N** 1 *(= noise)* petit coup *m* sec ; *(= blow)* tape *f* ◆ **there was a ~ at the door** on a frappé bruyamment à la porte ◆ **to give sb a ~ on the knuckles** donner un coup sur les doigts à qn ; *(fig = rebuke)* taper sur les doigts de qn ◆ **I don't care a ~** * je m'en fiche * éperdument

2 *(esp US* * *)* *(= criminal charge)* inculpation *f* ; *(= prison sentence)* condamnation *f* ◆ **to beat the ~** échapper à une condamnation ◆ **to hang a murder ~ on sb** faire endosser un meurtre à qn ◆ **to take the ~** * *(= blame)* se faire taper sur les doigts * ◆ **to get the ~** * **for sth** *(US)* trinquer * *or* écoper * pour qch

3 *(Mus)* rap *m*

4 *(US* * *= chat)* causette * *f*, conversation *f*

VT *[+ door]* frapper bruyamment à ; *[+ table]* frapper sur ◆ **to ~ sb's knuckles, to ~ sb over the knuckles** taper sur les doigts de qn ◆ **to get one's knuckles ~ped, to be ~ped over the knuckles** *(fig)* se faire taper sur les doigts

VI 1 *(= knock)* frapper, donner un coup sec ; *(fig) (= rebuke)* blâmer, réprouver

2 *(esp US* * *= chat)* tailler une bavette *, bavarder

3 *(Mus)* rapper

COMP rap artist N rappeur *m*, -euse *f*

rap music N musique *f* rap

rap session * **N** *(US = chat)* discussion *f* à bâtons rompus

rap sheet N *(US = police record)* casier *m* judiciaire

► **rap out VT SEP** 1 *(= say curtly)* dire brusquement ; *[+ oath]* lâcher ; *[+ order, retort]* lancer

2 *(Spiritualism) [+ message]* communiquer *or* annoncer au moyen de coups

rapacious /rəˈpeɪʃəs/ **ADJ** rapace

rapaciously /rəˈpeɪʃəslɪ/ **ADV** avec rapacité *or* avidité

rapacity /rəˈpæsɪtɪ/ **N** rapacité *f*, avidité *f*

rape¹ /reɪp/ **N** (also *Jur*) viol *m* ; († *= abduction)* ravissement † *m*, rapt *m* **VT** violer **COMP rape crisis centre N** centre *m* d'aide aux victimes de viols

rape² /reɪp/ **N** *(= plant)* colza *m*

COMP rape oil N huile *f* de colza

rape seed N graine *f* de colza

rape³ /reɪp/ **N** *(= grape pulp)* marc *m* de raisin ; *(= wine)* râpé *m*

Raphael /ˈræfeɪəl/ **N** Raphaël *m*

rapid /ˈræpɪd/ **ADJ** rapide **NPL rapids** *(in river)* rapides *mpl* ◆ **they ran the ~s** ils ont franchi les rapides

COMP rapid deployment force N *(Mil)* ⇒ **rapid reaction force**

rapid eye movement N mouvements *mpl* oculaires rapides *(pendant le sommeil paradoxal)* ; → **REM**

rapid eye movement sleep N sommeil *m* paradoxal

rapid fire N *(Mil)* tir *m* rapide ◆ **a hail of ~ fire** une pluie *or* une grêle de balles ◆ **~ fire of questions** feu *m* roulant de questions

rapid reaction force N *(Mil)* force *f* d'intervention rapide

rapid transit (system) N *(US)* métro *m*

rapidity /rəˈpɪdɪtɪ/ **N** rapidité *f*

rapidly /ˈræpɪdlɪ/ **ADV** rapidement

rapier /ˈreɪpɪəʳ/ **N** rapière *f* **ADJ** *[wit etc]* mordant **COMP rapier thrust N** *(lit)* coup *m* de pointe ; *(fig)* remarque *f* mordante

rapine /ˈræpaɪn/ **N** rapine *f*

rapist /ˈreɪpɪst/ **N** *(Jur)* violeur *m*

rappel /ræ'pel/ (US) VI descendre en rappel N (descente f en) rappel m

rapper /'ræpəʳ/ N (Mus) rappeur m, -euse f

rapping /'ræpɪŋ/ N (NonC) 1 (= noise) coups mpl secs et durs 2 (Mus) rap m

rapport /ræ'pɔːʳ/ N bonnes relations fpl (with avec ; between entre) ; ◆ **to establish a ~ with sb** établir une relation avec qn ◆ **I had a real ~ with my uncle** mon oncle et moi étions très complices or avions une relation très complice ◆ **in ~ with** en harmonie avec

> ⚠ In French, the word **rapport** simply means 'relationship', and does not have the connotations **rapport** has in English.

rapprochement /ræ'prɒʃmɑːŋ/ N rapprochement m (fig)

rapscallion † /ræp'skælɪən/ N vaurien m, mauvais garnement m

rapt /ræpt/ ADJ [concentration, silence] profond ; [interest] profond, intense ; [person, expression] captivé ◆ **~ in contemplation/in thought** plongé dans la contemplation/dans ses pensées ◆ **~ with wonder** émerveillé ◆ **~ with attention** captivé ◆ **she listened with ~ attention** elle écoutait, captivée

raptor /'ræptəʳ/ N (= bird of prey) rapace m

rapture /'ræptʃəʳ/ N (= delight) ravissement m, enchantement m ◆ **to be in ~s over** or **about** [+ object] être ravi or enchanté de ; [+ person] être en extase devant ◆ **to go into ~s over** or **about sth/sb** s'extasier sur qch/qn

rapturous /'ræptʃərəs/ ADJ [applause] frénétique ; [reception] enthousiaste ; [welcome] enthousiaste, délirant ; (liter) [exclamation] de ravissement, d'extase

rapturously /'ræptʃərəslɪ/ ADV [greet, listen] avec ravissement ; [applaud] avec frénésie

ra-ra skirt /'rɑːrɑː,skɜːt/ N jupe f à falbalas

rare /reəʳ/ ADJ 1 (= uncommon, infrequent) (gen) rare ; [opportunity] unique ◆ **on the ~ occasions when he spoke** les rares fois où il a parlé ◆ **with ~ exceptions** à de rares exceptions près ◆ **it is ~ for her to come** il est rare qu'elle vienne ◆ **to grow ~(r)** [animals, plants] se raréfier ; [visits] s'espacer ◆ **a man who remembers birthdays is a ~ bird indeed** un homme qui se souvient des anniversaires est un oiseau rare ◆ **to have a ~ old time** †* (Brit) s'amuser comme un fou or une folle* 2 (Culin) [meat] saignant ◆ **a very ~ steak** un bifteck bleu ; → **medium** 3 (= rarefied) [atmosphere] raréfié ◆ **to grow ~(r)** se raréfier COMP **rare earth** N (Chem) terre f rare

rarebit /'reəbɪt/ N → **Welsh**

rarefaction /,reərɪ'fækʃən/ N raréfaction f

rarefied /'reərɪfaɪd/ ADJ (lit) raréfié ; (fig) (= isolated) à part ; (= insular) très fermé ◆ **the ~ world of particle physics** le monde à part de la physique des particules ◆ **outside the rarified world of architecture** en dehors de l'univers très fermé de l'architecture ◆ **the ~ atmosphere of university** le milieu élitiste de l'université ◆ **to become ~** se raréfier

rarefy /'reərɪfaɪ/ VT raréfier VI se raréfier

rarely /'reəlɪ/ ADV rarement

rareness /'reənɪs/ N rareté f

raring * /'reərɪŋ/ ADJ ◆ **to be ~ to go** être très impatient de commencer, ronger son frein ◆ **to be ~ to do sth** être très impatient or brûler de faire qch

rarity /'reərɪtɪ/ N (= scarcity) rareté f ; (= rare thing) chose f rare ◆ **the ~ of such attacks** la rareté de telles attaques ◆ **rain is a ~ here** la pluie est rare ici COMP **rarity value** N ◆ **to have ~ value** avoir de la valeur de par sa rareté

rascal /'rɑːskəl/ N 1 (= scamp) polisson(ne) m(f), fripon(ne) m(f) 2 († = scoundrel) coquin m, vaurien m

rascally /'rɑːskəlɪ/ ADJ ◆ **a ~ lawyer/merchant** un gredin d'avocat/de marchand ◆ **a ~ trick** un tour pendable

rash¹ /ræʃ/ N 1 (Med: gen) rougeur f, éruption f ; (from food etc) (plaques fpl d')urticaire f ; (in measles etc) éruption f, taches fpl rouges ◆ **to come out** or **break out in a ~** avoir une éruption ; → **heat, nettlerash** 2 (fig) [of strikes, attacks etc] éruption f

rash² /ræʃ/ ADJ [person] imprudent ; [action, behaviour, words, decision, promise] imprudent, irréfléchi ◆ **don't be ~!** sois prudent ! ◆ **don't do anything ~!** ne commets pas d'imprudences ! ◆ **in a ~ moment** dans un moment d'égarement ◆ **it was ~ of him to do that** il s'est montré très imprudent en faisant cela

rasher /'ræʃəʳ/ N (Brit) (mince) tranche f (de bacon)

rashly /'ræʃlɪ/ ADV [behave, act, offer, promise] imprudemment, sans réfléchir

rashness /'ræʃnɪs/ N imprudence f

rasp /rɑːsp/ N (= tool) râpe f ; (= noise) grincement m VT 1 (with tool) râper 2 (= speak: also **rasp out**) dire or crier d'une voix râpeuse VI grincer

raspberry /'rɑːzbərɪ/ N (= fruit) framboise f ◆ **to blow a ~*** faire pfft (pour exprimer son mépris) ◆ **to blow a ~ at sth*** descendre qch en flammes* ◆ **to get a ~ from*** se faire rabrouer or rembarrer par COMP [ice cream, tart] (à la) framboise inv ; [jam] de framboise
raspberry bush, raspberry cane N framboisier m

rasping /'rɑːspɪŋ/ ADJ [sound] de râpe ; [voice] râpeux ; [breath] haletant N (= sound) grincement m

Rasputin /ræ'spjuːtɪn/ N Raspoutine m

raspy /'rɑːspɪ/ ADJ ⇒ **rasping adj**

Rasta /'ræstə/ N, ADJ (abbrev of **Rastafarian**) rasta mf inv

Rastafarian /,ræstə'feərɪən/ N, ADJ rastafari mf inv

Rastafarianism /,ræstə'feərɪənɪzəm/ N rastafarianisme m

rat /ræt/ N (= animal) rat m ; (* pej = person) dégueulasse* m, salaud‡ m ; (= informer) mouchard(e) m(f) ; (* = blackleg) jaune m ; (*: abandoning friends) lâcheur* m, -euse* f ◆ **he's a dirty ~*** c'est un salaud‡ or une ordure‡ ◆ **you ~!*** espèce de dégueulasse !‡, espèce de salaud !‡ ◆ **~s!** † * (Brit expressing irritation) zut alors !* ◆ **the ~s are leaving the sinking ship** (fig) les rats quittent le navire ; → **smell**
VI 1 ◆ **to go ~ting** faire la chasse aux rats
2 **to ~ on sb** * (= inform on) donner qn, balancer qn* ; (= desert) lâcher qn*
COMP **rat-arsed** *‡ ADJ (Brit) bituré‡ ◆ **to get ~-arsed** se biturer‡
rat-catcher N chasseur m de rats
rat-catching N chasse f aux rats ; (= extermination) dératisation f
rat fink ‡ N (US) salaud‡ m, vache* f
rat poison N mort-aux-rats f inv
rat race N ambiance f de compétition acharnée ◆ **I decided I had to get out of the ~ race** j'ai décidé que je devais quitter cette vie de fou
rat run * N (Brit fig) raccourci m
rats' tails * NPL (pej) ◆ **her hair was in ~s' tails** des mèches de cheveux pendaient dans son cou
rat-trap N piège m à rats, ratière f

ratable /'reɪtəbl/ ADJ ⇒ **rateable**

rat-a-tat /'rætə'tæt/, **rat-a-tat-tat** /'rætə,tæt'tæt/ N (at door) toc toc m ; (of gunfire) ta ta ta ta m ; (on drum) rantanplan m

ratatouille /,rætə'twiː/ N ratatouille f

ratbag ‡ /'rætbæg/ N peau f de vache*

ratchet /'rætʃɪt/ N (= mechanism) rochet m COMP **ratchet wheel** N roue f à rochet
► **ratchet up** VI, VT SEP (esp US) augmenter

rate¹ /reɪt/ N 1 (= ratio, proportion) taux m ; (= speed) vitesse f, rythme m ◆ **birth/death ~** taux m de natalité/mortalité ◆ **the failure/success ~ for this exam is high** il y a un pourcentage élevé d'échecs/de réussites à cet examen ◆ **~ of consumption** taux m de consommation ◆ **~ of flow** [of electricity, water] débit m (moyen) ◆ **~ of climb** [of aircraft] vitesse f ascensionnelle ◆ **at the ~ of 100 litres an hour** à raison de 100 litres par heure ◆ **to pay sb at the ~ of €10 per hour** payer qn à raison de 10 € de l'heure ◆ **at a ~ of ...** (= speed) à une vitesse de ... ◆ **at a great ~, at a ~ of knots*** à fond de train*, à toute allure ◆ **to go at a terrific ~** aller à un train d'enfer ◆ **the population is growing at an alarming ~** la population augmente à un rythme inquiétant ◆ **if you continue at this ~** si vous continuez à ce train-là or à ce rythme-là ◆ **at his ~ of working, he'll never finish** au rythme auquel il travaille, il n'aura jamais terminé ◆ **at the ~ you're going, you'll be dead before long** (fig) du train où vous allez, vous ne ferez pas de vieux os ◆ **at this ~, I'll never find a job** si ça continue comme ça, je ne trouverai jamais de travail ◆ **at any ~** en tout cas, de toute façon ◆ **at that ~** à ce compte-là, dans ce cas ; → **first-rate, pulse¹**
2 (Comm, Fin, Econ, Med) taux m ; (Fin) cours m ; (Telec, Post, Transport) tarif m ◆ **~ of exchange** taux m de change, cours m du change ◆ **~ of growth** (Econ) ◆ **growth ~** taux m de croissance ◆ **~ of interest/pay/taxation** taux m d'intérêt/de rémunération/d'imposition ◆ **postage/advertising ~s** tarifs mpl postaux/de publicité ◆ **insurance ~s** primes fpl d'assurance ◆ **there is a reduced ~ for children** les enfants bénéficient d'un tarif réduit or d'une réduction ◆ **basic salary ~** traitement m de base ; → **basic**
NPL **rates** (Brit Fin: formerly = municipal tax) impôts mpl locaux ◆ **~s and taxes** impôts mpl et contributions fpl ◆ **a penny on/off the ~s** une augmentation/réduction d'un pour cent des impôts locaux ; → **water**
VT 1 (= estimate worth of, appraise) [+ object] évaluer (at à) ; (fig = consider) considérer (as comme) ◆ **to ~ sb/sth highly** faire grand cas de qn/qch ◆ **how does he ~ that film?** que pense-t-il de ce film ? ◆ **how do you ~ yourself as an administrator?** comment vous évaluez-vous en tant qu'administrateur ? ◆ **I ~ him amongst my best pupils** je le considère comme un de mes meilleurs élèves, je le compte parmi mes meilleurs élèves ◆ **I really ~ him*** je le trouve vraiment très bon ◆ **I don't really ~ him*** je ne le trouve pas très bon ◆ **I don't ~ any of his family*** je n'ai pas une très haute opinion des membres de sa famille ◆ **how would you ~ your chances of getting a job?** quelles sont vos chances de trouver un emploi, à votre avis ?
2 (Local Govt: formerly) établir le montant des impôts locaux sur
3 (= deserve) mériter ◆ **I think he ~s a pass (mark)** je pense qu'il mérite la moyenne
VI ◆ **he hardly ~s as a strong leader** on ne le considère pas vraiment comme un chef qui a de la poigne ◆ **reading does not ~ highly among children as a hobby** la lecture n'est pas un passe-temps très prisé des enfants
COMP **rate-cap** VT (Brit: formerly) fixer un plafond aux impôts locaux de
rate-capping N (Brit: formerly) plafonnement m des impôts locaux

rate collector N (*Brit: formerly*) receveur *m* municipal
rate rebate N (*Brit: formerly*) dégrèvement *m* (d'impôts locaux)

rate² /reɪt/ VT (*liter*) ⇒ **berate**

rateable /'reɪtəbl/ ADJ [*property*] imposable
COMP **rateable value** N (*Brit: formerly*) loyer *m* matriciel (*Admin*), valeur *f* locative imposable

ratepayer /'reɪtpeɪəʳ/ N (*Brit: formerly*) contribuable *mf* (*payant les impôts locaux*)

rather /'rɑːðəʳ/ LANGUAGE IN USE 7.4 ADV 1 (= *for preference*) plutôt ◆ **I would ~ have the blue dress** je préférerais *or* j'aimerais mieux avoir la robe bleue ◆ **I would much ~ …** je préférerais de beaucoup … ◆ **I would ~ be happy than rich** j'aimerais mieux être heureux que riche ◆ **I would ~ wait here than go** je préférerais attendre ici plutôt que de partir ◆ **I would ~ you came yourself** je préférerais que vous veniez (*subj*) vous-même ◆ **do you mind if I smoke? – I'd ~ you didn't** est-ce que je peux fumer ? – j'aimerais mieux pas ◆ **I'd ~ not** je préfère pas*, j'aime mieux pas* ◆ **I'd ~ not go** j'aimerais mieux ne pas y aller ◆ **I'd ~ die!** plutôt mourir ! ◆ **~ you than me** je ne t'envie pas, je n'irai pas te disputer la place*
◆ **rather than** ◆ **~ than wait, he went away** plutôt que d'attendre, il est parti ◆ **I use the bike if I can ~ than the car** si je peux, je prends le vélo plutôt que la voiture ◆ **the problem was psychological ~ than physiological** le problème était moins physiologique que psychologique, le problème était psychologique et non physiologique ◆ **solid ~ than hollow** plein et non creux
2 (= *more accurately*) plus exactement, plutôt ◆ **a car, or ~ an old banger** une voiture, ou plus exactement *or* ou plutôt une vieille guimbarde ◆ **he isn't on holiday, but ~ out of work** il n'est pas en vacances, mais bien plutôt au chômage
3 (= *to a considerable degree*) plutôt ; (= *to some extent*) un peu ; (= *somewhat*) quelque peu ; (= *fairly*) assez ; (= *slightly*) légèrement ◆ **he's a ~ clever person, he's ~ a clever person** il est plutôt intelligent ◆ **he felt ~ better** il se sentait un peu mieux ◆ **he looked ~ silly** il a eu l'air plutôt stupide ◆ **it's ~ more difficult than you think** c'est un peu plus difficile que vous ne croyez ◆ **Latin is ~ too difficult for me** le latin est un peu trop difficile pour moi ◆ **it's ~ a pity** c'est plutôt dommage ◆ **his book is ~ good** son livre est plutôt bon ◆ **that costs ~ a lot** cela coûte assez cher ◆ **I ~ think he's wrong** je crois bien *or* j'ai l'impression qu'il a tort ◆ **~!** † * (*esp Brit*) et comment !*

ratification /ˌrætɪfɪ'keɪʃən/ N ratification *f*

ratify /'rætɪfaɪ/ VT ratifier

rating¹ /'reɪtɪŋ/ N 1 (= *assessment*) estimation *f*, évaluation *f* ◆ **the government's low ~ in the opinion polls** la mauvaise cote *or* la faiblesse du gouvernement dans les sondages 2 (*Brit Fin* = *tax on property*) montant *m* des impôts locaux 3 (= *placing*) classement *m* 4 (*Brit Naut*) (= *classification*) classe *f* ; (= *sailor*) marin *m*, matelot *m* ◆ **the ~s** les matelots et gradés *mpl* NPL **ratings** ◆ **the (audience** *or* **TV) ~s** l'indice *m* d'écoute, l'audimat® *m* ◆ **to get good ~s** [*programme*] avoir un bon indice d'écoute ◆ **high/low ~s** forts/faibles indices *mpl* d'écoute ◆ **to boost ~s** faire grimper l'indice d'écoute *or* l'audimat®

rating² /'reɪtɪŋ/ N réprimande *f*, semonce *f*

ratio /'reɪʃɪəʊ/ N proportion *f*, rapport *m* ◆ **in the ~ of 100 to 1** dans la proportion de 100 contre 1, dans le rapport de 100 contre *or* à 1 ◆ **inverse** *or* **indirect ~** raison *f* inverse ◆ **in direct ~ to …** en raison directe de …

ratiocinate /ˌrætɪ'ɒsɪneɪt/ VI (*frm*) raisonner, ratiociner (*pej*)

ratiocination /ˌrætɪɒsɪ'neɪʃən/ N (*frm*) raisonnement *m*, ratiocination *f* (*pej*)

ration /'ræʃən/ N (= *allowance: of food, goods etc*) ration *f* ◆ **it's off the ~*** ce n'est plus rationné ◆ **~s** (= *food*) vivres *mpl* ◆ **to put sb on short ~s** réduire les rations de qn ; → **iron** VT [+ *goods, food, people*] rationner ◆ **he was ~ed to 1kg of meat** sa ration était de 1 kg de viande ◆ **motorists were ~ed to 30 litres of petrol a month** les automobilistes n'avaient droit qu'à 30 litres d'essence par mois
COMP **ration book** N carnet *m* de rationnement
ration card N carte *f* *or* ticket *m* de rationnement

► **ration out** VT SEP [+ *food etc*] rationner

rational /'ræʃənl/ ADJ [*person, argument, behaviour*] raisonnable, sensé ; [*creature, being*] doué de raison ; [*action, thinking, explanation, decision*] (*also Math*) rationnel, logique ; [*activity*] rationnel, conforme à la raison ; (*Med*) (= *lucid*) lucide ◆ **that wasn't very ~ of him** il n'a pas agi de façon très logique *or* rationnelle

rationale /ˌræʃə'nɑːl/ N (= *reasoning*) raisons *fpl* ; (= *statement*) exposé *m* raisonné ◆ **what is the ~ behind this decision?** quelles sont les raisons de cette décision ?

rationalism /'ræʃnəlɪzəm/ N rationalisme *m*

rationalist /'ræʃnəlɪst/ ADJ, N rationaliste *mf*

rationalistic /ˌræʃnə'lɪstɪk/ ADJ rationaliste

rationality /ˌræʃə'nælɪtɪ/ N rationalité *f*

rationalization /ˌræʃnəlaɪ'zeɪʃən/ N rationalisation *f*

rationalize /'ræʃnəlaɪz/ VT 1 [+ *event, conduct etc*] (tenter de) trouver une explication logique à ; (*Psych*) justifier *or* motiver après coup 2 (= *organize efficiently*) [+ *industry, production, problems*] rationaliser 3 (*Math*) rendre rationnel VI (*Psych*) chercher une justification après coup

rationally /'ræʃnəlɪ/ ADV [*think, behave, discuss, speak*] rationnellement, de façon rationnelle ◆ **~, it should be possible** logiquement, ça devrait être possible

rationing /'ræʃnɪŋ/ N rationnement *m* ◆ **food ~** rationnement *m* de l'alimentation

ratline /'rætlaɪn/ N (*Naut*) enfléchure *f*

ratpack /'rætpæk/ N (*gen*) jeunes loups *mpl* ; (= *journalists*) paparazzi *mpl*

rattan /ræ'tæn/ N rotin *m* COMP de *or* en rotin

rat-tat-tat /'rætə'tæt/ N ⇒ **rat-a-tat**

ratter /'rætəʳ/ N (= *dog*) ratier *m*

rattiness* /'rætɪnɪs/ N (= *bad temper*) (*in general*) caractère *m* grincheux ; (*on one occasion*) mauvaise humeur *f*

rattle /'rætl/ N 1 (= *sound*) [*of vehicle*] bruit *m* (de ferraille) ; [*of chains, typewriter*] cliquetis *m* ; [*of door*] vibrations *fpl* ; [*of hailstones, machine gun*] crépitement *m* ; [*of rattlesnake*] sonnettes *fpl* ; (*Med*: also **death rattle**) râle *m*
2 (*baby's, gen*) hochet *m* ; (*strung on pram*) boulier *m* (de bébé) ; [*of sports fan*] crécelle *f*
VI [*box, container, object*] faire du bruit ; [*articles in box*] s'entrechoquer ; [*vehicle*] faire un bruit de ferraille ; [*bullets, hailstones*] crépiter ; [*machinery*] cliqueter ; [*window*] trembler ◆ **to ~ at the door** cogner à la porte ◆ **there is something rattling** il y a quelque chose qui cogne ◆ **to ~ along/away** *etc* [*vehicle*] rouler/partir *etc* dans un bruit de ferraille
VT 1 [+ *box*] agiter (avec bruit) ; [+ *cans*] faire s'entrechoquer ; [+ *dice*] agiter, secouer ; [+ *keys*] faire cliqueter ◆ **to ~ sb's cage*** enquiquiner* qn
2 (* = *alarm*) [+ *person*] déconcerter, ébranler ◆ **to get ~d** perdre son sang-froid, paniquer* ◆ **don't get ~d!** pas de panique !*

► **rattle around** VI (*fig*) ◆ **I hate to think of her rattling around on her own in that big house** ça me fait mal au cœur de l'imaginer perdue dans cette grande maison

► **rattle away** VI ⇒ **rattle on**

► **rattle down** VI [*falling stones etc*] dégringoler *or* tomber avec fracas

► **rattle off** VT SEP [+ *poem, speech, apology*] débiter à toute allure

► **rattle on** VI parler sans arrêt (*about sth* de qch), jacasser

► **rattle through** VT FUS faire (*or* écrire *or* lire *etc*) à toute vitesse *or* au grand galop

rattler* /'rætləʳ/ N (*esp US* = *rattlesnake*) serpent *m* à sonnette, crotale *m*

rattlesnake /'rætlsneɪk/ N serpent *m* à sonnette, crotale *m*

rattletrap* /'rætltræp/ N guimbarde *f*, tacot* *m*

rattling /'rætlɪŋ/ N ⇒ **rattle noun 1** ADJ 1 (= *knocking*) bruyant ◆ **I heard a ~ noise** [*of chains, bottles*] j'ai entendu un cliquetis ; (= *knocking sound*) j'ai entendu quelque chose qui cognait 2 (= *fast*) ◆ **at a ~ pace** *or* **speed*** à toute *or* vive allure ADV (*esp Brit*) ◆ **~ good*** sacrément* bon ◆ **a ~ good yarn*** un récit rondement mené

rattrap /'rættræp/ N piège *m* à rats, ratière *f*

ratty* /'rætɪ/ ADJ 1 (*Brit* = *bad-tempered*) grincheux ◆ **don't get ~ with me!** ne passe pas tes nerfs sur moi !* 2 (*US* = *shabby*) [*person, coat*] miteux

raucous /'rɔːkəs/ ADJ [*laughter*] gros (grosse *f*) ; [*song*] bruyant ; [*party, evening*] bruyant, un peu trop animé ; [*person, crowd*] braillard*, tapageur ; [*bird cry*] rauque

raucously /'rɔːkəslɪ/ ADV [*laugh*] bruyamment ◆ **to shout ~** brailler*

raucousness /'rɔːkəsnɪs/ N [*of sound*] son *m* rauque

raunch* /rɔːntʃ/ N (*US*) [*of story, film*] ambiance *f* torride ; [*of song*] paroles *fpl* torrides

raunchy* /'rɔːntʃɪ/ ADJ [*person, clothing*] sexy *inv* ; [*story, film*] torride ; [*song*] paillard, grivois

ravage /'rævɪdʒ/ VT (= *ruin*) ravager, dévaster ; (= *plunder*) ravager, piller ◆ **body ~d by disease** corps *m* ravagé par la maladie NPL **ravages** [*of war etc*] ravages *mpl*, dévastation *f* ◆ **the ~s of time** les ravages *mpl* du temps, l'outrage *m* des ans

rave /reɪv/ VI (= *be delirious*) délirer, divaguer ; (= *talk wildly*) divaguer, déraisonner ; (= *speak furiously*) s'emporter, tempêter (*at, against* contre) ; (= *speak enthusiastically*) s'extasier (*about, over* sur), parler avec enthousiasme (*about, over* de) → **rant** N (*Brit* = *Acid House party*) rave *f*
COMP **rave culture** N (*NonC: Mus*) culture *f* rave
rave notice*, **rave review*** N critique *f* dithyrambique
rave-up* N (*Brit* = *wild party*) ◆ **to have a ~-up** faire la foire* *or* la fête*

► **rave up*** VT SEP ◆ **to rave it up** faire la foire* *or* la fête* N ◆ **rave-up*** → **rave**

ravel /'rævəl/ VT 1 (= *entangle: lit, fig*) emmêler, embrouiller, enchevêtrer 2 (= *disentangle*) ⇒ **ravel out vt sep** VI (= *become tangled*) s'embrouiller, s'enchevêtrer ; (= *fray*) s'effilocher

► **ravel out** VI s'effilocher VT SEP [+ *material*] effilocher ; [+ *threads*] démêler ; [+ *knitting*] défaire ; (*fig*) [+ *difficulty*] débrouiller ; [+ *plot*] dénouer

raven /'reɪvn/ N corbeau *m*
COMP (*in colour*) noir comme (du) jais *or* comme l'ébène
raven-haired ADJ aux cheveux de jais

ravening /'rævnɪŋ/ ADJ vorace, rapace

Ravenna /rə'venə/ N Ravenne

ravenous /ˈrævənəs/ ADJ *[animal]* vorace ; *[appetite]* vorace, féroce ; *[hunger]* de loup ◆ **I'm ~** * j'ai une faim de loup

ravenously /ˈrævənəslɪ/ ADV *[eat]* voracement, avec voracité ; *[look at]* d'un air vorace ◆ **to be ~ hungry** * avoir une faim de loup

raver * /ˈreɪvəʳ/ N *(Brit)* 1 *(gen)* noceur* *m*, -euse* *f*, fêtard(e)* *m(f)* 2 *(= person attending a rave)* raver* *m*

ravine /rəˈviːn/ N ravin *m*

raving /ˈreɪvɪŋ/ ADJ * ◆ **~ lunatic** fou *m* furieux, folle *f* furieuse ◆ **she's a ~ beauty** elle est d'une beauté éblouissante ; → **mad** N ◆ **~(s)** délire *m*, divagations *fpl*

ravioli /ˌrævɪˈəʊlɪ/ N raviolis *mpl*

ravish /ˈrævɪʃ/ VT 1 *(liter = delight)* ravir, transporter 2 (†† *or liter*) *(= rape)* violer ; *(= abduct)* ravir

ravisher /ˈrævɪʃəʳ/ N (†† *or liter*) ravisseur *m*

ravishing /ˈrævɪʃɪŋ/ ADJ *[woman]* ravissant ; *[man]* beau comme un dieu ; *[sight, beauty]* enchanteur (-teresse *f*) ; *[smile]* ravageur ◆ **to be ~ to look at** être un régal pour les yeux

ravishingly /ˈrævɪʃɪŋlɪ/ ADV ◆ **she is ~ beautiful** elle est d'une beauté éblouissante ◆ **the scenery is ~ beautiful** le paysage est magnifique ◆ **the film is ~ photographed** les prises de vue du film sont superbes

ravishment /ˈrævɪʃmənt/ N 1 *(liter = delight)* enchantement *m*, ravissement *m* 2 (†† *or liter*) *(= rape)* viol *m* ; *(= abduction)* ravissement † *m*, rapt *m*

raw /rɔː/ ADJ 1 *(= uncooked)* *[meat, fish, vegetables, egg]* cru

2 *(= unprocessed)* *[cotton, rubber, sugar, data, facts]* brut ; *[cloth]* écru ; *[alcohol, spirits]* pur ; *[sewage]* non traité ◆ **~ colour** couleur *f* crue ◆ **~ edge** *(Sewing)* bord *m* coupé

3 *(= basic)* *[emotion, ambition, energy, talent]* à l'état brut

4 *(= sore)* *[hands, back, skin]* abîmé ; *[wound, nerves]* à vif ; *[throat]* très irrité ◆ **his wife's words touched a ~ nerve** les paroles de sa femme ont touché la corde sensible

5 *(= inexperienced)* *[person]* sans expérience, inexpérimenté ; *[troops]* non aguerri ◆ **a ~ recruit** *(Mil)* un bleu

6 *(= cold)* *[night, day, climate]* glacial ; *[wind]* âpre ; *[air]* vif

7 *(= frank)* *[account]* sans complaisance ; *[story]* sans fard

8 *(= bawdy)* *[humour]* cru, grossier

9 (* *= unfair*) ◆ **he got a ~ deal** on ne lui a vraiment pas fait de cadeaux* ◆ **he's had a ~ deal from life** il n'a pas été gâté par la vie*

N ◆ **to touch sb on the ~** toucher *or* piquer qn au vif ◆ **life/nature in the ~** la vie/la nature telle qu'elle est ◆ **in the ~** * *(= naked)* nu, à poil*

COMP **raw material** N *(lit, fig)* matière *f* première

raw score N *(US Scol)* première approximation *f* de note

raw silk N soie *f* grège

rawboned /ˈrɔːbəʊnd/ ADJ *[person]* maigre, décharné ; *[horse]* efflanqué

rawhide /ˈrɔːhaɪd/ N *(= whip)* fouet *m* à lanières ; *(= material)* cuir *m* brut *or* vert

Rawlbolt ® /ˈrɔːlbəʊlt/ N *cheville d'ancrage en métal*

Rawlplug ® /ˈrɔːlplʌg/ N *cheville en plastique*

rawness /ˈrɔːnɪs/ N 1 *(= lack of experience)* inexpérience *f* 2 *(= primitive nature)* ◆ **the ~ of the music** le caractère primitif de la musique 3 *(on skin)* écorchure *f* 4 *[of climate]* froid *m* humide ◆ **the ~ of the wind** l'âpreté *f* du vent

ray[1] /reɪ/ N *[of light, heat, sun]* rayon *m* ; *(fig)* rayon *m*, lueur *f* ◆ **a ~ of hope** une lueur d'espoir ; → **cathode, death, X-ray** COMP **ray gun** N fusil *m* à rayons laser

ray[2] /reɪ/ N *(= fish)* raie *f* ; → **stingray**

ray[3] /reɪ/ N *(Mus)* ré *m*

rayon /ˈreɪɒn/ N *(= fabric)* rayonne *f*, soie *f* artificielle ADJ en rayonne

raze /reɪz/ VT raser ◆ **to ~ to the ground** *[+ town]* raser ; *[+ building]* raser, abattre à ras de terre

razor /ˈreɪzəʳ/ N rasoir *m* ◆ **electric ~** rasoir *m* électrique ◆ **on the ~'s edge** *(fig)* sur le fil du rasoir ; → **safety**

COMP **razor blade** N lame *f* de rasoir

razor burn N feu *m* du rasoir

razor clam N *(US)* couteau *m*

razor cut N *(Hairdressing)* coupe *f* au rasoir

razor-edged ADJ *[knife etc]* tranchant comme un rasoir ; *(fig)* *[wit]* acéré

razor-sharp ADJ *[knife etc]* tranchant comme un rasoir ; *(fig)* *[person, mind]* délié, vif ; *[wit]* acéré

razor shell N *(Brit)* couteau *m*

razor-slashing N taillades *fpl* à coup de rasoir

razor wire N fil *m* de fer barbelé acéré

razorbill /ˈreɪzəbɪl/ N petit pingouin *m*

razz ‡ /ræz/ VT *(US)* mettre en boîte*

razzle * /ˈræzl/ N ◆ **to go (out) on the ~** (sortir) faire la bringue ‡ *or* la nouba ‡ COMP **razzle-dazzle** * N tape-à-l'œil *m inv*

razzmatazz * /ˈræzməˈtæz/ N 1 *(= glitter)* tape-à-l'œil *m inv* 2 *(= double talk)* propos *mpl* trompeurs

RC /ɑːˈsiː/ *(Rel)* (abbrev of **Roman Catholic**) → **Roman**

RCAF /ˌɑːsiːeɪˈef/ N abbrev of **Royal Canadian Air Force**

RCMP /ˌɑːsiːemˈpiː/ N (abbrev of **Royal Canadian Mounted Police**) → **royal**

RCN /ˌɑːsiːˈen/ N abbrev of **Royal Canadian Navy**

Rd abbrev of **Road**

RDA /ˌɑːdiːˈeɪ/ N (abbrev of **recommended daily allowance** *or* **amount**) AQR *mpl*

RDC /ˌɑːdiːˈsiː/ N *(Brit Local Govt)* (abbrev of **Rural District Council**) → **rural**

RE /ɑːrˈiː/ N 1 *(Brit Scol)* (abbrev of **religious education**) → **religious** 2 *(Brit Mil)* (abbrev of **Royal Engineers**) → **royal**

re[1] /reɪ/ N *(Mus)* ré *m*

re[2] /riː/ PREP 1 *(= referring to)* concernant ◆ **re: household insurance** objet : assurance logement 2 *(Jur: also* **in re***)* en l'affaire de

re... /riː/ PREF *(before consonant)* re..., ré... ; *(before vowel)* r..., ré... ◆ **to redo** refaire ◆ **to reheat** réchauffer ◆ **to reopen** rouvrir ◆ **to re-elect** réélire

reach /riːtʃ/ N 1 *(= accessibility)* portée *f*, atteinte *f* ◆ **within ~** à portée ◆ **out of ~** hors de portée *or* d'atteinte ◆ **within sb's ~** à (la) portée de qn ◆ **out of sb's ~** hors de (la) portée de qn ◆ **within arm's ~** à portée de la main ◆ **cars are within everyone's ~ nowadays** de nos jours les voitures sont à la portée de toutes les bourses *or* de tous ◆ **out of the children's ~** hors de (la) portée des enfants ◆ **I keep it within easy ~** *or* **within my ~** je le garde à portée de main *or* sous la main ◆ **within easy ~ of the sea** à proximité de la mer, proche de la mer ◆ **beyond the ~ of the law** à l'abri de la justice ◆ **this subject is beyond his ~** ce sujet le dépasse

2 *(esp Boxing)* allonge *f* ◆ **he has a long ~** *(gen)* il peut allonger le bras loin ; *(Boxing)* il a une bonne allonge, il a de l'allonge

3 *(= length)* *[of beach, river]* étendue *f* ; *[of canal]* bief *m* ◆ **further to the north, there are great ~es of forest** plus au nord, il y a de grandes étendues de forêt ◆ **the upper/lower ~es of the river** le cours supérieur/inférieur de la rivière

VT 1 *(= get as far as)* *[+ place, age, goal, limit, perfection]* atteindre ; *[+ agreement, understanding]* aboutir à, arriver à ; *[+ conclusion]* arriver à ; *[+ compromise, decision]* parvenir à ◆ **when we ~ed him he was dead** quand nous sommes arrivés auprès de lui, il était mort ◆ **to ~ the terrace you have to cross the garden** pour accéder à la terrasse, il faut traverser le jardin ◆ **I hope this letter ~es him** j'espère que cette lettre lui parviendra ◆ **the news ~ed us too late** nous avons appris *or* reçu la nouvelle trop tard ◆ **to ~ page 50** arriver *or* en être à la page 50 ◆ **not a sound ~ed our ears** aucun bruit ne parvenait à nos oreilles ◆ **he is tall enough to ~ the top shelf** il est assez grand pour atteindre l'étagère d'en haut ◆ **he ~es her shoulder** il lui arrive à l'épaule ◆ **her dress ~es the floor** sa robe descend jusqu'à terre ◆ **the cancer has ~ed her liver** le cancer a atteint le foie ◆ **you can ~ me at my hotel** vous pouvez me joindre à mon hôtel ◆ **we hope to ~ a wider audience** nous espérons toucher un public plus large

2 *(= get and give)* passer ◆ **~ me (over) that book** passez-moi ce livre ◆ **~ (over) the salt for Richard** passez le sel à Richard

3 *(US Jur = suborn)* *[+ witness]* corrompre, suborner

VI 1 *[territory etc]* s'étendre ; *[voice, sound]* porter *(to* jusqu'à)

2 *(= stretch out hand:* also **reach across, reach out, reach over***)* tendre le bras ◆ **to ~ for sth** essayer de prendre qch, tendre le bras pour prendre qch ◆ **he ~ed into his pocket for his pencil** il mit la main dans sa poche pour prendre son crayon ◆ **to ~ for the stars** viser haut ◆ **~ for the sky!** ‡ *(US)* haut les mains !

COMP **reach-me-down** N ◆ **it is a ~-me-down from my sister** c'est un vêtement que ma sœur m'a passé

► **reach back** VI *(fig)* remonter *(to* à) ◆ **to ~ back to Victorian times** remonter à l'époque victorienne

► **reach down** VI *[clothes, curtains etc]* descendre *(to* jusqu'à)

VT SEP *(from hook)* décrocher ; *(from shelf)* descendre ◆ **will you ~ me down the book?** voulez-vous me descendre le livre ?, voulez-vous me passer le livre qui est là-haut ?

► **reach out** VT SEP tendre ◆ **he ~ed out his hand for the cup** il a étendu le bras pour prendre la tasse

► **reach up** VI 1 lever le bras ◆ **he ~ed up to get the book from the shelf** il a levé le bras pour atteindre le livre sur le rayon

2 monter ◆ **the flood water ~ed up to the windows** la crue (des eaux) est montée jusqu'aux fenêtres

reachable /ˈriːtʃəbl/ ADJ *[place, object]* accessible ◆ **he is ~ * at ...** on peut le joindre à ...

react /riːˈækt/ VI 1 *(gen)* réagir *(against* contre ; *on* sur ; *to* à) 2 *(Phys, Chem)* réagir *(with* avec)

reaction /riːˈækʃən/ LANGUAGE IN USE 6.1 N *(gen)* réaction *f* ◆ **the driver's ~s** les réflexes du conducteur ◆ **to have quick ~s** réagir vite ◆ **what was his ~ to your suggestion?** comment a-t-il réagi *or* quelle a été sa réaction à votre proposition ? ◆ **this decision was a ~ against violence** cette décision a été une manière de riposter à la violence ◆ **forces of ~** *(Pol)* forces *fpl* de la réaction, forces *fpl* réactionnaires ; → **chain**

COMP **reaction engine** N moteur *m* à réaction

reaction time N temps *m* de réaction

reactionary /riːˈækʃənrɪ/ ADJ, N réactionnaire *mf*

reactivate /riːˈæktɪveɪt/ VT réactiver

reactivation /riːˌæktɪˈveɪʃən/ N réactivation *f*

reactive /riːˈæktɪv/ ADJ *(gen, Chem, Phys)* réactif ; *(Psych)* réactionnel ◆ **to be too** ~ ne pas prendre assez d'initiatives

reactor /riːˈæktəʳ/ N *(Chem, Elec, Phys)* réacteur *m* ; → **nuclear**

read /riːd/ (pret, ptp **read** /red/) VT 1 *[+ book, letter etc]* lire ; *[+ music, bad handwriting]* déchiffrer, lire ; *[+ hieroglyphs]* déchiffrer ; *[+ proofs]* corriger ◆ **to ~ sb sth, to ~ sth to sb** lire qch à qn ◆ **I read him to sleep** je lui ai fait la lecture jusqu'à ce qu'il s'endorme ◆ **I brought you something to** ~ je vous ai apporté de la lecture ◆ **to ~ sb's lips** lire sur les lèvres de qn ◆ **~ my lips!** vous m'avez bien compris ? ◆ **to ~ the Riot Act** *(Jur)* ≈ faire les trois sommations ◆ **he read them the riot act*** *(fig)* il leur a remonté les bretelles* ◆ **to ~ sb a lesson*** faire la leçon à qn, sermonner qn ◆ **to take sth as read** *(= as self-evident)* considérer qch comme allant de soi ; *(= as agreed)* considérer qch comme convenu ◆ **they took the minutes as read** *(Admin)* ils sont passés à l'ordre du jour (sans revenir sur le procès-verbal de la dernière séance) ◆ **for "meet" ~ "met"** *(in errata)* au lieu de "meet" prière de lire "met" ◆ **read and approved** *(Jur: on document)* lu et approuvé ; → **well²**

2 *(= interpret) [+ dream]* interpréter, expliquer ; *(= understand)* comprendre ◆ **to ~ sb's palm** lire les lignes de la main à qn ◆ **to ~ the tea leaves** *or* **the teacups** ≈ lire dans le marc de café ◆ **to ~ the wind** *(US fig)* flairer le vent ◆ **these words can be read in several ways** ces mots peuvent s'interpréter de plusieurs façons ◆ **to ~ between the lines** *(fig)* lire entre les lignes ◆ **to ~ something into a text** faire dire à un texte quelque chose qu'il ne dit pas, solliciter un texte ◆ **we mustn't ~ too much into this** nous ne devons pas y attacher trop d'importance ◆ **to ~ sb's thoughts** lire (dans) la pensée de qn ◆ **I can ~ him like a book** je sais *or* devine toujours ce qu'il pense ◆ **I read disappointment in his eyes** j'ai lu la déception dans ses yeux

3 *(esp Brit Univ = study)* étudier, faire ◆ **to ~ medicine/law** faire (des études de) médecine/droit, faire sa médecine/son droit ◆ **he is ~ing English/geography** *etc* il fait de l'anglais/de la géographie *etc*

4 *[+ thermometer, barometer etc]* lire ◆ **to ~ a meter** relever un compteur

5 *[instruments]* marquer, indiquer ◆ **the thermometer ~s 37°** le thermomètre indique (une température de) 37°

6 *(Telec)* recevoir ◆ **do you ~ me?** est-ce que vous me recevez ? ; *(fig)* vous me comprenez ? ; → **loud**

7 *(Comput)* lire

VI 1 lire ◆ **he can ~ and write** il sait lire et écrire ◆ **she ~s well** elle lit bien, elle fait bien la lecture ; *[learner, beginner]* elle sait bien lire ◆ **he likes ~ing** il aime lire, il aime la lecture ◆ **to ~ aloud** lire à haute voix ◆ **to ~ to oneself** lire ◆ **do you like being read to?** aimez-vous qu'on vous fasse la lecture ? ◆ **I read about it in the paper** je l'ai lu *or* je l'ai vu dans le journal ◆ **I've read about him** j'ai lu quelque chose à son sujet

2 ◆ **the letter ~s thus ...** voici ce que dit la lettre ..., voici comment la lettre est rédigée ... ◆ **the quotation ~s as follows ...** voici les termes exacts de la citation ... ◆ **this book ~s well/badly** ce livre se lit bien/mal ◆ **his article ~s like an official report** le style de son article fait penser à celui d'un rapport officiel, son article a l'allure d'un rapport officiel

3 *(esp Univ = study)* étudier, faire des études ◆ **to ~ for an examination** préparer un examen ; → **bar¹**

N * lecture *f* ◆ **she enjoys a good** ~ elle aime bouquiner*, elle aime bien la lecture ◆ **it's a good** ~ ça se lit facilement, ça se laisse lire ◆ **to have a quiet/a little** ~ lire *or* bouquiner* tranquillement/un peu

COMP **read head** N *(Comput)* tête *f* de lecture
read-only ADJ *(Comput) [file]* à lecture seule
read-only memory N mémoire *f* morte
read-out *(Comput)* N *(on screen)* affichage *m* ; *(on paper)* sortie *f* papier *or* sur imprimante
read-write head N *(Comput)* tête *f* de lecture-écriture
read-write memory N *(Comput)* mémoire *f* lecture-écriture
read-write window N *(Comput)* fenêtre *f* d'inscription-lecture

► **read back** VT SEP *[+ one's notes etc]* relire

► **read off** VT SEP 1 *[+ text] (without pause)* lire d'un trait ; *(at sight)* lire à livre ouvert
2 *[+ instrument readings]* relever

► **read on** VI continuer à lire, poursuivre sa lecture ◆ **"now read on"** "suite du feuilleton"

► **read out** VT SEP 1 *[+ text]* lire à haute voix ; *[+ instrument readings]* relever à haute voix
2 *(Comput)* extraire de la mémoire, sortir
N ◆ **read-out** → **read**

► **read over** VT SEP relire

► **read through** VT SEP *(rapidly)* parcourir ; *(thoroughly)* lire en entier *or* d'un bout à l'autre

► **read up** VT SEP étudier (à fond), potasser* ◆ **I must ~ up the Revolution** il faut que j'étudie *(subj) or* que je potasse* *(subj)* la Révolution

► **read up on** VT FUS ⇒ **read up**

readability /ˌriːdəˈbɪlɪtɪ/ N lisibilité *f*

readable /ˈriːdəbl/ ADJ 1 *(= interesting) [book, account, style]* agréable à lire ◆ **it's very** ~ ça se lit facilement 2 *(= legible) [handwriting]* lisible ; see also **machine**

readdress /ˌriːəˈdres/ VT *[+ letter, parcel]* réadresser ; *(= forward)* faire suivre

reader /ˈriːdəʳ/ N 1 lecteur *m*, -trice *f* ◆ **publisher's** ~ lecteur *m*, -trice *f* dans une maison d'édition ◆ **he's a great** ~ il aime beaucoup lire, c'est un grand liseur ; → **lay⁴, proofreader** 2 *(Brit Univ)* ≈ chargé(e) *m(f)* d'enseignement ; *(US Univ)* directeur *m*, -trice *f* de thèse *or* d'études 3 *(= schoolbook) (to teach reading)* livre *m* de lecture ; *(= anthology)* recueil *m* de textes ◆ **first French** ~ recueil *m* de textes français pour première année 4 ◆ **(microfiche)** ~ lecteur *m* (de microfiche)

readership /ˈriːdəʃɪp/ N 1 *[of newspaper, magazine] (= number)* nombre *m* de lecteurs ; *(= type)* lectorat *m* ◆ **this paper has a big ~/a ~ of millions** ce journal a beaucoup de lecteurs/des millions de lecteurs ◆ **a magazine with a predominantly white, middle-class** ~ un magazine dont le lectorat est en majorité blanc et de classe moyenne 2 *(Brit Univ)* ≈ poste *m* (*or* fonctions *fpl*) de chargé(e) d'enseignement ; *(US Univ)* fonctions *fpl* (*or* responsabilités *fpl*) de directeur *m*, -trice *f* de thèse *or* d'études

readily /ˈredɪlɪ/ ADV 1 *(= willingly) [accept, agree]* volontiers, de bon cœur ; *[admit]* volontiers 2 *(= easily) [understand]* facilement, aisément ◆ **~ accessible** *[place, data]* facilement accessible ◆ **to be ~ apparent** se voir (facilement) ◆ **exotic vegetables are ~ available these days** on trouve facilement des légumes exotiques de nos jours

readiness /ˈredɪnɪs/ N 1 *(= preparedness)* **to be (kept) in** ~ être (tenu) prêt (*for* à, pour) 2 *(= willingness)* empressement *m*, bonne volonté *f* ◆ **his ~ to help us** son empressement à nous aider, l'empressement qu'il a montré à nous aider

reading /ˈriːdɪŋ/ N 1 *(NonC)* lecture *f* ; *[of proofs]* correction *f* ◆ **she likes** ~ elle aime bien lire *or* la lecture ◆ **this book is** *or* **makes very interesting** ~ ce livre est très intéressant (à lire) ◆ **I'd prefer some light** ~ je préférerais qch de distrayant *or* de facile à lire

2 *(= recital)* (séance *f* de) lecture *f* ; → **play, poetry**

3 *(= interpretation)* interprétation *f*, explication *f* ◆ **my ~ of the sentence** mon explication *or* interprétation de cette phrase ◆ **his ~ of the part** *(Cine, Theat)* son interprétation du rôle

4 *(= variant)* variante *f*, leçon *f*

5 *(from instrument)* **to take a** ~ lire un instrument, relever les indications d'un instrument ◆ **the ~ is ...** l'instrument indique ...

6 *(Parl) [of bill]* discussion *f*, lecture *f* ◆ **the House gave the bill its first** ~ la Chambre a examiné le projet de loi en première lecture ◆ **the third ~ of the bill was debated** le projet de loi a été discuté en troisième lecture

7 *(NonC = knowledge)* culture *f*, connaissances *fpl* ◆ **of wide** ~ instruit, cultivé

COMP **reading age** N *(Scol)* ◆ **he has a ~ age of eight** il a le niveau de lecture d'un enfant de huit ans ◆ **she has a low/advanced ~ age** son niveau de lecture est bas/élevé pour son âge ◆ **child of ~ age** enfant *mf* en âge de lire
reading book N livre *m* de lecture
reading desk N pupitre *m* ; *(Rel)* lutrin *m*
reading glass N loupe *f*
reading glasses NPL lunettes *fpl* pour lire
reading knowledge N ◆ **to have a ~ knowledge of Spanish** savoir lire l'espagnol
reading lamp, reading light N *(gen)* lampe *f* de travail *or* de bureau ; *(in train, plane etc)* liseuse *f*
reading list N bibliographie *f*, (liste *f* d')ouvrages *mpl* recommandés
reading matter N ◆ **I've got some ~ matter** j'ai des choses à lire *or* de quoi lire
reading room N salle *f* de lecture *or* de travail
reading speed N vitesse *f* de lecture

readjust /ˌriːəˈdʒʌst/ VT *[+ position of sth, salary]* rectifier ; *[+ clothes]* rajuster ; *[+ strategy, approach]* modifier ; *[+ one's life]* réorganiser ; *[+ instrument]* régler (de nouveau) VI se réadapter (*to* à)

readjustment /ˌriːəˈdʒʌstmənt/ N réadaptation *f* ; *[of salary]* rajustement *or* réajustement *m* ◆ **a period of** ~ une période de transition ◆ **the effects of economic** ~ les effets de la réforme économique

readvertise /ˌriːˈædvətaɪz/ VT repasser une annonce pour

ready /ˈredɪ/ ADJ 1 *(= prepared) [person, thing]* prêt ; *[answer, excuse]* tout fait ◆ **to be ~ to do sth** être prêt à *or* pour faire qch ◆ **are you ~ to order?** *(in restaurant)* puis-je prendre votre commande ? ◆ **dinner is** ~ le dîner est prêt ◆ **dinner's ~!** à table ! ◆ **your glasses will be ~ (for you) in a fortnight** vos lunettes seront prêtes dans quinze jours ◆ **the doctor's ~ for you now** le docteur est prêt à vous recevoir ◆ **everything is ~ for his visit** tout est prêt pour sa visite ◆ **~ for a challenge** préparé à un défi ◆ **~ for an emergency** prêt à intervenir en cas d'urgence ◆ **the troops were ~ for action** les troupes étaient prêtes à intervenir ◆ **~ for anything** prêt à tout ◆ **the contract will be ~ for signing tomorrow** le contrat sera prêt pour la signature demain ◆ **"flight 211 is now ready for boarding"** "vol 211, embarquement immédiat" ◆ **the wine is ~ for drinking** ce vin est bon à boire tout de suite ◆ **the crops are ~ for harvesting** c'est le moment de faire la récolte ◆ **~ for use** prêt à l'emploi ◆ **I'm ~ for him!** je l'attends de pied ferme ! ◆ **"now ready"** *(Publishing)* "vient de paraître" ◆ **~, steady** *(Brit) or* **set** *(US)*, **go!** *(Sport)* à vos marques ! prêts ? partez ! ◆ **~ and waiting** fin prêt ◆ **~ when you are** quand tu veux ◆ **to be ~ with a joke/an excuse** avoir une plaisanterie/excuse toute prête *or* en réserve

◆ **get + ready** ◆ **to get (o.s.) ~ (for sth)** se préparer (pour qch) ◆ **get ~ for it!** tenez-vous prêt ! ; *(before momentous news etc)* tenez-vous bien ! ◆ **to get sb/sth ~ (for sth/to do sth)** préparer qn/qch (pour qch/pour faire qch) ◆ **to get ~ to do sth** s'apprêter à faire qch, se préparer à faire qch

◆ **make + ready** ◆ **to make ~ (for sth/to do sth)** se préparer (pour qch/à faire qch) ◆ **to make sth ~** préparer qch

[2] *(Comm)* ◆ **we have the goods you ordered ~ to hand** nous tenons à votre disposition les marchandises que vous avez commandées ◆ **~ money, ~ cash** (argent *m*) liquide *m* ◆ **to pay in ~ cash** payer en espèces ◆ **how much have you got in ~ money** *or* **~ cash?** combien avez-vous en liquide ?

[3] *(= willing)* ◆ **~ to do sth** prêt à faire qch ◆ **he is always ~ to help** il est toujours prêt à rendre service ◆ **I am quite ~ to see him** je suis tout à fait disposé à le voir ◆ **I'm ~, willing and able to do the job** je suis prêt à faire ce travail ◆ **to be only too ~ to do sth** n'être que trop disposé à faire qch

[4] *(= needing)* ◆ **I'm ~ for bed** j'irais bien me coucher ◆ **I'm ~ for a break/drink** je ferais bien une pause/prendrais bien un verre

[5] *(= about to)* ◆ **he was ~ to hit her** il était sur le point de la frapper ◆ **he was ~ to cry** il était au bord des larmes

[6] *(= prompt) [wit]* vif ; *[reply]* prompt ; *[solution, explanation]* tout fait ; *[market]* tout trouvé ; *[availability]* immédiat ◆ **don't be so ~ to criticize** ne soyez pas si prompt à critiquer ◆ **to have a ~ smile** sourire facilement ◆ **to have a ~ tongue** avoir la langue déliée, avoir la parole facile ◆ **a ~ supply of sth** une réserve de qch facilement accessible *or* à portée de main ◆ **to have a ~ sale** *[goods]* se vendre facilement, être de vente courante

[7] *(Naut)* **~ about!** pare à virer !

N [1] *(Mil)* **to come to the ~** apprêter l'arme ◆ **at the ~** *(Mil)* prêt à faire feu ; *(Naut)* paré à faire feu ; *(fig)* fin prêt

[2] **the ~*** *or* **readies*** *(= money)* le fric*

COMP **ready-cooked** ADJ *[meal, dish]* cuisiné
ready-cut ADJ *[shelves]* prédécoupé
ready-furnished ADJ tout meublé
ready-made ADJ *[curtains]* tout fait ; *[clothes]* de confection, prêt à porter ; *[solution, answer]* tout prêt ◆ **~-made ideas** des idées banales *or* toutes faites
ready meal N plat *m* cuisiné
ready-mix N ◆ **~-mix for cakes/pancakes** *etc* préparation *f* instantanée pour gâteaux/crêpes *etc* ADJ ◆ **she made a ~-mix cake** elle a fait un gâteau à partir d'une préparation *or* d'un sachet
ready-mixed ADJ *[concrete]* prêt à l'emploi
ready-prepared ADJ *[meal]* tout préparé
ready reckoner N barème *m*
ready-to-eat, ready-to-serve ADJ cuisiné
ready-to-wear ADJ prêt à porter N prêt-à-porter *m*

reaffirm /ˌriːəˈfɜːm/ VT réaffirmer

reaffirmation /ˌriːæfəˈmeɪʃən/ N réaffirmation *f*

reafforestation /ˈriːəˌfɒrɪsˈteɪʃən/, **reforestation** (US) /ˌriːfɒrɪsˈteɪʃən/ N reboisement *m*

reagent /riːˈeɪdʒənt/ N *(Chem)* réactif *m*

real /rɪəl/ ADJ [1] *(gen)* vrai *before n* ; *(as opposed to apparent)* véritable, vrai *before n* ; *(Philos, Math)* réel ◆ **the danger was very ~** le danger était très réel ◆ **she wanted to see the ~ Africa** elle voulait voir l'Afrique, la vraie ◆ **he is the ~ boss** c'est lui le véritable *or* vrai patron ◆ **my ~ home is in Paris** c'est à Paris que je me sens chez moi ◆ **to show ~ interest** se montrer vraiment intéressé ◆ **in ~ life** dans la réalité ◆ **in the ~ world** dans la réalité ◆ **in ~ terms** en termes réels ◆ **we have no ~ reason to suspect him** nous n'avons pas de véritable raison de le soupçonner ◆ **there was no ~ evidence that ...** il n'y avait pas de véritable preuve que ... ◆ **it came as no ~ surprise to him** ça n'a pas vraiment été une surprise pour lui ◆ **I'm in ~ trouble** j'ai de gros problèmes ◆ **I had ~ trouble getting them to leave** j'ai eu un mal fou à les faire partir ◆ **to make ~ money*** gagner des mille et des cents* ◆ **get ~!*** sois réaliste !, faut pas rêver !* ◆ **it's the ~ McCoy*** c'est du vrai de vrai*

◆ **for real*** pour de vrai* ◆ **is this guy for ~?!*** il est incroyable, ce type* !

[2] *(= not fake) [jewels]* vrai *before n*, véritable ; *[flowers]* vrai *before n*, naturel ; *[silk]* naturel ; *[leather, gold]* véritable

◆ **the real thing** ◆ **it is a poor copy of the ~ thing** c'est une pâle copie de l'original ◆ **you're being recorded now – is this the ~ thing?** on vous enregistre – pour de bon ? ◆ **when you've tasted the ~ thing, this whisky ...** quand on a goûté du vrai whisky, celui-ci ... ◆ **climbing this hill isn't much when you've done the ~ thing** pour ceux qui ont fait de l'alpinisme, cette colline n'est rien du tout ◆ **this is love, the ~ thing** c'est l'amour avec un grand A ◆ **he's the ~ thing** *(= real film star, lion-tamer etc)* c'en est un vrai ; *(* = he's great)* il est super*

ADV *(esp US *)* vraiment ◆ **~ soon** très bientôt

N *(Philos)* ◆ **the ~** le réel

COMP **real ale** N *(Brit)* bière *f* traditionnelle
real estate N *(US Jur)* immobilier *m* ◆ **to work in ~ estate** *or* **the ~ estate business** travailler dans l'immobilier
real-estate agent N *(US)* agent *m* immobilier
real-estate developer N *(US)* promoteur *m* immobilier
real-estate office N *(US)* agence *f* immobilière
real-estate register N *(US)* cadastre *m*
Real Presence N *(Rel)* présence *f* réelle
real property N *(US Jur)* biens *mpl* immobiliers
real tennis N jeu *m* de paume
real time N *(Comput)* temps *m* réel
real-time computer N ordinateur *m* exploité en temps réel
real-time processing N *(Comput)* traitement *m* immédiat
real-time system N *(Comput)* système *m* temps réel

realign /ˌriːəˈlaɪn/ VT réaligner

realism /ˈrɪəlɪzəm/ N réalisme *m*

realist /ˈrɪəlɪst/ ADJ, N réaliste *mf*

realistic /rɪəˈlɪstɪk/ ADJ réaliste ◆ **we had no ~ chance of winning** nous n'avions aucune chance réelle de gagner ◆ **it is not ~ to expect that ...** nous ne pouvons pas raisonnablement espérer que ...

realistically /rɪəˈlɪstɪkəlɪ/ ADV *[expect, hope for]* d'une façon réaliste ; *[think, depict]* d'une façon réaliste, avec réalisme ; *[possible]* d'un point de vue réaliste ◆ **they are ~ priced** leur prix est réaliste ◆ **~, he had little chance of winning** soyons réalistes, il avait peu de chances de gagner

reality /riːˈælɪtɪ/ LANGUAGE IN USE 26.3 N [1] réalité *f* ◆ **to bring sb back to ~** ramener qn à la réalité ◆ **the harsh ~ of war** la dure réalité de la guerre ◆ **in ~** en réalité, en fait [2] *(= trueness to life)* réalisme *m*

COMP *[show, programm]* de téléréalité
reality check N ◆ **take a ~ check !** sois réaliste ! ◆ **we need a ~ check** gardons les pieds sur terre
reality TV N téléréalité *f*

realizable /ˈrɪəlaɪzəbl/ ADJ réalisable

realization /ˌrɪəlaɪˈzeɪʃən/ N [1] *[of assets, hope, plan]* réalisation *f* [2] *(= awareness)* prise *f* de conscience ◆ **he was hit by the sudden ~ that ...** il s'est subitement rendu compte que ...

realize /ˈrɪəlaɪz/ VT [1] *(= become aware of)* se rendre compte de ; *(= understand)* comprendre ◆ **does he ~ the problems?** se rend-il compte des problèmes ? ◆ **the committee ~s the gravity of the situation** le comité se rend compte de la gravité de la situation ◆ **he had not fully ~d that his illness was so serious** il ne s'était pas vraiment rendu compte de la gravité de sa maladie ◆ **I ~d it was raining** je me suis rendu compte qu'il pleuvait ◆ **I made her ~ that I was right** je lui ai bien fait comprendre que j'avais raison ◆ **this made me ~ how lucky I'd been** c'est là que je me suis rendu compte de la chance que j'avais eue ◆ **I ~ that ...** je me rends compte du fait que ... ◆ **yes, I ~ that!** oui, je sais bien !, oui, je m'en rends bien compte ! ◆ **I ~d how he had done it** j'ai compris comment *or* je me suis rendu compte de la façon dont il l'avait fait ◆ **I ~d why ...** j'ai compris pourquoi ... ◆ **I ~ it's too late, but ...** je sais bien qu'il est trop tard, mais ...

[2] *[+ ambition, hope, plan]* réaliser ◆ **to ~ one's (full) potential** réaliser son plein potentiel ◆ **my worst fears were ~d** mes pires craintes se sont réalisées

[3] *(Fin) [+ assets]* réaliser ; *[+ price]* atteindre ; *[+ interest]* rapporter ◆ **how much did your Rembrandt ~?, how much did you ~ on your Rembrandt?** combien votre Rembrandt vous a-t-il rapporté ?

reallocate /riːˈæləʊkeɪt/ VT *[+ money, tasks]* réallouer, réaffecter ; *[+ time]* réallouer

reallocation /ˌriːæləˈkeɪʃən/ N *[of resources, land, time]* réaffectation *f*

really /ˈrɪəlɪ/ ADV vraiment, réellement ◆ **I ~ don't know what to think** je ne sais vraiment pas quoi penser ◆ **he ~ is an idiot** c'est un véritable imbécile, il est vraiment idiot ◆ **it won't ~ last** ça ne durera guère ◆ **I don't REALLY like ...** je ne peux vraiment pas dire que j'aime ..., je n'aime guère ... ◆ **you ~ MUST visit Paris** il faut absolument que vous visitiez *(subj)* Paris EXCL *(in doubt)* vraiment ?, sans blague !* ; *(in surprise)* c'est vrai ? ; *(in protest:* also **well really!**) vraiment !, ça alors ! ◆ **not ~!** pas vraiment ! ; *(in disbelief)* pas possible !

realm /relm/ N *(liter = kingdom)* royaume *m* ; *(fig)* domaine *m* ; → **coin**

realpolitik /reɪˈɑːlpɒlɪtiːk/ N realpolitik *f*

realtor /ˈrɪəltɔːʳ/ N *(US)* agent *m* immobilier

realty /ˈrɪəltɪ/ N *(Jur)* biens *mpl* immobiliers *or* immeubles

ream¹ /riːm/ N *[of paper]* ≈ rame *f* (de papier) ◆ **he always writes ~s*** *(fig)* il écrit toujours des volumes *or* toute une tartine*

ream² /riːm/ VT *(Tech)* fraiser

reamer /ˈriːməʳ/ N *(Tech)* fraise *f*

reanimate /ˌriːˈænɪmeɪt/ VT ranimer, raviver

reanimation /ˈriːˌænɪˈmeɪʃən/ N *(Med)* réanimation *f*

reap /riːp/ VT *(Agr)* moissonner, faucher ; *(fig) [+ profit]* récolter, tirer ◆ **to ~ the fruit of one's labours** recueillir le fruit de son labeur ◆ **to ~ the benefits of one's kindness** être récompensé de sa bonté, récolter les fruits de sa bonté ◆ **to ~ what one has sown** *(fig)* récolter ce qu'on a semé ◆ **they left him to ~ the bitter harvest of his corruption** *(liter)* ils l'ont laissé payer le prix de sa corruption ; → **sow²** VI moissonner, faire la moisson

reaper /ˈriːpəʳ/ N *(= person)* moissonneur *m*, -euse *f* ; *(= machine)* moissonneuse *f* ◆ **~ and binder** moissonneuse-lieuse *f* ◆ **the (Grim) Reaper** *(liter = death)* la Faucheuse

reaping /ˈriːpɪŋ/ N moisson *f*
COMP **reaping hook** N faucille *f*
reaping machine N moissonneuse *f*

reappear /ˌriːəˈpɪəʳ/ VI réapparaître, reparaître

reappearance /ˌriːəˈpɪərəns/ N réapparition *f*

reappoint /ˌriːəˈpɔɪnt/ VT renommer (*to* à)

reappointment /ˌriːəˈpɔɪntmənt/ N renouvellement *m* de nomination (*to* à)

reapportion /ˌriːəˈpɔːʃən/ VT réassigner, répartir à nouveau ; (*US Pol*) redécouper, procéder à une révision du découpage électoral de VI (*US Pol*) subir un redécoupage électoral

reapportionment /ˌriːəˈpɔːʃənmənt/ N (*US Pol*) redécoupage *m* électoral

reappraisal /ˌriːəˈpreɪzəl/ N [*of situation, problem*] réévaluation *f*, réexamen *m* ; [*of author, film etc*] réévaluation *f*

reappraise /ˌriːəˈpreɪz/ VT réévaluer

rear[1] /rɪəʳ/ N 1 (*= back part*) arrière *m*, derrière *m* ; (** = buttocks*) derrière* *m* ◆ **in** *or* **at the ~** à l'arrière ◆ **at the ~ of ...** derrière ..., à l'arrière de ... ◆ **from the ~, he looks like Chaplin** (vu) de dos, il ressemble à Charlot ◆ **from the ~ the car looks like ...** par l'arrière *or* vue de derrière la voiture ressemble à ...

2 (*Mil*) arrière-garde *f*, arrières *mpl* ; [*of squad*] dernier rang *m* ; [*of column*] queue *f* ◆ **to attack an army in the ~** attaquer une armée à revers ◆ **to bring up the ~** (*Mil, gen*) fermer la marche

ADJ de derrière, arrière *inv*

COMP **rear admiral** N vice-amiral *m*
rear bumper N pare-chocs *m* arrière *inv*
rear door N [*of house*] porte *f* de derrière ; [*of car*] portière *f* arrière *inv*
rear-end VT (*US*) [*+ car*] emboutir (l'arrière de)
rear-engined ADJ [*car*] avec moteur *m* à l'arrière
rear gunner N mitrailleur *m* arrière *inv*
rear-mounted ADJ installé à l'arrière
rear projection N (*Cine*) projection *f* par transparence
rear-view mirror N [*of car*] rétroviseur *m*
rear wheel N [*of car*] roue *f* arrière *inv* or de derrière
rear-wheel drive N traction *f* arrière
rear window N [*of car*] vitre *f* arrière *inv*

rear[2] /rɪəʳ/ VT 1 [*+ animal, family*] élever ; [*+ plant*] faire pousser, cultiver 2 ◆ **to ~ one's head** relever *or* dresser la tête ◆ **the snake ~ed its head** le serpent s'est dressé ◆ **violence ~s its ugly head again** la violence fait sa réapparition (dans toute son horreur), on voit poindre à nouveau l'horrible violence 3 (*= set up*) [*+ monument*] dresser, ériger VI (also **rear up**) [*animal*] se cabrer ; [*mountain, snake*] se dresser

rearguard /ˈrɪəɡɑːd/ N (*Mil*) arrière-garde *f*
COMP **rearguard action** N (*lit, fig*) combat *m* d'arrière-garde ◆ **to fight a ~ action** (*fig*) mener un combat d'arrière-garde

rearm /ˌriːˈɑːm/ VT réarmer VI se réarmer

rearmament /ˌriːˈɑːməmənt/ N réarmement *m*

rearmost /ˈrɪəməʊst/ ADJ [*carriage*] dernier, de queue ; [*rank*] dernier

rearrange /ˌriːəˈreɪndʒ/ VT réarranger

rearrangement /ˌriːəˈreɪndʒmənt/ N réarrangement *m*, nouvel arrangement *m*

rearward /ˈrɪəwəd/ N arrière *m* ADJ [*part*] arrière *inv* ; [*position*] (situé) à l'arrière, de l'arrière ; [*movement*] en arrière ADV (also **rearwards**) vers l'arrière, par derrière

reason /ˈriːzn/ LANGUAGE IN USE 17.1, 26.3

N 1 (*= cause, justification*) (*for behaviour*) raison *f*, motif *m* ; (*for event*) raison *f*, cause *f* ◆ **~ for living** *or* **being** raison *f* d'être ◆ **the ~s are ...** les raisons en sont ... ◆ **the ~ for my lateness/the ~ why I am late is that ...** la raison de mon retard/pour laquelle je suis en retard, c'est que ... ◆ **my ~ for leaving, the ~ for my leaving** la raison de mon départ *or* pour laquelle je pars (*or* suis parti *etc*) ◆ **I want to know the ~ why** je veux savoir (le) pourquoi ◆ **and that's the ~ why** et voilà pourquoi, et voilà la raison ◆ **for no apparent ~** sans raison apparente ◆ **I have (good** *or* **every) ~ to believe that ...** j'ai (tout) lieu *or* j'ai de bonnes raisons de croire que ... ◆ **he doesn't trust her - with good ~!** il ne lui fait pas confiance, et il a bien raison !, il ne lui fait pas confiance, et pour cause ! ◆ **there is ~ to believe that he is dead** il y a lieu de croire qu'il est mort ◆ **for the simple ~ that ...** pour la simple *or* bonne raison que ... ◆ **for the very ~ that ...** précisément parce que ... ◆ **for that very ~** pour cette raison, pour cela même ◆ **for no ~** sans raison, sans motif ◆ **for some ~ (or another)** pour une raison ou pour une autre ◆ **for ~s best known to himself** pour des raisons qu'il est seul à connaître, pour des raisons connues de lui seul ◆ **all the more ~ for doing it** *or* **to do it** raison de plus pour le faire ◆ **with ~** avec (juste) raison, à juste titre ◆ **by ~ of** en raison de, à cause de ◆ **for personal/health** *etc* **~s** pour des raisons personnelles/de santé *etc*

2 (*NonC = mental faculty*) raison *f* ◆ **to lose one's ~** perdre la raison

3 (*NonC = common sense*) raison *f*, bon sens *m* ◆ **to see ~** entendre raison ◆ **to make sb see ~** raisonner qn, faire entendre raison à qn ◆ **he listened to ~** il s'est rendu à la raison ◆ **he won't listen to ~** on ne peut pas lui faire entendre raison ◆ **that stands to ~** cela va sans dire, cela va de soi ◆ **it stands to ~ that ...** il va sans dire que ... ◆ **I will do anything in** *or* **within ~** je ferai tout ce qu'il est raisonnablement possible de faire ; → **rhyme**

VI 1 (*= think logically*) raisonner

2 (*= argue*) **to ~ with sb** raisonner avec qn ◆ **one can't ~ with her** il n'y a pas moyen de lui faire entendre raison

VT (*= work out*) calculer (*that* que) ; (*= argue*) soutenir (*that* que) ; ◆ **I ~ed that changing my diet would lower my cholesterol level** je me suis dit que si je changeais mon alimentation, mon taux de cholestérol diminuerait ◆ **"listen," he ~ed, "I think Adam's up to no good"** "écoute, dit-il, j'ai l'impression qu'Adam trame quelque chose" ; see also **reasoned**

► **reason out** VT SEP [*+ problem*] résoudre (en raisonnant)

reasonable /ˈriːznəbl/ ADJ 1 [*person, behaviour, decision, explanation, request, price, rate, offer*] raisonnable ◆ **to be ~ about sth** être raisonnable à propos de qch ◆ **within a ~ time** dans un délai raisonnable ◆ **it is ~ to suppose that ...** on peut raisonnablement supposer que ... 2 [*standard, results, essay*] honnête ; [*distance*] appréciable ◆ **there is a ~ chance that ...** il y a des chances *or* de bonnes chances que ... + *subj* 3 (*Jur*) ◆ **~ doubt** doute *m* bien fondé ◆ **to prove guilt beyond (a) ~ doubt** prouver la culpabilité de l'accusé avec quasi-certitude ◆ **to use ~ force** (*Jur*) faire un usage modéré de la force ◆ **~ grounds for divorce** (*esp Jur*) des motifs *mpl* valables de divorcer

reasonableness /ˈriːznəblnɪs/ N caractère *m or* nature *f* raisonnable

reasonably /ˈriːznəblɪ/ ADV 1 (*= sensibly*) [*behave*] d'une façon raisonnable ; [*say, expect*] raisonnablement ◆ **~ priced** à un prix raisonnable *or* acceptable ◆ **one can ~ think that ...** il est raisonnable de penser que ... 2 (*= fairly*) [*good, happy, easy, sure, safe*] assez, relativement ◆ **to be ~ successful** réussir assez *or* relativement bien

reasoned /ˈriːznd/ ADJ rationnel

reasoning /ˈriːznɪŋ/ N raisonnement *m* ◆ **she was not really convinced by this line of ~.** elle n'était pas vraiment convaincue par ce raisonnement ADJ [*mind*] doué de raison

reassemble /ˌriːəˈsembl/ VT [*+ people, troops*] rassembler ; [*+ tool, machine*] reconstituer VI se rassembler ◆ **the committee ~s on 5 September** le comité se rassemblera le 5 septembre

reassembly /ˌriːəˈsemblɪ/ N [*of machine*] remontage *m*

reassert /ˌriːəˈsɜːt/ VT réaffirmer ◆ **to ~ o.s.** s'imposer à nouveau ◆ **the government's effort to ~ its control in the region** les efforts du gouvernement pour consolider son emprise sur la région ◆ **his sense of humour was beginning to ~ itself** il commençait à retrouver son sens de l'humour

reassess /ˌriːəˈses/ VT [*+ situation*] réexaminer ; (*for taxation*) [*+ person*] réviser la cote de ; (*Jur*) [*+ damages*] réévaluer

reassessment /ˌriːəˈsesmənt/ N [*of situation*] réexamen *m* ; (*for taxation*) [*of person*] réévaluation *f* (fiscale) ; (*Jur*) (*damages*) réévaluation *f*

reassurance /ˌriːəˈʃʊərəns/ N 1 (*emotional*) réconfort *m* 2 (*factual*) assurance *f*, garantie *f* ◆ **to seek ~ that ...** chercher à obtenir l'assurance *or* la garantie que ...

reassure /ˌriːəˈʃʊəʳ/ VT rassurer

reassuring /ˌriːəˈʃʊərɪŋ/ ADJ rassurant ◆ **it is ~ to know that ...** il est rassurant de savoir que ...

reassuringly /ˌriːəˈʃʊərɪŋlɪ/ ADV [*say*] d'un ton rassurant ; [*smile, nod, look at*] d'une manière rassurante ◆ **~ familiar** familier et rassurant ◆ **~ simple** d'une simplicité rassurante

reawaken /ˌriːəˈweɪkən/ VT [*+ person*] réveiller de nouveau ; [*+ interest*] réveiller de nouveau, faire renaître VI se réveiller de nouveau

reawakening /ˌriːəˈweɪknɪŋ/ N réveil *m* ; [*of ideas*] renouveau *m* ; [*of interest*] regain *m*

Reb*, **reb*** /reb/ N (*US*) soldat *m* confédéré

rebarbative /rɪˈbɑːbətɪv/ ADJ (*frm*) rébarbatif, rebutant

rebate /ˈriːbeɪt/ N (*= discount*) rabais *m*, remise *f* ; (*= money back*) remboursement *m* ; (*on tax, rates*) dégrèvement *m* ; (*on rent*) réduction *f* ; → **rate**[1], **rent**[1], **tax**

rebel /ˈrebl/ N (*also fig*) rebelle *mf*, insurgé *m* ; (*Pol*) dissident *m* ◆ **the ~s want another cut in interest rates** les dissidents réclament une nouvelle réduction des taux d'intérêt ADJ rebelle ; (*Pol*) dissident ◆ **~ forces in the region** les troupes rebelles présentes dans la région ◆ **~ MPs** les députés dissidents VI /rɪˈbel/ 1 (*gen: lit, fig*) se rebeller, se révolter (*against* contre) 2 (*fig*) ◆ **my feet ~led** mes pieds n'en pouvaient plus ◆ **at the sight of all that food, his stomach ~led** à la vue de toute cette nourriture, il a eu un haut-le-cœur

rebellion /rɪˈbeljən/ N rébellion *f*, révolte *f* ◆ **to rise in ~** se rebeller, se révolter

rebellious /rɪˈbeljəs/ ADJ (*Mil, fig*) rebelle

rebelliously /rɪˈbeljəslɪ/ ADV [*say*] avec révolte ; [*act*] de manière rebelle

rebelliousness /rɪˈbeljəsnɪs/ N esprit *m* de rébellion

rebirth /ˌriːˈbɜːθ/ N renaissance *f*

rebirthing /ˌriːˈbɜːθɪŋ/ N rebirth *m*

reboot /ˌriːˈbuːt/ VT (*Comput*) réinitialiser, relancer VI redémarrer

rebore /ˌriːˈbɔːʳ/ (*Tech*) VT réaléser N /ˈriːˌbɔːʳ/ réalésage *m* ◆ **this engine needs a ~** ce moteur a besoin d'être réalésé

reborn /ˌriːˈbɔːn/ ADJ ◆ **to be ~** [*person*] (*= reincarnated*) se réincarner (*as sth* en qch) ; (*= redeemed, saved*) renaître ; [*city*] renaître ; [*hatred*] se réveiller ; [*racism, fascism*] renaître, resurgir

rebound /rɪ'baʊnd/ VI 1 *[ball]* rebondir *(against* sur) ◆ **she realised her trick had ~ed on her** elle s'est rendu compte que sa ruse s'était retournée contre elle 2 *(after setback)* reprendre du poil de la bête* N /'ri:baʊnd/ *[of ball]* rebond *m* ; *[of bullet]* ricochet *m* ; *[of sales, economy]* reprise *f* ; *(in prices)* remontée *f (in* de) ◆ **to hit a ball on the ~** frapper une balle après le premier rebond ◆ **to be on the ~ from a setback** *etc (fig) (= feeling effects)* être sous le coup d'un échec (*or* d'une déception *etc*) ; *(= recovering)* reprendre du poil de la bête* après un échec (*or* une déception *etc*) ◆ **she married him on the ~*** elle était encore sous le coup d'une déception (sentimentale) quand elle l'a épousé

rebrand /ri:'brænd/ VT *(= change image of)* changer l'image de ; *(= change name of)* rebaptiser

rebranding /ri:'brændɪŋ/ N *[of company, product]* relookage* *m*

rebroadcast /,ri:'brɔ:dkɑ:st/ N retransmission *f* VT retransmettre

rebuff /rɪ'bʌf/ N rebuffade *f* ◆ **to meet with a ~** essuyer une rebuffade VT *[+ person]* repousser, rabrouer ; *[+ offering, suggestion]* repousser

rebuild /,ri:'bɪld/ (pret, ptp **rebuilt**) VT rebâtir, reconstruire ; *(Med) [+ sb's face, nose]* refaire

rebuilding /,ri:'bɪldɪŋ/ N *(NonC)* reconstruction *f*

rebuilt /,ri:'bɪlt/ VB pt, ptp of **rebuild**

rebuke /rɪ'bju:k/ N reproche *m*, réprimande *f* VT réprimander, faire des reproches à ◆ **to ~ sb for sth** reprocher qch à qn ◆ **to ~ sb for having done** reprocher à qn d'avoir fait

rebus /'ri:bəs/ N (pl **rebuses**) rébus *m*

rebut /rɪ'bʌt/ VT réfuter

rebuttal /rɪ'bʌtl/ N réfutation *f*

recalcitrance /rɪ'kælsɪtrəns/ N caractère *m or* esprit *m* récalcitrant

recalcitrant /rɪ'kælsɪtrənt/ ADJ récalcitrant

recalculate /ri:'kælkjʊleɪt/ VT *(gen)* recalculer ; *[+ risk, probability]* réévaluer

recall /rɪ'kɔ:l/ LANGUAGE IN USE 5.3, 26.3

VT 1 *(= summon back) [+ ambassador]* rappeler ; *(Sport) [+ player]* rappeler, sélectionner de nouveau ; *[+ library book]* demander le retour de ; *(Comm) [+ faulty products] (already sold)* rappeler ; *(in shop)* retirer de la vente ; *(Fin) [+ capital]* faire rentrer ◆ **to ~ sb to life** *(lit, fig)* rappeler qn à la vie ◆ **to ~ Parliament** convoquer le Parlement (en session extraordinaire)

2 *(= remember)* se rappeler *(that* que), se souvenir de ◆ **I cannot ~ meeting him** *or* **whether I met him** je ne me rappelle pas l'avoir rencontré ◆ **I ~ my mother telling me about it** je me souviens que *or* me rappelle que ma mère m'a parlé de ça ◆ **can you ~ how you felt at the time?** vous rappelez-vous ce que *or* vous souvenez-vous de ce que vous ressentiez à l'époque ? ◆ **as I ~** si mes souvenirs sont bons, si je me souviens bien ◆ **as far as I can ~** (pour) autant que je m'en souvienne, (pour) autant que je me rappelle *subj* ◆ **as you may** *or* **might ~** comme vous vous en souvenez peut-être

N rappel *m (also Mil)* ◆ **the company ordered the ~ of more than 900,000 cars** la société a demandé que 900 000 voitures soient renvoyées en usine ◆ **this book is on ~** *(in library)* on a demandé le retour de ce livre ◆ **they are demanding the ~ of parliament** ils demandent que le Parlement soit convoqué en session extraordinaire ◆ **lost beyond ~** *(fig)* perdu à tout jamais ◆ **to have total ~ of an incident** se souvenir d'un incident dans ses moindres détails

COMP **recall slip** N *[of library]* fiche *f* de rappel

recant /rɪ'kænt/ VT *[+ statement]* rétracter ; *[+ religious belief]* abjurer ◆ **to ~ one's opinion** se déjuger, changer d'avis VI se rétracter ; *(Rel)* abjurer

recantation /,ri:kæn'teɪʃən/ N rétractation *f*, reniement *m* ; *(Rel)* abjuration *f*

recap[1]* /'ri:kæp/ N abbrev of **recapitulation** VTI /rɪ'kæp/ (abbrev of **recapitulate**) ◆ **well, to ~, ...** eh bien, en résumé ...

recap[2] /'ri:kæp/ *(US)* N *(= tyre)* pneu *m* rechapé VT rechaper

recapitalization /,ri:kæpɪtəlaɪ'zeɪʃən/ N plan *m* de recapitalisation

recapitalize /,ri:'kæpɪtəlaɪz/ VT recapitaliser

recapitulate /,ri:kə'pɪtjʊleɪt/ VT *[+ argument]* récapituler, faire le résumé de ; *[+ facts]* reprendre VI récapituler, faire un résumé

recapitulation /'ri:kə,pɪtjʊ'leɪʃən/ N récapitulation *f*

recapture /,ri:'kæptʃə^r/ VT *[+ animal, prisoner]* reprendre, capturer ; *(esp Sport) [+ title]* reconquérir ; *[+ emotion, enthusiasm, form]* retrouver ; *[film, play, book] [+ atmosphere, period]* recréer ; *[+ vote]* récupérer N *[of town, territory]* reprise *f* ; *[of escapee]* arrestation *f*, capture *f* ; *[of escaped animal]* capture *f*

recast /,ri:'kɑ:st/ VT 1 *(Metal)* refondre 2 *[+ play, film]* changer la distribution (des rôles) de ; *[+ actor]* donner un nouveau rôle à 3 *(= rewrite)* refondre, remanier N *(Metal)* refonte *f*

recce* /'rekɪ/ *(gen, Brit Mil)* abbrev of **reconnaissance, reconnoitre**

recd *(Comm)* (abbrev of **received**) reçu

recede /rɪ'si:d/ VI 1 *[tide]* descendre ; *(fig) [coast, person, threat, danger]* s'éloigner ; *[memories, fear]* s'estomper ; *[hopes of rescue]* s'amenuiser ; *[lights]* s'évanouir (peu à peu) ◆ **the footsteps ~d** les pas se sont éloignés, le bruit des pas s'est estompé ◆ **to ~ into the distance** s'éloigner, disparaître dans le lointain ◆ **if untreated the gums ~** si les gencives ne sont pas traitées, les dents se déchaussent 2 *[chin, forehead]* être fuyant ◆ **his hair(line) is receding** son front se dégarnit 3 *[price]* baisser 4 *(frm)* ◆ **to ~ from** *[+ opinion, promise]* revenir sur

COMP **receding chin** N menton *m* fuyant

receding forehead N front *m* fuyant

receding hairline N front *m* dégarni ◆ **he has a receding hairline** son front se dégarnit

receipt /rɪ'si:t/ N 1 *(NonC: esp Comm)* réception *f* ◆ **to acknowledge ~ of** accuser réception de ◆ **on ~ of** dès réception de ◆ **I am in ~ of ...** j'ai reçu ... ◆ **to pay on ~** payer à la réception 2 *(= paper) (for payment)* reçu *m*, récépissé *m (for* de) ; *(for parcel, letter)* accusé *m* de réception ; *(for object purchased)* ticket *m* de caisse ; *(for services)* reçu *m* ; *(for taxi)* fiche *f*, reçu *m* NPL **receipts** *(Comm, Fin = money taken)* recette(s) *f(pl)* ◆ **tax ~s** recettes *fpl* fiscales, rentrées *fpl* de l'impôt VT *[+ bill]* acquitter COMP **receipt book** N livre *m or* carnet *m* de quittances, quittancier *m*

receivable /rɪ'si:vəbl/ ADJ recevable NPL **receivables** *(Fin)* créances *fpl* (recouvrables)

receive /rɪ'si:v/ VT 1 *(= get) [+ letter, present, punch]* recevoir ; *[+ money, salary]* recevoir, toucher ; *[+ refusal, setback]* essuyer ; *(Jur) [+ stolen goods]* receler ; *[+ medical care]* recevoir ; *[+ medical treatment]* subir ◆ **to ~ two years** *or* **two years' imprisonment** *(Jur)* être condamné à deux ans de prison ◆ **we ~d nothing but abuse** nous n'avons reçu que des insultes ◆ **we ~d your request yesterday** *(Comm)* votre demande nous est parvenue hier ◆ **~d with thanks** *(Comm)* pour acquit

2 *(= welcome)* recevoir, accueillir ◆ **to ~ sb with open arms** recevoir qn à bras ouverts ◆ **his suggestion was well/not well ~d** sa suggestion a reçu un accueil favorable/défavorable ◆ **to be ~d into the Church** *(Rel)* être reçu dans l'Église

3 *(Rad, TV) [+ transmission]* capter, recevoir ◆ **are you receiving me?** me recevez-vous ? ; → **loud**

VI 1 *(frm)* recevoir ◆ **the countess ~s on Mondays** Madame la comtesse reçoit le lundi

2 *(Jur)* être coupable de recel

received /rɪ'si:vd/ ADJ *[opinion]* reçu ◆ **the ~ wisdom** l'opinion *f* la plus répandue COMP **Received Pronunciation** N *(Ling)* prononciation *f* standard *(de l'anglais)* ; → ENGLISH

receiver /rɪ'si:və^r/ N 1 receveur *m*, -euse *f* ; *[of letter]* destinataire *mf* ; *[of goods]* consignataire *m*, réceptionnaire *mf* ; *(Jur) [of stolen property]* receleur *m*, -euse *f* 2 *(Fin, Jur)* ≈ administrateur *m* provisoire ◆ **official ~** *(in bankruptcy)* syndic *m* de faillite, administrateur *m* judiciaire ◆ **to call in the (official) ~** placer la société en règlement judiciaire 3 *[of telephone]* récepteur *m*, combiné *m* ◆ **to pick up** *or* **lift the ~** décrocher ◆ **to put down** *or* **replace the ~** raccrocher 4 *(= radio set)* (poste *m*) récepteur *m*

COMP **receiver rest** N commutateur *m*

receivership /rɪ'si:vəʃɪp/ N *(Fin)* ◆ **in ~** en redressement judiciaire ◆ **the company has gone into ~** la société a été placée en redressement judiciaire

receiving /rɪ'si:vɪŋ/ ADJ récepteur (-trice *f*), de réception ◆ **he blew his top and I was on the ~ end*** il s'est mis dans une colère noire, et c'est moi qui ai écopé* *or* qui en ai fait les frais* ◆ **he was on the ~ end* of their abuse/hatred/violence** il a fait les frais* de leurs insultes/leur haine/leur violence N *[of stolen goods]* recel *m*

COMP **receiving line** N *(US) rangée de personnes accueillant les invités à une réception*

receiving set N *(Rad)* poste récepteur *m*

recension /rɪ'senʃən/ N 1 *(NonC)* révision *f* 2 *(= text)* texte *m* révisé

recent /'ri:snt/ ADJ *[event, change, invention, survey, history, winner]* récent ; *[acquaintance]* de fraîche date, nouveau (nouvelle *f*) ◆ **a ~ arrival** *(= person)* un nouveau venu, une nouvelle venue ◆ **his ~ arrival** *(= action)* son arrivée récente ◆ **in ~ years** ces dernières années ◆ **in the ~ past** ces derniers temps ◆ **his most ~ book** son tout dernier livre

recently /'ri:sntlɪ/ ADV *(= not long ago)* récemment ; *(= lately)* dernièrement, récemment ◆ **as ~ as ...** pas plus tard que ... ◆ **until (quite) ~** jusqu'à ces derniers temps, il y a peu de temps encore

receptacle /rɪ'septəkl/ N récipient *m* ; *(fig)* réceptacle *m*

reception /rɪ'sepʃən/ N 1 *(NonC)* réception *f* 2 *(= ceremony)* réception *f* 3 *(= welcome)* réception *f*, accueil *m* ◆ **to get a favourable ~** être bien accueilli *or* reçu ◆ **to give sb a warm/chilly ~** faire un accueil chaleureux/froid à qn 4 *(Rad, TV)* réception *f* 5 *(Brit: in hotel)* réception *f* ◆ **at ~** à la réception

COMP **reception area** N *(gen)* accueil *m* ; *[of hotel]* réception *f*

reception centre N centre *m* d'accueil

reception class N *(Brit Scol)* cours *m* préparatoire

reception clerk N *(Brit)* réceptionniste *mf*

reception committee N *(lit, fig)* comité *m* d'accueil

reception desk N bureau *m* de réception

reception room N *(in public building)* salle *f* de réception ; *(in private house)* pièce *f* commune, salon *m*

receptionist /rɪ'sepʃənɪst/ N réceptionniste *mf*

receptive /rɪ'septɪv/ ADJ *[person, mood]* réceptif *(to sth* à qch) ◆ **~ to new ideas** réceptif *or* ouvert aux nouvelles idées

receptiveness /rɪ'septɪvnɪs/, **receptivity** /,ri:sep'tɪvɪtɪ/ N réceptivité *f*

receptor /rɪ'septə^r/ N *(Physiol)* récepteur *m*

recess /rɪ'ses/ N 1 (= *holidays*) (*Jur*) vacances *fpl* (judiciaires) ; (*Parl*) vacances *fpl* (parlementaires) ◆ **in ~** (*Parl*) en vacances 2 (= *short break*) (*US Jur*) suspension *f* d'audience ; (*esp US Scol*) récréation *f* ◆ **the court is in ~** (*US Jur*) l'audience est suspendue 3 (= *alcove*) renfoncement *m* ; [*of bed*] alcôve *f* ; [*of door, window*] embrasure *f* ; [*of statue*] niche *f* 4 (= *secret place*) recoin *m* ; (*fig* = *depths*) recoin *m*, repli *m* ◆ **in the ~es of his mind** dans les recoins de son esprit VT (= *make an alcove in*) pratiquer un renfoncement dans ; (= *put in alcove*) [+ *bed etc*] mettre dans un renfoncement VI (*US Jur, Parl*) suspendre les séances, être en vacances COMP
recess appointment N (*US Pol*) *nomination effectuée par le chef de l'exécutif pendant les vacances parlementaires*

recessed /'riːsesd/ ADJ [*doorway, cupboard, shelves*] en retrait ; [*window*] en retrait, encastré ; [*lighting*] encastré

recession /rɪ'seʃən/ N 1 (*NonC*) recul *m*, régression *f* 2 (*Econ*) récession *f*

recessional /rɪ'seʃənl/ (*Rel*) N hymne *m* de sortie du clergé ADJ de sortie

recessionary /rɪ'seʃənərɪ/ ADJ de récession

recessive /rɪ'sesɪv/ ADJ rétrograde ; (*Genetics*) récessif

recharge /'riː'tʃɑːdʒ/ VT [+ *battery, gun*] recharger ◆ **to ~ one's batteries** (*fig*) recharger ses batteries* *or* ses accus* VI [*battery*] se recharger

rechargeable /riː'tʃɑːdʒəbl/ ADJ [*battery, torch*] rechargeable

recherché /rə'ʃeəʃeɪ/ ADJ (= *special: whisky, wine, tea*) pour connaisseurs ; (= *unusual: topic, knowledge*) insolite

recidivism /rɪ'sɪdɪvɪzəm/ N récidive *f*

recidivist /rɪ'sɪdɪvɪst/ ADJ, N récidiviste *mf*

recipe /'resɪpɪ/ N 1 (*Culin, Pharm*) recette *f* 2 (*fig*) **~ for happiness** secret *m* du bonheur ◆ **what is your ~ for success?** quelle est votre recette pour réussir ? ◆ **lifting restrictions would be a ~ for disaster/anarchy/chaos** la levée des restrictions, c'est le meilleur moyen de s'attirer de gros ennuis/de tomber dans l'anarchie/de tomber dans le chaos COMP
recipe book N livre *m* de cuisine *or* de recettes

recipient /rɪ'sɪpɪənt/ N (*gen*) personne *f* qui reçoit (*or* a reçu *etc*) ; [*of letter*] destinataire *mf* ; [*of cheque*] bénéficiaire *mf* ; [*of award, decoration*] récipiendaire *m* ; (*Jur*) donataire *mf* ; (*Med*) [*of donated organ*] receveur *m*, -euse *f*

reciprocal /rɪ'sɪprəkəl/ ADJ (= *mutual*) [*agreement*] réciproque, mutuel ; [*action, arrangement, feeling*] réciproque ; (*Math*) réciproque, inverse ; (*Gram*) réciproque ◆ **~ visits** des échanges *mpl* de visites N (*Math*) réciproque *f*

reciprocally /rɪ'sɪprəkəlɪ/ ADV réciproquement, mutuellement ; (*Math*) inversement

reciprocate /rɪ'sɪprəkeɪt/ VT 1 [+ *smiles, wishes*] rendre ; [+ *help*] donner *or* offrir en retour ; [+ *kindness*] retourner 2 (*Tech*) donner un mouvement alternatif à VI 1 ◆ **he insulted me and I ~d** il m'a injurié, et je lui ai rendu la pareille ◆ **he called me a fool and I ~d** il m'a traité d'imbécile et je lui ai retourné le compliment 2 (*Tech*) avoir un mouvement alternatif *or* de va-et-vient
COMP **reciprocating device** N dispositif *m* de va-et-vient
reciprocating engine N moteur *m* alternatif

reciprocation /rɪˌsɪprə'keɪʃən/ N 1 [*of help, kindness*] échange *m* 2 (*Tech*) alternance *f*, va-et-vient *m inv*

reciprocity /ˌresɪ'prɒsɪtɪ/ N réciprocité *f*

recital /rɪ'saɪtl/ N 1 (= *account*) récit *m* ; [*of details*] énumération *f* 2 [*of poetry*] récitation *f*, récital *m* ; [*of music*] récital *m* NPL **recitals** (*Jur: in contract*) préambule *m*

recitation /ˌresɪ'teɪʃən/ N récitation *f* ◆ **to give a poetry ~** dire des vers

recitative /ˌresɪtə'tiːv/ N récitatif *m*

recite /rɪ'saɪt/ VT 1 [+ *poetry*] réciter, déclamer 2 [+ *facts*] exposer ; [+ *details*] énumérer VI réciter, déclamer

reckless /'reklɪs/ ADJ [*person, behaviour*] (= *heedless*) insouciant ; (= *rash*) imprudent ; [*disregard*] irresponsable ◆ **with ~ abandon** avec une désinvolture imprudente ◆ **~ of the consequences** insouciant des conséquences
COMP **reckless driver** N conducteur *m*, -trice *f* imprudent(e)
reckless driving N conduite *f* imprudente
reckless endangerment N (*US Jur*) *mise en danger d'autrui par imprudence*

recklessly /'reklɪslɪ/ ADV imprudemment

recklessness /'reklɪsnɪs/ N [*of person, behaviour*] (= *heedlessness*) insouciance *f* ; (= *rashness*) imprudence *f* ; [*of driving*] imprudence *f*

reckon /'rekən/ VT 1 (= *calculate*) [+ *time, numbers, points*] compter ; [+ *cost, surface*] calculer
2 (= *judge*) considérer, estimer ◆ **I ~ him among my friends** je le compte parmi *or* au nombre de mes amis ◆ **she is ~ed (to be) a beautiful woman** elle est considérée comme une femme très belle ◆ **the price is ~ed to be too high** on considère *or* estime le prix trop élevé ◆ **her chances of survival cannot now be ~ed good** à l'heure actuelle on estime qu'elle a de faibles chances de survivre ◆ **the number of victims was ~ed at around 300** on a estimé le nombre de victimes à environ 300 personnes
3 (* = *think*) penser ◆ **what do you ~ one of these houses would cost?** d'après vous *or* à votre avis, combien coûte une maison comme celle-ci ? ◆ **I ~ we can start** je pense qu'on peut commencer ◆ **I ~ he must be about forty** je lui donnerais la quarantaine ◆ **about thirty, I ~** une trentaine, à mon avis
VI 1 calculer, compter ◆ **~ing from tomorrow** en comptant à partir de demain, à compter de demain
2 (*fig*) **you can ~ on 30** tu peux compter sur 30 ◆ **I was ~ing on doing that tomorrow** j'avais prévu de faire *or* je pensais faire cela demain ◆ **I wasn't ~ing on having to do that** je ne m'attendais pas à devoir faire cela ◆ **they ~ to sell most of them abroad** ils comptent en vendre la majorité à l'étranger ◆ **you'll have to ~ with six more** il faudra compter avec six de plus ◆ **she had not ~ed on** *or* **with an objection from them** elle ne s'attendait pas à une objection de leur part ◆ **he's a person to be ~ed with** c'est une personne avec laquelle il faut compter ◆ **if you insult him you'll have to ~ with the whole family** si vous l'insultez, vous aurez affaire à toute la famille ◆ **he was ~ing without his secretary** il avait compté sans sa secrétaire ◆ **he ~ed without the fact that ...** il n'avait pas prévu que ..., il n'avait pas tenu compte du fait que ...

▸ **reckon in** VT SEP prendre en compte

▸ **reckon up** VT SEP (*gen*) calculer ; (= *add*) ajouter, additionner

reckoner /'rekənə^r/ N → **ready**

reckoning /'reknɪŋ/ N 1 (*Math etc*) (= *evaluation*) compte *m* ; (= *calculation*) calcul *m* ◆ **to be out in one's ~** s'être trompé dans ses calculs 2 (*Comm*) règlement *m* de compte(s) (*lit*) [*of hotel*] note *f* ; [*of restaurant*] addition *f* ◆ **the day of ~** (*Rel*) le jour du Jugement ◆ **the day of ~ can't be far away** (*fig*) un de ces jours ça va lui (*or* nous *etc*) retomber dessus 3 (= *judgement*) estimation *f* ◆ **to the best of my ~** (pour) autant que je puisse en juger ◆ **in your ~** d'après vous, à votre avis 4 (*Naut*) estime *f* ; → **dead**

reclaim /rɪ'kleɪm/ VT [+ *land*] (*gen*) reconquérir ; (*from forest, bush*) défricher ; (*with manure etc*) amender, bonifier ; [+ *by-product*] récupérer ; (= *demand back*) réclamer (*sth from sb* qch à qn) ; [+ *language, term*] récupérer ; [+ *title*] reprendre ; [+ *tax*] se faire rembourser ◆ **the land has been ~ed from the sea** la terre a été gagnée sur la mer ◆ **the land has been ~ed by the sea** les terres ont été reconquises par la mer ◆ **the land has been ~ed by the desert** les terres sont retournées à l'état de désert ◆ **a campaign to ~ the night** une campagne pour protester contre l'insécurité de la ville la nuit N ◆ **past** *or* **beyond ~** perdu à tout jamais ◆ **he is beyond ~** il ne se corrigera jamais

reclaimable /rɪ'kleɪməbl/ ADJ [*land*] amendable ; [*by-products*] récupérable

reclamation /ˌreklə'meɪʃən/ N 1 (= *conversion*) [*of land*] (*gen*) mise *f* en valeur ; (*from sea*) assèchement *m* ; (*from marsh*) assèchement *m*, assainissement *m* ; (*from forest, bush*) défrichement *m* ; [*of marshland*] assèchement *m*, assainissement *m* ; [*of desert*] reconquête *f* ; [*of mine*] reconversion *f* 2 (= *recovery*) récupération *f*

reclassify /ˌriː'klæsɪfaɪ/ VT reclasser, reclassifier

recline /rɪ'klaɪn/ VT [+ *head, arm*] reposer, appuyer VI [*person*] être allongé, être étendu ◆ **she was reclining in the armchair** elle était allongée *or* étendue sur le fauteuil ◆ **reclining in his bath** étendu *or* allongé dans son bain ◆ **the seat ~s** le siège est inclinable, le dossier (du siège) est réglable
COMP **reclining chair** N chaise *f* longue
reclining seat N [*of coach, plane, car*] siège *m* inclinable *or* à dossier réglable

recluse /rɪ'kluːs/ N reclus(e) *m(f)*, solitaire *mf*

reclusive /rɪ'kluːsɪv/ ADJ reclus

recognition /ˌrekəg'nɪʃən/ N 1 (*gen, Pol* = *acknowledgement*) reconnaissance *f* ◆ **in ~ of ...** en reconnaissance de ...
2 (= *fame etc*) **he seeks ~** il veut être reconnu ◆ **this brought him ~ at last** c'est ce qui lui a enfin permis d'être reconnu ◆ **his exploits have gained world-wide ~** ses exploits ont été reconnus dans le monde entier ◆ **to receive no ~** passer inaperçu
3 (= *identification*) reconnaissance *f* ; [*of aircraft type*] identification *f* ◆ **he has changed beyond** *or* **out of all ~** il est devenu méconnaissable ◆ **he has changed it beyond** *or* **out of all ~** il l'a rendu méconnaissable ◆ **to improve beyond** *or* **out of (all) ~** s'améliorer jusqu'à en être méconnaissable
4 (*Comput*) reconnaissance *f* ◆ **speech ~** reconnaissance *f* de la parole

recognizable /'rekəgnaɪzəbl/ ADJ reconnaissable ◆ **she was easily ~ by her walk** elle était facilement reconnaissable à sa démarche ◆ **it was instantly ~ to him** il l'a reconnu immédiatement ◆ **he was hardly ~ as the boy who ...** c'est à peine si l'on reconnaissait en lui le garçon qui ...

recognizably /ˌrekəg'naɪzəblɪ/ ADV ◆ **it is ~ different/better** on voit que c'est différent/meilleur ◆ **he was ~ a genius** on voyait bien que c'était un génie ◆ **it was ~ a woman's face** on reconnaissait bien un visage de femme

recognizance /rɪ'kɒgnɪzəns/ N (*esp US*) (*Jur*) engagement *m* ; (= *sum of money*) caution *f* (personnelle) ◆ **to enter into ~s (for sb)** se porter caution (pour qn) ◆ **bail in his own ~ of £1,000** mise *f* en liberté sous caution personnelle de 1 000 livres

recognize /'rekəgnaɪz/ LANGUAGE IN USE 15.1, 26.3
VT 1 (*gen*) reconnaître (*by* à ; *as* comme étant ; *that* que) ; ◆ **their independence was ~d by the Treaty of Berlin** leur indépendance a été reconnue par le traité de Berlin ◆ **I ~ my own**

shortcomings je reconnais *or* j'admets que j'ai des défauts ◆ **the company ~d him as a very able engineer** la société a reconnu en lui un ingénieur très compétent ◆ **it is generally ~d that ...** il est communément admis que... 2 *(US) [chairman of meeting]* donner la parole à

recognized /'rekəgnaɪzd/ ADJ *(gen)* reconnu ; *(Comm)* attitré ◆ **a directory of ~ teachers** une liste de professeurs agréés ◆ **anyone who is not a member of a ~ organisation** toute personne non membre d'une organisation agréée *or* reconnue

recoil /rɪ'kɔɪl/ VI 1 *[person]* reculer, avoir un mouvement de recul *(from* devant) ◆ **to ~ in disgust** reculer de dégoût ◆ **to ~ from doing sth** reculer devant l'idée de faire qch, se refuser à faire qch 2 *[gun]* reculer ; *[spring]* se détendre ; *(fig) [actions etc]* retomber *(on* sur) N *[of gun]* recul *m* ; *[of spring]* détente *f* ; *(fig) (from disgusting sight)* dégoût *m (from* pour, de), horreur *f (from* de) ; *(from idea)* répugnance *f (from* pour)

recollect /,rekə'lekt/ VT se rappeler, se souvenir de ◆ **to ~ o.s.** se recueillir VI se souvenir ◆ **as far as I (can) ~** autant que je m'en souvienne

recollection /,rekə'lekʃən/ N souvenir *m* ◆ **to the best of my ~** autant que je m'en souvienne ◆ **his ~ of it is vague** il ne s'en souvient que vaguement ◆ **I have some ~ of it** j'en ai un vague souvenir ◆ **I have no ~ of it** je ne m'en souviens pas, je n'en ai aucun souvenir

recommence /,ri:kə'mens/ VTI recommencer *(doing sth* à faire qch)

recommend /,rekə'mend/ LANGUAGE IN USE 19.4

VT 1 *(= speak well of)* recommander ◆ **to ~ sth/sb to sb** recommander qch/qn à qn ◆ **to ~ sb for a job** recommander qn pour un emploi ◆ **to come highly ~ed** être vivement recommandé

2 *(= advise)* recommander, conseiller ◆ **to ~ doing sth** recommander de faire qch ◆ **to ~ against sth** déconseiller qch, se prononcer contre qch ◆ **what do you ~ for a sore throat?** que recommandez-vous pour guérir un mal de gorge ? ◆ **he was ~ed to accept** on lui a recommandé *or* conseillé d'accepter ◆ **I ~ that you should accept the offer** je vous conseille d'accepter la proposition ◆ **it is to be ~ed** c'est à conseiller ◆ **it is not to be ~ed** c'est à déconseiller

3 *(= make acceptable)* ◆ **she has a lot to ~ her** elle a beaucoup de qualités en sa faveur, il y a beaucoup à dire en sa faveur ◆ **she has little to ~ her** elle n'a pas grand-chose pour elle ◆ **the apartment has little to ~ it** l'appartement est sans grand intérêt ◆ **this biography has much to ~ it** cette biographie est vraiment à recommander

4 *(frm = commit) [+ child, one's soul]* recommander, confier *(to* à)

COMP **recommended daily allowance, recommended daily amount, recommended daily intake** N apport *m* quotidien *or* journalier recommandé

recommended reading N *(NonC)* ouvrages *mpl* recommandés

recommended retail price N prix *m* conseillé

recommendable /,rekə'mendəbl/ ADJ recommandable ◆ **it is not ~** c'est à déconseiller

recommendation /,rekəmen'deɪʃən/ N recommandation *f* ◆ **on the ~ of ...** sur la recommandation de ...

recommendatory /,rekə'mendətərɪ/ ADJ de recommandation

recommittal /,ri:kə'mɪtl/ N *(US Parl)* renvoi *m* en commission *(d'un projet de loi)*

recompense /'rekəmpens/ N 1 *(= reward)* récompense *f* ◆ **in ~ for** en récompense de 2 *(Jur: for damage)* dédommagement *m*, compensation *f* VT 1 *(= reward)* récompenser *(for* de) 2 *(Jur etc = repay) [+ person]* dédommager ; *[+ damage, loss]* compenser, réparer

recompose /,ri:kəm'pəʊz/ VT 1 *(= rewrite)* recomposer 2 *(= calm)* **to ~ o.s.** se ressaisir, retrouver son calme *or* son sang-froid

reconcilable /'rekənsaɪləbl/ ADJ *[ideas, opinions]* conciliable, compatible *(with* avec)

reconcile /'rekənsaɪl/ VT *[+ person]* réconcilier *(to* avec) ; *[+ two facts, ideas, demands]* concilier ◆ **is it possible to ~ these two perspectives?** est-il possible de concilier ces deux perspectives ? ◆ **they were ~d** ils se sont réconciliés ◆ **to ~ o.s. to sth** se résigner à qch, se faire à qch ◆ **to ~ sb to sth** faire accepter qch à qn

reconciliation /,rekənsɪlɪ'eɪʃən/ N *[of persons]* réconciliation *f* ; *[of opinions, principles]* conciliation *f*

recondite /rɪ'kɒndaɪt/ ADJ *(frm)* abscons *(frm)*

recondition /,ri:kən'dɪʃən/ VT remettre à neuf *or* en état ◆ **~ed engine** moteur *m* refait à neuf *or* entièrement révisé ◆ **~ed fridge/vacuum cleaner** réfrigérateur *m*/aspirateur *m* remis en état

reconnaissance /rɪ'kɒnɪsəns/ N *(in armed forces)* reconnaissance *f*

COMP **reconnaissance flight** N vol *m* de reconnaissance

reconnaissance patrol N patrouille *f* de reconnaissance

reconnect /,ri:kə'nekt/ VT *[+ electricity, gas, water]* rétablir ; *[+ phone]* remettre en service ; *[+ person, home]* rebrancher sur le réseau ◆ **he wants to ~ the Tories with contemporary realities** il veut remettre les conservateurs en prise avec les réalités actuelles VI se remettre en prise *(with* avec)

reconnection /,ri:kə'nekʃən/ N *[of electricity, telephone]* remise *f* en service COMP **reconnection fee** N *(Elec, Telec etc)* reprise *f* d'abonnement

reconnoitre, reconnoiter (US) /,rekə'nɔɪtəʳ/ VT *[+ region]* reconnaître VI faire une reconnaissance

reconnoitring /,rekə'nɔɪtərɪŋ/ N *(Aviat, Mil)* reconnaissance *f*

reconquer /,ri:'kɒŋkəʳ/ VT reconquérir

reconquest /,ri:'kɒŋkwest/ N reconquête *f*

reconsider /,ri:kən'sɪdəʳ/ VT *[+ decision, opinion]* reconsidérer, réexaminer ; *[+ judgement]* réviser ◆ **won't you ~ it?** est-ce que vous seriez prêt à reconsidérer la question ? ◆ **to ~ whether to resign** reconsidérer la possibilité de démissionner VI *(gen)* reconsidérer *or* réexaminer la question ; *(= change one's mind)* changer d'avis

reconsideration /'ri:kən,sɪdə'reɪʃən/ N remise *f* en cause, nouvel examen *m*

reconstitute /,ri:'kɒnstɪtju:t/ VT *(gen)* reconstituer ; *(Culin)* réhydrater

reconstitution /'ri:,kɒnstɪ'tju:ʃən/ N reconstitution *f*

reconstruct /,ri:kən'strʌkt/ VT *[+ building]* reconstruire, rebâtir ; *[+ crime]* reconstituer ; *[+ policy, system]* reconstruire

reconstruction /,ri:kən'strʌkʃən/ N *[of building, policy, system]* reconstruction *f* ; *[of crime]* reconstitution *f* ◆ **the Reconstruction** *(US Hist)* la Reconstruction de l'Union *(après 1865)*

reconstructive surgery /,ri:kən'strʌktɪv 'sɜ:dʒərɪ/ N chirurgie *f* réparatrice

reconvene /,ri:kən'vi:n/ VT reconvoquer VI *[committee, jury etc]* se réunir *or* s'assembler de nouveau ; *[meeting]* reprendre ◆ **we will ~ at 10 o'clock** la réunion *(or* l'audience *etc)* reprendra à 10 heures

record /rɪ'kɔ:d/ LANGUAGE IN USE 27.3

VT 1 *(= register) [+ facts, story]* enregistrer ; *[+ protest, disapproval]* prendre acte de ; *[+ event etc] (in journal, log)* noter, consigner ; *(= describe)* décrire ◆ **to ~ the proceedings of a meeting** tenir le procès-verbal d'une assemblée ◆ **to ~ one's vote** *(Parl)* voter ◆ **his speech as ~ed in the newspapers ...** son discours, tel que le rapportent les journaux ... ◆ **history/the author ~s that ...** l'histoire/l'auteur rapporte que ... ◆ **it's not ~ed anywhere** ce n'est pas attesté ◆ **to ~ the population** recenser la population

2 *[instrument, thermometer]* enregistrer, marquer

3 *[+ speech, music]* enregistrer ◆ **to ~ sth on tape** enregistrer qch sur bande ◆ **to ~ sth on video** magnétoscoper qch ◆ **this is a ~ed message** *(Telec)* ceci est or vous écoutez un message enregistré ; → **tape**

VI enregistrer ◆ **he is ~ing at 5 o'clock** il enregistre à 5 heures ◆ **his voice does not ~ well** sa voix ne se prête pas bien à l'enregistrement

N /'rekɔ:d/ 1 *(= account, report)* rapport *m*, récit *m* ; *(of attendance)* registre *m* ; *(of act, decision)* minute *f* ; *(of evidence, meeting)* procès-verbal *m* ; *(= official report)* rapport *m* officiel ; *(Jur)* enregistrement *m* ; *(= historical report)* document *m* ◆ **the society's ~s** les actes *mpl* de la société ◆ **(public) ~s** archives *fpl*, annales *fpl* ◆ **to make** *or* **keep a ~** noter, consigner ◆ **this statue is a ~ of a past civilization** cette statue est un témoin d'une civilisation passée ◆ **it is on ~ that ...** *(fig)* c'est un fait établi *or* il est établi que ... ◆ **there is no similar example on ~** aucun exemple semblable n'est attesté ◆ **to go/be on ~ as saying that ...** déclarer/avoir déclaré publiquement que ... ◆ **to put on ~** consigner, mentionner (par écrit) ◆ **the highest temperatures on ~** les plus fortes températures enregistrées ◆ **there is no ~ of his having said it** il n'est noté *or* consigné nulle part qu'il l'ait dit ◆ **there is no ~ of it in history** l'histoire n'en fait pas mention ◆ **to put** *or* **set the ~ straight** mettre les choses au clair, dissiper toute confusion possible ◆ **just to put** *or* **set the ~ straight, let me point out that ...** pour qu'il n'y ait aucune confusion possible, disons bien que ... ◆ **for the ~, they refuse ...** *(fig)* il faut noter *or* signaler qu'ils refusent ... ◆ **this is strictly off the ~*** ceci est à titre (purement) confidentiel *or* officieux, ceci doit rester strictement entre nous ◆ **the interview was off the ~*** l'interview n'était pas officielle ◆ **off the ~*, he did come!** il est effectivement venu, mais que ceci reste entre nous *or* mais je ne vous ai rien dit ◆ **on the ~, he admitted that ...** *(Press etc)* dans ses déclarations officielles, il a reconnu que ...

2 *(= case history)* dossier *m* ; *(= card)* fiche *f* ◆ **service ~** *(Mil)* états *mpl* de service ◆ **(police) ~** *(Jur)* casier *m* judiciaire ◆ **~ of previous convictions** dossier *m* du prévenu ◆ **he's got a clean ~, he hasn't got a ~*** *(Jur, Police)* il a un casier (judiciaire) vierge ◆ **he's got a long ~** il a un casier judiciaire chargé ◆ **France's splendid ~** les succès *mpl* glorieux de la France ◆ **his past ~** sa conduite passée ◆ **his war ~** son passé militaire ◆ **his attendance ~ is bad** *(Scol)* il a été souvent absent ◆ **to have a good ~ at school** avoir un bon dossier scolaire ◆ **this airline has a good safety ~** cette compagnie aérienne a une bonne tradition de sécurité ◆ **he left a splendid ~ of achievements** il avait à son compte de magnifiques réussites ; → **police, track**

3 *(Comput)* article *m*

4 *(= recording) [of voice etc]* enregistrement *m*

5 *(Audio)* disque *m* ◆ **to make** *or* **cut a ~** graver un disque

6 *(Sport, fig)* record *m* ◆ **to beat** *or* **break the ~** battre le record ◆ **to hold the ~** détenir le

record ◆ **long-jump** ~ record *m* du saut en longueur ; → **world**

7 *[of seismograph etc]* courbe *f* enregistrée

COMP *[amount, attendance, result]* record *inv*

record breaker N *(= person) (gen)* nouveau champion *or* nouvelle championne en titre ; *(Sport)* nouveau recordman *m*, nouvelle recordwoman *f* ; *(= achievement)* performance *f* qui établit un nouveau record

record-breaking ADJ qui bat tous les records

record cabinet N casier *m* à disques, discothèque *f (meuble)*

record card N fiche *f*

record company N maison *f* de disques

record dealer N disquaire *mf*

record deck N platine *f* disques

record holder N détenteur *m*, -trice *f* du record

record library N discothèque *f (collection)*

record player N tourne-disque *m*

record producer N producteur *m*, -trice *f* de disques

record time N ◆ **to do sth in ~ time** faire qch en un temps record

record token N chèque-cadeau *m (à échanger contre un disque)*, chèque-disque *m*

recorded /rɪˈkɔːdɪd/ ADJ 1 *[music, message]* enregistré ; *[programme]* préenregistré, transmis en différé 2 *(= noted) [fact, occurrence]* attesté, noté ; *[crime]* signalé ; *[history]* écrit COMP **recorded delivery** N *(Brit Post) (= service)* ≃ recommandé *m (avec accusé de réception)* ; *(= letter, parcel)* envoi *m* en recommandé ◆ **to send sth by ~ delivery** ≃ envoyer qch en recommandé

recorder /rɪˈkɔːdəʳ/ N 1 *[of official facts]* archiviste *mf* ; *(= registrar)* greffier *m* 2 *(Brit Jur)* ≃ avocat *m* nommé à la fonction de juge ; *(US Jur)* ≃ juge *m* suppléant 3 *[of sounds] (= apparatus)* appareil *m* enregistreur ; *(= tape recorder)* magnétophone *m* ; *(= cassette recorder)* magnétophone *m* à cassettes ; → **video** 4 *(= person)* artiste *mf* qui enregistre 5 *(Mus)* flûte *f* à bec ◆ **descant/treble/tenor/bass** ~ flûte *f* à bec soprano/alto/ténor/basse

recording /rɪˈkɔːdɪŋ/ N *[of sound, facts]* enregistrement *m* ◆ **"this programme is a recording"** *(Rad)* "ce programme a été enregistré" ADJ *[artist]* qui enregistre ; *[apparatus]* enregistreur

COMP **the Recording Angel** N *(Rel) l'ange qui tient le grand livre des bienfaits et des méfaits*

recording equipment N matériel *m* d'enregistrement

recording session N séance *f* d'enregistrement

recording studio N studio *m* d'enregistrement

recording tape N bande *f or* ruban *m* magnétique

recording van N *(Rad, TV)* car *m* de reportage

recount /rɪˈkaʊnt/ VT *(= relate)* raconter, narrer ◆ **to ~ how an accident happened** retracer les circonstances d'un accident

re-count /ˌriːˈkaʊnt/ VT recompter, compter de nouveau N /ˈriːkaʊnt/ *[of votes]* recomptage *m or* nouveau comptage *m* des voix

recoup /rɪˈkuːp/ VT 1 *(= make good) [+ losses]* récupérer ◆ **to ~ costs** *[person]* rentrer dans ses fonds ; *[earnings]* couvrir les frais ; *[course of action]* permettre de couvrir les frais 2 *(= reimburse)* dédommager *(for* de*)* ◆ **to ~ o.s.** se dédommager, se rattraper 3 *(Jur)* déduire, défalquer VI récupérer ses pertes

recourse /rɪˈkɔːs/ N recours *m (to* à*)* ◆ **to have ~ to ...** avoir recours à ..., recourir à ...

recover /rɪˈkʌvəʳ/ VT *[+ sth lost, one's appetite, reason, balance]* retrouver ; *[+ sth lent]* reprendre *(from sb* à qn*)*, récupérer ; *[+ lost territory]* regagner, reconquérir ; *[+ sth floating]* repêcher ; *[+ space capsule, wreck]* récupérer ; *(Ind etc) [+ materials]* récupérer ; *(Fin) [+ debt]* recouvrer, récupérer ; *[+ goods, property]* rentrer en possession de ◆ **to ~ one's breath** reprendre haleine *or* sa respiration ◆ **to ~ one's strength** reprendre des forces ◆ **to ~ consciousness** revenir à soi, reprendre connaissance ◆ **to ~ one's sight/health** retrouver *or* recouvrer la vue/la santé ◆ **to ~ land from the sea** conquérir du terrain sur la mer ◆ **to ~ lost ground** *(fig)* se rattraper ◆ **to ~ o.s.** *or* **one's composure** se ressaisir, se reprendre ◆ **to ~ expenses** rentrer dans ses frais, récupérer ses débours ◆ **to ~ one's losses** réparer ses pertes ◆ **to ~ damages** *(Jur)* obtenir des dommages-intérêts

VI 1 *(after shock, accident)* se remettre *(from* de*)* ; *(from illness)* guérir, se rétablir *(from* de*)* ; *(= regain consciousness)* revenir à soi, reprendre connaissance ; *(after error)* se ressaisir ; *[economy, currency]* se rétablir, se redresser ; *[stock market]* reprendre ; *[shares]* remonter ◆ **she has completely ~ed** elle est tout à fait rétablie

2 *(Jur)* obtenir gain de cause ◆ **right to ~** droit *m* de reprise

re-cover /ˌriːˈkʌvəʳ/ VT recouvrir

recoverable /rɪˈkʌvərəbl/ ADJ *[goods, knowledge]* récupérable ; *[costs, debts]* recouvrable ; *[losses]* réparable

recovered /rɪˈkʌvəd/ ADJ *(after illness)* guéri, remis COMP **recovered memory** N *(Psych) (= thing remembered) souvenir d'une expérience traumatisante rappelé par psychothérapie* ; *(NonC) (= ability to remember) rappel d'expériences traumatisantes par psychothérapie*

recovery /rɪˈkʌvərɪ/ LANGUAGE IN USE 23.4

N 1 *(from illness)* guérison *f (from sth* de qch*)* ; *(from operation)* rétablissement *m* ◆ **he is making a good ~** *(gen)* il se remet bien ; *(from illness)* il est en bonne voie de guérison ; *(from operation)* il est en bonne voie de rétablissement ◆ **to make a full ~** *(from illness)* guérir complètement ; *(from operation)* se remettre complètement ◆ **he made a good ~ from his stroke** il s'est bien remis de son attaque ◆ **best wishes for a speedy ~** meilleurs vœux de prompt rétablissement ◆ **to be (well) on the road** *or* **way to ~** être en (bonne) voie de guérison ◆ **to be in ~** *(from alcohol, drug addiction)* être en cure de désintoxication ◆ **to be past ~** *[sick person]* être dans un état désespéré ; *[situation]* être sans remède, être irrémédiable ◆ **to make a ~** *(Sport)* se ressaisir

2 *(Fin, Econ) [of economy, market]* reprise *f*, redressement *m* ; *[of shares]* remontée *f* ◆ **a ~ in sales/in the housing market** une reprise des ventes/du marché de l'immobilier ◆ **to engineer the ~ of the economy** relancer l'économie ◆ **to be on the road to ~** être sur la voie de la reprise

3 *(= retrieval) (gen)* récupération *f* ; *[of body] (from water)* repêchage *m* ◆ **a reward for the ~ of the Turner painting** une récompense à la personne qui permettra de retrouver *or* récupérer le tableau de Turner

4 *(= regaining) [of memory, sight, health]* recouvrement *m* ; *[of consciousness, breath, strength]* reprise *f* ; *[of territory]* reconquête *f* ◆ **to bring about the ~ of sb's equanimity/reason/appetite** faire retrouver à qn sa sérénité/sa raison/son appétit

5 *(Fin) [of expenses]* remboursement *m* ; *[of debt]* recouvrement *m* ; *[of losses]* réparation *f* ; *(Jur) [of damages]* obtention *f*

COMP **recovery operation** N opération *f* de récupération *(d'un vaisseau spatial etc)*

recovery position N *(Med)* position *f* latérale de sécurité ◆ **to put sb in the ~ position** mettre qn en position latérale de sécurité

recovery room N *(Med)* salle *f* de réveil

recovery ship N navire *m* de récupération

recovery team N équipe *f* de sauvetage

recovery vehicle N dépanneuse *f*

recovery vessel N ⇒ **recovery ship**

recreant /ˈrekrɪənt/ ADJ, N *(liter)* lâche *mf*, traître(sse) *m(f)*

recreate /ˌriːkrɪˈeɪt/ VT recréer

recreation /ˌrekrɪˈeɪʃən/ N 1 loisir *m* ◆ **he listed his ~s as fishing and shooting** comme loisirs, il a donné la pêche et la chasse ◆ **for ~ I go fishing** je vais à la pêche pour me détendre 2 *(Scol)* récréation *f*, récré* *f*

COMP **recreation ground** N terrain *m* de jeux

recreation room N *[of school, hospital etc]* salle *f* de récréation ; *(US) [of home]* salle *f* de jeux

recreational /ˌrekrɪˈeɪʃənəl/ ADJ *(gen)* pour les loisirs ◆ **~ facilities** équipements *mpl* de loisirs COMP **recreational drug** N drogue *f* euphorisante

recreational sex N rapports *mpl* sexuels purement physiques

recreational therapist N ludothérapeute *mf*

recreational therapy N ludothérapie *f*

recreational vehicle N *(US)* camping-car *m*, autocaravane *f*

recreative /ˈrekrɪˌeɪtɪv/ ADJ récréatif, divertissant

recriminate /rɪˈkrɪmɪneɪt/ VI récriminer *(against* contre*)*

recrimination /rɪˌkrɪmɪˈneɪʃən/ N récrimination *f*

recriminatory /rɪˈkrɪmɪnətərɪ/ ADJ *[argument]* récriminateur (-trice *f*), plein de récriminations ; *[shout]* de protestation ◆ **~ remark** récrimination *f*

rec room* /ˈrekrʊm/ N *(US)* (abbrev of **recreation room**) salle *f* de jeux

recrudesce /ˌriːkruːˈdes/ VI *(liter)* être en recrudescence

recrudescence /ˌriːkruːˈdesns/ N *(liter)* recrudescence *f*

recrudescent /ˌriːkruːˈdesnt/ ADJ *(liter)* recrudescent

recruit /rɪˈkruːt/ N *(Mil, fig)* recrue *f* ◆ **the party gained ~s from the middle classes** le parti faisait des recrues dans la bourgeoisie ; → **raw** VT *[+ member, soldier, staff]* recruter ◆ **the party was ~ed from the middle classes** le parti se recrutait dans la bourgeoisie ◆ **he ~ed me to help** il m'a embauché* pour aider

recruiting /rɪˈkruːtɪŋ/ N recrutement *m* COMP **recruiting office** N *(Mil)* bureau *m* de recrutement

recruiting officer N (officier *m*) recruteur *m*

recruitment /rɪˈkruːtmənt/ N recrutement *m* COMP **recruitment agency** N agence *f* de recrutement

recruitment consultant N conseil *m* en recrutement

recta /ˈrektə/ NPL of **rectum**

rectal /ˈrektəl/ ADJ rectal

rectangle /ˈrekˌtæŋgl/ N rectangle *m*

rectangular /rekˈtæŋgjʊləʳ/ ADJ rectangulaire

rectifiable /ˈrektɪfaɪəbl/ ADJ rectifiable

rectification /ˌrektɪfɪˈkeɪʃən/ N *(gen, Chem, Math)* rectification *f* ; *(Elec)* redressement *m*

rectifier /ˈrektɪfaɪəʳ/ N *(Elec)* redresseur *m*

rectify /ˈrektɪfaɪ/ VT 1 *[+ error]* rectifier, corriger ◆ **to ~ an omission** réparer une négligence *or* un oubli 2 *(Chem, Math)* rectifier 3 *(Elec)* redresser

rectilineal /ˌrektɪˈlɪnɪəl/, **rectilinear** /ˌrektɪˈlɪnɪəʳ/ ADJ rectiligne

rectitude /ˈrektɪtjuːd/ N rectitude *f*

rector /ˈrektəʳ/ N 1 *(Rel)* pasteur *m (anglican)* 2 *(Scot Scol)* proviseur *m* (de lycée) ; *(Univ)* ≃ recteur *m*

rectorship /ˈrektəʃɪp/ N *(Scot Scol)* provisorat *m* ; *(Univ)* ≃ rectorat *m*

rectory /ˈrektərɪ/ N presbytère *m (anglican)*

rectum /ˈrektəm/ N (pl **rectums** *or* **recta**) rectum *m*

recumbent /rɪˈkʌmbənt/ ADJ *(liter) [person]* allongé, étendu ◆ ~ **figure** *(Art) (gen)* figure *f* couchée *or* allongée ; *(on tomb)* gisant *m* COMP **recumbent bicycle** N vélo *m* couché

recuperate /rɪˈkuːpəreɪt/ VI *(Med)* se rétablir, récupérer VT *[+ object]* récupérer ; *[+ losses]* réparer

recuperation /rɪˌkuːpəˈreɪʃən/ N *(Med)* rétablissement *m* ; *[of materials etc]* récupération *f*

recuperative /rɪˈkuːpərətɪv/ ADJ *[powers]* de récupération ; *[holiday, effect]* réparateur (-trice *f*)

recur /rɪˈkɜːʳ/ VI 1 *(= happen again) [error, event]* se reproduire ; *[idea, theme]* se retrouver, revenir ; *[illness, infection]* réapparaître ; *[opportunity, problem]* se représenter 2 *(= come to mind again)* revenir à la mémoire (to sb de qn) 3 *(Math)* se reproduire périodiquement

recurrence /rɪˈkʌrəns/ N *[of problem, event, idea, theme]* répétition *f* ; *[of headache, symptom]* réapparition *f* ; *[of opportunity, problem]* réapparition *f*, retour *m* ◆ **a ~ of the illness** un nouvel accès de la maladie, une rechute ◆ **let there be no ~ of this** que ceci ne se reproduise plus

recurrent /rɪˈkʌrənt/ ADJ 1 *(= recurring)* récurrent ◆ **~ nightmares** des cauchemars *mpl* récurrents ◆ **a ~ feature** un phénomène récurrent ◆ **~ bouts of tonsillitis** des angines *fpl* à répétition ◆ **~ miscarriages** des fausses couches *fpl* répétées ◆ **~ bouts of malaria** des crises *fpl* de paludisme intermittentes 2 *(Anat)* récurrent COMP **recurrent expenditure** N dépenses *fpl* courantes

recurring /rɪˈkɜːrɪŋ/ ADJ 1 ⇒ **recurrent 1** 2 *(Math)* ◆ **3.3333 ~** 3,3 à l'infini ◆ **0.2727 ~** 0,27 périodique COMP **recurring decimal** N fraction *f* décimale récurrente *or* périodique

recursion /rɪˈkɜːʃən/ N *(Math, Gram)* récurrence *f*

recursive /rɪˈkɜːsɪv/ ADJ *(Gram)* récursif

recursively /rɪˈkɜːsɪvlɪ/ ADV de façon récursive

recursiveness /rɪˈkɜːsɪvnɪs/ N récursivité *f*

recusant /ˈrekjʊzənt/ ADJ *(Rel)* réfractaire

recyclable /ˌriːˈsaɪkləbl/ ADJ recyclable

recycle /ˌriːˈsaɪkl/ VT *(gen)* recycler ; *[+ waste, water]* retraiter ; *[+ revenue]* réinvestir COMP **recycled paper** N papier *m* recyclé

recycling /ˌriːˈsaɪklɪŋ/ N recyclage *m*
COMP **recycling plant** N *(gen)* usine *f* de recyclage ; *(for large-scale or toxic waste)* usine *f* de traitement des déchets
recycling scheme N programme *m* de recyclage

red /red/ ADJ 1 *(in colour)* rouge ; *[hair]* roux (rousse *f*) ◆ **~ as a beetroot** *(Brit) or* **a beet** *(US)* rouge comme une tomate ◆ **to go as ~ as a beetroot** *(Brit) or* **a beet** *(US) (gen, from effort, sun, alcohol, embarrassment)* devenir rouge comme une tomate *or* une pivoine ; *(from anger)* devenir rouge de colère ◆ **he was rather ~ in the face** *(naturally)* il était rougeaud, il avait le teint rouge ◆ **her face was ~** *(gen, from anger, effort, sun, heat, alcohol)* elle avait le visage rouge ; *(= ashamed, embarrassed)* elle était rouge jusqu'aux oreilles ◆ **was I ~ in the face!** *, **was my face ~!** *, **did I have a ~ face!** * j'étais rouge jusqu'aux oreilles ! ◆ **he went ~ in the face** son visage est devenu tout rouge ◆ **~ with anger** rouge de colère ◆ **to go** *or* **turn ~ with embarrassment** rougir de confusion *or* d'embarras ◆ **nature ~ in tooth and claw** la nature impitoyable *or* sauvage ◆ **to go into ~ ink** * *(US) [company]* être dans le rouge ; *[individual]* se mettre à découvert ◆ **to bleed ~ ink** * *[business, company]* battre de l'aile ◆ **it's like a ~ rag to a bull** *(Brit)* c'est comme le rouge pour les taureaux ◆ **that is like a ~ rag to him** *(Brit)* il voit rouge quand on lui en parle *(or* quand on le lui montre *etc)* ◆ **to see ~** voir rouge ◆ **it's not worth a ~ cent** * *(US)* ça ne vaut pas un rond * ◆ **I didn't get a ~ cent!** *(US)* je n'ai pas touché un centime *or* un rond ! * ◆ **~ sky at night, shepherd's delight, ~ sky in the morning, shepherd's warning** *(Prov)* ciel rouge le soir, signe de beau temps, ciel rouge le matin, signe de mauvais temps ; see also **comp** ; → **blood, brick, man, paint**

2 *(Pol * pej)* rouge ◆ **better ~ than dead** plutôt rouge que mort

N 1 *(= colour, wine)* rouge *m*

2 *(Pol = person)* rouge *mf*, communiste *mf* ◆ **he sees ~s under the bed** il voit des communistes partout

3 *(Billiards)* bille *f* rouge ; *(Roulette)* rouge *m*

4 *(fig)* **to be in the ~** * être dans le rouge * ◆ **to get out of the ~** sortir du rouge * ◆ **to be £100 in the ~** avoir un découvert *or* un déficit de 100 livres

5 *(US Hist = Indians)* **the Reds** les Peaux-Rouges *mpl*

COMP **red admiral (butterfly)** N vulcain *m*
red alert N alerte *f* maximale *or* rouge ◆ **to be on ~ alert** *(Mil)* être en état d'alerte maximale
the Red Army N l'Armée *f* rouge
Red Army Faction N Fraction *f* armée rouge
red-blooded ADJ vigoureux
red-brick ADJ en briques rouges N *(Brit)* (also **red-brick university**) université *f* de fondation assez récente
the Red Brigades NPL *(Pol)* les Brigades *fpl* rouges
red cabbage N chou *m* rouge
red cap N *(Brit Mil *)* policier *m* militaire ; *(US Rail)* porteur *m*
red card N *(Ftbl)* carton *m* rouge ◆ **to be shown the ~ card** *(lit, fig)* recevoir un carton rouge
red-card VT donner un carton rouge à
red carpet N *(fig)* ◆ **to roll out the ~ carpet for sb** dérouler le tapis rouge pour recevoir qn, recevoir qn en grande pompe
red-carpet treatment N **to give sb the ~-carpet treatment** recevoir qn en grande pompe
Red China N Chine *f* rouge
Red Crescent N Croissant-Rouge *m*
Red Cross (Society) N Croix-Rouge *f*
red deer N cerf *m* noble *or* élaphe
red duster *, **red ensign** N *(Naut)* pavillon *m* de la marine marchande (britannique)
red-eye N *(Phot)* (effet *m*) yeux *mpl* rouges ; *(US)* mauvais whisky *m* ; *(* = night flight:* also **red-eye flight**) avion *m or* vol *m* de nuit
red-eyed ADJ aux yeux rouges
red-faced ADJ *(lit)* rougeaud, rubicond ; *(fig)* gêné, rouge de confusion
Red Flag N drapeau *m* rouge ◆ **"The Red Flag"** *hymne du parti travailliste*
red flag N *(= danger signal)* avertissement *m*
red giant N *(Astron)* géante *f* rouge
red grouse N grouse *f*, lagopède *m* d'Écosse
the Red Guard N *(in former USSR)* la garde rouge
the Red Guards NPL *(in China)* les gardes *mpl* rouges
red-haired ADJ roux (rousse *f*)
red-handed ADJ ◆ **to be caught ~-handed** être pris en flagrant délit *or* la main dans le sac
red hat N *(Rel)* chapeau *m* de cardinal
red-headed ADJ ⇒ **red-haired**
red heat N ◆ **to raise iron to ~ heat** chauffer le fer au rouge
red herring N *(lit)* hareng *m* saur ◆ **that's a ~ herring** c'est pour brouiller les pistes, c'est une diversion
red-hot ADJ *(lit)* chauffé au rouge, brûlant ; *(fig = enthusiastic)* ardent, enthousiaste ; *(fig = up to the moment) [news, information]* de dernière minute ; *(fig = very popular)* excellent N *(US Culin *)* hot-dog *m*
Red Indian N Peau-Rouge *mf*
red lead N minium *m*
red-letter day N jour *m* mémorable, jour *m* à marquer d'une pierre blanche
red light N *(= traffic light)* feu *m* rouge ◆ **to go through the ~ light** passer au rouge, griller * *or* brûler un feu rouge
red-light district N quartier *m* chaud *, quartier *m* des prostituées
red man N (pl **red men**) *(US)* Indien *m (aux USA)* ◆ **it's the ~ man** *(Brit: at pedestrian crossing)* c'est rouge (pour les piétons)
red meat N viande *f* rouge
red mist * N ◆ **he saw the ~ mist** il a vu rouge *
red mullet N rouget *m* barbet
Red Nose Day N *journée de collecte d'argent pour les œuvres charitables, où certains portent un nez rouge en plastique*
red ochre N *(Miner)* ocre *f* rouge
red pepper N poivron *m* rouge
Red Riding Hood N (also **Little Red Riding Hood**) le Petit Chaperon rouge
red salmon N saumon *m* rouge
Red Sea N mer *f* Rouge
red sea bream N daurade *f (or* dorade *f)* rose
red shank N chevalier *m* gambette
red snapper N vivaneau *m*
Red Square N *(in Moscow)* la place Rouge
red squirrel N écureuil *m*
red tape N *(fig)* paperasserie *f*, bureaucratie *f* tatillonne
red wine N vin *m* rouge

redact /rɪˈdækt/ VT *(frm) (= draw up)* rédiger ; *(= edit)* éditer

redaction /rɪˈdækʃən/ N *(frm) (= version)* rédaction *f* ; *(= editing)* édition *f*

redbreast /ˈredbrest/ N rouge-gorge *m*

redcoat /ˈredkəʊt/ N *(Hist)* soldat *m* anglais ; *(Brit) (in holiday camp)* animateur *m*, -trice *f*

redcurrant /redˈkʌrənt/ N groseille *f* (rouge)

redden /ˈredn/ VT rendre rouge, rougir VI *[person]* rougir ; *[foliage]* roussir, devenir roux

reddish /ˈredɪʃ/ ADJ *(gen)* tirant sur le rouge, rougeâtre *(pej)* ; *[hair]* tirant sur le roux, roussâtre *(pej)* ◆ **~-brown** *(gen)* d'un brun rouge, brun-rougeâtre *inv (pej)* ; *[hair]* d'un brun roux, brun-roussâtre *inv (pej)*

redecorate /ˌriːˈdekəreɪt/ VT *[+ room, house]* *(= repaint)* repeindre ; *(= redesign)* refaire la décoration de VI *(= repaint)* refaire les peintures ; *(= redesign)* refaire la décoration

redecoration /riːˌdekəˈreɪʃən/ N remise *f* à neuf des peintures, remplacement *m* des papiers peints

redeem /rɪˈdiːm/ VT *(= buy back)* racheter ; *(from pawn)* dégager ; *(Fin) [+ debt]* amortir, rembourser ; *[+ bill]* honorer ; *[+ mortgage]* purger ; *[+ insurance policy]* encaisser ; *(Comm) [+ coupon, token]* échanger *(for* contre) ; *(US) [+ banknote]* convertir en espèces ; *[+ promise]* tenir ; *[+ obligation]* s'acquitter de, satisfaire à ; *(Rel) [+ sinner]* racheter, rédimer *(frm)* ; *(= compensate for) [+ failing]* racheter, compenser ; *[+ fault]* réparer ◆ **to ~ o.s.** *or* **one's honour** se racheter ◆ **to ~ sb/sth from sth** sauver qn/qch de qch

redeemable /rɪˈdiːməbl/ ADJ *[voucher]* échangeable *(against sth* contre qch) ; *[bond, bill]* remboursable ; *[mortgage]* remboursable, amortissable ; *[debt]* amortissable ; *[insurance policy]* encaissable ; *(from pawn)* qui peut être dégagé ◆ **the vouchers are ~ on selected items** les bons sont à valoir sur l'achat de certains articles ◆ **the catalogue costs £5, ~ against a first order** le catalogue coûte 5 livres, remboursées à la première commande

Redeemer /rɪˈdiːməʳ/ N *(Rel)* Rédempteur *m*

redeeming /rɪˈdiːmɪŋ/ ADJ ◆ **to have some ~ features** avoir des qualités qui rachètent *or* compensent les défauts ◆ **I could not find a single ~ feature in this book** je n'ai pas trouvé la moindre qualité à ce livre ◆ **a book with no ~ qualities** un livre qu'aucune qualité ne vient sauver, un livre sans la moindre qualité pour racheter ses défauts ◆ **his one ~ quality is ...** la seule chose qui peut le racheter est ...

redefine /ˌriːdɪˈfaɪn/ VT *(gen)* redéfinir ◆ **to ~ the problem** modifier les données du problème

redemption /rɪˈdempʃən/ N [1] *(= salvation) (gen)* rédemption *f*, rachat *m* ; *(Rel)* rédemption *f* ◆ **the plants were crushed beyond ~** les plantes étaient tellement écrasées qu'elles étaient irrécupérables ◆ **to be beyond** *or* **past ~** *[person]* être définitivement perdu *(fig) [object]* être irréparable ; *[environment, plant]* être irrécupérable ; *[situation]* être irrémédiable [2] *(Fin) [of mortgage]* remboursement *m*, purge *f* (SPEC) ; *[of bond]* remboursement *m* ; *[of debt]* remboursement *m*, amortissement *m* ; *(from pawn)* dégagement *m*
COMP **redemption value** N valeur *f* de remboursement

redemptive /rɪˈdemptɪv/ ADJ rédempteur (-trice *f*)

redeploy /ˌriːdɪˈplɔɪ/ VT *[+ troops]* redéployer ; *[+ workers, staff] (gen)* redéployer ; *(to new location)* réaffecter ; *(Econ) [+ sector etc]* redéployer

redeployment /ˌriːdɪˈplɔɪmənt/ N *[of troops, weapons, resources, funds]* redéploiement *m* *((in)to sth* dans qch) ; *[of workers, staff] (gen)* redéploiement *m (to sth* dans qch) ; *(to new location)* réaffectation *f*

redesign /ˌriːdɪˈzaɪn/ VT reconcevoir

redevelop /ˌriːdɪˈveləp/ VT *[+ area]* rénover, réaménager

redevelopment /ˌriːdɪˈveləpmənt/ N *[of area]* rénovation *f*, réaménagement *m*
COMP **redevelopment area** N zone *f* de rénovation *or* de réaménagement

redhead /ˈredhed/ N roux *m*, rousse *f*, rouquin(e)* *m(f)*

redial /ˌriːˈdaɪəl/ *(Telec)* VT recomposer VI recomposer le numéro
COMP /ˈriːdaɪəl/ **redial button** N touche *f* bis
redial facility N rappel *m* du dernier numéro composé

redid /ˌriːˈdɪd/ VB pt of **redo**

redirect /ˌriːdaɪˈrekt/ VT *[+ letter, parcel]* faire suivre, réadresser ; *[+ funds, resources]* réallouer ; *[+ traffic]* dévier ◆ **to ~ one's energies** réorienter *or* rediriger son énergie *(towards* vers)

rediscover /ˌriːdɪsˈkʌvəʳ/ VT redécouvrir

redistribute /ˌriːdɪsˈtrɪbjuːt/ VT redistribuer

redistrict /ˌriːˈdɪstrɪkt/ VT *(US Pol, Admin)* soumettre à un redécoupage électoral (*or* administratif) VI *(US Pol, Admin)* se soumettre à un redécoupage électoral (*or* administratif)

redistricting /ˌriːˈdɪstrɪktɪŋ/ N *(US Pol, Admin)* redécoupage *m* électoral (*or* administratif)

redline /ˈredlaɪn/ VT *(US Fin)* pratiquer une discrimination financière envers

redneck* /ˈrednek/ N *(esp US)* rustre *m*, péquenaud(e)‡ *m(f)*

redness /ˈrednɪs/ N rougeur *f* ; *[of hair]* rousseur *f*

redo /ˌriːˈduː/ (pret **redid**, ptp **redone**) VT refaire

redolence /ˈredəʊləns/ N *(liter)* parfum *m*, odeur *f* agréable

redolent /ˈredəʊlənt/ ADJ *(liter)* [1] *(= evocative)* ◆ **~ of sth** évocateur (-trice *f*) de qch ◆ **to be ~ of sth** évoquer qch [2] *(= smelling)* ◆ **to be ~ of sth** sentir qch ◆ **the air was ~ with the smell of freshly-baked bread** l'air embaumait le pain frais

redone /ˌriːˈdʌn/ VB ptp of **redo**

redouble /ˌriːˈdʌbl/ VT [1] redoubler ◆ **to ~ one's efforts** redoubler ses efforts *or* d'efforts [2] *(Bridge)* surcontrer VI redoubler N *(Bridge)* surcontre *m*

redoubt /rɪˈdaʊt/ N *(Mil)* redoute *f*

redoubtable /rɪˈdaʊtəbl/ ADJ redoutable, formidable

redound /rɪˈdaʊnd/ VI *(frm)* contribuer *(to* à) ◆ **to ~ upon** retomber sur ◆ **to ~ to sb's credit** être (tout) à l'honneur de qn

redraft /ˌriːˈdrɑːft/ VT rédiger de nouveau

redress /rɪˈdres/ VT *[+ situation]* redresser ; *[+ wrong, grievance]* réparer ◆ **to ~ the balance (between)** rétablir l'équilibre (entre) N réparation *f* *(for sth* pour qch) ◆ **~ against sb** recours *m* contre qn ◆ **~ of grievances** réparation *f* ◆ **to have no ~** n'avoir aucun recours ◆ **to seek ~** exiger *or* demander réparation

redskin /ˈredskɪn/ N Peau-Rouge *mf*

redstart /ˈredstɑːt/ N *(= bird)* rouge-queue *m*

reduce /rɪˈdjuːs/ VT [1] *(= lessen)* réduire *(to* à ; *by* de) diminuer ; *(= shorten)* raccourcir ; *(= weaken)* affaiblir ; *(= lower)* abaisser ; *[+ drawing, plan]* réduire ; *[+ expenses]* réduire, restreindre ; *[+ price]* baisser, diminuer ; *[+ swelling]* résorber, résoudre ; *[+ temperature]* faire descendre, abaisser ; *[+ sauce]* faire réduire ; *[+ output]* ralentir ; *(Mil etc: in rank)* rétrograder, réduire à un grade inférieur ◆ **to ~ sb to the ranks** *(Mil)* casser qn ◆ **to ~ unemployment** réduire le chômage ; *(gradually)* résorber le chômage ◆ **to ~ speed** *(in car)* diminuer la vitesse, ralentir ◆ **"reduce speed now"** "ralentir" ◆ **to ~ the age of retirement to 58** ramener l'âge de la retraite à 58 ans ◆ **to ~ a prisoner's sentence** *(Jur)* réduire la peine d'un prisonnier
[2] *(Chem, Math, fig)* réduire *(to* en, à) ◆ **to ~ sth to a powder/to pieces/to ashes** réduire qch en poudre/en morceaux/en cendres ◆ **to ~ an argument to its simplest form** réduire un raisonnement à sa plus simple expression, simplifier un raisonnement au maximum ◆ **it has been ~d to nothing** cela a été réduit à zéro ◆ **he's ~d to a skeleton** il n'est plus qu'un squelette ambulant ◆ **to ~ sb to silence/obedience/despair** réduire qn au silence/à l'obéissance/au désespoir ◆ **to ~ sb to begging/to slavery** réduire qn à la mendicité/en esclavage ◆ **to be ~d to begging** être réduit *or* contraint à mendier ◆ **to ~ sb to submission** soumettre qn ◆ **to ~ sb to tears** faire pleurer qn ◆ **to ~ sth to writing** *(Admin, Jur)* consigner qch par écrit
VI *(esp US = slim)* maigrir ◆ **to be reducing** être au régime

reduced /rɪˈdjuːst/ ADJ *(gen)* réduit ◆ **to buy at a ~ price** *[+ ticket]* acheter à prix réduit ; *[+ goods]* acheter au rabais *or* en solde ◆ **to be ~** *[item on sale]* être soldé *or* en solde ◆ **"reduced"** *(on ticket)* "prix réduit" ◆ **on a ~ scale** *[reproduce]* à échelle réduite ; *[act, plan]* sur une plus petite échelle ◆ **in ~ circumstances** *(frm)* dans la gêne
COMP **reduced instruction set computer** N ordinateur *m* à jeu d'instructions réduit
reduced instruction set computing N traitement *m* avec jeu d'instructions réduit

reducer /rɪˈdjuːsəʳ/ N *(= slimming device)* appareil *m* d'amaigrissement ; *(Phot)* réducteur *m*

reducible /rɪˈdjuːsəbl/ ADJ réductible

reductio ad absurdum /rɪˈdʌktɪəʊ ædəbˈsɜːdəm/ N réduction *f* à l'absurde

reduction /rɪˈdʌkʃən/ N [1] réduction *f* ; *(in length)* raccourcissement *m* ; *(in width)* diminution *f* ; *[of expenses, staff]* réduction *f*, compression *f* ; *[of prices, wages]* diminution *f*, baisse *f* ; *[of temperature]* baisse *f* ; *[of voltage]* diminution *f* ; *[of sentence]* réduction *f*, modération *f* ; *[of swelling]* résorption *f*, résolution *f* ; *(Phot)* réduction *f* ; *(in gear system)* démultiplication *f* ◆ **to make a ~ on an article** *(in shop)* faire une remise sur un article ◆ **~ of taxes** dégrèvement *m* d'impôts ◆ **~ of speed** ralentissement *m* ◆ **~ in strength** *(Mil etc)* réduction *f* or diminution *f* des effectifs ◆ **~ in rank** rétrogradation *f* [2] *(Culin)* réduction *f*

reductionism /rɪˈdʌkʃəˌnɪzəm/ N [1] *(pej)* approche *f* réductrice [2] *(Philos)* réductionnisme *m*

reductionist /rɪˈdʌkʃənɪst/ ADJ [1] *(pej)* réducteur [2] *(Philos)* réductionniste N [1] *(pej)* personne *f* aux vues réductrices [2] *(Philos)* réductionniste *mf*

reductive /rɪˈdʌktɪv/ ADJ *(pej = simplistic)* réducteur (-trice *f*), simplificateur (-trice *f*)

redundance /rɪˈdʌndəns/ N ⇒ **redundancy**

redundancy /rɪˈdʌndənsɪ/ N [1] *(Brit: lay off)* licenciement *m* (économique), mise *f* au *or* en chômage (pour raisons économiques) ◆ **it caused a lot of redundancies** cela a causé de nombreux licenciements *or* la mise au chômage de nombreux employés ◆ **he feared ~** il redoutait d'être licencié *or* mis au chômage ◆ **he went in the last round of redundancies** il a perdu son emploi lors de la dernière série de licenciements, il fait partie de la dernière charrette* ◆ **compulsory ~** licenciement *m* ◆ **voluntary ~** départ *m* volontaire [2] *(= excess)* excès *m* [3] *(Literat)* redondance *f*
COMP **redundancy money, redundancy payment** N *(Brit)* indemnité *f* de licenciement

redundant /rɪˈdʌndənt/ ADJ [1] *(Brit: unemployed)* licencié *or* au *or* en chômage (pour raisons économiques) ◆ **to make sb ~** licencier qn *or* mettre qn au chômage (pour raisons économiques) [2] *(= superfluous) [object, example, detail]* superflu ; *[building]* désaffecté ; *[word, term, information]* redondant ; *(Brit) [person]* en surnombre

reduplicate /rɪˈdjuːplɪkeɪt/ VT redoubler ; *(Ling)* rédupliquer ADJ /rɪˈdjuːplɪkɪt/ redoublé, rédupliqué

reduplication /rɪˌdjuːplɪˈkeɪʃən/ N redoublement *m* ; *(Ling)* réduplication *f*

reduplicative /rɪˈdjuːplɪkətɪv/ ADJ *(Ling)* réduplicatif

redux /rɪˈdʌks/ ADJ *(esp US)* nouvelle formule *inv*

redwing /ˈredwɪŋ/ N *(= bird)* mauvis *m*

redwood /ˈredwʊd/ N *(= tree)* séquoia *m*

re-echo /riːˈekəʊ/ VI retentir, résonner (de nouveau *or* plusieurs fois) VT répéter, renvoyer en écho

reed /riːd/ N *(= plant)* roseau *m* ; *[of wind instrument]* anche *f* ; *(liter = pipe)* chalumeau *m*, pipeau *m* ◆ **the ~s** *(Mus)* les instruments *mpl* à anche ; → **broken**
COMP *[basket etc]* de *or* en roseau(x)
reed bed N roselière *f*
reed bunting N *(= bird)* bruant *m* des roseaux
reed instrument N *(Mus)* instrument *m* à anche
reed stop N *(Mus)* jeu *m* d'anches *or* à anches

re-educate /ˌriːˈedjʊkeɪt/ VT rééduquer

re-education /ˈriːˌedjʊˈkeɪʃən/ N rééducation *f*

reedy /ˈriːdɪ/ ADJ [1] *[bank]* couvert de roseaux ; *[pond]* envahi par les roseaux [2] *(pej = high-pitched) [voice, sound, instrument]* aigu (-guë *f*)

reef¹ /riːf/ N [1] récif *m*, écueil *m* ; *(fig)* écueil *m* ◆ **coral ~** récif *m* de corail [2] *(Min)* filon *m*

reef² /riːf/ N *(Naut)* ris *m* VT *(Naut) [+ sail]* prendre un ris dans
COMP **reef knot** N nœud *m* plat

reefer /ˈriːfəʳ/ **N** [1] (= *jacket*) caban *m* [2] * (= *joint*) joint * *m* [3] (US * = *truck etc*) camion *m* (*or* wagon *m*) frigorifique

reek /riːk/ **N** puanteur *f*, relent *m* **VI** [1] (~ *smell*) puer, empester **♦ to ~ of sth** puer *or* empester qch [2] (*Scot*) [*chimney*] fumer

reel /riːl/ **N** [1] [*of thread, tape etc*] bobine *f* ; (*Fishing*) moulinet *m* ; [*of film*] (*Cine*) bande *f* ; (*Phot*) bobine *f*, rouleau *m* ; (*for cable, hose*) dévidoir *m* ; (*Tech*) dévidoir *m*, touret *m*, bobine *f* ; → **inertia**

[2] (= *dance*) reel *m*, quadrille *m* écossais

VT [+ *thread*] bobiner

VI [1] (*gen*) chanceler ; [*drunkenly*] tituber **♦ he lost his balance and ~ed back** il a perdu l'équilibre et il a reculé en chancelant *or* titubant **♦ he went ~ing down the street** il a descendu la rue en chancelant *or* titubant **♦ the blow made him ~** le coup l'a fait chanceler, il a chancelé sous le coup

[2] (*fig*) **my head is ~ing** la tête me tourne **♦ the news made him** *or* **his mind ~** la nouvelle l'a ébranlé **♦ I ~ed at the very thought** cette pensée m'a donné le vertige **♦ I'm still ~ing from the shock of it** je ne me suis pas encore remis du choc **♦ to leave sb ~ing** ébranler qn **♦ the news left us ~ing with disbelief** la nouvelle nous a ébranlés et nous a laissés incrédules **♦ the news sent markets ~ing** la nouvelle a (profondément) perturbé les marchés

COMP reel holder N porte-bobines *m inv*
reel-to-reel ADJ à bobines

► **reel in VT SEP** (*Fishing, Naut*) ramener, remonter

► **reel off VT SEP** [+ *verses, list*] débiter ; [+ *thread*] dévider

► **reel up VT SEP** enrouler

re-elect /ˌriːɪˈlekt/ **VT** réélire

re-election /ˌriːɪˈlekʃən/ **N** (*Pol*) **♦ to stand** (*Brit*) *or* **run for ~** se représenter (aux élections)

re-embark /ˌriːɪmˈbɑːk/ **VTI** rembarquer

re-embarkation /ˈriːˌembɑːˈkeɪʃən/ **N** rembarquement *m*

re-emerge /ˌriːɪˈmɜːdʒ/ **VI** [*object, swimmer*] resurgir ; [*facts*] ressortir

re-employ /ˌriːɪmˈplɔɪ/ **VT** réembaucher

re-enact /ˌriːɪˈnækt/ **VT** [1] (*Jur*) remettre en vigueur [2] [+ *scene, crime*] reconstituer, reproduire

re-enactment /ˌriːɪˈnæktmənt/ **N** (*Jur*) [*of law*] remise *f* en vigueur ; [*of crime*] reconstitution *f*

re-engage /ˌriːɪnˈgeɪdʒ/ **VT** [+ *employee*] rengager, réembaucher **♦ to ~ the clutch** rengréner, rengrener

re-engagement /ˌriːɪnˈgeɪdʒmənt/ **N** [1] [*of employee*] rengagement *m*, réengagement *m*, réemploi *m* [2] [*of clutch*] rengrènement *m*

re-engineer /ˌriːendʒɪˈnɪəʳ/ **VT** [+ *machine*] redessiner, relooker * ; [+ *department, process, system*] redéfinir

re-enlist /ˌriːɪnˈlɪst/ **VI** se rengager **VT** rengager

re-enter /ˌriːˈentəʳ/ **VI** [1] rentrer [2] **♦ to ~ for an exam** se représenter à *or* se réinscrire pour un examen **VT** rentrer dans **♦ to ~ the Earth's atmosphere** (*Space*) rentrer dans l'atmosphère

re-entry /ˌriːˈentrɪ/ **N** (*gen, Space*) rentrée *f* **♦ her ~ into politics** son retour à la politique

COMP re-entry permit N permis *m* de rentrée (*dans un pays où l'on voyage avec un visa*)
re-entry point N (*Space*) point *m* de rentrée

re-erect /ˌriːɪˈrekt/ **VT** [+ *building, bridge*] reconstruire ; [+ *scaffolding, toy*] remonter

re-establish /ˌriːɪsˈtæblɪʃ/ LANGUAGE IN USE 26.3 **VT** [+ *relations, links, order, stability, monarchy, service*] rétablir ; [+ *person*] réhabiliter ; [+ *custom*] restaurer **♦ to ~ itself** [*species*] se réimplanter **♦ to ~ o.s. (as)** [*person*] (*after failure, setback*) retrouver sa place (de) **♦ the Conservatives are trying to ~ themselves in Scotland** les conservateurs essaient de retrouver leur place *or* de regagner du terrain en Écosse

re-establishment /ˌriːɪsˈtæblɪʃmənt/ **N** [*of relations, links, order, stability, monarchy, service*] rétablissement *m* ; [*of species*] réintroduction *f* ; [*of refugees*] réinstallation *f*

re-evaluate /ˌriːɪˈvæljʊeɪt/ **VT** réévaluer

reeve¹ /riːv/ **N** (*Hist*) premier magistrat *m* ; (*Can*) président *m* du conseil municipal

reeve² /riːv/ **VT** (*Naut*) [+ *rope*] passer dans un anneau *or* une poulie, capeler ; [+ *shoal*] passer au travers de

re-examination /ˈriːɪgˌzæmɪˈneɪʃən/ **N** nouvel examen *m* ; (*Jur: of witness*) nouvel interrogatoire *m*

re-examine /ˌriːɪgˈzæmɪn/ **VT** examiner de nouveau ; (*Jur*) [+ *witness*] interroger de nouveau

re-export /ˌriːɪkˈspɔːt/ **VT** réexporter **N** /ˌriːˈekspɔːt/ réexportation *f*

ref¹ (*Comm*) (abbrev of **with reference to**) → **reference**

ref² * /ref/ **N** (*Sport*) (abbrev of **referee**) arbitre *m*

refection /rɪˈfekʃən/ **N** (*frm*) (= *light meal*) collation *f*, repas *m* léger ; (= *refreshment*) rafraîchissements *mpl*

refectory /rɪˈfektərɪ/ **N** réfectoire *m* **COMP refectory table N** table *f* de réfectoire

refer /rɪˈfɜːʳ/ **VT** [1] (= *pass*) [+ *matter, question, file*] soumettre (*to* à) **♦ the problem was ~red to the UN** le problème a été soumis *or* renvoyé à l'ONU **♦ the dispute was ~red to arbitration** le litige a été soumis à l'arbitrage **♦ it was ~red to us for (a) decision** on nous a demandé de prendre une décision là-dessus **♦ I have to ~ it to my boss** je dois le soumettre à *or* en parler à mon patron **♦ I ~red him to the manager** je lui ai dit de s'adresser au gérant, je l'ai renvoyé au directeur **♦ the doctor ~red me to a specialist** le médecin m'a adressé à un spécialiste **♦ the patient was ~red for tests** on a envoyé le patient subir des examens **♦ to ~ sb to the article on ...** renvoyer qn à l'article sur ..., prier qn de se reporter *or* se référer à l'article sur ... **♦ "the reader is referred to page 10"** "prière de se reporter *or* se référer à la page 10" **♦ to ~ a cheque to drawer** (*Banking*) refuser d'honorer un chèque

[2] (*Jur*) [+ *accused*] déférer

[3] (*Univ*) [+ *student*] refuser **♦ his thesis has been ~red** on lui a demandé de revoir *or* de reprendre sa thèse

[4] (*liter, frm* = *attribute*) attribuer (*to* à)

VI [1] (= *allude*) (*directly*) parler (*to* de), faire référence (*to* à) ; (*indirectly*) faire allusion (*to* à) **♦ I am not ~ring to you** je ne parle pas de vous **♦ we shall not ~ to it again** nous n'en reparlerons pas, nous n'en parlerons plus **♦ he never ~s to that evening** il ne parle jamais de ce soir-là **♦ what can he be ~ring to?** de quoi parle-t-il ?, à quoi peut-il bien faire allusion ? **♦ he ~red to her as his assistant** il l'a appelée son assistante **♦ ~ring to your letter** (*Comm*) (comme) suite *or* en réponse à votre lettre **♦ ~ to drawer** (*Banking*) voir le tireur

[2] (= *apply*) s'appliquer (*to* à) **♦ does that remark ~ to me?** est-ce que cette remarque s'applique à moi ? **♦ this ~s to you all** cela vous concerne tous

[3] (= *consult*) se reporter, se référer (*to sth* à qch) **♦ to ~ to one's notes** consulter ses notes, se reporter *or* se référer à ses notes **♦ "please refer to section 3"** "prière de se reporter *or* se référer à la section 3" **♦ you must ~ to the original** vous devez vous reporter *or* vous référer à l'original

COMP referred pain N (*Med*) irradiation *f* douloureuse

► **refer back VT SEP** [+ *decision*] remettre (à plus tard), ajourner **♦ to ~ sth back to sb** consulter qn sur *or* au sujet de qch

referable /rɪˈfɜːrəbl/ **ADJ** attribuable (*to* à)

referee /ˌrefəˈriː/ **N** [1] (*Ftbl etc, also fig*) arbitre *m* ; (*Tennis*) juge-arbitre *m* [2] (*Brit: giving a reference*) répondant(e) *m(f)* **♦ to act as** *or* **be (a) ~ for sb** fournir des références *or* une attestation à qn **♦ to give sb as a ~** donner qn en référence **♦ may I give your name as a ~?** puis-je donner votre nom en référence ? **VT** (*Sport, fig*) arbitrer **VI** (*Sport, fig*) servir d'arbitre, être arbitre

reference /ˈrefrəns/ LANGUAGE IN USE 19.1

N [1] (*NonC*) référence *f* (*to* à) ; [*of question for judgement*] renvoi *m* **♦ outside the ~ of** hors de la compétence de **♦ keep these details for ~** gardez ces renseignements pour information ; → **future, term**

[2] (= *allusion*) (*direct*) mention *f* (*to* de) ; (*indirect*) allusion *f* (*to* à) **♦ a ~ was made to his illness** on a fait allusion à *or* on a fait mention de sa maladie **♦ in** *or* **with ~ to** quant à, en ce qui concerne ; (*Comm*) (comme) suite à **♦ without ~ to** sans tenir compte de, sans égard pour

[3] (= *testimonial*) **~(s)** références *fpl* **♦ to give sb a good ~** *or* **good ~s** fournir de bonnes références à qn **♦ a banker's ~** des références bancaires **♦ I've been asked for a ~ for him** on m'a demandé de fournir des renseignements sur lui

[4] ⇒ **referee noun 2**

[5] (*in book, article* = *note redirecting reader*) renvoi *m*, référence *f* ; (*on map*) coordonnées *fpl* ; (*Comm: on letter*) référence *f* **♦ please quote this ~** prière de rappeler cette référence ; → **cross**

[6] (= *connection*) rapport *m* (*to* avec) **♦ this has no ~ to ...** cela n'a aucun rapport avec ...

[7] (*Ling*) référence *f*

VT [1] [+ *quotation*] référencer ; [+ *book*] fournir les références de

[2] (= *refer to*) faire référence à

COMP reference book N ouvrage *m* de référence
reference library N bibliothèque *f* d'ouvrages de référence
reference mark N renvoi *m*
reference number N (*Comm*) numéro *m* de référence
reference point N point *m* de référence
reference strip N (*Phot*) bande *f* étalon

referendum /ˌrefəˈrendəm/ **N** (pl **referendums** *or* **referenda** /ˌrefəˈrendə/) référendum *m* **♦ to hold a ~** organiser un référendum **♦ a ~ will be held** un référendum aura lieu

referent /ˈrefərənt/ **N** référent *m*

referential /ˌrefəˈrenʃəl/ **ADJ** référentiel

referral /rɪˈfɜːrəl/ **N** [1] (*Med, Psych*) (= *act*) orientation *f* d'un patient (*vers des services spécialisés*) ; (= *person*) patient(e) *m(f)* (*orienté(e) vers des services spécialisés*) **♦ ask your doctor for a ~ to a dermatologist** demandez à votre médecin de vous envoyer chez un dermatologue **♦ letter of ~** *lettre par laquelle un médecin adresse un patient à un spécialiste* [2] (*Jur*) **♦ the ~ of the case to the Appeal Courts** le renvoi de l'affaire en appel **♦ the ~ of the case to the Director of Public Prosecutions** la soumission de l'affaire au procureur général [3] (*NonC: to higher authority*) **♦ he sanctioned the deal without ~** il a approuvé le marché sans en référer à une autorité supérieure

refill /ˌriːˈfɪl/ **VT** [+ *glass, bottle*] remplir à nouveau ; [+ *pen, lighter*] recharger **N** /ˈriːfɪl/ (*gen*) recharge *f* ; (= *cartridge*) cartouche *f* ; (*for propelling pencil*) mine *f* de rechange ; (*for notebook*) feuilles *fpl* de rechange **♦ would you like a ~ *?** (*for drink*) encore un verre (*or* une tasse) ?

refinance /riːˈfaɪnæns/ VT refinancer

refine /rɪˈfaɪn/ VT 1 *[+ ore]* affiner ; *[+ oil]* épurer ; *[+ crude oil, sugar]* raffiner 2 *(= improve)* *[+ language]* châtier ; *[+ manners]* réformer ; *[+ theory, technique, process, taste]* affiner ; *[+ model, engine]* perfectionner ; *[+ essay etc]* peaufiner* VI ◆ **to ~ upon sth** raffiner sur qch

refined /rɪˈfaɪnd/ ADJ 1 *(= processed)* *[food, ore]* traité ; *[sugar, oil]* raffiné ; *[flour]* bluté ; *[metal]* affiné ◆ **~ products** *(St Ex, Econ)* produits *mpl* raffinés 2 *(= genteel)* *[person, manners, taste]* raffiné 3 *(= sophisticated)* *[model, engine]* perfectionné

refinement /rɪˈfaɪnmənt/ N 1 *(NonC = refining)* *[of crude oil, sugar]* raffinage *m* ; *[of ore]* affinage *m* ; *[of oil]* épuration *f* 2 *(NonC)* *[of person]* raffinement *m*, délicatesse *f* ; *[of language, style]* raffinement *m* 3 *(= improvement: in technique, machine etc)* perfectionnement *m* *(in* de*)*

refiner /rɪˈfaɪnəʳ/ N *[of crude oil, sugar]* raffineur *m* ; *[of metals]* affineur *m* ; *[of oil]* épureur *m*

refinery /rɪˈfaɪnərɪ/ N *(for crude oil, sugar)* raffinerie *f* ; *(for metals)* affinerie *f*

refit /ˌriːˈfɪt/ VT *[+ ship etc]* *(also gen)* remettre en état ; *[+ factory]* équiper de nouveau, renouveler l'équipement de VI *[ship]* être remis en état N /ˈriːfɪt/ *[of ship]* remise *f* en état ; *[of factory]* nouvel équipement *m* COMP **refit yard** N chantier *m* de réarmement

refitting /ˌriːˈfɪtɪŋ/, **refitment** /ˌriːˈfɪtmənt/ N ⇒ **refit noun**

reflate /ˌriːˈfleɪt/ VT *(Econ)* relancer

reflation /riːˈfleɪʃən/ N *(Econ)* relance *f*

reflationary /riːˈfleɪʃnərɪ/ ADJ *(Econ)* de relance

reflect /rɪˈflekt/ VT 1 *(= show)* refléter ; *[+ credit, discredit]* faire rejaillir, faire retomber ◆ **a price that ~s the real costs of production** un prix qui reflète les coûts de production réels ◆ **concern at the economic situation was ~ed in the government's budget** le budget du gouvernement traduisait une certaine inquiétude face à la situation économique ◆ **the many difficulties are ~ed in his report** son rapport rend compte des multiples difficultés

♦ **to reflect on** ◆ **this kind of behaviour ~s on the school** ce genre d'attitude rejaillit sur l'école ◆ **the affair did not ~ well on the company** ce scandale a terni l'image de la société

2 *[+ light, image]* refléter ; *[mirror]* réfléchir ; *[+ heat, sound]* renvoyer ◆ **the moon is ~ed in the lake** la lune se reflète dans le lac ◆ **I saw him ~ed in the mirror** j'ai vu son image dans le miroir *or* réfléchie par le miroir ◆ **he saw himself ~ed in the mirror** le miroir a réfléchi *or* lui a renvoyé son image ◆ **he basked** *or* **bathed in the ~ed glory of his friend's success** il tirait gloire *or* fierté de la réussite de son ami

3 *(= think)* ◆ **to ~ that ...** se dire que ...

VI 1 *(= meditate)* réfléchir *(on* à*)*, méditer *(on* sur*)*

2 ◆ **to ~ off** être réfléchi par

COMP **reflecting prism** N prisme réflecteur

► **reflect (up)on** VT FUS *(= affect)* *[+ person]* avoir des répercussions *or* des incidences sur la réputation de ; *[+ reputation]* avoir des répercussions *or* des incidences sur ◆ **to ~ well/badly (up)on sb** faire honneur à/nuire à la réputation de qn

reflectingly /rɪˈflektɪŋlɪ/ ADV ⇒ **reflectively**

reflection /rɪˈflekʃən/ N 1 *(NonC = reflecting)* *[of light, heat, sound]* réflexion *f* 2 *(= image: in mirror etc)* reflet *m*, image *f* ◆ **to see one's ~ in a mirror** voir son reflet dans un miroir ◆ **a pale ~ of former glory** un pâle reflet de la gloire passée 3 *(NonC = consideration)* réflexion *f* ◆ **on ~** (toute) réflexion faite, à la réflexion ◆ **on serious ~** après mûre réflexion ◆ **he did it without sufficient ~** il l'a fait sans avoir suffisamment réfléchi 4 *(= thoughts, comments)* ◆ **~s** réflexions *fpl* *(on, upon* sur*)* 5 *(= adverse criticism)* critique *f* *(on* de*)*, réflexion *f* désobligeante *(on* sur*)* ; *(on sb's honour)* atteinte *f* *(on* à*)* ◆ **this is no ~ on ...** cela ne porte pas atteinte à ...

reflective /rɪˈflektɪv/ ADJ 1 *(= pensive)* *[person, expression]* *(by nature)* réfléchi ; *(on one occasion)* pensif ; *[powers]* de réflexion ◆ **to be in a ~ mood** être d'humeur pensive ◆ **it was a ~ occasion** ce fut une occasion propice à la méditation 2 *(= typical)* ◆ **to be ~ of sth** refléter qch 3 *[surface, material, clothing]* réfléchissant ; *[light]* réfléchi 4 *(Gram)* ⇒ **reflexive 1**

reflectively /rɪˈflektɪvlɪ/ ADV *[look]* d'un air pensif ; *[say]* d'un ton pensif

reflectiveness /rɪˈflektɪvnɪs/ N caractère *m* réfléchi *or* pensif

reflector /rɪˈflektəʳ/ N *(gen)* réflecteur *m* ; *[of car, bicycle]* réflecteur *m*, cataphote ® *m*

reflex /ˈriːfleks/ ADJ *(Physiol, Psych, fig)* réflexe ; *(Math)* *[angle]* rentrant ; *(Phys)* réfléchi ◆ **~ (camera)** *(Phot)* (appareil *m*) reflex *m* N réflexe *m* ; → **condition**

reflexion /rɪˈflekʃən/ N ⇒ **reflection**

reflexive /rɪˈfleksɪv/ ADJ 1 *(Gram)* réfléchi 2 *(= reactive)* ◆ **a ~ movement** un réflexe N *(Gram)* verbe *m* réfléchi

COMP **reflexive pronoun** N pronom *m* réfléchi
reflexive verb N verbe *m* (pronominal) réfléchi

reflexively /rɪˈfleksɪvlɪ/ ADV 1 *(Gram)* à la forme réfléchie 2 *(= instinctively)* *[move]* d'instinct

reflexology /ˌriːflekˈsɒlədʒɪ/ N réflexologie *f*

refloat /ˌriːˈfləʊt/ VT *[+ ship, business etc]* renflouer, remettre à flot VI être renfloué, être remis à flot

reflux /ˈriːflʌks/ N reflux *m*

reforest /riːˈfɒrɪst/ VT reboiser

reforestation /ˌriːfɒrɪsˈteɪʃən/ (US) N ⇒ **reafforestation**

reform /rɪˈfɔːm/ N réforme *f* ; → **land** VT *[+ law]* réformer ; *[+ institution, service]* réformer, faire des réformes dans ; *[+ conduct]* corriger ; *[+ person]* faire prendre de meilleures habitudes à ◆ **to ~ spelling** faire une réforme de *or* réformer l'orthographe VI *[person]* s'amender, se réformer†

COMP *[measures etc]* de réforme
Reform Judaism N judaïsme *m* non orthodoxe
the Reform Laws NPL *(Brit Hist)* les lois *fpl* de réforme parlementaire
reform school N *(US)* maison *f* de redressement

re-form /ˌriːˈfɔːm/ VT 1 *(= form again)* reformer, rendre sa première forme à ; *(Mil)* *[+ ranks]* reformer ; *[+ troops]* rallier, remettre en rangs 2 *(= give new form to)* donner une nouvelle forme à VI se reformer ; *(Mil)* se reformer, reprendre sa formation

reformable /rɪˈfɔːməbl/ ADJ réformable

reformat /ˌriːˈfɔːmæt/ VT *(Comput)* reformater

reformation /ˌrefəˈmeɪʃən/ N *(NonC)* *[of church, spelling, conduct]* réforme *f* ; *[of person]* assagissement *m*, retour *m* à une vie plus sage ◆ **the Reformation** *(Hist)* la Réforme, la Réformation

reformative /rɪˈfɔːmətɪv/ ADJ de réforme, réformateur (-trice *f*)

reformatory /rɪˈfɔːmətərɪ/ N *(Brit ††)* maison *f* de correction *or* de redressement ; *(US Jur)* centre *m* d'éducation surveillée

reformed /rɪˈfɔːmd/ ADJ 1 *[alcoholic]* ancien *before n* ; *[criminal]* repenti ; *[spelling]* réformé ◆ **he's a ~ character** il s'est rangé *or* assagi 2 *(Rel)* *[church]* réformé ; *[Jew]* non orthodoxe

reformer /rɪˈfɔːməʳ/ N réformateur *m*, -trice *f*

reformist /rɪˈfɔːmɪst/ ADJ, N réformiste *mf*

reformulate /riːˈfɔːmjʊˌleɪt/ VT reformuler

refract /rɪˈfrækt/ VT réfracter

refracting /rɪˈfræktɪŋ/ ADJ *(Phys)* réfringent COMP **refracting angle** N angle *m* de réfringence
refracting telescope N lunette *f* d'approche

refraction /rɪˈfrækʃən/ N réfraction *f*

refractive /rɪˈfræktɪv/ ADJ réfractif, réfringent COMP **refractive index** N indice *m* de réfraction

refractometer /ˌriːfrækˈtɒmɪtəʳ/ N réfractomètre *m*

refractor /rɪˈfræktəʳ/ N 1 *(Phys)* milieu *m* réfringent, dispositif *m* de réfraction 2 *(= telescope)* lunette *f* d'approche

refractory /rɪˈfræktərɪ/ ADJ réfractaire

refrain¹ /rɪˈfreɪn/ VI se retenir, s'abstenir *(from doing sth* de faire qch*)* ◆ **he ~ed from comment** il s'est abstenu de tout commentaire ◆ **they ~ed from measures leading to ...** ils se sont abstenus de toute mesure menant à ... ◆ **please ~ from smoking** *(on notice)* prière de ne pas fumer ; *(spoken)* ayez l'obligeance de ne pas fumer

refrain² /rɪˈfreɪn/ N *(Mus, Poetry, fig)* refrain *m*

refrangible /rɪˈfrændʒəbl/ ADJ réfrangible

refresh /rɪˈfreʃ/ VT *[drink, bath]* rafraîchir ; *[food]* revigorer, redonner des forces à ; *[sleep, rest etc]* délasser, détendre ; *(Comput)* *[+ screen]* rafraîchir ◆ **to ~ o.s.** *(with drink)* se rafraîchir ; *(with food)* se restaurer ; *(with sleep)* se reposer, se délasser ◆ **to feel ~ed** se sentir revigoré ◆ **to ~ one's memory** se rafraîchir la mémoire ◆ **to ~ one's memory about sth** se remettre qch en mémoire ◆ **let me ~ your memory!** je vais vous rafraîchir la mémoire !* ◆ **they must ~ and update their skills** ils doivent actualiser leurs connaissances

refresher /rɪˈfreʃəʳ/ N 1 *(= drink etc)* boisson *f etc* pour se rafraîchir 2 *(Jur)* honoraires *mpl* supplémentaires COMP **refresher course** N stage *m or* cours *m* de remise à niveau

refreshing /rɪˈfreʃɪŋ/ ADJ *[honesty, idea, approach, drink, fruit, taste, bath]* rafraîchissant ; *[change, sight, news]* agréable ; *[sleep]* réparateur (-trice *f*) ◆ **it's ~ to see that ...** ça fait du bien de voir que ..., c'est agréable de voir que ...

refreshingly /rɪˈfreʃɪŋlɪ/ ADV *[different]* agréablement ◆ **~ honest/frank/new** d'une honnêteté/franchise/originalité qui fait plaisir à voir ◆ **~ cool** d'une fraîcheur vivifiante ◆ **a ~ dry wine** un vin sec et agréable

refreshment /rɪˈfreʃmənt/ N 1 *[of mind, body]* repos *m*, délassement *m* 2 *(= food, drink)* **(light) ~s** rafraîchissements *mpl* ◆ **~s** *(= place)* ⇒ **refreshment room**

COMP **refreshment bar** N buvette *f*
refreshment room N *(Rail)* buffet *m*
refreshment stall N ⇒ **refreshment bar**

refried beans /ˌriːfraɪdˈbiːnz/ NPL *préparation mexicaine à base de haricots*

refrigerant /rɪˈfrɪdʒərənt/ ADJ, N réfrigérant *m* ; *(Med)* fébrifuge *m*

refrigerate /rɪˈfrɪdʒəreɪt/ VT réfrigérer ; *(in cold room etc)* frigorifier

refrigeration /rɪˌfrɪdʒəˈreɪʃən/ N réfrigération *f*

refrigerator /rɪˈfrɪdʒəreɪtəʳ/ N *(= cabinet)* réfrigérateur *m*, frigidaire ® *m*, frigo* *m* ; *(= room)* chambre *f* frigorifique ; *(= apparatus)* condenseur *m* COMP *[truck etc]* frigorifique

refrigeratory /rɪˈfrɪdʒərətərɪ/ ADJ, N *(Chem)* réfrigérant *m*

refringent /rɪˈfrɪndʒənt/ ADJ réfringent

refuel /ˌriːˈfjʊəl/ VI se ravitailler en carburant *or* en combustible VT ravitailler

refuelling, refueling (US) /ˌriːˈfjʊəlɪŋ/ N ravitaillement *m* (en carburant *or* en combustible) COMP **refuelling stop** N (*for plane*) escale *f* technique

refuge /ˈrefjuːdʒ/ N (*lit, fig*) refuge *m*, abri *m* (*from* contre) ; (*for climbers, pedestrians etc*) refuge *m* ◆ **place of ~** asile *m* ◆ **a ~ for battered women** un foyer pour femmes battues ◆ **to seek ~** chercher refuge *or* asile ◆ **they sought ~ from the fighting in the city** ils ont cherché un refuge pour échapper aux combats dans la ville ◆ **to seek ~ in silence** chercher refuge dans le silence ◆ **to take ~ in** (*lit, fig*) se réfugier dans ◆ **he took ~ in alcohol and drugs** il se réfugia dans l'alcool et la drogue ◆ **she found ~ in a book** elle a trouvé refuge dans un livre ◆ **God is my ~** Dieu est mon refuge

refugee /ˌrefjʊˈdʒiː/ N réfugié(e) *m(f)*
COMP **refugee camp** N camp *m* de réfugiés
refugee status N statut *m* de réfugié

refulgence /rɪˈfʌldʒəns/ N (*liter*) splendeur *f*, éclat *m*

refulgent /rɪˈfʌldʒənt/ ADJ (*liter*) resplendissant, éclatant

refund /rɪˈfʌnd/ VT 1 rembourser (*to sb* à qn) ◆ **to ~ sb's expenses** rembourser qn de ses frais *or* dépenses ◆ **to ~ postage** rembourser les frais de port 2 (*Fin*) [*+ excess payments*] ristourner N /ˈriːfʌnd/ remboursement *m* ; (*Fin*) ristourne *f* ◆ **tax ~** bonification *f* de trop-perçu ◆ **to get a ~** se faire rembourser

refundable /rɪˈfʌndəbl/ ADJ remboursable

refurbish /ˌriːˈfɜːbɪʃ/ VT [*+ building*] réaménager, remettre à neuf ; [*+ furniture*] remettre à neuf ; [*+ image*] moderniser

refurbishment /ˌriːˈfɜːbɪʃmənt/ N réaménagement *m*, remise *f* à neuf

refurnish /ˌriːˈfɜːnɪʃ/ VT remeubler

refusal /rɪˈfjuːzəl/ N refus *m* (*to do sth* de faire qch) ◆ **~ of justice** (*Jur*) déni *m* de justice ◆ **to get a ~, to meet with a ~** se heurter à *or* essuyer un refus ◆ **to give a flat ~** refuser net ◆ **three ~s** (*Horse-riding*) trois refus ◆ **to give** *or* **offer sb first ~ of sth** accorder à qn l'option sur qch ◆ **to have (the) first ~ of sth** recevoir la première offre de qch, avoir le droit de préemption sur qch

refuse¹ /rɪˈfjuːz/ LANGUAGE IN USE 8.3, 9.3, 12 VT (*gen*) refuser (*sb sth* qch à qn ; *to do sth* de faire qch) se refuser (*to do sth* à faire qch) ; [*+ offer, invitation*] refuser, décliner ; [*+ request*] rejeter, repousser ◆ **I absolutely ~ to do it** je me refuse catégoriquement à le faire ◆ **to be ~d** essuyer un refus ◆ **to be ~d sth** se voir refuser qch ◆ **they were ~d permission to leave** on leur a refusé *or* ils se sont vu refuser la permission de partir ◆ **she ~d him** elle l'a rejeté ◆ **she ~d his proposal** elle a rejeté son offre ◆ **to ~ a fence** [*horse*] refuser l'obstacle VI refuser, opposer un refus ; [*horse*] refuser l'obstacle

refuse² /ˈrefjuːs/ N détritus *mpl*, ordures *fpl* ; (= *industrial or food waste*) déchets *mpl* ◆ **household ~** ordures *fpl* ménagères ◆ **garden ~** détritus *mpl* de jardin
COMP **refuse bin** N poubelle *f*, boîte *f* à ordures
refuse chute N (*at dump*) dépotoir *m* ; (*in building*) vide-ordures *m inv*
refuse collection N ramassage *m or* collecte *f* des ordures
refuse collector N éboueur *m*
refuse destructor N incinérateur *m* (d'ordures)
refuse disposal N traitement *m* des ordures ménagères
refuse disposal service N service *m* de voirie
refuse disposal unit N broyeur *m* d'ordures
refuse dump N (*public*) décharge *f* (publique), dépotoir *m* ; (*in garden*) monceau *m* de détritus
refuse lorry N camion *m* des éboueurs

refus(e)nik /rɪˈfjuːznɪk/ N (*Pol*) refuznik *mf*

refutable /rɪˈfjuːtəbl/ ADJ réfutable

refutation /ˌrefjʊˈteɪʃən/ N réfutation *f*

refute /rɪˈfjuːt/ LANGUAGE IN USE 26.3 VT (= *disprove*) réfuter ; (= *deny*) nier ◆ **she was quick to ~ the accusation** elle a tout de suite nié cette accusation

reg. /redʒ/ N (*Brit* *) (abbrev of **registration number**) → **registration** ADJ (abbrev of **registered**) ◆ **~ no.** n°

-reg * /redʒ/ ADJ, N (*Brit*) (abbrev of **-registration**) ◆ **P-reg (car)** *voiture dont l'immatriculation commence ou finit par un P (la lettre indiquant l'année de mise en circulation)*

regain /rɪˈgeɪn/ VT [*+ one's composure, balance, self-confidence*] retrouver ; [*+ sb's confidence*] regagner, reconquérir ; [*+ one's health, sight etc*] recouvrer ; [*+ title, initiative*] reprendre ; [*+ independence, territory*] reconquérir ; (*liter* = *arrive back at*) [*+ place*] regagner ◆ **to ~ one's strength** récupérer (ses forces), recouvrer ses forces ◆ **to ~ consciousness** revenir à soi, reprendre connaissance ◆ **to ~ lost time** regagner *or* rattraper le temps perdu ◆ **to ~ one's footing** reprendre pied ◆ **to ~ possession (of)** rentrer en possession (de)

regal /ˈriːgəl/ ADJ [*suite, staircase, manner, bearing, gesture*] royal ; [*splendour, dignity*] majestueux ; [*disdain*] souverain

regale /rɪˈgeɪl/ VT régaler (*sb with sth* qn de qch)

regalia /rɪˈgeɪlɪə/ N [*of monarch*] prérogatives *fpl* royales ; (= *insignia*) insignes *mpl* royaux ; [*of Freemasons etc*] insignes *mpl* ◆ **she was in full ~** (*hum*) elle était dans ses plus beaux atours *or* en grand tralala *

regally /ˈriːgəlɪ/ ADV (*lit, fig*) royalement

regard /rɪˈgɑːd/ LANGUAGE IN USE 21.2
VT 1 (= *consider*) considérer (*as* comme) ; ◆ **he was ~ed as an outstanding prime minister** il était considéré comme un premier ministre d'exception ◆ **we ~ it as worth doing** à notre avis ça vaut la peine de le faire ◆ **we don't ~ it as necessary** nous ne le considérons pas comme nécessaire ◆ **I ~ him highly** je le tiens en grande estime ◆ **without ~ing his wishes** sans tenir compte de ses souhaits
◆ **to regard + with** ◆ **to ~ with favour** voir d'un bon œil ◆ **to ~ with loathing** détester, haïr ◆ **millions ~ed this prospect with horror** cette perspective faisait horreur à des millions de gens ◆ **displays of emotion are ~ed with suspicion** les démonstrations d'émotion sont vues d'un mauvais œil *or* sont mal vues
◆ **as regards ...** pour *or* en ce qui concerne ..., pour ce qui regarde ...
2 (*liter*) (= *look at*) observer
N 1 (= *concern*) considération *f* ◆ **the economy was developed without ~ for the interests of farmers** on a développé l'économie sans aucune considération *or* aucun égard pour les intérêts des agriculteurs ◆ **to have ~ to sb/sth** tenir compte de qn/qch ◆ **to have** *or* **show little ~ for sb/sth** faire peu de cas de qn/qch ◆ **to have** *or* **show no ~ for sb/sth** ne faire aucun cas de qn/qch ◆ **out of ~ for sb/sth** par égard pour qn/qch ◆ **having ~ to sb/sth** si l'on tient compte de qn/qch
◆ **in this** *or* **that regard** à cet égard, sous ce rapport
◆ **with** *or* **in regard to** (= *concerning*) pour *or* en ce qui concerne, quant à
◆ **without regard to sth** (= *irrespective of*) sans distinction de qch
2 (*NonC* = *esteem*) respect *m*, estime *f* ◆ **I have a very high ~ for him** j'ai beaucoup de respect *or* d'estime pour lui ◆ **he had a high ~ for Kemp's abilities** il pensait que Kemp était très capable ◆ **to hold sb/sth in high ~** tenir qn/qch en haute estime ◆ **to hold sb/sth in low ~** tenir qn/qch en piètre estime
3 (*liter* = *look*) regard *m*
NPL **regards** (*in messages*) ◆ **give him my ~s** transmettez-lui mon bon *or* meilleur souvenir ◆ **Paul sends his kind ~s** Paul vous envoie son bon souvenir ◆ **(kindest) ~s** (*as letter-ending*) meilleurs souvenirs

> ⚠ **to regard** is rarely translated by **regarder**, which usually means 'to look at'.

regardful /rɪˈgɑːdfʊl/ ADJ ◆ **~ of** [*feelings, duty*] attentif à ; [*interests*] soucieux de, soigneux de

regarding /rɪˈgɑːdɪŋ/ PREP (= *with regard to*) pour *or* en ce qui concerne, quant à ◆ **information ~ sb/sth** des informations concernant qn/qch *or* relatives à qn/qch

regardless /rɪˈgɑːdlɪs/ ADJ ◆ **~ of** [*sb's feelings, fate*] indifférent à ; [*future, danger*] insouciant de ; [*sb's troubles*] inattentif à ◆ **~ of the consequences** sans se soucier des conséquences ◆ **~ of expense** *or* **cost** quel que soit le prix ◆ **~ of rank** sans distinction de rang ◆ **~ of what the law says** indépendamment de ce que dit la loi ADV [*carry on*] quand même

regatta /rɪˈgætə/ N (*one event*) régate *f* ; (*regular event*) régates *fpl* ◆ **to take part in a ~** régater, prendre part à une régate

Regency /ˈriːdʒənsɪ/ ADJ [*furniture, style*] style Regency *inv* (*anglaise*)

regency /ˈriːdʒənsɪ/ N régence *f*

regenerate /rɪˈdʒenəreɪt/ VT régénérer VI se régénérer ADJ /rɪˈdʒenərɪt/ (*frm*) régénéré

regeneration /rɪˌdʒenəˈreɪʃən/ N régénération *f*

regenerative /rɪˈdʒenərətɪv/ ADJ régénérateur (-trice *f*)

regent /ˈriːdʒənt/ N régent(e) *m(f)* ; (*US Univ*) membre *m* du conseil d'université ◆ **prince ~** prince régent

reggae /ˈregeɪ/ N reggae *m*

regicide /ˈredʒɪsaɪd/ N (= *person*) régicide *mf* ; (= *act*) régicide *m*

régime, regime (US) /reɪˈʒiːm/ N régime *m* ◆ **~ change** changement de régime

regimen /ˈredʒɪmen/ N (*Med: frm*) régime *m*

regiment /ˈredʒɪmənt/ N (*Mil, fig*) régiment *m* VT /ˈredʒɪment/ (*fig pej*) imposer une discipline trop stricte à, enrégimenter

regimental /ˌredʒɪˈmentl/ ADJ [*duties, insignia, car, tie*] régimentaire ; [*life, tradition, headquarters, commander*] du régiment ; [*system*] de régiments NPL **regimentals** (*Mil*) uniforme *m* ◆ **in full ~s** en grand uniforme, en grande tenue
COMP **regimental band** N fanfare *f* du régiment
regimental sergeant major N ≈ adjudant-chef *m*

regimentation /ˌredʒɪmenˈteɪʃən/ N (*pej*) discipline *f* excessive

regimented /ˈredʒɪmentɪd/ ADJ (*pej*) [*people, way of life, institution, society*] enrégimenté ; [*appearance*] trop strict

region /ˈriːdʒən/ N région *f* ◆ **the lower ~s** (*fig*) les enfers *mpl* ◆ **in the ~ of 5kg/10 euros** environ *or* dans les 5 kg/10 €, aux alentours de 5 kg/10 € NPL **the regions** (*Brit*) les provinces *fpl* ◆ **in the ~s** en province

regional /ˈriːdʒənl/ ADJ régional ◆ **on a ~ basis** sur le plan régional
COMP **regional council** N (*Scot*) ≃ conseil *m* général
regional development N aménagement *m* régional

regionalism /ˈriːdʒənəlɪzəm/ N régionalisme *m*

regionalist /ˈriːdʒənəlɪst/ ADJ, N régionaliste *mf*

register /ˈredʒɪstəʳ/ N 1 *(gen)* registre *m* ; *(of members etc)* liste *f* ; *(Scol:* also **attendance register)** registre *m* d'absences ◆ **electoral** ~ liste *f* électorale ◆ ~ **of births, marriages and deaths** registre *m* d'état civil

2 *(Tech = gauge of speed, numbers etc)* compteur *m*, enregistreur *m*

3 *[of voice, organ etc]* registre *m*

4 *(Ling)* registre *m* ◆ **it's the wrong** ~ ce n'est pas le bon registre

5 *(Typ)* registre *m*

6 *(US = air vent)* registre *m*

7 *(US = cash register)* caisse *f* (enregistreuse)

VT 1 *(= record formally)* *[+ fact, figure]* enregistrer ; *[+ birth, death, marriage]* déclarer ; *[+ vehicle]* (faire) immatriculer ◆ **to** ~ **a trademark** déposer une marque de fabrique ◆ **he ~ed his disapproval by refusing ...** il a manifesté sa désapprobation en refusant ... ◆ **to** ~ **a protest** protester ; see also **registered**

2 *(= take note of)* *[+ fact]* enregistrer ; * *(= realize)* se rendre compte de, réaliser* ◆ **I ~ed the fact that he had gone** je me suis rendu compte *or* j'ai réalisé* qu'il était parti

3 *(= indicate)* *[machine]* *[+ speed, quantity]* indiquer, marquer ; *[+ rainfall]* enregistrer ; *[+ temperature]* marquer ; *[face, expression]* *[+ happiness, sorrow]* exprimer, refléter ◆ **he ~ed** *or* **his face ~ed surprise** son visage *or* il a exprimé l'étonnement, il a paru étonné ◆ **he ~ed** *or* **his face ~ed no emotion** il n'a pas exprimé d'émotion, il n'a pas paru ému

4 *(Post)* *[+ letter]* recommander ; *(Rail)* *[+ luggage]* (faire) enregistrer ◆ **to** ~ **one's luggage through to London** (faire) enregistrer ses bagages jusqu'à Londres ; see also **registered**

5 *(Tech)* *[+ parts]* faire coïncider ; *(Typ)* mettre en registre

VI 1 *(on electoral list etc)* se faire inscrire, s'inscrire ; *(in hotel)* s'inscrire sur *or* signer le registre ◆ **to** ~ **with a doctor** se faire inscrire comme patient chez un médecin ◆ **to** ~ **with the police** se déclarer à la police ◆ **to** ~ **for military service** se faire recenser, se faire porter sur les tableaux de recensement ◆ **to** ~ **for a course/for French literature** s'inscrire à un cours/en littérature française

2 *(Tech)* *[two parts of machine]* coïncider exactement ; *(Typ)* être en registre

3 *(* = be understood)* être compris ◆ **it hasn't ~ed (with him)** cela ne lui est pas entré dans la tête, il n'a pas saisi ◆ **her death hadn't ~ed with him** il n'avait pas vraiment réalisé qu'elle était morte

COMP **register office** N *(Brit)* ⇒ **registry office** ; → **registry**

register ton N *(Naut)* tonneau *m* de jauge

registered /ˈredʒɪstəd/ ADJ 1 *(= listed)* *[voter]* inscrit (sur les listes électorales) ; *[student]* inscrit ; *[drug addict]* inscrit *(pour une cure de désintoxication)* ; *[nursing home]* agréé ◆ **a** ~ **childminder** une nourrice agréée ◆ ~ **to vote** inscrit sur les listes électorales ◆ **to be** ~ **(as) blind/disabled** ≃ être titulaire d'une carte de cécité/d'invalidité ◆ **a Greek-~ ship** un navire immatriculé en Grèce, un navire battant pavillon grec ◆ **a British-~ car** une voiture immatriculée en Grande-Bretagne ◆ **J-~ car** *(Brit)* *voiture dont l'immatriculation commence or finit par un J (la lettre indiquant l'année de mise en circulation)* ; → **state**

2 *(Post)* *[letter, mail]* recommandé ; *(Rail)* *[luggage]* enregistré

COMP **registered charity** N ≃ association *f* caritative reconnue d'utilité publique

registered company N société *f* inscrite au registre du commerce

Registered General Nurse N *(Brit)* ≃ infirmier *m*, -ière *f* diplômé(e)

registered name N nom *m* déposé

registered nurse N *(US)* ≃ infirmier *m*, -ière *f* diplômé(e) d'État

registered office N siège *m* social

registered post N ◆ **by** ~ **post** par envoi recommandé

registered share N *(Stock Exchange)* action *f* nominative

registered shareholder N *(Stock Exchange)* ≃ actionnaire *mf* inscrit(e)

registered stocks NPL *(Stock Exchange)* actions *fpl or* valeurs *fpl* nominatives, titres *mpl* nominatifs

registered trademark N marque *f* déposée

registrar /ˌredʒɪˈstrɑːʳ/ N 1 *(Brit Admin)* officier *m* de l'état civil ◆ **to be married by the** ~ se marier civilement *or* à la mairie 2 *(Univ)* *(Brit)* secrétaire *mf* (général(e)) ; *(US)* chef *m* du service des inscriptions 3 *(Brit Med)* chef *m* de clinique 4 *(Jur)* *(in court)* greffier *m* ◆ **(companies')** ~ *(Fin)* conservateur *m* (du registre des sociétés) COMP **registrar's office** N bureau *m* de l'état civil

registration /ˌredʒɪˈstreɪʃən/ N 1 *(= listing)* *[of voters]* inscription *f* ; *[of dog]* déclaration *f* ; *[of trademark]* dépôt *m* ; *(Univ)* inscription *f* ◆ **for VAT** assujettissement *m* à la TVA *(au-delà d'un certain chiffre d'affaires)* ◆ **J-~ car** *(Brit)* *voiture dont l'immatriculation commence ou finit par un J (la lettre indiquant l'année de mise en circulation)*

2 *(Post)* *[of letter]* recommandation *f* ; *(Rail)* *[of luggage]* enregistrement *m*

3 *(Brit Scol:* also **registration period)** appel *m*

COMP **registration document** N *(Brit: for vehicle)* ≃ carte *f* grise

registration fee N *(Post)* taxe *f* de recommandation ; *(Rail: for luggage)* frais *mpl* d'enregistrement ; *(Univ)* droits *mpl* d'inscription

registration number N *(Brit Aut)* numéro *m* minéralogique *or* d'immatriculation ◆ **car (with)** ~ **number R971 VBW** voiture *f* immatriculée R971 VBW

registry /ˈredʒɪstrɪ/ N *(= act)* enregistrement *m*, inscription *f* ; *(= office)* *(gen)* bureau *m* de l'enregistrement ; *(Brit Admin)* bureau *m* de l'état civil ; *(Naut)* certificat *m* d'immatriculation ◆ **port of** ~ *(Naut)* port *m* d'attache COMP **registry office** N *(Brit)* bureau *m* d'état civil ◆ **to get married in a** ~ **office** se marier civilement *or* à la mairie

regius professor /ˈriːdʒəsprəˈfesəʳ/ N *(Brit Univ)* professeur *m (titulaire d'une chaire de fondation royale)*

regnal /ˈregnl/ ADJ ◆ ~ **year** année *f* du règne

regnant /ˈregnənt/ ADJ régnant ◆ **queen** ~ reine *f* régnante

regorge /rɪˈgɔːdʒ/ VT vomir, régurgiter VI refluer

regress /rɪˈgres/ VI 1 *(Bio, Psych, fig)* régresser *(to* au stade de), rétrograder 2 *(= move backwards)* retourner en arrière, reculer N /ˈriːgres/ ⇒ **regression**

regression /rɪˈgreʃən/ N *(lit)* retour *m* en arrière, recul *m* ; *(Bio, Psych, fig)* régression *f*

regressive /rɪˈgresɪv/ ADJ régressif COMP **regressive tax** N impôt *m* dégressif, taxe *f* dégressive

regret /rɪˈgret/ LANGUAGE IN USE 12.3, 14, 18.2, 20.4, 24.4, 25.1

VT regretter *(doing sth, to do sth* de faire qch ; *that* que *+ subj)* ; *[+ mistake, words, event]* regretter, être désolé *or* navré de ; *[+ one's youth, lost opportunity]* regretter ◆ **I** ~ **what I said** je regrette ce que j'ai dit ◆ **I** ~ **to say that** ... j'ai le regret de dire que ... ◆ **he is very ill, I** ~ **to say** il est très malade, hélas *or* je regrette de le dire ◆ **we** ~ **to hear that** ... nous sommes désolés d'apprendre que ... ◆ **we** ~ **that it was not possible to** ... *(gen)* nous sommes désolés de n'avoir pu ... ; *(Comm)* nous sommes au regret de vous informer qu'il n'a pas été possible de ... ◆ **it is to be ~ted that** ... il est regrettable que ... *+ subj* ◆ **you won't** ~ **it!** vous ne le regretterez pas ! ◆ **the President ~s he cannot see you today** le Président est au regret *or* exprime ses regrets de ne pouvoir vous recevoir aujourd'hui ◆ **he is much ~ted** on le regrette beaucoup

N regret *m* *(for* de) ◆ **much to my** ~ à mon grand regret ◆ **I have no ~s** je ne regrette rien, je n'ai aucun regret ◆ **to do sth with** ~ faire qch à regret *or* à contrecœur ◆ **to send (one's) ~s** envoyer ses excuses ◆ **please give her my ~s that I cannot come** dites-lui, s'il vous plaît, combien je regrette de ne pouvoir venir

regretful /rɪˈgretfʊl/ ADJ plein de regret ◆ **to be** ~ **about sth** regretter qch

regretfully /rɪˈgretfəlɪ/ ADV 1 *(= with regret)* *[say, decide, decline]* à regret 2 *(= unfortunately)* ◆ ~, **nationalism is flourishing again** malheureusement, le nationalisme est en pleine recrudescence

regrettable /rɪˈgretəbl/ LANGUAGE IN USE 14, 26.3 ADJ regrettable, fâcheux ◆ **it is** ~ **that** ... il est regrettable que ... (+ *subj*)

regrettably /rɪˈgretəblɪ/ ADV *[poor, ignorant, true]* malheureusement, tristement ◆ ~ **few people came** il est regrettable que si peu de gens soient venus ◆ ~, **he refused** malheureusement, il a refusé

regroup /ˌriːˈgruːp/ VT regrouper VI se regrouper ; *(fig)* se ressaisir

regrouping /ˌriːˈgruːpɪŋ/ N regroupement *m*

regs* /regz/ NPL (abbrev of **regulations**) règlement *m*

Regt. abbrev of **Regiment**

regular /ˈregjʊləʳ/ ADJ 1 *(gen)* *[pulse, reminders, features, flight, order, meals]* régulier ◆ **on a** ~ **basis** régulièrement ◆ **as** ~ **as clockwork** *[person]* réglé comme une horloge ; *[occurrence]* très régulier ◆ **to be in** *or* **have** ~ **contact with sb/sth** avoir des contacts réguliers avec qn/qch ◆ **to be in** ~ **employment** avoir un emploi fixe ◆ **to take** ~ **exercise** faire régulièrement de l'exercice ◆ **a** ~ **feature of sth** un aspect courant de qch ◆ **to be a** ~ **feature on the menu** figurer régulièrement au menu ◆ **to be** ~ **in one's habits** être régulier dans ses habitudes ◆ **to keep** ~ **hours** mener une vie réglée, avoir des horaires très réguliers ◆ **at** ~ **intervals** à intervalles réguliers ◆ **to hold** ~ **meetings** se réunir régulièrement ◆ **life took on a** ~ **pattern** la vie a commencé à prendre un cours normal ◆ **to make** ~ **payments** effectuer des versements réguliers ◆ **to have a** ~ **place on the team** avoir régulièrement sa place dans l'équipe ◆ **to run** ~ **advertisements in the press** faire paraître régulièrement des publicités dans la presse ◆ **to make** ~ **trips to** se rendre régulièrement à ◆ **to be in** ~ **use** être régulièrement utilisé

2 *(= even)* *[surface]* uni

3 *(= habitual)* *[reader]* assidu, fidèle *before n* ; *[listener]* fidèle *before n* ◆ **to be a** ~ **listener to sth** écouter régulièrement qch ◆ **a** ~ **customer/visitor** un(e) habitué(e) ◆ **to be a** ~ **churchgoer** être pratiquant, aller régulièrement à l'église

4 *(esp US = customary)* *[event]* habituel ; *[partner]* régulier ◆ **it's past his** ~ **bedtime** on a dépassé l'heure à laquelle il va habituellement se coucher ◆ **the** ~ **staff** le personnel permanent ◆ **our** ~ **cleaning woman** notre femme de ménage habituelle ◆ **my** ~ **dentist** mon dentiste habituel ◆ **my** ~ **doctor** mon médecin traitant

5 *(esp US)* *(= ordinary)* ordinaire ; *(Comm)* *[size]* normal ; *[price]* normal, courant ◆ **I'm just a** ~ **guy** * *(US)* je ne suis qu'un type* comme un autre ◆ **he's a** ~ **guy** * *(US)* c'est un chic type* ◆ **would you like** ~, **large, or extra-large?**

normal, grand ou super* ? ◆ ~ **fries** portion *f* de frites normale ◆ **he's an acupuncturist, not a ~ doctor** ce n'est pas un médecin normal, c'est un acupuncteur ◆ **it is quite ~ to apply in person** il est tout à fait courant de faire sa demande en personne

[6] *(Mil) (= not conscripted) [army, troops]* régulier ; *[officer]* de l'armée régulière ; *(Police) [officer]* de carrière ◆ ~ **soldier** soldat *m* de métier ◆ **the ~ police force** les forces *fpl* de police régulières *(par rapport aux forces auxiliaires et spéciales)*

[7] *(* = real)* véritable ◆ **this is turning into a ~ epidemic** ça tourne à l'épidémie

[8] *(Math, Gram, Rel)* régulier

[9] * *(in menstruation)* ◆ **I'm quite ~** mes règles sont assez régulières ; *(= not constipated)* ◆ **to be ~** aller régulièrement à la selle ◆ **to keep sb ~** permettre à qn d'aller régulièrement à la selle ◆ ~ **bowel movements** selles *fpl* régulières

N [1] *(Mil)* soldat *m* de métier ; *(= police officer)* policier *m* (de métier)

[2] *(= habitual customer etc)* habitué(e) *m(f)*, bon(ne) client(e) *m(f)* ◆ **he's one of the ~s on that programme** *(Rad, TV)* il participe *or* prend part régulièrement à ce programme

[3] *(Rel)* régulier *m*, religieux *m*

[4] *(US = gas)* essence *f* (ordinaire), ordinaire *m*

COMP **regular gas(oline)** N *(US)* essence *f*, *(ordinaire)* ordinaire *m*

regularity /ˌregjʊˈlærɪtɪ/ N régularité *f*

regularize /ˈregjʊləraɪz/ VT régulariser

regularly /ˈregjʊləlɪ/ ADV régulièrement

regulate /ˈregjʊleɪt/ VT [1] *(= control systematically) [+ amount, flow]* régler ; *[+ expenditure]* régler, calculer ◆ **to ~ one's life by sth** se régler sur qch ◆ **a well-~d life** une vie bien réglée [2] *[+ machine]* régler, ajuster

regulation /ˌregjʊˈleɪʃən/ N [1] *(= rule)* règlement *m*, arrêté *m*

◆ **regulations** réglementation *f* ; *[of club, school]* règlement *m* ◆ **against (the) ~s** *[of club]* contraire au règlement ; → **fire, safety**

◆ **rules and regulations** règles *fpl* ◆ **these activities do not conform with diplomatic rules and ~s** ces activités ne sont pas conformes aux règles de la diplomatie

[2] *(= controlling)* réglementation *f* ◆ **free markets require tight ~** l'économie de marché nécessite une réglementation stricte

ADJ *[style, size, colour]* réglementaire ◆ ~ **boots** brodequins *mpl* d'ordonnance

COMP **regulation time** N *(Sport)* temps *m* réglementaire

regulative /ˈregjʊlətɪv/ ADJ régulateur (-trice *f*)

regulator /ˈregjʊleɪtəʳ/ N *(= body)* organisme *m* de contrôle ; *(= person)* régulateur *m*, -trice *f* ; *(= instrument, mechanism)* régulateur *m* ◆ **acidity ~** correcteur *m* d'acidité

regulatory /ˌregjʊˈleɪtərɪ/ ADJ *[body, authority, system, role, changes]* de réglementation ; *[control, framework]* réglementaire ◆ ~ **reform** réforme *f* de la réglementation

Regulo ® /ˈregjʊləʊ/ N ◆ ~ **(mark) 6** thermostat 6

regurgitate /rɪˈgɜːdʒɪteɪt/ VT *[animal, bird, person]* régurgiter ; *[drainpipe etc]* dégorger VI refluer

regurgitation /rɪˌgɜːdʒɪˈteɪʃən/ N régurgitation *f*

rehab* /ˈriːhæb/ N (abbrev of **rehabilitation**) *[of disabled, ill person]* rééducation *f* ; *[of alcoholic, drug user] (= drying-out)* désintoxication *f* ; *(to everyday life)* réintégration *f*

rehabilitate /ˌriːəˈbɪlɪteɪt/ VT *[+ disabled, ill person]* rééduquer ; *[+ refugees]* réadapter ; *[+ demobilized troops]* réintégrer (dans la vie civile) ; *[+ ex-prisoner]* réinsérer ; *[+ drug user, alcoholic]* réhabiliter ; *[+ disgraced person, sb's memory]* réhabiliter

rehabilitation /ˈriːəˌbɪlɪˈteɪʃən/ N *[of disabled, ill person] (to everyday life)* rééducation *f* ; *(to work)* réadaptation *f* ; *[of ex-prisoner]* réinsertion *f* ; *[of refugee]* réadaptation *f* ; *[of drug user, alcoholic]* réhabilitation *f* ; *[of demobilized troops]* réintégration *f* (dans la vie civile) ; *[of area, building, disgraced person]* réhabilitation *f* COMP **rehabilitation centre** N *(for disabled, ill person)* centre *m* de réadaptation ; *(for drug user, alcoholic)* centre *m* de réhabilitation ; *(for prisoner)* centre *m* de réinsertion

rehash* /ˌriːˈhæʃ/ VT *[+ literary material etc]* remanier, réarranger N /ˈriːhæʃ/ resucée* *f*

rehearsal /rɪˈhɜːsəl/ N [1] *(Theat)* répétition *f* ; *(fig) (= preparation)* préparation *f (for sth* de qch) ◆ **this play is in ~** on répète cette pièce ; → **dress** [2] *(NonC) [of facts etc]* énumération *f*, récit *m* détaillé

rehearse /rɪˈhɜːs/ VT *(Theat)* répéter ; *(gen) [+ facts, grievances]* énumérer ◆ **to ~ what one is going to say** préparer ce qu'on va dire ◆ **well ~d** *[+ play]* répété avec soin ; *[+ actor]* qui a soigneusement répété son texte ; *(fig) [+ intervention, protest]* soigneusement étudié

reheat /ˌriːˈhiːt/ VT réchauffer

re-home, rehome /ˌriːˈhəʊm/ VT *[+ pet]* trouver qn pour adopter

rehouse /ˌriːˈhaʊz/ VT reloger

reign /reɪn/ N *(lit, fig)* règne *m* ◆ **in the ~ of** sous le règne de ◆ **the Reign of Terror** *(Hist)* la Terreur ◆ ~ **of terror** *(fig)* régime *m* de terreur VI *(lit, fig)* régner *(over* sur) ◆ **silence ~s** le silence règne ◆ **to ~ supreme** *[monarch]* régner en *or* être le maître absolu ; *[champion]* être sans rival ; *[justice, peace]* régner en souverain(e)

reigning /ˈreɪnɪŋ/ ADJ *[monarch]* régnant ; *[champion]* en titre ; *(fig) [attitude]* actuel, dominant

reiki /ˈreɪkɪ/ N reiki *m*

reimburse /ˌriːɪmˈbɜːs/ VT rembourser *(sb for sth* qch à qn, qn de qch) ◆ **to ~ sb (for) his expenses** rembourser qn de ses dépenses

reimbursement /ˌriːɪmˈbɜːsmənt/ N remboursement *m*

reimpose /ˌriːɪmˈpəʊz/ VT réimposer

rein /reɪn/ N *(often pl: lit, fig)* rêne *f* ; *[of horse in harness]* guide *f* ◆ **~s** *[of child]* rênes *fpl* ◆ **to hold the ~s (of power)** *(lit, fig)* tenir les rênes (du pouvoir) ◆ **to keep a ~ on sb/sth** *(lit, fig)* tenir qn/qch en bride ◆ **to give (a) free ~ to** *(fig) [+ anger, passions, one's imagination]* donner libre cours à ◆ **to give sb free ~ (to do sth)** donner carte blanche à qn (pour faire qch)

► **rein back** VT SEP *[+ horse]* faire reculer VI reculer

► **rein in** VI *(fig)* ralentir VT SEP *[+ horse]* serrer la bride à, ramener au pas ; *(fig) [+ passions]* contenir, maîtriser

► **rein up** VI s'arrêter

reincarnate /ˌriːɪnˈkɑːneɪt/ VT réincarner ADJ /ˌriːɪnˈkɑːnɪt/ *(frm)* réincarné

reincarnation /ˌriːɪnkɑːˈneɪʃən/ N réincarnation *f*

reindeer /ˈreɪndɪəʳ/ N (pl **reindeer** or **reindeers**) renne *m*

reinforce /ˌriːɪnˈfɔːs/ VT renforcer ; *[+ one's demands etc]* appuyer COMP **reinforced concrete** N béton *m* armé

reinforcement /ˌriːɪnˈfɔːsmənt/ N [1] *(= action)* renforcement *m* ; *(= thing)* renfort *m* [2] *(Mil = action)* renforcement *m* ◆ **~s** *(also fig)* renforts *mpl* COMP *[troops, supplies]* de renfort

reinsert /ˌriːɪnˈsɜːt/ VT réinsérer

reinstate /ˌriːɪnˈsteɪt/ VT *[+ employee]* réintégrer, rétablir dans ses fonctions ; *[+ text]* rétablir *(in* dans)

reinstatement /ˌriːɪnˈsteɪtmənt/ N réintégration *f*, rétablissement *m*

reinstitute /ˌriːˈɪnstɪtjuːt/ VT rétablir

reinstitution /ˌriːɪnstɪˈtjuːʃən/ N rétablissement *m*

reinsurance /ˌriːɪnˈʃʊərəns/ N réassurance *f* ; *[of underwriter etc] (against possible losses)* contre-assurance *f*

reinsure /ˌriːɪnˈʃʊəʳ/ VT *[+ policy, contract]* réassurer, contracter une contre-assurance sur ; *[insurance company]* réassurer ◆ **to ~ o.s.** se réassurer, contracter une contre-assurance

reintegrate /ˌriːˈɪntɪgreɪt/ VT réintégrer

reintegration /ˌriːɪntɪˈgreɪʃən/ N réintégration *f*

reintroduce /ˌriːɪntrəˈdjuːs/ VT réintroduire

reintroduction /ˌriːɪntrəˈdʌkʃən/ N *[measure, bill, scheme, death penalty]* réintroduction *f* ; *[plant, animal, species]* réintroduction *f*

reinvent /ˌriːɪnˈvent/ VT [1] ◆ **to ~ the wheel** réinventer la roue [2] ◆ **to ~ o.s.** faire peau neuve ◆ **to ~ o.s. as sth** se métamorphoser en qch

reinvention /ˌriːɪnˈvenʃən/ N *[of person, thing]* réinvention *f*

reinvest /ˌriːɪnˈvest/ VT *(Fin)* réinvestir

reinvestment /ˌriːɪnˈvestmənt/ N *(Fin)* nouveau placement *m*, nouvel investissement *m*

reinvigorate /ˌriːɪnˈvɪgəreɪt/ VT revigorer

reissue /ˌriːˈɪʃjuː/ VT *[+ book]* donner une nouvelle édition de, rééditer ; *[+ film]* ressortir, redistribuer N *(= act) [of book]* réédition *f* ; *[of film]* redistribution *f* ◆ **it is a ~** *[book]* il a été réédité ; *[film]* il est ressorti

reiterate /riːˈɪtəreɪt/ VT *[+ statement, view]* réaffirmer ; *[+ promise, claim]* réitérer ◆ **he ~d his demand for more proof** il a redemandé de nouvelles preuves

reiteration /riːˌɪtəˈreɪʃən/ N réitération *f*, répétition *f*

reiterative /riːˈɪtərətɪv/ ADJ réitératif

reject /rɪˈdʒekt/ LANGUAGE IN USE 12.1 VT [1] *(gen)* rejeter, repousser ; *[+ damaged goods etc] [customer, shopkeeper]* refuser ; *[maker, producer]* mettre au rebut ; *[+ suitor]* repousser, éconduire ; *[+ candidate, manuscript]* refuser ; *[+ offer, proposal, application]* rejeter ; *[+ plea, advances]* repousser ; *[+ possibility]* rejeter, repousser ; *[+ coins] [machine]* refuser [2] *(Med) [body] [+ medication, transplant]* rejeter [3] *(Comput)* rejeter N /ˈriːdʒekt/ [1] *(Comm)* pièce *f or* article *m* de rebut ; → **export** [2] *(Comput)* rejet *m* COMP /ˈriːdʒekt/ *[goods]* de rebut **reject shop** N boutique *f* d'articles de second choix

rejection /rɪˈdʒekʃən/ N rejet *m (also Med)* ◆ **the ~ of such initiatives** le rejet de telles initiatives ◆ **be prepared for many ~s before you land a job** préparez-vous à essuyer de nombreux refus avant d'obtenir un emploi COMP **rejection slip** N *(Publishing)* lettre *f* de refus

rejig* /ˌriːˈdʒɪg/, **rejigger*** (US) /ˌriːˈdʒɪgəʳ/ VT réorganiser, réarranger

rejoice /rɪˈdʒɔɪs/ VT réjouir ◆ **it ~d his heart to see ...** *(frm, liter)* il s'est félicité du fond du cœur de voir ... VI se réjouir *(at, over, in* de) ◆ **they ~d to see peace return to their country at last** ils se sont réjouis de voir enfin la paix revenir dans leur pays ◆ **he ~s in the name of Marmaduke** *(hum, iro)* il a le privilège de s'appeler Marmaduke *(iro)*

rejoicing /rɪˈdʒɔɪsɪŋ/ N [1] *(NonC)* réjouissance *f*, jubilation *f* [2] ◆ **~s** réjouissances *fpl*, fête *f*

rejoin[1] /ˌriːˈdʒɔɪn/ VT *[+ party, club]* adhérer à nouveau à ; *[+ person, army]* rejoindre ◆ **they ~ed the motorway at junction 15** ils ont rejoint l'autoroute à l'entrée nº 15 VI se rejoindre

rejoin[2] /rɪˈdʒɔɪn/ VI *(= reply)* répliquer, répondre

rejoinder /rɪˈdʒɔɪndəʳ/ N réplique *f*, repartie *f* ; *(Jur)* réplique *f*, réponse *f* à une réplique

rejuvenate /rɪˈdʒuːvɪneɪt/ VTI rajeunir

rejuvenating /rɪˈdʒuːvɪneɪtɪŋ/ ADJ rajeunissant

rejuvenation /rɪˌdʒuːvɪˈneɪʃən/ N rajeunissement *m*

rekindle /ˌriːˈkɪndl/ VT *[+ fire]* rallumer, attiser ; *(fig) [+ hope, enthusiasm, tensions, enmities]* ranimer, raviver VI se rallumer, se ranimer

relapse /rɪˈlæps/ N *(Med, fig)* rechute *f* ◆ **to have a ~** avoir *or* faire une rechute, rechuter VI *(gen)* retomber *(into* dans) ; *[ill person]* rechuter

Relate /rɪˈleɪt/ N *(Brit) centre de consultation conjugale*

relate /rɪˈleɪt/ VT 1 *(= recount) [+ story]* raconter, relater ; *[+ details]* rapporter ◆ **strange to ~ ...** chose curieuse (à dire) ...

2 *(= associate)* établir un rapport entre, rapprocher ; *[+ breeds]* apparenter ; *(to a category)* rattacher, lier ◆ **it is often difficult to ~ the cause to the effect** il est souvent difficile d'établir un rapport de cause à effet *or* d'établir un lien entre la cause et l'effet

VI 1 *(= refer)* se rapporter, toucher *(to* à)

2 *(Psych)* **to ~ to sb** *(= form relationship)* établir des rapports avec qn ; *(= maintain relationship)* entretenir des rapports avec qn ◆ **how do you ~ to your parents?** quels rapports entretenez-vous avec vos parents ? ◆ **he doesn't ~ to other people** il n'a pas le sens des contacts ◆ **women ~ more to this than men** les femmes sentent mieux cela que les hommes ◆ **I can ~ to that** * je comprends ça

related /rɪˈleɪtɪd/ ADJ 1 *(in family) [person]* parent ; *[animal, species, language]* apparenté *(to sth* à qch) ◆ **he is ~ to Jane** il est parent de Jane ◆ **she is ~ to us** elle est notre parente ◆ **they are ~ to each other** ils sont parents ◆ **he is ~ to the Royal family** c'est un parent de la famille royale ◆ **he is ~ by marriage to our great aunt/the Royal family** c'est un parent *or* il est parent par alliance de notre grand-tante/de la famille royale ◆ **they are closely/distantly ~** ce sont de proches parents/des parents éloignés ◆ **two closely ~ species/languages** deux espèces/langues très proches

2 *(= connected) (Chem)* apparenté ; *(Philos)* connexe ; *(Mus)* relatif ◆ **to be ~ to sth** être lié à qch ◆ **food allergies and ~ problems** les allergies alimentaires et les problèmes qui y sont liés ◆ **cookware, cutlery, and ~ products** les ustensiles de cuisine, les couverts et les produits du même ordre ◆ **geometry and other ~ subjects** la géométrie et les sujets connexes *or* qui s'y rattachent ◆ **another ~ issue which this film deals with is ...** ce film aborde aussi un problème apparenté, à savoir ... ◆ **the two events are not ~** ces deux événements n'ont pas de rapport ◆ **two closely ~ questions** deux questions fort proches l'une de l'autre *or* étroitement liées ◆ **two distantly ~ questions** deux questions fort éloignées l'une de l'autre

ADJ ◆ **-related** *(in compounds)* qui est lié à ◆ **health-~ problems** problèmes *mpl* liés à la santé ◆ **earnings-~ pensions** retraites *fpl* ramenées au salaire

relating /rɪˈleɪtɪŋ/ ADJ ◆ **~ to** concernant, relatif à

relation /rɪˈleɪʃən/ N 1 *(family = person)* parent(e) *m(f)* ; *(= kinship)* parenté *f* ◆ **I've got some ~s coming to dinner** j'ai de la famille à dîner ◆ **is he any ~ to you?** est-il de vos parents ? ◆ **he is no ~ (of mine** *or* **to me)** il n'est pas de ma famille, il n'y a aucun lien de parenté entre nous ◆ **what ~ is she to you?** quelle est sa parenté avec vous ?

2 *(= relationship)* rapport *m*, relation *f* ◆ **to bear a ~ to** avoir rapport à ◆ **to bear no ~ to** n'avoir aucun rapport avec, être sans rapport avec ◆ **in** *or* **with ~ to** par rapport à, relativement à ◆ **~s** relations *fpl*, rapports *mpl* ; *(= personal ties)* rapports *mpl* ◆ **to have business ~s with** être en rapports *mpl* *or* relations *fpl* d'affaires avec ◆ **diplomatic/friendly/international ~s** relations *fpl* diplomatiques/d'amitié/internationales ◆ **~s are rather strained** les relations *or* les rapports sont assez tendu(e)s ◆ **sexual ~s** rapports *mpl* (sexuels) ; → **public**

3 *(= telling) [of story]* récit *m*, relation *f* ; *[of details]* rapport *m*

relational /rɪˈleɪʃənl/ ADJ *(gen, Ling)* relationnel

relationship /rɪˈleɪʃənʃɪp/ N 1 *(= family ties)* liens *mpl* de parenté ◆ **what is your ~ to him?** quels sont les liens de parenté entre vous ?, quels sont vos liens de parenté avec lui ?

2 *(= connection)* rapport *m* ; *(= relations)* relations *fpl*, rapports *mpl* ; *(= personal ties)* rapports *mpl* ◆ **to see a ~ between two events** voir un rapport *or* un lien entre deux événements ◆ **to have a ~ with sb** *(gen)* avoir des relations *or* être en relations avec qn ; *(sexual)* avoir une liaison avec qn ◆ **to be in a ~** avoir quelqu'un dans sa vie ◆ **he has a good ~ with his clients** il est en bons rapports avec ses clients ◆ **they have a good ~** ils s'entendent bien ◆ **friendly/business ~** relations *fpl* d'amitié/d'affaires ◆ **his ~ with his father was strained** ses rapports avec son père étaient tendus ◆ **the ~ between mother and child** les rapports entre la mère et l'enfant

relative /ˈrelətɪv/ ADJ 1 *(= comparative) [safety, peace, comfort, luxury, weakness]* relatif ◆ **with ~ ease** avec une relative facilité ◆ **he is a ~ newcomer** c'est plus ou moins un nouveau venu ◆ **her ~ lack of experience** sa relative inexpérience ◆ **in ~ terms** en termes relatifs ◆ **petrol consumption is ~ to speed** la consommation d'essence est fonction de *or* relative à la vitesse ◆ **there is a shortage of labour ~ to demand** il y a une pénurie de main d'œuvre par rapport à la demande ◆ **all human values are ~** toutes les valeurs humaines sont relatives ◆ **it's all ~** tout est relatif

2 *(= respective) [importance, merits, strengths]* respectif

3 *(= relevant)* ◆ **~ to sth** relatif à qch, qui se rapporte à qch ◆ **the documents ~ to the problem** les documents relatifs au problème *or* qui se rapportent au problème

4 *(Gram, Mus)* relatif

N 1 *(= person)* parent(e) *m(f)* ◆ **one of my ~s** un(e) parent(e) à moi, un membre de ma famille ◆ **all my ~s came** toute ma famille est venue

2 *(Gram)* relatif *m*

COMP **relative clause** N *(Gram)* (proposition *f*) relative *f*

relative conjunction N *(Gram)* conjonction *f* de subordination

relative major (key) N *(Mus)* (ton *m*) majeur *m* relatif

relative minor (key) N *(Mus)* (ton *m*) mineur *m* relatif

relative pronoun N *(Gram)* pronom *m* relatif

relatively /ˈrelətɪvlɪ/ ADV relativement ◆ **~ speaking** comparativement

relativism /ˈrelətɪvɪzəm/ N relativisme *m*

relativist /ˈrelətɪvɪst/ ADJ, N relativiste *mf*

relativistic /ˌrelətɪˈvɪstɪk/ ADJ relativiste

relativity /ˌreləˈtɪvɪtɪ/ N *(gen, Ling, Philos, Phys)* relativité *f* ◆ **theory of ~** théorie *f* de la relativité

relativization /ˌrelətɪvaɪˈzeɪʃən/ N relativisation *f*

relativize /ˈrelətɪvaɪz/ VT relativiser

relaunch /riːˈlɔːntʃ/ VT *[+ organization, scheme]* relancer N *[of organization, scheme]* nouveau lancement *m*

relax /rɪˈlæks/ VT *[+ hold, grip]* relâcher, desserrer ; *(Med) [+ bowels]* relâcher ; *[+ muscles]* relâcher, décontracter ; *[+ discipline, attention, effort]* relâcher ; *[+ restrictions]* modérer ; *[+ measures, tariffs]* assouplir ; *[+ person, one's mind]* détendre, délasser ; see also **relaxed** VI 1 *(= rest)* se détendre, se relaxer ◆ **let's just ~!** *(* = calm down)* restons calmes !, du calme ! 2 *[hold, grip]* se relâcher, se desserrer ; *[muscles]* se relâcher, se décontracter

relaxant /rɪˈlæksənt/ N décontractant *m* ◆ **muscle ~** décontractant *m* musculaire

relaxation /ˌriːlækˈseɪʃən/ N 1 *(NonC) [of muscles, discipline, attention]* relâchement *m* ; *[of mind]* détente *f*, relaxation *f* ; *[of body]* décontraction *f*, relaxation *f* ; *[of restrictions, measures, tariffs]* assouplissement *m* ◆ **measures of ~** *(Jur)* mesures *fpl* d'assouplissement 2 *(= recreation)* détente *f*, délassement *m* ; *(= rest)* repos *m* ◆ **you need some ~ after work** on a besoin d'une détente après le travail ◆ **books are her ~** pour se délasser *or* se détendre elle lit

relaxed /rɪˈlækst/ ADJ *[person, mood, discussion, attitude, approach, smile]* détendu, décontracté ; *[discipline, muscle]* relâché ◆ **to feel ~** se sentir détendu ◆ **I feel fairly ~ about it** * *(fig)* je ne m'en fais pas pour ça

relaxing /rɪˈlæksɪŋ/ ADJ *[weekend, holiday, place]* reposant ; *[atmosphere]* reposant, relaxant ; *[music, massage]* relaxant ; *[bath]* relaxant, délassant ◆ **to have a ~ time** passer des moments reposants

relay /ˈriːleɪ/ N 1 *[of horses, men etc]* relais *m* ◆ **to work in ~s** travailler par relais, se relayer 2 *(Rad, TV)* émission *f* relayée 3 *(Sport)* ⇒ **relay race** 4 *(Elec, Phys, Tech)* relais *m* VT *(Elec, Rad, TV etc) [+ programme]* relayer, retransmettre ; *[+ signal]* transmettre, retransmettre ; *[+ message, information]* relayer

COMP **relay race** N course *f* de relais

relay station N *(Rad, TV)* relais *m*

re-lay /ˌriːˈleɪ/ VT (pret, ptp **re-laid**) *[+ carpet]* reposer

release /rɪˈliːs/ N 1 *(NonC, from captivity, prison, custody, obligation, responsibility)* libération *f* ; *(from service)* dispense *f*, exemption *f* ; *(Comm: from customs, bond)* congé *m* ◆ **on his ~ from prison he ...** dès sa sortie de prison, il ... ◆ **the ~ of the prisoners by the allied forces** la libération des prisonniers par les forces alliées ◆ **death was a happy ~ for him** pour lui la mort a été une délivrance

2 *(NonC) [of goods]* mise *f* en vente ; *[of news]* autorisation *f* de publier ; *[of film, record]* sortie *f* ; *[of book]* parution *f*, sortie *f* ◆ **this film is now on general ~** ce film n'est plus en exclusivité

3 *(= item just brought out)* **new ~** *(= record, CD)* nouvel album *m* ; *(= film)* nouveau film *m* ; *(= book)* nouveauté *f* ; *(= video)* nouvelle vidéo *f* ◆ **their latest ~** leur dernier album (*or* film *etc*) ; → **press**

4 *(NonC) [of bomb]* largage *m* ; *(Phot etc)* déclenchement *m* ; *[of steam]* échappement *m*

5 (also **release switch/button**) touche *f* de déclenchement

VT 1 *(= set free) [+ person] (from prison)* libérer, relâcher *(from* de), élargir *(Jur)* ; *(from hospital)* autoriser à sortir *(from* de) ; *(from chains)* libérer *(from* de) ; *(from rubble, wreckage)* dégager *(from* de) ; *(from obligation, debt)* dégager, libérer *(from* de) ; *(from promise, vow)* relever *(from* de) ; *[+ cap-*

tive animal] relâcher ◆ **to ~ sb on bail** *(Jur)* mettre qn en liberté provisoire sous caution ◆ **death ~d him from pain** la mort mit fin à ses souffrances ◆ **his employer agreed to ~ him** son patron lui a permis de cesser son travail ◆ **can you ~ him for a few hours each week?** pouvez-vous le libérer quelques heures par semaine ?

2 *(= let go) [+ object, sb's hand, pigeon]* lâcher ; *[+ bomb]* larguer, lâcher ; *(Chem) [+ gas]* dégager ; *[+ anger]* donner libre cours à ◆ **to ~ one's anger on sb** passer sa colère sur qn ◆ **to ~ one's hold** *or* **grip** lâcher prise ◆ **to ~ one's hold of** *or* **one's grip on sth** lâcher qch ◆ **humour is wonderful for releasing tension** l'humour est idéal pour libérer les tensions ◆ **massage helps to ~ the tension in your shoulders and neck** les massages aident à décrisper les épaules et le cou

3 *(= issue) [+ book, record]* sortir, faire paraître ; *[+ film]* (faire) sortir ; *[+ goods]* mettre en vente ; *(= publish, announce) [+ news]* autoriser la publication de ; *[+ details of sth]* publier ◆ **to ~ a statement** publier un communiqué *(about* au sujet de)

4 *(Jur) [+ property]* céder

5 *[+ spring, clasp, catch]* faire jouer ; *(Phot) [+ shutter]* déclencher ; *[+ handbrake]* desserrer ◆ **to ~ the clutch** débrayer

COMP *[switch, knob, catch etc]* de déclenchement *or* de sortie *etc*

release date N *[of film, record]* date *f* de sortie ; *[of book]* date *f* de parution ; *[of prisoner]* date *f* de libération, date *f* de sortie

release print N *(Cine)* copie *f* d'exploitation

release valve N soupape *f* de sûreté

relegate /ˈrelɪgeɪt/ VT 1 *(= demote) [+ person]* reléguer ; *(Sport) [+ team]* reléguer *(to* à, en), déclasser ◆ **to be ~d** *(Brit Ftbl)* descendre en seconde *etc* division ◆ **to ~ old furniture to the attic** reléguer de vieux meubles au grenier 2 *(= hand over) [+ matter, question]* renvoyer *(to* à), se décharger de *(to* sur)

relegation /ˌrelɪˈgeɪʃən/ N relégation *f (also Sport)* ; *[of matter, question]* renvoi *m (to* à)

relent /rɪˈlent/ VI s'adoucir, se laisser toucher, se laisser fléchir ; *(= reverse one's decision)* revenir sur une décision ; *(fig) [weather]* s'améliorer

relentless /rɪˈlentlɪs/ ADJ *[search, pursuit, noise, demands, attacks, criticism]* incessant ; *[pressure, energy, determination, pace, growth]* implacable ; *(iro) [optimism, cheerfulness]* incorrigible ; *[person]* implacable, impitoyable ◆ **to be ~ in doing sth** *or* **in one's efforts to do sth** ne pas relâcher ses efforts pour faire qch ◆ **the ~ march of technology** l'avancée *f* inexorable de la technologie

relentlessly /rɪˈlentlɪslɪ/ ADV 1 *(= tirelessly) [fight, pursue]* avec acharnement ; *[advance, march]* inexorablement ◆ **the sun beat down ~** le soleil était implacable 2 *(= unremittingly) [cheerful, happy, grim]* incurablement, incorrigiblement

relet /ˌriːˈlet/ VT relouer

relevance /ˈreləvəns/, **relevancy** /ˈreləvənsɪ/ N *[of question, remark, argument]* pertinence *f*, intérêt *m* ; *[of fact, information]* importance *f*, intérêt *m* ◆ **I don't see the ~ of your question/that remark (to the issue)** je ne vois pas l'intérêt de votre question/cette remarque ◆ **to be of particular ~ (to sb)** être particulièrement pertinent (pour qn) ◆ **a curriculum which is of ~ to all pupils** un programme qui intéresse tous les élèves ◆ **to have no ~ to sth** n'avoir aucun rapport avec qch ◆ **outdated concepts which have no ~ to the present day** des concepts démodés qui sont sans rapport avec la réalité d'aujourd'hui

relevant /ˈreləvənt/ ADJ 1 *(= pertinent) [information, fact, question, remark, argument]* pertinent ; *[law, regulation]* applicable *(to* à) ◆ **that is not ~** ce n'est pas pertinent ◆ **Molière's plays are still ~ today** les pièces de Molière sont toujours d'actualité ◆ **Ancient History may be fascinating but it's hardly ~ when it comes to finding a job** l'histoire ancienne est peut-être fascinante mais ne sert pas à grand-chose quand il s'agit de trouver du travail ◆ **the ~ year** *(Jur, Fin)* l'année *f* de référence ◆ **to be ~ to sth** *(gen)* être en rapport avec qch ◆ **questions that are ~ to management** des questions qui ont à voir *or* qui sont en rapport avec la gestion ◆ **poetry ~ to people's lives** une poésie dans laquelle les gens se reconnaissent ◆ **it's particularly ~ to people who have recently lost their jobs** c'est particulièrement utile pour les gens qui viennent de perdre leur emploi ◆ **to be ~ to sb/sth** *[law, regulation]* être applicable à qn/qch, concerner qn/qch

2 *(= appropriate) [+ details, information]* voulu, nécessaire ; *[law, regulation]* qui convient ; *[official, authority]* compétent ◆ **make sure you enclose all the ~ certificates** n'oubliez pas de joindre tous les certificats nécessaires

reliability /rɪˌlaɪəˈbɪlɪtɪ/ N *[of person, character]* sérieux *m* ; *[of memory, description]* sûreté *f*, précision *f* ; *[of device, machine]* fiabilité *f*

reliable /rɪˈlaɪəbl/ ADJ *[person]* digne de confiance, sérieux ; *[account, report]* digne de foi, sérieux ; *[firm]* sérieux ; *[ally, source, information]* sûr ; *[machine, method, service, figures, guide, memory, description]* fiable ; *[evidence]* solide ◆ **he's very ~** on peut compter sur lui

reliably /rɪˈlaɪəblɪ/ ADV *[work, measure, date]* de manière fiable ◆ **I am ~ informed that ...** j'ai appris de source sûre que ...

reliance /rɪˈlaɪəns/ N *(= trust)* confiance *f (on* en) ; *(= dependence)* dépendance *f (on* de), besoin *m (on* de) ; ◆ **to place ~ on sb/sth** avoir confiance en qn/qch

reliant /rɪˈlaɪənt/ ADJ ◆ **to be ~ on sb (for sth)** être dépendant de qn (pour qch), dépendre de qn (pour qch) ◆ **to be ~ on sth** dépendre de qch ; → **self**

relic /ˈrelɪk/ N relique *f (also Rel)* ◆ **~s** *(= human remains)* dépouille *f* (mortelle) ; *[of past]* reliques *fpl*, vestiges *mpl*

relict †† /ˈrelɪkt/ N veuve *f*

relief /rɪˈliːf/ N 1 *(from pain, anxiety)* soulagement *m* ◆ **to bring ~ (to sb)** apporter *or* procurer du soulagement (à qn) ◆ **I felt great ~ when ...** j'ai éprouvé un grand *or* vif soulagement quand ... ◆ **he laughed with ~** il rit de soulagement ◆ **to my ~** à mon grand soulagement ◆ **that's a ~!** ouf ! je respire !, j'aime mieux ça ! ◆ **(to me) it was a ~ to find it** j'ai été soulagé de le retrouver ◆ **it's a ~ to get out of the office once in a while** ça fait du bien de sortir du bureau de temps en temps ; → **comic**

2 *(= assistance)* secours *m*, aide *f* ◆ **to go to the ~ of ...** aller au secours de ... ◆ **to come to the ~ of ...** venir en aide à ... ◆ **to send ~ to ...** envoyer des secours à ...

3 *(US Admin)* aides *fpl* sociales ◆ **to be on** *or* **getting ~** bénéficier d'aides sociales

4 *(Mil) [of town]* libération *f* ; *[of guard]* relève *f*

5 *(= substitute or extra workers)* relève *f*

6 *(= exemption) (Jur)* exonération *f* ; *(fiscal)* dégrèvement *m*

7 *(Art, Geog)* relief *m* ◆ **high/low ~** haut-/bas-relief ◆ **to stand out in (bold** *or* **sharp** *or* **clear) ~ against ...** se détacher sur ... ◆ **to bring** *or* **throw sth into ~** *(lit, fig)* mettre qch en relief, faire ressortir qch

COMP *[train, coach]* supplémentaire ; *[typist, clerk]* suppléant

relief agency N organisation *f* humanitaire

relief fund N caisse *f* de secours

relief map N carte *f* en relief

relief organization N *[of refugees, earthquakes etc]* organisation *f* humanitaire

relief road N *(Brit)* itinéraire *m* de délestage

relief supplies NPL secours *mpl*

relief troops NPL relève *f*, troupes *fpl* de secours

relief valve N soupape *f* de sûreté

relief work N travail *m* humanitaire

relief worker N représentant *m* d'un organisme humanitaire

relieve /rɪˈliːv/ VT 1 *[+ person]* soulager ◆ **to feel/look ~d** se sentir/avoir l'air soulagé ◆ **he was ~d to learn that ...** il a été soulagé d'apprendre que ... ◆ **to be ~d at sth** être soulagé par qch ◆ **to be ~d that ...** être soulagé que ... + *subj* ◆ **to ~ sb of a burden** soulager qn d'un fardeau ◆ **to ~ sb of a coat/suitcase** débarrasser qn d'un manteau/d'une valise ◆ **to ~ sb of a duty** décharger qn d'une obligation ◆ **to ~ sb of a post, to ~ sb of a command** *(Mil)* relever qn de ses fonctions ◆ **a thief has ~d me of my purse** *(hum)* un voleur m'a soulagé de *or* délesté de mon porte-monnaie

2 *(= mitigate) [+ anxiety, pain, stress, mental suffering]* soulager ; *[+ pressure]* diminuer ; *[+ fear, boredom]* dissiper ; *[+ poverty]* remédier à, pallier ◆ **to ~ sb's mind** tranquilliser (l'esprit de) qn ◆ **to ~ one's feelings** *(sorrow)* s'épancher ; *(anger)* décharger sa colère *or* sa bile ◆ **to ~ the symptoms of sth** soulager les symptômes de qch ◆ **to ~ a situation** remédier à une situation ◆ **the black of her dress was ~d by a white collar** un col blanc égayait sa robe noire ◆ **the new road ~s peak-hour congestion** la nouvelle route facilite la circulation aux heures de pointe ◆ **the new road ~s congestion in the town centre** la nouvelle route décongestionne le centre-ville ◆ **to ~ congestion** *(Med)* décongestionner ◆ **to ~ o.s.** *(euph)* se soulager, faire ses besoins *

3 *(= help)* secourir, venir en aide à

4 *(= take over from)* relayer ◆ **Paul will ~ you at six** Paul vous relayera à six heures ◆ **to ~ the guard** *(Mil)* relever la garde

5 *(Mil) [+ town, fort, garrison]* libérer

relievo /rɪˈliːvəʊ/ N *(Art)* relief *m*

religion /rɪˈlɪdʒən/ N *(= belief)* religion *f* ; *(= form of worship)* culte *m* ; *(on form etc)* confession *f* ◆ **the Christian ~** la religion chrétienne ◆ **this new ~ already has many adherents** ce nouveau culte a déjà de nombreux adeptes ◆ **wars of ~** guerres *fpl* de religion ◆ **to make a ~ of doing sth** se faire une obligation (absolue) de faire qch ◆ **it's against my ~ (to do that)** *(lit)* c'est contraire à ma religion (de faire cela) ◆ **it's against my ~ to clean windows** * *(hum)* je ne fais jamais les vitres, c'est contraire à ma religion *(hum)* ◆ **to enter ~** entrer en religion ◆ **her name in ~** son nom de religion ◆ **to get ~** * *(hum)* découvrir Dieu

religiosity /rɪˌlɪdʒɪˈɒsɪtɪ/ N *(pej)* religiosité *f*

religious /rɪˈlɪdʒəs/ ADJ *[beliefs, practice, order, service, music, book, leader]* religieux ; *[freedom]* religieux, de religion ; *[person]* religieux, croyant ; *[war]* de religion ◆ **a ~ maniac** *or* **lunatic** * un fanatique religieux N *(pl inv)* religieux *m*, -ieuse *f*

COMP **religious education** N *(Scol)* éducation *f* religieuse

religious instruction N *(Scol)* instruction *f* religieuse

religiously /rɪˈlɪdʒəslɪ/ ADV 1 *(Rel)* ◆ **a ~ diverse country** un pays qui présente une grande diversité religieuse ◆ **~ minded people** gens *mpl* religieux ◆ **~ motivated** motivé par la religion 2 *(= conscientiously)* religieusement

religiousness /rɪˈlɪdʒəsnɪs/ N piété *f*, dévotion *f*

reline /ˌriːˈlaɪn/ VT *[+ coat, jacket]* mettre une nouvelle doublure à, redoubler ◆ **to ~ the brakes** *[of car]* changer les garnitures de freins

relinquish /rɪˈlɪŋkwɪʃ/ VT 1 *(= give up) [+ hope, power]* abandonner ; *[+ plan, right]* renoncer à *(to sb* en faveur de qn) ; *[+ habit]* renoncer à ; *[+ post]* quitter, abandonner ; *[+ goods, property* *etc]* se dessaisir de, abandonner 2 *(= let go)* *[+ object]* lâcher ◆ **to ~ one's hold on sth** lâcher qch

relinquishment /rɪˈlɪŋkwɪʃmənt/ N abandon *m* *(of sth* de qch)

reliquary /ˈrelɪkwərɪ/ N reliquaire *m*

relish /ˈrelɪʃ/ N 1 *(= enjoyment)* goût *m* *(for* pour) ◆ **to do sth with (great) ~, to take ~ in doing sth** faire qch avec délectation ◆ **he ate with ~** il mangeait de bon appétit ◆ **he rubbed his hands with ~ at the prospect of ...** il se frotta les mains de plaisir à la perspective de ... 2 *(Culin) (= flavour)* goût *m*, saveur *f* ; *(= pickle: for hamburger etc)* achards *mpl* ; *(= seasoning)* condiment *m*, assaisonnement *m* ; *(= trace: of spices etc)* soupçon *m* ; *(fig = charm)* attrait *m*, charme *m* ◆ **it had lost all ~** *(fig)* cela avait perdu tout attrait VT *[+ food, wine]* savourer ◆ **to ~ doing sth** se délecter à faire qch, trouver du plaisir à faire qch ◆ **I don't ~ the idea** *or* **prospect** *or* **thought of getting up at five** l'idée de me lever à cinq heures ne me sourit guère *or* ne me dit rien

relive /ˌriːˈlɪv/ VT revivre

reload /ˌriːˈləʊd/ VT, VI recharger

relocate /ˌriːləʊˈkeɪt/ VT *(gen)* installer ailleurs ; *[+ company]* délocaliser ; *[+ worker] (in a new place)* transférer, muter ; *(in a new job)* reconvertir VI *(= move house)* déménager, s'installer ailleurs ; *[company]* se réimplanter ; *[worker] (in a new place)* changer de lieu de travail ; *(in a new job)* se reconvertir ◆ **to ~ to ...** déménager à ..., s'installer à

relocation /ˌriːləʊˈkeɪʃən/ N *(gen)* déménagement *m* ; *[of company]* délocalisation *f* ; *[of worker] (in a new place)* transfert *m*, mutation *f* ; *(in a new job)* reconversion *f* ; *[of household]* déménagement *m*

COMP **relocation allowance** N prime *f* de relogement

relocation expenses NPL *(paid to employee)* frais *mpl* de déménagement

reluctance /rɪˈlʌktəns/ N 1 répugnance *f* *(to do sth* à faire qch) ◆ **to do sth with ~** faire qch à regret *or* à contrecœur ◆ **to make a show of ~** se faire prier, se faire tirer l'oreille 2 *(Elec)* réluctance *f*

reluctant /rɪˈlʌktənt/ ADJ *[person, animal]* réticent *(to do sth* à faire qch) ; *[acceptance]* peu enthousiaste ; *[praise, consent, permission, response]* peu enthousiaste, donné à contrecœur ◆ **the ~ soldier** le soldat malgré lui ◆ **to give one's ~ approval to sth** donner son accord à qch avec réticence *or* à contrecœur ◆ **to take the ~ decision to do sth** prendre avec réticence *or* à contrecœur la décision de faire qch

reluctantly /rɪˈlʌktəntlɪ/ ADV à contrecœur

rely /rɪˈlaɪ/ VI ◆ **to ~ (up)on sb/sth** compter sur qn/qch ◆ **she relied on the trains being on time** elle comptait *or* tablait sur le fait que les trains seraient à l'heure ◆ **I ~ on him for my income** je dépends de lui pour mes revenus ◆ **you can ~ upon it** vous pouvez y compter ◆ **you can ~ on me not to say anything about it** vous pouvez compter sur moi pour ne pas en parler, comptez sur ma discrétion ◆ **she is not to be relied upon** on ne peut pas compter sur elle ◆ **he relies increasingly on his assistants** il se repose de plus en plus sur ses assistants ◆ **you mustn't ~ on other people for everything** il faut se prendre en charge ◆ **to ~ on sth** *(Jur)* invoquer qch

REM /rem/ N (abbrev of **rapid eye movement**) → **rapid**

remain /rɪˈmeɪn/ VI 1 *(= be left)* rester ◆ **much ~s to be done** il reste beaucoup à faire ◆ **nothing ~s to be said** il ne reste plus rien à dire ◆ **nothing ~s but to accept** il ne reste plus qu'à accepter ◆ **it ~s to be seen whether ...** reste à savoir si ... ◆ **that ~s to be seen** c'est ce que nous verrons, c'est ce qu'il reste à voir ◆ **the fact ~s that he is wrong** il n'en est pas moins vrai *or* toujours est-il qu'il a tort ◆ **take 2 from 4, 2 ~ 4** moins 2, il reste 2

2 *(= stay)* rester, demeurer ◆ **to ~ faithful** demeurer *or* rester fidèle ◆ **~ seated** restez assis ◆ **to ~ out/in** *etc* rester (en) dehors/(en) dedans *etc* ◆ **to ~ up** rester levé ◆ **let the matter ~ as it is** laissez l'affaire comme cela ◆ **it ~s the same** ça ne change pas ◆ **to ~ silent** garder le silence ◆ **it ~s unsolved** ce n'est toujours pas résolu ◆ **if the weather ~s fine** si le temps se maintient (au beau) ◆ **I ~, yours faithfully** *(in letters)* je vous prie d'agréer *or* veuillez agréer l'expression de mes sentiments distingués

► **remain behind** VI rester

remainder /rɪˈmeɪndəʳ/ N 1 *(= sth left over)* reste *m* ; *(= remaining people)* autres *mfpl* ; *(Math)* reste *m* ; *(Jur)* usufruit *m* avec réversibilité ◆ **for the ~ of the week** pendant le reste *or* le restant de la semaine 2 ◆ **~s** *(Comm) (= books etc)* invendus *mpl* soldés, soldes *mpl* d'éditeur ; *(= clothes, articles)* fin(s) *f(pl)* de série VT *[+ books etc]* solder

remaining /rɪˈmeɪnɪŋ/ ADJ *[people, objects]* qui reste (*or* restait), restant ◆ **use up the ~ olives in the sauce** utiliser le reste des olives dans la sauce ◆ **she's one of his few ~ friends** elle fait partie des rares amis qui lui restent

remains /rɪˈmeɪnz/ NPL *[of meal]* restes *mpl* ; *[of fortune, army]* débris *mpl* ; *[of building]* vestiges *mpl*, ruines *fpl* ◆ **literary ~** œuvres *fpl* posthumes ◆ **his (mortal) ~** ses restes *mpl*, sa dépouille mortelle ◆ **human ~** restes *mpl* humains

remake /ˌriːˈmeɪk/ VT refaire ; *(Cine) [+ film]* faire un remake de N /ˈriːmeɪk/ *(Cine)* remake *m*

remand /rɪˈmɑːnd/ VT *(gen, Jur) [+ case, accused person]* déférer, renvoyer *(to* à) ◆ **to ~ sb to a higher court** *(Jur)* renvoyer qn à une instance supérieure ◆ **to ~ sb in custody** mettre qn en détention provisoire ◆ **to ~ sb on bail** mettre qn en liberté sous caution ◆ **case ~ed for a week** affaire *f* renvoyée à huitaine ; → **further** N renvoi *m* (à une autre audience) ◆ **to be on ~** *(= in custody)* être en détention provisoire ; *(= on bail)* être en liberté provisoire

COMP **remand centre** N *(Brit)* centre *m* de détention provisoire

remand home † N *(Brit)* ≃ maison *f* d'arrêt

remand prisoner N personne *f* en détention provisoire

remand wing N quartier *m* de détention provisoire

remark /rɪˈmɑːk/ N 1 *(= comment)* remarque *f* ◆ **to make** *or* **pass the ~ that ...** faire remarquer *or* observer que ... ◆ **I have a few ~s to make on that subject** j'ai quelques remarques à vous communiquer à ce sujet ◆ **to make** *or* **pass unkind ~s about sb/sth** faire des remarques désagréables sur qn/qch ◆ **~s were made about your absence** votre absence a fait l'objet de remarques 2 *(NonC)* ◆ **worthy of ~** digne d'attention, remarquable VT 1 *(= say)* (faire) remarquer, (faire) observer ◆ **"it's raining" he ~ed** "il pleut" observa-t-il 2 *(= notice)* remarquer, observer VI faire des remarques *or* des observations *(on* sur) ◆ **he ~ed on it to me** il m'en a fait l'observation *or* la remarque

remarkable /rɪˈmɑːkəbl/ ADJ remarquable *(for sth* par qch) ◆ **it is ~ that ...** il est remarquable que ... + *subj* ◆ **there's nothing ~ about that** cela n'a rien de remarquable ◆ **it is ~ how quickly children grow up** la vitesse à laquelle les enfants grandissent est incroyable, c'est incroyable ce que les enfants grandissent vite

remarkably /rɪˈmɑːkəblɪ/ ADV extrêmement ◆ **this has been a ~ difficult year for him** cette année a été extrêmement difficile pour lui ◆ **~, the factory had escaped the bombing** fait étonnant *or* par miracle, l'usine avait échappé aux bombardements

remarriage /ˌriːˈmærɪdʒ/ N remariage *m*

remarry /ˌriːˈmærɪ/ VI se remarier VT remarier

remaster /ˌriːˈmɑːstəʳ/ VT *[+ recording]* remixer ; → **digitally**

rematch /ˈriːmætʃ/ N *(gen)* match *m* retour ; *(Boxing)* deuxième combat *m* VT /ˌriːˈmætʃ/ opposer à nouveau

remediable /rɪˈmiːdɪəbl/ ADJ remédiable

remedial /rɪˈmiːdɪəl/ ADJ 1 *(Med) [treatment]* curatif ◆ **~ exercises** gymnastique *f* corrective 2 *(Educ) [class]* de rattrapage ◆ **~ education** soutien *m* scolaire ◆ **~ teaching** cours *mpl* de rattrapage *or* de soutien ◆ **~ help** soutien *m* ◆ **~ (course in) English** cours *mpl* de rattrapage *or* de soutien en anglais 3 *(= corrective) [work]* de réparation ◆ **~ action** *or* **measures** mesures *fpl* de redressement

remedy /ˈremədɪ/ N *(Med)* remède *m* *(for* contre *or* pour) ; *(fig)* solution *f*, remède *m* ; *(Jur)* recours *m* ◆ **the ~ lies in the hands of the government** c'est le gouvernement qui détient la solution ◆ **divorce is not a ~ for a marriage problem** le divorce n'est pas une solution aux problèmes conjugaux ◆ **the ~ for despair** le remède contre le désespoir ◆ **to seek ~** *(legal)* chercher à obtenir réparation ◆ **a natural ~** un remède naturel ◆ **beyond ~** sans remède VT *(Med)* remédier à ; *(fig)* remédier à, porter remède à ◆ **the situation cannot be remedied** la situation est sans remède

remember /rɪˈmembəʳ/ VT 1 *(= recall) [+ person, date, occasion]* se souvenir de, se rappeler ◆ **to ~ that ...** se rappeler que ... ◆ **I ~ doing it** je me rappelle l'avoir fait, je me souviens de l'avoir fait ◆ **I ~ed to do it** j'ai pensé à le faire, je n'ai pas oublié de le faire ◆ **I ~ when an egg cost one penny** je me souviens de l'époque où un œuf coûtait un penny ◆ **I cannot ~ your name** je ne me rappelle plus votre nom, je ne me souviens pas de votre nom ◆ **don't you ~ me?** *(face to face)* vous ne me reconnaissez pas ? ; *(phone)* vous ne vous souvenez pas de moi ? ◆ **I ~ your face** je me souviens de votre visage, je vous reconnais ◆ **I don't ~ a thing about it** je n'en ai pas le moindre souvenir, je ne me souviens de rien ◆ **I can never ~ phone numbers** je n'ai aucune mémoire pour les *or* je ne me souviens jamais des numéros de téléphone ◆ **let us ~ that ...** n'oublions pas que ... ◆ **a night/occasion to ~** une soirée/un moment mémorable *or* inoubliable ◆ **here's something to ~ him by** voici un souvenir de lui ◆ **he is ~ed as a fine violinist** il a laissé le souvenir d'un violoniste talentueux ◆ **she will be ~ed by millions (for her honesty/for supporting this cause)** des millions de gens se souviendront d'elle (pour son honnêteté/pour son soutien à cette cause) ◆ **I can't ~ the word at the moment** le mot m'échappe pour le moment ◆ **we can't always ~ everything** on ne peut pas toujours songer à tout ◆ **~ where you are!** ressaisissez-vous ! ◆ **to ~ o.s.** se reprendre ◆ **to ~ sb in one's prayers** ne pas oublier qn dans ses prières ◆ **that's worth ~ing** c'est bon à savoir

2 *(= commemorate) [+ the fallen, a battle]* commémorer

3 *(= give good wishes to)* rappeler *(to* au bon souvenir de) ◆ **~ me to your mother** rappelez-moi au bon souvenir de votre mère ◆ **he asked to be ~ed to you** il vous envoie son meilleur souvenir

4 *(= give money or a present to)* ne pas oublier ◆ **to ~ sb in one's will** ne pas oublier qn dans son testament

VI se souvenir ◆ **I can't ~** je ne me souviens pas, je ne sais plus ◆ **as far as I ~** autant que je m'en souvienne ◆ **not as far as I ~** pas à ma connaissance, pas que je m'en souvienne ◆ **if I**

~ **right(ly)** si j'ai bonne mémoire, si je m'en *or* me souviens bien ◆ **the last time we had a party, if you ~, it took us days to clear up** la dernière fois que nous avons organisé une soirée, je te rappelle qu'il nous a fallu des jours pour tout ranger ◆ **he was, you ~, a great man** il était, comme vous le savez, un grand homme

remembered /rɪˈmembəd/ ADJ *(liter)* *[happiness etc]* inscrit dans la mémoire

remembrance /rɪˈmembrəns/ N *(= memory, thing remembered)* souvenir *m*, mémoire *f* ; *(= act of remembering, keepsake)* souvenir *m* ◆ **Remembrance Day** *(Brit)* ◆ **Remembrance Sunday** ≈ (le jour de) l'Armistice *m*, le 11 Novembre ; → POPPY DAY ◆ **in ~ of** en souvenir de ◆ **to the best of my ~** pour autant que je m'en souvienne ◆ **within the ~ of man** de mémoire d'homme ◆ **to have no ~ of sth** ne pas se souvenir de qch, n'avoir aucun souvenir de qch

remind /rɪˈmaɪnd/ LANGUAGE IN USE 5.1 VT rappeler *(sb of sth* qch à qn ; *sb that* à qn que) ◆ **you are ~ed that ...** nous vous rappelons que ... ◆ **to ~ sb to do sth** faire penser à qn à faire qch ◆ **must I ~ you (again)?** faut-il que je (vous) le redise *or* le rappelle *subj* encore une fois ? ◆ **she ~ed him of his mother** elle lui rappelait sa mère ◆ **that ~s me!** à propos !, j'y pense !

reminder /rɪˈmaɪndəʳ/ N *(= note, knot etc)* mémento *m*, pense-bête *m* ◆ **as a ~ that ...** pour (vous *or* lui *etc*) rappeler que ... ◆ **his presence was a ~ of ...** sa présence rappelait ... ◆ **a gentle ~** un rappel discret ◆ **give him a gentle ~** rappelez-le-lui discrètement ◆ **(letter of) ~** *(Comm)* lettre *f* de rappel COMP **reminder call** N *(Telec)* mémo appel *m*

reminisce /ˌremɪˈnɪs/ VI évoquer *or* raconter ses souvenirs ◆ **to ~ about sth** évoquer qch

reminiscence /ˌremɪˈnɪsəns/ N réminiscence *f*

reminiscent /ˌremɪˈnɪsənt/ ADJ 1 *(= similar)* ◆ **to be ~ of sth** rappeler qch, faire penser à qch 2 *(= nostalgic)* *[person, mood, smile]* nostalgique

reminiscently /ˌremɪˈnɪsəntlɪ/ ADV ◆ **he smiled ~** il sourit à ce souvenir ◆ **he talked ~ of the war** il évoquait des souvenirs de la guerre

remiss /rɪˈmɪs/ ADJ *(frm)* négligent ◆ **he has been ~ in not finishing his work** il s'est rendu coupable de négligence en ne terminant pas son travail ◆ **that was very ~ of you** vous vous êtes montré très négligent ◆ **it would be ~ of me to do that** ce serait négligent de ma part que de faire cela

remission /rɪˈmɪʃən/ N *(gen, Med, Rel)* rémission *f* ; *(Jur)* remise *f* ◆ **the ~ of sins** la rémission des péchés ◆ **he earned three years' ~ (for good conduct)** *(Brit Jur)* on lui a accordé trois ans de remise de peine (pour bonne conduite) ◆ **~ from a debt** *(Jur)* remise *f* d'une dette ◆ **there can be no ~ of registration fees** il ne peut y avoir de dispense *or* d'exemption des droits d'inscription ◆ **to be in ~** *(Med)* *[disease, person]* être en rémission ◆ **to go into ~** *[disease, person]* entrer en rémission

remissness /rɪˈmɪsnɪs/ N négligence *f*

remit[1] /rɪˈmɪt/ LANGUAGE IN USE 20.6 VT 1 *(frm = send)* *[+ money]* envoyer, verser 2 *(Jur)* *[+ case]* renvoyer 3 *[+ sin]* pardonner, remettre ; *[+ fee, debt, penalty, punishment]* remettre ◆ **to have part of one's sentence ~ted** bénéficier d'une remise de peine ◆ **to ~ sb's sentence** faire bénéficier qn d'une remise de peine ◆ **the prisoner's sentence was ~ted** le détenu a reçu une remise de peine VI *(= become less)* diminuer

remit[2] /ˈriːmɪt/ N *(Brit)* domaine *m* de compétence, attributions *fpl* ◆ **their ~ covers terrorism and spying** leurs attributions comprennent *or* leur domaine de compétence comprend le terrorisme et l'espionnage ◆ **to have a ~ to do sth** avoir pour mission *or* tâche de faire qch ◆ **is it within your ~?** est-ce que cela relève de votre compétence ?, est-ce que cela entre dans vos attributions ?

remittal /rɪˈmɪtl/ N *(Jur)* renvoi *m* (à une instance inférieure)

remittance /rɪˈmɪtəns/ N 1 *(of money, gen)* versement *m* ; *(Banking, Econ, Fin)* remise *f* de fonds ; *(Comm etc = payment)* paiement *m*, règlement *m* ◆ **enclose your ~** joignez votre règlement 2 *(of documents)* remise *f*
COMP **remittance advice** N *(Comm)* avis *m* de versement
remittance man N (pl **remittance men**) *(US)* *résident étranger entretenu (par ses parents etc)*

remittee /remɪˈtiː/ N destinataire *mf (d'un envoi de fonds)*

remittent /rɪˈmɪtənt/ ADJ *(Med)* rémittent ; *(fig)* intermittent

remitter /rɪˈmɪtəʳ/ N 1 remetteur *m*, -euse *f* ; *[of money]* envoyeur *m*, -euse *f* ; *(Comm)* remettant *m* 2 *(Jur)* renvoi *m* (à une instance inférieure)

remix /ˈriːmɪks/ N *(Mus)* remix *m* VT /ˌriːˈmɪks/ *(Mus)* remixer

remnant /ˈremnənt/ N *(= anything remaining)* reste *m*, restant *m* ; *(= piece)* débris *m*, bout *m* ; *[of custom, splendour]* vestige *m* ; *[of food, fortune]* bribe *f*, débris *m* ; *[of cloth]* coupon *m* ◆ **~s** *(Comm)* soldes *mpl* (de fins de série) ◆ **the ~ of the army** ce qui restait (*or* reste) de l'armée
COMP **remnant day** N *(Comm)* jour *m* de soldes
remnant sale N solde *m* (de coupons *or* d'invendus *or* de fins de série)

remodel /ˌriːˈmɒdl/ VT *[+ building]* remanier ; *(fig)* *[+ society]* réorganiser ; *[+ constitution]* remanier

remold /ˌriːˈməʊld/ VT, N *(US)* ⇒ **remould**

remonstrance /rɪˈmɒnstrəns/ N 1 *(NonC)* remontrance *f* 2 *(= protest)* protestation *f* ; *(= reproof)* reproche *m*

remonstrant /rɪˈmɒnstrənt/ ADJ *[tone]* de remontrance, de protestation N protestataire *mf*

remonstrate /ˈremənstreɪt/ VI protester *(against* contre) ◆ **to ~ with sb about sth** faire des remontrances à qn au sujet de qch VT faire observer *or* remarquer *(avec l'idée de reproche ou de contradiction)* (that que)

remorse /rɪˈmɔːs/ N *(NonC)* remords *m* (*at* de ; *for* pour) ◆ **a feeling of ~** un remords ◆ **without ~** sans pitié

remorseful /rɪˈmɔːsfʊl/ ADJ plein de remords ◆ **he was not ~ (about** *or* **for)** il n'avait aucun remords (pour)

remorsefully /rɪˈmɔːsfəlɪ/ ADV avec remords ◆ **... he said ~** ... dit-il, plein de remords

remorsefulness /rɪˈmɔːsfʊlnɪs/ N *(NonC)* remords *m*

remorseless /rɪˈmɔːslɪs/ ADJ 1 *(= merciless)* *[person]* sans pitié, impitoyable 2 *(= relentless)* *[pressure]* implacable, impitoyable (*in sth* dans qch) ; *[ambition]* dévorant

remorselessly /rɪˈmɔːslɪslɪ/ ADV *(= mercilessly)* *[tease, pursue]* sans pitié, impitoyablement ; *(= relentlessly)* implacablement, impitoyablement

remorselessness /rɪˈmɔːslɪsnɪs/ N absence *f* *or* manque *m* de pitié *or* de remords

remote /rɪˈməʊt/ ADJ 1 *[place]* *(= distant)* éloigné, lointain ; *(= isolated)* isolé ; *[relative, ancestor, descendant]* éloigné, lointain *before n* ◆ **in ~ country districts** dans les régions rurales isolées ◆ **in a ~ spot** dans un lieu isolé ◆ **in the ~ past/future** dans un passé/avenir lointain ◆ **~ antiquity** la plus haute antiquité ◆ **a village ~ from the world** un village à l'écart du monde ◆ **a house ~ from a main road** une maison située loin *or* à l'écart des grands axes
2 *(= distanced)* éloigné *(from sth* de qch) ◆ **what he said was rather ~ from the subject in hand** ce qu'il a dit n'avait pas beaucoup de rapport avec le sujet ◆ **subjects that seem ~ from our daily lives** des questions qui paraissent sans rapport avec notre vie quotidienne
3 *(= slight)* *[hope]* mince *before n* ; *[resemblance, chance, possibility]* vague ; *[prospect]* lointain ; *[risk]* ténu ◆ **the odds of that happening are ~** il y a très peu de chances que cela se produise ◆ **I haven't the ~st idea** je n'en ai pas la moindre idée
4 *(= aloof)* *[person]* distant
5 *(= remote-controlled)* à distance ◆ **~ handset** télécommande *f*
N (also **remote control**) télécommande *f*
COMP **remote access** N *(Comput)* accès *m* à distance, téléconsultation *f*
remote control N télécommande *f*
remote-controlled ADJ télécommandé
remote job entry N *(Comput)* télésoumission *f* de travaux
remote sensing N télédétection *f*

remotely /rɪˈməʊtlɪ/ ADV 1 *(= vaguely)* **her cooking is not even ~ edible** sa cuisine est tout à fait immangeable ◆ **it isn't ~ possible that ...** il est absolument impossible que ... + *subj* ◆ **he failed to say anything ~ interesting** il n'a rien dit d'un tant soit peu intéressant ◆ **I'm not ~ interested in art** l'art ne m'intéresse pas le moins du monde ◆ **it doesn't ~ resemble ...** cela ne ressemble en rien à ... ◆ **avoid saying anything ~ likely to upset him** évitez de dire quoi que ce soit qui puisse l'agacer ◆ **I've never seen anything ~ like it** jamais de ma vie je n'ai vu une chose pareille ◆ **the only person present even ~ connected with show business** la seule personne présente qui ait un rapport quelconque avec le monde du spectacle
2 *(= distantly)* ◆ **to be ~ situated** être situé loin de tout, être isolé ◆ **we are ~ related** nous sommes (des) parents éloignés
3 *(= aloofly)* *[say]* d'un ton distant ; *[behave]* d'un air distant
4 *(= from a distance)* *[control, detonate]* à distance

remoteness /rɪˈməʊtnɪs/ N 1 *(in space)* éloignement *m*, isolement *m* ; *(in time)* éloignement *m* 2 *(= aloofness)* attitude *f* distante *or* réservée *(from sb* envers qn)

remould, remold *(US)* /ˌriːˈməʊld/ VT *(Tech)* remouler ; *[+ tyre]* rechaper ; *(fig)* *[+ sb's character]* corriger N /ˈriːməʊld/ *(= tyre)* pneu *m* rechapé

remount /ˌriːˈmaʊnt/ VT 1 *[+ horse]* remonter sur ; *[+ bicycle]* enfourcher de nouveau ; *[+ ladder]* grimper de nouveau sur 2 *[+ picture]* rentoiler ; *[+ photo]* faire un nouveau montage de VI remonter à cheval (*or* à bicyclette)

removable /rɪˈmuːvəbl/ ADJ amovible, détachable ◆ **a sofa/cushion with a ~ cover** un canapé/coussin déhoussable

removal /rɪˈmuːvəl/ N 1 *(= taking away)* enlèvement *m* ; *(esp Brit)* *[of furniture, household]* déménagement *m* ; *[of abuse, evil]* suppression *f* ; *[of pain]* soulagement *m* ; *(from a job)* *(= demotion)* déplacement *m* ; *(= sacking)* renvoi *m*, révocation *f* ; *(Med)* ablation *f* ◆ **stain ~** détachage *m* 2 († *: from house*) déménagement *m* ◆ **after our ~** après notre déménagement ◆ **our ~ to this house** notre emménagement *m* dans cette maison ◆ **our ~ from London** notre déménagement de Londres
COMP **removal expenses** NPL *(Brit)* frais *mpl* de déménagement
removal man N (pl **removal men**) déménageur *m*
removal van N *(Brit)* voiture *f* *or* camion *m* *or* fourgon *m* de déménagement

remove /rɪ'muːv/ VT *[+ object]* enlever *(from* de) ; *[+ clothes]* enlever, ôter ; *[+ furniture, lid]* enlever ; *[+ stain, graffiti]* enlever, faire partir ; *[+ paragraph, word, item on list, threat, tax]* supprimer ; *[+ objection]* réfuter ; *[+ difficulty, problem]* résoudre ; *(lit, fig) [+ obstacle]* écarter ; *[+ doubt]* chasser ; *[+ suspicion, fear]* dissiper ; *[+ employee]* destituer, révoquer ; *[+ official]* déplacer ; *(Med) [+ lung, kidney]* enlever ; *[+ tumour]* extirper, enlever ; *[+ splint, bandage]* enlever ◆ **he was ~d to the cells** on l'a emmené en cellule ◆ **to ~ sb to hospital** hospitaliser qn ◆ **to ~ a child from school** retirer un enfant de l'école ◆ **~ the prisoner!** *(Jur: in court)* faites sortir l'accusé ! ◆ **he ~d himself to another room** il s'est retiré dans une autre pièce ◆ **to ~ sb's name** rayer qn, radier qn ◆ **to ~ one's make-up** se démaquiller ◆ **make-up removing cream** lait *m* démaquillant ◆ **to ~ unwanted hair from one's legs** s'épiler les jambes ◆ **to be far ~d from sth** *(fig)* être loin de qch ◆ **cousin once/twice ~d** cousin(e) *m(f)* au deuxième/troisième degré

VI † déménager, changer de domicile ◆ **to ~ to London** aller habiter à Londres, aller s'installer à Londres

N 1 *(in relationship)* degré *m* de parenté

2 *(frm: fig)* **to be only a few ~s from ...** être tout proche de ... ◆ **this is but one ~ from disaster** nous frisons *(or* ils frisent *etc)* la catastrophe ◆ **it's a far ~ from ...** c'est loin d'être ...

remover /rɪ'muːvəʳ/ N 1 *(= removal man)* déménageur *m* 2 *(= substance) (for varnish)* dissolvant *m* ; *(for stains)* détachant *m* ◆ **paint ~** décapant *m* (pour peintures) ; → **cuticle, hair, make-up**

remunerate /rɪ'mjuːnəreɪt/ VT rémunérer

remuneration /rɪˌmjuːnə'reɪʃən/ N rémunération *f (for* de)

remunerative /rɪ'mjuːnərətɪv/ ADJ *(frm) [scheme, investment]* rémunérateur (-trice *f*), lucratif ; *[job, employment]* rémunéré

Renaissance /rɪ'neɪsɑ̃ːns/ *(Art, Hist)* N ◆ **the ~** la Renaissance

COMP *[art, scholar]* de la Renaissance ; *[style, palace]* Renaissance *inv*

Renaissance man N (pl **Renaissance men**) homme *m* aux talents multiples

renaissance /rɪ'neɪsɑ̃ːns/ N renaissance *f*

renal /'riːnl/ ADJ rénal COMP **renal failure** N défaillance *f or* insuffisance *f* rénale

rename /ˌriː'neɪm/ VT *[+ person, street, town]* rebaptiser *(fig) (Comput) [+ file]* renommer

renascence /rɪ'næsns/ N ⇒ **renaissance**

renascent /rɪ'næsnt/ ADJ renaissant

rend /rend/ (pret, ptp **rent**) VT *(liter) [+ cloth]* déchirer ; *[+ armour]* fendre ; *(fig)* déchirer, fendre ◆ **to ~ sth from ...** *(lit, fig)* arracher qch à *or* de ... ◆ **a country rent by civil war** un pays déchiré par la guerre civile ◆ **to ~ sb's heart** fendre le cœur à qn

render /'rendəʳ/ VT 1 *(frm = give) [+ service, homage, judgement]* rendre ; *[+ help]* donner ; *[+ explanation]* donner, fournir ◆ **~ unto Caesar the things which are Caesar's** il faut rendre à César ce qui est à César ◆ **to ~ thanks to sb** remercier qn ◆ **to ~ thanks to God** rendre grâce à Dieu ◆ **to ~ assistance (to sb)** prêter assistance *or* secours (à qn) ◆ **to ~ an account of sth** rendre compte de qch ◆ **for services ~ed** pour services rendus

2 *(Comm) [+ account]* remettre, présenter

3 *[+ music]* interpréter ; *[+ text]* rendre, traduire *(into* en)

4 *(= make)* rendre ◆ **his accident ~ed him helpless** son accident l'a rendu complètement infirme ◆ **the blow ~ed him unconscious** *or* **insensible** le coup lui a fait perdre connaissance

5 *(Culin) [+ fat]* faire fondre

6 *(Constr)* enduire *(with* de)

▸ **render down** VT SEP *[+ fat]* faire fondre

▸ **render up** VT SEP *(liter) [+ fortress]* rendre ; *[+ prisoner, treasure]* livrer

rendering /'rendərɪŋ/ N 1 *[of music, poem]* interprétation *f* ; *[of text, phrase]* traduction *f (into* en) ; ◆ **the film is a startling visual ~ of the biblical text** le film donne une interprétation visuelle étonnante du texte biblique 2 *(Constr)* enduit *m* COMP **rendering plant** N usine *f* de transformation de déchets animaux

rendez-vous /'rɒndɪvuː/ N (pl **rendez-vous** /'rɒndɪvuːz/) rendez-vous *m* ◆ **let's make a ~ for next week** prenons rendez-vous pour la semaine prochaine VI *(= meet)* se retrouver ; *(= assemble)* se réunir ◆ **to ~ with sb** rejoindre qn ◆ **they ~ed with the patrol at dawn** *(Mil etc)* ils ont rejoint la patrouille à l'aube

rendition /ren'dɪʃən/ N ⇒ **rendering**

reneague /rɪ'niːg/ VI ⇒ **renege**

renegade /'renɪgeɪd/ N renégat(e) *m(f)* ADJ *[forces, faction, person]* rebelle

renege /rɪ'neɪg/ VI manquer à sa parole ; *(Cards)* faire une renonce ◆ **to ~ on a promise** manquer à sa promesse

renegotiate /ˌriːnɪ'gəʊʃɪeɪt/ LANGUAGE IN USE 19.5 VT renégocier

renegue /rɪ'neɪg/ VI ⇒ **renege**

renew /rɪ'njuː/ VT *[+ appointment, attack, contract, passport, promise, one's strength]* renouveler ; *[+ lease]* renouveler, reconduire ; *[+ supplies]* remplacer, renouveler ◆ **to ~ negotiations/discussions** reprendre des négociations/discussions ◆ **to ~ one's subscription** renouveler son abonnement, se réabonner ◆ **to ~ one's acquaintance with sb** renouer connaissance avec qn ; see also **renewed**

renewable /rɪ'njuːəbl/ ADJ *[contract, resources, energy]* renouvelable NPL **renewables** énergies *fpl* renouvelables

renewal /rɪ'njuːəl/ N 1 *(= resumption) [of hostilities]* reprise *f* ; *[of society]* renouveau *m* ; *[of attack]* renouvellement *m* ; *[of interest, strength]* regain *m* 2 *(= improvement) [of city]* rénovation *f* ; *[of district, area]* rénovation *f*, réhabilitation *f* ; → **urban** 3 *(= revalidating) [of licence, visa, passport, policy]* renouvellement *m* ; *[of contract, lease]* renouvellement *m* reconduction *f* ◆ **~ of subscription** réabonnement *m* 4 *(Rel)* renouveau *m*

renewed /rɪ'njuːd/ ADJ ◆ **~ interest/hope/enthusiasm** un regain d'intérêt/d'espoir/d'enthousiasme ◆ **with ~ vigour** avec une vitalité accrue ◆ **~ fighting** une recrudescence des combats ◆ **he has come under ~ pressure to resign** on fait de nouveau pression sur lui pour qu'il démissionne ◆ **to make ~ efforts to do sth** renouveler ses efforts pour faire qch ◆ **to feel a ~ sense of well-being** se sentir revivre

rennet /'renɪt/ N *(for junket)* présure *f*

renounce /rɪ'naʊns/ VT *[+ liberty, opinions, ideas, title]* renoncer à ; *[+ religion]* abjurer ; *[+ right]* renoncer à, abandonner ; *[+ treaty]* dénoncer ; *[+ friend]* renier ; *[+ cause, party]* renier, désavouer ; *[+ principles]* répudier ◆ **to ~ the flesh** *(Rel)* renoncer à la *or* aux plaisirs de la chair VI *(Bridge)* défausser

renouncement /rɪ'naʊnsmənt/ N ⇒ **renunciation**

renovate /'renəʊveɪt/ VT *[+ clothes, house]* remettre à neuf, rénover ; *[+ building, painting, statue]* restaurer

renovation /ˌrenəʊ'veɪʃən/ N 1 *(NonC = doing up) [of house, flat]* rénovation *f*, remise *f* à neuf ; *(= restoration) [of historic building, painting, statue]* restauration *f* ◆ **to be in need of ~** être en mauvais état 2 *(to building)* ◆ **~s** travaux *mpl*

renown /rɪ'naʊn/ N renommée *f*, renom *m* ◆ **a wine of ~** un vin renommé ◆ **a scholar of great** *or* **high ~** un érudit renommé *or* de renom

renowned /rɪ'naʊnd/ ADJ *[artist, scientist]* renommé *(for sth* pour qch), célèbre *(for sth* pour qch) ; *[expert, place]* réputé *(for sth* pour qch), célèbre *(for sth* pour qch) ◆ **internationally ~ writers** des écrivains de renommée internationale ◆ **garlic is ~ as an antiseptic** l'ail est réputé pour ses vertus antiseptiques

rent¹ /rent/ N *[of house, room]* loyer *m* ; *[of farm]* fermage *m* ; *[of television etc]* (prix *m* de) location *f* ◆ **for ~** *(US)* à louer ◆ **quarter's ~** terme *m* ◆ **(one week) late** *or* **behind with one's ~** en retard (d'une semaine) sur son loyer ◆ **to pay a high/low ~ for sth** payer un gros/petit loyer pour qch

VT 1 *(= take for rent)* louer ◆ **we don't own it, we only ~ it** nous ne sommes pas propriétaires, mais locataires seulement ◆ **~ed accommodation/flat** *etc* logement *m*/appartement *m etc* en location ◆ **"rent-a-bike"** "location de vélos"

2 (also **rent out**) louer, donner en location

COMP **rent-a-car** N *(= firm)* société *f* de location de voitures

rent-a-crowd* N ⇒ **rent-a-mob**

rent allowance N *(Brit)* indemnité *f or* allocation *f* (de) logement

rent-a-mob* N *(Brit) (gen)* agitateurs *mpl* professionnels ; *(= supporters: at meeting etc)* claque *f*

rent book N *(for accommodation)* carnet *m* de quittances de loyer

rent boy* N jeune prostitué *m*

rent collector N personne *f* chargée d'encaisser les loyers

rent control N encadrement *m* des loyers

rent-controlled ADJ à loyer plafonné

rent-free ADJ exempt de loyer, gratuit ADV sans payer de loyer

rent rebate N réduction *f* de loyer

rent review N *(Brit Admin)* réajustement *m* des loyers

rent strike N grève *f* des loyers ◆ **to go on ~ strike, to stage a ~ strike** faire la grève des loyers

> ⚠ In French, the word **rente** means 'pension', 'allowance' or 'private income'.

rent² /rent/ VB pt, ptp of **rend** N *(= tear) (in cloth)* déchirure *f*, accroc *m* ; *(in rock)* fissure *f* ; *(in clouds)* déchirure *f*, trouée *f* ; *(in party etc)* rupture *f*, scission *f*

rental /'rentl/ N *(esp Brit)* 1 *(= amount paid) [of house, land]* (montant *m* du) loyer *m* ; *(esp for holiday accommodation)* prix *m* de location ; *[of television etc]* (prix *m* de) location *f* ; *[of telephone]* abonnement *m* ; *(= income from rents)* revenu *m* en loyers *or* fermages 2 *(= activity)* location *f* ◆ **car/bike ~** location *f* de voitures/vélos

COMP **rental car** N voiture *f* de location

rental library N *(US)* bibliothèque *f* de prêt *(payante)*

renumber /ˌriː'nʌmbəʳ/ VT numéroter de nouveau, renuméroter

renunciation /rɪˌnʌnsɪ'eɪʃən/ N *(frm) [of violence, religion, citizenship, title, right, claim]* renonciation *f (of sth* à qch) ; *[of wife, husband, friend]* reniement *m (of sb* de qn) ; *[of cause, party]* reniement *m (of sth* de qch), désaveu *m (of sth* de qch) ; *[of treaty]* dénonciation *f (of sth* de qch) ; *[of principles] (also Jur)* répudiation *f (of sth* de qch)

reoccupy /ˌriː'ɒkjʊpaɪ/ VT réoccuper

reopen /ˌriː'əʊpən/ VT *[+ box, door]* rouvrir ; *[+ fight, battle, hostilities]* reprendre ; *[+ debate,* *discussion]* rouvrir ◆ **to ~ a case** *(Jur)* rouvrir une affaire VI *[school]* reprendre ; *[shop, theatre etc]* rouvrir ; *[wound]* se rouvrir

reopening /ˌriːˈəʊpnɪŋ/ N réouverture *f*

reorder /ˌriːˈɔːdəʳ/ VT 1 *[+ goods, supplies]* commander de nouveau 2 *(= reorganize)* reclasser, réorganiser

reorganization /ˈriːˌɔːgənaɪˈzeɪʃən/ N réorganisation *f*

reorganize /ˌriːˈɔːgənaɪz/ VT réorganiser VI se réorganiser

rep¹ * /rep/ N abbrev of **repertory**

rep² /rep/ N *(= fabric)* reps *m*

rep³ * /rep/ N (abbrev of **representative**) 1 *(Comm)* représentant(e) *m(f)* (de commerce) 2 *(Admin, Pol = official)* porte-parole *m inv*

Rep. *(US Pol)* 1 abbrev of **Representative** 2 abbrev of **Republican**

repackage /ˌriːˈpækɪdʒ/ VT *[+ product]* reconditionner ; *[+ parcel]* remballer ; *(fig) [+ proposal, scheme]* reformuler

repaid /rɪˈpeɪd/ VB pt, ptp of **repay**

repaint /ˌriːˈpeɪnt/ VT repeindre

repair¹ /rɪˈpɛəʳ/ VT *[+ tyre, shoes, chair]* réparer ; *[+ clothes]* réparer, raccommoder ; *[+ machine, watch]* réparer, arranger ; *[+ roof, road]* réparer, refaire ; *(Naut) [+ hull]* radouber ; *(fig) [+ error, wrong]* réparer, remédier à N 1 *(gen)* réparation *f* ; *[of clothes]* raccommodage *m* ; *[of shoes]* ressemelage *m* ; *[of roof, road]* réfection *f* ; *(Naut) [of hull]* radoub *m* ◆ **to be under ~** être en réparation ◆ **to be beyond ~** être irréparable ◆ **damaged** *or* **broken beyond ~** irréparable ◆ **closed for ~s** fermé pour cause de travaux 2 *(NonC = condition)* **to be in good/bad ~** être en bon/mauvais état ◆ **to keep sth in (good) ~** entretenir qch

COMP **repair kit** N trousse *f* de réparation
repair man N (pl **repair men**) réparateur *m*
repair outfit N ⇒ **repair kit**
repair shop N atelier *m* de réparations

repair² /rɪˈpɛəʳ/ VI *(liter)* ◆ **to ~ to** *(= go)* aller à, se rendre à ; *(= return)* retourner à

repairable /rɪˈpɛərəbl/ ADJ réparable

repairer /rɪˈpɛərəʳ/ N réparateur *m*, -trice *f* ; → **clock, shoe**

repaper /ˌriːˈpeɪpəʳ/ VT retapisser, refaire les papiers peints de

reparable /ˈrepərəbl/ ADJ réparable

reparation /ˌrepəˈreɪʃən/ N réparation *f* ◆ **to make ~s for sth** *(fig)* réparer qch *(une injure etc)*

repartee /ˌrepɑːˈtiː/ N *(NonC)* repartie *or* répartie *f*

repast /rɪˈpɑːst/ N *(liter)* repas *m*, banquet *m*

repatriate /riːˈpætrɪeɪt/ VT rapatrier N /riːˈpætrɪət/ rapatrié(e) *m(f)*

repatriation /riːˌpætrɪˈeɪʃən/ N rapatriement *m*

repay /riːˈpeɪ/ (pret, ptp **repaid**) VT 1 *(= pay back) [+ money]* rendre, rembourser ; *[+ person]* rembourser ; *[+ debt, obligation]* s'acquitter de ◆ **if you lend me the money, I'll ~ you on Saturday** si tu me prêtes l'argent, je te le rendrai *or* je te rembourserai samedi ◆ **to ~ sb's expenses** rembourser *or* indemniser qn de ses frais ◆ **how can I ever ~ you?** *(fig)* comment pourrais-je jamais vous remercier ? ◆ **and this is how they ~ me!** *(fig)* c'est comme ça qu'ils me remercient !

2 *(= give in return)* récompenser ◆ **to ~ sb's kindness** payer de retour la gentillesse de qn, récompenser qn de sa gentillesse ◆ **he repaid their kindness by stealing their camera** *(iro)* il les a remerciés de leur gentillesse en leur volant leur appareil photo, en guise de remerciement, il leur a volé leur appareil photo ◆ **to be repaid for one's efforts** être récompensé de ses efforts

repayable /riːˈpeɪəbl/ ADJ remboursable ◆ **the loan is ~ at any time** le créancier peut exiger le remboursement de cette dette à tout moment ◆ **~ in ten monthly instalments** remboursable en dix mensualités ◆ **~ over ten years** remboursable sur dix ans

repayment /riːˈpeɪmənt/ N *[of money]* remboursement *m* ; *[of effort]* récompense *f* ◆ **~s can be spread over three years** les remboursements peuvent s'échelonner sur trois ans

COMP **repayment mortgage** N *(Brit)* *emprunt logement sans capital différé*
repayment schedule N *(Fin)* échéancier *m* de remboursement

repeal /rɪˈpiːl/ VT *[+ law]* abroger, annuler ; *[+ sentence]* annuler ; *[+ decree]* révoquer N abrogation *f*, annulation *f*, révocation *f*

repeat /rɪˈpiːt/ LANGUAGE IN USE 27.5

VT *(= say again)* répéter ; *[+ demand, promise]* réitérer ; *(Mus)* reprendre ; *(= recite) [+ poem etc]* réciter (par cœur) ; *(= do again) [+ action, attack]* répéter, renouveler ; *[+ pattern, motif]* répéter, reproduire ; *(Comm) [+ order]* renouveler ◆ **this offer will never be ~ed** *(Comm)* (c'est une) offre unique *or* exceptionnelle ◆ **you must not ~ what I tell you** il ne faut pas répéter ce que je vous dis ◆ **to ~ o.s.** se répéter

VI 1 répéter ◆ **I ~, it is impossible** je le répète, c'est impossible

2 *(Math)* se reproduire périodiquement ◆ **0.054 ~ing** 0,054 périodique

3 **radishes ~ on me** * les radis me donnent des renvois *

N répétition *f* ; *(Mus)* reprise *f* ; *(esp Brit Rad, TV)* reprise *f*, rediffusion *f*

ADJ *[business, customer]* ◆ **to get ~ business** réussir à fidéliser la clientèle ◆ **we give reductions to ~ customers** nous accordons des réductions à nos fidèles clients

COMP **repeat mark(s)** N(PL) *(Mus)* barre *f* de reprise, renvoi *m*
repeat offender N *(Jur)* récidiviste *mf*
repeat order N *(Brit Comm)* commande *f* renouvelée
repeat performance N *(Theat)* deuxième représentation *f* ◆ **he gave a ~ performance** *(fig)* il a fait exactement la même chose ; *(pej)* il a fait la même comédie
repeat prescription N *(Brit Med)* *renouvellement d'une ordonnance*
repeat sign N *(Mus)* ⇒ **repeat mark(s)**

repeated /rɪˈpiːtɪd/ ADJ *[attacks, requests, warnings, criticism, efforts]* répété, renouvelé ◆ **after ~ attempts** après plusieurs tentatives ◆ **his plans have suffered ~ delays** ses projets ont subi une accumulation de retards

repeatedly /rɪˈpiːtɪdlɪ/ ADV à plusieurs reprises, sans cesse ◆ **he had been ~ kicked in the head** il avait reçu plusieurs coups de pied à la tête

repeater /rɪˈpiːtəʳ/ N 1 *(= gun/watch/alarm clock)* fusil *m*/montre *f*/réveil *m* à répétition 2 *(Math)* fraction *f* périodique 3 *(US Scol)* redoublant(e) *m(f)* ; *(US Jur)* récidiviste *mf* COMP **repeater loan** N *(Econ, Fin)* prêt-relais *m*

repeating /rɪˈpiːtɪŋ/ ADJ *[gun]* à répétition

repeg /ˌriːˈpeg/ VT *(Econ, Fin)* ne plus faire flotter, redonner une parité fixe à

repel /rɪˈpel/ VT *[+ enemy, sb's advances, magnetic pole]* repousser ; *(fig = disgust)* dégoûter, inspirer de la répulsion à ◆ **to be ~led by ...** *(fig)* être dégoûté par ..., éprouver de la répulsion pour ... VI *[magnets, magnetic poles]* se repousser

repellant /rɪˈpelənt/ N ⇒ **repellent noun**

repellent /rɪˈpelənt/ ADJ *(frm) [person, animal, character, sight, smell]* repoussant, répugnant ; *[view, opinion]* abject ◆ **to be ~ to sb** *(lit, fig)* dégoûter qn ◆ **I find him ~** je le trouve répugnant, il me dégoûte ; → **water** N → **insect**

repent /rɪˈpent/ VI se repentir *(of* de) VT se repentir de, regretter

repentance /rɪˈpentəns/ N repentir *m*

repentant /rɪˈpentənt/ ADJ *[person, expression]* repentant ◆ **to be ~** *(= repent)* se repentir

repercussion /ˌriːpəˈkʌʃən/ N *[of sounds]* répercussion *f* ; *[of shock]* répercussion *f*, contrecoup *m* ; *(fig)* répercussion *f* ◆ **to have ~s on sth** se répercuter sur qch, avoir des répercussions sur qch ◆ **the ~s of this defeat** le contrecoup *or* les répercussions de cet échec ◆ **there will be no ~s** il n'y aura pas de répercussions ◆ **the ~ on prices of the rise in costs** la répercussion sur les prix de la hausse du coût

repertoire /ˈrepətwɑːʳ/ N *(Theat, fig)* répertoire *m*

repertory /ˈrepətərɪ/ N 1 *(Theat, fig)* ⇒ **repertoire** 2 (also **repertory theatre**) théâtre *m* de répertoire ◆ **to act in ~, to play ~** faire partie d'une troupe de répertoire ◆ **he did three years in ~** il a joué pendant trois ans dans un théâtre de répertoire COMP **repertory company** N compagnie *f or* troupe *f* (de théâtre) de répertoire

repetition /ˌrepɪˈtɪʃən/ N 1 *(= recurrence)* répétition *f* ◆ **I don't want a ~ of this!** que cela ne se reproduise pas ! ◆ **he didn't want a ~ of the scene with his mother** il ne voulait pas que cette scène avec sa mère se reproduise 2 *(NonC = duplication)* répétition *f* ◆ **to learn by ~** apprendre en répétant

repetitious /ˌrepɪˈtɪʃəs/ ADJ *(frm) [text, speech]* plein de répétitions *or* de redites ; *[drumming, job]* répétitif

repetitive /rɪˈpetɪtɪv/ ADJ *[writing]* plein de redites ; *[work, movements, rhythms]* répétitif COMP **repetitive strain injury** N *(Med)* troubles *mpl* musculo-squelettiques *(dus à une activité répétée)*, lésion *f* de surmenage

rephrase /ˌriːˈfreɪz/ VT reformuler ◆ **let me ~ that, I'll ~ that** je vais m'exprimer autrement

repine /rɪˈpaɪn/ VI se plaindre, murmurer

replace /rɪˈpleɪs/ VT 1 *(= put back)* remettre à sa place ◆ **to ~ the receiver** *(Telec)* raccrocher 2 *(= take the place of)* remplacer, tenir la place de 3 *(= provide substitute for)* remplacer *(by, with* par)

replaceable /rɪˈpleɪsəbl/ ADJ remplaçable

replacement /rɪˈpleɪsmənt/ N 1 *(NonC = putting back)* remise *f* en place, replacement *m* 2 *(NonC = substituting)* remplacement *m*, substitution *f* 3 *(= person)* remplaçant(e) *m(f)* ; *(= product)* produit *m* de remplacement

COMP **replacement engine** N moteur *m* de rechange ◆ **to fit a ~ engine** faire l'échange standard du moteur
replacement part N pièce *f* de rechange

replant /ˌriːˈplɑːnt/ VT replanter

replay /ˈriːpleɪ/ *(esp Brit) (Sport)* N ◆ **the ~ is on 15 October** le match sera rejoué le 15 octobre ; → **action, instant** VT /ˌriːˈpleɪ/ *[+ match]* rejouer ; *[+ cassette, video]* repasser

replenish /rɪˈplenɪʃ/ VT remplir de nouveau *(with* de) ◆ **to ~ one's supplies of sth** se réapprovisionner en qch

replenishment /rɪˈplenɪʃmənt/ N remplissage *m* ◆ **~ of supplies** réapprovisionnement *m*

replete /rɪˈpliːt/ ADJ 1 *(= full up) [person]* rassasié, repu 2 *(= fully supplied)* ◆ **~ with sth** rempli de qch, plein de qch

repletion /rɪˈpliːʃən/ N satiété *f*

replica /ˈreplɪkə/ N *(gen)* copie *f* exacte ; *[of painting]* réplique *f* ; *[of document]* fac-similé *m*

replicate /ˈreplɪˌkeɪt/ VT 1 *(= reproduce) (gen)* reproduire ; *(Bio)* se reproduire par mitose ou méiose 2 (= *fold back*) replier ADJ /'replɪkɪt/ [*leaf etc*] replié

replication /ˌreplɪ'keɪʃən/ N (*gen*) reproduction *f* ; (*Bio*) reproduction *f* par mitose

reply /rɪ'plaɪ/ LANGUAGE IN USE 20.2, 21.1, 27 N réponse *f* ; (*quick*) réplique *f* ; (*Jur*) réplique *f* ◆ **in ~ (to)** en réponse (à) ◆ **he made no ~** (*liter*) il n'a pas répondu VTI répondre ; (*quickly*) répliquer

COMP **reply coupon** N (*Post*) coupon-réponse *m*
reply-paid ADJ préaffranchi

repoint /ˌriː'pɔɪnt/ VT [+ *building etc*] rejointoyer

repointing /ˌriː'pɔɪntɪŋ/ N rejointoiement *m*

repo man * /'riːpəʊˌmæn/ (pl **repo men**) N (*US*) ⇒ **repossession man** ; → **repossession**

repopulate /ˌriː'pɒpjuleɪt/ VT repeupler

report /rɪ'pɔːt/ LANGUAGE IN USE 26.3

N 1 (= *account, statement*) rapport *m* ; [*of speech*] compte rendu *m* ; [*of debate, meeting*] compte rendu *m*, procès-verbal *m* ; (*Press, Rad, TV*) reportage *m* (*on* sur) ; (*official*) rapport *m* (d'enquête) ; (*at regular intervals: on weather, sales, etc*) bulletin *m* ◆ **monthly ~** bulletin *m* mensuel ◆ **school ~** (*Brit*) bulletin *m* scolaire ◆ **to make a ~ on ...** faire un rapport sur ... ; (*Press, Rad, TV*) faire un reportage sur ... ◆ **annual ~** (*Comm*) rapport *m* annuel (de gestion) ◆ **chairman's ~** rapport *m* présidentiel ◆ **law ~s** (*Jur*) recueil *m* de jurisprudence *or* de droit ◆ **to make a ~ against ...** (*Jur*) dresser un procès-verbal à ... ; → **progress, weather**

2 (= *rumour*) rumeur *f* ◆ **there is a ~ that ...** le bruit court que ..., on dit que ... ◆ **as ~ has it** selon les bruits qui courent, selon la rumeur publique ◆ **there are ~s of rioting** il y aurait (*or* il y aurait eu) des émeutes ◆ **the ~s of rioting have been proved** les rumeurs selon lesquelles il y aurait eu des émeutes se sont révélées fondées ◆ **I have heard a ~ that ...** j'ai entendu dire que ...

3 († = *repute*) [*of person*] réputation *f* ; [*of product*] renom *m*, renommée *f* ◆ **of good ~** de bonne réputation, dont on dit du bien ◆ **to know sth only by ~** ne savoir qch que par ouï-dire

4 (= *explosion*) détonation *f*, explosion *f* ◆ **with a loud ~** avec une forte détonation

VT 1 (= *give account of*) rapporter, rendre compte de ; (= *bring to notice esp of authorities*) signaler ; (*Press, Rad, TV*) rapporter ◆ **to ~ a speech** faire le compte rendu d'un discours ◆ **to ~ one's findings** [*scientist etc*] rendre compte de l'état de ses recherches ; [*commission*] présenter ses conclusions ◆ **to ~ progress** rendre compte (des progrès) ◆ **only one paper ~ed his death** un seul journal a signalé *or* mentionné sa mort ◆ **the papers ~ed the crime as solved** les journaux ont présenté le crime comme résolu ◆ **our correspondent ~s from Rome that ...** notre correspondant à Rome nous apprend que ... ◆ **he is ~ed as having said ...** il aurait dit ... ◆ **it is ~ed that a prisoner has escaped, a prisoner is ~ed to have escaped** un détenu se serait évadé ◆ **to ~ a bill** (*Parl*) présenter un projet de loi ◆ **to move to ~ progress** (*Parl*) demander la clôture des débats

2 (= *announce*) déclarer, annoncer ◆ **it is ~ed from the White House that ...** on annonce à la Maison-Blanche que ...

3 (= *notify authorities of*) [+ *accident, crime, suspect*] signaler ; [+ *criminal, culprit*] dénoncer (*often pej*) ◆ **all accidents must be ~ed to the police** tous les accidents doivent être signalés à la police ◆ **to ~ a theft to the police** signaler un vol à la police ◆ **to ~ sb for bad behaviour** signaler qn pour mauvaise conduite ◆ **to ~ sb's bad behaviour** signaler la mauvaise conduite de qn ◆ **her colleague ~ed her to the boss out of jealousy** sa collègue l'a dénoncée au patron par jalousie

4 (*Mil, Naut*) signaler ◆ **to ~ sb sick** signaler que qn est malade ◆ **~ed missing** porté manquant *or* disparu ◆ **nothing to ~** rien à signaler ◆ **to ~ one's position** signaler *or* donner sa position

VI 1 (= *announce o.s. ready*) se présenter ◆ **~ to the director on Monday** présentez-vous chez le directeur lundi ◆ **to ~ for duty** se présenter au travail, prendre son service

2 (*Mil*) **to ~ to one's unit** rallier son unité ◆ **to ~ sick** se faire porter malade

3 (= *give a report*) rendre compte (*on* de), faire un rapport (*on* sur) ; (*Press, Rad, TV*) faire un reportage (*on* sur) ◆ **the committee is ready to ~** le comité est prêt à faire son rapport ◆ **Michael Brown ~ing from Rome** (*Rad, TV*) de Rome, (le reportage de) Michael Brown

4 (*Admin: in hierarchy*) **to ~ to** travailler sous l'autorité de ◆ **he ~s to the sales manager** il est sous les ordres (directs) du directeur des ventes ◆ **who do you ~ to?** qui est votre supérieur hiérarchique ?

COMP **report card** N (*Scol*) bulletin *m* scolaire
reported speech N (*Gram*) style *m* *or* discours *m* indirect
report stage N (*Brit Parl*) *examen d'un projet de loi avant la troisième lecture* ◆ **the bill has reached the ~ stage** le projet de loi vient de passer en commission

► **report back** VI 1 (= *return*) (*Mil etc*) rentrer au quartier ◆ **you must ~ back at 6 o'clock** (*gen*) il faut que vous soyez de retour à 6 heures

2 (= *give report*) donner *or* présenter son rapport (*to* à) ◆ **the committee was asked to investigate the complaint and ~ back to the assembly** le comité a été chargé d'examiner la plainte et de faire un rapport à l'assemblée

> ⚠ The noun **report** is not translated by the French word **report**, one of whose meanings is 'postponement'.

reportage /ˌrepɔː'tɑːʒ/ N reportage *m*

reportedly /rɪ'pɔːtɪdlɪ/ ADV ◆ **he had ~ seen her** il l'aurait vue ◆ **~, several prisoners had escaped** plusieurs prisonniers se seraient échappés ◆ **he was shot dead, ~ by one of his own men** il a été abattu, et le meurtrier serait l'un de ses propres hommes

reporter /rɪ'pɔːtəʳ/ N 1 (*Press*) journaliste *mf* ; (*on the spot*) reporter *m* ; (*Rad, TV*) reporter *m* ◆ **special ~** envoyé(e) *m(f)* spécial(e) 2 (*Parl*) (= *stenographer*) sténographe *mf* ; (*Jur*) greffier *m* COMP **reporters' gallery** N (*Jur, Parl*) tribune *f* de la presse

reporting /rɪ'pɔːtɪŋ/ N (*NonC: Press, Rad, TV*) reportages *mpl* COMP **reporting restrictions** NPL (*Jur*) restrictions *fpl* imposées aux médias (*lors de la couverture d'un procès*)

repose /rɪ'pəʊz/ N (= *rest*) repos *m* ; (= *sleep*) sommeil *m* ; (= *peace*) repos *m*, tranquillité *f* ◆ **in ~** au repos VT (*frm*) [+ *confidence, trust*] mettre, placer (*in* en) ◆ **to ~ o.s.** (= *rest*) se reposer VI 1 (= *rest*) se reposer ; [*the dead*] reposer 2 (= *be based*) reposer, être fondé (*on* sur)

reposition /ˌriːpə'zɪʃən/ VT repositionner

repository /rɪ'pɒzɪtərɪ/ N (*gen, also Comm*) (= *warehouse*) dépôt *m*, entrepôt *m* ; (*fig*) [*of knowledge, experience, facts etc*] mine *f* ; (= *person*) dépositaire *mf* (*d'un secret etc*)

repossess /ˌriːpə'zes/ VT reprendre possession de, rentrer en possession de

repossession /ˌriːpə'zeʃən/ N reprise *f* de possession

COMP **repossession man** * N (*US*) récupérateur * *m* (*huissier chargé de saisir un bien non payé*)
repossession order N (avis *m* de) saisie *f*

repot /ˌriː'pɒt/ VT rempoter

repp /rep/ N ⇒ **rep²**

reprehend /ˌreprɪ'hend/ VT [+ *person*] réprimander ; [+ *action, behaviour*] blâmer, condamner

reprehensible /ˌreprɪ'hensɪbl/ ADJ répréhensible

reprehensibly /ˌreprɪ'hensɪblɪ/ ADV de manière répréhensible

represent /ˌreprɪ'zent/ VT 1 (= *stand for, symbolize*) représenter ◆ **a drawing ~ing prehistoric man** un dessin qui représente l'homme préhistorique ◆ **phonetic symbols ~ sounds** les symboles phonétiques représentent des sons ◆ **he ~s all that is best in his country's culture** il représente *or* personnifie le meilleur de la culture de son pays ◆ **£200 doesn't ~ a good salary these days** 200 livres ne représentent *or* ne constituent plus un bon salaire de nos jours

2 (= *declare to be*) [+ *person, event*] représenter ; [+ *grievance, risk etc*] présenter (*as* comme étant) ◆ **he ~ed me to be a fool** *or* **as a fool** il m'a représenté *or* dépeint comme un imbécile ◆ **I am not what you ~ me to be** je ne suis pas tel que vous me décrivez *or* dépeignez ◆ **he ~s himself as a doctor** il se fait passer pour un médecin ◆ **it is exactly as ~ed in the advertisement** cela est exactement conforme à la description de l'annonce (publicitaire)

3 (= *explain*) exposer, représenter (*liter*) ; (= *point out*) faire remarquer, signaler ◆ **can you ~ to him how much we need his help?** pouvez-vous lui faire comprendre à quel point nous avons besoin de son aide ?

4 (= *act or speak for*) représenter (*also Parl*) ; (*Jur*) représenter (en justice), postuler pour ◆ **he ~s Warrington in Parliament** il représente Warrington au Parlement, c'est le député de Warrington ◆ **the delegation ~ed the mining industry** la délégation représentait l'industrie minière ◆ **he ~s their firm in London** il représente leur maison à Londres ◆ **to ~ one's country** (*esp Sport*) représenter son pays ◆ **many countries were ~ed at the ceremony** de nombreux pays étaient représentés à la cérémonie ◆ **women artists were well/strongly ~ed at the exhibition** les femmes artistes étaient bien/fortement représentées à l'exposition ◆ **I ~ Mr Thomas** je représente M. Thomas

5 (*Theat*) [+ *character*] jouer (le rôle de) ; [+ *part*] jouer, interpréter

6 (*Jur: in contracts etc*) déclarer

re-present /ˌriːprɪ'zent/ VT présenter de nouveau

representation /ˌreprɪzen'teɪʃən/ N 1 (*Theat, gen*) représentation *f* ; [*of role*] interprétation *f* ◆ **proportional ~** (*Parl*) représentation *f* proportionnelle 2 (= *protest*) **~s** protestation *f* officielle ◆ **the ambassador made ~s to the government** l'ambassadeur a adressé une protestation officielle au gouvernement

representational /ˌreprɪzen'teɪʃənl/ ADJ (*frm: Art*) figuratif ; [*model, system*] représentatif

representative /ˌreprɪ'zentətɪv/ ADJ (*also Govt*) représentatif (*of sth* de qch) N représentant(e) *m(f)* ; (*esp Brit Comm*) représentant *m* (de commerce) ; (*US Pol*) député *m* ; (= *spokesperson*) porte-parole *m inv* ; → **house**

repress /rɪ'pres/ VT [+ *revolt, sneeze, feelings, smile*] réprimer ; (*Psych*) refouler

repressed /rɪ'prest/ ADJ [*person, impulse*] refoulé ; [*feeling*] refoulé, réprimé

repression /rɪ'preʃən/ N 1 (*political, social*) répression *f* 2 (*Psych*) (*voluntary*) répression *f* ; (*involuntary*) refoulement *m*

repressive /rɪ'presɪv/ ADJ [*regime, law, policy, measures, action*] répressif ; [*forces*] de répression

reprieve /rɪ'priːv/ N 1 (*Jur*) (lettres *fpl* de) grâce *f*, commutation *f* de la peine capitale ;

(= delay) sursis m 2 (fig = respite) répit m, sursis m ◆ **they won a ~ for the house** ils ont obtenu un sursis pour la maison VT (Jur) accorder une commutation de la peine capitale a ; (= delay) surseoir à l'exécution de ; (fig) accorder un répit à ◆ **the building has been ~d for a while** le bâtiment bénéficie d'un sursis

reprimand /ˈreprɪmɑːnd/ N (from parents, teachers) réprimande f ; (from employer) blâme m VT réprimander, blâmer

reprint /ˌriːˈprɪnt/ VT [+ book] réimprimer ; [+ article] reproduire ◆ **this book is being ~ed** ce livre est en réimpression ◆ **newspapers worldwide had ~ed the story** les journaux du monde entier ont repris la nouvelle VI [book] être en réimpression N /ˈriːprɪnt/ [of book] réimpression f ◆ **cheap ~** réimpression f bon marché

reprisal /rɪˈpraɪzəl/ N ◆ **~s** représailles fpl ◆ **to take ~s** user de représailles ◆ **as a** or **in ~ for ...** en représailles à ... ◆ **by way of ~** par représailles

reprise /rɪˈpriːz/ N (Mus) reprise f

repro* /ˈriːprəʊ/ N abbrev of **reprographics, reprography** COMP (abbrev of **reproduction**) ◆ **~ furniture** copie(s) f(pl) de meuble(s) ancien(s)

reproach /rɪˈprəʊtʃ/ N 1 (= rebuke) reproche m ◆ **to heap ~es on sb** accabler qn de reproches ◆ **term of ~** parole f de reproche 2 (NonC = discredit) honte f, opprobre m ◆ **to be a ~ to ...** (fig) être la honte de ... ◆ **to bring ~ on ...** jeter le discrédit sur ..., discréditer ... ◆ **above** or **beyond ~** sans reproche(s), irréprochable VT faire des reproches à ◆ **to ~ sb for sth** reprocher qch à qn ◆ **to ~ sb for having done sth** reprocher à qn d'avoir fait qch ◆ **he has nothing to ~ himself with** il n'a rien à se reprocher

reproachful /rɪˈprəʊtʃfʊl/ ADJ [look, tone] réprobateur (-trice f) ; [remark] lourd de reproches ; [eyes] chargé de réprobation ◆ **he was ~** il avait une attitude pleine de reproches

reproachfully /rɪˈprəʊtʃfəlɪ/ ADV [say] sur un ton réprobateur or de reproche ; [look at, shake one's head] d'un air réprobateur

reprobate /ˈreprəʊbeɪt/ ADJ, N (frm or hum) dépravé(e) m(f) VT réprouver

reprobation /ˌreprəʊˈbeɪʃən/ N réprobation f

reprocess /ˌriːˈprəʊses/ VT retraiter

reprocessing /ˌriːˈprəʊsesɪŋ/ N retraitement m ; → **nuclear**

reproduce /ˌriːprəˈdjuːs/ VT reproduire VI se reproduire

reproducible /ˌriːprəˈdjuːsɪbl/ ADJ reproductible

reproduction /ˌriːprəˈdʌkʃən/ N (gen, Art, Bio) reproduction f ◆ **sound ~** reproduction f sonore ◆ **this picture is a ~** ce tableau est une reproduction COMP **reproduction furniture** N (NonC) copie(s) f(pl) de meuble(s) ancien(s)

reproductive /ˌriːprəˈdʌktɪv/ ADJ reproducteur (-trice f)

reprographic /ˌriːprəˈgræfɪk/ ADJ de reprographie

reprographics /ˌriːprəˈgræfɪks/, **reprography** /rɪˈprɒgrəfɪ/ N reprographie f

reproof /rɪˈpruːf/ N reproche m, réprimande f ◆ **a tone of ~** un ton de reproche ◆ **in ~** en signe de désapprobation

re-proof /ˌriːˈpruːf/ VT [+ garment] réimperméabiliser

reproval /rɪˈpruːvəl/ N reproche m, blâme m

reprove /rɪˈpruːv/ VT [+ person] blâmer (for de), réprimander (for sur) ; [+ action] réprouver, condamner

reproving /rɪˈpruːvɪŋ/ ADJ [look, shake of one's head, tone] réprobateur (-trice f) ; [letter] de reproche(s)

reprovingly /rɪˈpruːvɪŋlɪ/ ADV d'un air or ton de reproche

reptile /ˈreptaɪl/ N (lit, fig) reptile m COMP **reptile house** N vivarium m

reptilian /repˈtɪlɪən/ ADJ (lit, fig) reptilien N reptile m (also fig)

republic /rɪˈpʌblɪk/ N république f ◆ **the Republic** (US) les États-Unis d'Amérique

republican /rɪˈpʌblɪkən/ ADJ, N républicain(e) m(f) COMP **Republican party** N (Pol) parti m républicain

republicanism /rɪˈpʌblɪkənɪzəm/ N (gen) républicanisme m ; (US) ◆ **Republicanism** politique f du parti républicain

republication /ˌriːpʌblɪˈkeɪʃən/ N [of book] réédition f, republication f ; [of law, banns] nouvelle publication f

republish /ˌriːˈpʌblɪʃ/ VT [+ book] rééditer ; [+ banns] publier de nouveau

repudiate /rɪˈpjuːdɪeɪt/ VT [+ friend, ally] renier, désavouer ; [+ accusation] récuser, repousser ; [government etc] [+ debt, treaty, obligation] refuser de respecter ; [+ remarks] désavouer ; [+ agreement] renier ◆ **to ~ one's wife** répudier sa femme ◆ **the group's refusal to ~ violence** le refus du groupe de renoncer à la violence ◆ **he called on the American government to ~ the vote** il a demandé au gouvernement américain de ne pas reconnaître les résultats du vote

repudiation /rɪˌpjuːdɪˈeɪʃən/ N [of violence, doctrine, remarks] condamnation f ; [of charge, evidence] rejet m ◆ **~ of a treaty/a debt** refus m de respecter un traité/d'honorer une dette

repugnance /rɪˈpʌgnəns/ N répugnance f, aversion f (to pour) ◆ **he shows ~ to accepting charity** il répugne à accepter la charité

repugnant /rɪˈpʌgnənt/ ADJ répugnant ◆ **to be ~ to sb** répugner à qn

repulse /rɪˈpʌls/ VT (Mil) repousser, refouler ; (fig) [+ help, offer] repousser, rejeter N (Mil) échec m ; (fig) refus m, rebuffade f ◆ **to meet with** or **suffer a ~** essuyer un refus or une rebuffade

repulsion /rɪˈpʌlʃən/ N (also Phys) répulsion f

repulsive /rɪˈpʌlsɪv/ ADJ [person, behaviour, sight, idea] repoussant ; (Phys) [force] répulsif ◆ **I found it ~ to think that ...** il me répugnait de penser que ...

repulsively /rɪˈpʌlsɪvlɪ/ ADV ◆ **~ ugly/large** etc d'une laideur/grosseur etc repoussante

repulsiveness /rɪˈpʌlsɪvnɪs/ N aspect m or caractère m repoussant

repurchase /ˌriːˈpɜːtʃɪs/ N rachat m VT racheter

reputable /ˈrepjʊtəbl/ ADJ [person, company] de bonne réputation ; [brand, product] réputé

reputably /ˈrepjʊtəblɪ/ ADV ◆ **to be ~ employed (as)** gagner honorablement sa vie (comme) ◆ **~ established in the business world** honorablement établi dans le monde des affaires

reputation /ˌrepjʊˈteɪʃən/ N réputation f ◆ **to have a good/bad ~** avoir (une) bonne/(une) mauvaise réputation ◆ **a good ~ as a singer** une bonne réputation de chanteur ◆ **to have a ~ for honesty** avoir la réputation d'être honnête, être réputé pour son honnêteté ◆ **to live up to one's ~** soutenir sa réputation ◆ **she was by ~ a good organizer** elle avait la réputation d'être une bonne organisatrice ◆ **to know sb by ~** connaître qn de réputation ◆ **your ~ has gone before you** votre réputation vous a précédé

repute /rɪˈpjuːt/ N réputation f, renom m ◆ **to know sb by ~** connaître qn de réputation ◆ **to be of good ~** avoir (une) bonne réputation ◆ **a restaurant of ~** un restaurant réputé or en renom ◆ **place of ill ~** endroit m mal famé ◆ **a house of ill ~** (euph = brothel) une maison close ◆ **to hold sb in high ~** avoir une très haute opinion de qn

reputed /rɪˈpjuːtɪd/ ADJ 1 (= supposed) [love affair, author] soi-disant ◆ **he bought the painting for a ~ $2,000,000** on dit qu'il a acheté le tableau 2 millions de dollars ◆ **the buildings were ~ to be haunted** ces bâtiments étaient réputés hantés ◆ **the story's ~ to be true** l'histoire est réputée authentique ◆ **he is ~ to have worked miracles** à ce qu'on dit, il aurait fait des miracles 2 (= esteemed) [person, organization] réputé 3 (Jur) ◆ **~ father** père m putatif

reputedly /rɪˈpjuːtɪdlɪ/ ADV à ce que l'on dit + cond ◆ **events that ~ took place thousands of years ago** des événements qui, d'après ce qu'on dit, auraient eu lieu il y a des milliers d'années

request /rɪˈkwest/ LANGUAGE IN USE 4, 10.1, 20.2, 25.1

N 1 demande f ; (official) requête f ◆ **at sb's ~** sur or à la demande de qn ; (official) sur la requête de qn ◆ **by general** or **popular ~** à la demande générale ◆ **on** or **by ~** sur demande ◆ **to make a ~ for sth** faire une demande de qch ◆ **to make a ~ to sb for sth** demander qch à qn ◆ **to grant a ~** accéder à une demande or à une requête

2 (Rad) disque m des auditeurs or demandé par un auditeur ◆ **to play a ~ for sb** passer un disque à l'intention de qn

VT demander ◆ **to ~ sth from sb** demander qch à qn ◆ **to ~ sb to do sth** demander à qn de faire qch, prier qn de faire qch ◆ **"you are requested not to smoke"** "prière de ne pas fumer" ◆ **as ~ed in your letter of ...** comme vous (nous) l'avez demandé dans votre lettre du ... ◆ **herewith, as ~ed, my cheque for £50** ci-joint, comme vous l'avez demandé, un chèque de 50 livres ◆ **it's all I ~ of you** c'est tout ce que je vous demande

COMP **request programme** N (Rad) programme m composé par les auditeurs
request stop N (Brit) [of bus] arrêt m facultatif

requiem /ˈrekwɪem/ N requiem m COMP **requiem mass** N messe f de requiem

require /rɪˈkwaɪəʳ/ LANGUAGE IN USE 10.1, 20.2 VT 1 (= need) [person] avoir besoin de ; [thing, action] demander, requérir ◆ **I have all I ~** j'ai tout ce qu'il me faut or tout ce dont j'ai besoin ◆ **the journey will ~ three hours** le voyage prendra or demandera trois heures ◆ **it ~s great care** cela demande or requiert beaucoup de soin ◆ **this plant ~s frequent watering** cette plante doit être arrosée souvent ◆ **if ~d** au besoin, si besoin est ◆ **when (it is) ~d** quand il le faut ◆ **what qualifications are ~d?** quels sont les diplômes nécessaires or exigés ?

2 (= demand) exiger ; (= order) exiger, réclamer ◆ **to ~ sb to do sth** exiger de qn qu'il fasse qch ◆ **you are ~d to present yourself here tomorrow** vous êtes prié de vous présenter ici demain ◆ **to ~ sth of sb** exiger qch de qn ◆ **as ~d by law** comme la loi l'exige ◆ **we ~ two references** nous exigeons deux références

required /rɪˈkwaɪəd/ ADJ [conditions, amount] requis ◆ **by the ~ date** en temps voulu ◆ **to meet the ~ standards** [machine] être conforme aux normes ; [student] avoir le niveau requis ◆ **in the ~ time** dans les délais prescrits

COMP **required course** N (US Scol) matière f obligatoire
required reading N (Scol, Univ) ouvrage(s) m(pl) au programme ◆ **his latest article is ~ reading for all those interested in the subject** (fig) tous ceux qui sont intéressés par ce sujet doivent absolument lire son dernier article

requirement /rɪˈkwaɪəmənt/ N 1 *(= need)* exigence *f*, besoin *m* ◆ **to meet sb's ~s** satisfaire aux exigences *or* aux besoins de qn ◆ **there isn't enough to meet the ~** il n'y en a pas assez pour satisfaire la demande 2 *(= condition)* condition *f* requise ◆ **to fit the ~s** remplir les conditions 3 *(US Univ)* cursus *m* obligatoire

requisite /ˈrekwɪzɪt/ *(frm)* N 1 *(= thing required)* chose *f* nécessaire *or* requise *(for* pour*)* ◆ **all the ~s** tout ce qui est nécessaire 2 **travel/toilet ~s** accessoires *mpl* de voyage/toilette ADJ requis

requisition /ˌrekwɪˈzɪʃən/ N demande *f* ; *(gen Mil)* réquisition *f* ◆ **to put in a ~ for ...** faire une demande de ... ◆ **to obtain sth by ~** *(Mil)* réquisitionner qch VT *(gen)* faire une demande de ; *(Mil)* réquisitionner

requital /rɪˈkwaɪtl/ N *(= repayment)* récompense *f* ; *(= revenge)* revanche *f*

requite /rɪˈkwaɪt/ VT 1 **~d love** amour *m* partagé 2 *(frm = repay) [+ person, action]* récompenser, payer *(for* de*)* 3 *(frm = avenge) [+ action]* venger ; *[+ person]* se venger de

reran /ˌriːˈræn/ VB pt of **rerun**

reread /ˌriːˈriːd/ (pret, ptp **reread** /ˌriːˈred/) VT relire

reredos /ˈrɪədɒs/ N retable *m*

reroof /ˌriːˈruːf/ VT refaire la toiture de

reroute /ˌriːˈruːt/ VT *[+ train, coach]* changer l'itinéraire de, dérouter ◆ **our train was ~d through Leeds** on a fait faire à notre train un détour par Leeds, notre train a été dérouté sur Leeds

rerun /ˈriːrʌn/ (vb : pret **reran**, ptp **rerun**) N *[of film, tape]* reprise *f* ; *[of TV programme, series]* rediffusion *f* ◆ **the opposition has demanded a ~ of the elections** l'opposition a demandé que l'on organise de nouvelles élections ◆ **a ~ of the contest is almost certain** on va très certainement devoir recommencer l'épreuve ◆ **the result could have been a ~ of 1931** le résultat aurait pu être la répétition de ce qui s'est passé en 1931 VT /ˌriːˈrʌn/ *[+ film, tape]* passer de nouveau ; *[+ race]* courir de nouveau ◆ **to ~ an election** organiser de nouvelles élections ◆ **to ~ a program** *(Comput)* réexécuter un programme

resale /ˌriːˈseɪl/ N *(gen)* revente *f* ◆ **"not for resale"** *(on package etc)* "échantillon gratuit"
COMP **resale price** N prix *m* à la revente
resale price maintenance N prix *m* de vente imposé
resale value N *[of car]* cote *f or* prix *m* à l'Argus ◆ **what's the ~ value?** *(gen)* ça se revend combien ? ; *(car)* elle est cotée combien à l'Argus ?

resat /ˌriːˈsæt/ VB pt, ptp of **resit**

reschedule /ˌriːˈʃedjuːl, (US) riːˈskedjuːl/ VT *[+ meeting, visit]* changer l'heure (or la date) de ; *[+ train service etc]* changer l'horaire de ; *[+ repayments, debt]* rééchelonner ; *[+ plans, course]* changer le programme de ; *[+ TV programme]* reprogrammer

rescind /rɪˈsɪnd/ VT *[+ judgement]* rescinder, casser ; *[+ law]* abroger ; *[+ act]* révoquer ; *[+ contract]* résilier, dissoudre ; *[+ decision, agreement]* annuler

rescission /rɪˈsɪʒən/ N *[of law]* abrogation *f* ; *[of agreement]* annulation *f* ; *[of contract]* résiliation *f*

rescript /ˈriːskrɪpt/ N *(Hist, Rel)* rescrit *m*

rescriptions /rɪˈskrɪpʃənz/ NPL *(Stock Exchange)* bons *mpl* du Trésor, emprunts *mpl* des collectivités publiques

rescue /ˈreskjuː/ N *(= help)* secours *mpl* ; *(= saving)* sauvetage *m* ; *(= freeing)* délivrance *f* ◆ **~ was difficult** le sauvetage a été difficile ◆ **~ came too late** les secours sont arrivés trop tard ◆ **to go to sb's ~** aller au secours *or* à la rescousse de qn ◆ **to come to sb's ~** venir en aide à qn *or* à la rescousse de qn ◆ **to the ~** à la rescousse ; → **air**
VT *(= save)* sauver, secourir ; *(= free)* délivrer *(from* de*)* ◆ **you ~d me from a difficult situation** vous m'avez tiré d'une situation difficile ◆ **the ~d were taken to hospital** les rescapés ont été emmenés à l'hôpital
COMP **rescue attempt** N tentative *f or* opération *f* de sauvetage
rescue operations NPL opérations *fpl* de sauvetage
rescue party N *(gen)* équipe *f* de secours ; *(Ski, Climbing)* colonne *f* de secours
rescue services NPL services *mpl* de secours
rescue worker N sauveteur *m*, secouriste *mf*

rescuer /ˈreskjʊəʳ/ N sauveteur *m*

resealable /ˌriːˈsiːləbl/ ADJ *[container]* refermable

research /rɪˈsɜːtʃ/ N recherche(s) *f(pl)* ◆ **a piece of ~** un travail de recherche ◆ **to do ~** faire des recherches *or* de la recherche ◆ **to carry out ~ into the effects of ...** faire des recherches sur les effets de ...
VI faire des recherches *(into, on* sur*)*
VT *[+ article, book etc]* faire des recherches pour *or* en vue de, se documenter sur ◆ **well-~ed** bien documenté
COMP **research and development** N *(Ind etc)* recherche *f* et développement *m*, recherche-développement *f*
research assistant, research associate N *(Univ)* ≈ étudiant(e) *m(f)* en maîtrise *(ayant le statut de chercheur)*
research establishment N centre *m* de recherches
research fellow N *(Univ)* ≈ chercheur *m*, -euse *f* attaché(e) à l'université ; see also **researcher**
research fellowship N *(Univ)* poste *m* de chercheur (-euse *f*) attaché(e) à l'université
research laboratory N laboratoire *m* de recherches
research scientist N chercheur *m*, -euse *f* ; see also **researcher**
research student N *(Univ)* étudiant(e) *m(f)* qui fait de la recherche, étudiant(e) *m(f)* de doctorat *(ayant statut de chercheur)*
research work N travail *m* de recherche, recherches *fpl*
research worker N chercheur *m*, -euse *f* ; see also **researcher**

researcher /rɪˈsɜːtʃəʳ/ N chercheur *m*

reseat /ˌriːˈsiːt/ VT 1 *[+ person]* faire changer de place à ◆ **to ~ o.s.** se rasseoir 2 *[+ chair]* rempailler, refaire le siège de ; *[+ trousers]* mettre un fond à

resection /riːˈsekʃən/ N résection *f*

reselect /ˌriːsɪˈlekt/ VT *(Pol) [party]* accorder de nouveau son investiture à ◆ **to be ~ed** *[candidate]* recevoir de nouveau l'investiture de son parti

reselection /ˌriːsɪˈlekʃən/ N *(Pol)* investiture *f* renouvelée ◆ **to stand for ~** se porter candidat à l'investiture

resell /ˌriːˈsel/ (pret, ptp **resold**) VT revendre

resemblance /rɪˈzembləns/ N ressemblance *f* ◆ **to bear a strong/faint ~ (to)** avoir une grande/vague ressemblance (avec) ◆ **this bears no ~ to the facts** ceci n'a aucune ressemblance avec les faits ◆ **there's not the slightest ~ between them** il n'y a pas la moindre ressemblance entre eux, ils ne se ressemblent pas du tout

resemble /rɪˈzembl/ LANGUAGE IN USE 5.1 VT *[person]* ressembler à ; *[thing]* ressembler à, être semblable à ◆ **they ~ each other** ils se ressemblent

resent /rɪˈzent/ VT *[+ sb's reply, look, attitude]* être contrarié par ; *(stronger)* être indigné de ◆ **I ~ that!** je proteste ! ◆ **I ~ your tone** votre ton me déplaît fortement ◆ **he ~ed my promotion** il n'a jamais pu accepter *or* admettre ma promotion ◆ **he ~ed having lost his job/the fact that I married her** il n'acceptait pas la perte de son emploi/mon mariage avec elle, la perte de son emploi/mon mariage avec elle lui restait en travers de la gorge* ◆ **he really ~ed this** ça lui est resté en travers de la gorge* ◆ **he may ~ my being here** il n'appréciera peut-être pas ma présence

resentful /rɪˈzentfʊl/ ADJ *[person, reply, look]* plein de ressentiment ◆ **to be** *or* **feel ~ of** *or* **towards sb (for doing sth)** en vouloir à qn (d'avoir fait qch) ◆ **to be ~ of sb's success** mal accepter le succès de qn

resentfully /rɪˈzentfəlɪ/ ADV avec ressentiment

resentment /rɪˈzentmənt/ N ressentiment *m*

reservation /ˌrezəˈveɪʃən/ LANGUAGE IN USE 26.3
N 1 *(= restriction)* réserve *f* ; *(Jur)* réservation *f* ◆ **mental ~** restriction *f* mentale ◆ **without ~** sans réserve, sans arrière-pensée ◆ **with ~s** avec certaines réserves, sous réserve ◆ **to have ~s about ...** faire *or* émettre des réserves sur ... 2 *(= booking)* réservation *f* ◆ **to make a ~ at the hotel/on the boat** réserver *or* retenir une chambre à l'hôtel/une place sur le bateau ◆ **to have a ~** avoir une réservation 3 *(= area of land)* réserve *f* ; *(US)* réserve *f* (indienne) 4 *(Brit)* **(central) ~** *(on roadway)* bande *f* médiane 5 *(Rel)* **Reservation (of the Sacrament)** les Saintes Réserves *fpl* COMP **reservation desk** N *(in airport, hotels etc)* comptoir *m* des réservations

reserve /rɪˈzɜːv/ VT 1 *(= keep)* réserver, garder ◆ **to ~ one's strength** ménager *or* garder ses forces ; *(Sport)* se réserver ◆ **to ~ o.s. for ...** se réserver pour ... ◆ **to ~ the best wine for one's friends** réserver *or* garder le meilleur vin pour ses amis ◆ **to ~ judgement** réserver son jugement ◆ **to ~ the right to do sth** se réserver le droit de faire qch ◆ **to ~ a warm welcome for sb** ménager *or* réserver un accueil chaleureux à qn
2 *(= book in advance) [+ room, seat]* réserver, retenir
N 1 *(= sth stored)* réserve *f*, stock *m* ◆ **to have great ~s of energy** avoir une grande réserve d'énergie ◆ **cash ~** réserve *f* en devises ◆ **gold ~s** réserves *fpl* d'or *or* en or ◆ **world ~s of pyrites** réserves *fpl* mondiales de pyrite ◆ **to keep** *or* **hold in ~** tenir en réserve
2 *(= restriction)* réserve *f*, restriction *f* ◆ **without ~** sans réserve, sans restriction ◆ **with all ~** *or* **all proper ~s** sous toutes réserves
3 *(Brit:* also **reserve price***)* prix *m* minimum
4 *(= piece of land)* réserve *f* ; → **game¹, nature**
5 *(NonC = attitude)* réserve *f*, retenue *f* ◆ **he treated me with some ~** il s'est tenu sur la réserve avec moi ◆ **to break through sb's ~** amener qn à se départir de sa réserve *or* retenue
6 *(Mil)* **the Reserve** la réserve ◆ **the ~s** la réserve, les réservistes *mpl*
7 *(Sport)* ◆ **the ~s** l'équipe *f* B
COMP *[currency, fund]* de réserve
reserve bank N *(US)* banque *f* de réserve
reserve list N *(Mil)* cadre *m* de réserve
reserve player N *(esp Brit Sport)* remplaçant(e) *m(f)*
reserve price N *(Brit)* prix *m* minimum
reserve tank N (also **reserve petrol tank**) réservoir *m* (d'essence) de secours, nourrice *f*
reserve team N *(Brit)* équipe *f* B

reserved /rɪˈzɜːvd/ ADJ *[person, behaviour, room, table, seat]* réservé ◆ **to be ~ about sth** se montrer réservé sur qch ; → **copyright, right**

reservedly /rɪˈzɜːvɪdlɪ/ ADV avec réserve, avec retenue

reservist /rɪˈzɜːvɪst/ N *(Mil)* réserviste *m*

reservoir /ˈrezəvwɑːʳ/ N *(lit, fig)* réservoir *m*

reset /ˌriːˈset/ (pret, ptp **reset**) VT [1] *[+ precious stone]* remonter [2] *[+ clock, watch]* remettre à l'heure ◆ **to ~ the alarm** remettre l'alarme [3] *(Comput)* redémarrer [4] *(Med) [+ limb]* remettre ◆ **to ~ a broken bone** réduire une fracture [5] *(Typ)* recomposer COMP **reset button, reset switch** N *(Comput)* bouton *m* de redémarrage

resettle /ˌriːˈsetl/ VT *[+ refugees]* établir (ailleurs), relocaliser ; *[+ land]* repeupler VI s'établir (ailleurs)

resettlement /ˌriːˈsetlmənt/ N *[of land]* repeuplement *m* ; *[of people]* déplacement *m*, relocalisation *f* COMP **resettlement programme** N *programme visant à relocaliser une population dans une nouvelle région*

reshape /ˌriːˈʃeɪp/ VT *[+ dough, clay]* refaçonner, modeler de nouveau ; *[+ text, policy, society, system]* réorganiser

reshuffle /ˌriːˈʃʌfl/ VT [1] *[+ cards]* battre de nouveau [2] *(fig) [+ cabinet, board of directors]* remanier N [1] *(Cards)* **to have a ~** rebattre [2] *(in command etc)* remaniement *m* ; *(Pol)* ◆ **Cabinet ~** remaniement *m* ministériel

reside /rɪˈzaɪd/ VI *(lit, fig)* résider ◆ **the power ~s in** *or* **with the President** le pouvoir est entre les mains du Président

residence /ˈrezɪdəns/ N [1] *(frm = house)* résidence *f*, demeure *f* ◆ **the President's official ~** la résidence officielle du Président

[2] *(US)* (also **university residence, residence hall**) résidence *f* (universitaire)

[3] *(NonC = stay)* séjour *m*, résidence *f* ◆ **to take up ~ in the country** élire domicile *or* s'installer à la campagne ◆ **after five years' ~ in Britain** après avoir résidé en Grande-Bretagne pendant cinq ans ◆ **place/country of ~** *(Admin)* lieu *m*/pays *m* de résidence

◆ **in residence** *[monarch, governor etc]* en résidence ◆ **the students are now in ~** les étudiants sont maintenant rentrés ◆ **there is always a doctor in ~** il y a toujours un médecin à demeure

COMP **residence hall** N *(US Univ)* résidence *f* universitaire

residence permit N *(Brit)* permis *m or* carte *f* de séjour

residency /ˈrezɪdənsɪ/ N *(gen)* résidence *f* officielle ; *(US Med)* internat *m* de deuxième et de troisième années ◆ **they've got a ~ at Steve's Bar** *(Mus = regular engagement)* ils jouent régulièrement au Steve's Bar

resident /ˈrezɪdənt/ N [1] habitant(e) *m(f)* ; *(in foreign country)* résident(e) *m(f)* ; *(in street)* riverain(e) *m(f)* ; *(in hostel)* pensionnaire *mf* ◆ **"parking for residents only"** "parking privé" ◆ **"residents only"** "interdit sauf aux riverains"

[2] *(US Med)* interne *mf* de deuxième et de troisième années

ADJ [1] *[landlord]* occupant ; *[chaplain, tutor, caretaker]* à demeure ; *[doctor, dramatist, DJ]* attitré ◆ **to be ~ abroad/in France** résider à l'étranger/en France ◆ **the ~ population** la population fixe ◆ **our ~ expert (on sth)** *(hum)* notre spécialiste (de qch)

[2] *[animal]* non migrateur (-trice *f*)

COMP **resident head** N *(US Univ)* directeur *m*, -trice *f* d'une résidence universitaire

resident physician N *(Med)* interne *mf*

residents' association N association *f* de riverains

resident student N *(US Univ)* *étudiant(e) d'une université d'État dont le domicile permanent est situé dans cet État*

residential /ˌrezɪˈdenʃəl/ ADJ [1] *(= not industrial) [area]* d'habitation ◆ **~ accommodation** logements *mpl* [2] *(= live-in) [post, job, course]* avec hébergement, résidentiel ; *[staff]* logé sur place COMP **residential care** N ◆ **to be in ~ care** être pris en charge en établissement spécialisé

residua /rɪˈzɪdjʊə/ NPL of **residuum**

residual /rɪˈzɪdjʊəl/ ADJ restant ; *(Chem)* résiduaire ; *[radiation, fault]* résiduel ◆ **the ~ powers of the British sovereign** les pouvoirs qui restent au souverain britannique N *(Chem)* résidu *m* ; *(Math)* reste *m* NPL **residuals** *(= royalties) droits versés aux acteurs et à l'auteur à l'occasion d'une rediffusion d'un programme télévisé ou d'un film*

COMP **residual current** N courant *m* résiduel

residual current device N disjoncteur *m* différentiel

residual heat N chaleur *f* résiduelle

residual income N revenu *m* net

residual unemployment N chômage *m* résiduel

residuary /rɪˈzɪdjʊərɪ/ ADJ restant ; *(Chem)* résiduaire ◆ **~ estate** *(Jur)* montant *m* net d'une succession ◆ **~ legatee** *(Jur)* ≈ légataire *mf* universel(le)

residue /ˈrezɪdjuː/ N reste(s) *m(pl)* ; *(Chem)* résidu *m* ; *(Math)* reste *m* ; *(Jur)* reliquat *m*

residuum /rɪˈzɪdjʊəm/ N (pl **residua**) résidu *m*, reste *m*

resign /rɪˈzaɪn/ VT [1] *(= give up)* se démettre de ; *[+ one's job]* démissionner de ; *(= hand over)* céder *(to* à) ◆ **he ~ed the leadership to his colleague** il a cédé la direction à son collègue ◆ **to ~ one's commission** *(Mil etc)* démissionner *(se dit d'un officier)* [2] *(= accept)* **to ~ o.s. to (doing) sth** se résigner à (faire) qch VI démissionner, donner sa démission *(from* de)

resignation /ˌrezɪgˈneɪʃən/ N [1] *(from job)* démission *f* ◆ **to tender one's ~** donner sa démission [2] *(mental state)* résignation *f* [3] *(NonC) [of a right]* abandon *m (of* de), renonciation *f (of* à)

> ⚠ **resignation** is only translated by the French word **résignation** when it refers to a state of mind.

resigned /rɪˈzaɪnd/ ADJ résigné ◆ **to be ~ to (doing) sth** s'être résigné à (faire) qch ◆ **to become ~ to (doing) sth** se résigner à (faire) qch

resignedly /rɪˈzaɪnɪdlɪ/ ADV *[say]* avec résignation, d'un ton résigné ; *[shrug, sigh]* avec résignation, d'un air résigné

resilience /rɪˈzɪlɪəns/ N *[of person, character]* résistance *f*, faculté *f* de récupération ; *[of rubber]* élasticité *f*

resilient /rɪˈzɪlɪənt/ ADJ *[object, material, currency, market]* résistant ◆ **he is very ~** *(physically)* il a beaucoup de résistance, il récupère bien ; *(mentally)* il a du ressort, il ne se laisse pas abattre

resin /ˈrezɪn/ N résine *f*

resinous /ˈrezɪnəs/ ADJ résineux

resist /rɪˈzɪst/ VT *[+ attack, arrest, person]* résister à, s'opposer à ; *[+ temptation]* résister à ; *[+ order]* refuser d'obéir *or* d'obtempérer à ; *[+ change]* s'opposer à ◆ **I couldn't ~ (eating) another cake** je n'ai pas pu résister à l'envie de *or* je n'ai pas pu m'empêcher de manger encore un gâteau ◆ **he ~s any advice** il s'oppose à *or* il est rebelle à tout conseil VI résister, offrir de la résistance

resistance /rɪˈzɪstəns/ N *(gen, Elec, Med, Mil, Phys)* résistance *f* ◆ **the Resistance** *(Hist)* la Résistance ◆ **to meet with ~** se heurter à une résistance ◆ **to offer ~ to sth** résister à qch ◆ **to put up** *or* **offer stiff ~ to sth** opposer une vive résistance à qch ◆ **he offered no ~** il n'opposa aucune résistance *(to* à) ◆ **his ~ was very low** *(Med)* il n'offrait presque plus de résistance ◆ **that's the line of least ~** c'est la solution de facilité ◆ **to take the line of least ~** choisir la solution de facilité ; → **passive**

COMP **resistance fighter** N résistant(e) *m(f)*

resistance movement N mouvement *m* de résistance *m*

resistant /rɪˈzɪstənt/ ADJ *[person]* hostile *(to sth* à qch) ; *[virus, plant, material]* résistant *(to sth* à qch) ◆ **~ to penicilin** pénicillorésistant ; → **water**

-resistant /rɪˈzɪstənt/ ADJ *(in compounds)* ◆ **disease-resistant** *[plant]* résistant aux maladies ◆ **fire-resistant** *[paint, cloth]* ignifugé ◆ **heat-resistant** résistant à la chaleur

resister /rɪˈzɪstəʳ/ N réfractaire *m*

resistor /rɪˈzɪstəʳ/ N *(Elec)* résistance *f*

resit /ˌriːˈsɪt/ (pret, ptp **resat**) *(Brit)* VT se représenter à, repasser VI se présenter à la deuxième session N /ˈriːsɪt/ deuxième session *f (d'un examen)* ◆ **to have a ~ in law** devoir se représenter en droit ◆ **to fail one's ~s/one's ~ in chemistry** échouer une deuxième fois à ses examens/à son examen de chimie

resite /ˌriːˈsaɪt/ VT *[+ factory]* réimplanter, transférer

resize /ˌriːˈsaɪz/ VT *(Comput) [+ window]* redimensionner

reskill /riːˈskɪl/ VI se recycler VT recycler

resold /ˌriːˈsəʊld/ VB pt, ptp of **resell**

resole /ˌriːˈsəʊl/ VT ressemeler

resolute /ˈrezəluːt/ ADJ *[person]* résolu, déterminé ; *[opposition]* résolu ; *[refusal]* ferme ; *[faith]* solide ◆ **to take ~ action** agir avec résolution *or* détermination ◆ **to be ~ in doing sth** faire qch avec résolution *or* détermination ◆ **to be ~ in one's opposition to sth** s'opposer résolument à qch ◆ **to remain ~ in the fight against sb/sth** continuer résolument à se battre contre qn/qch

resolutely /ˈrezəluːtlɪ/ ADV *[resist, oppose, stride, stare]* résolument ; *[refuse]* fermement ◆ **the Government remains ~ committed to the fight against unemployment** le gouvernement poursuit résolument son combat contre le chômage

resoluteness /ˈrezəluːtnɪs/ N résolution *f*, détermination *f*

resolution /ˌrezəˈluːʃən/ N [1] *(= decision)* résolution *f* ◆ **to make a ~ to do sth** prendre la résolution de faire qch ◆ **good ~s** bonnes résolutions *fpl* ; → **New Year** [2] *(Admin, Pol)* résolution *f* ◆ **to make a ~** prendre une résolution ◆ **to adopt/reject a ~** adopter/rejeter une résolution [3] *(NonC = resoluteness)* fermeté *f*, résolution *f* ◆ **to show ~** faire preuve de fermeté, faire preuve de décision [4] *(NonC = solving) [of problem, puzzle]* résolution *f* [5] *(NonC: Chem, Med, Mus, Phot)* résolution *f (into* en)

resolvable /rɪˈzɒlvəbl/ ADJ résoluble

resolve /rɪˈzɒlv/ VT [1] *[+ problem, difficulty]* résoudre ; *[+ doubt]* dissiper

[2] *(= break up)* résoudre, réduire *(into* en) ◆ **to ~ sth into its elements** ramener *or* réduire qch à ses éléments ◆ **water ~s itself into steam** l'eau se résout *or* se transforme en vapeur ◆ **the meeting ~d itself into a committee** l'assemblée se constitua en commission

[3] *(Med, Mus)* résoudre

VI [1] *(= decide)* résoudre, décider *(to do sth* de faire qch), se résoudre, se décider *(to do sth* à faire qch) ◆ **to ~ (up)on sth** se résoudre à qch ◆ **to ~ that ...** décider que ... ◆ **it has been ~d that ...** il a été décidé que ...

② *(= break up)* se résoudre *(into* en) ◆ **the question ~s into four points** la question se divise en quatre points
N ① *(NonC = resoluteness)* résolution *f*, fermeté *f* ◆ **to do sth with** ~ faire qch avec détermination
② *(= decision)* résolution *f*, décision *f* ◆ **to make a ~ to do sth** prendre la résolution de faire qch, résoudre de faire qch

resolved /rɪˈzɒlvd/ ADJ résolu *(to do sth* à faire qch), décidé *(to do sth* à faire qch)

resonance /ˈrezənəns/ N *(gen, Mus, Phon, Phys)* résonance *f* ; *[of voice]* résonance *f*, sonorité *f*

resonant /ˈrezənənt/ ADJ ① *(= sonorous, echoing) [voice, room]* sonore ; *[sound]* retentissant ② *(= evocative)* ◆ **to be ~ of sth** rappeler qch ◆ **it is a place ~ with memories for him** c'est un endroit qui éveille en lui une foule de souvenirs ◆ **it was a place ~ with memories of him** c'est un endroit qui évoquait des souvenirs de lui

resonate /ˈrezəneɪt/ VI ① *[sound]* résonner ② ◆ **the room ~d with the sound of laughter** la pièce résonnait de rires ③ *(fig)* ◆ **that ~s with me** je suis tout à fait d'accord là-dessus

resonator /ˈrezəneɪtəʳ/ N résonateur *m*

resorption /rɪˈzɔːpʃən/ N résorption *f*

resort /rɪˈzɔːt/ N ① *(= recourse)* recours *m* ◆ **without ~ to violence** sans recourir *or* avoir recours à la violence ◆ **as a last** *or* **final ~, in the last** *or* **final ~** en dernier ressort ◆ **it was/you were my last ~** c'était/tu étais mon dernier recours ② *(= place)* lieu *m* de séjour *or* de vacances ◆ **coastal ~** plage *f* ◆ **seaside/summer ~** station *f* balnéaire/estivale ◆ **winter sports ~** station *f* de sports d'hiver ◆ **a ~ of thieves** *(fig liter)* un repaire de voleurs ; → **health, holiday** VI ◆ **to ~ to sth** avoir recours à qch, recourir à qch ◆ **to ~ to sb** avoir recours à qn ◆ **to ~ to doing sth** en venir à faire qch

resound /rɪˈzaʊnd/ VI retentir, résonner *(with* de) ◆ **his speech will ~ throughout France/history** son discours retentira dans toute la France/à travers l'histoire VT faire retentir *or* résonner

resounding /rɪˈzaʊndɪŋ/ ADJ ① *(= loud) [thud, crack, crash, laugh]* sonore ; *[voice]* sonore, tonitruant ◆ ~ **applause** un tonnerre d'applaudissements ② *(= great) [triumph, victory, success]* retentissant ; *[defeat]* écrasant ◆ **a ~ silence** un silence pesant ◆ **a ~ no** un non catégorique

resoundingly /rɪˈzaʊndɪŋlɪ/ ADV ① *(= loudly) [fall, crash]* bruyamment ② *(= convincingly) [beat, defeat]* à plate(s) couture(s) ◆ **to be ~ successful** *[plan]* être couronné de succès ; *[person]* remporter un succès retentissant

resource /rɪˈsɔːs/ N ① *(= wealth, supplies etc)* ressource *f* ◆ **financial/mineral/natural ~s** ressources *fpl* pécuniaires/en minerais/naturelles ◆ **~s of men and materials** ressources *fpl* en hommes et en matériel ◆ **the total ~s of a company** *(Fin)* l'ensemble des ressources d'une société ◆ **he has no ~s against boredom** il ne sait pas lutter *or* se défendre contre l'ennui ◆ **left to his own ~s** livré à ses propres ressources *or* à lui-même ② *(Comput)* ressources *fpl* ③ *(= resort)* ressource *f* ◆ **you are my last ~** vous êtes ma dernière ressource *or* mon dernier espoir COMP **resource centre** N *(Scol, Univ etc)* centre *m* de documentation

resourced /rɪˈsɔːst/ ADJ *(Brit)* ◆ **well ~** qui dispose de bonnes ressources ◆ **under-~** qui ne dispose pas des ressources nécessaires

resourceful /rɪˈsɔːsfʊl/ ADJ *[person]* plein de ressources, ingénieux

resourcefully /rɪˈsɔːsfəlɪ/ ADV d'une manière ingénieuse

resourcefulness /rɪˈsɔːsfʊlnɪs/ N *(NonC)* ingéniosité *f* ◆ **one's own inner ~** ses ressources *fpl* intérieures

resourcing /rɪˈsɔːsɪŋ/ N *(NonC = resources)* ressources *fpl*

respect /rɪsˈpekt/ N ① *(NonC = esteem)* respect *m* ◆ **to have ~ for** *[+ person]* avoir du respect pour, respecter ; *[+ the law, sb's intelligence]* respecter ◆ **I have the greatest ~ for him** j'ai infiniment de respect pour lui ◆ **to treat with ~** traiter avec respect ◆ **to be held in ~** être tenu en haute estime ◆ **he can command ~** il impose le respect, il sait se faire respecter ◆ **she has no ~ for other people's feelings** elle n'a aucune considération *or* aucun respect pour les sentiments d'autrui ◆ **out of ~ for ...** par respect *or* égard pour ... ◆ **with (due** *or* **the greatest) ~ I still think that ...** sans vouloir vous contredire *or* sauf votre respect je crois toujours que ... ◆ **without ~ of persons** *(frm)* sans acception de personne ◆ **without ~ to the consequences** sans tenir compte *or* se soucier des conséquences, sans s'arrêter aux conséquences
② *(= reference, aspect)*
♦ **in ... respect(s)** ◆ **in some ~s** à certains égards, sous certains rapports ◆ **in many ~s** à bien des égards ◆ **in this ~** à cet égard, sous ce rapport ◆ **in one ~** d'un certain côté ◆ **in other ~s** à d'autres égards ◆ **in what ~?** sous quel rapport ?, à quel égard ? ◆ **good in ~ of content** bon sous le rapport du contenu *or* quant au contenu
♦ **with respect to ...** pour *or* en ce qui concerne ..., quant à ..., relativement à ...
③ **~s** *(= regards)* respects *mpl* ; *(man to woman)* hommages *mpl* ◆ **to pay one's ~s to sb** présenter ses respects à qn ◆ **give my ~s to ...** présentez mes respects (*or* mes hommages) à ... ◆ **to pay one's last ~s to sb** rendre un dernier hommage à qn
VT ① *[+ person, customs, sb's wishes, opinions, grief, the law]* respecter ◆ **to ~ o.s.** se respecter
② *(frm)* ◆ **as ~s ...** quant à ..., en ce qui concerne ...

respectability /rɪˌspektəˈbɪlɪtɪ/ N respectabilité *f*

respectable /rɪsˈpektəbl/ ADJ *[person, behaviour, motives, size, amount, piece of work]* respectable ; *[clothes]* convenable, comme il faut ◆ **young people from ~ homes** des jeunes gens venant de foyers respectables ◆ **he was outwardly ~ but ...** il avait l'apparence de la respectabilité mais ... ◆ **in ~ society** entre gens respectables ◆ **a ~ writer** un écrivain qui n'est pas sans talent ◆ **to finish a ~ second/third** finir honorablement deuxième/troisième ◆ **it is ~ to do sth** il est respectable de faire qch

respectably /rɪsˈpektəblɪ/ ADV ① *(= decently) [dress, behave]* convenablement, comme il faut ◆ **a ~ married man** un homme marié et respectable ② *(= adequately)* ◆ **he finished ~ in fourth place** il a fini honorablement à la quatrième place

respecter /rɪsˈpektəʳ/ N ◆ **death/the law is no ~ of persons** tout le monde est égal devant la mort/la loi ◆ **death is no ~ of wealth** les riches et les pauvres sont égaux devant la mort ◆ **he is no ~ of persons** il ne s'en laisse imposer par personne

respectful /rɪsˈpektfʊl/ ADJ respectueux *(of sth* de qch ; *to(wards) sb* envers qn, à l'égard de qn)

respectfully /rɪsˈpektfəlɪ/ ADV *[speak, bow, listen]* respectueusement, avec respect ; *[stand, wait, ask, suggest]* respectueusement ; *[treat]* avec respect ◆ **I would ~ disagree with Mr Brown** avec tout le respect que je lui dois, je suis en désaccord avec M. Brown ◆ **I remain ~ yours** *or* **yours ~** *(in letters)* je vous prie d'agréer l'expression de mes sentiments respectueux ; *(man to woman)* je vous prie d'agréer l'expression de mes très respectueux hommages

respectfulness /rɪsˈpektfʊlnɪs/ N *[of person]* attitude *f* respectueuse ; *[of tone, manner]* caractère *m* respectueux

respecting /rɪsˈpektɪŋ/ PREP concernant, relatif à

respective /rɪsˈpektɪv/ ADJ respectif

respectively /rɪsˈpektɪvlɪ/ ADV respectivement

respiration /ˌrespɪˈreɪʃən/ N *(Bot, Med)* respiration *f*

respirator /ˈrespəˌreɪtəʳ/ N *(Med)* respirateur *m* ; *(Mil)* masque *m* à gaz

respiratory /ˈrespərətərɪ/ ADJ respiratoire
COMP **respiratory arrest** N arrêt *m* respiratoire
respiratory failure N insuffisance *f* or défaillance *f* respiratoire
respiratory system N système *m* respiratoire
respiratory tract N appareil *m* respiratoire

respire /rɪsˈpaɪəʳ/ VTI respirer

respite /ˈrespaɪt/ N répit *m*, relâche *m* or *f* ; *(Jur)* sursis *m* ◆ **without (a) ~** sans répit, sans relâche COMP **respite care** N ◆ **to provide ~ care** *héberger temporairement des personnes invalides pour soulager leurs proches*

resplendence /rɪsˈplendəns/ N splendeur *f*

resplendent /rɪsˈplendənt/ ADJ resplendissant ◆ **to look ~** être resplendissant ◆ **~ in a silk dress** resplendissant dans sa robe de soie ◆ **to be ~ with sth** resplendir de qch, être resplendissant de qch

resplendently /rɪsˈplendəntlɪ/ ADV splendidement

respond /rɪsˈpɒnd/ VI ① *(= reply)* répondre *(to* à ; *with* par) ; *(Rel)* chanter les répons ◆ **to ~ to a toast** répondre à un toast ② *(= show reaction to)* répondre *(to* à) ◆ **brakes that ~ well** freins *mpl* qui répondent bien ◆ **car that ~s well to controls** voiture *f* qui a de bonnes réactions *or* qui répond bien aux commandes ◆ **the patient ~ed to treatment** le malade a bien réagi au traitement ◆ **the illness ~ed to treatment** le traitement a agi sur la maladie

respondent /rɪsˈpɒndənt/ N ① *(Jur)* défendeur *m*, -deresse *f* ② *(in opinion poll etc)* personne *f* interrogée, sondé *m* ADJ qui répond *or* réagit *(to* à)

response /rɪsˈpɒns/ N ① *(lit, fig)* réponse *f* ; *(to treatment)* réaction *f* ◆ **in ~ to** en réponse à ◆ **in ~ to the radio appeal, the sum of £10,000 was raised** à la suite de *or* en réponse à l'appel radiodiffusé, on a recueilli la somme de 10 000 livres ◆ **his only ~ was to nod** pour toute réponse, il a hoché la tête ◆ **we had hoped for a bigger ~ from the public** nous n'avons pas reçu du public la réponse escomptée ② *(Rel)* répons *m* COMP **response time** N *[of machine, person, police, ambulance etc]* temps *m* de réponse

responsibility /rɪˌspɒnsəˈbɪlɪtɪ/ LANGUAGE IN USE 18.3
N responsabilité *f* ◆ **to lay** *or* **put** *or* **place the ~ for sth on sb** tenir qn pour responsable de qch, faire porter la responsabilité de qch à qn ◆ **the report placed ~ for the accident on the company** le rapport a déclaré la société responsable de cet accident ◆ **to take ~ for sth** prendre *or* assumer la responsabilité de qch ◆ **"the company takes no responsibility for objects left here"** = "la compagnie décline toute responsabilité pour les objets en dépôt" ◆ **to take on the ~** accepter *or* assumer la responsabilité ◆ **the group which claimed ~ for the attack** le groupe qui a revendiqué l'attentat ◆ **that's his ~** c'est à lui de s'en occuper ◆ **it's not my ~ to do that** ce n'est pas à moi de faire ça ◆ **on my own ~** sous ma responsabilité

◆ **he wants a position with more ~** il cherche un poste offrant plus de responsabilités ◆ **he has too many responsibilities** il a trop de responsabilités ◆ **it is a big ~ for him** c'est une lourde responsabilité pour lui

COMP **responsibility allowance, responsibility payment** N prime *f* de fonction

responsible /rɪ'spɒnsəbl/ ADJ 1 (*= trustworthy*) [*person, attitude, organization*] responsable

2 (*= in charge*) responsable (*to sb* devant qn ; *for sb* de qn) ◆ **~ for sth** responsable de qch, chargé de qch ◆ **~ for doing sth** chargé de faire qch ◆ **who is ~ here?** qui est le responsable ici ?

3 (*= the cause*) **she is ~ for the success of the project** c'est à elle que l'on doit le succès du projet ◆ **he was ~ for improving standards of service** c'est grâce à lui que le service s'est amélioré ◆ **who is ~ for breaking the window?** qui a cassé la vitre ? ◆ **CFCs are ~ for destroying the ozone layer** les CFC sont responsables de la destruction de la couche d'ozone ◆ **I demand to know who is ~ for this!** j'exige de savoir qui est responsable *or* de connaître le responsable ! ◆ **to hold sb ~ for sth** tenir qn responsable de qch

4 (*= involving or demanding responsibility*) ◆ **a ~ job** un travail à responsabilité(s)

responsibly /rɪ'spɒnsəblɪ/ ADV avec sérieux, de façon responsable

responsive /rɪ'spɒnsɪv/ ADJ 1 (*= receptive*) [*audience, class, pupil*] réceptif ◆ **he wasn't very ~ when I spoke to him about it** quand je lui en ai parlé, il ne s'est pas montré très réceptif *or* il n'a pas beaucoup réagi 2 (*= ready to react*) [*person*] sensible, réceptif ◆ **to be ~ to sb's needs** être sensible *or* réceptif aux besoins de qn ◆ **to be ~ to criticism** être sensible à la critique ◆ **to be ~ to sb's request** accueillir favorablement la demande de quelqu'un 3 (*Med*) ◆ **to be ~ to antibiotics/treatment** réagir aux antibiotiques/au traitement 4 (*= easily controlled*) [*machine, car, steering*] sensible 5 (*= answering*) ◆ **to give a ~ smile/nod** faire un sourire/hocher la tête en guise de réponse

responsiveness /rɪ'spɒnsɪvnɪs/ N (*NonC = receptiveness*) capacité *f* de réaction ◆ **the government's ~ to social pressures** l'aptitude *f* du gouvernement à réagir aux pressions sociales

respray /,riː'spreɪ/ VT [*+ car*] refaire la peinture de N /'riːspreɪ/ ◆ **the car needs a ~** il faut refaire la peinture de la voiture

rest /rest/ N 1 (*gen = relaxation etc*) repos *m* ◆ **a day of ~** un jour de repos ◆ **to need ~** avoir besoin de repos ◆ **to need a ~** avoir besoin de se reposer ◆ **to have a ~** se reposer ◆ **she took** *or* **had an hour's ~** elle s'est reposée pendant une heure ◆ **we had a couple of ~s during the walk** pendant la promenade nous nous sommes arrêtés deux fois pour nous reposer ◆ **no ~ for the wicked** pas de repos pour les braves ◆ **~ and recuperation** (*US Mil = leave*) permission *f* ◆ **take a ~!** reposez-vous ! ◆ **to have a good night's ~** passer une bonne nuit ◆ **to retire to ~** (*liter*) se retirer ◆ **at ~** au repos ◆ **to be at ~** (*= peaceful*) être tranquille *or* calme ; (*= immobile*) être au repos ; (*euph = dead*) reposer en paix ◆ **to lay to ~** (*lit*) porter en terre ◆ **to lay** *or* **put to ~** (*fig*) [*+ idea, notion*] enterrer ◆ **to set at ~** [*+ fears, doubts*] dissiper ◆ **to put** *or* **set sb's mind** *or* **heart at ~** tranquilliser qn, rassurer qn ◆ **you can set** *or* **put your mind at ~** tu peux être tranquille ◆ **to come to ~** [*ball, car etc*] s'arrêter, s'immobiliser ; [*bird, insect*] se poser ◆ **give it a ~!*** (*= change the subject*) change de disque !* ; (*= stop working*) laisse tomber !*

2 (*= support for instrument, back, arm etc*) support *m*, appui *m* ; → **armrest, receiver**

3 (*= remainder*) **the ~ of the money** le reste *or* ce qui reste de l'argent, l'argent qui reste ◆ **the ~ of the boys** les garçons qui restent, les autres garçons ◆ **I will take half of the money and you keep the ~** je prends la moitié de l'argent et tu gardes le reste *or* le restant ◆ **I will take this book and you keep the ~** je prends ce livre et tu gardes le reste ◆ **you go off and the ~ of us will wait here** pars, nous (autres) nous attendrons ici ◆ **he was as drunk as the ~ of them** il était aussi ivre que les autres ◆ **all the ~ of the money** tout ce qui reste de l'argent, tout l'argent qui reste ◆ **all the ~ of the books** tous les autres livres ◆ **and all the ~ (of it)*** et tout ça*, et tout ce qui s'ensuit ◆ **for the ~** quant au reste

4 (*Mus*) pause *f* ; (*Poetry*) césure *f* ◆ **crotchet** (*Brit*) *or* **quarter-note** (*US*) **~** (*Mus*) soupir *m*

VI 1 (*= repose*) se reposer ; [*the dead*] reposer ◆ **she never ~s** elle ne se repose jamais ◆ **you must ~ for an hour** il faut vous reposer pendant une heure ◆ **he won't ~ till he finds out the truth** (*fig*) il n'aura de cesse qu'il ne découvre *subj* la vérité ◆ **to ~ easy** dormir sur ses deux oreilles ◆ **to ~ on one's oars** (*lit*) lever les avirons *or* les rames ; (*fig*) prendre un repos bien mérité ◆ **to ~ on one's laurels** se reposer *or* s'endormir sur ses lauriers ◆ **to be ~ing** (*euph*) [*actor*] se trouver sans engagement ◆ **may he ~ in peace** qu'il repose en paix ◆ **to let a field ~** (*Agr*) laisser reposer un champ, laisser un champ en jachère ◆ **"the defence/prosecution rests"** (*Jur*) *formule utilisée par les avocats pour conclure leur plaidoyer ou réquisitoire*

2 (*= remain*) rester, demeurer ◆ **~ assured that ...** soyez certain *or* assuré que ... ◆ **he refused to let the matter ~** il refusait d'en rester là ◆ **they agreed to let the matter ~** ils ont convenu d'en rester là ◆ **the matter must not ~ there** l'affaire ne doit pas en rester là ◆ **and there the matter ~s for the moment** l'affaire en est là pour le moment ◆ **the authority ~s with him** c'est lui qui détient l'autorité ◆ **the decision ~s with him, it ~s with him to decide** la décision lui appartient, il lui appartient de décider ◆ **it doesn't ~ with me** cela ne dépend pas de moi

3 (*= lean, be supported*) [*person*] s'appuyer (*on* sur ; *against* contre) ; [*ladder*] être appuyé (*on* sur ; *against* contre) ; [*roof etc*] reposer (*on* sur) ; (*fig*) [*argument, reputation, case*] reposer (*on* sur) ; [*eyes, gaze*] se poser, s'arrêter (*on* sur) ◆ **her elbows were ~ing on the table** ses coudes reposaient sur la table ◆ **a heavy responsibility ~s on him** (*fig*) il a une lourde responsabilité

VT 1 faire *or* laisser reposer, donner du repos à ◆ **to ~ o.s.** se reposer ◆ **I am quite ~ed** je me sens tout à fait reposé ◆ **to ~ the horses** laisser reposer les chevaux ◆ **God ~ his soul!** que Dieu ait son âme !, paix à son âme !

2 (*Jur*) **to ~ one's case** conclure sa plaidoirie ◆ **I ~ my case!** (*hum*) CQFD !

3 (*= lean*) poser, appuyer (*on* sur ; *against* contre) ; (*fig = base*) [*+ suspicions*] fonder (*on* sur) ◆ **to ~ one's hand on sb's shoulder** poser la main sur l'épaule de qn ◆ **to ~ one's elbows on the table** poser les coudes sur la table ◆ **to ~ a ladder against a wall** appuyer une échelle contre un mur

COMP **rest area** N aire *f* de repos
rest camp N (*Mil*) cantonnement *m*
rest centre N centre *m* d'accueil
rest cure N cure *f* de repos
rest day N jour *m* de repos
rest home, rest house N maison *f* de repos
resting place N [*of the dead*] dernière demeure *f*
rest room N (*US*) toilettes *fpl*
rest stop N (*US*) (*= place*) aire *f* de repos ; (*= break in journey*) pause *f* (*pendant un trajet en voiture ou en bus*)

► **rest up*** VI se reposer

restart /,riː'stɑːt/ VT [*+ work, activity, race*] reprendre, recommencer ; [*+ engine*] relancer, remettre en marche ; [*+ machine*] remettre en marche VI reprendre, recommencer ; [*engine, machine*] se remettre en marche N (*of race, career*) nouveau départ *m*

restate /,riː'steɪt/ VT [*+ argument, reasons, commitment, objection*] répéter ; [*+ opposition, view, one's position*] réaffirmer ; [*+ demand*] redemander ; [*+ problem*] énoncer de nouveau ; [*+ theory, case*] exposer de nouveau ◆ **he continued to ~ his opposition to violence** il a continué de réaffirmer son opposition à la violence

restatement /,riː'steɪtmənt/ N (*gen*) répétition *f* ; [*of plan, theory*] nouvel énoncé *m* ◆ **~ of the law** (*Jur*) réexposé *m* du droit ◆ **he denied that it was simply a ~ of existing government policy** il a nié qu'il s'agisse simplement d'une réaffirmation de la politique gouvernementale existante ◆ **his remarks amount to a ~ of the party's hardline position** ses remarques ne font que réaffirmer la position dure adoptée par le parti ◆ **his speech ended with a clear ~ of the party's demands** il a terminé son discours en réitérant clairement les exigences du parti

restaurant /'restərɔ̃ːŋ/ N restaurant *m*

COMP [*food, prices*] de restaurant
restaurant car N (*Brit Rail*) wagon-restaurant *m*

restaurateur /,restərə'tɜːr/ N restaurateur *m*, -trice *f*

restful /'restfʊl/ ADJ [*sleep*] (paisible et) réparateur (-trice *f*) ; [*atmosphere, lighting, colour, holiday*] reposant ; [*place*] paisible, tranquille ◆ **he's a very ~ person** c'est quelqu'un avec qui on se sent détendu

restfully /'restfəlɪ/ ADV [*sleep*] paisiblement, tranquillement

restitution /,restɪ'tjuːʃən/ N 1 (*NonC*) restitution *f* ◆ **to make ~ of sth** restituer qch ◆ **~ of conjugal rights** (*Jur*) ordre *m* de réintégration du domicile conjugal 2 (*= reparation*) réparation *f*

restive /'restɪv/ ADJ 1 (*= restless*) [*horse*] rétif ; [*person*] agité ◆ **to grow ~** [*horse*] devenir rétif ; [*person*] s'agiter 2 (*= discontented*) [*group, crew*] agité, indocile ◆ **to grow ~** s'agiter, devenir difficile à contrôler

restiveness /'restɪvnɪs/ N agitation *f* ; [*of horse*] rétivité *f*, nature *f* rétive

restless /'restlɪs/ ADJ 1 (*= unsettled, fidgety*) [*person, mind, attitude*] agité ; [*child*] agité, remuant ; [*curiosity*] insatiable ◆ **to grow ~** [*person*] s'agiter ◆ **to be ~ (in one's sleep)** avoir un sommeil agité ◆ **to have** *or* **spend a ~ night** avoir une nuit agitée 2 (*= discontented*) [*group*] agité, indocile ◆ **to get** *or* **grow** *or* **become ~** s'agiter, devenir difficile à contrôler ◆ **the natives are ~** (*hum*) il y a de l'orage dans l'air, il y a de l'eau dans le gaz 3 (*liter = moving*) [*wind*] impétueux (*liter*) ; [*sea*] agité COMP **restless spirit** N (*lit, fig*) âme *f* errante

restlessly /'restlɪslɪ/ ADV avec agitation, nerveusement ◆ **to walk ~ up and down** faire nerveusement les cent pas, tourner comme un lion *or* un ours en cage

restlessness /'restlɪsnɪs/ N [*of person*] agitation *f* ; [*of manner*] agitation *f*, nervosité *f* ; [*of crowd*] impatience *f*

restock /,riː'stɒk/ VT [*+ shop*] réapprovisionner ; [*+ freezer, shelves*] remplir ses étagères ; [*+ pond, river*] repeupler, empoissonner

restoration /,restə'reɪʃən/ N 1 (*NonC = return*) rétablissement *m* ; (*Jur*) [*of property*] restitution *f* ◆ **the Restoration** (*Brit Hist*) la Restauration (*de la monarchie en 1660*) ◆ **the ~ of diplomatic relations** le rétablissement des relations diplomatiques ◆ **I owe the ~ of my hearing to this new technique** j'ai retrouvé l'audition grâce à cette nouvelle technique 2 [*of text*] rétablissement *m* ; [*of monument, work of art*] restauration *f* COMP **Restoration comedy** N

(Brit Theat) théâtre *m* de la Restauration anglaise

restorative /rɪˈstɔːrətɪv/ ADJ, N fortifiant *m*, reconstituant *m*

restore /rɪˈstɔːʳ/ VT 1 *(= give or bring back) [+ sth lost, borrowed, stolen]* rendre, restituer *(to à)* ; *[+ sb's sight etc]* rendre ; *(Jur) [+ rights, law etc]* rétablir ; *[+ confidence]* redonner *(to sb à qn ; in dans)* ; *[+ order, calm]* rétablir ◆ **to ~ sb's health** rétablir la santé de qn, rendre la santé à qn ◆ **~d to health** rétabli, guéri ◆ **to ~ sb to life** ramener qn à la vie ◆ **the brandy ~d my strength** *or* **me** le cognac m'a redonné des forces ◆ **he was ~d to them safe and sound** il leur a été rendu sain et sauf ◆ **to ~ a monarch to the throne** restaurer un monarque ◆ **to ~ sb to power** ramener qn au pouvoir 2 *(= repair) [+ building, painting, furniture etc]* restaurer ; *[+ leather goods]* rénover ; *[+ text]* restituer, rétablir ◆ **to ~ sth to its former condition** remettre qch en état

restorer /rɪˈstɔːrəʳ/ N *(Art etc)* restaurateur *m*, -trice *f* ; → **hair**

restrain /rɪˈstreɪn/ VT 1 *(= prevent: gen)* retenir ◆ **I was going to do it but he ~ed me** j'allais le faire mais il m'a retenu *or* m'en a empêché ◆ **to ~ sb from doing sth** empêcher qn de faire qch 2 *[+ dangerous person etc] (= overcome)* maîtriser ; *(= control)* contenir 3 *(= control) [+ one's anger, feelings etc]* réprimer, refréner ◆ **please ~ yourself!** je vous en prie dominez-vous ! 4 *(= restrict) [+ trade etc]* restreindre COMP **restraining order** N *(Jur)* injonction *f* de ne pas faire, ordonnance *f* restrictive

restrained /rɪˈstreɪnd/ ADJ *[person]* maître (maîtresse *f*) de soi ; *[tone, manner, response, reaction, performance, speech]* mesuré ; *[emotion]* contenu ; *[style, décor]* sobre ◆ **he was very ~ when he heard the news** quand il a appris la nouvelle, il est resté très maître de lui

restraint /rɪˈstreɪnt/ N 1 *(= restriction)* limitation *f (on sth* de qch), contrainte *f* ◆ **without ~** sans contrainte

2 *(NonC = limiting)* frein *m*, contrôle *m* ◆ **price ~** contrôle *m* des prix ◆ **fiscal ~** contrôle *m* de la fiscalité ; → **wage**

3 *(NonC = moderation) [of person, behaviour]* modération *f*, mesure *f* ; *[of style, speech]* retenue *f*, mesure *f* ◆ **his ~ was admirable** il se maîtrisait admirablement ◆ **sexual ~** modération *f* sexuelle ◆ **to exercise** *or* **show ~** faire preuve de modération or de retenue ◆ **to show a lack of ~** manquer de retenue ◆ **with/without ~** *[say]* avec/sans retenue ; *[act]* avec/sans retenue *or* modération ; → **self**

4 *(= restraining device) (in prison, hospital)* entrave *f* ◆ **to be in ~s** être entravé *or* attaché ◆ **to put sb in ~s** *or (frm)* **under ~** entraver qn, attacher qn

5 *(= safety device: in car etc) dispositif de sécurité, par exemple ceinture de sécurité, siège pour bébé* ◆ **head ~** appuie-tête *m*

COMP **restraint of trade** N *(Jur, Fin)* atteinte *f or* entraves *fpl* à la liberté du commerce

restrict /rɪˈstrɪkt/ VT restreindre, limiter *(to à)* ◆ **visiting is ~ed to one hour per day** les visites sont limitées à une heure par jour ◆ **to ~ sb's authority/freedom** restreindre *or* limiter l'autorité/la liberté de qn ◆ **access ~ed to members of staff** accès réservé au personnel, accès interdit aux personnes étrangères à l'établissement

restricted /rɪˈstrɪktɪd/ ADJ 1 *(= limited) [visibility]* réduit ; *[number, choice, group, circulation]* restreint, limité ; *[space, range, viewpoint, horizon]* restreint ; *[access] (= partial)* limité ; *(= forbidden to some people)* réservé ◆ **on a ~ diet** au régime 2 *(= hindered)* ◆ **to feel ~** *[person] (physically)* se sentir à l'étroit ; *(by clothes)* se sentir engoncé ; *(mentally)* avoir l'impression d'étouffer 3 *(= classified) [document, information]* confidentiel

COMP **restricted area** N *(Admin, Mil = prohibited)* zone *f* interdite ; *(Brit: on road)* zone *f* à vitesse limitée ◆ **within a ~ area** *(= delimited)* dans une zone restreinte *or* limitée

restricted code N *(Ling)* code *m* restreint

restriction /rɪˈstrɪkʃən/ N restriction *f*, limitation *f* ◆ **to place ~s on ...** imposer des restrictions à ... ◆ **speed ~** limitation *f* de vitesse ◆ **price ~** contrôle *m* de prix

restrictive /rɪˈstrɪktɪv/ ADJ 1 *(= limiting) [measures]* de restriction ; *[law, policy]* restrictif ; *[environment]* étouffant 2 *(= tight) [clothing]* qui gêne le mouvement

COMP **restrictive clause** N *(Gram)* proposition *f* déterminative

restrictive practices NPL *(Brit) (by trade unions)* pratiques *fpl* syndicales restrictives ; *(by manufacturers)* atteintes *fpl* à la libre concurrence

restrictive relative clause N proposition *f* déterminative

re-string /ˌriːˈstrɪŋ/ (pret, ptp **re-strung** /ˌriːˈstrʌŋ/) VT *[+ pearls, necklace]* renfiler ; *(Mus) [+ violin]* remplacer les cordes de ; *(Sport) [+ racket]* recorder ; *[+ bow]* remplacer la corde de, remettre une corde à

restructure /riːˈstrʌktʃəʳ/ VT restructurer VI se restructurer

restructuring /riːˈstrʌktʃərɪŋ/ N restructuration *f*

restyle /ˌriːˈstaɪl/ VT *[+ product]* donner un nouveau look* à ◆ **to have one's hair ~d** changer de coiffure ◆ **to ~ sb's hair** changer la coiffure de qn

result /rɪˈzʌlt/ LANGUAGE IN USE 17, 26.3 N résultat *m* ◆ **to demand ~s** exiger des résultats ◆ **to get ~s** *[person]* obtenir de bons résultats ; *[action]* donner de bons résultats, aboutir ◆ **to get a ~*** *(Brit)* arriver à quelque chose* ◆ **as a ~ he failed** en conséquence il a échoué, résultat : il a échoué* ◆ **to be the ~ of sth** être la conséquence de qch, être dû à qch, résulter de qch ◆ **as a ~ of** *(gen)* à la suite de ; *(= directly because of: esp Admin)* par suite de ◆ **he died as a ~ of his injuries** il est décédé des suites de ses blessures ◆ **without ~** sans résultat *m* VI résulter *(from de)* ◆ **it ~s that ...** il s'ensuit que ...

► **result in** VT FUS *[+ higher/lower level, increased efficiency, changes, loss]* entraîner, conduire à ; *[+ damage, injury, death]* occasionner ; *[+ failure]* se solder par

resultant /rɪˈzʌltənt/ ADJ ◆ **victims of the war and the ~ famine** les victimes de la guerre et de la famine qui en a résulté *or* qui s'est ensuivie N *(Math)* résultante *f*

resume /rɪˈzjuːm/ VT 1 *(= restart etc) [+ tale, account]* reprendre ; *[+ activity, discussions]* reprendre, recommencer ; *[+ relations]* renouer ◆ **to ~ work** reprendre le travail, se remettre au travail ◆ **to ~ one's journey** reprendre la route, continuer son voyage ◆ **I ~d digging the garden** je me suis remis à bêcher le jardin ◆ **"well" he ~d "eh bien"** reprit-il ◆ **to ~ one's seat** *(frm)* se rasseoir ◆ **to ~ possession of sth** *(frm)* reprendre possession de qch VI *[classes, work etc]* reprendre, recommencer

⚠ **résumer** means 'to sum up', not **to resume**.

résumé /ˈreɪzjuːmeɪ/ N résumé *m* ; *(US)* curriculum vitæ *m inv*

resumption /rɪˈzʌmpʃən/ N reprise *f* ; *[of diplomatic relations]* rétablissement *m*

resurface /ˌriːˈsɜːfɪs/ VT *[+ road]* refaire la surface de VI *[diver, submarine]* remonter à la *or* en surface, faire surface ; *(fig = reappear)* refaire surface ◆ **she ~d* after a year of mourning** elle a recommencé à sortir après un an de deuil

resurgence /rɪˈsɜːdʒəns/ N *(gen)* résurgence *f* ; *(Econ)* reprise *f*

resurgent /rɪˈsɜːdʒənt/ ADJ *[nationalism, fundamentalism]* renaissant, qui connaît un nouvel essor ; *(Econ) [spending]* en nette augmentation

resurrect /ˌrezəˈrekt/ VT *(Rel)* ressusciter ; *(fig) [+ fashion, ideas]* ressortir du placard ; *[+ career, debate]* reprendre ; *(* hum) [+ dress, chair etc]* remettre en service

resurrection /ˌrezəˈrekʃən/ N *(Rel, fig)* résurrection *f*

resus*, **Resus*** /ˈriːsʌs/ N abbrev of **resuscitation room** → **resuscitation**

resuscitate /rɪˈsʌsɪteɪt/ VT *(gen)* faire revivre ; *(Med)* réanimer

⚠ **ressusciter** means 'to bring back to life', not **to resuscitate**.

resuscitation /rɪˌsʌsɪˈteɪʃən/ N réanimation *f*

COMP **resuscitation room** N salle *f* de réanimation

resuscitator /rɪˈsʌsɪteɪtəʳ/ N *(Med* réanimateur *m*

retail /ˈriːteɪl/ N (vente *f* au) détail *m* VT vendre au détail ; *(fig) [+ gossip]* colporter, répandre VI *[goods]* se vendre (au détail) *(at à)* ADV ◆ **to buy/sell ~** acheter/vendre au détail

COMP **retail banking** N *(Fin) opérations bancaires portant sur les comptes personnels*

retail business N commerce *m* de détail

retail dealer N détaillant(e) *m(f)*

retail outlet N ◆ **they are looking for a ~ outlet for ...** ils cherchent un débouché pour ... ◆ **50 ~ outlets** 50 points *mpl* de vente

retail park N *(Brit)* centre *m* commercial

retail price N prix *m* de détail ◆ **~ price index** ≃ indice *m* des prix de l'INSEE

retail shop *(Brit)*, **retail store** *(US)* N magasin *m* de détail, détaillant *m*

retail therapy ◆ **she indulged in a bit of ~ therapy in London** elle est allée faire un peu de shopping à Londres pour se remonter le moral

the retail trade N *(= traders)* les détaillants *mpl* ; *(= selling)* la vente au détail

retailer /ˈriːteɪləʳ/ N détaillant(e) *m(f)*

retain /rɪˈteɪn/ VT 1 *(= keep)* conserver, garder ; *(= hold)* retenir, maintenir ; *[+ heat]* conserver ◆ **~ing wall** mur *m* de soutènement ◆ **to ~ control (of)** garder le contrôle (de) ◆ **~ed earnings** *(Fin)* bénéfices *mpl* non distribués 2 *(= remember)* garder en mémoire 3 *(= engage) [+ lawyer]* retenir, engager ◆ **~ing fee** ⇒ **retainer 2**

retainer /rɪˈteɪnəʳ/ N 1 *(†, liter = servant)* serviteur *m* 2 *(= fee)* acompte *m*, avance *f* sur honoraires ; *(to lawyer)* provision *f* ; *(= rent)* caution *f (versée à titre de loyer réduit par un locataire lors de son absence)* ◆ **to be on a ~** être sous contrat *(garantissant une disponibilité future)*

retake /ˈriːteɪk/ (vb : pret **retook**, ptp **retaken**) N 1 *(Cine)* nouvelle prise *f* (de vues) 2 *(= exam)* deuxième session *f (d'un examen)* ◆ **to fail one's (chemistry) ~s** échouer une deuxième fois à ses examens (de chimie) VT /ˌriːˈteɪk/ 1 reprendre ; *[+ prisoner]* reprendre, rattraper 2 *(Cine)* faire une nouvelle prise de 3 *[+ exam]* se représenter à, repasser

retaliate /rɪˈtælɪeɪt/ VI se venger *(against sb/sth* de qn/qch), user de représailles *(against sb* envers qn) ◆ **he ~d by breaking a window** pour se venger il a brisé une fenêtre ◆ **he ~d by pointing out that ...** il a riposté *or* rétorqué que ..., pour sa part il a fait observer que ... ◆ **to ~ (up)on sb** rendre la pareille à qn, user de représailles envers qn

retaliation /rɪˌtælɪˈeɪʃən/ N représailles *fpl* ◆ **in ~** par mesure de représailles ◆ **in ~ for ...** pour venger ..., pour se venger de ... ◆ **policy of ~** politique *f* de représailles

retaliatory /rɪ'tælɪətərɪ/ ADJ *(frm)* de représailles ◆ **~ measures** *(gen, Mil)* (mesures *fpl* de) représailles *fpl* ; *(Econ)* mesures *fpl* de rétorsion ◆ **a ~ blockade** un blocus en guise de représailles

retard /rɪ'tɑːd/ VT retarder N retard *m*

retarded /rɪ'tɑːdɪd/ ADJ (also **mentally retarded**) arriéré NPL **the retarded** (also **the mentally retarded**) les attardés *mpl* (mentaux)
COMP **retarded acceleration** N *(Tech)* accélération *f* négative
retarded ignition N *(in vehicle)* retard *m* à l'allumage

retch /retʃ/ VI avoir des haut-le-cœur N haut-le-cœur *m inv*

retching /'retʃɪŋ/ N haut-le-cœur *m inv*

retd abbrev of **retired**

retell /ˌriː'tel/ (pret, ptp **retold**) VT raconter encore une fois

retention /rɪ'tenʃən/ N (NonC) *(= keeping)* maintien *m* ; *(Med)* rétention *f* ; *(= memory)* mémoire *f*

retentive /rɪ'tentɪv/ ADJ ◆ **a ~ memory** *or* **mind** une mémoire fidèle ; → **anal, anally**

retentiveness /rɪ'tentɪvnɪs/ N faculté *f* de retenir, mémoire *f*

rethink /ˌriː'θɪŋk/ (pret, ptp **rethought** /ˌriː'θɔːt/) VT repenser N /'riːθɪŋk/ ◆ **we'll have to have a ~** nous allons devoir y réfléchir encore un coup *

reticence /'retɪsəns/ N réticence *f*

reticent /'retɪsənt/ ADJ réservé ◆ **~ about sth** réticent à parler de qch ◆ **officials have been ~ about giving details of exactly what did happen** les responsables se sont montrés réticents *or* peu enclins à expliquer ce qui s'était passé exactement ◆ **she is very ~ about her past** elle n'aime pas parler de son passé

reticently /'retɪsəntlɪ/ ADV avec réticence, avec réserve

reticle /'retɪkl/ N *(Opt)* réticule *m*

reticulate /rɪ'tɪkjʊlɪt/, **reticulated** /rɪ'tɪkjʊleɪtɪd/ ADJ réticulé

reticule /'retɪkjuːl/ N 1 ⇒ **reticle** 2 *(= handbag)* réticule † *m*

retina /'retɪnə/ N (pl **retinas** *or* **retinae** /'retɪniː/) rétine *f*

retinal /'retɪnl/ ADJ rétinien

retinue /'retɪnjuː/ N escorte *f*

retire /rɪ'taɪəʳ/ VI 1 *(= withdraw)* se retirer, partir ; *(Mil)* reculer, se replier ; *[jury]* se retirer ; *(Sport)* abandonner ◆ **to ~ from the room** quitter la pièce ◆ **to ~ to the lounge** se retirer au salon, passer au salon ◆ **to ~ hurt** *(Sport)* abandonner à la suite d'une blessure ◆ **to ~ into o.s.** rentrer en *or* se replier sur soi-même ◆ **to ~ from the world/from public life** se retirer du monde/de la vie publique 2 († *= go to bed*) (aller) se coucher 3 *(= give up one's work)* prendre sa retraite ◆ **to ~ from business** se retirer des affaires VT *[+ worker, employee]* mettre à la retraite ; *(Fin) [+ bond]* retirer de la circulation ◆ **to be compulsorily ~d** être mis à la retraite d'office

retired /rɪ'taɪəd/ ADJ 1 *(= no longer working)* à la retraite ◆ **a ~ person** un(e) retraité(e) 2 *(= secluded) [life, spot]* retiré
COMP **retired list** N *(Mil)* état *m* des mises à la retraite
retired pay N pension *f* de retraite

retiree /rɪtaɪ'riː/ N *(US)* retraité(e) *m(f)*

retirement /rɪ'taɪəmənt/ N 1 *(= stopping work)* retraite *f* ◆ **~ at 60** (mise *f* à la) retraite à 60 ans ◆ **to announce one's ~** annoncer que l'on prend sa retraite ◆ **to come out of ~** reprendre ses activités *or* une occupation *or* du service *(après avoir pris sa retraite)* ◆ **how will you spend your ~?** qu'est-ce que vous ferez quand vous aurez pris votre retraite ? ; → **early**
2 *(= seclusion)* isolement *m*, solitude *f* ◆ **to live in ~** vivre retiré du monde
3 *(Mil)* retraite *f*, repli *m* ; *(Sport)* abandon *m*
COMP **retirement age** N âge *m* de la retraite
retirement benefit N prime *f* or indemnité *f* de départ en retraite
retirement community N *(US)* communauté *f* de retraités
retirement home N *(personal)* maison *f* pour sa retraite ; *(communal)* maison *f* de retraite
retirement pay N retraite *f*
retirement pension N (pension *f* de) retraite *f* ; *(Mil)* solde *f* de retraite
retirement relief N *(Brit) exonération, dont bénéficient les retraités, sur les plus-values en capital* ; see also **pension**

retiring /rɪ'taɪərɪŋ/ ADJ 1 *(= shy) [person]* réservé 2 *(= outgoing) [chairman, president]* sortant 3 *(= taking retirement)* qui part en retraite 4 ◆ **~ room** cabinet *m* particulier COMP **retiring age** N âge *m* de la retraite

retold /ˌriː'təʊld/ VB pt, ptp of **retell**

retook /ˌriː'tʊk/ VB pt of **retake**

retool /ˌriː'tuːl/ VT *[+ factory]* rééquiper ; *[+ machine]* renouveler VI se rééquiper

retort /rɪ'tɔːt/ N 1 *(= answer)* réplique *f*, riposte *f* 2 *(Chem)* cornue *f* VT répliquer *(that* que) ◆ **"not at all" he ~ed** "pas du tout" répliqua-t-il

retouch /ˌriː'tʌtʃ/ VT *(Art, Phot)* retoucher

retrace /rɪ'treɪs/ VT *[+ developments etc] (= research into)* reconstituer ; *(= give account of)* retracer ◆ **to ~ one's path** *or* **steps** revenir sur ses pas, rebrousser chemin

retract /rɪ'trækt/ VT 1 *(= withdraw) [+ offer, evidence]* retirer ; *[+ statement]* rétracter, revenir sur 2 *(= draw back) [+ undercarriage, aerial]* rentrer ; *[+ claws]* rentrer, rétracter ; *[+ tentacles, snail's horns]* rétracter VI 1 *(= withdraw statement etc)* se rétracter 2 *(= draw back)* se rétracter ; *[undercarriage, blade, aerial]* rentrer

retractable /rɪ'træktəbl/ ADJ *[undercarriage, aerial, roof]* escamotable ; *[blade]* rentrant ; *[claws, tentacles etc]* rétractile ; *[ball-point pen]* à pointe rétractable ◆ **~ tape measure** mètre *m* ruban (à enrouleur)

retraction /rɪ'trækʃən/ N *[of statement, offer]* rétractation *f* ; *[of claws etc]* rétraction *f* ; *[of undercarriage]* escamotage *m*

retrain /ˌriː'treɪn/ VT recycler VI se recycler

retraining /ˌriː'treɪnɪŋ/ N recyclage *m*

retransmit /ˌriːtrænz'mɪt/ VT réexpédier ; *(Phys, Rad, TV)* retransmettre

retread /ˌriː'tred/ VT *[+ tyre]* rechaper N /'riːtred/ 1 *(= tyre)* pneu *m* rechapé 2 *(fig)* nouvelle mouture *f*

retreat /rɪ'triːt/ N 1 *(also Mil)* retraite *f* ◆ **the army is in ~** l'armée bat en retraite ◆ **to sound the ~** battre la retraite ◆ **to make** *or* **beat a hasty ~** battre en retraite 2 *(St Ex: of currency)* repli *m* ◆ **the pound went into ~** la livre a cédé du terrain 3 *(= place: also Rel)* retraite *f* ◆ **to go on a ~** faire une retraite ◆ **a country ~** un endroit (*or* une maison *etc*) tranquille à la campagne VI *(Mil)* battre en retraite ; *(= withdraw)* se retirer *(from* de) ; *[flood, glacier]* reculer ; *[chin, forehead]* être fuyant ◆ **to ~ within o.s.** se replier sur soi-même ◆ **~ing** *[army, troops]* en retraite ◆ **to ~ from** *(fig) [+ promise, belief etc]* abandonner, se défaire de VT *(Chess)* ramener

retrench /rɪ'trentʃ/ VT réduire ses dépenses VI restreindre, réduire

retrenchment /rɪ'trentʃmənt/ N 1 *(= cutting back)* réduction *f* (des dépenses) 2 *(Mil)* retranchement *m*

retrial /ˌriː'traɪəl/ N *(Jur)* révision *f* de procès

retribution /ˌretrɪ'bjuːʃən/ N châtiment *m*

⚠ The French word **rétribution** means 'payment', not **retribution**.

retributive /rɪ'trɪbjʊtɪv/ ADJ *(frm)* punitif

retrievable /rɪ'triːvəbl/ ADJ *[object, material]* récupérable ; *[money]* recouvrable ; *[error, loss]* réparable ; *(Comput)* accessible

retrieval /rɪ'triːvəl/ N 1 *(Comput)* extraction *f* ◆ **data ~** extraction *f* de données ; see also **information** 2 *(= recovery) [of object]* récupération *f* ; *[of money]* recouvrement *m* ; *[of memories]* rappel *m*

retrieve /rɪ'triːv/ VT *(= recover) [+ object]* récupérer *(from* de) ; *[dog]* rapporter ; *(Fin)* recouvrer ; *(Comput)* retrouver ; *[+ information]* rechercher et extraire ; *[+ fortune, honour, position]* rétablir ; *(= set to rights) [+ error]* réparer ; *[+ situation]* redresser, sauver ; *(= rescue)* sauver, tirer *(from* de) ◆ **we shall ~ nothing from this disaster** *(lit, fig)* nous ne sauverons *or* récupérerons rien de ce désastre VI *[dog]* rapporter

retriever /rɪ'triːvəʳ/ N retriever *m*, chien *m* d'arrêt

retro /'retrəʊ/ ADJ *[fashion, music]* rétro *inv*

retro... /'retrəʊ/ PREF rétro...

retroactive /ˌretrəʊ'æktɪv/ ADJ *(frm) [pay rise, legislation]* rétroactif ◆ **~ to 1 October** avec effet rétroactif au 1er octobre ◆ **~ payment** *(on salary)* rappel *m*

retroactively /ˌretrəʊ'æktɪvlɪ/ ADV rétroactivement

retroengine /'retrəʊˌendʒɪn/ N rétrofusée *f*

retrofit /'retrəʊfɪt/ VT *[+ machine, system]* modifier les équipements de ; *[+ building]* mettre aux normes

retroflex(ed) /'retrəʊfleks(t)/ ADJ *(Ling)* apical, rétroflexe

retroflexion /ˌretrəʊ'flekʃən/ N *(Med)* rétroflexion *f*

retrograde /'retrəʊgreɪd/ ADJ *(also Astron)* rétrograde VI rétrograder

retrogress /ˌretrəʊ'gres/ VI rétrograder

retrogression /ˌretrəʊ'greʃən/ N régression *f*

retrogressive /ˌretrəʊ'gresɪv/ ADJ rétrograde ; *(Bio)* régressif

retropack /'retrəʊpæk/ N système *m* de rétrofusées

retrorocket /'retrəʊˌrɒkɪt/ N rétrofusée *f*

retrospect /'retrəʊspekt/ N examen *m* or coup *m* d'œil rétrospectif ◆ **in ~** rétrospectivement

retrospection /ˌretrəʊ'spekʃən/ N examen *m* rétrospectif

retrospective /ˌretrəʊ'spektɪv/ ADJ *[survey, emotion]* rétrospectif ; *[pay rise, effect, legislation]* rétroactif ◆ **~ exhibition** *(Art)* rétrospective *f* N *(Art)* rétrospective *f*

retrospectively /ˌretrəʊ'spektɪvlɪ/ ADV *(gen)* rétrospectivement ; *(Admin, Jur)* rétroactivement

retroviral /ˌretrəʊ'vaɪrəl/ ADJ rétroviral

retrovirus /'retrəʊˌvaɪərəs/ N rétrovirus *m*

retry /ˌriː'traɪ/ VT *(Jur)* juger de nouveau

retune /ˌriː'tjuːn/ VI *(Rad) (= adjust tuning)* rajuster le réglage ; *(= change station/frequency)* changer de station/fréquence ◆ **to ~ to FM** passer sur FM VT *[+ musical instrument]* réaccorder ; *[+ engine]* modifier le réglage de ; *(Rad) [+ set]* régler N /'riːtjuːn/ *[of engine]* révision *f*

return /rɪ'tɜːn/ VI *[person, vehicle etc] (= come back)* revenir ; *(= go back)* retourner ; *[property]* retourner, revenir (*to* à) ; *[symptoms, doubts, fears]* réapparaître ◆ **to ~ home** rentrer ◆ **have they ~ed?** sont-ils revenus *or* rentrés ? ◆ **his good spirits ~ed** sa bonne humeur est revenue ◆ **to ~ to one's work** se remettre à *or* reprendre son travail ◆ **to ~ to school** rentrer (en classe) ◆ **to ~ to a subject/an idea** revenir à un sujet/une idée ◆ **to ~ to what we were talking about, he …** pour en revenir à la question, il … ◆ **to ~ to one's bad habits** reprendre ses mauvaises habitudes

VT [1] *(= give back) (gen)* rendre ; *[+ sth borrowed, stolen, lost]* rendre, restituer ; *(= bring back)* rapporter ; *[+ goods to shop]* rendre, rapporter ; *(= put back)* remettre ; *(= send back)* renvoyer, retourner ; *[+ ball, sound, light]* renvoyer ; *[+ compliment, salute, blow, visit]* rendre ; *[+ sb's love]* répondre à ◆ **to ~ money to sb** rembourser qn ◆ **he ~ed the $5 to him** il lui a remboursé les 5 dollars, il l'a remboursé des 5 dollars ◆ **to ~ a book to the library** rapporter *or* rendre un livre à la bibliothèque ◆ **to ~ a book to the shelf** remettre un livre sur le rayon ◆ **he ~ed it to his pocket** il l'a remis dans sa poche ◆ **to ~ a call** rappeler ◆ **"return to sender"** *(on letter)* "retour à l'envoyeur" ◆ **to ~ thanks** *(liter)* rendre grâce, remercier ◆ **to ~ the favour** renvoyer l'ascenseur* *(fig)*, rendre la pareille ◆ **to ~ sb's favour** rendre service à qn (en retour) ◆ **I hope to ~ your kindness** j'espère pouvoir vous rendre service en retour ◆ **his love was not ~ed** elle n'a pas répondu à son amour ◆ **to ~ good for evil** rendre le bien pour le mal ◆ **to ~ like for like** rendre la pareille ◆ **to ~ hearts** *(Bridge)* rejouer du cœur, renvoyer cœur ◆ **to ~ the ball** *(Tennis etc)* renvoyer la balle ◆ **backhand well ~ed by …** revers bien repris par … ; → **fire**

[2] *(= reply)* répondre, répliquer

[3] *(= declare) [+ income, details]* déclarer ◆ **to ~ a verdict** *(Jur)* rendre *or* prononcer un verdict ◆ **to ~ a verdict of guilty on sb** déclarer qn coupable ◆ **to ~ a verdict of murder** conclure au meurtre

[4] *(Fin) [+ profit, income]* rapporter, donner

[5] *(Parl) [+ candidate]* élire ◆ **he was ~ed by an overwhelming majority** il a été élu à *or* avec une très forte majorité

N [1] *(= coming, going back) [of person, illness, seasons]* retour *m* ◆ **on my ~** à mon retour ◆ **my ~ home** mon retour ◆ **after their ~ to school** après la rentrée (des classes) ◆ **by ~ of post** par retour du courrier ◆ **a ~ to one's old habits** un retour à ses vieilles habitudes ◆ **many happy ~s (of the day)!** bon anniversaire ! ; → **point**

[2] *(= giving back)* retour *m* ; *(= sending back)* renvoi *m* ; *(= putting back)* remise *f* en place ; *[of sth lost, stolen, borrowed]* restitution *f* ; *[of money]* remboursement *m* ; → **sale**

[3] (Brit: also **return ticket**) aller et retour *m*, aller-retour *m* ◆ **two ~s to London** deux allers et retours pour Londres, deux allers-retours pour Londres

[4] *(= recompense)* récompense *f* (*for* de) ; *(from land, business, mine)* rendement *m*, rapport *m* ; *(from investments, shares)* rapport *m* ◆ **~s** *(= profits)* bénéfice *m*, profit *m* ; *(= receipts)* rentrées *fpl*, recettes *fpl* ◆ **small profits and quick ~s** de bas prix et un gros chiffre d'affaires ◆ **~ on capital** *(Fin)* rapport *m* de capital ◆ **~ on investments** rentabilité *f* des investissements ◆ **to get a poor ~ for one's kindness** être mal récompensé *or* mal payé de sa gentillesse

♦ **in return** en retour ◆ **they want something in ~** ils veulent quelque chose en retour ◆ **in ~ for** en récompense de, en échange de

[5] *(= act of declaring) [of verdict]* déclaration *f* ; *[of election results]* proclamation *f* ; *(= report)* rapport *m*, relevé *m* ; *(= statistics)* statistique *f* ◆ **official ~s** statistiques *fpl* officielles ◆ **the population ~s show that …** le recensement montre que … ◆ **the election ~s** les résultats *mpl* de l'élection ◆ **tax ~** (feuille *f* de) déclaration *f* de revenus *or* d'impôts

[6] *(Parl) [of candidate]* élection *f*

[7] *(Sport)* riposte *f* ; *(Tennis)* retour *m* ◆ **~ of service** retour *m* de service

[8] *(Comput etc)* **~ (key)** (touche *f*) "retour"

COMP **return fare** N *(Brit)* (prix *m*) aller-retour *m*, aller et retour *m*

return flight N *(Brit) (= journey back)* vol *m* (de) retour ; *(= two-way journey)* vol *m* aller-retour

return half N *[of ticket]* coupon *m* de retour

returning officer N *(Pol)* président *m* du bureau de vote

return item N *(Fin)* impayé *m*

return journey N *(Brit)* (voyage *m or* trajet *m* de) retour *m*

return match N *(Brit)* revanche *f*, match *m* retour

return stroke N *(Tech)* mouvement *m* de retour

return ticket N *(Brit)* (billet *m* d')aller (et) retour *m*

return visit N → **return visit**

returnable /rɪˈtɜːnəbl/ ADJ *[bottle, container]* consigné ◆ **~ deposit** caution *f*

returnee /rɪtɜːˈniː/ N *(Pol) personne qui retourne dans son pays après une longue absence*

returner /rɪˈtɜːnəʳ/ N *(= working woman) femme qui reprend le travail après avoir élevé ses enfants*

return visit /rɪˈtɜːnˈvɪzɪt/ N [1] *(= repeat visit)* deuxième *or* nouvelle visite *f* ; *(for check-up)* visite *f* de contrôle ◆ **to make** *or* **pay a ~** *(= go back)* retourner ; *(= come back)* revenir ◆ **in 1979, the Pope made his first ~ to Poland** en 1979, le pape est retourné (*or* revenu) pour la première fois en Pologne ◆ **towards the end of his career he made a nostalgic ~ to Germany** vers la fin de sa carrière, il est retourné (*or* revenu) en Allemagne par nostalgie

[2] *(= returning sb's visit: to person who has visited you)* ◆ **it is hoped that a ~ by our German friends can be arranged** on espère que nos amis allemands pourront nous rendre visite à leur tour ◆ **the exchange went well and Moscow was invited to send an economist on a ~** l'échange s'est bien passé et on a invité Moscou à envoyer à son tour un économiste

retype /ˌriːˈtaɪp/ VT retaper (à la machine)

reunification /ˌriːjuːnɪfɪˈkeɪʃən/ N réunification *f* ◆ **since German ~** depuis la réunification allemande

reunify /ˌriːˈjuːnɪfaɪ/ VT réunifier

reunion /riːˈjuːnjən/ N réunion *f*

Réunion /riːˈjuːnjən/ N ◆ **~ (Island)** (l'île *f* de) la Réunion

reunite /ˌriːjuːˈnaɪt/ VT réunir ◆ **they were ~d at last** ils se sont enfin retrouvés VI se réunir

re-up* /ˌriːˈʌp/ VI *(US Mil)* rempiler*, se réengager

re-usable /ˌriːˈjuːzəbl/ ADJ réutilisable

re-use /ˌriːˈjuːz/ VT réutiliser

rev /rev/ N (abbrev of **revolution**) tour *m* ◆ **~ counter** compte-tours *m inv* ◆ **4,000 ~s per minute** 4 000 tours minute VT ⇒ **rev up vt sep 1** VI ⇒ **rev up vi 1**

▸ **rev up*** VI [1] *[engine]* s'emballer ; *[driver]* emballer le moteur [2] *(= prepare)* se préparer (*for* pour) VT SEP [1] *[+ engine]* emballer [2] *(fig) [+ production]* accélérer ◆ **to be ~ved up for sth** *(= eager)* être fin prêt pour qch

Rev. abbrev of **Reverend**

revaluation /ˌriːvæljʊˈeɪʃən/ N *(Fin)* réévaluation *f*

revalue /ˌriːˈvæljuː/ VT *(Fin)* réévaluer

revamp* /ˌriːˈvæmp/ VT *[+ company, department]* réorganiser ; *[+ house, room, object]* retaper*

revanchism /rɪˈvæntʃɪzəm/ N revanchisme *m*

revanchist /rɪˈvæntʃɪst/ N, ADJ revanchiste *mf*

Revd abbrev of **Reverend**

reveal /rɪˈviːl/ VT *(gen)* révéler ; *(= make visible) [+ hidden object etc]* découvrir, laisser voir ; *(= make known)* révéler *(that* que) ; *[+ truth, facts]* révéler, faire connaître ; *[+ corruption]* révéler, mettre à jour ◆ **I cannot ~ to you what he said** je ne peux pas vous révéler ce qu'il a dit ◆ **to ~ one's identity** se faire connaître, révéler son identité ◆ **he ~ed himself as being …** il s'est révélé comme étant … ◆ **his condition ~ed itself as (being) psychological in origin** ses problèmes se sont avérés avoir une cause psychologique ◆ **~ed religion** religion *f* révélée

revealing /rɪˈviːlɪŋ/ ADJ [1] *(= telling) [insight, glimpse, book, comment]* révélateur (-trice *f*) [2] *[dress, blouse etc] (gen)* suggestif ; *(= see-through)* transparent ; *(= low-cut)* très décolleté

revealingly /rɪˈviːlɪŋlɪ/ ADV ◆ **~, most of his clients are women** il est révélateur que la plupart de ses clients soient des femmes ◆ **he ~ remarked that he'd never read the book in question** il a eu une remarque révélatrice lorsqu'il a dit qu'il n'avait jamais lu le livre en question

reveille /rɪˈvælɪ/ N *(Mil)* réveil *m* ; → **sound¹**

revel /ˈrevl/ VI [1] *(= make merry)* s'amuser, se divertir ; *(= carouse)* faire la fête [2] *(= delight)* se délecter (*in sth* de qch) ◆ **to ~ in doing sth** se délecter à faire qch, prendre grand plaisir à faire qch NPL **revels** *(= entertainment)* divertissements *mpl* ; *(= carousing)* festivités *fpl*

revelation /ˌrevəˈleɪʃən/ N révélation *f* ◆ **his criminal activities were a complete ~ to me** j'ignorais tout de ses activités criminelles ◆ **(the Book of) Revelation** *(Rel)* l'Apocalypse *f*

revelatory /ˌrevəˈleɪtərɪ/ ADJ révélateur (-trice *f*) ; → **self**

reveller, reveler (US) /ˈrevləʳ/ N fêtard *m*, joyeux convive *m* ◆ **the ~s** les gens *mpl* de la fête, les fêtards *mpl*

revelry /ˈrevlrɪ/ N *(NonC)* festivités *fpl*

revenge /rɪˈvendʒ/ N *(lit)* vengeance *f* ; *(fig, Sport etc)* revanche *f* ◆ **to take ~ on sb for sth** se venger de qch sur qn ◆ **to get one's ~** se venger ◆ **to do sth out of** *or* **in ~** faire qch par vengeance ◆ **in ~ he killed him** pour se venger il l'a tué VT *[+ insult, murder]* venger ◆ **to ~ o.s., to be ~d** *(gen)* se venger *(on sb* de qn ; *on sb for sth* de qch sur qn) ; *(in sport competition etc)* prendre sa revanche *(on sb* sur qn ; *for sth* de qch)

revengeful /rɪˈvendʒfʊl/ ADJ *[person]* vindicatif ; *[act]* vengeur (-geresse *f*)

revengefully /rɪˈvendʒfəlɪ/ ADV vindicativement

revenger /rɪˈvendʒəʳ/ N vengeur *m*, -geresse *f*

revenue /ˈrevənjuː/ N *[of state]* recettes *fpl* ; *[of individual]* revenu *m* ; → **inland**

COMP **revenue man** † N (pl **revenue men**) douanier *m*

revenue officer N agent *m or* employé(e) *m(f)* des douanes

revenue sharing N *(US Econ) redistribution d'une partie des impôts fédéraux aux autorités locales*

revenue stamp N timbre *m* fiscal

revenue stream N source *f* de revenus

reverb* /rɪˈvɜːb/ N *(NonC = effect)* écho *m*

reverberate /rɪˈvɜːbəreɪt/ VI *[sound]* retentir, résonner, se répercuter ; *[room]* résonner (*with* de) ; *(fig) [protests etc]* se propager VT *[+ sound]* renvoyer, répercuter ; *[+ light]* réverbérer, réfléchir ; *[+ heat]* réverbérer

reverberation /rɪˌvɜːbəˈreɪʃən/ N *[of sound]* répercussion *f* ; *[of room]* résonance *f* ; *(fig = effect)* retentissements *mpl* ◆ **to send ~s around the world** *(fig)* avoir des répercussions dans le monde entier

reverberator /rɪˈvɜːbəreɪtəʳ/ N réflecteur *m*

revere /rɪˈvɪəʳ/ VT révérer, vénérer

revered /rɪˈvɪəd/ ADJ vénéré

reverence /ˈrevərəns/ N 1 (= respect) vénération f ◆ **to have ~ for sb, to hold sb in ~** révérer qn ◆ **to show** or **pay ~ to** rendre hommage à 2 ◆ **your Reverence** ≈ mon (révérend) père VT révérer

reverend /ˈrevərənd/ ADJ 1 (Rel) (Anglican) ◆ **the ~ gentleman** le révérend ◆ **the Reverend (Robert) Martin** (in titles, Anglican) le révérend (Robert) Martin ; (Nonconformist) le pasteur (Robert) Martin ◆ **yes, Reverend** ^ (Anglican, Nonconformist) oui, mon révérend ◆ **the Most Reverend** le Révérendissime ◆ **the Very** or **Right Reverend Robert Martin** (Anglican) le très révérend Robert Martin ◆ **Reverend Mother** révérende mère f 2 († = venerable) vénérable N (*: Protestant) pasteur m

reverent /ˈrevərənt/ ADJ (frm) déférent

reverential /ˌrevəˈrenʃəl/ ADJ (frm) [tone, attitude, respect] révérencieux

reverently /ˈrevərəntlɪ/ ADV (frm) [say] révérencieusement, avec déférence ; [speak, look at] avec déférence

reverie /ˈrevərɪ/ N rêverie f

revers /rɪˈvɪəʳ/ N (pl **revers** /rɪˈvɪəz/) revers m (d'un vêtement)

reversal /rɪˈvɜːsəl/ N 1 (= turning upside down) (also fig) [of policy, roles, trend] renversement m ; (= switching over of two objects) interversion f ; [of opinion, view etc] revirement m ; (Jur) [of judgement] arrêt m d'annulation, réforme f 2 (= failure) revers m

reverse /rɪˈvɜːs/ LANGUAGE IN USE 27.6

ADJ [process, situation, motion] inverse ; [effect] inverse, contraire ◆ **in the ~ direction** en sens inverse ◆ **in ~ order** dans l'ordre inverse ◆ **~ side** [of coin, medal] revers m ; [of sheet of paper] verso m ; [of cloth] envers m ; [of painting] dos m

N 1 (= opposite) contraire m ◆ **quite the ~!** au contraire ! ◆ **it is quite the ~** c'est tout le contraire ◆ **he is the ~ of polite** il est tout sauf poli ◆ **in ~** (fig) dans l'ordre inverse ; see also noun 4

2 (= back) [of coin, medal] revers m ; [of sheet of paper] verso m ; [of cloth] envers m ; [of painting] dos m

3 (= setback, loss) revers m, échec m ; (= defeat) revers m, défaite f

4 (Driving) **in ~** en marche arrière ◆ **to put a car in ~** enclencher la marche arrière ◆ **to go into ~** (fig) [process, one's fortunes etc] renverser la vapeur

VT 1 (= turn the other way round) renverser, retourner ; [+ garment] retourner ; [+ situation] renverser, changer complètement ; [+ photo, result] inverser ◆ **to ~ the order of things** inverser l'ordre des choses ◆ **to ~ one's policy** faire volte-face (fig) ◆ **to ~ a procedure** procéder par ordre inverse ◆ **to ~ a decision** revenir sur une décision ◆ **to ~ a trend** renverser une tendance ◆ **to ~ the charges** (Brit Telec) téléphoner en PCV ◆ **to ~ the position(s) of two objects** intervertir or inverser deux objets

2 (= cause to move backwards) [+ moving belt] renverser la direction or la marche de ; [+ typewriter ribbon] changer de sens ◆ **to ~ the engine** (Tech) faire machine arrière ◆ **to ~ one's car into the garage/down the hill** rentrer dans le garage/descendre la côte en marche arrière ◆ **he ~d the car into a tree** il a heurté un arbre en faisant une marche arrière ◆ **to ~ one's car across the road** faire une marche arrière en travers de la route

3 (Jur = annul) [+ decision, verdict] réformer, annuler ; [+ judgement] réformer, déjuger ; [+ sentence] révoquer, casser

VI (Brit) (= move backwards) [car] faire marche arrière ; [dancer] renverser ◆ **to ~ into the garage/out of the driveway/down the hill** (Aut) rentrer dans le garage/sortir de l'allée/descendre la côte en marche arrière ◆ **to ~ into a tree** heurter un arbre en faisant une marche arrière ◆ **to ~ across the road** faire une marche arrière en travers de la route

COMP **reverse-charge call** N (Brit Telec) (appel m or communication f en) PCV m

reverse discrimination N (US) discrimination f en faveur des minorités

reverse gear N marche f arrière

reverse racism N (US) racisme m à l'envers

reverse turn N (in car) virage m en marche arrière ; (Dancing) renversement m

reversing light N (Brit) feu m de marche arrière, feu m de recul

► **reverse out** VT FUS (Typ) passer du noir au blanc

reversibility /rɪˌvɜːsɪˈbɪlɪtɪ/ N réversibilité f

reversible /rɪˈvɜːsəbl/ ADJ [process, effect, operation, coat, jacket] réversible ; [decision] révocable

reversion /rɪˈvɜːʃən/ N 1 (= return to former state) retour m (to à) ; (Bio) réversion f ◆ **~ to type** (Bio) réversion f au type primitif 2 (Jur) réversion f, droit m de retour 3 (Phot) inversion f

reversionary /rɪˈvɜːʃnərɪ/ ADJ 1 (Jur) de réversion, réversible 2 (Bio) atavique, régressif

revert /rɪˈvɜːt/ VI 1 (= return) revenir (to à) ; (Jur) revenir, retourner (to à) ; [property] faire retour (to à) ◆ **he has ~ed to smoking marijuana** il a recommencé à fumer de la marijuana ◆ **to ~ to the question** pour en revenir à la question ◆ **to ~ to type** (Bio) retourner or revenir au type primitif ◆ **he has ~ed to type** (fig) le naturel a repris le dessus 2 (= become again) **fields ~ing to woodland** des champs qui retournent à l'état de forêt

review /rɪˈvjuː/ N 1 [of situation, events, the past] examen m, bilan m ; [of wages, prices, contracts] révision f ; (= printed etc report) rapport m d'enquête ◆ **under ~** [salaries, policy] en cours de révision ◆ **the agreement comes up for ~** or **comes under ~ next year** l'accord doit être révisé l'année prochaine ◆ **I shall keep your case under ~** je suivrai votre cas de très près ◆ **he gave a ~ of recent developments in photography** il a passé en revue les progrès récents de la photographie

2 (Mil, Naut = inspection) revue f ◆ **to hold a ~** passer une revue

3 (US Scol etc = revision) révision f

4 (= critical article) [of book, film, play etc] critique f, compte rendu m ◆ **~ copy** [of book] exemplaire m de service de presse

5 (= magazine) revue f, périodique m

VT 1 (= consider again) [+ the past] passer en revue ; [+ one's life] passer en revue, faire le point sur ; [+ progress] faire le point sur ; [+ options] envisager ; [+ procedures] réviser ◆ **we shall ~ the situation next year** nous réexaminerons la situation l'année prochaine ◆ **the Supreme Court will ~ that decision** la Cour suprême réexaminera cette décision ◆ **to ~ the situation** réexaminer la situation

2 [+ troops] passer en revue

3 (US Scol etc) revoir, réviser

4 [+ book, play, film] faire la critique de, donner or faire un compte rendu de

COMP **review board** N commission f d'évaluation

review body N office m d'évaluation

reviewing stand N tribune f des officiels

review panel N ⇒ **review board**

reviewer /rɪˈvjuːəʳ/ N critique mf ◆ **book/film etc ~** critique mf littéraire/de cinéma etc

revile /rɪˈvaɪl/ VT honnir (liter), vilipender VI proférer des injures (at, against contre)

revise /rɪˈvaɪz/ VT 1 (= change) [+ opinion, estimate] réviser, modifier ◆ **to ~ sth upward(s)** réviser qch en hausse ◆ **to ~ sth downward(s)** réviser qch à la baisse 2 (= update) [+ text, dictionary etc] réviser ; (= correct) [+ proof] corriger, revoir ◆ **~d edition** édition f revue et corrigée ◆ **Revised Standard Version** [of Bible] traduction anglaise de la bible de 1953 ◆ **Revised Version** (Brit) [of Bible] traduction anglaise de la Bible de 1884 3 (Brit Scol) revoir, réviser VI (Brit Scol) réviser ◆ **to ~ for exams** réviser or faire des révisions pour des examens ◆ **to start revising** commencer à réviser or (à faire) ses révisions N (Typ) (épreuve f de) mise f en pages, seconde épreuve f

reviser /rɪˈvaɪzəʳ/ N [of text] réviseur m ; [of proof] correcteur m, -trice f

revision /rɪˈvɪʒən/ N révision f

revisionism /rɪˈvɪʒənɪzəm/ N révisionnisme m

revisionist /rɪˈvɪʒənɪst/ ADJ, N révisionniste mf

revisit /ˌriːˈvɪzɪt/ VT 1 (= study, discuss again) [+ issue] réexaminer ; [+ author, one's past] revisiter ; [+ book] relire ; [+ film] revoir 2 [+ place] revisiter ; [+ person] retourner voir

revitalization /riːˌvaɪtəlaɪˈzeɪʃən/ N [of area, industry etc] revitalisation f

revitalize /ˌriːˈvaɪtəlaɪz/ VT (gen) redonner de la vitalité à, revitaliser ◆ **to ~ the economy** revitaliser l'économie

revival /rɪˈvaɪvəl/ N 1 (= bringing back) [of custom, ceremony] reprise f ; [of interest] renouveau m, regain m ; [of movement] retour m en force ; (in sales) reprise f, relance f ; (Jur) remise f en vigueur 2 (Theat) [of play] reprise f ; (Rel) [of faith] renouveau m, réveil m ◆ **~ meeting** réunion f pour le renouveau de la foi

revivalism /rɪˈvaɪvəlɪzəm/ N (Rel) revivalisme m

revivalist /rɪˈvaɪvəlɪst/ ADJ, N revivaliste mf

revive /rɪˈvaɪv/ VT 1 [+ person] (from fainting) ranimer ; (from near death, esp Med) réanimer ◆ **a glass of brandy will ~ you** un verre de cognac vous remontera or vous requinquera 2 [+ fire, feeling, pain, memory] ranimer, raviver ; [+ conversation] ranimer ; [+ hope, interest] faire renaître, raviver ; [+ trade, business] relancer, réactiver ; [+ fashion] remettre en vogue ; [+ law] remettre en vigueur ; [+ custom, usage] rétablir ; [+ play] reprendre ◆ **to ~ sb's spirits** remonter le moral à qn VI [person] reprendre connaissance ; [hope, feelings] renaître ; [business, trade] reprendre

reviver /rɪˈvaɪvəʳ/ N (= drink) remontant m

revivify /ˌriːˈvɪvɪfaɪ/ VT revivifier (liter)

revocation /ˌrevəˈkeɪʃən/ N [of order, promise, edict] révocation f ; [of law, bill] abrogation f ; [of licence] retrait m ; [of decision] annulation f

revoke /rɪˈvəʊk/ VT [+ law] rapporter, abroger ; [+ order, edict] révoquer ; [+ promise] revenir sur, révoquer ; [+ decision] revenir sur, annuler ; [+ licence] retirer VI (Cards) faire une (fausse) renonce N (Cards) (fausse) renonce f

revolt /rɪˈvəʊlt/ N révolte f ◆ **to break out in ~, to rise in ~** se révolter, se soulever ◆ **to be in ~ (against)** se révolter or être révolté (contre) ; → stir¹ VI 1 (= rebel) se révolter, se soulever (against contre) 2 (= be disgusted) se révolter (at contre), être dégoûté (at par) VT révolter, dégoûter ◆ **to be ~ed by sth/sb** être révolté or dégoûté par qch/qn

revolting /rɪˈvəʊltɪŋ/ ADJ 1 (= repulsive, disgusting) dégoûtant, répugnant 2 (* = unpleasant) [weather, colour] épouvantable ; [dress] affreux

revoltingly /rɪˈvəʊltɪŋlɪ/ ADV ◆ **~ dirty** d'une saleté révoltante or repoussante ◆ **~ ugly** d'une laideur repoussante

revolution /ˌrevəˈluːʃən/ N 1 (= turn) [of planet] révolution f ; [of wheel] révolution f, tour m 2

(Pol etc = uprising) révolution *f*, coup *m* d'État ; *(fig)* révolution *f* ◆ **the French Revolution** *(Hist)* la Révolution française ◆ **a ~ in farming methods** une révolution dans les méthodes d'exploitation agricole ◆ **Industrial/Agricultural Revolution** *(Hist)* Révolution *f* industrielle/agricole

revolutionary /ˌrevəˈluːʃnərɪ/ ADJ, N *(lit, fig)* révolutionnaire *mf*

revolutionize /ˌrevəˈluːʃənaɪz/ VT révolutionner, transformer radicalement

revolve /rɪˈvɒlv/ VT *(lit)* faire tourner ◆ **to ~ a problem in one's mind** tourner et retourner un problème dans son esprit VI tourner ◆ **to ~ on an axis/around the sun** tourner sur un axe/autour du soleil ◆ **the discussion ~d around two topics** la discussion tournait autour de deux sujets ◆ **everything ~s around him** tout dépend de lui

revolver /rɪˈvɒlvəʳ/ N revolver *m*

revolving /rɪˈvɒlvɪŋ/ ADJ *[chair, bookcase, stand]* pivotant ; *[stage]* tournant ; *(Astron)* en rotation, qui tourne ; *(Tech)* rotatif, à rotation ◆ **~ light** *(gen)* feu *m* tournant, feu *m* à éclats ; *(on police car etc)* gyrophare *m*
COMP **revolving credit** N *(US)* crédit *m* documentaire renouvelable
revolving door N tambour *m* ◆ **the ~ door of senior executives** *(fig)* la valse* des cadres supérieurs ◆ **the ~ door between government and the private sector** les chassés-croisés *mpl* de personnel entre le service public et le secteur privé ◆ **the ~ door of the justice system** le cercle vicieux du système judiciaire
revolving presidency N présidence *f* tournante

revue /rɪˈvjuː/ N *(Theat)* *(satirical)* revue *f* ; *(spectacular)* revue *f*, spectacle *m* de music-hall ◆ **~ artist** artiste *mf* de music-hall

revulsion /rɪˈvʌlʃən/ N 1 *(= disgust)* écœurement *m*, répugnance *f* (at devant) 2 *(= sudden change)* revirement *m* ; *(= reaction)* réaction *f* *(against* contre)

reward /rɪˈwɔːd/ N récompense *f* ◆ **as a ~ for your honesty** en récompense de votre honnêteté ◆ **as (a) ~ for helping me** pour vous *(or le etc)* récompenser de m'avoir aidé ◆ **200 euros' ~** 200 € de récompense ◆ **to offer a ~** offrir une récompense ◆ **to reap the ~s** récolter les dividendes ◆ **high financial ~s** des avantages financiers conséquents VT récompenser *(for* de) ; *(with money)* récompenser, rémunérer *(for* de) ◆ **"finder will be rewarded"** "récompense à qui rapportera l'objet" ◆ **to ~ sb with a smile** remercier qn d'un sourire ◆ **to ~ attention/investigation** *(fig)* mériter de l'attention/des recherches

rewarding /rɪˈwɔːdɪŋ/ ADJ *(financially)* rémunérateur (-trice *f*) ; *(morally)* gratifiant ; *(mentally)* enrichissant ◆ **this is a very ~ book** c'est un livre très enrichissant ◆ **a ~ film** un film enrichissant ◆ **bringing up a child is exhausting but ~** élever un enfant est une occupation exténuante mais gratifiante

rewind /ˌriːˈwaɪnd/ (pret, ptp **rewound**) VT *[+ thread]* rebobiner, rembobiner ; *[+ film, ribbon, tape]* rembobiner ; *[+ watch]* remonter

rewinding /ˌriːˈwaɪndɪŋ/ N *[of film, tape, video, thread]* rembobinage *m* ; *[of clock, watch]* remontage *m*

rewire /ˌriːˈwaɪəʳ/ VT ◆ **to ~ a house** refaire l'installation électrique d'une maison ◆ **the house needs rewiring** l'installation électrique de la maison doit être refaite

reword /ˌriːˈwɜːd/ VT *[+ paragraph, question]* reformuler ; *[+ idea]* exprimer en d'autres termes

rework /ˌriːˈwɜːk/ VT retravailler ◆ **~ the choreography a bit** retravaillez un peu la chorégraphie ◆ **they have thoroughly ~ed the show twice** ils ont remanié le spectacle en profondeur à deux reprises ◆ **she later ~ed the idea for her first book** elle a repris l'idée en la modifiant dans son premier roman ◆ **see if you can ~ your schedule** essayez de revoir votre emploi du temps

rewound /ˌriːˈwaʊnd/ VB pt, ptp of **rewind**

rewritable /ˌriːˈraɪtəbl/ ADJ *[CD, disk]* réinscriptible, réenregistrable

rewrite /ˌriːˈraɪt/ (pret **rewrote**, ptp **rewritten**) VT *(gen)* récrire ; *(= rework)* remanier ; *(= copy)* recopier N * remaniement *m* COMP **rewrite rule, rewriting rule** N *(Gram)* règle *f* de réécriture

rewriter /ˌriːˈraɪtəʳ/ N *(US Press)* rewriter *m*, rédacteur-réviseur *m*

rewritten /ˌriːˈrɪtn/ VB ptp of **rewrite**

rewrote /ˌriːˈrəʊt/ VB pt of **rewrite**

Reykjavik /ˈreɪkjəviːk/ N Reykjavik

RGN /ˌɑːdʒiːˈen/ N (abbrev of **Registered General Nurse**) → **registered**

Rh N (abbrev of **rhesus**) Rh COMP **Rh factor** N facteur *m* Rhésus

rhapsodic /ræpˈsɒdɪk/ ADJ *(Mus)* *[passage, style]* r(h)apsodique ; *(fig = lyrical)* *[account, description, verse]* dithyrambique

rhapsodize /ˈræpsədaɪz/ VI s'extasier *(over, about* sur)

rhapsody /ˈræpsədɪ/ N *(Mus)* r(h)apsodie *f* ; *(fig)* éloge *m* dithyrambique ◆ **she went into rhapsodies over** *or* **about her trip to Florence** elle a parlé de son voyage à Florence en termes dithyrambiques ◆ **"Rhapsody in Blue"** *(Mus)* "Rhapsodie en bleu"

rhea /ˈriːə/ N nandou *m*

rheme /riːm/ N rhème *m*

Rhenish /ˈrenɪʃ/ ADJ *[wine]* du Rhin

rhenium /ˈriːnɪəm/ N rhénium *m*

rheostat /ˈriːəʊstæt/ N rhéostat *m*

rhesus /ˈriːsəs/ N rhésus *m*
COMP **rhesus baby** N enfant *mf* rhésus
rhesus factor N facteur *m* Rhésus
rhesus monkey N (singe *m*) rhésus *m*
rhesus negative ADJ rhésus négatif
rhesus positive ADJ rhésus positif

rhetic /ˈriːtɪk/ ADJ *(Ling)* rhétique

rhetoric /ˈretərɪk/ N rhétorique *f* ; *(pej)* discours *m* ; *(= art)* art *m* oratoire ◆ **the general's anti-Western ~** le discours anti-occidental du général

rhetorical /rɪˈtɒrɪkəl/ ADJ (de) rhétorique ; *[style]* ampoulé *(pej)* ◆ **~ question** question *f* de pure forme *or* purement rhétorique ◆ **he didn't answer her question, which had been ~ in any case** il n'a pas répondu à sa question, qui était de toute façon purement rhétorique

rhetorically /rɪˈtɒrɪkəlɪ/ ADV *[ask]* pour la forme ; *[speak, declaim]* en orateur

rhetorician /ˌretəˈrɪʃən/ N rhétoricien *m*, -ienne *f*, rhéteur *m* *(also pej)*

rheumatic /ruːˈmætɪk/ N *(= person)* rhumatisant(e) *m(f)* ADJ *[pain]* rhumatismal ; *[person]* rhumatisant, qui souffre de rhumatismes ; *[hands, fingers]* plein de rhumatismes COMP **rheumatic fever** N rhumatisme *m* articulaire aigu

rheumaticky * /ruːˈmætɪkɪ/ ADJ *[person]* rhumatisant ; *[hands, fingers]* plein de rhumatismes ; *[pain]* rhumatismal

rheumatics * /ruːˈmætɪks/ NPL rhumatismes *mpl*

rheumatism /ˈruːmətɪzəm/ N rhumatisme *m*

rheumatoid /ˈruːmətɔɪd/ ADJ ◆ **~ arthritis** polyarthrite *f* chronique évolutive, rhumatisme *m* chronique polyarticulaire

rheumatologist /ˌruːməˈtɒlədʒɪst/ N rhumatologue *mf*

rheumatology /ˌruːməˈtɒlədʒɪ/ N rhumatologie *f*

rheumy /ˈruːmɪ/ ADJ *(liter)* *[eyes]* chassieux *(frm)*

Rhine /raɪn/ N Rhin *m*

Rhineland /ˈraɪnlænd/ N ◆ **the ~** la Rhénanie

rhinestone /ˈraɪnstəʊn/ N diamant *m* fantaisie

rhinitis /raɪˈnaɪtɪs/ N *(Med)* rhinite *f*

rhino * /ˈraɪnəʊ/ N (pl **rhino** *or* **rhinoes**) abbrev of **rhinoceros**

rhinoceros /raɪˈnɒsərəs/ N (pl **rhinoceros** *or* **rhinoceroses**) rhinocéros *m*

rhizome /ˈraɪzəʊm/ N rhizome *m*

Rhode Island /ˈrəʊdˈaɪlənd/ N Rhode Island *m* ◆ **in ~** dans le Rhode Island

Rhodes /rəʊdz/ N *(Geog)* Rhodes *f* ◆ **in ~** à Rhodes

Rhodesia /rəʊˈdiːʒə/ N Rhodésie *f*

Rhodesian /rəʊˈdiːʒən/ ADJ rhodésien N Rhodésien *m*, -ienne *f*

rhodium /ˈrəʊdɪəm/ N rhodium *m*

rhododendron /ˌrəʊdəˈdendrən/ N rhododendron *m*

rhomb /rɒm/ N ⇒ **rhombus**

rhombi /ˈrɒmbaɪ/ NPL of **rhombus**

rhombic /ˈrɒmbɪk/ ADJ rhombique

rhomboid /ˈrɒmbɔɪd/ N rhomboïde *m* ADJ rhomboïdal

rhombus /ˈrɒmbəs/ N (pl **rhombuses** *or* **rhombi**) losange *m*, rhombe *m*

Rhône /rəʊn/ N Rhône *m*

rhubarb /ˈruːbɑːb/ N 1 *(= plant)* rhubarbe *f* 2 *(Theat)* **"rhubarb, rhubarb, rhubarb"** ≈ brouhaha *m* *(mot employé pour reconstituer un murmure de fond)* 3 *(US* * *= quarrel)* prise *f* de bec, éclats *mpl* de voix COMP *[jam]* de rhubarbe ; *[tart]* à la rhubarbe

rhyme /raɪm/ N 1 *(= identical sound)* rime *f* ◆ **for (the sake of) the ~** pour la rime ◆ **without ~ or reason** sans rime ni raison ◆ **there seems to be neither ~ nor reason to it** cela ne rime à rien, cela n'a ni rime ni raison 2 *(= poetry)* vers *mpl* ; *(= a poem)* poème *m* ◆ **in ~** en vers (rimés) ◆ **to put sth into ~** mettre qch en vers ; → **nursery** VT faire rimer *(with* avec) VI 1 *[word]* rimer *(with* avec) 2 *(pej = write verse)* faire de mauvais vers, rimailler *(pej)* COMP **rhyme scheme** N agencement *m* des rimes

rhymed /raɪmd/ ADJ rimé

rhymer /ˈraɪməʳ/, **rhymester** /ˈraɪmstəʳ/ N *(pej)* rimailleur *m*, -euse *f* *(pej)*

rhyming /ˈraɪmɪŋ/ ADJ qui rime
COMP **rhyming couplet** N *strophe composée de deux vers qui riment*
rhyming dictionary N dictionnaire *m* des rimes
rhyming game N jeu *m* de rimes
rhyming slang N *argot des Cockneys*

RHYMING SLANG

L'"argot rimé" est une forme d'argot utilisée par les Cockneys ; il consiste à remplacer un mot par une expression qui rime avec ce mot : par exemple, on dira "apples and pears" pour "stairs". Cette forme de langage est parfois difficile à comprendre, surtout lorsque la rime est supprimée ; ainsi, à la place de "butcher's hook" (pour "look"), les Cockneys vont simplement dire "butcher's", par exemple dans "let's take a butcher's" (jetons un coup d'œil). Certaines expressions de ce **rhyming slang** sont passées dans la langue courante et sont comprises par tous les Britanniques ; pour "use your head" (réfléchis un peu), on entendra ainsi "use your loaf", "loaf" étant une réduction de "loaf of bread" (pour "head").

rhythm /ˈrɪðəm/ N rythme *m* ◆ ~ **and blues** *(Mus)* rhythm and blues *m*
COMP **rhythm guitar** N guitare *f* rythmique
rhythm method N *[of contraception]* méthode *f* Ogino *or* des températures
rhythm section N *(Mus)* section *f* rythmique

rhythmic(al) /ˈrɪðmɪk(əl)/ ADJ *[movement, beat]* rythmique ; *[music]* rythmé, cadencé

rhythmically /ˈrɪðmɪkəlɪ/ ADV de façon rythmique, en rythme

RI /ɑːrˈaɪ/ N 1 (abbrev of **religious instruction**) → **religious** 2 abbrev of **Rhode Island**

rib /rɪb/ N 1 *(Anat, Culin)* côte *f* ◆ **true/false** ~ vraie/fausse côte *f* ; → **dig, floating, poke², stick** 2 *[of leaf, ceiling]* nervure *f* ; *[of ship]* membre *m*, membrure *f* ; *[of shell]* strie *f* ; *[of umbrella]* baleine *f* ; *[of knitting]* côte *f* VT (* = *tease)* taquiner, mettre en boîte *
COMP **rib cage** N cage *f* thoracique
rib roast N *(Culin)* côte *f* de bœuf
rib-tickler * N blague * *f*
rib-tickling * ADJ tordant *

ribald /ˈrɪbəld/ ADJ *[comment, joke]* grivois, égrillard ; *[laughter]* égrillard

ribaldry /ˈrɪbəldrɪ/ N (NonC) grivoiserie *f* ; (= *comments)* grivoiseries *fpl*

riband † /ˈrɪbənd/ N ⇒ **ribbon** ; → **blue**

ribbed /rɪbd/ ADJ *[cotton, sweater, socks]* à côtes ; *[shell]* strié ; *[ceiling]* à nervures

ribbing /ˈrɪbɪŋ/ N 1 *(NonC: Knitting)* côtes *fpl* 2 (* = *teasing)* **to give sb a** ~ taquiner qn ◆ **to get a** ~ se faire taquiner

ribbon /ˈrɪbən/ N 1 *[of dress, hair, typewriter, decoration]* ruban *m* ◆ **velvet** ~ ruban *m* de velours ; → **bunch** 2 ◆ **in** ~**s** (= *in tatters)* en lambeaux ◆ **to tear sth to** ~**s** *(lit)* mettre qch en lambeaux ; *(fig) [+ play etc]* éreinter qch COMP **ribbon development** N (NonC) croissance *f* urbaine linéaire *(le long des grands axes routiers)*

riboflavin /ˌraɪbəʊˈfleɪvɪn/ N riboflavine *f*

ribonucleic /ˈraɪbəʊnjuːˈkliːɪk/ ADJ ◆ ~ **acid** acide *m* ribonucléique

rice /raɪs/ N riz *m*
COMP **rice bowl** N (= *bowl)* bol *m* à riz ; (= *region)* région *f* rizicole
rice growing N riziculture *f*
rice-growing ADJ rizicole, producteur (-trice *f*) de riz
rice paper N papier *m* de riz
rice pudding N riz *m* au lait
rice wine N saké *m*

ricefield /ˈraɪsfiːld/ N rizière *f*

ricer /ˈraɪsəʳ/ N *(US Culin)* presse-purée *m inv*

rich /rɪtʃ/ ADJ 1 *(gen) [person, country, variety, life, soil, food, sound, colour]* riche ; *[smell]* riche, puissant ; *[tapestries]* riche, somptueux ; *[gift, clothes, banquet]* somptueux ; *[voice]* chaud, aux tonalités riches ; *[profit]* gros (grosse *f*) ; *[wine]* généreux ◆ ~ **people** les riches *mpl* ◆ ~ **and famous** riche et célèbre ◆ **to grow** *or* **get** ~**(er)** s'enrichir ◆ **to make sb** ~ enrichir qn ◆ **to get** ~ **quick** (*, *gen pej)* s'enrichir rapidement ; see also **get** ◆ **to be (all) the** ~**er for sth** gagner beaucoup à faire qch ◆ ~ **in minerals/vitamins/detail/history** *etc* riche en minéraux/vitamines/détails/histoire *etc* ◆ **the sauce was too** ~ **for me** j'ai trouvé la sauce écœurante ◆ **for** ~**er, for poorer** *(in marriage service)* ≈ pour le meilleur et pour le pire ; → **Croesus, picking**
2 (= *unreasonable)* ◆ **that's** ~**!** * c'est un peu fort !, elle est bonne, celle-là !
3 († = *funny) [humour, tale]* savoureux
N ◆ ~**es** richesse(s) *f(pl)*
NPL **the rich** les riches *mpl*
COMP **rich tea biscuit** N ≈ petit-beurre *m*

-rich /rɪtʃ/ ADJ *(in compounds)* ◆ **calcium-/protein-rich** riche en calcium/protéines ◆ **oil-rich** *[nation, region]* riche en pétrole

Richard /ˈrɪtʃəd/ N Richard *m* ◆ ~ **(the) Lionheart** Richard *m* Cœur de Lion

richly /ˈrɪtʃlɪ/ ADV *[decorated, flavoured, scented, coloured]* richement ; *[dressed]* richement, somptueusement ; *[illustrated]* abondamment ; *[deserved]* largement ; *[rewarded]* généreusement ; *[satisfying]* profondément ◆ **to be** ~ **endowed with courage/talent** avoir du courage/talent à revendre ◆ ~ **patterned** à riches motifs ◆ **a** ~ **rewarding experience** une expérience extrêmement enrichissante

richness /ˈrɪtʃnɪs/ N *[of person, life, culture, soil, voice, food, colour]* richesse *f* ; *[of tapestries]* richesse *f*, somptuosité *f* ; *[of gift, clothes, banquet]* somptuosité *f* ◆ ~ **in oil/vitamins** richesse *f* en pétrole/vitamines

Richter /ˈrɪxtəʳ/ N ◆ **the** ~ **scale** l'échelle *f* de Richter

rick¹ /rɪk/ N *(Agr)* meule *f (de foin etc)*

rick² /rɪk/ VT, N ⇒ **wrick**

rickets /ˈrɪkɪts/ N *(NonC)* rachitisme *m* ◆ **to have** ~ être rachitique

rickety /ˈrɪkɪtɪ/ ADJ *(Med)* rachitique ; *(fig) [building, fence, stairs]* branlant ; *[furniture]* bancal ; *[vehicle]* bringuebalant

rickey /ˈrɪkɪ/ N *(US) cocktail au citron vert*

rickrack /ˈrɪkræk/ N *(NonC: US)* ganse *f* en zigzag

rickshaw /ˈrɪkʃɔː/ N *(pulled by man)* pousse (-pousse) *m inv* ; *(pulled by bicycle etc)* rickshaw *m*

ricky-tick * /ˈrɪkɪtɪk/ ADJ *(US)* démodé, vieillot

ricochet /ˈrɪkəʃeɪ/ N ricochet *m* VI ricocher

ricotta /rɪˈkɒtə/ N ricotte *f*

rictus /ˈrɪktəs/ N (pl **rictus** *or* **rictuses**) rictus *m*

rid /rɪd/ (pret, ptp **rid** *or* **ridded**) VT *(of pests, disease)* débarrasser ; *(of bandits etc)* délivrer (of de) ◆ **to be** ~ **of sb/sth** être débarrassé de qn/qch
◆ **to get rid of, to rid o.s. of** *(frm) [+ spots, cold, cough, fleas, possessions, rubbish]* se débarrasser de ; *[+ habit, illusion, desire, tendency]* perdre, se défaire de ; *[+ fears, doubts]* perdre ; *[+ unwanted goods]* se débarrasser de, se défaire de ; *[+ boyfriend, girlfriend]* laisser tomber *, se débarrasser de ◆ **to get** ~ **of one's debts** liquider *or* régler ses dettes ◆ **the body gets** ~ **of waste** l'organisme élimine les déchets

riddance /ˈrɪdəns/ N débarras *m* ◆ **good** ~ **(to bad rubbish)!** * bon débarras ! *

ridden /ˈrɪdn/ VB ptp of **ride** ADJ ◆ ~ **by** tourmenté *or* hanté par ◆ ~ **by fears** hanté par la peur ◆ ~ **by remorse** tourmenté par le remords

-ridden /ˌrɪdn/ ADJ *(in compounds)* ◆ **disease-/guilt-/remorse-ridden** accablé par la maladie/la culpabilité/le remords ◆ **angst-/fear-ridden** tourmenté par l'angoisse/la peur ; → **debt, hag**

riddle¹ /ˈrɪdl/ N crible *m*, claie *f* VT 1 *[+ coal, soil etc]* cribler, passer au crible ; *[+ stove]* agiter la grille de 2 *[+ person, target]* cribler ◆ ~**d with holes/bullets** criblé de trous/balles ◆ **the council is** ~**d with corruption** la corruption règne au conseil ◆ **the committee is** ~**d with troublemakers** le comité grouille de provocateurs

riddle² /ˈrɪdl/ N (= *puzzle)* énigme *f*, devinette *f* ; (= *mystery)* énigme *f*, mystère *m* ◆ **to speak** *or* **talk in** ~**s** parler par énigmes ◆ **to ask sb a** ~ poser une devinette à qn

ride /raɪd/ (vb : pret **rode**, ptp **ridden**) N 1 (= *outing)* promenade *f*, tour *m* ; (= *distance covered)* trajet *m* ◆ **he gave the child a** ~ **on his back** il a promené l'enfant sur son dos ◆ **to go for a** ~ **in a car** faire un tour en voiture ◆ **he gave me a** ~ **into town in his car** il m'a emmené en ville dans sa voiture ◆ **it's my first** ~ **in a Rolls** c'est la première fois que je me promène *or* que je roule en Rolls ◆ **we went for a** ~ **in a train** nous avons fait un voyage en train ◆ **can I have a** ~ **on your bike?** est-ce que je peux emprunter ton vélo ? ◆ **to have a** ~ **in a helicopter** faire un tour en hélicoptère ◆ **we got a** ~ **in a taxi** nous avons pris un taxi ◆ **it was the taxi** ~ **they liked best** c'est le tour en taxi qu'ils ont préféré ◆ **bike** ~ tour *m or* promenade *f* à vélo ◆ **car** ~ tour *m* en voiture ◆ **coach** ~ tour *m or* excursion *f* en car ◆ **it's a short taxi** ~ **to the airport** ce n'est pas loin en taxi jusqu'à l'aéroport ◆ **he has a long (car/bus)** ~ **to work** il a un long trajet (en voiture/en autobus) jusqu'à son lieu de travail ◆ **it's only a short** ~ **by bus/coach/train/car/taxi** il n'y en a pas pour longtemps *or* c'est tout près en bus/en car/en train/en voiture/en taxi ◆ **it's a 60p** ~ **from the station** le trajet depuis la gare coûte 60 pence ◆ **three** ~**s on the merry-go-round** trois tours de manège ◆ **to steal a** ~ voyager sans billet *or* sans payer ◆ **I just came along for the** ~ *(fig)* je suis venu pour voir ◆ **to take sb for a** ~ *(in car etc)* emmener qn faire un tour ; *(fig)* (= *make fool of)* faire marcher qn *, mener qn en bateau * ; (= *swindle)* rouler qn *, posséder qn * ; *(US * euph = kill)* emmener qn faire un tour ; → **joy-ride, Valkyrie**
2 *(on horseback)* promenade *f or* tour *m* à cheval ; (= *long journey)* chevauchée *f* ◆ **after a hard** ~ **across country** après une chevauchée pénible à travers la campagne
3 *(at fairground)* tour *m* ◆ **a** ~ **on the rollercoaster** un tour de montagnes russes
4 * *(fig)* ◆ **motherhood was no easy** ~ la maternité n'était pas facile à assumer ◆ **he faces a rough** ~ **from the media** il risque de se faire malmener par les médias ◆ **he was given a rough** ~ **over his remarks about the homeless** on lui a fait payer ses remarques sur les SDF ◆ **the company has not had a smooth** *or* **an easy** ~ **lately** tout n'a pas été rose pour l'entreprise ces derniers temps, l'entreprise a eu sa part d'ennuis ces derniers temps
5 (= *path for horses)* allée *f* cavalière
6 *(Horse-riding = mount)* ◆ **Castilian Queen is a difficult** ~ Castilian Queen est difficile à monter
VI 1 (= *ride a horse)* monter à cheval, faire du cheval ◆ **can you** ~**?** savez-vous monter à cheval ? ◆ **she** ~**s a lot** elle fait beaucoup d'équitation ◆ **he has ridden since childhood** il monte à cheval *or* il fait de l'équitation depuis son enfance ◆ **she learnt to** ~ **on Oscar** elle a appris à monter (à cheval) sur Oscar ◆ **to go riding** faire du cheval, monter à cheval ◆ **to** ~ **astride/sidesaddle** monter à califourchon/en amazone ◆ **he** ~**s well** il est bon cavalier ◆ **the**

jockey was riding just under 65 kilos (en tenue) le jockey pesait un peu moins de 65 kilos ; → **hound**

[2] *(= go on horseback/by bicycle/by motorcycle)* aller à cheval/à bicyclette/à *or* en moto ◆ **to ~ down/away** *etc* descendre/s'éloigner *etc* à cheval (*or* à bicyclette *or* à *or* en moto *etc*) ◆ **he stopped then rode on** il s'est arrêté puis a repris sa route ◆ **they had ridden all day** ils avaient passé toute la journée à cheval *or* en selle ◆ **he rode to London** il est allé à Londres à cheval (*or* à bicyclette *etc*) ◆ **he was riding on a bicycle/a camel** il était à bicyclette/à dos de chameau ◆ **the child was riding on his father's back** le père portait l'enfant sur son dos ◆ **he was riding on his mother's shoulders** sa mère le portait sur ses épaules ◆ **the witch was riding on a broomstick** la sorcière était à cheval *or* à califourchon sur un balai ◆ **they were riding on a bus/in a car/in a train** ils étaient en autobus/en voiture/en train ◆ **they rode in a bus to …** ils sont allés en bus à … ◆ **she ~s to work on a bike** elle va au travail à bicyclette ◆ **the seagull ~s on the wind** *(fig liter)* la mouette est portée par le vent ◆ **the moon was riding high in the sky** la lune voguait haut dans le ciel ◆ **he's riding high** *(fig)* il a le vent en poupe ◆ **he was riding high in public opinion** il avait la cote (auprès du public) ◆ **he was riding high on his latest success** tout baignait* pour lui après son dernier succès ◆ **we'll just have to let the matter** *or* **to let things ~ for a while** nous allons devoir laisser l'affaire suivre son cours *or* laisser courir* pendant un certain temps ◆ **she had to let things ~** elle a dû laisser courir* ; → **anchor, fall, roughshod, punch¹, shank**

[3] **to ~ well** *[horse]* être une bonne monture

[4] *(Tech etc) (= overlap)* chevaucher ; *(= work out of place)* travailler

VT [1] ◆ **to ~ a horse** monter à cheval ◆ **have you ever ridden a horse?** êtes-vous déjà monté à cheval ? ◆ **I have never ridden Flash** je n'ai jamais monté Flash ◆ **he rode Cass at Newmarket** il montait Cass à Newmarket ◆ **he rode Buster into town** il a pris Buster pour aller en ville, il est allé en ville sur Buster ◆ **Jason will be ridden by J. Bean** Jason sera monté par J. Bean ◆ **he rode his horse straight at me** il a dirigé son cheval droit sur moi ◆ **he rode his horse up the stairs** il a fait monter l'escalier à son cheval ◆ **he rode his horse away/back** *etc* il est parti/revenu *etc* à cheval ◆ **to ~ two horses at the same time** *(Brit fig)* courir deux lièvres à la fois ◆ **he ~s his pony to school** il va à l'école à dos de poney ◆ **have you ever ridden a donkey/camel?** êtes-vous déjà monté à dos d'âne/de chameau ? ◆ **he was riding a donkey** il était à dos d'âne ◆ **he was riding a motorbike** il était à *or* en moto ◆ **he rode his motorbike to the station** il est allé à la gare à *or* en moto ◆ **I have never ridden a bike/a motorbike** je ne suis jamais monté à vélo/à moto ◆ **can I ~ your bike?** est-ce que je peux emprunter ton vélo ? ◆ **he was riding a bicycle** il était à bicyclette ◆ **he rode his cycle into town** il est allé en ville à bicyclette ◆ **he always ~s a bicycle** il va partout à *or* il se déplace toujours à bicyclette ◆ **witches ~ broomsticks** les sorcières chevauchent des balais ◆ **she was riding a broomstick** elle était à cheval *or* à califourchon sur un balai ◆ **they had ridden 10km** ils avaient fait 10 km à cheval (*or* à bicyclette *or* à *or* en moto *etc*) ◆ **they had ridden all the way** ils avaient fait tout le trajet à cheval (*or* à bicyclette *etc*) ◆ **he rode the country looking for …** il a parcouru le pays à la recherche de … ◆ **to ~ sb on a rail** *(US)* expulser qn de la ville *(en l'emmenant à califourchon sur un poteau)* ◆ **the birds rode the wind** *(fig)* les oiseaux se laissaient porter par le vent ◆ **the ship rode the waves** *(liter)* le bateau voguait sur les vagues ◆ **he's riding (on) a wave of personal popularity** il jouit d'une excellente cote de popularité ; see also **ride on** ; → **herd, race¹**

[2] *(esp US * = nag etc)* être toujours sur le dos de*, ne pas ficher la paix à* *(about* au sujet de) ◆ **don't ~ him too hard** ne soyez pas trop dur avec lui

► **ride about, ride around** VI se déplacer *or* faire un tour (à cheval *or* à bicyclette *or* en voiture *etc*)

► **ride behind** VI *(on same horse)* monter en croupe ; *(on motorcycle)* monter derrière *or* en croupe ; *(in car)* être assis à l'arrière ; *(different horse, motorcycle, car)* être derrière

► **ride down** VT SEP [1] *(= trample)* renverser, piétiner

[2] *(= catch up with)* rattraper

► **ride on** VT FUS dépendre de ◆ **billions of dollars are riding on the outcome of the election** de l'issue des élections dépendent des milliards de dollars ◆ **his reputation's riding on the outcome of the trial** sa réputation dépend de l'issue du procès, c'est sa réputation qui est en jeu dans ce procès

► **ride out** VI sortir (à cheval *or* à bicyclette *etc*)

VT SEP *(fig)* surmonter ◆ **to ~ out the storm** *(Naut)* étaler la tempête ; *(fig)* surmonter la crise ◆ **to ~ out a difficult time** se tirer d'une *or* surmonter une mauvaise passe ◆ **the company managed to ~ out the depression** la société a réussi à survivre à la dépression

► **ride up** VI [1] *[horseman, cyclist etc]* arriver

[2] *[skirt, trousers]* remonter ◆ **her underskirt had ridden up (a)round her hips** son jupon lui était remonté sur les hanches

rider /ˈraɪdəʳ/ N [1] *(= person) [of horse]* cavalier *m*, -ière *f* ; *[of racehorse]* jockey *m* ; *[of circus horse]* écuyer *m*, -ère *f* ; *[of bicycle]* cycliste *mf* ; *[of motorcycle]* motocycliste *mf* ◆ **a good ~** un bon cavalier, une bonne cavalière ; → **dispatch, outrider** [2] *(= addition: to document)* annexe *f* ; *(to bill)* clause *f* additionnelle ; *(to insurance policy, jury's verdict)* avenant *m* ◆ **the committee added a ~ condemning …** la commission ajouta une clause condamnant …

ridesharing /ˈraɪdʃɛərɪŋ/ N *(US)* covoiturage *m*

ridge /rɪdʒ/ N [1] *(= top of a line of hills or mountains)* arête *f*, crête *f* ; *(= extended top of a hill)* faîte *m* ; *(= ledge on hillside)* corniche *f* ; *(= chain of hills, mountains)* chaîne *f* ; *(in sea = reef)* récif *m* [2] *(of roof, on nose)* arête *f* ; *(on sand)* ride *f* ; *(in ploughed land)* billon *m* ; *(on cliff, rock face)* strie *f* ◆ **a ~ of high pressure** une ligne de hautes pressions ◆ **~ and furrow (formation)** *(Agr)* crêtes *fpl* de labours ; → **alveolar** VT *[+ roof]* enfaîter ; *[+ earth]* billonner ; *[+ rock face]* strier ; *[+ sand]* rider

COMP **ridge piece, ridge pole** N poutre *f* de faîte *m*, faîtage *m*

ridge tent N tente *f* (à toit en arête)

ridge tile N (tuile *f*) faîtière *f*, enfaîteau *m*

ridge way N chemin *m or* route *f* de crête

ridicule /ˈrɪdɪkjuːl/ N raillerie *f*, ridicule *m* ◆ **to hold sb/sth up to ~** tourner qn/qch en ridicule *or* en dérision ◆ **to lay o.s. open to ~** s'exposer aux railleries ◆ **she's an object of ~** elle est un objet de risée VT ridiculiser, tourner en ridicule *or* en dérision

ridiculous /rɪˈdɪkjʊləs/ ADJ ridicule ◆ **she was made to look ~** elle a été ridiculisée ◆ **to make o.s. (look) ~** se rendre ridicule, se ridiculiser ◆ **to take things to ~ extremes** pousser les choses trop loin ◆ **to go to ~ lengths** trop en faire ◆ **to go to ~ lengths to do sth** se ridiculiser à force de faire qch ; → **sublime**

ridiculously /rɪˈdɪkjʊləslɪ/ ADV ridiculement ◆ **~, he blamed himself for the accident** il se sentait responsable de l'accident, ce qui est ridicule

ridiculousness /rɪˈdɪkjʊləsnɪs/ N ridicule *m*

riding /ˈraɪdɪŋ/ N (also **horse-riding**) équitation *f* ; *(= horsemanship)* monte *f*

COMP **riding boots** NPL bottes *fpl* de cheval

riding breeches NPL culotte *f* de cheval

riding crop N ⇒ **riding whip**

riding habit N habit *m or* tenue *f* d'amazone

riding jacket N veste *f* de cheval *or* d'équitation

riding master N professeur *m* d'équitation

riding school N manège *m*, école *f* d'équitation

riding stable(s) N(PL) centre *m* d'équitation, manège *m*

riding whip N cravache *f*

rife /raɪf/ ADJ ◆ **to be ~** *[disease, racism, crime, unemployment]* sévir ◆ **rumours are/speculation is ~ (that)** les rumeurs/les spéculations vont bon train (comme quoi) ◆ **corruption is ~** la corruption est monnaie courante

◆ **rife with** ◆ **a city ~ with violence** une ville en proie à la violence, une ville où sévit la violence ◆ **the whole company is ~ with corruption/jealousy** la corruption/jalousie sévit dans toute l'entreprise ◆ **the media is ~ with rumours/speculation** les rumeurs/spéculations vont bon train dans les médias

riff /rɪf/ N *(Mus)* riff *m*

riffle /ˈrɪfl/ VT (also **riffle through**) *[+ pages, papers]* feuilleter rapidement, parcourir

riffraff /ˈrɪfˌræf/ N racaille *f*

rifle¹ /ˈraɪfl/ VT *[+ town]* piller ; *[+ tomb]* violer ; *[+ drawer, till]* vider ; *[+ house]* dévaliser, vider ◆ **to ~ sb's pockets** faire les poches à qn ◆ **she ~d through the papers** elle feuilletait rapidement les documents

rifle² /ˈraɪfl/ N *(= gun)* fusil *m* (rayé) ; *(for hunting)* carabine *f* de chasse ◆ **the Rifles** *(Mil)* ≈ les chasseurs *mpl* à pied, (le régiment de) l'infanterie *f* légère

COMP **rifle butt** N crosse *f* de fusil

rifle range N *(outdoor)* champ *m* de tir ; *(indoor)* stand *m* de tir ◆ **within ~ range** à portée de fusil

rifle shot N coup *m* de fusil ; *(= marksman)* tireur *m* ◆ **within ~ shot** à portée de fusil

rifleman /ˈraɪflmən/ N (pl **-men**) fusilier *m*

rift /rɪft/ N [1] *(lit)* fissure *f* ; *(deeper)* crevasse *f* ; *(in clouds)* trouée *f* [2] *(fig = disagreement)* désaccord *m* ; *(Pol) (in party)* division *f* ; *(in cabinet, group)* division *f*, désaccord *m* ◆ **this caused a ~ in their friendship** ceci a causé une faille dans leur amitié ◆ **the ~ between them was widening** ils s'éloignaient de plus en plus l'un de l'autre COMP **rift valley** N *(Geol)* graben *m*

rig /rɪg/ N [1] *(Naut)* gréement *m* [2] (also **oil rig**) *(on land)* derrick *m* ; *(at sea:* also **floating rig**) plateforme *f* (pétrolière) flottante [3] *(* = outfit:* also **rig out**) tenue *f*, accoutrement *m (pej)* [4] *(US = tractor-trailer)* semi-remorque *m* VT [1] *(Naut)* gréer [2] *(= fix dishonestly) [+ election, competition, game]* truquer ; *[+ prices]* fixer illégalement ◆ **it was ~ged** c'était un coup monté ◆ **to ~ the market** *(Stock Exchange)* manipuler le marché, provoquer une hausse (*or* une baisse) factice dans les cours VI *(Naut)* être gréé

► **rig out** VT SEP *(= clothe)* habiller *(with* de ; *as* en)

► **rig up** VT *[+ boat]* gréer ; *(with mast)* mâter ; *[+ equipment]* monter, installer ; *(fig) (= make hastily)* faire avec des moyens de fortune *or* avec les moyens du bord ; *(= arrange)* arranger

rigger /ˈrɪgəʳ/ N [1] *(for ship)* gréeur *m* ; *(for plane)* monteur-régleur *m* [2] *(on Stock Exchange)* agioteur *m*, manipulateur *m*

rigging /ˈrɪgɪŋ/ N [1] *(Naut) (= ropes etc)* gréement *m* ; *(= action)* gréage *m* [2] *(US = clothes)* vêtements *mpl*, fringues** *fpl* [3] *(* = dishonest interference) [of election, competition]* truquage *m* ; *[of prices]* fixation *f* illégale ; *(on Stock Exchange)* agiotage *m* manipulation *f*

right /raɪt/

LANGUAGE IN USE 11, 13, 26.3

1 ADJECTIVE	4 PLURAL NOUN
2 ADVERB	5 TRANSITIVE VERB
3 NOUN	6 COMPOUNDS

1 - ADJECTIVE

1 [= morally good] bien *inv* ◆ **it isn't ~ to lie, lying isn't ~** ce n'est pas bien de mentir ◆ **it's not ~, leaving her like this** ce n'est pas bien de la laisser comme ça ◆ **I have always tried to do what was ~** j'ai toujours essayé de bien agir ◆ **to do what is ~ by sb** agir pour le bien de qn ◆ **you were ~ to refuse** vous avez bien fait de *or* vous avez eu raison de refuser ◆ **he thought it ~ to warn me** il a cru *or* jugé bon de m'avertir ◆ **would it be ~ to tell him?** est-ce que ce serait une bonne chose de le lui dire ? ◆ **to do the ~ thing by sb** bien agir *or* agir honorablement envers qn

◆ **only right** ◆ **it seemed only ~ to give him the money** il paraissait normal de lui donner l'argent ◆ **it is only ~ for her to go** *or* **that she should go** il n'est que juste qu'elle y aille ◆ **it is only ~ to point out that ...** il faut néanmoins signaler que ... ◆ **that's only ~ and proper!** ce n'est que justice !, c'est bien le moins ! ◆ **it's only ~ and proper that ...** il n'est que juste que ... (+ *subj*)

2 [= accurate] juste, exact ◆ **that's ~** c'est juste, c'est exact ◆ **that can't be ~!** ce n'est pas possible ! ◆ **is that ~?** *(checking)* c'est bien ça ? ; *(expressing surprise)* vraiment ? ◆ **the ~ time** *(by the clock)* l'heure exacte *or* juste ; see also **adjective 3** ◆ **is the clock ~?** est-ce que la pendule est à l'heure ? ◆ **my guess was ~** j'avais deviné juste

◆ **to be right** *[person]* avoir raison ◆ **you're quite ~** vous avez parfaitement raison ◆ **how ~ you are!*** je suis entièrement d'accord avec vous !, et comment !*

◆ **to get sth right** ◆ **I got all the answers ~** j'ai répondu juste à toutes les questions ◆ **to get one's sums ~** ne pas se tromper dans ses calculs ◆ **to get one's facts ~** ne pas se tromper ◆ **let's get it ~ this time!** cette fois-ci, il s'agit de ne pas nous tromper !

◆ **to put** *or* **set right** *[+ error]* corriger, rectifier ; *[+ situation]* redresser ; *[+ clock]* remettre à l'heure ; *[+ sth broken]* réparer, remettre en état ◆ **that can easily be put ~** on peut (facilement) arranger ça ◆ **I tried to put things ~ after their quarrel** j'ai essayé d'arranger les choses après leur dispute ◆ **the plumber came and put things ~** le plombier est venu et a fait les réparations nécessaires

◆ **to put** *or* **set sb right** *(= correct)* corriger qn ; *(= disabuse)* détromper qn ; *(= cure)* guérir qn ◆ **the medicine soon put** *or* **set him ~** ce médicament l'a vite guéri ◆ **put me ~ if I'm wrong** corrigez-moi si je me trompe

3 [= correct] bon *(before noun)* ◆ **the ~ answer** la bonne réponse ◆ **it is just the ~ size** c'est la bonne taille ◆ **on the ~ road** *(lit)* sur le bon chemin ◆ **is this the ~ road for Lyons?** est-ce que c'est bien la route de Lyon *or* la bonne route pour Lyon ? ◆ **on the ~ road, on the ~ track** *(fig)* sur la bonne voie ◆ **to come at the ~ time** arriver au bon moment, bien tomber ◆ **to do sth at the ~ time** faire qch au bon moment ◆ **the ~ word** le mot juste ◆ **she is on the ~ side of forty** elle n'a pas encore quarante ans ◆ **to get on the ~ side of sb*** s'attirer les bonnes grâces de qn ◆ **to know the ~ people** avoir des relations ◆ **your assumption was ~** tu avais vu juste

4 [= best] meilleur (-eure *f*) ◆ **what's the ~ thing to do?** quelle est la meilleure chose à faire ? ◆ **I don't know what's the ~ thing to do** je ne sais pas ce qu'il faut faire *or* ce qu'il convient de faire ◆ **we will do what is ~ for the country** nous ferons ce qui est dans l'intérêt du pays ◆ **the ~ man for the job** l'homme de la situation, l'homme qu'il nous (*or* leur *etc*) faut

5 [= necessary] ◆ **I haven't got the ~ papers with me** je n'ai pas les documents nécessaires sur moi ◆ **I didn't have the ~ books for the course** je n'avais pas les livres qu'il fallait pour ce cours

6 [= proper] ◆ **to do sth the ~ way** faire qch comme il faut ◆ **that is the ~ way of looking at it** c'est bien ainsi qu'il faut aborder la question ◆ **she wasn't wearing the ~ clothes** *(socially inappropriate)* elle n'avait pas la tenue requise, elle n'était pas habillée comme il fallait ◆ **if you go hiking you must wear the ~ shoes** lorsque l'on fait de la randonnée, il faut porter des chaussures adaptées

7 [= in proper state] *[person]* guéri, rétabli ; *[part of body]* guéri ◆ **David's ankle is still not ~** la cheville de David n'est pas encore guérie ◆ **I don't feel quite ~ today** je ne me sens pas très bien *or* pas dans mon assiette aujourd'hui ◆ **the brakes aren't ~** les freins ne fonctionnent pas bien, il y a quelque chose qui cloche dans les freins ◆ **to be in one's ~ mind** avoir toute sa raison ◆ **he's not ~ in the head*** il déraille* ◆ **to be as ~ as rain*** *(Brit: after illness)* se porter comme un charme ; → **all right**

8 [= real : esp Brit*] ◆ **it's a ~ mess in there** c'est la pagaille* complète là-dedans ◆ **I felt a ~ fool** je me suis senti complètement idiot ◆ **she gave them a ~ telling off** elle les a enguirlandés* quelque chose de bien

9 [agreeing, confirming etc] ~!, ~ **you are!*** d'accord !, entendu ! ◆ **~ on!‡ (approvingly)** c'est ça ! ◆ **~, who's next?** bon, c'est à qui le tour ? ◆ **(oh) ~!* (= I see)** ah, d'accord ! ◆ **she was the last to leave, ~?** elle est partie la dernière, c'est bien ça ? ◆ **too ~!** et comment !

◆ **right enough** ◆ **it was him ~ enough!** c'était bien lui, aucun doute là-dessus !

10 [= opposite of left] droit ◆ **~ hand** main *f* droite ◆ **on my ~ hand you see the bridge** sur ma droite vous voyez le pont ◆ **it's a case of the ~ hand not knowing what the left hand's doing** il y a un manque total de communication et de coordination ; see also **compounds** ◆ **I'd give my ~ arm to know the truth** je donnerais n'importe quoi pour connaître la vérité

2 - ADVERB

1 [= straight, directly] droit ◆ **~ ahead of you** droit devant vous ◆ **~ in front of you** sous vos yeux ◆ **the blow hit me ~ in the face** j'ai reçu le coup en pleine figure ◆ **~ behind you** *(gen)* juste derrière vous ◆ **you'll have the wind ~ behind you** vous aurez le vent dans le dos ◆ **public opinion would be ~ behind them** ils auraient l'opinion publique pour eux ◆ **go ~ on** continuez tout droit ◆ **I'll be ~ back** je reviens tout de suite

◆ **right away** *(= immediately)* tout de suite, sur-le-champ ; *(= at the first attempt)* du premier coup

◆ **right off*** du premier coup

2 [= exactly] ◆ **~ then** sur-le-champ ◆ **I had to decide ~ then** j'ai dû décider sur-le-champ ◆ **~ now** *(= at the moment)* en ce moment ; *(= at once)* tout de suite ◆ **~ here** ici même ◆ **~ in the middle** au beau milieu, en plein milieu ◆ **~ at the start** au tout début ◆ **from the start** dès le début

3 [= completely, all the way] tout ◆ **~ round the house** tout autour de la maison ◆ **to fall ~ to the bottom** tomber tout au fond ◆ **~ (up) against the wall** tout contre le mur ◆ **~ at the top of the mountain** tout en haut de la montagne ◆ **~ at the back, ~ at the bottom** tout au fond ◆ **pierced ~ through** transpercé *or* percé de part en part ◆ **to turn ~ round** se retourner, faire volte-face ◆ **push it ~ in** enfoncez-le complètement ◆ **he's ~ up there** *(in race)* il est en tête

4 [= correctly, well] bien ◆ **you haven't put the lid on ~** tu n'as pas bien mis le couvercle ◆ **if I remember ~** si je me souviens bien ◆ **to guess ~** deviner juste ◆ **to answer ~** répondre correctement, bien répondre ◆ **you did ~ to refuse** vous avez bien fait *or* eu raison de refuser ◆ **if everything goes ~** si tout va bien ◆ **nothing goes ~ for them** rien ne leur réussit ◆ **if I get you ~*** si je vous comprends bien

5 [†, dial = very] très ◆ **she's doing ~ well** elle va très bien

6 [= opposite of left] à droite ◆ **to look ~** regarder à droite ◆ **the party has now moved ~ of centre** le parti se situe maintenant à la droite du centre, c'est devenu un parti de centre droit ◆ **eyes ~!** *(Mil)* tête droite ! ◆ **~ about turn!** *(Mil)* demi-tour *m* (à) droite !

◆ **right and left** *(= on every side)* ◆ **to be cheated ~ and left** se faire avoir* par tout le monde ◆ **to owe money ~ and left** devoir de l'argent à tout le monde

◆ **right, left and centre*** *(= everywhere)* partout, de tous côtés

3 - NOUN

1 [= moral] bien *m* ◆ **he doesn't know ~ from wrong** il ne sait pas discerner le bien du mal ◆ **to be in the ~** avoir raison, être dans le vrai ◆ **to know the ~s and wrongs of a question** connaître les tenants et les aboutissants d'une question

2 [= entitlement] droit *m* ◆ **by ~** de droit ◆ **to have a ~ to sth** avoir droit à qch ◆ **to have a** *or* **the ~ to do sth** avoir le droit de faire qch ◆ **he has no ~ to sit here** il n'a pas le droit de s'asseoir ici ◆ **what ~ have you to say that?** de quel droit dites-vous cela ? ◆ **by what ~?** de quel droit ? ◆ **he has no ~ to the money** il n'a pas droit à cet argent ◆ **he is within his ~s** il est dans son droit ◆ **I know my ~s** je connais mes droits ◆ **to stand on** *or* **assert one's ~s** faire valoir ses droits ◆ **I won't stand on my ~ to do so** je ne ferai pas valoir mon droit à le faire ◆ **women's ~s** les droits *mpl* de la femme *or* des femmes ◆ **women's ~s movement** mouvement *m* pour les droits de la femme ◆ **~ of appeal** *(Jur)* droit *m* d'appel ; see also **plural noun**

◆ **by rights** en toute justice

◆ **in one's own right** ◆ **Taiwan wants membership in its own ~** Taïwan veut adhérer indépendamment ◆ **she's a poet in her own ~** elle est elle-même poète

3 [= opposite of left] droite *f* ◆ **to drive on the ~** conduire à droite ◆ **to keep to the ~** tenir la *or* sa droite, serrer à droite ◆ **on my ~** à ma droite ◆ **on** *or* **to the ~ of the church** à droite de l'église ◆ **by the ~, march!** *(Mil)* à droite, droite ! ◆ **to take a ~** *(US)* tourner à droite ◆ **the Right** *(Pol)* la droite

4 [Boxing] droite *f*

4 - PLURAL NOUN

rights

1 [Comm] droits *mpl* ◆ **manufacturing/publication ~s** droits *mpl* de fabrication/publication ◆ **TV/film ~s** droits *mpl* d'adaptation pour la télévision/le cinéma ◆ **"all rights reserved"** "tous droits réservés" ◆ **to have the (sole) ~s of** *or* **to sth** avoir les droits (exclusifs) de qch

2 [= proper state] ◆ **to put** *or* **set sth to ~s** mettre qch en ordre ◆ **to put the world** *or* **things to ~s** refaire le monde

3 [set phrase] ◆ **to have sb bang** *or* **dead to ~s*** *(= have evidence against sb)* avoir coincé* qn ; *(= understand sb well)* avoir bien cerné qn

5 - TRANSITIVE VERB

1 = return to normal [+ car, ship] redresser ♦ **the car ~ed itself** la voiture s'est redressée (toute seule) ♦ **the problem should ~ itself** le problème devrait s'arranger tout seul *or* se résoudre de lui-même
2 = make amends for [+ wrong] redresser ; [+ injustice] réparer

6 - COMPOUNDS

right angle N angle *m* droit ♦ **to be at ~ angles (to)** être perpendiculaire à
right-angled ADJ à angle droit
right-angled triangle N triangle *m* rectangle
right-click (Comput) VI cliquer à droite VT cliquer à droite sur
right-hand ADJ ♦ **~-hand drive car** voiture *f* avec (la) conduite à droite ♦ **his ~-hand man** son bras droit (*fig*) ♦ **the ~-hand side** le côté droit
right-handed ADJ [person] droitier ; [punch, throw] du droit ; [screw] fileté à droite ; [scissors, tin-opener etc] pour droitiers
right-hander N (Motor Racing) virage *m* à droite ; (Boxing) droite *f* ; (= person) droitier *m*, -ière *f*
right-ho * EXCL ⇒ **righto**
Right Honourable ADJ (Brit) le Très Honorable
right-minded ADJ ⇒ **right-thinking**
right-of-centre ADJ (Pol) (de) centre droit
right of way N (across property) droit *m* de passage ; (= priority for driver) priorité *f* ♦ **it's his ~ of way** c'est lui qui a la priorité ♦ **he has (the) ~ of way** il a la priorité
right-oh EXCL ⇒ **righto**
right-on * ADJ vertueux
rights issue N (Stock Exchange) émission *f* de droits de souscription
right-thinking ADJ sensé
right-to-life ADJ [movement, group] (gen) pour le droit à la vie ; (anti-abortion) antiavortement *inv*
right-to-lifer N (US) adversaire *mf* de l'avortement
right triangle N (US) ⇒ **right-angled triangle**
right whale N baleine *f* franche
right wing N (Sport) ailier *m* droit ; (Pol) droite *f* ♦ **the ~ wing of the party** l'aile droite du parti
right-wing ADJ (Pol) de droite ♦ **to be ~-wing** être de droite
right-winger N (Pol) homme *m* or femme *f* de droite ; (Sport) ailier *m* droit

righteous /ˈraɪtʃəs/ ADJ 1 (frm) (= virtuous) vertueux ; (= honest) droit, intègre 2 (= self-righteous: esp pej) [person, manner, tone, article] moralisateur (-trice *f*) ; [indignation, anger] justifié ♦ **stop being so ~!** cesse de faire la morale ! ; → **self** NPL **the righteous** (Bible) les justes *mpl*

righteously /ˈraɪtʃəslɪ/ ADV vertueusement

righteousness /ˈraɪtʃəsnɪs/ N droiture *f*, vertu *f*

rightful /ˈraɪtfʊl/ ADJ [owner, heir, inheritance, position, claim] légitime ♦ **one day all minorities will take their ~ place in society** un jour, toutes les minorités obtiendront la place qui leur revient dans la société ♦ **~ claimant** ayant droit *m*

rightfully /ˈraɪtfəlɪ/ ADV légitimement ♦ **we demand only what is ~ ours** nous n'exigeons que ce qui nous appartient légitimement

rightism /ˈraɪtɪzəm/ N droitisme *m*, opinions *fpl* de droite

rightist /ˈraɪtɪst/ (Pol) N homme *m* or femme *f* de droite ADJ de droite

rightly /ˈraɪtlɪ/ LANGUAGE IN USE 13, 26.3 ADV 1 (= correctly) bien, avec raison ♦ **he ~ assumed that ...** il supposait avec raison que ... ♦ **she hoped she'd chosen ~** elle espérait qu'elle avait bien choisi *or* qu'elle avait fait le bon choix ♦ **I don't ~ know** * je ne sais pas très bien ♦ **it shouldn't ~ do that** cela ne devrait vraiment pas faire ça 2 (= justifiably) à juste titre ♦ **~ or wrongly** à tort ou à raison ♦ **~ so** à juste titre

righto * /ˌraɪtˈəʊ/ EXCL (Brit) d'accord, OK

rightsizing /ˈraɪtˌsaɪzɪŋ/ N [of company] dégraissage *m* des effectifs

rightward(s) /ˈraɪtwəd(z)/ ADJ, ADV à droite, vers la droite

righty ho * /ˌraɪtɪˈhəʊ/ EXCL (Brit) ⇒ **righto**

rigid /ˈrɪdʒɪd/ ADJ 1 (lit) [material, structure] rigide ; [muscle] raide ♦ **~ with fear** paralysé par la peur ♦ **~ with rage** *or* **anger** blême de colère ♦ **to be bored ~** * s'ennuyer à mourir ♦ **this kind of music bores me ~** * ce genre de musique m'ennuie à mourir 2 [specifications, interpretation, principles, rule, discipline] strict ; [system, hierarchy, adherence, person, approach, attitude] rigide ; [control, censorship] rigoureux

rigidity /rɪˈdʒɪdɪtɪ/ N 1 (lit) [of material, structure] rigidité *f* ; [of muscle] raideur *f* 2 [of control, censorship, principles, rule, discipline] rigueur *f* ; [of specifications, interpretation, system, person, attitude] rigidité *f*

rigidly /ˈrɪdʒɪdlɪ/ ADV 1 (= stiffly) [stand, move, gesture] avec raideur ♦ **~ constructed** construit de manière rigide ♦ **to stand ~ to attention** être figé dans un garde-à-vous impeccable ♦ **to sit ~ erect** *or* **upright** être assis droit comme un i 2 (fig) [enforce, control, disciplined, organized etc] rigoureusement ♦ **to stick ~ to sth** s'en tenir rigoureusement à qch ♦ **~ authoritarian/conformist/dogmatic** d'un autoritarisme/conformisme/dogmatisme rigide ♦ **nursing is still a ~ hierarchical profession** la profession d'infirmière reste très hiérarchisée

rigmarole /ˈrɪgmərəʊl/ N comédie *f*, cinéma *m* ♦ **to go through the whole** *or* **same ~ again** recommencer le même cinéma *

rigor /ˈrɪgəʳ/ N (US) ⇒ **rigour**

rigor mortis /ˈrɪgəˈmɔːtɪs/ N rigidité *f* cadavérique

rigorous /ˈrɪgərəs/ ADJ [examination, test, control, person] rigoureux ♦ **he is ~ about quality** il est très strict sur la qualité ♦ **to be ~ in doing sth** faire qch rigoureusement

rigorously /ˈrɪgərəslɪ/ ADV [enforce, control, observe, define, test] rigoureusement

rigour, rigor (US) /ˈrɪgəʳ/ N rigueur *f*

rile * /raɪl/ VT agacer, mettre en boule *

Riley /ˈraɪlɪ/ N (Brit) ♦ **to live the life of ~** * avoir *or* mener la belle vie

rill /rɪl/ N (liter) ruisselet *m*

rim /rɪm/ N (gen) bord *m* ; [of wheel] jante *f* ; [of spectacles] monture *f* ♦ **a ~ of dirt** *or* **a dirty ~ around the bath** une trace sale sur le bord de la baignoire VT border ; [+ wheel] janter, cercler

rimaye /rɪˈmeɪ/ N (Climbing) rimaye *f*

rime¹ † /raɪm/ ⇒ **rhyme**

rime² /raɪm/ N (liter) givre *m*

rimless /ˈrɪmlɪs/ ADJ [spectacles] sans monture

rind /raɪnd/ N [of orange, lemon] peau *f*, pelure *f* ; (= grated zest) zeste *m* ; (= peel) écorce *f* ; (= peelings) pelure *f* ; [of cheese] croûte *f* ; [of bacon] couenne *f* ♦ **melon ~** écorce *f* de melon

ring¹ /rɪŋ/ N 1 (gen) anneau *m* ; (on finger) anneau *m* ; (with stone) bague *f* ; [of bishop] anneau *m* ; (on bird's foot) bague *f* ; (for napkin) rond *m* ; (for swimmer) bouée *f* de natation ; (for invalid to sit on) rond *m* (pour malade) ; [of piston] segment *m* ; [of turbine] couronne *f* ♦ **diamond ~** bague *f* de diamant(s) ♦ **wedding ~** alliance *f*, anneau *m* de mariage ♦ **electric ~** (for cooking) plaque *f* électrique ♦ **gas ~** brûleur *m* (de cuisinière à gaz) ; → **earring, key, signet**

2 (= circle) cercle *m*, rond *m* ; [of people] cercle *m* ; [of smoke] rond *m* ; (in water) rond *m* ; (in tree trunk) cercle *m* ; (= round sun, moon) auréole *f*, halo *m* ♦ **the ~s of Saturn** les anneaux *mpl* de Saturne ♦ **to have ~s round the eyes** avoir les yeux cernés *or* battus ♦ **to stand in a ~** se tenir en cercle *or* en rond, former un cercle ♦ **to run ~s round sb** * dominer qn de la tête et des épaules

3 (= group) (gen, Pol) coterie *f*, clique *f* (pej) ; [of dealers] groupe *m*, cartel *m* ; [of gangsters] bande *f*, gang *m* ; [of spies] réseau *m* ♦ **there is a ~ operating** (at auction) il y a un système d'enchères privées

4 (= enclosure) (at circus) piste *f* ; (at exhibition) arène *f*, piste *f* ; (Racing) enceinte *f* des bookmakers ; (Boxing) ring *m* ♦ **the ~** (Boxing) la boxe, le ring

VT (= surround) entourer ; (with quoit, hoop) jeter un anneau sur ; (= circle) [+ item on list etc] entourer d'un cercle ; [+ bird, tree] baguer ; [+ bull] mettre un anneau au nez de

COMP **ring-a-ring-a-roses** N *ronde enfantine*
ring binder N classeur *m* à anneaux
ring exercise N (Gym) exercice *m* aux anneaux
ring-fence VT [+ money] allouer ♦ **to ~-fence a local authority** *obliger une municipalité à utiliser l'argent destiné à un usage particulier*
ring finger N annulaire *m*
ring ouzel N merle *m* à plastron
ring-pull N (Brit: on can) anneau *m* (d'ouverture), bague *f* ♦ **~-pull can** boîte *f* avec anneau (d'ouverture)
ring road N (Brit) rocade *f* ; (motorway-type) périphérique *m*
ring spanner N clef *f* polygonale
ring-tailed ADJ à queue zébrée

ring² /rɪŋ/ LANGUAGE IN USE 27.2, 27.5 (vb : pret **rang**, ptp **rung**)

N 1 (= sound) son *m* ; [of bell] sonnerie *f* ; (lighter) tintement *m* ; [of electric bell] retentissement *m* ; [of coins] tintement *m* ♦ **there was a ~ at the door** on a sonné à la porte ♦ **to hear a ~ at the door** entendre sonner à la porte ♦ **give two ~s for the maid** sonne deux coups *or* deux fois pour (appeler) la bonne ♦ **his voice had an angry ~ (to it)** il y avait un accent *or* une note de colère dans sa voix ♦ **that has the ~ of truth (to it)** ça sonne juste

2 (esp Brit * = phone call) coup *m* de téléphone *or* de fil * ♦ **to give sb a ~** donner *or* passer un coup de téléphone *or* de fil * à qn

3 ♦ **~ of bells** jeu *m* de cloches

VI 1 [bell] sonner, retentir ; (lightly) tinter ; [alarm clock, telephone] sonner ♦ **the bell rang** la cloche a sonné *or* tinté, la sonnette a retenti ♦ **the bell rang for dinner** la cloche a sonné le dîner ♦ **to ~ for sb** sonner qn ♦ **to ~ for sth** sonner pour demander qch ♦ **please ~ for attention** prière de sonner ♦ **to ~ for the lift** appeler l'ascenseur ♦ **to ~ at the door** sonner à la porte ♦ **you rang, sir?** Monsieur a sonné ?

2 (= telephone) téléphoner

3 (= sound) [words] retentir, résonner ; [voice] vibrer ; [coin] sonner, tinter ; (= resound) résonner, retentir ; [ears] tinter, bourdonner ♦ **the room rang with their shouts** la pièce résonnait de leurs cris ♦ **the town rang with his praises** la ville entière chantait ses louanges ♦ **the news set the town ~ing** toute la ville parlait de la nouvelle, dans toute la ville il n'était bruit que de la nouvelle † ♦ **his voice rang with emotion** sa voix vibrait d'émotion ♦ **his words still ~ in my ears** ses mots retentissent encore à mes oreilles

♦ **to ring hollow** *or* **false** sonner faux ♦ **these claims ~ hollow** *or* **false** ces affirmations *or* protestations sonnent faux

♦ **to ring true** *[statement]* avoir l'air sincère ♦ **her denial rang true** sa dénégation avait l'air sincère ♦ **the story didn't ~ true** l'histoire sonnait faux

VT 1 *(= sound: gen)* sonner ; *[+ coin]* faire sonner, faire tinter ♦ **to ~ the doorbell** sonner (à la porte) ♦ **to ~ the bell** *(lit)* sonner, donner un coup de sonnette ; *(handbell)* agiter la sonnette ; (* *fig* = *succeed*) décrocher la timbale*, réussir magnifiquement ♦ **they rang the church bells** *(gen)* ils ont fait sonner les cloches ; *[bell ringers]* ils ont sonné les cloches ♦ **his name ~s a bell*** son nom me dit quelque chose *or* me rappelle quelque chose ♦ **he/it ~s my bell** * (US) il/ça me botte* ♦ **to ~ the knell (of)** sonner le glas (de) ♦ **to ~ the hours** sonner les heures ♦ **to ~ the changes** *[bells]* carillonner *(en variant l'ordre des cloches)* ♦ **to do sth to ~ the changes** faire qch pour changer ♦ **to ~ the changes on an outfit/the menu** *etc* varier un ensemble/le menu *etc*

2 *(Telec)* (also **ring up**) téléphoner à, donner *or* passer un coup de téléphone *or* de fil* à

COMP **ring tone** N sonnerie *f*

► **ring around** ⇒ **ring round**

► **ring back** VI, VT SEP *(Brit Telec)* rappeler

► **ring down** VT SEP *(Theat)* ♦ **to ring down the curtain** (faire) baisser le rideau ♦ **to ~ down the curtain on sth** marquer la fin de qch

► **ring in**

VI *(Brit = report by telephone)* téléphoner un reportage

VT SEP ♦ **to ring in the New Year** carillonner le Nouvel An

► **ring off** VI *(Brit Telec)* raccrocher

► **ring out** VI *[bell]* sonner ; *[voice]* résonner ; *[shot]* éclater, retentir

► **ring round** *(Brit)*

VI *(Telec)* donner des coups de téléphone

VT FUS ♦ **I'll ring round my friends** je vais appeler (tous) mes amis

► **ring up** VT SEP 1 *(Brit Telec)* donner un coup de téléphone *or* de fil* à

2 *(Theat)* **to ~ up the curtain** frapper les trois coups, (sonner pour faire) lever le rideau ♦ **to ~ up the curtain on a new career** *etc* marquer le début d'une nouvelle carrière *etc*

3 *(on cash register)* *[+ amount]* enregistrer ; *(fig)* *[+ profits, sales]* réaliser

ringbolt /ˈrɪŋbəʊlt/ N piton *m* ; *(on boat)* anneau *m* (d'amarrage)

ringdove /ˈrɪŋdʌv/ N ramier *m*

ringer /ˈrɪŋəʳ/ N 1 (also **bell ringer**) sonneur *m*, carillonneur *m* 2 *(= lookalike)* sosie *m* ♦ **he is a dead ~* for the President** c'est le sosie du président

ringing /ˈrɪŋɪŋ/ ADJ *[bell]* qui sonne *or* tinte ; *[voice, tone]* sonore ; *[endorsement]* vibrant ; *[declaration]* retentissant ♦ **in ~ tones** avec des accents vibrants N *[of bell]* sonnerie *f*, son *m* ; *(lighter)* tintement *m* ; *[of electric bell]* retentissement *m* ; *[of telephone]* sonnerie *f* ; *(in ears)* tintement *m*, bourdonnement *m* COMP **ringing tone** N *(Brit Telec)* tonalité *f* d'appel

ringleader /ˈrɪŋliːdəʳ/ N chef *m*, meneur *m*

ringlet /ˈrɪŋlɪt/ N frisette *f* ; *(long)* anglaise *f*

ringmaster /ˈrɪŋmɑːstəʳ/ N ♦ **the** ~ ≈ Monsieur Loyal

ringside /ˈrɪŋsaɪd/ N ♦ **at the** ~ au premier rang ♦ **to have a ~ seat** *(fig)* être aux premières loges

ringway /ˈrɪŋweɪ/ N ⇒ **ring road** ; → **ring¹**

ringworm /ˈrɪŋwɜːm/ N teigne *f*

rink /rɪŋk/ N *(for ice-hockey, ice-skating)* patinoire *f* ; *(for roller-skating)* skating *m*

rinky-dink * /ˈrɪŋkɪˈdɪŋk/ ADJ *(US)* *(old-fashioned, also small-time)* ringard* ; *(= poor quality)* de camelote* ; *(= broken down)* déglingué*, démoli

rinse /rɪns/ N 1 *(= act)* rinçage *m* ♦ **give the cup a ~** rincez la tasse, passez la tasse sous le robinet 2 *(for hair)* rinçage *m* VT 1 *[+ clothes etc]* rincer ♦ **to ~ one's hands** se passer les mains à l'eau ♦ **to ~ the soap off one's hands** se rincer les mains 2 *(= colour with a rinse)* **to ~ one's hair** se faire un *or* des rinçage(s) ♦ **she ~d her hair black** elle s'est fait un rinçage noir

► **rinse out** VT SEP 1 *[+ hair tint, colour, dirt]* faire partir à l'eau 2 *[+ cup]* rincer ♦ **to ~ out one's mouth** se rincer la bouche

Rio /ˈriːəʊ/ N ♦ ~ **(de Janeiro)** Rio (de Janeiro) ♦ ~ **Grande** Rio Grande *m*

riot /ˈraɪət/ N 1 *(= uprising)* émeute *f* ; *(Jur)* actes *mpl* séditieux ♦ **the ~s against the régime** les émeutes *fpl* contre le régime

2 *(fig)* **a ~ of colour(s)** une débauche de couleurs ♦ **a ~ of reds and blues** une profusion de rouges et de bleus ♦ **a ~ of flowers** une profusion de fleurs ♦ **he's a ~** ‡ c'est un (type) rigolo* ♦ **she's a ~** ‡ elle est rigolote* ♦ **the film is a ~** ‡ *(= funny)* le film est tordant* ♦ **to run ~** *[people, imagination]* être déchaîné ; *[vegetation]* pousser dans tous les sens

VI faire une émeute ; *(Jur)* se livrer à des actes séditieux

COMP **Riot Act** N *(Hist)* loi *f* contre les attroupements séditieux ; see also **read**

riot control N *(NonC)* répression *f* des émeutes

riot-control ADJ antiémeute

riot gear N *(NonC)* tenue *f* antiémeute

the riot police N les unités *fpl* antiémeute

riot shield N bouclier *m* antiémeute

the Riot Squad N ⇒ **the riot police**

rioter /ˈraɪətəʳ/ N émeutier *m*, -ière *f* ; *(vandalizing)* casseur *m*

rioting /ˈraɪətɪŋ/ N *(NonC)* émeutes *fpl* ADJ *[mob, youths etc]* en émeute

riotous /ˈraɪətəs/ ADJ 1 *(= uproarious)* *[party, evening]* très animé ; *[performance, comedy, welcome]* délirant* ♦ **they had a ~ time*** ils se sont amusés comme des fous ♦ **she burst into ~ laughter** elle s'est mise à hurler de rire 2 *(= disorderly)* *[behaviour]* séditieux ; *[crowd]* déchaîné ♦ **to engage in ~ living** mener une vie dissipée *or* de débauche ♦ ~ **assembly** *(Jur)* attroupements *mpl* séditieux

riotously /ˈraɪətəslɪ/ ADV 1 *[behave, act]* *(= noisily)* de façon tapageuse ; *(Jur)* de façon séditieuse 2 ♦ **it was ~ funny** * c'était tordant*

RIP /ˌɑːraɪˈpiː/ (abbrev of **rest in peace**) R.I.P.

rip /rɪp/ N déchirure *f*

VT déchirer, fendre ♦ **to ~ open a letter** ouvrir une lettre en hâte, fendre une enveloppe ♦ **to ~ the buttons from a shirt** arracher les boutons d'une chemise

VI 1 *[cloth]* se déchirer, se fendre

2 * **the fire/explosion ~ped through the house** l'incendie a fait rage à travers la maison/l'explosion a soufflé la maison de part en part ♦ **the jet ~ped through the sky** le jet a fendu le ciel ♦ **the car ~s along** la voiture roule à toute vitesse *or* roule à toute biture* ♦ **let her** *or* **it ~!*** *[boat, car]* appuie !, fonce !* ♦ **to ~ into sb** *(= criticize, tell off)* descendre qn en flammes*

♦ **to let rip** * *(= let o.s. go)* se laisser aller* ; *(in anger)* éclater, exploser *(de colère etc)* ♦ **I need to really let ~ for once** j'ai besoin de me laisser vraiment aller pour une fois ♦ **he let ~ at me** il m'a passé un bon savon* ♦ **turn the guitars up full and let ~** mettez le volume des guitares au maximum et allez-y à fond ♦ **she let ~ with a string of four-letter words** elle a lâché un chapelet de jurons

♦ **to let sth rip** * ♦ **he will not let inflation ~** il ne laissera pas l'inflation s'emballer

COMP **rip off** ‡ N → **rip-off**

rip-roaring * ADJ *(gen)* d'une gaieté bruyante, exubérant ; *[success]* monstre*

► **rip off** VT SEP 1 *(lit)* arracher *(from* de)

2 (‡ = *steal*) *[+ object, goods]* voler ; *(= defraud etc)* *[+ customer]* arnaquer*, filouter* ; *[+ employee]* exploiter ♦ **they're ~ping you off!** c'est du vol manifeste *or* de l'arnaque* !

N ♦ **rip-off** ‡ → **rip-off**

► **rip out** VT SEP arracher

► **rip up** VT SEP déchirer

riparian /raɪˈpeərɪən/ ADJ, N riverain(e) *m(f)*

ripcord /ˈrɪpkɔːd/ N poignée *f* d'ouverture

ripe /raɪp/ ADJ 1 *(lit)* *[fruit]* mûr ; *[cheese]* fait 2 *(fig = mature)* *[age, judgement]* mûr ♦ **to live to a ~ old age** vivre vieux *or* jusqu'à un âge avancé ♦ **to live to the ~ old age of 88** atteindre l'âge respectable de 88 ans ♦ **wait until the time is ~** attendez le moment opportun ♦ **the market is ~ for the picking** ce marché vous tend les bras* ♦ **the time is ~ to begin afresh** il est temps de tout reprendre à zéro ♦ **the time is ~ for revolution** le temps est venu de faire la révolution ♦ **conditions were ~ for an outbreak of cholera/a military uprising** toutes les conditions étaient réunies pour une épidémie de choléra/une insurrection armée 3 (* = *fetid*) *[smell]* fétide ♦ **he smelled rather ~** il ne sentait pas la rose 4 (* = *crude*) *[language, humour]* égrillard ; → **overripe**

ripen /ˈraɪpən/ VT (faire) mûrir VI mûrir ; *[cheese]* se faire

ripeness /ˈraɪpnɪs/ N maturité *f*

rip-off ‡ /ˈrɪpɒf/ N 1 *(= swindle)* escroquerie *f* ♦ **it's a ~!** c'est du vol *or* de l'arnaque* ! 2 *(= copy)* imitation *f* COMP **rip-off artist** ‡ N escroc *m*

riposte /rɪˈpɒst/ N *(Fencing: also fig)* riposte *f* VI riposter

ripper /ˈrɪpəʳ/ N *(= murderer)* éventreur *m* ♦ **Jack the Ripper** Jack l'éventreur

ripping †‡ /ˈrɪpɪŋ/ ADJ *(Brit)* épatant*, sensationnel*

ripple /ˈrɪpl/ N 1 *(= movement)* *[of water]* ride *f*, ondulation *f* ; *[of crops]* ondulation *f* 2 *(= noise)* *[of waves]* clapotis *m* ; *[of voices]* murmure(s) *m(pl)*, gazouillement *m* ; *[of laughter]* cascade *f* 3 *(= ice-cream)* **chocolate/raspberry ~** *glace à la vanille marbrée de glace au chocolat/à la framboise* VI *[water]* se rider ; *[crops, hair]* onduler ; *[waves]* clapoter VT *[+ water]* rider ; *[+ crops]* faire onduler COMP **ripple effect** N effets *mpl* *or* répercussions *fpl* en chaîne

ripsaw /ˈrɪpsɔː/ N scie *f* à refendre

riptide /ˈrɪptaɪd/ N contre-courant *m*, turbulence *f*

RISC /ˌɑːraɪesˈsiː/ N *(Comput)* 1 (abbrev of **reduced instruction set computer**) → **reduced** 2 (abbrev of **reduced instruction set computing**) → **reduced**

rise /raɪz/ (vb : pret **rose**, ptp **risen**) N 1 *[of theatre curtain, sun]* lever *m* ; *(Mus)* hausse *f* ; *(= increase)* *(in temperature)* élévation *f*, hausse *f* ; *(in pressure)* hausse *f* ; *[of tide]* flux *m*, flot *m* ; *[of river]* crue *f* ; *(Brit: in wages)* augmentation *f*, relèvement *m* *(Admin)* ; *(in prices)* hausse *f*, augmentation *f* ; *(in bank rate)* relèvement *m* ♦ **prices are on the ~** les prix sont en hausse ♦ **to ask for a ~** *(Brit)* *[employee]* demander une augmentation (de salaire) ♦ **there has been a ~ in the number of people looking for work** le nombre des demandeurs d'emploi a augmenté ♦ **his meteoric ~** son ascension *f* fulgurante ♦ **her ~ to power** son ascension *f* au pouvoir ◆ **his ~ to fame took 20 years** il a mis 20 ans à parvenir à la gloire *or* à devenir célèbre ◆ **the ~ of Bristol/the steel industry** l'essor *m* de Bristol/de l'industrie de l'acier ◆ **the ~ of the working classes** l'ascension du prolétariat ◆ **the ~ and fall of an empire** l'essor et la chute d'un empire, la grandeur et la décadence d'un empire ◆ **to get a ~ out of sb***, **to take the ~ out of sb** * *(fig)* se payer la tête de qn*

[2] *(= small hill)* éminence *f*, hauteur *f* ; *(= slope)* côte *f*, pente *f*

[3] *(= origin) [of river]* source *f* ◆ **the river has** *or* **takes its ~ (in)** la rivière prend sa source *or* a son origine (dans)

♦ **to give rise to** *[+ problems, pain, symptoms]* causer, provoquer ; *[+ speculation, rumour]* donner lieu à, engendrer ; *[+ fear, suspicions, concern, anxiety]* susciter ; *[+ impression]* donner

VI [1] *(= get up) (from sitting, lying)* se lever, se mettre debout ; *(from bed)* se lever ; *(after falling)* se relever ◆ **he ~s early/late** il se lève tôt/tard ◆ **~ and shine!** allez, lève-toi !, debout, là-dedans !* ◆ **he rose to go** il s'est levé pour partir ◆ **to ~ to one's feet** se mettre debout, se lever ◆ **to ~ on tiptoe** se mettre sur la pointe des pieds ◆ **to ~ from (the) table** se lever de table ◆ **he rose from his chair** il s'est levé de sa chaise ◆ **he rose from his sickbed to go and see her** il a quitté son lit pour aller la voir ◆ **to ~ from the dead** ressusciter (des morts) ◆ **the horse rose on its hind legs** le cheval s'est dressé (sur ses jambes de derrière) *or* s'est cabré

[2] *(= go up, ascend) [smoke, mist]* s'élever, monter ; *[balloon]* s'élever ; *[aircraft, lift]* monter ; *[theatre curtain, sun, moon, wind]* se lever ; *[dough, bread]* lever ; *[hair]* se dresser ; *[ground]* monter (en pente) ; *[voice]* monter, devenir plus aigu ; *[sea]* devenir houleux ; *[water, river, tide, blood pressure, temperature, exchange rate]* monter ; *[barometer]* remonter, être en hausse ; *[hopes, anger]* croître, grandir ; *[prices]* monter, augmenter ; *[cost of living]* augmenter, être en hausse ; *[stocks, shares]* monter, être en hausse ◆ **to ~ to the surface** *[swimmer, object, fish]* remonter à la *or* en surface ◆ **the fish are rising well** les poissons mordent bien ◆ **the mountain ~s to 3,000 metres** la montagne a une altitude de 3 000 mètres ◆ **the mountains rising before him** les montagnes qui se dressaient *or* s'élevaient devant lui ◆ **he won't ~ to any of your taunts** il ne réagira à aucune de vos piques ◆ **his eyebrows rose at the sight of her** quand il l'a vue il a levé les sourcils (d'étonnement) ◆ **the idea/image rose in his mind** l'idée/l'image s'est présentée à son esprit ◆ **great cheers rose from the audience** de nombreux hourras s'élevèrent de la foule ◆ **to ~ to the occasion** se montrer à la hauteur de la situation *or* des circonstances ◆ **I can't ~ to £50** je ne peux pas aller jusqu'à 50 livres ◆ **to ~ in price** augmenter (de prix) ◆ **to ~ above a certain temperature/a certain level** dépasser une température donnée/un niveau donné ◆ **her spirits rose** son moral a remonté ◆ **the colour rose to her cheeks** ses joues se sont empourprées, le rouge lui est monté aux joues ; → **bait, challenge, gorge**

[3] *(fig: in society, rank)* s'élever ◆ **to ~ in the world** réussir, faire son chemin dans le monde ◆ **to ~ from nothing** partir de rien ◆ **to ~ from the ranks** *(Mil)* sortir du rang ◆ **he rose to be President/a captain** il s'est élevé jusqu'à devenir Président/jusqu'au grade de capitaine ◆ **to ~ to fame** connaître la célébrité

[4] *(= adjourn) [assembly]* clore la session ; *[meeting]* lever la séance ◆ **the House rose at 2am** *(Parl)* l'Assemblée a levé la séance à 2 heures du matin ◆ **Parliament will ~ on Thursday next** les vacances parlementaires commenceront jeudi prochain

[5] *(= originate) [river]* prendre sa source *or* sa naissance *(in* dans)

[6] *(= rebel:* also **rise up**) se soulever, se révolter *(against* contre) ◆ **to ~ (up) in revolt** se révolter *(against* contre) ◆ **they rose (up) in anger and assassinated the tyrant** emportés par la colère ils se sont soulevés et ont assassiné le tyran ◆ **a feeling of inadequacy rose (up) within him** un sentiment de médiocrité montait en lui

risen /ˈrɪzn/ VB ptp of **rise** ADJ *(Rel)* ◆ **the ~ Christ** *or* **Lord** le Christ ressuscité

riser /ˈraɪzəʳ/ N [1] *(= person)* **to be an early ~** être lève-tôt *inv or* matinal ◆ **to be a late ~** être lève-tard *inv* [2] *[of stair]* contremarche *f*

risibility /ˌrɪzɪˈbɪlɪtɪ/ N *(frm)* risibilité *f*

risible /ˈrɪzɪbl/ ADJ *(frm)* risible

rising /ˈraɪzɪŋ/ N [1] *(= rebellion)* soulèvement *m*, insurrection *f*

[2] *(NonC) [of sun, star]* lever *m* ; *[of barometer]* hausse *f* ; *[of prices]* augmentation *f*, hausse *f* ; *[of river]* crue *f* ; *[of person from dead]* résurrection *f* ; *(Theat) [of curtain]* lever *m* ; *[of ground]* élévation *f* ◆ **the ~ and falling of the waves** le mouvement des vagues ◆ **the ~ and falling of the boat on the water** le mouvement du bateau qui danse sur les flots

[3] *[of Parliament, court]* ajournement *m*, clôture *f* de séance

ADJ [1] *[sun]* levant ; *[barometer, prices, temperature]* en hausse ; *[tide]* montant ; *[wind]* qui se lève ; *[tone]* qui monte ; *[anger, fury]* croissant ; *[ground]* qui monte en pente ◆ **the ~ sap** la sève ascendante *or* brute

[2] *(fig)* nouveau (nouvelle *f*) ◆ **a ~ young doctor** un jeune médecin d'avenir ◆ **the ~ generation** la nouvelle génération, les jeunes *mpl* ; see also **comp**

ADV * ◆ **she's ~ six** elle va sur ses six ans ◆ **the ~ fives** *(Brit Scol)* les enfants qui auront cinq ans dans l'année

COMP **rising damp** N humidité *f* (par capillarité)

rising star N *(lit, fig)* étoile *f* montante

risk /rɪsk/ LANGUAGE IN USE 2.3

N [1] *(= possible danger)* risque *m* ◆ **to take** *or* **run ~s** courir des risques ◆ **to take** *or* **run the ~ of doing sth** courir le risque de faire qch ◆ **you're running the ~ of being arrested** *or* **of arrest** vous risquez de vous faire arrêter ◆ **that's a ~ you'll have to take** c'est un risque à courir ◆ **there's too much ~ involved** c'est trop risqué ◆ **it's not worth the ~** ça ne vaut pas la peine de courir un tel risque ◆ **there is no ~ of his coming** *or* **that he will come** il n'y a pas de risque qu'il vienne, il ne risque pas de venir ◆ **you do it at your own ~** vous le faites à vos risques et périls ◆ **goods sent at sender's ~** *(Comm)* envois *mpl* faits aux risques de l'expéditeur ◆ **at the ~ of seeming stupid** au risque de *or* quitte à paraître stupide ◆ **at the ~ of his life** au péril de sa vie ; → **occupational, owner**

♦ **at risk** *[person, life]* en danger ◆ **millions of lives are at ~** des millions de vies sont en danger ◆ **children at ~** les enfants *mpl* en danger ◆ **some jobs are at ~** des emplois risquent d'être supprimés *or* sont menacés

♦ **to put sth** *or* **sb at risk** mettre qch *or* qn en danger ◆ **they are putting people's lives at ~** ils mettent des vies en danger

[2] *(Insurance)* risque *m* ◆ **fire ~** risque *m* d'incendie ◆ **he is a bad accident ~** il présente des risques élevés d'accident ◆ **he is a bad ~** on court trop de risques avec lui

VT [1] *[+ life, career, future, reputation, savings]* risquer ◆ **you ~ falling** vous risquez de tomber ◆ **he ~ed life and limb to rescue the drowning child** il a risqué sa vie pour sauver l'enfant qui se noyait ; → **neck**

[2] *[+ battle, defeat, quarrel]* s'exposer aux risques de ; *[+ accident]* risquer d'avoir, courir le risque de ; *(= venture) [+ criticism, remark]* risquer, hasarder ◆ **she won't ~ coming today** elle ne se risquera pas à venir aujourd'hui ◆ **I'll ~ it** je vais risquer *or* tenter le coup* ◆ **I can't ~ it** je ne peux pas prendre un tel risque

COMP **risk assessment** N évaluation *f* des risques

risk capital N capitaux *mpl* à risques

risk factor N facteur *m* de risque

risk management N gestion *f* des risques

risk-taking N ◆ **he does not like ~-taking** il n'aime pas prendre de risques, il n'a pas le goût du risque

riskily /ˈrɪskɪlɪ/ ADV de manière risquée ◆ **~, he's decided to resign** il a décidé de démissionner, ce qui est risqué

riskiness /ˈrɪskɪnɪs/ N risques *mpl*, aléas *mpl*

risky /ˈrɪskɪ/ ADJ *[enterprise, deed]* risqué ; *[joke, story]* risqué, osé ◆ **it's ~, it's a ~ business** c'est risqué

risotto /rɪˈzɒtəʊ/ N risotto *m*

risqué /ˈriːskeɪ/ ADJ *[story, joke]* risqué, osé

rissole /ˈrɪsəʊl/ N *(Brit)* rissole *f*

rite /raɪt/ N rite *m* ◆ **funeral ~s** rites *mpl* funèbres ◆ **the Rite of Spring** *(Mus)* le Sacre du printemps ; → **last¹** COMP **rite of passage** N rite *m* de passage ◆ **a ~(s)-of-passage novel** un roman d'initiation

ritual /ˈrɪtjʊəl/ ADJ rituel N rituel *m* ◆ **he went through the ~(s)** *(fig)* il a fait les gestes rituels, il s'est conformé aux rites ◆ **he went through the ~ of apologizing** il a fait les excuses rituelles, il s'est excusé comme de coutume

ritualism /ˈrɪtjʊəlɪzəm/ N ritualisme *m*

ritualist /ˈrɪtjʊəlɪst/ ADJ, N ritualiste *mf*

ritualistic /ˌrɪtjʊəˈlɪstɪk/ ADJ ritualiste

ritualize /ˈrɪtjʊəlaɪz/ VT ritualiser

ritually /ˈrɪtjʊəlɪ/ ADV rituellement

ritzy* /ˈrɪtsɪ/ ADJ luxueux

rival /ˈraɪvəl/ N rival(e) *m(f)* ADJ *[firm, enterprise]* rival, concurrent ; *[attraction]* rival ◆ **two ~ firms** deux entreprises rivales, deux concurrents VT *(gen)* rivaliser avec *(in* de) ; *(Comm)* être en concurrence avec ; *(= equal)* égaler (in en) ◆ **he can't ~ her in intelligence** pour ce qui est de l'intelligence, elle le domine de la tête et des épaules ◆ **his achievements ~ even yours** ses réussites sont presque égales aux vôtres

rivalry /ˈraɪvəlrɪ/ N rivalité *f (between* entre)

rive /raɪv/ (pret **rived**, ptp **riven**) /ˈrɪvən/ *(liter)* VT fendre VI se fendre ◆ **riven by** fendu par ; *(fig)* déchiré par

river /ˈrɪvəʳ/ N rivière *f* ; *(flowing into sea)* fleuve *m (also fig)* ◆ **down ~** en aval ◆ **up ~** en amont ◆ **the ~ Seine** *(Brit)* ◆ **the Seine ~** *(US)* la Seine ◆ **the accident has resulted in several ~s being polluted** à la suite de cet accident, plusieurs cours d'eau ont été pollués ◆ **~s of blood** *(fig)* des fleuves *mpl* de sang ; → **sell**

COMP *[police, port, system]* fluvial

river basin N bassin *m* fluvial

river blindness N *(Med)* cécité *f* des rivières, onchocercose *f*

river estuary N estuaire *m*

river fish N poisson *m* d'eau douce *or* de rivière

river fishing N *(NonC)* pêche *f* fluviale *or* en eau douce

river head N source *f* (de rivière *or* de fleuve)

river horse* N hippopotame *m*

river lamprey N lamproie *f* de rivière

river-mouth N bouche *f* d'une rivière (*or* d'un fleuve), embouchure *f*

river traffic N *(NonC)* trafic *m* fluvial, navigation *f* fluviale

riverbank /ˈrɪvəbæŋk/ N rive *f*, berge *f*

riverbed /ˈrɪvəbed/ N lit *m* de rivière *or* de fleuve

riverboat /ˈrɪvəbəʊt/ N embarcation *f* fluviale ♦ **a Mississippi** ~ un bateau du Mississippi ♦ **by** ~ en bateau

riverine /ˈrɪvəraɪn/ ADJ fluvial ; *[person]* riverain

riverside /ˈrɪvəsaɪd/ N bord *m* de l'eau (*or* de la rivière *or* du fleuve), rive *f* ♦ **by the** ~ au bord de l'eau (*or* de la rivière *etc*) ♦ **along the** ~ le long de la rivière (*or* du fleuve) ADJ (situé) au bord de la rivière *etc*

rivet /ˈrɪvɪt/ N rivet *m* VT (*Tech*) riveter, river ♦ **it ~ed our attention** ça nous a fascinés ♦ **~ed with fear** rivé *or* cloué sur place par la peur COMP **rivet joint** N rivetage *m*

riveter /ˈrɪvɪtəʳ/ N (*= person*) riveur *m* ; (*= machine*) riveuse *f*

rivet(t)ing /ˈrɪvɪtɪŋ/ N rivetage *m* ADJ (*= fascinating*) fascinant

Riviera /ˌrɪvɪˈeərə/ N ♦ **the (French)** ~ la Côte d'Azur ♦ **the Italian** ~ la Riviera (italienne)

rivulet /ˈrɪvjʊlɪt/ N (petit) ruisseau *m*

Riyadh /rɪˈjɑːd/ N Riyad

riyal /rɪˈjɑːl/ N riyal *m*

RL N (abbrev of **Rugby League**) → **rugby**

RM /ɑːrˈem/ N (*Brit Mil*) (abbrev of **Royal Marines**) → **royal**

RMT /ˌɑːremˈtiː/ N (*Brit*) (abbrev of **National Union of Rail, Maritime and Transport Workers**) *syndicat*

RN 1 (*Brit Mil*) (abbrev of **Royal Navy**) → **royal** 2 (*US*) abbrev of **registered nurse**

RNA /ˌɑːrenˈeɪ/ N (*Med*) (abbrev of **ribonucleic acid**) ARN *m*

RNAS /ˌɑːrenerˈes/ N (*Brit*) (abbrev of **Royal Naval Air Services**) *aéronavale britannique*

RNLI /ˌɑːrenelˈaɪ/ N (*Brit*) (abbrev of **Royal National Lifeboat Institution**) ≈ Société *f* nationale de sauvetage en mer

RNR /ˌɑːrenˈɑːʳ/ N (*Brit Mil*) (abbrev of **Royal Naval Reserve**) → **royal**

RNZAF abbrev of **Royal New Zealand Air Force**

RNZN abbrev of **Royal New Zealand Navy**

roach[1] /rəʊtʃ/ N (pl **roach** *or* **roaches**) (*= fish*) gardon *m*

roach[2] /rəʊtʃ/ N 1 (*esp US* *) (abbrev of **cockroach**) cafard *m*, blatte *f* 2 (*for joint, cigarette*) filtre *m* COMP **roach clip** N (*US: for joint*) *pince métallique servant à tenir un joint*

road /rəʊd/ N 1 (*gen*) route *f* ; (*minor*) chemin *m* ; (*in town*) rue *f* ; (*fig*) chemin *m*, voie *f* ♦ **trunk** ~ (route *f*) nationale *f*, grande route *f* ♦ **country** ~ route *f* de campagne, (route *f*) départementale *f* ♦ **"road up"** "attention travaux" ♦ **I prefer to travel by** ~ je préfère voyager en voiture ♦ **to take (to) the** ~ prendre la route, se mettre en route ♦ **is this the** ~ **to London** *or* **the London** ~? c'est (bien) la route de Londres ? ♦ **London Road** (*in towns*) rue *f* de Londres ♦ **you're on the right** ~ vous êtes sur la bonne route ; (*fig*) vous êtes sur la bonne voie ♦ **the** ~ **to hell is paved with good intentions** (*Prov*) l'enfer est pavé de bonnes intentions (*Prov*) ♦ **somewhere along the** ~ **he changed his mind** (*fig*) il a changé d'avis à un moment donné *or* en cours de route * ♦ **you're in my** ~ * vous me barrez le passage ♦ **(get) out of the** ~! * dégagez ! *, ôtez-vous de là ! ♦ **any** ~ * (*dial*) de toute façon ♦ **to have one for the** ~ * prendre un dernier verre avant de partir, boire le coup de l'étrier ♦ **to take the high/low** ~ (*US fig*) se comporter de façon irréprochable/malhonnête ♦ **~s** (*Naut*) rade *f* ♦ **in Yarmouth ~s** en rade de Yarmouth ; → **arterial, end, hit, main, Rome**

♦ **across the road** ♦ **she lives across the** ~ **(from us)** elle habite en face de chez nous ♦ **just across the** ~ **is a bakery** il y a une boulangerie juste en face

♦ **off the road** ♦ **my car is off the** ~ **just now** ma voiture est au garage ♦ **the car went off the** ~ la voiture a quitté la route

♦ **on the road** ♦ **I hope to get my car back on the** ~ **soon** j'espère que ma voiture sera bientôt en état (de rouler) ♦ **my car is (back) on the** ~ **again** ma voiture est à nouveau en état de marche ♦ **this vehicle shouldn't be on the** ~ on ne devrait pas laisser circuler un véhicule dans cet état ♦ **he is a danger on the** ~ (au volant) c'est un danger public ♦ **to be on the** ~ *[salesman, theatre company]* être en tournée ♦ **we were on the** ~ **at 6 in the morning** nous étions sur la route à 6 heures du matin ♦ **we've been on the** ~ **since this morning** nous voyageons depuis ce matin ♦ **we were on the** ~ **to Paris** nous étions en route pour Paris ♦ **on the** ~ **to ruin/success** sur le chemin de la ruine/du succès ♦ **on-the-~ price, price on the** ~ (*Brit: car sales*) prix *m* clés en mains

2 (*US*) abbrev of **railroad**

COMP **road accident** N accident *m* de la route *or* de la circulation
road atlas N recueil *m* de cartes routières
road bike N vélo *m* de route
road book N guide *m* routier
road bridge N pont *m* routier
road construction N construction *f* routière *or* de routes
road fund licence N (*Brit*) vignette *f* (automobile)
road gang N (*US*) équipe *f* de forçats (employés à construire des routes)
road haulage N transports *mpl* routiers
road haulier N entrepreneur *m* de transports routiers
road hog N chauffard * *m*
road hump N ralentisseur *m*
road manager N (*Mus*) organisateur *m*, -trice *f* de tournées
road map N (*= map*) carte *f* routière ; (*= plan for future actions*) feuille *f* de route ♦ ~ **map to peace** feuille de route pour la paix
road metal N empierrement *m*
road movie N road movie *m*
road pricing N (*Brit*) *système de péage*
road race N course *f* sur route
road racer N (*Cycling*) routier *m*, -ière *f*
road racing N compétition *f* sur route
road rage * N agressivité *f* au volant
road rider N (*Cycling*) ⇒ **road racer**
road runner N (*US = bird*) coucou *m* terrestre (du Sud-Ouest)
road safety N sécurité *f* routière
road sense N ♦ **he has no** ~ **sense** *[driver]* il n'a aucun sens de la conduite ; *[pedestrian]* il ne fait jamais attention à la circulation ♦ **to teach a child** ~ **sense** apprendre à un enfant à faire attention à la circulation
road show N (*Theat*) spectacle *m* en tournée ; (*Rad, TV*) émission *f* itinérante
road sign N panneau *m* indicateur *or* de signalisation ♦ **international** ~ **signs** signalisation *f* routière internationale
road stability N *[of vehicle]* tenue *f* de route
road surveyor N agent *m* des Ponts et Chaussées, agent *m* voyer
road sweeper N (*= person*) balayeur *m*, -euse *f* ; (*= vehicle*) balayeuse *f*
road tax N (*Brit*) taxe *f* sur les véhicules à moteur ♦ ~ **tax disc** (*Brit*) vignette *f* (automobile)
road test N essai *m* sur route
road-test VT ♦ **they are ~-testing the car tomorrow** ils vont faire les essais sur route demain
road traffic N (*NonC*) circulation *f* routière
road traffic accident N accident *m* de la route
road transport N transports *mpl* routiers
road-trials NPL (*= road test*) essais *mpl* sur route ; (*= rally*) épreuves *fpl* sur route
road-user N (*gen*) usager *m* de la route ♦ **~-user charges** taxation *f* des usagers de la route

ROADS

Les Britanniques et les Américains n'utilisent pas les mêmes termes pour désigner les différents types de routes. En Grande-Bretagne, les routes nationales sont des "A-roads" ou "trunk roads", les routes secondaires des "B-roads". Dans la première catégorie, certaines sont des quatre voies séparées par un terre-plein central : elles portent alors le nom de "dual carriageways" (le terme américain équivalent est "divided highways"). Les autoroutes ("motorways") sont gratuites.

Aux États-Unis, le terme générique pour une autoroute est "superhighway", mais l'on distingue les "interstate highways", qui vont d'un État à l'autre - certaines étant gratuites ("freeways"), les autres payantes ("toll roads" ou "turnpikes") - et les "expressways", qui sont les autoroutes urbaines ou périurbaines.

roadbed /ˈrəʊdbed/ N (*US*) *[of railroad]* ballast *m* ; *[of road]* empierrement *m*

roadblock /ˈrəʊdblɒk/ N barrage *m* routier

roadholding /ˈrəʊdhəʊldɪŋ/ N tenue *f* de route

roadhouse /ˈrəʊdhaʊs/ N (*US*) relais *m* routier

roadie * /ˈrəʊdɪ/ N roadie * *m*

roadkill /ˈrəʊdkɪl/ N cadavre *m* d'animal (*tué sur la route*)

roadmaking /ˈrəʊdmeɪkɪŋ/ N (*NonC*) construction *f* routière *or* des routes

roadman /ˈrəʊdmən/ N (pl **-men**) cantonnier *m*

roadmender /ˈrəʊdmendəʳ/ N ⇒ **roadman**

roadroller /ˈrəʊdrəʊləʳ/ N rouleau *m* compresseur

roadside /ˈrəʊdsaɪd/ N (*gen*) bord *m* de la route ; (*= verge*) bas-côté *m*, accotement *m* ♦ **along** *or* **by the** ~ au bord de la route COMP *[inn]* (situé) au bord de la route
roadside repairs NPL (*professional*) dépannage *m* ; (*done alone*) réparations *fpl* de fortune

roadstead /ˈrəʊdsted/ N (*Naut*) rade *f*

roadster /ˈrəʊdstəʳ/ N (*= car*) roadster *m* ; (*= cycle*) bicyclette *f* routière

roadway /ˈrəʊdweɪ/ N chaussée *f* ; (*on bridge*) tablier *m*

roadwork /ˈrəʊdwɜːk/ N (*NonC: Sport*) jogging *m* sur route NPL **roadworks** travaux *mpl* (d'entretien des routes) ♦ **"roadworks ahead"** "attention travaux"

roadworthy /ˈrəʊdwɜːðɪ/ ADJ ♦ **a** ~ **car** une voiture conforme aux normes de sécurité

roam /rəʊm/ VT *[+ streets, countryside]* parcourir, errer dans *or* par ♦ **to** ~ **the (seven) seas** courir *or* écumer les mers, bourlinguer sur toutes les mers ♦ **to** ~ **the streets** traîner dans les rues VI errer ; *[thoughts]* vagabonder ♦ **the right to** ~ (*Brit*) la liberté de se promener où on veut ♦ **to** ~ **about the house** errer dans la maison ♦ **to** ~ **about the world** parcourir le monde ♦ **to** ~ **about the streets** traîner dans les rues

► **roam about, roam around** VI (*= wander*) errer, vagabonder ; (*= travel*) bourlinguer *, rouler sa bosse *

roamer /ˈrəʊməʳ/ N vagabond *m*

roaming /ˈrəʊmɪŋ/ ADJ *[person]* errant, vagabond ; *[dog]* errant ; *[thoughts]* vagabond N 1 (*gen*) vagabondage *m* 2 (*Telec*) roaming *m*

roan[1] /rəʊn/ ADJ, N (*= horse*) rouan *m* ; → **strawberry**

roan[2] /rəʊn/ N (*= leather*) basane *f*

roar /rɔːʳ/ VI *[person, crowd]* hurler, pousser de grands cris ; (*with anger*) rugir ; *[lion, wind, sea]* rugir ; *[bull]* mugir, beugler ; *[thunder, guns, waterfall, storm, forest fire]* gronder ; *[engine, vehicle]* vrombir, ronfler ; *[fire in hearth]* ronfler ◆ **to ~ with pain** hurler de douleur ◆ **to ~ with laughter** rire à gorge déployée, hurler de rire ◆ **this will make you ~!*** tu vas hurler de rire !, tu vas rigoler !* ◆ **the trucks ~ed past us** les camions nous ont dépassés dans un ronflement *or* hurlement de moteur ◆ **the car ~ed up the street** la voiture remonta la rue dans un ronflement *or* hurlement de moteur ◆ **he ~ed away on his motorbike** il est parti en faisant vrombir sa moto

VT 1 (also **roar out**) *[+ order, one's disapproval]* hurler ; *[+ song]* chanter à tue-tête

2 **to ~ the engine*** faire ronfler *or* faire vrombir le moteur

N *[of crowd]* clameur *f*, hurlement *m* ; *[of lion]* rugissement *m* ; *[of bull]* mugissement *m* ; *[of river, waterfall, traffic]* grondement *m* ; *[of engine]* vrombissement *m* ; *[of furnace]* ronflement *m* ◆ **~s of laughter** une explosion de rires ◆ **the ~s of the crowd** les clameurs *fpl* de la foule

roaring /ˈrɔːrɪŋ/ ADJ 1 *[lion, engine]* rugissant ; *[wind, sea]* mugissant ; *[traffic]* assourdissant ; *[crowd]* hurlant ; *[guns, waterfall, storm]* grondant ; *[forest fire]* ronflant ◆ **a ~ fire** *(in hearth)* une belle flambée 2 *(Brit * fig)* ◆ **a ~ success** un succès fou* ◆ **to be doing a ~ trade (in sth)** faire des affaires en or (en vendant qch) ADV *(Brit)* ◆ **~ drunk** * soûl comme une bourrique

N *[of crowd]* hurlements *mpl*, clameur *f* ; *[of lion]* rugissement *m* ; *[of bull]* mugissement *m* ; *[of river, waterfall, traffic]* grondement *m*

COMP **the Roaring Forties** NPL *(Geog)* les quarantièmes *mpl* rugissants

the Roaring Twenties NPL (= *1920s*) les années *fpl* folles

roast /rəʊst/ N 1 rôti *m* ◆ **~ of veal/pork** *etc* rôti *m* de veau/porc *etc* ◆ **~ of beef** rôti *m* de bœuf, rosbif *m* ◆ **a slice off the ~** une tranche de *or* du rôti 2 *(US = barbecue)* barbecue *m* ADJ *[pork, veal, chicken]* rôti ◆ **~ beef** rôti *m* de bœuf, rosbif *m* ◆ **~ potatoes** pommes *fpl* de terre rôties VT 1 *[+ meat]* (faire) rôtir ; *[+ chestnuts]* griller, rôtir ; *[+ coffee beans]* griller, torréfier ; *[+ minerals]* calciner, griller ◆ **to ~ o.s. by the fire** se rôtir au coin du feu 2 *(US ‡ = criticize)* éreinter VI *[meat]* rôtir ; see also **roasting**

roaster /ˈrəʊstəʳ/ N *(= device)* rôtissoire *f* ; *(= bird)* volaille *f* à rôtir

roasting /ˈrəʊstɪŋ/ N *(lit)* rôtissage *m* ◆ **to give sb a ~‡** sonner les cloches à qn* ADJ 1 *(* = hot) [day, weather]* torride ◆ **it's ~ in here*** on crève* (de chaleur) ici, on rôtit* ici ◆ **I'm ~!*** je crève* de chaleur ! 2 *(Culin) [chicken etc]* à rôtir

COMP **roasting jack, roasting spit** N tournebroche *m*

rob /rɒb/ VT 1 *(= steal from) [+ person]* voler, dévaliser ; *[+ shop]* dévaliser ; *[+ orchard]* piller ◆ **to ~ sb of sth** *(purse etc)* voler qch à qn ; *(rights, privileges)* dépouiller *or* priver qn de qch ◆ **to ~ an orchard** piller un verger ◆ **to ~ the till** voler de l'argent dans la caisse ◆ **to ~ Peter to pay Paul** déshabiller Pierre pour habiller Paul ◆ **I've been ~bed of my watch** on m'a volé ma montre ◆ **I've been ~bed** j'ai été volé ◆ **the bank was ~bed** la banque a été dévalisée, il y a eu un vol à la banque ◆ **we were ~bed*** *(Sport)* on nous a volé la victoire ◆ **he has been ~bed of the pleasure of seeing her** il a été privé du plaisir de la voir ◆ **the shock ~bed him of speech** *(briefly)* le choc lui a fait perdre la parole ; *(long-term)* le choc lui a ôté l'usage de la parole 2 *(* = steal)* piquer*

robber /ˈrɒbəʳ/ N voleur *m*, -euse *f* ; *(= burglar)* cambrioleur *m* COMP **robber baron** N *(US)* requin *m* de l'industrie *or* de la finance

robbery /ˈrɒbərɪ/ N vol *m* ◆ **~ with violence** *(Jur)* vol *m* avec voies de fait *or* coups et blessures ◆ **at that price it's sheer ~!*** à ce prix-là c'est du vol manifeste *or* de l'escroquerie ! ; → **armed, daylight, highway**

robe /rəʊb/ N 1 *(= loose garment)* robe *f* ; *(= ceremonial garment)* robe *f* de cérémonie ◆ **he was wearing his ~ of office** il portait la robe de sa charge ◆ **ceremonial ~s** vêtements *mpl* de cérémonie ◆ **christening ~** robe *f* de baptême ; → **coronation** 2 *(= dressing gown)* peignoir *m* ◆ **a towelling ~** un peignoir en éponge 3 *(US = rug)* couverture *f* VT revêtir (d'une robe) ; *(fig, liter)* parer, revêtir (in de) VI *[judge etc]* revêtir sa robe

robin /ˈrɒbɪn/ N 1 *(in Europe:* also **robin redbreast**) rouge-gorge *m* 2 *(in North America)* merle *m* américain ; → **round**

robot /ˈrəʊbɒt/ N robot *m* ; *(fig)* robot *m*, automate *m*

COMP *[worker, guidance, pilot]* automatique, -robot

robot bomb N bombe *f* volante

robot plane N avion-robot *m*

robotic /rəʊˈbɒtɪk/ ADJ *[manner, movements]* d'automate, de robot

robotics /rəʊˈbɒtɪks/ N *(NonC)* robotique *f*

robotization /ˌrəʊbɒtaɪˈzeɪʃən/ N robotisation *f*

robotize /ˈrəʊbɒtaɪz/ VT robotiser

robust /rəʊˈbʌst/ ADJ 1 *(= strong) [person, appetite, economy]* robuste ; *[plant]* robuste, résistant ; *[material]* résistant ; *[object, structure, design]* solide ; *[economic growth]* soutenu ◆ **to have a ~ constitution** avoir une constitution robuste ◆ **to be in ~ health** avoir une santé robuste 2 *(= vigorous) [activity, attitude, speech]* énergique ; *[humour]* jovial ◆ **to put up** *or* **make a ~ defence of sb/sth** défendre vigoureusement *or* énergiquement qn/qch 3 *(= intense) [flavour, wine]* corsé, robuste

robustly /rəʊˈbʌstlɪ/ ADV 1 *(= strongly)* ◆ **~ built** *[person]* de robuste constitution ; *[object]* solide 2 *(= vigorously) [oppose, attack, defend]* vigoureusement, énergiquement ; *[reply]* avec vigueur ◆ **to campaign ~ (for/against sth)** mener une campagne vigoureuse *or* énergique (en faveur de/contre qch)

robustness /rəʊˈbʌstnɪs/ N robustesse *f*, vigueur *f*

ROC /ˌɑːrəʊˈsiː/ N (abbrev of **Republic of China**) République *f* de Chine *f*

roc /rɒk/ N roc(k) *m*

rock¹ /rɒk/ VT 1 *(= swing to and fro) [+ child]* bercer ; *[+ cradle]* balancer ◆ **to ~ a child to sleep** endormir un enfant en le berçant ◆ **a boat ~ed by the waves** un bateau bercé par les vagues ; see also **vt 2** ◆ **to ~ o.s. in a rocking chair** se balancer dans un rocking-chair

2 *(= shake)* ébranler, secouer ; *[+ ship] [waves]* ballotter ; *[explosion]* ébranler ; *(fig * = startle)* ébranler, secouer ◆ **town ~ed by an earthquake** ville *f* ébranlée par un tremblement de terre ◆ **country ~ed by rioting** *etc* pays *m* ébranlé par des émeutes *etc* ◆ **to ~ the boat** * *(fig)* jouer les trouble-fête, semer le trouble *or* la perturbation ◆ **don't ~ the boat*** ne compromets pas les choses, ne fais pas l'empêcheur de danser en rond* ◆ **that bit of news will ~ her!*** cette nouvelle va la bouleverser *or* lui faire un choc !

VI 1 *(= sway gently) [cradle, hammock]* (se) balancer ; *[person, ship]* se balancer ◆ **he was ~ing back and forth** il se balançait d'avant en arrière

2 *(= sway violently) [person]* chanceler ; *[building]* être ébranlé *or* secoué ◆ **the mast was ~ing in the wind** le mât oscillait dans le vent ◆ **the ground ~ed beneath our feet** le sol a tremblé sous nos pieds ◆ **they ~ed with laughter*** ils étaient écroulés *or* pliés de rire*

N (also **rock music**) rock *m* ; see also **glam, punk**

ADJ *(Mus) [ballet, musical etc]* rock *inv* ◆ **~ musician** rocker *m*

COMP **rock 'n' roll, rock-and-roll** N rock (and roll) *or* rock 'n' roll *m* ◆ **to do the ~-and-roll** danser le rock (and roll) ADJ rock *inv*

rock star N *(Mus)* rock star *f*

rock² /rɒk/ N 1 *(NonC = substance) (any kind)* roche *f* ; *(hard)* roc *m* ; (also **rock face**) rocher *m*, paroi *f* rocheuse ◆ **caves hewn out of the ~** des cavernes *fpl* creusées dans la roche *or* le roc ◆ **hewn out of solid ~** creusé à même le roc, creusé dans le roc ◆ **built on ~** *(lit, fig)* bâti sur le roc ◆ **they were drilling into ~ and not clay** ils foraient la roche *or* le roc et non l'argile ◆ **porous/volcanic** *etc* **~** roche *f* poreuse/volcanique *etc* ◆ **the study of ~s** l'étude *f* des roches

2 *(= large mass, huge boulder)* rocher *m*, roc *m (liter)* ; *(smaller)* roche *f* ◆ **these plants grow on ~s** ces plantes poussent sur les rochers *or* sur la roche ◆ **a huge ~ blocked their way** un énorme rocher leur bouchait le passage ◆ **fallen ~s** éboulis *mpl* ◆ **the Rock (of Gibraltar)** le rocher de Gibraltar ◆ **as solid as a ~** solide comme un roc ◆ **to be between a ~ and a hard place** être pris dans un dilemme

◆ **on the rocks** *[drink]* avec des glaçons ◆ **to be on the rocks** *[marriage]* être en difficulté ; *[business, economy]* être au bord de la faillite ◆ **to go on the rocks** *[ship]* s'échouer sur les rochers ; *[marriage]* échouer ; *[business, economy]* faire faillite

3 *(US = stone)* caillou *m*

4 *‡ (= diamond)* diam* *m* ◆ **~s** *(= jewels)* quincaillerie* *f*

5 *(Brit = sweet)* ≃ sucre *m* d'orge ◆ **Blackpool ~** *bâton de sucre d'orge marqué au nom de Blackpool*

6 ◆ **to get one's ~s off‡** prendre son pied‡

COMP **rock bass** N perche *f*, achigan *m*

rock bottom N *(Geol)* fond *m* rocheux ◆ **this is ~ bottom** * *(fig)* c'est la fin de tout, c'est la catastrophe ◆ **her spirits reached ~ bottom*** elle avait le moral à zéro* ◆ **prices were at ~ bottom** les prix étaient au plus bas

rock-bottom ADJ *(Comm)* ◆ **"rock-bottom prices"** "prix sacrifiés", "prix défiant toute concurrence"

rock bun, rock cake N *(Brit)* rocher *m (Culin)*

rock candy N *(US)* ≃ sucre *m* d'orge

rock carving N sculpture *f* sur roc

rock-climber N varappeur *m*, -euse *f*, rochassier *m*, -ière *f*

rock-climbing N varappe *f*, escalade *f*

rock crystal N cristal *m* de roche

rock dove N pigeon *m* biset

rock face N paroi *f* rocheuse

rock fall N chute *f* de pierres *or* de rochers

rock garden N (jardin *m* de) rocaille *f*

rock-hard ADJ *(lit)* dur comme la pierre ◆ **she's ~-hard*** *(= tough)* c'est une coriace

rock painting N *(Art)* peinture *f* rupestre *or* pariétale

rock plant N plante *f* alpestre *or* de rocaille

rock pool N flaque *f or* flache *f* laissée par la marée *(en bord de mer)*

rock-ribbed ADJ *(US)* inébranlable, à toute épreuve

rock rose N hélianthème *m*

rock salmon N *(Brit)* roussette *f*

rock salt N sel *m* gemme

rock-solid ADJ *(lit, fig)* solide comme un roc

rock-steady ADJ *[hand, voice]* parfaitement ferme ; *[camera, gun, moving car]* parfaitement stable

rockabilly /ˈrɒkəbɪlɪ/ N *(Mus)* rockabilly *m*

rocker /ˈrɒkəʳ/ N 1 *[of cradle etc]* bascule *f* ; *(esp US = rocking chair)* rocking-chair *m*, berceuse *f* ◆ **to be off one's ~‡** être cinglé*, avoir une case en moins* ◆ **to go off one's ~‡** perdre la boule* 2 *(= person)* rockeur *m*, -euse *f*

rockery /ˈrɒkərɪ/ N (jardin *m* de) rocaille *f*

rocket /ˈrɒkɪt/ N 1 *(= weapon)* fusée *f*, roquette *f* ; *(= spacecraft, firework)* fusée *f* ◆ **to fire** *or* **send up a ~** lancer une fusée ◆ **distress ~** fusée *f* de détresse ◆ **space** ~ fusée *f* interplanétaire ◆ **he's just had a** ~ * **from the boss** *(Brit fig)* le patron vient de lui passer un savon * *or* de l'enguirlander *

② *(= plant)* roquette *f*

VI *[prices]* monter en flèche ◆ **he went ~ing * past my door** il est passé en trombe devant ma porte ◆ **to ~ to fame** devenir célèbre du jour au lendemain

COMP **rocket attack** **N** attaque *f* à la roquette
rocket base **N** ⇒ **rocket range**
rocket fuel **N** *(NonC)* propergol *m*
rocket gun **N** fusil *m* lance-roquettes *inv* *or* lance-fusées *inv*
rocket launcher **N** lance-roquettes *m inv*, lance-fusées *m inv*
rocket plane **N** avion-fusée *m*
rocket-propelled **ADJ** autopropulsé
rocket propulsion **N** propulsion *f* par fusée, autopropulsion *f*
rocket range **N** base *f* de lancement de missiles ◆ **within ~ range** à portée de missiles
rocket research **N** recherches *fpl* aérospatiales
rocket science **N** technologie *f* des fusées ◆ **it's not ~ science** ce n'est vraiment pas sorcier *
rocket scientist **N** spécialiste *mf* des fusées ◆ **it doesn't take a ~ scientist to ...** pas besoin d'être un génie pour ...
rocket ship **N** vaisseau *m* spatial
rocket technology **N** technologie *f* des fusées

rocketry /ˈrɒkɪtrɪ/ **N** *(= science)* technologie *f* des fusées ; *(= rockets collectively)* (panoplie *f* de) fusées *fpl*

rockfish /ˈrɒkfɪʃ/ **N** (pl **rockfish** *or* **rockfishes**) rascasse *f*

rocking /ˈrɒkɪŋ/ **N** balancement *m*, ballottement *m*

COMP **rocking chair** **N** rocking-chair *m*, berceuse *f*
rocking horse **N** cheval *m* à bascule

rockling /ˈrɒklɪŋ/ **N** (pl **rockling** *or* **rocklings**) loche *f* de mer

rocky¹ /ˈrɒkɪ/ **ADJ** ① *(* = precarious) [marriage]* fragile, instable ; *[health]* précaire, chancelant ◆ **his finances are ~** sa situation financière est précaire ◆ **to be going through a ~ patch** traverser une période difficile ② *(= unsteady) [table, chair]* branlant

rocky² /ˈrɒkɪ/ **ADJ** *(lit) [shore, mountain]* rocheux ; *[road, path]* rocailleux ◆ **I knew it would be a ~ road to recovery** je savais que mon rétablissement n'était pas du tout cuit * *or* que mon rétablissement serait long et difficile ◆ **on the ~ road to fame** sur le dur chemin de la gloire **COMP** **the Rocky Mountains** **NPL** (also **the Rockies**) les (montagnes *fpl*) Rocheuses *fpl*

rococo /rəʊˈkəʊkəʊ/ **N** rococo *m* **ADJ** rococo *inv*

rod /rɒd/ **N** ① *(wooden)* baguette *f* ; *(metallic)* tringle *f* ; *[of machinery]* tige *f* ; *(for punishment)* baguette *f*, canne *f* ; *(symbol of authority)* verge *f* ◆ **curtain/stair ~** tringle *f* à rideaux/d'escalier ◆ **to make a ~ for one's own back** donner des verges pour se faire battre *or* fouetter ◆ **to rule with a ~ of iron** *[+ country]* gouverner d'une main de fer ; *[+ person, family]* mener à la baguette *or* à la trique * ; → **black, connecting, piston, spare** ② (also **fishing rod**) canne *f* (à pêche) ◆ **to fish with ~ and line** pêcher à la ligne ③ *(= measure)* perche *f* (= 5,03 m) ④ *[of eye]* bâtonnet *m* ⑤ *(US ‡ = gun)* flingue‡ *m* ⑥ *(* = hotrod)* hotrod *m*, voiture *f* gonflée ⑦ *(**‡= penis)* bite**‡ *f* **COMP** **rod bearing** **N** *(Tech)* manchon *m* de bielle

rode /rəʊd/ **VB** pt of **ride**

rodent /ˈrəʊdənt/ **N** rongeur *m* **ADJ** rongeur ◆ **~ cancer, ~ ulcer** *(Med)* cancer *m* de la peau

rodeo /ˈrəʊdɪəʊ/ **N** rodéo *m*

rodomontade /ˌrɒdəmɒnˈteɪd/ **N** rodomontade *f*

roe¹ /rəʊ/ **N** (pl **roe** *or* **roes**) *(species: also* **roe deer***)* chevreuil *m*

COMP **roe buck** **N** chevreuil *m* mâle
roe deer **N** *(female)* chevreuil *m* femelle chevrette *f*

roe² /rəʊ/ **N** *[of fish]* ◆ **hard ~** œufs *mpl* de poisson ◆ **soft ~** laitance *f* ◆ **herring ~** œufs *mpl* *or* laitance *f* de hareng

roentgen /ˈrɒntjən/ **N** Roentgen *or* Röntgen *m*

rogation /rəʊˈgeɪʃən/ *(Rel)* **N** *(gen pl)* rogations *fpl*

COMP **Rogation Days** **NPL** *les trois jours qui précèdent l'Ascension*
Rogation Sunday **N** dimanche *m* des Rogations

rogatory /ˈrɒgətərɪ/ **ADJ** *(Jur)* rogatoire ; → **letter**

Roger /ˈrɒdʒəʳ/ **N** Roger *m* ◆ **"roger!"** *(Telec)* "compris !" ; → **jolly**

roger **‡ /ˈrɒdʒəʳ/ **VT** tringler**‡

rogue /rəʊg/ **N** ① *(= scoundrel)* voyou *m* ; *(= scamp)* coquin(e) *m(f)* ◆ **a loveable ~** une sympathique fripouille ◆ **you little ~!** petit coquin ! ② *(= solitary animal)* solitaire *m* **ADJ** *[elephant, lion, male]* solitaire ; *[gene]* aberrant ◆ **~ element** *(= maverick)* franc-tireur *m* ◆ **mysterious ~ programmes known as viruses** de mystérieux programmes incontrôlables connus sous le nom de virus ◆ **these one-time ~ states seeking respectability** ces États autrefois en marge et qui se cherchent aujourd'hui une respectabilité ◆ **~ cop** * flic * *m* solitaire **COMP** **rogues' gallery** **N** *(Police)* photographies *fpl* de l'identité judiciaire *or* des sommiers * ◆ **they look like a ~s' gallery** ils ont des têtes de repris de justice

roguery /ˈrəʊgərɪ/ **N** *(= wickedness)* coquinerie *f*, malhonnêteté *f* ; *(= mischief)* espièglerie *f*

roguish /ˈrəʊgɪʃ/ **ADJ** *(= mischievous) [person, smile, charm, humour]* malicieux ; *(= rascally) [person]* coquin

roguishly /ˈrəʊgɪʃlɪ/ **ADV** *[smile, say]* malicieusement ◆ **he winked at me ~** il m'a fait un clin d'œil malicieux

ROI /ˌɑːrəʊˈaɪ/ **N** (abbrev of **Republic of Ireland**) République *f* d'Irlande

roil /rɔɪl/ *(esp US)* **VI** *[water]* bouillonner **VT** *(fig)* perturber ◆ **to ~ the waters** semer le trouble

roily /ˈrɔɪlɪ/ **ADJ** *(esp US) [water, sea]* troublé, agité ; *(fig) [person]* exaspéré

roister /ˈrɔɪstəʳ/ **VI** s'amuser bruyamment

roisterer /ˈrɔɪstərəʳ/ **N** fêtard(e) * *m(f)*

Roland /ˈrəʊlənd/ **N** Roland *m* ◆ **a ~ for an Oliver** un prêté pour un rendu

role, rôle /rəʊl/ **N** *(Theat, fig)* rôle *m* ; → **leading¹**

COMP **role model** **N** modèle *m*
role play **N** *(NonC)* jeu(x) *m(pl)* de rôle **VT** traiter sous forme de jeu de rôle ◆ **~-play one of the following situations** traitez l'une des situations suivantes sous forme de jeu de rôle **VI** faire des jeux de rôle
role reversal **N** inversion *f* des rôles

roll /rəʊl/ **N** ① *[of cloth, paper, netting, wire, hair etc]* rouleau *m* ; *[of banknotes]* liasse *f* ; *[of tobacco]* carotte *f* ; *[of butter]* coquille *f* ; *[of flesh, fat]* bourrelet *m* ◆ **~ of film** *(Phot)* (rouleau *m* de) pellicule *f*

② (also **bread roll**) petit pain *m* ; → **sausage, Swiss**

③ *(= movement) [of ship]* roulis *m* ; *[of sea]* houle *f* ; *[of plane]* tonneau *m* ◆ **to walk with a ~** se balancer en marchant, avoir une démarche chaloupée ◆ **the ship gave a sudden ~** le bateau roula brusquement ◆ **the horse was having a ~ on the grass** le cheval se roulait dans l'herbe ◆ **to have a ~ in the hay with sb** * batifoler * dans l'herbe avec qn ; → **rock¹**

④ *(= sound) [of thunder, drums]* roulement *m* ; *[of organ]* ronflement *m*

⑤ *(= list, register)* liste *f*, tableau *m* ; *(for court, ship's crew etc)* rôle *m* ◆ **class ~** *(Scol)* liste *f* (nominative) des élèves ◆ **we have 60 pupils on our ~(s)** nous avons 60 élèves inscrits ◆ **falling ~s** *(Scol)* diminutions *fpl* des effectifs ◆ **to call the ~** faire l'appel ◆ **~ of honour** *(Brit)* *(Mil)* noms *mpl* des combattants morts pour la patrie *or* tombés au champ d'honneur ; *(Scol)* tableau *m* d'honneur ◆ **to strike sb or sb's name off the ~s** *(Jur)* radier qn des listes *or* du tableau ; → **electoral**

⑥ **to be on a ~** * *(= prospering)* avoir le vent en poupe

VI ① *(= turn over)* rouler ◆ **to ~ over and over** *[object]* rouler sur soi-même ; *[person]* se rouler ◆ **the coin ~ed under the table** la pièce a roulé sous la table ◆ **stones ~ed down the hill** des pierres ont roulé *or* déboulé jusqu'au pied de la colline ◆ **the car ~ed down the hill** *(brakes off)* la voiture a descendu la pente toute seule ; *(over and over)* la voiture a dévalé la pente en faisant une série de tonneaux ◆ **the lorries ~ed through the streets** les camions roulaient dans les rues ◆ **his car ~ed to a stop** sa voiture s'arrêta doucement ◆ **to ~ headlong down a slope** dégringoler une pente ◆ **the children were ~ing down the slope** les enfants dévalaient la pente en roulant ◆ **tears were ~ing down her cheeks** les larmes coulaient sur ses joues ◆ **the waves were ~ing on to the beach** les vagues déferlaient sur la plage ◆ **the newspapers were ~ing off the presses** les journaux tombaient des rotatives ◆ **the wheels kept ~ing** les roues continuaient à tourner ◆ **heads will ~** il y aura des limogeages *, des têtes vont tomber ◆ **we were ~ing along at 100km/h** *(in car)* nous roulions à 100 (km) à l'heure ◆ **the horse ~ed in the mud** le cheval s'est roulé dans la boue ◆ **he's ~ing in money** * *or* **in it** * il roule sur l'or ◆ **they were ~ing in the aisles** * ils se tordaient de rire, ils se tenaient les côtes * ◆ **she is trainer and manager ~ed into one** elle est entraîneur et manager tout à la fois *or* en même temps ◆ **to ~ with the punches** encaisser les coups

② *[ship]* rouler ◆ **he ~ed from side to side as he walked** il se balançait en marchant ◆ **his eyes were ~ing** ses yeux roulaient, il roulait les yeux

③ *[thunder]* gronder, rouler ; *[drums, words]* rouler ; *[voice]* retentir ; *[organ]* rendre un son grave et prolongé ; *[noises]* se répercuter

④ *(= function, operate) [machine]* marcher, fonctionner ; *[film cameras]* tourner ◆ **cameras ~!** on tourne ! ◆ **to keep the show ~ing** * *(Theat)* s'arranger pour que le spectacle continue *subj* ◆ **you must keep the ball** *or* **things ~ing while I'm away** * arrangez-vous pour que tout marche pendant mon absence

VT ① *[+ barrel, hoop, ball]* faire rouler ; *[+ umbrella, cigarette]* rouler ; *[+ pastry, dough]* étendre *or* abaisser au rouleau ; *[+ metal]* laminer ; *[+ lawn]* rouler ; *[+ road]* cylindrer ◆ **to ~ one's eyes** rouler des yeux ◆ **to ~ one's r's** rouler les r ◆ **to ~ sth between one's fingers** rouler qch avec *or* entre ses doigts ◆ **to ~ string into a ball** enrouler de la ficelle en pelote ◆ **the hedgehog ~ed itself up into a ball** le hérisson s'est roulé en boule ◆ **he ~ed himself in a blanket** il s'est enroulé dans une couverture ◆ **they ~ed the car to the side of the road** ils ont poussé la voiture sur le bas-côté ; see also **rolled**

② *(US ‡ = rob)* dévaliser

COMP **roll bar** **N** *(on car)* arceau *m* de sécurité
roll call **N** *(gen, Mil, Scol)* appel *m* ◆ **a ~ call of sporting giants** une belle brochette de sommités du sport
roll-collar **N** *(Brit)* ⇒ **roll-neck**
roll film **N** rouleau *m* *or* bobine *f* de pellicule photo(graphique)

roll-neck N (Brit) *[of sweater]* col *m* roulé ADJ ◆ **~-neck(ed)** à col roulé
roll-on N, ADJ → **roll-on**
roll-top desk N bureau *m* à cylindre
roll-up*, **roll-your-own*** N (Brit) cigarette *f* roulée

► **roll about** VI *[coins, marbles]* rouler çà et là ; *[ship]* rouler ; *[person, dog]* se rouler par terre

► **roll along** VI 1 *[ball, vehicle]* rouler
2 *(* = arrive)* s'amener*, se pointer*
VT SEP *[+ ball]* faire rouler ; *[+ car]* pousser

► **roll around** VI ⇒ **roll about**

► **roll away** VI *[clouds, mist, vehicle]* s'éloigner ; *[ball]* rouler au loin ◆ **the ball ~ed away from me** le ballon a roulé loin de moi
VT SEP *[+ trolley, table]* pousser

► **roll back** VI *[object]* rouler en arrière ; *[eyes]* chavirer
VT SEP 1 *[+ object]* rouler en arrière ; *[+ carpet]* rouler ; *[+ sheet]* enlever (en roulant)
2 *(= bring back)* ramener ◆ **if only we could ~ back the years** si seulement nous pouvions ramener le temps passé
3 *(US = reduce)* réduire ◆ **to ~ back the State** diminuer le pouvoir de l'État
4 *(= undo) [+ reform]* défaire
N ◆ **rollback*** → **rollback**

► **roll by** VI *[vehicle, procession]* passer ; *[clouds]* traverser le ciel, dériver dans le ciel ; *[time, years]* s'écouler, passer

► **roll down** VI *[ball, person]* rouler de haut en bas ; *[tears]* couler
VT SEP 1 *[+ cart]* descendre (en roulant)
2 *(= wind down) [+ car window]* descendre, baisser
3 *[+ socks, sleeves]* baisser ; *[+ stockings]* rouler

► **roll in** VI *[waves]* déferler ; * *[letters, contributions, suggestions]* affluer ; * *[person]* s'amener*, se pointer* ◆ **he ~ed in* half an hour late** il s'est amené* *or* pointé* avec une demi-heure de retard ◆ **the money keeps ~ing in*** l'argent continue à affluer
VT SEP *[+ barrel, trolley]* faire entrer (en roulant)

► **roll off** VI 1 *[vehicle, procession]* s'ébranler, se mettre en marche
2 *(= fall off)* dégringoler

► **roll on** VI *[vehicle etc]* continuer de rouler ; *[time]* s'écouler ◆ **~ on the holidays!*** (Brit) vivement les vacances ! ◆ **~ on Tuesday!*** (Brit) vivement mardi !
VT SEP *[+ stockings]* enfiler
N ◆ **roll-on** → **roll-on**
◆ **roll-on-roll-off** (Brit) → **roll-on**

► **roll out** VT SEP 1 *[+ barrel, trolley]* rouler *or* pousser dehors
2 *[+ sentence, verse]* débiter
3 *[+ pastry]* étendre *or* abaisser au rouleau ; *[+ metal]* laminer
4 *(= introduce) [+ system, offer]* introduire
N ◆ **roll-out** → **roll-out**

► **roll over** VI *[person, animal] (once)* se retourner (sur soi-même) ; *(several times* : also **roll over and over)** se rouler
VT SEP *[+ person, animal, object]* retourner

► **roll past** VI ⇒ **roll by**

► **roll up** VI 1 *[animal]* se rouler *(into* en)
2 *(* = arrive)* arriver, s'amener* ◆ **~ up and see the show!** *(at fairground)* approchez, venez voir le spectacle !
VT SEP *[+ cloth, paper, map]* rouler ◆ **to ~ up one's sleeves** retrousser ses manches
N ◆ **roll-up*** → **roll**

rollaway bed /ˈrəʊləweɪˈbed/ N (US) lit *m* pliant (sur roulettes)

rollback /ˈrəʊlbæk/ N (US) *(gen)* réduction *f* ; *(Econ)* baisse *f* forcée des prix (sur ordre du gouvernement)

rolled /rəʊld/ ADJ 1 (also **rolled up**) *[carpet, newspaper, blanket, garment]* roulé, enroulé ; *[trousers, sleeves]* retroussé ; *[umbrella]* plié 2 *(Phon)* roulé
COMP **rolled gold** N plaqué *m* or
rolled-gold ADJ *[bracelet]* (en) plaqué or
rolled oats NPL flocons *mpl* d'avoine
rolled-steel joist N poutrelle *f*
rolled tobacco N tabac *m* en carotte

Roller* /ˈrəʊləʳ/ N (Brit) Rolls *f*

roller /ˈrəʊləʳ/ N 1 *(gen)* rouleau *m* ; *(for pastry)* rouleau *m* à pâtisserie ; *(for roads)* rouleau *m* compresseur ; *(for lawn)* rouleau *m* de jardin ; *(for metal)* laminoir *m*, cylindre *m* lamineur ; *(in papermaking, textiles)* calandre *f*
2 *(for painting and decorating)* rouleau *m* (à peinture) ; *(for inking)* rouleau *m* (encreur)
3 *(for winding sth round)* rouleau *m* ; *[of blind]* enrouleur *m* ; *(for hair)* bigoudi *m*, rouleau *m* à mise en plis ◆ **to put one's hair in ~s** se mettre des bigoudis
4 *(for moving things)* rouleau *m* ; *(= wheel)* roulette *f*, galet *m* ◆ **table on ~s** table *f* à roulettes
5 *(part of harness)* surfaix *m*
6 *(= wave)* lame *f* de houle
COMP **roller bandage** N bande *f* (roulée)
roller blade N, VI ⇒ **rollerblade**
roller blind N store *m*
roller coaster N montagnes *fpl* russes
roller skate N patin *m* à roulettes
roller-skate VI faire du patin à roulettes
roller-skating N patinage *m* à roulettes
roller towel N rouleau *m* essuie-main(s)

rollerball /ˈrəʊləˌbɔːl/ N stylo *m* à bille

Rollerblade ® /ˈrəʊləˌbleɪd/ N roller *m* VI faire du roller

rollerdrome /ˈrəʊləˌdrəʊm/ N (US) piste *f* de patin à roulettes

rollick* /ˈrɒlɪk/ VI (also **rollick about**) s'amuser bruyamment

rollicking* /ˈrɒlɪkɪŋ/ ADJ *[person]* d'une gaieté exubérante, joyeux ; *[play, farce]* bouffon ; *[occasion]* (bruyant et) joyeux ◆ **to lead a ~ life** mener joyeuse vie *or* une vie de patachon* ◆ **to have a ~ time** s'amuser follement *or* comme des fous ◆ **it was a ~ party** nous nous sommes amusés comme des petits fous à la soirée N *(= telling off)* savon* *m* ◆ **to give sb a (real) ~** passer un (sacré *or* bon) savon à qn* ◆ **to get a (real) ~** recevoir un (sacré *or* bon) savon*

rolling /ˈrəʊlɪŋ/ ADJ 1 *(= undulating) [countryside, landscape]* vallonné ; *[hills, lawns]* onduleux
2 *(= pitching) [ship]* qui roule ; *[sea]* houleux ◆ **~ waves** (vagues *fpl*) déferlantes *fpl*
3 *(= swaying) [gait, walk]* chaloupé
4 *(= ongoing) [contract]* révisable ; *[programme]* constamment remis à jour ◆ **~ news service** service *m* d'informations permanentes
ADV ◆ **to be ~ drunk*** être rond comme une queue de pelle*
COMP **rolling mill** N *(= factory)* laminerie *f*, usine *f* de laminage ; *(= machine)* laminoir *m*
rolling pin N rouleau *m* à pâtisserie
rolling plan N *(Fin)* plan *m* pluriannuel (révisable chaque année)
rolling stock N *(Rail)* matériel *m* roulant
rolling stone N **a ~ stone gathers no moss** *(Prov)* pierre qui roule n'amasse pas mousse *(Prov)* ◆ **he's a ~ stone** il mène une vie nomade
rolling targets NPL *(US Econ)* objectifs *mpl* économiques révisables

rollmop /ˈrəʊlmɒp/ N (Brit) (also **rollmop herring**) rollmops *m*

roll-on /ˈrəʊlɒn/ N *(= corset)* gaine *f* ADJ *[deodorant etc]* à bille
COMP **roll-on-roll-off** N (manutention *f* par) roulage *m*
roll-on-roll-off ferry N ferry *m* roulier *or* roll-on roll-off
roll-on-roll-off ship N roulier *m*

roll-out /ˈrəʊlaʊt/ N *[of new technology, system]* lancement *m*

rollover /ˈrəʊləʊvəʳ/ N 1 *(NonC: Fin) [of loan, debt]* refinancement *m* 2 *(Brit: in lottery)* remise *f* en jeu du prix 3 *[of mobile phone time]* report *m* de minutes ADJ 1 *(Brit: in lottery)* ◆ **it's a ~ week** le gros lot de la semaine précédente a été remis en jeu 2 ◆ **~ minutes** *(for mobile phone)* report *m* de minutes

Rolodex ® /ˈrəʊlədeks/ N fichier *m* Rolodex ®

roly-poly /ˈrəʊlɪˈpəʊlɪ/ ADJ * *[person, figure]* rondelet ; *[child]* potelé N 1 *(Brit:* also **roly-poly pudding)** (gâteau *m*) roulé *m* à la confiture 2 *(* = plump child)* poupard *m*

ROM /rɒm/ N *(Comput)* (abbrev of **Read-Only-Memory**) → **read**

Roma (gypsy) /ˈrəʊmə(ˈdʒɪpsɪ)/ N Rom *mf inv*

Romagna /ˈromaɲa/ N Romagne *f*

romaine /rəʊˈmeɪn/ N *(US:* also **romaine lettuce)** (laitue *f*) romaine *f*

Roman /ˈrəʊmən/ N 1 *(= person)* Romain(e) *m(f)* ◆ **the Epistle to the ~s** *(Bible)* l'épître *f* aux Romains 2 *(Typ)* romain *m* ADJ *(Archit, Geog, Hist, Rel, Typ)* romain ; → **holy**
COMP **the Roman alphabet** N l'alphabet *m* romain
Roman arch N voûte *f* (en) plein cintre, arc *m* plein cintre
the Roman calendar N le calendrier romain
Roman candle N chandelle *f* romaine
Roman Catholic ADJ, N catholique *mf* (romain)
the Roman Catholic Church N l'Église *f* catholique (romaine)
Roman Catholicism N catholicisme *m*
the Roman Empire N l'Empire *m* romain
Roman law N droit *m* romain
Roman letters NPL *(Typ)* caractères *mpl* romains
Roman nose N nez *m* aquilin
Roman numeral N chiffre *m* romain
the Roman Rite N *(Rel)* le rite romain

⚠ In French, the noun **roman** means 'novel'.

romance /rəʊˈmæns/ N 1 *(= tale of chivalry)* roman *m* ; *(= love story/film)* roman *m*/film *m* sentimental ; *(Mus)* romance *f* ; *(= love affair)* idylle *f* ; *(= love)* amour *m* ; *(NonC = charm, attraction)* charme *m* ◆ **it's quite a ~** c'est un vrai roman ◆ **it's pure ~** *(fig = lies)* c'est de la pure invention, c'est du roman ◆ **their ~ lasted six months** leur idylle a duré six mois ◆ **he was her first ~** il était son premier amoureux *or* amour ◆ **they had a beautiful ~** ils ont vécu un beau roman (d'amour) ◆ **the ~ of the sea/of foreign lands** la poésie de la mer/des pays étrangers 2 *(Ling)* **Romance** roman *m* ADJ *(Ling)* ◆ **Romance** roman VI enjoliver, broder *(fig)* VT *(= woo)* faire la cour à, courtiser

romancer /rəʊˈmænsəʳ/ N conteur *m*, -euse *f* ◆ **he's a ~** *(fig)* il enjolive toujours tout

Romanesque /ˌrəʊməˈnesk/ ADJ *[architecture]* roman

Romania /rəʊˈmeɪnɪə/ N Roumanie *f*

Romanian /rəʊˈmeɪnɪən/ ADJ *(gen)* roumain ; *[ambassador, embassy]* de Roumanie N 1 Roumain(e) *m(f)* 2 *(= language)* roumain *m*

Romanic /rəʊˈmænɪk/ ADJ *[language]* roman

Romanize /ˈrəʊmənaɪz/ VT *(Hist)* romaniser ; *(Rel)* convertir au catholicisme

Romans(c)h /rəʊˈmænʃ/ N romanche *m*

romantic /rəʊˈmæntɪk/ ADJ 1 *(= amorous) [relationship, interlude, assignation]* amoureux ; *[novel, film]* sentimental ; *[novelist, holiday, dinner]* romantique 2 *(= picturesque, glamorous) [appearance, landscape, castle]* romantique ◆ **a ~ figure like Lawrence of Arabia** un personnage romantique comme Lawrence d'Arabie 3 *(= unrealistic) [person]* romantique, sentimental ;

[idea, view, image] romantique [4] *(Art, Literat, Mus)* ◆ **Romantic** romantique N romantique *mf*, sentimental(e) *m(f)* ; *(Art, Literat, Mus)* romantique *mf*

COMP **romantic comedy** N comédie *f* sentimentale

romantic fiction N *(NonC)* les romans *mpl* roses

romantic lead N *(Cine, Theat)* jeune premier *m*, -ière *f*

romantic love N amour *m* romantique

the Romantic Movement N le Mouvement romantique, le romantisme

romantically /rəʊˈmæntɪkəlɪ/ ADV [1] *(= picturesquely, glamorously)* ◆ **the castle is ~ sited on a cliff top** le château occupe une situation très romantique au sommet d'une falaise ◆ **~ named ...** au nom romantique de ... [2] *(= amorously)* *[behave, kiss]* amoureusement ◆ **~ inclined** *or* **minded** romantique ◆ **to be ~ involved with sb** avoir une liaison avec qn ◆ **she has been ~ linked with the prince** on a parlé d'une idylle entre le prince et elle ◆ **~, things are looking up** sur le plan sentimental, les choses s'annoncent bien [3] *(= unrealistically)* *[talk, describe]* sentimentalement

romanticism /rəʊˈmæntɪsɪzəm/ N romantisme *m*

romanticist /rəʊˈmæntɪsɪst/ N romantique *mf*

romanticize /rəʊˈmæntɪsaɪz/ VTI romancer

romanticized /rəʊˈmæntɪsaɪzd/ ADJ *[idea, view, depiction]* très romantique

Romany /ˈrɒmənɪ/ N [1] Rom *mf inv*, tzigane *or* tsigane *mf* [2] *(= language)* romani *m* ADJ *[person, society, culture, language]* rom *inv*, tzigane *or* tsigane ◆ **a ~ caravan** une roulotte de tziganes *or* tsiganes

Rome /rəʊm/ N Rome ◆ **when in ~ (do as the Romans do)** *(Prov)* à Rome il faut vivre comme les Romains ◆ **~ wasn't built in a day** *(Prov)* Paris *or* Rome ne s'est pas fait en un jour ◆ **all roads lead to ~** *(Prov)* tous les chemins mènent à Rome ◆ **the Church of ~** l'Église *f* (catholique) romaine ◆ **to go over to ~** *(Rel)* se convertir au catholicisme

Romeo /ˈrəʊmɪəʊ/ N Roméo *m*

Romish /ˈrəʊmɪʃ/ ADJ *(pej)* catholique

romp /rɒmp/ N [1] *(hum = sex)* ébats *mpl* amoureux [2] *(= energetic play)* jeux *mpl* bruyants, ébats *mpl* ◆ **the play was just a ~** la pièce n'était (guère) qu'une farce VI *[children, puppies]* jouer bruyamment, s'ébattre ◆ **the horse ~ed home** le cheval est arrivé dans un fauteuil* ◆ **to ~ through an exam** bien se débrouiller à un examen

rompers /ˈrɒmpəz/ NPL, **romper suit** /ˈrɒmpəsuːt/ N barboteuse *f*

Romulus /ˈrɒmjʊləs/ N ◆ **~ and Remus** Romulus *m* et Remus *m*

Roncesvalles /ˈrɒnsəvælz/ N Roncevaux

rondeau /ˈrɒndəʊ/ (pl **rondeaux** /ˈrɒndəʊz/, **rondel** /ˈrɒndl/) N *(Mus, Poetry)* rondeau *m*

rondo /ˈrɒndəʊ/ N *(Mus)* rondeau *m*

Roneo ® /ˈrəʊnɪəʊ/ VT polycopier, ronéoter

rood /ruːd/ N [1] *(Rel Archit)* crucifix *m* [2] *(Brit = measure)* quart *m* d'arpent COMP **rood screen** N jubé *m*

roof /ruːf/ N *[of building, car]* toit *m (also Climbing)* ; *[of cave, tunnel]* plafond *m* ; *(fig: of sky, branches)* voûte *f* ◆ **the ~ of the mouth** *(Anat)* la voûte du palais ◆ **without a ~ over one's head** sans abri *or* toit ◆ **a room in the ~** une chambre sous les combles *or* sous les toits ◆ **I couldn't live under her ~** je ne pourrais pas vivre chez elle ◆ **to live under the same ~ as sb** vivre sous le même toit que qn ◆ **under one ~** *(gen)* sous le même toit ; *(in shopping arcade, hypermarket etc)* réuni(s) au même endroit ◆ **to go through** *or* **to hit the ~** * *[person]* exploser, piquer une crise* ; *[price, claim]* crever le plafond ; → **flat¹, raise, sunshine**

VT *[+ house]* couvrir (d'un toit) ◆ **red-~ed** à toit rouge

COMP **roof garden** N jardin *m* sur le toit

roof light N plafonnier *m*

roof rack N *(esp Brit)* galerie *f*

roof terrace N terrasse *f* sur le toit

► **roof in** VT SEP couvrir d'un toit

► **roof over** VT SEP recouvrir d'un toit

roofer /ˈruːfəʳ/ N couvreur *m*

roofing /ˈruːfɪŋ/ N [1] *(on house)* toiture *f*, couverture *f* [2] *(= act)* pose *f* de la toiture *or* de la couverture COMP **roofing felt** N couverture *f* bitumée *or* goudronnée

roofless /ˈruːflɪs/ ADJ sans toit

rooftop /ˈruːftɒp/ N toit *m* ◆ **to shout** *or* **proclaim sth from the ~s** *(fig)* crier qch sur tous les toits *(fig)*

rook¹ /rʊk/ N *(= bird)* (corbeau *m*) freux *m* VT (* = *swindle)* rouler (dans la farine)*, escroquer

rook² /rʊk/ N *(Chess)* tour *f*

rookery /ˈrʊkərɪ/ N colonie *f* de freux ; *[of seals, penguins]* colonie *f* ; *(fig pej = overcrowded slum)* taudis *m* surpeuplé

rookie * /ˈrʊkɪ/ N *(US esp Mil)* bleu* *m*

room /rʊm/ N [1] *(in house)* pièce *f* ; *(large)* salle *f* ; *(= bedroom)* chambre *f* ; *(= office, study)* bureau *m* ; *(in hotel)* chambre *f* ◆ **~s to let** chambres *fpl* à louer ◆ **~ and board** pension *f* ◆ **his ~s** son appartement ◆ **come to my ~s for coffee** venez prendre le café chez moi ◆ **they live in ~s** ils habitent un meublé *or* un garni *(pej)* ; → **double, lecture, roof**

[2] *(NonC = space)* place *f* ◆ **is there ~?** y a-t-il de la place ? ◆ **there is ~ for two people** il y a de la place pour deux personnes ◆ **there's no ~** il n'y a pas de place ◆ **there's not enough** *or* **no ~ to swing a cat** * c'est grand comme un mouchoir de poche ◆ **to take up ~/too much ~** prendre de la place/trop de place ◆ **to make ~ for sb** faire une place pour qn ◆ **to make ~ for sth** faire de la place pour qch ◆ **there is still ~ for hope** il y a encore lieu d'espérer ◆ **there is little ~ for hope** il ne reste pas beaucoup d'espoir ◆ **there is no ~ for doubt** il n'y a pas de doute possible ◆ **there is ~ for improvement in your work** votre travail laisse à désirer

VI *(US)* partager une chambre (*with* avec) ; ◆ **to ~ with a landlady** louer une chambre meublée

COMP **room clerk** N *(US)* réceptionniste *mf*

room divider N meuble *m* de séparation

rooming house N *(US)* immeuble *m (avec chambres à louer)* ◆ **he lives in a ~ing house** il habite un meublé

rooming-in N *(in maternity wards) possibilité pour les accouchées de garder leur nouveau-né dans leur chambre*

room service N service *m* des chambres (d'hôtel), room-service *m* ◆ **ring for ~ service** appelez le garçon d'étage

room temperature N température *f* ambiante ◆ **to bring a wine to ~ temperature** chambrer un vin ◆ **wine at ~ temperature** vin *m* chambré

-roomed /rʊmd/ ADJ *(in compounds)* ◆ **a six-roomed house** une maison de six pièces ◆ **a two-roomed flat** un deux-pièces

roomer /ˈrʊməʳ/ N *(US)* locataire *mf*

roomette /ruːˈmet/ N *(US Rail)* compartiment *m* individuel de wagons-lits

roomful /ˈrʊmfʊl/ N pleine salle *f*

roominess /ˈrʊmɪnɪs/ N dimensions *fpl* spacieuses

roommate /ˈrʊmmeɪt/ N camarade *mf* de chambre ; *(US: sharing lodgings)* personne *f* avec laquelle on partage un appartement

roomy /ˈrʊmɪ/ ADJ *[flat, car]* spacieux ; *[bag]* grand ; *[garment]* ample

roost /ruːst/ N perchoir *m*, juchoir *m* ; → **rule** VI *(= settle)* se percher, se jucher ; *(= sleep)* jucher ◆ **all her little schemes are coming home to ~** toutes ses petites combines vont lui retomber dessus *or* se retourner contre elle

rooster /ˈruːstəʳ/ N *(esp US)* coq *m*

root /ruːt/ N [1] *(gen, Bot, Math etc)* racine *f* ; *(fig)* *[of trouble etc]* origine *f*, cause *f* ◆ **to pull up** *or* **out by the ~s** déraciner, extirper ◆ **to take ~** *(lit, fig)* prendre racine ◆ **to pull up one's ~s** *(fig)* se déraciner ◆ **her ~s are in France** elle est restée française de cœur *or* d'esprit ◆ **she has no ~s** elle n'a pas de racines, c'est une déracinée ◆ **to put down ~s in a country** s'enraciner dans un pays ◆ **the ~ of the matter** la vraie raison ◆ **to get to the ~ of the problem** trouver la cause *or* aller au fond du problème ◆ **that is at the ~ of ...** cela est à l'origine de ... ◆ **what lies at the ~ of his attitude?** quelle est la raison fondamentale de son attitude ? ; → **cube, grass, square**

◆ **root and branch** ◆ **to change sth ~ and branch** modifier qch de fond en comble ◆ **to destroy sth ~ and branch** détruire qch complètement ◆ **a ~-and-branch reform** une réforme radicale

[2] *(Ling)* *(gen)* racine *f* ; *(Gram)* *[of verb]* radical *m* ; *[of non-verb]* base *f*

[3] *[of tooth]* racine *f* ; *[of tongue]* base *f*

[4] *(Mus)* fondamentale *f*

VT *(Bot)* enraciner ◆ **a deeply ~ed belief** une croyance profondément enracinée ◆ **to be** *or* **stand ~ed to the spot** être cloué sur place

VI [1] *[plants etc]* s'enraciner, prendre racine

[2] *[pigs]* fouiller (avec le groin)

COMP **root beer** N *(US) boisson gazeuse à base d'extraits végétaux*

root canal N *[of tooth]* canal *m* dentaire

root-canal therapy, root-canal work N *(Dentistry)* dévitalisation *f*, pulpectomie *f*

root cause N cause *f* première

root crops NPL racines *fpl* comestibles

root ginger N gingembre *m* frais

root sign N *(Math)* radical *m*

roots music N *(= world music)* world music *f* ; *(= reggae)* reggae *m* (des origines)

root vegetable N racine *f* (comestible)

root word N *(Ling)* mot *m* souche *inv*

► **root about** VI fouiller *(among* dans ; *for sth* pour trouver qch)

► **root among** VI fouiller dans

► **root around** VI ⇒ **root about**

► **root for** * VT FUS *[+ team]* encourager, applaudir

► **root out** VT SEP *(fig)* *(= find)* dénicher ; *(= remove)* extirper

► **root through** VI ⇒ **root among**

► **root up** VT SEP *[+ plant]* déraciner ; *[pigs]* déterrer ; *(fig)* extirper

rootless /ˈruːtlɪs/ ADJ *(lit, fig)* sans racine(s)

rootstock /ˈruːtstɒk/ N *(Bot)* rhizome *m*

rope /rəʊp/ N [1] *(gen)* corde *f* ; *(Naut)* cordage *m* ; *[of bell]* cordon *m* ◆ **to give sb more ~** *(fig)* lâcher la bride à qn ◆ **give him enough ~ and he'll hang himself** si on le laisse faire il se passera lui-même la corde au cou *or* il creusera sa propre tombe ◆ **the ~s** *(Boxing etc)* les cordes *fpl* ◆ **on the ~s** *(Boxing)* dans les cordes ; * *(fig)* *[person]* sur le flanc* ; *[business]* qui bat de l'aile* ◆ **to know the ~s** * *(fig)* connaître toutes les ficelles* ◆ **to show sb the ~s** * mettre qn au courant ◆ **to learn the ~s** * se mettre au courant ◆ **to be at the end of one's ~** *(US)* *(= annoyed, impatient)* être à bout de nerfs ;

(= *desperate*) être sur le point de craquer ◆ **a ~ of pearls** un collier de perles ◆ **a ~ of onions** un chapelet d'oignons ◆ **a ~ of hair** une torsade de cheveux ; → **clothes, skipping, tightrope**

2 (*Climbing*) corde *f* ; (*people on rope*) cordée *f* ◆ **a ~ of climbers** une cordée d'alpinistes ◆ **to put on the ~** s'encorder ◆ **there were three of them on the ~** ils formaient une cordée de trois

VT 1 [*+ box, case*] corder ◆ **to ~ sb to a tree** lier qn à un arbre ◆ **to ~ climbers (together)** encorder des alpinistes ◆ **~d party** (*Climbing*) cordée *f*

2 (*US = catch*) [*+ cattle*] prendre au lasso

COMP **rope burn** N brûlure *f* (*provoquée par une corde*)

rope ladder N échelle *f* de corde

rope-length N (*Climbing*) longueur *f* de corde

rope maker N cordier *m*

rope trick N ◆ **Indian ~ trick** *tour de prestidigitation réalisé avec une corde*

roping-off N (*Climbing*) rappel *m*

► **rope in** VT SEP [*+ area*] entourer de cordes, délimiter par une corde ◆ **to ~ sb in** * (*fig*) enrôler qn, embringuer qn * ◆ **he got himself ~d in * to help at the fête** il s'est laissé embringuer * pour aider à la fête ◆ **I don't want to get ~d in * for anything** je ne veux pas me laisser embringuer *

► **rope off** VT SEP (= *section off*) réserver par une corde ; (= *block off*) interdire l'accès de

► **rope up** (*Climbing*) VI s'encorder

VT SEP encorder ◆ **to be ~d up** être encordé

ropedancer /ˈrəʊpdɑːnsəʳ/, **ropewalker** /ˈrəʊpwɔːkəʳ/ N funambule *mf*, danseur *m*, -euse *f* de corde

rop(e)y /ˈrəʊpɪ/ ADJ 1 (*Brit* * = *mediocre*) pas terrible * 2 (*Brit = ill*) ◆ **to feel a bit rop(e)y** * être *or* se sentir patraque * 3 (= *rope-like*) [*muscles, arm, neck*] noueux

RORO N (abbrev of **roll-on-roll-off**) → **roll-on**

rosary /ˈrəʊzərɪ/ N 1 (*Rel*) chapelet *m* ; (= *fifteen decades*) rosaire *m* ◆ **to say the ~** dire *or* réciter son chapelet 2 (*in garden*) roseraie *f*

rose¹ /rəʊz/ VB pt of **rise**

rose² /rəʊz/ N 1 (= *flower*) rose *f* ; (also **rose-bush, rose tree**) rosier *m* ◆ **wild ~** églantine *f* ◆ **life isn't all ~s** la vie n'est pas rose tous les jours ◆ **it isn't all ~s** tout n'est pas rose ◆ **there is no ~ without a thorn** (*Prov*) il n'y a pas de roses sans épines ◆ **she's an English ~** elle est belle comme une fleur *or* fraîche comme une rose ◆ **that will put ~s back in your cheeks** cela va te rendre tes belles couleurs ◆ **under the ~** (*fig liter*) en confidence ◆ **the Wars of the Roses** (*Brit Hist*) la guerre des Deux-Roses ◆ **everything is coming up ~s** * tout marche comme sur des roulettes * ◆ **to come up smelling of ~s** * s'en sortir très bien ; → **bed, Christmas, rock²**

2 [*of hose, watering can*] pomme *f* ; (*on hat, shoe*) rosette *f* ; [*of pump*] crépine *f* ; (*on ceiling*) rosace *f* (de plafond) ; → **compass**

3 (= *colour*) rose *m*

ADJ rose

COMP [*leaf, petal*] de rose

rose-coloured ADJ rose, couleur de rose *inv* ◆ **to see everything/life through ~-coloured spectacles** voir tout/la vie en rose

rose diamond N (diamant *m* en) rose *f*

rose garden N roseraie *f*

rose grower N rosiériste *mf*

rose pink ADJ rose, rosé

rose-red ADJ vermeil

rose-tinted ADJ ⇒ **rose-coloured**

rose water N eau *f* de rose (*lit*)

rose window N rosace *f*, rose *f*

rosé /ˈrəʊzeɪ/ N rosé *m* (*vin*)

roseate /ˈrəʊzɪɪt/ ADJ (*liter*) 1 (= *pink*) rose 2 (*pej* = *rose-tinted*) [*picture, vision*] idyllique

rosebay /ˈrəʊzbeɪ/ N laurier-rose *m*

rosebed /ˈrəʊzbed/ N parterre *m or* massif *m* de roses

rosebowl /ˈrəʊzbəʊl/ N coupe *f* à fleurs

rosebud /ˈrəʊzbʌd/ N bouton *m* de rose COMP **rosebud mouth** N bouche *f* en cerise

rosebush /ˈrəʊzbʊʃ/ N rosier *m*

rosehip /ˈrəʊzhɪp/ N cynorhodon *m*, gratte-cul *m* COMP **rosehip syrup** N sirop *m* d'églantine

roselike /ˈrəʊzlaɪk/ ADJ rosacé

rosemary /ˈrəʊzmərɪ/ N romarin *m*

roseola /rəʊˈziːələ/ N roséole *f*

rosette /rəʊˈzet/ N (= *ribbons etc*) rosette *f* ; (*Sport: as prize*) cocarde *f* ; (*Archit*) rosace *f*

rosewood /ˈrəʊzwʊd/ N bois *m* de rose COMP en bois de rose

Rosh Hashanah /ˌrɒʃhəˈʃɑːnə/ N Rosh ha-Shana, Roch ha-Shana

Rosicrucian /ˌrəʊzɪˈkruːʃən/ ADJ, N rosicrucien(ne) *m(f)*

rosin /ˈrɒzɪn/ N colophane *f*

RoSPA /ˈrɒspə/ N (*Brit*) (abbrev of **Royal Society for the Prevention of Accidents**) *société pour la prévention des accidents*

roster /ˈrɒstəʳ/ N liste *f*, tableau *m* (de service) ; → **duty**

rostrum /ˈrɒstrəm/ N (pl **rostrums** *or* **rostra** /ˈrɒstrə/) [*for speaker*] tribune *f*, estrade *f* ; estrade *f* (*Roman Hist*) rostres *mpl* ◆ **on the ~** à la tribune COMP **rostrum camera** N banc-titre *n*

rosy /ˈrəʊzɪ/ ADJ 1 (= *pink*) [*colour*] rosé ; [*face, cheeks, complexion, light*] rose 2 (= *optimistic*) [*view*] optimiste ◆ **the situation looks ~ (for her)** la situation se présente bien (pour elle) ◆ **things don't look very ~ for her** la situation n'est pas rose pour elle ◆ **his future looks ~** l'avenir se présente bien pour lui ◆ **the party seemed to have a ~ future ahead of it** l'avenir du parti était prometteur ◆ **to paint a ~ picture of sth** faire *or* brosser un tableau idyllique de qch

rot /rɒt/ N (*NonC*) 1 pourriture *f* ; (*Bot, Med*) carie *f* ◆ **he worked well at the beginning then the ~ set in** * au début il travaillait bien mais par la suite il a flanché * *or* les problèmes ont commencé ◆ **to stop the ~** redresser la situation ; → **dry** 2 (*esp Brit* † * = *nonsense*) balivernes *fpl* ◆ **to talk ~** dire *or* débiter des balivernes ◆ **that's utter ~, that's a lot of ~** ce ne sont que des balivernes VI pourrir ; (*fig*) [*person*] croupir ◆ **to ~ in jail** croupir en prison ◆ **let him ~!** * qu'il aille se faire pendre ! * VT (faire) pourrir

► **rot away** VI pourrir

rota /ˈrəʊtə/ N 1 (*esp Brit*) liste *f*, tableau *m* (de service) 2 (*Rel*) **Rota** rote *f*

Rotarian /rəʊˈtɛərɪən/ ADJ, N rotarien *m*

rotary /ˈrəʊtərɪ/ ADJ 1 [*tin-opener, dial, control, movement*] rotatif 2 ◆ **Rotary (Club)** Rotary Club *m*

COMP **rotary clothes dryer** N séchoir *m* rotatif

rotary cultivator N motoculteur *m*

rotary engine N moteur *m* rotatif

rotary kiln N four *m* rotatif

rotary (lawn)mower N tondeuse *f* à lame rotative

rotary press N rotative *f*

rotary printer N tireuse *m* rotative

rotary printing press N ⇒ **rotary press**

rotary shutter N (*Phot*) obturateur *m* rotatif

rotary-wing aircraft N aéronef *m* à voilure tournante

rotate /rəʊˈteɪt/ VT (= *revolve*) faire tourner ; (*on pivot*) faire pivoter ; (= *change round*) [*+ crops*] alterner ; [*two people*] [*+ work, jobs*] faire à tour de rôle VI tourner ; (*on pivot*) pivoter ; [*crops*] être alterné

rotating /rəʊˈteɪtɪŋ/ ADJ (*gen*) tournant ; (= *pivoting*) pivotant

rotation /rəʊˈteɪʃən/ N (= *turning*) rotation *f* ; (= *turn*) rotation *f*, tour *m* ◆ **in** *or* **by ~** à tour de rôle ◆ **~ of crops** assolement *m*, rotation *f* (des cultures)

rotatory /rəʊˈteɪtərɪ/ ADJ rotatoire

Rotavator ® /ˈrəʊtəveɪtəʳ/ N (*Brit*) ⇒ **Rotovator**

rote /rəʊt/ N ◆ **by ~** [*learn*] machinalement, sans essayer de comprendre ; [*recite*] comme un perroquet COMP **rote learning** N apprentissage *m* par cœur

rotgut ‡ /ˈrɒtgʌt/ N (*pej*) tord-boyaux ‡ *m inv*

rotisserie /rəʊˈtɪsərɪ/ N (= *grill or oven*) rôtissoire *f* ; (= *fitment*) tournebroche *m* ; (= *restaurant*) rôtisserie *f*

rotogravure /ˌrəʊtəʊgrəˈvjʊəʳ/ N rotogravure *f*

rotor /ˈrəʊtəʳ/ N [*of machine, generator, helicopter*] rotor *m*

COMP **rotor arm** N rotor *m*

rotor blade N pale *f* de rotor

rotorcraft /ˈrəʊtəkrɑːft/ N giravion *m*, hélicoptère *m*

rototill /ˈrəʊtəʊtɪl/ VT (*US*) labourer avec un motoculteur

Rototiller ® /ˈrəʊtəʊtɪləʳ/ N (*US*) motoculteur *m*

rotovate /ˈrəʊtəveɪt/ VT (*Brit*) labourer avec un motoculteur

Rotovator ® /ˈrəʊtəveɪtəʳ/ N (*Brit*) motoculteur *m*

rotproof /ˈrɒtpruːf/ ADJ imputrescible

rotten /ˈrɒtn/ ADJ 1 (= *decayed*) [*wood, vegetation, vegetable, egg*] pourri ; [*meat*] pourri, avarié ; [*fruit, tooth*] pourri, gâté

2 (= *corrupt*) véreux, corrompu ◆ **~ to the core** pourri jusqu'à la moelle ; → **comp**

3 (* = *useless*) nul (*at sth* en qch ; *at doing sth* pour faire qch)

4 (* = *unpleasant*) ◆ **what ~ weather !** quel temps pourri ! * ◆ **what ~ luck!** quelle guigne ! *, quelle poisse ! * ◆ **we had a ~ time** on ne s'est pas marrés * ◆ **what a ~ trick!** quel sale tour ! * ◆ **that's a ~ thing to say/do!** c'est moche * de dire/faire ça ! ◆ **it's a ~ business** c'est une sale affaire ◆ **isn't it ~ about poor Anne?** pauvre Anne ! quel sale coup ! * ◆ **to feel/look ~** * (= *ill*) se sentir/avoir l'air mal fichu * ◆ **to feel ~ * (about doing sth)** (= *guilty*) se sentir minable * (de faire qch)

5 (*: *expressing annoyance*) fichu *, sale * *before n* ◆ **you can keep your ~ bike** tu peux te le garder, ton sale vélo *

ADV * ◆ **to spoil sb ~** pourrir qn ◆ **to fancy sb ~** (*Brit*) être entiché de qn

COMP **rotten apple** N (*fig*) brebis *f* galeuse ◆ **one ~ apple spoils the (whole) barrel** (*Prov*) il ne faut qu'une brebis galeuse pour infecter le troupeau

rottenness /ˈrɒtnnɪs/ N (état *m* de) pourriture *f*

rotter † * /ˈrɒtəʳ/ N (*Brit*) sale type * *m*

rotting /ˈrɒtɪŋ/ ADJ en pourriture, qui pourrit

Rottweiler /ˈrɒtˌvaɪləʳ/ N Rottweiler *m*

rotund /rəʊˈtʌnd/ ADJ 1 (= *round*) [*person, body*] replet (-ète *f*), rondelet ; [*object, building*] arrondi ◆ **his ~ stomach** son ventre rebondi 2 (= *sonorous*) [*voice, tone*] sonore

rotunda /rəʊˈtʌndə/ N rotonde *f*

rotundity /rəʊˈtʌndɪtɪ/ N [*of person*] embonpoint *m* ; (*fig*) [*of style*] grandiloquence *f* ; [*of voice*] sonorité *f*

rouble, ruble (US) /ˈruːbl/ N rouble *m*

roué /ˈruːeɪ/ N roué *m*, débauché *m*

rouge /ruːʒ/ N rouge *m* (à joues) VT ◆ **to ~ one's cheeks** se farder les joues, se mettre du rouge aux joues

rough /rʌf/ ADJ 1 (= *not smooth*) [*skin, hands, cloth*] rêche ; (*harder*) rugueux ; [*bark*] rugueux ; [*ground, road, track*] raboteux ◆ **~ edges** aspérités *fpl* ◆ **the proposal still has some ~ edges** le projet n'est pas encore tout à fait au point ◆ **he'll be a good salesman once we knock off the ~ edges** il fera un bon vendeur lorsque nous l'aurons un peu dégrossi ◆ **to give sb the ~ side of one's tongue** * (*Brit*) passer un savon * à qn

2 (= *harsh*) [*sound*] rude, âpre ; [*voice*] rude ; [*taste*] âpre ; [*wine*] grossier ◆ **to taste ~** avoir un goût âpre

3 (= *unrefined*) [*person, speech, manners*] rude ; [*tone, voice*] brusque

4 (* = *difficult*) [*life*] dur ◆ **to have a ~ time (of it)** en voir de rudes *or* de dures * ◆ **to give sb a ~ time** en faire voir de toutes les couleurs à qn * ◆ **it's ~ on him** c'est dur pour lui ◆ **don't be too ~ on him** ne sois pas trop dur avec lui ; → **ride**

5 (*Brit* * = *ill*) ◆ **to feel ~** ne pas se sentir bien, être mal fichu * ◆ **you sound ~!** tu as l'air mal fichu !

6 (= *violent*) [*person, game, treatment*] rude ; [*sex*] brutal ◆ **to be ~ with sb** (*physically*) malmener qn ; (*verbally*) être dur avec qn ◆ **a ~ customer** * un dur * ◆ **~ handling** rudoiement *m* ◆ **a ~ neighbourhood** un quartier difficile ◆ **~ play** (*Sport*) jeu *m* brutal ◆ **~ stuff** * brutalités *fpl* ◆ **no ~ stuff!** mollo ! *

7 (= *stormy*) [*weather*] gros (grosse *f*) ; [*sea*] agité, mauvais ; [*crossing*] agité ◆ **it was very ~** la mer était très agitée *or* mauvaise

8 (= *rudimentary*) [*shelter*] rudimentaire ; [*clothes*] grossier ; (= *approximate*) [*calculation, translation, estimate, description*] approximatif ; [*plan*] vague, approximatif ◆ **a ~ guess** une approximation ◆ **at a ~ estimate** *or* **guess** à vue de nez ◆ **can you give me a ~ idea (of) how long it will take?** à votre avis, ça prendra combien de temps environ ? ◆ **I've got a ~ idea (of) what it looks like** je vois à peu près à quoi ça ressemble ◆ **as a ~ guide** à titre indicatif ◆ **he gave a ~ outline of the proposals** il a donné les grandes lignes des propositions ◆ **~ draft** brouillon *m* ◆ **~ sketch** croquis *m* ébauche *f*

9 (= *uncultivated*) ◆ **~ pasture** prés *mpl* incultes ◆ **a piece of ~ ground** un terrain vague

ADV ◆ **to sleep ~** coucher sur la dure ◆ **to live ~** vivre à la dure ◆ **to play ~** [*child, sportsperson*] jouer de manière brutale ; [*gangster*] avoir des méthodes brutales ◆ **we can either keep it friendly, or we can play ~** soit on continue à l'amiable, soit on devient méchants ◆ **to cut up ~** * (*Brit*) (*angry*) se mettre en rogne * ; (*violent*) devenir violent

N 1 (= *ground*) terrain *m* accidenté *or* rocailleux ; (*Golf*) rough *m* ◆ **to take the ~ with the smooth** (*fig*) prendre les choses comme elles viennent

2 (= *draft*) brouillon *m*, premier jet *m* ◆ **to write sth out in ~** rédiger qch au brouillon ◆ **a diamond in the ~** (*US*) ⇒ **rough diamond**

3 (* = *person*) voyou *m*

VT ◆ **to ~ it** * vivre à la dure

COMP **rough-and-ready** ADJ [*method*] fruste, rudimentaire ; [*work*] grossier, fait à la hâte ; [*installation, equipment*] rudimentaire, de fortune ; [*person*] fruste

rough-and-tumble ADJ [*play, game*] désordonné ◆ **the ~-and-tumble atmosphere of ...** l'ambiance *f* de foire d'empoigne de ... N 1 (= *cut and thrust*) **he enjoys the ~-and-tumble of Washington** il aime l'ambiance mouvementée de Washington ◆ **the ~-and-tumble of political life** l'univers *m* mouvementé de la politique 2 (= *rough play*) jeux *mpl* désordonnés

rough diamond N (*lit*) diamant *m* brut ◆ **he's a ~ diamond** (*Brit*) sous ses dehors frustes, il a un cœur d'or

rough-dry VT sécher sans repasser

rough-hewn ADJ dégrossi, ébauché

rough justice N justice *f* sommaire

rough paper N (*NonC: Brit*) papier *m* de brouillon

rough puff pastry N pâte *f* feuilletée (simplifiée)

rough sleeper N sans-abri *m*

rough-spoken ADJ au langage grossier

rough trade ‡ N partenaire homosexuel des bas-fonds

rough work N (*NonC*) brouillon *m*

► **rough out** VT SEP [+ *plan, drawing*] ébaucher

► **rough up** VT SEP [+ *hair*] ébouriffer ◆ **to ~ sb up** * malmener qn ; (*stronger*) tabasser ‡ qn

roughage /ˈrʌfɪdʒ/ N (*NonC*) fibres *fpl*

roughcast /ˈrʌfkɑːst/ ADJ, N crépi *m* VT crépir

roughen /ˈrʌfn/ VT rendre rude *or* rugueux VI devenir rude *or* rugueux

roughhouse * /ˈrʌfhaʊs/ N bagarre *f*

roughly /ˈrʌflɪ/ ADV 1 (= *violently*) [*pull, push, play*] brutalement ◆ **to treat sb/sth ~** malmener qn/qch

2 (= *brusquely*) [*speak, answer, order*] durement

3 (= *crudely*) [*make, sew, chop, slice*] grossièrement

4 (= *approximately*) à peu près ◆ **~ comparable/equal** à peu près comparable/égal ◆ **it costs ~ 25 euros** ça coûte environ 25 € ◆ **~ half of the population** environ la moitié de la population ◆ **he was ~ the same age as me** il avait environ *or* à peu près le même âge que moi ◆ **tell me ~ what it's all about** dites-moi grosso modo *or* en gros de quoi il s'agit ◆ **he ~ outlined the proposals** il a donné les grandes lignes des propositions ◆ **to sketch sth ~** faire un croquis de qch ◆ **to fall ~ into two categories** se répartir approximativement en deux catégories ◆ **~ translated, the name means ...** traduit approximativement, ce nom veut dire ... ◆ **~ speaking** en gros, grosso modo

roughneck * /ˈrʌfnek/ N (*esp US*) voyou *m*, dur *m* à cuire *

roughness /ˈrʌfnɪs/ N (*NonC*) 1 [*of skin, hands, cloth*] rudesse *f* ; [*of ground, road, track*] mauvais état *m* ; [*of edges*] rugosité *f* 2 (= *harshness*) [*of sound, voice, taste, wine*] rudesse *f* 3 (= *lack of refinement*) [*of person, manners, speech*] rudesse *f* ; [*of tone, voice*] brusquerie *f* 4 (= *violence*) [*of person, game, treatment*] brutalité *f* ; [*of neighbourhood*] caractère *m* dangereux 5 (= *storminess*) [*of sea*] agitation *f* ◆ **the ~ of the weather** le mauvais temps 6 (= *rudimentary nature*) [*of shelter*] caractère *m* rudimentaire ; [*of clothes*] grossièreté *f* 7 (= *approximate nature*) [*of calculation, translation, estimate, description*] caractère *m* approximatif ; [*of plan*] manque *m* de détails

roughrider /ˌrʌfˈraɪdəʳ/ N dresseur *m*, -euse *f* *or* dompteur *m*, -euse *f* de chevaux

roughshod /ˈrʌfʃɒd/ ADV ◆ **to ride ~ over** [+ *objection, person*] faire peu de cas de

roulette /ruːˈlet/ N roulette *f* ; → **Russian**

COMP **roulette table** N table *f* de roulette

roulette wheel N roulette *f*

Roumania /ruːˈmeɪnɪə/ N ⇒ **Rumania**

Roumanian /ruːˈmeɪnɪən/ ADJ, N ⇒ **Rumanian**

round /raʊnd/

When **round** is an element in a phrasal verb, eg **ask round, call round, rally round**, look up the verb.

ADV 1 (= *around*) autour ◆ **there was a wall right ~** il y avait un mur tout autour ◆ **he went ~ by the bridge** il a fait le détour *or* il est passé par le pont ◆ **you can't get through here, you'll have to go ~** vous ne pouvez pas passer par ici, il faut faire le tour ◆ **the long way ~** le chemin le plus long ◆ **it's a long way ~** ça fait un grand détour *or* un grand crochet ◆ **spring will soon be ~ again** le printemps reviendra bientôt ; → **gather round, look round**

◆ **all + round** ◆ **there was a wall all ~** il y avait un mur tout autour ◆ **this ought to make life much easier all ~** (= *for everybody*) cela devrait simplifier la vie de tout le monde ◆ **this called for drinks all ~** cela méritait une tournée générale ◆ **she ordered drinks all ~ to celebrate** elle a commandé une tournée générale pour fêter ça ◆ **taking things all ~, taken all ~** tout compte fait ◆ **all (the) year ~** pendant toute l'année

◆ **round and round** en rond ◆ **to go (*or* drive *or* ride) ~ and ~** (*looking for sth*) tourner en rond ◆ **the idea was going ~ and ~ in his head** il tournait et retournait l'idée dans sa tête

2 (*to sb's place*) ◆ **she ran ~ to her mother's** elle a couru chez sa mère ◆ **come ~ and see me** venez me voir ◆ **I asked him ~ for a drink** je l'ai invité à (passer) prendre un verre chez moi ◆ **I'll be ~ at 8 o'clock** je serai là à 8 heures

3 (*set structure*)

◆ **round about** (= *approximately*) autour de, environ ◆ **~ about 7 o'clock** autour de 7 heures, vers (les) 7 heures ◆ **~ about £800** 800 livres environ

PREP 1 (*of place etc*) autour de ◆ **sitting ~ the table** assis autour de la table ◆ **sitting ~ the fire** assis au coin du feu *or* auprès du feu ◆ **all ~ the house** tout autour de la maison ◆ **the villages ~ Brighton** les villages *mpl* des environs *or* des alentours de Brighton ◆ **she knows everybody ~ about** elle connaît tout le monde dans le coin ◆ **the house is just ~ the corner** la maison est au coin de la rue *or* juste après le coin de la rue ; (*fig*) la maison est tout près ◆ **come and see me if you're ~ this way** viens me voir si tu passes par ici *or* si tu es dans le coin * ◆ **to go ~ a corner** tourner un coin ; (*driving*) prendre un virage ◆ **to go ~ an obstacle** contourner un obstacle ◆ **to look ~ a house** visiter une maison ◆ **to show sb ~ a town** faire visiter une ville à qn ◆ **they went ~ the castle** ils ont visité le château ◆ **they went ~ the cafés looking for ...** ils ont fait le tour des cafés à la recherche de ... ◆ **she's 75cm ~ the waist** elle fait 75 cm de tour de taille ◆ **put a blanket ~ him** enveloppez-le dans une couverture ; → **clock, world**

2 (*esp Brit* = *approximately*) autour de, environ ◆ **~ 7 o'clock** autour de 7 heures, vers (les) 7 heures ◆ **~ £800** 800 livres environ

ADJ 1 (= *circular*) rond, circulaire ; (= *rounded*) rond, arrondi ◆ **to have ~ shoulders** avoir le dos rond *or* voûté ◆ **~ handwriting** écriture *f* ronde

2 (= *complete*) **a ~ dozen** une douzaine tout rond ◆ **~ figure, ~ number** chiffre *m* rond ◆ **in ~ figures that will cost 20 million** cela coûtera 20 millions en chiffres ronds *or* pour donner un chiffre rond

3 (*fig uses*) ◆ **in rich ~ tones** d'une voix riche et sonore ◆ **at a ~ pace** à vive allure ◆ **a (good) ~ sum** une somme rondelette *or* coquette * ◆ **he told me in ~ terms why ...** il m'a expliqué tout net pourquoi ... ; see also **comp**

N 1 (= *circle etc*) rond *m*, cercle *m* ; (*Brit*) (= *slice*) [*of bread, meat*] tranche *f* ◆ **a ~ of toast** un toast, une tranche de pain grillé

2 (*esp Brit:* also **delivery round**) tournée *f* ◆ **to do** *or* **make one's ~(s)** *[watchman, policeman]* faire sa ronde *or* sa tournée ; *[postman, milkman]* faire sa tournée ; *[doctor]* faire ses visites ◆ **to do** *or* **make the ~s of …** faire le tour de … ◆ **to go** *or* **do the ~s** *[infection, a cold etc]* faire des ravages ; *[news, joke etc]* courir, circuler ◆ **the story is going the ~s that …** le bruit court que …, on raconte *or* on dit que … ◆ **the story went the ~s of the club** l'histoire a fait le tour du club ◆ **this coat has gone the ~s of the family*** ce manteau a fait le tour de la famille ◆ **the daily ~** (*fig*) la routine quotidienne, le train-train quotidien ◆ **your life is just one long ~ of pleasures** tu ne penses qu'à t'amuser

3 *[of cards, golf, competition, tournament]* partie *f* ; (*Boxing*) round *m*, reprise *f* ; (*Horse-riding*) tour *m* de piste, parcours *m* ; *[of election]* tour *m* ; *[of talks, discussions]* série *f* ◆ **to have a clear ~** (*Horse-riding*) faire un tour de piste *or* un parcours sans fautes ◆ **a new ~ of negotiations** une nouvelle série de négociations ; → **ammunition, applause, shot**

4 *[of drinks]* tournée *f* ◆ **to pay for a ~ (of drinks)** payer une tournée* ◆ **it's my ~** c'est ma tournée*

5 (*Mus*) canon *m* ; (*Dancing*) ronde *f*

6 ◆ **in the ~** (*Sculp*) en ronde-bosse ; (*Theat*) en rond ; (*fig = taken as a whole*) globalement

VT 1 (= *make round*) arrondir

2 (*Comput, Math*) *[+ figure]* arrondir

3 (= *go round*) *[+ corner]* tourner ; *[+ bend]* prendre ; (*Naut*) *[+ cape]* doubler ; *[+ obstacle]* contourner

COMP **round arch** N (*Archit*) (arc *m* en) plein cintre *m*, arc *m* roman

round-cheeked ADJ aux joues rondes, joufflu

round dance N ronde *f*

round-eyed ADJ (*lit*) aux yeux ronds ; (*with surprise*) avec des yeux ronds

round-faced ADJ au visage rond

rounding error N erreur *f* d'arrondi

round-necked pullover N pull(-over) *m* ras du cou

round robin N (= *petition*) pétition *f* (*où les signatures sont disposées en rond*) ; (*esp US Sport*) *tournoi où tous les joueurs se rencontrent*

round-shouldered ADJ voûté

Round Table N (*Myth*) Table *f* ronde

round-table ADJ ◆ **~-table discussion** table *f* ronde

round-table discussion N table *f* ronde

round-the-clock ADJ 24 heures sur 24 ; see also **clock**

round trip N aller *m* et retour ◆ **Concorde does three ~ trips a week** le Concorde effectue trois rotations *fpl* par semaine

round trip ticket N billet *m* aller-retour

► **round down** VT SEP *[+ prices etc]* arrondir (au chiffre inférieur)

► **round off** VT SEP *[+ speech, list, series]* terminer ; *[+ sentence]* parachever ; *[+ debate, meeting]* mettre fin à, clore ; *[+ meal]* terminer, finir (*with* par) ◆ **and now, to ~ off, I must say …** et maintenant, pour conclure *or* en dernier lieu, je dois dire …

► **round on** VT FUS ⇒ **round upon**

► **round up** VT SEP 1 (= *bring together*) *[+ people]* rassembler, réunir ; *[+ cattle]* rassembler ; *[+ criminals]* ramasser*

2 *[+ prices etc]* arrondir (au chiffre supérieur)

N ◆ **roundup** → **roundup**

► **round upon** VT FUS (*in words*) s'en prendre à ; (*in actions*) sauter sur, attaquer

roundabout /ˈraʊndəbaʊt/ ADJ *[route]* détourné, indirect ◆ **we came (by) a ~ way** nous avons fait un détour ◆ **by ~ means** par des moyens détournés ◆ **~ phrase** circonlocution *f* ◆ **what a ~ way of doing things!** quelle façon contournée *or* compliquée de faire les choses !

N (*Brit = merry-go-round*) manège *m* ; (*esp Brit = playground apparatus*) tourniquet *m* ; (*at road junction*) rond-point *m* (à sens giratoire) ; (*on traffic sign*) sens *m* giratoire ; → **swing**

rounded /ˈraʊndɪd/ ADJ 1 (= *curved*) *[shape, edge, hill]* arrondi ; *[face, breasts, hips, handwriting]* rond ; *[shoulders]* voûté ; *[spine]* courbé 2 (= *complete*) *[education]* complet (-ète *f*) et équilibré ; *[film, book]* étoffé ; *[wine, tone]* rond ; *[flavour]* plein ; *[person, character]* équilibré ; *[character in book]* étoffé ◆ **a ~ picture of the situation** une description complète et impartiale de la situation 3 (*Culin*) *[tablespoon]* gros (grosse *f*) 4 (*Phon*) *[vowel]* arrondi

roundel /ˈraʊndl/ N (= *decoration*) rond *m* ; (= *symbol, logo*) insigne *m* rond ; (*on warplane*) cocarde *f*

roundelay †† /ˈraʊndɪleɪ/ N (*Mus*) rondeau *m*

rounder /ˈraʊndəʳ/ N (*US*) fêtard* *m*, noceur* *m*

rounders /ˈraʊndəz/ N (*Brit*) *sorte de baseball*

Roundhead /ˈraʊndhed/ N (*Brit Hist*) Tête *f* ronde

roundhouse /ˈraʊndhaʊs/ N (*US Rail*) rotonde *f*

roundly /ˈraʊndlɪ/ ADV *[condemn, criticize]* sans ambages ; *[reject]* catégoriquement ; *[defeat]* à plate(s) couture(s)

roundness /ˈraʊndnɪs/ N rondeur *f*

roundsman /ˈraʊndzmən/ N (pl **-men**) (*Brit*) livreur *m* ◆ **milk ~** laitier *m*

roundup /ˈraʊndʌp/ N *[of cattle, people]* rassemblement *m* ; *[of criminals, suspects]* rafle *f* ; (= *meeting*) tour *m* d'horizon ; (= *news summary*) résumé *m* de l'actualité

roundworm /ˈraʊndwɜːm/ N ascaride *m*

rouse /raʊz/ VT (= *awaken*) réveiller, éveiller ; (= *stimulate*) activer, éveiller ; *[+ feeling]* exciter, stimuler ; *[+ admiration, interest]* susciter ; *[+ indignation]* provoquer, soulever ; *[+ suspicions]* éveiller ◆ **~ yourself!** secouez-vous !* ◆ **to ~ the masses** soulever les masses ◆ **to ~ sb to action** inciter *or* pousser qn à agir ◆ **to ~ sb (to anger)** mettre qn en colère ◆ **he's a terrible man when he's ~d** il est redoutable quand il est en colère VI (= *waken*) se réveiller ; (= *become active*) sortir de sa torpeur

rousing /ˈraʊzɪŋ/ ADJ *[cheers, applause, chorus, reception]* enthousiaste ; *[speech]* enthousiasmant ; *[music]* entraînant

roust /raʊst/, **roust out** VT (*US*) (= *evict*) chasser ; (= *call out*) faire venir ◆ **to ~ sb out of bed/his home** arracher qn de son lit/de sa maison

roustabout /ˈraʊstəbaʊt/ N (*US*) débardeur *m* ; (*Austral*) manœuvre *m*

rout¹ /raʊt/ N 1 (*Mil = defeat*) déroute *f*, débâcle *f* ◆ **to put to ~** mettre en déroute 2 († † = *revels*) raout † *m*, fête *f* mondaine 3 (*Jur = mob*) attroupement *m* illégal VT (= *defeat*) mettre en déroute

rout² /raʊt/ VI (= *search:* also **rout about**) fouiller

► **rout out** VT (= *find*) dénicher ; (= *force out*) déloger ◆ **to ~ sb out of bed** tirer qn de son lit

route /ruːt/ N 1 (*gen, also of train, plane, ship etc*) itinéraire *m* ; (*Climbing*) itinéraire *m*, voie *f* ◆ **shipping/air ~s** routes *fpl* maritimes/aériennes ◆ **all ~s** (= *road sign*) toutes directions ◆ **what ~ does the 39 bus take?** par où passe le 39 ?, quel est l'itinéraire du 39 ? ◆ **we're on a bus ~** nous sommes sur une ligne d'autobus ◆ **the ~ to the coast goes through …** pour aller à la côte on passe par … ◆ **I know a good ~ to London** je connais un bon itinéraire pour aller à Londres ◆ **en ~ (for)** en route (pour) ; → **sea, trade**

2 /*often* raʊt/ (*Mil*) ordres *mpl* de marche, route *f* à suivre

3 (*US*) /*often* raʊt/ (= *delivery round*) tournée *f* ◆ **he has a paper ~** il distribue des journaux

4 (*US*) /*often* raʊt/ **Route 39** (*in highway names*) ≃ la nationale 39

VT (= *plan route of*) *[+ train, coach, bus]* fixer le parcours *or* l'itinéraire de ; *[+ phone call]* acheminer ◆ **to ~ a train through Leeds** faire passer un train par Leeds ◆ **my luggage was ~d through Amsterdam** mes bagages ont été expédiés via Amsterdam ◆ **they've ~d the train by Leeds** le train passe maintenant par Leeds

COMP **route map** N (= *road map*) carte *f* routière ; (*for ramblers*) topo* *m* ; (*for trains etc*) carte *f* du réseau

route march N (*Mil*) marche *f* d'entraînement

route planner N (= *map*) carte *f* routière ; (= *road atlas*) recueil *m* de cartes routières

> ⚠ The commonest meaning of the French word **route** is 'road'. It only translates the English word **route** in a few contexts.

router /ˈruːtəʳ/ N (*Comput*) routeur *m*

routine /ruːˈtiːn/ N 1 routine *f* ◆ **daily ~** (*gen*) occupations *fpl* journalières routine *f* quotidienne ; (*pej*) train-train *m inv* de la vie quotidienne ; (*Mil, Naut*) emploi *m* du temps ◆ **business** *or* **office ~** travail *m* courant du bureau ◆ **as a matter of ~** automatiquement, systématiquement

2 (*Theat*) numéro *m* ◆ **dance ~** numéro *m* de danse ◆ **he gave me the old ~* about his wife not understanding him** il m'a ressorti la vieille rengaine du mari incompris, il a mis le disque* du mari incompris

ADJ 1 (= *normal*) *[work, matter, check, maintenance, flight]* de routine ; *[procedure, questions]* de routine, d'usage ◆ **it was quite ~** c'était de la simple routine ◆ **on a ~ basis** de façon routinière ◆ **~ duties** obligations *fpl* courantes ◆ **to make ~ inquiries** mener une enquête de routine

2 (= *predictable*) *[report, problem, banter]* banal

routinely /ruːˈtiːnlɪ/ ADV couramment ◆ **to be ~ tested** *[person]* passer un examen de routine ; *[blood]* être systématiquement examiné

rove /rəʊv/ VI errer, vagabonder ; *[eyes]* errer VT *[+ countryside]* parcourir, errer dans *or* sur ; *[+ streets]* errer dans, aller au hasard dans

rover /ˈrəʊvəʳ/ N vagabond(e) *m(f)*

roving /ˈrəʊvɪŋ/ ADJ *[reporter]* volant ; *[ambassador, musician]* itinérant ; *[gang]* errant ◆ **to have a ~ commission to do sth** avoir carte blanche *or* toute latitude pour faire qch ◆ **to have a ~ eye** être toujours à l'affût d'une aventure (amoureuse) N vagabondage *m*

row¹ /rəʊ/ N *[of objects, people]* (*beside one another*) rang *m*, rangée *f* ; (*behind one another*) file *f*, ligne *f* ; *[of seeds, plants]* rayon *m*, rang *m* ; *[of houses, trees, figures]* rangée *f* ; *[of cars]* file *f* ; (*Knitting*) rang *m* ◆ **in the front ~** au premier rang ◆ **the front/second/back ~ (of the scrum)** (*Rugby*) la première/deuxième/troisième ligne (de mêlée) ◆ **a hard** *or* **long** *or* **tough ~ to hoe** une rude besogne ◆ **they were sitting in a ~** ils étaient assis en rang ◆ **four failures in a ~** quatre échecs d'affilée *or* de suite ◆ **in ~s** en rangs COMP **row house** N (*US*) *maison qui fait partie d'une rangée de maisons identiques et contiguës* ; → HOUSE

row² /rəʊ/ VT *[+ boat]* faire avancer à la rame *or* à l'aviron ; *[+ person, object]* transporter en canot (*to* à) ◆ **to ~ sb across** faire traverser qn en canot ◆ **to ~ a race** faire une course d'aviron ; → **stroke** VI (*gen*) ramer ; (*Sport*) faire de l'aviron ◆ **he ~ed across the Atlantic** il a traversé l'Atlantique à la rame *or* à l'aviron ◆ **to go ~ing** (*for pleasure*) canoter, faire du canotage ; (*Sport*) faire de l'aviron ◆ **to ~ away** s'éloigner à la rame ◆ **to ~ back** (*lit*) revenir à la rame ; (*fig*) revenir en arrière ◆ **to ~ back on sth** *(fig)* revenir sur qch N promenade *f* en canot ◆ **to go for a ~** canoter, faire un tour en canot ◆ **it will be a hard ~ upstream** ce sera dur de remonter la rivière à la rame *or* à l'aviron

row³ * /raʊ/ *(esp Brit)* N *(= noise)* vacarme *m*, boucan * *m* ; *(= quarrel)* dispute *f* ◆ **to make a ~** faire du vacarme *or* du boucan * ◆ **what a ~!** quel vacarme *or* boucan * ! ◆ **to have a ~ with sb** se disputer avec qn, s'engueuler‡ avec qn ◆ **to give sb a ~** passer un savon à qn *, sonner les cloches à qn * ◆ **to get (into) a ~** se faire passer un savon * *or* sonner les cloches * VI se disputer, s'engueuler‡ *(with* avec)

rowan /'raʊən/ N *(= tree)* sorbier *m* des oiseleurs ; *(= berry)* sorbe *f*

rowboat /'rəʊbəʊt/ N *(US)* canot *m* (à rames)

rowdiness /'raʊdɪnɪs/ N tapage *m*, chahut *m*

rowdy /'raʊdɪ/ ADJ *[person, behaviour]* chahuteur ; *[party]* un peu trop animé ; *[demonstration]* bruyant ◆ **~ scenes in Parliament** scènes *fpl* de chahut au parlement ◆ **to be ~** *[person]* chahuter N * bagarreur * *m*, voyou *m* ◆ **football rowdies** hooligans *mpl* (des matchs de football)

rowdyism /'raʊdɪɪzəm/ N tapage *m*, chahut *m*

rower /'rəʊəʳ/ N rameur *m*, -euse *f* ; *(in navy)* nageur *m*, -euse *f*

rowing /'rəʊɪŋ/ N *(for pleasure)* canotage *m* ; *(Sport)* aviron *m* ; *(in navy)* nage *f*
COMP **rowing boat** N *(Brit)* canot *m* (à rames)
rowing club N club *m* d'aviron
rowing machine N rameur *m*

rowlock /'rɒlək/ N *(esp Brit)* dame *f* de nage, tolet *m*

royal /'rɔɪəl/ ADJ 1 *(lit, fig)* royal ◆ **the ~ household** la maison royale ◆ **~ occasion** *événement honoré de la présence d'un membre de la famille royale* ◆ **the ~ "we"** le pluriel de majesté ◆ **the ~ road to freedom/success** la voie royale de la liberté/du succès ◆ **to give sb a (right) ~ welcome** réserver à qn un accueil royal ◆ **he's a ~ pain in the backside** * c'est le roi des enquiquineurs * ; → **prerogative, princess**
2 *[paper]* de format grand raisin ◆ **~ octavo** in-huit raisin
N * membre *m* de la famille royale ◆ **the ~s** la famille royale
COMP **the Royal Academy (of Arts)** N *(Brit)* l'Académie *f* royale des Beaux-Arts
the Royal Air Force N *(Brit)* la Royal Air Force
royal assent N *(Brit)* sanction *f* royale *(d'un projet de loi)* ◆ **to receive** *or* **be given ~ assent** être approuvé par le souverain
royal blue N bleu roi *m inv*
royal-blue ADJ bleu roi *inv*
the Royal Canadian Mounted Police N la Gendarmerie royale canadienne
Royal Commission N *(Brit)* commission *f* d'enquête parlementaire
royal correspondent N *correspondant(e) chargé(e) des affaires royales*
the Royal Engineers NPL *(Brit Mil)* le génie (militaire britannique)
royal family N famille *f* royale
royal flush N *(Cards)* flush *m* royal
Royal Highness N ◆ **Your/His Royal Highness** Votre/Son Altesse Royale
royal jelly N gelée *f* royale
the Royal Mail N *(Brit)* le service postal britannique
the Royal Marines NPL *(Brit Mil)* l'infanterie *f* de marine ◆ **a Royal Marine** un soldat de l'infanterie de marine
the Royal Mint N *(Brit)* l'hôtel *m* des Monnaies
the Royal Naval Reserve N *(Brit Mil) le corps de réservistes de la marine*
the Royal Navy N *(Brit Mil)* la marine nationale
royal pardon N grâce *f* royale
the Royal Shakespeare Company N *(Brit) troupe de théâtre spécialisée dans le répertoire shakespearien*
the Royal Society N *(Brit)* ≃ l'Académie *f* des sciences
the Royal Society for the Prevention of Cruelty to Animals N *(Brit)* → **RSPCA**
the Royal Ulster Constabulary N *(Brit Police)* la police de l'Irlande du Nord
royal warrant N *(Brit) autorisation que reçoit un commerçant de fournir la famille royale*

> **ROYAL SHAKESPEARE COMPANY**
>
> La **Royal Shakespeare Company**, ou **RSC**, est une troupe de théâtre fondée en 1960 à Stratford-on-Avon, lieu de naissance de Shakespeare. Basée à Stratford et au Barbican à Londres, elle présente naturellement des pièces de Shakespeare mais aussi d'autres auteurs classiques ou contemporains. La **RSC** fait chaque année des tournées de six mois dans toute la Grande-Bretagne et elle a acquis une solide réputation internationale.

royalism /'rɔɪəlɪzəm/ N royalisme *m*

royalist /'rɔɪəlɪst/ ADJ, N royaliste *mf*

royally /'rɔɪəlɪ/ ADV 1 *(= lavishly) [entertain, treat]* royalement 2 *(* = completely)* ◆ **to get ~ drunk** se soûler à mort * ◆ **to be ~ pissed off (with sb)** ‡ en avoir sa claque * (de qn) ◆ **to have ~ screwed up** ‡ avoir merdé en beauté *‡

royalty /'rɔɪəltɪ/ N 1 *(= position, dignity, rank)* royauté *f* 2 *(= royal person)* membre *m* de la famille royale ; *(= royal persons)* (membres *mpl* de) la famille royale ◆ **when speaking to ~** quand on s'adresse à un membre de la famille royale ◆ **we were treated like ~** nous avons été accueillis comme des princes 3 (also **royalties**) *(from book)* royalties *fpl*, droits *mpl* d'auteur ; *(from oil well, patent)* royalties *fpl*

rozzer ‡ /'rɒzəʳ/ N *(Brit)* flic * *m*, poulet * *m*

RP /ɑː'piː/ N *(Ling)* (abbrev of **Received Pronunciation**) → **received** ; → ENGLISH

RPI /ˌɑːpiː'aɪ/ N *(Brit)* (abbrev of **retail price index**) → **retail**

rpm /ˌɑːpiː'em/ N 1 (abbrev of **revolutions per minute**) tr/min 2 *(Comm)* (abbrev of **resale price maintenance**) → **resale**

RR *(US)* abbrev of **railroad**

RRP /ˌɑːrɑː'piː/ N *(Comm)* (abbrev of **recommended retail price**) → **recommend**

RSA /ˌɑːresˌeɪ/ N 1 (abbrev of **Royal Society of Arts**) *organisme britannique habilité à conférer des diplômes* 2 (abbrev of **Royal Scottish Academy**) Académie *f* royale d'Écosse 3 (abbrev of **Republic of South Africa**) (République *f* d')Afrique *f* du Sud

RSC /ˌɑːres'siː/ N *(Brit)* (abbrev of **Royal Shakespeare Company**) → **royal**

RSI /ˌɑːres'aɪ/ N (abbrev of **repetitive strain injury**) TMS *mpl*

RSM /ˌɑːres'em/ N *(Mil)* (abbrev of **Regimental Sergeant Major**) → **regimental**

RSPB /ˌɑːrespiː'biː/ N *(Brit)* (abbrev of **Royal Society for the Protection of Birds**) *société britannique de protection des oiseaux*

RSPCA /ˌɑːrespiːsiː'eɪ/ N *(Brit)* (abbrev of **Royal Society for the Prevention of Cruelty to Animals**) ≃ SPA *f*

RSV /ˌɑːres'viː/ N (abbrev of **Revised Standard Version**) → **revise**

RSVP /ˌɑːresviː'piː/ (abbrev of **please reply**) RSVP

RTA /ˌɑːtiː'eɪ/ N (abbrev of **road traffic accident**) → **road**

Rt Hon. *(Brit Pol)* (abbrev of **Right Honourable**) → **right**

Rt Rev. (abbrev of **Right Reverend**) → **reverend**

RU N (abbrev of **Rugby Union**) → **rugby**

rub /rʌb/ N 1 *(on thing)* frottement *m* ; *(on person)* friction *f* ; *(with duster etc)* coup *m* de chiffon *or* de torchon ◆ **to give sth a ~** *[+ furniture, shoes, silver]* donner un coup de chiffon *or* de torchon à qch ; *[+ sore place, one's arms]* frotter qch ◆ **to give sb a ~** frictionner qn
2 *(= obstacle)* **there's the ~!** c'est là la difficulté !, voilà le hic ! * ◆ **the ~ is that ...** l'ennui *or* le hic *, c'est que ... ◆ **we didn't have the ~ of the green** *(esp Brit)* nous n'avons pas été vernis * *or* pas eu de chance
3 *(= massage cream)* crème *f* de massage ; *(= massage oil)* huile *f* de massage
VT frotter ; *(= polish)* astiquer, frotter ; *(Art) [+ brass, inscription]* prendre un frottis de ◆ **~ yourself and you'll soon be dry** frictionne-toi *or* frotte-toi, tu seras bientôt sec ◆ **to ~ one's nose** se frotter le nez ◆ **to ~ sb's nose in sth** *(fig)* ne jamais laisser oublier qch à qn ◆ **to ~ one's hands (together)** se frotter les mains ◆ **to ~ one's hands with glee** *(esp Brit)* se frotter les mains ◆ **to ~ sth dry** sécher qch en le frottant ◆ **to ~ a hole in sth** faire un trou dans qch à force de frotter ◆ **to ~ sth through a sieve** passer qch au tamis ◆ **to ~ lotion into the skin** faire pénétrer de la lotion dans la peau ◆ **to ~ shoulders** *(Brit) or* **elbows** *(US)* **with all sorts of people** côtoyer toutes sortes de gens ◆ **to ~ sb the wrong way** *(US)* prendre qn à rebrousse-poil ; → **salt**
VI *[thing]* frotter *(against* contre) ; *[person, cat]* se frotter *(against* contre)
COMP **rub-down** N ◆ **to give a horse a ~-down** bouchonner un cheval ◆ **to give sb a ~-down** faire une friction à qn, frictionner qn
rub-up N ◆ **to give sth a ~-up** frotter *or* astiquer qch

► **rub along** * VI *(Brit)* faire *or* poursuivre son petit bonhomme de chemin ◆ **to ~ along (together)** *[two people]* vivre *or* s'accorder tant bien que mal ◆ **he can ~ along in French, he knows enough French to ~ along with** il sait assez de français pour se tirer d'affaire tant bien que mal *or* pour se débrouiller

► **rub away** VT SEP *[+ mark]* faire disparaître (en frottant), effacer ◆ **she ~bed her tears away** elle a essuyé ses larmes

► **rub down** VT SEP *[+ horse]* bouchonner ; *[+ person]* frictionner *(with* avec) ; *[+ wall, paintwork] (= clean)* frotter, nettoyer du haut en bas ; *(= sandpaper)* poncer, polir
N ◆ **rub-down** → **rub**

► **rub in** VT SEP *[+ oil, liniment]* faire pénétrer en frottant ; *(fig) [+ idea]* insister sur ; *[+ lesson]* faire entrer *(to* à) ◆ **don't ~ it in!** * *(fig)* pas besoin de me le rappeler ! ◆ **he's always ~bing in how rich he is** il ne vous laisse jamais oublier à quel point il est riche

► **rub off** VI *[mark]* partir, s'en aller ; *[writing]* s'effacer, disparaître ◆ **the blue will ~ off on to your hands** tu vas avoir les mains toutes bleues ◆ **I hope some of his politeness will ~ off on to his brother** * j'espère qu'il passera un peu de sa politesse à son frère, j'espère que sa politesse déteindra un peu sur son frère
VT SEP *[+ writing on blackboard]* effacer ; *[+ dirt]* enlever en frottant

► **rub on** VT SEP *[+ cream, polish etc]* passer

► **rub out** VI *[mark, writing]* s'effacer, s'en aller ◆ **that ink won't ~ out** cette encre ne s'effacera pas
VT SEP *(= erase)* effacer ; *(* = kill)* descendre *, liquider *

► **rub up** VI ◆ **to ~ up against all sorts of people** côtoyer toutes sortes de gens
VT SEP *[+ vase, table]* frotter, astiquer ◆ **to ~ sb up the right way** savoir (comment) s'y prendre avec qn ◆ **to ~ sb up the wrong way** *(Brit)* prendre qn à rebrousse-poil ◆ **to ~ up one's French** *(* = revise)* dérouiller* son français
N ◆ **rub-up** → **rub**

rubato /ruːˈbɑːtəʊ/ N, ADV rubato *m*

rubber¹ /ˈrʌbəʳ/ N 1 *(= material: no pl)* caoutchouc *m* ◆ **synthetic ~** caoutchouc *m* synthétique ◆ **to burn ~*** *(= start)* démarrer sur les chapeaux de roue ; *(= pass)* passer en trombe ; → **foam**
2 *(Brit = eraser)* gomme *f*
3 *(esp US* ⁑ *= condom)* préservatif *m*, capote *f*
NPL **rubbers** *(= shoes)* caoutchoucs *mpl*
ADJ de *or* en caoutchouc ; see also **comp**
COMP **rubber band** N élastique *m*
rubber boots NPL *(US)* bottes *fpl* de *or* en caoutchouc
rubber bullet N balle *f* de *or* en caoutchouc
rubber cement N dissolution *f* de caoutchouc
rubber cheque* *(Brit)*, **rubber check*** *(US)* N chèque *m* en bois* *or* sans provision
rubber gloves NPL gants *mpl* de *or* en caoutchouc
rubber plant N caoutchouc *m (plante verte)*
rubber plantation N plantation *f* d'hévéas
rubber ring N *(for swimming)* bouée *f* (de natation) ; *(for sitting on)* rond *m* (pour malade)
rubber solution N dissolution *f*
rubber stamp N tampon *m* en caoutchouc
rubber-stamp* VT *(lit)* tamponner ; *(fig)* approuver sans discussion
rubber tree N arbre *m* à gomme, hévéa *m*
rubber-tyred ADJ sur pneus

rubber² /ˈrʌbəʳ/ N *(Cards)* rob *m*, robre *m* ◆ **to play a ~** faire un robre *or* une partie ◆ **that's game and ~** *(Bridge)* c'est la partie

rubberized /ˈrʌbəraɪzd/ ADJ caoutchouté

rubberneck †⁑ /ˈrʌbənek/ *(US)* N *(= tourist)* touriste *mf* ; *(= onlooker)* badaud(e) *m(f)* VI faire le badaud

rubbery /ˈrʌbərɪ/ ADJ *[object, substance, skin, food]* caoutchouteux ; *[lips]* lippu ; *[legs]* en coton

rubbing /ˈrʌbɪŋ/ N *(= action)* frottement *m*, friction *f* ; *(Art)* frottis *m*, reproduction *f* par frottage ; → **brass** COMP **rubbing alcohol** N *(US)* alcool *m* à 90°

rubbish /ˈrʌbɪʃ/ N 1 *(= waste material)* détritus *mpl* ; *(Brit = household rubbish)* ordures *fpl*, immondices *fpl* ; *[of factory]* déchets *mpl* ; *[of building site]* décombres *mpl* ; *(pej = worthless things)* camelote* *f* ◆ **household ~** ordures *fpl* ménagères ◆ **garden ~** détritus *mpl* de jardin ◆ **this shop sells a lot of ~** ce magasin ne vend que de la camelote* ◆ **it's just ~** ça ne vaut rien ; see also **noun 2**
2 *(fig = nonsense)* bêtises *fpl* ◆ **to talk ~** dire des bêtises *or* des inepties ◆ **(what a lot of) ~!*** n'importe quoi !* ◆ **this book is ~** ce livre ne vaut strictement rien ◆ **that's just ~** ça ne veut rien dire, ça n'a aucun sens ◆ **it is ~ to say that ...** c'est idiot de dire que ...
ADJ *(* = useless)* nul ◆ **I'm ~ at golf** je suis nul en golf
VT *(* = denigrate)* débiner*
COMP **rubbish bin** N *(Brit)* poubelle *f*, boîte *f* à ordures
rubbish chute N *(at dump)* dépotoir *m* ; *(in building)* vide-ordures *m inv*
rubbish collection N ramassage *m or* collecte *f* des ordures
rubbish dump, rubbish heap N *(public)* décharge *f* publique, dépotoir *m* ; *(in garden)* monceau *m* de détritus

rubbishy* /ˈrʌbɪʃɪ/ ADJ *(esp Brit) [film, book, magazine]* nul, débile* ; *[goods]* de mauvaise qualité, qui ne vaut rien ◆ **this is ~ stuff** ça ne vaut rien

rubble /ˈrʌbl/ N *[of ruined house, bomb site, demolition site]* décombres *mpl* ; *(smaller pieces)* gravats *mpl* ; *(in road-building)* blocaille *f*, blocage *m* ◆ **the building was reduced to a heap of ~** il ne restait du bâtiment qu'un tas de décombres

rube⁑ /ruːb/ N *(US)* péquenaud⁑ *m*

Rube Goldberg /ˈruːbˈgəʊldbɜːg/ N *(US)* ◆ **a ~ machine** un engin bricolé avec les moyens du bord

rubella /ruːˈbelə/ N rubéole *f*

Ruben(s)esque* /ˌruːbɪn(z)ˈesk/ ADJ *(= plump)* aux formes généreuses

Rubicon /ˈruːbɪkən/ N Rubicon *m* ◆ **to cross the ~** passer *or* franchir le Rubicon

rubicund /ˈruːbɪkənd/ ADJ *(liter)* rubicond

rubidium /ruːˈbɪdɪəm/ N rubidium *m*

ruble /ˈruːbl/ N *(US)* ⇒ **rouble**

rubric /ˈruːbrɪk/ N rubrique *f*

ruby /ˈruːbɪ/ N rubis *m* ; *(= colour)* couleur *f* rubis
COMP *(= colour) [wine]* (de couleur) rubis *inv* ; *[lips]* vermeil ; *(= made of rubies) [necklace, ring]* de rubis
ruby grapefruit N pomelo *m* rose
ruby wedding N noces *fpl* de rubis

RUC /ˌɑːjuːˈsiː/ N *(Brit Police)* (abbrev of **Royal Ulster Constabulary**) → **royal**

ruche /ruːʃ/ N ruche *f*

ruched /ruːʃt/ ADJ ruché

ruck¹ /rʌk/ N *(Racing)* peloton *m* ; *(Rugby)* mêlée *f* ouverte *or* spontanée ; *(Brit = fight)* bagarre *f* ◆ **the (common) ~** *(fig)* les masses *fpl*, la foule, le peuple ◆ **to get out of the ~** se distinguer du commun des mortels

ruck² /rʌk/ N *(= crease)* faux pli *m*, godet *m*

► **ruck up** VI *[skirt, blouse]* remonter en faisant des plis

ruckle /ˈrʌkl/ N ⇒ **ruck²**

rucksack /ˈrʌksæk/ N *(esp Brit)* sac *m* à dos

ruckus* /ˈrʌkəs/ N (pl **ruckuses**) *(US)* grabuge* *m*

ruction* /ˈrʌkʃən/ N *(gen pl) (= rows)* disputes *fpl*, grabuge* *m* ; *(= riots)* troubles *mpl*, bagarres *fpl* ◆ **there'll be ~s if you break that glass** si tu casses ce verre tu vas te faire sonner les cloches* *or* il va y avoir du grabuge*

rudder /ˈrʌdəʳ/ N *[of aircraft, boat]* gouvernail *m* ◆ **vertical/horizontal ~** *[of aircraft]* gouvernail *m* de direction/de profondeur

rudderless /ˈrʌdəlɪs/ ADJ *[boat]* sans gouvernail ; *[government, country]* à la dérive

ruddiness /ˈrʌdɪnɪs/ N ◆ **the ~ of her complexion** son teint rose ; *(pej)* son teint rougeaud

ruddy /ˈrʌdɪ/ ADJ 1 *[face]* rose ; *(pej)* rougeaud ; *[complexion]* rose ; *(pej)* rougeaud, coloré ; *[sky, glow]* rougeoyant ◆ **her face had a ~ glow** elle avait les joues roses 2 *(Brit † * euph = bloody)* satané* ◆ **he's a ~ fool** c'est un imbécile fini ◆ **you're a ~ nuisance** tu me casses vraiment les pieds* ◆ **what the ~ hell are you doing?** mais qu'est-ce que tu fiches ?* ADV *(Brit † * euph = bloody)* bougrement †* ◆ **how could you be so ~ stupid?** comment as-tu pu être aussi bougrement †* idiot ?

rude /ruːd/ ADJ 1 *(= impolite) [person, behaviour, reply]* impoli *(to sb* avec qn ; *about sth* à propos de qch) ; *[remark]* impoli ◆ **he's always ~** c'est un grossier personnage ◆ **it's ~ to stare/to speak with your mouth full** c'est mal élevé de dévisager les gens/de parler la bouche pleine 2 *(= obscene) [noise]* incongru ; *[joke]* grossier ; *[story]* scabreux ; *[song]* grivois ; *[gesture]* obscène 3 *(= unexpected) [shock]* brutal ◆ **to have or get a ~ awakening** *(fig)* être brutalement rappelé à la réalité 4 *(liter = primitive) [shelter, table, implement]* rudimentaire 5 *(= vigorous) [health]* de fer ◆ **to be in ~ health** avoir une santé de fer COMP **rude word** N gros mot *m*

⚠ In French, **rude** means 'rough' or 'tough'.

rudely /ˈruːdlɪ/ ADV 1 *(= impolitely) [say]* impoliment ; *[push, interrupt]* impoliment, brutalement ◆ **before I was so ~ interrupted** avant qu'on ne m'interrompe aussi impoliment 2 *(= unexpectedly) [awaken]* en sursaut, brusquement ; *[shatter]* brutalement 3 *(liter = primitively) [carved, shaped]* grossièrement

rudeness /ˈruːdnɪs/ N 1 *(= impoliteness) [of person, behaviour, reply]* impolitesse *f* ; *[of remark]* impolitesse *f*, grossièreté *f* 2 *(= obscenity) [of joke]* grossièreté *f* ; *[of story]* côté *m* scabreux ; *[of song]* grivoiserie *f* ; *[of gesture]* obscénité *f* 3 *(= unexpectedness) [of shock]* brutalité *f*

rudiment /ˈruːdɪmənt/ N *(Anat)* rudiment *m* ◆ **~s** *(fig)* rudiments *mpl*, éléments *mpl*, notions *fpl* élémentaires

rudimentary /ˌruːdɪˈmentərɪ/ ADJ rudimentaire ◆ **I've only got ~ French** je n'ai que quelques rudiments de français, mon français est rudimentaire

rue¹ /ruː/ VT *(liter)* se repentir de, regretter amèrement ◆ **to ~ the day (when)** maudire le jour (où)

rue² /ruː/ N *(= plant)* rue *f*

rueful /ˈruːfʊl/ ADJ contrit

ruefully /ˈruːfəlɪ/ ADV *[say, admit]* avec regret ; *[smile]* d'un air contrit

ruff¹ /rʌf/ N 1 *(Dress)* collerette *f* ; *(Hist)* fraise *f* ; *[of bird, animal]* collier *m*, collerette *f* 2 *(= sandpiper)* combattant *m* ; *(= pigeon)* pigeon *m* capucin

ruff² /rʌf/ *(Cards)* N action *f* de couper (avec un atout) VTI couper (avec un atout)

ruffian /ˈrʌfɪən/ N voyou *m*, brute *f* ◆ **you little ~!*** petit polisson !

ruffianly /ˈrʌfɪənlɪ/ ADJ *[person]* brutal ; *[behaviour]* de voyou, de brute ; *[looks, appearance]* de brigand, de voyou

ruffle /ˈrʌfl/ N *(on wrist)* manchette *f (en dentelle etc)* ; *(on chest)* jabot *m* ; *(round neck)* fraise *f* ; *(= ripple: on water)* ride *f*, ondulation *f* VT 1 *(= disturb) [+ hair, feathers]* ébouriffer ; *[+ surface, water]* agiter, rider ; *[+ one's clothes]* déranger, froisser ◆ **the bird ~d (up) its feathers** l'oiseau a hérissé ses plumes 2 *(fig) (= upset)* froisser ; *(= annoy)* contrarier, irriter ◆ **she wasn't at all ~d** elle était restée parfaitement calme ◆ **to ~ sb's feathers** froisser qn

Rufflette ® /rʌˈflet/ N (also **Rufflette tape**) galon *m* fronceur, ruflette ® *f*

rug /rʌg/ N 1 *(for floor)* petit tapis *m* ; *(bedside)* descente *f* de lit, carpette *f* ; *(fireside)* carpette *f* ◆ **to pull the ~ out from under sb's feet, to pull the ~ from under sb** *(fig)* couper l'herbe sous le pied de qn 2 *(esp Brit = blanket)* couverture *f* ; *(in tartan)* plaid *m* ; → **travelling** 3 *(⁑ = wig)* moumoute* *f*, postiche *m* COMP **rug rat*** N *(esp US = baby)* pitchoun(e)* *m(f)*, poupon *m*

rugby /ˈrʌgbɪ/ N (also **rugby football**) rugby *m*
COMP **rugby league** N (le) rugby à treize
rugby player N rugbyman *m*, joueur *m* de rugby
rugby tackle N plaquage *m* VT plaquer
rugby union N (le) rugby à quinze

rugged /ˈrʌgɪd/ ADJ 1 *(= rough) [terrain]* accidenté ; *[coastline, cliffs]* déchiqueté ; *[mountains]* aux contours déchiquetés ; *[landscape, beauty]* sauvage 2 *(= masculine) [man]* rude ; *[features]* rude, taillé à coups de serpe 3 *(= tough) [person, personality, character, manners]* rude ; *[individualism, independence, determination]* farouche ; *[resistance]* acharné ◆ **hill farmers are a ~ breed**

les éleveurs des montagnes sont de solides gaillards [4] *(= durable) [machine, construction, clothing]* solide

ruggedness /ˈrʌɡɪdnɪs/ **N** *[of landscape]* aspect *m* sauvage ; *[of character, features]* rudesse *f*

rugger * /ˈrʌɡəʳ/ **N** *(Brit)* rugby *m*

Ruhr /rʊəʳ/ **N** Ruhr *f*

ruin /ˈruːɪn/ **N** [1] *(= destruction, cause of destruction)* ruine *f* ◆ **the palace was going to ~** *or* **falling into ~** le palais tombait en ruine *or* menaçait ruine ◆ **he was on the brink of ~, ~ stared him in the face** il était au bord de la ruine ◆ **the ~ of my hopes** la ruine *or* la faillite de mes espérances ◆ **drink was his ~** l'alcool a été sa perte ◆ **it will be the ~ of him** ça sera sa ruine ◆ **you will be the ~ of me** tu seras ma perte *or* ma ruine ; → **rack[2]** [2] *(gen pl = remains)* ruine(s) *f(pl)* ◆ **in ~s** *(lit, fig)* en ruine ◆ **the castle is now a ~** le château est maintenant une ruine **VT** *[+ building, reputation, hopes, health, person]* ruiner ; *[+ clothes]* abîmer ; *[+ event, enjoyment]* gâter ◆ **he's going to ~ himself** il va se ruiner

ruination /ˌruːɪˈneɪʃən/ **N** ruine *f*, perte *f* ◆ **to be the ~ of** être la ruine de

ruined /ˈruːɪnd/ **ADJ** *[building, city]* en ruine ; *[economy]* délabré, en ruine ; *[person] (morally)* perdu ; *(financially)* ruiné ; *[career]* ruiné

ruinous /ˈruːɪnəs/ **ADJ** [1] *(= expensive) [cost]* exorbitant ; *[expense]* exorbitant, ruineux [2] *(= disastrous) [effects, consequences]* dévastateur (-trice *f*) ; *[war, policy]* désastreux ◆ **to be ~ for sb/sth** entraîner la ruine de qn/qch, ruiner qn/qch [3] *(liter = dilapidated) [building]* délabré ◆ **to be in a ~ state** être délabré

ruinously /ˈruːɪnəslɪ/ **ADV** ◆ **~ expensive** ruineux ◆ **~ high interest rates** des taux *mpl* d'intérêt ruineux *or* exorbitants

rule /ruːl/ **N** [1] *(= guiding principle)* règle *f* ; *(= regulation)* règlement *m* ; *(Gram)* règle *f* ◆ **the ~s of the game** la règle du jeu ◆ **school ~s** règlement *m* intérieur de l'école (*or* du lycée *etc*) ◆ **it's against the ~s** c'est contraire à la règle *or* au règlement ◆ **running is against the ~s, it's against the ~s to run** il est contraire à la règle *or* il n'est pas permis de courir ◆ **to play by the ~s** *(lit, fig)* jouer suivant *or* selon les règles, respecter les règles *(fig)* ◆ **to bend** *or* **stretch the ~s** faire une entorse au règlement ◆ **~s and regulations** statuts *mpl* ◆ **standing ~** règlement *m* ◆ **it's a ~ that ...** il est de règle que ... + *subj* ◆ **~ of the road** *(on roads)* règle *f* générale de la circulation ; *(at sea)* règles *fpl* générales du trafic maritime ◆ **to do sth by ~** faire qch selon les règles ◆ **the ~ of three** *(Math)* la règle de trois ◆ **a rough ~ of thumb is that it is best to ...** en règle générale il vaut mieux ... ◆ **by ~ of thumb** à vue de nez ◆ **golden ~** règle *f* d'or ; → **exception, work**

[2] *(= custom)* coutume *f*, habitude *f* ◆ **ties are the ~ in this hotel** les cravates sont de règle dans cet hôtel ◆ **bad weather is the ~ in winter** le mauvais temps est habituel *or* normal en hiver ◆ **he makes it a ~ to get up early** il a pour règle de se lever tôt ◆ **to make tidiness a ~** faire de l'ordre une règle

◆ **as a rule** en règle générale

[3] *(NonC = authority)* autorité *f*, empire *m* ◆ **under British ~** sous l'autorité britannique ◆ **under a tyrant's ~** sous l'empire *or* la domination d'un tyran ◆ **majority ~, the ~ of the majority** *(Pol etc)* le gouvernement par la majorité ◆ **they will enforce the ~ of law** ils feront respecter la loi ; → **home**

[4] *(for measuring)* règle *f* (graduée) ◆ **a foot ~** une règle d'un pied ◆ **folding ~** mètre *m* pliant ; → **slide**

[5] *(Rel)* règle *f*

VT [1] *[+ country]* gouverner ; *(fig) [+ passions, emotion]* maîtriser ; *[+ person]* dominer, mener ◆ **to ~ the roost** faire la loi ◆ **he ~d the company for 30 years** il a dirigé la compagnie *or* il a été à la tête de la compagnie pendant 30 ans ◆ **to be ~d by jealousy** être mené *or* dominé par la jalousie ◆ **to ~ one's passions** maîtriser ses passions ◆ **he is ~d by his wife** il est dominé par sa femme ◆ **if you would only be ~d by what I say ...** si seulement tu voulais consentir à écouter mes conseils ... ◆ **I won't be ~d by what he wants** je ne veux pas me plier à ses volontés

[2] *[judge, umpire etc]* décider, déclarer (*that* que) ◆ **the judge ~d the defence out of order** *(Jur)* le juge a déclaré non recevables les paroles de l'avocat pour la défense ◆ **the judge ~d that the child should go to school** le juge a décidé que l'enfant irait à l'école

[3] *(= draw lines on) [+ paper]* régler, rayer ; *[+ line]* tirer à la règle ◆ **~d paper** papier *m* réglé *or* rayé

VI [1] *(= reign)* régner (*over* sur) ◆ **United ~ OK** *(in graffiti)* United vaincra

[2] ◆ **the prices ruling in Paris** les cours pratiqués à Paris

[3] *(Jur)* statuer (*against* contre ; *in favour of* en faveur de ; *on* sur)

COMP **the rule book** **N** le règlement ◆ **to do sth by the ~ book** *(fig)* faire qch dans les règles ◆ **to throw the ~ book at sb** * remettre qn à sa place, rembarrer qn *

► **rule in** **VT SEP** ◆ **he was ruling nothing in or out** il ne s'est pas avancé

► **rule off** **VT** *(Comm) [+ account]* clore, arrêter ◆ **to ~ off a column of figures** tirer une ligne sous une colonne de chiffres

► **rule out** **VT SEP** *[+ word, sentence]* barrer, rayer ; *(fig) [+ possibility, suggestion, date, person]* exclure, écarter ◆ **the age limit ~s him out** il est exclu du fait de la limite d'âge ◆ **murder can't be ruled out** il est impossible d'écarter *or* d'exclure l'hypothèse d'un meurtre ; → **rule in**

ruler /ˈruːləʳ/ **N** [1] *(= sovereign)* souverain(e) *m(f)* ; *(= political leader)* chef *m* (d'État) ◆ **the country's ~s** les dirigeants *mpl* du pays [2] *(for measuring)* règle *f*

ruling /ˈruːlɪŋ/ **ADJ** *[class, body]* dirigeant ; *[elite]* dirigeant, au pouvoir ; *[party]* au pouvoir ; *[principle]* souverain ; *[passion]* dominant ; *[price]* en vigueur **N** *(Admin, Jur)* décision *f*, jugement *m* ; *[of judge]* décision *f* ◆ **to give a ~** rendre un jugement

rum[1] /rʌm/ **N** rhum *m*

COMP **rum-running** **N** contrebande *f* d'alcool

rum toddy **N** grog *m*

rum[2] † * /rʌm/ **ADJ** *(Brit) [person, situation]* loufoque * ; *[idea]* loufoque *, biscornu *

Rumania /ruːˈmeɪnɪə/ **N** Roumanie *f*

Rumanian /ruːˈmeɪnɪən/ **ADJ** roumain **N** [1] *(= person)* Roumain(e) *m(f)* [2] *(= language)* roumain *m*

rumba /ˈrʌmbə/ **N** rumba *f*

rumble /ˈrʌmbl/ **N** [1] *(= noise) [of thunder, cannon]* grondement *m* ; *[of train, lorry]* roulement *m*, grondement *m* ; *[of pipe, stomach]* gargouillement *m*, borborygme *m* [2] (*‡ = fight*) bagarre *f*, baston * *m* or *f* **VI** *[thunder, cannon]* gronder ; *[stomach, pipes]* gargouiller ◆ **to ~ past** *[vehicle]* passer avec fracas **VT** [1] *(Brit ‡ = see through) [+ swindle]* flairer, subodorer * ; *[+ trick]* piger * ; *[+ person]* voir venir ; *(= find out)* piger * (*what/why etc* ce que/pourquoi *etc*) ◆ **I soon ~d him** *or* **his game** *or* **what he was up to!** j'ai tout de suite pigé sa combine ! * [2] (also **rumble out**) *[+ comments, remarks]* dire en grondant, grommeler

COMP **rumble seat** **N** strapontin *m*

rumble strip **N** *(on road)* bande *f* rugueuse

► **rumble on** **VI** *(Brit) [argument, controversy]* traîner en longueur

rumbling /ˈrʌmblɪŋ/ **N** *[of thunder]* grondement *m* ; *[of vehicle]* roulement *m*, grondement *m* ; *[of stomach, pipe]* gargouillement *m* ◆ **~s of discontent** murmures *mpl* de mécontentement ◆ **tummy ~s** * gargouillis *mpl*, borborygmes *mpl*

rumbustious /rʌmˈbʌstʃəs/ **ADJ** *(Brit)* exubérant

ruminant /ˈruːmɪnənt/ **ADJ, N** ruminant *m*

ruminate /ˈruːmɪneɪt/ **VI** ruminer ◆ **to ~ over** *or* **about** *or* **on sth** *(fig)* ruminer qch, retourner qch dans sa tête **VT** ruminer

rumination /ˌruːmɪˈneɪʃən/ **N** rumination *f*

ruminative /ˈruːmɪnətɪv/ **ADJ** *[person]* pensif ; *[mood]* méditatif, pensif

ruminatively /ˈruːmɪnətɪvlɪ/ **ADV** d'un air pensif, pensivement

rummage /ˈrʌmɪdʒ/ **N** [1] *(= action)* **to have a good ~ round** fouiller partout [2] *(US = jumble)* bric-à-brac *m* **VI** (also **rummage about, rummage around**) farfouiller *, fouiller (*among, in* dans ; *for* pour trouver) **COMP** **rummage sale** **N** *(US)* vente *f* de charité *(de bric-à-brac)*

rummy[1] * /ˈrʌmɪ/ **ADJ** ⇒ **rum[2]** **N** *(US * = drunk)* poivrot * *m*

rummy[2] /ˈrʌmɪ/ **N** *(Cards)* rami *m*

rumour, rumor *(US)* /ˈruːməʳ/ **N** rumeur *f* (*that* selon laquelle) ◆ **there is a disturbing ~ (to the effect) that ...** il court un bruit inquiétant selon lequel ... ◆ **all these nasty ~s** toutes ces rumeurs pernicieuses ◆ **~ has it that ...** on dit que ..., le bruit court que ... ◆ **there is a ~ of war** le bruit court *or* on dit qu'il va y avoir la guerre ◆ **the ~ mill** la rumeur publique **VT** ◆ **it is ~ed that ...** on dit que ..., le bruit court que ... ◆ **he is ~ed to be in London** il serait à Londres, le bruit court qu'il est à Londres ◆ **he is ~ed to be rich** on le dit riche

COMP **rumour-monger** **N** colporteur *m*, -euse *f* de rumeurs

rumour-mongering **N** *(NonC)* commérages *mpl*, colportage *m* de rumeurs

rump /rʌmp/ **N** [1] *[of animal]* croupe *f* ; *[of fowl]* croupion *m* ; *(Culin)* culotte *f* (de bœuf) ; * *[of person]* derrière *m*, postérieur * *m* [2] *(esp Brit pej) [of group, organization]* derniers vestiges *mpl* **ADJ** *(Pol)* ◆ **a ~ party/opposition** *etc* un parti/une opposition *etc* croupion ◆ **~ Yugoslavia** ce qui reste de la Yougoslavie ◆ **the Rump Parliament** *(Brit Hist)* le Parlement croupion

rumple /ˈrʌmpl/ **VT** *[+ clothes, paper]* froisser ; *[+ hair]* ébouriffer

rumpsteak /ˈrʌmpsteɪk/ **N** rumsteck *m*

rumpus * /ˈrʌmpəs/ **N** (pl **rumpuses**) chahut *m* ; *(= noise)* tapage *m*, boucan * *m* ; *(= quarrel)* prise *f* de bec * ◆ **to make** *or* **kick up a ~** faire du chahut *or* du boucan * ◆ **to have a ~ with sb** se chamailler * avec qn, avoir une prise de bec * avec qn **COMP** **rumpus room** **N** *(esp US)* salle *f* de jeux

rumpy-pumpy * /ˈrʌmpɪˈpʌmpɪ/ **N** *(NonC)* partie *f* de jambes en l'air *

rumrunner /ˈrʌmrʌnəʳ/ **N** *(Hist) (= person)* contrebandier *m (d'alcool)* ; *(= ship)* bateau *m* servant à la contrebande d'alcool

run /rʌn/

vb : pret **ran**, ptp **run**

1 NOUN	4 TRANSITIVE VERB
2 PLURAL NOUN	5 COMPOUNDS
3 INTRANSITIVE VERB	6 PHRASAL VERBS

1 – NOUN

[1] = act of running action *f* de courir, course *f* ◆ **to go for a ~** aller courir ◆ **to go for a 2-km ~**

faire 2 km de course à pied ◆ **at a** ~ en courant ◆ **to break into a** ~ se mettre à courir ◆ **to make a** ~ **for it** se sauver, filer* ◆ **I'll give them a (good)** ~ **for their money!** ils vont voir à qui ils ont affaire ! ◆ **he's had a good** ~ *(on sb's death)* il a bien profité de l'existence

2 = outing tour *m* ◆ **to go for a** ~ **in the car** faire un tour en voiture ◆ **they went for a** ~ **in the country** ils ont fait un tour à la campagne ◆ **we had a pleasant** ~ **down** le voyage a été agréable

3 = distance travelled trajet *m* ; *(= route)* ligne *f* ◆ **it's a 30-minute** ~ il y a une demi-heure de trajet ◆ **it's a 30-minute bus** ~ il y a une demi-heure de bus ◆ **it's a short car** ~ le trajet n'est pas long en voiture ◆ **the boat no longer does that** ~ le bateau ne fait plus cette traversée, ce service n'existe plus ◆ **the ferries on the Dover-Calais** ~ les ferrys sur la ligne Douvres-Calais ◆ **the ships on the China** ~ les paquebots qui font la Chine

4 = series série *f* ; *(Cards)* séquence *f* ◆ **a** ~ **of misfortunes** une série de malheurs, une série noire ◆ **a** ~ **of bad luck** une période de malchance ◆ **she's having a** ~ **of luck** la chance lui sourit ◆ **a** ~ **on the red** *(Roulette)* une série à la rouge ◆ **the** ~ **of the cards** le hasard du jeu

5 Theat, TV = period of performance ◆ **when the London** ~ **was over** une fois la saison à Londres *or* la série de représentations à Londres terminée ◆ **the play had a long** ~ la pièce a tenu longtemps l'affiche ◆ **her new series begins a** ~ **on BBC1** sa nouvelle série d'émissions va bientôt passer sur BBC1

6 = great demand *(Econ)* ruée *f* ◆ **there was a** ~ **on the pound** il y a eu une ruée sur la livre ◆ **a** ~ **on shares** une ruée sur les actions ◆ **there was a** ~ **on the banks** les guichets (des banques) ont été assiégés ◆ **there has been a** ~ **on sugar** les gens se sont précipités (dans les magasins) pour acheter du sucre, il y a une ruée sur le sucre

7 = use ◆ **they have the** ~ **of the garden** ils ont la jouissance du jardin ◆ **they gave us the** ~ **of the garden** ils nous ont donné la jouissance du jardin

8 of tide flux *m*

9 = trend *[of market]* tendance *f* ; *[of events]* tournure *f* ◆ **the decisive goal arrived, against the** ~ **of play** le but décisif a été marqué contre le cours du jeu ◆ **against the** ~ **of the polls, he was re-elected** contrairement à la tendance indiquée par les sondages, il a été réélu

10 = type ◆ **he was outside the common** ~ **of lawyers** ce n'était pas un avocat ordinaire ◆ **he didn't fit the usual** ~ **of petty criminals** il n'avait pas le profil du petit malfaiteur ordinaire ◆ **the usual** ~ **of problems** les problèmes *mpl* habituels

11 = track for sledging, skiing piste *f* ◆ **ski** ~ piste *f* de ski

12 = animal enclosure enclos *m*

13 in tights échelle *f*

14 Mus roulade *f*

15 Printing tirage *m* ◆ **a** ~ **of 5,000 copies** un tirage de 5 000 exemplaires

16 Cricket course *f* ◆ **to make a** ~ marquer une course

17 Mil = raid, mission raid *m* (aérien) ◆ **a bombing** ~ un bombardement

18 US Pol = bid for leadership candidature *f (for à)*

19 set structures

◆ **in the long run** à long terme ◆ **it will be more economical in the long** ~ ce sera plus économique à long terme ◆ **things will sort themselves out in the long** ~ les choses s'arrangeront avec le temps

◆ **in the short run** à court terme ◆ **the most effective policy in the short** ~ les mesures les plus efficaces à court terme ◆ **no improvement is likely in the short** ~ il y a peu de chances que la situation s'améliore à court terme *or* dans l'immédiat

◆ **on the run** ◆ **a criminal on the** ~ **(from the police)** un criminel recherché par la police ◆ **he is still on the** ~ il court toujours, il est toujours en cavale* ◆ **he was on the** ~ **for several months** il n'a été repris qu'au bout de plusieurs mois ◆ **to have the enemy on the** ~ mettre l'ennemi en fuite ◆ **to keep the enemy on the** ~ harceler l'ennemi ◆ **I knew I had him on the** ~ je savais que j'avais réussi à le mettre en mauvaise posture ◆ **she has so much to do she's always on the** ~* elle a tant à faire qu'elle est toujours en train de courir

2 - PLURAL NOUN

runs ** ◆ **to have the** ~**s** avoir la courante* *or* la chiasse**

3 - INTRANSITIVE VERB

1 gen courir ; *(= hurry)* courir, se précipiter ◆ **don't** ~ **across the road** ne traverse pas la rue en courant ◆ **he's trying to** ~ **before he can walk** *(Brit)* il essaie de brûler les étapes ◆ **to** ~ **behind sb** *(fig)* avoir du retard par rapport à qn ◆ **to** ~ **down/off** descendre/partir en courant ◆ **to** ~ **down a slope** dévaler une pente *or* descendre une pente en courant ◆ **to** ~ **for the bus** courir pour attraper le bus ◆ **he used to** ~ **for his school** il représentait son lycée dans les épreuves de course à pied ◆ **it** ~**s in the family** *[disease]* c'est héréditaire ; *[characteristic]* c'est de famille ◆ **my thoughts ran on Jenny** je pensais à Jenny ◆ **she came** ~**ning out** elle est sortie en courant ◆ **she ran over to her neighbour's** elle a couru *or* s'est précipitée chez son voisin ◆ **three men ran past him** trois hommes l'ont dépassé en courant ◆ **laughter ran round the room** le rire gagnait toute la salle ◆ **a rumour ran through the school** un bruit courait à l'école ◆ **this theme** ~**s through the whole Romantic movement** c'est un thème récurrent chez les romantiques ◆ **all sorts of thoughts were** ~**ning through my head** toutes sortes d'idées me venaient à l'esprit ◆ **that tune is** ~**ning through my head** cet air me trotte dans la tête ◆ **the rope ran through his fingers** la corde lui a filé entre les doigts ◆ **money simply** ~**s through his fingers** c'est un panier percé, l'argent lui file entre les doigts ◆ **she ran to meet him** elle a couru *or* s'est précipitée à sa rencontre ◆ **she ran to help him** elle a couru l'aider, elle a volé à son secours ; see also phrasal verbs

2 = flee fuir, prendre la fuite ◆ ~ **for it!** sauvez-vous !

3 drawer, curtains coulisser ◆ **the drawer** ~**s smoothly** le tiroir coulisse facilement

4 = flow, leak *[river, tears, tap, cheese]* couler ; *[sore, abscess]* suppurer ; *[colour]* déteindre ; *[dye, ink]* baver ◆ **to** ~ **into the sea** *[river]* se jeter dans la mer ◆ **the river** ~**s between wooded banks** la rivière coule entre des berges boisées ◆ **your bath is** ~**ning now** votre bain est en train de couler ◆ **to leave a tap** ~**ning** laisser un robinet ouvert ◆ **tears ran down her cheeks** les larmes coulaient sur ses joues ◆ **his eyes are** ~**ning** il a les yeux qui coulent *or* pleurent ◆ **his nose was** ~**ning** il avait le nez qui coulait ◆ **the milk ran all over the floor** le lait s'est répandu sur le sol ◆ **a heavy sea was** ~**ning** la mer était grosse ◆ **where the tide is** ~**ning strongly** là où les marées sont fortes

◆ **to run high** *[river]* être haut ; *[sea]* être gros ◆ **feelings were** ~**ning high** les passions étaient exacerbées ◆ **tension was** ~**ning high** l'atmosphère était très tendue

◆ **to run with** *(= be saturated)* ◆ **the floor was** ~**ning with water** le plancher était inondé ◆ **the walls were** ~**ning with moisture** les murs ruisselaient (d'humidité) ◆ **his face was** ~**ning with sweat** son visage ruisselait de sueur

5 words, text ◆ **how does the last sentence** ~ **?** quelle est la dernière phrase ? ◆ **so the story** ~**s** c'est ce que l'on raconte

6 Pol *etc* = stand être candidat, se présenter ◆ **he isn't** ~**ning this time** il n'est pas candidat *or* il ne se présente pas cette fois-ci ◆ **he won't** ~ **again** il ne se représentera plus ◆ **to** ~ **for President** *or* **the Presidency** être candidat à la présidence

7 = be ◆ **I'm** ~**ning a bit late** j'ai un peu de retard, je suis un peu en retard ◆ **to** ~ **wild** *[person]* être déchaîné ; *[animal]* courir en liberté ; *[plants, garden]* retourner à l'état sauvage

◆ **to run at** *[amount]* ◆ **inflation is** ~**ning at 3%** le taux d'inflation est de 3% ◆ **the deficit is now** ~**ning at 300 million dollars a year** le déficit est maintenant de 300 millions de dollars par an

8 = extend, continue *[play]* être à l'affiche, se jouer ; *[film]* passer ; *[contract]* valoir, être valide ◆ **the play has been** ~**ning for a year** la pièce est à l'affiche *or* se joue depuis un an ◆ **this contract has ten months to** ~ ce contrat expire dans dix mois *or* vaut (encore) pour dix mois ◆ **the two sentences to** ~ **concurrently/consecutively** *(Jur)* avec/sans confusion des deux peines ◆ **the programme ran for an extra ten minutes** *(Rad, TV)* l'émission a duré dix minutes de plus que prévu ◆ **the programme is** ~**ning to time** *(TV, Rad)* l'émission passera à l'heure prévue ◆ **the book has** ~ **into five editions** ce livre en est à sa cinquième édition

9 bus, train, coach, ferry assurer le service ◆ **this train** ~**s between London and Manchester** ce train assure le service Londres-Manchester *or* entre Londres et Manchester ◆ **the buses** ~ **once an hour** les bus passent toutes les heures ◆ **the buses are** ~**ning early/late/to** *or* **on time** les bus sont en avance/en retard/à l'heure ◆ **there are no trains** ~**ning today** il n'y a pas de trains aujourd'hui ◆ **that train doesn't** ~ **on Sundays** ce train n'assure pas le service *or* n'est pas en service le dimanche

10 = function *[machine]* marcher ; *[factory]* fonctionner, marcher ; *[wheel]* tourner ◆ **the car is** ~**ning smoothly** la voiture marche bien ◆ **you mustn't leave the engine** ~**ning** il ne faut pas laisser tourner le moteur ◆ **this car** ~**s on diesel** cette voiture marche au gazole ◆ **the radio** ~**s off the mains/off batteries** cette radio marche sur secteur/sur piles ◆ **things are** ~**ning smoothly** tout se passe bien

11 = pass *[road, river etc]* passer *(through* à travers) ; *[mountain range]* s'étendre ◆ **the road** ~**s past our house** la route passe devant notre maison ◆ **the road** ~**s right into town** la route va jusqu'au centre-ville ◆ **the main road** ~**s north and south** la route principale va du nord au sud ◆ **he has a scar** ~**ning across his chest** il a une cicatrice en travers de la poitrine ◆ **a wall** ~**s round the garden** un mur entoure le jardin ◆ **the river** ~**s through the valley** la rivière coule dans la vallée ◆ **the roots** ~ **under the house** les racines passent sous la maison

12 = unravel *[knitting]* se démailler ; *[tights]* filer

4 - TRANSITIVE VERB

1 gen courir ◆ **he ran 2km non-stop** il a couru (pendant) 2 km sans s'arrêter ◆ **he** ~**s 15km every day** il fait 15 km de course à pied tous les jours ◆ **he ran the distance in under half an hour** il a couvert la distance en moins d'une demi-heure ◆ **to** ~ **the 100 metres** courir le 100 mètres ◆ **to** ~ **a race** participer à une (épreuve de) course ◆ **you ran a good race** vous avez fait une excellente course ◆ **the first race will be** ~ **at 2 o'clock** la première épreuve se

courra à 2 heures ◆ **but if it really happened he'd ~ a mile*** mais si ça se produisait, il aurait vite fait de se débiner* ◆ **to ~ the streets** *[child, dog]* traîner dans les rues ◆ **to ~ a red** *or* **a stoplight**(US) brûler *or* griller un feu rouge ◆ **they beat Wales and ran Scotland very close** ils ont battu le pays de Galles et ont bien failli battre l'Écosse ◆ **you're ~ning things a bit close*** *or* **fine***! ça va être juste !, tu calcules un peu juste !

2 = chase, hunt *[+ fox, deer]* chasser ; *(= make run) [+ person]* chasser ; *[+ animal]* poursuivre, pourchasser ; *(Sport) [+ horse]* faire courir ◆ **to ~ a horse in the Derby** engager *or* faire courir un cheval dans le Derby ◆ **the sheriff ran him out of town** le shérif l'a chassé de la ville ◆ **they ran him out of the house** ils l'ont chassé de la maison ◆ **to ~ sb into debt** endetter qn

3 Pol *[+ candidate]* présenter ◆ **the party is ~ning 100 candidates this year** le parti présente 100 candidats (aux élections) cette année

4 = transport *[+ person]* conduire ; *[+ goods]* transporter ◆ **to ~ sb into town** conduire qn en ville ◆ **he ran her home** il l'a ramenée chez elle ◆ **I'll ~ your luggage to the station** j'apporterai vos bagages à la gare

5 = smuggle *[+ guns, whisky]* passer en contrebande ◆ **he was ~ning guns to the island** il faisait passer *or* il passait des fusils dans l'île en contrebande

6 = operate : esp Brit *[+ machine]* faire marcher ; *(Comput) [+ program]* exécuter ◆ **to ~ a radio off the mains** faire marcher une radio sur secteur ◆ **it would be cheaper to ~ the heating system on gas** ce serait plus économique si le chauffage fonctionnait en gaz ◆ **I can't afford to ~ a car** je ne peux pas me permettre d'avoir une voiture ◆ **he ~s a Rolls** il a une Rolls ◆ **this car is very cheap to ~** cette voiture est très économique

7 = organize, manage *[+ business, company, organization, school]* diriger, gérer ; *[+ mine]* gérer, administrer ; *[+ shop, hotel, club]* tenir ; *[+ newspaper]* être directeur de ; *[+ competition]* organiser ; *[+ public transport]* gérer ◆ **the company ~s extra buses at rush hours** la société met en service des bus supplémentaires aux heures de pointe ◆ **the school is ~ning courses for foreign students** le collège organise des cours pour les étudiants étrangers ◆ **to ~ a house** tenir une maison ◆ **I want to ~ my own life** je veux mener ma vie comme je l'entends ◆ **she's the one who really ~s everything** en réalité c'est elle qui dirige tout

8 = put, move ◆ **he ran a line of stitches along the hem** il a fait une série de points le long de l'ourlet ◆ **to ~ a boat ashore** pousser un bateau sur le rivage ◆ **to ~ one's finger down a list** suivre une liste du doigt ◆ **to ~ the car into/out of the garage** rentrer la voiture au/sortir la voiture du garage ◆ **he ran the car into a tree** sa voiture est rentrée dans un arbre, il a percuté un arbre (avec sa voiture) ◆ **to ~ a pipe into a room** faire passer un tuyau dans une pièce ◆ **to ~ wires under the floorboards** faire passer des fils électriques sous le plancher ◆ **to ~ one's eye over a page** jeter un coup d'œil sur une page ◆ **he ran the vacuum cleaner over the carpet** il a passé l'aspirateur sur le tapis ◆ **to ~ one's hand over sth** passer la main sur qch ◆ **to ~ one's fingers over the piano keys** promener ses doigts sur le clavier ◆ **to ~ one's fingers through one's hair** se passer la main dans les cheveux

9 = publish publier ◆ **the paper ran a series of articles on genetic engineering** le journal a publié une série d'articles sur les manipulations génétiques ◆ **the papers ran the story on the front page** les journaux ont publié l'article en première page, cette histoire a fait la une des journaux

10 = present *[+ film]* présenter, donner ; *(Comm)* vendre ◆ **the supermarket is ~ning a new line in fresh pasta** le supermarché vend une nouvelle gamme de pâtes fraîches

11 = cause to flow faire couler ◆ **to ~ water into a bath** faire couler de l'eau dans une baignoire ◆ **I'll ~ you a bath** je vais te faire couler un bain ◆ **he ~s his words together** il mange ses mots

5 - COMPOUNDS

run-around* N ◆ **he gave me the ~-around** il s'est défilé*

run-down ADJ *[person]* à plat*, mal fichu* ; *[building, area]* délabré ; *[factory]* en perte de vitesse ◆ **I feel a little ~-down** je ne me sens pas très bien ; see also **rundown**

run-in N *(* = quarrel)* engueulade* f, prise f de bec *(over à propos de)* ; *(= rehearsal)* répétition f ; *(= approach)* approche f

run-off N *[of contest] (= second round)* deuxième tour ; *(= last round)* dernier tour ; *(Sport)* finale f (d'une course) ; *(Agr) [of pollutants]* infiltrations fpl ◆ **there was nothing to stop the ~-off of rainwater** rien ne pouvait empêcher le ruissellement pluvial *or* des eaux de pluie

run-of-the-mill ADJ banal, ordinaire

run-on ADJ *(Typ) [text]* composé sans alinéa ◆ **~-on line** enjambement m

run-resist ADJ ⇒ **runproof**

run-through N *(before test)* essai m ; *(Theat)* filage m

run time N *(Comput)* durée f d'exploitation

run-up N 1 *(= time)* période f préparatoire *(to à)* ◆ **the ~-up to the launch of Channel 5** la période préparatoire au lancement de Channel 5 ◆ **he handled the ~-up to the general election** c'est lui qui s'est occupé des préparatifs des élections législatives ◆ **in the ~-up to the elections/to Christmas** à l'approche des élections/de Noël 2 *(US = increase)* augmentation f *(in de)* 3 *Sport* course f d'élan

6 - PHRASAL VERBS

► **run about** VI *(gen)* courir çà et là ; *(looking for sth, working etc)* courir dans tous les sens ◆ **the children were ~ning about all over the house** les enfants couraient partout dans la maison ◆ **she has been ~ning about* with him for several months** *(fig)* elle sort avec lui depuis plusieurs mois

► **run across** VI traverser en courant
VT FUS *(= meet) [+ person]* rencontrer par hasard, tomber sur ; *(= find) [+ object, quotation, reference]* trouver par hasard, tomber sur

► **run after** VT FUS courir après ◆ **he doesn't ~ after women** *(fig)* ce n'est pas un coureur ◆ **I'm not going to spend my days ~ning after you!** je ne suis pas ta bonne !

► **run against** VT FUS ◆ **the game was ~ning against them** ils étaient en train de perdre la partie ◆ **to ~ against sb** *(Pol)* se présenter contre qn

► **run along** VI courir ; *(= go away)* s'en aller ◆ **~ along!** sauvez-vous !, filez !*

► **run around** VI ⇒ **run about**

► **run at** VT FUS *(= attack)* se jeter *or* se précipiter sur

► **run away** VI 1 partir en courant ; *(= flee) [person]* se sauver, s'enfuir ; *[horse]* s'emballer ◆ **to ~ away from home** faire une fugue ◆ **don't ~ away, I need your advice** ne te sauve pas, j'ai besoin d'un conseil ◆ **she ran away with another man** *(= elope)* elle est partie avec un autre homme ◆ **he ran away with the funds** *(= steal)* il est parti avec la caisse

2 *[water]* s'écouler ◆ **he let the bath water ~ away** il a laissé la baignoire se vider
VT SEP *[+ water]* vider

► **run away with** VT FUS 1 *(= win easily) [+ race, match]* gagner haut la main ; *[+ prize]* remporter haut la main
2 *(= use up) [+ funds, money, resources]* épuiser
3 ◆ **you're letting your imagination ~ away with you** tu te laisses emporter par ton imagination ◆ **don't let your emotions ~ away with you** ne te laisse pas dominer par tes émotions ◆ **don't ~ away with the idea that ...** n'allez pas vous mettre dans la tête que ... ; see also **run away vi 1**

► **run back** VI revenir *or* retourner en courant
VT SEP 1 *[+ person]* ramener (en voiture)
2 *(= rewind) [+ tape, film]* rembobiner

► **run by** ⇒ **run past**

► **run down** VI 1 *[person]* descendre en courant
2 *[watch etc]* s'arrêter *(faute d'être remonté)* ; *[battery]* se décharger
VT SEP 1 *(= knock over)* renverser ; *(= run over)* écraser
2 *(Naut) [+ ship]* heurter *or* aborder par l'avant *or* par l'étrave ; *(in battle)* éperonner
3 *(esp Brit = limit, reduce) [+ production]* diminuer ; *[+ factory]* diminuer la production de ◆ **they are ~ning down their DIY stores** ils vont réduire le nombre (*or* la taille) de leurs magasins de bricolage
4 *(* = disparage)* critiquer, dire du mal de
5 *(= pursue and capture) [+ criminal]* découvrir la cachette de ; *[+ stag etc]* mettre aux abois
6 *[+ list, page]* parcourir

► **run in** VI entrer en courant ; *(* = call)* passer ◆ **I'll ~ in and see you tomorrow*** je passerai vous voir demain
VT SEP 1 *(Brit) [+ car]* roder ◆ **"running in, please pass"** "en rodage"
2 *(* = arrest)* emmener au poste

► **run into** VT FUS 1 *(= meet)* rencontrer par hasard, tomber sur ◆ **to ~ into difficulties** *or* **trouble** se heurter à des difficultés ◆ **to ~ into danger** se trouver dans une situation dangereuse ◆ **to ~ into debt** s'endetter ◆ **we've ~ into a problem** il y a un problème
2 *(= collide with)* rentrer dans ◆ **the car ran into a tree** la voiture est rentrée dans un arbre
3 *(= merge)* ◆ **the colours are ~ning into each other** les couleurs déteignent les unes sur les autres ◆ **I was so tired, my words began to ~ into one another** j'étais si fatigué que je commençais à bredouiller
4 *(= amount to)* s'élever à ◆ **the cost will ~ into thousands of pounds** le coût va s'élever *or* se chiffrer à des milliers de livres

► **run off** VI ⇒ **run away vi**
VT SEP 1 ⇒ **run away vt sep**
2 *(Typ)* tirer ◆ **to ~ off 600 copies** tirer 600 exemplaires
3 *(Sport)* ◆ **to ~ off the heats** *[runner]* disputer les éliminatoires

► **run on** VI 1 continuer de courir ; *(fig *: in talking)* parler sans arrêt ◆ **but here am I ~ning on, and you're in a hurry** mais je parle, je parle, alors que vous êtes pressé ◆ **it ran on for four hours** ça a duré quatre heures
2 *[letters, words]* ne pas être séparés, être liés ; *[line of writing]* suivre sans alinéa ; *[verse]* enjamber ; *[time]* passer, s'écouler
VT SEP *[+ letters, words, sentences]* faire suivre sur la même ligne

► **run out** VI 1 *[person]* sortir en courant ; *[rope, chain]* se dérouler ; *[liquid]* couler ◆ **the pier ~s out into the sea** la jetée s'avance dans la mer
2 *(= come to an end) [lease, contract]* expirer ; *[supplies]* être épuisé, venir à manquer ; *[period of time]* être écoulé, tirer à sa fin ◆ **my patience**

is ~ning out ma patience est à bout, je suis à bout de patience ◆ **when the money ~s out** quand il n'y aura plus d'argent, quand l'argent sera épuisé ◆ **their luck ran out** la chance les a lâchés

VT SEP *[+ rope, chain]* laisser filer

► **run out of** VT FUS *[+ supplies, money]* venir à manquer de, être à court de ; *[+ patience]* être à bout de ◆ **we're ~ning out of time** il ne nous reste plus beaucoup de temps ◆ **we've ~ out of time** *(TV, Rad)* il est temps de rendre l'antenne, le temps qui nous était imparti est écoulé ◆ **to ~ out of petrol** *(Brit)* or **gas** *(US)* tomber en panne d'essence ◆ **to ~ out of gas** * *(US fig)* s'essouffler

► **run out on*** VT FUS *[+ person]* laisser tomber *

► **run over** VI 1 *(= overflow) [liquid, container]* déborder ◆ **the play ran over by ten minutes** *(Rad, TV etc)* la pièce a duré dix minutes de plus que prévu ◆ **we're ~ning over** *(Rad, TV etc)* nous avons pris du retard

2 *(= go briefly)* passer ◆ **I'll ~ over tomorrow** je passerai demain ◆ **she ran over to her neighbours'** elle a fait un saut chez ses voisins

VT FUS 1 *(= recapitulate) [+ story, part in play]* revoir, reprendre ◆ **I'll ~ over your part with you** je vous ferai répéter votre rôle ◆ **let's just ~ over it again** reprenons cela encore une fois

2 *(= reread) [+ notes]* parcourir

VT SEP *(in car etc) [+ person, animal]* écraser

► **run past** VI passer en courant

VT SEP * *[+ idea]* expliquer ◆ **could you ~ that past me again?** est-ce que tu pourrais m'expliquer ça encore une fois ?

► **run through** VI passer or traverser en courant

VT FUS 1 *(= use up) [+ fortune]* gaspiller

2 *(= read quickly) [+ notes, text]* parcourir, jeter un coup d'œil sur

3 *(= rehearse) [+ play]* répéter ; *[+ verse, movement]* reprendre ; *(= recapitulate)* récapituler, reprendre ◆ **let's ~ through the chorus again** reprenons le refrain encore une fois ◆ **if I may just ~ through the principal points once more?** pourrais-je reprendre or récapituler les points principaux ?

VT SEP 1 ◆ **to ~ sb through (with a sword)** passer qn au fil de l'épée, transpercer qn d'un coup d'épée

2 *(Comput) [+ data]* passer (en revue)

► **run to** VT FUS 1 *(= seek help from)* faire appel à ; *(= take refuge with)* se réfugier dans les bras de ◆ **as usual she ran to her parents** comme d'habitude elle a fait appel à papa et maman or elle est allée se réfugier dans les bras de or chez ses parents ◆ **I wouldn't go ~ning to the police** je ne me précipiterais pas au commissariat de police ◆ **go on then, ~ to mummy!** c'est ça, va te réfugier dans les jupes de ta mère !

2 *(= afford)* ◆ **I can't ~ to a new car** je ne peux pas me payer une nouvelle voiture ◆ **the funds won't ~ to a meal in a restaurant** il n'y a pas assez d'argent pour un repas au restaurant

3 *(= develop)* ◆ **to ~ to fat** grossir

4 *(= amount to)* ◆ **the article ~s to several hundred pages** l'article fait plusieurs centaines de pages

► **run up** VI *(= climb quickly)* monter en courant ; *(= approach quickly)* s'approcher en courant ◆ **a man ran up and fired several shots** un homme est arrivé en courant et a tiré plusieurs coups de feu

VT SEP 1 ◆ **to ~ up a hill** monter une colline en courant

2 *[+ flag]* hisser

3 *[+ bills]* accumuler ◆ **to ~ up a debt** s'endetter *(of de)* ◆ **she's ~ up a huge bill at the garage** ça va lui coûter cher chez le garagiste

4 *(* = make quickly) [+ garment]* faire or coudre rapidement ◆ **she can ~ up a dress in no time** elle peut faire or coudre une robe en un rien de temps

► **run up against** VT FUS *[+ problem, difficulty]* se heurter à

---

runabout /ˈrʌnəbaʊt/ N *(= car)* petite voiture f ; *(= boat)* runabout m COMP **runabout ticket** N *(Rail etc)* billet m circulaire

runaway /ˈrʌnəweɪ/ N *(gen)* fuyard m, fugitif m, -ive f ; *(= teenager, pupil etc)* fugueur m, -euse f

ADJ *[slave, person]* fugitif ; *[horse]* emballé ; *[of car]* fou (folle f) ◆ **~ wedding** mariage m clandestin ◆ **the ~ couple** le couple clandestin, les amants mpl ◆ **~ inflation** *(Fin)* inflation f galopante ◆ **~ success** *(fig)* succès m à tout casser*, succès m monstre* ◆ **he had a ~ victory** il a remporté la victoire haut la main

rundown /ˈrʌndaʊn/ N 1 *(= reduction: gen)* réduction f, diminution f ; *[of industry, organization]* réductions fpl de personnel ◆ **there will be a ~ of staff** il y aura une réduction de personnel ◆ **the ~ of key areas of the economy** la réduction de l'activité dans certains domaines-clés de l'économie 2 *(* = summary)* récapitulatif m ◆ **here's a ~ of the options** voici un récapitulatif des diverses possibilités ◆ **to give sb a ~ on sth** * mettre qn au courant or au parfum‡ de qch ◆ **give me a quick ~ on who is involved** dites-moi brièvement qui sont les participants

rune /ruːn/ N rune f ◆ **to read the ~s** *(Brit fig)* interpréter la situation ◆ **they read the ~s correctly** ils ont vu juste

rung¹ /rʌŋ/ VB ptp of **ring²**

rung² /rʌŋ/ N *[of ladder]* barreau m, échelon m ; *[of chair]* bâton m, barreau m

runic /ˈruːnɪk/ ADJ runique

runnel /ˈrʌnl/ N *(= brook)* ruisseau m ; *(= gutter)* rigole f

runner /ˈrʌnəʳ/ N 1 *(= athlete)* coureur m ; *(= horse)* partant m ; *(= messenger)* messager m, courrier m ; *(= smuggler)* contrebandier m ◆ **to do a ~** * déguerpir*, mettre les bouts‡ ◆ **Bow Street Runner** *(Brit Hist)* sergent m (de ville) ; → **blockade, gunrunner** 2 *(= sliding part) [of car seat, door etc]* glissière f ; *[of curtain]* suspendeur m ; *[of sledge]* patin m ; *[of skate]* lame f ; *[of turbine]* couronne f mobile ; *[of drawer]* coulisseau m 3 *(= hall carpet)* chemin m de couloir ; *(= stair carpet)* chemin m d'escalier ; (also **table-runner**) chemin m de table 4 *(Bot = plant)* coulant m, stolon m

COMP **runner bean** N *(Brit)* haricot m grimpant or à rames

runner-up N (pl **runners-up**) *(coming second)* second(e) m(f) ◆ **~s-up will each receive ...** *(after first, second, third place)* les autres gagnants recevront chacun ...

running /ˈrʌnɪŋ/ N 1 *(= action: in race etc)* course f ◆ **to make the ~** *(Brit) (Sport)* faire le lièvre ; *(fig) (in work)* mener la course ; *(in relationship)* prendre l'initiative ◆ **to be in the ~** avoir des chances de réussir ◆ **to be out of the ~** * ne plus être dans la course ◆ **to be in the ~ for promotion/for the job** être sur les rangs pour obtenir de l'avancement/pour avoir le poste

2 *(NonC = functioning) [of machine]* marche f, fonctionnement m ; *[of train]* marche f

3 *(NonC: gen)* gestion f ; *[of competition]* organisation f

4 *(NonC = smuggling)* contrebande f ; → **gunrunning**

ADJ 1 *(= flowing) [tap]* ouvert ◆ **~ water, a ~ stream** un petit cours d'eau, un ruisseau ◆ **~ water** *(from tap)* eau f courante ◆ **~ water in every room** eau f courante dans toutes les chambres ◆ **hot and cold ~ water** eau f courante chaude et froide ◆ **to wash sth under hot/cold ~ water** laver qch sous le robinet d'eau chaude/froide ◆ **to have a ~ nose** avoir le nez qui coule ◆ **~ cold** *(Med)* rhume m de cerveau

2 *(= continuous)* ◆ **to become a ~ joke between ...** devenir un inépuisable or perpétuel sujet de plaisanterie entre ... ◆ **a ~ argument** une vieille querelle ◆ **~ battle** *(lit) combat où l'un des adversaires bat en retraite* ; *(fig)* lutte f continuelle ◆ **to keep up a ~ battle (with sb)** mener un combat de harcèlement (contre qn) ◆ **~ sore** *(Med)* plaie f suppurante ; *(fig)* véritable plaie f ; → **long¹**

ADV de suite ◆ **four days/times ~** quatre jours/fois de suite ◆ **(for) three years ~** pendant trois ans ◆ **for the third year ~** pour la troisième année consécutive

COMP **running account** N *(Fin)* compte m courant *(entre banques etc)* ◆ **to have** or **keep a ~ account with sb** être en compte avec qn

running board N *[of car, train]* marchepied m

running bowline N *(Naut)* laguis m

running commentary N *(Rad, TV)* commentaire m suivi *(on sth* de qch) ◆ **she gave us a ~ commentary on what was happening** *(fig)* elle nous a fait un commentaire détaillé de ce qui se passait

running costs NPL *(esp Brit) [of business]* frais mpl de fonctionnement or d'exploitation, dépenses fpl courantes ; *[of machine]* frais mpl d'entretien ◆ **the ~ costs of the car/the central heating are high** la voiture/le chauffage central revient cher

running fire N *(Mil)* feu m roulant

running hand N écriture f cursive

running head N *(Typ)* ⇒ **running title**

running jump N saut m avec élan ◆ **(go and) take a ~ jump!** * va te faire cuire un œuf ! *

running kick N coup m de pied donné en courant

running knot N nœud m coulant

running mate N *(US Pol)* candidat(e) m(f) à la vice-présidence

running order N *[of programme]* ordre m de passage ◆ **we reversed the ~ order** nous avons inversé l'ordre de passage

◆ **in running order** en état de marche

running repairs NPL réparations fpl courantes

running shoe N chaussure f de course

running stitch N *(Sewing)* point m de devant

running tally N ⇒ **running total**

running time N *[of film]* durée f

running title N *(Typ)* titre m courant

running total N cumul m, total m cumulé ◆ **to keep a ~ total (of sth)** tenir un compte régulier (de qch)

running track N *(Sport)* piste f

runny* /ˈrʌnɪ/ ADJ *[sauce, honey, consistency]* liquide ; *[omelette]* baveux ; *[eyes]* qui pleure ◆ **a ~ egg** *(boiled)* un œuf à la coque ; *(fried, poached)* un œuf dont le jaune est crémeux ◆ **to have a ~ nose** avoir le nez qui coule

runproof /ˈrʌnpruːf/ ADJ *[tights]* indémaillable ; *[mascara]* waterproof

runt /rʌnt/ N *(= animal)* avorton m ; *(pej) (= person)* nabot(e) m(f), avorton m ◆ **a little ~ of a man** un bonhomme tout riquiqui *

runway /ˈrʌnweɪ/ N *(for planes)* piste f ; *(Tech)* chemin m or piste f de roulement

rupee /ruːˈpiː/ N roupie f

rupture /ˈrʌptʃəʳ/ N *(lit, fig)* rupture f ; *(Med * = hernia)* hernie f VT rompre ◆ **~d aneurism** *(Med)* rupture f d'anévrisme ◆ **to ~ o.s.** se donner une hernie VI se rompre

rural /ˈrʊərəl/ ADJ *[area, village, school, life, economy, poverty]* rural ; *[setting, landscape]* rural, champêtre *(liter)* ; *[household]* paysan ; *[policeman, services, crime]* en milieu rural ; *[postmaster, housing]* en zone rurale ; *[accent]* campagnard ◆ **~ England** l'Angleterre f rurale ◆ **~ dean** *(Brit*

Rel) doyen m rural ◆ ~ **depopulation** exode m rural
COMP **rural development** N développement m rural
rural district council N (Brit) conseil m municipal rural
rural planning N aménagement m rural

ruse /ruːz/ N ruse f, stratagème m

rush¹ /rʌʃ/ N 1 (= rapid movement) course f précipitée, ruée f ; [of crowd] ruée f ; (with jostling) bousculade f ; (Mil = attack) bond m, assaut m ◆ **he was caught in the ~ for the door** il a été pris dans la ruée vers la porte ◆ **it got lost in the ~** ça s'est perdu dans la bousculade ◆ **to make a ~ at** se précipiter sur ◆ **there was a ~ for the empty seats** il y a eu une ruée vers les places libres, on s'est rué vers or sur les places libres ◆ **gold ~** ruée f vers l'or ◆ **there's a ~ on matches** (Comm) on se rue sur les allumettes ◆ **we have a ~ on in the office just now** c'est le coup de feu en ce moment au bureau ◆ **the Christmas ~** (in shops) la bousculade dans les magasins avant Noël ◆ **we've had a ~ of orders** on nous a submergés de commandes ◆ **a ~ of warm air** une bouffée d'air tiède ◆ **there was a ~ of water** l'eau a jailli ◆ **he had a ~ of blood to the head** il a eu un coup de sang
2 (= hurry) hâte f ◆ **the ~ of city life** le rythme effréné de la vie urbaine ◆ **to be in a ~** être extrêmement pressé ◆ **I had a ~ to get here in time** j'ai dû me dépêcher pour arriver à l'heure ◆ **I did it in a ~** je l'ai fait à toute vitesse or en quatrième vitesse* ◆ **what's all the ~?** pourquoi est-ce que c'est si pressé ? ◆ **is there any ~ for this?** est-ce que c'est pressé ? or urgent ? ◆ **it all happened in a ~** tout est arrivé or tout s'est passé très vite
3 (Cine) rush m (pl inv)
4 (Drugs ‡) flash* m
5 (US Univ: of fraternity etc) campagne f de recrutement
VI [person] se précipiter ; [car] foncer ◆ **the train went ~ing into the tunnel** le train est entré à toute vitesse dans le tunnel ◆ **they ~ed to help her** ils se sont précipités pour l'aider ◆ **I ~ed to her side** je me suis précipité à ses côtés ◆ **they ~ed to her defence** ils se sont précipités pour la défendre ◆ **I'm ~ing to finish it** je me presse or je me dépêche pour le finir ◆ **to ~ through** [+ book] lire à la hâte or en diagonale ; [+ meal] prendre sur le pouce* ; [+ museum] visiter au pas de course ; [+ town] traverser à toute vitesse ; [+ work] expédier ◆ **to ~ in/out/back** etc entrer/sortir/rentrer etc précipitamment or à toute vitesse ; see also **rush in, rush out** ◆ **to ~ to the attack** se jeter or se ruer à l'attaque ◆ **to ~ to conclusions** tirer des conclusions hâtives ◆ **the blood ~ed to his face** le sang lui est monté au visage ◆ **memories ~ed into his mind** des souvenirs lui affluèrent à l'esprit ◆ **he ~ed into marriage** il s'est marié hâtivement or à la hâte ◆ **the wind ~ed through the stable** le vent s'engouffrait dans l'écurie ◆ **a torrent of water ~ed down the slope** un véritable torrent a dévalé la pente ; → **headlong**
VT 1 (= cause to move quickly) entraîner or pousser vivement ◆ **to ~ sb to hospital** transporter qn d'urgence à l'hôpital ◆ **they ~ed more troops to the front** ils ont envoyé or expédié d'urgence des troupes fraîches sur le front ◆ **they ~ed him out of the room** ils l'ont fait sortir précipitamment or en toute hâte de la pièce ◆ **I don't want to ~ you** je ne voudrais pas vous bousculer ◆ **don't ~ me!** laissez-moi le temps de souffler ! ◆ **to ~ sb off his feet** ne pas laisser à qn le temps de souffler ◆ **to ~ sb into a decision** forcer or obliger qn à prendre une décision à la hâte ◆ **to ~ sb into doing sth** forcer or obliger qn à faire qch à la hâte ◆ **they ~ed the bill through Parliament** ils ont fait voter la loi à la hâte ; see also **rushed**
2 (= take by storm: Mil) [+ town, position] prendre d'assaut ; [+ fence, barrier] franchir (sur son élan) ◆ **her admirers ~ed the stage** ses admirateurs ont envahi la scène ◆ **the mob ~ed the line of policemen** la foule s'est élancée contre le cordon de police
3 (= do hurriedly) [+ job, task] dépêcher ; [+ order] exécuter d'urgence ◆ **"please rush me three tickets"** (Comm) "envoyez-moi de toute urgence trois billets"
4 ‡ (= charge) faire payer ; (= swindle) faire payer un prix exorbitant à, estamper* ◆ **how much were you ~ed for it?** combien on te l'a fait payer ? ◆ **you really were ~ed for that!** tu t'es vraiment fait estamper* pour ça !
5 (US Univ: of fraternity etc) recruter
COMP **rush hour** N heures fpl de pointe or d'affluence
rush-hour traffic N circulation f aux heures de pointe
rush job N (gen) travail m urgent ◆ **that was a ~ job** (= urgent) c'était urgent ; (pej) (= too rushed) c'était fait à la va-vite*
rush order N (Comm) commande f pressée or urgente

► **rush about, rush around** VI courir çà et là

► **rush at** VT FUS se jeter sur, se ruer sur ; [+ enemy] se ruer sur, fondre sur ◆ **don't ~ at the job, take it slowly** ne fais pas ça trop vite, prends ton temps

► **rush down** VI [person] descendre précipitamment ; [stream] dévaler

► **rush in** VI (lit) entrer précipitamment or à toute vitesse ; (fig) se précipiter (to pour) see also **rush¹ vi**

► **rush out** VI sortir précipitamment or à toute vitesse
VT SEP (= produce quickly) [+ goods] sortir rapidement ◆ **we'll ~ it out to you right away** (= deliver) nous vous le livrerons directement dans les plus brefs délais

► **rush through** VT SEP [+ order] exécuter d'urgence ; [+ goods, supplies] envoyer or faire parvenir de toute urgence ; [+ bill, legislation] faire voter à la hâte ◆ **they ~ed medical supplies through to him** on lui a fait parvenir des médicaments de toute urgence ; see also **rush¹ vi**

► **rush up** VI (= arrive) accourir
VT SEP [+ help, reinforcements] faire parvenir or (faire) envoyer d'urgence (to à)

rush² /rʌʃ/ N (= plant) jonc m ; (for chair) jonc m, paille f
COMP **rush light** N chandelle f à mèche de jonc
rush mat N natte f de jonc
rush matting N (NonC) natte f de jonc

rushed /rʌʃt/ ADJ 1 (= hurried) [meal] expédié ; [decision] hâtif, précipité ; [work] fait à la va-vite* 2 (= busy) [person] débordé ◆ **to be ~ off one's feet** être (complètement) débordé ◆ **she was ~ off her feet trying to get everything ready** elle était complètement débordée avec tous les préparatifs

rusk /rʌsk/ N (esp Brit) biscotte f

russet /ˈrʌsɪt/ N 1 (= colour) couleur f feuille-morte inv, brun roux inv 2 (= apple) reinette f grise ADJ brun roux inv

Russia /ˈrʌʃə/ N Russie f

Russian /ˈrʌʃən/ ADJ (gen) russe ; [ambassador, embassy] de Russie ; [teacher] de russe N 1 Russe mf 2 (= language) russe m
COMP **Russian doll** N poupée f russe or gigogne
Russian dressing N (Culin) sauce f rouge relevée (pour la salade)
the Russian Federation N la Fédération de Russie
Russian Orthodox ADJ (Rel) orthodoxe russe
Russian Orthodox Church N Église f orthodoxe russe
Russian roulette N roulette f russe
Russian salad N salade f russe

Russkie*, Russky* /ˈrʌskɪ/ (esp US † pej or hum) N Rus(s)kof* m inv, Popov* mf inv ADJ russe

Russo- /ˈrʌsəʊ/ PREF russo- ◆ **~Japanese** russo-japonais

rust /rʌst/ N (on metal, also plant disease) rouille f ; (= colour) couleur f rouille, roux m VT (lit, fig) rouiller VI (lit, fig) se rouiller
COMP **the Rust Belt** N (US) la région industrielle des États-Unis ◆ **the Rust Belt states** les États mpl industriels américains
rust bucket* N (= car, boat) tas m de rouille*
rust-coloured ADJ (couleur) rouille inv
rust-resistant ADJ ⇒ **rustproof adj**

► **rust in** VI [screw] se rouiller dans son trou

► **rust up** VI se rouiller

rusted /ˈrʌstɪd/ (esp US) ADJ rouillé

rustic /ˈrʌstɪk/ N campagnard(e) m(f), paysan(ne) m(f) ADJ 1 (= rural) [scene, charm, simplicity, appearance] rustique, champêtre (liter) ; [restaurant] rustique ; [novel] pastoral 2 (= roughly-made) [furniture] rustique ; [wall] grossier 3 (pej = crude) frustre (pej), grossier (pej)

rusticate /ˈrʌstɪkeɪt/ VI habiter la campagne VT (Brit Univ) exclure (temporairement)

rusticity /rʌsˈtɪsɪtɪ/ N rusticité f

rustiness /ˈrʌstɪnɪs/ N rouillure f, rouille f

rustle /ˈrʌsl/ N [of leaves] bruissement m ; [of silk, skirt] bruissement m, froufrou m ; [of paper] froissement m VI [leaves, wind] bruire ; [paper] produire un froissement or un bruissement ; [clothes, skirt] faire froufrou ◆ **she ~d into the room** elle est entrée en froufroutant dans la pièce ◆ **something ~d in the cupboard** il y a eu un froissement or un bruissement dans le placard VT 1 [+ leaves] faire bruire ; [+ paper] froisser ; [+ programme] agiter avec un bruissement ; [+ petticoat, skirt] faire froufrouter 2 (esp US = steal) [+ cattle] voler

► **rustle up*** VT SEP se débrouiller* pour trouver (or faire), préparer (à la hâte) ◆ **can you ~ me up a cup of coffee?** tu pourrais me donner un café en vitesse ?

rustler /ˈrʌsləʳ/ N 1 (esp US = cattle thief) voleur m de bétail 2 (US * = energetic person) type* m énergique or expéditif

rustling /ˈrʌslɪŋ/ N 1 (= cattle theft) vol m de bétail 2 ⇒ **rustle noun**

rustproof /ˈrʌstpruːf/ ADJ [metal, alloy] inoxydable, qui ne rouille pas ; [paint, treatment] antirouille inv, anticorrosion inv ; [bodywork] traité contre la rouille or la corrosion VT traiter contre la rouille or la corrosion

rustproofing /ˈrʌstpruːfɪŋ/ N traitement m antirouille or anticorrosion

rusty /ˈrʌstɪ/ ADJ 1 (lit, fig) rouillé ◆ **to go** or **get ~** [metal] rouiller ; [person] se rouiller ◆ **my English is pretty ~** mon anglais est un peu rouillé ◆ **his ~ typing skills** ses notions de dactylographie, qui ne datent pas d'hier ◆ **your skills are a little ~** vous avez un peu perdu la main ◆ **I'm very ~ on criminal law** il y a longtemps que je n'ai plus pratiqué le droit pénal 2 (in colour) (also **rusty brown**) brun roux inv

rut¹ /rʌt/ (= sexual readiness of animal) N rut m VI être en rut COMP **rutting season** N saison f du rut

rut² /rʌt/ N (in track, path) ornière f ; (fig) routine f, ornière f ◆ **to be (stuck) in** or **to get into a ~** (fig) [person] s'encroûter ; [mind] devenir routinier ◆ **to get out of the ~** sortir de l'ornière VT sillonner ◆ **~ted** [road, path] défoncé

rutabaga /ˌruːtəˈbeɪɡə/ N (US) rutabaga m

ruthenium /ruːˈθiːnɪəm/ **N** ruthénium *m*

ruthless /ˈruːθlɪs/ **ADJ** *[person]* impitoyable, sans pitié (*in sth* dans qch) ; *[treatment, determination, investigation, deed]* impitoyable ◆ **to be ~ in doing sth** faire qch impitoyablement

ruthlessly /ˈruːθlɪslɪ/ **ADV** *[suppress, crush]* impitoyablement, sans pitié ◆ **~ efficient** d'une efficacité redoutable ◆ **she was a ~ ambitious woman** c'était une femme dont l'ambition n'épargnait rien ni personne

ruthlessness /ˈruːθlɪsnɪs/ **N** caractère *m or* nature *f* impitoyable

RV /ɑːˈviː/ **N** 1 *(Bible)* (abbrev of **Revised Version**) → **revise** 2 *(US)* (abbrev of **recreational vehicle**) camping-car *m* ◆ **~ park** terrain *m* pour camping-cars

Rwanda /rʊˈændə/ **N** Rwanda *m* ◆ **in ~** au Rwanda

Rwandan /rʊˈændən/ **ADJ** rwandais **N** Rwandais(e) *m(f)*

rye /raɪ/ **N** 1 (= *grain*) seigle *m* 2 *(US)* ⇒ **rye whisky, rye bread**

COMP **rye bread** **N** pain *m* de seigle

rye whisky **N** whisky *m* (de seigle)

ryegrass /ˈraɪgrɑːs/ **N** ray-grass *m inv*

Ss

S, s /es/ **N** 1 *(= letter)* S, s *m* ◆ **S for sugar** ≈ S comme Suzanne 2 *(abbrev of* **south***)* S 3 ◆ **S** *(Rel)* *(abbrev of* **Saint***)* St(e) 4 ◆ **S** *(abbrev of* **small***)* (taille *f*) S *m*

SA /es'eɪ/ **N** 1 *(abbrev of* **South Africa, South America, South Australia***)* → **south** 2 *(abbrev of* **Salvation Army***)* Armée *f* du Salut

Saar /zɑːʳ/ **N** *(= river, region)* ◆ **the ~** la Sarre

sab * /sæb/ **N** *(Brit) activiste cherchant à saboter les chasses à courre*

sabbatarian /ˌsæbə'tɛərɪən/ **N** *(= Christian)* partisan *m* de l'observance stricte du dimanche ; *(= Jew)* personne *f* qui observe le sabbat **ADJ** *(= Jewish Rel)* de l'observance du sabbat

Sabbath /'sæbəθ/ **N** *(Jewish)* sabbat *m* ; *(Christian)* repos *m* dominical ; († *= Sunday)* dimanche *m* ◆ **to keep** *or* **observe/break the ~** observer/ne pas observer le sabbat *or* le repos dominical ◆ **(witches') sabbath** sabbat *m*

sabbatical /sə'bætɪkəl/ **N** congé *m* sabbatique ◆ **to be on ~** être en congé sabbatique ◆ **to take a ~** prendre un congé sabbatique
COMP **sabbatical leave N** congé *m* sabbatique
sabbatical term N trois mois *mpl* de congé sabbatique
sabbatical year N année *f* sabbatique

sabbing * /'sæbɪŋ/ **N** *(NonC: Brit)* (also **hunt-sabbing**) sabotage *m* des chasses à courre

saber /'seɪbəʳ/ **N** *(US)* ⇒ **sabre**

sable /'seɪbl/ **N** 1 *(= animal)* zibeline *f*, martre *f* 2 *(Heraldry)* sable *m* **COMP** 1 *[fur]* de zibeline, de martre ; *[brush]* en poil de martre 2 *(liter = black)* noir

sabotage /'sæbətɑːʒ/ **N** *(NonC)* sabotage *m* ◆ **an act of ~** un sabotage **VT** *(lit, fig)* saboter

saboteur /ˌsæbə'tɜːʳ/ **N** saboteur *m*, -euse *f*

sabre, saber *(US)* /'seɪbəʳ/ **N** sabre *m*
COMP **sabre rattling N** *(esp Pol)* tentatives *fpl* d'intimidation
sabre-toothed tiger N tigre *m* à dents de sabre

sac /sæk/ **N** *(Anat, Bio)* sac *m*

saccharin /'sækərɪn/ **N** *(US)* ⇒ **saccharine noun**

saccharine /'sækəriːn/ **ADJ** 1 *(Culin) [product]* à la saccharine ; *[pill, flavour]* de saccharine 2 *(= sentimental) [story, ending]* mièvre ; *[ballad, melody]* sirupeux ; *[sweetness, smile]* mielleux ◆ **~ sentimentality** mièvrerie *f* **N** saccharine *f*

sacerdotal /ˌsæsə'dəʊtl/ **ADJ** sacerdotal

sachet /'sæʃeɪ/ **N** sachet *m* ; *[of shampoo]* dosette *f*

sack¹ /sæk/ **N** 1 *(= bag)* sac *m* ◆ **coal ~** sac *m* à charbon ◆ **~ of coal** sac *m* de charbon ◆ **a ~ of potatoes** un sac de pommes de terre ◆ **that dress makes her look like a ~ of potatoes** elle ressemble à un sac de pommes de terre dans cette robe ◆ **she flopped down on to the sofa like a ~ of potatoes** elle s'est affalée sur le canapé 2 *(* = dismissal)* **to give sb the ~** renvoyer qn, virer * qn ◆ **to get the ~** être renvoyé, se faire virer * ◆ **he got the ~ for stealing** il s'est fait virer * parce qu'il avait volé 3 *(esp US * = bed)* pieu ‡ *m*, plumard ‡ *m* ◆ **to hit the ~** aller se pieuter ‡ ◆ **he's hot in the ~** c'est un bon coup ‡ **VT** *(= dismiss) [+ employee]* renvoyer, virer *
COMP **sack dress N** robe *f* sac
sack race N course *f* en sac
▸ **sack out** ‡, **sack up** ‡ **VI** *(US = go to bed)* aller se pieuter ‡

sack² /sæk/ *(liter)* **N** *(= plundering)* sac *m*, pillage *m* **VT** *[+ town]* mettre à sac, piller

sack³ /sæk/ **N** *(= wine)* vin *m* blanc sec

sackbut /'sækbʌt/ **N** *(Mus)* saquebute *f*

sackcloth /'sækklɒθ/ **N** grosse toile *f*, toile *f* à sac ◆ **~ and ashes** *(Rel)* le sac et la cendre ◆ **to be in ~ and ashes** *(fig)* être contrit

sacking¹ /'sækɪŋ/ **N** 1 *(NonC = fabric)* grosse toile *f*, toile *f* à sac 2 *(= dismissal)* renvoi *m* ◆ **large scale ~s** renvois *mpl* massifs

sacking² /'sækɪŋ/ **N** *(= plundering)* sac *m*, pillage *m*

sacra /'sækrə/ **NPL** of **sacrum**

sacral /'seɪkrəl/ **ADJ** *(Anat)* sacré

sacrament /'sækrəmənt/ **N** sacrement *m* ◆ **to receive the ~s** communier ; → **blessed**

sacramental /ˌsækrə'mentl/ **ADJ** sacramentel **N** sacramental *m*

sacred /'seɪkrɪd/ **ADJ** 1 *(= holy) [place, object, animal, symbol]* sacré *(to* pour) 2 *(= religious) [art, music, rite]* sacré, religieux ◆ **~ writings** livres *mpl* sacrés ◆ **~ and profane love** l'amour *m* sacré et l'amour *m* profane 3 *(= sacrosanct) [principle, duty, promise]* sacré *(to* pour) ◆ **~ to the memory of sb** consacré à la mémoire de qn ◆ **is nothing ~?** les gens ne respectent plus rien ! ◆ **to her nothing was ~** elle ne respectait rien (ni personne)
COMP **sacred cow N** *(lit, fig)* vache *f* sacrée
the Sacred Heart N le Sacré-Cœur
Sacred History N Histoire *f* sainte

sacredness /'seɪkrɪdnɪs/ **N** caractère *m* sacré

sacrifice /'sækrɪfaɪs/ **N** *(all senses)* sacrifice *m* ◆ **the ~ of the mass** *(Rel)* le saint sacrifice (de la messe) ◆ **to make great ~s** *(fig)* faire *or* consentir de grands sacrifices *(for sb* pour qn ; *to do sth* pour faire qch) → **self** **VT** *(all senses)* sacrifier *(to* à) ◆ **to ~ o.s. for sb** se sacrifier pour qn ◆ **"cost £25: sacrifice for £5"** * *(in small ads)* "prix 25 livres : sacrifié à 5 livres"

sacrificial /ˌsækrɪ'fɪʃəl/ **ADJ** *[rite]* sacrificiel ; *[animal]* du sacrifice
COMP **sacrificial lamb N** *(Bible)* agneau *m* pascal ; *(fig)* bouc *m* émissaire
sacrificial victim N *(lit)* victime *f* du sacrifice ; *(fig)* victime *f* expiatoire

sacrilege /'sækrɪlɪdʒ/ **N** *(lit, fig)* sacrilège *m* ◆ **that would be ~** ce serait un sacrilège

sacrilegious /ˌsækrɪ'lɪdʒəs/ **ADJ** sacrilège ◆ **it would be ~ to do such a thing** ce serait (un) sacrilège de faire une chose pareille

sacrist(an) /'sækrɪst(ən)/ **N** sacristain(e) *m(f)*, sacristine *f*

sacristy /'sækrɪstɪ/ **N** sacristie *f*

sacroiliac /ˌseɪkrəʊ'ɪlɪæk/ **ADJ** sacro-iliaque **N** articulation *f* sacro-iliaque

sacrosanct /'sækrəʊsæŋkt/ **ADJ** sacro-saint

sacrum /'sækrəm/ **N** (pl **sacra**) sacrum *m*

SAD /sæd/ **N** *(abbrev of* **seasonal affective disorder***)* → **seasonal**

sad /sæd/ LANGUAGE IN USE 24.4
ADJ 1 *(= unhappy) [person, expression, eyes]* triste ; *[feeling]* de tristesse ◆ **to become ~** devenir triste ◆ **the more he thought about it, the ~der he became** plus il y pensait, plus ça le rendait triste ◆ **to make sb ~** attrister qn, rendre qn triste ◆ **it makes me ~ to think that ...** ça me rend triste *or* ça m'attriste de penser que ... ◆ **he eventually departed a ~der and (a) wiser man** finalement il partit, mûri par la dure leçon de l'expérience ◆ **I'm ~ that I/you won't be able to come** je suis désolé de ne pouvoir venir/que vous ne puissiez pas venir ◆ **I shall be ~ to leave** je serai désolé de partir ◆ **he was ~ to see her go** il était triste de la voir partir ◆ **(I'm) ~ to say he died five years ago** malheureusement, il est mort il y a cinq ans
2 *(= saddening) [story, news, situation, duty, occasion]* triste ; *[loss]* douloureux ◆ **it's a ~ business** c'est une triste affaire ◆ **it's a ~ state of affairs** c'est un triste état de choses ◆ **the ~ fact** *or* **truth is that ...** la triste vérité est que ... ◆ **it's ~ that they can't agree** c'est désolant qu'ils n'arrivent pas à se mettre d'accord ◆ **it's ~ to see such expertise wasted** c'est désolant de voir ce talent gâché ◆ **~ to say, he died soon after** c'est triste à dire *or* malheureusement, il est mort peu après
3 *(* pej = pathetic) [person]* minable *, pitoyable ◆ **that ~ little man** ce pauvre type

COMP **sad bastard** ** N pauvre con ** m
sad case * N ◆ **he's a real ~ case** c'est vraiment un cas navrant
sad-eyed ADJ aux yeux tristes
sad-faced ADJ au visage triste
sad sack * N (US) (gen) nullité f ; (= soldier) mauvais soldat m

sadden /'sædn/ VT attrister, rendre triste ◆ **it ~s me to hear that he has gone** je suis peiné d'apprendre qu'il est parti ◆ **it ~s me that …** cela m'attriste que … + subj

saddening /'sædnɪŋ/ ADJ attristant, triste ◆ **it is ~ to think that …** c'est triste de penser que …

saddle /'sædl/ N 1 [of horse, cycle] selle f ◆ **to be in the ~** (= on horse) être en selle ; (= in power) tenir les rênes ◆ **he leaped into the ~** il sauta en selle ; → **sidesaddle**
2 [of hill] col m
3 (Culin) ~ **of lamb** selle f d'agneau ◆ ~ **of hare** râble m de lièvre
VT 1 (also **saddle up**) [+ horse] seller
2 (* fig) ◆ **to ~ sb with sth** [person] [+ job, debts, responsibility] refiler * qch à qn ◆ **I've been ~d with organizing the meeting** je me retrouve avec l'organisation de la réunion sur les bras ◆ **the war ~d the country with a huge debt** à cause de la guerre le pays s'est retrouvé lourdement endetté ◆ **we're ~d with it** nous voilà avec ça sur les bras ◆ **to ~ o.s. with sth** s'encombrer de qch
COMP **saddle-backed** ADJ [horse] ensellé
saddle horse N cheval m de selle
saddle joint N (of mutton or lamb) selle f
saddle shoes NPL (US) chaussures basses bicolores
saddle-sore ADJ meurtri à force d'être en selle
saddle-stitched ADJ cousu à longs points

saddlebag /'sædlbæg/ N [of horse] sacoche f (de selle) ; [of cycle] sacoche f (de bicyclette)

saddlebow /'sædlbəʊ/ N pommeau m de selle

saddlecloth /'sædlklɒθ/ N tapis m de selle

saddler /'sædləʳ/ N sellier m

saddlery /'sædlərɪ/ N (= articles, business) sellerie f

saddo ** /'sædəʊ/ (pl **saddos** or **saddoes**) ADJ minable * N (= person) pauvre type m **, minable * mf

Sadducee /'sædjʊsiː/ N Sad(d)ucéen(ne) m(f)

sadism /'seɪdɪzəm/ N sadisme m

sadist /'seɪdɪst/ ADJ, N sadique mf

sadistic /sə'dɪstɪk/ ADJ sadique

sadistically /sə'dɪstɪkəlɪ/ ADV sadiquement, avec sadisme

sadly /'sædlɪ/ ADV 1 (= sorrowfully) [say, smile, look at, shake one's head] tristement, avec tristesse 2 (= woefully) [familiar, evident, neglected] tristement ; [disappointed] profondément ◆ **to be ~ lacking in sth** manquer cruellement de qch ◆ **to be ~ in need of sth** avoir bien besoin de qch ◆ **to be ~ mistaken** se tromper lourdement ◆ **he will be ~ missed** il sera regretté de tous 3 (= unfortunately) malheureusement ◆ ~ **for sb/sth** malheureusement pour qn/qch ◆ **Jim, who ~ died in January …** Jim, qui, à notre grande tristesse, est mort en janvier …

sadness /'sædnɪs/ N (NonC) tristesse f, mélancolie f

sadomasochism /ˌseɪdəʊ'mæsəkɪzəm/ N sadomasochisme m

sadomasochist /ˌseɪdəʊ'mæsəkɪst/ N sadomasochiste mf

sadomasochistic /ˌseɪdəʊmæsə'kɪstɪk/ ADJ sadomasochiste

SAE, s.a.e. /ˌeseɪ'iː/ N (Brit) 1 (abbrev of **stamped addressed envelope**) → **stamp** 2 (abbrev of **self-addressed envelope**) → **self**

safari /sə'fɑːrɪ/ N safari m ◆ **to be/go on (a) ~** faire/aller faire un safari
COMP **safari hat** N chapeau m de brousse
safari jacket N saharienne f
safari park N (Brit) parc m animalier ; (in Africa) réserve f animalière
safari shirt N saharienne f
safari suit N ensemble m saharien

safe /seɪf/ ADJ 1 (= not risky) [substance, toy] sans danger ; [nuclear reactor] sûr, sans danger ; [place, vehicle] sûr ; [ladder, structure] solide ◆ **in a ~ place** en lieu sûr ◆ **a ~ anchorage** un bon mouillage ◆ **the ice isn't ~** la glace n'est pas solide ◆ **he's a ~ pair of hands** c'est quelqu'un de sûr ◆ **to be in ~ hands** être en de bonnes mains ◆ **is that dog ~?** ce chien n'est pas méchant ? ◆ **that dog isn't ~ with** or **around children** ce chien peut présenter un danger pour les enfants ◆ **he's ~ in jail** * **for the moment** pour le moment on est tranquille, il est en prison ◆ **the ~st thing (to do) would be to wait here** le plus sûr serait d'attendre ici ; → **house, play**

◆ **to make sth safe** ◆ **to make a bomb ~** désamorcer une bombe ◆ **to make a building ~** assurer la sécurité d'un bâtiment ◆ **to make a place ~ for sb/sth** éliminer tous les dangers qu'un endroit pourrait présenter pour qn/qch ◆ **to make it ~, the element is electrically insulated** pour plus de sécurité, l'élément est isolé

◆ **safe to …** ◆ **the water is ~ to drink** on peut boire cette eau sans danger, l'eau est potable ◆ **this food is perfectly ~ to eat** la consommation de cet aliment ne présente aucun danger ◆ **it is ~ to say/assume that …** on peut affirmer/supposer sans trop s'avancer que … ◆ **is it ~ to come out?** est-ce qu'on peut sortir sans danger ? ◆ **is it ~ to use rat poison with children around?** n'est-ce pas dangereux d'utiliser de la mort-aux-rats là où il y a des enfants ? ◆ **they assured him that it was ~ to return** ils lui ont assuré qu'il pouvait revenir en toute sécurité ◆ **it might be ~r to wait** il serait peut-être plus prudent d'attendre ◆ **it's not ~ to go out after dark** il est dangereux de sortir la nuit

2 [choice, job] sûr ; [method] sans risque ; [limit, level] raisonnable ◆ **keep your alcohol consumption (to) within ~ limits** buvez avec modération ◆ **a ~ margin** une marge de sécurité ◆ **to keep a ~ distance from sb/sth** or **between o.s. and sb/sth** (gen) se tenir à bonne distance de qn/qch ; (while driving) maintenir la distance de sécurité par rapport à qn/qch ◆ **to follow sb at a ~ distance** suivre qn à une distance respectueuse ◆ **(just) to be on the ~ side** * par précaution, pour plus de sûreté

3 (= successful, problem-free) ◆ **to wish sb a ~ journey** souhaiter bon voyage à qn ◆ **(have a) ~ journey!** bon voyage ! ◆ **a ~ landing** un atterrissage réussi ◆ **he wrote to acknowledge the ~ arrival of the photographs** il a écrit pour dire que les photos étaient bien arrivées ◆ **to ensure the ~ delivery of supplies** veiller à ce que les vivres arrivent subj à bon port ◆ **let us pray for the ~ return of the troops** prions pour que nos troupes reviennent saines et sauves ◆ **to ensure the ~ return of the hostages** faire en sorte que les otages soient libérés sains et saufs ◆ **a reward for the ~ return of the stolen equipment** une récompense à qui rapportera en bon état l'équipement volé

4 (= likely to be right) ◆ **it is a ~ assumption that …** on peut dire sans trop s'avancer que … ◆ **this was a pretty ~ guess** on ne s'avançait pas trop en supposant cela

◆ **a safe bet** (safe choice) un bon choix ◆ **the house wine is always a ~ bet** choisir la cuvée du patron, c'est sans risque ◆ **it is a ~ bet that …** il y a toutes les chances pour que … + subj ◆ **it's a ~ bet he'll win** il gagnera à coup sûr

5 (= not in danger) [person] en sécurité ; (= no longer in danger) hors de danger ; [object] en sécurité ◆ **I don't feel very ~ on this ladder** je ne me sens pas très en sécurité sur cette échelle ◆ **I won't feel ~ until he is behind bars** je ne serai pas tranquille tant qu'il ne sera pas derrière les barreaux ◆ **I feel so ~ here with you** je me sens tellement en sécurité ici auprès de toi ◆ **he's ~ for re-election** il sera réélu à coup sûr ◆ ~ **in the knowledge that …** avec la certitude que … ◆ ~ **and sound** sain et sauf ◆ **a ~ winner** (Sport) un gagnant certain or assuré ◆ **to be ~ with sb** être en sécurité avec qn ◆ **I'll keep it ~ for you** je vais vous le garder en lieu sûr ◆ **your reputation is ~** votre réputation ne craint rien ◆ **your secret is ~ (with me)** je ne le répéterai pas, (avec moi) votre secret ne risque rien ◆ **no girl is ~ with him** (fig) c'est un séducteur impénitent ◆ **better ~ than sorry** (Prov) deux précautions valent mieux qu'une (Prov)

◆ **to be safe from sth** être à l'abri de qch ◆ **the town is now ~ from attack** la ville est maintenant à l'abri de toute attaque ◆ **I'm ~ from him now** il ne peut plus me nuire or me faire de mal maintenant ◆ **to be ~ from being sued** ne pas risquer de procès ◆ **he's ~ from harm** il n'est pas en danger ◆ **to keep sb ~ from harm** protéger qn
N (for money, valuables) coffre-fort m ; → **meat**
COMP **safe area** N (Pol) zone f de sécurité
safe-blower N perceur m de coffre-fort (qui utilise des explosifs)
safe-breaker N perceur m de coffre-fort
safe-conduct N (Mil etc) sauf-conduit m
safe-cracker N ⇒ **safe-breaker**
safe deposit N (= vault) chambre f forte, salle f des coffres ; (also **safe deposit box**) coffre(-fort) m (à la banque)
safe haven N 1 (Mil, Pol) zone f de refuge 2 (= refuge) (gen) abri m sûr ; (for terrorists, criminals) repaire m ; (for people in danger) refuge m ◆ **to provide ~ haven for sb, to offer ~ haven to sb** offrir un abri sûr or un refuge à qn 3 (fig = escape) refuge m (from contre) ◆ **the idea of the family as a ~ haven from the brutal outside world** la famille perçue comme un refuge contre la brutalité du monde extérieur ◆ **the district was once a ~ haven from Manhattan's hustle and bustle** le quartier était autrefois à l'abri du tourbillon d'activité de Manhattan
safe house N lieu m sûr
safe passage N ◆ **to guarantee sb/sth (a) ~ passage to/from a country** assurer la protection de qn/qch à son entrée dans un pays/à sa sortie d'un pays
the safe period * N (Med) la période sans danger
safe seat N siège m sûr ; (Brit Pol) ◆ **it was a ~ Conservative seat** c'était un siège acquis au parti conservateur ; → MARGINAL SEAT
safe sex N rapports mpl sexuels sans risque ; (specifically with condom) rapports mpl sexuels protégés

safeguard /'seɪfgɑːd/ VT sauvegarder, protéger (against contre) N sauvegarde f, garantie f (against contre) ◆ **as a ~ against** comme sauvegarde contre, pour éviter COMP **safeguard clause** N (Jur) clause f de sauvegarde

safekeeping /ˌseɪf'kiːpɪŋ/ N ◆ **in ~** sous bonne garde, en sécurité ◆ **I gave it to him for ~, I put it in his ~** je le lui ai donné à garder ◆ **the key is in his ~** on lui a confié la clé

safely /'seɪflɪ/ ADV 1 (= without risk) sans risque or danger, en toute sécurité ◆ **you can walk about quite ~ in the town centre** vous pouvez vous promener sans risque or sans danger dans le centre-ville ◆ **most food can ~ be frozen for months** on peut congeler la plupart des aliments sans risque or sans danger pendant plusieurs mois ◆ **drive ~!** sois prudent !

◆ **he was ~ tucked up in bed** il était en sécurité *or* bien au chaud dans son lit

2 (= *without mishap*) [*return, land*] sans encombre ; [*arrive*] bien, à bon port ◆ **give me a ring to let me know you've got home** ~ passe-moi un coup de fil pour que je sache que tu es bien rentré ◆ **the consignment reached us** ~ nous avons bien reçu les marchandises

3 (= *securely*) [*shut, locked, stowed*] bien ◆ **to put sth away** ~ ranger qch en lieu sûr

4 (= *well and truly*) **now that the election is ~ out of the way, the government can ...** maintenant que le gouvernement n'a plus à se soucier des élections, il peut ... ◆ **he's ~ through to the semi-final** il est arrivé sans encombre en demi-finale

5 (= *confidently*) **one can ~ say that ...** on peut, sans risque de se tromper, affirmer que ... ◆ **I think I can ~ say that ...** je pense pouvoir dire sans trop m'avancer que ...

safeness /'seɪfnɪs/ **N** (= *freedom from danger*) sécurité *f* ; [*of construction, equipment*] solidité *f*

safety /'seɪftɪ/ **N** 1 (= *not being in danger*) sécurité *f* ◆ **his ~ must be our first consideration** sa sécurité doit être notre premier souci ◆ **for his (own) ~** pour sa (propre) sécurité ◆ **for ~'s sake** pour plus de sûreté, par mesure de sécurité ◆ **to ensure sb's ~** veiller sur *or* assurer la sécurité de qn ◆ **he sought ~ in flight** il chercha le salut dans la fuite ◆ **they went back to the ~ of the house** ils sont retournés se réfugier dans la maison ◆ **they watched from the ~ of the embassy** en lieu sûr *or* loin du danger dans l'ambassade, ils regardaient la scène ◆ **there is ~ in numbers** plus on est nombreux, moins il y a de danger ◆ **in a place of ~** en lieu sûr ◆ **in ~** en sécurité ◆ **he reached ~ at last** il fut enfin en sûreté *or* en sécurité ◆ **to play for ~** ne pas prendre de risques ◆ **~ first!** la sécurité d'abord ! ; see also **comp**, road

2 (= *not presenting any danger*) [*of drug*] innocuité *f* ; [*of machine, power plant*] sécurité *f* ◆ **they are concerned about the ~ of the equipment** ils s'interrogent sur la sécurité du matériel

COMP **safety belt N** ceinture *f* de sécurité
safety blade N lame *f* de sûreté
safety bolt N verrou *m* de sûreté
safety catch N cran *m* de sûreté
safety chain N chaîne *f* de sûreté
safety curtain N (*Theat*) rideau *m* de fer
safety-deposit box N (*US*) coffre(-fort) *m* (*à la banque*)
safety device N ⇒ **safety feature**
safety factor N coefficient *m* de sécurité
safety feature N dispositif *m* de sécurité
safety glass N verre *m* securit ® *or* de sécurité
safety island N (*US: on road*) refuge *m*
safety lamp N lampe *f* de mineur
safety lock N serrure *f* de sécurité
safety margin N marge *f* de sécurité
safety match N allumette *f* de sûreté *or* suédoise
safety measure N mesure *f* de sécurité ◆ **as a ~ measure** pour plus de sûreté, par mesure de sécurité
safety mechanism N dispositif *m* de sécurité
safety net N (*lit*) filet *m* (de protection) ; (*fig*) filet *m* de sécurité
safety pin N épingle *f* de nourrice
safety precaution N mesure *f* de sécurité
safety razor N rasoir *m* mécanique *or* de sûreté
safety regulations NPL règles *fpl* de sécurité
safety screen N écran *m* de sécurité
safety valve N (*lit, fig*) soupape *f* de sûreté
safety zone N (*US: on road*) refuge *m* (*pour piétons*)

saffron /'sæfrən/ **N** safran *m* **ADJ** [*colour, robe*] safran *inv* ; [*flavour*] safrané, de safran
COMP **saffron-coloured ADJ** safran *inv*
saffron powder N safran *m*
saffron rice N riz *m* safrané *or* au safran
saffron strands, saffron threads NPL pistils *mpl* de safran, stigmates *mpl* de safran
saffron yellow ADJ jaune *inv* safran *inv*

sag /sæg/ **VI** [*roof, chair*] s'affaisser ; [*beam, floorboard*] s'arquer, fléchir ; [*cheeks, breasts, hemline*] pendre ; [*rope*] être détendu ; [*gate*] être affaissé ; [*prices*] fléchir, baisser **N** [*of prices, sales, credibility*] baisse *f* ; [*of roof*] affaissement *m* ◆ **the ~ in the market** la contraction du marché

saga /'sɑːgə/ **N** (*Literat*) saga *f* ; (= *film, story*) aventure *f* épique ; (= *novel*) roman-fleuve *m* ◆ **he told me the whole ~ of what had happened** il m'a raconté tout ce qui était arrivé *or* toutes les péripéties en long et en large ◆ **the hostage ~** la saga de la prise d'otages ◆ **the long-running ~ of education reform** le long feuilleton de la réforme du système scolaire

sagacious /sə'geɪʃəs/ **ADJ** (*frm*) [*person, remark*] sagace ; [*choice*] judicieux

sagaciously /sə'geɪʃəslɪ/ **ADV** (*frm*) avec sagacité

sagaciousness /sə'geɪʃəsnɪs/, **sagacity** /sə'gæsɪtɪ/ **N** sagacité *f*

sage[1] /seɪdʒ/ **N** (= *plant*) sauge *f* ◆ **~ and onion stuffing** farce *f* à l'oignon et à la sauge COMP **sage green N, ADJ** vert *m* cendré *inv*

sage[2] /seɪdʒ/ (*liter*) **ADJ** [*person, advice*] sage ◆ **~ words of warning** une sage mise en garde **N** sage *m*

sagebrush /'seɪdʒbrʌʃ/ **N** (*US*) armoise *f* ◆ **the Sagebrush State** le Nevada

sagely /'seɪdʒlɪ/ **ADV** (= *wisely*) [*say*] avec sagesse ; (*iro*) (= *importantly*) avec componction ◆ **to nod ~** opiner de la tête avec componction

sagging /'sægɪŋ/ **ADJ** 1 (= *drooping*) [*armchair, ceiling, beam*] affaissé ; [*rope*] détendu ; [*stomach*] qui s'affaisse ; [*breasts*] qui tombent, flasque ; [*cheeks, hemline*] pendant ; [*skin*] distendu 2 (= *flagging*) [*morale, spirits*] défaillant ; [*stock market, dollar*] mou (molle *f*) ◆ **to bolster one's ~ popularity** soutenir sa popularité en baisse ◆ **the president's ~ ratings** la cote de popularité en baisse du président

saggy* /'sægɪ/ **ADJ** [*mattress, sofa*] défoncé ; [*garment*] avachi ; [*bottom, breasts*] flasque

Sagittarian /,sædʒɪ'teərɪən/ **N** ◆ **to be (a) ~** être (du) Sagittaire **ADJ** [*person*] du Sagittaire ; [*character trait*] propre au Sagittaire

Sagittarius /,sædʒɪ'teərɪəs/ **N** (*Astron*) Sagittaire *m* ◆ **I'm (a) ~** (*Astrol*) je suis (du) Sagittaire

sago /'seɪgəʊ/ **N** sagou *m*
COMP **sago palm N** sagoutier *m*
sago pudding N sagou *m* au lait

Sahara /sə'hɑːrə/ **N** ◆ **the ~ (Desert)** le (désert du) Sahara

sahib /'sɑːhɪb/ **N** (*in India*) sahib *m* ◆ **yes, ~** oui, sahib ◆ **Smith Sahib** Monsieur Smith

said /sed/ **VB** pt, ptp of **say** **ADJ** (*frm, Jur*) ◆ **the ~ newspaper** ledit journal ◆ **the circulation of the ~ newspaper** le tirage dudit journal ◆ **the ~ letter** ladite lettre ◆ **the said Daphne** ladite Daphne

Saigon /saɪ'gɒn/ **N** Saïgon

sail /seɪl/ **N** 1 [*of boat*] voile *f* ; → **hoist, wind**[1]
◆ **to set sail** [*boat*] prendre la mer ; [*person*] partir en bateau ◆ **to set ~ for** [*boat*] partir à destination de ◆ **he has set ~ for America** il est parti pour l'Amérique (en bateau) ◆ **he set ~ from Dover** il est parti de Douvres (en bateau)
◆ **under + sail** à la voile ◆ **under full ~** toutes voiles dehors
2 (= *trip*) **to go for a ~** faire un tour en bateau *or* en mer ◆ **Spain is two days' ~ from here** l'Espagne est à deux jours de mer
3 [*of windmill*] aile *f*

VI 1 [*boat*] ◆ **the steamer ~s at 6 o'clock** le vapeur prend la mer *or* part à 6 heures ◆ **the boat ~ed up/down the river** le bateau remonta/descendit la rivière ◆ **the ship ~ed into Cadiz** le bateau entra dans le port de Cadix ◆ **the ship ~ed away into the distance** le bateau s'éloigna ◆ **to ~ into harbour** entrer au port ◆ **the ship ~ed out of Southampton/round the cape** le bateau a quitté le port de Southampton/a doublé le cap ◆ **to ~ at 10 knots** filer 10 nœuds
2 ◆ **he ~s** *or* **goes sailing every weekend** il fait du bateau *or* de la voile tous les week-ends ◆ **to ~ away/back** *etc* partir/revenir *etc* en bateau ◆ **we ~ at 6 o'clock** nous partons à 6 heures, le bateau part à 6 heures ◆ **we ~ed into Southampton** nous sommes entrés dans le port de Southampton ◆ **we ~ed for Australia** nous sommes partis pour l'Australie (en bateau) ◆ **to ~ round the world** faire le tour du monde en bateau ◆ **to ~ into the wind** avancer contre le vent ◆ **to ~ close to the wind** (*Naut*) naviguer au plus près ◆ **to ~ close** *or* **near to the wind** (*fig*) (= *take a risk*) jouer un jeu dangereux ; (= *nearly break law*) friser l'illégalité ; (*in jokes etc*) friser la vulgarité ◆ **to ~ under false colours** (*fig*) agir sous de faux prétextes
3 [*swan etc*] glisser ◆ **clouds were ~ing across the sky** des nuages glissaient *or* couraient dans le ciel ◆ **she ~ed into the room*** elle est entrée dans la pièce d'un pas majestueux ◆ **the plate ~ed past my head and hit the door** l'assiette est passée à côté de ma tête et a heurté la porte

VT 1 (*liter*) ◆ **to ~ the seas** parcourir les mers ◆ **he ~ed the Atlantic last year** l'année dernière il a fait la traversée de *or* il a traversé l'Atlantique (en bateau)
2 [*+ boat*] (= *manoeuvre*) manœuvrer ◆ **she ~ed her boat into the harbour** elle a manœuvré (son bateau) pour entrer dans le port ◆ **he ~ed his boat round the cape** il a doublé le cap ◆ **he ~s his own yacht** (= *owns it*) il a son propre yacht ; (= *captains it*) il barre *or* pilote son yacht lui-même

COMP **sail maker N** voilier *m* (*personne*)

► **sail into*** **VT FUS** (= *scold*) ◆ **he really sailed into me** il m'a volé dans les plumes*

► **sail through*** **VI** réussir haut la main
VT FUS ◆ **to sail through one's degree/one's driving test** avoir sa licence/son permis de conduire haut la main

sailboard /'seɪlbɔːd/ **N** planche *f* à voile

sailboarder /'seɪl,bɔːdə[r]/ **N** véliplanchiste *mf*

sailboarding /'seɪl,bɔːdɪŋ/ **N** planche *f* à voile ◆ **to go ~** faire de la planche à voile

sailboat /'seɪlbəʊt/ **N** (*US*) bateau *m* à voiles, voilier *m*

sailcloth /'seɪlklɒθ/ **N** toile *f* à voile

sailing /'seɪlɪŋ/ **N** 1 (*NonC* = *activity, hobby*) (*dinghies etc*) navigation *f* à voile ; (*yachts*) navigation *f* de plaisance ◆ **a day's ~** une journée de voile *or* en mer ◆ **his hobby is ~** son passe-temps favori est la voile ; → **plain** 2 (= *departure*) départ *m*
COMP **sailing boat N** (*Brit*) bateau *m* à voiles, voilier *m*
sailing date N date *f* de départ (d'un bateau)
sailing dinghy N canot *m* à voiles, dériveur *m*
sailing orders NPL instructions *fpl* de navigation
sailing ship N grand voilier *m*, navire *m* à voiles

sailor /'seɪlə[r]/ **N** (*gen*) marin *m* ; (*before the mast*) matelot *m* ◆ **to be a good/bad ~** avoir/ne pas avoir le pied marin
COMP **sailor hat N** chapeau *m* de marin
sailor suit N costume *m* marin

sailplane /'seɪlpleɪn/ **N** planeur *m*

sainfoin /'sænfɔɪn/ **N** sainfoin *m*

saint /seɪnt/ N saint(e) *m(f)* ◆ **~'s day** fête *f* (de saint) ◆ **All Saints' (Day)** la Toussaint ◆ **he's no ~** * ce n'est pas un petit saint
COMP **Saint Bernard** N (= *dog*) saint-bernard *m*
Saint Helena N *(Geog)* Sainte-Hélène *f* ◆ **on Saint Helena** à Sainte-Hélène
Saint John N saint *m* Jean
Saint John's wort N mille-pertuis *m or* mille-pertuis *m inv*
the Saint Lawrence N le Saint-Laurent ◆ **the Saint Lawrence Seaway** la voie maritime du Saint-Laurent
saint-like ADJ ⇒ **saintly**
Saint Lucia N *(Geog)* Sainte-Lucie *f* ◆ **in Saint Lucia** à Sainte-Lucie
Saint Lucian ADJ saint-lucien N Saint-Lucien(ne) *m(f)*
Saint Patrick's Day N la Saint-Patrick
Saint Peter's Church N (l'église *f*) Saint-Pierre
Saint Pierre and Miquelon N *(Geog)* Saint-Pierre-et-Miquelon
Saint Vincent and the Grenadines N *(Geog)* Saint-Vincent-et-Grenadines
Saint Vitus' dance N *(Med)* danse *f* de Saint-Guy

sainted /ˈseɪntɪd/ ADJ († *or hum*) ◆ **your father** votre saint homme de père ◆ **my ~ aunt!** * *(esp Brit)* sacrebleu ! *

sainthood /ˈseɪnthʊd/ N sainteté *f*

saintliness /ˈseɪntlɪnɪs/ N sainteté *f*

saintly /ˈseɪntlɪ/ ADJ *[man, woman]* saint *before n* ; *[quality, behaviour, generosity]* digne d'un saint ; *[smile] (false)* angélique, de sainte nitouche ◆ **to be ~** *[person]* être un(e) saint(e)

saithe /seɪθ/ *(Brit)* N lieu noir *m*, colin *m*

sake¹ /seɪk/ N ◆ **for the ~ of sb** pour qn, par égard pour qn ◆ **for the ~ of your career/my health** pour ta carrière/ma santé ◆ **for God's ~** pour l'amour de Dieu ◆ **for my ~** pour moi, par égard pour moi ◆ **for your own ~** pour ton bien ◆ **for their ~(s)** pour eux ◆ **do it for both our ~s** fais-le (par égard) pour nous deux ◆ **to eat for the ~ of eating** manger pour (le plaisir de) manger ◆ **for old times' ~** en souvenir du passé ◆ **let's do it for old times' ~** faisons-le, en souvenir du passé ◆ **for argument's ~** à titre d'exemple ◆ **art for art's ~** l'art pour l'art ◆ **for the ~ of peace** pour avoir la paix ; → **goodness, heaven, pity, safety**
◆ **for its own sake** ◆ **to acquire knowledge for its own ~** acquérir des connaissances pour le plaisir ◆ **pleasure for its own ~** le plaisir pour le plaisir ◆ **he loves money for its own ~** il aime l'argent pour l'argent
◆ **for the sake of it** pour le plaisir ◆ **I'm not making changes for the ~ of it** je ne fais pas des changements pour le plaisir (d'en faire) ◆ **you're being destructive just for the ~ of it** tu détruis pour (le plaisir de) détruire

sake², saké, saki /ˈsɑːkɪ/ N saké *m*

Sakhalin (Island) /ˈsækəliːn(ˌaɪlənd)/ N (l'île *f* de) Sakhaline *f*

sal /sæl/ N sel *m*
COMP **sal ammoniac** N sel *m* ammoniac
sal volatile N sel *m* volatil

salaam /səˈlɑːm/ N salutation *f* (à l'orientale) VI saluer (à l'orientale) EXCL salam

salability /ˌseɪləˈbɪlɪtɪ/ N *(US)* ⇒ **saleability**

salable /ˈseɪləbl/ ADJ *(US)* ⇒ **saleable**

salacious /səˈleɪʃəs/ ADJ *(frm)* salace, lubrique

salaciousness /səˈleɪʃəsnɪs/ N salacité *f*

salad /ˈsæləd/ N salade *f* ◆ **ham ~** jambon *m* accompagné de salade ◆ **tomato ~** salade *f* de tomates ; → **fruit, potato**
COMP **salad bar** N buffet *m* de crudités
salad bowl N saladier *m*
salad cream N *(Brit)* (sorte *f* de) mayonnaise *f (en bouteille etc)*
salad days NPL années *fpl* de jeunesse et d'inexpérience
salad dish N ⇒ **salad bowl**
salad dressing N *(oil and vinegar)* vinaigrette *f* ; *(made with egg)* mayonnaise *f*
salad oil N huile *f* de table
salad servers NPL couverts *mpl* à salade
salad shaker N panier *m* à salade
salad spinner N essoreuse *f* à salade

salamander /ˈsæləˌmændəʳ/ N (= *lizard, legendary beast*) salamandre *f*

salami /səˈlɑːmɪ/ N salami *m*

salaried /ˈsælərɪd/ ADJ *[employment, post]* salarié ◆ **a ~ employee** un(e) salarié(e)

salary /ˈsælərɪ/ LANGUAGE IN USE 19.2 N salaire *m* ◆ **he couldn't do that on his ~** il ne pourrait pas faire ça avec ce qu'il gagne *or* avec son salaire
COMP **salary bracket** N fourchette *f* des salaires
salary earner N personne *f* qui touche un salaire
salary range N éventail *m* des salaires
salary scale N échelle *f* des salaires

salaryman /ˈsælərɪmæn/ N (pl **-men**) employé *m* de bureau *(surtout au Japon)*

sale /seɪl/ N 1 (= *act*) vente *f* ◆ **we made a quick ~** la vente a été vite conclue ◆ **he finds a ready ~ for his vegetables** il n'a aucun mal à vendre ses légumes ◆ **on ~ or return, on a ~-or-return basis** avec possibilité de retour ◆ **~s are up/down** les ventes ont augmenté/baissé ◆ **she is in ~s** elle est *or* travaille dans la vente ◆ **~ by auction** vente *f* publique, vente *f* aux enchères ; → **cash, quick**
◆ **for sale** à vendre ◆ **"not for sale"** "cet article n'est pas à vendre" ◆ **to put sth up for ~** mettre qch en vente ◆ **our house is up for ~** notre maison est à vendre *or* en vente
◆ **on sale** *(Brit)* en vente ◆ **on ~ at all good chemists** en vente dans toutes les bonnes pharmacies ◆ **to go on ~** être mis en vente
2 (= *event: gen*) vente *f* ; (also **auction sale**) vente *f* (aux enchères) ; *(Comm:* also **sales**) soldes *mpl* ◆ **the ~s are on** c'est la saison des soldes ◆ **the ~ begins** *or* **the ~s begin next week** les soldes commencent la semaine prochaine ◆ **this shop is having a ~ just now** il y a des soldes dans ce magasin en ce moment ◆ **to put sth in the ~** solder qch ◆ **in a ~** en solde ◆ **they are having a ~ in aid of the blind** on organise une vente (de charité) en faveur des aveugles ; → **bring, clearance, jumble**
COMP **sale of produce** N vente *f* de produits
sale of work N vente *f* de charité
sale price N prix *m* soldé
sales assistant N *(Brit)* vendeur *m*, -euse *f*
sales clerk N *(US)* ⇒ **sales assistant**
sales conference N réunion *f* de la force de vente
sales department N service *m* des ventes
sales director N directeur *m*, -trice *f or* chef *m* des ventes
sales drive N campagne *f* de promotion des ventes
sales figures NPL chiffres *mpl* de vente
sales force N force *f* de vente
sales leaflet N argumentaire *m*
sales manager N directeur *m*, -trice *f* commercial(e)
sales office N bureau *m* de vente
sales pitch N baratin * *m* publicitaire, boniment *m*
sales promotion N promotion *f* des ventes
sales rep *, **sales representative** N représentant(e) *m(f)* (de commerce), VRP *m*
sales resistance N réaction *f* défavorable (à la publicité), résistance *f* de l'acheteur
sales revenue N chiffre *m* d'affaires
sales slip N *(in shops)* ticket *m* (de caisse)
sales talk * N baratin * *m* publicitaire, boniment *m*
sales target N objectif *m* des ventes
sales tax N taxe *f* à l'achat
sale value N valeur *f* marchande
sales volume N volume *m* des ventes

saleability /ˌseɪləˈbɪlɪtɪ/ N ◆ **establish the ~ of the property before you buy it** avant d'acheter la propriété, vérifiez si elle est facile à vendre

saleable, salable *(US)* /ˈseɪləbl/ ADJ *[object]* vendable ; *[skill]* monnayable ; *[artist]* dont les œuvres sont vendables ◆ **a highly ~ commodity** un produit qui se vend très bien ◆ **small cars are more ~ than big ones at the moment** les petites voitures se vendent mieux que les grosses en ce moment

Salerno /səˈlɜːnəʊ/ N Salerne

saleroom /ˈseɪlrʊm/ N *(Brit)* salle *f* des ventes

salesgirl /ˈseɪlzgɜːl/ N vendeuse *f*

salesman /ˈseɪlzmən/ N (pl **-men**) *(in shop)* vendeur *m* ; (= *representative*) représentant *m* (de commerce), VRP *m* ◆ **he's a good ~** il sait vendre ; see also **door**

salesmanship /ˈseɪlzmənʃɪp/ N art *m* de la vente

salesperson /ˈseɪlzpɜːsn/ N vendeur *m*, -euse *f*

salesroom /ˈseɪlzrʊm/ N *(US)* ⇒ **saleroom**

saleswoman /ˈseɪlzwʊmən/ N (pl **-women**) *(in shop)* vendeuse *f* ; (= *representative*) représentante *f* (de commerce), VRP *m*

salient /ˈseɪlɪənt/ ADJ saillant ◆ **~ feature** aspect *m* fondamental ◆ **to make ~ points about sth** faire des remarques pertinentes à propos de qch

salina /səˈliːnə/ N 1 (= *marsh*) (marais *m*) salant *m*, salin *m*, saline *f* ; (= *saltworks*) saline(s) *f(pl)*, raffinerie *f* de sel 2 (= *mine*) mine *f* de sel

saline /ˈseɪlaɪn/ ADJ salin N 1 ⇒ **salina 1** 2 (= *solution*) solution *f* saline
COMP **saline drip** N perfusion *f* de sérum physiologique *or* isotonique
saline solution N solution *f* saline

salinity /səˈlɪnɪtɪ/ N salinité *f*

saliva /səˈlaɪvə/ N salive *f*

salivary /ˈsælɪvərɪ/ ADJ salivaire

salivate /ˈsælɪveɪt/ VI saliver ◆ **to ~ over sth** *(fig)* se lécher les babines *or* saliver en pensant à qch

salivation /ˌsælɪˈveɪʃən/ N salivation *f*

sallow¹ /ˈsæləʊ/ ADJ *[complexion, face, skin]* cireux ; *[person]* au teint cireux

sallow² /ˈsæləʊ/ N (= *willow*) saule *m*

sallowness /ˈsæləʊnɪs/ N teint *m* jaunâtre

sally /ˈsælɪ/ N 1 *(Mil)* sortie *f* 2 (= *flash of wit*) saillie *f*, boutade *f* ◆ **to make a ~** dire une boutade
► **sally forth, sally out** VI sortir gaiement

Sally Army * /ˌsælɪˈɑːmɪ/ N *(Brit)* (abbrev of **Salvation Army**) → **salvation**

salmon /ˈsæmən/ N (pl **salmons** *or* **salmon**) saumon *m* ; → **rock², smoke**
COMP **salmon farm** N élevage *m* de saumons
salmon fishing N pêche *f* au saumon
salmon pink N, ADJ (rose *m*) saumon *m inv*
salmon steak N darne *f* de saumon
salmon trout N truite *f* saumonée

salmonella /ˌsælməˈnelə/ N (pl **salmonellae** /ˌsælməˈneliː/) salmonelle *f* COMP **salmonella poisoning** N salmonellose *f*

salmonellosis /ˌsælmɒneˈləʊsɪs/ N salmonellose *f*

Salome /səˈləʊmɪ/ N Salomé *f*

salon /ˈsælɒn/ N *(all senses)* salon *m* ; → **beauty, hair**

saloon /səˈluːn/ N 1 (= *large room*) salle *f*, salon *m* ; *(on ship)* salon *m* 2 *(Brit:* also **saloon bar**) bar

m ; (US = bar) bar m, saloon m [3] (Brit = car) berline f
COMP **saloon bar** N (Brit) bar m
saloon car N (Brit = car) berline f ; (US = railway carriage) voiture-salon f

salsa /'sɑːlsə/ N [1] (Culin) sauce froide à base d'oignons, de tomates et de poivrons [2] (Mus) salsa f

salsify /'sælsɪfɪ/ N salsifis m

SALT /sɔːlt/ ABBR abbrev of **Strategic Arms Limitation Talks** COMP **SALT negotiations** NPL négociations fpl SALT

salt /sɔːlt/ N sel m ◆ **kitchen/table** ~ sel m de cuisine/de table ◆ **there's too much ~ in the potatoes** les pommes de terre sont trop salées ◆ **I don't like ~ in my food** je n'aime pas manger salé ◆ **to rub ~ in(to) the wound** (fig) retourner le couteau dans la plaie ◆ **he's not worth his** ~ il ne vaut pas grand-chose ◆ **any teacher/politician worth his** ~ tout professeur/homme politique qui se respecte ◆ **to take sth with a pinch** or **grain of** ~ ne pas prendre qch au pied de la lettre ◆ **the ~ of the earth** le sel de la terre ◆ **below the** ~ † socialement inférieur (-eure f) ◆ **an old (sea)** ~ un vieux loup de mer ; → **bath, smell**
ADJ [1] (= salty) [taste] salé ; [air] marin ◆ **to shed ~ tears** (liter) verser des larmes amères [2] (= salted) [fish, meat, porridge] salé
VT [+ meat, one's food] saler
COMP **salt beef** N bœuf m salé
salt box N (US = house) maison à deux étages et à toit dissymétrique
salt flat N salant m
salt-free ADJ sans sel
salt lake N lac m salé
salt lick N (= block of salt) pierre f à lécher ; (= place) salant m
salt marsh N marais m salant
salt mine N mine f de sel ◆ **back to the ~ mines!** * allez, il faut reprendre le collier !*
salt pan N puits m salant
salt pork N porc m salé
salt shaker N salière f
salt spoon N cuiller f or cuillère f à sel
salt tax N (Hist) gabelle f
salt water N eau f salée
► **salt away** VT SEP [+ meat] saler ; (fig) [+ money] mettre à gauche*
► **salt down** VT FUS saler, conserver dans le sel

saltcellar /'sɔːlt,seləʳ/ N salière f

saltine /sɔːl'tiːn/ N (US = cracker) petit biscuit m salé

saltiness /'sɔːltɪnɪs/ N [of water] salinité f ; [of food] goût m salé

salting /'sɔːltɪŋ/ N [1] (= act of putting salt on) salaison f [2] (= place: esp Brit) (marais m) salant m

saltpetre, saltpeter (US) /'sɔːlt,piːtəʳ/ N salpêtre m

saltwater /'sɔːltwɔːtəʳ/ ADJ [fish] de mer

saltworks /'sɔːltwɜːks/ N (NonC) saline(s) f(pl)

salty /'sɔːltɪ/ ADJ [1] (= containing salt) [food, water, taste] salé ; [soil] salin ; [deposit] de sel [2] († = risqué) [language, story] salé

salubrious /sə'luːbrɪəs/ ADJ (frm) (= healthy) [place] salubre ; [climate] sain ◆ **it's not a very ~ district** c'est un quartier un peu malsain

salubrity /sə'luːbrɪtɪ/ N salubrité f

saluki /sə'luːkɪ/ N sloughi m

salutary /'sæljʊtərɪ/ ADJ salutaire

salutation /,sæljʊ'teɪʃən/ N salut m ; (exaggerated) salutation f ◆ **in** ~ pour saluer

salutatorian /sə,luːtə'tɔːrɪən/ N (US Scol) deuxième mf de la promotion (qui prononce un discours de fin d'année)

salute /sə'luːt/ N (with hand) salut m ; (with guns) salve f ◆ **military** ~ salut m militaire ◆ **to give (sb) a** ~ faire un salut (à qn) ◆ **to take the** ~ passer les troupes en revue ◆ **to raise one's hand in** ~ saluer de la main ; → **fire, gun** VT (Mil etc) saluer (de la main) ; (fig = acclaim) saluer (as comme) ◆ **to ~ the flag** saluer le drapeau ◆ **he ~d the historic achievement of the government** il a salué ce succès historique du gouvernement VI (Mil etc) faire un salut

Salvador(i)an /,sælvə'dɔːr(ɪ)ən/ ADJ salvadorien N Salvadorien(ne) m(f)

salvage /'sælvɪdʒ/ N (NonC) [1] (= saving) [of ship, cargo] sauvetage m ; (for re-use) récupération f [2] (= things saved from fire, wreck) objets mpl récupérés ; (= things for re-use) objets mpl récupérables ◆ **to collect old newspapers for** ~ récupérer les vieux journaux [3] (= payment) prime f or indemnité f de sauvetage VT [1] (= save) sauver ; [+ pride, reputation] préserver ◆ **to ~ one's marriage** sauver son mariage ◆ **we'll have to ~ what we can from the situation** il nous faudra sauver ce que nous pourrons de la situation ◆ **she was lucky to (be able to) ~ her career** c'est tout juste si elle a pu sauver sa carrière [2] [+ ship] sauver, effectuer le sauvetage de ; [+ material, cargo] sauver (from de) [3] [+ objects for re-use] récupérer COMP [operation, work, company, vessel] de sauvetage

salvation /sæl'veɪʃən/ N (Rel etc) salut m ; (economic) relèvement m ◆ **work has been his** ~ c'est le travail qui l'a sauvé, il a trouvé son salut dans le travail COMP **Salvation Army** N Armée f du Salut ◆ **Salvation Army band** fanfare f de l'Armée du Salut

salvationist /sæl'veɪʃənɪst/ N salutiste mf

salve[1] /sælv/ N (lit, fig) baume m VT [+ pain] soulager, apaiser ◆ **to ~ his conscience he ...** pour soulager sa conscience, il ...

salve[2] /sælv/ VT (= salvage) sauver

salver /'sælvəʳ/ N plateau m (de métal)

salvia /'sælvɪə/ N sauge f à fleurs rouges, salvia f

salvo[1] /'sælvəʊ/ N (pl **salvos** or **salvoes**) (Mil) salve f ; → **fire**

salvo[2] /'sælvəʊ/ N (pl **salvos**) (Jur) réserve f, réservation f

salvor /'sælvəʳ/ N sauveteur m (en mer)

Salzburg /'sæltsbɜːg/ N Salzbourg

SAM /sæm/ N (Mil) (abbrev of **surface-to-air missile**) SAM m

Sam /sæm/ N (dim of **Samuel**) → **uncle** COMP **Sam Browne (belt)** N (Mil) ceinturon m et baudrier m ; (for cyclist) bande f fluorescente

Samaria /sə'meərɪə/ N Samarie f

Samaritan /sə'mærɪtən/ N Samaritain(e) m(f) ◆ **the Good** ~ (Rel) le bon Samaritain ◆ **he was a good** ~ il faisait le bon Samaritain ◆ **Good ~ Laws** (US) lois mettant un sauveteur à l'abri des poursuites judiciaires qui pourraient être engagées par le blessé ◆ **the ~s** (= organization) ≈ SOS-Amitié ADJ samaritain

samarium /sə'meərɪəm/ N samarium m

samba /'sæmbə/ N samba f

sambo** /'sæmbəʊ/ N (pej) moricaud(e)** m(f) (pej)

same /seɪm/ LANGUAGE IN USE 5.3, 7.5, 26.2
ADJ même (as que) ◆ **to be the ~ age/shape** avoir le même âge/la même forme ◆ **the carpet was the ~ colour as the wall** la moquette était de la même couleur que le mur ◆ **we come from the ~ place** nous venons du même endroit ◆ **he reads the ~ paper as me** il lit le même journal que moi ◆ **is that the ~ man (that) I saw yesterday?** est-ce bien l'homme que j'ai vu hier ? ◆ **the ~ woman that spoke to me** la femme qui m'a parlé ◆ **the ~ girl as I saw yesterday** la fille que j'ai vue hier ◆ **but in the ~ breath he said ...** mais il a ajouté ... ◆ **the ~ day** le même jour ◆ **the very ~ day** le jour même ◆ **the ~ day as last year** le même jour que l'année dernière ◆ **that ~ day** ce même jour ◆ **~ difference!** * c'est du pareil au même !*, c'est kif-kif !* ◆ **it's the ~ old rubbish on TV tonight** il y a les bêtises habituelles à la télé ce soir ◆ **I'm still the ~ person I was before** je n'ai pas changé ◆ **for the ~ reason** pour la même raison ◆ **it comes to the ~ thing** cela revient au même ◆ **we sat at the ~ table as usual** nous avons pris notre table habituelle ◆ **how are you? – ~ as usual!*** comment vas-tu ? – comme d'habitude ! ◆ **in the ~ way** de même ◆ **in the ~ way as** or **that ...** de la même façon que ... ; → **one, story**[1], **token, way**
◆ **at the same time** ◆ **they both arrived at the ~ time** ils sont arrivés en même temps ◆ **don't all talk at the ~ time** ne parlez pas tous en même temps or à la fois ◆ **at the ~ time we must remember that ...** il ne faut cependant pas oublier que ... ◆ **at the very ~ time as ...** au moment même or précis où ...
PRON [1] ◆ **the** ~ (gen) la même chose ; (specific reference) le or la même ; (Jur = aforementioned) le susdit, la susdite ◆ **we must all write the** ~ il faut que nous écrivions tous la même chose ◆ **he left and I did the** ~ il est parti et j'ai fait de même or j'en ai fait autant ◆ **I'll do the ~ for you** je te le revaudrai ◆ **she's much** or **about the** ~ (in health) son état est inchangé ◆ **I still feel the ~ about you** mes sentiments à ton égard n'ont pas changé ◆ **it's not the ~ at all** ce n'est pas du tout la même chose, ce n'est pas du tout pareil ◆ **it's the ~ everywhere** c'est partout pareil ◆ **and the ~ to you!** (good wishes) à vous aussi !, vous de même ! ; (as retort) je te souhaite la pareille ! ◆ **you idiot! – ~ to you!** * idiot ! – toi-même ! ◆ **~ here!*** moi aussi ! ◆ **it's the ~ with us** (et) nous aussi
◆ **the same + as** ◆ **their house is the ~ as before** leur maison est la même qu'avant ◆ **the price is the ~ as last year** c'est le même prix que l'année dernière ◆ **do the ~ as your brother** fais comme ton frère ◆ **I don't feel the ~ about it as I did** maintenant je vois la chose différemment ◆ **it's not the ~ as before** ce n'est plus pareil, ce n'est plus comme avant
◆ **all the same, just the same** ◆ **it's all** or **just the ~ to me** cela m'est égal ◆ **thanks all** or **just the** ~ merci tout de même or quand même* ◆ **all** or **just the ~, he refused** il a refusé quand même or tout de même, n'empêche qu'il a refusé ◆ **things go on just the** ~ (= monotonously) rien ne change ; (= in spite of everything) rien n'a changé, la vie continue (quand même) ◆ **I'll leave now if it's all the ~ to you** je pars maintenant, si ça ne te dérange pas
◆ **(the) same again** ◆ **I would do the ~ again** (si c'était à refaire,) je recommencerais ◆ **he'll never be the ~ again** (after accident, bereavement) il ne sera plus jamais le même ◆ **things can never be the ~ again** les choses ne seront plus jamais comme avant ◆ **(the) ~ again please** * (in bar) la même chose, s'il vous plaît, remettez-moi (or remettez-nous) ça*
[2] (Comm: frm) le or la même ◆ **"to repairing same, £20"** "réparation du même (or de la même), 20 livres"
COMP **same-day** ADJ [delivery, service] (garanti) le jour même or dans la journée
same-sex ADJ [relationship, marriage] homosexuel

sameness /'seɪmnɪs/ N identité f, similitude f ; (= monotony) monotonie f, uniformité f

samey * /'seɪmɪ/ ADJ (Brit) répétitif ◆ **her songs are very** ~ ses chansons se ressemblent toutes

Sami /'sɑːmɪ/ N Sami mf

samizdat /,sæmɪz'dæt/ N samizdat m ◆ **~ publication** samizdat m

Samoa /sə'məʊə/ N les Samoa fpl ◆ **in** ~ aux Samoa

Samoan /sə'məʊən/ ADJ samoan N Samoan(e) *m(f)*

samosa /sə'məʊsə/ N (pl **samosas** or **samosa**) samosa *m*

samovar /,sæməʊ'vɑːʳ/ N samovar *m*

sampan /'sæmpæn/ N sampan(g) *m*

samphire /'sæm,faɪəʳ/ N criste-marine *f*

sample /'sɑːmpl/ N *(gen)* échantillon *m* ; *[of urine]* échantillon *m* ; *[of blood, tissue]* prélèvement *m* ◆ **as a** ~ à titre d'échantillon ◆ **to take a** ~ prélever un échantillon, faire un prélèvement *(also Geol)* ◆ **to take a blood** ~ faire une prise or un prélèvement de sang *(from* à) ◆ **to choose from** ~**s** choisir sur échantillons ◆ **free** ~ *(Comm)* échantillon *m* gratuit ◆ **a** ~ **of his poetry** un exemple de sa poésie ; → **random**

VT 1 *[+ food, wine]* goûter ; *(fig) [+ lifestyle]* goûter à

2 *(Mus)* sampler

3 *[+ opinion]* sonder ◆ **the newspaper has** ~**d public opinion on ...** le journal a fait un sondage sur ...

COMP ◆ **a** ~ **selection** un échantillon ◆ **a** ~ **sentence** un exemple de phrase

sample book N *(Comm)* catalogue *m* d'échantillons

sample case N *(used by salesperson)* valise *f* d'échantillons

sample letter N lettre *f* modèle

sample section N ◆ **a** ~ **section of the population** un échantillon représentatif de la population

sample survey N enquête *f* par sondage

sampler /'sɑːmpləʳ/ N *(Sewing)* échantillon *m* de broderie ; *(Mus)* sampler *m*, échantillonneur *m*

sampling /'sɑːmplɪŋ/ N *(gen)* échantillonnage *m* ; *(Mus)* sampling *m* ◆ ~ **technique** *(Comm etc)* technique *f* d'échantillonnage

Samson /'sæmsn/ N Samson *m*

Samuel /'sæmjʊəl/ N Samuel *m*

samurai /'sæmʊ,raɪ/ N *(pl inv)* samouraï or samurai *m*

COMP **samurai bond** N *(Fin)* obligation *f* libellée en yens émise par des emprunteurs étrangers

samurai sword N épée *f* de samouraï

samurai tradition N tradition *f* samouraï

samurai warrior N (guerrier *m*) samouraï *m*

San Andreas /sænæn'dreɪəs/ N ◆ **the** ~ **Fault** la faille de San Andreas

sanatorium /,sænə'tɔːrɪəm/ N (pl **sanatoriums** or **sanatoria** /,sænə'tɔːrɪə/) *(Brit)* sanatorium *m* ; *(Scol)* infirmerie *f*

Sancho Panza /,sæntʃəʊ'pænzə/ N Sancho Pança *m*

sancta /'sæŋktə/ NPL of **sanctum**

sanctification /,sæŋktɪfɪ'keɪʃən/ N sanctification *f*

sanctify /'sæŋktɪfaɪ/ VT sanctifier

sanctimonious /,sæŋktɪ'məʊnɪəs/ ADJ *[person, comment, speech]* moralisateur (-trice *f*)

sanctimoniously /,sæŋktɪ'məʊnɪəslɪ/ ADV d'une manière moralisatrice ; *[speak]* d'un ton moralisateur or prêcheur

sanctimoniousness /,sæŋktɪ'məʊnɪəsnɪs/ N *[of comment, speech]* ton *m* moralisateur ; *[of person]* attitude *f* moralisatrice

sanction /'sæŋkʃən/ N 1 *(NonC = authorization)* sanction *f*, approbation *f* ◆ **he gave it his** ~ il a donné son approbation ◆ **with the** ~ **of sb** avec le consentement de qn 2 *(= enforcing measure)* sanction *f* ◆ **to impose economic** ~**s against** or **on ...** prendre des sanctions économiques contre ... ◆ **to lift the** ~**s on ...** lever les sanctions contre ... VT 1 *[+ law]* autoriser, approuver ◆ **to** ~ **the use of force** autoriser le recours à la force ◆ **I will not** ~ **such a thing** je ne peux pas approuver or sanctionner une chose pareille 2 *(= impose sanctions on)* prendre des sanctions contre COMP **sanctions-busting** N violation *f* de sanctions

> ⚠ Be cautious about translating **to sanction** by **sanctionner**, which can mean 'to punish'.

sanctity /'sæŋktɪtɪ/ N *[of person, behaviour]* sainteté *f* ; *[of oath, place]* caractère *m* sacré ; *[of property, marriage]* inviolabilité *f* ◆ **odour of** ~ odeur *f* de sainteté

sanctuary /'sæŋktjʊərɪ/ N *(= holy place)* sanctuaire *m* ; *(= refuge)* asile *m* ; *(for wildlife)* réserve *f* ◆ **right of** ~ droit *m* d'asile ◆ **to seek** ~ chercher asile ◆ **to take** ~ trouver asile, se réfugier ; → **bird**

sanctum /'sæŋktəm/ N (pl **sanctums** or **sancta**) 1 *(= holy place)* sanctuaire *m* 2 *(* = sb's study etc)* retraite *f*, tanière *f* ◆ **the (inner)** ~ *(hum)* le saint des saints *(hum)*

sand /sænd/ N 1 sable *m* ◆ **a grain of** ~ un grain de sable ◆ ~**s** *[of beach]* plage *f* (de sable) ; *[of desert]* désert *m* (de sable) ◆ **this resort has miles and miles of golden** ~**(s)** cette station balnéaire a des kilomètres de plages de sable doré ◆ **to be built on** ~ *[plan, agreement]* être construit sur du sable ◆ **the** ~**s of time** les grains *mpl* du sablier ◆ **the** ~**s (of time) are running out** les jours sont comptés

2 *(US * = courage)* cran * *m*

VT 1 *[+ path]* sabler, couvrir de sable ; *(against ice)* sabler

2 (also **sand down**) poncer

COMP **sand bar** N barre *f (de rivière)*

sand blind ADJ *(US)* qui a mauvaise vue

sand castle N château *m* de sable

sand desert N désert *m* de sable

sand dollar N *(US = animal)* oursin *m* plat

sand dune N dune *f* (de sable)

sand eel N anguille *f* de sable, lançon *m*

sand flea N *(= beach flea)* puce *f* de mer ; *(tropical)* chique *f*

sand martin N hirondelle *f* de rivage

sand trap N *(US Golf)* bunker *m*

sand yacht N char *m* à voile

sand-yachting N ◆ **to go** ~**-yachting** faire du char à voile

sandal /'sændl/ N sandale *f*

sandal(wood) /'sændl(wʊd)/ N santal *m* COMP *[box, perfume]* de santal

sandbag /'sændbæg/ N sac *m* de sable or de terre VT 1 *(* = stun)* assommer 2 *[+ wall, door, dam]* renforcer avec des sacs de sable or de terre

sandbank /'sændbæŋk/ N banc *m* de sable

sandblast /'sændblɑːst/ N jet *m* de sable VT décaper à la sableuse

sandblaster /'sænd,blɑːstəʳ/ N sableuse *f*

sandblasting /'sænd,blɑːstɪŋ/ N décapage *m* à la sableuse ◆ ~ **machine** sableuse *f*

sandbox /'sændbɒks/ N bac *m* à sable ; *(Rail)* sablière *f*

sandboy /'sændbɔɪ/ N ◆ **happy as a** ~ heureux comme un poisson dans l'eau or comme un roi

sander /'sændəʳ/ N *(= tool)* ponceuse *f*

sandfly /'sændflaɪ/ N phlébotome *m* ; *(= biting midge)* simulie *f*

sandglass /'sændglɑːs/ N sablier *m*

Sandhurst /'sændhɜːst/ N *(Brit)* école militaire

sanding /'sændɪŋ/ N *[of road]* sablage *m* ; *(= sandpapering)* ponçage *m* au papier de verre

S & L /,esənd'el/ N *(US Fin)* (abbrev of **savings and loan association**) → **saving**

sandlot /'sændlɒt/ *(US)* N terrain *m* vague N **sandlot baseball** N baseball *m* pratiqué dans les terrains vagues

S & M /,esənd'em/ N abbrev of **sadomasochism** ADJ (abbrev of **sadomasochistic**) sadomaso *, SM *

sandman /'sændmæn/ N (pl **-men**) *(fig)* marchand *m* de sable

sandpaper /'sænd,peɪpəʳ/ N papier *m* de verre VT (also **sandpaper down**) poncer

sandpapering /'sænd,peɪpərɪŋ/ N ponçage *m*

sandpile /'sændpaɪl/ N *(US)* tas *m* de sable

sandpiper /'sænd,paɪpəʳ/ N *(= bird)* bécasseau *m*, chevalier *m*

sandpit /'sændpɪt/ N *(esp Brit)* sablonnière *f*, carrière *f* de sable ; *(for children)* bac *m* à sable

sandshoes /'sændʃuːz/ NPL *(rubber-soled)* tennis *mpl or fpl* ; *(rope-soled)* espadrilles *fpl*

sandstone /'sændstəʊn/ N grès *m* COMP **sandstone quarry** N carrière *f* de grès, grésière *f*

sandstorm /'sændstɔːm/ N tempête *f* de sable

sandwich /'sænwɪdʒ/ N sandwich *m* ◆ **cheese** ~ sandwich *m* au fromage ◆ **open** ~ canapé *m* ◆ **he's the meat** or **filling in the** ~ * *(Brit)* il est pris entre deux feux VT (also **sandwich in**) *[+ person, appointment]* intercaler ◆ **to be** ~**ed (between)** être pris en sandwich (entre) * ◆ **three pieces of wood,** ~**ed together** trois couches de bois superposées

COMP **sandwich bar** N sandwicherie *f*

sandwich board N panneau *m* publicitaire *(porté par un homme-sandwich)*

sandwich cake N *(Brit)* gâteau *m* fourré

sandwich course N formation *f* en alternance

sandwich loaf N pain *m* de mie

sandwich man N (pl **sandwich men**) homme-sandwich *m*

sandworm /'sændwɜːm/ N arénicole *f*

sandy /'sændɪ/ ADJ 1 *(= covered with, containing sand) [soil, ground]* sablonneux ; *[beach]* de sable ; *[water, deposit]* sableux 2 *(= light-brown)* couleur (de) sable *inv* ; *[hair, moustache]* blond roux *inv*

sane /seɪn/ ADJ 1 *(Psych) [person]* sain d'esprit ; *[behaviour]* sain 2 *(= sensible) [system, policy, advice]* sensé ; *[person]* sensé, raisonnable

sanely /'seɪnlɪ/ ADV sainement, raisonnablement

Sanforized ® /'sænfəraɪzd/ ADJ irrétrécissable, qui ne rétrécit pas au lavage

San Francisco /,sænfræn'sɪskəʊ/ N San Francisco

sang /sæŋ/ VB pt of **sing**

sangfroid /'sɑːŋ'frwɑː/ N sang-froid *m inv*

sangria /sæŋ'griːə/ N sangria *f*

sanguinary /'sæŋgwɪnərɪ/ ADJ *(frm)* 1 *(= bloody) [battle, struggle]* sanglant ; *[violence]* sanguinaire 2 *(= bloodthirsty) [person]* sanguinaire

sanguine /'sæŋgwɪn/ ADJ 1 *(frm = optimistic) [person, view, temperament]* optimiste *(about* quant à) ◆ **of (a)** ~ **disposition** d'un naturel optimiste, porté à l'optimisme 2 *(liter) [complexion]* sanguin 3 *(Med Hist) [person, temperament]* sanguin

sanguinely /'sæŋgwɪnlɪ/ ADV avec optimisme

sanguineous /sæŋ'gwɪnɪəs/ ADJ sanguinolent

sanitarium /,sænɪ'tɛərɪəm/ N (pl **sanitariums** or **sanitaria** /,sænɪ'tɛərɪə/) *(esp US)* ⇒ **sanatorium**

sanitary /'sænɪtərɪ/ ADJ 1 *(= hygienic) [place]* hygiénique 2 *(= to do with hygiene) [conditions, system, services]* sanitaire ◆ ~ **facilities** (installations *fpl*) sanitaires *mpl* ◆ ~ **arrangements** dispositions *fpl* sanitaires

COMP **sanitary engineer** N ingénieur *m* des services sanitaires

sanitary inspector N inspecteur *m*, -trice *f* de la santé publique
sanitary napkin N *(US)* ⇒ **sanitary towel**
sanitary protection N *(NonC)* protections *fpl* périodiques
sanitary towel N *(Brit)* serviette *f* hygiénique

sanitation /ˌsænɪˈteɪʃən/ N *(in house)* installations *fpl* sanitaires, sanitaires *mpl* ; *(in town)* système *m* sanitaire ; *(= science)* hygiène *f* publique COMP **sanitation man** N (pl **sanitation men**) *(US)* éboueur *m* (municipal)

sanitize /ˈsænɪtaɪz/ VT *(lit)* assainir, désinfecter ; *(fig)* assainir, expurger

sanitized /ˈsænɪtaɪzd/ ADJ *[account, view of events]* édulcoré, expurgé

sanity /ˈsænɪtɪ/ N *[of person]* santé *f* mentale ◆ **he was restored to** ~ il a retrouvé sa raison ◆ **the voice of** ~ la voix de la raison ◆ **fortunately** ~ **prevailed** heureusement le bon sens l'emporta ◆ **these measures may bring some** ~ **back into the housing market** ces mesures contribueront peut-être à modérer la folie qui s'est emparée du marché de l'immobilier

sank /sæŋk/ VB pt of **sink¹**

San Marinese /ˌsænˌmærɪˈniːz/ ADJ san-marinais N San-Marinais(e) *m(f)*

San Marino /ˌsænməˈriːnəʊ/ N Saint-Marin ◆ **in** ~ à Saint-Marin

San Salvador /ˌsænˈsælvədɔːʳ/ N San Salvador

sansevieria /ˌsænsɪˈvɪərɪə/ N sansevière *f*

Sanskrit /ˈsænskrɪt/ ADJ, N sanscrit *m*

Santa * /ˈsæntə/ N ⇒ **Santa Claus**

Santa Claus /ˌsæntəˈklɔːz/ N le père Noël

Santiago /ˌsæntɪˈɑːgəʊ/ N (also **Santiago de Chile**) Santiago (du Chili) ; (also **Santiago de Compostela**) Saint-Jacques-de-Compostelle

Saone /soːn/ N Saône *f*

sap¹ /sæp/ N *[of plant]* sève *f*

sap² /sæp/ N *(Mil = trench)* sape *f* VT *[+ strength, confidence]* saper, miner

sap³ ‡ /sæp/ N *(= fool)* cruche * *f*, andouille * *f*

saphead ‡ /ˈsæphed/ N *(US)* cruche * *f*, andouille * *f*

sapless /ˈsæplɪs/ ADJ *[plant]* sans sève

sapling /ˈsæplɪŋ/ N jeune arbre *m* ; *(fig liter)* jeune homme *m* ◆ **~s** boisage *m*

sapper /ˈsæpəʳ/ N *(Brit Mil)* soldat *m* du génie ◆ **the Sappers** * le génie

sapphic /ˈsæfɪk/ ADJ saphique

sapphire /ˈsæfaɪəʳ/ N *(= jewel, gramophone needle)* saphir *m* COMP *[ring]* de saphir(s) ; *[sky]* (also **sapphire blue**) de saphir

sappy¹ /ˈsæpɪ/ ADJ *[leaves]* plein de sève ; *[wood]* vert

sappy² ‡ /ˈsæpɪ/ ADJ *(= foolish)* cruche *

saraband /ˈsærəbænd/ N sarabande *f*

Saracen /ˈsærəsn/ ADJ sarrasin N Sarrasin(e) *m(f)*

Saragossa /ˌsærəˈgɒsə/ N Saragosse

Saranwrap ® /səˈrænræp/ N *(US)* film *m* alimentaire (transparent), Scellofrais ® *m*

Saratoga /ˌsærəˈtəʊgə/ N Saratoga COMP **Saratoga trunk** N *(US)* grosse malle *f* à couvercle bombé

sarcasm /ˈsɑːkæzəm/ N *(NonC)* sarcasme *m*, raillerie *f*

sarcastic /sɑːˈkæstɪk/ ADJ sarcastique

sarcastically /sɑːˈkæstɪkəlɪ/ ADV *[say]* d'un ton sarcastique

sarcoma /sɑːˈkəʊmə/ N (pl **sarcomas** or **sarcomata** /sɑːˈkəʊmətə/) *(Med)* sarcome *m*

sarcomatosis /sɑːˌkəʊməˈtəʊsɪs/ N sarcomatose *f*

sarcophagus /sɑːˈkɒfəgəs/ N (pl **sarcophaguses** or **sarcophagi** /sɑːˈkɒfəgaɪ/) sarcophage *m*

sardine /sɑːˈdiːn/ N sardine *f* ◆ **tinned** or *(US)* **canned ~s** sardines *fpl* en boîte or en conserve ◆ **packed like ~s** serrés comme des sardines

Sardinia /sɑːˈdɪnɪə/ N Sardaigne *f* ◆ **in** ~ en Sardaigne

Sardinian /sɑːˈdɪnɪən/ ADJ sarde N 1 *(= person)* Sarde *mf* 2 *(= language)* sarde *m*

sardonic /sɑːˈdɒnɪk/ ADJ sardonique

sardonically /sɑːˈdɒnɪkəlɪ/ ADV *[smile]* d'un air sardonique, sardoniquement ; *[say]* d'un ton sardonique, sardoniquement ◆ **to laugh** ~ avoir un rire sardonique

Sargasso Sea /sɑːˈgæsəʊˌsiː/ N mer *f* des Sargasses

sarge ‡ /sɑːdʒ/ N (abbrev of **sergeant**) sergent *m*

sari /ˈsɑːrɪ/ N sari *m*

sarin /ˈsɑːrɪn/ N sarin *m*

Sark /sɑːk/ N (île *f* de) Sercq

sarky ‡ /ˈsɑːkɪ/ ADJ sarcastique

sarnie * /ˈsɑːnɪ/ N *(Brit)* sandwich *m*

sarong /səˈrɒŋ/ N sarong *m*

SARS /sɑːz/ N (abbrev of **severe acute respiratory syndrome**) SRAS *m*, syndrome *m* respiratoire aigu sévère

sarsaparilla /ˌsɑːsəpəˈrɪlə/ N *(= plant)* salsepareille *f* ; *(= drink)* boisson *f* à la salsepareille

sartorial /sɑːˈtɔːrɪəl/ ADJ *(frm) [elegance, habits, matters]* vestimentaire ◆ ~ **art** art *m* du tailleur

sartorius /sɑːˈtɔːrɪəs/ N (pl **sartorii** /sɑːˈtɔːrɪaɪ/) *(Anat)* muscle *m* couturier

SAS /ˌeseɪˈes/ N *(Brit Mil)* (abbrev of **Special Air Service**) ≃ GIGN *m*

SASE /ˌeseɪesˈiː/ N *(US)* (abbrev of **self-addressed stamped envelope**) → **self**

sash¹ /sæʃ/ N *(on uniform)* écharpe *f* ; *(on dress)* large ceinture *f* à nœud

sash² /sæʃ/ N *[of window]* châssis *m* à guillotine COMP **sash cord** N corde *f (d'une fenêtre à guillotine)*
sash window N fenêtre *f* à guillotine

sashay * /sæˈʃeɪ/ VI *(= walk stylishly)* évoluer d'un pas léger, glisser ◆ **she ~ed in/out** elle entra/sortit d'un pas léger

sashimi /ˈsæʃɪmɪ/ N sashimi *m*

Sask. abbrev of **Saskatchewan**

Saskatchewan /sæsˈkætʃɪˌwən/ N *(= province)* Saskatchewan *m* ◆ **in** ~ dans le Saskatchewan

Sasquatch /ˈsæskwætʃ/ N *animal hypothétique des forêts du nord-est des États-Unis et du Canada*

sass * /sæs/ *(US)* N toupet * *m*, culot * *m* VT être insolent avec

Sassenach /ˈsæsənæx/ N *(Scot: gen pej) nom donné aux Anglais par les Écossais*, ≃ Angliche ‡ *mf*

sassy * /ˈsæsɪ/ ADJ *(US) (= cheeky)* insolent, impertinent

SAT /ˌeseɪˈtiː/ N *(US Educ)* (abbrev of **Scholastic Aptitude test**) examen *m* d'entrée à l'université

SAT

Aux États-Unis, les **SAT** (**Scholastic Aptitude Tests**) sont un examen national de fin d'enseignement secondaire, composé surtout de tests de logique permettant d'évaluer le raisonnement verbal et mathématique des élèves. La note maximale est de 1 600 points et la moyenne tourne généralement autour de 900 points. Les résultats obtenus à cet examen (**SAT** scores) sont adressés aux universités dans lesquelles le lycéen a fait une demande d'inscription, et celles-ci font leur sélection sur la base à la fois de ces notes et du dossier scolaire de l'élève. Il est possible de se présenter aux **SAT** autant de fois qu'on le désire.

sat /sæt/ VB pt, ptp of **sit**

Sat. abbrev of **Saturday**

Satan /ˈseɪtn/ N Satan *m* ; → **limb**

satanic /səˈtænɪk/ ADJ 1 *(Rel, Occultism) [ritual, cult, forces]* satanique 2 *(= evil) [reputation]* démoniaque COMP **satanic abuse** N *(NonC)* sévices *mpl* sexuels associés à des rites sataniques

satanically /səˈtænɪkəlɪ/ ADV d'une manière satanique

Satanism /ˈseɪtənɪzəm/ N satanisme *m*

Satanist /ˈseɪtənɪst/ N sataniste *mf* ADJ ⇒ **satanic**

satay /ˈsæteɪ/ N ◆ **chicken/pork** ~ *petite brochette de poulet/porc accompagnée d'une sauce aux cacahuètes* COMP **satay sauce** N sauce *f* aux cacahuètes, sauce *f* satay

satchel /ˈsætʃəl/ N cartable *m*

Satcom /ˈsætˌkɒm/ N centre *m* de communications par satellite

sate /seɪt/ VT ⇒ **satiate**

sated /ˈseɪtɪd/ ADJ ⇒ **satiated**

sateen /sæˈtiːn/ N satinette *f* COMP en satinette

satellite /ˈsætəlaɪt/ N 1 *(Astron, Space, Telec)* satellite *m* ◆ **artificial** ~ satellite *m* artificiel, satellite-relais *m* 2 *(Pol)* satellite *m* 3 *(US = dormitory town)* ville *f* satellite VT *(= transmit via satellite)* transmettre par satellite
COMP *[town, country etc]* satellite
satellite broadcasting N diffusion *f* par satellite
satellite dish N antenne *f* parabolique
satellite link(-up) N liaison *f* satellite
satellite nation N *(Pol)* nation *f* satellite
satellite navigation system N système *m* de navigation par satellite
satellite photograph N photo *f* satellite
satellite telephone N téléphone *m* (par) satellite
satellite television N télévision *f* par satellite

satiate /ˈseɪʃɪeɪt/ VT *(lit)* assouvir, rassasier *(with* de) ; *(fig)* blaser *(with* par)

satiated /ˈseɪʃɪeɪtɪd/ ADJ *(with food)* repu, rassasié ; *(with pleasures)* comblé, blasé *(pej)*

satiation /ˌseɪʃɪˈeɪʃən/ N *(lit, fig)* assouvissement *m* ◆ **to** ~ **(point)** (jusqu')à satiété

satiety /səˈtaɪətɪ/ N *(frm)* satiété *f*

satin /ˈsætɪn/ N satin *m* ; → **silk**
COMP *[dress, slipper]* en or de satin ; *[paper, finish]* satiné **satin-smooth** ADJ satin
satin stitch N plumetis *m*

satinette /ˌsætɪˈnet/ N satinette *f* COMP en satinette

satinwood /ˈsætɪnwʊd/ N bois *m* de citronnier

satire /ˈsætaɪəʳ/ N satire *f (on* contre)

satiric(al) /səˈtɪrɪk(əl)/ ADJ satirique

satirically /səˈtɪrɪkəlɪ/ ADV d'une manière satirique

satirist /ˈsætərɪst/ **N** (= *writer*) satiriste *mf* ; (= *cartoonist*) caricaturiste *mf* ; (*in cabaret etc*) ≃ chansonnier *m* ◆ **he's TV's greatest** ~ il n'a pas son pareil à la télévision pour la satire

satirize /ˈsætəraɪz/ **VT** faire la satire de

satisfaction /ˌsætɪsˈfækʃən/ **N** 1 (*NonC* = *pleasure*) satisfaction *f* ◆ **to feel ~/great ~** éprouver de la satisfaction/une satisfaction profonde ◆ **his ~ at having completed his book** la satisfaction qu'il éprouvait d'avoir terminé son livre ◆ **he expressed his ~ at the results of the vote** il a exprimé sa satisfaction devant les résultats de l'élection ◆ **sexual ~** satisfaction *f* sexuelle ◆ **it gave us great ~ to hear that ...** nous avons appris avec beaucoup de satisfaction que ... ◆ **to my (great) ~ he ...** à ma grande satisfaction il ... ◆ **to everybody's ~** à la satisfaction de tous ◆ **has the repair been done to your ~?** est-ce que vous êtes satisfait de la réparation ? ◆ **his innocence has not been proved to my ~** on n'a pas réussi à me convaincre de son innocence ◆ **she would not give him the ~ of seeing how annoyed she was** elle ne voulait pas lui faire le plaisir de lui montrer à quel point elle était contrariée ; → **job**

2 (*NonC*) [*of demand, need*] satisfaction *f* ; [*of wrong*] réparation *f*, dédommagement *m* ; [*of appetite*] assouvissement *m* ; [*of debt*] règlement *m*, acquittement *m* ◆ **to give/obtain ~** donner/obtenir satisfaction ◆ **I demand ~** † je demande réparation

3 (= *satisfying experience*) satisfaction *f* ◆ **one of her greatest ~s comes from her work with children** son travail avec les enfants lui apporte l'une de ses plus grandes satisfactions

satisfactorily /ˌsætɪsˈfæktərɪlɪ/ **ADV** de manière satisfaisante

satisfactory /ˌsætɪsˈfæktərɪ/ **ADJ** satisfaisant ◆ **to bring sth to a ~ conclusion** mener qch à bon terme, conclure qch de manière satisfaisante ◆ **he's in a ~ condition** (*Med*) son état est satisfaisant ◆ **to make a ~ recovery** (*Med*) se rétablir *or* se remettre de manière satisfaisante ◆ **we are sorry it was not ~** (*in commercial letters*) nous regrettons que vous n'en soyez pas satisfait *or* que cela ne vous ait pas donné (entière) satisfaction

satisfied /ˈsætɪsfaɪd/ **ADJ** 1 (= *content*) [*person*] satisfait (*with* de ; *to do sth* de faire qch) ◆ **in a ~ voice** d'un ton satisfait ◆ **some people are never ~!** il y en a qui ne sont jamais contents ! ◆ **I'll stay then: (are you) ~?** (*angrily*) alors je reste : tu es content ? ◆ **you've made her cry: (are you) ~?** tu l'as fait pleurer : tu es content de toi *or* satisfait ? 2 (= *convinced*) [*person*] satisfait (*with* de), convaincu (*with* par) ◆ **I'm ~ that her death was accidental** je suis convaincu que sa mort a été accidentelle ◆ **I'm ~ that I'm right** je suis convaincu d'avoir raison ; see also **satisfy**

satisfy /ˈsætɪsfaɪ/ **VT** 1 [+ *person*] satisfaire, contenter ◆ **to ~ the examiners (in History)** (*Scol, Univ: frm*) être reçu (en histoire *or* à l'examen d'histoire) ; see also **satisfied** 2 [+ *hunger, need, want, creditor*] satisfaire ; [+ *condition*] satisfaire à, remplir ; [+ *objection*] répondre à ; [+ *debt, obligation*] s'acquitter de ; (*Comm*) [+ *demand*] satisfaire à 3 (= *convince*) convaincre, assurer (*sb that* qn que ; *of* de) ◆ **to ~ o.s. of sth** s'assurer de qch ◆ **I am satisfied that you have done your best** je suis convaincu *or* persuadé que vous avez fait de votre mieux **VI** donner satisfaction

satisfying /ˈsætɪsfaɪɪŋ/ **ADJ** [*life, relationship, work, career*] satisfaisant ; [*task, experience*] gratifiant ; [*food, meal*] substantiel

satrap /ˈsætrəp/ **N** satrape *m*

satsuma /ˌsætˈsuːmə/ **N** satsuma *f*

saturate /ˈsætʃəreɪt/ **VT** saturer (*with* de) ◆ **to ~ the market** saturer le marché ◆ **my shoes are ~d** mes chaussures sont trempées **COMP saturated fat N** graisse *f* saturée

saturation /ˌsætʃəˈreɪʃən/ **N** saturation *f* **COMP saturation bombing N** bombardement *m* intensif

saturation point N point *m* de saturation ◆ **to reach ~ point** arriver à saturation

Saturday /ˈsætədɪ/ **N** samedi *m* ◆ **on ~** samedi ◆ **on ~s** le samedi ◆ **next ~, ~ next** samedi prochain *or* qui vient ◆ **last ~** samedi dernier ◆ **the first/last ~ of the month** le premier/dernier samedi du mois ◆ **every ~** tous les samedis, chaque samedi ◆ **every other ~, every second ~** un samedi sur deux ◆ **it is ~ today** nous sommes samedi aujourd'hui, on est samedi ◆ **~ 18 December** samedi 18 décembre ◆ **on ~ 23 January** le samedi 23 janvier ◆ **the ~ after next** samedi en huit ◆ **a week on ~, ~ week** samedi en huit ◆ **a fortnight on ~, ~ fortnight** samedi en quinze ◆ **a week/fortnight past on ~** il y a huit/quinze jours samedi dernier ◆ **the following ~** le samedi suivant ◆ **the ~ before last** l'autre samedi ◆ **~ morning** samedi matin ◆ **~ afternoon** samedi après-midi ◆ **~ evening** samedi soir ◆ **~ night** samedi soir ; (*overnight*) la nuit de samedi ◆ **~ closing** fermeture *f* le samedi ◆ **the ~ edition** (*Press*) l'édition *f* de *or* du samedi ◆ **~ night special** * (*US* = *gun*) revolver *m* bon marché ; → **holy**

Saturn /ˈsætən/ **N** (*Myth*) Saturne *m* ; (*Astron*) Saturne *f*

Saturnalia /ˌsætəˈneɪlɪə/ **N** (pl **Saturnalia** *or* **Saturnalias**) saturnale(s) *f(pl)*

saturnine /ˈsætənaɪn/ **ADJ** (*liter*) [*man, face*] ténébreux ; [*features*] sombre

satyr /ˈsætəʳ/ **N** satyre *m*

sauce /sɔːs/ **N** 1 (*Culin*) sauce *f* ◆ **what's ~ for the goose is ~ for the gander** (*Prov*) ce qui est bon pour l'un l'est pour l'autre ; → **apple, mint², tomato, white** 2 († * = *impudence*) toupet* *m* ◆ **none of your ~!** (*to child*) petit(e) impertinent(e) ! ; (*to adult*) assez d'impertinence ! 3 (*US* ✱ = *drink*) **the ~** l'alcool *m* ◆ **to hit the ~, to be on the ~** picoler* **COMP sauce boat N** saucière *f*

saucepan /ˈsɔːspən/ **N** casserole *f* ; → **double**

saucer /ˈsɔːsəʳ/ **N** soucoupe *f*, sous-tasse *f* ◆ **~-eyed, with eyes like ~s** avec des yeux comme des soucoupes ; → **flying**

saucily * /ˈsɔːsɪlɪ/ **ADV** [*behave, speak*] avec impertinence, impertinemment ; [*dress*] avec coquetterie ; [*look*] d'un air coquin

sauciness * /ˈsɔːsɪnɪs/ **N** (= *cheekiness*) toupet* *m*, impertinence *f* ; (= *smartness*) coquetterie *f*

saucy * /ˈsɔːsɪ/ **ADJ** 1 (= *cheeky*) [*person*] impertinent (*with* avec) ; [*look*] coquin 2 (*esp Brit* = *suggestive*) [*joke, humour*] grivois ; [*postcard, photo*] osé ; [*clothes*] suggestif

Saudi /ˈsaʊdɪ/ **ADJ** (*gen*) saoudien ; [*ambassador, embassy*] d'Arabie Saoudite ; [*capital*] de l'Arabie Saoudite **N** Saoudien(ne) *m(f)* **COMP Saudi Arabia N** Arabie *f* Saoudite

Saudi Arabian ADJ saoudien **N** Saoudien(ne) *m(f)*

sauerkraut /ˈsaʊəkraʊt/ **N** (*NonC*) choucroute *f*

Saul /sɔːl/ **N** Saül *m*

sauna /ˈsɔːnə/ **N** (also **sauna bath**) sauna *m* ◆ **at the ~** au sauna ◆ **in the ~** dans le sauna

saunter /ˈsɔːntəʳ/ **VI** flâner ◆ **to ~ in/out/away** *etc* entrer/sortir/s'éloigner *etc* d'un pas nonchalant **N** ◆ **to go for a ~** * faire une petite promenade *or* une balade*

saurian /ˈsɔːrɪən/ **ADJ, N** saurien *m*

sausage /ˈsɒsɪdʒ/ **N** saucisse *f* ; (*pre-cooked*) saucisson *m* ◆ **beef/pork ~** saucisse *f* de bœuf/de porc ◆ **not a ~** ✱ (*Brit*) rien, des clous ✱ ; → **cocktail, garlic, liver, comp** **COMP sausage dog** * **N** teckel *m*, saucisson *m* à pattes* (*hum*)

sausage machine N machine *f* à faire les saucisses

sausage meat N chair *f* à saucisse

sausage roll N (*esp Brit*) ≃ friand *m*

sauté /ˈsəʊteɪ/ **VT** [+ *potatoes, meat*] faire sauter **ADJ** ◆ **~ potatoes** pommes *fpl* (de terre) sautées

savage /ˈsævɪdʒ/ **ADJ** 1 (= *violent, harsh*) [*person*] féroce, brutal ; [*animal, attack, criticism, look*] féroce ; [*blow*] brutal ; [*temper*] sauvage 2 (= *drastic*) ◆ **a ~ pay cut** une très forte réduction de salaire ◆ **~ cuts in the education budget** des coupes *fpl* claires dans le budget de l'éducation 3 († = *primitive*) [*tribe*] sauvage **N** sauvage *mf* **VT** [*animal*] attaquer férocement ; [*critics etc*] éreinter, attaquer violemment

savagely /ˈsævɪdʒlɪ/ **ADV** 1 (= *violently, harshly*) [*beat*] sauvagement ; [*criticize*] violemment, férocement ; [*say*] brutalement ; [*funny*] férocement ◆ **~ beautiful** d'une beauté sauvage ◆ **to attack sb/sth ~** (*lit*) attaquer qn/qch sauvagement ; (*fig*) attaquer qn/qch violemment 2 (= *drastically*) ◆ **the film has been ~ cut** *or* **edited** ce film a été monstrueusement coupé ◆ **to cut staff/a budget ~** faire des coupes claires dans un budget/parmi le personnel

savageness /ˈsævɪdʒnɪs/, **savagery** /ˈsævɪdʒrɪ/ **N** (= *cruelty*) sauvagerie *f*, brutalité *f*, férocité *f* ; (= *primitiveness*) barbarie *f*

savanna(h) /səˈvænə/ **N** savane *f*

savant /ˈsævənt/ **N** érudit(e) *m(f)*, homme *m* de science, lettré(e) *m(f)*

save¹ /seɪv/ **VT** 1 (= *rescue*) [+ *person, animal, jewels, building, marriage*] sauver (*from* de) ◆ **surgeons could not ~ his leg** les chirurgiens n'ont pas pu sauver sa jambe ◆ **a campaign to ~ the hospital** une campagne pour le maintien *or* la survie de l'hôpital ◆ **we must ~ the planet for future generations** il faut préserver *or* sauvegarder la planète pour les générations à venir ◆ **to ~ the situation** sauver la situation ◆ **~ the whales/seals** (*as slogan*) sauvez les baleines/phoques ◆ **I couldn't do it to ~ my soul** je ne pourrais pas le faire, même si ma vie en dépendait ◆ **to ~ one's (own) skin** * *or* **neck** * *or* **hide** * sauver sa peau* ◆ **to ~ one's (own) bacon** * (*esp Brit*) se tirer du pétrin ◆ **to ~ sb's bacon** *or* **neck** tirer qn d'affaire ◆ **to ~ sb's ass** ✱ *or* **butt** ✱ (*US*) sortir qn de la merde ✱ ◆ **to be ~d by the bell** être sauvé par le gong ◆ **to ~ the day** sauver la mise ◆ **to ~ face** sauver la face ◆ **God ~ the Queen!** vive la reine ! ; → **wreckage**

◆ **to save sb's life** sauver la vie à *or* de qn ◆ **thanks, you ~d my life!** (*fig*) merci, tu m'as sauvé la vie ! ◆ **I couldn't do it to ~ my life** je ne pourrais pas le faire, même si ma vie en dépendait ◆ **she can't cook to ~ her life** * elle est nulle* en cuisine ◆ **he can't sing to ~ his life** * il chante comme un pied*

◆ **to save ... from** (= *protect, prevent*) ◆ **to ~ sb from death/drowning** sauver qn de la mort/de la noyade ◆ **to ~ sb from falling** empêcher qn de tomber ◆ **to ~ sb from himself** protéger qn de *or* contre lui-même ◆ **to ~ a building from demolition** sauver un bâtiment de la démolition, empêcher la démolition d'un bâtiment

2 (*Rel*) [+ *sinner*] sauver, délivrer ◆ **to ~ one's soul** sauver son âme

3 (also **save up**) [+ *money*] mettre de côté ; [+ *food*] mettre de côté, garder ◆ **he has money ~d** il a de l'argent de côté ◆ **I've ~d you a piece of cake** je t'ai gardé un morceau de gâteau ◆ **to ~ o.s. (up) for sth** se réserver pour qch ◆ **he ~d the last sweet for himself** il s'est gardé le dernier bonbon ◆ **I was saving the wine for later** je gardais le vin pour plus tard ◆ **to ~ sth**

till (the) last garder qch pour la bonne bouche ◆ **to ~ the best for last** garder le meilleur pour la fin ◆ **to ~ (up) old newspapers for charity** garder les vieux journaux pour les bonnes œuvres ◆ **to ~ stamps/matchboxes** *etc (= collect)* collectionner les timbres/les boîtes d'allumettes *etc* ◆ **will you ~ me a place at your table?** me garderez-vous une place à votre table ?

4 *(= not spend, not use) [+ money, labour]* économiser ; *[+ time]* (faire) gagner ; *(= avoid) [+ difficulty etc]* éviter *(sb sth* qch à qn) ◆ **you have ~d me a lot of trouble** vous m'avez évité bien des ennuis ◆ **to ~ time let's assume that ...** pour aller plus vite *or* pour gagner du temps admettons que ... *+ subj* ◆ **this route will ~ you 10 miles** cet itinéraire vous fera gagner 16 kilomètres ◆ **going by plane will ~ you four hours (on the train journey)** vous gagnerez quatre heures en prenant l'avion (au lieu du train) ◆ **that will ~ my going** *or* **me from going** cela m'évitera d'y aller ◆ **think of all the money you'll ~** pensez à tout l'argent que vous économiserez *or* à toutes les économies que vous ferez ◆ **"save 10p on this packet"** "10 pence d'économie sur ce paquet" ◆ **you ~ £1 if you buy three packets** en achetant trois paquets vous économisez une livre ◆ **to ~ petrol** faire des économies d'essence, économiser l'essence ◆ **industry must be encouraged to ~ energy** il faut encourager l'industrie à faire des économies d'énergie ◆ **he's saving his strength** *or* **himself for tomorrow's race** il se ménage pour la course de demain ◆ **to ~ o.s. for sb** *(euph, hum)* se réserver pour qn ; → **penny, stitch**

5 *(Sport)* **to ~ a goal/penalty** arrêter un but/penalty

6 *(Comput)* sauvegarder

VI 1 (also **save up**) mettre (de l'argent) de côté, faire des économies ◆ **to ~ for the holidays/for a new bike** mettre de l'argent de côté pour les vacances/pour (acheter) un nouveau vélo

◆ **to save on sth** économiser sur qch, faire des économies sur qch

2 *(Sport)* faire une parade

N 1 *(Sport)* parade *f*

2 *(Comput)* sauvegarde *f*

► **save up** VI ⇒ **save¹ vi 1**

VT SEP ⇒ **save¹ vt 3**

save² /seɪv/ PREP *(liter)* ◆ **~ (for)** sauf, à l'exception de ◆ **~ that ...** sauf que ..., à ceci près que ...

saveloy /ˈsævəlɔɪ/ N cervelas *m*

saver /ˈseɪvəʳ/ N épargnant(e) *m(f)*

Savile Row /ˈsævɪlˈrəʊ/ N *(Brit) rue de Londres où se trouvent les plus grands tailleurs* COMP **a Savile Row suit** N un costume de Savile Row

saving /ˈseɪvɪŋ/ N 1 *(= rescue)* sauvetage *m* ; → **face, life**

2 *(Rel) [of sinner]* salut *m*

3 *[of time, money]* économie *f* ; *(Banking)* épargne *f* ◆ **we must make ~s** il faut économiser *or* faire des économies ◆ **this means a great ~ of time/petrol** *etc* cela représente une grande économie de temps/d'essence *etc* ◆ **a ~ of $12** une économie de 12 dollars ◆ **a considerable ~ in time and money** une économie considérable de temps et d'argent ◆ **the government is trying to encourage ~** le gouvernement cherche à encourager l'épargne

4 *(Comput)* sauvegarde *f*

NPL **savings** économies *fpl* ◆ **small ~s** la petite épargne ◆ **to live on one's ~s** vivre de ses économies ; → **national, post office**

PREP † sauf ◆ **~ your presence** sauf votre respect

COMP **saving clause** N *(Jur)* clause *f* de sauvegarde

saving grace N ◆ **the film's/John's only ~ grace is ...** la seule chose qui rachète *or* sauve le film/John est ...

savings account N *(Brit)* compte *m* d'épargne ; *(US)* compte *m* de dépôt

savings and loan association N *(US)* ≃ société *f* de crédit immobilier

savings bank N caisse *f* d'épargne

savings stamp N timbre-épargne *m*

saviour /ˈseɪvjəʳ/, **savior** *(US)* /ˈseɪvjəʳ/ N sauveur *m* ◆ **the Saviour** *(Rel)* le Sauveur ◆ **Our Saviour** Notre Sauveur

savoir-faire /ˈsævwɑːfeəʳ/ N savoir-vivre *m inv*

savor /ˈseɪvəʳ/ *(US)* ⇒ **savour**

savoriness /ˈseɪvərɪnɪs/ N *(US)* ⇒ **savouriness**

savorless /ˈseɪvəlɪs/ ADJ *(US)* ⇒ **savourless**

savory /ˈseɪvərɪ/ N 1 *(= herb)* sarriette *f* 2 *(US)* ⇒ **savoury noun** ADJ *(US)* ⇒ **savoury adj**

savour, savor *(US)* /ˈseɪvəʳ/ N *(= flavour: lit, fig)* saveur *f* VT *[+ food, drink]* savourer, déguster ; *[+ triumph]* savourer ◆ **to ~ every moment** savourer chaque instant *or* chaque moment ◆ **to ~ the delights of ...** goûter aux plaisirs de ... ◆ **he was ~ing the excitement of the competition** il était pris par la fièvre de la compétition VI 1 *(lit, liter)* ◆ **to ~ of sth** sentir qch 2 *(fig)* **to ~ of fascism/heresy** sentir le fascisme/l'hérésie, avoir des relents de fascisme/d'hérésie ◆ **she hated anything that ~ed of the supernatural** elle détestait tout ce qui avait trait au surnaturel

savouriness, savoriness *(US)* /ˈseɪvərɪnɪs/ N saveur *f*, succulence *f*

savourless, savorless *(US)* /ˈseɪvəlɪs/ ADJ sans saveur

savoury, savory *(US)* /ˈseɪvərɪ/ ADJ 1 *(Brit = not sweet) [food, dish]* salé *(par opposition à sucré)* ◆ **a ~ pie** une tourte 2 *(= appetizing) [smell]* appétissant ; *[taste]* savoureux 3 *(= respectable)* ◆ **not a very ~ subject** un sujet peu appétissant *or* peu ragoûtant ◆ **some not very ~ episodes in her past** des épisodes pas très reluisants de son passé ◆ **the main square is none too ~ at night** la place principale est assez mal fréquentée la nuit ◆ **one of the book's less ~ characters** l'un des personnages les moins recommandables du roman N *(Culin)* mets *m* salé ; *(on toast)* canapé *m* chaud

Savoy /səˈvɔɪ/ N Savoie *f* ADJ savoyard ◆ **~ cabbage** *(Brit)* chou *m* frisé de Milan

Savoyard /səˈvɔɪɑːd/ N Savoyard(e) *m(f)* ADJ savoyard

savvy /ˈsævɪ/ N * jugeote * *f*, bon sens *m* VI 1 *(= know)* **no ~** †‡ sais pas, moi * 2 (‡ *= understand)* piger ‡, comprendre ◆ **I can take care of myself, ~?** je me débrouille tout seul, tu piges ? ‡ ADJ ‡ calé *, futé

saw¹ /sɔː/ (vb : pret **sawed**, ptp **sawed** *or* **sawn**) N scie *f* ; → **circular** VT scier, débiter à la scie ◆ **to ~ wood** (‡, *US fig = sleep)* roupiller * ; *(= snore)* ronfler ; see also **sawn** VI ◆ **to ~ through a plank/the bars of a cell** scier une planche/les barreaux d'une cellule

COMP **saw edge** N lame *f* dentée

saw-edged knife N (pl **saw-edged knives**) couteau-scie *m*

► **saw away** * VI *(pej)* ◆ **to saw away at the violin** racler du violon

► **saw off** VT SEP enlever à la scie ADJ ◆ **sawed-off** → **sawed** ADJ ◆ **sawn-off** → **sawn**

► **saw up** VT SEP débiter à la scie

saw² /sɔː/ N *(= saying)* dicton *m*

saw³ /sɔː/ VB pt of **see¹**

sawbones † * /ˈsɔːbəʊnz/ N *(pej)* chirurgien *m*, charcutier ‡ *m (pej)*

sawbuck /ˈsɔːbʌk/ N *(US) (= sawhorse)* chevalet *m* de scieur de bois ; ‡ *(= ten-dollar bill)* billet *m* de dix dollars

sawdust /ˈsɔːdʌst/ N *(NonC)* sciure *f* (de bois)

sawed /sɔːd/ VB pt, ptp of **saw¹**

COMP **sawed-off** * ADJ *(US pej = short)* court sur pattes *, petit

sawed-off shotgun N carabine *f* à canon scié

sawfish /ˈsɔːfɪʃ/ N (pl **sawfish** *or* **sawfishes**) poisson-scie *m*

sawhorse /ˈsɔːhɔːs/ N chevalet *m* de scieur de bois

sawmill /ˈsɔːmɪl/ N scierie *f*

sawn /sɔːn/ VB ptp of **saw¹** ADJ scié ◆ **~ timber** bois *m* de sciage COMP **sawn-off shotgun** N *(Brit)* carabine *f* à canon scié

sawyer /ˈsɔːjəʳ/ N scieur *m*

sax * /sæks/ N (abbrev of **saxophone**) saxo * *m*

saxhorn /ˈsækshɔːn/ N saxhorn *m*

saxifrage /ˈsæksɪfrɪdʒ/ N saxifrage *f*

Saxon /ˈsæksn/ ADJ saxon N 1 *(= person)* Saxon(ne) *m(f)* 2 *(= language)* saxon *m*

Saxony /ˈsæksənɪ/ N Saxe *f*

saxophone /ˈsæksəfəʊn/ N saxophone *m*

saxophonist /ˌsækˈsɒfənɪst/ N saxophoniste *mf*, saxo * *m*

say /seɪ/ LANGUAGE IN USE 6.2, 26.1, 26.2 (pret, ptp **said**)

VT 1 *(= speak, utter, pronounce)* dire *(sth to sb* qch à qn ; *about* au sujet de, à propos de) ; *[+ lesson, poem]* réciter ; *[+ prayer]* faire, dire ◆ **to ~ mass** *(Rel)* dire la messe ◆ **as I said yesterday** comme je l'ai dit hier ◆ **as I said in my letter/on the phone** comme je vous l'ai (*or* le lui ai *etc*) dit dans ma lettre/au téléphone ◆ **the Prime Minister said that ...** le Premier ministre a dit *or* a déclaré que ... ◆ **well said!** bien dit ! ◆ **something was said about it** on en a parlé, il en a été question ◆ **all of that can be said in two sentences** tout cela tient en deux phrases ◆ **~ after me ...** répétez après moi ... ◆ **so ~ing, he sat down** sur ces mots *or* sur ce, il s'assit ◆ **to ~ one's piece** dire ce qu'on a à dire ◆ **it's easier** *or* **sooner said than done!** c'est plus facile à dire qu'à faire !, facile à dire ! ◆ **though I ~ it myself ..., though I ~s‡ it as shouldn't ...** ce n'est pas à moi de dire ça mais ... ; → **least, less, nothing, word**

◆ **not to say ...** ◆ **interesting, not to ~ encouraging** intéressant, pour ne pas dire encourageant ◆ **that's not to ~ that our relationship can't improve** cela ne veut pas dire que nos relations ne peuvent pas s'améliorer

◆ **to say sth again** redire qch ◆ **could you ~ that again?** pourriez-vous répéter (ce que vous venez de dire) ? ◆ **~ again?** * pardon ? ◆ **you can ~ that again!** * c'est le cas de le dire !

◆ **... to say for oneself** ◆ **she hasn't much to ~ for herself** elle n'a jamais grand-chose à dire ◆ **he always has a lot to ~ for himself** il parle toujours beaucoup, il a toujours quelque chose à dire ◆ **what have you (got) to ~ for yourself?** * qu'est-ce que tu as comme excuse ?

◆ **to say yes/no** dire oui/non ◆ **he ~s yes to everything** il dit oui à tout ◆ **to ~ yes/no to an invitation** accepter/refuser une invitation ◆ **your father said no** *(= said it wasn't/didn't etc)* ton père a dit que non ; *(= refused)* ton père a dit non *or* a refusé ◆ **I invited him but he said no** je l'ai invité (à venir) mais il a refusé ◆ **he just can't ~ no** il ne sait pas dire non ◆ **I wouldn't ~ no!** je ne dirais pas non !

◆ **when all is said and done** tout compte fait, au bout du compte

2 *(direct speech)* **"yes" she said** "oui" dit-elle ◆ **"10 o'clock" he said to himself** "10 heures" se dit-il

3 (= *state*) dire ◆ **it ~s in the rules (that), the rules ~ (that)** il est dit dans le règlement (que) ◆ **it ~s on the radio there's going to be snow** la radio annonce de la neige ◆ **it ~s here that you need a password** c'est écrit ici qu'on a besoin d'un mot de passe ◆ **it is said that ...** on dit que ... ◆ **he is said to be seriously ill** on dit qu'il est gravement malade

4 (= *claim*) dire, prétendre ◆ **he got home at 6 so he ~s** il est rentré à 6 heures à ce qu'il dit *or* prétend ◆ **that's what you ~!, so you ~!** (*expressing doubt*) c'est ce que vous dites !, c'est vous qui le dites !

5 (*giving instructions*) dire ◆ **he said to wait here** il a dit d'attendre ici ◆ **he said I was to give you this** il m'a dit de vous donner ceci

6 (*expressing opinions, estimating*) dire ◆ **what will people ~?** qu'est-ce que les gens vont dire ? ◆ **he doesn't care what people ~** il se moque du qu'en-dira-t-on ◆ **you might as well ~ the earth is flat!** autant dire que la terre est plate ! ◆ **I ~ he should do it** je suis d'avis qu'il le fasse ◆ **I can't ~ I'm fond of anchovies** je ne peux pas dire que j'aime *subj* les anchois ◆ **to see him you would ~ he was ill** à le voir on dirait qu'il est malade ◆ **what would you ~ is the population of Paris?** à votre avis *or* d'après vous, combien y a-t-il d'habitants à Paris ? ◆ **I would ~ she's intelligent** je dirais qu'elle est intelligente ◆ **I would ~ she was 50** je dirais qu'elle a 50 ans, je lui donnerais 50 ans ◆ **would you really ~ so?** (le pensez-vous) vraiment ? ◆ **I'll ~ this** *or* **I'll ~ one thing for him, he's clever** je dirai ceci en sa faveur, il est intelligent ◆ **~ what you like** *or* **will (about him), he's not a bad guy** * tu peux dire ce que tu veux (de lui), ce n'est pas un mauvais bougre*

◆ **say + much/a lot** ◆ **that doesn't ~ much for him** ce n'est pas à son honneur ◆ **that doesn't ~ much for his intelligence** cela en dit long (*iro*) sur son intelligence ◆ **it ~s much** *or* **a lot for his courage that he stayed** le fait qu'il soit resté en dit long sur son courage ◆ **his clothes ~ a lot about him** ses vêtements en disent long sur lui *or* sa personnalité ◆ **that's ~ing a lot*** ce n'est pas peu dire ◆ **he's cleverer than his brother but that isn't ~ing much** *or* **a lot*** il est plus intelligent que son frère, mais ça ne veut rien dire

◆ **something to be said for ...** ◆ **there's something to be said for it** cela a du bon *or* des avantages ◆ **there's something to be said for being obstinate** cela peut avoir du bon *or* des avantages d'être têtu ◆ **he stuck to what he believes in and there's something to be said for that** il est resté fidèle à ses convictions et on ne peut pas lui en vouloir ◆ **there's something to be said for waiting** il y aurait peut-être intérêt à attendre, on ferait peut-être mieux d'attendre

7 (= *imagine*) imaginer ◆ **~ someone left you a fortune, what would you do with it?** imaginons que vous héritiez d'une fortune, qu'en feriez-vous ? ◆ **(let's) ~ for argument's sake that ...** mettons à titre d'exemple que ... ; see also **vt 6** ◆ **there's no ~ing what he'll do next** (il est) impossible de dire *or* on ne peut pas savoir ce qu'il va faire ensuite

8 (= *admit*) dire, reconnaître ◆ **I must ~ (that) she's very pretty** je dois dire *or* reconnaître qu'elle est très jolie

9 (*proposals*) ◆ **shall we ~ £5/Tuesday ?** disons *or* mettons 5 livres/mardi ? ◆ **what do you ~ to a cup of tea?** que diriez-vous d'une tasse de thé ? ◆ **what would you ~ to a round of golf?** si on faisait une partie de golf ? ◆ **what (do you) ~ we have some lunch?** que dirais-tu de déjeuner ? ◆ **what do you ~?*** qu'en dis-tu ?

10 (= *register*) [*dial, gauge*] marquer, indiquer ◆ **my watch ~s 10 o'clock** ma montre marque *or* indique 10 heures ◆ **the thermometer ~s 30°** le thermomètre marque *or* indique 30°

11 (*emphatic*) ◆ **you('ve) said it !*** tu l'as dit !* ◆ **don't ~ it's broken!*** ne me dis pas que c'est cassé ! ◆ **enough said!*, 'nuff said!*** (ça) suffit !, assez parlé ! ◆ **~ no more** (= *I understand*) ça va, j'ai compris ◆ **let's ~ no more about it!** n'en parlons plus ! ◆ **it goes without ~ing that ...** il va sans dire que ..., il va de soi que ... ◆ **is he right? – I should ~ he is** *or* **I should ~ so** (*expressing certainty*) est-ce qu'il a raison ? – et comment *or* pour avoir raison il a raison ! ; (*expressing doubt*) est-ce qu'il a raison ? – il me semble *or* je pense que oui ◆ **didn't I ~ so?** je l'avais bien dit, n'est-ce pas ? ◆ **and so ~ all of us!** * nous sommes tous d'accord là-dessus ◆ **I should ~ he is right!** il a bien raison, c'est moi qui vous le dis ! ; → **goodbye, nothing, thank**

VI dire ◆ **so to ~** pour ainsi dire ◆ **that is to ~** c'est-à-dire ◆ **it is (as) one** *or* **you might ~ a new method** c'est comme qui dirait* une nouvelle méthode ◆ **(I) ~!*** dites donc ! ◆ **you don't ~!*** (*iro*) sans blague !* (*iro*), pas possible ! (*iro*) ◆ **~*, what time is it?** (*US*) dites, quelle heure est-il ? ◆ **if there were, ~, 500 people** s'il y avait, mettons *or* disons, 500 personnes ◆ **~s you!** (*, *iro*) que tu dis !* ◆ **~s who?*** ah oui ? (*iro*) ◆ **as they ~** comme on dit, comme dirait l'autre* ◆ **it seems rather rude, I must ~** cela ne me paraît guère poli, je l'avoue ◆ **well, I must ~!** (*expressing indignation*) ça alors !* ◆ **I'll ~!** † ça, c'est sûr ! ◆ **it's not for me to ~** (= *not my responsibility*) ce n'est pas à moi de décider *or* de juger ; (= *not my place*) ce n'est pas à moi de le dire

N ◆ **to have a** *or* **one's ~** (= *say one's piece*) dire ce qu'on a à dire ◆ **to have a ~/no ~ in the matter** avoir/ne pas avoir voix au chapitre, avoir/ne pas avoir son mot à dire ◆ **let him have his ~!** laissez-le s'exprimer ! ◆ **I will have my ~!** je dirai ce que j'ai à dire ! ◆ **to have a ~ in selecting ...** avoir son mot à dire dans la sélection de ... ◆ **to have the final ~** être celui qui décide *or* qui prend les décisions ◆ **to have a strong ~ in sth** jouer un rôle déterminant dans qch

COMP **say-so*** **N** ◆ **on your ~-so** parce que vous le dites (*or* l'aviez dit *etc*) ◆ **on his ~-so** parce qu'il le dit (*or* l'a dit *etc*), sur ses dires ◆ **it's his ~-so** c'est lui qui décide, c'est à lui de dire

saying /'seɪɪŋ/ **N** dicton *m* ◆ **as the ~ goes** comme dit le proverbe, comme on dit ◆ **~s of the week** les mots *mpl* *or* les citations *fpl* de la semaine

SBU /ˌesbiːˈjuː/ **N** (abbrev of **strategic business unit**) → **strategic**

SC abbrev of **South Carolina**

s/c (abbrev of **self-contained**) → **self**

scab /skæb/ **N** 1 [*of wound*] croûte *f*, escarre *f* 2 (* *pej* = *strikebreaker*) jaune *m* (*pej*), briseur *m* de grève **VI** 1 (also **scab over**) se cicatriser, former une croûte 2 (* *pej* = *strikebreaker*) refuser de faire grève, faire le jaune

scabbard /'skæbəd/ **N** [*of dagger*] gaine *f* ; [*of sword*] fourreau *m*

scabby /'skæbɪ/ **ADJ** 1 (= *covered with scabs*) [*knees, hands, skin*] couvert de croûtes 2 (= *having scabies*) [*person, animal*] galeux, scabieux (*Med*) 3 (*Brit* * = *despicable*) [*person*] minable* ; [*behaviour*] dégueulasse*

scabies /'skeɪbiːz/ **N** (*NonC: Med*) gale *f*

scabious¹ /'skeɪbɪəs/ **ADJ** (= *having scabies*) scabieux

scabious² /'skeɪbɪəs/ **N** (=*plant*) scabieuse *f*

scabrous /'skeɪbrəs/ **ADJ** 1 [*question, topic*] scabreux, risqué 2 (= *scaly*) rugueux

scads* /skædz/ **NPL** ◆ **~ of** beaucoup de, plein* de

scaffold /'skæfəld/ **N** 1 (= *gallows*) échafaud *m* 2 (*Constr*) échafaudage *m*

scaffolding /'skæfəldɪŋ/ **N** (*NonC*) (= *structure*) échafaudage *m* ; (= *material*) matériel *m* pour échafaudages

scag* /skæg/ **N** (*Drugs*) héro* *f*

scalable* /'skeɪləbl/ **ADJ** (*network, technology, computing*) modulable ◆ **~ font** police à taille variable

scalawag* /'skæləwæg/ **N** (*US*) ⇒ **scallywag**

scald /skɔːld/ **VT** [+ *jar, teapot, tomatoes*] ébouillanter ; (= *sterilize*) stériliser ◆ **to ~ one's hand** s'ébouillanter la main ◆ **to ~ o.s.** s'ébouillanter ◆ **to ~ the milk** (*Culin*) chauffer le lait sans le faire bouillir ◆ **to run off** *or* **set off like a ~ed cat** (*Brit*) filer comme un zèbre, prendre ses jambes à son cou **N** brûlure *f* (*causée par un liquide bouillant*)

scalding /'skɔːldɪŋ/ **ADJ** 1 (= *hot*) [*water, steam, coffee, sun, tears*] brûlant ; [*heat*] torride ◆ **a bath of ~ water** un bain brûlant ◆ **I have a ~ pain when urinating** j'ai une sensation de brûlure quand j'urine 2 (= *severe*) [*criticism*] virulent **ADV** ◆ **~ hot** [*water, coffee, sun*] brûlant ; [*weather*] terriblement chaud ◆ **it is ~ hot today** il fait terriblement chaud aujourd'hui, il fait une chaleur torride aujourd'hui

scale¹ /skeɪl/ **N** 1 [*of thermometer, ruler*] graduation *f*, échelle *f* (graduée) ; [*of numbers*] série *f* ; [*of wages*] barème *m*, grille *f* ◆ **~ of charges** liste *f* des tarifs ◆ **social ~** échelle *f* sociale ; → **centigrade, Fahrenheit, sliding**

2 [*of map, drawing*] échelle *f* ◆ **(drawn** *or* **true) to ~** à l'échelle ◆ **drawn to a ~ of ...** rapporté à l'échelle de ... ◆ **on a ~ of 1cm to 5km** à une échelle de 1 cm pour 5 km ◆ **this map is not to ~** les distances ne sont pas respectées sur cette carte

3 (= *scope*) échelle *f* ; (= *size etc*) importance *f*, ampleur *f* ◆ **on a large/small ~** sur une grande/petite échelle ◆ **on a national ~** à l'échelle nationale, à l'échelon national ◆ **a disaster of** *or* **on this ~** une catastrophe de cette importance *or* de cette ampleur ◆ **the ~ and intensity of the fighting** l'ampleur *f* et l'intensité *f* des combats ◆ **grand in ~** [*plans, programme*] à grande échelle, de grande envergure

4 (*Mus*) gamme *f* ◆ **the ~ of C** la gamme de do ◆ **to practise one's ~s** faire ses gammes

VT 1 (= *climb*) [+ *wall, mountain*] escalader

2 [+ *map*] dessiner à l'échelle

COMP **scale drawing** **N** dessin *m* à l'échelle

scale model **N** modèle *m* réduit ; → **full-scale**

► **scale back** **VT SEP** (*US*) ⇒ **scale down**

► **scale down** **VT SEP** (*gen*) réduire ; [+ *salary*] (*Scol*) [+ *marks*] réduire proportionnellement ; [+ *drawing*] réduire l'échelle de ; [+ *production*] réduire, baisser

► **scale up** **VT SEP** augmenter proportionnellement

scale² /skeɪl/ **N** → **scales** **VTI** peser

COMP **scale maker** **N** fabricant *m* de balances

scale pan **N** plateau *m* de balance

scale³ /skeɪl/ **N** 1 [*of fish, reptile, rust*] écaille *f* ; [*of skin*] squame *f* ◆ **metal ~** écaille *f* métallique ◆ **the ~s fell from his eyes** les écailles lui sont tombées des yeux 2 (*NonC, of water pipes, kettle*) tartre *m*, dépôt *m* calcaire ; (*of teeth*) tartre *m* **VT** 1 [+ *fish*] écailler 2 [+ *teeth, kettle*] détartrer

► **scale off** **VI** s'en aller en écailles, s'écailler

scales /skeɪlz/ **NPL** (*for weighing, gen: in kitchen, shop*) balance *f* ; (*in bathroom*) pèse-personne *m inv*, balance *f* ; (*for babies*) pèse-bébé *m inv* ; (*for luggage, heavy goods*) bascule *f* ; (*for letters*) pèse-lettre *m inv* ; (*manual, with weight on a rod*) balance *f* romaine ◆ **kitchen** *or* **household ~** balance *f* de ménage ◆ **pair of ~** balance *f* (à plateaux) ◆ **the Scales** (*Astrol, Astron*) la Balance ◆ **to turn the ~ at 80 kilos** peser 80 kilos ◆ **to tip the ~ (in sb's favour/against sb)** faire pencher la balance (en faveur/défaveur de qn) ; → **platform**

scallion /'skæljən/ N *(gen)* oignon *m* ; *(US = shallot)* échalote *f* ; *(US = leek)* poireau *m*

scallop /'skɒləp/ N 1 coquille *f* Saint-Jacques, pétoncle *m* 2 *(Sewing)* **~s** festons *mpl* VT 1 ◆ **~ed fish/lobster** coquille *f* de poisson/de homard 2 *[+ hem etc]* festonner ◆ **~ed edge** *(Sewing)* bordure *f* festonnée *or* à festons ; *(Culin)* ◆ **to ~ (the edges of) a pie** canneler le bord d'une tourte COMP **scallop shell** N coquille *f*

scallywag * /'skælɪwæg/ N 1 *(= rascal)* petit(e) polisson(ne) *m(f)* 2 *(US Hist pej) Sudiste républicain favorable à l'émancipation des Noirs et considéré comme traître par les autres Sudistes*

scalp /skælp/ N cuir *m* chevelu ; *(= trophy)* scalp *m* VT 1 *[+ person]* scalper 2 *(US *)* *[+ tickets]* revendre *(au marché noir)* VI *(Stock Exchange *)* boursicoter

scalpel /'skælpəl/ N *(Med)* scalpel *m* ; *(for paper etc)* cutter *m*

scalper * /'skælpə^r/ N 1 *(Stock Exchange)* spéculateur *m* sur la journée 2 *(= ticket tout)* vendeur *m*, -euse *f* de billets à la sauvette

scaly /'skeɪlɪ/ ADJ 1 *(= covered in scales) [creature, body]* écailleux, couvert d'écailles 2 *(= peeling) [skin]* qui pèle, qui se desquame *(Med)*, squameux *(Med)* ; *[paint]* écaillé, qui s'écaille 3 *(= having limescale deposits) [kettle, pipe]* entartré

scam * /skæm/ N arnaque‡ *f*, escroquerie *f* VI faire de la gratte * *or* des bénefs‡

scamp[1] * /skæmp/ N *(= child)* polisson(ne) *m(f)*, galopin * *m* ; *(= adult)* coquin(e) *m(f)*

scamp[2] /skæmp/ VT *[+ one's work etc]* bâcler *

scamper /'skæmpə^r/ N galopade *f* ; *[of mice]* trottinement *m* VI *[children]* galoper ; *[mice]* trottiner ◆ **to ~ in/out** *etc [children]* entrer/sortir *etc* en gambadant

► **scamper about** VI *[children]* gambader ; *[mice]* trottiner çà et là

► **scamper away, scamper off** VI *[children, mice]* s'enfuir, détaler *

scampi /'skæmpɪ/ NPL langoustines *fpl* (frites), scampi *mpl*

scan /skæn/ VT 1 *(= examine closely) [+ horizon, sb's face]* scruter ; *[+ crowd]* scruter du regard ; *[+ newspaper]* lire attentivement *(for sth* pour y trouver qch) 2 *(= glance quickly over) [+ horizon]* promener son regard sur ; *[+ crowd]* parcourir des yeux ; *[+ newspaper]* parcourir rapidement, feuilleter 3 *(Comput)* scruter 4 *(TV, Radar)* balayer ; *(Med) [machine]* balayer ; *[person]* faire une scanographie de 5 *(Poetry)* scander VI se scander ◆ **this line does not ~** ce vers est faux N 1 *(Rad, TV)* balayage *m* 2 *(Med) (= scanning)* scanographie *f*, tomodensitométrie *f* ; *(= picture)* scanner *m*, scanographie *f* ◆ **(ultrasound) ~** *(Med)* échographie *f* ◆ **to have a ~** passer un scanner ; *(ultra-sound)* passer une échographie

scandal /'skændl/ N 1 *(= disgrace)* scandale *m* ; *(Jur)* diffamation *f* ◆ **we can't afford another ~** nous ne pouvons pas nous permettre d'être impliqués dans un nouveau scandale ◆ **to cause a ~** causer un scandale ◆ **the Webb ~** le scandale Webb ◆ **a financial ~** un scandale financier ◆ **it's a (real) ~** c'est scandaleux, c'est une honte ◆ **it's a ~ that ...** c'est un scandale *or* une honte que ... + *subj* 2 *(NonC = gossip)* cancans *mpl*, ragots * *mpl* ◆ **there's a lot of ~ going around about him** il y a beaucoup de ragots * qui circulent sur son compte COMP **scandal sheet** * N *(pej)* journal *m* à scandale

scandalize /'skændəlaɪz/ VT scandaliser, indigner ◆ **I was ~d by their behaviour** j'ai été scandalisé par leur comportement

scandalmonger /'skændl,mʌŋgə^r/ N mauvaise langue *f*, colporteur *m*, -euse *f* de ragots * ; *(US Press)* torchon * *m*

scandalous /'skændələs/ ADJ scandaleux ◆ **it's ~ that ...** c'est un scandale *or* une honte que ... + *subj*, c'est scandaleux que ... + *subj* ◆ **I think it's a ~ price to charge (for)** je trouve scandaleux qu'on demande ce prix-là (pour)

scandalously /'skændələslɪ/ ADV *[behave]* de façon scandaleuse ; *[expensive, rich, poor]* scandaleusement

Scandinavia /,skændɪ'neɪvɪə/ N Scandinavie *f*

Scandinavian /,skændɪ'neɪvɪən/ ADJ scandinave N Scandinave *mf*

scandium /'skændɪəm/ N scandium *m*

scanner /'skænə^r/ N 1 *(Med)* (also **CAT scanner**) scanner *m*, tomodensitomètre *m* ; (also **ultrasound scanner**) échographe *m* 2 *(Rad, Telec)* scanner *m* 3 *(Radar)* antenne *f* 4 *(Comput)* (also **optical scanner**) scanner *or* scanneur *m*

scanning /'skænɪŋ/ N *(electronic)* balayage *m* ; *(Med) (by ultrasound)* échographie *f* COMP **scanning device** N *(Telec)* organe *m* explorateur ; *(Med)* dispositif *m* de scanographie **scanning electron microscope** N microscope *m* électronique à balayage

scansion /'skænʃən/ N scansion *f*

scant /skænt/ ADJ 1 *(= insufficient) [reward]* (bien) maigre ; *[information]* (bien *or* très) insuffisant ◆ **to pay ~ attention to sth** ne guère prêter attention à qch ◆ **there is ~ evidence of the success they talk about** il n'y a guère de preuves du succès dont ils parlent ◆ **to receive ~ praise (from sb) (for sth)** recevoir des éloges parcimonieux (de qn) (pour qch) ◆ **to have ~ regard for sth** peu se soucier de qch ◆ **to show ~ respect for sth** ne pas manifester beaucoup de respect pour qch 2 *(= bare)* ◆ **it measures a ~ 2cm** ça fait à peine 2 cm ◆ **a ~ two months later** à peine deux mois plus tard

scantily /'skæntɪlɪ/ ADV *[furnished]* chichement ◆ **~ clad** *or* **dressed** en tenue légère ◆ **~ clad in a light cotton blouse** légèrement vêtu d'un fin chemisier de coton ◆ **a ~ cut blouse** un chemisier très échancré

scantiness /'skæntɪnɪs/ N *(= insufficiency)* insuffisance *f*

scanty /'skæntɪ/ ADJ *[information]* maigre, sommaire ; *[evidence]* maigre ; *[news]* sommaire ; *[knowledge]* limité, sommaire ; *[swimsuit]* minuscule ; *[blouse]* échancré ◆ **a ~ income** de maigres revenus

scapegoat /'skeɪpgəʊt/ N bouc *m* émissaire VT ◆ **to ~ sb** faire de qn un bouc émissaire

scapegrace /'skeɪpgreɪs/ N coquin(e) *m(f)*, vaurien(ne) *m(f)*

scapula /'skæpjʊlə/ N (pl **scapulas** *or* **scapulae** /'skæpjʊli:/) omoplate *f*

scapular /'skæpjʊlə^r/ ADJ, N scapulaire *m*

scar[1] /skɑ:^r/ N *(= mark: lit, fig)* cicatrice *f* ; *(from knife wound, esp on face)* balafre *f* ◆ **the quarrying left a ~ on the hillside** l'exploitation de la carrière a laissé une cicatrice sur *or* a mutilé le flanc de la colline ◆ **emotional ~s** cicatrices *fpl* psychologiques ◆ **the ~s of war** les cicatrices *fpl* de la guerre VT marquer d'une cicatrice ; *(with knife)* balafrer ◆ **his face was ~red by smallpox** son visage était grêlé par la petite vérole ◆ **war-~red town** ville qui porte des cicatrices de la guerre ◆ **walls ~red by bullets** des murs portant des traces de balles ◆ **this is something that's going to ~ him forever** *(fig)* c'est quelque chose qui va le marquer profondément ◆ **she was ~red by the death of her parents** elle avait été profondément marquée par la mort de ses parents COMP **scar tissue** N tissus *mpl* cicatrisés

scar[2] /skɑ:^r/ N *(= crag)* rocher *m* escarpé

scarab /'skærəb/ N *(= beetle, gem)* scarabée *m*

scarce /skεəs/ ADJ *[food, water, money]* peu abondant, rare ; *[people, jobs]* rare, peu nombreux ; *[goods]* rare ; *[resources]* limité ◆ **to become** *or* **get ~** commencer à manquer, se faire rare ◆ **to make o.s. ~** * *(= leave)* s'éclipser * ADV † ⇒ **scarcely**

scarcely /'skεəslɪ/ ADV à peine ◆ **they could ~ have imagined that ...** ils auraient à peine pu imaginer que ..., ils n'auraient guère pu imaginer que ... ◆ **the landscape has ~ altered** le paysage a à peine changé *or* n'a presque pas changé ◆ **I could ~ believe it** je pouvais à peine le croire ◆ **I ~ know what to say** je ne sais trop que dire ◆ **they were ~ ever apart** ils étaient presque toujours ensemble ◆ **he was ~ more than a boy** il sortait à peine *or* tout juste de l'enfance ◆ **it is ~ surprising that ...** il n'est guère surprenant que ... ◆ **with ~ a sound** pratiquement *or* presque sans faire de bruit ◆ **there was ~ a ripple on the sea** il n'y avait pratiquement aucune ride sur la mer ◆ **there was ~ a building left undamaged** il ne restait pratiquement aucun bâtiment intact ◆ **it could ~ have been a less promising start** ça aurait difficilement pu commencer plus mal ◆ **the press is ~ an advertisement for self-restraint** on ne peut guère dire que la presse soit un modèle de retenue ◆ **~ had the car stopped when the police surrounded it** à peine la voiture s'était-elle arrêtée que les policiers l'encerclèrent

scarceness /'skεəsnɪs/ N ⇒ **scarcity**

scarcity /'skεəsɪtɪ/ N *[of product, foodstuff]* rareté *f*, pénurie *f* ; *[of money]* manque *m* ◆ **there is a ~ of good artists today** il n'y a plus guère de bons artistes COMP **scarcity value** N valeur *f* de rareté

scare /skεə^r/ N 1 *(* = fright)* ◆ **to give sb a ~** faire peur à qn, ficher la frousse à qn * ◆ **what a ~ he gave me!** il m'a fait une de ces peurs *or* frousses ! *
2 *(= rumour)* bruit *m* alarmant *or* alarmiste ◆ **to raise a ~** semer la panique, faire courir des bruits alarmants ◆ **the invasion ~** les bruits *mpl* alarmistes d'invasion ◆ **bomb/gas/typhoid ~** alerte *f* à la bombe/au gaz/à la typhoïde ◆ **food ~** alerte *f* à l'intoxication alimentaire ◆ **health ~** alerte *f* aux risques sanitaires ◆ **because of the war ~** à cause des rumeurs de guerre
VT effrayer, faire peur à ◆ **to ~ sb stiff** * *or* **out of their wits** * faire une peur bleue à qn, ficher la frousse * *or* la trouille * à qn ◆ **to ~ the life** *or* **wits out of sb** * faire une peur bleue à qn, ficher la frousse * *or* la trouille * à qn ; see also **scared** ; → **hell, shit**
VI s'effrayer ◆ **to ~ easily** avoir peur d'un rien
COMP *[headlines]* alarmiste **scare story** N rumeur *f* alarmiste

► **scare away, scare off** VT SEP ◆ **the dog/the price scared him away** le chien/le prix l'a fait fuir

► **scare up** * VT SEP *(US) [+ food, money]* arriver à trouver

scarecrow /'skεəkrəʊ/ N *(lit, fig)* épouvantail *m*

scared /skεəd/ ADJ effrayé ◆ **he was terribly ~** il était terrifié *or* épouvanté ◆ **to be running ~** * avoir la frousse * ◆ **to be ~ (of sb/sth)** avoir peur (de qn/qch) ◆ **to be ~ of doing sth** *or* **to do sth** avoir peur de faire qch ◆ **too ~ to move** trop effrayé pour bouger ◆ **to be ~ that ...** avoir peur que ... + *subj* ◆ **I'm ~ that he'll try to find me** j'ai peur qu'il n'essaie *subj* de me trouver ◆ **to be ~ to death** * être mort de frousse * *or* trouille * ◆ **he's ~ to death of women** * il a une peur bleue des femmes ◆ **to be ~ out of one's wits** * avoir une peur bleue ; → **stiff**

scaredy* /'skɛədɪ/ N *(baby talk)* ◆ ~ **(cat)** trouillard(e)* *m(f)*, poule *f* mouillée*

scarehead* /'skɛəhed/ N *(US Press)* manchette *f* à sensation

scaremonger /'skɛə,mʌŋgəʳ/ N alarmiste *mf*, oiseau *m* de malheur

scaremongering /'skɛə,mʌŋgərɪŋ/ N alarmisme *m*

scarf[1] /skɑːf/ N (pl **scarfs** *or* **scarves**) écharpe *f* ; *(square)* foulard *m* COMP **scarf-ring** N coulant *m* *or* anneau *m* pour foulard ; → **headscarf**

scarf[2]* /skɑːf/ VT (US: also **scarf down**) engloutir, s'enfiler*

Scarface /'skɑːfeɪs/ N le Balafré

scarify /'skɛərɪfaɪ/ VT *(Agr, Med)* scarifier ; *(fig)* éreinter

scarlatina /,skɑːlə'tiːnə/ N scarlatine *f*

scarlet /'skɑːlɪt/ ADJ écarlate ◆ **to go** *or* **blush ~ (with shame/embarrassment)** devenir écarlate *or* cramoisi (de honte/de gêne) N écarlate *f* COMP **scarlet fever** N scarlatine *f*
scarlet pimpernel N mouron *m*
scarlet runner (bean) N haricot *m* grimpant
scarlet woman † N (pl **scarlet women**) *(pej)* femme *f* de mauvaise vie

scarp /skɑːp/ N escarpement *m*

scarper* /'skɑːpəʳ/ VI *(Brit)* ficher le camp*

scarves /skɑːvz/ NPL of **scarf**

scary* /'skɛərɪ/ ADJ *[person, monster]* effrayant ; *[moment, feeling]* effrayant, angoissant ; *[experience]* effrayant, angoissant, qui fiche la frousse* ; *[movie]* qui donne le frisson *or* la chair de poule ◆ **that's a ~ thought** c'est une idée qui fait peur

scat[1]* /skæt/ EXCL allez ouste !*

scat[2] /skæt/ N *(Jazz)* scat *m* *(style d'improvisation vocale)*

scathing /'skeɪðɪŋ/ ADJ *[person, remark, criticism]* cinglant *(about* au sujet de) ◆ **to give sb a ~ look** jeter un regard plein de mépris à qn

scathingly /'skeɪðɪŋlɪ/ ADV *[say]* sur un ton cinglant ; *[write]* sur un ton cinglant, en termes cinglants ◆ **to look ~ at sb** jeter un regard plein de mépris à qn

scatological /,skætə'lɒdʒɪkəl/ ADJ scatologique

scatter /'skætəʳ/ VT 1 (also **scatter about, scatter around**) *[+ crumbs, papers, seeds]* éparpiller ; *[+ sand, salt, sawdust, nails]* répandre ◆ **to ~ sth to the four winds** semer qch aux quatre vents ◆ **to ~ cushions on a divan** jeter des coussins çà et là sur un divan
2 *[+ clouds, crowd]* disperser ; *[+ enemy]* mettre en déroute ; *[+ light]* diffuser ◆ **my relatives are ~ed all over the country** ma famille est dispersée aux quatre coins du pays
VI *[clouds, crowd]* se disperser ◆ **the robbers ~ed at the approach of the police** les voleurs se sont dispersés *or* enfuis dans toutes les directions à l'arrivée de la police
N *(Math, Tech)* dispersion *f* ◆ **a ~ of houses** des maisons dispersées *or* éparses ◆ **a ~ of raindrops** quelques gouttes de pluie éparses
COMP **scatter cushion** NPL petits coussin *m*
scatter-gun N fusil *m* de chasse ADJ *(fig)* *[approach]* tous azimuts*
scatter rugs NPL carpettes *fpl*

scatterbrain /'skætəbreɪn/ N écervelé(e) *m(f)*, hurluberlu* *m*

scatterbrained /'skætəbreɪnd/ ADJ écervelé, hurluberlu*

scattered /'skætəd/ ADJ 1 *(= dispersed)* *[books]* éparpillé ; *[buildings, trees]* dispersé, éparpillé ; *[population]* dispersé, disséminé ; *[light]* diffus ; *[riots]* sporadique, intermittent ◆ **~ fighting** combats *mpl* sporadiques *or* intermittents ◆ **the village is very ~** les maisons du village sont très dispersées 2 ◆ **~ with sth** *(= strewn with: gen)* parsemé de qch ; *[+ nails, flowers, corpses]* jonché de qch COMP **scattered showers** NPL averses *fpl* intermittentes *or* éparses

scattering /'skætərɪŋ/ N *[of clouds, crowd]* dispersion *f* ; *[of light]* diffusion *f* ◆ **there was a ~ of people in the hall** il y avait quelques personnes dispersées *or* çà et là dans la salle

scattershot /'skætəʃɒt/ ADJ ◆ **the money has been spent in (a) ~ fashion** l'argent a été dépensé à tort et à travers ◆ **he fielded the committee's ~ questions** il a répondu aux questions du comité, qui partaient dans tous les sens

scattiness* /'skætɪnɪs/ N *(NonC: Brit)* *[of person]* étourderie *f*

scatty* /'skætɪ/ ADJ *(Brit)* 1 *(= scatterbrained)* *[person]* étourdi ◆ **she's so ~!** quelle tête de linotte ! 2 *(= distracted)* ◆ **to drive sb ~** rendre qn zinzin* *inv*

scavenge /'skævɪndʒ/ VT *[+ streets]* enlever les ordures de ; *[+ object]* récupérer VI ◆ **to ~ in the dustbins (for sth)** faire les poubelles (pour trouver qch)

scavenger /'skævɪndʒəʳ/ N 1 *(= animal)* charognard *m* 2 *(= street cleaner)* éboueur *m* 3 *(= person: on rubbish dumps, in bins)* pilleur *m* de poubelles COMP **scavenger hunt** N chasse *f* au trésor, rallye *m*

SCE /,essiː'iː/ N (abbrev of **Scottish Certificate of Education**) *examen de fin d'études secondaires en Écosse*

scenario /sɪ'nɑːrɪəʊ/ N 1 *(Cine)* scénario *m* 2 *(= sequence of events)* scénario *m* ; *(= plan of action)* plan *m* d'action, stratégie *f* *(for* pour) ◆ **best-/worst-case ~** *(Mil, Pol etc)* meilleure/pire hypothèse *f* ◆ **in the worst-case ~** dans le pire des cas *or* la pire des hypothèses

scenarist /'siːnərɪst/ N scénariste *mf*

scene /siːn/ N 1 *(= part of play, film)* scène *f* ; *(= setting)* scène *f*, décor *m* ◆ **a bedroom ~** une scène de lit ◆ **the garden ~ in "Richard II"** la scène du jardin dans "Richard II" ◆ **the balcony ~ from "Romeo and Juliet"** la scène du balcon de "Roméo et Juliette" ◆ **outdoor** *or* **outside ~** *(Cine, TV)* extérieur *m* ◆ **~ from a film** scène *f* *or* séquence *f* (tirée) d'un film ◆ **the big ~ in the film** la grande scène du film ◆ **it was his big ~** c'était sa grande scène ◆ **the ~ is set in Paris** la scène se passe à Paris, l'action se déroule à Paris ◆ **the ~ was set for their romance** toutes les conditions étaient réunies pour leur idylle ◆ **this set the ~ for the discussion** ceci a préparé le terrain pour les discussions ◆ **now let our reporter set the ~ for you** notre reporter va maintenant vous mettre au courant de la situation
♦ **behind the scenes** *(Theat, fig)* dans les coulisses ◆ **to work behind the ~s** *(fig)* travailler dans l'ombre *or* dans les coulisses
2 *(= sight)* spectacle *m*, tableau *m* ; *(= view)* vue *f* ; *(fig)* scène *f* ; *(= happening)* incident *m* ◆ **the hills make a lovely ~** les collines offrent un très joli spectacle *or* tableau ◆ **the ~ spread out before you** la vue *or* le panorama qui s'offre à vous ◆ **picture the ~ ...** imaginez la scène ... ◆ **~s of violence** scènes *fpl* de violence ◆ **there were angry ~s at the meeting** des incidents violents ont eu lieu au cours de la réunion ◆ **it was a ~ of utter destruction/chaos/horror** c'était une scène de destruction totale/de chaos total/d'horreur totale ◆ **it's a bad ~*** *(fig)* c'est pas brillant*, la situation n'est pas brillante
3 *(= place)* lieu(x) *m(pl)*, endroit *m* ◆ **the ~ of the crime/accident** le lieu du crime/de l'accident ◆ **the town had once been the ~ of a great battle** la ville avait été jadis le théâtre d'une grande bataille ◆ **~ of operations** *(Mil)* théâtre *m* des opérations ◆ **he needs a change of ~** il a besoin de changer d'air *or* de décor ◆ **they were soon on the ~** ils furent vite sur les lieux ◆ **to appear** *or* **come on the ~** faire son apparition ◆ **when I came on the ~** quand je suis arrivé
4 *(* = fuss)* scène *f* ◆ **he made a ~** il a fait toute une histoire ◆ **to have a ~ with sb** avoir une scène avec qn ; see also **noun 6** ◆ **I hate ~s** je déteste les scènes
5 *(= sphere of activity)* scène *f*, monde *m* ◆ **the political ~** la scène politique ◆ **the (gay) ~** le milieu gay ◆ **"non-scene"** *(in personal ad)* "hors ghetto" ◆ **the jazz/pop/rave ~** le monde du jazz/de la pop/des raves ◆ **the drug(s) ~ in our big cities** le milieu de la drogue dans nos grandes villes ◆ **it's not my ~*** ce n'est pas mon truc*
6 *(sexually)* **to have a ~* with sb** avoir une liaison avec qn ; see also **noun 4**
COMP **scene change** N *(Theat)* changement *m* de décor(s)
scene painter N peintre *m* de décors
scene shift N changement *m* de décor(s)
scene shifter N machiniste *mf*

scenery /'siːnərɪ/ N 1 paysage *m* ◆ **mountain ~** paysage *m* de montagnes ◆ **a change of ~ will do you good** un changement d'air *or* de décor* vous fera du bien 2 *(Theat)* décor(s) *m(pl)*

scenic /'siːnɪk/ ADJ pittoresque ◆ **to take the ~ route** *(lit)* prendre l'itinéraire touristique ; *(fig hum)* prendre le chemin des écoliers*
COMP **scenic car** N *(esp US Rail)* voiture *f* panoramique
scenic design N *(Theat)* *(= sets)* décors *mpl* ; *(= profession)* conception *f* de décors
scenic designer N *(Theat)* décorateur *m*, -trice *f* de théâtre
scenic railway N *(= miniature railway)* petit train *m* (d'agrément) ; *(Brit)* *(= roller coaster)* montagnes *fpl* russes, scenic railway *m*

scenography /siː'nɒgrəfɪ/ N scénographie *f*

scent /sent/ N 1 *(= odour)* parfum *m*, senteur *f* *(liter)*
2 *(esp Brit = perfume)* parfum *m* ◆ **to use ~** se parfumer
3 *(= animal's track)* fumet *m* ; *(fig)* piste *f*, voie *f* ◆ **to lose the ~** *(Hunting, fig)* perdre la piste ◆ **to throw** *or* **put sb off the ~** faire perdre la piste à qn ◆ **to put** *or* **throw dogs off the ~** dépister les chiens, faire perdre la piste aux chiens ◆ **to be on the (right) ~** être sur la bonne piste *or* voie ◆ **he got the ~ of something suspicious** il a flairé quelque chose de louche
4 *(= sense of smell)* *[of person]* odorat *m* ; *[of animal]* flair *m*
VT 1 *(= put scent on)* *[+ handkerchief, air]* parfumer *(with* de)
2 *(= smell)* *[+ game]* flairer ; *[+ danger, trouble]* flairer, pressentir ◆ **to ~ blood** *(fig)* deviner une faille chez son adversaire
COMP **scent bottle** N *(esp Brit)* flacon *m* à parfum
scent spray N *(esp Brit)* vaporisateur *m* (à parfum) ; *(= aerosol)* atomiseur *m* (à parfum)

scented /'sentɪd/ ADJ parfumé

scentless /'sentlɪs/ ADJ inodore, sans odeur

scepter /'septəʳ/ N *(US)* ⇒ **sceptre**

sceptic, skeptic *(US)* /'skeptɪk/ ADJ, N sceptique *mf*

sceptical, skeptical *(US)* /'skeptɪkəl/ ADJ *[person, attitude]* sceptique *(about, of* sur) ◆ **to cast a ~ eye on** *or* **over sth** porter un regard sceptique sur qch ◆ **I'm ~ about it** cela me laisse sceptique ◆ **to be ~ about doing sth** douter qu'il soit bon de faire qch ◆ **to be ~ that** *or* **about whether ...** douter que ... + *subj* ◆ **they are ~ about how genuine his commitment is** ils ont des doutes sur la sincérité de son engagement

sceptically, skeptically (US) /ˈskeptɪkəlɪ/ ADV *[ask]* d'un ton sceptique, avec scepticisme ; *[look at]* d'un air sceptique, avec scepticisme ◆ **he raised his eyebrows** ~ il haussa les sourcils d'un air sceptique

scepticism, skepticism (US) /ˈskeptɪsɪzəm/ N scepticisme *m*

sceptre, scepter (US) /ˈseptəʳ/ N sceptre *m*

Schadenfreude /ˈʃɑːdən,frɔɪdə/ N joie *f* malsaine *(éprouvée face au malheur d'autrui)*

schedule /ˈʃedjuːl, (US) ˈskedjuːl/ N 1 *(= timetable) [of work, duties]* programme *m*, planning *m* ; *[of trains etc]* horaire *m* ; *[of events]* calendrier *m* ◆ **production/building** *etc* ~ calendrier *m or* planning *m* pour la production/la construction *etc* ◆ **to make out a** ~ établir un programme *or* un plan *or* un horaire ◆ **our** ~ **does not include the Louvre** notre programme ne comprend pas le Louvre ◆ **I've got a very hectic** ~ j'ai un emploi du temps très chargé

2 *(= forecasted timings)* ◆ **to be ahead of** ~ *(in work)* avoir de l'avance sur son programme ; *[train]* avoir de l'avance ◆ **the train is behind** ~ le train a du retard ◆ **the preparations are behind** ~ il y a du retard dans les préparatifs ◆ **our work has fallen behind** ~ nous sommes en retard dans notre travail ◆ **the train is on** ~ le train est à l'heure ◆ **the preparations are on** ~ il n'y a pas de retard dans les préparatifs ◆ **the work is on** ~ les travaux avancent conformément aux prévisions *or* au calendrier ◆ **the ceremony will take place on** ~ la cérémonie aura lieu à l'heure prévue *(or* à la date prévue *etc)* ◆ **the ceremony went off according to** ~ la cérémonie s'est déroulée comme prévu ◆ **it all went (off) according to** ~ tout s'est passé comme prévu ◆ **to work to a very tight** ~ avoir un programme très serré

3 *(= list) [of goods, contents]* liste *f*, inventaire *m* ; *[of prices]* barème *m*, tarif *m* ◆ ~ **of charges** liste *f or* barème *m* des prix

4 *(Jur: to contract)* annexe *f (to* à)

VT 1 *(gen pass) [+ activity]* programmer, prévoir ◆ **his ~d speech** le discours qu'il doit *(or* devait *etc)* prononcer ◆ **his ~d departure** son départ prévu ◆ **at the ~d time/date** *etc* à l'heure/à la date *etc* prévue *or* indiquée ◆ **~d price** prix *m* tarifé ◆ **as ~d** comme prévu ◆ **~d service** *[train, bus etc]* service régulier ◆ **~d flight** vol *m* régulier ◆ **this stop is not ~d** cet arrêt n'est pas prévu ◆ **he is ~d to leave at midday** son départ est fixé pour midi ◆ **you are ~d to speak after him** d'après le programme vous parlez après lui ◆ **the talks are ~d for this weekend** les pourparlers sont prévus *or* programmés pour ce week-end ◆ **the train is ~d for 11 o'clock** *or* **to arrive at 11 o'clock** (selon l'horaire) le train doit arriver à 11 heures, le train arrive normalement à 11 heures ◆ **the government has ~d elections for 5 January** le gouvernement a prévu des élections pour le 5 janvier, le gouvernement a fixé les élections au 5 janvier ◆ **~d territories** zone *f* sterling

2 *[+ object]* inscrire sur une liste ◆ **~d building** *(Brit)* bâtiment *m* classé *(comme monument historique)*

schema /ˈskiːmə/ N (pl **schemata** /skiːˈmɑːtə/) schéma *m*

schematic /skɪˈmætɪk/ ADJ schématique

schematically /skɪˈmætɪkəlɪ/ ADV schématiquement

scheme /skiːm/ N 1 *(= plan)* plan *m* ; *(= project)* projet *m* ; *(= method)* procédé *m (for doing sth* pour faire qch) ◆ **he's got a** ~ **for re-using plastic bottles** il a un projet *or* un procédé pour réutiliser les bouteilles en plastique ◆ **a** ~ **of work** un plan de travail ◆ **profit-sharing** ~ système *m* de participation (aux bénéfices) ◆ **pension** ~ régime *m* de retraite ◆ **a** ~ **for greater productivity** un plan destiné à augmenter la productivité ◆ **man's place in the** ~ **of things** le rôle de l'homme dans l'ordre des choses ◆ **where does he stand in the** ~ **of things?** où se situe-t-il dans tout cela ? ◆ **where does he stand in the great** *or* **grand** ~ **of things?** *(iro)* quelle place occupe-t-il dans le grand ordre de l'univers ? ◆ **in my/your** *etc* ~ **of things** dans ma/votre *etc* vision des choses ◆ **it's some crazy** ~ **of his** c'est une de ses idées invraisemblables ◆ **it's not a bad** ~ * ça n'est pas une mauvaise idée ; → **supplementary**

2 *(= plot)* complot *m*, machination(s) *f(pl)* ; *(= dishonest plan)* procédé *m* malhonnête, combine * *f* ◆ **it's a** ~ **to get him out of the way** c'est un complot pour l'éliminer

3 *(= arrangement)* arrangement *m*, combinaison *f* ; → **colour, rhyme**

VT combiner, machiner

VI *[group]* comploter, conspirer ; *[individual]* intriguer *(to do sth* pour faire qch)

schemer /ˈskiːməʳ/ N *(pej)* intrigant(e) *m(f)*

scheming /ˈskiːmɪŋ/ ADJ *(pej) [person]* intrigant N machinations *fpl*, intrigues *fpl*

scherzo /ˈskɜːtsəʊ/ N (pl **scherzos** *or* **scherzi** /ˈskɜːtsiː/) scherzo *m*

schilling /ˈʃɪlɪŋ/ N schilling *m*

schism /ˈsɪzəm/ N schisme *m*

schismatic /sɪzˈmætɪk/ ADJ, N schismatique *mf*

schist /ʃɪst/ N schiste *m* cristallin

schistosomiasis /ˌʃɪstəsəʊˈmaɪəsɪs/ N schistosomiase *f*, bilharziose *f*

schizo ‡ /ˈskɪtsəʊ/ ADJ, N (abbrev of **schizophrenic**) schizo ‡ *mf*

schizoid /ˈskɪtsɔɪd/ ADJ, N schizoïde *mf*

schizophrenia /ˌskɪtsəʊˈfriːnɪə/ N schizophrénie *f*

schizophrenic /ˌskɪtsəʊˈfrenɪk/ ADJ, N schizophrène *mf*

schlemiel ‡, **schlemihl** ‡ /ʃləˈmiːl/ N (US) pauvre bougre * *m*, minable *mf*

schlep(p) ‡ /ʃlep/ (US) VI se traîner, crapahuter ‡ VT trimballer *, (se) coltiner *

schlock ‡ /ʃlɒk/ N pacotille *f* ADJ de pacotille

schlong *‡ /ʃlɒŋ/ N (US) bite *‡ *f*

schmaltz * /ʃmɔːlts/ N (NonC) sentimentalisme *m* excessif

schmaltzy * /ˈʃmɔːltsɪ/ ADJ à la guimauve, à l'eau de rose

schmear * /ʃmɪəʳ/ N (US) ◆ **the whole** ~ tout le bataclan *

schmo /ʃməʊ/ N (pl **schmoes**) (US) ballot * *m*, andouille * *f*

schmooze * /ʃmuːz/ VI (US) *(= gossip)* jaser * ; *(= bootlick)* faire de la lèche ‡

schmuck ‡ /ʃmʌk/ N (US) con ‡ *m*, connard ‡ *m*, connasse ‡ *f*

schmutter * /ˈʃmʌtəʳ/ N *(= cloth)* textile *m* ; *(= clothing)* vêtement *m*

schnapps /ʃnæps/ N schnaps *m*

schnook /ʃnʊk/ N (US) ballot * *m*, pauvre type * *m*

schnorkel /ˈʃnɔːkl/ N ⇒ **snorkel**

schnorrer ‡ /ˈʃnɔːrəʳ/ N (US) mendigot *m*, tapeur * *m*

schnozzle ‡ /ˈʃnɒzl/ N (US) gros pif * *m*, tarin * *m*

scholar /ˈskɒləʳ/ N 1 lettré(e) *m(f)*, érudit(e) *m(f)* ◆ **a** ~ **and a gentleman** un homme cultivé et raffiné ◆ **a Dickens** ~ un(e) spécialiste de Dickens ◆ **I'm not much of a** ~ je ne suis pas bien savant *or* instruit 2 *(= scholarship holder)* boursier *m*, -ière *f* ; († *= pupil)* écolier *m*, -ière *f*

scholarly /ˈskɒləlɪ/ ADJ *[person, publication, account]* érudit, savant ; *[approach]* érudit ; *[debate]* d'érudits ◆ **to have a** ~ **interest in a subject** s'intéresser à un sujet en tant que spécialiste

scholarship /ˈskɒləʃɪp/ N 1 érudition *f*, savoir *m* 2 *(= award)* bourse *f* (d'études) ; *(US Univ)* bourse *f (pour étudiant de licence)* ◆ **to win a** ~ **to Cambridge** obtenir une bourse pour Cambridge *(par concours)* COMP **scholarship holder** N boursier *m*, -ière *f*

scholastic /skəˈlæstɪk/ ADJ 1 *(= educational) [work, level]* scolaire ◆ ~ **achievement** réussite *f* scolaire 2 *(among scholars) [debate, controversy]* parmi les érudits N *(Philos)* scolastique *m*

COMP **scholastic aptitude test** N (US) examen *m* d'entrée à l'université ; → **SAT**

scholastic philosophy N philosophie *f* scolastique

the scholastic profession N *(gen)* l'enseignement *m* ; *(= teachers collectively)* les enseignants *mpl*

scholasticism /skəˈlæstɪsɪzəm/ N scolastique *f*

school¹ /skuːl/ N 1 *(gen)* école *f* ; *(in formal contexts)* établissement *m* scolaire ; *(= primary school)* école *f* ; *(= secondary school) (gen)* lycée *m* ; *(up to 16 only)* collège *m* ; *[of dancing]* école *f*, académie *f* ; *[of music]* école *f*, conservatoire *m* ; (US * *= university)* fac * *f* ◆ **to go to** ~ aller à l'école *(or* au collège *or* au lycée *etc)* ◆ **to leave** ~ quitter l'école *etc* ◆ **to send a child to** ~ *[parent]* envoyer un enfant à l'école ; *[local authority]* scolariser un enfant ◆ **she gave a talk to the** ~ *(= pupils collectively)* elle a fait un exposé à l'école *(or* au collège *or* au lycée *etc)* ◆ **to go camping/sailing with the** ~ aller faire du camping/de la voile avec l'école *etc* ◆ **to go skiing with the** ~ ≈ partir en classe de neige ◆ **television for ~s** télévision *f* scolaire ◆ **programmes** *or* **broadcasts for ~s** émissions *fpl* éducatives ; → **boarding, high, old, summer**

◆ **at** *or* **in school** à l'école *(or* au collège *etc)* ◆ **we were at** ~ **together** nous étions à la même école *(or* au même collège *etc)* ◆ **he wasn't at** ~ **yesterday** il n'était pas à l'école *or* en classe hier

2 *(= lessons)* classe(s) *f(pl)* ; *(gen secondary)* cours *mpl* ◆ ~ **reopens in September** la rentrée scolaire *or* la rentrée des classes est en septembre ◆ **there's no** ~ **this morning** il n'y a pas classe ce matin, il n'y a pas (de) cours ce matin ◆ **we met every day after** ~ nous nous retrouvions tous les jours après l'école

3 *(Univ)* faculté *f* ◆ **Schools** *(at Oxford and Cambridge) (= building)* salle *d'examen* ; *(= finals)* ≈ examens *mpl* de licence ◆ **he's at law/medical** ~ il fait son droit/sa médecine, il est en droit/médecine ◆ **I went to art/business** ~ je suis allé dans une école d'art/de commerce

4 *(= institute)* institut *m* ; *(= department)* département *m* ◆ **School of Linguistics/African Studies** *etc* Institut *m or* Département *m* de Linguistique/d'Études africaines *etc*

5 *(fig)* école *f* ◆ **the** ~ **of life** l'école *f* de la vie ◆ **he graduated from the** ~ **of hard knocks** il a été à rude école

6 *(Hist) (= scholasticism)* **the ~s** l'École *f*, la scolastique

7 *[of painting, philosophy]* école *f* ◆ **the Dutch** ~ *(Art)* l'école *f* hollandaise ◆ **the Freudian** ~ l'école *f* freudienne ◆ **a** ~ **of thought** une école de pensée ◆ **an aristocrat/doctor** *etc* **of the old** ~ un aristocrate/un médecin *etc* de la vieille école ◆ **he's one of the old** ~ il est de la vieille école

VT *[+ person]* éduquer ; *[+ animal]* dresser ; *[+ feelings, reactions]* contrôler ◆ **his father ~ed him in the basics of carpentry** son père lui a appris *or* enseigné les rudiments de la menuiserie ◆ **to** ~ **o.s. to do sth** s'astreindre à faire qch

COMP *[equipment, edition, television, doctor]* scolaire

school-age child N (pl **school-age children**) enfant *mf* d'âge scolaire

school attendance N scolarisation *f*, scolarité *f*
school board N *(US) [of school]* conseil *m* d'établissement ; *(= local authority)* conseil *m* d'administration des établissements scolaires
school bus N car *m* de ramassage scolaire ♦ ~ **bus service** service *m* de ramassage scolaire
school certificate N *(formerly)* ≈ BEPC *m*
school council N *(Brit)* comité *m* des délégués de classe
school counsellor N *(US)* conseiller *m*, -ère *f* général(e) d'éducation
school crossing patrol N → **crossing**
school dinner N ⇒ **school lunch**
school district N *(US)* secteur *m* scolaire
school fees NPL frais *mpl* de scolarité
school fund N *fonds collectés grâce à diverses opérations organisées par les élèves d'une école*
school holidays NPL vacances *fpl* scolaires
school hours NPL ♦ **during ~ hours** pendant les heures de cours *or* de classe ♦ **out of ~ hours** en dehors des heures de cours *or* de classe
school inspector N *(Brit Scol) (secondary)* ≈ inspecteur *m*, -trice *f* d'académie ; *(primary)* ≈ inspecteur *m*, -trice *f* primaire
school leaver N *(Brit)* jeune *mf* qui a terminé ses études secondaires
school-leaving age N âge *m* de fin de scolarité ♦ **to raise the ~-leaving age** prolonger la scolarité *(to* jusqu'à)
school librarian N *(books only)* bibliothécaire *mf* scolaire ; *(books and other resources)* documentaliste *mf* scolaire
school life N vie *f* scolaire
school lunch, school meal N déjeuner *m* à la cantine (scolaire) ♦ **he hates ~ lunches** *or* **meals** il déteste manger à la cantine
school medical officer N *(Brit)* médecin *m* scolaire
school night N veille *f* d'une journée d'école
school of education N *(US)* école *f* normale (primaire)
school of motoring N auto-école *f*
school outing N *(Brit)* sortie *f* (éducative) scolaire
school phobia N phobie *f* de l'école
school record N dossier *m* scolaire
school report N bulletin *m* (scolaire)
school run N ♦ **to do the ~ run** emmener les enfants à l'école
schools inspector N ⇒ **school inspector**
schools medical officer N ⇒ **school medical officer**
school superintendent N *(US)* inspecteur *m*, -trice *f (responsable du bon fonctionnement des établissements scolaires)*
school tie N cravate *f* de l'école ; → **old**
school time N ♦ **in ~ time** pendant les heures de cours *or* de classe
school trip N ⇒ **school outing**
school uniform N uniforme *m* scolaire
school year N année *f* scolaire

school² /sku:l/ N *[of fish]* banc *m*

schoolbag /'sku:lbæg/ N cartable *m*

schoolbook /'sku:lbʊk/ N livre *m* scolaire *or* de classe

schoolboy /'sku:lbɔɪ/ N *(gen)* élève *m* ; *(at primary school)* écolier *m* ; *(at secondary school)* lycéen *m* ; *(up to age 16 only)* collégien *m* ; see also **public**
COMP **schoolboy crush*** N béguin* *m* (on pour)
schoolboy slang N argot *m* des écoles *or* des lycées

schoolchild /'sku:ltʃaɪld/ N (pl **-children**) *(gen)* élève *mf* ; *(at primary school)* écolier *m*, -ière *f* ; *(at secondary school)* lycéen(ne) *m(f)* ; *(up to age 16 only)* collégien(ne) *m(f)*

schooldays /'sku:ldeɪz/ NPL années *fpl* de scolarité *or* d'école ♦ **during my ~** du temps où j'allais en classe

schooled /sku:ld/ ADJ ♦ **to be ~ in sth** avoir l'expérience de qch ♦ **to be well ~ in sth** être rompu à qch

schoolfellow /'sku:lfeləʊ/, **schoolfriend** /'sku:lfrend/ N camarade *mf* de classe

schoolgirl /'sku:lgɜ:l/ N *(gen)* élève *f* ; *(at primary school)* écolière *f* ; *(at secondary school)* lycéenne *f* ; *(up to age 16 only)* collégienne *f*
COMP **schoolgirl complexion** N teint *m* de jeune fille
schoolgirl crush* N béguin* *m* (on pour)

schoolhouse /'sku:lhaʊs/ N *(US) (= school building)* école *f* ; *(for head teacher)* maison *f* du directeur

schooling /'sku:lɪŋ/ N 1 *(Scol)* instruction *f*, études *fpl* ♦ **~ is free** les études sont gratuites ♦ **compulsory ~** scolarité *f* obligatoire ♦ **~ is compulsory up to age 16** la scolarité est obligatoire jusqu'à 16 ans ♦ **he had very little formal ~** il n'a pas fait une scolarité complète ♦ **he lost a year's ~** il a perdu une année (d'école) 2 *[of horse]* dressage *m*

schoolkid* /'sku:lkɪd/ N écolier *m*, -ière *f*

schoolmarm /'sku:lmɑ:m/ N *(pej)* institutrice *f*, maîtresse *f* d'école

schoolmarmish /'sku:l,mɑ:mɪʃ/ ADJ *(pej)* ♦ **she is very ~** elle fait *or* est très maîtresse d'école

schoolmaster /'sku:l,mɑ:stəʳ/ N *(primary)* instituteur *m* ; *(secondary)* professeur *m*

schoolmate /'sku:lmeɪt/ N ⇒ **schoolfellow**

Schoolmen /'sku:lmən/ NPL *(Philos)* scolastiques *mpl*

schoolmistress /'sku:l,mɪstrɪs/ N *(primary)* institutrice *f* ; *(secondary)* professeur *m*

schoolroom /'sku:lrʊm/ N salle *f* de classe ♦ **in the ~** dans la (salle de) classe, en classe

schoolteacher /'sku:l,ti:tʃəʳ/ N *(primary)* instituteur *m*, -trice *f* ; *(secondary)* professeur *m*

schoolteaching /'sku:l,ti:tʃɪŋ/ N enseignement *m*

schoolwork /'sku:lwɜ:k/ N travail *m* scolaire

schoolyard /'sku:ljɑ:d/ N *(esp US)* cour *f* d'école

schooner /'sku:nəʳ/ N 1 *(Naut)* schooner *m*, goélette *f* 2 *(Brit = sherry glass)* grand verre *m* (à Xérès) ; *(US = beer glass)* demi *m* (de bière)

schtick /ʃtɪk/ N *(US)* numéro *m (de comédien)*

schuss /ʃʊs/ N *(Ski)* schuss *m*

schwa /ʃwɑ:/ N *(Phon)* schwa *m*

sciatic /saɪ'ætɪk/ ADJ sciatique

sciatica /saɪ'ætɪkə/ N sciatique *f*

science /'saɪəns/ N 1 science(s) *f(pl)* ♦ **we study ~ at school** nous étudions les sciences au lycée ♦ **gardening for him is quite a ~** pour lui le jardinage est une véritable science ♦ **the Faculty of Science, the Science Faculty** *(Univ)* la faculté des Sciences ♦ **Secretary (of State) for Science, Minister of Science** *(Brit)* ministre *m* de la Recherche scientifique ♦ **Department** *or* **Ministry of Science** ministère *m* de la Recherche scientifique ; → **applied, natural, social** 2 († = *knowledge)* science † *f* ♦ **to blind sb with ~** éblouir qn de sa science
COMP *[equipment, subject]* scientifique ; *[exam]* de sciences **science fiction** N science-fiction *f* ADJ de science-fiction
science park N parc *m* scientifique
science teacher N professeur *m* de sciences

scientific /,saɪən'tɪfɪk/ ADJ 1 scientifique ♦ **the ~ community** la communauté scientifique ♦ **she received her ~ training in the US** elle a fait ses études de sciences aux États-Unis 2 *(= methodical)* méthodique ♦ **to be ~ about sth** être méthodique par rapport à qch
COMP **the scientific method** N la méthode scientifique
scientific officer N *(Brit Police)* expert *m* (de la police)

scientifically /,saɪən'tɪfɪkəlɪ/ ADV 1 *[prove, explain]* scientifiquement ♦ **to be ~ based** reposer sur des bases scientifiques ♦ **to be ~ trained** avoir une formation scientifique ♦ **~ speaking** d'un point de vue scientifique 2 *(= methodically) [search]* de manière méthodique ; *[plan]* de manière systématique

scientist /'saɪəntɪst/ N *(as career)* scientifique *mf* ; *(= scientific scholar)* savant *m* ♦ **my daughter is a ~** ma fille est une scientifique ♦ **one of our leading ~s** l'un de nos plus grands savants ; → **Christian, social**

scientologist /,saɪən'tɒlədʒɪst/ ADJ, N scientologue *mf*

scientology /'saɪən'tɒlədʒɪ/ N scientologie *f*

sci-fi* /'saɪ'faɪ/ (abbrev of **science-fiction**) N science-fiction *f*, SF *f* ADJ de science-fiction, de SF

Scillies /'sɪlɪz/ NPL ♦ **the ~, the Scilly Isles** les Sorlingues *fpl*, les îles *fpl* Scilly

scimitar /'sɪmɪtəʳ/ N cimeterre *m*

scintilla /sɪn'tɪlə/ N ♦ **not a ~ of evidence** pas l'ombre d'une preuve, pas la moindre preuve ♦ **not a ~ of (a) doubt** pas l'ombre d'un doute, pas le moindre doute

scintillate /'sɪntɪleɪt/ VI *[star, jewel]* scintiller ; *(fig) [person]* briller, pétiller d'esprit

scintillating /'sɪntɪleɪtɪŋ/ ADJ *[person, performance, wit]* brillant ; *[conversation]* brillant, spirituel ♦ **in ~ form** dans une forme éblouissante

scion /'saɪən/ N *(= person)* descendant(e) *m(f)* ; *(Bot)* scion *m*

Scipio /'sɪpɪəʊ/ N Scipion *m*

scissor /'sɪzəʳ/ NPL **scissors** ciseaux *mpl* ♦ **a pair of ~s** une paire de ciseaux ; → **kitchen, nail** VT * couper avec des ciseaux
COMP **scissor bill** N bec *m* en ciseaux
scissor(s) jump N *(Sport)* saut *m* en ciseaux
scissor(s) kick N *(Swimming)* ciseaux *mpl*
scissors-and-paste job N *(lit)* montage *m* ; (* fig) compilation *f*

sclera /'sklɪərə/ N *(Anat)* sclérotique *f*

sclerosis /sklɪ'rəʊsɪs/ N (pl **scleroses** /sklɪ'rəʊsi:z/) sclérose *f* ; → **multiple**

sclerotic /sklɪ'rɒtɪk/ ADJ sclérotique

SCM /,essi:'em/ N *(Brit)* (abbrev of **State-Certified Midwife**) → **state**

scoff¹ /skɒf/ VI se moquer ♦ **to ~ at sb/sth** se moquer de qn/qch, mépriser qn/qch ♦ **he was ~ed at by the whole town** il a été l'objet de risée de toute la ville

scoff²* /skɒf/ VTI *(esp Brit = eat)* bouffer⁑

scoffer /'skɒfəʳ/ N moqueur *m*, -euse *f*, railleur *m*, -euse *f*

scoffing /'skɒfɪŋ/ ADJ *[remark, laugh]* moqueur, railleur N moqueries *fpl*, railleries *fpl*

scofflaw /'skɒflɔ:/ N *(US)* personne *f* qui se moque des lois et des règlements

scold /skəʊld/ VT réprimander *(for doing sth* pour avoir fait qch) ; *[+ child]* gronder *(for doing sth* pour avoir fait qch) ♦ **he got ~ed** il s'est fait réprimander ; *[child]* il s'est fait gronder VI grogner, rouspéter* N *(= woman)* mégère *f*, chipie *f*

scolding /'skəʊldɪŋ/ N gronderie *f*, réprimande *f* ♦ **to get a ~ from sb** se faire gronder par qn ♦ **to give sb a ~** réprimander *or* gronder qn

scoliosis /,skɒlɪ'əʊsɪs/ N scoliose *f*

scollop /'skɒləp/ N, VT ⇒ **scallop**

sconce /skɒns/ N *(on wall)* applique *f* ; *(for carrying candle)* bougeoir *m*

scone /skɒn/ N scone *m (petit pain au lait)*

scoop /sku:p/ N 1 *(for flour, sugar)* pelle *f* *(à main)* ; *(for water)* écope *f* ; *(for ice cream)* cuiller *f* à glace ; *(for mashed potatoes)* cuiller *f* à purée ; *[of bulldozer]* lame *f* ; *[of dredger]* benne *f* preneuse ; (also **scoopful**) pelletée *f*

2 *(Press)* scoop *m*, exclusivité *f* ; *(Comm)* bénéfice *m* important ◆ **to make a ~** *(Comm)* faire un gros bénéfice ; *(Press)* publier une exclusivité, faire un scoop ◆ **it was a ~ for the "Globe"** *(Press)* le "Globe" l'a publié en exclusivité, cela a été un scoop pour le "Globe"

VT *(Comm)* *[+ market]* s'emparer de ; *[+ competitor]* devancer ; *[+ profit]* ramasser ; *[+ prize, award]* décrocher* ; *(Press)* *[+ story]* publier en exclusivité ◆ **to ~ the pool*** tout rafler

► **scoop out** VT SEP ◆ **to scoop water out of a boat** écoper un bateau ◆ **he ~ed the sand out (of the bucket)** il a vidé le sable (du seau) ◆ **he ~ed out a hollow in the soft earth** il a creusé un trou dans la terre molle

► **scoop up** VT SEP *[+ earth, sweets]* ramasser ; *(with instrument)* ramasser à la pelle ◆ **the eagle ~ed up the rabbit** l'aigle a saisi le lapin dans ses serres ◆ **he ~ed up the child and ran for his life** il a ramassé l'enfant en vitesse et s'est enfui à toutes jambes

scoot* /sku:t/ VI se sauver*, filer* ◆ **~!** fichez le camp !*, filez !* ◆ **to ~ in/out** *etc* entrer/sortir *etc* rapidement *or* en coup de vent

► **scoot away***, **scoot off*** VI se sauver*, filer*

scooter /ˈsku:təʳ/ N (also **motor scooter**) scooter *m* ; *(child's)* trottinette *f*

scope /skəʊp/ N 1 *(= range)* *[of law, regulation]* étendue *f*, portée *f* ; *[of undertaking]* envergure *f* ; *[of powers, disaster]* étendue *f* ; *[of changes]* ampleur *f* ◆ **reforms of considerable ~** des réformes d'une portée considérable ◆ **a programme of considerable ~** un programme d'une envergure considérable ◆ **to extend the ~ of one's activities** élargir le champ de ses activités, étendre son rayon d'action

◆ **in scope** ◆ **limited in ~** d'une portée limitée ◆ **this project is more limited in ~** ce projet est de moins grande envergure *or* est moins ambitieux ◆ **to be broad in ~** *[project]* être de grande envergure ; *[research]* être d'une portée considérable ; *[book]* être ambitieux ◆ **his evaluation of the situation is very broad in ~** son évaluation de la situation porte sur de nombreux aspects ◆ **the service is comprehensive in ~** ce service est très complet

2 *(= possibility, potential)* *(for activity, action etc)* possibilité *f*, occasion *f* ◆ **he wants a job with more ~** *(more varied)* il voudrait un travail plus varié ; *(with more prospects)* il voudrait un travail offrant davantage de perspectives d'évolution ◆ **his job gave him plenty of ~ to show his ability** son travail lui a amplement permis de faire la preuve de ses compétences ◆ **it gave him full ~ to decide for himself** cela le laissait entièrement libre de *or* cela lui laissait toute latitude pour prendre les décisions lui-même ◆ **the subject is within/beyond the ~ of this book** ce sujet entre dans le cadre/dépasse le cadre de ce livre ◆ **that is within the ~ of the new regulations** ceci est prévu par le nouveau règlement

3 *(= competences, capabilities)* compétences *fpl* ◆ **this work is within/beyond his ~** ce travail entre dans ses compétences/dépasse ses compétences

◆ **scope for** ◆ **there's not much ~ for originality/creativity** ça ne laisse pas beaucoup de place à l'originalité/la créativité ◆ **there is ~ for improvement** ça pourrait être mieux ◆ **there is ~ for increasing our share of the market** il nous est possible d'augmenter notre part du marché ◆ **there is little ~ for reducing our costs** il ne nous est pas vraiment possible de réduire nos coûts, nous n'avons pas beaucoup de marge de manœuvre pour réduire nos coûts

scorbutic /skɔ:ˈbju:tɪk/ ADJ scorbutique

scorch /skɔ:tʃ/ N (also **scorch mark**) brûlure *f* (légère) ◆ **there was a ~ on her dress** sa robe avait été roussie VT *[+ linen]* roussir, brûler (légèrement) ; *[+ grass]* *[fire etc]* brûler ; *[sun]* dessécher, roussir VI 1 *[linen]* brûler (légèrement) 2 *(Brit * = drive fast:* also **scorch along**) *[driver]* conduire à un train d'enfer ; *[car]* rouler à toute vitesse ; *[cyclist]* pédaler à fond de train *or* comme un fou* *(or* une folle*) COMP **scorched earth policy** N tactique *f* de la terre brûlée

scorcher* /ˈskɔ:tʃəʳ/ N journée *f* de canicule ◆ **today's going to be a ~** aujourd'hui ça va être la canicule ◆ **it was a (real) ~ (of a day)** il faisait une chaleur caniculaire *or* une de ces chaleurs*

scorching* /ˈskɔ:tʃɪŋ/ ADJ 1 *(= hot)* *[day]* de canicule ; *[heat]* caniculaire ; *[sand]* brûlant ; *[sun]* de plomb ◆ **~ weather** canicule *f* 2 *(= fast)* ◆ **at a ~ pace** à une vitesse folle ADV ◆ **~ hot** *[food]* brûlant ; *[liquid]* bouillant ◆ **~ hot weather** canicule *f* ◆ **it was a ~ hot day** il faisait une chaleur caniculaire *or* une de ces chaleurs* ◆ **the sun is ~ hot** il fait un soleil de plomb

score /skɔ:ʳ/ N 1 *(= amount won etc)* *(Sport)* score *m* ; *(Cards)* marque *f* ; *(US Scol = mark)* note *f* ◆ **to keep (the) ~** *(gen)* compter *or* marquer les points ; *(Cards)* tenir la marque ; *(Tennis)* tenir le score ◆ **there's no ~ yet** *(Ftbl)* aucun but n'a encore été marqué, le score est toujours vierge ◆ **there was no ~ in the match between Leeds and York** Leeds et York ont fait match nul ◆ **what's the ~?** *(Sport)* quel est le score ? ; *(* fig)* où en sont les choses ? ◆ **to know the ~*** *(fig)* savoir de quoi il retourne ; → **half**

2 *(= debt)* compte *m*, dette *f* ◆ **to settle a ~ with sb** *(fig)* régler ses comptes avec qn ◆ **I've got a ~ or an old ~ to settle with him** j'ai un compte à régler avec lui ◆ **this was more than just a settling of old ~s** c'était plus qu'un simple règlement de comptes

3 *(= subject, account)* ◆ **on the ~ of ...** pour cause de ..., en raison de ... ◆ **on more ~s than one** à plus d'un titre ◆ **on this** *or* **that ~** à cet égard, à ce sujet ◆ **on what ~?** à quel titre ? ◆ **on several ~s** à plusieurs titres

4 *(= mark, cut)* *(on metal, wood)* rayure *f* ; *(deeper)* entaille *f* ; *(on rock)* strie *f* ; *(on skin, leather, accidental)* éraflure *f* ; *(deliberate)* incision *f*

5 *[of film]* musique *f* ◆ **who wrote the ~?** qui est l'auteur de la musique *or* de la bande originale ?

6 *(Mus = sheets of music)* partition *f* ◆ **piano ~** partition *f* de piano ◆ **to follow the ~** suivre la partition ; → **vocal**

7 *(= twenty)* **a ~** vingt ◆ **a ~ of people** une vingtaine de personnes ◆ **three ~ and ten** †† soixante-dix ◆ **~s of times** des dizaines de fois ◆ **there were ~s of mistakes** il y avait un grand nombre de *or* des tas* de fautes

VT 1 *[+ goal, point]* marquer ◆ **to ~ 70% (in an exam)** avoir 70 sur 100 (à un examen) ◆ **he went five games without scoring a point** *(Tennis)* il n'a pas marqué un seul point pendant cinq jeux ◆ **they had 14 goals ~d against them** leurs adversaires ont marqué 14 buts ◆ **to ~ a hit** *(Fencing)* toucher ; *(Shooting)* viser juste ; *(Drugs* ‡*)* se procurer de la dope* ◆ **to ~ a hit of crack/speed/smack**‡ se procurer sa dose de crack/de speed*/d'héro* ◆ **to ~ a great success** *or* **a hit** *(fig)* remporter *or* se tailler un grand succès ◆ **he certainly ~d a hit with her*** il lui a vraiment fait bonne impression ◆ **to ~ points** *(fig)* marquer des points ◆ **to ~ a point over** *or* **off sb** marquer un point sur qn

2 *(= cut)* *[+ stick]* entailler ; *[+ rock]* strier ; *[+ ground]* entamer ; *[+ wood, metal]* rayer ; *[+ leather, skin]* *(deliberately)* inciser ; *(accidentally)* érafler ; *(Culin)* inciser ◆ **lines had been ~d on the wall** des lignes avaient été tracées sur le mur

3 *(Mus)* *(= arrange)* adapter *(for* pour) ; *(= orchestrate)* orchestrer *(for* pour) ; *(= compose)* composer ◆ **the film was ~d by Michael Nyman** la musique *or* la bande originale du film a été composée par Michael Nyman ◆ **it is ~d for piano and cello** c'est écrit pour piano et violoncelle

VI 1 *(Sport)* *(= win points)* marquer un *or* des point(s) ; *(= score goal)* marquer un but ; *(= keep the score)* marquer les points ◆ **to ~ well in a test** avoir *or* obtenir un bon résultat à un test ◆ **they failed to ~** *(Ftbl)* ils n'ont pas réussi à marquer (un but) ◆ **Barnes ~d from a distance of twenty feet** *(Ftbl)* Barnes a marqué à sept mètres ◆ **that is where he ~s** *(fig)* c'est là qu'il a le dessus *or* l'avantage ◆ **to ~ over** *or* **off sb** marquer un point aux dépens de qn

2 *(‡ = succeed)* *(gen)* avoir du succès ; *(= get off with)* lever* ; *(with woman)* lever* une nana‡ ; *(with man)* lever* un mec‡ ; *(in buying drugs)* se procurer de la dope*

COMP **score draw** N *(Brit Ftbl)* match *m* nul *(avec un minimum de un but)*

► **score out, score through** VT SEP rayer, barrer

► **score up** VT SEP *[+ points]* marquer, faire ; *[+ debt]* porter en compte, inscrire

scoreboard /ˈskɔ:bɔ:d/ N *(gen)* tableau *m* d'affichage *(des scores)* ; *(Billiards)* boulier *m*

scorecard /ˈskɔ:kɑ:d/ N *[of game]* carte *f or* fiche *f* de score ; *(Shooting)* carton *m* ; *(Golf)* carte *f* de parcours ; *(Cards)* feuille *f* de marque

scorekeeper /ˈskɔ:ˌki:pəʳ/ N *(= person)* marqueur *m*, -euse *f*

scoreless /ˈskɔ:lɪs/ ADJ *(Sport)* ◆ **the game was ~, it was a ~ game** aucun point n'a été marqué pendant le jeu ◆ **a ~ draw** un match nul zéro à zéro

scoreline /ˈskɔ:laɪn/ N *(Sport)* score *m*

scorer /ˈskɔ:rəʳ/ N 1 *(keeping score)* marqueur *m* 2 (also **goal scorer**) marqueur *m* (de but) ◆ **to be the top ~** être le meilleur marqueur

scoresheet /ˈskɔ:ʃi:t/ N *(in games)* feuille *f* de match ◆ **they're ahead on the ~** *(Ftbl)* ils mènent à la marque

scoring /ˈskɔ:rɪŋ/ N *(NonC)* 1 *(Sport)* buts *mpl* ; *(Cards)* points *mpl* ◆ **all the ~ was in the second half** tous les buts ont été marqués pendant la deuxième mi-temps ◆ **to open the ~** ouvrir la marque ◆ **"rules for scoring"** "comment marquer les points" 2 *(= cut)* incision *f*, striage *m* ; *(Culin)* incision *f* 3 *(Mus)* arrangement *m*

scorn /skɔ:n/ N *(NonC)* mépris *m*, dédain *m* ◆ **to be filled with ~ (for)** n'avoir que du mépris *or* du dédain (pour) ◆ **to heap** *or* **pour ~ on sb/sth** traiter qn/qch avec mépris ◆ **my suggestion was greeted with ~** ma proposition a été accueillie avec mépris *or* dédain ; → **laugh** VT *[+ person, action]* mépriser ; *[+ advice]* faire fi de ; *[+ suggestion, idea]* dédaigner ◆ **he was ~ed as ineffectual/as an amateur** on le méprisait parce qu'on le considérait comme incompétent/comme un simple amateur ◆ **he ~s telling lies** *or* **to tell a lie** *(liter)* il ne s'abaisserait pas à mentir

scornful /ˈskɔ:nfʊl/ ADJ méprisant, dédaigneux ◆ **to be ~ of sb/sth** mépriser qn/qch ◆ **to be ~ about sth** manifester son mépris *or* son dédain pour qch

scornfully /ˈskɔ:nfəlɪ/ ADV avec mépris, avec dédain

Scorpio /ˈskɔ:pɪəʊ/ N *(Astron)* Scorpion *m* ◆ **I'm (a) ~** *(Astrol)* je suis (du) Scorpion

scorpion /ˈskɔːpɪən/ **N** scorpion *m* ◆ **the Scorpion** *(Astrol, Astron)* le Scorpion **COMP scorpion fish N** rascasse *f*

Scorpionic /ˌskɔːpɪˈɒnɪk/ **N** ◆ **to be a ~** être (du) Scorpion

Scot /skɒt/ **N** Écossais(e) *m(f)* ◆ **the ~s** les Écossais *mpl* ; see also **Scots**

Scotch /skɒtʃ/ **N** (also **Scotch whisky**) whisky *m*, scotch *m* **NPL the Scotch** * les Écossais *mpl* **ADJ** écossais

COMP Scotch broth N *potage écossais à base de mouton, de légumes et d'orge*
Scotch egg N *(esp Brit) œuf dur enrobé de chair à saucisse et pané*
Scotch-Irish ADJ *(US)* irlando-écossais
Scotch mist N bruine *f*, crachin *m*
Scotch pine N pin *m* sylvestre
Scotch tape ® **N** *(US)* scotch ® *m*, ruban *m* adhésif
Scotch terrier N scotch-terrier *m*
Scotch woodcock N *(Culin)* toast *m* aux œufs brouillés et aux anchois

scotch /skɒtʃ/ **VT** *[+ rumour]* étouffer ; *[+ plan, attempt]* faire échouer ; *[+ revolt, uprising]* réprimer ; *[+ claim]* démentir

scot-free /ˈskɒtˈfriː/ **ADV** ◆ **to get off ~** s'en tirer à bon compte

Scotland /ˈskɒtlənd/ **N** Écosse *f* ◆ **Secretary of State for ~** ministre *m* des Affaires écossaises ; → **yard²**

Scots /skɒts/ **N** *(= dialect)* écossais *m* **ADJ** écossais

COMP the Scots Guards NPL *(Mil)* la Garde écossaise
Scots law N droit *m* écossais
Scots pine N pin *m* sylvestre

Scotsman /ˈskɒtsmən/ **N** (pl **-men**) Écossais *m*

Scotswoman /ˈskɒtsˌwʊmən/ **N** (pl **-women**) Écossaise *f*

Scotticism /ˈskɒtɪsɪzəm/ **N** expression *f* écossaise

Scottie /ˈskɒtɪ/ **N** (abbrev of **Scotch terrier**) → **Scotch**

Scottish /ˈskɒtɪʃ/ **ADJ** écossais

COMP Scottish country dancing N danses *fpl* folkloriques écossaises
Scottish Nationalism N nationalisme *m* écossais
Scottish Nationalist N nationaliste *mf* écossais(e) **ADJ** de *or* des nationaliste(s) écossais
the Scottish National Party N *(Brit Pol)* le Parti national écossais
the Scottish Office N *(Brit Pol)* le ministère des Affaires écossaises
Scottish Secretary N *(Brit Pol)* ministre *m* des Affaires écossaises
Scottish terrier N scotch-terrier *m*

scoundrel /ˈskaʊndrəl/ **N** fripouille *f*, vaurien *m* ; *(stronger)* crapule *f* ; *(= child)* coquin(e) *m(f)*, (petit) chenapan *m* ◆ **you little ~!** (espèce de) petit coquin *or* chenapan !

scour /ˈskaʊəʳ/ **VT** ① *[+ pan, sink]* récurer ; *[+ metal]* décaper ; *[+ table, floor]* frotter ② *[+ channel]* creuser, éroder ③ *(= search)* fouiller ◆ **I ~ed the newspaper for the article** j'ai cherché partout dans le journal pour trouver l'article ◆ **they ~ed the neighbourhood in search of the murderer** ils ont fouillé le quartier pour trouver l'assassin ◆ **to ~ the area/the woods/the countryside** battre le secteur/les bois/la campagne ◆ **I've ~ed the house and I can't see my keys anywhere** j'ai fouillé la maison de fond en comble et je n'arrive pas à trouver mes clés

COMP scouring pad N tampon *m* à récurer *or* abrasif
scouring powder N poudre *f* à récurer

► **scour off VT SEP** enlever en frottant

► **scour out VT SEP** récurer

scourer /ˈskaʊərəʳ/ **N** *(= powder)* poudre *f* à récurer ; *(= pad)* tampon *m* à récurer

scourge /skɜːdʒ/ **N** *(fig)* fléau *m* ; *(= whip)* discipline *f*, fouet *m* **VT** *(fig)* châtier, être un fléau pour ; *(= whip)* fouetter ◆ **to ~ o.s.** se flageller

scouse * /skaʊs/ *(Brit)* **N** ① *(= person)* originaire *mf* de Liverpool ② *(= dialect)* dialecte *m* de Liverpool **ADJ** de Liverpool

Scouser * /ˈskaʊsəʳ/ **N** *(Brit)* originaire *mf* de Liverpool ◆ **Janet's dad is a ~** le père de Janet est (originaire) de Liverpool

scout /skaʊt/ **N** ① *(Mil)* éclaireur *m* ◆ **he's a good ~** † * c'est un chic type * ; → **talent**
② *(gen Catholic)* scout *m* ; *(gen non-Catholic)* éclaireur *m* ; → **cub**
③ * **to have a ~ round** reconnaître le terrain ◆ **have a ~ round to see if he's there** allez jeter un coup d'œil pour voir s'il est là
④ (also **talent scout**) *(Sport)* découvreur *m*, -euse *f* or dénicheur *m*, -euse *f* de futurs grands joueurs ; *(Cine, Theat)* découvreur *m*, -euse *f* or dénicheur *m*, -euse *f* de talents
⑤ *(Brit Univ)* domestique *mf*
VI *(Mil)* aller en reconnaissance
VT explorer ◆ **to ~ an area for sth** explorer un endroit pour trouver qch

COMP scout camp N camp *m* scout
scout car N *(Mil)* voiture *f* de reconnaissance
scout movement N mouvement *m* scout
scout uniform N uniforme *m* de scout

► **scout about, scout around VI** *(Mil)* aller en reconnaissance ◆ **to ~ about for sth** *(fig)* chercher qch, aller *or* être à la recherche de qch

scouting /ˈskaʊtɪŋ/ **N** *(NonC)* ① *(= youth movement)* scoutisme *m* ② *(Mil)* reconnaissance *f*

scoutmaster /ˈskaʊtˌmɑːstəʳ/ **N** chef *m* scout

scow /skaʊ/ **N** chaland *m*

scowl /skaʊl/ **N** air *m* de mauvaise humeur, mine *f* renfrognée ◆ **... he said with a ~** ... dit-il en se renfrognant *or* d'un air renfrogné
VI se renfrogner ◆ **to ~ at sb/sth** jeter un regard mauvais à qn/qch **VT** ◆ **"shut up!" he ~ed** "tais-toi !" dit-il en se renfrognant *or* l'œil mauvais

scowling /ˈskaʊlɪŋ/ **ADJ** *[face, look]* renfrogné, maussade

SCR /ˌesiːˈɑːʳ/ **N** *(Brit Univ)* (abbrev of **senior common room**) → **senior**

scrabble /ˈskræbl/ **VI** ① (also **scrabble about, scrabble around**) **to ~ in the ground for sth** gratter la terre pour trouver qch ◆ **she ~d (about** *or* **around) in the sand for the keys she had dropped** elle cherchait à tâtons dans le sable les clés qu'elle avait laissé tomber ◆ **he ~d (about** *or* **around) for a pen in the drawer** il a tâtonné dans le tiroir à la recherche d'un stylo ② *(= scramble)* ◆ **to ~ to do sth** chercher à faire qch au plus vite ◆ **his mind ~d for alternatives** il se creusait la tête pour trouver au plus vite d'autres solutions **N** *(= game)* ◆ **Scrabble** ® Scrabble ® *m*

scrag /skræg/ **N** *(Brit Culin:* also **scrag end***)* collet *m* (de mouton) **VT** ⁑ *[+ person]* tordre le cou à *

scragginess /ˈskrægɪnɪs/ **N** *(= scrawniness)* maigreur *f*

scraggly * /ˈskræglɪ/ **ADJ** *(US) [beard, hair]* en bataille ; *[plant]* difforme

scraggy /ˈskrægɪ/ **ADJ** ① *(= scrawny)* maigre ② *(= unkempt, scanty) [hair, beard, fur]* peu fourni et hérissé

scram ⁑ /skræm/ **VI** ficher le camp * ◆ **~!** fiche(-moi) le camp ! * ◆ **I'd better ~** je dois filer *

scramble /ˈskræmbl/ **VI** ① *(= clamber)* **to ~ up/down** *etc* grimper/descendre *etc* tant bien que mal ◆ **he ~d along the cliff** il a avancé avec difficulté le long de la falaise ◆ **they ~d over the rocks/up the cliff** en s'aidant des pieds et des mains ils ont avancé sur les rochers/escaladé la falaise ◆ **he ~d into/out of the car** il est monté dans/est descendu de la voiture à toute vitesse, il s'est précipité dans/hors de la voiture ◆ **he ~d down off the wall** il a dégringolé du mur ◆ **he ~d through the hedge** il s'est frayé tant bien que mal un passage à travers la haie ◆ **to ~ for** *[+ coins, seats]* se bousculer pour (avoir), se disputer ; *[+ jobs etc]* faire des pieds et des mains pour (avoir)
② *(Brit Sport)* **to go scrambling** faire du trial
③ *[planes]* décoller sur alerte
VT *[+ eggs, signal]* brouiller ; *(TV)* coder, crypter
N ① ruée *f* ◆ **the ~ for seats** la ruée pour les places ◆ **there was a ~ for seats** *(to sit down)* on s'est rué sur les places ; *(to buy seats)* on s'est arraché les places
② (also **motorcycle scramble**) (réunion *f* de) trial *m*

COMP scrambled eggs NPL œufs *mpl* brouillés

scrambler /ˈskræmbləʳ/ **N** ① *(Telec = device)* brouilleur *m* ; *(TV)* brouilleur *m*, codeur *m* ② *(Brit = motorcyclist)* trialiste *mf*

scrambling /ˈskræmblɪŋ/ **N** *(Brit Sport)* trial *m*

scrap¹ /skræp/ **N** ① *(= small piece) [of paper, cloth, bread, string]* (petit) bout *m* ; *[of verse, writing]* quelques lignes *fpl* ; *[of conversation]* bribe *f* ; *[of news]* fragment *m* ◆ **~s** *(= broken pieces)* débris *mpl* ; *(= food remnants)* restes *mpl* ◆ **there isn't a ~ of evidence** il n'y a pas la moindre preuve ◆ **it wasn't a ~ of use** cela n'a servi absolument à rien ◆ **there wasn't a ~ of truth in it** il n'y avait pas un brin de vérité là-dedans ◆ **not a ~** pas du tout
② *(NonC = scrap iron)* ferraille *f* ◆ **to collect ~** récupérer de la ferraille ◆ **I put it out for ~** je l'ai envoyé à la ferraille ◆ **to sell a car/ship for ~** vendre une voiture/un bateau comme épave *or* à la casse ◆ **what is it worth as ~?** qu'est-ce que cela vaudrait (vendu) comme épave *or* à la casse ?
VT jeter, bazarder * ; *[+ car, ship]* envoyer à la ferraille *or* à la casse ; *[+ equipment]* mettre au rebut ; *[+ project]* abandonner, mettre au rancart * ◆ **let's ~ the idea** laissons tomber cette idée

COMP scrap car N voiture *f* mise en épave *or* à la casse
scrap dealer N marchand *m* de ferraille, ferrailleur *m*
scrap iron N ferraille *f*
scrap merchant N ⇒ **scrap dealer**
scrap metal N ⇒ **scrap iron**
scrap paper N *(for scribbling on)* (papier *m* de) brouillon *m* ; *(= old newspapers etc)* vieux papiers *mpl*
scrap value N ◆ **its ~ value is £10** (vendu) à la casse cela vaut 10 livres

scrap² * /skræp/ **N** *(= fight)* bagarre *f* ◆ **to get into** *or* **have a ~** se bagarrer * *(with avec)* **VI** se bagarrer *

scrapbook /ˈskræpbʊk/ **N** album *m* *(de coupures de journaux etc)*

scrape /skreɪp/ **N** ① *(= action)* coup *m* de grattoir *or* de racloir ; *(= sound)* grattement *m*, raclement *m* ; *(= mark)* éraflure *f*, égratignure *f* ◆ **to give sth a ~** gratter *or* racler qch ◆ **to give one's knee a ~** s'érafler *or* s'égratigner le genou
② *[of butter etc]* fine couche *f*, lichette * *f*
③ *(* = trouble)* **to get (o.s.) into a ~** s'attirer des ennuis ◆ **he's always getting into ~s** il lui arrive toujours des histoires * ◆ **to get (o.s.) out of a ~** se tirer d'affaire *or* d'embarras ◆ **to get sb into a ~** attirer des ennuis à qn, mettre qn dans un mauvais pas ◆ **to get sb out of a ~** tirer qn d'affaire *or* d'embarras
VT *(= graze)* érafler, égratigner ; *(= just touch)* frôler, effleurer ; *(= clean: gen)* gratter, racler ; *[+ vegetables]* gratter ◆ **to ~ (the skin off) one's knees** s'érafler les genoux ◆ **to ~ one's plate**

clean tout manger, nettoyer *or* racler* son assiette ◆ **I ~d his bumper** je lui ai frôlé *or* éraflé le pare-chocs ◆ **to ~ a living** vivoter ◆ **to ~ a violin*** racler du violon ◆ **to ~ the bottom** *(Naut)* talonner (le fond) ◆ **to ~ (the bottom of) the barrel** *(fig)* en être réduit aux raclures *(fig)* see also **scrape up**

VI *(= make scraping sound)* racler, gratter ; *(= rub)* frotter *(against* contre) ◆ **to ~ along the wall** frôler le mur ◆ **the car ~d past the lamppost** la voiture a frôlé le réverbère ◆ **to ~ through the doorway** réussir de justesse à passer par la porte ◆ **to ~ through an exam** réussir un examen de justesse ◆ **he just ~d into university** il a été admis de justesse à l'université ; → **bow²**

▸ **scrape along** VI ⇒ **scrape by**

▸ **scrape away** VI ◆ **to ~ away* at the violin** racler du violon

VT SEP enlever en grattant *or* en raclant

▸ **scrape by** VI *(financially)* vivoter ◆ **she ~d by on £30 per week** elle vivotait avec 30 livres par semaine

▸ **scrape off** VT SEP ⇒ **scrape away vt sep**

▸ **scrape out** VT SEP *[+ contents]* enlever en grattant *or* en raclant ; *[+ pan]* nettoyer en raclant, récurer

▸ **scrape through** VI passer de justesse ; *(fig = succeed)* réussir de justesse

▸ **scrape together** VT SEP 1 ◆ **to scrape two bits of metal together** frotter deux morceaux de métal l'un contre l'autre

2 *[+ objects]* rassembler, ramasser ; *[+ money]* rassembler à grand-peine *or* en raclant les fonds de tiroirs*

▸ **scrape up** VT SEP *[+ earth, pebbles]* ramasser, mettre en tas ; *[+ money]* rassembler à grand-peine *or* en raclant les fonds de tiroirs*

scraper /ˈskreɪpəʳ/ N racloir *m*, grattoir *m* ; *(at doorstep)* décrottoir *m*, gratte-pieds *m inv*

scraperboard /ˈskreɪpəbɔːd/ N carte *f* à gratter

scrapheap /ˈskræphiːp/ N tas *m* de ferraille ◆ **to throw** *or* **toss sth on the ~** *(fig)* mettre qch au rebut, bazarder qch* ◆ **to throw** *or* **toss sb on the ~*** mettre qn au rancart* ◆ **only fit for the ~*** bon à mettre au rancart* ◆ **to end up on the ~** *(fig)* être mis au rebut

scrapie /ˈskreɪpɪ/ N *(= disease)* tremblante *f*

scraping /ˈskreɪpɪŋ/ ADJ *[noise]* de grattement, de raclement N 1 *[of butter]* fine couche *f*, lichette* *f* ◆ **~s** *[of food]* restes *mpl* ; *[of dirt, paint]* raclures *fpl* 2 *(= action)* grattement *m*, raclement *m* ; → **bow²**

scrappy /ˈskræpɪ/ ADJ 1 *(= disjointed) [conversation, essay, film]* décousu ; *[education]* incomplet (-ète *f*) ; *[football match]* confus ◆ **a ~ goal** un but marqué à la suite d'un cafouillage 2 *[piece of paper]* en piteux état

scrapyard /ˈskræpjɑːd/ N *(esp Brit)* dépôt *m* de ferraille ; *(for cars)* cimetière *m* de voitures, casse* *f*

scratch /skrætʃ/ N 1 *(= mark) (on skin)* égratignure *f*, éraflure *f* ; *(on paint)* éraflure *f* ; *(on glass, record)* rayure *f* ◆ **they came out of it without a ~** ils s'en sont sortis indemnes *or* sans une égratignure ◆ **it's only a ~** ce n'est qu'une égratignure

2 *(= action)* grattement *m* ; *(by claw)* coup *m* de griffe ; *(by fingernail)* coup *m* d'ongle ◆ **the cat gave her a ~** le chat l'a griffée ◆ **to have a good ~*** se gratter un bon coup*

3 *(= noise)* grattement *m*, grincement *m*

4 *(set phrases)*

◆ **from scratch** ◆ **to be on** *or* **start from ~** *(Sport)* être scratch *inv* ◆ **to start from ~** *(fig)* partir de zéro* ◆ **I studied Spanish from ~** j'ai appris l'espagnol en partant de zéro ◆ **we'll have to start from ~ again** il nous faudra repartir de zéro*

◆ **up to scratch** ◆ **he didn't come up to ~** il ne s'est pas montré à la hauteur ◆ **his work doesn't come up to ~** son travail n'est pas à la hauteur *or* au niveau ◆ **to bring up to ~** amener au niveau voulu ◆ **to keep sb up to ~** maintenir qn au niveau voulu

VT 1 *(with nail, claw)* griffer ; *[+ varnish]* érafler ; *[+ record, glass]* rayer ◆ **to ~ a hole in sth** creuser un trou en grattant qch ◆ **he ~ed his hand on a nail** il s'est éraflé *or* écorché la main sur un clou ◆ **he ~ed his name on the wood** il a gravé son nom dans le bois ◆ **it only ~ed the surface** *(fig) (gen)* c'était très superficiel ; *[report, lecture]* ça n'a fait qu'effleurer la question, c'était très superficiel ◆ **we've only managed to ~ the surface of the problem** nous n'avons fait qu'effleurer *or* aborder le problème ◆ **to ~ a few lines** *(= write)* griffonner quelques mots

2 *(= to relieve itch)* gratter ◆ **to ~ o.s.** se gratter ◆ **to ~ one's head** *(lit, fig)* se gratter la tête ◆ **you ~ my back and I'll ~ yours** un petit service en vaut un autre

3 *(= cancel) [+ meeting]* annuler ; *(Comput)* effacer ; *(Sport etc) [+ competitor, horse]* scratcher ; *[+ match, game]* annuler ; *(US Pol) [+ candidate]* rayer de la liste ◆ **to ~ a ballot** *(US Pol)* modifier un bulletin de vote *(en rayant un nom etc)*

VI 1 *(with nail, claw)* griffer ; *(= to relieve itch)* se gratter ; *[hen]* gratter le sol ; *[pen]* gratter, grincer ◆ **the dog was ~ing at the door** le chien grattait à la porte

2 *(Sport etc) [competitor]* se faire scratcher ; *[candidate]* se désister

COMP *[crew, team]* de fortune, improvisé ; *[vote]* par surprise ; *[golfer]* scratch *inv*, de handicap zéro

scratch and sniff ADJ *que l'on gratte pour sentir un parfum*

scratch file N *(Comput)* fichier *m* de travail *or* de manœuvre

scratch 'n' sniff N ⇒ **scratch and sniff**

scratch pad N *(gen)* bloc-notes *m* ; *(Comput)* mémoire *f* bloc-notes

scratch paper N *(US)* ⇒ **scrap paper** ; → **scrap¹**

scratch race N course *f* scratch

scratch score N *(Golf)* scratch score *m*, score *m* ramené à zéro

scratch sheet* N *(US Racing)* journal *m* des courses *(hippiques)*

scratch tape N *(Comput)* bande *f* de travail *or* de manœuvre

scratch test N *(Med)* cuti(-réaction) *f*, test *m* cutané

▸ **scratch out** VT SEP 1 *(from list)* rayer, effacer

2 *[+ hole]* creuser en grattant ◆ **to ~ sb's eyes out** arracher les yeux à qn

▸ **scratch together** VT SEP *(fig) [+ money]* réussir à amasser (en raclant les fonds de tiroirs*)

▸ **scratch up** VT SEP *[+ bone]* déterrer ; *(fig) [+ money]* ⇒ **scratch together**

scratchcard /ˈskrætʃkɑːd/ N *(Brit)* carte *f* à gratter

scratchy /ˈskrætʃɪ/ ADJ *[surface, material]* rêche, qui accroche ; *[pen]* qui grince, qui gratte ; *[handwriting]* en pattes de mouche ; *[record]* rayé, éraillé

scrawl /skrɔːl/ N 1 *(gen)* gribouillage *m*, griffonnage *m* ◆ **I can't read her ~** je ne peux pas déchiffrer son gribouillage ◆ **the word finished in a ~** le mot se terminait par un gribouillage ◆ **her letter was just a ~** sa lettre était griffonnée 2 *(= brief letter, note)* mot *m* griffonné à la hâte VT gribouiller, griffonner ◆ **to ~ a note to sb** griffonner un mot à qn ◆ **there were rude words ~ed all over the wall** il y avait des mots grossiers gribouillés sur tout le mur VI gribouiller

scrawny /ˈskrɔːnɪ/ ADJ maigre

scream /skriːm/ N 1 *[of pain, fear]* cri *m* aigu *or* perçant, hurlement *m* ; *[of laughter]* éclat *m* ◆ **to give a ~** pousser un cri

2 ***it was a ~** c'était à se tordre*, c'était vraiment marrant* ◆ **he's a ~** il est désopilant *or* impayable*

VI *(also* **scream out***) [person]* crier ; *(stronger)* hurler ; *[baby]* crier, brailler ; *[siren, brakes, wind]* hurler ◆ **to ~ with laughter** rire aux éclats *or* aux larmes ◆ **to ~ with pain/with rage** hurler de douleur/de rage ◆ **to ~ for help** crier à l'aide *or* au secours ◆ **to ~ at sb** crier après qn

VT *(also* **scream out***)* 1 *[+ abuse etc]* hurler *(at* à) ◆ **"shut up" he ~ed** "taisez-vous" hurla-t-il ◆ **to ~ o.s. hoarse** s'enrouer à force de crier, s'égosiller

2 *[headlines, posters]* annoncer en toutes lettres

▸ **scream down** VT SEP ◆ **to scream the place down** crier comme un damné *or* sourd

▸ **scream out** VI ⇒ **scream vi**

VT SEP ⇒ **scream vt**

screamer* /ˈskriːməʳ/ N *(US)* 1 *(= headline)* énorme manchette *f* 2 *(= joke)* histoire *f* désopilante ◆ **he's a ~** il est désopilant *or* impayable*

screamingly* /ˈskriːmɪŋlɪ/ ADV ◆ **~ funny** à mourir de rire, tordant* ◆ **~ boring** à mourir d'ennui

scree /skriː/ N éboulis *m (en montagne)*

screech /skriːtʃ/ N *(gen)* cri *m* strident ; *(from pain, fright, rage)* hurlement *m* ; *[of brakes]* grincement *m* ; *[of tyres]* crissement *m* ; *[of owl]* cri *m* (rauque et perçant) ; *[of siren]* hurlement *m* ◆ **she gave a ~ of laughter** elle est partie d'un rire perçant VI *[person]* pousser des cris stridents, hurler ; *[brakes]* grincer ; *[tyres]* crisser ; *[singer, owl]* crier ; *[siren]* hurler VT crier à tue-tête COMP **screech owl** N chouette *f* effraie, chat-huant *m*

screed /skriːd/ N 1 *(= discourse)* laïus* *m*, topo* *m (about* sur) ; *(= letter)* longue missive *f (about* sur) ◆ **to write ~s*** *(= a lot)* écrire des volumes *or* toute une tartine* 2 *(Constr) (= depth guide strip)* guide *m* ; *(= levelling device)* règle *f* à araser le béton ; *(NonC = surfacing material)* matériau *m* de ragréage

screen /skriːn/ N 1 *(in room)* paravent *m* ; *(for fire)* écran *m* de cheminée ; *(fig: of troops, trees)* rideau *m* ; *(= pretence)* masque *m* ; → **safety, silk, smoke**

2 *(Cine, TV, Comput etc)* écran *m* ◆ **to show sth on a ~** projeter qch ◆ **a 50-cm ~** *(TV)* un écran de 50 cm ◆ **the ~** *(Cine)* l'écran *m*, le cinéma ◆ **the big** *or* **large ~** *(Cine)* le grand écran ◆ **the small ~** *(TV)* le petit écran ◆ **to write for the ~** écrire des scénarios ◆ **stars of the ~** les vedettes *fpl* de l'écran ◆ **the violence children see on ~** la violence que les enfants voient à l'écran ◆ **they are married off ~ as well as on** ils sont mari et femme à la scène *or* à l'écran comme à la ville ◆ **information can be accessed on ~** *(Comput)* on peut afficher les renseignements à l'écran ◆ **to work on ~** *(Comput)* travailler sur écran ; → **panoramic, television, wide**

3 *(= sieve)* crible *m*, tamis *m*

VT 1 *(= hide)* masquer, cacher ; *(= protect)* faire écran à, protéger ◆ **the trees ~ed the house** les arbres masquaient *or* cachaient la maison ◆ **to ~ sth from sight** *or* **view** dérober *or* masquer qch aux regards ◆ **to ~ sth from the wind/sun** protéger qch du vent/du soleil ◆ **to ~ one's eyes** se protéger les yeux avec la main, faire écran de sa main pour se protéger les yeux ◆ **in order to ~ our movements from the enemy** pour cacher *or* masquer nos mouvements à l'ennemi

2 *[+ film]* projeter

3 *(= check)* *[+ candidates]* présélectionner ; *[+ phone call]* filtrer ; *[+ luggage, passengers]* contrôler ◆ **to ~ sb (for a job)** passer au crible la candidature de qn ◆ **the candidates were carefully ~ed** les candidats ont été passés au crible ◆ **to ~ women for breast cancer** proposer aux femmes un dépistage du cancer du sein

COMP **screen actor** N acteur *m* de cinéma, vedette *f* de l'écran

screen door N porte *f* grillagée

screen dump N *(Comput)* impression *f* d'écran

screen memory N *(Psych)* souvenir-écran *m*

screen name N *(Cine)* nom *m* d'acteur/d'actrice

screen rights NPL droits *mpl* d'adaptation cinématographique

screen saver N économiseur *m* d'écran

screen test N bout *m* d'essai ◆ **to do a ~ test** tourner un bout d'essai

screen wash N *(Brit: of vehicle)* liquide *m* lave-glace

screen washer N *(Brit: of vehicle)* lave-glace *m*

screen writer N scénariste *mf*

► **screen off** VT SEP ◆ **the kitchen was screened off from the rest of the room** la cuisine était séparée du reste de la pièce par un rideau *(or* un paravent) ◆ **the nurses ~ed off his bed** les infirmiers ont mis un paravent autour de son lit ◆ **the trees ~ed off the house from the road** les arbres cachaient la maison de la route, les arbres faisaient écran entre la maison et la route ◆ **a cordon of police ~ed off the accident from the onlookers** les agents de police ont formé un cordon pour cacher l'accident aux badauds

screenful /ˈskriːnfʌl/ N *(Comput)* écran *m*

screening /ˈskriːnɪŋ/ N 1 *[of film]* projection *f* 2 *[of person]* *(= selection)* tri *m*, procédure *f* de sélection sur dossier ; *(Med)* *[of person]* examen *m* de dépistage *(of sb* pratiqué sur qn) ◆ **the ~ of women for breast cancer** le dépistage du cancer du sein chez les femmes ◆ **the ~ of luggage and passengers** le contrôle des bagages et des passagers 3 *[of coal]* criblage *m* COMP **screening room** N *(Cine)* salle *f* de projection

screenplay /ˈskriːnpleɪ/ N scénario *m*

screenwriting /ˈskriːnraɪtɪŋ/ N écriture *f* de scénarios

screw /skruː/ N 1 vis *f* ; *(= action)* tour *m* de vis ◆ **a ~ of tea/sweets/tobacco** *etc* † *(Brit)* un cornet de thé/de bonbons/de tabac *etc* ◆ **he's got a ~ loose** * il lui manque une case * ◆ **to put** *or* **tighten the ~(s) on sb** *, **to turn the ~ on sb** * augmenter la pression sur qn ; → **thumbscrew**

2 *(= propeller)* hélice *f* ; → **airscrew, twin**

3 *(*‡ = sex)* **it was a good ~** on a bien baisé*‡ ◆ **she's a good ~** c'est un bon coup‡

4 *(‡ = prison warder)* maton(ne)‡ *m(f)*

5 *(Brit* † ‡ *= income)* salaire *m* ◆ **he gets a good ~** son boulot paie bien *

VT 1 visser *(on* sur ; *to* à) fixer avec une vis ◆ **to ~ sth tight** visser qch à bloc

2 *(= twist)* ◆ **to ~ one's face into a smile** grimacer un sourire

3 *(= extort)* *[+ money]* extorquer, soutirer *(out of* à) ; *[+ information]* arracher *(out of* à) ; *(‡ = defraud)* *[+ person]* arnaquer *, pigeonner *

4 *(*‡= have sex with)* baiser*‡

5 *(‡: in exclamations)* **~ you!** va te faire voir * *or* foutre*‡! ◆ **~ the cost/the neighbours!** on se fout du prix/des voisins !‡

VI se visser

COMP **screw bolt** N boulon *m* à vis

screw joint N joint *m* à vis

screw propeller N hélice *f*

screw thread N filet *m or* filetage *m* de vis

screw top N couvercle *m* à pas de vis

screw-top(ped) ADJ avec couvercle à pas de vis

screw-up ‡ N *(fig = muddle)* pagaille * *f* complète

► **screw around** VI 1 *(‡ = waste time)* glander‡, glandouiller‡

2 *(*‡ sexually)* coucher à droite à gauche *

► **screw down** VI se visser

VT SEP visser (à fond)

► **screw off** VI se dévisser

VT SEP dévisser

► **screw on** VI se visser

VT SEP visser, fixer avec des vis ; *[+ lid]* visser ◆ **he's got his head ~ed on all right** * *or* **the right way** * il a la tête sur les épaules

► **screw round** VT SEP tourner, visser ◆ **to ~ one's head round** se dévisser la tête *or* le cou

► **screw together** VT SEP *[+ two parts]* fixer avec une vis ◆ **to ~ sth together** assembler qch avec des vis

► **screw up** VT SEP 1 visser (à fond), resserrer (à fond)

2 *[+ paper]* chiffonner, froisser ; *[+ handkerchief]* rouler, tortiller ◆ **to ~ up one's eyes** plisser les yeux ◆ **to ~ up one's face** faire la grimace ◆ **to ~ up (one's) courage** prendre son courage à deux mains * *(to do sth* pour faire qch)

3 *(‡ = spoil)* foutre en l'air*‡, bousiller‡

4 **to ~ sb up** ‡ détraquer * *or* perturber qn ◆ **he is ~ed up** ‡ il est paumé‡

VI ‡ merder*‡

N ◆ **screw-up** ‡ → **screw**

screwball ‡ /ˈskruːbɔːl/ ADJ, N cinglé(e) * *m(f)*, tordu(e)‡ *m(f)*

screwdriver /ˈskruːˌdraɪvəʳ/ N *(= tool)* tournevis *m* ; *(= drink)* vodka-orange *f*

screwed ‡ /skruːd/ ADJ *(Brit = drunk)* paf * *inv*, bourré‡ ; see also **screw up**

screwy ‡ /ˈskruːɪ/ ADJ *[person]* cinglé * ; *[idea, situation]* tordu *

scribble /ˈskrɪbl/ VI gribouiller ◆ **he was scribbling in a notebook** il gribouillait sur un carnet ◆ **we were scribbling away furiously, trying to finish the exam** nous écrivions frénétiquement pour essayer de terminer l'épreuve ◆ **someone has ~d all over the wall** quelqu'un a gribouillé sur le mur

VT griffonner, gribouiller ◆ **to ~ a note to sb** griffonner *or* gribouiller un mot à qn ◆ **there were comments ~d all over the page** il y avait des commentaires griffonnés *or* gribouillés sur toute la page

N gribouillage *m* ◆ **I can't read her ~** je ne peux pas déchiffrer son gribouillage ◆ **the word ended in a ~** le mot se terminait par un gribouillage ◆ **her letter was just a ~** sa lettre était griffonnée

► **scribble down** VT SEP *[+ notes]* griffonner

► **scribble out** VT SEP 1 *(= erase)* rayer, raturer

2 *[+ essay, draft]* jeter sur le papier, ébaucher

scribbler /ˈskrɪbləʳ/ N *(lit)* gribouilleur *m*, -euse *f* ; *(fig = bad author)* plumitif *m*

scribbling /ˈskrɪblɪŋ/ N gribouillage *m*, gribouillis *m* COMP **scribbling pad** N *(Brit)* bloc-notes *m*

scribe /skraɪb/ N scribe *m*

scrimmage /ˈskrɪmɪdʒ/ N *(gen, Sport)* mêlée *f*

scrimp /skrɪmp/ VI lésiner *(on* sur), être chiche *(on* de) ◆ **to ~ and save** économiser sur tout

scrimshank * /ˈskrɪmʃæŋk/ *(Brit Mil)* N ⇒ **scrimshanker** VI ‡ tirer au flanc *

scrimshanker * /ˈskrɪmˌʃæŋkəʳ/ N *(Brit Mil)* tire-au-flanc * *mf inv*

scrip /skrɪp/ N *(Fin)* titre *m* provisoire (d'action)

scripholder /ˈskrɪphəʊldəʳ/ N *(Fin)* détenteur *m*, -trice *f* de titres (provisoires)

script /skrɪpt/ N 1 *(Cine)* scénario *m* ; *(Rad, Theat, TV)* texte *m* 2 *(in exam)* copie *f* ; *(Jur)* document *m* original 3 *(NonC)* *(= handwriting)* script *m*, écriture *f* script ; *(Typ)* scriptes *fpl* ; → **italic** VT *[+ film]* écrire le scénario de

scripted /ˈskrɪptɪd/ ADJ *[talk, discussion]* préparé d'avance ; *[speech]* écrit à l'avance

scriptural /ˈskrɪptʃərəl/ ADJ biblique

Scripture /ˈskrɪptʃəʳ/ N (also **Holy Scripture(s)**) Écriture *f* sainte, Saintes Écritures *fpl* ◆ **~ (lesson)** *(Scol)* (cours *m* d')instruction *f* religieuse

scripture /ˈskrɪptʃəʳ/ N texte *m* sacré

scriptwriter /ˈskrɪptˌraɪtəʳ/ N *(Cine, TV)* scénariste *mf*

scrivener †† /ˈskrɪvnəʳ/ N *(= scribe)* scribe *m* ; *(= notary)* notaire *m*

scrod /skrɒd/ N *(US)* jeune morue *f or* cabillaud *m (spécialité du Massachusetts)*

scrofula /ˈskrɒfjʊlə/ N scrofule *f*

scrofulous /ˈskrɒfjʊləs/ ADJ scrofuleux

scroll /skrəʊl/ N 1 *[of parchment]* rouleau *m* ; *(= ancient book)* manuscrit *m* ; → **dead** 2 *(Archit)* volute *f*, spirale *f* ; *(in writing)* enjolivement *m* ; *[of violin]* volute *f* VI *(Comput)* défiler VT *(Comput)* ◆ **to ~ sth up/down** dérouler *or* faire défiler qch vers le haut/le bas COMP **scroll bar** N *(Comput)* barre *f* de défilement

Scrooge /skruːdʒ/ N harpagon *m*

scrotum /ˈskrəʊtəm/ N (pl **scrotums** *or* **scrota** /ˈskrəʊtə/) scrotum *m*

scrounge * /skraʊndʒ/ VT *[+ meal, clothes etc]* réussir à se faire offrir *(from or off sb* par qn) ◆ **to ~ money from sb** taper qn * ◆ **he ~d £5 off him** il l'a tapé de 5 livres * ◆ **can I ~ your pen?** je peux te piquer * ton stylo ? VI ◆ **to ~ on sb** vivre aux crochets de qn ◆ **he's always scrounging** c'est un parasite ; *(for meals)* c'est un pique-assiette N ◆ **to be on the ~ for sth** essayer d'emprunter qch ◆ **he's always on the ~** c'est un parasite

scrounger * /ˈskraʊndʒəʳ/ N parasite *m*, profiteur *m*, -euse *f* ; *(for meals)* pique-assiette *mf inv*

scroungy ‡ /ˈskraʊndʒɪ/ ADJ *(US = scruffy)* dépenaillé *, débraillé

scrub¹ /skrʌb/ N nettoyage *m* à la brosse, bon nettoyage *m* ◆ **to give sth a good ~** bien nettoyer qch (à la brosse *or* avec une brosse) ◆ **give your face a ~!** lave-toi bien la figure ! ◆ **it needs a ~** cela a besoin d'être bien nettoyé

VT 1 *[+ floor]* nettoyer *or* laver à la brosse ; *[+ washing]* frotter ; *[+ pan]* récurer ◆ **to ~ one's hands** se brosser les mains, bien se nettoyer les mains ◆ **she ~bed the walls clean** elle a nettoyé les murs à fond ◆ **he ~bed the walls with bleach** il a nettoyé les murs à fond avec de l'eau de Javel ◆ **to ~ o.s. (all over)** se frotter vigoureusement (tout le corps)

2 *(* = cancel)* *[+ match etc]* annuler ◆ **let's ~ that** laissons tomber

VI frotter ◆ **she's been on her knees ~bing all day** elle a passé sa journée à genoux à frotter les planchers ◆ **to ~ at sth** récurer qch ◆ **he was ~bing away at the oven** il récurait le four ◆ **let's ~ round it** ‡ *(fig)* laissons tomber *, n'en parlons plus

COMP **scrubbing brush** *(Brit)*, **scrub brush** *(US)* N brosse *f* à récurer

► **scrub away** VT SEP *[+ dirt]* enlever en frottant ; *[+ stain]* faire partir (en frottant)

► **scrub down** VT SEP *[+ room, walls]* nettoyer à fond ◆ **to ~ o.s. down** faire une toilette en règle

► **scrub off** VT SEP ⇒ **scrub away**

► **scrub out** VT SEP *[+ name]* effacer ; *[+ stain]* faire partir ; *[+ pan]* récurer

► **scrub up** VI [surgeon etc] se brosser les mains avant d'opérer

scrub² /skrʌb/ N (NonC = brushwood) broussailles fpl

scrubber¹ /ˈskrʌbəʳ/ N (also **pan-scrubber**) tampon m à récurer

scrubber²* /ˈskrʌbəʳ/ N (= woman) pute* f

scrubby /ˈskrʌbɪ/ ADJ [land] broussailleux ; [trees, grass] rabougri

scrubland /ˈskrʌblænd/ N (gen) brousse f ; (in Austral) scrub m

scrubwoman /ˈskrʌb,wʊmən/ N (pl **-women**) (US) femme f de ménage

scruff /skrʌf/ N 1 ◆ **by the ~ of the neck** par la peau du cou 2 (* = untidy person) individu m débraillé or peu soigné

scruffily /ˈskrʌfɪlɪ/ ADV ◆ **~ dressed** débraillé, dépenaillé*

scruffiness /ˈskrʌfɪnɪs/ N [of person] tenue f débraillée or dépenaillée* ; [of clothes, building] miteux m

scruffy /ˈskrʌfɪ/ ADJ [person, appearance, clothes] débraillé, dépenaillé* ; [building] miteux ; [hair] en désordre

scrum /skrʌm/ N 1 (Rugby) mêlée f ◆ **to put the ball into the ~** introduire le ballon dans la or en mêlée 2 (* fig = pushing) bousculade f, mêlée f ◆ **the ~ of reporters** la bousculade or la mêlée des journalistes ◆ **she pushed through the ~ of photographers** elle s'est frayé un chemin à travers la mêlée des photographes
COMP **scrum half** N demi m de mêlée

scrummage /ˈskrʌmɪdʒ/ N ⇒ **scrum** VI (Rugby) jouer en mêlée ; (fig) se bousculer

scrummy* /ˈskrʌmɪ/ ADJ [food] délicieux ; [person] craquant*

scrump* /skrʌmp/ VT (Brit) [+ apples etc] chaparder

scrumptious* /ˈskrʌmpʃəs/ ADJ délicieux ◆ **it smells ~** ça sent délicieusement bon

scrumpy /ˈskrʌmpɪ/ N (Brit) cidre m fermier

scrunch /skrʌntʃ/ VI ◆ **her feet ~ed on the gravel** ses pas crissaient sur le gravier VT (also **scrunch up**) (= crush) écraser ◆ **to ~ sth into a ball** faire une boule de qch

scrunchie /ˈskrʌntʃɪ/ N (for hair) chouchou m

scruple /ˈskruːpl/ N scrupule m ◆ **moral/religious ~s** scrupules mpl moraux/religieux ◆ **to have ~s about sth** avoir des scrupules au sujet de qch ◆ **he has no ~s** il est sans scrupules, il est dénué de scrupules ◆ **to have no ~s about sth** n'avoir aucun scrupule au sujet de qch ◆ **to have no ~s about doing sth** n'avoir aucun scrupule à faire qch, ne pas avoir scrupule à faire qch VI (frm) ◆ **I did not ~ to accept his offer** je n'ai pas hésité à accepter or je n'ai pas eu scrupule (liter) à accepter son offre

scrupulous /ˈskruːpjʊləs/ ADJ 1 (= honest) [person, organization, honesty] scrupuleux ◆ **it is not ~ to do that** ce n'est pas honnête de faire cela 2 (= meticulous) [person, research, care] scrupuleux, méticuleux ; [attention] scrupuleux ◆ **he was ~ about paying his debts** il payait scrupuleusement ses dettes ◆ **he is ~ about hygiene** il fait très attention aux questions d'hygiène ◆ **he spoke with the most ~ politeness** il s'exprimait avec une extrême politesse

scrupulously /ˈskruːpjʊləslɪ/ ADV 1 (= honestly) [behave] d'une manière scrupuleuse ◆ **~ honest/fair** d'une honnêteté/équité scrupuleuse 2 (= meticulously) [avoid] soigneusement ◆ **~ clean** d'une propreté irréprochable ◆ **to be ~ careful** faire preuve d'un soin méticuleux

scrupulousness /ˈskruːpjʊləsnɪs/ N (NonC) (= honesty) scrupules mpl, esprit m scrupuleux ; (= exactitude) minutie f

scrutineer /,skruːtɪˈnɪəʳ/ N (Brit) scrutateur m, -trice f

scrutinize /ˈskruːtɪnaɪz/ VT [+ writing, document] scruter, examiner minutieusement ; [+ votes] pointer

scrutiny /ˈskruːtɪnɪ/ N 1 (= act of scrutinizing) [of document, conduct] examen m minutieux or rigoureux ; [of votes] pointage m ◆ **it should be open to public ~** les gens devraient avoir un droit de regard ◆ **they want to increase parliamentary ~ over these activities** ils veulent augmenter le droit de regard du parlement sur ces activités ◆ **to keep sb under close ~** surveiller qn de près ◆ **to come under intense ~** être examiné de très près 2 (= watchful gaze) regard m insistant or scrutateur (frm) ◆ **under his ~, she felt nervous** son regard insistant or scrutateur la mettait mal à l'aise

SCSI /ˈskʌzɪ/ N (Comput) (abbrev of **small computer systems interface**) SCSI f

scuba /ˈskuːbə/ N scaphandre m autonome
COMP **scuba dive** VI faire de la plongée sous-marine
scuba diver N plongeur m, -euse f
scuba diving N plongée f sous-marine (autonome)

scud /skʌd/ VI (also **scud along**) [clouds, waves] courir (à toute allure) ; [boat] filer (vent arrière) ◆ **the clouds were ~ding across the sky** les nuages couraient (à toute allure) dans le ciel

scuff /skʌf/ VT [+ shoes, furniture] érafler ◆ **~ed shoes** chaussures fpl éraflées ◆ **to ~ one's feet** traîner les pieds VI traîner les pieds COMP **scuff marks** NPL (on shoes) éraflures fpl, marques fpl d'usure

scuffle /ˈskʌfl/ N bagarre f, échauffourée f, rixe f VI 1 se bagarrer* (with avec) 2 (= shuffle) traîner les pieds

scull /skʌl/ N 1 (= one of a pair of oars) aviron m ; (= single oar for stern) godille f 2 (= boat) outrigger m VI (with two oars) ramer (en couple) ; (with single oar) godiller ◆ **to go ~ing** faire de l'aviron VT (with two oars) faire avancer à l'aviron ; (with single oar) faire avancer à la godille

scullery /ˈskʌlərɪ/ N (esp Brit) arrière-cuisine f
COMP **scullery maid** N fille f de cuisine

sculpt /skʌlp(t)/ VT sculpter (out of dans) VI sculpter, faire de la sculpture

sculptor /ˈskʌlptəʳ/ N sculpteur m

sculptress /ˈskʌlptrɪs/ N femme f sculpteur, sculpteur m ◆ **I met a ~** j'ai rencontré une femme sculpteur ◆ **she is a ~** elle est sculpteur

sculptural /ˈskʌlptʃərəl/ ADJ sculptural

sculpture /ˈskʌlptʃəʳ/ N sculpture f ◆ **a (piece of) ~** une sculpture VT sculpter

scum /skʌm/ N 1 (gen) écume f ; (foamy) écume f, mousse f ; (dirty) couche f de saleté ; (on bath) crasse f ◆ **to remove the ~ (from)** (= foam) écumer ; (= dirt) décrasser, nettoyer 2 (pej = people) **they're just ~** c'est de la racaille ◆ **the ~ of the earth** le rebut du genre humain 3 (* pej = person: also **scumbag**) salaud* m, ordure* f

scummy /ˈskʌmɪ/ ADJ (lit) écumeux, couvert d'écume, mousseux ; (* pej) de salaud*

scunner* /ˈskʌnəʳ/ (Scot) N ◆ **what a ~ !** quelle barbe !* VI ◆ **to be ~ed** en avoir marre*

scupper /ˈskʌpəʳ/ N (Naut) dalot or daleau m VT (Brit *) [+ plan, negotiations] faire capoter* ; [+ effort] saboter ◆ **we're ~ed** nous sommes fichus*

scurf /skɜːf/ N (on scalp) pellicules fpl (du cuir chevelu) ; (on skin) peau f morte

scurfy /ˈskɜːfɪ/ ADJ [scalp] pelliculeux ; [skin] dartreux

scurrility /skʌˈrɪlɪtɪ/ N 1 (= slander) caractère m calomnieux 2 (= obscenity) obscénité f

scurrilous /ˈskʌrɪləs/ ADJ 1 (= defamatory) [rumour, article] calomnieux 2 (= obscene) obscène

scurrilously /ˈskʌrɪləslɪ/ ADV 1 (= slanderously) [suggest, abuse] calomnieusement 2 (= obscenely) ◆ **~ funny jokes** des plaisanteries fpl obscènes

scurry /ˈskʌrɪ/ N débandade f, sauve-qui-peut m inv ◆ **a ~ of footsteps** des pas précipités VI se précipiter, filer* (à toute allure)

► **scurry away, scurry off** VI [person] détaler, se sauver (à toutes jambes) ; [animal] détaler

scurvy /ˈskɜːvɪ/ N scorbut m ADJ († or liter) bas (basse f), mesquin, vil (vile f)

scut /skʌt/ N [of rabbit, deer] queue f

scutcheon /ˈskʌtʃən/ N écu m, écusson m

scuttle¹ /ˈskʌtl/ N (for coal) seau m (à charbon)

scuttle² /ˈskʌtl/ VI courir précipitamment ◆ **to ~ in/out/through** etc entrer/sortir/traverser etc précipitamment

► **scuttle away, scuttle off** VI déguerpir, filer*

scuttle³ /ˈskʌtl/ N 1 (Naut) écoutille f 2 (US: in ceiling) trappe f VT 1 (Naut) saborder ◆ **to ~ one's own ship** se saborder 2 (fig) [+ hopes, plans] faire échouer

scuttlebutt /ˈskʌtlbʌt/ N 1 (Naut = water cask) baril m d'eau douce 2 (US fig = gossip) ragots mpl, commérages mpl

scuzzy* /ˈskʌzɪ/ ADJ (= dirty) dégueulasse* ; (= seedy) louche

Scylla /ˈsɪlə/ N Scylla ◆ **to be between ~ and Charybdis** tomber de Charybde en Scylla

scythe /saɪð/ N faux f VT faucher

► **scythe down** VT SEP [+ opponents, critics] descendre en flammes*

► **scythe through** VT FUS [+ troops, army] décimer ; [+ building] pulvériser

SD abbrev of **South Dakota**

SDI /,esdiːˈaɪ/ N (US Mil, Space) (abbrev of **Strategic Defense Initiative**) → **strategic**

SDLP /,esdiːelˈpiː/ N (Ir Pol) (abbrev of **Social Democratic and Labour Party**) → **social**

SDP /,esdiːˈpiː/ N (Brit Pol: formerly) (abbrev of **Social Democratic Party**) → **social**

SE (abbrev of **south-east**) S.-E.

sea /siː/ N 1 (not land) mer f ◆ **to swim in the ~** nager or se baigner dans la mer ◆ **on the ~** [boat] en mer ; [town] au bord de la mer ◆ **by** or **beside the ~** au bord de la mer ◆ **by ~** par mer, en bateau ◆ **to be swept** or **carried out to ~** être emporté par la mer ◆ **to go to ~** [boat] prendre la mer ; [person] devenir or se faire marin ◆ **to put to ~** prendre la mer ◆ **look out to ~** regardez au or vers le large ◆ **over** or (liter) **beyond the ~(s)** outre-mer ◆ **from over** or (liter) **beyond the ~(s)** d'outre-mer ◆ **(out) at ~** (lit) en mer ◆ **I'm all at ~*** (= unable to understand, follow) je nage complètement* ; (= unable to get used to new situation) je suis complètement désorienté or déboussolé* ◆ **he was all at ~ in the discussion** il était complètement perdu dans la discussion ◆ **it left him all at ~** cela l'a complètement désorienté ; → **burial, call, follow, half, high**
2 (= particular area) mer f ◆ **the Sea of Galilee** la mer de Galilée ; → **dead, red, seven**
3 (NonC = state of the sea) (état m de la) mer f ◆ **what's the ~ like?** comment est la mer ? ◆ **a rough** or **heavy ~** une mer houleuse ◆ **a calm ~** une mer calme ◆ **to ship a ~** (Naut) embarquer un paquet de mer
4 (fig) [of flowers, corn] mer f ; [of blood] mare f, mer f ; [of difficulties, troubles, doubts, confusion]

océan *m* ◆ **a ~ of faces** une multitude de visages

COMP **sea air** N air *m* marin *or* de la mer
sea anchor N ancre *f* flottante
sea anemone N anémone *f* de mer
sea bathing N bains *mpl* de mer
sea battle N bataille *f* navale
sea bed N fond *m* de la mer
sea bird N oiseau *m* de mer, oiseau *m* marin
sea biscuit N biscuit *m* de mer
sea boot N botte *f* de caoutchouc
sea bream N dorade *or* daurade *f*
sea breeze N brise *f* de mer *or* du large
sea captain N capitaine *m* (de la marine marchande)
sea change N profond changement *m*
sea chest N malle-cabine *f*
sea coast N côte *f*
sea cow N vache *f* marine
sea crossing N traversée *f* (*par mer*)
sea cucumber N concombre *m* de mer
sea defences NPL ouvrages *mpl* de défense (contre la mer)
sea dog N (= *fish*) roussette *f*, chien *m* de mer ; (= *seal*) phoque *m* commun ◆ **(old) ~ dog** (= *sailor*) (vieux) loup *m* de mer
sea eagle N aigle *m* de mer
sea eel N anguille *f* de mer
sea elephant N éléphant *m* de mer
sea fight N combat *m* naval
sea fish N poisson *m* de mer
sea fish farming N aquaculture *f* marine
sea floor N fond *m* de la mer
sea front N bord *m* de (la) mer, front *m* de mer
sea god N dieu *m* marin
sea-green N vert *m* glauque *inv* ADJ glauque
sea horse N hippocampe *m*
sea kale N chou *m* marin, crambe *m*
sea lane N couloir *m* *or* voie *f* de navigation maritime
sea legs NPL ◆ **to find** *or* **get one's ~ legs** s'amariner, s'habituer à la mer ◆ **he's got his ~ legs** il a retrouvé le pied marin
sea level N niveau *m* de la mer ◆ **100 metres above/below ~ level** 100 mètres au-dessus/au-dessous du niveau de la mer
sea lift N (*Mil*) évacuation *f* par mer
sea lion N otarie *f*
sea loch N (*Scot*) bras *m* de mer
Sea Lord N (*Brit*) ≃ amiral *m* ◆ **First Sea Lord** ≃ amiral *m* chef d'état-major de la Marine
sea mile N mille *m* marin
sea otter N loutre *f* de mer
sea power N puissance *f* navale
sea route N route *f* maritime
sea rover N (= *ship*) bateau *m* pirate ; (= *person*) pirate *m*
sea salt N sel *m* de mer
Sea Scout N scout *m* marin
sea serpent N serpent *m* de mer
sea shanty N chanson *f* de marins
sea shell N coquillage *m*
sea transport N transports *mpl* maritimes
sea trout N truite *f* de mer
sea urchin N oursin *m*
sea view N (*esp Brit*) vue *f* sur la mer
sea wall N digue *f*
sea water N eau *f* de mer

Seabee /ˈsiːˌbiː/ N (*US Mil*) militaire *m* du Génie maritime

seaboard /ˈsiːbɔːd/ N littoral *m*, côte *f*

seaborne /ˈsiːbɔːn/ ADJ [*goods*] transporté par mer ; [*trade*] maritime

seafarer /ˈsiːˌfɛərəʳ/ N marin *m*

seafaring /ˈsiːˌfɛərɪŋ/ N (also **seafaring life**) vie *f* de marin COMP **seafaring man** N marin *m*

seafood /ˈsiːfuːd/ N fruits *mpl* de mer

seagirt /ˈsiːgɜːt/ ADJ (*liter*) ceint par la mer

seagoing /ˈsiːgəʊɪŋ/ ADJ (*Naut*) long-courrier ; [*theme, experience*] maritime ◆ **~ man** marin *m* ◆ **~ ship** (navire *m*) long-courrier *m*, navire *m* de mer

seagull /ˈsiːgʌl/ N mouette *f*

seal¹ /siːl/ N phoque *m* VI ◆ **to go ~ing** chasser le phoque COMP **seal cull** N abattage *m* de phoques

seal² /siːl/ N 1 (= *stamping device*) sceau *m*, cachet *m* ; (*on document*) sceau *m*, cachet *m* ; (*on envelope*) cachet *m* ; (*on package*) plomb *m* ; (*Jur: on door etc*) scellé *m* ◆ **to be under ~** (*frm*) [*document*] être sous scellés ◆ **under ~ of secrecy** sous le sceau du secret ◆ **under the ~ of confession** dans le secret de la confession ◆ **~ of quality** (*Comm*) label *m* de qualité ◆ **given under my hand and ~** (*Jur*) signé et scellé par moi ◆ **to put** *or* **set one's ~ to sth** apposer son sceau à qch ◆ **to set** *or* **give one's ~ of approval to sth** donner son approbation à qch ◆ **this set the ~ on their alliance** ceci a scellé leur alliance ; → **privy, self**
2 (= *ornamental stamp*) **Christmas ~** timbre *m* ornemental de Noël
3 (= *device for sealing: also Aut*) joint *m* (d'étanchéité) ◆ **the ~ is not very good** ce n'est pas très étanche
VT 1 (= *put seal on*) [+ *document*] sceller, apposer un sceau sur ; (= *stick down*) [+ *envelope, packet*] coller, fermer ; (= *close with seal*) [+ *envelope*] cacheter ; [+ *package*] plomber ; [+ *jar*] sceller, fermer hermétiquement ; [+ *tin*] souder ◆ **~ed orders** instructions *fpl* secrètes ◆ **my lips are ~ed** (*hum*) mes lèvres sont scellées ◆ **to ~ a steak** (*Culin*) saisir un bifteck ; → **hermetically**
2 (= *close off*) [+ *area*] boucler ; [+ *border*] fermer
3 (= *decide*) [+ *fate*] régler, décider (de) ; [+ *bargain*] conclure ◆ **this ~ed his fate** cela a décidé (de) *or* a réglé son sort
COMP **seal ring** N chevalière *f*

▸ **seal in** VT SEP enfermer (hermétiquement) ◆ **our special process ~s the flavour in** notre procédé spécial garde *or* conserve toute la saveur

▸ **seal off** VT SEP (= *close up*) [+ *door, room*] condamner ; (= *forbid entry to*) [+ *passage, road, room*] interdire l'accès de ; (*with troops, police etc*) [+ *area*] boucler

▸ **seal up** VT SEP [+ *window, door, jar*] fermer hermétiquement, sceller ; [+ *tin*] souder

sealant /ˈsiːlənt/ N (= *device*) joint *m* ; (= *substance*) enduit *m* étanche

sealer /ˈsiːləʳ/ N (= *person*) chasseur *m* de phoques ; (= *ship*) navire *m* équipé pour la chasse au(x) phoque(s)

sealing¹ /ˈsiːlɪŋ/ N chasse *f* aux phoques

sealing² /ˈsiːlɪŋ/ N [*of document*] scellage *m* ; [*of letter*] cachetage *m* ; [*of package*] plombage *m* COMP **sealing wax** N cire *f* à cacheter

sealskin /ˈsiːlskɪn/ N peau *f* de phoque ADJ en peau de phoque

seam /siːm/ N 1 (*in cloth, canvas*) couture *f* ; (*in plastic, rubber*) couture *f*, joint *m* ; (*in planks, metal*) joint *m* ; (*in welding*) soudure *f* ◆ **to fall** *or* **come apart at the ~s** [*garment*] se découdre ; [*relationship*] battre de l'aile ; [*system, country*] s'écrouler ◆ **to be bursting at the ~s*** [*suitcase, room*] être plein à craquer 2 (*Min*) filon *m*, veine *f* ; (*Geol*) couche *f* 3 (*on face*) (= *wrinkle*) ride *f* ; (= *scar*) balafre *f*, couture *f* VT faire une couture *or* un joint à

seaman /ˈsiːmən/ N (pl **-men**) (*gen*) marin *m* ; (*US Navy*) quartier-maître *m* de 2e classe ; → **able, ordinary**
COMP **seaman apprentice** N (*US Navy*) matelot *m* breveté
seaman recruit N (*US Navy*) matelot *m*

seamanlike /ˈsiːmənlaɪk/ ADJ de bon marin

seamanship /ˈsiːmənʃɪp/ N habileté *f* dans la manœuvre, qualités *fpl* de marin

seamed /siːmd/ ADJ 1 [*stockings, tights*] à couture 2 [*face*] sillonné de rides ◆ **a face ~ with wrinkles** un visage sillonné de rides ◆ **the cave was ~ with crevices** la paroi de la caverne était entaillée de fissures ◆ **grey rock ~ with white** de la roche grise veinée de blanc

seamen /ˈsiːmən/ NPL of **seaman**

seamless /ˈsiːmlɪs/ ADJ 1 [*stockings, bra, garment*] sans couture 2 (= *smooth*) [*transition*] sans heurts, en douceur ; [*blend*] homogène ◆ **a ~ whole** un ensemble homogène

seamstress /ˈsemstrɪs/ N couturière *f*

seamy /ˈsiːmɪ/ ADJ [*event, details*] sordide ; [*district*] mal famé, louche ◆ **the ~ side of life** le côté sordide de la vie

séance /ˈseɪɑːns/ N [*of spiritualists*] séance *f* de spiritisme ; [*of committee etc*] séance *f*, réunion *f*

seaplane /ˈsiːpleɪn/ N hydravion *m* COMP **seaplane base** N hydrobase *f*

seaport /ˈsiːpɔːt/ N port *m* de mer

sear /sɪəʳ/ ADJ desséché, flétri VT 1 (= *wither*) [+ *flower, grain, leaves*] flétrir ; (= *burn*) brûler ; (= *cauterize*) cautériser ; (= *brand*) marquer au fer rouge 2 (*Culin*) griller 3 (*fig* = *make callous*) [+ *person, conscience, feelings*] endurcir

▸ **sear through** VT FUS [+ *walls, metal*] traverser, percer

search /sɜːtʃ/ N 1 (*for sth lost*) recherche(s) *f(pl)* ◆ **in ~ of** à la recherche de ◆ **a ~ was made for the child** on a entrepris des recherches pour retrouver l'enfant ◆ **the ~ for the missing man** les recherches entreprises pour retrouver l'homme ◆ **to begin a ~ for** [+ *person*] partir à la recherche de ; [+ *thing*] se mettre à la recherche de ◆ **in my ~ I found an interesting book** au cours de mes recherches j'ai découvert un livre intéressant ; → **house**
2 [*of drawer, box, pocket, district*] fouille *f* ; (*Admin*) [*of luggage etc*] visite *f* ; (*Jur*) [*of building etc*] perquisition *f* ◆ **the ~ did not reveal anything** la fouille n'a rien donné ◆ **his ~ of the drawer revealed nothing** il a fouillé le tiroir sans rien trouver *or* pour ne rien trouver ◆ **the thieves' ~ of the house** la fouille de la maison par les voleurs ◆ **house ~** (*Police*) perquisition *f* à domicile, visite *f* domiciliaire ◆ **right of ~** (*Jur*) droit *m* de visite ◆ **passengers must submit to a ~** les passagers doivent se soumettre à une fouille
3 (*Comput*) recherche *f* ◆ **~ and replace** recherche *f* et remplacement *m*
VT 1 (= *hunt through*) [+ *house, park, woods, district*] fouiller ; (*Jur*) [+ *house etc*] perquisitionner ◆ **they ~ed the woods for the child** ils ont fouillé les bois *or* ils ont passé les bois au peigne fin à la recherche de l'enfant ◆ **we have ~ed the library for it** nous l'avons cherché partout dans la bibliothèque
2 (= *examine*) [+ *pocket, drawer, suitcase*] fouiller (dans) (*for* pour essayer de retrouver) ; [+ *luggage*] (*gen*) fouiller ; (*Customs, Police etc*) visiter ; [+ *suspect*] fouiller ◆ **they ~ed him for a weapon** ils l'ont fouillé pour s'assurer qu'il n'avait pas d'arme ◆ **~ me!*** je n'en sais rien !, je n'en ai pas la moindre idée !
3 (= *scan*) [+ *documents, records, photograph*] examiner (en détail) (*for* pour trouver) ◆ **he ~ed her face for some sign of affection** il a cherché sur son visage un signe d'affection ◆ **to ~ one's conscience** sonder sa conscience ◆ **to ~ one's memory** chercher dans *or* fouiller dans ses souvenirs
4 (*Comput*) [+ *file*] consulter ◆ **to ~ a file for sth** rechercher qch dans un fichier
VI 1 (*gen*) chercher ◆ **to ~ after** *or* **for sth** chercher *or* rechercher qch ◆ **to ~ through sth** fouiller qch, chercher dans qch ◆ **they ~ed through his belongings** ils ont fouillé ses affaires
2 (*Comput*) **to ~ for** rechercher

COMP **search-and-destroy** ADJ *(Mil)* *[mission, operation]* de recherche et destruction
search and rescue N sauvetage *m*
search engine N *(Comput)* moteur *m* de recherche
search party N équipe *f* de secours
search warrant N *(Jur)* mandat *m* de perquisition

► **search about, search around** VI ◆ **to search about for sth** chercher qch un peu partout, fouiller un peu partout pour trouver qch

► **search out** VI SEP chercher partout ; *(and find)* trouver

searcher /ˈsɜːtʃəʳ/ N chercheur *m*, -euse *f* *(for, after* en quête de)

searching /ˈsɜːtʃɪŋ/ ADJ *[look, glance, eyes]* scrutateur (-trice *f*), inquisiteur (-trice *f*) ; *[mind]* pénétrant ; *[question]* perspicace ; *[examination]* rigoureux ◆ **it was a ~ test of his ability** cela a mis ses compétences à rude épreuve ; → **heart**

searchingly /ˈsɜːtʃɪŋlɪ/ ADV *[look]* d'un air inquisiteur

searchlight /ˈsɜːtʃlaɪt/ N projecteur *m*

searing /ˈsɪərɪŋ/ ADJ 1 *(= intense)* *[heat]* torride ; *[sun]* brûlant, de plomb ; *[light]* aveuglant ; *[pain]* fulgurant 2 *(= forceful)* *[indictment, criticism, article]* virulent

seascape /ˈsiːskeɪp/ N *(= view)* paysage *m* marin ; *(Art)* marine *f*

seashore /ˈsiːʃɔːʳ/ N rivage *m*, bord *m* de (la) mer ◆ **by** *or* **on the ~** au bord de la mer ◆ **children playing on the ~** des enfants qui jouent sur la plage

seasick /ˈsiːsɪk/ ADJ ◆ **to be ~** avoir le mal de mer ◆ **to feel ~** avoir le mal de mer

seasickness /ˈsiːsɪknɪs/ N mal *m* de mer

seaside /ˈsiːsaɪd/ N *(NonC)* bord *m* de la mer ◆ **at** *or* **beside** *or* **by the ~** au bord de la mer, à la mer ◆ **we're going to the ~** nous allons à la mer *or* au bord de la mer

COMP *[town]* au bord de la mer ; *[holiday]* à la mer ; *[hotel]* en bord de mer, au bord de la mer
seaside resort N station *f* balnéaire

season /ˈsiːzn/ LANGUAGE IN USE 23.2

N 1 *(spring, summer etc)* saison *f* ◆ **the dry ~** la saison sèche ; → **monsoon, rainy**

2 *(Sport, Comm, Zool, Agr, Hunting etc)* saison *f* ; *(= period of activity, availability etc)* époque *f*, saison *f* ; (also **social season**) saison *f* des réunions mondaines ◆ **it isn't the ~ for lily of the valley** ce n'est pas la saison du muguet ◆ **the hay fever ~** la saison du rhume des foins ◆ **when does the new ~ begin?** *(Sport)* quand commence la nouvelle saison ? ◆ **his first ~ in the Celtic team** *(Sport)* sa première saison dans l'équipe du Celtic ◆ **the start of the ~** *(for tourism, hotels etc)* le début de (la) saison ; *(Shooting)* l'ouverture de la chasse ; *(social)* le commencement de la saison (mondaine) ◆ **early in the ~** *(gen)* en début de saison ; *(very beginning)* au début de la saison ◆ **late in the ~** dans l'arrière-saison, tard dans la saison ◆ **the busy ~** *(for shops etc)* la période de grande activité ; *(for hotels etc)* la pleine saison ◆ **the peak/high/low ~** *(Brit)* la pleine/haute/basse saison ◆ **the hunting/fishing** *etc* **~** la saison de la chasse/de la pêche *etc* ◆ **the strawberry/sweetcorn ~** la saison des fraises/du maïs ◆ **the football ~** la saison de football ◆ **the tourist ~** la saison touristique ◆ **the holiday ~** la période *or* la saison des vacances ◆ **the Christmas ~** la période de Noël *or* des fêtes ◆ **"Season's greetings"** "Joyeux Noël et bonne année" ◆ **to be out of/in ~** *[food]* ne pas être/être de saison ; *(for hunting)* être fermé/ouvert ; see also **noun 6** ◆ **are pheasants in ~ now?** les faisans sont-ils en saison ? ◆ **to go somewhere out of/in ~** aller quelque part hors saison *or* en basse saison/en haute saison ◆ **strawberries out of/in ~** fraises hors de/de saison ; → **breeding, festive, silly**

3 *(fig)* moment *m* opportun ◆ **a word in ~** un mot dit à propos *or* au moment opportun ◆ **in (~) and out of ~** à tout bout de champ ◆ **in due ~** en temps utile, au moment opportun

4 *(Theat)* saison *f* (théâtrale) ◆ **he did a ~ at the Old Vic** il a joué à l'Old Vic pendant une saison ◆ **the film is here for a short ~** le film sera projeté quelques semaines ◆ **for a ~, Peter Knight in "Macbeth"** pour quelques semaines, Peter Knight dans "Macbeth" ◆ **a Dustin Hoffman ~, a ~ of Dustin Hoffman films** *(TV)* un cycle Dustin Hoffman

5 ⇒ **season ticket**

6 *[animals]* *(for mating)* ◆ **to be out of/in ~** *[males]* ne pas être/être en (période de) rut ; *[females]* ne pas être/être en chaleur

VT 1 *[+ wood]* faire sécher, dessécher ; *[+ cask]* abreuver ; see also **seasoned**

2 *(Culin)* *(with condiments)* assaisonner ; *(with spice)* épicer, relever ◆ **a highly ~ed dish** un plat relevé ◆ **a speech ~ed with humour** un discours assaisonné *or* pimenté d'humour

COMP **season ticket** N *(Rail, Theat etc)* carte *f* d'abonnement ◆ **to take out a ~ ticket** prendre un abonnement, s'abonner *(for* à)
season ticket holder N abonné(e) *m(f)*

seasonable /ˈsiːznəbl/ ADJ 1 *[weather]* de saison 2 *(frm = timely)* *[advice, arrival]* opportun

seasonal /ˈsiːzənl/ ADJ *[work, migration]* saisonnier ; *[changes, fruit, vegetable]* de saison ◆ **the holiday business is ~** le tourisme est une industrie saisonnière

COMP **seasonal adjustment** N *(Econ, Pol)* correction *f* des variations saisonnières ◆ **after ~ adjustments** en données corrigées des variations saisonnières, après correction des variations saisonnières
seasonal affective disorder N dépression *f* saisonnière
seasonal variation N *(gen, Econ)* variation *f* saisonnière
seasonal worker N (ouvrier *m*, -ière *f*) saisonnier *m*, -ière *f*

seasonally /ˈsiːzənəlɪ/ ADV *[migrate]* de manière saisonnière ◆ **~ available fruit and vegetables** les fruits *mpl* et légumes *mpl* de saison ◆ **~ adjusted figures** données *fpl* corrigées des variations saisonnières ◆ **according to the ~ adjusted figures** en données corrigées des variations saisonnières, après correction des variations saisonnières

seasoned /ˈsiːznd/ ADJ 1 *(= experienced)* *[professional, performer]* chevronné, expérimenté ; *[observer, traveller]* expérimenté ; *[troops]* aguerri ◆ **~ campaigner** *(fig)* vieux routier *m* ◆ **a ~ campaigner for civil rights** un vétéran des campagnes pour les droits civils 2 *[wood, timber]* séché ; see also **season**

seasoning /ˈsiːznɪŋ/ N assaisonnement *m* ◆ **add ~** assaisonnez ◆ **there wasn't enough ~ in the soup** la soupe manquait d'assaisonnement ◆ **with a ~ of humour** avec un grain *or* une pointe d'humour

seat /siːt/ N 1 *(= chair etc)* *(gen)* siège *m* ; *(in theatre, cinema)* fauteuil *m* ; *(in bus, train)* banquette *f* ; *(in car)* *(individual)* siège *m* ; *(for several people)* banquette *f* ; *[of cycle]* selle *f* ; → **back, driver, hot**

2 *(= place or right to sit)* place *f* ◆ **to take a ~** s'asseoir ◆ **to take one's ~** prendre place ; see also **noun 4** ◆ **to keep one's ~** rester assis ◆ **to lose one's ~** perdre sa place ; see also **noun 4** ◆ **have a ~** asseyez-vous, prenez place ◆ **I'd like two ~s for ...** *(Cine, Theat)* je voudrais deux places pour ... ◆ **keep a ~ for me** gardez-moi une place ◆ **there are ~s for 70 people** il y a 70 places assises ; → **book**

3 *(= part of chair)* siège *m* ; *[of trousers]* fond *m* ; *(* = buttocks)* derrière *m*, postérieur* *m* ◆ **he was flying by the ~ of his pants** *(fig)* il a dû faire appel à toute la présence d'esprit dont il était capable

4 *(Parl)* siège *m* ◆ **to keep/lose one's ~** être/ne pas être réélu ◆ **to take one's ~ in the Commons/in the Lords** *(Brit)* prendre son siège aux Communes/à la Chambre des lords, ≃ être validé comme député à l'Assemblée nationale/comme sénateur ◆ **the socialists won/lost ten ~s** les socialistes ont gagné/perdu dix sièges ◆ **they won the ~ from the Conservatives** ils ont pris le siège aux conservateurs ◆ **a majority of 50 ~s** une majorité de 50 (députés *etc*) ; → **safe**

5 *(on company board, committee)* siège *m*

6 *(= location, centre)* *[of government]* siège *m* ; *[of commerce]* centre *m* ; *(Med)* *[of infection]* foyer *m* ◆ **~ of learning** haut lieu *m* du savoir ◆ **he has a (country) ~ in the north** il a un manoir *or* un château dans le nord

7 *(Horse-riding)* **to have a good ~** avoir une bonne assiette, bien se tenir en selle ◆ **to keep one's ~** rester en selle ◆ **to lose one's ~** être désarçonné, vider les étriers

VT 1 *[+ child]* (faire) asseoir ; *(at table)* *[+ guest]* placer ◆ **to ~ o.s.** s'asseoir ◆ **please be ~ed** veuillez vous asseoir, asseyez-vous je vous prie ◆ **to remain ~ed** rester assis ◆ **the waiter ~ed him at my table** le garçon l'a placé à ma table ; → **deep**

2 *(= have or find room for)* **we cannot ~ them all** nous n'avons pas assez de sièges pour tout le monde ◆ **how many does the hall ~?** combien y a-t-il de places assises *or* à combien peut-on s'asseoir dans la salle ? ◆ **this car ~s six in comfort** on tient confortablement à six dans cette voiture ◆ **this table ~s eight** on peut tenir à huit à cette table, c'est une table pour huit personnes *or* couverts

3 (also **reseat**) *[+ chair]* refaire le siège de ; *[+ trousers]* (re)mettre un fond à

VI *(frm)* ◆ **this skirt won't ~** cette jupe ne va pas se déformer à l'arrière

COMP **seat back** N dossier *m* (de chaise *etc*)
seat belt N ceinture *f* de sécurité
seat cover N housse *f* *(de siège)*

-seater /ˈsiːtəʳ/ ADJ, N *(in compounds)* ◆ **a two-seater** *(= car)* une deux places ◆ **two-seater car/plane** voiture *f*/avion *m* biplace *or* à deux places ◆ **a 50~ coach** un car de 50 places

seating /ˈsiːtɪŋ/ N *(NonC)* 1 *(= act)* répartition *f or* allocation *f* des places ◆ **is the ~ (of the guests) all right?** est-ce qu'on a bien placé les invités ? 2 *(= seats)* sièges *mpl* ; *(as opposed to standing room)* places *fpl* assises ◆ **~ for 600** 600 places assises

COMP **seating accommodation** N nombre *m* de places assises
seating arrangements NPL ◆ **we must think about the ~ arrangements** nous devons réfléchir à la manière dont nous allons placer les gens ◆ **what are the ~ arrangements?** comment va-t-on placer les gens ?
seating capacity N ⇒ **seating accommodation**
seating plan N *(at dinner)* plan *m* de table

seatmates /ˈsiːtmeɪts/ NPL *(US)* ◆ **we were ~** nous étions assis l'un(e) à côté de l'autre

SEATO /ˈsiːtəʊ/ N (abbrev of **South East Asia Treaty Organisation**) OTASE *f*

seatwork /ˈsiːtwɜːk/ N *(US Scol)* travail *m* fait en classe

seaward /ˈsiːwəd/ ADJ 1 *(= towards the sea)* *[side, face, end]* qui fait face à la mer, côté mer ; *[journey]* vers la mer 2 *(= from the sea)* *[wind]* (venant) du large ADV (also **seawards**) *(= towards sea)* vers la mer ; *(= out to sea)* vers le large

seaway /ˈsiːweɪ/ N route *f* maritime

seaweed /ˈsiːwiːd/ N algue(s) *f(pl)*

seaworthiness /ˈsiːˌwɜːðɪnɪs/ N navigabilité *f* ; → **certificate**

seaworthy /ˈsiːˌwɜːðɪ/ ADJ en état de naviguer
sebaceous /sɪˈbeɪʃəs/ ADJ sébacé
Sebastian /sɪˈbæstjən/ N Sébastien *m*
seborrhoea /ˌsebəˈrɪə/ N séborrhée *f*
sebum /ˈsiːbəm/ N sébum *m*
SEC /ˌesiːˈsiː/ N (US) (abbrev of **Securities and Exchange Commission**) ≈ COB *f*
sec* /sek/ N abbrev of **second**
SECAM /ˈsiːˌkæm/ (TV) (abbrev of **séquentiel à mémoire**) SECAM *m*
secant /ˈsiːkənt/ N sécante *f* ADJ sécant
secateurs /ˌsekəˈtɜːz/ NPL (esp Brit: also **pair of secateurs**) sécateur *m*
secede /sɪˈsiːd/ VI faire sécession, se séparer (*from* de)
secession /sɪˈseʃən/ N sécession *f*, séparation *f*
secessionist /sɪˈseʃnɪst/ ADJ, N sécessionniste *mf*
seclude /sɪˈkluːd/ VT éloigner *or* isoler (du monde)
secluded /sɪˈkluːdɪd/ ADJ [*place, beach, house*] retiré, à l'écart ; [*valley, garden*] retiré ; [*life*] retiré (du monde) ; [*village*] isolé
seclusion /sɪˈkluːʒən/ N solitude *f* ◆ **to live in ~** vivre en solitaire, vivre retiré du monde
second¹ /ˈsekənd/ ADJ 1 (*one of many*) deuxième ; (*one of two*) second ◆ **a ~ chance** une seconde *or* autre chance ◆ **you may not get a ~ chance** l'occasion ne se représentera peut-être pas ◆ **Britain's ~ city** la deuxième ville de Grande-Bretagne ◆ **the ~ day I was there** le lendemain de mon arrivée ◆ **every ~ day** tous les deux jours, un jour sur deux ◆ **every ~ Thursday** un jeudi sur deux ◆ **on the ~ floor** (*Brit*) au deuxième (étage) ; (*US*) au premier (étage) ◆ **to hear** *or* **learn sth at ~ hand** (= *indirectly*) apprendre qch de seconde main ; see also **secondhand** ◆ **to be ~ in the queue** être le (*or* la) deuxième dans la queue ◆ **he was ~ in French** (*Scol*) il était deuxième en français ◆ **this is her ~ marriage** c'est la deuxième fois qu'elle se marie, c'est son second mariage ◆ **in the ~ place** deuxièmement, en second lieu ◆ **in the first place ... in the ~ place ...** d'abord ... ensuite ... ◆ **to be** *or* **lie in ~ place** être en deuxième position, occuper la deuxième place ◆ **to finish in ~ place** terminer deuxième ◆ **that's the ~ time you've asked me that** c'est la deuxième fois que vous me posez la question ◆ **a ~ time** une deuxième fois ◆ **for the** *or* **a ~ time** pour la deuxième fois ◆ **for the ~ and last time** pour la seconde et dernière fois ◆ **~ time around** la deuxième fois ◆ **to be ~ to none** être sans pareil, être sans égal ◆ **San Francisco is ~ only to New York as the tourist capital of the States** San Francisco se place tout de suite après New York comme capitale touristique des États-Unis ; → **helping, look, row¹** ; *for other phrases see* **sixth**

2 (= *additional*) [*car*] deuxième ◆ **to have a ~ home** avoir une résidence secondaire

3 (*in comparisons*) second ◆ **there are fears of a ~ Chernobyl** on craint un second Tchernobyl ◆ **England is like a ~ home to him** l'Angleterre est une seconde patrie pour lui ◆ **she's like a ~ mother to me** elle est (comme) une deuxième mère pour moi ◆ **~ self** autre soi-même *m* ◆ **my ~ self** un(e) autre moi-même

4 (*Mus*) ◆ **~ violin** second violon *m* ◆ **to play ~ violin** être second violon ◆ **she's singing ~ soprano in the concert** elle est seconde soprano pour ce concert

5 (*in titles*) ◆ **Queen Elizabeth the Second** la reine Élisabeth II ◆ **Pope John Paul the Second** le pape Jean-Paul II ; *for other phrases see* **sixth**

ADV 1 (*one of many*) deuxième ; (*one of two*) second ◆ **to come ~** (*in poll, league table*) arriver deuxième *or* second, arriver en deuxième *or* seconde position ◆ **to come** *or* **finish ~** (*in race, competition, election*) arriver *or* terminer deuxième *or* second ◆ **Lowry came ~ to Everett** Lowry est arrivée en seconde position derrière Everett ◆ **he was placed ~** il s'est classé deuxième *or* second ◆ **he arrived ~** (*at meeting, party etc*) il a été le deuxième à arriver

2 (= *secondly*) deuxièmement

3 (+ *superl adj*) ◆ **the ~ tallest building in the world** le deuxième immeuble du monde par sa hauteur ◆ **the ~ largest shareholder** le deuxième actionnaire par ordre d'importance ◆ **the ~ most common question** la deuxième parmi les questions les plus souvent posées ; see also **second-best**

N 1 deuxième *mf*, second(e) *m(f)* ◆ **he came a good** *or* **close ~** il a été battu de justesse ◆ **he came a poor ~** il est arrivé deuxième, loin derrière le vainqueur

2 (*Boxing*) soigneur *m* ; (*in duel*) second *m*, témoin *m* ◆ **~s out (of the ring)!** (*Boxing*) soigneurs hors du ring !

3 (*Brit Univ*) ≈ licence *f* avec mention (assez) bien ◆ **he got an upper/a lower ~** ≈ il a eu sa licence avec mention bien/assez bien ◆ **many students get a lower ~** de nombreux étudiants sont reçus avec la mention assez bien

4 (also **second gear**) seconde *f* ◆ **in ~** en seconde

5 (*Mus* = *interval*) seconde *f*

NPL **seconds** 1 (*Comm* = *imperfect goods*) articles *mpl* de second choix, articles *mpl* comportant un défaut

2 (* = *second helping*) rab‡ *m*, rabiot* *m* ◆ **anyone for ~s?*** qui en reveut ?, qui veut du rab ?‡

VT 1 [+ *motion*] appuyer ; [+ *speaker*] appuyer la motion de ◆ **I'll ~ that** (*at meeting*) j'appuie cette proposition *or* cette demande ; (*gen*) je suis d'accord *or* pour*

2 /sɪˈkɒnd/ (*Brit Admin, Mil*) affecter provisoirement (*to* à), détacher (*to* à)

COMP **second-best** → **second-best**
second chamber N (*Parl*) deuxième chambre *f* ◆ **the ~ chamber** (*Brit*) la Chambre haute, la Chambre des lords
second childhood N ◆ **to be in one's ~ childhood** être retombé en enfance
second-class → **second-class**
the second coming N (*Rel*) le second avènement (du Christ)
second cousin N petit(e) cousin(e) *m(f)* (*issu(e) de germains*)
second fiddle N (*fig*) ◆ **to play ~ fiddle** jouer les seconds rôles (*to sb* à côté de qn)
second gear N seconde *f*
second-guess* VT (*esp US*) [+ *sb's reaction*] essayer d'anticiper ◆ **to ~-guess sb** essayer d'anticiper ce que qn va faire
the second house N (*Theat*) la deuxième *or* seconde représentation (de la journée)
second-in-command N (*Mil*) commandant *m* en second ; (*Naut*) second *m* ; (*gen*) second *m*, adjoint *m* ◆ **to be ~ in command** être deuxième dans la hiérarchie
second language N (*in education system*) première langue *f* (étrangère) ; (*of individual*) deuxième langue *f*
second lieutenant N (*Mil etc*) sous-lieutenant *m*
second mate N (*Merchant Navy*) commandant *m* en second
second mortgage N hypothèque *f* de second rang
second name N nom *m* de famille
second nature N ◆ **it's ~ nature (to him)** c'est une seconde nature (chez lui) ◆ **it was ~ nature for him to help his friends** aider ses amis était chez lui une seconde nature
second officer N ⇒ **second mate**
a second opinion N (*gen*) un autre avis, l'avis *m* de quelqu'un d'autre ; (*from doctor, lawyer, etc*) un deuxième avis ◆ **I'd like a ~ opinion** j'aimerais avoir un autre avis *or* l'avis de quelqu'un d'autre
the second person N (*Gram*) la deuxième personne ◆ **in the ~ person** à la deuxième personne ◆ **the ~ person singular/plural** la deuxième personne du singulier/du pluriel
second-rate ADJ [*goods*] de qualité inférieure ; [*work*] médiocre ; [*writer*] de seconde zone
second-rater* N médiocre *mf*, médiocrité *f*
second sight N ◆ **to have ~ sight** avoir le don de double vue
second string N (*esp US Sport*) (= *player*) remplaçant(e) *m(f)* ; (= *team*) équipe *f* de réserve ◆ **he has a ~ string to his bow** il a plus d'une corde à son arc
second teeth NPL seconde dentition *f*
second thought N ◆ **without** *or* **with hardly a ~ thought** sans hésiter ◆ **not to give sb/sth a ~ thought** ne plus penser à qn/qch ◆ **he didn't give it a ~ thought** il l'a fait sans hésiter ◆ **on ~ thoughts** (*Brit*) *or* **thought** (*US*) réflexion faite, à la réflexion ◆ **to have ~ thoughts (about sth)** (= *be doubtful*) avoir des doutes (sur qch) ; (= *change mind*) changer d'avis (à propos de qch) ◆ **to have ~ thoughts about doing sth** (= *be doubtful*) se demander si l'on doit faire qch ; (= *change mind*) changer d'avis et décider de ne pas faire qch
second wind N ◆ **to get one's ~ wind** trouver un *or* son second souffle

second² /ˈsekənd/ N (*in time*) seconde *f* ◆ **it won't take a ~** il y en a pour une seconde ◆ **at that very ~** à cet instant précis ◆ **just a ~!, half a ~!*** un instant !, une seconde ! ◆ **I'm coming in half a ~** j'arrive tout de suite *or* dans une seconde ◆ **I'll be with you in (just) a ~** je suis à vous dans une seconde ; → **split** COMP **second hand** N trotteuse *f*

secondarily /ˈsekəndərɪlɪ/ ADV 1 (= *in the second place*) en second lieu 2 (= *less importantly*) accessoirement

secondary /ˈsekəndərɪ/ ADJ 1 (= *less important*) [*character, role, effect, source*] secondaire ◆ **of ~ importance** (d'une importance) secondaire ◆ **the cost is a ~ consideration** la question du coût est secondaire ◆ **my desire to have children was always ~ to my career** ma carrière a toujours primé sur mon désir d'avoir des enfants

2 (*Educ*) [*education*] secondaire, du second degré ; [*schooling*] secondaire ; [*student, teacher*] du secondaire ◆ **after five years of ~ education** après cinq années d'enseignement secondaire, après cinq années dans le secondaire ◆ **subjects taught at ~ level** les matières *fpl* enseignées dans le secondaire

N 1 (*Univ etc* = *minor subject*) matière *f* secondaire, sous-dominante *f*

2 (also **secondary school**) (*gen*) établissement *m* d'enseignement secondaire ; (*age 11 to 15*) collège *m* (d'enseignement secondaire) ; (*from age 15 to 18*) lycée *m*

3 (*Med*) (also **secondary tumour**) tumeur *f* secondaire, métastase *f*

COMP **secondary action** N (*Pol*) mouvement *m* de solidarité
secondary cancer N (*Med*) métastase *f* du cancer
secondary cause N (*Philos*) cause *f* seconde
secondary era N (*Geol*) (ère *f*) secondaire *m*
secondary infection N (*Med*) surinfection *f*
secondary modern (school) N (*Brit: formerly*) *établissement secondaire d'enseignement général et technique*
secondary picketing N (*Pol*) *mise en place de piquets de grève autour d'établissements traitant avec une entreprise en grève*
secondary product N sous-produit *m*

secondary road N ≈ route *f* départementale, route *f* secondaire
secondary school N ⇒ noun 2
secondary sex(ual) characteristics NPL caractères *mpl* sexuels secondaires
secondary stress N *(Phon)* accent *m* secondaire
secondary tumour N ⇒ noun 3

second-best /ˈsekəndˈbest/ N ◆ **it is the ~** *(gen)* c'est ce qu'il y a de mieux après ; *(= poor substitute)* c'est un pis-aller ◆ **as a ~** faute de mieux, au pis-aller ADJ *[jacket etc]* de tous les jours ◆ **his ~ novel** de tous ses romans celui qui vient en second du point de vue de la qualité ADV ◆ **to come off ~** perdre, se faire battre

second-class /ˈsekəndˈklɑːs/ ADJ *(lit)* de deuxième classe ; *(Rail) [ticket, compartment]* de seconde (classe) ; *[hotel]* de seconde catégorie, de second ordre ; *(pej) [food, goods etc]* de qualité inférieure ◆ **~ citizen** citoyen(ne) *m(f)* de seconde zone *or* de deuxième ordre ◆ **~ degree** *(Univ)* ⇒ **second**[1] **noun 3** ◆ **~ mail** *(Brit)* courrier *m* à tarif réduit ; *(US)* imprimés et périodiques *mpl* ◆ **~ stamp** *(Brit)* timbre *m* à tarif réduit ◆ **a ~ return to London** *(Rail)* un aller et retour en seconde (classe) pour Londres ◆ **~ seat** *(Rail)* seconde *f* ADV *(Rail etc)* ◆ **to travel ~** voyager en seconde ◆ **to send sth ~** envoyer qch en courrier ordinaire

seconder /ˈsekəndəʳ/ N *[of motion]* personne *f* qui appuie une motion ; *[of candidate]* deuxième parrain *m*

secondhand /ˈsekəndˈhænd/ ADJ *[clothes, car]* d'occasion, de seconde main ; *(fig) [information, account]* de seconde main ADV *[buy]* d'occasion ◆ **to hear sth ~** entendre dire qch, entendre qch de quelqu'un d'autre
COMP **secondhand bookseller** N bouquiniste *mf*
secondhand bookshop N bouquiniste *m*, magasin *m* de livres d'occasion
secondhand dealer N marchand(e) *m(f)* d'occasion
secondhand smoke * N la fumée des cigarettes *(des autres)*

secondly /ˈsekəndlɪ/ LANGUAGE IN USE 26.2 ADV deuxièmement ◆ **firstly ... ~ ...** premièrement ... deuxièmement ... ; *(Admin, Comm, Jur)* primo ... secundo ...

secondment /sɪˈkɒndmənt/ N *(Brit)* affectation *f* provisoire, détachement *m* ◆ **on ~** *(at home)* en détachement, détaché *(to* à*)* ; *(abroad)* en mission *(to* à*)*

secrecy /ˈsiːkrəsɪ/ N *(NonC)* secret *m* ◆ **in ~** en secret, secrètement ◆ **in strict ~** en grand secret, dans le plus grand secret ◆ **under pledge of ~** *(frm)* sous le sceau du secret ◆ **a veil of ~** un voile de mystère ◆ **there's no ~ about it** on n'en fait pas (un) mystère ◆ **there was an air of ~ about her** elle avait un petit air mystérieux ◆ **a country where ~ reigns** un pays qui a la manie du secret ◆ **I rely on your ~** † je compte sur votre discrétion ; → **swear**

secret /ˈsiːkrɪt/ N secret *m* ◆ **to keep a ~** garder un secret ◆ **to keep sth a ~** garder *or* tenir qch secret ◆ **to keep sth a ~ from sb** cacher qch à qn ◆ **I told it you as a ~** je vous l'ai dit en confidence ◆ **to let sb into the ~** mettre qn dans le secret ◆ **to let sb into a ~** révéler *or* confier un secret à qn ◆ **to be in (on) the ~** être au courant ◆ **there's no ~ about it** cela n'a rien de secret ◆ **to have no ~s from sb** ne pas avoir de secrets pour qn ◆ **to make no ~ of** *or* **about sth** ne pas cacher qch ◆ **he makes no ~ of the fact that ...** il ne cache pas que ... ◆ **lovers' ~** confidence *f* d'amoureux ◆ **the ~ of success** le secret du succès ◆ **the ~ of being a good teacher is listening** *or* **is to listen to one's pupils** le secret, pour être un bon professeur, c'est de savoir écouter ses élèves ; → **open, state**

◆ **in secret** en secret
ADJ 1 *(= clandestine) [talks, plan, life, ingredient]* secret (-ète *f*) ◆ **it's all highly ~** tout cela est top secret ◆ **~ funds** caisse *f* noire ◆ **to be sent on a ~ mission** être envoyé en mission secrète ◆ **to keep sth ~** tenir *or* garder qch secret ◆ **to keep sth ~ from sb** cacher qch à qn ; → **top**[1]
2 *(= concealed) [drawer, passage]* secret (-ète *f*) ; *[entrance]* secret (-ète *f*), dérobé
3 *(Pol) [ballot, vote, voting, election]* à bulletin secret
4 *(= private)* ◆ **you've got a ~ admirer !** vous avez un admirateur ! ◆ **I'm a ~ admirer of her novels** j'avoue que j'apprécie ses romans ◆ **to be a ~ drinker/drug user** boire/se droguer en cachette
COMP **secret agent** N agent *m* secret
secret police N police *f* secrète
the Secret Service N *(Brit)* les services *mpl* secrets ; *(US)* les services *mpl* chargés de la protection du président
secret society N société *f* secrète
secret weapon N *(lit, fig)* arme *f* secrète

secretaire /ˌsekrɪˈtɛəʳ/ N secrétaire *m*

secretarial /ˌsekrəˈtɛərɪəl/ ADJ *[course, work]* de secrétariat ; *[job]* de secrétaire ; *[skills]* en secrétariat ◆ **his duties are mostly ~** il fait essentiellement un travail de secrétaire, ses tâches sont avant tout administratives
COMP **secretarial agency** N agence *f* de placement de secrétaires
secretarial college, secretarial school N école *f* de secrétariat

secretariat /ˌsekrəˈtɛərɪət/ N secrétariat *m*

secretary /ˈsekrətrɪ/ N 1 *(in office, of club etc)* secrétaire *mf* ; (also **company secretary**) secrétaire *mf* général(e) *(d'une société)* ; → **foreign, parliamentary, under** 2 *(= writing desk)* secrétaire *m*
COMP **secretary-general** N (pl **secretaries-general**) secrétaire *mf* général(e)
Secretary of State N *(Pol) (Brit)* ministre *m* (*of, for* de) ; *(US)* secrétaire *m* d'État, ≈ ministre *m* des Affaires étrangères
Secretary of State for Education and Employment N *(Brit)* ministre *mf* de l'Éducation et de l'Emploi
Secretary of State for Scotland N *(Brit Pol)* ministre *m* des Affaires écossaises
secretary to the board N secrétaire *mf* (auprès) du comité de gestion

secrete /sɪˈkriːt/ VT 1 *(= produce)* sécréter 2 *(= hide)* cacher

secretion /sɪˈkriːʃən/ N 1 *(= process, fluid)* sécrétion *f* 2 *(NonC = hiding)* action *f* de cacher

secretive /ˈsiːkrətɪv/ ADJ *[person, behaviour, air]* secret (-ète *f*), cachottier ; *[organization]* impénétrable ◆ **to be ~ about sth** faire mystère de qch

secretively /ˈsiːkrətɪvlɪ/ ADV *[smile]* d'une manière impénétrable ◆ **she's been behaving very ~ lately** elle est très renfermée ces derniers temps, on dirait qu'elle nous cache quelque chose ces derniers temps

secretiveness /ˈsiːkrətɪvnɪs/ N *(NonC)* réserve *f*, cachotteries *fpl*

secretly /ˈsiːkrətlɪ/ ADV *[meet, marry, plan]* en secret ; *[film]* en cachette, secrètement ; *[hope, want]* secrètement ◆ **she was ~ relieved** en son for intérieur, elle était soulagée ◆ **he was ~ pleased** il était content, mais ne le montrait pas, en son for intérieur, il n'était pas mécontent

sect /sekt/ N secte *f*

sectarian /sekˈtɛərɪən/ ADJ *[violence, killings]* motivé par le sectarisme ; *[motive, divisions, organization]* sectaire ◆ **~ school** école *f* confessionnelle N sectaire *mf*

sectarianism /sekˈtɛərɪənɪzəm/ N sectarisme *m*

section /ˈsekʃən/ N 1 *[of book, document, law, population, text]* section *f*, partie *f* ; *[of country]* partie *f* ; *[of road, pipeline]* section *f*, tronçon *m* ; *[of town]* quartier *m* ; *[of machine, furniture]* élément *m* ; *(Mil)* groupe *m* (de combat) ◆ **the brass/string ~** *[of orchestra]* les cuivres *mpl*/les cordes *fpl* ◆ **the financial ~** *(Press)* la *or* les page(s) financière(s) ◆ **~ two of the municipal by-laws** l'article deux des arrêtés municipaux ◆ **this bookcase comes in ~s** cette bibliothèque se vend par éléments ◆ **there is a ~ of public opinion which maintains ...** il y a une partie *or* une section de l'opinion publique qui maintient ...
2 *[of company, government]* service *m* ; *[of store]* rayon *m* ; → **consular**
3 *(Rail) (= part of network)* canton *m* (de voie ferrée) ; *(US) (= extra train)* train *m* supplémentaire, train-bis *m* ; *(in sleeping car)* compartiment-lits *m*
4 *(= cut)* coupe *f*, section *f* ; *(for microscope)* coupe *f*, lamelle *f* ◆ **longitudinal/vertical ~** coupe *f* longitudinale/verticale ; → **cross**
5 *(= act of cutting)* section *f*, sectionnement *m*
VT 1 *(= divide)* diviser
2 *[+ mentally ill person]* interner
COMP **section hand** N *(US Rail)* cantonnier *m* (des chemins de fer), agent *m* de la voie
section mark N paragraphe *m* *(signe typographique)*

► **section off** VT SEP séparer

sectional /ˈsekʃənl/ ADJ 1 *(= factional) [interests]* d'un groupe, particulier ; *[conflict]* interne 2 *(= made of several parts) [bookcase, furniture]* modulaire 3 *(Archit) [drawing]* en coupe N *(US)* ⇒ **sectional sofa** COMP **sectional sofa** N *(US)* canapé *m* d'angle

sectionalism /ˈsekʃənəlɪzəm/ N défense *f* des intérêts d'un groupe

sector /ˈsektəʳ/ N 1 secteur *m* ; *(Mil)* secteur *m*, zone *f* ; *(Comput)* secteur *m* ; *(fig)* secteur *m*, domaine *m* ◆ **private/public ~** secteur *m* privé/public 2 *(Geom)* secteur *m* ; *(= instrument)* compas *m* (de proportions) VT sectoriser

sectoral /ˈsektərəl/ ADJ *(Econ)* sectoriel

sectorial /sekˈtɔːrɪəl/ ADJ sectoriel

secular /ˈsekjʊləʳ/ ADJ *[society, education, school]* laïque ; *[life, priest, clergy]* séculier ; *[matter, music, writer]* profane

secularism /ˈsekjʊlərɪzəm/ N *(= policy)* laïcité *f* ; *(= doctrine)* laïcisme *m*

secularization /ˌsekjʊləraɪˈzeɪʃən/ N *(NonC) [of society, education, art]* sécularisation *f*, laïcisation *f*

secularize /ˈsekjʊləraɪz/ VT *[+ society, schools, education]* séculariser

secure /sɪˈkjʊəʳ/ ADJ 1 *(= stable) [job, position]* sûr ; *[career, future]* assuré ; *[relationship]* solide ; *[environment]* sécurisant
2 *(= unworried) [person]* tranquille, sans inquiétude ◆ **to feel ~** se sentir en sécurité *or* sécurisé ◆ **to feel ~ about sth** ne pas avoir d'inquiétudes quant à qch ◆ **to make sb feel ~** sécuriser qn ◆ **a child must be (emotionally) ~** un enfant a besoin de sécurité affective, un enfant a besoin d'être sécurisé ◆ **to be financially ~** être à l'abri des soucis financiers ◆ **~ in the knowledge that ...** avec la certitude que ...
3 *(= impregnable) [building, car, computer system]* protégé, à l'abri des effractions ; *[code]* inviolable ◆ **I want to make my home ~ against burglars** je veux protéger ma maison des cambrioleurs *or* contre les cambrioleurs
4 *[door, window, base, knot, lock, rope]* solide ; *[structure, ladder]* stable ◆ **to get a ~ foothold in a market** prendre solidement pied sur un marché ◆ **to be on ~ ground** *(fig)* être en terrain connu

VT 1 *(= get) [+ object]* se procurer, obtenir ; *[+ staff, performer]* engager ; *[+ agreement, deal, ceasefire, sb's freedom, support]* obtenir ◆ **to ~ sth for sb, to ~ sb sth** obtenir qch pour qn ◆ **I did everything possible to ~ him the job** j'ai fait tout ce que j'ai pu pour lui obtenir ce travail ◆ **a win that ~d them a place in the final** une victoire qui leur a valu une place en finale ◆ **to ~ victory** remporter la victoire
2 *(= fix) [+ rope]* fixer, attacher ; *[+ door, window]* bien fermer ; *[+ tile]* fixer ; *(= tie up) [+ person, animal]* attacher ◆ **to ~ X to Y** fixer X à Y
3 *(= make safe: from danger)* protéger *(against, from* contre) ; *[+ debt, loan]* garantir ; *[+ future]* assurer
4 *(Mil = capture)* prendre (le contrôle de) ◆ **their troops have ~d the bridge/the airport** leurs troupes ont pris le contrôle du pont/de l'aéroport *or* ont pris le pont/l'aéroport
COMP secure accommodation N *(Brit Jur)* ≃ centre *m* d'éducation surveillée
secure unit N *(Brit) (for young offenders)* ≃ centre *m* d'éducation surveillée ; *(for mental patients) pavillon d'hôpital psychiatrique réservé aux malades dangereux*

securely /sɪˈkjʊəlɪ/ **ADV** 1 *(= firmly) [fasten, fix]* solidement, bien ; *[lock]* bien 2 *(= safely)* ◆ **he remains ~ in power** il est solidement installé au pouvoir ◆ **the strike was ~ under the union's control** le syndicat avait la grève bien en main ◆ **~ established** solidement établi

Securicor ® /sɪˈkjʊərɪkɔːʳ/ **N** *société de surveillance et de convoi de fonds* **COMP Securicor guard N** employé *m* du service de surveillance, convoyeur *m* de fonds

securitization /sɪˌkjʊərɪtaɪˈzeɪʃən/ **N** *(Fin)* titrisation *f*

securitize /sɪˈkjʊərɪtaɪz/ **VT** *[+ loan]* titriser

security /sɪˈkjʊərɪtɪ/ **N** 1 *(= safety, confidence)* sécurité *f* ◆ **in ~** en sécurité ◆ **job ~** sécurité *f* de l'emploi ◆ **~ of tenure** *(in one's job)* sécurité *f* totale de l'emploi ; *(Jur: of tenant)* bail *m* assuré ◆ **a child needs ~** un enfant a besoin de sécurité sur le plan affectif, un enfant a besoin d'être sécurisé
2 *(against spying, escape etc)* sécurité *f* ◆ **~ was very lax** les mesures de sécurité étaient très relâchées ◆ **maximum** *or* **top** *or* **high ~ wing** *[of jail]* quartier *m* de haute surveillance ; see also **maximum**
3 *(for loan)* caution *f*, garantie *f* ◆ **loans without ~** crédit *m* à découvert ◆ **up to £10,000 without ~** jusqu'à 10 000 livres sans caution *or* sans garantie ◆ **to go** *or* **stand ~ for sb** se porter garant pour *or* de qn
NPL securities *(Stock Exchange)* valeurs *fpl*, titres *mpl* ◆ **government securities** fonds *mpl* d'État ◆ **securities fraud** fraudes *fpl* boursières
COMP securities analyst N analyste *m* financier
Securities and Investment Board N *(Brit)* ≃ commission *f* des opérations de Bourse
securities market N marché *m* des valeurs
security agreement N accord *m* de sécurité
security blanket N *[of child]* doudou* *f* ; *(Psych)* objet *m* transitionnel ; *[of police]* dispositif *m* de sécurité ◆ **he's my ~ blanket** c'est quelqu'un sur qui je peux compter
security camera N caméra *f* de surveillance
security clearance N *autorisation officielle accordée par les services de sécurité*
Security Council N Conseil *m* de sécurité
security firm N société *f* de surveillance
securities firm, securities house N maison *f* de courtage
security forces NPL forces *fpl* de sécurité
security guard N *(gen)* garde *m* chargé de la sécurité ; *(transporting money)* convoyeur *m* de fonds
security leak N fuite *f (de documents, de secrets etc)*
security officer N *(in armed forces)* officier *m* chargé de la sécurité ; *(in factory, workplace)* inspecteur *m* (chargé) de la sécurité
security police N services *mpl* de la sûreté
security risk N *personne susceptible de compromettre la sûreté de l'État, la sécurité d'une organisation etc* ◆ **that man is a ~ risk** cet homme constitue un risque *or* n'est pas sûr
security vetting N enquête *f* de sécurité *(of sb* sur qn) ◆ **a policy of ~ vetting** une politique d'enquêtes de sécurité

sedan /sɪˈdæn/ **N** 1 *(also* **sedan chair***)* chaise *f* à porteurs 2 *(US = car)* conduite *f* intérieure, berline *f*

sedate /sɪˈdeɪt/ **ADJ** 1 *[person]* posé, calme ; *[behaviour]* calme, pondéré ; *[place, event]* tranquille, paisible ◆ **the ~ world of antique dealing** le monde tranquille du commerce des antiquités ◆ **at a ~ pace** *or* **speed** posément, sans se presser ◆ **in a ~ manner** posément 2 *(= conservative) [dress, furnishings]* conventionnel **VT** *(Med)* donner des sédatifs à, mettre sous sédation

sedately /sɪˈdeɪtlɪ/ **ADV** 1 *(= slowly) [walk, drive]* posément, sans se presser 2 *(= conservatively) [dressed, furnished]* de manière conventionnelle

sedateness /sɪˈdeɪtnɪs/ **N** *[of person]* calme *m* ; *[of place, dancing]* calme *m*, tranquillité *f* ; *[of pace]* lenteur *f*

sedation /sɪˈdeɪʃən/ **N** sédation *f* ◆ **under ~** sous calmants

sedative /ˈsedətɪv/ **ADJ, N** calmant *m*, sédatif *m*

sedentary /ˈsedntrɪ/ **ADJ** sédentaire

sedge /sedʒ/ **N** laîche *f*, carex *m* **COMP sedge warbler N** phragmite *m* des joncs, rousserolle *f*

sediment /ˈsedɪmənt/ **N** *(Geol, Med)* sédiment *m* ; *(in boiler, liquids)* dépôt *m* ; *(in wine)* dépôt *m*

sedimentary /ˌsedɪˈmentərɪ/ **ADJ** sédimentaire

sedimentation /ˌsedɪmenˈteɪʃən/ **N** sédimentation *f*

sedition /səˈdɪʃən/ **N** sédition *f*

seditious /səˈdɪʃəs/ **ADJ** séditieux

seduce /sɪˈdjuːs/ **VT** *(gen, sexually)* séduire ◆ **to ~ sb (away) from sth** détourner qn de qch ◆ **to ~ sb into doing sth** convaincre qn de faire qch

seducer /sɪˈdjuːsəʳ/ **N** séducteur *m*, -trice *f*

seduction /sɪˈdʌkʃən/ **N** séduction *f*

seductive /sɪˈdʌktɪv/ **ADJ** *[person, voice, notion, argument, smile]* séduisant ; *[offer]* séduisant, alléchant ; *[message]* attrayant ; *[garment]* sexy* ◆ **the ~ charms of sth** les séductions *fpl* *or* les charmes *mpl* irrésistibles de qch

seductively /sɪˈdʌktɪvlɪ/ **ADV** 1 *(= alluringly) [smile, look at, dress]* de manière séduisante 2 *(= temptingly)* ◆ **~ simple** d'une simplicité exquise ◆ **a ~ domestic atmosphere** une ambiance cosy* ◆ **a ~ illustrated book** un livre avec de ravissantes illustrations

seductiveness /sɪˈdʌktɪvnɪs/ **N** caractère *m* séduisant, séduction *f*

seductress /sɪˈdʌktrɪs/ **N** séductrice *f*

sedulous /ˈsedjʊləs/ **ADJ** assidu, persévérant, attentif

sedulously /ˈsedjʊləslɪ/ **ADV** assidûment, avec persévérance

sedum /ˈsiːdəm/ **N** sedum *m*

see[1] /siː/ **LANGUAGE IN USE 26.3** (pret **saw**, ptp **seen**)
VT 1 *(gen)* voir ◆ **I can ~ him** je le vois ◆ **I saw him read/reading the letter** je l'ai vu lire/qui lisait la lettre ◆ **he was seen to read the letter** on l'a vu lire la lettre ◆ **she saw him knocked down** elle l'a vu se faire renverser ◆ **there was not a house to be seen** il n'y avait pas une seule maison en vue ◆ **there was no one at all** *or* **not a soul to be seen** il n'y avait pas âme qui vive, il n'y avait pas un chat* ◆ **to ~ sth with one's own eyes** voir qch de ses propres yeux ◆ **~ page 10** voir (à la) page 10 ◆ **I could ~ it** *or* **that one coming** * *(fig)* je le sentais venir, je m'y attendais ◆ **can you ~ your way without a torch?** est-ce que vous pouvez trouver votre chemin *or* est-ce que vous y voyez assez sans lampe de poche ?
♦ **to see one's way to doing sth** ◆ **can you ~ your way to helping us?** est-ce que vous trouveriez le moyen de nous aider ? ◆ **I can't ~ my way to doing that** je ne vois pas comment je pourrais le faire
2 *(= understand, conceive)* voir ◆ **I fail to ~** *or* **I can't ~ how you're going to do it** je ne vois pas du tout *or* je ne vois vraiment pas comment vous allez le faire ◆ **the French ~ it differently** les Français voient la chose différemment ◆ **the way I ~ it, as I ~ it** à mon avis, selon moi ◆ **this is how** *or* **the way I ~ it** voici comment je vois la chose ◆ **do you ~ what I mean?** vous voyez ce que je veux dire ? ◆ **I ~ what you're getting at** je vois où vous voulez en venir ◆ **I don't ~ why** je ne vois pas pourquoi ◆ **I don't ~ why not** *(granting permission)* je n'y vois aucune objection ; *(not understanding sb's refusal)* je ne vois pas pourquoi ◆ **to ~ the joke** comprendre *or* saisir la plaisanterie
3 *(= notice, learn, discover)* voir ◆ **I saw in the paper that he had died** j'ai vu dans le journal qu'il était décédé ◆ **I ~ they've bought a new car** je vois qu'ils ont acheté une nouvelle voiture ◆ **~ who's at the door** allez voir qui est à la porte ◆ **not until I ~ how many there are** pas avant de savoir *or* de voir combien il y en a ◆ **I'll ~ what I can do** je verrai *or* je vais voir ce que je peux faire ◆ **let's ~ what you're capable of** voyons (un peu) ce que vous savez faire
4 *(= have an opinion)* trouver ◆ **I ~ nothing wrong in it** je n'y trouve rien à redire ◆ **I don't know what she sees in him** je ne sais pas ce qu'elle lui trouve
5 *(= meet, speak to)* voir ; *[+ doctor, lawyer]* voir, consulter ◆ **to go and** *or* **to ~ sb** aller voir qn ◆ **I'm seeing the doctor tomorrow** je vais chez le docteur *or* je vois le docteur demain ◆ **the manager wants to ~ you** le directeur veut vous voir, le directeur vous demande ◆ **I can't ~ you today** je ne peux pas vous voir aujourd'hui ◆ **I want to ~ you about my son** je voudrais vous voir *or* vous parler au sujet de mon fils ◆ **how nice to ~ you!** *(greeting)* ça me fait plaisir de vous voir ! ◆ **I'll ~ you in hell first!** * jamais de la vie !, il faudra que vous me passiez sur le corps d'abord !
6 *(= visit) [+ country, town]* visiter ◆ **to ~ the sights** *[of town]* visiter la ville ; *[of country]* visiter le pays ◆ **to ~ the sights of Paris** visiter ce qu'il y a à voir à Paris ◆ **I want to ~ the world** je veux voyager
7 *(= have relationship with) (social)* voir, fréquenter ; *(romantic)* sortir avec, fréquenter ◆ **they ~ a lot of him** ils le voient souvent ◆ **we've seen less of him lately** on l'a moins vu ces derniers temps ◆ **she's seeing John just now** elle sort avec John en ce moment
8 *(saying goodbye)* **(it was) nice to ~ you!** ça m'a fait plaisir de vous voir ! ◆ **~ you!** * à bientôt ! * ◆ **~ you later!** * à tout à l'heure ! ◆ **~ you some time!** * à un de ces jours ! ◆ **~ you soon!** à bientôt ! ◆ **~ you (on) Sunday** à dimanche ◆ **~ you next week** à la semaine prochaine
9 *(= experience, know)* voir ◆ **1963 saw the assassination of John F. Kennedy** (l'année) 1963 a vu l'assassinat de John F. Kennedy ◆ **I've seen some things in my time but ...** j'en ai vu (des choses) dans ma vie mais ... ◆ **he saw service in Libya** *(Mil)* il a servi en Libye, il a fait la campagne de Libye ◆ **since she's started going round with that crowd she has certainly seen life** depuis qu'elle fait partie de cette

bande elle en a vu des choses ◆ **I'm going to Australia because I want to ~ life** je pars en Australie parce que je veux voir *or* découvrir le monde ◆ **since becoming a social worker she's certainly seen life** depuis qu'elle est assistante sociale elle a pu se rendre compte de ce que c'est que la vie ◆ **he's not easily shocked, he's seen it all** il ne se choque pas facilement, il en a vu d'autres

⑩ *(= accompany, escort)* (re)conduire, (r)accompagner ◆ **to ~ sb to the station** accompagner *or* conduire qn à la gare ◆ **to ~ sb home/to the door** reconduire *or* raccompagner qn jusque chez lui/jusqu'à la porte ◆ **to ~ the children to bed** coucher les enfants ◆ **he was so drunk we had to ~ him to bed** il était tellement ivre que nous avons dû l'aider à se coucher ; see also **see off, see out**

⑪ *(= allow to be)* ◆ **I couldn't ~ her left alone** je ne pouvais pas supporter *or* permettre qu'on la laisse *subj* toute seule

⑫ *(= ensure)* s'assurer ◆ **~ that he has all he needs** veillez à ce qu'il ne manque de rien ◆ **~ that you have it ready for Monday** faites en sorte que ce soit prêt pour lundi ◆ **I'll ~ he gets the letter** je ferai le nécessaire pour que la lettre lui parvienne, je me charge de lui faire parvenir la lettre ◆ **I'll ~ you (all) right** * je veillerai à ce que vous n'y perdiez *subj* pas, vous n'en serez pas de votre poche* ; see also **see to**

⑬ *(= imagine)* voir, (s')imaginer ◆ **I can't ~ myself doing that** je me vois mal *or* je m'imagine mal faire cela ◆ **I can't ~ myself being elected** je ne vois pas très bien comment je pourrais être élu

⑭ *(Poker etc)* **(I'll) ~ you** je demande à vous voir, je vous vois

VI ① voir ◆ **to ~ in/out/through** *etc* voir à l'intérieur/à l'extérieur/à travers *etc* ◆ **let me ~** *(= show me)* montre-moi, fais voir ; *(at window etc)* laisse-moi regarder ; see also **vi d** ◆ **~ for yourself** voyez vous-même ◆ **he couldn't ~ to read** il n'y voyait pas assez clair pour lire ◆ **I can hardly ~ without my glasses** je n'y vois pas grand-chose sans mes lunettes ◆ **cats can ~ in the dark** les chats voient clair la nuit ◆ **you can ~ for miles** on y voit à des kilomètres ; → **eye**

② *(= find out)* voir ◆ **I'll go and ~** je vais (aller) voir ◆ **I'll go and ~ if dinner's ready** je vais (aller) voir si le dîner est prêt

③ *(= understand)* voir, comprendre ◆ **as far as I can ~** à ce que je vois ◆ **I ~!** je vois !, ah bon ! ◆ **as you can ~** comme vous pouvez (le) constater ◆ **so I ~** c'est bien ce que je vois ◆ **now ~ here!** *(in anger)* non, mais dites donc !* ◆ **... you ~** *(in explanations etc)* ... voyez-vous, ... vous voyez ◆ **it's all over now, ~?*** c'est fini, compris ?* ◆ **she was bound to win, don't you ~?** tu ne comprends pas qu'elle allait forcément gagner ?

④ *(= think, deliberate)* voir ◆ **let me ~, let's ~** voyons (un peu) ◆ **let me ~** *or* **let's ~, what have I got to do?** voyons, qu'est-ce que j'ai à faire ? ◆ **I'll have to ~ (if)** je vais voir (si) ◆ **we'll soon ~** nous le saurons bientôt ◆ **we'll soon ~ if ...** nous saurons bientôt si ... ◆ **can I go out? – we'll ~** est-ce que je peux sortir ? – on verra

COMP **see-through** ADJ transparent

► **see about** VT FUS ① *(= deal with)* s'occuper de ◆ **he came to ~ about buying the house** il est venu voir s'il pouvait acheter la maison ◆ **he came to ~ about the washing machine** il est venu au sujet de la machine à laver

② *(= consider)* **to ~ about sth** voir si qch est possible ◆ **can I go? – we'll ~ about it** est-ce que je peux y aller ? – on va voir *or* on verra (ça) ◆ **he said he wouldn't do it – we'll ~ about that!** il a dit qu'il ne le ferait pas – c'est ce qu'on va voir ! ◆ **we must ~ about (getting) a new television** il va falloir songer à s'acheter une nouvelle télévision

► **see after** VT FUS s'occuper de

► **see in** VT SEP *[+ person]* faire entrer ◆ **to ~ the New Year in** fêter la nouvelle année, faire le réveillon du nouvel an

► **see into** VT FUS *(= study, examine)* s'enquérir de, examiner ◆ **we shall have to ~ into this** il va falloir examiner la question *or* se renseigner là-dessus

► **see off** VT SEP ① *(= accompany)* ◆ **I saw him off at the station/airport** *etc* je l'ai accompagné au train *or* à la gare/à l'avion *or* à l'aéroport *etc* ◆ **we'll come and ~ you off** on viendra vous dire au revoir

② *(* fig = defeat)* damer le pion à

► **see out** VT SEP ① *[+ person]* reconduire *or* raccompagner à la porte ◆ **I'll ~ myself out** ce n'est pas la peine de me raccompagner ◆ **he saw himself out** il est sorti sans qu'on le raccompagne *subj*

② ◆ **this coat will have to see the winter out** il faut que ce manteau lui *(or* me *etc)* fasse l'hiver ◆ **he was so ill we wondered whether he'd ~ the week out** il était si malade que nous nous demandions s'il passerait la semaine ◆ **I saw the third act out then left** je suis resté jusqu'à la fin du troisième acte puis je suis parti

► **see over** VT FUS *[+ house, factory, gardens]* visiter

► **see through**

VT FUS *[+ person]* voir clair en, deviner les intentions de ; *[+ behaviour, promises]* ne pas se laisser tromper *or* duper par ◆ **I saw through him at once** j'ai tout de suite vu clair dans son jeu *or* deviné ses intentions ◆ **she saw through his scheming** elle ne s'est pas laissé tromper *or* duper par ses machinations

VT SEP *(never fus) [+ project, deal]* mener à bonne fin ◆ **£50 should ~ you through** 50 livres devraient vous suffire ◆ **don't worry, I'll ~ you through** ne vous inquiétez pas, vous pouvez compter sur moi ◆ **she saw me through all the hard times** elle m'a aidé dans tous les moments difficiles

ADJ ◆ **see-through** → **see¹**

► **see to** VT FUS *(= mend)* réparer ; *(= deal with)* s'occuper de ◆ **to ~ to it that ...** veiller à ce que ... + *subj* ◆ **I'll ~ to the car** je m'occuperai de la voiture ◆ **please ~ to it that ...** veillez s'il vous plaît à ce que ... + *subj* ◆ **~ to it that they are paid on time** veillez à ce qu'ils soient payés à temps ◆ **I'll ~ to it** j'y veillerai ◆ **the sweets didn't last long, the children saw to that!** les bonbons n'ont pas fait long feu, les enfants se sont chargés de les faire disparaître !

see² /siː/ N *[of bishop]* siège *m* épiscopal, évêché *m* ; *[of archbishop]* archevêché *m* ; → **holy**

seed /siːd/ N ① *(Agr, Bot etc)* graine *f* ; *(collective n: for sowing)* graines *fpl*, semence *f* ; *(in apple, grape etc)* pépin *m* ◆ **to run** *or* **go to ~** *[plant]* monter en graine ; *[person] (= grow slovenly)* se négliger, se laisser aller ; *(= lose vigour)* se décatir

② *(fig = source, origin)* germe *m* ◆ **the ~s of discontent** les germes *mpl* du mécontentement ◆ **to sow ~s of doubt in sb's mind** semer le doute dans l'esprit de qn

③ *(liter) (= sperm)* semence *f*, sperme *m* ; *(= offspring)* progéniture *f*

④ *(Tennis etc:* also **seeded player***)* tête *f* de série ◆ **first** *or* **number one ~** tête *f* de série numéro un ◆ **number two ~** tête de série numéro deux ◆ **the top ~s** les premières têtes *fpl* de série

VT ① *[+ lawn]* ensemencer ; *[+ raisin, grape]* épépiner ◆ **to ~ clouds** ensemencer les nuages

② *(Tennis)* **he was ~ed third** il était (classé) troisième tête de série ; see also **noun d**

VI monter en graine

COMP **seed box** N germoir *m*

seed corn N blé *m* de semence ◆ **they are eating their ~ corn** ils mangent leur blé en herbe

seeding machine N semoir *m*

seed merchant N grainetier *m*

seed money N *(Econ, Fin)* capital *m* initial, mise *f* de fonds initiale

seed pearls NPL semence *f* de perles, très petites perles *fpl*

seed pod N tégument *m*

seed potato N pomme *f* de terre de semence

seed tray N ⇒ **seed box**

seedbed /ˈsiːdbed/ N semis *m*, couche *f*

seedcake /ˈsiːdkeɪk/ N gâteau *m* au carvi

seedily /ˈsiːdɪlɪ/ ADV *[dress]* minablement, de façon minable

seediness /ˈsiːdɪnɪs/ N *(= shabbiness)* aspect *m* minable *or* miteux

seedless /ˈsiːdlɪs/ ADJ sans pépins

seedling /ˈsiːdlɪŋ/ N semis *m*, (jeune) plant *m*

seedsman /ˈsiːdzmən/ N (pl **-men**) ⇒ **seed merchant**

seedy /ˈsiːdɪ/ ADJ ① *(= shabby) [clothes]* râpé, miteux ; *[person, hotel]* minable, miteux ② *(* = ill)* **I'm feeling ~** je suis *or* je me sens mal fichu*, je me sens patraque* ◆ **he looks rather ~** il a l'air mal fichu*

seeing /ˈsiːɪŋ/ LANGUAGE IN USE 26.3 N vue *f*, vision *f* ◆ **~ is believing** *(Prov)* voir c'est croire

CONJ ◆ **~ that** *or* **as*** vu que, étant donné que

COMP **Seeing Eye dog** N *(US)* chien *m* d'aveugle

seek /siːk/ (pret, ptp **sought**) VT ① *(= look for) [+ object, person, solution, death]* chercher ; *[+ fame, honours]* rechercher ; *[+ happiness, peace]* chercher, rechercher ◆ **to ~ one's fortune in Canada** chercher *or* tenter fortune au Canada ◆ **to ~ work** chercher du travail ◆ **they sought shelter from the storm** ils ont cherché un abri *or* un refuge contre la tempête ◆ **we sought shelter in the embassy/under a big tree** nous nous sommes réfugiés à l'ambassade/sous un grand arbre ◆ **the reason is not far to ~** la raison n'est pas difficile à trouver, on n'a pas à chercher loin pour trouver la raison ◆ **candidates are urgently sought for the post of chef** *(in advertisements)* on recherche de toute urgence un chef de cuisine ◆ **American male, ~s attractive, intelligent female** Américain désire faire connaissance belle femme intelligente

② *(= ask)* demander *(from sb* à qn*)* ◆ **to ~ advice/help from sb** demander conseil/de l'aide à qn ◆ **to ~ (political) asylum** demander l'asile politique ◆ **to ~ compensation for sth** demander à être indemnisé de qch ◆ **the prosecutors are ~ing the death penalty** l'accusation réclame la peine de mort

③ *(frm = attempt)* chercher *(to do sth* à faire qch*)* ◆ **they sought to kill him** ils ont cherché à le tuer

VI ◆ **to ~ for** *or* **after sth/sb** rechercher qch/qn ◆ **much sought after** très recherché, très demandé

► **seek out** VT SEP *[+ person]* aller voir, (aller) s'adresser à ; *[+ trouble etc]* (re)chercher

seeker /ˈsiːkəʳ/ N ① *(= person)* chercheur *m*, -euse *f* ◆ **to be a ~ after** *[+ truth, knowledge etc]* être en quête de ; → **asylum, job, self** ② *(Mil = device)* autodirecteur *m*

seem /siːm/ LANGUAGE IN USE 6.2, 15.2, 26.3 VI sembler, avoir l'air ◆ **he ~s honest** il semble (être) honnête, il a l'air honnête ◆ **he ~ed nice enough** il semblait *or* avait l'air plutôt gentil ◆ **further strikes ~ unlikely** il semble peu probable qu'il y ait de nouvelles grèves ◆ **she makes it ~ so simple!** avec elle tout paraît si simple ! ◆ **she ~s to know you** elle semble vous connaître, elle a l'air de vous connaître ◆ **she ~s not to want to leave** elle semble ne pas vouloir partir, elle n'a pas l'air de vouloir partir ◆ **we ~ to have met before** il me semble *or* j'ai l'impression que nous nous sommes déjà rencontrés ◆ **I ~ to have heard that before** il me semble avoir déjà entendu ça ◆ **I can't ~ to do it** je n'arrive pas à le faire ◆ **I ~ed to be floating** j'avais l'impression de flotter ◆ **the noise ~ed to be coming from the basement** on avait l'impression que le bruit venait du sous-sol ◆ **how did she ~ to you?** comment l'as-tu trouvée ? ◆ **how does it ~ to you?** qu'en penses-tu ? ◆ **it all ~s like a dream** on croit rêver ◆ **I did what ~ed best** j'ai fait ce que j'ai jugé bon ◆ **there doesn't ~ to be any wine left** on dirait qu'il ne reste plus de vin ◆ **there ~s to be a mistake in this translation** il semble y avoir une erreur dans cette traduction ◆ **there ~s to be a mistake, I'm the one who booked this room** il semble y avoir erreur, c'est moi qui ai retenu cette chambre

♦ **it seems (that) …** (= *looks as if*) il semble que … ; (= *people say*) il paraît que … ◆ **it ~s that the** *or* **as if the government is going to fall** (= *looks as if*) il semble bien que le gouvernement va tomber ◆ **it ~s that the government is going to fall** (= *people say*) il paraît que le gouvernement va tomber ◆ **I've checked and it ~s she's right** j'ai vérifié et il semble qu'elle a raison *or* elle semble avoir raison ◆ **it ~s she's right for everybody says so** il semble bien qu'elle a raison puisque tout le monde est d'accord là-dessus ◆ **I've checked and it doesn't ~ she's right** *or* **it ~s she's not right** j'ai vérifié et il ne semble pas qu'elle ait raison ◆ **from what people say it doesn't ~ she's right** d'après ce qu'on dit il ne semble pas qu'elle ait raison ◆ **does it ~ that she is right?** est-ce qu'elle semble avoir raison ? ◆ **it ~s to me that we should leave at once** il me semble que nous devrions partir tout de suite ◆ **it does not ~ to me that we can accept** il ne me semble pas que nous puissions accepter ◆ **does it ~ to you as though it's going to rain?** est-ce qu'il te semble qu'il va pleuvoir ?, est-ce que tu crois qu'il va pleuvoir ? ◆ **they're getting married next week, so it ~s** ils se marient la semaine prochaine à ce qu'il paraît *or* semble-t-il ◆ **it ~s not** il paraît que non ◆ **it ~s so** il paraît que oui ◆ **it ~s that he died yesterday** il paraît qu'il est mort hier ◆ **he died yesterday it ~s** il est mort hier, paraît-il ◆ **it ~s ages since we last met** j'ai l'impression que ça fait des siècles* que nous ne nous sommes pas vus

seeming /ˈsiːmɪŋ/ ADJ apparent, soi-disant *inv*

seemingly /ˈsiːmɪŋlɪ/ ADV apparemment ◆ **there has ~ been a rise in inflation** à ce qu'il paraît il y a eu une hausse de l'inflation ◆ **he's left then? – ~** il est donc parti ? – (à ce qu')il paraît *or* d'après ce qu'on dit

seemliness /ˈsiːmlɪnɪs/ N [*of behaviour*] bienséance *f* ; [*of dress*] décence *f*

seemly /ˈsiːmlɪ/ ADJ [*behaviour*] convenable, bienséant ; [*dress*] décent, correct

seen /siːn/ VB ptp of **see¹**

seep /siːp/ VI suinter, filtrer ◆ **water was ~ing through the walls** l'eau suintait des murs *or* filtrait à travers les murs, les murs suintaient

► **seep away** VI s'écouler peu à peu *or* goutte à goutte

► **seep in** VI s'infiltrer

► **seep out** VI 1 [*fluid*] suinter
2 [*information, news*] filtrer

seepage /ˈsiːpɪdʒ/ N [*of water, blood*] suintement *m* ; (*from tank*) fuite *f*, déperdition *f*

seer /sɪəʳ/ N (*liter*) voyant(e) *m(f)*, prophète *m*, prophétesse *f*

seersucker /ˈsɪəˌsʌkəʳ/ N crépon *m* de coton

seesaw /ˈsiːsɔː/ N (jeu *m* de) bascule *f* ADJ (*fig*) en yoyo® VI (*lit*) jouer à la bascule ; (*fig*) osciller COMP **seesaw motion** N mouvement *m* de bascule, va-et-vient *m inv*

seethe /siːð/ VI 1 ◆ **to ~ with anger/rage** bouillir de colère/rage ◆ **he was (positively) seething*** il était fumasse* *or* furibard* ◆ **a country seething with discontent** un pays où le mécontentement couve *or* fermente ◆ **resentment ~d in him** il était rongé par le ressentiment ◆ **the crowd ~d round the film star** la foule se pressait autour de la vedette ◆ **the streets were seething with people** les rues grouillaient de monde ◆ **a seething mass of people** une masse grouillante de gens, une foule grouillante 2 [*boiling liquid, sea*] bouillonner

segment /ˈsegmənt/ N (*gen*) segment *m* ; [*of orange etc*] quartier *m*, morceau *m* VT /segˈment/ segmenter, couper en segments VI /segˈment/ se segmenter

segmental /segˈmentl/ ADJ (*gen*) segmentaire ; (*Ling*) segmental

segmentation /ˌsegmənˈteɪʃən/ N segmentation *f*

segregate /ˈsegrɪgeɪt/ VT séparer, isoler (*from* de) ; (*Pol*) séparer ◆ **to ~ the sexes** séparer les sexes ◆ **they decided to ~ the contagious patients** ils ont décidé d'isoler les (malades) contagieux ◆ **the political prisoners were ~d from the others** les prisonniers politiques ont été séparés *or* isolés des autres

segregated /ˈsegrɪgeɪtɪd/ ADJ (*Pol*) [*school, club, bus*] où la ségrégation est appliquée ◆ **a ~ school system** un système d'enseignement où la ségrégation est appliquée

segregation /ˌsegrɪˈgeɪʃən/ N (*Pol*) ségrégation *f* ; [*of group, person, object*] séparation *f*, isolement *m* (*from* de)

segregationist /ˌsegrɪˈgeɪʃnɪst/ N ségrégationniste *mf* ADJ [*riot, demonstration*] ségrégationniste ; [*policy*] de ségrégation, ségrégationniste

segue /ˈsegweɪ/ VI ◆ **the band ~d from "These Foolish Things" into "Blue Moon"** après "These Foolish Things" l'orchestre a enchaîné "Blue Moon" ◆ **the film attempts to ~ (from tragedy) into comedy** le film essaie de passer subtilement (de la tragédie) à la comédie N (*Mus*) enchaînement *m* (*from* de ; *into* à)

Seine /seɪn/ N Seine *f*

seine /seɪn/ N (also **seine net**) seine *f*

seismic /ˈsaɪzmɪk/ ADJ (*lit*) sismique ; (*fig*) [*events, changes, effects, efforts*] cataclysmique ◆ **~ shift** (*fig*) changement *m* radical

seismograph /ˈsaɪzməgrɑːf/ N sismographe *m*

seismography /saɪzˈmɒgrəfɪ/ N sismographie *f*

seismologist /saɪzˈmɒlədʒɪst/ N sismologue *mf*

seismology /saɪzˈmɒlədʒɪ/ N sismologie *f*

seize /siːz/ VT 1 (= *clutch, grab*) saisir, attraper ◆ **she ~d (hold of) his hand, she ~d him by the hand** elle lui a saisi la main ◆ **he ~d her by the hair** il l'a empoignée par les cheveux ◆ **to ~ sb bodily** attraper qn à bras-le-corps ◆ **to ~ the opportunity to do sth** saisir l'occasion *or* sauter sur l'occasion de faire qch ◆ **to ~ the day** vivre dans l'instant ◆ **to be ~d with rage** avoir un accès de rage ◆ **to be ~d with fear** être saisi de peur ◆ **she was ~d with the desire to see him** un désir soudain de le voir s'est emparé d'elle *or* l'a saisie ◆ **he was ~d with a bout of coughing** il a été pris d'un accès de toux, il a eu un accès de toux ; → **bull¹**

2 (= *get possession of by force*) s'emparer de, se saisir de ; (*Mil*) [+ *territory*] s'emparer de ; [+ *person, gun, ship*] capturer, s'emparer de ◆ **to ~ power** s'emparer du pouvoir

3 (*Jur*) [+ *person*] arrêter, détenir ; [+ *property, contraband*] confisquer, saisir

VI [*mechanism*] se gripper

► **seize on** VT FUS ⇒ **seize upon**

► **seize up** VI [*mechanism*] se gripper ; [*limb joint*] s'ankyloser ; (*fig*) [*traffic*] se paralyser, s'immobiliser

► **seize upon** VT FUS [+ *opportunity, chance*] saisir ; [+ *idea*] se saisir de ◆ **his opponents ~d upon these revelations** ses opposants se sont saisis de ces révélations

seizure /ˈsiːʒəʳ/ N 1 (NonC) [*of goods, gun, property*] saisie *f* ; [*of city, ship*] capture *f* ; [*of power, territory*] prise *f* ; [*of criminal*] capture *f*, arrestation *f* ; (*Jur*) appréhension *f* (au corps) ; [*of contraband*] saisie *f*, confiscation *f* 2 (*Med*) crise *f*, attaque *f* ◆ **to have a ~** avoir une crise *or* une attaque

seldom /ˈseldəm/ ADV rarement, peu souvent ◆ **he ~ worked** il travaillait rarement, il ne travaillait pas souvent ◆ **~ if ever** rarement pour ne pas dire jamais

select /sɪˈlekt/ VT [+ *team, candidate*] sélectionner (*from, among* parmi) ; [+ *gift, book, colour*] choisir (*from, among* parmi) ◆ **to ~ a sample of** [+ *rock*] prélever un échantillon de ; [+ *colours, materials*] choisir un échantillon de ◆ **~ed poems** poèmes *mpl* choisis ◆ **~ed works** œuvres *fpl* choisies ◆ **~ed tomatoes** tomates *fpl* de premier choix ADJ [*audience*] choisi, d'élite ; [*club*] fermé ; [*restaurant*] chic *inv*, sélect ◆ **a ~ few** quelques privilégiés ◆ **a ~ group of friends** quelques amis choisis ◆ **they formed a small ~ group** ils formaient un petit groupe fermé COMP **select committee** N (*Brit Parl*) commission *f* (d'enquête) parlementaire

selectee /sɪlekˈtiː/ N (*US Mil*) appelé *m*

selection /sɪˈlekʃən/ N sélection *f*, choix *m* ◆ **to make a ~** faire une sélection *or* un choix ◆ **they've got a good ~ of cookery books** ils ont un choix assez large de livres de cuisine ◆ **~s from …** (*Literat, Mus*) morceaux *mpl* choisis de … ; → **natural** COMP **selection committee** N comité *m* de sélection

selective /sɪˈlektɪv/ ADJ [*recruitment, classification, memory*] sélectif ◆ **one must be ~** il faut savoir faire un choix ◆ **~ breeding** élevage *m* à base de sélection ◆ **~ entry** (*Brit*) ◆ **~ admissions** (*US*) (*Scol*) sélection *f* ◆ **~ school** (*Brit*) école *f* (*or* lycée *m or* collège *m*) à recrutement sélectif ◆ **~ service** (*US Mil*) service *m* militaire obligatoire, conscription *f* ◆ **~ strike** (*by workers*) grève *f* ponctuelle *or* limitée

selectively /sɪˈlektɪvlɪ/ ADV [*terrorists etc*] ◆ **to strike ~** se livrer à des actions ponctuelles

selectivity /ˌsɪlekˈtɪvɪtɪ/ N 1 [*of procedure, system*] sélectivité *f* ; (*Scol*) sélection *f* 2 (*Elec, Rad*) sélectivité *f*

selectman /sɪˈlektmən/ N (pl **-men**) (*US*) conseiller *m* municipal (en Nouvelle-Angleterre)

selector /sɪˈlektəʳ/ N (= *person*) sélectionneur *m*, -euse *f* ; (*Tech*) sélecteur *m*

selenium /sɪˈliːnɪəm/ N sélénium *m*

self /self/ N (pl **selves**) 1 (*gen, Philos, Psych*) **the ~** le moi *inv* ◆ **the cult of ~** le culte du moi ◆ **the conscious ~** le moi conscient ◆ **his better ~** le meilleur de lui-même ◆ **her real ~** son vrai moi ◆ **my former ~** le moi *or* la personne que j'étais auparavant ◆ **she's her old ~ again** elle est redevenue complètement elle-même ◆ **he'll soon be his usual ~ again** il retrouvera bientôt sa santé (*or* sa gaieté *etc*) ◆ **she had no thought of ~** elle ne pensait pas à elle-même *or* à son intérêt personnel ◆ **to thine own ~ be true** (*Prov*) demeure fidèle à toi-même ; → **second¹, shadow**

2 (*Comm etc*) moi-même *etc* ◆ **your good ~** vous-même ◆ **your good selves** vous-mêmes

◆ **pay** ~ *(on cheque)* payez à l'ordre de moi-même

COMP **self-abasement** N abaissement *m* de soi, avilissement *m*
self-absorbed ADJ égocentrique
self-absorption N égocentrisme *m*
self-abuse N († *= masturbation)* masturbation; *f (= destructive behaviour)* autodestruction *f*
self-accusation N autoaccusation *f*
self-acting ADJ automatique
self-addressed envelope N enveloppe *f* à son nom et adresse
self-addressed stamped envelope N enveloppe *f* affranchie à son nom et adresse
self-adhesive ADJ autoadhésif
self-adjusting ADJ à réglage automatique
self-advertisement N ◆ **to indulge in ~-advertisement** faire sa propre réclame
self-aggrandizement N autoglorification *f*
self-analysis N autoanalyse *f*
self-apparent ADJ évident, qui va de soi
self-appointed ADJ autoproclamé ◆ **he was a ~-appointed critic of ...** il a pris sur lui de critiquer ...
self-appraisal N autoévaluation *f*
self-assembly ADJ en kit
self-assertion N affirmation *f* de soi
self-assertive ADJ très sûr de soi
self-assessment N autoévaluation *f* ◆ **~-assessment system** *(Brit Fin)* le système de déclaration des revenus *(avec autoévaluation des impôts à payer)*
self-assurance N assurance *f*, confiance *f* en soi
self-assured ADJ sûr de soi, plein d'assurance
self-aware ADJ ◆ **to be ~-aware** avoir pris conscience de soi
self-awareness N (prise *f* de) conscience *f* de soi
self-belay, self-belaying system N *(Climbing)* autoassurance *f*
self-belief N *(NonC)* confiance *f* en soi
self-betterment N amélioration *f* de soi-même *or* de sa condition
self-catering N appartement *m etc* indépendant (avec cuisine) ADJ indépendant (avec cuisine)
self-censorship N *(NonC)* autocensure *f*
self-centred ADJ égocentrique
self-centredness N égocentrisme *m*
self-certification N *(NonC: Brit Admin) justification par l'employé d'un arrêt de travail de sept jours maximum pour cause de maladie*
self-cleaning ADJ autonettoyant
self-closing ADJ à fermeture automatique
self-coloured ADJ uni
self-composed ADJ posé, calme
self-composure N calme *m*, sang-froid *m*
self-conceit N vanité *f*, suffisance *f*
self-conceited ADJ vaniteux, suffisant
self-confessed ADJ ◆ **he is a ~-confessed thief** il avoue être voleur, il reconnaît être voleur
self-confidence N confiance *f* en soi
self-confident ADJ sûr de soi, plein d'assurance
self-congratulation N autosatisfaction *f*
self-congratulatory ADJ satisfait de soi
self-conscious ADJ *(= shy) [person, manner]* emprunté, embarrassé, gauche ; *(= aware of oneself or itself) [art, person, political movement]* conscient (de son image) ◆ **to be ~-conscious about sth** être gêné *or* embarrassé par qch
self-consciously ADV *(= shyly)* de façon empruntée, timidement ; *(= deliberately)* volontairement
self-consciousness N *(= shyness)* gêne *f*, timidité *f* ; *(= awareness)* conscience *f* (de son image)
self-contained ADJ *[person]* indépendant ; *(Brit) [flat]* indépendant, avec entrée particulière
self-contempt N mépris *m* de soi
self-contradiction N contradiction *f* avec soi-même
self-contradictory ADJ *[text]* contradictoire *(en soi)* ; *[person]* qui se contredit
self-control N maîtrise *f* de soi, sang-froid *m*
self-controlled ADJ maître (maîtresse *f*) de soi
self-correcting ADJ autocorrecteur (-trice *f*)
self-critical ADJ qui se critique ; *(Pol, Rel)* qui fait son autocritique
self-criticism N critique *f* de soi ; *(Pol, Rel)* autocritique *f*
self-deception N aveuglement *m*
self-declared ADJ ⇒ **self-proclaimed**
self-defeating ADJ *[action, plan]* qui va à l'encontre du but recherché
self-defence N *(= skill, art)* autodéfense *f* ◆ **in ~-defence** *(Jur)* pour se défendre, en légitime défense *(Jur)*
self-delusion N aveuglement *m*
self-denial N abnégation *f*, sacrifice *m* de soi
self-denying ADJ *[person]* qui fait preuve d'abnégation, qui se sacrifie ; *[decision etc]* qui impose le sacrifice de ses intérêts
self-deprecating ADJ ◆ **to be ~-deprecating** *[person]* se dénigrer soi-même
self-deprecatory ADJ *[thoughts]* qui s'autodénigre
self-destruct VI s'autodétruire, se désintégrer ADJ *[device, program]* autodestructeur (-trice *f*)
self-destruction N autodestruction *f*
self-destructive ADJ *[person, behaviour]* autodestructeur (-trice *f*) ◆ **she has a tendency to be ~-destructive** elle a tendance à s'autodétruire
self-determination N autodétermination *f*
self-determined ADJ autodéterminé
self-determining ADJ qui s'autodétermine
self-discipline N autodiscipline *f*
self-disciplined ADJ qui fait preuve d'autodiscipline
self-discovery N *(Psych)* découverte *f* de soi
self-doubt N fait *m* de douter de soi-même
self-doubting ADJ qui doute de soi-même
self-drive ADJ *(Brit) [car]* sans chauffeur
self-educated ADJ autodidacte
self-effacement N modestie *f*, effacement *m*
self-effacing ADJ effacé, modeste
self-elected ADJ *(Pol)* qui s'est élu lui-même ◆ **he was a ~-elected critic of ...** il avait pris sur lui de critiquer ...
self-employed ADJ indépendant, qui travaille à son compte
the self-employed NPL les travailleurs *mpl* indépendants
self-employment N ◆ **in ~-employment** ⇒ **self-employed**
self-esteem N respect *m* de soi, amour-propre *m* ◆ **to have low/high ~-esteem** avoir une mauvaise/bonne opinion de soi-même
self-evaluation N autoévaluation *f*
self-evident ADJ évident, qui va de soi
self-evidently ADV fort *or* bien évidemment
self-examination N examen *m* de conscience ; *(Med) [of breasts, testicles]* autopalpation *f*
self-explanatory ADJ qui se passe d'explication, évident
self-expression N expression *f* (libre)
self-fertilization N autofécondation *f*
self-fertilizing ADJ autofertile
self-filling ADJ à remplissage automatique
self-financing N autofinancement *m* ADJ qui s'autofinance
self-flattery N louanges *fpl* que l'on s'adresse à soi-même
self-forgetful ADJ désintéressé
self-forgetfulness N désintéressement *m*
self-fulfilling prophecy N prédiction *f* qui se réalise
self-fulfilment N *(NonC)* accomplissement *m* de soi
self-glorification N autoglorification *f*
self-governing ADJ autonome
self-government N autonomie *f*
self-harm, self-harming N automutilation *f*
self-hate N haine *f* de soi
self-hating ADJ qui se déteste
self-hatred N ⇒ **self-hate**
self-help N *(gen)* efforts *mpl* personnels, débrouillardise * *f* ; *(Econ)* autoassistance *f*
self-help group N groupe *m* d'entraide
self-hypnosis N autohypnose *f*
self-ignite VI s'enflammer spontanément
self-ignition N *(gen)* combustion *f* spontanée ; *(in vehicle)* autoallumage *m*
self image N image *f* de soi-même
self-importance N suffisance *f*
self-important ADJ suffisant, m'as-tu-vu * *inv*
self-imposed ADJ auto-imposé, que l'on s'impose à soi-même
self-improvement N progrès *mpl* personnels
self-induced ADJ *[illness, misery, problems]* que l'on a provoqué soi-même
self-indulgence N *(gen)* amour *m* de son propre confort ; *(= self-pity)* apitoiement *m* sur soi-même
self-indulgent ADJ *(gen)* qui ne se refuse rien ; *(= self-pitying)* qui s'apitoie sur son (propre) sort
self-inflicted ADJ que l'on s'inflige à soi-même, volontaire
self-interest N intérêt *m* (personnel)
self-interested ADJ intéressé, qui recherche son avantage personnel
self-justification N autojustification *f*
self-justifying ADJ justificatif
self-knowledge N connaissance *f* de soi
self-levelling foot N (pl **self-levelling feet**) *(on furniture)* pied *m* de nivellement, pied *m* autoréglable
self-loader N arme *f* automatique
self-loading ADJ *[gun]* automatique
self-loathing N dégoût *m* de soi-même ADJ qui a horreur de soi-même
self-locking ADJ à fermeture automatique
self-love N narcissisme *m*, amour *m* de soi-même
self-lubricating ADJ autolubrifiant
self-lubrication N autolubrification *f*
self-made ADJ qui a réussi par ses propres moyens
self-made man N self-made man *m* fils *m* de ses œuvres *(frm)*
self-maintenance N entretien *m* automatique
self-mastery N maîtrise *f* de soi
self-mockery N autodérision *f*
self-mocking ADJ *[person]* qui se moque de soi-même ; *[humour]* empreint d'autodérision
self-mockingly ADV par autodérision
self-motivated ADJ très motivé (de par soi-même)
self-murder N suicide *m*
self-mutilation N *(NonC)* automutilation *f*
self-neglect N négligence *f* de soi
self-obsessed ADJ égocentrique
self-obsession N égocentrisme *m*
self-opinionated ADJ entêté, opiniâtre
self-ordained ADJ ◆ **he was a ~-ordained critic of ...** il avait pris sur lui de critiquer ...
self-parody N autoparodie *f*
self-perpetuating ADJ ◆ **it's ~-perpetuating** ça se perpétue
self-pity N apitoiement *m* sur soi-même
self-pitying ADJ qui s'apitoie sur son (propre) sort
self-poisoning N empoisonnement *m* ◆ **paracetamol ~-poisoning** suicide *m* par surdose de paracétamol
self-portrait N autoportrait *m*
self-possessed ADJ qui garde son sang-froid, maître (maîtresse *f*) de soi
self-possession N sang-froid *m*, maîtrise *f* de soi
self-praise N éloge *m* de soi-même, autolouange *f*
self-preoccupied ADJ égocentrique
self-preservation N instinct *m* de conservation

self-pride N orgueil *m* personnel, fierté *f*
self-proclaimed ADJ autoproclamé ◆ **he was a ~-proclaimed critic of ...** il avait pris sur lui de critiquer ...
self-promotion N autopromotion *f*
self-propelled ADJ autopropulsé
self-protection N ◆ **from ~-protection** pour sa propre protection
self-publicist N spécialiste *mf* de la publicité personnelle
self-punishment N autopunition *f*
self-raising flour N *(Brit)* farine *f* pour gâteaux *(avec levure incorporée)*
self-realization N épanouissement *m* personnel
self-referential ADJ autoréférentiel (-le *f*)
self-regard N ⇒ **self-esteem**
self-regulating ADJ autorégulateur (-trice *f*)
self-regulation N autorégulation *f*
self-regulatory ADJ ⇒ **self-regulating**
self-reliance N autonomie *f*
self-reliant ADJ autonome ◆ **to be ~-reliant** être autonome, ne pas avoir besoin des autres
self-renewal N renouvellement *m* automatique
self-renewing ADJ qui se renouvelle automatiquement
self-replicating ADJ *[computer, machine etc]* autoreproducteur (-trice *f*)
self-reproach N repentir *m*, remords *m*
self-reproachful ADJ plein de reproches à l'égard de soi-même
self-respect N respect *m* de soi
self-respecting ADJ qui se respecte ◆ **no ~-respecting teacher would agree that ...** aucun professeur qui se respecte *subj* ne conviendrait que ...
self-restraint N retenue *f*
self-revelation N révélation *f* de soi-même
self-revelatory ADJ d'inspiration autobiographique
self-ridicule N autodérision *f*
self-righteous ADJ pharisaïque, satisfait de soi
self-righteousness N pharisaïsme *m*, autosatisfaction *f*
self-righting ADJ inchavirable
self-rising flour N *(US)* ⇒ **self-raising flour**
self-rule N *(Pol)* autonomie *f*
self-ruling ADJ *(Pol)* autonome
self-sacrifice N abnégation *f*, dévouement *m*
self-sacrificing ADJ qui se sacrifie, qui a l'esprit de sacrifice
self-satisfaction N contentement *m* de soi, fatuité *f*
self-satisfied ADJ *[person]* content de soi, suffisant ; *[smile]* suffisant, de satisfaction
self-sealing ADJ *[envelope]* autocollant, autoadhésif ; *[container]* à obturation automatique
self-seeker N égoïste *mf*
self-seeking ADJ égoïste
self-service N, ADJ libre-service *m inv* ◆ **~-service shop/restaurant** (magasin *m*/restaurant *m*) libre-service *m inv* or self-service *m inv* ◆ **~-service garage** station *f* (d'essence) libre-service
self-serving ADJ égoïste, intéressé
self-standing ADJ *(lit)* autoportant ; *(fig) [of company, organization]* autonome
self-starter N *(in vehicle)* démarreur *m* (automatique *or* électrique) ; *(fig) (= hard-working person)* personne *f* motivée (et pleine d'initiative)
self-steering ADJ à pilotage automatique
self-study N apprentissage *m* autonome
self-styled ADJ soi-disant *inv*, prétendu
self-sufficiency N *(economic)* autarcie *f* ; *(= self-confidence)* autosuffisance *f*
self-sufficient ADJ *(economically)* autarcique ; *(= self-confident)* autosuffisant
self-supporting ADJ *[person]* qui subvient à ses (propres) besoins ; *[firm]* financièrement indépendant
self-sustaining growth N *(Econ)* croissance *f* autonome
self-tapping ADJ *[screw]* autotaraudeur
self-taught ADJ autodidacte ◆ **"French self-taught"** "apprenez le français par vous-même"
self-timer N *(Phot)* retardateur *m*
self-torture N torture *f* délibérée de soi-même
self-treatment N *(Med)* automédication *f*
self-will N volonté *f* inébranlable
self-willed ADJ entêté, volontaire
self-winding ADJ (à remontage) automatique
self-worship N adulation *f* de soi-même
self-worth N ◆ **feeling of ~-worth** confiance en soi

selfhood /ˈselfhʊd/ N *(Psych)* individualité *f*

selfish /ˈselfɪʃ/ ADJ *[person, behaviour]* égoïste ; *[motive]* intéressé

selfishly /ˈselfɪʃlɪ/ ADV égoïstement, en égoïste

selfishness /ˈselfɪʃnɪs/ N égoïsme *m*

selfless /ˈselflɪs/ ADJ désintéressé, altruiste

selflessly /ˈselflɪslɪ/ ADV sans penser à soi, d'une façon désintéressée, par altruisme

selflessness /ˈselflɪsnɪs/ N désintéressement *m*, altruisme *m*

selfsame /ˈselfseɪm/ ADJ même ◆ **this is the ~ book** c'est bien le même livre ◆ **I reached Paris the ~ day** je suis arrivé à Paris le même jour *or* le jour même

sell /sel/ (pret, ptp **sold**) VT 1 *[+ goods, item]* vendre ; *[+ stock]* écouler ◆ **"to be sold"** "à vendre" ◆ **to ~ sth for $25** vendre qch 25 dollars ◆ **he sold it (to) me for £10** il me l'a vendu 10 livres ◆ **he sold the books at $10 each** il a vendu les livres 10 dollars pièce *or* chaque ◆ **he was ~ing them at** *or* **for £10 a dozen** il les vendait 10 livres la douzaine ◆ **do you ~ stamps?** est-ce que vous vendez des timbres ? ◆ **are stamps sold here?** est-ce qu'on vend des timbres ici ? ◆ **I was sold this in Grenoble** on m'a vendu cela à Grenoble ◆ **it's our reputation that ~s our products** c'est notre réputation qui fait vendre nos produits ◆ **to ~ o.s.** *(sexually)* se vendre ; see also **vt b** ◆ **to ~ one's body** vendre son corps ◆ **to ~ sb into slavery** vendre qn comme esclave ◆ **to ~ one's life dearly** vendre chèrement sa vie ◆ **to ~ the pass** *(fig)* abandonner *or* trahir la cause ◆ **to ~ a secret** vendre *or* trahir un secret ◆ **to ~ sb short** *(= cheat)* avoir qn*, posséder qn* ; *(= belittle)* ne pas faire *or* rendre justice à qn ◆ **to ~ o.s. short** ne pas savoir se vendre ◆ **he sold his soul for political power** il a vendu son âme contre le pouvoir (politique) ◆ **I'd ~ my soul for a coat/body like that!*** je donnerais n'importe quoi *or* je vendrais mon âme pour avoir un manteau/un corps comme ça ! ◆ **he'd ~ his own mother** il vendrait père et mère ; → **bill**[1], **pup**
2 *(* = put across)* ◆ **to ~ sb an idea** vendre une idée à qn ◆ **if we can ~ coexistence to the two countries** si nous arrivons à faire accepter le principe de la coexistence aux deux pays ◆ **he doesn't ~ himself very well** il n'arrive pas à se faire valoir *or* à se mettre en valeur ◆ **if you can ~ yourself to the voters** si vous arrivez à convaincre les électeurs ◆ **to be sold on*** **an idea** *etc* être emballé* *or* enthousiasmé par une idée *etc* ◆ **to be sold on sb*** être complètement emballé* par qn
3 *(* = betray)* vendre* ◆ **I've been sold!** on m'a vendu !* ◆ **to ~ sb down the river** trahir qn
VI se vendre ◆ **these books ~ at** *or* **for $10 each** ces livres se vendent 10 dollars pièce *or* chaque ◆ **they ~ at £10 a dozen** ils se vendent 10 livres la douzaine ◆ **your car should ~ for £8,000** votre voiture devrait se vendre 8 000 livres ◆ **it ~s well** cela se vend bien ◆ **these books aren't ~ing** ces livres se vendent mal ◆ **to ~ short** *(on Stock Exchange)* vendre à découvert ◆ **the idea didn't ~** l'idée n'a pas été acceptée ; → **cake**
N 1 *(* = disappointment)* déception *f* ; *(= fraud)* attrape-nigaud *m* ◆ **what a ~!** ce que je me suis *(or* tu t'es *etc)* fait avoir !*
2 *(Comm)* → **hard, soft**
COMP **sell-by date** N date *f* limite de vente ◆ **to be past one's ~-by date*** avoir fait son temps
sell-off N ⇒ **selloff**
sell-through ADJ *[video]* réservé à la vente
▸ **sell back** VT SEP revendre *(à la même personne etc)*
▸ **sell off** VT SEP *[+ stock]* liquider ; *[+ goods]* solder ; *[+ shares]* vendre, liquider ; *[+ company]* brader
▸ **sell on** VT SEP revendre
▸ **sell out** VI 1 *(US = sell up) (business)* vendre son fonds *or* son affaire ; *(stock)* liquider son stock
2 *(= be used up) [product, tickets]* se vendre tous
3 *[shopkeeper etc]* **to ~ out of sth** *(temporarily)* être à court de qch ; *(= use up supply of)* épuiser son stock de qch
4 *(fig)* renier ses principes ◆ **to ~ out to the enemy** passer à l'ennemi ◆ **to ~ out on sb** trahir qn
VT SEP 1 *(on Stock Exchange)* vendre
2 *(= sell remaining stock of)* vendre tout son stock de ◆ **this item is sold out** cet article est épuisé ◆ **we are sold out of everything** nous avons tout vendu ◆ **we are sold out of milk** nous n'avons plus de lait, nous sommes à court de lait ◆ **the house was sold out** *(Theat)* toutes les places étaient louées ◆ **tickets for the ballet were sold out** il n'y avait plus de billets pour le ballet, tous les billets pour le ballet avaient été vendus ◆ **the concert is sold out** il n'y a plus de billets pour le concert, le concert se jouera à guichets fermés
▸ **sell up** *(esp Brit)* VI 1 *(gen)* se défaire de *or* vendre toutes ses possessions ; *(= sell one's house)* vendre sa maison
2 *(= sell business)* ⇒ **sell out vi 1**
VT SEP 1 *(Jur) [+ goods]* opérer la vente forcée de, saisir ; *[+ debtor]* vendre les biens de
2 *(Comm) [+ business]* vendre, liquider

seller /ˈseləʳ/ N 1 *(in compounds)* vendeur *m*, -euse *f*, marchand(e) *m(f)* ◆ **newspaper-~** vendeur *m*, -euse *f* de journaux ◆ **onion-~** marchand(e) *m(f)* d'oignons ; → **bookseller** 2 *(as opposed to buyer)* vendeur *m* ◆ **~'s market** marché *m* favorable au vendeur 3 **this book is a (good) ~*** ce livre se vend bien *or* comme des petits pains* ; → **bestseller**

selling /ˈselɪŋ/ N vente(s) *f(pl)*
COMP **selling point** N *(Comm)* avantage *m* pour le client ; *(fig)* atout *m*
selling price N prix *m* de vente
selling rate N *(Fin)* cours *m* vendeur

selloff /ˈselɒf/ N vente *f*

Sellotape ® /ˈseləʊteɪp/ *(Brit)* N scotch ® *m*, ruban *m* adhésif VT ◆ **sellotape** scotcher, coller avec du ruban adhésif

sellout /ˈselaʊt/ N 1 *(Cine, Theat etc)* **the play was a ~** tous les billets (pour la pièce) ont été vendus, on a joué à guichets fermés *or* à bureaux fermés 2 *(= betrayal)* trahison *f*, capitulation *f* ◆ **a ~ of minority opinion** une trahison de l'opinion de la minorité ◆ **a ~ to the left** *(Pol)* une capitulation devant la gauche

seltzer /ˈseltsəʳ/ N *(US:* also **seltzer water)** eau *f* de Seltz

selvage, selvedge /ˈselvɪdʒ/ N lisière *f (d'un tissu)*

selves /selvz/ NPL of **self**

semantic /sɪˈmæntɪk/ ADJ sémantique ◆ **~ field** champ *m* sémantique

semantically /sɪˈmæntɪkəlɪ/ ADV sémantiquement, d'un point de vue sémantique

semanticist /sɪˈmæntɪsɪst/ N sémanticien(ne) *m(f)*

semantics /sɪˈmæntɪks/ N *(NonC)* sémantique *f*

semaphore /ˈseməfɔːʳ/ N 1 signaux *mpl* à bras ◆ **in ~** par signaux à bras 2 *(Rail)* sémaphore *m* VT transmettre par signaux à bras

semblance /ˈsembləns/ N semblant *m*, apparence *f* ◆ **without a ~ of respect** sans le moindre semblant de respect ◆ **to put on a ~ of sorrow** faire semblant d'avoir de la peine

seme /siːm/ N *(Ling)* sème *m*

semen /ˈsiːmən/ N sperme *m*, semence *f*

semester /sɪˈmestəʳ/ N *(esp US)* semestre *m*

semi /ˈsemɪ/ PREF 1 → **comp** 2 *(= not completely: + adj)* plus ou moins ◆ **it's ~ tidy** c'est plus ou moins bien rangé N 1 *(Brit *)* abbrev of **semi-detached** 2 * abbrev of **semifinal** 3 *(US)* abbrev of **semitrailer**

COMP **semi-annual** ADJ *(US)* semestriel (-le *f*)

semi-detached *(Brit)* N (also **semi-detached house**) maison *f* jumelle ADJ ◆ **~-detached houses** maisons *fpl* mitoyennes

semi-monthly ADJ, N *(US Press)* bimensuel *m*

semi-skimmed ADJ demi-écrémé

semiautomatic /ˌsemɪɔːtəˈmætɪk/ ADJ semi-automatique

semibasement /ˌsemɪˈbeɪsmənt/ N ≈ rez-de-jardin *m*

semibreve /ˈsemɪbriːv/ *(esp Brit Mus)* N ronde *f*

COMP **semibreve rest** N pause *f*

semicircle /ˈsemɪsɜːkl/ N demi-cercle *m*

semicircular /ˌsemɪˈsɜːkjʊləʳ/ ADJ demi-circulaire, semi-circulaire, en demi-cercle

semicolon /ˌsemɪˈkəʊlən/ N point-virgule *m*

semicommercial /ˌsemɪkəˈmɜːʃəl/ ADJ semi-commercial

semiconductor /ˌsemɪkənˈdʌktəʳ/ N semi-conducteur *m*

semiconscious /ˌsemɪˈkɒnʃəs/ ADJ à demi conscient

semiconsonant /ˌsemɪˈkɒnsənənt/ N semi-consonne *f*, semi-voyelle *f*

semidarkness /ˌsemɪˈdɑːknɪs/ N pénombre *f*, demi-jour *m*

semidesert /ˌsemɪˈdezət/ ADJ semi-désertique

semifinal /ˌsemɪˈfaɪnl/ N demi-finale *f* ◆ **to go out in the ~s** être éliminé en demi-finale

semifinalist /ˌsemɪˈfaɪnəlɪst/ N demi-finaliste *mf* ; *(= team)* équipe *f* demi-finaliste

semiliquid /ˌsemɪˈlɪkwɪd/ ADJ semi-liquide

semiliterate /ˌsemɪˈlɪtərɪt/ ADJ quasiment illettré

seminal /ˈsemɪnl/ ADJ *(Physiol)* séminal ; *(fig)* majeur

seminar /ˈsemɪnɑːʳ/ N séminaire *m*, colloque *m* ; *(Univ)* séminaire *m*, séance *f* de travaux pratiques *or* de TP

seminarian /ˌsemɪˈneərɪən/, **seminarist** /ˈsemɪnərɪst/ N séminariste *m*

seminary /ˈsemɪnərɪ/ N *(= priests' college)* séminaire *m* ; *(= school)* petit séminaire *m*

semiofficial /ˌsemɪəˈfɪʃəl/ ADJ semi-officiel, officieux

semiologist /ˌsemɪˈɒlədʒɪst/ N sémiologue *mf*

semiology /ˌsemɪˈɒlədʒɪ/ N sémiologie *f*

semiotic /ˌsemɪˈɒtɪk/ ADJ sémiotique

semiotics /ˌsemɪˈɒtɪks/ N *(NonC)* sémiotique *f*

semipolitical /ˌsemɪpəˈlɪtɪkəl/ ADJ semi-politique

semiprecious /ˌsemɪˈpreʃəs/ ADJ semi-précieux ◆ **~ stone** pierre *f* semi-précieuse

semiprivate room /ˌsemɪpraɪvɪtˈrʊm/ N *(US Med)* chambre *f* d'hôpital à plusieurs lits

semiprofessional /ˌsemɪprəˈfeʃənl/ ADJ semi-professionnel

semiquaver /ˈsemɪkweɪvəʳ/ N *(esp Brit Mus)* double croche *f*

semiskilled /ˌsemɪˈskɪld/ ADJ *[work]* d'ouvrier spécialisé ◆ **~ worker** ouvrier *m*, -ière *f* spécialisé(e), OS *mf*

semisolid /ˌsemɪˈsɒlɪd/ ADJ semi-solide

Semite /ˈsiːmaɪt/ N Sémite *or* sémite *mf*

Semitic /sɪˈmɪtɪk/ ADJ *[language]* sémitique ; *[people]* sémite

semitone /ˈsemɪtəʊn/ N demi-ton *m*

semitrailer /ˌsemɪˈtreɪləʳ/ N *(= truck)* semi-remorque *m*

semitropical /ˌsemɪˈtrɒpɪkəl/ ADJ semi-tropical

semivowel /ˈsemɪvaʊəl/ N semi-voyelle *f*, semi-consonne *f*

semiweekly /ˌsemɪˈwiːklɪ/ ADJ, N *(US Press)* bihebdomadaire *m*

semolina /ˌseməˈliːnə/ N semoule *f* ; (also **semolina pudding**) semoule *f* au lait

sempiternal /ˌsempɪˈtɜːnl/ ADJ *(liter)* éternel, perpétuel

sempstress /ˈsempstrɪs/ N ⇒ **seamstress**

SEN /ˌesiːˈen/ N *(Brit)* (abbrev of **State-Enrolled Nurse**) → **state**

Sen. *(US)* abbrev of **Senator**

sen. abbrev of **senior**

senate /ˈsenɪt/ N 1 *(Pol)* sénat *m* ◆ **the Senate** *(in US, Can, Austral)* le Sénat 2 *(Univ)* conseil *m* d'université

senator /ˈsenɪtəʳ/ N sénateur *m*

senatorial /ˌsenəˈtɔːrɪəl/ ADJ sénatorial

send /send/ (pret, ptp **sent**) VT 1 *(= dispatch)* *[+ object, letter, e-mail]* envoyer *(to sb* à qn) ; ◆ **I filled in the form but I didn't ~ it** j'ai rempli le formulaire mais je ne l'ai pas envoyé ◆ **to press '~'** *(for e-mail)* appuyer sur 'envoi' ◆ **to ~ help** envoyer des secours ◆ **I'll ~ a car (for you)** j'enverrai une voiture (vous chercher) ◆ **to ~ washing to the laundry** donner *or* envoyer du linge au blanchissage ◆ **God sent a plague to punish the Egyptians** Dieu envoya un fléau aux Égyptiens pour les punir ◆ **this decision ~s the wrong signal** *or* **message** cette décision risque d'être mal interprétée ◆ **these things are sent to try us!** *(hum)* c'est le ciel qui nous envoie ces épreuves ! ; → **regard, wish, word**

2 *(= cause to go)* *[+ person]* envoyer ◆ **to ~ sb for sth** envoyer qn chercher qch ◆ **to ~ sb to do sth** envoyer qn faire qch ◆ **I sent him (along) to see her** je l'ai envoyé la voir ◆ **~ him (along) to see me** dis-lui de venir me voir, envoie-le-moi ◆ **to ~ sb to bed** envoyer qn se coucher ◆ **to ~ sb home** renvoyer qn chez lui ; *(to a different country)* rapatrier qn ◆ **to ~ workers home** *(= lay off)* mettre des employés en chômage technique ◆ **to ~ a child to school** *[parent]* envoyer un enfant à l'école ; *[local authority]* scolariser un enfant ◆ **they sent him to school in London** ils l'ont mis en pension à Londres ◆ **I won't ~ you to school today** je ne t'envoie pas à l'école aujourd'hui ◆ **children are sent to school at the age of five** les enfants doivent aller à l'école à partir de cinq ans ◆ **some children are sent to school without breakfast** il y a des enfants qui vont à l'école sans avoir pris de petit déjeuner ◆ **the rain sent us indoors** la pluie nous a fait rentrer ◆ **they sent the dogs after the escaped prisoner** ils ont envoyé les chiens à la poursuite *or* à la recherche du prisonnier évadé ◆ **to ~ sb to sleep** *(lit, fig)* endormir qn ◆ **to ~ sb into fits of laughter** faire éclater qn de rire ◆ **to ~ sb packing*** *or* **about his business*** envoyer promener qn*, envoyer paître qn* ◆ **to ~ prices/shares** *etc* **soaring** faire monter les prix/les actions *etc* en flèche ; → **Coventry, prison**

3 *(= propel, cause to move)* *[+ ball]* envoyer, lancer ; *[+ stone, arrow]* lancer ◆ **to ~ an astronaut/a rocket into space** lancer *or* envoyer un astronaute/une fusée dans l'espace ◆ **he sent the ball over the trees** il a envoyé *or* lancé le ballon par-dessus les arbres ◆ **he screwed up the paper and sent it straight into the basket** il a froissé le papier et l'a envoyé *or* l'a lancé tout droit dans la corbeille ◆ **the explosion sent a cloud of smoke into the air** l'explosion a projeté un nuage de fumée (en l'air) ◆ **the news sent a thrill through her** la nouvelle l'a électrisée ◆ **the sight of the dog sent her running to her mother** en voyant le chien elle s'est précipitée vers sa mère ◆ **the blow sent him sprawling** le coup l'a envoyé par terre ◆ **he sent the plate flying** il a envoyé voler* l'assiette ◆ **to ~ sb flying** envoyer qn rouler à terre

4 *(= cause to become)* rendre ◆ **the noise is ~ing me mad** le bruit me rend fou

5 († *⁎ = make ecstatic)* emballer* ◆ **this music ~s me** cette musique m'emballe* ◆ **he ~s me** je le trouve sensationnel

VI *(frm, liter)* ◆ **they sent to ask if …** ils envoyèrent demander si …

COMP **sending-off** N *(Ftbl etc)* expulsion *f*

send-off N ◆ **they were given a warm ~-off** on leur a fait des adieux chaleureux ◆ **they gave him a big ~-off** ils sont venus nombreux lui souhaiter bon voyage

send-up* N *(Brit)* parodie *f*

► **send away** VI ◆ **to send away for sth** *(= order by post)* commander qch par correspondance ; *(= order and receive)* se faire envoyer qch

VT SEP 1 envoyer ; *(= expel: from country, town)* expulser ◆ **to ~ one's children away to school** mettre ses enfants en pension ◆ **to ~ a radio/car away to be fixed** donner une radio/une voiture à réparer

2 *(= dismiss)* *[+ person]* congédier

3 *[+ parcel, letter, goods]* envoyer ; *(= post)* envoyer (par la poste)

► **send back** VT SEP *[+ person, thing]* renvoyer

► **send down** VT SEP 1 *(lit)* *[+ person]* faire descendre, envoyer en bas

2 *[+ prices, sb's temperature, blood pressure]* faire baisser

3 *(Brit Univ)* renvoyer (de l'université)

4 *(* = jail)* coffrer*⁎, envoyer en prison

► **send for** VT FUS 1 *[+ doctor, police etc]* faire venir, appeler ; *(= send sb to get)* faire appeler, envoyer chercher ◆ **to ~ for help** envoyer chercher de l'aide, se faire envoyer des secours

2 *(= order by post)* commander par correspondance ; *(= order and receive)* se faire envoyer

► **send forth** VT SEP *(liter)* *[+ light]* diffuser ; *[+ leaf]* produire ; *[+ smell]* répandre, exhaler ; *[+ army]* envoyer

► **send in** VT SEP 1 *[+ person]* faire entrer ; *[+ troops]* envoyer

2 *[+ resignation]* envoyer, donner ; *[+ report, entry form]* envoyer, soumettre ◆ **to ~ in an application** faire une demande ; *(for job)* poser sa candidature ◆ **to ~ in a request** envoyer *or* faire une demande ◆ **~ in your name and address if you wish to receive …** envoyez vos nom et adresse si vous désirez recevoir …

► **send off** VI ⇒ **send away vi**

VT SEP 1 *[+ person]* envoyer ◆ **I sent him off to think it over/get cleaned up** *etc* je l'ai envoyé méditer là-dessus/se débarbouiller *etc* ◆ **she sent the child off to the grocer's** elle a envoyé l'enfant chez l'épicier

2 *(= say goodbye to)* dire au revoir à ◆ **there was a large crowd to ~ him off** une foule de gens était venue lui dire au revoir

3 *[+ letter, parcel, goods]* envoyer, expédier ; *(= post)* mettre à la poste

4 *(Ftbl etc) [+ player]* expulser

N ◆ **send-off** → **send**

► **send on** VT SEP *(Brit) [+ letter]* faire suivre ; *[+ luggage] (in advance)* expédier à l'avance ; *(afterwards)* faire suivre ; *[+ object left behind]* renvoyer

► **send out** VI ◆ **to send out for sth** *(= order by phone) [+ pizza etc]* commander qch par téléphone ; *(= send sb to fetch)* envoyer chercher qch

VT SEP 1 *[+ person]* faire sortir ◆ **she sent the children out to play** elle a envoyé les enfants jouer dehors ◆ **I sent her out for a breath of air** je l'ai envoyée prendre l'air ◆ **they were sent out for talking too loudly** on les a mis à la porte parce qu'ils parlaient trop fort

2 *(= post) [+ correspondence, leaflets]* envoyer (par la poste)

3 *[+ scouts, messengers, emissary]* envoyer

4 *(= emit) [+ smell]* répandre, exhaler ; *[+ heat]* diffuser, répandre ; *[+ light]* diffuser, émettre ; *[+ smoke]* répandre ; *[+ signal] (gen)* émettre ; *(Rad)* diffuser

5 *(= put out) [+ shoots, roots]* produire, donner

► **send round** VT SEP 1 *(= circulate) [+ document, bottle etc]* faire circuler

2 faire parvenir ◆ **I'll ~ it round to you as soon as it's ready** je vous le ferai parvenir *or* porter dès que cela sera prêt

3 *[+ person]* envoyer ◆ **I sent him round to the grocer's** je l'ai envoyé chez l'épicier

► **send up** VT SEP 1 *[+ person, luggage]* faire monter ; *[+ aeroplane]* envoyer ; *[+ spacecraft, flare]* lancer ; *[+ smoke]* envoyer ; *[+ prices]* faire monter en flèche

2 *(Brit* = make fun of) [+ person]* mettre en boîte* ; *(= imitate) [+ person, book]* parodier

3 *[+ entry form]* envoyer

4 *(= blow up)* faire sauter*, faire exploser

5 *(* = jail)* coffrer*, envoyer en prison

N ◆ **send-up** * *(Brit)* → **send**

sender /ˈsendəʳ/ N expéditeur *m*, -trice *f*, envoyeur *m*, -euse *f* ; → **return**

Seneca /ˈsenɪkə/ N Sénèque *m*

Senegal /ˌsenɪˈɡɔːl/ N Sénégal *m* ◆ **in ~** au Sénégal

Senegalese /ˈsenɪɡəˈliːz/ ADJ sénégalais N *(pl inv)* Sénégalais(e) *m(f)*

senile /ˈsiːnaɪl/ ADJ sénile ◆ **~ decay** dégénérescence *f* sénile COMP **senile dementia** N démence *f* sénile

senility /sɪˈnɪlɪtɪ/ N sénilité *f*

senior /ˈsiːnɪəʳ/ ADJ 1 *(= older)* aîné, plus âgé ◆ **he is three years ~ to me, he is ~ to me by three years** il est mon aîné de trois ans, il est plus âgé que moi de trois ans ◆ **(Mr) Smith Senior** (M.) Smith père ◆ **Mrs Smith Senior** Mme Smith mère

2 *(= of higher rank) [employee]* de grade supérieur ; *[officer]* supérieur (-eure *f*) ; *[position, rank]* supérieur (-eure *f*), plus élevé ◆ **at ~ level** *(Sport)* en senior ◆ **he is ~ to me in the firm** *(in rank)* il est au-dessus de moi dans l'entreprise, son poste dans l'entreprise est plus élevé que le mien ; *(in service)* il a plus d'ancienneté que moi dans la maison ◆ **~ officer** *(Mil)* officier *m* supérieur ◆ **a ~ official** *(Admin)* un haut fonctionnaire ; *(in private firm)* un cadre supérieur *or* haut placé ◆ **~ CID officer** *(Brit)* officier *m* de police judiciaire haut placé ◆ **~ police officer** officier *m* de police haut placé

3 *(hum)* ◆ **a ~ moment** un trou de mémoire

N 1 *(in age)* aîné(e) *m(f)* ◆ **he is my ~ by three years, he is three years my ~** *(in age)* il est mon aîné de trois ans, il est plus âgé que moi de trois ans ; *(in service)* il a trois ans d'ancienneté de plus que moi

2 *(US Univ)* étudiant(e) *m(f)* de licence ; *(US Scol)* élève *mf* de terminale ◆ **the ~s** *(Brit Scol)* les grands *mpl*, les grandes *fpl*

COMP **senior aircraftman** N (pl **senior aircraftmen**) *(Brit Air Force)* ≈ soldat *m*

senior aircraftwoman N (pl **senior aircraftwomen**) *(Brit Air Force)* ≈ soldat *m*

senior airman N (pl **senior airmen**) *(US Air Force)* caporal-chef *m*

senior chief petty officer N *(US Navy)* premier maître *m*

senior citizen N personne *f* du troisième âge, senior *m* ◆ **~ citizens' club** club *m* du troisième age

senior clerk N premier commis *m*, commis *m* principal

senior common room N *(Brit Univ)* salle *f* des professeurs

senior editor N rédacteur *m*, -trice *f* en chef

senior executive N cadre *m* supérieur

senior high school N *(US)* ≈ lycée *m*

senior master N *(Brit Scol)* professeur *m* principal

senior master sergeant N *(US Air Force)* adjudant *m*

senior partner N associé *m* principal

senior prom N *(US)* bal *m* des classes de terminale

senior school N *(= oldest classes)* grandes classes *fpl* ; *(= secondary school)* collège *m* d'enseignement secondaire

Senior Service N *(Brit)* marine *f* (de guerre)

senior year N *(US Scol)* (classe *f*) terminale *f*, dernière année *f* d'études (scolaires)

seniority /ˌsiːnɪˈɒrɪtɪ/ N *(in age)* priorité *f* d'âge ; *(in rank)* rang *m*, niveau *m* de responsabilité ; *(in years of service)* ancienneté *f* ◆ **promotion by ~** avancement *m* à l'ancienneté

senna /ˈsenə/ N séné *m* COMP **senna pod** N gousse *f* de séné

sensation /senˈseɪʃən/ N 1 *(= feeling)* sensation *f* ◆ **to lose all ~ in one's arm** perdre toute sensation dans le bras ◆ **to have a dizzy ~** avoir une sensation de vertige 2 *(= impression)* sensation *f* ◆ **to have the ~ of doing sth** avoir la sensation de faire qch ◆ **I felt a ~ of being watched** j'avais l'impression *or* le sentiment que l'on m'observait 3 *(= excitement, success)* sensation *f* ; *(Press)* sensation *f* ◆ **to create** *or* **cause a ~** faire sensation ◆ **it was a ~ in Paris** cela a fait sensation à Paris ◆ **it's a ~!** c'est sensationnel ! ◆ **the film that turned her into an overnight ~** le film qui a fait d'elle une star du jour au lendemain

sensational /senˈseɪʃənl/ ADJ 1 *[event]* qui fait sensation, sensationnel ; *[fashion]* qui fait sensation ◆ **~ murder** meurtre *m* qui fait sensation 2 *[film, novel, newspaper]* à sensation ◆ **he gave a ~ account of the accident** il a fait un récit dramatique de l'accident 3 *(* = marvellous)* sensationnel*, formidable*

sensationalism /senˈseɪʃnəlɪzəm/ N *(NonC)* 1 *(Press etc)* recherche *f* or exploitation *f* du sensationnel 2 *(Philos)* sensualisme *m*

sensationalist /senˈseɪʃnəlɪst/ N colporteur *m*, -euse *f* de nouvelles à sensation ; *(= writer)* auteur *m* à sensation ADJ à sensation ◆ **they described it in ~ terms** ils l'ont décrit en recherchant le sensationnel

sensationalize /senˈseɪʃnəlaɪz/ VT dramatiser

sensationally /senˈseɪʃnəlɪ/ ADV ◆ **it was ~ successful/popular** *etc* cela a connu un succès/une popularité *etc* inouï(e) *or* fantastique ◆ **he was ~ dropped from the team** à la surprise générale, il a été écarté de l'équipe

sense /sens/ N 1 *(= faculty)* sens *m* ◆ **~ of hearing** ouïe *f* ◆ **~ of smell** odorat *m* ◆ **~ of sight** vue *f* ◆ **~ of taste** goût *m* ◆ **~ of touch** toucher *m* ; see also **noun 4** ; → **sixth**

2 *(= awareness)* sens *m*, sentiment *m* ◆ **~ of colour** sens *m* de la couleur ◆ **~ of direction** sens *m* de l'orientation ◆ **~ of duty** sentiment *m* du devoir ◆ **~ of humour** sens *m* de l'humour ◆ **he has no ~ of humour** il n'a pas le sens de l'humour ◆ **to lose all ~ of time** perdre toute notion de l'heure ◆ **to have no ~ of shame** ne pas savoir ce que c'est que la honte ; → **business, road, strong, occasion**

3 *(= sensation, impression) (physical)* sensation *f* ; *(mental)* sentiment *m* ◆ **a ~ of achievement** le sentiment d'avoir accompli quelque chose ◆ **a ~ of warmth** une sensation de chaleur ◆ **a ~ of guilt** un sentiment de culpabilité ◆ **we tried to get a ~ of what was going on** on a essayé de comprendre ce qui se passait ◆ **to get** *or* **have a ~ that ...** avoir le sentiment que ... ◆ **there's no ~ that they might have done it for the money** on n'a pas l'impression qu'ils ont fait ça pour l'argent

4 *(= sanity)* **to take leave of one's ~s** perdre la tête *or* la raison ◆ **to come to one's ~s** *(= become reasonable)* revenir à la raison ◆ **to bring sb to his ~s** ramener qn à la raison

5 *(= wisdom, sound judgement)* (also **common-sense**) bon sens *m* ◆ **haven't you enough ~** *or* **the (good) ~ to refuse?** n'avez-vous pas assez de bon sens pour refuser ? ◆ **there is some ~ in what he says** il y a du bon sens dans ce qu'il dit ◆ **to have more ~ than to do sth** avoir trop de bon sens pour faire qch, être trop sensé pour faire qch ◆ **you should have had more ~ than to tell them that** vous auriez dû avoir assez de bon sens pour ne pas le leur dire ◆ **they should have more ~!** ils devraient avoir un peu plus de jugeote ! *

6 *(= reasonable quality)* sens *m* ◆ **there's no ~ in (doing) that** cela n'a pas de sens, cela ne rime à rien ◆ **what's the ~ of** *or* **in (doing) that?** à quoi bon (faire) cela ? ◆ **to see ~** entendre raison ◆ **he won't see ~** il ne veut pas entendre raison ◆ **try to make him see ~** essaie de lui faire entendre raison ; → **sound², talk**

7 *(= meaning) [of word, phrase, writing, text etc]* sens *m* (also *Ling*), signification *f* ◆ **in the literal/figurative ~** au sens propre/figuré ◆ **in every ~ of the word** dans tous les sens du terme ◆ **alcoholism is not a disease in the usual ~ of the word** l'alcoolisme n'est pas une maladie au sens habituel du terme

◆ **in a + sense** ◆ **in a ~** dans un (certain) sens, dans une certaine mesure ◆ **in a very real ~** de fait

◆ **in no sense** en aucune manière ◆ **this is in no ~ a criminal offence** ceci ne constitue en aucune manière un délit

◆ **to make sense** *[words, speech etc]* avoir du sens ◆ **it doesn't make ~** cela n'a pas de sens ◆ **what she did makes ~** ce qu'elle a fait est logique *or* se tient ◆ **what she did just doesn't make ~** ce qu'elle a fait n'est pas logique ◆ **why did he do it? – I don't know, it doesn't make ~** pourquoi est-ce qu'il a fait ça ? – je n'en sais rien, c'est à n'y rien comprendre ◆ **do you think it makes ~ to start now?** pensez-vous que c'est une bonne idée de commencer maintenant ? ◆ **yes, that makes ~** oui, ça paraît raisonnable

◆ **to make sense of sth** arriver à comprendre qch, saisir la signification de qch

8 *(= opinion)* **the general ~ of the meeting** l'opinion générale *or* le sentiment de ceux présents ◆ **the ~ of the Senate** *(US Pol)* la recommandation du Sénat

VT 1 *(= become aware of, feel) [+ sb's uneasiness, grief, happiness etc]* sentir (intuitivement) ; *[+ trouble]* pressentir ◆ **to ~ danger** pressentir le danger ◆ **they ~ victory** ils ont le sentiment qu'ils vont gagner ◆ **to ~ somebody's pres-**

ence sentir une présence, se rendre compte d'une présence ◆ **I could ~ his eyes on me** je sentais qu'il me regardait ◆ **I ~d his interest in what I was saying** j'ai senti que ce que je disais l'intéressait ◆ **to ~ that one is unwelcome** sentir *or* deviner qu'on n'est pas le bienvenu ◆ **she can ~ when her children are unhappy** elle le sent *or* devine quand ses enfants sont malheureux

[2] *[machine, sensor device] [+ movement, heat, change]* détecter ◆ **the camera ~s when a film has reached the end** la caméra le détecte quand un film est arrivé au bout

COMP **sense organ** N organe *m* des sens *or* sensoriel

senseless /ˈsenslɪs/ ADJ [1] *(= stupid) [person]* insensé ; *[action, idea]* stupide, qui ne tient pas debout ; *(stronger)* absurde, insensé ◆ **a ~ waste of energy resources** un gâchis insensé des ressources d'énergie ◆ **it was a ~ waste of human life** il (*or* elle *etc*) est mort(e) pour rien ◆ **what a ~ thing to do! (*or* to say! *etc*)** c'est d'une stupidité sans nom !, ça n'a pas le sens commun ! [2] *(= unconscious)* sans connaissance ◆ **to fall ~ (to the floor)** tomber sans connaissance ; → **knock**

senselessly /ˈsenslɪslɪ/ ADV stupidement, d'une façon insensée

senselessness /ˈsenslɪsnɪs/ N *[of person]* manque *m* de bon sens ; *[of action, idea]* absurdité *f* ◆ **the absolute ~ of war** l'absurdité *f* totale de la guerre

sensibility /ˌsensɪˈbɪlɪtɪ/ N [1] *(NonC)* sensibilité *f* [2] ◆ **sensibilities** susceptibilité *f*

sensible /ˈsensəbl/ ADJ [1] *(= wise, of sound judgement) [person]* sensé, raisonnable ◆ **she's a ~ person *or* type** elle est très raisonnable *or* sensée ◆ **try to be ~ about it** sois raisonnable ◆ **that was ~ of you** tu as très bien fait, c'était la chose à faire [2] *(= reasonable, practicable) [act, decision, choice]* sage, raisonnable ; *[clothes]* pratique ◆ **the most ~ thing (to do) would be to see her** le plus sage *or* raisonnable serait de la voir [3] *(frm = perceptible) [change, difference, rise in temperature]* sensible [4] *(frm = aware)* **I am ~ † of the honour you do me** je suis sensible à *or* conscient de l'honneur que vous me faites

> ⚠ When **sensible** means 'wise' or 'reasonable', it does not correspond to the French word **sensible**.

sensibleness /ˈsensəblnɪs/ N bon sens *m*, jugement *m*

sensibly /ˈsensəblɪ/ ADV [1] *(= reasonably) [act, decide]* raisonnablement, sagement ◆ **to be ~ dressed** porter des vêtements pratiques [2] *(= perceptibly)* sensiblement

sensitive /ˈsensɪtɪv/ ADJ [1] *[person] (= emotionally aware, responsive)* sensible ; *(= easily hurt)* sensible (*to* à) ; *(= easily offended)* facilement blessé (*to* par), susceptible ; *(= easily influenced)* impressionnable, influençable ◆ **she is ~ about her nose** elle fait une fixation sur son nez ◆ **she's a ~ soul** c'est quelqu'un de très sensible *or* émotif

[2] *(= delicate) [eyes, matter, skin, subject, topic]* délicat, sensible ; *[situation]* névralgique, délicat ; *(Phot) [film]* sensible (*to* à) ; *(Phot) [paper]* sensibilisé ◆ **public opinion is very ~ to hints of corruption** l'opinion publique réagit vivement à tout soupçon de corruption ◆ **this is politically very ~** sur le plan politique ceci est très délicat ◆ **that is a very ~ area** *(= place)* c'est un point chaud ; *(fig = subject matter)* c'est un domaine très délicat *or* sensible

[3] *(= sore) [tooth, skin, sore place]* sensible

[4] *(affecting national security) [document etc]* sensible

[5] *(Stock Exchange, Comm) [market]* nerveux

ADJ *(in compounds)* ◆ **heat-/light-~** sensible à la chaleur/la lumière

sensitively /ˈsensɪtɪvlɪ/ ADV avec sensibilité, d'une manière sensible

sensitiveness /ˈsensɪtɪvnɪs/ N *(= responsiveness) (physical, emotional)* sensibilité *f* ; *(to criticism)* susceptibilité *f*

sensitivity /ˌsensɪˈtɪvɪtɪ/ N [1] *[of person, instrument, gauge, machine]* sensibilité *f* ◆ **their ~ to this problem** leur sensibilisation à ce problème ◆ **~ to pain** sensibilité à la douleur ◆ **if you experience any ~, discontinue use** *(= soreness)* en cas de réaction (allergique), cesser l'utilisation [2] *(= delicacy) [of subject]* caractère *m* délicat ; *[of information]* caractère *m* sensible ◆ **an issue of great ~** un sujet très délicat

sensitize /ˈsensɪtaɪz/ VT *(gen, Phot)* sensibiliser

sensor /ˈsensəʳ/ N détecteur *m* ◆ **heat ~** palpeur *m*

sensory /ˈsensərɪ/ ADJ des sens ; *[organ, nerve]* sensoriel

sensual /ˈsensjʊəl/ ADJ sensuel

sensualism /ˈsensjʊəlɪzəm/ N sensualité *f* ; *(Philos)* sensualisme *m*

sensualist /ˈsensjʊəlɪst/ N personne *f* sensuelle, voluptueux *m*, -euse *f* ; *(Philos)* sensualiste *mf*

sensuality /ˌsensjʊˈælɪtɪ/ N sensualité *f*

sensually /ˈsensjʊəlɪ/ ADV sensuellement

sensuous /ˈsensjʊəs/ ADJ *[person, temperament, poetry, music]* voluptueux, sensuel

sensuously /ˈsensjʊəslɪ/ ADV avec volupté, voluptueusement

sensuousness /ˈsensjʊəsnɪs/ N *[of poetry, music]* qualité *f* voluptueuse *or* sensuelle ; *[of person, temperament]* sensualité *f*

sent /sent/ VB pt, ptp of **send**

sentence /ˈsentəns/ N [1] *(Gram)* phrase *f* [2] *(Jur) (= judgement)* condamnation *f*, sentence *f* ; *(= punishment)* peine *f* ◆ **to pass ~ on sb** *(lit, fig)* prononcer une condamnation *or* une sentence contre qn ◆ **~ of death** arrêt *m* de mort, condamnation *f* à mort ◆ **under ~ of death** condamné à mort ◆ **he got a five-year ~** il a été condamné à cinq ans de prison ◆ **a long ~** une longue peine ◆ **a jail ~** une peine *f* de prison ◆ **a heavy/light ~** une peine sévère/légère ; → **commute, life, serve** VT prononcer une condamnation *or* une sentence contre ◆ **to ~ sb to death/to five years** condamner qn à mort/à cinq ans de prison COMP **sentence structure** N structure *f* de la phrase

sententious /senˈtenʃəs/ ADJ sentencieux, pompeux

sententiously /senˈtenʃəslɪ/ ADV sentencieusement

sententiousness /senˈtenʃəsnɪs/ N *[of speech]* ton *m* sentencieux ; *[of person]* caractère *m* sentencieux

sentient /ˈsenʃənt/ ADJ sensible, doué de sensation

sentiment /ˈsentɪmənt/ N [1] *(NonC = feeling)* sentiment *m* ◆ **public ~** le sentiment général ◆ **there is growing nationalist ~ in the country** on observe dans le pays une montée du sentiment nationaliste ◆ **his actions were motivated by religious ~** ses actes ont été motivés par un sentiment religieux ◆ **anti-government ~ was strong** il y avait un fort sentiment antigouvernemental [2] *(= opinion, thought)* sentiment *m* ◆ **what are your ~s on this?** quels sont vos sentiments à ce sujet ? ◆ **what a marvellous ~!** quelle idée charmante ! ◆ **my ~s exactly!** c'est exactement ce que je pense ! [3] *(= emotion)* sentiment *m* ◆ **my ~s towards your daughter** les sentiments que j'éprouve pour votre fille [4] *(NonC = sentimentality)* sentimentalité *f*, sensiblerie *f* *(pej)*

sentimental /ˌsentɪˈmentl/ ADJ *[person, novel]* sentimental *(also pej)* ◆ **it's of ~ value only** sa valeur est purement sentimentale ◆ **~ comedy** *(Literat)* comédie *f* larmoyante

sentimentalism /ˌsentɪˈmentəlɪzəm/ N sentimentalisme *m*, sensiblerie *f* *(pej)*

sentimentalist /ˌsentɪˈmentəlɪst/ N sentimental(e) *m(f)*

sentimentality /ˌsentɪmenˈtælɪtɪ/ N sentimentalité *f*, sensiblerie *f* *(pej)*

sentimentalize /ˌsentɪˈmentəlaɪz/ VT rendre sentimental VI faire du sentiment *

sentimentally /ˌsentɪˈmentəlɪ/ ADV sentimentalement, d'une manière (*or* d'une voix *etc*) sentimentale

sentinel /ˈsentɪnl/ N sentinelle *f*, factionnaire *m*

sentry /ˈsentrɪ/ N *(Mil)* sentinelle *f*, factionnaire *m* ; *(fig)* sentinelle *f*

COMP **sentry box** N guérite *f*

sentry duty N ◆ **to be on ~ duty** être en *or* de faction

Seoul /səʊl/ N Séoul

Sep. abbrev of **September**

sepal /ˈsepəl/ N sépale *m*

separable /ˈsepərəbl/ ADJ séparable

separate /ˈseprət/ ADJ *[section, piece]* séparé, distinct ; *[treaty, peace]* séparé ; *[career, existence]* indépendant ; *[organization, unit]* distinct, indépendant ; *[entrance]* particulier ; *[occasion, day]* différent ; *[question, issue]* différent, autre ◆ **the children have ~ rooms** les enfants ont chacun leur (propre) chambre ◆ **Paul and his wife sleep in ~ beds/rooms** Paul et sa femme font lit/chambre à part ◆ **they live completely ~ lives** ils mènent des vies complètement séparées ◆ **we want ~ bills** *(in restaurant etc)* nous voudrions des additions séparées, nous voudrions chacun notre addition ◆ **the two houses though semi-detached are quite ~** les deux maisons bien que jumelées sont tout à fait indépendantes (l'une de l'autre) ◆ **I wrote it on a ~ sheet** je l'ai écrit sur une feuille séparée *or* sur une feuille à part ◆ **take a ~ sheet for each answer** prenez une nouvelle feuille pour chaque réponse ◆ **there will be ~ discussions on this question** cette question sera discutée à part *or* séparément ◆ **there is a ~ department for footwear** il y a un rayon séparé *or* spécial pour les chaussures ◆ **"with separate toilet"** "avec WC séparé" ◆ **keep the novels ~ from the textbooks** ne mélangez pas les romans et les livres de classe

NPL **separates** *(= clothes)* vêtements *mpl* à coordonner

VT /ˈsepəreɪt/ séparer (*from* de) ; *(= sort out)* séparer, trier ; *(= divide up)* diviser ; *[+ strands]* dédoubler ; *[+ milk]* écrémer ◆ **to ~ truth from error** distinguer le vrai du faux ◆ **only three points now ~ the two teams** trois points seulement séparent maintenant les deux équipes ; → **separated, sheep, wheat**

VI /ˈsepəreɪt/ [1] *[liquids]* se séparer (*from* de) ; *[metals etc]* se séparer, se détacher (*from* de)

[2] *[people]* se séparer, se quitter ; *[fighters]* rompre ; *[married couple]* se séparer ; *[non-married couple]* rompre

COMP **separate opinion** N *(US Jur)* avis *m* divergeant de la minorité des juges

separate school N *(Can)* école *f* *or* collège *m* privé(e)

▸ **separate out** VT SEP séparer, trier

separated /ˈsepəreɪtɪd/ ADJ *[couple, person]* séparé

separately /ˈseprətlɪ/ ADV séparément

separateness /ˈseprətnɪs/ N séparation *f* (*from* de) ◆ **feeling of ~** sentiment *m* de séparation *or* d'être à part

separation /ˌsepəˈreɪʃən/ N séparation *f* ; *[of ore]* triage *m* ; *(Pol, Rel)* scission *f*, séparation *f* ; *(after marriage)* séparation *f (from d'avec)* ◆ **judicial** ~ séparation *f* de corps COMP **separation allowance** N *(Mil)* allocation *f* militaire ; *(= alimony)* pension *f* alimentaire

separatism /ˈsepərətɪzəm/ N séparatisme *m*

separatist /ˈsepərətɪst/ ADJ, N séparatiste *mf*

separator /ˈsepəreɪtəʳ/ N *(all senses)* séparateur *m*

Sephardi /seˈfɑːdɪ/ N (pl **Sephardim** /seˈfɑːdɪm/) séfarade *mf*

Sephardic /seˈfɑːdɪk/ ADJ séfarade

sepia /ˈsiːpjə/ N 1 *(= colour)* sépia *f* 2 *(= fish)* seiche *f* COMP **sepia drawing** N sépia *f*

sepoy /ˈsiːpɔɪ/ N cipaye *m*

sepsis /ˈsepsɪs/ N *(Med)* septicité *f*, état *m* septique

Sept. abbrev of **September**

septa /ˈseptə/ NPL of **septum**

September /sepˈtembəʳ/ N septembre *m*, mois *m* de septembre ◆ **the first of** ~ le premier septembre ◆ **the tenth of** ~ le dix septembre ◆ **on the tenth of** ~ le dix septembre ◆ **in** ~ en septembre ◆ **in the month of** ~ au mois de septembre ◆ **each** *or* **every** ~ tous les ans *or* chaque année en septembre ◆ **at the beginning of** ~ au début (du mois) de septembre, début septembre ◆ **in the middle of** ~, **in mid** ~ au milieu (du mois) de septembre, à la mi-septembre ◆ **at the end of** ~ à la fin (du mois) de septembre, fin septembre ◆ **during** ~ pendant le mois de septembre ◆ **there are 30 days in** ~ il y a 30 jours au mois de septembre, septembre a 30 jours ◆ ~ **was cold** septembre a été froid, il a fait froid en septembre ◆ **early in** ~, **in early** ~ au début de septembre ◆ **late in** ~, **in late** ~ vers la fin de septembre ◆ **last/next** ~ septembre dernier/prochain

COMP **September holidays** NPL congés *mpl* (du mois) de septembre

September Massacre N *(Hist)* massacres *mpl* de septembre

September rains NPL pluies *fpl* (du mois) de septembre

September weather N ◆ **it's ~ weather** il fait un temps de septembre

Septembrist /sepˈtembrɪst/ N septembriseur *m*

septet /sepˈtet/ N septuor *m*

septic /ˈseptɪk/ ADJ septique ; *[wound]* infecté ◆ **to go** *or* **become** ~ s'infecter

COMP **septic poisoning** N septicémie *f*

septic tank N fosse *f* septique

septicaemia, septicemia (US) /ˌseptɪˈsiːmɪə/ N septicémie *f*

septuagenarian /ˌseptjʊədʒɪˈneərɪən/ ADJ, N septuagénaire *mf*

Septuagesima /ˌseptjʊəˈdʒesɪmə/ N Septuagésime *f*

Septuagint /ˈseptjʊədʒɪnt/ N version *f* des Septante

septum /ˈseptəm/ N (pl **septa**) *(Anat, Bot)* cloison *f*, septum *m*

septuplet /sepˈtʌplɪt/ N septuplé(e) *m(f)*

sepulcher /ˈsepəlkəʳ/ N (US) ⇒ **sepulchre**

sepulchral /sɪˈpʌlkrəl/ ADJ sépulcral ; *(fig = gloomy)* funèbre, sépulcral

sepulchre, sepulcher (US) /ˈsepəlkəʳ/ N sépulcre *m*, tombeau *m* ; *(Rel)* sépulcre *m* ; → **holy, white**

sequel /ˈsiːkwəl/ N 1 *(= consequence)* suite *f*, conséquence *f* ; *(to illness etc)* séquelles *fpl* ◆ **there was a tragic** ~ cela a eu des suites *or* des conséquences tragiques 2 *[of book, film etc]* suite *f*

sequence /ˈsiːkwəns/ N 1 *(= order)* ordre *m*, suite *f* ◆ **in** ~ par ordre ◆ **out of** ~ dans le désordre, les uns à la suite des autres ◆ **in historical** ~ par ordre chronologique ◆ **logical** ~ ordre *m or* enchaînement *m* logique 2 *(= series)* suite *f*, succession *f* ; *(Cards)* séquence *f* ◆ **a** ~ **of events** un enchaînement d'événements ◆ **the** ~ **of events was always the same** les choses se déroulaient toujours de la même façon 3 ◆ **(film)** ~ séquence *f* ◆ **(dance)** ~ numéro *m* (de danse) 4 *(Mus)* séquence *f* 5 *(Comput)* séquence *f* 6 *(Ling) (gen)* suite *f* ◆ ~ **of tenses** *(Gram)* concordance *f* des temps VT *[+ genes, DNA]* séquencer

sequencer /ˈsiːkwənsəʳ/ N *(Mus)* séquenceur *m*

sequential /sɪˈkwenʃəl/ ADJ 1 *(= in regular sequence)* séquentiel 2 *(= following)* qui suit ◆ ~ **upon** *or* **from ...** qui résulte de ... 3 *(Comput)* séquentiel ◆ ~ **access/processing** accès *m*/traitement *m* séquentiel

sequester /sɪˈkwestəʳ/ VT 1 *(= isolate)* isoler ; *(= shut up)* enfermer, séquestrer 2 *(Jur) [+ property]* séquestrer

sequestered /sɪˈkwestəd/ ADJ 1 *[life]* isolé, retiré ; *[spot]* retiré, peu fréquenté 2 *(Jur) [property]* mis *or* placé sous séquestre

sequestrate /sɪˈkwestreɪt/ VT *(Jur)* 1 ⇒ **sequester 2** 2 *(= confiscate)* confisquer, saisir

sequestration /ˌsiːkwesˈtreɪʃən/ N *(Jur)* 1 *[of property]* séquestration *f*, mise *f* sous séquestre 2 *(= confiscation)* confiscation *f*, saisie *f* conservatoire

sequin /ˈsiːkwɪn/ N paillette *f*

sequinned, sequined (US) /ˈsiːkwɪnd/ ADJ pailleté, cousu de paillettes

sequoia /sɪˈkwɔɪə/ N séquoia *m*

sera /ˈsɪərə/ NPL of **serum**

seraglio /seˈrɑːlɪəʊ/ N sérail *m*

serape /səˈrɑːpɪ/ N (US) poncho *m*, couverture *f* mexicaine

seraph /ˈserəf/ N (pl **seraphs** *or* **seraphim**) *(Rel, liter etc)* séraphin *m*

seraphic /səˈræfɪk/ ADJ *(lit, fig)* séraphique

seraphim /ˈserəfɪm/ NPL of **seraph**

Serb /sɜːb/ ADJ serbe N 1 Serbe *mf* 2 *(Ling)* serbe *m*

Serbia /ˈsɜːbɪə/ N Serbie *f*

Serbian /ˈsɜːbɪən/ ADJ, N ⇒ **Serb**

Serbo-Croat /ˈsɜːbəʊˈkrəʊæt/, **Serbo-Croatian** /ˈsɜːbəʊkrəʊˈeɪʃən/ ADJ serbo-croate N 1 Serbo-Croate *mf* 2 *(= language)* serbo-croate *m*

sere /sɪəʳ/ ADJ ⇒ **sear adj**

serenade /ˌserəˈneɪd/ N sérénade *f* VT donner une sérénade à

serendipitous /ˌserənˈdɪpɪtəs/ ADJ *[discovery etc]* heureux ◆ **his timing was** ~ il ne pouvait pas mieux tomber

serendipity /ˌserənˈdɪpɪtɪ/ N *(NonC: hum)* hasard *m* heureux

serene /səˈriːn/ ADJ *[person, smile, place, atmosphere]* serein, paisible ; *[face]* serein ; *[sky]* serein, clair ; *[sea, river]* calme ◆ **to become** *or* **grow** ~ *[person]* devenir serein, se rasséréner ; *[sky]* redevenir serein ; *[sea, river]* redevenir calme ◆ **His Serene Highness** Son Altesse *f* Sérénissime

serenely /səˈriːnlɪ/ ADV *[smile]* avec sérénité, sereinement ; *[say]* d'un ton serein ◆ ~ **indifferent to the noise** suprêmement indifférent au bruit

serenity /sɪˈrenɪtɪ/ N *[of person, place, smile, lifestyle]* sérénité *f*

serf /sɜːf/ N serf *m*, serve *f*

serfdom /ˈsɜːfdəm/ N servage *m*

serge /sɜːdʒ/ N serge *f* COMP de serge **serge suit** N complet *m* en serge ◆ **blue** ~ **suit** complet *m* en serge bleue

sergeant /ˈsɑːdʒənt/ N 1 *(Brit Mil, Air Force)* sergent *m* ◆ **yes,** ~ oui, chef ; see also **colour, drill², flight²** 2 *(US Air Force)* caporal-chef *m* 3 *(Police)* ≈ brigadier *m* ; → **detective**

COMP **sergeant at arms** N huissier *m* d'armes

sergeant first class N *(US Mil)* sergent-chef *m*

sergeant-major N *(Mil) (Brit)* sergent-major *m* ; *(US)* adjudant-chef *m* ; → **company, regimental**

serial /ˈsɪərɪəl/ N 1 *(Rad, TV)* feuilleton *m* ; *(in magazine etc:* also **serial story***)* roman-feuilleton *m*, feuilleton *m* ◆ **television/radio** ~ feuilleton *m* à la télévision/à la radio, feuilleton *m* télévisé/radiophonique ◆ **13-part** ~ feuilleton *m* en 13 épisodes

2 *(= publication, journal)* publication *f* périodique, périodique *m*

ADJ 1 *(Comput) [disk, transmission, processing, programming etc]* série *inv* ; *[access]* séquentiel

2 *[music]* sériel

COMP **serial killer** N tueur *m* en série

serial killing(s) N(PL) meurtres *mpl* en série

serial monogamy N *série de liaisons monogamiques*

serial murder N meurtres *mpl* en série

serial number N *[of goods, car engine]* numéro *m* de série ; *[of soldier]* (numéro *m*) matricule *m* ; *[of cheque, bank-note]* numéro *m*

serial port N *(Comput)* port *m* série

serial rapist N violeur *m* en série

serial rights NPL droits *mpl* de reproduction en feuilleton

serial writer N feuilletoniste *mf*

serialism /ˈsɪərɪəˌlɪzəm/ N *(Mus)* sérialisme *m*

serialization /ˌsɪərɪəlaɪˈzeɪʃən/ N *(Press)* publication *f* en feuilleton ; *(Rad, TV)* adaptation *f* en feuilleton

serialize /ˈsɪərɪəlaɪz/ VT *(Press)* publier en feuilleton ; *(Rad, TV)* adapter en feuilleton ◆ **it was ~d in six parts** cela a été publié *or* adapté en six épisodes ◆ **it has been ~d in the papers** cela a paru *or* été publié en feuilleton dans les journaux

serially /ˈsɪərɪəlɪ/ ADV 1 *[number]* en série 2 ◆ **to appear/be published** ~ *[story]* paraître/être publié en feuilleton ; *[magazine, journal]* paraître/être publié en livraisons périodiques

seriatim /ˌsɪərɪˈeɪtɪm/ ADV *(frm)* successivement, point par point

sericulture /ˌserɪˈkʌltʃəʳ/ N sériciculture *f*

series /ˈsɪərɪz/ N *(pl inv)* 1 *(gen)* série *f* ; *(Math)* série *f*, suite *f* ◆ **a** ~ **of volumes on this subject** une série de volumes sur ce sujet ◆ **there has been a** ~ **of incidents** il y a eu une série *or* une suite d'incidents ◆ **it will be one of a** ~ **of measures intended to ...** cette mesure entrera dans le cadre d'une série de mesures destinées à ...

◆ **in series** *(Elec)* en série

2 *(Rad, TV)* série *f* (d'émissions) ; *(= set of books)* collection *f* ; *(= set of stamps)* série *f* ◆ **this is the last in the present** ~ *(Rad, TV)* voilà la dernière émission de notre série ◆ **a new paperback** ~ *(Publishing)* une nouvelle collection de poche ◆ ~ **director** *(in publishing)* directeur (-trice *f*) *(d'une collection)* ◆ ~ **editor** rédacteur (-trice *f*) en chef *(d'une série d'émissions)* ; → **world**

COMP **series connection** N *(Elec)* montage *m* en série

serio-comic /ˌsɪərɪəʊˈkɒmɪk/ ADJ mi-sérieux mi-comique

serious /ˈsɪərɪəs/ ADJ 1 *(= in earnest, not frivolous) [person, offer, suggestion, interest]* sérieux, sincère ; *[publication, conversation, discussion, occasion]* sérieux, important ; *[report, information,* account] sérieux, sûr ; [literature, music] respectable ; [attitude, voice, smile, look] plein de sérieux, grave ; [tone] sérieux, grave ; (= unsmiling) [person] sérieux, grave ; [look] grave, sévère ; (= thoughtful) sérieux ; [pupil] sérieux, appliqué ◆ **are you ~?** (parlez-vous) sérieusement ? ◆ **I'm quite** ~ je suis sérieux, je parle sérieusement ◆ **to give ~ thought to sth** (= ponder) bien réfléchir à qch ; (= intend) songer sérieusement à qch ◆ **to be ~ about one's work** être sérieux dans son travail ◆ **the ~ student of jazz will maintain that ...** quelqu'un qui s'intéresse sérieusement au jazz affirmera que ... ◆ **marriage is a ~ business** le mariage est une affaire sérieuse ◆ **she earns ~ money*** elle gagne un bon paquet* ◆ **~ wine*** vin m décent

2 (= causing concern) [illness, injury, mistake, situation] grave, sérieux ; [damage] important, considérable ; [threat] sérieux ; [loss] grave, lourd ◆ **I have ~ doubts about ...** je doute sérieusement de ..., j'ai de graves doutes sur ... ◆ **the patient's condition is** ~ le patient est dans un état grave

COMP **Serious Fraud Office** N (Brit) service de la répression des fraudes majeures

seriously /ˈsɪərɪəslɪ/ ADV 1 (= in earnest) sérieusement, avec sérieux ; (= not jokingly) sérieusement, sans plaisanter ◆ **he said it all quite** ~ il l'a dit tout à fait sérieusement ◆ **yes, but ~ ...** oui, mais sérieusement ... ◆ **~ now ...** sérieusement ..., toute plaisanterie (mise) à part ... ◆ **to take sth/sb** ~ prendre qch/qn au sérieux ◆ **to think ~ about sth** (= ponder) bien réfléchir à qch ; (= intend) songer sérieusement à qch 2 (= dangerously) gravement, sérieusement ; [ill] gravement ; [wounded] grièvement ; [worried] sérieusement 3 (= very) ◆ **to be ~ rich** * avoir beaucoup de fric*

seriousness /ˈsɪərɪəsnɪs/ N 1 [of offer, suggestion, interest] sérieux m, sincérité f ; [of occasion] sérieux m, importance f ◆ **this shows the ~ of their intentions** cela montre le sérieux de leurs intentions ◆ **he spoke with great** ~ il a parlé avec beaucoup de sérieux ◆ **this issue is viewed with great ~ by the government** le gouvernement prend cette question très au sérieux

◆ **in all seriousness** sérieusement, en toute sincérité

2 [of situation, illness, mistake, threat, loss, injury] gravité f ; [of damage] importance f, ampleur f

serjeant /ˈsɑːdʒənt/ N ⇒ **sergeant**

sermon /ˈsɜːmən/ N (Rel) sermon m ; (fig pej) sermon m, laïus* m ◆ **the Sermon on the Mount** le Sermon sur la Montagne ◆ **to give sb a** ~ (fig pej) faire un sermon à qn

sermonize /ˈsɜːmənaɪz/ (fig pej) VT sermonner VI prêcher, faire des sermons

sermonizing /ˈsɜːmənaɪzɪŋ/ (fig pej) N propos mpl moralisateurs

seropositive /ˌsɪərəʊˈpɒzɪtɪv/ ADJ séropositif

serotonin /ˌserəˈtəʊnɪn/ N (Bio) sérotonine f

serous /ˈsɪərəs/ ADJ séreux

serpent /ˈsɜːpənt/ N (lit, fig) serpent m ; → **sea**

serpentine /ˈsɜːpəntaɪn/ ADJ (liter) [river, road] sinueux, tortueux, qui serpente ; (= treacherous) perfide ; (= of snake) de serpent N (Miner) serpentine f, ophite m

SERPS /sɜːps/ N (Brit) (abbrev of **state earnings-related pension scheme**) assurance-vieillesse de la Sécurité sociale

serrate /seˈreɪt/ VT denteler, découper en dents de scie

serrated /seˈreɪtɪd/ ADJ [edge, blade] en dents de scie ◆ **~ knife** couteau-scie m

serration /seˈreɪʃən/ N dentelure f

serried /ˈserɪd/ ADJ serré ◆ **in ~ ranks** en rangs serrés

serum /ˈsɪərəm/ N (pl **serums** or **sera**) sérum m ◆ **tetanus** ~ sérum m antitétanique

servant /ˈsɜːvənt/ N (in household) domestique mf ; (= maid) bonne f ; (fig) serviteur m, servante f ◆ **to keep a** ~ avoir un(e) domestique ◆ **a large staff of ~s** une nombreuse domesticité ◆ **the ~s' hall** l'office m or f ◆ **I'm not your** ~ je ne suis pas votre domestique ◆ **the government is the ~ of the people** le gouvernement est le serviteur or est au service du peuple ◆ **your obedient** ~ † (in letters) ≈ veuillez agréer, Monsieur (or Madame etc), l'assurance de ma considération distinguée ; → **civil, humble, man-servant, public** COMP **servant girl** N servante f, bonne f

serve /sɜːv/ VT 1 (= work for) [+ master, employer, family] servir, être au service de ; [+ God, one's country] servir ◆ **he ~d his country well** il a bien servi son pays, il a bien mérité de la patrie (frm) ◆ **he has ~d the firm well** il a bien servi l'entreprise, il a rendu de grands services à l'entreprise ◆ **he has ~d our cause well** il a bien servi notre cause ◆ **to ~ two masters** servir deux maîtres à la fois ◆ **if my memory ~s me (right)** si j'ai bonne mémoire, si je me souviens bien ◆ **his knowledge of history ~d him well** ses connaissances en histoire lui ont bien servi

2 (Rel) **to ~ mass** servir la messe

3 (= be used as) [object etc] servir (as de) ; (= be useful to) rendre service à, être utile à ◆ **it ~s her as a table** ça lui sert de table ◆ **it will ~ my** (or **your** etc) **purpose** or **needs** cela fera l'affaire ◆ **it ~s its purpose** or **turn** cela fait l'affaire, cela suffit bien ◆ **it ~s a variety of purposes** cela sert à divers usages ◆ **it ~s no useful purpose** cela ne sert à rien (de spécial)

◆ **to serve sb right** ◆ **(it) ~s him right** c'est bien fait pour lui, il ne l'a pas volé ◆ **(it) ~s you right for being so stupid** cela t'apprendra à être si stupide ◆ **it would have ~d them right if they hadn't got any** ça aurait été bien fait pour eux s'ils n'en avaient pas reçu

4 (in shop, restaurant) servir ◆ **to ~ sb (with) sth** servir qch à qn ◆ **are you being ~d?** est-ce qu'on s'occupe de vous ? ◆ **dinner is ~d** le dîner est servi ; (as formal announcement) Madame est servie (or Monsieur est servi) ◆ **this fish should be ~d with mustard sauce** ce poisson se sert or se mange avec une sauce à la moutarde ◆ **"serves five"** (in recipe etc) "pour cinq personnes" ; see also **first, serving**

5 (with transport, church services) desservir ; (with gas, electricity) alimenter ◆ **the bus ~s six villages** le car dessert six villages ◆ **the power station ~s a large district** la centrale alimente une zone étendue

6 (= work out) **to ~ one's apprenticeship** or **time (as)** faire son apprentissage (de) ◆ **to ~ one's time** (Mil) faire son temps de service ; (Prison) faire son temps de prison ◆ **to ~ time** faire de la prison ◆ **to ~ (out) a prison sentence** purger une peine (de prison) ◆ **he has ~d over 25 years altogether** en tout il a fait plus de 25 ans de prison

7 (Jur) **to ~ legal process** signifier or notifier un acte judiciaire ◆ **to ~ notice on sb (to the effect) that ...** notifier or signifier à qn que ... ◆ **to ~ a summons on sb, to ~ sb with a summons** remettre une assignation à qn ◆ **to ~ a warrant on sb, to ~ sb with a warrant** délivrer à qn un mandat ◆ **to ~ a writ on sb, to ~ sb with a writ** assigner qn

8 (Tennis etc) servir

9 [bull, stallion etc] servir

VI 1 [servant, waiter] servir ◆ **to ~ at table** servir à table ◆ **is there anyone serving at this table?** est-ce que quelqu'un fait le service or s'occupe du service à cette table ?

2 (= work, do duty) **to ~ on a committee/jury** être membre d'un comité/d'un jury ◆ **he has ~d for two years as chairman of this society** cela fait deux ans qu'il exerce la fonction de président de cette société ; see also **serving**

3 (Mil) servir ◆ **to ~ in the army** servir dans l'armée ◆ **he ~d in Germany** il a servi en Allemagne ◆ **he ~d as a Sapper in the Engineers** il a servi comme simple soldat dans le génie ◆ **to ~ under sb** servir sous (les ordres de) qn ◆ **he ~d with my brother** mon frère et lui ont été soldats ensemble

4 (= be useful) servir (for, as de), être utile ◆ **it's not exactly what I want, but it'll** ~ ce n'est pas exactement ce que je veux, mais ça fera l'affaire ◆ **it ~s to show/explain ...** cela sert à montrer/expliquer ...

5 (Rel) servir

6 (Tennis) servir, être au service

N (Tennis etc) service m ◆ **he has a strong** ~ il a un service puissant ◆ **it's your** ~ c'est à vous de servir

► **serve out** VT SEP 1 [+ meal, soup] servir ; [+ rations, provisions] distribuer

2 [+ term of office, contract] finir ; [+ prison sentence] purger ; see also **serve vt 6**

► **serve up** VT SEP servir, mettre sur la table

server /ˈsɜːvəʳ/ N 1 (Comput) serveur m 2 (= person) (Rel) servant m ; (Tennis etc) serveur m, -euse f 3 (= tray) plateau m ; (= utensil) couvert m à servir ; → **salad**

servery /ˈsɜːvərɪ/ N (Brit) office m

service /ˈsɜːvɪs/ N 1 (NonC = act of serving person, country etc) service m ◆ **the ~ is very poor** (in shop, hotel etc) le service est très mauvais ◆ **15% ~ included** (Brit: on bill) service 15% compris ◆ **~ at sea** (Mil) service m dans la marine ◆ **to see ~ (as)** (Mil) avoir du service or servir (comme) ◆ **this coat has given good** ~ ce manteau a fait de l'usage ◆ **ten years'** ~ dix ans de service ◆ **on Her Majesty's** ~ au service de Sa Majesté ◆ **at your** ~ à votre service or disposition ; ◆ **to be in sb's** ~ être au service de qn; → **active, military**

◆ **in(to)/out of service** ◆ **to be in** ~ [domestic servant] être domestique or en service ◆ **how long has this machine been in ~?** depuis quand cette machine fonctionne-t-elle ? ◆ **to bring/come into** ~ mettre/entrer en service ◆ **this machine is out of** ~ cette machine est hors service

◆ **of service** ◆ **to be of ~ to sb** être utile à qn, rendre service à qn ◆ **can I be of ~?** est-ce que je peux vous aider ? ; (in shop) qu'y a-t-il pour votre service ? ◆ **anything to be of ~!** à votre service !

2 (= department, system) service m ◆ **medical/public/social** etc **~s** services mpl médicaux/publics/sociaux etc ◆ **customs** ~ service m des douanes ; → **civil, health, postal**

3 (= transport system) **the train ~ to London is excellent** il y a d'excellentes liaisons ferroviaires avec Londres, Londres est très bien desservi par le train ◆ **the number 4 bus** ~ la ligne (de bus numéro) 4

4 (= help given) service m ◆ **to do sb a** ~ rendre service à qn ◆ **for ~s rendered (to)** pour services rendus (à) ◆ **they dispensed with his ~s** ils se sont passés or privés de ses services ◆ **do you need the ~s of a lawyer?** avez-vous besoin (des services) d'un avocat ?

5 (Rel) (gen) service m ; (Catholic) service m, office m ; (Protestant) service m, culte m ; → **evening, funeral**

6 (= maintenance work) [of car etc] révision f ; [of household machine] service m après-vente ◆ **30,000-km** ~ (for car) révision des 30 000 km ◆ **to put one's car in for** ~ donner sa voiture à réviser ; → **after**

7 (= set of crockery) service m ◆ **coffee** ~ service m à café ; → **dinner, tea**

8 *(Tennis etc)* service *m* ◆ **whose ~ is it?** c'est à qui de servir ?

9 **~ of documents** *(Jur)* signification *f or* notification *f* d'actes ◆ **~ of process** *(Jur)* signification *f* d'un acte judiciaire *or* d'une citation

NPL **services** 1 *(on motorway)* ⇒ **service station**

2 ◆ **the (armed) ~s** les forces *fpl* armées ◆ **when I was in the ~s** quand j'étais dans l'armée *(or* la marine *or* l'aviation *etc)* ◆ **the ~s were represented** il y avait des représentants des forces armées

VT *[+ car, washing machine]* réviser ; *(Fin) [+ debt]* servir les intérêts de ; *[+ organization, group]* offrir ses services à ◆ **I took my car in to be ~d** j'ai donné ma voiture à réviser

COMP **service academy** N *(US Mil)* école *f* militaire

service agreement N *(Brit)* contrat *m* de service après-vente

service area N *[of motorway]* aire *f* de services

service break N *(Tennis)* break *m*

service bus N autobus *m* régulier

service charge N service *m*

service department N *(= office etc)* service *m* des réparations *or* d'entretien ; *(= repair shop)* atelier *m* de réparations

service dress N *(Brit Mil)* tenue *f* de gala

service elevator N *(US)* ⇒ **service lift**

service families NPL *(Mil)* familles *fpl* de militaires

service flat N *(Brit)* appartement *m* avec service *(assuré par le personnel de l'immeuble)*

service game N *(Tennis)* jeu *m* de service

service hatch N passe-plat *m*

service industries NPL services *mpl*, industries *fpl* de service

service lift N *(Brit) (for goods)* monte-charge *m inv* ; *(for personnel)* ascenseur *m* de service

service line N *(Tennis)* ligne *f* de service

service module N *(Space)* module *m* de service

service provider N prestataire *m* de services

service rifle N *(Mil)* fusil *m* de guerre

service road N *(Brit) (= access road)* voie *f or* chemin *m* d'accès ; *(for works traffic)* voie *f* de service

service sector N *(Econ)* secteur *m* tertiaire

service station N station-service *f*

service tunnel N tunnel *m* de service

serviceable /'sɜːvɪsəbl/ ADJ 1 *(= practical)* fonctionnel ◆ **the furniture was plain but ~** les meubles étaient simples mais fonctionnels 2 *(= usable, operative)* utilisable ◆ **an old but still ~ washing machine** une vieille machine à laver encore utilisable *or* qui marche encore

serviceman /'sɜːvɪsmən/ N (pl **-men**) *(Mil)* militaire *m*

servicewoman /'sɜːvɪs,wʊmən/ N (pl **-women**) *(Mil)* femme *f* soldat

servicing /'sɜːvɪsɪŋ/ N *[of car]* révision *f* ; *[of washing machine etc]* entretien *m*

serviette /,sɜːvɪ'et/ *(esp Brit)* N serviette *f* (de table) COMP **serviette ring** N rond *m* de serviette

servile /'sɜːvaɪl/ ADJ *[person, behaviour]* servile, obséquieux ; *[flattery etc]* servile

servility /sɜː'vɪlɪtɪ/ N servilité *f*

serving /'sɜːvɪŋ/ N 1 *(= action)* service *m* 2 *(= portion)* portion *f*, part *f* ADJ *(in office)* ◆ **the ~ chairman** *etc* le président *etc* en exercice

COMP **serving dish** N plat *m*

serving hatch N passe-plat *m*

serving spoon N grande cuillère *or* cuiller *f (pour servir)*

servitude /'sɜːvɪtjuːd/ N servitude *f*, asservissement *m* ; *(= slavery)* esclavage *m* ; → **penal**

servo /'sɜːvəʊ/ N (abbrev of **servo-mechanism, servo-motor**) → **servo-**

servo- /'sɜːvəʊ/ PREF servo … ◆ **~assisted** assisté ◆ **~control** servocommande *f* ◆ **~mechanism** servomécanisme *m* ◆ **~motor** servomoteur *m*

sesame /'sesəmɪ/ N sésame *m* ◆ **open Sesame!** Sésame, ouvre-toi !

COMP **sesame oil** N huile *f* de sésame

sesame seeds NPL graines *fpl* de sésame

sesh * /seʃ/ N *(= session)* séance *f*

session /'seʃən/ N 1 *(= single sitting)* séance *f* ; *(= period when sittings take place)* session *f* ; *(= lesson)* cours *m* ◆ **a yoga ~, a ~ of yoga** un cours *or* une séance de yoga ◆ **two afternoon ~s a week** deux séances *(or* cours) par semaine l'après-midi ◆ **the morning/afternoon ~** *(Brit Scol)* les cours *mpl* du matin/de l'après-midi ◆ **a photo ~** une séance de photos ◆ **I had a ~ with him yesterday** *(working)* nous avons travaillé ensemble hier ; *(in discussion)* nous avons eu une (longue) discussion hier ◆ **we're in for a long ~** nous n'aurons pas fini de sitôt ◆ **to go into secret ~** siéger en séance secrète *or* à huis clos ; → **jam², quarter, recording**

◆ **in session** *(Parl, Jur)* en session ◆ **this court is now in ~** le tribunal est en session *or* en séance, l'audience est ouverte

◆ **out of session** *(Parl)* hors session

2 *(Scol, Univ) (= year)* année *f* (universitaire *or* scolaire) ; *(US) (= term)* trimestre *m* (universitaire)

COMP **session musician** N *(Mus)* musicien(ne) *m(f)* de studio

set /set/ (vb : pret, ptp **set**) N 1 *[of objects]* jeu *m*, série *f*, assortiment *m* ; *(= kit)* trousse *f* ; *[of sails, oars, keys, golf clubs, knives, spanners]* jeu *m* ; *[of ties, pens]* jeu *m*, assortiment *m* ; *[of chairs, saucepans, weights, numbers, stamps]* série *f* ; *[of books, ornaments, toy cars]* collection *f* ; *[of bracelets, magazines]* collection *f*, série *f* ; *[of dishes, plates, mugs]* service *m* ; *[of tyres]* train *m* ; *[of jewels]* parure *f* ; *[of theories]* corps *m*, ensemble *m* ◆ **I need two more to make up the ~** il m'en manque deux pour avoir le jeu complet *or* toute la série ◆ **in ~s of three** par séries *or* jeux de trois ◆ **in ~s** en jeux complets, en séries complètes ◆ **it makes a ~ with those over there** cela forme un ensemble avec les autres là-bas ◆ **a ~ of rooms** un appartement ◆ **a ~ of kitchen utensils** une batterie de cuisine ◆ **~ of teeth** *(natural)* dentition *f*, denture *f* ; *(false)* dentier *m* ◆ **top/bottom ~** *[of false teeth]* appareil *m* pour la mâchoire supérieure/inférieure ◆ **a ~ of dining-room furniture** une salle à manger *(meubles)* ◆ **he had a whole ~ of telephones on his desk** il avait toute une collection *or* batterie *(hum)* de téléphones sur son bureau ◆ **sewing ~** trousse *f* de couture ◆ **painting ~** boîte *f* de peinture ◆ **chess/draughts ~** jeu *m* d'échecs/de dames ; → **tea**

2 *(Tennis)* set *m* ◆ **~ to Henman** set Henman

3 *(Math, Philos)* ensemble *m*

4 *(Elec)* appareil *m* ; *(Rad, TV)* poste *m* ; → **headset, transistor, wireless**

5 *(= group of people)* groupe *m*, bande *f (also pej)* ; *(larger)* monde *m*, milieu *m* ◆ **the golfing ~** le monde du golf ◆ **the literary ~** le monde des lettres, les milieux *mpl* littéraires ◆ **I'm not in their ~, we're not in the same ~** nous ne sommes pas du même monde *or* milieu ◆ **a ~ of thieves/gangsters** *etc* une bande de voleurs/gangsters *etc* ◆ **they're just a ~ of fools!** ce n'est qu'une bande d'imbéciles ! ; → **jet¹**

6 *(Brit Scol)* groupe *m* de niveau

7 *(= stage) (Cine)* plateau *m* ; *(Theat)* scène *f* ; *(= scenery)* décor *m* ◆ **on (the) ~** *(Cine)* sur le plateau ; *(Theat)* en scène

8 *(Mus = part of concert)* set *m*, partie *f*

9 *(Hairdressing)* mise *f* en plis ◆ **to have a ~** se faire faire une mise en plis ; → **shampoo**

10 *(NonC = position, posture, direction etc) [of body]* position *f*, attitude *f* ; *[of head]* port *m* ; *[of shoulders]* position *f* ; *[of tide, wind]* direction *f* ; *[of opinion, sb's mind etc]* tendance *f*

11 *(liter)* ◆ **at ~ of sun** au coucher du soleil

12 *(Hunting)* arrêt *m* ; → **dead**

13 *(= plant)* plante *f* à repiquer ◆ **onion ~s** oignons *mpl* à repiquer

ADJ 1 *(= unchanging) [rule, price, time]* fixe ; *[smile]* figé ; *[purpose, dogma]* fixe, (bien) déterminé ; *[opinion, idea]* (bien) arrêté ; *[lunch]* à prix fixe ◆ **~ in one's ways** conservateur (-trice *f*), routinier, qui tient à ses habitudes ◆ **~ in one's opinions** immuable dans ses convictions ◆ **the ~ meal, the ~ menu** *(in restaurant)* le menu ◆ **~ expression, ~ phrase** expression *f* consacrée *or* toute faite, locution *f* figée *(frm)* ; → **stone**

2 *[fruit]* ◆ **the fruit is ~** les fruits ont (bien) noué ; → **fair¹**

3 *(= prearranged) [time, date]* fixé, décidé d'avance ; *(Scol etc) [book, subject]* au programme ; *[speech, talk]* préparé d'avance ; *[prayer]* liturgique

4 *(= determined)* **to be ~ (up)on sth** vouloir qch à tout prix ◆ **since you are so ~ on it** puisque vous y tenez tant ◆ **to be ~ on doing sth** être résolu à faire qch, vouloir à tout prix faire qch ◆ **to be (dead) ~ against sth** s'opposer (absolument *or* formellement) à qch

5 *(= ready)* prêt ◆ **they're all ~!** ils sont fin prêts ! ◆ **to be all ~ to do sth** être prêt à *or* pour faire qch ◆ **on your marks, get ~, go !** *(Sport)* à vos marques, prêts, partez ! ; → **scene**

VT 1 *(= place, put) [+ object]* mettre, poser, placer ; *[+ signature]* apposer ; *[+ sentry, guard]* poster ◆ **~ it on the table/beside the window/over there** mettez-le *or* posez-le sur la table/près de la fenêtre/là-bas ◆ **the house is ~ on a hill** la maison est située sur une colline ◆ **his stories, ~ in the Paris of 1890, …** ses histoires, qui se passent *or* qui se déroulent dans le Paris de 1890, … ◆ **he ~ the scheme before the committee** il a présenté le projet au comité ◆ **I ~ him above Wordsworth** je le place *or* mets au-dessus de Wordsworth, je le considère supérieur à Wordsworth ◆ **what value do you ~ on this?** *(lit)* à quelle valeur *or* à quel prix estimez-vous cela ? ; *(fig)* quelle valeur accordez-vous à cela ? ◆ **we must ~ the advantages against the disadvantages** il faut peser le pour et le contre, il faut mettre en balance les avantages et les inconvénients ; *for other phrases see* **fire, foot, heart, store**

2 *(= arrange, adjust) [+ clock, mechanism]* régler ; *[+ alarm]* mettre ; *(on display) [+ specimen, butterfly etc]* monter ; *[+ hen]* faire couver ; *[+ plant]* repiquer ; *(Typ) [+ type, page]* composer ; *(Med) [+ arm, leg] (in plaster)* plâtrer ; *(with splint)* mettre une attelle à ; *[+ fracture]* réduire ◆ **he ~s his watch by the radio** il règle sa montre sur la radio ◆ **~ your watch to the right time/to 2pm** mettez votre montre à l'heure/à 14 heures ◆ **have you ~ the alarm clock?** est-ce que tu as mis le réveil ? ◆ **I've ~ the alarm for six** *or* **to wake me at six** j'ai mis le réveil à *or* pour six heures ◆ **he ~ the controls to automatic** il a mis les commandes sur automatique ◆ **to ~ sb's hair** faire une mise en plis à qn ◆ **to have one's hair ~** se faire faire une mise en plis ; *for other phrases see* **sail, table**

3 *(= fix, establish) [+ date, deadline, limit]* fixer ◆ **let's ~ a time for the meeting** fixons l'heure de la réunion ◆ **I've ~ myself a time limit** je me suis fixé une limite (de temps) *or* un délai ◆ **he ~ a new record for the 100 metres** il a établi un nouveau record pour le 100 mètres ◆ **they ~ the pass mark at ten** on a fixé la moyenne à dix ; *for other phrases see* **agenda, course, fashion, pace¹**

4 *(= give, assign) [+ task, subject]* donner ; *[+ exam, test]* composer *or* choisir les questions de ; *[+ texts, books]* mettre au programme ◆ **I ~ them a difficult translation** je leur ai donné

une traduction difficile (à faire) ◆ **to ~ sb a problem** poser un problème à qn ◆ **Molière is not ~ this year** Molière n'est pas au programme cette année ◆ **I ~ him the task of clearing up** je l'ai chargé de ranger *or* du rangement ; → **example**

5 *(Brit Scol)* ◆ **to ~ pupils for** *or* **in maths** répartir les élèves en groupes de niveau en maths

6 *(= cause to be, do, begin etc)* **to ~ a dog on sb** lâcher *or* lancer un chien contre qn ; see also **set upon** ◆ **they ~ the police on to him** ils l'ont signalé à la police ◆ **she ~ my brother against me** elle a monté mon frère contre moi ◆ **to ~ sth going** mettre qch en marche ◆ **the news ~ me thinking** la nouvelle m'a fait réfléchir *or* m'a donné à réfléchir ◆ **that ~ him wondering whether ...** cela l'a porté *or* poussé à se demander si ... ◆ **this ~ everyone laughing** cela a fait rire tout le monde, à cela tout le monde s'est mis à rire ◆ **to ~ sb to do sth** faire faire qch à qn, donner à qn la tâche de faire qch ◆ **I ~ him to work at once** je l'ai mis au travail aussitôt ◆ **they ~ him to work mending the fence** ils lui ont fait réparer la barrière ◆ **to ~ o.s. to do sth** entreprendre de faire qch

7 *[+ gem]* sertir *(in* dans*)*, monter *(in* sur*)* ◆ **to ~ sth with jewels** orner *or* incruster qch de pierres précieuses

8 *[+ jelly, jam]* faire prendre ; *[+ concrete]* faire prendre, faire durcir ; *[+ dye, colour]* fixer

VI 1 *[sun, moon]* se coucher ◆ **the ~ting sun** le soleil couchant

2 *[broken bone, limb]* se ressouder ; *[jelly, jam]* prendre ; *[glue]* durcir ; *[concrete]* prendre, durcir ; *[fruit]* nouer ; *[character]* se former, s'affermir ◆ **quick-~ting cement** ciment *m* prompt *or* à prise rapide ◆ **his face ~ in a hostile expression** son visage s'est figé dans une expression hostile

3 *(= begin)* se mettre, commencer *(to doing sth* à faire qch*)* ◆ **to ~ to work** se mettre au travail, s'y mettre* ◆ **to ~ to work mending** *or* **to mend the lawnmower** entreprendre de *or* se mettre à réparer la tondeuse à gazon

COMP set-aside N *(EU)* jachère *f* obligatoire

set designer N *(Theat)* décorateur *m*, -trice *f* de théâtre

set-in sleeve N manche *f* rapportée

set piece N *(= fireworks)* pièce *f* (de feu) d'artifice ; *(Art, Literat, Mus)* morceau *m* traditionnel ; *(in music competition etc)* morceau *m* de concours ; *(Sport)* combinaison *f* calculée ◆ **a ~-piece speech** un discours savamment préparé ◆ **a ~-piece debate** un débat-spectacle

set point N *(Tennis)* balle *f* de set

set square N équerre *f* (à dessin)

set theory N *(Math)* théorie *f* des ensembles

set-to* N *(= fight)* bagarre *f* ; *(= quarrel)* prise *f* de bec* ◆ **to have a ~-to with sb** se bagarrer avec qn*, avoir une prise de bec avec qn*

set-top box N *(TV)* décodeur *m*

► **set about** VT FUS 1 *(= begin) [+ task, essay]* se mettre à ◆ **to ~ about doing sth** se mettre à faire qch, entreprendre de faire qch ◆ **I don't know how to ~ about it** je ne sais pas comment m'y prendre

2 *(= attack)* attaquer ◆ **they ~ about each other** *(blows)* ils en sont venus aux coups *or* aux mains ; *(words)* ils ont commencé à s'injurier

VT SEP *[+ rumour etc]* faire courir ◆ **he ~ it about that ...** il a fait courir le bruit que ...

► **set apart** VT SEP *[+ object etc]* mettre de côté *or* à part ◆ **his eyes are ~ wide apart** il a les yeux très écartés ◆ **that ~s him apart from the others** *(fig)* cela le distingue des autres

► **set aside** VT SEP 1 *(= keep, save)* mettre de côté, garder en réserve

2 ◆ **she set her book aside when I came in** elle a posé son livre quand je suis entré

3 *(= reject, annul) [+ request, objection, proposal, petition]* rejeter ; *[+ decree, will]* annuler ; *(Jur) [+ judgement, verdict]* casser

► **set back** VT SEP 1 *(= replace)* remettre ◆ **~ it back on the shelf** remets-le sur l'étagère

2 ◆ **the house was set back from the road** la maison était (construite) en retrait de la route

3 *(= retard) [+ development, progress]* retarder ; *[+ clock]* retarder *(by* de*)* ◆ **the disaster ~ back the project by ten years** le désastre a retardé de dix ans la réalisation du projet

4 *(* = cost)* coûter ◆ **that car must have ~ him back a packet*** *or* **a good deal** cette voiture a dû lui coûter les yeux de la tête ◆ **how much did all that ~ you back?** combien tu as casqué* pour tout ça ?

► **set by** VT SEP ⇒ **set aside 1**

► **set down** VT SEP 1 *(= put down) [+ object]* poser, déposer ; *[+ passenger]* laisser, déposer

2 *[+ plane]* poser

3 *(= record)* noter, inscrire ; *[+ rules, guidelines]* établir, définir ◆ **the 1990 convention ~ down rules for the treatment of asylum seekers** la convention de 1990 a établi *or* défini des règles relatives au traitement des demandeurs d'asile ◆ **to ~ sth down in writing** *or* **on paper** coucher *or* mettre qch par écrit ◆ **~ it down on** *or* **to my account** *(Comm)* mettez-le *or* portez-le sur mon compte

4 *(= attribute)* attribuer *(sth to sth* qch à qch*)* ◆ **the accident must be ~ down to negligence** l'accident doit être imputé à la négligence ◆ **we ~ it all down to the fact that he was tired** nous avons expliqué tout cela par sa fatigue, nous avons attribué tout cela à sa fatigue

5 *(= assess, estimate)* **I had already ~ him down as a liar** je le tenais déjà pour menteur

► **set forth** VI ⇒ **set off vi**

VT SEP *[+ idea, plan, opinion]* faire connaître, exposer ; *[+ conditions, rules]* inclure

► **set in** VI *(= begin) [complications, difficulties]* survenir, surgir ; *[disease]* se déclarer ◆ **a reaction ~ in after the war** une réaction s'est amorcée après la guerre ◆ **the rain will soon ~ in** il va bientôt commencer à pleuvoir ◆ **the rain has ~ in for the night** il va pleuvoir toute la nuit ◆ **the rain has really ~ in now!** la pluie a l'air bien installée !

VT SEP *(Sewing) [+ sleeve]* rapporter

ADJ ◆ **set-in** → **set**

► **set off** VI *(= leave)* se mettre en route, partir ◆ **to ~ off on a journey/an expedition** partir en voyage/en expédition ◆ **he ~ off on a long explanation** *(fig)* il s'est lancé dans une longue explication

VT SEP 1 *[+ bomb]* faire exploser ; *[+ firework]* faire partir ; *[+ mechanism, alarm, rise in inflation]* déclencher ◆ **to ~ sb off (laughing/crying etc)** faire rire/pleurer *etc* qn ◆ **her remark ~ him off and she couldn't get a word in edgeways** après sa remarque il s'est lancé et elle n'a pas pu placer un mot

2 *(= enhance) [+ hair, eyes, picture, furnishings]* mettre en valeur, faire valoir ; *[+ complexion, colour]* rehausser, mettre en valeur

3 *(= balance etc)* ◆ **to set off profits against losses** balancer les pertes et les profits, opposer les pertes aux profits ◆ **we must ~ off the expenses against the profits** il faut déduire les dépenses des bénéfices ◆ **the profit on hats will ~ off the loss on ties** le bénéfice sur les chapeaux compensera le déficit sur les cravates

► **set on** VT FUS ⇒ **set upon**

► **set out** VI 1 *(= leave, depart)* se mettre en route *(for* pour*)*, partir *(for* pour ; *from* de ; *in search of* à la recherche de*)*

2 *(= intend, propose)* **he ~ out to explain why it had happened** il a cherché à *or* s'est proposé d'expliquer pourquoi cela s'était produit ◆ **I didn't ~ out to prove you were wrong** il n'était pas dans mon intention de prouver *or* mon but n'était pas de prouver que vous aviez tort ◆ **I ~ out to convince him he should change his mind** j'ai entrepris de le persuader de changer d'avis ◆ **the book ~s out to show that ...** ce livre a pour objet *or* but de montrer que ...

VT SEP *[+ books, goods]* exposer ; *[+ chessmen etc on board]* disposer ; *(fig) [+ reasons, ideas]* présenter, exposer ◆ **the conditions are ~ out in paragraph three** les modalités sont indiquées *or* prévues au paragraphe trois ◆ **it's very clearly ~ out here** c'est expliqué *or* exposé ici de façon très claire ◆ **the information is well ~ out on the page** l'information est bien présentée sur la page

► **set to** VI *(= start)* commencer, se mettre *(to do sth* à faire qch*)* ; *(= start work)* s'y mettre* ◆ **they ~ to with their fists** ils en sont venus aux coups (de poing)

N ◆ **set-to*** → **set**

► **set up** VI *(Comm etc)* ◆ **to ~ up in business as a grocer** s'établir épicier ◆ **he ~ up in business in London** il a monté une affaire *or* une entreprise à Londres

VT SEP 1 *(= place in position) [+ chairs, table, stall]* placer, installer ; *[+ tent]* dresser ; *[+ monument, statue]* ériger, dresser ◆ **to ~ up type** *(Typ)* assembler les caractères, composer ◆ **to ~ up camp** établir un camp

2 *(= start, establish) [+ school, institution]* fonder ; *[+ business, company, fund]* créer, lancer ; *[+ tribunal, government, committee]* constituer ; *[+ fashion]* lancer ; *[+ record]* établir ; *[+ theory]* avancer ◆ **to ~ up an inquiry** ouvrir une enquête ◆ **to ~ up house** *or* **home** s'installer ◆ **they've ~ up home in Toulon/Spain** ils se sont installés à Toulon/en Espagne ◆ **they ~ up house** *or* **home together** ils se sont mis en ménage ◆ **to ~ up shop** *(Comm)* ouvrir un commerce *or* un magasin, s'établir ; *(fig)* s'établir, s'installer ◆ **he ~ up shop as a grocer** il s'est établi épicier, il a ouvert une épicerie ◆ **he ~ up shop as a doctor** * *(fig)* il s'est installé comme médecin ◆ **to ~ sb up in business** établir *or* lancer qn dans les affaires ◆ **he's all ~ up now** il est bien établi *or* lancé maintenant ◆ **I've ~ it all up for you** je vous ai tout installé *or* préparé

3 *(= pose)* **I've never ~ myself up as a scholar** je n'ai jamais prétendu être savant

4 *(after illness)* rétablir, remettre sur pied

5 *(= equip)* munir, approvisionner *(with* de*)*

6 *(* = falsely incriminate)* monter un coup contre ◆ **I've been ~ up** je suis victime d'un coup monté

7 *(* = lure into a trap)* piéger

N ◆ **setting-up** → **setting**

► **set upon** VT FUS *(= attack) (physically)* attaquer, se jeter sur ; *(verbally)* attaquer

setback /ˈsetbæk/ N *(= hitch)* contretemps *m* ; *(more serious)* revers *m*, échec *m* ; *(in health)* rechute *f* ◆ **there has been a new ~ to the peace process** le processus de paix est à nouveau menacé ◆ **there has been another ~ to hopes of an early release of the prisoners** l'espoir d'une libération prochaine des prisonniers a de nouveau été déçu ◆ **to suffer a ~** essuyer un revers

sett /set/ N 1 *(in roadway etc)* pavé *m* 2 *[of badger]* terrier *m*

settee /seˈtiː/ N canapé *m* COMP **settee bed** N canapé-lit *m*

setter /ˈsetəʳ/ N 1 *(= dog)* setter *m*, chien *m* d'arrêt 2 *(= person) [of gems]* sertisseur *m* ; → **typesetter**

setting /ˈsetɪŋ/ N 1 *(= surroundings, background)* cadre *m* 2 *[of jewel]* monture *f* 3 *(Mus) [of poem etc]* mise *f* en musique ◆ **~ for piano** arrangement *m* pour piano 4 *(NonC) [of sun, moon]* coucher *m* ; *(= act of placing)* mise *f* ; *[of machine etc]* réglage *m* ; *(Typ)* composition *f* ; *(Med) [of fracture]* réduction *f* ; *[of limb, bone]* pose *f* d'un plâtre *or* d'une attelle *(of* à*)* 5 *(= hardening) [of jam]* épaississement *m* ; *[of cement]* solidification *f*, durcissement *m* 6 *(Brit Scol)* répartition *f* par groupes de niveaux

COMP **setting lotion** N lotion *f or* fixateur *m* pour mise en plis
setting ring N *(Phot)* bague *f* de réglage
setting-up N *[of institution, company etc]* création *f*, lancement *m* ; *(Typ)* composition *f*
setting-up exercises NPL exercices *mpl* d'assouplissement

settle[1] /'setl/ N banc *m* à haut dossier

settle[2] /'setl/ VT 1 *(= install, make comfortable) [+ child, patient]* installer ◆ **to ~ a child for the night** installer un enfant pour la nuit ◆ **she ~d her head back against the head-rest** elle a reposé sa tête sur l'appui-tête ◆ **he ~d himself in an armchair** il s'est installé (confortablement) dans un fauteuil ◆ **he ~d himself in the saddle** il s'est installé sur la selle ◆ **he is a difficult horse to ~** c'est un cheval nerveux ◆ **he ~d his gaze** *or* **his eyes on my face** son regard se posa *or* s'arrêta sur mon visage ; see also **settled**

2 *(= sort out, resolve) [+ question, matter, argument, legal dispute, case]* régler ; *[+ problem]* résoudre ; *[+ one's affairs]* régler, mettre en ordre ; *(= fix, agree on) [+ conditions, terms, details, date]* fixer ◆ **to ~ one's difficulties** résoudre ses problèmes ◆ **they have ~d their differences** ils ont réglé leurs différends ◆ **several points remain to be ~d** il reste encore plusieurs points à régler ◆ **the result was ~d in the first half** *(Ftbl etc)* la première mi-temps a décidé du résultat ◆ **that ~s it** *(= no more problem)* comme ça le problème est réglé ; *(= that's made my mind up)* ça me décide ◆ **~ it among yourselves** réglez *or* arrangez ça entre vous ◆ **that's ~d then?** alors c'est entendu ? ◆ **nothing is ~d** on n'a encore rien décidé ◆ **I'll ~ him!** * je vais lui régler son compte ! * ; see also **settled** ; → **score**

3 *(= pay) [+ debt]* rembourser, s'acquitter de ; *[+ bill, account]* régler ; see also **account**

4 *(= calm, stabilize) [+ nerves]* calmer ; *[+ doubts]* apaiser, dissiper ◆ **he sprinkled water on the floor to ~ the dust** il a aspergé le sol d'eau pour empêcher la poussière de voler ◆ **this will ~ your stomach** ceci calmera *or* soulagera tes douleurs d'estomac

5 *(Jur = bequeath)* ◆ **to ~ sth on sb** faire don de qch à qn ; *(in will)* léguer qch à qn

6 *[+ land] (= colonize)* coloniser ; *(= inhabit)* peupler ; see also **settled**

VI 1 *(= land, alight) [bird, insect]* se poser *(on* sur*)*

2 *(= sink) [sediment, coffee grounds, tea leaves]* se déposer ; *[wall]* se tasser ; *[building]* s'affaisser ◆ **contents of the packet may ~ during transit** *(Comm)* le contenu du paquet peut se tasser pendant le transport

3 *(= become permanent) [snow]* tenir ; *[dust etc]* retomber ; see also **vi 5** ◆ **to ~ on sth** *[dust, snow]* couvrir qch ◆ **the weather has ~d** le temps s'est mis au beau fixe ◆ **the cold has ~d on his chest** son rhume s'est transformé en bronchite ◆ **her eyes** *or* **gaze ~d on him** son regard s'arrêta *or* se posa sur lui ; see also **settled**

4 *(= get comfortable)* ◆ **to ~ into an armchair** s'installer (confortablement) dans un fauteuil ◆ **to ~ into one's new job** s'habituer *or* se faire à son nouvel emploi ◆ **to ~ into a routine** adopter une routine ◆ **to ~ to sth** se mettre (sérieusement) à qch, s'appliquer à qch ◆ **I can't ~ to anything** je suis incapable de me concentrer ◆ **let your meal ~ before you go swimming** attends d'avoir digéré avant de te baigner

5 *(= calm down) [emotions]* s'apaiser ; *[conditions]* redevenir normal ; *[situation]* redevenir normal, s'arranger ◆ **when the dust has ~d** *(fig)* quand les choses se seront tassées *

6 *(= go to live)* s'installer, se fixer ; *(as colonist)* s'établir ◆ **he ~d in London/in France** il s'est installé *or* fixé à Londres/en France ◆ **the Dutch ~d in South Africa** les Hollandais se sont établis en Afrique du Sud

7 *(= sort out, accept)* ◆ **to ~ with sb for the cost of the meal** régler qn pour le prix du repas, régler le prix du repas à qn ◆ **to ~ out of court** *(Jur)* arriver à un règlement à l'amiable ◆ **he ~d for $200** il s'est contenté de 200 dollars, il a accepté 200 dollars ◆ **they ~d on $200** ils se sont mis d'accord sur 200 dollars ◆ **will you ~ for a draw?** accepteriez-vous un match nul ?

8 *(= choose, decide on)* **to ~ on sth** fixer son choix sur qch, opter *or* se décider pour qch

► **settle down** VI *[person] (in armchair, sofa)* s'installer *(in* dans*)* ; *(= take up one's residence)* s'installer, se fixer ; *(= become calmer)* se calmer ; *(after wild youth)* se ranger, s'assagir ; *[excitement, emotions]* s'apaiser ; *[situation, conditions]* s'arranger ◆ **he ~d down to read the document** il s'est installé pour lire tranquillement le document ◆ **to ~ down to work** se mettre (sérieusement) au travail ◆ **he has ~d down in his new job** il s'est adapté *or* s'est fait à son nouvel emploi ◆ **to ~ down at school** s'habituer *or* s'adapter à l'école ◆ **it's time he got married and ~d down** il est temps qu'il se marie *subj* et qu'il ait une vie stable ◆ **he can't ~ down anywhere** il n'arrive à se fixer nulle part ◆ **he took some time to ~ down in Australia/to civilian life** il a mis du temps à s'habituer *or* à s'adapter à la vie en Australie/à la vie civile ◆ **when things have ~d down again** quand les choses se seront calmées *or* se seront tassées *

VT SEP installer ◆ **to ~ o.s. down in an armchair** s'installer confortablement dans un fauteuil ◆ **he ~d the child down on the sofa** il a installé l'enfant sur le canapé

► **settle in** VI *(= get things straight)* s'installer ; *(= get used to things)* s'adapter ◆ **the house is finished and they're quite ~d in** la maison est terminée et ils sont tout à fait installés ◆ **we took some time to ~ in** nous avons mis du temps à nous adapter

► **settle up** VI régler (la note) ◆ **to ~ up with sb** *(financially)* régler qn ; *(fig)* régler son compte à qn * ◆ **let's ~ up** faisons nos comptes

VT SEP *[+ bill]* régler

settled /'setld/ VB pret, ptp of **settle[2]** ADJ 1 *[weather]* stable ◆ **the weather is ~** le temps est stable 2 *[land, area] (= colonized)* colonisé ; *(= inhabited)* habité, peuplé 3 *(= unchanging) [social order, life, team]* établi ◆ **a man of ~ habits** un homme aux habitudes régulières 4 *(= at ease: in new job, home)* **I feel ~** je me sens bien ◆ **to get ~** s'installer 5 *[question, matter]* réglé

settlement /'setlmənt/ N 1 *(NonC) [of question, argument, bill, debt]* règlement *m* ; *[of conditions, terms, details, date]* décision *f* (of concernant) ; *[of problem]* solution *f* ◆ **in ~ of an account** pour *or* en règlement d'un compte 2 *(= agreement)* accord *m* ◆ **to reach a ~** arriver à *or* conclure un accord ; → **negotiate, wage** 3 *(Jur)* donation *f* *(on sb* en faveur de qn*)* ; *(= act of settling)* constitution *f* ; *(= income)* rente *f* ; *(= dowry)* dot *f* ; → **marriage** 4 *(= colonization)* colonisation *f* ; *(= colony)* colonie *f* ; *(= village)* village *m*, hameau *m* ; *(= homestead)* ferme *f or* habitation *f* (isolée) ◆ **the first ~ on the island** le premier établissement humain dans l'île ; → **penal** 5 *(for social work:* also **settlement house***)* centre *m* d'œuvres sociales 6 *(Constr: of building)* tassement *m*

settler /'setlə[r]/ N colon *m*, colonisateur *m*, -trice *f*

settlor /'setlə[r]/ N *(Fin, Jur)* constituant *m*

setup /'setʌp/ N 1 *(= way sth is organised)* **what's the ~?** comment est-ce que c'est organisé *or* que ça marche ? ◆ **it's an odd ~** c'est une drôle de situation ◆ **I don't like that ~ at all** je n'aime pas l'allure de tout ça * ◆ **when did he join the ~?** quand est-ce qu'il est entré là-dedans ? 2 * *(= trick)* coup *m* monté, machination *f* ; *(= trap)* piège *m* COMP **setup file** N *(Comput)* fichier *m* de configuration

seven /'sevn/ ADJ sept *inv* N sept *m inv* ; *for phrases see* **six** PRON sept ◆ **there are ~** il y en a sept

COMP **the seven deadly sins** NPL *(liter)* les sept péchés *mpl* capitaux
seven-league boots NPL bottes *fpl* de sept lieues
the seven seas NPL *(liter)* toutes les mers *fpl* (du globe) ◆ **to sail the ~ seas** parcourir les mers
the Seven Sisters NPL *(Astron, Myth)* les Pléiades *fpl* ; *(US Univ) groupe de sept universités pour jeunes filles dans le nord-est des États-Unis*
the seven wonders of the world NPL les sept merveilles *fpl* du monde
the seven-year itch * N *sentiment d'insatisfaction après sept ans de mariage*

sevenfold /'sevn,fəʊld/ ADJ septuple ADV au septuple

seventeen /,sevn'tiːn/ ADJ dix-sept *inv* N dix-sept *m inv* ; *for phrases see* **six** PRON dix-sept ◆ **there are ~** il y en a dix-sept

seventeenth /,sevn'tiːnθ/ ADJ dix-septième N dix-septième *mf* ; *(= fraction)* dix-septième *m* ; *for phrases see* **sixth**

seventh /'sevnθ/ ADJ septième N 1 septième *mf* ; *(= fraction)* septième *m* ; *for phrases see* **sixth** 2 *(Mus)* septième *f* COMP **Seventh Day Adventist** N adventiste *mf* du septième jour ; → **heaven**

seventieth /'sevntɪɪθ/ ADJ soixante-dixième, septantième *(Belg, Helv)* N soixante-dixième *mf* ; *(= fraction)* soixante-dixième *m* ; *for phrases see* **sixth**

seventy /'sevntɪ/ ADJ soixante-dix *inv*, septante *inv (Belg, Helv)* N soixante-dix *m inv* ◆ **he's in his seventies** il est septuagénaire, il a plus de soixante-dix ans ; *for other phrases see* **sixty** PRON soixante-dix ◆ **there are ~** il y en a soixante-dix

sever /'sevə[r]/ VT *[+ rope]* couper, trancher ; *(fig) [+ relations]* rompre, cesser ; *[+ communications]* interrompre ◆ **to ~ all connections with sb** cesser toutes relations avec qn ; *(Comm)* se dissocier de qn VI *[rope]* se rompre

severability /,sevərə'bɪlɪtɪ/ N *(Jur)* autonomie *f* des dispositions d'un contrat

several /'sevrəl/ ADJ 1 *(in number)* plusieurs ◆ **~ times** plusieurs fois ◆ **~ hundred people** plusieurs centaines de personnes 2 *(frm = separate)* ◆ **they went their ~ ways** *(lit)* ils sont partis chacun de leur côté ; *(fig)* la vie les a séparés ◆ **their ~ occupations** leur diverses *or* différentes occupations *fpl* ; → **joint** PRON plusieurs *mfpl* ◆ **~ of them** plusieurs d'entre eux (*or* elles) ◆ **~ of us saw the accident** plusieurs d'entre nous ont vu l'accident, nous sommes plusieurs à avoir vu l'accident ◆ **~ of us passed the exam** nous sommes plusieurs à avoir été reçus à l'examen

severally /'sevrəlɪ/ ADV séparément, individuellement

severance /'sevərəns/ N séparation *f* *(from* de*)* ; *[of relations]* rupture *f* ; *[of communications]* interruption *f*

COMP **severance motion** N *(US Jur)* demande *f* de procès séparés *(par des coaccusés)*
severance package, severance pay N indemnité *f* de licenciement

severe /sɪ'vɪə[r]/ ADJ 1 *(= serious, intense) [problem, consequences, damage, shortage, injury, illness, disability]* grave ; *[blow, defeat]* sévère ; *[loss]* sévère, lourd ; *[hardship, setback]* sérieux ; *[competition]* serré, acharné ; *[pain]* vif *before n* ; *[migraine, pressure]* fort ; *[storm]* violent ; *[frost]* fort ; *[climate, winter]* rigoureux ; *[cold]* intense ◆ **a ~ cold** un gros rhume 2 *(= strict) [person, expression, penalty, measure]* sévère ◆ **it was a ~ test of her patience** cela a mis sa patience à rude épreuve 3 *(= austere) [clothes]* sévère ◆ **her style of dress was somewhat ~** elle s'habillait de façon un peu austère COMP **severe acute respiratory syndrome** N syndrome *m* respiratoire aigu sévère

severely /sɪˈvɪəlɪ/ ADV 1 *[damage, disrupt, injure, affect]* gravement ; *[strain, limit, hamper]* sérieusement ◆ **~ ill/depressed/disabled** gravement malade/déprimé/handicapé ◆ **he's ~ subnormal** c'est un débile profond 2 *[punish, reprimand, criticize, look]* sévèrement 3 *[dress]* sévèrement

severity /sɪˈverɪtɪ/ N *(NonC) [of problem, crisis, recession, illness, injury]* gravité *f* ; *[of punishment, criticism, building, clothes, tone]* sévérité *f* ; *[of pain, storm]* violence *f* ; *[of winter]* rigueur *f*

Seville /səˈvɪl/ N Séville
COMP **Seville orange** N *(Brit)* orange *f* amère, bigarade *f*
Seville orange tree N *(Brit)* bigaradier *m*

sew /səʊ/ (pret **sewed**, ptp **sewn, sewed**) VT coudre ◆ **to ~ a button on sth** coudre un bouton à qch ; *(if button missing)* recoudre un bouton à qch VI coudre, faire de la couture

► **sew on** VT SEP *(gen)* coudre ; *(also* **sew back on***)* recoudre

► **sew up** VT SEP *[+ tear]* recoudre ; *[+ seam]* faire ; *[+ sack]* fermer par une couture ; *[+ wound]* (re)coudre, suturer ◆ **to ~ sth up in a sack** coudre qch dans un sac ◆ **we've got the contract all ~n up** * le contrat est dans le sac* *or* dans la poche* ◆ **the French market is pretty well ~n up** * le marché français est pratiquement verrouillé ◆ **they've got the match all ~n up** * ils ont le match dans leur poche* ◆ **it's all ~n up now** * l'affaire est dans le sac*

sewage /ˈsjuːɪdʒ/ N *(NonC)* eaux *fpl* d'égout *or* usées
COMP **sewage disposal** N évacuation *f* des eaux usées
sewage farm N champ *m* d'épandage
sewage pipe N égout *m*
sewage works N ⇒ **sewage farm**

sewer /ˈsjʊəʳ/ N égout *m* ; → **main**
COMP **sewer gas** N gaz *m* méphitique (d'égouts)
sewer rat N rat *m* d'égout

sewerage /ˈsjʊərɪdʒ/ N 1 *(= disposal)* évacuation *f* des vidanges ; *(= system)* (système *m* d')égouts *mpl* ; *(= cost of service)* frais *mpl* de vidange 2 ⇒ **sewage**

sewing /ˈsəʊɪŋ/ N *(NonC) (= activity, skill)* couture *f* ; *(= piece of work)* ouvrage *m* ◆ **I like ~** j'aime coudre *or* la couture ◆ **she put her ~ down** elle a posé son ouvrage
COMP **sewing basket** N boîte *f* à couture
sewing bee N *(US)* ◆ **they have a ~ bee on Thursdays** elles se réunissent pour coudre le jeudi
sewing cotton N fil *m* de coton, fil *m* à coudre
sewing machine N machine *f* à coudre
sewing silk N fil *m* de soie

sewn /səʊn/ VB ptp of **sew**

sex /seks/ N 1 sexe *m* ◆ **the gentle** *or* **weaker ~** *(† or hum)* le sexe faible
2 *(NonC = sexual act)* rapports *mpl* sexuels, relations *fpl* sexuelles ◆ **to have ~ (with sb)** faire l'amour (avec qn), avoir des rapports (sexuels) avec qn ◆ **all he ever thinks about is ~** * ◆ **he's got ~ on the brain** * il ne pense qu'au sexe *or* qu'à ça* ◆ **~ outside marriage** relations *fpl* (sexuelles) hors mariage
VT *[+ chick etc]* déterminer le sexe de
COMP *[education, instinct]* sexuel(le)
sex act N acte *m* sexuel
sex aid N gadget *m* érotique
sex-and-shopping ADJ *(Brit)* ◆ **~-and-shopping novel** *roman de gare, érotique et superficiel*
sex appeal N sex-appeal *m*
sex change (operation) N (opération *f* de) changement *m* de sexe ◆ **to have** *or* **undergo a ~ change (operation)** se faire opérer pour changer de sexe
sex clinic N clinique *f* de sexologie
sex-crazy * ADJ ◆ **he is ~-crazy** c'est un obsédé (sexuel)
sex discrimination N discrimination *f* sexuelle
sex drive N pulsion *f* sexuelle
sex fiend N satyre* *m*
sex goddess N bombe *f* sexuelle
sex hormone N hormone *f* sexuelle
sex hygiene N *(US)* hygiène *f* sexuelle
the sex industry N l'industrie *f* du sexe
sex kitten * N minette *f* très sexy
sex life N vie *f* sexuelle
sex-linked ADJ *(Bio)* lié au sexe
sex-mad * ADJ ⇒ **sex-crazy**
sex maniac N obsédé(e) sexuel(le) *m(f)*
sex manual N ouvrage *m* sur le sexe
sex object N objet *m* sexuel
sex offender N délinquant(e) sexuel(le) *m(f)*
sex organ N organe *m* sexuel
sex partner N partenaire *mf* sexuel(le)
sex pot * N fille *f or* femme *f* très sexy*
sex scene N *(Cine, Theat)* scène *f* érotique
sex selection N *[of baby]* choix *m* du sexe
sex shop N sex-shop *m*, boutique *f* porno *inv*
sex show N spectacle *m* érotique
sex-starved * ADJ (sexuellement) frustré*
sex symbol N sex-symbol *m*
sex therapist N sexologue *mf*
sex therapy N sexologie *f*
sex tourism N tourisme *m* sexuel
sex toy N gadget *m*
sex urge N ⇒ **sex drive**
sex worker N travailleur (-euse) *m(f)* sexuel(le)

► **sex up** * VT SEP donner du piquant à

sexagenarian /ˌseksədʒɪˈneərɪən/ ADJ, N sexagénaire *mf*

Sexagesima /ˌseksəˈdʒesɪmə/ N Sexagésime *f*

sexed /sekst/ ADJ 1 *[organism]* sexué 2 ◆ **to be highly ~** avoir une forte libido

sexiness /ˈseksɪnɪs/ N *(NonC) [of person, voice, eyes]* sex-appeal *m* ; *(* fig) [of subject, issue]* côté *m* excitant

sexism /ˈseksɪzəm/ N sexisme *m*

sexist /ˈseksɪst/ ADJ sexiste

sexless /ˈsekslɪs/ ADJ *[person] (also Bio)* asexué ◆ **a ~ marriage** une vie conjugale sans rapports sexuels

sexologist /sekˈsɒlədʒɪst/ N sexologue *mf*

sexology /sekˈsɒlədʒɪ/ N sexologie *f*

sexploitation * /ˌseksplɔɪˈteɪʃən/ N *utilisation de l'image de la femme-objet dans la publicité etc*

sextant /ˈsekstənt/ N sextant *m*

sextet /seksˈtet/ N *(= players, composition)* sextuor *m*

sexton /ˈsekstən/ N sacristain *m*, bedeau *m*

sextuplet /seksˈtjuːplɪt/ N sextuplé(e) *m(f)*

sexual /ˈseksjʊəl/ ADJ sexuel
COMP **sexual abuse** N sévices *mpl* sexuels, abus *m* sexuel
sexual equality N égalité *f* des sexes
sexual harassment N harcèlement *m* sexuel
sexual health N précautions *fpl* en matière sexuelle
sexual intercourse N rapports *mpl* sexuels
sexual orientation N orientation *f* sexuelle
sexual politics N *conventions définissant la place des individus dans la société en fonction de leur sexe ou de leurs préférences sexuelles*
sexual preference N ⇒ **sexual orientation**
sexual services NPL commerce *m* sexuel tarifé
sexual stereotyping N catégorisation *f* en stéréotypes sexuels

sexuality /ˌseksjʊˈælɪtɪ/ N sexualité *f*

sexualize /ˈseksjʊəlaɪz/ VT sexualiser

sexually /ˈseksjʊəlɪ/ ADV 1 *[attractive, exciting, explicit, available, inadequate]* sexuellement ; *[threatening]* du point de vue sexuel ◆ **to be ~ abused** subir des sévices sexuels ◆ **to be ~ active** avoir une activité sexuelle ◆ **~ aroused** excité sexuellement ◆ **to be ~ attracted to sb** avoir une attirance sexuelle pour qn ◆ **~ harassed** soumis à un harcèlement sexuel 2 *(= by sex) [segregated]* par le sexe
COMP **sexually transmitted disease** N maladie *f* sexuellement transmissible
sexually transmitted infection N infection *f* sexuellement transmissible

sexy /ˈseksɪ/ ADJ 1 *(= sexually exciting) [person, clothes]* sexy* *inv* ; *[voice]* séduisant ; *[image]* de séducteur (-trice *f*) ◆ **to look ~** avoir l'air sexy* *or* séduisant 2 *(= interested in sex)* ◆ **to be** *or* **feel ~** avoir des envies ◆ **to make sb feel ~** donner des envies à qn, exciter qn 3 *(* = exciting) [subject, issue]* excitant

Seychelles /seɪˈʃel(z)/ NPL ◆ **the ~** les Seychelles *fpl*

Seychellois /ˌseɪʃelˈwɑː/ ADJ seychellois N Seychellois(e) *m(f)*

sez* /sez/ ⇒ **says ;** → **say ~ you!** *(iro)* que tu dis !* ◆ **~ who?*** ah oui ? *(iro)*

SF /esˈef/ N (abbrev of **science fiction**) SF *f*

SFA /ˌesefˈeɪ/ (abbrev of **Scottish Football Association**) fédération *f* écossaise de football

SFO /ˌesefˈəʊ/ N *(Brit)* (abbrev of **Serious Fraud Office**) → **serious**

sfx /ˌesefˈeks/ NPL *(Cine)* (abbrev of **special effects**) → **special**

sgd (abbrev of **signed**) → **sign vt 1**

SGML /ˌesdʒiːemˈel/ N *(Comput)* (abbrev of **Standard Generalized Mark-up Language**) SGML *m*

Sgt N (abbrev of **Sergeant**) ~ **J. Smith** *(on envelopes)* le Sergent J. Smith

shabbily /ˈʃæbɪlɪ/ ADV 1 *(= tattily) [dressed]* pauvrement 2 *(= unfairly) [behave]* mesquinement ; *[treat]* avec mesquinerie

shabbiness /ˈʃæbɪnɪs/ N *[of dress]* aspect *m* élimé *or* râpé ; *[of person]* mise *f* pauvre ; *[of behaviour, treatment]* mesquinerie *f*, petitesse *f*

shabby /ˈʃæbɪ/ ADJ 1 *(= tatty) [person, clothes, district, house, furnishings]* miteux 2 *(= unfair) [treatment, behaviour, compromise]* mesquin ◆ **a ~ trick** un vilain tour, une mesquinerie
COMP **shabby-genteel** ADJ pauvre mais digne
shabby-looking ADJ de pauvre apparence

shack /ʃæk/ N cabane *f*, hutte *f*

► **shack up*** VI *(= live)* se mettre en ménage *(with sb* avec qn*)* ◆ **to ~ up together** vivre ensemble

shackle /ˈʃækl/ NPL **shackles** chaînes *fpl*, fers *mpl* ; *(fig)* chaînes *fpl*, entraves *fpl* VT mettre aux fers, enchaîner ; *(fig)* entraver

shad /ʃæd/ N (pl **shad** *or* **shads**) alose *f*

shade /ʃeɪd/ N 1 *(NonC)* ombre *f* ◆ **in the ~ of a tree** à l'ombre *or* sous l'ombrage d'un arbre ◆ **40° in the ~** 40° à l'ombre ◆ **to put sb/sth in the ~** *(fig)* éclipser qn/qch
2 *[of colour]* nuance *f*, ton *m* ; *[of opinion]* nuance *f* ◆ **several ~s darker than that** plus sombre de plusieurs tons (que cela) ◆ **several ~s of red** plusieurs nuances *or* tons de rouge ◆ **a new ~ of lipstick** un nouveau ton *or* une nouvelle couleur de rouge à lèvres ◆ **a ~ of meaning** une nuance
3 *(= hint, small amount)* **a ~ of vulgarity** un soupçon de vulgarité ◆ **there's not a ~ of difference between them** il n'y a pas la moin-

dre différence entre eux ◆ **a ~ bigger** un tout petit peu *or* légèrement plus grand ◆ **~s of Sartre!** voilà qui fait penser à Sartre !, ça rappelle Sartre !

4 *(= lampshade)* abat-jour *m inv* ; *(= eyeshade)* visière *f* ; *(= blind)* store *m*

5 *(liter = ghost)* ombre *f*, fantôme *m*

NPL **shades** * *(= sunglasses)* lunettes *fpl* de soleil

VT 1 *[trees, parasol]* donner de l'ombre à ; *[person] [+ one's work etc]* abriter du soleil *or* de la lumière ◆ **~d place** endroit *m* ombragé *or* à l'ombre ◆ **he ~d his eyes with his hands** il s'abrita les yeux de la main ◆ **to ~ a light** voiler une lampe

2 (also **shade in**) *[+ painting etc]* ombrer, nuancer ; *(by hatching) [+ outline, drawing etc]* hachurer ; *(= colour in)* colorer *(in en)*

3 *[+ price]* baisser *or* diminuer progressivement ◆ **prices ~d for quantities** tarif *m* dégressif pour commandes en gros ◆ **~d charges tariff** tarif *m* dégressif

4 *(= narrowly win)* gagner de justesse

VI (also **shade off**) 1 se dégrader *(into* jusqu'à), se fondre *(into* en) ◆ **the red ~s (off) into pink** le rouge se fond en rose

2 *[prices]* baisser

► **shade off** VI ⇒ **shade vi**

VT SEP *[+ colours etc]* estomper

shadiness /ˈʃeɪdɪnɪs/ N (NonC) 1 *(= shade)* ombre *f* 2 *(fig)* caractère *m* suspect *or* louche

shading /ˈʃeɪdɪŋ/ N 1 *(NonC, in painting etc)* ombres *fpl*, noirs *mpl* ; *(= hatching)* hachure(s) *f(pl)* ; *(fig)* nuance *f* 2 *(for plants)* ◆ **to provide ~** faire de l'ombre

shadow /ˈʃædəʊ/ N 1 *(= shade)* ombre *f* ◆ **in the ~ of the tree** à l'ombre de l'arbre ◆ **in the ~ of the porch** dans l'ombre du porche ◆ **he was standing in (the) ~** il se tenait dans l'ombre ◆ **I could see his ~ on the wall** je voyais son ombre (projetée) sur le mur ◆ **he's afraid** *or* **frightened** *or* **scared of his own ~** il a peur de son ombre ◆ **to live in sb's ~** vivre dans l'ombre de qn ◆ **he's only a ~ of his former self** il n'est plus que l'ombre de lui-même ◆ **to have (dark) ~s under one's eyes** avoir les yeux cernés, avoir des cernes *mpl* sous les yeux ; → **cast**

2 *(= darkness)* ◆ **the ~s** l'obscurité *f*, les ténèbres *fpl*

3 *(= hint)* ◆ **without a ~ of doubt** sans l'ombre d'un doute ◆ **not a ~ of truth** pas le moindre atome de vérité

4 *(= detective etc)* personne *f* (*or* détective *m etc*) qui file quelqu'un ◆ **to put a ~ on sb** faire filer qn, faire prendre qn en filature

5 *(= inseparable companion)* ombre *f*

VT *(= follow)* filer, prendre en filature

COMP **shadow-box** VI boxer dans le vide
shadow-boxing N *(Sport)* boxe *f* dans le vide ; *(fig)* attaque *f* de pure forme, attaque *f* purement rituelle
shadow cabinet N *(Brit Parl)* cabinet *m* fantôme
shadow Foreign Secretary N *(Brit Parl)* ◆ **he is (the) ~ Foreign Secretary** il est le porte-parole de l'opposition pour les Affaires étrangères
shadow minister N *(Brit Pol)* ministre *m* fantôme
shadow play N spectacle *m* d'ombres chinoises

Shadow Cabinet

Dans le système parlementaire britannique, le « cabinet fantôme » (**Shadow Cabinet**) se compose des députés du principal parti d'opposition qui deviendraient ministres si leur parti était élu. Chaque ministre en fonction a donc un homologue dans l'opposition : au ministre de l'Intérieur (Home Secretary) ou des Finances (Chancellor) correspond donc un « **Shadow** Home Secretary » et un « **Shadow** Chancellor ». Leur rôle est d'interroger le gouvernement sur sa politique dans leurs domaines de spécialité et d'être les porte-parole des opinions de leur parti.

shadowy /ˈʃædəʊɪ/ ADJ 1 *(= shady) [place]* ombragé ; *[woods]* sombre, ombreux 2 *(= indistinct) [figure, shape, outline, form]* confus, vague, indistinct ; *[idea, plan]* vague, indistinct 3 *(= mysterious) [figure, group]* indéfini ◆ **the ~ world of espionage** le monde mystérieux de l'espionnage

shady /ˈʃeɪdɪ/ ADJ 1 *(= shadowy) [place]* ombragé ◆ **under a ~ tree** à l'ombre d'un arbre 2 *(= dishonest) [person, behaviour]* louche ; *[lawyer, deal]* véreux ◆ **to have a ~ past** avoir un passé louche

shaft /ʃɑːft/ N 1 *(= stem, handle) [of arrow, spear]* hampe *f* ; *[of tool, golf club]* manche *m* ; *[of feather]* tuyau *m* ; *[of column]* fût *m* ; *[of bone]* diaphyse *f* ; *(on cart, carriage, plough etc)* brancard *m* ; *[of vehicle, machine]* arbre *m* ; → **camshaft** 2 *(liter = arrow)* flèche *f* ◆ **Cupid's ~s** les flèches *fpl* de Cupidon ◆ **~ of light** rayon *m or* trait *m* de lumière 3 *[of mine]* puits *m* ; *[of lift, elevator]* cage *f* ; *(for ventilation)* puits *m*, cheminée *f* VT (**** = have sex with) baiser** ◆ **we'll be ~ed if that happens** *(fig = defeat, ruin)* si ça arrive, on sera baisés‡ *or* niqués**

shag¹ /ʃæg/ N *(= tobacco)* tabac *m* très fort

shag² /ʃæg/ N *(= bird)* cormoran *m* huppé

shag³ /ʃæg/ N *(Brit)* ◆ **to have a ~**** baiser** VT *(Brit ** = have sex with)* baiser** VI 1 *(Brit ** = have sex)* baiser** 2 *(US)* **to ~ off‡** se tirer‡, foutre le camp‡

shag⁴ * /ʃæg/ VT *(US = retrieve) [+ ball]* récupérer

shag⁵ /ʃæg/ N *(= napped fabric)* laine *f* à longues mèches

COMP **shag (pile) carpet** N moquette *f* à longues mèches
shag (pile) rug N tapis *m* à longues mèches

shagged ** /ʃægd/ ADJ ◆ **to be ~ (out)** être claqué* *or* crevé‡

shaggy /ˈʃægɪ/ ADJ *[hair, beard]* hirsute ; *[eyebrows, mane]* broussailleux ; *[animal, fur]* à longs poils hirsutes ; *[carpet, rug]* à longs poils COMP **shaggy dog story** N histoire *f* sans queue ni tête

shagreen /ʃæˈgriːn/ N chagrin *m (cuir)*

Shah /ʃɑː/ N schah *or* chah *m*

shake /ʃeɪk/ (vb : pret **shook**, ptp **shaken**) N 1 *(= movement)* **to give sth a ~** secouer qch ◆ **with a ~ of his head** en refusant d'un hochement de tête, en hochant la tête en signe de refus ◆ **with a ~ in his voice** la voix tremblante, d'une voix tremblante ◆ **to be all of a ~*** être tout tremblant ◆ **to have the ~s*** *(from nerves)* avoir la tremblote* ; *(from drink)* trembler, être agité de tremblements ◆ **in a brace** *or* **couple of ~s***, **in two ~s (of a lamb's tail)*** en un clin d'œil, en moins de deux* ◆ **he/it is no great ~s*** il/cela ne casse rien* ◆ **he's no great ~s*** **at swimming** *or* **as a swimmer** il n'est pas fameux *or* il ne casse rien* comme nageur

2 *(= drink)* milk-shake *m* ; → **handshake, milk**

VT 1 *[+ duster, rug, person]* secouer ; *[+ dice, bottle, medicine, cocktail]* agiter ; *[+ house, windows etc]* faire trembler ; *(= brandish) [+ stick etc]* brandir ◆ **"shake the bottle"** "agiter avant emploi" ◆ **to ~ one's head** *(in refusal)* dire *or* faire non de la tête, hocher la tête en signe de refus ; *(at bad news)* secouer la tête ◆ **he shook his finger at me** *(playfully, warningly)* il m'a fait signe du doigt ; *(threateningly)* il m'a menacé du doigt ◆ **to ~ one's fist/stick at sb** menacer qn du poing/de sa canne ◆ **to ~ hands with sb, to ~ sb's hand** serrer la main à qn ◆ **they shook hands** ils se sont serré la main ◆ **they shook hands on it** ils se sont serré la main en signe d'accord ◆ **~ a leg!** * *(fig)* remue-toi !, bouge-toi !* ◆ **to ~ o.s. (or itself)** *[person, animal]* se secouer ; *(to remove sand, water etc)* s'ébrouer ◆ **a man with more medals than you can ~ a stick at*** un homme qui avait des tonnes* de médailles

2 ◆ **to ~ apples from a tree** secouer un arbre pour en faire tomber les pommes ◆ **he shook the sand out of his shoes** il a secoué ses chaussures pour en vider le sable ◆ **he shook two aspirins into his hand** il a fait tomber deux comprimés d'aspirine dans sa main ◆ **he shook pepper on to his steak** il a saupoudré son bifteck de poivre ◆ **he shook himself free** il s'est libéré d'une secousse ◆ **he shook (off) the dust of that country from his feet** *(liter)* il a décidé de ne plus remettre les pieds dans le pays

3 *[+ confidence, belief, resolve]* ébranler ; *[+ opinion]* affecter ◆ **even torture could not ~ him** même la torture ne l'a pas fait céder

4 *(fig) (= amaze)* stupéfier ; *(= disturb)* secouer, bouleverser ◆ **this will ~ you!** tu vas en être soufflé !*, ça va t'en boucher un coin !‡ ◆ **four days which shook the world** quatre jours qui ébranlèrent le monde ◆ **he needs to be ~n out of his smugness** il faudrait qu'il lui arrive *subj* quelque chose qui lui fasse perdre de sa suffisance ; see also **shaken**

5 *(US *)* ⇒ **shake off 2**

VI 1 *[person, hand, table]* trembler ; *[building, windows, walls]* trembler, être ébranlé ; *[leaves, grasses]* trembler, être agité ; *[voice]* trembler, trembloter ◆ **he was shaking with laughter, his sides were shaking** il se tordait (de rire) ◆ **to ~ with cold** trembler de froid, grelotter ◆ **to ~ with fear** trembler de peur ◆ **the walls shook at the sound** le bruit a fait trembler les murs ; → **boot¹, shoe**

2 *(= shake hands)* **they shook on the deal** ils ont scellé leur accord d'une poignée de main ◆ **(let's) ~ on it!** tope là !, topez là !

COMP **shake-out** N *(US Econ)* tassement *m*
shake-up N grande réorganisation *f*, grand remaniement *m*

► **shake down** VI 1 (* = *settle for sleep)* se coucher, se pieuter‡ ◆ **I can ~ down anywhere** je peux pioncer‡ *or* me pieuter‡ n'importe où

2 *(= learn to work etc together)* **they'll be a good team once they've ~n down** ils formeront une bonne équipe quand ils se seront habitués *or* faits les uns aux autres

3 *(= settle) [contents of packet etc]* se tasser

4 (* = *develop)* évoluer

5 *(= succeed)* réussir

VT SEP 1 ◆ **to shake down apples from a tree** faire tomber des pommes en secouant l'arbre, secouer l'arbre pour en faire tomber les pommes ◆ **to ~ down the contents of a packet** secouer un paquet pour en tasser le contenu

2 *(US)* **to ~ sb down for $50** ‡ soutirer *or* faire cracher‡ 50 dollars à qn

3 *(US* ‡ *= frisk, search) [+ person]* fouiller

► **shake off** VT SEP 1 ◆ **to shake off dust/sand/water from sth** secouer la poussière/le sable/l'eau de qch

2 *(fig = get rid of) [+ cold, cough]* se débarrasser de ; *[+ yoke etc]* se libérer de, s'affranchir de ; *[+ habit]* se défaire de, perdre ; *[+ pursuer]* se débarrasser de, semer*

► **shake out** VT SEP 1 *[+ flag, sail]* déployer ; *[+ blanket]* bien secouer ; *[+ bag]* vider en secouant ◆ **she picked up the bag and shook out its contents** elle a pris le sac et l'a vidé en le secouant ◆ **she shook 50p out of her bag** elle a secoué son sac et en a fait tomber 50 pence

2 *[+ workforce]* dégraisser

VI (* = *turn out*) évoluer

N ◆ **shake-out** → **shake**

► **shake up** VT SEP 1 *[+ pillow, cushion]* secouer, taper ; *[+ bottle, medicine]* agiter

2 *(fig = disturb)* bouleverser, secouer ◆ **he was considerably ~n up by the news** il a été très secoué *or* il a été bouleversé par la nouvelle, la nouvelle lui a fait un coup* ; see also **shook**

3 *(fig = rouse, stir) [+ person]* secouer, secouer les puces à* ; *[+ firm, organization]* réorganiser de fond en comble

N ◆ **shake-up** → **shake**

shakedown /ˈʃeɪkdaʊn/ N (= *bed*) lit *m* de fortune ; *(US ‡)* (= *search*) fouille *f* ; (= *extortion*) extorsion *f*, chantage *m*

shaken /ˈʃeɪkn/ ADJ *(by being in accident)* secoué ; *(by seeing accident)* bouleversé ; *(by news)* ébranlé ◆ **~ but not stirred** *[martini] préparé en secouant plutôt qu'en mélangeant* ; *(hum) [person]* secoué mais pas franchement ému

Shaker /ˈʃeɪkəʳ/ N, ADJ *(Rel)* Shaker *mf*

shaker /ˈʃeɪkəʳ/ N *(for cocktails)* shaker *m* ; *(for dice)* cornet *m* ; *(for salad)* panier *m* à salade ; → **flour**

Shakespearean, Shakespearian /ʃeɪksˈpɪərɪən/ ADJ shakespearien

shakily /ˈʃeɪkɪlɪ/ ADV *[stand up]* en chancelant ; *[walk]* d'un pas mal assuré ; *[speak]* d'une voix mal assurée ; *[write]* d'une main tremblante

shakiness /ˈʃeɪkɪnɪs/ N *(NonC) [of hand]* tremblement *m* ; *[of table, chair etc]* manque *m* de stabilité *or* solidité ; *[of building]* manque *m* de solidité ; *[of voice]* chevrotement *m* ; *(fig) [of position]* instabilité *f* ; *[of health]* faiblesse *f* ; *[of knowledge]* insuffisance *f*, faiblesse *f*

shako /ˈʃækəʊ/ N (pl **shakos** *or* **shakoes**) s(c)hako *m*

shaky /ˈʃeɪkɪ/ ADJ 1 (= *weak*) *[person] (from illness)* chancelant ; *(from nerves)* mal à l'aise 2 (= *trembling*) *[person, legs] (from fear, illness)* flageolant, tremblant ; *(from age)* tremblant ; *[voice] (from fear, illness)* tremblant ; *(from age)* chevrotant ; *(from nerves)* mal assuré ; *[hand]* tremblant ; *[handwriting]* tremblé ◆ **her legs were** ~ elle flageolait sur ses jambes 3 (= *wobbly*) *[table, building]* branlant, peu solide 4 (= *uncertain*) *[start]* incertain ; *[business, firm, deal]* à l'avenir incertain ; *[argument]* boiteux ; *[knowledge]* hésitant ; *[health]* chancelant ; *[prospects]* précaire ◆ **~ finances** une situation financière incertaine ◆ **my Spanish is very** ~ mon espagnol est très hésitant ◆ **to get off to a ~ start** partir sur un mauvais pied

shale /ʃeɪl/ N argile *f* schisteuse, schiste *m* argileux COMP **shale oil** N huile *f* de schiste

shall /ʃæl/ MODAL AUX VB (neg **shall not** *often abbr to* **shan't**) see also **should** 1 *(in 1st person future tense)* **I ~** *or* **I'll arrive on Monday** j'arriverai lundi ◆ **we ~ not** *or* **we shan't be there before 6 o'clock** nous n'y serons pas avant 6 heures ◆ **I'll come in a minute** je vais venir *or* je viens dans un instant

2 *(in 1st person questions)* **~ I open the door?** dois-je ouvrir la porte ?, voulez-vous que j'ouvre *subj* la porte ?, j'ouvre la porte ?* ◆ **I'll buy three, ~ I?** je vais en acheter trois, n'est-ce pas *or* d'accord* ? ◆ **let's go in, ~ we?** entrons, voulez-vous ? ◆ **~ we ask him to come with us?** si on lui demandait de venir avec nous ?

3 *(indicating command, guarantee etc)* **it ~ be done this way and no other** cela sera fait *or* doit être fait de cette façon et d'aucune autre ◆ **thou shalt not kill** *(Bible)* tu ne tueras point ◆ **you ~ obey me** vous m'obéirez, vous devez m'obéir ◆ **you shan't have that job!** tu n'auras pas ce poste !

shallot /ʃəˈlɒt/ N échalote *f*

shallow /ˈʃæləʊ/ ADJ 1 (= *not deep*) *[water, lake, grave, depression, container]* peu profond ; *[soil]* mince ; *[breathing]* superficiel ◆ **the ~ end of the pool** le petit bain *or* bassin de la piscine 2 *(pej = superficial) [person, mind, character, argument, novel, film]* superficiel ; *[conversation]* futile NPL **shallows** bas-fond *m*, haut-fond *m*

shallowly /ˈʃæləʊlɪ/ ADV *[breathe]* superficiellement

shallowness /ˈʃæləʊnɪs/ N 1 *(lit)* manque *m* de profondeur 2 *(pej) [of person]* esprit *m* superficiel ; *[of character]* manque *m* de profondeur ; *[of conversation]* futilité *f* ; *[of knowledge]* caractère *m* superficiel

shalt †† /ʃælt/ VB 2nd person sg of **shall**

sham /ʃæm/ N (= *pretence*) comédie *f*, imposture *f* ; (= *person*) imposteur *m* ; (= *jewellery, furniture*) imitation *f* ◆ **this diamond is a ~** ce diamant est faux *or* du toc* ◆ **the election was a ~** l'élection n'était qu'une comédie ◆ **his promises were a ~** ses promesses n'étaient que du vent ◆ **the whole organization was a ~** l'organisation tout entière n'était qu'une imposture

ADJ *[jewellery, doctor, priest, title]* faux (fausse *f*) ; *[deal]* fictif ; *[piety]* feint ; *[illness]* feint, simulé ; *[fight]* simulé ◆ **a ~ marriage** une simulacre de mariage ◆ **a ~-Tudor house** une maison pseudo-Tudor ◆ **~ olde-worlde decor** décor *m* en faux ancien ◆ **~ Louis XVI** de l'imitation *or* du faux Louis XVI

VT feindre, simuler ◆ **to ~ ill** *or* **illness** feindre *or* simuler une maladie, faire semblant d'être malade ◆ **she ~med dead** elle a fait la morte, elle a fait semblant d'être morte

VI faire semblant, jouer la comédie ◆ **he's only ~ming** il fait seulement semblant

shaman /ˈʃæmən/ N chaman *m*

shamanism /ˈʃæməˌnɪzəm/ N chamanisme *m*

shamateur* /ˈʃæmətəʳ/ N *(Sport)* sportif *m*, -ive *f* prétendu(e) amateur *(qui se fait rémunérer)*

shamble /ˈʃæmbl/ VI marcher en traînant les pieds ◆ **to ~ in/out/away** *etc* entrer/sortir/s'éloigner *etc* en traînant les pieds

shambles /ˈʃæmblz/ N *(NonC, gen = muddle)* confusion *f*, désordre *m* ; *(stronger: after battle, disaster)* scène *f* or spectacle *m* de dévastation ◆ **what a ~!** quelle (belle) pagaille !* ◆ **his room was (in) a ~** sa chambre était sens dessus dessous *or* tout en l'air ◆ **the match degenerated into a ~** le match s'est terminé dans la pagaille* ◆ **your essay is a ~*** votre dissertation est un fouillis sans nom* ◆ **it's a bloody ~‡** c'est complètement bordélique‡

shambolic* /ʃæmˈbɒlɪk/ ADJ *(Brit)* bordélique‡

shame /ʃeɪm/ N 1 *(NonC)* (= *feeling*) honte *f*, confusion *f* ; (= *humiliation*) honte *f* ◆ **to my eternal** *or* **lasting ~** à ma très grande honte ◆ **he hung his head in ~** il a baissé la tête de honte *or* de confusion ◆ **to bring ~ (up)on sb** être *or* faire la honte de qn, déshonorer qn ◆ **to put sb/sth to ~** faire honte à qn/qch ◆ **~ on you!** quelle honte !, c'est honteux de votre part ! ◆ **the ~ of it!** quelle honte !, c'est honteux ! ◆ **the ~ of that defeat** la honte de cette défaite, cette défaite déshonorante ◆ **she has no sense of ~** elle ne sait pas ce que c'est que la honte, elle n'a aucune pudeur ◆ **he has lost all sense of ~** il a perdu toute honte, il a toute honte bue *(liter)* ; → **cry, crying**

2 *(NonC = pity)* dommage *m* ◆ **it's a ~** c'est dommage *(that que + subj ; to do sth de faire qch)* ◆ **it's a dreadful ~!** c'est tellement dommage ! ◆ **it would be a ~ if he were to refuse** *or* **if he refused** il serait dommage qu'il refuse *subj* ◆ **(what a) ~!** (quel) dommage ! ◆ **(what a) ~ he isn't here!** (quel) dommage qu'il ne soit pas ici ! ◆ **nice legs, ~ about the face!** jolies jambes, on ne peut pas en dire autant de son visage !

VT (= *bring disgrace on*) couvrir de honte, faire la honte de ; (= *make ashamed*) faire honte à ◆ **to ~ sb into doing sth** obliger qn à faire qch en lui faisant honte, piquer l'amour-propre de qn pour qu'il fasse qch ◆ **to be ~d into doing sth** faire qch par amour-propre *or* pour conserver son amour-propre

shamefaced /ˈʃeɪmfeɪst/ ADJ (= *ashamed*) honteux, penaud ; (= *confused*) confus, timide ◆ **he was rather ~ about it** il en était tout honteux *or* penaud

shamefacedly /ˈʃeɪmfeɪsɪdlɪ/ ADV d'un air penaud *or* honteux

shamefacedness /ˈʃeɪmfeɪstnɪs/ N *(NonC)* air *m* penaud *or* honteux

shameful /ˈʃeɪmfʊl/ ADJ *[behaviour, attitude, event, experience, secret]* honteux ; *[record]* déplorable ◆ **there is nothing ~ about it** il n'y a pas de honte à cela ◆ **it is ~ that ...** c'est une honte que ... + *subj* ◆ **it's ~ to do that** c'est une honte de faire cela

shamefully /ˈʃeɪmfəlɪ/ ADV *[act, behave, treat]* de façon honteuse ; *[bad, late]* scandaleusement ◆ **~ lazy/ignorant** si paresseux/ignorant que c'en est une honte ◆ **the government have ~ neglected this sector** le gouvernement a négligé ce secteur d'une façon scandaleuse

shameless /ˈʃeɪmlɪs/ ADJ 1 (= *brazen*) *[person, liar, behaviour, attempt]* éhonté ; *[lie]* éhonté, sans vergogne ◆ **~ hussy** († *or hum*) petite effrontée *f* ◆ **to be quite ~ about (doing) sth** ne pas avoir du tout honte de (faire) qch 2 (= *immodest*) *[person]* sans pudeur, impudique ; *[act]* impudique

shamelessly /ˈʃeɪmlɪslɪ/ ADV 1 (= *brazenly*) *[declare, lie, cheat, flirt]* sans vergogne, sans la moindre gêne ; *[steal]* sans vergogne ◆ **~ sentimental/theatrical** d'une sentimentalité/théâtralité éhontée 2 (= *immodestly*) *[act, behave]* sans pudeur, de façon impudique

shamelessness /ˈʃeɪmlɪsnɪs/ N *(NonC) [of person, behaviour]* (= *brazenness*) effronterie *f*, impudence *f* ; (= *immodesty*) impudeur *f*

shaming /ˈʃeɪmɪŋ/ ADJ mortifiant, humiliant ◆ **it's too ~!** quelle humiliation !

shammy* /ˈʃæmɪ/ N (also **shammy leather**) peau *f* de chamois

shampoo /ʃæmˈpuː/ N (= *product, process*) shampooing *or* shampoing *m* ◆ **~ and set** shampooing *m* (et) mise *f* en plis ◆ **to give o.s. a ~** se faire un shampooing, se laver la tête ; → **dry** VT *[+ person]* faire un shampooing à ; *[+ hair, carpet]* shampouiner ◆ **to have one's hair ~ed and set** se faire faire un shampooing (et) mise en plis

shamrock /ˈʃæmrɒk/ N trèfle *m* *(emblème national de l'Irlande)*

shamus‡ /ˈʃeɪməs/ N *(US)* (= *policeman*) flic* *m* ; (= *detective*) détective *m* privé

shandy /ˈʃændɪ/ N *(Brit)* panaché *m*

Shanghai /ʃæŋˈhaɪ/ N Shanghai

shanghai /ʃæŋˈhaɪ/ VT *(Naut* ††*)* embarquer de force comme membre d'équipage ◆ **to ~ sb into doing sth*** contraindre qn à faire qch

Shangri-la /ˈʃæŋrɪˈlɑː/ N paradis *m* terrestre

shank /ʃæŋk/ N *(Anat)* jambe *f* ; *[of horse]* canon *m* ; *(Culin)* jarret *m* ; (= *handle*) manche *m* COMP **Shanks's pony** N ◆ **to go** *or* **ride on Shanks's pony** aller à pinces‡

shan't /ʃɑːnt/ ⇒ **shall not** ; → **shall**

shantung /ʃænˈtʌŋ/ N shant(o)ung *m*

shanty¹ /ˈʃæntɪ/ N *(= hut)* baraque *f*, cabane *f*

shanty² /ˈʃæntɪ/ N *(Brit)* (also **sea shanty**) chanson *f* de marins

shantytown /ˈʃæntɪˌtaʊn/ N bidonville *m*

SHAPE /ʃeɪp/ N (abbrev of **Supreme Headquarters Allied Powers Europe**) SHAPE *m (quartier général des forces alliées de l'OTAN en Europe)*

shape /ʃeɪp/ N [1] *(= form, outline)* forme *f* ◆ **what ~ is the room?, what is the ~ of the room?** quelle est la forme de la pièce ?, de quelle forme est la pièce ? ◆ **vases of all ~s** des vases de toutes formes ◆ **of all ~s and sizes** de toutes les formes et de toutes les tailles ◆ **children of all ~s and sizes** des enfants d'allures diverses ◆ **they come in all ~s and sizes** *(lit)* il y en a de toutes sortes et de toutes les tailles ; *(fig)* il y en a une variété infinie ◆ **a monster in human ~** un monstre à figure humaine ◆ **his nose is a funny ~** son nez a une drôle de forme ◆ **this jumper has lost its ~** ce pull s'est déformé ◆ **this tradition has existed for centuries in some ~ or form** cette tradition existe depuis des siècles sous une forme ou sous une autre ◆ **I can't stand racism in any ~ or form** je ne peux pas tolérer le racisme sous quelque forme que ce soit ◆ **that's the ~ of things to come** cela donne une idée de ce qui nous attend ◆ **who knows what ~ the future will take?** qui sait comment se présentera l'avenir ? ◆ **to take the ~ of sth** *(lit, fig)* prendre la forme de qch

♦ **in shape** *(describing something)* ◆ **it's like a mushroom in ~** cela a la forme d'un champignon, cela ressemble à un champignon ◆ **it's triangular in ~** c'est en forme de triangle, c'est triangulaire

♦ **in the shape of** ◆ **in the ~ of a cross** en forme de croix ◆ **a prince in the ~ of a swan** un prince sous la forme d'un cygne ◆ **the news reached him in the ~ of a telegram from his brother** c'est par un télégramme de son frère qu'il a appris la nouvelle ◆ **perks in the ~ of luncheon vouchers** des avantages sous la forme de chèques-restaurant

♦ **into shape** ◆ **he carved the wood into ~** il a façonné le bois ◆ **he beat the silver into ~** il a façonné l'argent ◆ **to pull/squeeze/twist sth back into ~** redonner sa forme initiale à qch en le tirant/en le serrant/en le tordant ◆ **to knock** *or* **lick* into ~** *(fig)* *[+ assistant, new arrival]* former, dresser* ; *[+ soldier]* entraîner, dresser* ◆ **to knock** *or* **lick* sth into ~** arranger qch, rendre qch présentable ◆ **he managed to knock** *or* **lick* the team into ~** il a réussi à mettre l'équipe au point

♦ **out of shape** *(= misshapen)* déformé ◆ **to pull/squeeze/twist sth out of ~** déformer qch en le tirant/en le serrant/en le tordant

♦ **to take shape** *[thing being made, project, idea]* prendre forme *or* tournure

[2] *(= human figure)* forme *f*, figure *f* ; *(= silhouette)* forme *f*, silhouette *f* ; *(= thing dimly seen)* forme *f* vague *or* imprécise ; *(= ghost etc)* fantôme *m*, apparition *f* ◆ **a ~ loomed up out of the darkness** une forme imprécise surgit de l'obscurité

[3] *(describing health, fitness)* **what kind of ~ is he in?** est-ce qu'il est en forme ? ◆ **what kind of ~ is the company in?** quel est l'état de santé de l'entreprise ? ◆ **to be in (good) ~** *[person]* être en (bonne) forme ; *[business]* être en bonne santé ◆ **to keep o.s. in good ~** rester *or* se maintenir en forme ◆ **I'm trying to get back in ~** j'essaie de me remettre en forme, j'essaie de retrouver la forme ◆ **to get (o.s.) into ~** (re)trouver la forme ◆ **in poor ~** *[person, business]* mal en point ◆ **she's in really bad ~** elle ne va vraiment pas bien ◆ **I'm out of ~** je ne suis pas en forme

[4] *(for jellies etc)* moule *m* ; *(in hat-making)* forme *f*

VT *[+ clay]* façonner, modeler ; *[+ stone, wood]* façonner, tailler ; *(fig) [+ statement, explanation]* formuler ◆ **he ~d the clay into a tree, he ~d a tree out of the clay** il a façonné un arbre dans l'argile ◆ **oddly ~d** d'une forme bizarre ◆ **a nicely ~d stone** une pierre d'une jolie forme ◆ **~d canvas** *(Phot)* détourage *m* ◆ **~d like a fish** en forme de poisson ◆ **to ~ sb's ideas/character** modeler *or* former les idées/le caractère de qn ◆ **to ~ sb's life** déterminer le destin de qn ◆ **to ~ the course of events** influencer la marche des événements

VI *(fig)* prendre forme *or* tournure ; → **shape up**

► **shape up** VI [1] *(= get on)* progresser ; *(= progress) [project]* prendre forme *or* tournure ◆ **our plans are shaping up well** nos projets prennent tournure *or* sont en bonne voie ◆ **things are shaping up well** tout marche bien, on avance ◆ **how is he shaping up?** comment s'en sort-il ?*, est-ce qu'il se fait ? ◆ **he is shaping up nicely as a goalkeeper** il est en train de devenir un bon gardien de but ◆ **~ up!*** secoue-toi un peu !* ◆ **~ up or ship out!*** rentre dans le rang ou fiche le camp !*

[2] *(esp US = slim etc)* retrouver la forme

-shaped /ʃeɪpt/ ADJ *(in compounds)* en forme de ◆ **heart-shaped** en forme de cœur ; → **egg**

shapeless /ˈʃeɪplɪs/ ADJ *[dress, hat, cardigan]* informe, sans forme ; *[mass, lump, bundle]* informe ; *[person]* aux formes lourdes ; *[book, plan, monologue]* sans aucune structure ◆ **to become ~** *[clothes]* se déformer, s'avachir

shapelessness /ˈʃeɪplɪsnɪs/ N absence *f* de forme

shapeliness /ˈʃeɪplɪnɪs/ N belles proportions *fpl*, beauté *f* (de forme), galbe *m*

shapely /ˈʃeɪplɪ/ ADJ *[woman]* bien proportionné ; *[legs]* bien galbé ; *[body]* harmonieux ◆ **her ~ figure** sa silhouette harmonieuse *or* bien proportionnée

shard /ʃɑːd/ N tesson *m* (de poterie)

share /ʃɛəʳ/ LANGUAGE IN USE 11.1, 12.1, 26.3

N [1] part *f* ◆ **here's your ~** voici votre part, voici ce qui vous est dû ◆ **my ~ is $5** ma (quote-)part s'élève à 5 dollars ◆ **his ~ of the inheritance** sa part *or* sa portion de l'héritage ◆ **his ~ of** *or* **in the profits** sa part des bénéfices ◆ **he will get a ~ of** *or* **in the profits** il aura part aux bénéfices ◆ **he has a ~ in the business** il est l'un des associés dans cette affaire ◆ **he has a half-~ in the firm** il possède la moitié de l'entreprise ◆ **to have a ~ in doing sth** contribuer à faire qch ◆ **he had some ~ in it** il y était pour quelque chose ◆ **I had no ~ in that** je n'y étais pour rien ◆ **to take a ~ in sth** participer à qch ◆ **to pay one's ~** payer sa (quote-)part ◆ **to bear one's ~ of the cost** participer aux frais ◆ **he wants more than his ~** il veut plus qu'il ne lui est dû, il tire la couverture à lui ◆ **he isn't doing his ~** il ne fournit pas sa part d'efforts ◆ **he's had more than his (fair) ~ of misfortune** il a eu plus que sa part de malheurs ◆ **to take one's ~ of the blame** accepter sa part de responsabilité ◆ **he does his full ~ of work** il fournit toute sa (quote-)part de travail ; → **fair¹, lion**

[2] *(Stock Exchange)* action *f* ◆ **he has 500 ~s in an oil company** il a 500 actions d'une compagnie de pétrole ; → **ordinary, preference, qualifying**

[3] *(Agr = ploughshare)* soc *m (de charrue)*

VT [1] *(gen)* partager ; *[+ room, prize]* partager *(with sb* avec qn) ; *[+ expenses, work]* partager *(with sb* avec qn) ; *[+ profits]* avoir part à ; *[+ sorrow, joy]* partager, prendre part à ; *[+ responsibility, blame, credit]* partager ◆ **they ~d the money (between them)** ils se sont partagé l'argent ◆ **you can ~ Anne's book** *(in school etc)* tu peux suivre avec Anne ◆ **they ~ certain characteristics** ils ont certaines caractéristiques en commun ◆ **I do not ~ that view** je ne partage pas cette opinion ◆ **I ~ your hope that ...** j'espère avec *or* comme vous que ...

[2] (also **share out**) partager, répartir *(among, between* entre)

VI partager ◆ **~ and ~ alike** à chacun sa part

♦ **to share in** *[+ sorrow, joy]* partager, prendre part à ; *[+ responsibility]* partager ; *[+ profits]* avoir part à ; *[+ expenses, work]* participer à, partager

COMP **share capital** N capital *m* actions
share certificate N titre *m or* certificat *m* d'actions
shared facility N *(Comput)* installation *f* commune
shared line N *(Telec)* ligne *f* partagée
share index N indice *m* de la Bourse
share issue N émission *f* d'actions
share option N *possibilité de prise de participation des employés dans leur entreprise*
share-out N partage *m*, distribution *f*
share premium N prime *f* d'émission
share price N cours *m* d'une action
share shop N *(Brit) guichet où sont vendues les actions émises lors de la privatisation des entreprises publiques*

► **share out**
VT SEP ⇒ **share vt 2**
N ◆ **share-out** → **share**

sharecropper /ˈʃɛəˌkrɒpəʳ/ N *(esp US Agr)* métayer *m*, -ère *f*

sharecropping /ˈʃɛəˌkrɒpɪŋ/ N *(esp US)* métayage *m*

shareholder /ˈʃɛəˌhəʊldəʳ/ N *(Fin etc)* actionnaire *mf*

shareholding /ˈʃɛəˌhəʊldɪŋ/ N *(Fin)* actionnariat *m*

shareware /ˈʃɛəwɛəʳ/ N *(NonC: Comput)* shareware *m*

Sharia, sharia /ʃəˈriːə/ N charia *f* ◆ **~ law** loi de la charia

shark /ʃɑːk/ N *(= fish: gen)* requin *m* ; *(generic name)* squale *m* ; *(fig pej = sharp businessman)* requin *m* ; *(= swindler)* escroc *m*, aigrefin *m*

sharkskin /ˈʃɑːkskɪn/ N *(= fabric)* peau *f* d'ange

sharon /ˈʃærən/ N (also **sharon fruit**) charon *or* sharon *m*

sharp /ʃɑːp/ ADJ [1] *(= good for cutting) [knife, razor, blade]* (bien) aiguisé *or* affûté ; *[piece of glass, tin, edge]* coupant ◆ **the ~ edge** *[of knife]* le (côté) tranchant

[2] *(= pointed) [pencil]* bien taillé ; *[needle, pin]* très pointu ; *[teeth, fingernails, beak, nose, chin]* pointu ; *[fang]* acéré ; *[point]* acéré, aigu (-guë *f*) ; *[corner]* aigu (-guë *f*) ; *[features]* anguleux ◆ **to be at the ~ end of sth** *(fig)* être en première ligne de *or* pour qch

[3] *(= well-defined) [contrast]* vif, net ; *[image, TV picture]* net ; *[distinction, difference]* net, marqué ; *[outline]* net, distinct ; *[division]* fort ◆ **to be in ~ contrast to sth** contraster vivement *or* nettement avec qch ◆ **to bring into ~ focus** *(Phot)* bien mettre au point ; *[+ problem, issue]* faire ressortir nettement ; see also **relief**

[4] *(= acute) [person]* dégourdi, malin (-igne *f*) ; *[intelligence]* vif, pénétrant ; *[wit]* vif ; *[mind]* pénétrant ; *[awareness]* aigu (-guë *f*) ; *[eyesight]* perçant ; *[hearing]* fin ◆ **to have ~ ears** avoir l'oreille *or* l'ouïe fine ◆ **to have ~ eyes** ne pas avoir les yeux dans sa poche ◆ **he has a ~ eye for a bargain** il sait repérer *or* flairer une bonne affaire ◆ **to keep a ~ look-out for sb/sth** guetter qn/qch avec vigilance *or* d'un œil attentif ◆ **he's (as) ~ as a needle** *or* **razor** *(= clever)* il a l'esprit très vif ; *(= missing nothing)* rien ne lui échappe ◆ **his mind is (as) ~ as a razor** il a l'esprit très vif

5 *(= abrupt) [rise, fall, decline, reduction, cut]* fort ; *[increase, drop]* brusque, soudain ; *[bend, corner]* serré ; *[angle]* aigu ; *[change]* brutal ◆ **the motorcycle made a ~ right turn** la moto a pris un virage serré à droite ◆ **he gave the handle a ~ turn** il a tourné la poignée brusquement

6 *(= intense) [pain]* cuisant, vif ; *[sensation]* vif ; *[wind, cold]* vif, pénétrant ; *[frost]* fort ; *[blow]* sec (sèche *f*) ; *[cry]* perçant, aigu (-guë *f*)

7 *(= severe) [criticism, attack]* mordant, incisif ; *[retort, words]* mordant, cinglant ; *[rebuke]* vif ; *[order, tone, voice]* cassant ◆ **to be a ~ reminder of sth** rappeler qch de façon brutale ◆ **to have a ~ tongue** *(fig)* avoir la langue acérée, être caustique

8 *(pej = unscrupulous) [business practices]* déloyal ; see also **comp**

9 *(* = stylish) [person]* classe * *inv* ; *[suit]* chic *inv* ◆ **to be a ~ dresser** s'habiller très classe * *inv*

10 *(= acrid) [smell, perfume]* piquant, âcre *(pej)* ; *[taste, sauce]* piquant, âpre *(pej)* ; *[cheese]* au goût prononcé

11 *(= brisk) [pace]* vif ◆ **look** *or* **be ~ (about it)!** * *(esp Brit)* grouille-toi ! *

12 *(Mus) [note]* trop haut ◆ **C ~** do dièse ◆ **you were a little ~** vous avez chanté (or joué) un peu trop haut

ADV 1 *(= abruptly) [stop]* brusquement, net ◆ **to turn ~ left/right** prendre un virage serré à gauche/à droite

2 *(Mus) [sing, play]* trop haut

3 *(= precisely)* ◆ **at 8 (o'clock) ~** à 8 heures précises *or* pile

N 1 *(Mus)* dièse *m*

2 *(Med = hypodermic)* aiguille *f*

COMP **sharp-eared** ADJ *(fig)* qui a l'oreille *or* l'ouïe fine

sharp-eyed ADJ qui a un œil de lynx, à qui rien n'échappe

sharp-faced, sharp-featured ADJ aux traits anguleux

sharp practice N pratique *f* déloyale

sharp-sighted ADJ ⇒ **sharp-eyed**

sharp-tempered ADJ coléreux, soupe au lait * *inv*

sharp-tongued ADJ caustique

sharp-witted ADJ à l'esprit vif *or* prompt

sharpen /ˈʃɑːpən/ VT (also **sharpen up**) 1 *[+ blade, knife, razor, tool]* affûter, aiguiser ; *[+ scissors]* aiguiser ; *[+ pencil]* tailler ◆ **the cat was ~ing its claws on the chair leg** le chat aiguisait ses griffes *or* se faisait les griffes sur le pied de la chaise 2 *(fig) [+ outline, picture, focus]* rendre plus net ; *[+ difference, contrast]* rendre plus marqué ; *[+ appetite]* aiguiser ; *[+ desire]* exciter ; *[+ pain]* aggraver, aviver ; *[+ feeling]* aviver ; *[+ intelligence]* affiner, rendre plus fin ◆ **to ~ one's wits** se dégourdir 3 *(esp Brit: Mus)* diéser VI *[voice]* devenir plus perçant ; *[desire, pain]* devenir plus vif, s'aviver

sharpener /ˈʃɑːpnəʳ/ N *(= knife sharpener) (on wall, on wheel etc)* aiguisoir *m* à couteaux, affiloir *m* ; *(long, gen with handle)* fusil *m* à repasser les couteaux ; *(= pencil sharpener)* taille-crayons *m inv*

sharpening /ˈʃɑːpnɪŋ/ N aiguisage *m*, affilage *m*, affûtage *m*

sharper /ˈʃɑːpəʳ/ N escroc *m*, filou *m*, aigrefin *m* ; *(= card sharper)* tricheur *m*, -euse *f (professionnel(le))*

sharpie ⁑ /ˈʃɑːpɪ/ N *(US) (= alert person)* petit(e) futé(e) *m(f)* ; *(= crook)* filou *m*, escroc *m*

sharpish /ˈʃɑːpɪʃ/ ADJ 1 *(= good for cutting) [knife, razor, blade]* assez aiguisé *or* affûté ; *[edge]* assez coupant 2 *(= pointed) [pencil]* assez bien taillé ; *[teeth, fingernails, beak, nose, chin]* assez pointu ; *[point]* assez aigu (-guë *f*) ; *[features]* assez anguleux ; → **sharp** ADV *(Brit * = quickly)* en vitesse *

sharply /ˈʃɑːplɪ/ ADV 1 *(= abruptly) [fall, drop, increase, decline, change]* brusquement ; *[stop]* brusquement, net ; *[reduce]* nettement ◆ **prices have risen ~** les prix ont monté en flèche ◆ **to turn ~ to the left** tourner tout de suite à gauche ◆ **to corner ~** *(in country)* prendre un virage à la corde ; *(in town)* prendre un tournant serré

2 *(= clearly) [show up, stand out, differ, divide]* nettement ◆ **~ defined** *[image]* qui se détache nettement ◆ **~ in focus** *(Phot, fig)* parfaitement net ◆ **a ~ focused strategy** une stratégie bien ciblée ◆ **to bring ~ into focus** *(Phot)* bien mettre au point ; *[+ issue, differences]* faire ressortir nettement ◆ **to contrast ~ with sth** contraster vivement avec qch

3 *(= severely) [criticise, react]* vivement ; *[say, ask, comment, reply]* avec brusquerie ; *[look at]* sévèrement ◆ **a ~ worded attack** une attaque mordante *or* incisive ◆ **to speak ~ to sb about sth** parler à qn de qch en termes sévères

4 *(= acutely, alertly) [say, ask]* vivement, avec intérêt ◆ **he looked at me ~** il m'a regardé soudain avec intérêt

5 *(= distinctly) [click, tap]* sèchement

6 ◆ **~ pointed** *[knife, scissors]* effilé, (très) pointu ; *[nose]* pointu

7 *(= quickly)* rapidement

sharpness /ˈʃɑːpnɪs/ N 1 *[of razor, knife]* tranchant *m* ; *[of pencil, needle, nail]* pointe *f* aiguë 2 *[of turn, bend]* angle *m* brusque ; *[of outline etc]* netteté *f* ; *[of pain]* violence *f*, acuité *f* ; *[of criticism, reproach, rebuke]* sévérité *f*, tranchant *m* ; *[of tone, voice]* brusquerie *f*, aigreur *f* ; *[of taste, smell]* piquant *m*, âcreté *f (pej)* ; *[of wind, cold]* âpreté *f* ◆ **there's a ~ in the air** il fait frais

sharpshooter /ˈʃɑːpʃuːtəʳ/ N *(esp US)* tireur *m* d'élite

shat *⁎* /ʃæt/ VB pt, ptp of **shit**

shatter /ˈʃætəʳ/ VT *[+ window, door]* fracasser *(against* contre*)* ; *[+ health]* ruiner ; *[+ self-confidence, career]* briser ; *[+ faith, life]* détruire ; *[+ hopes, chances]* ruiner, détruire ◆ **the sound ~ed the glass** le son a brisé le verre ◆ **to ~ sb's nerves** démolir les nerfs de qn ◆ **she was ~ed by his death** sa mort l'a anéantie ; see also **shattered** VI *[glass, windscreen, cup]* voler en éclats ; *[box etc]* se fracasser

shattered /ˈʃætəd/ ADJ 1 *(= grief-stricken)* anéanti, consterné ; *(= aghast, overwhelmed)* bouleversé 2 *(= ruined) [country, economy]* détruit ; *[dream, life, confidence]* brisé ◆ **the ~ remains of the building** les débris *mpl* du bâtiment 3 *(* = exhausted)* crevé *, éreinté

shattering /ˈʃætərɪŋ/ ADJ 1 *(= devastating) [experience, news]* bouleversant ; *[blow, effect]* dévastateur (-trice *f*) ; *[defeat]* écrasant 2 *(Brit * = exhausting) [day, journey]* crevant *

shatterproof glass /ʃætəpruːfˈglɑːs/ N verre *m* securit ® *inv*

shave /ʃeɪv/ (vb : pret **shaved**, ptp **shaved, shaven**) N ◆ **to give sb a ~** raser qn ◆ **to have** *or* **give o.s. a ~** se raser, se faire la barbe ◆ **to have a close** *or* **narrow ~** *(fig)* l'échapper belle, y échapper de justesse ◆ **that was a close** *or* **narrow ~!** il était moins une ! *, on l'a échappé belle ! ; → **aftershave** VT *[+ person, face, legs etc]* raser ; *[+ wood]* raboter, planer ; *(fig = brush against)* raser, frôler ◆ **to ~ the price of sth** faire un rabais sur le prix de qch VI se raser ◆ **to ~ under one's arms** se raser les aisselles

► **shave off** VT SEP 1 ◆ **to shave off one's beard** se raser la barbe 2 ◆ **the joiner shaved some of the wood off** le menuisier a enlevé un peu du bois au rabot ◆ **to ~ off a few pounds** faire un rabais de quelques livres

shaven /ˈʃeɪvn/ VB †† ptp of **shave** ADJ rasé ; → **clean**

shaver /ˈʃeɪvəʳ/ N 1 rasoir *m* électrique 2 ◆ **(young) ~** † * gosse * *m*, gamin *m*

COMP **shaver outlet** N *(US)* ⇒ **shaver point**

shaver point N prise *f* pour rasoir électrique

Shavian /ˈʃeɪvɪən/ ADJ à la *or* de George Bernard Shaw

shaving /ˈʃeɪvɪŋ/ N 1 *(= piece of wood, metal etc)* copeau *m* 2 *(NonC: with razor etc)* rasage *m* ◆ **~ is a nuisance** c'est embêtant * de se raser

COMP **shaving brush** N blaireau *m*

shaving cream N crème *f* à raser

shaving foam N mousse *f* à raser

shaving gel N gel *m* à raser

shaving soap N savon *m* à barbe

shaving stick N bâton *m* de savon à barbe

shawl /ʃɔːl/ N châle *m*

she /ʃiː/ PERS PRON 1 elle ◆ **~ has arrived** elle est arrivée ◆ **~ is a doctor** elle est médecin, c'est un médecin ◆ **~ is a small woman** elle est petite ◆ **it is ~** c'est elle ◆ **if I were ~** *(frm)* si j'étais elle, si j'étais à sa place ◆ **SHE didn't do it** ce n'est pas elle qui l'a fait ◆ **younger than ~** plus jeune qu'elle ◆ **~'s a fine boat/car** c'est un beau bateau/une belle voiture ◆ **here ~ is** la voici 2 *(+ rel pron)* celle ◆ **~ who** *or* **that can ...** celle qui peut ... N * femelle *f* ◆ **it's a ~** *[animal]* c'est une femelle ; *[baby]* c'est une fille

COMP *(gen: with names of animals)* femelle *after n*

she-bear N ourse *f*

she-cat N *(fig)* mégère *f*, furie *f*

she-devil N *(fig)* démon *m*, furie *f*

she-goat N chèvre *f* ; → **wolf**

s/he (abbrev of **he or she**) il ou elle

shea /ʃɪə/ N karité *m*

sheaf /ʃiːf/ N (pl **sheaves**) *[of corn]* gerbe *f* ; *[of papers]* liasse *f* ; *[of arrows]* faisceau *m*

shear /ʃɪəʳ/ (vb : pret **sheared**, ptp **sheared** *or* **shorn**)

NPL **shears** *(for gardening)* cisaille(s) *f(pl)* ; *(= large scissors)* grands ciseaux *mpl* ◆ **a pair of ~s** une paire de cisailles ; → **pruning** VT *[+ sheep]* tondre ◆ **shorn of** *(fig)* dépouillé de

► **shear off** VI *[branch etc]* partir, se détacher VT SEP *[+ wool]* tondre ; *[+ projecting part, nail]* faire partir, arracher ; *[+ branch]* couper, élaguer ◆ **the ship had its bow shorn off in the collision** dans la collision l'avant du navire a été emporté

► **shear through** VT FUS *[+ paper, cloth]* trancher ; *[+ wood, metal]* fendre ; *(fig) [+ the waves, the crowd]* fendre

shearer /ˈʃɪərəʳ/ N *(= person)* tondeur *m*, -euse *f* ; *(= machine)* tondeuse *f*

shearing /ˈʃɪərɪŋ/ N *(= process)* tonte *f* ◆ **~s** *(= wool etc)* tonte

sheath /ʃiːθ/ N (pl **sheaths** /ʃiːðz/) 1 *[of dagger]* gaine *f* ; *[of sword]* fourreau *m* ; *[of scissors etc]* étui *m* ; *[of electric cable, flex]* gaine *f* ; *(Bio)* gaine *f*, enveloppe *f* ; *(Bot)* enveloppe *f* ; *(Brit = contraceptive)* préservatif *m* 2 (also **sheath dress**) fourreau *m (robe)* COMP **sheath knife** N (pl **sheath knives**) couteau *m* à gaine

sheathe /ʃiːð/ VT 1 *[+ sword, dagger]* rengainer ; *[+ cable]* gainer ; *[cat etc] [+ claws]* rentrer 2 *(= cover)* recouvrir, revêtir *(with* de*)*

sheaves /ʃiːvz/ NPL of **sheaf**

Sheba /ˈʃiːbə/ N Saba ◆ **the Queen of ~** la reine de Saba

shebang * /ʃəˈbæŋ/ N ◆ **the whole ~** toute l'affaire, tout le tremblement *

shebeen /ʃɪˈbiːn/ N *(Ir)* débit *m* de boissons clandestin

shed¹ /ʃed/ N 1 *(gen)* abri *m* ; *(smallish)* abri *m*, cabane *f* ; *(larger)* remise *f*, resserre *f* ; *(large open-sided: Rail, Agr etc)* hangar *m* ; *(= lean-to)* appentis *m* ◆ **bicycle ~** abri *m* à vélos, remise *f* pour les vélos ◆ **garden ~** abri *m* de jardin, cabane *f* ; → **cowshed, toolshed** 2 *(= part of factory)* atelier *m*

shed² /ʃed/ (pret, ptp **shed**) VT 1 *(= lose, get rid of)* *[+ petals, leaves, fur, horns]* perdre ; *[+ shell]* dépouiller ; *[truck]* *[+ load]* déverser, perdre ; *(Space) [+ section of craft]* larguer, éjecter ; *[+ tears]* verser, répandre ; *[+ coat etc]* enlever, se dépouiller de *(frm)* ; *[+ unwanted thing]* se débarrasser de, se défaire de ; *[+ assistant, employee]* se défaire de, se séparer de ◆ **to ~ hairs** *[dog, cat]* perdre ses poils ◆ **the snake ~s its skin** le serpent mue ◆ **to ~ blood** *(one's own)* verser son sang ; *(other people's)* faire couler le sang, verser *or* répandre le sang ◆ **I'm trying to ~ 5 kilos** j'essaie de perdre 5 kilos ◆ **this fabric ~s water** ce tissu ne laisse pas pénétrer l'eau

2 *(= send out)* *[+ light]* répandre, diffuser ; *[+ warmth, happiness]* répandre ◆ **to ~ light on** *(lit)* éclairer ; *[+ sb's motives etc]* jeter de la lumière sur ; *[+ problem]* éclaircir ; *[+ little-known subject]* éclairer

she'd /ʃiːd/ ⇒ **she had, she would** ; → **have, would**

sheen /ʃiːn/ N *(on silk)* lustre *m*, luisant *m* ; *(on hair)* brillant *m*, éclat *m* ◆ **to take the ~ off sth** *(lit)* délustrer qch ; *(fig)* diminuer l'éclat de qch

sheep /ʃiːp/ N *(pl inv)* mouton *m* *(animal)* ; *(= ewe)* brebis *f* ◆ **they followed him like ~** ils l'ont suivi comme des moutons, ils l'ont suivi comme les moutons de Panurge ◆ **to make ~'s eyes at sb** faire les yeux doux à qn ◆ **there are so many computers on the market it's hard to sort out** *or* **to separate the ~ from the goats** il y a tellement d'ordinateurs sur le marché que c'est difficile de faire le tri ; → **black, lost**

COMP **sheep-dip** N bain *m* parasiticide *(pour moutons)*

sheep farm N ferme *f* d'élevage de moutons

sheep farmer N éleveur *m* de moutons

sheep farming N élevage *m* de moutons

sheep track N piste *f* à moutons

sheep-worrying N harcèlement *m* des moutons *(par des chiens)*

sheepdog /ˈʃiːpdɒg/ N chien *m* de berger ; → **trial**

sheepfold /ˈʃiːpfəʊld/ N parc *m* à moutons, bergerie *f*

sheepherder /ˈʃiːp,hɜːdəʳ/ N *(US)* berger *m*, gardien *m* de moutons

sheepish /ˈʃiːpɪʃ/ ADJ penaud *(about sth* de qch*)*

sheepishly /ˈʃiːpɪʃlɪ/ ADV d'un air penaud

sheepishness /ˈʃiːpɪʃnɪs/ N timidité *f*, air *m* penaud

sheepshank /ˈʃiːpʃæŋk/ N *(Naut)* jambe *f* de chien

sheepshearer /ˈʃiːp,ʃɪərəʳ/ N *(= person)* tondeur *m*, -euse *f* (de moutons) ; *(= machine)* tondeuse *f* (à moutons)

sheepshearing /ˈʃiːp,ʃɪərɪŋ/ N *(NonC)* tonte *f* (des moutons)

sheepskin /ˈʃiːpskɪn/ N 1 peau *f* de mouton 2 *(US Univ * fig)* peau *f* d'âne, diplôme *m*

COMP *[waistcoat etc]* en peau de mouton

sheepskin jacket N canadienne *f*

sheer¹ /ʃɪəʳ/ ADJ 1 *(= utter)* *[beauty, terror, boredom, stupidity, joy, delight]* (à l'état) pur ; *[waste, carelessness, survival]* pur et simple ; *[variety]* même *after n* ; *[impossibility, necessity]* absolu ◆ **by ~ accident** tout à fait par hasard ◆ **by ~ coincidence** par pure coïncidence ◆ **in ~ desperation** en désespoir de cause ◆ **by ~ force of will** par la seule force de la volonté ◆ **to succeed through ~ hard work** réussir grâce à *or* par son seul travail ◆ **by ~ luck** tout à fait par hasard ◆ **it was ~ luck I was there** c'était tout à fait par hasard que j'étais là ◆ **it's ~ madness** c'est de la folie pure ◆ **a sigh of ~ pleasure** un soupir de pur plaisir ◆ **the ~ pleasure of reading a good story** le simple plaisir de lire une bonne histoire ◆ **the ~ scale of the disaster/size of the job** l'importance même du désastre/du travail ◆ **the ~ strength of the animal** la force même de l'animal ◆ **delays are occurring because of the ~ volume of traffic** il y a des ralentissements dus uniquement à la densité de la circulation

2 *(= fine)* *[tights, stockings, fabric etc]* très fin

3 *(= smooth)* *[make-up]* satiné

4 *(= vertical)* *[cliff, rock]* à pic, abrupt ◆ **a ~ drop** un à-pic, un abrupt

ADV à pic, abruptement

sheer² /ʃɪəʳ/ *(Naut = swerve)* N embardée *f* VI faire une embardée

► **sheer off** VI *[ship]* faire une embardée ; *(gen)* changer de direction

sheet /ʃiːt/ N 1 *(on bed)* drap *m* ; *(= shroud)* linceul *m* ; *(= dust sheet)* housse *f* ; *(= tarpaulin)* bâche *f* ; → **white**

2 *(= piece)* *[of plastic, rubber]* morceau *m* ; *[of paper, notepaper]* feuille *f* ; *[of iron, steel]* tôle *f* ; *[of glass, metal etc]* feuille *f*, plaque *f* ◆ **a ~ of stamps** une planche de timbres ◆ **an odd** *or* **loose ~** une feuille volante ◆ **order ~** *(Comm)* bulletin *m* de commande ; → **balance**

3 *(= expanse)* *[of water, snow etc]* étendue *f* ◆ **a ~ of ice** *(large)* une plaque de glace ; *(thin film)* une couche de glace ; *(on road)* une plaque de verglas ◆ **a ~ of flame** un rideau de flammes ◆ **~s of rain** des trombes *fpl* d'eau ◆ **the rain came down in ~s** il pleuvait à seaux

4 *(= periodical)* périodique *m* ; *(= newspaper)* journal *m*

5 *(Naut)* écoute *f* ◆ **he's three ~s to** *or* **in the wind** †* *(fig)* il est gris † ; → **main**

COMP **sheet anchor** N *(Naut)* ancre *f* de veille ; *(fig)* ancre *f* de salut

sheet ice N verglas *m*

sheet lightning N *(NonC)* éclair *m* en nappe(s)

sheet metal N *(NonC: gen)* tôle *f* ◆ **~ metal (work)shop** tôlerie *f*

sheet music N *(NonC)* partitions *fpl*

► **sheet down*** VI *(Brit)* *[rain]* tomber à seaux ; *[snow]* tomber à gros flocons ◆ **it's ~ing down** *(rain)* il pleut à seaux ; *(snow)* il neige à gros flocons

sheeting /ˈʃiːtɪŋ/ N *(NonC)* *[paper, plastic]* feuilles *fpl* ; *(= sheet metal)* tôle *f*

Sheherazade /ʃə,herəˈzɑːdə/ N Schéhérazade *f*

sheik(h) /ʃeɪk/ N 1 cheik *m* ; → **oil** 2 *(US fig)* séducteur *m*, Roméo *m*

sheik(h)dom /ˈʃeɪkdəm/ N *tribu ou territoire sous l'autorité d'un cheik*

sheila* /ˈʃiːlə/ N *(Austral)* nana* *f*

shekel /ˈʃekl/ N *(modern)* shekel *m* ; *(Hist: Bible etc)* sicle *m* ; *(US * fig = coin)* pièce *f* de monnaie ◆ **~s** * *(fig)* fric* *m*, sous* *mpl* ◆ **to be in the ~s**‡ *(fig US)* avoir du fric*

sheldrake /ˈʃel,dreɪk/, **shelduck** /ˈʃel,dʌk/ N tadorne *m* de Bellon

shelf /ʃelf/ (pl **shelves**) N 1 étagère *f* ; *(in shop)* rayon *m* ; *(in oven)* plaque *f* ◆ **a ~ of books** un rayon de livres ◆ **a set of shelves** une étagère, un rayonnage ◆ **there are more luxury goods on the shelves nowadays** *(Comm)* il y a plus d'articles de luxe sur les rayons *or* dans les magasins aujourd'hui ◆ **to buy sth off the ~** acheter qch tout fait ; see also **off** ◆ **to leave sth on the ~** *(= postpone)* laisser qch de côté *or* au placard* ◆ **she doesn't want to be (left) on the ~** elle voudrait se caser* ; → **bookshelf**

2 *(= edge)* *(in rock)* rebord *m*, saillie *f* ; *(underwater)* écueil *m* ; → **continental**

COMP **shelf life** N *(Comm)* durée *f* de conservation en stock ◆ **most pop stars have a short ~ life** *(hum)* la plupart des stars de la pop ne durent pas longtemps ◆ **her relationships have limited ~ life** ses relations sont éphémères

shelf mark N *(in library)* cote *f*

shell /ʃel/ N 1 *[of egg, nut, oyster, snail]* coquille *f* ; *[of tortoise, lobster, crab]* carapace *f* ; *(on beach, in collection)* coquillage *m* ; *[of peas]* cosse *f* ◆ **to come out of/go back into one's ~** *(lit, fig)* sortir de/rentrer dans sa coquille ◆ **"clam on the shell"** *(US)* ≃ "dégustation de clams" ; → **cockle**

2 *[of building]* carcasse *f* ; *[of ship]* coque *f* ◆ **pastry ~** *(Culin)* fond *m* de tarte

3 *(Mil)* obus *m* ; *(US = cartridge)* cartouche *f*

4 *(= racing boat)* outrigger *m*

VT 1 *[+ peas]* écosser ; *[+ nut]* décortiquer, écaler ; *[+ oyster]* écailler, retirer de sa coquille ; *[+ crab, prawn, shrimp, lobster]* décortiquer ; see also **shelled**

2 *(Mil)* bombarder (d'obus)

COMP *[necklace, ornament etc]* de *or* en coquillages

shell game N *(US)* *(= trick)* bonneteau *m* (pratiqué avec des coques de noix) ; *(fig)* *(= fraud)* escroquerie *f*

shell-like‡ N *(Brit = ear)* oreille *f* ◆ **can I have a word in your ~-like?** je peux te dire deux mots ?

shell shock N *(Med)* psychose *f* traumatique *(du soldat)*, commotion *f (due aux combats)*

shell-shocked ADJ *(lit)* commotionné ; *(fig)* abasourdi

shell suit N survêtement *m*

► **shell out*** VI casquer‡, payer ◆ **to ~ out for sth** payer qch, casquer‡ pour qch

VT SEP cracher‡, aligner*

she'll /ʃiːl/ ⇒ **she will** ; → **will**

shellac /ʃəˈlæk/ N (gomme *f*) laque *f* VT 1 *(lit)* laquer 2 *(US * = beat)* battre à plates coutures

shellacking* /ʃəˈlækɪŋ/ N *(US)* 1 *(Sport = defeat)* raclée *f*, déculottée *f* 2 *(= telling-off)* **to get** *or* **take a ~ (from)** se faire enguirlander (par)

shelled /ʃeld/ ADJ *[nut, prawn]* décortiqué ; *[pea]* écossé

shellfire /ˈʃelfaɪəʳ/ N *(Mil)* tirs *mpl* d'obus, pilonnage *m* à l'artillerie

shellfish /ˈʃelfɪʃ/ N (pl **shellfish** or **shellfishes**) *(= lobster, crab)* crustacé *m* ; *(= mollusc)* coquillage *m* NPL *(Culin)* fruits *mpl* de mer

shelling /ˈʃelɪŋ/ N *(NonC: Mil)* bombardement *m* (par obus), pilonnage *m* d'artillerie

shellproof /ˈʃelpruːf/ ADJ *(Mil)* blindé

shelter /ˈʃeltəʳ/ N 1 *(NonC)* abri *m*, couvert *m* ◆ **under the ~ of ...** à l'abri sous ... ◆ **to take ~, to get under ~** se mettre à l'abri *or* à couvert ◆ **to take ~ from/under** s'abriter de/sous ◆ **to seek/offer ~** chercher/offrir un abri *(from* contre*)* ◆ **she gave him ~ for the night** elle lui a donné (un) asile pour la nuit ◆ **we must find ~ for the night** nous devons trouver un abri pour cette nuit ; *(Brit)* ◆ **Shelter** *organisation bénévole d'aide aux SDF*

2 *(= hut etc)* *(on mountain)* abri *m*, refuge *m* ; *(for sentry)* guérite *f* ; *(= bus shelter)* Abri-bus ® *m* ; *(= air-raid shelter)* abri *m*

3 *(for homeless)* asile *m*, refuge *m*

VT 1 *(= protect)* *(from wind, rain, sun, shells etc)* abriter *(from* de*)*, protéger *(from* de, contre*)* ; *(from blame etc)* protéger *(from* de*)* ; *[+ criminal etc]* protéger ; *(= hide)* cacher ◆ **~ed from the wind** à l'abri du vent ; see also **sheltered**

2 *(= give lodging to)* recueillir, donner un asile *or* le couvert à ; *[+ fugitive etc]* donner asile à, recueillir

VI s'abriter *(from* de ; *under* sous*)* se mettre à l'abri *or* à couvert

sheltered /ˈʃeltəd/ ADJ 1 *(= protected from weather)* *[place, garden, harbour, waters]* abrité 2 *(= protected)* *[life, upbringing, environment etc]* protégé 3 *(Brit = supervised)* *[work, employment]* en milieu protégé 4 *(Econ)* *[industry]* protégé *(contre la concurrence étrangère)*

COMP **sheltered accommodation, sheltered housing** N (NonC) (Brit) (for elderly) logement-foyer m ; (for disabled) foyer m d'hébergement pour handicapés
sheltered workshop N (Brit) atelier m protégé

shelve /ʃelv/ VT 1 (fig - postpone) [+ plan, project, problem] mettre en sommeil or en suspens 2 (lit) (= put on shelf) [+ book] mettre (or remettre) en place ; (= fit with shelves) [+ cupboard, wall] garnir de rayons or d'étagères VI (= slope: also **shelve down**) descendre en pente douce

shelves /ʃelvz/ NPL of **shelf**

shelving /ˈʃelvɪŋ/ N (NonC) rayonnage(s) m(pl), étagères fpl ; [of project etc] mise f en sommeil or en suspens

shemozzle * /ʃəˈmɒzl/ N (Brit) bagarre * f, chamaillerie * f ◆ **there was quite a ~!** ça a bardé ! *

shenanigan(s) * /ʃəˈnænɪgən(z)/ N (NonC) (= trickery) manigances fpl, entourloupettes * fpl ; (= rowdy fun) chahut m

shepherd /ˈʃepəd/ N 1 berger m ; (Rel) pasteur m ◆ **the Good Shepherd** (Rel) le bon Pasteur or Berger 2 (also **shepherd dog**) chien m de berger VT [+ sheep] garder, soigner ◆ **the dog ~ed the flock into the field** le chien a fait entrer le troupeau dans le pré ◆ **to ~ sb in** faire entrer qn ◆ **to ~ sb out** conduire qn jusqu'à la porte ◆ **he ~ed us round Paris** il nous a escortés or nous a servi de guide dans Paris
COMP **shepherd boy** N jeune pâtre m (liter), jeune berger m
shepherd's check N ⇒ **shepherd's plaid**
shepherd's crook N houlette f
shepherd's pie N (esp Brit) ≃ hachis m Parmentier
shepherd's plaid N plaid m noir et blanc
shepherd's purse N (= plant) bourse-à-pasteur f

shepherdess /ˈʃepədɪs/ N bergère f

sherbet /ˈʃɜːbət/ N 1 (Brit) (= fruit juice) jus m de fruit glacé ; (fizzy) boisson f gazeuse ; (= powder) poudre f acidulée or de sorbet 2 (US = water ice) sorbet m

sheriff /ˈʃerɪf/ N 1 (Brit Jur) shérif m 2 (US) shérif m, ≃ capitaine m de gendarmerie COMP **Sheriff Court** N (Scot) ≃ tribunal m de grande instance ; (US) ≃ tribunal m de police

Sherpa /ˈʃɜːpə/ N (pl **Sherpas** or **Sherpa**) sherpa m

sherry /ˈʃerɪ/ N xérès m, sherry m

she's /ʃiːz/ ⇒ **she is, she has** ; → **be, have**

Shetland /ˈʃetlənd/ N ◆ **the ~s** les îles fpl Shetland ADJ (gen) [people, customs, village] des îles Shetland ; [sweater] en shetland
COMP **the Shetland Islands, the Shetland Isles** NPL ⇒ **the Shetlands**
Shetland pony N poney m des Shetland
Shetland pull-over N pull-over m en shetland
Shetland wool N shetland m

Shetlander /ˈʃetləndəʳ/ N Shetlandais(e) m(f)

shew †† /ʃəʊ/ VTI ⇒ **show**

shhh /ʃː/ EXCL chut !

Shiah /ˈʃiːə/ N 1 (= doctrine) chiisme m 2 (= follower: also **Shiah Muslim**) chiite mf ADJ chiite

shiatsu /ʃiːˈætsuː/ N shiatsu m

shibboleth /ˈʃɪbəleθ/ N (Bible) schibboleth m ; (fig) (= doctrine) doctrine f or principe m arbitraire ; (= password) mot m de passe ; (= characteristic) caractéristique f, signe m distinctif

shield /ʃiːld/ N (gen) bouclier m ; (not round) écu m ; (Her) écu m, blason m ; (on gun) bouclier m ; (on or around machine) écran m de protection, tôle f protectrice ; (against radiation) écran m ; (fig) (= safeguard) sauvegarde f, bouclier m (liter) (against contre) ; (= person) protecteur m, -trice f ◆ **thermal ~** (Space) bouclier m thermique ; → **dress, windshield** VT protéger (from de, contre) ; [+ fugitive, criminal] protéger, couvrir ; [+ machine operator] protéger ; [+ gun, machine] fixer un écran de protection à ◆ **to ~ one's eyes from the sun** se protéger les yeux du soleil ◆ **to ~ sb with one's body** faire à qn un bouclier or un rempart de son corps

shift /ʃɪft/ N 1 (= change) changement m (in de), modification f (in de) ◆ **there has been a ~ in policy/attitude** la politique/l'attitude a changé ◆ **a sudden ~ in policy/attitude** un retournement or un bouleversement de la politique/de l'attitude ◆ **~ of emphasis** changement m d'éclairage ◆ **a sudden ~ in the wind** une saute de vent ; → **scene, vowel**

2 (= period of work) poste m, période f de travail ; (= people) poste m, équipe f (de relais) ◆ **he works ~s, he's on ~s** il travaille par équipes, il fait un travail posté ◆ **they used to work a ten-hour ~ in that factory** ils avaient des postes de dix heures dans cette usine ◆ **I work an eight-hour ~** je fais les trois-huit, je fais un poste de huit heures ◆ **this factory operates on three ~s per 24-hour period** dans cette usine ils font les trois-huit, dans cette usine trois équipes se relaient sur 24 heures ◆ **to be on day/night ~** être (au poste) de jour/de nuit ◆ **which ~ do you prefer?** quel poste préférez-vous ? ◆ **the next ~ was late coming on** l'équipe suivante était en retard pour prendre la relève ◆ **they worked in ~s to release the injured man** ils se sont relayés pour dégager le blessé ; → **day, night**

3 (frm) ◆ **to make ~ with sth/sb** se contenter de or s'accommoder de qch/qn ◆ **to make ~ without sth/sb** se passer de qch/qn ◆ **to make ~ to do sth** s'arranger pour faire qch ◆ **as a last desperate ~ he ...** en désespoir de cause il ...

4 (= gearshift) changement m de vitesse

5 (= straight dress) robe f droite ; († = woman's slip) chemise f

6 (Comput) décalage m

7 (Ling) mutation f

VT 1 (= move) [+ object, furniture] déplacer, changer de place ; [+ one's head, arm etc] bouger, remuer ; (Theat) [+ scenery] changer ; [+ screw] débloquer, faire bouger ; [+ lid, top, cap] faire bouger ; [+ stain] enlever, faire disparaître ; [+ employee] (to another town) muter (to à) ; (to another job, department) affecter (to à) ; [+ blame, responsibility] rejeter (on, on to sur) ◆ **he ~ed his chair nearer the fire** il a approché sa chaise du feu ◆ **to ~ sth in/out/away** etc rentrer/sortir/écarter etc qch ◆ **we couldn't ~ him (from his opinion)** nous n'avons pas réussi à le faire changer d'avis or à l'ébranler ◆ **I can't ~ this cold** * je n'arrive pas à me débarrasser de ce rhume

2 (= change, exchange) changer de ◆ **to ~ position** (lit, fig) changer de position ◆ **to ~ gears** changer de vitesse, passer les vitesses ; → **ground¹**

VI 1 (= go) aller ; (= move house) déménager ; (= change position, stir) [person, animal, planet etc] changer de place or de position, bouger ; [limb] remuer, bouger ; [wind] tourner ; [ballast, cargo, load] se déplacer ; [opinions, ideas] changer, se modifier ; [stain] s'en aller, disparaître ◆ **~ (over) a minute to let me past** * pousse-toi or bouge-toi * une minute pour me laisser passer ◆ **~ off the rug** * dégage * du tapis ◆ **can you ~ down or up or along a little?** (on seat etc) pourriez-vous vous pousser un peu ? ◆ **to ~ into second (gear)** passer la deuxième ◆ **he won't ~** il ne bougera pas ◆ **the government has not ~ed from its original position** le gouvernement est resté sur sa première position ◆ **that car certainly ~s** * (= goes fast) elle fonce, cette voiture ! ◆ **come on, ~!** * (= hurry) allez, remue-toi * or grouille-toi * !

2 ◆ **to ~ for o.s.** se débrouiller * tout seul

COMP **shift key** N [of keyboard] touche f de majuscule
shift lock N [of keyboard] touche f de verrouillage des majuscules
shift register N (Comput) registre m à décalage
shift work N (Brit) travail m en or par équipes ; (in factory) travail m posté ◆ **to do ~ work, to be on ~ work** travailler en équipes ; (in factory) faire du travail posté
shift worker N travailleur m, -euse f posté(e)

► **shift about, shift around** VI 1 (= change job) changer souvent d'emploi ; (within same firm) être muté plusieurs fois 2 (= fidget) bouger, remuer
VT SEP [+ furniture etc] déplacer, changer de place

► **shift back** VI (= withdraw) (se) reculer
VT SEP [+ chair etc] reculer

► **shift over** VI s'écarter, se pousser ◆ **~ over!** * pousse-toi !

shiftily /ˈʃɪftɪlɪ/ ADV [say] d'un ton faux ; [tell] sournoisement ; [look] d'un air sournois

shiftiness /ˈʃɪftɪnɪs/ N [of person, behaviour] sournoiserie f ; [of look, eyes] aspect m fuyant ; [of answer] caractère m évasif

shifting /ˈʃɪftɪŋ/ ADJ [winds, currents] variable ; [attitudes, pattern, colours] changeant ; [alliances, population, balance of power] instable
COMP **shifting cultivation** N culture f itinérante
shifting sands NPL (lit) sables mpl mouvants ; (fig) terrain m mouvant

shiftless /ˈʃɪftlɪs/ ADJ (frm) apathique, indolent

shiftlessness /ˈʃɪftlɪsnɪs/ N manque m de ressources

shifty * /ˈʃɪftɪ/ ADJ [person, behaviour] sournois ; [look, eyes] fuyant ; [answer] évasif
COMP **shifty-eyed** * ADJ aux yeux fuyants
shifty-looking * ADJ à l'aspect fuyant

shiitake mushroom /ʃiːˌtækɪˈmʌʃrʊm/ N champignon m shiitaké

Shiite, Shi'ite /ˈʃiːaɪt/ (also **Shiite Muslim**) N, ADJ chiite mf

shiksa, shikse(h) /ˈʃɪksə/ N (esp US: gen pej) jeune fille f goy

shill /ʃɪl/ N (US: at fairground etc) compère m

shillelagh /ʃəˈleɪlə/ N gourdin m irlandais

shilling /ˈʃɪlɪŋ/ N (Brit) shilling m

shilly-shally /ˈʃɪlɪˌʃælɪ/ VI hésiter ; (deliberately) tergiverser, atermoyer ◆ **stop ~ing!** décide-toi enfin ! N ⇒ **shilly-shallying**

shilly-shallying /ˈʃɪlɪˌʃælɪɪŋ/ N (NonC) hésitations fpl, valse-hésitation f ; (deliberate) tergiversations fpl, atermoiements mpl

shimmer /ˈʃɪməʳ/ VI [satin, jewels] chatoyer ; [water, lake, heat haze, road surface] miroiter ◆ **the moonlight ~ed on the lake** le clair de lune faisait miroiter le lac N [of satin, jewels] chatoiement m ; [of water, lake] miroitement m

shimmering /ˈʃɪmərɪŋ/, **shimmery** /ˈʃɪmərɪ/ ADJ [material, jewel] chatoyant ; [water, lake] miroitant ◆ **the ~ moonlight on the lake** le clair de lune qui faisait miroiter le lac

shimmy /ˈʃɪmɪ/ N 1 (US: in car) shimmy m 2 (= dance) shimmy m VI (US) [car] avoir du shimmy

shin /ʃɪn/ N 1 tibia m 2 (Brit Culin) ◆ **of beef** jarret m de bœuf VI ◆ **to ~ up a tree** grimper à un arbre ◆ **to ~ down a tree** descendre d'un arbre ◆ **to ~ over a wall** escalader un mur COMP **shin guard, shin pad** N protège-tibia m

shinbone /ˈʃɪnbəʊn/ N tibia m

shindig * /ˈʃɪndɪg/ N (= dance, party etc) fiesta f, soirée f joyeuse

shindy * /ˈʃɪndɪ/ N 1 (= brawl) bagarre f ; (= row, commotion) tapage m, boucan * m ◆ **to kick up or make a ~** faire du boucan * 2 ⇒ **shindig**

shine /ʃaɪn/ (vb : pret, ptp **shone**) N *[of sun]* éclat *m* ; *[of metal]* éclat *m*, brillant *m* ; *[of shoes]* brillant *m* ◆ **to give sth a ~** faire briller qch, faire reluire qch ◆ **to take the ~ off** *[+ brass, shoes]* rendre mat *or* terne *(pej)* ; *(fig) [+ success, news]* diminuer l'attrait de, faire tomber à plat ; *[+ sb else's achievement]* éclipser ◆ **the ~ on his trousers** son pantalon lustré ◆ **to take a ~ to sb** * se toquer de qn * ; → **moonshine, rain**
VI *[sun, stars, lamp]* briller ; *[metal, shoes]* briller, reluire ; *(fig = excel)* briller ◆ **the sun is shining** il fait (du) soleil, il y a du soleil, le soleil brille ◆ **the moon is shining** il y a clair de lune ◆ **to ~ on sth** éclairer *or* illuminer qch ◆ **the light was shining in my eyes** j'avais la lumière dans les yeux ◆ **her face shone with happiness** son visage rayonnait de bonheur ◆ **her eyes shone with pleasure/envy** ses yeux brillaient de plaisir/luisaient d'envie ◆ **to ~ at football/Spanish** *(fig)* briller *or* faire des étincelles * au football/en espagnol
VT 1 ◆ **~ your torch** *or* **the light over here** éclairez par ici ◆ **he shone his torch on the car** il a braqué sa lampe de poche sur la voiture, il a éclairé la voiture
2 (pret, ptp **shone** *or* **shined**) *[+ furniture, brass, shoes]* astiquer, faire briller
► **shine down** VI *[sun, moon, stars]* briller
► **shine through** VI *[light etc]* passer, filtrer ; *(fig) [courage etc]* transparaître
► **shine up** VI *(US)* ◆ **to shine up to sb** * *(to girl)* faire du plat * à qn ; *(to boss)* faire de la lèche * à qn

shiner /ˈʃaɪnəʳ/ N (‡ *= black eye)* œil *m* au beurre noir *

shingle /ˈʃɪŋgl/ N *(NonC: on beach etc)* galets *mpl* ; *(on roof)* bardeau *m* ; *(coated in tar)* shingle *m* ; *(US * = signboard)* petite enseigne *f (de docteur, de notaire etc)* ; *(† = hairstyle)* coupe *f* à la garçonne VT † *[+ hair]* couper à la garçonne
COMP **shingle beach** N plage *f* de galets

shingles /ˈʃɪŋglz/ N *(NonC)* zona *m* ◆ **to have ~** avoir un zona

shingly /ˈʃɪŋglɪ/ ADJ *[beach]* (couvert) de galets

shininess /ˈʃaɪnɪnɪs/ N éclat *m*, brillant *m*

shining /ˈʃaɪnɪŋ/ ADJ 1 *(= gleaming) [eyes, hair]* brillant ; *[face]* rayonnant ; *[furniture, floor, metal]* luisant 2 *(= outstanding) [success, moment]* remarquable ◆ **she was a ~ example to everyone** c'était un modèle pour tout le monde ◆ **~ light (in sth)** *(fig) (person)* lumière *f* (en qch) ; *(thing)* phare *f* (de qch) ; → **improve**

shinny /ˈʃɪnɪ/ VI ⇒ **shin vi**

Shinto /ˈʃɪntəʊ/ N shinto *m*

Shintoism /ˈʃɪntəʊɪzəm/ N shintoïsme *m*

Shintoist /ˈʃɪntəʊɪst/ ADJ, N shintoïste *mf*

shinty /ˈʃɪntɪ/ N *sorte de hockey sur gazon*

shiny /ˈʃaɪnɪ/ ADJ *[surface, hair, shoes, coin]* brillant ; *[car]* rutilant ; *[furniture, metal, fabric]* luisant ; *[nose]* qui brille (*or* brillait) ◆ **the company's ~ new offices** les nouveaux bureaux rutilants de la société

ship /ʃɪp/ N *(gen)* bateau *m* ; *(large)* navire *m* ; *(= vessel)* vaisseau *m*, bâtiment *m* ◆ **His (***or* **Her) Majesty's Ship Maria/Falcon** la Maria/le Falcon ◆ **the good ~ Caradoc** (†, *liter*) la nef † Caradoc, le Caradoc ◆ **when my ~ comes in** *(fig)* quand j'aurai fait fortune ◆ **he runs** *or* **keeps a tight ~** *(fig)* il ne plaisante pas sur l'organisation (*or* la discipline) ◆ **it was a case of "ships that pass in the night"** ce fut une rencontre sans lendemain ◆ **the ~ of the desert** le vaisseau du désert, le chameau ; → **board, jump, warship**
VT 1 *(= transport)* transporter ; *(= send by ship)* expédier (par bateau) ; *(= send by any means)* expédier ◆ **the goods were ~ped on SS Wallisdown** la marchandise a été expédiée à bord du Wallisdown
2 *(= put or take on board) [+ cargo]* embarquer, charger ; *[+ water]* embarquer ◆ **to ~ the oars** rentrer les avirons
COMP **ship canal** N canal *m* maritime *or* de navigation
ship chandler N ⇒ **ship's chandler**
ship of the line N *(Hist)* bâtiment *m* de ligne
ship's biscuit N *(NonC)* biscuit *m* (de mer)
ship's boat N chaloupe *f*
ship's boy N mousse *m*
ship's chandler N fournisseur *m* d'équipement pour bateaux, shipchandler *m*
ship's company N équipage *m*, hommes *mpl* du bord
ship's papers N papiers *mpl* de bord *or* d'un navire
ship-to-shore radio N liaison *f* radio avec la côte
► **ship off, ship out** VI s'embarquer (*to* pour)
VT SEP 1 *(= send by ship)* [+ *goods, troops etc*] envoyer (par bateau *or* par mer)
2 (* *= send*) *[+ goods, person]* expédier *

shipboard /ˈʃɪpbɔːd/ ADJ *[task]* à bord ; *[personnel]* de bord ◆ **a ~ romance** une histoire d'amour le temps d'une croisière N ◆ **on ~** à bord

shipbuilder /ˈʃɪpˌbɪldəʳ/ N constructeur *m* naval

shipbuilding /ˈʃɪpˌbɪldɪŋ/ N construction *f* navale

shipload /ˈʃɪpləʊd/ N *(lit)* charge *f* ; *(fig)* grande quantité *f*, masse * *f* ◆ **tourists were arriving by the ~** les touristes arrivaient par bateaux entiers

shipmate /ˈʃɪpmeɪt/ N camarade *m* de bord

shipment /ˈʃɪpmənt/ N *(= load)* cargaison *f* ; *(= act of shipping)* expédition *f (par bateau)* ◆ **ready for ~** *(Comm)* prêt à l'expédition

shipowner /ˈʃɪpˌəʊnəʳ/ N armateur *m*

shipper /ˈʃɪpəʳ/ N *(organizing transport)* chargeur *m* ; *(transporter)* expéditeur *m*, affréteur *m*

shipping /ˈʃɪpɪŋ/ N *(NonC)* 1 *(= ships collectively)* navires *mpl* ; *(= traffic)* navigation *f* ◆ **attention all ~!** *(Rad)* avis à la navigation ! ◆ **it was a danger to ~** cela constituait un danger pour la navigation ◆ **the canal is closed to British ~** le canal est fermé aux navires britanniques 2 *(= sending)* expédition *f* ; *(= act of loading)* chargement *m*, embarquement *m* 3 *(= charges for transporting cargo)* frais *mpl* de transport
COMP **shipping agent** N agent *m* maritime
shipping clerk N expéditionnaire *mf*
shipping company N compagnie *f* de navigation
shipping forecast N météo *f* marine
shipping lane N voie *f* de navigation
shipping line N ⇒ **shipping company**
shipping losses NPL ◆ **~ losses during 1944** les pertes en navires au cours de l'année 1944

shipshape /ˈʃɪpʃeɪp/ ADJ bien rangé, en ordre ◆ **all ~ and Bristol fashion** arrangé d'une façon impeccable

shipwreck /ˈʃɪprek/ N *(= event)* naufrage *m* ; *(= wrecked ship)* épave *f* VT *(lit)* faire sombrer ; *(fig)* ruiner, anéantir ◆ **to be ~ed** faire naufrage ◆ **~ed on a desert island** *[vessel]* échoué sur une île déserte ; *[person]* naufragé sur une île déserte ◆ **a ~ed person** un(e) naufragé(e) ◆ **a ~ed sailor/vessel** un marin/vaisseau naufragé

shipwright /ˈʃɪpraɪt/ N *(= builder)* constructeur *m* naval ; *(= carpenter)* charpentier *m* (de chantier naval)

shipyard /ˈʃɪpjɑːd/ N chantier *m* naval

shire /ˈʃaɪəʳ/ N *(Brit)* comté *m* COMP **shire horse** N shire *m* cheval *m* de gros trait

shirk /ʃɜːk/ VT *[+ task, work]* éviter de faire, s'arranger pour ne pas faire ; *[+ obligation, duty]* esquiver, se dérober à ; *[+ difficulty, problem, issue]* éluder, esquiver ◆ **to ~ doing sth** éviter de faire qch, s'arranger pour ne pas faire qch VI tirer au flanc *

shirker /ˈʃɜːkəʳ/ N tire-au-flanc * *mf inv*

shirr /ʃɜːʳ/ VT 1 *(Sewing)* froncer 2 *(US Culin)* **~ed eggs** œufs *mpl* en cocotte *or* au four

shirring /ˈʃɜːrɪŋ/ N fronces *fpl* COMP **shirring elastic** N (fil *m*) élastique *m* à froncer, ≃ Lastex ® *m*

shirt /ʃɜːt/ N *(man's)* chemise *f* ; *(woman's)* chemisier *m* ; *(footballer's etc)* maillot *m* ◆ **keep your ~ on!** ‡ *(fig)* ne vous mettez pas en rogne * *or* en pétard ‡ ! ◆ **to put one's ~ on sth** *(Betting etc)* jouer (toute) sa fortune *or* tout ce qu'on a sur qch ◆ **to lose one's ~** *(Betting etc)* perdre (toute) sa fortune *or* tout ce qu'on a, y laisser sa chemise ; → **boil**[1], **nightshirt, stuff**
COMP **shirt front** N plastron *m*
shirt-lifter *‡ N *(pej)* pédé ‡ *m*
shirt sleeves NPL ◆ **in (one's) ~ sleeves** en bras *or* manches de chemise
shirt-tail N pan *m* de chemise ◆ **in (one's) ~-tails** en chemise
shirt-tail cousin * N *(US)* cousin(e) *m(f)* éloigné(e), cousin(e) *m(f)* à la mode de Bretagne

shirtdress /ˈʃɜːtdres/ N robe *f* chemisier

shirting /ˈʃɜːtɪŋ/ N *(NonC)* shirting *m*

shirtwaist /ˈʃɜːtweɪst/ N *(US)* (*= blouse*) chemisier *m* ; (*= dress*) robe *f* chemisier COMP **shirtwaist(ed) dress** N ⇒ **shirtwaister**

shirtwaister /ˈʃɜːtˌweɪstəʳ/ N robe *f* chemisier

shirty * /ˈʃɜːtɪ/ ADJ *(Brit) [person, reply]* vache * ◆ **to get ~ (with sb) (about sth)** se mettre en rogne * (contre qn) (à propos de qch)

shish kebab /ˈʃiːʃkəˈbæb/ N chiche-kebab *m*

shit *‡ /ʃɪt/ (vb : pret, ptp **shat**) N 1 *(lit, fig) (= excrement, rubbish)* merde *‡ *f* ; *(= nonsense)* conneries ‡ *fpl* ◆ **~!** merde ! ‡ ◆ **no ~?** sans blague ? * ◆ **to be in the ~** être dans la merde *‡ ◆ **in deep ~** dans la merde *‡ jusqu'au cou ◆ **don't give me that ~!** arrête de déconner ! ‡ ◆ **to have** *or* **take a ~** chier *‡ un coup ◆ **I don't give a ~!** j'en ai rien à branler ! *‡, je m'en contrefous ! ‡ *(about de)* ◆ **to scare the ~ out of sb** flanquer une de ces trouilles * à qn ◆ **to beat** *or* **kick** *or* **knock the ~ out of sb** passer qn à tabac *, dérouiller qn ‡ ◆ **then the ~ really hit the fan** alors ça a bardé * *or* chié *‡
2 *(= person)* salaud ‡ *m*
3 *(Drugs = resin)* shit *m*
VI chier *‡ ◆ **it's time to ~ or get off the pot** *(US)* il est temps de s'y mettre ou bien de passer la main
VT 1 *(lit, fig)* **to ~ o.s.** chier *‡ dans son froc ◆ **to ~ a brick** *or* **bricks** chier *‡ *or* faire dans son froc
2 *(US = talk nonsense to)* raconter des conneries ‡ à ◆ **you're ~ting me** tu déconnes ‡
ADJ merdique ‡, nul à chier *‡
COMP **shit-hole** *‡ N endroit *m* de merde *‡
shit-hot *‡ ADJ vachement bon ‡
shit-scared *‡ ADJ ◆ **to be ~-scared** avoir une trouille bleue ‡
shit-stirrer *‡ N fouteur *m*, -euse *f* de merde *‡

shite *‡ /ʃaɪt/ N *(Brit)* merde *‡ *f*

shitface *‡ /ˈʃɪtfeɪs/ N ⇒ **shithead**

shitfaced *‡ /ˈʃɪtfeɪst/ ADJ pété ‡, cassé ‡

shithead *‡ /ˈʃɪthed/ N connard ‡ *m*, connasse ‡ *f*

shithouse *‡ /ˈʃɪthaʊs/ N *(= lavatory)* chiottes ‡ *fpl* ◆ **this ~ of a country** ce pays de merde *‡ ; → **built**

shitless** /ˈʃɪtlɪs/ ADJ ◆ **to scare sb ~** flanquer une de ces trouilles* à qn ◆ **to be scared ~** avoir une peur bleue* ◆ **to bore sb ~** casser les couilles à qn** ◆ **to be bored ~** se faire chier**

shitlist** /ˈʃɪtlɪst/ N liste f noire

shitload** /ˈʃɪtləʊd/ N ◆ **a ~** or **~s of sth** (= lots) des tonnes de qch* ◆ **a ~ of trouble** un merdier pas possible**

shitty** /ˈʃɪtɪ/ ADJ *[person, mood, food]* dégueulasse*; *[place, job]* merdique* ◆ **what a ~ thing to do/say!** c'est dégueulasse* de faire/dire ça !

shitwork** /ˈʃɪtwɜːk/ N (NonC: US) boulot m merdique*

shiver¹ /ˈʃɪvəʳ/ VI (*with cold, fear*) frissonner, trembler (*with* de) ; (*with pleasure*) frissonner, tressaillir (*with* de) → **boot¹**, **shoe** N (*from cold*) frisson m ; (*from fear, pleasure*) frisson m, tressaillement m ◆ **it sent ~s down his spine** cela lui a donné froid dans le dos ◆ **he gave a ~** il a frissonné, il a eu un frisson ◆ **to give sb the ~s** donner le frisson à qn

shiver² /ˈʃɪvəʳ/ N (= *fragment*) éclat m, fragment m VI (= *shatter*) voler en éclats, se fracasser VT fracasser ◆ **~ my timbers!** mille sabords !

shivery /ˈʃɪvərɪ/ ADJ (*from cold*) frissonnant, grelottant ; (*from emotion, fever*) frissonnant, tremblant

shoal¹ /ʃəʊl/ N [*of fish*] banc m (*de poissons*) ◆ **~s of applications** une avalanche de demandes

shoal² /ʃəʊl/ N (= *shallows*) haut-fond m, basfond m ; (= *sandbank*) banc m de sable, écueil m

shock¹ /ʃɒk/ N 1 (= *impact*) [*of collision etc*] choc m, heurt m ; [*of earthquake, explosion*] secousse f
2 (*Elec*) décharge f (électrique) ◆ **to get a ~** recevoir une décharge (électrique), prendre le jus* ◆ **she got a ~ from the refrigerator, the refrigerator gave her a ~** elle a reçu une décharge en touchant le réfrigérateur
3 (*to sensibilities etc*) choc m, coup m ; (= *feeling, emotion*) horreur f ◆ **he got such a ~ when he heard that ...** cela lui a donné un tel choc or coup d'apprendre que ... ◆ **he hasn't yet got over the ~ of her death** il ne s'est pas encore remis du choc que lui a causé sa mort ◆ **the ~ killed him** le choc l'a tué ◆ **the ~ of the election results** les résultats mpl stupéfiants des élections ◆ **their refusal came as a ~ to me** leur refus m'a stupéfié or ébahi ◆ **it comes as a ~ to hear that ...** il est stupéfiant d'apprendre que ... ◆ **you gave me a ~!** vous m'avez fait peur ! ◆ **I got such a ~!** j'en étais tout retourné !* ◆ **~ horror!*** (*hum*) quelle horreur ! ; ◆ **pale with ~** pâle de saisissement ◆ **my feeling is one of ~ at the idea that ...** j'éprouve un sentiment d'horreur à l'idée que ..., je suis bouleversé à l'idée que ...
4 (*Med*) commotion f, choc m ◆ **anaphylactic ~** choc m anaphylactique ◆ **to be suffering from ~** être en état de choc, être commotionné ◆ **in a state of ~** en état de choc, commotionné ; → **shell**
NPL **shocks** * (*US* = *shock absorbers*) amortisseurs mpl
ADJ [*defeat, victory, news, resignation, decision*] surprise
VT 1 (= *take aback*) secouer, retourner* ; (*stronger*) bouleverser ; (= *disgust*) dégoûter ; (= *scandalize*) choquer, scandaliser ◆ **to ~ sb out of his complacency** déstabiliser qn ◆ **he's easily ~ed** il se choque facilement or pour un rien
2 (*Culin*) plonger dans de l'eau glacée
COMP [*tactics*] de choc
shock absorber N amortisseur m
shock-horror* ADJ [*story, film*] d'épouvante ; [*headline*] sensationnel, à sensation
shock jock* N (*esp US*) *présentateur de radio qui cherche à provoquer de vives controverses en exprimant des opinions extrémistes*
shock resistant ADJ résistant aux chocs
shock therapy, shock treatment N (*Med*) (traitement m par) électrochoc m
shock troops NPL troupes fpl de choc
shock wave N (*Phys*) onde f de choc ◆ **the news sent ~ waves through Congress** la nouvelle a provoqué de vifs remous au sein du Congrès

shock² /ʃɒk/ N ◆ **a ~ of hair** une tignasse*

shocked /ʃɒkt/ ADJ 1 (= *unpleasantly surprised*) [*person, voice, expression, face*] abasourdi (*at sth* par qch) ; [*reaction*] choqué ◆ **a ~ silence** un silence consterné ◆ **to listen in ~ silence** écouter muet de stupéfaction ◆ **~ to see/hear/learn sth** abasourdi de voir/d'entendre/d'apprendre qch 2 (= *scandalized*) choqué 3 (*Med*) commotionné

shocker* /ˈʃɒkəʳ/ N 1 **he's a ~** il est impossible or imbuvable* ◆ **last week was a ~** (= *stressful*) j'ai eu une semaine affreuse 2 (= *cheap book*) livre m à sensation

shocking /ˈʃɒkɪŋ/ ADJ 1 (= *scandalous*) [*act, behaviour, book*] choquant, scandaleux ; [*sight*] choquant, atroce ; [*decision, waste of money*] scandaleux ; [*price*] scandaleux, exorbitant ; [*murder, cruelty*] odieux, atroce ; [*crime*] odieux, atroce, affreux ; [*news*] atroce, bouleversant ◆ **the film wasn't really ~** le film n'avait rien de vraiment choquant ◆ **it may be ~ to the older generation** cela pourrait choquer les générations plus âgées ◆ **it is ~ to think that ...** il est scandaleux de penser que ... + *subj* ◆ **it is ~ that ...** il est scandaleux que ... + *subj* ◆ **the ~ truth** la terrible vérité 2 (*Brit* * = *dreadful*) [*weather, results, cold, cough*] affreux, épouvantable ; [*quality, handwriting*] épouvantable ◆ **in a ~ state** dans un état épouvantable COMP **shocking pink** ADJ, N rose m shocking inv

shockingly /ˈʃɒkɪŋlɪ/ ADV 1 (= *disturbingly*) [*effective, frank*] terriblement ◆ **~, children are more likely to be killed in an accident in the home** chose terrible, un enfant a plus de chances d'être tué dans un accident domestique 2 (* = *badly*) [*play, act*] de façon lamentable ; [*behave*] affreusement mal ; (= *scandalously*) scandaleusement, de façon choquante 3 (*Brit* * = *extremely*) [*bad, unfair, expensive, difficult*] terriblement, affreusement

shockproof /ˈʃɒkpruːf/ ADJ (*lit*) antichoc inv ; (* fig) [*person*] difficile à choquer

shod /ʃɒd/ VB pt, ptp of **shoe**

shoddily /ˈʃɒdɪlɪ/ (*pej*) ADV [*made, built*] mal ; [*behave, treat*] très mal

shoddiness /ˈʃɒdɪnɪs/ N [*of work, goods*] mauvaise qualité f ; [*of behaviour*] bassesse f, mesquinerie f

shoddy /ˈʃɒdɪ/ ADJ (*pej*) [*workmanship, goods*] de mauvaise qualité ; [*service*] de mauvaise qualité, mauvais ; [*treatment*] indigne ; [*behaviour, attempt*] mesquin ; [*building*] miteux N (= *cloth*) lirette f

shoe /ʃuː/ (vb : pret, ptp **shod**) N chaussure f ; (= *horseshoe*) fer m (à cheval) ; (= *brake shoe*) sabot m (de frein) ◆ **to have one's ~s on/off** être chaussé/déchaussé ◆ **to put on one's ~s** mettre ses chaussures, se chausser ◆ **to take off one's ~s** enlever ses chaussures, se déchausser ◆ **to quake** or **shake** or **tremble** or **shiver in one's ~s** (*fig*) avoir une peur bleue ◆ **I wouldn't like to be in his ~s** (*fig*) je n'aimerais pas être à sa place ◆ **to step into** or **fill sb's ~s** (*fig*) succéder à qn ◆ **he's waiting for dead men's ~s** il attend que quelqu'un meure pour prendre sa place ◆ **you'll know where the ~ pinches when ...** (*fig*) vous vous trouverez serré or à court quand ... ◆ **that's another pair of ~s** (*fig*) c'est une autre paire de manches ◆ **that's where the ~ pinches** c'est là que le bât blesse ◆ **to drop the other ~** (*US fig*) finir ce que l'on a commencé ◆ **if the ~ fits, wear it** (*US*) qui se sent morveux (qu'il) se mouche, il n'y a que la vérité qui blesse ; → **court**
VT [*+ horse*] ferrer ◆ **to be well/badly shod** [*person*] être bien/mal chaussé ◆ **the cobbler's children are always the worst shod** (*Prov*) ce sont les cordonniers qui sont les plus mal chaussés (*Prov*)
COMP **shoe cream** N crème f pour chaussures
shoe leather N cuir m pour chaussures ◆ **I wore out a lot of ~ leather, it cost me a lot in ~ leather** ça m'est revenu cher en chaussures, j'ai dû faire des kilomètres à pied
shoe polish N cirage m
shoe repairer N cordonnier m ◆ **~ repairer's (shop)** cordonnerie f
shoe repairing N (*NonC*) cordonnerie f
shoe repairs NPL cordonnerie f
shoe size N pointure f ◆ **what ~ size are you?** quelle est votre pointure ?, quelle pointure faites-vous ?

shoeblack † /ˈʃuːblæk/ N cireur m, -euse f de chaussures

shoebrush /ˈʃuːbrʌʃ/ N brosse f à chaussures

shoehorn /ˈʃuːhɔːn/ N chausse-pied m VT ◆ **the cars are ~ed into tiny spaces** les voitures sont casées dans des emplacements minuscules ◆ **I was ~ing myself into a skin-tight ball gown** j'enfilais non sans mal une robe de bal moulante

shoelace /ˈʃuːleɪs/ N lacet m (de chaussure) ◆ **you are not fit** or **worthy to tie his ~s** vous n'êtes pas digne de délier le cordon de ses souliers

shoemaker /ˈʃuːˌmeɪkəʳ/ N (= *cobbler*) cordonnier m ; (= *manufacturer*) fabricant m de chaussures ; (= *shoeshop owner*) chausseur m COMP **shoemaker's shop** N cordonnerie f

shoeshine boy /ˈʃuːʃaɪnˈbɔɪ/ N cireur m de chaussures

shoeshop /ˈʃuːʃɒp/ N magasin m de chaussures

shoestring /ˈʃuːstrɪŋ/ N (*US: lit*) ⇒ **shoelace** ◆ **to do sth on a ~** faire qch à peu de frais or avec peu d'argent ◆ **they're living on a ~** ils sont gênés, ils doivent se serrer la ceinture* COMP **shoestring budget** N budget m minime or infime

shoetree /ˈʃuːtriː/ N embauchoir m

shone /ʃɒn/ VB pt, ptp of **shine**

shoo /ʃuː/ EXCL (*to animals*) pschtt ! ; (*to person*) ouste !* VT (also **shoo away, shoo off**) chasser COMP **shoo-in*** N (*US*) ◆ **it's a ~-in** c'est du tout cuit*, c'est du gâteau* ◆ **the president looks a ~-in for a second term** le président sera réélu à coup sûr

shook /ʃʊk/ VB pt of **shake** COMP **shook-up*** ADJ ◆ **to be ~-up about sth** être secoué par qch ◆ **a ~-up generation** une génération de paumés*

shoot /ʃuːt/ (vb : pret, ptp **shot**) N 1 (*on branch etc*) pousse f, rejeton m (*Bio*) ; (= *seedling*) pousse f
2 (= *chute*) glissière f, déversoir m
3 (= *shooting party*) partie f de chasse ; (= *land*) (terrain m de) chasse f ◆ **the whole (bang) ~*** (= *all of them*) tout le tremblement*
4 (= *photo assignment*) séance f (de photos) ; (= *filming session*) séance f (de tournage)
5 (*expletive*) **~!*** zut !*, mercredi !*
VT 1 [*+ animal*] (= *hunt*) chasser ; (= *kill*) abattre, tirer ; [*+ injured horse etc*] abattre ; [*+ person*] (= *hit*) atteindre d'un coup de feu ; (= *wound*) blesser par balle(s) ; (= *kill*) tuer par balle(s), abattre ; (= *execute*) fusiller ◆ **~ him!** tire !, descends-le !* ◆ **to be shot in the head** être atteint d'une balle dans la tête ◆ **he had been shot through the heart** il avait reçu une balle en plein cœur ◆ **to ~ sb dead** abattre qn ◆ **he was shot as a spy** il a été fusillé pour espionnage ◆ **people have been shot for less!** (*hum*)

on en a tué pour moins que ça ! ◆ **you'll get shot for that!** * *(hum)* tu vas te faire incendier pour ça ! * ◆ **to ~ from the hip** *(lit)* tirer l'arme à la hanche ; *(fig) (challenging sb)* attaquer impulsivement ; *(answering sb)* riposter impulsivement ◆ **to ~ the lights** griller *or* brûler le feu rouge ◆ **to ~ o.s. in the foot** * *(fig)* se tirer une balle dans le pied *(fig)* ◆ **it's a case of ~ the messenger** c'est se tromper de cible ◆ **it's like ~ing fish in a barrel** * c'est un combat gagné d'avance

2 *(= fire)* *[+ gun]* tirer un coup de *(at* sur) ; *[+ arrow]* décocher, tirer *(at* sur) ; *[+ bullet]* tirer *(at* sur) ; *[+ rocket, missile]* lancer *(at* sur) ; ◆ **the volcano shot lava high into the air** le volcan projetait de la lave dans les airs ◆ **to ~ a goal, to ~ the ball into the net** marquer un but ◆ **he shot the bolt** *(fastened)* il a mis *or* poussé le verrou ; *(opened)* il a tiré le verrou ◆ **he has shot his bolt** *(fig)* il a joué sa dernière carte, il a brûlé ses dernières cartouches ◆ **to ~ the breeze** * *(US)* bavarder ◆ **to ~ the bull** ‡ *(US)* raconter des conneries ‡ ◆ **to ~ a line** ‡ faire de l'épate *, en mettre plein la vue * ◆ **to ~ a line about sth** ‡ *(Brit)* raconter des histoires *or* des bobards * à propos de qch ◆ **to ~ the works** * **on sth** *(US = spend all)* claquer * tout son argent pour acheter qch ◆ **to ~ dice** jeter les dés ◆ **to ~ (for) the moon** viser (très) haut ; → **pool²**

3 *(= direct)* *[+ look, glance]* décocher, lancer *(at* à) ; *[sun]* *[+ ray of light]* darder ◆ **he shot her a smile** il lui a lancé *or* décoché un sourire ◆ **to ~ questions at sb** bombarder *or* mitrailler qn de questions

4 *(Cine etc)* *[+ film, scene]* tourner ; *[+ subject of snapshot etc]* prendre (en photo)

5 *[+ rapids]* franchir, descendre ; *[+ bridge]* passer rapidement sous

6 * *(= send)* envoyer, expédier ; *(= give)* donner ; *(= throw)* jeter, flanquer *

7 *(Drugs)* **to ~ heroin** * se shooter * à l'héroïne

VI 1 *(with gun, bow)* tirer *(at* sur) ; *(Sport: at target)* tirer (à la cible) ◆ **to go ~ing** *(Brit = hunt)* chasser, aller à la chasse ◆ **to ~ to disable/kill** tirer pour blesser/tuer ◆ **to ~ on sight** tirer à vue ◆ **he can't ~ straight** il tire mal *or* comme un pied * ◆ **they're both ~ing for** *or* **at the same target** *(fig)* ils travaillent de concert

2 *(= move quickly)* **to ~ in/out/past** *etc* *[person, car, ball etc]* entrer/sortir/passer *etc* en flèche ◆ **to ~ along** filer ◆ **he shot to the door** il s'est précipité vers la porte ◆ **to ~ to fame/stardom** devenir très vite célèbre/une star ◆ **the car shot out of a side street** la voiture a débouché à toute vitesse d'une rue transversale ◆ **he shot across the road** il a traversé la rue comme une flèche ◆ **the bullet shot past his ears** la balle lui a sifflé aux oreilles ◆ **the cat shot up the tree** le chat a grimpé à l'arbre à toute vitesse ◆ **the pain went ~ing up his arm** la douleur au bras le lancinait, son bras l'élançait ◆ **he has shot ahead in the last few weeks** *(in class etc)* il a fait des progrès énormes depuis quelques semaines

3 *(Ftbl etc)* shooter, tirer ◆ **to ~ at goal** shooter, faire un shoot ◆ **~!** ‡ *(in conversation)* vas-y !, dis ce que tu as à dire !

4 *(Bot)* bourgeonner, pousser

COMP shoot-'em-up * **N** *(Cine)* film *m* de violence ; *(= video game)* jeu *m* vidéo violent

shoot-out N *(= fight)* fusillade *f* ; *(Ftbl)* épreuve *f* des tirs au but

shoot-the-chute N *(US)* toboggan *m* *(appareil de manutention)*

shoot-to-kill ADJ *[policy]* qui consiste à tirer avec l'intention de tuer

► **shoot away VI** 1 *(Mil etc = fire)* continuer à tirer, tirer sans arrêt

2 *(= move)* partir comme une flèche, s'enfuir à toutes jambes

VT SEP ⇒ **shoot off vt sep 2**

► **shoot back VI** 1 *(Mil etc)* retourner le *(or* son *etc)* feu *(at* à)

2 *(= move)* retourner *or* rentrer *or* revenir en flèche

► **shoot down VT SEP** 1 *[+ plane]* abattre, descendre ◆ **he was shot down in flames** *[pilot]* son avion s'est abattu en flammes ◆ **to ~ down in flames** * *[+ project]* démolir ; *[+ person]* descendre en flammes *

2 *(= kill)* *[+ person]* abattre, descendre *

► **shoot off VI** ⇒ **shoot away vi 2**

VT SEP 1 *[+ gun]* décharger, faire partir ◆ **he's always ~ing his mouth off** ‡ *(fig)* il faut toujours qu'il ouvre *subj* le bec * *or* sa grande gueule ‡ ◆ **to ~ one's mouth off about sth** ‡ raconter des histoires *or* des bobards * au sujet de qch

2 ◆ **he had a leg shot off** il a eu une jambe emportée par un éclat d'obus

► **shoot out VI** *[person, car etc]* sortir comme une flèche ; *[flame, water]* jaillir

VT SEP 1 ◆ **to shoot out one's tongue** *[person]* tirer la langue ; *[snake]* darder sa langue ◆ **he shot out his arm and grabbed my stick** il a avancé brusquement le bras et a attrapé ma canne ◆ **he was shot out of the car** il a été éjecté de la voiture

2 ◆ **to shoot it out** avoir un règlement de compte (à coups de revolvers *or* de fusils), s'expliquer à coups de revolvers *or* de fusils

N ◆ **shoot-out** * → **shoot**

► **shoot up VI** 1 *[flame, water]* jaillir ; *[rocket, price etc]* monter en flèche

2 *(= grow quickly)* *[tree, plant]* pousser vite ; *[child]* bien pousser *

3 *(Drugs *)* se shooter *

VT SEP (*: *with gun)* flinguer ‡, tirer sur

ADJ ◆ **shot up** ‡ → **shot adj 4**

shooter /ˈʃuːtəʳ/ **N** 1 (‡ *= gun)* flingue * *m* 2 *(also* **target shooter***)* *personne qui pratique le tir* ; → **peashooter, sharpshooter, six, troubleshooter**

shooting /ˈʃuːtɪŋ/ **N** 1 *(NonC = shots)* coups *mpl* de feu ; *(continuous)* fusillade *f* ◆ **I heard some ~ over there** j'ai entendu des coups de feu par là-bas ◆ **the ~ caused ten deaths** la fusillade a fait dix morts

2 *(= act) (murder)* meurtre *m or* assassinat *m* (avec une arme à feu) ; *(execution)* fusillade *f*, exécution *f* ◆ **the ~ of a policeman in the main street** le meurtre d'un agent de police abattu dans la grand-rue

3 *(esp Brit = hunting)* chasse *f* ◆ **rabbit ~** la chasse au lapin ◆ **there's good ~ there** il y a une bonne chasse là-bas

4 *(Cine)* *[of film, scene]* tournage *m*

ADJ *[pain]* lancinant

COMP shooting brake † **N** *(Brit = car)* break *m*

shooting-down N ◆ **the ~-down of the diplomat** l'attentat *m* à l'arme à feu contre le diplomate ◆ **the ~-down of the plane (by the enemy)** la perte *or* la destruction de l'avion (abattu par l'ennemi)

shooting gallery N tir *m*, stand *m* (de tir)

shooting incident N ◆ **there were a few ~ incidents last night** la nuit dernière il y a eu quelques échanges de coups de feu

shooting iron † ‡ **N** *(US)* flingue * *m*

shooting match * **N** *(Brit fig)* ◆ **the whole ~ match** tout le bataclan *, tout le tremblement *

shooting party N partie *f* de chasse

shooting range N tir *m*, stand *m* (de tir) ◆ **within ~ range** à portée (de tir)

shooting script N *(Cine)* découpage *m*

shooting spree N ◆ **to go on a ~ spree** être pris d'un accès *or* d'une crise de folie meurtrière

shooting star N étoile *f* filante

shooting stick N canne-siège *f*

shooting war N lutte *f* armée

shop /ʃɒp/ **N** 1 *(esp Brit Comm)* magasin *m* ; *(small)* boutique *f* ◆ **wine ~** marchand *m* de vins ◆ **at the butcher's ~** à la boucherie, chez le boucher ◆ **"The Toy Shop"** "la Maison du Jouet" ◆ **mobile** *or* **travelling ~** épicerie *f etc* roulante ◆ **he's just gone (round) to the ~s** il est juste sorti faire des courses ◆ **to set up ~** *(lit, fig)* s'établir, s'installer ◆ **to shut up ~** *(lit, fig)* fermer boutique ◆ **you've come to the wrong ~** * *(fig)* tu te trompes d'adresse * *(fig)* ◆ **to talk ~** *(fig)* parler boutique *or* affaires ◆ **all over the ~** * *(= everywhere)* partout ; *(= in confusion)* en désordre, bordélique * ; → **back, corner, grocer**

2 *(Brit = shopping)* ◆ **to do one's weekly ~** faire ses courses de la semaine

3 *(= workshop)* atelier *m*

4 *(= part of factory)* atelier *m* ◆ **assembly ~** atelier *m* de montage ; → **closed, machine**

VI ◆ **to ~ at Harrods** faire ses courses *or* ses achats chez Harrods ◆ **"shop at Brown's"** *(sign)* "achetez chez Brown" ◆ **to go ~ping** *(specific errands)* faire les courses ; *(leisurely browsing)* faire les magasins, faire du shopping * ◆ **I was ~ping for a winter coat** je cherchais un manteau d'hiver ◆ **she's ~ping for a husband/a new sales director** elle cherche un mari/un nouveau directeur des ventes

VT *(esp Brit* ‡ *= betray)* vendre, donner *

COMP *(= bought in shop)* *[cakes etc]* acheté dans le commerce

shop assistant N *(Brit)* vendeur *m*, -euse *f*, employé(e) *m(f)* (de magasin)

the shop floor N *(Brit = place)* l'atelier *m* ; *(= workers)* les ouvriers *mpl* ◆ **he works on the ~ floor** c'est un ouvrier

shop front N *(Brit)* devanture *f*

shop steward N *(Brit)* délégué(e) *m(f)* syndical(e)

shop talk * **N** *(= jargon)* jargon *m* (de métier) ◆ **I'm getting tired of ~ talk** je commence à en avoir assez de parler affaires *or* boulot *

shop window N vitrine *f*

► **shop around VI** *(= go around shops)* faire les magasins ; *(= compare prices)* comparer les prix ◆ **to ~ around for sth** faire les magasins *or* comparer les prix avant d'acheter qch ◆ **it's worth ~ping around before you decide on a university** ça vaut la peine de comparer *or* se renseigner avant de choisir une université

shopaholic * /ˌʃɒpəˈhɒlɪk/ **N** accro *mf* du shopping *

shopfitter /ˈʃɒpˌfɪtəʳ/ **N** *(esp Brit)* décorateur *m* de magasin

shopgirl /ˈʃɒpgɜːl/ **N** *(Brit)* vendeuse *f*

shopkeeper /ˈʃɒpˌkiːpəʳ/ **N** commerçant(e) *m(f)*, marchand(e) *m(f)* ◆ **small ~** petit commerçant *m*

shoplift /ˈʃɒplɪft/ **VTI** voler à l'étalage

shoplifter /ˈʃɒpˌlɪftəʳ/ **N** voleur *m*, -euse *f* à l'étalage

shoplifting /ˈʃɒpˌlɪftɪŋ/ **N** *(NonC)* vol *m* à l'étalage

shopper /ˈʃɒpəʳ/ **N** 1 *(= person)* personne *f* qui fait ses courses ; *(= customer)* client(e) *m(f)* 2 *(= bag)* sac *m* (à provisions), cabas *m* ; *(on wheels)* caddie ® *m*

shopping /ˈʃɒpɪŋ/ **N** *(NonC)* 1 courses *fpl* ◆ **to do the/some ~** faire les/des courses ◆ **~ is very tiring** faire les courses est très fatigant ◆ **"open Thursdays for late evening shopping"** "ouvert le jeudi en nocturne", "nocturne le jeudi" ; → **mall, window, shop**

2 *(= goods)* achats *mpl*

COMP *[street, district]* commerçant

shopping bag N sac *m* (à provisions), cabas *m*

shopping basket N panier *m* (à provisions)

shopping cart N (US) ⇒ **shopping trolley**
shopping centre N centre *m* commercial
shopping channel N chaîne *f* de téléachat
shopping complex N ⇒ **shopping centre**
shopping list N liste *f* de(s) courses ◆ **a ~ list of requests/demands** une liste de requêtes/ revendications
shopping mall N centre *m* commercial
shopping precinct N *(Brit)* zone *f* commerciale (piétonnière)
shopping spree N ◆ **to go on a ~ spree** aller faire du shopping
shopping trip N ◆ **to go on a ~ trip** partir faire les magasins *or* les boutiques
shopping trolley N *(Brit)* caddie ® *m*

shopsoiled /ˈʃɒpsɔɪld/ ADJ *(Brit)* qui a fait l'étalage *or* la vitrine, défraîchi

shopwalker † /ˈʃɒpˌwɔːkəʳ/ N *(Brit)* chef *m* de rayon

shopworn /ˈʃɒpwɔːn/ ADJ *(US)* ⇒ **shopsoiled**

shore¹ /ʃɔːʳ/ N *[of sea]* rivage *m*, bord *m* ; *[of lake]* rive *f*, bord *m* ; *(= coast)* côte *f*, littoral *m* ; *(= beach)* plage *f* ◆ **these ~s** *(fig liter)* ces rives ◆ **on ~** *(esp Naut)* à terre ◆ **to go on ~** *(Naut)* débarquer
COMP **shore leave** N *(Naut)* permission *f* à terre
shore patrol N *(US Navy)* détachement *m* de police militaire (de la Marine)

shore² /ʃɔːʳ/ N *(for wall, tunnel)* étai *m*, étançon *m* ; *(for tree)* étai *m* ; *(for ship)* accore *m*, étançon *m* VT étayer, étançonner, accorer
► **shore up** VT SEP 1 ⇒ **shore²** vt 2 *(fig)* consolider

shoreline /ˈʃɔːlaɪn/ N littoral *m*

shoreward(s) /ˈʃɔːwəd(z)/ ADJ, ADV *(from sea)* vers le rivage *or* la côte ; *(from river, lake)* vers la rive

shorn /ʃɔːn/ VB ptp of **shear**

short /ʃɔːt/

LANGUAGE IN USE 26.2

1 ADJECTIVE
2 ADVERB
3 NOUN
4 PLURAL NOUN
5 TRANSITIVE VERB
6 INTRANSITIVE VERB
7 COMPOUNDS

1 - ADJECTIVE

1 size, distance court ; *[person] (= not tall)* petit, de petite taille ; *[step, walk]* petit ; *[visit, message, conversation]* court, bref ; *[programme]* court ◆ **the ~est route** le chemin le plus court ◆ **the ~est distance between two points** le plus court chemin d'un point à un autre ◆ **a ~ distance away, a ~ way off** à peu de distance, à une faible distance ◆ **he's got rather ~ legs** *[person]* il a les jambes plutôt courtes ; *[dog etc]* il est plutôt court sur pattes ◆ **these trousers are ~ in the leg** ce pantalon est court de jambes ◆ **~ ski** *(Ski)* ski *m* court ; see also **compounds** ◆ **make the skirt ~er** raccourcis la jupe ◆ **the ~ answer is that he ...** *(fig)* tout simplement il ... ◆ **I'd like a ~ word** *or* **a few ~ words with you** j'aimerais vous dire un mot ◆ **~ and to the point** bref et précis ◆ **that was ~ and sweet** *(hum)* ça n'a pas traîné *(hum)*, ça a été du vite fait* ◆ **to have sb by the ~ hairs**‡ *or* **~ and curlies**‡ tenir qn à la gorge *or* par les couilles*‡ ◆ **he got the ~ end of the stick** c'est lui qui en a pâti ◆ **to win by a ~ head** *(Racing)* gagner d'une courte tête ; *(fig)* gagner de justesse ◆ **to make ~ work of sth** ne pas mettre beaucoup de temps à faire qch ◆ **to make ~ work of sb*** envoyer promener qn* ; → **shrift, story, term**

2 period, time ◆ **a ~ time** *or* **while ago** il y a peu de temps ◆ **in a ~ time** *or* **while** dans peu de temps, bientôt ◆ **time is getting ~** il ne reste plus beaucoup de temps ◆ **the days are getting ~er** les jours raccourcissent ◆ **one ~ year of happiness** une petite *or* brève année de bonheur ◆ **to take a ~ holiday** prendre quelques jours de vacances ◆ **~er hours and better pay** une réduction du temps de travail et une augmentation de salaire ◆ **they want a ~er working week** ils veulent réduire la durée du travail hebdomadaire ◆ **to be on ~ time, to work ~ time** être au chômage partiel ; see also **compounds** ◆ **to put sb on ~ time** mettre qn au chômage partiel ; → **notice**

◆ **in short** en bref

3 Ling *[vowel, syllable]* bref

4 = abbreviated ◆ **"TV" is ~ for "television"** "TV" est l'abréviation de "télévision" ◆ **Fred is ~ for Frederick** Fred est le diminutif de Frederick ◆ **he's called Fred for ~** son diminutif est Fred

5 = lacking **I'm a bit ~ this month*** je suis un peu fauché* *or* à court ce mois-ci ◆ **petrol is ~** *or* **in ~ supply at the moment** on manque d'essence en ce moment ◆ **to give sb ~ change** ne pas rendre la monnaie juste à qn, ne pas rendre assez à qn ; *(deliberately)* tricher en rendant la monnaie à qn ◆ **to give ~ weight** *or* **measure** ne pas donner le poids juste ; *(deliberately)* tricher sur le poids ; → **commons**

◆ **to be short of sth** *(= lack)* manquer de qch ◆ **we are £2,000 ~ of our target** il nous manque encore 2 000 livres pour atteindre notre objectif ◆ **he's one sandwich ~ of a picnic** *or* **several cards ~ of a full deck*** il lui manque une case*, il a une case vide* ◆ **we're not ~ of volunteers** nous ne manquons pas de volontaires ◆ **to be ~ of sugar** être à court de sucre, manquer de sucre ; → **breath**

◆ **to be short on sth** manquer de qch ◆ **the report is ~ on details** le rapport manque de détails ◆ **he's long on muscle but a bit ~ on brains*** *(hum)* il a beaucoup de muscle mais pas tellement de cervelle

6 = curt *[reply, manner]* brusque, sec (sèche *f*) ◆ **he was rather ~ with me** il a été assez sec *or* brusque avec moi

7 Fin *[bill]* à courte échéance ; *[loan]* à court terme ◆ **~ sale** vente *f* à découvert

2 - ADVERB

1 **to take sb up ~** couper la parole à qn ◆ **to be taken** *or* **caught ~*** être pris d'un besoin pressant ; → **bring up, cut**

◆ **to fall + short** ◆ **the ball fell ~** le ballon n'est pas tombé assez loin ◆ **his work fell ~ of what we had expected** son travail n'a pas répondu à notre attente ◆ **the copy fell far ~ of the original** la copie était loin de valoir l'original ◆ **to fall ~ of perfection** ne pas atteindre la perfection

◆ **to stop short** ◆ **the car stopped ~ of the house** la voiture s'est arrêtée avant (d'arriver au niveau de) la maison ◆ **I'd stop ~ of murder** je n'irais pas jusqu'au meurtre

2 = lacking **we're three ~** il nous en manque trois ◆ **I'm £2 ~** il me manque 2 livres ; → **sell**

◆ **to go short** ◆ **we never went ~** nous n'avons jamais manqué du nécessaire ◆ **to go ~ of sth** *(= lack sth)* manquer de qch ; *(= deprive o.s. of sth)* se priver de qch

◆ **to run short** ◆ **supplies are running ~** les provisions s'épuisent *or* commencent à manquer ◆ **to run ~ of sth** se trouver à court de qch, venir à manquer de qch

◆ **short of** *(= less than)* moins de, en dessous de ; *(= except)* sauf ; *(= before)* avant ◆ **£10 ~ of what they needed** 10 livres de moins que ce dont ils avaient besoin ◆ **it's well ~ of the truth** c'est bien en deçà de la vérité ◆ **a week ~ of their arrival/his birthday** *etc* une semaine avant leur arrivée/son anniversaire *etc* ◆ **not far ~ of £100** pas loin de 100 livres, presque 100 livres ◆ **he fell down 10 metres ~ of the winning post** il est tombé à 10 mètres du poteau d'arrivée ◆ **I don't see what you can do ~ of asking him yourself** je ne vois pas ce que vous pouvez faire à moins de *or* si ce n'est lui demander vous-même ◆ **he did everything ~ of asking her to marry him** il a tout fait sauf *or* hormis lui demander de l'épouser

◆ **nothing short of** ◆ **it's nothing ~ of robbery** c'est du vol ni plus ni moins ◆ **nothing ~ of a revolution will satisfy them** seule une révolution saura les satisfaire, il ne leur faudra rien moins qu'une révolution pour les satisfaire

◆ **little short of** ◆ **it's little ~ of suicide** c'est presque un suicide, peu s'en faut que ce ne soit un suicide ◆ **it's little ~ of folly** cela frise la folie

3 - NOUN

1 = short film court métrage *m* ; → **long¹**
2 = short-circuit court-circuit *m*
3 Brit = drink alcool *m* fort

4 - PLURAL NOUN

shorts *(= garment) (gen)* short *m* ; *[of footballer etc]* culotte *f* ; *(US = men's underwear)* caleçon *m* ◆ **a pair of ~s** un short (*or* une culotte *etc*)

5 - TRANSITIVE VERB

Elec court-circuiter

6 - INTRANSITIVE VERB

Elec se mettre en court-circuit

7 - COMPOUNDS

short-acting ADJ *[drug]* à effet rapide
short-arse‡ N *(Brit)* demi-portion* *f* *(pej)* ◆ **to be a ~-arse** être bas du cul‡
short back-and-sides N *coupe très courte derrière et sur les côtés*
short-change VT ◆ **to ~-change sb** *(lit: in shop etc)* ne pas rendre assez à qn ; *(fig)* rouler* qn
short-circuit N *(Elec)* court-circuit *m* VT *(Elec, fig = bypass)* court-circuiter ; *(fig) (= cause to fail)* faire capoter VI se mettre en court-circuit
short corner N *(Hockey)* corner *m*
short covering N *(Stock Exchange)* rachat *m* pour couvrir un découvert
short cut N *(lit, fig)* raccourci *m* ◆ **I took a ~ cut through the fields** j'ai pris un raccourci *or* j'ai coupé à travers champs ◆ **you'll have to do it all with no ~ cuts** il faudra que tu fasses tout sans rien omettre
short-dated ADJ *(Fin)* à courte échéance
short division N *(Math)* division *f* simple
short-haired ADJ *[person]* aux cheveux courts ; *[animal]* à poil ras
short-handed ADJ à court de personnel *or* de main-d'œuvre
short-haul N *[of truck]* camionnage *m* à *or* sur courte distance ; *[of plane]* vol *m* à *or* sur courte distance ADJ à courte distance
short-life ADJ *(Brit Comm) [food]* à durée de conservation limitée ; *[garment]* qui n'est pas fait pour durer
short-list *(Brit)* N liste *f* de(s) candidats sélectionnés VT mettre sur la liste de(s) candidats sélectionnés, présélectionner ◆ **he was ~-listed for the post of ...** il était parmi les candidats sélectionnés pour le poste de ...
short-lived ADJ *[animal]* à la vie éphémère ; *[happiness]* de courte durée
short message service N système *m* or service *m* de minimessages
short-order ADJ *(US)* ◆ **~-order cook** cuisinier *m*, -ière *f* préparant des plats rapides ◆ **~-order service** service *m* de plats rapides
short pastry N ⇒ **shortcrust pastry**

short-range ADJ *[shot, gun]* de *or* à courte portée ; *[aircraft]* à court rayon d'action ; *(fig) [plan, weather forecast]* à court terme
short seller N *(Stock Exchange)* vendeur *m* à découvert
short sharp shock N *(Brit = punishment)* sanction *f* sévère *(mais de courte durée)* ; *(fig)* électrochoc *m*
short sharp shock treatment N *(Brit)* traitement *m* brutal *(visant à dissuader les jeunes délinquants de récidiver)*
short sight N myopie *f*
short-sighted ADJ *(lit)* myope ; *(fig) [person]* myope, qui manque de perspicacité ; *[policy, measure]* qui manque de vision
short-sightedness N *(lit)* myopie *f* ; *(fig) [of person]* myopie *f* intellectuelle, manque *m* de perspicacité ; *[of policy, measure]* manque *m* de vision
short ski method N ski *m* évolutif
short-sleeved ADJ à manches courtes
short-staffed ADJ ◆ **to be ~-staffed** manquer de personnel, souffrir d'une pénurie de personnel
short-stay ADJ *[parking, visa]* de courte durée ; *[hospital ward]* pour séjours de courte durée
short-stay car park N parc *m* de stationnement de courte durée
short story N nouvelle *f*
short story writer N nouvelliste *mf*
short-tempered ADJ ◆ **to be ~-tempered** *(in general)* être coléreux, s'emporter facilement ; *(= in a bad temper)* être de mauvaise humeur
short-term ADJ *[parking etc]* de courte durée ; *[loan, planning, solution]* à court terme
short-term car park N ⇒ **short-stay car park**
short-termism N *(pej)* vision *f* à court terme
short-term memory N mémoire *f* à court terme
short-time working N chômage *m* partiel
short trousers NPL culottes *fpl* courtes *(de petit garçon)* ◆ **when he was still in ~ trousers** quand il était encore en culottes courtes
short-winded ADJ qui manque de souffle, au souffle court

shortage /ˈʃɔːtɪdʒ/ N *[of corn, coal, energy, cash]* manque *m*, pénurie *f* ; *[of resources]* manque *m*, insuffisance *f* ◆ **in times of ~** en période de pénurie ◆ **there was no ~ of water** on ne manquait pas d'eau ◆ **owing to the ~ of staff** à cause du manque de personnel ◆ **the food ~** la pénurie de vivres, la disette ◆ **the housing ~** la crise du logement

shortbread /ˈʃɔːtbred/ N sablé *m*

shortcake /ˈʃɔːtkeɪk/ N *(US)* ◆ **strawberry** *etc* **~** tarte *f* sablée aux fraises *etc*

shortcoming /ˈʃɔːtˌkʌmɪŋ/ N défaut *m*

shortcrust pastry /ˌʃɔːtkrʌstˈpeɪstrɪ/ N *(Culin)* pâte *f* brisée

shorten /ˈʃɔːtn/ VT *[+ skirt, rope]* raccourcir ; *[+ visit, holiday, journey]* écourter ; *[+ life]* abréger ; *[+ book, programme, letter]* raccourcir, abréger ; *[+ syllabus]* alléger ; *[+ distance, time]* réduire VI *[days etc]* raccourcir ◆ **the odds are ~ing** *(lit)* la cote baisse ; *(fig)* les chances augmentent

shortening /ˈʃɔːtnɪŋ/ N *(NonC)* 1 *(= action) [of skirt, rope, days]* raccourcissement *m* ; *[of book, programme, letter]* raccourcissement *m*, abrégement *m* ; *[of life, visit, holiday, journey]* abrégement *m* ; *[of syllabus]* allégement *m* ; *[of distance, time]* réduction *f* 2 *(esp US Culin)* matière *f* grasse

shortfall /ˈʃɔːtfɔːl/ N *(in payments, profits, savings)* montant *m* insuffisant *(in* de*)* ; *(in numbers)* nombre *m* insuffisant *(in* de*)* ◆ **a ~ in earnings** manque *m* à gagner ◆ **there is a ~ of £5,000** il manque 5 000 livres ◆ **the ~ of £5,000** les 5 000 livres qui manquent ◆ **there is a ~ of 200 in the registrations for this course** il manque 200 inscriptions à ce cours

shorthand /ˈʃɔːthænd/ N 1 *(lit)* sténographie *f* ◆ **to take sth down in ~** prendre qch en sténo, sténographier qch 2 *(fig) (= abbreviation)* abréviation *f* ; *(= code of behaviour, coded message)* code *m* ◆ **"motivation essential": that's ~ for "you'll be working 24 hours a day"** *(hum)* "motivation indispensable" : c'est une façon de dire que tu vas travailler 24 heures sur 24 ADJ *(fig = abbreviated) [term, version, formula]* abrégé
COMP **shorthand notebook** N carnet *m* de sténo
shorthand notes NPL notes *fpl* en *or* de sténo
shorthand typing N sténodactylo *f*
shorthand typist N sténodactylo *mf*
shorthand writer N sténo(graphe) *mf*

shorthorn /ˈʃɔːthɔːn/ N *(= cow)* race *f* shorthorn *(race bovine)*

shortie /ˈʃɔːtɪ/ N ⇒ **shorty**

shortish /ˈʃɔːtɪʃ/ ADJ *[person]* assez petit ; *[hair, skirt]* plutôt court ; *[period]* assez bref

shortly /ˈʃɔːtlɪ/ ADV 1 *(= soon) [go, visit]* bientôt ; *(= in a few days)* prochainement ◆ **details will be released ~** des précisions seront communiquées prochainement ◆ **more of that ~** nous reviendrons sur ce sujet d'ici peu ◆ **~ before/after sth** peu avant/après qch ◆ **~ after seven** peu après sept heures ◆ **~ before half past two** peu avant deux heures et demie ◆ **~ afterwards** peu (de temps) après 2 *(= curtly) [say, speak]* sèchement, brusquement 3 *(= concisely) [explain]* brièvement

shortness /ˈʃɔːtnɪs/ N 1 *[of stick, skirt, hair, grass, arms]* peu *m or* manque *m* de longueur ; *[of person]* petite taille *f*, petitesse *f* ; *[of visit, message, conversation, programme]* brièveté *f*, courte durée *f* ; *[of vowel, syllable]* brévité *f* ◆ **because of its ~** parce que c'est (or c'était) si court 2 *(= curtness)* brusquerie *f*, sécheresse *f*

shortsheet /ˈʃɔːtʃiːt/ VT *(US) [+ bed]* mettre en portefeuille

shortstop /ˈʃɔːtstɒp/ N *(Baseball)* bloqueur *m*

shortwave /ˈʃɔːtweɪv/ *(Rad)* N ondes *fpl* courtes ADJ *[radio]* à ondes courtes ; *[transmission]* sur ondes courtes

shorty * /ˈʃɔːtɪ/ N courtaud(e) *m(f)*, nabot(e) *m(f) (pej)* ◆ **hey ~!** hé toi le *or* la petit(e) !

Shostakovich /ˌʃɒstəˈkəʊvɪtʃ/ N Chostakovitch *m*

shot /ʃɒt/ N 1 *(from gun)* coup *m* (de feu) ; *(= bullet)* balle *f* ; *(NonC:* also **lead shot***)* plomb *m* ◆ **not a single ~ was fired** pas un seul coup de feu n'a été tiré ◆ **to take** *or* **have** *or* **fire a ~ at sb/sth** tirer sur qn/qch ◆ **good ~!** (c'était) bien visé ! ; see also **noun 3** ◆ **a ~ across the bows** *(lit, fig)* un coup de semonce ◆ **at the first ~** du premier coup ◆ **the first ~ killed him** la première balle l'a tué ◆ **I've got four ~s left** il me reste quatre coups *or* balles ◆ **a round of five ~s** une salve de cinq coups ◆ **he is a good/bad ~** il est bon/mauvais tireur ◆ **to make a ~ in the dark** tenter le coup, deviner à tout hasard ◆ **that was just a ~ in the dark** c'était dit à tout hasard ◆ **he was off like a ~** il est parti comme une flèche ◆ **he agreed like a ~** * il y a consenti sans hésiter *or* avec empressement ◆ **would you go? - like a ~!** * est-ce que tu irais ? – sans hésiter *or* et comment ! * ◆ **he's only got one ~ (left) in his locker** c'est sa dernière chance *or* cartouche * ; → **crack, long¹, Parthian, parting**
2 *(Space)* lancement *m* ; → **moon, space**
3 *(Sport, Ftbl, Hockey)* tir *m* ; *(Golf, Tennis etc)* coup *m* ; *(= throw)* lancer *m* ◆ **good ~!** bien joué ! ◆ **a ~ at goal** un shoot, un tir au but ◆ **to put the ~** *(Sport)* lancer le poids ◆ **the biggest by a long ~** de loin le plus grand ◆ **to call the ~s** * *(fig)* mener la barque
4 *(= attempt)* essai *m* ; *(= guess)* hypothèse *f* ; *(= turn to play)* tour *m* ◆ **to have a ~ at (doing) sth** essayer de faire qch ◆ **to give something one's best ~** * mettre le paquet *, faire de son mieux ◆ **have a ~ at it!** *(= try it)* tentez le coup ! ; *(= guess)* devinez !, dites voir ! *
5 *(Phot)* photo(graphie) *f* ; *(Cine)* prise *f* de vue(s), plan *m*
6 *(= injection)* piqûre *f (against* contre*)* ◆ **a ~ in the arm** *(fig)* un coup de fouet, un stimulant
7 *[of whisky etc]* coup *m* ◆ **put a ~ of gin in it** ajoute donc un peu *or* une goutte de gin
ADJ 1 *(= iridescent) [silk]* changeant
2 *(= suffused)* ◆ **black hair ~ (through) with silver** des cheveux noirs striés d'argent ◆ **his work is ~ through with humour** son œuvre est imprégnée d'humour
3 *(* = rid)* ◆ **~ of sb/sth** débarrassé de qn/qch ◆ **to get ~ of sb/sth** se débarrasser de qn/qch
4 *(* = destroyed:* also **shot to pieces***)* *[object, machine]* bousillé * ◆ **my nerves are totally ~** j'ai les nerfs en capilotade ◆ **her confidence was ~ to pieces** sa confiance était totalement anéantie ◆ **to get/be ~ of ...** se débarrasser/être débarrassé de ... ◆ **to be (all) ~ up** ** *(= exhausted)* être exténué *or* sur les rotules **
COMP **shot angle** N *(Cine, Phot)* angle *m* de prise de vue(s)
shot put N *(Sport)* lancer *m* du poids
shot putter N lanceur *m*, -euse *f* de poids

shotgun /ˈʃɒtgʌn/ N fusil *m* de chasse ◆ **to ride ~** *(US)* voyager comme passager, accompagner COMP **shotgun marriage, shotgun wedding** N *(fig)* régularisation *f* (précipitée), mariage *m* forcé

should /ʃʊd/ LANGUAGE IN USE 1.1, 2, 15.2 MODAL AUX VB (cond of **shall**) (neg **should not,** *abbr* **shouldn't**) 1 *(indicating obligation, advisability, desirability)* **I ~ go and see her** je devrais aller la voir, il faudrait que j'aille la voir ◆ **~ I go too? - yes you ~** devrais-je y aller aussi ? – oui vous devriez *or* ça vaudrait mieux ◆ **he thought he ~ tell you** il a pensé qu'il ferait bien de vous le dire *or* qu'il devrait vous le dire ◆ **you ~ know that we have spoken to him** *(frm)* il faut que vous sachiez que nous lui avons parlé ◆ **you ~ have been a teacher** vous auriez dû être professeur ◆ **~n't you go and see her?** est-ce que vous ne devriez pas aller la voir ?, est-ce que vous ne feriez pas bien d'aller la voir ? ◆ **everything is as it ~ be** tout est comme il se doit, tout est en ordre ◆ **... which is as it ~ be** ... comme il se doit ◆ **how ~ I know?** comment voulez-vous que je (le) sache ?
2 *(indicating probability)* **he ~ win the race** il devrait gagner la course, il va probablement gagner la course ◆ **he ~ have got there by now I expect** je pense qu'il est arrivé, il a dû arriver à l'heure qu'il est ◆ **that ~ be Marie at the door now** ça doit être Marie (qui frappe *or* qui sonne) ◆ **this ~ do the trick** * ça devrait faire l'affaire ◆ **why ~ he suspect me?** pourquoi me soupçonnerait-il ?
3 *(often used to form conditional in 1st pers)* **I ~** *or* **I'd go if he invited me** s'il m'invitait, j'irais ◆ **we ~ have come if we had known** si nous avions su, nous serions venus ◆ **will you come? - I ~ like to** est-ce que vous viendrez ? – j'aimerais bien ◆ **I ~n't be surprised if he comes** *or* **came** *or* **were to come** ça ne m'étonnerait pas qu'il vienne ◆ **I ~ think there were about 40** (je pense qu')il devait y en avoir environ 40 ◆ **was it a good film? - I ~ think it was!** est-ce que c'était un bon film ? – je pense bien *or* et comment ! * ◆ **he's coming to apologize - I ~ think so too!** il vient présenter ses excuses – j'espère bien ! ◆ **I ~ hope not!** il ne manquerait plus que ça ! * ◆ **I ~ say so!** et comment ! *
4 *(subj uses: frm)* **it is necessary that he ~ be told** il faut qu'on le lui dise ◆ **lest he ~ change his mind** de crainte qu'il ne change *subj* d'avis

◆ **it is surprising that he ~ be so young** c'est étonnant qu'il soit si jeune ◆ **who ~ come in but Paul!** et devinez qui est entré ? Paul !

shoulder /ˈʃəʊldəʳ/ **N** 1 *[of person, animal, garment]* épaule *f* ◆ **to have broad ~s** *(lit)* être large d'épaules *or* de carrure ; *(fig)* avoir les reins solides *(fig)* ◆ **the ~s are too wide, it's too wide across the ~s** c'est trop large d'épaules *or* de carrure ◆ **put my jacket round your ~s** mets ma veste sur tes épaules *or* sur ton dos ◆ **to cry** *or* **weep on sb's ~** *(lit, fig)* pleurer sur l'épaule de qn ◆ **she had her bag on** *or* **over one ~** elle portait son sac à l'épaule ◆ **they stood ~ to ~** *(lit)* ils étaient coude à coude *or* côte à côte ; *(fig)* ils se serraient les coudes ◆ **all the responsibilities had fallen on his ~s** toutes les responsabilités étaient retombées sur lui *or* sur ses épaules ◆ **to put** *or* **set one's ~ to the wheel** s'atteler à la tâche ; → **cold, head, look, rub, straighten**

2 *[of road]* accotement *m*, bas-côté *m* ; *[of hill]* contrefort *m*, épaulement *m* ; *(Climbing)* épaule *f* ; → **hard**

VT 1 *[+ load, case]* charger sur son épaule ; *[+ child etc]* hisser sur ses épaules ; *(fig) [+ responsibility]* endosser ; *[+ task]* se charger de ◆ **to ~ arms** *(Mil)* porter l'arme ◆ **~ arms!** portez arme !

2 ◆ **to ~ sb aside** *or* **out of the way** écarter qn d'un coup d'épaule ◆ **to ~ one's way through the crowd** se frayer un chemin à travers *or* dans la foule à coups d'épaules

COMP **shoulder bag** **N** sac *m* à bandoulière
shoulder blade **N** omoplate *f* ◆ **it hit him between the ~ blades** cela l'a atteint entre les épaules
shoulder-high **ADJ** *[grass, hedge, wall]* à hauteur d'épaule ◆ **to carry sb ~-high** porter qn en triomphe
shoulder holster **N** étui *m* de revolver *(porté à l'épaule)*
shoulder joint **N** *(Anat)* articulation *f* de l'épaule
shoulder-length hair **N** *(NonC)* cheveux *mpl* mi-longs *or* jusqu'aux épaules
shoulder pad **N** épaulette *f* *(rembourrage d'épaules de vêtement)*
shoulder strap **N** *[of garment]* bretelle *f* ; *[of bag]* bandoulière *f* ; *(Mil)* patte *f* d'épaule

shouldn't /ˈʃʊdnt/ ⇒ **should not** ; → **should**

should've /ˈʃʊdv/ ⇒ **should have** ; → **should**

shout /ʃaʊt/ **N** cri *m* ◆ **a ~ of joy** un cri de joie ◆ **there were ~s of applause/protest/laughter** des acclamations/des protestations bruyantes/des éclats de rire ont retenti ◆ **he gave a ~ of laughter** il a éclaté de rire ◆ **to give sb a ~** appeler qn ◆ **~s of "long live the queen" could be heard** on entendait crier "vive la reine" ◆ **it's my ~*** *(Brit = round of drinks)* c'est ma tournée*

VT *[+ order, slogan]* crier ◆ **"no" he ~ed** "non" cria-t-il ◆ **to ~ o.s. hoarse** s'enrouer à force de crier ; → **head**

VI 1 crier, pousser des cris ◆ **stop ~ing, I'm not deaf!** ne crie pas comme ça, je ne suis pas sourd ! ◆ **to ~ for joy** crier de joie, pousser des cris de joie ◆ **to ~ with laughter** éclater de rire ◆ **to ~ for help** crier *or* appeler au secours ◆ **she ~ed for Jane to come** elle a appelé Jane en criant *or* à grands cris ◆ **she ~ed for someone to come and help her** elle a appelé pour qu'on vienne l'aider ◆ **he ~ed to** *or* **at me to throw him the rope** il m'a crié de lui lancer la corde ◆ **it's nothing to ~ about*** *(fig)* ça n'a rien d'extraordinaire, il n'y a pas de quoi en faire un plat*

2 *(= scold etc)* **to ~ at sb** engueuler* qn, crier après* qn

► **shout after** **VT FUS** *[+ person]* crier à

► **shout down** **VT SEP** 1 *(= boo, express disagreement) [+ speaker]* huer ◆ **they ~ed down the proposal** ils ont rejeté la proposition avec de hauts cris

2 *(= shout loudly)* **to ~ the place** *or* **house down** crier comme un damné *or* un sourd ◆ **I thought she was going to ~ the place down** elle criait tellement que j'ai crû que tout allait s'écrouler

► **shout out** **VI** *(gen)* pousser un cri ◆ **to ~ out to sb** interpeller qn

VT SEP *[+ order]* crier ; *[+ slogan]* crier, lancer

shouting /ˈʃaʊtɪŋ/ **N** *(NonC)* cris *mpl*, clameur *f* ; *(= noise of quarrelling)* éclats *mpl* de voix ◆ **it's all over bar the ~** *(fig)* l'important est fait (il ne reste plus que les détails) **COMP** **shouting match*** **N** engueulade* *f*

shove /ʃʌv/ **N** poussée *f* ◆ **to give sb/sth a ~** pousser qn/qch ◆ **give it a good ~** poussez-le un bon coup

VT 1 *(= push)* pousser ; *(with effort)* pousser avec peine *or* effort ; *(= thrust) [+ stick, finger etc]* enfoncer *(into* dans ; *between* entre) ; *[+ rag]* fourrer *(into* dans) ; *(= jostle)* bousculer ◆ **to ~ sth in/out/down** *etc* faire entrer/sortir/descendre *etc* qch en le poussant ◆ **to ~ sth/sb aside** pousser qch/qn de côté, écarter qch/qn (d'un geste) ◆ **to ~ sth into a drawer/one's pocket** fourrer qch dans un tiroir/sa poche ◆ **stop shoving me!** arrêtez de me pousser *or* bousculer ! ◆ **to ~ sb into a room** pousser qn dans une pièce ◆ **to ~ sb against a wall** pousser *or* presser qn contre un mur ◆ **to ~ sb off the pavement** pousser qn du trottoir ; *(by jostling)* obliger qn à descendre du trottoir (en le bousculant) ◆ **to ~ sb/sth out of the way** écarter qn/qch en le poussant, pousser qn/qch pour l'écarter ◆ **he ~d the box under the table** *(= moved)* il a poussé *or* fourré la boîte sous la table ; *(= hid)* il a vite caché la boîte sous la table ◆ **they ~d the car off the road** ils ont poussé la voiture sur le bas-côté ◆ **she ~d the books off the table** elle a poussé *or* balayé les livres de dessus la table ◆ **he ~d his finger into my eye** il m'a mis le doigt dans l'œil ◆ **he ~d his head through the window** il a mis *or* passé la tête par la fenêtre ◆ **he ~d the book into my hand** il m'a fourré le livre dans la main ◆ **to ~ a door open** ouvrir une porte en la poussant *or* d'une poussée, pousser une porte (pour l'ouvrir) ◆ **to ~ one's way through the crowd** se frayer un chemin dans *or* à travers la foule, s'ouvrir un passage dans la foule en poussant

2 *(* = put)* fourrer*, mettre

VI pousser ◆ **stop shoving!** arrêtez de pousser !, ne bousculez pas ! ◆ **he ~d (his way) past me** il m'a dépassé en me bousculant ◆ **two men ~d (their way) past** deux hommes sont passés en jouant des coudes *or* en bousculant les gens ◆ **he ~d (his way) through the crowd** il s'est frayé un chemin dans *or* à travers la foule

COMP **shove-ha'penny** **N** *(Brit)* jeu *m* de palet de table

► **shove about, shove around** **VT SEP** *(lit) [+ object]* pousser çà et là *or* dans tous les sens ; *[+ person]* bousculer ; *(* fig = treat high-handedly)* en prendre à son aise avec

► **shove away** **VT SEP** *[+ person, object]* repousser

► **shove back** **VT SEP** *(= push back) [+ person, chair]* repousser ; *(= replace)* remettre (à sa place) ; *(into pocket etc)* fourrer de nouveau, remettre

► **shove down*** **VT SEP** *[+ object]* poser ◆ **he ~d down a few notes before he forgot** il a griffonné *or* gribouillé quelques notes pour ne pas oublier

► **shove off** **VI** *(Naut)* pousser au large ; *(* = leave)* ficher le camp*, filer*

VT SEP *[+ boat]* pousser au large, déborder

► **shove on*** **VT SEP** 1 *[+ one's coat etc]* enfiler ; *[+ hat]* enfoncer

2 ◆ **shove on another record** mets donc un autre disque

► **shove out** **VT SEP** *[+ boat]* pousser au large, déborder ; *[+ person]* mettre à la porte

► **shove over** **VI** *(* = move over)* se pousser

VT SEP 1 *(= knock over) [+ chair etc]* renverser ; *[+ person]* faire tomber (par terre)

2 *(over cliff etc)* pousser

3 ◆ **shove it over to me*** passe-le-moi

► **shove up*** **VI** ⇒ **shove over vi**

shovel /ˈʃʌvl/ **N** pelle *f* ; *(mechanical)* pelleteuse *f*, pelle *f* mécanique **VT** *[+ coal, grain]* pelleter ; *(also* **shovel out***) [+ snow, mud]* enlever à la pelle ◆ **to ~ earth into a pile** pelleter la terre pour en faire un tas ◆ **he ~led the food into his mouth*** il fourrait* *or* enfournait* la nourriture dans sa bouche

► **shovel up** **VT SEP** *[+ sth spilt etc]* ramasser avec une pelle *or* à la pelle ; *[+ snow]* enlever à la pelle

shoveler /ˈʃʌvələʳ/ **N** (canard *m*) souchet *m*

shovelful /ˈʃʌvlfʊl/ **N** pelletée *f*

show /ʃəʊ/ (vb : pret **showed**, ptp **shown** *or* **showed**) **N** 1 *[of hatred etc]* manifestation *f*, démonstration *f* ; *[of affection etc]* démonstration *f*, témoignage *m* ; *(= semblance)* apparence *f*, semblant *m* ; *(= ostentation)* parade *f* ◆ **an impressive ~ of strength** un impressionnant étalage de force, une impressionnante démonstration de force ◆ **the dahlias make** *or* **are a splendid ~** les dahlias sont splendides (à voir) *or* offrent un spectacle splendide ◆ **they make a great ~ of their wealth** ils font parade *or* étalage de leur richesse ◆ **with a ~ of emotion** en affectant l'émotion, en affectant d'être ému ◆ **they made a ~ of resistance** ils ont fait semblant de résister, ils ont offert un simulacre de résistance ◆ **to make a ~ of doing sth** faire semblant *or* mine de faire qch

◆ **(just) for show** pour l'effet

2 *(= exhibition)* exposition *f* ; *(= trade fair)* foire *f* ; *(for dogs, cats)* concours *m* ; *(agricultural)* salon *m* ◆ **flower ~** floralies *fpl* ; *(smaller)* exposition *f* de fleurs ◆ **dress ~** défilé *m* de couture ◆ **he's holding his first London ~** *[artist, sculptor]* il expose à Londres pour la première fois ◆ **the Boat Show** le Salon de la Navigation ; → **dog-show, fashion, motor**

◆ **on show** exposé ◆ **there were some fine pieces on ~** quelques beaux objets étaient exposés ◆ **to put sth on ~** exposer qch

3 *(Theat etc)* spectacle *m* ; *(= variety show)* show *m* ◆ **there are several good ~s on in London** on donne plusieurs bons spectacles à Londres en ce moment ◆ **I often go to a ~** je vais souvent au spectacle ◆ **the last ~ starts at 9** *(Theat)* la dernière représentation commence à 21 heures ; *(Cine)* la dernière séance commence à 21 heures ◆ **on with the ~!** *(= start)* que la représentation commence *subj* ! ; *(= continue)* que la représentation continue *subj* ! ◆ **the ~ must go on** *(Theat, fig)* il faut continuer malgré tout ◆ **let's get this ~ on the road*** *(fig)* il faut faire démarrer* tout ça, passons à l'action ◆ **this is Paul's ~*** *(= Paul is in charge)* c'est Paul qui commande ici ◆ **to run the ~*** tenir les rênes ◆ **he runs the whole ~*** *(fig)* c'est lui qui commande *or* a tout en main ◆ **to give the ~ away*** vendre la mèche* ◆ **to put up a good ~** *(fig)* faire bonne figure, bien se défendre* ◆ **to make a poor ~** faire triste *or* piètre figure ◆ **it's a poor ~*** c'est lamentable, il n'y a pas de quoi être fier ◆ **it's a poor ~* that ...** il est malheureux que ... + *subj* ◆ **good ~!*** *(esp Brit)* bravo ! ; → **steal**

VT 1 *(= display, make visible)* montrer, faire voir ; *[+ ticket, passport]* montrer, présenter ; *(= exhibit) [+ goods for sale, picture, dog]* exposer ◆ **~ it me!** faites voir !, montrez-le-moi ! ◆ **we're going to ~ (you) some slides** nous allons (vous) passer *or* projeter quelques diapositives ◆ **they ~ a film during the flight** on passe un film *or* il y a une projection de cinéma pendant le vol ◆ **what is ~ing at that cinema/at the Odeon?** qu'est-ce qu'on donne *or* qu'est-ce qui passe dans ce cinéma/à l'Odéon ? ◆ **the film was first ~n in 1974** ce film est sorti en 1974 ◆ **it has been ~n on television** c'est passé à la télévision ◆ **what can I ~ you?** *(in shop)* que puis-je vous montrer ?, que désirez-vous voir ? ◆ **as ~n by the graph** comme le montre *or* l'indique le graphique ◆ **as ~n in the illustration on page 4** voir l'illustration page 4 ◆ **there's nothing to ~ for it** *(fig)* on ne le dirait pas, ça ne se voit *or* ne se remarque pas ◆ **he has nothing to ~ for it** il n'en a rien tiré, ça ne lui a rien donné *or* apporté ◆ **he has nothing to ~ for all the effort he has put into it** les efforts qu'il y a consacrés n'ont rien donné ◆ **I ought to ~ myself** *or* **my face at Paul's party** il faudrait que je fasse acte de présence à la soirée de Paul ◆ **he daren't ~ himself** *or* **his face there again** il n'ose plus s'y montrer *or* montrer son nez là-bas* ◆ **to ~ one's hand** *or* **cards** *(fig)* dévoiler ses intentions, abattre son jeu *or* ses cartes ◆ **to ~ a clean pair of heels** se sauver à toutes jambes ◆ **~ a leg!*** *(Brit)* lève-toi !, debout ! ◆ **to ~ one's teeth** *(lit, fig)* montrer les dents ◆ **to ~ sb the door** montrer la porte à qn, mettre qn à la porte ◆ **to ~ the flag** *(fig)* être là pour le principe, faire acte de présence

2 *(= indicate)* *[dial, clock etc]* indiquer, marquer ; *(gen)* montrer, indiquer ◆ **what time does your watch ~?** quelle heure est-il à votre montre ? ◆ **to ~ a loss/profit** indiquer une perte/un bénéfice ◆ **the figures ~ a rise over last year's sales** les chiffres montrent *or* indiquent que les ventes ont augmenté par rapport à l'année dernière ◆ **the roads are ~n in red** les routes sont marquées en rouge

3 *(= demonstrate)* montrer, faire voir ; *(= reveal)* montrer, laisser voir ; *(= explain)* montrer, expliquer ; *(= prove)* montrer, prouver ; *[+ one's intelligence, kindness, courage, tact]* montrer, faire preuve de ; *[+ one's interest, enthusiasm, surprise, agreement]* montrer, manifester ; *[+ one's approval]* montrer, indiquer ; *[+ one's gratitude, respect]* témoigner ◆ **to ~ loyalty** se montrer loyal *(to sb* envers qn) ; ◆ **if they were afraid, they didn't ~ it** s'ils avaient peur, ils ne l'ont pas montré ◆ **that dress ~s her bra** cette robe laisse voir son soutien-gorge ◆ **this skirt ~s the dirt** cette jupe est salissante ◆ **it's ~ing signs of wear** cela porte des signes d'usure ◆ **he was ~ing signs of tiredness** il montrait des signes de fatigue ◆ **it ~ed signs of having been used** il était visible qu'on s'en était servi, manifestement on s'en était servi ◆ **to ~ fight** se montrer combatif ◆ **her choice of clothes ~s good taste** sa façon de s'habiller témoigne de son bon goût ◆ **he ~ed that he was angry** il a manifesté *or* laissé voir sa colère ◆ **he's beginning to ~ his age** il commence à faire son âge ◆ **this ~s great intelligence** cela révèle *or* dénote beaucoup d'intelligence ◆ **he ~ed himself (to be) a coward** il s'est montré *or* révélé lâche ◆ **to ~ sth to be true** démontrer la vérité de qch, montrer que qch est vrai ◆ **it all goes to ~ that ...** tout cela montre *or* prouve bien que ... ◆ **it only** *or* **just goes to ~!*** tu m'en diras tant !*, c'est bien ça la vie ! ◆ **I ~ed him that it was impossible** je lui ai prouvé *or* démontré que c'était impossible ◆ **he ~ed me how it works** il m'a montré *or* il m'a fait voir comment cela fonctionne ◆ **I'll ~ him!** * *(fig)* je lui apprendrai ! ◆ **to ~ sb the way** montrer *or* indiquer le chemin à qn ◆ **I'll ~ you the way** suivez-moi (je vais vous montrer le chemin) ; → **willing**

4 *(= guide, conduct)* **to ~ sb into the room** faire entrer qn dans la pièce ◆ **to ~ sb to his seat** placer qn ◆ **to ~ sb to the door** reconduire qn jusqu'à la porte ◆ **to ~ sb over** *or* **round a house** faire visiter une maison à qn

VI 1 *[emotion]* être visible ; *[stain, scar]* se voir ; *[underskirt etc]* dépasser ◆ **it doesn't ~** cela ne se voit pas, on ne dirait pas ◆ **don't worry, it won't ~** ne t'inquiète pas, ça ne se verra pas ◆ **his fear ~ed on his face** la peur se lisait sur son visage

2 *(esp US = arrive)* ⇒ **show up vi 2**

COMP **show bill** N *(Theat)* affiche *f* de spectacle
show biz* N le monde du spectacle, le show-biz*
show business N le monde du spectacle, le show business
show flat N *(Brit)* appartement *m* témoin
show girl N girl *f*
show home, show house N *(Brit)* maison *f* témoin
show jumping N *(NonC)* concours *m* hippique, jumping *m*
show-me attitude* N *(US)* scepticisme *m*
the Show-Me State N *(US)* le Missouri
show-off N frimeur *m*, -euse *f*, m'as-tu-vu(e)* *m(f) pl inv*
show of hands N vote *m* à main levée ◆ **to vote by ~ of hands** voter à main levée
show-stopper N ◆ **it was a ~-stopper** * c'était le clou* du spectacle
show-stopping* ADJ sensationnel*
show trial N *(Jur) procès pour l'exemple*
show window N *(lit, fig)* vitrine *f*

► **show about, show around** VT SEP faire visiter les lieux *mpl* (*or* la ville *or* la maison *etc*) à

► **show in** VT SEP *[+ visitor etc]* faire entrer

► **show off** VI *(gen)* frimer*, poser (pour la galerie) ; *[child]* chercher à se rendre intéressant, faire l'intéressant ◆ **she's always ~ing off** c'est une frimeuse* *or* une poseuse ◆ **stop ~ing off** *(gen)* arrête de frimer* ; *(showing off knowledge)* arrête d'étaler ta science*

VT SEP 1 *[+ sb's beauty, complexion etc]* faire valoir, mettre en valeur

2 *(pej)* *[+ one's wealth, knowledge etc]* faire étalage de, étaler ◆ **he wanted to ~ off his new car** il voulait faire admirer sa nouvelle voiture

N ◆ **show-off** → **show**

N ◆ **showing-off** → **showing**

► **show out** VT SEP *[+ visitor etc]* accompagner *or* reconduire (jusqu'à la porte)

► **show round** VT SEP ⇒ **show about, show around**

► **show through** VI *(= be visible)* se voir au travers

► **show up** VI 1 *(= stand out)* *[feature]* ressortir ; *[mistake]* être visible *or* manifeste ; *[stain]* se voir (nettement) ◆ **the tower ~ed up clearly against the sky** la tour se détachait nettement sur le ciel

2 *(* = arrive, appear)* se pointer*, s'amener*

VT SEP 1 *[+ visitor etc]* faire monter

2 *[+ fraud, impostor]* démasquer, dénoncer ; *[+ flaw, defect]* faire ressortir

3 *(= embarrass)* faire honte à (en public)

showboat /ˈʃəʊbəʊt/ *(US)* N *(lit)* bateau-théâtre *m* ; *(‡ fig = person)* m'as-tu-vu(e)* *m(f) pl inv* VI crâner*, en mettre plein la vue

showcase /ˈʃəʊkeɪs/ N *(lit, fig)* vitrine *f* VT présenter COMP **showcase project** N opération *f* de prestige

showdown /ˈʃəʊdaʊn/ N épreuve *f* de force

shower /ˈʃaʊəʳ/ N 1 *[of rain]* averse *f* ; *(fig)* *[of blows]* volée *f*, grêle *f* ; *[of sparks, stones, arrows]* pluie *f* ; *[of blessings]* déluge *m* ; *[of insults]* torrent *m*, flot *m*

2 douche *f* ◆ **to have** *or* **take a ~** prendre une douche ◆ **to send sb to the ~s*** *(US) (Sport)* expulser qn ; *(fig)* mettre qn sur la touche *(fig)*

3 *(Brit ‡ pej = people)* bande *f* de crétins*

4 *(before wedding etc)* **to give a ~ for sb** organiser une soirée pour donner ses cadeaux à qn

VT *(fig)* ◆ **to ~ sb with gifts/praise, to ~ gifts/praise on sb** combler qn de cadeaux/de louanges ◆ **to ~ blows on sb** faire pleuvoir des coups sur qn ◆ **to ~ abuse** *or* **insults on sb** accabler *or* couvrir qn d'injures ◆ **invitations were/advice was ~ed (up)on him** les invitations/les conseils pleuvaient (sur lui)

VI 1 *(= wash)* se doucher, prendre une douche

2 *(= fall)* **small stones/hailstones ~ed (down) on to the car** des petites pierres/grêlons pleuvaient sur la voiture ◆ **advice ~ed upon him** les conseils pleuvaient sur lui

COMP **shower attachment** N douchette *f* à main, douchette *f* de lavabo
shower cap N bonnet *m* de douche
shower cubicle N cabine *f* de douche
shower curtain N rideau *m* de douche
shower gel N gel *m* douche
shower stall N ⇒ **shower cubicle**
shower unit N bloc-douche *m*

showerproof /ˈʃaʊəpruːf/ ADJ imperméable

showery /ˈʃaʊərɪ/ ADJ *[weather, day]* pluvieux ◆ **~ rain** averses *fpl* ◆ **it will be ~** il y aura des averses

showground /ˈʃəʊgraʊnd/ N champ *m* de foire

showing /ˈʃəʊɪŋ/ N 1 *[of pictures etc]* exposition *f* ; *[of film]* projection *f* ◆ **the first ~ is at 8pm** *(Cine)* la première séance est à 20 heures ◆ **another ~ of this film** *(Cine, TV)* une nouvelle projection de ce film 2 *(= performance)* performance *f*, prestation* *f* ◆ **on this ~ he doesn't stand much chance** si c'est tout ce dont il est capable *or* à en juger d'après cette prestation, il n'a pas de grandes chances ◆ **he made a good ~** il s'en est bien tiré ◆ **he made a poor ~** il ne s'est vraiment pas distingué 3 ◆ **on his own ~** de son propre aveu COMP **showing-off** N *(NonC)* frime *f*, pose *f*

showjumper /ˈʃəʊˌdʒʌmpəʳ/ N *(= rider)* cavalier *m*, -ière *f* de concours hippique ; *(= horse)* cheval *m* (de saut) d'obstacles

showman /ˈʃəʊmən/ N (pl **-men**) *(in fair, circus etc)* forain *m* ◆ **he's a real ~** *(fig)* il a vraiment le sens de la mise en scène *(fig)*

showmanship /ˈʃəʊmənʃɪp/ N art *m or* sens *m* de la mise en scène

shown /ʃəʊn/ VB ptp of **show**

showpiece /ˈʃəʊpiːs/ N 1 *[of exhibition etc]* trésor *m*, joyau *m* 2 *(fig)* **Arran's ~ is Brodick Castle** le joyau d'Arran est Brodick Castle ◆ **the new school is a ~** la nouvelle école est un modèle du genre ◆ **the capital's ~ art gallery** la plus prestigieuse galerie d'art de la capitale

showplace /ˈʃəʊpleɪs/ N 1 *(= tourist attraction)* lieu *m* de grand intérêt touristique 2 *(fig)* ⇒ **showpiece 2** COMP **showplace home** N *(US)* maison *f* de rêve

showroom /ˈʃəʊrʊm/ N salle *f* d'exposition, showroom *m* ◆ **in ~ condition** à l'état *m* neuf

showtime /ˈʃəʊtaɪm/ N ◆ **it's ~!** le spectacle commence ! ◆ **ten minutes till ~!** le spectacle commence dans dix minutes !

showy* /ˈʃəʊɪ/ ADJ *(pej)* *[clothes, jewellery, décor]* voyant, tape-à-l'œil *inv* ; *[colour]* voyant, criard ; *[person, manner]* plein d'ostentation

shrank /ʃræŋk/ VB pt of **shrink**

shrapnel /ˈʃræpnl/ N *(Mil)* 1 obus *m* à balles, shrapnel *m* 2 *(NonC)* éclats *mpl* d'obus

shred /ʃred/ N *[of cloth, paper, skin, plastic sheeting]* lambeau *m* ; *(fig)* *[of truth]* parcelle *f*, grain *m* ; *[of common sense]* grain *m*, once *f* ◆ **not a ~ of evidence** pas la moindre *or* plus petite preuve ◆ **her dress hung in ~s** sa robe était en lambeaux ◆ **to tear** *or* **rip into ~s** mettre en lambeaux ◆ **without a ~ of clothing on** nu comme un ver, complètement nu VT 1 *[+ paper]* *(gen)* mettre en lambeaux, déchiqueter ; *(in shredder)* détruire (par lacération), déchiqueter [2] *[+ carrots]* râper ; *[+ cabbage, lettuce]* couper en lanières

shredder /ˈʃredəʳ/ N [1] *[of food processor]* (disque *m*) râpeur *m* [2] (also **paper** *or* **document shredder**) destructeur *m* (de documents), déchiqueteuse *f* ◆ **to put sth through the ~** détruire qch, passer qch à la déchiqueteuse

shrew /ʃruː/ N [1] *(= animal)* musaraigne *f* [2] *(= woman)* mégère *f* ; → **taming**

shrewd /ʃruːd/ ADJ *[person] (= clear-sighted)* perspicace ; *(= cunning)* astucieux ; *[plan]* astucieux ; *[businessman, politician]* habile ; *[assessment, reasoning, investment, move]* judicieux ◆ **a ~ judge of character** un fin psychologue ◆ **I can make a ~ guess at what he wanted** je crois que je devine ce qu'il voulait ◆ **to have a ~ suspicion that ...** être assez perspicace pour soupçonner que ...

shrewdly /ˈʃruːdlɪ/ ADV *[look at]* d'un air perspicace ; *[say, ask, assess, suspect]* avec perspicacité ; *[realize, recognize, perceive, comment]* judicieusement ; *[reason]* habilement ; *[guess]* astucieusement

shrewdness /ˈʃruːdnɪs/ N *[of person]* perspicacité *f*, habileté *f*, sagacité *f* ; *[of assessment]* perspicacité *f* ; *[of plan]* astuce *f*

shrewish /ˈʃruːɪʃ/ ADJ *(pej) [woman]* acariâtre ; *[behaviour]* de mégère ◆ **a ~ woman** une mégère

shriek /ʃriːk/ N hurlement *m*, cri *m* perçant *or* aigu ◆ **to let out** *or* **give a ~** pousser un hurlement *or* un cri ◆ **~s of laughter** de grands éclats *mpl* de rire ◆ **with ~s of laughter** en riant à gorge déployée VI hurler, crier *(with* de) ◆ **to ~ with laughter** rire à gorge déployée, se tordre de rire ◆ **the colour simply ~s at you** *(fig)* cette couleur hurle *or* est vraiment criarde VT hurler, crier ◆ **to ~ abuse at sb** hurler des injures à qn ◆ **"no" he ~ed** "non" hurla-t-il

shrift /ʃrɪft/ N ◆ **to give sb short ~** expédier qn sans ménagement, envoyer promener qn * ◆ **I got short ~ from him** il m'a traité sans ménagement, il m'a envoyé promener *

shrike /ʃraɪk/ N pie-grièche *f*

shrill /ʃrɪl/ ADJ *(pej)* [1] *(= piercing) [voice, cry]* strident, perçant ; *[laughter, music]* strident ; *[whistle]* strident, aigu (-guë *f*) [2] *(= vehement) [demand]* outrancier ; *[protest]* violent VI *[whistle, telephone]* retentir VT ◆ **"stop !" she ~ed** "arrête !" cria-t-elle d'une voix perçante *or* stridente

shrillness /ˈʃrɪlnɪs/ N *(NonC)* ton *m* aigu *or* perçant

shrilly /ˈʃrɪlɪ/ ADV *(pej)* [1] *(= piercingly) [say, sing]* d'une voix stridente *or* perçante ◆ **her voice sounded ~ from the corridor** on entendait sa voix perçante dans le couloir ◆ **to whistle ~** émettre un sifflement strident *or* aigu [2] *(= vehemently) [demand]* de façon outrancière ; *[protest, condemn]* violemment

shrimp /ʃrɪmp/ N crevette *f* ◆ **he's just a little ~** *(fig)* il n'est pas plus haut que trois pommes VI ◆ **to go ~ing** aller pêcher la crevette
COMP **shrimp cocktail** N *(Culin)* cocktail *m* de crevettes
shrimp sauce N sauce *f* crevette

shrine /ʃraɪn/ N *(= place of worship)* lieu *m* saint, lieu *m* de pèlerinage ; *(= reliquary)* châsse *f* ; *(= tomb)* tombeau *m* ; *(fig)* haut lieu *m*

shrink /ʃrɪŋk/ (pret **shrank**, ptp **shrunk**) VI [1] *(= get smaller) [clothes]* rétrécir ; *[area]* se réduire ; *[boundaries]* se resserrer ; *[piece of meat]* réduire ; *[body, person]* se ratatiner, rapetisser ; *[wood]* se contracter ; *[quantity, amount]* diminuer ◆ **"will not shrink"** *(on label)* "irrétrécissable" [2] (also **shrink away, shrink back**) reculer, se dérober *(from sth* devant qch ; *from doing sth* devant l'idée de faire qch) ◆ **she shrank (away** *or* **back) from him** elle a eu un mouvement de recul ◆ **he did not ~ from saying that ...** il n'a pas craint de dire que ... VT *[+ wool]* (faire) rétrécir ; *[+ metal]* contracter N *(* = psychiatrist)* psychiatre *mf*, psy * *mf*
COMP **shrink-wrap** VT emballer sous film plastique
shrink-wrapped ADJ emballé sous film plastique

shrinkage /ˈʃrɪŋkɪdʒ/ N *(NonC) [of clothes]* rétrécissement *m* ; *[of wood, market]* contraction *f* ; *[of industry]* recul *m* ; *[of quantity, amount]* diminution *f* ; *[of metal]* retrait *m* ◆ **to allow for ~** *(in material)* prévoir un rétrécissement

shrinking /ˈʃrɪŋkɪŋ/ ADJ craintif COMP **shrinking violet** N sensitive *f*, personne *f* sensible et timide

shrive †† /ʃraɪv/ (pret **shrived** *or* **shrove**, ptp **shrived** *or* **shriven**) VT confesser et absoudre

shrivel /ˈʃrɪvl/ (also **shrivel up**) VI *[apple, body]* se ratatiner ; *[skin]* se rider, se flétrir ; *[leaf]* se flétrir, se racornir ; *[steak]* se racornir, se ratatiner ◆ **her answer made him ~ (up)** sa réponse lui a donné envie de rentrer sous terre VT dessécher, flétrir

shriven /ˈʃrɪvn/ VB ptp of **shrive**

shroud /ʃraʊd/ N [1] linceul *m*, suaire *m (liter)* ; *(fig) [of mist]* voile *m*, linceul *m (liter)* ; *[of snow]* linceul *m (liter)* ; *[of mystery]* voile *m* [2] *[of mast]* hauban *m* ; *[of parachute]* suspentes *fpl* [3] *(Space: of rocket)* coiffe *f* VT *[+ corpse]* envelopper dans un linceul, ensevelir ◆ **~ed in mist/snow** enseveli sous la brume/la neige, sous un linceul de brume/de neige *(liter)* ◆ **~ed in mystery/secrecy** enveloppé de mystère/d'une atmosphère de secret

shrove /ʃrəʊv/ VB pt of **shrive** COMP **Shrove Tuesday** N (le) Mardi gras

Shrovetide /ˈʃrəʊvtaɪd/ N les jours *mpl* gras *(les trois jours précédant le Carême)*

shrub /ʃrʌb/ N arbrisseau *m* ; *(small)* arbuste *m* ; → **flowering**

shrubbery /ˈʃrʌbərɪ/ N (massif *m* d')arbustes *mpl*

shrubby /ˈʃrʌbɪ/ ADJ arbustif ◆ **a ~ tree** un arbuste

shrug /ʃrʌg/ N haussement *m* d'épaules ◆ **to give a ~ of contempt** hausser les épaules (en signe) de mépris ◆ **... he said with a ~** ... dit-il en haussant les épaules *or* avec un haussement d'épaules VTI ◆ **to ~ (one's shoulders)** hausser les épaules

► **shrug off** VT SEP *[+ suggestion, warning]* dédaigner, faire fi de ; *[+ remark]* ignorer, ne pas relever ; *[+ infection, a cold]* se débarrasser de

shrunk /ʃrʌŋk/ VB ptp of **shrink**

shrunken /ˈʃrʌŋkən/ ADJ *[person, body]* ratatiné, rabougri ◆ **~ head** tête *f* réduite

shtick /ʃtɪk/ N ⇒ **schtick**

shtoom *, **stumm** * /ʃtʊm/ ADJ ◆ **to keep shtoom** la boucler *

shuck /ʃʌk/ (US) N *(= pod)* cosse *f* ; *[of nut]* écale *f* ; *[of chestnut]* bogue *f* ; *[of corn]* spathe *f* EXCL ◆ **~s !** * mince alors ! *, zut alors ! * VT *[+ bean]* écosser ; *[+ nut]* écaler ; *[+ chestnut]* éplucher ; *[+ corn]* égrener ◆ **to ~ one's clothes** se désaper *

► **shuck off** * VT SEP *(US) [+ garment]* enlever ◆ **to ~ off one's clothes** se désaper * ◆ **to ~ off one's jacket** tomber la veste *

shudder /ˈʃʌdəʳ/ N *(from cold)* frisson *m* ; *(from horror)* frisson *m*, frémissement *m* ; *[of vehicle, ship, engine]* vibration *f*, trépidation *f* ◆ **to give a ~** *[person]* frissonner, frémir ; *[vehicle, ship]* avoir une forte secousse, être ébranlé ◆ **it gives me the ~s** * ça me donne des frissons ◆ **he realized with a ~ that ...** il a frissonné *or* frémi, comprenant que ... VI *(from cold)* frissonner ; *(from horror)* frémir, frissonner ; *[engine, motor]* vibrer, trépider ; *[vehicle, ship] (on striking sth)* avoir une forte secousse, être ébranlé ; *(for mechanical reasons)* vibrer, trépider ◆ **I ~ to think what might have happened** je frémis rien qu'à la pensée de ce qui aurait pu se produire ◆ **what will he do next? – I ~ to think!** qu'est-ce qu'il va encore faire ? – j'en frémis d'avance !

shuffle /ˈʃʌfl/ N [1] ◆ **the ~ of footsteps** le bruit d'une démarche traînante
[2] *(Cards)* battage *m* ; *(fig)* réorganisation *f* ◆ **give the cards a good ~** bats bien les cartes ◆ **a cabinet (re)~** *(Parl)* un remaniement ministériel ◆ **to get lost in the ~** *(US) [person]* passer inaperçu ; *[fact, issue etc]* être mis aux oubliettes *or* au placard
VT [1] ◆ **to ~ one's feet** *(while sitting or standing)* bouger les pieds ; *(when nervous)* agiter nerveusement les pieds
[2] *[+ cards]* battre ; *[+ dominoes]* mêler, brouiller ; *[+ papers]* remuer, déranger
VI [1] traîner les pieds ◆ **to ~ in/out/along** *etc* entrer/sortir/avancer *etc* d'un pas traînant *or* en traînant les pieds
[2] *(Cards)* battre (les cartes)

► **shuffle off** VI s'en aller *or* s'éloigner d'un pas traînant *or* en traînant les pieds
VT SEP *[+ garment]* enlever maladroitement ; *(fig) [+ responsibility]* rejeter *(on to sb* sur qn), se dérober à

► **shuffle out of** VT FUS *(fig) [+ duty, responsibility]* se dérober à

shuffleboard /ˈʃʌflbɔːd/ N jeu *m* de palets

shufti, shufty * /ˈʃʌftɪ, ˈʃʊftɪ/ N *(Brit)* ◆ **to have** *or* **take a ~ (at sth)** jeter un œil * *or* coup d'œil (à qch)

shun /ʃʌn/ VT *[+ place, temptation]* fuir ; *[+ person, publicity]* fuir, éviter ; *[+ work, obligation]* éviter, esquiver ◆ **I ~ned his company** j'ai fui sa présence ◆ **to ~ doing sth** éviter de faire qch

shunt /ʃʌnt/ VT [1] *(Rail) (= direct)* aiguiller ; *(= divert)* dériver, détourner ; *(= move about)* manœuvrer ; *(= position)* garer [2] *(* fig) [+ conversation, discussion]* aiguiller, détourner *(on to* sur) ; *[+ person]* expédier * *(to* à) ◆ **they ~ed the visitors to and fro between the factory and the offices** * ils ont fait faire la navette aux visiteurs entre l'usine et les bureaux ◆ **~ that book over to me!** * passe-moi *or* file-moi ce bouquin ! * [3] *(Elec)* shunter, dériver VI *(fig)* ◆ **to ~ (to and fro)** * *[person, object, document]* faire la navette *(between* entre) N *(Rail)* aiguillage *m* ; *(* fig)* collision *f*

shunter /ˈʃʌntəʳ/ N *(Brit Rail) (= person)* aiguilleur *m* (de train) ; *(= engine)* locomotive *f* de manœuvre

shunting /ˈʃʌntɪŋ/ *(Rail)* N manœuvres *fpl* d'aiguillage
COMP **shunting operation** N *(Brit)* opération *f* de triage
shunting yard N voies *fpl* de garage et de triage

shush /ʃʊʃ/ EXCL chut ! VT * faire chut à ; *(= silence:* also **shush up**) faire taire

shut /ʃʌt/ (pret, ptp **shut**) VT *[+ eyes, door, factory, shop]* fermer ; *[+ drawer]* (re)fermer, repousser ◆ **the shop is ~ now** le magasin est fermé maintenant ◆ **the shop is ~ on Sundays** le magasin ferme *or* est fermé le dimanche ◆ **we're ~ting the office for two weeks in July** nous fermons le bureau pour deux semaines au mois de juillet ◆ **to ~ one's finger in a drawer** se pincer *or* se prendre le doigt dans un tiroir ◆ **to ~ sb in a room** enfermer qn dans une pièce ◆ **~ your mouth!** * ferme-la ! *, boucle-la ! * ◆ **~ your face!** * ta gueule ! *, la ferme ! * ; → **door, ear¹, eye, open, stable²**
VI *[door, box, lid, drawer]* se fermer, fermer ; *[museum, theatre, shop]* fermer ◆ **the door ~** la porte s'est (re)fermée ◆ **the door ~s badly** la porte

ferme mal ◆ **the shop ~s on Sundays/at 6 o'clock** le magasin ferme le dimanche/à 18 heures

COMP **shut-eye**‡ N ◆ **to get a bit of ~-eye** *or* **some ~-eye** piquer un roupillon‡, dormir un peu

shut-in ADJ *(esp US)* enfermé, confiné

shut-out N *(at factory)* lock-out *m inv* ; *(US Sport)* victoire *f (remportée du fait que l'équipe adverse n'a marqué aucun point)*

shut-out bid N *(Bridge)* (annonce *f* de) barrage *m*

► **shut away** VT SEP *[+ person, animal]* enfermer ; *[+ valuables]* mettre sous clé ◆ **he ~s himself away** il s'enferme chez lui, il vit en reclus

► **shut down** VI *[business, shop, theatre]* fermer (définitivement), fermer ses portes

VT SEP *[+ lid]* fermer, rabattre ; *[+ business, shop, theatre]* fermer (définitivement) ; *[+ machine]* arrêter

► **shut in** VT SEP *[+ person, animal]* enfermer ; *(= surround)* entourer *(with* de*)* ◆ **to feel ~ in** se sentir enfermé *or* emprisonné *(fig)*

ADJ ◆ **shut-in** → **shut**

► **shut off** VT SEP 1 *(= stop, cut) [+ electricity, gas]* couper, fermer ; *[+ engine]* couper ; *[+ supplies]* arrêter, couper

2 *(= isolate) [+ person]* isoler, séparer *(from* de*)* ◆ **we're very ~ off here** nous sommes coupés de tout ici *or* très isolés ici

► **shut out** VT SEP 1 ◆ **he found that they had shut him out, he found himself shut out** il a trouvé qu'il était à la porte *or* qu'il ne pouvait pas entrer ◆ **don't ~ me out, I haven't got a key** ne ferme pas la porte, je n'ai pas de clé ◆ **I ~ the cat out at night** je laisse *or* mets le chat dehors pour la nuit ◆ **close the door and ~ out the noise** ferme la porte pour qu'on n'entende pas le bruit ◆ **he ~ them out of his will** il les a exclus de son testament ◆ **you can't ~ him out of your life** tu ne peux pas l'exclure *or* le bannir de ta vie

2 *(= block) [+ view]* boucher ; *[+ memory]* chasser de son esprit

3 *(US Sport) [+ opponent]* bloquer

N ◆ **shut-out** → **shut**

► **shut to** VI *[door]* se (re)fermer

VT SEP (re)fermer

► **shut up** VI *(* = be quiet)* se taire ◆ **~ up!** tais-toi !, la ferme !‡ ◆ **better just ~ up and get on with it** mieux vaut se taire *or* la boucler* et continuer

VT SEP 1 *[+ factory, business, theatre, house]* fermer ; → **shop**

2 *[+ person, animal]* enfermer ; *[+ valuables]* mettre sous clé ◆ **to ~ sb up in prison** emprisonner qn, mettre qn en prison

3 *(* = silence)* faire taire, clouer le bec à*

shutdown /ˈʃʌtdaʊn/ N fermeture *f*

shutoff /ˈʃʌtɒf/ N (also **shutoff device**) interrupteur *m* automatique, dispositif *m* d'arrêt automatique

shutter /ˈʃʌtəʳ/ N volet *m* ; *(Phot)* obturateur *m* ◆ **to put up the ~s** mettre les volets ; *(= close shop)* fermer (le magasin) ; *(fig: permanently)* fermer boutique, fermer définitivement

COMP **shutter release** N *(Phot)* déclencheur *m* d'obturateur

shutter speed N vitesse *f* d'obturation

shuttered /ˈʃʌtəd/ ADJ *[house, window] (= fitted with shutters)* muni de volets ; *(= with shutters closed)* aux volets clos ◆ **the windows were ~** les fenêtres étaient munies de volets *or* avaient leurs volets fermés

shuttle /ˈʃʌtl/ N 1 *[of loom, sewing machine]* navette *f*

2 *(= plane, train etc)* navette *f* ◆ **air ~** navette *f* aérienne ◆ **space ~** navette *f* spatiale

3 *(*: in badminton = shuttlecock)* volant *m*

VI *[person, vehicle, boat, documents]* faire la navette *(between* entre*)*

VT ◆ **to ~ sb to and fro** envoyer qn à droite et à gauche ◆ **he was ~d (back and forth) between the factory and the office** on l'a renvoyé de l'usine au bureau et vice versa, il a dû faire la navette entre l'usine et le bureau ◆ **the papers were ~d (backwards and forwards) from one department to another** les documents ont été renvoyés d'un service à l'autre

COMP **shuttle bus** N navette *f*

shuttle diplomacy N navettes *fpl* diplomatiques

shuttle movement N *(Tech)* mouvement *m* alternatif

shuttle service N *(Aviat, Rail etc)* (service *m* de) navettes *fpl*

shuttlecock /ˈʃʌtlkɒk/ N *(in badminton)* volant *m*

shy¹ /ʃaɪ/ ADJ 1 *(= nervous) [person, smile, look]* timide ◆ **he's a ~ person, he's ~ of people** c'est un timide ◆ **to be ~ with people** être timide avec les gens ◆ **don't be ~** ne sois pas timide, ne fais pas le *(or* la*)* timide ◆ **to make sb (feel) ~** intimider qn ◆ **she went all ~* when asked to give her opinion** elle a été tout intimidée quand on lui a demandé de donner son avis

2 *(= wary)* **to be ~ of sb/sth** avoir peur de qn/qch ◆ **he was so ~ about his private life** il craignait tellement de parler de sa vie privée ◆ **to be ~ of doing sth** avoir peur de faire qch ; → **bite, camera, fight, workshy**

3 *[animal, bird]* craintif ; → **gun**

4 *(esp US = short)* ◆ **he is two days ~ of his 95th birthday** il va avoir 95 ans dans deux jours ◆ **I'm $5 ~** il me manque 5 dollars ◆ **they are $65,000 ~ of the $1 million that's needed** il leur manque 65 000 dollars pour avoir le million nécessaire

VI *[horse]* broncher *(at* devant*)*

► **shy away** VI *(fig)* ◆ **to shy away from doing sth** répugner à faire qch, s'effaroucher à l'idée de faire qch

shy² /ʃaɪ/ *(Brit)* VT *(= throw)* lancer, jeter N *(lit)* ◆ **to take** *or* **have a ~ at sth** lancer un projectile *(or* une pierre *etc)* vers qch ◆ **"20p a shy"** "20 pence le coup" ◆ **to have a ~ at doing sth** *(fig = try)* tenter de faire qch ; → **coconut**

shyly /ˈʃaɪlɪ/ ADV timidement

shyness /ˈʃaɪnɪs/ N (NonC) *[of person]* timidité *f* ; *[of animal, bird]* caractère *m* craintif

shyster* /ˈʃaɪstəʳ/ N *(US) (gen)* escroc *m* ; *(= lawyer)* avocat *m* véreux *or* marron

SI /esˈaɪ/ N (abbrev of **Système international (d'unités)**) SI *m*

si /siː/ N *(Mus)* si *m*

Siam /saɪˈæm/ N Siam *m* ◆ **in ~** au Siam

Siamese /ˌsaɪəˈmiːz/ ADJ *(gen)* siamois N 1 *(pl inv)* Siamois(e) *m(f)* 2 *(= language)* siamois *m*

COMP **Siamese cat** N chat *m* siamois

Siamese twins NPL (frères *mpl*) siamois *mpl*, (sœurs *fpl*) siamoises *fpl*

SIB /ˌesaɪˈbiː/ N *(Brit)* (abbrev of **Securities and Investments Board**) ≃ COB *f*

Siberia /saɪˈbɪərɪə/ N Sibérie *f*

Siberian /saɪˈbɪərɪən/ ADJ sibérien, de Sibérie N Sibérien(ne) *m(f)*

sibilant /ˈsɪbɪlənt/ ADJ *(frm, also Phon)* sifflant N *(Phon)* sifflante *f*

sibling /ˈsɪblɪŋ/ N ◆ **~s** enfants *mfpl* de mêmes parents, fratrie *f* ◆ **one of his ~s** l'un de ses frères et sœurs ◆ **Paul and Julie are ~s** Paul et Julie sont frère et sœur ◆ **she's my ~** c'est ma sœur COMP **sibling rivalry** N rivalité *f* fraternelle

sibyl /ˈsɪbɪl/ N sibylle *f*

sibylline /ˈsɪbɪlaɪn/ ADJ sibyllin

sic /sɪk/ ADV sic

Sicilian /sɪˈsɪlɪən/ ADJ *(gen)* sicilien N 1 Sicilien(ne) *m(f)* 2 *(= dialect)* sicilien *m*

Sicily /ˈsɪsɪlɪ/ N Sicile *f* ◆ **in ~** en Sicile

sick /sɪk/ ADJ 1 *(= ill) [person]* malade ◆ **he's a ~ man** il est (très) malade ◆ **to fall** *or* **take † ~** tomber malade ◆ **to be off ~** *(= off work)* être en congé maladie ; *(= off school)* être absent pour maladie ◆ **she's off ~ with 'flu** elle n'est pas là *or* elle est absente, elle a la grippe ◆ **to go ~** se faire porter malade ◆ **to call in** *or* **phone in ~** téléphoner pour dire que l'on est malade ◆ **to be ~ of a fever** † avoir la fièvre ; → **homesick**

2 ◆ **to be ~** *(= vomit)* vomir ◆ **to be as ~ as a dog** * être malade comme un chien ◆ **to make sb ~** faire vomir qn ◆ **to make o.s. ~** se faire vomir ; *(= nauseous)* ◆ **to feel ~** avoir mal au cœur, avoir envie de vomir ◆ **I get ~ in planes** j'ai mal au cœur *or* je suis malade en avion, j'ai le mal de l'air ◆ **a ~ feeling** *(lit)* un haut-le-cœur ; *(fig)* une (sensation d')angoisse ◆ **worried ~*, ~ with worry** fou *or* malade d'inquiétude ; → **airsick, car, seasick, travel**

3 *(= disgusted)* **to make sb ~** rendre qn malade, écœurer qn ◆ **you make me ~!** tu m'écœures !, tu me dégoûtes ! ◆ **it's enough to make you ~** il y a de quoi vous écœurer *or* dégoûter ◆ **it makes me ~ to my stomach** ça m'écœure, ça me fait gerber‡ ◆ **he felt ~ about the whole business** toute l'affaire le rendait malade ◆ **it makes me ~ to think that ...** ça me rend malade de penser que ... ◆ **he was really ~ at failing the exam** * ça l'a vraiment rendu malade d'avoir échoué à l'examen ◆ **to be as ~ as a parrot** en être malade* ◆ **to be ~ at heart** *(liter = unhappy)* avoir la mort dans l'âme

4 *(= fed up)* ◆ **to be ~ of sb/sth/doing sth** en avoir assez *or* marre* de qn/qch/faire qch ◆ **to be ~ of the sight of sb** en avoir assez *or* marre* de voir qn ◆ **to be/get ~ and tired*** *or* **~ to death*** *or* **~ to the (back) teeth* of ...** en avoir/finir par en avoir par-dessus la tête* *or* ras le bol* de ...

5 *(pej = offensive) [person, mind, joke, humour, suggestion]* malsain ◆ **~ comedian** comique *m* porté sur l'humour malsain

6 *(US = inferior)* ◆ **they made our team look ~** à côté d'eux, notre équipe avait l'air nulle *or* minable

N *(Brit * = vomit)* vomi* *m*, vomissure *f*

NPL **the sick** les malades *mfpl*

COMP **sick bag** N sac *m* vomitoire

sick bay N infirmerie *f*

sick building syndrome N syndrome *m* du bâtiment malsain

sick headache N migraine *f*

sick leave N ◆ **on ~ leave** en congé *m* (de) maladie

sick list N ◆ **to be on the ~ list** *(Admin)* être porté malade ; *(* = ill)* être malade

sick-making‡ ADJ dégoûtant, gerbant‡

sick note* N *(for work)* certificat *m* médical ; *(for school)* billet *m* d'excuse

sick-out N *(US= workers' protest) mouvement de protestation où tous les travailleurs se font porter malade*

sick pay N indemnité *f* de maladie *(versée par l'employeur)*

► **sick up*** VT SEP *(Brit)* dégueuler‡, vomir

sickbed /ˈsɪkbed/ N lit *m* de malade

sicken /ˈsɪkn/ VT rendre malade, donner mal au cœur à ; *(fig)* dégoûter, écœurer VI tomber malade ◆ **to ~ for sth** *[person]* couver qch ◆ **to ~ of ...** *(fig)* se lasser de ..., en avoir assez de ...

sickening /ˈsɪknɪŋ/ ADJ 1 *(= disgusting) [sight, smell]* écœurant, qui soulève le cœur ; *[cruelty]* révoltant ; *[waste]* révoltant, dégoûtant ; *[crime]* ignoble, révoltant ◆ **a ~ feeling of failure** un écœurant sentiment d'échec ◆ **a ~**

feeling of panic une affreuse sensation de panique ◆ **a ~ feeling of foreboding** un horrible sentiment d'appréhension [2] (* = *annoying*) *[person, behaviour, situation]* agaçant, énervant [3] (= *unpleasant*) *[blow]* mauvais ; *[crunch]* sinistre ◆ **with a ~ thud** avec un bruit sourd et sinistre

sickeningly /ˈsɪknɪŋlɪ/ **ADV** *[familiar]* tristement ◆ **~ violent/polite** d'une violence/d'une politesse écœurante ◆ **it is ~ sweet** c'est si sucré que c'est écœurant ◆ **he made it all look ~ easy** avec lui, tout paraissait d'une facilité écœurante ◆ **he seems ~ happy** il semble si heureux que c'en est écœurant ◆ **he stood at the top of a ~ steep gully** il se tenait au sommet d'une ravine vertigineuse ◆ **the ship was rolling ~** le roulis du bateau soulevait le cœur

sickie* /ˈsɪkɪ/ **N** *(Brit, Austral)* ◆ **he threw a ~** il n'est pas venu au travail sous prétexte qu'il était malade

sickle /ˈsɪkl/ **N** faucille *f* **COMP sickle-cell anaemia N** *(Med)* anémie *f* à hématies falciformes

sickliness /ˈsɪklɪnɪs/ **N** *[of person]* état *m* maladif ; *[of cake]* goût *m* écœurant

sickly /ˈsɪklɪ/ **ADJ** [1] (= *unhealthy*) *[person, face, complexion, pallor]* maladif ; *[business, company]* mal en point ; *[climate]* malsain ; *[plant]* étiolé ◆ **she gave a ~ smile** elle eut un pâle sourire [2] *(Brit = nauseating)* *[smell, colour, cake]* écœurant ; *[smile]* mielleux **ADV** ◆ **~ green** d'un vert nauséeux ◆ **~ yellow** cireux ◆ **~ sweet** *[smell, taste]* douceâtre ; *[book]* mièvre ; *[person, expression]* mielleux

sickness /ˈsɪknɪs/ **N** *(NonC)* (= *illness*) maladie *f* ◆ **there's a lot of ~ in the village** il y a beaucoup de malades dans le village ◆ **there's ~ on board** il y a des malades à bord ◆ **bouts of ~** (= *vomiting*) vomissements *mpl* ◆ **mountain ~** mal *m* des montagnes ◆ **in ~ and in health** *(in marriage service)* ≈ pour le meilleur et pour le pire ; → **travel**

COMP sickness benefit N *(Brit)* (prestations *fpl* de l') assurance-maladie *f*

sickness insurance N assurance-maladie *f*

sicko‡ /ˈsɪkəʊ/ *(esp US pej)* **N** taré(e)* *m(f)* **ADJ** *[person]* taré* ; *[group]* de tarés*

sickroom /ˈsɪkrʊm/ **N** *(in school etc)* infirmerie *f* ; *(at home)* chambre *f* de malade

side /saɪd/ **N** [1] *[of person]* côté *m* ◆ **wounded in the ~** blessé au côté ◆ **to sleep on one's ~** dormir sur le côté ◆ **to hold one's ~s with laughter** se tenir les côtes ; → **split**

◆ **at/by one's side** ◆ **he had the telephone by his ~** il avait le téléphone à côté de lui *or* à portée de la main ◆ **his assistant was at** *or* **by his ~** son assistant était à ses côtés ◆ **she remained by his ~ through thick and thin** elle est restée à ses côtés *or* elle l'a soutenu à travers toutes leurs épreuves

◆ **side by side** *(lit)* côte à côte ; *(fig: in agreement)* en parfait accord *(with* avec)

[2] *[of animal]* flanc *m* ◆ **a ~ of bacon** une flèche de lard ◆ **a ~ of beef/mutton** un quartier de bœuf/mouton

[3] *(as opposed to top, bottom)* *[of box, house, car, triangle]* côté *m* ; *[of ship]* flanc *m*, côté *m* ; *[of mountain] (gen)* versant *m* ; (= *flank*) flanc *m* ; *(inside) [of cave, ditch, box]* paroi *f* ◆ **the north ~** *[of mountain]* le versant nord ◆ **vines growing on the ~ of the hill** des vignes qui poussent sur le flanc de la colline ◆ **by the ~ of the church** à côté de *or* tout près de l'église ◆ **set the box on its ~** pose la caisse sur le côté ◆ **go round the ~ of the house** contournez la maison ◆ **you'll find him round the ~ of the house** tournez le coin de la maison et vous le verrez ◆ **she's (built) like the ~ of a house‡** c'est un monument*, elle est colossale ; → **near, off**

[4] *[of cube, record, coin]* côté *m*, face *f* ; *[of garment, cloth, slice of bread, sheet of paper, shape]* côté *m* ; *(fig) [of matter, problem etc]* aspect *m* ; *[of sb's character]* facette *f* ◆ **the right ~** *[of garment, cloth]* l'endroit *m* ◆ **the wrong ~** *[of garment, cloth]* l'envers *m* ◆ **right/wrong ~ out** *[of cloth]* à l'endroit/l'envers ◆ **right/wrong ~ up** dans le bon/mauvais sens ◆ **"this side up"** *(on box etc)* "haut" ◆ **write on both ~s of the paper** écrivez des deux côtés de la feuille, écrivez recto verso ◆ **I've written six ~s** j'ai écrit six pages ◆ **the other ~ of the coin** *or* **picture** *(fig)* le revers de la médaille ◆ **they are two ~s of the same coin** *(fig) [issues]* ce sont deux facettes d'un même problème ; *[people]* ils représentent deux facettes d'une même tendance ◆ **there are two ~s to every quarrel** dans toute querelle il y a deux points de vue ◆ **look at it from his ~ (of it)** considère cela de son point de vue ◆ **now listen to my ~ of the story** maintenant écoute ma version des faits ◆ **he's got a nasty ~* to him** *or* **to his nature** il a un côté méchant ; → **bright, flip, right**

[5] (= *edge*) *[of road, lake, river]* bord *m* ; *[of wood, forest]* lisière *f* ; *[of field, estate]* bord *m*, côté *m* ◆ **by the ~ of the road/lake** *etc* au bord de la route/du lac *etc*

[6] (= *part away from centre*) côté *m* ◆ **on the other ~ of the street/room** de l'autre côté de la rue/la pièce ◆ **he crossed to the other ~ of the room** il a traversé la pièce ◆ **he was on the wrong ~ of the road** il était du mauvais côté de la route ◆ **the east ~ of the town** la partie est *or* les quartiers est de la ville ◆ **he got out of the train on the wrong ~** il est descendu du train à contre-voie ◆ **he is paralysed down one ~ of his face** il a un côté du visage paralysé ◆ **it's on this ~ of London** c'est dans cette partie de Londres ; *(between here and London)* c'est avant Londres, c'est entre ici et Londres ◆ **the science ~ of the college** la section sciences du collège ◆ **members on the other ~ of the House** *(Brit Parl)* (= *the government*) les députés *mpl* de la majorité ; (= *the opposition*) les députés *mpl* de l'opposition ◆ **he got out of bed on the wrong ~, he got out of the wrong ~ of the bed** il s'est levé du pied gauche ◆ **he's on the wrong ~ of 50** il a passé la cinquantaine ◆ **he's on the right ~ of 50** il n'a pas encore 50 ans ◆ **this ~ of Christmas** avant Noël ◆ **he makes a bit (of money) on the ~ by doing ...*** il se fait un peu d'argent en plus *or* il arrondit ses fins de mois en faisant ... ◆ **a cousin on his mother's ~** un cousin du côté de sa mère ◆ **my grandfather on my mother's ~** mon grand-père maternel ◆ **on the other ~** *(TV)* sur l'autre chaîne ◆ **it's on the heavy/big ~** c'est plutôt lourd/grand ◆ **it's on the hot/chilly ~** *[weather]* il fait plutôt chaud/froid ; → **safe, sunny** ◆ **from all ~s, from every ~** de tous côtés, de toutes parts

◆ **from side to side** ◆ **the boat rocked from ~ to ~** le bateau se balançait ◆ **to sway** *or* **swing from ~ to ~** balancer ◆ **he moved his jaw from ~ to ~** il bougeait sa mâchoire d'un côté et de l'autre

◆ **on/to one side** ◆ **he moved to one ~** il s'est écarté ◆ **to take sb on** *or* **to one ~** prendre qn à part ◆ **to put sth to** *or* **on one ~** mettre qch de côté ◆ **leaving that question to one ~ for the moment ...** laissant la question de côté pour le moment ...

[7] (= *group, team, party*) *(gen)* camp *m* ; *(Sport)* équipe *f* ; *(Pol etc)* parti *m* ◆ **he's on our ~** il est dans notre camp *or* avec nous ◆ **God was on their ~** Dieu était avec eux ◆ **to be on the ~ of the angels** avoir raison d'un point de vue moral ◆ **we have time on our ~** nous avons le temps pour nous, le temps joue en notre faveur ◆ **whose ~ are you on?** dans quel camp êtes-vous ?, qui soutenez-vous ? ◆ **to get on the wrong ~ of sb** se faire mal voir de qn ◆ **there are faults on both ~s** les deux camps ont des torts *or* sont fautifs ◆ **with a few concessions on the government ~** avec quelques concessions de la part du gouvernement ◆ **to take ~s (with sb)** prendre parti (pour qn) ◆ **to pick** *or* **choose ~s** (= *decide one's viewpoint*) choisir son camp ; *(for game etc)* faire *or* tirer les équipes ◆ **they've picked** *or* **chosen the England ~** *(Sport)* on a sélectionné l'équipe d'Angleterre ; → **change**

[8] *(Brit * = conceit)* **he's got no ~, there's no ~ to him** c'est un homme très simple, ce n'est pas un crâneur* ◆ **to put on ~** prendre des airs supérieurs, crâner*

COMP *[chapel, panel, elevation, seat]* latéral

side arms NPL armes *fpl* de poing

side dish N plat *m* d'accompagnement

side door N entrée *f* latérale, petite porte *f*

side drum N tambour *m* plat, caisse *f* claire

side effect N effet *m* secondaire

side entrance N entrée *f* latérale

side face ADJ, ADV *(Phot)* de profil

side-foot VT *[ball]* frapper de l'extérieur du pied

side glance N regard *m* oblique *or* de côté

side-impact bars NPL ⇒ **side-impact protection**

side-impact protection N *(NonC: on car)* protections *fpl* latérales, renforts *mpl* latéraux

side issue N question *f* secondaire, à-côté *m*

side judge N *(US Jur)* juge *m* adjoint

side-on ADJ *[collision, crash]* latéral ; *[view]* latéral, de côté

side order N *(Culin)* garniture *f*

side plate N petite assiette *f* *(que l'on place à la gauche de chaque convive)*

side road N *(Brit)* petite route *f*, route *f* transversale ; *(in town)* petite rue *f*, rue *f* transversale

side salad N salade *f* *(pour accompagner un plat)*

side show N *(at fair)* attraction *f* ; *(fig = minor point)* détail *m*

side-slipping N *(Ski)* dérapage *m*

side-splitting* ADJ tordant*, gondolant*

side street N petite rue *f*, rue *f* transversale

side stroke N *(Swimming)* nage *f* indienne

side trim N *(on car)* moulure *f* latérale

side view N vue *f* latérale

side-wheeler N *(US)* bateau *m* à aubes

side whiskers NPL favoris *mpl*

▸ **side against VT FUS** ◆ **to side against sb** prendre parti contre qn

▸ **side with VT FUS** ◆ **to side with sb** se ranger du côté de qn, prendre parti pour qn

sidebar /ˈsaɪdbɑːʳ/ **N** [1] *(Press)* encadré *m* [2] *(US Jur)* entretien *m* en aparté [3] *(fig = sidelight)* aspect *m* [4] *(at festival etc)* événement *m* annexe

sideboard /ˈsaɪdbɔːd/ **N** buffet *m*

sideboards *(Brit)* /ˈsaɪdbɔːdz/, **sideburns** /ˈsaɪdbɜːnz/ **NPL** pattes *fpl*, favoris *mpl*

sidecar /ˈsaɪdkɑːʳ/ **N** side-car *m*

-sided /ˈsaɪdɪd/ **ADJ** *(in compounds)* ◆ **three-sided** à trois côtés, trilatéral ◆ **many-sided** multilatéral ; → **one**

sidekick* /ˈsaɪdkɪk/ **N** (= *assistant*) acolyte *m* ; (= *friend*) copain* *m*, copine* *f*

sidelight /ˈsaɪdlaɪt/ **N** *(Brit: on car)* feu *m* de position, veilleuse *f* ◆ **it gives us a ~ on ...** cela projette un éclairage particulier sur ..., cela révèle un côté *or* aspect inattendu de ...

sideline /ˈsaɪdlaɪn/ **N** [1] *(Sport)* (ligne *f* de) touche *f* ◆ **on the ~s** *(Sport)* sur la touche ; *(fig)* dans les coulisses ◆ **he stayed** *or* **stood on the ~s** *(fig)* il n'a pas pris position, il n'est pas intervenu ◆ **to be relegated to the ~s** être mis sur la touche [2] activité *f* (*or* travail *m etc*) secondaire ◆ **he sells wood as a ~** il a aussi un petit commerce de bois ◆ **it's just a ~** *(Comm)* ce n'est pas notre spécialité **VT** *(Sport, fig)* mettre sur la touche

sidelong /ˈsaɪdlɒŋ/ **ADJ** oblique, de côté **ADV** de côté, en oblique

sidereal /saɪˈdɪərɪəl/ ADJ sidéral

sidesaddle /ˈsaɪdsædl/ ADV ◆ **to ride ~** monter en amazone

sideslip /ˈsaɪdslɪp/ *(Flying)* N glissade *f or* glissement *m* sur l'aile VI glisser sur l'aile

sidesman /ˈsaɪdzmæn/ N (pl **-men**) *(Brit Rel)* ≃ bedeau *m*

sidestep /ˈsaɪdstep/ VT *[+ blow]* éviter, esquiver ; *[+ question]* éluder ; *[+ rules etc]* ne pas tenir compte de VI *(lit)* faire un pas de côté ; *(Ski)* monter en escalier ; *(fig)* rester évasif ; *(Boxing)* esquiver

sidestepping /ˈsaɪdstepɪŋ/ N *(Ski)* montée *f* en escalier ; *(Boxing)* esquives *fpl*

sideswipe /ˈsaɪdswaɪp/ N (= *blow*) coup *m* oblique ; *(fig)* allusion *f* désobligeante

sidetable /ˈsaɪdteɪbl/ N desserte *f*

sidetrack /ˈsaɪdtræk/ VT *[+ train]* dériver, dérouter ; *(fig) [+ person]* faire s'écarter de son sujet ◆ **to get ~ed** *(fig)* s'écarter de son sujet

sidewalk /ˈsaɪdwɔːk/ N *(US)* trottoir *m*
COMP **sidewalk artist** N *(US)* artiste *mf* de rue
sidewalk café N *(US)* café *m* avec terrasse *(sur le trottoir)*

sideways /ˈsaɪdweɪz/ ADV [1] (= *to one side, side-on) [glance, look]* de biais, de côté ; *[move]* latéralement ; *[walk]* en crabe ; *[stand]* de profil ; *[sit]* de côté ; *[fall]* sur le côté ◆ **to slide ~** déraper ◆ **to turn ~** se tourner ◆ **it goes in ~** ça rentre de côté ◆ **~ on** de côté ◆ **a car parked ~ on to the kerb** une voiture garée le long du trottoir ; see also **knock** [2] *(in career)* ◆ **to move ~** changer de poste au même niveau hiérarchique ADJ [1] (= *to one side) [glance, look, movement]* de biais, de côté [2] *(in career)* ◆ **~ move** *or* **step** changement *m* de poste au même niveau hiérarchique ◆ **the Justice Minister's recent ~ move to Defence** la récente mutation du ministre de la Justice au ministère de la Défense

siding /ˈsaɪdɪŋ/ N [1] *(Rail)* voie *f* de garage *or* d'évitement ; → **goods** [2] *(US* = *wall covering)* revêtement *m* extérieur

sidle /ˈsaɪdl/ VI ◆ **to ~ along** marcher de côté, avancer de biais ◆ **to ~ in/out** *etc* entrer/sortir *etc* furtivement ◆ **he ~d into the room** il s'est faufilé dans la pièce ◆ **he ~d up to me** il s'est glissé jusqu'à moi

Sidon /ˈsaɪdən/ N Sidon

SIDS /ˌesaɪdiːˈes/ N *(Med)* (abbrev of **sudden infant death syndrome**) MSN *f*

siege /siːdʒ/ N *(Mil, fig)* siège *m* ◆ **in a state of ~** en état de siège ◆ **to lay ~ to a town** assiéger une ville ◆ **to be under ~** *[town]* être assiégé ; *(fig: by questioning etc)* être sur la sellette, être en butte à de nombreuses critiques ◆ **to raise** *or* **lift the ~** lever le siège *(lit)*
COMP **siege economy** N économie *f* de siège
siege mentality N ◆ **to have a ~ mentality** être toujours sur la défensive
siege warfare N guerre *f* de siège

Siena, Sienna /sɪˈenə/ N Sienne

Sienese /sɪəˈniːz/ ADJ siennois

sienna /sɪˈenə/ N (= *earth*) terre *f* de Sienne *or* d'ombre ; (= *colour*) ocre *m* brun ; → **burnt**

sierra /sɪˈerə/ N sierra *f*

Sierra Leone /sɪˈerəlɪˈəʊn/ N Sierra Leone *f*

Sierra Leonean /sɪˈerəlɪˈəʊnɪən/ ADJ sierra-léonais N Sierra-Léonais(e) *m(f)*

siesta /sɪˈestə/ N sieste *f* ◆ **to have** *or* **take a ~** faire une *or* la sieste

sieve /sɪv/ N *(for coal, stones)* crible *m* ; *(for sugar, flour, sand, soil)* tamis *m* ; *(for wheat)* van *m* ; *(for liquids)* passoire *f* ◆ **to rub** *or* **put through a ~** *(Culin)* passer au tamis ◆ **he's got a head** *or* **memory** *or* **brain like a ~** * il a la tête comme une passoire * VT *[+ fruit, vegetables]* passer ; *[+ sugar, flour, sand, soil]* tamiser ; *[+ coal, stones]* passer au crible, cribler

sift /sɪft/ VT [1] *[+ flour, sugar, sand]* tamiser, passer au tamis ; *[+ coal, stones]* cribler, passer au crible ; *[+ wheat]* vanner ; *(fig) [+ evidence]* passer au crible ◆ **to ~ flour on to sth** saupoudrer qch de farine (au moyen d'un tamis) [2] (also **sift out**) *(lit)* séparer (à l'aide d'un crible) ; *(fig) [+ facts, truth]* dégager *(from* de) VI *(fig)* ◆ **to ~ through sth** passer qch en revue, examiner qch

sifter /ˈsɪftəʳ/ N *(for flour, sugar, sand)* tamis *m* ; *(for soil)* cribleuse *f*, crible *m*

sigh /saɪ/ N soupir *m* ◆ **to heave** *or* **give a ~** soupirer, pousser un soupir VT ◆ **"if only he had come" she ~ed** "si seulement il était venu" dit-elle dans un soupir *or* soupira-t-elle VI soupirer, pousser un soupir ; *[wind]* gémir ◆ **he ~ed with relief** il a poussé un soupir de soulagement ◆ **to ~ for sth** soupirer après *or* pour qch ; *(for sth lost)* regretter qch ◆ **to ~ over sth** se lamenter sur qch, regretter qch

sighing /ˈsaɪɪŋ/ N *[of person]* soupirs *mpl* ; *[of wind]* gémissements *mpl*

sight /saɪt/ N [1] (= *faculty, range of vision*) vue *f* ◆ **to have good/poor ~** avoir une bonne/mauvaise vue ◆ **to lose one's ~** perdre la vue ◆ **to get back** *or* **regain one's ~** recouvrer la vue ◆ **to catch ~ of sb/sth** apercevoir qn/qch ◆ **to lose ~ of sb/sth** perdre qn/qch de vue ◆ **to keep ~ of sth** surveiller qch

◆ *preposition +* **sight** ◆ **to shoot on** *or* **at ~** tirer à vue ◆ **he translated it at ~** il l'a traduit à livre ouvert ◆ **he played the music at ~** il a déchiffré le morceau de musique ◆ **at the ~ of ...** à la vue de ..., au spectacle de ... ◆ **to know sb by ~** connaître qn de vue ◆ **the train was still in ~** on voyait encore le train, le train était encore visible ◆ **the end is (with)in ~** la fin est en vue, on entrevoit la fin ◆ **we are within ~ of a solution** nous entrevoyons une solution ◆ **we live within ~ of the sea** de chez nous on voit *or* aperçoit la mer ◆ **to come into ~** apparaître ◆ **keep the luggage in ~** surveillez les bagages

[2] (= *glimpse, act of seeing*) **it was my first ~ of Paris** c'était la première fois que je voyais Paris ◆ **I got my first ~ of that document yesterday** j'ai vu ce document hier pour la première fois ◆ **their first ~ of land came after 30 days at sea** la terre leur est apparue pour la première fois au bout de 30 jours en mer ◆ **the ~ of the cathedral** la vue de la cathédrale ◆ **I can't bear** *or* **stand the ~ of blood** je ne peux pas supporter la vue du sang ◆ **I can't bear** *or* **stand the ~ of him, I hate the ~ of him** je ne peux pas le voir (en peinture*) *or* le sentir* ◆ **to buy/accept sth ~ unseen** *(Comm)* acheter/accepter qch sans l'avoir examiné ◆ **to find favour in sb's ~** *(liter)* trouver grâce aux yeux de qn ◆ **all men are equal in the ~ of God** tous les hommes sont égaux devant Dieu ◆ **in the ~ of the law** aux yeux de la loi, devant la loi ; → **heave, second[1], short**

◆ **at first sight** à première vue, au premier abord ◆ **love at first ~** le coup de foudre

◆ **out of + sight** ◆ **out of ~** hors de vue ◆ **don't let the luggage out of your ~** ne perdez pas les bagages de vue ◆ **to keep out of ~** VI se cacher, ne pas se montrer VT cacher, ne pas montrer ◆ **it is out of ~** on ne le voit pas, ce n'est pas visible ◆ **he never lets it out of his ~** il le garde toujours sous les yeux ; *(liter)* ◆ **out of my ~!** hors de ma vue ! ◆ **keep out of his ~!** qu'il ne te voie pas ! ◆ **out of ~ out of mind** *(Prov)* loin des yeux loin du cœur *(Prov)*

[3] (= *spectacle*) spectacle *m (also pej)* ◆ **the tulips are a wonderful ~** les tulipes sont magnifiques ◆ **it is a ~ to see** *or* **a ~ to be seen** cela vaut la peine d'être vu, il faut le voir ◆ **the Grand Canyon is one of the ~s of the world** le Grand Canyon est l'un des plus beaux paysages *or* offre l'un des plus beaux spectacles au monde ◆ **it's one of the ~s of Paris** c'est l'une des attractions touristiques de Paris, c'est l'une des choses à voir à Paris ◆ **it's a sad ~** c'est triste (à voir), ça fait pitié ◆ **it's not a pretty ~** ça n'est pas beau à voir ◆ **it was a ~ for sore eyes** *(welcome)* cela réchauffait le cœur ; (* *pej*) c'était à pleurer ◆ **his face was a ~!** *(amazed etc)* il faisait une de ces têtes ! * ; *(after injury etc)* il avait une tête à faire peur ! * ◆ **I must look a ~!** je dois avoir une de ces allures ! * ◆ **doesn't she look a ~ in that hat!** elle a l'air d'un épouvantail avec ce chapeau ! ; → **see[1]**

[4] *(on gun)* mire *f* ◆ **to take ~** viser ◆ **to have sth in one's ~s** avoir qch dans sa ligne de mire ◆ **to have sb in one's ~s** *(fig)* avoir qn dans le collimateur *or* dans sa ligne de mire ◆ **to set one's ~s too high** *(fig)* viser trop haut *(fig)* ◆ **to set one's ~s on sth** avoir des vues sur qch

[5] *(phrases)* **not by a long ~** loin de là, loin s'en faut ◆ **it's a (far** *or* **long) ~ better than the other** * c'est infiniment mieux que l'autre ◆ **he's a ~ too clever** * il est par *or* bien trop malin

VT [1] (= *see*) *[+ land, person]* apercevoir

[2] ◆ **to ~ a gun** (= *aim*) prendre sa mire, viser ; (= *adjust*) régler le viseur d'un canon

COMP **sight draft** N *(Comm, Fin)* effet *m* à vue
sight-read VT *(Mus)* déchiffrer
sight-reading N déchiffrage *m*

sighted /ˈsaɪtɪd/ ADJ qui voit ◆ **partially ~** malvoyant NPL **the sighted** les voyants *mpl (lit)*, ceux *mpl* qui voient

-sighted /ˈsaɪtɪd/ ADJ *(in compounds)* ◆ **weak-sighted** à la vue faible ; → **clear, short**

sighting /ˈsaɪtɪŋ/ N ◆ **numerous ~s of the monster have been reported** le monstre aurait été aperçu à plusieurs reprises

sightless /ˈsaɪtlɪs/ ADJ *[person, eyes]* aveugle

sightline /ˈsaɪtlaɪn/ N champ *m* de vision

sightly /ˈsaɪtlɪ/ ADJ ◆ **it's not very ~** ce n'est pas beau à voir

sightseeing /ˈsaɪtsiːɪŋ/ N tourisme *m* ◆ **to go ~, to do some ~** *(gen)* faire du tourisme ; *(in town)* visiter la ville

sightseer /ˈsaɪtsiːəʳ/ N touriste *mf*

sign /saɪn/ N [1] *(with hand etc)* signe *m*, geste *m* ◆ **he made a ~ of recognition** il m'a *(or* lui a *etc)* fait signe qu'il me *(or* le *etc)* reconnaissait ◆ **they communicated by ~s** ils communiquaient par signes ◆ **to make a ~ to sb** faire signe à qn *(to do sth* de faire qch) ◆ **to make the ~ of the Cross** faire le signe de la croix *(over sb/sth* sur qn/qch) ; (= *cross o.s.*) se signer ◆ **he made a rude ~** il a fait un geste grossier

[2] (= *symbol*) signe *m* ◆ **the ~s of the zodiac** les signes *mpl* du zodiaque ◆ **born under the ~ of Leo** né sous le signe du Lion ◆ **air/earth/fire/water ~** signe *m* d'air/de terre/de feu/d'eau ; → **minus**

[3] (= *indication*) signe *m*, indication *f* ; *(Med)* signe *m* ; (= *trace*) signe *m*, trace *f* ◆ **as a ~ of ...** en signe de ... ◆ **it's a good/bad ~** c'est bon/mauvais signe ◆ **all the ~s are that ...** tout laisse à penser *or* indique que ... ◆ **those clouds are a ~ of rain** ces nuages annoncent la pluie *or* sont signe de pluie ◆ **violence is a ~ of fear** la violence est signe de peur ◆ **it's a ~ of the times** c'est un signe des temps ◆ **it's a sure ~** c'est un signe infaillible ◆ **at the slightest ~ of disagreement** au moindre signe de désaccord

◆ **any/no sign of** ◆ **has there been any ~ of him?** est-ce que quelqu'un l'a vu ? ◆ **any ~ of the dog?** on a retrouvé le chien ? ◆ **there's no ~ of him anywhere** on ne le trouve nulle part, il n'y a aucune trace de lui ◆ **there's no ~ of it anywhere** c'est introuvable, je *(or* il *etc)* n'arrive pas à le (re)trouver ◆ **there is no ~ of his agreeing** rien ne laisse à penser *or* rien n'indique qu'il va accepter ◆ **he gave no ~ of wishing to come with us** il ne donnait aucun signe de *or* il n'avait pas du tout l'air de vouloir venir avec nous ◆ **he gave no ~ of having heard us** rien n'indiquait qu'il nous avait entendus ◆ **there was no ~ of life** il n'y avait aucun signe de vie ◆ **he gave no ~ of life** *(lit, fig)* il n'a pas donné signe de vie ; → **show**

4 *(= notice)* panneau *m* ; *(on inn, shop)* enseigne *f* ; *(= traffic warnings etc)* panneau *m* (de signalisation) ; *(= directions on motorways etc)* panneau *m* (indicateur) ; *(= writing on signpost)* direction *f*, indication *f* ◆ **I can't read the ~** *(on road)* je n'arrive pas à lire le panneau

VT 1 *[+ letter, document, register, visitors' book]* signer ◆ **to ~ one's name** signer (son nom) ◆ **he ~s himself John Smith** il signe "John Smith" ◆ **~ed John Smith** *(in letters)* signé John Smith ◆ **~ed and sealed** *[agreement]* conclu en bonne et due forme ; *[new law]* voté en bonne et due forme ◆ **it was ~ed, sealed and delivered by twelve noon** *(fig)* à midi, l'affaire était entièrement réglée ; → **pledge**

2 *(Sport) [+ player]* engager

3 *[+ spoken language]* traduire en langue des signes

VI 1 signer ◆ **you have to ~ for the key** vous devez signer pour obtenir la clé ◆ **he ~ed for the parcel** il a signé le reçu pour le colis ◆ **Smith has ~ed for Celtic** *(Ftbl)* Smith a signé (un contrat) avec le Celtic ; → **dotted**

2 ◆ **to ~ to sb to do sth** faire signe à qn de faire qch

3 *(= use sign language)* s'exprimer dans le langage des signes, signer

COMP **sign language** N langage *m* des signes ◆ **to talk in ~ language** parler *or* communiquer par signes

sign writer N peintre *mf* d'enseignes

► **sign away** VT SEP ◆ **to sign sth away** signer sa renonciation à qch, signer l'abandon de son droit sur qch ◆ **to ~ one's life away** *(fig)* hypothéquer son avenir

► **sign in** VI *(in factory)* pointer *(en arrivant)* ; *(in hotel, club etc)* signer le registre *(en arrivant)*

VT SEP *(at club)* ◆ **to ~ sb in** faire entrer qn en tant qu'invité *(en signant le registre)*

► **sign off** VI 1 *(Rad, TV)* terminer l'émission ◆ **this is Jacques Dupont ~ing off** ici Jacques Dupont qui vous dit au revoir

2 *(on leaving work)* pointer en partant ; *(Brit: DSS) informer la sécurité sociale que l'on a retrouvé du travail*

3 *(at end of letter)* terminer sa lettre

VT FUS *(fig) (= conclude) [+ deal, career etc]* conclure

► **sign on** VI 1 *(= enrol) (for course etc)* s'inscrire ; *(for job)* se faire embaucher *(as* comme, en tant que) ; *(Mil)* s'engager *(as* comme, en tant que) ; *(Brit) (at employment office)* pointer au chômage, pointer à la sécurité sociale ◆ **I've ~ed on for German conversation** je me suis inscrit au cours de conversation allemande

2 *(on arrival at work)* pointer en arrivant

VT SEP *[+ employee]* embaucher ; *(Mil)* engager

► **sign out** VT SEP *[+ library book, sports equipment etc]* signer pour emprunter

VI *(in hotel, club etc)* signer le registre *(en partant)* ; *(in office)* pointer *(en partant)*

► **sign over** VT SEP céder par écrit *(to* à)

► **sign up** VI ⇒ **sign on vi 1**

VT SEP ⇒ **sign on vt sep**

signage /ˈsaɪnɪdʒ/ N signalisation *f*

signal /ˈsɪgnl/ N 1 *(gen, Ling, Naut, Psych, Rail)* signal *m* ◆ **at a prearranged ~** à un signal convenu ◆ **the ~ for departure** le signal du départ ◆ **flag ~s** *(Naut)* signaux *mpl* par pavillons ◆ **(traffic) ~s** feux *mpl* de circulation ◆ **the ~ is at red** *(Rail)* le signal est au rouge ◆ **I didn't see his ~** *(driver)* je n'ai pas vu son clignotant ; → **distress, hand**

2 *(= electronic impulse, message: Rad, Telec, TV)* signal *m* ◆ **I'm getting the engaged ~** ça sonne occupé *or* pas libre ◆ **send a ~ to HQ to the effect that ...** envoyez un signal *or* message au QG pour dire que ... ◆ **the ~ is very weak** *(Rad, Telec, TV)* le signal est très faible ◆ **station ~** *(Rad, TV)* indicatif *m* de l'émetteur ◆ **the Signals** *(Mil)* les Transmissions *fpl*

ADJ *[success, triumph]* éclatant, insigne *(liter)* ; *[failure]* notoire, insigne *(liter)* ; *[contribution]* remarquable, insigne *(liter)* ; *[importance]* capital

VT *[+ message]* communiquer par signaux ◆ **to ~ sb on/through** *etc* faire signe à qn d'avancer/de passer *etc* ◆ **to ~ a turn** *(while driving)* indiquer *or* signaler un changement de direction ◆ **to ~ that ...** signaler que ...

VI *(gen)* faire des signaux ; *(while driving)* mettre son clignotant ◆ **to ~ to sb** faire signe à qn *(to do sth* de faire qch)

COMP **signal book** N *(Naut)* code *m* international de signaux, livre *m* des signaux

signal box N *(Rail)* cabine *f* d'aiguillage, poste *m* d'aiguillage *or* de signalisation

signal flag N *(Naut)* pavillon *m* de signalisation

signalize /ˈsɪgnəlaɪz/ VT *(= mark, make notable)* marquer ; *(= point out)* distinguer, signaler

signally /ˈsɪgnəlɪ/ ADV manifestement ◆ **a task they have ~ failed to accomplish** une tâche qu'ils n'ont manifestement pas su accomplir ◆ **the present law has ~ failed** la loi actuelle a manifestement échoué

signalman /ˈsɪgnəlmæn/ N (pl **-men**) *(Rail)* aiguilleur *m* ; *(Naut)* signaleur *m*, sémaphoriste *m*

signatory /ˈsɪgnətərɪ/ ADJ signataire N signataire *mf (to* de)

signature /ˈsɪgnətʃəʳ/ N 1 signature *f* ◆ **to set** *or* **put one's ~ to sth** apposer sa signature à qch 2 *(Mus = key signature)* armature *f* COMP **signature tune** N *(esp Brit)* indicatif *m (musical)*

signboard /ˈsaɪnbɔːd/ N *(for advertisements)* panneau *m* publicitaire

signer /ˈsaɪnəʳ/ N signataire *mf*

signet /ˈsɪgnɪt/ N sceau *m*, cachet *m* COMP **signet ring** N chevalière *f* ; → **writer**

significance /sɪgˈnɪfɪkəns/ N *(= meaning)* signification *f* ; *(= importance) [of event, speech]* importance *f*, portée *f* ◆ **a look of deep ~** un regard lourd de sens ◆ **what he thinks is of no ~** peu importe ce qu'il pense ◆ **it was of great ~** c'était très significatif ◆ **this is of particular ~** ceci est particulièrement important *or* significatif

significant /sɪgˈnɪfɪkənt/ LANGUAGE IN USE 26.1

ADJ 1 *(= appreciable) [number, amount, difference, factor, role, implications]* significatif ; *[event]* significatif, d'une grande portée ◆ **a ~ number of people** un nombre significatif de personnes, un grand nombre de gens 2 *(= meaningful: gen)* significatif ; *[look, sigh, tone]* lourd de sens ◆ **it is ~ that ...** il est significatif que ... + *subj* ◆ **statistically/politically/historically ~** statistiquement/politiquement/historiquement significatif

COMP **significant figure** N *(Math)* chiffre *m* significatif

significant other N partenaire *mf*

significantly /sɪgˈnɪfɪkəntlɪ/ ADV 1 *(= appreciably) [higher, lower, different, better, reduced]* considérablement ; *[contribute]* fortement ◆ **to change/improve/increase ~** changer/s'améliorer/augmenter considérablement 2 *(= notably)* ◆ **he was ~ absent** son absence a été remarquée ◆ **~, most applicants are men** il est significatif que la plupart des candidats soient des hommes ◆ **~, he refused** il est significatif qu'il ait refusé 3 *(= meaningfully)* ◆ **to look at sb ~** jeter à qn un regard lourd de sens ◆ **to smile ~** avoir un sourire lourd de sens

signification /ˌsɪgnɪfɪˈkeɪʃən/ N signification *f*, sens *m*

signify /ˈsɪgnɪfaɪ/ VT 1 *(= mean)* signifier, vouloir dire *(that* que) ; *(= indicate)* indiquer, dénoter ◆ **it signifies intelligence** cela indique *or* dénote de l'intelligence 2 *(= make known)* signifier, indiquer *(that* que) ; *[+ one's approval]* signifier ; *[+ one's opinion]* faire connaître VI avoir de l'importance ◆ **it does not ~** cela n'a aucune importance, cela importe peu

signing /ˈsaɪnɪŋ/ N 1 *[of letter, contract, treaty etc]* signature *f* 2 *(Sport)* **Clarke, their recent ~ from Liverpool** Clarke, leur récent transfert de Liverpool 3 *(= sign language)* langage *m* des signes

signpost /ˈsaɪnpəʊst/ N poteau *m* indicateur VT *[+ direction, place]* indiquer ◆ **Lewes is ~ed at the crossroads** Lewes est indiqué au carrefour ◆ **the road is badly ~ed** *(= not indicated)* la route est mal indiquée ; *(= no signposts on it)* la route est mal signalisée

signposting /ˈsaɪnpəʊstɪŋ/ N signalisation *f* (verticale)

Sikh /siːk/ N Sikh *mf* ADJ sikh

Sikhism /ˈsiːkɪzəm/ N sikhisme *m*

silage /ˈsaɪlɪdʒ/ N *(= fodder)* fourrage *m* ensilé *or* vert ; *(= method)* ensilage *m*

silence /ˈsaɪləns/ N silence *m* ◆ **he called for ~** il a demandé *or* réclamé le silence ◆ **when he finished speaking, there was ~** quand il a eu fini de parler, le silence s'est installé ◆ **the ~ was broken by a cry** un cri a rompu *or* déchiré le silence ◆ **they listened in ~** ils ont écouté en silence ◆ **a two minutes' ~** deux minutes de silence ◆ **the right to ~** *(Jur)* le droit au silence ◆ **your ~ on this matter ...** le mutisme dont vous faites preuve à ce sujet ... ◆ **there is ~ in official circles** dans les milieux autorisés on garde le silence ◆ **to pass sth over in ~** passer qch sous silence ◆ **~ gives** *or* **means consent** *(Prov)* qui ne dit mot consent *(Prov)* ◆ **~ is golden** *(Prov)* le silence est d'or *(Prov)* → **dead, radio, reduce**

VT 1 *[+ person, critic, guns] (gen)* faire taire ; *(by force etc)* réduire au silence ; *[+ noise]* étouffer ; *[+ conscience]* faire taire ◆ **to ~ criticism** faire taire les critiques ◆ **to ~ the opposition** faire taire l'opposition, réduire l'opposition au silence

2 *(= kill)* ◆ **to ~ sb** faire taire qn définitivement

silencer /ˈsaɪlənsəʳ/ N *(on gun, Brit: on car)* silencieux *m*

silent /ˈsaɪlənt/ ADJ 1 *(= making no noise) [person, machine, place, prayer, demonstration, tribute]* silencieux ◆ **to be** *or* **keep ~** garder le silence, rester silencieux ◆ **to fall** *or* **become ~** se taire ◆ **be ~!** taisez-vous !, silence ! ◆ **~ tears rolled down his cheeks** des larmes coulaient en silence sur ses joues ◆ **to look at sb in ~ contempt** dévisager qn en silence et avec mépris ◆ **she looked at me in ~ admiration** elle me regarda, muette d'admiration ◆ **to watch in ~ despair** observer avec un désespoir muet ◆ **to sit in ~ contemplation of sth** rester assis à contempler qch en silence ◆ **his mouth was open in a ~ scream** il avait la bouche ouverte pour crier mais aucun son n'en sortait ◆ **to make a ~ protest** protester en silence ◆ **it was (as) ~ as the grave** *or* **the tomb** il régnait un silence de mort ; see also **adj 2**

2 *(= saying nothing)* ◆ **to be ~ (on** *or* **about sth)** *[person, organization]* garder le silence (sur qch), rester muet (sur qch) ◆ **the law is ~ on this point** la loi ne dit rien à ce sujet ◆ **to keep** *or* **remain** *or* **stay ~ (on** *or* **about sth)** garder le silence (sur qch) ◆ **he was (as) ~ as the grave** *or*

tomb il était muet comme une tombe ; see also adj 1 ◆ **you have the right to remain ~** *(Police)* vous avez le droit de garder le silence ◆ **to give sb the ~ treatment** ne plus parler à qn

3 *(= taciturn)* *[person]* taciturne ◆ **he's the strong, ~ type** il est du genre géant taciturne

4 *(Cine)* *[film, movie]* muet ◆ **the ~ era** l'époque *f* du (cinéma) muet

5 *(Ling = not pronounced)* *[letter]* muet ◆ **~ "h"** "h" muet

N *(Cine)* ◆ **the ~s** *(gen pl)* les films *mpl* muets, le (cinéma) muet

COMP **silent killer** N *maladie mortelle aux symptômes indécelables*
the silent majority N la majorité silencieuse
silent partner N *(US Comm)* (associé *m*) commanditaire *m*
silent revolution N révolution *f* silencieuse
the silent screen *(Cine)* N le (cinéma) muet
silent witness N témoin *m* muet

silently /ˈsaɪləntlɪ/ ADV *(= without speaking)* en silence ; *(= without making any noise)* silencieusement

Silesia /saɪˈliːʃɪə/ N Silésie *f*

silex /ˈsaɪleks/ N silex *m*

silhouette /ˌsɪluːˈet/ N *(gen, Art)* silhouette *f* ◆ **to see sth in ~** voir la silhouette de qch, voir qch en silhouette VT ◆ **to be ~d against** se découper contre, se profiler sur ◆ **~d against** se découpant contre, se profilant sur

silica /ˈsɪlɪkə/ N silice *f* COMP **silica gel** N gel *m* de silice

silicate /ˈsɪlɪkɪt/ N silicate *m*

siliceous /sɪˈlɪʃəs/ ADJ siliceux

silicon /ˈsɪlɪkən/ N silicium *m*

COMP **Silicon Alley** N Silicon Alley *f* *(quartier contenant de nombreuses entreprises d'informatique)*
silicon carbide N carbure *m* de silicium
silicon chip N puce *f* électronique
Silicon Valley N Silicon Valley *f*

silicone /ˈsɪlɪkəʊn/ N silicone *f*

silicosis /ˌsɪlɪˈkəʊsɪs/ N silicose *f*

silk /sɪlk/ N 1 *(= material)* soie *f* ; *(= thread)* (fil *m* de) soie *f* ◆ **they were all in their ~s and satins** elles étaient toutes en grande toilette ◆ **the shelves were full of ~s and satins** les rayonnages regorgeaient de soieries et de satins ; → **artificial, raw, sewing**

2 *(Brit Jur = barrister)* avocat *m* de la couronne ◆ **to take ~** être nommé avocat de la couronne

ADJ de *or* en soie ◆ **you can't make a ~ purse out of a sow's ear** *(Prov)* on ne peut pas arriver à un excellent résultat sans de bonnes bases

COMP **silk factory** N fabrique *f* de soie
silk finish N ◆ **with a ~ finish** *[cloth, paintwork]* satiné
silk hat N *(= top hat)* haut-de-forme *m*
silk industry N soierie *f*
silk manufacturer N fabricant *m* en soierie ; *(in Lyons)* soyeux *m*
silk-screen printing N *(NonC)* sérigraphie *f*
silk stocking N bas *m* de soie
silk thread N fil *m* de soie

silken /ˈsɪlkən/ ADJ 1 *(= made of silk)* *[ribbon, fabric]* de soie, en soie 2 *(= like silk)* *[hair, eyelashes, skin]* soyeux ; *[voice]* suave ◆ **a ~ sheen** un lustre soyeux COMP **the Silken Ladder** N *(Mus)* l'Échelle *f* de soie

silkiness /ˈsɪlkɪnɪs/ N soyeux *m*

silkworm /ˈsɪlkwɜːm/ N ver *m* à soie ◆ **breeding** sériciculture *f* *(SPÉC)*, élevage *m* des vers à soie

silky /ˈsɪlkɪ/ ADJ *[hair, skin, fabric]* soyeux ; *[voice]* suave ◆ **a ~ sheen** un lustre soyeux ◆ **~ smooth** *or* **soft** d'une douceur soyeuse

sill /sɪl/ N *[of window]* rebord *m*, appui *m* ; *[of door]* seuil *m* ; *[of car]* bas *m* de marche

silliness /ˈsɪlɪnɪs/ N sottise *f*

silly /ˈsɪlɪ/ ADJ 1 *(= foolish)* *[person, behaviour, mistake]* bête ; *[remark, idea, game]* idiot ◆ **I hope he won't do anything ~** j'espère qu'il ne va pas faire de bêtises ◆ **don't be ~!** ne fais pas l'idiot(e) ! ◆ **to drink o.s. ~** * boire à en devenir idiot ◆ **you ~ fool!** espèce d'idiot(e) ! ◆ **the ~ idiot!** quel(le) imbécile ! ◆ **you're a ~ little boy** tu es un gros bêta * ◆ **shut up, you ~ old fool!** tais-toi, vieux fou ! ◆ **(if you) ask a ~ question, (you) get a ~ answer** à question idiote, réponse idiote ◆ **I'm sorry, it was a ~ thing to say** excusez-moi, j'ai dit une bêtise ◆ **that was a ~ thing to do** c'était bête de faire ça ◆ **it's the silliest thing I ever heard** c'est la plus grosse bêtise que j'aie jamais entendue ◆ **I used to worry about the silliest little things** je m'inquiétais des moindres vétilles ◆ **he was ~ to resign** il a été bête de démissionner

2 *(= ridiculous)* *[name, hat, price]* ridicule ◆ **I feel ~ in this hat** je me sens ridicule avec ce chapeau ◆ **to make sb look ~** rendre qn ridicule

N * idiot(e) *m(f)* ◆ **you big ~!** espèce d'imbécile !

COMP **silly billy** * N gros bêta *, grosse bêtasse *
silly money N sommes *fpl* ridiculement élevées
the silly season N *(Brit Press)* la période creuse *(pour la presse)*

silo /ˈsaɪləʊ/ N *(gen, Mil)* silo *m*

silt /sɪlt/ N *(gen)* limon *m* ; *(= mud)* vase *f*

► **silt up** VI *(with mud)* s'envaser ; *(with sand)* s'ensabler VT SEP engorger

silting /ˈsɪltɪŋ/ N envasement *m*, ensablement *m*

Silurian /saɪˈlʊərɪən/ ADJ, N *(Geol)* silurien *m*

silver /ˈsɪlvəʳ/ N *(NonC)* 1 *(= metal)* argent *m* ; *(= silverware, cutlery etc)* argenterie *f*

2 *(= money)* argent *m* (monnayé), monnaie *f* *(en pièces d'argent or de nickel)* ◆ **have you got any ~? – sorry, only notes** est-ce que vous avez de la monnaie ? – désolé, je n'ai que des billets ◆ **£2 in ~** 2 livres en pièces d'argent

ADJ 1 *(= made of silver)* en argent ◆ **to be born with a ~ spoon in one's mouth** naître avec une cuiller d'argent dans la bouche

2 *(in colour)* argenté ; *[car]* gris métallisé *inv* ; → **cloud**

VT *[+ mirror, fork]* argenter

COMP **silver age** N âge *m* d'argent
silver birch N bouleau *m* argenté
silver collection N *(at meeting etc)* quête *f* ◆ **"there will be a silver collection"** "vous êtes priés de contribuer généreusement à la quête"
silver disc N *(Brit Mus)* disque *m* d'argent
silver fir N sapin *m* argenté
silver foil N ⇒ **silver paper**
silver fox N renard *m* argenté
silver gilt N plaqué *m* argent
silver-grey ADJ gris argenté *inv*
silver-haired ADJ aux cheveux argentés
silver jubilee N (fête *f* du) vingt-cinquième anniversaire *m* *(d'un événement)*
silver lining N *(fig)* ◆ **to have a ~ lining** avoir de bons côtés ◆ **to look for the ~ lining in sth** chercher le bon côté de qch ; → **cloud**
silver medal N médaille *f* d'argent
silver medallist N médaillé(e) *m(f)* d'argent
silver paper N papier *m* d'argent
silver plate N *(NonC)* *(= solid silver articles)* argenterie *f* ; *(= electroplate)* plaqué *m* argent
silver-plated ADJ argenté, plaqué argent *inv*
silver plating N argenture *f*
the silver screen N *(Cine)* le grand écran
the Silver State N *(US)* le Nevada
silver surfers * NPL *(esp US)* internautes *mfpl* aux tempes grisonnantes
silver tongue N ◆ **to have a ~ tongue** être beau parleur ◆ **his ~ tongue** ses belles paroles
silver-tongued ADJ à la langue déliée, éloquent
silver wedding N noces *fpl* d'argent

silverback /ˈsɪlvəbæk/ N *(= gorilla)* dos *m* argenté

silverfish /ˈsɪlvəfɪʃ/ N (pl **silverfish**) poisson *m* d'argent, lépisme *m*

silverside /ˈsɪlvəsaɪd/ N *(Brit Culin)* ≃ gîte *m* à la noix

silversmith /ˈsɪlvəsmɪθ/ N orfèvre *mf*

silverware /ˈsɪlvəwɛəʳ/ N argenterie *f* ; (* *= trophies*) trophées *mpl*

silvery /ˈsɪlvərɪ/ ADJ *[colour, light, hair]* argenté ; *[sound, voice, laugh]* argentin ◆ **~ grey/white** gris/blanc argenté *inv*

silviculture /ˈsɪlvɪˌkʌltʃəʳ/ N sylviculture *f*

SIM card /ˈsɪmkɑːd/ N (abbrev of **Subscriber Identity Module card**) carte *f* SIM

simian /ˈsɪmɪən/ ADJ, N simien(ne) *m(f)*

similar /ˈsɪmɪləʳ/ ADJ semblable *(to sb/sth* à qn/qch) ; *(= roughly similar)* similaire *(to sb/sth* à qn/qch) ◆ **we have a ~ house** notre maison est presque la même *or* presque pareille ◆ **your case is ~** votre cas est semblable *or* similaire ◆ **the two houses are so ~ that ...** les deux maisons sont si semblables que *or* se ressemblent à tel point que ... ◆ **on a ~ occasion** dans des circonstances analogues ◆ **in a ~ situation** dans une situation analogue *or* de ce genre ◆ **in a ~ way** de façon analogue ◆ **everyone is of a ~ age** tout le monde a à peu près le même âge ◆ **they all taste somewhat ~** ils ont tous à peu près le même goût ◆ **paint removers and ~ products** les décapants et les produits similaires ◆ **he asked for 38 ~ offences to be considered** il a demandé à ce que 38 délits similaires soient pris en considération ◆ **vehicles ~ to the bicycle** véhicules *mpl* voisins de *or* apparentés à la bicyclette ◆ **the feeling is ~ to being drunk** la sensation est semblable à celle de l'ivresse

◆ **similar in ...** ◆ **they are ~ in appearance** ils se ressemblent ◆ **the two cars are ~ in design** les deux voitures sont de conception similaire ◆ **the two houses are ~ in size** les deux maisons sont de dimensions similaires *or* comparables ◆ **he is ~ in character to his father** il a un peu le même caractère que son père ◆ **it is ~ in colour** c'est à peu près de la même couleur ◆ **it is ~ in colour to a ruby** c'est d'une couleur semblable à celle du rubis

COMP **similar triangles** NPL *(Geom)* triangles *mpl* semblables

similarity /ˌsɪmɪˈlærɪtɪ/ LANGUAGE IN USE 5.3 N ressemblance *f (to* avec ; *between* entre), similitude *f (between* entre), similarité *f (between* entre)

similarly /ˈsɪmɪləlɪ/ ADV *[treat, behave etc]* de la même façon, de façon similaire ; *[pleasant, unpleasant, angry etc]* tout aussi ◆ **they were ~ dressed** ils étaient habillés de façon similaire, leurs vêtements se ressemblaient ◆ **~, we don't agree with ...** de même, nous ne sommes pas d'accord avec ...

simile /ˈsɪmɪlɪ/ N *(Literat)* comparaison *f* ◆ **style rich in ~** style *m* riche en comparaisons

similitude /sɪˈmɪlɪtjuːd/ N similitude *f*, ressemblance *f* ; *(Literat etc)* comparaison *f*

SIMM (chip) /ˈsɪm(tʃɪp)/ (abbrev of **single in-line memory module**) N barrette *f* SIMM

simmer /ˈsɪməʳ/ N *(= slight boil)* faible ébullition *f* ◆ **the stew was just on the ~** le ragoût cuisait à feu doux *or* mijotait VI *[water]* frémir ; *[vegetables]* cuire à feu doux ; *[soup, stew]* mijoter, cuire à feu doux ; *(fig)* *(with excitement)* être en ébullition ; *(with anticipation)* être tout excité d'avance ; *(with discontent)* bouillir de mécontentement ; *[revolt]* couver ; *[anger]* couver, monter ◆ **he was ~ing (with rage)** il bouillait (de rage) VT *[+ water, dye]* faire cuire à petits bouillons ; *[+ soup, stew]* faire mijoter *or* cuire à feu doux ; *[+ vegetables]* faire cuire à feu doux

► **simmer down** * VI *(fig)* s'apaiser, se calmer ◆ **~ down!** calme-toi !, un peu de calme !

simnel cake /ˈsɪmnlkeɪk/ N *(Brit)* gâteau *m* aux raisins recouvert de pâte d'amandes *(généralement servi à Pâques)*

Simon /ˈsaɪmən/ N Simon *m* ◆ **~ says ...** *(= game)* Jacques a dit ...

simonize /ˈsaɪmənaɪz/ VT lustrer, polir

simony /ˈsaɪmənɪ/ N simonie *f*

simper /ˈsɪmpəʳ/ N sourire *m* affecté ◆ **~s** minauderie(s) *f(pl)* VTI minauder ◆ **"yes" she ~ed** "oui" dit-elle en minaudant

simpering /ˈsɪmpərɪŋ/ N minauderies *fpl*, mignardises *fpl* ADJ *[person]* minaudier ; *[smile]* affecté ◆ **to give sb a ~ smile** sourire à qn en minaudant

simperingly /ˈsɪmpərɪŋlɪ/ ADV d'une manière affectée, avec affectation

simple /ˈsɪmpl/ ADJ 1 *(= uncomplicated) [question, task, machine, food, person, substance, life form]* simple *after n* ◆ **it's as ~ as ABC** c'est simple comme bonjour* ◆ **a dangerously ~ way of ...** une façon dangereusement simpliste de ... ◆ **a ~ black dress** une robe noire toute simple ◆ **in ~ English, in ~ language** en termes simples, en langage clair ◆ **the ~ life** la vie simple ◆ **she likes the ~ life** elle aime vivre simplement *or* avec simplicité ◆ **the ~ things in** *or* **of life** les choses simples de la vie ◆ **they're ~ people** ce sont des gens simples ◆ **I'm a ~ soul** je suis tout simple ◆ **in ~ terms** en termes simples ◆ **to make simple(r)** simplifier ◆ **it's a ~ matter to have the clock repaired** c'est très simple de faire réparer la pendule ; → **adj 2** ◆ **nothing could be simpler!** c'est tout ce qu'il y a de plus simple ! ◆ **it is ~ to fix** c'est facile à réparer ◆ **the camcorder is ~ to use** ce caméscope est simple à utiliser ◆ **the ~ truth** la vérité pure ; → **pure**

2 *(= mere)* simple *before n* ◆ **the ~ fact that ...** le simple fait que ... ◆ **the ~ fact is I haven't the time** je n'ai tout simplement pas le temps ◆ **the ~ fact is he's a liar** c'est tout simplement un menteur ◆ **he's a ~ labourer** c'est un simple manœuvre ◆ **it's a ~ matter of money/practice** c'est une simple question d'argent/de pratique ◆ **it's a ~ matter of buying another key** il s'agit tout simplement d'acheter une autre clé ; → **adj 1** ◆ **a ~ phone call could win you a week's holiday in Florida** un simple appel et vous pourriez gagner une semaine de vacances en Floride ◆ **for the ~ reason that...** pour la simple raison que ...

3 *(*: mentally) [person]* simplet

COMP **simple division** N *(Math)* division *f* simple

simple equation N *(Math)* équation *f* du premier degré

simple fraction N *(Math)* fraction *f* simple

simple fracture N *(Med)* fracture *f* simple

simple-hearted ADJ candide, franc (franche *f*), ouvert

simple interest N *(Fin)* intérêts *mpl* simples

simple majority N majorité *f* simple

simple-minded ADJ simplet, simple d'esprit

simple-mindedness N simplicité *f* d'esprit, naïveté *f*

simple sentence N phrase *f* simple

Simple Simon N nigaud *m*, naïf *m*

simple tense N temps *m* simple

simple time N *(Mus)* mesure *f* simple

simpleton /ˈsɪmpltən/ N nigaud(e) *m(f)*, niais(e) *m(f)*

simplicity /sɪmˈplɪsɪtɪ/ N simplicité *f* ◆ **it's ~ itself** c'est la simplicité même, c'est tout ce qu'il y a de plus simple

simplifiable /ˈsɪmplɪfaɪəbl/ ADJ simplifiable

simplification /ˌsɪmplɪfɪˈkeɪʃən/ N simplification *f*

simplify /ˈsɪmplɪfaɪ/ VT simplifier

simplistic /sɪmˈplɪstɪk/ ADJ *(pej)* simpliste ◆ **it is ~ to say that ...** il est simpliste de dire que ...

Simplon Pass /ˈsɪmplɒn,pɑːs/ N col *m* du Simplon

simply /ˈsɪmplɪ/ ADV 1 *(= merely)* simplement ◆ **I ~ said that ...** j'ai simplement dit que ... ◆ **she could ~ refuse** elle pourrait refuser purement et simplement ◆ **he was known ~ as Jay** on l'appelait simplement Jay ◆ **it ~ isn't possible, it's ~ impossible** c'est absolument *or* tout simplement impossible ◆ **that's ~ the way it is** c'est comme ça ◆ **it's ~ a question of money** c'est simplement une question d'argent ◆ **they sacked her ~ because she's pregnant** ils l'ont renvoyée simplement parce qu'elle était enceinte

2 *(= absolutely)* ◆ **you ~ must come !** il faut absolument que vous veniez *subj* ! ◆ **I ~ can't believe it** je n'arrive vraiment pas à y croire ◆ **that is ~ not true** c'est tout simplement faux ◆ **that is ~ not good enough!** c'est lamentable ! ◆ **he is quite ~ the best** il est tout simplement le meilleur, il est le meilleur, cela ne fait aucun doute ◆ **it was quite ~ the worst moment of my life** ce fut sans aucun doute le pire moment de ma vie

3 *(= straightforwardly) [speak]* simplement ◆ **very ~, he was short of money** il était tout simplement à court d'argent ◆ **to put it ~, we've got a problem** en deux mots, nous avons un problème

4 *(= modestly) [live, dress, furnish]* simplement, avec simplicité

simulacrum /ˌsɪmjʊˈleɪkrəm/ N (pl **simulacra** /sɪmjʊˈleɪkrə/) simulacre *m*

simulate /ˈsɪmjʊleɪt/ VT simuler ; *[+ emotion, illness]* simuler, feindre COMP **simulated leather** N imitation *f* cuir

simulation /ˌsɪmjʊˈleɪʃən/ N simulation *f*

simulator /ˈsɪmjʊleɪtəʳ/ N simulateur *m* ; (also **flight simulator**) simulateur *m* de vol

simulcast /ˈsɪməlkɑːst/ VT diffuser simultanément à la radio et à la télévision N émission *f* radiotélévisée

simultaneity /ˌsɪməltəˈniːɪtɪ/ N simultanéité *f*

simultaneous /ˌsɪməlˈteɪnɪəs/ ADJ simultané COMP **simultaneous broadcast** N émission *f* simultanée

simultaneous equations NPL *(Math)* système *m* d'équations

simultaneous translation N traduction *f* simultanée

simultaneously /ˌsɪməlˈteɪnɪəslɪ/ ADV simultanément ◆ **~ with sb/sth** en même temps que qn/qch

sin /sɪn/ N péché *m* ◆ **~s of omission/commission** péchés *mpl* par omission/par action ◆ **a ~ against (the law of) God** un manquement à la loi de Dieu ◆ **it's a ~ to do that** *(Rel)* c'est un péché de faire cela ; *(hum)* c'est une honte *or* un crime de faire cela ◆ **to live in ~** † *(unmarried)* vivre dans le péché *(with sb* avec qn) → **seven, ugly** VI pécher *(against* contre) ◆ **he was more ~ned against than ~ning** il était plus victime que coupable

COMP **sin bin** N *(US Ice Hockey etc)* prison *f* ; *(Brit = institution) établissement pour enfants en difficulté*

sin tax * N *(US)* taxe *f* sur le tabac et l'alcool

Sinai /ˈsaɪneɪaɪ/ N ◆ **(the) ~** le Sinaï ◆ **the ~ Desert** le désert du Sinaï ◆ **Mount ~** le mont Sinaï

Sinbad /ˈsɪnbæd/ N ◆ **~ the Sailor** Sinbad le Marin

since /sɪns/ LANGUAGE IN USE 17.1

CONJ 1 *(in time)* depuis que ◆ **~ he'd moved there his health had improved** depuis qu'il s'y était installé sa santé s'était améliorée

> When **since** is followed by the present perfect in English, use the present in French.

◆ **~ I have been here** depuis que je suis ici ◆ **~ she's been working for us** depuis qu'elle travaille pour nous

> When **since** is followed by the past in English, use the passé composé in French.

◆ **ever ~ I met him** depuis que *or* depuis le jour où je l'ai rencontré ◆ **it's a week ~ I saw him** cela fait une semaine que je ne l'ai (pas) vu, je ne l'ai pas vu depuis une semaine ◆ **it is a long time ~ I last saw you** il y a longtemps que je ne vous ai vu ◆ **it's ages ~ I saw you** cela fait des siècles qu'on ne s'est pas vus*

2 *(= because)* puisque ◆ **why don't you buy it, ~ you are so rich!** achète-le donc, puisque tu es si riche !

ADV depuis ◆ **he has not been here ~** il n'est pas venu depuis ◆ **he has been my friend ever ~** il est resté mon ami depuis (ce moment-là) ◆ **not long ~** il y a peu de temps ◆ **it's many years ~** il y a bien des années de cela, cela fait bien des années

PREP depuis ◆ **~ arriving** *or* **his arrival** depuis son arrivée, depuis qu'il est arrivé ◆ **I have been waiting ~ 10 o'clock** j'attends depuis 10 heures ◆ **I'd been waiting ~ 10 o'clock** j'attendais depuis 10 heures ◆ **~ then** depuis (lors) ◆ **~ when has he had a car?** depuis quand a-t-il une voiture ? ◆ **~ when?** (*, *iro*) depuis quand ?* ◆ **he left in June, ~ when we have not heard from him** il est parti en juin et nous sommes sans nouvelles depuis *or* et depuis lors nous sommes sans nouvelles ◆ **ever ~ 1900 France has attempted to ...** depuis 1900 la France tente de ... ◆ **ever ~ then** *or* **that time she's never gone out alone** depuis ce temps-là elle ne sort plus jamais seule ◆ **how long is it ~ the accident?** il s'est passé combien de temps depuis l'accident ?, l'accident remonte à quand ?

sincere /sɪnˈsɪəʳ/ LANGUAGE IN USE 22, 23.6 ADJ sincère *(about sth* à propos de qch) ◆ **my ~ good wishes** mes vœux les plus sincères ◆ **it is my ~ belief that ...** je crois sincèrement que ... ◆ **to be ~ in one's desire to do sth** *or* **in wanting to do sth** désirer *or* vouloir sincèrement faire qch

sincerely /sɪnˈsɪəlɪ/ ADV 1 *(= genuinely) [hope, believe, regret, say]* sincèrement ◆ **his ~ held religious beliefs** les croyances religieuses auxquelles il est sincèrement attaché 2 *(in letters)* ◆ **Yours ~** *(Brit)*, **Sincerely yours** *(US)* Veuillez agréer, Monsieur *(or* Madame *etc)*, l'expression de mes salutations distinguées

sincerity /sɪnˈserɪtɪ/ N *[of person, emotion]* sincérité *f* ◆ **in all ~** en toute sincérité

sine /saɪn/ N *(Math)* sinus *m*

sinecure /ˈsaɪnɪkjʊəʳ/ N sinécure *f*

sine qua non /ˈsaɪnɪkweɪˈnɒn/ N condition *f* sine qua non

sinew /ˈsɪnjuː/ N *(Anat)* tendon *m* ◆ **~s** *(= muscles)* muscles *mpl* ; *(= strength)* force(s) *f(pl)* ; *(= energy)* vigueur *f*, nerf *m* ◆ **money is the ~s of war** l'argent est le nerf de la guerre ◆ **a man of great moral ~** un homme d'une grande force morale

sinewy /ˈsɪnjʊɪ/ ADJ *(= muscular) [person]* musclé ; *[body, arms]* nerveux ; *[muscles]* bien dessiné ; *(Culin) [meat]* tendineux ; *(= vigorous) [music, performance]* vigoureux ; *[writing, style]* nerveux

sinfonietta /ˌsɪnfən'jetə/ **N** (= *short symphony*) sinfonietta *f* ; (= *small symphony orchestra*) sinfonietta *m*

sinful /'sɪnfʊl/ **ADJ** *[behaviour]* honteux, immoral ; *[city, world]* plein de péchés, de perdition ; *[act, waste, system]* honteux ; *[thought, pleasure, desire]* coupable ◆ **a ~ act** un péché ◆ **he was taught that sex was ~** on lui a appris que les rapports sexuels étaient un péché ◆ **her ~ past** son passé dissolu *or* de pécheresse *(hum)* ◆ **a fridge filled with ~ goodies** un réfrigérateur rempli de tentations ◆ **it was ~ to ...** on considérait cela comme un péché de ...

sinfully /'sɪnfəlɪ/ **ADV** *[behave, think]* d'une façon coupable ; *[waste]* scandaleusement

sinfulness /'sɪnfʊlnɪs/ **N** (NonC) *[of person]* péchés *mpl* ; *[of deed]* caractère *m* honteux

sing /sɪŋ/ (pret **sang**, ptp **sung**) **VT** *[person, bird]* chanter ; *(fig)* *[+ sb's beauty etc]* chanter, célébrer ◆ **she sang the child to sleep** elle a chanté jusqu'à ce que l'enfant s'endorme ◆ **she was ~ing the child to sleep** elle chantait pour que l'enfant s'endorme ◆ **to ~ mass** chanter la messe ◆ **sung mass** messe *f* chantée, grand-messe *f* ◆ **to ~ another tune** *(fig)* déchanter, changer de ton ◆ **to ~ sb's/sth's praises** chanter les louanges de qn/qch ◆ **to ~ one's own praises** vanter ses propres mérites

VI [1] *[person, bird, violin]* chanter ; *[ears]* bourdonner, tinter ; *[wind, kettle]* siffler ◆ **to ~ like a lark** chanter comme un rossignol ◆ **to ~ soprano** chanter soprano ◆ **to ~ small*** se faire tout petit, filer doux* ◆ **they are ~ing from the same hymn sheet** *or* **song sheet** *(Brit fig)* ils ont le même discours

[2] (US *) moucharder*, se mettre à table*

COMP sing-along N ◆ **to have a ~-along** chanter tous en chœur

► **sing along VI** ◆ **he invited the audience to sing along** il a invité la salle à chanter en chœur avec lui ◆ **I like records that get people ~ing along** j'aime les disques qui incitent les gens à chanter en chœur ◆ **to ~ along with** *or* **to a record/a song/the radio** accompagner un disque/une chanson/la radio de la voix ◆ **the audience was ~ing along to his latest hit** la salle chantait son dernier tube en chœur avec lui

► **sing out VI** chanter fort ; (* *fig*) crier ◆ **if you want anything just ~ out*** si vous voulez quoi que ce soit vous n'avez qu'à appeler (bien fort) ◆ **to ~ out for sth*** réclamer qch à grands cris

► **sing up VI** chanter plus fort ◆ **~ up!** plus fort !

sing. (abbrev of **singular**) sing.

Singapore /ˌsɪŋgə'pɔːʳ/ **N** Singapour ◆ **in ~** à Singapour

Singaporean /ˌsɪŋgə'pɔːrɪən/ **ADJ** *(gen)* singapourien ; *[ambassador, embassy]* de Singapour **N** Singapourien(ne) *m(f)*

singe /sɪndʒ/ **VT** brûler légèrement ; *[+ cloth, clothes]* roussir ; *[+ poultry]* flamber ◆ **to ~ one's wings** *(fig)* se brûler les ailes *or* les doigts **N** (also **singe mark**) légère brûlure *f* ; (= *scorch mark on cloth*) tache *f* de roussi, roussissure *f*

singer /'sɪŋəʳ/ **N** chanteur *m*, -euse *f* ; → **opera**

COMP singer-songwriter N auteur-compositeur *m* *(de chansons)*

Singhalese /ˌsɪŋgə'liːz/ **ADJ** cing(h)alais **N** [1] (pl **Singhaleses** *or* **Singhalese**) Cing(h)alais(e) *m(f)* [2] (= *language*) cing(h)alais *m*

singing /'sɪŋɪŋ/ **N** (NonC) *[of person, bird, violin]* chant *m* ; *[of kettle, wind]* sifflement *m* ; *(in ears)* bourdonnement *m*, tintement *m*

COMP singing lesson N ◆ **to have ~ lessons** prendre des cours de chant, apprendre le chant

singing teacher N professeur *m* de chant

singing telegram N *service qui consiste à envoyer des filles chanter des compliments à des gens dont c'est l'anniversaire*

singing voice N ◆ **to have a good ~ voice** avoir de la voix, avoir une belle voix

single /'sɪŋgl/ **ADJ** [1] (= *just one*) *[rose, shot, survivor]* seul ◆ **in a ~ day** en un seul jour ◆ **a ~ diamond** *(on ring)* un diamant monté seul ; (= *ring itself*) un solitaire ◆ **every ~ day** tous les jours sans exception ◆ **every ~ house was damaged** il n'y a pas une maison qui n'ait été endommagée ◆ **every ~ one (of them)** tous *(or* toutes) sans exception ◆ **to drink sth in a ~ gulp** boire qch d'un seul coup *or* en une seule gorgée ◆ **I did not, for a ~ moment, doubt her sincerity** je n'ai pas douté un seul instant de sa sincérité ◆ **there isn't a ~ moment to lose** il n'y a pas une minute à perdre ◆ **not a ~ person had come** absolument personne n'était venu, pas une seule personne n'était venue ◆ **she didn't mention it to a ~ one of her friends** elle ne l'a mentionné à aucun des ses amis ◆ **if there is a ~** *or* **one ~ objection to this proposal** s'il y a une seule *or* la moindre objection à cette proposition ◆ **I didn't see a ~ soul** je n'ai vu absolument personne, je n'ai pas vu âme qui vive ◆ **I couldn't think of a ~ thing to say** je ne savais absolument pas quoi dire

[2] (= *not several*) **a** *or* **one ~ department should deal with all of these matters** un service unique *or* un même service devrait traiter toutes ces affaires

[3] *(intensifying = individual)* ◆ **the biggest ~ issue in the election campaign** le sujet principal de la campagne électorale ◆ **the ~ biggest producer of coal** le plus grand producteur de charbon ◆ **the ~ greatest problem** le plus grand problème ◆ **the ~ most important invention since the wheel** la plus grande invention depuis la roue

[4] (= *not double or multiple*) *[knot, flower, thickness, wardrobe]* simple ; *[garage]* pour une voiture ◆ **a ~ sheet** un drap pour un lit d'une personne ◆ **a ~ whisky/gin** un whisky/gin simple ◆ **to be in ~ figures** *[number, score]* être inférieur (-eure *f*) à dix ; *[rate]* être inférieur (-eure *f*) à 10% ◆ **in ~ file** en file indienne ; see also **spacing**

[5] (= *unmarried*) *[person]* célibataire ; *[life]* de célibataire ◆ **she's a ~ woman** elle est célibataire, c'est une célibataire ◆ **~ people** célibataires *mpl* ◆ **the ~ homeless** les gens *mpl* seuls et sans abri ◆ **"marital status?" – "single"** "situation familiale ?" – "célibataire"

[6] *(Brit Rail etc)* ◆ **~ ticket** aller *m* simple ◆ **how much is the ~ fare to London?** combien coûte l'aller simple pour Londres ?

N [1] *(Cricket = one run)* **a ~** une seule course, un seul point ◆ **three ~s** trois fois une course *or* un point

[2] *(Brit Rail etc = ticket)* aller *m* (simple)

[3] *(in cinema, theatre)* **there are only ~s left** il ne reste que des places séparées *or* isolées

[4] (= *record*) **a ~** un 45 tours ◆ **his latest ~** son dernier 45 tours

[5] *(Brit = pound coin or note)* billet *m or* pièce *f* d'une livre ; *(US = dollar note)* billet *m* d'un dollar

[6] (also **single room**) chambre *f* simple *or* d'une personne

[7] *(drink = one measure)* **make mine a ~** donnez-moi un simple ◆ **double or ~?** double ou simple ?

NPL singles [1] *(Tennis etc)* simple *m* ◆ **ladies' ~s** simple *m* dames

[2] (* = *unmarried people*) célibataires *mpl* ◆ **~s bar/club** bar *m*/club *m* de rencontres pour célibataires

COMP single-barrelled ADJ à un canon

single bed N lit *m* d'une personne

single-breasted ADJ *[jacket, coat]* droit

single-celled ADJ unicellulaire

single combat N ◆ **in ~ combat** en combat singulier

single cream N *(Brit)* crème *f* fraîche liquide

single-crop farming N monoculture *f*

single currency N monnaie *f* unique

single-decker *(Brit)* **ADJ** sans impériale **N** autobus *m (or tramway m etc)* sans impériale

single-density ADJ → **density**

single-engined ADJ monomoteur (-trice *f*)

single-entry book-keeping N comptabilité *f* en partie simple

single European currency N monnaie *f* unique européenne

the Single European Market N le marché unique européen

single-handed ADV tout seul, sans aucune aide **ADJ** *[achievement]* fait sans aucune aide ; *[sailing, voyage, race]* en solitaire ◆ **to be ~-handed** *[person]* n'avoir aucune aide, être tout seul

single-handedly ADV tout(e) seul(e), à lui *etc* tout seul

single honours N *(Brit Univ:* also **single honours degree**) ≃ licence *f* préparée dans une seule matière

single lens reflex N (also **single lens reflex camera**) reflex *m* (à un objectif)

single malt N (also **single malt whisky**) (whisky *m*) single malt *m*

single-masted ADJ à un mât

single-minded ADJ *[person]* résolu, ferme ; *[attempt]* énergique, résolu ; *[determination]* tenace ◆ **to be ~-minded about sth** concentrer tous ses efforts sur qch ◆ **to be ~-minded in one's efforts to do sth** tout faire en vue de faire qch

single-mindedly ADV résolument

single-mindedness N détermination *f*, ténacité *f*

single mother N mère *f* célibataire

single parent N père *m or* mère *f* célibataire

single-parent family N famille *f* monoparentale

single-party ADJ *(Pol)* *[state, government]* à parti unique

single person supplement N ⇒ **single supplement**

single room N chambre *f* simple *or* individuelle

single room supplement N ⇒ **single supplement**

single-seater N (also **single-seater aeroplane**) (avion *m*) monoplace *m*

single-sex ADJ *(Brit)* *[school, education, class]* non mixte

single-sided disk N *(Comput)* disque *m* simple face

single-storey ADJ de plain-pied

single supplement N supplément *m* chambre individuelle

single track N *(Rail)* voie *f* unique

single-track ADJ *(Rail)* à voie unique ◆ **to have a ~-track mind** (= *one thing at a time*) ne pouvoir se concentrer que sur une seule chose à la fois ; (= *obsessive idea*) n'avoir qu'une idée en tête

Single Transferable Vote N ≃ scrutin *m* de liste à représentation proportionnelle

single-use ADJ *[camera, syringe]* à usage unique

► **single out VT SEP** (= *distinguish*) distinguer ; (= *pick out*) choisir ◆ **I don't want to ~ anyone out** je ne veux pas faire de distinctions ◆ **he's ~d out for all the nasty jobs** on le choisit pour toutes les corvées ◆ **to ~ o.s. out** se singulariser

singleness /'sɪŋglnɪs/ **N** ◆ **~ of purpose** persévérance *f*, ténacité *f*

singlet /'sɪŋglɪt/ **N** *(Brit)* maillot *m or* tricot *m* de corps, débardeur *m*

singleton /'sɪŋgltən/ **N** *(Cards)* singleton *m*

singly /'sɪŋglɪ/ **ADV** séparément

singsong /'sɪŋsɒŋ/ **N** *(Brit)* ◆ **to have a ~** chanter en chœur **ADJ** ◆ **~ voice** voix *f* qui psalmodie ◆ **to repeat sth in a ~ voice** répéter qch d'une voix chantante

singular /ˈsɪŋgjʊləʳ/ ADJ 1 *(Gram)* *[noun, verb, form, ending]* au singulier 2 *(= exceptional, unusual)* *[lack of success]* singulier ◆ **a woman of ~ beauty** une femme d'une singulière beauté ◆ **his ~ manner of dress** sa manière singulière de s'habiller N *(Gram)* singulier *m* ◆ **in the ~** au singulier ◆ **in the masculine ~** au masculin singulier

singularity /ˌsɪŋgjʊˈlærɪtɪ/ N singularité *f*

singularize /ˈsɪŋgjʊləraɪz/ VT singulariser

singularly /ˈsɪŋgjʊləlɪ/ ADV singulièrement

Sinhalese /ˌsɪnəˈliːz/ ADJ, N ⇒ **Singhalese**

sinister /ˈsɪnɪstəʳ/ ADJ 1 *(= ominous)* sinistre 2 *(Her)* sénestre, senestre

sinisterly /ˈsɪnɪstəlɪ/ ADV sinistrement

sink[1] /sɪŋk/ (pret **sank**, ptp **sunk**) VI 1 *(= go under)* *[ship]* couler, sombrer ; *[person, object]* couler ◆ **to ~ to the bottom** couler *or* aller au fond ◆ **to ~ like a stone** couler à pic ◆ **they left him to ~ or swim** ils l'ont laissé s'en sortir* *or* s'en tirer* tout seul ◆ **it was ~ or swim** il fallait bien s'en sortir* *or* s'en tirer* tout seul

2 *[ground]* s'affaisser ; *[foundation, building]* s'affaisser, se tasser ; *[level, river, fire]* baisser ◆ **the land ~s towards the sea** le terrain descend en pente vers la mer ◆ **the sun was ~ing** le soleil se couchait ◆ **the sun sank below the horizon** le soleil a disparu au-dessous de l'horizon ◆ **to ~ out of sight** disparaître ◆ **to ~ to one's knees** tomber à genoux ◆ **to ~ to the ground** s'affaisser, s'écrouler ◆ **he sank into a chair** il s'est laissé tomber dans un fauteuil ◆ **he sank into the mud up to his knees** il s'est enfoncé dans la boue jusqu'aux genoux ◆ **she let her head ~ into the pillow** elle a laissé retomber sa tête sur l'oreiller ◆ **the water slowly sank into the ground** l'eau a pénétré *or* s'est infiltrée lentement dans le sol ◆ **he is ~ing fast** *(= dying)* il décline *or* il baisse rapidement

3 *(fig)* **to ~ into a deep sleep** tomber *or* sombrer dans un profond sommeil ◆ **to ~ into despondency** tomber dans le découragement, se laisser aller au découragement ◆ **to ~ into insignificance/poverty/ despair** sombrer dans l'insignifiance/la misère/le désespoir ◆ **he has sunk in my estimation** il a baissé dans mon estime ◆ **his voice sank** sa voix s'est faite plus basse ◆ **his voice sank to a whisper** il s'est mis à chuchoter, sa voix n'était plus qu'un murmure ◆ **his heart** *or* **his spirits sank** le découragement *or* l'accablement s'est emparé de lui, il en a eu un coup de cafard* ◆ **his heart sank at the thought** son cœur s'est serré à cette pensée ◆ **it's enough to make your heart ~** c'est à vous démoraliser *or* à vous donner le cafard*

4 *[prices, value, temperature, sales, numbers]* chuter ◆ **the shares have sunk to three dollars** les actions ont chuté jusqu'à trois dollars ◆ **the pound has sunk to a new low** la livre est tombée plus bas que jamais *or* a atteint sa cote la plus basse

VT 1 *[+ ship]* couler, faire sombrer ; *[+ object]* immerger ; *(fig)* *[+ theory]* démolir ; *[+ business, project]* ruiner, couler ; *[+ play, book]* couler, démolir ; * *[+ person]* couler, ruiner la réputation de ◆ **they sank their differences** ils ont enterré *or* oublié leurs querelles ◆ **to be sunk in thought/depression/despair** être plongé dans ses pensées/la dépression/le désespoir ◆ **I'm sunk*** je suis fichu* *or* perdu

2 *[+ mine, well]* creuser, forer ; *[+ foundations]* creuser ; *[+ pipe]* noyer ◆ **to ~ a post 2 metres in the ground** enfoncer un pieu 2 mètres dans le sol ◆ **the dog sank his fangs into my leg** le chien a enfoncé *or* planté ses crocs dans ma jambe ◆ **he sank his teeth into the sandwich** il a mordu (à belles dents) dans le sandwich ◆ **he can ~ a glass of beer in five seconds*** *(Brit)* il peut avaler *or* descendre* une bière en cinq secondes ◆ **to ~ the ball** *(Golf)* faire entrer la balle dans le trou ◆ **to ~ a lot of money in a project** *(= invest)* investir *or* placer beaucoup d'argent dans une entreprise ; *(= lose)* perdre *or* engloutir beaucoup d'argent dans une entreprise

► **sink back** VI *[person]* (se laisser) retomber ◆ **it sank back into the water** c'est retombé dans l'eau ◆ **he managed to sit up but soon sank back exhausted** il a réussi à s'asseoir mais s'est bientôt laissé retomber épuisé ◆ **he sank back into his chair** il s'est enfoncé dans son fauteuil

► **sink down** VI *[building]* s'enfoncer, s'affaisser ; *[post]* s'enfoncer ◆ **to ~ down into a chair** s'enfoncer dans un fauteuil ◆ **to ~ down on one's knees** tomber à genoux ◆ **he sank down (out of sight) behind the bush** il a disparu derrière le buisson

► **sink in** VI 1 *[person, post etc]* s'enfoncer ; *[water, ointment etc]* pénétrer

2 *[explanation]* rentrer* ; *[remark]* faire son effet ◆ **when the facts sank in, he ...** quand il a eu pleinement compris les faits, il ... ◆ **as it hadn't really sunk in yet he ...** comme il ne réalisait pas encore, il ... ◆ **my explanation took a long time to ~ in** mon explication a eu du mal à rentrer*, il a *(or* ils ont *etc)* mis longtemps à comprendre mon explication

sink[2] /sɪŋk/ N 1 *(in kitchen)* évier *m* ; *(US: in bathroom)* lavabo *m* ◆ **double ~** évier *m* à deux bacs ◆ **a ~ of iniquity** un lieu de perdition *or* de débauche ; → **kitchen** 2 *(= forest)* puits *m* de carbone ADJ *[school, estate]* défavorisé COMP **sink unit** N bloc-évier *m*

sinker /ˈsɪŋkəʳ/ N 1 *(= lead)* plomb *m* ; → **hook** 2 *(US * = doughnut)* beignet *m*

sinking /ˈsɪŋkɪŋ/ ADJ 1 *(= foundering)* ◆ **a ~ ship** *(lit)* un bateau qui sombre ; *(fig)* *[organization, cause]* un navire en perdition *(fig)* see also **rat** 2 ◆ **to have a ~ feeling that ...** *(= dread)* avoir le sentiment angoissant que ... ◆ **that ~ feeling** ce sentiment d'angoisse ◆ **with a ~ heart** la mort dans l'âme 3 *(Fin)* ◆ **a ~ pound/dollar** une livre/un dollar en (forte) baisse N ◆ **the ~ of a ship** *(accidental)* le naufrage d'un navire ; *(in battle)* la destruction d'un navire COMP **sinking fund** N *(Fin)* fonds *mpl* d'amortissement

sinless /ˈsɪnlɪs/ ADJ sans péché, pur, innocent

sinner /ˈsɪnəʳ/ N pécheur *m*, -eresse *f*

Sinn Féin /ʃɪnˈfeɪn/ N Sinn Fein *m*

Sino- /ˈsaɪnəʊ/ PREF sino- ◆ **~Soviet** sino-soviétique

Sinologist /ˌsaɪˈnɒlədʒɪst/ N sinologue *mf*

Sinology /ˌsaɪˈnɒlədʒɪ/ N sinologie *f*

Sinophobia /ˌsaɪnəʊˈfəʊbɪə/ N sinophobie *f*

sinuosity /ˌsɪnjʊˈɒsɪtɪ/ N sinuosité *f*

sinuous /ˈsɪnjʊəs/ ADJ *[shape, curve, road, roots]* sinueux ; *[snake, dance, music, style]* ondulant ; *[movement]* onduleux ◆ **with ~ grace** avec une grâce ondoyante

sinus /ˈsaɪnəs/ N (pl **sinuses**) sinus *m inv* ◆ **to have ~ trouble** avoir de la sinusite

sinusitis /ˌsaɪnəˈsaɪtɪs/ N *(NonC)* sinusite *f* ◆ **to have ~** avoir de la sinusite

Sioux /suː/ ADJ sioux *inv* ◆ **the ~ State** *(US)* le Dakota du Nord N 1 *(pl inv)* Sioux *mf* 2 *(= language)* sioux *m*

sip /sɪp/ N petite gorgée *f* ◆ **do you want a ~ of rum?** voulez-vous une goutte de rhum ? ◆ **he took a ~** il a bu une petite gorgée VT *(= drink a little at a time)* boire à petites gorgées *or* à petits coups ; *(= take a sip)* boire une petite gorgée de ; *(with enjoyment)* siroter* VI ◆ **he ~ped at his whisky** *(= drank a little at a time)* il a bu son whisky à petites gorgées ; *(= took a sip)* il a bu une petite gorgée de son whisky

siphon /ˈsaɪfən/ N siphon *m* ; → **soda** VT siphonner

► **siphon off** VT SEP *(lit)* siphonner ; *(fig)* *[+ people]* mettre à part ; *[+ profits, funds]* canaliser ; *(illegally)* détourner

sir /sɜːʳ/ N monsieur *m* ◆ **yes ~** oui, Monsieur ; *(to officer in Army, Navy, Air Force)* oui, mon commandant *(or* mon lieutenant *etc)* ; *(to surgeon)* oui docteur ◆ **yes/no ~!*** *(emphatic)* ça oui/non ! ◆ **Dear Sir** *(in letter)* (Cher) Monsieur ◆ **Sir** *(to newspaper editor)* Monsieur (le Directeur) ◆ **my dear/good ~** *(iro)* mon cher/bon Monsieur ◆ **Sir John Smith** sir John Smith

sire /ˈsaɪəʳ/ N *(= animal)* père *m* ; *(†† = father)* père *m* ; *(†† = ancestor)* aïeul *m* ◆ **yes ~** *(to king)* oui sire VT engendrer

siree* /sɪˈriː/ N *(US: emphatic)* ◆ **yes/no ~!** ça oui/non !

siren /ˈsaɪərən/ N 1 *(= device)* sirène *f* 2 *(Myth)* **the Sirens** les sirènes *fpl* ADJ *(liter)* *[charms]* séducteur (-trice *f*) ; *[song]* de sirène, enchanteur (-teresse *f*)

sirloin /ˈsɜːlɔɪn/ N aloyau *m* COMP **sirloin steak** N bifteck *m* dans l'aloyau *or* d'aloyau

sirocco /sɪˈrɒkəʊ/ N sirocco *m*

sis‡ /sɪs/ N (abbrev of **sister**) sœurette *f*, frangine‡ *f*

sisal /ˈsaɪsəl/ N sisal *m* COMP en *or* de sisal

sissy* /ˈsɪsɪ/ *(pej)* N *(= coward)* poule *f* mouillée ◆ **he's a bit of a ~** *(= effeminate)* il est un peu efféminé ADJ *[boy]* efféminé ; *[voice, clothes, sport]* de fille ◆ **a ~ man** une chochotte* ◆ **Mummy's little ~ boy** le petit chéri à sa maman ◆ **poetry is ~ stuff** la poésie est un truc de filles ◆ **it's ~ doing** *or* **to do that** c'est un truc* de fille

sister /ˈsɪstəʳ/ N 1 sœur *f* ◆ **her younger ~** sa (sœur) cadette, sa petite sœur ; → **half, stepsister** 2 *(Rel)* religieuse *f*, (bonne) sœur *f* ◆ **yes ~** oui, ma sœur ◆ **Sister Mary Margaret** sœur Marie Marguerite ◆ **the Sisters of Charity** les sœurs de la Charité 3 *(Brit Med:* also **nursing sister**) infirmière *f* chef ◆ **yes ~** oui Madame *(or* Mademoiselle) 4 *(US)* **listen ~!**‡ écoute ma vieille !* ADJ *[company, party]* frère (sœur *f*) ; *[publication, hotel, radio station]* jumeau (-elle *f*) ◆ **~ organization** organisation *f* sœur ◆ **~ country** pays *m* frère ◆ **~ ship** sistership *m* COMP **sister-in-law** N (pl **sisters-in-law**) belle-sœur *f*

sister school N *(US Univ)* *université pour femmes jumelée avec une université pour hommes*

sisterhood /ˈsɪstəhʊd/ N *(= solidarity)* solidarité *f* féminine ; *(Rel)* communauté *f* (religieuse) ◆ **the ~** *(= group of women)* la communauté (des femmes)

sisterly /ˈsɪstəlɪ/ ADJ fraternel, de sœur

Sistine /ˈsɪstiːn/ ADJ ◆ **the ~ Chapel** la chapelle Sixtine

Sisyphus /ˈsɪsɪfəs/ N Sisyphe *m*

sit /sɪt/ (pret, ptp **sat**) VI 1 (also **sit down**) s'asseoir ◆ **to be ~ting** être assis ◆ **~!** *(to dog)* assis ! ◆ **~ by me** assieds-toi près de moi ◆ **he was ~ting at his desk/at table** il était (assis) à son bureau/à table ◆ **they spent the evening ~ting at home** ils ont passé la soirée (tranquillement) à la maison ◆ **he just ~s at home all day** il reste chez lui toute la journée à ne rien faire ◆ **he was ~ting over his books all evening** il a passé toute la soirée dans ses livres ◆ **to ~ through a lecture/play** assister à une conférence/à une pièce jusqu'au bout ◆ **don't just ~ there, do something!** ne reste pas là à ne rien faire ! ◆ **to ~ still** rester *or* se tenir tranquille, ne pas bouger ◆ **to ~ straight** *or* **upright** se tenir droit ◆ **to ~ for one's portrait** poser pour son portrait ◆ **she sat for Picasso** elle a posé pour Picasso ◆ **to ~ on a committee/jury** être membre *or* faire partie d'un comité/jury ◆ **to ~ for an exam** passer un examen, se présenter à un examen ◆ **he sat for Sandhurst** il s'est présenté au concours d'entrée de Sandhurst ◆ **he ~s for Brighton** *(Brit Parl)* il est (le) député de Brighton ◆ **to be ~ting pretty*** avoir le bon filon*, tenir le bon bout* ◆ **to ~ at sb's feet** *(hum or liter)* suivre l'enseignement de qn ; → **tight**

2 *[bird, insect]* se poser, se percher ◆ **to be ~ting** être perché ; *(on eggs)* couver ◆ **the hen is ~ting on three eggs** la poule couve trois œufs

3 *[committee, assembly etc]* être en séance, siéger ◆ **the committee is ~ting now** le comité est en séance ◆ **the House ~s from November to June** la Chambre siège de novembre à juin ◆ **the House sat for 16 hours** la Chambre a été en séance pendant 16 heures

4 *[dress, coat etc]* tomber *(on sb* sur qn) ◆ **the jacket ~s badly across the shoulders** la veste tombe mal aux épaules ◆ **this policy would ~ well with their allies** cette politique serait bien vue de leurs alliés ◆ **it sat heavy on his conscience** *(liter)* cela lui pesait sur la conscience ◆ **how ~s the wind?** *(liter)* d'où vient *or* souffle le vent ?

VT 1 (also **sit down**) asseoir, installer ; *(invite to sit)* faire asseoir ◆ **he sat the child (down) on his knee** il a assis *or* installé l'enfant sur ses genoux ◆ **they sat him (down) in a chair** *(= placed him in it)* ils l'ont assis *or* installé dans un fauteuil ; *(= invited him to sit)* ils l'ont fait asseoir dans un fauteuil

2 ◆ **to ~ a horse well/badly** monter bien/mal, avoir une bonne/mauvaise assiette

3 *(esp Brit) [+ exam]* passer, se présenter à

COMP **sit-down*** N ◆ **he had a ten-minute ~-down** il s'est assis dix minutes (pour se reposer) ADJ ◆ **we had a ~-down lunch** nous avons déjeuné à table ◆ **~-down strike** grève *f* sur le tas
sit-in N → **sit-in**
sit-up N *(Gym)* redressement *m* assis

► **sit about, sit around** VI rester assis (à ne rien faire), traîner

► **sit back** VI ◆ **to sit back in an armchair** se carrer *or* se caler dans un fauteuil ◆ **to ~ back on one's heels** s'asseoir sur les talons ◆ **just ~ back and listen to this** installe-toi bien et écoute un peu (ceci) ◆ **he sat back and did nothing about it** *(fig)* il s'est abstenu de faire quoi que ce soit, il n'a pas levé le petit doigt ◆ **~ back and enjoy yourself** détends-toi et profite du moment ◆ **I can't just ~ back and do nothing!** je ne peux quand même pas rester là à ne rien faire *or* à me croiser les bras ! ◆ **the Government sat back and did nothing to help them** le gouvernement n'a pas fait le moindre geste pour les aider

► **sit by** VI rester sans rien faire ◆ **to ~ (idly) by (while ...)** rester sans rien faire (pendant que ...)

► **sit down** VI s'asseoir ◆ **to be ~ting down** être assis ◆ **he sat down to a huge dinner** il s'est attablé devant un repas gigantesque ◆ **to take sth ~ting down** * *(fig)* rester les bras croisés devant qch

VT SEP ⇒ **sit vt 1**

N ◆ **sit-down** * ADJ → **sit**

► **sit in** VI 1 ◆ **she sat in all day waiting for him to come** elle est restée à la maison toute la journée à l'attendre, elle a passé la journée chez elle à l'attendre ◆ **to ~ in on a discussion** assister à une discussion (sans y prendre part) ◆ **to ~ in for sb** *(fig = replace)* remplacer qn

2 *(as protest)* ◆ **the demonstrators sat in in the director's office** les manifestants ont occupé le bureau du directeur

N ◆ **sit-in** → **sit-in**

► **sit on** * VT FUS 1 *(= keep to oneself) [+ news, facts, report]* garder secret, garder le silence sur ; *(= not pass on) [+ file, document]* garder (pour soi), accaparer ◆ **the committee sat on the proposals for weeks, then decided to ...** le comité a laissé de côté les propositions pendant des semaines, puis a décidé de ...

2 *(= silence) [+ person]* faire taire, fermer *or* clouer le bec à* ◆ **he won't be sat on** il ne se laisse pas marcher sur les pieds

3 *(= reject) [+ idea, proposal]* rejeter, repousser

► **sit out** VI *(= sit outside)* (aller) s'asseoir dehors, se mettre *or* s'installer dehors

VT SEP 1 ◆ **to sit a lecture/play out** rester jusqu'à la fin d'une conférence/d'une pièce, assister à une conférence/à une pièce jusqu'au bout

2 ◆ **she sat out the waltz** elle n'a pas dansé la valse

► **sit up** VI 1 *(= sit upright)* se redresser, s'asseoir bien droit ◆ **to be ~ting up** être assis bien droit, se tenir droit ◆ **he was ~ting up in bed** il était assis dans son lit ◆ **you can ~ up now** vous pouvez vous asseoir maintenant ◆ **to make sb ~ up** *(fig)* secouer *or* étonner qn ◆ **to ~ up (and take notice)** *(fig: gen)* se secouer, se réveiller ◆ **he began to ~ up and take notice** *(after illness)* il a commencé à reprendre intérêt à la vie *or* à refaire surface

2 *(= stay up)* rester debout, ne pas se coucher ◆ **to ~ up late** se coucher tard, veiller tard ◆ **to ~ up all night** ne pas se coucher de la nuit ◆ **don't ~ up for me** couchez-vous sans m'attendre ◆ **the nurse sat up with him** l'infirmière est restée à son chevet *or* l'a veillé

VT SEP *[+ doll, child]* asseoir, redresser

N ◆ **sit-up** → **sit**

► **sit upon** * VT FUS ⇒ **sit on**

sitar /sɪ'tɑːʳ/ N sitar *m*

sitcom * /'sɪtkɒm/ N *(Rad, TV)* (abbrev of **situation comedy**) sitcom *f*, comédie *f* de situation

site /saɪt/ N *[of town, building]* emplacement *m* ; *(Archeol, Comput)* site *m* ; *(Constr)* chantier *m* (de construction *or* de démolition *etc*) ; *(Camping)* (terrain *m* de) camping *m* ◆ **the ~ of the battle** le champ de bataille ; → **building, launching**

◆ **off site** au dehors, à l'extérieur ◆ **the work is carried out off ~** le travail est effectué au dehors *or* à l'extérieur

◆ **on site** sur place ◆ **they live on ~** ils habitent sur place

VT *[+ town, building, gun]* placer ◆ **they want to ~ the steelworks in that valley** on veut placer *or* construire l'aciérie dans cette vallée ◆ **the factory is very badly ~d** l'usine est très mal située *or* placée

COMP **site measuring** N *(Civil Engineering)* métré *m*
Site of Special Scientific Interest N *(Brit)* site *m* d'intérêt scientifique, ≃ réserve *f* naturelle

sit-in /'sɪtɪn/ N *[of demonstrators]* sit-in *m*, manifestation *f* avec occupation de locaux ; *[of workers]* grève *f* sur le tas ◆ **the workers held a ~** les ouvriers ont organisé une grève sur le tas ◆ **the students held a ~ in the university offices** les étudiants ont occupé les bureaux de l'université ◆ **the ~ at the offices** l'occupation *f* des bureaux

siting /'saɪtɪŋ/ N implantation *f* ◆ **the ~ of the new town there was a mistake** l'implantation de la ville nouvelle à cet endroit était une erreur ◆ **the ~ of the new factories has given rise to many objections** l'implantation des nouvelles usines a soulevé de nombreuses objections

sitter /'sɪtəʳ/ N *(Art)* modèle *m* ; *(= baby-sitter)* baby-sitter *mf* ; *(= hen)* couveuse *f* ◆ **he missed a ~*‡** *(Sport)* il a raté un coup enfantin ◆ **it's a ~!*‡** tu ne peux pas (or il ne peut pas *etc*) le rater !

sitting /'sɪtɪŋ/ N *[of committee, assembly etc]* séance *f* ; *(for portrait)* séance *f* de pose ; *(in canteen etc)* service *m* ◆ **they served 200 people in one ~/in two ~s** ils ont servi 200 personnes à la fois/en deux services ◆ **second ~ for lunch** deuxième service pour le déjeuner ◆ **at one** *or* **a single ~** *(= in one go)* d'une seule traite ADJ *[committee]* en séance ; *[official]* en exercice ; *[game bird]* posé, au repos

COMP **sitting and standing room** N places *fpl* debout et assises
sitting duck* N *(fig)* cible *f* facile
sitting room N salon *m*
sitting target N *(lit, fig)* cible *f* facile

situate /'sɪtjʊeɪt/ VT *(= locate) [+ building, town]* placer ; *(= put into perspective) [+ problem, event]* situer ◆ **the house is ~d in the country** la maison se trouve *or* est située à la campagne ◆ **the shop is well ~d** le magasin est bien situé *or* bien placé ◆ **we are rather badly ~d as there is no bus service** nous sommes assez mal situés car il n'y a pas d'autobus ◆ **he is rather badly ~d at the moment** *(fig)* il est dans une situation assez défavorable *or* en assez mauvaise posture en ce moment ; *(financially)* il est assez gêné *or* il a des ennuis d'argent en ce moment ◆ **I am well ~d to appreciate the risks** je suis bien placé pour apprécier les risques ◆ **how are you ~d for money?** ça va du point de vue argent ?, où en es-tu question argent ?

situation /ˌsɪtjʊ'eɪʃən/ N 1 *(= location) [of town, building etc]* situation *f*, emplacement *m* ◆ **the house has a fine ~** la maison est bien située 2 *(= circumstances)* situation *f* (also *Literat*) ◆ **he was in a very difficult ~** il se trouvait dans une situation très difficile ◆ **they managed to save the ~** ils ont réussi à sauver *or* redresser la situation ◆ **the international ~** la situation internationale, la conjoncture internationale ◆ **they're in a waiting/discussion** *etc* **~** ils sont en situation d'attente/de dialogue *etc* ◆ **in an exam ~, you must ...** à un examen, il faut ... 3 *(= job)* situation *f* ◆ **"situations vacant/wanted"** "offres/demandes d'emploi"

COMP **situation comedy** N comédie *f* de situation

situational /ˌsɪtjʊ'eɪʃənl/ ADJ situationnel

Situationism /sɪtjʊ'eɪʃəˌnɪzəm/ N *(Philos)* situationnisme *m*

Situationist /sɪtjʊ'eɪʃəˌnɪst/ ADJ, N *(Philos)* situationniste *mf*

six /sɪks/ ADJ six *inv* ◆ **he is ~ (years old)** il a six ans ; see also **comp** ◆ **he'll be ~ on Saturday** il aura six ans samedi ◆ **he lives in number ~** il habite au (numéro) six ◆ **~ times ~** six fois six

N 1 six *m inv* ◆ **it is ~ o'clock** il est six heures ◆ **come at ~** venez à six heures ◆ **it struck ~** six heures ont sonné ◆ **they are sold in ~es** c'est vendu par (lots *or* paquets de) six ◆ **the children arrived in ~es** les enfants sont arrivés par groupes de six ◆ **he lives at ~ Churchill Street** il habite (au) six Churchill Street ◆ **the ~ of diamonds** *(Cards)* le six de carreaux ◆ **two ~es are twelve** deux fois six douze

2 *(fig phrases)* **~ of the best*** *(Brit)* six grands coups ◆ **to be (all) at ~es and sevens** *[books, house etc]* être en désordre *or* en pagaille*, être sens dessus dessous ; *[person]* être tout retourné* ◆ **to be ~ foot under*** *(hum)* manger les pissenlits par la racine* ◆ **it's ~ of one and half a dozen of the other*, it's ~ and half a dozen*** c'est blanc bonnet et bonnet blanc, c'est du pareil au même*

3 *(Cricket)* **to hit a ~** marquer six courses *fpl or* points *mpl (d'un seul coup)* ◆ **he hit three ~es** il a marqué trois fois six courses *or* points ; → **knock**

PRON six ◆ **there were about ~** il y en avait six environ *or* à peu près ◆ **~ of the girls came** six des filles sont venues ◆ **there are ~ of us** nous sommes *or* on est* six ◆ **all ~ (of us) left** nous sommes partis tous les six ◆ **all ~ (of them) left** tous les six sont partis, ils sont partis tous les six

COMP **the Six Counties** NPL *(Brit)* les six comtés *mpl* de l'Irlande du Nord
six-cylinder ADJ *[car, engine]* à six cylindres N (voiture *f* à) six cylindres *f*
six-eight time N *(Mus)* mesure *f* à six-huit
six-footer* N personne *f* qui mesure plus d'un mètre quatre-vingts
six-gun* N ⇒ **six-shooter**
Six Nations N *(Rugby)* ◆ **the Six Nations** le Tournoi des six nations
six-pack N pack *m* de six ◆ **to have a ~-pack stomach*** avoir des tablettes de chocolat*
six-seater ADJ à six places N *(= car etc)* (voiture *f etc* à) six places *f* ; *(= plane etc)* (avion *m etc* à) six places *m*
six-shooter* N six-coups *m inv*
six-sided ADJ hexagonal
six-speed gearbox N boîte *f* (à) six vitesses
six-storey N à six étages
six-yard box N *(Ftbl)* surface *f* de but
six-year-old ADJ *[child, horse]* de six ans ; *[house, car]* vieux (vieille *f*) de six ans N *(= child)* enfant *mf* (âgé(e)) de six ans ; *(= horse)* cheval *m* de six ans

sixfold /ˈsɪksfəʊld/ ADJ sextuple ADV au sextuple

sixish /ˈsɪksɪʃ/ ADJ ◆ **he is ~** il a dans les six ans, il a six ans environ ◆ **he came at ~** il est venu vers (les) six heures

sixpence /ˈsɪkspəns/ N *(Brit)* *(= coin)* (ancienne) pièce *f* de six pence ; *(= value)* six pence *mpl*

sixpenny /ˈsɪkspənɪ/ ADJ à six pence

sixteen /ˈsɪksˈtiːn/ ADJ seize *inv* ◆ **she was sweet ~** c'était une fraîche jeune fille (de seize ans) N seize *m inv* ; *for phrases see* **six** PRON seize ◆ **there are ~** il y en a seize

sixteenth /ˈsɪksˈtiːnθ/ ADJ seizième N seizième *mf* ; *(= fraction)* seizième *m* ; *for phrases see* **sixth**

sixth /sɪksθ/ ADJ sixième ◆ **to be ~ in an exam/in German** être sixième à un concours/en allemand ◆ **she was the ~ to arrive** elle est arrivée la sixième ◆ **Charles the Sixth** Charles six ◆ **the ~ of November, November the ~** le six novembre

N sixième *mf* ; *(= fraction)* sixième *m* ; *(Mus)* sixte *f* ◆ **he wrote the letter on the ~** il a écrit la lettre le six, sa lettre est du six ◆ **your letter of the ~** votre lettre du six (courant) ◆ **the ~** *(Brit Scol)* ⇒ **sixth form**

ADV 1 *(in race, exam, competition)* en sixième position *or* place ◆ **he came** *or* **was placed ~** il s'est classé sixième

2 ⇒ **sixthly**

COMP **sixth form** N *(Brit Scol)* ≈ classes *fpl* de première et terminale ◆ **to be in the ~ form** ≈ être en première *or* en terminale
sixth-form college N *lycée n'ayant que des classes de première et de terminale*
sixth-former, sixth-form pupil N ≈ élève *mf* de première *or* de terminale
the sixth grade N *(US Scol)* ≈ le CM2
sixth sense N sixième sens *m*

sixthly /ˈsɪksθlɪ/ ADV sixièmement, en sixième lieu

sixtieth /ˈsɪkstɪɪθ/ ADJ soixantième N soixantième *mf* ; *(= fraction)* soixantième *m* ; *for phrases see* **sixth**

sixty /ˈsɪkstɪ/ ADJ soixante *inv* ◆ **he is about ~** il a une soixantaine d'années, il a dans les soixante ans ◆ **about ~ books** une soixantaine de livres

N soixante *m inv* ◆ **about ~** une soixantaine, environ soixante ◆ **to be in one's sixties** avoir entre soixante et soixante-dix ans, être sexagénaire ◆ **he is in his early sixties** il a un peu plus de soixante ans ◆ **he is in his late sixties** il approche de soixante-dix ans ◆ **she's getting on** *or* **going on for ~** elle approche de la soixantaine, elle va sur ses soixante ans ◆ **in the sixties** *(= 1960s)* dans les années soixante ◆ **in the early/late sixties** au début/vers la fin des années soixante ◆ **the temperature was in the sixties** ≈ il faisait entre quinze et vingt degrés ◆ **the numbers were in the sixties** le nombre s'élevait à plus de soixante ◆ **to do ~*** *(in car)* faire du soixante milles (à l'heure), ≈ faire du cent (à l'heure) ; *for other phrases see* **six**

PRON soixante ◆ **there are ~** il y en a soixante

COMP **sixty-first** ADJ soixante et unième N soixante et unième *mf* ; *(= fraction)* soixante et unième *m* PRON soixante et unième
sixty-four (thousand) dollar question* N ◆ **that's the ~-four (thousand) dollar question** c'est la question à mille francs
sixty-odd* PRON ◆ **there were ~-odd** il y en avait soixante et quelques*, il y en avait une soixantaine ◆ **~-odd books** un peu plus de soixante livres, soixante et quelques livres
sixty-one ADJ soixante et un(e) PRON soixante et un
sixty-second ADJ soixante-deuxième N soixante-deuxième *mf* ; *(= fraction)* soixante-deuxième *m*
sixty-two ADJ soixante-deux *inv* N soixante-deux *m inv* PRON soixante-deux ◆ **there are ~-two** il y en a soixante-deux

sizable /ˈsaɪzəbl/ ADJ ⇒ **sizeable**

sizably /ˈsaɪzəblɪ/ ADV ⇒ **sizeably**

size¹ /saɪz/ N *(for plaster, paper)* colle *f* ; *(for cloth)* apprêt *m* VT encoller, apprêter

size² /saɪz/ N 1 *[of person, animal, sb's head, hands]* taille *f* ; *[of room, building]* grandeur *f*, dimensions *fpl* ; *[of car, chair]* dimensions *fpl* ; *[of egg, fruit, jewel]* grosseur *f* ; *[of parcel]* grosseur *f*, dimensions *fpl* ; *[of book, photograph, sheet of paper, envelope]* taille *f*, dimensions *fpl* ; *(= format)* format *m* ; *[of sum]* montant *m* ; *[of estate, park, country]* étendue *f*, superficie *f* ; *[of problem, difficulty, obstacle]* ampleur *f*, étendue *f* ; *[of operation, campaign]* ampleur *f*, envergure *f* ◆ **the small/large ~** *[of packet, tube etc]* le petit/grand modèle ◆ **the ~ of the town** l'importance *f* de la ville ◆ **a building of vast ~** un bâtiment de belles dimensions ◆ **the ~ of the farm** *(building)* les dimensions *fpl* de la ferme ; *(land)* l'étendue *f* de la ferme ◆ **the ~ of the fish you caught** la taille du poisson que tu as attrapé ◆ **the ~ of the sum involved was so large that ...** la somme en question était d'une telle importance que ... ◆ **sort them according to ~** triez-les selon la grosseur (or le format *etc*) ◆ **to alter/cut/make sth to ~** transformer/couper/faire qch sur mesure ◆ **it's the ~ of a brick** c'est de la taille d'une brique ◆ **it's the ~ of a walnut** c'est de la grosseur d'une noix ◆ **it's the ~ of a house/elephant** c'est grand comme une maison/un éléphant ◆ **he's about your ~** il est à peu près de la même taille que vous ◆ **that's about the ~ of it!** c'est à peu près ça ! ◆ **he cut the wood to ~** il a coupé le bois à la dimension voulue ◆ **they are all of a ~*** ils sont tous de la même grosseur (or de la même taille *etc*) ; → **cut down, shape**

2 *[of coat, skirt, dress, trousers etc]* taille *f* ; *[of shoes, gloves]* pointure *f* ; *[of shirt]* encolure *f* ◆ **what ~ are you?, what ~ do you take?** *(in dress etc)* quelle taille faites-vous ? ; *(in shoes, gloves)* quelle pointure faites-vous ? ; *(in shirts)* vous faites combien d'encolure *or* de tour de cou ? ; *(in hats)* quel est votre tour de tête ? ◆ **what ~ of collar** *or* **shirt?** quelle encolure ? ◆ **I take ~ 12** je prends du 12 *or* la taille 12 ◆ **what ~ (of) shoes do you take?** quelle pointure faites-vous ?, vous chaussez du combien ? ◆ **I take ~ 5 (shoes)** ≈ je chausse *or* je fais du 38 ◆ **what ~ of waist are you?** quel est votre tour de taille ? ◆ **we are out of ~ 5** ≈ nous n'avons plus de 38 ◆ **we haven't got your ~** nous n'avons pas votre taille (*or* pointure *etc*) ; → **try** ◆ **"one size"** "taille unique" ◆ **I need a ~ smaller** il me faut la taille (*or* la pointure *etc*) en-dessous ◆ **it's two ~s too big for me** c'est deux tailles (*or* pointures *etc*) au-dessus de ce qu'il me faut ◆ **hip ~** tour *m* de hanches

VT classer *or* trier selon la grosseur (*or* la dimension *or* la taille *etc*)

► **size up** VT SEP *[+ person]* juger, jauger ; *[+ situation]* mesurer ◆ **to ~ up the problem** mesurer l'étendue du problème ◆ **I can't quite ~ him up** *(= don't know what he is worth)* je n'arrive pas vraiment à le juger *or* à décider ce qu'il vaut ; *(= don't know what he wants)* je ne vois pas vraiment où il veut en venir

-size /saɪz/ ADJ *(in compounds)* ⇒ **-sized**

sizeable /ˈsaɪzəbl/ ADJ *[amount, number, problem, operation, proportion]* assez important, assez considérable ; *[object, building, estate]* assez grand ; *[majority]* assez large, assez confortable

sizeably /ˈsaɪzəblɪ/ ADV considérablement, de beaucoup

-sized /saɪzd/ ADJ *(in compounds)* → **size²** ◆ **medium-sized** de taille (*or* grandeur *or* grosseur *etc*) moyenne ; → **life**

sizeist /ˈsaɪzɪst/ ADJ antigros *inv* N raciste *mf* antigros

sizzle /ˈsɪzl/ VI grésiller N grésillement *m*

sizzler* /ˈsɪzləʳ/ N journée *f* torride *or* caniculaire

sizzling /ˈsɪzlɪŋ/ ADJ *[fat, bacon]* grésillant ◆ **a ~ noise** un grésillement ADV ◆ **~ hot** brûlant ◆ **it was a ~ hot day*** il faisait une chaleur torride *or* caniculaire ce jour-là

ska /skɑː/ N *(Mus)* ska *m*

skate¹ /skeɪt/ N (pl **skate** *or* **skates**) *(= fish)* raie *f*

skate² /skeɪt/ N patin *m* ◆ **put** *or* **get your ~s on!*** *(fig)* grouille-toi !*, magne-toi !* ; → **ice, roller**

VI patiner ◆ **to go skating** *(ice)* faire du patin *or* du patinage ; *(roller)* faire du patin à roulettes *or* du skating ◆ **he ~d across the pond** il a traversé l'étang (en patinant *or* à patins) ◆ **it went skating across the room** cela a glissé à travers la pièce ; → **ice, roller**

► **skate around, skate over, skate round** VT FUS *[+ problem, difficulty, objection]* esquiver autant que possible

skateboard /ˈskeɪtbɔːd/ N skateboard *m*, planche *f* à roulettes VI faire de la planche à roulettes

skateboarder /ˈskeɪtbɔːdəʳ/ N skateur *m*, -euse *f*

skateboarding /ˈskeɪtbɔːdɪŋ/ N skateboard *m*, planche *f* à roulettes

skater /ˈskeɪtəʳ/ N *(ice)* patineur *m*, -euse *f* ; *(roller)* personne *f* qui fait du skating *or* du patinage à roulettes

skating /ˈskeɪtɪŋ/ N *(ice)* patinage *m* ; *(roller)* skating *m*, patinage *m* à roulettes

COMP *[champion, championship, display]* *(ice)* de patinage ; *(roller)* de skating, de patinage à roulettes **skating rink** N *(ice)* patinoire *f* ; *(roller)* skating *m*
skating turn N *(Ski)* pas *m* du patineur

skean dhu /ˈskiːənˈduː/ N *(Scot)* poignard *m* *(porté dans la chaussette)*

skedaddle* /skɪˈdædl/ VI *(= run away)* décamper*, déguerpir* ; *(= flee in panic)* fuir en catastrophe

skeet shooting /ˈskiːtˌʃuːtɪŋ/ N skeet *m*, tir *m* au pigeon d'argile, ball-trap *m*

skein /skeɪn/ N *[of wool etc]* écheveau *m*

skeletal /ˈskelɪtl/ ADJ 1 *(Anat)* *[structure, development]* du squelette ; *[remains]* de squelette ◆ **~ structure** *or* **system** squelette *m* 2 *(= emaci-*

ated) *[person, body]* squelettique ; *[face]* émacié 3 *(= schematic) [timetable]* schématique

skeleton /'skelɪtn/ N *(Anat)* squelette *m* ; *[of building, ship, model etc]* squelette *m*, charpente *f* ; *[of plan, scheme, suggestion, novel etc]* schéma *m*, grandes lignes *fpl* ◆ **he was a mere** *or* **a walking** *or* **a living** ~ c'était un véritable cadavre ambulant ◆ **he was reduced to a** ~ il n'était plus qu'un squelette, il était devenu (d'une maigreur) squelettique ◆ **the staff was reduced to a** ~ le personnel était réduit au strict minimum ◆ **a** ~ **in the cupboard** *(Brit) or* **closet** *(US)* un cadavre dans le placard* ◆ **the family** ~ le secret de famille ; → **feast**
COMP *[army, crew, staff]* squelettique, réduit au strict minimum
skeleton key N passe *m*, passe-partout *m inv*
skeleton law N *(Ind)* loi-cadre *f*
skeleton map N carte *f* schématique
skeleton outline N *[of drawing, map, plan]* schéma *m* simplifié ; *[of proposals, report]* résumé *m*, grandes lignes *fpl*

skep /skep/ N 1 *(= beehive)* ruche *f* 2 *(= basket)* panier *m*

skeptic /'skeptɪk/ ADJ, N *(US)* ⇒ **sceptic**

skeptical /'skeptɪkəl/ ADJ *(US)* ⇒ **sceptical**

skeptically /'skeptɪkəlɪ/ ADJ *(US)* ⇒ **sceptically**

skepticism /'skeptɪsɪzəm/ N *(US)* ⇒ **scepticism**

sketch /sketʃ/ N 1 *(= drawing) (rough)* croquis *m* ; *(preliminary)* esquisse *f* ; *[of ideas, proposals etc]* aperçu *m*, ébauche *f* ◆ **a rough** ~ *(= drawing)* une ébauche ◆ **he gave me a (rough)** ~ **of what he planned to do** *(fig)* il m'a donné un aperçu de *or* il m'a dit en gros ce qu'il comptait faire
2 *(Theat)* sketch *m*, saynète *f*
VI *(roughly)* faire des croquis ; *(= make preliminary drawing)* faire des esquisses ◆ **to go ~ing** aller *or* partir faire des croquis
VT *[+ view, castle, figure] (roughly)* faire un croquis de, croquer ; *(= make preliminary drawing)* faire une esquisse de, esquisser ; *[+ map]* faire à main levée ; *(fig) [+ ideas, proposals, novel, plan]* ébaucher, esquisser
COMP **sketch(ing) book** N carnet *m* à croquis *or* à dessins
sketching pad N bloc *m* à dessins
sketch map N carte *f* faite à main levée
sketch pad N ⇒ **sketching pad**
► **sketch in** VT SEP *[+ detail in drawing]* ajouter, dessiner ; *(fig) [+ details]* ajouter ; *[+ facts]* indiquer
► **sketch out** VT SEP *[+ plans, proposals, ideas]* ébaucher, esquisser ◆ **to** ~ **out a picture of sth** *(lit, fig)* ébaucher qch, dessiner les grandes lignes de qch

sketchily /'sketʃɪlɪ/ ADV sommairement ◆ **the ideas are** ~ **developed** les idées sont (sommairement) esquissées

sketchy /'sketʃɪ/ ADJ *[details]* incomplet (-ète *f*), lacunaire ; *[account, report]* peu détaillé, sommaire ; *[piece of work]* peu détaillé ; *[knowledge]* rudimentaire, sommaire

skew /skjuː/ N ◆ **to be on the** ~ être de travers *or* en biais ADJ de travers ADV *[hang]* de travers VI 1 (also **skew round**) obliquer ◆ **negotiations ~ed off course** *(fig)* les négociations ont dévié de leur but initial 2 *(= squint)* loucher
COMP **skew-eyed*** ADJ qui louche, qui a un œil qui dit merde à l'autre*
skew-whiff* ADJ *(Brit)* ◆ **(on the) ~-whiff** de travers, de guingois*, de traviole*

skewbald /'skjuːbɔːld/ ADJ pie *inv* N cheval *m* pie *inv*

skewed /skjuːd/ ADJ 1 *(= slanting)* de travers 2 *(= distorted) [conception, view, graph]* déformé ; *[statistics]* faussé

skewer /'skjʊəʳ/ N *(for roast etc)* broche *f* ; *(for kebabs)* brochette *f* VT *[+ chicken]* embrocher ; *[+ pieces of meat]* mettre en brochette ; *(fig)* transpercer, embrocher*

ski /skiː/ N (pl **skis** *or* **ski**) ski *m*, planche* *f* ; *[of seaplane]* patin *m* ; → **water**
VI faire du ski, skier ◆ **to go ~ing** *(as holiday)* partir aux sports d'hiver ; *(= go out skiing)* (aller) faire du ski ◆ **I like ~ing** j'aime faire du ski *or* skier ◆ **to** ~ **down a slope** descendre une pente à *or* en skis
COMP *[school, clothes]* de ski
ski binding N fixation *f*
ski boot N chaussure *f* de ski
ski bunny* N *(US = girl)* minette *f* de station de ski
ski instructor N moniteur *m*, -trice *f* de ski
ski jump N *(= action)* saut *m* à skis ; *(= place)* tremplin *m* (de ski)
ski-jumping N saut *m* à skis
ski lift N télésiège *m*, remonte-pente *m inv*
ski-mountaineering N ski *m* de haute montagne
ski pants NPL fuseau *m* (de ski)
ski-pass N forfait *m* skieur(s)
ski pole N ⇒ **ski stick**
ski-rack N *[of car]* porte-skis *m*
ski resort N station *f* de ski *or* de sports d'hiver
ski run N piste *f* de ski
ski slope N pente *f or* piste *f* de ski
ski stick N bâton *m* de ski
ski-suit N combinaison *f* (de ski)
ski-touring N ski *m* de randonnée, randonnée *f* à ski
ski tow N téléski *m*, remonte-pente *m inv*
ski trousers NPL fuseau *m* (de ski)
ski wax N fart *m*
ski-wear N vêtements *mpl* de ski

skibob /'skiːbɒb/ N ski-bob *m*, véloski *m*

skid /skɪd/ N 1 *[of car etc]* dérapage *m* ◆ **to get** *or* **go into a** ~ déraper, faire un dérapage ◆ **to get out of a ~, to correct a** ~ redresser *or* contrôler un dérapage
2 *(on wheel)* cale *f*
3 *(under heavy object, rollers, logs etc)* traîneau *m* ◆ **to put the ~s*** **on** *or* **under** *(= cause to fail) [+ person]* faire un croc-en-jambe à *(fig) [+ plan etc]* faire tomber à l'eau* ◆ **her marriage/career is on the ~s*** son mariage/sa carrière bat de l'aile ◆ **to hit the ~s*** *(US)* devenir clochard(e)
VI *(in car etc)* déraper ; *[person]* déraper, glisser ◆ **the car ~ded to a halt** *or* **stop** la voiture a dérapé et s'est immobilisée ◆ **I ~ded into a tree** j'ai dérapé et percuté un arbre ◆ **he went ~ding into the bookcase** il a glissé *or* dérapé et est allé se cogner contre la bibliothèque ◆ **the toy ~ded across the room** le jouet a glissé jusqu'à l'autre bout de la pièce ◆ **prices ~ded*** *(US)* les prix ont dérapé
COMP **skid row** N *(esp US)* quartier *m* de clochards, cour *f* des miracles ◆ **he's heading for** ~ **row** *(fig)* il finira clochard*

skidlid* /'skɪdlɪd/ N casque *m* (de moto)

skidmark /'skɪdmɑːk/ N trace *f* de pneu, trace *f* de dérapage

skidoo /skɪ'duː/ N skidoo *m*, motoneige *f*, scooter *m* des neiges

skidpad /'skɪdpæd/, **skidpan** /'skɪdpæn/ N piste *f* d'entraînement au dérapage *(pour apprendre à contrôler un véhicule)*

skidproof /'skɪdpruːf/ ADJ antidérapant

skier /'skiːəʳ/ N skieur *m*, -euse *f*

skiff /skɪf/ N skiff *m*, yole *f*

skiffle /'skɪfl/ N *(Mus)* skiffle *m*

skiing /'skiːɪŋ/ N *(NonC)* ski *m* ; → **water**
COMP *[clothes, school]* de ski
skiing holiday N vacances *fpl* aux sports d'hiver, vacances *fpl* de neige ◆ **to go on a** ~ **holiday** partir aux sports d'hiver
skiing instructor N moniteur *m*, -trice *f* de ski
skiing pants NPL fuseau *m* (de ski)
skiing resort N station *f* de ski *or* de sports d'hiver
skiing trousers NPL ⇒ **skiing pants**

skilful, skillful *(US)* /'skɪlfʊl/ ADJ *[person, player]* habile *(at doing sth* à faire qch), adroit ; *[use, choice, management]* intelligent ◆ ~ **at hunting** habile à la chasse ◆ **to be** ~ **in doing sth** faire preuve d'habileté *or* d'adresse pour faire qch ◆ **to be** ~ **with sth** savoir se servir de qch

skilfully, skillfully *(US)* /'skɪlfəlɪ/ ADV *[organize, carry out, use]* habilement, intelligemment ; *[avoid]* adroitement ; *[write]* avec habileté

skilfulness, skillfulness *(US)* /'skɪlfʊlnɪs/ N *(NonC)* habileté *f*, adresse *f*

skill /skɪl/ N 1 *(NonC = competence, ability)* habileté *f*, adresse *f* ; *(gen manual)* dextérité *f* ; *(= talent)* savoir-faire *m*, talent *m* ◆ **the** ~ **of the dancers** l'adresse *f or* le talent des danseurs ◆ **the** ~ **of the juggler** l'adresse *f or* la dextérité du jongleur ◆ **his** ~ **at billiards** son habileté *or* son adresse au billard ◆ **his** ~ **in negotiation** son talent de négociateur ◆ **her** ~ **in persuading them** l'habileté dont elle a fait preuve pour les persuader ◆ **lack of** ~ maladresse *f*
2 *(in craft etc)* technique *f* ◆ **~s** *(gen)* capacités *fpl*, compétences *fpl* ; *(Scol: innate)* aptitudes *fpl* ; *(Scol: learnt)* savoir *m* ◆ **it's a** ~ **that has to be acquired** c'est une technique qui s'apprend ◆ **we could make good use of his ~s** ses capacités *or* ses compétences nous seraient bien utiles ◆ **what ~s do you have?** quelles sont vos compétences ? ◆ **learning a language is a question of learning new ~s** apprendre une langue consiste à acquérir de nouvelles compétences

Skillcentre /'skɪlsentəʳ/ N *(Brit) centre de formation professionnelle pour demandeurs d'emploi*

skilled /skɪld/ ADJ 1 *(= skilful) [person, driver]* habile, adroit ◆ **to be** ~ **in the use of sth** savoir bien se servir de qch, faire un usage habile de qch ◆ **to be** ~ **in diplomacy** être un habile diplomate ◆ ~ **in the art of negotiating** maître dans l'art de la négociation ◆ ~ **in** *or* **at doing sth** habile à faire qch ◆ **to be** ~ **in reading and writing** savoir bien lire et écrire 2 *[job, worker]* qualifié ◆ **a low-~ clerical job** un emploi *or* un travail peu qualifié dans un bureau ◆ ~ **nursing care** *(US) soins dispensés par un personnel médical qualifié* ◆ ~ **nursing facility** *(US) centre de soins dispensés par un personnel médical qualifié* ; see also **semiskilled**

skillet /'skɪlɪt/ N poêlon *m*

skillful /'skɪlfʊl/ ADJ *(US)* ⇒ **skilful**

skillfully /'skɪlfəlɪ/ ADV *(US)* ⇒ **skilfully**

skillfulness /'skɪlfʊlnɪs/ N *(US)* ⇒ **skilfulness**

skim /skɪm/ VT 1 *[+ milk]* écrémer ; *[+ soup]* écumer ◆ **to** ~ **the cream/scum/grease from sth** écrémer/écumer/dégraisser qch
2 **to** ~ **the ground/water** *[bird etc]* raser *or* effleurer *or* frôler le sol/la surface de l'eau ◆ **to** ~ **a stone across the pond** faire ricocher une pierre sur l'étang
3 *(US * fig) [+ one's income]* ne pas déclarer en totalité au fisc
VI 1 ◆ **to** ~ **across the water/along the ground** raser l'eau/le sol ◆ **the stone ~med across the pond** la pierre a ricoché d'un bout à l'autre de l'étang ◆ **to** ~ **through a book** parcourir *or* feuilleter un livre ◆ **he ~med over the difficult passages** il s'est contenté de parcourir rapidement les passages difficiles
2 *(US * = cheat on taxes)* frauder (le fisc)
COMP **skim(med) milk** N lait *m* écrémé
► **skim off** VT SEP *[+ cream, grease, money]* enlever ◆ **rich Italian clubs** ~ **off all Europe's stars** les clubs italiens volent toutes les stars européennes ◆ **private schools** ~ **off the cream**

from state schools les écoles privées dépouillent les écoles publiques de leurs meilleurs éléments

skimmer /ˈskɪməʳ/ N 1 (= *bird*) rhyncops *m*, bec-en-ciseaux *m* 2 (= *kitchen utensil*) écumoir *m* 3 (*for swimming pool*) skimmer *m*

skimming /ˈskɪmɪŋ/ N (*US* * = *tax fraud*) ≃ fraude *f* fiscale

skimp /skɪmp/ VI lésiner, économiser ◆ **to ~ on** [*+ butter, cloth, paint etc*] lésiner sur ; [*+ money*] économiser ; [*+ praise, thanks*] être avare de ; [*+ piece of work*] faire à la va-vite, bâcler*

skimpily /ˈskɪmpɪlɪ/ ADV [*serve, provide*] avec parcimonie ; [*live*] chichement

skimpiness /ˈskɪmpɪnɪs/ N [*of meal, helping, allowance*] insuffisance *f*

skimpy /ˈskɪmpɪ/ ADJ [*bikini, underwear*] minuscule ; [*meal*] frugal, maigre *before n* ; [*pay*] maigre *before n* ◆ **she was wearing a ~ dress** elle portait une robe qui dévoilait presque tout

skin /skɪn/ N 1 [*of person, animal*] peau *f* ◆ **she has (a) good/bad ~** elle a une jolie/vilaine peau ◆ **to wear wool next to the ~** porter de la laine sur la peau *or* à même la peau ◆ **wet** *or* **soaked to the ~** trempé jusqu'aux os ◆ **the snake casts** *or* **sheds its ~** le serpent mue ◆ **rabbit ~** peau *f* de lapin

2 (*phrases*) ◆ **to be (all** *or* **only) ~ and bone** n'avoir que la peau sur les os ◆ **with a whole ~** indemne, sain et sauf, sans une écorchure ◆ **to escape by the ~ of one's teeth** l'échapper belle ◆ **we caught the last train by the ~ of our teeth** nous avons attrapé le dernier train de justesse ◆ **to have a thick ~** avoir une peau d'éléphant, être insensible ◆ **to have a thin ~** être susceptible, avoir l'épiderme sensible ◆ **to get under sb's ~*** (= *annoy*) porter *or* taper* sur les nerfs à qn ; (= *understand*) se mettre à la place de qn ◆ **I've got you under my ~*** je suis amoureux fou de toi ◆ **it's no ~ off my nose!‡** (= *does not hurt me*) pour ce que ça me coûte ! ; (= *does not concern me*) ce n'est pas mon problème ! ; → **pigskin, save¹**

3 [*of fruit, vegetable, milk pudding, sausage, drum*] peau *f* ; (*peeled*) pelure *f* ; [*of boat, aircraft*] revêtement *m* ; (*for duplicating*) stencil *m* ; (*for wine*) outre *f* ◆ **to cook potatoes in their ~(s)** faire cuire des pommes de terre en robe des champs *or* en robe de chambre ◆ **a banana ~** une peau de banane

4 (*Ski*) **~s** peaux *fpl* (de phoque)

5 (‡ = *cigarette paper*) papier *m* à cigarette

VT 1 [*+ animal*] dépouiller ; [*+ fruit, vegetable*] éplucher ◆ **I'll ~ him alive!*** je vais l'écorcher tout vif ! ◆ **to ~ one's knee** s'érafler *or* s'écorcher le genou ◆ **there are more ways than one** *or* **there is more than one way to ~ a cat*** il y a plusieurs façons de plumer un canard ; → **eye**

2 (‡ = *steal from*) estamper*, plumer*

COMP [*colour, texture*] de (la) peau

skin cancer N cancer *m* de la peau

skin care N soins *mpl* pour la peau

skin-deep ADJ superficiel ◆ **it's only ~-deep** ça ne va pas (chercher) bien loin ; see also **beauty**

skin disease N maladie *f* de (la) peau

skin diver N plongeur *m*, -euse *f* sous-marin(e)

skin diving N plongée *f* sous-marine

skin flick‡ N (*Cine*) (film *m*) porno* *m inv*

skin game* N (*US*) escroquerie *f*

skin graft N greffe *f* de (la) peau

skin grafting N greffe *f* de la peau

skin mag(azine)* N (*US*) revue *f* porno*

skin patch N (*Med*) patch *m*, timbre *m* transdermique

skin test N (*Med*) cuti(-réaction) *f*

▸ **skin up‡** VI rouler un joint*

skinflint /ˈskɪnflɪnt/ N grippe-sou *m*, radin(e)* *m(f)*

skinful‡ /ˈskɪnfʊl/ N ◆ **to have (had) a ~** être bourré‡ ◆ **he's got a ~ of whisky** il s'est soûlé* *or* il a pris une biture‡ au whisky

skinhead /ˈskɪnhed/ N (*Brit* = *thug*) skinhead *m*

skinless /ˈskɪnlɪs/ ADJ [*meat, sausage, fish*] sans (la) peau

-skinned /skɪnd/ ADJ (*in compounds*) ◆ **fair-skinned** à (la) peau claire ; → **thick, thin**

skinner /ˈskɪnəʳ/ N peaussier *m*

skinny /ˈskɪnɪ/ ADJ 1 (= *thin*) [*person, legs, arms*] maigre ◆ **the ~ look** (*Fashion*) la mode ultra-mince 2 (= *close-fitting*) [*sweater*] moulant

COMP **skinny-dip*** N baignade *f* à poil* VI se baigner à poil*

skinny-dipping* N (*NonC*) baignade *f* à poil* ◆ **to go ~-dipping** se baigner à poil*

skinny-rib (sweater *or* **jumper)*** N pull-chaussette *m*

skint‡ /skɪnt/ ADJ (*Brit*) fauché*

skintight /skɪnˈtaɪt/ ADJ collant, ajusté

skip¹ /skɪp/ N petit bond *m*, petit saut *m* ◆ **to give a ~** faire un petit bond *or* saut

VI 1 gambader, sautiller ; (*with rope*) sauter à la corde ◆ **to ~ with joy** sauter *or* bondir de joie ◆ **the child ~ped in/out** *etc* l'enfant est entré/sorti *etc* en gambadant *or* en sautillant ◆ **she ~ped lightly over the stones** elle sautait légèrement par-dessus les pierres ◆ **he ~ped out of the way of the cycle** il a fait un bond pour éviter le vélo ◆ **he ~ped over that point** il est passé sur ce point, il a sauté par-dessus *or* a glissé sur ce point ◆ **to ~ from one subject to another** sauter d'un sujet à un autre ◆ **the author** *or* **book ~s about a lot** l'auteur papillonne beaucoup dans ce livre

2 (*fig*) **I ~ped up to London yesterday** j'ai fait un saut à Londres hier ◆ **I ~ped round to see her** j'ai fait un saut chez elle

VT (= *omit*) [*+ chapter, page, paragraph*] sauter, passer ; [*+ class, meal*] sauter ◆ **I'll ~ lunch** je vais sauter le déjeuner, je vais me passer de déjeuner ◆ **~ it!*** laisse tomber !* ◆ **~ the details!** laisse tomber les détails !*, épargne-nous les détails ! ◆ **to ~ school** sécher les cours

COMP **skip rope** N (*US*) corde *f* à sauter

skip² /skɪp/ N (*Brit* = *container*) benne *f*

skipper /ˈskɪpəʳ/ N (*Naut*) capitaine *m*, patron *m* ; (*Sport* *) capitaine *m*, chef *m* d'équipe ; (*in race*) skipper *m* VT * [*+ boat*] commander ; [*+ team*] être le chef de, mener

skipping /ˈskɪpɪŋ/ N saut *m* à la corde COMP **skipping rope** N (*Brit*) corde *f* à sauter

skirl /skɜːl/ N son *m* aigu (*de la cornemuse*)

skirmish /ˈskɜːmɪʃ/ N (*gen*) échauffourée *f* ; (*Mil*) escarmouche *f* ; (*fig*) escarmouche *f*, accrochage* *m* VI (*Mil*) s'engager dans une escarmouche ◆ **to ~ with sb** (*fig*) avoir un accrochage* avec qn

skirt /skɜːt/ N 1 (= *garment*) jupe *f* ; [*of frock coat*] basque *f* 2 (= *girl*) **a bit of ~‡** une nana‡ 3 (*on machine, vehicle*) jupe *f* 4 (= *steak*) flanchet *m* VT (also **skirt round**) (= *go round*) contourner, longer ; (= *miss, avoid*) [*+ town, obstacle*] contourner, éviter ; [*+ problem, difficulty*] esquiver, éluder ◆ **the road ~s (round) the forest** la route longe *or* contourne la forêt ◆ **we ~ed (round) Paris to the north** nous sommes passés au nord de Paris, nous avons contourné Paris par le nord ◆ **to ~ (round) the issue (of whether)** esquiver *or* éluder la question (de savoir si) VI ◆ **to ~ round** → vt COMP **skirt length** N hauteur *f* de jupe

skirting /ˈskɜːtɪŋ/ N (*Brit*: also **skirting board**) plinthe *f*

skit /skɪt/ N parodie *f* (*on* de) ; (*Theat*) sketch *m* satirique

skitter /ˈskɪtəʳ/ VI ◆ **to ~ across the water/along the ground** [*bird*] voler en frôlant l'eau/le sol ; [*stone*] ricocher sur l'eau/le sol

skittish /ˈskɪtɪʃ/ ADJ (= *frivolous*) capricieux ; (= *nervous*) nerveux ; (= *coquettish*) coquet ; (= *excitable*) [*horse*] ombrageux

skittishly /ˈskɪtɪʃlɪ/ ADV (= *coquettishly*) en faisant la coquette

skittle /ˈskɪtl/ N quille *f* ◆ **~s** (*esp Brit*) (jeu *m* de) quilles *fpl* ; → **beer** COMP **skittle alley** N (piste *f* de) jeu *m* de quilles, bowling *m*

skive* /skaɪv/ (*Brit*) VI (also **skive off**) tirer au flanc* N ◆ **to be on the ~** tirer au flanc*

skiver* /ˈskaɪvəʳ/ N (*Brit*) tire-au-flanc* *m inv*

skivvy* /ˈskɪvɪ/ N 1 (*Brit pej* = *servant*) boniche *f* (*pej*), bonne *f* à tout faire 2 (*US*) **skivvies*** (= *underwear*) sous-vêtements *mpl* (d'homme) VI (*Brit*) faire la boniche

Skopje /ˈskɔːpje/ N Skopje

skua /ˈskjuːə/ N stercoraire *m*, labbe *m*

skulduggery* /skʌlˈdʌgərɪ/ N (*NonC*) maquignonnage *m*, trafic *m* ◆ **a piece of ~** un maquignonnage

skulk /skʌlk/ VI (also **skulk about**) rôder en se cachant, rôder furtivement ◆ **to ~ in/away** *etc* entrer/s'éloigner *etc* furtivement

skull /skʌl/ N crâne *m* ◆ **~ and crossbones** (= *emblem*) tête *f* de mort ; (= *flag*) pavillon *m* à tête de mort ◆ **I can't get it into his (thick) ~* that ...** pas moyen de lui faire comprendre que ..., je n'arrive pas à lui faire entrer dans le crâne* que ...

skullcap /ˈskʌlkæp/ N calotte *f*

skunk /skʌŋk/ N (pl **skunk** *or* **skunks**) 1 (= *animal*) mouffette *f* ; (= *fur*) sconse *m* ; (* *pej* = *person*) mufle* *m*, canaille *f*, salaud‡ *m* 2 *(*Drugs*) **~ (weed)** skunk *m*

sky /skaɪ/ N ciel *m* ◆ **the skies** le(s) ciel(s) ; (*fig*) les cieux *mpl* ◆ **there was a clear blue ~** le ciel était clair et bleu ◆ **in the ~** dans le ciel ◆ **under the open ~** à la belle étoile ◆ **under a blue ~, under blue skies** sous un ciel bleu ◆ **the skies over** *or* **of England** les ciels *mpl* d'Angleterre ◆ **the skies of Van Gogh** les ciels *mpl* de Van Gogh ◆ **under warmer skies** sous des cieux plus cléments ◆ **to praise sb to the skies** porter qn aux nues ◆ **it came out of a clear (blue) ~** (*fig*) c'est arrivé de façon tout à fait inattendue, on ne s'y attendait vraiment pas ◆ **the ~'s the limit*** tout est possible

VT [*+ ball*] envoyer très haut *or* en chandelle

COMP **sky ad** N publicité *f or* annonce *f* aérienne

sky blue N bleu *m* ciel

sky-blue ADJ bleu ciel *inv*

sky-high ADJ très haut (dans le ciel) ; (*fig*) extrêmement haut ◆ **he hit the ball ~-high** il a envoyé le ballon très haut (dans le ciel) ◆ **the bridge was blown ~-high** le pont a sauté, le pont a volé en morceaux ◆ **to blow a theory ~-high** démolir une théorie ◆ **prices are ~-high** les prix sont exorbitants ◆ **the crisis sent sugar prices ~-high** la crise a fait monter en flèche le prix du sucre

sky marshal N *agent de police ou de sécurité embarqué sur un vol pour en assurer sa protection*

sky pilot †‡ N (= *priest*) curé *m*

sky-surfing N sky-surfing *m*

sky train N *avion qui remorque un ou plusieurs planeurs*

skycap /ˈskaɪkæp/ N (*US*) porteur *m* (*dans un aéroport*)

skydive /ˈskaɪdaɪv/ N saut *m* (en parachute) en chute libre VI faire du parachutisme en chute libre

skydiver /ˈskaɪdaɪvəʳ/ N parachutiste *mf* (faisant de la chute libre)

skydiving /ˈskaɪdaɪvɪŋ/ N parachutisme *m* (en chute libre)

Skye /skaɪ/ N (île f de) Skye f

skyjack* /ˈskaɪˌdʒæk/ VT [+ plane] détourner, pirater

skyjacker* /ˈskaɪˌdʒækəʳ/ N pirate m de l'air

skyjacking* /ˈskaɪˌdʒækɪŋ/ N détournement m d'avion, piraterie f aérienne

Skylab /ˈskaɪlæb/ N (Space) laboratoire m spatial, Skylab m

skylark /ˈskaɪlɑːk/ N (= bird) alouette f (des champs) VI * chahuter, faire le fou

skylarking* /ˈskaɪlɑːkɪŋ/ N rigolade * f, chahut m

skylight /ˈskaɪlaɪt/ N lucarne f, tabatière f

skyline /ˈskaɪlaɪn/ N ligne f d'horizon ; [of city] ligne f des toits ; [of buildings] profil m, silhouette f

skyrocket /ˈskaɪrɒkɪt/ N fusée f VI [prices] monter en flèche

skyscraper /ˈskaɪskreɪpəʳ/ N gratte-ciel m inv

skyward /ˈskaɪwəd/ ADJ, ADV vers le ciel

skywards /ˈskaɪwədz/ ADV [soar, point] vers le ciel ; [gaze] en l'air

skyway /ˈskaɪweɪ/ N (US) (= air corridor) route f or voie f aérienne ; (= road) route f surélevée

skywriting /ˈskaɪraɪtɪŋ/ N publicité f aérienne (tracée dans le ciel par un avion)

slab /slæb/ N 1 (large piece) [of stone, wood, slate] bloc m ; (flat) plaque f ; [of meat] pièce f ; (smaller) carré m, pavé m ; [of cake] pavé m ; (smaller) grosse tranche f ; [of chocolate] plaque f ; (smaller) tablette f 2 (= paving slab) dalle f ; (= table, surface) (in butcher's etc) étal m ; (in mortuary) table f de dissection or d'autopsie COMP **slab cake** N grand cake m rectangulaire

slack /slæk/ ADJ 1 (= loose) [skin, sail] flasque, mou (molle f) ; [rope] lâche, mal tendu ; [joint, knot] desserré ; [hold, grip] faible ; [muscle] relâché ◆ **to be ~** [screw] avoir du jeu ; [rope] avoir du mou ◆ **keep it ~!** [rope] laissez du mou ! ◆ **to have a ~ mouth/jaw** avoir la lèvre inférieure/la mâchoire pendante

2 (= not busy) [time, season, month] creux ; [demand] faible ; [market, trade] faible, stagnant ◆ **during ~ periods** (weeks, months etc) pendant les jours or mois creux, pendant les périodes creuses ; (in the day) aux heures creuses ◆ **business is ~ this week** les affaires marchent au ralenti or ne vont pas fort * cette semaine

3 (= lax) [discipline, security] relâché ; [student] inappliqué, peu sérieux ; [worker] peu sérieux, peu consciencieux ◆ **to be ~ in** or **about one's work** se relâcher dans son travail

N 1 (in rope: Climbing) mou m ; (in cable) ballant m ; (in joint etc) jeu m ◆ **to take up the ~ in a rope** raidir un cordage ◆ **to take up the ~ in the economy** relancer les secteurs affaiblis de l'économie ◆ **to cut sb some ~** (fig) faciliter les choses à qn

2 (= coal) poussier m

NPL **slacks** (= trousers) pantalon m ◆ **a pair of ~s** un pantalon

VI * ne pas travailler comme il le faudrait

COMP **slack water** N étale mf

▸ **slack off** VI 1 (* = stop working/trying etc) se relâcher (dans son travail/dans ses efforts etc) 2 [business, trade, demand] ralentir
VT SEP [+ rope, cable] détendre, donner du mou à

▸ **slack up*** VI ralentir (ses efforts or son travail)

slacken /ˈslækn/ VT (also **slacken off**) [+ rope] relâcher, donner du mou à ; [+ cable] donner du ballant à ; [+ reins] relâcher ; [+ screw] desserrer ; [+ pressure etc] diminuer, réduire ◆ **to ~ one's pace** ralentir l'allure ◆ **to ~ speed** (in car) diminuer de vitesse, ralentir VI (also **slacken off**) [rope] se relâcher, prendre du mou ; [cable] prendre du ballant ; [screw] se desserrer ; [gale] diminuer de force ; [speed] diminuer ; [activity, business, trade] ralentir, diminuer ; [effort, enthusiasm, pressure] diminuer, se relâcher

▸ **slacken off** (esp Brit) VI 1 ⇒ **slacken** VI 2 [person] se relâcher, se laisser aller VT SEP ⇒ **slacken** VT

▸ **slacken up** VI ⇒ **slacken off** VI 2

slackening /ˈslæknɪŋ/ N (NonC) [of effort, grip, rope, muscles] relâchement m ; [of output, pace] ralentissement m ◆ **a ~ of demand** une diminution or baisse de la demande ◆ **a ~ in sb's determination** un fléchissement de la détermination de qn

slacker* /ˈslækəʳ/ N flemmard(e) * m(f), fainéant(e) m(f)

slackly /ˈslæklɪ/ ADV 1 (= loosely) [hang] lâchement, mollement 2 (= laxly) [work, play] négligemment ; [supervise] sans fermeté

slackness /ˈslæknɪs/ N [of rope etc] manque m de tension ; * [of person] négligence f, laisser-aller m inv ◆ **the ~ of trade** le ralentissement or la stagnation des affaires

slag /slæg/ N 1 (Metal) scories fpl, crasses fpl 2 (Min) stériles mpl 3 (Brit ‡ = slut) salope ‡ f VT (Brit) → **slag off** COMP **slag heap** N (Metal) crassier m ; (Min) terril m

▸ **slag off** ‡ VT SEP (esp Brit) ◆ **to slag sb off** (= scold, insult) engueuler ‡ qn ; (= speak badly of) débiner * qn

slain /sleɪn/ (liter) VB ptp of **slay** NPL **the slain** (Mil) les morts mpl, les soldats mpl tombés au champ d'honneur

slake /sleɪk/ VT [+ lime] éteindre ; [+ one's thirst] étancher ; (fig) [+ desire for revenge etc] assouvir, satisfaire

slalom /ˈslɑːləm/ N slalom m VI slalomer COMP **slalom descent** N descente f en slalom **slalom racer, slalom specialist** N slalomeur m, -euse f

slam /slæm/ N 1 [of door] claquement m ◆ **to shut the door with a ~** claquer la porte 2 (Bridge) chelem m ◆ **to make a grand/little ~** faire un grand/petit chelem

VT 1 [+ door] (faire) claquer, fermer violemment ; [+ lid] (faire) claquer, rabattre violemment ◆ **to ~ the door shut** claquer la porte ◆ **she ~med the books on the table** elle a jeté brutalement or a flanqué * les livres sur la table ◆ **he ~med the ball into the grandstand** d'un coup violent il a envoyé le ballon dans la tribune ◆ **our team ~med yours** * (fig) notre équipe a écrasé la vôtre

2 (‡ = criticize) éreinter *, descendre en flammes *

VI 1 [door, lid] claquer ◆ **the door ~med shut** la porte s'est refermée en claquant 2 ◆ **to ~ into** (or **against**) **sth** s'écraser contre qch

COMP **slam dancing** N (NonC) slam m (danse punk qui consiste à se jeter contre les autres spectateurs) **slam-dunk** (US Basketball) N slam-dunk m, smash m VT, VI smasher

▸ **slam down** VT SEP (gen) poser or jeter brutalement, flanquer * ; [+ lid] rabattre brutalement ◆ **to ~ the phone down** raccrocher brutalement ◆ **he ~med the phone down on me** il m'a raccroché au nez

▸ **slam on** VT SEP ◆ **to slam on the brakes** freiner à mort ◆ **to ~ the brakes on sth** * (fig = put a stop to) mettre le holà à qch

▸ **slam to** VI se refermer en claquant
VT SEP refermer en claquant

slammer /ˈslæməʳ/ N (= prison) ◆ **the ~** ‡ la taule ‡, la prison

slander /ˈslɑːndəʳ/ N calomnie f ; (Jur) diffamation f ◆ **it's a ~ to suggest that ...** c'est de la calomnie que de suggérer que ... VT calomnier, dire du mal de ; (Jur) diffamer

slanderer /ˈslɑːndərəʳ/ N calomniateur m, -trice f ; (Jur) diffamateur m, -trice f

slanderous /ˈslɑːndərəs/ ADJ calomnieux ; (Jur) diffamatoire

slanderously /ˈslɑːndərəslɪ/ ADV calomnieusement ; (Jur) de façon diffamatoire

slang /slæŋ/ N (NonC) argot m ◆ **in ~** en argot ◆ **in army/school ~** en argot militaire/d'écolier, dans l'argot des armées/des écoles ◆ **that word is ~** c'est un mot d'argot or argotique, c'est un argotisme ◆ **to talk ~** parler argot ◆ **he uses a lot of ~** il emploie beaucoup d'argot, il s'exprime dans une langue très verte ; → **rhyming** ADJ [phrase, word] d'argot, argotique ◆ **a ~ expression** un argotisme VT * traiter de tous les noms COMP **slanging match*** N (Brit) prise f de bec *

slangily* /ˈslæŋɪlɪ/ ADV ◆ **to talk ~** parler argot, employer beaucoup d'argot

slangy* /ˈslæŋɪ/ ADJ [style, language, expression] argotique ; [person] qui emploie beaucoup d'argot

slant /slɑːnt/ N 1 inclinaison f, aspect m penché ; (fig = point of view) point m de vue (on sur), angle m, perspective f ; (= bias) parti m pris ◆ **what's his ~ on it?** quel est son point de vue sur la question ? ◆ **to give a ~ to sth** présenter qch avec parti pris ◆ **to give/get a new ~ * on sth** présenter/voir qch sous un angle or jour nouveau 2 (Typ) (also **slant mark**) (barre f) oblique f VI [line, handwriting] pencher, être incliné ; [light, sunbeam] passer obliquement VT [+ line, handwriting] faire pencher, incliner ; (fig) [+ account, news] présenter avec parti pris ◆ **~ed eyes** yeux mpl bridés ◆ **a ~ed report** un rapport orienté or tendancieux COMP **slant-eyed** ADJ aux yeux bridés

slanting /ˈslɑːntɪŋ/ ADJ [line, rays, light, rain] oblique ; [roof, surface] en pente, incliné ; [handwriting] penché, couché ; [eyes] bridé

slantwise /ˈslɑːntwaɪz/ ADV, ADJ obliquement, de biais

slanty* /ˈslɑːntɪ/ ADJ ◆ **~-eyed** aux yeux bridés ◆ **~ eyes** yeux mpl bridés

slap /slæp/ N claque f ; (on face) gifle f ; (on back) grande tape f ; (stronger) grande claque f ◆ **a ~ on the bottom** une fessée ◆ **a ~ in the face** (lit, fig) une gifle ◆ **a ~ on the back** une grande tape or claque dans le dos ◆ **to give sb a ~** donner une gifle à qn ◆ **to give sb a ~ on the wrist** (fig) réprimander qn ◆ **to get a ~ on the wrist** se faire taper sur les doigts

ADV * en plein, tout droit ◆ **he ran ~ into the wall** il est rentré en plein dans or tout droit dans le mur ◆ **~ in the middle** en plein or au beau milieu

VT 1 (= hit) [+ person] donner une tape à ; (stronger) donner une claque à ◆ **to ~ sb on the back** donner une tape or une claque dans le dos à qn ◆ **to ~ a child's bottom** donner une fessée à un enfant ◆ **to ~ sb's face** or **sb in the face** gifler qn ◆ **to ~ one's knees** or **thighs** (in amusement etc) se taper les cuisses

2 (= put) flanquer * ◆ **he ~ped the book on the table** il a flanqué * le livre sur la table ◆ **he ~ped £50 on to the price** * il a gonflé son prix de 50 livres

COMP **slap and tickle** ‡ N (Brit) ◆ **they were having a bit of the old ~ and tickle** ils étaient en train de se peloter *
slap-bang * ADV (Brit) ◆ **~-bang into the wall** en plein or tout droit dans le mur ◆ **he ran ~-bang(-wallop) into his mother** il a heurté sa mère de plein fouet ; (= met) il s'est retrouvé nez à nez avec sa mère

slap-happy* ADJ *(= carelessly cheerful)* insouciant, décontracté*, relaxe* ; *(US = punch-drunk)* groggy, abruti par les coups

slap-up meal* N *(Brit)* repas *m* fameux *or* extra*

▸ **slap around** VT SEP donner des claques à ◆ **he ~s his wife around** il bat sa femme

▸ **slap down** VT SEP *[+ object]* poser brusquement *or* violemment ◆ **to ~ sb down** * *(fig)* rembarrer* qn, envoyer qn sur les roses*

▸ **slap on** VT SEP *[+ paint etc]* appliquer à la va-vite *or* n'importe comment ; * *[+ tax]* flanquer*, coller* ◆ **to ~ on make-up** se maquiller à la va-vite ◆ **she ~ped some foundation on her face*** elle s'est collé vite fait du fond de teint sur la figure* ◆ **he ~ped a coat of paint on the wall** il a flanqué* une couche de peinture sur le mur

slapdash* /ˈslæpdæʃ/ ADJ *[person]* négligent ; *[work]* bâclé* ADV à la va-vite, n'importe comment

slaphead‡ /ˈslæphed/ N *(pej or hum = bald person)* ◆ **he's a ~** c'est un crâne d'œuf*, il est chauve comme un œuf*

slapper‡ /ˈslæpəʳ/ N garce‡ *f*

slapstick /ˈslæpstɪk/ N (also **slapstick comedy**) grosse farce *f*, comédie *f* bouffonne

slash /slæʃ/ N ① *(= cut: gen)* entaille *f*, taillade *f* ; *(on face)* entaille *f*, balafre *f* ; *(Sewing: in sleeve)* crevé *m*

② *(Typ:* also **slash mark**) (barre *f*) oblique *f*

③ **to go for a ~***‡ *(= urinate)* aller pisser un coup‡

VT ① *(with knife, sickle etc)* entailler ; *(several cuts)* taillader ; *[+ rope]* couper net, trancher ; *[+ face]* balafrer ; *(with whip, stick)* cingler ; *(Sewing) [+ sleeve]* faire des crevés dans ◆ **~ed sleeves** manches *fpl* à crevés ◆ **to ~ sb** taillader qn ◆ **his attacker ~ed his face/his jacket** son assaillant lui a balafré le visage/a tailladé sa veste ◆ **to ~ one's wrists** s'ouvrir les veines

② *(fig) [+ prices]* casser*, écraser* ; *[+ costs, expenses]* réduire radicalement ; *[+ speech, text]* couper *or* raccourcir radicalement ◆ **"prices slashed"** "prix cassés", "prix sacrifiés"

③ *(* = condemn) [+ book, play]* éreinter*, démolir*

VI ◆ **he ~ed at me with his stick** il m'a flanqué* un *or* des coup(s) de bâton ◆ **he ~ed at the grass with his stick** il cinglait l'herbe de sa canne

COMP **slash-and-burn** ADJ *(Agr)* ◆ **~-and-burn agriculture** *or* **farming** culture *f* sur brûlis

slasher film* /ˈslæʃəfɪlm/, **slasher movie*** /ˈslæʃəmuːvɪ/ N film *m* d'horreur *(particulièrement violent)*

slashing /ˈslæʃɪŋ/ ADJ *(fig) [criticism, attack]* cinglant, mordant

slat /slæt/ N lame *f* ; *(wooden)* latte *f* ; *[of blind]* lamelle *f*

slate /sleɪt/ N *(= substance, object: Constr, Scol etc)* ardoise *f* ; *(fig: Pol)* liste *f* provisoire de candidats ◆ **they've got a full ~ there** *(Pol)* ils ont des candidats dans toutes les circonscriptions ◆ **put it on the ~*** *(Brit Comm)* mettez-le sur mon compte, ajoutez ça à mon ardoise* ◆ **to start with a clean ~** repartir sur une bonne base ; → **wipe** VT ① *[+ roof]* ardoiser ② *(US Pol) [+ candidate]* proposer ③ *(Brit *) (= criticize)* éreinter*, démolir* ; *(= scold)* attraper*, engueuler‡ ④ *(US)* **to be ~d* for sth** *(= destined)* être désigné pour qch

COMP *[deposits]* d'ardoise, ardoisier ; *[industry]* ardoisier, de l'ardoise ; *[roof]* en ardoise, d'ardoise

slate-blue ADJ, N bleu ardoise *m inv*

slate-coloured ADJ ardoise *inv*

slate-grey ADJ, N gris ardoise *m inv*

slate quarry N ardoisière *f*, carrière *f* d'ardoise

slater /ˈsleɪtəʳ/ N *(in quarry)* ardoisier *m* ; *[of roof]* couvreur *m*

slather /ˈslæðəʳ/ VT ◆ **to ~ sth on** appliquer une couche épaisse de qch ◆ **to ~ sth with sth** enduire qch de qch

slatted /ˈslætɪd/ ADJ à lames ; *(wooden)* à lattes ; *[blind]* à lamelles

slattern /ˈslætən/ N souillon *f*

slatternly /ˈslætənlɪ/ ADJ *[woman, appearance]* négligé ; *[behaviour, habits]* de souillon

slaty /ˈsleɪtɪ/ ADJ *(in texture)* ardoisier, semblable à l'ardoise ; *(in colour)* (couleur) ardoise *inv*

slaughter /ˈslɔːtəʳ/ N *[of animals]* abattage *m* ; *[of people]* massacre *m* ◆ **the ~ on the roads** les hécatombes *fpl* sur la route ◆ **there was great ~** cela a été un carnage *or* un massacre VT *[+ animal]* abattre ; *[+ person]* tuer sauvagement ; *[+ people]* massacrer ◆ **our team really ~ed them*** *(= beat)* notre équipe les a écrasés *or* massacrés*

slaughterer /ˈslɔːtərəʳ/ N *[of animals]* tueur *m*, assommeur *m* ; *[of person]* meurtrier *m* ; *[of people]* massacreur *m*

slaughterhouse /ˈslɔːtəhaʊs/ N abattoir *m*

Slav /slɑːv/ ADJ, N slave *mf*

slave /sleɪv/ N *(lit, fig)* esclave *mf* ◆ **to be a ~ to** *(fig)* être (l')esclave de ; → **white** VI (also **slave away**) travailler comme un nègre, trimer ◆ **to ~ (away) at sth/at doing sth** s'escrimer sur qch/à faire qch

COMP **slave driver** N *(lit)* surveillant *m* d'esclaves ; *(fig)* négrier *m*, -ière *f*

slave labour N *(NonC) (= exploitation)* exploitation *f* des esclaves ; *(= work)* travail *m* fait par les esclaves ; *(* fig)* travail *m* de forçat *or* de galérien ◆ **~ labour camp** camp *m* de travaux forcés

slave ship N (vaisseau *m*) négrier *m*

slave trade N commerce *m* des esclaves, traite *f* des Noirs

slave trader N marchand *m* d'esclaves, négrier *m*

slave traffic N trafic *m* d'esclaves

slaver[1] /ˈsleɪvəʳ/ N *(= person)* marchand *m* d'esclaves, négrier *m* ; *(= ship)* (vaisseau *m*) négrier *m*

slaver[2] /ˈslævəʳ/ *(= dribble)* N bave *f* VI baver ◆ **to ~ over sth** *(fig)* baver* devant qch

slavery /ˈsleɪvərɪ/ N *(lit, fig)* esclavage *m* ◆ **housework is nothing but ~** le ménage est un véritable esclavage *or* une perpétuelle corvée ; → **sell**

slavey* /ˈsleɪvɪ/ N boniche* *f*

Slavic /ˈslɑːvɪk/ ADJ, N slave *m*

slavish /ˈsleɪvɪʃ/ ADJ *[imitation]* servile ; *[devotion]* béat ; *[remake]* sans aucune originalité ◆ **to be a ~ follower of sb/sth** suivre qn/qch aveuglément

slavishly /ˈsleɪvɪʃlɪ/ ADV *[follow]* servilement, aveuglément ; *[copy]* bêtement ◆ **their ~ pro-American attitude** leur attitude aveuglément pro-américaine ◆ **the film is ~ faithful to the novel** le film est trop proche du roman

Slavonic /sləˈvɒnɪk/ ADJ, N slave *m*

slavophile /ˈslævəʊ,faɪl/ N, ADJ slavophile *mf*

slaw /slɔː/ N *(esp US)* salade *f* de chou cru

slay /sleɪ/ (pret **slew**, ptp **slain**) VT *(liter)* tuer ◆ **he ~s me!** ‡ *(fig)* il me fait mourir *or* crever* de rire ! ; see also **slain**

slayer /ˈsleɪəʳ/ N *(liter)* tueur *m*, -euse *f*

SLD /ˌesel'diː/ N *(Brit Pol)* (abbrev of **Social and Liberal Democrats**) → **social**

sleaze* /sliːz/ N ① *(Pol = corruption)* corruption *f* ② *(= filth)* sordidité *f* ◆ **that film is pure ~** ce film est complètement sordide

sleazebag‡ /ˈsliːzbæg/, **sleazeball**‡ /ˈsliːzbɔːl/ N ordure‡ *f*

sleaziness* /ˈsliːzɪnɪs/ N aspect *m* sordide ; *[of person]* air *m* louche

sleazy* /ˈsliːzɪ/ ADJ *[place, atmosphere, behaviour]* sordide ; *[person]* louche ; *[magazine]* cochon

sled /sled/ N *(US)* ⇒ **sledge noun**

sledding /ˈsledɪŋ/ N *(US)* ◆ **hard** *or* **tough ~*** période *f (or* tâche *f)* difficile

sledge /sledʒ/ N traîneau *m* ; *(child's)* luge *f* VI ◆ **to go sledging** faire de la luge, se promener en traîneau ◆ **to ~ down/across** *etc* descendre/traverser *etc* en luge *or* en traîneau

sledgehammer /ˈsledʒ,hæməʳ/ N marteau *m* de forgeron ◆ **to strike sb/sth a ~ blow** *(fig)* assener un coup violent *or* magistral à qn/qch

sleek /sliːk/ ADJ *[hair, fur]* lustré, lisse et brillant ; *[cat]* au poil lustré ; *[person]* soigné ; *[car, boat, aircraft, furniture]* aux lignes pures

▸ **sleek down** VT SEP ◆ **to sleek one's hair down** se lisser les cheveux

sleekly /ˈsliːklɪ/ ADV *[smile, reply]* doucereusement, avec onction

sleekness /ˈsliːknɪs/ N *[of person]* allure *f* soignée ; *[of car, plane]* lignes *fpl* profilées ; *[of structure, building]* finesse *f or* pureté *f* (de lignes)

sleep /sliːp/ (vb : pret, ptp **slept**) N ① sommeil *m* ◆ **to be in a deep** *or* **sound ~** dormir profondément ◆ **to be in a very heavy ~** dormir d'un sommeil de plomb ◆ **to talk in one's ~** parler en dormant *or* dans son sommeil ◆ **to walk in one's ~** marcher en dormant ◆ **to sleep the ~ of the just** dormir du sommeil du juste ◆ **overcome by ~** ayant succombé au sommeil ◆ **to have a ~, to get some ~** dormir ; *(for a short while)* faire un somme ◆ **to get** *or* **go to ~** s'endormir ◆ **my leg has gone to ~** j'ai la jambe engourdie ◆ **I didn't get a wink of ~** *or* **any ~ all night** je n'ai pas fermé l'œil de la nuit ◆ **she sang the child to ~** elle a chanté jusqu'à ce que l'enfant s'endorme ◆ **to put** *or* **send sb to ~** endormir qn ◆ **to put a cat to ~** *(euph = put down)* faire piquer un chat ◆ **I need eight hours' ~ a night** il me faut (mes) huit heures de sommeil chaque nuit ◆ **a three-hour ~** trois heures de sommeil ◆ **I haven't had enough ~ lately** je manque de sommeil ces temps-ci ◆ **I had a good ~ last night** j'ai bien dormi la nuit dernière ◆ **to have a good night's ~** passer une bonne nuit ◆ **a ~ will do you good** cela vous fera du bien de dormir ◆ **let him have his ~ out** laisse-le dormir tant qu'il voudra ; → **beauty, lose**

② *(* = matter in eyes)* chassie *f*

VI ① dormir ◆ **to ~ tight** *or* **like a log** *or* **like a top** dormir à poings fermés *or* comme une souche *or* comme un loir ◆ **~ tight!** dors bien ! ◆ **to ~ heavily** dormir d'un sommeil de plomb ◆ **he was ~ing deeply** *or* **soundly** il dormait profondément, il était profondément endormi ◆ **to ~ soundly** *(= without fear)* dormir sur ses deux oreilles ◆ **to ~ lightly** *(regularly)* avoir le sommeil léger ; *(on one occasion)* dormir d'un sommeil léger ◆ **I didn't ~ a wink all night** je n'ai pas fermé l'œil de la nuit ◆ **to ~ the clock round** faire le tour du cadran ◆ **he was ~ing on his feet** *(fig)* il dormait debout

② *(= spend night)* coucher ◆ **he slept in the car** il a passé la nuit *or* dormi dans la voiture ◆ **he slept at his aunt's** il a couché chez sa tante ◆ **he ~s on a hard mattress** il couche *or* dort sur un matelas dur

③ *(= have sex)* ◆ **to ~ with sb** coucher* avec qn

VT ◆ **the house ~s eight (people)** on peut loger *or* coucher huit personnes dans cette maison ◆ **this room will ~ four (people)** on peut coucher quatre personnes *or* coucher à quatre dans cette chambre ◆ **the hotel ~s 500** l'hôtel peut loger *or* contenir 500 personnes ◆ **can you ~ us all?** pouvez-vous nous coucher tous ?

COMP **sleep deprivation** N privation f de sommeil
sleep-learning N hypnopédie f

► **sleep around** * VI coucher* avec n'importe qui, coucher* à droite et à gauche

► **sleep away** VT SEP ◆ **to sleep the morning away** passer la matinée à dormir, ne pas se réveiller de la matinée

► **sleep in** VI 1 *(= lie late)* faire la grasse matinée, dormir tard ; *(= oversleep)* ne pas se réveiller à temps, dormir trop tard
2 *[nurse, servant etc]* être logé sur place

► **sleep off** VT SEP ◆ **to sleep sth off** dormir pour faire passer qch, se remettre de qch en dormant ◆ **go to bed and ~ it off** va te coucher et cela te passera en dormant ◆ **to ~ off a hangover, to ~ it off*** dormir pour faire passer sa gueule de bois*, cuver son vin*

► **sleep on** VI ◆ **he slept on till ten** il a dormi jusqu'à dix heures, il ne s'est pas réveillé avant dix heures ◆ **let him ~ on for another hour** laisse-le dormir encore une heure
VT FUS ◆ **to sleep on a problem/a letter/a decision** attendre le lendemain pour résoudre un problème/répondre à une lettre/prendre une décision ◆ **let's ~ on it** nous verrons demain, la nuit porte conseil ◆ **I'll have to ~ on it** il faut que j'attende demain pour décider

► **sleep out** VI 1 *(in open air)* coucher à la belle étoile ; *(in tent)* coucher sous la tente
2 *[nurse, servant etc]* ne pas être logé (sur place)

► **sleep over** VI passer la nuit, coucher

► **sleep through** VI ◆ **I slept through till the afternoon** j'ai dormi comme une souche *or* sans me réveiller jusqu'à l'après-midi
VT FUS ◆ **he slept through the storm** l'orage ne l'a pas réveillé ◆ **he slept through the alarm clock** il n'a pas entendu son réveil (sonner)

► **sleep together** VI *(= have sex)* coucher ensemble

sleeper /ˈsliːpəʳ/ N 1 *(= person)* dormeur *m*, -euse *f* ; *(fig = spy)* espion(ne) *m(f)* en sommeil ◆ **to be a light/heavy ~** avoir le sommeil léger/lourd ◆ **that child is a good ~** cet enfant dort très bien *or* fait sa nuit sans se réveiller 2 *(Brit Rail) (on track)* traverse *f* ; *(= berth)* couchette *f* ; *(= rail car)* voiture-lit *f* ; *(= train)* train-couchettes *m* ◆ **I took a ~ to Marseilles** j'ai pris un train-couchettes pour aller à Marseille, je suis allé à Marseille en train-couchettes 3 *(esp Brit = earring)* clou *m (boucle d'oreille)* 4 *(fig = sudden success)* révélation *f*

sleepily /ˈsliːpɪlɪ/ ADV *[smile, blink etc]* d'un air endormi ; *[say, ask]* d'un ton endormi

sleepiness /ˈsliːpɪnɪs/ N *[of person]* envie *f* de dormir, torpeur *f* ; *[of town]* somnolence *f*, torpeur *f*

sleeping /ˈsliːpɪŋ/ ADJ *[person, village]* endormi ◆ **let ~ dogs lie** *(Prov)* il ne faut pas réveiller le chat qui dort *(Prov)* ◆ **to let ~ dogs lie** ne pas réveiller le chat qui dort ◆ **(the) Sleeping Beauty** la Belle au bois dormant
COMP **sleeping accommodation** N *(in house)* place *f* pour dormir, lits *mpl* ; *(on train)* couchettes *fpl*
sleeping area N *(in house)* chambres *fpl* à coucher ; *(in studio flat)* coin *m* à dormir
sleeping bag N sac *m* de couchage
sleeping berth N couchette *f*
sleeping car N *(Rail)* wagon-lit *m*, voiture-lit *f*
sleeping draught N soporifique *m*
sleeping partner N *(Brit Comm)* (associé *m*) commanditaire *m*
sleeping pill N somnifère *m*
sleeping policeman N (pl **sleeping policemen**) *(Brit: in road)* ralentisseur *m*, gendarme *m* couché
sleeping porch N *(US)* chambre-véranda *f*
sleeping position N position *f* pour dormir
sleeping problems NPL troubles *mpl* du sommeil ◆ **I have terrible ~ problems** je dors très mal
sleeping quarters NPL chambres *fpl* (à coucher) ; *(in barracks)* chambrées *fpl* ; *(= dormitory)* dortoir *m*
sleeping sickness N maladie *f* du sommeil
sleeping suit N grenouillère *f*
sleeping tablet N ⇒ **sleeping pill**

sleepless /ˈsliːplɪs/ ADJ *[person]* qui ne dort pas, insomniaque ◆ **a ~ baby can be very tiring** ça peut être très fatigant d'avoir un bébé qui ne dort pas ◆ **(to have) a ~ night** (passer) une nuit blanche ◆ **he arrived exhausted after a ~ journey** il est arrivé épuisé, n'ayant pas dormi de tout le trajet ◆ **he spent many ~ hours worrying** il a passé de longues heures sans sommeil à se faire du souci

sleeplessly /ˈsliːplɪslɪ/ ADV sans pouvoir dormir

sleeplessness /ˈsliːplɪsnɪs/ N insomnie *f*

sleepover /ˈsliːpəʊvəʳ/ N *[of child]* nuit *f* chez un ami

sleepwalk /ˈsliːpwɔːk/ VI être somnambule

sleepwalker /ˈsliːpwɔːkəʳ/ N somnambule *mf*

sleepwalking /ˈsliːpwɔːkɪŋ/ N *(NonC)* somnambulisme *m*

sleepwear /ˈsliːpwɛəʳ/ N *(NonC: Comm etc)* vêtements *mpl or* lingerie *f* de nuit

sleepy /ˈsliːpɪ/ ADJ 1 *(= drowsy) [person]* qui a sommeil ; *[voice, look]* endormi ◆ **to be** *or* **feel ~** avoir sommeil 2 *(= quiet) [village, town]* somnolent

sleepyhead * /ˈsliːpɪhed/ N endormi(e) *m(f)*

sleepyheaded * /sliːpɪˈhedɪd/ ADJ (à moitié) endormi

sleet /sliːt/ N neige *f* fondue VI ◆ **it is ~ing** il tombe de la neige fondue

sleeve /sliːv/ N *[of garment]* manche *f* ; *[of record]* pochette *f* ; *[of cylinder etc]* chemise *f* ◆ **he's always got something up his ~** il a plus d'un tour dans son sac ◆ **he's bound to have something up his ~** il a certainement quelque chose en réserve, il garde certainement un atout caché ◆ **I don't know what he's got up his ~** je ne sais pas ce qu'il nous réserve (comme surprise) ◆ **I've got an idea up my ~** j'ai une petite idée en réserve *or* dans la tête ◆ **to have** *or* **wear one's heart on one's ~** laisser voir ses sentiments, être transparent ; → **laugh, shirt**
COMP **sleeve board** N jeannette *f*
sleeve note N *(Brit: on record sleeve)* texte *m (sur pochette de disque)*

-sleeved /sliːvd/ ADJ *(in compounds)* ◆ **long-sleeved** à manches longues

sleeveless /ˈsliːvlɪs/ ADJ sans manches ◆ **~ T-shirt** tee-shirt *m* sans manches

sleigh /sleɪ/ N traîneau *m* VI aller en traîneau
COMP **sleigh bell** N grelot *m or* clochette *f* (de traîneau)
sleigh ride N ◆ **to go for a ~ ride** faire une promenade en traîneau

sleight /slaɪt/ N ◆ **~ of hand** *(= skill)* habileté *f*, dextérité *f* ; *(= trick)* tour *m* de passe-passe ◆ **by (a) ~ of hand** par un tour de passe-passe

slender /ˈslendəʳ/ ADJ 1 *(lit) [person, figure]* svelte, mince ; *[legs, arms, fingers, waist]* fin ; *[neck]* fin, gracieux ; *[column]* élancé 2 *(fig) [hope, chance, margin]* faible ; *[income, means, resources]* maigre

slenderize /ˈslendəraɪz/ VT *(US)* amincir

slenderly /ˈslendəlɪ/ ADV ◆ **~ built** svelte, mince

slenderness /ˈslendənɪs/ N 1 *(lit) [of figure, person]* sveltesse *f*, minceur *f* ; *[of legs, arms, fingers, waist, neck]* finesse *f* 2 *(fig) [of income, means, resources]* maigreur *f* ◆ **the ~ of the Conservative majority** la faible majorité des conservateurs ◆ **the ~ of his chances of winning** le peu de chances qu'il a de gagner

slept /slept/ VB pt, ptp of **sleep**

sleuth /sluːθ/ N *(= dog:* also **sleuth hound***)* limier *m* ; *(* = detective)* limier *m*, détective *m* VI *(*:* also **sleuth around**) fureter, fouiner*

slew¹ /sluː/ VB pt of **slay**

slew² /sluː/ (also **slew round**) VI virer, pivoter ; *(Naut)* virer ; *[car]* déraper par l'arrière ; *(right round)* faire un tête-à-queue ◆ **the car ~ed (round) to a stop** la voiture s'est arrêtée après un tête-à-queue VT faire pivoter, faire virer ◆ **he ~ed the car (round)** il a fait déraper la voiture par l'arrière ; *(= right round)* il a fait un tête-à-queue

slew³ /sluː/ N *(esp US)* ◆ **a ~ of ...** un tas* de ..., un grand nombre de ...

slewed †* /sluːd/ ADJ *(Brit = drunk)* paf* *inv*, soûl*

slice /slaɪs/ N 1 *[of cake, bread, meat]* tranche *f* ; *[of lemon, cucumber, sausage]* rondelle *f*, tranche *f* ◆ **~ of bread and butter** tranche *f* de pain beurré, tartine *f* beurrée
2 *(= part)* partie *f* ; *(= share)* part *f* ◆ **it took quite a ~ of our profits** cela nous a pris une bonne partie de nos bénéfices ◆ **a large ~ of the credit** une grande part du mérite ◆ **~ of life** tranche *f* de vie ◆ **~ of luck** coup *m* de chance
3 *(= kitchen utensil)* spatule *f*, truelle *f*
4 *(Sport)* balle *f* coupée, slice *m*
VT 1 *[+ bread, cake, meat]* couper (en tranches) ; *[+ lemon, sausage, cucumber]* couper (en rondelles) ; *[+ rope etc]* couper net, trancher ◆ **to ~ sth thin** couper qch en tranches *or* rondelles fines ◆ **~d bread** le pain en tranches ◆ **a ~d loaf** un pain en tranches ◆ **it's the best thing since ~d bread*** on n'a pas vu mieux depuis l'invention du fil à couper le beurre
2 *(Sport) [+ ball]* couper, slicer
VI ◆ **this knife won't ~** ce couteau coupe très mal ◆ **this bread won't ~** ce pain se coupe très mal *or* est très difficile à couper

► **slice off** VT SEP *[+ piece of rope, finger etc]* couper net ◆ **to ~ off a piece of sausage** couper une rondelle de saucisson ◆ **to ~ off a steak** couper *or* tailler un bifteck

► **slice through** VT FUS *[+ rope]* couper net, trancher ; *(fig) [+ restrictions etc]* (réussir à) passer au travers de, court-circuiter* ◆ **to ~ through the air/the waves** fendre l'air/les flots

► **slice up** VT SEP couper *or* débiter en tranches *or* en rondelles

slicer /ˈslaɪsəʳ/ N *(= knife)* couteau *m* électrique ; *(= machine)* trancheuse *f*

slick /slɪk/ ADJ 1 *(= efficient, skilful)* ◆ **the robbery was an extremely ~ operation** le braquage a été rondement mené 2 *(pej = superficial, glib) [person]* qui a du bagout* ; *[explanation]* trop prompt ; *[excuse]* facile ; *[style]* superficiel ; *[manner]* doucereux, mielleux ◆ **he always has a ~ answer** il a toujours réponse à tout 3 *(= shiny, slippery) [hair]* lissé ; *[road, surface]* glissant ◆ **~ tyres** pneus *mpl* lisses N (also **oil slick**) nappe *f* de pétrole ; *(on beach)* marée *f* noire VT ◆ **to ~ (down) one's hair** *(with comb etc)* se lisser les cheveux ; *(with hair cream)* mettre de la brillantine ◆ **~ed-back hair** cheveux *mpl* lissés en arrière

slicker /ˈslɪkəʳ/ N *(US)* combinard(e)* *m(f)* ; → **city**

slickly /ˈslɪklɪ/ ADV élégamment, habilement

slickness /ˈslɪknɪs/ N 1 *(= efficiency, skill)* habileté *f* 2 *(pej = superficiality, glibness)* caractère *m* superficiel 3 *(= shininess, slipperiness) [of hair]* brillant *m* ; *[of road]* surface *f* glissante

slid /slɪd/ ptp of **slide**

slide /slaɪd/ (vb : pret, ptp **slid**) N [1] *(= action)* glissade *f* ; (also **landslide**) glissement *m* (de terrain) ; *(fig: in prices, temperature etc)* baisse *f*, chute *f* (in de)

[2] *(in playground, pool etc)* toboggan *m* ; *(= polished ice etc)* glissoire *f* ; *(for logs etc)* glissoir *m*

[3] *(Phot)* diapositive *f*, diapo * *f* ; *[of microscope]* porte-objet *m* ◆ **illustrated with ~s** accompagné de diapositives ◆ **a film for ~s** une pellicule à diapositives ; → **colour, lantern**

[4] *(Tech = runner)* coulisse *f* ; *(on trombone etc)* coulisse *f* ; *(Mus: between notes)* coulé *m* ; *(= hair slide)* barrette *f*

VI [1] *[person, object]* glisser ; *(on ice etc) [person]* faire des glissades, glisser ◆ **to ~ down the bannisters** descendre en glissant sur la rampe ◆ **to ~ down a slope** descendre une pente en glissant, glisser le long d'une pente ◆ **the drawer ~s in and out easily** le tiroir glisse bien, le tiroir s'ouvre et se ferme facilement ◆ **the top ought to ~ gently into place** on devrait pouvoir mettre le haut en place en le faisant glisser doucement ◆ **the book slid off my knee** le livre a glissé de mes genoux ◆ **to let things ~** laisser les choses aller à la dérive ◆ **he let his studies ~** il a négligé ses études

[2] *(= move silently)* se glisser ◆ **he slid into the room** il s'est glissé dans la pièce ◆ **to ~ into bad habits** prendre insensiblement de mauvaises habitudes

VT faire glisser, glisser ◆ **he slid the chair across the room** il a fait glisser la chaise à travers la pièce ◆ **he slid the packing case into a corner** il a glissé la caisse dans un coin ◆ **he slid the photo into his pocket** il a glissé la photo dans sa poche ◆ **to ~ the top (back) onto a box** remettre le couvercle sur une boîte en le faisant glisser ◆ **~ the drawer into place** remets le tiroir en place ◆ **he slid the gun out of the holster** il a sorti le revolver de l'étui

COMP **slide box** N *(Phot)* classeur *m* pour diapositives, boîte *f* à diapositives
slide changer N *(Phot)* passe-vue *m*
slide fastener N *(Dress etc)* fermeture *f* éclair ®, fermeture *f* à glissière
slide guitar N slide guitar *f*
slide magazine N *(Phot)* panier *m*
slide projector N *(Phot)* projecteur *m* de diapositives
slide rule N règle *f* à calcul
slide show N projection *f* de diapositives

► **slide down** VI *[person, animal, vehicle]* descendre en glissant ; *[object]* glisser

► **slide off** VI [1] *[top, lid etc]* s'enlever facilement *or* en glissant

[2] *(fig = leave quietly) [guest]* s'en aller discrètement, s'éclipser* ; *[thief]* s'éloigner furtivement

sliding /ˈslaɪdɪŋ/ ADJ *[movement]* glissant ; *[part]* qui glisse, mobile ; *[panel, door, seat]* coulissant ◆ **~ roof** toit *m* ouvrant ◆ **~ scale** *(for payments, taxes etc)* échelle *f* mobile ◆ **~ time** *(US)* horaire *m* flexible N glissement *m*

slight /slaɪt/ ADJ [1] *(= minor) (gen)* petit, léger *before n* ; *[error]* petit ◆ **to be at a ~ angle** être légèrement incliné ◆ **it doesn't make the ~est bit of difference** *(= is unimportant)* cela n'a aucune importance ; *(= is useless)* ça ne sert à rien ◆ **without the ~est hint of embarrassment/disappointment** sans manifester la moindre gêne/la moindre déception ◆ **I haven't the ~est idea** je n'en ai pas la moindre idée ◆ **I haven't the ~est idea (of) where he's gone/what to do** je n'ai pas la moindre idée de l'endroit où il est allé/de ce qu'il faut faire ◆ **nobody showed the ~est interest** personne n'a manifesté le moindre intérêt ◆ **not in the ~est** pas le moins du monde ◆ **he takes offence at the ~est thing** il se vexe pour un rien ◆ **just the ~est bit short** un tout petit peu trop court

[2] *(= slim) [person, figure]* mince, menu ◆ **to be of ~ build** être menu, avoir les attaches fines

[3] *(= inconsiderable)* insignifiant ◆ **a book of very ~ scholarship** un livre vraiment peu érudit ◆ **it is no ~ accomplishment** c'est un exploit, et non des moindres

VT *(= ignore)* ignorer, manquer d'égards envers ; *(= offend)* blesser, offenser ◆ **he felt (himself) ~ed** il s'est senti blessé *or* offensé

N *(= insult)* affront *m* ◆ **this is a ~ on all of us** c'est un affront qui nous touche tous

slighting /ˈslaɪtɪŋ/ ADJ offensant

slightingly /ˈslaɪtɪŋlɪ/ ADV d'une manière blessante

slightly /ˈslaɪtlɪ/ ADV [1] *[different, deaf, injured, damaged]* légèrement ; *[expensive, more, less, better etc]* un peu ; *[change, rise, fall, improve etc]* légèrement ◆ **~ unfair** un peu injuste, pas très juste ◆ **~ uneasy** pas très à l'aise ◆ **I know her ~** je la connais un peu ◆ **ever so ~** * un tout petit peu [2] ◆ **~ built** *[person]* menu, aux attaches fines

slightness /ˈslaɪtnɪs/ N *(= slimness)* minceur *f* ; *(= frailty)* fragilité *f* ; *[of difference, increase etc]* caractère *m* insignifiant *or* négligeable

slim /slɪm/ ADJ [1] *[person]* *(= thin)* mince, svelte [2] *(fig) [majority]* faible ; *[chance, hope]* faible, mince ◆ **(the) chances are ~ of England winning** *or* **that England will win** il y a peu de chances que l'Angleterre gagne *subj* ◆ **his chances of winning are ~, he has only a ~ chance of winning** il a peu de chances de gagner, ses chances de gagner sont minces VI maigrir ; *(= diet)* suivre un régime amaigrissant ◆ **she's ~ming** elle suit un régime (amaigrissant) VT (also **slim down**) *[diet etc]* faire maigrir ; *[dress etc]* amincir N *(East African name for AIDS)* ◆ **Slim** * sida *m*

► **slim down** VI [1] *[person]* maigrir, perdre du poids [2] *[business, company]* réduire ses effectifs, dégraisser* VT SEP [1] ⇒ **slim vt** [2] *(fig)* **~med down** *[business, company]* allégé, dégraissé*

slime /slaɪm/ N *(= mud)* vase *f* ; *(on riverbeds)* limon *m* ; *(= sticky substance)* dépôt *m* visqueux *or* gluant ; *(from snail)* bave *f*

sliminess /ˈslaɪmɪnɪs/ N [1] *(lit) [of substance, creature, surface]* viscosité *f* [2] *(fig) [of person]* obséquiosité *f*

slimline /ˈslɪmlaɪn/ ADJ *[drink]* light, hypocalorique ; *[body, person]* mince, svelte ; *[dishwasher, freezer etc]* mini *inv*

slimmer /ˈslɪməʳ/ N personne *f* au régime ◆ **if you are a ~** si vous suivez un régime

slimming /ˈslɪmɪŋ/ N fait *m* de suivre un régime amaigrissant, amaigrissement *m* ◆ **~ can be very tiring** un régime amaigrissant peut être très fatigant, ça peut être très fatigant d'être au régime ADJ *[garment]* qui amincit ; *[food]* amincissant ; *[pills, tablets]* pour maigrir

COMP **slimming aid** N *(= food)* (produit *m*) amincissant *m*
slimming club N centre *m* d'amaigrissement
slimming diet N régime *m* amaigrissant

slimness /ˈslɪmnɪs/ N [1] *(lit = thinness)* minceur *f* [2] *(fig)* ◆ **the ~ of their majority** leur faible majorité ◆ **the ~ of his chances** le peu de chances *or* les faibles chances qu'il a

slimy /ˈslaɪmɪ/ ADJ [1] *(lit) [substance, creature, surface]* visqueux [2] *(Brit fig) [person]* mielleux, obséquieux ◆ **he's a ~ toad** c'est un lécheur *or* un lèche-bottes*

sling /slɪŋ/ (vb : pret, ptp **slung**) N [1] *(= weapon)* fronde *f* ; *(child's)* lance-pierre(s) *m inv* ◆ **they were quite unable to cope with the ~s and arrows of outrageous fortune** ils n'étaient pas à même de faire face à l'adversité

[2] *(= hoist)* cordages *mpl*, courroies *fpl* ; *(for oil drums etc)* courroie *f* ; *(Naut) (for loads, casks, boats)* élingue *f* ; *(for mast)* cravate *f* ; *(for rifle)* bretelle *f* ; *(Med)* écharpe *f* ◆ **to have one's arm in a ~** avoir le bras en écharpe

[3] *(Climbing)* anneau *m* (de corde) ; (also **gear sling**) baudrier *m*

VT [1] *(= throw) [+ objects, stones]* lancer, jeter (*at or to sb* à qn ; *at sth* sur qch) ; *[+ insults, accusations]* lancer (*at sb* à qn) ◆ **~ your hook!** * *(Brit)* fiche le camp !*

[2] *(= hang) [+ hammock etc]* suspendre ; *[+ load etc]* hisser ; *(Naut)* élinguer ◆ **to ~ across one's shoulder** *[+ rifle]* mettre en bandoulière *or* à la bretelle ; *[+ satchel]* mettre en bandoulière ; *[+ load, coat]* jeter par derrière l'épaule ◆ **with his rifle slung across his shoulder** avec son fusil en bandoulière *or* à la bretelle

► **sling away** * VT SEP *(= get rid of)* bazarder*

► **sling out** * VT SEP *(= put out) [+ person]* flanquer* à la porte *or* dehors ; *[+ object]* bazarder*

► **sling over** * VT SEP *(= pass)* balancer*, envoyer

► **sling up** VT SEP suspendre

slingbacks /ˈslɪŋbæks/ NPL escarpins *mpl* à bride (arrière)

slingshot /ˈslɪŋʃɒt/ N *(US)* lance-pierre(s) *m inv*

slink /slɪŋk/ (pret, ptp **slunk**) VI ◆ **to ~ away/out** s'en aller/sortir furtivement *or* sournoisement

slinkily * /ˈslɪŋkɪlɪ/ ADV d'une démarche ondoyante *or* ondulante

slinking /ˈslɪŋkɪŋ/ ADJ furtif

slinky * /ˈslɪŋkɪ/ ADJ *[dress, skirt]* moulant, sinueux ; *[figure]* ondoyant ; *[walk]* ondoyant, ondulant

slip /slɪp/ N [1] *(= mistake)* bévue *f*, erreur *f* ; *(= oversight)* étourderie *f*, oubli *m* ; *(moral)* écart *m*, faute *f* légère ◆ **~ of the tongue, ~ of the pen** lapsus *m* ◆ **it was a ~ of the tongue** c'était un lapsus, la langue lui a (*or* m'a *etc*) fourché ◆ **he made several ~s** il a fait *or* commis plusieurs lapsus ◆ **there's many a ~ 'twixt cup and lip** *(Prov)* il y a loin de la coupe aux lèvres *(Prov)*

[2] *(= paper: in filing system)* fiche *f* ◆ **a ~ of paper** *(= small sheet)* un bout *or* un morceau de papier ; *(= strip)* une bande de papier ◆ **credit card ~** facture *f* de carte de crédit

[3] *(set phrase)*

◆ **to give sb the slip** fausser compagnie à qn

[4] *(= underskirt)* combinaison *f* ; → **gym**

[5] ◆ **the ~s** *(Naut)* la cale ; *(Theat)* les coulisses *fpl* ; *(Cricket) partie du terrain se trouvant diagonalement derrière le batteur* ◆ **in the ~s** *(Naut)* sur cale ; *(Theat)* dans les coulisses

[6] *(= plant-cutting)* bouture *f*

[7] **a (mere) ~ of a boy/girl** un gamin/une gamine

[8] *(NonC: Pottery)* engobe *m*

VI [1] *(= slide) [person, foot, hand, object]* glisser ◆ **he ~ped on the ice** il a glissé *or* dérapé sur la glace ◆ **my foot/hand ~ped** mon pied/ma main a glissé ◆ **the clutch ~ped** *(Driving)* l'embrayage a patiné ◆ **the knot has ~ped** le nœud a glissé *or* coulissé ◆ **the fish ~ped off the hook** le poisson s'est détaché de l'hameçon ◆ **the drawer ~s in and out easily** le tiroir glisse bien, le tiroir s'ouvre et se ferme facilement ◆ **the top ought to ~ gently into place** on devrait pouvoir mettre le haut en place en le faisant glisser doucement ◆ **the saw ~ped and cut my hand** la scie a glissé *or* dérapé et m'a entaillé la main ◆ **the book ~ped out of his hand/off the table** le livre lui a glissé des doigts/a glissé de la table ◆ **the beads ~ped through my fingers** les perles m'ont glissé entre les doigts ◆ **money ~s through her fingers** l'argent lui file entre les doigts ◆ **to let sth ~ through one's fingers** laisser qch filer entre ses doigts ◆ **the thief ~ped through their fingers** le voleur leur a filé entre les doigts ◆ **several errors had ~ped into the report** plusieurs erreurs s'étaient glissées dans le rapport ◆ **to let an opportunity ~, to let ~ an opportunity** laisser passer *or* laisser échapper une occasion ◆ **he let ~ an oath** il a laissé échapper un juron ◆ **he let (it) ~ that ...** il a laissé échapper que ... ◆ **he's ~ping*** *(= getting old, less efficient)* il baisse, il n'est plus ce qu'il était ; *(= making more mistakes)* il ne fait plus assez attention, il ne se concentre plus assez ; → **net¹**

2 *(= move quickly) [person]* se glisser, passer ; *[vehicle]* se faufiler, passer ◆ **he ~ped into/out of the room** il s'est glissé *or* coulé dans/hors de la pièce ◆ **he ~ped through the corridors** il s'est faufilé dans les couloirs ◆ **I'll just ~ through the garden** je vais passer par le jardin ◆ **the motorbike ~ped through the traffic** la motocyclette s'est faufilée à travers la circulation ◆ **he ~ped over** *or* **across the border** il se faufila de l'autre côté de la frontière ◆ **to ~ into bed** se glisser *or* se couler dans son lit ◆ **to ~ into a dress** *etc* se glisser dans *or* enfiler (rapidement) une robe *etc* ◆ **to ~ out of a dress** *etc* enlever (rapidement) une robe *etc* ◆ **he ~ped easily into his new role** il s'est adapté *or* il s'est fait facilement à son nouveau rôle ◆ **to ~ into bad habits** prendre insensiblement de mauvaises habitudes

VT 1 *(= slide)* glisser ◆ **to ~ a coin to sb/into sb's hand** glisser une pièce à qn/dans la main de qn ◆ **he ~ped the book back on the shelf** il a glissé *or* remis le livre à sa place sur l'étagère ◆ **he ~ped the ring on her finger** il lui a glissé *or* passé la bague au doigt ◆ **he ~ped the photo into his pocket** il a glissé la photo dans sa poche ◆ **to ~ the top (back) onto a box** remettre le couvercle sur une boîte en le faisant glisser ◆ **~ the drawer (back) into place** remets le tiroir en place ◆ **he ~ped the gun out of its holster** il a retiré *or* sorti le revolver de son étui ◆ **to ~ the clutch** *(Driving)* faire patiner l'embrayage ◆ **a question on Proust was ~ped into the exam** l'épreuve a comporté une question inattendue sur Proust ◆ **to ~ a stitch** *(Knitting)* glisser une maille

2 *(= escape from)* échapper à ; *(Naut) [+ anchor, cable, moorings]* filer ◆ **the dog ~ped its collar** le chien s'est dégagé de son collier ◆ **he ~ped the dog's leash** il a lâché le chien ◆ **that ~ped his attention** *or* **his notice** cela lui a échappé ◆ **it ~ped his notice that ...** il ne s'est pas aperçu que ..., il n'a pas remarqué que ..., il lui a échappé que ... ◆ **it ~ped my memory** *or* **my mind** j'avais complètement oublié cela, cela m'était complètement sorti de la tête

COMP **slip-on** ADJ facile à mettre *or* à enfiler*
slip-ons, slip-on shoes NPL chaussures *fpl* sans lacets
slipped disc N *(Med)* hernie *f* discale
slip road N *(Brit) (to motorway)* bretelle *f* d'accès ; *(= bypass road)* voie *f* de déviation
slip stitch N *(Knitting)* maille *f* glissée
slip-up* N bévue *f*, cafouillage* *m* ◆ **there has been a ~-up somewhere** quelqu'un a dû faire une gaffe*, quelque chose a cafouillé* ◆ **a ~-up in communication(s)** un cafouillage* dans les communications

► **slip along** VI faire un saut, passer ◆ **he has just ~ped along to the shops** il a fait un saut jusqu'aux magasins ◆ **~ along to Mary's and ask her ...** fais un saut *or* passe chez Marie et demande-lui ...

► **slip away** VI *[car, boat]* s'éloigner doucement ; *[guest]* partir discrètement, s'esquiver ; *[thief]* filer*, s'esquiver ◆ **I ~ped away for a few minutes** je me suis esquivé *or* éclipsé* pour quelques minutes ◆ **her life was ~ping away (from her)** la vie la quittait

► **slip back** VI *[guest]* revenir *or* retourner discrètement ; *[thief, spy]* revenir *or* retourner furtivement ◆ **I'll just ~ back and get it** je retourne le chercher ◆ **they ~ped back into bad habits** ils ont peu à peu repris leurs mauvaises habitudes

VT SEP → **slip vt 1**

► **slip by** VI ⇒ **slip past**

► **slip down** VI 1 *[object, car]* glisser ; *[person]* glisser et tomber ◆ **I'll just ~ down and get it** je descends le chercher

2 *[food, drink]* descendre* tout seul

► **slip in** VI *[car, boat]* entrer doucement ; *[person]* entrer discrètement *or* sans se faire remarquer ; *[thief]* entrer furtivement *or* subrepticement ; *[cat etc]* entrer inaperçu ◆ **several errors have ~ped in** plusieurs erreurs s'y sont glissées ◆ **I'll just ~ in and tell him** je vais juste entrer le lui dire ◆ **I've only ~ped in for a minute** je ne fais que passer, je ne fais qu'entrer et sortir

VT SEP *[+ object]* glisser, placer ; *[+ part, drawer]* glisser à sa place ; *[+ remark, comment]* glisser, placer ◆ **to ~ in the clutch** *(Driving)* embrayer

► **slip off** VI 1 ⇒ **slip away**

2 *[coat, lid, cover]* glisser

VT SEP *[+ cover, ring, bracelet, glove, shoe]* enlever ; *[+ garment]* enlever, ôter

► **slip on** **VT SEP** *[+ garment]* passer, enfiler* ; *[+ ring, bracelet, glove]* mettre, enfiler ; *[+ shoe]* mettre ; *[+ lid, cover]* (re)mettre, placer

ADJ ◆ **slip-on** → **slip**

► **slip out** VI *[guest]* sortir discrètement, s'esquiver ; *[thief]* sortir furtivement, filer* ◆ **I must just ~ out for some cigarettes** il faut que je sorte un instant chercher des cigarettes ◆ **she ~ped out to the shops** elle a fait un saut jusqu'aux magasins ◆ **the secret ~ped out** le secret a été révélé par mégarde ◆ **the words ~ped out before he realized it** les mots lui ont échappé avant même qu'il ne s'en rende compte

VT SEP sortir doucement (*or* discrètement *etc*)

► **slip over** VI 1 ⇒ **slip along**

2 *(= fall)* glisser et tomber

VT SEP ◆ **to slip one over on sb*** rouler qn*

► **slip past** VI *[person, vehicle]* passer, se faufiler ◆ **the years ~ped past** les années passèrent

► **slip round** VI ⇒ **slip along**

► **slip through** VI *[person, error]* passer, s'introduire

► **slip up*** VI *(= make mistake)* se ficher dedans*

N ◆ **slip-up** → **slip**

slipcase /ˈslɪpkeɪs/ N *[of book]* coffret *m*

slipcover /ˈslɪpkʌvəʳ/ N *(esp US) (on book)* jaquette *f* ; *(on furniture)* housse *f*

slipknot /ˈslɪpnɒt/ N nœud *m* coulant

slipover* /ˈslɪpəʊvəʳ/ N pull-over *m* sans manches

slippage /ˈslɪpɪdʒ/ N *[of output]* dérapage *m* (*in* de) ; *(in schedule)* retard *m*

slipper /ˈslɪpəʳ/ N pantoufle *f* ; *(warmer)* chausson *m* ; *(= mule)* mule *f* ; → **glass**

slippery /ˈslɪpərɪ/ ADJ 1 *(lit) [surface, road, soap, mud, shoes]* glissant ◆ **it's ~ underfoot** le sol est glissant ◆ **his fingers were ~ with blood/sweat** le sang/la sueur rendait ses doigts glissants ◆ **the roads were ~ with ice** les routes étaient verglacées ◆ **to be on the ~ slope** *(fig)* être sur la pente savonneuse 2 *(pej) [person] (= evasive)* fuyant, insaisissable ; *(= unreliable)* sur qui on ne peut pas compter ◆ **he's a ~ customer** il est retors

slippy* /ˈslɪpɪ/ ADJ glissant ◆ **look ~ (about it)!**** *(Brit)* grouille-toi !*

slipshod /ˈslɪpʃɒd/ ADJ *[person] (in dress etc)* débraillé, négligé ; *(in work)* négligent ; *[work, style]* négligé, peu soigné

slipslop* /ˈslɪpslɒp/ N *(= liquor)* lavasse* *f*, bibine* *f* ; *(= talk, writing)* bêtises *fpl*

slipstream /ˈslɪpstriːm/ N *[of plane]* sillage *m*

slipway /ˈslɪpweɪ/ N *(Naut) (for building, repairing)* cale *f* (de construction) ; *(for launching)* cale *f* de lancement

slit /slɪt/ (vb : pret, ptp **slit**) **N** 1 *(= opening)* fente *f* ; *(= cut)* incision *f* ; *(= tear)* déchirure *f* ◆ **to make a ~ in sth** *(= cut)* fendre *or* entailler qch ; *(= tear)* déchirer qch ◆ **the skirt has a ~ up the side** la jupe a une fente *or* est fendue sur le côté 2 (*** = *vagina*) fente*** *f* **ADJ** ◆ **to have ~ eyes** *(= slanting)* avoir les yeux bridés ◆ **he looked at me through ~ eyes** *(concentrating)* il m'a regardé en plissant les yeux **VT** *(= make an opening in)* fendre ; *(= cut)* inciser, faire une fente dans ; *(= tear)* déchirer ◆ **to ~ sb's throat** trancher la gorge à qn, égorger qn ◆ **to ~ one's wrists** s'ouvrir les veines ◆ **to ~ a letter open** ouvrir une lettre ◆ **to ~ a sack open** éventrer *or* fendre un sac ◆ **a ~ skirt** une jupe fendue **COMP** **slit-eyed** ADJ *(= with eyes nearly closed)* aux yeux plissés ; *(= with slanting eyes)* aux yeux bridés

slither /ˈslɪðəʳ/ VI *[person, animal]* glisser ; *[snake]* onduler ◆ **he ~ed about on the ice** il dérapait sur la glace, il essayait de se tenir en équilibre sur la glace ◆ **the car ~ed (about) all over the place** la voiture dérapait dans tous les sens ◆ **he ~ed down the slope/down the rope** il a dégringolé* la pente/le long de la corde ◆ **the snake ~ed across the path** le serpent a traversé le sentier en ondulant

slithery /ˈslɪðərɪ/ ADJ glissant

sliver /ˈslɪvəʳ/ N *[of glass, wood]* éclat *m* ; *[of cheese, ham etc]* lamelle *f*

slivovitz /ˈslɪvəʊvɪts/ N *(NonC)* slivowitz *m*

Sloane Ranger* /ˌsləʊnˈreɪndʒəʳ/ N *(Brit)* ≃ personne *f* BCBG

slob* /slɒb/ N rustaud(e) *m(f)*, plouc** *mf*

► **slob out*** VI glander*

slobber /ˈslɒbəʳ/ **VI** *[person, dog etc]* baver ◆ **to ~ over sth** *(lit)* baver sur qch ; *(fig pej)* s'attendrir *or* s'extasier exagérément sur qch ◆ **to ~ over sb** *[dog]* couvrir qn de grands coups de langue ; *(pej = kiss) [person]* faire des mamours* à qn, donner une fricassée de museau à qn** **N** *(NonC)* bave *f*, salive *f* ; *(fig pej)* sensiblerie *f*, attendrissement *m* exagéré

slobbery /ˈslɒbərɪ/ ADJ *(pej)* baveux

sloe /sləʊ/ **N** prunelle *f* ; *(= bush)* prunellier *m*

COMP **sloe-eyed** ADJ aux yeux de biche
sloe gin N gin *m* à la prunelle

slog /slɒg/ **N** *(= work)* long travail *m* pénible, travail *m* de Romain ; *(= effort)* gros effort *m* ◆ **the programme was one long ~** le programme exigeait un grand effort *or* représentait un travail de Romain ◆ **it was a (hard) ~ to pass the exam** il a fallu fournir un gros effort pour réussir à l'examen ◆ **after a long ~ he reached the top of the hill** il a atteint le sommet de la colline après une ascension pénible ◆ **he found it nothing but a ~** c'était une vraie corvée pour lui

VT *[+ ball]* donner un grand coup à ; *[+ opponent]* donner un grand coup à, donner un gnon** à ◆ **we left them to ~ it out** nous les avons laissé s'expliquer à coups de poing

VI 1 *(= work etc)* travailler très dur ◆ **he ~ged (his way) through the book** il a peiné pour lire ce livre

2 *(= walk etc)* marcher d'un pas lourd, avancer avec obstination ◆ **he ~ged up the hill** il a gravi la colline avec effort

► **slog along** VI marcher d'un pas lourd, avancer avec difficulté ◆ **we ~ged along for 10km** nous nous traînés sur 10 km

► **slog away** VI travailler dur *or* comme un nègre* ◆ **to ~ away at sth** trimer* sur qch

► **slog on** VI ⇒ **slog along**

slogan /ˈsləʊgən/ N slogan *m*

sloganeering /ˌsləʊgəˈnɪərɪŋ/ N *(NonC: pej)* ◆ **politics should be about ideas, rather than** ~ en politique, il faut des idées, pas des slogans

slogger * /ˈslɒgəʳ/ N *(= hard worker)* bourreau *m* de travail ; *(Boxing)* cogneur *m*

slo-mo * /ˌsləʊˈməʊ/ N (abbrev of **slow-motion**) ralenti *m* ◆ **in** ~ au ralenti

sloop /sluːp/ N sloop *m*

slop /slɒp/ VT *[+ liquid] (= spill)* renverser, répandre ; *(= tip carelessly)* répandre *(on to* sur ; *into* dans) ◆ **you've ~ped paint all over the floor** tu as éclaboussé tout le plancher de peinture

VI (also **slop over**) *[water, tea etc]* déborder, se renverser *(into* dans ; *on to* sur) ; *[bowl, bucket]* déborder

NPL **slops** *(= dirty water)* eaux *fpl* sales ; *(in teacup etc)* fond *m* de tasse ; *(= liquid food) (for invalids etc)* bouillon *m*, aliment *m* liquide ; *(for pigs)* pâtée *f*, soupe *f*

COMP **slop basin** N vide-tasses *m inv*

slop bucket, slop pail N *(in kitchen etc)* poubelle *f* ; *(in bedroom)* seau *m* de toilette ; *(on farm)* seau *m* à pâtée

slopping out N *(NonC: Brit Prison)* corvée *f* de tinettes

► **slop about, slop around** VI 1 ◆ **the water was slopping about in the bucket** l'eau clapotait dans le seau ◆ **they were ~ping about in the mud** ils pataugeaient dans la boue

2 *(fig)* **she ~s about in a dressing gown all day** * elle traîne *or* traînasse * toute la journée en robe de chambre

VT SEP renverser *or* mettre un peu partout

► **slop out** VI *(Brit Prison)* faire la corvée de tinettes, vider les seaux hygiéniques

► **slop over** VI ⇒ **slop** vi

VT SEP renverser

slope /sləʊp/ N 1 *[of roof, floor, ground, surface]* inclinaison *f*, pente *f* ; *[of handwriting etc]* inclinaison *f* ◆ **roof with a slight/steep** ~ toit *m* (qui descend) en pente douce/raide ◆ **road with a** ~ **of 1 in 8** route *f* avec une pente de 12,5% ◆ **rifle at the** ~ *(Mil)* fusil *m* sur l'épaule

2 *(= rising ground, gentle hill)* côte *f*, pente *f* ; *(= mountainside)* versant *m*, flanc *m* ◆ ~ **up** montée *f* ◆ ~ **down** descente *f* ◆ **the car got stuck on a** ~ la voiture est restée en panne dans une côte ◆ **halfway up** *or* **down the** ~ à mi-côte, à mi-pente ◆ **on the ~s of Mount Etna** sur les flancs de l'Etna ◆ **the southern ~s of the Himalayas** le versant sud de l'Himalaya ◆ **on the (ski) ~s** sur les pistes (de ski)

VI *[ground, roof]* être en pente, être incliné ; *[handwriting]* pencher ◆ **the garden ~s towards the river** le jardin descend en pente vers la rivière

VT incliner, pencher ◆ **to** ~ **arms** *(Mil)* mettre l'arme sur l'épaule ◆ **"slope arms!"** "portez arme !"

► **slope away, slope down** VI *[ground]* descendre en pente *(to* jusqu'à ; *towards* vers)

► **slope off** * VI se tirer ⁑, se barrer ⁑

► **slope up** VI *[road, ground]* monter

sloping /ˈsləʊpɪŋ/ ADJ *[ground, roof]* en pente, incliné ; *[handwriting]* penché ; *[shoulders]* tombant

sloppily /ˈslɒpɪlɪ/ ADV *(= carelessly) [dress, work]* sans soin, n'importe comment ; *[eat, drink]* salement ; *[speak]* mal ◆ ~ **acted/written** écrit/joué n'importe comment

sloppiness /ˈslɒpɪnɪs/ N 1 *(= carelessness) (gen)* négligence *f*, manque *m* de soin ; *(in thinking, logic)* manque *m* de rigueur ◆ **the** ~ **of his work** son travail peu soigné ◆ **the** ~ **of their English** leur anglais très relâché 2 *(= sentimentality)* sensiblerie *f* 3 *(= sloppy consistency) [of cement, paste, food etc]* consistance *f* trop liquide

sloppy /ˈslɒpɪ/ ADJ 1 *(= careless) [work, handwriting, spelling]* négligé, peu soigné ; *[language]* relâché ; *[thinking, logic]* qui manque de rigueur ; *[appearance]* négligé, débraillé ◆ **his** ~ **attitude** son je-m'en-foutisme * ◆ **their** ~ **English** leur anglais *m* très relâché ◆ **to get** ~ *[person]* se relâcher ◆ **to be a** ~ **worker** travailler n'importe comment ◆ **to be a** ~ **eater** manger salement 2 *(= sentimental) [film, book, story]* à l'eau de rose ◆ **a big** ~ **kiss** un gros baiser mouillé 3 *(gen pej) [cement, paste, food]* trop liquide 4 *[garment]* lâche, ample COMP **sloppy Joe** N *(= sweater)* grand pull *m* ; *(US = sandwich)* hamburger *m*

slosh /slɒʃ/ VT 1 *(Brit ⁑ = hit)* flanquer * un coup *or* un gnon ⁑ à 2 * *(= spill)* renverser, répandre ; *(= apply lavishly)* répandre *(on to, over* sur ; *into* dans) ◆ **to** ~ **paint on a wall** barbouiller un mur de peinture, flanquer * de la peinture sur un mur ◆ **he ~ed water over the floor** *(deliberately)* il a répandu de l'eau par terre ; *(accidentally)* il a renversé *or* fichu * de l'eau par terre VI ◆ **water was ~ing everywhere** l'eau se répandait partout ◆ **to** ~ **through mud/water** patauger dans la boue/ l'eau

► **slosh about** *, **slosh around** * VI ⇒ **slop about vi 1** VT SEP ⇒ **slop about vt sep**

sloshed ⁑ /slɒʃt/ ADJ *(esp Brit = drunk)* beurré ⁑, rond ⁑ ◆ **to get** ~ prendre une biture ⁑

slot /slɒt/ N 1 *(= slit)* fente *f* ; *(= groove)* rainure *f* ; *(in door, for mail)* ouverture *f* pour les lettres ◆ **to put a coin in the** ~ mettre *or* introduire une pièce dans la fente

2 *(fig = space in schedule etc) (gen, also Rad, TV)* créneau *m*, tranche *f* horaire ; *(Scol etc: in timetable)* heure *f*, plage *f* horaire ◆ **they are looking for something to fill the early-evening comedy** ~ *(Rad, TV etc)* on cherche quelque chose pour la tranche comédie du début de soirée ◆ **who will fit this ~?** *(= job etc)* qui fera l'affaire pour ce créneau ?

VT ◆ **to** ~ **a part into another part** emboîter *or* encastrer une pièce dans une autre pièce ◆ **to** ~ **sth into a programme/timetable** insérer *or* faire rentrer qch dans une grille de programmes/d'horaires

VI ◆ **this part ~s into that part** cette pièce-ci s'emboîte *or* s'encastre dans celle-là ◆ **the song will** ~ **into the programme here** on peut insérer *or* faire figurer la chanson à ce moment-là du programme

COMP **slot car** N *(US)* petite voiture *f (de circuit électrique)*

slot machine N *(for tickets, cigarettes etc)* distributeur *m* (automatique) ; *(in fair etc)* appareil *m or* machine *f* à sous

slot meter N compteur *m* (de gaz etc) (à pièces)

slotted spoon N écumoire *f*

► **slot in** VI *[piece, part]* s'emboîter, s'encastrer ; *(fig) [item on programme etc]* s'insérer, figurer

VT SEP *[+ piece, part]* emboîter, encastrer ; *(fig) [+ item on programme]* insérer, faire figurer

► **slot together** VI *[pieces, parts]* s'emboîter *or* s'encastrer les un(e)s dans les autres

VT SEP *[+ pieces, parts]* emboîter *or* encastrer les un(e)s dans les autres

sloth /sləʊθ/ N 1 *(NonC) (= laziness)* paresse *f* 2 *(= animal)* paresseux *m*

slothful /ˈsləʊθfʊl/ ADJ *(liter)* paresseux

slothfully /ˈsləʊθfəlɪ/ ADV paresseusement

slouch /slaʊtʃ/ N 1 ◆ **to walk with a** ~ mal se tenir en marchant 2 ◆ **he's no** ~ * il n'est pas empoté * VI ◆ **he was ~ing in a chair** il était affalé dans un fauteuil ◆ **she always ~es** elle ne se tient jamais droite, elle est toujours avachie ◆ **stop ~ing!** redresse-toi !, tiens-toi droit ! ◆ **he ~ed in/out** *etc* il entra/sortit *etc* en traînant les pieds, le dos voûté COMP **slouch hat** N chapeau *m* (mou) à larges bords

► **slouch about, slouch around** VI traîner à ne rien faire

slough[1] /slaʊ/ N *(= swamp)* bourbier *m*, marécage *m* ◆ **the Slough of Despond** *(fig)* l'abîme *m* du désespoir

slough[2] /slʌf/ N *[of snake]* dépouille *f*, mue *f* VT (also **slough off**) ◆ **the snake ~ed (off) its skin** le serpent a mué

► **slough off** VT SEP 1 ⇒ **slough**[2] **vt** 2 *(fig) [+ habit etc]* perdre, se débarrasser de

Slovak /ˈsləʊvæk/ ADJ slovaque N 1 Slovaque *mf* 2 *(= language)* slovaque *m* COMP **the Slovak Republic** N la République slovaque

Slovakia /sləʊˈvækɪə/ N Slovaquie *f*

Slovakian /sləʊˈvækɪən/ ADJ, N ⇒ **Slovak**

sloven /ˈslʌvn/ N souillon *f*

Slovene /ˈsləʊviːn/ ADJ slovène N 1 Slovène *mf* 2 *(= language)* slovène *m*

Slovenia /sləʊˈviːnɪə/ N Slovénie *f*

Slovenian /sləʊˈviːnɪən/ ADJ, N ⇒ **Slovene**

slovenliness /ˈslʌvnlɪnɪs/ N *(= untidiness)* aspect *m* négligé *or* débraillé ; *(= carelessness)* je-m'en-foutisme * *m*

slovenly /ˈslʌvnlɪ/ ADJ *[person, appearance, work]* négligé ◆ **his** ~ **attitude** son je-m'en-foutisme *

slow /sləʊ/ ADJ 1 *(gen)* lent ◆ **the** ~ **movement of the symphony** le mouvement lent de la symphonie ◆ **after a** ~ **start** après un départ laborieux ◆ **the pace of life there is** ~ là-bas on vit au ralenti ◆ **it's** ~ **but sure** on (*or* ça) avance lentement mais sûrement ◆ **a** ~ **train** *(Brit = stopping-train)* un (train) omnibus ◆ **at a** ~ **speed** à petite vitesse ◆ **it's** ~ **going** *(lit, fig)* cela n'avance pas vite ◆ **it's** ~ **work** c'est un travail qui avance lentement ◆ **he's a** ~ **learner** il n'apprend pas vite ◆ **to be** ~ **of speech** *(frm)* parler lentement ◆ **to be** ~ **to do sth** *or* **in doing sth** mettre du temps à faire qch ◆ **she was not** ~ **to notice** *or* **in noticing ...** il ne lui a pas fallu longtemps pour remarquer ... ; → **mark**[2], **progress, uptake**

2 *[pitch, track, surface]* lourd

3 *(euph = stupid)* lent, qui a l'esprit lent ◆ **he's a bit** ~ il a l'esprit un peu lent

4 *(= boring) [party, evening, play, film etc]* ennuyeux

5 *(pej = slack, sluggish) [market, trading, demand]* stagnant ; *[growth]* lent ◆ **business is** ~ les affaires stagnent

6 *[watch, clock]* ◆ **my watch is** ~ ma montre retarde ◆ **my watch is ten minutes** ~ ma montre retarde de dix minutes

7 *(Culin)* ◆ **in a** ~ **oven** à feu doux ◆ **over a** ~ **heat** à feu doux

8 *(Phot) [film]* lent

ADV *(= slowly)* lentement ◆ **to go ~er** ralentir ◆ **to go** ~ *[workers]* faire la grève perlée ; → **astern, dead**

VT (also **slow down, slow up**) *[+ person] (in walk)* faire ralentir ; *(in activity)* ralentir, retarder ; *[+ vehicle, machine]* ralentir (la marche de) ; *[+ traffic]* ralentir ; *[+ horse]* ralentir l'allure *or* le pas de ; *[+ progress, production, negotiations]* ralentir, retarder ; *[+ reaction]* rendre moins rapide ◆ **his injury ~ed him down** *or* **up** sa blessure l'a ralenti ◆ **all these interruptions have ~ed us down** *or* **up** toutes ces interruptions nous ont retardés

VI (also **slow down, slow off, slow up**) *[driver, worker, walker, vehicle, machine, production, progress]* ralentir ; *[reactions]* devenir plus lent *or* moins rapide ◆ **"slow"** *(road sign)* "ralentir" ◆ **a "slow" signal** un panneau "attention, ralentir" ◆ **you must** ~ **down or you will**

make yourself ill *(fig)* il faut que vous travailliez moins, sinon vous allez tomber malade ◆ **since his retirement his life has ~ed down** depuis qu'il a pris sa retraite il vit au ralenti

COMP **slow-acting** ADJ à action lente ◆ **it is ~-acting** cela agit lentement

slow burn‡ N *(US)* ◆ **he did a ~ burn** il a fini par péter les plombs‡

slow-burning ADJ à combustion lente ◆ **it is ~-burning** cela brûle lentement

slow cooker N *(Culin)* cocotte *f* électrique

slow handclap N *(Brit: by audience)* applaudissements *mpl* rythmés *(pour exprimer le mécontentement)*

slow lane * N *(in countries where they drive on right)* voie *f* de droite ; *(in other countries)* voie *f* de gauche ; → **life**

slow match N mèche *f* à combustion lente

slow motion N *(Cine etc)* ◆ **in ~ motion** au ralenti ADJ ◆ **~-motion film/shot** *etc* (film *m*/prise *f* de vues *etc* au) ralenti *m*

slow-moving ADJ *[person, animal]* lent, aux mouvements lents ; *[vehicle]* lent ; *[play]* lent, dont l'action est lente

slow puncture N *(Brit) pneu qui se dégonfle lentement*

slow-speaking, slow-spoken ADJ qui parle lentement

slow virus N virus *m* lent

slow-witted ADJ lourdaud, qui a l'esprit lent *or* lourd

slow worm N orvet *m*

► **slow down** VT SEP ⇒ **slow vt**

VI ⇒ **slow vi**

► **slow off** VI ⇒ **slow vi**

► **slow up** VT SEP ⇒ **slow vt**

VI ⇒ **slow vi**

slowcoach /ˈsləʊkəʊtʃ/ N *(Brit = dawdler)* lambin(e)* *m(f)*

slowdown /ˈsləʊdaʊn/ N ralentissement *m* ; *(US = strike)* grève *f* perlée

slowly /ˈsləʊlɪ/ ADV *(gen)* lentement ; *[realize, start, increase]* peu à peu ◆ **~ but surely** lentement mais sûrement

slowness /ˈsləʊnɪs/ N *[of person, vehicle, movement etc]* lenteur *f* ; *[of pitch, track]* lourdeur *f* ; *[of party, evening]* manque *m* d'entrain *or* d'intérêt ; *[of novel, plot, play]* lenteur *f*, manque *m* de mouvement *or* d'action ; *(= lack of energy etc)* allure *f* posée ◆ **~ (of mind)** lenteur *f or* lourdeur *f* d'esprit ◆ **his ~ to act** *or* **in acting** la lenteur avec laquelle *or* le retard avec lequel il a agi

slowpoke * /ˈsləʊpəʊk/ N *(US)* ⇒ **slowcoach**

SLR /ˌeselˈɑːʳ/ N *(Phot)* (abbrev of **single lens reflex (camera)**) → **single**

sludge /slʌdʒ/ N *(NonC) (= mud)* boue *f*, vase *f* ; *(= sediment)* boue *f*, dépôt *m* ; *(= sewage)* vidanges *fpl* ; *(= melting snow)* neige *f* fondue

slug /slʌg/ N *(= animal)* limace *f* ; *(= bullet)* balle *f* ; *(= blow)* coup *m* ; *(Min, Typ)* lingot *m* ; *(esp US = metal token)* jeton *m* ; *(US ‡ = false coin)* fausse pièce *f* ◆ **a ~ of whisky**‡ *(US)* un peu *or* un coup* de whisky sec VT *(* = hit)* frapper (comme une brute)

► **slug out** * VT SEP ◆ **to slug it out** se taper dessus* *(pour régler une question)*

slugfest‡ /ˈslʌgfest/ N bagarre *f*, rixe *f*

sluggard /ˈslʌgəd/ N paresseux *m*, -euse *f*, fainéant(e) *m(f)*

slugger /ˈslʌgəʳ/ N *(Baseball)* joueur *m* qui frappe fort

sluggish /ˈslʌgɪʃ/ ADJ *[person, temperament]* mou (molle *f*), léthargique ; *(= slow-moving)* lent ; *(= lazy)* paresseux ; *[growth, reaction, movement, circulation, digestion]* lent ; *[liver]* paresseux ; *[market, business]* stagnant ◆ **the engine is ~** le moteur manque de reprise *or* de nervosité ◆ **sales are ~** les ventes ne vont pas fort

sluggishly /ˈslʌgɪʃlɪ/ ADV *[move]* lentement ; *[react, respond, flow]* mollement ; *(Econ, Fin) [trade, perform]* faiblement

sluggishness /ˈslʌgɪʃnɪs/ N *[of person]* mollesse *f*, lenteur *f* ; *[of engine]* manque *m* de nervosité

sluice /sluːs/ N 1 *(whole structure)* écluse *f* ; *(= gate:* also **sluice gate, sluice valve***)* vanne *f or* porte *f* d'écluse ; *(= channel:* also **sluiceway***)* canal *m* (à vannes) ; *(= water)* éclusée *f* 2 ◆ **to give sth/o.s. a ~ (down)** laver qch/se laver à grande eau VT (also **sluice down**) laver à grande eau COMP **sluice gate, sluice valve** N vanne *f or* porte *f* d'écluse

sluiceway /ˈsluːsweɪ/ N canal *m* (à vannes)

slum /slʌm/ N *(= house)* taudis *m* ◆ **the ~s** les quartiers *mpl* pauvres ; *(in suburb)* la zone ; *(= shanty towns)* les bidonvilles *mpl* VI *(* = live cheaply:* also **slum it***) (esp Brit)* vivre à la dure, manger de la vache enragée* ◆ **we don't see you often round here – I'm ~ming (it) today!** *(iro)* on ne te voit pas souvent ici – aujourd'hui je m'encanaille ! VT ◆ **to ~ it** * → **vi**

COMP **slum area** N quartier *m* pauvre

slum clearance N aménagement *m* des quartiers insalubres

slum clearance area N zone *f* de quartiers insalubres en voie d'aménagement

slum clearance campaign N campagne *f* pour la démolition des taudis

slum-dweller N habitant(e) *m(f)* de taudis

slum dwelling N taudis *m*

slumber /ˈslʌmbəʳ/ N *(liter:* also **slumbers***)* sommeil *m* (paisible) VI dormir paisiblement

COMP **slumber party** N *(US) soirée entre adolescentes qui restent dormir chez l'une d'entre elles*

slumber wear N *(NonC: Comm)* vêtements *mpl* de nuit

slumb(e)rous /ˈslʌmb(ə)rəs/ ADJ *(liter) (= drowsy)* somnolent ; *(= soporific)* assoupissant *(liter)*

slumgullion /slʌmˈgʌljən/ N *(US)* ragoût *m*

slumlord * /ˈslʌmlɔːd/ N *(US pej)* marchand* *m* de sommeil

slummy * /ˈslʌmɪ/ ADJ sordide

slump /slʌmp/ N *(in numbers, popularity, morale etc)* forte baisse *f*, baisse *f* soudaine (in de) ; *(Econ)* dépression *f* ; *(on Stock Exchange)* effondrement *m* (des cours) ; *(in sales etc)* baisse *f* soudaine (in de) ; *(in prices)* effondrement *m* (in de) ◆ **the 1929 ~** la crise (économique) de 1929

VI 1 *[popularity, morale, production, trade]* baisser brutalement ; *[prices, rates]* s'effondrer ◆ **business has ~ed** les affaires sont en baisse, c'est le marasme (économique) 2 (also **slump down**) s'effondrer, s'écrouler *(into* dans ; *onto* sur) ◆ **he lay ~ed on the floor** il gisait effondré *or* écroulé par terre ◆ **he was ~ed over the wheel** il était affaissé sur le volant 3 *(= stoop)* avoir le dos rond *or* voûté

► **slump back** VI *[person]* retomber en arrière

► **slump down** VI ⇒ **slump vi 2**

► **slump forward** VI *[person]* tomber en avant

slung /slʌŋ/ VB pt, ptp of **sling**

slunk /slʌŋk/ VB pt, ptp of **slink**

slur /slɜːʳ/ N 1 *(= insult)* insulte *f* ; *(= calumny)* atteinte *f (on* à) ; ◆ **to be a ~ on sb's reputation** porter atteinte à *or* être une tache sur la réputation de qn ◆ **that is a ~ on him** cela porte atteinte à son intégrité ◆ **to cast a ~ on sb** porter atteinte à la réputation de qn ◆ **it's no ~ on him to say ...** ce n'est pas le calomnier que de dire ... 2 *(Mus)* liaison *f* VT *(= join) [+ several sounds, words]* lier à tort ; *(Mus)* lier ; *(= enunciate indistinctly) [+ word etc]* mal articuler, ne pas articuler ◆ **his speech was ~red, he ~red his words** il n'arrivait pas à articuler, il n'articulait pas VI *[sounds etc]* être *or* devenir indistinct

► **slur over** VT FUS *[+ incident, mistake, differences, discrepancies]* passer sous silence, glisser sur

slurp /slɜːp/ VTI boire à grand bruit N slurp *m*

slurry /ˈslʌrɪ/ N boue *f*, pâte *f*

slush /slʌʃ/ N *(NonC) (= snow)* neige *f* fondue ; *(= mud)* gadoue *f* ; *(fig = sentiment)* sensiblerie *f*

COMP **slush fund** N fonds *mpl* secrets, caisse *f* noire

the slush pile * N *(Publishing)* les manuscrits *mpl* refusés

slushy /ˈslʌʃɪ/ ADJ 1 *[snow]* fondu ; *[road, street]* couvert de neige fondue 2 *(* = sentimental) [film, book, story]* à l'eau de rose ; *[song]* sentimental

slut /slʌt/ N *(pej) (dirty)* souillon *f* ; *(immoral)* salope‡ *f*, pute‡ *f*

sluttish /ˈslʌtɪʃ/ ADJ *[appearance]* sale, de souillon ; *[morals, behaviour]* de salope‡ ◆ **a ~ woman** une souillon

sly /slaɪ/ ADJ 1 *(= crafty, roguish) [person, animal]* rusé ; *[plan]* astucieux ; *[smile, look]* entendu, narquois ; *[remark, reference, suggestion]* narquois ◆ **he's a ~ dog** *or* **a ~ (old) fox*** c'est une fine mouche ◆ **(as) ~ as a fox** rusé comme un renard 2 *(pej = underhand, cunning) [person, trick]* sournois *(pej)* 3 *(* = secretive)* ◆ **she gave me a ~ kick under the table** elle m'a donné un coup de pied en douce* sous la table ◆ **they were having a ~ cigarette in the toilets** ils fumaient en douce* dans les toilettes N ◆ **on the ~** en cachette, en douce*

slyboots * /ˈslaɪbuːts/ N malin *m*, -igne *f*

slyly /ˈslaɪlɪ/ ADV 1 *(= craftily, roguishly) [say, smile, look, suggest]* d'un air entendu, d'un air narquois 2 *(pej = cunningly)* sournoisement *(pej)*

slyness /ˈslaɪnɪs/ N 1 *(= craftiness, roguishness) [of person, look]* ruse *f* ◆ **the ~ of her smile/comment** son sourire/commentaire narquois 2 *(pej = underhandedness, cunning)* sournoiserie *f (pej)*

smack¹ /smæk/ VI *(lit, fig)* ◆ **to ~ of sth** sentir qch N 1 *(= small taste)* léger *or* petit goût *m* ; *(fig)* soupçon *m* 2 *(‡ = heroin)* héroïne *f*, blanche‡ *f*

smack² /smæk/ N *(= slap)* tape *f* ; *(stronger)* claque *f* ; *(on face)* gifle *f* ; *(= sound)* bruit *m* sec, claquement *m* ; *(* fig = kiss)* gros baiser *m* (qui claque) ◆ **he gave the ball a good ~** il a donné un grand coup dans le ballon ◆ **it was a ~ in the eye for them*** *(esp Brit) (= snub)* c'était une gifle pour eux ; *(= setback)* c'était un revers pour eux

VT *[+ person]* donner une tape à ; *(stronger)* donner une claque à ; *(on face)* gifler ◆ **to ~ sb's face** gifler qn, donner une paire de gifles à qn ◆ **I'll ~ your bottom!** je vais te donner la fessée !, tu vas avoir la fessée ! ◆ **he ~ed the table (with his hand)** il a frappé sur la table (de la main) ◆ **to ~ a kiss on sb's face** plaquer un baiser sur le visage de qn ◆ **to ~ one's lips** se lécher les babines

ADV * en plein ◆ **~ in the middle** en plein milieu ◆ **he kissed her ~ on the lips** il l'a embrassée en plein sur la bouche ◆ **he ran ~ into the tree** il est rentré en plein *or* tout droit dans l'arbre

smack³ /smæk/ N (also **fishing smack**) smack *m*, sémaque *m*

smacker‡ /ˈsmækəʳ/ N *(= kiss)* gros baiser *m*, grosse bise* *f* ; *(= blow)* grand coup *m* (retentissant) ; *(Brit = pound)* livre *f* ; *(US = dollar)* dollar *m*

smackhead‡ /ˈsmækhed/ N héroïnomane *mf*, camé(e) *m(f)*‡

smacking /ˈsmækɪŋ/ N fessée *f* ◆ **to give sb a ~** donner une *or* la fessée à qn ADJ ◆ **a ~ kiss** un baiser sonore, un gros baiser

small /smɔːl/ ADJ 1 *(gen)* petit ; *[family, audience, population]* peu nombreux ; *[waist]* mince ; *[meal]* léger ◆ **the ~est possible number of books** le moins de livres possible ◆ **a ~ proportion of the business is international** une faible proportion des transactions commerciales sont internationales ◆ **"I'm sorry" he said in a ~ voice** "je suis désolé" dit-il d'une petite voix ◆ **he is a ~ eater** il mange très peu, il a un petit appétit ◆ **in ~ letters** en minuscules *fpl* ◆ **with a ~ "e"** avec un "e" minuscule ◆ **~ shopkeeper/farmer/businessman** petit commerçant *m*/agriculteur *m*/entrepreneur *m* ◆ **to feel ~** *(fig)* être dans ses petits souliers, se sentir honteux ◆ **to make sb feel ~** humilier qn ◆ **to make sb look ~** rabaisser qn devant tout le monde ◆ **it's a ~ world!** le monde est petit ! ◆ **to get** *or* **grow ~er** *[income, difficulties, population, amount, supply]* diminuer ; *[object]* rapetisser ◆ **mobile phones are getting ~er** les téléphones portables sont de plus en plus petits *or* compacts ◆ **to make sth ~er** *[+ income, amount, supply]* diminuer qch ; *[+ organization]* réduire qch ; *[+ garment]* reprendre qch ; see also **comp** ; → **hour, print, way**

2 *(= young) [child]* petit, jeune ◆ **I was very ~ at the time** j'étais tout petit *or* jeune à l'époque

3 *(frm = slight, scant)* ◆ **a matter of ~ importance** une affaire de peu d'importance ◆ **it's ~ comfort to them to know that ...** cela ne les consolera guère de savoir que ... ◆ **to have ~ cause** *or* **reason to do sth** n'avoir guère de raison de faire qch ◆ **a matter of no ~ consequence** une affaire d'une grande importance ◆ **they paid ~ attention to his suggestion** ils ont prêté peu d'attention à sa suggestion ◆ **this is of ~ concern to them** cela ne les préoccupe guère ; → **wonder**

ADV ◆ **to cut sth up ~** *[+ paper]* couper qch en petits morceaux ; *[+ meat]* hacher qch menu

N 1 ◆ **the ~ of the back** le creux des reins

2 *(Brit: npl)* **~s** † * *(= underwear)* dessous *mpl*, sous-vêtements *mpl*

COMP **small ads** NPL *(Brit Press)* petites annonces *fpl*
small-arms NPL *(Mil)* armes *fpl* portatives, armes *fpl* légères
small beer N *(Brit fig)* ◆ **it's ~ beer** c'est de la petite bière* ◆ **he's ~ beer** il ne compte pas beaucoup
small-bore ADJ de petit calibre
small business N petite entreprise *f*
small change N *(NonC)* petite *or* menue monnaie *f*
small claims court N *(Jur)* tribunal *m* d'instance *(s'occupant d'affaires mineures)*
small end N *(in car)* pied *m* de bielle
the smallest room N († , *hum*) le petit coin*
small fry N menu fretin *m* ; *(= children)* les gosses* *mfpl* ◆ **they're just ~ fry** c'est du menu fretin
small intestine N *(Anat)* intestin *m* grêle
small-minded ADJ mesquin
small-mindedness N petitesse *f* d'esprit, mesquinerie *f*
small-mouth bass N *(= fish)* achigan *m* à petite bouche
small potatoes NPL *(esp US)* ⇒ **small beer**
small-scale ADJ peu important ; *[undertaking]* de peu d'importance, de peu d'envergure ; *[map]* à petite échelle
the small screen N *(TV)* le petit écran
small-size(d) ADJ petit
small talk N *(NonC)* papotage *m*, menus propos *mpl* ◆ **he's got plenty of ~ talk** il a la conversation facile
small-time ADJ peu important, de troisième ordre ◆ **a ~-time crook** un escroc à la petite semaine
small-timer * N moins *m* que rien, individu *m* insignifiant
small town N *(US)* petite ville *f*
small-town ADJ *(esp US pej)* provincial ; → **print**

SMALL TOWN

Aux États-Unis, une ville de moins de 10 000 habitants est une « petite ville » (**small town**). Le terme « village », peu utilisé, évoque plutôt l'ancien continent ou les pays du tiers-monde. Les populations des petites villes sont généralement appréciées pour les valeurs qu'elles incarnent : gentillesse, honnêteté, politesse, rapports de bon voisinage et patriotisme. Cependant, on peut aussi parler des « **small-town** attitudes » dans un sens péjoratif pour désigner une tendance aux préjugés et une certaine étroitesse d'esprit.

smallholder /ˈsmɔːlhəʊldəʳ/ N *(Brit)* ≃ petit agriculteur *m*

smallholding /ˈsmɔːlhəʊldɪŋ/ N *(Brit)* ≃ petite ferme *f*

smallish /ˈsmɔːlɪʃ/ ADJ *(in size)* plutôt *or* assez petit ; *(in importance)* peu important ◆ **a ~ number of ...** un nombre restreint de ...

smallness /ˈsmɔːlnɪs/ N *[of object]* petitesse *f* ; *[of sum of money]* petitesse *f*, modicité *f*

smallpox /ˈsmɔːlpɒks/ N variole *f*, petite vérole *f*

smarm * /smɑːm/ VI *(Brit)* flatter, flagorner ◆ **to ~ over sb** lécher les bottes* à qn, passer de la pommade* à qn

smarmy * /ˈsmɑːmɪ/ ADJ *(Brit) [person]* lèche-bottes* *inv*, obséquieux* ; *[manner]* de lèche-bottes*

smart /smɑːt/ ADJ 1 *(= not shabby) [hotel, restaurant, club, neighbourhood, party, dinner]* chic *inv* ; *[person, clothes, appearance]* élégant ; *[house, car]* beau (belle *f*) ; *[garden, lawn]* soigné ◆ **you're looking very ~** tu es très élégant

2 *(= fashionable)* à la mode, dernier cri *inv* ◆ **the ~ set** le beau monde ◆ **the Paris/London ~ set** le tout Paris/le tout Londres

3 *(esp US * = clever) [person]* intelligent ; *[idea]* astucieux, malin (-igne *f*) ; *[deed, act]* intelligent, astucieux ◆ **that wasn't very ~ (of you)** ce n'était pas très malin (de ta part) ◆ **he's too ~ for me** il est trop malin pour moi ◆ **(that was) ~ work!** *(= clever)* beau travail ! ; *(= swift)* ça n'a pas traîné ! *

4 *(* pej = cheeky)* culotté* ◆ **don't get ~ with me!** ne la ramène pas !* ◆ **she's got a ~ answer to everything** elle a toujours réponse à tout

5 *(= brisk) [pace]* vif ◆ **give the nail a ~ tap** tapez un bon coup sur le clou ◆ **look ~ (about it)!*** grouille-toi !*, remue-toi !

VI 1 *[cut, graze]* brûler ; *[iodine etc]* piquer ◆ **my eyes were ~ing** j'avais les yeux qui me piquaient ◆ **the smoke made his throat ~** la fumée lui irritait la gorge

2 *(fig)* être piqué au vif ◆ **he was ~ing under the insult** l'insulte l'avait piqué au vif ◆ **you'll ~ for this!** il vous en cuira !, vous me le payerez !

NPL *(US)* ◆ **~s*** *(= brains)* jugeote* *f*

COMP **smart alec(k)** *, **smart ass** * *(US)* N *(pej)* (Monsieur *or* Madame *or* Mademoiselle) je-sais-tout* *mf inv*
smart bomb N bombe *f* intelligente, bombe *f* guidée
smart card N carte *f* à mémoire *or* à puce
smart drug N smart drug *f*, médicament *m* psychoénergétique
smart money N réserve *f* d'argent *(destinée à faire des investissements au moment opportun)* ◆ **the ~ money is on him winning** dans les milieux bien informés, on le donne gagnant
smart phone N smartphone *m*, téléphone *m* intelligent

smartarse * /ˈsmɑːtɑːs/, **smartass** * *(US)* /ˈsmɑːtæs/ N bêcheur* *m*, -euse* *f*

smarten /ˈsmɑːtn/ VT → **smarten up** VT SEP

► **smarten up** VI 1 *(= make o.s. tidy etc) [person]* devenir plus élégant *or* soigné ; *[town]* devenir plus élégant *or* pimpant ◆ **you'd better ~ up for dinner** il faut que tu t'arranges *subj* (un peu) *or* que tu te fasses beau (belle *f*) pour le dîner

2 *(= speed up) [production, pace]* s'accélérer

VT SEP 1 *(= tidy up) [+ person]* rendre plus élégant *or* plus soigné ; *[+ child]* pomponner, bichonner ; *[+ house, room, town]* (bien) arranger, rendre élégant *or* pimpant ◆ **to ~ o.s. up** se faire beau (belle *f*) *or* élégant

2 *(= speed up)* accélérer

smartly /ˈsmɑːtlɪ/ ADV 1 *(= elegantly) [dress]* élégamment, avec beaucoup d'élégance ◆ **~ dressed** *or* **turned out** élégamment vêtu ◆ **she wore a ~ tailored suit** elle portait un tailleur bien coupé 2 *(= briskly) [move] (gen)* rapidement ; *(person)* vivement ; *[reply]* du tac au tac ◆ **to tap sth ~** taper sur qch un bon coup

smartness /ˈsmɑːtnɪs/ N *(NonC) [of person, clothes]* chic *m*, élégance *f* ; *(= cleverness)* intelligence *f* ; *(= skilfulness)* habileté *f* ; *(= quickness)* rapidité *f*

smarty * /ˈsmɑːtɪ/ N (also **smarty-pants** *) bêcheur* *m*, -euse* *f*, (Monsieur *or* Madame *or* Mademoiselle) je-sais-tout* *mf inv*

smash /smæʃ/ N 1 *(= sound)* fracas *m* ; *(= blow)* coup *m* violent ; *(Tennis etc)* smash *m* ◆ **the ~ as the car hit the lamppost** le choc quand la voiture a percuté le réverbère ◆ **the cup fell with a ~** la tasse s'est fracassée (en tombant) par terre ◆ **he fell and hit his head a nasty ~ on the kerb** en tombant il s'est violemment cogné la tête contre le trottoir

2 (also **smash-up** *) *(= accident)* accident *m* ; *(= collision)* collision *f*, tamponnement *m* ; *(very violent)* télescopage *m* ◆ **car/rail ~** accident *m* de voiture/de chemin de fer

3 *(Econ, Fin = collapse)* effondrement *m* (financier), débâcle *f* (financière) ; *(on Stock Exchange)* krach *m* ; *(= bankruptcy)* faillite *f* ; *(= ruin)* ruine *f*, débâcle *f* complète

4 ⇒ **smash hit**

5 ◆ **whisky/brandy ~** whisky *m*/cognac *m* glacé à la menthe

ADV * ◆ **to run ~ into a wall** heurter un mur de front *or* de plein fouet, rentrer en plein dans un mur ◆ **the cup fell ~ to the ground** la tasse s'est fracassée par terre ◆ **to go ~** *(Fin)* faire faillite

VT 1 *(= break)* casser, briser ; *(= shatter)* fracasser ◆ **I've ~ed my watch** j'ai cassé ma montre ◆ **the waves ~ed the boat on the rocks** les vagues ont fracassé le bateau contre les rochers ◆ **to ~ sth to pieces** *or* **to bits** briser qch en mille morceaux, mettre qch en miettes ◆ **when they ~ed the atom*** quand on a désintégré *or* fissionné l'atome ◆ **to ~ a door open** enfoncer une porte ◆ **he ~ed the glass with the hammer, he ~ed the hammer through the glass** il a fracassé la vitre avec le marteau ◆ **he ~ed his fist into Paul's face** il a envoyé *or* balancé* son poing dans la figure de Paul ◆ **to ~ the ball** *(Tennis)* faire un smash, smasher ◆ **he ~ed the ball into the net** il a envoyé son smash dans le filet

2 *[+ spy ring etc]* briser, détruire ; *[+ hopes]* ruiner ; *[+ enemy]* écraser ; *[+ opponent]* battre à plate(s) couture(s), pulvériser* ◆ **he ~ed* the record in the high jump** *(Sport etc)* il a pulvérisé* le record du saut en hauteur

VI 1 se briser (en mille morceaux), se fracasser ◆ **the cup ~ed against the wall** la tasse s'est fracassée contre le mur ◆ **the car ~ed into the tree** la voiture s'est écrasée contre l'arbre ◆ **his fist ~ed into my face** il a envoyé *or* balancé* son poing sur ma figure, il m'a asséné son poing sur la figure

2 *(= go bankrupt)* faire faillite

COMP **smash-and-grab** N (also **smash-and-grab raid**) cambriolage *m* (commis en brisant une devanture) ◆ **there was a ~-and-grab (raid) at the jeweller's** des bandits ont brisé la vitrine du bijoutier et raflé les bijoux

smash hit* N ◆ **it was a ~ hit** cela a fait un malheur*, cela a eu un succès foudroyant ◆ **it was the ~ hit of the year** c'était le succès de l'année

smash-up* N → **noun 2**

▸ **smash down** VT SEP *[+ door, fence]* fracasser

▸ **smash in** VT SEP *[+ door]* enfoncer ◆ **to ~ sb's face** *or* **head in*** casser la gueule à qn*

▸ **smash up** VT SEP *[+ room, house, shop]* tout casser dans, tout démolir dans ; *[+ car]* accidenter, bousiller* ◆ **he was ~ed up* in a car accident** il a été grièvement blessé *or* sérieusement amoché* dans un accident de voiture

N ◆ **smash-up** * → **smash noun 2**

smashed /smæʃt/ ADJ 1 (* = *drunk*) pété*, bourré* ◆ **to get ~** se soûler* 2 (*: *on drugs*) défoncé* ◆ **to get ~** se défoncer* 3 *(= broken) [vehicle]* bousillé* ; *[skull, limb, bone]* fracassé

smasher †* /ˈsmæʃəʳ/ N *(Brit)* ◆ **he's a ~** *(in appearance)* il est vachement* beau ◆ **she's a ~** elle est vachement* jolie *or* bien roulée* ◆ **to be a ~** *(in character etc)* être épatant* *or* vachement chouette* ◆ **it's a ~** c'est épatant*

smashing* /ˈsmæʃɪŋ/ ADJ *(Brit)* super* ◆ **we had a ~ time** on s'est amusé comme des fous*

smattering /ˈsmætərɪŋ/ N connaissances *fpl* vagues *or* superficielles ◆ **a ~ of** un petit nombre de ◆ **he has a ~ of German** il sait un peu l'allemand, il sait quelques mots d'allemand ◆ **I've got a ~ of maths** j'ai quelques connaissances vagues *or* quelques notions en maths

SME /ˌesemˈiː/ N (abbrev of **small and medium (-sized) enterprise**) PME *f inv*

smear /smɪəʳ/ N 1 *(= mark)* trace *f* ; *(longer)* traînée *f* ; *(= stain)* (légère) tache *f*, salissure *f* ◆ **a long ~ of ink** une traînée d'encre ◆ **there is a ~ on this page** il y a une légère tache *or* une salissure sur cette page, cette page est tachée *or* salie

2 *(= defamation)* diffamation *f* *(on, against* de) ◆ **this ~ on his honour/reputation** cette atteinte à son honneur/sa réputation

3 *(Med)* frottis *m*, prélèvement *m* ; → **cervical**

VT 1 *(= wipe)* ◆ **to ~ cream on one's hands, to ~ one's hands with cream** s'enduire les mains de crème ◆ **he ~ed his face with mud, he ~ed mud on his face** il s'est barbouillé le visage de boue ◆ **his hands were ~ed with ink** il avait les mains barbouillées *or* tachées d'encre, il avait des traînées d'encre sur les mains ◆ **you've ~ed it all over the place** tu en a mis partout ◆ **he ~ed butter on the slice of bread** il a étalé du beurre sur la tranche de pain

2 *[+ page of print]* maculer ; *[+ wet paint]* faire une trace *or* une marque sur ; *[+ lettering]* étaler (accidentellement)

3 *(fig) [+ reputation, integrity]* salir, entacher ◆ **to ~ sb** *[story, report]* salir *or* entacher la réputation de qn ; *[person]* calomnier qn

4 *(US* * = *defeat)* battre à plates coutures

VI *[ink, paint]* se salir

COMP **smear campaign** N campagne *f* de diffamation

smear tactics NPL procédés *mpl* diffamatoires

smear test N *(Med)* ⇒ **noun 3**

smear word N ◆ **it is a ~ word** c'est de la diffamation

smeary /ˈsmɪərɪ/ ADJ *[face]* barbouillé ; *[window]* couvert de taches *or* de traînées ; *[ink, paint]* sali

smell /smel/ (vb : pret, ptp **smelled** *or* **smelt**) N *(= sense of smell)* odorat *m* ; *[of animal]* odorat *m*, flair *m* ; *(= odour)* odeur *f* ; *(= bad smell)* mauvaise odeur *f* ◆ **he has a keen sense of ~** il a l'odorat très développé, il a le nez très fin ◆ **he has no sense of ~** il n'a pas d'odorat ◆ **the mixture has no ~** le mélange est inodore *or* n'a pas d'odeur ◆ **a gas with no ~** un gaz inodore *or* sans odeur ◆ **it has a nice/nasty ~** cela sent bon/mauvais ◆ **what a ~ in here!** ce que ça sent mauvais ici ! ◆ **there was a ~ of burning in the room** il y avait une odeur de brûlé dans la pièce, la pièce sentait le brûlé ◆ **to have a ~ at sth** *[person]* sentir qch ; *(more carefully)* renifler qch ; *[dog etc]* flairer *or* renifler qch

VT sentir ; *(= sniff at)* sentir, renifler ◆ **he could ~ or he smelt something burning** il sentait que quelque chose brûlait ◆ **he smelt the meat to see if it was bad** il a senti *or* reniflé la viande pour voir si elle était encore bonne ◆ **the dog could ~ or the dog smelt the bone** le chien a flairé *or* éventé l'os ◆ **the dog smelt the bone suspiciously** le chien a flairé *or* reniflé l'os d'un air soupçonneux ◆ **I ~ a rat!** il y a anguille sous roche !, il y quelque chose de louche là-dedans *or* là-dessous ! ◆ **he ~ed danger** il a flairé *or* deviné le danger ◆ **I (can) ~ danger!** je pressens un danger !

VI 1 ◆ **since the accident he cannot ~** depuis l'accident il n'a plus d'odorat ◆ **to ~ at sth** *[person]* sentir *or* renifler qch ; *[dog etc]* renifler *or* flairer qch

2 ◆ **that mixture doesn't ~ (at all)** ce mélange ne sent rien *or* n'a pas (du tout) d'odeur ◆ **this gas doesn't ~** ce gaz est inodore ◆ **these socks ~!** ces chaussettes sentent mauvais ! ◆ **this room ~s!** cette pièce sent mauvais *or* pue ! ◆ **his breath ~s** il a mauvaise haleine ◆ **that ~s like chocolate** ça sent le chocolat, on dirait du chocolat ◆ **to ~ of onions/burning** *etc* sentir l'oignon/le brûlé *etc* ◆ **to ~ good** *or* **sweet** sentir bon ◆ **to ~ bad** sentir mauvais ◆ **to ~ foul** empester ◆ **it ~s delicious!** quelle odeur délicieuse ! ◆ **it ~s dreadful!** ça pue ! ◆ **the deal ~s a bit*** cette affaire semble plutôt louche *or* ne semble pas très catholique* ◆ **that idea ~s!** * *(fig)* cette idée ne vaut rien !, c'est une idée catastrophique !* ◆ **I think he ~s!** * *(fig)* je trouve que c'est un sale type !*

COMP **smelling salts** NPL sels *mpl*

▸ **smell out** VT SEP 1 *(= discover) [dog etc]* découvrir en flairant *or* en reniflant ; *[person] [+ criminal, traitor]* découvrir, dépister ; *[+ treachery, plot]* découvrir

2 ◆ **it's smelling the room out** ça empeste la pièce

smelliness /ˈsmelɪnɪs/ N *(NonC)* mauvaise odeur *f*

smelly /ˈsmelɪ/ ADJ *[person, feet, armpits]* qui sent mauvais ; *[breath]* mauvais ; *[cheese]* qui sent fort ◆ **it's rather ~ in here** ça sent mauvais ici

smelt¹ /smelt/ VB pt, ptp of **smell**

smelt² /smelt/ N (pl **smelt** *or* **smelts**) *(= fish)* éperlan *m*

smelt³ /smelt/ VT *[+ ore]* fondre ; *[+ metal]* extraire par fusion

smelter /ˈsmeltəʳ/ N haut fourneau *m*

smelting /ˈsmeltɪŋ/ N *(= process)* extraction *f* par fusion

COMP **smelting furnace** N haut-fourneau *m*

smelting works N *(pl inv)* fonderie *f*

smidgen*, **smidgin*** /ˈsmɪdʒən/ N ◆ **a ~ of** *(gen)* un tout petit peu de ; *[+ truth]* un grain de, un brin de

smile /smaɪl/ N sourire *m* ◆ **with a ~ on his lips** le sourire aux lèvres ◆ **... he said with a ~** ... dit-il en souriant ◆ **... he said with a nasty ~** ... dit-il en souriant méchamment *or* avec un mauvais sourire ◆ **he had a happy ~ on his face** il avait un sourire heureux, il souriait d'un air heureux ◆ **to give sb a ~** faire *or* adresser un sourire à qn, sourire à qn ◆ **she gave a little ~** elle a eu un petit sourire ◆ **to be all ~s** être tout souriant *or* tout sourire ◆ **take that ~ off your face!** arrête donc de sourire comme ça ! ◆ **I'll wipe** *or* **knock the ~ off his face!** il verra s'il a encore envie de sourire !, je vais lui faire passer l'envie de sourire ! ; → **raise, wear, wreathe**

VI sourire *(at or to sb* à qn) ◆ **to ~ to oneself** sourire intérieurement ◆ **to ~ sadly** avoir un sourire triste, sourire tristement *or* d'un air triste ◆ **to keep smiling** garder le sourire ◆ **he ~d at my efforts** il a souri de mes efforts ◆ **fortune ~d (up)on him** la fortune lui sourit

VT ◆ **to ~ a bitter smile** avoir un sourire amer, sourire amèrement *or* avec amertume ◆ **to ~ one's thanks** remercier d'un sourire

smiley /ˈsmaɪlɪ/ ADJ (* = *smiling, friendly) [person, face]* souriant ; *[eyes]* rieur N *(Comput)* emoticon *m*, smiley *m* ; *(as badge)* badge *m* de tête souriante

smiling /ˈsmaɪlɪŋ/ ADJ *[person, face, eyes, mouth]* souriant

smilingly /ˈsmaɪlɪŋlɪ/ ADV en souriant, avec un sourire

smirch /smɜːtʃ/ VT *(lit)* salir, souiller ; *(fig liter)* ternir, entacher N *(lit, fig)* tache *f*

smirk /smɜːk/ N *(= self-satisfied smile)* petit sourire *m* satisfait *or* suffisant ; *(knowing)* petit sourire *m* narquois ; *(affected)* petit sourire *m* affecté VI sourire d'un air satisfait (*or* suffisant *or* narquois *or* affecté)

smite /smaɪt/ (pret **smote**, ptp **smitten**) VT († † *or liter*) *(= strike)* frapper (d'un grand coup) ; *(= punish)* châtier *(liter)* ; *(fig) [pain]* déchirer ; *[one's conscience]* tourmenter ; *[light]* frapper ; → **smitten** N coup *m* violent

smith /smɪθ/ N *(shoes horses)* maréchal-ferrant *m* ; *(forges iron)* forgeron *m* ; → **goldsmith, silversmith**

smithereens /ˌsmɪðəˈriːnz/ NPL ◆ **to smash sth to ~** briser qch en mille morceaux, faire voler qch en éclats ◆ **it lay in ~** cela s'était brisé en mille morceaux, cela avait volé en éclats

Smithsonian Institution /smɪθˈsəʊnɪən,ɪnstɪˈtjuːʃən/ N *(US)* ◆ **the ~** la Smithsonian Institution

SMITHSONIAN INSTITUTION

La **Smithsonian Institution**, située dans la ville de Washington, est le plus grand musée du monde. Créé par le Congrès en 1846 grâce au don d'un scientifique anglais, James Smithson, ce complexe aujourd'hui financé par le Congrès réunit quatorze musées consacrés notamment à l'aviation et à l'espace, à l'histoire de l'Amérique, aux Indiens d'Amérique, aux beaux-arts. Riche de 100 millions de pièces, il est surnommé « le grenier de la nation » (the nation's attic). Il comporte également un zoo et un institut de recherche scientifique.

smithy /ˈsmɪðɪ/ N forge *f*

smitten /ˈsmɪtn/ VB ptp of **smite** ADJ *(= in love)* amoureux ◆ **he was really ~ with her** il en était vraiment amoureux, il était fou d'elle ◆ **to be ~ with** *or* **by** *[+ remorse, desire, urge]* être pris de ; *[+ terror, deafness]* être frappé de ; * *[+ sb's beauty]* être enchanté par ; * *[+ idea]* s'enthousiasmer pour

smock /smɒk/ N *(= dress, peasant's garment etc)* blouse *f* ; *(= protective overall)* blouse *f*, sarrau *m* ; *(= maternity top)* blouse *f* de grossesse ; *(= maternity dress)* robe *f* de grossesse VT faire des smocks à

smocking /ˈsmɒkɪŋ/ N *(NonC)* smocks *mpl*

smog /smɒg/ N smog *m* ♦ **~ mask** masque *m* antibrouillard

smoggy /ˈsmɒgɪ/ ADJ *[city, air]* pollué par le smog ; *[sky]* obscurci par le smog

smoke /sməʊk/ N 1 *(NonC)* fumée *f* ♦ **to go up in ~** *[house etc]* brûler ; *[plans, hopes etc]* partir en fumée, tomber à l'eau ♦ **the ~ is beginning to clear** *(fig)* on commence à y voir plus clair ♦ **it's all ~ and mirrors** *(US)* on n'y voit que du feu ♦ **there's no ~ without fire** *(Prov)* il n'y a pas de fumée sans feu *(Prov)* ♦ **the (Big) Smoke**⁑ *(Brit)* Londres ; → **cloud, holy, puff**
2 ♦ **to have a ~** fumer ♦ **have a ~!** prends une cigarette ! ♦ **I've no ~s**⁑ je n'ai plus de sèches⁑
VI 1 *[chimney, lamp etc]* fumer
2 *[person]* fumer ♦ **he ~s like a chimney*** il fume comme un sapeur
VT 1 *[+ cigarette etc]* fumer ♦ **he ~s cigarettes/a pipe** il fume la cigarette/la pipe
2 *[+ meat, fish, glass]* fumer ♦ **~d salmon/trout** *etc* saumon *m*/truite *f etc* fumé(e) ♦ **~d glass** verre *m* fumé ♦ **~d-glass** *[window, windscreen etc]* en verre fumé ; → **haddock**
COMP **smoke alarm** N détecteur *m* de fumée
smoke bomb N bombe *f* fumigène
smoke detector N détecteur *m* de fumée
smoke-dry VT fumer
smoke-filled ADJ *(during fire)* rempli de fumée ; *(from smoking etc)* enfumé ♦ **~-filled room** *(fig)* salle *f* de réunion très animée, PC *m* de crise
smoke-free ADJ *[area, environment, workplace]* non-fumeur
smoke pollution N *(from factory)* pollution *f* par les fumées ; *(tobacco)* pollution *f* par la fumée de tabac
smoke ring N rond *m* de fumée ♦ **to blow ~ rings** faire des ronds de fumée
smoke screen N *(Mil)* rideau *m* or écran *m* de fumée ; *(fig)* paravent *m (fig)*
smoke shop N *(US)* tabac *m*
smoke signal N signal *m* de fumée ♦ **~ signals** *(fig)* (vagues) indications *fpl*
► **smoke out** VT SEP *[+ insects, snake etc]* enfumer ; *(fig)* *[+ traitor, culprit etc]* dénicher, débusquer ♦ **it was smoking the room out** c'était en train d'enfumer la pièce

smokeless /ˈsməʊklɪs/ ADJ ♦ **~ fuel** combustible *m* non fumigène ♦ **~ zone** *zone où l'on n'a le droit d'utiliser que des combustibles non fumigènes* ♦ **the ~ cigarette** la cigarette sans fumée

smoker /ˈsməʊkəʳ/ N 1 *(= person)* fumeur *m*, -euse *f* ♦ **he has a ~'s cough** il a une toux de fumeur 2 *(Rail)* wagon *m* fumeurs

smokestack /ˈsməʊkstæk/ N cheminée *f (extérieure)* ADJ ♦ **~ America** l'Amérique *f* industrielle ♦ **~ industries** industries *fpl* traditionnelles

smokey /ˈsməʊkɪ/ ADJ, N ⇒ **smoky**

smoking /ˈsməʊkɪŋ/ N tabagisme *m* ♦ **I hate ~** *(other people)* je déteste qu'on fume, je déteste le tabagisme ; *(myself)* je déteste fumer ♦ **"no smoking"** "défense de fumer" ♦ **campaign against ~** campagne *f* contre le tabac or le tabagisme ♦ **"smoking can seriously damage your health"** "le tabac nuit gravement à la santé" ♦ **to give up ~** arrêter de fumer ADJ ♦ **a ~ fireplace** une cheminée qui fume ; see also **comp**
COMP **smoking car** N *(US)* wagon *m* fumeurs
smoking compartment N *(Rail)* wagon *m* fumeurs
smoking gun* N *(esp US fig = proof)* preuve *f* tangible ♦ **we don't have a ~ gun** nous n'avons pas de preuve tangible
smoking-jacket N veste *f* d'intérieur
smoking-related ADJ *[diseases]* lié à la tabagie
smoking room N fumoir *m*

smoky /ˈsməʊkɪ/ ADJ *[atmosphere, room]* enfumé ; *[fire]* qui fume ; *[flame]* fumeux ; *[surface] (= smoke-covered)* sali or noirci par la fumée ; *[glass] (= smoked)* fumé ; *[taste]* fumé ♦ **~ grey** gris cendré *inv* ♦ **~ blue** bleu ardoise *inv* N *(US*⁑*)* motard *m* (de la police routière)

smolder /ˈsməʊldəʳ/ VI *(US)* ⇒ **smoulder**

smoldering /ˈsməʊldərɪŋ/ ADJ *(US)* ⇒ **smouldering**

smooch* /smuːtʃ/ VI *(= kiss)* se bécoter* ; *(= pet)* se peloter⁑ ; *(= dance)* se frotter l'un contre l'autre N ♦ **to have a ~** ⇒ **vi**

smoochy* /ˈsmuːtʃɪ/ ADJ *[record, song]* langoureux

smooth /smuːð/ ADJ 1 *(= not rough) (gen) [sea, surface, texture, road, stone, tyre, hair]* lisse ; *[lake]* d'huile ; *[fabric]* lisse, soyeux ; *[skin]* lisse, doux (douce *f*) ; *(= unwrinkled) [cheek, brow]* lisse, sans rides ; *(= hairless) [face, chin]* glabre, lisse ♦ **the flagstones had been worn ~ by centuries of use** les dalles étaient patinées par les années ♦ **as ~ as silk** or **satin** *[skin, fabric, hair]* doux comme de la soie ♦ **the sea was as ~ as glass** la mer était d'huile
2 *(= not lumpy) [paste, sauce, mixture, consistency]* onctueux, homogène
3 *(= not harsh) [flavour, wine, whisky etc]* moelleux ; *[voice, sound]* doux (douce *f*)
4 *(= even, not jerky) [flow, stride, breathing]* régulier ; *[takeoff, landing, transition]* en douceur ; *[sea crossing]* calme, par mer calme ; *[flight]* sans heurts ; *[engine]* qui tourne parfaitement ♦ **~ running** *[of machinery]* bon fonctionnement *m* ; *[of organization, business, economy]* bonne marche *f* ♦ **the takeoff/landing was ~** le décollage/l'atterrissage s'est fait en douceur ♦ **the bill had a ~ passage through Parliament** le Parlement n'a pas fait obstacle au projet de loi
5 *(slightly pej = suave) [person, manners]* doucereux *(pej)*, suave ; *[talk]* mielleux *(pej)* ♦ **he's a ~ talker** c'est un beau parleur ♦ **he's a ~ operator*** il sait s'y prendre ; see also **satin, silky**
VT 1 *[+ sheets, cloth, piece of paper, skirt]* lisser, défroisser ; *[+ pillow, hair, feathers]* lisser ; *[+ wood]* rendre lisse, planer ; *[+ marble]* rendre lisse, polir ♦ **to ~ cream into one's skin** faire pénétrer la crème dans la peau (en massant doucement) ♦ **that ~ed her ruffled** or **rumpled feathers** cela lui a rendu le sourire
2 *(fig)* ♦ **to ~ sb's way** or **path to the top** faciliter le chemin de qn vers le sommet ♦ **to ~ the way** or **path of an application/request** faciliter l'acceptation d'une candidature/demande
COMP **smooth-faced** ADJ au visage glabre or lisse ; *(fig: slightly pej)* trop poli, doucereux
smooth-running ADJ *[engine, machinery]* qui fonctionne sans à-coups ; *[car]* qui ne secoue pas, qui ne donne pas d'à-coups ; *[business, organization, scheme]* qui marche bien or sans heurts
smooth-shaven ADJ rasé de près
smooth-spoken, smooth-talking, smooth-tongued ADJ enjôleur, doucereux
► **smooth back** VT SEP *[+ one's hair]* ramener doucement en arrière ; *[+ sheet]* rabattre en lissant or en défroissant
► **smooth down** VT SEP *[+ hair, feathers]* lisser ; *[+ sheet, cover]* lisser, défroisser ; *(fig)* *[+ person]* calmer, apaiser
► **smooth out** VT SEP *[+ material, dress]* défroisser ; *[+ wrinkles, creases]* faire disparaître ; *(fig)* *[+ anxieties]* chasser, faire disparaître ; *[+ difficulties]* aplanir, faire disparaître
► **smooth over** VT SEP *[+ soil]* aplanir, égaliser ; *[+ sand]* égaliser, rendre lisse ; *[+ wood]* rendre lisse, planer ♦ **to ~ things over** *(fig)* arranger les choses

smoothie /ˈsmuːðɪ/ N 1 *(* pej)* beau parleur *m* 2 *(= drink)* lait *m* frappé aux fruits *(au yaourt ou à la glace)*

smoothly /ˈsmuːðlɪ/ ADV 1 *(= evenly, not jerkily) [move]* en douceur, sans à-coups ♦ **to run ~** *[engine]* (bien) tourner 2 *(= efficiently, suavely) [act]* habilement ; *(pej) [speak]* d'un ton doucereux *(pej)* ♦ **to run** or **go ~** *[event, operation]* bien se passer ♦ **the move to the new house went off** or **passed off ~** le déménagement s'est bien passé

smoothness /ˈsmuːðnɪs/ N *(NonC)* 1 *[of surface, texture, road, stone, tyre, hair, sea, skin]* aspect *m* lisse ; *[of fabric]* aspect *m* lisse or soyeux ; *[of paste, sauce, mixture]* onctuosité *f* ; *[of flavour, wine, whisky etc]* rondeur *f*, moelleux *m* ; *[of voice, sound]* douceur *f* 2 *(= evenness) [of flow, stride, breathing]* régularité *f* ; *[of sea crossing]* calme *m* ♦ **the ~ of the landing** l'atterrissage *m* en douceur ♦ **listen to the ~ of the engine!** écoutez comme le moteur tourne bien ! 3 *(pej = suaveness) [of person, manners]* caractère *m* doucereux or mielleux

smoothy⁑ /ˈsmuːðɪ/ N ⇒ **smoothie**

smorgasbord /ˈsmɔːgəsˌbɔːd/ N *(Culin)* smorgasbord *m*, buffet *m* scandinave

smote /sməʊt/ VB pt of **smite**

smother /ˈsmʌðəʳ/ VT 1 *(= stifle) [+ person, flames]* étouffer ; *[+ noise]* étouffer, amortir ; *(fig) [+ scandal, feelings]* étouffer ; *[+ criticism, doubt, yawn]* étouffer, réprimer ; *[+ one's anger]* contenir, réprimer 2 *(= cover)* (re) couvrir *(with* de) ♦ **she ~ed the child with kisses** elle a couvert or dévoré l'enfant de baisers ♦ **books ~ed in dust** des livres enfouis sous la poussière or tout (re)couverts de poussière ♦ **a child ~ed in dirt** un enfant tout sale or tout couvert de crasse ♦ **a face ~ed in make-up** une figure toute emplâtrée de maquillage ♦ **he was ~ed in blankets** il était tout emmailloté de couvertures, il était tout emmitouflé dans ses couvertures VI *[person]* être étouffé, mourir étouffé COMP **smother-love*** N *(iro)* amour *m* maternel possessif or dévorant

smoulder, smolder *(US)* /ˈsməʊldəʳ/ VI *[fire, emotion]* couver ; *[woman]* être très sexy* ♦ **to ~ with rage** être blême de rage

smouldering, smoldering *(US)* /ˈsməʊldərɪŋ/ ADJ 1 *(lit) [fire]* qui couve ; *[ashes, rubble]* qui fume 2 *(fig) [expression, look]* provocant, aguichant ; *[emotion]* qui couve ♦ **his ~ hatred** la haine qui couve en lui

SMP /ˌesemˈpiː/ N *(Brit)* (abbrev of **Statutory Maternity Pay**) → **statutory**

SMS /ˌesemˈes/ N (abbrev of **Short Message Service**) SMS *m*

smudge /smʌdʒ/ N *(on paper, cloth)* (légère) tache *f*, traînée *f* ; *(in text, print etc)* bavure *f*, tache *f* VT *[+ face]* salir ; *[+ print]* maculer ; *[+ paint]* faire une trace or une marque sur ; *[+ lettering, writing]* étaler accidentellement VI s'étaler

smudgy /ˈsmʌdʒɪ/ ADJ *[photo]* indistinct ; *[page]* sali, taché ; *[writing]* à moitié effacé ♦ **~ newsprint** papier *m* journal salissant

smug /smʌg/ ADJ *[person, voice, attitude, smile]* suffisant ; *[optimism, satisfaction]* béat ; *[remark, speech]* plein de suffisance

smuggle /ˈsmʌgl/ VT *[+ tobacco, drugs]* faire la contrebande de, passer en contrebande or en fraude ♦ **to ~ in/out** *etc* *[+ contraband]* faire entrer/sortir *etc* ; *[+ goods]* faire entrer/sortir *etc* en contrebande ; *(fig)* *[+ letters etc]* faire entrer/sortir *etc* clandestinement or en fraude ; *[+ person, animal]* faire entrer/sortir *etc* clandestinement ♦ **to ~ sth past** or **through the customs** passer qch en contrebande, passer qch sans le déclarer à la douane ♦ **~d goods** contrebande *f* ♦ **~d whisky** whisky *m* de contrebande VI faire de la contrebande

smuggler /ˈsmʌgləʳ/ N contrebandier *m*, -ière *f*

smuggling /ˈsmʌglɪŋ/ **N** (NonC) *[of goods]* contrebande *f* **COMP smuggling ring N** réseau *m* de contrebandiers

smugly /ˈsmʌglɪ/ **ADV** *[say]* d'un ton suffisant ; *[behave, smile]* d'un air suffisant

smugness /ˈsmʌgnɪs/ **N** *[of person]* suffisance *f* ; *[of voice, reply]* ton *m* suffisant

smut /smʌt/ **N** (= *dirt*) petite saleté *f* ; (= *soot*) flocon *m* de suie ; (*in eye*) escarbille *f* ; (= *dirty mark*) tache *f* de suie ; (*Bot*) charbon *m* du blé ; (*NonC* = *obscenity*) obscénité(s) *f(pl)*, cochonneries* *fpl* ◆ **programme full of** ~ (*TV*) émission *f* cochonne*

smuttiness /ˈsmʌtɪnɪs/ **N** (*NonC: fig*) obscénité *f*, grossièreté *f*

smutty /ˈsmʌtɪ/ **ADJ** 1 (* = *rude*) *[joke, film, book]* cochon* ; *[person]* grossier 2 (= *smudged with dirt*) *[face, object]* sali

snack /snæk/ **N** 1 (*gen*) casse-croûte *m inv* ◆ **to have a** ~ casser la croûte, manger (un petit) quelque chose 2 (= *party snack*) amuse-gueule *m inv* **VI** ⇒ **to have a snack noun 1 COMP snack bar N** snack-bar *m*, snack *m*

snaffle /ˈsnæfl/ **N** (also **snaffle bit**) mors *m* brisé **VT** (*Brit* * = *steal*) chiper*, faucher*

snafu ✱ /snæˈfuː/ (*US*) **ADJ** en pagaille* **VT** mettre la pagaille* dans

snag /snæg/ **N** (= *drawback*) inconvénient *m* ; (= *hidden obstacle*) obstacle *m* caché ; (= *stump of tree, tooth etc*) chicot *m* ; (= *tear*) (*in cloth*) accroc *m* ; (*in stocking*) fil *m* tiré ◆ **there's a** ~ **in it somewhere** il y a sûrement un os* ◆ **to run into** *or* **hit a** ~ tomber sur un os* ◆ **that's the** ~**!** voilà le hic !* ◆ **the** ~ **is that you must ...** l'embêtant* c'est que vous devez ... **VT** *[+ cloth]* faire un accroc à ; *[+ stockings, tights]* accrocher (*on sth* contre qch), tirer un fil à **VI** *[rope etc]* s'accrocher (à quelque chose) ; *[stockings, tights etc]* s'accrocher

snail /sneɪl/ **N** escargot *m* ◆ **at a** ~**'s pace** *[walk]* comme un escargot, à un pas de tortue ; (*fig*) *[progress, continue]* à un pas de tortue ; → **pace[1]** **COMP snail mail** * **N** (*NonC: hum*) ◆ **to send sth by** ~ **mail** envoyer qch par la poste
snail shell N coquille *f* d'escargot

snake /sneɪk/ **N** serpent *m* ; (*fig pej* = *person*) traître(sse) *m(f)*, faux frère *m* ◆ ~ **in the grass** (*fig*) (= *person*) ami(e) *m(f)* perfide, traître(sse) *m(f)* ; (= *danger*) serpent *m* caché sous les fleurs ◆ **the Snake** (*Pol Econ*) le serpent (monétaire) ; → **grass, water**
VI *[road, river]* serpenter (*through* à travers) ◆ **the road** ~**d down the mountain** la route descendait en lacets *or* en serpentant au flanc de la montagne ◆ **the whip** ~**d through the air** la lanière du fouet a fendu l'air en ondulant
COMP snake charmer N charmeur *m* de serpent
snake eyes ✱ **NPL** (*US: at dice*) double un *m*, deux *m* (aux dés)
snake fence N (*US*) barrière *f* en zigzag, barrière *f* pliante
snake oil N (*US*) (= *quack remedy*) remède *m* de charlatan ; (= *nonsense*) inepties *fpl*, foutaises* *fpl*
snake pit N fosse *f* aux serpents
snakes and ladders N *sorte de jeu de l'oie*

► **snake along VI** *[road, river]* serpenter ; *[rope, lasso etc]* fendre l'air en ondulant

snakebite /ˈsneɪkbaɪt/ **N** morsure *f* de serpent

snakeskin /ˈsneɪkskɪn/ **N** peau *f* de serpent **COMP** *[handbag etc]* en (peau de) serpent

snaky * /ˈsneɪkɪ/ **ADJ** 1 (= *winding*) *[road, river]* sinueux 2 (= *treacherous*) *[person, behaviour, remark]* sournois

snap /snæp/ **N** 1 (= *noise*) *[of fingers, whip, elastic]* claquement *m* ; *[of sth breaking]* bruit *m* sec, craquement *m* ; *[of sth shutting]* bruit *m* sec, claquement *m* ; (= *action*) *[of whip]* claquement *m* ; *[of breaking twig etc]* rupture *f* or cassure *f* soudaine ◆ **he closed the lid with a** ~ il a refermé le couvercle avec un bruit sec *or* d'un coup sec ◆ **with a** ~ **of his fingers he ...** faisant claquer ses doigts il ... ◆ **the dog made a** ~ **at my leg** le chien a essayé de me mordre la jambe ◆ **put some** ~ **into it!** allons, un peu de nerf *or* d'énergie ! ◆ **he has plenty of** ~ il a du nerf*, il est très dynamique ; → **brandy, ginger**
2 (*Weather*) **a cold** ~ une brève vague de froid, un coup de froid
3 (also **snapshot**) photo *f* (d'amateur) ; (*not posed*) instantané *m* ◆ **here are our holiday** ~**s** voici nos photos de vacances ◆ **it's only a** ~ ce n'est qu'une photo d'amateur
4 (*US:* also **snap fastener**) pression *f*, bouton-pression *m*
5 (*Brit Cards*) ≃ bataille *f*
6 (*US*) **it's a** ~ * (= *easy*) c'est du gâteau*, c'est facile comme tout, c'est un jeu d'enfant
ADJ 1 (= *sudden*) *[vote, strike]* subit, décidé à l'improviste ; *[judgement, answer, remark]* fait sans réflexion, irréfléchi ◆ **to make a** ~ **decision** (se) décider tout d'un coup *or* subitement
2 (*US* * = *easy*) facile comme tout, facile comme pas deux*
ADV ◆ **to go** ~ se casser net *or* avec un bruit sec
EXCL (*gen*) tiens ! on est *or* fait pareil ! ; (*Cards*) ≃ bataille !
VI 1 (= *break*) se casser net *or* avec un bruit sec
2 *[whip, elastic, rubber band]* claquer ◆ **to** ~ **shut/open** se fermer/s'ouvrir avec un bruit sec *or* avec un claquement ◆ **the rubber band** ~**ped back into place** l'élastique est revenu à sa place avec un claquement
3 ◆ **to** ~ **at sb** *[dog]* essayer de mordre qn ; *[person]* parler à qn d'un ton brusque, rembarrer* qn ◆ **the dog** ~**ped at the bone** le chien a essayé de happer l'os
VT 1 (= *break*) casser net *or* avec un bruit sec
2 *[+ whip, rubber band etc]* faire claquer ◆ **to** ~ **one's fingers** faire claquer ses doigts ◆ **to** ~ **one's fingers at** *[+ person]* faire la nique à ; (*fig*) *[+ suggestion, danger]* se moquer de ◆ **to** ~ **sth open/shut** ouvrir/fermer qch d'un coup sec *or* avec un bruit sec
3 (*Phot*) prendre en photo
4 ◆ **"shut up !" he** ~**ped** "silence !" fit-il d'un ton brusque
COMP snap fastener N (*US*) (*on clothes*) pression *f*, bouton-pression *m* ; (*on handbag, bracelet etc*) fermoir *m*
snap-in, snap-on ADJ *[hood, lining]* amovible (à pressions)

► **snap back VI** 1 *[elastic, rope etc]* revenir en place brusquement *or* avec un claquement
2 (*fig: after illness, accident*) se remettre très vite
3 (*in answering*) répondre d'un ton brusque

► **snap off VI** se casser *or* se briser net
VT SEP casser net ◆ **to** ~ **sb's head off** (*fig*) rabrouer qn, rembarrer* qn

► **snap out VI** * ◆ **to** ~ **out of** *[+ gloom, lethargy, self-pity]* se sortir de, se tirer de ; *[+ bad temper]* contrôler, dominer ◆ ~ **out of it!** *[+ gloom etc]* secoue-toi !*, réagis ! ; *[+ bad temper]* contrôle-toi *or* domine-toi un peu !
VT SEP *[+ question/order]* poser/lancer d'un ton brusque *or* cassant

► **snap up VT SEP** *[dog etc]* happer, attraper ◆ **to** ~ **up a bargain** sauter sur *or* se jeter sur une occasion ◆ **they are** ~**ped up as soon as they come on the market** on se les arrache *or* on saute dessus dès qu'ils sont mis en vente

snapdragon /ˈsnæpdrægən/ **N** gueule-de-loup *f*

snapper /ˈsnæpəʳ/ **N** (pl **snapper** *or* **snappers**) (= *fish*) lutjanidé *m* ; (= *red snapper*) vivaneau *m*

snappish /ˈsnæpɪʃ/ **ADJ** (= *irritable*) *[person, reply, tone]* cassant ; *[dog]* hargneux

snappishness /ˈsnæpɪʃnɪs/ **N** *[of person]* caractère *m* cassant ; (*temporary*) brusquerie *f* ; *[of voice, reply]* ton *m* brusque *or* cassant

snappy /ˈsnæpɪ/ **ADJ** 1 (= *punchy*) *[title, phrase, slogan]* qui a du punch* ; *[dialogue]* nerveux ; *[reply]* bien envoyé 2 (= *snazzy*) *[clothes]* chic *inv* ◆ **he's a** ~ **dresser** il est toujours bien sapé* 3 * ◆ **make it** ~ **!, look** ~ **(about it) !** grouille-toi !*, remue-toi ! 4 ⇒ **snappish**

snapshot /ˈsnæpʃɒt/ **N** → **snap noun 3**

snare /snɛəʳ/ **N** piège *m* ; (*fig*) piège *m*, traquenard *m* ◆ **these promises are a** ~ **and a delusion** ces promesses ne servent qu'à allécher *or* appâter **VT** (*lit, fig*) attraper, prendre au piège **COMP snare drum N** tambour *m* à timbre

snarky ✱ /ˈsnɑːkɪ/ **ADJ** râleur*

snarl[1] /snɑːl/ **N** *[of dog]* grondement *m* féroce ◆ **to give a** ~ **of fury** *[dog]* gronder férocement ; *[person]* pousser un rugissement de fureur ◆ **... he said with a** ~ ... dit-il d'une voix rageuse *or* avec hargne **VI** *[dog]* gronder en montrant les dents *or* férocement ; *[person]* lancer un grondement (*at sb* à qn), gronder ◆ **when I went in the dog** ~**ed at me** quand je suis entré le chien a grondé en montrant les dents **VT** *[+ order]* lancer d'un ton hargneux *or* d'une voix rageuse ◆ **to** ~ **a reply** répondre d'un ton hargneux *or* d'une voix rageuse ◆ **"no" he** ~**ed** "non" dit-il avec hargne *or* d'une voix rageuse

snarl[2] /snɑːl/ **N** (*in wool, rope, hair etc*) nœud *m*, enchevêtrement *m* ◆ **a traffic** ~ un embouteillage ; see also **snarl-up VI** (also **snarl up, get snarled up**) *[wool, rope, hair]* s'emmêler, s'enchevêtrer ; *[traffic]* se bloquer ; * *[plans, programme]* cafouiller* **VT** (also **snarl up**) *[+ wool, rope, hair]* emmêler, enchevêtrer **COMP snarl-up N** ◆ **a traffic** ~**-up, a** ~**-up (in the traffic)** un embouteillage ◆ **there's been a** ~**-up** * (*fig: in plans etc*) il y a eu du cafouillage* *or* quelques anicroches

► **snarl up VI** ⇒ **snarl[2] vi VT SEP** 1 ⇒ **snarl[2] vt** 2 *[+ traffic]* bloquer ; * *[+ plans, programme]* mettre la pagaille* dans **N** ◆ **snarl-up** → **snarl[2]**

snatch /snætʃ/ **N** 1 (= *action*) geste *m* vif (*pour saisir quelque chose*) ; *[of child]* enlèvement *m* ◆ **there was a wages** ~ **yesterday** un fourgon convoyant des paies a été attaqué hier
2 (= *small piece*) fragment *m* ◆ **a** ~ **of music/poetry** quelques mesures *fpl*/vers *mpl* ◆ **a** ~ **of conversation** des bribes *fpl* de conversation ◆ **a few** ~**es of Mozart** quelques mesures de Mozart ◆ **to sleep in** ~**es** dormir par intermittence
3 (*Weight Lifting*) arraché *m*
4 (*✱= *vagina*) chatte*✱ *f*
VT (= *grab*) *[+ object]* saisir, s'emparer (brusquement) de ; *[+ a few minutes' peace, a holiday]* réussir à avoir ; *[+ opportunity]* saisir, sauter sur ; *[+ kiss]* voler, dérober (*from sb* à qn) ; *[+ sandwich, drink]* avaler à la hâte ; (= *steal*) voler, chiper* (*from sb* à qn), saisir ; (= *kidnap*) enlever ◆ **she** ~**ed the book from him** elle lui a arraché le livre ◆ **he** ~**ed the child from the railway line just in time** il a attrapé *or* empoigné l'enfant et l'a éloigné de la voie juste à temps ◆ **Cantona** ~**ed victory from the jaws of defeat with two last-minute goals** Cantona a arraché la victoire en marquant deux buts à la dernière minute ◆ **to** ~ **some sleep/rest** (réussir à) dormir/se reposer un peu ◆ **to** ~ **a meal** déjeuner (*or* dîner) à la hâte
VI ◆ **to** ~ **at** *[+ object, end of rope etc]* essayer de saisir, faire un geste vif pour saisir ; *[+ opportunity, chance]* saisir, sauter sur
COMP snatch squad N (*Brit*) *forces de l'ordre chargées d'appréhender les meneurs de manifestations*

► **snatch away, snatch off** VT SEP enlever d'un geste vif *or* brusque

► **snatch up** VT SEP *[+ object, child]* saisir

-snatcher /'snætʃəʳ/ N *(in compounds)* → **cradle**

snazzy * /'snæzɪ/ ADJ qui en jette⁑, chouette* ◆ **she's a ~ dresser** elle est toujours bien sapée*

sneak /sni:k/ (vb : pret, ptp **sneaked** *or US** **snuck**) N *(* = underhand person)* faux jeton* *m* ; *(Brit Scol = telltale)* mouchard(e)* *m(f)*, rapporteur* *m*, -euse* *f*
ADJ *[attack, visit]* furtif, subreptice ◆ **~ preview** *(Cine)* avant-première *f* ; *(gen)* avant-goût *m* ◆ **~ thief** chapardeur* *m*, -euse* *f*
VI 1 ◆ **to ~ in/out** *etc* entrer/sortir *etc* furtivement ◆ **he ~ed into the house** il s'est faufilé *or* s'est glissé dans la maison ◆ **he ~ed up behind** *or* **on me** il s'est approché de moi sans faire de bruit ◆ **success can ~ up on you** le succès peut arriver sans crier gare
2 *(Brit Scol *)* moucharder*, cafarder* *(on sb* qn)
VT 1 ◆ **I ~ed the letter onto his desk** j'ai glissé la lettre discrètement *or* en douce* sur son bureau ◆ **he ~ed the envelope from the table** il a enlevé furtivement *or* subrepticement l'enveloppe de la table ◆ **to ~ a look at sth** lancer un coup d'œil furtif à qch, regarder qch à la dérobée ◆ **he was ~ing* a cigarette** il était en train de fumer en cachette
2 *(* = pilfer)* faucher*, piquer*

► **sneak away, sneak off** VI s'esquiver, s'éclipser*

sneaker /'sni:kəʳ/ N *(esp US)* tennis *m*, basket *f*

sneaking /'sni:kɪŋ/ ADJ *(= grudging) [dislike, preference etc]* inavoué ◆ **I had a ~ feeling that ...** je ne pouvais m'empêcher de penser que ... ◆ **to have a ~ suspicion that ...** soupçonner que ... ◆ **I have a ~ admiration/respect for him** je ne peux pas m'empêcher de l'admirer/de le respecter

sneaky * /'sni:kɪ/ ADJ *[person, character, action]* sournois

sneer /snɪəʳ/ VI ricaner, sourire d'un air méprisant *or* sarcastique ◆ **to ~ at sb** se moquer de qn d'un air méprisant ◆ **to ~ at sth** tourner qch en ridicule N *(= act)* ricanement *m* ; *(= remark)* sarcasme *m*, raillerie *f* ◆ **... he said with a ~** ... dit-il d'un air méprisant

sneerer /'snɪərəʳ/ N ricaneur *m*, -euse *f*

sneering /'snɪərɪŋ/ ADJ *[person, contempt, remark]* sarcastique ; *[tone]* railleur N *(NonC)* raillerie(s) *f(pl)*

sneeringly /'snɪərɪŋlɪ/ ADV sarcastiquement

sneeze /sni:z/ N éternuement *m* VI éternuer ◆ **it is not to be ~d at** *(fig)* ce n'est pas à dédaigner, il ne faut pas cracher dessus* ◆ **when America ~s, Britain catches cold** *(Brit)* quand l'Amérique éternue, la Grande-Bretagne s'enrhume

snick /snɪk/ N petite entaille *f*, encoche *f* VT *[+ stick etc]* faire une petite entaille *or* une encoche dans ; *(Sport) [+ ball]* juste toucher

snicker /'snɪkəʳ/ N 1 *[of horse]* petit hennissement *m* 2 ⇒ **snigger noun** VI 1 *[horse]* hennir doucement 2 ⇒ **snigger vi**

snide /snaɪd/ ADJ narquois

sniff /snɪf/ N 1 *(from cold, crying etc)* reniflement *m* ◆ **to give a ~** renifler (une fois) ; *(disdainfully)* faire la grimace *or* la moue ◆ **... he said with a ~** ... dit-il en reniflant ; *(disdainfully)* ... dit-il en faisant la grimace *or* la moue ◆ **I got a ~ of gas** j'ai senti l'odeur du gaz ◆ **to have** *or* **take a ~ at sth** *[person]* renifler qch ; *(suspiciously)* flairer qch ; *[dog]* renifler *or* flairer qch ◆ **one ~ of that is enough to kill you** il suffit de respirer cela une fois pour en mourir ◆ **I didn't get a ~* of the whisky** *(fig)* je n'ai pas eu droit à une goutte de whisky
2 *(* = hint)* ◆ **to get a ~ of sth** flairer qch ◆ **at the first ~ of danger** au moindre danger
VI *(from cold, crying)* renifler ; *(disdainfully)* faire la grimace *or* la moue ; *[dog]* renifler ◆ **to ~ at sth** *[dog]* renifler *or* flairer qch ; *[person]* renifler qch ; *(fig)* faire la grimace *or* la moue à qch ◆ **it's not to be ~ed at** ce n'est pas à dédaigner, il ne faut pas cracher dessus*
VT *[dog etc]* renifler, flairer ; *[person] [+ food, bottle]* renifler, sentir l'odeur de ; *(suspiciously)* flairer ; *[+ air, perfume, aroma]* humer ; *[+ drug]* aspirer ; *[+ smelling salts]* respirer ; *(Pharm) [+ inhalant etc]* aspirer ◆ **to ~ glue** respirer de la colle, sniffer⁑

► **sniff out** VT *(= discover)* flairer

sniffer dog /'snɪfədɒg/ N chien *m* renifleur

sniffle /'snɪfl/ N *(= sniff)* reniflement *m* ; *(= slight cold)* petit rhume *m* de cerveau ◆ **... he said with a ~** ... dit-il en reniflant ◆ **to have a ~** *or* **the ~s*** avoir un petit rhume, être légèrement enrhumé VI *[person, dog]* renifler ; *(from catarrh etc)* avoir le nez bouché, renifler

sniffy * /'snɪfɪ/ ADJ *(= disdainful)* dédaigneux, méprisant ◆ **to be ~ about sth** se montrer désagréable à propos de qch

snifter /'snɪftəʳ/ N 1 *(Brit ⁑ = drink)* petit (verre *m* d')alcool *m* ◆ **to have a ~** prendre un petit verre, boire la goutte* 2 *(US = glass)* verre *m* ballon

snigger /'snɪgəʳ/ N rire *m* en dessous ; *(cynical)* ricanement *m* VI pouffer de rire ; *(cynically)* ricaner ◆ **to ~ at** *[+ remark, question]* pouffer de rire *or* ricaner en entendant ; *[+ sb's appearance etc]* se moquer de ◆ **stop ~ing!** arrête de rire *or* de ricaner comme ça !

sniggering /'snɪgərɪŋ/ N ricanements *mpl* ADJ qui n'arrête pas de pouffer de rire *or* de ricaner

snip /snɪp/ N 1 *(= cut)* petit coup *m* (de ciseaux *etc*), petite entaille *f* ; *(= small piece)* petit bout *m* *(d'étoffe etc)*, échantillon *m* ◆ **to have the ~*** se faire faire une vasectomie 2 *(Brit * = bargain)* bonne affaire *f*, (bonne) occasion *f* ; *(Racing)* gagnant *m* sûr VT couper (à petits coups de ciseaux *etc*) VI ◆ **to ~ at sth** donner des petits coups dans qch

► **snip off** VT SEP couper *or* enlever *or* détacher (à coups de ciseaux *etc*)

snipe /snaɪp/ N (*pl* **snipe** *or* **snipes**) *(= bird)* bécassine *f* VI *(= shoot)* tirer (en restant caché), canarder* ◆ **to ~ at sb/sth** canarder* qn/qch ; *(fig) (verbally)* critiquer qn/qch par en dessous *or* sournoisement

sniper /'snaɪpəʳ/ N tireur *m* isolé, sniper *m*

snippet /'snɪpɪt/ N *[of cloth, paper]* petit bout *m* ; *[of conversation, news, information]* fragment *m*, bribes *fpl*

snippy * /'snɪpɪ/ ADJ *(US) [person, tone]* hargneux ◆ **to be in a ~ mood** être de mauvais poil*

snitch ⁑ /snɪtʃ/ VI moucharder* *(on sb* qn) VT chiper*, piquer* N 1 *(= nose)* pif⁑ *m* 2 *(= telltale)* mouchard(e)* *m(f)*, rapporteur* *m*, -euse* *f* 3 *(* US = tad)* ◆ **a snitch** un tout petit peu

snivel /'snɪvl/ VI *(= whine)* pleurnicher, larmoyer ; *(= sniff)* renifler ; *(= have a runny nose)* avoir le nez qui coule, avoir la morve au nez *(pej)*

sniveler /'snɪvləʳ/ N *(US)* ⇒ **sniveller**

sniveling /'snɪvlɪŋ/ ADJ *(US)* ⇒ **snivelling**

sniveller /'snɪvləʳ/ N pleurnicheur *m*, -euse *f*

snivelling /'snɪvlɪŋ/ ADJ pleurnicheur, larmoyant N pleurnicherie(s) *f(pl)*, reniflement(s) *m(pl)*

snob /snɒb/ N snob *mf* ◆ **he's a terrible ~** il est terriblement snob ◆ **she's a musical/wine ~** c'est une snob en matière de musique/vin

snobbery /'snɒbərɪ/ N snobisme *m*

snobbish /'snɒbɪʃ/ ADJ snob *inv* ◆ **to be ~ about sb/sth** faire preuve de snobisme à l'égard de qn/en matière de qch

snobbishness /'snɒbɪʃnɪs/ N snobisme *m*

snobby * /'snɒbɪ/ ADJ snob *inv*

snog ⁑ /snɒg/ *(Brit)* VI se bécoter* N ◆ **to have a ~** se bécoter*

snood /snu:d/ N résille *f*

snook¹ /snu:k/ N (*pl* **snook** *or* **snooks**) *(= fish)* brochet *m* de mer

snook² /snu:k/ N → **cock vt 2**

snooker /'snu:kəʳ/ N *(= game)* snooker *m* ≃ jeu *m* de billard ; *(= shot)* snooker *m* VT *(lit)* faire un snooker à ; *(US = hoodwink)* tromper, avoir* ◆ **to be ~ed**⁑ *(Brit = be in difficulty)* être coincé*, être dans le pétrin*

snoop /snu:p/ N 1 ◆ **to have a ~ around** jeter un coup d'œil discret ◆ **I had a ~ around the kitchen** j'ai fureté discrètement *or* sans être vu dans la cuisine 2 ⇒ **snooper** VI se mêler des affaires des autres ◆ **to ~ (around)** fureter en essayant de passer inaperçu ◆ **he's been ~ing (around) here again** il est revenu fourrer son nez* par ici ◆ **to ~ on sb** surveiller qn, espionner qn ◆ **he was ~ing into her private life** il fourrait son nez* dans *or* il se mêlait de sa vie privée

snooper /'snu:pəʳ/ N *(pej)* fouineur* *m*, -euse* *f* ◆ **all the ~s from the Ministry** tous les espions du ministère, tous les enquêteurs du ministère qui fourrent leur nez* partout

snoot * /snu:t/ N pif⁑ *m*, nez *m*

snooty * /'snu:tɪ/ ADJ snob *inv*

snooze * /snu:z/ N petit somme *m*, roupillon* *m* ◆ **afternoon ~** sieste *f* ◆ **to have a ~** ⇒ **to snooze vi** VI piquer un roupillon* COMP **snooze button** N bouton *m* d'arrêt momentané *(d'un radio-réveil)*

snore /snɔ:ʳ/ N ronflement *m* *(d'un dormeur)* VI ronfler

snorer /'snɔ:rəʳ/ N ronfleur *m*, -euse *f*

snoring /'snɔ:rɪŋ/ N *(NonC)* ronflement(s) *m(pl)*

snorkel /'snɔ:kl/ N *[of submarine]* schnorkel *or* schnorchel *m* ; *[of swimmer]* tuba *m* VI nager avec un masque et un tuba

snorkelling /'snɔ:kəlɪŋ/ N plongée *f* (avec un masque et un tuba)

snort /snɔ:t/ N 1 *[of person]* grognement *m* ; *[of horse etc]* ébrouement *m* 2 ⁑ ⇒ **snorter 2** 3 *(Drugs *)* sniff⁑ *m*, prise *f* VI 1 *[horse etc]* s'ébrouer ; *[person] (angrily, contemptuously)* grogner, ronchonner ; *(laughing)* s'étrangler de rire 2 *(Drugs *)* sniffer⁑ de la drogue VT 1 *(= say) (angrily etc)* grogner, dire en grognant ; *(laughing)* dire en s'étranglant de rire 2 *(Drugs *)* sniffer⁑

snorter ⁑ /'snɔ:təʳ/ N 1 ◆ **a (real) ~ of a question/problem** une question/un problème vache⁑ ◆ **a ~ of a game** un match formidable* 2 *(= drink)* petit (verre *m* d')alcool *m* ◆ **to have a ~** prendre un petit verre, boire la goutte*

snot * /snɒt/ N 1 *(NonC: in nose)* morve *f* 2 *(* = snooty person)* morveux⁑ *m*, -euse⁑ *f*

snotty * /'snɒtɪ/ ADJ 1 *(= covered in snot) [nose]* qui coule ; *[face, child]* morveux ; *[handkerchief]* plein de morve 2 *(= snooty)* snob *inv* N *(= midshipman)* midship *m* ≃ aspirant *m*
COMP **snotty-faced** * ADJ morveux, qui a le nez qui coule
snotty-nosed * ADJ *(lit, fig)* snob *inv*

snout /snaʊt/ N 1 *(gen)* museau *m* ; *[of pig]* museau *m*, groin *m* ; *(* pej) [of person]* pif‡ *m* 2 *(NonC: Police *)* tabac *m*, perlot‡ *m*

snow /snəʊ/ N 1 neige *f* ◆ **hard/soft ~** neige *f* dure/molle ◆ **the eternal ~s** les neiges *fpl* éternelles ; → **fall, white**
2 *(fig: on TV screen)* neige *f*
3 *(Culin)* **apple** *etc* **~** purée *f* de pommes *etc (aux blancs d'œufs battus en neige)*
4 *(Drugs * = cocaine)* neige* *f*
VI neiger ◆ **it is ~ing** il neige, il tombe de la neige
VT *(US ‡ = charm glibly)* avoir qn au charme* ◆ **she ~ed‡ him into believing that he would win** elle a réussi à lui faire croire qu'il allait gagner
COMP **snow bank** N talus *m* de neige, congère *f*
snow-blind ADJ ◆ **to be ~-blind** souffrir de *or* être atteint de cécité des neiges
snow blindness N cécité *f* des neiges
snow blower N chasse-neige *m inv* à soufflerie, souffleuse *f (Can)*
snow-boot N *(Ski)* après-ski *m*
snow buggy N skidoo *m*, autoneige *f*
snow bunny* N *(US = girl)* minette *f* de station de ski
snow cap N couronne *f or* couverture *f* de neige
snow-capped ADJ couronné de neige
snow-clad, snow-covered ADJ *(liter)* enneigé, enfoui sous la neige
snow goose N (pl **snow geese**) oie *f* des neiges
snow job* N *(US)* ◆ **it's a ~ job** c'est du baratin* ◆ **to give sb a ~ job** baratiner* qn
snow leopard N léopard *m* des neiges, once *f*
snow line N limite *f* des neiges éternelles
snow pea N *(US, Austral)* mange-tout *m inv*
the Snow Queen N *(Myth)* la Reine des neiges
snow report N bulletin *m* d'enneigement
snow tyre N pneu-neige *m*, pneu *m* clouté
snow-white ADJ blanc (blanche *f*) comme neige, d'une blancheur de neige
Snow White (and the Seven Dwarfs) N Blanche-Neige *f* (et les sept nains)

► **snow in** VT *(pass only)* ◆ **to be snowed in** être bloqué par la neige

► **snow under** VT *(fig: pass only)* ◆ **he was snowed under with work** il était complètement submergé *or* débordé de travail, il avait tellement de travail qu'il ne savait pas où donner de la tête ◆ **to be ~ed under with letters/offers** être submergé de lettres/d'offres, recevoir une avalanche de lettres/d'offres

► **snow up** VT *(Brit)* ◆ **to be snowed up** *[road, village, farm, person]* être bloqué par la neige

snowball /ˈsnəʊbɔːl/ N boule *f* de neige ◆ **it hasn't got a ~'s chance in hell*** ça n'a pas l'ombre d'une chance ◆ **~(ing) effect** effet *m* boule de neige ◆ **~ fight** bataille *f* de boules de neige VI *(lit)* se lancer des boules de neige ; *[project]* faire boule de neige ◆ **her business ~ed** son entreprise s'est développée très rapidement ◆ **it has a ~ing effect** ça fait boule de neige

snowbelt /ˈsnəʊbelt/ N *(US)* régions *fpl* neigeuses

snowboard /ˈsnəʊbɔːd/ N surf *m* des neiges VI faire du surf sur neige

snowboarding /ˈsnəʊbɔːdɪŋ/ N surf *m* des neiges

snowbound /ˈsnəʊbaʊnd/ ADJ *[road, country]* complètement enneigé ; *[village, house, person]* bloqué par la neige

snowcat /ˈsnəʊkæt/ N *(= vehicle)* autoneige *f*

Snowdon /ˈsnəʊdən/ N *(Brit)* le (mont) Snowdon

Snowdonia /snəʊˈdəʊnɪə/ N le massif *or* le parc national du Snowdon

snowdrift /ˈsnəʊdrɪft/ N congère *f*, amoncellement *m* de neige

snowdrop /ˈsnəʊdrɒp/ N *(= plant)* perce-neige *m inv*

snowfall /ˈsnəʊfɔːl/ N chute *f* de neige

snowfield /ˈsnəʊfiːld/ N champ *m* de neige

snowflake /ˈsnəʊfleɪk/ N flocon *m* de neige

snowman /ˈsnəʊmæn/ N (pl **-men**) bonhomme *m* de neige ; → **abominable**

snowmobile /ˈsnəʊməˌbiːəl/ N *(US)* autoneige *f*, motoneige *f*

snowplough, snowplow *(US)* /ˈsnəʊplaʊ/ N *(also Ski)* chasse-neige *m inv* ◆ **~ (turn)** *(Ski)* stem *m*

snowshoe /ˈsnəʊʃuː/ N raquette *f*

snowslide /ˈsnəʊslaɪd/ N *(US)* avalanche *f*

snowstorm /ˈsnəʊstɔːm/ N tempête *f* de neige

snowsuit /ˈsnəʊsuːt/ N combinaison *f* de ski

snowy /ˈsnəʊɪ/ ADJ 1 *[weather, climate, winter]* neigeux ; *[valley, region, landscape, mountain, street]* enneigé ; *[roof]* couvert de neige ◆ **a ~ day/morning** une journée/matinée de neige ◆ **it was very ~ yesterday** il a beaucoup neigé hier 2 *(in colour)* (also **snowy white**) *[linen, shirt]* blanc (blanche *f*) comme neige ; *[hair, beard]* de neige COMP **snowy owl** N harfang *m*

SNP /esenˈpiː/ N *(Brit Pol)* (abbrev of **Scottish National Party**) → **Scottish**

Snr *(esp US)* abbrev of **senior**

snub¹ /snʌb/ N rebuffade *f* VT *[+ person]* snober ; *[+ offer]* repousser, rejeter ◆ **to be ~bed** essuyer une rebuffade

snub² /snʌb/ ADJ *[nose]* retroussé, camus *(pej)* ◆ **~-nosed** au nez retroussé *or* camus *(pej)*

snuck* /snʌk/ *(US)* VB pt, ptp of **sneak**

snuff¹ /snʌf/ N tabac *m* à priser ◆ **pinch of ~** prise *f* ◆ **to take ~** priser ◆ **he/his work isn't up to ~** †* *(Brit)* il/son travail n'est pas à la hauteur ◆ **his lectures didn't come up to ~** †* *(Brit)* ses cours ne valaient pas grand-chose VTI ⇒ **sniff vi, vt**

snuff² /snʌf/ VT *[+ candle]* moucher ◆ **to ~ it‡** *(Brit euph = die)* claquer*, casser sa pipe* COMP **snuff film, snuff movie** N film *m* porno sadique *(dont la scène principale est un meurtre filmé en direct)*

► **snuff out** VI *(‡ = die)* mourir, casser sa pipe* VT SEP 1 *[+ candle]* moucher 2 *[+ interest, hopes, enthusiasm, sb's life]* mettre fin à 3 *(‡ = kill)* zigouiller‡

snuffbox /ˈsnʌfbɒks/ N tabatière *f*

snuffer /ˈsnʌfəʳ/ N (also **candle-snuffer**) éteignoir *m* ◆ **~s** mouchettes *fpl*

snuffle /ˈsnʌfl/ N 1 ⇒ **sniffle noun** 2 ◆ **to speak in a ~** parler du nez *or* d'une voix nasillarde, nasiller VI 1 ⇒ **sniffle vi** 2 parler *(or* chanter) d'une voix nasillarde, nasiller VT dire *or* prononcer d'une voix nasillarde

snug /snʌg/ ADJ 1 *(= cosy) [house, bed, garment]* douillet ◆ **it's nice and ~ here** on est bien ici ◆ **he was ~ in bed** il était bien au chaud dans son lit ◆ **to be as ~ as a bug in a rug*** être bien au chaud, être douillettement installé 2 *(= close-fitting)* bien ajusté ◆ **it's a ~ fit** *[garment]* ça va, mais juste ; *[object]* cela rentre juste bien N *(Brit: in pub)* petite arrière-salle *f*

snuggery /ˈsnʌgərɪ/ N *(Brit)* ⇒ **snug noun**

snuggle /ˈsnʌgl/ VI se blottir, se pelotonner *(into sth* dans qch ; *beside sb* contre qn) VT *[+ child etc]* serrer *or* attirer contre soi

► **snuggle down** VI se blottir, se pelotonner *(beside sb* contre qn), se rouler en boule ◆ **~ down and go to sleep** installe-toi bien confortablement et dors

► **snuggle together** VI se serrer *or* se blottir l'un contre l'autre

► **snuggle up** VI se serrer, se blottir *(to sb* contre qn)

snugly /ˈsnʌglɪ/ ADV 1 *(= cosily)* douillettement ◆ **~ tucked in** bien au chaud sous ses couvertures 2 *(= tightly)* ◆ **these trousers fit ~** ce pantalon va juste bien ◆ **the washing machine fitted ~ into the space** la machine à laver s'encastrait parfaitement

so /səʊ/

LANGUAGE IN USE 17.2, 26.3

1 ADVERB	3 COMPOUNDS
2 CONJUNCTION	

1 - ADVERB

1 degree = to such an extent si, tellement, aussi ◆ **~ easy/quickly** tellement facile/rapidement ◆ **is it really ~ tiring?** est-ce vraiment si *or* tellement fatigant ?, est-ce vraiment aussi fatigant (que cela) ? ◆ **do you really need ~ long?** vous faut-il vraiment autant de temps *or* aussi longtemps (que cela) ? ◆ **~ early** si tôt, tellement tôt, d'aussi bonne heure

♦ **so ... (that)** si *or* tellement ... que ◆ **he was ~ clumsy (that) he broke the cup** il était si *or* tellement maladroit qu'il a cassé la tasse ◆ **the body was ~ decomposed that it was unidentifiable** le cadavre était tellement décomposé qu'il était impossible de l'identifier

♦ **so ... as to do sth** assez ... pour faire qch ◆ **he was ~ stupid as to tell her what he'd done** il a eu la stupidité de *or* il a été assez stupide pour lui raconter ce qu'il avait fait ◆ **would you be ~ kind as to open the door?** *(frm)* auriez-vous l'amabilité *or* la gentillesse *or* l'obligeance d'ouvrir la porte ?

♦ **not so ... as** pas aussi ... que ◆ **he is not ~ clever as his brother** il n'est pas aussi *or* si intelligent que son frère ◆ **it's not ~ big as all that!** ce n'est pas si grand que ça ! ◆ **it's not ~ big as I thought it would be** ce n'est pas aussi grand que je le pensais *or* que je l'imaginais ◆ **it's not nearly ~ difficult as you think** c'est loin d'être aussi difficile que vous le croyez ◆ **it's not ~ early as you think** il n'est pas aussi tôt que vous le croyez ◆ **he's not ~ good a teacher as his father** il n'est pas aussi bon professeur que son père, il ne vaut pas son père comme professeur ◆ **he's not ~ stupid as he looks** il n'est pas aussi *or* si stupide qu'il en a l'air ◆ **he was not ~ stupid as to say that to her** il n'a pas été bête au point de lui dire cela, il a eu l'intelligence de ne pas lui dire cela

2 = very, to a great extent si, tellement ◆ **I'm ~ tired!** je suis si *or* tellement fatigué ! ◆ **I'm ~ very tired!** je suis vraiment si *or* tellement fatigué ! ◆ **there's ~ much to do** il y a tellement *or* tant (de choses) à faire ◆ **thanks ~ much*, thanks ever ~‡** merci beaucoup *or* mille fois ◆ **it's not ~ very difficult!** cela n'est pas si difficile que ça ! ◆ **Elizabeth, who ~ loved France ...** Elizabeth, qui aimait tant la France ...

3 unspecified amount **how tall is he? – oh, about ~ tall** *(accompanied by gesture)* quelle taille fait-il ? – oh, à peu près (grand) comme ça ◆ **~ much per head** tant par tête ◆ **their skulls were crushed like ~ many eggshells** leurs crânes furent écrasés comme autant de coquilles d'œufs ◆ **his speech was ~ much nonsense** son discours était complètement stupide ◆ **how long will it take? – a week or ~** combien de temps cela va-t-il prendre ? – une semaine environ *or* à peu près ◆ **twenty or ~** à peu près vingt, une vingtaine

4 manner = thus, in this way ainsi, comme ceci *or* cela, de cette façon ◆ **you should stand (just *or* like) ~** vous devriez vous tenir comme ceci,

voici comment vous devriez vous tenir ◆ **as A is to B ~ C is to D** C est à D ce que A est à B ◆ **as he failed once ~ he will fail again** il échouera comme il a déjà échoué ◆ **you don't believe me but it is ~** vous ne me croyez pas mais il en est bien ainsi ◆ ~ **it was that ...** c'est ainsi que ... ◆ ~ **be it** *(frm)* soit ◆ **it ~ happened that ...** il s'est trouvé que ...

◆ **so (that)** *(intention)* pour + *infin*, afin de + *infin*, pour que + *subj*, afin que + *subj* ; *(result)* si bien que + *indic*, de (telle) sorte que + *indic* ◆ **I'm going early ~ (that) I'll get a ticket** j'y vais tôt pour obtenir *or* afin d'obtenir un billet ◆ **I brought it ~ (that) you could read it** je l'ai apporté pour que *or* afin que vous puissiez le lire ◆ **he arranged the timetable ~ (that) the afternoons were free** il a organisé l'emploi du temps de façon à laisser les après-midi libres *or* de (telle) sorte que les après-midi soient libres ◆ **he refused to move, ~ (that) the police had to carry him away** il a refusé de bouger, si bien que *or* de sorte que les agents ont dû l'emporter de force

◆ **so as to ...** afin de faire, pour faire ◆ **he stood up ~ as to see better** il s'est levé pour mieux voir

◆ **so as not to ...** ◆ **she put it down gently ~ as not to break it** elle l'a posé doucement pour ne pas le casser ◆ **he hurried ~ as not to be late** il s'est dépêché pour ne pas être *or* afin de ne pas être en retard

[5] used as substitute for phrase, word etc ~ **saying ...** ce disant ..., sur ces mots ... ◆ ~ **I believe** c'est ce que je crois, c'est ce qu'il me semble ◆ **is that ~?** pas possible !, tiens ! ◆ **that is ~** c'est bien ça, c'est exact ◆ **if that is ~ ...** s'il en est ainsi ... ◆ **just ~!, quite ~!** exactement !, tout à fait ! ◆ **I told you ~ yesterday** je vous l'ai dit hier ◆ ~ **it seems!** à ce qu'il paraît ! ◆ **he certainly said ~** c'est ce qu'il a dit, il a bien dit ça ◆ **please do ~** faites-le, faites ainsi ◆ **I think ~** je (le) crois, je (le) pense ◆ **I hope ~ (answering sb)** j'espère que oui ; (agreeing with sb) je l'espère, j'espère bien ◆ **how ~?** comment (ça se fait) ? ◆ **why~?** pourquoi (donc) ? ◆ **he said they would be there and ~ they were** il a dit qu'ils seraient là, et en effet ils y étaient ◆ ~ **do I!, ~ have I!, ~ am I!** *etc* moi aussi ! ◆ **he's going to bed and ~ am I** il va se coucher et moi aussi *or* et je vais en faire autant ◆ **if you do that ~ will I** si tu fais ça, j'en ferai autant ◆ **I'm tired – ~ am I!** je suis fatigué – moi aussi ! ◆ **he said he was French – ~ he did!** il a dit qu'il était français – c'est vrai *or* en effet ! ◆ **it's raining – ~ it is!** il pleut – en effet *or* c'est vrai ! ◆ **I want to see that film – ~ you shall!** je veux voir ce film – eh bien, tu le verras ! ◆ **I didn't say that! – you did ~!** * je n'ai pas dit ça ! – mais si, tu l'as dit ! * ◆ ~ **to speak, ~ to say** pour ainsi dire ◆ **and ~ forth, and ~ on (and ~ forth)** et ainsi de suite ◆ ~ **long!** * tchao ! *, salut ! * ◆ **I'm not going, ~ there!** je n'y vais pas, voilà !

2 – CONJUNCTION

[1] = therefore donc, par conséquent ◆ **he was late, ~ he missed the train** il est arrivé en retard, donc *or* par conséquent il a manqué le train ◆ **the roads are busy ~ be careful** il y a beaucoup de circulation, alors fais bien attention

[2] exclamatory ◆ ~ **there he is!** le voilà donc ! ◆ ~ **you're selling it?** alors vous le vendez ? ◆ ~ **he's come at last!** il est donc enfin arrivé ! ◆ **and ~ you see ...** alors comme vous voyez ... ◆ **I'm going home – ~?** * je rentre – et alors ? ◆ ~ **(what)?** * et alors ?, et après ?

3 – COMPOUNDS

so-and-so * N (pl **so-and-sos**) ◆ **Mr/Mrs So-and-so** Monsieur/Madame Untel ◆ **then if so-and-so says ...** alors si quelqu'un *or* Machin Chouette * dit ... ◆ **he's an old so-and-so** c'est un vieux schnock ⁑ ◆ **if you ask him to do so-and-so** si vous lui demandez de faire quoi que ce soit

so-called ADJ soi-disant *inv*, prétendu

so-so * ADJ comme ci comme ça, couci-couça * ◆ **his work is only so-so** son travail n'est pas fameux *

s/o *(Banking)* (abbrev of **standing order**) → **standing**

soak /səʊk/ N [1] ◆ **to give sth a (good) ~** (bien) faire tremper qch, (bien) laisser tremper qch ◆ **the sheets are in ~** les draps sont en train de tremper

[2] *(⁑ = drunkard)* soûlard * *m*, poivrot ⁑ *m*

VT [1] faire *or* laisser tremper *(in* dans) ◆ **to be/get ~ed to the skin** être trempé/se faire tremper jusqu'aux os *or* comme une soupe * ◆ **to ~ o.s. in the bath** faire trempette dans la baignoire ◆ **bread ~ed in milk** pain *m* imbibé de lait *or* qui a trempé dans du lait ◆ **he ~ed himself in the atmosphere of Paris** il s'est plongé dans l'atmosphère de Paris

[2] *(⁑ = take money from) (by overcharging)* estamper * ; *(by taxation)* faire payer de lourds impôts à ◆ **the government's policy is to ~ the rich** la politique du gouvernement est de faire casquer * les riches

VI [1] tremper *(in* dans) ◆ **to put sth in to ~** faire tremper qch, mettre qch à tremper

[2] *(⁑ = drink)* boire comme une éponge, avoir la dalle en pente *

COMP **soak test** N *(Comput)* rodage *m*

► **soak in** VI *[liquid]* pénétrer, être absorbé

► **soak out** VI *[stain etc]* partir *(au trempage)*

VT SEP *[+ stains]* faire partir en trempant

► **soak through** VI *[liquid]* traverser, filtrer au travers

VT SEP ◆ **to be soaked through** *[person]* être trempé (jusqu'aux os) ; *[object, garment]* être trempé

► **soak up** VT SEP *(lit, fig)* absorber

soaking /ˈsəʊkɪŋ/ N trempage *m* ◆ **to get a ~** se faire tremper (jusqu'aux os) ◆ **to give sth a ~** faire *or* laisser tremper qch ADJ (also **soaking wet**) *[person]* trempé (jusqu'aux os) ; *[object, garment]* trempé

soap /səʊp/ N [1] savon *m* ; (* fig: also **soft soap**) flatterie(s) *f(pl)*, flagornerie *f (pej)* ◆ **no ~!** *(⁑ fig US)* rien à faire !, des clous ! ⁑ ; → **shaving, toilet** [2] ⇒ **soap opera** VT savonner

COMP **soap bubble** N bulle *f* de savon

soap opera N *(fig: Rad, TV)* soap-opéra *m*, soap * *m*, feuilleton *m* mélo * *or* à l'eau de rose

soap powder N lessive *f* (en poudre), poudre *f* à laver

► **soap down** VT SEP savonner

soapbox /ˈsəʊpbɒks/ N [1] *(lit)* caisse *f* à savon ; *(fig: for speaker)* tribune *f* improvisée [2] *(= gocart)* auto *f* sans moteur (pour enfants), caisse *f* à savon *

COMP **soapbox derby** N course *f* en descente d'autos sans moteur (pour enfants)

soapbox orator N orateur *m* de carrefour, harangueur *m*, -euse *f* de foules

soapbox oratory N harangue(s) *f(pl)* de démagogue

soapdish /ˈsəʊpdɪʃ/ N porte-savon *m*

soapflakes /ˈsəʊpfleɪks/ NPL savon *m* en paillettes, paillettes *fpl* de savon

soapstone /ˈsəʊpstəʊn/ N stéatite *f*

soapsuds /ˈsəʊpsʌdz/ NPL *(= lather)* mousse *f* de savon ; *(= soapy water)* eau *f* savonneuse

soapy /ˈsəʊpɪ/ ADJ [1] *(lit) [water, taste, smell]* savonneux ; *[floor, object]* recouvert de savon ; *[cloth, hands, face]* plein de savon [2] *(Brit * = sentimental)* mièvre

soar /sɔːʳ/ VI (also **soar up**) *[bird, aircraft]* monter (en flèche) ; *[ball etc]* voler *(over* par-dessus) ; *(fig) [tower, cathedral]* s'élancer (vers le ciel) ; *[voice, music]* s'élever *(above* au-dessus de) ; *[prices, costs, profits]* monter en flèche ; *[ambitions, hopes]* grandir démesurément ; *[spirits, morale]* remonter en flèche ; see also **send**

► **soar up** VI → **soar**

soaraway * /ˈsɔːrəweɪ/ ADJ *[success, career etc]* fulgurant

soaring /ˈsɔːrɪŋ/ N *[of bird]* essor *m* ; *[of plane]* envol *m* ADJ [1] *(= increasing) [prices, costs, profits, unemployment]* qui monte en flèche ; *[inflation]* galopant ◆ **Britain's ~ crime rate** la forte hausse de la criminalité en Grande-Bretagne [2] *(= tall) [spire, skyscraper]* qui s'élance vers le ciel

sob /sɒb/ N sanglot *m* ◆ **... he said with a ~** ... dit-il en sanglotant

VI sangloter

VT ◆ **"no" she ~bed** "non" dit-elle en sanglotant ◆ **to ~ o.s. to sleep** s'endormir à force de sangloter *or* en sanglotant

COMP **sob sister** * N *(US)* journaliste *f* qui se spécialise dans les histoires larmoyantes

sob story * N histoire *f* mélodramatique *or* larmoyante ◆ **the main item was a ~ story about a puppy** *(Press etc)* l'article principal était une histoire à vous fendre le cœur concernant un chiot ◆ **he told us a ~ story about his sister's illness** il a cherché à nous apitoyer *or* à nous avoir au sentiment * en nous parlant de la maladie de sa sœur

sob stuff * N ◆ **there's too much ~ stuff in that film** il y a trop de sensiblerie *or* de mélo * dans ce film ◆ **he gave us a lot of ~ stuff** il nous a fait tout un baratin * larmoyant

► **sob out** VT SEP *[+ story]* raconter en sanglotant ◆ **to ~ one's heart out** pleurer à chaudes larmes *or* à gros sanglots

s.o.b. ⁑ /ˌesəʊˈbiː/ N *(US)* (abbrev of **son of a bitch**) salaud ⁑ *m*

sobbing /ˈsɒbɪŋ/ N sanglots *mpl* ADJ sanglotant

sober /ˈsəʊbəʳ/ ADJ [1] *(= not drunk)* pas ivre *or* soûl ; *(= sobered-up)* dessoûlé * ◆ **I'm perfectly ~** je ne suis pas du tout soûl ◆ **he's stone cold ~, he's (as) ~ as a judge** * il n'est pas du tout soûl ◆ **are you ~ yet?** tu as dessoûlé ?

[2] *(= abstinent)* sobre ◆ **she has been ~ now for three years** cela fait maintenant trois ans qu'elle ne boit plus *or* qu'elle est sobre

[3] *(= serious) [person, attitude]* pondéré ; *[expression]* grave ; *[assessment, statement, judgement]* mesuré ; *[fact, reality]* sans fard ◆ **upon ~ reflection** après mûre réflexion

[4] *(= plain) [suit, tie, colour, style]* sobre

VT [1] *(fig: also* **sober up***) (= calm)* calmer ; *(= deflate)* dégriser

[2] (also **sober up**) *(= stop being drunk)* dessoûler *, désenivrer

COMP **sober-headed** ADJ *[person]* sérieux, posé ; *[decision]* réfléchi, posé

sober-minded ADJ sérieux, sensé

sober-sided ADJ sérieux, grave, qui ne rit pas souvent

► **sober up** VI dessoûler *, désenivrer

VT SEP ⇒ **sober vt**

sobering /ˈsəʊbərɪŋ/ ADJ *(fig) [experience]* qui fait réfléchir ◆ **a ~ reminder of sth** un brusque rappel à la réalité de qch ◆ **it is a ~ thought** cela fait réfléchir ◆ **it had a ~ effect on him** cela l'a fait réfléchir

soberly /ˈsəʊbəlɪ/ ADV [1] *(= seriously) [speak, behave]* avec pondération [2] *(= plainly) [dress]* sobrement, avec sobriété

soberness /ˈsəʊbənɪs/ N [1] *(= seriousness)* pondération *f*, sérieux *m* [2] *(= plainness) [of style, design]* sobriété *f*

sobersides* /ˈsəʊbəsaɪdz/ N bonnet *m* de nuit *(fig)*

sobriety /səʊˈbraɪətɪ/ N ① ⇒ **soberness** ② *(= abstinence)* ◆ **the struggle for ~** la lutte constante pour rester sobre ◆ **she maintained her ~ for seven years** elle a réussi à rester sobre pendant sept ans ◆ **his ~ was in question** *(frm or hum)* on le soupçonnait d'avoir bu

sobriquet /ˈsəʊbrɪkeɪ/ N sobriquet *m*

soc. /sɒk/ N abbrev of **society**

soccer /ˈsɒkəʳ/ N football *m*, foot* *m*
COMP *[match, pitch, team]* de football, de foot*
soccer player N footballeur *m*
soccer season N saison *f* de football *or* de foot*

sociability /ˌsəʊʃəˈbɪlɪtɪ/ N sociabilité *f*

sociable /ˈsəʊʃəbl/ ADJ *[person, mood]* sociable ◆ **I'll have a drink just to be ~** je vais prendre un verre juste pour vous *(or lui etc)* faire plaisir ◆ **I'm not feeling very ~ this evening** je n'ai pas envie de voir des gens ce soir

sociably /ˈsəʊʃəblɪ/ ADV *[behave]* de façon sociable, aimablement ; *[invite, say]* amicalement

social /ˈsəʊʃəl/ ADJ ① *[class, status, problem, customs]* social ◆ **she's a ~ acquaintance** c'est une relation (personnelle) ◆ **~ event** *or* **activity** activité *f* socioculturelle ◆ **we work together but we don't have a ~ relationship** nous travaillons ensemble mais nous ne nous voyons pas en dehors du travail ◆ **he has little ~ contact with his business colleagues** il a peu de contacts avec ses collègues en dehors du travail ◆ **this isn't a ~ visit** *or* **call** il ne s'agit pas d'une visite de courtoisie ◆ **she didn't regard him as her ~ equal** pour elle, il n'appartenait pas au même milieu social ◆ **~ mobility** mobilité *f* sociale ◆ **upward ~ mobility** ascension *f* sociale ◆ **~ research** recherches *fpl* en sciences sociales ◆ **~ scale** échelle *f* sociale ; see also **comp**
② *[insect, animal]* social ◆ **man is a ~ animal** l'homme est un animal social *or* sociable ; see also **comp**
N *(= party)* (petite) fête *f*
COMP **social administration** N gestion *f* sociale
Social and Liberal Democrats N *(Brit Pol)* parti *m* social et libéral-démocrate
social anthropologist N spécialiste *mf* de l'anthropologie sociale
social anthropology N anthropologie *f* sociale
social benefits NPL prestations *fpl* sociales
Social Charter N *(Brit Pol)* charte *f* sociale
social circle N sphère *f* de la société
social climber N *(still climbing)* arriviste *mf* ; *(arrived)* parvenu(e) *m(f)*
social climbing N arrivisme *m*
social-climbing ADJ *[wife]* arriviste
social club N club *m (de rencontres)*
social column N *(Press)* carnet *m* mondain, mondanités *fpl*
social conscience N conscience *f* sociale
social contract N contrat *m* social
Social Democracy N social-démocratie *f*
Social Democrat N social-démocrate *mf*
Social Democratic ADJ social-démocrate
Social Democratic and Labour Party N *(Ir Pol)* parti *m* social-démocrate et travailliste
Social Democratic Party N *(Brit Pol: formerly)* parti *m* social-démocrate
social disease N *(gen)* maladie *f* due à des facteurs socioéconomiques ; *(venereal)* maladie *f* honteuse
social drinker N ◆ **to be a ~ drinker** boire seulement en compagnie
social drinking N fait *m* de boire seulement en compagnie
social engineering N manipulation *f* des structures sociales
social evening N soirée *f (entre amis)*
social exclusion N exclusion *f* sociale
social fund N *(Brit)* ≃ fonds *m* de solidarité
social gathering N réunion *f* entre amis
social history N histoire *f* sociale
social housing N *(NonC: Brit)* logements *mpl* sociaux
social inclusion N inclusion *f* sociale
social insurance N *(US)* sécurité *f* sociale
social life N ◆ **to have an active ~ life** *(= go out frequently)* sortir beaucoup ; *(= see people frequently)* voir du monde ; *(in high society)* avoir une vie mondaine active
social misfit N inadapté(e) *m(f)* social(e)
social order N ordre *m* social
social realism N ① réalisme *m* social ② ⇒ **socialist realism** ; → **socialist**
the social register N *(US)* ≃ le bottin ® mondain
social science N sciences *fpl* humaines ◆ **Faculty of Social Science** *(Univ)* faculté *f* des sciences humaines
social scientist N spécialiste *mf* des sciences humaines
social secretary N *[of organization]* responsable *mf* des programmes de loisirs ; *[of person]* secrétaire *mf* particulier (-ière)
social security N *(gen)* aide *f* sociale ; (also **social security benefits**) prestations *fpl* sociales ◆ **to be on ~ security** recevoir l'aide sociale ◆ **Department of Social Security** *(Brit)* ≃ Sécurité *f* sociale
Social Security Administration N *(US) service des pensions*
social security card N *(US)* ≃ carte *f* d'assuré social
social security number N *(US)* numéro *m* de Sécurité sociale
social service N ⇒ **social work**
social services NPL services *mpl* sociaux ◆ **Secretary of State for/Department of Social Services** ministre *m*/ministère *m* des Affaires sociales
social skills NPL savoir-vivre *m inv* ◆ **he's got no ~ skills** il ne sait pas se comporter en société ◆ **poor ~ skills** manque *m* de savoir-vivre ◆ **to develop one's ~ skills** améliorer son comportement en société
social spending N dépenses *fpl* d'aide sociale
social studies NPL sciences *fpl* sociales
social welfare N sécurité *f* sociale
social work N assistance *f* sociale
social worker N assistant(e) *m(f)* social(e), travailleur *m*, -euse *f* social(e)

SOCIAL SECURITY NUMBER

Aux États-Unis, le numéro de Sécurité sociale, formé de neuf chiffres, est indispensable pour bénéficier des prestations sociales, mais il est également utilisé de plus en plus comme numéro d'identité à l'échelle nationale : il figure sur les carnets de chèques ; certains États l'utilisent comme numéro de permis de conduire et certaines universités comme numéro d'inscription des étudiants. Depuis 1987, tous les enfants se voient attribuer un **social security number**.

socialism /ˈsəʊʃəlɪzəm/ N socialisme *m*

socialist /ˈsəʊʃəlɪst/ ADJ socialiste ◆ **the Socialist Republic of ...** la République socialiste de ... N socialiste *mf*
COMP **socialist realism** N réalisme *m* socialiste
Socialist Workers' Party N *(in Brit) parti d'extrême gauche*

socialistic /ˌsəʊʃəˈlɪstɪk/ ADJ socialisant

socialite /ˈsəʊʃəlaɪt/ N mondain(e) *m(f)* ◆ **a Paris ~** un membre du Tout-Paris

sociality /ˌsəʊʃɪˈælɪtɪ/ N socialité *f*, sociabilité *f*

socialization /ˌsəʊʃəlaɪˈzeɪʃən/ N socialisation *f (Pol)*

socialize /ˈsəʊʃəlaɪz/ VT *(Pol, Psych)* socialiser VI *(= be with people)* fréquenter des gens ; *(= make friends)* se faire des amis ; *(= chat)* s'entretenir, bavarder *(with sb* avec qn)

socializing /ˈsəʊʃəlaɪzɪŋ/ N ◆ **he doesn't like ~** il n'aime pas fréquenter les gens ◆ **there isn't much ~ on campus** on ne se fréquente pas beaucoup sur le campus

socially /ˈsəʊʃəlɪ/ ADV ① *(= not professionally etc) [meet, interact]* en société ◆ **I don't really mix with him ~** je ne le fréquente guère (en dehors du travail) ◆ **to know sb ~** fréquenter qn en dehors du travail ② *[disadvantaged, acceptable, conservative]* socialement ◆ **~ prominent** en vue dans la société ◆ **~ superior/inferior** d'un rang social supérieur/inférieur ◆ **to be ~ aware** *or* **conscious** avoir conscience des problèmes sociaux ◆ **~ adept** qui sait se comporter en société ◆ **to be ~ inadequate** être un(e) inadapté(e) social(e) ◆ **to be ~ conditioned to do sth** être conditionné par son milieu social à faire qch COMP **socially excluded** ADJ exclu de la société N ◆ **the ~ excluded** les exclus de la société

societal /səˈsaɪətl/ ADJ sociétal

society /səˈsaɪətɪ/ N ① *(= social community)* société *f* ◆ **to live in ~** vivre en société ◆ **for the good of ~** dans l'intérêt de la société *or* de la communauté ◆ **it is a danger to ~** cela constitue un danger social, cela met la société en danger ◆ **modern industrial societies** les sociétés *fpl* industrielles modernes
② *(NonC = high society)* (haute) société *f*, grand monde *m* ◆ **polite ~** la bonne société ◆ **the years she spent in ~** ses années de vie mondaine
③ *(NonC = company, companionship)* société *f*, compagnie *f* ◆ **in the ~ of ...** dans la société de ..., en compagnie de ... ◆ **I enjoy his ~** je me plais en sa compagnie, j'apprécie sa compagnie
④ *(= organized group)* société *f*, association *f* ; *(= charitable society)* œuvre *f* de charité, association *f* de bienfaisance ; *(Scol, Univ etc)* club *m*, association *f* ◆ **dramatic ~** club *m* théâtral, association *f* théâtrale ◆ **learned ~** société *f* savante ◆ **the Society of Friends** *(Rel)* la Société des Amis, les Quakers *mpl* ◆ **the Society of Jesus** *(Rel)* la Société de Jésus ; → **royal**
COMP *[correspondent, news, photographer, wedding]* mondain, de la haute société
society column N *(Press)* chronique *f* mondaine, carnet *m* mondain

socio... /ˈsəʊsɪəʊ/ PREF socio... ◆ **sociocultural** socioculturel ◆ **socioeconomic** socioéconomique ◆ **sociopolitical** sociopolitique ; see also **sociological**

sociobiology /ˌsəʊsɪəʊbaɪˈɒlədʒɪ/ N sociobiologie *f*

sociolect /ˈsəʊsɪəʊˌlekt/ N *(Ling)* sociolecte *m*

sociolinguistic /ˌsəʊsɪəʊlɪŋˈgwɪstɪk/ ADJ sociolinguistique

sociolinguistics /ˌsəʊsɪəʊlɪŋˈgwɪstɪks/ N *(NonC)* sociolinguistique *f*

sociological /ˌsəʊsɪəˈlɒdʒɪkəl/ ADJ sociologique

sociologically /ˌsəʊsɪəˈlɒdʒɪkəlɪ/ ADV *[important, significant]* sociologiquement

sociologist /ˌsəʊsɪˈɒlədʒɪst/ N sociologue *mf*

sociology /ˌsəʊsɪˈɒlədʒɪ/ N sociologie *f*

sociometry /ˌsəʊsɪˈɒmɪtrɪ/ N sociométrie *f*

sociopath /ˈsəʊsɪəʊpæθ/ N inadapté(e) *m(f)* social(e)

sociopathic /ˌsəʊsɪəʊˈpæθɪk/ ADJ socialement inadapté, sociopathe

sock¹ /sɒk/ N ① *(= short stocking)* chaussette *f* ; *(shorter)* socquette *f* ; *(= inner sole)* semelle *f* (intérieure) ; *[of footballer etc]* bas *m* ◆ **to pull one's ~s up** * *(fig Brit)* se secouer*, faire un effort

◆ **put a ~ in it!**‡ la ferme !‡, ta gueule !‡ ◆ **this will knock** *or* **blow your ~s off!** * ça va t'en mettre plein la vue ! * ◆ **it knocks the ~s off most science fiction films** * ça dame le pion à la plupart des films de science-fiction ◆ **to work one's ~s off** * s'éreinter (au travail) ◆ **to dance/act one's ~s off** * se défoncer* en dansant/jouant, danser/jouer en se donnant à fond [2] *(= windsock)* manche *f* à air

sock² * /sɒk/ N *(= slap)* beigne* *f* ; *(= punch)* gnon* *m* ◆ **to give sb a ~ on the jaw** flanquer un coup *or* son poing sur la gueule‡ à qn VT *(= strike)* flanquer une beigne‡ *or* un gnon‡ à ◆ **~ him one!** cogne dessus ! *, fous-lui une beigne !‡ ◆ **~ it to me!** vas-y envoie ! * ◆ **~ it to them!** montre-leur un peu !

sockdolager * /sɒk'dɒlədʒəʳ/ N (US) [1] *(= decisive event)* coup *m* décisif [2] *(= great person/thing)* personne *f*/chose *f* fantastique

socket /'sɒkɪt/ N *(gen)* cavité *f*, trou *m* *(où qch s'emboîte)* ; *[of hipbone]* cavité *f* articulaire ; *[of eye]* orbite *f* ; *[of tooth]* alvéole *f* ; *(Elec: for light bulb)* douille *f* ; *(Elec:* also **wall socket**) prise *f* de courant, prise *f* femelle ; *(Carpentry)* mortaise *f* ; *(in candlestick etc)* trou *m* ◆ **to pull sb's arm out of its ~** désarticuler *or* démettre l'épaule à qn
COMP **socket joint** N *(Tech)* joint *m* à rotule ; *(Anat)* énarthrose *f*
socket wrench N clé *f* à pipe *or* à douille

socko * /'sɒkəʊ/ (US) ADJ fantastique, du tonnerre

Socrates /'sɒkrətiːz/ N Socrate *m*

Socratic /sɒ'krætɪk/ ADJ socratique ◆ **~ irony** ironie *f* socratique ◆ **the ~ method** la maïeutique

sod¹ /sɒd/ N *(NonC: = turf)* gazon *m* ; *(= piece of turf)* motte *f* (de gazon)

sod² **/sɒd/ (Brit) N con** *m*, couillon** *m* ; *(pej)* salaud‡ *m*, salopard‡ *m* ◆ **the poor ~s who tried** les pauvres couillons** *or* bougres* qui ont essayé ◆ **poor little ~!** pauvre petit bonhomme ! ◆ **he's a real ~** c'est un salaud‡ *or* un salopard‡ ◆ **~ all** que dalle‡ VT ◆ **~ it !** merde (alors) !** ◆ **~ him!** il m'emmerde !**, qu'il aille se faire foutre !** COMP **Sod's Law** * N *(Brit)* loi *f* de l'emmerdement‡ maximum ◆ **that's Sod's Law** un emmerdement‡ n'arrive jamais seul

► **sod off** ** VI foutre le camp‡ ◆ **~ off!** fous le camp !‡, va te faire foutre !**

soda /'səʊdə/ N [1] *(Chem)* soude *f* ; (also **washing soda, soda crystals**) cristaux *mpl* de soude ; → **baking, caustic** [2] (also **soda water**) eau *f* de Seltz ◆ **whisky and ~** whisky *m* soda *or* à l'eau de Seltz ; → **club, ice** [3] *(US:* also **soda pop**) boisson *f* gazeuse *(sucrée)*
COMP **soda ash** N *(Chem)* soude *f* du commerce
soda biscuit N *(US)* petit gâteau *m* à la levure chimique
soda bread N pain *m* à la levure chimique
soda cracker N *(US)* gâteau *m* sec à la levure chimique
soda crystals NPL cristaux *mpl* de soude
soda fountain N *(US)* *(= siphon)* siphon *m* d'eau de Seltz ; *(= place)* buvette *f*
soda jerk(er) N *(US)* serveur *m*, -euse *f* *(dans une buvette)*
soda pop N *(US)* soda *m*
soda siphon N siphon *m* (d'eau de Seltz)
soda water N eau *f* de Seltz

sodality /səʊ'dælɪtɪ/ N camaraderie *f* ; *(= association, also Rel)* confrérie *f*

sodden /'sɒdn/ ADJ *[ground]* détrempé ; *[clothes, paper]* trempé *(with* de) ◆ **~ with drink, drink-~** abruti par l'alcool

sodding **/'sɒdɪŋ/ (Brit) ADJ ◆ **her ~ dog** son foutu chien‡, son putain de chien** ◆ **shut the ~ door!** ferme cette putain de porte !** ◆ **it's a ~ disgrace!** c'est une honte, nom de Dieu !‡ ◆ **~ hell!** bordel de merde !**
ADV ◆ **it's ~ difficult** c'est foutrement‡ difficile ◆ **he's ~ crazy!** il déconne‡ complètement !

sodium /'səʊdɪəm/ N sodium *m*
COMP **sodium bicarbonate** N bicarbonate *m* de soude
sodium carbonate N carbonate *m* de sodium
sodium chloride N chlorure *m* de sodium
sodium light N lampe *f* (à vapeur) de sodium
sodium nitrate N nitrate *m* de soude
sodium sulphate N sulfate *m* de soude
sodium-vapor lamp N *(US)* ⇒ **sodium light**

Sodom /'sɒdəm/ N Sodome

sodomite /'sɒdəmaɪt/ N sodomite *m*

sodomize /'sɒdəmaɪz/ VT sodomiser

sodomy /'sɒdəmɪ/ N sodomie *f*

sofa /'səʊfə/ N sofa *m*, canapé *m* COMP **sofa bed** N canapé-lit *m*

Sofia /'səʊfɪə/ N Sofia

soft /sɒft/ ADJ [1] *(= not hard) [ground, snow, butter, penis]* mou (molle *f*) ; *[fabric, skin, hand, breasts, body]* doux (douce *f*) ; *[food, bread, fruit, pencil, wood]* tendre ; *[bed, carpet, texture]* moelleux ; *[fur, hair, beard]* soyeux ; *[brush, toothbrush]* doux (douce *f*), souple ; *[leather]* souple ◆ **as ~ as silk** *or* **velvet** doux comme (de) la soie ◆ **to get** *or* **become ~(er)** *[ground, pitch]* devenir mou ; *[butter]* se ramollir ; *[leather]* s'assouplir ; *[skin]* s'adoucir ◆ **to make ~(er)** *[+ leather]* assouplir ; *[+ skin]* adoucir ◆ **to go ~** *[onions, biscuits]* ramollir ; see also **comp** ; → **roe², soap, solder**

[2] *(= gentle, not intense) [breeze, wind, kiss, light, colour]* doux (douce *f*) ; *[rain, touch, tap]* léger ; *[accent]* mélodieux ; *[lighting]* doux (douce *f*), tamisé

[3] *(= quiet) [sound, voice, laugh, music]* doux (douce *f*) ◆ **the music is too ~** la musique n'est pas assez forte, on n'entend pas assez la musique

[4] *(in shape) [outline, lines]* doux (douce *f*) ; *[pleat, fold]* souple

[5] *(pej = unfit) [person, body, muscles]* mou (molle *f*) ◆ **this sort of life makes you ~** ce genre de vie vous ramollit ◆ **to get** *or* **go ~** *[body]* s'avachir ; *[muscles]* se ramollir

[6] *(= kind) [person]* doux (douce *f*) ◆ **she had another, ~er side to her** il y avait une autre facette, plus douce, de sa personnalité ◆ **to have a ~ heart** avoir le cœur tendre

[7] *(pej) (= lenient) [person]* indulgent ; *[sentence]* léger ◆ **to get ~** *[person]* devenir trop indulgent *or* trop bon ◆ **to be (too) ~ on sb** être trop indulgent envers qn ◆ **to be (too) ~ on sth** *[+ crime, drugs]* être trop laxiste en matière de qch ◆ **to go ~ (on sth)** devenir plus laxiste (en matière de qch) ◆ **to have a ~ spot for sb/sth** avoir un faible pour qn/qch ◆ **to be a ~ touch** * être une (bonne) poire *

[8] *(= moderate) [approach]* modéré ◆ **to take a ~ line (on sth)** adopter une ligne modérée (en matière de qch) ◆ **the ~ left** *(Pol)* la gauche modérée

[9] *(* = easy) [life, job]* pépère*, peinard* ◆ **to take the ~ option** choisir la solution de facilité

[10] *(* = stupid)* débile* ◆ **to be ~ in the head** *(= stupid)* avoir le cerveau ramolli* ; *(= mad)* avoir perdu la boule* ; *(= senile)* être gâteux

[11] ◆ **to be ~ on sb** †* *(= attracted to)* avoir le béguin †* pour qn

[12] *[water]* non calcaire, doux

[13] *(Ling) [consonant]* doux (douce *f*)

[14] *(Econ, Fin, Stock Exchange) [prices, stocks, market]* mou (molle *f*), qui tend à la baisse ; *[economy]* amorphe ; *[currency]* faible ◆ **sales are ~** les ventes ne marchent pas très fort ◆ **~ loan** prêt *m* à taux bonifié

ADV [1] *(liter = quietly)* doucement

[2] *(= stupidly)* ◆ **don't talk ~ !** * tu dis n'importe quoi !

EXCL †† *(= wait)* un instant ! ; *(= be quiet)* silence !

COMP **soft-boiled egg** N œuf *m* à la coque
soft-bound book N livre *m* broché ; *(= paperback)* livre *m* de poche
soft brown sugar N sucre *m* roux
soft centre N *(Brit)* chocolat *m* fourré
soft-centred ADJ *(Brit)* [1] *[chocolate, boiled sweet]* fourré [2] *[person]* tendre sous des dehors austères ; *[comedy]* à l'eau de rose
soft cheese N fromage *m* à pâte molle
soft contact lens N lentille *f* (de contact) souple
soft copy N *(Comput)* visualisation *f* sur écran
soft-core ADJ *[pornography]* soft* *inv*
soft-cover ADJ → **softback**
soft currency N *(Fin)* devise *f* faible
soft drinks NPL boissons *fpl* non alcoolisées
soft drugs NPL drogues *fpl* douces
soft focus N flou *m* artistique
soft-focus ADJ *[image, picture]* (artistiquement) flou ◆ **~-focus filter** filtre *m* pour flou artistique ◆ **~-focus lens** objectif *m* pour flou artistique
soft-footed ADJ à la démarche légère, qui marche à pas feutrés *or* sans faire de bruit
soft fruit N *(Brit)* baies *fpl* comestibles, ≃ fruits *mpl* rouges
soft furnishings NPL *(Brit)* tissus *mpl* d'ameublement *(rideaux, tentures, housses etc)*
soft goods NPL *(Brit)* textiles *mpl*, tissus *mpl*
soft hat N chapeau *m* mou
soft-headed * ADJ faible d'esprit, cinglé‡
soft-hearted ADJ au cœur tendre, compatissant
soft ice-cream N glace *f* à l'italienne
soft iron N fer *m* doux
soft landing N *(lit, fig)* atterrissage *m* en douceur
soft margarine N pâte *f* à tartiner
soft palate N *(Anat)* voile *m* du palais
soft pedal N *(Mus)* pédale *f* douce
soft-pedal VI *(Mus, also fig)* mettre la pédale douce VT *(esp US = play down)* ◆ **they seem to be ~-pedalling the issue** ils semblent vouloir minimiser l'importance de la question ◆ **I would advise you to ~-pedal your over-assertive tactics** je vous conseille de mettre un bémol à vos tactiques, qui sont trop péremptoires ◆ **the government is now ~-pedalling on its previous promise** le gouvernement est en train de revenir sur sa promesse
soft pencil N crayon *m* à mine grasse
soft porn N soft porn *m*
soft sell N *(Comm)* technique *f* (de vente) non agressive ◆ **he's a master of the ~ sell** *(fig)* il est maître dans l'art de persuader les clients en douceur
soft-shelled ADJ *[egg, mollusc]* à coquille molle ; *[crustacean, turtle]* à carapace molle
soft shoulder N *[road]* accotement *m* non stabilisé
soft skills NPL compétences *fpl* relationnelles
soft soap N *(lit)* savon *m* vert ; *(* fig pej = flattery)* flatterie *f*
soft-soap * VT *(fig pej)* caresser dans le sens du poil*, passer de la pommade à
soft-spoken ADJ à la voix douce
soft steel N acier *m* doux
soft target N cible *f* facile
soft toilet paper N papier *m* hygiénique doux
soft top N *(= car)* décapotable *f*
soft toy N (jouet *m* en) peluche *f*
soft verge N *(on road)* accotement *m* non stabilisé
soft X-rays NPL rayons *mpl* X diffus

softback /'sɒftbæk/ N livre *m* broché ; *(= paperback)* livre *m* de poche

softball /'sɒftbɔːl/ N *(US)* sorte de base-ball, softball *m*

soften /'sɒfn/ VT *[+ butter, clay, ground, pitch]* (r)amollir ; *[+ collar, leather]* assouplir ; *[+ skin, colour, outline]* adoucir ; *[+ sound]* adoucir, atténuer ; *[+ lights, lighting]* adoucir, tamiser ; *[+ pain, anxiety]* atténuer ; *[+ sb's anger, reaction, effect, impression]* adoucir, atténuer ; *[+ resistance]* amoindrir, réduire ◆ **to ~ the blow** *(fig)* adoucir *or* amortir le choc

VI *[butter, clay, ground, pitch]* devenir mou (molle *f*), se ramollir ; *[collar, leather]* s'assouplir ; *[skin]* s'adoucir ; *[colour]* s'adoucir, s'atténuer ; *[sb's anger]* s'atténuer ◆ **his heart ~ed at the sight of her** il s'attendrit en la voyant ◆ **his eyes ~ed as he looked at her** son regard s'est adouci à sa vue

▸ **soften up** VI *[butter, clay, ground, pitch]* devenir mou, se ramollir ; *[collar, leather]* s'assouplir ; *[skin]* s'adoucir ; *(= grow less stern)* s'adoucir ◆ **we must not ~ up towards** *or* **on these offenders** nous ne devons pas faire preuve d'indulgence envers ces délinquants

VT SEP ① *[+ butter, clay, pitch, ground]* (r)amollir ; *[+ collar, leather]* assouplir ; *[+ skin]* adoucir

② *[+ person]* attendrir ; *(*: by cajoling) [+ customer etc]* bonimenter*, baratiner* ; *(*: by bullying)* intimider, malmener ; *[+ resistance, opposition]* réduire ; *(Mil: by bombing etc)* affaiblir par bombardement intensif

softener /'sɒfnəʳ/ N (also **water softener**) adoucisseur *m* ; (also **fabric softener**) produit *m* assouplissant

softening /'sɒfnɪŋ/ N ① *[of leather]* assouplissement *m* ; *[of skin]* adoucissement *m* ② *(Med)* ◆ **~ of the brain** ramollissement *m* cérébral ③ *(= moderating) [of attitude, position, policy]* assouplissement *m* ④ *(Ling) [of consonant]* adoucissement *m*

softie* /'sɒftɪ/ N *(too tender-hearted)* tendre *mf* ; *(no stamina etc)* mauviette *f*, mollasson(ne) *m(f)* ; *(= coward)* poule *f* mouillée, dégonflé(e)* *m(f)* ◆ **you silly ~, stop crying!** ne pleure plus, grand(e) nigaud(e) !

softly /'sɒftlɪ/ ADV ① *(= quietly) [say, call, sing, whistle]* doucement ; *[swear]* à voix basse ; *[walk]* à pas feutrés ◆ **a ~ spoken man** un homme à la voix douce ◆ **~, ~, catchee monkey*** vas-y mollo* ② *(= gently) [touch, tap]* légèrement ; *[kiss]* tendrement ③ *(= not brightly) [shine, glow, gleam]* faiblement ◆ **~ lit** à la lumière tamisée COMP **softly-softly** ADJ précautionneux ◆ **he adopted a ~-~ approach** il a pris beaucoup de précautions

softness /'sɒftnɪs/ N ① *[of ground, snow, butter]* mollesse *f* ; *[of fabric, skin, hand, breasts, body]* douceur *f* ; *[of bread, wood, fruit]* tendreté *f* ; *[of bed, carpet]* moelleux *m* ; *[of fur, hair, beard]* soyeux *m* ; *[of brush, toothbrush, leather]* souplesse *f* ◆ **the ~ of its consistency** sa consistance moelleuse

② *(= gentleness) [of breeze, wind, kiss]* douceur *f* ; *[of rain, touch, tap]* légèreté *f*

③ *(= lack of brightness) [of light, lighting, colour]* douceur *f*

④ *(= quietness) [of sound, accent, laugh, music]* douceur *f*

⑤ *(in shape) [of outline, lines]* douceur *f* ; *[of pleat, fold]* souplesse *f*

⑥ *(pej = unfitness) [of person, body, muscles]* mollesse *f*

⑦ *(= leniency) [of person]* indulgence *f* ; *[of sentence]* légèreté *f*

⑧ *(= moderation) [of approach, line]* modération *f*

⑨ *(* = easiness) [of life, job]* tranquillité *f*

⑩ *(* = stupidity)* débilité *f* ◆ **~ in the head** *(= stupidity, madness)* débilité *f* ; *(= senility)* gâtisme *m*

⑪ *[of water]* douceur *f*

software /'sɒft,weəʳ/ *(Comput)* N *(NonC)* software* *m*, logiciel *m*

COMP **software engineer** N ingénieur-conseil *m* en informatique, ingénieur *m* (en) logiciel
software engineering N génie *m* logiciel
software house N société *f* de services et de conseils en informatique, SSCI *f*
software library N logithèque *f*
software package N progiciel *m*

softwood /'sɒftwʊd/ N bois *m* tendre

softy* /'sɒftɪ/ N ⇒ **softie**

soggy /'sɒgɪ/ ADJ *[clothes]* trempé ; *[ground]* détrempé ; *[vegetables, pasta]* trop cuit, ramolli ; *[bread]* pâteux, ramolli

soh /səʊ/ N *(Mus)* sol *m*

soil[1] /sɔɪl/ N sol *m*, terre *f* ◆ **rich/chalky ~** sol *m or* terre *f* riche/calcaire ◆ **cover it over with ~** recouvre-le de terre ◆ **a man of the ~** *(liter)* un terrien, un homme de la terre ◆ **my native ~** ma terre natale, mon pays natal ◆ **on French ~** sur le sol français, en territoire français

soil[2] /sɔɪl/ VT *(lit)* salir ; *(fig) [+ reputation, honour]* souiller *(frm)* ◆ **this dress is easily ~ed** cette robe se salit vite *or* est salissante ◆ **~ed linen** linge *m* sale ◆ **~ed copy/item** *(Comm)* exemplaire *m*/article *m* défraîchi ; → **shopsoiled** VI *[material, garment]* se salir, être salissant N *(= excrement)* excréments *mpl*, ordures *fpl* ; *(= sewage)* vidange *f* COMP **soil pipe** N tuyau *m* d'écoulement ; *(vertical)* tuyau *m* de descente

soirée /'swɑːreɪ/ N soirée *f*

sojourn /'sɒdʒɜːn/ *(liter)* N séjour *m* VI séjourner, faire un séjour

solace /'sɒlɪs/ *(liter)* N consolation *f*, réconfort *m* ◆ **to be a ~ to sb** être un réconfort pour qn VT *[+ person]* consoler ; *[+ pain]* soulager, adoucir ◆ **to ~ o.s.** se consoler

solanum /səʊ'leɪnəm/ N solanacée *f*

solar /'səʊləʳ/ ADJ solaire

COMP **solar battery** N batterie *f* solaire, photopile *f*
solar calendar N calendrier *m* solaire
solar cell N pile *f* solaire, photopile *f*
solar collector N capteur *m* solaire
solar eclipse N éclipse *f* de soleil
solar flare N facule *f* solaire
solar furnace N four *m* solaire
solar heating N chauffage *m* (à l'énergie) solaire
solar panel N panneau *m* solaire
solar plexus N *(Anat)* plexus *m* solaire
solar power N énergie *f* solaire
solar-powered ADJ (à énergie) solaire
solar system N système *m* solaire
solar wind N vent *m* solaire
solar year N année *f* solaire

solarium /səʊ'leərɪəm/ N (pl **solariums** *or* **solaria** /səʊ'leərɪə/) solarium *m*

sold /səʊld/ VB pt, ptp of **sell**

solder /'səʊldəʳ/ N soudure *f* ◆ **hard ~** brasure *f* ◆ **soft ~** claire soudure *f* VT souder COMP **soldering iron** N fer *m* à souder

soldier /'səʊldʒəʳ/ N ① soldat *m (also fig)*, militaire *m* ◆ **woman ~** femme *f* soldat ◆ **~s and civilians** (les) militaires *mpl* et (les) civils *mpl* ◆ **Montgomery was a great ~** Montgomery était un grand homme de guerre *or* un grand soldat ◆ **he wants to be a ~** il veut être soldat *or* entrer dans l'armée ◆ **to play (at) ~s** *(pej)* jouer à la guerre ; *[children]* jouer aux (petits) soldats ◆ **~ of fortune** soldat *m* de fortune, mercenaire *m* ◆ **old ~** vétéran *m* ; → **foot, private**

② *(Brit * = finger of bread or toast)* mouillette *f*

VI servir dans l'armée, être soldat ◆ **he ~ed for ten years in the East** il a servi (dans l'armée) pendant dix ans en Orient ◆ **after six years' ~ing** après six ans de service dans l'armée ◆ **to be tired of ~ing** en avoir assez d'être soldat *or* d'être dans l'armée

COMP **soldier ant** N (fourmi *f*) soldat *m*

▸ **soldier on** VI *(Brit fig)* persévérer (malgré tout)

soldierly /'səʊldʒəlɪ/ ADJ *[values, bravery, discipline]* de soldat ; *[person]* à l'allure militaire

soldiery /'səʊldʒərɪ/ N *(collective)* soldats *mpl*, militaires *mpl*

sole[1] /səʊl/ N (pl **sole** *or* **soles**) *(= fish)* sole *f* ; → **Dover, lemon**

sole[2] /səʊl/ N *[of shoe, sock, stocking]* semelle *f* ; *[of foot]* plante *f* ; → **inner** VT ressemeler ◆ **to have one's shoes ~d** faire ressemeler ses chaussures ◆ **crepe-/rubber-/leather-~d** avec semelles de crêpe/caoutchouc/cuir

sole[3] /səʊl/ ADJ ① *(= only, single)* unique, seul ◆ **for the ~ purpose of ...** dans l'unique *or* le seul but de ... ◆ **the ~ reason** la seule *or* l'unique raison ◆ **their ~ surviving daughter** la seule de leurs filles qui soit encore en vie

② *(= exclusive) [right, possession]* exclusif ; *[responsibility]* entier ; *[heir]* universel ; *[owner]* unique ◆ **for the ~ use of ...** à l'usage exclusif de ... ◆ **to have ~ ownership of sth** être l'unique propriétaire de qch ◆ **~ supplier** *(Comm)* fournisseur *m* exclusif

COMP **sole agent** N *(Comm)* concessionnaire *mf* exclusif(-ive), dépositaire *mf* exclusif(-ive) ◆ **~ agent for Australia/for Collins dictionaries** distributeur *m* exclusif en Australie/des dictionnaires Collins
sole beneficiary N *(Jur)* légataire *m* universel
sole legatee N *(Jur)* légataire *mf* universel(le)
sole stockholder N unique actionnaire *mf*
sole trader N *(Comm)* gérant *m or* propriétaire *m* unique

solecism /'sɒləsɪzəm/ N *(Ling)* solécisme *m* ; *(= social offence)* manque *m* de savoir-vivre, faute *f* de goût

solei /'sɒlɪaɪ/ NPL of **soleus**

solely /'səʊllɪ/ ADV uniquement ◆ **to be ~ responsible for sth** être seul(e) responsable de qch ◆ **I am ~ to blame** je suis seul coupable, c'est entièrement de ma faute

solemn /'sɒləm/ ADJ *[mood, occasion, promise, music, warning]* solennel ; *[silence]* plein de solennité *or* de gravité ; *[face, expression]* grave ; *[person]* grave, solennel ◆ **it is my ~ duty to inform you that ...** il est de mon devoir de vous informer que ... *(frm)*

solemnity /sə'lemnɪtɪ/ N ① *(NonC = solemnness) [of person, tone, occasion, music]* solennité *f* ② *(= occasion)* solennité *f* ◆ **the solemnities** les solennités *fpl*

solemnization /'sɒləmnaɪ'zeɪʃən/ N *[of marriage]* célébration *f*

solemnize /'sɒləmnaɪz/ VT *[+ marriage]* célébrer ; *[+ occasion, event]* solenniser

solemnly /'sɒləmlɪ/ ADV *[swear, promise, utter]* solennellement ; *[say]* gravement, d'un ton solennel ; *[smile, nod, look at]* gravement

solenoid /'səʊlənɔɪd/ N *(Elec)* solénoïde *m*

soleus /'sɒlɪəs/ N (pl **solei**) muscle *m* soléaire

sol-fa /'sɒl'fɑː/ N (also **tonic sol-fa**) solfège *m*

soli /'səʊliː/ NPL of **solo**

solicit /sə'lɪsɪt/ VT solliciter *(sb for sth, sth from sb* qch de qn) ; *[+ vote]* solliciter, briguer ; *[+ alms]* quémander VI *[prostitute]* racoler

solicitation /sə,lɪsɪ'teɪʃən/ N sollicitation *f*

soliciting /sə'lɪsɪtɪŋ/ N racolage *m*

solicitor /sə'lɪsɪtəʳ/ N ① *(Jur) (Brit) (for sales, wills)* ≃ notaire *m* ; *(in divorce, police, court cases)* ≃ avocat *m* ; → **LAWYER** *(US)* ≃ juriste *m* conseil *or* avocat *m* conseil attaché à une municipalité *etc* ② *(US) (for contribution)* solliciteur *m*, -euse *f* ; *(for trade)* courtier *m*, placier *m*

COMP **Solicitor General** N (pl **Solicitors General**) *(Brit)* adjoint *m* du procureur général ; *(US)* adjoint *m* du ministre de la Justice

solicitous /sə'lɪsɪtəs/ ADJ *(frm)* plein de sollicitude *(of sb* envers qn) ◆ **to be ~ of sb's interests/wishes** se soucier des intérêts/désirs de qn

solicitously /sə'lɪsɪtəslɪ/ ADV *(frm)* avec sollicitude

solicitude /sə'lɪsɪtjuːd/ N *(frm)* sollicitude *f*

solid /'sɒlɪd/ ADJ 1 *(= not liquid or gas)* solide ◆ **~ food** aliments *mpl* solides ◆ **to freeze ~** *(gen)* geler ; *[water, lake, pond, pipes]* geler ; *[oil]* se congeler ◆ **frozen ~** complètement gelé ◆ **to go** *or* **become ~** se solidifier ; see also **adv**

2 *(= not hollow or plated) [tyre, ball, block]* plein ; *[layer, mass]* compact ; *[rock, oak, mahogany, gold, silver]* massif ◆ **the chain is made of ~ gold** la chaîne est en or massif ◆ **the door is made of ~ steel** la porte est tout en acier ◆ **cut in** *or* **out of (the) ~ rock** taillé à même le roc *or* dans la masse ◆ **the garden was a ~ mass of colour** le jardin resplendissait d'une profusion de couleurs ◆ **the square was ~ with cars*** la place était complètement embouteillée ◆ **the room was ~ with people*** la pièce était noire de monde ; see also **comp**

3 *(= continuous) [row, line]* continu, ininterrompu ; *[rain]* ininterrompu ◆ **he was six foot six of ~ muscle** c'était un homme de deux mètres tout en muscles ◆ **I waited a ~ hour** j'ai attendu une heure entière ◆ **he slept 18 ~ hours** il a dormi 18 heures d'affilée ◆ **they worked for two ~ days** ils ont travaillé deux jours sans s'arrêter *or* sans relâche ◆ **it will take a ~ day's work** cela exigera une journée entière de travail ◆ **a rug like this would take three ~ weeks to make** un tapis comme celui-ci demande bien trois semaines de travail

4 *(= substantial, reliable) [building, bridge, structure, grip, basis, relationship, majority, evidence, reasons]* solide ; *[meal]* consistant ; *[scholarship, piece of work, character, advice]* sérieux ; *[support]* indéfectible, ferme ; *[gains]* substantiel ; *[information]* sûr ◆ **a ~ grounding in mathematics** des connaissances *or* des bases solides en mathématiques ◆ **a man of ~ build** un homme solidement *or* bien bâti ◆ **a ~ citizen** un bon citoyen ◆ **~ middle-class values** les bonnes valeurs *fpl* bourgeoises ◆ **the Solid South** *(US Pol, Hist) États du Sud des États-Unis qui, depuis la guerre de Sécession, votaient traditionnellement pour le parti démocrate* ◆ **(as) ~ as a rock** *(lit) [structure, substance]* dur comme la pierre ; *(fig) [person]* solide comme un roc ; *[relationship]* indestructible ; see also **rock²** ; → **ground¹**

5 *(US* ✱ *= excellent)* super*

ADV ◆ **jammed ~** complètement bloqué *or* coincé ◆ **rusted ~** bloqué par la rouille, complètement rouillé ◆ **he was stuck ~ in the mud** il était complètement enlisé dans la boue ◆ **packed ~ (with people)** noir de monde ◆ **to be booked ~ (for three weeks)** *[hotel, venue, performer]* être complet (pendant trois semaines) ◆ **he slept for 18 hours ~** il a dormi 18 heures d'affilée ◆ **they worked for two days ~** ils ont travaillé deux jours de suite sans s'arrêter *or* sans relâche

N *(gen, Chem, Math, Phys)* solide *m* ◆ **~s** *(= food)* aliments *mpl* solides

COMP **solid angle** N *(Math)* angle *m* solide
solid compound N *(Ling)* mot *m* composé
solid figure N *(Math)* solide *m*
solid fuel N *(= coal etc)* combustible *m* solide ; *(for rockets etc)* (also **solid propellant**) propergol *m* solide
solid-fuel heating N chauffage *m* central au charbon *or* à combustibles solides
solid geometry N *(Math)* géométrie *f* dans l'espace
solid propellant N ⇒ **solid fuel**
solid-state ADJ *[physics]* des solides ; *[electronic device]* à circuits intégrés
solid word N *(Ling)* mot *m* simple

solidarity /,sɒlɪ'dærɪtɪ/ N *(NonC)* solidarité *f* ◆ **~ strike** grève *f* de solidarité

solidi /'sɒlɪ,daɪ/ NPL of **solidus**

solidification /sə,lɪdɪfɪ'keɪʃən/ N *[of liquid, gas]* solidification *f* ; *[of oil]* congélation *f*

solidify /sə'lɪdɪfaɪ/ VT *[+ liquid, gas]* solidifier ; *[+ oil]* congeler VI se solidifier, se congeler

solidity /sə'lɪdɪtɪ/ N solidité *f*

solidly /'sɒlɪdlɪ/ ADV 1 *(= firmly) [made, constructed]* solidement ◆ **~ built** *[structure]* solidement construit ; *[person]* solidement *or* bien bâti ◆ **Russia was ~ under communist rule** le communisme exerçait fermement son emprise sur la Russie ◆ **the idea was ~ based on the best psychological theory** cette idée était solidement fondée sur la meilleure théorie psychologique 2 *(= continuously)* sans arrêt 3 *[vote]* massivement, en masse ◆ **to be ~ behind sb/sth** soutenir qn/qch sans réserve ◆ **a ~ middle-class area** un quartier tout ce qu'il y a de bourgeois ◆ **the district of Morningside is ~ Conservative** le quartier de Morningside est un bastion conservateur

solidus /'sɒlɪdəs/ N (pl **solidi**) *(Typ)* barre *f* oblique

soliloquize /sə'lɪləkwaɪz/ VI soliloquer, monologuer ◆ **"perhaps" he ~d** "peut-être" dit-il, se parlant à lui-même

soliloquy /sə'lɪləkwɪ/ N soliloque *m*, monologue *m*

solipsism /'səʊlɪpsɪzəm/ N solipsisme *m*

solitaire /,sɒlɪ'teəʳ/ N 1 *(= stone, board game)* solitaire *m* 2 *(US Cards)* réussite *f*, patience *f*

solitariness /'sɒlɪtərɪnɪs/ N *[of life, task]* solitude *f*

solitary /'sɒlɪtərɪ/ ADJ 1 *(= lone, lonely) [person, life, activity, childhood]* solitaire ; *[place]* solitaire, retiré ◆ **a ~ hour** une heure de solitude ◆ **a ~ journey** un voyage en solitaire ◆ **she ate a ~ dinner** elle a pris son dîner seule *or* en solitaire ◆ **in ~ splendour** dans un splendide isolement 2 *(= sole)* seul, unique ◆ **one ~ tourist** un seul *or* unique touriste ◆ **with the ~ exception of ...** à la seule *or* l'unique exception de ... ◆ **not a ~ one*** pas un seul N * ⇒ **solitary confinement** COMP **solitary confinement** N ◆ **(in) ~ confinement** *(Jur)* (en) isolement *m* cellulaire

solitude /'sɒlɪtjuːd/ N solitude *f* ◆ **in ~** dans la solitude

solo /'səʊləʊ/ (pl **solos** *or* **soli**) N 1 *(Mus)* solo *m* ◆ **piano ~** solo *m* de piano 2 *(Cards:* also **solo whist)** whist-solo *m* ADV *[play, sing]* en solo ; *[fly]* en solo, en solitaire ◆ **to go ~** voler de ses propres ailes ◆ **he left the band to go ~** il a quitté le groupe pour entamer une carrière (en) solo ADJ *[instrument, album, artist]* solo *inv* ; *[performance]* en solo ; *[voice]* seul ; *[flight, crossing, journey]* en solitaire ◆ **a ~ piece** *or* **passage** un solo ◆ **his ~ career** sa carrière (en) solo

soloist /'səʊləʊɪst/ N soliste *mf*

Solomon /'sɒləmən/ N Salomon *m* ◆ **the judgement of ~** le jugement de Salomon ; → **song** COMP **the Solomon Islands** NPL les îles *fpl* Salomon

solon /'səʊlən/ N *(US)* législateur *m*

solstice /'sɒlstɪs/ N solstice *m* ◆ **summer/winter ~** solstice *m* d'été/d'hiver

solubility /,sɒljʊ'bɪlɪtɪ/ N solubilité *f*

soluble /'sɒljʊbl/ ADJ *[substance]* soluble ; *[problem]* résoluble, soluble ; → **water**

solus /'səʊləs/ *(Advertising)* ADJ *[advertisement, site, position]* isolé N annonce *f* isolée

solution /sə'luːʃən/ LANGUAGE IN USE 1.2 N 1 *(to problem etc)* solution *f* (to de) 2 *(Chem) (= act)* solution *f*, dissolution *f* ; *(= liquid)* solution *f* ; *(Pharm)* solution *f*, soluté *m* ◆ **in ~** en solution ; → **rubber¹**

solvable /'sɒlvəbl/ ADJ soluble, résoluble

solve /sɒlv/ VT *[+ equation, difficulty, problem]* résoudre ; *[+ crossword puzzle]* réussir ; *[+ murder]* élucider, trouver l'auteur de ; *[+ mystery]* élucider ◆ **to ~ a riddle** trouver la solution d'une énigme *or* d'une devinette, trouver la clé d'une énigme ◆ **that question remains to be ~d** cette question est encore en suspens

solvency /'sɒlvənsɪ/ N solvabilité *f*

solvent /'sɒlvənt/ ADJ 1 *(Fin) [company, client]* solvable 2 * *[person]* qui a une bonne situation 3 *(Chem)* dissolvant N *(Chem)* solvant *m*, dissolvant *m* COMP **solvent abuse** N usage *m* de solvants

Solzhenitsyn /,sɒlʒə'nɪtsɪn/ N Soljenitsyne *m*

Som. abbrev of **Somerset**

soma /'səʊmə/ N (pl **somas** *or* **somata**) *(Physiol)* soma *m*

Somali /səʊ'mɑːlɪ/ ADJ somalien, somali ; *[ambassador, embassy]* de Somalie N 1 Somali(e) *m(f)*, Somalien(ne) *m(f)* 2 *(= language)* somali *m* 3 *(= cat)* somali *m*

Somalia /səʊ'mɑːlɪə/ N Somalie *f*

Somalian /səʊ'mɑːlɪən/ ADJ somalien, somali N Somalien(ne) *m(f)*, Somali(e) *m(f)*

Somaliland /səʊ'mɑːlɪlænd/ N Somaliland *m* ◆ **in ~** au Somaliland

somata /'səʊmətə/ NPL of **soma**

somatic /səʊ'mætɪk/ ADJ somatique

sombre, somber *(US)* /'sɒmbəʳ/ ADJ *[colour, clothes, mood, outlook, prediction, prospect]* sombre ; *[person, thoughts, expression, voice]* sombre, morne ; *[message, speech, news]* pessimiste ; *[day, weather]* morne, maussade ; *[atmosphere]* lugubre ◆ **on a ~ note** sur un ton pessimiste ◆ **to be in ~ mood** être d'humeur sombre ◆ **her face grew ~** son visage s'assombrit

sombrely, somberly *(US)* /'sɒmbəlɪ/ ADV *[say]* d'un ton morne ; *[look, nod]* d'un air sombre ◆ **~ dressed** habillé de sombre

sombreness, somberness *(US)* /'sɒmbənɪs/ N caractère *m or* aspect *m* sombre ; *(= colour)* couleur *f* sombre ; *(= darkness)* obscurité *f*

sombrero /sɒm'breərəʊ/ N sombrero *m*

some /sʌm/

1 ADJECTIVE	3 ADVERB
2 PRONOUN	

1 - ADJECTIVE

1 = a certain amount of, a little du, de la, de l' ◆ **~ tea/ice cream/water** du thé/de la glace/de l'eau ◆ **have you got ~ money?** est-ce que tu as de l'argent ? ◆ **will you have ~ more meat?** voulez-vous encore de la viande *or* encore un peu de viande ?

2 = a certain number of des ◆ **~ cakes** des gâteaux ◆ **there are ~ children outside** il y a des enfants dehors ◆ **I haven't seen him for ~ years** cela fait des années que je ne l'ai pas vu

Before an adjective **de** is often used without the article:

◆ **~ wonderful memories** de merveilleux souvenirs ◆ **I found ~ small mistakes** j'ai trouvé de petites erreurs

3 indefinite un, une ◆ **~ woman was asking for her** il y avait une dame qui la demandait ◆ **give it to ~ child** donnez-le à un enfant ◆ **there must be ~ solution** il doit bien y avoir une solution ◆ **~ other day** un autre jour ◆ **at ~ restaurant in London** dans un restaurant de Londres ◆ **~ time last week** (un jour) la semaine dernière ◆ **in ~ way or (an)other** d'une façon ou d'une autre ◆ **~ other time maybe!**

une autre fois peut-être ! ◆ ~ **day** un de ces jours, un jour (ou l'autre) ◆ ~ **more talented person** quelqu'un de plus doué ◆ **I read it in ~ book (or other)** je l'ai lu quelque part dans un livre

4 = a certain ◆ **if you are worried about ~ aspect of your health** ... si un aspect quelconque de votre santé vous préoccupe ...

5 as opposed to others ◆ ~ **children like school** certains enfants aiment l'école ◆ ~ **coffee is bitter** certains cafés sont amers ◆ **in ~ ways, he's right** dans un sens, il a raison ◆ ~ **people like spinach, others don't** certains aiment les épinards, d'autres pas, il y a des gens qui aiment les épinards et d'autres non ◆ ~ **people just don't care** il y a des gens qui ne s'en font pas ◆ ~ **people say that** ... il y a des gens qui disent que ..., on dit que ... ◆ ~ **people!** *(in exasperation)* il y en a qui exagèrent !, il y a des gens, je vous jure !

6 = a considerable amount of ◆ **it took ~ courage to do that !** il a fallu du courage pour faire ça ! ◆ **he spoke at ~ length** il a parlé assez longuement ◆ **it's a matter of ~ importance** c'est une question assez importante ◆ ~ **distance away, a shepherd was shouting to his dog** au loin, un berger criait après son chien

7 = a limited ◆ **this will give you ~ idea of ...** cela vous donnera une petite idée de ... ◆ **that's ~ consolation!** c'est quand même une consolation ! ◆ **surely there's ~ hope she will recover?** il doit quand même y avoir une chance qu'elle guérisse ? ◆ **the book was ~ help, but not much** le livre m'a aidé un peu mais pas beaucoup

8 * : in exclamations, admiring ◆ **that's ~ fish !** ça c'est ce qu'on appelle un poisson ! ◆ **she's ~ girl!** c'est une fille formidable !* ◆ **that was ~ party!** ça a été une super fête !* ◆ **you're ~ help!** *(iro)* tu parles d'une aide !* ◆ **I'm trying to help! – ~ help!** j'essaie de t'aider ! – tu parles !* ◆ **he says he's my friend – ~ friend!** il dit être mon ami – drôle d'ami !*

2 – PRONOUN

1 = as opposed to others certains *mpl*, certaines *fpl* ◆ ~ **cheered, others shouted questions** certains applaudissaient, d'autres posaient des questions en criant à tue-tête ◆ ~ **of my friends** certains de mes amis

Note the use of **d'entre** with personal pronouns:

◆ ~ **of them were late** certains d'entre eux étaient en retard ◆ ~ **of us knew him** certains d'entre nous le connaissaient

2 as opposed to all of them quelques-uns *mpl*, quelques-unes *fpl* ◆ **I don't want them all, but I'd like ~** je ne les veux pas tous mais j'en voudrais quelques-uns

Even if not expressed, **of them** must be translated in French by **en**:

◆ **I've still got ~ (of them)** j'en ai encore quelques-uns ◆ ~ **(of them) have been sold** on en a vendu quelques-uns *or* un certain nombre

3 = a certain amount or number: when object en ◆ **I've got ~** j'en ai ◆ **have ~!** prenez-en ! ◆ **have ~ more** reprenez-en ◆ **give me ~!** donnez-m'en ! ◆ **if you find ~ tell me** si vous en trouvez dites-le-moi ◆ **do you need stamps? – it's okay, I've got ~** est-ce que tu as besoin de timbres ? – non, ça va, j'en ai

4 = a part une partie ◆ ~ **(of it) has been eaten** on en a mangé une partie ◆ **put ~ of the sauce into a bowl** versez une partie de la sauce dans un bol ◆ **have ~ of this cake** prenez un peu de gâteau ◆ ~ **of this essay is interesting** cette dissertation est intéressante par endroits, il y a des choses intéressantes dans cette dissertation ◆ **I agree with ~ of what you said** je suis d'accord avec certaines des choses que vous avez dites ◆ ~ **of what you say is true** il y a du vrai dans ce que vous dites

◆ **... and then some** * ◆ **it would cost twice that much and then ~** ça coûterait deux fois plus et même davantage ◆ **they accomplished all their objectives, and then ~** ils ont atteint tous leurs objectifs et les ont même dépassés

3 – ADVERB

1 = about environ ◆ **there were ~ twenty houses** il y avait environ vingt maisons, il y avait une vingtaine de maisons

2 esp US * = a bit ◆ **you'll feel better when you've slept ~** tu te sentiras mieux une fois que tu auras dormi un peu ◆ **I'll kill time by looking round ~** en attendant, je vais faire un petit tour

3 * : emphatic ◆ **that's going ~ !** c'est quelque chose ! ◆ **Edinburgh-London in five hours, that's going ~!** Édimbourg-Londres en cinq heures, c'est quelque chose !

...some /səm/ **N** *(in compounds)* groupe *m* de... ◆ **threesome** groupe de trois personnes ◆ **we went in a threesome** nous y sommes allés à trois ; → **foursome**

somebody /ˈsʌmbədɪ/ **PRON** 1 *(= some unspecified person)* quelqu'un ◆ **there is ~ at the door** il y a quelqu'un à la porte ◆ **there is ~ knocking at the door** on frappe à la porte ◆ **he was talking to ~ tall and dark** il parlait à quelqu'un de grand aux cheveux sombres ◆ **we need ~ really strong to do that** il nous faut quelqu'un de vraiment fort *or* quelqu'un qui soit vraiment fort pour faire cela ◆ **ask ~ French** demande à un Français (quelconque) ◆ **they've got ~ French staying with them** ils ont un Français *or* quelqu'un de français chez eux en ce moment ◆ ~ **from the audience** quelqu'un dans l'auditoire *or* l'assemblée ◆ ~ **or other** quelqu'un, je ne sais qui ◆ ~ **up there loves me*/hates me*** *(hum)* c'est/ce n'est pas mon jour de veine* ◆ **Mr Somebody-or-other** Monsieur Chose *or* Machin* ◆ **you must have seen ~!** tu as bien dû voir quelqu'un ! ; → **else**

2 *(= important person)* personnage *m* important ◆ **she thinks she's ~** elle se prend pour quelqu'un, elle se croit quelqu'un ◆ **they think they are ~** *or* **somebodies** ils se prennent pour *or* ils se croient des personnages importants

somehow /ˈsʌmhaʊ/ **ADV** ◆ ~ **or other** *(= in some way)* d'une manière ou d'une autre ; *(= for some reason)* pour une raison ou pour une autre ◆ **it must be done ~** il faut que ce soit fait d'une manière ou d'une autre ◆ **I managed it ~** j'y suis arrivé je ne sais comment ◆ **we'll manage ~** on se débrouillera* ◆ ~ **we must find $500** d'une manière ou d'une autre nous devons nous procurer 500 dollars, nous devons nous débrouiller* pour trouver 500 dollars ◆ **Taiwan is ~ different from the rest of China** Taïwan est différente, d'une certaine manière, du reste de la Chine ◆ **I ~ doubt it** je ne sais pas pourquoi, mais j'en doute ◆ **it seems odd ~** je ne sais pas pourquoi mais ça semble bizarre ◆ ~ **he's never succeeded** pour une raison ou pour une autre *or* je ne sais pas pourquoi, il n'a jamais réussi

someone /ˈsʌmwʌn/ **PRON** ⇒ **somebody**

someplace /ˈsʌmpleɪs/ **ADV** *(US)* ⇒ **somewhere**

somersault /ˈsʌməsɔːlt/ **N** 1 *(on ground, also accidental)* culbute *f* ; *(by child)* galipette *f* ; *(in air)* saut *m* périlleux ; *(by car)* tonneau *m* ◆ **to turn a ~** faire la culbute *or* un saut périlleux *or* un tonneau 2 *(fig = change of policy)* volte-face *f inv* ◆ **to do a ~** faire volte-face **VI** *[person]* faire la culbute, faire un *or* des saut(s) périlleux ; *[car]* faire un *or* plusieurs tonneau(x)

something /ˈsʌmθɪŋ/ **PRON** quelque chose *m* ◆ ~ **moved over there** il y a quelque chose qui a bougé là-bas ◆ ~ **must have happened to him** il a dû lui arriver quelque chose ◆ ~ **unusual** quelque chose d'inhabituel ◆ **there must be ~ wrong** il doit y avoir quelque chose qui ne va pas ◆ **did you say ~?** pardon ?, comment ?, vous dites ? ◆ **I want ~ to read** je veux quelque chose à lire ◆ **I need ~ to eat** j'ai besoin de manger quelque chose ◆ **would you like ~ to drink?** voulez-vous boire quelque chose ? ◆ **give him ~ to drink** donnez-lui (quelque chose) à boire ◆ **he has ~ to live for at last** il a enfin une raison de vivre ◆ **you can't get ~ for nothing** on n'a rien pour rien ◆ **I'll have to tell him ~ or other** il faudra que je lui dise quelque chose *or* que je trouve *subj* quelque chose à lui dire ◆ **he whispered ~ or other in her ear** il lui a chuchoté quelque chose *or* on ne sait quoi à l'oreille ◆ ~ **of the kind** quelque chose dans ce genre-là ◆ **there's ~ about her** *or* **she's got ~ about her I don't like** il y a chez elle *or* en elle quelque chose que je n'aime pas ◆ **there's ~ in what you say** il y a du vrai dans ce que vous dites ◆ ~ **tells me that ...** j'ai l'impression que ... ◆ **here's ~ for your trouble** voici pour votre peine ◆ **give him ~ for himself** donnez-lui la pièce* *or* un petit quelque chose ◆ **you've got ~ there!*** là tu n'as pas tort !, c'est vrai ce que tu dis là ! ◆ **do you want to make ~ (out) of it?** *(challengingly)* tu cherches la bagarre ?* ◆ **that's (really) ~!*, that really is ~!*** c'est pas rien !*, ça se pose là !* ◆ **she has a certain ~*** elle a un petit quelque chose, elle a un certain je ne sais quoi ◆ **that certain ~* which makes all the difference** ce petit je ne sais quoi qui fait toute la différence ◆ **the 4-~* train** le train de 4 heures et quelques ◆ **it's sixty-~** c'est soixante et quelques ◆ **he's called Paul ~** il s'appelle Paul Chose *or* Paul quelque chose ◆ **that has ~ to do with accountancy** ça a quelque chose à voir avec la comptabilité ◆ **he's got ~ to do with it** *(= is involved)* il a quelque chose à voir là-dedans *(or* avec ça) ; *(= is responsible)* il y est pour quelque chose ◆ **he is ~ to do with Brown and Co** il a quelque chose à voir avec Brown et Cie ◆ **he is ~ (or other) in aviation** il est quelque chose dans l'aéronautique ◆ **I hope to see ~ of you** j'espère vous voir un peu ◆ **it is really ~ to find good coffee nowadays** ça n'est pas rien* de trouver du bon café aujourd'hui ◆ **he scored 300 points, and that's ~!** il a marqué 300 points et ça c'est quelque chose* *or* et ça n'est pas rien !* ◆ **that's always ~** c'est toujours quelque chose, c'est toujours ça, c'est mieux que rien ◆ **he thinks he's ~*** il se croit quelque chose, il se prend pour quelqu'un ; → **else**

◆ **or something** ou quelque chose dans ce genre-là, ou quelque chose comme ça ◆ **he's got flu or ~** il a la grippe ou quelque chose comme ça *or* dans ce genre-là ◆ **do you think you're my boss or ~?** tu te prends pour mon patron ou quoi ?* ◆ **he fell off a wall or ~** il est tombé d'un mur ou quelque chose dans ce genre-là*, je crois qu'il est tombé d'un mur

◆ **something of** ◆ **he is ~ of a miser** il est quelque peu *or* plutôt avare ◆ **he is ~ of a pianist** il est assez bon pianiste, il joue assez bien du piano ◆ **it was ~ of a failure** c'était plutôt un échec

ADV 1 ◆ **he left ~ over £5,000** il a laissé plus de 5 000 livres, il a laissé dans les 5 000 livres et plus ◆ ~ **under £10** un peu moins de 10 livres ◆ **he won ~ like 2,000 euros** il a gagné quelque chose comme 2 000 €, il a gagné dans les 2 000 € ◆ **it's ~ like 10 o'clock** il est 10 heures environ, il est quelque chose comme 10 heures ◆ **it weighs ~ around 5 kilos** ça pèse 5 kilos environ, ça pèse dans les 5 kilos, ça fait quelque chose comme 5 kilos ◆ **there were ~ like 80 people there** 80 personnes environ étaient présentes, il y avait quelque chose comme 80 personnes ◆ **he talks ~ like his father** il parle un peu comme son père ◆ **now that's ~ like a claret!** voilà ce que j'appelle un bordeaux !, ça au moins c'est du bordeaux ! ◆ **now that's ~ like it!*** ça au moins c'est bien *or* c'est vraiment pas mal !*

[2] (*: *emphatic*) **it was ~ dreadful!** c'était vraiment épouvantable ! ◆ **the weather was ~ shocking!** comme mauvais temps ça se posait là !* ◆ **the dog was howling ~ awful** le chien hurlait que c'en était abominable*, le chien hurlait fallait voir comme‡

-something /ˈsʌmθɪŋ/ ADJ (*in compounds*) ◆ **he's thirty-something** il a une trentaine d'années ◆ **thirty-something couples** les couples *mpl* d'une trentaine d'années N (*in compounds*) ◆ **most American twenty-somethings do not vote** la plupart des Américains d'une vingtaine d'années ne votent pas

sometime /ˈsʌmtaɪm/ ADV [1] (*in past*) ◆ **last month** le mois dernier, au cours du mois dernier ◆ **it was ~ last May** c'était en mai, je ne sais plus exactement quand ◆ **it was ~ last winter** c'était l'hiver dernier, je ne sais plus exactement quand ◆ **it was ~ before 1950** c'était avant 1950, je ne sais plus exactement quand [2] (*in future*) un de ces jours, un jour ou l'autre ◆ **~ soon** bientôt, avant peu ◆ **~ before January** d'ici janvier ◆ **~ next year** (dans le courant de) l'année prochaine ◆ **~ after my birthday** après mon anniversaire ◆ **~ or (an-)other it will have to be done** il faudra bien le faire à un moment donné ADJ [1] (*= former*) ancien *before n* ◆ **it's a ~ thing*** (*US*) cela appartient au passé [2] (*US = occasional*) intermittent

sometimes /ˈsʌmtaɪmz/ ADV quelquefois, parfois ◆ **Burma, ~ known as Myanmar** la Birmanie, parfois appelée Myanmar ◆ **it is ~ difficult to ...** il est parfois difficile de ..., il peut être difficile de ... ◆ **he ~ forgets his glasses** il lui arrive d'oublier ses lunettes ◆ **you can be a real pain ~!*** qu'est-ce que tu peux être embêtant des fois !* ◆ **~ he agrees, ~ not** tantôt il est d'accord et tantôt non

somewhat /ˈsʌmwɒt/ ADV (*frm*) quelque peu ; (*with comparatives*) un peu ◆ **~ surprising** quelque peu *or* relativement surprenant ◆ **~ easier** un peu plus facile ◆ **it amused him ~** cela l'a quelque peu amusé ◆ **he greeted me ~ brusquely** il m'a salué avec une certaine brusquerie ◆ **it was ~ of a failure** c'était plutôt un échec, c'était plus ou moins un échec ◆ **more than ~** vraiment ◆ **I was more than ~ annoyed** (*hum*) j'étais plus qu'irrité

somewhere /ˈsʌmweəʳ/ ADV quelque part ◆ **~ or other** quelque part, je ne sais où ◆ **~ in France** quelque part en France ◆ **~ near Paris** (quelque part) près de *or* dans les environs de Paris ◆ **~ about** *or* **around here** quelque part par ici, pas loin d'ici ◆ **~ around 10 million people** environ *or* à peu près 10 millions de personnes ◆ **~ else** ailleurs ◆ **let's go ~ nice/cheap** allons dans un endroit agréable/bon marché ◆ **he's in the garden or ~** il est dans le jardin je crois ◆ **have you got ~ to stay?** avez-vous un endroit où loger ? ◆ **now we're getting ~!** enfin nous faisons des progrès !

Somme /sɒm/ N (*= river*) Somme *f* ◆ **the Battle of the ~** la bataille de la Somme

somnambulism /sɒmˈnæmbjʊlɪzəm/ N somnambulisme *m*

somnambulist /sɒmˈnæmbjʊlɪst/ N somnambule *mf*

somniferous /sɒmˈnɪfərəs/ ADJ somnifère, soporifique

somnolence /ˈsɒmnələns/ N somnolence *f*

somnolent /ˈsɒmnələnt/ ADJ somnolent

son /sʌn/ N fils *m* ◆ **I've got three ~s** j'ai trois fils *or* trois garçons ◆ **Son of God/Man** (*Rel*) Fils de Dieu/de l'Homme ◆ **his ~ and heir** son héritier ◆ **the ~s of men** (*liter*) les hommes *mpl* ◆ **he is his father's ~** (*in looks*) c'est tout le portrait de son père ; (*in character*) c'est bien le fils de son père ◆ **every mother's ~ of them** tous tant qu'ils sont (*or* étaient *etc*) ◆ **come here ~!*** viens ici mon garçon ! ; → **father**

COMP **son-in-law** N (pl **sons-in-law**) gendre *m*, beau-fils *m*

son-of-a-bitch*‡ N (pl **sons-of-bitches**) salaud‡ *m*, fils *m* de pute‡

son-of-a-gun‡ N (pl **sons-of-guns**) (espèce *f* de) vieille fripouille *f or* vieux coquin *m*

sonar /ˈsəʊnɑːʳ/ N sonar *m*

sonata /səˈnɑːtə/ N sonate *f* COMP **sonata form** N forme *f* sonate

sonatina /ˌsɒnəˈtiːnə/ N sonatine *f*

sonde /sɒnd/ N sonde *f*

sone /səʊn/ N sone *f*

song /sɒŋ/ N (*gen*) chanson *f* ; (*more formal*) chant *m* ; [*of birds*] chant *m*, ramage *m* ◆ **festival of French ~** festival *m* de chant français *or* de la chanson française ◆ **to break** *or* **burst into ~** se mettre à chanter (une chanson *or* un air), entonner une chanson *or* un air ◆ **give us a ~** chante-nous quelque chose ◆ **it was going for a ~** c'était à vendre pour presque rien *or* pour une bouchée de pain ◆ **what a ~ and dance* there was!** ça a fait une de ces histoires !* ◆ **there's no need to make a ~ and dance* about it** il n'y a pas de quoi en faire toute une histoire* *or* tout un plat* ◆ **to give sb the same old ~ and dance*** (*US = excuse*) débiter les excuses habituelles à qn ◆ **to be on ~** (*Brit*) être en pleine forme ; → **marching, singsong**

COMP **song cycle** N cycle *m* de chansons

song hit N chanson *f* à succès, tube* *m*

the Song of Solomon, the Song of Songs N le cantique des cantiques

song sheet N feuillet *m* de chanson ◆ **to be singing from the same ~ sheet** (*fig*) parler d'une même voix

song thrush N grive *f* musicienne

song without words N romance *f* sans paroles

song writer N (*words*) parolier *m*, -ière *f*, auteur *m* de chansons ; (*music*) compositeur *m*, -trice *f* de chansons ; (*both*) auteur-compositeur *m*

songbird /ˈsɒŋbɜːd/ N oiseau *m* chanteur

songbook /ˈsɒŋbʊk/ N recueil *m* de chansons

songfest /ˈsɒŋfest/ N (*US*) festival *m* de chansons

songsmith /ˈsɒŋsmɪθ/ N parolier *m*, -ière *f*

songster /ˈsɒŋstəʳ/ N (*= singer*) chanteur *m* ; (*= bird*) oiseau *m* chanteur

songstress /ˈsɒŋstrɪs/ N chanteuse *f*

sonic /ˈsɒnɪk/ ADJ [*speed*] sonique ; [*wave*] sonore N (*NonC*) ◆ **~s** l'acoustique *f* (*dans le domaine transsonique*)

COMP **sonic barrier** N mur *m* du son

sonic boom N bang *m inv* (supersonique)

sonic depth-finder N sonde *f* à ultra-sons

sonic mine N mine *f* acoustique

sonnet /ˈsɒnɪt/ N sonnet *m*

sonny* /ˈsʌnɪ/ N mon (petit) gars*, fiston* *m* ◆ **~ boy, ~ Jim** mon gars*, fiston*

sonority /səˈnɒrɪtɪ/ N sonorité *f*

sonorous /ˈsɒnərəs/ ADJ [*voice*] sonore ; [*sound*] éclatant, retentissant ; [*language, rhetoric*] grandiloquent

sonorously /ˈsɒnərəslɪ/ ADV [*say*] d'une voix sonore

sonorousness /ˈsɒnərəsnɪs/ N sonorité *f*

soon /suːn/ ADV [1] (*= before long*) bientôt ; (*= quickly*) vite ◆ **we shall ~ be in Paris** nous serons bientôt à Paris, nous serons à Paris dans peu de temps *or* sous peu ◆ **you would ~ get lost** vous seriez vite perdu ◆ **he ~ changed his mind** il a vite changé d'avis, il n'a pas mis longtemps *or* il n'a pas tardé à changer d'avis ◆ **I'll ~ finish this!** ça sera vite terminé ! ◆ **(I'll) see you ~!** à bientôt ! ◆ **very ~** très vite, très bientôt* ◆ **quite ~** dans assez peu de temps, assez vite ◆ **~ afterwards** peu après ◆ **quite ~ afterwards** assez peu de temps après ◆ **all too ~ it was over** ce ne fut que trop vite fini ◆ **all too ~ it was time to go** malheureusement il a bientôt fallu partir ◆ **the holidays can't come ~ enough!** vivement les vacances ! ◆ **they'll find out ~ enough!** ils le sauront bien assez tôt !

[2] (*= early*) tôt ◆ **why have you come so ~?** pourquoi êtes-vous venu si tôt ? ◆ **I expected you much ~er than this** je vous attendais bien plus tôt (que cela) *or* bien avant ◆ **I couldn't get here any ~er** je n'ai pas pu arriver plus tôt ◆ **how ~ can you get here?** dans combien de temps au plus tôt peux-tu être ici ?, quel jour (*or* à quelle heure *etc*) peux-tu venir au plus tôt ? ◆ **how ~ will it be ready?** dans combien de temps *or* quand est-ce que ce sera prêt ? ◆ **Friday is too ~** vendredi c'est trop tôt ◆ **we were none too ~** il était temps que nous arrivions *subj*, nous sommes arrivés juste à temps ◆ **and none too ~ at that!** et ce n'est pas trop tôt ! ◆ **must you leave so ~?** faut-il que vous partiez *subj* déjà *or* si tôt ?, quel dommage que vous deviez *subj* partir déjà *or* si tôt ! ◆ **so ~?** déjà ? ◆ **on Friday at the ~est** vendredi au plus tôt, pas avant vendredi ◆ **in five years or at his death, whichever is the ~er** dans cinq ans ou à sa mort, s'il meurt avant cinq ans *or* si celle-ci survient avant ◆ **he could (just) as ~ fly to the moon as pass that exam** il a autant de chances de réussir cet examen que d'aller sur la lune

[3] (*set structures*)

◆ **as soon as** ◆ **as ~ as possible** dès que possible, aussitôt que possible ◆ **I'll do it as ~ as I can** je le ferai dès que je pourrai *or* aussitôt que possible ◆ **let me know as ~ as you've finished** prévenez-moi dès que *or* aussitôt que vous aurez fini ◆ **as ~ as he spoke to her he knew ...** aussitôt qu'il lui a parlé il a su ... ◆ **as ~ as 7 o'clock** dès 7 heures

◆ **no sooner ...** ◆ **no ~er had he finished than his brother arrived** à peine avait-il fini que son frère est arrivé ◆ **no ~er said than done!** aussitôt dit aussitôt fait !

◆ **the sooner ...** ◆ **the ~er we get started the ~er we'll be done** plus tôt nous commencerons plus tôt nous aurons fini, plus tôt commencé plus tôt fini ◆ **the ~er the better!** le plus tôt sera le mieux ! ; (*iro*) il serait grand temps !, ça ne serait pas trop tôt !

◆ **sooner or later** tôt ou tard

[4] (*expressing preference*) **I'd ~er you didn't tell him** je préférerais que vous ne le lui disiez *subj* pas ◆ **I'd as ~ you ...** j'aimerais autant que vous ... + *subj* ◆ **I would ~er stay here than go** je préférerais rester ici (plutôt) que d'y aller ◆ **I would just as ~ stay here with you** j'aimerais tout autant rester ici avec vous, cela me ferait tout autant plaisir de rester ici avec vous ◆ **he would as ~ die as betray his friends** il préférerait mourir plutôt que de trahir ses amis ◆ **will you go? – I'd ~er not** *or* **I'd as ~ not!** est-ce que tu iras ? – je n'y tiens pas *or* je préférerais pas !* ◆ **I'd ~er die!** plutôt mourir ! ◆ **what would you ~er do?** qu'est-ce que vous aimeriez mieux (faire) *or* vous préféreriez (faire) ? ◆ **~er than have to speak to her, he left** plutôt que d'avoir à lui parler il est parti ◆ **she'd marry him as ~ as not** elle l'épouserait volontiers, elle aimerait bien l'épouser ◆ **~er you than me!*** je n'aimerais pas être à ta place, je te souhaite bien du plaisir !* (*iro*)

sooner /ˈsuːnəʳ/ ADV compar of **soon** N (*US*) pionnier *m* de la première heure (*dans l'Ouest* *des États-Unis)* COMP **the Sooner State** N *(US)* l'Oklahoma *m*

soonish /ˈsuːnɪʃ/ ADV bientôt (mais pas tout de suite)

soot /sʊt/ N *(NonC)* suie *f*

► **soot up** VI s'encrasser VT SEP encrasser

sooth †† /suːθ/ N ◆ **in ~** en vérité

soothe /suːð/ VT *[+ person]* calmer, apaiser ; *[+ nerves, mind, pain]* calmer ; *[+ anger, anxieties]* apaiser ; *[+ sb's vanity]* flatter ◆ **to ~ sb's fears** apaiser les craintes de qn, tranquilliser qn

soothing /ˈsuːðɪŋ/ ADJ *[bath, massage]* relaxant ; *[voice, words, music, manner]* apaisant ; *[drink]* calmant ; *[lotion, ointment]* adoucissant ; *[presence]* rassurant, réconfortant ◆ **the ~ effect of lavender oil/a glass of sherry** l'effet apaisant de l'huile de lavande/d'un verre de sherry

soothingly /ˈsuːðɪŋlɪ/ ADV *[say, whisper]* d'un ton apaisant ◆ **~ familiar** familier et réconfortant ◆ **~ cool** frais et apaisant

soothsayer /ˈsuːθseɪəʳ/ N devin *m*, devineresse *f*

soothsaying /ˈsuːθseɪɪŋ/ N divination *f*

sooty /ˈsʊtɪ/ ADJ *[object, surface]* couvert or noir de suie ; *[fumes, exhaust]* chargé de suie ; *[chimney, flue]* plein de suie ; *[flame]* fuligineux ; *[powder]* qui a l'aspect de la suie ◆ **~ particles** particules *fpl* de suie ◆ **a ~ black colour** un noir charbonneux *or* fuligineux

SOP /ˌesəʊˈpiː/ N (abbrev of **standard operating procedure**) → **standard**

sop /sɒp/ N [1] *(Culin)* morceau *m* de pain *(trempé dans du lait, du jus de viande etc)*, mouillette *f* ◆ **he can eat only ~s** il ne peut rien manger de trop solide, il doit se nourrir d'aliments semi-liquides ◆ **it's just a ~ to Cerberus** c'est simplement pour le *(or* les *etc)* ramener à de meilleures dispositions ◆ **he gave the guard £10 as a ~** il a donné 10 livres au gardien pour s'acheter ses bons services *or* pour lui graisser la patte* ◆ **it's a ~ to my conscience** c'est pour faire taire ma conscience ◆ **as a ~ to his pride, I agreed** j'ai accepté pour flatter son amour-propre ◆ **he only said that as a ~ to the unions** il a dit cela uniquement pour amadouer les syndicats

[2] *(* = sissy) (man)* poule *f* mouillée, lavette* *f* ; *(woman)* femme *f* très fleur bleue

► **sop up** VT SEP *[+ spilt liquid] [sponge, rag]* absorber ; *[person]* éponger *(with* avec*)* ◆ **he ~ped up the gravy with some bread** il a saucé son assiette avec un morceau de pain

Sophia /səʊˈfaɪə/ N Sophie *f*

sophism /ˈsɒfɪzəm/ N ⇒ **sophistry**

sophist /ˈsɒfɪst/ N sophiste *mf* ◆ **Sophists** *(Hist Philos)* sophistes *mpl*

sophistical /səˈfɪstɪkəl/ ADJ sophistique, captieux

sophisticate /səˈfɪstɪkeɪt/ N raffiné(e) *m(f)*, élégant(e) *m(f)*

sophisticated /səˈfɪstɪkeɪtɪd/ ADJ [1] *(= complex, advanced) [equipment, system, technique]* sophistiqué, (très) élaboré [2] *(= refined) [person, tastes, lifestyle]* raffiné [3] *(= intelligent, subtle) [person]* averti ; *[approach, analysis, understanding]* subtil ; *[play, film, book]* subtil, complexe

sophistication /səˌfɪstɪˈkeɪʃən/ N [1] *(= complexity) [of equipment, system, technique]* sophistication *f* [2] *(= refinement) [of person, tastes, lifestyle]* raffinement *m* [3] *(= intelligence, subtlety)* raffinement *m* ; *[of approach, analysis, understanding]* subtilité *f* ; *[of film, novel]* subtilité *f*, complexité *f* ◆ **the job demands a high level of political ~** cet emploi exige une grande subtilité politique *or* un grand sens politique

sophistry /ˈsɒfɪstrɪ/ N *(NonC)* sophistique *f* ◆ **(piece of) ~** sophisme *m* ◆ **Sophistry** *(Hist Philos)* sophistique *f*

Sophocles /ˈsɒfəkliːz/ N Sophocle *m*

sophomore /ˈsɒfəmɔːʳ/ N *(US)* étudiant(e) *m(f)* de seconde année

sophomoric /ˌsɒfəˈmɔːrɪk/ ADJ *(US pej)* aussi prétentieux qu'ignorant

soporific /ˌsɒpəˈrɪfɪk/ ADJ [1] *(= sedative)* soporifique ◆ **too much wine can be ~** trop de vin peut avoir un effet soporifique [2] *(* = boring)* soporifique* N somnifère *m*

sopping * /ˈsɒpɪŋ/ ADJ (also **sopping wet**) *[person]* trempé (jusqu'aux os) ; *[clothes]* à tordre

soppy * /ˈsɒpɪ/ ADJ *(Brit)* [1] *(= sentimental) [person]* fleur bleue *inv*, sentimental ; *[film, book, story]* à l'eau de rose, sentimental ◆ **people who are ~ about cats** les gens qui sont gagas* avec les chats [2] *(= silly) [person]* bébête* ; *[action]* bête ◆ **don't be so ~!** ne sois pas si bête ! [3] *(† = feeble, weedy)* mollasson* ◆ **he's a ~ git** c'est une mauviette *or* un mollasson*

soprano /səˈprɑːnəʊ/ N (pl **sopranos** *or* **soprani** /səˈprɑːniː/) *(= singer)* soprano *mf*, soprane *mf* ; *(= voice, part)* soprano *m* ◆ **to sing ~** avoir une voix de soprano ; → **boy** ADJ *[part, voice, repertoire]* de soprano ; *[aria]* pour soprano ; *[instrument]* soprano *inv* ◆ **the ~ saxophone** le saxophone soprano ◆ **the ~ clef** la clef d'ut dernière ligne

sorb /sɔːb/ N *(= tree)* sorbier *m* ; *(= fruit)* sorbe *f*

sorbet /ˈsɔːbeɪ, ˈsɔːbɪt/ N [1] *(= water ice)* sorbet *m* ◆ **lemon ~** sorbet *m* au citron [2] *(US)* ⇒ **sherbet 1**

sorbic /ˈsɔːbɪk/ ADJ ◆ **~ acid** acide *m* sorbique

sorbitol /ˈsɔːbɪtɒl/ N sorbitol *m*

sorcerer /ˈsɔːsərəʳ/ N sorcier *m* ◆ **the Sorcerer's Apprentice** *(Mus etc)* l'Apprenti sorcier *m*

sorceress /ˈsɔːsəres/ N sorcière *f*

sorcery /ˈsɔːsərɪ/ N sorcellerie *f*

sordid /ˈsɔːdɪd/ ADJ *[conditions, surroundings, affair, episode, detail]* sordide ; *[motive, action]* sordide, honteux ; *[behaviour]* abject, honteux

sordidly /ˈsɔːdɪdlɪ/ ADV sordidement

sordidness /ˈsɔːdɪdnɪs/ N *[of conditions, surroundings]* aspect *m* sordide ; *(fig) [of behaviour, motive, method]* bassesse *f* ; *[of agreement, deal]* caractère *m* honteux ; *[of crime, greed, gains]* caractère *m* sordide ; *[of film, book]* saleté *f*

sore /sɔːʳ/ ADJ [1] *(= inflamed)* irrité

[2] *(= painful)* douloureux ◆ **to have a ~ throat** avoir mal à la gorge ◆ **I'm ~ all over** j'ai mal partout ◆ **to have a ~ head** *(= headache)* avoir mal à la tête ◆ **to stick out** *or* **stand out like a ~ thumb*** *(= be obvious)* crever les yeux ; *(= stand out visually)* faire tache, détonner ◆ **a ~ spot** *(lit)* une zone sensible ; *(fig)* un sujet délicat ◆ **it's a ~ point (with him)** c'est un sujet qu'il vaut mieux éviter (avec lui) ; → **bear², sight**

[3] *(esp US * = offended, resentful)* vexé ◆ **I really feel ~ about it** ça m'a vraiment vexé ◆ **to get ~** se vexer ◆ **don't get ~!** ne te vexe pas ! ◆ **to be** *or* **feel ~ at** *or* **with sb** en vouloir à qn ◆ **to get ~ at** *or* **with sb** s'emporter contre qn

[4] *(†† or liter)* ◆ **to be in ~ need of sth** avoir grandement besoin de qch ◆ **to be ~ at heart** être affligé *or* désolé

ADV ◆ **to be ~ afraid** †† avoir grand-peur

N *(Med)* plaie *f* ◆ **to open up old ~s** rouvrir *or* raviver d'anciennes blessures *(fig)* → **running**

sorehead * /ˈsɔːhed/ N *(US)* râleur* *m*, -euse* *f*, rouspéteur* *m*, -euse* *f*

sorely /ˈsɔːlɪ/ ADV *(frm) [wounded]* gravement, grièvement ; *[disappointed]* cruellement ◆ **~ tempted** fortement tenté ◆ **modern equipment is ~ lacking** on manque cruellement de matériel moderne, le matériel moderne fait cruellement défaut ◆ **reform is ~ needed** on a grand besoin de réformes ◆ **to be ~ tested** *or* **tried** *[person, patience]* être mis à rude épreuve ◆ **she will be ~ missed** elle nous *(or* leur *etc)* manquera énormément

soreness /ˈsɔːnɪs/ N [1] *(= pain)* douleur *f* ◆ **muscle ~** douleurs *fpl* musculaires [2] * *(= annoyance)* contrariété *f*, irritation *f* ; *(= bitterness)* amertume *f* ; *(= anger)* colère *f*, rogne* *f*

sorghum /ˈsɔːgəm/ N sorgho *m*

soroptimist /sɒˈrɒptɪmɪst/ N *membre d'une association internationale pour les femmes dans les professions libérales*

sorority /səˈrɒrɪtɪ/ N *(US Univ)* association *f* d'étudiantes

Sorority, Fraternity

Beaucoup d'universités américaines possèdent des associations d'étudiants très sélectives, appelées **sororities** pour les femmes et **fraternities** pour les hommes, qui organisent des soirées, récoltent des fonds pour des œuvres de bienfaisance et cherchent à se distinguer des autres fraternités du même type. Le nom de ces associations est souvent formé à partir de deux ou trois lettres de l'alphabet grec : par exemple, « Kappa Kappa Gamma **sorority** » ou « Sigma Chi **fraternity** ».

sorrel /ˈsɒrəl/ N [1] *(= plant)* oseille *f* [2] *(= horse)* alezan *m* clair ; *(= colour)* roux *m*, brun rouge *m* ADJ *[horse]* alezan *inv*

sorrow /ˈsɒrəʊ/ LANGUAGE IN USE 24.4 N peine *f*, chagrin *m* ; *(stronger)* douleur *f* ◆ **his ~ at the loss of his son** le chagrin qu'il a éprouvé à la mort de son fils ◆ **to my (great) ~** à mon grand chagrin, à ma grande douleur ◆ **this was a great ~ to me** j'en ai eu beaucoup de peine *or* de chagrin ◆ **he was a great ~ to her** il lui a causé beaucoup de peine *or* de chagrin ◆ **more in ~ than in anger** avec plus de peine que de colère ◆ **the Man of Sorrows** *(Rel)* l'Homme *m* de douleur ; → **drown** VI ◆ **to ~ over** *[+ sb's death, loss]* pleurer ; *[+ news]* déplorer, se lamenter de ◆ **she sat ~ing by the fire** elle était assise au coin du feu toute à son chagrin

sorrowful /ˈsɒrəʊfʊl/ ADJ triste

sorrowfully /ˈsɒrəʊfəlɪ/ ADV *[look, shake head]* tristement, d'un air triste ; *[say]* d'un ton triste

sorrowing /ˈsɒrəʊɪŋ/ ADJ affligé

sorry /ˈsɒrɪ/ LANGUAGE IN USE 12.1, 18.1, 18.2 ADJ [1] *(= regretful)* désolé ◆ **I was ~ to hear of your accident** j'ai été désolé *or* navré d'apprendre que vous aviez eu un accident ◆ **I am ~ I cannot come** je regrette *or* je suis désolé de ne (pas) pouvoir venir ◆ **I am ~ she cannot come** je regrette *or* je suis désolé qu'elle ne puisse (pas) venir ◆ **I am ~ to have to tell you that ...** je regrette d'avoir à vous dire que ... ◆ **we are ~ to inform you ...** *(frm)* nous avons le regret de vous informer ... ◆ **he didn't pass, I'm ~ to say** il a échoué hélas *or* malheureusement ◆ **(I'm) ~ I am late, I'm ~ to be late** excusez-moi *or* je suis désolé d'être en retard ◆ **say you're ~!** dis *or* demande pardon ! ◆ **~!, ~ about that!*** pardon !, excusez-moi !, je suis désolé ! ◆ **I'm very** *or* **terribly ~** je suis vraiment désolé *or* navré ◆ **awfully ~!, so ~!** oh pardon !, excusez-moi !, je suis vraiment désolé ! ◆ **will you go? – I'm ~ I can't** est-ce que tu vas y aller ? – impossible hélas *or* (je suis) désolé mais je ne peux pas ◆ **can you do it? – no, ~** est-ce que tu peux le faire ? – non, désolé *or* désolé, je ne peux pas *or* malheureusement pas ◆ **~?** *(requesting repetition)* pardon ? ◆ **I am ~ to disturb you** je suis désolé de vous déranger, excusez-moi de vous déranger ◆ **I am** *or* **feel ~**

about all the noise yesterday je regrette beaucoup qu'il y ait eu tellement de bruit hier ♦ **~ about that vase!** excusez-moi pour ce vase ! ♦ **you'll be ~ for this!** vous le regretterez !, vous vous en repentirez !

[2] *(= pitying)* **to be** *or* **feel ~ for sb** plaindre qn ♦ **I feel so ~ for her since her husband died** elle me fait pitié depuis la mort de son mari ♦ **I'm ~ for you but you should have known better** je suis désolé pour vous *or* je vous plains mais vous auriez dû être plus raisonnable ♦ **if he can't do better than that then I'm ~ for him** *(iro)* s'il ne peut pas faire mieux, je regrette pour lui *or* je le plains ♦ **there's no need to feel** *or* **be ~ for him** il est inutile de le plaindre, il n'est pas à plaindre ♦ **to be** *or* **feel ~ for o.s.** se plaindre (de son sort), s'apitoyer sur soi-même *or* sur son propre sort ♦ **he looked very ~ for himself** il faisait piteuse mine

[3] *(= woeful) [condition]* triste ; *[excuse]* piètre ♦ **to be in a ~ plight** être dans une triste situation, être en fâcheuse posture ♦ **to be in a ~ state** être dans un triste état, être en piteux état ♦ **he was a ~ figure** il faisait triste *or* piteuse figure ♦ **a ~ sight** un triste spectacle, un spectacle désolant *or* affligeant ♦ **it was a ~ tale of mismanagement and inefficiency** c'était une lamentable *or* déplorable histoire de mauvaise gestion et d'inefficacité

sort /sɔːt/ **N** [1] *(= class, variety, kind, type) (gen)* sorte *f*, genre *m* ; *[of animal, plant]* sorte *f*, espèce *f* ; *(= make) [of car, machine, coffee etc]* marque *f* ♦ **this ~ of book** cette sorte *or* ce genre de livre ♦ **books of all ~s** des livres de toutes sortes *or* de tous genres ♦ **... and all ~s of things** ... et toutes sortes de choses encore, ... et j'en passe, ... et que sais-je ♦ **this ~ of thing(s)** ce genre de chose(s) ♦ **what ~ of flour do you want? – the ~ you gave me last time** quelle sorte de farine voulez-vous ? – la même que celle que vous m'avez donnée la dernière fois ♦ **what ~ of car is it?** quelle marque de voiture est-ce ? ♦ **what ~ of man is he?** quel genre *or* type d'homme est-ce ? ♦ **what ~ of dog is he?** qu'est-ce que c'est comme (race de) chien ? ♦ **he is not the ~ of man to refuse** ce n'est pas le genre d'homme à refuser, il n'est pas homme à refuser ♦ **he's not that ~ of person** ce n'est pas son genre ♦ **I'm not that ~ of girl!** ce n'est pas mon genre !, mais pour qui me prenez-vous ? ♦ **that's the ~ of person I am** c'est comme ça que je suis (fait) ♦ **what ~ of people does he think we are?** (mais enfin) pour qui nous prend-il ? ♦ **what ~ of a fool does he take me for?** (non mais *) il me prend pour un imbécile ! ♦ **what ~ of behaviour is this?** qu'est-ce que c'est que cette façon de se conduire ? ♦ **what ~ of an answer do you call that?** vous appelez ça une réponse ? ♦ **classical music is the ~ she likes most** c'est la musique classique qu'elle préfère ♦ **and all that ~ of thing** et autres choses du même genre, et tout ça * ♦ **you know the ~ of thing I mean** vous voyez (à peu près) ce que je veux dire ♦ **I don't like that ~ of talk/behaviour** je n'aime pas ce genre de conversation/de conduite ♦ **he's the ~ that will cheat** il est du genre à tricher ♦ **I know his ~!** je connais les gens de son genre *or* espèce ! ♦ **your ~ * never did any good** les gens de votre genre *or* espèce ne font rien de bien ♦ **they're not our ~ *** ce ne sont pas des gens comme nous ♦ **it's my ~ * of film** c'est le genre de film que j'aime *or* qui me plaît

[2] *(in phrases)* **something of the ~** quelque chose de ce genre(-là) *or* d'approchant ♦ **this is wrong – nothing of the ~!** c'est faux – pas le moins du monde ! ♦ **I shall do nothing of the ~!** je n'en ferai rien !, certainement pas ! ♦ **I will have nothing of the ~!** je ne tolérerai pas cela ! ♦ **it was beef of a ~** *(pej)* c'était quelque chose qui pouvait passer pour du bœuf ♦ **he is a painter of ~s** c'est un peintre si l'on peut dire ♦ **after a ~, in some ~** dans une certaine mesure, en quelque sorte ♦ **to be out of ~s** ne pas être dans son assiette ♦ **it takes all ~s (to make a world)** *(Prov)* il faut de tout pour faire un monde *(Prov)* ♦ **a good ~ *** un brave garçon, un brave type *, une brave fille ♦ **he's the right ~ *** c'est un type bien *

[3] ♦ **a ~ of** une sorte *or* espèce de, un genre de ♦ **there was a ~ of box in the middle of the room** il y avait une sorte *or* une espèce de boîte au milieu de la pièce, il y avait quelque chose qui ressemblait à une boîte au milieu de la pièce ♦ **there was a ~ of tinkling sound** il y avait une sorte *or* une espèce de bruit de grelot, on entendait quelque chose qui ressemblait à un bruit de grelot ♦ **in a ~ of way * I'm sorry** d'une certaine façon je le regrette ♦ **I had a ~ of fear that ...** j'avais un peu peur que ... + ne + *subj*

♦ **sort of *** ♦ **I ~ of thought that he would come** j'avais un peu l'idée qu'il viendrait ♦ **he was ~ of worried-looking** il avait un peu l'air inquiet, il avait l'air comme qui dirait inquiet ♦ **it's ~ of blue** c'est plutôt bleu ♦ **aren't you pleased? – ~ of!** tu n'es pas content ? – ben si ! *

VT [1] (also **sort out**) *(= classify) [+ documents, stamps]* classer ; *(= select those to keep) [+ documents, clothes, apples]* trier, faire le tri de ; *(= separate)* séparer *(from* de) ♦ **he spent the morning ~ing (out) his stamp collection** il a passé la matinée à classer *or* trier les timbres de sa collection ♦ **to ~ things (out) into sizes** *or* **according to size** trier des objets selon leur taille ♦ **to ~ out one's cards** *or* **one's hand** *(Cards)* arranger ses cartes, mettre de l'ordre dans ses cartes ♦ **to ~ (out) the clothes into clean and dirty** séparer les vêtements sales des propres, mettre les vêtements sales à part ♦ **can you ~ out the green ones and keep them aside?** pourriez-vous les trier et mettre les verts à part ?

[2] *(Post) [+ letters etc] (Comput) [+ data, file]* trier

[3] ♦ **to get sth ~ed *** *[+ problem, situation]* régler qch

[4] *(Scot * = mend)* arranger ♦ **I've ~ed your bike** j'ai arrangé ton vélo

COMP **sort code N** *(Banking)* code *m* guichet

sort-out * N ♦ **to have a ~-out** faire du rangement ♦ **I've had a ~-out of all these old newspapers** j'ai trié tous ces vieux journaux

► **sort out** **VT SEP** [1] ⇒ **sort vt 1**

[2] *(= tidy) [+ papers, toys, clothes]* ranger, mettre de l'ordre dans ; *[+ ideas]* mettre de l'ordre dans ; *(= solve) [+ problem]* régler, résoudre ; *[+ difficulties]* venir à bout de ; *(= fix, arrange)* arranger ♦ **I just can't ~ the twins out * (one from the other)** je ne peux pas distinguer les jumeaux (l'un de l'autre) ♦ **can you ~ this out for me?** est-ce que vous pourriez débrouiller ça pour moi ? ♦ **we've got it all ~ed out now** nous avons réglé *or* résolu la question ♦ **we'll soon ~ it out** nous aurons vite fait d'arranger ça *or* de régler ça ♦ **things will ~ themselves out** les choses vont s'arranger d'elles-mêmes ♦ **he was so excited I couldn't ~ out what had happened** il était tellement excité que je n'ai pas pu débrouiller *or* comprendre ce qui s'était passé ♦ **did you ~ out with him when you had to be there?** est-ce que tu as décidé *or* fixé avec lui l'heure à laquelle tu dois y être ? ♦ **to ~ o.s. out** se reprendre, résoudre ses problèmes ♦ **to ~ sb out *** *(Brit) (by punishing, threatening)* régler son compte à qn * ; *(= get out of difficulty)* tirer qn d'affaire ; *(after depression, illness)* aider qn à reprendre pied *(fig)*

[3] *(= explain)* **to ~ sth out for sb** expliquer qch à qn

N ♦ **sort-out * → sort**

sorted * /ˈsɔːtɪd/ **ADJ** [1] *(= arranged)* arrangé ♦ **in a few months everything should be ~** dans quelques mois tout devrait être arrangé [2] *(Drugs sl)* **are you ~?** tu as ce qu'il te faut ?

sorter /ˈsɔːtəʳ/ **N** [1] *(= person)* trieur *m*, -euse *f* [2] *(= machine) (for letters)* trieur *m* ; *(for punched cards)* trieuse *f* ; *(for grain)* trieur *m* ; *(for wool, coke)* trieur *m*, trieuse *f*

sortie /ˈsɔːtɪ/ **N** *[of planes, soldiers]* sortie *f* ♦ **they made** *or* **flew 400 ~s** ils ont fait 400 sorties

sorting /ˈsɔːtɪŋ/ **N** *(Comput, Post)* tri *m* **COMP** **sorting office N** *(Post)* bureau *m or* centre *m* de tri

SOS /ˌesəʊˈes/ **N** *(= signal)* SOS *m* ; *(fig)* SOS *m*, appel *m* au secours *(for sth* pour demander qch)

sot /sɒt/ **N** ivrogne *m* invétéré

sottish /ˈsɒtɪʃ/ **ADJ** abruti par l'alcool

sotto voce /ˈsɒtəʊˈvəʊtʃɪ/ **ADV** tout bas, à mi-voix ; *(Mus)* sotto voce

sou' /saʊ/ **ADJ** *(in compounds) (Naut)* ⇒ **south**

soubriquet /ˈsuːbrɪkeɪ/ **N** → **sobriquet**

Soudan /suˈdɑːn/ **N** ⇒ **Sudan**

Soudanese /ˌsuːdəˈniːz/ **ADJ, N** ⇒ **Sudanese**

soufflé /ˈsuːfleɪ/ **N** soufflé *m* ♦ **cheese/fish ~** soufflé *m* au fromage/au poisson

COMP **soufflé dish N** moule *m* à soufflé

soufflé omelette N omelette *f* soufflée

sough /saʊ/ *(liter)* **N** murmure *m* (du vent) **VI** *[wind]* murmurer

sought /sɔːt/ **VB** pt, ptp of **seek**

souk /suːk/ **N** souk *m*

soul /səʊl/ **N** [1] âme *f* ♦ **with all one's ~** de toute son âme, de tout son cœur ♦ **All Souls' Day** le jour des Morts ♦ **upon my ~! † *** grand Dieu ! ♦ **he cannot call his ~ his own** il ne s'appartient pas, il est complètement dominé ♦ **he was the ~ of the movement** *(fig)* c'était lui l'âme *or* l'animateur du mouvement ♦ **he is the ~ of discretion** c'est la discrétion même *or* personnifiée ♦ **he has no ~** il est trop terre à terre, il a trop les pieds sur terre ♦ **it lacks ~** cela manque de sentiment ; → **bare, body, heart, sell**

[2] *(= person)* âme *f*, personne *f* ♦ **a village of 300 ~s** un village de 300 âmes ♦ **the ship sank with 200 ~s** le bateau a sombré avec 200 personnes à bord ♦ **the ship sank with all ~s** le bateau a péri corps et biens ♦ **I didn't see a (single** *or* **living) ~** je n'ai pas vu âme qui vive ♦ **don't tell a ~** surtout n'en soufflez mot à personne ♦ **(you) poor ~!** mon (*or* ma) pauvre ! ♦ **(the) poor ~!** le (*or* la) pauvre ! ♦ **he's a good ~** il est bien brave * ♦ **she's a kind** *or* **kindly ~** elle est la gentillesse même ♦ **lend me your pen, there's a good ~ *** sois gentil *or* sois un ange, prête-moi ton stylo ; → **simple**

[3] *(US: esp of black Americans)* soul *m (façon de ressentir des Noirs)*

[4] *(US *)* abbrev of **soul brother, soul food, soul music**

ADJ *(US *: of black Americans)* ♦ **~ brother/sister** frère *m*/sœur *f* de race *(terme employé par les Noirs entre eux)* ♦ **Soul City** Harlem ♦ **~ food** nourriture *f* soul *(nourriture traditionnelle des Noirs du sud des États-Unis)* ♦ **~ band** groupe *m* de (musique) soul ♦ **~ music** musique *f* soul

COMP **soul-destroying ADJ** *(= boring)* abrutissant ; *(= depressing)* démoralisant

soul mate * N âme *f* sœur

soul-searching N introspection *f* ♦ **after a lot of ~-searching** après un long examen de conscience

soul-stirring ADJ très émouvant

soulful /ˈsəʊlfʊl/ **ADJ** *[eyes, look]* expressif ; *[expression]* attendrissant ; *[person, music]* sentimental

soulfully /ˈsəʊlfəlɪ/ **ADV** *[sing, write]* de façon sentimentale *or* attendrissante ; *[look]* d'un air expressif *or* éloquent

soulless /ˈsəʊllɪs/ ADJ *[place, building, music]* sans âme ; *[work]* abrutissant ; *[system]* inhumain ; *[eyes, look]* insensible, inexpressif ; *[existence]* vide

sound¹ /saʊnd/ N *(gen)* son *m* ; *[of sea, storm, breaking glass, car brakes]* bruit *m* ; *[of voice, bell, violins]* son *m* ◆ **the speed of ~** la vitesse du son ◆ **to the ~(s) of the national anthem** au(x) son(s) de l'hymne national ◆ **there was not a ~ to be heard** on n'entendait pas le moindre bruit ◆ **without (making) a ~** sans bruit, sans faire le moindre bruit ◆ **we heard the ~ of voices** nous avons entendu un bruit de voix ◆ **he lives within the ~ of the cathedral bells** depuis chez lui, on entend les cloches de la cathédrale ◆ **the Glenn Miller ~** la musique de Glenn Miller ◆ **I don't like the ~ of it** *(= it doesn't attract me)* ça ne me dit rien, ça ne me plaît pas ; *(= it's worrying)* ça m'inquiète ◆ **I don't like the ~ of his plans** ses projets ne me disent rien qui vaille ◆ **the news has a depressing ~** les nouvelles semblent déprimantes

VI 1 *[bell, trumpet, voice]* sonner, retentir ; *[car horn, siren, signal, order]* retentir ◆ **footsteps/a gun ~ed a long way off** on a entendu un bruit de pas/un coup de canon dans le lointain ◆ **a note of warning ~s through his writing** un avertissement retentit dans ses écrits ◆ **it ~s better if you read it slowly** c'est mieux *or* ça sonne mieux si vous le lisez lentement

2 *(= suggest by sound)* **that instrument ~s like a flute** le son de cet instrument ressemble à celui de la flûte, on dirait le son de la flûte ◆ **it ~s empty** (au son) on dirait que c'est vide ◆ **a language which ~ed (to me) like Dutch** une langue qui aurait pu être *or* qui (me) semblait être du hollandais ◆ **he ~s (like an) Australian** à l'entendre parler on dirait un Australien ◆ **the train ~ed a long way off, it ~ed as if** *or* **as though the train were a long way off** le train semblait être encore bien loin ◆ **it ~ed as if someone were coming in** on aurait dit que quelqu'un entrait ◆ **that ~s like Paul arriving** ça doit être Paul qui arrive ◆ **she ~s tired** elle semble fatiguée ◆ **you ~ like your mother when you say things like that** quand tu parles comme ça, tu me rappelles ta mère *or* on croirait entendre ta mère ◆ **you ~ terrible** *(to sick person)* (à t'entendre) tu sembles en triste état

3 *(= seem, appear)* sembler (être) ◆ **that ~s like an excuse** cela a l'air d'une excuse, cela ressemble à une excuse ◆ **how does it ~ to you?** qu'en penses-tu ? ◆ **it ~s like a good idea** ça a l'air d'(être) une bonne idée, ça semble être une bonne idée ◆ **it doesn't ~ too good** cela n'annonce rien de bon, ce n'est pas très prometteur ◆ **it ~s as if she isn't coming** j'ai l'impression qu'elle ne viendra pas ◆ **you don't ~ like the kind of person we need** (à en juger par ce que vous dites) vous ne semblez pas être le genre de personne qu'il nous faut

VT 1 *[+ bell, alarm]* sonner ; *[+ trumpet, bugle]* sonner de ; *(Mil) [+ reveille, retreat]* sonner ◆ **to ~ the last post** *(Mil)* envoyer la sonnerie aux morts ◆ **to ~ the** *or* **one's horn** *[of car]* klaxonner ◆ **to ~ a (note of) warning** *(fig)* lancer un avertissement ◆ **to ~ sb's praises** faire l'éloge de qn, chanter les louanges de qn

2 *(Ling)* **to ~ one's "t"s** faire sonner ses "t" ◆ **the "n" in "hymn" is not ~ed** le "n" de "hymn" ne se prononce pas

3 *(= examine) [+ rails, train wheels]* vérifier au marteau ◆ **to ~ sb's chest** *(Med)* ausculter qn

COMP *[film, recording]* sonore

sound archives NPL phonothèque *f*

sound barrier N mur *m* du son ◆ **to break the ~ barrier** franchir le mur du son

sound bite N petite phrase *f (prononcée par un homme politique pour être citée dans les médias)* ◆ **to talk in ~ bites** parler à coups de petites phrases

sound board N ⇒ **sounding board** ; → **sounding¹**

sound box N *(Mus)* caisse *f* de résonance

sound card N *(Comput)* carte *f* son

sound change N *(Phon)* changement *m* phonétique

sound check N *(Mus)* sound check *m*

sound effects NPL *(Rad etc)* bruitage *m*

sound effects man N (pl **sound effects men**) *(Cine, TV, Rad)* bruiteur *m*

sound engineer N *(Cine, Rad etc)* ingénieur *m* du son

sound file N *(Comput)* fichier *m* son

sound hole N *(Mus)* ouïe *f*

sound law N *(Phon)* loi *f* phonétique

sound library N phonothèque *f*

sound mixer N ⇒ **sound engineer**

sound pollution N nuisance *f* due au bruit

sound-producing ADJ *(Phon)* phonatoire

sound recordist N preneur (-euse *m(f)*) de son

sound shift N *(Phon)* mutation *f* phonétique

sound stage N *(Recording)* salle *f* de tournage

sound system N *(Ling)* système *m* de sons ; *(= hi-fi)* chaîne *f* hi-fi ; *(for disco, concert)* sonorisation *f*, sono* *f*

sound truck N *(US)* camionnette *f* équipée d'un haut-parleur

sound wave N *(Phys)* onde *f* sonore

► **sound off** VI 1 ⁑ *(= proclaim one's opinions)* faire de grands laïus* *(about* sur) ; *(= boast)* se vanter *(about* de), la ramener⁑ *(about* à propos de) ; *(= grumble)* rouspéter*, râler* *(about* à propos de) ◆ **to ~ off at sb** engueuler⁑ qn

2 *(US Mil = number off)* se numéroter

sound² /saʊnd/ ADJ 1 *(= healthy, robust) [person]* en bonne santé, bien portant ; *[heart]* solide ; *[constitution, teeth, lungs, fruit, tree]* sain ; *[timber]* sain, solide ; *[structure, floor, bridge]* solide, en bon état ; *(fig) [firm, business, financial position]* sain, solide ; *[bank, organization]* solide ; *[investment]* sûr ◆ **the bullet struck his ~ leg** la balle a atteint sa jambe valide ◆ **of ~ mind** sain d'esprit ◆ **~ in body and mind** sain de corps et d'esprit ◆ **to be ~ in wind and limb** avoir bon pied bon œil ◆ **to be as ~ as a bell** être en parfait état ; → **safe**

2 *(= competent, judicious, sensible) [judgement]* sain ; *[doctrine]* orthodoxe, solide ; *[argument, reasoning]* solide, valable ; *[decision, advice, opinion]* sensé ; *[case, training]* solide ; *[rule, policy, behaviour, tactics]* sensé, valable ; *[claim, title]* valable, sérieux ; *[statesman, player etc]* compétent ◆ **he is a ~ worker** il sait travailler, il est compétent dans son travail ◆ **he is a ~ socialist** c'est un bon socialiste, c'est un socialiste bon teint ◆ **he is ~ enough on theory ...** il connaît très bien la théorie ... ◆ **he's a ~ guy** * *(= sensible)* il est très sérieux *or* sensé ; *(= we can trust him)* c'est un type fiable* ◆ **~ sense** bon sens *m*, sens *m* pratique ◆ **that was a ~ move** c'était une action judicieuse *or* sensée

3 *(= thorough) [defeat]* complet (-ète *f*), total ; *[sleep]* profond ◆ **a ~ thrashing** une bonne *or* belle correction ◆ **he is a ~ sleeper** il a un bon sommeil, il dort bien

ADV ◆ **to be ~ asleep** être profondément endormi, dormir à poings fermés ◆ **to sleep ~** bien dormir

sound³ /saʊnd/ N *(Med = probe)* sonde *f* VT *(gen, Med, Naut etc)* sonder ; *(fig)* (also **sound out**) *[+ person]* sonder *(on, about* sur) ◆ **to ~ sb's opinions/feelings on sth** sonder qn sur ses opinions/ses sentiments à propos de qch VI sonder COMP **sound line** N ligne *f* de sonde

sound⁴ /saʊnd/ N *(Geog)* détroit *m*, bras *m* de mer

soundalike * /ˈsaʊndəlaɪk/ N ◆ **he's an Elvis ~** il a la voix d'Elvis

sounding¹ /ˈsaʊndɪŋ/ N 1 *[of trumpet, bell etc]* son *m* ◆ **the ~ of the retreat/the alarm** le signal de la retraite/de l'alerte 2 *(Med)* auscultation *f* COMP **sounding board** N *(Mus)* table *f* d'harmonie ; *(behind rostrum etc)* abat-voix *m inv* ◆ **he used the committee as a ~ board for his new idea** il a d'abord essayé sa nouvelle idée sur les membres du comité

sounding² /ˈsaʊndɪŋ/ N *(= act of measuring)* sondage *m* ◆ **~s** *(= measurement, data)* sondages *mpl* ◆ **to take ~s** *(lit, fig)* faire des sondages COMP **sounding line** N ligne *f* de sonde

-sounding /ˈsaʊndɪŋ/ ADJ *(in compounds)* qui sonne ◆ **foreign-sounding name** nom *m* à consonance étrangère ◆ **strange-/respectable-sounding** qui sonne étrange/respectable *or* bien

soundless /ˈsaʊndlɪs/ ADJ silencieux

soundlessly /ˈsaʊndlɪslɪ/ ADV *[move]* sans bruit, en silence ; *[laugh, cry]* en silence ; *[say]* sans émettre un son

soundly /ˈsaʊndlɪ/ ADV 1 *(= thoroughly) [defeat]* à plate(s) couture(s) ; *[condemn]* sévèrement ◆ **to whip sb ~** donner de bons coups de fouet à qn ◆ **he was ~ beaten** *or* **thrashed** *(= defeated)* il a été battu à plate(s) couture(s) ; *(= punished)* il a reçu une bonne *or* belle correction 2 *(= deeply) [asleep]* profondément ◆ **to sleep ~** *(lit)* dormir profondément *or* à poings fermés ; *(fig)* dormir sur ses deux oreilles 3 *(= firmly)* ◆ **~ based** *[business, financial position]* sain, solide ; *[decision]* qui repose sur des bases solides 4 *(= strongly) [constructed]* solidement 5 *(= safely) [invest]* bien, judicieusement 6 *(= competently) [organize, manage]* bien, de façon saine *or* sûre ; *[play]* correctement, bien, comme il faut 7 *(= sensibly, logically) [advise, reason, argue]* judicieusement

soundness /ˈsaʊndnɪs/ N (NonC) 1 *(= health) [of body, horse]* santé *f* ; *[of mind]* équilibre *m* 2 *(= stability) [of company, economy]* bonne santé *f* 3 *(= strength) [of structure]* solidité *f* 4 *(= sensibleness, logicality) [of judgement]* justesse *f* ; *[of advice, proposal, argument, philosophy, policy]* bon sens *m* 5 *(= deepness) [of sleep]* profondeur *f*

soundpost /ˈsaʊndpəʊst/ N *(Mus)* âme *f*

soundproof /ˈsaʊndpruːf/ VT insonoriser ADJ insonorisé

soundproofing /ˈsaʊndpruːfɪŋ/ N insonorisation *f*

soundtrack /ˈsaʊndtræk/ N *(Cine)* bande *f* sonore

soup /suːp/ N 1 soupe *f* ; *(thinner or sieved)* potage *m* ; *(very smooth)* velouté *m* ◆ **clear ~** potage *m* clair ◆ **mushroom/tomato ~** velouté *m* de champignons/de tomate ◆ **onion ~** soupe *f* à l'oignon ◆ **vegetable ~** soupe *f or* potage *m* aux légumes ◆ **to be in the ~*** être dans le pétrin* *or* dans de beaux draps ; → **pea** 2 *(US* ⁑ *= nitroglycerine)* nitroglycérine *f* COMP **soup cube** N potage *m* en cube ; *(= stock cube)* bouillon *m* Kub ® *or* en cube

soup kitchen N soupe *f* populaire

soup plate N assiette *f* creuse *or* à soupe

soup spoon N cuiller *f* à soupe

soup tureen N soupière *f*

► **soup up** * VT SEP *[+ engine]* gonfler* ◆ **he was driving a ~ed-up Mini** ® il conduisait une Mini ® au moteur gonflé* *or* poussé

soupçon /ˈsuːpsɔ̃ːn/ N *[of garlic, malice]* soupçon *m*, pointe *f*

soupy /ˈsuːpɪ/ ADJ *[liquid] (= thick)* épais (-aisse *f*) ; *(= unclear)* trouble ; *[fog, atmosphere]* épais (-aisse *f*), dense ; (* *fig = sentimental*) *[film, story, voice]* sirupeux

sour /ˈsaʊəʳ/ ADJ 1 *(in taste, smell) [fruit, wine, beer, cream, smell, taste]* aigre ; *[milk]* tourné, aigre ◆ **to go** *or* **turn ~** *[milk]* tourner ; *[cream]* devenir aigre ◆ **this milk tastes ~** ce lait a tourné

2 *(Agr) [soil]* trop acide

3 *(= embittered) [person, voice]* aigre ; *[face, expression, mood]* revêche ; *[comment]* acerbe ◆ **to**

give sb a ~ look lancer un regard mauvais à qn ◆ **to turn** *or* **go ~** *[situation, relationship]* mal tourner, tourner à l'aigre

VT *(lit, fig)* aigrir ; *[+ milk]* faire tourner

VI 1 *(lit)* s'aigrir ; *[milk]* tourner

2 *(fig) [person, character]* s'aigrir ; *[relations]* se dégrader ; *[situation]* mal tourner, se dégrader ◆ **to ~ on sb/sth** se brouiller avec qn/qch

N ◆ **whisky** *etc* **~** cocktail *m* de whisky *etc* au citron

COMP **sour(ed) cream** N *(for cooking)* crème *f* fermentée

sour-faced ADJ à la mine revêche *or* rébarbative

sour grapes NPL *(fig)* dépit *m* ◆ **it was clearly ~ grapes on his part** c'était évidemment du dépit de sa part ◆ **it sounds like ~ grapes** ça ressemble à du dépit

sour milk N *(for cooking)* lait *m* fermenté

source /sɔːs/ N *[of river]* source *f* ; *(fig)* source *f*, origine *f* ◆ **~s** *(Literat etc)* sources *fpl* ◆ **a ~ of heat** une source de chaleur ◆ **a ~ of infection** *(Med)* un foyer d'infection ◆ **we have other ~s of supply** nous avons d'autres sources d'approvisionnement, nous pouvons nous approvisionner ailleurs ◆ **what is the ~ of this information?** quelle est l'origine *or* la provenance de cette nouvelle ? ◆ **I have it from a reliable ~ that ...** je tiens de bonne source *or* de source sûre que ... ◆ **at ~** à la source VT *(Comm = find supplier for)* rechercher des fournisseurs de ◆ **to be ~d from** provenir de

COMP **source language** N *(Ling)* langue *f* de départ, langue *f* source ; *(Comput)* langage *m* source

source materials NPL *(Literat etc)* sources *fpl*

source program N *(Comput)* programme *m* source

sourcing /ˈsɔːsɪŋ/ N *(Comm)* approvisionnement *m*

sourdine /sʊəˈdiːn/ N sourdine *f*

sourdough /ˈsaʊədəʊ/ N *(US)* levain *m*

sourish /ˈsaʊərɪʃ/ ADJ *(lit, fig)* aigrelet

sourly /ˈsaʊəlɪ/ ADV 1 *(= disagreeably) [say, complain, think]* avec aigreur, aigrement ; *[look]* d'un air revêche 2 ◆ **to smell ~ of sth** avoir une odeur aigre de qch

sourness /ˈsaʊənɪs/ N *(NonC) [of fruit, flavour, milk, cream, wine, beer, person, comment]* aigreur *f* ◆ **the ~ of her expression/mood/tone** son expression *f*/humeur *f*/ton *m* revêche

sourpuss * /ˈsaʊəpʊs/ N grincheux *m*, -euse *f*

sousaphone /ˈsuːzəfəʊn/ N sousaphone *m*

souse /saʊs/ VT 1 *(= immerse)* tremper *(in* dans) ; *(= soak)* faire *or* laisser tremper *(in* dans) ◆ **to ~ sth with water** inonder qch d'eau ◆ **~d** ‡ *(fig = drunk)* rond*, noir‡ 2 *(Culin)* mariner ◆ **~d herrings** harengs *mpl* marinés ; *(rolled up)* rollmops *mpl* N 1 *(Culin)* marinade *f (à base de vinaigre)* 2 *(‡ = drunkard)* poivrot* *m*, ivrogne *mf*

south /saʊθ/ N sud *m* ◆ **to the ~ of** au sud de ◆ **in the ~ of Scotland** dans le sud de l'Écosse ◆ **the house faces the ~** la maison est exposée au sud ◆ **to veer to the ~, to go into the ~** *[wind]* tourner au sud ◆ **the wind is in the ~** le vent est au sud ◆ **the wind is (coming** *or* **blowing) from the ~** le vent vient *or* souffle du sud ◆ **to live in the ~** habiter dans le Sud ; *(in France)* habiter dans le Midi ◆ **the South of France** le Sud de la France, le Midi ◆ **the South** *(US Hist)* le Sud, les États *mpl* du Sud ; → **deep**

ADJ sud *inv*, du *or* au sud ◆ **~ wind** vent *m* du sud ◆ **~ coast** côte *f* sud *or* méridionale ◆ **on the ~ side** du côté sud ◆ **the room has a ~ aspect** la pièce est exposée au sud ◆ **~ transept/door** *(Archit)* transept *m*/portail *m* sud *or* méridional ◆ **in ~ Devon** dans le sud du Devon ◆ **in the South Atlantic** dans l'Atlantique Sud ; see also **comp**

ADV *[go]* vers le sud, en direction du sud ; *[be, lie]* au sud, dans le sud ◆ **~ of the island** *[go, sail]* au sud de l'île ; *[be, lie]* dans le sud de l'île ◆ **the town lies ~ of the border** la ville est située au sud de la frontière ◆ **further ~** plus au sud ◆ **we drove ~ for 100km** nous avons roulé pendant 100 km en direction du sud *or* du midi ◆ **go ~ till you get to Crewe** allez en direction du sud jusqu'à Crewe ◆ **to sail due ~** aller droit vers le sud ; *(Naut)* avoir le cap au sud ◆ **~ by ~-west** sud quart sud-ouest

COMP **South Africa** N Afrique *f* du Sud

South African ADJ sud-africain, d'Afrique du Sud N Sud-Africain(e) *m(f)*

South America N Amérique *f* du Sud

South American ADJ sud-américain, d'Amérique du Sud N Sud-Américain(e) *m(f)*

South Australia N Australie-Méridionale *f*

South Carolina N Caroline *f* du Sud ◆ **in South Carolina** en Caroline du Sud

South Dakota N Dakota *m* du Sud ◆ **in South Dakota** dans le Dakota du Sud

south-east N sud-est *m* ADJ (du *or* au) sud-est *inv* ADV vers le sud-est

South-East Asia N le Sud-Est asiatique, l'Asie *f* du sud-est

south-easter N vent *m* du sud-est

south-easterly ADJ *[wind, direction]* du sud-est ; *[situation]* au sud-est ADV vers le sud-est

south-eastern ADJ (du *or* au) sud-est

south-eastward(s) ADV vers le sud-est

south-facing ADJ exposé au sud *or* au midi

South Georgia N Géorgie *f* du Sud

South Moluccan N Moluquois(e) *m(f)* du Sud

the South Pacific N le Pacifique Sud

South Pole N pôle *m* Sud

the South Sea Islands NPL l'Océanie *f*

the South Seas NPL les mers *fpl* du Sud

south-south-east N sud-sud-est *m* ADJ (du *or* au) sud-sud-est *inv* ADV vers le sud-sud-est

south-south-west N sud-sud-ouest *m* ADJ (du *or* au) sud-sud-ouest *inv* ADV vers le sud-sud-ouest

south-west N sud-ouest *m* ADJ (du *or* au) sud-ouest *inv* ADV vers le sud-ouest

South West Africa N l'Afrique *f* du sud-ouest

south-wester N vent *m* du sud-ouest, suroît *m*

south-westerly ADJ *[wind, direction]* du sud-ouest ; *[situation]* au sud-ouest ADV vers le sud-ouest

south-western ADJ (du *or* au) sud-ouest *inv*

south-westward(s) ADV vers le sud-ouest ; → **Korea, Vietnam**

southbound /ˈsaʊθbaʊnd/ ADJ *[traffic, vehicles]* (se déplaçant) en direction du sud ; *[carriageway]* sud *inv* ◆ **to be ~ on the M1** être sur la M1 en direction du sud

southerly /ˈsʌðəlɪ/ ADJ *[wind]* du sud ; *[situation]* au sud ◆ **in a ~ direction** en direction du sud *or* du midi, vers le sud *or* le midi ◆ **~ latitudes** latitudes *fpl* australes ◆ **~ aspect** exposition *f* au sud *or* au midi ADV vers le sud

southern /ˈsʌðən/ ADJ sud *inv*, du sud ◆ **the ~ coast** la côte sud *or* méridionale ◆ **house with a ~ outlook** maison *f* exposée au sud *or* au midi ◆ **~ wall** mur *m* exposé au sud *or* au midi ◆ **~ hemisphere** hémisphère *m* sud *inv or* austral ◆ **Southern Africa** Afrique *f* australe ◆ **~ France** le Sud de la France, le Midi ◆ **in ~ Spain** dans le Sud de l'Espagne, en Espagne méridionale COMP **the Southern Cross** N la Croix-du-Sud

southerner /ˈsʌðənəʳ/ N 1 homme *m or* femme *f* du Sud, habitant(e) *m(f)* du Sud ; *(in France)* Méridional(e) *m(f)* ◆ **he is a ~** il vient du Sud ◆ **the ~s** les gens *mpl* du Sud 2 *(US Hist)* sudiste *mf*

southernmost /ˈsʌðənməʊst/ ADJ le plus au sud, à l'extrême sud

southpaw /ˈsaʊθpɔː/ N *(Sport)* gaucher *m*

southward /ˈsaʊθwəd/ ADJ au sud ADV (also **southwards**) vers le sud

souvenir /ˌsuːvəˈnɪəʳ/ N souvenir *m (objet)*

sou'wester /saʊˈwestəʳ/ N *(= hat)* suroît *m* ; *(= wind)* ⇒ **south-wester** ; → **south**

sovereign /ˈsɒvrɪn/ N souverain(e) *m(f)* ; *(Brit = coin)* souverain *m (ancienne pièce d'or qui valait 20 shillings)* ADJ *[state, independence, body, law, powers]* souverain *after n* ; *[contempt, indifference]* souverain *before n* ◆ **a ~ remedy for** *or* **against sth** † un remède souverain contre qch

sovereignty /ˈsɒvrəntɪ/ N souveraineté *f*

soviet /ˈsəʊvɪət/ N soviet *m* ◆ **the Supreme Soviet** le Soviet suprême ◆ **the Soviets** *(= people)* les Soviétiques *mpl* ADJ soviétique

COMP **Soviet Russia** N la Russie soviétique

the Soviet Union N l'Union *f* soviétique

sovietize /ˈsəʊvɪətaɪz/ VT soviétiser

Sovietologist /ˌsəʊvɪəˈtɒlədʒɪst/ N soviétologue *mf*

sow[1] /saʊ/ N *(= pig)* truie *f* COMP **sow thistle** N laiteron *m*

sow[2] /səʊ/ (pret **sowed**, ptp **sown** *or* **sowed**) VT *[+ seed, grass]* semer ; *[+ field]* ensemencer *(with* en) ; *(fig) [+ mines, pebbles, doubt, discord]* semer ◆ **~ the wind and reap the whirlwind** *(Prov)* qui sème le vent récolte la tempête *(Prov)* → **seed, wild** VI semer

sowbelly /ˈsaʊbelɪ/ N *(US)* petit salé *m*

sower /ˈsəʊəʳ/ N *(= person)* semeur *m*, -euse *f* ; *(= machine)* semoir *m*

sowing /ˈsəʊɪŋ/ N 1 *(= work)* semailles *fpl* ; *(= period, seeds)* semailles *fpl* ; *(= young plants)* semis *mpl* 2 *(NonC = act) [of field]* ensemencement *m* ◆ **the ~ of seeds** les semailles COMP **sowing machine** N semoir *m*

sown /səʊn/ VB ptp of **sow**[2]

soy /sɔɪ/ N 1 (also **soy sauce**) sauce *f* de soja 2 *(US)* ⇒ **soya**

soya /ˈsɔɪə/ N *(esp Brit:* also **soya bean**) *(= plant)* soja *or* soya *m* ; *(= bean)* graine *f* de soja

COMP **soya flour** N farine *f* de soja

soya sauce N sauce *f* soja

soybean /ˈsɔɪbiːn/ N *(US)* ⇒ **soya bean** ; → **soya**

sozzled † * /ˈsɒzld/ ADJ *(Brit)* paf* *inv*, noir*

SP /esˈpiː/ N *(Brit)* (abbrev of **starting price**) 1 *(Racing)* cote *f* de départ 2 *(* = information)* ◆ **what's the ~ on him ?** qu'est-ce qui se dit sur lui ? ◆ **to give sb the ~ on sb/sth** donner des infos* à qn sur qn/qch

spa /spɑː/ N 1 *(= town)* station *f* thermale, ville *f* d'eau ; *(= spring)* source *f* minérale 2 *(US:* also **health spa**) établissement *m* de cure de rajeunissement

space /speɪs/ N 1 *(NonC: gen, Astron, Phys)* espace *m* ◆ **the rocket vanished into ~** la fusée a disparu dans l'espace ◆ **he was staring into ~** il regardait dans l'espace *or* dans le vide ; → **outer**

2 *(NonC = room)* espace *m*, place *f* ◆ **to clear (a** *or* **some) ~** *or* **make ~ for sb/sth** faire de la place pour qn/qch ◆ **to take up a lot of ~** *[car, books, piece of furniture]* prendre une grande place *or* beaucoup de place, être encombrant ; *[building]* occuper un grand espace ◆ **the ~ occupied by a car/a building** l'encombrement *m* d'une voiture/d'un bâtiment ◆ **there isn't enough ~ for it** il n'y a pas assez de place pour ça ◆ **I haven't enough ~ to turn the car** je n'ai pas assez de place pour *or* je n'ai pas la place de tourner la voiture ◆ **to buy ~ in a newspaper (for an advertisement)** acheter de l'espace (publicitaire) dans un journal

3 *(fig = freedom)* ◆ **she needed a bit of ~** elle avait besoin qu'on la laisse un peu tranquille

♦ **we give each other** ~ nous nous accordons une certaine liberté

4 (= *gap, empty area*) espace *m*, place *f NonC* ; (*Mus*) interligne *m* ; (*Typ: between two words etc*) espace *m*, blanc *m* ; (*Typ*) (= *blank type*) espace *m* ♦ **in the ~s between the trees** (dans les espaces) entre les arbres ♦ **a ~ of 10 metres between the buildings** un espace *or* une distance de 10 mètres entre les bâtiments ♦ **leave a ~ for the name** laisse de la place *or* un espace pour le nom ♦ **in the ~ provided** dans la partie (*or* la case) réservée à cet effet ♦ **in an enclosed ~** dans un espace clos *or* fermé ♦ **I'm looking for a ~ to park the car in** *or* **a parking ~** je cherche une place (pour me garer) ; → **blank, open**

5 (= *interval, period*) espace *m* (de temps), intervalle *m* ♦ **after a ~ of ten minutes** après un intervalle de dix minutes ♦ **for the ~ of a month** pendant une durée *or* une période d'un mois ♦ **a ~ of five years** une période de cinq ans ♦ **in the ~ of three generations/one hour** en l'espace de trois générations/d'une heure ♦ **a short ~ of time** un court laps de temps *or* espace de temps ♦ **for a ~** pendant un certain temps

VT 1 (also **space out**) [+ *chairs, words, visits, letters*] espacer ; [+ *payments*] échelonner (*over* sur) ♦ **~ the posts (out) evenly** espacez les poteaux régulièrement, plantez les poteaux à intervalles réguliers ♦ **you'll have to ~ them further out** *or* **further apart, you'll have to ~ them out more** il faudra laisser plus d'espace entre eux *or* les espacer davantage ♦ **to be single-/ double-~d** [*text*] avoir des interlignes *mpl* simples/doubles ♦ **to ~ type out to fill a line** espacer *or* répartir les caractères sur toute une ligne ♦ **the houses were well ~d (out)** les maisons étaient bien *or* largement espacées

2 ♦ **to be ~d (out)**‡ être défoncé‡

COMP [*journey, programme, research, rocket*] spatial
the Space Age **N** l'ère *f* spatiale
space-age **ADJ** de l'ère spatiale, futuriste
space bar **N** [*of typewriter, keyboard*] barre *f* d'espacement
space cadet‡ **N** (*esp US*) allumé(e)‡ *m(f)*
space capsule **N** capsule *f* spatiale
space fiction **N** science-fiction *f* (*sur le thème des voyages dans l'espace*)
space-filler **N** (*Press*) article *m* bouche-trou *inv*
space flight **N** (= *journey*) voyage *m* spatial *or* dans l'espace ; (*NonC*) voyages *mpl* *or* vols *mpl* spatiaux
space heater **N** radiateur *m*
space helmet **N** casque *m* d'astronaute *or* de cosmonaute
Space Invaders ® **N** Space Invaders *mpl* (*jeu vidéo mettant en scène des envahisseurs extraterrestres*) ♦ **Space Invaders machine** Space Invaders *m*
space lab **N** laboratoire *m* spatial
space opera* **N** space opera *m* (*film ou série de science-fiction sur le thème des voyages dans l'espace*)
space plane **N** ⇒ **space shuttle**
space platform **N** ⇒ **space station**
space probe **N** sonde *f* spatiale
the space race **N** la course à l'espace
space-saving **ADJ** qui économise *or* gagne de la place
space science **N** spatiologie *f*
space scientist **N** spécialiste *mf* en spatiologie, spatiologue *mf*
space shot **N** (= *launching*) lancement *m* d'un engin spatial ; (= *flight*) vol *m* spatial
space shuttle **N** navette *f* spatiale
space sickness **N** mal *m* de l'espace
space station **N** station *f* orbitale *or* spatiale
space-time **N** espace-temps *m*
space-time continuum **N** continuum *m* espace-temps
space travel **N** voyages *mpl* spatiaux *or* interplanétaires *or* dans l'espace
space writer **N** (*Press*) journaliste *mf* payé(e) à la ligne

spacecraft /ˈspeɪskrɑːft/ **N** engin *m* *or* vaisseau *m* spatial

spaceman /ˈspeɪsmæn/ **N** (pl **-men**) (*gen*) spationaute *m* ; (*American*) astronaute *m* ; (*Russian*) cosmonaute *m*

spaceport /ˈspeɪspɔːt/ **N** base *f* de lancement (*d'engins spatiaux*)

spaceship /ˈspeɪsʃɪp/ **N** ⇒ **spacecraft**

spacesuit /ˈspeɪssuːt/ **N** combinaison *f* spatiale

spacewalk /ˈspeɪswɔːk/ **N** marche *f* dans l'espace **VI** marcher dans l'espace

spacewalker /ˈspeɪswɔːkəʳ/ **N** marcheur *m*, -euse *f* de l'espace

spacewoman /ˈspeɪswʊmən/ **N** (pl **-women**) (*gen*) spationaute *f* ; (*American*) astronaute *f* ; (*Russian*) cosmonaute *f*

spacey* /ˈspeɪsɪ/ **ADJ** [*music*] planant* ; [*person*] qui plane*

spacing /ˈspeɪsɪŋ/ **N** (*esp Typ*) espacement *m* ; (*between two objects*) espacement *m*, écartement *m* ; (also **spacing out** : *of payments, sentries*) échelonnement *m* ♦ **to type sth in single/double ~** taper qch avec un interligne simple/double

spacious /ˈspeɪʃəs/ **ADJ** [*room, house, car*] spacieux ; [*garden*] grand ; [*garment*] ample ♦ **~ accommodation** logement *m* spacieux

spaciousness /ˈspeɪʃəsnɪs/ **N** grandes dimensions *fpl*, grandeur *f*

spacy* /ˈspeɪsɪ/ **ADJ** ⇒ **spacey**

spade /speɪd/ **N** 1 bêche *f*, pelle *f* ; (*child's*) pelle *f* ♦ **to call a ~ a ~** appeler un chat un chat, ne pas avoir peur des mots 2 (*Cards*) pique *m* ♦ **the six of ~s** le six de pique ♦ **in ~s** * (*fig*) par excellence ; *for other phrases see* **club** 3 (**‡ *pej*) nègre *m*, négresse *f*

spadeful /ˈspeɪdfʊl/ **N** pelletée *f* ♦ **by the ~** (*fig*) en grandes quantités

spadework /ˈspeɪdwɜːk/ **N** (*NonC: fig*) travail *m* préliminaire

spag bol‡ /ˌspægˈbɒl/ **N** (*Brit*) spaghettis *mpl* bolognaise

spaghetti /spəˈgetɪ/ **N** spaghettis *mpl*
COMP **spaghetti bolognese** **N** spaghettis *mpl* bolognaise
spaghetti junction **N** échangeur *m* à niveaux multiples
spaghetti western* **N** western-spaghetti* *m*, western *m* italien

Spain /speɪn/ **N** Espagne *f*

spake †† /speɪk/ **VB** pt of **speak**

Spam ® /spæm/ **N** ≈ mortadelle *f*

spam /spæm/ (*Internet*) **N** spam *m* **VT** spammer

spammer /ˈspæməʳ/ **N** (*Internet*) spamme(u)r *m*

span¹ /spæn/ **N** 1 [*of hands, arms*] envergure *f* ; [*of girder*] portée *f* ; [*of bridge*] travée *f* ; [*of arch*] portée *f*, ouverture *f* ; [*of roof*] portée *f*, travée *f* ; [*of plane, bird*] (also **wingspan**) envergure *f* ♦ **a bridge with three ~s** un pont à trois travées ♦ **single-~ bridge** pont à travée unique ♦ **the bridge has a ~ of 120 metres** le pont a une travée *or* une portée de 120 mètres

2 (*in time*) espace *m* (de temps), durée *f* ♦ **the average ~ of life** la durée moyenne de vie ♦ **man's ~ is short** (*liter*) la vie humaine est brève ♦ **for a brief** *or* **short ~ (of time)** pendant un bref moment, pendant un court espace de temps ; → **life**

3 (†† = *measure*) empan *m*

4 (= *yoke*) [*of oxen etc*] paire *f*

VT 1 [*bridge, rope, plank etc*] [+ *stream, ditch*] enjamber ; [+ *bridge-builder*] jeter *or* construire un pont sur ♦ **Christianity ~s almost 2,000 years** le christianisme embrasse presque 2 000 ans ♦ **his life ~s almost the whole of the 18th century** sa vie s'étend sur *or* couvre presque tout le 18e siècle ♦ **his compositions ~ all types of music** ses compositions couvrent *or* embrassent tous les types de musique

2 (= *measure*) mesurer à l'empan

span² †† /spæn/ **VB** pt of **spin**

spandex /ˈspændeks/ **N** Lycra ®

spangle /ˈspæŋgl/ **N** paillette *f* ♦ **dress with ~s on it** robe *f* pailletée *or* à paillettes **VT** orner de paillettes ♦ **~d with** (*fig*) pailleté de ; → **star**

spangly* /ˈspæŋglɪ/ **ADJ** à paillettes, pailleté

Spaniard /ˈspænjəd/ **N** Espagnol(e) *m(f)*

spaniel /ˈspænjəl/ **N** épagneul *m*

Spanish /ˈspænɪʃ/ **ADJ** (*gen*) espagnol ; [*ambassador, embassy, monarch*] d'Espagne ; [*teacher*] d'espagnol ♦ **the ~ way of life** la vie espagnole, la façon de vivre des Espagnols ♦ **the ~ people** les Espagnols *mpl*
N (= *language*) espagnol *m*
NPL **the Spanish** les Espagnols *mpl*
COMP **Spanish America** **N** Amérique *f* hispanophone
Spanish-American **ADJ** hispano-américain
the Spanish Armada **N** (*Hist*) l'Invincible Armada *f*
Spanish chestnut **N** châtaigne *f*, marron *m*
the Spanish Civil War **N** la guerre civile espagnole, la guerre d'Espagne
Spanish fly **N** (*NonC*) (poudre *f* de) cantharide *f*
Spanish guitar **N** guitare *f* classique
the Spanish Main **N** la mer des Antilles *or* des Caraïbes
Spanish moss **N** (*US*) mousse *f* espagnole
Spanish omelette **N** omelette *f* aux pommes de terre et aux légumes
Spanish onion **N** oignon *m* d'Espagne
Spanish rice **N** riz *m* à l'espagnole

spank /spæŋk/ **N** ♦ **to give sb a ~** donner un coup *or* une claque à qn sur les fesses **VT** (*gen, for sexual pleasure*) donner une fessée à **VI** ♦ **to be** *or* **go ~ing along** [*horse, vehicle, ship*] aller *or* filer à bonne allure

spanking /ˈspæŋkɪŋ/ **N** fessée *f* ♦ **to give sb a ~** donner une fessée à qn **ADJ** * 1 (= *excellent*) super* ♦ **in ~ condition** en excellent état 2 (= *fast*) [*pace*] fulgurant ♦ **to move at a ~ pace** [*film, events*] se dérouler à un rythme échevelé ♦ **to speed along at a ~ pace** [*car*] passer à toute berzingue* 3 (= *fresh*) [*breeze*] fort, bon **ADV** †* ♦ **~ new** flambant neuf ♦ **~ white/clean** d'une blancheur/d'une propreté éclatante

spanner /ˈspænəʳ/ **N** (*Brit*) clé *f* (à écrous) ♦ **to put a ~ in the works** mettre des bâtons dans les roues **COMP** **spanner wrench** **N** clé *f* à ergots

spar¹ /spɑːʳ/ **N** (*Geol*) spath *m*

spar² /spɑːʳ/ **N** (*Naut*) espar *m*

spar³ /spɑːʳ/ **VI** (*Boxing*) s'entraîner (à la boxe) (*with sb* avec qn) ; (*rough and tumble*) se bagarrer* amicalement (*with sb* avec qn) ; [*two people*] échanger des coups de poing pour rire ; (*fig*) (= *argue*) se disputer (*with sb* avec qn) ; [*two people*] se défier en paroles
COMP **sparring match** **N** (*Boxing*) combat *m* d'entraînement ; (*fig*) échange *m* verbal
sparring partner **N** (*Boxing*) sparring-partner *m*, partenaire *mf* d'entraînement ; (*fig*) adversaire *mf*

spare /speəʳ/ **ADJ** 1 (= *reserve*) de réserve ; (= *replacement*) de rechange ; (= *surplus*) de *or* en trop ♦ **take a ~ pen in case that one runs out** prends un stylo de rechange *or* de réserve au cas où celui-ci n'aurait plus d'encre ♦ **I've a ~ pen if you want it** j'ai un autre stylo *or* un stylo en trop, si tu veux ◆ **have you any ~ cups?** *(in case you need more)* est-ce que tu as des tasses de réserve ? ; *(which you're not using)* est-ce que tu as des tasses de ou en trop ? ◆ **take some ~ clothes** prends des vêtements de rechange ◆ **there were no ~ chairs** *or* **no chairs ~** il n'y avait pas de chaise libre ◆ **a ~ bed** *(gen)* un lit de libre ; *(for houseguests)* un lit d'amis ◆ **~ cash** *(small amount)* argent *m* de reste ; *(larger)* argent *m* disponible ◆ **I'll lend you my ~ key** je vais te prêter mon double (de clé) ◆ **I've got a ~ ticket for the play** j'ai une place en plus pour la pièce de théâtre ◆ **there are two going ~** * il en reste deux ◆ **thousands of tickets are going ~** * il reste des milliers de billets ◆ **I felt like a ~ prick***⁑ **at a wedding** *(hum)* je me demandais ce que je foutais là⁑

② *(= lean) [person, body]* sec (sèche *f*)

③ *(= austere) [prose, style, design, room]* dépouillé ; *[music]* sobre ; *[diet, meal]* frugal

④ *(Brit* ⁑ *= crazy)* ◆ **to go ~** devenir dingue * ◆ **to drive sb ~** rendre qn dingue *

N *(= part)* pièce *f* de rechange, pièce *f* détachée ; *(= tyre)* pneu *m* de rechange ; *(= wheel)* roue *f* de secours

VT ① *(= do without)* se passer de ◆ **we can't ~ him just now** nous ne pouvons pas nous passer de lui en ce moment ◆ **can you ~ it?** vous n'en avez pas besoin ? ◆ **can you ~ £10?** est-ce que tu aurais 10 livres ? ◆ **can you ~ me £5?** est-ce que tu peux me passer 5 livres ? ◆ **I can only ~ a few minutes, I can't ~ the time (to do it)** je n'ai pas le temps (de le faire), je n'ai pas une minute (à y consacrer) ◆ **I can only ~ an hour for my piano practice** je peux seulement consacrer une heure à *or* je ne dispose que d'une heure pour mes exercices de piano ◆ **I can ~ you five minutes** je peux vous accorder *or* consacrer cinq minutes ◆ **to ~ a thought for** penser à, avoir une pensée pour

◆ **to spare** ◆ **he had time to ~ so he went to the pictures** il n'était pas pressé *or* il avait du temps devant lui, alors il est allé au cinéma ◆ **did you have a rush to get here? – no, I had time (and) to ~** est-ce que tu as dû te dépêcher pour arriver ? – non, j'ai eu plus de temps qu'il ne m'en fallait ◆ **I've only a few minutes to ~** je ne dispose que de quelques minutes, je n'ai que quelques minutes de libres *or* devant moi ◆ **there are three to ~** il en reste trois ◆ **I've got none** *or* **nothing to ~** j'ai juste ce qu'il me faut, je n'en ai pas trop ◆ **I've enough and to ~** j'en ai plus qu'il ne m'en faut ◆ **she had a metre to ~** elle en avait un mètre de trop *or* de plus que nécessaire ◆ **with two minutes to ~** avec deux minutes d'avance ◆ **we did it with $5 to ~** nous l'avons fait et il nous reste encore 5 dollars

② *(= show mercy to) [+ person, sb's life, tree]* épargner ◆ **he ~d no one** *(lit, fig)* il n'a épargné personne, il n'a fait grâce à personne ◆ **the plague ~d no one** la peste n'a épargné personne ◆ **if I'm ~d** † si Dieu me prête vie ◆ **to ~ sb's feelings** ménager (les sentiments de) qn ◆ **~ my blushes!** épargnez ma modestie !, ne me faites pas rougir !

③ *[+ suffering, grief]* éviter, épargner *(to sb* à qn) ◆ **to ~ sb embarrassment** épargner *or* éviter de l'embarras à qn ◆ **I wanted to ~ him trouble** je voulais lui éviter de se déranger ◆ **you could have ~d yourself the trouble** vous auriez pu vous épargner tout ce mal ◆ **I'll ~ you the details** je vous fais grâce des détails

④ *(= refrain from using) [+ one's strength, efforts]* ménager ◆ **we have ~d no expense to make her stay a pleasant one** nous n'avons pas reculé devant la dépense pour que son séjour soit agréable ◆ **he ~d no expense to modernize the house** il a dépensé sans compter pour moderniser la maison ◆ **no expense ~d** peu importe le prix ◆ **he didn't ~ himself, he ~d no pains** il s'est donné beaucoup de mal, il n'a pas épargné sa peine ◆ **he could have ~d his pains, he could have ~d himself the trouble** il s'est donné du mal pour rien ◆ **~ your pains, it's too late now** pas la peine de te donner du mal, c'est trop tard maintenant ◆ **~ the rod and spoil the child** *(Prov)* qui aime bien châtie bien *(Prov)*

COMP spare bedroom N ⇒ **spare room**

spare part N pièce *f* de rechange, pièce *f* détachée

spare-part surgery* N chirurgie *f* de transplantation

spare room N chambre *f* d'amis

spare time N temps *m* libre ◆ **to do sth in one's ~ time** faire qch pendant son temps libre *or* ses moments de libre

spare-time ADJ (fait) à temps perdu *or* pendant les moments de loisir ◆ **~-time activities** (activités *fpl* de) loisirs *mpl*

spare tyre N *[of car]* roue *f* de secours ; (* *fig* = fat) bourrelet *m* (de graisse) *(à la taille)* ◆ **to get a ~ tyre** * prendre de l'embonpoint ◆ **to get rid of one's ~ tyre** * se débarrasser de son bourrelet (de graisse)

spare wheel N *[of car]* roue *f* de secours

sparerib /ˈspɛərɪb/ **N** *(Culin)* travers *m* (de porc)

sparing /ˈspɛərɪŋ/ **ADJ** *[person]* économe ; *[use]* modéré ; *[amount]* limité, modéré ◆ **she was ~ with heat and light** elle faisait des économies de chauffage et d'électricité ◆ **I've not been ~ with the garlic** je n'ai pas lésiné sur l'ail ◆ **he was ~ with** *or* *(frm)* **of the wine** il a lésiné sur le vin ◆ **~ of words** *(frm)* avare *or* chiche de paroles ◆ **you must be more ~ of your strength** vous devez ménager vos forces ◆ **~ in one's praise (for sb)** avare de ses louanges (à l'égard de qn) ◆ **to be ~ in one's use of sth** utiliser qch avec modération

sparingly /ˈspɛərɪŋlɪ/ **ADV** *[use, apply]* avec modération ; *[eat]* frugalement ; *[drink]* peu ; *[spend, praise]* avec parcimonie

spark /spɑːk/ **N** *(Elec)* étincelle *f* ; *(fig) [of intelligence, wit, life]* étincelle *f* ; *[of commonsense, interest]* lueur *f* ◆ **to make the ~s fly** *(fig) (= start a row)* mettre le feu aux poudres *(fig) (= fight)* se bagarrer un bon coup * ◆ **they'll strike ~s off each other** ils se stimuleront (l'un l'autre) ; → **bright NPL sparks** *(Brit = electrician)* électricien *m* ; *(= radio operator)* radio *m* (de bord) **VI** jeter des étincelles **VT** (also **spark off**) *[+ rebellion, complaints, quarrel]* provoquer, déclencher ; *[+ interest, enthusiasm]* susciter, éveiller *(in sb* chez qn) ◆ **to ~ a fire** provoquer un incendie

COMP spark gap N *(Elec)* écartement *m* des électrodes

spark(ing) plug N bougie *f*

sparkle /ˈspɑːkl/ **N** (NonC) *[of stars, dew, tinsel]* scintillement *m*, étincellement *m* ; *[of diamond]* éclat *m*, feux *mpl* ; *(in eye)* étincelle *f*, éclair *m* ; *(fig)* vie *f*, éclat *m* **VI** *[glass, drops of water, snow]* étinceler, briller ; *[surface of water, lake]* scintiller, miroiter ; *[diamond]* étinceler, jeter des feux, scintiller ; *[fabric]* chatoyer ; *[wine]* pétiller ; *[eyes]* étinceler, pétiller *(with* de) ; *[person]* briller ; *[conversation, play, book]* étinceler, pétiller *(with* de), être brillant *or* étincelant

sparkler /ˈspɑːkləʳ/ **N** ① *(= firework)* cierge *m* magique ② (* *= sparkling wine)* vin *m* pétillant ③ (⁑ *= diamond)* diam⁑ *m*

sparkling /ˈspɑːklɪŋ/ **ADJ** ① *(= bright) [glass, diamond, snow, sand, sea, eyes]* étincelant *(with sth* de qch) ; *[day, sky]* radieux ; *[surface of water, lake]* scintillant, miroitant ② *(= scintillating) [person, conversation, script, performance, results]* brillant ◆ **he was in ~ form** il était dans une forme éblouissante ③ *(= fizzy) [wine]* mousseux ; *[water] (naturally)* gazeux naturel ; *(artificially)* gazéifié ◆ **~ cider** cidre *m* **ADV** ◆ **~ clean** d'une propreté éclatante

sparkly* /ˈspɑːklɪ/ **ADJ** brillant

sparky* /ˈspɑːkɪ/ **ADJ** plein d'entrain

sparrow /ˈspærəʊ/ **N** moineau *m* ; → **hedgesparrow**

sparrowgrass /ˈspærəʊgrɑːs/ **N** *(dial)* asperge(s) *f(pl)*

sparrowhawk /ˈspærəʊhɔːk/ **N** épervier *m*

sparse /spɑːs/ **ADJ** *[population, hair, vegetation]* clairsemé ; *[traffic]* léger ; *[furniture]* rare ; *[dialogue]* entrecoupé de longs silences

sparsely /ˈspɑːslɪ/ **ADV** *[wooded, furnished]* peu ◆ **~ populated** peu peuplé

Sparta /ˈspɑːtə/ **N** Sparte

Spartacus /ˈspɑːtəkəs/ **N** Spartacus *m*

Spartan /ˈspɑːtən/ **N** Spartiate *mf* **ADJ** ① *(= from Sparta)* spartiate ② *(= austere:* also **spartan)** *[lifestyle, accommodation, conditions, diet]* spartiate

spasm /ˈspæzəm/ **N** *(Med)* spasme *m* ; *(fig)* accès *m (of* de) ◆ **a ~ of coughing** un accès *or* une quinte de toux ◆ **to work in ~s** travailler par à-coups *or* par accès

spasmodic /spæzˈmɒdɪk/ **ADJ** ① *(= intermittent) [work, movements, attempts, service]* intermittent, irrégulier ◆ **the team had only ~ success** l'équipe n'a connu que des succès intermittents ◆ **to mount ~ raids** lancer des raids répétés ② *(Med)* spasmodique

spasmodically /spæzˈmɒdɪkəlɪ/ **ADV** ① *(= intermittently) [continue, campaign]* de façon intermittente ; *[work, try]* par à-coups, de façon intermittente *or* irrégulière ② *(Med)* ◆ **to jerk ~** *[person, body, chest]* être agité de spasmes irréguliers

spastic /ˈspæstɪk/ **ADJ** ① († *= handicapped) [person]* handicapé moteur (handicapée moteur *f*) ② *(Med) [movement, paralysis]* spasmodique ③ *(pej = clumsy) [movement]* convulsif **N** *(Med* †) handicapé(e) *m(f)* moteur *f inv* **COMP spastic colon N** colopathie *f* spasmodique

spasticity /spæsˈtɪsɪtɪ/ **N** *(Med)* paralysie *f* spasmodique

spat¹ /spæt/ **VB** pt, ptp of **spit¹**

spat² /spæt/ **N** *(= gaiter)* demi-guêtre *f*

spat³ /spæt/ **N** *(= oyster)* naissain *m*

spat⁴* /spæt/ *(US = quarrel)* **N** prise *f* de bec * **VI** avoir une prise de bec *

spate /speɪt/ **N** *(Brit)* ① *[of river]* crue *f* ② *[of letters, orders]* avalanche *f* ; *[of words, abuse]* torrent *m* ◆ **a ~ of bombings** une vague d'attentats ◆ **in ~** en crue ◆ **to be in full ~** *(= talking at length)* être parti (dans son sujet) ◆ **to have a ~ of work** être débordé *or* submergé de travail ◆ **a fresh ~ of sabotage/attacks** une recrudescence d'actes de sabotage/d'attaques

spatial /ˈspeɪʃəl/ *(frm)* **ADJ** ① *(= physical) [relationship, variation]* spatial ; *[constraints]* d'espace ◆ **~ distribution of employment** répartition *f* or distribution *f* géographique de l'emploi ② *(Psych)* ◆ **~ awareness/ability/skills** perception *f* spatiale **COMP spatial frequency N** *(Elec)* fréquence *f* spatiale

spatiotemporal /ˌspeɪʃɪəʊˈtempərəl/ **ADJ** spatiotemporel

spatter /ˈspætəʳ/ **VT** *(accidentally)* éclabousser *(with* de) ; *(deliberately)* asperger *(with* de) ◆ **to ~ mud on** *or* **over a dress** éclabousser de boue une robe **VI** *(= splash)* gicler *(on* sur) ; *(= sound)* crépiter *(on* sur) **N** *(= mark)* éclaboussure(s) *f(pl)* ; *(= sound)* crépitement *m*

-spattered /ˈspætəd/ **ADJ** *(in compounds)* ◆ **the butcher's blood-spattered apron** le tablier éclaboussé de sang du boucher ◆ **mud-spattered car** voiture *f* éclaboussée de boue

spatula /ˈspætjʊlə/ **N** *(Culin)* spatule *f* ; *(Med)* abaisse-langue *m inv*

spavin /ˈspævɪn/ **N** éparvin *m*

spawn /spɔːn/ N *[of fish, frog]* frai *m*, œufs *mpl* ; *[of mushroom]* mycélium *m* ; *(pej = person)* progéniture *f (iro)* VT pondre ; *(fig pej)* engendrer, faire naître VI frayer ; *(fig pej)* se reproduire, se multiplier

spawning /ˈspɔːnɪŋ/ N *(NonC)* frai *m* COMP **spawning ground** N frayère *f*

spay /speɪ/ VT *[+ animal]* enlever les ovaires de

SPCA /ˌespiːsiːˈeɪ/ N *(US)* (abbrev of **Society for the Prevention of Cruelty to Animals**) ≈ SPA *f*

SPCC /ˌespiːsiːˈsiː/ N *(US)* (abbrev of **Society for the Prevention of Cruelty to Children**) *association pour la protection de l'enfance*

speak /spiːk/ (pret **spoke**, ptp **spoken**) VI 1 *(= talk)* parler *(to* à ; *of, about* de) ; *(= converse)* parler, s'entretenir *(with* avec) ; *(= be on speaking terms)* parler, adresser la parole *(to* à) ; *(fig) [gun, trumpet etc]* retentir, se faire entendre ◆ **to ~ in a whisper** chuchoter ◆ **~ normally, don't shout!** parle normalement, ne crie pas ! ◆ **to ~ to o.s.** parler tout seul ◆ **I'll ~ to him about it** je vais lui en parler, je vais lui en toucher un mot *or* deux mots ◆ **I don't know him to ~ to** je ne le connais pas assez bien pour lui parler *or* pour lui adresser la parole ◆ **I'll never ~ to him again** je ne lui adresserai plus jamais la parole ◆ **did you ~?*** pardon ?, tu m'as parlé ? ◆ **you have only to ~** tu n'as qu'un mot à dire ◆ **~ing personally ...** pour ma part ..., personnellement ... ◆ **~ing as a member of the society I ...** en tant que membre de la société je ...

◆ **so to speak** pour ainsi dire

◆ *adverb* **+ speaking** ◆ **biologically/philosophically ~ing** biologiquement/philosophiquement parlant

2 *(Telec)* ◆ **who's (that) ~ing ?** qui est à l'appareil ? ; *(passing on call)* c'est de la part de qui ? ◆ **(this is) Paul ~ing** ici Paul, (c'est) Paul à l'appareil ◆ **~ing!** lui-même *(or* elle-même) !, c'est moi-même ! ; → **action, badly, roughly**

3 *(= make a speech)* parler *(on or about sth* de qch) ; *(= begin to speak)* prendre la parole ◆ **to ~ in public** parler en public ◆ **he rose to ~** il s'est levé pour prendre la parole *or* pour parler ◆ **Mr Latimer will ~ next** ensuite c'est M. Latimer qui prendra la parole ◆ **the chairman asked him to ~** le président lui a donné la parole ◆ **Mr King will now ~ on "The Incas"** M. King va maintenant (nous) parler des Incas ◆ **to ~ in a debate** *[proposer, seconder]* faire un discours *or* prendre la parole au cours d'un débat ; *(from floor of house)* participer à un débat, intervenir dans un débat

4 *(phrases)* ◆ **to ~ for sb** *(= be spokesman for)* parler pour qn *or* au nom de qn ; *(= give evidence for)* parler *or* témoigner en faveur de qn ◆ **~ing for myself ...** personnellement ..., pour ma part ..., en ce qui me concerne ... ◆ **~ for yourself!*** parle pour toi !* ◆ **let him ~ for himself** laisse-le s'exprimer, laisse-le dire lui-même ce qu'il a à dire ◆ **it ~s for itself** c'est évident, c'est tout ce qu'il y a de plus clair ◆ **the facts ~ for themselves** les faits parlent d'eux-mêmes *or* se passent de commentaires ◆ **I can ~ for** *or* **to his honesty** je peux témoigner de *or* répondre de son honnêteté ◆ **it ~s to the chaos that was inside me** cela dit *or* montre bien la confusion qui régnait en moi ◆ **that ~s well for his generosity** ceci montre bien *or* prouve bien qu'il est généreux ◆ **to ~ of sth as sth** appeler qch qch ◆ **he always ~s well of her** il dit toujours du bien d'elle ◆ **he is very well spoken of** on dit beaucoup de bien de lui ◆ **everything spoke of wealth** tout indiquait la richesse ◆ **everything spoke of fear/hatred** tout révélait *or* trahissait la peur/la haine ◆ **to ~ to a motion** *(Parl etc)* soutenir une motion

◆ **speaking of ...** ◆ **~ing of holidays ...** à propos de vacances ..., puisqu'on parle de vacances ... ◆ **~ing of which ...** à propos ...

◆ **... to speak of** ◆ **he has no friends/money to ~ of** il n'a pour ainsi dire pas d'amis/d'argent ◆ **nobody to ~ of** pour ainsi dire personne ◆ **it's nothing to ~ of** ce n'est pas grand-chose, cela ne vaut pas la peine qu'on en parle *subj*, c'est trois fois rien*

◆ **spoken for** ◆ **that is already spoken for** c'est déjà réservé *or* retenu ◆ **she is already spoken for** elle est déjà prise

VT 1 *[+ language]* parler ◆ **"English spoken"** "ici on parle anglais" ◆ **French is spoken all over the world** le français se parle dans le monde entier

2 *(liter) [+ a poem, one's lines, the truth]* dire ◆ **I didn't ~ a word** je n'ai rien dit ◆ **to ~ one's mind** dire ce que l'on pense

N *(in compounds)* langage *m* de ..., jargon *m* de ... ◆ **computerspeak** langage *m or* jargon *m* de l'informatique, langage *m or* jargon *m* des informaticiens

▸ **speak out** VI ⇒ **speak up 2**

▸ **speak up** VI 1 *(= talk loudly)* parler fort *or* haut ; *(= raise one's voice)* parler plus fort *or* plus haut ◆ **~ up!** (parle) plus fort *or* plus haut ! ; *(= don't mumble)* parle plus clairement !

2 *(fig)* parler franchement, ne pas mâcher ses mots ◆ **he's not afraid to ~ up** il n'a pas peur de dire ce qu'il pense *or* de parler franchement, il ne mâche pas ses mots ◆ **I think you ought to ~ up** je crois que vous devriez dire franchement ce que vous pensez ◆ **to ~ up for sb** parler en faveur de qn, défendre qn ◆ **to ~ up against sth** s'élever contre qch

speakeasy * /ˈspiːkiːzɪ/ N *(US Hist)* bar *m* clandestin *(pendant la prohibition)*

speaker /ˈspiːkəʳ/ N 1 *(gen)* celui *m* (*or* celle *f*) qui parle ; *(in dialogue, discussion)* interlocuteur *m*, -trice *f* ; *(in public)* orateur *m*, -trice *f* ; *(= lecturer)* conférencier *m*, -ière *f* ◆ **he's a good/poor ~** il parle bien/mal, c'est un bon/mauvais orateur *or* conférencier ◆ **the previous ~** la personne qui a parlé la dernière, l'orateur *or* le conférencier précédent

2 ◆ **Speaker (of the House)** *(Brit)* président(e) *m(f)* de la Chambre des communes ; *(US)* président(e) *m(f)* de la Chambre des représentants

3 ◆ **French ~** personne *f* qui parle français ; *(as native or official language)* francophone *mf* ◆ **he is not a Welsh ~** il ne parle pas gallois ; → **native**

4 (also **loudspeaker**) *(for PA system, musical instruments)* haut-parleur *m*, enceinte *f* ; *[of hi-fi]* baffle *m*, enceinte *f*

SPEAKER (OF THE HOUSE)

En Grande-Bretagne, le **Speaker** est le président de la Chambre des communes, qui veille au respect du règlement et au bon déroulement des séances. Élu au début de chaque législature, il n'appartient pas nécessairement au parti au pouvoir, mais il perd son droit de vote et se doit de rester impartial. Au début de chacune de leurs interventions, les députés s'adressent au président de l'assemblée par ces mots : « Mister/Madam **Speaker** ».

Aux États-Unis le président de la Chambre des représentants est le **Speaker of the House** : il est le leader du parti majoritaire et joue le rôle de porte-parole de son parti. Politiquement, il vient en seconde position, après le vice-président des États-Unis, pour remplacer le président en cas de vacance du pouvoir.

speaking /ˈspiːkɪŋ/ ADJ *(= talking) [doll, machine]* parlant N *(= skill)* art *m* de parler ; → **public**

COMP **the speaking clock** N *(Brit)* l'horloge *f* parlante

speaking part, speaking role N *(Cine, Theat)* rôle *m (autre que de figuration)*

speaking terms NPL ◆ **they're on ~ terms again** ils se parlent à nouveau, ils s'adressent à nouveau la parole ◆ **they're not on ~ terms** ils ne s'adressent plus la parole, ils ne se parlent plus ◆ **she's on ~ terms with him again** elle lui parle à nouveau, elle lui adresse à nouveau la parole

speaking tube N tuyau *m* acoustique

speaking voice N ◆ **his ~ voice** le timbre de sa voix quand il parle ◆ **he has a pleasant ~ voice** il a une voix agréable (à entendre)

-speaking /ˈspiːkɪŋ/ ADJ *(in compounds)* ◆ **English-speaking** *[country]* anglophone, de langue anglaise ; *[person]* anglophone, parlant anglais ◆ **slow-speaking** au débit lent, à la parole lente

spear /spɪəʳ/ N 1 *[of warrior, hunter]* lance *f* 2 *[of broccoli, asparagus]* pointe *f* VT transpercer d'un coup de lance ◆ **he ~ed a potato with his fork** il a piqué une pomme de terre avec sa fourchette

COMP **spear grass** N *(Brit)* chiendent *m*

spear gun N fusil *m* sous-marin *or* à harpon

spearcarrier /ˈspɪəkærɪəʳ/ N *(Theat) (lit)* soldat *m* ◆ **he started as a ~** *(fig)* il a débuté en jouant les hallebardiers, il a commencé par être figurant

spearfish /ˈspɪəfɪʃ/ VI *(US)* (also **go spearfishing**) pratiquer la pêche sous-marine

spearhead /ˈspɪəhed/ N *(Mil, fig)* fer *m* de lance VT *[+ attack, offensive]* être le fer de lance de ; *[+ campaign]* mener

spearmint /ˈspɪəmɪnt/ N *(= plant)* menthe *f* verte ; *(= chewing gum)* chewing-gum *m* (à la menthe) COMP *[sweet]* à la menthe ; *[flavour]* de menthe

spec * /spek/ N (abbrev of **speculation**) ◆ **to buy sth on ~** risquer *or* tenter le coup* en achetant qch ◆ **I went along on ~** j'y suis allé à tout hasard NPL **specs** (abbrev of **specifications**) spécifications *fpl*, caractéristiques *fpl* (techniques)

special /ˈspeʃəl/ ADJ 1 *(= particular, exceptional) [occasion, assignment, permission, arrangements, adviser, price, study, skill]* spécial ; *[purpose, use, equipment]* spécial, particulier ; *[day]* grand, exceptionnel ; *[event, situation, goods]* exceptionnel ; *[circumstances]* exceptionnel, extraordinaire ; *[powers, meeting]* extraordinaire ; *[case]* particulier, à part ; *[status, interest]* particulier ; *[effort, pleasure, attention]* (tout) particulier ; *[treatment]* de faveur ◆ **what is so ~ about it?** qu'est-ce que cela a de si exceptionnel *or* extraordinaire ? ◆ **is there anything ~ you would like?** as-tu envie de quelque chose de particulier *or* de spécial ? ◆ **to take ~ care** faire (tout) particulièrement attention ◆ **take ~ care of it** fais-y (tout) particulièrement attention, prends-en un soin tout particulier ◆ **by ~ command of ...** sur ordre spécial *or* exprès de ... ◆ **are you thinking of any ~ date?** est-ce que tu penses à une date particulière *or* en particulier ? ◆ **this is rather a ~ day for me** c'est une journée particulièrement importante pour moi ◆ **can I ask a ~ favour?** peux-tu me rendre un grand service ? ◆ **it's a ~ feature of the village** c'est une caractéristique *or* une particularité du village ◆ **in this one ~ instance** dans ce cas bien particulier ◆ **my ~ chair** mon fauteuil préféré, le fauteuil que je me réserve ◆ **what are you doing this weekend? – nothing ~** que fais-tu ce week-end ? – rien de spécial *or* de particulier ◆ **there is nothing ~ about being a journalist** le fait d'être journaliste n'a rien d'extraordinaire ◆ **I've no ~ person in mind** je ne pense à personne en particulier ◆ **to have a ~ place in sb's heart** occuper une place à part dans le cœur de qn ◆ **he has a ~ place in our affections** nous sommes tout particulièrement attachés à lui ◆ **Britain had its own ~ problems** la Grande-

Bretagne avait ses propres problèmes ♦ **I had no ~ reason for suspecting him** je n'avais aucune raison particulière de le soupçonner ♦ **why do you say that? – oh, no ~ reason** pourquoi as-tu dit ça ? – oh, j'ai dit ça sans raison particulière ♦ **with ~ responsibility for sth** *(Pol)* chargé du dossier de qch ♦ **I've cooked something ~ for dinner** j'ai préparé quelque chose de spécial pour le dîner ♦ **she is something ~** elle n'est pas comme tout le monde ♦ **~ to that country** particulier *or* propre à ce pays ♦ **as a ~ treat my grandfather would take me to the zoo** quand il voulait me gâter, mon grand-père m'emmenait au zoo ♦ **we had roast beef as a ~ treat** nous nous sommes offert un extra et avons mangé du rosbif ♦ **he has his own ~ way with the children** il a une façon toute particulière *or* bien à lui de s'y prendre avec les enfants

2 *(= dear) [person]* ♦ **is there anyone ~ in your life ?** y a-t-il quelqu'un dans votre vie ? ♦ **"professional woman seeks someone special to share her life with"** "femme exerçant profession libérale cherche âme sœur" ♦ **tender moments with a ~ person** moments de tendresse avec une personne qu'on aime ♦ **her ~ friend** son meilleur ami, un ami intime ♦ **you're extra ~!*** tu es vraiment tout pour moi ! ♦ **she's very ~ to us** elle nous est très chère

N *(= train)* train *m* supplémentaire ; *(= newspaper)* édition *f* spéciale ; *(= policeman)* auxiliaire *m* de police ; *(Rad, TV * = programme)* émission *f* spéciale ♦ **the chef's ~** la spécialité du chef *or* de la maison ♦ **today's ~** *(on menu)* le plat du jour ♦ **this week's ~** *(on item in shop)* l'affaire *f* de la semaine ; → **football**

COMP **special agent** N *(= spy)* agent *m* secret

Special Air Service N *(Brit Mil)* ≃ Groupement *m* d'intervention de la gendarmerie nationale

Special Branch N *(Brit Police)* les renseignements *mpl* généraux

special constable N *(Brit)* auxiliaire *m* de police

special correspondent N *(Press, Rad, TV)* envoyé(e) *m(f)* spécial(e)

special delivery N *(Post)* ♦ **by ~ delivery** en exprès

special-delivery letter N *(Post)* lettre *f* exprès

special edition N *[of book]* édition *f* spéciale ; *[of programme]* diffusion *f* spéciale ; *[of car]* modèle *m* spécial

special education N *(Brit)* ⇒ **special schooling**

special effects NPL effets *mpl* spéciaux

special feature N *(Press)* article *m* spécial

special handling N *(US Post)* acheminement *m* rapide

special interest group N *(Pol etc)* groupe *m* de pression

special jury N *(Jur)* jury *m* spécial

special licence N *(Jur) (gen)* dispense *f* spéciale ; *(for marriage)* dispense *f* de bans

special messenger N ♦ **by ~ messenger** par messager spécial

special needs NPL *(Educ, Admin)* problèmes *mpl* de scolarité ♦ **children with ~ needs, ~ needs children** enfants *mpl* ayant des problèmes de scolarité ♦ **~ needs teacher** enseignant(e) *m(f)* spécialisé(e) pour enfants ayant des problèmes de scolarité

special offer N promotion *f*, offre *f* spéciale ♦ **on ~ offer** en promotion

Special Patrol Group N *(Brit Police)* ≃ brigade *f* antiémeute

special relationship N *(Pol)* lien *m* privilégié *(with* avec*)*

special school N *(Brit)* établissement *m* scolaire spécialisé

special schooling N *(Brit)* enseignement *m* spécialisé *(pour handicapés mentaux)*

special school teacher N *(Brit)* instituteur *m*, -trice *f* spécialisé(e)

special slalom N *(Ski)* slalom *m* spécial

special student N *(US Univ)* auditeur *m*, -trice *f* libre *(ne préparant pas de diplôme)*

special subject N *(Scol, Univ)* option *f* ; *(advanced)* sujet *m* spécialisé

specialism /ˈspeʃəlɪzəm/ N 1 *(= subject, skill)* spécialité *f* 2 *(= specialization)* spécialisation *f*

specialist /ˈspeʃəlɪst/ N *(gen, Med)* spécialiste *mf (in* de*)* ♦ **an eye/heart ~** *(Med)* un(e) ophtalmologue/cardiologue ♦ **you need a ~ to tell you that** seul un spécialiste *or* un expert peut vous dire cela

COMP *[knowledge, dictionary]* spécialisé, spécial

specialist teacher N *(primary)* instituteur *m*, -trice *f* (spécialisé(e) dans une matière) ; *(secondary)* professeur *m* (spécialisé(e) dans une matière)

specialist work N ♦ **it's ~ work** cela requiert un spécialiste *or* un professionnel, un amateur ne peut pas le faire

speciality /ˌspeʃɪˈælɪtɪ/ N spécialité *f* ♦ **to make a ~ of sth** se spécialiser dans qch ♦ **his ~ is Medieval English** c'est un spécialiste de l'anglais médiéval ♦ **it is a ~ of the village** c'est une spécialité du village ♦ **armchairs are this firm's ~** cette firme se spécialise dans les fauteuils ♦ **the chef's ~** la spécialité du chef *or* de la maison

specialization /ˌspeʃəlaɪˈzeɪʃən/ N spécialisation *f (in* dans*)*

specialize /ˈspeʃəlaɪz/ VI *[student, firm, chef]* se spécialiser *(in* dans*)* ♦ **he ~s in making a fool of himself** *(hum)* il se fait un point de passer pour un imbécile

specialized /ˈspeʃəlaɪzd/ ADJ *[knowledge, equipment]* spécial ; *[vocabulary, department, training]* spécialisé ; *[tools]* à usage spécial COMP **specialized subject** N *(Scol, Univ)* option *f* ; *(advanced)* sujet *m* spécialisé

specially /ˈspeʃəlɪ/ ADV 1 *(= expressly) [designed, made, built, adapted]* spécialement ; *[commissioned, prepared, selected, formulated]* (tout) spécialement ♦ **to be ~ trained** avoir reçu une formation spéciale ♦ **~ written for children** écrit spécialement pour les enfants ♦ **I asked for it ~** je l'ai demandé exprès *or* tout spécialement 2 *(* = exceptionally) [good, difficult]* particulièrement ; *[important]* spécialement, particulièrement 3 *(= in particular) [think]* surtout, tout particulièrement ♦ **he is ~ interested in Proust** il s'intéresse tout spécialement *or* tout particulièrement à Proust ♦ **we would ~ like to see the orchard** nous aimerions particulièrement *or* surtout voir le verger

specialty /ˈspeʃəltɪ/ N *(US)* ⇒ **speciality**

specie /ˈspiːʃiː/ N *(Fin)* espèces *fpl* (monnayées)

species /ˈspiːʃiːz/ N *(pl inv: all senses)* espèce *f*

specific /spəˈsɪfɪk/ ADJ *[person, description, instructions, meaning, reason, plan]* précis ; *[issue, charge, case]* précis, particulier ; *[area, conditions, group, need]* spécifique, particulier ♦ **he refused to be more ~** il a refusé d'être plus précis ♦ **he was very ~ on that point** il s'est montré très explicite sur ce point ♦ **nothing very ~** rien de bien précis ♦ **~ to sb/sth** propre à qn/qch N 1 *(Med)* (remède *m*) spécifique *m (for* de, contre*)* ; *(fig)* remède *m* spécifique 2 *(pl)* **let's get down to ~s** *(= details etc)* entrons dans les détails, prenons des exemples précis

COMP **specific gravity** N *(Phys)* densité *f*

specific heat N *(Phys)* chaleur *f* massique *or* spécifique

specific name N *(Bio)* nom *m* d'espèce

-specific /spəˈsɪfɪk/ ADJ *(in compounds)* ♦ **most predators are species-specific** la plupart des prédateurs sont spécifiques à certaines espèces ♦ **most societies impose gender-specific clothing** la plupart des sociétés imposent des habitudes vestimentaires propres à chaque sexe

specifically /spəˈsɪfɪkəlɪ/ ADV 1 *(= especially) [design]* tout spécialement, expressément ; *[aim at, relate to]* tout spécialement ; *[intend, plan]* expressément, particulièrement 2 *(= in particular)* en particulier ♦ **more ~** plus particulièrement 3 *(= explicitly) [mention, refer to, authorize, warn, recommend]* expressément ♦ **to state sth ~** préciser qch ♦ **I told you quite ~** je vous l'avais bien précisé *or* spécifié ♦ **he ~ asked us not to mention the fact** il nous a bien spécifié de ne pas mentionner ce fait, il nous a expressément demandé de ne pas mentionner ce fait 4 *(= uniquely)* ♦ **~ medical/socialist/political** spécifiquement médical/socialiste/politique

specification /ˌspesɪfɪˈkeɪʃən/ N 1 *(NonC = act of specifying)* spécification *f*, précision *f* 2 *(= item in contract etc)* stipulation *f*, prescription *f* ♦ **this ~ was not complied with** cette stipulation *or* cette prescription n'a pas été respectée ♦ **~s** *(for building, machine etc)* spécifications *fpl*, caractéristiques *fpl* (techniques) ; *(in contract etc)* cahier *m* des charges ; → **outline**

specify /ˈspesɪfaɪ/ VT spécifier, préciser ♦ **unless otherwise specified** sauf indication contraire ♦ **at a specified time** à un moment précis, à une heure précise

specimen /ˈspesɪmɪn/ N *[of rock, species, style]* spécimen *m* ; *[of blood, tissue]* prélèvement *m* ; *[of urine]* échantillon *m* ; *(fig = example)* spécimen *m*, exemple *m (of* de*)* ♦ **that trout is a fine ~** cette truite est un magnifique spécimen *or* est magnifique ♦ **an odd ~*** un drôle d'individu ♦ **you're a pretty poor ~*** tu es un *(or* une*)* pas grand-chose*

COMP **specimen copy** N spécimen *m*

specimen page N page *f* spécimen

specimen signature N spécimen *m* de signature

specious /ˈspiːʃəs/ ADJ *(frm)* spécieux

speciousness /ˈspiːʃəsnɪs/ N *(NonC: frm)* caractère *m* spécieux

speck /spek/ N *[of dust, soot]* grain *m* ; *[of blood, dirt, mud, ink]* toute petite tache *f* ; *(on fruit, leaves, skin)* tache *f*, tavelure *f* ♦ **it has got black ~s all over it** c'est entièrement couvert de toutes petites taches noires ♦ **I've got a ~ in my eye** j'ai une poussière dans l'œil ♦ **just a ~ on the horizon/in the sky** rien qu'un point noir à l'horizon/dans le ciel ♦ **cream? – just a ~*, thanks** de la crème ? – juste un petit peu, merci VT tacheter, moucheter ; *[+ fruit]* tacheter, taveler

speckle /ˈspekl/ N tacheture *f*, moucheture *f* VT tacheter, moucheter

speckled /ˈspekld/ ADJ *[egg]* tacheté, moucheté *(with sth* de qch*)* ♦ **~ with (patches of) brown and white** tacheté *or* moucheté de brun et de blanc ♦ **the sky was ~ with stars** le ciel était constellé d'étoiles ♦ **the beach was ~ with people** il y avait des gens éparpillés sur la plage

specs* /speks/ NPL 1 abbrev of **spectacles** 2 → **spec**

spectacle /ˈspektəkl/ N *(= sight)* spectacle *m* ; *(= show)* revue *f* à grand spectacle ♦ **the coronation was a great ~** le couronnement a été un spectacle somptueux ♦ **to make a ~ of o.s.** *(pej)* se donner en spectacle COMP **spectacle case** N *(Brit)* étui *m* à lunettes

spectacled /ˈspektəkld/ ADJ *(gen, in animal names)* à lunettes

spectacles /ˈspektəkəlz/ NPL *(Brit)* ♦ **(pair of) ~** lunettes *fpl*

spectacular /spekˈtækjʊləʳ/ ADJ *(gen)* spectaculaire ; *[sight]* impressionnant ; *[failure, collapse]* retentissant N *(Cine/Theat)* superproduction *f*, film *m*/revue *f* à grand spectacle

spectacularly /spek'tækjʊlǝlɪ/ ADV *[good, bad, beautiful, handsome]* extraordinairement ; *[crash, increase, grow, fail]* de manière spectaculaire ◆ **to prove ~ successful** connaître un succès spectaculaire ◆ **her ~ successful career** sa spectaculaire réussite professionnelle ◆ **everything went ~ wrong** tout s'est extraordinairement mal passé ◆ **in ~ bad taste** d'un extraordinaire mauvais goût ◆ **they beat us ~ easily** ils nous ont battus avec une facilité spectaculaire

spectate /spek'teɪt/ VI être présent en tant que spectateur (*or* spectatrice)

spectator /spek'teɪtǝʳ/ N spectateur *m*, -trice *f* ◆ **the ~s** les spectateurs *mpl* COMP **spectator sport** N ◆ **I don't like ~ sports** je n'aime pas le sport en tant que spectacle ◆ **rugby, the most exciting of ~ sports** le rugby, le sport le plus passionnant à regarder ◆ **this tends to be rather a ~ sport** c'est un sport qui attire plus de spectateurs que de joueurs

specter /'spektǝʳ/ N (US) ⇒ **spectre**

spectra /'spektrǝ/ NPL of **spectrum**

spectral /'spektrǝl/ ADJ 1 *(liter = ghostly)* spectral *(liter)* 2 *(Phys)* spectral

spectre, specter (US) /'spektǝʳ/ N spectre *m*, fantôme *m*

spectrogram /'spektrǝʊgræm/ N spectrogramme *m*

spectrograph /'spektrǝʊgrɑːf/ N spectrographe *m*

spectroscope /'spektrǝʊskǝʊp/ N spectroscope *m*

spectroscopic /'spektrǝskɒpɪk/ ADJ spectroscopique

spectroscopy /spek'trɒskǝpɪ/ N spectroscopie *f*

spectrum /'spektrǝm/ N (pl **spectra**) 1 *(Phys)* spectre *m* 2 *[of views, services]* éventail *m* ◆ **the political ~** l'échiquier *m* politique ◆ **people from across the political ~** l'ensemble de l'échiquier politique ◆ **at the other end/both ends of the political ~** à l'autre extrémité/aux deux extrémités de l'échiquier politique ◆ **a broad ~ of opinion exists on this issue** les opinions sont très diverses sur le sujet ◆ **a wide ~ of people** un large échantillon *or* éventail de gens COMP *[analysis, colours]* spectral

specula /'spekjʊlǝ/ NPL of **speculum**

speculate /'spekjʊleɪt/ VI 1 *(= make guesses)* avancer des hypothèses, conjecturer *(about, on* sur) ◆ **I'm not going to ~** je ne veux pas avancer des hypothèses *or* conjecturer ◆ **doctors ~d that he died of natural causes** les médecins ont avancé l'hypothèse qu'il était mort de causes naturelles 2 *(Fin)* spéculer 3 *(Philos)* spéculer *(about, on* sur)

speculation /ˌspekjʊ'leɪʃǝn/ N 1 *(= guessing)* conjecture(s) *f(pl) (about* sur) ; *(scientific)* hypothèse *f* ◆ **it is the subject of much ~** cela donne lieu à bien des conjectures ◆ **that is pure ~** ce ne sont que des conjectures ◆ **the news prompted widespread ~ that the hostages may be freed** la nouvelle a laissé penser à beaucoup de gens que les otages allaient être libérés 2 *(Fin)* spéculation *f (in, on* sur) 3 *(Philos)* spéculation *f*

speculative /'spekjʊlǝtɪv/ ADJ 1 *(Fin)* spéculatif ; *[builder, developer]* qui spécule ◆ **~ investors** spéculateurs *mpl* 2 *[story]* basé sur des suppositions 3 *(= inquiring) [look]* inquisiteur (-trice *f*)

speculatively /'spekjʊlǝtɪvlɪ/ ADV 1 *(= inquiringly) [look at]* d'un air inquisiteur 2 *(Fin)* dans un but spéculatif

speculator /'spekjʊleɪtǝʳ/ N spéculateur *m*, -trice *f*

speculum /'spekjʊlǝm/ N (pl **speculums** *or* **specula**) *[of telescope]* miroir *m* ; *(Med)* spéculum *m*

sped /sped/ VB pt, ptp of **speed**

speech /spiːtʃ/ N 1 *(NonC) (= faculty)* parole *f* ; *(= enunciation)* articulation *f*, élocution *f* ; *(= manner of speaking)* façon *f* de parler, langage *m* ; *(as opposed to writing)* parole *f* ; *(= language) [of district, group]* parler *m*, langage *m* ◆ **to lose the power of ~** perdre (l'usage de) la parole ◆ **his ~ was very indistinct** il parlait *or* articulait très indistinctement ◆ **he expresses himself better in ~ than in writing** il s'exprime mieux oralement que par écrit ◆ **his ~ betrays his origins** son langage *or* sa façon de s'exprimer trahit ses origines ◆ **~ is silver but silence is golden** *(Prov)* la parole est d'argent mais le silence est d'or *(Prov)* ◆ **free ~, freedom of ~** liberté *f* de parole *or* d'expression ; → **figure, part**

2 *(= formal address)* discours *m (on* sur) ◆ **to make a ~** faire un discours ◆ **~, ~!** un discours ! ; → **king, maiden, queen**

3 *(Ling) (= utterances)* parole *f* ; *(= spoken language)* langage *m* parlé ◆ **direct/indirect ~** *(Gram)* discours *m* direct/indirect

COMP **speech act** N *(Ling)* acte *m* de parole
speech bubble N *(in comic, cartoon)* bulle *f*
speech clinic N centre *m* d'orthophonie
speech community N *(Ling)* communauté *f* linguistique
speech day N *(Brit Scol)* (jour *m* de la) distribution *f* des prix
speech defect N défaut *m* de langage
speech difficulty N défaut *m* d'élocution
speech disorder N ⇒ **speech defect**
speech from the throne N *(Britain and Commonwealth)* discours *m* du Trône *(discours du monarque pour l'ouverture de la saison parlementaire)*
speech impediment N ⇒ **speech difficulty**
speech maker N orateur *m*, -trice *f*
speech making N *(NonC: slightly pej)* discours *mpl*, beaux discours *mpl (pej)*
speech organ N *(Anat)* organe *m* de la parole
speech recognition N *(Comput)* reconnaissance *f* de la parole
speech sound N *(Ling)* phonème *m*
speech synthesis N *(Comput)* synthèse *f* vocale
speech synthesizer N *(Comput)* synthétiseur *m* de parole
speech therapist N orthophoniste *mf*, phoniatre *mf*
speech therapy N orthophonie *f*, phoniatrie *f*
speech training N leçons *fpl* d'élocution
speech writer N ◆ **her ~ writer** la personne qui écrit ses discours

speechify /'spiːtʃɪfaɪ/ VI *(pej)* faire des laïus, laïusser

speechifying /'spiːtʃɪfaɪɪŋ/ N *(pej)* laïus* *mpl*, beaux discours *mpl*

speechless /'spiːtʃlɪs/ ADJ *[person]* muet ◆ **I'm ~!*** je suis sans voix ! ◆ **I was so happy I was ~** j'étais si heureux que j'en suis resté muet *or* sans voix ◆ **to leave sb ~** laisser qn sans voix ◆ **she was left ~** elle en est restée sans voix ◆ **she stared at him in ~ disbelief/horror** elle le fixa, muette d'incrédulité/d'horreur ◆ **~ with astonishment/fear/rage/shock** muet d'étonnement/de peur/de rage/de stupeur

speed /spiːd/ (vb : pret, ptp **sped** *or* **speeded**) N 1 *(= rate of movement)* vitesse *f* ; *(= rapidity)* rapidité *f* ; *(= promptness)* promptitude *f* ◆ **the ~ of light/sound** la vitesse de la lumière/du son ◆ **his reading ~ is low** il lit lentement ◆ **shorthand/typing ~s** nombre *m* de mots-minute en sténo/en dactylo ◆ **a secretary with good ~s** une secrétaire qui a une bonne vitesse (de frappe et de sténo) ◆ **what ~ were you going at** *or* **doing?** quelle vitesse faisiez-vous ?, à quelle vitesse rouliez-vous ? ◆ **at a ~ of 80km/h** à une vitesse de 80 km/h ◆ **at a great ~** à toute vitesse ◆ **at top ~** *[go, run, move, drive]* à toute vitesse *or* allure ; *[do sth]* très vite, en quatrième vitesse* ◆ **with all possible ~** le plus vite possible ◆ **with such ~** si vite ◆ **to pick up** *or* **gather ~** prendre de la vitesse ◆ **to be up to ~** *(= functioning properly)* être opérationnel ◆ **to bring up to ~** *[+ student]* mettre au niveau ; → **airspeed, cruise, full, high**

2 *(Aut, Tech = gear)* vitesse *f* ◆ **four forward ~s** quatre vitesses avant ◆ **a three-~ gear** une boîte à trois vitesses

3 *(NonC: Phot) [of film]* rapidité *f* ; *(= width of aperture)* degré *m* d'obturation ; *(= length of exposure)* durée *f* d'exposition

4 *(* = drug)* speed* *m*, amphétamines *fpl*

5 ◆ **good ~!** †† Dieu vous garde ! †

VT (pret, ptp **sped** *or* **speeded**) *(liter) [+ arrow etc]* lancer, décocher ◆ **to ~ sb on his way** souhaiter bon voyage à qn ◆ **God ~ you!** †† Dieu vous garde ! †

VI 1 (pret, ptp **sped**) *(= move fast) [person, vehicle, horse, boat, plane]* **to ~ along** aller à toute vitesse *or* à toute allure, filer comme un éclair ◆ **the arrow sped from his bow** *(liter)* la flèche jaillit de son arc

2 (pret, ptp **speeded**) *(in car etc = go too fast)* conduire trop vite, excéder la limitation de vitesse ◆ **you're ~ing!** tu vas trop vite !, tu fais un *or* des excès de vitesse !

COMP **speed bump** N ralentisseur *m*
speed camera N *(Brit Police)* radar *m*
speed check N contrôle *m* de vitesse
speed chess N blitz *m*
speed cop* N *(Brit)* motard* *m (policier)*
speed dating N dating *m (soirée de rencontres pour célibataires durant laquelle les participants n'ont que quelques minutes pour faire connaissance)*
speed-dial N *(esp US)* numérotation *f* abrégée
speed limit N ◆ **there's no ~ limit** il n'y a pas de limitation de vitesse ◆ **the ~ limit is 80km/h** la vitesse est limitée à 80 km/h ◆ **to keep within the ~ limit** respecter la limitation de vitesse ◆ **to go over the ~ limit** dépasser la limitation de vitesse
speed merchant* N mordu(e)* *m(f)* de vitesse
speed reading N lecture *f* rapide
speed restriction N limitation *f* de vitesse
speed skating N *(Sport)* patinage *m* de vitesse
speed trap N *(on road)* contrôle *m* radar ◆ **to go through a ~ trap** passer devant un contrôle radar ◆ **to get caught by a ~ trap** être pris au radar*
speed-up N accélération *f* ◆ **the president has ordered a ~-up of aid for the unemployed** le président a demandé qu'on accélère l'aide aux chômeurs
speed zone N *(US)* zone *f* à vitesse limitée

► **speed along** VI (pret, ptp **sped along**) *[person, vehicle]* aller à toute allure *or* à toute vitesse, filer comme l'éclair
VT SEP (pret, ptp **speeded along**) *[+ work, production]* activer

► **speed up** (pret, ptp **speeded up**) VI *(gen)* aller plus vite ; *[car]* accélérer ; *[engine, machine]* tourner plus vite ◆ **do ~ up!** plus vite !
VT SEP *[+ machine]* faire tourner plus vite ; *[+ service, work, delivery, production]* accélérer ; *[+ person]* faire aller plus vite, presser ; *[+ film]* accélérer ◆ **to ~ things up** activer les choses
N ◆ **speed-up** → **speed**

speedball /'spiːdbɔːl/ N 1 *(= game)* speedball *m* 2 *(* = drug) mélange m de cocaïne, d'héroïne et d'amphétamines*, pot *m* belge *(arg)*

speedboat /'spiːdbǝʊt/ N vedette *f* ; *(with outboard motor)* hors-bord *m inv*

speeder /'spiːdǝʳ/ N *(= fast driver)* fou *m*, folle *f* de la vitesse ; *(convicted)* automobiliste *mf* coupable d'excès de vitesse

speedily /'spiːdɪlɪ/ ADV *[react, move, deal with, finish, work]* rapidement ; *[reply, return]* rapidement, promptement ◆ **as ~ as possible** aussi rapidement *or* vite que possible

speediness /ˈspiːdɪnɪs/ N *[of service, decision, recovery]* rapidité *f*, promptitude *f*

speeding /ˈspiːdɪŋ/ N *(in car etc)* excès *m* de vitesse
COMP **speeding conviction** N condamnation *f* pour excès de vitesse
speeding fine N amende *f* pour excès de vitesse
speeding ticket N PV *m* pour excès de vitesse

speedo* /ˈspiːdəʊ/ N *(Brit)* compteur *m* (de vitesse)

speedometer /spɪˈdɒmɪtəʳ/ N compteur *m* (de vitesse), indicateur *m* de vitesse

speedster* /ˈspiːdstəʳ/ N fou *m*, folle *f* de la route *(pej)*, mordu(e)* *m(f)* de la vitesse

speedwalk /ˈspiːdwɔːk/ N *(US)* tapis *m* roulant

speedway /ˈspiːdweɪ/ N *(Sport = racetrack)* piste *f* de vitesse pour motos ; *(US = road)* voie *f* express ; *(NonC) (Sport)* (also **speedway racing**) course(s) *f(pl)* de motos

speedwell /ˈspiːdwel/ N *(= plant)* véronique *f*

speedy /ˈspiːdɪ/ LANGUAGE IN USE 23.4 ADJ *[action, movement, process, solution, decision, service, car]* rapide ; *[response, reply]* rapide, prompt ◆ **to bring sth to a ~ conclusion** mener rapidement qch à terme ◆ **there is little prospect of a ~ end to the recession** il est peu probable que la récession touche à sa fin ◆ **we wish her a ~ recovery** nous lui souhaitons un prompt rétablissement

speleologist /ˌspiːlɪˈɒlədʒɪst/ N spéléologue *mf*

speleology /ˌspiːlɪˈɒlədʒɪ/ N spéléologie *f*

spell[1] /spel/ N *(= magic power)* charme *m (also fig)*, sortilège *m* ; *(= magic words)* formule *f* magique, incantation *f* ◆ **an evil ~** un maléfice ◆ **to put** *or* **cast a ~ on** *or* **over sb, to put sb under a ~** jeter un sort à qn, ensorceler qn ; *(fig)* ensorceler qn, envoûter qn ◆ **under a ~** ensorcelé, envoûté ◆ **under the ~ of sb/sth, under sb's/sth's ~** *(fig)* ensorcelé *or* envoûté par qn/qch ◆ **to break the ~** *(lit, fig)* rompre le charme ◆ **the ~ of the East** le charme *or* les sortilèges *mpl* de l'Orient

spell[2] /spel/ N 1 *(= period of work, turn)* tour *m* ◆ **we each took a ~ at the wheel** nous nous sommes relayés au volant, nous avons conduit chacun à notre tour ◆ **~ of duty** tour *m* de service 2 *(= brief period)* (courte) période *f* ◆ **cold/sunny ~s** périodes *fpl* de froid/ensoleillées ◆ **for/after a ~** pendant/après un certain temps ◆ **for a short ~** pendant un petit moment ◆ **he has done a ~ in prison** il a été en prison pendant un certain temps, il a fait de la prison ◆ **he's going through a bad ~** il traverse une mauvaise période, il est dans une mauvaise passe ◆ **to have a dizzy** *or* **giddy ~** avoir un vertige 3 *(Scot, Austral = short rest)* petite sieste *f*

spell[3] /spel/ (pret, ptp **spelt** *or* **spelled**) VT 1 *(in writing)* écrire, orthographier ; *(aloud)* épeler ◆ **how do you ~ it?** comment est-ce que cela s'écrit ? ◆ **can you ~ it for me?** pouvez-vous me l'épeler ? ◆ **he spelt "address" with one "d"** il a écrit "address" avec un seul "d"
2 *[letters]* former, donner ◆ **d-o-g ~s "dog"** d-o-g donnent *or* font (le mot) "dog"
3 *(fig = mean)* signifier ; *(= entail)* mener à ◆ **that would ~ ruin for him** cela signifierait *or* serait la ruine pour lui ◆ **effort ~s success** l'effort mène au succès
VI épeler ◆ **to learn to ~** apprendre à épeler, apprendre l'orthographe ◆ **he can't ~, he ~s badly** il fait des fautes d'orthographe, il ne sait pas l'orthographe, il a une mauvaise orthographe
COMP **spell-check** *(Comput)* N correcteur *m or* vérificateur *m* orthographique VT effectuer la vérification orthographique de
spell-checker N *(Comput)* correcteur *m or* vérificateur *m* orthographique
► **spell out** VT SEP 1 *(= read letter by letter)* épeler ; *(= decipher)* déchiffrer
2 *[+ consequences, alternatives]* expliquer bien clairement *(for sb* à qn) ◆ **let me ~ it out for you** laissez-moi vous expliquer cela bien clairement ◆ **do I have to ~ it out for you?** faut-il que je mette les points sur les i ?

spellbinder /ˈspelbaɪndəʳ/ N *(= speaker)* orateur *m*, -trice *f* fascinant(e) ◆ **that film was a ~** ce film vous tenait en haleine

spellbinding /ˈspelbaɪndɪŋ/ ADJ envoûtant

spellbound /ˈspelbaʊnd/ ADJ *(lit, fig)* envoûté ◆ **to hold sb ~** *(with a story)* tenir qn sous le charme ; *(with one's charm)* subjuguer qn

speller /ˈspeləʳ/ N 1 **to be a good/bad ~** *[person]* savoir/ne pas savoir l'orthographe 2 *(= book)* livre *m* d'orthographe

spelling /ˈspelɪŋ/ N orthographe *f* ◆ **reformed ~** nouvelle orthographe *f*
COMP *[test, practice]* d'orthographe
spelling bee N concours *m* d'orthographe
spelling book N livre *m* d'orthographe
spelling checker N *(Comput)* correcteur *m* orthographique
spelling error, spelling mistake N faute *f* d'orthographe
spelling pronunciation N prononciation *f* orthographique

spelt[1] /spelt/ VB *(esp Brit)* pt, ptp of **spell**[3]

spelt[2] /spelt/ N *(= cereal)* épeautre *m*

spelunker /spɪˈlʌŋkəʳ/ N *(US)* spéléologue *mf*

spelunking /spɪˈlʌŋkɪŋ/ N *(US)* spéléologie *f*

spend /spend/ (pret, ptp **spent**) VT 1 *[+ money]* dépenser ◆ **he ~s a lot (of money) on food/bus fares/clothes** il dépense beaucoup en nourriture/tickets d'autobus/vêtements ◆ **he ~s a lot (of money) on his house/car/girlfriend** il dépense beaucoup *or* il fait de grosses dépenses pour sa maison/sa voiture/sa petite amie ◆ **he spent a fortune on having the roof repaired** il a dépensé une somme folle *or* une fortune pour faire réparer le toit ◆ **without ~ing a penny** sans dépenser un sou, sans bourse délier ◆ **to ~ a penny*** *(Brit = go to the toilet)* aller au petit coin* ; see also **money**
2 *(= pass) [+ time, holiday, evening, one's life]* passer ◆ **to ~ time on sth** passer du temps sur qch, consacrer du temps à qch ◆ **to ~ time (in) doing sth** passer *or* consacrer du temps à faire qch ◆ **he ~s his time reading** il passe son temps à lire ◆ **I spent two hours on that letter** j'ai passé deux heures sur cette lettre, cette lettre m'a pris deux heures ◆ **they've spent a lot of effort on improving the service** ils ont fait beaucoup d'efforts pour améliorer le service
3 *(= consume, exhaust) [+ ammunition, provisions]* épuiser ◆ **to be spent** *[hatred, enthusiasm]* être tombé ◆ **her fury was now spent** sa fureur était maintenant apaisée ◆ **the storm had spent its fury** *(liter)* la tempête s'était calmée ; see also **spent**
VI dépenser
N dépenses *fpl* ◆ **the total ~ is $5,000** au total, les dépenses s'élèvent à 5 000 dollars ◆ **our total ~ on advertising, our total advertising ~** le total de nos dépenses publicitaires

spender /ˈspendəʳ/ N ◆ **to be a big ~** dépenser beaucoup ◆ **the store attracts big ~s** le magasin attire des gens prêts à dépenser beaucoup d'argent ◆ **the country is the world's biggest ~ on defence** c'est le pays qui dépense le plus au monde pour la défense

spending /ˈspendɪŋ/ N *(NonC)* dépenses *fpl* ◆ **government ~** dépenses *fpl* publiques
COMP **spending money** N *(NonC)* argent *m* de poche
spending power N pouvoir *m* d'achat
spending spree N ◆ **to go on a ~ spree** faire des folies

spendthrift /ˈspendθrɪft/ N dépensier *m*, -ière *f*, panier *m* percé* ◆ **he's a ~** il est très dépensier ADJ dépensier

spent /spent/ VB pt, ptp of **spend** ADJ 1 *(= burnt out) [cartridge, match]* utilisé ; *[fuel, fuel rod, uranium]* épuisé ◆ **to be a ~ force** *(fig)* ne plus avoir d'influence, ne plus avoir l'influence que l'on avait 2 *(liter = exhausted) [person]* recru *(liter)* ◆ **they collapsed, their energy ~** ils se sont effondrés, à bout de forces

sperm /spɜːm/ N *(pl inv, single)* spermatozoïde *m* ; *(= semen)* sperme *m*
COMP **sperm bank** N banque *f* de sperme
sperm count N nombre *m* de spermatozoïdes
sperm oil N huile *f* de baleine
sperm whale N cachalot *m*

spermaceti /ˌspɜːməˈsetɪ/ N spermaceti *m*, blanc *m* de baleine

spermatozoon /ˌspɜːmətəʊˈzəʊɒn/ N (pl **spermatozoa** /ˌspɜːmətəʊˈzəʊə/) spermatozoïde *m*

spermicidal /ˌspɜːmɪˈsaɪdl/ ADJ spermicide

spermicide /ˈspɜːmɪsaɪd/ N spermicide *m*

spew /spjuː/ VT 1 (*: also **spew up**) dégueuler*, vomir ◆ **it makes me ~** ça (me) donne envie de dégueuler* *or* vomir, c'est dégueulasse* 2 (also **spew forth, spew out**) *[+ fire, lava, curses]* vomir

SPF /ˌespiːˈef/ N (abbrev of **sun protection factor**) → **sun**

SPG /ˌespiːˈdʒiː/ N *(Brit Police)* (abbrev of **Special Patrol Group**) → **special**

sphagnum /ˈsfægnəm/ N (also **sphagnum moss**) sphaigne *f*

sphere /sfɪəʳ/ N *(gen, Astron, Math etc)* sphère *f* ; *(fig)* sphère *f*, domaine *m* ◆ **the music of the ~s** la musique des sphères célestes ◆ **~ of interest/influence** sphère *f* d'intérêt/d'influence ◆ **the ~ of poetry** le domaine de la poésie ◆ **in the social ~** dans le domaine social ◆ **distinguished in many ~s** renommé dans de nombreux domaines ◆ **that is outside my ~** cela n'entre pas dans mes compétences ◆ **within a limited ~** dans un cadre *or* domaine restreint

spherical /ˈsferɪkəl/ ADJ sphérique

spheroid /ˈsfɪərɔɪd/ N sphéroïde *m* ADJ sphéroïdal

sphincter /ˈsfɪŋktəʳ/ N sphincter *m*

sphinx /sfɪŋks/ N (pl **sphinxes**) sphinx *m* ◆ **the Sphinx** le Sphinx

spic** /spɪk/ N *(US pej)* ⇒ **spick**

spice /spaɪs/ N 1 *(Culin)* épice *f* ◆ **mixed ~(s)** épices *fpl* mélangées ◆ **there's too much ~ in it** c'est trop épicé 2 *(fig)* piquant *m*, sel *m* ◆ **the papers like a story with a bit of ~ to it** les journaux aiment les nouvelles qui ont du piquant *or* qui ne manquent pas de sel ◆ **a ~ of irony/humour** une pointe d'ironie/d'humour ◆ **the ~ of adventure** le piment de l'aventure VT *(Culin)* épicer, relever *(with* de) ; *(fig)* pimenter *(with* de)
COMP **spice rack** N casier *m or* étagère *f* à épices
the Spice Route N la Route des épices
► **spice up** VT *(fig)* pimenter

spiciness /ˈspaɪsɪnɪs/ N *(NonC) [of food]* goût *m* épicé *or* relevé ; *[of story]* piquant *m*

spick** /spɪk/ N *(US pej)* Latino *mf*

spick-and-span /ˈspɪkənˈspæn/ ADJ *[room, object]* impeccable, reluisant de propreté, nickel* ; *[person]* impeccable

spicy /ˈspaɪsɪ/ ADJ [1] *[food, flavour, smell]* épicé [2] *(= racy) [story]* croustillant, épicé ; *[detail]* piquant, croustillant ; *[language]* salé

spider /ˈspaɪdəʳ/ N [1] *(= animal)* araignée *f* [2] *(for luggage)* pieuvre *f (à bagages)* [3] *(US = fry-pan)* poêle *f* (à trépied)

COMP **spider crab** N araignée *f* de mer
spider plant N chlorophytum *m*
spider's web N toile *f* d'araignée

spiderman /ˈspaɪdəmæn/ N (pl **-men**) *(Constr) ouvrier travaillant en hauteur, sur un échafaudage, un toit etc*

spiderweb /ˈspaɪdəweb/ N *(US)* ⇒ **spider's web** ; → **spider**

spidery /ˈspaɪdərɪ/ ADJ *[writing]* en pattes de mouche ; *[shape]* en forme d'araignée

spiel * /spiːl/ N laïus * *m inv*, baratin * *m* ; *(Advertising etc)* boniment(s) * *m(pl)*, baratin * *m*

► **spiel off** * VT SEP *(US)* débiter, réciter à toute allure

spiffing † * /ˈspɪfɪŋ/ ADJ *(Brit)* épatant *

spigot /ˈspɪgət/ N [1] *(= plug for barrel)* fausset *m* [2] *(Brit = part of tap)* clé *f (d'un robinet)* ; *(US = faucet)* robinet *m*

spik ** /spɪk/ N *(US pej)* ⇒ **spick**

spike /spaɪk/ N [1] *(= sharp point) (wooden, metal)* pointe *f* ; *(on railing)* pointe *f* de fer, (fer *m* de) lance *f* ; *(on shoe)* pointe *f* ; *(for letters, bills)* pique-notes *m inv* ; *(= nail)* gros clou *m* à large tête ; *(= tool)* pointe *f* ; *[of antler]* dague *f* ; *(Bot)* épi *m* ; *(on graph)* pointe *f*, haut *m*

[2] *(= sports shoes)* **~s** * chaussures *fpl* à pointes

[3] *(Climbing)* **rocky** ~ becquet *m*

[4] *(Volleyball)* smash *m*

VT [1] *(= pierce)* transpercer ; *(= put spikes on)* garnir de pointes *or* de clous ; *(fig = frustrate) [+ plan, hope]* contrarier ◆ **~d shoes** *(Sport)* chaussures *fpl* à pointes ◆ **to ~ sb's guns** *(fig)* mettre des bâtons dans les roues à qn

[2] * *[+ drink]* corser (with de) ◆ **~d coffee** café *m* arrosé d'alcool

[3] *(Press = suppress) [+ article, story, quote]* supprimer

[4] ◆ **~d hair** cheveux *mpl* hérissés

VI *(Volleyball)* smasher

COMP **spike heels** NPL *(US)* talons *mpl* aiguilles
spike lavender N (lavande *f*) aspic *m*

spikenard /ˈspaɪknɑːd/ N *(NonC)* nard *m* (indien)

spiky /ˈspaɪkɪ/ ADJ [1] *(= pointed) [shape, flower, leaf]* pointu ; *[hair]* hérissé [2] *(= covered with spikes) [cactus, leaf]* couvert d'épines [3] *(Brit * = irritable) [person]* irascible, irritable

spill[1] /spɪl/ (vb : pret, ptp **spilt** *or* **spilled**) N [1] *(= act of spilling)* fait *m* de renverser, renversement *m* ; → **oil**

[2] *(from horse, cycle)* chute *f* ; *(in car)* accident *m* ◆ **to have a** ~ *[rider]* faire une chute ; *[driver]* avoir un accident

VT *[+ water, sand, salt]* renverser, répandre ; *[+ rider, passenger]* jeter à terre ◆ **she spilt the salt** elle a renversé le sel ◆ **she spilt wine all over the table** elle a renversé *or* répandu du vin sur toute la table ◆ **you're ~ing water from that jug** tu renverses de l'eau de la cruche ◆ **to ~ blood** verser *or* faire couler le sang ◆ **to ~ the beans** * *(gen)* vendre la mèche *(about* à propos de) ; *(under interrogation)* se mettre à table *, parler ◆ **to ~ one's guts** * *(= talk) (gen)* raconter sa vie ; *(under interrogation)* se mettre à table *, parler ◆ **to ~ (wind from) a sail** *(Naut)* étouffer une voile

VI *[liquid, salt]* se répandre ◆ **the light was ~ing under the door** un filet de lumière passait sous la porte

► **spill out** VI se répandre ; *(fig) [people]* sortir en masse ◆ **the crowd ~ed out into the streets** la foule s'est déversée dans la rue

VT SEP *[+ contents, sand, liquid]* répandre ; *(fig) [+ story, truth, details]* révéler, raconter (précipitamment)

► **spill over** VI *[liquids]* déborder, se répandre ; *[population]* se déverser *(into* dans) ◆ **these problems ~ed over into his private life** ces problèmes ont envahi sa vie privée

spill[2] /spɪl/ N *(for lighting with)* longue allumette *f (de papier etc)*

spillage /ˈspɪlɪdʒ/ N *[of oil, toxic waste, chemicals]* déversement *m* accidentel ◆ **he swerved to avoid an oil** ~ il a donné un coup de volant pour éviter une flaque d'huile

spillikins /ˈspɪlɪkɪnz/ N *(Brit)* (jeu *m* de) jonchets *mpl*, mikado *m*

spillover /ˈspɪləʊvəʳ/ N [1] ~ **(effect)** *(Econ)* retombées *fpl*, effet *m* d'entraînement ◆ **the army is trying to avoid a possible** ~ *(= spread of conflict)* l'armée essaie d'éviter le débordement du conflit ◆ **they want to prevent a ~ of refugees into neighbouring territories** ils veulent éviter que certains réfugiés ne gagnent les régions voisines [2] *(= quantity spilt)* quantité *f* renversée

spillway /ˈspɪlweɪ/ N *(US)* déversoir *m*

spilt /spɪlt/ VB *(esp Brit)* pt, ptp of **spill**[1]

spin /spɪn/ (vb : pret **spun** *or* **span**, ptp **spun**) N [1] *(= turning motion)* tournoiement *m* ; *(Aviat)* (chute *f* en) vrille *f* ◆ **to give a wheel a** ~ faire tourner une roue ◆ **long/short** ~ *(on washing machine)* essorage *m* complet/léger ◆ **to put (a) ~ on a ball** donner de l'effet à une balle ◆ **to go into a** ~ *[plane]* tomber en vrille ◆ **to pull** *or* **get out of a** ~ *[plane]* se sortir d'une (chute en) vrille ◆ **to get into a** ~ *(fig) [person]* s'affoler, paniquer * ◆ **everything was in such a** ~ c'était la pagaille * complète ◆ **to give sth a** ~ * *(fig = try out)* essayer qch ; → **flat**[1]

[2] *(* = ride)* petit tour *m*, balade * *f* ◆ **to go for a** ~ faire un petit tour *or* une balade * (en voiture *or* à bicyclette *etc*)

[3] ◆ **to put a new/different ~ on sth** * présenter qch sous un nouvel angle/un angle différent ◆ **they tried to put a positive ~ on the results** ils ont essayé de présenter les résultats sous un angle positif

[4] *(political)* manipulation *f*

VT [1] *[+ wool, yarn, fibres, glass]* filer *(into* en, pour en faire) ; *[+ thread etc]* fabriquer, produire ; *[spider, silkworm]* filer, tisser ◆ **to ~ a yarn** *or* **story** inventer *or* raconter une histoire ◆ **spun glass** verre *m* filé ◆ **hair like spun gold** des cheveux ressemblant à de l'or filé ◆ **spun silk** schappe *m or f* ◆ **spun yarn** *(Naut)* bitord *m* ; → **fine**[2]

[2] *[+ wheel, nut, revolving stand etc]* faire tourner ; *[+ top]* lancer ; *(Sport) [+ ball]* donner de l'effet à ◆ **to ~ a coin** jouer à pile ou face ◆ **he's just ~ning his wheels** * *(US)* il loupe * tout ce qu'il tente

[3] *(Brit)* ⇒ **spin-dry**

VI [1] *[spinner etc]* filer ; *[spider]* filer *or* tisser sa toile

[2] (also **spin round**) *[suspended object, top, dancer]* tourner, tournoyer ; *[planet, spacecraft]* tourner (sur soi-même) ; *[machinery wheel]* tourner ; *[car wheel]* patiner ; *[aircraft]* vriller, tomber en vrillant ; *(Sport) [ball]* tournoyer ◆ **to ~ round and round** continuer à tourner (*or* tournoyer *etc*) ◆ **to send sth/sb ~ning** envoyer rouler qch/qn ◆ **the disc went ~ning away over the trees** le disque s'envola en tournoyant pardessus les arbres ◆ **he spun round as he heard me come in** il s'est retourné vivement en m'entendant entrer ◆ **my head is ~ning (round)** j'ai la tête qui tourne ◆ **the room was ~ning (round)** la chambre tournait (autour de moi *or* lui *etc*)

[3] *(= move quickly)* **to ~** *or* **go ~ning along** *[vehicle]* rouler à toute vitesse, filer (à toute allure)

[4] *(Fishing)* **to ~ for trout** *etc* pêcher la truite *etc* à la cuiller

COMP **spin doctor** * N *(Pol) spécialiste en communication chargé de l'image d'un parti politique*
spin-dry VT essorer (à la machine)
spin-dryer N *(Brit)* essoreuse *f*
spin-drying N *(NonC)* essorage *m* à la machine
spin-off N → **spin-off**

► **spin off** VI ◆ **to ~ off from** *(= arise as result of)* résulter de

N ◆ **spin-off** → **spin-off**

► **spin out** VT SEP *[+ story, explanation]* faire durer, délayer ; *[+ visit, money, food]* faire durer

► **spin round** VI → **spin vi 2**

VT SEP *[+ wheel, nut, revolving stand]* faire tourner ; *[+ person]* faire pivoter ; *[+ dancing partner]* faire tourner *or* tournoyer

spina bifida /ˈspaɪnəˈbɪfɪdə/ N spina-bifida *m*

spinach /ˈspɪnɪdʒ/ N *(= plant)* épinard *m* ; *(Culin)* épinards *mpl*

spinal /ˈspaɪnl/ ADJ *(Anat) [injury]* à la colonne vertébrale ; *[surgery, disorder, deformity, tumour, problem]* de la colonne vertébrale ; *[nerve, muscle]* spinal ; *[ligament, disc]* vertébral ◆ **a very painful ~ condition** une affection de la colonne vertébrale très douloureuse

COMP **spinal anaesthesia** N rachianesthésie *f*
spinal anaesthetic N ◆ **to give sb a ~ anaesthetic** faire une rachianesthésie à qn
spinal column N colonne *f* vertébrale
spinal cord N moelle *f* épinière
spinal fluid N liquide *m* rachidien
spinal meningitis N méningite *f* cérébrospinale

spindle /ˈspɪndl/ N [1] *(Spinning)* fuseau *m* ; *(on machine)* broche *f* [2] *(Tech) [of pump]* axe *m* ; *[of lathe]* arbre *m* ; *[of valve]* tige *f*

COMP **spindle-legged** *, **spindle-shanked** * ADJ qui a de longues échasses * *(fig)*
spindle-shanks * N ⇒ **spindlelegs**

spindlelegs * /ˈspɪndllegz/ N *(= person)* grand échalas * *m*

spindly /ˈspɪndlɪ/ ADJ grêle

spindrift /ˈspɪndrɪft/ N *(= spray from sea)* embrun(s) *m(pl)*, poudrin *m*

spine /spaɪn/ N [1] *(= backbone)* colonne *f* vertébrale, épine *f* dorsale ; *[of fish]* épine *f* ; *(= spike) [of hedgehog]* piquant *m*, épine *f* ; *[of plant]* épine *f*, piquant *m* ; *[of book]* dos *m* ; *[of hill etc]* crête *f* [2] *(US = courage)* courage *m* ◆ **he has no** ~ c'est un lâche

COMP **spine-chiller** N roman *m or* film *m etc* à vous glacer le sang
spine-chilling ADJ à vous glacer le sang
spine-tingling ADJ *(= frightening)* à vous glacer le sang ; *(= moving)* prenant

spineless /ˈspaɪnlɪs/ ADJ [1] *(= cowardly) [person]* sans caractère, mou (molle *f*) ; *[attitude]* mou (molle *f*) ◆ **he's** ~ il manque de caractère [2] *[organism]* invertébré

spinelessly /ˈspaɪnlɪslɪ/ ADV *(fig)* lâchement, mollement

spinet /spɪˈnet/ N *(Mus)* épinette *f*

spinnaker /ˈspɪnəkəʳ/ N spinnaker *m*, spi *m*

spinner /ˈspɪnəʳ/ N *(= person)* fileur *m*, -euse *f* ; *(Fishing)* cuiller *f* ; *(= spin-dryer)* essoreuse *f* ; *(= revolving display stand)* tourniquet *m* ◆ **he sent down a** ~ * *(Baseball, Cricket)* il a donné de l'effet à la balle ; → **money**

spinneret /ˌspɪnəˈret/ N *(in spinning, of spider)* filière *f*

spinney /ˈspɪnɪ/ N *(Brit)* bosquet *m*, petit bois *m*

spinning /ˈspɪnɪŋ/ N *(by hand)* filage *m* ; *(by machine)* filature *f* ; *(Fishing)* pêche *f* à la cuiller

COMP **spinning jenny** N jenny *f*

spinning machine N machine *f or* métier *m* à filer
spinning mill N filature *f*
spinning top N toupie *f*
spinning wheel N rouet *m*

spin-off /ˈspɪnɒf/ N *(gen)* profit *m or* avantage *m* inattendu ; *[of industrial process, technology]* application *f* secondaire ◆ ~ **effect** *(Fin)* retombées *fpl*, effet *m* d'entraînement ◆ **this tool is a direct ~ from nuclear technology** cet outil est directement dérivé de la technologie nucléaire ◆ **this TV series is a ~ from the famous film** ce feuilleton télévisé est tiré du célèbre film

Spinoza /spɪˈnəʊzə/ N Spinoza *m*

spinster /ˈspɪnstəʳ/ N célibataire *f* ; *(pej)* vieille fille *f* ◆ **she is a ~** elle est célibataire, elle n'est pas mariée

spinsterhood † /ˈspɪnstəhʊd/ N célibat *m (pour une femme)* ◆ **a last attempt to avoid ~** une dernière tentative pour éviter de rester vieille fille *(pej) or* pour éviter le célibat ◆ **a life of ~** une vie de vieille fille *(pej)*

spiny /ˈspaɪnɪ/ ADJ épineux
COMP **spiny anteater** N échidné *m*
spiny lobster N langouste *f*

spiracle /ˈspɪrəkl/ N *(= air hole)* orifice *m* d'aération ; *[of whale etc]* évent *m* ; *[of insect etc]* stigmate *m* ; *(Geol)* cassure *f*

spiral /ˈspaɪərəl/ ADJ *[pattern, movement, dive]* en spirale ; *[spring]* en spirale, à boudin ; *[curve, shell]* en spirale, spiroïdal ; *[nebula]* spiral N spirale *f* ◆ **in a ~** en spirale ◆ **the wage-price ~** la montée inexorable des salaires et des prix ◆ **the inflationary ~** la spirale inflationniste
VI *[staircase, smoke]* monter en spirale ; *[ball, missile etc]* tourner en spirale ; *[plane]* vriller ; *(fig) [prices]* monter en flèche ; *[prices and wages]* former une spirale
COMP **spiral galaxy** N galaxie *f* spirale
spiral notebook N carnet *m* à spirale
spiral staircase, spiral stairway N escalier *m* en colimaçon

► **spiral down** VI *[plane]* descendre en vrille

► **spiral up** VI *[plane]* monter en vrille ; *[staircase, smoke, missile]* monter en spirale ; *[prices]* monter en flèche

spirally /ˈspaɪərəlɪ/ ADV en spirale, en hélice

spire /ˈspaɪəʳ/ N *(Archit)* flèche *f*, aiguille *f* ; *[of tree, mountain]* cime *f* ; *[of grass, plant]* brin *m*, pousse *f*

spirit /ˈspɪrɪt/ N 1 *(= soul)* esprit *m* ◆ **the life of the ~** la vie de l'esprit, la vie spirituelle ◆ **he was there in ~** il était présent en esprit *or* de cœur ◆ **the ~ is willing but the flesh is weak** l'esprit est prompt mais la chair est faible ◆ **God is pure ~** Dieu est un pur esprit ; → **holy, move**

2 *(= supernatural being)* esprit *m* ◆ **evil ~** esprit *m* malin *or* du mal

3 *(= person)* esprit *m* ◆ **one of the greatest ~s of his day** un des plus grands esprits de son temps ◆ **the courageous ~ who ...** l'esprit courageux *or* l'âme courageuse qui ... ◆ **a few restless ~s** quelques mécontents ◆ **the leading ~ in the party** l'âme *m* du parti ; → **kindred, moving**

4 *(= attitude, approach)* esprit *m* ◆ **the ~, not the letter of the law** l'esprit *m* et non la lettre de la loi ◆ **the ~ of the age** *or* **the times** l'esprit *m* des temps *or* de l'époque ◆ **he's got the right ~** il a l'attitude qu'il faut ◆ **he has great fighting ~** il ne se laisse jamais abattre ◆ **that's the ~!** c'est ça !, voilà comment il faut réagir ! ; → **community, public, team**

◆ **in(to) + spirit** ◆ **in a ~ of forgiveness** dans un esprit de pardon ◆ **the film is certainly in the ~ of the book** le film est certainement conforme à l'esprit du livre ◆ **you must take it in the ~ in which it was meant** prenez-le dans l'esprit où c'était dit *or* voulu ◆ **to take sth in the right/wrong ~** prendre qch en bonne/mauvaise part *or* du bon/mauvais côté ◆ **in a ~ of revenge** par esprit de vengeance ◆ **in a ~ of mischief** *etc* par espièglerie *etc* ◆ **you must enter into the ~ of the thing** il faut y participer de bon cœur

5 *(= courage)* courage *m*, cran* *m* ; *(= energy)* énergie *f* ; *(= passion)* fougue *f* ; *(= vitality)* entrain *m* ◆ **man of ~** homme *m* énergique *or* de caractère ◆ **he replied with ~** il a répondu avec fougue ◆ **he sang/played with ~** il a chanté/joué avec fougue

6 *(Chem)* alcool *m* ◆ **preserved in ~(s)** conservé dans de l'alcool ◆ **~(s) of ammonia** sel *m* ammoniaque ◆ **~(s) of salt** esprit-de-sel *m* ◆ **~(s) of turpentine** (essence *f* de) térébenthine *f* ◆ **~s** *(= drink)* spiritueux *mpl*, alcool *m* ◆ **raw ~s** alcool *m* pur ; → **methylated spirit(s), surgical**

NPL **spirits** (– *frame of mind*) humeur *f*, état *m* d'esprit ; *(= morale)* moral *m* ◆ **in good ~s** de bonne humeur ◆ **in high ~s** enjoué ◆ **in poor** *or* **low ~s, out of ~s** déprimé, qui n'a pas le moral ◆ **depression can alternate with high ~s** des périodes de dépression peuvent alterner avec des moments d'exaltation ◆ **to keep one's ~s up** ne pas se laisser abattre, garder le moral ◆ **my ~s rose** j'ai repris courage ◆ **to raise sb's ~s** remonter le moral à qn

VT ◆ **he was ~ed out of the castle** on l'a fait sortir du château comme par enchantement *or* magie ◆ **the documents were mysteriously ~ed off his desk** les documents ont été mystérieusement escamotés *or* subtilisés de son bureau

COMP *[lamp, stove, varnish]* à alcool ; *(Spiritualism) [help, world]* des esprits
spirit gum N colle *f* gomme
spirit level N niveau *m* à bulle

► **spirit away, spirit off** VT SEP *[+ person]* faire disparaître comme par enchantement ; *[+ object, document etc]* escamoter, subtiliser

spirited /ˈspɪrɪtɪd/ ADJ *[person]* plein d'entrain ; *[horse]* fougueux ; *[reply, speech]* plein de verve, fougueux ; *[defence]* plein de verve ; *[attempt, attack]* courageux ; *[conversation]* animé ; *[music]* plein d'allant ◆ **to put up** *or* **make a ~ defence of sth** défendre qch avec vigueur ◆ **he gave a ~ performance** *(Mus, Theat, Cine, Sport)* il a joué avec brio ; → **free, high, low¹, mean³, public**

spiritless /ˈspɪrɪtlɪs/ ADJ *[person]* sans entrain, sans énergie, sans vie ; *[acceptance, agreement]* veule, lâche

spiritual /ˈspɪrɪtjʊəl/ ADJ *(gen)* spirituel ; *[person]* d'une grande spiritualité ◆ **his ~ home** sa patrie spirituelle *or* d'adoption *(fig)* ◆ **the lords ~** *(Brit)* les lords *mpl* spirituels *(évêques siégeant à la Chambre des pairs)* N chant *m* religieux ; (also **Negro spiritual**) (negro-)spiritual *m* COMP **spiritual adviser** N *(Rel)* conseiller *m*, -ère *f* spirituel(le), directeur *m*, -trice *f* de conscience

spiritualism /ˈspɪrɪtjʊəlɪzəm/ N *(Rel)* spiritisme *m* ; *(Philos)* spiritualisme *m*

spiritualist /ˈspɪrɪtjʊəlɪst/ ADJ, N *(Rel)* spirite *mf* ; *(Philos)* spiritualiste *mf*

spirituality /ˌspɪrɪtjʊˈælɪtɪ/ N 1 *(NonC)* spiritualité *f*, qualité *f* spirituelle 2 *(Rel)* **spiritualities** biens *mpl* et bénéfices *mpl* ecclésiastiques

spiritually /ˈspɪrɪtjʊəlɪ/ ADV spirituellement

spirituous /ˈspɪrɪtjʊəs/ ADJ spiritueux, alcoolique ◆ **~ liquor** spiritueux *mpl*

spirt /spɜːt/ ⇒ **spurt**

spit¹ /spɪt/ (vb : pret, ptp **spat**) N *(= spittle)* crachat *m* ; *(= saliva) [of person]* salive *f* ; *[of animal]* bave *f* ; *(Bot)* écume *f* printanière, crachat *m* de coucou ; *(= action)* crachement *m* ◆ **~ and polish** *(esp Mil)* briquage *m*, astiquage *m* ◆ **there was just a ~ of rain** il tombait quelques gouttes de pluie ◆ **a ~ and sawdust pub** * *(Brit)* un pub miteux ◆ **he's the dead** *or* **very ~* of his uncle** c'est le portrait craché* de son oncle, son oncle et lui se ressemblent comme deux gouttes d'eau

VT *[+ blood, curses, flames etc]* cracher ◆ **to ~ (out) the dummy** * *(Austral fig)* bouder comme un gamin*

VI *[person, cat etc]* cracher *(at sb* sur qn) ; *[fire, fat]* crépiter ◆ **she spat in his face** elle lui a craché à la figure ◆ **it was ~ting (with rain)** *(Brit)* il tombait quelques gouttes de pluie ◆ **to ~ in the wind** * *(fig)* pisser dans un violon‡ ◆ **to ~ in sb's eye** *(fig)* faire face à qn

► **spit out** VT SEP *[+ pip, pill]* (re)cracher ; *[+ tooth, curses, information]* cracher ◆ **~ it out!** * *(= say it)* allons, accouche‡ *or* vide ton sac ! *

► **spit up** VT SEP *[+ blood etc]* cracher

spit² /spɪt/ N *(Culin)* broche *f* ; *(Geog)* pointe *f or* langue *f* (de terre) VT embrocher

spit³ /spɪt/ N *(in gardening)* ◆ **to dig sth two ~s deep** creuser qch à une profondeur de deux fers de bêche

spite /spaɪt/ N 1 *(NonC) (= ill feeling)* rancune *f*, dépit *m* ◆ **out of pure ~** par pure rancune *or* malveillance ◆ **to have a ~ against sb** * avoir une dent contre qn, en vouloir à qn

2 *(set structure)*

◆ **in spite of** malgré, en dépit de ◆ **in ~ of it** malgré cela, en dépit de cela ◆ **in ~ of the fact that he has seen me** bien qu'il m'ait vu, malgré qu'il m'ait vu ◆ **in ~ of everyone** envers et contre tous

VT vexer, contrarier

spiteful /ˈspaɪtfʊl/ ADJ *[person]* méchant, malveillant ; *[behaviour, story]* malveillant ; *[tongue]* venimeux ◆ **a ~ remark** *or* **comment** une méchanceté, une remarque malveillante

spitefully /ˈspaɪtfəlɪ/ ADV méchamment

spitefulness /ˈspaɪtfʊlnɪs/ N méchanceté *f*, malveillance *f*

spitfire /ˈspɪtfaɪəʳ/ N ◆ **to be a ~** *[person]* s'emporter pour un rien, être soupe au lait

spitroast /ˈspɪtrəʊst/ VT faire rôtir à la broche

spitroasted /ˈspɪtrəʊstɪd/ ADJ (rôti) à la broche

spitting /ˈspɪtɪŋ/ N ◆ **"spitting prohibited"** "défense de cracher" ◆ **within ~ distance** * *(fig)* à deux pas (*of* de) → **image**

spittle /ˈspɪtl/ N *(ejected)* crachat *m* ; *(dribbled) [of person]* salive *f* ; *[of animal]* bave *f*

spittoon /spɪˈtuːn/ N crachoir *m*

spitz /spɪts/ N loulou *m (chien)*

spiv* /spɪv/ N *(Brit)* chevalier *m* d'industrie

splash /splæʃ/ N 1 *(= act)* éclaboussement *m* ; *(= sound)* floc *m*, plouf *m* ; *(= series of sounds)* clapotement *m* ; *(= mark)* éclaboussure *f*, tache *f* ; *[of colour]* tache *f* ◆ **he dived in with a ~** il a plongé dans un grand éclaboussement ◆ **it made a great ~ as it hit the water** c'est tombé dans l'eau avec un gros plouf *or* en faisant une grande gerbe ◆ **to make a ~** * *(fig)* faire sensation, faire du bruit

2 *(in drinks etc)* **a ~ of** *(= small amount) (gen)* un petit peu de ; *[+ soda water]* une giclée de

ADV ◆ **it went ~ into the stream** c'est tombé dans l'eau (en faisant floc *or* plouf)

VT 1 *(gen)* éclabousser *(sth over sb/sth* qch sur qn/qch ; *sb/sth with sth* qn/qch de qch) ◆ **to ~ milk on the floor** renverser du lait par terre ◆ **he ~ed paint on the floor** il a fait des éclaboussures de peinture par terre ◆ **don't ~ me!** *(in swimming etc)* ne m'éclabousse pas ! ◆ **to ~ one's way through a stream** traverser un ruisseau en éclaboussant *or* en pataugeant ◆ **~ed with red/colour** avec des taches rouges/de couleur

2 (= *apply hastily*) **to ~ o.s. with water, to ~ water on o.s.** s'asperger d'eau ◆ **he ~ed paint on the wall** il a barbouillé le mur de peinture

3 (*fig*) [*+ headlines*] mettre en manchette ◆ **the news was ~ed across the front page** (*Press*) la nouvelle était en manchette, la nouvelle a fait cinq colonnes à la une

VI 1 [*liquid, mud etc*] faire des éclaboussures ◆ **the milk ~ed on** *or* **over the tablecloth** le lait a éclaboussé la nappe ◆ **tears ~ed on to her book** les larmes s'écrasaient sur son livre

2 [*person, animal*] barboter, patauger ◆ **to ~ across a stream** traverser un ruisseau en éclaboussant *or* en pataugeant ◆ **the dog ~ed through the mud** le chien pataugeait dans la boue ◆ **to ~ into the water** [*person*] plonger dans l'eau dans un grand éclaboussement *or* en faisant une grande gerbe ; [*stone etc*] tomber dans l'eau avec un gros floc *or* plouf

COMP **splash guard** N [*of car etc*] garde-boue *m inv*

► **splash about** VI [*person, animal*] barboter, patauger (*in* dans)

VT SEP [*+ ink, mud*] faire des éclaboussures de ; (*fig*) [*+ money*] faire étalage de

► **splash down** VI [*spacecraft*] amerrir

► **splash out** * (*Brit*) VI (= *spend money*) faire une folie

VT SEP [*+ money*] claquer*, dépenser

► **splash up** VI gicler (*on sb* sur qn)

VT SEP faire gicler

splashback /ˈsplæʃbæk/ N revêtement *m* (*au dessus d'un évier etc*)

splashboard /ˈsplæʃbɔːd/ N [*of car etc*] garde-boue *m inv*

splashdown /ˈsplæʃdaʊn/ N (*Space*) amerrissage *m*

splashy * /ˈsplæʃɪ/ ADJ (*US*) tape-à-l'œil *inv*

splat /splæt/ N ◆ **with a ~** avec un flac *or* floc

EXCL flac !, floc !

splatter /ˈsplætəʳ/ ⇒ **spatter**

splay /spleɪ/ VT [*+ window frame*] ébraser ; [*+ end of pipe etc*] évaser ; [*+ feet, legs*] tourner en dehors VI (also **splay out**) [*window frame*] s'ébraser ; [*end of pipe etc*] se tourner en dehors

splayfeet /ˈspleɪfiːt/ NPL pieds *mpl* tournés en dehors

splayfooted /ˌspleɪˈfʊtɪd/ ADJ [*person*] aux pieds plats ; [*horse*] panard

spleen /spliːn/ N (*Anat*) rate *f* ; (*fig = bad temper*) mauvaise humeur *f*, humeur *f* noire ; († † = *melancholy*) spleen *m* ◆ **to vent one's ~ on ...** décharger sa bile sur ...

splendid /ˈsplendɪd/ ADJ [*view, collection, building, painting, performance*] magnifique, splendide ; [*idea*] magnifique ; [*book*] (*in content*) merveilleux ; (*in appearance*) splendide ; [*meal*] merveilleux ; [*example*] superbe ; [*person*] (= *excellent*) excellent ; (= *imposing*) magnifique ; [*player, teacher*] excellent ◆ **~!** formidable ! ◆ **to do a ~ job** faire un travail formidable ◆ **~ isolation** splendide isolement *m*

splendidly /ˈsplendɪdlɪ/ ADV [*play, sing*] magnifiquement, à merveille ; [*dressed, carved, restored, appointed*] magnifiquement, superbement ; [*get along, come along*] à merveille, merveilleusement ◆ **~ named** merveilleusement nommé ◆ **~ arrogant/vulgar/ugly** d'une arrogance/vulgarité/laideur réjouissante ◆ **you did ~** tu as été magnifique ◆ **everything is going ~** tout se passe à merveille

splendiferous † * /splenˈdɪfərəs/ ADJ (*Brit hum*) mirobolant*, mirifique † (*also hum*)

splendour, splendor (*US*) /ˈsplendəʳ/ N splendeur *f*, magnificence *f*, éclat *m*

splenetic /splɪˈnetɪk/ ADJ 1 (*frm = bad-tempered*) hargneux, atrabilaire † 2 († † = *melancholy*) porté au spleen

splice /splaɪs/ VT [*+ rope, cable*] épisser ; [*+ film, tape*] coller ; [*+ timbers*] enter, abouter ◆ **to ~ the mainbrace** (*Naut*) distribuer une ration de rhum ; (* *fig* = *have a drink*) boire un coup* ◆ **to get ~d** * (= *married*) convoler N (*in rope*) épissure *f* ; (*in film*) collure *f* ; (*in wood*) enture *f*

splicer /ˈsplaɪsəʳ/ N (*for film*) colleuse *f* (*à bandes adhésives*)

spliff * /splɪf/ N (*Drugs*) pétard* *m*, joint* *m*

splint /splɪnt/ N (*Med*) éclisse *f*, attelle *f* ◆ **to put sb's arm in ~s** éclisser le bras de qn ◆ **she had her leg in ~s** elle avait la jambe éclissée

splinter /ˈsplɪntəʳ/ N [*of glass, shell, wood*] éclat *m* ; [*of bone*] esquille *f* ; (*in one's finger etc*) écharde *f* VT 1 [*+ wood*] fendre en éclats ; [*+ glass, bone*] briser en éclats 2 [*+ political party*] scinder, fragmenter VI 1 [*wood*] se fendre en éclats ; [*glass, bone*] se briser en éclats 2 [*political party*] se scinder, se fragmenter COMP **splinter group** N groupe *m* dissident *or* scissionniste, faction *f* dissidente

splinterproof glass /ˈsplɪntəpruːfˈglɑːs/ N verre *m* sécurit ® *inv*

split /splɪt/ (vb : pret, ptp **split**) N 1 (*in garment, fabric, canvas, at seam*) fente *f* ; (= *tear*) déchirure *f* ; (*in wood, rock*) crevasse *f*, fente *f* ; (*in earth's surface*) fissure *f* ; (*in skin*) fissure *f*, déchirure *f* ; (*from cold*) gerçure *f*, crevasse *f* ; (*fig = quarrel*) rupture *f* ; (*Pol*) scission *f*, schisme *m* ◆ **there was a three-way ~ in the committee** le comité s'est trouvé divisé en trois clans

2 (= *share*) **I want my ~** * je veux ma part (du gâteau*) ◆ **they did a four-way ~ of the profits** ils ont partagé les bénéfices en quatre

3 (= *small bottle*) **soda/lemonade ~** petite bouteille *f* d'eau gazeuse/de limonade ◆ **jam/cream ~** (= *cake*) gâteau *m* fourré à la confiture/à la crème ◆ **banana ~** banana split *m inv*

NPL **splits** ◆ **to do the ~s** faire le grand écart

VT 1 (= *cleave*) [*+ wood, pole*] fendre ; [*+ slate, diamond*] cliver ; [*+ stones*] fendre, casser ; [*+ fabric, garment*] déchirer ; [*+ seam*] fendre ; [*lightning, frost, explosion, blow*] fendre ; (*fig*) [*+ party*] diviser, créer une scission *or* un schisme dans ◆ **to ~ the atom** fissionner l'atome ◆ **to ~ sth open** ouvrir qch en le coupant en deux *or* en fendant ◆ **he ~ his head open as he fell** il s'est fendu le crâne en tombant ◆ **the sea had ~ the ship in two** la mer avait brisé le bateau en deux ◆ **he ~ it in two** il l'a fendu (en deux) ◆ **he ~ it into three** il l'a coupé en trois ◆ **~ the loaf lengthwise** fendez le pain dans le sens de la longueur ◆ **to ~ hairs** couper les cheveux en quatre, chercher la petite bête, chinoiser ◆ **to ~ an infinitive** (*Gram*) *intercaler un adverbe entre "to" et le verbe* ◆ **to ~ one's sides (laughing** *or* **with laughter)** se tordre de rire ◆ **this decision ~ the radical movement** cette décision a divisé le mouvement radical, cette décision a provoqué une scission *or* un schisme dans le mouvement radical ◆ **it ~ the party down the middle** cela a littéralement divisé le parti en deux ◆ **the voters were ~ down the middle** l'électorat était divisé *or* coupé en deux

2 (= *divide, share*) [*+ work, profits, booty, bill*] (se) partager, (se) répartir ◆ **let's ~ a bottle of wine** si on prenait une bouteille de vin à deux (*or trois etc*) ? ◆ **they ~ the money three ways** ils ont divisé l'argent en trois ◆ **to ~ the difference** (*lit*) partager la différence ; (*fig*) couper la poire en deux ◆ **they ~ the work/the inheritance** ils se sont partagé le travail/l'héritage

VI 1 [*wood, pole, seam*] se fendre ; [*stones*] se fendre, se casser ; [*fabric, garment*] se déchirer ; (*fig*) [*party, Church, government*] se diviser, se désunir ◆ **to ~ open** se fendre ◆ **my head is ~ting** j'ai atrocement mal à la tête ◆ **the party ~ over nationalization** le parti s'est divisé sur la question des nationalisations, il y a eu une scission *or* un schisme dans le parti à propos de la question des nationalisations

2 (= *divide*) (also **split up**) [*cells*] se diviser ; [*people, party etc*] se diviser, se séparer ◆ **the crowd ~ into smaller groups** la foule s'est divisée *or* séparée en petits groupes ◆ **Latin ~ into the Romance languages** le latin s'est divisé *or* ramifié en langues romanes

3 (*Brit* * = *tell tales, inform*) vendre la mèche* ◆ **to ~ on sb** cafarder qn*

4 (* = *depart*) filer*, mettre les bouts*

COMP **split cane** N osier *m* ADJ en osier

split decision N (*Boxing*) décision *f* prise à la majorité

split ends NPL (*in hair*) fourches *fpl*

split infinitive N (*Gram*) *infinitif où un adverbe est intercalé entre "to" et le verbe*

split-level cooker N cuisinière *f* à éléments de cuisson séparés

split-level house N maison *f* à deux niveaux

split-new ADJ tout neuf (neuve *f*)

split-off N séparation *f*, scission *f* (*from* de)

split peas NPL pois *mpl* cassés

split-pea soup N soupe *f* de pois cassés

split personality N double personnalité *f*

split pin N (*Brit*) goupille *f* fendue

split ring N bague *f* fendue

split screen N (*Cine, TV, Comput*) écran *m* divisé

split-screen facility N (*Comput*) écran *m* divisible en fenêtres, fonction *f* écran divisé

split second N fraction *f* de seconde ◆ **in a ~ second** en un rien de temps

split-second timing N [*of military operation etc*] précision *f* à la seconde près ; [*of actor, comedian*] sens *m* du moment

split-site ADJ [*school etc*] sur différents sites

split ticket N (*US Pol*) ◆ **to vote a ~ ticket** voter pour une liste avec panachage

split-up N [*of engaged couple, friends*] rupture *f* ; [*of married couple*] séparation *f* ; [*of political party*] scission *f*

► **split off** VI [*piece of wood, branch etc*] se détacher (en se fendant) (*from* de) ; (*fig*) [*group, department, company etc*] se séparer (*from* de) ◆ **a small group of children ~ off and wandered away** un petit groupe d'enfants s'est séparé des autres et est parti de son côté

VT SEP [*+ branch, splinter, piece*] enlever (en fendant *or* en cassant) (*from* de) ; (*fig*) [*+ company, group, department*] séparer (*from* de)

N ◆ **split-off** → **split**

► **split up** VI 1 [*ship*] se briser ; [*boulder, block of wood*] se fendre

2 [*meeting, crowd*] se disperser ; [*party, movement*] se diviser, se scinder ; [*friends*] rompre, se brouiller ; [*married couple*] se séparer ; [*engaged couple*] rompre

VT SEP 1 [*+ wood, stones*] fendre (*into* en) ; [*+ chemical compound*] diviser (*into* en) ◆ **to ~ up a book into six chapters** diviser un livre en six chapitres

2 [*+ money, work*] partager, répartir (*among* entre), diviser (*into* en) ◆ **we must ~ up the work amongst us** nous devons nous partager *or* nous répartir le travail

3 [*+ party, group, organization*] diviser, scinder (*into* en) ; [*+ meeting*] mettre fin à ; [*+ crowd*] disperser ; [*+ friends*] séparer ◆ **you'll have to ~ up those two boys if you want them to do any work** il faut que vous sépariez ces deux garçons si vous voulez qu'ils travaillent

N ◆ **split-up** → **split**

splitting /ˈsplɪtɪŋ/ N [*of nation, organization*] division *f* ; [*of roles*] partage *m* ◆ **the ~ of an infinitive** (*Gram*) *l'insertion d'un adverbe entre "to" et le verbe* ◆ **the ~ of the atom** la fission de l'atome ; → **hair** ADJ ◆ **to have a ~ headache** avoir un mal de tête atroce ; → **ear¹, side**

splodge /splɒdʒ/, **splotch** /splɒtʃ/ N [of ink, paint, colour, dirt, mud] éclaboussure f, tache f ◆ **strawberries with a great ~ of cream** des fraises avec un monceau de crème VT [+ windows, dress etc] éclabousser, barbouiller (with de) ; [+ mud, ink etc] faire des taches or des éclaboussures de (on sur) VI [mud etc] gicler (on sur)

splurge * /splɜːdʒ/ N (= ostentation) tralala * m ; (= spending spree) folles dépenses fpl, folie f ◆ **the wedding reception was** or **made a great ~** la réception de mariage était à grand tralala * ◆ **she went on a** or **had a ~ and bought a Rolls** elle a fait une vraie folie et s'est payé une Rolls VI (also **splurge out**) faire une or des folie(s) (on en achetant) VT dépenser (en un seul coup) (on sth pour qch), engloutir (on sth dans qch)

splutter /ˈsplʌtəʳ/ N [of person] (= spitting) crachotement m ; (= stuttering) bredouillement m, bafouillage * m ; [of engine] bafouillage * m ; [of fire, frying pan, fat, candle] crépitement m VI [person] (= spit) crachoter, postillonner ; (= stutter) bredouiller, bafouiller * ; [pen] cracher ; [engine] bafouiller *, tousser ; [fire, frying pan, fat, candle] crépiter ◆ **he ~ed indignantly** il a bredouillé or bafouillé * d'indignation VT (also **splutter out**) [+ words, excuse] bredouiller, bafouiller *

spoil /spɔɪl/ (vb : pret, ptp **spoiled** or **spoilt**) N 1 (gen pl) ~(s) (= booty) butin m ; (fig: after business deal etc) bénéfices mpl, profits mpl ; (US Pol) poste m or avantage m reçu en récompense de services politiques rendus ◆ **the ~s of war** le butin or les dépouilles fpl de la guerre ◆ **he wants his share of the ~s** (fig) il veut sa part du gâteau *

2 (NonC: from excavations etc) déblais mpl

VT 1 (= damage) abîmer ◆ **to ~ one's eyes** s'abîmer la vue ◆ **fruit ~ed by insects** des fruits abîmés par les insectes ◆ **the drought has really ~t the garden** la sécheresse a vraiment fait des dégâts dans le jardin ◆ **to ~ a ballot paper** rendre un bulletin de vote nul

2 (= detract from) [+ view, style, effect] gâter ; [+ holiday, occasion, pleasure] gâter, gâcher ◆ **these weeds quite ~ the garden** ces mauvaises herbes enlaidissent or défigurent le jardin ◆ **his peace of mind was ~t by money worries** sa tranquillité était empoisonnée par des soucis d'argent ◆ **to ~ one's appetite** s'enlever or se couper l'appétit ◆ **if you eat that now you'll ~ your lunch** si tu manges ça maintenant tu n'auras plus d'appétit pour le déjeuner ◆ **don't ~ your life by doing that** ne gâche pas ta vie en faisant cela ◆ **if you tell me the ending you'll ~ the film for me** si vous me racontez la fin vous me gâcherez tout l'intérêt du film ◆ **she ~t the meal by overcooking the meat** elle a gâté le repas en faisant trop cuire la viande ◆ **she ~t the meal by telling him the bad news** elle a gâché le repas en lui racontant la triste nouvelle ◆ **the weather ~ed our holiday** le temps nous a gâté or gâché nos vacances ◆ **to ~ the ship for a ha'p'orth of tar** (Prov) tout gâcher en faisant des économies de bout de chandelle ; → **fun**

3 (= pamper) [+ child, one's spouse, dog etc] gâter ◆ **to ~ o.s.** se gâter soi-même, se faire plaisir ◆ **to ~ sb rotten** * pourrir qn ; → **spare**

VI 1 [food] s'abîmer ; (in ship's hold, warehouse, shop) s'avarier

2 ◆ **to be ~ing for a fight** brûler de se battre, chercher la bagarre *

COMP **spoils system** N (US Pol) système m des dépouilles (consistant à distribuer des postes administratifs à des partisans après une victoire électorale)

spoilage /ˈspɔɪlɪdʒ/ N (NonC) (= process) détérioration f ; (= thing, amount spoilt) déchet(s) m(pl)

spoiled /spɔɪld/ ADJ ⇒ **spoilt**

spoiler /ˈspɔɪləʳ/ N 1 (on car) becquet m ; (on plane) aérofrein m 2 (= person) empêcheur m de danser en rond ◆ **a rival publisher brought out a ~** (Press) un éditeur concurrent leur a coupé l'herbe sous le pied

spoilsport /ˈspɔɪlspɔːt/ N trouble-fête mf inv, rabat-joie m inv ◆ **don't be such a ~!** ne joue pas les trouble-fête or les rabat-joie !

spoilt /spɔɪlt/ VB pt, ptp of **spoil** ADJ 1 (= indulged) [child] gâté ◆ **to be ~ for choice** avoir l'embarras du choix 2 (= invalid) [ballot paper] nul 3 (= rotten) [food] abîmé

spoke¹ /spəʊk/ N [of wheel] rayon m ; [of ladder] barreau m, échelon m ◆ **to put a ~ in sb's wheel** (Brit) mettre des bâtons dans les roues à qn

spoke² /spəʊk/ VB pt of **speak**

spoken /ˈspəʊkən/ VB ptp of **speak** ADJ [dialogue, recitative] parlé ◆ **a robot capable of understanding ~ commands** un robot capable de comprendre la commande vocale ◆ **the ~ language** la langue parlée ◆ **the ~ word** l'oral m, la langue parlée ◆ **~ English** l'anglais m parlé ; → **well²**

spokeshave /ˈspəʊkʃeɪv/ N vastringue f

spokesman /ˈspəʊksmən/ N (pl **-men**) porte-parole m inv (of, for de)

spokesperson /ˈspəʊks,pɜːsən/ N porte-parole m inv

spokeswoman /ˈspəʊks,wʊmən/ N (pl **-women**) porte-parole m inv (femme)

Spoleto /spəʊˈletəʊ/ N Spolète

spoliation /,spəʊlɪˈeɪʃən/ N (esp Naut) pillage m, spoliation f

spondaic /spɒnˈdeɪɪk/ ADJ spondaïque

spondee /ˈspɒndiː/ N spondée m

spondulicks *, **spondulix** * /spɒnˈduːlɪks/ NPL († or hum) pépètes † * fpl

sponge /spʌndʒ/ N 1 (= animal, object, substance) éponge f ◆ **to give sth a ~** donner un coup d'éponge à or sur qch ◆ **to throw in** or **up the ~** * (fig) s'avouer vaincu, abandonner la partie

2 (Culin: also **sponge cake**) gâteau m or biscuit m de Savoie

VT 1 [+ face, person, carpet] éponger, essuyer or nettoyer à l'éponge ; [+ wound] éponger ; [+ liquid] éponger, étancher

2 (* = cadge) [+ meal] se faire payer * (from or off sb par qn) ◆ **to ~ money from sb** taper * qn ◆ **he ~d £10 off his father** il a tapé * son père de 10 livres

VI (* = cadge) ◆ **to ~ on sb** vivre aux crochets de qn ◆ **he's always sponging** c'est un parasite ; (for meals) c'est un pique-assiette

COMP **sponge bag** N (Brit) trousse f de toilette
sponge bath N toilette f à l'éponge
sponge cake N gâteau m or biscuit m de Savoie
sponge-down N [of person] toilette f à l'éponge ; [of walls] coup m d'éponge
sponge finger N boudoir m
sponge mop N balai m éponge
sponge pudding N ≈ pudding m (sorte de gâteau de Savoie)
sponge rubber N caoutchouc m mousse ®

► **sponge down** VT SEP [+ person] laver à l'éponge ; [+ horse] éponger ; [+ walls etc] nettoyer or laver or essuyer à l'éponge ◆ **to ~ o.s. down** se laver à l'éponge, s'éponger
N ◆ **sponge-down** → **sponge**

► **sponge out** VT SEP [+ wound] éponger ; [+ stain, writing] effacer à l'éponge

► **sponge up** VT SEP [+ liquid] éponger, étancher

sponger * /ˈspʌndʒəʳ/ N (pej) parasite m ; (for meals) pique-assiette mf inv

sponginess /ˈspʌndʒɪnɪs/ N spongiosité f

spongy /ˈspʌndʒɪ/ ADJ spongieux

sponsor /ˈspɒnsəʳ/ N 1 [of appeal, proposal, announcement etc] personne f qui accorde son patronage, membre m d'un comité de patronage ; (for club membership) parrain m, marraine f ; [of concert, event] sponsor m ; (individual: for fund-raising event) donateur m, -trice f (à l'occasion d'une "sponsored walk" etc) ; (US) [of club] animateur m, -trice f ◆ **the bank is one of the exhibition's ~s** la banque est un des partenaires de l'exposition

2 (Fin: for loan etc) caution f ; (for commercial enterprise) parrain m ◆ **to be sb's ~, to stand ~ to sb, to act as ~ for sb** se porter caution pour qn

3 (Rel = godparent) parrain m, marraine f

VT 1 [+ sporting event, concert, radio programme, exhibition] sponsoriser ; [+ commercial enterprise, club member] parrainer ; [+ fund-raising walker, swimmer] s'engager à rémunérer (en fonction de sa performance) ; [+ proposal] promouvoir ◆ **~ed walk** (in fund-raising) marche entreprise pour récolter des dons en faveur d'une œuvre de bienfaisance

2 (Fin) [+ borrower] se porter caution pour

3 (Rel) être le parrain (or la marraine) de

4 [+ terrorism] soutenir ; [+ negotiations] organiser ◆ **peace talks ~ed by the UN** des pourparlers de paix organisés sous l'égide de l'ONU

SPONSORED

Les « **sponsored** events » sont un moyen souvent employé pour récolter des dons en faveur d'une œuvre de bienfaisance. Ils consistent à prendre part à un événement sportif (course à pied, course cycliste, saut en parachute) après avoir demandé à sa famille, ses amis ou ses collègues de s'engager à faire un don si on finit la course. Pour une « **sponsored** walk », on promet généralement de donner une certaine somme par kilomètre parcouru.

-sponsored /ˈspɒnsəd/ ADJ (in compounds) ◆ **government-sponsored entreprises** (= financed) des entreprises financées par le gouvernement ◆ **government-sponsored programmes** (= financed) des programmes financés par le gouvernement ◆ **state-sponsored** financé par l'État ◆ **United Nations-sponsored** (= organized) organisé par l'ONU

sponsorship /ˈspɒnsəʃɪp/ N [of sporting event, concert, radio programme, exhibition] sponsoring m ; (Rad, TV) commande f publicitaire ; [of appeal, announcement] patronage m ; (Comm) mécénat m d'entreprise ; [of loan] cautionnement m ; [of child, member] parrainage m ◆ **they must end their ~ of terrorism** ils doivent arrêter de soutenir le terrorisme

spontaneity /,spɒntəˈneɪətɪ/ N spontanéité f

spontaneous /spɒnˈteɪnɪəs/ ADJ spontané
COMP **spontaneous abortion** N avortement m spontané
spontaneous combustion N combustion f spontanée
spontaneous generation N génération f spontanée
spontaneous miscarriage N avortement m spontané
spontaneous remission N rémission f spontanée

spontaneously /spɒnˈteɪnɪəslɪ/ ADV [behave, abort, combust] spontanément ; [arise] spontanément, soudainement ◆ **to miscarry ~** avoir un avortement spontané ◆ **to be ~ warm/friendly** se montrer spontanément chaleureux/amical

spoof * /spuːf/ N (= hoax) blague * f, canular m ; (= parody) parodie f, satire f (on de) ADJ ◆ **a ~ horror film/documentary** une parodie de film d'épouvante/de documentaire ◆ **a ~ announcement** une déclaration bidon * VT

[+ reader, listener etc] faire marcher ; *(= parody)* *[+ book etc]* parodier

spook /spuːk/ N 1 (* *hum = ghost)* apparition *f*, revenant *m* 2 *(US* ⁑ *= secret agent)* barbouze* *f* VT *(US)* 1 *(= haunt)* *[+ person, house]* hanter 2 *(= frighten)* effrayer, faire peur à

spooky* /ˈspuːkɪ/ ADJ *[person, place, atmosphere, music]* sinistre ; *[film]* qui fait froid dans le dos, qui donne la chair de poule ; *[feeling]* à vous faire froid dans le dos, à vous donner la chair de poule ◆ **to bear a ~ resemblance to sb/sth** ressembler d'une manière étrange à qn/qch

spool /spuːl/ N *[of camera, film, tape, thread, typewriter ribbon]* bobine *f* ; *[of fishing reel]* tambour *m* ; *[of sewing machine, weaving machine]* canette *f* ; *[of wire]* rouleau *m*

spoon /spuːn/ N cuillère *or* cuiller *f* ; *(= spoonful)* cuillerée *f*, cuiller *f* ; *(Golf)* spoon *m*, bois *m* trois ; → **dessertspoon, silver** VT ◆ **to ~ sth into a plate/out of a bowl** *etc* verser qch dans une assiette/enlever qch d'un bol *etc* avec une cuiller VI († * *fig)* flirter COMP **spoon-feed** VT *(lit)* ◆ **to ~-feed sb** nourrir qn à la cuiller ◆ **he needs to be ~-fed all the time** *(fig)* il faut toujours qu'on lui mâche *subj* le travail

► **spoon off** VT SEP *[+ fat, cream etc]* enlever avec une cuiller

► **spoon out** VT SEP *(= take out)* verser avec une cuiller ; *(= serve out)* servir avec une cuiller

► **spoon up** VT SEP *[+ food, soup]* manger avec une cuiller ; *[+ spillage]* ramasser avec une cuiller

spoonbill /ˈspuːnbɪl/ N spatule *f*

spoonerism /ˈspuːnərɪzəm/ N contrepèterie *f*

spoonful /ˈspuːnfʊl/ N cuillerée *f*, cuiller *f*

spoor /spʊəʳ/ N *(NonC)* *[of animal]* foulées *fpl*, trace *f*, piste *f*

sporadic /spəˈrædɪk/ ADJ sporadique ◆ **~ fighting** combats *mpl* sporadiques, échauffourées *fpl*

sporadically /spəˈrædɪkəlɪ/ ADV sporadiquement

spore /spɔːʳ/ N spore *f*

sporran /ˈspɒrən/ N *(Scot)* escarcelle *f* en peau *(portée avec le kilt)*

sport /spɔːt/ N 1 sport *m* ◆ **he is good at ~** il est doué pour le sport, il est très sportif ◆ **he is good at several ~s** il est doué pour plusieurs sports ◆ **outdoor/indoor ~s** sports *mpl* de plein air/d'intérieur ◆ **~s** *(meeting)* réunion *f* sportive ◆ **school ~s** réunion *f or* compétition *f* sportive scolaire ; → **field**

2 † *(NonC = fun, amusement)* divertissement *m*, amusement *m* ; *(liter = plaything)* jouet *m* ◆ **it was great ~** c'était très divertissant *or* amusant ◆ **in ~** pour rire, pour s'amuser ◆ **we had (some) good ~** *(gen)* nous nous sommes bien divertis *or* amusés ; *(Hunting/Fishing)* nous avons fait bonne chasse/bonne pêche ◆ **to make ~ of sb** *(liter)* se moquer de qn, tourner qn en ridicule ; → **spoilsport**

3 (* *= person)* **(good) ~** chic* *or* brave type* *m*, chic* *or* brave fille *f* ◆ **be a ~!** sois chic !* ◆ **come on, ~!** *(Austral)* allez, mon vieux* *or* mon pote⁑ !

4 *(Bio) (= mutation)* variété *f* anormale

VI *(liter)* folâtrer, batifoler

VT *[+ tie, hat, beard, buttonhole]* arborer, exhiber ; *[+ black eye]* exhiber

COMP **sport coat, sport jacket** N *(US)* ⇒ **sports jacket** ; → **sports**

sportiness /ˈspɔːtɪnɪs/ N *(lit, fig)* caractère *m* sportif

sporting /ˈspɔːtɪŋ/ ADJ 1 *(Sport)* *[event, activity, organization, career, prowess]* sportif ◆ **a ~ injury** une blessure *or* un traumatisme du sport ◆ **the ~ world** le monde du sport ◆ **~ goods** articles *mpl* de sport 2 *(= fair)* *[gesture]* généreux ; *[person]* chic* *inv* ◆ **that's very ~ of you** c'est très chic* de votre part ◆ **to have a ~ chance (of winning)** avoir de bonnes chances (de gagner) ◆ **to give sb a ~ chance (of winning)** donner à qn une chance (de gagner)

COMP **sporting gun** N fusil *m* de chasse
sporting house † N *(US euph)* maison *f* de passe

sportingly /ˈspɔːtɪŋlɪ/ ADV très sportivement

sportive /ˈspɔːtɪv/ ADJ folâtre, badin

sports /spɔːts/ ADJ *[programme, reporting, newspaper etc]* de sport, sportif ; *[commentator, reporter, news, editor, club]* sportif ; *[clothes]* sport *inv*

COMP **sports bra** N soutien-gorge *m* de sport
sports car N voiture *f* de sport
sports coat N ⇒ **sports jacket**
sports day N *(Brit Scol)* réunion *f or* compétition *f* sportive scolaire
sports desk N *(Press)* rédaction *f* sportive
sports enthusiast N ⇒ **sports fan**
sports equipment N *(NonC)* équipement *m* sportif, matériel *m* de sport
sports fan* N fanatique *mf* de sport
sports ground N terrain *m* de sport, stade *m*
sports injuries clinic N clinique *f* du sport
sports injury N blessure *f* sportive, traumatisme *m* du sport
sports jacket N veste *f* sport *inv*
sports medicine N médecine *f* sportive
sports page N *(Press)* page *f* sportive *or* des sports
sports shop N magasin *m* de sports

sportscast /ˈspɔːtskɑːst/ N *(US Rad, TV)* émission *f* sportive

sportscaster /ˈspɔːtskɑːstəʳ/ N *(US Rad, TV)* reporter *m* sportif

sportsman /ˈspɔːtsmən/ N (pl **-men**) sportif *m* ◆ **he's a real ~** *(fig)* il est beau joueur, il est très sport *inv*

sportsmanlike /ˈspɔːtsmənlaɪk/ ADJ *(lit, fig)* sportif, chic* *inv*

sportsmanship /ˈspɔːtsmənʃɪp/ N *(lit, fig)* sportivité *f*, esprit *m* sportif

sportsperson /ˈspɔːtspɜːsən/ N sportif *m*, -ive *f*

sportswear /ˈspɔːtswɛəʳ/ N *(NonC)* vêtements *mpl* de sport

sportswoman /ˈspɔːtswʊmən/ N (pl **-women**) sportive *f*

sportswriter /ˈspɔːtsraɪtəʳ/ N rédacteur *m* sportif

sporty* /ˈspɔːtɪ/ ADJ 1 *(= fast)* *[car]* de sport 2 *(Sport)* *[person]* sportif 3 *(Fashion)* *[clothes]* sport *inv*

spot /spɒt/ N 1 *[of blood, ink, paint]* *(= mark, dot etc)* tache *f* ; *(= splash)* éclaboussure *f* ; *(on fruit)* tache *f*, tavelure *f* ; *(= polka dot)* pois *m* ; *(on dice, domino)* point *m* ; *[of leopard]* tache *f*, moucheture *f* ; *(on reputation)* tache *f*, souillure *f* *(on sur)* ◆ **a ~ of dirt** une tache, une salissure ◆ **a ~ of red** une tache *or* un point rouge ◆ **a dress with red ~s** une robe à pois rouges ◆ **~s of rain** *(Brit)* quelques gouttes *fpl* de pluie ◆ **to have ~s before one's eyes** *or* **the eyes** voir des mouches volantes devant les yeux ◆ **the ten ~ of spades** *(Cards)* le dix de pique ◆ **a five/ten ~**⁑ *(US = money)* un billet de cinq/dix dollars ◆ **without a ~ or stain** *(fig liter)* sans la moindre tache *or* souillure ; → **beauty, knock, sunspot**

2 *(= pimple)* bouton *m* ; *(freckle-type)* tache *f* (de son) ◆ **he came out in ~s** il a eu une éruption de boutons ◆ **these ~s are measles** ce sont des taches de rougeole

3 *(esp Brit = small amount)* **a ~ of** un peu de ; *[+ whisky, coffee etc]* une goutte de ; *[+ irony, jealousy]* une pointe de ; *[+ truth, commonsense]* un grain de ◆ **he did a ~ of work** il a travaillé un peu ◆ **brandy? – just a ~** du cognac ? – juste une goutte *or* un soupçon ◆ **there's been a ~ of trouble** il y a eu un petit incident *or* un petit problème ◆ **how about a ~ of lunch?*** et si on déjeunait ?, et si on mangeait un morceau ? ◆ **we had a ~ of lunch** nous avons mangé un morceau ; → **bother**

4 *(= place)* endroit *m* ◆ **show me the ~ on the map** montrez-moi l'endroit sur la carte ◆ **a good ~ for a picnic** un bon endroit *or* coin pour un pique-nique ◆ **it's a lovely ~!** c'est un endroit *or* un coin ravissant ! ◆ **there's a tender ~ on my arm** j'ai un point sensible au bras ◆ **the ~ in the story where ...** l'endroit *or* le moment dans l'histoire où ... ◆ **to be in a (bad** *or* **tight) ~*** être dans le pétrin*, être dans de beaux draps ; → **high, hit, soft**

◆ **on the spot** ◆ **the police were on the ~ in two minutes** la police est arrivée sur les lieux en deux minutes ◆ **it's easy if you're on the ~** c'est facile si vous êtes sur place *or* si vous êtes là ◆ **leave it to the man on the ~ to decide** laissez décider la personne qui est sur place ◆ **our man on the ~** *(Press)* notre envoyé spécial ◆ **an on-the-~ broadcast/report** une émission/un reportage sur place ◆ **an on-the-~ enquiry** une enquête sur le terrain ◆ **an on-the-~ fine** une amende payable sur-le-champ *or* avec paiement immédiat ◆ **he was fined on the ~** on lui a infligé une amende sur-le-champ ◆ **he decided on the ~** il s'est décidé sur-le-champ *or* tout de suite ◆ **he was killed on the ~** il a été tué sur le coup ◆ **to put sb on the ~** mettre qn en difficulté *or* dans l'embarras

5 *(in show)* numéro *m* ◆ **a solo ~ in cabaret** un numéro individuel dans une revue ◆ **he got a ~ in the Late Show** il a fait un numéro dans le Late Show

6 *(= advertisement)* spot *m or* message *m* publicitaire ◆ **Glo-Kleen had a ~ (ad*) before the news** il y a eu un spot publicitaire de Glo-Kleen avant les informations

7 (also **spot announcement**) **there was a ~ (announcement) about the referendum** il y a eu une brève annonce au sujet du référendum

8 (* : also **nightspot**) boîte *f* de nuit

9 ⇒ **spotlight noun**

10 *(Billiards, Snooker)* mouche *f*

11 *(Ftbl) (= penalty spot)* point *m* de penalty

VT 1 *(= speckle, stain)* tacher (with de) ◆ **a tie ~ted with fruit stains** une cravate portant des taches de fruit ; see also **spotted**

2 *(= recognize, notice)* *[+ person, object, vehicle]* apercevoir, repérer* ; *[+ mistake]* trouver, repérer ; *[+ bargain, winner, sb's ability]* déceler, découvrir ◆ **can you ~ any bad apples in this tray?** est-ce que tu vois *or* tu trouves des pommes gâtées sur cette claie ?

VI 1 *[material, garment etc]* se tacher, se salir

2 ◆ **it is ~ting (with rain)** il commence à pleuvoir, il tombe quelques gouttes de pluie

3 *(Mil etc = act as spotter)* observer

COMP *[transaction, goods, price]* payé comptant ; *[count, test]* intermittent, fait à l'improviste
spot ad*, spot advertisement, spot announcement N spot *m or* message *m* publicitaire
spot cash N *(NonC)* argent *m* comptant *or* liquide
spot check N contrôle *m* inopiné *or* impromptu
spot-check VT contrôler *or* vérifier de façon impromptue
spot fine N amende *f* à régler immédiatement
spot kick N *(Ftbl) (= penalty kick)* penalty *m*
spot market N marché *m* au comptant
spot-on* ADJ *(Brit) (= right)* ◆ **what he said was ~-on** ce qu'il a dit était en plein dans le mille* ◆ **he guessed ~-on** il a mis en plein dans le mille* ◆ **your new jacket is ~-on** *(= very good)* ta nouvelle veste est super*
spot rate N *(Fin)* cours *m* du disponible

spot remover N détachant *m*
spot survey N sondage *m*
spot-weld VT souder par points

spotless /ˈspɒtlɪs/ ADJ 1 *(= clean)* *[room, street, beach, clothes]* impeccable ◆ **she keeps the house ~** elle entretient impeccablement la maison 2 *(= flawless)* *[reputation, image]* sans tache ADV * ⇒ **spotlessly**

spotlessly /ˈspɒtlɪslɪ/ ADV ◆ **~ clean** impeccable, reluisant de propreté

spotlessness /ˈspɒtlɪsnɪs/ N propreté *f* (impeccable *or* immaculée)

spotlight /ˈspɒtlaɪt/ N *(Theat = beam)* rayon *m* or feu *m* de projecteur ; *(Theat = lamp)* projecteur *m*, spot *m* ; *(in home)* spot *m* ; *(= headlamp)* phare *m* auxiliaire ◆ **the ~ was on him** *(fig)* il était en vedette ; *(in the public eye)* les feux de l'actualité étaient braqués sur lui ◆ **to turn the ~ on sb/sth** *(Theat, fig)* ⇒ **to spotlight sb/sth** → **vt**

◆ **in the spotlight** *(Theat)* sous le feu du *or* des projecteur(s) ; *(fig)* en vedette, sous le feu des projecteurs

VT *(Theat)* diriger les projecteurs sur ; *(fig)* *[+ sb's success, achievements]* mettre en vedette ; *[+ changes, differences, a fact]* mettre en lumière

spotlit /ˈspɒtlɪt/ ADJ illuminé

spotted /ˈspɒtɪd/ ADJ 1 *(= patterned)* *[handkerchief, tie, dress, crockery]* à pois ; *[animal]* tacheté ◆ **blue eggs ~ with brown** œufs *mpl* bleus tachetés de marron ◆ **a yellow tie ~ with grey** une cravate jaune à pois gris 2 *(= blemished)* ◆ **~ with paint** taché de peinture ◆ **~ with stains** couvert de taches ◆ **~ with nasty green mould** couvert d'horribles taches de moisissure verte

COMP **spotted dick** N *(Brit Culin)* *pudding aux raisins de Corinthe*
spotted fever N fièvre *f* éruptive
spotted flycatcher N gobe-mouches *m* gris

spotter /ˈspɒtəʳ/ N 1 *(Brit)* **train/plane ~** *(as hobby)* passionné(e) *m(f)* de trains/d'avions 2 *(Mil etc)* *(for enemy aircraft)* guetteur *m* ; *(during firing)* observateur *m* 3 *(US Comm *)* surveillant(e) *m(f)* du personnel COMP **spotter plane** N avion *m* d'observation

spotting /ˈspɒtɪŋ/ N 1 repérage *m* ; *(Brit)* ◆ **train/plane ~** *passe-temps consistant à identifier le plus grand nombre possible de trains/d'avions* 2 *(Med)* traces *fpl* (de sang)

spotty /ˈspɒtɪ/ ADJ 1 *[person, face, skin]* boutonneux 2 *(esp US = patchy)* *[support]* irrégulier, inégal ; *[bus service]* irrégulier ; *[knowledge]* inégal 3 *(* = patterned)* *[handkerchief, shirt, crockery]* à pois 4 *(= dirty)* *[garment]* taché

spousal /spaʊzl/ ADJ *(esp US)* *[duties, violence]* conjugal ; *[consent]* du conjoint

spouse /spaʊz/ N *(frm or hum)* époux *m*, épouse *f* ; *(Jur)* conjoint(e) *m(f)*

spout /spaʊt/ N *[of teapot, jug, can]* bec *m* ; *(for tap)* brise-jet *m inv* ; *[of gutter, pump etc]* dégorgeoir *m* ; *[of pipe]* orifice *m* ; *[of fountain]* jet *m*, ajutage *m* ; *(= stream of liquid)* jet *m*, colonne *f* ◆ **to be up the ~** ‡ *(Brit)* *[plans, timetable etc]* être fichu * *or* foutu ‡ ; *[person]* *(= in trouble)* être dans un mauvais cas, être dans de beaux draps ; *(= pregnant)* être en cloque ‡ ◆ **that's another £50 (gone) up the ~** ‡ voilà encore 50 livres de foutues en l'air ‡ ; → **waterspout**

VI 1 *[liquid]* jaillir, sortir en jet *(from, out of* de) ; *[whale]* lancer un jet d'eau, souffler

2 (* fig pej = harangue) pérorer, laïusser * *(about* sur)

VT (also **spout out**) 1 *[+ liquid]* faire jaillir, laisser échapper un jet de ; *[+ smoke, lava]* lancer *or* émettre un jet de, vomir

2 *(* = recite)* débiter, déclamer ◆ **he can ~ columns of statistics** il peut débiter *or* dévider des colonnes entières de statistiques

sprain /spreɪn/ N entorse *f* ; *(less serious)* foulure *f* VT *[+ muscle, ligament]* fouler, étirer ◆ **to ~ one's ankle** se faire *or* se donner une entorse à la cheville ; *(less serious)* se fouler la cheville ◆ **to have a ~ed ankle** s'être fait une entorse à la cheville ; *(less serious)* s'être foulé la cheville

sprang /spræŋ/ VB pt of **spring**

sprat /spræt/ N sprat *m* ◆ **it was a ~ to catch a mackerel** c'était un appât

sprawl /sprɔːl/ VI (also **sprawl out**) *(= fall)* tomber, s'étaler * ; *(= lie)* être affalé *or* vautré ; *[handwriting]* s'étaler (dans tous les sens) ; *[plant]* ramper, s'étendre *(over* sur) ; *[town]* s'étaler *(over* dans) ◆ **he was ~ing *or* lay ~ed in an armchair** il était affalé *or* vautré dans un fauteuil ◆ **to send sb ~ing** faire tomber qn de tout son long *or* les quatre fers en l'air, envoyer qn rouler par terre N *(position)* attitude *f* affalée , *[of building, town]* étendue *f* ◆ **an ugly ~ of buildings down the valley** d'affreux bâtiments qui s'étalent dans la vallée ◆ **London's suburban ~** l'étalement *m* *or* l'extension *f* de la banlieue londonienne ◆ **the seemingly endless ~ of suburbs** l'étendue *f* apparemment infinie des banlieues, les banlieues *fpl* tentaculaires

sprawling /ˈsprɔːlɪŋ/ ADJ *[person, position, body]* affalé ; *[house]* grand et informe ; *[city]* tentaculaire ; *[novel, handwriting]* qui part (*or* partait) dans tous les sens

spray¹ /spreɪ/ N 1 *(gen)* (nuage *m* de) gouttelettes *fpl* ; *(from sea)* embruns *mpl* ; *(from hosepipe)* pluie *f* ; *(from atomizer)* spray *m* ; *(from aerosol)* pulvérisation *f* ◆ **wet with the ~ from the fountain** aspergé par le jet de la fontaine

2 *(= container, aerosol)* bombe *f*, aérosol *m* ; *(for scent etc)* atomiseur *m*, spray *m* ; *(refillable)* vaporisateur *m* ; *(for lotion)* brumisateur *m* ; *(larger: for garden etc)* pulvérisateur *m* ◆ **insecticide ~** *(= aerosol)* bombe *f* (d')insecticide ; *(contents)* insecticide *m* *(en bombe)* ; → **hair**

3 (also **spray attachment, spray nozzle**) pomme *f*, ajutage *m*

VT 1 *[+ roses, garden, crops]* faire des pulvérisations sur ; *[+ room]* faire des pulvérisations dans ; *[+ hair]* vaporiser *(with* de) ; *(= spray-paint)* *[+ car]* peindre à la bombe ◆ **to ~ the lawn with weedkiller** pulvériser du désherbant sur la pelouse ◆ **they ~ed the oil slick with detergent** ils ont répandu du détergent sur la nappe de pétrole ◆ **to ~ sth/sb with bullets** arroser qch/qn de balles, envoyer une grêle de balles sur qch/qn

2 *[+ water]* vaporiser, pulvériser *(on* sur) ; *[+ scent]* vaporiser ; *[+ insecticide, paint]* pulvériser ◆ **they ~ed foam on the flames** ils ont projeté de la neige carbonique sur les flammes

VI 1 ◆ **it ~ed everywhere** ça a tout arrosé ◆ **it ~ed all over the carpet** ça a arrosé tout le tapis

2 *(= spray insecticide)* pulvériser des insecticides

COMP *[deodorant, insecticide etc]* (présenté) en bombe
spray can N bombe *f*
spray gun N pistolet *m* *(à peinture etc)*
spraying machine N *(Agr)* pulvérisateur *m*
spray-on ADJ *(lit)* en aérosol, en bombe ; *(* hum)* *[jeans, dress]* hyper moulant *
spray-paint N peinture *f* en bombe VT peindre à la bombe

► **spray out** VI *[liquid]* jaillir *(on to, over* sur) ◆ **water ~ed out all over them** ils ont été complètement aspergés *or* arrosés d'eau

spray² /spreɪ/ N *[of flowers]* gerbe *f* ; *[of greenery]* branche *f* ; *(= brooch)* aigrette *f*

sprayer /ˈspreɪəʳ/ N 1 ⇒ **spray¹ noun 2** 2 *(= aircraft:* also **crop-sprayer**) avion-pulvérisateur *m*

spread /spred/ (vb : pret, ptp **spread**) N 1 *(NonC)* *[of fire, disease, infection]* propagation *f*, progression *f* ; *[of nuclear weapons]* prolifération *f* ; *[of idea, knowledge]* diffusion *f*, propagation *f* ◆ **to stop the ~ of a disease** empêcher une maladie de s'étendre, arrêter la propagation d'une maladie ◆ **the ~ of education** le progrès de l'éducation ◆ **the ~ of risk** *(Insurance)* la division des risques

2 *(= extent, expanse)* *[of wings]* envergure *f* ; *[of arch]* ouverture *f*, portée *f* ; *[of bridge]* travée *f* ; *[of marks, prices, ages]* gamme *f*, échelle *f* ; *[of wealth]* répartition *f*, distribution *f* ◆ **a ~ of canvas *or* of sail** *(Naut)* un grand déploiement de voiles ◆ **he's got middle-age(d) ~** il a pris de l'embonpoint avec l'âge

3 *(= cover)* *(for table)* dessus *m* *or* tapis *m* de table ; *(for meals)* nappe *f* ; *(= bedspread)* dessus-de-lit *m inv*, couvre-lit *m*

4 *(Culin)* pâte *f* (à tartiner) ◆ **cheese ~** fromage *m* à tartiner

5 *(* = meal)* festin *m* ◆ **what a lovely ~!** c'est un vrai festin !

6 *(Cards)* séquence *f*

7 *(Press, Typ)* *(= two pages)* double page *f* ; *(across columns)* deux (*or* trois *etc*) colonnes *fpl*

ADJ *(Ling)* *[vowel]* non arrondi ; *[lips]* étiré

VT 1 (also **spread out**) *[+ cloth, sheet, map]* étendre, étaler *(on sth* sur qch) ; *[+ carpet, rug]* étendre, dérouler ; *[+ wings, bird's tail, banner, sails]* déployer ; *[+ net]* étendre, déployer ; *[+ fingers, toes, arms, legs]* écarter ; *[+ fan]* ouvrir ◆ **the peacock ~ its tail** le paon a fait la roue ◆ **to ~ one's wings** *(fig)* élargir ses horizons ◆ **to ~ o.s.** *(lit:* also **spread o.s. out**) s'étaler, prendre plus de place ; *(= speak at length)* s'étendre, s'attarder *(on* sur) ; *(= extend one's activities)* s'étendre

2 *[+ bread]* tartiner *(with* de) ; *[+ butter, jam, glue]* étaler *(on* sur) ; *[+ face cream]* étendre *(on* sur) ◆ **~ both surfaces with glue, ~ glue on both surfaces** étalez de la colle sur les deux surfaces, enduisez de colle les deux surfaces ◆ **to ~ butter on a slice of bread, to ~ a slice of bread with butter** tartiner de beurre une tranche de pain, beurrer une tartine

3 *(= distribute)* *[+ sand etc]* répandre *(on, over* sur) ; *[+ fertilizer]* épandre, étendre *(over, on* sur) ; (also **spread out**) *[+ objects, cards, goods]* étaler *(on* sur) ; *[+ soldiers, sentries]* disposer, échelonner *(along* le long de) ◆ **he ~ sawdust on the floor** il a répandu de la sciure sur le sol, il a couvert le sol de sciure ◆ **he ~ his books (out) on the table** il a étalé ses livres sur la table ◆ **there were policemen ~ (out) all over the hillside** il y avait des agents de police éparpillés *or* dispersés sur toute la colline ◆ **the wind ~ the flames** le vent a propagé les flammes

4 *(= diffuse)* *[+ disease, infection]* propager ; *[+ germs]* disséminer ; *[+ wealth]* distribuer ; *[+ rumours]* faire courir ; *[+ news]* faire circuler, communiquer ; *[+ knowledge]* répandre, diffuser ; *[+ panic, fear, indignation]* répandre, semer ; *(in time:* also **spread out**) *[+ payment, studies]* échelonner, étaler *(over* sur) ◆ **his visits were ~ (out) over three years** ses visites se sont échelonnées *or* étalées sur une période de trois ans ◆ **he ~ his degree (out) over five years** il a échelonné ses études de licence sur cinq ans ◆ **his research was ~ over many aspects of the subject** ses recherches embrassaient *or* recouvraient de nombreux aspects du sujet ◆ **our resources are ~ very thinly** nous n'avons plus aucune marge dans l'emploi de nos ressources ◆ **the new regulations ~ the tax burden more evenly** les nouveaux règlements répartissent la charge fiscale plus uniformément ◆ **to ~ o.s. too thin** trop disperser ses efforts ◆ **to ~ the word** *(= propagate ideas)* prêcher la bonne parole ◆ **to ~ the word about sth** *(= announce)* annoncer qch

VI 1 *(= widen, extend further)* *[river, stain]* s'élargir, s'étaler ; *[flood, oil slick, weeds, fire, infection, disease]* gagner du terrain, s'étendre ; *[water]* se répandre ; *[pain]* s'étendre ; *[panic, indignation]*

se propager ; *[news, rumour, knowledge]* se propager, se répandre ◆ **to ~ into** *or* **over sth** *[river, flood, water, oil slick]* se répandre dans *or* sur qch ; *[fire, pain]* se communiquer à qch, atteindre qch ; *[weeds, panic]* envahir qch ; *[disease]* atteindre qch, contaminer qch ; *[news, education]* atteindre qch, se répandre dans *or* sur qch ◆ **under the ~ing chestnut tree** sous les branches étendues du marronnier

2 *(= stretch, reach)* (also **spread out**) *[lake, plain, oil slick, fire]* s'étendre *(over* sur) ◆ **the desert ~s over 500 square miles** le désert s'étend sur *or* recouvre 500 miles carrés ◆ **his studies ~ (out) over four years** ses études se sont étendues sur quatre ans

3 *[butter, paste etc]* s'étaler

COMP **spread betting** N pari *m* diversifié *(pour répartir ses chances et limiter les pertes)*

spread eagle N *(Her)* aigle *f* éployée

spread-eagle ADJ *(US)* chauvin VT ◆ **to ~-eagle sb** envoyer qn rouler par terre ◆ **to be** *or* **lie ~-eagled** être étendu bras et jambes écartés

► **spread out** VI 1 *[people, animals]* se disperser, s'éparpiller ◆ **~ out!** dispersez-vous !

2 *(= open out) [fan]* s'ouvrir ; *[wings]* se déployer ; *[valley]* s'élargir

3 ⇒ **spread vi 2**

VT SEP ◆ **the valley lay spread out before him** la vallée s'étendait à ses pieds ◆ **he was ~ out on the floor** il était étendu de tout son long par terre ; see also **spread vt 1, 3, 4**

spreader /ˈspredə^r/ N *(for butter)* couteau *m* à tartiner ; *(for glue)* couteau *m* à palette ; *(Agr: for fertilizer)* épandeur *m*, épandeuse *f*

spreadsheet /ˈspredʃiːt/ N *(Comput) (= chart)* tableau *m* ; *(= software)* tableur *m*

spree /spriː/ N fête *f* ◆ **to go on** *or* **have a ~** faire la fête *or* la noce* ; → **buying, crime, drinking, spending, shooting, shopping**

sprig /sprɪg/ N brin *m*

sprightliness /ˈspraɪtlɪnɪs/ N *(NonC, physical)* vivacité *f*, vitalité *f* ; *(mental)* vivacité *f*

sprightly /ˈspraɪtlɪ/ ADJ *(= physically)* alerte ; *(= mentally)* alerte, vif

spring /sprɪŋ/ (vb : pret **sprang**, ptp **sprung**) N

1 *(= leap)* bond *m*, saut *m* ◆ **in** *or* **with** *or* **at one ~** d'un bond, d'un saut

2 *(for chair, mattress, watch, machine)* ressort *m* ◆ **the ~s** *[of car]* la suspension ; → **hairspring, mainspring**

3 *(NonC = resilience) [of mattress]* élasticité *f* ; *[of bow, elastic band]* détente *f* ◆ **he had a ~ in his step** il marchait d'un pas élastique *or* souple

4 *[of water]* source *f* ◆ **hot ~** source *f* chaude

5 *(fig)* **~s** *(= cause, motive)* mobile *m*, motif *m*, cause *f* ; *(= origin)* source *f*, origine *f*

6 *(= season)* printemps *m* ◆ **in (the) ~** au printemps ◆ **~ is in the air** on sent venir le printemps

VI 1 *(= leap)* bondir, sauter ◆ **to ~ in/out/across** *etc* entrer/sortir/traverser *etc* d'un bond ◆ **to ~ at sth/sb** bondir *or* sauter *or* se jeter sur qch/qn ◆ **to ~ to one's feet** se lever d'un bond

2 *(fig)* **to ~ to attention** bondir au garde-à-vous ◆ **to ~ to sb's help** bondir *or* se précipiter à l'aide de qn ◆ **to ~ to the rescue** se précipiter pour porter secours ◆ **he sprang into action** il est passé à l'action ◆ **they sprang into the public eye** ils ont tout à coup attiré l'attention du public ◆ **to ~ into existence** apparaître du jour au lendemain ◆ **to ~ into view** apparaître soudain, surgir ◆ **to ~ to mind** venir *or* se présenter à l'esprit ◆ **tears sprang to her eyes** les larmes lui sont venues aux yeux, les larmes lui sont montées aux yeux ◆ **the first name that sprang to his lips** le premier nom qui lui est venu aux lèvres ◆ **his hand sprang to his gun** il a saisi *or* attrapé son pistolet ◆ **the door sprang open** la porte s'est brusquement ouverte ◆ **where did you ~ from?** d'où est-ce que tu sors ? ◆ **hope ~s eternal** l'espoir fait vivre

3 *(= originate from)* provenir, découler *(from* de) ◆ **the oak sprang from a tiny acorn** le chêne est sorti d'un tout petit gland ◆ **all his actions ~ from the desire to ...** toutes ses actions proviennent *or* découlent de son désir de ... ◆ **it sprang from his inability to cope with the situation** c'est venu *or* né de son incapacité à faire face à la situation

4 *[timbers etc] (= warp)* jouer, se gondoler ; *(= split)* se fendre

VT 1 *[+ trap, lock]* faire jouer ; *[+ mine]* faire sauter ◆ **to ~ a surprise on sb** surprendre qn ◆ **to ~ a question on sb** poser une question à qn à brûle-pourpoint *or* de but en blanc ◆ **to ~ a piece of news on sb** annoncer une nouvelle à qn de but en blanc ◆ **he sprang the suggestion on me suddenly** il me l'a suggéré de but en blanc *or* à l'improviste ◆ **he sprang it on me** il m'a pris de court *or* au dépourvu

2 *(= put springs in) [+ mattress]* pourvoir de ressorts ; *[+ car]* suspendre ◆ **well-sprung** *[car]* bien suspendu

3 *(Hunting) [+ game]* lever ; ‡ *[+ prisoner]* aider à se faire la belle‡ ◆ **he was sprung‡ from Dartmoor** on l'a aidé à se cavaler‡ de Dartmoor

4 *(= leap over) [+ ditch, fence etc]* sauter, franchir d'un bond

5 *[+ timbers, mast] (= warp)* gondoler, faire jouer ; *(= split)* fendre ; → **leak**

COMP *[weather, day, flowers]* printanier, de printemps ; *[mattress]* à ressorts

spring balance N balance *f* à ressort

spring binder N *(= file)* classeur *m* à ressort

spring binding N *[of file]* reliure *f* à ressort

spring chicken N *(Culin)* poussin *m* ◆ **he/she is no ~ chicken** il/elle n'est pas de toute première jeunesse

spring-clean N *(NonC)* (also **spring-cleaning**) grand nettoyage *m* (de printemps) VT nettoyer de fond en comble

spring fever N fièvre *f* printanière

spring greens NPL *(Brit)* choux *mpl* précoces

spring-like ADJ printanier, de printemps

spring-loaded ADJ tendu par un ressort

spring lock N serrure *f* à fermeture automatique

spring onion N *(Brit)* ciboule *f*

spring roll N *(Culin)* rouleau *m* de printemps

spring snow N *(Ski)* neige *f* de printemps

spring tide N *(gen)* grande marée *f* ; *(at equinox)* marée *f* d'équinoxe (de printemps)

spring water N eau *f* de source

► **spring up** VI *[person]* se lever d'un bond *or* précipitamment ; *[flowers, weeds]* surgir de terre ; *[corn]* lever brusquement ; *[new buildings, settlements]* pousser comme des champignons ; *[wind, storm]* se lever brusquement ; *[rumour]* naître, s'élever ; *[doubt, fear]* naître, jaillir ; *[friendship, alliance]* naître, s'établir ; *[problem, obstacle, difficulty]* se présenter, surgir

springboard /ˈsprɪŋbɔːd/ N *(lit, fig)* tremplin *m*

springbok /ˈsprɪŋbɒk/ N (pl **springbok** *or* **springboks**) springbok *m*

springe /sprɪndʒ/ N collet *m*

springiness /ˈsprɪŋɪnɪs/ N *[of rubber, mattress]* élasticité *f* ; *[of ground, turf, step, hair]* souplesse *f* ; *[of plank]* flexibilité *f* ; *[of carpet]* moelleux *m*

springtide /ˈsprɪŋtaɪd/ N *(liter)* ⇒ **springtime**

springtime /ˈsprɪŋtaɪm/ N printemps *m*

springy /ˈsprɪŋɪ/ ADJ *[rubber, mattress, texture]* élastique, souple ; *[carpet]* moelleux ; *[plank]* flexible ; *[ground, turf, step]* souple ; *[step]* alerte, souple ; *[hair]* frisé

sprinkle /ˈsprɪŋkl/ VT ◆ **to ~ sth with water, to ~ water on sth** asperger qch d'eau ◆ **to ~ water on the garden** arroser légèrement le jardin ◆ **a rose ~d with dew** une rose couverte de rosée ◆ **to ~ sand on** *or* **over sth, to ~ sth with sand** répandre une légère couche de sable sur qch, couvrir qch d'une légère couche de sable ◆ **to ~ sand/grit on the roadway** sabler/cendrer la route ◆ **to ~ sugar over a cake, to ~ a cake with sugar** *(Culin)* saupoudrer un gâteau de sucre ◆ **lawn ~d with daisies** pelouse parsemée *or* émaillée *(liter)* de pâquerettes ◆ **they are ~d about here and there** ils sont éparpillés *or* disséminés ici et là

sprinkler /ˈsprɪŋklə^r/ N *(for lawn)* arroseur *m* ; *(for sugar etc)* saupoudreuse *f* ; *(larger)* saupoudroir *m* ; *(in ceiling: for fire-fighting)* diffuseur *m* (d'extincteur automatique d'incendie), sprinkler *m* COMP **sprinkler system** N *(for lawn)* combiné *m* d'arrosage ; *(for fire-fighting)* installation *f* d'extinction automatique d'incendie

sprinkling /ˈsprɪŋklɪŋ/ N 1 *(= act) (with water, gen, Rel)* aspersion *f* ; *(on garden, road, street)* arrosage *m* ; *(with sugar)* saupoudrage *m* ◆ **to give sth a ~ (of water)** *(gen)* asperger qch (d'eau) ; *[+ garden, road, street]* arroser qch ◆ **to give sth a ~ (of sugar)** saupoudrer qch (de sucre) 2 *(= quantity) [of sand, snow]* mince couche *f* ◆ **top off with a ~ of icing sugar/grated Parmesan** terminer en saupoudrant de sucre glace/parmesan râpé ◆ **a ~ of water** quelques gouttes *fpl* d'eau ◆ **a ~ of freckles** quelques taches *fpl* de rousseur ◆ **a ~ of sightseers** quelques rares touristes *mpl* ◆ **a ~ of women ministers** un petit nombre de femmes ministres ◆ **a ~ of literary allusions in the text** des allusions littéraires émaillant le texte

sprint /sprɪnt/ N *(Sport)* sprint *m* ◆ **to make a ~ for the bus** piquer* un sprint *or* foncer pour attraper l'autobus VI *(Sport)* sprinter ; *(gen)* foncer, piquer* un sprint ◆ **to ~ down the street** descendre la rue à toutes jambes

sprinter /ˈsprɪntə^r/ N *(Sport)* sprinter *m*, sprinteur *m*, -euse *f*

sprit /sprɪt/ N *(Naut)* livarde *f*, balestron *m*

sprite /spraɪt/ N lutin *m*, farfadet *m* ; *(Comput = icon in game)* joueur *m*, lutin *m*

spritz /sprɪts/ N N *(= fizz)* ◆ **it has a slight ~** c'est légèrement pétillant VT *(= spray)* vaporiser *(with* de) ◆ **I ~ed myself with water** je me suis aspergé d'eau

spritzer /ˈsprɪtsə^r/ N *boisson à base de vin blanc et d'eau gazeuse*

sprocket /ˈsprɒkɪt/ N pignon *m* COMP **sprocket wheel** N pignon *m* (d'engrenage)

sprog‡ /sprɒg/ N *(Brit)* 1 *(= child)* morpion* *m*, -ionne* *f (pej)* 2 *(Mil)* bleu *m*

sprout /spraʊt/ N *(on plant, branch etc)* pousse *f* ; *(from bulbs, seeds)* germe *m* ◆ **(Brussels) ~** chou *m* de Bruxelles VI 1 *[bulbs, onions etc]* germer, pousser 2 (also **sprout up** = *grow quickly*) *[plants, crops, weeds]* bien pousser ; *[child]* grandir *or* pousser vite 3 (also **sprout up** = *appear*) *[mushrooms etc]* pousser ; *[weeds]* surgir de terre ; *[new buildings]* surgir de terre, pousser comme des champignons VT ◆ **to ~ new leaves** pousser *or* produire de nouvelles feuilles ◆ **to ~ shoots** *[potatoes, bulbs]* germer ◆ **the wet weather has ~ed the barley** le temps humide a fait germer l'orge ◆ **the deer has ~ed horns** les cornes du cerf ont poussé, le cerf a mis ses bois ◆ **Paul has ~ed* a moustache** Paul s'est laissé pousser la moustache

spruce[1] /spruːs/ N (also **spruce tree**) épicéa *m* spruce ◆ **white/black ~** *(Can)* épinette *f* blanche/noire

spruce[2] /spruːs/ ADJ *[person]* pimpant, soigné ; *[garment]* net, impeccable ; *[house]* coquet, pimpant

► **spruce up** VT SEP *[+ child]* faire beau ; *[+ house]* bien astiquer ◆ **all ~d up** *[person]* tiré à quatre épingles ; *[house]* bien astiqué, reluisant de propreté ◆ **to ~ o.s. up** se faire tout beau (toute belle *f*)

sprucely /ˈspruːslɪ/ ADV ◆ **~ dressed** tiré à quatre épingles, sur son trente et un

spruceness /ˈspruːsnɪs/ N *[of person]* mise *f* soignée ; *[of house]* aspect *m* coquet

sprung /sprʌŋ/ VB ptp of **spring** ADJ *[seat, mattress]* à ressorts

spry /spraɪ/ ADJ alerte, plein d'entrain

SPUC /ˌespiːjuːˈsiː/ N *(Brit)* (abbrev of **Society for the Protection of the Unborn Child**) *association anti-avortement*

spud /spʌd/ N (= *tool*) sarcloir *m* ; (* = *potato*) patate * *f* COMP **spud-bashing** ⁎ N *(Mil)* corvée *f* de patates *

spume /spjuːm/ N *(liter)* écume *f*

spun /spʌn/ VB pt, ptp of **spin**

spunk /spʌŋk/ N 1 *(NonC* ⁎ *= courage)* cran * *m*, courage *m* 2 *(Brit* *⁎ *= semen)* foutre *⁎ *m*

spunky ⁎ /ˈspʌŋkɪ/ ADJ plein de cran *

spur /spɜːʳ/ N 1 *[of horse, fighting cock, mountain, masonry]* éperon *m* ; *[of bone]* saillie *f* ; *(fig)* aiguillon *m* ◆ **to dig in one's ~s** enfoncer ses éperons, éperonner son cheval ◆ **to win** *or* **earn one's ~s** *(Brit) (Hist)* gagner ses éperons ; *(fig)* faire ses preuves ◆ **on the ~ of the moment** sous l'impulsion du moment, sur un coup de tête ◆ **the ~ of hunger** l'aiguillon *m* de la faim ◆ **it will be a ~ to further efforts** cela nous *(or les etc)* incitera à faire des efforts supplémentaires

2 *(Rail:* also **spur track**) (= *siding*) voie *f* latérale, voie *f* de garage ; (= *branch*) voie *f* de desserte, embranchement *m*

3 *(on motorway etc)* embranchement *m*

VT (also **spur on**) *[+ horse]* éperonner ; *(fig)* éperonner, aiguillonner ◆ **he ~red his horse on** (= *applied spurs once*) il a éperonné son cheval, il a donné de l'éperon à son cheval ; (= *sped on*) il a piqué des deux ◆ **~red on by ambition** éperonné *or* aiguillonné par l'ambition ◆ **to ~ sb (on) to do sth** encourager *or* inciter qn à faire qch ◆ **this ~red him (on) to greater efforts** ceci l'a encouragé à redoubler d'efforts

COMP **spur gear** N ⇒ **spur wheel**
spur-of-the-moment ADJ fait sur l'impulsion du moment
spur wheel N roue *f* à dents droites

spurge /spɜːdʒ/ N euphorbe *f* COMP **spurge laurel** N daphné *m*

spurious /ˈspjʊərɪəs/ ADJ *(gen)* faux (fausse *f*) ; *[document, writings]* faux (fausse *f*), apocryphe ; *[claim]* fallacieux ; *[interest, affection, desire]* simulé, feint

spuriously /ˈspjʊərɪəslɪ/ ADV faussement

spurn /spɜːn/ VT *[+ help, offer]* repousser, rejeter ; *[+ lover]* éconduire

spurt /spɜːt/ N *[of water, flame]* jaillissement *m*, jet *m* ; *[of anger, enthusiasm, energy]* sursaut *m*, regain *m* ; (= *burst of speed*) accélération *f* ; *(fig: at work etc)* effort *m* soudain, coup *m* de collier ◆ **final ~** *(Racing)* emballage *m*, rush *m* ◆ **to put on a ~** *(Sport)* démarrer, sprinter ; *(in running for bus)* piquer * un sprint, foncer ; *(fig: in work)* donner un coup de collier, faire un soudain effort ◆ **in ~s** (= *sporadically*) par à-coups VI 1 (also **spurt out, spurt up**) *[water, blood]* jaillir, gicler *(from* de) ; *[flame]* jaillir *(from* de) 2 *[runner]* piquer * un sprint, foncer ; *(Sport)* démarrer, sprinter VT (also **spurt out**) *[+ flame, lava]* lancer, vomir ; *[+ water]* laisser jaillir, projeter

sputa /ˈspjuːtə/ NPL of **sputum**

sputnik /ˈspʊtnɪk/ N spoutnik *m*

sputter /ˈspʌtəʳ/ VI (= *progress unevenly*) piétiner ◆ **the economy is already ~ing** l'économie piétine déjà ◆ **the battle ~ed to a halt** la bataille s'est enlisée et a pris fin ; see also **splutter vi, vt**

sputum /ˈspjuːtəm/ N (pl **sputa**) crachat *m*, expectorations *fpl*

spy /spaɪ/ N *(gen, Ind, Pol)* espion(ne) *m(f)* ◆ **police ~** indicateur *m*, -trice *f* de police

VI *(gen)* espionner, épier ; *(Ind, Pol)* faire de l'espionnage ◆ **to ~ for a country** faire de l'espionnage au service *or* pour le compte d'un pays ◆ **to ~ on sb** espionner qn ◆ **to ~ on sth** épier qch ◆ **stop ~ing on me!** arrête de m'espionner *or* de me surveiller ! ◆ **to ~ into sth** chercher à découvrir qch subrepticement

VT (= *catch sight of*) apercevoir ◆ **I spied him coming** je l'ai vu qui arrivait *or* s'approchait ◆ **I ~, with my little eye, something beginning with A** je vois quelque chose qui commence par A, essaie de deviner *(jeu d'enfant)*

COMP *[film, story etc]* d'espionnage
spy-in-the-sky * N satellite-espion *m*
spy plane N avion-espion *m*
spy ring N réseau *m* d'espionnage
spy satellite N satellite-espion *m*

► **spy out** VT SEP reconnaître ◆ **to ~ out the land** *(lit, fig)* reconnaître le terrain

spycatcher /ˈspaɪkætʃəʳ/ N *(Brit)* chasseur *m* d'espions

spyglass /ˈspaɪglɑːs/ N lunette *f* d'approche

spyhole /ˈspaɪhəʊl/ N judas *m*

spying /ˈspaɪɪŋ/ N *(NonC)* espionnage *m*

spymaster /ˈspaɪmɑːstəʳ/ N chef *m* des services secrets

spyware /ˈspaɪweəʳ/ N logiciel *m* espion

Sq abbrev of **Square**

sq. (abbrev of **square**) carré ◆ **4~ m** 4 m²

squab /skwɒb/ N (pl **squabs** *or* **squab**) 1 (= *pigeon*) pigeonneau *m* 2 *(Brit: in car)* assise *f*

squabble /ˈskwɒbl/ N chamaillerie * *f*, prise *f* de bec * VI se chamailler *, se disputer *(over sth* à propos de qch)

squabbler * /ˈskwɒbləʳ/ N chamailleur * *m*, -euse * *f*

squabbling /ˈskwɒblɪŋ/ N *(NonC)* chamaillerie(s) * *f(pl)*

squad /skwɒd/ N *[of soldiers, policemen, workmen, prisoners]* escouade *f*, groupe *m* ; *(Sport)* équipe *f* ◆ **the England ~** *(Sport)* l'équipe *f* d'Angleterre ; → **firing, flying** COMP **squad car** N *(esp US Police)* voiture *f* de police

squaddie, squaddy * /ˈskwɒdɪ/ N *(Brit = private soldier)* deuxième classe *m inv*

squadron /ˈskwɒdrən/ N *(in army)* escadron *m* ; *(in navy, airforce)* escadrille *f* COMP **squadron leader** N *(Brit Aviat)* commandant *m*

squalid /ˈskwɒlɪd/ ADJ *[place, conditions, love affair, experience]* sordide ; *[motive]* bas (basse *f*), ignoble ◆ **it was a ~ business** c'était une affaire sordide

squall /skwɔːl/ N 1 *(Weather)* rafale *f or* bourrasque *f* (de pluie) ; *(at sea)* grain *m* ◆ **there are ~s ahead** *(fig)* il y a de l'orage dans l'air, il va y avoir du grabuge * 2 (= *cry*) hurlement *m*, braillement *m* VI *[baby]* hurler, brailler

squalling /ˈskwɔːlɪŋ/ ADJ criard, braillard *

squally /ˈskwɔːlɪ/ ADJ *[wind]* qui souffle en rafales ; *[weather]* à bourrasques, à rafales ; *[day]* entrecoupé de bourrasques

squalor /ˈskwɒləʳ/ N *(NonC)* conditions *fpl* sordides, misère *f* noire ◆ **to live in ~** vivre dans des conditions sordides *or* dans la misère noire ; *(pej)* vivre comme un cochon *(or* des cochons) *

squander /ˈskwɒndəʳ/ VT *[+ time, money, talents]* gaspiller ; *[+ fortune, inheritance]* dissiper, dilapider ; *[+ opportunity, chances]* laisser filer, laisser passer

square /skweəʳ/ N 1 (= *shape*) carré *m* ; *[of chessboard, crossword, graph paper]* case *f* ; (= *square piece*) *[of fabric, chocolate, toffee]* carré *m* ; *[of cake]* part *f* (carrée) ; (= *window pane*) carreau *m* ◆ **to fold paper into a ~** plier une feuille de papier en carré ◆ **divide the page into ~s** divisez la page en carrés, quadrillez la page ◆ **linoleum with black and white ~s on it** du linoléum en damier noir et blanc *or* à carreaux noirs et blancs ◆ **the troops were drawn up in a ~** les troupes avaient formé le carré ◆ **form (yourselves into) a ~** placez-vous en carré, formez un carré ◆ **to start again from ~ one** * repartir à zéro *, repartir de la case départ ◆ **now we're back to ~ one** * nous nous retrouvons à la case départ *, nous repartons à zéro *

2 *(in town)* place *f* ; *(with gardens)* square *m* ; *(esp US = block of houses)* pâté *m* de maisons ; *(Mil:* also **barrack square**) cour *f* (de caserne) ◆ **the town ~** la (grand-)place

3 (= *drawing instrument*) équerre *f* ◆ **it's out of ~** ce n'est pas d'équerre ◆ **to cut sth on the ~** équarrir qch ◆ **to be on the ~** * *[offer, deal]* être honnête *or* régulier * ; *[person]* jouer franc jeu, jouer cartes sur table ; → **set, T**

4 *(Math)* carré *m* ◆ **four is the ~ of two** quatre est le carré de deux

5 (* *pej = conventional person*) **he's a real ~** il est vraiment ringard * ◆ **don't be such a ~!** ne sois pas si ringard ! *

ADJ 1 *(in shape) [object, shape, hole, face, jaw, shoulders]* carré ◆ **a ~ corner** un coin à angle droit ◆ **of ~ build** trapu, ramassé ◆ **to be a ~ peg in a round hole** * ne pas être dans son élément

2 ◆ **~ with** *or* **to sth** (= *parallel*) parallèle à qch ; (= *at right angles*) à angle droit avec qch, perpendiculaire à qch

3 *(Math)* ◆ **6 ~ metres** 6 mètres carrés ◆ **6 metres ~** (de) 6 mètres sur 6 ◆ **a 25-cm ~ baking dish** un moule de 25 centimètres sur 25

4 *(Fin) [accounts, books, figures]* en ordre ◆ **to get one's accounts ~** mettre ses comptes en ordre, balancer ses comptes ◆ **to get ~ with sb** *(financially)* régler ses comptes avec qn ; *(fig = get even with)* rendre la pareille à qn ◆ **to be (all) ~** être quitte

5 *(Sport)* ◆ **to be all ~** être à égalité

6 (= *honest*) *[dealings]* honnête ◆ **a ~ deal** un arrangement équitable *or* honnête ◆ **to get a ~ deal** être traité équitablement ◆ **to give sb a ~ deal** agir honnêtement avec qn ◆ **to be ~ with sb** être honnête avec qn ; → **fair¹**

7 (* *pej = conventional*) *[person, habit, attitude]* ringard * ◆ **be there or be ~!** *(hum)* tous les gens branchés * y seront

8 (= *unequivocal*) *[refusal, denial]* net, catégorique

9 *(Cricket)* à angle droit ◆ **to be ~ of the wicket** être placé perpendiculairement au guichet

ADV 1 (= *squarely*) ◆ **to hit** *or* **catch sb ~ on the forehead/on the jaw** atteindre qn en plein front/en pleine mâchoire ◆ **to hit sb ~ in the chest** frapper qn en pleine poitrine ◆ **a huge wave hit the ship ~ on** une énorme lame a frappé le bateau de plein fouet ◆ **to kiss sb ~ on the mouth** embrasser qn à pleine bouche ◆ **~ in the middle** en plein milieu ◆ **to be ~ in the middle of sth** être au beau milieu de qch ◆ **to look sb ~ in the face** regarder qn bien en face ◆ **to stand ~** être bien campé sur ses jambes ◆ **the bomb landed ~ on target** la bombe est tombée en plein sur l'objectif ; → **fair¹**

2 (= *parallel*) ◆ **~ to** *or* **with sth** parallèlement à qch ◆ **he turned to face me ~ on** il s'est tourné pour être juste en face de moi ◆ **to stand ~ on to the camera** se tenir bien en face de la caméra

3 (= *at right angles*) ◆ **to cut sth ~** équarrir qch, couper qch au carré *or* à angle droit ◆ **~ to** *or*

with sth à angle droit avec qch, d'équerre avec qch ◆ **the ship ran ~ across our bows** le navire nous a complètement coupé la route

VT 1 (= *make square*) *[+ figure, shape]* rendre carré, carrer ; *[+ stone, timber]* équarrir, carrer ; *[+ corner]* couper au carré *or* à angle droit ◆ **to ~ one's shoulders** redresser les épaules ◆ **to try to ~ the circle** *(fig)* chercher à faire la quadrature du cercle

2 (= *settle, sort out*) *[+ books, accounts]* mettre en ordre, balancer ; *[+ debts]* acquitter, régler ; *[+ creditors]* régler, payer ; (= *reconcile*) concilier, faire cadrer (*with* avec) ◆ **to ~ one's account with sb** régler ses comptes avec qn ◆ **to ~ o.s. with sb** régler ses comptes avec qn ◆ **I can't ~ that with what he told me yesterday** ça ne cadre pas avec ce qu'il m'a dit hier ◆ **he managed to ~ it with his conscience** il s'est arrangé avec sa conscience ◆ **can you ~* it with the boss?** est-ce que vous pouvez arranger ça avec le patron ? ◆ **I can ~* him** (= *get him to agree*) je m'occupe de lui, je me charge de lui

3 *(Math)* *[+ number]* élever au carré ◆ **four ~d is sixteen** quatre au carré fait seize

VI cadrer, correspondre ◆ **that doesn't ~ with the facts** cela ne cadre pas avec les faits, cela ne correspond pas aux faits ◆ **that ~s!** * ça cadre !, ça colle ! *

COMP **square-bashing** * N *(Brit Mil)* exercice *m*
square bracket N *(Typ)* crochet *m*
square-built ADJ trapu
square-cut ADJ coupé à angle droit, équarri
square dance N ≈ quadrille *m*
square-dancing N *(NonC)* quadrille *m*
square-faced ADJ au visage carré
square-jawed ADJ à la mâchoire carrée
square knot N *(US)* nœud *m* plat
square leg N *(Cricket) position du joueur de champ lorsqu'il est placé à angle droit avec le batteur*
square meal N repas *m* substantiel
the Square Mile N *(in London)* la City
square number N *(Math)* carré *m*
square-rigged ADJ *(Naut)* gréé (en) carré
square rigger N *(Naut)* navire *m* gréé en carré
square root N racine *f* carrée
square-shouldered ADJ aux épaules carrées, carré d'épaules
square-toed ADJ *[shoes]* à bout carré

► **square off** VI *(in quarrel)* se faire face ; *(in fist fight)* se mettre en garde (*to sb* devant qn)

VT SEP *[+ paper, plan]* diviser en carrés, quadriller ; *[+ wood, edges]* équarrir

► **square up** VI 1 *[boxers, fighters]* se mettre en garde (*to sb* devant qn) ◆ **to ~ up to a problem** *(fig)* faire face à un problème

2 (= *pay debts*) régler ses comptes (*with sb* avec qn)

VT SEP 1 (= *make square*) *[+ paper]* couper au carré *or* à angle droit ; *[+ wood]* équarrir

2 *[+ account, debts]* régler, payer ◆ **I'll ~ things up* for you** ne vous en faites pas, je vais arranger ça

squarely /ˈskweəlɪ/ ADV 1 (= *completely*) complètement ◆ **responsibility rests ~ with the President** la responsabilité incombe complètement au président ◆ **to lay** *or* **place the blame for sth ~ on sb** rejeter complètement la responsabilité de qch sur qn

2 (= *directly*) ◆ **to look at sb ~** regarder qn droit dans les yeux ◆ **to look sb ~ in the eye** regarder qn dans le blanc des yeux ◆ **a film that looks ~ at social problems** un film qui traite sans détour des problèmes sociaux ◆ **to face one's guilt ~** assumer sa culpabilité sans détour ◆ **she faced her mother ~** elle s'est campée devant sa mère d'un air résolu ◆ **a film aimed ~ at family audiences** un film visant directement un public familial ◆ **to hit sb ~ in the stomach** frapper qn en plein dans le ventre ◆ **set ~ in the middle of the wall** placé en plein milieu du mur

3 (= *honestly*) *[deal with]* honnêtement ; → **fairly**

squash[1] /skwɒʃ/ N 1 *(Brit)* **lemon/orange ~** citronnade *f*/orangeade *f* (concentrée)

2 *(Sport)* squash *m*

3 (= *crowd*) cohue *f*, foule *f* ; (= *crush*) cohue *f*, bousculade *f* ◆ **we all got in, but it was a ~** on est tous entrés mais on était serrés ◆ **a great ~ of people** une cohue, une foule ◆ **I lost him in the ~ at the exit** je l'ai perdu dans la cohue *or* dans la bousculade à la sortie

VT *[+ fruit, beetle, hat, box]* écraser ; *(fig)* *[+ argument]* réfuter ; (= *snub*) *[+ person]* rabrouer ◆ **to ~ flat** *[+ fruit, beetle]* écraser, écrabouiller* ; *[+ hat, box]* aplatir ◆ **he ~ed his nose against the window** il a écrasé son nez contre la vitre ◆ **you're ~ing me!** tu m'écrases ! ◆ **she ~ed the shoes into the suitcase** elle a réussi à caser* les chaussures dans la valise ◆ **can you ~ two more people in the car?** est-ce que tu peux faire tenir *or* caser* deux personnes de plus dans la voiture ?

VI 1 *[people]* **they ~ed into the elevator** ils se sont serrés *or* entassés dans l'ascenseur ◆ **they ~ed through the gate** ils ont franchi le portail en se bousculant

2 *[fruit, parcel etc]* s'écraser ◆ **will it ~?** est-ce que cela risque de s'écraser ?

COMP **squash court** N *(Sport)* court *m* de squash
squash player N joueur *m*, -euse *f* de squash
squash racket N raquette *f* de squash

► **squash in** VI *[people]* s'empiler, s'entasser ◆ **when the car arrived they all ~ed in** quand la voiture est arrivée ils se sont tous empilés *or* entassés dedans ◆ **can I ~ in?** est-ce que je peux me trouver une petite place ?

VT SEP *(into box, suitcase etc)* réussir à faire rentrer

► **squash together** VI *[people]* se serrer (les uns contre les autres)

VT SEP *[+ objects]* serrer, tasser ◆ **we were all ~ed together** nous étions très serrés *or* entassés

► **squash up** VI *[people]* se serrer, se pousser ◆ **can't you ~ up a bit?** pourriez-vous vous serrer *or* vous pousser un peu ?

VT SEP *[+ object]* écraser ; *[+ paper]* chiffonner en boule

squash[2] /skwɒʃ/ N (pl **squashes** *or* **squash**) (= *gourd*) gourde *f* ; *(US* = *marrow)* courge *f*

squashy * /ˈskwɒʃɪ/ ADJ *[fruit, sofa]* mou (molle *f*)

squat[1] /skwɒt/ ADJ *[person]* trapu, courtaud ; *[building]* ramassé, trapu ; *[armchair, jug, teapot]* trapu ; *[glass]* court VI 1 (also **squat down**) *[person]* s'accroupir, s'asseoir sur ses talons ; *[animal]* se tapir, se ramasser ◆ **to be ~ting (down)** *[person]* être accroupi, être assis sur ses talons ; *[animal]* être tapi *or* ramassé 2 *[squatters]* squatter ◆ **to ~ in a house** squatter *or* squattériser une maison N (= *act of squatting, place*) squat *m* COMP **squat thrust** N *(Gym)* saut *m* de main

squat[2] ‡ /skwɒt/ N *(US:* also **diddly-squat)** ◆ **you don't know ~ (about that)** t'y connais que dalle‡ ◆ **that doesn't mean ~ (to me)** (pour moi,) ça veut dire que dalle‡

squatter /ˈskwɒtəʳ/ N squatter *m* COMP **squatter's rights** N droit *m* de propriété par occupation du terrain

squatting /ˈskwɒtɪŋ/ N squat *m*, squattage *m*

squaw /skwɔː/ N squaw *f*, femme *f* peau-rouge

squawk /skwɔːk/ VI *[hen, parrot]* pousser un *or* des gloussement(s) ; *[baby]* brailler ; *[person]* pousser un *or* des cri(s) rauque(s) ; (* fig = complain) râler*, gueuler‡ N gloussement *m*, braillement *m*, cri *m* rauque COMP **squawk box** * N *(US* = *loudspeaker)* haut-parleur *m*

squeak /skwiːk/ N *[of hinge, wheel, pen, chalk]* grincement *m* ; *[of shoes]* craquement *m* ; *[of mouse, doll]* petit cri *m* aigu, vagissement *m* ; *[of person]* petit cri *m* aigu, glapissement *m* ◆ **to let out** *or* **give a ~ of fright/surprise** *etc* pousser un petit cri *or* glapir de peur/de surprise *etc* ◆ **not a ~*, mind!** (= *be quiet*) pas de bruit, hein ! ; (= *keep it secret*) pas un mot !, motus et bouche cousue !* ◆ **I don't want another ~ out of you** je ne veux plus t'entendre ; → **narrow** VI 1 (= *make sound*) *[hinge, wheel, chair, gate, pen, chalk]* grincer ; *[shoe]* craquer ; *[mouse, doll]* vagir, pousser un *or* des petit(s) cri(s) ; *[person]* glapir 2 *(in exam, election)* ◆ **to ~ through** être accepté de justesse VT ◆ **"no" she ~ed** "non" glapit-elle

squeaker /ˈskwiːkəʳ/ N *(in toy etc)* sifflet *m*

squeaky /ˈskwiːkɪ/ ADJ *[hinge, gate, wheel, chair]* grinçant ; *[pen]* qui crisse ; *[toy]* qui grince ; *[shoes]* qui craque ; *[voice]* aigu (-guë *f*) COMP **squeaky-clean** * ADJ *(lit)* (= *very clean*) *[hair]* tout propre ; *[office, home]* ultrapropre ; (= *above reproach*) *[person]* blanc comme neige ; *[reputation, image]* irréprochable ; *[company]* à la réputation irréprochable

squeal /skwiːl/ N *[of person, animal]* cri *m* aigu *or* perçant ; *[of brakes]* grincement *m*, hurlement *m* ; *[of tyres]* crissement *m* ◆ **to let out** *or* **give a ~ of pain** pousser un cri de douleur ◆ **... he said with a ~ of laughter** ... dit-il avec un rire aigu VI 1 *[person, animal]* pousser un *or* des cri(s) (aigu(s) *or* perçant(s)) ; *[brakes]* grincer, hurler ; *[tyres]* crisser ◆ **he ~ed like a (stuck) pig** il criait comme un cochon qu'on égorge ◆ **she tickled the child and he ~ed** elle a chatouillé l'enfant et il a poussé un petit cri 2 (‡ = *inform*) vendre la mèche* ◆ **to ~ on sb** balancer* *or* donner* qn ◆ **somebody ~ed to the police** quelqu'un les (*or* nous etc) a balancés* *or* donnés* à la police VT ◆ **"help" he ~ed** "au secours" cria-t-il (d'une voix perçante)

squeamish /ˈskwiːmɪʃ/ ADJ facilement dégoûté (*about sth* par qch) ◆ **I'm not ~ about blood** je ne suis pas facilement dégoûté par la vue du sang ◆ **don't be so ~!** ne fais pas le délicat !

squeamishness /ˈskwiːmɪʃnɪs/ N *(NonC)* délicatesse *f* exagérée

squeegee /ˌskwiːˈdʒiː/ N *(for windows)* raclette *f* (à bord de caoutchouc) ; (= *mop*) balai-éponge *m* COMP **squeegee merchant** * N *(Brit)* laveur *m* de pare-brise

squeeze /skwiːz/ N 1 *(NonC: in crowd)* cohue *f*, bousculade *f* ◆ **to give sth a ~** ⇒ **to squeeze sth vt 1** ◆ **he gave her a big ~** il l'a serrée très fort dans ses bras ◆ **he gave her hand a tender ~** il lui serra tendrement la main ◆ **a ~ of lemon** quelques gouttes *fpl* de citron ◆ **a ~ of toothpaste** un peu de dentifrice ◆ **it was a real ~ in the bus** on était serrés comme des sardines* *or* on était affreusement tassés dans l'autobus ◆ **it was a (tight) ~ to get through** il y avait à peine la place de passer ◆ **to put the ~ on sb**‡ presser qn, harceler qn

2 *(Econ)* (also **credit squeeze**) restrictions *fpl* de crédit ◆ **spending ~** réduction *f* des dépenses

3 *(Bridge)* squeeze *m* (*in* à)

4 (* = *romantic partner*) (petit) copain *m*, (petite) copine *f*

VT 1 (= *press*) *[+ handle, tube, plastic bottle, lemon, sponge]* presser ; *[+ cloth]* tordre ; *[+ doll, teddy bear]* appuyer sur ; *[+ sb's hand, arm]* serrer ◆ **he ~d his finger in the door** il s'est pris *or* pincé le doigt dans la porte ◆ **she ~d another sweater into the case** elle a réussi à caser* un autre chandail dans la valise ◆ **to ~ one's eyes shut** fermer les yeux en serrant fort ◆ **he ~d his victim dry** * il a saigné sa victime à blanc

2 (= *extract*) ◆ **~ the water from the sponge** essorez l'éponge ◆ **~ the air from the tyre** faites sortir l'air du pneu en appuyant dessus

3 *[+ prices, profits]* réduire

VI ◆ **he ~d past me** il s'est glissé devant moi en me poussant un peu ◆ **he managed to ~ into the bus** il a réussi à se glisser *or* à s'introduire dans l'autobus en poussant ◆ **they all ~d into the car** ils se sont entassés *or* empilés dans la voiture ◆ **can you ~ underneath the fence?** est-ce que tu peux te glisser sous la barrière ? ◆ **he ~d through the crowd** il a réussi à se faufiler à travers la foule ◆ **she ~d through the window** elle s'est glissée par la fenêtre ◆ **the car ~d into the empty space** il y avait juste assez de place pour se garer

COMP **squeeze bottle** N *(US)* flacon *m* en plastique déformable

squeeze-box* N *(= accordion)* accordéon *m* ; *(= concertina)* concertina *m*

► **squeeze in** VI *[person]* trouver une petite place ; *[car etc]* rentrer tout juste, avoir juste la place ◆ **can I ~ in?** est-ce qu'il y a une petite place pour moi ?

VT SEP *[+ object into box, item on programme]* trouver une petite place pour ◆ **can you ~ two more people in?** est-ce que vous avez de la place pour deux autres personnes ?, est-ce que vous pouvez prendre deux autres personnes ? ◆ **I can ~ you in* tomorrow at nine** je peux vous prendre (en vitesse) *or* vous caser* demain à neuf heures

► **squeeze out** VI ◆ **he managed to squeeze out of the window** à force de contorsions, il a réussi à sortir par la fenêtre

VT 1 *(= extract) [+ water, juice, toothpaste, air]* faire sortir (en pressant) (*of* de)

2 *[+ information, names, contribution]* soutirer, arracher ; *[+ money]* soutirer (*of* à) ◆ **you won't ~ a penny out of me** tu ne me feras pas lâcher* un sou ◆ **the government hopes to ~ more money out of the taxpayers** le gouvernement espère soutirer encore de l'argent aux contribuables

3 *(= get rid of) [+ person]* évincer ◆ **his brother tried to ~ him out of the company** son frère a essayé de l'évincer de l'entreprise

► **squeeze past** VI *[person]* passer en se faufilant *or* en poussant ; *[car]* se faufiler, se glisser

► **squeeze through** VI *[person]* se faufiler, se frayer un chemin ; *[car]* se faufiler, se glisser (*between* entre)

► **squeeze up*** VI *[person]* se serrer, se pousser

squeezer /ˈskwiːzəʳ/ N presse-fruits *m inv* ◆ **lemon ~** presse-citron *m inv*

squelch /skweltʃ/ N 1 bruit *m* de succion *or* de pataugeage ◆ **I heard the ~ of his footsteps in the mud** je l'ai entendu patauger dans la boue ◆ **the tomato fell with a ~** la tomate s'est écrasée par terre avec un bruit mat 2 *(‡ = crushing retort)* réplique *f* qui coupe le sifflet* VI *[mud etc]* faire un bruit de succion ◆ **to ~ in/out** *etc [person]* entrer/sortir *etc* en pataugeant ◆ **to ~ (one's way) through the mud** avancer en pataugeant dans la boue ◆ **the water ~ed in his boots** l'eau faisait flic flac* dans ses bottes VT *(= crush underfoot)* piétiner, écraser

squib /skwɪb/ N pétard *m* ; → **damp**

squid /skwɪd/ N (pl **squid** *or* **squids**) calmar *m*, encornet *m*

squidgy* /ˈskwɪdʒɪ/ ADJ *(Brit)* visqueux

squiffy †* /ˈskwɪfɪ/ ADJ *(Brit)* éméché* ◆ **to get ~** se noircir †*

squiggle /ˈskwɪgl/ N *(= scrawl)* gribouillis *m* ; *(= wriggle)* tortillement *m* VI *(in writing etc)* gribouiller, faire des gribouillis ; *[worm etc]* se tortiller

squiggly /ˈskwɪglɪ/ ADJ ondulé

squillion* /ˈskwɪlɪən/ N *(Brit)* myriade *f* ◆ **~s of pounds** des millions et des millions de livres ◆ **a ~ reasons** une myriade de raisons

squinch /skwɪntʃ/ *(US)* VT *[+ eyes]* plisser ◆ **he ~ed his eyes at the sunlight** il a plissé les yeux à cause du soleil, le soleil lui a fait plisser les yeux VI plisser les yeux

squint /skwɪnt/ N 1 *(Med)* strabisme *m* ◆ **to have a ~** loucher, être atteint de strabisme

2 *(= sidelong look)* regard *m* de côté ; *(* = quick glance)* coup *m* d'œil ◆ **to have** *or* **take a ~ at sth** * *(obliquely)* regarder qch du coin de l'œil, lorgner qch ; *(quickly)* jeter un coup d'œil à qch ◆ **let's have a ~!*** donne voir !, montre voir !* ◆ **have a ~* at this** jette un coup d'œil là-dessus, zieute ‡ ça

VI 1 *(Med)* loucher

2 *(= screw up eyes)* ◆ **he ~ed in the sunlight** il a plissé les yeux à cause du soleil, le soleil lui a fait plisser les yeux

3 *(= take a look)* jeter un coup d'œil ◆ **he ~ed down the tube** il a jeté un coup d'œil dans le tube ◆ **to ~ at sth** *(obliquely)* regarder qch du coin de l'œil, lorgner qch ; *(quickly)* jeter un coup d'œil à qch ◆ **he ~ed at me quizzically** il m'a interrogé du regard

COMP **squint-eyed** ADJ qui louche

squirarchy /ˈskwaɪərɑːkɪ/ N ⇒ **squirearchy**

squire /ˈskwaɪəʳ/ N *(= landowner)* propriétaire *m* terrien ≃ châtelain *m* ; *(Hist = knight's attendant)* écuyer *m* ◆ **the ~ told us ...** le châtelain nous a dit ... ◆ **the ~ of Barcombe** le seigneur † *or* le châtelain de Barcombe ◆ **yes ~!‡** *(Brit)* oui chef *or* patron !* VT *[+ lady]* escorter, servir de cavalier à ◆ **she was ~d by ...** elle était escortée par ...

squirearchy /ˈskwaɪərɑːkɪ/ N *(NonC)* hobereaux *mpl*, propriétaires *mpl* terriens

squirm /skwɜːm/ VI 1 *[worm etc]* se tortiller ◆ **to ~ through a window** *[person]* passer par une fenêtre en faisant des contorsions 2 *(fig) [person] (from embarrassment)* ne pas savoir où se mettre, être au supplice ; *(from distaste)* avoir un haut-le-corps ◆ **spiders make me ~** j'ai un haut-le-corps quand je vois une araignée ◆ **her poetry makes me ~** ses poèmes me mettent mal à l'aise

squirrel /ˈskwɪrəl/ N écureuil *m* ◆ **red ~** écureuil *m* roux ◆ **grey ~** écureuil *m* gris COMP *[coat etc]* en petit-gris

► **squirrel away** VT SEP *[+ nuts etc]* amasser

squirt /skwɜːt/ N 1 *[of water]* jet *m* ; *[of detergent]* giclée *f* ; *[of scent]* quelques gouttes *fpl* 2 *(* pej = person)* petit morveux* *m*, petite morveuse* *f* VT *[+ water]* faire jaillir, faire gicler (*at, on, onto* sur ; *into* dans) ; *[+ detergent]* verser une giclée de ; *[+ oil]* injecter ; *[+ scent]* faire tomber quelques gouttes de ◆ **he ~ed the insecticide onto the roses** il a pulvérisé de l'insecticide sur les roses ◆ **to ~ sb with water** asperger *or* arroser qn d'eau ◆ **to ~ scent on sb, to ~ sb with scent** asperger qn de parfum VI *[liquid]* jaillir, gicler ◆ **the water ~ed into my eye** j'ai reçu une giclée d'eau dans l'œil ◆ **water ~ed out of the broken pipe** l'eau jaillissait du tuyau cassé COMP **squirt gun** N *(US)* pistolet *m* à eau

squirter /ˈskwɜːtəʳ/ N poire *f* (en caoutchouc)

squishy* /ˈskwɪʃɪ/ ADJ *[fruit]* mollasson ; *[ground, texture]* spongieux

Sr (abbrev of **Senior**) Sr

SRC /esɑːˈsiː/ N *(Brit)* 1 (abbrev of **Science Research Council**) ≃ CNRS *m* 2 (abbrev of **students' representative council**) *comité d'étudiants*

Sri Lanka /ˌsriːˈlæŋkə/ N Sri Lanka *m* ◆ **in ~** au Sri Lanka

Sri Lankan /ˌsriːˈlæŋkən/ ADJ *(gen)* sri-lankais ; *[ambassador, embassy]* du Sri Lanka N Sri-Lankais(e) *m(f)*

SRN /esɑːrˈen/ N *(Brit)* (abbrev of **State-Registered Nurse**) → **state**

SS /esˈes/ N 1 (abbrev of **steamship**) *navire de la marine marchande britannique* ◆ **~ Charminster** le Charminster 2 (abbrev of **Saints**) Sts *mpl*, Stes *fpl* 3 *(= Nazi)* SS *m inv*

SSA /ˌesesˈeɪ/ N *(US)* (abbrev of **Social Security Administration**) → **social**

SSP /ˌesesˈpiː/ N *(Brit)* (abbrev of **statutory sick pay**) → **statutory**

SSSI /ˌesesesˈaɪ/ N *(Brit)* (abbrev of **Site of Special Scientific Interest**) → **site**

St N 1 (abbrev of **Street**) rue *f* ◆ **Churchill ~** rue Churchill 2 (abbrev of **Saint**) St(e) ◆ **~ Peter** saint Pierre ◆ **~ Anne** sainte Anne

COMP **St John Ambulance** N *(Brit) association bénévole de secouristes*

St Lawrence N *(Geog = river)* Saint-Laurent *m*

St Lawrence Seaway N *(Geog)* voie *f* maritime du Saint-Laurent

st abbrev of **stone(s)**

stab /stæb/ N 1 *(with dagger/knife etc)* coup *m* (de poignard/de couteau *etc*) ◆ **a ~ in the back** *(fig)* un coup bas *or* déloyal ◆ **a ~ of pain** un élancement ◆ **a ~ of remorse/grief** un remords/une douleur lancinant(e)

2 *(* = attempt)* **to have** *or* **make a ~ at (doing) sth** s'essayer à (faire) qch ◆ **I'll have a ~ at it** je vais tenter le coup

VT *(with knife etc) (= kill)* tuer d'un coup de *or* à coups de couteau *etc* ; *(= wound)* blesser d'un coup de *or* à coups de couteau *etc* ; *(= kill or wound with dagger)* poignarder ◆ **to ~ sb with a knife** frapper qn d'un coup de couteau, donner un coup de couteau à qn ◆ **to ~ sb to death** tuer qn d'un coup de *or* à coups de couteau *etc* ◆ **he was ~bed through the heart** il a reçu un coup de couteau *etc* dans le cœur ◆ **to ~ sb in the back** *(lit, fig)* poignarder qn dans le dos ◆ **he ~bed his penknife into the desk** il a planté son canif dans le bureau ◆ **he ~bed the pencil through the map** il a transpercé la carte d'un coup de crayon

VI ◆ **he ~bed at the book with his finger** il a frappé le livre du doigt

COMP **stab-wound** N coup *m* de poignard (*or* couteau *etc*) ; *(= mark)* trace *f* de coup de poignard (*or* couteau *etc*) ◆ **to die of ~-wounds** mourir poignardé

stabbing /ˈstæbɪŋ/ N agression *f* (à coups de couteau *etc*) ◆ **there was another ~ last night** la nuit dernière une autre personne a été attaquée à coups de couteau *etc* ADJ *[gesture]* comme pour frapper ; *[sensation]* lancinant ◆ **~ pain** douleur *f* lancinante, élancement *m*

stabile /ˈsteɪbaɪl/ N *(Art)* stabile *m*

stability /stəˈbɪlɪtɪ/ N *(NonC: gen)* stabilité *f* ; *[of marriage]* solidité *f*

stabilization /ˌsteɪbəlaɪˈzeɪʃən/ N stabilisation *f*

stabilize /ˈsteɪbəlaɪz/ VT stabiliser

stabilizer /ˈsteɪbəlaɪzəʳ/ N *(on car, plane, boat)* stabilisateur *m* ; *(in food)* stabilisant *m* NPL **stabilizers** *(Brit) [of bicycle]* stabilisateurs *mpl*

COMP **stabilizer bar** N *(US: on car)* barre *f* antiroulis, stabilisateur *m*

stable¹ /ˈsteɪbl/ ADJ *(gen)* stable ; *[marriage]* solide ; *(Med)* stationnaire, stable ◆ **to be in a ~ relationship** avoir une relation stable ◆ **he is not a very ~ character** il est plutôt instable ◆ **to be in a serious but ~ condition** *(Med)* être dans un état grave mais stationnaire *or* stable ◆ **sterling has remained ~ against the euro** la livre sterling est restée stable par rapport à l'euro

stable² /ˈsteɪbl/ N *(= building)* écurie *f* ; (also **racing stable**) écurie *f* (de courses) ◆ **(riding) ~(s)** centre *m* d'équitation, manège *m* ◆ **another bestseller from the HarperCollins ~** un nouveau best-seller qui sort de chez HarperCollins VT *[+ horse]* mettre dans une *or* à l'écurie

COMP **stable-boy** N garçon *m or* valet *m* d'écurie

stable companion N *(Brit)* ⇒ **stablemate**
stable door N **to shut** *or* **close the ~ door after the horse has bolted** *or* **has gone** *(Prov)* prendre des précautions après coup
stable girl N valet *m* d'écurie
stable lad N *(Brit)* lad *m*

stablemate /ˈsteɪblmeɪt/ N *(= horse)* compagnon *m* de stalle ; *(= person)* camarade *mf* d'études (*or* de travail *etc*)

stabling /ˈsteɪblɪŋ/ N écuries *fpl* ◆ **we have ~ for twenty horses** nos écuries peuvent accueillir vingt chevaux

staccato /stəˈkɑːtəʊ/ ADV *(Mus)* staccato ADJ *(Mus) [notes]* piqué ; *[passage]* joué en staccato ; *[gunfire, voice, style]* saccadé

stack /stæk/ N 1 *(Agr)* meule *f* ; *[of rifles]* faisceau *m* ; *[of wood, books, papers]* tas *m*, pile *f* ; *(US) [of tickets]* carnet *m* ◆ **~s* of** un tas* de, plein* de ◆ **I've got ~s*** *or* **a ~* of things to do** j'ai des tas* de choses *or* plein* de choses à faire ◆ **to have ~s* of money** rouler sur l'or, être bourré de fric‡ ◆ **we've got ~s* of time** on a tout le temps ; → **haystack**

2 *(= group of chimneys)* souche *f* de cheminée ; *(on factory, boat etc)* (tuyau *m* de) cheminée *f*

3 *(in library, bookshop)* **~s** rayons *mpl*, rayonnages *mpl*

4 *(Comput)* pile *f*

VT 1 *[+ hay, straw]* mettre en meule ; (also **stack up**) *[+ books, wood]* empiler, entasser ; *[+ dishes]* empiler ◆ **the table was ~ed with books** la table était couverte de piles de livres ◆ **she's well-~ed‡** *(hum)* il y a du monde au balcon*

2 *[+ supermarket shelves]* remplir ◆ **she ~ed the shelf with books** *(gen)* elle a entassé des livres sur le rayon

3 *(= hold waiting) [+ incoming calls, applications etc]* mettre en attente ; *(Aviat) [+ aircraft]* mettre en attente (à différentes altitudes)

4 *(*, pej)* ◆ **to ~ a jury** composer un jury favorable ◆ **he had ~ed the committee with his own supporters** il avait noyauté le comité en y plaçant ses partisans ◆ **to ~ the cards** *or* *(US)* **the deck** tricher (en battant les cartes) ◆ **the cards** *or* **odds are ~ed against me** tout joue contre moi

► **stack up** VI *(US = measure, compare)* se comparer *(with, against* à)

VT SEP *(gen)* empiler, entasser ; *[+ wheat, barrels]* gerber ; see also **stack vt 1**

stadium /ˈsteɪdɪəm/ N (pl **stadiums** *or* **stadia** /ˈsteɪdɪə/) stade *m (sportif)*

staff¹ /stɑːf/ N (pl **staffs**) *(= work force) (Comm, Ind)* personnel *m* ; *(Scol, Univ)* personnel *m* enseignant, professeurs *mpl* ; *(= servants)* domestiques *mfpl* ; *(Mil)* état-major *m* ◆ **a large ~** un personnel *etc* nombreux ◆ **to be on the ~** faire partie du personnel ◆ **we have 30 typists on the ~** notre personnel comprend 30 dactylos ◆ **15 ~** *(gen)* 15 employés ; *(teachers)* 15 professeurs *or* enseignants ◆ **he's left our ~** il ne fait plus partie de notre personnel ◆ **he joined our ~ in 1984** il est entré chez nous en 1984, il a commencé à travailler chez nous en 1984 ◆ **he's ~** il fait partie du personnel ; → **chief, editorial**

VT *[+ school, hospital etc]* pourvoir en personnel ◆ **it is ~ed mainly by immigrants** le personnel se compose surtout d'immigrants ◆ **the hotel is well-~ed** l'hôtel est pourvu d'un personnel nombreux ; → **overstaffed, short, understaffed**

COMP **staff association** N association *f* du personnel, ≃ comité *m* d'entreprise
staff canteen N restaurant *m* d'entreprise, cantine *f* (des employés)
staff college N *(Mil)* école *f* supérieure de guerre
staff corporal N *(Brit)* ≃ adjudant *m*
staff discount N remise *f* pour le personnel
staff meeting N *(Scol, Univ)* conseil *m* des professeurs
staff nurse N *(Med)* infirmier *m*, -ière *f*
staff officer N *(Mil)* officier *m* d'état-major
staff sergeant N *(Brit, US Army)* ≃ sergent-chef *m* ; *(US Air Force)* sergent *m*
staff-student ratio N ⇒ **staffing ratio** ; → **staffing**
staff training N formation *f* du personnel

staff² /stɑːf/ N (pl **staves** *or* **staffs**) *(liter = rod, pole)* bâton *m* ; *(longer)* perche *f* ; *(= walking stick)* bâton *m* ; *(shepherd's)* houlette *f* ; *(= weapon)* bâton *m*, gourdin *m* ; *(= symbol of authority)* bâton *m* de commandement ; *(Rel)* crosse *f*, bâton *m* pastoral ; (also **flagstaff**) mât *m* ; †† *[of spear, lance etc]* hampe *f* ; *(fig = support)* soutien *m* ◆ **a ~ for my old age** *(fig)* mon bâton de vieillesse ◆ **bread is the ~ of life** le pain est l'aliment vital *or* le soutien de la vie

staff³ /stɑːf/ N (pl **staves**) *(Mus)* portée *f*

staffed /ˈstɑːft/ ADJ *(permanently)* où il y a du personnel en permanence

staffer /ˈstɑːfəʳ/ N *(esp US) (in journalism)* membre *m* de la rédaction ; *(in organization)* membre *m* du personnel

staffing /ˈstɑːfɪŋ/ N effectifs *mpl*
COMP *[problems etc]* de personnel ◆ **to reduce ~ levels** réduire les effectifs
staffing ratio N *(Scol etc)* taux *m* d'encadrement ◆ **the ~ ratio is good/bad** le taux d'encadrement est élevé/faible

staffroom /ˈstɑːfrʊm/ N *(Scol, Univ)* salle *f* des professeurs

Staffs abbrev of **Staffordshire**

stag /stæg/ N 1 *(= deer)* cerf *m* ; *(= other animal)* mâle *m* 2 *(Brit St Ex)* loup *m* ADJ 1 *(= men only) [event, evening]* entre hommes ◆ **~ night** *or* **party** *(gen = men-only party)* soirée *f* entre hommes ; *(before wedding)* enterrement *m* de la vie de garçon ◆ **he's having a ~ night** *or* **party** il enterre sa vie de garçon ◆ **the ~ line** *(US)* le coin des hommes seuls *(dans une soirée)* 2 *(US * = pornographic) [film]* porno* *inv* ◆ **~ show** spectacle *m* porno
COMP **stag beetle** N cerf-volant *m (scarabée)*, lucane *m*
stag hunt(ing) N chasse *f* au cerf

stage /steɪdʒ/ N 1 *(Theat = place)* scène *f* ◆ **the ~** *(= profession)* le théâtre ◆ **to write for the ~** écrire des pièces de théâtre ◆ **the book was adapted for the ~** le livre a été adapté pour le théâtre *or* porté à la scène ◆ **his play never reached the ~** sa pièce n'a jamais été jouée ◆ **to set the ~ for sth** *(fig)* préparer le terrain pour qch ◆ **the ~ is set for a memorable match** tout annonce un match mémorable ◆ **to hold the ~** être le point de mire ◆ **he has disappeared from the political ~** il a disparu de la scène politique ; → **downstage**

♦ **on (the) stage** sur scène ◆ **to come on ~** entrer en scène ◆ **to go on the ~** monter sur la scène ; *(as career)* monter sur les planches, commencer à faire du théâtre ◆ **on the ~ as in real life** à la scène comme à la ville ◆ **she has appeared on the ~** elle a fait du théâtre

2 *(= platform: in hall etc)* estrade *f* ; *(Constr = scaffolding)* échafaudage *m* ; (also **landing stage**) débarcadère *m* ; *[of microscope]* platine *f*

3 *(= point, section) [of journey]* étape *f* ; *[of road, pipeline]* section *f* ; *[of rocket]* étage *m* ; *[of operation]* étape *f*, phase *f* ; *[of process, disease]* stade *m*, phase *f* ◆ **a four-~ rocket** une fusée à quatre étages ◆ **the second ~ fell away** le deuxième étage s'est détaché ◆ **a critical ~** une phase *or* un stade critique ◆ **the first ~ of his career** le premier échelon de sa carrière ◆ **in the early ~s** au début ◆ **at an early ~ in its history** vers le début de son histoire ◆ **at this ~ in the negotiations** à ce point *or* à ce stade des négociations ◆ **what ~ is your project at?** à quel stade *or* où en est votre projet ? ◆ **it has reached the ~ of being translated** c'en est au stade de la traduction ◆ **we have reached a ~ where ...** nous (en) sommes arrivés à un point *or* à un stade où ... ◆ **the child has reached the talking ~** l'enfant en est au stade où il commence à parler ◆ **he's going through a difficult ~** il passe par une période difficile ◆ **it's just a ~ in his development** ce n'est qu'une phase *or* un stade dans son développement ; → **fare**

♦ **at some stage** ◆ **we'll need to meet at some ~ to talk about it** il faudra que nous nous voyions pour en discuter à un moment ou à un autre ◆ **at some ~ during the year** au cours de l'année ◆ **everybody in the party was ill at some ~ of the tour** tout le monde dans le groupe a été malade au cours du voyage

♦ **in stages, by stages** par étapes ◆ **in** *or* **by easy ~s** *[travel]* par petites étapes ; *[study]* par degrés ◆ **the reform was carried out in ~s** la réforme a été appliquée en plusieurs étapes *or* temps

♦ **stage by stage** étape par étape

4 (also **stagecoach**) diligence *f*

VT *(Theat)* monter, mettre en scène ◆ **they ~d an accident/a reconciliation** *(= organize)* ils ont organisé un accident/une réconciliation ; *(= feign)* ils ont monté un accident/fait semblant de se réconcilier ◆ **they ~d a demonstration** *(= organize)* ils ont organisé une manifestation ; *(= carry out)* ils ont manifesté ◆ **to ~ a strike** *(= organize)* organiser une grève ; *(= go on strike)* faire la grève ◆ **that was no accident, it was ~d** ce n'était pas un accident, c'était un coup monté

COMP **stage designer** N décorateur *m*, -trice *f* de théâtre
stage direction N *(= instruction)* indication *f* scénique ; *(NonC) (= art, activity)* (art *m* de la) mise *f* en scène
stage director N metteur *m* en scène
stage door N entrée *f* des artistes
stage effect N effet *m* scénique
stage fright N trac* *m*
stage left N côté *m* cour
stage-manage VT *[+ play, production]* s'occuper de la régie de ; *[+ event, demonstration]* orchestrer
stage manager N *(Theat)* régisseur *m*
stage name N nom *m* de scène
stage play N *(Theat)* pièce *f* de théâtre
stage production N production *f* théâtrale
stage race N *(Sport)* course *f* par étapes
stage right N côté *m* jardin
stage set N *(Theat)* décor *m*
stage show N ⇒ **stage production**
stage-struck ADJ ◆ **to be ~-struck** mourir d'envie de faire du théâtre
stage whisper N *(fig)* aparté *m* ◆ **in a ~ whisper** en aparté

> ⚠ **stage** in French means 'training course'.

stagecraft /ˈsteɪdʒkrɑːft/ N *(NonC: Theat)* technique *f* de la scène

stagehand /ˈsteɪdʒhænd/ N machiniste *m*

stager /ˈsteɪdʒəʳ/ N ◆ **old ~** vétéran *m*, vieux routier *m*

stagey /ˈsteɪdʒɪ/ ADJ ⇒ **stagy**

stagflation /stægˈfleɪʃən/ N *(Econ)* stagflation *f*

stagger /ˈstægəʳ/ VI chanceler, tituber ◆ **he ~ed to the door** il est allé à la porte d'un pas chancelant *or* titubant ◆ **to ~ along/in/out** *etc* avancer/entrer/sortir *etc* en chancelant *or* titubant ◆ **he was ~ing about** il se déplaçait en chancelant *or* titubant, il vacillait sur ses jambes

VT 1 *(= amaze)* stupéfier, renverser ; *(= horrify)* atterrer ◆ **this will ~ you** tu vas trouver cela stupéfiant *or* renversant ◆ **I was ~ed to learn that ...** *(= amazed)* j'ai été absolument stupéfait d'apprendre que ... ; *(= horrified)* j'ai été atterré d'apprendre que ...

2 *[+ spokes, objects]* espacer ; *[+ visits, payments]* échelonner ; *[+ holidays]* étaler ◆ **they work ~ed hours** leurs heures de travail sont étalées *or* échelonnées ◆ **~ed start** *(Sport)* départ *m* décalé

N allure *f* chancelante *or* titubante

NPL **staggers** *(Vet)* vertigo *m*

staggering /ˈstæɡərɪŋ/ ADJ 1 *(= astounding) [number, amount, losses, success, news]* stupéfiant, ahurissant ; *[increase]* stupéfiant 2 *(= powerful) (lit)* ◆ **~ blow** coup *m* de massue ◆ **to be a ~ blow (to sb/sth)** *(fig)* être un coup de massue (pour qn/qch) N 1 *(= action)* démarche *f* chancelante *or* titubante 2 *[of hours, visits etc]* échelonnement *m* ; *[of holidays]* étalement *m*

staggeringly /ˈstæɡərɪŋlɪ/ ADJ *[difficult]* extraordinairement ◆ **~ beautiful** d'une beauté stupéfiante ◆ **the team's ~ bad performance** la prestation extrêmement décevante de l'équipe ◆ **~ high prices** des prix exorbitants

staghound /ˈstæɡhaʊnd/ N *espèce de fox-hound*

staging /ˈsteɪdʒɪŋ/ N 1 *(= scaffolding)* (plate-forme *f* d')échafaudage *m* 2 *(Theat: of play)* mise *f* en scène 3 *(Space)* largage *m* (d'un étage de fusée) COMP **staging post** N *(Mil, also gen)* relais *m*, point *m* de ravitaillement

stagnancy /ˈstæɡnənsɪ/ N stagnation *f*

stagnant /ˈstæɡnənt/ ADJ *[water]* stagnant ; *[pond]* à l'eau stagnante ; *[air]* confiné ; *[mind]* inactif ; *[economy, market, business, output, society]* stagnant ◆ **~ growth** stagnation *f*

stagnate /stæɡˈneɪt/ VI *[water]* être stagnant, croupir ; *[economy, business, market, person, production]* stagner

stagnation /stæɡˈneɪʃən/ N stagnation *f*

stagy /ˈsteɪdʒɪ/ ADJ *(pej) [appearance, diction, mannerisms]* théâtral ; *[person]* cabotin

staid /steɪd/ ADJ *(pej) [person, appearance]* collet monté *inv* ; *[behaviour, place, community]* sclérosé ; *[image]* guindé ; *[car, suit]* très ordinaire

staidness /ˈsteɪdnɪs/ N *(pej) [of person, appearance]* aspect *m* collet monté ; *[of institution, community]* sclérose *f* ; *[of place, behaviour]* caractère *m* sclérosé ; *[of image]* caractère *m* guindé ; *[of car, suit]* caractère *m* très ordinaire

stain /steɪn/ N 1 *(lit, fig = mark)* tache *f* *(on sur)* ◆ **blood/grease ~** tache *f* de sang/graisse ◆ **without a ~ on his character** sans une tache à sa réputation 2 *(= colouring)* colorant *m* ◆ **wood ~** couleur *f* pour bois VT 1 *(= mark, soil)* tacher ; *[+ reputation]* ternir, entacher ; *[+ career]* porter atteinte à, nuire à ◆ **~ed with blood** taché de sang 2 *(= colour) [+ wood]* teinter, teindre ; *[+ glass]* colorer VI ◆ **this material will ~** ce tissu se tache facilement *or* est très salissant

COMP **stained glass** N *(= substance)* verre *m* coloré ; *(= windows collectively)* vitraux *mpl*

stained-glass window N vitrail *m*, verrière *f*

stain remover N détachant *m*

stain resistant ADJ antitaches

-stained /steɪnd/ ADJ *(in compounds)* ◆ **grease-stained** taché de graisse ◆ **nicotine-stained** taché par la nicotine *or* le tabac ◆ **oil-stained** taché d'huile ; see also **bloodstained, tear²**

stainless /ˈsteɪnlɪs/ ADJ sans tache, pur COMP **stainless steel** N acier *m* inoxydable, inox *m*

stair /steəʳ/ N *(= step)* marche *f* ; (also **stairs, flight of stairs**) escalier *m* ◆ **to pass sb on the ~(s)** rencontrer qn dans l'escalier ◆ **below ~s** à l'office

COMP *[carpet]* d'escalier

stair rod N tringle *f* d'escalier

staircase /ˈsteəkeɪs/ N escalier *m* ; → **moving, spiral**

stairlift /ˈsteəlɪft/ N ascenseur-escalier *m* *(pour personnes handicapées)*

stairway /ˈsteəweɪ/ N escalier *m*

stairwell /ˈsteəwel/ N cage *f* d'escalier

stake /steɪk/ N 1 *(for fence, tree)* pieu *m*, poteau *m* ; *(as boundary mark)* piquet *m*, jalon *m* ; *(for plant)* tuteur *m* ; *(Hist)* bûcher *m* ◆ **to die** *or* **be burnt at the ~** mourir sur le bûcher ◆ **I would go to the ~ to defend their rights** *(Brit)* je serais prêt à mourir pour défendre leurs droits ◆ **to pull up ~s** * *(US)* déménager

2 *(Betting)* enjeu *m* ; *(fig = share)* intérêt *m* ◆ **~s** *(= horse-race)* course *f* de chevaux ◆ **the Newmarket ~s** *(Racing)* le Prix de Newmarket ◆ **to play for high ~s** *(lit, fig)* jouer gros jeu ◆ **to raise the ~s** *(fig)* faire monter les enchères ◆ **to have a ~ in sth** avoir des intérêts dans qch ◆ **he has got a ~ in the success of the firm** il est intéressé matériellement *or* financièrement au succès de l'entreprise ◆ **Britain has a big ~ in North Sea oil** la Grande-Bretagne a de gros investissements *or* a engagé de gros capitaux dans le pétrole de la mer du Nord

◆ **at stake** ◆ **the issue at ~** ce dont il s'agit, ce qui est en jeu, ce qui se joue ici ◆ **our future is at ~** notre avenir est en jeu, il s'agit de *or* il y va de notre avenir ◆ **there is a lot at ~** l'enjeu est considérable, il y a gros à perdre ◆ **there is a lot at ~ for him** il a gros à perdre ◆ **he has got a lot at ~** il joue gros jeu, il risque gros, il a misé gros

VT 1 *[+ territory, area]* marquer *or* délimiter (avec des piquets *etc*) ; *[+ path, line]* marquer, jalonner ; *[+ claim]* établir ◆ **to ~ one's claim to sth** revendiquer qch, établir son droit à qch

2 (also **stake up**) *[+ fence]* soutenir à l'aide de poteaux *or* de pieux ; *[+ plants]* mettre un tuteur à, soutenir à l'aide d'un tuteur

3 *(= bet) [+ money, jewels etc]* jouer, miser *(on sur)* ; *[+ one's reputation, life]* risquer, jouer *(on sur)* ◆ **he ~d everything** *or* **his all on the committee's decision** il a joué le tout pour le tout *or* il a joué son va-tout sur la décision du comité ◆ **I'd ~ my life on it** j'en mettrais ma tête à couper

4 *(= back financially) [+ show, project, person]* financer, soutenir financièrement

▸ **stake out** VT SEP 1 *[+ piece of land]* marquer *or* délimiter (avec des piquets *etc*) ; *[+ path, line]* marquer, jalonner ; *(fig) [+ section of work, responsibilities etc]* s'approprier, se réserver ◆ **to ~ out a position as ...** *(fig)* se tailler une position de ...

2 *(Police) [+ person, house]* mettre *or* garder sous surveillance, surveiller

stakeholder /ˈsteɪkhəʊldəʳ/ N partie *f* prenante COMP **stakeholder pension** N *(Brit)* *système d'épargne-retraite (par capitalisation)*

stakeout /ˈsteɪkaʊt/ N *(Police)* surveillance *f* ◆ **to be on a ~** effectuer une surveillance

stalactite /ˈstæləktaɪt/ N stalactite *f*

stalagmite /ˈstæləɡmaɪt/ N stalagmite *f*

stale /steɪl/ ADJ 1 *(= not fresh) [food]* qui n'est plus frais (fraîche *f*) ; *[bread, cake]* rassis (rassie *f*) ; *[biscuit]* vieux (vieille *f*) ; *[cheese]* desséché ; *[beer, perfume]* éventé ; *[air]* confiné ; *[breath, sweat, urine]* fétide ◆ **to smell of ~ cigarette smoke** sentir le tabac froid ◆ **to go ~** *[bread, cake]* rassir ; *[biscuit]* s'abîmer ; *[beer]* s'éventer ◆ **to smell ~** *[room]* sentir le renfermé 2 *[person]* qui a perdu tout enthousiasme, las (lasse *f*) ; *[idea, joke]* éculé ; *[news]* dépassé ◆ **to become ~** *[person]* perdre tout enthousiasme ; *[relationship]* s'étioler ; *[situation]* stagner 3 *(Fin)* ◆ **~ cheque** chèque *m* prescrit VI *(liter) [pleasures etc]* perdre de sa (*or* leur) fraîcheur *or* nouveauté

stalemate /ˈsteɪlmeɪt/ N *(Chess)* pat *m* ; *(fig)* impasse *f* ◆ **the discussions have reached ~** les discussions sont dans l'impasse ◆ **the ~ is complete** c'est l'impasse totale ◆ **to break the ~** sortir de l'impasse VT *(Chess)* faire pat *inv* ; *(fig) [+ project]* contrecarrer ; *[+ adversary]* paralyser, neutraliser

stalemated /ˈsteɪlmeɪtɪd/ ADJ *[discussions]* au point mort *(on sth* en ce qui concerne qch*)*, dans l'impasse *(on sth* en ce qui concerne qch*)* ; *[project]* au point mort

staleness /ˈsteɪlnɪs/ N *(NonC)* 1 *(= lack of freshness) [of food]* manque *m* de fraîcheur ; *[of air]* mauvaise qualité *f* ; *[of breath, sweat, urine]* mauvaise odeur *f* 2 *[of person]* manque *m* d'enthousiasme ; *[of news, situation]* manque *m* de fraîcheur ; *[of relationship]* étiolement *m*

Stalin /ˈstɑːlɪn/ N Staline *m*

Stalinism /ˈstɑːlɪnɪzəm/ N stalinisme *m*

Stalinist /ˈstɑːlɪnɪst/ N stalinien(ne) *m(f)* ADJ stalinien

stalk¹ /stɔːk/ N *[of plant]* tige *f* ; *[of fruit]* queue *f* ; *[of cabbage]* trognon *m* ; *[of animal's eyes]* pédoncule *m* ◆ **his eyes were out on ~s** * il ouvrait des yeux ronds, il écarquillait les yeux COMP **stalk-eyed** ADJ *[animal]* aux yeux pédonculés

stalk² /stɔːk/ VT 1 *[+ game, prey]* traquer ; *[+ victim]* suivre partout ; *[+ suspect]* filer 2 **to ~ the streets/town** *etc* *[fear, disease, death]* régner dans les rues/la ville *etc* VI ◆ **to ~ in/out/off** *etc* entrer/sortir/partir *etc* d'un air digne *or* avec raideur ◆ **he ~ed in haughtily/angrily/indignantly** il est entré d'un air arrogant/furieux/indigné COMP **stalking-horse** N *(fig)* prétexte *m* ◆ **I've no intention of standing as a ~ing-horse candidate** *(Pol)* je n'ai aucunement l'intention de me présenter comme candidat bidon *

stalker /ˈstɔːkəʳ/ N ◆ **she complained of being followed by a ~** elle s'est plainte d'un désaxé qui la suit partout

stalking /ˈstɔːkɪŋ/ N *(Jur)* traque *f* *(forme de harcèlement sexuel pathologique consistant à suivre partout sa victime)*

stall /stɔːl/ N 1 *(in stable, cowshed)* stalle *f* ◆ **(starting) ~s** *(Racing)* stalles *fpl* de départ

2 *(in market, street, at fair)* éventaire *m*, étal *m* ; *(in exhibition)* stand *m* ◆ **newspaper/flower ~** kiosque *m* à journaux/de fleuriste ◆ **bookstall** petite librairie *f* ◆ **coffee ~** buvette *f* ◆ **to set out one's ~** *(fig)* définir ses objectifs ◆ **to set out one's ~ to achieve sth** faire en sorte d'arriver à qch

3 *(Brit Theat)* (fauteuil *m* d')orchestre *m* ◆ **the ~s** l'orchestre *m*

4 *(in showers etc)* cabine *f* ; *(in church)* stalle *f* ; → **choir**

5 *(US: in car park)* place *f*, emplacement *m*

6 *(= finger stall)* doigtier *m*

7 *(Driving)* fait *m* de caler ◆ **in a ~** *(US fig)* au point mort

VI 1 *[car, engine, driver]* caler ; *[aircraft]* être en perte de vitesse, décrocher

2 *(fig)* **to ~ (for time)** essayer de gagner du temps, atermoyer ◆ **he managed to ~ until ...** il a réussi à trouver des faux-fuyants jusqu'à ce que ... ◆ **stop ~ing!** cesse de te dérober !

VT 1 *[+ engine, car]* caler ; *[+ plane]* causer une perte de vitesse *or* un décrochage à ◆ **to be ~ed** *[car]* avoir calé ; *(fig) [project etc]* être au point mort

2 *[+ person]* tenir à distance ◆ **I managed to ~ him until ...** j'ai réussi à le tenir à distance *or* à esquiver ses questions jusqu'à ce que ... ◆ **try to ~ him for a while** essaie de gagner du temps

COMP **stall-fed** ADJ *[animal]* engraissé à l'étable

stallholder /ˈstɔːlhəʊldəʳ/ N marchand(e) *m(f)* (à l'étal) ; *(at fair)* forain(e) *m(f)* ; *(at exhibition)* exposant(e) *m(f)*

stallion /ˈstæljən/ N étalon *m* *(cheval)*

stalwart /ˈstɔːlwət/ ADJ 1 *(= dependable) [person]* loyal ; *[supporter, ally]* inconditionnel ; *[work]* exemplaire 2 *(= sturdy) [person]* vigoureux, robuste N brave homme *m* (*or* femme *f*) ; *[of party etc]* fidèle *mf*

stamen /'steɪmen/ **N** (pl **stamens** or **stamina** /'stæmɪnə/) (*Bot*) étamine *f*

stamina /'stæmɪnə/ **N** (*NonC, physical*) résistance *f*, endurance *f* ; (*intellectual*) vigueur *f* ; (*moral*) résistance *f* ◆ **he's got ~** il est résistant, il a de l'endurance ; see also **stamen**

stammer /'stæməʳ/ **N** bégaiement *m*, balbutiement *m* ; (*Med*) bégaiement *m* ◆ **to have a ~** bégayer, être bègue **VI** bégayer, balbutier ; (*Med*) bégayer, être bègue **VT** (also **stammer out**) [*+ name, facts*] bégayer, balbutier ◆ **to ~ (out) a reply** bégayer or balbutier une réponse, répondre en bégayant or balbutiant ◆ **"n-not t-too m-much" he ~ed** "p-pas t-trop" bégaya-t-il

stammerer /'stæmərəʳ/ **N** bègue *mf*

stammering /'stæmərɪŋ/ **N** (*NonC*) bégaiement *m*, balbutiement *m* ; (*Med*) bégaiement *m* **ADJ** [*person*] (*from fear, excitement*) bégayant, balbutiant ; (*Med*) bègue ; [*answer*] bégayant, hésitant

stammeringly /'stæmərɪŋlɪ/ **ADV** en bégayant, en balbutiant

stamp /stæmp/ **N** 1 timbre *m* ; (*= postage stamp*) timbre(-poste) *m* ; (*= fiscal stamp, revenue stamp*) timbre *m* (fiscal) ; (*= savings stamp*) timbre(-épargne) *m* ; (*= trading stamp*) timbre(-prime) *m* ◆ **(National) Insurance ~** cotisation *f* à la Sécurité sociale ◆ **to put** or **stick a ~ on a letter** coller un timbre sur une lettre, timbrer une lettre ◆ **used/unused ~** timbre *m* oblitéré/non oblitéré

2 (*= implement*) (*for metal*) étampe *f*, poinçon *m* ; (*= rubber stamp*) timbre *m*, tampon *m* ; (*= date stamp*) timbre dateur *m*

3 (*= mark, impression*) (*on document*) cachet *m* ; (*on metal*) empreinte *f*, poinçon *m* ; (*Comm = trademark*) estampille *f* ◆ **look at the date ~** regardez la date sur le cachet ◆ **here's his address ~** voici le cachet indiquant son adresse ◆ **it's got a receipt ~ on it** il y a un cachet accusant paiement ◆ **he gave the project his ~ of approval** il a donné son aval au projet ◆ **the ~ of genius/truth** la marque or le sceau du génie/de la vérité ◆ **men of his ~** des hommes de sa trempe or de son acabit (*pej*)

4 [*of foot*] (*from cold*) battement *m* de pied ; (*from rage*) trépignement *m* ◆ **with a ~ (of his foot)** en tapant du pied

VT 1 ◆ **to ~ one's foot** taper du pied ◆ **to ~ one's feet** (*in rage*) trépigner ; (*in dance*) frapper du pied ; (*to keep warm*) battre la semelle ◆ **he ~ed the peg into the ground** il a tapé du pied sur le piquet pour l'enfoncer en terre

2 (*= stick a stamp on*) [*+ letter, parcel*] timbrer, affranchir ; [*+ savings book, insurance card*] timbrer, apposer un or des timbre(s) sur ; (*= put fiscal stamp on*) timbrer ◆ **this letter is not sufficiently ~ed** cette lettre n'est pas suffisamment affranchie

3 (*= mark with stamp*) tamponner, timbrer ; [*+ passport, document*] viser ; [*+ metal*] estamper, poinçonner ◆ **to ~ a visa on a passport** apposer un visa sur un passeport ◆ **to ~ the date on a form, to ~ a form with the date** apposer la date sur un formulaire (*avec un timbre dateur*) ◆ **he ~ed a design on the metal** il a estampillé le métal d'un motif ◆ **to ~ sth on one's memory** graver qch dans sa mémoire ◆ **his accent ~s him as (a) Belgian** son accent montre bien or indique bien qu'il est belge ◆ **to ~ o.s. on sth** laisser sa marque or son empreinte sur qch ; → **die²**

VI 1 taper du pied ; (*angrily*) taper du pied, trépigner ; [*horse*] piaffer ◆ **he ~ed on my foot** il a fait exprès de me marcher sur le pied ◆ **he ~ed on the burning wood** il a piétiné les braises ◆ **to ~ on a suggestion** rejeter une suggestion

2 (*angrily*) **to ~ in/out** *etc* entrer/sortir *etc* en tapant du pied ◆ **to ~ about** or **around** (*angrily*) taper du pied ; (*to keep warm*) battre la semelle

COMP **Stamp Act N** (*Hist*) loi *f* sur le timbre
stamp album N album *m* de timbres (-poste)
stamp-book N carnet *m* de timbres(-poste)
stamp collecting N (*NonC*) philatélie *f*
stamp collection N collection *f* de timbres(-poste)
stamp collector N collectionneur *m*, -euse *f* de timbres(-poste), philatéliste *mf*
stamp dealer N marchand(e) *m(f)* de timbres (-poste)
stamp duty N droit *m* de timbre
stamped addressed envelope N (*Brit*) enveloppe *f* affranchie à son nom et adresse ◆ **I enclose a ~ed addressed envelope (for your reply)** veuillez trouver ci-joint une enveloppe affranchie pour la réponse
stamping ground* N lieu *m* favori, royaume *m*
stamp machine N distributeur *m* (automatique) de timbres (-poste)

► **stamp down VT SEP** [*+ peg etc*] enfoncer du pied ; [*+ rebellion*] écraser, étouffer ; [*+ protests*] refouler

► **stamp out VT SEP** 1 [*+ fire*] piétiner, éteindre en piétinant ; [*+ cigarette*] écraser sous le pied ; (*fig*) [*+ rebellion*] enrayer, juguler ; [*+ custom, belief, tendency*] éradiquer

2 [*+ coin etc*] frapper ; [*+ design*] découper à l'emporte-pièce

3 [*+ rhythm*] marquer en frappant du pied

stampede /stæm'piːd/ **N** (*aimless*) [*of animals*] débandade *f*, fuite *f* précipitée ; [*of people*] sauve-qui-peut *m inv* ; [*of retreating troops*] débâcle *f*, déroute *f* ; (*fig: with purpose = rush*) ruée *f* ◆ **there was a ~ for the door** on s'est précipité or rué vers la porte ◆ **he got knocked down in the ~ for seats** il a été renversé dans la ruée vers les sièges

VI [*animals, people*] s'enfuir en désordre or à la débandade (*from de*), fuir en désordre or à la débandade (*towards* vers) ; (*fig = rush*) se ruer (*for sth* pour obtenir qch) ◆ **to ~ for the door** se ruer vers la porte

VT [*+ animals, people*] jeter la panique parmi ◆ **they ~d him into agreeing** il a accepté parce qu'ils ne lui ont pas laissé le temps de la réflexion ◆ **we mustn't let ourselves be ~d** il faut que nous prenions *subj* le temps de réfléchir

stance /stæns/ **N** (*lit, fig*) position *f* ; (*Climbing*) relais *m* ◆ **(bus) ~** quai *m* ◆ **to take up a ~** (*lit*) prendre place or position ; (*fig*) prendre position (*on* sur ; *against* contre)

stanch /stɑːntʃ/ **VT** ⇒ **staunch¹**

stanchion /'stɑːnʃən/ **N** (*as support*) étançon *m*, étai *m* ; (*for cattle*) montant *m*

stand /stænd/
vb : pret, ptp **stood**
LANGUAGE IN USE 7.3, 14

1 NOUN
2 TRANSITIVE VERB
3 INTRANSITIVE VERB
4 COMPOUNDS
5 PHRASAL VERBS

1 - NOUN

1 [= position : lit, fig] position *f* ◆ **to take (up) one's ~** (*lit*) prendre place or position ; (*fig*) prendre position (*on* sur ; *against* contre) ◆ **he took (up) his ~ beside me** il s'est placé or mis à côté de moi, il a pris position à côté de moi ◆ **I admired the firm ~ he took on that point** j'ai admiré sa fermeté sur cette question ◆ **I make my ~ upon these principles** je me base sur ces principes ◆ **to make** or **take a ~ against sth** (*fig = fight*) lutter contre qch ◆ **we must take a ~ against racism** nous devons lutter contre le racisme ◆ **they turned and made a ~** (*Mil*) ils ont fait volte-face et se sont défendus ◆ **the ~ of the Australians at Tobruk** (*Mil*) la résistance des Australiens à Tobrouk ◆ **Custer's last ~** le dernier combat de Custer

2 [also **taxi stand**] station *f* (de taxis)

3 [Comm : for displaying goods] étal *m*, étalage *m* ; (also **newspaper stand**) kiosque *m* à journaux ; (*= market stall*) étal *m* (étals *pl*), éventaire *m* ; (*at exhibition, funfair, trade fair*) stand *m*

4 [= seating area] tribune *f* ◆ **I've got a ticket for the ~(s)** j'ai une tribune, j'ai un billet de tribune(s)

5 [= witness stand] barre *f* ◆ **to take the ~** venir à la barre

6 [= holder, support] (*for plant, bust etc*) guéridon *m* ; (*for lamp*) pied *m* (de lampe) ; (*= hat stand*) porte-chapeaux *m inv* ; (*= coat stand*) portemanteau *m* ; (*= music stand*) pupitre *m* à musique

7 [of trees] bouquet *m*, bosquet *m* ◆ **a ~ of grass** une étendue d'herbe

8 [Cricket] **the ~ between Gooch and Hussein** le nombre de points que Gooch et Hussein ont marqué

9 ⇒ **standstill**

2 - TRANSITIVE VERB

1 [= place] [*+ object*] mettre ◆ **~ the plant in a sunny spot** mettez cette plante dans un endroit ensoleillé ◆ **he stood the child on the chair** il a mis l'enfant debout sur la chaise ◆ **to ~ sth (up) against a wall** mettre qch debout contre le mur ◆ **to ~ sth on its end** mettre qch debout

2 [= tolerate] [*+ heat, pain, criticism, insolence, attitude*] supporter ◆ **I can't ~ it any longer** (*pain etc*) je ne peux plus le supporter ; (*boredom etc*) j'en ai assez, j'en ai par-dessus la tête* ◆ **I can't ~ (the sight of) her** je ne peux pas la supporter or la sentir* ◆ **she can't ~ being laughed at** elle ne supporte pas qu'on se moque *subj* d'elle ◆ **I can't ~ gin/Wagner/wet weather** je déteste le gin/Wagner/la pluie

3 [= withstand] [*+ pressure, heat*] supporter, résister à ◆ **she stood the journey quite well** elle a bien supporté le voyage ◆ **these shoes won't ~ much wear** ces chaussures ne vont pas faire beaucoup d'usage ◆ **it won't ~ close examination** cela ne résistera pas à un examen approfondi ◆ **that doll won't ~ much more of that treatment** cette poupée ne va pas faire long feu à ce rythme-là

4 [* = pay for] payer, offrir ◆ **to ~ sb a drink** offrir un verre à qn, payer un pot à qn* ◆ **he stood the next round of drinks** il a payé la tournée suivante ◆ **to ~ sb a meal** inviter qn au restaurant ◆ **to ~ the cost of sth** payer qch ◆ **they agreed to ~ the cost of my course** ils ont accepté de payer mon stage

3 - INTRANSITIVE VERB

1 [= be upright : also **stand up**] [*person, animal*] être or se tenir debout ◆ **he is too weak to ~** il est trop faible pour se tenir debout or tenir sur ses jambes ◆ **my niece has just learnt to ~** ça ne fait pas longtemps que ma nièce sait se tenir debout ◆ **we had to ~ as far as Calais** nous avons dû rester debout or voyager debout jusqu'à Calais ◆ **you must ~ (up)** or **stay ~ing (up) till the music stops** vous devez rester debout jusqu'à ce que la musique s'arrête *subj* ◆ **~ (up) straight!** tiens-toi droit ! ◆ **we couldn't get the tent to ~ (up)** nous n'arrivions pas à monter la tente or à faire tenir la tente debout ◆ **the post must ~ upright** le poteau doit être bien droit ◆ **the house is still ~ing** la maison est encore debout or est toujours là ◆ **not much still ~s of the walls** il ne

reste plus grand-chose des murs ◆ **not a stone was left ~ing in the old town** la vieille ville a été complètement détruite

◆ **to stand or fall** ◆ **the project will ~ or fall by ...** le succès du projet repose sur ... ◆ **I ~ or fall by this** il en va de ma réputation

2 [= rise : also **stand up**] se lever ◆ **all ~!** levez-vous s'il vous plaît ! ◆ **to ~ (up) and be counted** *(fig)* déclarer ouvertement sa position

3 [= stay, stand still] rester (debout) ◆ **we stood talking for an hour** nous sommes restés debout à bavarder pendant une heure ◆ **don't just ~ there, do something!** ne reste pas là à ne rien faire *or* les bras ballants ! ◆ **~ over there till I'm ready** mets-toi *or* reste là-bas jusqu'à ce que je sois prêt ◆ **I left him ~ing on the bridge** je l'ai laissé sur le pont ◆ **they stood patiently in the rain** ils attendaient patiemment sous la pluie ◆ **he left the others ~ing** *(fig)* il dépassait les autres de la tête et des épaules *(fig)* ◆ **~ and deliver!** la bourse ou la vie !

4 [= be positioned, be] *[person]* être, se tenir ; *[object, vehicle, tree]* être, se trouver ; *[town, building]* se trouver ◆ **he stood there ready to shoot** il était *or* se tenait là, prêt à tirer ◆ **the man ~ing over there** cet homme là-bas ◆ **I like to know where I ~** *(fig)* j'aime savoir où j'en suis ◆ **where do you ~ with him?** où en êtes-vous avec lui ? ◆ **as things ~ at the moment** dans l'état actuel des choses ◆ **how do things ~ between them?** comment ça va entre eux ? ◆ **how do things** *or* **matters ~?** où en sont les choses ?

◆ **to stand** *+ preposition* ◆ **three chairs stood against the wall** il y avait trois chaises contre le mur ◆ **nothing ~s between you and success** rien ne s'oppose à votre réussite ◆ **this is all that ~s between him and ruin** sans cela il aurait déjà fait faillite ◆ **he stood in the doorway** il était debout dans l'embrasure de la porte ◆ **they stood in a circle around the grave** ils se tenaient en cercle autour de la tombe ◆ **tears stood in her eyes** elle avait les larmes aux yeux ◆ **the village ~s in the valley** le village se trouve *or* est (situé) dans la vallée ◆ **the house ~s in its own grounds** la maison est entourée d'un parc ◆ **a lamp stood in the middle of the table** il y avait une lampe au milieu de la table ◆ **where do you ~ on this question?** quelle est votre position sur cette question ? ◆ **beads of perspiration stood on his brow** des gouttes de sueur perlaient sur son front ◆ **he was ~ing over the stove, stirring a sauce** il était penché au-dessus du fourneau, occupé à remuer une sauce ◆ **she looked up to see Faith ~ing over her** elle leva les yeux et vit que Faith se tenait près d'elle ; see also **phrasal verbs**

◆ **to stand in the way** ◆ **to ~ in sb's way** bloquer *or* barrer le passage à qn ; *(fig)* se mettre en travers du chemin de qn ◆ **I won't ~ in your way** je ne me mettrai pas en travers de votre chemin, je ne vous ferai pas obstacle ◆ **nothing now ~s in our way** maintenant la voie est libre ◆ **his age ~s in his way** son âge est un handicap ◆ **to ~ in the way of sth** faire obstacle à qch ◆ **to ~ in the way of progress** faire obstacle au progrès

◆ **to stand to do sth** ◆ **to ~ to lose** risquer de perdre ◆ **the managers ~ to gain millions if the company is sold** les directeurs devraient gagner des millions si l'entreprise est vendue ◆ **he ~s to make a fortune on it** ça va sans doute lui rapporter une fortune

◆ **to stand** *+ past participle/adjective/adverb* ◆ **the car stood abandoned by the roadside** la voiture était abandonnée au bord de la route ◆ **to ~ accused of murder** être accusé de meurtre ◆ **he ~s alone in this matter** personne ne partage son avis sur cette question ◆ **this ~s alone** c'est unique en son genre ◆ **to ~ clear** s'écarter, se tenir à distance ◆ **~ clear of the doors!** ≈ attention, fermeture des portes ! ◆ **to ~ convicted of manslaughter** être condamné pour homicide ◆ **I ~ corrected** je reconnais mon erreur ◆ **to ~ opposed to sth** être opposé à qch, s'opposer à qch ◆ **they were ~ing ready to leave** ils se tenaient prêts à partir ◆ **the record ~s unbeaten** le record n'a pas encore été battu ◆ **to ~ well with sb** être bien vu de qn

5 [= tread] marcher ◆ **you're ~ing on my foot** tu me marches sur le pied ◆ **he stood on the beetle** il a marché sur *or* écrasé le scarabée ◆ **to ~ on the brakes** piler *

6 [= measure] *[person]* faire, mesurer ; *[building, tree]* faire ◆ **he ~s over six feet in his socks** il mesure *or* fait plus de 1 mètre 80 sans chaussures ◆ **the tree ~s 30 metres high** l'arbre fait 30 mètres de haut

7 [= be mounted, based] *[statue etc]* reposer *(on* sur) ; *[argument, case]* reposer, être basé *(on* sur) ◆ **the lamp ~s on an alabaster base** la lampe a un pied d'albâtre

8 [= be at the moment, have reached] **to ~ at** *[thermometer, clock]* indiquer ; *[price, value]* s'élever à ; *[score]* être de ◆ **you must accept the offer as it ~s** cette offre n'est pas négociable ◆ **the record stood at four minutes for several years** pendant plusieurs années le record a été de quatre minutes ◆ **sales ~ at 5% up on last year** les ventes sont en hausse de 5% par rapport à l'année dernière ◆ **to have £500 ~ing to one's account** *(Banking)* avoir 500 livres sur son compte ◆ **the amount ~ing to your account** le solde de votre compte, la somme que vous avez sur votre compte

9 [= remain undisturbed, unchanged] *[liquid, mixture, dough]* reposer ; *[tea, coffee]* infuser ◆ **the offer/agreement still ~s** l'offre/l'accord tient toujours ◆ **the objection still ~s** l'objection demeure ◆ **they agreed to let the regulation ~** ils ont décidé de ne rien changer au règlement

10 [Brit Parl = be candidate] se présenter, être candidat ◆ **he stood for Neath** il s'est présenté *or* il était candidat à Neath ◆ **to ~ against sb in an election** se présenter contre qn à des élections ◆ **to ~ for election** se présenter *or* être candidat aux élections ◆ **to ~ for re-election** se représenter ◆ **he stood for the council but wasn't elected** il était candidat au poste de conseiller municipal mais n'a pas été élu

11 [Naut] **to ~ (out) to sea** *(= move)* mettre le cap sur le large ; *(= stay)* être *or* rester au large

4 - COMPOUNDS

stand-alone ADJ *[system]* autonome, indépendant
stand-by N → **stand-by**
stand-in N remplaçant(e) *m(f)* ; *(Cine)* doublure *f*
stand-off N *(= pause : in negotiations etc)* temps *m* d'arrêt; *(= stalemate)* impasse *f* ; *(= counterbalancing situation)* contrepartie *f*
stand-off half N *(Rugby)* demi *m* d'ouverture
stand-offish ADJ distant
stand-offishness N froideur *f*, réserve *f*
stand-to N *(Mil)* alerte *f*
stand-up ADJ → **stand-up**

5 - PHRASAL VERBS

► **stand about, stand around** VI rester là ◆ **don't ~ about doing nothing!** ne reste pas là à ne rien faire ! ◆ **they were ~ing about wondering what to do** ils restaient là à se demander ce qu'ils pourraient bien faire ◆ **they kept us ~ing about for hours** ils nous ont fait attendre debout pendant des heures

► **stand aside** VI s'écarter, se pousser ◆ **he stood aside to let me pass** il s'est écarté pour me laisser passer ◆ **~ aside!** écartez-vous ! ◆ **to ~ aside in favour of sb** laisser la voie libre à qn, ne pas faire obstacle à qn ◆ **to ~ aside from something** *(fig)* rester en dehors de qch, ne pas se mêler de qch

► **stand back** VI *(= move back)* reculer, s'écarter ; *(fig)* prendre du recul ◆ **you must ~ back and get the problem into perspective** il faut que vous preniez *subj* du recul pour voir le problème dans son ensemble ◆ **the farm ~s back from the road** la ferme est en retrait de la route

► **stand by**
VI 1 *(pej = be onlooker)* rester là (à ne rien faire) ◆ **how could you ~ (idly) by while they attacked him?** comment avez-vous pu rester sans rien faire alors qu'ils l'attaquaient ? ◆ **we will not ~ (idly) by and let democracy be undermined** nous n'allons pas laisser attaquer la démocratie sans rien faire

2 *(= be ready for action) [troops]* être en état d'alerte ; *[person, ship, vehicle]* être *or* se tenir prêt ; *(= be at hand)* attendre *or* être sur place ◆ **~ by for takeoff** paré pour le décollage ◆ **~ by for further revelations** apprêtez-vous à entendre d'autres révélations

VT FUS 1 *(= support) [+ friend]* ne pas abandonner ; *[+ colleague, spouse]* soutenir, épauler ◆ **she stood by her husband** elle a soutenu son mari

2 *(= keep to) [+ promise]* tenir ; *[+ sb else's decision]* respecter, se conformer à ; *[+ one's own decision]* s'en tenir à ◆ **I ~ by what I have said** je m'en tiens à ce que j'ai dit

► **stand down**
VI *(= resign) [official, chairman]* se démettre de ses fonctions, démissionner ; *(= withdraw) [candidate]* se désister ; *(Jur) [witness]* quitter la barre ◆ **he stood down as chairman last January** il a démissionné de ses fonctions *or* de son poste de président en janvier dernier ◆ **he stood down in favour of his brother** il s'est désisté en faveur de son frère

VT FUS *(= withdraw) [+ troops]* donner l'ordre de se retirer ◆ **to be made to ~ down** être contraint de démissionner

► **stand for** VT FUS 1 *(= represent)* représenter ◆ **what does UNO ~ for?** à quoi correspond l'abréviation UNO ? ◆ **I dislike all he ~s for** je déteste tout ce qu'il représente *or* incarne

2 *(= support)* être pour, défendre ◆ **our party ~s for equality of opportunity** notre parti milite pour l'égalité des chances ; see also **stand vi 10**

3 *(= tolerate)* supporter, tolérer ◆ **I won't ~ for it!** je ne le tolérerai pas !

► **stand in** VI ◆ **to stand in for sb** remplacer qn ◆ **I offered to ~ in when he was called away** j'ai proposé de le remplacer quand il a dû s'absenter

► **stand off**
VI 1 *(= move away)* s'écarter ; *(= keep one's distance)* se tenir à l'écart *(from* de), garder ses distances *(from* par rapport à) ; *(= remain uninvolved)* ne pas intervenir

2 *(= reach stalemate)* aboutir à une impasse

VT SEP *(Brit) [+ workers]* mettre temporairement au chômage

► **stand out** VI 1 *(= project) [ledge, buttress]* avancer *(from* sur), faire saillie ; *[vein]* saillir *(on* sur)

2 *(= be conspicuous, clear)* ressortir, se détacher ◆ **to ~ out against the sky** ressortir *or* se détacher sur le ciel ◆ **the yellow ~s out against the dark background** le jaune ressort sur le fond sombre ◆ **his red hair stood out in the crowd** ses cheveux roux le faisaient remarquer dans la foule ◆ **that ~s out a mile!** * cela saute aux yeux !, cela crève les yeux !

[3] *(= be outstanding)* se distinguer ◆ **he ~s out from all the other students** il se distingue de tous les autres étudiants ◆ **he ~s out above all the rest** il surpasse tout le monde

[4] *(= remain firm)* tenir bon, tenir ferme ◆ **how long can you ~ out?** combien de temps peux-tu tenir ? ◆ **to ~ out for sth** revendiquer qch ◆ **to ~ out against** *[+ attack, domination, attacker]* résister à ; *[+ demand, change, proposal]* s'élever contre

► **stand over**

VI *[items for discussion]* ◆ **these questions can stand over until ...** ces questions peuvent attendre jusqu'à ce que ...

VT FUS *[+ person]* surveiller, être derrière le dos de ◆ **I hate people ~ing over me while I work** je déteste avoir toujours quelqu'un derrière *or* sur le dos quand je travaille ◆ **he would never have done it if I hadn't stood over him** il ne l'aurait jamais fait si je n'avais pas été constamment derrière lui ◆ **stop ~ing over him!** laisse-le donc un peu tranquille !

► **stand to** *(Mil)* VI être en état d'alerte

► **stand up**

VI [1] *(= rise)* se lever, se mettre debout ; *(= be standing) [person]* être debout ; *[tent, structure]* tenir debout ◆ **she had nothing but the clothes she was ~ing up in** elle ne possédait que les vêtements qu'elle avait sur le dos ◆ **to ~ up and be counted** *(fig)* déclarer ouvertement sa position

[2] *(= resist challenge)* tenir debout ◆ **they made accusations that did not ~ up** les accusations qu'ils avaient faites ne tenaient pas debout ◆ **that argument won't ~ up in court** cet argument va être facilement réfuté par la partie adverse

VT SEP [1] *(= place upright)* mettre ◆ **to ~ sth up against a wall** mettre *or* appuyer qch contre un mur ◆ **the soup was so thick you could ~ a spoon up in it** la soupe était si épaisse qu'on pouvait y faire tenir une cuiller debout

[2] *(* = fail to meet) [+ friend]* faire faux bond à ; *[+ boyfriend, girlfriend]* poser un lapin à*

► **stand up for** VT FUS *[+ person, principle, belief]* défendre ◆ **you must ~ up for what you think is right** vous devez défendre ce qui vous semble juste ◆ **~ up for me if he asks you what you think** prenez ma défense *or* soutenez-moi s'il vous demande votre avis ◆ **to ~ up for o.s.** savoir se défendre

► **stand up to** VT FUS *[+ opponent, bully, superior]* affronter ; *[+ person in argument]* tenir tête à ; *[+ use, conditions]* résister à ◆ **it won't ~ up to that sort of treatment** cela ne résistera pas à ce genre de traitement ◆ **the report won't ~ up to close examination** ce rapport ne résiste pas à l'analyse

standard /ˈstændəd/ N [1] *(= flag)* étendard *m* ; *(Naut)* pavillon *m*

[2] *(= norm)* norme *f* ; *(= criterion)* critère *m* ; *(for weights and measures)* étalon *m* ; *(for silver)* titre *m* ◆ **the metre is the ~ of length** le mètre est l'unité de longueur ◆ **monetary ~** titre *m* de monnaie ; → **gold**

[3] *(intellectual, qualitative)* niveau *m* (voulu) ◆ **to be** *or* **come up to ~** *(fig) [person]* être à la hauteur ; *[thing]* être de la qualité voulue ◆ **I'll never come up to his ~** je n'arriverai jamais à l'égaler ◆ **judging by that ~** selon ce critère ◆ **you are applying a double ~** vous avez deux poids, deux mesures ◆ **his ~s are high** il recherche l'excellence, il ne se contente pas de l'à-peu-près ◆ **he has set us a high ~** *(morally, artistically)* il a établi un modèle difficile à surpasser ◆ **the exam sets a high ~** cet examen exige un niveau élevé ◆ **the ~ of the exam was low** le niveau de l'examen était bas ◆ **to have high moral ~s** avoir un sens moral très développé ◆ **high/low ~ of living** niveau *m* de vie élevé/bas ◆ **to be first-year university ~** être du niveau de première année d'université ◆ **their ~ of culture** leur niveau de culture ◆ **I couldn't accept their ~s** je ne pouvais pas accepter leur échelle de valeurs

◆ **by any standard** à tout point de vue ◆ **it was mediocre/excellent by any ~** c'était incontestablement médiocre/excellent

[4] *(= support)* support *m* ; *(for lamp, street light)* pied *m* ; *(= actual streetlight)* réverbère *m* ; *(= water/gas pipe)* tuyau *m* vertical d'eau/de gaz ; *(= tree, shrub)* arbre *m* de haute tige ; → **lamp**

[5] *(Mus) (= jazz tune)* standard *m* ; *(= pop tune)* classique *m*

ADJ [1] *(= regular) [size, height]* normal, standard *inv* ; *[amount, charge, procedure]* normal ; *[measure, weight]* étalon *inv* ; *[model, design, feature]* standard *inv* ; *[product]* ordinaire ◆ **a ~ car** une voiture de série ◆ **it's ~ equipment on all their cars** c'est monté en série sur toutes leurs voitures ◆ **he's below ~ height for the police** il n'a pas la taille requise pour être agent de police ◆ **~ operating procedure** procédure *f* à suivre ◆ **~ practice** pratique *f* courante ◆ **the ~ rate of income tax** le taux d'imposition ordinaire pour l'impôt sur le revenu

[2] *(Ling = orthodox) [spelling, pronunciation, grammar, usage]* correct

[3] *(= recommended) [text, book]* de base, classique

[4] *[shrub]* de haute tige

COMP **standard bearer** N *(lit)* porte-étendard *m*, porte-drapeau *m* ; *(fig)* porte-drapeau *m*
standard class N *(Rail)* seconde classe *f*
standard clause N *(Jur)* clause-type *f*
standard deviation N *(Stat)* écart *m* type
Standard English N anglais *m* correct ; → ENGLISH
standard error N *(Stat)* erreur *f* type
standard gauge N *(Rail)* écartement *m* normal
standard-gauge ADJ *(Rail)* à écartement normal
Standard Grade N *(Scot Scol)* ≃ épreuve *f* du brevet des collèges
standard issue N ◆ **to be ~ issue** *(Mil)* être standard *inv* ; *(gen)* être la norme
standard-issue ADJ *(Mil)* réglementaire ; *(gen)* standard *inv*
standard lamp N *(Brit)* lampadaire *m*
standard rose N rosier *m* à haute tige
standard time N heure *f* légale

standardization /ˌstændədaɪˈzeɪʃən/ N *(NonC: gen)* standardisation *f* ; *(of product, terminology)* normalisation *f*

standardize /ˈstændədaɪz/ VT *(gen)* standardiser ; *[+ product, terminology]* normaliser ◆ **~d test** *(US Scol)* test de connaissances commun à tous les établissements

stand-by /ˈstændbaɪ/ N *(= person)* remplaçant(e) *m(f)* ; *(US Theat = understudy)* doublure *f* ; *(= car/battery)* voiture *f*/pile *f* de réserve *or* de secours ◆ **if you are called away you must have a ~** si vous vous absentez, vous devez avoir un remplaçant *or* quelqu'un qui puisse vous remplacer en cas de besoin ◆ **aspirin is a useful ~** c'est toujours utile d'avoir de l'aspirine ◆ **lemon is a useful ~ if you have no vinegar** le citron peut être utilisé à la place du vinaigre le cas échéant ◆ **to be on ~** *[troops]* être sur pied d'intervention ; *[plane]* se tenir prêt à décoller ; *[doctor]* être de garde ◆ **to be on 24-hour ~** *(Mil)* être prêt à intervenir 24 heures sur 24 ◆ **to put on ~** mettre sur pied d'intervention

ADJ *[car, battery etc]* de réserve ; *[generator, plan]* de secours ◆ **~ ticket** billet *m* stand-by ◆ **~ passenger** (passager *m*, -ère *f* en) stand-by *mf inv* ◆ **~ credit** *(Jur, Fin)* crédit *m* d'appoint *or* stand-by ◆ **~ loan** prêt *m* conditionnel *or* stand-by

standee * /stænˈdiː/ N *(US) (at match etc)* spectateur *m*, -trice *f* debout ; *(on bus etc)* voyageur *m*, -euse *f* debout

standing /ˈstændɪŋ/ ADJ [1] *(= upright) [passenger]* debout *inv* ; *[statue]* en pied ; *[corn, crop]* sur pied

[2] *(= permanent) [invitation]* permanent ; *[rule]* fixe ; *[grievance, reproach]* constant, de longue date ◆ **it's a ~ joke** c'est un sujet de plaisanterie continuel ◆ **it's a ~ joke that he wears a wig** on dit qu'il porte une perruque, c'est un sujet de plaisanterie continuel

N [1] *(= position, importance etc) [of person]* rang *m* ; *(= social status)* standing *m* ; *(= reputation)* réputation *f* ; *[of restaurant, business]* réputation *f*, standing *m* ; *[of newspaper]* réputation *f* ◆ **social ~** rang *m or* position *f* social(e), standing *m* ◆ **professional ~** réputation *f* professionnelle ◆ **what's his financial ~?** quelle est sa situation financière ? ◆ **his ~ in public opinion polls** sa cote de popularité ◆ **what's his ~?** quelle est sa réputation ?, que pense-t-on de lui ? ◆ **firms of that ~** des compagnies aussi réputées ◆ **a man of (high** *or* **some** *or* **good) ~** un homme considéré *or* estimé ◆ **he has no ~ in this matter** il n'a aucune autorité *or* il n'a pas voix au chapitre dans cette affaire

[2] *(= duration)* durée *f* ◆ **of ten years' ~** *[friendship]* qui dure depuis dix ans ; *[agreement, contract]* qui existe depuis dix ans ; *[doctor, teacher]* qui a dix ans de métier ◆ **of long ~** de longue date ◆ **friends of long ~** des amis de longue date ◆ **he has 30 years' ~ in the firm** il a 30 ans d'ancienneté dans l'entreprise, il travaille dans l'entreprise depuis 30 ans ; → **long**¹

[3] *(US Sport)* **the ~** le classement

[4] *(US Driving)* **"no standing"** "stationnement interdit"

COMP **standing army** N armée *f* de métier
standing charge N (frais *mpl* d')abonnement *m*
standing committee N comité *m* permanent
standing expenses NPL frais *mpl* généraux
standing jump N *(Sport)* saut *m* à pieds joints
standing order N *(Banking)* virement *m* automatique ; *(Admin, Parl)* règlement *m* intérieur ; *(Comm)* commande *f* permanente ◆ **to place a ~ order for a newspaper** passer une commande permanente pour un journal ◆ **~ orders** *(Mil)* règlement *m*
standing ovation N ovation *f* ◆ **to get a ~ ovation** se faire ovationner ◆ **to give sb a ~ ovation** se lever pour ovationner qn
standing room N *(NonC, in bus, theatre)* places *fpl* debout ◆ **"standing room only"** *(= seats all taken)* "il n'y a plus de places assises" ; *(= no seats provided)* "places debout seulement"
standing start N *(Sport)* départ *m* debout ; *(in car)* départ *m* arrêté
standing stone N pierre *f* levée
standing wave N *(Phys)* onde *f* stationnaire

standout /ˈstændaʊt/ *(US, Austral)* N *(= person)* as *m* ADJ exceptionnel (-elle *f*)

standpat * /ˈstændpæt/ ADJ *(US esp Pol)* immobiliste

standpipe /ˈstændpaɪp/ N colonne *f* d'alimentation

standpoint /ˈstændpɔɪnt/ N *(lit, fig)* point *m* de vue

standstill /ˈstændstɪl/ N arrêt *m* ◆ **to come to a ~** *[person, car]* s'immobiliser ; *[production]* s'arrêter ; *[discussions]* aboutir à une impasse ◆ **to bring to a ~** *[+ car]* arrêter ; *[+ production]* paralyser ; *[+ discussion]* aboutir ◆ **to be at a ~** *[person, car]* être immobile ; *[production]* être interrompu ; *[discussion]* être au point mort ◆ **trade is at a ~** les affaires sont au point mort

stand-up /ˈstændʌp/ ADJ *[collar]* droit ; *[meal etc]* (pris) debout ◆ **~ comedian** *or* **comic** comique *m* (qui se produit en solo) ◆ **a ~ fight** *(physical)* une bagarre violente ; *(= argument)* une discussion violente **N** * (= comedian) comique *mf* (qui se produit seul sur scène) ; *(NonC)* (= stand-up comedy) one man show(s) *m(pl)* comique(s)

stank /stæŋk/ **VB** pt of **stink**

Stanley ® /ˈstænliː/ **N** ◆ ~ **knife** cutter *m*

stannic /ˈstænɪk/ **ADJ** stannique

stanza /ˈstænzə/ **N** *(Poetry)* strophe *f* ; *(in song)* couplet *m*

stapes /ˈsteɪpiːz/ **N** (pl **stapes** or **stapedes** /stæˈpiːdiːz/) étrier *m*

staphylococcus /ˌstæfɪləˈkɒkəs/ **N** (pl **staphylococci** /ˌstæfɪləˈkɒkaɪ/) staphylocoque *m*

staple¹ /ˈsteɪpl/ **ADJ** *[product, food, industry]* de base ; *[crop]* principal ◆ ~ **commodity** article *m* de première nécessité ◆ ~ **diet** nourriture *f* de base ◆ **their ~ meals of fish and rice** leurs repas à base de poisson et de riz **N** 1 *(Econ)* (= chief commodity) produit *m* or article *m* de base ; (= raw material) matière *f* première 2 (= chief item) *(Comm: held in stock)* produit *m* or article *m* de base ; *(gen: of conversation etc)* élément *m* or sujet *m* principal ; *(in diet etc)* aliment *m* or denrée *f* de base 3 (= fibre) fibre *f*

staple² /ˈsteɪpl/ **N** *(for papers)* agrafe *f* ; *(Tech)* crampon *m*, cavalier *m* **VT** (also **staple together**) *[+ papers]* agrafer ; *[+ wood, stones]* cramponner ◆ **to ~ sth on to sth** agrafer qch à qch **COMP staple gun N** agrafeuse *f* d'artisan or d'atelier

stapler /ˈsteɪpləʳ/ **N** agrafeuse *f*

star /stɑːʳ/ **N** 1 *(Astron)* étoile *f* ; (= asterisk) astérisque *m* ; *(for merit at school)* bon point *m* ◆ **morning/evening** ~ étoile *f* du matin/du soir ◆ **the Stars and Stripes** *(US)* la Bannière étoilée ◆ **the Stars and Bars** *(US Hist)* le drapeau des États confédérés ◆ **Star of David** étoile *f* de David ◆ **the ~ of Bethlehem** l'étoile *f* de Bethléem ; see also **comp** ◆ **to have ~s in one's eyes** être naïvement plein d'espoir ◆ **to see ~s** *(fig)* voir trente-six chandelles ◆ **he was born under a lucky/an unlucky** ~ il est né sous une bonne/une mauvaise étoile ◆ **you can thank your (lucky) ~s * that ...** tu peux remercier le ciel de ce que ... ◆ **the ~s** (= horoscope) l'horoscope *m* ◆ **it was written in his ~s that he would do it** il était écrit qu'il le ferait ◆ **three-/five-~ hotel** hôtel *m* trois/cinq étoiles ; see also **five** ; → **four, guiding, pole², shooting, two**

2 (= famous person) vedette *f*, star *f* ◆ **the film made him into a** ~ le film en a fait une vedette or l'a rendu célèbre ◆ **the ~ of the show** la vedette du spectacle ; → **all, film**

VT 1 (= decorate with stars) étoiler ◆ **lawn ~red with daisies** pelouse *f* parsemée or émaillée *(liter)* de pâquerettes

2 (= put asterisk against) marquer d'un astérisque

3 *(Cine, Theat)* avoir pour vedette ◆ **the film ~s John Wayne** John Wayne est la vedette du film ◆ **~ring Mel Gibson as ...** avec Mel Gibson dans le rôle de ...

VI *(Cine, Theat)* être la vedette ; *(fig)* briller ◆ **to ~ in a film** être la vedette d'un film ◆ **he ~red as Hamlet** c'est lui qui a joué le rôle de Hamlet

COMP star anise N (= fruit) anis *m* étoilé ; (= plant) badiane *f*
star-chamber ADJ *(fig)* arbitraire
star-crossed ADJ maudit par le sort
star fruit N carambole *f*
star grass N herbe *f* étoilée
star-of-Bethlehem N (= plant) ornithogale *m*, dame-d'onze-heures *f*
star part N *(Cine, Theat)* premier rôle *m*
star prize N premier prix *m*
starring role, star role N *(Cine, Theat)* premier rôle *m*
star route N *(US Post)* liaison *f* postale
star shell N *(Mil)* fusée *f* éclairante
star sign N signe *m* zodiacal or du zodiaque
star-spangled ADJ parsemé d'étoiles, étoilé ◆ **the Star-Spangled Banner** *(US = flag, anthem)* la Bannière étoilée
star-studded ADJ *[sky]* parsemé d'étoiles ; *[cast]* prestigieux ; *[play]* à la distribution prestigieuse
star system N 1 *(Astron)* système *m* stellaire 2 *(Cine)* ◆ **the ~ system** le star-système or star-system
the star turn N la vedette
Star Wars N la Guerre des étoiles ◆ **the "Star Wars" * plan** or **program** *(US Mil)* le projet or le programme de la "Guerre des étoiles"

starboard /ˈstɑːbəd/ *(Naut)* **N** tribord *m* ◆ **to ~** à tribord ◆ **land to ~!** terre par tribord ! **ADJ** *[wing, engine, guns, lights]* de tribord ◆ **on the ~ beam** par le travers tribord ◆ **~ bow** tribord *m* avant ◆ **on the ~ bow** par tribord avant ◆ **~ side** tribord *m* ◆ **on the ~ side** à tribord, → **watch² VT** ◆ **to ~ the helm** mettre la barre à tribord

starburst /ˈstɑːbɜːst/ **N** *(liter)* étoile *f*

starch /stɑːtʃ/ **N** 1 *(in food)* amidon *m*, fécule *f* ; *(for stiffening)* amidon *m* ◆ **he was told to cut out all ~(es)** on lui a dit de supprimer tous les féculents ◆ **it took the ~ out of him** * *(US)* cela l'a mis à plat, cela lui a ôté toute son énergie 2 *(pej = formal manner)* raideur *f*, manières *fpl* apprêtées or empesées **VT** *[+ collar]* amidonner, empeser **COMP starch-reduced ADJ** *[bread]* de régime ; *[diet]* pauvre en féculents

starchy /ˈstɑːtʃɪ/ **ADJ** 1 *[food]* féculent ◆ **~ foods** féculents *mpl* 2 *(pej = formal) [person, attitude]* guindé

stardom /ˈstɑːdəm/ **N** *(NonC)* vedettariat *m*, célébrité *f* ◆ **to rise to ~, to achieve ~** devenir une vedette or une star

stardust /ˈstɑːdʌst/ **N** *(fig)* la vie en rose

stare /steəʳ/ **N** regard *m* (fixe) ◆ **cold/curious/vacant ~** (long) regard *m* froid/curieux/vague **VI** ◆ **to ~ at sb** dévisager qn, fixer qn du regard, regarder qn fixement ◆ **to ~ at sth** regarder qch fixement, fixer qch du regard ◆ **to ~ at sb/sth in surprise** regarder qn/qch avec surprise or d'un air surpris, écarquiller les yeux devant qn/qch ◆ **they all ~d in astonishment** ils ont tous regardé d'un air ébahi or en écarquillant les yeux ◆ **he ~d at me stonily** il m'a regardé d'un air dur ◆ **what are you staring at?** qu'est-ce que tu regardes comme ça ? ◆ **it's rude to ~** il est mal élevé de regarder les gens fixement ◆ **to ~ into space** regarder dans le vide or dans l'espace, avoir le regard perdu dans le vague

VT ◆ **to ~ sb in the face** dévisager qn, fixer qn du regard, regarder qn dans le blanc des yeux ◆ **where are my gloves? – here, they're staring you in the face!** où sont mes gants ? – ils sont sous ton nez or tu as le nez dessus ! ◆ **they're certainly in love, that ~s you in the face** ils sont vraiment amoureux, cela crève les yeux ◆ **ruin ~d him in the face, he was staring ruin in the face** il était au bord de la ruine ◆ **the truth ~d him in the face** la vérité lui crevait les yeux or lui sautait aux yeux

► **stare out VT SEP** faire baisser les yeux à

starfish /ˈstɑːfɪʃ/ **N** (pl inv) étoile *f* de mer

stargazer /ˈstɑːgeɪzəʳ/ **N** 1 (= astronomer) astronome *mf* ; (= astrologer) astrologue *mf* 2 (= fish) uranoscope *m*

stargazing /ˈstɑːgeɪzɪŋ/ **N** contemplation *f* des étoiles ; (= predictions) prédictions *fpl* astrologiques ; *(fig = dreaming)* rêverie *f*, rêvasserie *f (pej)*

staring /ˈsteərɪŋ/ **ADJ** *[crowd]* curieux ◆ **his ~ eyes** son regard fixe ; *(in surprise)* son regard étonné or ébahi ; *(in fear)* son regard effrayé

stark /stɑːk/ **ADJ** 1 (= austere) *[landscape, beauty, building, décor, colour]* austère ; *[cliff]* désolé, morne 2 (= harsh) *[choice]* difficile ; *[warning, reminder]* sévère ; *[reality]* dur ◆ **those are the ~ facts of the matter** voilà les faits bruts or tels qu'ils sont ◆ **the ~ fact is that ...** le fait est que ... 3 (= absolute) *[terror]* pur ◆ **in ~ contrast** tout à l'opposé ◆ **to be in ~ contrast to sb/sth** contraster vivement avec qn/qch **ADV** ◆ **~ naked** tout nu

starkers * /ˈstɑːkəz/ **ADJ** *(Brit)* à poil *

starkly /ˈstɑːklɪ/ **ADV** 1 (= austerely) *[furnished]* de façon austère ◆ **~ beautiful** d'une beauté sauvage 2 (= clearly) *[illustrate, outline]* crûment ; *[stand out]* âprement ; *[different]* carrément ; *[apparent]* nettement ◆ **to contrast ~ with sth** contraster de façon frappante avec qch ◆ **to be ~ exposed** être exposé sans ambages

starkness /ˈstɑːknɪs/ **N** *(NonC)* 1 (= austerity) *[of landscape, beauty, building, décor, colour]* austérité *f* ; *[of desert]* désolation *f* 2 (= harshness) *[of choice]* difficulté *f* ; *[of warning, reminder]* sévérité *f* ; *[of facts]* caractère *m* brut ; *[of reality]* dureté *f* 3 (= absoluteness) ◆ **the ~ of the contrast between ...** le contraste absolu entre ...

starless /ˈstɑːlɪs/ **ADJ** sans étoiles

starlet /ˈstɑːlɪt/ **N** *(Cine)* starlette *f*

starlight /ˈstɑːlaɪt/ **N** ◆ **by ~** à la lumière des étoiles

starling /ˈstɑːlɪŋ/ **N** étourneau *m*, sansonnet *m*

starlit /ˈstɑːlɪt/ **ADJ** *[night, sky]* étoilé ; *[countryside, scene]* illuminé par les étoiles

starry /ˈstɑːrɪ/ **ADJ** *[sky, night]* étoilé **COMP starry-eyed ADJ** *[person]* (= idealistic) idéaliste ; (= innocent) innocent, ingénu ; *(from wonder)* éberlué ; *(from love)* éperdument amoureux, ébloui ◆ **in ~-eyed wonder** le regard plein d'émerveillement, complètement ébloui

starstruck /ˈstɑːstrʌk/ **ADJ** ébloui *(devant une célébrité)*

START /stɑːt/ **N** (abbrev of **Strategic Arms Reduction Talks**) (traité *m*) START *m*

start /stɑːt/

LANGUAGE IN USE 26.1

1 NOUN	4 COMPOUNDS
2 TRANSITIVE VERB	5 PHRASAL VERBS
3 INTRANSITIVE VERB	

1 – NOUN

1 (= beginning) *[of speech, book, film, career etc]* commencement *m*, début *m* ; *[of negotiations]* début *m* ; *(Sport) [of race etc]* départ *m* ; (= starting line) (point *m* de) départ *m* ◆ **that was the ~ of all the trouble** c'est là que tous les ennuis ont commencé ◆ **to get off to a good** or **brisk** or **fast ~** bien commencer, bien démarrer ◆ **to get a good ~ in life** bien débuter dans la vie ◆ **they gave their son a good ~ in life** ils ont fait ce qu'il fallait pour que leur fils débute *subj* bien dans la vie ◆ **that was a good ~ to his career** cela a été un bon début or un début prometteur pour sa carrière ◆ **to get off to a bad** or **slow ~** *(lit, fig)* mal démarrer, mal commencer ◆ **it's off to a good/bad ~** c'est bien/mal parti ◆ **to be lined up for the ~** *(Sport)* être sur la ligne de départ ◆ **the whistle blew for the ~ of the race** le coup de sifflet a annoncé le départ de la course ◆ **wait for the ~** attendez le signal du départ

◆ **at the start** au commencement, au début

◆ **for a start** d'abord, pour commencer

◆ **from start to finish** du début à la fin

◆ **from the start** dès le début, dès le commencement

♦ **to make + start** ♦ **to make a ~** commencer ♦ **to make a ~ on sth** commencer qch, se mettre à qch ♦ **to make an early ~** commencer de bonne heure ; *(in journey)* partir de bonne heure ♦ **to make a fresh ~** recommencer (à zéro*)

2 = advantage *(Sport)* avance *f* ; *(fig)* avantage *m* ♦ **will you give me a ~?** est-ce que vous voulez bien me donner une avance ? ♦ **to give sb 10 metres' ~** *or* **a 10-metre ~** donner 10 mètres d'avance à qn ♦ **that gave him a ~ over the others in the class** cela lui a donné un avantage sur les autres élèves de sa classe, cela l'a avantagé par rapport aux autres élèves de sa classe

3 = sudden movement sursaut *m*, tressaillement *m* ♦ **to wake with a ~** se réveiller en sursaut ♦ **to give a ~** sursauter, tressaillir ♦ **to give sb a ~** faire sursauter *or* tressaillir qn ♦ **you gave me such a ~!** ce que vous m'avez fait peur !

2 - TRANSITIVE VERB

1 = begin commencer *(to do sth, doing sth* à faire qch, de faire qch), se mettre *(to do sth, doing sth* à faire qch) ; *[+ work]* commencer, se mettre à ; *[+ task]* entreprendre ; *[+ song]* commencer (à chanter), entonner ; *[+ attack]* déclencher ; *[+ bottle]* entamer, déboucher ♦ **to ~ a cheque book/a new page** commencer *or* prendre un nouveau carnet de chèques/une nouvelle page ♦ **to ~ a journey** partir en voyage ♦ **he ~ed the day with a glass of milk** il a bu un verre de lait pour bien commencer la journée ♦ **to ~ the day right** bien commencer la journée, se lever du pied droit ♦ **to ~ life as ...** débuter dans la vie comme ... ♦ **that doesn't (even) ~ to compare with ...** cela est loin d'être comparable à ..., cela n'a rien de comparable avec ... ♦ **it soon ~ed to rain** il n'a pas tardé à pleuvoir ♦ **I'd ~ed to think you weren't coming** je commençais à croire que tu ne viendrais pas ♦ **to ~ again** *or* **afresh** recommencer *(to do sth* à faire qch), recommencer à zéro* ♦ **don't ~ that again!** tu ne vas pas recommencer ! ♦ **"it's late" he ~ed** "il est tard" commença-t-il

♦ **to get started** commencer, démarrer ♦ **to get ~ed on (doing) sth** commencer (à faire) qch ♦ **let's get ~ed!** allons-y !, on s'y met !* ♦ **once I get ~ed I work very quickly** une fois lancé je travaille très vite ♦ **just to get ~ed, they ...** rien que pour mettre l'affaire en route *or* rien que pour démarrer, ils ...

2 = originate, initiate : also **start off, start up** *[+ discussion]* commencer, ouvrir ; *[+ conversation]* amorcer, engager ; *[+ quarrel, argument, dispute]* déclencher, faire naître ; *[+ reform, movement, series of events]* déclencher ; *[+ fashion]* lancer ; *[+ phenomenon, institution]* donner naissance à ; *[+ custom, policy]* inaugurer ; *[+ war]* causer ; *[+ rumour]* donner naissance à, faire naître ♦ **to ~ (up) a fire** *(in grate etc)* allumer un feu, faire du feu ; *(accidentally)* mettre le feu, provoquer un incendie ♦ **you'll ~ a fire if you go on doing that!** tu vas mettre le feu à la maison *or* tu vas provoquer un incendie si tu fais ça ! ♦ **she has ~ed a baby*** elle est enceinte

3 = cause to start (also **start up**) *[+ engine, vehicle]* mettre en marche, démarrer ; *[+ clock]* mettre en marche ; (also **start off**) *[+ race]* donner le signal du départ de ♦ **he ~ed the ball rolling by saying ...** pour commencer, il a dit ... ♦ **he blew the whistle to ~ the runners (off)** il a sifflé pour donner le signal du départ ♦ **he ~ed the new clerk (off) in the sales department** il a d'abord mis *or* affecté le nouvel employé au service des ventes ♦ **they ~ed her (off) as a typist** d'abord *or* pour commencer ils l'ont employée comme dactylo ♦ **to ~ sb (off** *or* **out) on a career** lancer *or* établir qn dans une carrière ♦ **if you ~ him (off) on that subject ...** si tu le lances sur ce sujet ... ♦ **that ~ed him (off) sneezing/remembering** *etc* alors il s'est mis à éternuer/à se souvenir *etc* ♦ **to ~ a hare** *(lit, fig)* lever un lièvre

♦ **to get sth started** *[+ engine, vehicle]* mettre qch en marche, faire démarrer qch ; *[+ clock]* mettre qch en marche ; *[+ project]* faire démarrer qch

♦ **to get sb started** *(gen)* mettre qn en selle ; *[+ film star, pop star etc]* lancer qn ♦ **to get sb ~ed on (doing) sth** faire commencer qch à qn

3 - INTRANSITIVE VERB

1 = begin : also **start off, start out, start up** *[person]* commencer, s'y mettre ; *[speech, programme, meeting, ceremony]* commencer ♦ **let's ~!** commençons !, allons-y !, on s'y met !* ♦ **we must ~ at once** il faut commencer *or* nous y mettre immédiatement ♦ **well, to ~ at the beginning** eh bien, pour commencer par le commencement ♦ **it's ~ing (off) rather well/badly** cela s'annonce plutôt bien/mal ♦ **to ~ (off) well in life** bien débuter dans la vie ♦ **to ~ (out** *or* **up) in business** se lancer dans les affaires ♦ **to ~ again** *or* **afresh** recommencer (à zéro*) ♦ **classes ~ on Monday** les cours commencent *or* reprennent lundi ♦ **the classes ~ (up) again soon** les cours reprennent bientôt, c'est bientôt la rentrée ♦ **~ing from Monday** à partir de lundi ♦ **to ~ (off) by doing sth** commencer par faire qch ♦ **~ by putting everything away** commence par tout ranger ♦ **~ on a new page** prenez une nouvelle page ♦ **he ~ed (off) in the sales department/as a secretary** il a débuté dans le service des ventes/comme secrétaire ♦ **he ~ed (off** *or* **out) as a Marxist** il a commencé par être marxiste, au début *or* au départ il a été marxiste ♦ **don't ~!*** *(= start complaining etc)* ne commence pas !

♦ **to start with** commencer par ♦ **to ~ with sth** commencer *or* débuter par qch ♦ **~ with me!** commencez par moi ! ♦ **to ~ with, there were only three of them, but later ...** (tout) d'abord ils n'étaient que trois, mais plus tard ... ♦ **to ~ with, this is untrue** pour commencer *or* d'abord, c'est faux ♦ **we only had 20 euros to ~ with** nous n'avions que 20 euros pour commencer *or* au début ♦ **he ~ed with the intention of writing a thesis** au début son intention était d'écrire *or* il avait l'intention d'écrire une thèse

2 = broach **to ~ on a book** commencer un livre ♦ **to ~ on a course of study** commencer *or* entreprendre un programme d'études ♦ **they had ~ed on a new bottle** ils avaient débouché *or* entamé une nouvelle bouteille ♦ **I ~ed on the job last week** *(employment)* j'ai commencé à travailler la semaine dernière ; *(task)* je m'y suis mis la semaine dernière ; see also **start on**

3 = originate, initiate : also **start up** *[music, noise, guns]* commencer, retentir ; *[fire]* commencer, prendre ; *[river]* prendre sa source ; *[road]* partir (at de) ; *[political party, movement, custom]* commencer, naître ♦ **that's when the trouble ~s** c'est alors *or* là que les ennuis commencent ♦ **it all ~ed when he refused to pay** toute cette histoire a commencé *or* tout a commencé quand il a refusé de payer

4 = leave : also **start off, start out** *[person]* partir, se mettre en route ; *[ship]* partir ; *[train]* démarrer, se mettre en marche ♦ **to ~ (off** *or* **out) from London/for Paris/on a journey** partir de Londres/pour Paris/en voyage ♦ **ten horses ~ed and only three finished** *(Sport)* dix chevaux ont pris le départ mais trois seulement ont fini la course ♦ **he ~ed (off) along the corridor** il s'est engagé dans le couloir ♦ **he ~ed (off) down the street** il a commencé à descendre la rue

5 = get going : also **start up** *[car, engine, machine]* démarrer, se mettre en route ; *[clock]* se mettre à marcher ♦ **my car won't ~** ma voiture ne veut pas démarrer*

6 = jump nervously *[person]* sursauter, tressaillir ; *[animal]* tressaillir, avoir un soubresaut ♦ **to ~ to one's feet** sauter sur ses pieds, se lever brusquement ♦ **he ~ed forward** il a fait un mouvement brusque en avant ♦ **his eyes were ~ing out of his head** les yeux lui sortaient de la tête ♦ **tears ~ed to her eyes** les larmes lui sont montées aux yeux

7 timbers jouer

4 - COMPOUNDS

starting block N *(Athletics)* starting-block *m*, bloc *m* de départ ♦ **to be fast/slow off the ~ing blocks** *(fig)* être rapide/lent à démarrer
starting gate N *(Racing)* starting-gate *m*
starting grid N *(Motor Racing)* grille *f* de départ
starting handle N *(Brit: for engine)* manivelle *f*
starting line N *(Sport)* ligne *f* de départ
starting pistol N pistolet *m* de starter
starting point N point *m* de départ
starting post N *(Sport)* ligne *f* de départ
starting price N *(Stock Exchange)* prix *m* initial ; *(Racing)* cote *f* de départ
starting salary N salaire *m* d'embauche
starting stalls NPL *(Racing)* stalles *fpl* de départ
start-up N *[of machine]* démarrage *m*, mise *f* en route ; *[of business]* lancement *m*, mise *f* en route ; *(= company)* start-up *m*, jeune pousse *f*
start-up costs N frais *mpl* de lancement *or* de démarrage
start-up money N capital *m* initial

5 - PHRASAL VERBS

► **start back** VI 1 *(= return)* prendre le chemin du retour, repartir
2 *(= recoil) [person, horse etc]* reculer soudainement, faire un bond en arrière

► **start in** VI s'y mettre, s'y coller* ♦ **~ in!** allez-y !

► **start off** VI → **start vi 1, 4**
VT SEP → **start vt 2, 3**

► **start on*** VT FUS *(= pick on)* s'en prendre à ; see also **start vi 2**

► **start out** VI → **start vi 1, 4**

► **start over** VI *(esp US)* repartir à zéro
VT recommencer

► **start up** VI → **start vi 1, 3, 5**
VT SEP → **start vt 2, vi 3**

---

starter /ˈstɑːtəʳ/ N 1 *(Sport) (= official)* starter *m* ; *(= horse)* partant *m* ♦ **to be under ~'s orders** *[runner]* être à ses marques ; *[horse]* être sous les ordres (du starter) ; *(fig)* être sur *or* dans les starting-blocks ♦ **to be a slow ~** *(fig)* être lent au départ *or* à démarrer ♦ **the child was a late ~** *(Scol etc)* cet enfant a mis du temps à se développer ; → **nonstarter** 2 *(in car)* démarreur *m* ; *(on machine etc)* bouton *m* de démarrage ; (also **starter motor**) démarreur *m* 3 *(Brit: in meal)* hors-d'œuvre *m inv* ♦ **for ~s*** *(= food)* comme hors-d'œuvre ; *(fig = for a start)* pour commencer, d'abord
COMP **starter flat** N *(Brit) appartement idéal pour une personne souhaitant accéder à la propriété*
starter home N *(Brit) logement idéal pour une personne souhaitant accéder à la propriété*
starter pack N *(Comm)* kit *m* de base

startle /ˈstɑːtl/ VT *[sound, sb's arrival]* faire sursauter *or* tressaillir ; *[news, telegram]* alarmer ♦ **it ~d him out of his sleep** cela l'a réveillé en sursaut ♦ **to ~ sb out of his wits** donner un (drôle* de) choc à qn ♦ **you ~d me!** tu m'as fait sursauter !, tu m'as fait peur !

startled /ˈstɑːtld/ ADJ *[animal]* effarouché ; *[person]* très surpris ; *[expression]* de saisissement ♦ **in a ~ voice** d'une voix qui montrait sa surprise ♦ **he gave her a ~ look** il lui lança un regard interloqué ♦ **she was ~ to see him** elle fut très surprise de le voir

startling /ˈstɑːtlɪŋ/ ADJ *[success, conclusion, results, evidence, news]* surprenant ; *[contrast]* saisissant

startlingly /ˈstɑːtlɪŋlɪ/ ADV *[different, similar]* étonnamment ◆ ~ **original** d'une originalité surprenante ◆ ~ **beautiful/modern** d'une beauté/modernité saisissante ◆ **his ~ blue eyes** ses yeux d'un bleu saisissant

starvation /stɑːˈveɪʃən/ N *(NonC)* inanition *f* ◆ **they are threatened with ~** ils risquent de mourir d'inanition *or* de faim, la famine les menace

COMP *[rations, wages]* de famine
starvation diet N ◆ **to be on a ~ diet** *(lit)* être sérieusement *or* dangereusement sous-alimenté ; *(fig)* suivre un régime draconien
starvation level N ◆ **to be living at ~ level** ⇒ **to be on a starvation diet**

starve /stɑːv/ VT 1 affamer ◆ **to ~ sb to death** laisser qn mourir de faim ◆ **to ~ o.s. to death** se laisser mourir de faim ◆ **she ~d herself to feed her children** elle s'est privée de nourriture pour donner à manger à ses enfants ◆ **you don't have to ~ yourself in order to slim** tu peux maigrir sans te laisser mourir de faim ◆ **to ~ sb into submission** soumettre qn par la faim ◆ **to ~ a town into surrender** *(Mil)* amener une ville à se rendre par la famine 2 *(= deprive)* priver *(sb of sth* qn de qch) ◆ **~d of affection** privé d'affection ◆ **engine ~d of petrol** moteur *m* à sec VI manquer de nourriture, être affamé ◆ **to ~ (to death)** mourir de faim ; *(deliberately)* se laisser mourir de faim ; see also **starving**

► **starve out** VT SEP *[+ person, animal]* obliger à sortir en affamant

starveling /ˈstɑːvlɪŋ/ N *(= person)* affamé(e) *m(f)*

starving /ˈstɑːvɪŋ/ ADJ *(lit)* affamé, famélique ◆ **I'm ~** * *(fig)* je meurs de faim, j'ai une faim de loup

stash * /stæʃ/ VT (also **stash away**) *(= hide)* cacher, planquer* ; *(= save up, store away)* mettre à gauche*, mettre de côté ◆ **he had $500 ~ed away** *(= saved up)* il avait mis 500 dollars de côté ; *(= in safe place)* il avait 500 dollars en lieu sûr N *(= place)* planque* *f*, cachette *f* ◆ **a ~ of jewellery/drugs** des bijoux cachés/des drogues cachées ◆ **a ~ of money** un magot, un bas de laine

stasis /ˈsteɪsɪs/ N *(Med, Literat)* stase *f*

state /steɪt/ N 1 *(= condition)* état *m* ◆ **~ of alert/emergency/siege/war** état *m* d'alerte/d'urgence/de siège/de guerre ◆ **the ~ of the art** l'état *m* actuel de la technique *or* des connaissances ; see also **comp** ◆ **in your ~ of health/mind** dans votre état de santé/d'esprit ◆ **he was in an odd ~ of mind** il était d'une humeur étrange ◆ **you're in no ~ to reply** vous n'êtes pas en état de répondre ◆ **I'd like to know the ~ of my account** *(in bank)* j'aimerais connaître la position de mon compte ◆ **what's the ~ of play?** *(fig)* où en est-on ? ◆ **in a good/bad ~ of repair** bien/mal entretenu ◆ **to be in a good/bad ~** *[chair, car, house]* être en bon/mauvais état ; *[person, relationship, marriage]* aller bien/mal ◆ **you should have seen the ~ the car was in** vous auriez dû voir l'état de la voiture ◆ **it wasn't in a (fit) ~ to be used** c'était hors d'état de servir, c'était inutilisable ◆ **he's not in a (fit) ~ to drive** il est hors d'état *or* il n'est pas en état de conduire ◆ **what a ~ you're in!** vous êtes dans un bel état ! ◆ **he got into a terrible ~ about it** * ça l'a mis dans tous ses états ◆ **don't get into such a ~!** * ne vous affolez pas ! ; → **affair, declare**

2 *(Pol)* État *m* ◆ **the State** l'État *m* ◆ **the States** * les États-Unis *mpl* ◆ **the State of Virginia** l'État *m* de Virginie ◆ **the affairs of ~** les affaires *fpl* de l'État ◆ **a ~ within a ~** un État dans l'État ; → **evidence, minister, police, secretary**

3 *(US = State Department)* **State** le Département d'État

4 *(= rank)* rang *m* ◆ **every ~ of life** tous les rangs sociaux

5 *(NonC = pomp)* pompe *f*, apparat *m* ◆ **the robes of ~** les costumes *mpl* d'apparat

◆ **in state** en grande pompe, en grand apparat ◆ **to live in ~** mener grand train ; → **lie¹**

VT déclarer, affirmer *(that* que) ; *[+ one's views, the facts]* exposer ; *[+ time, place]* fixer, spécifier ; *[+ conditions]* poser, formuler ; *[+ theory, restrictions]* formuler ; *[+ problem]* énoncer, poser ◆ **I also wish to ~ that ...** je voudrais ajouter que ... ◆ **it is ~d in the records that ...** il est écrit *or* mentionné dans les archives que ... ◆ **I have seen it ~d that ...** j'ai lu quelque part que ... ◆ **as ~d above** ainsi qu'il est dit plus haut ◆ **~ your name and address** déclinez vos nom, prénoms et adresse ; *(written)* inscrivez vos nom, prénoms et adresse ◆ **cheques must ~ the sum clearly** les chèques doivent indiquer la somme clairement ◆ **he was asked to ~ his case** on lui a demandé de présenter ses arguments ◆ **to ~ the case for the prosecution** *(Jur)* présenter le dossier de l'accusation

COMP *[business, documents, secret]* d'État ; *[security, intervention]* de l'État ; *[medicine]* étatisé ; *(US:* also **State**) *[law, policy, prison, university]* de l'État
state apartments NPL appartements *mpl* officiels
state banquet N banquet *m* de gala
State Capitol N *(US)* Capitole *m*
state-certified midwife N *(Brit Med)* sage-femme *f* diplômée d'État
state coach N *(Brit)* carrosse *m* d'apparat *(de cérémonie officielle)*
state control N contrôle *m* de l'État ◆ **under ~ control** ⇒ **state-controlled**
state-controlled ADJ étatisé
State Department N *(US)* Département *m* d'État, ≃ ministère *m* des Affaires étrangères
state education N *(Brit)* enseignement *m* public
state-enrolled nurse N *(Brit)* infirmier *m*, -ière *f* auxiliaire, aide-soignant(e) *mf*
state funeral N funérailles *fpl* nationales
State legislature N *(US Jur)* législature *f* de l'État
State line N *(US)* frontière *f* entre les États
state-maintained ADJ *(Brit Scol)* public
state militia N *(US)* milice *f (formée de volontaires d'un État)*
state-of-the-art ADJ *(fig = up-to-date) [computer, video]* dernier cri ◆ **it's ~-of-the-art** c'est ce qui se fait de mieux, c'est le dernier cri
State of the Union Address N *(US Pol)* discours *m* sur l'état de l'Union
state-owned ADJ étatisé
State police N *(NonC: US)* police *f* de l'État ◆ **Michigan State police** la police de l'État du Michigan
state-registered nurse N *(Brit: formerly)* infirmier *m*, -ière *f* diplômé(e) d'État
State Representative N *(US Pol)* membre *m* de la Chambre des représentants d'un État
State rights NPL *(US)* ⇒ **State's rights**
state-run ADJ d'état
State's attorney N *(US)* procureur *m*
state school N *(Brit)* école *f* publique
state sector N *(Econ etc)* secteur *m* public
State Senator N *(US Pol)* membre *m* du Sénat d'un État
state socialism N *(NonC: Pol Econ)* socialisme *m* d'État
State's rights NPL *(US)* droits *mpl* des États
state-subsidized ADJ subventionné par l'État
state-trading countries NPL *(Econ)* pays *mpl* à commerce d'État
state trooper N *(US)* ≃ gendarme *m*
State university N *(US)* université *f* d'État
state visit N ◆ **to go on** *or* **make a ~ visit to a country** se rendre en visite officielle *or* faire un voyage officiel dans un pays
state-wide ADJ, ADV *(US)* d'un bout à l'autre de l'État

STATE OF THE UNION ADDRESS

Le discours sur l'état de l'Union est l'allocution que prononce le président des États-Unis devant le Congrès en janvier de chaque année, au début de la session parlementaire. Dans cette intervention, diffusée à la radio et à la télévision, le président dresse un bilan de son action, expose ses projets et donne au Congrès des « informations sur l'état de l'Union », comme le demande la Constitution.

STATE'S RIGHTS

Le dixième amendement de la Constitution américaine accorde aux États un certain nombre de droits (**State's rights**) sur toutes les questions qui ne relèvent pas des prérogatives du gouvernement fédéral : enseignement, fiscalité, lois et réglementations diverses. Cependant, l'interprétation de ce texte a provoqué de nombreuses controverses : les États du Sud l'ont utilisé pour justifier la sécession avant la guerre civile, puis pour s'opposer à l'intégration raciale dans les années 1950. La question du degré d'autonomie dont disposent les États par rapport au pouvoir fédéral reste un sujet politiquement sensible.

statecraft /ˈsteɪtkrɑːft/ N *(NonC)* habileté *f* politique

stated /ˈsteɪtɪd/ ADJ *[date, sum]* fixé ; *[interval]* fixe ; *[limit]* prescrit ◆ **on ~ days** à jours fixes ◆ **at the ~ time, at the time ~** à l'heure dite

statehood /ˈsteɪthʊd/ N *(NonC)* ◆ **to achieve ~** devenir un État

statehouse /ˈsteɪthaʊs/ N *(US)* siège *m* de la législature d'un État

stateless /ˈsteɪtlɪs/ ADJ apatride ◆ **~ person** apatride *mf*

statelet /ˈsteɪtlɪt/ N *(Pol)* mini-État *m*

stateliness /ˈsteɪtlɪnɪs/ N majesté *f*, caractère *m* imposant

stately /ˈsteɪtlɪ/ ADJ *[person]* plein de dignité ; *[building, pace]* majestueux ◆ **to make ~ progress** progresser majestueusement COMP
stately home N *(Brit)* manoir *m or* château *m (ouvert au public)*

statement /ˈsteɪtmənt/ N 1 *(NonC) [of one's views, the facts]* exposition *f*, formulation *f* ; *[of time, place]* spécification *f* ; *[of theory, restrictions, conditions]* formulation *f* ; *[of problem]* énonciation *f* 2 *(written, verbal)* déclaration *f* ; *(Jur)* déposition *f* ◆ **official ~** communiqué *m* officiel ◆ **to make a ~** *(gen, Press)* faire une déclaration ; *(Jur)* faire une déposition, déposer ◆ **the painting makes a ~ about war** le tableau constitue une prise de position sur la guerre ◆ **~ of grounds** *(Jur)* exposé *m* des motifs 3 *(Fin) [of accounts etc] (= bill)* relevé *m* ; *(Comm = bill)* facture *f* ; (also **bank statement**) relevé *m* de compte 4 *(Ling)* assertion *f* VT *(Social Work)* ◆ **to ~ a child** évaluer les besoins spécifiques d'un enfant handicapé

stateroom /ˈsteɪtrʊm/ N *(Brit) [of palace]* grande salle *f* de réception ; *[of ship, train]* cabine *f* de luxe

stateside * /ˈsteɪtsaɪd/ ADJ *(US)* aux États-Unis, ≃ chez nous

statesman /ˈsteɪtsmən/ N (pl **-men**) homme *m* d'État ◆ **he is a real ~** *(fig)* il est extrêmement diplomate ; → **elder¹**

statesmanlike /ˈsteɪtsmənlaɪk/ **ADJ** *[qualities]* d'homme d'État ◆ **he's cultivating a more ~ image** il essaie de renforcer son image d'homme d'État

statesmanship /ˈsteɪtsmənʃɪp/ **N** *(NonC)* qualités *fpl* d'homme d'État

statesmen /ˈsteɪtsmən/ **NPL** of **statesman**

static /ˈstætɪk/ **ADJ** 1 *(= stationary)* statique ◆ **a series of ~ images** une série d'images fixes *or* statiques 2 *(= unchanging)* immuable ◆ **the ~ quality of their lives** leur vie immuable 3 *(= fixed) [population, output]* stationnaire **N** *(NonC)* 1 ◆ **~s** statique *f* 2 *(Elec, Rad, TV etc)* parasites *mpl* ◆ **he gave me a lot of ~ about ...** *(US)* il m'a passé un savon * à propos de ... **COMP**
static electricity **N** électricité *f* statique

station /ˈsteɪʃən/ **N** 1 *(= place)* poste *m*, station *f* ; *(= fire station)* caserne *f* de pompiers ; *(= lifeboat station)* centre *m or* poste *m* (de secours en mer) ; *(Mil)* poste *m* (militaire) ; *(Police)* poste *m or* commissariat *m* (de police), gendarmerie *f* ; *(Elec = power station)* centrale *f* (électrique) ; *(Rad)* station *f* de radio, poste *m* émetteur ; *(in Australia = sheep/cattle ranch)* élevage *m* (de moutons/de bétail), ranch *m* ◆ **naval ~** station *f* navale ◆ **foreign ~s** *(Rad)* stations *fpl* étrangères ◆ **calling all ~s** *(Telec)* appel *m* à tous les émetteurs ◆ **the Stations of the Cross** *(Rel)* les stations *fpl* de la Croix, le chemin de (la) Croix ; → **frontier, petrol, pump[1], service**
2 *(Rail)* gare *f* ; *[of underground]* station *f* ◆ **bus** *or* **coach ~** gare *f* routière ◆ **the train came into the ~** le train est entré en gare ; *(in underground)* la rame est entrée dans la station ; → **change**
3 *(= position)* poste *m (also Mil)*, position *f* ◆ **to take up one's ~** prendre position, se placer ◆ **from my ~ by the window** de la fenêtre où je m'étais posté *or* où je me trouvais
4 *(= rank)* condition *f*, rang *m* ◆ **one's ~ in life** son rang *or* sa situation social(e), sa place dans la société ◆ **to get ideas above one's ~** avoir des idées de grandeur ◆ **to marry beneath one's ~** † faire une mésalliance, se mésallier ◆ **to marry above one's ~** se marier au-dessus de sa condition
5 *(US Telec)* poste *m* ◆ **give me ~ 101** je voudrais le poste 101
VT *[+ people]* placer ; *[+ guards, observers, look-out, troops, ship]* poster ; *[+ tanks, guns]* placer, installer ◆ **to ~ o.s.** se placer, se poster ◆ **to be ~ed at** *[troops, regiment]* être en *or* tenir garnison à ; *[ships, sailors]* être en station à
COMP *(Rail) [staff, bookstall etc]* de (la) gare
station break **N** *(US Rad, TV)* page *f* de publicité
station house **N** *(US) (for police)* commissariat *m* ; *(for firefighters)* caserne *f* de pompiers
station master **N** *(Rail)* chef *m* de gare
station officer **N** *(Brit Police)* responsable *mf* d'un poste de police
station wag(g)on **N** *(US = car)* break *m*

stationary /ˈsteɪʃənəri/ **ADJ** 1 *(= motionless) [vehicle]* à l'arrêt ; *[person, ship]* stationnaire, immobile ; *[target]* immobile 2 *(= fixed) [crane]* fixe **COMP** **stationary bicycle** **N** bicyclette *f* fixe

stationer /ˈsteɪʃənəʳ/ **N** papetier *m*, -ière *f* ◆ **~'s (shop)** papeterie *f*

stationery /ˈsteɪʃənəri/ **N** *(NonC)* papeterie *f*, papier *m* et petits articles *mpl* de bureau ; *(= writing paper)* papier *m* à lettres **COMP** **Stationery Office** **N** *(Brit)* ◆ **His (or Her) Majesty's Stationery Office** ≈ l'Imprimerie *f* nationale *(fournit aussi de la papeterie à l'administration et publie une gamme étendue d'ouvrages et de brochures didactiques)*

statist /ˈsteɪtɪst/ **ADJ** *(Pol)* étatiste *mf*

statistic /stəˈtɪstɪk/ **N** statistique *f*, chiffre *m* ◆ **a set of ~s** une statistique ◆ **these ~s are not reliable** on ne peut pas se fier à ces chiffres *or* à ces statistiques ◆ **~s suggest that ...** la statistique *or* les statistiques suggère(nt) que ... ◆ **(vital) ~s** *(hum: woman's)* mensurations *fpl* ; → **statistics** **ADJ** ⇒ **statistical**

statistical /stəˈtɪstɪkəl/ **ADJ** *[analysis, evidence, data, probability, table, significance]* statistique ; *[error]* de statistiques ; *[expert]* en statistique(s)

statistically /stəˈtɪstɪkəlɪ/ **ADV** statistiquement

statistician /ˌstætɪsˈtɪʃən/ **N** statisticien(ne) *m(f)*

statistics /stəˈtɪstɪks/ **N** *(NonC)* statistique *f*

stative /ˈsteɪtɪv/ **ADJ** *(Ling)* ◆ **~ verb** verbe *m* d'état

stator /ˈsteɪtəʳ/ **N** stator *m*

stats /stæts/ **NPL** (abbrev of **statistics**) stats * *fpl*

statuary /ˈstætjʊəri/ **ADJ** statuaire **N** *(= art)* statuaire *f* ; *(= statues collectively)* statues *fpl*

statue /ˈstætjuː/ **N** statue *f* ◆ **the Statue of Liberty** la statue de la Liberté

statuesque /ˌstætjʊˈesk/ **ADJ** sculptural

statuette /ˌstætjʊˈet/ **N** statuette *f*

stature /ˈstætʃəʳ/ **N** stature *f*, taille *f* ; *(fig) [of person]* envergure *f*, stature *f* ; *(fig) [of institution]* envergure *f* ◆ **to be of small ~, to be small in** *or* **of ~** être petit *or* fluet ◆ **of short ~** court de stature *or* de taille ◆ **he is a writer of some ~** c'est un écrivain d'une certaine envergure *or* d'une certaine stature ◆ **his ~ as a painter increased when ...** il a pris de l'envergure en tant que peintre quand ... ◆ **moral/intellectual ~** envergure *f* sur le plan moral/intellectuel

status /ˈsteɪtəs/ **N** (pl **statuses**) 1 *(= economic etc position)* situation *f*, position *f* ; *(Admin, Jur)* statut *m* ◆ **social ~** standing *m* ◆ **civil ~** état *m* civil ◆ **what is his (official) ~?** quel est son titre officiel ?, quelle est sa position officielle ? ◆ **the economic ~ of the country** la situation *or* position économique du pays ◆ **the financial ~ of the company** l'état financier de la compagnie ◆ **the ~ of the black population** la condition sociale *or (Admin)* le statut de la population noire ◆ **his ~ as an assistant director** son standing de directeur adjoint
2 *(= prestige) [of person]* prestige *m*, standing *m* ; *[of job, post]* prestige *m* ◆ **it is the ~ more than the salary that appeals to him** c'est le prestige plus que le salaire qui a de l'attrait pour lui ◆ **he hasn't got enough ~ for the job** il ne fait pas le poids * pour le poste
COMP **status report** **N** *(gen, Mil etc)* ◆ **to make a ~ report on ...** faire le point sur ...
status symbol **N** *(gen)* signe *m* extérieur de (la) réussite ; *(marking financial success)* signe *m* extérieur de richesse

status quo /ˈsteɪtəsˈkwəʊ/ **N** statu quo *m inv*

statute /ˈstætjuːt/ **N** *(Jur etc)* loi *f* ◆ **by ~** selon la loi ◆ **the ~ of limitations is seven years** *(US Jur)* au bout de sept ans il y a prescription **COMP** **statute book** **N** *(esp Brit)* ≈ code *m* ◆ **to be on the ~ book** figurer dans les textes de loi, ≈ être dans le code
statute law **N** droit *m* écrit

statutorily /ˈstætjʊtərəlɪ/ **ADV** légalement

statutory /ˈstætjʊtəri/ **ADJ** 1 *(= legal) [duty, powers, provision, right, control]* légal ; *[offence]* prévu *or* défini par la loi ◆ **to have ~ effect** faire force de loi 2 *(pej = token) [woman etc]* de service *(pej)* ◆ **I was the ~ pensioner on the committee** j'étais le retraité-alibi *or* le retraité de service au comité
COMP **statutory body** **N** organisme *m* de droit public
statutory change **N** *(US Jur)* modification *f* législative
statutory corporation **N** société *f* d'État
statutory holiday **N** jour *m* férié ◆ **Monday is a ~ holiday** lundi est (un jour) férié
statutory maternity pay **N** *(Brit)* allocation *f* minimum de maternité
statutory meeting **N** assemblée *f* statutaire
statutory rape **N** *(Jur)* détournement *m* de mineur
statutory sick pay **N** *(Brit)* indemnité *f* de maladie *(versée par l'État)*

staunch[1] /stɔːntʃ/ **VT** *[+ flow]* contenir, arrêter ; *[+ blood]* étancher ; *[+ wound]* étancher le sang de

staunch[2] /stɔːntʃ/ **ADJ** *[supporter, defender, Republican, Protestant]* ardent ; *[friend]* loyal ; *[ally]* sûr ; *[support]* fidèle

staunchly /ˈstɔːntʃlɪ/ **ADV** *[oppose]* fermement ; *[defend, support]* vigoureusement ; *[conservative, Protestant]* résolument

staunchness /ˈstɔːntʃnɪs/ **N** dévouement *m*, loyauté *f*

stave /steɪv/ (vb : pret, ptp **stove** *or* **staved**) **N** *[of barrel etc]* douve *f* ; *(Mus)* portée *f* ; *(Poetry)* stance *f*, strophe *f*
► **stave in** **VT SEP** défoncer, enfoncer
► **stave off** **VT SEP** *[+ danger]* écarter, conjurer ; *[+ threat]* dissiper, conjurer ; *[+ ruin, disaster, defeat]* éviter, conjurer ; *[+ hunger]* tromper ; *[+ attack]* parer ◆ **in an attempt to ~ off the time when ...** en essayant de retarder le moment où ...

staves /steɪvz/ **NPL** of **staff[2], staff[3]**

stay[1] /steɪ/ **N** 1 séjour *m* ◆ **he is in Rome for a short ~** il est à Rome pour une courte visite *or* un bref séjour ◆ **a ~ in hospital** un séjour à l'hôpital ◆ **will it be a long ~?** est-ce qu'il restera *(or* vous resterez *etc)* longtemps ?
2 *(Jur)* suspension *f* ◆ **~ of execution** sursis *m* à l'exécution (d'un jugement) ◆ **to put a ~ on proceedings** surseoir aux poursuites
VT 1 *(= check)* arrêter ; *[+ disease, epidemic]* enrayer ; *[+ hunger]* tromper ; *(= delay)* retarder ; *(Jur) [+ judgement]* surseoir à, différer ; *[+ proceedings]* suspendre ; *[+ decision]* ajourner, remettre ◆ **to ~ one's hand** se retenir
2 *(= last out) [+ race]* terminer, aller jusqu'au bout de ; *[+ distance]* tenir ◆ **to ~ the course** *(Sport)* aller jusqu'au bout ; *(fig)* tenir bon, tenir le coup *
VI 1 *(= remain)* rester ◆ **~ there!** restez là ! ◆ **here I am and here I ~** j'y suis j'y reste ◆ **to ~ still, to ~ put** * ne pas bouger ◆ **to ~ for** *or* **to dinner** rester (à) dîner ◆ **to ~ faithful** rester *or* demeurer fidèle ◆ **~ tuned!** *(Rad)* restez à l'écoute !, ne quittez pas l'écoute ! ◆ **to ~ ahead of the others** garder son avance sur les autres ◆ **it is here to ~** c'est bien établi ◆ **he is here to ~** il est là pour de bon ◆ **things can't be allowed to ~ that way** on ne peut pas laisser les choses comme ça ◆ **if the weather ~s fine** si le temps se maintient (au beau) ◆ **he ~ed (for) the whole week** il est resté toute la semaine ◆ **he ~ed a year in Paris** il est resté un an à Paris, il a séjourné un an à Paris ◆ **to ~ with a company** *[customers, employees]* rester fidèle à une entreprise ◆ **to ~ off school/work** ne pas aller à l'école/au travail ◆ **to ~ off drugs/alcohol** ne plus prendre de drogue/d'alcool
2 *(on visit)* **has she come to ~?** est-ce qu'elle est venue avec l'intention de rester ? ◆ **she came to ~ (for) a few weeks** elle est venue passer quelques semaines ◆ **I'm ~ing with my aunt** je loge chez ma tante ◆ **to ~ in a hotel** être à l'hôtel ◆ **where do you ~ when you go to London?** où logez-vous quand vous allez à Londres ? ◆ **he was ~ing in Paris when he fell ill** il séjournait à Paris quand il est tombé malade
3 *(Scot = live permanently)* habiter
4 *(= persevere)* tenir ◆ **to ~ to the finish** tenir jusqu'à la ligne d'arrivée ◆ **to ~ with a**

scheme* ne pas abandonner un projet ◆ **~ with it!*** tenez bon !

5 (*liter* = *pause*) s'arrêter

COMP **stay-at-home** N, ADJ casanier *m*, -ière *f*, pantouflard(e) * *m(f)*

staying power N résistance *f*, endurance *f* ◆ **he hasn't a lot of ~ing power** il se décourage facilement

► **stay away** VI ◆ **he stayed away for three years** il n'est pas rentré avant trois ans ◆ **he ~ed away from the meeting** il n'est pas allé (*or* venu) à la réunion, il s'est abstenu d'aller à la réunion ◆ **to ~ away from school** ne pas aller à l'école, manquer l'école

► **stay behind** VI rester en arrière ◆ **you'll ~ behind after school!** tu resteras après la classe !

► **stay down** VI 1 rester en bas ; (*bending*) rester baissé ; (*lying down*) rester couché ; (*under water*) rester sous l'eau

2 (*Scol*) redoubler

3 (*food etc*) **nothing he eats will ~ down** il n'assimile rien *or* il ne garde rien de ce qu'il mange

► **stay in** VI 1 [*person*] (*at home*) rester à la maison, ne pas sortir ; (*Scol*) être en retenue

2 [*nail, screw, tooth filling*] tenir

► **stay out** VI 1 [*person*] (*away from home*) ne pas rentrer ; (= *outside*) rester dehors ◆ **get out and ~ out!** sortez et ne revenez pas ! ◆ **he always ~s out late on Fridays** il rentre toujours tard le vendredi ◆ **he ~ed out all night** il n'est pas rentré de la nuit ◆ **don't ~ out after 9 o'clock** rentrez avant 9 heures

2 (*on strike*) rester en grève

3 (*fig*) **to ~ out of** [+ *argument*] ne pas se mêler de ; [+ *prison*] éviter ◆ **to ~ out of trouble** se tenir tranquille ◆ **you ~ out of this!** mêlez-vous de vos (propres) affaires !

► **stay over** VI s'arrêter (un *or* plusieurs jour(s)), faire une halte ◆ **can you ~ over till Thursday?** est-ce que vous pouvez rester jusqu'à jeudi ?

► **stay up** VI 1 [*person*] rester debout, ne pas se coucher ◆ **don't ~ up for me** ne m'attendez pas pour aller vous coucher ◆ **you can ~ up to watch the programme** vous pouvez voir l'émission avant de vous coucher ◆ **we always ~ up late on Saturdays** nous veillons *or* nous nous couchons toujours tard le samedi

2 (= *not fall*) [*trousers, fence etc*] tenir ◆ **this zip won't ~ up** cette fermeture éclair ® ne veut pas rester fermée

stay² /steɪ/ N (*for pole, flagstaff etc: Naut*) étai *m*, hauban *m* ; (*for wall*) étai *m*, étançon *m* ; (*fig*) soutien *m*, support *m* NPL **stays** † (= *corsets*) corset *m* VT (also **stay up**) (*Naut*) haubaner, étayer

stayer /ˈsteɪəʳ/ N (= *horse*) stayer *m*, cheval *m* qui a du fond ; (= *runner*) coureur *m*, -euse *f* qui a du fond *or* de la résistance physique ◆ **he's a ~** (*Sport*) il a du fond, il est capable d'un effort prolongé ; (*fig*) il n'abandonne pas facilement, il va jusqu'au bout de ce qu'il entreprend

STD /ˌestiːˈdiː/ 1 (*Brit Telec*) (abbrev of **subscriber trunk dialling**) automatique *m* ◆ **to phone ~** téléphoner par l'automatique ◆ **~ code** indicatif *m* de zone 2 (abbrev of **sexually transmitted disease**) MST *f* ◆ **~ clinic** ≈ service *m* de (dermato-)vénérologie

stead /sted/ N ◆ **in my/his** *etc* **~** à ma/sa *etc* place ◆ **to stand sb in good ~** rendre grand service à qn, être très utile à qn

steadfast /ˈstedfəst/ (*liter*) ADJ 1 (= *unshakable*) [*person, refusal, belief*] inébranlable ; [*loyalty, support*] inébranlable, indéfectible ; [*intention, desire*] ferme ; [*gaze*] ferme, résolu ◆ **~ in adversity/danger** inébranlable au milieu des infortunes/du danger ◆ **to be ~ in one's belief that …** rester fermement persuadé que … ◆ **to be ~ in one's praise of sb/sth** ne pas tarir d'éloges sur qn/qch ◆ **to be ~ in one's opposition to sth** rester fermement opposé à qch 2 (= *loyal*) [*person*] constant, loyal ◆ **~ in love** constant en amour

steadfastly /ˈstedfəstlɪ/ ADV [*refuse, reject, deny, maintain*] inébranlablement ◆ **~ loyal** d'une loyauté inébranlable ◆ **to remain ~ at one's post** rester ferme à son poste

steadfastness /ˈstedfəstnɪs/ N fermeté *f*, résolution *f* (*liter*) ◆ **~ of purpose** ténacité *f*

Steadicam ® /ˈstedɪkæm/ N (TV) Steady cam ® *m*

steadily /ˈstedɪlɪ/ ADV 1 (= *continuously*) [*increase, worsen, improve, work*] régulièrement ; [*breathe, beat*] avec régularité ; [*advance, rain, sob*] sans interruption ◆ **a ~ increasing number of people** un nombre toujours croissant de personnes ◆ **the poor are ~ getting poorer** les pauvres deviennent de plus en plus pauvres *or* toujours plus pauvres ◆ **the engine ran ~** le moteur tournait sans à-coups 2 [*look at*] (= *without flinching*) sans détourner les yeux ; (= *intimidatingly*) droit dans les yeux, avec insistance ; [*reply*] (= *calmly*) fermement, avec fermeté 3 (= *firmly*) [*walk*] d'un pas ferme ; [*hold, grasp*] d'une main ferme

steadiness /ˈstedɪnɪs/ N (NonC) 1 (= *regularity*) [*of progress, supply, pace, breath, beat, demand*] régularité *f* ; [*of prices, sales, market, economy*] stabilité *f* 2 (= *composure*) [*of voice*] fermeté *f* ◆ **the ~ of her look** *or* **gaze** (= *unflinching*) son regard qui ne cillait pas ; (= *intimidating*) l'insistance de son regard ◆ **the ~ of his game** la régularité de son jeu ◆ **~ of nerve** sang-froid *m* ◆ **~ of purpose** détermination *f* inébranlable 3 (= *firmness*) [*of chair, table, ladder, boat*] stabilité *f* ; [*of hand*] (*in drawing*) sûreté *f* ; (*in holding*) fermeté *f* ; [*gait*] fermeté *f* 4 (= *dependability*) [*of person*] sérieux *m*

steady /ˈstedɪ/ ADJ 1 (= *regular*) [*supply, rain, breathing, beat, demand, income*] régulier ; [*prices, sales, market*] stable ; [*temperature, wind*] constant ◆ **to make ~ progress** progresser régulièrement, faire des progrès constants ◆ **there was a ~ downpour for three hours** il n'a pas cessé de pleuvoir pendant trois heures ◆ **at a ~ pace** à une allure régulière ◆ **a ~ stream** *or* **flow of sth** un flux régulier de qch ◆ **we were doing a ~ 60km/h** nous roulions à une vitesse régulière *or* constante de 60 km/h ◆ **to hold** *or* **keep sth ~** [+ *prices, demand*] stabiliser qch ; see also **adj 3** ◆ **a ~ job** un emploi stable ◆ **~ boyfriend** petit ami *m* attitré ◆ **~ girlfriend** petite amie *f* attitrée ◆ **to have a ~ relationship with sb** avoir une relation stable avec qn

2 (= *composed*) [*voice*] ferme ; [*nerves*] solide ; [*look, gaze*] (= *unflinching*) calme ; (= *intimidating*) soutenu, insistant ◆ **to look at sb with a ~ gaze, to give sb a ~ look** (= *unflinching*) regarder qn sans détourner les yeux ; (= *intimidating*) regarder qn droit dans les yeux *or* avec insistance ◆ **he plays a very ~ game** il a un jeu très régulier

3 (= *firm*) [*chair, table*] stable, solide ; [*boat*] stable ; [*hand*] (*in drawing*) sûr ; (*in holding*) ferme ◆ **to hold** *or* **keep sth ~** maintenir fermement qch ; see also **adj 1** ◆ **to hold ~** se maintenir ◆ **to be ~ (on one's feet)** être solide sur ses jambes ◆ **the car is not very ~ on corners** la voiture ne tient pas très bien la route dans les tournants

4 (= *dependable*) [*person*] sérieux

EXCL 1 (*Brit*: also **steady on!**) (= *be careful*) doucement ! ; (= *calm down*) du calme ! ; → **ready**

2 (*Naut*) **~ as she goes!, keep her ~!** comme ça droit !

ADV †* ◆ **they've been going ~ for six months** ils sortent ensemble depuis six mois ◆ **to go ~ with sb** sortir avec qn

N * (*male*) copain * *m* ; (*female*) copine * *f*

VT [+ *wobbling object*] stabiliser ; [+ *chair, table*] (*with hand*) maintenir ; (= *wedge*) caler ; [+ *nervous person, horse*] calmer ◆ **to ~ o.s.** se remettre d'aplomb ◆ **to ~ one's nerves** se calmer (les nerfs) ◆ **to have a ~ing effect on sb** (= *make less nervous*) calmer qn ; (= *make less wild*) assagir qn

VI (also **steady up**) (= *regain balance*) se remettre d'aplomb ; (= *grow less nervous*) se calmer ; (= *grow less wild*) se ranger, s'assagir ; [*prices, market*] se stabiliser

COMP **steady-state theory** N (*Phys*) théorie *f* de la création continue

steak /steɪk/ N (= *beef*) bifteck *m*, steak *m* ; (*of other meat*) tranche *f* ; (*of fish*) tranche *f*, darne *f* ; → **fillet, frying, rumpsteak, stew**

COMP **steak and kidney pie** N tourte *f* à la viande de bœuf et aux rognons

steak and kidney pudding N pudding *m* à la viande de bœuf et aux rognons

steak house N ⇒ **steakhouse**

steak knife N (pl **steak knives**) couteau *m* à viande *or* à steak

steakhouse /ˈsteɪkhaʊs/ N ≈ grill-room *m*

steal /stiːl/ (pret **stole**, ptp **stolen**) VT [+ *object, property*] voler, dérober (*liter*) (*from sb* à qn) ; (*fig*) [+ *kiss*] voler (*from sb* à qn) ◆ **he stole a book from the library** il a volé un livre à la bibliothèque ◆ **he stole money from the till/drawer** *etc* il a volé de l'argent dans la caisse/dans le tiroir *etc* ◆ **to ~ the credit for sth** s'attribuer tout le mérite de qch ◆ **to ~ a glance at …** jeter un coup d'œil furtif à …, lancer un regard furtif à … ◆ **to ~ a march on sb*** gagner *or* prendre qn de vitesse ◆ **to ~ the show from sb** (*Theat, also fig*) ravir la vedette à qn ◆ **he stole the show** il n'y en a eu que pour lui, on n'a eu d'yeux que pour lui ◆ **to ~ sb's thunder** voler la vedette à qn ◆ **Labour have stolen the Tories' clothes** (*Brit*) les travaillistes se sont appropriés les idées des conservateurs

VI 1 voler ◆ **thou shalt not ~** (*Bible*) tu ne voleras point

2 (= *move silently*) **to ~ up/down/out** *etc* monter/descendre/sortir *etc* furtivement ◆ **he stole into the room** il s'est glissé *or* faufilé dans la pièce ◆ **a smile stole across her lips** un sourire erra sur ses lèvres ◆ **a tear stole down her cheek** une larme furtive glissa sur sa joue ◆ **the light was ~ing through the shutters** la lumière filtrait à travers les volets

N (*US* = *theft*) vol *m* ◆ **it's a ~** * (*fig* = *bargain*) c'est une bonne affaire

► **steal away** VI s'esquiver

VT SEP [+ *child etc*] prendre, enlever (*from sb* à qn) ; [+ *sb's husband*] voler, prendre (*from sb* à qn) ; [+ *sb's affections*] détourner

stealing /ˈstiːlɪŋ/ N (NonC) vol *m* ◆ **~ is wrong** c'est mal de voler

stealth /stelθ/ N ◆ **by ~** furtivement, à la dérobée

COMP **Stealth bomber** N bombardier *m* furtif

stealth tax N (*pej*) impôt *m* indirect

stealthily /ˈstelθɪlɪ/ ADV [*move, remove, exchange*] furtivement, à la dérobée ; [*creep, enter, leave*] furtivement, à pas furtifs

stealthiness /ˈstelθɪnɪs/ N caractère *m* furtif, manière *f* furtive

stealthy /ˈstelθɪ/ ADJ furtif

steam /stiːm/ N (NonC) vapeur *f* ; (= *condensation: on window etc*) buée *f* ◆ **it works by ~** ça marche *or* fonctionne à la vapeur ◆ **full ~ ahead!** (*Naut*) en avant toute ! ◆ **the building project is going full ~ ahead** le projet de construction va de l'avant à plein régime ◆ **to get up** *or* **pick up ~** [*train, ship*] prendre de la vitesse ; [*driver etc*] faire monter la pression ; (*fig*) [*worker, programme, project*] démarrer vraiment * (*fig*) ◆ **when she gets up** *or* **picks up ~**

she can ... quand elle s'y met *or* quand elle est lancée elle peut ... ◆ **to run out of ~** *[speaker, worker]* s'essouffler ; *[programme, project]* tourner court, s'essouffler ◆ **the strike is running out of ~** le mouvement de grève commence à s'essouffler ◆ **under one's own ~** par ses propres moyens ◆ **to let off** *or* **blow off ~** * *(= energy)* se défouler * ; *(= anger)* épancher sa bile

VT *(for cleaning, disinfecting purposes)* passer à la vapeur ; *(Culin)* cuire à la vapeur ◆ **to ~ open an envelope** décacheter une enveloppe à la vapeur ◆ **to ~ off a stamp** décoller un timbre à la vapeur

VI 1 *[kettle, liquid, horse, wet clothes]* fumer

2 ◆ **to ~ along/away** *etc [steamship, train]* avancer/partir *etc* ; (* *fig*) *[person, car]* avancer/partir *etc* à toute vapeur * ◆ **they were ~ing along at 12 knots** ils filaient 12 nœuds ◆ **the ship ~ed up the river** le vapeur remontait la rivière ◆ **the train ~ed out of the station** le train est sorti de la gare dans un nuage de fumée ◆ **to ~ ahead** *[steamship]* avancer ; * *[person]* avancer à toute vapeur * ; (* *fig = make great progress*) faire des progrès à pas de géant

COMP *[boiler, iron, turbine]* à vapeur ; *[bath]* de vapeur

steam-driven ADJ à vapeur

steamed pudding N pudding *m* cuit à la vapeur

steamed up * ADJ *(fig)* ◆ **to get ~ed up** se mettre dans tous ses états *(about sth* à propos de qch) ◆ **don't get so ~ed up about it!** ne te mets pas dans tous tes états pour ça !

steam engine N *(Rail)* locomotive *f* à vapeur

steam heat N chaleur *f* fournie par la vapeur

steam organ N orgue *m* à vapeur

steam room N hammam *m*

steam shovel N *(US)* excavateur *m*

► **steam up** VI *[window, mirror]* se couvrir de buée ; *[bathroom]* se remplir de buée

VT SEP embuer

ADJ ◆ **steamed up** * → **steam**

steamboat /'stiːmbəʊt/ N (bateau *m* à) vapeur *m*

steamer /'stiːməʳ/ N 1 *(Naut)* (bateau *m* à) vapeur *m* ; *(= liner)* paquebot *m* 2 *(= saucepan)* cuit-vapeur *m inv*

steaming /'stiːmɪŋ/ ADJ 1 (also **steaming hot**) fumant 2 (* *= angry*) *[person]* fumasse * ; *[letter]* furibond * 3 *(Scot* * *= drunk)* bourré *

steamroller /'stiːmrəʊləʳ/ N rouleau *m* compresseur VT *(fig)* *[+ opposition etc]* écraser, briser ; *[+ obstacles]* aplanir ◆ **to ~ a bill through Parliament** *faire approuver un projet de loi au Parlement sans tenir compte de l'opposition* COMP

steamroller tactics NPL technique *f* du rouleau compresseur

steamship /'stiːmʃɪp/ N paquebot *m* COMP

steamship company N ligne *f* de paquebots

steamy /'stiːmɪ/ ADJ 1 *(= humid) [room, city, air]* plein de vapeur ; *[window]* embué 2 (* *= erotic*) *[affair, film, novel]* torride

steed /stiːd/ N *(liter)* coursier *m (liter)*

steel /stiːl/ N 1 *(NonC)* acier *m* ◆ **to be made of ~** *(fig)* avoir une volonté de fer ◆ **nerves of ~** nerfs *mpl* d'acier ; → **stainless**

2 *(= sharpener)* aiguisoir *m*, fusil *m* ; *(for striking sparks)* briquet † *m*, fusil † *m* ; *(liter = sword, dagger)* fer *m* ; → **cold**

VT *(fig)* ◆ **to ~ o.s.** *or* **one's heart to do sth** s'armer de courage pour faire qch ◆ **to ~ o.s. against sth** se cuirasser contre qch

COMP *(= made of steel) [knife, tool]* en acier ; *[manufacture]* de l'acier ; *(gen, also of steel production)* sidérurgique ; *[dispute, strike]* des sidérurgistes, des (ouvriers) métallurgistes ; *(Stock Exchange) [shares, prices]* de l'acier

steel band N steel band *m*

steel-clad ADJ bardé de fer

steel engraving N gravure *f* sur acier

steel grey ADJ gris acier *inv*, gris métallisé *inv*

steel guitar N steel-guitar *f*, guitare *f* à cordes métalliques

steel helmet N casque *m*

steel industry N sidérurgie *f*, industrie *f* sidérurgique

steel maker, steel manufacturer N métallurgiste *m*, aciériste *m*

steel mill N ⇒ **steelworks**

steel-plated ADJ revêtu d'acier

steel tape N *(Carpentry etc)* mètre *m* à ruban métallique

steel wool N *(NonC, for floors)* paille *f* de fer ; *(for saucepans)* tampon *m* métallique

steelworker /'stiːlˌwɜːkəʳ/ N (ouvrier *m*, -ière *f*) sidérurgiste *mf*, (ouvrier *m*, -ière *f*) métallurgiste *mf*

steelworks /'stiːlwɜːks/ N aciérie *f*

steely /'stiːlɪ/ ADJ 1 *[sky] (= blue)* bleu acier *inv* ; *(= grey)* gris acier *inv* ; *[colour]* acier *inv* 2 *(= grim) [person, smile]* dur et menaçant ; *[look, stare]* d'acier ; *[determination]* inébranlable ; *[refusal, attitude]* inébranlable, inflexible ◆ **his look of ~ concentration** son regard d'intense concentration 3 *(= like steel) [material, substance]* dur comme l'acier ; *[appearance]* de l'acier

COMP **steely blue** ADJ bleu acier *inv*

steely-eyed ADJ au regard d'acier

steely grey ADJ gris acier *inv*, gris métallisé *inv*

steely-hearted ADJ au cœur de pierre

steelyard /'stiːljɑːd/ N balance *f* romaine

steep[1] /stiːp/ ADJ 1 *[slope, incline, road, street, stairs]* raide ; *[hill, bank]* escarpé ; *[cliff]* abrupt ; *[roof]* pentu ; *[descent]* rapide ; *[ascent, climb]* rude ; *[dive]* à la verticale ◆ **a ~ path** un raidillon, un sentier raide 2 *(= great) [rise, fall]* fort 3 (* *= expensive*) *[price, fees]* élevé, raide * ; *[bill]* salé * 4 *(Brit* * *= unreasonable)* ◆ **that's** *or* **it's a bit ~** c'est un peu raide * *or* fort * ◆ **it's a bit ~ to expect us to do that!** c'est un peu raide * *or* fort * de s'attendre à ce qu'on fasse ça !

steep[2] /stiːp/ VT *(in water, dye etc)* tremper *(in* dans) ; *[+ washing]* faire tremper, mettre à tremper ; *(Culin)* macérer, mariner *(in* dans) ◆ **~ed in ignorance/vice** croupissant dans l'ignorance/le vice ◆ **~ed in prejudice** imbu de préjugés ◆ **a town ~ed in history** une ville imprégnée d'histoire ◆ **a scholar ~ed in the classics** un érudit imprégné des auteurs classiques VI *[clothes etc]* tremper ; *(Culin)* macérer, mariner

steepen /'stiːpən/ VI *(lit) [slope, ground]* devenir plus raide ; *(fig) [slump, decline]* s'accentuer

steeple /'stiːpl/ N clocher *m*, flèche *f*

steeplechase /'stiːpltʃeɪs/ N steeple(-chase) *m*

steeplechaser /'stiːplˌtʃeɪsəʳ/ N *(= horse)* coureur *m*, -euse *f* de steeple

steeplechasing /'stiːplˌtʃeɪsɪŋ/ N steeple (-chase) *m*

steeplejack /'stiːpldʒæk/ N réparateur *m* de hautes cheminées et de clochers

steeply /'stiːplɪ/ ADV 1 *(= precipitously) [rise, climb, fall, drop]* en pente raide ◆ **to bank ~** faire un virage serré sur l'aile ◆ **the lawn slopes ~ down to the river** la pelouse descend en pente raide vers la rivière ◆ **~ sloping roof/land** toit *m*/terrain *m* en pente raide ◆ **~ terraced vineyards** des vignobles en terrasses escarpées 2 *(= greatly)* ◆ **to rise/fall ~** *[prices, costs, profits]* monter en flèche/baisser fortement

steepness /'stiːpnɪs/ N *[of road etc]* pente *f* (raide) ; *[of slope]* abrupt *m*

steer[1] /stɪəʳ/ N *(= ox)* bœuf *m* ; *(esp US: castrated)* bouvillon *m*

steer[2] /stɪəʳ/ VT 1 *(= handle controls of) [+ ship]* gouverner ; *[+ boat]* barrer

2 *(= move, direct) [+ ship, car]* diriger *(towards* vers) ; *(fig) [+ person]* guider ; *[+ conversation]* diriger ◆ **to ~ a** *or* **one's course to** *(Naut)* faire route vers *or* sur ◆ **to ~ one's way through a crowd** se frayer un passage à travers une foule ◆ **he ~ed her over to the bar** il l'a guidée vers le bar ◆ **he ~ed me into a good job** c'est lui qui m'a permis de trouver un bon boulot *

VI *(Naut)* tenir le gouvernail *or* la barre, gouverner ◆ **to ~ by the stars** se guider sur les étoiles ◆ **he ~ed for the lighthouse** il a fait route vers *or* il a mis le cap sur le phare ◆ **~ due north!** cap au nord ! ◆ **this car/boat doesn't ~ well** cette voiture n'a pas une bonne direction/ce bateau gouverne mal ◆ **to ~ clear of sth** *(in boat)* passer au large de qch ; *(in car)* passer à l'écart de qch ◆ **to ~ clear of sb/sth** *(fig)* éviter qn/qch

N *(US* * *= tip)* tuyau * *m*, conseil *m* ◆ **a bum ~** un tuyau qui ne vaut rien

steerage /'stɪərɪdʒ/ *(Naut)* N entrepont *m* ADV dans l'entrepont, en troisième classe

steerageway /'stɪərɪdʒweɪ/ N erre *f*

steering /'stɪərɪŋ/ N *(NonC) [of car] (= action)* conduite *f* ; *(= mechanism)* direction *f* ; *[of boat]* conduite *f*, pilotage *m*

COMP **steering arm** N *[of car]* bras *m* de direction

steering column N *[of car]* colonne *f* de direction

steering committee N comité *m* de pilotage

steering gear N *[of car]* boîte *f* de direction ; *[of boat]* servomoteur *m* de barre *or* de gouvernail ; *[of plane]* direction *f*

steering lock N *(when driving)* rayon *m* de braquage ; *(= anti-theft device)* antivol *m* de direction

steering system N *[of car]* direction *f*

steering wheel N *[of car]* volant *m* ; *[of boat]* barre *f* à roue

steersman /'stɪəzmən/ N (pl **-men**) *(Naut)* timonier *m*, homme *m* de barre

stegosaurus /ˌstegəˈsɔːrəs/ N stégosaure *m*

stellar /'steləʳ/ ADJ 1 *(Astron)* stellaire 2 *(Cine, Theat etc) [person, cast]* brillant ; *[talent, quality, reputation]* sublime 3 *(= superb) [profits, education]* excellent

stem[1] /stem/ VT 1 *(= stop) [+ flow]* contenir, endiguer ; *[+ flood, river]* contenir, endiguer ; *[+ course of disease]* enrayer, juguler ; *[+ attack]* juguler, stopper ◆ **to ~ the course of events** endiguer la marche des événements ◆ **to ~ the tide** *or* **flow of ...** *(fig)* endiguer (le flot de) ... 2 *[+ ski]* ramener *or* écarter en chasse-neige

COMP **stem parallel** N *(Ski)* stem(m) *m* parallèle

stem turn N *(Ski)* (virage *m* en) stem(m) *m*

stem[2] /stem/ LANGUAGE IN USE 17.1 N 1 *[of flower, plant]* tige *f* ; *[of tree]* tronc *m* ; *[of fruit, leaf]* queue *f* ; *[of glass]* pied *m* ; *[of tobacco pipe]* tuyau *m* ; *[of feather]* tige *f*, tuyau *m* ; *(in handwriting, Printing: of letter)* hampe *f* ; *(Mus: of note)* queue *f* ; *(Ling: of word)* radical *m* 2 *(Naut) (= timber)* étrave *f* ; *(= part of ship)* avant *m*, proue *f* ◆ **from ~ to stern** de bout en bout VI ◆ **to ~ from ...** provenir de ..., découler de ..., dériver de ...

COMP **stem cell** N *(Bio)* cellule *f* souche ◆ **~ cell research** recherche *f* sur les cellules souches

stem ginger N gingembre *m* confit

stem-winder N montre *f* à remontoir

-stemmed /stemd/ ADJ *(in compounds)* ◆ **short-/thick-stemmed** *[pipe]* à tuyau court/épais ◆ **thin-/green-stemmed** *[plant]* à tige fine/verte ◆ **slim-/thick-stemmed** *[glass]* au pied fin/épais

stench /stentʃ/ N puanteur *f*, odeur *f* nauséabonde *or* fétide

stencil /'stensl/ N *(of metal, cardboard)* pochoir *m* ; *(of paper)* poncif *m* ; *(in typing etc)* stencil *m* ; *(= decoration)* peinture *f or* décoration *f* au pochoir ◆ **to cut a ~** *(Typing)* préparer un stencil VT *[+ lettering, name]* peindre *or* marquer au pochoir ; *(in typing etc) [+ document]* polycopier, tirer au stencil

Sten gun /'stengʌn/ **N** *(Brit Hist)* mitraillette *f* légère

steno* /'stenəʊ/ **N** *(US)* ⇒ **stenographer, stenography**

stenographer /ste'nɒgrəfə^r/ **N** sténographe *mf*

stenography /ste'nɒgrəfi/ **N** *(US)* sténographie *f*

stentorian /sten'tɔːrɪən/ **ADJ** *(liter)* *[voice, tones]* de stentor ; *[shout]* puissant

step /step/ **N** 1 *(= movement, sound, track)* pas *m* ◆ **to take a ~ back/forward** faire un pas en arrière/en avant ◆ **with slow ~s** à pas lents ◆ **at every ~** *(lit, fig)* à chaque pas ◆ **~ by ~** *(lit)* pas à pas ; *(fig)* petit à petit ; see also **comp** ◆ **he didn't move a ~** il n'a pas bougé d'un pas ◆ **we heard ~s in the lounge** nous avons entendu des pas *or* un bruit de pas dans le salon ◆ **we followed his ~s in the snow** nous avons suivi (la trace de) ses pas dans la neige ◆ **to follow in sb's ~s** *(fig)* marcher sur les pas *or* suivre les brisées de qn ◆ **it's a good ~*** *or* **quite a ~* to the village** *(= distance)* il y a un bon bout de chemin *or* ça fait une bonne trotte* d'ici au village ◆ **every ~ of the way** *[complain etc]* continuellement, constamment ; *[argue, object]* point par point ◆ **I'll fight this decision every ~ of the way** je combattrai cette décision jusqu'au bout ◆ **to be** *or* **stay one ~ ahead of sb** avoir une longueur d'avance sur qn ; → **retrace, watch²**

2 *(fig)* pas *m* *(towards* vers) ; *(= measure)* disposition *f*, mesure *f* ◆ **it is a great ~ for the nation to take** c'est pour la nation un grand pas à faire *or* à franchir ◆ **the first ~s in one's career** les premiers pas *or* les débuts *mpl* de sa carrière ◆ **it's a ~ up in his career** c'est une promotion pour lui ◆ **to take ~s (to do sth)** prendre des dispositions *or* des mesures (pour faire qch) ◆ **to take legal ~s** avoir recours à la justice, engager des poursuites *(to do sth* pour faire qch) ◆ **what's the next ~?** qu'est-ce qu'il faut faire maintenant *or* ensuite ? ◆ **the first ~ is to decide ...** la première chose à faire est de décider ... ; → **false**

3 *(NonC: in marching, dancing)* pas *m* ◆ **a waltz ~** un pas de valse ◆ **to keep ~** *(in marching)* marcher au pas ; *(in dance)* danser en mesure ◆ **to keep ~ with sb** *(lit, fig)* ne pas se laisser distancer par qn ◆ **to break ~** *(Mil)* rompre le pas

♦ **in(to) step** ◆ **to keep in ~** *(marching)* marcher au pas ; *(dancing)* danser en mesure ◆ **to fall into ~** *(marching)* se mettre au pas ◆ **to be in ~ with** *(fig)* *[+ person, values]* être en phase avec ; *[+ regulations]* être conforme à ◆ **they're in ~ with each other** ils sont en phase ◆ **Britain's economy has fallen into ~ with the rest of Europe** l'économie de la Grande-Bretagne est maintenant en phase avec celle du reste de l'Europe

♦ **out of step** ◆ **to get out of ~** *(marching)* rompre le pas ◆ **to be/march** *etc* **out of ~** ne pas être/marcher *etc* au pas ◆ **to be out of ~ with** *(fig)* *[+ person]* être déphasé *or* en déphasage par rapport à ; *[+ regulations]* ne pas être conforme à ◆ **the unions and their leaders are out of ~** il y a déphasage entre les syndicats et leurs dirigeants ◆ **the country is out of ~ with the rest of Europe** le pays est déphasé *or* en déphasage par rapport au reste de l'Europe

4 *(= stair)* marche *f* *(also Climbing)* ; *(= doorstep)* pas *m* de la porte, seuil *m* ; *(on bus etc)* marchepied *m* ◆ **(flight of) ~s** *(indoors)* escalier *m* ; *(outdoors)* perron *m*, escalier *m* ◆ **(pair of) ~s** *(Brit)* escabeau *m* ◆ **mind the ~** attention à la marche

5 (also **step aerobics**) step *m*

VT 1 *(= place at intervals)* échelonner

2 *(Naut)* *[+ mast]* arborer, mettre dans son emplanture

VI ◆ **~ this way** venez par ici ◆ **to ~ off sth** descendre de qch, quitter qch ◆ **he ~ped into the car/onto the pavement** il est monté dans la voiture/sur le trottoir ◆ **he ~ped into his slippers/trousers** il a mis ses pantoufles/son pantalon ◆ **to ~ into sb's boots** *(Brit)* succéder à qn ◆ **to ~ on sth** marcher sur qch ◆ **to ~ on the brakes** donner un coup de frein ◆ **to ~ on the gas*** *(US)* appuyer sur le champignon* ◆ **~ on it!*** dépêche-toi !, grouille-toi !* ◆ **to ~ out of line** *(gen)* sortir des rangs ; *(morally)* s'écarter du droit chemin ◆ **to ~ over sth** enjamber qch ; → **shoe**

COMP **step aerobics** **N** *(NonC: Sport)* step *m*

step-by-step **ADJ** *[instructions]* point par point

step change **N** changement *m* majeur *or* radical

step-parent **N** beau-père *m*/belle-mère *f* ◆ **~-parents** beaux-parents *mpl*

stepped-up **ADJ** *[campaign, efforts]* intensifié ; *[production, sales]* augmenté, accru

stepping stone **N** *(lit)* pierre *f* de gué ; *(fig)* marchepied *m*

► **step aside** **VI** *(lit)* faire un pas de côté ; *(= give up position)* s'effacer

► **step back** **VI** *(lit)* faire un pas en arrière, reculer ◆ **we ~ped back into Shakespeare's time** nous nous sommes retrouvés à l'époque de Shakespeare

► **step down** **VI** *(lit)* descendre *(from* de) ; *(fig)* se retirer, se désister *(in favour of sb* en faveur de qn)

► **step forward** **VI** faire un pas en avant ; *(= show o.s., make o.s. known)* s'avancer, se faire connaître ; *(= volunteer)* se présenter

► **step in** **VI** entrer ; *(fig)* intervenir, s'interposer

► **step inside** **VI** entrer

► **step out** **VI** *(= go outside)* sortir ; *(= hurry)* allonger le pas ; *(US * fig)* faire la bombe*

VT SEP *(= measure)* *[+ distance]* mesurer en comptant les pas

► **step up** **VI** ◆ **to step up to sb/sth** s'approcher de qn/qch

VT SEP *[+ production, sales]* augmenter, accroître ; *[+ campaign]* intensifier ; *[+ attempts, efforts]* intensifier, multiplier ; *(Elec)* *[+ current]* augmenter

ADJ ◆ **stepped-up** → **step**

stepbrother /'step,brʌðə^r/ **N** demi-frère *m*

stepchild /'steptʃaɪld/ **N** beau-fils *m*, belle-fille *f*

stepchildren /'step,tʃɪldrən/ **NPL** beaux-enfants *mpl*

stepdaughter /'step,dɔːtə^r/ **N** belle-fille *f*

stepfather /'step,fɑːðə^r/ **N** beau-père *m*

Stephen /'stiːvn/ **N** Étienne *m*, Stéphane *m*

stepladder /'step,lædə^r/ **N** escabeau *m*

stepmother /'step,mʌðə^r/ **N** belle-mère *f*

steppe /step/ **N** steppe *f*

Step Reebok ® /,step'riːbɒk/ **N** step *m*

stepsister /'step,sɪstə^r/ **N** demi-sœur *f*

stepson /'stepsʌn/ **N** beau-fils *m*

stereo /'stɪərɪəʊ/ **N** 1 (abbrev of **stereophonic**) *(= system)* stéréo *f*, stéréophonie *f* ; *(= record player/radio etc)* chaîne *f*/radio *f etc* stéréophonique *or* stéréo *inv* ; *(= record/tape etc)* disque *m*/bande *f* magnétique *etc* stéréophonique *or* stéréo ◆ **recorded in ~** enregistré en stéréo(phonie) 2 abbrev of **stereoscope, stereotype** *etc*

COMP *[record player, cassette recorder, tape etc]* stéréophonique, stéréo *inv* ; *[broadcast, recording]* en stéréophonie

stereo effect **N** effet *m* stéréo(phonique)

stereo sound **N** son *m* stéréo

stereo system **N** chaîne *f* hi-fi

stereo... /'stɪərɪəʊ/ **PREF** stéréo...

stereochemistry /,stɪərɪə'kemɪstrɪ/ **N** stéréochimie *f*

stereogram /'stɪərɪəgræm/, **stereograph** /'stɪərɪəgræf/ **N** stéréogramme *m*

stereophonic /,stɪərɪə'fɒnɪk/ **ADJ** stéréophonique

stereoscope /'stɪərɪəskəʊp/ **N** stéréoscope *m*

stereoscopic /,stɪərɪəs'kɒpɪk/ **ADJ** stéréoscopique

stereoscopy /,stɪərɪ'ɒskəpɪ/ **N** stéréoscopie *f*

stereotype /'stɪərɪətaɪp/ **N** 1 *(fig)* stéréotype *m* 2 *(Typ)* cliché *m* ; *(= process)* clichage *m* **VT** 1 *(fig)* stéréotyper 2 *(Printing)* clicher

stereotypical /,stɪərɪə'tɪpɪkl/ **ADJ** stéréotypé

stereovision /,stɪərɪə'vɪʒən/ **N** vision *f* stéréoscopique

sterile /'steraɪl/ **ADJ** *(all senses)* stérile

sterility /ste'rɪlɪtɪ/ **N** stérilité *f*

sterilization /,sterɪlaɪ'zeɪʃən/ **N** stérilisation *f*

sterilize /'sterɪlaɪz/ **VT** stériliser

sterling /'stɜːlɪŋ/ **N** *(NonC)* 1 *(Econ)* livres *fpl* sterling *inv* 2 (also **sterling silver**) argent *m* fin *or* de bon aloi **ADJ** 1 *(Metal)* *[gold, silver]* fin 2 (also **sterling silver**) *[bracelet]* d'argent fin *or* de bon aloi 3 *(esp Brit = excellent)* *[qualities, work, service, efforts]* remarquable ; *[advice]* excellent ◆ **a man of ~ worth** un homme de très grande valeur 4 *(Fin)* ◆ **pound ~** livre *f* sterling *inv*

COMP **the sterling area, the sterling bloc** **N** la zone sterling

stern¹ /stɜːn/ **N** *(Naut)* arrière *m*, poupe *f* ; * *[of horse etc]* croupe *f* ; * *[of person]* derrière *m*, postérieur* *m* ◆ **~ foremost** *(Naut)* par l'arrière, en marche arrière ; → **stem²**

stern² /stɜːn/ **ADJ** *[person, look, measure, rebuke, test]* sévère ; *[task]* rude ; *[opposition, resistance]* farouche ; *[warning]* sévère, sérieux ◆ **to be made of ~er stuff** être d'une autre trempe

sterna /'stɜːnə/ **NPL** of **sternum**

sternly /'stɜːnlɪ/ **ADV** 1 *(= severely)* *[say, rebuke]* sévèrement ; *[look at]* d'un air sévère ; *[warn]* sur un ton comminatoire ◆ **to deal ~ with sb/sth** se montrer sévère à l'égard de qn/qch ◆ **a ~ worded statement** une déclaration au ton comminatoire ◆ **a ~ factual account** un récit rigoureux basé sur les faits 2 *(= firmly)* *[forbid]* strictement ; *[oppose]* farouchement ; *[resist]* avec opiniâtreté

sternness /'stɜːnnɪs/ **N** *[of person, look, speech, measure, reprimand, test]* sévérité *f* ; *[of task]* difficulté *f* ; *[of opposition, resistance]* fermeté *f*

Sterno ® /'stɜːnəʊ/ *(US)* **N** ≈ méta ® *m* **COMP** **Sterno can** **N** *récipient pour tablette de méta*

sternum /'stɜːnəm/ **N** (pl **sternums** *or* **sterna**) sternum *m*

steroid /'stɪərɔɪd/ **N** stéroïde *m*

stertorous /'stɜːtərəs/ **ADJ** *(frm)* *[breathing]* stertoreux

stet /stet/ **IMPERS VB** *(Typ)* bon, à maintenir **VT** maintenir

stethoscope /'steθəskəʊp/ **N** stéthoscope *m*

Stetson ® /'stetsən/ **N** Stetson ® *m*

stevedore /'stiːvɪdɔː^r/ **N** arrimeur *m*, débardeur *m*, docker *m*

Steven /'stiːvn/ **N** Étienne *m*

stew /stjuː/ **N** *(meat)* ragoût *m* ; *(rabbit, hare)* civet *m* ◆ **to be/get in a ~*** *(= trouble)* être/se mettre dans le pétrin* ; *(= worry)* être/se mettre dans tous ses états ; → **Irish** **VT** *[+ meat]* (faire) cuire en ragoût, faire en daube ; *[+ rabbit, hare]* cuire en civet ; *[+ fruit]* faire cuire ◆ **~ed fruit** *(gen)* fruits *mpl* cuits ◆ **~ed apples/rhubarb** *etc* *(mushy)* compote *f* de pommes/de rhubarbe *etc* ◆ **~ed tea** thé *m* trop infusé ◆ **to be ~ed*** *(fig = drunk)* être pinté* **VI** *[meat]* cuire

en ragoût *or* à l'étouffée ; *[fruit]* cuire ; *[tea]* devenir trop infusé ◆ **to let sb ~ in his own juice** laisser qn cuire *or* mijoter dans son jus
COMP **stewing steak** *(Brit)*, **stew meat** *(US)* N bœuf *m* à braiser

steward /ˈstjuːəd/ N *(on ship, plane)* steward *m* ; *(on estate etc)* intendant *m*, régisseur *m* ; *(in club, college)* intendant *m*, économe *m* ; *(at meeting)* membre *m* du service d'ordre ; *(at dance)* organisateur *m* ; *(= doorman)* videur *m* ◆ **the ~s** *(at meeting etc)* le service d'ordre ; → **shop**

stewardess /ˈstjuədes/ N hôtesse *f*

stewardship /ˈstjuədʃɪp/ N *(= duties)* intendance *f* ◆ **under his ~** *(in club, college)* quand il était intendant *or* économe ; *(on estate)* quand il était intendant *or* régisseur

stewpan /ˈstjuːpæn/, **stewpot** /ˈstjuːpɒt/ N cocotte *f*

stg *(Fin)* abbrev of **sterling**

STI /ˌestiːˈaɪ/ N (abbrev of **sexually transmitted infection**) IST *f*

stick /stɪk/
vb : pret, ptp **stuck**

1 NOUN	4 INTRANSITIVE VERB
2 PLURAL NOUN	5 COMPOUNDS
3 TRANSITIVE VERB	6 PHRASAL VERBS

1 - NOUN

1 = length of wood bâton *m* ; *(= twig)* brindille *f* ; *(= walking stick)* canne *f* ; *(= stake for peas, flowers etc)* bâton *m*, tuteur *m* ; *(taller)* rame *f* ; *(for lollipop etc)* bâton *m* ; *(Mil, Mus)* baguette *f* ; *(= joystick)* manche *m* à balai ; *(Hockey, Lacrosse)* crosse *f* ; *(Ice Hockey)* stick *m* ◆ **a few ~s of furniture** quelques pauvres meubles ◆ **every ~ of furniture** chaque meuble ◆ **to carry a big ~** *(fig)* avoir le bras long ◆ **to use** *or* **wield the big ~** manier la trique ; *(Pol)* faire de l'autoritarisme ◆ **the policy of the big ~** la politique du bâton ◆ **to find a ~ to beat sb with** *(fig)* profiter de l'occasion pour s'en prendre à qn ◆ **to get (hold of) the wrong end of the ~** mal comprendre ◆ **to get on the ~**‡ *(fig US)* s'y coller*, s'y mettre

2 of charcoal, sealing wax morceau *m* ; *[of chalk, candy]* morceau *m*, bâton *m* ; *[of dynamite]* bâton *m* ; *[of chewing gum]* tablette *f* ; *[of celery]* branche *f* ; *[of rhubarb]* tige *f* ◆ **a ~ of bombs** un chapelet de bombes ◆ **a ~ of parachutists** un groupe de saut

3 esp Brit * = criticism **to give sb a lot of ~** éreinter qn *(for, over* à propos de) ◆ **to take** *or* **get a lot of ~** se faire éreinter *(for, over* à propos de)

4 Brit * = person **he is a dull** *or* **dry old ~** il est rasoir* ◆ **he's a funny old ~** c'est un numéro*

5 Drugs * stick *m*

2 - PLURAL NOUN

sticks

1 = firewood petit bois *m*

2 Sport = hurdles haies *fpl*

3 pej = backwoods ◆ **(out) in the ~s** * en pleine cambrousse*

4 ◆ **one summer they upped ~s and left for Canada** * un été, ils ont tout plaqué* et sont partis au Canada

3 - TRANSITIVE VERB

1 = thrust, stab *[+ pin, needle, fork]* piquer, planter *(into* dans) ; *[+ knife, dagger, bayonet]* plonger, planter *(into* dans) ; *[+ spade, rod]* planter, enfoncer *(into* dans) ◆ **to ~ a pin through sth** transpercer qch avec une épingle ◆ **I stuck the needle into my finger** je me suis piqué le doigt avec l'aiguille ◆ **we found this place by ~ing a pin in the map** nous avons trouvé ce coin en plantant une épingle au hasard sur la carte ◆ **a board stuck with drawing pins/nails** un panneau couvert de punaises/hérissé de clous ◆ **to ~ a pig** égorger un cochon ◆ **to squeal like a stuck pig** brailler comme un cochon qu'on égorge

2 * = put mettre ; *(inside sth)* mettre, fourrer* ◆ **he stuck it on the shelf/under the table** il l'a mis sur l'étagère/sous la table ◆ **to ~ sth into a drawer** mettre *or* fourrer* qch dans un tiroir ◆ **to ~ one's hands in one's pockets** mettre *or* fourrer* ses mains dans ses poches ◆ **he stuck his finger into the hole** il a mis *or* fourré* son doigt dans le trou ◆ **he stuck the lid on the box** il a mis le couvercle sur la boîte ◆ **he stuck his head through the window/round the door** il a passé la tête par la fenêtre/dans l'embrasure de la porte ◆ **to ~ one's hat on one's head** mettre son chapeau sur sa tête ◆ **I'll have to ~ a button on that shirt** il faudra que je mette un bouton à cette chemise ◆ **he had stuck £30 on the price** il avait majoré le prix de 30 livres ◆ **to ~ an advertisement in the paper** mettre *or* passer une annonce dans le journal ◆ **they stuck him on the committee** ils l'ont mis *or* collé* au comité ◆ **you know where you can ~ that!**‡, **~ it up your ass!***‡ tu sais où tu peux te le mettre ?‡ ◆ **she told him to ~ his job**‡ elle lui a dit d'aller se faire voir‡ avec son boulot*

3 with glue etc coller ◆ **to ~ a poster on the wall/a door** coller une affiche au mur/sur une porte ◆ **to ~ a stamp on a letter** coller un timbre sur une lettre ◆ **"stick no bills"** "défense d'afficher" ◆ **it was stuck fast** c'était bien collé *or* indécollable ◆ **he tried to ~ the murder on his brother**‡ il a essayé de mettre le meurtre sur le dos de son frère ◆ **you can't ~ that on me!**‡ vous ne pouvez pas me mettre ça sur le dos ! ◆ **he stuck me with the bill** il m'a laissé régler la note ◆ **he stuck**‡ **me (for) £10 for that old book** il m'a fait payer *or* il m'a pris 10 livres pour ce vieux bouquin*

◆ **to be stuck** *[key, lock, door, drawer, gears, valve, lid]* être coincé, être bloqué ; *[vehicle, wheels]* être coincé, être bloqué ; *(in mud)* être embourbé ; *(in sand)* être enlisé ; *[machine, lift]* être bloqué, être en panne ◆ **to be stuck in the lift** être coincé *or* bloqué dans l'ascenseur ◆ **the train was stuck at the station** le train était bloqué *or* immobilisé en gare ◆ **the car was stuck between two trucks** la voiture était bloquée *or* coincée entre deux camions ◆ **I was stuck in a corner and had to listen to him all evening** j'étais bloqué dans un coin et j'ai dû l'écouter toute la soirée ◆ **he was stuck in town all summer** il a été obligé de rester en ville tout l'été ◆ **I'm stuck at home all day** je suis cloué à la maison toute la journée ◆ **we're stuck here for the night** nous allons être obligés de passer la nuit ici ◆ **he's really stuck* on her** il est vraiment entiché d'elle ◆ **to be stuck for an answer** ne pas savoir que répondre ◆ **I'm stuck*** *(in crossword puzzle, guessing game, essay etc)* je sèche* ◆ **I'll help you if you're stuck*** je t'aiderai si tu n'y arrives pas ◆ **I'm stuck for £10*** il me manque 10 livres ◆ **he's not stuck for money*** ce n'est pas l'argent qui lui manque ◆ **I was stuck* with the job of organizing it all** je me suis retrouvé avec toute l'organisation sur les bras* *or* à devoir tout organiser ◆ **I was stuck* with the bill** c'est moi qui ai dû casquer* ◆ **I was stuck* with him all evening** je l'ai eu sur le dos *or* sur les bras toute la soirée

◆ **to get stuck** ◆ **to get stuck in the mud** s'embourber, s'enliser dans la boue ◆ **to get stuck in the sand** s'enliser dans le sable ◆ **a bone got stuck in my throat** une arête s'est mise en travers de ma gorge

4 esp Brit = tolerate *[+ sb's presence, mannerisms etc]* supporter ◆ **I can't ~ it any longer** j'en ai marre, j'en ai ras le bol‡ ◆ **I wonder how he ~s it at all** je me demande comment il peut tenir le coup ◆ **I can't ~ her** * je ne peux pas la blairer‡

4 - INTRANSITIVE VERB

1 = embed itself etc *[needle, spear]* se planter, s'enfoncer *(into* dans) ◆ **he had a knife ~ing in(to) his back** il avait un couteau planté dans le dos

2 = adhere *[glue, paste]* tenir ; *[stamp, label]* être collé, tenir *(to* à) ; *(fig) [habit, name etc]* rester ◆ **the paper stuck to the table** le papier est resté collé à la table ◆ **the eggs have stuck to the pan** les œufs ont attaché (à la poêle) ◆ **it ~s to your ribs*** *[food]* ça tient au corps *or* à l'estomac ◆ **the nickname stuck (to him)** le surnom lui est resté ◆ **to make a charge ~** prouver la culpabilité de quelqu'un

3 = remain, stay rester ◆ **to ~ close to sb** rester aux côtés de qn, ne pas quitter qn

◆ **to stick to sb/sth** ◆ **she stuck to him all through the holiday** elle ne l'a pas lâché d'une semelle pendant toutes les vacances ◆ **to ~ to sb like a limpet** *or* **a leech** se cramponner à qn ◆ **they stuck to the fox's trail** ils sont restés sur les traces du renard ◆ **to ~ to one's word** *or* **promise** tenir parole ◆ **to ~ to one's principles** rester fidèle à ses principes ◆ **to ~ to one's post** rester à son poste ◆ **to ~ to one's guns*** camper sur ses positions ◆ **he stuck to his story** il a maintenu ce qu'il avait dit ◆ **decide what you're going to say then ~ to it** décidez ce que vous allez dire et tenez-vous-y ◆ **to ~ to the facts** s'en tenir aux faits ◆ **~ to the point!** ne vous éloignez pas *or* ne sortez pas du sujet ! ◆ **to ~ to one's knitting** * *(fig)* se cantonner dans ce que l'on sait faire

◆ **to stick to/by sb** ◆ **to ~ to** *or* **by sb through thick and thin** rester fidèle à qn envers et contre tout ◆ **will you ~ by me?** est-ce que vous me soutiendrez ?

◆ **to stick to/at/in sth** ◆ **to ~ to** *or* **at a job** rester dans un emploi ◆ **I'll ~ in the job for a bit longer** pour le moment je garde ce boulot* *or* je vais rester où je suis ◆ **~ at it!** persévère !, tiens bon !

◆ **to stick with sb/sth** *[+ person]* *(= stay beside)* rester avec, ne pas quitter ; *[+ person, brand]* *(= stay loyal)* rester fidèle à ; *[+ activity, sport]* s'en tenir à ◆ **~ with him!*** ne le perdez pas de vue !

4 = get jammed etc *[wheels, vehicle]* se coincer, se bloquer ; *(= get stuck in mud)* s'embourber ; *(= get stuck in sand)* s'enliser ; *[key, lock, door, drawer, gears, valve, lid]* se coincer, se bloquer ; *[machine, lift]* se bloquer, tomber en panne ◆ **the car stuck in the mud** la voiture s'est embourbée ◆ **a bone stuck in my throat** une arête s'est mise en travers de ma gorge ◆ **that ~s in my throat** *or* **gizzard** * *(fig)* je n'arrive pas à le digérer* ◆ **the word "please" seems to ~ in her throat** on dirait qu'elle n'arrive pas à dire "s'il te plaît" ◆ **the bidding stuck at £100** les enchères se sont arrêtées à 100 livres ◆ **I got halfway through and stuck there** je suis resté coincé à mi-chemin ◆ **he stuck halfway through the second verse** il s'est arrêté *or* il a eu un trou au milieu de la deuxième strophe ◆ **it may ~ for a few weeks, but it'll sell in the end** *(house for sale)* ça risque de traîner quelques semaines, mais ça finira par se vendre ; → **fast**[1]

5 = balk reculer, regimber *(at, on* devant) ◆ **he will ~ at nothing to get what he wants** il ne recule devant rien pour obtenir ce qu'il veut ◆ **they may ~ on** *or* **at that clause** il se peut qu'ils regimbent *subj* devant cette clause

6 = extend, protrude ◆ **the nail was ~ing through the plank** le clou dépassait *or* sortait de la planche ◆ **the rod was ~ing into the next garden** la barre dépassait dans le jardin d'à côté ◆ **a narrow finger of land ~ing into enemy territory** une étroite bande de terre s'enfonçant en territoire ennemi

7 Cards **(I) ~!, I'm ~ing** (je suis) servi

5 - COMPOUNDS

stick figure N bonhomme *m*
sticking plaster N sparadrap *m*
sticking point N *(fig)* point *m* de friction
stick insect N phasme *m* ◆ **she's like a ~ insect** elle est maigre comme un clou
stick-in-the-mud * ADJ, N sclérosé(e) *m(f)*, encroûté(e) *m(f)*
stick-on ADJ adhésif
stick shift N *(US = gearstick)* levier *m* de vitesses
stick-toitiveness * N *(US)* ténacité *f*, persévérance *f*
stick-up * N braquage * *m*, hold-up *m*

6 - PHRASAL VERBS

► **stick around** * VI rester dans les parages ; *(= be kept waiting)* attendre, poireauter * ◆ **~ around for a few minutes** restez dans les parages un moment ◆ **I was tired of ~ing around doing nothing** j'en avais assez de poireauter * sans rien faire

► **stick away** VT SEP cacher, planquer‡ ◆ **he stuck it away behind the bookcase** il l'a caché *or* planqué‡ derrière la bibliothèque

► **stick back** VT SEP 1 *(= replace)* remettre *(into* dans ; *on to* sur)
2 *(with glue etc)* recoller

► **stick down** VI *[envelope etc]* (se) coller
VT SEP 1 *[+ envelope etc]* coller
2 *(* = put down)* poser, mettre ◆ **he stuck it down on the table** il l'a posé *or* mis sur la table
3 * *[+ notes, details]* noter en vitesse ◆ **he stuck down a few dates before he forgot** avant d'oublier il a rapidement noté quelques dates

► **stick in** VI * *(= make an effort)* s'y mettre sérieusement ; *(= persevere)* persévérer ◆ **you'll have to ~ in if you want to succeed** vous devrez vous y mettre sérieusement si vous voulez réussir ◆ **he stuck in at his maths** il a fait un gros effort en maths
VT SEP 1 *(= put in) [+ needle, pin, fork]* piquer ; *(forcefully)* planter ; *[+ dagger, knife, bayonet, spade]* planter, enfoncer ; *[+ photo in album etc]* coller ◆ **he stuck in a few quotations** * il a collé * quelques citations par-ci par-là ◆ **try to ~ in a word about our book** essaie de glisser un mot sur notre livre
2 *(fig)* **to get stuck in** * s'y mettre sérieusement

► **stick on** VI *[label, stamp etc]* rester collé
VT SEP 1 *[+ label]* coller ; *[+ stamp]* mettre, coller
2 *(* = put on) [+ hat, coat, lid]* mettre ◆ **~ on another CD** mets un autre CD ◆ **to ~ it on**‡ *(= put the price up)* augmenter le prix

► **stick out** VI 1 *(= protrude) [shirttails]* dépasser, sortir ; *[rod etc]* dépasser ; *[balcony etc]* faire saillie ◆ **his ears ~ out** il a les oreilles décollées ◆ **his teeth ~ out** il a les dents en avant ◆ **I could see his legs ~ing out from under the car** je voyais ses jambes qui sortaient de sous la voiture ◆ **to ~ out beyond sth** dépasser qch ◆ **it ~s out a mile** * ça crève les yeux *(that* que)
2 *(= persevere etc)* tenir (bon) ◆ **can you ~ out a little longer?** est-ce que vous pouvez tenir un peu plus longtemps ? ◆ **to ~ out for more money** tenir bon dans ses revendications pour une augmentation de salaire

VT SEP 1 *[+ rod etc]* faire dépasser ; *[+ one's arm, head]* sortir ◆ **to ~ one's chest out** bomber la poitrine ◆ **to ~ one's tongue out** tirer la langue
2 *(* = tolerate)* supporter ◆ **to ~ it out** tenir le coup

► **stick through** VI *(= protrude)* dépasser
VT SEP *[+ pen, rod, one's finger etc]* passer à travers

► **stick together** VI 1 *[labels, pages, objects]* être collés ensemble ◆ **the pieces won't ~ together** les morceaux ne veulent pas rester collés *or* se coller ensemble
2 *(= stay together)* rester ensemble ; *(fig)* se serrer les coudes ◆ **~ together till you get through the park** restez ensemble jusqu'à la sortie *or* ne vous séparez pas avant la sortie du parc ◆ **we must all ~ together!** nous devons nous serrer les coudes !
VT SEP coller (ensemble)

► **stick up** VI 1 ◆ **there was a rock sticking up out of the water** il y avait un rocher qui sortait *or* émergeait de l'eau ◆ **his head was ~ing up above the crowd** sa tête était visible au-dessus de la foule ◆ **your hair is ~ing up** vos cheveux rebiquent *
2 * ◆ **to stick up for sb** prendre la défense *or* le parti de qn ◆ **to ~ up for o.s.** défendre ses intérêts, ne pas se laisser faire ◆ **to ~ up for one's rights** défendre ses droits, ne pas se laisser faire
VT SEP 1 *[+ notice etc]* afficher
2 ◆ **to stick up one's hand** lever la main ◆ **~ 'em up!** * haut les mains ! ◆ **to ~ sb up**‡ dévaliser qn (sous la menace d'un revolver) ◆ **they stuck up the bank**‡ ils ont braqué * la banque

► **stick with** VT FUS → **stick vi 3**

stickball /ˈstɪkbɔːl/ N *(US) sorte de base-ball*

sticker /ˈstɪkəʳ/ N 1 *(= label)* autocollant *m* ◆ **a ban the bomb ~** un autocollant antinucléaire ; → **billsticker** 2 *(fig)* **he's a ~** * il n'abandonne pas facilement, il n'est pas du genre à baisser les bras * COMP **sticker price** N *(US: in car sales)* prix *m* clés en mains

stickiness /ˈstɪkɪnɪs/ N *(NonC)* 1 *(Brit)* **the label has lost its ~** *(= gumminess)* l'étiquette ne colle plus 2 *[of substance, toffee, dough, clay]* consistance *f* collante ; *[of object, paste]* consistance *f* collante *or* poisseuse ; *[of paint, syrup]* consistance *f* poisseuse ; *[of road, surface]* caractère *m* gluant 3 *(Sport) [of ground]* lourdeur *f* 4 *(= sweatiness, mugginess) [of hands, heat]* moiteur *f* ; *[of weather, climate, day]* chaleur *f* humide, moiteur *f* 5 *(* = difficulty) [of situation, problem, moment, conversation]* difficulté *f*

stickleback /ˈstɪklbæk/ N épinoche *f*

stickler /ˈstɪkləʳ/ N ◆ **to be a ~ for** *[+ discipline, obedience, correct clothing, good manners]* insister sur, tenir rigoureusement à ; *[+ etiquette]* être à cheval sur, être pointilleux sur ; *[+ grammar, spelling]* être rigoriste en matière de ; *[+ figures, facts]* être pointilleux sur le chapitre de, insister sur ◆ **to be a ~ for detail** être tatillon

stickpin /ˈstɪkpɪn/ N *(US)* épingle *f* de cravate

stickweed /ˈstɪkwiːd/ N *(US)* jacobée *f*

stickwork /ˈstɪkwɜːk/ N *(NonC)* ◆ **his ~ is very good** *[of hockey player etc]* il manie bien la crosse *or* le stick ; *[of drummer]* il manie bien les baguettes

sticky /ˈstɪkɪ/ ADJ 1 *(Brit = gummed) [label]* adhésif ◆ **to be ~ on both sides** avoir deux faces adhésives
2 *(= clinging) [substance, toffee, dough, clay]* collant ; *[object, fingers]* collant, poisseux ; *[paste]* collant, gluant ; *[syrup]* poisseux ; *[road, surface]* gluant ; *[blood, paint, oil]* visqueux ◆ **a ~ mark** une tache collante ◆ **to have ~ eyes** avoir des yeux chassieux ◆ **to have ~ fingers** *(*, euph)* être clepto(mane) *
3 *(Sport) [ground]* lourd ◆ **to find the going ~** *(Racing)* trouver le terrain lourd
4 *(= sweaty, muggy) [person, palms, heat]* moite ; *[weather, climate, day]* chaud et humide ◆ **his shirt was wet and ~ at the back** sa chemise pleine de sueur lui collait au dos ◆ **to feel hot and ~** *[person]* transpirer ◆ **it was hot and ~** l'atmosphère était moite
5 *(* = difficult) [situation, problem, moment]* délicat, difficile ; *[conversation]* pénible ◆ **to go through a ~ patch, to be** *or* **to bat on a ~ wicket** *(Brit)* être dans le pétrin * ◆ **to have a ~ time** passer un mauvais quart d'heure
6 *(Brit = violent)* ◆ **to come to** *or* **meet a ~ end** * mal finir
7 *(Brit = unhelpful)* ◆ **to be ~ about doing sth** * faire des histoires * pour faire qch
COMP **sticky-fingered** *, **sticky-handed** * ADJ *(fig = dishonest)* clepto(mane) *
sticky tape N *(Brit)* ruban *m* adhésif, scotch ® *m*

stiff /stɪf/ ADJ 1 *(= rigid, hard to move) [card, paper]* rigide ; *[material]* raide ; *[collar, brush, door, drawer, lock]* dur
2 *(Culin) [mixture, paste]* ferme ◆ **whisk the egg whites until ~** battre les blancs en neige ferme
3 *(Physiol) [person] (gen)* raide ; *(from exercise)* courbaturé ; *[limb, muscle]* raide ; *[corpse]* raide, rigide ; *[joint]* ankylosé ; *[finger]* engourdi ; *[movement]* difficile ◆ **to have a ~ neck** avoir un torticolis ; see also **comp** ◆ **to have a ~ back** avoir des courbatures dans le dos ◆ **you'll be** *or* **feel ~ tomorrow** vous aurez des courbatures demain ◆ **my back felt very ~** j'avais très mal au dos, j'avais des courbatures dans le dos ◆ **~ with cold** frigorifié * ◆ **to go ~ with terror** être paralysé par la peur ◆ **her face was ~ with tension** elle avait les traits crispés ◆ **(as) ~ as a board** *or* **as a poker** raide comme un piquet ◆ **to keep a ~ upper lip** rester impassible, garder son flegme
4 * ◆ **to be bored ~** s'ennuyer à mourir ◆ **to bore sb ~** raser * qn ◆ **to be frozen ~** être frigorifié * ◆ **to be scared ~** être mort de trouille * ◆ **to scare sb ~** ficher la trouille * à qn ◆ **worried ~** mort d'inquiétude
5 *(= severe) [penalty, sentence, fine, warning]* sévère ; *[competition]* rude ; *[challenge]* sérieux ; *[opposition, resistance]* tenace ; *[test, exam]* difficile ; *[climb]* raide, pénible
6 *(= formal) [person]* guindé ; *[smile]* contraint ; *[bow]* raide ◆ **to give a ~ bow** s'incliner avec raideur ◆ **~ and formal** *[person, manner, letter, atmosphere]* guindé
7 *(= high) [price]* élevé ; *[price rise]* fort ; *[bill]* salé *
8 *(= strong) [whisky]* bien tassé ◆ **I could use a ~ drink** j'ai besoin d'un (petit) remontant
9 *[breeze, wind]* fort
N 1 *(‡ = corpse)* macchabée‡ *m*
2 *(= fool)* **big ~**‡ gros balourd *m or* bêta *m*
3 *(US *) (= tramp)* vagabond *m* ; *(= laborer:* also **working stiff)** ouvrier *m*
COMP **stiff arm** N *(US)* ◆ **to give sb the ~ arm** écarter qn (d'un geste) du bras
stiff-arm VT *(US)* ◆ **to ~-arm sb** écarter qn (d'un geste) du bras
stiff-necked ADJ *(fig)* opiniâtre, entêté

stiffen /ˈstɪfn/ (also **stiffen up**) VT 1 *[+ card, fabric]* rendre rigide ; *(= starch)* empeser 2 *[+ dough, paste]* donner de la consistance à 3 *[+ limb]* raidir ; *[+ joint]* ankyloser 4 *(fig) [+ morale, resistance etc]* affermir VI 1 *[card, fabric]* devenir raide *or* rigide 2 *[dough, paste]* prendre de la consistance, devenir ferme 3 *[limb]* se raidir ; *[joint]* s'ankyloser ; *[door, lock]* devenir dur ◆ **he ~ed when he heard the noise** il s'est raidi quand il a entendu le bruit 4 *[breeze]* augmenter d'intensité, fraîchir 5 *(fig) [resistance]* devenir opiniâtre ; *[morale]* s'affermir

stiffener /ˈstɪfənəʳ/ N 1 *(= starch etc)* amidon *m* 2 *(= plastic strip: in collar etc)* baleine *f*

stiffening /ˈstɪfənɪŋ/ N *(= cloth)* toile *f (pour raidir les revers etc)*

stiffly /ˈstɪflɪ/ ADV *[move, say, smile, greet]* avec raideur ◆ **to stand ~** se tenir raide ◆ **~ starched** très amidonné ◆ **~ sprung** bien suspendu ◆ **~ beaten** *or* **whipped** *[egg white]* battu en neige ferme ; *[cream]* fouetté en chantilly ferme

stiffness /ˈstɪfnɪs/ N *(NonC)* 1 *(= lack of suppleness) [of person, knees, back etc]* raideur *f* ; *[of joints]* raideur *f*, ankylose *f* ◆ **~ in** *or* **of the neck** torticolis *m* ◆ **the ~ you feel after exercise** les courbatures *fpl* causées par l'exercice physique 2 *(= formality) [of manner]* raideur *f* 3 *(= rigidity) [of card, paper]* rigidité *f* ; *[of material]* raideur *f* ; *[of collar, brush]* dureté *f* 4 *(= difficulty of operating) [of door, drawer, lock]* résistance *f* 5 *(= severity) [of penalty, sentence, fine, warning]* sévérité *f* ; *[of competition]* âpreté *f* ; *[of challenge]* sérieux *m* ; *[of opposition, resistance]* ténacité *f* ; *[of climb]* caractère *m* ardu, difficulté *f* ; *[of test, exam]* difficulté *f* 6 *(Culin) [of mixture, paste]* fermeté *f* 7 *[of breeze, wind]* âpreté *f*

stifle /ˈstaɪfl/ VT *[+ person]* étouffer, suffoquer ; *[+ fire]* étouffer ; *[+ sobs]* réprimer, étouffer ; *[+ anger, smile, desire]* réprimer ◆ **to ~ a yawn/sneeze** réprimer une envie de bâiller/d'éternuer VI étouffer, suffoquer N *(Anat) [of horse etc]* grasset *m*

stifling /ˈstaɪflɪŋ/ ADJ *[heat, atmosphere]* étouffant, suffocant ; *[situation, place]* étouffant ; *[smoke, fumes]* suffocant ◆ **it's ~ today/in here** on étouffe aujourd'hui/ici

stigma /ˈstɪgmə/ N (pl **stigmas** or **stigmata** /stɪgˈmɑːtə/) stigmate *m* ◆ **the ~ta** *(Rel)* les stigmates *mpl* ◆ **there's a certain (social) ~ attached to being unemployed** le chômage est un peu considéré comme une tare (sociale) ◆ **in order to remove the ~ associated with AIDS** pour que le sida ne soit plus considéré comme une maladie honteuse

stigmatic /stɪgˈmætɪk/ ADJ, N *(Rel)* stigmatisé(e) *m(f)*

stigmatize /ˈstɪgmətaɪz/ VT *(all senses)* stigmatiser

stile /staɪl/ N 1 *(= steps over fence, wall)* échalier *m* ; *(= turnstile)* tourniquet *m (porte)* 2 *(Constr etc = upright)* montant *m*

stiletto /stɪˈletəʊ/ N (pl **stilettos** or **stilettoes**) *(= weapon)* stylet *m* ; (also **stiletto heel**) talon *m* aiguille

still¹ /stɪl/ ADV 1 *(= up to this time)* encore, toujours ◆ **he was ~ wearing his coat** il n'avait pas encore *or* toujours pas enlevé son manteau ◆ **she ~ lives in London** elle vit toujours à Londres ◆ **he's ~ as stubborn as ever** il est toujours aussi entêté ◆ **I can ~ remember it** je m'en souviens encore ◆ **he ~ hasn't arrived** il n'est toujours pas arrivé ◆ **I ~ don't understand** je ne comprends toujours pas ◆ **you could ~ change your mind** vous pouvez encore changer d'avis, il est encore temps de changer d'avis

2 *(stating what remains)* encore ◆ **I've got three left** il m'en reste encore trois ◆ **there's ~ time** il y a *or* on a encore le temps

◆ **still to ...** ◆ **the details have ~ to be worked out** il reste encore à régler les détails ◆ **there are further redundancies ~ to come** il y aura encore d'autres licenciements ◆ **there are many things ~ to do** il y a encore beaucoup de choses à faire ◆ **there are many questions ~ to be answered** il reste encore beaucoup de questions sans réponse ◆ **there are ten weeks ~ to go** il reste encore dix semaines ◆ **~ to come, the financial news ...** dans quelques instants, les informations financières ...

3 *(= nonetheless)* quand même, tout de même ◆ **he's ~ your brother** c'est quand même *or* tout de même ton frère ◆ **I didn't win; ~, it's been good experience** je n'ai pas gagné, mais ça a quand même *or* tout de même été une bonne expérience ◆ **~ and all** * tout compte fait

4 *(= however)* ◆ **I've got to find the money from somewhere ; ~, that's my problem** il faut que je trouve l'argent quelque part, mais ça, c'est mon problème ◆ **I failed; ~, that's life!** j'ai échoué, mais c'est la vie ! ◆ **~, never mind!** bon, tant pis !

5 *(in comparisons = even)* encore ◆ **he was ~ more determined after the debate** il était encore plus résolu après le débat ◆ **living standards have fallen ~ further** les niveaux de vie sont tombés encore plus bas ◆ **more serious ~** *or* **~ more serious is the problem of ethnic unrest** il y a le problème autrement plus sérieux des troubles ethniques

6 *(= yet)* encore ◆ **there is ~ another reason** il y a encore une autre raison

still² /stɪl/ ADJ 1 *(= motionless) [person, hands, air, water]* immobile

2 *(= calm) [place, night, day]* calme ◆ **all was ~** tout était calme ◆ **the ~ waters of the lake** les eaux calmes du lac ◆ **~ waters run deep** *(Prov)* il n'est pire eau que l'eau qui dort *(Prov)* ◆ **a ~, small voice** une petite voix insistante

3 *(Brit = not fizzy) [drink, orange]* non gazeux ; *[water]* plat

4 *(= silent)* ◆ **be ~ !** †† paix ! ††

ADV ◆ **hold ~ !** *(gen)* ne bouge pas ! ; *(= don't fidget)* reste tranquille ! ◆ **to keep** *or* **stay** *or* **stand ~** *[person] (gen)* ne pas bouger ; *(= not fidget)* rester tranquille ◆ **to sit ~** *[person] (gen)* rester assis sans bouger ; *(= not fidget)* rester tranquillement assis ◆ **time stood ~** le temps s'est arrêté ◆ **her heart stood ~** son cœur a cessé de battre

N 1 *(liter)* silence *m*, calme *m* ◆ **in the ~ of the night** dans le silence de la nuit

2 *(Cine)* ⇒ **still photograph**

VT *[+ anger, fear]* calmer ; *[+ person]* apaiser, tranquilliser ; *(= silence)* faire taire

COMP **still life** N (pl **still lifes**) *(Art)* nature *f* morte

still photograph N *(Cine)* photo *f* de film

still³ /stɪl/ N *(= apparatus)* alambic *m* ; *(= place)* distillerie *f* VT distiller

stillbirth /ˈstɪlbɜːθ/ N *(= birth)* mort *f* à la naissance ; *(= child)* enfant *mf* mort-né(e)

stillborn /ˈstɪlbɔːn/ ADJ mort-né (mort-née *f*)

stillness /ˈstɪlnɪs/ N *[of person, hands, air, water]* immobilité *f* ; *(= calm) [of place, night, day]* calme *m* ◆ **an eerie ~** un calme inquiétant

stilt /stɪlt/ N échasse *f* ; *(Archit)* pilotis *m*

stilted /ˈstɪltɪd/ ADJ *[person, conversation, language, manner]* guindé ◆ **the actors' ~ performances** le manque de naturel des acteurs

stimulant /ˈstɪmjʊlənt/ ADJ stimulant N *(lit, fig)* stimulant *m* ◆ **to be a ~ to ...** *(fig)* stimuler ...

stimulate /ˈstɪmjʊleɪt/ VT *(gen, Physiol)* stimuler ◆ **to ~ sb to sth/to do sth** inciter *or* pousser qn à qch/à faire qch

stimulating /ˈstɪmjʊleɪtɪŋ/ ADJ *(gen)* stimulant ; *(sexually)* excitant

stimulation /ˌstɪmjʊˈleɪʃən/ N *(= stimulus)* stimulant *m* ; *(= state)* stimulation *f*

stimulative /ˈstɪmjʊlətɪv/ ADJ stimulant

stimulus /ˈstɪmjʊləs/ N (pl **stimuli** /ˈstɪmjʊlaɪ/) *(Physiol)* stimulus *m* ; *(fig)* stimulant *m* ◆ **to be a ~ to** *or* **for** *(fig) [+ exports, efforts, imagination]* stimuler ◆ **it gave trade a new ~** cela a donné une nouvelle impulsion *or* un coup de fouet au commerce ◆ **under the ~ of ...** stimulé par ...

stimy /ˈstaɪmɪ/ N, VT ⇒ **stymie**

sting /stɪŋ/ (vb : pret, ptp **stung**) N 1 *[of insect]* dard *m*, aiguillon *m* ◆ **but there's a ~ in the tail** mais il y a une mauvaise surprise à la fin ◆ **it's had its ~ removed** *(of plan, draft, legislation etc)* on l'a rendu inopérant ◆ **to take the ~ out of** *[+ words]* adoucir ; *[+ situation]* désamorcer

2 *(= pain, wound, mark) [of insect, nettle etc]* piqûre *f* ; *[of iodine etc]* brûlure *f* ; *[of whip]* douleur *f* cuisante ; *(fig) [of attack]* mordant *m*, vigueur *f* ; *[of criticism, remark]* causticité *f*, mordant *m* ◆ **I felt the ~ of the rain on my face** la pluie me cinglait le visage ◆ **the ~ of salt water in the cut** la brûlure de l'eau salée dans la plaie

3 *(esp US* ‡ *= confidence trick)* arnaque * *f*, coup *m* monté

VT 1 *[insect, nettle, antiseptic]* piquer ; *[rain, hail, whip]* cingler, fouetter ; *[remark, criticism]* piquer au vif ◆ **stung by remorse** bourrelé de remords ◆ **my remark stung him into action** ma remarque (l'a piqué au vif et) l'a poussé à agir ◆ **he was stung into replying brusquely** piqué *or* blessé, il répondit brusquement ; → **quick**

2 ‡ avoir *, estamper * ◆ **he stung me for £10 for that meal** il m'a eu * *or* estampé * en me faisant payer ce repas 10 livres ◆ **I've been stung!** je me suis fait avoir *or* estamper ! *

VI *[insect, nettle, antiseptic, eyes]* piquer ; *[blow, slap, whip]* faire mal ◆ **that remark really stung** cette remarque m'a vraiment blessé ◆ **that ~s!** ça pique ! ◆ **the smoke made his eyes ~** la fumée lui piquait les yeux

stinger /ˈstɪŋgəʳ/ N 1 *(= cocktail) cocktail à base de crème de menthe* 2 *(US) [of insect]* piqûre *f* 3 *(US * = remark)* pique *f*, pointe *f*

stingily /ˈstɪndʒɪlɪ/ ADV *[praise]* chichement ; *[spend]* avec avarice ; *[serve]* en lésinant

stinginess /ˈstɪndʒɪnɪs/ N *[of person]* ladrerie *f*, avarice *f* ; *[of portion]* insuffisance *f*

stinging /ˈstɪŋɪŋ/ ADJ *[blow, slap, pain]* cuisant ; *[sensation]* cuisant, de piqûre ; *[rain, wind, comment, attack, criticism]* cinglant N *(= sensation)* sensation *f* cuisante COMP **stinging nettle** N ortie *f*

stingray /ˈstɪŋreɪ/ N pastenague *f*

stingy /ˈstɪndʒɪ/ ADJ *[person]* radin * ; *[portion, amount]* misérable, mesquin ◆ **to be ~ with** *[+ food, wine]* lésiner sur ; *[+ praise]* être chiche de ◆ **~ with money** avare (de ses sous)

stink /stɪŋk/ (vb : pret **stank**, ptp **stunk**) N 1 puanteur *f*, odeur *f* infecte ◆ **what a ~!** ce que ça pue ! ◆ **there's a ~ of corruption** cela pue la corruption, cela sent la corruption à plein nez

2 (* fig = row, trouble) esclandre *m*, grabuge * *m* ◆ **there was a dreadful ~ about the broken windows** il y a eu du grabuge * à propos des carreaux cassés ◆ **to kick up** *or* **cause** *or* **make a ~** faire toute une scène, râler * ◆ **to kick up a ~ about sth** causer un esclandre à propos de qch, faire du grabuge * à cause de qch

VI 1 puer, empester ◆ **it ~s of fish** cela pue *or* empeste le poisson ◆ **it ~s in here!** cela pue *or* empeste ici ! ◆ **it ~s to high heaven** * *(lit)* cela empeste, ça fouette * ◆ **it ~s of corruption** cela pue la corruption, cela sent la corruption à plein nez ◆ **the whole business ~s** c'est une sale affaire ◆ **they're ~ing with money** ‡ ils sont bourrés de fric ‡

2 *(‡ = be very bad) [person, thing]* être dégueulasse ‡

VT *[+ room etc]* empester

COMP **stink-bomb** N boule *f* puante

stink-horn N satyre *m* puant

► **stink out** VT SEP *[+ fox etc]* enfumer ; *[+ room]* empester

stinker ‡ /ˈstɪŋkəʳ/ N *(pej) (= person)* salaud ‡ *m*, salope ‡ *f* ; *(= angry letter)* lettre *f* d'engueulade‡ ◆ **to be a ~** *[person]* être salaud (*or* salope)‡ ; *[problem, question]* être un casse-tête

stinking /ˈstɪŋkɪŋ/ ADJ 1 *(= smelly) [person, lavatory, rubbish]* puant 2 (* *= horrible*) sale * *before n* ◆ **take your ~ hands off me!** retire tes sales pattes ! *, bas les pattes ! * ◆ **this ~ little town** cette sale * petite ville ◆ **what a ~ thing to do!** quelle vacherie ! * ◆ **a ~ letter** une lettre de réclamation virulente 3 *(Brit = bad)* ◆ **a ~ cold** * un sale rhume, un rhume carabiné * ◆ **a ~ hangover** une gueule de bois carabinée * ADV ◆ **~ rich** * bourré de fric *, plein aux as *

stinkpot‡ /ˈstɪŋkpɒt/ N salaud‡ *m*, salope‡ *f*

stinkweed /ˈstɪŋkwiːd/ N diplotaxis *m*

stinky * /ˈstɪŋkɪ/ ADJ puant

stint /stɪnt/ N 1 ration *f* de travail, besogne *f* assignée ◆ **to do one's ~** *(= daily work)* faire son travail quotidien ; *(= do one's share)* faire sa part de travail ◆ **he does a ~ in the gym/at the typewriter every day** il passe un certain temps chaque jour au gymnase/à la machine ◆ **I've done my ~ at the wheel** j'ai pris mon tour au volant ◆ **I've finished my ~ for today** j'ai fini ce que j'avais à faire aujourd'hui

2 ◆ **without ~** *[spend]* sans compter ; *[give, lend]* généreusement, avec largesse

VT *[+ food]* lésiner sur ; *[+ compliments]* être chiche de ◆ **to ~ sb of sth** mesurer qch à qn ◆ **he ~ed himself in order to feed the children** il s'est privé afin de nourrir les enfants ◆ **he didn't ~ himself** il ne s'est privé de rien

VI ◆ **to ~ on** *[+ food]* lésiner sur ; *[+ compliments]* être chiche de ◆ **to ~ on money** être avare *or* ladre

stipend /ˈstaɪpend/ N *(esp Rel)* traitement *m*

stipendiary /staɪˈpendɪərɪ/ ADJ *[services, official]* rémunéré ; *[priest]* qui reçoit un traitement N *personne qui reçoit une rémunération or un traitement fixe* ; (*Brit Jur*: also **stipendiary magistrate**) juge *m* au tribunal de police

stipple /ˈstɪpl/ VT pointiller

stipulate /ˈstɪpjʊleɪt/ VT stipuler (*that* que) ; *[+ price]* stipuler, convenir expressément de ; *[+ quantity]* stipuler, prescrire VI ◆ **to ~ for sth** stipuler qch, spécifier qch, convenir expressément de qch

stipulation /ˌstɪpjʊˈleɪʃən/ N stipulation *f* ◆ **on the ~ that ...** à la condition expresse que ... + *fut or subj*

stir¹ /stɜːʳ/ N 1 ◆ **to give sth a ~** remuer *or* tourner qch

2 *(= commotion)* agitation *f*, sensation *f* ◆ **there was a great ~ in Parliament about ...** il y a eu beaucoup d'agitation au Parlement à propos de ... ◆ **it caused** *or* **made quite a ~** cela a fait du bruit ◆ **he caused quite a ~ when he announced his resignation** cela a fait beaucoup de bruit quand il a annoncé sa démission

VT 1 *[+ tea, soup, mixture]* remuer ; *[+ fire]* tisonner ◆ **he ~red sugar into his tea** il a mis du sucre dans son thé et l'a remué ◆ **she ~red milk into the mixture** elle a ajouté du lait au mélange

2 *(= move)* remuer ; *(quickly)* agiter ◆ **the wind ~red the leaves** le vent a agité *or* a fait trembler les feuilles ◆ **nothing could ~ him from his chair** rien ne pouvait le tirer de son fauteuil ◆ **to ~ o.s.** * se secouer, se bouger‡ ◆ **to ~ one's stumps** * se grouiller‡

3 *(fig) [+ curiosity, passions]* exciter ; *[+ emotions]* éveiller ; *[+ imagination]* stimuler ; *[+ person]* émouvoir ◆ **to ~ sb to do sth** inciter qn à faire qch ◆ **to ~ a people to revolt** inciter un peuple à la révolte ◆ **to ~ sb to pity** émouvoir la compassion de qn ◆ **it ~red his heart** cela lui a remué le cœur ◆ **to ~ sb's blood** réveiller l'enthousiasme de qn ◆ **it was a song to ~ the blood** c'était une chanson enthousiasmante

VI 1 *[person]* remuer, bouger ; *[leaves, curtains etc]* remuer, trembler ; *[feelings]* être excité ◆ **I will not ~ from here** je ne bougerai pas d'ici ◆ **he hasn't ~red from the spot** il n'a pas quitté l'endroit ◆ **he wouldn't ~ an inch** *(lit)* il ne voulait pas bouger d'un centimètre ; *(fig)* il ne voulait pas faire la moindre concession ◆ **to ~ in one's sleep** bouger en dormant *or* dans son sommeil ◆ **nobody is ~ring yet** personne n'est encore levé, tout le monde dort encore ◆ **nothing was ~ring in the forest** rien ne bougeait dans la forêt ◆ **the curtains ~red in the breeze** la brise a agité les rideaux ◆ **anger ~red within her** la colère est montée en elle

2 (* *= try to cause trouble*) essayer de mettre la pagaille * *or* de causer des problèmes

COMP **stir-fry** VT faire sauter (en remuant) ADJ *[vegetables]* sauté N *(= dish) légumes (et/ou viande) sautés*

► **stir in** VT SEP *[+ milk etc]* ajouter en tournant

► **stir round** VT SEP *(Culin etc)* tourner

► **stir up** VT SEP *[+ soup etc]* tourner, remuer ; *[+ fire]* tisonner ; *(fig) [+ curiosity, attention, anger]* exciter ; *[+ imagination]* exciter, stimuler ; *[+ memories, the past]* réveiller ; *[+ revolt]* susciter ; *[+ hatred]* attiser ; *[+ mob]* ameuter ; *[+ opposition, discord]* fomenter ; *[+ trouble]* provoquer ; *[+ person]* secouer ◆ **to ~ sb up to sth/to do sth** pousser *or* inciter qn à qch/à faire qch

stir² ‡ /stɜːʳ/ *(esp US)* N *(= prison)* taule‡ *or* tôle‡ *f* ◆ **in ~** en taule‡ COMP **stir-crazy**‡ ADJ rendu dingue‡ par la réclusion

stirrer * /ˈstɜːrəʳ/ N *(= troublemaker)* fauteur *m* de troubles, fouteur *m*, -euse *f* de merde‡

stirring /ˈstɜːrɪŋ/ ADJ *[speech]* vibrant ; *[tale]* passionnant ; *[music]* entraînant ; *[performance]* enthousiasmant ; *[victory]* grisant N *(= first sign) [of discontent, revolt]* frémissement *m* ; *[of love]* frisson *m* ◆ **a ~ of interest** un début d'intérêt

stirrup /ˈstɪrəp/ N 1 *[of rider]* étrier *m* ◆ **to put one's feet in the ~s** chausser les étriers 2 *(US Climbing)* escarpolette *f*, étrier *m* 3 *(Med)* ◆ **~s** étriers *mpl*

COMP **stirrup cup** N coup *m* de l'étrier
stirrup leather N étrivière *f*
stirrup pump N pompe *f* à main portative
stirrup strap N ⇒ **stirrup leather**

stitch /stɪtʃ/ N *(Sewing)* point *m* ; *(Knitting)* maille *f* ; *(Surgery)* point *m* de suture ; *(= sharp pain)* point *m* de côté ◆ **she put a few ~es in the tear** elle a fait un point à la déchirure ◆ **to drop a ~** *(Knitting)* sauter une maille ◆ **to put ~es in a wound** suturer *or* recoudre une plaie ◆ **he had ten ~es** on lui a fait dix points de suture ◆ **to get one's ~es out** se faire retirer ses fils (de suture) ◆ **a ~ in time saves nine** *(Prov)* un point à temps en vaut cent ◆ **he hadn't a ~ (of clothing) on** * il était nu comme un ver ◆ **he hadn't a dry ~ on him** il n'avait pas un fil de sec sur le dos ◆ **to be in ~es** * se tenir les côtes, se tordre de rire ◆ **her stories had us in ~es** * ses anecdotes nous ont fait rire aux larmes ; → **cable**

VT *[+ seam, hem, garment] (gen)* coudre ; *(on machine)* piquer ; *[+ book]* brocher ; *[+ wound]* suturer ; → **hand, machine**

VI coudre

COMP **stitch-up**‡ N *(Brit)* coup *m* monté

► **stitch down** VT SEP rabattre

► **stitch on** VT SEP *[+ pocket, button]* coudre ; *(= mend)* recoudre

► **stitch up** VT SEP 1 *(Sewing)* coudre ; *(= mend)* recoudre ; *(Med)* suturer

2 (* *= arrange, finalize) [+ agreement]* (réussir à) conclure

3 (‡ *fig = frame*) monter un coup contre ◆ **I was ~ed up** j'ai été victime d'un coup monté

stitching /ˈstɪtʃɪŋ/ N couture *f*, points *mpl*

stoat /stəʊt/ N hermine *f*

stock /stɒk/ N 1 *(= supply) [of cotton, sugar, books, goods]* réserve *f*, provision *f*, stock *m* *(Comm)* ; *[of money]* réserve *f* ◆ **in ~** *(Comm)* en stock, en magasin ◆ **out of ~** épuisé ◆ **the shop has a large ~** le magasin est bien approvisionné ◆ **coal ~s are low** les réserves *or* les stocks de charbon sont réduit(e)s ◆ **~ of plays** *(Theat)* répertoire *m* ◆ **I've got a ~ of cigarettes** j'ai une provision *or* un stock * de cigarettes ◆ **to get in** *or* **lay in a ~ of** s'approvisionner en, faire provision de ◆ **it adds to our ~ of facts** cela complète les données en notre possession ◆ **a great ~ of learning** un grand fonds d'érudition ◆ **the linguistic** *or* **word ~** *(Ling)* le fonds lexical ; → **dead, surplus**

◆ **to take stock** *(Comm)* faire l'inventaire ; *(fig)* faire le point ◆ **to take ~ of** *[+ situation, prospects etc]* faire le point de ; *[+ person]* jauger

2 *(Agr = animals and equipment)* cheptel *m* (vif et mort) ; (*Agr*: also **livestock**) cheptel *m* vif, bétail *m* ; *(Rail)* matériel *m* roulant ; *(= raw material)* matière *f* première ; *(for paper-making)* pâte *f* à papier ; → **fatstock, livestock, rolling**

3 *(Fin)* valeurs *fpl*, titres *mpl* ; *(= company shares)* actions *fpl* ◆ **~s and shares** valeurs *fpl* (mobilières), titres *mpl* ◆ **railway ~(s)** actions *fpl* des chemins de fer ◆ **to put ~ in sth** *(fig)* faire cas de qch ◆ **his ~ has risen** *(fig)* sa cote a remonté ; → **preference, registered**

4 *(= tree trunk)* tronc *m* ; *(= tree stump)* souche *f* ; *(for grafting)* porte-greffe *m*, ente *f* ; → **laughing**

5 *(= base, stem) [of anvil]* billot *m* ; *[of plough]* fût *m* ; *[of rifle]* fût *m* et crosse *f* ; *[of plane]* fût *m*, bois *m* ; *[of whip]* manche *m* ; *[of fishing rod]* gaule *f* ; *[of anchor]* jas *m* ; → **lock¹**

6 *(= descent, lineage)* origine *f*, souche *f* ◆ **of good Scottish ~** de bonne souche écossaise ◆ **he comes of farming ~** il vient d'une famille d'agriculteurs, il est d'origine *or* de souche paysanne

7 *(Cards)* talon *m*

8 *(Culin)* bouillon *m* ◆ **chicken ~** bouillon *m* de poulet

9 *(= flower)* giroflée *f*, matthiole *f*

10 *(Hist)* **the ~s** le pilori

11 ◆ **to be on the ~s** *[ship]* être sur cale ; *[book, piece of work, scheme]* être en chantier

12 *(= tie)* cravate *f* foulard

ADJ 1 *(Comm) [goods, model]* courant, de série ◆ **~ line** article *m* suivi ◆ **~ size** taille *f* courante *or* normalisée ◆ **she is not ~ size** elle n'est pas une taille courante

2 *(Theat) [play]* du répertoire ◆ **~ character** personnage *m* type

3 *(= standard, hackneyed) [argument, joke, excuse, comment, response]* classique ◆ **~ phrase** cliché *m*, expression *f* toute faite

4 *(for breeding)* destiné à la reproduction ◆ **~ mare** jument *f* poulinière

VT 1 *(= supply) [+ shop, larder, cupboard]* approvisionner (*with* en) ; *[+ library/farm]* monter en livres/en bétail ; *[+ river, lake]* peupler (*with* de), empoissonner ◆ **well-~ed** *[shop etc]* bien approvisionné ; *[library, farm]* bien fourni *or* pourvu

2 *(Comm = hold in stock) [+ milk, hats, tools etc]* avoir, vendre

COMP **stock book** N livre *m* d'inventaire(s)
stock car N *(Rail)* wagon *m* à bestiaux ; *(Aut Sport)* stock-car *m*
stock car racing N course *f* de stock-cars
stock certificate N *(Fin)* titre *m*
stock company N *(Fin)* société *f* par actions, société *f* anonyme ; see also **joint** *(US Theat)* compagnie *f or* troupe *f* (de théâtre) de répertoire
stock control N *(Comm)* ⇒ **stock management**
stock cube N *(Culin)* bouillon *m* Kub ®
stock dividend N dividende *m* sous forme d'actions

stock exchange N Bourse *f* (des valeurs) ◆ **on the ~ exchange** à la Bourse
stock-in-trade N ◆ **irony was part of Shakespeare's ~-in-trade** Shakespeare maniait volontiers l'ironie dans son œuvre ◆ **jokes about religion are part of his ~-in-trade** les histoires sur la religion font partie de son répertoire de base ◆ **ruins were the ~-in-trade of Romantic painters** les ruines étaient un des thèmes habituels des peintres romantiques
stock level N (*Comm*) niveau *m* des stocks
stock list N (*Fin*) cours *m* de la Bourse ; (*Comm*) liste *f* des marchandises en stock, inventaire *m* commercial
stock management N gestion *f* des stocks
stock market N Bourse *f*, marché *m* financier
stock option N (*Fin*) stock-option *m*
stock-still ADJ ◆ **to stand** *or* **be ~-still** rester planté comme un piquet ; (*in fear, amazement*) rester cloué sur place

► **stock up** VI s'approvisionner (*with, on* en, de ; *for* pour) faire ses provisions (*with, on* de ; *for* pour)
VT SEP *[+ shop, larder, cupboard, freezer]* garnir ; *[+ library]* accroître le stock de livres de ; *[+ farm]* accroître le cheptel de ; *[+ river, lake]* aleviner, empoissonner

stockade /stɒˈkeɪd/ N 1 (= *fencing, enclosure*) palissade *f* 2 (*US: for military prisoners*) salle *f* de police (*d'une caserne*), bloc* *m* VT palanquer

stockbreeder /ˈstɒk,briːdəʳ/ N éleveur *m*, -euse *f*

stockbreeding /ˈstɒk,briːdɪŋ/ N élevage *m*

stockbroker /ˈstɒkbrəʊkəʳ/ N agent *m* de change
COMP **the stockbroker belt** N (*Brit*) la banlieue résidentielle
stockbroker Tudor N (*Brit*) *style Tudor des banlieues résidentielles*

stockbroking /ˈstɒkbrəʊkɪŋ/ N commerce *m* des valeurs en Bourse, transactions *fpl* boursières

stockfish /ˈstɒkfɪʃ/ N stockfisch *m inv*

stockholder /ˈstɒkhəʊldəʳ/ N (*US*) actionnaire *mf*

stockholding /ˈstɒkhəʊldɪŋ/ N 1 (*Comm*) stockage *m* 2 (*Fin*) actions *fpl*

Stockholm /ˈstɒkhəʊm/ N Stockholm

stockily /ˈstɒkɪlɪ/ ADV ◆ **~ built** trapu, râblé

stockiness /ˈstɒkɪnɪs/ N aspect *m* trapu *or* râblé

stockinet(te) /,stɒkɪˈnet/ N (= *fabric*) jersey *m* ; (= *knitting stitch*) (point *m* de) jersey *m*

stocking /ˈstɒkɪŋ/ N bas *m* ; → **Christmas, nylon**
COMP **stocking feet** NPL ◆ **in one's ~ feet** sans chaussures
stocking-filler N tout petit cadeau *m* de Noël
stocking mask N bas *m* (*d'un bandit masqué*)
stocking stitch N (*Knitting*) (point *m* de) jersey *m*

stockist /ˈstɒkɪst/ N (*Brit*) revendeur *m*

stockjobber /ˈstɒkdʒɒbəʳ/ N (*Brit*) *intermédiaire qui traite directement avec l'agent de change* ; (*US: often pej*) agent *m* de change, agioteur *m*

stockman /ˈstɒkmən/ N (pl **-men**) gardien *m* de bestiaux

stockpile /ˈstɒkpaɪl/ VT *[+ food etc]* stocker, faire *or* constituer des stocks de ; *[+ weapons]* amasser, accumuler VI faire des stocks N stock *m*, réserve *f*

stockpiling /ˈstɒkpaɪlɪŋ/ N (*NonC*) stockage *m*, constitution *f* de stocks

stockpot /ˈstɒkpɒt/ N (*Culin*) marmite *f* de bouillon

stockroom /ˈstɒkrum/ N magasin *m*, réserve *f*

stocktaking /ˈstɒkteɪkɪŋ/ N (*Brit Comm*) (= *action*) inventaire *m* ◆ **to do ~** (*Comm*) faire l'inventaire ; (*fig*) faire le point

stocky /ˈstɒkɪ/ ADJ 1 (= *thickset*) *[man]* trapu, râblé ◆ **his ~ build** sa forte carrure 2 *[plant, growth]* dense

stockyard /ˈstɒkjɑːd/ N parc *m* à bestiaux

stodge* /stɒdʒ/ N (*NonC: Brit*) 1 (= *food*) aliment *m* bourratif, étouffe-chrétien* *m inv* 2 (*in book etc*) littérature *f* indigeste

stodgy /ˈstɒdʒɪ/ ADJ (*pej*) 1 (*Culin*) *[food, meal, pudding]* bourratif ; *[cake]* pâteux, lourd 2 (* = *dull*) *[person]* rasant*, barbant* ; *[writing, book]* indigeste

stogie, stogy /ˈstəʊgɪ/ N (*US*) cigare *m*

stoic /ˈstəʊɪk/ N stoïque *mf* ◆ **Stoic** (*Philos*) stoïcien *m* ADJ 1 (= *uncomplaining*) *[person, acceptance]* stoïque ◆ **to be ~ about sth** accepter qch stoïquement 2 (*Philos*) ◆ **Stoic** stoïcien

stoical /ˈstəʊɪkəl/ ADJ stoïque

stoically /ˈstəʊɪklɪ/ ADV stoïquement

stoicism /ˈstəʊɪsɪzəm/ N stoïcisme *m*

stoke /stəʊk/ VT (also **stoke up**) *[+ fire, furnace]* alimenter ; *[+ engine, boiler]* chauffer ◆ **this will ~ fears of civil war** cela va alimenter *or* renforcer la crainte d'une guerre civile

► **stoke up** VI (*furnace*) alimenter la chaudière ; (*open fire*) entretenir le feu ; (* = *eat*) se remplir la panse*
VT SEP ⇒ **stoke**

stokehole /ˈstəʊkhəʊl/ N (*Naut*) chaufferie *f* ; *[of boiler, furnace]* porte *f* de chauffe

stoker /ˈstəʊkəʳ/ N (*Naut, Rail etc*) chauffeur *m*

STOL /stɒl/ (abbrev of **short take-off and landing**) ADAC *m*

stole¹ /stəʊl/ N (*Dress*) étole *f*, écharpe *f* ; (*Rel*) étole *f*

stole² /stəʊl/ VB pt of **steal**

stolen /ˈstəʊlən/ VB ptp of **steal**

stolid /ˈstɒlɪd/ ADJ *[person, manner, expression, face]* impassible

stolidity /stɒˈlɪdɪtɪ/ N flegme *m*, impassibilité *f*

stolidly /ˈstɒlɪdlɪ/ ADV *[say, stare, ignore, stand, sit]* impassiblement ◆ **to be ~ British (in one's attitudes)** être d'un flegme tout britannique (dans ses attitudes)

stolidness /ˈstɒlɪdnɪs/ N ⇒ **stolidity**

stomach /ˈstʌmək/ N (*Anat*) estomac *m* ; (= *belly*) ventre *m* ◆ **he was lying on his ~** il était couché *or* allongé sur le ventre, il était à plat ventre ◆ **to have a pain in one's ~** avoir mal à l'estomac *or* au ventre ◆ **I have no ~ for this journey** je n'ai aucune envie de faire ce voyage ◆ **an army marches on its ~** une armée ne se bat pas le ventre creux ; → **empty, full** VT *[+ food]* digérer ; *[+ behaviour, sb's jokes]* digérer*, encaisser* ◆ **he couldn't ~ this** il n'a pas pu l'encaisser*
COMP *[disease]* de l'estomac ; *[ulcer]* à l'estomac
stomach ache N mal *m* de ventre ◆ **I have (a) ~ ache** j'ai mal au ventre
stomach pump N pompe *f* (*pour lavage d'estomac*) ◆ **he was given a ~ pump** on lui a fait un lavage d'estomac
stomach stapling N gastroplastie *f*
stomach trouble N (*NonC*) ennuis *mpl* gastriques

stomatologist /,stəʊməˈtɒlədʒɪst/ N stomatologiste *mf*, stomatologue *mf*

stomatology /,stəʊməˈtɒlədʒɪ/ N stomatologie *f*

stomp /stɒmp/ VI ◆ **to ~ in/out** *etc* entrer/sortir *etc* d'un pas lourd et bruyant ◆ **we could hear him ~ing about** on entendait le bruit lourd de ses pas VT (*esp US*) ◆ **to ~ one's feet** (*in rage*) trépigner ; (*in dance*) frapper du pied N 1 *[of feet]* martèlement *m* 2 (= *dance*) swing *m*

stone /stəʊn/ N 1 (= *substance, gem: single piece*) pierre *f* ; (= *pebble*) caillou *m* ; (*on beach*) galet *m* ; (*commemorative*) stèle *f* (commémorative) ; (= *gravestone*) pierre *f* tombale, stèle *f* ◆ **(made) of ~** de pierre ◆ **within a ~'s throw (of)** à deux pas (de) ◆ **to leave no ~ unturned** remuer ciel et terre (*to do sth* pour faire qch) ◆ **to turn to ~, to change into ~** VT pétrifier, changer en pierre VI se pétrifier ◆ **it isn't set** *or* **cast** *or* **carved in ~** cela n'a rien d'immuable ; → **paving, precious, rolling, stand, tombstone**
2 (*esp Brit: in fruit*) noyau *m*
3 (*Med*) calcul *m* ◆ **to have a ~ in the kidney** avoir un calcul rénal ◆ **to have a ~ removed from one's kidney** se faire enlever un calcul rénal ; → **gallstone**
4 (*pl gen inv: Brit* = *weight*) = 14 livres, = 6,348 kg ; → **Imperial System**
VT 1 *[+ person, object]* lancer *or* jeter des pierres sur, bombarder de pierres ◆ **to ~ sb to death** lapider qn, tuer qn à coups de pierre ◆ **~ the crows!*** (*Brit*) vingt dieux !
2 *[+ date, olive]* dénoyauter
COMP *[building, wall]* en pierre
Stone Age N l'âge *m* de (la) pierre ADJ de l'âge de la pierre
stone-blind ADJ complètement aveugle
stone-broke* ADJ (*US*) ⇒ **stony-broke** ; → **stony**
stone circle N (*Brit*) cromlech *m*
stone-cold ADJ complètement froid ◆ **~-cold sober*** pas du tout ivre
stone-dead ADJ raide mort
stone-deaf ADJ sourd comme un pot
stone fruit N fruit *m* à noyau
stone-ground ADJ *[flour, wheat]* meulé à la pierre

stonebreaker /ˈstəʊn,breɪkəʳ/ N (= *person*) casseur *m* de pierres ; (= *machine*) casse-pierre(s) *m*, concasseur *m*

stonechat /ˈstəʊntʃæt/ N (= *bird*) traquet *m* (pâtre)

stonecrop /ˈstəʊnkrɒp/ N (= *plant*) orpin *m*

stonecutter /ˈstəʊnkʌtəʳ/ N (= *person*) tailleur *m*, -euse *f* de pierres précieuses, lapidaire *m* ; (= *machine*) sciotte *f*, scie *f* (de carrier)

stoned* /ˈstəʊnd/ ADJ (*on drugs*) défoncé* (*on sth* à qch) ; (= *drunk*) complètement bourré* *or* beurré* ◆ **to get ~** (*on drugs*) se défoncer* ; (*on alcohol*) prendre une cuite*

stonemason /ˈstəʊnmeɪsən/ N tailleur *m* de pierre(s)

stonewall /ˈstəʊnwɔːl/ VI (*Cricket*) jouer très prudemment ; (*fig*) donner des réponses évasives

stoneware /ˈstəʊnweəʳ/ N (*NonC*) pots *mpl* de grès

stonewashed /ˈstəʊnwɒʃt/ ADJ *[jeans]* délavé

stonework /ˈstəʊnwɜːk/ N (*NonC*) maçonnerie *f*

stonily /ˈstəʊnɪlɪ/ ADV avec froideur, froidement ; *[stare, look]* d'un œil froid

stonking* /ˈstɒŋkɪŋ/ ADJ (= *fantastic*) génial*

stony /ˈstəʊnɪ/ ADJ 1 (= *containing stones, stone-like*) *[soil, path, floor, tiles]* pierreux ; *[beach]* de galets ◆ **her words fell on ~ ground** ses paroles n'ont pas trouvé d'écho ◆ **his pleas fell on ~ ground** ses demandes n'ont pas trouvé de réponse 2 (= *made of stone*) *[outcrop, cliff]* rocheux 3 (= *unsympathetic*) *[person]* dur, insensible ; *[look, stare, expression]* dur ; *[face]* de marbre ; *[silence]* glacial
COMP **stony-broke*** ADJ (*Brit*) fauché comme les blés*
stony-faced ADJ au visage impassible

stood /stʊd/ VB pt, ptp of **stand**

stooge /stuːdʒ/ N (*Theat*) comparse *mf*, faire-valoir *m* ; (*gen: pej*) laquais *m*

stook /stuːk/ N moyette *f* VI moyetter

stool /stuːl/ N 1 tabouret *m* ; (*folding*) pliant *m* ; (= *footstool*) tabouret *m*, marchepied † *m* ◆ **to fall between two ~s** se retrouver le bec dans l'eau* ; → **music, piano** 2 (*fig*) *[of window]* rebord *m* 3 (*Med*) **~s** selles *fpl* 4 (*Bot*) pied *m* *(de plante)*, plante *f* mère COMP **stool pigeon** * N indicateur *m*, -trice *f*, mouchard(e) *m(f)* ; *(in prison)* mouton *m*

stoolie*, **stooly*** /ˈstuːlɪ/ N *(US)* ⇒ **stool pigeon** ; → **stool**

stoop¹ /stuːp/ N 1 ◆ **to have** *or* **walk with a** ~ avoir le dos voûté *or* rond 2 *[of bird of prey]* attaque *f* plongeante VI 1 *(= have a stoop)* avoir le dos voûté 2 (also **stoop down**) se pencher, se baisser ; *(fig)* s'abaisser *(to sth* jusqu'à qch ; *to do sth, to doing sth* jusqu'à faire qch) ◆ **he would ~ to anything** il est prêt à toutes les bassesses 3 *[bird of prey]* plonger

stoop² /stuːp/ N *(US)* véranda *f*

stooping /ˈstuːpɪŋ/ ADJ *[person, back]* voûté ; *[shoulders]* tombant ; *[posture]* courbé

stop /stɒp/ N 1 *(= halt)* arrêt *m* *(also Ski)* ; *(= short stay)* halte *f* ◆ **we had a ~ of a few days in Arles** nous avons fait une halte de quelques jours à Arles ◆ **we had a ~ for coffee** nous avons fait une pause-café ◆ **they worked for six hours without a ~** ils ont travaillé six heures d'affilée *or* sans s'arrêter ◆ **a five-minute ~, five minutes' ~** cinq minutes d'arrêt ◆ **to be at a ~** *[vehicle]* être à l'arrêt ; *[traffic]* être bloqué ; *[work, progress, production]* s'être arrêté, avoir cessé ◆ **to come to a ~** *[traffic, vehicle]* s'arrêter ; *[work, progress, production]* cesser ◆ **to bring to a ~** *[+ traffic, vehicle]* arrêter ; *[+ work, progress, production]* arrêter, faire cesser ◆ **to make a ~** *[bus, train]* s'arrêter ; *[plane, ship]* faire escale ◆ **to put a ~ to sth** mettre fin à qch, mettre un terme à qch ◆ **I'll put a ~ to all that!** je vais mettre un terme *or* le holà à tout ça !

2 *(= stopping place)* *[of bus, train]* arrêt *m* ; *[of plane, ship]* escale *f* ; → **bus, request**

3 *[of organ]* jeu *m* ◆ **to pull out all the ~s** *(fig)* faire un suprême effort, remuer ciel et terre *(to do sth* pour faire qch)

4 *(Punctuation)* point *m* ; *(in telegrams)* stop *m* ; see also **full**

5 *(= device)* *(on drawer, window)* taquet *m* ; *(= door stop)* butoir *m* de porte ; *(on typewriter:* also **margin stop**) margeur *m* ; *(Tech)* mentonnet *m*

6 *(Phon)* (consonne *f*) occlusive *f*

7 *(Phot)* diaphragme *m*

VT 1 *(= block)* *[+ hole, pipe]* boucher, obturer ; *(accidentally)* boucher, bloquer ; *[+ leak]* boucher, colmater ; *[+ jar, bottle]* boucher ; *[+ tooth]* plomber ◆ **to ~ one's ears** se boucher les oreilles ◆ **to ~ one's ears to sth** *(fig)* rester sourd à qch ◆ **to ~ a gap** *(lit)* boucher un trou ; *(fig)* combler une lacune ; see also **stopgap** ◆ **to ~ the way** barrer le chemin

2 *(= halt)* *[+ person, vehicle, ball, machine, process]* arrêter ; *[+ traffic]* arrêter, interrompre ; *[+ progress]* interrompre ; *[+ light]* empêcher de passer ; *[+ pain, worry, enjoyment]* mettre fin à ; *(fig, Sport etc = beat)* battre ◆ **he ~ped the show with his marvellous medley of old hits** il a fait un tabac* avec son merveilleux pot-pourri de vieilles chansons à succès ◆ **to ~ sb short** *(lit)* arrêter qn net *or* brusquement ; *(= interrupt)* interrompre qn ◆ **to ~ sb (dead) in his tracks** *(lit)* arrêter qn net *or* brusquement ; *(fig)* couper qn dans son élan ◆ **to ~ sth (dead) in its tracks** *(fig)* interrompre qch ◆ **he ~ped a bullet*** il a reçu une balle ◆ **the walls ~ some of the noise** les murs étouffent *or* absorbent une partie du bruit

3 *(= cease)* arrêter, cesser *(doing sth* de faire qch) ◆ ~ **it!** assez !, ça suffit ! ◆ ~ **that noise!** assez de bruit ! ◆ **to ~ work** arrêter *or* cesser de travailler, cesser le travail

4 *(= interrupt)* *[+ activity, building, production]* interrompre, arrêter ; *(= suspend)* suspendre ; *(Boxing)* *[+ fight]* suspendre ; *[+ allowance, leave, privileges]* supprimer ; *[+ wages]* retenir ; *[+ gas, electricity, water supply]* couper ◆ **rain ~ped play** la pluie a interrompu *or* arrêté la partie ◆ **they ~ped £15 out of his wages** ils ont retenu 15 livres sur son salaire ◆ **to ~ one's subscription** résilier son abonnement ◆ **to ~ (payment on) a cheque** faire opposition au paiement d'un chèque ◆ **to ~ payment** *[bank]* suspendre ses paiements ◆ **he ~ped the milk for a week** il a fait interrompre *or* il a annulé la livraison du lait pendant une semaine

5 *(= prevent)* empêcher *(sb's doing sth, sb from doing sth* qn de faire qch ; *sth happening, sth from happening* que qch n'arrive *(subj)*) ◆ **there's nothing to ~ you** rien ne vous en empêche ◆ **he ~ped the house (from) being sold** il a empêché que la maison (ne) soit vendue *or* la vente de la maison

6 *(Mus)* *[+ string]* presser ; *[+ hole of trumpet etc]* boucher, mettre le doigt sur

VI 1 *[person, vehicle, machine, clock, sb's heart]* s'arrêter ◆ **to ~ to do sth** s'arrêter pour faire qch ◆ ~ **thief!** au voleur ! ◆ **you can ~ now** *(in work etc)* vous pouvez (vous) arrêter maintenant ◆ **we'll ~ here for today** *(in lesson etc)* nous nous arrêterons *or* nous nous en tiendrons là pour aujourd'hui ◆ **he ~ped (dead) in his tracks** il s'est arrêté net *or* pile* ◆ **he ~ped in mid sentence** il s'est arrêté au beau milieu d'une phrase ◆ ~ **and think** réfléchissez bien ◆ ~ **and consider if** *or* **whether ...** réfléchissez si ... ◆ **he never knows where to ~** il ne sait pas s'arrêter ◆ **he will ~ at nothing** il est prêt à tout, il ne recule devant rien *(to do sth* pour qch) → **dead, shortstop**

2 *[supplies, production, process, music]* s'arrêter, cesser ; *[attack, pain, worry, enjoyment, custom]* cesser ; *[allowance, privileges]* être supprimé ; *[play, programme, concert]* finir, se terminer ; *[conversation, discussion, struggle]* cesser, se terminer

3 * *(= remain)* rester ; *(= live temporarily)* loger ◆ ~ **where you are!** restez là où vous êtes ! ◆ **I'm ~ping with my aunt** je loge chez ma tante

COMP *[button, lever, signal]* d'arrêt ; *(Phot)* *[bath, solution]* d'arrêt

stop-and-go N *(US)* → **stop-go**

stop consonant N *(Phon)* (consonne *f*) occlusive *f*

stop-frame ADJ *[animation, photography]* image par image *inv*

stop-go N → **stop-go**

stop-off N arrêt *m*, courte halte *f*

stop order N *(on Stock Exchange)* ordre *m* stop

stop-press N *(Brit Press)* *(= news)* nouvelles *fpl* de dernière heure ; *(as heading)* "dernière heure"

stop sign N (panneau *m*) stop *m*

► **stop away*** VI ◆ **he stopped away for three years** il est resté trois ans sans revenir *or* trois ans absent ◆ **he ~ped away from the meeting** il n'est pas allé à la réunion

► **stop behind*** VI rester en arrière *or* à la fin

► **stop by*** VI s'arrêter en passant

► **stop down*** VI *(bending)* rester baissé ; *(lying down)* rester couché ; *(under water)* rester sous l'eau

► **stop in*** VI 1 *(at home)* rester à la maison *or* chez soi, ne pas sortir

2 ⇒ **stop by**

► **stop off** VI s'arrêter ; *(on journey)* s'arrêter, faire une halte ◆ **let's ~ off and get a pizza** arrêtons-nous pour acheter une pizza

N ◆ **stop-off** → **stop**

► **stop out*** VI rester dehors, ne pas rentrer ◆ **he always ~s out late on Fridays** il rentre toujours tard le vendredi

► **stop over** VI s'arrêter (un *or* plusieurs jour(s)), faire une halte

► **stop up** VI *(Brit *)* ne pas se coucher, rester debout ◆ **don't ~ up for me** ne m'attendez pas pour aller vous coucher

VT SEP *[+ hole, pipe, jar, bottle]* boucher ◆ **my nose is ~ped up** j'ai le nez bouché

stopcock /ˈstɒpkɒk/ N robinet *m* d'arrêt

stopgap /ˈstɒpgæp/ N bouche-trou *m* ADJ *[measure, solution]* provisoire

stop-go /ˌstɒpˈgəʊ/ N *(gen, Econ)* ◆ **a period of ~** une période d'activité intense suivie de relâchement, une période de "stop and go" COMP **stop-go policy** N politique *f* en dents de scie

stoplight /ˈstɒplaɪt/ N *(US)* *(= traffic light)* feu *m* rouge ; *(= brake light)* feu *m* de stop

stopover /ˈstɒpəʊvəʳ/ N halte *f*

stoppage /ˈstɒpɪdʒ/ N 1 *(in traffic, work)* arrêt *m*, interruption *f* ; *(Sport)* arrêt *m* de jeu ; *(= strike)* arrêt *m* de travail, grève *f* ; *[of leave, wages, payment]* suspension *f* ; *(= amount deducted)* retenue *f* 2 *(= blockage)* obstruction *f*, engorgement *m* ; *(Med)* occlusion *f* COMP **stoppage time** N *(Sport)* arrêts *mpl* de jeu ◆ **to play ~ time** jouer les arrêts de jeu

stopper /ˈstɒpəʳ/ N *[of bottle, jar]* bouchon *m* ; *[of bath, basin]* bouchon *m*, bonde *f* ◆ **to take the ~ out of a bottle** déboucher une bouteille ◆ **to put the ~ into a bottle** boucher une bouteille ◆ **to put a ~ on sth*** mettre un terme *or* le holà à qch ; → **conversation** VT boucher

stopping /ˈstɒpɪŋ/ N 1 *(NonC = halting)* *[of activity, progress, vehicle, process]* arrêt *m* ; *[of cheque]* opposition *f* au paiement ; *[of match, game, payment]* suspension *f* ; *[of allowance, leave, privileges]* suppression *f* ; *[of wages]* retenue *f* *(of* sur) 2 *(NonC = blocking)* *[of hole, pipe]* obturation *f*, bouchage *m* ; *[of leak]* colmatage *m*, bouchage *m* ; *(Mus)* → **double** 3 *[of tooth]* plombage *m*

COMP **stopping place** N *(= lay-by etc)* endroit *m* où s'arrêter ◆ **we were looking for a ~ place** nous cherchions un endroit où nous arrêter

stopping train N (train *m*) omnibus *m*

stopwatch /ˈstɒpwɒtʃ/ N chronomètre *m*

storage /ˈstɔːrɪdʒ/ N 1 *(NonC)* *[of goods, fuel]* entreposage *m*, emmagasinage *m* ; *[of furniture]* entreposage *m* ; *[of food, wine]* rangement *m*, conservation *f* ; *[of radioactive waste]* stockage *m* ; *[of heat, electricity]* accumulation *f* ; *[of documents]* conservation *f* ◆ **to put in(to) ~** entreposer, emmagasiner ; *[+ furniture]* mettre au garde-meuble ; → **cold**

2 *(Comput)* *(= state)* mémoire *f* ; *(= action)* mise *f* en mémoire

COMP *[problems]* d'entreposage, d'emmagasinage ; *[charges]* de magasinage

storage battery N accumulateur *m*, accu* *m*

storage capacity N *(gen, Comput)* capacité *f* de stockage

storage heater (also **electric storage heater**) N radiateur *m* électrique à accumulation, accumulateur *m* de chaleur

storage space N *(in house)* espace *m* de rangement ; *(in firm etc)* espace *m* de stockage

storage tank N *(for oil etc)* réservoir *m* de stockage ; *(for rainwater)* citerne *f*

storage unit N *(= furniture)* meuble *m* de rangement

store /stɔːʳ/ N 1 *(= supply, stock, accumulation)* provision *f*, réserve *f*, stock *m* *(Comm)* ; *[of learning, information]* fonds *m* ◆ **to get in** *or* **lay in a ~ of sth** faire provision de qch ◆ **to keep a ~ of sth** avoir une provision de qch ◆ **to set great ~/little ~ by sth** faire grand cas/peu de cas de qch, attacher du prix/peu de prix à qch

2 **~s** *(= supplies)* provisions *fpl* ◆ **to take on** *or* **lay in ~s** s'approvisionner, faire des provisions

3 *(Brit = depot, warehouse)* entrepôt *m* ; *(= furniture store)* garde-meuble *m* ; *(in office, factory etc:* also **stores**) réserve *f* ; *(larger)* service *m* des approvisionnements ◆ **ammunition ~** dépôt *m* de munitions

♦ **in store, into store** ♦ **to put in(to)** ~ *[+ goods]* entreposer ; *[+ furniture]* mettre au garde-meuble ♦ **I am keeping this in ~ for winter** je garde cela en réserve pour l'hiver ♦ **I've got a surprise in ~ for you** j'ai une surprise en réserve pour vous, je vous réserve une surprise ♦ **what does the future hold** *or* **have in ~ for him?, what is** *or* **lies in ~ for him?** que lui réserve l'avenir ?

4 *(esp US = shop)* magasin *m*, commerce *m* ; *(large)* grand magasin *m* ; *(small)* boutique *f* ♦ **book ~** magasin *m* de livres, librairie *f* ; → **chain, department, general**

VT 1 *(= keep in reserve, collect:* also **store up**) *[+ food, fuel, goods]* mettre en réserve ; *[+ documents]* conserver ; *[+ electricity, heat]* accumuler, emmagasiner ; *(fig) (in one's mind) [+ facts, information]* noter *or* enregistrer dans sa mémoire ♦ **this cellar can ~ enough coal for the winter** cette cave peut contenir assez de charbon pour passer l'hiver

2 *(= place in store:* also **store away**) *[+ food, fuel, goods]* emmagasiner, entreposer ; *[+ furniture]* mettre au garde-meuble ; *[+ crops]* mettre en grange, engranger ; *(Comput)* mettre en réserve ♦ **he ~d the information (away)** *(in filing system etc)* il a rangé les renseignements ; *(in his mind)* il a noté les renseignements ♦ **I've got the camping things ~d (away) till we need them** j'ai rangé *or* mis de côté les affaires de camping en attendant que nous en ayons besoin ♦ **where do you ~ your wine?** où est-ce que vous entreposez *or* conservez votre vin ?

3 *(Comput)* mémoriser

VI ♦ **these apples ~ well/badly** ces pommes se conservent bien/mal

COMP *(gen: esp US) [item, line]* de série ; *(US:* also **store-bought**) *[clothes]* de confection *or* de série ; *[cake]* du commerce

store card N *(Comm)* carte *f* privative

store detective N vigile *m* en civil *(dans un grand magasin)*

► **store away** VT SEP → **store vt 2**

► **store up** VT SEP → **store vt 1**

storefront /ˈstɔːfrʌnt/ N *(US)* devanture *f*

storehouse /ˈstɔːhaʊs/ N entrepôt *m* ; *(fig: of information etc)* mine *f*

storekeeper /ˈstɔːˌkiːpəʳ/ N magasinier *m* ; *(esp US = shopkeeper)* commerçant(e) *m(f)*

storeroom /ˈstɔːrʊm/ N réserve *f*, magasin *m*

storey, story *(US)* /ˈstɔːrɪ/ N étage *m* ♦ **on the 3rd** *or (US)* **4th ~** au troisième (étage) ♦ **a four-~(ed)** *or (US)* **four-storied building** un bâtiment de quatre étages

-storeyed, -storied *(US)* /ˈstɔːrɪd/ ADJ *(in compounds)* → **storey**

stork /stɔːk/ N cigogne *f*

storm /stɔːm/ N 1 tempête *f* ; *(= thunderstorm)* orage *m* ; *(on Beaufort scale)* tempête *f* ♦ **~ of rain/snow** tempête *f* de pluie/de neige ♦ **magnetic ~** orage *m* magnétique ♦ **it was a ~ in a teacup** *(Brit)* c'était une tempête dans un verre d'eau ; → **dust, hailstorm, sandstorm**

2 *[of arrows, missiles]* pluie *f*, grêle *f* ; *[of insults, abuse]* torrent *m* ; *[of cheers, protests, applause, indignation]* tempête *f* ♦ **there was a political ~** les passions politiques se sont déchaînées ♦ **his speech caused** *or* **raised quite a ~** son discours a provoqué une véritable tempête *or* un ouragan ♦ **to bring a ~ about one's ears** soulever un tollé (général) ♦ **a period of ~ and stress** une période très orageuse *or* très tourmentée

3 *(Mil)* **to take by ~** prendre d'assaut ♦ **this product has taken the market by ~** ce produit a pris le marché d'assaut ♦ **the play took London by ~** la pièce a obtenu un succès foudroyant *or* fulgurant à Londres

VT *(Mil)* prendre *or* emporter d'assaut ♦ **angry ratepayers ~ed the town hall** les contribuables en colère ont pris d'assaut *or* ont envahi la mairie

VI *[wind]* souffler en tempête, faire rage ; *[rain]* tomber à torrents, faire rage ; *(fig) [person]* fulminer ♦ **to ~ at sb** tempêter *or* fulminer contre qn ♦ **to ~ (one's way) in/out** *etc* entrer/sortir *etc* comme un ouragan

COMP *[signal, warning]* de tempête

storm belt N zone *f* des tempêtes

storm cellar N *(US)* abri *m* contre les tempêtes *or* cyclones

storm centre N centre *m* de dépression, œil *m* du cyclone ; *(fig)* centre *m* de l'agitation

storm cloud N nuage *m* orageux ; *(fig)* nuage *m* noir *or* menaçant ♦ **the ~ clouds are gathering** *(fig)* l'avenir est sombre

storm cone N cône *m* de tempête

storm damage N dégâts *mpl* occasionnés par la tempête

storm door N double porte *f (à l'extérieur)*

storm drain N collecteur *m* d'eaux pluviales

storm force N ♦ **to reach ~ force** *[wind]* atteindre force 10

storm-force ADJ *[wind]* de force 10

storm lantern N lampe-tempête *f*, lanterne-tempête *f*

storm-lashed ADJ battu par l'orage *or* la tempête

storm petrel N ⇒ **stormy petrel** ; → **stormy**

storm sewer N collecteur *m* d'eaux pluviales

storm-tossed ADJ ballotté *or* battu par la tempête

storm trooper N *(Mil) (gen)* membre *m* d'une troupe d'assaut ; *(= Nazi)* membre *m* des sections d'assaut nazies

storm troops NPL troupes *fpl* d'assaut

storm water N eau(x) *f(pl)* pluviale(s)

storm window N double fenêtre *f (à l'extérieur)*

stormbound /ˈstɔːmbaʊnd/ ADJ bloqué par la tempête

storming /ˈstɔːmɪŋ/ N *(= attack, invasion)* assaut *m* ♦ **the ~ of the Bastille** la prise de la Bastille ADJ *(* = impressive)* spectaculaire, impressionnant

stormproof /ˈstɔːmpruːf/ ADJ à l'épreuve de la tempête

stormy /ˈstɔːmɪ/ ADJ 1 *[weather, night, skies]* orageux ; *[seas, waters]* démonté ♦ **on a ~ night** par une nuit d'orage 2 *(= turbulent) [meeting, scene, relationship]* orageux, houleux ; *[period]* tumultueux ; *[career]* mouvementé ; *[temperament, person]* violent, emporté ♦ **~ waters** période *f* tumultueuse ♦ **the bill had a ~ passage through Parliament** l'adoption du projet de loi au Parlement a donné lieu à des débats houleux COMP **stormy petrel** N *(= bird)* pétrel *m* ; *(fig)* enfant *mf* terrible

story¹ /ˈstɔːrɪ/ N 1 *(= account)* histoire *f* ♦ **it's a long ~** c'est toute une histoire, c'est une longue histoire ♦ **that's only part of the ~** mais ce n'est pas tout ♦ **you're not telling me the whole** *or* **full ~, you're only telling me part of the ~** tu ne me dis pas tout, tu me caches quelque chose ♦ **a different ~** *(fig)* une autre histoire ♦ **but that's another ~** mais ça c'est une autre histoire ♦ **it's quite another ~** *or* **a very different ~** c'est une tout autre histoire ♦ **it's the same old ~** c'est toujours la même histoire *or* la même chanson* ♦ **these scars tell their own ~** ces cicatrices parlent d'elles-mêmes *or* en disent long ♦ **what the police found in the truck told a different ~** ce que la police a trouvé dans le camion indiquait tout autre chose ♦ **so, what's the ~?** alors, raconte ! ♦ **that's the ~ of my life!** *(hum)* ça m'arrive tout le temps !

2 *(= version of events)* **I've heard his ~** j'ai entendu sa version des faits ♦ **he changed his ~** il est revenu sur ce qu'il avait dit ♦ **let's get our ~ straight** mettons-nous bien d'accord sur ce que nous allons dire ♦ **according to your ~** d'après ce que vous dites, selon vous

3 *(= tale)* histoire *f*, conte *m* ; *(= legend)* histoire *f*, légende *f* ; *(Literat)* histoire *f*, récit *m* ; *(short)* nouvelle *f* ; *(= anecdote, joke)* histoire *f*, anecdote *f* ♦ **there's an interesting ~ attached to that** on raconte une histoire intéressante à ce sujet ♦ **or so the ~ goes** ou du moins c'est ce que l'on raconte, d'après les on-dit ♦ **he writes stories** il écrit des histoires *or* des nouvelles ♦ **she told the children a ~** elle a raconté une histoire aux enfants ♦ **do you know the ~ about ...?** connaissez-vous l'histoire de ... ? ♦ **what a ~ this house could tell!** que de choses cette maison pourrait nous *(or vous etc)* raconter ! ♦ **what's the ~ behind that song/that picture?** quelle est l'histoire de cette chanson/de ce tableau ? ; → **bedtime, fairy, short**

4 *(= plot) [of film]* scénario *m* ; *[of book]* intrigue *f* ; *[of play]* intrigue *f*, action *f* ♦ **the ~ of the film is taken from his book** le scénario du film est tiré de son roman ♦ **he did the ~ for the film** il a écrit le scénario du film

5 *(Press, Rad, TV) (= event etc)* affaire *f* ; *(= article)* article *m* ♦ **they devoted two pages to the ~ of ...** ils ont consacré deux pages à l'affaire de ... ♦ **did you read the ~ on ...?** avez-vous lu l'article sur ... ? ♦ **I don't know if there's a ~ in it** je ne sais pas s'il y a matière à un article ♦ **he was sent to cover the ~ of the refugees** on l'a envoyé faire un reportage sur les réfugiés

6 *(* = fib)* histoire *f* ♦ **to tell stories** raconter des histoires

COMP **story line** N *[of film]* scénario *m* ; *[of book]* intrigue *f* ; *[of play]* intrigue *f*, action *f*

story-writer N nouvelliste *mf*

story² /ˈstɔːrɪ/ N *(US)* ⇒ **storey**

storyboard /ˈstɔːrɪbɔːd/ N *(Cine, TV)* story-board *m*

storybook /ˈstɔːrɪbʊk/ N livre *m* de contes *or* d'histoires ADJ *(fig) [situation, love affair]* romanesque ♦ **a meeting with a ~ ending** une rencontre qui se termine comme dans les romans

storyteller /ˈstɔːrɪteləʳ/ N conteur *m*, -euse *f* ; *(* = fibber)* menteur *m*, -euse *f*

storytelling /ˈstɔːrɪtelɪŋ/ N *(NonC)* ♦ **they pass on their tradition through ~** leurs traditions se transmettent à travers les contes

stoup /stuːp/ N *(Rel)* bénitier *m* ; *(†† = tankard)* pichet *m*

stout /staʊt/ ADJ 1 *(= fat) [person]* corpulent, gros (grosse *f*) ♦ **to get** *or* **grow ~** prendre de l'embonpoint 2 *(= sturdy) [legs]* solide, robuste ; *[stick, door, rope, shoes]* solide ; *[horse]* vigoureux ; *[branch]* gros (grosse *f*) 3 *(= resolute) [soldier, defence, resistance, opposition, heart]* vaillant ; *[support]* résolu ♦ **he is a ~ fellow** † c'est un brave type* N *(= beer)* stout *m or f*, bière *f* brune COMP **stout-hearted** ADJ vaillant, intrépide

stoutly /ˈstaʊtlɪ/ *(liter)* ADV 1 *(= resolutely) [fight, defend, resist]* vaillamment ; *[deny]* vigoureusement ; *[believe, maintain]* dur comme fer 2 ♦ **~ built** *[hut]* solidement bâti

stoutness /ˈstaʊtnɪs/ N *(NonC)* 1 *(= fatness) [of person]* corpulence *f*, embonpoint *m* 2 *(= sturdiness) [of horse, branch]* vigueur *f* ; *[of stick, door, rope, shoes]* solidité *f* 3 *(= resoluteness) [of defence, resistance, opposition]* vaillance *f* ; *[of support]* détermination *f* ♦ **the ~ of his resolve** sa résolution inébranlable ♦ **~ of heart** vaillance *f*

stove¹ /stəʊv/ N 1 *(= heater)* poêle *m* ; → **wood** 2 *(= cooker) (solid fuel)* fourneau *m* ; *(gas, electric)* cuisinière *f* ; *(small)* réchaud *m* 3 *(= industrial oven)* four *m*, étuve *f*

stove² /stəʊv/ VB pt, ptp of **stave**

stovepipe /ˈstəʊvpaɪp/ **N** *(lit, also fig = hat)* tuyau *m* de poêle

stow /stəʊ/ **VT** ranger, mettre ; *(out of sight:* also **stow away**) faire disparaître, cacher ; *(Naut) [+ cargo]* arrimer ; (also **stow away**) *[+ ropes, tarpaulins etc]* ranger ◆ **where can I ~ this?** où puis-je déposer ceci ? ◆ **~ it!*** la ferme !*, ferme-la !*

► **stow away** **VI** s'embarquer clandestinement ◆ **he ~ed away to Australia** il s'est embarqué clandestinement pour l'Australie **VT SEP** *(= put away)* ranger ; *(= put in its place)* ranger, placer ; *(= put out of sight)* faire disparaître, cacher ; (* *fig) [+ meal, food]* enfourner * ; see also **stow**

stowage /ˈstəʊɪdʒ/ **N** *(Naut) (= action)* arrimage *m* ; *(= space)* espace *m* utile ; *(= costs)* frais *mpl* d'arrimage

stowaway /ˈstəʊəweɪ/ **N** passager *m* clandestin, passagère *f* clandestine

strabismus /strəˈbɪzməs/ **N** strabisme *m*

strabotomy /strəˈbɒtəmɪ/ **N** strabotomie *f*

straddle /ˈstrædl/ **VT** *[+ horse, cycle]* enfourcher ; *[+ chair]* se mettre à califourchon *or* à cheval sur ; *[+ fence, ditch, bridge]* enjamber ; *[+ two periods, two cultures]* être à cheval sur ◆ **to be straddling sth** être à califourchon *or* à cheval sur qch ◆ **the village ~s the border** le village est à cheval sur la frontière ◆ **the town ~s the river Avon** la ville s'étend sur les deux rives de l'Avon ◆ **to ~ an issue** *(US)* ménager la chèvre et le chou **VI** être à califourchon ; *(US * fig)* nager entre deux eaux, ménager la chèvre et le chou

strafe /strɑːf/ **VT** *(with machine guns)* mitrailler au sol ; *(with shellfire, bombs)* bombarder, marmiter

strafing /ˈstrɑːfɪŋ/ **N** *(on ground, from plane)* mitraillage *m* au sol

straggle /ˈstrægl/ **VI** 1 *[vines, plants]* pousser tout en longueur, pousser au hasard ; *[hair]* être *or* retomber en désordre ; *[houses, trees]* être épars *or* disséminés ; *[village]* s'étendre en longueur ◆ **the branches ~d along the wall** les branches tortueuses grimpaient le long du mur ◆ **the village ~s for miles along the road** les maisons du village s'égrènent *or* le village s'étend sur des kilomètres le long de la route ◆ **her hair was straggling over her face** ses cheveux rebelles *or* des mèches folles retombaient en désordre sur son visage 2 **to ~ in/out** *[people, cars]* entrer/sortir petit à petit

► **straggle away, straggle off** **VI** se débander *or* se disperser petit à petit

straggler /ˈstræglәʳ/ **N** 1 *(= person)* traînard(e) *m(f)* ; *(= plane etc)* avion *m etc* à la traîne * 2 *(Bot)* branche *f* gourmande, gourmand *m*

straggling /ˈstræglɪŋ/, **straggly** /ˈstræglɪ/ **ADJ** *[hair, beard]* hirsute ; *[plant]* (qui pousse) tout en longueur ; *[village]* tout en longueur ◆ **a ~ row of houses** un rang de maisons disséminées ◆ **a long ~ line** une longue ligne irrégulière

straight /streɪt/ **ADJ** 1 *(= not curved) [road, edge, stick, nose, skirt, trousers]* droit ; *[course, route]* en ligne droite ; *[chair]* à dossier droit ; *[hair]* raide ◆ **a ~ line** *(gen)* une ligne droite ; *(Math)* une droite ◆ **to walk in a ~ line** marcher en ligne droite ◆ **on a ~ course** en ligne droite ◆ **to have a ~ back** avoir le dos droit ◆ **to keep one's back ~** se tenir droit ◆ **to play (with) a ~ bat** *(Cricket)* jouer avec la batte verticale ; *(Brit = act decently)* jouer franc jeu

2 *(= not askew) [picture, rug, tablecloth, tie, hat, hem]* droit ◆ **the picture isn't ~** le tableau n'est pas droit *or* est de travers ◆ **to put** *or* **set ~** *[+ picture, hat, tie]* redresser, remettre droit ; *[+ rug, tablecloth]* remettre droit

3 *(= frank) [person, answer, question]* franc (franche *f*) *(with sb* avec qn) ; *[dealing]* loyal, régulier ; *[denial, refusal]* net, catégorique ◆ **to be ~ about sth** exprimer franchement qch ◆ **let's be ~ about this** soyons francs, ne nous leurrons pas ◆ **~ talk(ing), ~ speaking** franc-parler *m* ◆ **it's time for some ~ talking** soyons francs ◆ **to play a ~ game** jouer franc jeu ◆ **~ tip** *(Racing, St Ex etc)* tuyau * *m* sûr

4 *(= unambiguous)* clair ◆ **say nothing, is that ~?** tu ne dis rien, c'est clair ? ◆ **have you got that ~?** est-ce bien clair ? ◆ **let's get this ~** entendons-nous bien sur ce point ◆ **let's get that ~ right now** mettons cela au clair tout de suite ◆ **to get things ~ in one's mind** mettre les choses au clair dans son esprit ◆ **to put sth ~** mettre qch au clair ◆ **to put** *or* **set sb ~ (about sth)** éclairer qn (sur qch) ◆ **to keep sb ~ (about sth)** empêcher qn de se tromper (sur qch) ◆ **to put** *or* **set o.s. ~ with sb** faire en sorte de ne pas être en reste avec qn ; → **record**

5 *(= tidy) [house, room, books, affairs, accounts]* en ordre ◆ **to put** *or* **set** *or* **get sth ~** *[+ house, room, books]* mettre qch en ordre, mettre de l'ordre dans qch ; *[+ affairs, accounts]* mettre de l'ordre dans qch

6 *(= pure, simple)* ◆ **it was a ~ choice between A and B** il n'y avait que deux solutions, A ou B ◆ **the election was a ~ fight between the Tories and Labour** l'élection a mis aux prises conservateurs et travaillistes ◆ **her latest novel is ~ autobiography** son dernier roman est de l'autobiographie pure ◆ **to get ~ As** *(US)* obtenir les notes les plus élevées ◆ **a ~ A student** *(US)* un étudiant qui obtient les notes les plus élevées partout

7 *(= consecutive) [victories, defeats, games, months]* consécutif ◆ **to win ten ~ victories** remporter dix victoires d'affilée *or* consécutives ◆ **for five ~ days** pendant cinq jours d'affilée *or* consécutifs ◆ **in ~ sets** *(Tennis)* en deux/trois sets *(pour les matchs en trois/cinq sets)* ◆ **to win/lose in ~ sets** gagner/perdre tous les sets

8 *(* = not owed or owing money)* quitte ◆ **if I give you £5, then we'll be ~** si je te donne cinq livres, nous serons quittes

9 *(= unmixed) [whisky, vodka]* sec (sèche *f*), sans eau

10 *(Theat) (= mainstream) [theatre]* traditionnel ; *(= non-comic) [play, role, actor]* sérieux

11 *(= unsmiling)* ◆ **to keep a ~ face** garder son sérieux ◆ **to say sth with a ~ face** dire qch sans sourire *or* avec un grand sérieux ; see also **comp**

12 *(Geom) [angle]* plat

13 *(* = conventional) [person]* conventionnel, conformiste

14 *(* = heterosexual)* hétéro *

15 * *(= not criminal) [person]* honnête, régulier ◆ **I've been ~ for three years** *(not on drugs)* ça fait trois ans que je n'ai pas pris de drogue

N 1 **the ~** *[of racecourse, railway line, river]* la ligne droite ◆ **now we're in the ~** *(fig)* nous sommes maintenant dans la dernière ligne droite

2 ◆ **to cut sth on the ~** couper qch (de) droit fil ◆ **out of the ~** de travers, en biais

3 **to follow** *or* **keep to the ~ and narrow** rester dans le droit chemin ◆ **to keep sb on the ~ and narrow** faire suivre le droit chemin à qn

4 * *(= heterosexual)* hétéro * *mf*

ADV 1 *(= in a straight line) [walk]* droit ; *[grow]* (bien) droit ; *[fly]* en ligne droite ; *[shoot]* juste ◆ **~ above us** juste au-dessus de nous ◆ **~ across from the house** juste en face de la maison ◆ **to go ~ ahead** aller tout droit ◆ **he looked ~ ahead** il a regardé droit devant lui ◆ **he came ~ at me** il s'est dirigé droit sur moi ◆ **to look ~ at sb** regarder qn droit dans les yeux ◆ **to hold o.s. ~** se tenir droit ◆ **to look sb ~ in the face/the eye** regarder qn bien en face/droit dans les yeux ◆ **to go ~ on** aller tout droit ◆ **to sit ~** s'asseoir bien droit ◆ **to sit up ~** se redresser ◆ **to stand ~** se tenir droit ◆ **to stand up ~** se redresser ◆ **the bullet went ~ through his chest** la balle lui a traversé la poitrine de part en part ◆ **to go ~ towards sb/sth** se diriger droit vers qn/qch ◆ **the cork shot ~ up in the air** le bouchon est parti droit en l'air

2 *(= level)* ◆ **to hang ~** *[picture]* être bien droit

3 *(= directly)* ◆ **~ after this** tout de suite après ◆ **to come ~ back** *(= without detour)* revenir directement ; *(= immediately)* revenir tout de suite ◆ **~ from the horse's mouth** de source sûre ◆ **to go ~ home** *(= without detour)* rentrer directement chez soi ; *(= immediately)* rentrer chez soi tout de suite ◆ **he went ~ to London** *(= without detour)* il est allé directement *or* tout droit à Londres ; *(= immediately)* il s'est immédiatement rendu à Londres ◆ **to go ~ to bed** aller tout de suite se coucher ◆ **I may as well come ~ to the point** autant que j'en vienne droit au fait ◆ **give it to me** *or* **tell me ~** * dis-le-moi carrément ◆ **I let him have it ~ from the shoulder** * *(= told him)* je le lui ai dit carrément

◆ **straight away** tout de suite, sur-le-champ

◆ **straight off** *(= immediately)* tout de suite, sur-le-champ ; *(= without hesitation)* sans hésiter ; *(= without beating about the bush)* sans ambages, sans mâcher ses mots

◆ **straight out** *(= without hesitation)* sans hésiter ; *(= without beating about the bush)* sans ambages, sans mâcher ses mots ◆ **to tell sb sth ~ out** dire franchement qch à qn

◆ **straight up** * *(Brit) (= really)* ◆ **~ up, I got fifty quid for it** sans blaguer *, j'en ai tiré cinquante livres ◆ **I got fifty quid for it – ~ up?** j'en ai tiré cinquante livres – sans blague ? *

4 *(= neat)* ◆ **to drink one's whisky ~** boire son whisky sec *or* sans eau

5 *(= clearly)* ◆ **he couldn't think ~** il avait le cerveau brouillé, il n'avait plus les idées claires ◆ **I couldn't see ~** je n'y voyais plus clair

6 ◆ **to go ~** * *(= reform)* revenir dans le droit chemin

7 *(= consecutively)* ◆ **for five days ~** pendant cinq jours d'affilée *or* consécutifs

8 *(Theat)* ◆ **he played the role ~** il a joué le rôle avec mesure

COMP **straight-acting** * **ADJ** ◆ **to be ~-acting** avoir un look hétéro *

straight arrow **N** *(esp US = person)* bon citoyen *m*

straight-cut tobacco **N** tabac *m* coupé dans la longueur de la feuille

straight-faced **ADV** en gardant son sérieux, d'un air impassible **ADJ** qui garde son sérieux, impassible

straight flush **N** *(Cards)* quinte *f* flush

straight-laced **ADJ** ⇒ **strait-laced** ; → **strait**

straight-line **ADJ** *[depreciation]* constant

straight man **N** (pl **straight men**) *(Theat)* comparse *m*, faire-valoir *m*

straight-out * **ADJ** *[answer, denial, refusal]* net, catégorique ; *[supporter, enthusiast, communist]* pur jus * ; *[liar, thief]* fieffé *before n*

straight razor **N** *(US)* rasoir *m* à main *or* de coiffeur

straight ticket **N** *(US Pol)* ◆ **to vote a ~ ticket** choisir une liste sans panachage

straightedge /ˈstreɪtedʒ/ **N** règle *f (large et plate)* ; *(in carpentry)* limande *f*

straighten /ˈstreɪtn/ **VT** *[+ wire, nail]* redresser ; *[+ hair]* décrêper, défriser ; *[+ road]* refaire *(en éliminant les tournants)* ; *[+ tie, hat]* ajuster ; *[+ picture]* redresser, remettre d'aplomb ; *[+ room]* mettre de l'ordre dans, mettre en ordre ; *[+ papers]* ranger ◆ **to have one's teeth ~ed** se faire redresser les dents ◆ **to ~ one's back** *or* **shoulders** se redresser, se tenir droit ◆ **to ~ the hem of a skirt** arrondir une jupe

VI (also **straighten out**) *[road]* devenir droit ; (also **straighten out, straighten up**) *[growing plant]* pousser droit ; (also **straighten up**) *[person]* se redresser

▸ **straighten out** VI → **straighten vi**

VT SEP *[+ wire, nail]* redresser, défausser ; *[+ road]* refaire en éliminant les tournants ; *(fig) [+ situation]* débrouiller ; *[+ problem]* résoudre ; *[+ one's ideas]* mettre de l'ordre dans, débrouiller ◆ **he managed to ~ things out** * il a réussi à arranger les choses ◆ **I'm trying to ~ out how much I owe him** * j'essaie de trouver combien je lui dois ◆ **to ~ sb out**‡ remettre qn dans la bonne voie ◆ **I'll soon ~ him out!**‡ je vais aller le remettre à sa place !, je vais lui apprendre !

▸ **straighten up** VI 1 → **straighten vi**

2 *(= tidy up)* mettre de l'ordre, ranger

VT SEP *[+ room, books, papers]* ranger, mettre de l'ordre dans

straightforward /ˌstreɪtˈfɔːwəd/ ADJ *(= frank)* honnête, franc (franche *f*) ; *(= plain-spoken)* franc (franche *f*), direct ; *(= simple)* simple ◆ **it's very ~** c'est tout ce qu'il y a de plus simple ◆ **it was ~ racism** c'était du racisme pur et simple *or* du racisme à l'état pur

straightforwardly /ˌstreɪtˈfɔːwədlɪ/ ADV *[answer]* franchement, sans détour ; *[behave]* avec droiture, honnêtement ◆ **everything went quite ~** il n'y a pas eu de problèmes, tout s'est bien passé

straightforwardness /ˌstreɪtˈfɔːwədnɪs/ N *(= frankness)* honnêteté *f*, franchise *f* ; *(= plain-spokenness)* franchise *f* ; *(= simplicity)* simplicité *f*

straightjacket /ˈstreɪtdʒækɪt/ N ⇒ **straitjacket**

straightness /ˈstreɪtnɪs/ N 1 *(= frankness)* franchise *f* ; *(= honesty)* rectitude *f* 2 *(* = heterosexual attitudes)* attitudes *fpl* hétéro *

straightway †† /ˈstreɪtweɪ/ ADV incontinent, sur-le-champ

strain¹ /streɪn/ N 1 *(Tech etc)* tension *f*, pression *f* ◆ **the ~ on the rope** la tension de la corde, la force exercée sur la corde ◆ **it broke under the ~** cela s'est rompu sous la tension ◆ **that puts a great ~ on the beam** cela exerce une forte pression sur la poutre ◆ **to take the ~ off sth** diminuer la pression sur qch ◆ **it put a great ~ on their friendship** cela a mis leur amitié à rude épreuve ◆ **it was a ~ on the economy/their resources/his purse** cela grevait l'économie/leurs ressources/son budget ◆ **to stand the ~** *[rope, beam]* supporter la tension (*or* le poids *etc*) ; *[person]* tenir le coup * ; → **breaking**

2 *(physical)* effort *m* (physique) ; *(= overwork)* surmenage *m* ; *(= tiredness)* fatigue *f* ◆ **the ~(s) of city life** la tension de la vie urbaine ◆ **the ~ of six hours at the wheel** la fatigue nerveuse que représentent six heures passées au volant ◆ **listening for three hours is a ~** écouter pendant trois heures demande un grand effort ◆ **all the ~ and struggle of bringing up the family** toutes les tensions et les soucis que l'on a quand on élève des enfants ◆ **the ~ of climbing the stairs** l'effort requis pour monter l'escalier ◆ **he has been under a great deal of ~** ses nerfs ont été mis à rude épreuve ◆ **the situation put a great ~ on him** *or* **put him under a great ~** la situation l'a épuisé *or* l'a beaucoup fatigué nerveusement ; → **stress**

3 *(Med = sprain)* entorse *f*, foulure *f* ; → **eyestrain**

4 ◆ **~s** *(Mus)* accords *mpl*, accents *mpl* ; *(Poetry)* accents *mpl*, chant *m* ◆ **to the ~s of the "London March"** aux accents de la "Marche londonienne"

VT 1 *[+ rope, beam]* tendre fortement *or* excessivement ; *(Med) [+ muscle]* froisser ; *[+ arm, ankle]* fouler ; *(fig) [+ friendship, relationship, marriage]* mettre à rude épreuve ; *[+ resources, savings, budget, the economy]* grever ; *[+ meaning]* forcer ; *[+ word]* forcer le sens de ; *[+ sb's patience]* mettre à l'épreuve ; *[+ one's authority]* outrepasser, excéder ◆ **to ~ one's back** se donner un tour de reins ◆ **to ~ one's heart** se fatiguer le cœur ◆ **to ~ one's shoulder** se froisser un muscle dans l'épaule ◆ **to ~ one's voice** *(action)* forcer sa voix ; *(result)* se casser la voix ◆ **to ~ one's eyes** s'abîmer *or* se fatiguer les yeux ◆ **he ~ed his eyes to make out what it was** il a plissé les yeux pour mieux distinguer ce que c'était ◆ **to ~ one's ears to hear sth** tendre l'oreille pour entendre qch ◆ **to ~ every nerve to do sth** fournir un effort intense pour faire qch ◆ **to ~ o.s.** *(= damage muscle etc)* se froisser un muscle ; *(= overtire o.s.)* se surmener ◆ **don't ~ yourself!** *(iro)* surtout ne te fatigue pas !

2 *(†† or liter)* **to ~ sb to o.s.** *or* **to one's heart** serrer qn contre son cœur, étreindre qn

3 *(= filter) [+ liquid, soup, gravy]* passer ; *[+ vegetables]* (faire) égoutter

VI ◆ **to ~ to do sth** *(physically)* peiner pour faire qch, fournir un gros effort pour faire qch ; *(mentally)* s'efforcer de faire qch ◆ **to ~ at sth** *(pushing/pulling)* pousser/tirer qch de toutes ses forces ; *(fig = jib at)* renâcler à qch ◆ **to ~ at the leash** *[dog]* tirer fort sur sa laisse ◆ **to ~ at a gnat (and swallow a camel)** *(Prov)* faire une histoire pour une vétille et passer sur une énormité ◆ **to ~ after sth** *(fig)* faire un grand effort pour obtenir qch ◆ **to ~ under a weight** ployer sous un poids

▸ **strain off** VT SEP *[+ liquid]* vider

strain² /streɪn/ N *(= breed, lineage)* race *f*, lignée *f* ; *[of animal etc]* race *f* ; *[of virus]* souche *f* ; *(= tendency, streak)* tendance *f* ◆ **there is a ~ of madness in the family** il y a dans la famille des tendances à *or* une prédisposition à la folie ◆ **there was a lot more in the same ~** il y en avait encore beaucoup du même genre ◆ **he continued in this ~** il a continué sur ce ton *or* dans ce sens

strained /streɪnd/ ADJ 1 *(= tense) [person, voice, relations, atmosphere, silence]* tendu 2 *(= unnatural) [smile]* contraint ; *[laugh, jollity, politeness]* forcé ; *[manner]* emprunté ; *[style]* affecté 3 *(Physiol) (= damaged) [muscle]* froissé ; *[arm, ankle]* foulé ; *[eyes]* fatigué ; *[voice] (= overtaxed)* forcé ; *(= injured)* cassé ◆ **he has a ~ shoulder/back** il s'est froissé un muscle dans l'épaule/le dos 4 *(Culin) [baby food]* en purée ; *[vegetables]* égoutté ; *[liquid, soup, gravy]* passé

strainer /ˈstreɪnəʳ/ N *(Culin)* passoire *f* ; *(conical)* chinois *m* ; *(Tech)* épurateur *m* ◆ **put the sauce through a ~** passer la sauce au chinois

strait /streɪt/ N 1 *(Geog: also straits)* détroit *m* ◆ **the Strait of Gibraltar** le détroit de Gibraltar ◆ **the Straits of Dover** le Pas de Calais ◆ **the Strait of Hormuz** le détroit d'Hormuz *or* d'Ormuz 2 *(fig)* **~s** situation *f* difficile ◆ **to be in financial ~s** avoir des ennuis d'argent ; → **dire** ADJ (*††: esp Biblical*) étroit COMP **strait-laced** ADJ collet monté *inv*

straitened /ˈstreɪtnd/ ADJ *(frm) [times]* de gêne ◆ **in ~ circumstances** dans la gêne ◆ **the more ~ economic circumstances of the 1990s** la situation économique plus difficile des années 1990

straitjacket /ˈstreɪtdʒækɪt/ N camisole *f* de force

strand¹ /strænd/ N *(liter: = shore)* grève *f* VT *[+ ship]* échouer ; (also **to leave stranded**) *[+ person]* laisser en rade * *or* en plan * ◆ **they were (left) ~ed without passports or money** ils se sont retrouvés en rade * *or* coincés sans passeport ni argent ◆ **he took the car and left me ~ed** il a pris la voiture et m'a laissé en plan * *or* en rade *

strand² /strænd/ N *[of thread, wire]* brin *m* ; *[of rope]* toron *m* ; *[of fibrous substance]* fibre *f* ; *[of pearls]* rang *m* ; *(fig: in narrative etc)* fil *m*, enchaînement *m* ◆ **a ~ of hair** une mèche ◆ **the ~s of one's life** le fil de sa vie

strange /streɪndʒ/ ADJ 1 *(= peculiar) [person, behaviour, feeling, fact, event, place, situation]* étrange ◆ **there's something ~ about him** il a quelque chose de bizarre ◆ **the ~ thing is that ...** ce qu'il y a d'étrange, c'est que ... ◆ **it feels ~ (to do sth)** ça fait bizarre (de faire qch), ça paraît étrange (de faire qch) ◆ **it is ~ that ...** c'est étrange que ... + *subj* ◆ **it is ~ to do sth** c'est étrange de faire qch ◆ **to seem ~ to sb** paraître étrange à qn ◆ **~ as it may seem ...** aussi étrange que cela puisse paraître ... ◆ **~ to say I have never met her** chose étrange, je ne l'ai jamais rencontrée, ce qu'il y a d'étrange, c'est que je ne l'ai jamais rencontrée ; → **bedfellow, truth**

2 *(= unfamiliar) [country, city, house, language]* inconnu (*to sb* à qn) ◆ **a ~ man** un inconnu ◆ **there were several ~ people there** il y avait plusieurs personnes que je ne connaissais pas (*or* qu'il ne connaissait pas *etc*) ◆ **don't talk to any ~ men** n'adresse pas la parole à des inconnus ◆ **never get in a ~ car** ne monte jamais dans la voiture d'un inconnu ◆ **a ~ car was parked in front of my house** une voiture inconnue était garée devant chez moi ◆ **I awoke in a ~ bed** je me suis réveillé dans un lit qui n'était pas le mien

3 *(= unaccustomed) [work, activity]* inhabituel ◆ **you'll feel rather ~ at first** vous vous sentirez un peu dépaysé pour commencer

4 *(= unwell)* ◆ **to feel ~** *[person]* se sentir mal, ne pas se sentir bien

strangely /ˈstreɪndʒlɪ/ ADV *[act, behave]* de façon étrange, bizarrement ; *[familiar, quiet]* étrangement ◆ **~ named** au nom étrange ◆ **to be ~ reminiscent of sb/sth** rappeler étrangement qn/qch ◆ **~ (enough), I have never met her** chose étrange, je ne l'ai jamais rencontrée

strangeness /ˈstreɪndʒnɪs/ N étrangeté *f*, bizarrerie *f*

stranger /ˈstreɪndʒəʳ/ N *(unknown)* inconnu(e) *m(f)* ; *(from another place)* étranger *m*, -ère *f* ◆ **he is a perfect ~ (to me)** il m'est totalement inconnu ◆ **I'm a ~ here** je ne suis pas d'ici ◆ **I am a ~ to Paris** je ne connais pas Paris ◆ **a ~ to politics** un novice en matière de politique ◆ **he was no ~ to misfortune** *(liter)* il connaissait bien le malheur, il avait l'habitude du malheur ◆ **you're quite a ~!** vous vous faites *or* vous devenez rare !, on ne vous voit plus ! ◆ **hello ~!** tiens, un revenant ! * COMP **Strangers' Gallery** N *(Brit Parl)* tribune *f* réservée au public

strangle /ˈstræŋgl/ VT étrangler ; *(fig) [+ free speech]* étrangler, museler ; *[+ protests]* étouffer ◆ **~d** *[person, voice, cry, laugh]* étranglé ; *[sneeze, sob]* étouffé

stranglehold /ˈstræŋglhəʊld/ N 1 *(Sport)* étranglement *m* ◆ **to get sb in a ~** faire un étranglement à qn 2 *(fig)* **the country has been kept in an economic ~** le pays a été maintenu dans un étau économique ◆ **to break the Serbian ~ on the capital** pour briser l'étau serbe autour la capitale ◆ **the company's ~ on the market** la mainmise de cette entreprise sur le marché

strangler /ˈstræŋgləʳ/ N étrangleur *m*, -euse *f*

strangling /ˈstræŋglɪŋ/ N *(lit)* strangulation *f*, étranglement *m* ; *(fig)* étranglement *m* ◆ **there have been several ~s in Boston** plusieurs personnes ont été étranglées à Boston

strangulate /ˈstræŋgjʊleɪt/ VT *(Med)* étrangler

strangulation /ˌstræŋgjʊˈleɪʃən/ N (NonC) strangulation *f*

strap /stræp/ N 1 *(of leather, thin)* lanière *f* ; *(broader)* sangle *f* ; *(of cloth)* bande *f* ; *(on shoe, also Climbing)* lanière *f* ; *(on harness etc)* sangle *f*, courroie *f* ; *(on suitcase, around book)* sangle *f*, lanière *f* ; *(on garment)* bretelle *f* ; *(on shoulder bag, camera etc)* bandoulière *f* ; *(= watch strap)* bracelet *m*
2 *(for razor)* cuir *m*
3 *(in bus, tube)* poignée *f* de cuir
4 *(used for punishment)* lanière *f* de cuir ◆ **to give sb the ~** administrer une correction à qn (avec une lanière de cuir) ◆ **to get the ~** recevoir une correction (avec une lanière de cuir)
VT 1 *(= tie)* attacher *(sth to sth* qch à qch*)*
2 (also **strap up**) *[+ sb's ribs]* bander ; *[+ suitcase, books]* attacher avec une sangle
3 *[+ child etc]* administrer une correction à
COMP **strap-hang** VI voyager debout *(dans les transports en commun)*
strap-hanger N *(standing)* voyageur *m*, -euse *f* debout *inv (dans les transports en commun)* ; *(US) (public transport user)* usager *m* des transports en commun

► **strap down** VT SEP attacher avec une sangle *or* une courroie

► **strap in** VT SEP *[+ object]* attacher avec une sangle ; *[+ child in car, pram]* attacher *(avec une ceinture or un harnais)* ◆ **he isn't properly ~ped in** il est mal attaché

► **strap on** VT SEP *[+ object]* attacher ; *[+ watch]* mettre, attacher

► **strap up** VT SEP ⇒ **strap vt 2**

strapless /ˈstræplɪs/ ADJ *[dress, bra]* sans bretelles

strapline /ˈstræplaɪn/ N *(Press = headline)* gros titre *m*

strapped * /stræpt/ ADJ ◆ **to be financially ~, to be ~ for funds** *or* **for cash** être à court (d'argent)

strapper * /ˈstræpəʳ/ N gaillard(e) *m(f)*

strapping /ˈstræpɪŋ/ ADJ bien bâti, costaud * ◆ **a ~ fellow** un solide gaillard N (NonC) 1 *(for cargo)* courroies *fpl*, sangles *fpl* 2 *(Med)* bandages *mpl*

strappy * /ˈstræpɪ/ ADJ *[sandals]* à lanières

Strasbourg /ˈstræzbɜːg/ N Strasbourg

strata /ˈstrɑːtə/ NPL of **stratum**

stratagem /ˈstrætɪdʒəm/ N stratagème *m*

strategic /strəˈtiːdʒɪk/ ADJ stratégique ◆ **to put sth in a ~ position** *(Mil)* mettre qch à un endroit stratégique
COMP **Strategic Air Command** N *(US)* l'aviation *f* militaire stratégique (américaine)
strategic business unit N domaine *m* d'activité stratégique
Strategic Defense Initiative N *(US)* Initiative *f* de défense stratégique
strategic fit N *(= management strategy)* adaptation *f* stratégique

strategical /strəˈtiːdʒɪkəl/ ADJ stratégique

strategically /strəˈtiːdʒɪkəlɪ/ ADV *[important, sensitive]* stratégiquement ◆ **to be ~ placed** *or* **located** *or* **situated** être placé à un endroit stratégique ◆ **~, speed is vital in a desert campaign** la vitesse est un élément stratégique fondamental lors d'une campagne dans le désert ◆ **~, a merger would make sense** du point de vue stratégique, une fusion serait souhaitable

strategist /ˈstrætɪdʒɪst/ N stratège *m*

strategy /ˈstrætɪdʒɪ/ N stratégie *f*

stratification /ˌstrætɪfɪˈkeɪʃən/ N stratification *f*

stratificational /ˌstrætɪfɪˈkeɪʃənl/ ADJ *(Ling)* stratificationnel

stratify /ˈstrætɪfaɪ/ VTI stratifier

stratocruiser /ˈstrætəʊˌkruːzəʳ/ N avion *m* stratosphérique

stratosphere /ˈstrætəʊsfɪəʳ/ N stratosphère *f* ◆ **this would send oil prices into the ~** cela ferait exploser le prix du pétrole

stratospheric /ˌstrætəʊsˈferɪk/ ADJ stratosphérique

stratum /ˈstrɑːtəm/ N (pl **stratums** *or* **strata**) *(Geol)* strate *f*, couche *f* ; *(fig)* couche *f*

straw /strɔː/ N paille *f* ◆ **to drink sth through a ~** boire qch avec une paille ◆ **to draw ~s** tirer à la courte paille ◆ **to draw the short ~** *(lit)* tirer la paille la plus courte ; *(fig)* tirer le mauvais numéro ◆ **man of ~** *(fig)* homme *m* de paille ◆ **to clutch** *or* **catch** *or* **grasp at ~s** se raccrocher désespérément à un semblant d'espoir ◆ **it's a ~ in the wind** c'est une indication des choses à venir ◆ **when he refused, it was the last ~** quand il a refusé, ça a été la goutte d'eau qui fait déborder le vase ◆ **that's the last ~** *or* **the ~ that breaks the camel's back!** ça c'est le comble ! ◆ **I don't care a ~** * je m'en fiche *, j'en ai rien à cirer *
COMP *(= made of straw: gen)* de *or* en paille ; *[roof]* de paille, de chaume
straw boss N *(US)* sous-chef *m*
straw-coloured ADJ paille *inv*
straw hat N chapeau *m* de paille
straw man N (pl **straw men**) *(fig)* homme *m* de paille
straw mat N paillasson *m*
straw mattress N paillasse *f*
straw poll N sondage *m* d'opinion
straw-poll elections NPL *(US Pol)* élection-pilote *f*, élection-témoin *f*
straw vote N *(esp US)* ⇒ **straw poll**

strawberry /ˈstrɔːbərɪ/ N *(= fruit)* fraise *f* ; *(= plant)* fraisier *m* ◆ **wild ~** fraise *f* des bois, fraise *f* sauvage
COMP *[jam]* de fraises ; *[ice cream]* à la fraise ; *[tart]* aux fraises
strawberry bed N fraiseraie *f*, fraisière *f*
strawberry blonde ADJ blond vénitien *inv* N femme *f or* fille *f etc* aux cheveux blond vénitien
strawberry mark N *(Anat)* fraise *f*, envie *f*
strawberry roan N cheval *m* rouan, jument *f* rouanne

stray /streɪ/ N 1 *(= dog, cat, etc)* animal *m* errant *or* perdu ; *(= sheep, cow etc)* animal *m* égaré ; *(= child)* enfant *mf* perdu(e) *or* abandonné(e) ◆ **this dog is a ~** c'est un chien perdu *or* errant ; → **waif**
2 *(Rad)* **~s** parasites *mpl*, friture *f*
ADJ 1 *(= lost) [dog, cat]* errant ; *[cow, sheep]* égaré ; *[child]* perdu, abandonné
2 *(= random) [bullet]* perdu ; *[shot, fact, plane, taxi]* isolé ; *[thought]* vagabond ; *[hairs, bits of food]* épars ◆ **he picked a ~ hair off her shoulder** il a enlevé un cheveu de son épaule ◆ **~ strands of hair fell across her forehead** des mèches folles lui tombaient sur le front ◆ **a few ~ houses** quelques maisons éparses ◆ **a few ~ cars** quelques rares voitures ◆ **a ~ red sock had got into the white wash** une chaussette rouge s'était égarée dans le linge blanc
VI (also **stray away**) *[person, animal]* s'égarer ; *[thoughts]* vagabonder, errer ◆ **to ~ (away) from** *(lit, fig) [+ place, plan, subject]* s'écarter de ; *[+ course, route]* dévier de ◆ **they ~ed into enemy territory** ils se sont égarés *or* ont fait fausse route et se sont retrouvés en territoire ennemi ◆ **his thoughts ~ed to the coming holidays** il se prit à penser aux vacances prochaines

streak /striːk/ N 1 *(= line, band)* raie *f*, bande *f* ; *[of ore, mineral]* veine *f* ; *[of light]* rai *m*, filet *m* ; *[of blood, paint]* filet *m* ◆ **his hair had ~s of grey in it** ses cheveux commençaient à grisonner ◆ **he had (blond) ~s put in his hair** il s'est fait faire des mèches (blondes) ◆ **a ~ of cloud across the sky** une traînée nuageuse dans le ciel ◆ **a ~ of lightning** un éclair ◆ **he went past like a ~ (of lightning)** il est passé comme un éclair
2 *(= tendency)* tendance(s) *f(pl)*, propension *f* ◆ **he has a jealous ~** *or* **a ~ of jealousy** il a des tendances *or* une propension à la jalousie ◆ **she has a ~ of Irish blood** elle a du sang irlandais dans les veines ◆ **a lucky ~, a ~ of luck** une période de chance ◆ **an unlucky ~, a ~ of bad luck** une période de malchance ◆ **a winning ~** *(Sport)* une suite *or* une série de victoires ; *(Gambling)* une bonne passe ◆ **to be on a winning ~** *(Sport)* accumuler les victoires ; *(Gambling)* être dans une bonne passe
VT zébrer, strier *(with* de*)* ◆ **a mirror ~ed with dirt** un miroir zébré de traînées sales ◆ **sky ~ed with red** ciel *m* strié *or* zébré de bandes rouges ◆ **cheeks ~ed with tear-marks** joues *fpl* sillonnées de larmes ◆ **clothes ~ed with mud/paint** vêtements *mpl* maculés de traînées de boue/de peinture ◆ **his hair was ~ed with grey** ses cheveux commençaient à grisonner ◆ **she's got ~ed hair, she's had her hair ~ed** elle s'est fait faire des mèches ◆ **rock ~ed with quartz** roche *f* veinée de quartz ◆ **meat ~ed with fat** viande *f* persillée
VI 1 *(= rush)* **to ~ in/out/past** *etc* entrer/sortir/passer *etc* comme un éclair
2 *(* = dash naked)* courir tout nu en public

streaker * /ˈstriːkəʳ/ N streaker *m*, -euse *f*

streaky /ˈstriːkɪ/ ADJ *[glass, window, mirror]* plein de traînées ; *[pattern, sky]* strié, zébré ◆ **the first coat of paint looked rather ~** la première couche de peinture avait l'air plutôt irrégulière ◆ **he had ~ fair hair** il avait les cheveux blonds avec des mèches
COMP **streaky bacon** N *(Brit)* bacon *m* entrelardé

stream /striːm/ N 1 *(= brook)* ruisseau *m*
2 *(= current)* courant *m* ◆ **to go with the ~** *(lit, fig)* suivre le courant ◆ **to go against the ~** *(lit, fig)* aller contre le courant *or* à contre-courant ; → **downstream, upstream**
3 *(= flow) [of water]* flot *m*, jet *m* ; *[of lava]* flot *m*, torrent *m* ; *[of blood, light, oaths, excuses, cars, trucks]* flot *m* ; *[of tears]* torrent *m*, ruisseau *m* ; *[of curses]* flot *m*, torrent *m* ; *[of cold air etc]* courant *m* ◆ **a thin ~ of water** un mince filet d'eau ◆ **the water flowed out in a steady ~** l'eau s'écoulait régulièrement ◆ **to be/go on ~** être/entrer en service ◆ **to come on ~** être mis en service ◆ **to bring the oil on ~** mettre le pipeline en service ◆ **~s of people were coming out** des flots de gens sortaient, les gens sortaient à flots ◆ **the ~ of consciousness** *(Literat, Psych)* la vie mouvante et insaisissable de la conscience, le "stream of consciousness"
4 *(Brit Scol)* groupe *m* de niveau ◆ **divided into five ~s** *(Brit Scol)* réparti en cinq groupes de niveau ◆ **the top/middle/bottom ~** la section forte/moyenne/faible
VI 1 *[water, tears, oil, milk]* ruisseler ; *[blood]* ruisseler, dégouliner ◆ **to ~ with blood/tears** *etc* ruisseler de sang/de larmes *etc* ◆ **the fumes made his eyes ~** les émanations l'ont fait pleurer à chaudes larmes ◆ **cold air/sunlight ~ed through the window** l'air froid/le soleil entra à flots par la fenêtre
2 *(in wind etc)* (also **stream out**) flotter au vent
3 **to ~ in/out/past** *etc [people, cars etc]* entrer/sortir/passer *etc* à flots
VT 1 ◆ **to ~ blood/water** *etc* ruisseler de sang/d'eau *etc*
2 *(Scol) [+ pupils]* répartir par niveau ◆ **to ~ French** *or* **the French classes** répartir les élèves par niveaux en français

streamer /ˈstriːməʳ/ **N** *(of paper)* serpentin *m* ; *(= banner)* banderole *f* ; *(Astron)* flèche *f* lumineuse ; *(Press)* manchette *f*

streaming /ˈstriːmɪŋ/ **N** *(Scol)* répartition *f* des élèves par niveaux **ADJ** *(Brit)* ◆ **to have a ~ cold** avoir un gros rhume ◆ **to have a ~ nose** avoir le nez qui n'arrête pas de couler ◆ **to have ~ eyes** avoir les yeux qui pleurent

streamline /ˈstriːmlaɪn/ **VT** 1 *[+ car, boat, plane]* donner un profil aérodynamique à 2 *[+ organization, system, process]* rationaliser ; *(= downsize)* dégraisser les effectifs de

streamlined /ˈstriːmlaɪnd/ **ADJ** 1 *[plane, shape or body of plane]* aérodynamique ; *[car, shape or body of car]* caréné, profilé ; *[shape or body of animal, bird] (in air)* aérodynamique ; *(in water)* hydrodynamique 2 *[organization, system, process]* rationalisé ; *(through downsizing)* dégraissé 3 *(= uncluttered) [room, appearance]* dépouillé ◆ **a ~ new kitchen** une nouvelle cuisine aux lignes dépouillées 4 *(= slim) [silhouette]* svelte

streamlining /ˈstriːmlaɪnɪŋ/ **N** *[of organization, system, process]* rationalisation *f* ; *(= downsizing)* dégraissage *m*

street /striːt/ **N** 1 rue *f* ◆ **I saw him in the ~** je l'ai vu dans la rue ◆ **to take to the ~s** *[demonstrators, protesters]* descendre dans la rue ◆ **to turn** *or* **put sb (out) into the ~** mettre qn à la rue ◆ **to be out on the ~(s)** *(= homeless)* être à la rue, être SDF ◆ **a woman of the ~s** † une prostituée ◆ **she is on the ~s*, she works the ~s*** elle fait le trottoir

2 *(fig)* **that's right up my ~*** *(Brit)* c'est tout à fait dans mes cordes ◆ **he is not in the same ~ as you*** *(Brit)* il ne vous arrive pas à la cheville ◆ **to be ~s ahead of sb*** *(Brit)* dépasser qn de loin ◆ **they're ~s apart*** un monde *or* tout les sépare ◆ **~s better*** *(Brit)* beaucoup mieux ; → **back, high, man, queer, walk**

COMP *[noises etc]* de la rue ; *[singer etc]* des rues
street accident N accident *m* de la circulation
street arab † **N** gamin(e) *m(f)* des rues
street child N enfant *m* des rues
street cleaner N *(= person)* balayeur *m* ; *(= machine)* balayeuse *f*
street cred*, street credibility N ◆ **to have ~ cred** *or* **credibility** être branché* ◆ **this will do wonders for your ~ cred** *or* **credibility** c'est excellent pour ton image de marque
street directory N ⇒ **street guide**
street door N porte *f* donnant sur la rue, porte *f* d'entrée
street fighting N *(NonC: Mil)* combats *mpl* de rue
street furniture N mobilier *m* urbain
street guide N plan *m* de la ville, répertoire *m* des rues
street hawker N colporteur *m*
street level N ◆ **at ~ level** au rez-de-chaussée
street lighting N *(NonC)* éclairage *m* des rues *or* de la voie publique
street map N plan *m* de la ville, répertoire *m* des rues
street market N marché *m* en plein air *or* à ciel ouvert
street musician N musicien *m*, -ienne *f* des rues
street name N nom *m* de rue
street people NPL sans-abri *mpl*, SDF *mpl*
street person N SDF *mf*
street photographer N photographe *mf* de rue
street plan N plan *m* de la ville
street price N *(US Stock Exchange)* cours *m* après Bourse *or* hors Bourse ; *[of drugs]* prix *m* de vente *(au consommateur)*
street seller N marchand *m* ambulant
street smart* ADJ *(US = shrewd)* futé, dégourdi
street smarts NPL *(US)* débrouillardise *f*
street sweeper N *(= person)* balayeur *m* ; *(= machine)* balayeuse *f*
street theatre N *(NonC)* théâtre *m* de rue
street trading N *(NonC)* vente *f* ambulante
street urchin N gamin(e) *m(f)* des rues
street value N *[of drugs]* valeur *f* à la revente
street vendor N marchand *m* ambulant

streetcar /ˈstriːtkɑːʳ/ **N** *(US)* tramway *m*

streetlamp /ˈstriːtlæmp/, **streetlight** /ˈstriːtlaɪt/ **N** réverbère *m*

streetwalker /ˈstriːtˌwɔːkəʳ/ **N** prostituée *f*

streetwise /ˈstriːtwaɪz/ **ADJ** *(lit) [child]* conscient des dangers de la rue ; *(fig) [worker, policeman]* futé, dégourdi

strength /streŋθ/ **N** *(NonC)* 1 *[of person, animal, voice, magnet, lens]* force *f*, puissance *f* ; *[of wind, enemy, team, nation, one's position]* force *f* ; *(= health)* forces *fpl*, robustesse *f* ; *[of current]* intensité *f*

◆ **on the strength of** *(= as a result of)* grâce à ◆ **the group achieved stardom solely on the ~ of their videos** le groupe est devenu célèbre simplement grâce à ses clips ◆ **he was able to borrow money on the ~ of advances he had already received** il a pu emprunter de l'argent grâce à des avances qu'il avait déjà reçues ◆ **he was elected on the ~ of his personality** c'est sa personnalité qui l'a fait élire ◆ **he was convicted on the ~ of medical evidence** sa culpabilité a été établie sur des preuves médicales ◆ **shares have risen in value on the ~ of the merger** les actions ont monté à la suite de la fusion

2 *[building, wall, wood, shoes, material]* solidité *f*

3 *[of character, accent, emotion, influence, attraction]* force *f* ; *[of belief, opinion]* force *f*, fermeté *f* ; *[of arguments, reasons]* force *f*, solidité *f* ; *[of protests]* force *f*, vigueur *f* ; *[of claim, case]* solidité *f*

4 *[of tea, coffee, cigarette]* force *f* ; *[of sauce]* goût *m* relevé ; *[of drink]* teneur *f* en alcool ; *[of solution]* titre *m* ◆ **he hadn't the ~ to lift it** il n'avait pas la force de le soulever ◆ **with all my/his/our ~** de toutes mes/ses/nos forces ◆ **his ~ failed him** ses forces l'ont abandonné ◆ **give me ~!*** Dieu qu'il faut être patient ! ◆ **to get one's ~ back** reprendre des forces, recouvrer ses forces ◆ **to go from ~ to ~** devenir de plus en plus fort ◆ **~ of character** force de caractère ◆ **~ of purpose** résolution *f*, détermination *f* ◆ **he has great ~ of purpose** il est très résolu *or* déterminé ◆ **~ of will** volonté *f*, fermeté *f* ◆ **the ~ of the pound** la solidité de la livre ◆ **the pound has gained in ~** la livre s'est consolidée ◆ **to be bargaining from ~** être en position de force pour négocier ; → **show, tensile**

5 *(Mil, Naut)* effectif(s) *m(pl)* ◆ **fighting ~** effectif(s) *m(pl)* mobilisable(s) ◆ **they are below** *or* **under ~** leur effectif n'est pas au complet ◆ **to bring up to ~** compléter l'effectif de ◆ **his friends were there in ~** ses amis étaient là en grand nombre ◆ **to be on the ~** *(Mil)* figurer sur les contrôles ; *(gen)* faire partie du personnel

strengthen /ˈstreŋθən/ **VT** 1 *[+ person, muscle, limb]* fortifier ; *[+ building, table]* consolider, renforcer ; *[+ wall]* étayer ; *[+ fabric, material]* renforcer ; *[+ the pound, stock market]* consolider 2 *[+ team, opinion, affection, argument, emotion, belief, one's position, one's resolve]* renforcer ◆ **this has ~ed the case for reform** cela a renforcé les arguments en faveur de la réforme ◆ **to ~ sb's hand** *(fig)* renforcer la position de qn ◆ **to ~ one's grip on sth** renforcer son contrôle sur qch **VI** *[muscle, limb]* devenir fort *or* vigoureux, se fortifier ; *[wind]* augmenter, redoubler ; *[desire, influence, characteristic]* augmenter ; *[prices]* se raffermir

strengthening /ˈstreŋθənɪŋ/ **N** *[of nation, team, one's position, case, building, material]* renforcement *m* ; *[of currency, stock market]* consolidation *f* ; *[of affection]* augmentation *f* **ADJ** ◆ **~ exercises** exercices *mpl* de raffermissement ◆ **a ~ economy** une économie en croissance ◆ **to have a ~ effect on sth** consolider qch

strenuous /ˈstrenjʊəs/ **ADJ** *[exercise, life, holiday, game, march, campaign]* épuisant ; *[activity, work, job]* ardu ; *[efforts, attempts, opposition, resistance, attack]* acharné ; *[objection, protest, denial]* vigoureux ◆ **it was all too ~ for me** tout cela était trop ardu pour moi ◆ **I'd like to do something less ~** j'aimerais faire quelque chose de moins pénible ◆ **he mustn't do anything ~** *(Med)* il ne faut pas qu'il se fatigue *subj*

strenuously /ˈstrenjʊəslɪ/ **ADV** *[exercise, deny, oppose, object, protest]* vigoureusement ; *[resist, try]* avec acharnement

strenuousness /ˈstrenjʊəsnɪs/ **N** (degré *m* d')effort *m* requis (of par)

strep throat* /ˌstrepˈθrəʊt/ **N** *(NonC: Med)* angine *f* (streptococcique)

streptococcal /ˌstreptəʊˈkɒkl/, **streptococcic** /ˌstreptəʊˈkɒksɪk/ **ADJ** streptococcique

streptococcus /ˌstreptəʊˈkɒkəs/ **N** (pl **streptococci** /ˌstreptəʊˈkɒkaɪ/) streptocoque *m*

streptomycin /ˌstreptəʊˈmaɪsɪn/ **N** streptomycine *f*

stress /stres/ LANGUAGE IN USE 26.3

N 1 *(= pressure etc)* pression *f*, stress *m* ; *(Med)* stress *m* ; (also **mental stress, nervous stress**) tension *f* (nerveuse) ◆ **in times of ~** à des moments *or* à une période de grande tension ◆ **the ~es and strains of modern life** toutes les pressions et les tensions de la vie moderne, les agressions de la vie moderne ◆ **to be under ~** *[person]* être stressé ; *[relationship]* être tendu ◆ **this put him under great ~** ceci l'a considérablement stressé ◆ **he reacts well under ~** il réagit bien dans des conditions difficiles

2 *(= emphasis)* insistance *f* ◆ **to lay ~ on** insister sur

3 *(Ling, Poetry) (NonC: gen)* accentuation *f* ; *(= accent: on syllable)* accent *m* ; *(= accented syllable)* syllabe *f* accentuée ; *(Mus)* accent *m* ◆ **the ~ is on the first syllable** *(Ling)* l'accent tombe sur la première syllabe ; → **primary, secondary**

4 *(Tech, Mechanics, Constr)* effort *m*, contrainte *f* ; *(on rope, cable)* charge *f* ◆ **the ~ acting on a metal** l'effort qui agit sur un métal ◆ **the ~ produced in the metal** le travail du métal ◆ **to be in ~** *[beam, metal]* travailler ◆ **the ~ to which a beam is subjected** la charge qu'on fait subir à une poutre ◆ **a ~ of 500 kilos per square millimetre** une charge de 500 kilos par millimètre carré ; → **tensile**

VT 1 *(= emphasize) [+ good manners, one's innocence etc]* insister sur ; *[+ fact, detail]* faire ressortir, souligner

2 *(Ling, Mus, Poetry)* accentuer

3 *(Tech: natural process)* fatiguer, faire travailler ; *(Tech: industrial process) [+ metal]* mettre sous tension

COMP **stress fracture N** *(Med)* fracture *f* de marche
stress mark N *(Ling)* accent *m*
stress quotient N ◆ **this job has a high ~ quotient** ce travail provoque une grande tension nerveuse
stress-related ADJ *[illness]* causé par le stress

stressed /strest/ **ADJ** 1 *(= tense) [person]* stressé ◆ **what are you getting so ~ out* about?** pourquoi es-tu si stressé ?*, il n'y a pas de quoi stresser* 2 *(Ling, Poetry)* accentué 3 *(Phys)* soumis à une contrainte

stressful /ˈstresfʊl/ **ADJ** *[situation, environment, life, day, job]* stressant ; *[event]* stressant, éprouvant

stressor /ˈstresəʳ/ **N** *(= stress factor)* facteur *m* de stress

stretch /stretʃ/ **N** 1 *(= act, gesture)* étirement *m* ◆ **to have a ~** s'étirer

◆ **by** + **stretch** ◆ **by a ~ of the imagination** en faisant un effort d'imagination ◆ **by no** *or* **not by any ~ of the imagination can one say that ...** même en faisant un gros effort d'imagination, on ne peut pas dire que ... ◆ **not by a long ~!** loin de là !

◆ **to be at full stretch** *[arms, rope]* être complètement tendu ; *[engine, factory]* tourner à plein régime ; *[person]* être au maximum de ses capacités ◆ **we're at full ~ at the moment** nous sommes à plein régime en ce moment

[2] *(= elasticity)* **there's not much ~ left in this elastic** cet élastique a beaucoup perdu de son élasticité ◆ **there's a lot of ~ in this material** ce tissu donne *or* prête à l'usage

[3] *(= distance, span: of wing etc)* envergure *f*

[4] *(= period of time)* période *f* ◆ **for a long ~ of time** (pendant) longtemps ◆ **for hours at a ~** des heures durant ◆ **he read it all in one ~** il l'a lu d'une (seule) traite ◆ **to do a ~** * faire de la prison *or* de la taule‡ ◆ **he's done a ten-year ~** * il a fait dix ans de taule‡

[5] *(= area)* étendue *f* ; *(= part)* partie *f*, bout *m* ◆ **vast ~es of sand/snow** de vastes étendues de sable/de neige ◆ **there's a straight ~ (of road) after you pass the lake** la route est toute droite *or* il y a un bout tout droit une fois que vous avez dépassé le lac ◆ **a magnificent ~ of country** une campagne magnifique ◆ **in that ~ of the river** dans cette partie de la rivière ◆ **for a long ~ the road runs between steep hills** sur des kilomètres la route serpente entre des collines escarpées ◆ **to go into the final ~** *(Racing, Running, also fig)* entrer dans la dernière ligne droite ; → **home**

[6] *(Naut)* bordée *f* (courue sous les mêmes amures)

ADJ *[garment, fabric, cushion-cover]* extensible

VT [1] *(= make longer, wider etc) [+ rope, spring]* tendre ; *[+ elastic]* étirer ; *[+ shoe, glove, hat]* élargir ; *(Med) [+ muscle, tendon]* distendre ; *(fig) [+ law, rules]* tourner ; *[+ meaning]* forcer ; *[+ one's principles]* adapter ; *[+ one's authority]* outrepasser, excéder ◆ **(if you were) to ~ a point you could say that ...** on pourrait peut-être aller jusqu'à dire que ... ◆ **you could ~ a point and allow him to ...** vous pourriez faire une petite concession et lui permettre de ... ◆ **to ~ the truth** forcer la vérité, exagérer ◆ **to ~ one's imagination** faire un effort d'imagination

[2] *(= extend: also* **stretch out***) [+ wing]* déployer ; *[+ rope, net, canopy]* tendre *(between* entre ; *above* au-dessus de) ; *[+ rug]* étendre, étaler ; *[+ linen]* étendre ◆ **to ~ o.s.** *(after sleep etc)* s'étirer ; see also **vt 4** ◆ **he had to ~ his neck to see** il a dû tendre le cou pour voir ◆ **he ~ed (out) his arm to grasp the handle** il tendit *or* allongea le bras pour saisir la poignée ◆ **he ~ed his arms and yawned** il s'étira et bâilla ◆ **he ~ed his leg to ease the cramp** il a étendu *or* allongé sa jambe pour faire passer la crampe ◆ **I'm just going to ~ my legs** * *(= go for a walk)* je vais juste me dégourdir les jambes ◆ **the blow ~ed him (out) cold** le coup l'a mis KO * ◆ **to be fully ~ed** *[rope etc]* être tendu au maximum ◆ **to ~ one's wings** élargir ses horizons ; see also **vt 3, vt 4**

[3] *(fig) [+ resources, supplies, funds, income] (= make them last)* faire durer, tirer le maximum de ; *(= put demands on them)* mettre à rude épreuve ◆ **to be fully ~ed** *[engine]* tourner à plein régime ; *[factory]* tourner à plein régime *or* rendement ◆ **our supplies/resources** *etc* **are fully ~ed** nos provisions/ressources *etc* sont utilisées au maximum, nos provisions/ressources *etc* ne sont pas élastiques ◆ **we're very ~ed at the moment** on tourne à plein régime en ce moment ; see also **vt 2, vt 4**

[4] *(fig) [+ athlete, student etc]* pousser, exiger le maximum de ◆ **the work he is doing does not ~ him enough** le travail qu'il fait n'exige pas assez de lui ◆ **to be fully ~ed** travailler à la limite de ses possibilités ◆ **to ~ sb to the limits** pousser qn au maximum ◆ **to ~ o.s. too far** vouloir en faire trop ; see also **vt 2, 3**

VI [1] *[person, animal]* s'étirer ◆ **he ~ed lazily** il s'est étiré paresseusement ◆ **he ~ed across me to get the book** il a tendu le bras devant moi pour prendre le livre

[2] *(= lengthen)* s'allonger ; *(= widen)* s'élargir ; *[elastic]* s'étirer, se tendre ; *[fabric, jersey, gloves, shoes]* prêter, donner

[3] *(= extend, reach, spread out:* also often **stretch out***) [rope etc]* s'étendre, aller ; *[forest, plain, procession, sb's authority, influence]* s'étendre ◆ **the rope won't ~ to that post** la corde ne va pas jusqu'à ce poteau ◆ **how far will it ~?** jusqu'où ça va ? ◆ **my money won't ~ * to a new car** je n'ai pas les moyens de m'acheter une nouvelle voiture ◆ **the festivities ~ed (out) into January** les festivités se sont prolongées pendant une partie du mois de janvier ◆ **a life of misery ~ed (out) before her** une vie de misère s'étendait *or* s'étalait devant elle

COMP **stretch limo** * **N** limousine *f* extra-longue

stretch mark N vergeture *f*

► **stretch across VI** ◆ **he stretched across and touched her cheek** il a tendu la main et touché sa joue

► **stretch down VI** ◆ **she stretched down and picked up the book** elle a tendu la main et ramassé le livre, elle a allongé le bras pour ramasser le livre

► **stretch out VI** s'étendre ◆ **he ~ed out on the bed** il s'est étendu sur le lit ; see also **stretch vi 3**

VT SEP [1] *(= reach) [+ arm, hand, foot]* tendre ; *(= extend) [+ leg, rug, linen]* étendre ; *[+ wing]* déployer ; *[+ net, canopy, rope]* tendre ; *(= lengthen) [+ meeting, discussion]* prolonger ; *[+ story, explanation]* allonger ◆ **he ~ed himself out on the bed** il s'est étendu sur le lit

[2] ⇒ **stretch vt 2**

► **stretch over VI** ⇒ **stretch across**

► **stretch up VI** ◆ **he stretched up to reach the shelf** il s'est étiré pour atteindre l'étagère

stretcher /ˈstretʃəʳ/ **N** [1] *(Med)* brancard *m*, civière *f* [2] *(= device) (for gloves)* ouvre-gants *m inv* ; *(for shoes)* forme *f* ; *(for fabric)* cadre *m* ; *(for artist's canvas)* cadre *m*, châssis *m* ; *(on umbrella)* baleine *f* [3] *(Constr = brick)* panneresse *f*, carreau *m* ; *(= crosspiece in framework)* traverse *f* ; *(= crossbar in chair, bed etc)* barreau *m*, bâton *m* ; *(= cross-plank in canoe etc)* barre *f* de pieds **VT** porter sur un brancard *or* une civière ◆ **the goalkeeper was ~ed off** le gardien de but a été emmené sur un brancard *or* une civière

COMP **stretcher-bearer N** brancardier *m*

stretcher case N malade *mf or* blessé(e) *m(f)* qui ne peut pas marcher

stretcher party N équipe *f* de brancardiers

stretchy /ˈstretʃɪ/ **ADJ** extensible

strew /struː/ (pret **strewed**, ptp **strewed** *or* **strewn**) **VT** *[+ straw, sand, sawdust]* répandre, éparpiller *(on, over* sur) ; *[+ flowers, objects]* éparpiller, semer *(on, over* sur) ; *[+ wreckage etc]* éparpiller, disséminer *(over* sur) ; *[+ ground, floor]* joncher, parsemer *(with* de) ; *[+ room, table]* joncher *(also fig)*

strewth ‡ /struːθ/ **EXCL** ça alors ! *, bon sang ! *

striate /straɪˈeɪt/ **VT** strier

stricken /ˈstrɪkən/ **VB** *(rare)* ptp of **strike ADJ** [1] *[area, city, economy]* sinistré ; *(by war)* dévasté ; *[ship]* en détresse ; *[industry, firm]* gravement touché ◆ **to be ~ by famine/drought** être frappé par la famine/la sécheresse [2] *(= wounded)* gravement blessé ◆ **~ with grief** accablé de douleur ◆ **~ with** *or* **by panic** saisi de panique ◆ **to be ~ with** *or* **by polio/cancer** être atteint de polio/d'un cancer ◆ **I was ~ with** *or* **by guilt** j'ai été pris d'un sentiment de culpabilité [3] *(= afflicted) [person, look, expression]* affligé ; see also **strike**

-stricken /ˈstrɪkən/ **ADJ** *(in compounds)* frappé de, atteint de, accablé de ◆ **plague-stricken** touché par de la peste ; → **grief**

strict /strɪkt/ **ADJ** [1] *(= severe, inflexible)* strict ; *[person]* strict, sévère ; *[secrecy]* absolu ◆ **security was ~ for the President's visit** de strictes mesures de sécurité avaient été mises en place pour la visite du Président ◆ **to be under ~ orders (not) to do sth** avoir reçu l'ordre formel de (ne pas) faire qch ◆ **to reveal/treat sth in ~ confidence** révéler/traiter qch de façon strictement confidentielle ◆ **"write in strict confidence to Paul Jackson"** "écrire à Paul Jackson : discrétion assurée" ◆ **this is in the ~est confidence** c'est strictement confidentiel

[2] *[meaning, truth]* strict ◆ **in the ~ sense (of the word)** au sens strict (du mot), stricto sensu ◆ **in ~ order of precedence** suivant strictement l'ordre de préséance ◆ **a ~ time limit** un délai impératif

COMP **strict liability N** *(Jur)* responsabilité *f* inconditionnelle

strictly /ˈstrɪktlɪ/ **LANGUAGE IN USE 26.3 ADV** [1] *(= sternly, severely) [treat, bring up]* d'une manière stricte

[2] *[controlled, enforced, observed, adhered to]* rigoureusement ◆ **~ confidential/personal/limited** strictement confidentiel/privé/limité ◆ **~ prohibited** *or* **forbidden** *(gen)* formellement interdit ◆ **"smoking strictly prohibited"** "défense absolue de fumer" ◆ **~ between us** *or* **ourselves** *or* **you and me** strictement entre nous ◆ **this is ~ business** c'est strictement professionnel ◆ **our relationship is ~ professional** notre relation est strictement professionnelle ◆ **that's not ~ true** ce n'est pas tout à fait vrai ◆ **it's not ~ necessary** ce n'est pas absolument nécessaire ◆ **you should avoid medication unless ~ necessary** évitez de prendre des médicaments si ce n'est pas indispensable ◆ **fox-hunting is ~ for the rich** la chasse au renard est réservée aux riches ◆ **this car park is ~ for the use of residents** ce parking est exclusivement *or* strictement réservé aux résidents ◆ **~ speaking** à proprement parler ◆ **that's ~ for the birds!** * ça c'est bon pour les imbéciles ! *

strictness /ˈstrɪktnɪs/ **N** sévérité *f*

stricture /ˈstrɪktʃəʳ/ **N** *(= criticism)* critique *f* (hostile) *(on* de) ; *(= restriction)* restriction *f (on* de) ; *(Med)* sténose *f*, rétrécissement *m*

stridden /ˈstrɪdn/ **VB** ptp of **stride**

stride /straɪd/ (vb : pret **strode**, ptp **stridden**) **N** grand pas *m*, enjambée *f* ; *[of runner]* foulée *f* ◆ **with giant ~s** à pas de géant ◆ **in** *or* **with a few ~s he had caught up with the others** il avait rattrapé les autres en quelques enjambées *or* foulées ◆ **to make great ~s (in French/in one's studies)** faire de grands progrès (en français/dans ses études) ◆ **to get into one's ~, to hit one's ~** trouver son rythme (de croisière) ◆ **to take sth in one's ~** *(Brit)* ◆ **to take sth in ~** *(US)* accepter qch sans sourciller *or* sans se laisser démonter ◆ **he took it in his ~** *(Brit)* ◆ **he took it in ~** *(US)* il a continué sans se décontenancer, il ne s'est pas laissé démonter ◆ **to put sb off their ~** faire perdre sa concentration à qn, déboussoler * qn ◆ **to be caught off ~** *(US)* être pris au dépourvu

VI marcher à grands pas *or* à grandes enjambées ◆ **to ~ along/in/away** *etc* avancer/entrer/s'éloigner *etc* à grands pas *or* à grandes enjambées ◆ **he was striding up and down the room** il arpentait la pièce

VT [1] *[+ deck, yard, streets]* arpenter

[2] † ⇒ **bestride**

stridency /ˈstraɪdənsɪ/ **N** [1] *[of tone, rhetoric etc]* véhémence *f* [2] *[of sound, voice]* stridence *f*

strident /ˈstraɪdənt/ ADJ 1 *(gen pej = vociferous) [critic, criticism]* acharné, véhément ; *[tone, rhetoric, feminist]* véhément ◆ **there were ~ calls for his resignation/for him to resign** on a demandé à grands cris sa démission/qu'il démissionne 2 *[sound, voice]* strident *(also Phon)*

stridently /ˈstraɪdəntlɪ/ ADV 1 *(= noisily) [hoot, sound, whistle]* d'une façon stridente 2 *(= vociferously) [demand, declare]* à grands cris ◆ ~ **anti-American** farouchement anti-américain

strife /straɪf/ N *(NonC)* conflit *m*, dissensions *fpl* ; *(less serious)* querelles *fpl* ◆ **a party crippled by internal ~** *(Pol)* un parti paralysé par des dissensions *or* des querelles intestines ◆ **industrial ~** conflits *mpl* sociaux ◆ **domestic ~** querelles *fpl* de ménage, dissensions *fpl* domestiques ◆ **to cease from ~** *(liter)* déposer les armes COMP **strife-ridden, strife-torn** ADJ *[country]* déchiré par les conflits ; *[party]* déchiré par les dissensions

strike /straɪk/ LANGUAGE IN USE 15.2 (vb : pret **struck**, ptp **struck**, (**rare**) **stricken**)

N 1 *(= industrial action)* grève *f (of, by de)* ◆ **the coal ~** la grève des mineurs ◆ **the electricity/gas ~** la grève (des employés) de l'électricité/du gaz ◆ **the transport/hospital ~** la grève des transports/des hôpitaux ◆ **the Ford ~** la grève chez Ford ◆ **to call a ~** lancer un ordre de grève ; → **general, hunger, rail¹, steel, sympathy**

◆ **on strike** en grève ◆ **to be (out) on ~** être en grève, faire grève *(for* pour obtenir ; *against* pour protester contre) ◆ **to go on ~, to come out on ~** se mettre en grève, faire grève

2 *(= military attack)* frappe *f* ; *(by aircraft)* frappe *f* aérienne ◆ **first ~** *(Mil)* première frappe *f*

3 *(= act of hitting)* coup *m* (frappé)

4 *(Min, Miner etc = discovery)* découverte *f* ◆ **to make a ~** découvrir un gisement ◆ **a lucky ~** *(fig)* un coup de chance

5 *(Fishing: by angler)* ferrage *m* ; *(Fishing: by fish)* touche *f*, mordage *m* ; *(Baseball, Bowling)* strike *m* ◆ **you have two ~s against you** *(US fig)* tu es mal parti*, ça se présente mal pour toi ◆ **the building/government has three ~s against it** *(US)* les jours du bâtiment/du gouvernement sont comptés ◆ **three ~s and you're out** *(US Jur) principe selon lequel une troisième récidive entraîne une condamnation à perpétuité*

6 *[of clock]* sonnerie *f* des heures

VT 1 *(= hit) [+ person]* frapper, donner un *or* des coup(s) à ; *[+ ball]* toucher, frapper ; *[+ nail, table]* frapper sur, taper sur ; *(Mus) [+ string]* toucher, pincer ; *[snake]* mordre, piquer ◆ **to ~ sth with one's fist, to ~ one's fist on sth** frapper du poing *or* donner un coup de poing sur qch ◆ **to ~ sth with a hammer** frapper *or* taper sur qch avec un marteau ◆ **he struck me (a blow) on the chin** il m'a frappé au menton, il m'a donné un coup de poing au menton ◆ **to ~ the first blow** donner le premier coup, frapper le premier *(or* la première) ◆ **to ~ a blow for freedom** rompre une lance pour la liberté ◆ **he struck his rival a shrewd blow by buying the land** il a porté à son rival un coup subtil en achetant la terre ◆ **he struck the knife from his assailant's hand** d'un coup de poing il a fait tomber le couteau de la main de son assaillant ◆ **the pain struck him as he bent down** la douleur l'a saisi quand il s'est baissé ◆ **disease struck the city** la maladie s'est abattue sur la ville ◆ **to be stricken by** *or* **with remorse** être pris de remords ◆ **the city was struck** *or* **stricken by fear** la ville a été prise de peur, la peur s'est emparée de la ville ◆ **to ~ fear into sb** *or* **sb's heart** remplir (le cœur de) qn d'effroi ◆ **it struck terror and dismay into the whole population** cela a terrorisé la population tout entière ; → **heap**

2 *(= knock against) [person, one's shoulder etc, spade]* cogner contre, heurter ; *[car etc]* heurter, rentrer dans* ; *(Naut) [+ rocks, the bottom]* toucher, heurter ; *(fig) [lightning, light]* frapper ◆ **he struck his head on** *or* **against the table as he fell** sa tête a heurté la table quand il est tombé, il s'est cogné la tête à *or* contre la table en tombant ◆ **the stone struck him on the head** la pierre l'a frappé *or* l'a heurté à la tête ◆ **he was struck by two bullets** il a reçu deux balles ◆ **to be struck by lightning** être frappé par la foudre, être foudroyé ◆ **a piercing cry struck his ear** un cri perçant lui a frappé l'oreille *or* les oreilles ◆ **the horrible sight that struck his eyes** le spectacle horrible qui s'est présenté à lui

3 *(= find, discover) [+ gold]* découvrir, trouver ; *(fig) [+ hotel, road]* tomber sur, trouver ; *(fig) [+ difficulty, obstacle]* rencontrer ◆ **to ~ gold** *(fig)* trouver le filon* ◆ **to ~ oil** *(Miner)* trouver du pétrole ; *(fig)* trouver le filon* ◆ **to ~ it rich** *(fig)* faire fortune ; → **patch**

4 *(= make, produce etc) [+ coin, medal]* frapper ; *[+ sparks, fire]* faire jaillir *(from* de) ; *[+ match]* frotter, gratter ; *(fig) [+ agreement, truce]* arriver à, conclure ◆ **to ~ a light** allumer une allumette *(or* un briquet *etc)* ◆ **to ~ roots** *[plant]* prendre racine ◆ **to ~ cuttings** *(in gardening)* faire prendre racine à des boutures ◆ **to ~ an average** établir une moyenne ◆ **to ~ a balance** trouver un équilibre, trouver le juste milieu ◆ **to ~ a bargain** conclure un marché ◆ **to ~ an attitude** poser ; → **pose**

5 *[+ chord, note]* sonner, faire entendre ; *[clock]* sonner ◆ **to ~ a false note** sonner faux ◆ **to ~ a note of warning** donner *or* sonner l'alarme ◆ **the clock struck three** la pendule a sonné trois heures ◆ **it has just struck six** six heures viennent juste de sonner ◆ **to ~ four bells** *(Naut)* piquer quatre

6 *(= take down) [+ tent]* démonter, plier ; *[+ sail]* amener ; *[+ camp]* lever ; *[+ flag]* baisser, amener ◆ **to ~ the set** *(Theat)* démonter le décor

7 *(= delete) [+ name]* rayer *(from* de) ; *[+ person] (from list)* rayer ; *(from professional register)* radier *(from* de) ◆ **the judge ordered the remark to be struck** *or* **stricken from the record** le juge a ordonné que la remarque soit rayée du procès-verbal

8 *(= cause to be or become)* rendre (subitement) ◆ **to ~ sb dumb** *(lit, fig)* rendre qn muet ◆ **to be struck dumb** *(lit)* être frappé de mutisme ; *(fig)* rester muet, être sidéré* ◆ **to ~ sb dead** porter un coup mortel à qn ◆ **~ me pink!** ⁑ j'en suis soufflé !*

9 *(= make impression on)* sembler, paraître *(sb* à qn) ◆ **I was struck by his intelligence** j'ai été frappé par son intelligence ◆ **I wasn't very struck* with him** il ne m'a pas fait très bonne impression ◆ **to be struck on sb**⁑ *(= impressed by)* être très impressionné par qn ; *(= in love with)* être toqué* de qn ◆ **I'm not very struck on French films**⁑ je ne suis pas (un) fana* des films français ◆ **the funny side of it struck me later** le côté drôle de la chose m'est apparu *or* m'a frappé plus tard ◆ **that ~s me as a good idea** cela me semble *or* paraît une bonne idée ◆ **an idea suddenly struck him** soudain il a eu une idée, une idée lui est venue soudain à l'esprit ◆ **it ~s me that** *or* **~s me* he is lying** j'ai l'impression qu'il ment, à mon avis il ment ◆ **how did he ~ you?** quelle impression *or* quel effet vous a-t-il fait ? ◆ **how did the film ~ you?** qu'avez-vous pensé du film ?

10 *(Fishing) [angler]* ferrer ◆ **the fish struck the bait** le poisson a mordu à l'appât

VI 1 *(= hit)* frapper ; *(= attack) (Mil)* attaquer ; *[snake]* mordre, piquer ; *[tiger]* sauter sur sa proie ; *(fig) [disease etc]* frapper ; *[panic]* s'emparer des esprits ◆ **to ~ home** *(lit, fig)* frapper *or* toucher juste, faire mouche ◆ **to ~ lucky** *(esp Brit fig)* avoir de la chance ◆ **he struck at his attacker** il porta un coup à son assaillant ◆ **we must ~ at the root of this evil** nous devons attaquer *or* couper ce mal dans sa racine ◆ **it ~s at the root of our parliamentary system** cela porte atteinte aux fondements mêmes de notre système parlementaire ◆ **his speech ~s at the heart of the problem** son discours porte sur le fond même du problème ◆ **his foot struck against** *or* **on a rock** son pied a buté contre *or* heurté un rocher ◆ **when the ship struck** quand le bateau a touché ◆ **the sun was striking through the mist** le soleil perçait la brume ◆ **the chill struck through to his very bones** le froid a pénétré jusqu'à la moelle de ses os ; → **iron**

2 *[match]* s'allumer

3 *[clock]* sonner ◆ **has 6 o'clock struck?** est-ce que 6 heures ont sonné ?

4 *(= go on strike)* faire grève *(for* pour obtenir ; *against* pour protester contre)

5 *(= turn, move, go)* aller, prendre ◆ **~ left on leaving the forest** prenez à gauche en sortant de la forêt ◆ **to ~ uphill** se mettre à grimper la côte

6 *(Gardening = take root)* prendre racine ; *(Fishing = seize bait)* mordre

COMP *[committee, fund]* de grève

strike force N *(gen: of police etc)* brigade *f* d'intervention ; *(Mil)* force *f* de frappe

strike fund N caisse *f* syndicale de grève

strike leader N leader *m* de la grève

strike pay N salaire *m* de gréviste

► **strike back** VI *(Mil, gen)* rendre les coups *(at sb* à qn), se venger *(at sb* de qn), user de représailles *(at sb* à l'égard de qn)

► **strike down** VT SEP 1 abattre ; *(fig) [esp disease]* terrasser

2 *(US = abolish) [+ law]* abolir

► **strike in** VI *(fig = interrupt)* interrompre

► **strike off**

VI *(= change direction)* ◆ **he struck off across the fields** il a pris à travers champs

VT SEP 1 *[+ sb's head]* trancher, couper ; *[+ branch]* couper

2 *(= score out, delete: from list)* rayer ◆ **to be struck off** *[doctor etc]* être radié

3 *(Typ)* tirer

► **strike on** VT FUS *[+ idea]* avoir ; *[+ solution]* tomber sur, trouver

► **strike out**

VI 1 *(= hit out)* se débattre ◆ **he struck out wildly** il s'est débattu furieusement ◆ **he struck out at his attackers** il s'est débattu contre ses agresseurs

2 *(= set off)* ◆ **to strike out for the shore** *[swimmer]* se mettre à nager vers le rivage ; *[rower]* se mettre à ramer vers le rivage ◆ **he left the firm and struck out on his own** il a quitté l'entreprise et s'est mis à son compte

VT SEP *(= delete) [+ word, question]* rayer

► **strike through** VT SEP ⇒ **strike out vt sep**

► **strike up**

VI *[band etc]* commencer à jouer ; *[music]* commencer

VT SEP *[band]* se mettre à jouer ; *[singers]* se mettre à chanter ◆ **~ up the band!** faites jouer l'orchestre ! ◆ **to ~ up an acquaintance** faire *or* lier connaissance *(with sb* avec qn) ◆ **to ~ up a friendship** lier amitié *(with sb* avec qn)

► **strike upon** VT FUS ⇒ **strike on**

strikebound /ˈstraɪkbaʊnd/ ADJ bloqué par une (*or* la) grève

strikebreaker /ˈstraɪkˌbreɪkəʳ/ N briseur *m* de grève

strikebreaking /ˈstraɪkˌbreɪkɪŋ/ N ◆ **he was accused of ~** on l'a accusé d'être un briseur de grève

striker /ˈstraɪkəʳ/ N 1 *(= person on strike)* gréviste *mf* 2 *(= clapper)* frappeur *m* ; *(on clock)* marteau *m* ; *(on gun)* percuteur *m* 3 *(Ftbl)* buteur *m*

striking /ˈstraɪkɪŋ/ ADJ [1] *(= impressive, outstanding) [feature, contrast, similarity, difference]* frappant, saisissant ◆ **to be in ~ contrast to sth** offrir un contraste frappant *or* saisissant avec qch ◆ **to bear a ~ resemblance to sb** ressembler à qn de manière frappante, présenter une ressemblance frappante avec qn ◆ **his** (*or* **her**) **~ good looks** sa grande beauté ◆ **she was a ~ redhead** c'était une superbe rousse

[2] ◆ **to be within ~ distance (of sth)** être à proximité (de qch) ◆ **he had come within ~ distance of a medal/the presidency** une médaille/la présidence était maintenant à sa portée ◆ **to be within ~ distance of doing sth** être bien placé pour faire qch

[3] *[clock]* ◆ **a ~ clock** une horloge qui sonne les heures, une horloge à carillon ◆ **the ~ mechanism** le carillon

[4] *(Mil) [force, power]* de frappe

[5] *(= on strike) [workers]* en grève, gréviste

N [1] *[of coins]* frappe *f*

[2] *[of clock]* carillon *m*

strikingly /ˈstraɪkɪŋlɪ/ ADV [1] de façon frappante, de façon saisissante ◆ **~ different (from sth)** différent à tous points de vue (de qch) ◆ **~ beautiful** d'une beauté saisissante, d'une grande beauté ◆ **~ modern/bold** d'une modernité/audace saisissante, extrêmement moderne/audacieux ◆ **to be ~ similar to sb/sth** ressembler à qn/qch de façon frappante *or* saisissante ◆ **to be ~ evident** sauter aux yeux, crever les yeux [2] ◆ **to contrast ~ with sth** offrir un contraste frappant *or* saisissant avec qch ◆ **to differ ~ (from sth)** différer à tous points de vue (de qch) ◆ **~, inflation is now higher than ever** ce qui est frappant, c'est que l'inflation n'a jamais été aussi forte

Strimmer ® /ˈstrɪməʳ/ N *(small)* coupe-bordure *m* ; *(heavy-duty)* débroussailleuse *f*

string /strɪŋ/ (vb : pret, ptp **strung**) N [1] *(= cord)* ficelle *f* ; *[of violin, piano, bow, racket]* corde *f* ; *[of puppet]* ficelle *f*, fil *m* ; *[of apron, bonnet, anorak]* cordon *m* ; *(Bot: on bean etc)* fil(s) *m(pl)* ◆ **a piece of ~** un bout de ficelle ◆ **he has got her on a ~** il la tient, il la mène par le bout du nez ◆ **to have more than one ~ to one's bow** avoir plus d'une corde à son arc ◆ **his first ~** sa première ressource ◆ **his second ~** sa deuxième ressource, la solution de rechange ◆ **the ~s** *(Mus)* les cordes *fpl*, les instruments *mpl* à cordes ◆ **there are no ~s attached** cela ne vous (*or* nous *etc*) engage à rien ◆ **with no ~s attached** sans condition(s) ◆ **with ~s (attached)** assorti de conditions ; → **apron, heartstrings**

◆ **to pull strings** ◆ **he had to pull ~s to get the job** il a dû faire jouer le piston* pour obtenir le poste ◆ **to pull ~s for sb** exercer son influence pour aider qn, pistonner qn* ◆ **he's the one who pulls the ~s** *(= has control)* c'est lui qui tire les ficelles

[2] *[of beads, pearls]* rang *m* ; *[of onions]* chapelet *m* ; *[of garlic]* chaîne *f* ; *[of people, vehicles]* file *f* ; *[of racehorses]* écurie *f* ; *[of curses, lies, insults, excuses]* kyrielle *f*, chapelet *m*

[3] *(Ling)* séquence *f*

[4] *(Comput)* chaîne *f* ◆ **a numeric/character ~** une chaîne numérique/de caractères

[5] *(Sport)* équipe *f* (provisoire)

VT [1] *[+ musical instrument]* monter ; *[+ bow]* garnir d'une corde ; *[+ racket]* corder ; → **highly**

[2] *[+ beads, pearls]* enfiler ; *[+ rope]* tendre *(across* en travers de ; *between* entre*)* ◆ **they strung lights in the trees** ils ont suspendu des lampions dans les arbres

[3] *[+ beans]* enlever les fils de

COMP *(Mus) [orchestra, quartet]* à cordes ; *[serenade, piece]* pour cordes

string bag N filet *m* à provisions

string bean N *(= vegetable)* haricot *m* vert ; *(US * = tall thin person)* asperge* *f*, grande perche *f*

string correspondent N *(US Press)* correspondant(e) *m(f)* local(e) à temps partiel

string(ed) instrument N *(Mus)* instrument *m* à cordes

string player N *(Mus)* musicien(ne) *m(f)* qui joue d'un instrument à cordes

string-puller N ◆ **he's a ~-puller** il n'hésite pas à se faire pistonner *or* à faire jouer ses relations

string-pulling N piston *m* ◆ **he did a bit of ~-pulling for me** il m'a pistonné*

string tie N cravate-lacet *f*

string vest N tricot *m* de corps à grosses mailles

► **string along*** VI suivre ◆ **to ~ along with sb** *(= accompany)* accompagner qn ; *(= agree with)* se ranger à l'avis de qn

VT SEP *(pej)* faire marcher, bercer de fausses espérances

► **string out** VI *[people, things]* se déployer *(along* le long de*)* ◆ **~ out a bit more!** espacez-vous un peu plus !

VT SEP [1] *[+ lanterns, washing etc]* suspendre ; *[+ guards, posts]* échelonner ◆ **to be strung out along the road** *[people, things]* être déployé le long de la route

[2] *(fig)* **to be strung out*** *(= debilitated)* être à plat ; *(= disturbed)* être perturbé ; *(Drugs = addicted)* être accro* ; *(Drugs = under influence)* être défoncé* ; *(Drugs: with withdrawal symptoms)* être en manque

► **string together** VT SEP *[+ words, sentences]* enchaîner ◆ **he can barely ~ a sentence** *or* **two words together** il a du mal à aligner deux phrases

► **string up** VT SEP [1] *[+ lantern, onions, nets]* suspendre (au moyen d'une corde)

[2] *(fig)* **he had strung himself up to do it** il avait aiguisé toutes ses facultés en vue de le faire ◆ **to be strung up (about sth)** être très tendu *or* nerveux (à la pensée de qch)

[3] *(* = hang, lynch)* pendre

stringed /strɪŋd/ ADJ → **string comp**

-stringed /strɪŋd/ ADJ *(in compounds)* ◆ **four-stringed** à quatre cordes

stringency /ˈstrɪndʒənsɪ/ N *(= strictness) [of control, regulations, test]* rigueur *f* ; *[of reforms]* caractère *m* draconien ◆ **thanks to the ~ of the security** grâce aux strictes mesures de sécurité ◆ **financial** *or* **economic ~** austérité *f*

stringent /ˈstrɪndʒənt/ ADJ [1] *(= strict) [control, regulations, standards, test]* rigoureux ; *[reforms]* draconien ◆ **the meeting took place amid ~ security** de strictes mesures de sécurité ont été mises en place pour cette réunion [2] *(= compelling) [reasons, arguments]* solide ; *[necessity]* impérieux

stringently /ˈstrɪndʒəntlɪ/ ADV rigoureusement

stringer /ˈstrɪŋəʳ/ N *(= journalist)* correspondant(e) *m(f)* local(e) à temps partiel

stringy /ˈstrɪŋɪ/ ADJ *[beans, celery, meat]* filandreux ; *[molasses, cooked cheese]* filant, qui file ; *[plant, seaweed]* tout en longueur ; *(fig) [person]* filiforme

strip /strɪp/ N [1] *[of metal, wood, paper, grass]* bande *f* ; *[of fabric]* bande *f*, bandelette *f* ; *[of ground]* bande *f*, langue *f* ; *[of water, sea]* bras *m* ◆ **a ~ of garden** un petit jardin tout en longueur ◆ **to tear sb off a ~*, to tear a ~ off sb*** sonner les cloches à qn*

[2] (also **landing strip**) piste *f* d'atterrissage

[3] (also **comic strip**) ⇒ **strip cartoon**

[4] *(Brit Ftbl etc = clothes)* tenue *f* ◆ **the England ~** la tenue de l'équipe (de football) d'Angleterre

[5] * ⇒ **striptease**

VT [1] *(= remove everything from) [+ person]* déshabiller, dévêtir ; (also **strip down**) *[+ room, house]* vider ; *[thieves]* dévaliser, vider ; *[+ car, engine, gun]* démonter complètement ; *(Tech) [+ nut, screw, gears]* arracher le filet de ; *[wind, people, birds] [+ branches, bushes]* dépouiller, dégarnir ; *(= take paint etc off) [+ furniture, door]* décaper ◆ **to ~ sb naked** *or* **to the skin** déshabiller *or* dévêtir qn complètement ◆ **to ~ a bed (down)** défaire un lit complètement ◆ **to ~ (down) the walls** enlever *or* arracher le papier peint

[2] *(= remove) [+ old covers, wallpaper, decorations, ornaments]* enlever ; *[+ old paint]* décaper, enlever ◆ **to ~ the bark from the tree** dépouiller un arbre de son écorce

[3] *(= deprive etc) [+ person, object]* dépouiller *(of* de*)* ◆ **to ~ a tree of its bark** dépouiller un arbre de son écorce ◆ **to ~ a room of all its pictures** enlever tous les tableaux dans une pièce ◆ **to ~ sb of his titles/honours** dépouiller qn de ses titres/honneurs ◆ **to ~ a company of its assets** *(Fin)* cannibaliser* une compagnie ; see also **asset**

VI se déshabiller ; *[striptease artist]* faire du (*or* un) striptease ◆ **to ~ naked** *or* **to the skin** se mettre nu ◆ **to ~ to the waist** se mettre torse nu ◆ **to be ~ped to the waist** être nu jusqu'à la ceinture, être torse nu

COMP **strip cartoon** N *(Brit)* bande *f* dessinée

strip club N boîte *f* de striptease

strip cropping N *(Agr)* cultures alternées selon les courbes de niveaux

strip joint N *(US)* ⇒ **strip club**

strip light N (tube *m* au) néon *m*

strip lighting N *(Brit)* éclairage *m* au néon *or* fluorescent

strip mine N *(US)* mine *f* à ciel ouvert

strip mining N *(US)* extraction *f* à ciel ouvert

strip poker N strip-poker *m*

strip-search N fouille *f* corporelle VT ◆ **he was ~-searched at the airport** on l'a fait se déshabiller et soumis à une fouille corporelle à l'aéroport

strip show N striptease *m*

strip-wash N (grande) toilette *f* VT faire la (grande) toilette de

► **strip away** VT SEP *[+ paint, varnish]* décaper ; *[+ layer of dirt, turf, bark]* retirer ; *[+ pretence, hypocrisy, artifice]* démasquer ◆ **chemicals that ~ away the skin's protective outer layer** des produits qui attaquent la couche protectrice de l'épiderme ◆ **to ~ away sb's dignity** priver qn de sa dignité

► **strip down** VI ⇒ **strip off vi**

VT SEP *(Tech etc) [+ machine, engine, gun]* démonter complètement ; see also **strip vt 1**

► **strip off** VI se déshabiller

VT SEP *[+ buttons, ornaments]* enlever, ôter *(from* de*)* ; *[+ paper]* enlever, arracher *(from* de*)* ; *[+ leaves]* faire tomber *(from* de*)* ; *[+ berries]* prendre *(from* de*)*

stripe /straɪp/ N [1] *(of one colour)* raie *f*, rayure *f* ◆ **~s** *(pattern)* rayures *fpl* ◆ **yellow with a white ~** jaune rayé de blanc ; → **pinstripe, star** [2] *(Mil)* galon *m* ◆ **to get one's ~s** gagner ses galons ◆ **to lose one's ~s** être dégradé [3] † *(= lash)* coup *m* de fouet ; *(= weal)* marque *f* (d'un coup de fouet)

striped /straɪpt/ ADJ *[garment, wallpaper, fabric]* rayé, à rayures ; *[animal, insect]* rayé ◆ **a pair of ~ trousers** *(broad stripes)* un pantalon rayé ; *(pinstripes)* un pantalon à fines rayures ◆ **~ with red** rayé de rouge

stripey* /ˈstraɪpɪ/ ADJ ⇒ **stripy**

stripling /ˈstrɪplɪŋ/ N adolescent *m*, tout jeune homme *m*, gringalet *m* *(pej)*

strippagram /ˈstrɪpəgræm/ N *message envoyé à l'occasion d'une célébration par l'intermédiaire d'une personne qui fait un striptease ; cette personne*

stripper /ˈstrɪpəʳ/ N [1] (also **paint-stripper**) décapant *m* [2] *(= striptease artist)* strip-teaseuse *f* ◆ **male ~** strip-teaseur *m*

striptease /ˈstrɪptiːz/ N striptease *m*, effeuillage *m* ◆ ~ **artist** strip-teaseuse *f*

stripteaser /ˈstrɪptiːzəʳ/ N strip-teaseuse *f*

stripy* /ˈstraɪpɪ/ ADJ *[garment, wallpaper, fabric]* rayé, à rayures ; *[animal, insect]* rayé

strive /straɪv/ (pret **strove** /strəʊv/, ptp **striven** /ˈstrɪvn/) VI [1] (= *try hard*) s'efforcer (*to do sth* de faire qch), faire son possible (*to do sth* pour faire qch) ◆ **to ~ after** *or* **for sth** s'efforcer d'obtenir qch, faire son possible pour obtenir qch [2] (*liter* = *struggle, fight*) lutter, se battre (*against, with* contre)

striving /ˈstraɪvɪŋ/ N efforts *mpl* (*for* pour obtenir)

strobe /strəʊb/ ADJ *[lights]* stroboscopique N [1] (also **strobe light, strobe lighting**) lumière *f* stroboscopique [2] ⇒ **stroboscope**

stroboscope /ˈstrəʊbəskəʊp/ N stroboscope *m*

strode /strəʊd/ VB pt of **stride**

stroke /strəʊk/ N [1] (= *movement, blow: gen, Billiards, Cricket, Golf, Tennis etc*) coup *m* ; (*Swimming* = *movement*) mouvement *m* des bras (*pour nager*) ; (*Rowing, Swimming* = *style*) nage *f* ; (*Rowing* = *movement*) coup *m* de rame *or* d'aviron ◆ **he gave the cat a ~** il a fait une caresse au chat ◆ **with a ~ of his axe** d'un coup de hache ◆ **with a ~ of the pen** d'un trait de plume ◆ **~ of lightning** coup *m* de foudre ◆ **good ~!** (*Golf, Tennis etc*) bien joué ! ◆ **to row at 38 ~s to the minute** ramer *or* nager à une cadence de 38 coups d'aviron minute ◆ **to set the ~** (*Rowing, fig*) donner la cadence ◆ **to put sb off his ~** (*Sport*) faire perdre le rythme à qn ; (*fig*) faire perdre tous ses moyens à qn ◆ **he swam the pool with powerful ~s** il a traversé le bassin d'une manière puissante ; → **backstroke, breast**

[2] (*fig*) **at a (single) ~, at one ~** d'un (seul) coup ◆ **it was a tremendous ~ to get the committee's agreement** cela a été un coup de maître que d'obtenir l'accord du comité ◆ **he hasn't done a ~ (of work)** il n'a rien fait du tout, il n'en a pas fichu une rame* ◆ **~ of diplomacy** chef-d'œuvre *m* de diplomatie ◆ **~ of genius** trait *m* de génie ◆ **~ of luck** coup *m* de chance *or* de veine ; → **master**

[3] (= *mark*) *[of pen, pencil]* trait *m* ; *[of brush]* touche *f* ; (*Typ* = *oblique*) barre *f* ◆ **thick ~s of the brush** des touches *fpl* épaisses ◆ **5 ~ 6** (*Typ*) 5 barre 6 ; → **brush**

[4] *[of bell, clock]* coup *m* ◆ **on the ~ of ten** sur le coup de dix heures, à dix heures sonnantes ◆ **in the ~ of time** juste à temps

[5] (*Med*) attaque *f* (d'apoplexie) ◆ **to have a ~** avoir une attaque ; → **heatstroke, sunstroke**

[6] (*of piston*) course *f* ◆ **a two-/four-~ engine** un moteur à deux/quatre temps ; see also **two**

[7] (*Rowing* = *person*) chef *m* de nage ◆ **to row ~** être chef de nage, donner la nage

VT [1] *[+ cat, sb's hand, one's chin]* caresser ; *[+ sb's hair]* caresser, passer la main dans ◆ **to ~ sb (up) the wrong way** (*fig*) prendre qn à rebrousse-poil *or* à contre-poil

[2] (*Rowing*) **to ~ a boat** être chef de nage, donner la nage

[3] (= *draw line through:* also **stroke out**) biffer

[4] (*Sport*) *[+ ball]* frapper

VI (*Rowing*) être chef de nage, donner la nage

COMP **stroke play** N (*NonC: Golf*) *comptage des points au coup par coup*

stroke-play tournament N (*Golf*) stroke-play *m*

► **stroke down** VT SEP *[+ cat's fur]* caresser ; *[+ hair]* lisser ◆ **to ~ sb down** (*fig*) apaiser *or* amadouer qn

► **stroke out** VT SEP ⇒ **stroke vt 3**

► **stroke up** VT SEP → **stroke vt 1**

stroll /strəʊl/ N petite promenade *f* ◆ **to have** *or* **take a ~, to go for a ~** aller faire un tour VI se promener nonchalamment, flâner ◆ **to ~ in/out/away** *etc* entrer/sortir/s'éloigner *etc* sans se presser ◆ **to ~ up and down the street** descendre et remonter la rue en flânant *or* sans se presser ◆ **to ~ around** flâner

stroller /ˈstrəʊləʳ/ N [1] (= *person*) promeneur *m*, -euse *f*, flâneur *m*, -euse *f* [2] (*esp US* = *push chair*) poussette *f* ; (*folding*) poussette-canne *f*

strolling /ˈstrəʊlɪŋ/ ADJ *[player, minstrel]* ambulant

stroma /ˈstrəʊmə/ N (pl **stromata** /ˈstrəʊmətə/) stroma *m*

strong /strɒŋ/ ADJ [1] (*physically*) *[person, animal]* fort ; (= *healthy*) robuste ; *[heart, nerves]* solide ◆ **to be (as) ~ as an ox** *or* **a horse** *or* **a bull** (= *powerful*) être fort comme un bœuf ; (= *healthy*) avoir une santé de fer ◆ **to have ~ eyesight** avoir une très bonne vue ◆ **to have ~ legs** avoir de bonnes jambes ◆ **do you feel ~?** est-ce que vous vous sentez en forme ? ◆ **when you are ~ again** (*in health*) quand vous aurez repris des forces ◆ **she has never been very ~** elle a toujours eu une petite santé ◆ **you need a ~ stomach for that job** il faut avoir l'estomac solide *or* bien accroché* pour faire ce travail ; → **constitution**

[2] (*morally*) fort ◆ **you must be ~** (*in courage*) il faut que vous soyez courageux ◆ **he's a very ~ person** (*mentally*) c'est quelqu'un de très solide ; → **point, suit**

♦ **to be strong in sth** (= *good at sth*) être fort en qch

♦ **to be strong on sth** (= *good at sth*) être fort en qch ; (*emphasising*) mettre l'accent sur qch ◆ **the government is ~ on civil rights** le gouvernement fait beaucoup pour les droits civils ◆ **the local cuisine is ~ on seafood** les fruits de mer ont une place importante dans la cuisine locale ◆ **they're ~er on rhetoric than on concrete action** ils sont plus doués pour les discours que pour l'action

[3] (= *robust*) *[building, wall, table, shoes, bolt, nail, fabric]* solide

[4] (= *powerful*) *[magnet]* puissant ; *[electric current]* intense ; *[lens, spectacles]* fort, puissant ; *[light]* fort, vif ; *[glue, medicine]* fort

[5] (= *convincing*) *[reasons, candidate, contender]* sérieux ◆ **we are in a ~ position to make them obey** nous sommes bien placés pour les faire obéir ◆ **there is ~ evidence to suggest that …** il y a de nombreuses preuves qui laissent penser que … ◆ **there are ~ indications that …** tout semble indiquer que … ; → **case¹**

[6] (= *uncompromising, unequivocal*) *[measures, steps]* énergique ◆ **in ~ terms** en termes non équivoques ◆ **to write sb a ~ letter** écrire une lettre bien sentie à qn

[7] (= *intense*) *[influence, attraction]* fort, profond ; *[emotion, desire, interest, protest]* vif ◆ **to have a ~ effect on sth** avoir beaucoup d'effet sur qch ◆ **I had a ~ sense of …** je ressentais vivement … ◆ **I've a ~ feeling that …** j'ai bien l'impression que … ◆ **he's got ~ feelings on this matter** cette affaire lui tient à cœur ◆ **it is my ~ opinion** *or* **belief that …** je suis fermement convaincu *or* persuadé que …

[8] (= *fervent*) fervent ◆ **a ~ socialist** un socialiste fervent ◆ **~ supporters of …** d'ardents partisans de …, des fervents de … ◆ **I am a ~ believer in …** je crois fermement à *or* profondément à …

[9] *[flavour, odour, coffee, cheese, wine, cigarette]* fort ; (*pej*) *[butter]* rance ; *[sauce]* (= *concentrated*) concentré ; (= *highly seasoned*) relevé ; *[solution]* concentré ◆ **it has a ~ smell** ça sent fort

[10] (*in numbers*) **an army 500 ~** une armée (forte) de 500 hommes ◆ **they were 100 ~** ils étaient au nombre de 100

[11] (*Ling*) *[verb, form]* fort

ADV ◆ **to be going ~** *[person]* être toujours solide ; *[car etc]* marcher toujours bien ; *[relationship etc]* aller bien ; *[firm, business]* aller bien, être florissant ◆ **that's pitching it** *or* **coming it** *or* **going it a bit ~*** il pousse (*or* vous poussez *etc*) un peu*, il y va (*or* vous y allez *etc*) un peu fort ◆ **to come on ~*** (*gen* = *be overbearing*) insister lourdement ; (*sexually*) faire du rentre-dedans* ; (*US*) (= *make progress*) progresser fortement

COMP **strong-arm** ADJ → **strong-arm**

strong breeze N (*on Beaufort scale*) vent *m* frais

strong drink N (*NonC*) alcool *m*, boisson *f* alcoolisée

strong gale N (*on Beaufort scale*) fort coup *m* de vent

strong-minded ADJ → **strong-minded**

strong-willed ADJ résolu ◆ **to be ~-willed** avoir de la volonté

strong-arm* /ˈstrɒŋɑːm/ ADJ *[method, treatment]* brutal ◆ **~ man** gros bras *m* (*fig*) ◆ **~ tactics** la manière forte VT faire violence à ◆ **to ~ sb into doing sth** forcer la main à qn pour qu'il fasse qch

strongbox /ˈstrɒŋbɒks/ N coffre-fort *m*

stronghold /ˈstrɒŋhəʊld/ N (*Mil*) forteresse *f*, fort *m* ; (*fig*) bastion *m*

strongly /ˈstrɒŋlɪ/ ADV [1] *[influence, hint, accentuate, remind, indicate, imply]* fortement ; *[attract, recommend, advise, interest, desire]* fortement, vivement ; *[criticize, protest]* vivement ; *[deny, condemn, protest, defend]* vigoureusement ; *[fight, attack]* énergiquement ; *[support, oppose]* fermement ; *[feel, sense, believe]* profondément ◆ **to argue ~ for** *or* **in favour of sth** plaider vigoureusement *or* avec force pour qch ◆ **to argue ~ against sth** s'élever avec véhémence contre qch ◆ **to argue ~ that …** soutenir fermement que … ◆ **to taste ~ of sth** avoir un goût prononcé de qch ◆ **to smell ~ of sth** avoir une forte odeur de qch ◆ **the kitchen smelled ~ of smoke** il y avait une forte odeur de fumée dans la cuisine ◆ **fish features ~ in the Japanese diet** le poisson occupe une place importante dans l'alimentation des Japonais ◆ **if you feel ~ about this problem, write to us** si ce problème vous tient à cœur, écrivez-nous ◆ **I feel very ~ that …** je suis convaincu que …

[2] ◆ **~ recommended** vivement recommandé ◆ **you are ~ recommended** *or* **advised to leave the country** nous vous recommandons vivement de quitter le pays ◆ **~ held views** *or* **opinions** opinions *fpl* très arrêtées ◆ **to be ~ critical of sb/sth** critiquer vivement qn/qch ◆ **to be ~ in favour of sth** être très favorable à qch ◆ **to be ~ against** *or* **opposed to sth** s'opposer fermement à qch ◆ **~ anti-American/nationalist** farouchement anti-américain/nationaliste ◆ **a ~ worded letter** une lettre virulente ◆ **his accent was ~ northern** il avait un très net *or* fort accent du Nord ◆ **~ built** *[person]* costaud* ◆ **~ constructed** *or* **made** *or* **built** solide

strongman /ˈstrɒŋmæn/ N (pl **-men**) (*in circus etc*) hercule *m* ; (*fig, Comm, Pol etc*) homme *m* fort

strong-minded /ˌstrɒŋˈmaɪndɪd/ ADJ résolu, qui a beaucoup de volonté, qui sait ce qu'il veut

strong-mindedly /ˌstrɒŋˈmaɪndɪdlɪ/ ADV avec une persévérance tenace, avec ténacité

strong-mindedness /ˌstrɒŋˈmaɪndɪdnɪs/ N volonté *f*, force *f* de caractère

strongroom /ˈstrɒŋrʊm/ N (*gen*) chambre *f* forte ; (*in bank*) chambre *f* forte, salle *f* des coffres

strontium /ˈstrɒntɪəm/ N strontium *m* ◆ **~ 90** strontium *m* 90, strontium *m* radioactif

strop /strɒp/ N cuir *m* (à rasoir) VT *[+ razor]* repasser sur le cuir

strophe /ˈstrəʊfɪ/ N strophe *f*

stroppy* /ˈstrɒpɪ/ ADJ *(Brit)* buté et râleur* ◆ **to get ~** se mettre à râler* ◆ **to get ~ with sb** se mettre en rogne contre qn*

strove /strəʊv/ VB pt of **strive**

struck /strʌk/ VB pt, ptp of **strike**

structural /ˈstrʌktʃərəl/ ADJ 1 *(also Econ = relating to non-physical structure) [change, problem, reform etc]* structurel ◆ **~ complexity** complexité *f* de structure ◆ **~ unemployment** chômage *m* structurel
2 *(= relating to structuralism)* structural ◆ **~ psychology/linguistics** psychologie *f*/linguistique *f* structurale
3 *(= relating to physical structure) [repair, alteration, failure, integrity, weakness, damage, fault]* au niveau de la structure ◆ **~ defect** *(in building)* vice *f* de construction ◆ **the house was in good ~ condition** la structure de la maison était saine
COMP **structural engineer** N ingénieur *m* en génie civil
structural engineering N génie *m* civil
structural inspection N ⇒ **structural survey**
structural steel N acier *m* (de construction)
structural survey N *(Archit, Constr)* expertise *f* détaillée

structuralism /ˈstrʌktʃərəlɪzəm/ N structuralisme *m*

structuralist /ˈstrʌktʃərəlɪst/ ADJ, N structuraliste *mf*

structurally /ˈstrʌktʃərəlɪ/ ADV ◆ **the building is ~ sound/unsound** la structure du bâtiment est saine/peu saine ◆ **~, the film is quite complex** structurellement, c'est un film assez complexe

structure /ˈstrʌktʃəʳ/ N *(all senses)* structure *f* VT structurer

structured /ˈstrʌktʃəd/ ADJ structuré ◆ **~ activity** *(Educ)* activité *f* structurée

struggle /ˈstrʌgl/ N *(lit, fig)* lutte *f* *(for* pour ; *against* contre ; *with* avec ; *to do sth* pour faire qch) ; *(= fight)* bagarre *f* ◆ **to put up a ~** résister *(also fig)*, se débattre ◆ **he lost his glasses in the ~** il a perdu ses lunettes dans la bagarre ◆ **they surrendered without a ~** *(Mil)* ils n'ont opposé aucune résistance ◆ **you won't succeed without a ~** vous ne réussirez pas sans vous battre, il faudra vous battre si vous voulez réussir ◆ **her ~ to feed her children** sa lutte quotidienne pour nourrir ses enfants ◆ **the ~ to find somewhere to live** les difficultés qu'on a à trouver *or* le mal qu'il faut se donner pour trouver un logement ◆ **I had a ~ to persuade him** j'ai eu beaucoup de mal à le persuader, je ne l'ai persuadé qu'au prix de grands efforts ◆ **it was a ~ but we made it** cela nous a demandé beaucoup d'efforts mais nous y sommes arrivés
VI 1 *(gen)* lutter *(against* contre ; *for* pour) ; *(= fight)* se battre ; *(= thrash around)* se débattre, se démener ; *(= try hard)* se démener, se décarcasser* *(to do sth* pour faire qch), s'efforcer *(to do sth* de faire qch) ◆ **he was struggling with the thief** il était aux prises avec le voleur ◆ **he ~d fiercely as they put on the handcuffs** il a résisté avec acharnement quand on lui a passé les menottes ◆ **he ~d to get free** il s'est démené pour se libérer ◆ **they were struggling for power** ils se disputaient le pouvoir ◆ **he was struggling to make ends meet** il avait beaucoup de mal à joindre les deux bouts, il tirait le diable par la queue ◆ **he is struggling to finish it before tomorrow** il se démène *or* il se décarcasse* pour le terminer avant demain
2 *(= move with difficulty)* **to ~ in/out** *etc* entrer/sortir *etc* avec peine ◆ **he ~d up the cliff** il s'est hissé péniblement *or* à grand-peine jusqu'au sommet de la falaise ◆ **he ~d through the tiny window** il s'est contorsionné pour passer par la minuscule fenêtre ◆ **to ~ through the crowd** se frayer péniblement *or* tant bien que mal un chemin à travers la foule ◆ **he ~d to his feet** il s'est levé péniblement *or* à grand-peine ◆ **he ~d into a jersey** il a enfilé tant bien que mal un pull-over

► **struggle along** VI *(lit)* avancer avec peine *or* à grand-peine ; *(fig: financially)* subsister *or* se débrouiller tant bien que mal

► **struggle back** VI *(= return)* revenir *(or* retourner) avec peine *or* à grand-peine ◆ **to ~ back to solvency** s'efforcer de redevenir solvable

► **struggle on** VI 1 ⇒ **struggle along**
2 *(= continue the struggle)* continuer de lutter, poursuivre la lutte *(against* contre)

► **struggle through** VI *(fig)* venir à bout de ses peines, s'en sortir

struggling /ˈstrʌglɪŋ/ ADJ *[artist etc]* qui tire le diable par la queue

strum /strʌm/ VT 1 *[+ piano]* tapoter de ; *[+ guitar, banjo etc]* gratter de, racler (de) 2 (also **strum out**) *[+ tune] (on piano)* tapoter ; *(on guitar etc)* racler VI ◆ **to ~ on** ⇒ **vt 1** N (also **strumming**) *[of guitar etc]* raclement *m*

strumpet †† /ˈstrʌmpɪt/ N catin *f*

strung /strʌŋ/ VB (pt, ptp of **string**) see also **highly, string up**

strut¹ /strʌt/ VI (also **strut about, strut around**) se pavaner ◆ **to ~ in/out/along** *etc* entrer/sortir/avancer *etc* en se pavanant *or* d'un air important ◆ **to ~ one's stuff*** frimer*

strut² /strʌt/ N *(= support)* étai *m*, support *m* ; *(for wall, trench, mine)* étrésillon *m* ; *(more solid)* étançon *m* ; *(Carpentry)* contrefiche *f* ; *(between uprights)* lierne *f*, traverse *f*, entretoise *f* ; *(in roof)* jambe *f* de force

strychnine /ˈstrɪkniːn/ N strychnine *f*

stub /stʌb/ N *[of pencil, broken stick]* bout *m*, morceau *m* ; *[of cigarette, cigar]* mégot *m* ; *[of tail]* moignon *m* ; *[of cheque, ticket]* talon *m* VT ◆ **to ~ one's toe/one's foot** se cogner le doigt de pied/le pied *(against* contre) COMP **stub end** N *[of pencil etc]* bout *m* (de crayon *etc*)

► **stub out** VT SEP *[+ cigar, cigarette]* écraser

stubble /ˈstʌbl/ N (NonC) *(in field)* chaume *m*, éteule *f* ; *(on chin)* barbe *f* de plusieurs jours ◆ **field of ~** chaume *m*, éteule *f*

stubbly /ˈstʌblɪ/ ADJ *[field]* couvert de chaume ; *[chin, face]* mal rasé ; *[beard]* de plusieurs jours ; *[hair]* court et raide, en brosse

stubborn /ˈstʌbən/ ADJ 1 *[person]* têtu, entêté ; *[animal]* têtu, rétif ; *[opposition, campaign, resistance]* opiniâtre, acharné ; *[denial, refusal, defiance, insistence, determination]* opiniâtre ◆ **his ~ attitude** son entêtement ◆ **she has a ~ streak** elle a un côté têtu *or* entêté ; → **mule¹** 2 *[stain]* rebelle, récalcitrant ; *[cold, fever etc]* rebelle, persistant ; *[problem]* persistant, tenace

stubbornly /ˈstʌbənlɪ/ ADV obstinément ◆ **he ~ refused** il a refusé obstinément ◆ **he was ~ determined** sa détermination était inébranlable ◆ **interest rates have remained ~ high** les taux d'intérêt sont restés élevés

stubbornness /ˈstʌbənnɪs/ N *[of person]* entêtement *m* ; *[of animal]* caractère *m* rétif ; *[of opposition, campaign, resistance]* opiniâtreté *f*, acharnement *m* ; *[of denial, refusal, defiance, insistence]* obstination *f*, opiniâtreté *f*

stubby /ˈstʌbɪ/ ADJ *[person]* courtaud ; *[finger]* boudiné ; *[pencil, crayon]* gros et court ◆ **a dog with ~ legs** un chien court sur pattes

stucco /ˈstʌkəʊ/ N (pl **stuccoes** *or* **stuccos**) stuc *m* VT stuquer COMP de *or* en stuc, stuqué

stuccowork /ˈstʌkəʊwɜːk/ N stucs *mpl*

stuck /stʌk/ VB pt, ptp of **stick** COMP **stuck-up*** ADJ bêcheur*

stud¹ /stʌd/ N 1 *(= knob, nail)* clou *m* à grosse tête ; *(on door, shield)* clou *m* décoratif ; *(on boots)* clou *m* (à souliers) ; *(on football boots)* crampon *m* ; *(on tyre, roadway)* clou *m* ; *(= cat's-eye)* clou *m* à catadioptre ; (also **collar stud**) bouton *m* de col 2 *(in chain)* étai *m* ; *(= double-headed screw)* goujon *m* ; *(= pivot screw)* tourillon *m* 3 *(Constr)* montant *m* VT *[+ boots, shield, door]* clouter ◆ **~ded tyre** pneu *m* clouté *or* à clous ◆ **~ded with** *(fig)* parsemé de ◆ **sky ~ded with stars** ciel *m* parsemé d'étoiles

stud² /stʌd/ N 1 (also **racing stud**) écurie *f* (de courses) ; (also **stud farm**) haras *m* ◆ **to be at ~, to have been put (out) to ~** être au haras 2 (* = *man*) étalon* *m*
COMP **stud farm** N haras *m*
stud fee N prix *m* de la saillie
stud mare N (jument *f*) poulinière *f*
stud poker N *(Cards)* variété de poker

studbook /ˈstʌdbʊk/ N stud-book *m*

student /ˈstjuːdənt/ N *(Univ)* étudiant(e) *m(f)* ; *(esp US Scol)* élève *mf*, lycéen(ne) *m(f)* ◆ **medical ~** étudiant(e) *m(f)* en médecine ◆ **~'s book** livre *m* de l'élève ◆ **he is a ~ of bird life** il étudie la vie des oiseaux ◆ **he is a keen ~** il est très studieux
COMP *(Univ) [life]* étudiant, estudiantin ; *(Univ) [residence, restaurant]* universitaire ; *(Univ) [power, unrest]* étudiant ; *[attitudes, opinions] (Univ)* des étudiants ; *(Scol)* des élèves, des lycéens
the student community N les étudiants *mpl*
student council N *(Scol)* comité *m* des délégués de classe
student councillor N *(Scol, Univ)* délégué(e) *m(f)* de classe
student driver N *(US)* jeune conducteur *m*, -trice *f*
student file N *(US Scol)* dossier *m* scolaire
student grant N bourse *f*
student ID card N *(US Scol)* carte *f* d'étudiant
student lamp N *(US)* lampe *f* de bureau *(orientable)*
student loan N prêt *m* étudiant
student nurse N élève *mf* infirmier (-ière)
student participation N *(Univ)* participation *f* des étudiants ; *(Scol)* participation *f* (en classe)
students' union N ⇒ **Student Union**
student teacher N professeur *m* stagiaire ; *(in primary school)* instituteur *m*, -trice *f* stagiaire
student teaching N stage *m* pédagogique
Student Union N *(Univ) (= association)* association *f* d'étudiants ; *(= building) locaux d'une association d'étudiants*

studentship /ˈstjuːdəntʃɪp/ N bourse *f* (d'études)

studhorse /ˈstʌdhɔːs/ N étalon *m*

studied /ˈstʌdɪd/ ADJ 1 *[indifference, casualness, politeness, calm]* affecté, étudié ; *[elegance]* recherché ; *[insult]* délibéré, voulu ◆ **to maintain a ~ silence** garder délibérément le silence ◆ **to maintain a ~ neutrality** rester délibérément neutre 2 *(pej = affected) [pose, style]* affecté

studio /ˈstjuːdɪəʊ/ N *[of artist, photographer, musician etc]* studio *m*, atelier *m* ; *(Cine, Rad, Recording, TV etc)* studio *m* ; → **mobile, recording**
COMP **studio apartment** N *(US)* studio *m* *(logement)*
studio audience N *(Rad, TV)* public *m* *(invité à une émission)*
studio couch N divan *m*
studio flat N *(Brit)* studio *m* *(logement)*
studio portrait N *(Phot)* portrait *m* photographique

studious /ˈstjuːdɪəs/ ADJ 1 *[person]* studieux, appliqué 2 *(= deliberate, careful) [insult, avoidance]* délibéré, voulu ; *[politeness, calm]* affecté, étudié

studiously /ˈstjuːdɪəslɪ/ ADV *(= deliberately, carefully) [avoid, ignore]* soigneusement ◆ **~ polite/**

ambiguous d'une politesse/ambiguïté affectée *or* étudiée

studiousness /'stjuːdɪəsnɪs/ **N** application *f* (*à l'étude*), amour *m* de l'étude

study /'stʌdɪ/ LANGUAGE IN USE 26.1

N 1 (*gen*) étude *f* ◆ **to make a ~ of sth** faire une étude de qch, étudier qch ◆ **it is a ~ of women in industry** c'est une étude sur les femmes dans l'industrie ◆ **his studies showed that ...** ses recherches ont montré que ... ◆ **it is a ~ in social justice** (*= model, ideal*) c'est un modèle de justice sociale ◆ **his face was a ~** (*fig hum*) il fallait voir sa figure ; → **brown**

2 (*= act of studying*) étude *f* ; (*Scol*) études *fpl* ◆ **he spends all his time in ~** il consacre tout son temps à l'étude *or* à ses études, il passe tout son temps à étudier

3 (*= room*) bureau *m*

VT [*+ nature, an author, text*] étudier ; (*Scol, Univ*) [*+ maths etc*] faire des études de, étudier ; [*+ project, proposal, map, ground*] étudier, examiner soigneusement ; [*+ person, sb's face, reactions*] étudier, observer attentivement ; [*+ stars*] observer ; see also **studied**

VI (*gen*) étudier ; (*Scol, Univ etc*) étudier, faire ses études ◆ **to ~ hard** travailler dur ◆ **to ~ under sb** travailler sous la direction de qn ; [*painter, composer*] être l'élève de qn ◆ **to ~ for an exam** préparer un examen ◆ **he is ~ing to be a doctor/a pharmacist** il fait des études de médecine/de pharmacie ◆ **he is ~ing to be a teacher** il fait des études pour entrer dans l'enseignement *or* pour devenir professeur

COMP [*visit, hour*] d'étude ; [*group*] de travail
study hall **N** (*US Scol*) (*gen*) permanence *f* ; (*in boarding school*) (salle *f* d')étude *f*
study hall teacher **N** (*US Scol*) surveillant(e) *m(f)* d'étude
study period **N** (*Brit*) (heure *f* de) permanence *f*, (heure *f* d')étude *f* surveillée
study room **N** (*Scol*) permanence *f* ; (*in boarding school*) (salle *f* d')étude *f*
study tour **N** voyage *m* d'études

stuff /stʌf/ **N** (*NonC*) 1 * (*gen*) chose *f*, truc* *m* ◆ **look at that ~** regarde ça, regarde ce truc* ◆ **it's dangerous ~** c'est dangereux ◆ **what's this ~ in this jar?** qu'est-ce que c'est que ça *or* que ce truc* dans ce pot ? ◆ **his new book is good ~** son nouveau livre est bien ◆ **there's some good ~ in what he writes** il y a de bonnes choses dans ce qu'il écrit ◆ **his painting is poor ~** sa peinture ne vaut pas grand-chose ◆ **Joyce? I can't read his ~ at all** Joyce ? je ne supporte pas du tout (ses livres) ◆ **I can't listen to his ~ at all** je ne supporte pas sa musique ◆ **all that ~ about how he wants to help us** (*pej*) toutes ces promesses en l'air comme quoi il veut nous aider ◆ **that's the ~ (to give them *or* to give the troops)!** bravo !, c'est ça ! ◆ **~ and nonsense!**‡ balivernes ! ◆ **he knows his ~** il connaît son sujet *or* son métier ◆ **do your ~!** vas-y !, c'est à toi ! ◆ **he did his ~ very well** il s'en est bien sorti ◆ **she's a nice bit of ~**‡ elle est canon‡ *or* bien roulée‡ ; → **greenstuff, hot, stern²**

2 * (*= miscellaneous objects*) trucs* *mpl* ; (*= possessions*) affaires *fpl* ; (*= tools etc*) ◆ **he brought back a lot of ~ from China** il a rapporté des tas de choses de Chine ◆ **the workmen left some of their ~ behind** les ouvriers ont laissé une partie de leur matériel ◆ **put your ~ away** range tes affaires

3 (*= fabric, cloth*) étoffe *f* ◆ **it is the (very) ~ of life/politics** *etc* c'est l'essence même de la vie/la politique *etc* ◆ **he is the ~ that heroes are made from, he is the ~ of heroes** (*liter*) il a l'étoffe d'un héros

4 (* Drugs) came‡ *f*

VT 1 (*= fill, pack*) [*+ cushion, quilt, chair, toy, mattress*] rembourrer (*with* avec) ; (*Taxidermy*) [*+ animal*] empailler ; [*+ sack, box, pockets*] bourrer, remplir (*with* de) ; (*Culin*) [*+ chicken, tomato*] farcir (*with* avec) ; (*= stop up*) [*+ hole*] boucher (*with* avec) ; (*= cram, thrust*) [*+ objects, clothes, books*] fourrer (*in, into* dans) ◆ **to ~ one's ears** se boucher les oreilles ◆ **to ~ one's fingers into one's ears** fourrer ses doigts dans ses oreilles ◆ **he ~ed the papers down the drain** il a fourré *or* enfoncé les papiers dans le tuyau ◆ **he ~ed some money into my hand** il m'a fourré de l'argent dans la main ◆ **he is a ~ed shirt*** c'est un grand ponte* suffisant ◆ **to ~ o.s. with food, to ~ food into one's mouth** se gaver *or* se bourrer de nourriture ◆ **he was ~ing himself*** il s'empiffrait* ◆ **I'm ~ed*** (*= full up*) je n'en peux plus ◆ **they ~ed him with morphine*** ils l'ont bourré de morphine ◆ **to ~ one's head with useless facts** se farcir *or* se bourrer la tête de connaissances inutiles* ◆ **he's ~ing your head with silly ideas*** il te bourre le crâne *or* il te farcit la cervelle d'idées niaises ◆ **the museum is ~ed with interesting things*** le musée est bourré de choses intéressantes ◆ **to ~ a ballot box** (*US Pol*) mettre des bulletins de vote truqués dans une urne ◆ **get ~ed!**‡ (*Brit*) va te faire cuire un œuf !‡, va te faire foutre !*‡ ◆ **~ him!**‡ qu'il aille se faire voir‡ *or* foutre*‡ ! ◆ **~ the council tax/decency!**‡ j'en ai rien à foutre*‡ des impôts locaux/des convenances !

2 (* = *put*) mettre ◆ **~ your books on the table** mets *or* fous‡ tes livres sur la table ◆ **(you know where) you can ~ that!**‡ tu sais où tu peux te le mettre !‡

3 (‡ = *defeat, ruin*) baiser*‡, niquer*‡ ◆ **we'll be ~ed if that happens** si ça arrive, on sera baisés*‡ *or* niqués*‡

4 (*‡ = *have sex with*) baiser*‡

VI (* = *guzzle*) s'empiffrer*

COMP **stuffed animal, stuffed toy** **N** peluche *f*

► **stuff away*** **VT SEP** [*+ food*] enfourner*, engloutir

► **stuff up** **VT SEP** [*+ hole*] boucher ◆ **my nose is ~ed up*, I'm ~ed up*** j'ai le nez bouché

stuffily* /'stʌfɪlɪ/ **ADV** [*say etc*] d'un ton désapprobateur

stuffiness /'stʌfɪnɪs/ **N** (*in room*) manque *m* d'air ; [*of person*] pruderie *f*, esprit *m* étriqué *or* vieux jeu *inv*

stuffing /'stʌfɪŋ/ **N** (*NonC*) (*= padding material*) [*of quilt, cushion, mattress*] bourre *f*, rembourrage *m* ; [*of toy, chair*] rembourrage *m* ; (*Taxidermy*) paille *f* ; (*Culin*) farce *f* ◆ **he's got no ~** (*pej*) c'est une chiffe molle ◆ **to knock the ~ out of sb*** (*= demoralize*) démoraliser qn ; (*= take down a peg*) remettre qn à sa place

stuffy /'stʌfɪ/ **ADJ** 1 (*= airless*) [*room*] mal aéré ; [*atmosphere*] étouffant ◆ **it's ~ in here** on manque d'air ici ◆ **the room was ~ after the meeting** on manquait d'air dans la salle après la réunion 2 (*= stick-in-the-mud*) vieux jeu *inv* ; (*= snobby*) guindé ◆ **golf has a rather ~ image in England** le golf a une image assez vieux jeu et guindée en Angleterre ◆ **Delphine's father is a nice man, but rather ~** le père de Delphine est un homme gentil, mais il est un peu collet monté 3 (*= congested*) [*nose, sinuses*] bouché

stultify /'stʌltɪfaɪ/ **VT** [*+ person*] abrutir, déshumaniser ; [*+ sb's efforts, action*] rendre vain ; [*+ argument, reasoning, claim*] enlever toute valeur à

stultifying /'stʌltɪfaɪɪŋ/ **ADJ** [*work, system, regime*] abrutissant ; [*atmosphere, effect*] débilitant

stumble /'stʌmbl/ **N** 1 (*in walking*) faux pas *m*, trébuchement *m* ; [*of horse*] faux pas *m* 2 ◆ **he recited it without a ~** il l'a récité sans trébucher *or* se reprendre une seule fois **VI** 1 trébucher (*over* sur, contre), faire un faux pas ; [*horse*] broncher ◆ **he ~d against the table** il a trébuché *or* fait un faux pas et a heurté la table ◆ **to ~ in/out/along** *etc* entrer/sortir/avancer *etc* en trébuchant 2 (*in speech*) trébucher (*at, over* sur) ◆ **he ~d through the speech** il a prononcé le discours d'une voix hésitante *or* trébuchante **COMP** **stumbling block** **N** pierre *f* d'achoppement

► **stumble across, stumble (up)on** **VT FUS** (*fig*) tomber sur

stumblebum‡ /'stʌmbl,bʌm/ **N** (*US*) empoté(e)* *m(f)*, abruti(e)* *m(f)*

stumm‡ /ʃtʊm/ **ADJ** ⇒ **shtoom**

stump /stʌmp/ **N** 1 [*of tree*] souche *f*, chicot *m* ; [*of limb, tail*] moignon *m* ; [*of tooth*] chicot *m* ; [*of cigar*] bout *m*, mégot* *m* ; [*of pencil, chalk, sealing wax, crayon etc*] bout *m* (*qui reste de qch*) ◆ **to find o.s. up a ~*** (*US*) ne savoir que répondre, être perplexe

2 (*Cricket*) piquet *m*

3 (*US Pol*) estrade *f* (d'un orateur politique) ◆ **to be *or* go on the ~** faire campagne, faire une tournée de discours

4 ◆ **~s**‡ (*= legs*) guiboles‡ *fpl* ; → **stir¹**

VT 1 (* = *puzzle, nonplus*) coller*, faire sécher* ◆ **to be ~ed by a problem** buter sur un problème ◆ **to be ~ed by a question** sécher* sur une question ◆ **that's got me ~ed, I'm ~ed** (*during quiz, crossword etc*) je sèche*

2 (*Cricket*) éliminer

3 (*US Pol*) **to ~ a state** faire une tournée électorale dans un état

VI 1 ◆ **to ~ in/out/along** *etc* (*heavily*) entrer/sortir/avancer *etc* à pas lourds ; (*limping*) entrer/sortir/avancer *etc* clopin-clopant*

2 (*US Pol*) faire une tournée électorale

COMP **stump speech** **N** discours *m* électoral

► **stump up*** (*Brit*) **VI** casquer‡

VT SEP cracher*, y aller de

stumpy /'stʌmpɪ/ **ADJ** [*person, leg, tail*] courtaud ; [*object, plant*] court et épais (-aisse *f*)

stun /stʌn/ **VT** étourdir, assommer ; (*using stunning device*) paralyser ; (*fig = amaze*) abasourdir, stupéfier

COMP **stun grenade** **N** grenade *f* incapacitante *or* paralysante
stun gun **N** pistolet *m* paralysant

stung /stʌŋ/ **VB** pt, ptp of **sting**

stunk /stʌŋk/ **VB** ptp of **stink**

stunned /stʌnd/ **ADJ** 1 (*lit*) assommé 2 (*= flabbergasted*) abasourdi, stupéfait (*by sth* de qch) ◆ **in ~ silence** muet de stupeur ◆ **there was a ~ silence** tout le monde s'est tu, abasourdi *or* stupéfait ◆ **the news was received in ~ disbelief** la nouvelle a été accueillie avec stupéfaction et incrédulité

stunner‡ /'stʌnəʳ/ **N** (*= girl/dress/car etc*) fille *f*/robe *f*/voiture *f etc* superbe

stunning /'stʌnɪŋ/ **ADJ** 1 (* = *fantastic, impressive: gen*) remarquable, (très) étonnant ; [*woman*] superbe ◆ **a ~ blonde** une superbe blonde ◆ **a ~ success** un formidable succès ◆ **you look ~** tu es superbe 2 ◆ **he gave me a ~ blow on the jaw** il m'a envoyé un coup à la mâchoire qui m'a assommé 3 (*= amazing, overwhelming*) [*success, news, defeat*] stupéfiant ◆ **news of his death came as a ~ blow** la nouvelle de sa mort a été un coup terrible ◆ **it was a ~ blow to the government's credibility** ça a porté un coup terrible à la crédibilité du gouvernement

stunningly /'stʌnɪŋlɪ/ **ADV** [*simple, original etc*] remarquablement ◆ **~ beautiful** d'une beauté extraordinaire *or* incroyable

stunt¹ /stʌnt/ **N** (*= feat*) tour *m* de force, exploit *m* (*destiné à attirer l'attention du public*) ; [*of stuntman*] cascade *f* ; (*in plane*) acrobatie *f* ; [*of students*] canular* *m* ; (also **publicity stunt**) truc* *m* publicitaire ◆ **don't ever pull a ~ like that again*** ne recommence plus jamais un truc* pareil ◆ **it's a ~ to get your money** c'est un truc* *or* c'est un coup monté pour avoir votre argent ◆ **that was a good** ~ c'était un truc* ingénieux *or* une combine⁑ ingénieuse VI *[pilot]* faire des acrobaties ; *(Cine)* faire des cascades

COMP **stunt double** N cascadeur *m*, -euse *f*, doublure *f*

stunt flier N aviateur *m* de haute voltige

stunt flying N acrobatie *f* aérienne, haute voltige *f*

stunt kite N cerf-volant *m* pilotable

stunt² /stʌnt/ VT *[+ growth]* retarder, arrêter ; *[+ person, plant]* retarder la croissance *or* le développement de

stunted /'stʌntɪd/ ADJ *[person]* rachitique, chétif ; *[plant]* rabougri ; *[growth, development]* retardé

stuntman /'stʌntmæn/ N (pl **-men**) cascadeur *m*

stuntwoman /'stʌnt,wʊmən/ N (pl **-women**) cascadeuse *f*

stupefaction /,stju:pɪ'fækʃən/ N stupéfaction *f*, stupeur *f*

stupefy /'stju:pɪfaɪ/ VT *[blow]* étourdir ; *[drink, drugs, lack of sleep]* abrutir ; *(= astound)* stupéfier, abasourdir

stupefying /'stju:pɪfaɪɪŋ/ ADJ ① *(frm = stultifying)* abrutissant ② *(* = boring)* mortel* ③ *(* = stupendous)* stupéfiant

stupendous /stju:'pendəs/ ADJ ① *(= amazing, impressive: gen)* extraordinaire, remarquable ; *[sum, quantity]* prodigieux ; *[vulgarity, ignorance]* incroyable ② *(* = wonderful)* sensationnel*, formidable

stupendously /stju:'pendəslɪ/ ADV *[good]* extraordinairement ; *[rich]* prodigieusement ◆ ~ **vulgar/thick*** *etc* incroyablement *or* prodigieusement vulgaire/stupide *etc*, d'une vulgarité/stupidité *etc* incroyable *or* prodigieuse

stupid /'stju:pɪd/ ADJ ① *(= unintelligent) [person, question, idea, mistake]* stupide, idiot, bête ◆ **to make sb look** ~ ridiculiser qn ◆ **it was** ~ **of me to refuse, I refused, which was** ~ **of me** j'ai eu la bêtise de refuser, j'ai été assez bête pour refuser ◆ **how** ~ **of me!** que je suis bête ! ◆ **to do something** ~ faire une bêtise ◆ **what a** ~ **thing to do!** c'était vraiment idiot *or* bête (de faire ça) ! ◆ **that hat looks really** ~ **(on you)** tu as l'air vraiment idiot avec ce chapeau ◆ **don't be** ~**!** ne sois pas bête ! ◆ **to act** ~* faire l'imbécile ; → **bore²**

② *(*: expressing annoyance)* ◆ **I hate this** ~ **machine !** je déteste cette maudite *or* fichue* machine ! ◆ **it was just a** ~ **quarrel/misunderstanding** ce n'était qu'une querelle/un malentendu stupide ◆ **you can keep your** ~ **presents, I don't want them!** tu peux garder tes cadeaux débiles*, je n'en veux pas ! ◆ **even just** ~ **things like missing a bus get me depressed** un rien me déprime, même des bêtises comme manquer le bus ◆ **you** ~ **idiot!** espèce d'idiot(e) !* ◆ **you** ~ **moron*/bastard*⁑!** espèce d'idiot/de con⁑ ! ◆ **that** ~ **bitch!***⁑cette espèce de conne !*⁑

③ *(† = insensible, dazed) (from blow, drink etc)* abruti, hébété ◆ **to knock sb** ~ assommer qn ◆ **to knock o.s.** ~ s'assommer ◆ **to laugh o.s.** ~* rire comme un bossu *or* comme une baleine* ◆ **to drink o.s.** ~* s'abrutir d'alcool

stupidity /stju:'pɪdɪtɪ/ N stupidité *f*, sottise *f*, bêtise *f*

stupidly /'stju:pɪdlɪ/ ADV ① *(= foolishly) [behave]* stupidement, bêtement ◆ ~**, I told him your name, I** ~ **told him your name** j'ai eu la bêtise de *or* j'ai été assez bête pour lui dire votre nom ◆ ~ **generous/zealous** d'une générosité/d'un zèle stupide ② *(= absently, as if stunned) [smile, say]* d'un air hébété *or* stupide † ◆ **"but ... she's dead!" he said** ~ "mais ... elle est morte !" dit-il d'un air hébété *or* stupide †

stupidness /'stju:pɪdnɪs/ N ⇒ **stupidity**

stupor /'stju:pə^r^/ N stupeur *f* ◆ **to be in a drunken** ~ être ivre mort

sturdily /'stɜ:dɪlɪ/ ADV ① ◆ ~ **built** *[person]* de constitution robuste ; *[furniture, structure, vehicle, equipment]* solide, robuste ; *[building]* (de construction) solide ② *(= stoically) [say]* d'un air résolu *or* déterminé ◆ ~ **independent** résolument indépendant

sturdiness /'stɜ:dɪnɪs/ N ① *[of furniture, structure, vehicle, equipment]* solidité *f* ; *[of building]* construction *f* solide ; *[of plant, person]* robustesse *f*, vigueur *f* ② *[of resistance, defence, refusal]* caractère *m* énergique

sturdy /'stɜ:dɪ/ ADJ ① *[person, plant]* robuste, vigoureux ; *[object, structure, body]* solide ② *[resistance, defence, refusal]* énergique, vigoureux ◆ ~ **common sense** solide bon sens *m*

sturgeon /'stɜ:dʒən/ N (pl inv) esturgeon *m*

stutter /'stʌtə^r^/ N bégaiement *m* ◆ **to have a** ~ bégayer VI bégayer ◆ **to** ~ **on/along** *(fig)* progresser difficilement VT (also **stutter out**) bégayer, dire en bégayant

stutterer /'stʌtərə^r^/ N bègue *mf*

stuttering /'stʌtərɪŋ/ N *(NonC)* bégaiement *m* ADJ ① *(= stammering) [voice]* bégayant, qui bégaie ② *(fig = jerky)* hésitant ◆ **a** ~ **start** un début hésitant

Stuttgart /'ʃtʊtgɑ:t/ N Stuttgart

STV /,esti:'vi/ N *(Pol)* (abbrev of **Single Transferable Vote**) → **single**

sty¹ /staɪ/ N *[of pigs]* porcherie *f*

sty², stye /staɪ/ N *(Med)* orgelet *m*, compère-loriot *m*

Stygian /'stɪdʒɪən/ ADJ *(fig)* sombre *or* noir comme le Styx, ténébreux ◆ ~ **darkness** ténèbres *fpl* impénétrables, nuit *f* noire

style /staɪl/ N ① *(gen, Art, Literat, Mus, Sport, Typ etc)* style *m* ◆ **in the** ~ **of Mozart** dans le style *or* à la manière de Mozart ◆ **building in the Renaissance** ~ édifice *m* (de) style Renaissance ◆ ~ **of life** *or* **living** style *m* de vie ◆ **he won in fine** ~ il l'a emporté haut la main ◆ **I like his** ~ **of writing** j'aime sa manière d'écrire *or* son style ◆ **I don't like his** ~ *(fig)* je n'aime pas son genre ◆ **that house is not my** ~* ce n'est pas mon genre de maison ◆ **that's the** ~**!*** bravo ! ; → **cramp¹**

② *(Dress etc) (gen)* mode *f* ; *(specific)* modèle *m* ; *(Hairdressing)* coiffure *f* ◆ **in the latest** ~ ADV à la dernière mode ADJ du dernier cri ◆ **these coats are made in two** ~**s** ces manteaux sont disponibles en deux modèles ◆ **the four** ~**s are all the same price** les quatre modèles sont tous au même prix ◆ **I want something in that** ~ je voudrais quelque chose dans ce genre-là *or* dans ce goût-là

③ *(NonC = distinction, elegance) [of person]* allure *f*, chic *m* ; *[of building, car, film, book]* style *m*, cachet *m* ◆ **that writer lacks** ~ cet écrivain manque de style *or* d'élégance, le style de cet écrivain manque de tenue

♦ **in style** ◆ **to live in** ~ mener grand train, vivre sur un grand pied ◆ **he does things in** ~ il fait bien les choses ◆ **they got married in** ~ ils se sont mariés en grande pompe ◆ **he certainly travels in** ~ quand il voyage il fait bien les choses

④ *(= sort, type)* genre *m* ◆ **just the** ~ **of book/car I like** justement le genre de livre/de voiture que j'aime

⑤ *(= form of address)* titre *m*

VT ① *(= call, designate)* appeler ◆ **he** ~**s himself "Doctor"** il se fait appeler "Docteur" ◆ **the headmaster is** ~**d "rector"** le directeur a le titre de "recteur" ; → **self**

② *(= design etc) [+ dress, car, boat]* créer, dessiner ◆ **to** ~ **sb's hair** coiffer qn ◆ **to have one's hair** ~**d** se faire coiffer ◆ **it is** ~**d for comfort not elegance** c'est un modèle conçu en fonction du confort et non de l'élégance

③ *(Typ) [+ manuscript]* préparer *(selon le style de l'éditeur)*

COMP **style book** N *(Typ)* manuel *m* des règles typographiques

style sheet N *(Comput)* feuille *f* de style

-style /staɪl/ ADJ *(in compounds)* ◆ **western-style democracy** démocratie *f* de style occidental ◆ **to dress 1920s-style** s'habiller dans le style des années 20

styli /'staɪlaɪ/ NPL of **stylus**

styling /'staɪlɪŋ/ N *(NonC) [of dress]* forme *f*, ligne *f*, façon *f* ; *[of car]* ligne *f* ; *(Hairdressing)* coupe *f* COMP *[mousse, gel, lotion]* coiffant, structurant **styling brush** N brosse *f* ronde

stylish /'staɪlɪʃ/ ADJ *[person, car, clothes]* élégant, chic *inv* ; *[district, resort, bar, hotel etc]* chic *inv* ; *[film, book]* qui a du style ; *[performer, performance]* de grande classe

stylishly /'staɪlɪʃlɪ/ ADV *[dress]* élégamment ; *[write]* avec style ; *[designed, decorated]* avec élégance ◆ ~ **dressed** élégamment vêtu, habillé avec élégance ◆ **she wore a** ~**-cut black suit** elle portait un tailleur noir d'une coupe élégante

stylishness /'staɪlɪʃnɪs/ N *[of person, car, clothes]* élégance *f*, chic *m*

stylist /'staɪlɪst/ N *(Literat)* styliste *mf* ; *(Dress etc)* modéliste *mf* ; *(Hairdressing)* coiffeur *m*, -euse *f*, artiste *mf* (capillaire)

stylistic /staɪ'lɪstɪk/ ADJ *(Ling, Literat, Mus, Art, Cine etc)* stylistique ◆ **a** ~ **device** un procédé stylistique *or* de style

stylistically /staɪ'lɪstɪkəlɪ/ ADV d'un point de vue stylistique ◆ ~**, he owes much to Hemingway** d'un point de vue stylistique, il doit beaucoup à Hemingway

stylistics /staɪ'lɪstɪks/ N *(NonC)* stylistique *f*

stylize /'staɪlaɪz/ VT styliser

stylus /'staɪləs/ N (pl **styluses** *or* **styli**) *(= tool)* style *m* ; *[of record player]* saphir *m*

stymie /'staɪmɪ/ N *(Golf)* trou *m* barré VT *(Golf)* barrer le trou à ; *(* fig)* coincer* ◆ **I'm** ~**d*** je suis coincé*, je suis dans une impasse

styptic /'stɪptɪk/ ADJ styptique ◆ ~ **pencil** crayon *m* hémostatique N styptique *m*

Styrofoam ® /'staɪrə,fəʊm/ N *(US)* polystyrène *m* expansé COMP *[cup]* en polystyrène

Styx /stɪks/ N Styx *m*

suasion /'sweɪʒən/ N (also **moral suasion**) pression *f* morale

suave /swɑ:v/ ADJ affable ; *(= insincere)* mielleux

suavely /'swɑ:vlɪ/ ADV *[say]* d'un ton mielleux ◆ **to smile** ~ avoir un sourire mielleux

suavity /'swɑ:vɪtɪ/ N *(NonC)* manières *fpl* doucereuses *(pej)*

sub * /sʌb/ abbrev of **subaltern, subedit, subeditor, sub-lieutenant, submarine, subscription, substitute**

subagent /sʌb'eɪdʒənt/ N sous-agent *m*

subalpine /'sʌb'ælpaɪn/ ADJ subalpin

subaltern /'sʌbltən/ N *(Brit Mil) officier d'un rang inférieur à celui de capitaine* ADJ subalterne

subaqua /,sʌb'ækwə/ ADJ ◆ ~ **club** club *m* de plongée

subaqueous /'sʌb'eɪkwɪəs/ ADJ subaquatique, aquatique

subarctic /'sʌb'ɑ:ktɪk/ ADJ subarctique ; *(fig)* presque arctique

subassembly /,sʌbə'semblɪ/ N sous-assemblée *f*

subatomic /'sʌbə'tɒmɪk/ ADJ subatomique

sub-basement /sʌbˈbeɪsmənt/ N second sous-sol *m*

sub-branch /ˈsʌbˈbrɑːntʃ/ N sous-embranchement *m*

subclass /ˈsʌbˈklɑːs/ N sous-classe *f*

subcommittee /ˈsʌbkəˌmɪtɪ/ N sous-comité *m* ; *(larger)* sous-commission *f* ◆ **the Housing Subcommittee** la sous-commission du logement

subcompact /ˌsʌbˈkɒmpækt/ N *(US = car)* petite voiture *f*

subconscious /ˌsʌbˈkɒnʃəs/ ADJ, N subconscient *m*

subconsciously /ˌsʌbˈkɒnʃəslɪ/ ADV 1 *(= without realizing)* inconsciemment 2 *(Psych)* au niveau du subconscient, de manière subconsciente

subcontinent /ˌsʌbˈkɒntɪnənt/ N sous-continent *m* ◆ **the (Indian) Subcontinent** le sous-continent indien

subcontract /ˌsʌbˈkɒntrækt/ N sous-traité *m* VT /ˌsʌbkənˈtrækt/ sous-traiter

subcontracting /ˌsʌbkɒnˈtræktɪŋ/ N sous-traitance *f* ADJ *[firm]* qui sous-traite

subcontractor /ˌsʌbkənˈtræktəʳ/ N sous-entrepreneur *m*, sous-traitant *m*

subculture /ˈsʌbˌkʌltʃəʳ/ N *(Sociol)* subculture *f* ; *(Bacteriology)* culture *f* repiquée

subcutaneous /ˈsʌbkjʊˈteɪnɪəs/ ADJ sous-cutané

subcutaneously /ˌsʌbkjʊˈteɪnɪəslɪ/ ADV en sous-cutané

subdeacon /ˌsʌbˈdiːkən/ N sous-diacre *m*

subdeb* /ˈsʌbdeb/, **subdebutante** /ˈsʌbˌdebjuːtɑːnt/ N *(US)* jeune fille *f* qui n'a pas encore fait son entrée dans le monde

subdistrict /ˈsʌbˌdɪstrɪkt/ N subdivision *f* d'un quartier

subdivide /ˌsʌbdɪˈvaɪd/ VT subdiviser *(into* en*)* VI se subdiviser

subdivision /ˈsʌbdɪˌvɪʒən/ N subdivision *f*

subdominant /ˌsʌbˈdɒmɪnənt/ N *(Ecol)* (espèce *f*) sous-dominante *f* ; *(Mus)* sous-dominante *f*

subdue /səbˈdjuː/ VT *[+ people, country]* subjuguer, assujettir, soumettre ; *[+ feelings, passions, desire]* contenir, refréner, maîtriser ; *[+ light, colour]* adoucir, atténuer ; *[+ voice]* baisser ; *[+ pain]* atténuer, amortir

subdued /səbˈdjuːd/ ADJ 1 *(= morose) [person, mood, atmosphere]* sombre ; *[voice]* qui manque d'entrain ◆ **she was very** ~ elle avait perdu son entrain 2 *(= restrained, unobtrusive) [reaction, response]* prudent 3 *(= quiet, dim) [colour]* doux (douce *f*) ; *[light, lighting]* tamisé, voilé ; *[voice]* bas (basse *f*) ; *[conversation, discussion]* à voix basse

subedit /ˌsʌbˈedɪt/ VT *(Brit Press, Typ)* corriger, mettre au point, préparer pour l'impression

subeditor /ˌsʌbˈedɪtəʳ/ N *(Brit Press, Typ)* secrétaire *mf* de (la) rédaction

sub-entry /ˈsʌbˌentrɪ/ N *(Accounting)* sous-entrée *f*

subfamily /ˈsʌbˌfæmɪlɪ/ N sous-famille *f*

subfield /ˈsʌbfiːld/ N *(Math)* subdivision *f*

sub-frame /ˈsʌbfreɪm/ N *[of car]* faux-châssis *m*

subfusc /ˈsʌbfʌsk/ N toge *f* et mortier noirs

subgroup /ˈsʌbgruːp/ N sous-groupe *m*

subhead(ing) /ˈsʌbˌhed(ɪŋ)/ N sous-titre *m*

subhuman /ˌsʌbˈhjuːmən/ ADJ *[conditions]* inhumain ◆ **to treat/portray foreigners as** ~ traiter/dépeindre les étrangers comme des sous-hommes N sous-homme *m*

subject /ˈsʌbdʒɪkt/ N 1 *(esp Brit = citizen etc)* sujet(te) *m(f)* ◆ **the king and his** ~**s** le roi et ses sujets ◆ **British** ~ sujet *m* britannique ◆ **he is a French** ~ *(in France)* il est de nationalité française ; *(elsewhere)* c'est un ressortissant français

2 *(Med, Phot, Psych etc = person)* sujet *m* ◆ **he's a good** ~ **for treatment by hypnosis** c'est un sujet qui répond bien au traitement par l'hypnose ◆ **he's a good** ~ **for research into hypnosis** c'est un bon sujet pour une étude sur l'hypnose

3 *(= matter, topic: gen, Art, Literat, Mus etc)* sujet *m (of, for* de*)* ; *(Scol, Univ)* matière *f*, discipline *f* ◆ **to get off the** ~ sortir du sujet ◆ **that's off the** ~ c'est hors du sujet *or* à côté du sujet ◆ **let's get back to the** ~ revenons à nos moutons ◆ **on the** ~ **of ...** au sujet de ..., sur le sujet de ... ◆ **while we're on the** ~ **of ...** pendant que nous parlons de ..., à propos de ... ◆ **let's change the** ~ changeons de sujet ◆ **his best** ~ *(Scol, Univ)* sa matière *or* sa discipline forte ; → **drop**

4 *(= reason, occasion)* sujet *m*, motif *m (of, for* de*)* ◆ **it is not a** ~ **for rejoicing** il n'y a pas lieu de se réjouir

5 *(Gram, Logic, Philos)* sujet *m*

ADJ 1 *(frm = subservient) [people, tribes, state]* asservi, soumis ◆ **the police are** ~ **to the law, like the rest of us** la police doit obéir à la loi, comme nous tous

2 ◆ ~ **to** *(= prone to)* sujet à ◆ **the area is** ~ **to drought** la région est sujette à la sécheresse ◆ **he is** ~ **to back pain** il est sujet au mal de dos *or* à des maux de dos ◆ ~ **to French rule** sous (la) domination française ◆ **your gift will be** ~ **to VAT** votre cadeau sera soumis à la TVA

3 ◆ ~ **to** *(= depending on)* ◆ ~ **to the approval of the committee** sous réserve de l'accord du comité ◆ **you may leave the country** ~ **to producing the necessary documents** vous pouvez quitter le territoire à condition de fournir les documents nécessaires ◆ **the building is being sold** ~ **to certain conditions** le bâtiment est à vendre sous certaines conditions ◆ **my offer is** ~ **to the following conditions** mon offre est soumise aux conditions suivantes ◆ **the decision is** ~ **to approval/confirmation (by the minister)** cette décision doit être approuvée/confirmée (par le ministre) ◆ **they have authority to decide,** ~ **to the minister's approval** ils ont le pouvoir de décision, sous réserve de l'approbation du ministre ◆ **"subject to availability"** *[holiday, concert, flight]* "dans la limite des places disponibles" ; *[free gift]* "dans la limite des stocks disponibles" ◆ **"prices are subject to alteration"** "ces prix sont sujets à modifications" ◆ ~ **to prior sale** sauf vente (antérieure)

VT /səbˈdʒekt/ *(= subdue) [+ country]* soumettre, assujettir *(liter)* ◆ **to** ~ **sb to sth** soumettre qn à qch, faire subir qch à qn ◆ **to** ~ **sth to heat/cold** exposer qch à la chaleur/au froid ◆ **he was ~ed to much criticism** il a été en butte à de nombreuses critiques, il a fait l'objet de nombreuses critiques, il a été très critiqué ◆ **to** ~ **o.s. to criticism** s'exposer à la critique

COMP **subject heading** N rubrique *f*

subject index N *(in book)* index *m* thématique ; *(in library)* fichier *m* par matières

subject matter N *(= theme)* sujet *m* ; *(= content)* contenu *m*

subject pronoun N pronom *m* sujet

subjection /səbˈdʒekʃən/ N sujétion *f*, soumission *f* ◆ **to hold** *or* **keep in** ~ maintenir dans la sujétion *or* sous son joug ◆ **to bring into** ~ soumettre, assujettir *(liter)* ◆ **they were living in a state of complete** ~ ils étaient complètement assujettis *or* soumis

subjective /səbˈdʒektɪv/ ADJ 1 subjectif 2 *(Gram) [case, pronoun]* sujet N *(Gram)* nominatif *m*

subjectively /səbˈdʒektɪvlɪ/ ADV subjectivement

subjectivism /səbˈdʒektɪvɪzəm/ N subjectivisme *m*

subjectivity /ˌsəbdʒekˈtɪvɪtɪ/ N subjectivité *f*

subjoin /ˌsʌbˈdʒɔɪn/ VT adjoindre, ajouter

sub judice /ˌsʌbˈdʒuːdɪsɪ/ ADJ *(Jur)* ◆ **the matter is** ~ l'affaire est en instance *or* devant les tribunaux

subjugate /ˈsʌbdʒʊgeɪt/ VT *[+ people, country]* subjuguer, soumettre, assujettir ; *[+ animal, feelings]* dompter

subjugation /ˌsʌbdʒʊˈgeɪʃən/ N subjugation *f*, assujettissement *m*

subjunctive /səbˈdʒʌŋktɪv/ ADJ, N subjonctif *m* ◆ **in the** ~ **(mood)** au (mode) subjonctif

subkingdom /ˈsʌbˌkɪŋdəm/ N *(Bot, Zool etc)* embranchement *m*

sublease /ˈsʌbliːs/ N sous-location *f* VT sous-louer *(to* à ; *from* à*)*

sublet /ˌsʌbˈlet/ (vb : pret, ptp **sublet**) N sous-location *f* VT sous-louer *(to* à*)*

sub-librarian /ˌsʌblaɪˈbreərɪən/ N bibliothécaire *mf* adjoint(e)

sub-lieutenant /ˌsʌblefˈtenənt/ N *(Brit Naut)* enseigne *m* de vaisseau (de première classe)

sublimate /ˈsʌblɪmeɪt/ VT *(all senses)* sublimer ADJ /ˈsʌblɪmɪt/ N *(Chem)* sublimé *m*

sublimation /ˌsʌblɪˈmeɪʃən/ N sublimation *f*

sublime /səˈblaɪm/ ADJ 1 *[being, beauty, painting, scenery, music]* sublime ; *[moment]* divin 2 *(* = delightful) [dinner, hat, person]* divin, sensationnel* 3 *[indifference, disregard]* suprême *before n*, souverain *before n* ; *[innocence]* suprême *before n* ; *[incompetence]* prodigieux N sublime *m* ◆ **from the** ~ **to the ridiculous** du sublime au grotesque

sublimely /səˈblaɪmlɪ/ ADV 1 ◆ ~ **beautiful** d'une beauté sublime 2 *(* = delightfully) [dance, sing etc]* divinement 3 *[indifferent, ignorant]* souverainement, au plus haut point ◆ **the government seems** ~ **unaware of the danger** le gouvernement semble totalement inconscient du danger

subliminal /ˌsʌbˈlɪmɪnl/ ADJ subliminal

COMP **subliminal advertising** N publicité *f* subliminale

subliminal image N image *f* subliminale

subliminal message N message *m* subliminal

subliminally /ˌsʌbˈlɪmɪnəlɪ/ ADV *[evoke, influence etc]* de manière subliminale

sublimity /səˈblɪmɪtɪ/ N sublimité *f*

sublingual /ˌsʌbˈlɪŋgwəl/ ADJ sublingual

submachine gun /ˌsʌbməˈʃiːngʌn/ N mitraillette *f*

submarine /ˌsʌbməˈriːn/ N 1 *(Naut)* sous-marin *m* 2 *(US *: also* **submarine sandwich, sub sandwich***)* gros sandwich *m* mixte ADJ sous-marin

COMP **submarine chaser** N chasseur *m* de sous-marins

submarine pen N abri *m* pour sous-marins

submariner /ˌsʌbˈmærɪnəʳ/ N sous-marinier *m*

submaxillary /ˌsʌbˈmæksɪlərɪ/ ADJ sous-maxillaire

submediant /ˌsʌbˈmiːdɪənt/ N *(Mus)* sus-dominante *f*

sub-menu /ˈsʌbmenjuː/ N *(Comput)* sous-menu *m*

submerge /səbˈmɜːdʒ/ VT *[flood, tide, sea]* submerger ; *[+ field]* inonder, submerger ◆ **to** ~ **sth in sth** immerger qch dans qch ◆ **to** ~ **o.s. in sth** *(fig)* se plonger totalement dans qch VI *[submarine, diver etc]* s'immerger

submerged /səbˈmɜːdʒd/ ADJ submergé ◆ ~ **in work** *(fig)* submergé *or* débordé de travail

submergence /səbˈmɜːdʒəns/ N submersion *f*

submersible /səbˈmɜːsəbl/ ADJ, N submersible *m*

submersion /səbˈmɜːʃən/ N 1 *(in liquid)* submersion *f* 2 ◆ **total ~ in an interesting hobby can be very relaxing** se plonger totalement dans un hobby intéressant peut apporter une grande détente

submission /səbˈmɪʃən/ N 1 *(= submissiveness)* soumission *f* *(to* à*)* ◆ **she nodded her head in ~** elle a incliné la tête d'un air soumis ◆ **to starve/beat sb into ~** soumettre qn en le privant de nourriture/en le battant 2 *(Wrestling)* abandon *m* 3 *(NonC = handing in) [of documents, sample, application, report]* dépôt *m* ; *[of thesis]* remise *f* (au rapporteur) 4 *(= proposal)* proposition *f* 5 *(Jur)* **~s** conclusions *fpl (d'une partie)* ◆ **to file ~s with a court** déposer des conclusions auprès d'un tribunal 6 *(frm = assertion)* **it is my ~ that ...** ma thèse est que ... ◆ **in my/our ~** selon ma/notre thèse

submissive /səbˈmɪsɪv/ ADJ *[person, behaviour, attitude]* soumis, docile ◆ **children were expected to be ~ to their elders** on attendait des enfants qu'ils se soumettent à leurs aînés

submissively /səbˈmɪsɪvlɪ/ ADV docilement

submissiveness /səbˈmɪsɪvnɪs/ N soumission *f*, docilité *f*

submit /səbˈmɪt/ VT 1 ◆ **to ~ o.s. to sb/sth** se soumettre à qn/qch 2 *(= put forward) [+ documents, sample, proposal, report, evidence]* soumettre *(to* à*)*, présenter *(to* à*)* ◆ **to ~ that ...** suggérer que ... ◆ **I ~ that ...** ma thèse est que ... VI *(Mil)* se soumettre *(to* à*)* ; *(fig)* se soumettre, se plier *(to* à*)*

subnormal /ˌsʌbˈnɔːməl/ ADJ 1 (also **mentally subnormal**) *[person]* attardé, arriéré 2 *[weight, height, temperature etc]* inférieur (-eure *f*) à la normale NPL **the subnormal** ◆ **the mentally/educationally ~** les attardés *mpl or* retardés *mpl* (sur le plan intellectuel/éducatif)

suborbital /ˌsʌbˈɔːbɪtəl/ ADJ *(Space)* sous-orbital

sub-order /ˈsʌbɔːdəʳ/ N sous-ordre *m*

subordinate /səˈbɔːdnɪt/ ADJ 1 *[officer, role, position]* subalterne *(to* à*)* 2 *(Gram)* subordonné N subordonné(e) *m(f)*, subalterne *mf* VT /səˈbɔːdɪneɪt/ subordonner *(to* à*)* COMP **subordinating conjunction** N *(Gram)* subordonnant *m* conjonction *f* de subordination

subordination /səˌbɔːdɪˈneɪʃən/ N subordination *f*

suborn /sʌˈbɔːn/ VT suborner

subparagraph /ˈsʌbˌpærəgrɑːf/ N sous-paragraphe *m*

subplot /ˈsʌbˌplɒt/ N *(Literat)* intrigue *f* secondaire

subpoena /səˈpiːnə/ *(Jur)* N citation *f*, assignation *f (pour le témoin)* VT citer *or* assigner (à comparaître)

subpopulation /ˈsʌbˌpɒpjʊˈleɪʃən/ N subpopulation *f*

sub-postmaster /ˌsʌbˈpəʊstmæstəʳ/ N *(Brit)* receveur *m* des postes

sub-postmistress /ˌsʌbˈpəʊstmɪstrɪs/ N *(Brit)* receveuse *f* des postes

sub-post office /ˌsʌbˈpəʊstɒfɪs/ N agence *f* postale

subregion /ˈsʌbˌriːdʒən/ N sous-région *f*

subrogate /ˈsʌbrəgɪt/ ADJ subrogé ◆ **~ language** *(Ling)* langage *m* subrogé

sub rosa /ˌsʌbˈrəʊzə/ ADV en confidence, sous le sceau du secret

subroutine /ˈsʌbruːˌtiːn/ N *(Comput)* sous-programme *m*

sub-Saharan /ˌsʌbsəˈhɑːrən/ ADJ *(Geog)* subsaharien (-enne *f*) COMP **sub-Saharan Africa** N Afrique *f* subsaharienne *or* noire

subscribe /səbˈskraɪb/ LANGUAGE IN USE 11.2 VT 1 *[+ money]* donner, verser *(to* à*)* 2 *[+ one's signature, name]* apposer *(to* au bas de*)* ; *[+ document]* signer ◆ **he ~s himself John Smith** il signe John Smith VI 1 ◆ **to ~ to** *[+ book, new publication, fund]* souscrire à ; *[+ newspaper] (= become a subscriber)* s'abonner à ; *(= be a subscriber)* être abonné à ; *(Comput)* s'abonner à la liste de ; *[+ charity]* verser une somme d'argent à, apporter une contribution à ◆ **to ~ for shares** souscrire à des actions 2 *[+ opinion, project, proposal]* souscrire à ◆ **I don't ~ to the idea that money should be given to ...** je ne suis pas partisan de donner de l'argent à ... ◆ **I don't ~ to that point of view** je ne partage pas ce point de vue

subscriber /səbˈskraɪbəʳ/ N *(to fund, new publication etc)* souscripteur *m*, -trice *f (to* de*)* ; *(to newspaper, also Telec)* abonné(e) *m(f) (to* de*)* ; *(to opinion, idea)* adepte *mf*, partisan *m (to* de*)* COMP **subscriber trunk dialling** N *(Brit Telec)* automatique *m*

subscript /ˈsʌbskrɪpt/ *(Typ)* ADJ inférieur (-eure *f*) N indice *m*

subscription /səbˈskrɪpʃən/ N *(to fund, charity)* souscription *f* ; *(to club)* cotisation *f* ; *(to newspaper)* abonnement *m* ◆ **to pay one's ~** *(to club)* payer *or* verser sa cotisation ; *(to newspaper)* payer *or* régler son abonnement ◆ **to take out a ~ to ...** *(Press)* s'abonner à ... COMP **subscription rate** N *(Press)* tarif *m* d'abonnement

subsection /ˈsʌbˌsekʃən/ N *(Jur etc)* subdivision *f*, article *m*

subsequent /ˈsʌbsɪkwənt/ ADJ *(= later in past)* postérieur (-eure *f*), ultérieur (-eure *f*) ; *(= in future)* à venir ADV *(frm)* ◆ **~ to this** par la suite ◆ **~ to his arrival** à la suite de son arrivée ◆ **events that occurred ~ to March 1995** les événements postérieurs à mars 1995

subsequently /ˈsʌbsɪkwəntlɪ/ ADV par la suite, ultérieurement

subserve /səbˈsɜːv/ VT *(frm)* favoriser

subservience /səbˈsɜːvɪəns/ N 1 *(= submission) [of person, nation]* asservissement *m (to sb/sth* à qn/qch*)* 2 *(pej = servility) [of person, manner, behaviour]* servilité *f (pej) (to sb* envers qn*)* 3 *(frm = secondary role)* rôle *m* accessoire *or* secondaire *(to sb/sth* par rapport à qn/qch*)*

subservient /səbˈsɜːvɪənt/ ADJ 1 *(= submissive) [person, nation]* asservi, soumis *(to* à*)* 2 *(pej = servile) [person, manner, behaviour]* servile *(pej)* 3 *(frm = secondary)* accessoire, secondaire *(to sb/sth* par rapport à qn/qch*)*

subset /ˈsʌbˌset/ N sous-ensemble *m*

subside /səbˈsaɪd/ VI *[land, pavement, foundations, building]* s'affaisser, se tasser ; *[flood, river]* baisser, décroître ; *[wind, anger, excitement]* tomber, se calmer ; *[threat]* s'éloigner ; *[person] (into armchair etc)* s'affaisser, s'écrouler *(into* dans ; *on to* sur*)*

subsidence /ˈsʌbsɪdns, səbˈsaɪdəns/ N *[of land, pavement, foundations, building]* affaissement *m* ◆ **"road liable to subsidence"** "chaussée instable" ◆ **the crack in the wall is caused by ~** la faille dans le mur est due à l'affaissement du terrain

subsidiarity /ˌsəbsɪdɪˈærɪtɪ/ N subsidiarité *f*

subsidiary /səbˈsɪdɪərɪ/ ADJ 1 *[role]* secondaire, accessoire ; *[motive, reason, aim]* subsidiaire *(to* par rapport à*)* ; *(Theat, Literat) [character]* secondaire ; *[advantage, income]* accessoire 2 *(Univ) [subject, course]* optionnel ◆ **to do ~ Latin** étudier le latin en option 3 *(Fin, Comm)* ◆ **~ company/bank** filiale *f (d'une société/d'une banque)* N *(Fin)* filiale *f*

subsidize /ˈsʌbsɪdaɪz/ VT subventionner ◆ **heavily ~d** *[agriculture, housing]* fortement subventionné

subsidy /ˈsʌbsɪdɪ/ N subvention *f* ◆ **government** *or* **state ~** subvention *f* de l'État ◆ **there is a ~ on butter** l'État subventionne les producteurs *or* la production de beurre

subsist /səbˈsɪst/ VI subsister ◆ **to ~ on bread/$100 a week** vivre de pain/avec 100 dollars par semaine

subsistence /səbˈsɪstəns/ N 1 existence *f*, subsistance *f* ◆ **means of ~** moyens *mpl* d'existence *or* de subsistance 2 (also **subsistence allowance, subsistence benefit**) frais *mpl or* indemnité *f* de subsistance

COMP **subsistence crops** NPL cultures *fpl* vivrières de base

subsistence economy N économie *f* de subsistance

subsistence farmer N agriculteur *m* qui produit le minimum vital

subsistence farming N agriculture *f* de subsistance

subsistence level N minimum *m* vital ◆ **to live at ~ level** avoir tout juste de quoi vivre

subsistence wage N salaire *m* tout juste suffisant pour vivre, salaire *m* de subsistance

subsoil /ˈsʌbsɔɪl/ N *(Agr, Geol)* sous-sol *m*

subsonic /ˌsʌbˈsɒnɪk/ ADJ *[plane, speed etc]* subsonique

subspecies /ˈsʌbˌspiːʃiːz/ N *(pl inv)* sous-espèce *f*

substance /ˈsʌbstəns/ N *(= matter, material, essential meaning, gist)* substance *f (also Chem, Philos, Phys, Rel etc)* ; *(= solid quality)* solidité *f* ; *(= consistency)* consistance *f* ; *(= wealth etc)* biens *mpl*, fortune *f* ◆ **that is the ~ of his speech** voilà la substance *or* l'essentiel de son discours ◆ **I agree with the ~ of his proposals** je suis d'accord sur l'essentiel de ses propositions ◆ **the meal had not much ~ (to it)** le repas n'était pas très substantiel ◆ **to lack ~** *[film, book, essay]* manquer d'étoffe ; *[argument]* être plutôt mince ; *[accusation, claim, allegation]* être sans grand fondement ◆ **in ~** en substance ◆ **a man of ~** † *(= rich)* un homme riche *or* cossu ◆ **the ~ of the case** *(Jur)* le fond de l'affaire ; → **sum**

COMP **substance abuse** N abus *m* de substances toxiques

substandard /ˌsʌbˈstændəd/ ADJ 1 *(= low-quality) [goods, service, materials]* de qualité inférieure ; *[work]* médiocre 2 *(= below a certain standard) [housing, conditions, abattoir etc]* non conforme aux normes 3 *(Ling)* incorrect

substantial /səbˈstænʃəl/ ADJ 1 *(= considerable, sizeable)* important, considérable ; *[business]* gros (grosse *f*) ; *[house]* grand ◆ **to be in ~ agreement** être d'accord sur l'essentiel *or* dans l'ensemble 2 *(= durable) [object, structure]* solide 3 *(= sustaining) [meal]* substantiel 4 *(= convincing) [proof]* convaincant, solide ; *[objection]* fondé ; *[argument]* de poids 5 *(frm = real, tangible)* substantiel

substantially /səbˈstænʃəlɪ/ ADV 1 *(= considerably)* considérablement ◆ **~ bigger/higher** *etc* beaucoup plus grand/plus haut *etc* ◆ **~ more refugees** beaucoup plus de réfugiés ◆ **~ different** fondamentalement différent 2 *(= to a large extent) [correct, true, the same]* en grande partie ◆ **this is ~ true** c'est en grande partie vrai ◆ **to remain ~ unchanged** rester inchangé dans l'ensemble ◆ **it is ~ the same book** c'est en grande partie le même livre 3 ◆ **~ constructed** solidement construit

substantiate /səbˈstænʃɪeɪt/ VT fournir des preuves à l'appui de, justifier ◆ **he could not ~ it** il n'a pas pu fournir de preuves

substantiation /səbˌstænʃɪˈeɪʃən/ N preuve *f*, justification *f*

substantival /ˌsʌbstənˈtaɪvəl/ ADJ *(Gram)* substantif, à valeur de substantif

substantive /ˈsʌbstəntɪv/ N (Gram) substantif m ADJ 1 (frm = substantial) important 2 (Gram) substantif

substation /ˈsʌbˌsteɪʃən/ N sous-station f

substitute /ˈsʌbstɪtjuːt/ N (= person: gen, Sport) remplaçant(e) m(f), suppléant(e) m(f) (for de) ; (= thing) produit m de substitution or de remplacement (for de) ; (Gram) (terme m) substitut m ◆ **you must find a ~ (for yourself)** vous devez vous trouver un remplaçant, il faut vous faire remplacer ◆ **~s for rubber, rubber ~s** succédanés mpl or ersatz m inv de caoutchouc ◆ **"beware of substitutes"** (Comm) "se méfier des contrefaçons" ◆ **there is no ~ for wool** rien ne peut remplacer la laine ◆ **a correspondence course is no/a poor ~ for personal tuition** les cours par correspondance ne remplacent pas/remplacent mal les cours particuliers ; → **turpentine**

ADJ (Sport) (à titre de) remplaçant ◆ **~ coffee** ersatz m inv or succédané m de café

VT substituer (A for B A à B), remplacer (A for B B par A)

VI ◆ **to ~ for sb** remplacer or suppléer qn

COMP **substitute teacher** N (US) suppléant(e) m(f), remplaçant(e) m(f)

substitution /ˌsʌbstɪˈtjuːʃən/ N substitution f (also Chem, Ling, Math etc), remplacement m ◆ **~ of x for y** substitution de x à y, remplacement de y par x ◆ **to make a ~** (Sport) remplacer un joueur

substrata /ˈsʌbˌstrɑːtə/ NPL of **substratum**

substrate /ˈsʌbstreɪt/ N (Chem) substrat m

substratum /ˈsʌbˌstrɑːtəm/ N (pl **substrata** /ˈsʌbˌstrɑːtə/) (gen, Geol, Ling, Sociol etc) substrat m ; (Agr) sous-sol m ; (fig) fond m

substructure /ˈsʌbˌstrʌktʃəʳ/ N infrastructure f

subsume /səbˈsjuːm/ VT subsumer

subsystem /ˈsʌbˌsɪstəm/ N sous-système m

subteen /ˌsʌbˈtiːn/ N (esp US) préadolescent(e) m(f)

subtemperate /ˌsʌbˈtempərɪt/ ADJ subtempéré

subtenancy /ˌsʌbˈtenənsɪ/ N sous-location f

subtenant /ˌsʌbˈtenənt/ N sous-locataire mf

subtend /səbˈtend/ VT sous-tendre

subterfuge /ˈsʌbtəfjuːdʒ/ N subterfuge m

subterranean /ˌsʌbtəˈreɪnɪən/ ADJ (lit, fig) souterrain

subtext /ˈsʌbtekst/ N sujet m sous-jacent

subtilize /ˈsʌtɪlaɪz/ VTI subtiliser

subtitle /ˈsʌbˌtaɪtl/ N sous-titre m VT sous-titrer

subtitling /ˈsʌbˌtaɪtlɪŋ/ N sous-titrage m

subtle /ˈsʌtl/ ADJ (gen) subtil (subtile f) ; [mind, humour, irony, joke] subtil (subtile f), fin ; [perfume, flavour] subtil (subtile f), délicat ; [pressure, implication, suggestion, reminder, rebuke] discret (-ète f) ; [plan] ingénieux ; [flaw] léger ◆ **a ~ form of racism** une forme insidieuse de racisme ◆ **the ~ message of the film is that ...** le message implicite or en filigrane de ce film est que ...

subtleness /ˈsʌtlnɪs/ N ⇒ **subtlety 1**

subtlety /ˈsʌtltɪ/ N 1 (NonC: gen) subtilité f ; [of mind, humour, irony, joke] subtilité f, finesse f ; [of perfume, flavour] subtilité f, délicatesse f ; [of pressure, implication, suggestion, reminder, rebuke] discrétion f ; [of plan] ingéniosité f 2 (= detail) subtilité f

subtly /ˈsʌtlɪ/ ADV [imply, suggest, remind, rebuke] discrètement ; [change, enhance] de façon subtile ◆ **~ flavoured** au goût subtil or délicat ◆ **~ coloured** aux couleurs subtiles ◆ **~ spicy** délicatement épicé ◆ **~ erotic** d'un érotisme subtil

subtonic /ˌsʌbˈtɒnɪk/ N sous-tonique f

subtopic /ˌsʌbˈtɒpɪk/ N sous-thème m, subdivision f d'un thème

subtotal /ˈsʌbˌtəʊtl/ N total m partiel

subtract /səbˈtrækt/ VT soustraire, retrancher, déduire (from de)

subtraction /səbˈtrækʃən/ N soustraction f

subtropical /ˈsʌbˈtrɒpɪkəl/ ADJ subtropical

subtropics /sʌbˈtrɒpɪks/ NPL régions fpl subtropicales

suburb /ˈsʌbɜːb/ N faubourg m ◆ **the ~s** la banlieue ◆ **in the ~s** en banlieue ◆ **the outer ~s** la grande banlieue ◆ **it is now a ~ of London** c'est maintenant un faubourg de Londres, ça fait désormais partie de la banlieue de Londres

suburban /səˈbɜːbən/ ADJ 1 [house, street, community, train] de banlieue ◆ **a ~ area** une banlieue, une zone suburbaine (frm) ◆ **~ development** or **growth** développement m suburbain ◆ **~ sprawl** (NonC: pej) (= phenomenon) développement anarchique des banlieues ; (= particular suburb) banlieue f tentaculaire 2 (pej) [attitude, values, accent] banlieusard (pej) ◆ **his ~ lifestyle** sa vie étriquée (pej) de banlieusard

suburbanite /səˈbɜːbənaɪt/ N habitant(e) m(f) de la banlieue, banlieusard(e) m(f) (pej)

suburbanize /səˈbɜːbənaɪz/ VT donner le caractère or les caractéristiques de la banlieue à, transformer en banlieue

suburbia /səˈbɜːbɪə/ N (NonC) la banlieue

subvention /səbˈvenʃən/ N subvention f

subversion /səbˈvɜːʃən/ N subversion f

subversive /səbˈvɜːsɪv/ ADJ (lit, fig) subversif N élément m subversif

subvert /səbˈvɜːt/ VT [+ the law, tradition] bouleverser, renverser ; (= corrupt) [+ person] corrompre

subway /ˈsʌbweɪ/ N (= underpass: esp Brit) passage m souterrain ; (= railway: esp US) métro m ◆ **by ~** en métro

sub-zero /ˌsʌbˈzɪərəʊ/ ADJ [temperature] au-dessous de zéro

succeed /səkˈsiːd/ VI 1 (= be successful) réussir (in sth dans qch) ; (= prosper) réussir, avoir du succès ; [plan, attempt] réussir ◆ **to ~ in doing sth** réussir or parvenir à faire qch ◆ **he ~s in all he does** tout lui réussit, il réussit tout ce qu'il entreprend ◆ **nothing ~s like success** (Prov) un succès en entraîne un autre ◆ **to ~ in business/as a politician** réussir or avoir du succès en affaires/en tant qu'homme politique ◆ **to ~ in life/one's career** réussir dans la vie/sa carrière

2 (= follow) succéder (to à) ◆ **he ~ed (to the throne) in 1911** il a succédé (à la couronne) en 1911 ◆ **there ~ed a period of peace** il y eut ensuite une période de paix

VT [person] succéder à, prendre la suite de ; [event, storm, season etc] succéder à, suivre ◆ **he ~ed his father as leader of the party** il a succédé à or pris la suite de son père à la direction du parti ◆ **he was ~ed by his son** son fils lui a succédé ◆ **as year ~ed year** comme les années passaient, comme les années se succédaient

succeeding /səkˈsiːdɪŋ/ ADJ (in past) suivant ; (in future) à venir ◆ **each ~ year brought ...** chaque année qui passait apportait ... ◆ **many Armenians left their homeland in ~ years** beaucoup d'Arméniens ont quitté leur patrie pendant les années qui ont suivi ◆ **each ~ year will bring ...** chacune des années à venir apportera ... ◆ **this issue will need serious consideration in ~ weeks** il faudra sérieusement réfléchir à ce problème pendant les semaines à venir ◆ **my sight gets worse with each ~ year** ma vue baisse d'année en année ◆ **she returns to this idea in the ~ chapters** elle reprend cette idée dans les chapitres suivants

success /səkˈses/ LANGUAGE IN USE 23.5, 23.6

N [of plan, venture, attempt, person] succès m, réussite f ◆ **~ in an exam** le succès or la réussite à un examen ◆ **his ~ in doing sth** le fait qu'il ait réussi à faire qch ◆ **his ~ in his attempts** la réussite qui a couronné ses efforts ◆ **without ~** sans succès, en vain ◆ **to meet with ~** avoir du succès ◆ **he met with little ~** il a eu or obtenu peu de succès ◆ **to have great ~** avoir beaucoup de succès ◆ **to make a ~ of sth** (project, enterprise) faire réussir qch, mener qch à bien ; (job, meal, dish) réussir qch ◆ **we wish you every ~** nous vous souhaitons très bonne chance ◆ **congratulations on your ~** je vous félicite de votre succès, (toutes mes) félicitations pour votre succès ◆ **congratulations on your ~ in obtaining ...** je vous félicite d'avoir réussi à obtenir ... ◆ **he was a ~ at last** il avait enfin réussi, il était enfin arrivé, il avait enfin du succès ◆ **he was a great ~ at the dinner/as Hamlet/as a writer/in business** il a eu beaucoup de succès au dîner/dans le rôle de Hamlet/en tant qu'écrivain/en affaires ◆ **it was a ~** [holiday, meal, evening, attack] c'était une réussite, c'était réussi ; [play, book, record] ça a été couronné de succès ◆ **the hotel was a great ~** on a été très content de l'hôtel ; → **rate¹, succeed**

COMP **success story** N (histoire f d'une) réussite f

successful /səkˈsesfʊl/ ADJ 1 [plan, attempt, venture, treatment, policy] couronné de succès ; [campaign, deal, effort, mission, meeting] fructueux, couronné de succès ; [candidate in exam] reçu, admis ; [election candidate] victorieux ; [application] retenu ; [marriage] heureux ◆ **there have been only three ~ prosecutions so far** jusqu'ici, seules trois actions en justice ont abouti ◆ **to be ~** (= succeed) réussir ◆ **the tests were ~** les tests ont produit de bons résultats ◆ **the strike proved very ~** la grève a été couronnée de succès ◆ **(up)on** or **after ~ completion of** [+ course] après avoir été reçu à l'issue de ; [+ deal] après avoir conclu ◆ **her application was ~** sa candidature a été retenue ◆ **to be (very) ~ in** or **at doing sth** (très bien) réussir à faire qch ◆ **to be ~ in one's efforts** voir ses efforts aboutir ◆ **to be ~ in sth** (attempt, mission, exam) réussir qch ◆ **unfortunately your application has not been ~** nous avons le regret de vous faire savoir que votre candidature n'a pas été retenue ◆ **let us hope that the government will be ~ in its efforts to obtain ratification** espérons que le gouvernement parviendra à obtenir la ratification ◆ **to reach a ~ conclusion** or **outcome** aboutir ◆ **this option offers the best chance of a ~ outcome** ce choix offre la meilleure chance de réussite ◆ **the show had a ~ run on Broadway** ce spectacle a eu une bonne saison or a eu beaucoup de succès à Broadway

2 (= prosperous, popular etc) [businessman, business, company] prospère ; [doctor, surgeon, lawyer, barrister, academic] réputé ; [writer, painter, book, film] à succès ; [career] brillant ◆ **she has a ~ career as a novelist/journalist** elle mène une brillante carrière de romancière/journaliste ; → **bidder**

successfully /səkˈsesfəlɪ/ ADV avec succès ◆ **a certificate showing you ~ completed the course** un certificat indiquant que vous avez été reçu à l'issue de ce stage

succession /səkˈseʃən/ N 1 [of victories, disasters, delays, kings] succession f, série f ◆ **the ~ of days and nights** la succession or l'alternance f des jours et des nuits

♦ **in + succession** ♦ **in** ~ *(= one after the other)* successivement, l'un(e) après l'autre ; *(= by turns)* successivement, tour à tour, alternativement ; *(= on each occasion)* successivement, progressivement ♦ **four times in** ~ quatre fois de suite ♦ **for ten years in** ~ pendant dix années consécutives *or* dix ans de suite ♦ **in close** *or* **rapid** ~ *[walk]* à la file ; *[happen]* coup sur coup

2 *(NonC) (= act of succeeding: to title, throne, office, post)* succession *f (to* à) ; *(Jur = heirs collectively)* héritiers *mpl* ♦ **he is second in** ~ **(to the throne)** il occupe la deuxième place dans l'ordre de succession (à la couronne) ♦ **in** ~ **to his father** à la suite de son père

successive /sək'sesɪv/ **ADJ** successif ♦ **on three** ~ **occasions** trois fois de suite ♦ **on four** ~ **days** pendant quatre jours consécutifs *or* de suite ♦ **for the third** ~ **year/time** pour la troisième année/fois consécutive ♦ **with each** ~ **failure** à chaque nouvel échec

successively /sək'sesɪvlɪ/ **ADV** successivement ♦ ~ **higher levels of unemployment** des taux de chômage de plus en plus élevés

successor /sək'sesəʳ/ **N** *(= person, thing)* successeur *m (to, of* de) ♦ **the** ~ **to the throne** l'héritier *m*, -ière *f* de la couronne ♦ ~ **in title** *(Jur)* ayant droit *m*, ayant cause *m*

succinct /sək'sɪŋkt/ **ADJ** *[account, instructions etc]* concis, succinct ; *[person]* concis

succinctly /sək'sɪŋktlɪ/ **ADV** succinctement

succinctness /sək'sɪŋktnɪs/ **N** concision *f*

succor /'sʌkəʳ/ **N, VT** *(US)* ⇒ **succour**

succotash /'sʌkətæʃ/ **N** *(US Culin) plat de maïs en grain et de fèves de Lima*

succour, succor *(US)* /'sʌkəʳ/ *(liter)* **N** *(NonC)* secours *m*, aide *f* **VT** secourir, soulager, venir à l'aide de

succubus /'sʌkjʊbəs/ **N** (pl **succubi** /'sʌkjʊ,baɪ/) succube *m*

succulence /'sʌkjʊləns/ **N** succulence *f*

succulent /'sʌkjʊlənt/ **ADJ** *(also Bot)* succulent **N** *(= plant)* plante *f* grasse ♦ ~**s** plantes *fpl* grasses, cactées *fpl*

succumb /sə'kʌm/ **VI** *(to temptation etc)* succomber *(to* à) ; *(= die)* mourir *(to* de), succomber

such /sʌtʃ/ **ADJ** 1 *(= of that sort)* tel, pareil ♦ ~ **a book** un tel livre, un livre pareil, un pareil livre, un livre de cette sorte ♦ ~ **books** de tels livres, des livres pareils, de pareils livres, des livres de cette sorte ♦ ~ **people** de telles gens, des gens pareils, de pareilles gens ♦ **we had** ~ **a case last year** nous avons eu un cas semblable l'année dernière ♦ **in** ~ **cases** en pareil cas ♦ **did you ever hear of** ~ **a thing?** avez-vous jamais entendu une chose pareille ? ♦ **Robert was** ~ **a one** Robert était comme ça ♦ ~ **was my reply** telle a été ma réponse, c'est ce que j'ai répondu ♦ ~ **is not the case** ce n'est pas le cas ici ♦ **it was** ~ **weather!** quel temps il a fait !, il a fait un de ces temps ! ♦ **... or some** ~ **(thing)** ... ou une chose de ce genre ♦ **until** ~ **time** jusqu'à ce moment-là ♦ **it is not** ~ **as to cause concern** cela ne doit pas être une raison d'inquiétude ♦ **his health was** ~ **as to alarm his wife** son état de santé était de nature à alarmer sa femme ♦ **you can take my car,** ~ **as it is** vous pouvez prendre ma voiture pour ce qu'elle vaut

♦ **no such ...** ♦ **there's no** ~ **thing!** ça n'existe pas ! ; see also **adj 2** ♦ **there is no** ~ **thing in France** il n'y a rien de tel en France ♦ **there are no** ~ **things as unicorns** les licornes n'existent pas ♦ **I said no** ~ **thing!** je n'ai jamais dit cela !, je n'ai rien dit de la sorte ! ♦ **no** ~ **thing!** pas du tout ! ♦ **no** ~ **book exists** un tel livre n'existe pas

♦ **such as** *(= like, for example)* tel que, comme ♦ **a friend** ~ **as Paul** un ami tel que *or* comme Paul ♦ **a book** ~ **as this** un livre tel que *or* comme celui-ci ♦ **animals** ~ **as cats** les animaux tels que *or* comme les chats ♦ ~ **as?** * quoi, par exemple ?

♦ **such ... as** ♦ ~ **writers as Molière and Corneille** des écrivains tels (que) *or* comme Molière et Corneille ♦ **only** ~ **a fool as Martin would do that** il fallait un idiot comme Martin *or* quelqu'un d'aussi bête que Martin pour faire cela ♦ ~ **a book as this** un livre tel que celui-ci ♦ **he's not** ~ **a fool as you think** il n'est pas aussi *or* si bête que vous croyez ♦ **I'm not** ~ **a fool as to believe that!** je ne suis pas assez bête pour croire ça ! ♦ **have you** ~ **a thing as a penknife?** auriez-vous un canif par hasard ? ♦ **it caused** ~ **scenes of grief as are rarely seen** cela a provoqué des scènes de douleur telles qu'on *or* comme on en voit peu ♦ ~ **people as knew him** les gens qui le connaissaient ♦ ~ **books as I have** le peu de livres *or* les quelques livres que je possède ♦ **until** ~ **time as ...** jusqu'à ce que ... + *subj*, en attendant que ... + *subj*

2 *(= so much)* tellement, tant ♦ **embarrassed by** ~ **praise** embarrassé par tant *or* tellement de compliments ♦ **he was in** ~ **pain** il souffrait tellement ♦ **don't be in** ~ **a rush** ne soyez pas si pressé ♦ **we had** ~ **a surprise!** quelle surprise nous avons eue !, nous avons eu une de ces surprises !, nous avons été drôlement surpris ! * ♦ **there was** ~ **a noise that ...** il y avait tellement *or* tant de bruit que ... ♦ **his rage was** ~ **that ...**, ~ **was his rage that ...** il était tellement *or* si furieux que ...

ADV 1 *(= so very)* si, tellement ♦ **he gave us** ~ **good coffee** il nous a offert un si bon café ♦ ~ **big boxes** de si grandes boîtes ♦ ~ **a lovely present** un si joli cadeau ♦ **it was** ~ **a long time ago!** il y a si *or* tellement longtemps de ça ! ♦ **he bought** ~ **an expensive car that ...** il a acheté une voiture si *or* tellement chère que ...

2 *(in comparisons)* aussi ♦ **I haven't had** ~ **good coffee for years** ça fait des années que je n'ai pas bu un aussi bon café ♦ ~ **lovely children as his** des enfants aussi gentils que les siens

PRON ceux *mpl*, celles *fpl* ♦ ~ **as wish to go** ceux qui veulent partir ♦ **all** ~ tous ceux ♦ **I'll give you** ~ **as I have** je vous donnerai ceux que j'ai *or* le peu que j'ai ♦ **I know of no** ~ je n'en connais point

♦ **as such** *(= in that capacity)* à ce titre, comme tel(le), en tant que tel(le) ; *(= in itself)* en soi ♦ **the soldier, as** ~, **deserves respect** tout soldat, comme tel, mérite le respect ♦ **the work as** ~ **is boring, but the pay is good** le travail en soi est ennuyeux, mais le salaire est bon ♦ **and as** ~ **he was promoted** et en tant que tel il a obtenu de l'avancement ♦ **he was a genius but not recognized as** ~ c'était un génie mais il n'était pas reconnu pour tel *or* considéré comme tel ♦ **there are no houses as** ~ il n'y a pas de maisons à proprement parler

♦ **... and such(like)** * ♦ **teachers and doctors and** ~**(like)** les professeurs et les docteurs et autres (gens de la sorte) ♦ **rabbits and hares and** ~**(like)** les lapins, les lièvres et autres animaux de ce genre *or* de la sorte ♦ **shoes and gloves and** ~**(like)** les souliers, les gants et autres choses de ce genre *or* de la sorte

COMP **such-and-such ADJ** tel (et *or* ou tel) ♦ **Mr Such-and-**~ * Monsieur Untel ♦ **in** ~**-and-**~ **a street** dans telle (et *or* ou telle) rue

suchlike * /'sʌtʃlaɪk/ **ADJ** de la sorte, de ce genre **PRON** see **such pron**

suck /sʌk/ **VT** *[+ fruit, pencil]* sucer ; *[+ juice, poison]* sucer *(from* de) ; *(through straw) [+ drink]* aspirer *(through* avec) ; *[+ sweet]* sucer, suçoter ; *[baby breast, bottle]* téter ; *[leech]* sucer ; *[pump, machine]* aspirer *(from* de) ♦ **to** ~ **one's thumb** sucer son pouce ♦ **child** ~**ing its mother's breast** enfant qui tète sa mère ♦ **to** ~ **dry** *[+ orange etc]* sucer tout le jus de ; *(fig) [+ person] (of money)* sucer jusqu'au dernier sou ; *(of energy)* sucer jusqu'à la moelle ♦ **to be** ~**ed into a situation** être entraîné dans une situation ♦ ~ **it and see** * il faut se lancer * (pour savoir si ça marchera) ; → **teach**

VI 1 *[baby]* téter

2 ♦ **to** ~ **at** *[+ fruit, pencil, pipe]* sucer ; *[+ sweet]* sucer, suçoter

3 *(esp US* ✱*)* **it** ~**s!** *(= is very bad)* c'est nul ! ✱

N 1 ♦ **to have a** ~ **at sth, to give sth a** ~ sucer qch

2 *(at breast)* tétée *f* ♦ **to give** ~ **to ...** *(liter)* allaiter ..., donner le sein à ...

COMP **sucking-pig N** cochon *m* de lait

▸ **suck down VT SEP** *[sea, mud, sands]* engloutir

▸ **suck in VI** ✱ ♦ **to** ~ **in with sb** *(fig)* faire de la lèche à qn ✱, lécher les bottes de qn

VT SEP *[sea, mud, sands]* engloutir ; *[porous surface]* absorber ; *[pump, machine]* aspirer ; *(fig) [+ knowledge, facts]* absorber, assimiler

▸ **suck off** *✱* **VT SEP** tailler une pipe à *✱

▸ **suck out VT SEP** *[person]* sucer, faire sortir en suçant *(of, from* de) ; *[machine]* refouler à l'extérieur *(of, from* de)

▸ **suck up VI** ✱ ♦ **to** ~ **up to sb** *(fig)* faire de la lèche à qn ✱, lécher les bottes * de qn

VT SEP *[person]* aspirer, sucer ; *[pump, machine]* aspirer ; *[porous surface]* absorber

sucker /'sʌkəʳ/ **N** 1 *(on machine)* ventouse *f* ; *(= plunger)* piston *m* ; *(Bot)* surgeon *m*, drageon *m* ; *[of leech, octopus]* ventouse *f* ; *[of insect]* suçoir *m* 2 *(* ✱ *= person)* poire * *f*, gogo * *m* ♦ **to be a** ~ **for sth** ne pouvoir résister à qch ♦ **never give a** ~ **an even break** * *(US)* ne donne jamais une chance à un imbécile ♦ **to play sb for a** ~ mener qn en bateau *, rouler * qn **VT** *(US* ✱ *= swindle)* embobiner * ♦ **to get** ~**ed out of 500 dollars** se faire refaire de 500 dollars **COMP** **sucker punch** * **N** *(fig)* coup *m* bas

suckle /'sʌkl/ **VT** *[+ child]* allaiter, donner le sein à ; *[+ young animal]* allaiter **VI** téter

suckling /'sʌklɪŋ/ **N** *(= act)* allaitement *m* ; *(= child)* nourrisson *m*, enfant *mf* à la mamelle **COMP** **suckling pig N** cochon *m* de lait

sucky ✱ /'sʌkɪ/ **ADJ** *(US)* merdique ✱

sucrase /'sju:kreɪz/ **N** sucrase *f*, invertase *f*

sucrose /'su:krəʊz/ **N** saccharose *m*

suction /'sʌkʃən/ **N** succion *f* ♦ **it works by** ~ cela marche par succion ♦ **to adhere by** ~ **(on)** faire ventouse (sur) **VT** *[+ liquid]* aspirer

COMP *[apparatus, device]* de succion
suction cup N ventouse *f*
suction disc N ventouse *f*
suction pad N ventouse *f*
suction pump N pompe *f* aspirante
suction valve N clapet *m* d'aspiration

Sudan /sʊ'dɑ:n/ **N** ♦ **(the)** ~ le Soudan

Sudanese /,su:də'ni:z/ **ADJ** soudanais **N** *(pl inv) (= person)* Soudanais(e) *m(f)*

sudden /'sʌdn/ **ADJ** *(gen)* soudain ; *[death]* subit, soudain ; *[attack, marriage]* imprévu, inattendu ; *[inspiration]* subit ♦ **it's all so** ~**!** on s'y attendait tellement peu !, c'est arrivé tellement vite ! ♦ **all of a** ~ soudain, tout à coup **COMP** **sudden death N** *(Brit Ftbl, Golf:* also **sudden death play-off)** mort *f* subite ; *(US Sport:* also **sudden death overtime)** *prolongation où les ex æquo sont départagés dès le premier point marqué* **sudden infant death syndrome N** mort *f* subite du nourrisson

suddenly /'sʌdnlɪ/ **ADV** soudain, tout à coup ♦ **to die** ~ mourir subitement ♦ ~**, the door**

opened soudain *or* tout à coup, la porte s'est ouverte

suddenness /ˈsʌdnɪs/ N *(gen)* caractère *m* soudain, soudaineté *f* ; *[of death, inspiration]* caractère *m* subit ; *[of attack, marriage]* caractère *m* imprévu *or* inattendu

sudoku /suːˈdəʊkuː/ N sudoku *m*

suds /sʌdz/ NPL 1 (also **soapsuds**) *(= lather)* mousse *f* de savon ; *(= soapy water)* eau *f* savonneuse 2 *(US* ‡ *= beer)* bière *f*

sudsy /ˈsʌdzɪ/ ADJ savonneux

sue /suː/ VT *(Jur)* poursuivre en justice, intenter un procès à *(for sth* pour obtenir qch ; *over, about* au sujet de) ◆ **to ~ sb for damages** poursuivre qn en dommages-intérêts ◆ **to ~ sb for libel** intenter un procès en diffamation à qn ◆ **to be ~d for damages/libel** être poursuivi en dommages-intérêts/en diffamation ◆ **to ~ sb for divorce** entamer une procédure de divorce contre qn VI 1 *(Jur)* intenter un procès, engager des poursuites ◆ **to ~ for divorce** entamer une procédure de divorce 2 *(liter)* **to ~ for peace/pardon** solliciter la paix/le pardon

suede /sweɪd/ N daim *m*, cuir *m* suédé ◆ **imitation ~** suédine *f* COMP *[shoes, handbag, coat, skirt]* de daim ; *[gloves]* de suède ; *[leather]* suédé

suet /sʊɪt/ N *(Culin)* graisse *f* de rognon ◆ **~ pudding** *gâteau sucré ou salé à base de farine et de graisse de bœuf*

Suetonius /swiːˈtəʊnɪəs/ N Suétone *m*

Suez /ˈsuːɪz/ N ◆ **~ Canal** canal *m* de Suez ◆ **Gulf of ~** golfe *m* de Suez ◆ **before/after ~** *(Brit Hist)* avant/après l'affaire de Suez

suffer /ˈsʌfəʳ/ VT 1 *(= undergo) (gen)* subir ; *[+ hardship, bereavement, martyrdom, torture]* souffrir, subir ; *[+ punishment, change in circumstances, loss]* subir ; *[+ damage, setback]* essuyer, subir ; *[+ pain, headaches, hunger]* souffrir de ◆ **he ~ed a lot of pain** il a beaucoup souffert ◆ **to ~ the consequences** subir les conséquences ◆ **to ~ death** *(liter)* mourir ◆ **her popularity ~ed a decline** sa popularité a souffert *or* a décliné

2 *(= allow) [+ opposition, sb's rudeness, refusal etc]* tolérer, permettre ◆ **I can't ~ it a moment longer** je ne peux plus le souffrir *or* le tolérer, c'est intolérable, c'est insupportable ◆ **he doesn't ~ fools gladly** il n'a aucune patience pour les imbéciles ◆ **to ~ sb to do** *(liter)* souffrir que qn fasse

VI 1 *[person]* souffrir ◆ **to ~ in silence** souffrir en silence ◆ **to ~ for one's sins** expier ses péchés ◆ **he ~ed for it later** il en a souffert les conséquences *or* il en a pâti plus tard ◆ **you'll ~ for this!** vous me le paierez ! ◆ **I'll make him ~ for it!** il me le paiera !

2 *(= be afflicted by)*

◆ **to suffer from** *[+ rheumatism, heart trouble, the cold, hunger]* souffrir de ; *[+ deafness]* être atteint de ; *[+ a cold, influenza, frostbite, pimples, bad memory]* avoir ◆ **he ~s from a limp/stammer** *etc* il boite/bégaie *etc* ◆ **he was ~ing from shock** il était commotionné ◆ **to ~ from the effects of** *[+ fall, illness]* se ressentir de, souffrir des suites de ; *[+ alcohol, drug]* subir le contrecoup de ◆ **to be ~ing from having done sth** souffrir *or* se ressentir d'avoir fait qch ◆ **the child was ~ing from his environment** l'enfant souffrait de son environnement ◆ **she ~s from lack of friends** son problème c'est qu'elle n'a pas d'amis ◆ **the house is ~ing from neglect** la maison se ressent du manque d'entretien ◆ **his style ~s from being overelaborate** son style souffre d'un excès de recherche ; → **delusion**

3 *(= be injured, impaired) [eyesight, hearing, speech]* se détériorer ; *[health, reputation, plans, sales, wages]* souffrir ; *[car, town, house]* souffrir, être endommagé ; *[business]* souffrir, péricliter ◆ **your health will ~** votre santé en souffrira *or* en pâtira ◆ **the regiment ~ed badly** le régiment a essuyé de grosses pertes

sufferance /ˈsʌfərəns/ N tolérance *f*, souffrance *f (Jur)* ◆ **on ~** par tolérance

sufferer /ˈsʌfərəʳ/ N *(from illness)* malade *mf* ; *(from misfortune)* victime *f* ; *(from accident)* accidenté(e) *m(f)*, victime *f* ◆ **~ from diabetes/AIDS/asthma** *etc*, **diabetes/AIDS/asthma** *etc* **~** diabétique *mf*/sidéen(ne) *m(f)*/asthmatique *mf etc* ◆ **my fellow ~s at the concert** *(hum)* mes compagnons *mpl* d'infortune au concert

suffering /ˈsʌfərɪŋ/ N souffrance(s) *f(pl)* ◆ **"after much suffering patiently borne"** "après de longues souffrances patiemment endurées" ◆ **her ~ was great** elle a beaucoup souffert ADJ souffrant, qui souffre

suffice /səˈfaɪs/ *(frm)* VI suffire, être suffisant ◆ **~ it to say ...** qu'il (me) suffise de dire ..., je me contenterai de dire ... VT suffire à, satisfaire

sufficiency /səˈfɪʃənsɪ/ N (pl **sufficiencies**) *(frm)* quantité *f* suffisante ◆ **a ~ of coal** une quantité suffisante de charbon, suffisamment de charbon, du charbon en quantité suffisante *or* en suffisance ; → **self**

sufficient /səˈfɪʃənt/ ADJ *[number, quantity, cause, condition]* suffisant ◆ **~ time/money/evidence** suffisamment de temps/d'argent/de preuves ◆ **to be ~** être suffisant *(for* pour), suffire *(for* à) ◆ **I've got ~** j'en ai suffisamment ◆ **to have ~ to eat** avoir suffisamment à manger ◆ **he earns ~ to live on** il gagne de quoi vivre ◆ **one song was ~ to show he couldn't sing** une chanson a suffi à *or* pour démontrer qu'il ne savait pas chanter ◆ **~ unto the day (is the evil thereof)** *(Prov)* à chaque jour suffit sa peine *(Prov)* → **self**

sufficiently /səˈfɪʃəntlɪ/ ADV suffisamment ◆ **a ~ large number/quantity** un nombre/une quantité suffisant(e) ◆ **he is ~ clever to do that** il est suffisamment intelligent pour faire ça

suffix /ˈsʌfɪks/ N *[of word]* suffixe *m* ◆ **these ships were all numbered with the ~ LBK** ces bateaux avaient tous un numéro suivi des trois lettres LBK VT /sʌˈfɪks/ suffixer *(to* à)

suffocate /ˈsʌfəkeɪt/ VI suffoquer, étouffer ; *(with anger, indignation, surprise)* suffoquer *(with* de) VT suffoquer, étouffer ; *[anger, indignation, surprise]* suffoquer ◆ **he felt ~d in that small town atmosphere** il étouffait dans cette atmosphère de petite ville

suffocating /ˈsʌfəkeɪtɪŋ/ ADJ 1 *(= asphyxiating) [heat, atmosphere]* étouffant, suffocant ; *[fumes]* asphyxiant, suffocant ; *[smell]* suffocant ◆ **it's ~ in here** on étouffe ici ◆ **the room was ~** l'atmosphère de la pièce était étouffante *or* suffocante 2 *(= oppressive) [atmosphere, regime, relationship, life]* étouffant ; *[respectability]* oppressant

suffocation /ˌsʌfəˈkeɪʃən/ N suffocation *f*, étouffement *m* ; *(Med)* asphyxie *f* ◆ **to die from ~** mourir asphyxié

suffragan /ˈsʌfrəgən/ ADJ suffragant N ◆ **~ (bishop)** (évêque *m*) suffragant *m*

suffrage /ˈsʌfrɪdʒ/ N 1 *(= franchise)* droit *m* de suffrage *or* de vote ◆ **universal ~** suffrage *m* universel ◆ **elected by universal ~** élu au suffrage universel 2 *(frm = vote)* suffrage *m*, vote *m*

suffragette /ˌsʌfrəˈdʒet/ N suffragette *f* ◆ **the Suffragette Movement** *(Hist)* le Mouvement des Suffragettes

suffragist /ˈsʌfrədʒɪst/ N partisan(e) *m(f)* du droit de vote pour les femmes

suffuse /səˈfjuːz/ VT *[light]* baigner, se répandre sur ; *[emotion]* envahir ◆ **the room was ~d with light** la pièce baignait dans une lumière douce ◆ **~d with red** rougi, empourpré

sugar /ˈʃʊgəʳ/ N *(NonC)* sucre *m* ◆ **come here ~!*** viens ici chéri(e) ! ◆ **~!*** *(euph)* mercredi !* ; → **icing** VT *[+ food, drink]* sucrer ; → **pill**

COMP **sugar almond** N ⇒ **sugared almond**
sugar basin N *(Brit)* sucrier *m*
sugar beet N betterave *f* sucrière *or* à sucre
sugar bowl N ⇒ **sugar basin**
sugar cane N canne *f* à sucre
sugar-coated ADJ *(lit)* dragéifié ; *(fig = falsely pleasant)* doucereux, mielleux
sugar cube N morceau *m* de sucre
sugar daddy* N vieux protecteur *m*
sugar diabetes † * N diabète *m* sucré
sugar-free ADJ sans sucre
sugar loaf N pain *m* de sucre
sugar lump N ⇒ **sugar cube**
sugar maple N *(Can, US)* érable *m* à sucre
sugar pea N (pois *m*) mange-tout *m inv*
sugar plantation N plantation *f* de canne à sucre
sugar refinery N raffinerie *f* de sucre
sugar shaker N saupoudreuse *f*, sucrier *m* verseur
sugar tongs NPL pince *f* à sucre

sugared /ˈʃʊgəd/ ADJ *[food, drink]* sucré ; *[flowers etc]* en sucre COMP **sugared almond** N dragée *f*

sugarless /ˈʃʊgəlɪs/ ADJ sans sucre

sugarplum /ˈʃʊgəplʌm/ N bonbon *m*, dragée *f*

sugary /ˈʃʊgərɪ/ ADJ 1 *[food, drink, taste]* sucré 2 *(fig pej) [film, music, lyrics]* sirupeux ; *[person, voice, smile]* doucereux, mielleux

suggest /səˈdʒest/ LANGUAGE IN USE 1, 2.2 VT 1 *(= propose)* suggérer, proposer *(sth to sb* qch à qn) ; *(pej = hint)* insinuer *(sth to sb* qch à qn) ◆ **I ~ that we go to the museum** je suggère *or* je propose qu'on aille au musée ◆ **he ~ed that they went to London** il leur a suggéré *or* proposé d'aller à Londres ◆ **I ~ you ask him** tu devrais lui demander ◆ **I ~ed taking her out to dinner** j'ai suggéré *or* proposé qu'on l'emmène au restaurant ◆ **an idea ~ed itself (to me)** une idée m'est venue à l'esprit ◆ **what are you trying to ~?** que voulez-vous dire par là ?, qu'insinuez-vous ? *(pej)* ◆ **I ~ to you that ...** *(esp Jur)* mon opinion est que ...

2 *(= imply) [facts, data, sb's actions]* laisser entendre *(that* que) ; *(= evoke)* évoquer, faire penser à ◆ **what does that smell ~ to you?** à quoi cette odeur vous fait-elle penser ? ◆ **the coins ~ a Roman settlement** les pièces de monnaie semblent indiquer l'existence d'un camp romain ◆ **it doesn't exactly ~ a careful man** on ne peut pas dire que cela dénote un homme soigneux

> ⚠ When it means 'imply', **suggest** is not translated by **suggérer**.

suggestibility /səˌdʒestɪˈbɪlɪtɪ/ N suggestibilité *f*

suggestible /səˈdʒestɪbl/ ADJ influençable ; *(Psych)* suggestible

suggestion /səˈdʒestʃən/ LANGUAGE IN USE 1.1 N 1 *(gen)* suggestion *f* ; *(= proposal)* suggestion *f*, proposition *f* ; *(= insinuation)* allusion *f*, insinuation *f* ◆ **to make** *or* **offer a ~** faire une suggestion *or* une proposition ◆ **if I may make a ~** si je peux me permettre de faire une suggestion ◆ **have you any ~s?** avez-vous quelque chose à suggérer ? ◆ **my ~ is that ...** je suggère *or* je propose que ... ◆ **there is no ~ of corruption** rien n'indique qu'il y ait eu corruption 2 *(NonC: Psych etc)* suggestion *f* ◆ **the power of ~** la force de suggestion 3 *(= trace)* soupçon *m*, pointe *f* COMP **suggestion(s) box** N boîte *f* à idées

suggestive /sə'dʒestɪv/ ADJ [1] *(sexually) [remark, look, pose, clothing]* suggestif [2] *(= reminiscent)* ◆ **to be ~ of sth** suggérer qch

suggestively /sə'dʒestɪvlɪ/ ADV *[move, dance]* de façon suggestive ; *[say]* d'un ton suggestif ◆ **to wink ~** faire un clin d'œil suggestif

suggestiveness /sə'dʒestɪvnɪs/ N *(pej)* caractère *m* suggestif, suggestivité *f*

suicidal /ˌsʊɪ'saɪdl/ ADJ [1] *[person, feelings, tendencies]* suicidaire ◆ **he was not the ~ type** il n'était pas du genre suicidaire *or* à se suicider ◆ **I feel absolutely ~** j'ai vraiment envie de me tuer [2] *(fig = ruinous) [act, decision, carelessness]* suicidaire ◆ **it would be absolutely ~ (to do that)!** ce serait complètement suicidaire *or* un véritable suicide (de faire ça) !

suicide /'sʊɪsaɪd/ N *(= act; lit, fig)* suicide *m* ; *(= person)* suicidé(e) *m(f)* ◆ **there were two attempted ~s** il y a eu deux tentatives *fpl* de suicide, deux personnes ont tenté de se suicider ◆ **such an act was political ~** cet acte était un véritable suicide politique ◆ **economically it would be ~ to do so** ce serait du suicide (du point de vue économique) ; → **attempt, commit**

COMP *[attack etc]* suicide *inv*
suicide attempt, suicide bid N tentative *f* de suicide
suicide bomber N auteur *m* d'un (*or* de l')attentat-suicide, tueur-kamikaze *m*
suicide bombing N attentat *m* suicide
suicide note N lettre *f* de suicide
suicide pact N pacte *m* suicidaire

suit /suːt/ LANGUAGE IN USE 4, 7.4, 11.3, 19.2

N [1] *(tailored garment, for man)* costume *m*, complet *m* ; *(for woman)* tailleur *m* ; *(non-tailored, also for children)* ensemble *m* ; *[of racing driver, astronaut]* combinaison *f* ◆ **~ of clothes** tenue *f* ◆ **~ of armour** armure *f* complète ◆ **a ~ of sails** *(Naut)* un jeu de voiles ◆ **the men in (grey) ~s** *(Brit)* les décideurs *mpl* ; → **lounge, trouser**

[2] *(frm = request)* requête *f*, pétition *f* ; *(liter: for marriage)* demande *f* en mariage ; → **press**

[3] *(Jur)* poursuite *f*, procès *m*, action *f* en justice ◆ **to bring a ~** intenter un procès *(against sb* à qn), engager des poursuites *(against sb* contre qn) ◆ **criminal ~** action *f* pénale ; → **file², lawsuit, party**

[4] *(Cards)* couleur *f* ◆ **long** *or* **strong ~** couleur *f* longue ; *(fig)* fort *m* ◆ **geography is not his strong ~** la géographie n'est pas son fort ◆ **short ~** couleur *f* courte ; → **follow**

[5] *(* = business executive)* cadre sup * *m*

VT [1] *(= be convenient, satisfactory for) [arrangements, date, price, climate, food, occupation]* convenir à ◆ **it doesn't ~ me to leave now** cela ne m'arrange pas de partir maintenant ◆ **I'll do it when it ~s me** je le ferai quand ça m'arrangera ◆ **such a step ~ed him perfectly** *or* **just ~ed his book** * une telle mesure lui convenait parfaitement *or* l'arrangeait parfaitement ◆ **~ yourself!** * c'est comme vous voudrez !, faites comme vous voudrez *or* voulez ! ◆ **~s me!** * ça me va !, ça me botte ! ‡ ◆ **it ~s me here** je suis bien ici ◆ **that ~s me down to the ground** * ça me va tout à fait

[2] *(= be appropriate to)* convenir à, aller à ◆ **the job doesn't ~ him** l'emploi ne lui convient pas, ce n'est pas un travail fait pour lui ◆ **such behaviour hardly ~s you** une telle conduite ne vous va guère *or* n'est guère digne de vous ◆ **the part ~ed him perfectly** *(Theat)* le rôle lui allait comme un gant *or* était fait pour lui ◆ **he is not ~ed to teaching** il n'est pas fait pour l'enseignement ◆ **the hall was not ~ed to such a meeting** la salle n'était pas faite pour *or* ne se prêtait guère à une telle réunion ◆ **it ~s their needs** cela leur convient ◆ **they are well ~ed (to one another)** ils sont faits l'un pour l'autre, ils sont très bien assortis

[3] *[garment, colour, hairstyle]* aller à ◆ **it ~s her beautifully** cela lui va à merveille

[4] *(= adapt)* adapter, approprier *(sth to sth* qch à qch) ◆ **to ~ the action to the word** joindre le geste à la parole

[5] *(= dress)* ◆ **~ed and booted** élégamment vêtu, bien mis *

VI faire l'affaire, convenir ◆ **will tomorrow ~?** est-ce que demain vous conviendrait *or* vous irait ?

suitability /ˌsuːtə'bɪlɪtɪ/ N *[of action, remark, example, choice]* à-propos *m*, pertinence *f* ; *[of time, accommodation, clothes]* caractère *m* approprié ◆ **I have doubts about his ~ (as captain of England)** je doute qu'il possède *subj* les qualités requises (pour être capitaine de l'équipe d'Angleterre) ◆ **his ~ (for the position) is not in doubt** le fait qu'il possède les qualités requises (pour ce poste) n'est pas mis en doute

suitable /'suːtəbl/ ADJ *[place, time, action, clothes]* approprié *(for* à) ; *[remark, reply, example, choice]* approprié *(for* à), pertinent ; *[behaviour]* convenable *(for* pour) ; *[climate, job]* qui convient *(for* à) ; *[food, colour]* qui convient *(for* à), approprié *(for* à) ; *[size]* qui va *(for* à) ; *[donor, epitaph]* approprié *(for* à) ◆ **it's not ~** *(gen)* ça ne convient pas ◆ **an especially ~ form of exercise** une forme d'exercice particulièrement indiquée *or* appropriée ◆ **he is not at all a ~ person** ce n'est pas du tout quelqu'un comme lui qu'il faut ◆ **I can't find anything ~** je ne trouve rien qui convienne *or* qui fasse l'affaire ◆ **a ~ caption for the illustration** une légende qui aille avec *or* qui convienne à l'illustration ◆ **the most ~ man for the job** l'homme le plus apte à occuper ce poste, l'homme le plus indiqué pour ce poste ◆ **these products are ~ for all skin types** ces produits conviennent à tous les types de peau ◆ **these flats are not ~ for families** ces appartements ne conviennent pas aux familles *or* ne sont pas vraiment appropriés pour les familles ◆ **the 25th is the most ~ for me** c'est le 25 qui m'arrange *or* me convient le mieux ◆ **the film isn't ~ for children** ce n'est pas un film pour les enfants

suitably /'suːtəblɪ/ ADV *[reply, thank, apologize]* comme il convient, comme il se doit ; *[behave]* convenablement, comme il faut ; *[equipped]* comme il faut ◆ **I'm not ~ dressed for gardening** je ne suis pas habillé comme il faut pour jardiner ◆ **to be ~ qualified** posséder les compétences requises *or* qu'il faut ◆ **he was ~ impressed when I told him that ...** il a été assez impressionné quand je lui ai dit que ...

suitcase /'suːtkeɪs/ N valise *f* ◆ **to live out of a ~** vivre sans jamais vraiment défaire ses bagages

suite /swiːt/ N [1] *(= furniture)* mobilier *m* ; *(= rooms: in hotel etc)* appartement *m*, suite *f* ◆ **a dining-room ~** un mobilier *or* un ensemble de salle à manger, une salle à manger ; → **bedroom, bridal** [2] *(Mus)* suite *f* [3] *(= retainers)* suite *f*, escorte *f*

suiting /'suːtɪŋ/ N *(NonC = fabric)* tissu *m* pour complet

suitor /'suːtəʳ/ N soupirant *m*, prétendant *m* ; *(Jur)* plaideur *m*, -euse *f* ; *(Comm)* acquéreur *m* potentiel, repreneur *m* potentiel

Sulawesi /ˌsuːlə'weɪsɪ/ N Sulawesi, les Célèbes *fpl*

sulcus /'sʌlkəs/ N (pl **sulci** /'sʌlsaɪ/) scissure *f*

Suleiman /ˌsuːlɪ'mɑːn/ N ◆ **~ the Magnificent** Soliman *or* Suleyman le Magnifique

sulfa /'sʌlfə/ N *(US)* ⇒ **sulpha**

sulfate /'sʌlfeɪt/ N *(US)* ⇒ **sulphate**

sulfide /'sʌlfaɪd/ N *(US)* ⇒ **sulphide**

sulfonamide /sʌl'fɒnəmaɪd/ N *(US)* ⇒ **sulphonamide**

sulfur /'sʌlfəʳ/ N *(US)* ⇒ **sulphur**

sulfureous /sʌl'fjʊərɪəs/ ADJ *(US)* ⇒ **sulphureous**

sulfuric /sʌl'fjʊərɪk/ ADJ *(US)* ⇒ **sulphuric**

sulfurous /'sʌlfərəs/ ADJ *(US)* ⇒ **sulphurous**

sulk /sʌlk/ N bouderie *f*, maussaderie *f* ◆ **to be in a ~, to have (a fit of) the ~s** bouder, faire la tête VI bouder, faire la tête

sulkily /'sʌlkɪlɪ/ ADV *[behave, look, say]* d'un air boudeur

sulkiness /'sʌlkɪnɪs/ N *(= state)* bouderie *f* ; *(= temperament)* caractère *m* boudeur *or* maussade

sulky /'sʌlkɪ/ ADJ *[person, voice, expression, silence]* boudeur ◆ **to be** *or* **look ~ (about sth)** faire la tête (à propos de qch)

sullen /'sʌlən/ ADJ *[person, look, comment, silence, sky]* maussade ; *[clouds]* menaçant

sullenly /'sʌlənlɪ/ ADV *[say, reply]* d'un ton maussade ; *[look, stare]* d'un air maussade *or* renfrogné ; *[promise, agree]* de mauvaise grâce ◆ **the ~ resentful expression on her face** son air *or* son visage maussade et irrité ◆ **to be ~ silent** être enfermé dans un silence maussade

sullenness /'sʌlənnɪs/ N *[of person]* humeur *f* maussade, maussaderie *f* ; *[of attitude, voice, silence]* maussaderie *f* ◆ **the ~ of the sky/clouds** l'aspect menaçant du ciel/des nuages

sully /'sʌlɪ/ VT *(liter)* souiller ◆ **to ~ one's hands with sth/by doing sth** se salir les mains avec qch/en faisant qch

sulpha /'sʌlfə/ N ◆ **~ drug** sulfamide *m*

sulphate /'sʌlfeɪt/ N sulfate *m* ◆ **copper ~** sulfate *m* de cuivre

sulphide /'sʌlfaɪd/ N sulfure *m*

sulphonamide /sʌl'fɒnəmaɪd/ N sulfamide *m*

sulphur /'sʌlfəʳ/ N soufre *m* ADJ *(colour)* (also **sulphur yellow**) jaune soufre *inv*
COMP **sulphur bath** N bain *m* sulfureux
sulphur dioxide N anhydride *m* sulfureux
sulphur spring N source *f* sulfureuse

sulphureous /sʌl'fjʊərɪəs/ ADJ sulfureux ; *(in colour)* couleur *m* de soufre, soufré

sulphuric /sʌl'fjʊərɪk/ ADJ sulfurique

sulphurous /'sʌlfərəs/ ADJ sulfureux

sultan /'sʌltən/ N sultan *m*

sultana /sʌl'tɑːnə/ N [1] *(esp Brit = fruit)* raisin *m* de Smyrne [2] *(= woman)* sultane *f* COMP **sultana cake** N *(esp Brit)* cake *m* (aux raisins de Smyrne)

sultanate /'sʌltənɪt/ N sultanat *m*

sultriness /'sʌltrɪnɪs/ N *(= heat)* chaleur *f* étouffante ; *[of weather]* lourdeur *f*

sultry /'sʌltrɪ/ ADJ [1] *(= hot) [day]* étouffant ; *[weather, air]* lourd ; *[heat]* lourd, suffocant ; *[atmosphere]* étouffant, pesant ◆ **it was hot and ~** il faisait chaud et lourd [2] *(fig = sensual) [person, voice, look, smile]* sensuel

sum /sʌm/ LANGUAGE IN USE 20.6

N *(= total after addition)* somme *f*, total *m* *(of* de) ; *(= amount of money)* somme *f* (d'argent) ; *(Math = problem)* calcul *m*, opération *f* ; *(specifically adding)* addition *f* ◆ **~s** *(Scol = arithmetic)* le calcul ◆ **to do a ~ in one's head** faire un calcul mental *or* de tête ◆ **he is good at ~s** il est bon en calcul ◆ **the ~ of its parts** la somme de ses composants *or* parties ◆ **the ~ of our experience** la somme de notre expérience ◆ **the ~ and substance of what he said** les grandes lignes de ce qu'il a dit ◆ **in ~** en somme, somme *f* toute ; → **lump¹, round**

COMP **summing-up** N récapitulation *f*, résumé *m* (also Jur)
sum total N *(= amount)* somme *f* totale ; *(= money)* montant *m* (global) ◆ **the ~ total of all this was that he ...** le résultat de tout cela a été qu'il ...

► **sum up**
VI récapituler, faire un *or* le résumé ; *(Jur)* résumer ◆ **to ~ up, let me say that ...** en résumé *or* pour récapituler je voudrais dire que ...
VT SEP 1 *(= summarize) [+ speech, facts, arguments]* résumer, récapituler ; *[+ book etc]* résumer ◆ **that ~s up all I felt** cela résume tout ce que je ressentais
2 *(= assess) [+ person]* jauger, se faire une idée de ; *[+ situation]* apprécier d'un coup d'œil
N ◆ **summing-up** → **sum**

sumac(h) /'su:mæk/ N sumac *m*

Sumatra /sʊ'mɑ:trə/ N Sumatra

Sumatran /sʊ'mɑ:trən/ ADJ de Sumatra N habitant(e) *m(f) or* natif *m*, -ive *f* de Sumatra

summa cum laude /,sʊməkʊm'laʊdeɪ/ ADV *(US Univ)* ◆ **to graduate ~** ≈ obtenir son diplôme avec mention très honorable

summarily /'sʌmərɪlɪ/ ADV sommairement

summarize /'sʌməraɪz/ VT *[+ book, text, speech]* résumer ; *[+ facts, arguments]* résumer, récapituler VI faire un résumé

summary /'sʌmərɪ/ N 1 *(NonC)* résumé *m*, récapitulation *f* ◆ **in ~** en résumé 2 *(= printed matter, list etc)* sommaire *m*, résumé *m* ; *(Fin) [of accounts]* relevé *m* ◆ **here is a ~ of the news** *(Rad, TV)* voici les nouvelles *fpl* en bref ADJ sommaire

summat‡ /'sʌmət/ N *(dial)* ⇒ **something**

summation /sʌ'meɪʃən/ N *(= addition)* addition *f* ; *(= summing-up)* récapitulation *f*, résumé *m (also Jur)*

summer /'sʌmə^r/ N été *m* ◆ **in (the) ~** en été ◆ **in the ~ of 1997** pendant l'été (de) 1997 ◆ **a girl of 17 ~s** *(liter)* une jeune fille de 17 printemps ; → **high, Indian** VI passer l'été
COMP *[weather, heat, season, activities]* d'été, estival ; *[day, residence]* d'été
summer camp N *(US Scol)* colonie *f* de vacances
summer clothes NPL vêtements *mpl* d'été, tenue *f* estivale *or* d'été
summer holidays NPL grandes vacances *fpl*
summer house N maison *f* de vacances ; *(in country)* maison *f* de campagne ; see also **summerhouse**
summer lightning N éclair *m* de chaleur
summer resort N station *f* estivale
summer school N université *f* d'été
summer squash N *(US)* courgette *f*
summer time N *(Brit: by clock)* heure *f* d'été
summer visitor N estivant(e) *m(f)*

summerhouse /'sʌməhaʊs/ N pavillon *m* d'été

summertime /'sʌmətaɪm/ N *(= season)* été *m*

summery /'sʌmərɪ/ ADJ *[clothes]* d'été, estival ; *[colours, food]* d'été ◆ **the ~ weather** le temps estival

summit /'sʌmɪt/ N 1 *[of mountain]* sommet *m*, cime *f* 2 *(fig) [of power, honours, glory]* sommet *m* ; *[of ambition]* summum *m* 3 *(Pol)* sommet *m* ◆ **at ~ level** au plus haut niveau
COMP *(Pol) [talks]* au sommet
summit conference N (conférence *f* au) sommet *m*
summit meeting N rencontre *f* au sommet

summitry* /'sʌmɪtrɪ/ N *(esp US Pol)* tactique *f* de la rencontre au sommet

summon /'sʌmən/ VT *[+ servant, police]* appeler, faire venir ; *(to meeting)* convoquer (to à) ; *[+ monarch, president, prime minister]* mander (to à) ; *(Jur)* citer, assigner (as comme) ; *[+ help, reinforcements]* requérir ◆ **the Queen ~ed Parliament** la reine a convoqué le Parlement ◆ **to ~ sb to do sth** sommer qn de faire qch ◆ **to ~ sb to appear** *(Jur)* citer qn à comparaître, assigner qn ◆ **they ~ed the town to surrender** *(Mil)* ils ont sommé la ville de *or* ils ont mis la ville en demeure de se rendre ◆ **I was ~ed to his presence** j'ai été requis de paraître devant lui, il m'a mandé auprès de lui ◆ **to ~ sb in/down** *etc (Admin etc)* sommer qn d'entrer/de descendre *etc*

► **summon up** VT SEP *[+ one's energy, strength]* rassembler, faire appel à ; *[+ interest, enthusiasm]* faire appel à ◆ **to ~ up (one's) courage** faire appel à *or* rassembler tout son courage, s'armer de courage, prendre son courage à deux mains *(to do sth* pour faire qch) ◆ **he ~ed up the courage to fight back** il a trouvé le courage de riposter

summons /'sʌmənz/ N (pl **summonses**) sommation *f (also Mil)*, injonction *f* ; *(Jur)* citation *f*, assignation *f* ◆ **to take out a ~ against sb** *(Jur)* faire assigner qn ◆ **he got a ~ for drunken driving** il a reçu une citation à comparaître *or* une assignation pour conduite en état d'ivresse ◆ **they sent him a ~ to surrender** *(Mil)* ils lui ont fait parvenir une sommation de se rendre ; → **issue, serve** VT *(Jur)* citer, assigner *(à comparaître) (for sth* pour qch)

sumo /'su:məʊ/ N sumo *m*

sump /sʌmp/ N *(Tech)* puisard *m (pour eaux-vannes etc)* ; *(Brit: in car)* carter *m* ; *(= deep cave)* fosse *f* COMP **sump oil** N *(in car)* huile *f* de carter

sumptuary /'sʌmptjʊərɪ/ ADJ *(frm)* somptuaire ◆ **~ law** *(Hist)* loi *f* somptuaire

sumptuous /'sʌmptjʊəs/ ADJ somptueux

sumptuously /'sʌmptjʊəslɪ/ ADV somptueusement

sumptuousness /'sʌmptjʊəsnɪs/ N somptuosité *f*

sun /sʌn/ N soleil *m* ◆ **the ~ is shining** il fait (du) soleil, le soleil brille ◆ **in the ~** au soleil ◆ **right in the ~** en plein soleil ◆ **a place in the ~** *(lit)* un endroit ensoleillé *or* au soleil ; *(fig)* une place au soleil ◆ **this room certainly catches the ~** cette pièce reçoit beaucoup de soleil ◆ **to catch the ~** *(= get a tan)* prendre des bonnes couleurs ; *(= get sunburned)* prendre un coup de soleil ◆ **in the July ~** au soleil de juillet ◆ **come out of the ~** ne restez pas au soleil ◆ **the ~ is in my eyes** j'ai le soleil dans les yeux ◆ **he rose with the ~** il se levait avec le soleil ◆ **everything under the ~** tout ce qu'il est possible d'imaginer ◆ **nothing under the ~** rien au monde ◆ **there's no prettier place under the ~** il n'est pas de plus joli coin au monde *or* sur la terre ◆ **no reason under the ~** pas la moindre raison ◆ **there is nothing new under the ~** il n'y a rien de nouveau sous le soleil ; → **midnight**
VT ◆ **to ~ o.s.** *[lizard, cat]* se chauffer au soleil ; *[person]* prendre un bain de soleil, lézarder au soleil
COMP **sun bonnet** N capeline *f*
sun dance N danse *f* du soleil *(rituel du solstice chez les Indiens d'Amérique)*
sun deck N *[of house, hotel etc]* véranda *f* ; *[of ship]* pont *m* supérieur
sun-drenched ADJ inondé de soleil
sun dress N robe *f* bain de soleil
sun-filled ADJ ensoleillé, rempli de soleil
sun-god N dieu *m* soleil *or* Soleil
sun helmet N casque *m* colonial
sun hood N *[of camera]* pare-soleil *m*
the Sun King N *(Hist)* le Roi-Soleil
sun-kissed ADJ baigné de soleil
sun lamp N lampe *f* à bronzer *or* à ultraviolets
sun lotion N ⇒ **suntan lotion** ; → **suntan**
sun lounge N véranda *f* ; *(in health institution etc)* solarium *m*
sun-lounger N chaise *f* longue *(pour bronzer)*
sun oil N ⇒ **suntan oil** ; → **suntan**
sun porch N petite véranda *f*
sun-shield N *[of car]* pare-soleil *m inv*
sun umbrella N parasol *m*
sun visor N *(for eyes, on cap)* visière *f* ; *[of car]* pare-soleil *m inv*
sun-worship N *(Rel)* culte *m* du soleil
sun-worshipper N *(Rel)* adorateur *m*, -trice *f* du soleil ; *(gen)* adepte *mf or* fanatique *mf* du bronzage

Sun. abbrev of **Sunday**

sunbaked /'sʌnbeɪkt/ ADJ brûlé par le soleil

sunbath /'sʌnbɑ:θ/ N bain *m* de soleil

sunbathe /'sʌnbeɪð/ VI prendre un bain *or* des bains de soleil, se (faire) bronzer

sunbather /'sʌnbeɪðə^r/ N personne *f* qui prend un bain de soleil

sunbathing /'sʌnbeɪðɪŋ/ N bains *mpl* de soleil

sunbeam /'sʌnbi:m/ N rayon *m* de soleil

sunbed /'sʌnbed/ N *(with sunray lamp)* lit *m* solaire ; *(for outdoors)* lit *m* pliant

Sunbelt /'sʌnbelt/ N (US) ◆ **the ~** *les États du sud des États-Unis*

SUNBELT

La « région du soleil » désigne les États du sud des États-Unis (de la Caroline du Nord à la Californie), caractérisés par un climat chaud et ensoleillé et qui connaissent, depuis quelque temps, un fort développement économique dû notamment aux mouvements migratoires en provenance du nord du pays. Les États du nord, par opposition, sont parfois appelés « Frostbelt » (région du gel) ou « Rustbelt » (région de la rouille) à cause de leurs vieilles infrastructures industrielles.

sunblind /'sʌnblaɪnd/ N store *m*

sunblock /'sʌnblɒk/ N écran *m* (solaire) total

sunburn /'sʌnbɜ:n/ N coup *m* de soleil

sunburned /'sʌnbɜ:nd/, **sunburnt** /'sʌnbɜ:nt/ ADJ *(= tanned)* bronzé, hâlé ; *(painfully)* brûlé par le soleil ◆ **to get ~** *(= tan)* (se faire) bronzer ; *(painfully)* prendre un coup de soleil

sunburst /'sʌnbɜ:st/ N rayon *m* de soleil *(entre les nuages)* COMP **sunburst clock** N horloge *f* en forme de soleil

sundae /'sʌndeɪ/ N sundae *m*, coupe *f* glacée Chantilly

Sunday /'sʌndɪ/ N 1 dimanche *m* ; → **Easter, month, palm²** ; *for other phrases see* **Saturday**
2 **the ~s*** *(= Sunday papers)* les journaux *mpl* du dimanche
COMP *[clothes, paper]* du dimanche ; *[walk, rest, peace]* dominical
Sunday best N ◆ **in one's ~ best** tout endimanché, en habits du dimanche
Sunday driver N *(pej)* chauffeur *m* du dimanche
Sunday-go-to-meeting* ADJ *(US) [clothes]* du dimanche
Sunday motorist N *(pej)* ⇒ **Sunday driver**
Sunday observance N observance *f* du repos dominical
Sunday opening N *(Comm)* ouverture *f* des magasins le dimanche, commerce *m* dominical
Sunday papers NPL journaux *mpl* du dimanche
Sunday school N ≈ catéchisme *m*
Sunday school teacher N ≈ catéchiste *mf*
Sunday trading N *(Comm)* ⇒ **Sunday opening** ◆ **~ trading laws** réglementation *f* du commerce dominical

SUNDAY PAPERS

Les journaux du dimanche occupent une place essentielle dans les activités dominicales des Britanniques, qui en achètent souvent plusieurs. Il s'agit soit de journaux paraissant uniquement le dimanche (« Observer » et « News of the World », par exemple), soit d'éditions du dimanche de quotidiens (« Sunday Times », « Sunday Telegraph », Independent on Sunday », « Sunday Express », etc.). Un **Sunday paper** contient généralement des rubriques très variées sur les arts, les sports, les voyages ou les affaires, et s'accompagne d'un supplément magazine en couleurs.

Aux États-Unis, le plus grand journal du dimanche est l'édition dominicale du « New York Times », mais les Américains préfèrent généralement la presse locale à la presse nationale.

sunder /ˈsʌndəʳ/ *(liter)* VT fractionner, scinder N ◆ **in** ~ *(= apart)* écartés ; *(= in pieces)* en morceaux

sundial /ˈsʌndaɪəl/ N cadran *m* solaire

sundown /ˈsʌndaʊn/ N *(US)* ⇒ **sunset**

sundowner * /ˈsʌndaʊnəʳ/ N *(Austral = tramp)* chemineau *m*, clochard *m* ; *(Brit = drink) boisson alcoolisée prise en début de soirée*

sundried /ˌsʌnˈdraɪd/ ADJ séché au soleil

sundry /ˈsʌndrɪ/ ADJ divers ◆ **all and** ~ tout le monde NPL **sundries** articles *mpl* divers

sunfish /ˈsʌnfɪʃ/ N *(pl inv)* poisson *m* lune

sunflower /ˈsʌnˌflaʊəʳ/ N tournesol *m*, soleil *m* ◆ **the Sunflower State** *(US)* le Kansas
COMP **sunflower oil** N huile *f* de tournesol
sunflower seeds NPL graines *fpl* de tournesol

sung /sʌŋ/ VB ptp of **sing**

sunglasses /ˈsʌnˌglɑːsɪz/ NPL lunettes *fpl* de soleil

sunhat /ˈsʌnhæt/ N chapeau *m* de soleil *or* de plage

sunk /sʌŋk/ VB ptp of **sink¹** COMP **sunk costs** NPL *(= fixed costs)* frais *mpl or* coûts *mpl* fixes

sunken /ˈsʌŋkən/ ADJ *[ship, treasure]* englouti ; *[rock]* submergé ; *[garden, road]* en contrebas ; *[bath]* encastré ; *[eyes]* enfoncé ; *[cheeks]* creux

sunless /ˈsʌnlɪs/ ADJ sans soleil

sunlight /ˈsʌnlaɪt/ N (lumière *f* du) soleil *m* ◆ **in the** ~ au soleil, à la lumière du soleil

sunlit /ˈsʌnlɪt/ ADJ ensoleillé

Sunni /ˈsʌnɪ/ N *(= religion)* sunnisme *m* ; *(= person)* sunnite *mf* ADJ sunnite

sunny /ˈsʌnɪ/ ADJ 1 *(= bright) [climate, room, morning]* ensoleillé ; *[side] (of street, building etc)* exposé au soleil, ensoleillé ◆ **it's** ~ **today** il y a du soleil aujourd'hui ◆ **the outlook is** ~ on prévoit du soleil, on peut s'attendre à un temps ensoleillé ◆ ~ **intervals,** ~ **periods** *(Brit Met)* éclaircies *fpl* 2 *(= cheerful) [smile]* rayonnant, radieux ; *[person]* épanoui ; *[personality]* enjoué ◆ **to have a** ~ **disposition** avoir un naturel enjoué ◆ **to be in a** ~ **mood** être d'humeur enjouée ◆ **the** ~ **side of life** les bons côtés de la vie COMP **sunny side up** ADJ *(US Culin)* ◆ **eggs** ~ **side up** œufs *mpl* sur le plat *(frits sans avoir été retournés)*

sunray lamp /ˈsʌnreɪˌlæmp/ N *(Med)* ⇒ **sun lamp**; → **sun**

sunray treatment /ˈsʌnreɪˌtriːtmənt/ N héliothérapie *f*

sunrise /ˈsʌnraɪz/ N lever *m* de soleil ◆ **at** ~ au lever du jour COMP **sunrise industry** N industrie *f* en pleine expansion

sunroof /ˈsʌnruːf/ N *[of car]* toit *m* ouvrant

sunscreen /ˈsʌnskriːn/ N écran *m* solaire

sunseeker /ˈsʌnsiːkəʳ/ N amateur *m* de soleil

sunset /ˈsʌnset/ N coucher *m* de soleil ◆ **at** ~ à la tombée de la nuit *or* du jour
COMP **sunset clause** N *(US Jur)* clause *f* de révision
sunset industry N industrie *f* en déclin
sunset law N *(US) loi stipulant que le vote approuvant la création d'un organisme gouvernemental doit être périodiquement reconduit pour que l'organisme continue d'exister*

sunshade /ˈsʌnʃeɪd/ N *(for eyes)* visière *f* ; *(for table, on pram)* parasol *m* ; *(in car)* pare-soleil *m inv* ; *(= parasol)* ombrelle *f*

sunshine /ˈsʌnʃaɪn/ N *(NonC)* (lumière *f* du) soleil *m* ◆ **in the** ~ au soleil ◆ **five hours of** ~ cinq heures d'ensoleillement ◆ **a ray of** ~ *(fig) (= person, event)* un rayon de soleil ◆ **he's a real ray of** ~ **today** *(iro)* il est gracieux comme une porte de prison aujourd'hui ◆ **hallo** ~!* bonjour mon rayon de soleil !
COMP **sunshine law** N *(US) loi imposant la publicité des débats pour les décisions administratives*
sunshine roof N *[of car]* toit *m* ouvrant
the Sunshine State N *(US)* la Floride

sunspecs * /ˈsʌnspeks/ NPL ⇒ **sunglasses**

sunspot /ˈsʌnspɒt/ N tache *f* solaire

sunstroke /ˈsʌnstrəʊk/ N *(NonC: Med)* insolation *f* ◆ **to get** ~ attraper une insolation

sunsuit /ˈsʌnsuːt/ N bain *m* de soleil

suntan /ˈsʌntæn/ N bronzage *m* ◆ **to get a** ~ se (faire) bronzer
COMP **suntan lotion** N lotion *f or* lait *m* solaire
suntan oil N huile *f* solaire

suntanned /ˈsʌntænd/ ADJ bronzé

suntrap /ˈsʌntræp/ N coin *m* très ensoleillé

sunup /ˈsʌnʌp/ N *(US)* ⇒ **sunrise**

sup /sʌp/ VI souper *(on, off* de) VT *(also* **sup up**) boire *or* avaler à petites gorgées N petite gorgée *f*

super /ˈsuːpəʳ/ ADJ *(esp Brit *)* super* N 1 *(Police)* * abbrev of **superintendent** 2 *(Cine)* * abbrev of **supernumerary** 3 *(US = gasoline)* super(carburant) *m*
COMP **Super Bowl** N *(US Ftbl)* Super Bowl *m (championnat de football américain)*
super-class N superclasse *f*
super-duper * ADJ formid * *inv*, sensass * *inv*
Super Tuesday N *(US Pol)* super-mardi *m (second mardi du mois de mars, date-clé des élections primaires)*

super... /ˈsuːpəʳ/ PREF super... ◆ **super-salesman** super-vendeur *m* ; see also **superannuate**

superable /ˈsuːpərəbl/ ADJ surmontable

superabundance /ˌsuːpərəˈbʌndəns/ N surabondance *f*

superabundant /ˌsuːpərəˈbʌndənt/ ADJ surabondant

superannuate /ˌsuːpəˈrænjʊeɪt/ VT mettre à la retraite ◆ **~d** retraité, à la *or* en retraite ; *(fig)* suranné, démodé

superannuation /ˌsuːpəˌrænjʊˈeɪʃən/ N *(= act)* (mise *f* à la) retraite *f* ; *(Brit = pension)* pension *f* de retraite ; *(Brit:* also **superannuation contribution**) versements *mpl or* cotisations *fpl* pour la pension COMP **superannuation fund** N *(Brit)* caisse *f* de retraite

superb /suːˈpɜːb/ ADJ *[view, weather, day]* superbe ; *[quality, opportunity]* merveilleux, exceptionnel ◆ **in** ~ **condition** en excellent état

superblock /ˈsuːpəblɒk/ N *(US) zone urbaine aménagée en quartier piétonnier*

superbly /suːˈpɜːblɪ/ ADV superbement ◆ **they have done** ~ **well** ils ont superbement bien réussi ◆ **he is** ~ **fit** il est dans une forme (physique) éblouissante

superbug /ˈsuːpəbʌg/ N bactérie *f* multirésistante

supercargo /ˈsuːpəˌkɑːgəʊ/ N *(Naut)* subrécargue *m*

supercharged /ˈsuːpətʃɑːdʒd/ ADJ surcomprimé

supercharger /ˈsuːpəˌtʃɑːdʒəʳ/ N compresseur *m*

supercilious /ˌsuːpəˈsɪlɪəs/ ADJ *[person]* hautain, dédaigneux ; *[smile]* dédaigneux

superciliously /ˌsuːpəˈsɪlɪəslɪ/ ADV *[look at]* dédaigneusement, d'un air hautain ; *[say]* dédaigneusement, d'un ton hautain

superciliousness /ˌsuːpəˈsɪlɪəsnɪs/ N hauteur *f*, arrogance *f*

supercomputer /ˌsuːpəkəmˈpjuːtəʳ/ N supercalculateur *m*, superordinateur *m*

superconductive /ˌsuːpəkənˈdʌktɪv/ ADJ supraconducteur

superconductivity /ˈsuːpəˌkɒndʌkˈtɪvɪtɪ/ N supraconductivité *f*

superconductor /ˌsuːpəkənˈdʌktəʳ/ N supraconducteur *m*

supercool /ˌsuːpəˈkuːl/ VT *(Chem)* sous-refroidir

supercover /ˈsuːpəˌkʌvəʳ/ N *(Insurance)* garantie *f* totale, couverture *f* complète

superego /ˌsuːpərˈiːgəʊ/ N surmoi *m*

supererogation /ˈsuːpərˌerəˈgeɪʃən/ N surérogation *f*

superette /ˈsuːpəret/ N *(US)* petit supermarché *m*, supérette *f*

superficial /ˌsuːpəˈfɪʃəl/ ADJ superficiel

superficiality /ˈsuːpəˌfɪʃɪˈælɪtɪ/ N caractère *m* superficiel, manque *m* de profondeur

superficially /ˌsuːpəˈfɪʃəlɪ/ ADV *[discuss, examine]* superficiellement ; *[attractive]* en apparence

superficies /ˌsuːpəˈfɪʃiːz/ N *(pl inv)* superficie *f*

superfine /ˈsuːpəfaɪn/ ADJ *[goods, quality]* extrafin, superfin, surfin ; *(pej) [distinction]* trop ténu, bien mince

superfluity /ˌsuːpəˈflʊɪtɪ/ N 1 surabondance *f* *(of* de) 2 ⇒ **superfluousness**

superfluous /sʊˈpɜːflʊəs/ ADJ *[goods, explanation]* superflu ◆ **it is** ~ **to say that** ... inutile de dire que ... ◆ **he felt rather** ~ * il se sentait de trop

superfluously /sʊˈpɜːflʊəslɪ/ ADV d'une manière superflue

superfluousness /sʊˈpɜːflʊəsnɪs/ N caractère *m* superflu

supergiant /ˌsuːpəˈdʒaɪənt/ N *(Astron)* supergéante *f*

superglue /ˈsuːpəgluː/ N colle *f* extra-forte

supergrass * /ˈsuːpəgrɑːs/ N *(Brit)* super-indicateur *m* de police

supergroup /ˈsuːpəgruːp/ N *(Mus)* supergroupe *m*

superheat /ˌsuːpəˈhiːt/ VT surchauffer

superhero /ˈsuːpəˌhɪərəʊ/ N super-héros *m*

superhighway /ˈsuːpəˌhaɪweɪ/ N *(US)* voie *f* express (à plusieurs files) ; → ROADS ; → **information**

superhuman /ˌsuːpəˈhjuːmən/ ADJ surhumain N surhomme *m*

superimpose /ˌsuːpərɪmˈpəʊz/ VT superposer *(on* à) ◆ **~d** *(Cine, Phot, Typ)* en surimpression

superintend /ˌsuːpərɪnˈtend/ VT superviser ; *[+ exam]* surveiller

superintendence /ˌsuːpərɪnˈtendəns/ N *(NonC) [of activity]* contrôle *m* ; *[of child, prisoner]* surveillance *f* ◆ **under the** ~ **of sb** sous la surveillance de qn

superintendent /ˌsuːpərɪnˈtendənt/ N 1 *[of institution, orphanage]* directeur *m*, -trice *f* ; *[of department]* chef *m* 2 *(Brit)* (also **police superin-**

tendent, superintendent of police) ≈ commissaire *m* (de police)

Superior /sʊˈpɪərɪəʳ/ ADJ ◆ **Lake** ~ le lac Supérieur

superior /sʊˈpɪərɪəʳ/ LANGUAGE IN USE 5.2 ADJ 1 *(= better)* supérieur (-eure *f*) *(to* à) ◆ ~ **in number to** ... supérieur en nombre à ..., numériquement supérieur à ... ◆ **in ~ numbers** en plus grand nombre, plus nombreux ◆ **the vastly ~ numbers of the enemy** les effectifs largement supérieurs de l'ennemi 2 *(= high-quality) [product, goods]* de qualité supérieure ◆ **a very ~ model** un modèle très supérieur 3 *(pej = supercilious) [person]* hautain, dédaigneux ; *[air, smile]* supérieur (-eure *f*), de supériorité ◆ **to feel ~** se sentir supérieur 4 *(in hierarchy)* supérieur *(to* à) ◆ **his ~ officer** l'officier qui lui était supérieur ; → **mother** 5 *(Anat) [limb]* supérieur (-eure *f*) 6 *(Typ) [letter, number]* en exposant, supérieur (-eure *f*) N supérieur(e) *m(f)* COMP **superior court** N *(US Jur) juridiction intermédiaire*

superiority /sʊˌpɪərɪˈɒrɪtɪ/ N supériorité *f* *(to, over* par rapport à) COMP **superiority complex** N complexe *m* de supériorité

superjacent /ˈsuːpəˈdʒeɪsənt/ ADJ sus-jacent

superjumbo /ˌsuːpədʒʌmbəʊ/ N *(= plane)* superjumbo *m*, très gros porteur *m*

superlative /sʊˈpɜːlətɪv/ ADJ 1 *(= excellent) [artist, quality, achievement]* exceptionnel, extraordinaire 2 *(Gram)* superlatif N *(Gram)* superlatif *m* ◆ **in the ~** au superlatif ◆ **he tends to talk in ~s** il a tendance à exagérer

superlatively /sʊˈpɜːlətɪvlɪ/ ADV *[play, perform]* de façon extraordinaire ; *[rich, well]* extraordinairement

superman /ˈsuːpəmæn/ N (pl **-men**) surhomme *m* ◆ **Superman** *(on TV etc)* Superman *m*

supermarket /ˈsuːpəˌmɑːkɪt/ N supermarché *m*

supermen /ˈsuːpəmen/ NPL of **superman**

supermini /ˈsuːpəmɪnɪ/ N *(= car)* supermini *f*

supermodel /ˈsuːpəmɒdl/ N top model *m*

supernal /suːˈpɜːnəl/ ADJ *(liter)* céleste, divin

supernatural /ˌsuːpəˈnætʃərəl/ ADJ surnaturel N surnaturel *m*

supernormal /ˌsuːpəˈnɔːməl/ ADJ au-dessus de la normale

supernova /ˌsuːpəˈnəʊvə/ N (pl **supernovae** /ˌsuːpəˈnəʊviː/) *(Astron)* supernova *f*

supernumerary /ˌsuːpəˈnjuːmərərɪ/ ADJ *(Admin, Bio etc)* surnuméraire ; *(= superfluous)* superflu N *(Admin etc)* surnuméraire *mf* ; *(Cine)* figurant(e) *m(f)*

superorder /ˈsuːpərɔːdəʳ/ N superordre *m*

superordinate /ˌsuːpərˈɔːdənɪt/ ADJ dominant, supérieur N *(Ling)* terme *m* générique

superphosphate /ˌsuːpəˈfɒsfeɪt/ N superphosphate *m*

superpose /ˌsuːpəˈpəʊz/ VT *(also Geom)* superposer *(on* à)

superposition /ˌsuːpəpəˈzɪʃən/ N superposition *f*

superpower /ˈsuːpəpaʊəʳ/ N *(Pol)* superpuissance *f*, supergrand *m*

superscript /ˈsuːpəˌskrɪpt/ *(Typ)* ADJ supérieur (-eure *f*) N *(= number)* chiffre *m* supérieur ; *(= letter)* lettre *f* supérieure

superscription /ˌsuːpəˈskrɪpʃən/ N suscription *f*

supersede /ˌsuːpəˈsiːd/ VT *[+ belief, object, order]* remplacer ; *[+ person]* supplanter, prendre la place de ◆ **this edition ~s previous ones** cette édition remplace et annule les précédentes ◆ **~d idea/method** idée *f*/méthode *f* périmée

supersensitive /ˌsuːpəˈsensɪtɪv/ ADJ hypersensible

supersize /ˈsuːpəˌsaɪz/, **supersized** /ˈsuːpəˌsaɪzd/ ADJ *[portion, order]* géant

supersonic /ˌsuːpəˈsɒnɪk/ ADJ *[aircraft, vehicle, speed]* supersonique ; *[flight, travel]* en avion supersonique

supersonically /ˌsuːpəˈsɒnɪkəlɪ/ ADV en supersonique

superstar /ˈsuːpəstɑːʳ/ N superstar *f*

superstate /ˈsuːpəsteɪt/ N *(pej)* super-État *m*

superstition /ˌsuːpəˈstɪʃən/ N superstition *f*

superstitious /ˌsuːpəˈstɪʃəs/ ADJ superstitieux ◆ **to be ~ about walking under ladders** éviter de passer sous les échelles par superstition

superstitiously /ˌsuːpəˈstɪʃəslɪ/ ADV superstitieusement

superstore /ˈsuːpəstɔːʳ/ N *(esp Brit)* hypermarché *m*

superstratum /ˌsuːpəˈstrɑːtəm/ N (pl **superstratums** or **superstrata** /ˌsupəˈstrɑːtə/) *(Ling)* superstrat *m*

superstructure /ˈsuːpəˌstrʌktʃəʳ/ N superstructure *f*

supertanker /ˈsuːpəˌtæŋkəʳ/ N pétrolier *m* géant, supertanker *m*

supertax /ˈsuːpətæks/ N tranche *f* supérieure de l'impôt sur le revenu

supervene /ˌsuːpəˈviːn/ VI survenir

supervention /ˌsuːpəˈvenʃən/ N apparition *f*, manifestation *f*

supervise /ˈsuːpəvaɪz/ VT *[+ work]* superviser ; *[+ exam]* surveiller ; *[+ research]* diriger ◆ **UN-~d elections** des élections supervisées par l'ONU ◆ **the children were not adequately ~d** les enfants étaient mal encadrés ◆ **we offer ~d activities for children** nous proposons des activités surveillées or encadrées pour les enfants ◆ **~d play area** espace *m* de jeu surveillé VI *(at work)* superviser ; *(at school)* surveiller

supervision /ˌsuːpəˈvɪʒən/ N *(= watch)* surveillance *f* ; *(= monitoring)* supervision *f*, contrôle *m* ; *(= management)* direction *f* ◆ **under the ~ of** ... sous la surveillance *or* direction de ... ◆ **to keep sth under strict ~** exercer une surveillance *or* un contrôle sévère sur qch COMP **supervision order** N *(Brit Jur)* ordonnance *f* de surveillance

supervisor /ˈsuːpəvaɪzəʳ/ N *(gen)* surveillant(e) *m(f)* ; *(Comm)* chef *m* de rayon ; *(at exam)* surveillant(e) *m(f)* ; *(Univ)* directeur *m*, -trice *f* or patron *m* de thèse

supervisory /ˈsuːpəvaɪzərɪ/ ADJ *[post, role, powers, body]* de surveillance ◆ **~ staff** personnel *m* chargé de la surveillance ◆ **in a ~ capacity** à titre de surveillant(e)

superwoman /ˈsuːpəˌwʊmən/ N (pl **-women**) superwoman *f*

supine /ˈsuːpaɪn/ ADJ *(liter)* 1 *(lit = prostrate)* (also **lying supine, in a supine position**) allongé sur le dos 2 *(pej = passive) [person, attitude]* mollasse *(pej)*

supper /ˈsʌpəʳ/ N *(= main evening meal)* dîner *m* ; *(after theatre etc)* souper *m* ; *(= snack)* collation *f* ◆ **to have ~** dîner *(or* souper *etc)* ◆ **we made him sing for his ~** *(fig)* nous l'avons aidé *etc*, mais c'était donnant donnant ; → **lord** COMP **supper club** N *(US) petit restaurant nocturne, avec danse et éventuellement spectacle*

suppertime /ˈsʌpətaɪm/ N l'heure *f* du dîner *(or* du souper *etc)* ◆ **at ~** au dîner *(or* souper *etc)*

supplant /səˈplɑːnt/ VT *[+ person]* supplanter, évincer ; *[+ object]* supplanter, remplacer

supple /ˈsʌpl/ ADJ *(lit, fig)* souple ◆ **to become ~r** s'assouplir

supplement /ˈsʌplɪmənt/ N *(also Press)* supplément *m* *(to* à) → **colour** VT /ˈsʌplɪˌment/ *[+ income]* augmenter, arrondir *(by doing sth* en faisant qch) ; *[+ book, information, one's knowledge]* ajouter à, compléter

supplemental /ˌsʌplɪˈmentəl/ ADJ *(esp US)* supplémentaire

supplementary /ˌsʌplɪˈmentərɪ/ ADJ *(gen, Geom, Mus)* supplémentaire ; *[food, vitamins]* complémentaire ◆ **you may need ~ iron** vous pourriez avoir besoin d'un complément de fer ◆ **~ to** en plus de

COMP **supplementary benefit** N *(NonC: Brit Admin: formerly)* allocation *f* supplémentaire
supplementary question N *(Brit Parl)* question *f* orale
supplementary scheme N *(Jur)* régime *m* complémentaire

suppleness /ˈsʌplnɪs/ N souplesse *f*

suppletion /səˈpliːʃən/ N *(Ling)* suppléance *f*

suppletive /səˈpliːtɪv/ ADJ *(Ling)* supplétif

suppliant /ˈsʌplɪənt/, **supplicant** /ˈsʌplɪkənt/ ADJ, N suppliant(e) *m(f)*

supplicate /ˈsʌplɪkeɪt/ VT supplier, implorer *(sb to do sth* qn de faire qch) ; *[+ mercy etc]* implorer *(from sb* de qn) VI ◆ **to ~ for sth** implorer qch

supplication /ˌsʌplɪˈkeɪʃən/ N supplication *f* ; *(written)* supplique *f* ◆ **to kneel in ~** supplier à genoux

supplier /səˈplaɪəʳ/ N fournisseur *m*

supply¹ /səˈplaɪ/ N 1 *(= amount, stock)* provision *f*, réserve *f* ◆ **a good ~ of coal** une bonne provision *or* réserve de charbon ◆ **to get *or* lay in a ~ of** ... faire des provisions de ..., s'approvisionner de ... ◆ **to get in a fresh ~ of sth** renouveler sa provision *or* sa réserve de qch ◆ **supplies** *(gen)* provisions *fpl*, réserves *fpl* ; *(= food)* vivres *mpl* ; *(Mil)* subsistances *fpl*, approvisionnements *mpl* ◆ **electrical supplies** matériel *m* électrique ◆ **office supplies** fournitures *fpl* or matériel de bureau

2 *(NonC) (= act of supplying) [of fuel etc]* alimentation *f* ; *[of equipment, books etc]* fourniture *f* ◆ **the ~ of fuel to the engine** l'alimentation du moteur en combustible ◆ **the electricity/gas ~** l'alimentation en électricité/gaz ◆ **~ and demand** *(Econ)* l'offre *f* et la demande ◆ **Ministry of Supply** *(Brit)* ≈ services *mpl* de l'Intendance ; → **short, water**

3 *(person = temporary substitute)* remplaçant(e) *m(f)*, suppléant(e) *m(f)* ◆ **to teach *or* be on ~** faire des suppléances *or* des remplacements

4 *(Parl)* **supplies** crédits *mpl*

VT 1 *(= provide, furnish) [+ tools, books, goods]* fournir, procurer *(to sb* à qn) ; *(Comm)* fournir, approvisionner ; *(= equip) [+ person, city]* fournir, approvisionner *(with sth* en *or* de qch) ; *(Mil: with provisions)* ravitailler, approvisionner ◆ **we ~ most of the local schools** *(Comm)* nous fournissons *or* nous approvisionnons la plupart des écoles locales ◆ **to ~ from stock** *(Comm)* livrer sur stock ◆ **sheep ~ wool** les moutons donnent de la laine ◆ **we ~ the tools for the job** nous fournissons *or* nous procurons les outils nécessaires pour faire le travail ◆ **to ~ electricity/gas/water to the town** alimenter la ville en électricité/gaz/eau ◆ **to ~ sb with food** nourrir *or* alimenter qn ◆ **they kept us supplied with milk** grâce à eux nous n'avons jamais manqué de lait ◆ **the car was supplied with a radio** la voiture était munie *or* pourvue d'une radio ◆ **a battery is not supplied with the torch** la lampe de poche est livrée sans pile ◆ **to ~ sb with information/details** fournir des renseignements/des détails à qn

2 *(= make good) [+ need, deficiency]* suppléer à, remédier à ; *[+ sb's needs]* subvenir à ; *[+ loss]* réparer, compenser

COMP [train, wagon, truck, convoy] de ravitaillement, ravitailleur ; [pharmacist etc] intérimaire
supply chain N chaîne f logistique
supply line N voie f de ravitaillement
supply management N (Econ) régulation f de l'offre
supply ship N navire m ravitailleur
supply-side economics NPL théorie f de l'offre
supply teacher N (Brit) suppléant(e) m(f)

supply² /'sʌplɪ/ ADV [move, bend] avec souplesse, souplement

support /sə'pɔːt/ LANGUAGE IN USE 11.2, 13, 26.2
N 1 (NonC: lit, fig) appui m, soutien m ; (financial) aide f (financière) ◆ **he couldn't stand without ~** il ne pouvait pas se soutenir (sur ses jambes) ◆ **he leaned on me for ~** il s'est appuyé sur moi ◆ **to give ~ to sb/sth** soutenir qn/qch ◆ **this bra gives good ~** ce soutien-gorge maintient bien la poitrine ◆ **he depends on his father for (financial) ~** il dépend financièrement de son père ◆ **he has no visible means of ~** (financial) il n'a pas de moyens d'existence connus ◆ **what means of ~ has he got?** quelles sont ses ressources ? ◆ **he looked to his friends for ~** il a cherché un soutien or un appui auprès de ses amis ◆ **he needs all the ~ he can get** il a bien besoin de tout l'appui qu'on pourra lui donner ◆ **he got a lot of ~ from his friends** ses amis l'ont vraiment soutenu or appuyé ◆ **the proposal got no ~** personne n'a parlé en faveur de la proposition ◆ **have I your ~ in this?** est-ce que je peux compter sur votre appui or soutien en la matière ? ◆ **to give** or **lend one's ~ to ...** prêter son appui à ... ◆ **that lends ~ to his theory** ceci corrobore or vient corroborer sa théorie ◆ **they stopped work in ~** ils ont cessé le travail par solidarité ; → **moral**
◆ **in support of** ◆ **he spoke in ~ of the motion** il a parlé en faveur de la motion ◆ **in ~ of his theory/claim** à l'appui de sa théorie/revendication ◆ **they demonstrated in ~ of the prisoners** ils ont manifesté en faveur des prisonniers, ils ont fait une manifestation de soutien aux prisonniers ◆ **a collection in ~ of the accident victims** une quête au profit des victimes de l'accident
2 (= object) (gen) appui m ; (Constr, Tech) support m, soutien m ; (fig: moral, financial etc) soutien m ; (US Econ = subsidy) subvention f ◆ **use the stool as a ~ for your foot** prenez le tabouret comme appui pour votre pied ◆ **he is the sole (financial) ~ of his family** il est le seul soutien (financier) de sa famille ◆ **he has been a great ~ to me** il a été pour moi un soutien précieux
3 ⇒ **support act**
VT 1 (= hold up) [pillar, beam] supporter, soutenir ; [bridge] porter ; [person, neck] soutenir ◆ **the elements necessary to ~ life** les éléments nécessaires à l'entretien de la vie, les éléments vitaux
2 (= uphold) [+ motion, cause, party, candidate] (passively) être pour ; (actively) soutenir ; [+ sb's application, action, protest] soutenir, appuyer ; [+ team] être supporter de, supporter* ◆ **with only his courage to ~ him** avec son seul courage comme soutien, n'ayant de soutien que son courage ◆ **his friends ~ed him in his refusal to obey** ses amis l'ont soutenu or ont pris son parti lorsqu'il a refusé d'obéir ◆ **the socialists will ~ it** les socialistes seront or voteront pour ◆ **I cannot ~ what you are doing** je ne peux pas approuver ce que vous faites ◆ **~ed by a cast of thousands** (Cine, Theat) avec le concours de milliers d'acteurs et figurants ◆ **the proofs that ~ my case** les preuves à l'appui de ma cause ◆ **a subsidy to ~ the price of beef** une subvention pour maintenir le prix du bœuf ◆ **he ~s Celtic** (Ftbl) c'est un supporter du Celtic, il supporte* le Celtic
3 (= bear out, prove) [+ hypothesis, view, claim] conforter ◆ **this research ~s the hypothesis/the idea that ...** cette recherche conforte l'hypothèse/l'idée selon laquelle ...
4 (financially) subvenir aux besoins de ◆ **she has a husband and three children to ~** elle doit subvenir aux besoins de son mari et de ses trois enfants ◆ **to ~ o.s.** (gen) subvenir à ses propres besoins ; (= earn one's living) gagner sa vie ◆ **the school is ~ed by money from ...** l'école reçoit une aide financière de ...
5 (= endure) supporter, tolérer
COMP (Mil etc) [troops, convoy, vessel] de soutien
support act N (Mus) groupe m (or chanteur m, -euse f) en première partie or en vedette américaine ◆ **who was the ~ act?** qui était en première partie ?
support band N (Mus) groupe m en première partie (d'un concert) or en vedette américaine ◆ **who were the ~ band?** qui était en première partie ?
support group N groupe m d'entraide
support hose N (pl inv) bas mpl (or collants mpl) de contention or antifatigue
support price N (Econ) prix m de soutien
support stockings NPL bas mpl de contention or antifatigue

supportable /sə'pɔːtəbl/ ADJ supportable, tolérable

supporter /sə'pɔːtəʳ/ N 1 (Constr, Tech) soutien m, support m ; (Her) tenant m 2 (= person) [of party] sympathisant(e) m(f) ; [of theory, cause, opinion] partisan m ◆ **she's a ~ of ...** elle soutient ..., elle est pour ... ; (Sport) supporter m ◆ **football ~s** supporters mpl de football

supporting /sə'pɔːtɪŋ/ ADJ 1 (= corroborating) [document] de confirmation ◆ **~ evidence** preuves fpl à l'appui 2 (Cine, Theat) [role, part] second before noun ◆ **~ actor** (acteur m qui a un) second rôle m ◆ **she won an Oscar for Best Supporting Actress** elle a reçu l'Oscar du meilleur second rôle féminin ◆ **the ~ cast** les seconds rôles mpl ◆ **to be in the ~ cast** avoir un second rôle 3 (Constr) [wall] de soutènement, porteur ; → **self** COMP **supporting film** N (Cine) film m qui passe en première partie

supportive /sə'pɔːtɪv/ ADJ [role] de soutien ; [relationship] d'un grand soutien or secours ◆ **she has a very ~ family** sa famille lui est d'un grand soutien ◆ **to provide a ~ environment for sb** créer autour de qn un environnement favorable ◆ **my father was very ~ of the idea** mon père soutenait tout à fait cette idée

supportively /sə'pɔːtɪvlɪ/ ADV [act, behave] de façon très positive

supportiveness /sə'pɔːtɪvnɪs/ N soutien m, aide f

suppose /sə'pəʊz/ LANGUAGE IN USE 6.2, 26.3
VT 1 (= imagine) supposer (that que + subj) ; (= assume, postulate) supposer (that que + indic) ◆ **~ he doesn't come? – he will – yes but just ~!** et s'il ne vient pas ? – il viendra – oui, mais à supposer qu'il ne vienne pas or oui, mais au cas où il ne viendrait pas ? ◆ **if we ~ that the two are identical** si nous supposons que les deux sont identiques ◆ **~ A equals B** (Math) soit A égale B ◆ **~ ABC a triangle** soit un triangle ABC
2 (= believe) croire ; (= think) penser (that que) ◆ **what do you ~ he wants?** à votre avis que peut-il bien vouloir ? ◆ **I went in, and who do you ~ was there?** je suis entré et devine qui se trouvait là ? ◆ **he is (generally) ~d to be rich, it is (generally) ~d that he is rich** il passe pour être riche, on dit qu'il est riche ◆ **I never ~d him (to be) a hero** je n'ai jamais pensé or imaginé qu'il fût un héros ◆ **I don't ~ he'll agree, I ~ he won't agree** cela m'étonnerait qu'il soit d'accord, je ne pense pas qu'il sera d'accord, je suppose qu'il ne sera pas d'accord ◆ **I ~ so** probablement, je suppose que oui ◆ **I don't ~ so, I ~ not** je ne (le) pense or crois pas, probablement pas ◆ **do you ~ we could get together for dinner some evening?** accepteriez-vous de dîner avec moi un soir ?, pensez-vous que nous pourrions dîner ensemble un soir ? ◆ **wouldn't you ~ he'd be sorry?** n'auriez-vous pas pensé qu'il le regretterait ?
◆ **to be supposed to do sth** être censé faire qch ◆ **she was ~d to telephone this morning** elle était censée or elle devait téléphoner ce matin ◆ **he isn't ~d to know** il n'est pas censé le savoir ◆ **you're not ~d to do that** il ne vous est pas permis de faire cela ◆ **what's that ~d to mean?** qu'est-ce que tu veux dire par là ?
3 (in suggestions) **~ we go for a walk?** et si nous allions nous promener ? ◆ **~ I tell him myself?** et si c'était moi qui le lui disais ?
◆ **supposing ...** (hypothesis) si + indic, à supposer que + subj, supposé que + subj ◆ **supposing he can't do it?** et s'il ne peut pas le faire ?, et à supposer or et supposé qu'il ne puisse le faire ? ◆ **even supposing that ...** à supposer même que ... + subj ◆ **always supposing that ...** en supposant que ... + subj, en admettant que ... + subj
4 (= presuppose) supposer ◆ **that ~s unlimited resources** cela suppose des ressources illimitées
VI ◆ **you'll come, I ~ ?** vous viendrez, j'imagine or je suppose ? ◆ **don't spend your time supposing, do something!** ne passe pas ton temps à faire des suppositions, fais quelque chose !

supposed /sə'pəʊzd/ ADJ 1 (= so-called) prétendu, soi-disant inv ◆ **the ~ benefits of an expensive education** les prétendus avantages d'une éducation coûteuse 2 (= presumed) supposé ; see also **suppose**

supposedly /sə'pəʊzɪdlɪ/ ADV soi-disant ◆ **he had ~ gone to France** il était soi-disant allé en France ◆ **~ safe chemicals** des produits chimiques soi-disant sans danger ◆ **did he go? – ~!** est-ce qu'il y est allé ? – soi-disant ! ◆ **~, his last words were ...** ses dernières paroles auraient été ...

supposing /sə'pəʊzɪŋ/ CONJ → **suppose vt 3**

supposition /ˌsʌpə'zɪʃən/ N supposition f, hypothèse f ◆ **that is pure ~** c'est une pure supposition ◆ **on the ~ that ...** à supposer que ... + subj, dans la supposition que ... + subj ◆ **on this ~** dans cette hypothèse

suppositional /ˌsʌpə'zɪʃənl/, **suppositious** /ˌsʌpə'zɪʃəs/ ADJ hypothétique

supposititious /səˌpɒzɪ'tɪʃəs/ ADJ supposé, faux (fausse f), apocryphe

suppository /sə'pɒzɪtərɪ/ N suppositoire m

suppress /sə'pres/ VT [+ abuse, crime] supprimer, mettre fin à ; [+ revolt] réprimer, étouffer ; [+ one's feelings] réprimer, refouler ; [+ yawn] réprimer ; [+ scandal, facts, truth] étouffer ; [+ newspaper, publication] interdire ; [+ evidence] faire disparaître, supprimer ; (Psych) refouler ; (Med) [+ symptoms] supprimer ; (Elec, Rad etc) antiparasiter ; (* = silence) [+ heckler etc] faire taire ◆ **to ~ a cough/sneeze** etc se retenir de or réprimer une envie de tousser/d'éternuer etc

suppressant /sə'presnt/ N ◆ **appetite ~** anorexigène m

suppression /sə'preʃən/ N 1 [of document, evidence, information, human rights] suppression f ; [of revolt, protest, movement] répression f ; [of democracy] étouffement m ◆ **the ~ of dissidents/minorities** la répression des dissidents/minorités 2 (Psych) [of emotion] refoulement m 3 (Med) inhibition f 4 (Elec, Rad etc) antiparasitage m

suppressive /sə'presɪv/ ADJ répressif

suppressor /səˈpresəʳ/ N *(Elec etc)* dispositif *m* antiparasite

suppurate /ˈsʌpjʊəreɪt/ VI suppurer

suppuration /ˌsʌpjʊəˈreɪʃən/ N suppuration *f*

supranational /ˌsuːprəˈnæʃənl/ ADJ supranational

suprarenal /ˌsuːprəˈriːnl/ ADJ surrénal

suprasegmental /ˌsuːprəsegˈmentl/ ADJ *(Ling)* suprasegmental

supremacist /sʊˈpreməsɪst/ N personne *f* qui croit en la suprématie d'un groupe (*or* d'une race *etc*), suprémaciste *mf*

supremacy /sʊˈpreməsɪ/ N suprématie *f* (*over* sur) → **white**

supreme /sʊˈpriːm/ ADJ *(all senses)* suprême ◆ **the Supreme Being** *(Rel)* l'Être *m* suprême ◆ **Supreme Commander** *(Mil)* commandant *m* en chef *or* suprême, généralissime *m* ◆ **Supreme Court** *(Can Jur, US Jur)* Cour *f* suprême ◆ **to make the ~ sacrifice** faire le sacrifice de sa vie ; → **reign, soviet**

supremely /sʊˈpriːmlɪ/ ADV suprêmement

supremo /sʊˈpriːməʊ/ N *(Brit)* grand chef *m*

Supt. *(Brit Police)* abbrev of **Superintendent**

sura /ˈsʊərə/ N sourate *f*

surcharge /ˈsɜːtʃɑːdʒ/ N (= *extra payment, extra load, also Elec, Post* = *overprinting*) surcharge *f* ; (= *extra tax*) surtaxe *f* ◆ **import ~** surtaxe *f* à l'importation VT surcharger, surtaxer

surd /sɜːd/ ADJ *(Math)* irrationnel ; *(Ling)* sourd N *(Math)* quantité *f or* nombre *m* irrationnel(le) ; *(Ling)* sourde *f*

sure /ʃʊəʳ/ LANGUAGE IN USE 6.2, 15.1, 16.1

ADJ 1 (= *reliable, safe etc*) *[aim, shot, marksman, judgement, method, friend, footing]* sûr ; *[solution, remedy]* sûr, infaillible ; *[facts]* sûr, indubitable ; *[success]* assuré, certain

2 (= *definite, indisputable*) sûr, certain ◆ **it is ~ that he will come, he is ~ to come** il est certain qu'il viendra, il viendra, c'est sûr ◆ **it is not ~ that he will come, he is not ~ to come** il n'est pas sûr *or* certain qu'il vienne ◆ **it's not ~ yet** ça n'a encore rien de sûr ◆ **it's ~ to rain** il va pleuvoir à coup sûr *or* c'est sûr et certain* ◆ **be ~ to tell me, be ~ and tell me** ne manquez pas de me le dire ◆ **you're ~ of a good meal** un bon repas vous est assuré ◆ **he's ~ of success** il est sûr *or* certain de réussir ◆ **you can't be ~ of him** vous ne pouvez pas être sûr de lui ◆ **I want to be ~ of seeing him** je veux être sûr *or* certain de le voir ◆ **nothing is ~ in this life** dans cette vie on n'est sûr de rien ◆ **~ thing!*** oui bien sûr !, d'accord ! ◆ **he is, to be ~, rather tactless** il manque de tact, c'est certain ◆ **well, to be ~!*** bien, ça alors !

◆ **to make sure** ◆ **to make ~ of a seat** s'assurer (d')une place ◆ **to make ~ of one's facts** vérifier *or* s'assurer de ce qu'on avance ◆ **better get a ticket beforehand and make ~** il vaut mieux prendre un billet à l'avance pour plus de sûreté *or* pour être sûr* ◆ **make ~ you've locked the door** vérifie que tu as bien fermé la porte à clé ◆ **to make ~ to do sth** ne pas oublier de faire qch ◆ **did you lock it? – I think so but I'd better make ~** l'avez-vous fermé à clé ? – je crois, mais je vais vérifier *or* m'en assurer ◆ **I've made ~ of having enough coffee for everyone** j'ai veillé à ce qu'il y ait assez de café pour tout le monde ◆ **just to make ~** pour plus de sûreté

◆ **for sure** ◆ **he'll leave for ~** il partira sans aucun doute ◆ **and that's for ~*** ça ne fait aucun doute ◆ **I'll find out for ~** je me renseignerai pour savoir exactement ce qu'il en est ◆ **do you know for ~?** êtes-vous absolument sûr *or* certain ? ◆ **I'll do it next week for ~** je le ferai la semaine prochaine sans faute

3 (= *positive, convinced*) sûr (*of* de), certain ◆ **I'm *or* I feel ~ I've seen him** je suis sûr *or* certain de l'avoir vu ◆ **I'm ~ he'll help us** je suis sûr qu'il nous aidera ◆ **I'm not ~** je ne suis pas sûr *or* certain (*that* que + *subj*) ◆ **I'm not ~ how/why/when** *etc* je ne sais pas très bien comment/pourquoi/quand *etc* ◆ **I'm not ~ (if) he can** je ne suis pas sûr *or* certain qu'il puisse ◆ **I'm ~ I didn't mean to** je ne l'ai vraiment pas fait exprès ◆ **he says he did it but I'm not so ~ (about that)** il dit que c'est lui qui l'a fait mais je n'en suis pas si sûr (que ça) ◆ **I'm going alone! – I'm not so ~ about that *or* don't be so ~ about that!** j'irai seul ! – ne le dis pas si vite ! ◆ **to be/feel ~ of o.s.** être/se sentir sûr de soi

ADV 1 *(esp US* = *certainly)* **he can ~ play** il joue vachement* bien ◆ **he was ~ drunk, he ~ was drunk** il était complètement soûl ◆ **will you do it? – ~!** le ferez-vous ? – bien sûr ! ◆ **it's hot today – it ~ is!** il fait chaud aujourd'hui – ça, c'est vrai ! ◆ **are you leaving now? – I ~ am!** tu pars maintenant ? – ouais !*

2 *(set phrases)*

◆ **sure enough** *(confirming)* effectivement, en effet ; *(promising)* assurément, sans aucun doute ◆ **~ enough, he did come** comme je l'avais (*or* on l'avait *etc*) bien prévu, il est venu ◆ **and ~ enough he did arrive** et effectivement *or* en effet il est arrivé ◆ **~ enough*, I'll be there** j'y serai sans faute ◆ **it's petrol, ~ enough** c'est effectivement *or* bien de l'essence, c'est de l'essence en effet ◆ **~ enough!** assurément ! ◆ **he ~ enough made a hash of that*** *(US)* pour sûr qu'il a tout gâché*

◆ **as sure as** aussi sûr que ◆ **as ~ as my name's Smith** aussi sûr que je m'appelle Smith ◆ **as ~ as fate, as ~ as anything, as ~ as guns*, as ~ as eggs is eggs*** aussi sûr que deux et deux font quatre

COMP **sure-enough*** ADJ *(US* = *real, actual)* réel

sure-fire* ADJ certain, infaillible

sure-footed ADJ *(lit)* au pied sûr ◆ **to be ~-footed** *(fig* = *skilful)* faire preuve de doigté

sure-footedly ADV d'un pied sûr

surely /ˈʃʊəlɪ/ ADV 1 *(expressing confidence: assuredly)* sûrement, certainement ; *(expressing incredulity)* tout de même ◆ **~ we've met before?** je suis sûr que nous nous sommes déjà rencontrés ! ◆ **~ he didn't say that!** il n'a pas pu dire ça, tout de même ! ◆ **there is ~ some mistake** il doit sûrement *or* certainement y avoir quelque erreur ◆ **~ you can do something to help?** il doit bien y avoir quelque chose que vous puissiez faire pour aider ◆ **~ you didn't believe him?** vous ne l'avez pas cru, j'espère ◆ **~ to God‡ *or* to goodness*, you know that!** mais bon sang tu devrais bien le savoir !* ◆ **it must rain soon, ~** il va bien pleuvoir, tout de même ◆ **that's ~ not true** ça ne peut pas être vrai, ça m'étonnerait que ce soit vrai ◆ **~ not!** pas possible ! ◆ **~!** *(US* = *with pleasure)* bien volontiers !

2 (= *inevitably*) sûrement, à coup sûr ◆ **justice will ~ prevail** la justice prévaudra sûrement

3 *[advance, move]* (= *safely*) sûrement ; (= *confidently*) avec assurance ; → **slowly**

sureness /ˈʃʊənɪs/ N (= *certainty*) certitude *f* ; (= *sure-footedness*) sûreté *f* ; (= *self-assurance*) assurance *f*, sûreté *f* de soi ; *[of judgement, method, footing, grip]* sûreté *f* ; *[of aim, shot]* justesse *f*, précision *f* ◆ **the ~ of his touch** sa sûreté de main

surety /ˈʃʊərətɪ/ N 1 *(Jur)* (= *money*) caution *f* ; (= *person*) caution *f*, garant(e) *m(f)* ◆ **to go *or* stand ~ for sb** se porter caution *or* garant pour qn ◆ **in his own ~ of £1,000** après avoir donné une sûreté personnelle de 1 000 livres 2 †† certitude *f* ◆ **of a ~** certainement

surf /sɜːf/ N *(NonC)* (= *waves*) vagues *fpl* déferlantes, ressac *m* ; (= *foam*) écume *f* ; (= *spray*) embrun *m* VI (*also* **go surfing**) surfer, faire du surf VT *[+ waves]* surfer sur ◆ **to ~ the Net*** surfer sur Internet, surfer sur le net COMP **surf boat** N surf-boat *m*

surface /ˈsɜːfɪs/ N 1 *[of earth, sea, liquid, object etc]* surface *f* ◆ **under the ~** *[of sea, lake etc]* sous l'eau ◆ **to come *or* rise to the ~** remonter à la surface ; *(fig)* faire surface, se faire jour ◆ **to break ~** *[submarine]* faire surface ; *[diver]* réapparaître ◆ **on the ~** *(Naut)* en surface ; *(Min: also* **at the surface***)* au jour, à la surface ; *(fig)* à première vue, au premier abord ◆ **on the ~ of the table** sur la surface de la table ◆ **his faults are all on the ~** il a des défauts mais il a bon fond ◆ **I can't get below the ~ with him** je n'arrive pas à le connaître vraiment *or* à aller au-delà des apparences avec lui ◆ **prejudices just below *or* beneath the ~** préjugés prêts à faire surface *or* à se faire jour ◆ **the road ~ is icy** la chaussée est verglacée ◆ **social unrest, never far below the ~ …** les troubles sociaux, toujours prêts à éclater …

2 *(Math)* (= *area*) surface *f* ; (= *side: of solid*) côté *m*, face *f*

ADJ 1 *[tension]* superficiel *(also fig)* *(Naut)* *[vessel etc]* de surface ; *(Min)* *[work]* au jour, à la surface ◆ **it's only a ~ reaction** ce n'est qu'une réaction superficielle

2 *(Phon, Gram)* de surface

VT 1 *[+ road]* revêtir (*with* de) ; *[+ paper]* calandrer, glacer

2 *(Naut)* *[+ submarine, object, wreck]* amener à la surface

VI *[swimmer, diver, whale]* revenir *or* remonter à la surface ; *[submarine]* faire surface ; *(fig* = *emerge)* *[news, feeling etc]* faire surface, se faire jour ; (* *fig*) *(after absence)* réapparaître ; *(after hard work)* faire surface

COMP **surface area** N *(Math etc)* surface *f*, superficie *f*

surface grammar N grammaire *f* de surface

surface mail N *(Post)* courrier *m* par voie de terre ; *(by sea)* courrier *m* maritime ◆ **by ~ mail** par voie de terre ; *(by sea)* par voie maritime

surface noise N *(on record player)* grésillements *mpl*

surface structure N structure *f* de surface

surface-to-air ADJ *(Mil)* sol-air *inv*

surface-to-surface ADJ *(Mil)* sol-sol *inv*

surface water N eaux *fpl* de surface

surface workers NPL *(Min)* personnel *m* qui travaille au jour *or* à la surface

surfboard /ˈsɜːfbɔːd/ N planche *f* de surf VI surfer

surfboarder /ˈsɜːfˌbɔːdəʳ/ N ⇒ **surfer**

surfboarding /ˈsɜːfˌbɔːdɪŋ/ N ⇒ **surfing**

surfcasting /ˈsɜːfˌkɑːstɪŋ/ N *(US Sport)* pêche *f* au lancer en mer *(depuis le rivage)*

surfeit /ˈsɜːfɪt/ N excès *m* (*of* de) ; *(NonC* = *satiety)* satiété *f* ◆ **to have a ~ of …** avoir une indigestion de … *(fig)* ◆ **there is a ~ of …** il y a par trop de … VT ◆ **to be ~ed with pleasure** être repu de plaisir

surfer /ˈsɜːfəʳ/ N surfeur *m*, -euse *f* ; (*: *on Internet*) internaute *mf*

surfing /ˈsɜːfɪŋ/ N surf *m* ; → **surf vi**

surfride /ˈsɜːfraɪd/ VI surfer

surfrider /ˈsɜːfˌraɪdəʳ/ N ⇒ **surfer**

surfriding /ˈsɜːfˌraɪdɪŋ/ N ⇒ **surfing**

surge /sɜːdʒ/ N *(gen)* mouvement *m* puissant ; *[of rage, fear, enthusiasm]* vague *f*, montée *f* ; *(Elec)* saute *f* de courant ; *(fig: in sales etc)* afflux *m* ◆ **the ~ of the sea** la houle ◆ **he felt a ~ of anger** il a senti la colère monter en lui ◆ **there was a ~ of sympathy for him** il y a eu un vif mouvement *or* une vague de sympathie pour lui ◆ **the ~ of people around the car** la foule qui se pressait autour de la voiture ◆ **he was carried along by the ~ of the crowd** il était porté par le mouvement de la foule

VI 1 *[waves]* s'enfler ; *[flood, river]* déferler ◆ **the sea ~d against the rocks** la houle battait *or* heurtait les rochers ◆ **the surging sea** la mer houleuse ◆ **the ship ~d at anchor** le bateau amarré était soulevé par la houle ◆ **the power ~d suddenly** *(Elec)* il y a eu une brusque surtension de courant ◆ **the blood ~d to his cheeks** le sang lui est monté *or* lui a reflué au visage ◆ **anger ~d (up) within him** la colère monta en lui

2 *[crowd, vehicles etc]* déferler ◆ **to ~ in/out** *etc* entrer/sortir *etc* à flots ◆ **they ~d round the car** ils se pressaient autour de la voiture ◆ **they ~d forward** ils se sont lancés en avant ◆ **a surging mass of demonstrators** une foule déferlante de manifestants

surgeon /ˈsɜːdʒən/ **N** chirurgien *m* ◆ **she is a ~** elle est chirurgien ◆ **a woman ~** une femme chirurgien ; → **dental, house, veterinary COMP**

surgeon general N (pl **surgeons general**) *(Mil)* médecin *m* général ; *(US Admin)* ministre *m* de la Santé

surgery /ˈsɜːdʒərɪ/ **N** 1 *(NonC = skill, study, operation)* chirurgie *f* ◆ **it is a fine piece of ~** le chirurgien a fait du beau travail ◆ **to have ~** se faire opérer ; → **plastic** 2 *(Brit = consulting room)* cabinet *m* (de consultation) ; *(Brit = interview)* consultation *f* ◆ **come to the ~ tomorrow** venez à mon cabinet demain, venez à la consultation demain ◆ **when is his ~?** à quelle heure sont ses consultations ?, à quelle heure consulte-t-il ? ◆ **during his ~** pendant ses heures de consultation ◆ **there is an afternoon ~** il consulte l'après-midi **COMP surgery hours NPL** heures *fpl* de consultation

surgical /ˈsɜːdʒɪkəl/ **ADJ** *[operation, intervention, treatment]* chirurgical ; *[instruments]* chirurgical, de chirurgie

COMP surgical appliance N appareil *m* orthopédique

surgical cotton N coton *m* hydrophile

surgical dressing N pansement *m*

surgical shock N choc *m* opératoire

surgical spirit N *(Brit)* alcool *m* à 90 (degrés)

surgical strike N *(Mil)* frappe *f* chirurgicale

surgically /ˈsɜːdʒɪkəlɪ/ **ADV** chirurgicalement

Surinam /ˌsʊərɪˈnæm/ **N** Surinam *m* ◆ **in ~** au Surinam

Surinamese /ˌsʊərɪnæˈmiːz/ **ADJ** surinamais **N** Surinamais(e) *m(f)*

surliness /ˈsɜːlɪnɪs/ **N** caractère *m* revêche *or* maussade

surly /ˈsɜːlɪ/ **ADJ** revêche, maussade

surmise /ˈsɜːmaɪz/ **N** conjecture *f*, hypothèse *f* ◆ **it was nothing but ~** c'était entièrement conjectural **VT** /sɜːˈmaɪz/ conjecturer, présumer *(from sth* d'après qch) ◆ **to ~ that ...** *(= infer)* conjecturer que ..., présumer que ... ; *(= suggest)* émettre l'hypothèse que ... ◆ **I ~d as much** je m'en doutais

surmount /sɜːˈmaʊnt/ **VT** 1 *(Archit etc)* surmonter ◆ **~ed by a statue** surmonté d'une statue 2 *(= overcome)* *[+ obstacle, difficulties, problems]* surmonter, venir à bout de

surmountable /sɜːˈmaʊntəbl/ **ADJ** surmontable

surname /ˈsɜːneɪm/ **N** nom *m* de famille ◆ **name and ~** nom et prénoms **VT** ◆ **~d Jones** nommé *or* dénommé Jones, dont le nom de famille est Jones

surpass /sɜːˈpɑːs/ **LANGUAGE IN USE 5.2 VT** *[+ person]* surpasser *(in* en) ; *[+ hopes, expectations]* dépasser ◆ **to ~ o.s.** *(also iro)* se surpasser *(also iro)*

surpassing /sɜːˈpɑːsɪŋ/ **ADJ** incomparable, sans pareil

surplice /ˈsɜːpləs/ **N** surplis *m*

surpliced /ˈsɜːplɪst/ **ADJ** en surplis

surplus /ˈsɜːpləs/ **N** (pl **surpluses**) *(Comm, Econ, gen)* surplus *m*, excédent *m* ; *(Fin)* boni *m*, excédent *m* ◆ **a tea ~** un surplus *or* un excédent de thé **ADJ** *(gen)* *[food, boxes etc]* en surplus ; *(Comm, Econ)* en surplus, excédentaire ; *(Fin)* de boni, excédentaire ◆ **it is ~ to (our) requirements** cela excède nos besoins ◆ **~ copies** *[of book, document etc]* exemplaires *mpl* de passe ◆ **~ stock** surplus *mpl*, stocks *mpl* excédentaires ◆ **American ~ wheat** excédent *m or* surplus *m* de blé américain ◆ **his ~ energy** son surcroît d'énergie **COMP surplus store N** magasin *m* de surplus

surprise /səˈpraɪz/ **LANGUAGE IN USE 16.2**

N *(NonC) (= emotion)* surprise *f*, étonnement *m* ; *(= event etc)* surprise *f* ◆ **much to my ~, to my great ~** à ma grande surprise, à mon grand étonnement ◆ **he stopped in ~** il s'est arrêté sous l'effet de la surprise, étonné il s'est arrêté ◆ **to take by ~** *[+ person]* surprendre, prendre au dépourvu ; *(Mil)* *[+ fort, town]* prendre par surprise ◆ **a look of ~** un regard surpris *or* traduisant la surprise ◆ **imagine my ~ when ...** imaginez quel a été mon étonnement *or* quelle a été ma surprise quand ... ◆ **what a ~!** quelle surprise ! ◆ **~, ~!** *(when surprising sb)* surprise ! ; *(iro)* comme par hasard *(iro)* ◆ **to give sb a ~** faire une surprise à qn, surprendre qn ◆ **it was a lovely/nasty ~ for him** cela a été pour lui une agréable/mauvaise surprise ◆ **to have a ~** être surpris, avoir une surprise ◆ **it came as a ~ (to me) to learn that ...** j'ai eu la surprise d'apprendre que ...

ADJ *[defeat, gift, visit, decision]* inattendu, inopiné ◆ **~ attack** attaque *f* par surprise, attaque *f* brusquée

VT 1 *(= astonish)* surprendre, étonner ◆ **he was ~d to hear that ...** il a été surpris *or* étonné d'apprendre que ..., cela l'a surpris *or* étonné d'apprendre que ... ◆ **I shouldn't be ~d if it snowed** cela ne m'étonnerait pas qu'il neige *subj* ◆ **don't be ~d if he refuses** ne soyez pas étonné *or* surpris s'il refuse, ne vous étonnez pas s'il refuse ◆ **it's nothing to be ~d at** cela n'a rien d'étonnant, ce n'est pas *or* guère étonnant ◆ **I'm ~d at** *or* **by his ignorance** son ignorance me surprend ◆ **I'm ~d at you!** je ne m'attendais pas à cela de vous !, cela me surprend de votre part ! ◆ **it ~d me that he agreed** j'ai été étonné *or* surpris qu'il accepte *subj*, je ne m'attendais pas à ce qu'il accepte *subj* ◆ **go on, ~ me!** *(iro)* allez, étonne-moi ! ◆ **he ~d me into agreeing to do it** j'ai été tellement surpris que j'ai accepté de le faire ; see also **surprised**

2 *(= catch unawares)* *[+ army, sentry]* surprendre, attaquer par surprise ; *[+ thief]* surprendre, prendre sur le fait ; *(gen)* surprendre

surprised /səˈpraɪzd/ **ADJ** surpris, étonné ◆ **you'd be ~ how many people ...** si tu savais combien de gens ... ◆ **he'll surely be on time – you'd be ~!** il sera sûrement à l'heure – n'y compte pas ! ; see also **surprise**

surprising /səˈpraɪzɪŋ/ **LANGUAGE IN USE 16.2 ADJ** surprenant, étonnant ◆ **it is ~ that ...** il est surprenant *or* étonnant que ... + *subj*

surprisingly /səˈpraɪzɪŋlɪ/ **ADV** *[big, sad etc]* étonnamment, étrangement ◆ **you look ~ cheerful for someone who ...** vous m'avez l'air de bien bonne humeur pour quelqu'un qui ... ◆ **~ enough, ...** chose étonnante, ... ◆ **not ~ he didn't come** comme on pouvait s'y attendre il n'est pas venu, il n'est pas venu, ce qui n'a rien d'étonnant

surreal /səˈrɪəl/ **ADJ** surréaliste *(fig)*

surrealism /səˈrɪəlɪzəm/ **N** surréalisme *m*

surrealist /səˈrɪəlɪst/ **ADJ, N** surréaliste *mf*

surrealistic /səˌrɪəˈlɪstɪk/ **ADJ** surréaliste

surrender /səˈrendəʳ/ **VI** *(Mil)* se rendre *(to* à), capituler *(to* devant) ◆ **to ~ to the police** se livrer à la police, se constituer prisonnier ◆ **to ~ to despair** s'abandonner *or* se livrer au désespoir

VT 1 *(Mil)* *[+ town, hill]* livrer *(to* à)

2 *[+ firearms]* rendre *(to* à) ; *[+ stolen property, documents, photos]* remettre *(to* à) ; *[+ insurance policy]* racheter ; *[+ lease]* céder ; *[+ one's rights, claims, powers, liberty]* renoncer à, abdiquer ; *[+ hopes]* abandonner ◆ **to ~ o.s. to despair/to the delights of sth** s'abandonner *or* se livrer au désespoir/aux plaisirs de qch

N 1 *(Mil etc)* reddition *f* *(to* à), capitulation *f* *(to* devant) ◆ **no ~!** on ne se rend pas ! ; → **unconditional**

2 *(= giving up)* *[of firearms, stolen property, documents]* remise *f* *(to* à) ; *[of insurance policy]* rachat *m* ; *[of one's rights, claims, powers, liberty]* renonciation *f* *(of* à), abdication *f* *(of* de ; *to* en faveur de) ; *[of hopes]* abandon *m* ; *[of lease]* cession *f* ; *(= return)* restitution *f* *(of* de ; *to* à)

COMP surrender value N *(Insurance)* valeur *f* de rachat

surreptitious /ˌsʌrəpˈtɪʃəs/ **ADJ** *[entry, removal]* subreptice, clandestin ; *[movement, gesture]* furtif

surreptitiously /ˌsʌrəpˈtɪʃəslɪ/ **ADV** *[enter, remove]* subrepticement, clandestinement ; *[move]* furtivement, sournoisement *(pej)*

surrogacy /ˈsʌrəgəsɪ/ **N** *(in childbearing)* maternité *f* de substitution

surrogate /ˈsʌrəgɪt/ **N** 1 *(gen: frm)* substitut *m*, représentant *m* 2 *(Psych)* substitut *m* 3 *(Brit: also* **surrogate bishop**) *évêque auxiliaire à qui l'on délègue le pouvoir d'autoriser les mariages sans publication de bans* 4 *(US = judge)* *juge chargé de l'homologation de testaments etc* **ADJ** *[pleasure etc]* de remplacement **VI** /ˈsʌrəgeɪt/ *(be a surrogate mother)* être mère porteuse *or* mère de substitution **COMP surrogate mother N** *(Genetics)* mère *f* porteuse, mère *f* de substitution ; *(Psych)* substitut *m* maternel

surrogate motherhood N maternité *f* de substitution

surround /səˈraʊnd/ **VT** entourer ; *(totally)* cerner, encercler ◆ **~ed by** entouré de ◆ **you are ~ed** *(Mil, Police etc)* vous êtes cerné *or* encerclé ◆ **to ~ o.s. with friends/allies** s'entourer d'amis/d'alliés **N** bordure *f*, encadrement *m* ; *[of fireplace]* entourage *m* ; *(Brit: on floor: also* **surrounds**) bordure *f* *(entre le tapis et le mur)* **NPL surrounds** *(frm = surroundings)* cadre *m* **COMP surround sound N** *(Cine)* son *m* surround

surrounding /səˈraʊndɪŋ/ **ADJ** *[streets, countryside, villages]* alentour *inv*, environnant ◆ **Liège and the ~ area** Liège et ses alentours *or* environs ◆ **the ~ tissue is healthy** *(Med)* les tissus autour sont sains **NPL surroundings** *(= surrounding country)* alentours *mpl*, environs *mpl* ; *(= setting)* cadre *m*, décor *m* ◆ **the ~s of Glasgow are picturesque** les alentours *or* les environs de Glasgow sont pittoresques ◆ **he found himself in ~s strange to him** il s'est retrouvé dans un cadre *or* décor qu'il ne connaissait pas ◆ **animals in their natural ~s** des animaux dans leur cadre naturel

surtax /ˈsɜːtæks/ **N** *(gen)* surtaxe *f* ; *(= income tax)* tranche *f* supérieure de l'impôt sur le revenu ◆ **to pay ~** être dans les tranches supérieures d'imposition

surtitles /ˈsɜːˌtaɪtlz/ **NPL** surtitres *mpl*

surveillance /sɜːˈveɪləns/ **N** surveillance *f* ◆ **to keep sb under ~** surveiller qn ◆ **under constant ~** sous surveillance continue

survey /ˈsɜːveɪ/ **N** 1 *(= comprehensive view)* *[of countryside, prospects, development etc]* vue *f* générale *or* d'ensemble *(of* de) ◆ **he gave a general ~ of the situation** il a fait un tour d'horizon de la situation, il a passé la situation en revue

2 *(= investigation, study)* *[of reasons, prices, situation, sales, trends]* enquête *f* *(of* sur), étude *f* *(of* de) ◆ **to carry out** *or* **make a ~ of** enquêter sur,

faire une étude de ◆ ~ **of public opinion** sondage *m* d'opinion

3 *(in land surveying)* levé *m* ; → **aerial, ordnance**

4 *(Brit: in housebuying)* *(= act)* expertise *f* ; *(= report)* (rapport *m* d')expertise *f*

VT /sɜː'veɪ/ 1 *(via questionnaire)* *[+ people]* interroger ; *[+ attitudes, opinions]* faire une enquête sur ◆ **about half the people ~ed ...** la moitié environ des personnes interrogées ... ◆ **211 companies were ~ed for the report** l'enquête a porté sur 211 entreprises

2 *(= consider)* passer en revue ◆ **he ~ed the thirty years of his rule** il a passé en revue ses trente ans au pouvoir ◆ **the Prime Minister ~ed the situation** le Premier ministre a fait un tour d'horizon de *or* a passé en revue la situation ◆ **the book ~s the history of the motorcar** le livre passe en revue *or* étudie dans les grandes lignes l'histoire de l'automobile

3 *(= look around at)* *[+ countryside, view, crowd]* embrasser du regard ◆ **he ~ed the scene with amusement** il regardait la scène d'un œil amusé

4 *(Surv)* *[+ site, land]* faire le levé de ; *(Brit)* *[+ house, building]* inspecter, examiner ; *[+ country, coast]* faire le levé topographique de ; *[+ seas]* faire le levé hydrographique de

COMP **survey course** N *(US Univ)* cours *m* d'initiation

survey ship N navire *m* de recherche hydrographique

surveying /sɜː'veɪɪŋ/ N 1 *(NonC = action)* *[of site, land]* levé *m* ; *[of house]* expertise *f* ; *[of country, coast]* levé *m* topographique ; *[of seas]* levé *m* hydrographique 2 *(= science, occupation)* *[of site, land]* arpentage *m* ; *[of house]* expertise *f* ; *[of country, coast]* topographie *f* ; *[of seas]* topographie *f* marine, hydrographie *f* COMP *[instrument]* d'arpentage ; *[studies]* de topographie

surveyor /sə'veɪəʳ/ N *(Brit)* *[of property, buildings etc]* expert *m* ; *[of land, site]* (arpenteur *m*) géomètre *m* ; *[of country, coastline]* topographe *mf* ; *[of seas]* hydrographe *mf* ; → **quantity**

survival /sə'vaɪvəl/ N *(= act)* survie *f* *(also Jur, Rel)* ; *(= relic)* *[of custom, beliefs etc]* survivance *f*, vestige *m* ◆ **the ~ of the fittest** *(lit: in evolution)* la lutte pour la vie ; *(fig)* la loi du plus fort

COMP **survival bag** N ≈ couverture *f* de survie

survival course N cours *m* de survie

survival kit N trousse *f* de survie

survivalist /sə'vaɪvəlɪst/ N *écologiste extrême vivant en autarcie pour pouvoir survivre à une éventuelle catastrophe planétaire*

survive /sə'vaɪv/ VI *[person]* survivre *(on* avec*)* ; *[house, jewellery, book, custom]* survivre, subsister ◆ **he ~d to tell the tale** il a survécu et a pu raconter ce qui s'était passé ◆ **to ~ to fight another day** s'en sortir sans trop de dommages ◆ **only three volumes ~** il ne reste *or* il ne subsiste plus que trois tomes ◆ **you'll ~!** *(iro)* vous n'en mourrez pas ! ◆ **they don't eat/earn enough to ~ on** il ne mangent/gagnent pas assez pour survivre VT *[+ person]* survivre à ; *[+ injury, disease]* réchapper de ; *[+ fire, accident, experience, invasion]* survivre à, réchapper de ◆ **he is ~d by a wife and two sons** sa femme et deux fils lui survivent

surviving /sə'vaɪvɪŋ/ ADJ *[spouse, children]* survivant ◆ ~ **company** *(Fin after merger)* société *f* absorbante

survivor /sə'vaɪvəʳ/ N survivant(e) *m(f)* ; *[of accident]* survivant(e) *m(f)*, rescapé(e) *m(f)* ; *(fig)* *[of regime, earlier time]* rescapé(e) *m(f)* ; *[of abuse]* ancienne victime *f* ◆ **he's a real ~!** il surmonte toutes les crises !

sus* /sʌs/ *(Brit)* N (abbrev of **suspicion**) ◆ ~ **law** loi *f* autorisant à interpeller des suspects à discrétion VT ⇒ **suss**

susceptibility /sə,septə'bɪlɪtɪ/ N *(= sensitiveness)* émotivité *f*, sensibilité *f* ; *(= touchiness)* susceptibilité *f* ; *(Med)* prédisposition *f* *(to* à*)* ◆ **his ~ to hypnosis** la facilité avec laquelle on l'hypnotise ◆ **his susceptibilities** ses cordes *fpl* sensibles

susceptible /sə'septəbl/ ADJ 1 *(Med, Bot: to disease)* prédisposé *(to* à*)* ; *(= impressionable)* émotif ; *(= able to be affected)* ◆ ~ **to sb's influence** sensible à l'influence de qn ◆ ~ **to flattery/to (the) cold** sensible à la flatterie/au froid ◆ ~ **to advertising** influençable par la publicité 2 *(frm = capable)* ◆ ~ **of** *or* **to change/measurement/resolution** susceptible d'être modifié/mesuré/résolu

sushi /'suːʃɪ/ N *(NonC)* sushi *m*

COMP **sushi bar** N petit restaurant *m* de sushi

sushi restaurant N restaurant *m* de sushi

suspect /'sʌspekt/ N suspect(e) *m(f)* ◆ **the usual ~s** *(fig)* les suspects *mpl* habituels ADJ suspect VT /səs'pekt/ 1 soupçonner *(that* que*)* ; *[+ person]* soupçonner, suspecter *(pej)* *(of doing sth* de faire *or* d'avoir fait qch*)* ; *[+ ambush, swindle]* flairer, soupçonner ◆ **I ~ him of being the author** *[of book etc]* je le soupçonne d'en être l'auteur ; *[of anonymous letter]* je le soupçonne *or* je le suspecte d'en être l'auteur ◆ **he ~s nothing** il ne se doute de rien 2 *(= think likely)* soupçonner, avoir dans l'idée, avoir le sentiment *(that* que*)* ◆ **I ~ he knows who did it** je soupçonne *or* j'ai dans l'idée qu'il connaît le coupable ◆ **I ~ed as much** je m'en doutais ◆ **he'll come, I ~** il viendra, j'imagine 3 *(= have doubts about)* douter de ◆ **I ~ the truth of what he says** je doute de la vérité de ce qu'il dit

suspend /səs'pend/ VT 1 *(= hang)* suspendre *(from* à*)* ◆ **to be ~ed in sth** *[particles etc]* être en suspension dans qch ◆ **a column of smoke hung ~ed in the still air** une colonne de fumée flottait dans l'air immobile

2 *(= stop temporarily, defer etc)* *[+ publication]* suspendre, surseoir ; *[+ decision, payment, regulation, meetings, discussions]* suspendre ; *[+ licence, permission]* retirer provisoirement ; *[+ bus service]* interrompre provisoirement ◆ **to ~ judgement** suspendre son jugement

3 *[+ employee, office holder, officer etc]* suspendre *(from* de*)* ; *(Scol, Univ)* exclure temporairement

COMP **suspended animation** N *(fig hum)* ◆ **to be in a state of ~ed animation** ne donner aucun signe de vie

suspended sentence N *(Jur)* condamnation *f* avec sursis ◆ **he received a ~ed sentence of six months in jail** il a été condamné à six mois de prison avec sursis

suspender /səs'pendəʳ/ N *(Brit)* *(for stockings)* jarretelle *f* ; *(for socks)* fixe-chaussette *m* NPL **suspenders** *(US = braces)* bretelles *fpl* COMP **suspender belt** N *(Brit)* porte-jarretelles *m inv*

suspense /səs'pens/ N *(NonC)* 1 incertitude *f*, attente *f* ; *(in book, film, play)* suspense *m* ◆ **we waited in great ~** nous avons attendu haletants ◆ **to keep sb in ~** tenir qn en suspens, laisser qn dans l'incertitude ; *[film]* tenir qn en suspens *or* en haleine ◆ **to put sb out of (his) ~** mettre fin à l'incertitude *or* à l'attente de qn ◆ **the ~ is killing me!*** ce suspense me tue ! *(also iro)* 2 *(Admin, Jur)* **to be** *or* **remain in ~** être (laissé) *or* rester en suspens COMP **suspense account** N *(Accounting)* compte *m* d'ordre

suspenseful /səs'pensfʊl/ ADJ plein de suspense

suspension /səs'penʃən/ N 1 *(NonC)* *(= interruption)* *[of decision, payment, constitution, talks]* suspension *f* ; *[of licence, permission]* retrait *m* provisoire ; *[of programme, service]* interruption *f* provisoire ; *[of democracy]* abandon *m* provisoire ◆ ~ **of disbelief** *(Literat)* acceptation *f* des invraisemblances 2 *(= debarment)* *[of employee, official, player]* suspension *f* ; *[of pupil, student]* renvoi *m* or exclusion *f* temporaire 3 *(Jur)* *[of sentence]* sursis *m* 4 *[of vehicle]* suspension *f* 5 *(Chem, Phys)* suspension *f* *(of* de*)* ◆ **in ~** en suspension

COMP **suspension bridge** N pont *m* suspendu

suspension file N dossier *m* suspendu *(dans un tiroir)*

suspension points NPL *(Typ)* points *mpl* de suspension

suspensory /səs'pensərɪ/ ADJ *[ligament]* suspenseur *m only* ; *[bandage]* de soutien

suspicion /səs'pɪʃən/ N 1 soupçon *m* ; *(NonC)* soupçon(s) *m(pl)* ◆ **an atmosphere laden with ~** une atmosphère chargée de soupçons ◆ **above** *or* **beyond ~** au-dessus *or* à l'abri de tout soupçon ◆ **under ~** considéré comme suspect ◆ **he was regarded with ~** on s'est montré soupçonneux à son égard ◆ **to arrest sb on ~** *(Jur)* arrêter qn sur des présomptions ◆ **on ~ of murder** sur présomption de meurtre ◆ **I had a ~ that he wouldn't come back** quelque chose me disait *or* j'avais le sentiment qu'il ne reviendrait pas ◆ **I had no ~ that ...** je ne me doutais pas du tout que ... ◆ **I had (my) ~s about that letter** j'avais mes doutes quant à cette lettre ◆ **I have my ~s about it** j'ai des doutes là-dessus, cela me semble suspect ◆ **he was right in his ~ that ...** il avait raison de soupçonner que ..., c'est à juste titre qu'il soupçonnait que ...

2 *(fig = trace, touch)* soupçon *m*

suspicious /səs'pɪʃəs/ ADJ 1 *(= distrustful)* *[person, attitude, look]* méfiant, soupçonneux ◆ **you've got a ~ mind!** tu es très méfiant *or* soupçonneux ! ◆ **~ minds might think that ...** des esprits soupçonneux pourraient croire que ... ◆ **to be ~ of sb/sth** se méfier de qn/qch ◆ **to be ~ about sb/sth** avoir des soupçons sur qn/qch ◆ **to be ~ that ...** soupçonner que ... ◆ **to become** *or* **grow ~** commencer à se méfier 2 *(= causing suspicion:* also **suspicious-looking***)* *[person, object, action, death]* suspect ◆ **in ~ circumstances** dans des circonstances suspectes

suspiciously /səs'pɪʃəslɪ/ ADV 1 *(= with suspicion)* *[examine, glance, ask]* avec méfiance 2 *(= causing suspicion)* *[behave, act]* de manière suspecte ◆ ~ **similar** d'une ressemblance suspecte ◆ ~ **high/low prices** des prix étrangement élevés/bas ◆ **it looks ~ like measles** ça a tout l'air d'être la rougeole ◆ **it sounds ~ as though he ...** il y a tout lieu de soupçonner qu'il ... ◆ **he arrived ~ early** c'est louche qu'il soit arrivé si tôt

suspiciousness /səs'pɪʃəsnɪs/ N *(NonC)* 1 *(feeling suspicion)* caractère *m* soupçonneux *or* méfiant 2 *(causing suspicion)* caractère *m* suspect

suss* /sʌs/ VT *(Brit)* ◆ **to ~ (out)** *[+ situation, plan]* piger‡ ◆ **I can't ~ him out** je n'arrive pas à le cerner ◆ **he'll ~ you (out) straight away** il va tout de suite comprendre ton jeu ◆ **I've ~ed it out, I've got it ~ed** j'ai pigé‡

sussed* /sʌst/ ADJ *(Brit)* *[person]* branché*

sustain /səs'teɪn/ VT 1 *[+ weight, beam etc]* supporter ; *[+ body]* nourrir, sustenter † ; *[+ life]* maintenir ; *(Mus)* *[+ note]* tenir, soutenir ; *[+ effort, role]* soutenir ; *[+ pretence]* poursuivre, prolonger ; *[+ assertion, theory]* soutenir, maintenir ; *[+ charge]* donner des preuves à l'appui de ◆ **that food won't ~ you for long** ce n'est pas cette nourriture qui va vous donner beaucoup de forces ◆ **objection ~ed** *(Jur)* ≈ (objection *f*) accordée ◆ **the court ~ed his claim** *or* **~ed him in his claim** *(Jur)* le tribunal a fait droit à sa revendication ; see also **sustained** 2 *(= suffer)* *[+ attack]* subir ; *[+ loss]* éprouver, essuyer ; *[+ damage]* subir, souffrir ; *[+ injury]* recevoir ◆ **he ~ed concussion** il a été commotionné

sustainability /sə,steɪnə'bɪlɪtɪ/ N *[of resources, energy source etc]* durabilité *f*, pérennité *f* ; *[of policy, economy etc]* poursuite *f* dans le temps

sustainable /səs'teɪnəbəl/ ADJ 1 *(Econ)* *[rate, growth]* viable ; *[energy, source, forest, develop-*

ment] durable ; *[resource]* renouvelable 2 *[argument]* tenable

sustainably /səs'teɪnəblɪ/ ADV ◆ ~ **managed** géré durablement

sustained /səs'teɪnd/ ADJ *[campaign, pressure, wind]* soutenu ; *[effort, attack, applause]* prolongé ◆ ~ **growth** *(Econ)* expansion *f* soutenue ◆ **a ~ recovery** *(Econ)* une reprise soutenue

sustaining /səs'teɪnɪŋ/ ADJ *[food]* consistant, substantiel

COMP **sustaining pedal** N *(Mus)* pédale *f* forte
sustaining program N *(US Rad, TV)* émission *f* non sponsorisée

sustenance /'sʌstɪnəns/ N *(NonC)* 1 *(= nourishing quality)* valeur *f* nutritive ; *(= food and drink)* alimentation *f*, nourriture *f* ◆ **there's not much ~ in melon** le melon n'est pas très nourrissant *or* nutritif, le melon n'a pas beaucoup de valeur nutritive ◆ **they depend for ~ on ..., they get their ~ from ...** ils se nourrissent de ... ◆ **roots and berries were** *or* **provided their only ~** les racines et les baies étaient leur seule nourriture, pour toute nourriture ils avaient des racines et des baies 2 *(= means of livelihood)* moyens *mpl* de subsistance

suttee /sʌ'tiː/ N *(= widow)* (veuve *f*) sati *f inv* ; *(= rite)* sati *m*

suture /'suːtʃəʳ/ N suture *f*

SUV /ˌesjuː'viː/ N *(esp US) (Aut)* (abbrev of **sport utility vehicle**) SUV *m*

suzerain /'suːzəˌreɪn/ N suzerain(e) *m(f)*

suzerainty /'suːzərəntɪ/ N suzeraineté *f*

svelte /svelt/ ADJ svelte

Svengali /sven'gɑːlɪ/ N *homme aux pouvoirs malfaisants*

SVGA /ˌesviːdʒiː'eɪ/ N *(Comput)* (abbrev of **super video graphics array**) super-VGA *m*

SVQ /ˌesviː'kjuː/ N (abbrev of **Scottish Vocational Qualification**) *qualification professionnelle* ; → NVQ

SW 1 *(Rad)* (abbrev of **short wave**) OC *fpl* 2 (abbrev of **south-west**) S.-O.

swab /swɒb/ N *(= mop, cloth)* serpillière *f* ; *(Naut)* faubert *m* ; *(for gun-cleaning)* écouvillon *m* ; *(Med = cotton wool etc)* tampon *m* ; *(Med = specimen)* prélèvement *m* ◆ **to take a ~ of sb's throat** *(Med)* faire un prélèvement dans la gorge de qn VT 1 (also **swab down**) *[+ floor etc]* nettoyer, essuyer ; *(Naut) [+ deck]* passer le faubert sur 2 (also **swab out**) *[+ gun]* écouvillonner ; *(Med) [+ wound]* tamponner, essuyer *or* nettoyer avec un tampon

swaddle /'swɒdl/ VT *(in bandages)* emmailloter *(in* de) ; *(in blankets etc)* emmitoufler* *(in* dans) ; *[+ baby]* emmailloter, langer COMP **swaddling bands, swaddling clothes** NPL *(liter)* maillot *m*, lange *m*

swag /swæg/ N 1 *(* = loot)* butin *m* 2 *(Austral)* bal(l)uchon* *m*

swagger /'swægəʳ/ N air *m* fanfaron ; *(= gait)* démarche *f* assurée ◆ **to walk with a ~** marcher en plastronnant *or* d'un air important VI 1 (also **swagger about, swagger along**) plastronner, parader ◆ **to ~ in/out** *etc* entrer/sortir *etc* d'un air fanfaron *or* en plastronnant 2 *(= boast)* se vanter *(about* de)

COMP **swagger coat** N manteau *m* trois quarts
swagger stick N *(Mil)* badine *f*, jonc *m*

swaggering /'swægərɪŋ/ ADJ *[gait]* assuré ; *[person, look, gesture]* fanfaron N *(= strutting)* airs *mpl* importants ; *(= boasting)* fanfaronnades *fpl*

swagman* /'swægmæn/ N (pl **-men**) *(Austral)* ouvrier *m* agricole itinérant

Swahili /swɑː'hiːlɪ/ ADJ swahili, souahéli N (pl **Swahili** *or* **Swahilis**) *(= language)* swahili *m*, souahéli *m* NPL *(= people)* Swahilis *mpl*, Souahélis *mpl*

swain /sweɪn/ N *(†† or liter)* amant † *m*, soupirant † *m*

SWALK /swɔːlk/ (abbrev of **sealed with a loving kiss**) doux baisers *(message au dos d'une enveloppe)*

swallow¹ /'swɒləʊ/ N *(= bird)* hirondelle *f* ◆ **one ~ doesn't make a summer** *(Prov)* une hirondelle ne fait pas le printemps *(Prov)*

COMP **swallow dive** N *(Brit)* saut *m* de l'ange
swallow-tailed coat N (habit *m* à) queue *f* de pie

swallow² /'swɒləʊ/ N *(= act)* avalement *m* ; *(= amount)* gorgée *f* ◆ **at** *or* **with one ~** *[drink]* d'un trait, d'un seul coup ; *[food]* d'un seul coup VI avaler ◆ **he ~ed hard** *(with emotion)* sa gorge se serra VT 1 *[+ food, drink, pill]* avaler ; *[+ oyster]* gober 2 *(fig) [+ story]* avaler, gober ; *[+ insult]* avaler, encaisser* ; *[+ one's anger, pride]* ravaler ◆ **that's a bit hard to ~** c'est plutôt dur à avaler ◆ **they ~ed it whole** ils ont tout avalé *or* gobé

► **swallow down** VT SEP avaler

► **swallow up** VT SEP *(fig)* engloutir ◆ **the ground seemed to ~ them up** le sol semblait les engloutir ◆ **he was ~ed up in the crowd** il s'est perdu *or* il a disparu dans la foule ◆ **the mist ~ed them up** la brume les a enveloppés ◆ **taxes ~ up half your income** les impôts engloutissent *or* engouffrent la moitié de vos revenus

swallowtail (butterfly) /'swɒləʊteɪl('bʌtəflaɪ)/ N machaon *m*

swam /swæm/ VB pt of **swim**

swami /'swɑːmɪ/ N (pl **swamies** *or* **swamis**) pandit *m*

swamp /swɒmp/ N marais *m*, marécage *m* VT *(= flood)* inonder ; *[+ boat]* emplir d'eau ; *(= sink)* submerger ; *(fig)* submerger *(with* de) ◆ **he was ~ed with requests/letters** il était submergé de requêtes/lettres ◆ **I'm absolutely ~ed* (with work)** je suis débordé (de travail) ◆ **towards the end of the game they ~ed us** *(Ftbl etc)* vers la fin de la partie ils ont fait le jeu

COMP **swamp buggy** N *(US)* voiture *f* amphibie
swamp fever N paludisme *m*, malaria *f*

swampland /'swɒmplænd/ N *(NonC)* marécages *mpl*

swampy /'swɒmpɪ/ ADJ marécageux

swan /swɒn/ N cygne *m* ◆ **the Swan of Avon** le cygne de l'Avon *(Shakespeare)* VI *(Brit *)* ◆ **he ~ned off to London before the end of term** il est parti à Londres sans s'en faire* *or* il est tranquillement parti à Londres avant la fin du trimestre ◆ **he's ~ning around in Paris somewhere** il se balade* quelque part dans Paris sans s'en faire*

COMP **swan dive** N *(US)* saut *m* de l'ange
Swan Lake N *(Ballet)* le Lac des Cygnes
swan-necked ADJ *[woman]* au cou de cygne ; *[tool]* en col de cygne
swan song N *(fig)* chant *m* du cygne
swan-upping N *(Brit) recensement annuel des cygnes de la Tamise*

swank* /swæŋk/ N 1 *(NonC)* esbroufe* *f* ◆ **out of ~** pour épater*, pour faire de l'esbroufe* 2 *(† = person)* esbroufeur* *m*, -euse* *f* VI faire de l'esbroufe*, chercher à épater* *or* à en mettre plein la vue* ◆ **to ~ about sth** se vanter de qch

swanky* /'swæŋkɪ/ ADJ huppé*

swannery /'swɒnərɪ/ N colonie *f* de cygnes

swansdown /'swɒnzdaʊn/ N *(NonC) (= feathers)* (duvet *m* de) cygne *m* ; *(= fabric)* molleton *m*

swap* /swɒp/ N troc *m*, échange *m* ◆ **it's a fair ~** ça se vaut ◆ **~s** *(stamps etc)* doubles *mpl* VT échanger, troquer *(A for B* A contre B) ; *[+ stamps, stories]* échanger *(with sb* avec qn) ◆ **Paul and Martin have ~ped hats** Paul et Martin ont échangé leurs chapeaux ◆ **let's ~ places** changeons de place (l'un avec l'autre) ◆ **I'll ~ you!** tu veux échanger avec moi ? ; → **wife** VI échanger

COMP **swap meet** N *(US Comm) rassemblement où l'on vend ou troque divers objets usagés*
swap shop N *(Brit) lieu ou rassemblement où l'on troque divers objets usagés*

► **swap over, swap round** VT SEP, VI changer de place

SWAPO /'swɑːpəʊ/ N (abbrev of **South-West Africa People's Organization**) SWAPO *f*

sward †† /swɔːd/ N gazon *m*, pelouse *f*

swarm¹ /swɔːm/ N *[of bees, flying insects]* essaim *m* ; *[of ants, crawling insects]* fourmillement *m*, grouillement *m* ; *[of people]* nuée *f*, essaim *m* ◆ **in a ~, in ~s** *(fig)* en masse VI 1 *[bees]* essaimer 2 *[crawling insects]* grouiller ◆ **to ~ in/out** *etc [people]* entrer/sortir *etc* en masse ◆ **they ~ed round** *or* **over** *or* **through the palace** ils ont envahi le palais en masse ◆ **the children ~ed round his car** les enfants s'agglutinaient autour de sa voiture 3 *(lit, fig) [ground, town, streets]* fourmiller, grouiller *(with* de)

swarm² /swɔːm/ VT (also **swarm up**) *[+ tree, pole]* grimper à toute vitesse à *(en s'aidant des pieds et des mains)*

swarthiness /'swɔːðɪnɪs/ N teint *m* basané *or* bistré

swarthy /'swɔːðɪ/ ADJ *[person]* à la peau basanée, au teint basané ; *[complexion]* basané

swashbuckler /'swɒʃˌbʌkləʳ/ N fier-à-bras *m*

swashbuckling /'swɒʃˌbʌklɪŋ/ ADJ *[person]* truculent ; *[film, role]* de cape et d'épée

swastika /'swɒstɪkə/ N svastika *or* swastika *m* ; *(Nazi)* croix *f* gammée

SWAT /swɒt/ (abbrev of **Special Weapons and Tactics**) ~ **team** ≈ GIGN *m (groupe d'intervention de la gendarmerie nationale)*

swat /swɒt/ VT *[+ fly, mosquito]* écraser ; *(* = slap) [+ table etc]* donner un coup sur, taper sur N 1 ◆ **to give a fly a ~, to take a ~ at a fly** donner un coup de tapette à une mouche 2 (also **fly swat**) tapette *f*

swatch /'swɒtʃ/ N échantillon *m* (de tissu)

swath /swɔːθ/ N (pl **swaths** /swɔːðz/) ⇒ **swathe noun**

swathe /sweɪð/ VT *(= bind)* emmailloter *(in* de) ; *(= wrap)* envelopper *(in* dans) ◆ **~d in bandages** emmailloté de bandages ◆ **~d in blankets** enveloppé *or* emmitouflé* dans des couvertures N *(Agr)* andain *m* ◆ **to cut corn in ~s** couper le blé en javelles ◆ **to cut a ~ through** *(fig) [disease, epidemic]* décimer ; *[recession, cutbacks]* ravager

swatter /'swɒtəʳ/ N (also **fly swatter**) tapette *f*

sway /sweɪ/ N *(NonC)* 1 *(= motion) [of rope, hanging object, trees]* balancement *m*, oscillation *f* ; *[of boat]* balancement *m*, oscillations *fpl* ; *[of tower block, bridge]* mouvement *m* oscillatoire, oscillation *f*

2 *(liter)* emprise *f (over* sur), domination *f (over* de) ◆ **to hold ~ over** avoir de l'emprise sur, tenir sous son emprise *or* sa domination ◆ **to fall under the ~ of** tomber sous l'emprise de

VI *[tree, rope, hanging object, boat]* se balancer, osciller ; *[tower block, bridge]* osciller ; *[train]* tanguer ; *[person]* tanguer, osciller ; *(fig) (= vacillate)* osciller, balancer *(liter) (between* entre) ◆ **he stood ~ing (about** *or* **from side to side** *or* **backwards and forwards)** il oscillait (sur ses jambes or de droite à gauche or d'arrière en avant), il tanguait ◆ **to ~ in/out** *etc (from drink,* *injury)* entrer/sortir *etc* en tanguant ; *(regally)* entrer/sortir *etc* majestueusement ◆ **he ~ed towards leniency** il a penché pour la clémence

VT 1 *[+ hanging object]* balancer, faire osciller ; *[+ hips]* rouler, balancer ; *[wind]* balancer, agiter ; *[waves]* balancer, ballotter

2 *(= influence)* influencer, avoir une action déterminante sur ◆ **these factors finally ~ed the committee** ces facteurs ont finalement influencé le choix *or* la décision du comité ◆ **I allowed myself to be ~ed** je me suis laissé influencer ◆ **his speech ~ed the crowd** son discours a eu une action déterminante sur la foule

COMP **sway-back** N ensellure *f*, lordose *f*
sway-backed ADJ ensellé

Swazi /ˈswɑːzɪ/ ADJ swazi N Swazi(e) *m(f)*

Swaziland /ˈswɑːzɪ,lænd/ N Swaziland *m* ◆ **in ~** au Swaziland

swear /swɛəʳ/ (pret **swore**, ptp **sworn**) VT 1 jurer *(on sth* sur qch ; *that* que ; *to do sth* de faire qch) ; *[+ fidelity, allegiance]* jurer ◆ **I ~ it!** je le jure ! ◆ **to ~ an oath** *(solemnly)* prêter serment ; *(= curse)* lâcher *or* pousser un juron ◆ **to ~ (an oath) to do sth** faire (le) serment *or* jurer de faire qch ◆ **to ~ a charge against sb** *(Jur)* accuser qn sous serment ◆ **I could have sworn he touched it** j'aurais juré qu'il l'avait touché ◆ **I ~ he said so!** il l'a dit, je vous le jure !, je vous jure qu'il l'a dit ! ◆ **I ~ I've never enjoyed myself more** ma parole, je ne me suis jamais autant amusé ; see also **oath, sworn** ; → **black**

2 *[+ witness, jury]* faire prêter serment à ◆ **to ~ sb to secrecy** faire jurer le secret à qn

VI 1 *(= take solemn oath etc)* jurer ◆ **do you so ~?** – **I ~** *(Jur)* = dites "je le jure" – je le jure ◆ **he swore on the Bible** il a juré sur la Bible ◆ **I ~ by all I hold sacred** je jure sur ce que j'ai de plus sacré ◆ **to ~ to the truth of sth** jurer que qch est vrai ◆ **would you ~ to having seen him?** est-ce que vous jureriez que vous l'avez vu ? ◆ **I think he did but I couldn't** *or* **wouldn't ~ to it** il me semble qu'il l'a fait mais je n'en jurerais pas ◆ **to ~ blind** *(Brit) or* **up and down** *(US)* **that ...** jurer ses grands dieux que ...

2 *(= curse)* jurer, pester *(at* contre, après) ; *(= blaspheme)* jurer, blasphémer ◆ **don't ~!** ne jure pas !, ne sois pas grossier ! ◆ **to ~ like a trooper** jurer comme un charretier ◆ **it's enough to make you ~*** il y a de quoi vous faire râler*

▸ **swear by** VT FUS *(fig)* ◆ **he swears by vitamin C tablets** il ne jure que par la vitamine C ◆ **I ~ by whisky as a cure for flu** pour moi il n'y a rien de tel que le whisky pour guérir la grippe

▸ **swear in** VT SEP *[+ jury, witness, president etc]* assermenter, faire prêter serment à

▸ **swear off** VT FUS *[+ alcohol, tobacco]* jurer de renoncer à ◆ **he has sworn off stealing** il a juré de ne plus voler

▸ **swear out** VT SEP *(US Jur)* ◆ **to swear out a warrant for sb's arrest** obtenir un mandat d'arrêt contre qn en l'accusant sous serment

swearword /ˈswɛəwɜːd/ N gros mot *m*, juron *m*

sweat /swet/ N 1 sueur *f*, transpiration *f* ; *(fig: on walls etc)* humidité *f*, suintement *m* ; *(= state)* sueur(s) *f(pl)* ◆ **by the ~ of his brow** à la sueur de son front ◆ **to be dripping** *or* **covered with ~** ruisseler de sueur, être en nage ◆ **to work up** *or* **get up a ~, to break ~** se mettre à transpirer ◆ **to be in a ~** *(lit)* être en sueur, être couvert de sueur ; *(*fig)* avoir des sueurs froides ◆ **he was in a great ~ about it** ça lui donnait des sueurs froides ; → **cold**

2 *(* = piece of work etc)* corvée *f* ◆ **it was an awful ~** on a eu un mal de chien, on en a bavé‡ ◆ **no ~!‡** pas de problème !

3 **an old ~‡** un vétéran, un vieux routier

VI *[person, animal]* suer *(with, from* de), être en sueur ; *[walls]* suer, suinter ; *[cheese etc]* suer ◆ **he was ~ing profusely** il suait à grosses gouttes ◆ **to ~ like a bull** *or* **a pig** suer comme un bœuf ◆ **he was ~ing over his essay*** il suait *or* transpirait sur sa dissertation

VT 1 *[+ person, animal]* faire suer *or* transpirer ; *(fig) [+ workers]* exploiter

2 ◆ **to ~ blood** * *(= work hard)* suer sang et eau *(over sth* sur qch) ; *(= be anxious)* avoir des sueurs froides ◆ **he was ~ing blood over** *or* **about the exam*** l'examen lui donnait des sueurs froides ◆ **don't ~ it!‡** *(US fig)* calme-toi !, relaxe !*

COMP **sweated goods** NPL marchandises produites par une main-d'œuvre exploitée
sweated labour N main-d'œuvre exploitée
sweat gland N glande *f* sudoripare
sweat lodge N *sorte de sauna à usage religieux dans certaines tribus amérindiennes*
sweat pants NPL *(US)* jogging *m*
sweat-stained ADJ taché *or* maculé de sueur

▸ **sweat off** VT SEP ◆ **I've sweated off half a kilo** j'ai perdu un demi-kilo à force de transpirer

▸ **sweat out** VT SEP *[+ cold etc]* guérir en transpirant ◆ **you'll just have to ~ it out*** *(fig)* il faudra t'armer de patience ◆ **they left him to ~ it out*** ils n'ont rien fait pour l'aider

sweatband /ˈswetbænd/ N *(in hat)* cuir *m* intérieur ; *(Sport)* bandeau *m*

sweater /ˈswetəʳ/ N tricot *m*, pull-over *m*, pull* *m* COMP **sweater girl** N fille *f* bien roulée*

sweating /ˈswetɪŋ/ N *[of person, animal]* transpiration *f* ; *(Med)* sudation *f* ; *[of wall]* suintement *m*

sweats* /swets/ NPL *(esp US)* (tenue *f* de) jogging *m*

sweatshirt /ˈswetʃɜːt/ N sweat-shirt *m*

sweatshop /ˈswetʃɒp/ N *atelier où la main-d'œuvre est exploitée*

sweatsuit /ˈswetsuːt/ N *(US)* survêtement *m*, survêt* *m*

sweaty /ˈswetɪ/ ADJ *[person, body] (= sweating)* en sueur ; *(= sticky)* collant de sueur ; *[hand, skin]* moite (de sueur) ; *[hair, clothes]* collant de sueur ; *[smell]* de sueur ; *[place]* où l'on sue ◆ **I've got ~ feet** je transpire *or* sue des pieds ◆ **to get ~** *[person]* se mettre en sueur

Swede /swiːd/ N Suédois(e) *m(f)*

swede /swiːd/ N *(esp Brit)* rutabaga *m*

Sweden /ˈswiːdən/ N Suède *f*

Swedenborgian /,swiːdənˈbɔːdʒɪən/ ADJ swedenborgien

Swedish /ˈswiːdɪʃ/ ADJ *(gen)* suédois ; *[ambassador, embassy, monarch]* de Suède N *(= language)* suédois *m* NPL **the Swedish** les Suédois *mpl*

COMP **Swedish gymnastics** NPL gymnastique *f* suédoise
Swedish massage N massage *m* suédois
Swedish mile N mile *m* suédois (= 10 km)
Swedish movements NPL ⇒ **Swedish gymnastics**

sweep /swiːp/ (vb : pret, ptp **swept**) N 1 *(with broom etc)* coup *m* de balai ◆ **to give a room a ~ (out)** donner un coup de balai à *or* balayer une pièce ; → **clean**

2 (also **chimney sweep**) ramoneur *m* ; → **black**

3 *(= movement) [of arm]* grand geste *m* ; *[of sword]* grand coup *m* ; *[of scythe]* mouvement *m* circulaire ; *[of net]* coup *m* ; *[of lighthouse beam, radar beam]* trajectoire *f* ; *[of tide]* progression *f* irrésistible ; *[of progress, events]* marche *f* ◆ **in** *or* **with one ~** d'un seul coup ◆ **with a ~ of his arm** d'un geste large ◆ **to make a ~ of the horizon** *(with binoculars)* parcourir l'horizon ; *[lighthouse beam]* balayer l'horizon ◆ **to make a ~ for mines** draguer des mines ◆ **the police made a ~ of the district** la police a ratissé le quartier

4 *(= range) [of telescope, gun, lighthouse, radar]* champ *m* ◆ **with a ~ of 180°** avec un champ de 180°

5 *(= curve, line) [of coastline, hills, road, river]* grande courbe *f* ; *(Archit)* courbure *f*, voussure *f* ; *[of curtains, long skirt]* drapé *m* ◆ **a wide ~ of meadowland** une vaste étendue de prairie ◆ **the graceful ~ of her lines** *(car, ship, plane)* son élégante ligne aérodynamique

6 abbrev of **sweepstake**

VT 1 *[+ room, floor, street]* balayer ; *[+ chimney]* ramoner ; *(Naut) [+ river, channel]* draguer ; *(fig) [waves, hurricane, bullets, searchlights, skirts]* balayer ◆ **to ~ a room clean** donner un bon coup de balai dans une pièce ◆ **to ~ sth clean of mines** *(Naut)* déminer qch ◆ **he swept the horizon with his binoculars** il a parcouru l'horizon avec ses jumelles ◆ **his eyes/his glance swept the room** il a parcouru la pièce des yeux/du regard ◆ **their fleet swept the seas in search of ...** leur flotte a sillonné *or* parcouru les mers à la recherche de ... ◆ **a wave of panic swept the city** un vent de panique a soufflé sur la ville ; → **broom**

2 *[+ dust, snow etc]* balayer ; *(Naut) [+ mines]* draguer, enlever ◆ **he swept the rubbish off the pavement** il a enlevé les ordures du trottoir d'un coup de balai ◆ **she swept the snow into a heap** elle a balayé la neige et en a fait un tas ◆ **to ~ sth under the carpet** *or* **rug** *(fig)* tirer le rideau sur qch ◆ **to ~ sth off the table on to the floor** faire tomber qch de la table par terre d'un geste large ◆ **to ~ one's hair off one's face** écarter ses cheveux de son visage ◆ **to ~ sth into a bag** faire glisser qch d'un geste large dans un sac ◆ **to ~ everything before one** *(fig)* remporter un succès total, réussir sur toute la ligne ◆ **the army swept the enemy before them** l'armée a balayé l'ennemi devant elle ◆ **to ~ the board** remporter un succès complet, tout rafler* ◆ **the socialists swept the board at the election** les socialistes ont remporté l'élection haut la main ◆ **he swept the obstacles from his path** il a balayé *or* écarté les obstacles qui se trouvaient sur son chemin ◆ **the crowd swept him into the square** la foule l'a emporté *or* entraîné sur la place, il a été pris dans le mouvement de la foule et il s'est retrouvé sur la place ◆ **the wave swept him overboard** la vague l'a jeté pardessus bord ◆ **the wind swept the caravan over the cliff** le vent a emporté la caravane et l'a précipitée du haut de la falaise ◆ **the current swept the boat downstream** le courant a emporté le bateau ◆ **to be swept off one's feet** *(by wind, flood etc)* être emporté *(by* par) ; *(fig)* être enthousiasmé *or* emballé* *(by* par) ◆ **the water swept him off his feet** le courant lui a fait perdre pied ◆ **he swept her off her feet** *(fig)* elle a eu le coup de foudre pour lui ◆ **this election swept the socialists into office** *or* **power** cette élection a porté les socialistes au pouvoir avec une forte majorité

VI 1 *(= pass swiftly)* **to ~ in/out/along** *etc [person, vehicle, convoy]* entrer/sortir/avancer *etc* rapidement ◆ **the car swept round the corner** la voiture a pris le virage comme un bolide ◆ **the planes went ~ing across the sky** les avions sillonnaient le ciel ◆ **the rain swept across the plain** la pluie a balayé la plaine ◆ **panic swept through the city** la panique s'est emparée de la ville ◆ **plague swept through the country** la peste a ravagé le pays

2 *(= move impressively)* **to ~ in/out/along** *etc [person, procession]* entrer/sortir/avancer *etc* majestueusement ◆ **she came ~ing into the room** elle a fait une entrée majestueuse dans la pièce ◆ **to ~ into office** *(fig: Pol)* être porté au pouvoir ◆ **the royal car swept down the avenue** la voiture royale a descendu l'avenue d'une manière imposante ◆ **the motorway ~s**

across the hills l'autoroute s'élance à travers les collines ◆ **the forests ~ down to the sea** les forêts descendent en pente douce jusqu'au bord de la mer ◆ **the bay ~s away to the south** la baie décrit une courbe majestueuse vers le sud ◆ **the Alps ~ down to the coast** les Alpes descendent majestueusement vers la côte

COMP **sweep hand** N *[of clock etc]* trotteuse *f*

► **sweep along** VI → **sweep vi 1, 2**

VT SEP *[crowd, flood, current, gale]* emporter, entraîner ; *[+ leaves]* balayer

► **sweep aside** VT SEP *[+ object, person]* repousser, écarter ; *[+ suggestion, objection]* repousser, rejeter ; *[+ difficulty, obstacle]* écarter

► **sweep away** VI *(= leave) (rapidly)* s'éloigner rapidement ; *(impressively)* s'éloigner majestueusement *or* d'une manière imposante ; see also **sweep vi 2**

VT SEP *[+ dust, snow, rubbish]* balayer ; *[crowd, flood, current, gale]* entraîner ◆ **they swept him away to lunch** ils l'ont entraîné pour aller déjeuner

► **sweep down** VI → **sweep vi 2**

VT SEP *[+ walls etc]* nettoyer avec un balai ; *[flood, gale etc]* emporter ◆ **the river swept the logs down to the sea** les bûches ont flotté sur la rivière jusqu'à la mer

► **sweep off** ⇒ **sweep away**

► **sweep out** VI → **sweep vi 1, 2**

VT SEP *[+ room, dust, rubbish]* balayer

► **sweep up** VI 1 *(with broom etc)* **to ~ up after sb** balayer les débris *or* les saletés de qn ◆ **to ~ up after a party** balayer quand les invités sont partis

2 ◆ **he swept up to me** *(angrily)* il s'est approché de moi avec furie *or* majestueusement ; *(impressively)* il s'est approché de moi majestueusement ◆ **the car swept up to the house** *(rapidly)* la voiture a remonté rapidement l'allée jusqu'à la maison ; *(impressively)* la voiture a remonté l'allée jusqu'à la maison d'une manière imposante

VT SEP *[+ snow, leaves, dust etc]* balayer ◆ **she swept up the letters and took them away** elle a ramassé les lettres d'un geste brusque et les a emportées

sweepback /ˈswiːpbæk/ N *[of aircraft wing etc]* flèche *f*

sweeper /ˈswiːpəʳ/ N 1 *(= worker)* balayeur *m* 2 *(= machine)* balayeuse *f* ; (also **carpet sweeper**) balai *m* mécanique ; *(= vacuum cleaner)* aspirateur *m* 3 *(Ftbl)* libéro *m*

sweeping /ˈswiːpɪŋ/ ADJ 1 *[gesture, movement]* grand ; *[curve]* large ; *[glance]* circulaire ; *[coastline]* qui décrit une courbe majestueuse ; *[lawn]* qui descend en pente majestueuse ; *[staircase]* qui descend majestueusement ; *[bow]* profond ; *[skirts]* qui balaie le sol 2 *(= large-scale) [change, reorganization]* radical ; *[reduction, cuts, powers]* considérable ◆ **~ gains/losses** *(Pol: at election)* progression *f*/recul *m* considérable *or* très net(te) 3 *(= decisive) [victory]* écrasant 4 *(pej = indiscriminate)* ◆ **~ statement/generalization** déclaration *f*/généralisation *f* à l'emporte-pièce ◆ **that's pretty ~!** c'est beaucoup dire ! NPL **sweepings** balayures *fpl*, ordures *fpl* ; *(fig) [of society etc]* rebut *m*

sweepstake /ˈswiːpsteɪk/ N sweepstake *m*

sweet /swiːt/ ADJ 1 *(= not savoury) [taste, food, drink]* sucré ; *[smell]* doux (douce *f*), suave ; *[apple, orange]* doux (douce *f*), sucré ◆ **to taste ~** être sucré ◆ **to smell ~** avoir une odeur suave ◆ **I love ~ things** j'adore le sucré *or* les sucreries *fpl* ; → **sickly**

2 *(= not dry) [cider, wine]* doux (douce *f*) ; → **medium**

3 *(= kind) [person, face, smile]* doux (douce *f*) ◆ **she has such a ~ nature** elle est d'une nature si douce ◆ **she is a very ~ person** elle est vraiment très gentille ◆ **you're such a ~ guy!** t'es vraiment un chic type ! * ◆ **that was very ~ of her** c'était très gentil de sa part ◆ **how ~ of you to think of me!** comme c'est gentil de votre part d'avoir pensé à moi ! ◆ **to be ~ to sb** être gentil avec qn ◆ **to keep sb ~** * chercher à être dans les petits papiers de qn * ◆ **(as) ~ as pie** *(Brit) [person]* gentil comme tout ; *[situation]* qui marche parfaitement ◆ **Sweet Jesus!** ** nom de Dieu ! ** ; → **Fanny**

4 *(= cute) [child, dog, house, hat]* mignon ◆ **a ~ old lady** une adorable vieille dame ; → **sixteen**

5 *(= pleasant) [sound, voice, music]* harmonieux, mélodieux ◆ **revenge is ~!** la vengeance est douce ! ◆ **the ~ taste of victory/revenge** le goût exquis de la victoire/vengeance ◆ **the ~ smell of success** la douceur de la gloire, l'ivresse du succès ◆ **the news was ~ music to my ears** cette nouvelle a été douce à mes oreilles ◆ **~ dreams!** fais de beaux rêves ! ◆ **to whisper ~ nothings in sb's ear** conter fleurette à qn ; see also **bittersweet**

6 *(= pure) [air, breath]* frais (fraîche *f*) ; *[water]* pur ◆ **to smell ~** *[air]* être pur ; *[breath]* être frais

7 *(iro)* ◆ **he carried on in his own ~ way** il a continué comme il l'entendait ◆ **he'll do it in his own ~ time** il le fera quand bon lui semblera ◆ **she went her own ~ way** elle a fait comme il lui plaisait ◆ **to please one's own ~ self** n'en faire qu'à sa tête ◆ **at his own ~ will** à son gré

8 *(* = attracted)* ◆ **to be ~ on sb** avoir le béguin * pour qn

N *(esp Brit = candy)* bonbon *m* ; *(Brit = dessert)* dessert *m* ◆ **the ~s of success/solitude** *etc* les délices *fpl* de la réussite/de la solitude *etc* ◆ **come here, (my) ~** * viens ici, mon ange

COMP **sweet-and-sour** ADJ aigre-doux (aigre-douce *f*)

sweet chestnut N châtaigne *f*, marron *m*

sweet herbs NPL fines herbes *fpl*

sweet-natured ADJ d'un naturel doux

sweet pea N pois *m* de senteur

sweet pepper N piment *m* doux, poivron *m* (vert *or* rouge)

sweet potato N patate *f* douce

sweet-scented, sweet-smelling ADJ agréablement parfumé, odoriférant

sweet talk N flagorneries *fpl*

sweet-talk VT flagorner

sweet-tempered ADJ ⇒ **sweet-natured**

sweet tooth N ◆ **to have a ~ tooth** avoir un faible pour les sucreries

sweet trolley N *(Brit)* chariot *m* des desserts

sweet william N *(= plant)* œillet *m* de poète

sweetbread /ˈswiːtbred/ N ris *m* de veau *or* d'agneau

sweetbriar, sweetbrier /ˈswiːtbraɪəʳ/ N églantier *m* odorant

sweetcorn /ˈswiːtkɔːn/ N maïs *m* doux

sweeten /ˈswiːtn/ VT 1 *[+ coffee, sauce etc]* sucrer ; *[+ air]* purifier ; *[+ room]* assainir 2 *(fig) [+ person, sb's temper, task]* adoucir 3 (* : also **sweeten up**) *(= give incentive to)* amadouer ; *(= bribe)* graisser la patte à * ; → **pill** VI *[person, sb's temper]* s'adoucir

sweetener /ˈswiːtnəʳ/ N 1 *(for coffee, food)* édulcorant *m* 2 (* fig) *(= incentive)* carotte * *f* ; *(= bribe)* pot-de-vin *m* ; *(= compensation)* quelque chose *m* pour faire passer la pilule *, lot *m* de consolation

sweetening /ˈswiːtnɪŋ/ N *(NonC = substance)* édulcorant *m*

sweetheart /ˈswiːthɑːt/ N petit(e) ami(e) *m(f)*, bien-aimé(e) † *m(f)* ◆ **yes ~** oui chéri(e) *or* mon ange

sweetie * /ˈswiːtɪ/ N 1 *(= person:* also **sweetie-pie** *) **he's/she's a ~** il/elle est chou *, c'est un ange ◆ **yes ~** oui mon chou * *or* mon ange 2 *(esp Scot = candy)* bonbon *m*

sweetish /ˈswiːtɪʃ/ ADJ au goût sucré, douceâtre *(pej)*

sweetly /ˈswiːtlɪ/ ADV 1 *(= kindly) [smile, say, answer]* gentiment 2 *(= pleasantly) [sing, play]* mélodieusement 3 *(= efficiently)* ◆ **the engine is running ~** le moteur marche sans à-coups ◆ **he hit the ball ~** il a frappé la balle avec un timing parfait 4 ◆ **~ scented** agréablement parfumé, odoriférant

sweetmeat /ˈswiːtmiːt/ N sucrerie *f*, confiserie *f*

sweetness /ˈswiːtnɪs/ N *(to taste)* goût *m* sucré ; *(in smell)* odeur *f* suave ; *(to hearing)* son *m* mélodieux *or* harmonieux ; *[of person, nature, character, expression]* douceur *f* ◆ **to be all ~ and light** être tout douceur

sweetshop /ˈswiːtʃɒp/ N *(Brit)* confiserie *f (souvent avec papeterie, journaux et tabac)*

swell /swel/ (vb : pret **swelled**, ptp **swollen** *or* **swelled**) N 1 *[of sea]* houle *f* ◆ **heavy ~** forte houle *f* ; → **groundswell**

2 *(Mus)* crescendo *m inv* (et diminuendo *m inv*) ; *(on organ)* boîte *f* expressive

3 († * *= stylish person)* personne *f* huppée *, gandin *m (pej)* ◆ **the ~s** les gens *mpl* huppés *, le gratin *

ADJ * 1 *(esp US † = stylish, showy) [clothes, house, car, restaurant]* chic *inv* ; *[relatives, friends]* huppé *

2 *(US = wonderful)* super * *inv* ◆ **I had a ~ time** je me suis super * bien amusé

VI 1 (also **swell up**) *[balloon, tyre, air bed]* (se) gonfler ; *[sails]* se gonfler ; *[ankle, arm, eye, face]* enfler ; *[wood]* gonfler ◆ **to ~ (up) with pride** se gonfler d'orgueil ◆ **to ~ (up) with rage/indignation** bouillir de rage/d'indignation

2 *(= increase) [river]* grossir ; *[sound, music, voice]* s'enfler ; *[numbers, population, membership]* grossir, augmenter ◆ **the numbers soon ~ed to 500** le nombre a vite atteint 500 ◆ **the little group soon ~ed into a crowd** le petit groupe est vite devenu une foule ◆ **the murmuring ~ed to a roar** le murmure s'enfla pour devenir un rugissement

VT *[+ sail]* gonfler ; *[+ sound]* enfler ; *[+ river, lake]* grossir ; *[+ number]* grossir, augmenter ◆ **this ~ed the membership/population to 1,500** ceci a porté à 1 500 le nombre des membres/le total de la population ◆ **a population swollen by refugees** une population grossie par les réfugiés ◆ **a river swollen by rain** une rivière grossie par les pluies, une rivière en crue ◆ **a fifth edition swollen by a mass of new material** une cinquième édition augmentée d'une quantité de matière nouvelle ◆ **to be swollen with pride** être gonflé *or* bouffi d'orgueil ◆ **to be swollen with rage** bouillir de rage ; see also **swollen**

COMP **swell box** N *(Mus)* boîte *f* expressive

► **swell out** VI *[sails etc]* se gonfler

VT SEP gonfler

► **swell up** VI ⇒ **swell vi 1**

swellhead * /ˈswelhed/ N *(US)* bêcheur * *m*, -euse * *f*

swellheaded * /ˌswelˈhedɪd/ ADJ bêcheur *

swellheadedness * /ˌswelˈhedɪdnɪs/ N vanité *f*, suffisance *f*

swelling /ˈswelɪŋ/ N 1 *(= bulge, lump) (gen)* grosseur *f* ; *(on tyre)* hernie *f* ; *(Med)* bosse *f*, grosseur *f* 2 *(NonC: Med) [of limb, foot, finger, face, jaw]* enflure *f* ; *[of eye, stomach, breasts, tissue, organ]* gonflement *m* ◆ **it's to reduce the ~** c'est pour faire désenfler 3 *(NonC) [of balloon, tyre, sails, wood]* gonflement *m* ; *[of population]* accroissement *m* ADJ *[sound, chorus, voices, ankle, eye]* qui enfle ; *[sail]* gonflé

swelter /ˈsweltəʳ/ VI étouffer de chaleur

sweltering /ˈsweltərɪŋ/ ADJ *[weather]* étouffant ; *[heat]* étouffant, accablant ; *[day, afternoon]* torride ◆ **it's** ~ on étouffe (de chaleur)

swept /swept/ VB pt, ptp of **sweep**

sweptback /ˌsweptˈbæk/ ADJ *[plane wings]* en flèche ; *[hair]* rejeté en arrière

sweptwing aircraft /ˌsweptwɪŋˈɛəkrɑːft/ N avion *m* à ailes en flèche

swerve /swɜːv/ VI *[boxer, fighter]* faire un écart ; *[ball]* dévier ; *[vehicle, ship]* faire une embardée ; *[driver]* donner un coup de volant ; *(fig)* dévier *(from de)* ◆ **the car ~d away from the lorry on to the verge** la voiture a fait une embardée pour éviter le camion et est montée sur l'accotement ◆ **he ~d round the bollard** il a viré sur les chapeaux de roues autour de la borne lumineuse VT *[+ ball]* faire dévier ; *[+ vehicle]* faire faire une embardée à N *[of vehicle, ship]* embardée *f* ; *[of boxer, fighter]* écart *m*

swift /swɪft/ ADJ rapide ◆ **the river is ~ at this point** le courant (de la rivière) est rapide à cet endroit ◆ **to wish sb a ~ recovery** souhaiter à qn un prompt rétablissement ◆ **they were ~ to act/respond/obey** ils ont été prompts à agir/réagir/obéir N *(= bird)* martinet *m*
COMP **swift-flowing** ADJ *[river]* au courant rapide ; *[current]* rapide
swift-footed ADJ *(liter)* au pied léger

swiftly /ˈswɪftlɪ/ ADV *[move, react, walk, spread, become]* rapidement, vite ◆ **a ~ flowing river** une rivière au courant rapide ◆ **the company has moved** *or* **acted ~ to deny the rumours** l'entreprise a réagi promptement pour démentir les rumeurs

swiftness /ˈswɪftnɪs/ N rapidité *f*

swig * /swɪg/ N lampée * *f* ; *(larger)* coup *m* ◆ **to take a ~ at a bottle** boire un coup à même la bouteille VT lamper *

► **swig down** * VT SEP avaler d'un trait

swill /swɪl/ N 1 *(NonC, for pigs etc)* pâtée *f* ; *(= garbage, slops)* eaux *fpl* grasses 2 ◆ **to give sth a ~ (out** *or* **down)** ⇒ **to swill sth (out** *or* **down)** vt 1 VT 1 *(also* **swill out, swill down***)* *[+ floor]* laver à grande eau ; *[+ glass]* rincer 2 *(also* **swill around***)* *[+ liquid]* remuer 3 *(* = drink)* boire avidement, boire à grands traits VI *[liquid]* remuer

swim /swɪm/ (vb : pret **swam**, ptp **swum**) N ◆ **to go for a ~, to have** *or* **take a ~** *(in sea, lake, river)* aller nager *or* se baigner ; *(in swimming baths)* aller à la piscine ◆ **it's time for our ~** c'est l'heure de la baignade ◆ **after a 2km ~** après avoir fait 2 km à la nage ◆ **Channel ~** traversée *f* de la Manche à la nage ◆ **it's a long ~** voilà une bonne *or* longue distance à parcourir à la nage ◆ **I had a lovely ~** ça m'a fait du bien de nager comme ça ◆ **to be in the ~ (of things)** être dans le mouvement

VI 1 *[person]* nager ; *(as sport)* faire de la natation ; *[fish, animal]* nager ◆ **to go ~ming** *(in sea, lake, river)* aller nager *or* se baigner ; *(in swimming baths)* aller à la piscine ◆ **to ~ away/back** *etc [person]* s'éloigner/revenir *etc* à la nage ; *[fish]* s'éloigner/revenir *etc* ◆ **to ~ across a river** traverser une rivière à la nage ◆ **he swam under the boat** il est passé sous le bateau (à la nage) ◆ **to ~ under water** nager sous l'eau ◆ **he had to ~ for it** son seul recours a été de se sauver à la nage *or* de se jeter à l'eau et de nager ◆ **to ~ against the current** nager contre le courant ◆ **to ~ against the tide** *(fig)* nager à contre-courant ◆ **to ~ with the tide** *(fig)* suivre le courant

2 *(fig)* **the meat was ~ming in gravy** la viande nageait *or* baignait dans la sauce ◆ **her eyes were ~ming (with tears)** ses yeux étaient noyés *or* baignés de larmes ◆ **the bathroom was ~ming** la salle de bains était inondée ◆ **the room was ~ming round** *or* **~ming before his eyes** la pièce semblait tourner autour de lui ◆ **his head was ~ming** la tête lui tournait

VT *[+ race]* nager ; *[+ lake, river]* traverser à la nage ◆ **it was first swum in 1900** la première traversée à la nage a eu lieu en 1900 ◆ **he can ~ 10km** il peut faire 10 km à la nage ◆ **he can ~ two lengths** il peut nager *or* faire deux longueurs ◆ **before he had swum ten strokes** avant qu'il ait pu faire *or* nager dix brasses ◆ **I can't ~ a stroke** je suis incapable de faire une brasse ◆ **can you ~ the crawl?** savez-vous nager *or* faire le crawl ?

swimmer /ˈswɪməʳ/ N nageur *m*, -euse *f*

swimming /ˈswɪmɪŋ/ N *(gen)* nage *f* ; *(Sport, Scol)* natation *f*
COMP **swimming bath(s)** N(PL) *(Brit)* piscine *f*
swimming cap N bonnet *m* de bain
swimming costume N *(Brit)* maillot *m* (de bain) une pièce
swimming crab N étrille *f*
swimming gala N compétition *f* de natation
swimming instructor N maître *m* nageur
swimming pool N piscine *f*
swimming ring N bouée *f*
swimming suit N maillot *m* (de bain)
swimming trunks NPL caleçon *m or* slip *m* de bain

swimmingly †* /ˈswɪmɪŋlɪ/ ADV à merveille ◆ **they got on ~** ils se sont entendus à merveille ◆ **everything went ~** tout a marché comme sur des roulettes

swimsuit /ˈswɪmsuːt/ N maillot *m* (de bain)

swimwear /ˈswɪmweəʳ/ N *(NonC)* maillots *mpl* de bain

swindle /ˈswɪndl/ N escroquerie *f* ◆ **it's a ~** c'est du vol, nous nous sommes fait estamper * *or* rouler * VT escroquer ◆ **to ~ sb out of his money, to ~ sb's money out of him** escroquer de l'argent à qn

swindler /ˈswɪndləʳ/ N escroc *m*

swine /swaɪn/ N *(pl inv) (= pig)* pourceau *m*, porc *m* ; *(‡ fig = person)* salaud ‡ *m* ◆ **you ~!‡** espèce de salaud !‡

swineherd †† /ˈswaɪnhɜːd/ N porcher *m*, -ère *f*

swing /swɪŋ/ (vb : pret, ptp **swung**) N 1 *(= movement)* balancement *m* ; *[of pendulum] (= movement)* mouvement *m* de va-et-vient, oscillations *fpl* ; *(= arc, distance)* arc *m* ; *[of instrument pointer, needle]* oscillations *fpl* ; *(Boxing, Golf)* swing *m* ◆ **the ~ of the boom sent him overboard** le retour de la bôme l'a jeté pardessus bord ◆ **he gave the starting handle a ~** il a donné un tour de manivelle ◆ **the golfer took a ~ at the ball** le joueur de golf a essayé de frapper *or* a frappé la balle avec un swing ◆ **to take a ~ at sb** * décocher *or* lancer un coup de poing à qn ◆ **the ~ of the pendulum brought him back to power** le mouvement du pendule l'a ramené au pouvoir ◆ **the socialists need a ~ of 5% to win the election** *(Pol)* il faudrait aux socialistes un revirement d'opinion en leur faveur de l'ordre de 5% pour qu'ils remportent *subj* l'élection ◆ **a ~ to the left** *(Pol)* un revirement en faveur de la gauche ◆ **the ~s of the market** *(on Stock Exchange)* les fluctuations *fpl or* les hauts et les bas *mpl* du marché

2 *(= rhythm) [of dance etc]* rythme *m* ; *[of jazz music]* swing *m* ◆ **to walk with a ~ in one's step** marcher d'un pas rythmé ◆ **music/poetry with a ~ to it** *or* **that goes with a ~** musique *f*/poésie *f* rythmée *or* entraînante ◆ **to go with a ~** *[evening, party]* marcher du tonnerre * ◆ **to be in full ~** *[party, election, campaign]* battre son plein ; *[business]* être en plein rendement, gazer * ◆ **to get into the ~ of** *[+ new job, married life etc]* s'habituer *or* se faire à ◆ **to get into the ~ of things** se mettre dans le bain

3 *(= scope, freedom)* **they gave him full ~ in the matter** ils lui ont donné carte blanche en la matière ◆ **he was given full ~ to make decisions** on l'a laissé entièrement libre de prendre des décisions ◆ **he gave his imagination full ~** il a donné libre cours à son imagination

4 *(= seat for swinging)* balançoire *f* ◆ **to have a ~** se balancer, faire de la balançoire ◆ **to give a child a ~** pousser un enfant qui se balance ◆ **what you gain on the ~s you lose on the roundabouts *, (it's) ~s and round-abouts *** ce qu'on gagne d'un côté on le perd de l'autre

5 *(= music)* swing *m*

VI 1 *(= hang, oscillate) [arms, legs]* se balancer, être ballant ; *[object on rope, hammock]* se balancer ; *[pendulum]* osciller ; *(on a swing)* se balancer ; *(= pivot) (also* **swing round***)* tourner, pivoter ; *[person]* se retourner, virevolter ◆ **he was left ~ing by his hands** il s'est retrouvé seul suspendu par les mains ◆ **to ~ to and fro** se balancer ◆ **the load swung (round) through the air as the crane turned** comme la grue pivotait la charge a décrit une courbe dans l'air ◆ **the ship was ~ing at anchor** le bateau se balançait sur son ancre ◆ **he swung across on the rope** agrippé à la corde il s'est élancé et a *or* est passé de l'autre côté ◆ **the monkey swung from branch to branch** le singe se balançait de branche en branche ◆ **he swung up the rope ladder** il a grimpé prestement à l'échelle de corde ◆ **he swung (up) into the saddle** il a sauté en selle ◆ **the door swung open/shut** la porte s'est ouverte/s'est refermée ◆ **he swung (round) on his heel** il a virevolté

2 *(= move rhythmically)* **to ~ along/away** *etc* avancer/s'éloigner *etc* d'un pas rythmé *or* allègre ◆ **the regiment went ~ing past the king** le régiment a défilé au pas cadencé devant le roi ◆ **to ~ into action** *[army]* se mettre en branle ; *(fig)* passer à l'action ◆ **music that really ~s** musique *f* qui swingue

3 *(= change direction:* also **swing round***) [plane, vehicle]* virer ◆ **the convoy swung (round) into the square** le convoi a viré pour aller sur la place ◆ **the river ~s north here** ici la rivière décrit une courbe *or* oblique vers le nord ◆ **the country has swung to the right** *(Pol)* le pays a viré *or* effectué un virage à droite ◆ **to ~ both ways‡** *(= be bisexual)* marcher à voile et à vapeur *

4 ◆ **to ~ at a ball** frapper *or* essayer de frapper une balle avec un swing ◆ **to ~ at sb** décocher *or* lancer un coup de poing à qn ◆ **he swung at me with the axe** il a brandi la hache pour me frapper

5 *(* = be hanged)* être pendu ◆ **he'll ~ for it** on lui mettra la corde au cou pour cela ◆ **I'd ~ for him** je le tuerais si je le tenais

6 *(* = be fashionable)* être branché *, être dans le vent ◆ **the party was really ~ing** la soirée battait son plein

VT 1 *(= move to and fro) [+ one's arms, legs, umbrella, hammock]* balancer ; *[+ object on rope]* balancer, faire osciller ; *[+ pendulum]* faire osciller ; *[+ child on swing]* pousser ; *(= brandish)* brandir ◆ **he swung his sword above his head** il a fait un moulinet avec l'épée au-dessus de sa tête ◆ **he swung his axe at the tree** il a brandi sa hache pour frapper l'arbre ◆ **he swung his racket at the ball** il a ramené sa raquette pour frapper la balle ◆ **he swung the box (up) on to the roof of the car** il a envoyé la boîte sur le toit de la voiture ◆ **he swung the case (up) on to his shoulders** il a balancé la valise sur ses épaules ◆ **he swung himself across the stream/over the wall** *etc* il s'est élancé et a franchi le ruisseau/et a sauté pardessus le mur *etc* ◆ **to ~ o.s. (up) into the saddle** sauter en selle ◆ **to ~ one's hips** rouler *or* balancer les hanches, se déhancher ◆ **to ~ the lead** * *(Brit)* tirer au flanc * ; → **room**

2 (= *turn:* also **often swing round**) *[+ propeller]* lancer ; *[+ starting handle]* tourner ◆ **to ~ a door open/shut** ouvrir/fermer une porte ◆ **he swung the ship (round) through 180°** il a viré de 180°, il a fait virer (le bateau) de 180° ◆ **he swung the car round the corner** il a viré au coin

3 (= *influence*) *[+ election, decision]* influencer ; *[+ voters]* faire changer d'opinion ◆ **his speech swung the decision against us** son discours a provoqué un revirement et la décision est allée contre nous ◆ **he managed to ~ the deal*** il a réussi à emporter l'affaire ◆ **do you think you can ~ it for me?*** tu crois que tu peux m'arranger ça ? ◆ **to ~ it on sb*** tirer une carotte à qn *, pigeonner qn *

4 *(Mus) [+ a tune, the classics etc]* jouer de manière rythmée

COMP **swing band** N *(Mus)* orchestre *m* de swing

swing-bin N *(Brit)* poubelle *f* à couvercle pivotant

swing bridge N pont *m* tournant

swing door N porte *f* battante

swing music N swing *m*

swing shift* N *(US)* (= *period*) période *f* du soir *(pour un travail posté)* ; (= *workers*) équipe *f* du soir

swing vote N *(esp US)* vote *m* décisif ◆ **the Black community will be the ~ vote in the election** l'issue de ces élections dépendra du vote noir

swing voter N *(esp US) électeur dont le vote est décisif pour l'issue d'une élection*

swing-wing ADJ *[aircraft]* à géométrie variable

► **swing round** VI *[person]* se retourner, virevolter ; *[crane etc]* tourner, pivoter ; *[ship, plane, convoy, procession]* virer ; *[car, truck]* virer ; *(after collision etc)* faire un tête-à-queue ; *(fig) [voters]* virer de bord ; *[opinions]* connaître un revirement ; see also **swing vi 1, 3**

VT SEP *[+ object on rope etc]* faire tourner ; *[+ sword, axe]* brandir, faire des moulinets avec ; *[+ crane etc]* faire pivoter ; *[+ car, ship, plane, convoy, procession]* faire tourner *or* virer ; see also **swing vt 2**

► **swing to** VI *[door]* se refermer

swingeing /ˈswɪndʒɪŋ/ ADJ *(Brit) [attack]* violent ; *[increase]* considérable ; *[fine, tax]* fort ; *[defeat, majority]* écrasant ◆ **~ cuts** des coupes *fpl* sombres

swinger* /ˈswɪŋəʳ/ N ◆ **he's a ~** (= *with it*) il est branché * *or* dans le vent ; *(going to parties)* c'est un noceur * ; *(sexually)* il couche à droite et à gauche

swinging /ˈswɪŋɪŋ/ ADJ 1 (= *swaying, rocking*) *[rope, weight, pendulum, legs, hammock]* qui se balance ; *[door, shutter]* qui bat ◆ **a ~ weight on the end of a cord** un poids se balançant *or* qui se balance au bout d'une corde ◆ **the bar was full of ~ fists** dans le bar, les coups volaient 2 (= *syncopated*) *[music, rhythm]* entraînant, qui swingue * 3 (* = *modern, fashionable*) dans le vent 4 (* = *lively, exciting*) *[party etc]* animé ◆ **~ London** le "Swinging London" ◆ **the Swinging Sixties** les sixties, les années soixante

COMP **swinging door** N *(US)* ⇒ **swing door** ; → **swing**

swinging single* N *(US) célibataire qui a de nombreuses aventures sexuelles*

swingometer /swɪŋˈɒmɪtəʳ/ N *(at election)* indicateur *m* de tendances

swinish* /ˈswaɪnɪʃ/ ADJ dégueulasse *

swipe /swaɪp/ N * *(at ball etc)* grand coup *m* ; (= *slap*) baffe * *f* ◆ **to take a ~ at** *(lit)* ⇒ **to swipe at** → **vi** ◆ **to take a ~ at sb** *(fig)* s'en prendre à *or* attaquer qn (de façon détournée) VT 1 (* = *hit*) *[+ ball]* frapper à toute volée ; *[+ person]* gifler à toute volée 2 (* = *steal: often hum*) piquer * *(sth from sb* qch à qn) 3 *[+ card]* ◆ **you pay by swiping a credit card** on paie avec une carte magnétique VI ◆ **to ~ at** * *[+ ball etc]* frapper *or* essayer de frapper à toute volée ; *[+ person]* flanquer * une baffe * à COMP **swipe card** N carte *f* magnétique

swirl /swɜːl/ N *(in river, sea)* tourbillon *m*, remous *m* ; *[of dust, sand]* tourbillon *m* ; *[of smoke]* tourbillon *m*, volute *f* ; *(fig) [of cream, ice cream etc]* volute *f* ; *[of lace, ribbons etc]* tourbillon *m* ◆ **the ~ of the dancers' skirts** le tourbillon *or* le tournoiement des jupes des danseuses VI *[water, river, sea]* tourbillonner, faire des remous *or* des tourbillons ; *[dust, sand, smoke, skirts]* tourbillonner, tournoyer VT ◆ **to ~ sth along/away** *[river]* entraîner/emporter qch en tourbillonnant ◆ **he ~ed his partner round the room** il a fait tournoyer *or* tourbillonner sa partenaire autour de la salle

swish /swɪʃ/ N *[of whip]* sifflement *m* ; *[of water, person in long grass]* bruissement *m* ; *[of grass in wind]* frémissement *m*, bruissement *m* ; *[of tyres in rain]* glissement *m* ; *[of skirts]* bruissement *m*, froufrou *m* VT 1 *[+ whip, cane]* faire siffler 2 (* = *beat, cane*) administrer *or* donner des coups de trique à VI *[cane, whip]* siffler, cingler l'air ; *[water]* bruire ; *[long grass]* frémir, bruire ; *[skirts]* bruire, froufrouter ADJ 1 *(Brit* * = *grand) [hotel, house etc]* chic *inv* ; *(pej)* rupin * 2 *(US* * = *effeminate)* efféminé

swishy* /ˈswɪʃɪ/ ADJ 1 *(Brit = smart)* chic *inv* ; *(pej)* rupin * 2 *(US = effeminate)* efféminé

Swiss /swɪs/ N *(pl inv)* Suisse *m*, Suisse(sse) *f* NPL **the Swiss** les Suisses *mpl* ADJ *(gen)* suisse ; *[ambassador, embassy]* de Suisse

COMP **Swiss chard** N bette *f*

Swiss cheese N *gruyère ou emmenthal* ◆ **her argument has more holes than ~ cheese** *(esp US hum)* son argument ne tient pas debout

Swiss cheese plant N monstera *f*

Swiss-French ADJ (= *from French-speaking Switzerland*) suisse romand

Swiss-German ADJ (= *from German-speaking Switzerland*) suisse allemand N (= *person*) Suisse *mf* allemand(e) ; (= *language*) suisse *m* allemand

the Swiss Guards NPL la garde suisse, les suisses *mpl*

Swiss roll N *(Brit Culin)* gâteau *m* roulé

Swiss steak N *(US Culin) steak fariné et braisé aux tomates et aux oignons*

switch /swɪtʃ/ N 1 *(Elec) (gen)* bouton *m* électrique, commande *f (esp Tech)* ; *(for lights)* interrupteur *m*, commutateur *m* ; *[of car]* (also **ignition switch**) contact *m* ◆ **the ~ was on/off** le bouton était sur la position ouvert/fermé, c'était allumé/éteint

2 *(Rail = points)* aiguille *f*, aiguillage *m*

3 (= *transfer*) *[of opinion] (gen)* changement *m* ; *(radical)* revirement *m*, retournement *m* ; *[of allegiance]* changement *m* ; *[of funds]* transfert *m (from* de ; *to* en faveur de) ◆ **his ~ to Labour** son revirement en faveur des travaillistes ◆ **the ~ to hearts/clubs** *(Bridge: in bidding)* (le changement de couleur et) le passage à cœur/trèfle ◆ **the ~ of the 8.30 from platform four** le changement de voie du train de 8h30 attendu au quai numéro quatre ◆ **the ~ of the aircraft from Heathrow to Gatwick because of fog** le détournement sur Gatwick à cause du brouillard de l'avion attendu à Heathrow

4 (= *stick*) baguette *f* ; (= *cane*) canne *f* ; (= *riding crop*) cravache *f* ; (= *whip*) fouet *m*

5 *[of hair]* postiche *m*

VT 1 (= *transfer*) *[+ one's support, allegiance, attention]* reporter *(from* de ; *to* sur) ◆ **to ~ production to another factory** transférer la production dans une autre usine ◆ **to ~ production to another model** (cesser de produire l'ancien modèle et) se mettre à produire un nouveau modèle ◆ **to ~ the conversation to another subject** détourner la conversation, changer de sujet de conversation

2 (= *exchange*) échanger *(A for B* A contre B ; *sth with sb* qch avec qn) ; (also **switch over, switch round**) *[+ two objects, letters in word, figures in column]* intervertir, permuter ; (= *rearrange:* also **switch round**) *[+ books, objects]* changer de place ◆ **we had to ~ taxis when the first broke down** nous avons dû changer de taxi quand le premier est tombé en panne ◆ **to ~ plans** changer de projet ◆ **we have ~ed all the furniture round** nous avons changé tous les meubles de place

3 *(Rail)* aiguiller *(to* sur)

4 (= *change*) **to ~ the oven to "low"** mettre le four sur "doux" ◆ **to ~ the radio/TV to another programme** changer de station/de chaîne ; see also **switch back, switch on**

5 ◆ **to ~ the grass with one's cane** cingler l'herbe avec sa canne ◆ **the cow ~ed her tail** la vache fouettait l'air de sa queue ◆ **he ~ed it out of my hand** il me l'a arraché de la main

VI 1 (= *transfer*) (also **switch over**) **Paul ~ed (over) to Conservative** Paul a voté conservateur cette fois ◆ **we ~ed (over) to oil central heating** (nous avons changé et) nous avons maintenant fait installer le chauffage central au mazout ◆ **many have ~ed (over) to teaching** beaucoup se sont recyclés dans l'enseignement

2 *[tail]* battre l'air

COMP **switch-car** N *(for gangster: in escape etc)* voiture-relais *f*

switch hit VI *(Baseball)* frapper la balle indifféremment de la main droite ou de la main gauche

switch-hitter N *(Baseball)* batteur *m* ambidextre ; *(US* * = *bisexual)* bisexuel(le) *m(f)*

► **switch back** VI *(to original plan, product, allegiance)* revenir, retourner *(to* à) ◆ **to ~ back to the other programme** *(Rad, TV)* remettre l'autre émission

VT SEP ◆ **to switch the oven back to "low"** remettre le four sur "doux" ◆ **to ~ the light back on** rallumer ◆ **to ~ the heater/oven back on** rallumer le radiateur/le four

N ◆ **switchback** ADJ → **switchback**

► **switch off** VI 1 *(Elec)* éteindre ; *(Rad, TV)* éteindre *or* fermer le poste ; (= *lose interest, unwind*) décrocher * ◆ **when the conversation is boring, he just ~es off*** quand la conversation l'ennuie, il décroche *

2 **to ~ off automatically** *[heater, oven etc]* s'éteindre tout seul *or* automatiquement

VT SEP *[+ electricity, gas]* éteindre, fermer ; *[+ radio, television, heater]* éteindre ; *[+ alarm clock, burglar alarm]* arrêter ◆ **to ~ off the light** éteindre (la lumière) ◆ **he ~ed the programme off** *(Rad, TV)* il a éteint (le poste) ◆ **to ~ off the engine** *[of car]* couper *or* arrêter le moteur ◆ **the oven ~es itself off** le four s'éteint automatiquement ◆ **he seems to be ~ed off* most of the time** *(fig)* il semble être à côté de ses pompes * la plupart du temps

► **switch on** VI 1 *(Elec)* allumer ; *(Rad, TV)* allumer le poste

2 ◆ **to switch on automatically** *[heater, oven etc]* s'allumer tout seul *or* automatiquement

VT SEP *[+ gas, electricity]* allumer ; *[+ water supply]* ouvrir ; *[+ radio, television, heater]* allumer, brancher ; *[+ engine, machine]* mettre en marche ◆ **to ~ on the light** allumer (la lumière) ◆ **his music ~es me on*** sa musique me branche * ◆ **to be ~ed on*** *(fig)* (= *up-to-date*) être branché *, être dans le vent *or* à la page ; *(by drugs)* planer * ; *(sexually)* être excité

► **switch over** VI 1 ⇒ **switch vi 1**

2 *(TV, Rad)* changer de chaîne/de station ◆ **to ~ over to the other programme** mettre l'autre chaîne/station

VT SEP 1 → **switch vt 2**

2 (*TV, Rad*) **to ~ the programme over** changer de chaîne/de station

N ♦ **switchover** → **switchover**

► **switch round** VI [*two people*] changer de place (l'un avec l'autre)

VT SEP → **switch vt 2**

switchback /ˈswɪtʃbæk/ N (*Brit = road: also at fair*) montagnes *fpl* russes ADJ (*= up and down*) tout en montées et descentes ; (*= zigzag*) en épingles à cheveux

switchblade /ˈswɪtʃbleɪd/ N (*US*) (also **switchblade knife**) couteau *m* à cran d'arrêt

switchboard /ˈswɪtʃbɔːd/ N (*Elec*) tableau *m* de distribution ; (*Telec*) standard *m* COMP **switchboard operator** N (*Telec*) standardiste *mf*

switcheroo */ˌswɪtʃəˈruː/ N (*esp US*) volte-face *f inv*, revirement *m* ♦ **to pull a ~** faire volte-face, effectuer un revirement

switchgear /ˈswɪtʃgɪəʳ/ N (*NonC: Elec*) appareillage *m* de commutation

switchman /ˈswɪtʃmən/ N (pl **-men**) (*Rail*) aiguilleur *m*

switchover /ˈswɪtʃəʊvəʳ/ N ♦ **the ~ from A to B** le passage de A à B ♦ **the ~ to the metric system** l'adoption *f* du système métrique

switchyard /ˈswɪtʃjɑːd/ N (*US Rail*) gare *f* de triage

Swithin /ˈswɪðɪn/ N Swithin *or* Swithun *m* ♦ **St ~'s Day** (jour *m* de) la Saint-Swithin (*15 juillet : pluie de Saint-Swithin, pluie pour longtemps*)

Switzerland /ˈswɪtsələnd/ N Suisse *f* ♦ **French-/German-/Italian-speaking ~** Suisse *f* romande/allemande/italienne

swivel /ˈswɪvl/ N pivot *m*, tourillon *m* VT (also **swivel round**) faire pivoter, faire tourner VI [*object*] pivoter, tourner

COMP [*seat, mounting etc*] pivotant, tournant

swivel chair N fauteuil *m* pivotant

► **swivel round** VI pivoter VT SEP ⇒ **swivel vt**

swizz */swɪz/ N (*Brit = swindle*) escroquerie *f* ♦ **what a ~!** (*= disappointment*) on est eu !*, on s'est fait avoir !*

swizzle /ˈswɪzl/ N (*Brit* *) ⇒ **swizz** COMP **swizzle stick** N fouet *m*

swollen /ˈswəʊlən/ VB ptp of **swell** ADJ [*limb, foot, finger, face, jaw*] enflé ; [*eye, breasts, tissue, organ*] gonflé ; [*stomach*] ballonné ; [*river, lake, stream*] en crue ; [*population*] accru ♦ **~ with blood/pus** *etc* plein de sang/pus *etc* ♦ **eyes ~ with tears** *or* **weeping** yeux gonflés de larmes ♦ **the river was ~ with rain** la rivière était grossie par les crues ♦ **the capital is ~ with refugees** la capitale est envahie par les réfugiés ♦ **to have ~ glands** avoir (une inflammation) des ganglions ♦ **to get a ~ head** (*Brit fig*) attraper la grosse tête* ; see also **swell** COMP **swollen-headed** * ADJ bêcheur*

swoon /swuːn/ VI († *or hum = faint*) se pâmer † (*also hum*) ; (*fig*) se pâmer d'admiration (*over sb/sth* devant qn/qch) N († *or hum*) pâmoison *f* ♦ **in a ~** en pâmoison

swoop /swuːp/ N [*of bird, plane*] descente *f* en piqué ; (*= attack*) attaque *f* en piqué (*on* sur) ; [*of police etc*] descente *f*, rafle *f* (*on* dans) ♦ **at** *or* **in one (fell) ~** d'un seul coup VI (also **swoop down**) [*bird*] fondre, piquer ; [*aircraft*] descendre en piqué, piquer ; [*police etc*] faire une descente ♦ **the plane ~ed (down) low over the village** l'avion est descendu en piqué au-dessus du village ♦ **the eagle ~ed (down) on the rabbit** l'aigle a fondu *or* s'est abattu sur le lapin ♦ **the soldiers ~ed (down) on the terrorists** les soldats ont fondu sur les terroristes

swoosh */swuːʃ/ N [*of water*] bruissement *m* ; [*of stick etc through air*] sifflement *m* ; [*of tyres in rain*] glissement *m* VI [*water*] bruire ♦ **he went ~ing through the mud** il est passé avec un bruit de boue qui gicle *or* en faisant gicler bruyamment la boue

swop /swɒp/ ⇒ **swap**

sword /sɔːd/ N épée *f* ♦ **to wear a ~** porter l'épée ♦ **to put sb to the ~** passer qn au fil de l'épée ♦ **to put up one's ~** rengainer son épée, remettre son épée au fourreau ♦ **to cross ~s with sb** (*lit, fig*) croiser le fer avec qn ♦ **those that live by the ~ die by the ~** quiconque se servira de l'épée périra par l'épée ♦ **to turn** *or* **beat one's ~s into ploughshares** forger des socs de ses épées

COMP [*scar, wound*] d'épée **sword and sorcery** N (*Literat, Cine etc*) *genre de romans, films ou jeux électroniques mêlant barbarie et sorcellerie dans un cadre moyenâgeux*

sword arm N bras *m* droit

sword dance N danse *f* du sabre

sword-point N ♦ **at ~-point** à la pointe de l'épée

sword-swallower N avaleur *m* de sabres

swordfish /ˈsɔːdfɪʃ/ N (pl inv) espadon *m*

swordplay /ˈsɔːdpleɪ/ N ♦ **there was a lot of ~ in the film** il y avait beaucoup de duels *or* ça ferraillait dur* dans le film

swordsman /ˈsɔːdzmən/ N (pl **-men**) épéiste *m* ♦ **to be a good ~** être une fine lame

swordsmanship /ˈsɔːdzmənʃɪp/ N (habileté *f* dans le) maniement *m* de l'épée

swordstick /ˈsɔːdstɪk/ N canne *f* à épée

swore /swɔːʳ/ VB pt of **swear**

sworn /swɔːn/ VB ptp of **swear** ADJ [*evidence, statement*] donné sous serment ; [*enemy*] juré ; [*ally, friend*] à la vie et à la mort

swot */swɒt/ (*Brit*) N (*pej*) bûcheur *m*, -euse *f* VT bûcher*, potasser* VI bûcher*, potasser* ♦ **to ~ for an exam** bachoter ♦ **to ~ at maths** bûcher* *or* potasser* ses maths

► **swot up** * VI, VT SEP ♦ **to swot up (on) sth** potasser* qch

swotting * /ˈswɒtɪŋ/ N bachotage *m* ♦ **to do some ~** bosser*, bachoter

swotty * /ˈswɒtɪ/ ADJ (*Brit pej*) bûcheur

swum /swʌm/ VB ptp of **swim**

swung /swʌŋ/ VB pt, ptp of **swing** COMP **swung dash** N (*Typo*) tilde *m*

sybarite /ˈsɪbəraɪt/ N sybarite *mf*

sybaritic /ˌsɪbəˈrɪtɪk/ ADJ sybarite

sycamore /ˈsɪkəmɔːʳ/ N sycomore *m*, faux platane *m*

sycophancy /ˈsɪkəfənsɪ/ N flagornerie *f*

sycophant /ˈsɪkəfənt/ N flagorneur *m*, -euse *f*

sycophantic /ˌsɪkəˈfæntɪk/ ADJ [*person*] servile, flagorneur ; [*behaviour, laughter*] obséquieux

Sydney /ˈsɪdnɪ/ N Sydney

syllabary /ˈsɪləbərɪ/ N syllabaire *m*

syllabi /ˈsɪləˌbaɪ/ NPL of **syllabus**

syllabic /sɪˈlæbɪk/ ADJ syllabique

syllabification /sɪˌlæbɪfɪˈkeɪʃən/ N syllabation *f*

syllabify /sɪˈlæbɪfaɪ/ VT décomposer en syllabes

syllable /ˈsɪləbl/ N syllabe *f* ♦ **to explain sth in words of one ~** expliquer qch en petit nègre

syllabub /ˈsɪləbʌb/ N ≈ sabayon *m*

syllabus /ˈsɪləbəs/ N (pl **syllabuses** *or* **syllabi**) (*Scol, Univ*) programme *m* ♦ **on the ~** au programme

syllogism /ˈsɪlədʒɪzəm/ N syllogisme *m*

syllogistic /ˌsɪləˈdʒɪstɪk/ ADJ syllogistique

syllogize /ˈsɪlədʒaɪz/ VI raisonner par syllogismes

sylph /sɪlf/ N sylphe *m* ; (*fig = woman*) sylphide *f*

sylphlike /ˈsɪlflaɪk/ ADJ [*woman*] gracile, qui a une taille de sylphide ; [*figure*] de sylphide

sylvan /ˈsɪlvən/ ADJ (*liter*) sylvestre

sylviculture /ˈsɪlvɪkʌltʃəʳ/ N sylviculture *f*

symbiosis /ˌsɪmbɪˈəʊsɪs/ N (*also fig*) symbiose *f* ♦ **to live in ~ with** vivre en symbiose avec

symbiotic /ˌsɪmbɪˈɒtɪk/ ADJ (*lit, fig*) symbiotique

symbol /ˈsɪmbəl/ N symbole *m*

symbolic(al) /sɪmˈbɒlɪk(əl)/ ADJ symbolique

symbolically /sɪmˈbɒlɪkəlɪ/ ADV symboliquement ♦ **~ important** important sur le plan symbolique

symbolism /ˈsɪmbəlɪzəm/ N symbolisme *m*

symbolist /ˈsɪmbəlɪst/ ADJ, N symboliste *mf*

symbolization /ˌsɪmbəlaɪˈzeɪʃən/ N symbolisation *f*

symbolize /ˈsɪmbəlaɪz/ VT symboliser

symmetric(al) /sɪˈmetrɪk(əl)/ ADJ (*gen, Geom, Math*) symétrique

symmetrically /sɪˈmetrɪkəlɪ/ ADV symétriquement, avec symétrie

symmetry /ˈsɪmɪtrɪ/ N symétrie *f*

sympathetic /ˌsɪmpəˈθetɪk/ ADJ 1 (*= showing concern*) [*person, smile*] compatissant ♦ **to be a ~ listener** écouter avec compassion ♦ **they were ~ but could not help** ils ont compati mais n'ont rien pu faire pour aider ♦ **to be/feel ~ towards sb** montrer/ressentir de la compassion pour qn ♦ **she was ~ to the problems of single parents** elle comprenait les problèmes des parents célibataires 2 (*= kind*) [*person*] bien disposé, bienveillant ; [*response*] favorable 3 (*Literat, Theat, Cine = likeable*) [*character*] sympathique 4 (*Anat, Physiol*) sympathique ♦ **the ~ nervous system** le système nerveux sympathique

> ⚠ Be cautious about translating **sympathetic** by **sympathique**, which usually means 'nice'.

sympathetically /ˌsɪmpəˈθetɪkəlɪ/ ADV 1 (*= compassionately*) avec compassion 2 (*= kindly, favourably*) [*listen, consider, portray*] avec bienveillance ♦ **to be ~ disposed** *or* **inclined to sb/sth** être favorablement disposé envers qn/qch ♦ **the house has been ~ restored** la maison a été restaurée en respectant son caractère d'origine 3 (*Anat, Physiol*) par sympathie

sympathize /ˈsɪmpəθaɪz/ VI (*= feel sorry for*) compatir ♦ **I do ~ (with you)!** je compatis !, comme je vous comprends ! ♦ **her cousin called to ~** sa cousine est venue témoigner sa sympathie ♦ **I ~ with you in your grief** je m'associe *or* je compatis à votre douleur ♦ **I ~ with you** *or* **what you feel** *or* **what you say** je comprends votre point de vue ♦ **they ~d with the guerrillas** ils ont sympathisé avec les guérilleros

sympathizer /ˈsɪmpəθaɪzəʳ/ N 1 (*= supporter*) sympathisant(e) *m(f)* (*with* de) 2 (*with the unfortunate*) **he was a ~ with wronged women** il avait de la compassion pour les femmes traitées injustement

sympathy /ˈsɪmpəθɪ/ LANGUAGE IN USE 24.4

N 1 (*= pity*) compassion *f* ♦ **to feel ~ for** éprouver *or* avoir de la compassion pour ♦ **we expressed our ~ for her loss** nous lui avons fait nos condoléances ♦ **I've had little help and no ~** je n'ai reçu que peu de secours et aucune compassion ♦ **to show one's ~ for sb** exprimer sa compassion pour qn ♦ **please accept my (deepest) ~** *or* **sympathies** veuillez agréer mes condoléances

2 (*= agreement*) **I have some ~ with this point of view** je comprends assez ce point de vue ♦ **I am in ~ with your proposals but ...** je suis en

accord avec *or* je ne désapprouve pas vos propositions mais ...

[3] *(= feeling)* **he was suspected of pro-democracy sympathies** on le soupçonnait d'avoir des sympathies pro-démocratiques ◆ **the sympathies of the crowd were with him** il avait le soutien de la foule, la foule était pour lui

[4] *(= fellow feeling)* solidarité *f (for avec)* ◆ **I have no ~ with lazy people** je n'ai aucune indulgence pour les gens qui sont paresseux ◆ **to come out** *or* **strike in ~ with sb** faire grève en solidarité avec qn

COMP **sympathy strike** N grève *f* de solidarité

> ⚠ Be cautious about translating **sympathy** by **sympathie**, whose commonest meaning is 'liking'.

symphonic /sɪmˈfɒnɪk/ ADJ *[music, work, piece]* symphonique ◆ **a ~ composer** un compositeur de musique symphonique COMP **symphonic poem** N poème *m* symphonique

symphony /ˈsɪmfənɪ/ N symphonie *f*
COMP *[concert, orchestra]* symphonique
symphony writer N symphoniste *mf*

symposium /sɪmˈpəʊzɪəm/ N (pl **symposiums** *or* **symposia** /sɪmˈpəʊzɪə/) *(all senses)* symposium *m*

symptom /ˈsɪmptəm/ N *(Med, fig)* symptôme *m*, indice *m*

symptomatic /ˌsɪmptəˈmætɪk/ ADJ symptomatique *(of sth* de qch*)*

synaesthesia, synesthesia (US) /ˌsɪnəsˈθiːzɪə/ N *(NonC)* synesthésie *f*

synagogue /ˈsɪnəgɒg/ N synagogue *f*

synapse /ˈsaɪnæps/ N synapse *f*

sync * /sɪŋk/ N (abbrev of **synchronization**) ◆ **in ~** bien synchronisé, en harmonie ◆ **they are in ~** *(fig: of people)* ils sont en harmonie, le courant passe ◆ **out of ~** mal synchronisé, déphasé

synchro * /ˈsɪŋkrəʊ/ (abbrev of **synchromesh**) N synchroniseur *m* COMP **synchro gearbox** N boîte *f* de vitesses synchronisées

synchromesh /ˌsɪŋkrəʊˈmeʃ/ *(Aut)* N synchroniseur *m* COMP **synchromesh gearbox** N boîte *f* de vitesses synchronisées

synchronic /sɪŋˈkrɒnɪk/ ADJ *(gen)* synchrone ; *(Ling)* synchronique

synchronicity /sɪŋkrəˈnɪsɪtɪ/ N synchronisme *m*

synchronism /ˈsɪŋkrənɪzəm/ N synchronisme *m*

synchronization /ˌsɪŋkrənaɪˈzeɪʃən/ N synchronisation *f*

synchronize /ˈsɪŋkrənaɪz/ VT synchroniser VI *[events]* se passer *or* avoir lieu simultanément ; *[footsteps etc]* être synchronisés ◆ **to ~ with sth** être synchrone avec qch, se produire en même temps que qch COMP **synchronized swimming** N *(Sport)* natation *f* synchronisée

synchronous /ˈsɪŋkrənəs/ ADJ synchrone

syncline /ˈsɪŋklaɪn/ N synclinal *m*

syncopate /ˈsɪŋkəpeɪt/ VT syncoper

syncopation /ˌsɪŋkəˈpeɪʃən/ N *(Mus)* syncope *f*

syncope /ˈsɪŋkəpɪ/ N *(Ling, Med)* syncope *f*

syncretism /ˈsɪŋkrɪtɪzəm/ N syncrétisme *m*

syndic /ˈsɪndɪk/ N *(= government official)* administrateur *m*, syndic *m* ; *(Brit Univ)* membre *m* d'un comité administratif

syndicalism /ˈsɪndɪkəlɪzəm/ N syndicalisme *m*

syndicalist /ˈsɪndɪkəlɪst/ ADJ, N syndicaliste *mf*

syndicate /ˈsɪndɪkɪt/ N [1] *(Comm etc)* syndicat *m*, coopérative *f* [2] *[of criminals]* gang *m*, association *f* de malfaiteurs [3] *(US Press) agence spécialisée dans la vente par abonnements d'articles, de reportages etc* VT /ˈsɪndɪkeɪt/ [1] *(Press: esp US) [+ article etc]* vendre *or* publier par l'intermédiaire d'un syndicat de distribution ; *[+ TV or radio programme]* distribuer sous licence ◆ **~d columnist** *(Press)* journaliste *mf* d'agence [2] *(Fin)* **to ~ a loan** former un consortium de prêt ◆ **~d loan** prêt *m* consortial [3] *[+ workers]* syndiquer

syndrome /ˈsɪndrəʊm/ N *(lit, fig)* syndrome *m*

synecdoche /sɪˈnekdəkɪ/ N synecdoque *f*

synergism /ˈsɪnəˌdʒɪsəm/ N synergie *f*

synergy /ˈsɪnədʒɪ/ N synergie *f*

synesthesia /ˌsɪnəsˈθiːzɪə/ N (US) ⇒ **synaesthesia**

synod /ˈsɪnəd/ N synode *m*

synonym /ˈsɪnənɪm/ N synonyme *m*

synonymous /sɪˈnɒnɪməs/ ADJ *(lit, fig)* synonyme *(with sth* de qch*)*

synonymy /sɪˈnɒnəmɪ/ N synonymie *f*

synopsis /sɪˈnɒpsɪs/ N (pl **synopses** /sɪˈnɒpsiːz/) résumé *m*, précis *m* ; *(Cine, Theat)* synopsis *m or f*

synoptic /sɪˈnɒptɪk/ ADJ synoptique

synovial /saɪˈnəʊvɪəl/ ADJ synovial

syntactic(al) /sɪnˈtæktɪk(əl)/ ADJ syntaxique

syntagm /ˈsɪntæm/ (pl **syntagms**), **syntagma** /sɪnˈtægmə/ (pl **syntagmata** /sɪnˈtægmətə/) N syntagme *m*

syntagmatic /ˌsɪntægˈmætɪk/ ADJ syntagmatique

syntax /ˈsɪntæks/ N syntaxe *f* ◆ **~ error** *(Comput)* erreur *f* de syntaxe

synth /sɪnθ/ N (abbrev of **synthetizer**) synthé * *m*

synthesis /ˈsɪnθəsɪs/ N (pl **syntheses** /ˈsɪnθəsiːz/) synthèse *f*

synthesize /ˈsɪnθəsaɪz/ VT *(= combine)* synthétiser ; *(= produce)* produire synthétiquement *or* par une synthèse, faire la synthèse de

synthesizer /ˈsɪnθəsaɪzəʳ/ N synthétiseur *m* ; → **speech, voice**

synthetic /sɪnˈθetɪk/ ADJ [1] *(= man-made) [material, chemical, drug, fibre]* synthétique [2] *(pej = false) [person, behaviour, emotion, taste]* artificiel N *(gen)* produit *m* synthétique ◆ **~s** *(= fibres)* fibres *fpl* synthétiques

syphilis /ˈsɪfɪlɪs/ N syphilis *f*

syphilitic /ˌsɪfɪˈlɪtɪk/ ADJ, N syphilitique *mf*

syphon /ˈsaɪfən/ N, VT ⇒ **siphon**

Syria /ˈsɪrɪə/ N Syrie *f*

Syrian /ˈsɪrɪən/ ADJ *(gen)* syrien ; *[ambassador, embassy]* de Syrie N Syrien(ne) *m(f)*

syringe /sɪˈrɪndʒ/ N seringue *f* VT seringuer

syrup /ˈsɪrəp/ N *(also Med)* sirop *m* ; (also **golden syrup**) mélasse *f* raffinée

syrupy /ˈsɪrəpɪ/ ADJ *(lit, fig)* sirupeux

system /ˈsɪstəm/ N [1] *(= structured whole)* système *m* ◆ **a political/economic/social ~** un système politique/économique/social ◆ **nervous ~** système *m* nerveux ◆ **digestive ~** appareil *m* digestif ◆ **the railway ~** le réseau de chemin de fer ◆ **the Social Security ~** le régime de la Sécurité sociale ◆ **new teaching ~s** nouveaux systèmes *mpl* d'enseignement ◆ **the Bell ~** *(Comm)* la compagnie *or* le réseau Bell ◆ **the St. Lawrence ~** *[of rivers]* le système fluvial *or* le réseau hydrographique du Saint-Laurent ◆ **the urban ~** *(Geog)* la trame urbaine ◆ **it's all ~s go** * ça turbine (un max) * ; → **feudal**

[2] *(= the body)* organisme *m* ◆ **her ~ will reject it** son organisme le rejettera ◆ **it was a shock to his ~** cela a été une secousse pour son organisme, cela a ébranlé son organisme ◆ **to get sth out of one's ~** * *(fig gen)* trouver un exutoire à qch ◆ **let him get it out of his ~** * *(anger)* laisse-le décharger sa bile ; *(hobby, passion)* laisse-le faire, ça lui passera ◆ **he can't get her out of his ~** * il n'arrive pas à l'oublier

[3] *(= established order)* **the ~** le système ◆ **to get round** *or* **beat** *or* **buck the ~** trouver le joint *(fig)* ◆ **down with the ~!** à bas le système !

[4] *(Comput)* système *m* ; → **operating**

[5] *(NonC = order)* méthode *f NonC* ◆ **to lack ~** manquer de méthode

COMP **system disk** N *(Comput)* disque *m* système
system operator N *(Comput)* opérateur *m* du système, serveur *m*
systems analysis N analyse *f* fonctionnelle
systems analyst N analyste *mf* en système
systems desk N pupitre *m*
systems engineer N ingénieur *m* système
systems programmer N programmeur *m* d'étude
systems software N logiciel *m* de base *or* d'exploitation

systematic /ˌsɪstəˈmætɪk/ ADJ *(gen)* systématique ; *[person]* méthodique

systematically /ˌsɪstəˈmætɪkəlɪ/ ADV systématiquement

systematization /ˌsɪstəmətaɪˈzeɪʃən/ N systématisation *f*

systematize /ˈsɪstəmətaɪz/ VT systématiser

systemic /sɪˈstemɪk/ ADJ [1] *(gen)* du système ; *(Anat)* du système, de l'organisme ; *[insecticide]* systémique ◆ **~ circulation** circulation *f* générale ◆ **~ infection** infection *f* généralisée [2] *(Ling)* systémique

systole /ˈsɪstəlɪ/ N systole *f*

T t

T, t /tiː/ **N** (= *letter*) T, t *m* ◆ **T for Tommy** ≃ TÊ comme Thérèse ◆ **that's it to a T*** c'est exactement cela ◆ **he'd got everything down to a T*** il avait pensé à tout ◆ **it fits him to a T*** ça lui va comme un gant ; → **dot**

COMP **T-bar** **N** (*Ski:* also **T-bar lift**) téléski *m* (à archets)

T-bone **N** (*Culin:* also **T-bone steak**) steak *m* avec un os en T

T-cell **N** lymphocyte *m* T, cellume *f* T

T-junction **N** intersection *f* en T

T-shaped **ADJ** en forme de T, en équerre

T-shirt **N** T-shirt *or* tee-shirt *m*

T-square **N** équerre *f* en T

T-stop **N** (*Phot*) diaphragme *m*

TA /tiːˈeɪ/ **N** 1 (*Brit Mil*) (abbrev of **Territorial Army**) → **territorial** 2 (*US Univ*) (abbrev of **teaching assistant**) → **teaching**

ta* /tɑː/ **EXCL** (*Brit*) merci !

tab /tæb/ **N** 1 (= *part of garment*) patte *f* ; (= *loop on garment etc*) attache *f* ; (= *label*) étiquette *f* ; (*on shoelace*) ferret *m* ; (= *marker: on file etc*) onglet *m* ◆ **to keep ~s** *or* **a ~ on*** [*+ person*] avoir *or* tenir à l'œil* ; [*+ thing*] garder un œil sur* 2 (*esp US* * = *café check*) addition *f*, note *f* ◆ **to pick up the ~*** (*lit, fig*) payer la note *or* l'addition 3 (*Comput*) (abbrev of **tabulator**) **~ key** touche *f* de tabulation 4 (*Drugs* *) pilule *f*, comprimé *m* 5 abbrev of **tablet 1**

tabard /ˈtæbəd/ **N** tabard *m*

Tabasco ® /təˈbæskəʊ/ **N** Tabasco ® *m*

tabby /ˈtæbɪ/ **N** (also **tabby cat**) chat(te) *m(f)* tigré(e) *or* moucheté(e)

tabernacle /ˈtæbənækl/ **N** tabernacle *m* ◆ **the Tabernacle** (*Rel*) le tabernacle

table /ˈteɪbl/ **N** 1 (= *furniture, food on it*) table *f* ; (= *people at table*) tablée *f*, table *f* ◆ **ironing/bridge/garden** table *f* à repasser/de bridge/de jardin ◆ **at ~** à table ◆ **to sit down to ~** se mettre à table ◆ **to lay** *or* **set the ~** mettre la table *or* le couvert ◆ **to clear the ~** débarrasser la table, desservir ◆ **the whole ~ laughed** toute la tablée *or* la table a ri ◆ **to lay sth on the ~** (*Parl*) remettre *or* ajourner qch ◆ **the bill lies on the ~** (*Parl*) la discussion du projet de loi a été ajournée ◆ **to put sth on the ~** (*fig*) (*Brit* = *propose*) avancer qch, mettre qch sur la table ; (*US* = *postpone*) ajourner *or* remettre qch ◆ **he slipped me £5 under the ~*** (*fig*) il m'a passé 5 livres de la main à la main ◆ **he was nearly under the ~** (*fig*) un peu plus et il roulait sous la table* ◆ **to turn the ~s** (*fig*) renverser les rôles, retourner la situation (*on sb* aux dépens de qn)

2 [*of facts, statistics*] tableau *m* ; [*of prices, fares, names*] liste *f* ; (*Math*) table *f* ; (*Sport:* also **league table**) classement *m* ◆ **~ of contents** table *f* des matières ◆ **the two-times ~** (*Math*) la table de (multiplication par) deux ◆ **we are in fifth place in the ~** (*Sport*) nous sommes classés cinquièmes, nous sommes cinquièmes au classement ; → **log²**

3 (*Geog*) ⇒ **tableland**

4 (*Rel*) **the Tables of the Law** les Tables *fpl* de la Loi

VT 1 (*Brit Admin, Parl* = *present*) [*+ motion etc*] présenter, déposer

2 (*US Admin, Parl* = *postpone*) [*+ motion etc*] ajourner ◆ **to ~ a bill** reporter la discussion d'un projet de loi

3 (= *tabulate*) dresser une liste *or* une table de ; [*+ results*] classifier

COMP [*wine, grapes, knife, lamp*] de table

Table Bay **N** (*Geog*) la baie de la Table

table dancing **N** numéro *m* de strip-tease sur commande

table d'hôte **ADJ** à prix fixe **N** (pl **tables d'hôte**) table *f* d'hôte, repas *m* à prix fixe

table football **N** baby-foot *m*

table leg **N** pied *m* de table

table linen **N** linge *m* de table

table manners **NPL** ◆ **he has good ~ manners** il sait se tenir à table

Table Mountain **N** (*Geog*) la montagne de la Table

table napkin **N** serviette *f* (de table)

table runner **N** chemin *m* de table

table salt **N** sel *m* fin

table talk **N** (*NonC*) menus propos *mpl*

table tennis **N** ping-pong *m*, tennis *m* de table **COMP** de ping-pong

table-tennis player **N** joueur *m*, -euse *f* de ping-pong, pongiste *mf*

table turning **N** (*NonC*) spiritisme *m*, tables *fpl* tournantes

tableau /ˈtæbləʊ/ **N** (pl **tableaux** *or* **tableaus** /ˈtæbləʊz/) (*Theat*) tableau *m* vivant ; (*fig*) tableau *m*

tablecloth /ˈteɪblklɒθ/ **N** nappe *f*

tableland /ˈteɪbllænd/ **N** (*Geog*) (haut) plateau *m*

tablemat /ˈteɪblmæt/ **N** (*made of cloth*) set *m* de table ; (*heat-resistant*) dessous-de-plat *m inv*

tablespoon /ˈteɪblspuːn/ **N** cuiller *f* de service ; (= *measurement:* also **tablespoonful**) cuillerée *f* à soupe, ≃ 15 ml

tablet /ˈtæblɪt/ **N** 1 (*Pharm*) comprimé *m*, cachet *m* ; (*for sucking*) pastille *f* 2 (= *stone: inscribed*) plaque *f* (commémorative) ; (*Hist: of wax, slate etc*) tablette *f* 3 [*of chocolate*] tablette *f* ◆ **~ of soap** savonnette *f* 4 (*Comput*) tablette *f*

tabletop /ˈteɪbltɒp/ **N** dessus *m* de table

tableware /ˈteɪblweəʳ/ **N** (*NonC*) vaisselle *f*

tabloid /ˈtæblɔɪd/ **N** (*Press:* also **tabloid newspaper**) tabloïd(e) *m*, quotidien *m* populaire **ADJ** (also **in tabloid form**) en raccourci, condensé ◆ **~ television** (*pej*) télévision *f* à sensation

TABLOIDS, BROADSHEETS

Il existe deux formats de journaux en Grande-Bretagne : le grand format du type "Le Figaro" en France (**broadsheet**), qui caractérise la presse de qualité ("Times", "Guardian", "Independent", "Daily Telegraph") et les tabloïdes qui se distinguent par leurs gros titres accrocheurs, leurs articles courts, leurs nombreuses photographies, leurs opinions tranchées et leur goût pour les histoires à scandale. Parmi les titres représentatifs de cette presse à sensation, on peut citer le "Sun", le "Daily Mirror", le "Daily Express" et le "Daily Mail".

Aux États-Unis, le principal quotidien **broadsheet** est l'édition nationale du "New York Times". Les tabloïdes américains les plus connus comprennent le "New York Daily News" et le "Chicago Sun-Times".

taboo /təˈbuː/ **ADJ, N** (*Rel, fig*) tabou *m* **VT** proscrire, interdire

tabor /ˈteɪbəʳ/ **N** tambourin *m*

tabu /təˈbuː/ **ADJ, VT** ⇒ **taboo**

tabular /ˈtæbjʊləʳ/ **ADJ** tabulaire

tabulate /ˈtæbjʊleɪt/ **VT** [*+ facts, figures*] présenter sous forme de tableau ; [*+ results*] classifier ; (*Typo*) mettre en colonnes

tabulation /ˌtæbjʊˈleɪʃən/ **N** 1 (*NonC* = *act*) [*of information, results*] disposition *f* *or* présentation *f* en tableaux 2 (= *table*) tableau *m*

tabulator /ˈtæbjʊleɪtəʳ/ **N** [*of typewriter*] tabulateur *m*

tache* /tæʃ/ **N** (*Brit*) moustache *f*, bacchantes* *fpl*

tacheometer /ˌtækɪˈɒmɪtəʳ/ **N** tachéomètre *m*

tachograph /ˈtækəgrɑːf/ **N** (*Brit*) tachygraphe *m*

tachometer /tæˈkɒmɪtəʳ/ **N** tachymètre *m*

tachycardia /ˌtækɪˈkɑːdɪə/ **N** tachycardie *f*

tachycardiac /ˌtækɪˈkɑːdɪæk/ **ADJ** tachycardique

tachymeter /tæˈkɪmɪtəʳ/ **N** tachéomètre *m*

tacit /ˈtæsɪt/ **ADJ** [*approval, agreement, admission, understanding*] tacite ; [*knowledge*] implicite

tacitly /ˈtæsɪtlɪ/ ADV tacitement

taciturn /ˈtæsɪtɜːn/ ADJ taciturne

taciturnity /ˌtæsɪˈtɜːnɪtɪ/ N taciturnité *f*

Tacitus /ˈtæsɪtəs/ N Tacite *m*

tack /tæk/ N 1 *(for wood, linoleum, carpet)* punaise *f*, semence *f* ; *(for upholstery)* semence *f* ; *(US:* also **thumbtack**) punaise *f* ; → **brass**
2 *(Sewing)* point *m* de bâti
3 *(= tactic)* tactique *f* ◆ **a change of** ~ un changement de tactique ◆ **the government changed** ~ le gouvernement a changé de direction *or* d'orientation ◆ **this finding set them off on another** ~ cette découverte les a conduits à orienter différemment leurs recherches ◆ **to be on the right/wrong** ~ être sur la bonne/mauvaise voie ◆ **to try another** ~ essayer une autre tactique
4 *(Naut)* bord *m*, bordée *f* ◆ **to make a** ~ faire *or* courir *or* tirer un bord *or* une bordée ◆ **to be on a port/starboard** ~ être bâbord/tribord amures
5 *(NonC: for horse)* sellerie *f (articles)*
6 *(NonC: * = rubbishy things)* objets *mpl* kitsch
VT 1 (also **tack down**) *[+ wood, lino, carpet]* clouer ◆ **he ~ed a note to the door** il a punaisé un mot à la porte
2 *(Sewing)* faufiler, bâtir ◆ ~ **the two pieces of material together** assemblez les deux morceaux de tissu
VI *(Naut = make a tack)* faire *or* courir *or* tirer un bord *or* une bordée ◆ **they ~ed back to the harbour** ils sont rentrés au port en louvoyant

► **tack down** VT SEP *(Sewing)* maintenir en place au point de bâti ; see also **tack vt 1**

► **tack on** VT SEP 1 *(Sewing)* bâtir, appliquer au point de bâti
2 *(fig)* ajouter (après coup) *(to à)*

tackiness /ˈtækɪnɪs/ N *(NonC)* 1 *(* = bad taste) [of person, place, film, clothes, remark]* vulgarité *f* 2 *(= stickiness) [of glue, paint, surface]* viscosité *f*

tacking /ˈtækɪŋ/ *(Sewing)* N bâtissage *m*, faufilure *f* ◆ **to take out the ~ from sth** défaufiler qch COMP **tacking stitch** N point *m* de bâti

tackle /ˈtækl/ LANGUAGE IN USE 26.2 N 1 *(NonC) (Naut = ropes, pulleys)* appareil *m* de levage ; *(gen = gear, equipment)* équipement *m* ◆ **fishing** ~ matériel *m* de pêche 2 *(Ftbl, Hockey, Rugby etc = action)* tacle *m* ; *(US Ftbl = player)* plaqueur *m*
VT 1 *(physically: Ftbl, Hockey, Rugby etc)* tac(k)ler ; *[+ thief, intruder]* saisir à bras-le-corps 2 *(verbally)* **I'll ~ him about it at once** je vais lui en parler *or* lui en dire deux mots tout de suite ◆ **I ~d him about what he had done** je l'ai questionné sur ce qu'il avait fait 3 *[+ task]* s'attaquer à ; *[+ problem, question, subject]* aborder, s'attaquer à ; * *[+ meal, food]* attaquer* ◆ **firemen ~d the blaze** les pompiers se sont attaqués à l'incendie ◆ **he ~d Hebrew on his own** il s'est mis à l'hébreu tout seul

tackroom /ˈtækrʊm/ N sellerie *f*

tacky /ˈtækɪ/ ADJ 1 *(* = tasteless) [person, place, film, clothes, remark]* vulgaire 2 *(= sticky) [glue]* qui commence à prendre ; *[paint, varnish]* pas tout à fait sec ; *[surface]* poisseux, collant

taco /ˈtɑːkəʊ/ N (pl **tacos**) taco *m*

tact /tækt/ N *(NonC)* tact *m*, délicatesse *f*

tactful /ˈtæktfʊl/ ADJ *[person, remark, behaviour]* plein de tact, délicat ; *[silence]* diplomatique ; *[hint, inquiry, reference]* discret (-ète *f*) ◆ **that wasn't a very ~ question** cette question n'était pas très délicate ◆ **to be ~ (with sb/about sth)** faire preuve de tact (envers qn/à propos de qch) ◆ **she was too ~ to say what she thought** elle avait trop de tact pour dire ce qu'elle pensait

tactfully /ˈtæktfəlɪ/ ADV avec tact ◆ **as he so ~ puts it ...** comme il le dit avec tant de tact ... ◆ **he ~ refrained from further comment** il a été assez délicat pour s'abstenir de tout autre commentaire

tactfulness /ˈtæktfʊlnɪs/ N ⇒ **tact**

tactic /ˈtæktɪk/ N *(Mil, fig)* tactique *f* ◆ **~s** *(NonC: Mil)* la tactique

tactical /ˈtæktɪkəl/ ADJ *(Mil, fig)* tactique ◆ **a ~ plan** une stratégie ◆ **to play a brilliant ~ game** *(Sport)* jouer avec une habileté tactique hors pair COMP **tactical voting** N *(Brit)* vote *m* utile

tactically /ˈtæktɪkəlɪ/ ADV *(Mil, fig) [important, disastrous]* d'un *or* du point de vue tactique, sur le plan tactique ; *[use]* tactiquement ◆ **to vote** ~ voter utile

tactician /tækˈtɪʃən/ N *(Mil, fig)* tacticien *m*

tactile /ˈtæktaɪl/ ADJ 1 *(= physical) [person]* qui a le sens tactile développé 2 *(= pleasant to touch) [fabric]* agréable au toucher ◆ **the ~ quality of textiles** le toucher des textiles 3 *(through touch) [sense, experience]* tactile

tactless /ˈtæktlɪs/ ADJ *[person]* peu délicat, qui manque de tact ; *[hint]* grossier ; *[inquiry, reference]* indiscret (-ète *f*) ; *[answer]* qui manque de tact, peu diplomatique *(fig) [suggestion]* peu délicat

tactlessly /ˈtæktlɪslɪ/ ADV *[behave]* de façon peu délicate, sans tact *or* délicatesse ; *[say]* de façon peu délicate

tactlessness /ˈtæktlɪsnɪs/ N manque *m* de tact

tad* /tæd/ N ◆ **a ~ big/small** *etc* un chouïa* grand/petit *etc*

tadpole /ˈtædpəʊl/ N têtard *m*

Tadzhik /ˈtɑːdʒɪk/ ADJ tadjik N 1 Tadjik(e) *m(f)* 2 *(= language)* tadjik *m*

Tadzhikistan /tɑːˌdʒɪkɪˈstɑːn/ N Tadjikistan *m* ◆ **in** ~ au Tadjikistan

tae kwon do /ˈtaɪˈkwɒnˈdəʊ/ N taekwondo *m*

taffeta /ˈtæfɪtə/ N *(NonC)* taffetas *m*

taffrail /ˈtæfreɪl/ N *(Naut)* couronnement *m* ; *(= rail)* lisse *f* de couronnement

Taffy* /ˈtæfɪ/ N *(pej)* (also **Taffy Jones**) *sobriquet donné à un Gallois*

taffy /ˈtæfɪ/ N *(US)* bonbon *m* au caramel ; *(Can)* tire *f* d'érable

tag /tæg/ N 1 *[of shoelace, cord etc]* ferret *m* ; *(on garment etc)* patte *f*, marque *f* ; *(= label: also fig)* étiquette *f* ; *(= marker: on file etc)* onglet *m* ; *(= surveillance device)* bracelet-émetteur *m* de surveillance électronique ◆ **all uniforms must have name ~s** chaque uniforme doit être marqué au nom de son propriétaire ; → **price**
2 *(= quotation)* citation *f* ; *(= cliché)* cliché *m*, lieu *m* commun ; *(= catchword)* slogan *m* ◆ ~ **(question)** *(Ling)* question-tag *f*
3 *(NonC = game)* (jeu *m* du) chat *m*
4 *(Comput)* balise *f*
VT 1 *[+ garment]* marquer ; *[+ bag, box, file]* étiqueter ; *(US * fig) [+ car]* mettre un papillon* sur ; *[+ driver]* mettre une contravention à
2 *(* = follow)* suivre ; *[detective]* filer
3 *(= describe) [+ person]* appeler, étiqueter
4 *(Comput)* baliser
5 *[+ offender] doter d'une plaque d'identité électronique à des fins de surveillance*
COMP **tag day** N *(US)* journée *f* de vente d'insignes *(pour une œuvre)*
tag end N *[of speech, performance, programme etc]* fin *f* ; *[of goods for sale]* restes *mpl*
tag line N *[of play]* dernière réplique *f* ; *[of poem]* dernier vers *m*

► **tag along** VI suivre le mouvement* ◆ **she left and the children ~ged along behind her** elle est partie et les enfants l'ont suivie ◆ **the others came ~ging along behind** les autres traînaient derrière *or* étaient à la traîne derrière ◆ **she usually ~s along (with us)** la plupart du temps elle vient avec nous

► **tag on*** VI ◆ **to tag on to sb** coller aux talons de qn* ◆ **he came ~ging on behind** il traînait derrière
VT SEP *(fig)* ajouter (après coup) *(to à)*

► **tag out** VT SEP *(Baseball)* mettre hors jeu

Tagalog /təˈgɑːlɒg/ N *(= language)* tagal *m*, tagalog *m*

tagboard /ˈtægbɔːd/ N *(US)* carton *m* (pour étiquettes)

tagger /ˈtægəʳ/ N *(Comput)* étiqueteur *m*

tagging /ˈtægɪŋ/ N (also **electronic tagging** : *in penal system)* marquage *m* (électronique)

tagliatelle /ˌtæljəˈtelɪ, ˌtæglɪəˈtelɪ/ N *(NonC)* tagliatelles *fpl*

tagmeme /ˈtægmiːm/ N *(Ling)* tagmème *m*

tagmemics /tægˈmiːmɪks/ N *(Ling: NonC)* tagmémique *f*

Tagus /ˈteɪgəs/ N Tage *m*

tahini /təˈhiːnɪ/ N *(NonC)* crème *f* de sésame

Tahiti /təˈhiːtɪ/ N Tahiti *f* ◆ **in** ~ à Tahiti

Tahitian /təˈhiːʃɪən/ ADJ tahitien N 1 Tahitien(ne) *m(f)* 2 *(= language)* tahitien *m*

t'ai chi (ch'uan) /ˈtaɪdʒiː(ˈtʃwɑːn)/ N tai-chi(-chuan) *m*

tail /teɪl/ N 1 *[of animal, aircraft, comet, kite, procession, hair]* queue *f* ; *[of shirt]* pan *m* ; *[of coat]* basque *f* ; *[of ski]* talon *m* ◆ **with his ~ between his legs** *(lit, fig)* la queue entre les jambes ◆ **to keep one's ~ up** *(fig)* ne pas se laisser abattre ◆ **he was right on my ~** *(= following me)* il me suivait de très près ◆ **it is a case of the ~ wagging the dog** c'est une petite minorité qui se fait obéir ◆ **to turn ~ (and run)** prendre ses jambes à son cou ; → **sting**
2 *[of coin]* pile *f* ◆ **~s I win!** pile je gagne !
3 *(* hum = buttocks)* postérieur* *m* ◆ **a piece of ~**⁑ *(US)* une fille baisable⁑
4 ◆ **to put a ~ on sb**⁑ *[detective etc]* faire filer qn
NPL **tails** * *(Dress)* queue *f* de pie
VT 1 * *[+ suspect etc]* suivre, filer
2 *(= cut tail of animal)* couper la queue à ; → **top**[1]
VI ◆ **to ~ after sb** suivre qn tant bien que mal
COMP **tail assembly** N *[of plane]* dérive *f*
tail coat N queue *f* de pie
tail end N *[of piece of meat, roll of cloth etc]* bout *m* ; *[of procession]* queue *f* ; *[of storm, debate, lecture]* toutes dernières minutes *fpl*, fin *f*
tail feather N plume *f* rectrice
tail lamp, tail light N *[of vehicle, train etc]* feu *m* arrière *inv*
tail-off N diminution *f or* baisse *f* graduelle
tail section N *[of plane]* arrière *m*
tail skid N *[of plane]* béquille *f* de queue
tail unit N *[of plane]* empennage *m*

► **tail away** VI *[sounds]* se taire (peu à peu) ; *[attendance, interest, numbers]* diminuer, baisser (petit à petit) ; *[novel]* se terminer en queue de poisson

► **tail back** VI ◆ **the traffic tailed back to the bridge** le bouchon *or* la retenue remontait jusqu'au pont
N ◆ **tailback** → **tailback**

► **tail off** VI ⇒ **tail away**
N ◆ **tail-off** → **tail**

tailback /ˈteɪlbæk/ N *(Brit = traffic jam)* bouchon *m*

tailboard /ˈteɪlbɔːd/ N *[of vehicle]* hayon *m*

-tailed /teɪld/ ADJ *(in compounds)* ◆ **long-tailed** à la queue longue

tailgate /ˈteɪlgeɪt/ N *[of vehicle]* hayon *m* (arrière) VT ◆ **to ~ sb** coller au train* de qn

tailhopping /ˈteɪlhɒpɪŋ/ N *(Ski)* ruade *f*

tailor /ˈteɪləʳ/ N tailleur *m*

VT *[+ garment]* façonner ; *(fig) [+ speech, book, product, service]* adapter *(to, to suit* à ; *for* pour) ◆ **a ~ed skirt** une jupe ajustée ◆ **the software can be ~ed to meet your requirements** le logiciel peut être adapté à vos besoins

COMP **tailor-made** ADJ *[garment]* fait sur mesure ◆ **the building is ~-made for this purpose** le bâtiment est conçu spécialement pour cet usage ◆ **a lesson ~-made for that class** une leçon conçue *or* préparée spécialement pour cette classe ◆ **the job was ~-made for him** le poste était fait pour lui

tailor-make VT ◆ **the therapist will ~-make the session for you** le psychanalyste adaptera la séance à vos besoins ◆ **we can ~-make your entire holiday** nous pouvons vous organiser tout un voyage à la carte

tailor's chalk N craie *f* de tailleur

tailor's dummy N mannequin *m* ; *(fig pej)* fantoche *m*

tailoring /ˈteɪlərɪŋ/ N *(fig) [of product, service]* personnalisation *f*, adaptation *f (to* à)

tailpiece /ˈteɪlpiːs/ N *(to speech)* ajout *m* ; *(to document, book)* appendice *m* ; *(to letter)* post-scriptum *m* ; *(Typ)* cul-de-lampe *m* ; *[of violin]* cordier *m*

tailpipe /ˈteɪlpaɪp/ N *(US = exhaust)* tuyau *m* d'échappement

tailplane /ˈteɪlpleɪn/ N stabilisateur *m*

tailspin /ˈteɪlspɪn/ N *[of plane]* vrille *f* ; *[of prices]* chute *f* verticale ◆ **to be in a ~** *(Aviat)* vriller VI tomber en chute libre

tailwind /ˈteɪlwɪnd/ N vent *m* arrière *inv*

taint /teɪnt/ VT *[+ meat, food]* gâter ; *[+ water]* infecter, polluer ; *[+ air, atmosphere]* vicier, infecter, polluer ; *(fig liter) [+ sb's reputation]* salir, ternir ◆ **blood ~ed with the AIDS virus** du sang contaminé par le virus du sida N *(NonC)* infection *f*, souillure *f* ; *(= decay)* corruption *f*, décomposition *f* ; *(fig: of insanity, sin, heresy)* tare *f (fig)* ◆ **her government never shook off the ~ of corruption** son gouvernement ne s'est jamais débarrassé de l'image corrompue qui était la sienne

tainted /ˈteɪntɪd/ ADJ 1 *(= tarnished) [money]* sale ; *[evidence]* suspect, douteux ; *[reputation]* terni, sali ; *[action, motive]* impur ◆ **the system is ~ with corruption** le système est entaché de corruption ◆ **politicians ~ by scandal** des hommes politiques éclaboussés par des scandales 2 *(= contaminated) [food] (gen)* abîmé, gâté ; *(with chemicals)* pollué ; *[meat]* avarié ; *[blood]* contaminé ; *[water, air, atmosphere]* pollué ; *[breath]* chargé ; *[drug]* frelaté

Taiwan /ˈtaɪˈwɑːn/ N Taïwan ◆ **in ~** à Taïwan

Taiwanese /ˌtaɪwəˈniːz/ ADJ taïwanais N *(pl inv)* Taïwanais(e) *m(f)*

Tajik /ˈtɑːdʒɪk/ ADJ, N → **Tadzhik**

Tajikistan /tɑːdʒiːkɪstɑːn/ N Tadjikistan *m* ◆ **in ~** au Tadjikistan

take /teɪk/

vb : pret **took**, ptp **taken**

1 NOUN	4 COMPOUNDS
2 TRANSITIVE VERB	5 PHRASAL VERBS
3 INTRANSITIVE VERB	

1 - NOUN

1 Cine, Phot prise *f* de vue(s) ; *(Recording)* enregistrement *m*

2 Fishing, Hunting prise *f*

3 US Comm = takings recette *f* ◆ **to be on the ~*** *(= stealing)* se servir dans la caisse

4 esp US * = share part *f*, montant *m* perçu ◆ **the taxman's ~ is nearly 50%** la ponction fiscale s'élève à près de 50%

5 * = view point *m* de vue

2 - TRANSITIVE VERB

1 gen prendre ; *(= seize)* prendre, saisir ◆ **to ~ sb's hand** prendre la main de qn ◆ **he took me by the arm, he took my arm** il m'a pris (par) le bras ◆ **he took her in his arms** il l'a prise dans ses bras ◆ **to ~ sb by the throat** prendre *or* saisir qn à la gorge ◆ **I ~ a (size) 12 in dresses** je mets *or* fais du 42 ◆ **I ~ a (size) 5 in shoes** je chausse du 38 ◆ **the policeman took his name and address** l'agent a pris *or* relevé ses nom et adresse ◆ **he ~s "The Times"** il lit le "Times" ◆ **he took the cathedral from the square** *(Phot)* il a pris la cathédrale vue de la place ◆ **he ~s a good photo*** *(Phot)* il est très photogénique ◆ **to ~ a ticket for a concert** prendre un billet *or* une place pour un concert ◆ **I'll ~ that one** je prends *or* prendrai celui-là ◆ **to ~ a wife** † prendre femme † ◆ **~ your partners for a waltz** invitez vos partenaires et en avant pour la valse ◆ **to ~ sth (up)on o.s.** prendre qch sur soi ◆ **to ~ it (up)on o.s. to do sth** prendre sur soi *or* sous son bonnet de faire qch

2 = extract prendre *(from sth* dans qch), tirer *(from sth* de qch) ; *(= remove)* prendre, enlever, ôter *(from sb* à qn) ; *(without permission)* prendre ◆ **to ~ sth from one's pocket** prendre qch dans *or* tirer qch de sa poche ◆ **to ~ sth from a drawer** prendre qch dans un tiroir ◆ **he ~s his examples from real life** il tire ses exemples de la réalité ◆ **I took these statistics from a government report** j'ai tiré ces statistiques d'un rapport gouvernemental

3 Math etc = subtract soustraire, ôter *(from* de) ◆ **he took 5 euros off the price** il a fait un rabais *or* une remise de 5 €

4 = capture *(Mil) [+ city, district, hill]* prendre, s'emparer de ; *(gen) [+ suspect, wanted man]* prendre, capturer ; *[+ fish etc]* prendre, attraper ; *(sexually) [+ woman]* prendre ; *(Chess)* prendre ; *[+ prize]* obtenir, remporter ; *[+ degree]* avoir, obtenir ◆ **to ~ a trick** *(Cards)* faire une levée ◆ **my ace took his king** j'ai pris son roi avec mon as ◆ **the grocer ~s about £500 per day** *(Brit)* l'épicier fait à peu près 500 livres de recette par jour, l'épicier vend pour à peu près 500 livres de marchandises par jour ; → **fancy, prisoner, surprise**

5 = ingest, consume *[+ food, drink]* prendre ◆ **he ~s sugar in his tea** il prend du sucre dans son thé ◆ **to ~ tea** † **with sb** prendre le thé avec qn ◆ **to ~ drugs** *(= medicines)* prendre des médicaments ; *(= narcotics)* se droguer ◆ **to ~ morphine** prendre de la morphine ◆ **"not to be taken (internally)"** *(Med)* "à usage externe" ◆ **he took no food for four days** il n'a rien mangé *or* pris pendant quatre jours

6 = occupy *[+ chair, seat]* prendre, s'asseoir sur ; *(= rent) [+ house, flat etc]* prendre, louer ◆ **to ~ one's seat** s'asseoir ◆ **is this seat ~n?** cette place est-elle prise *or* occupée ?

7 = go by *[+ bus, train, plane, taxi]* prendre ; *[+ road]* prendre, suivre ◆ **~ the first on the left** prenez la première à gauche

8 = negotiate *[+ bend]* prendre ; *[+ hill]* grimper ; *[+ fence]* sauter ◆ **he took that corner too fast** il a pris ce virage trop vite

9 Scol, Univ *(= sit) [+ exam, test]* passer, se présenter à ; *(= study) [+ subject]* prendre, faire ◆ **what are you taking next year?** qu'est-ce que tu prends *or* fais l'an prochain (comme matière) ?

10 esp Brit = teach *[+ class, students]* faire cours à ◆ **the teacher who took us for economics** le professeur qui nous faisait cours en économie *or* qui nous enseignait l'économie

11 = tolerate *[+ behaviour, remark etc]* accepter ; *[+ alcohol, garlic]* supporter ◆ **he won't ~ that reply from you** il n'acceptera jamais une telle réponse venant de vous ◆ **I'll ~ no nonsense!** on ne me raconte pas d'histoires ! ◆ **I'm not taking any!*** je ne marche pas !* ◆ **I can't ~ it any more** je n'en peux plus ◆ **we can ~ it!** on ne se laissera pas abattre !, on (l')encaissera !* ◆ **I can't ~ alcohol** je ne supporte pas l'alcool

12 = have as capacity contenir, avoir une capacité de ◆ **the bus ~s 60 passengers** l'autobus a une capacité de 60 places ◆ **the hall will ~ 200 people** la salle contient jusqu'à 200 personnes ◆ **the bridge will ~ 10 tons** le pont supporte un poids maximal de 10 tonnes

13 = receive, accept *[+ gift, payment]* prendre, accepter ; *[+ a bet]* accepter ; *[+ news]* prendre, supporter ◆ **he won't ~ less than $50 for it** il en demande au moins 50 dollars ◆ **~ it from me!** croyez-moi !, croyez-moi sur parole ! ◆ **(you can) ~ it or leave it** c'est à prendre ou à laisser ◆ **whisky? I can ~ it or leave it*** le whisky ? j'aime ça mais sans plus ◆ **she took his death quite well** elle s'est montrée très calme en apprenant sa mort ◆ **she took his death very badly** elle a été très affectée par sa mort ◆ **I wonder how she'll ~ it** je me demande comment elle prendra cela ◆ **you must ~ us as you find us** vous devez nous prendre comme nous sommes ◆ **to ~ things as they come** prendre les choses comme elles viennent* ◆ **you must ~ things as they are** il faut prendre les choses comme elles sont* ◆ **will you ~ it from here?** *(handing over task etc)* pouvez-vous prendre la suite *or* la relève ? ◆ **~ five/ten!*** *(esp US = have a break)* repos !

14 = assume supposer, imaginer ◆ **I ~ it that …** je suppose *or* j'imagine que … ◆ **how old do you ~ him to be?** quel âge lui donnez-vous ? ◆ **what do you ~ me for?** pour qui me prenez-vous ? ◆ **do you ~ me for a fool?** vous me prenez pour un imbécile ? ◆ **I took you for a burglar** je vous ai pris pour un cambrioleur ◆ **I took him to be foreign** je le croyais étranger ◆ **to ~ A for B** prendre A pour B, confondre A et B

15 = consider prendre ◆ **now ~ Ireland** prenons par exemple l'Irlande ◆ **~ the case of …** prenons *or* prenez le cas de … ◆ **taking one thing with another …** tout bien considéré …

16 = require prendre, demander ; *(Gram)* être suivi de ◆ **it ~s time** cela prend *or* demande du temps ◆ **the journey ~s five days** le voyage prend *or* demande cinq jours ◆ **it took me two hours to do it, I took two hours to do it** j'ai mis deux heures (à *or* pour le faire) ◆ **~ your time!** prenez votre temps ! ◆ **it won't ~ long** cela ne prendra pas longtemps ◆ **that ~s a lot of courage** cela demande beaucoup de courage ◆ **it ~s a brave man to do that** il faut être courageux pour faire cela ◆ **it ~s some doing*** ce n'est pas évident ◆ **it ~s some believing*** c'est à peine croyable ◆ **it took three policemen to hold him down** il a fallu trois agents pour le tenir ◆ **it ~s two to make a quarrel** *(Prov)* il faut être au moins deux pour se battre ◆ **he's got what it ~s!*** il est à la hauteur ◆ **he's got what it ~s to do the job** il a toutes les qualités requises pour ce travail

17 = carry *[+ child, object]* porter, apporter, emporter ; *[+ one's gloves, umbrella]* prendre, emporter (avec soi) ; *(= lead)* emmener, conduire ; *(= accompany)* accompagner ◆ **he took her some flowers** il lui a apporté des fleurs ◆ **~ his suitcase upstairs** montez sa valise ◆ **he ~s home £200 a week** il gagne 200 livres net par semaine ◆ **he took her to the cinema** il l'a emmenée au cinéma ◆ **I'll ~ you to dinner** je vous emmènerai dîner ◆ **they took him over the factory** ils lui ont fait visiter l'usine ◆ **to ~ sb to hospital** transporter qn à l'hôpital ◆ **he took me home in his car** il m'a ramené *or* raccompagné dans sa voiture ◆ **this road will ~ you to Paris** cette route vous mènera à Paris ◆ **this bus will ~ you to the town hall** cet

autobus vous conduira à la mairie ◆ **£20 won't ~ you far these days** de nos jours on ne va pas loin avec 20 livres ◆ **what took you to Lille?** qu'est-ce qui vous a fait aller à Lille ?

[18] [= refer] **to ~ a matter to sb** soumettre une affaire à qn, en référer à qn ◆ **I took it to him for advice** je lui ai soumis le problème pour qu'il me conseille

3 - INTRANSITIVE VERB

[fire, vaccination, plant cutting etc] prendre

4 - COMPOUNDS

take-home pay N salaire *m* net
take-up N *(Brit)* souscription *f*

5 - PHRASAL VERBS

► **take aback** VT SEP → **aback**

► **take after** VT FUS ressembler à, tenir de ◆ **she ~s after her mother** elle ressemble à *or* tient de sa mère

► **take against** VT FUS prendre en grippe

► **take along** VT SEP *[+ person]* emmener ; *[+ camera etc]* emporter, prendre

► **take apart** VI *[toy, machine]* se démonter
VT SEP *[+ machine, engine, toy]* démonter, désassembler ; *(* fig = criticize harshly) [+ plan, suggestion]* démanteler, démolir * ◆ **I'll ~ him apart * if I get hold of him!** si je l'attrape je l'étripe *or* ça va être sa fête ! *

► **take aside** VT SEP *[+ person]* prendre à part, emmener à l'écart

► **take away** VI ◆ **it takes away from its value** cela diminue *or* déprécie sa valeur ◆ **that doesn't ~ away from his merit** cela n'enlève rien à son mérite
VT SEP [1] *(= carry or lead away) [+ object]* emporter ; *[+ person]* emmener ◆ **"not to be taken away"** *(on book etc)* "à consulter sur place"
[2] *(= remove) [+ object]* prendre, retirer, enlever *(from sb* à qn ; *from sth* de qch) ; *[+ sb's child, wife, sweetheart]* enlever *(from sb* à qn) ◆ **she took her children away from the school** elle a retiré ses enfants de l'école
[3] *(Math)* soustraire, ôter *(from* de) ◆ **if you ~ three away from six ...** six moins trois ...

► **take back** VT SEP [1] *(= accept back) [+ gift, one's wife, husband]* reprendre ◆ **to ~ back a** *or* **one's promise** reprendre sa parole ◆ **she took back all she had said about him** elle a retiré tout ce qu'elle avait dit à son sujet ◆ **I ~ it all back!** je n'ai rien dit !
[2] *(= return) [+ book, goods]* rapporter *(to* à) ; *(= accompany) [+ person]* raccompagner, reconduire *(to* à)
[3] *(= recall, evoke)* ◆ **it takes me back to my childhood** cela me rappelle mon enfance

► **take down** VT SEP [1] *[+ object from shelf etc]* descendre *(from, off* de) ; *[+ trousers]* baisser ; *[+ picture]* décrocher, descendre ; *[+ poster]* décoller ; → **peg**
[2] *(= dismantle) [+ scaffolding, tent]* démonter ; *[+ building]* démolir
[3] *(= write etc) [+ notes, letter]* prendre ; *[+ address, details]* prendre, noter, inscrire
[4] *(in courtroom)* ◆ **take him down!** qu'on emmène le prisonnier !

► **take from** VT FUS ⇒ **take away from** ; → **take away**

► **take in** VT SEP [1] *(into building) [+ garden furniture, harvest]* rentrer ; *[+ person]* faire entrer
[2] *(into one's home) [+ lodgers]* prendre ; *[+ friend]* recevoir ; *[+ homeless person, stray dog]* recueillir
[3] ◆ **she takes in sewing** elle fait *or* prend de la couture à domicile
[4] *(= make smaller) [+ skirt, dress, waistband]* reprendre ◆ **to ~ in the slack on a rope** *(Climbing)* avaler le mou d'une corde
[5] *(= include, cover)* couvrir, inclure, englober, embrasser ◆ **we cannot ~ in all the cases** nous ne pouvons pas couvrir *or* inclure tous les cas ◆ **this ~s in all possibilities** ceci englobe *or* embrasse toutes les possibilités ◆ **we took in Venice on the way home** *(fig)* nous avons visité Venise sur le chemin du retour ◆ **to ~ in a movie** aller au cinéma
[6] *(= grasp, understand)* saisir, comprendre ◆ **that child ~s everything in** rien n'échappe à cet enfant ◆ **the children were taking it all in** les enfants étaient tout oreilles ◆ **she couldn't ~ in his death at first** dans les premiers temps elle ne pouvait pas se faire à l'idée de sa mort ◆ **he hadn't fully ~n in that she was dead** il n'avait pas (vraiment) réalisé qu'elle était morte ◆ **he took in the situation at a glance** il a apprécié la situation en un clin d'œil
[7] *(* = cheat, deceive)* avoir *, rouler * ◆ **I've been ~n in** je me suis laissé avoir *, j'ai été roulé * ◆ **he's easily ~n in** il se fait facilement avoir * ◆ **to be ~n in by appearances** se laisser prendre aux *or* tromper par les apparences ◆ **I was ~n in by his disguise** je me suis laissé prendre à son déguisement

► **take off** VI *[person]* partir *(for* pour) ; *[aircraft, career, scheme]* décoller ◆ **the plane took off for Berlin** l'avion s'est envolé pour Berlin
VT SEP [1] *(= remove) [+ garment]* enlever, ôter, retirer ; *[+ buttons, price tag, lid]* enlever ; *[+ telephone receiver]* décrocher ; *[+ item on menu, train, bus]* supprimer ◆ **they had to ~ his leg off** *(= amputate)* on a dû l'amputer d'une jambe ◆ **he took £5 off** *(= lowered price)* il a baissé le prix de *or* il a fait un rabais de 5 livres, il a rabattu 5 livres sur le prix ◆ **I'll ~ something off the price for you** je vais vous faire un rabais *or* une remise (sur le prix) ◆ **her new hairstyle ~s five years off her** * sa nouvelle coiffure la rajeunit de cinq ans
[2] *(= lead etc away) [+ person, car]* emmener ◆ **he took her off to lunch** il l'a emmenée déjeuner ◆ **to ~ sb off to jail** emmener qn en prison ◆ **he was ~n off to hospital** on l'a transporté à l'hôpital ◆ **after the wreck a boat took the crew off** une embarcation est venue sauver l'équipage du navire naufragé ◆ **to ~ o.s. off** s'en aller
[3] *(Brit = imitate)* imiter, pasticher

► **take on** VI [1] *[idea, fashion etc]* prendre, marcher *
[2] *(Brit * = be upset)* s'en faire *
VT SEP [1] *(= accept etc) [+ work, responsibility]* prendre, accepter, se charger de ; *[+ bet]* accepter ; *[challenger in game/fight]* accepter d'affronter ◆ **I'll ~ you on!** *(Betting)* chiche ! ; *(Sport)* je te parie que je te bats ! ◆ **he has ~n on more than he bargained for** il n'avait pas compté prendre une si lourde responsabilité ◆ **to agree to ~ a job on** *(employment)* accepter un poste ; *(task)* accepter de se charger d'un travail
[2] *[+ employee]* prendre, embaucher ; *[+ cargo, passenger]* embarquer, prendre ; *[+ form, qualities]* prendre, revêtir
[3] *(= contend with) [+ enemy]* s'attaquer à ◆ **he took on the whole committee** *(= challenge etc)* il s'est attaqué *or* s'en est pris au comité tout entier

► **take out** VT SEP [1] *(= lead or carry outside) [+ chair etc]* sortir ; *[+ prisoner]* faire sortir ◆ **they took us out to see the sights** ils nous ont emmenés visiter la ville ◆ **he took her out to lunch/the theatre** il l'a emmenée déjeuner/au théâtre ◆ **he has often ~n her out** il l'a souvent sortie ◆ **I'm going to ~ the children/dog out** je vais sortir les enfants/le chien
[2] *(from pocket, drawer)* prendre *(from, of* dans) ; *(= remove)* sortir, retirer, enlever, ôter *(from, of* de) ; *[+ tooth]* arracher ; *[+ appendix, tonsils]* enlever ; *[+ stain]* ôter, enlever *(from* de) ◆ **~ your hands out of your pockets** sors *or* enlève *or* retire tes mains de tes poches ◆ **that will ~ you out of yourself a bit** *(fig)* cela vous changera les idées ◆ **that sort of work certainly ~s it out of you** * c'est vraiment un travail épuisant ◆ **when he got the sack he took it out on the dog** * quand il a été licencié, il s'est défoulé * sur le chien ◆ **don't ~ it out on me!** * ce n'est pas la peine de t'en prendre à moi ! ◆ **don't ~ your bad temper out on me** * ne passe pas ta mauvaise humeur sur moi
[3] *[+ insurance policy]* souscrire à, prendre ; *[+ patent]* prendre ; *[+ licence]* se procurer
[4] *(Mil *) [+ target]* descendre *, bousiller *

► **take over** VI *[dictator, army, political party]* prendre le pouvoir ◆ **to ~ over from sb** prendre la relève *or* le relais de qn ◆ **let him ~ over** cédez-lui la place
VT SEP [1] *(= escort or carry across)* **he took me over to the island in his boat** il m'a transporté jusqu'à l'île dans son bateau ◆ **will you ~ me over to the other side?** voulez-vous me faire traverser ?
[2] *(= assume responsibility for) [+ business, shop]* reprendre ; *[+ sb's debts]* prendre à sa charge ◆ **he took over the shop from his father** il a pris la suite de son père dans le magasin ◆ **he took over the job from Paul** il a succédé à Paul (à ce poste) ◆ **I took over his duties** je l'ai remplacé dans ses fonctions ◆ **he took over the leadership of the party when Smith resigned** il a remplacé Smith à la tête du parti après la démission de celui-ci
[3] *(Fin) [+ another company]* absorber, racheter ◆ **the tourists have ~n over Venice** les touristes ont envahi Venise

► **take to** VT FUS [1] *(= conceive liking for) [+ person]* se prendre d'amitié pour, se prendre de sympathie pour, sympathiser avec ; *[+ game, action, study]* prendre goût à, mordre à * ◆ **I didn't ~ to the idea** l'idée ne m'a rien dit ◆ **they took to each other at once** ils se sont plu immédiatement ◆ **I didn't ~ to him** il ne m'a pas beaucoup plu
[2] *(= start, adopt) [+ habit]* prendre ; *[+ hobby]* se mettre à ◆ **to ~ to drink/drugs** se mettre à boire/à se droguer ◆ **she took to telling everyone ...** elle s'est mise à dire à tout le monde ...
[3] *(= go to)* **to take to one's bed** s'aliter ◆ **to ~ to the woods** *[walker]* aller dans la forêt ; *[hunted man]* aller se réfugier *or* se cacher dans la forêt ◆ **to ~ to the boats** *(Naut)* abandonner *or* évacuer le navire ; → **heel[1]**

► **take up** VI ◆ **to take up with sb** se lier avec qn, se prendre d'amitié pour qn
VT SEP [1] *(= lead or carry upstairs, uphill etc) [+ person]* faire monter ; *[+ object]* monter
[2] *(= lift) [+ object from ground]* ramasser, prendre ; *[+ carpet]* enlever ; *[+ roadway, pavement]* dépaver ; *[+ dress, hem, skirt]* raccourcir ; *[+ passenger]* prendre ; *(fig: after interruption) [+ one's work, book]* reprendre, se remettre à, continuer ; *[+ conversation, discussion, story]* reprendre (le fil de) ◆ **she took up the story where she had left off** elle a repris l'histoire là où elle s'était arrêtée ; → **cudgel**
[3] *(= occupy) [+ space]* occuper, tenir, prendre ; *[+ time]* prendre, demander ; *[+ attention]* occuper, absorber ◆ **he is very ~n up** il est très pris ◆ **he is quite ~n up with her** il ne pense plus qu'à elle ◆ **he is completely ~n up with his plan** il est tout entier à son projet ◆ **it ~s up too much room** cela prend *or* occupe trop de place ◆ **it ~s up all my free time** cela (me) prend tout mon temps libre
[4] *(= absorb) [+ liquids]* absorber
[5] *(= raise question of) [+ subject]* aborder ◆ **I'll ~ that up with him** je lui en parlerai ◆ **I would like to ~ you up on something you said earlier** je voudrais revenir sur quelque chose que vous avez dit précédemment

6 *(= start, accept)* *[+ hobby, subject, sport, language]* se mettre à ; *[+ career]* embrasser ; *[+ method]* adopter, retenir ; *[+ challenge]* relever ; *[+ shares]* souscrire à ; *[+ person]* *(as friend)* adopter ; *(as protégé)* prendre en main ◆ **to ~ up one's new post** entrer en fonction ◆ **I'll ~ you up on your promise** je mettrai votre parole à l'épreuve ◆ **I'd like to ~ you up on your offer of free tickets** je voudrais accepter votre offre de places gratuites ◆ **I'll ~ you up on that some day** je m'en souviendrai à l'occasion, un jour je vous prendrai au mot

takeaway /'teɪkəweɪ/ N *(Brit = food shop)* magasin *m* de plats à emporter
COMP **takeaway food** N plats *mpl* préparés (à emporter)
takeaway meal N repas *m* à emporter

takedown* /'teɪkdaʊn/ ADJ *[toy, weapon]* démontable

taken /'teɪkən/ VB ptp of **take** ADJ 1 *[seat, place]* pris, occupé 2 ◆ **to be very ~ with sb/sth** être très impressionné par qn/qch ◆ **I'm not very ~ with him** il ne m'a pas fait une grosse impression ◆ **I'm quite ~ with** *or* **by that idea** cette idée me plaît énormément

takeoff /'teɪkɒf/ N *(in plane)* décollage *m* ; *(Gym, Ski)* envol *m* ; *(fig: Econ etc)* démarrage *m* ; *(= imitation)* imitation *f*, pastiche *m*

takeout /'teɪkaʊt/ N 1 *(US)* ⇒ **takeaway** 2 *(Bridge* also **takeout bid)** réponse *f* de faiblesse

takeover /'teɪkəʊvəʳ/ N *(Pol)* prise *f* du pouvoir ; *(Fin)* rachat *m* COMP **takeover bid** N offre *f* publique d'achat, OPA *f*

taker /'teɪkəʳ/ N ◆ **~s of snuff** les gens qui prisent ◆ **drug-~s** les drogués *mpl* ◆ **at $50 he found no ~s** il n'a pas trouvé d'acheteurs *or* trouvé preneur pour 50 dollars ◆ **this suggestion found no ~s** cette suggestion n'a été relevée par personne

taking /'teɪkɪŋ/ ADJ *[person, manners]* séduisant ; *[child]* mignon N 1 ◆ **it is yours for the ~** tu n'as qu'à (te donner la peine de) le prendre 2 *(Mil = capture)* prise *f* 3 *(Brit Jur)* **~ and driving away a vehicle** vol *m* de véhicule NPL **takings** *(Brit Comm)* recette *f*

talc /tælk/, **talcum (powder)** /tælkəm(paʊdəʳ)/ N talc *m*

tale /teɪl/ N *(= story)* conte *m*, histoire *f* ; *(= legend)* histoire *f*, légende *f* ; *(= account)* récit *m*, histoire *f* *(pej)* ◆ **"Tales of King Arthur"** *(Literat)* "La Légende du Roi Arthur" ◆ **he told us the ~ of his adventures** il nous a fait le récit de ses aventures ◆ **I've heard that ~ before** j'ai déjà entendu cette histoire-là quelque part ◆ **I've been hearing ~s about you** on m'a dit *or* raconté des choses sur vous ◆ **to tell ~s** *(= inform on sb)* rapporter, cafarder* ; *(= to lie)* mentir, raconter des histoires* ◆ **to tell ~s out of school** *(fig)* raconter ce qu'on devrait taire ◆ **he lived to tell the ~** il y a survécu ; → **fairy, old, tell, woe**

Taleban /'tælɪbæn/ N, ADJ ⇒ **Taliban**

talebearer /'teɪlbɛərəʳ/ N rapporteur *m*, -euse *f*, mouchard(e) *m(f)*

talebearing /'teɪlbɛərɪŋ/ N rapportage *m*, cafardage* *m*

talent /'tælənt/ N 1 *(= gift)* don *m*, talent *m* ; *(NonC)* talent *m* ◆ **to have a ~ for drawing** être doué pour le dessin, avoir un don *or* du talent pour le dessin ◆ **a writer of great ~** un écrivain de grand talent *or* très talentueux ◆ **he encourages young ~** il encourage les jeunes talents ◆ **he is looking for ~ amongst the schoolboy players** il cherche de futurs grands joueurs parmi les lycéens
2 *(‡ = attractive people)* **there's not much ~ here tonight** il n'y a pas grand-chose comme petits lots‡ ici ce soir
3 *(= coin)* talent *m*
COMP **talent competition** N ⇒ **talent show**
talent contest N *concours musical ayant pour but de détecter les jeunes talents*
talent scout N *(Cine, Theat)* découvreur *m*, -euse *f* *or* dénicheur *m*, -euse *f* de vedettes ; *(Sport)* dénicheur *m*, -euse *f* de futurs grands joueurs
talent show N concours *m* d'amateurs
talent spotter N ⇒ **talent scout**

talented /'tæləntɪd/ ADJ talentueux, doué

taletelling /'teɪltelɪŋ/ N ⇒ **talebearing**

tali /'teɪlaɪ/ NPL of **talus**

Taliban /'tælɪbæn/ N Taliban *m* ◆ **the Taliban** les Taliban ADJ taliban

talisman /'tælɪzmən/ N (pl **talismans**) talisman *m*

talk /tɔːk/ N 1 conversation *f*, discussion *f* ; *(more formal)* entretien *m* ; *(= chat)* causerie *f* ◆ **during his ~ with the Prime Minister** pendant son entretien avec le Premier ministre ◆ **~s** *(esp Pol)* discussions *fpl* ◆ **peace ~s** pourparlers *mpl* de paix ◆ **the Geneva ~s on disarmament** la conférence de Genève sur le désarmement ◆ **I enjoyed our (little) ~** notre causerie *or* notre petite conversation m'a été très agréable ◆ **we've had several ~s about this** nous en avons parlé *or* discuté plusieurs fois ◆ **I must have a ~ with him** *(gen)* il faut que je lui parle *subj* ; *(warning, threatening etc)* j'ai à lui parler ◆ **we must have a ~ some time** il faudra que nous nous rencontrions *subj* un jour pour discuter *or* causer
2 *(= informal lecture)* exposé *m* *(on sur)* ; *(less academic or technical)* causerie *f* *(on sur)* ◆ **to give a ~** faire un exposé, donner une causerie *(on sur)* ◆ **Mr Jones has come to give us a ~ on ...** M. Jones est venu nous parler de ... ◆ **to give a ~ on the radio** parler à la radio
3 *(NonC)* propos *mpl* ; *(= gossip)* bavardage(s) *m(pl)* ; *(pej)* racontars *mpl* ◆ **the ~ was all about the wedding** les propos tournaient autour du mariage ◆ **you should hear the ~!** si tu savais ce qu'on raconte ! ◆ **there is (some) ~ of his returning** *(= it is being discussed)* il est question qu'il revienne ; *(= it is being rumoured)* on dit qu'il va peut-être revenir, le bruit court qu'il va revenir ◆ **there was no ~ of his resigning** il n'a pas été question qu'il démissionne *subj* ◆ **it's common ~ that ...** on dit partout que ..., tout le monde dit que ... ◆ **it's just ~** ce ne sont que des on-dit *or* des racontars *or* des bavardages ◆ **there has been a lot of ~ about her** il a beaucoup été question d'elle ; *(pej)* on a raconté beaucoup d'histoires sur elle ◆ **I've heard a lot of ~ about the new factory** j'ai beaucoup entendu parler de la nouvelle usine ◆ **all that ~ about what he was going to do!** toutes ces vaines paroles sur ce qu'il allait faire ! ◆ **he's all ~** *(pej)* c'est un grand vantard *or* hâbleur ◆ **it was all (big) ~** *(pej)* tout ça c'était du vent* ◆ **she's/it's the ~ of the town** on ne parle que d'elle/de cela ; → **baby, idle, small**
VI 1 *(= speak)* parler *(about, of* de) ; *(= chatter)* bavarder, causer ◆ **he can't ~ yet** il ne parle pas encore ◆ **after days of torture he finally ~ed** après plusieurs jours de torture, il a enfin parlé ◆ **I'll make you ~!** (avec moi) tu vas parler ! ◆ **now you're ~ing!*** voilà qui devient intéressant ! ◆ **it's easy** *or* **all right for him to ~!** il peut parler ! ◆ **look who's ~ing!***, **YOU can ~!*** *(iro)* tu peux parler !*, tu es mal placé pour faire ce genre de remarque ! ◆ **to ~ through one's hat*** *or* **through a hole in one's head***, **to ~ out of one's arse***‡ *(Brit)* débloquer‡, dire des conneries‡ ◆ **he was just ~ing for the sake of ~ing** il parlait pour ne rien dire ◆ **he ~s too much** *(too chatty)* il parle trop ; *(indiscreet)* il ne sait pas se taire ◆ **he can ~ under water** *(Austral)* c'est un moulin à paroles ◆ **don't ~ to me like that!** ne me parle pas sur ce ton ! ◆ **do what he tells you because he knows what he's ~ing about** fais ce qu'il te demande parce qu'il sait ce qu'il dit ◆ **he knows what he's ~ing about when he's on the subject of cars** il s'y connaît quand il parle (de) voitures ◆ **he doesn't know what he's ~ing about** il ne sait pas ce qu'il dit ◆ **I'm not ~ing about you** ce n'est pas de toi que je parle, il ne s'agit pas de toi ◆ **he was ~ing of** *or* **about going to Greece** il parlait d'aller en Grèce ◆ **it's not as if we're ~ing about ...** ce n'est pas comme s'il s'agissait de ... ◆ **you're ~ing about a million dollars** ça coûterait un million de dollars ◆ **they ~ed of** *or* **about nothing except ...** ils ne parlaient que de ... ◆ **the marriage was much ~ed of in the town** toute la ville parlait du mariage ◆ **his much ~ed-of holiday never happened** ses fameuses vacances ne sont jamais arrivées ◆ **I'm not ~ing to him any more** je ne lui adresse plus la parole, je ne lui cause plus* ◆ **~ing of films, have you seen ...?** en parlant de *or* à propos de films, avez-vous vu ... ? ◆ **~ about a stroke of luck!*** ça tombe (*or* tombait *etc*) à pic !* ; → **big, tough**
2 *(= converse)* parler *(to* à ; *with* avec) discuter *(to, with* avec) ; *(more formally)* s'entretenir *(to, with* avec) ; *(= chat)* causer *(to, with* avec) ; *(= gossip)* parler, causer *(about* de), jaser *(pej)* *(about* sur) ◆ **who were you ~ing to?** à qui parlais-tu ? ◆ **I saw them ~ing (to each other)** je les ai vus en conversation l'un avec l'autre ◆ **to ~ to o.s.** se parler tout seul ◆ **I'll ~ to you about that tomorrow** je t'en parlerai demain ; *(threateningly)* j'aurai deux mots à te dire là-dessus demain ◆ **it's no use ~ing to you** je perds mon temps avec toi ◆ **we were just ~ing of** *or* **about you** justement nous parlions de toi ◆ **the Foreign Ministers ~ed about the crisis in China** les ministres des Affaires étrangères se sont entretenus de la crise chinoise ◆ **I have ~ed with him several times** j'ai eu plusieurs conversations avec lui ◆ **try to keep him ~ing** essaie de le faire parler aussi longtemps que possible ◆ **to get o.s. ~ed about** faire parler de soi ; → **nineteen**
VT 1 *[+ a language, slang]* parler ◆ **to ~ business/politics** parler affaires/politique ◆ **to ~ nonsense** *or* **rubbish*** *or* **tripe**‡ dire n'importe quoi *or* des conneries‡ ◆ **he's ~ing sense** c'est la voix de la raison qui parle, ce qu'il dit est le bon sens même ◆ **~ sense!** ne dis pas n'importe quoi ! ◆ **we're ~ing big money/serious crime here*** il s'agit de grosses sommes d'argent/de crimes graves* ; → **hind², shop, turkey**
2 ◆ **to ~ sb into doing sth** persuader qn de faire qch ◆ **I managed to ~ him out of doing it** je suis arrivé à le dissuader de le faire ◆ **she ~ed him into a better mood** elle a dissipé sa mauvaise humeur ◆ **he ~ed himself into the job** il a si bien parlé qu'on lui a offert le poste ◆ **to ~ sb through sth** bien expliquer qch à qn
COMP **talk radio** N *(NonC)* *radio qui donne la priorité aux interviews et aux débats*
talk show N *(Rad)* débat *m* (radiodiffusé) ; (TV) débat *m* (télévisé), talk-show *m*
talk time N *(on mobile phone)* temps *m* de communication

► **talk away** VI parler *or* discuter sans s'arrêter, ne pas arrêter de parler ◆ **we ~ed away for hours** nous avons passé des heures à parler *or* discuter ◆ **she was ~ing away about her plans when suddenly ...** elle était partie à parler de ses projets quand soudain ...

► **talk back** VI répondre (insolemment) *(to sb* à qn)

► **talk down** VI ◆ **to talk down to sb** parler à qn comme à un enfant
VT SEP 1 *(= silence)* **they ~ed him down** leurs flots de paroles l'ont réduit au silence
2 *[+ pilot, aircraft]* aider à atterrir par radio-contrôle
3 *[+ suicidal person]* persuader de ne pas sauter

4 (= *speak ill of*) dénigrer
5 (*esp Brit: in negotiations*) ◆ **to talk sb down** marchander avec qn (pour qu'il baisse son prix) ◆ **to ~ wages down** obtenir une baisse des salaires

► **talk on** VI parler *or* discuter sans s'arrêter, ne pas arrêter de parler ◆ **she ~ed on and on about it** elle en a parlé pendant des heures et des heures

► **talk out** VT SEP 1 (= *discuss thoroughly*) **to ~ it/things out** mettre les choses au clair
2 (*Parl*) **to ~ out a bill** prolonger la discussion d'un projet de loi jusqu'à ce qu'il soit trop tard pour le voter
3 ◆ **to talk o.s. out** parler jusqu'à l'épuisement

► **talk over** VT SEP 1 [*+ question, problem*] discuter (de), débattre ◆ **let's ~ it over** discutons-en entre nous ◆ **I must ~ it over with my wife first** je dois d'abord en parler à ma femme
2 ⇒ **talk round** vt sep

► **talk round** VT SEP (*Brit*) ◆ **to talk sb round** amener qn à changer d'avis, gagner qn à son avis, convaincre *or* persuader qn
VT FUS [*+ problem, subject*] tourner autour de ◆ **they ~ed round it all evening** ils ont tourné autour du pot toute la soirée

► **talk up** VI (*US = speak frankly*) ne pas mâcher ses mots
VT FUS [*+ project, book*] pousser, vanter ◆ **to ~ sb up** (*esp Brit: in negotiations*) marchander avec qn pour qu'il offre davantage ◆ **to ~ the price up** obtenir plus d'argent

talkathon /'tɔːkəθɒn/ N (*US*) débat-marathon *m*

talkative /'tɔːkətɪv/ ADJ bavard

talkativeness /'tɔːkətɪvnɪs/ N volubilité *f*, loquacité *f* (*liter*)

talker /'tɔːkəʳ/ N ◆ **he's a great ~** c'est un grand bavard, il a la langue bien pendue* ◆ **he's a terrible ~** (*talks too much*) c'est un vrai moulin à paroles

talkie* /'tɔːkɪ/ N (*Cine*) film *m* parlant ◆ **the ~s** le cinéma parlant ; → **walkie-talkie**

talking /'tɔːkɪŋ/ N bavardage *m* ◆ **he did all the ~** il a fait tous les frais de la conversation ◆ **that's enough ~!** assez de bavardages !, assez bavardé ! ◆ **no ~!** défense de parler !, silence (s'il vous plaît) ! ADJ [*doll, parrot, film*] parlant
COMP **talking book** N lecture *f* enregistrée d'un livre
talking head N (*TV*) présentateur *m*, -trice *f*
talking point N sujet *m* de discussion *or* de conversation
talking shop* N (*Brit*) parlot(t)e *f*
talking-to* N engueulade‡ *f* ◆ **to give sb a (good) ~-to** passer un savon à qn*

tall /tɔːl/ ADJ 1 (*in height*) [*building, tree, window*] haut ◆ **a ~ person** une personne de grande taille ◆ **a ~ man** un homme grand ◆ **a ~ woman/girl** une grande femme/fille ◆ **a ~ boy** un grand garçon ◆ **a ~ glass** un grand verre ◆ **how ~ is this building/that tree?** quelle est la hauteur de ce bâtiment/cet arbre ? ◆ **how ~ are you?** combien mesurez-vous ? ◆ **he hadn't realized how ~ she was** il ne s'était pas rendu compte qu'elle était aussi grande ◆ **he is six feet ~** ≈ il mesure 1 mètre 80 ◆ **a six-foot-~ man** ≈ un homme d'un mètre 80 *or* mesurant 1 mètre 80 ◆ **~ and slim** élancé ◆ **he is ~er than his brother** il est plus grand que son frère ◆ **she's 5cm ~er than me, she's ~er than me by 5cm** elle mesure 5 cm de plus que moi ◆ **she is ~er than me by a head** elle me dépasse d'une tête ◆ **she wears high heels to make herself look ~er** elle porte des talons hauts pour se grandir *or* pour avoir l'air plus grande ◆ **to get** *or* **grow ~er** grandir
2 ◆ **that's a ~ order !*** (= *difficult*) c'est beaucoup demander !
ADV ◆ **he stands six feet ~** ≈ il mesure bien 1 mètre 80 ◆ **to stand ~** (*US fig*) garder la tête haute ◆ **to walk ~** marcher la tête haute
COMP **tall ship** N grand voilier *m*
tall story, tall tale N histoire *f* à dormir debout

tallboy /'tɔːlbɔɪ/ N (*Brit*) commode *f*

tallness /'tɔːlnɪs/ N [*of person*] grande taille *f* ; [*of building etc*] hauteur *f*

tallow /'tæləʊ/ N suif *m* COMP **tallow candle** N chandelle *f*

tally /'tælɪ/ N (*Hist = stick*) taille *f* (*latte de bois*) ; (= *count*) compte *m* ◆ **to keep a ~ of** (= *count*) tenir le compte de ; (= *mark off on list*) pointer ◆ **the final ~ was 221 votes for the government and 124 against** le decompte final donnait 221 voix pour le gouvernement et 124 contre VI concorder (*with* avec), correspondre (*with* à) ; ◆ **this description didn't seem to ~ with what we saw** cette description ne semblait pas correspondre à ce que nous avons vu ◆ **the figures didn't seem to ~** les chiffres ne semblaient pas concorder VT (*also* **tally up**) (= *count*) compter

tallyho /'tælɪ'həʊ/ EXCL, N taïaut *m*

Talmud /'tælmʊd/ N (*Rel*) Talmud *m*

Talmudic /tæl'mʊdɪk/ ADJ talmudique

talon /'tælən/ N 1 [*of eagle etc*] serre *f* ; [*of tiger etc, person*] griffe *f* 2 (*Archit, Cards*) talon *m*

talus /'teɪləs/ N (pl **tali**) astragale *m*

Tamagotchi ® /tæmə'gɒtʃɪ/ N Tamagotchi ® *m*

tamarin /'tæmərɪn/ N tamarin *m* (*singe*)

tamarind /'tæmərɪnd/ N (= *fruit*) tamarin *m* ; (= *tree*) tamarinier *m*

tamarisk /'tæmərɪsk/ N tamaris *m*

tambour /'tæm,bʊəʳ/ N (*Archit, Mus*) tambour *m* ; (*Sewing*) métier *m* or tambour *m* à broder

tambourine /,tæmbə'riːn/ N tambour *m* de basque, tambourin *m*

Tamburlaine /'tæmbəleɪn/ N Tamerlan *m*

tame /teɪm/ ADJ 1 (= *not wild*) [*animal, bird*] apprivoisé ◆ **to become ~(r)** s'apprivoiser ◆ **let's ask our ~ American*** (*hum*) demandons à notre Américain de service 2 (*pej = compliant*) [*follower*] docile 3 (*pej = unexciting*) [*party, match, book*] insipide, fade ; [*place*] insipide ◆ **to be ~ stuff** être insipide VT [*+ bird, wild animal*] apprivoiser ; [*+ esp lion, tiger*] dompter ; (*fig*) [*+ passion*] maîtriser ; [*+ person*] mater, soumettre

tamely /'teɪmlɪ/ ADV [*agree, accept, surrender*] docilement ◆ **the story ends ~** le dénouement est plat

tamer /'teɪməʳ/ N dresseur *m*, -euse *f* ◆ **lion-~** dompteur *m*, -euse *f* (de lions)

Tamerlane /'tæməleɪn/ N Tamerlan *m*

Tamil /'tæmɪl/ N 1 Tamoul(e) *or* Tamil(e) *m(f)* 2 (= *language*) tamoul *or* tamil *m* ADJ tamoul *or* tamil

taming /'teɪmɪŋ/ N (*NonC: gen*) apprivoisement *m* ; [*of circus animals*] dressage *m*, domptage *m* ◆ **"The Taming of the Shrew"** "La Mégère apprivoisée"

Tammany /'tæmənɪ/ N (*US Hist*) *organisation démocrate de New York*

tammy* /'tæmɪ/, **tam o'shanter** /,tæmə'ʃæntəʳ/ N béret *m* écossais

tamoxifen /tə'mɒksɪfen/ N tamoxifène *m*

tamp /tæmp/ VT [*+ earth*] damer, tasser ; [*+ tobacco*] tasser ◆ **to ~ a drill hole** (*in blasting*) bourrer un trou de mine à l'argile *or* au sable

► **tamp down** 1 [*+ earth*] damer, tasser ; [*+ tobacco*] tasser 2 (*fig*) [*+ violence, looting, extremism*] réprimer ◆ **to ~ down expectations** modérer les attentes

Tampax ® /'tæmpæks/ N Tampax ® *m*

tamper /'tæmpəʳ/ VI ◆ **to ~ with** [*+ machinery, car, brakes, safe etc*] toucher à (*sans permission*) ; [*+ lock*] essayer de crocheter ; [*+ documents, accounts, evidence*] falsifier ; [*+ food*] frelater ; (*US*) [*+ jury*] soudoyer ; [*+ sb's papers, possessions*] toucher à, mettre le nez dans* ◆ **my computer has been ~ed with** quelqu'un a touché à mon ordinateur ◆ **the brakes had been ~ed with** les freins ont été trafiqués COMP **tamper-proof** ADJ [*bottle*] avec fermeture de sécurité ; [*envelope*] indécachetable ; [*ID card*] infalsifiable

tampon /'tæmpɒn/ N tampon *m*

tan /tæn/ N (*also* **suntan**) bronzage *m*, hâle *m* ◆ **she's got a lovely ~** elle a un beau bronzage, elle est bien bronzée ◆ **to get a ~** bronzer ADJ brun clair VT 1 [*+ skins*] tanner ◆ **to ~ sb*, to ~ sb's hide (for him)*** tanner le cuir à qn* 2 [*sun*] [*+ sunbather, holiday-maker*] bronzer ; [*+ sailor, farmer etc*] hâler ◆ **to get ~ned** bronzer VI bronzer

tandem /'tændəm/ N 1 (= *bicycle*) tandem *m* 2 (= *in collaboration*) ◆ **to do sth in ~** faire qch en tandem ◆ **to work in ~ with sb** travailler en collaboration *or* en tandem* avec qn 3 (= *simultaneously*) ◆ **to happen in ~** arriver simultanément ◆ **the two systems will run in ~** les deux systèmes seront appliqués simultanément ◆ **in ~ with sth** parallèlement à qch ADV ◆ **to ride ~** rouler en tandem

tandoori /tæn'dʊərɪ/ (*Culin*) ADJ, N tandoori *or* tandouri *m inv*

tang /tæŋ/ N 1 (= *taste*) saveur *f* forte (et piquante) ; (= *smell*) senteur *f* or odeur *f* forte (et piquante) ◆ **the salt ~ of the sea air** l'odeur caractéristique de la marée 2 [*of file, knife*] soie *f*

tanga /'tæŋgə/ N (= *briefs*) minislip *m*, tanga *m*

Tanganyika /,tæŋgə'njiːkə/ N Tanganyika *m* ◆ **Lake ~** le lac Tanganyika

tangent /'tændʒənt/ N (*Math*) tangente *f* ◆ **to go off** *or* **fly off at a ~** (*fig*) partir dans une digression

tangential /tæn'dʒenʃəl/ ADJ 1 (= *unconnected*) [*remark, issue*] sans rapport 2 (*Geom*) [*line, curve*] tangent (*to* à) 3 (*Phys*) [*force*] tangentiel

tangentially /tæn'dʒenʃəlɪ/ ADV 1 (= *indirectly*) [*relate to, touch on*] indirectement 2 (*Geom*) tangentiellement

tangerine /,tændʒə'riːn/ N (*also* **tangerine orange**) mandarine *f* ADJ [*colour, skirt*] mandarine *inv* ; [*flavour*] de mandarine

tangibility /,tændʒɪ'bɪlɪtɪ/ N tangibilité *f*

tangible /'tændʒəbl/ ADJ [*object, evidence, proof*] tangible ; [*results, benefits*] tangible, palpable ; [*assets*] corporel ◆ **~ net worth** (*Fin*) valeur *f* nette réelle

tangibly /'tændʒəblɪ/ ADV [*demonstrate, improve*] de manière tangible

Tangier /tæn'dʒɪəʳ/ N Tanger

tangle /'tæŋgl/ N [*of wool, string, rope*] enchevêtrement *m* ; (*Climbing: in rope*) nœud *m* ; [*of creepers, bushes, weeds*] fouillis *m*, enchevêtrement *m* ; (*fig = muddle*) confusion *f* ◆ **to get into a ~** [*string, rope, wool*] s'entortiller, s'enchevêtrer ; [*hair*] s'emmêler ; (*fig*) [*person, accounts*] s'embrouiller ; [*traffic*] se bloquer ◆ **he got into a ~ when he tried to explain** il s'est embrouillé dans ses explications ◆ **I'm in a ~ with the accounts** je suis empêtré dans les comptes ◆ **the whole affair was a hopeless ~** toute cette histoire était affreusement confuse *or* était affreusement embrouillée

VT (also **tangle up** : *lit*) enchevêtrer, embrouiller, emmêler ◆ **his tie got ~d up in the machine** sa cravate s'est entortillée dans la machine ◆ **to get ~d (up)** *(gen)* ⇒ **to get into a tangle** → **noun**

VI 1 *(= become tangled)* ⇒ **to get into a tangle** *(lit senses)* → **noun**

2 * ◆ **to ~ with sb** se frotter à qn, se colleter avec qn * ◆ **they ~d over whose fault it was** ils se sont colletés * sur la question de savoir qui était responsable

tango /ˈtæŋgəʊ/ **N** (pl **tangos**) tango *m* **VI** danser le tango ◆ **it takes two to ~** il faut être deux

tangy /ˈtæŋɪ/ **ADJ** acidulé

tank /tæŋk/ **N** 1 *(= container) (for storage)* réservoir *m*, cuve *f* ; *(for rainwater)* citerne *f* ; *(for gas)* réservoir *m* ; *[of car]* (also **petrol tank**) réservoir *m* (à essence) ; *(for transporting)* réservoir *m*, cuve *f* ; *(esp oil)* tank *m* ; *(for fermenting, processing etc)* cuve *f* *(also Phot)* ; *(for fish)* aquarium *m* ; → **fuel, septic**

2 *(Mil)* char *m* (d'assaut *or* de combat), tank *m*

COMP *(Mil) [commander]* de char d'assaut *or* de combat ; *[brigade]* de chars d'assaut *or* de combat

tank car **N** *(US Rail)* wagon-citerne *m*

tank top **N** pull-over *m* sans manches

tank town * **N** *(US fig)* petite ville *f* (perdue), trou * *m* *(fig)*

tank trap **N** *(Mil)* fossé *m* antichar

tank truck **N** *(US)* camion-citerne *m*

► **tank along** * **VI** *(esp on road)* foncer *, aller à toute allure *

► **tank up** **VI** (*) *(= get petrol)* faire le plein ; *(Brit* ‡ *fig = drink a lot)* se soûler la gueule ‡

VT SEP * *[+ car etc]* remplir d'essence ◆ **to be ~ed up** ‡ *(Brit fig)* être bituré ‡ ◆ **to get ~ed up** ‡ *(Brit fig)* se soûler la gueule ‡

tankard /ˈtæŋkəd/ **N** chope *f*, pot *m* à bière

tanker /ˈtæŋkəʳ/ **N** *(= truck)* camion-citerne *m* ; *(= ship)* pétrolier *m*, tanker *m* ; *(= aircraft)* avion *m* ravitailleur ; *(Rail)* wagon-citerne *m*

tankful /ˈtæŋkfʊl/ **N** ◆ **a ~ of petrol** un réservoir (plein) d'essence ◆ **a ~ of water** une citerne (pleine) d'eau

tanned /tænd/ **ADJ** *[sunbather, holiday-maker]* bronzé ; *(= weatherbeaten) [sailor, farmer]* hâlé

tanner[1] /ˈtænəʳ/ **N** tanneur *m*

tanner[2] † * /ˈtænəʳ/ **N** *(Brit)* (ancienne) pièce *f* de six pence

tannery /ˈtænərɪ/ **N** tannerie *f* *(établissement)*

tannic /ˈtænɪk/ **ADJ** tannique **COMP** **tannic acid** **N** ⇒ **tannin**

tannin /ˈtænɪn/ **N** tan(n)in *m*

tanning /ˈtænɪŋ/ **N** 1 (also **suntanning**) bronzage *m* 2 *[of hides]* tannage *m* 3 ‡ *(fig = beating)* raclée * *f*

Tannoy ® /ˈtænɔɪ/ *(Brit)* **N** système *m* de haut-parleurs ◆ **on** *or* **over the ~** par haut-parleur **VT** *[+ message]* annoncer par haut-parleur

tansy /ˈtænzɪ/ **N** tanaisie *f*

tantalize /ˈtæntəlaɪz/ **VT** ◆ **the dreams of democracy that so ~ them** les rêves de démocratie qui les attirent tant ◆ **it gave just enough details to ~ the reader** il donnait juste assez de détails pour intriguer le lecteur ◆ **~ your taste buds with ...** titillez vos papilles gustatives avec ...

tantalizing /ˈtæntəlaɪzɪŋ/ **ADJ** *[glimpse]* terriblement attrayant ; *[possibility]* terriblement excitant ; *[offer, smell]* terriblement alléchant ◆ **this ~ glimpse** ce fascinant aperçu

tantalizingly /ˈtæntəlaɪzɪŋlɪ/ **ADV** ◆ **~ slowly** avec une lenteur désespérante ◆ « **perhaps** », **she added ~** « peut-être », dit-elle d'un ton énigmatique ◆ **to get ~ close to doing sth** se retrouver à deux doigts de faire qch ◆ **the prize was ~ within my reach** le prix était là, à me tenter

tantalum /ˈtæntələm/ **N** tantale *m*

Tantalus /ˈtæntələs/ **N** Tantale *m*

tantamount /ˈtæntəmaʊnt/ **ADJ** ◆ **to be ~ to sth** être équivalent à qch ◆ **it's ~ to failure** cela équivaut à un échec ◆ **the attack was ~ to a declaration of war** cette attaque équivalait *or* revenait à une déclaration de guerre ◆ **the decision was ~ to protecting terrorist organisations** cette décision revenait à protéger les organisations terroristes

Tantric /ˈtæntrɪk/ **ADJ** tantrique

tantrum /ˈtæntrəm/ **N** (also **temper tantrum**) crise *f* de colère ; *[of child]* caprice *m* ◆ **to have** *or* **throw a ~** piquer une colère ; *[child]* faire un caprice

Tanzania /ˌtænzəˈnɪə/ **N** Tanzanie *f* ◆ **United Republic of ~** République *f* unie de Tanzanie

Tanzanian /ˌtænzəˈnɪən/ **ADJ** tanzanien **N** Tanzanien(ne) *m(f)*

Tao /ˈtaʊ/ **N** Tao *m*

Taoiseach /ˈtiːʃæx/ **N** *(Ir)* Premier ministre *m* *(irlandais)*

Taoism /ˈtaʊɪzəm/ **N** taoïsme *m*

Taoist /ˈtaʊɪst/ **ADJ, N** taoïste *mf*

tap[1] /tæp/ **N** 1 *(Brit: for water, gas etc)* robinet *m* ; *(Brit = tap on barrel etc)* cannelle *f*, robinet *m* ; *(= plug for barrel)* bonde *f* ◆ **the hot/cold ~** le robinet d'eau chaude/froide

◆ **on tap** ◆ **ale on ~** bière *f* (à la) pression ◆ **there are funds/resources on ~** il y a des fonds/des ressources disponibles ◆ **a wealth of information on ~** une mine d'informations à votre disposition *or* facilement accessibles ◆ **he has £3 million on ~** il dispose de 3 millions de livres

2 *(Telec)* écoute *f* téléphonique

3 (also **screw tap** : *Tech*) taraud *m*

VT 1 *[+ telephone, telephone line]* mettre *or* placer sur écoute ◆ **to ~ sb's phone** mettre qn sur écoute ◆ **my phone is being ~ped** mon téléphone est sur écoute

2 *(fig) [+ resources, supplies]* exploiter, utiliser ◆ **to ~ sb for money** * taper * qn ◆ **they ~ped her for a loan** * ils ont réussi à lui emprunter de l'argent ◆ **to ~ sb for £10** * taper * qn de 10 livres ◆ **to ~ sb for information** soutirer des informations à qn

3 *[+ cask, barrel]* percer, mettre en perce ; *[+ pine]* gemmer ; *[+ other tree]* inciser ; *(Elec) [+ current]* capter ; *[+ wire]* brancher ◆ **to ~ the rubber from a tree** saigner un arbre pour recueillir le latex

COMP **tap water** **N** eau *f* du robinet

► **tap into** **VT FUS** *(= gain access to) [+ system, network]* accéder à ; *(= exploit) [+ fear, enthusiasm]* exploiter

tap[2] /tæp/ **N** 1 petit coup *m*, petite tape *f* ◆ **there was a ~ at the door** on a frappé doucement *or* légèrement à la porte

2 *(NonC:* also **tap-dancing**) claquettes *fpl*

NPL **taps** *(Mil = end of the day)* (sonnerie *f* de) l'extinction *f* des feux ; *(at funeral)* sonnerie *f* aux morts

VI taper (doucement) ; *(repeatedly)* tapoter ◆ **to ~ on** *or* **at the door** frapper doucement à la porte

VT taper (doucement) ; *(repeatedly)* tapoter ◆ **she ~ped the child on the cheek** elle a tapoté la joue de l'enfant ◆ **he ~ped me on the shoulder** il m'a tapé sur l'épaule ◆ **to ~ in a nail** enfoncer un clou à petits coups ◆ **to ~ one's foot** taper du pied ◆ **he was ~ping an annoying rhythm on his glass** il tapotait sur son verre d'une manière agaçante ◆ **he ~ped his fingers on the steering wheel** il tapotait (sur) le volant

COMP **tap dance** **N** claquettes *fpl*

tap-dance **VI** faire des claquettes

tap-dancer **N** danseur *m*, -euse *f* de claquettes

tap-dancing **N** → **noun 2**

► **tap out** **VT SEP** 1 *[+ one's pipe]* débourrer

2 *[+ signal, code]* pianoter ◆ **to ~ out a message in Morse** transmettre un message en morse

tapas /ˈtæpəs/ **NPL** *(Culin)* tapas *fpl*

tape /teɪp/ **N** 1 *(gen: of cloth, paper, metal)* ruban *m*, bande *f* ; *(for parcels, documents)* bolduc *m* ; (also **sticky tape**) scotch ® *m*, ruban *m* adhésif ; *(Med)* sparadrap *m* ◆ **the message was coming through on the ~** le message nous parvenait sur la bande (perforée) ; → **paper, punch**[1]**, red**

2 *(Recording, Comput) (= actual tape)* bande *f* magnétique ; *(= audio cassette)* cassette *f* (audio *inv*) ; *(= video cassette)* cassette *f* vidéo *inv*, vidéocassette *f* ◆ **the ~ is stuck** la bande est coincée ◆ **I'm going to buy a ~** je vais acheter une cassette ; (also **video tape**) je vais acheter une cassette vidéo *or* une vidéocassette ◆ **bring your ~s** apporte tes cassettes ◆ **to get sth down on ~** enregistrer qch ◆ **to make a ~ of a song** enregistrer une chanson

3 *(Sport)* fil *m* *(d'arrivée)* ; *(at opening ceremonies)* ruban *m*

4 (also **tape measure**) mètre *m* à ruban ; *(esp Sewing)* centimètre *m*

5 *(Sewing) (decorative)* ruban *m*, ganse *f* ; *(for binding)* extrafort *m*

VT 1 (also **tape up**) *[+ parcel etc]* attacher avec du ruban *or* du bolduc ; *(with sticky tape)* scotcher *, coller avec du scotch ® *or* du ruban adhésif ◆ **to ~ sb's mouth** bâillonner qn avec du sparadrap ◆ **they ~d her legs and her feet** ils lui ont attaché les jambes et les pieds avec du sparadrap ◆ **he ~d up the hole in the radiator** il a bouché le trou du radiateur avec du scotch ® *or* du ruban adhésif

2 *(Brit fig)* **I've got him ~d** * je sais ce qu'il vaut ◆ **I've got it all ~d** * je sais parfaitement de quoi il retourne ◆ **they had the game/situation ~d** * ils avaient le jeu/la situation bien en main ◆ **he's got the job ~d** * il sait exactement ce qu'il y a à faire

3 *(= record) [+ song, message]* enregistrer (sur bande *or* au magnétophone) ; *[+ video material]* enregistrer ◆ **~d lesson** *(Scol etc)* leçon *f* enregistrée sur bande

COMP **tape deck** **N** platine *f* de magnétophone

tape drive **N** *(Comput)* dérouleur *m* de bande magnétique

tape head **N** tête *f* de lecture-enregistrement

tape machine **N** *(Brit = tape recorder)* magnétophone *m*

tape measure **N** mètre *m* à ruban ; *(esp Sewing)* centimètre *m*

tape-record **VT** enregistrer (sur bande)

tape recorder **N** magnétophone *m*

tape recording **N** enregistrement *m* (sur bande)

tape streamer **N** sauvegarde *f* sur bande

► **tape over** *(Recording)* **VT FUS** effacer *(en enregistrant autre chose)*

VT SEP ◆ **to tape sth over sth** enregistrer qch sur qch

taper /ˈteɪpəʳ/ **N** *(for lighting)* bougie *f* fine *(pour allumer les cierges, bougies etc)* ; *(Rel = narrow candle)* cierge *m*

VT *[+ column, table leg, trouser leg, aircraft wing]* fuseler ; *[+ stick, end of belt]* tailler en pointe, effiler ; *[+ hair]* effiler ; *[+ structure, shape]* terminer en pointe

VI *[column, table leg, trouser leg]* finir en fuseau ; *[stick, end of belt]* s'effiler ; *[hair]* être effilé ; *[structure, outline]* se terminer en pointe, s'effiler

► **taper off** **VI** *[sound]* se taire peu à peu ; *[storm]* aller en diminuant ; *[conversation]* tomber ◆ **the end ~s off to a point** le bout se termine en pointe ◆ **immigration is expected to ~ off** on s'attend à ce que l'immigration diminue progressivement ◆ **the snow has ~ed off** la neige a presque cessé de tomber ◆ **the president's popularity is ~ing off** la popularité du président est en baisse

VT SEP *(lit)* finir en pointe ; *(fig)* réduire progressivement

tapered /ˈteɪpəd/ ADJ *[column, table leg]* fuselé, en fuseau ; *[fingers]* fuselé ; *[trouser leg]* en fuseau ; *[stick]* pointu ; *[hair]* effilé ; *[structure, outline]* en pointe

tapering /ˈteɪpərɪŋ/ ADJ *[column, fingers]* fuselé ; see also **tapered**

tapestry /ˈtæpɪstrɪ/ N tapisserie *f* ◆ **the Bayeux Tapestry** la tapisserie de Bayeux ◆ **it's all part of life's rich** ~ tout cela fait partie de la trame complexe de l'existence, c'est la vie

tapeworm /ˈteɪpwɜːm/ N ténia *m*, ver *m* solitaire

tapioca /ˌtæpɪˈəʊkə/ N tapioca *m*

tapir /ˈteɪpəʳ/ N tapir *m*

tappet /ˈtæpɪt/ N *(Tech)* poussoir *m* (de soupape)

tapping¹ /ˈtæpɪŋ/ N *(NonC)* 1 *[of pine]* gemmage *m* ; *[of other trees]* incision *f* ; *[of electric current]* captage *m* 2 *(Telec)* **phone** ~ écoutes *fpl* téléphoniques

tapping² /ˈtæpɪŋ/ N *(NonC = noise, act)* tapotement *m* ◆ ~ **sound** tapotement *m*

taproom /ˈtæprʊm/ N *(Brit)* salle *f* (de bistro(t))

taproot /ˈtæprʊt/ N pivot *m*, racine *f* pivotante

tar¹ /tɑːʳ/ N *(NonC)* goudron *m* ; *(on roads)* goudron *m*, bitume *m* VT *[+ fence etc]* goudronner ; *[+ road]* goudronner, bitumer ◆ **~red felt** *(= roofing)* couverture *f* bitumée *or* goudronnée ◆ **to ~ and feather sb** passer qn au goudron et à la plume ◆ **they're all ~red with the same brush** ils sont tous à mettre dans le même sac *

tar² † * /tɑːʳ/ N *(= sailor)* mathurin † *m* ; → **jack**

taramasalata /ˌtærəməsəˈlɑːtə/ N tarama *m*

tarantella /ˌtærənˈtelə/ N tarentelle *f*

tarantula /təˈræntjʊlə/ N (pl **tarantulas** *or* **tarantulae** /təˈræntjʊˌliː/) tarentule *f*

tarboosh, tarbush /tɑːˈbuːʃ/ N tarbouch(e) *m*

tardily /ˈtɑːdɪlɪ/ ADV tardivement

tardiness /ˈtɑːdɪnɪs/ N *(NonC) (= slowness)* lenteur *f*, manque *m* d'empressement *(in doing sth* à faire qch) ; *(= unpunctuality)* manque *m* de ponctualité

tardy /ˈtɑːdɪ/ ADJ *(= late) [response]* tardif ; *(= slow) [progress]* lent ◆ **to be ~ in doing sth** faire qch avec du retard COMP **tardy slip** N *(US Scol)* billet *m* de retard

tare¹ /tɛəʳ/ N ◆ **~s** †† *(= weeds)* ivraie *f*

tare² /tɛəʳ/ N *(Comm = weight)* tare *f*

target /ˈtɑːɡɪt/ N *(Mil, Sport: for shooting practice, Mil: in attack or mock attack)* cible *f* ; *(fig = objective)* objectif *m* ◆ **an easy** ~ une cible facile ◆ **he was an obvious ~ for his enemies** il constituait une cible évidente pour ses ennemis ◆ **she was the ~ of a violent attack** elle a été victime d'une violente agression ◆ **the ~ of much criticism** la cible *or* l'objet *m* de nombreuses critiques ◆ **they set themselves a ~ of $1,000** ils se sont fixé 1 000 dollars comme objectif *or* un objectif de 1 000 dollars ◆ **the ~s for production** les objectifs de production ◆ **"on-target earnings £30,000"** "salaire jusqu'à £30 000 selon résultats" ◆ **our ~ is young people under 20** notre cible *or* le public ciblé, ce sont les jeunes de moins de 20 ans ◆ **the government met its ~ for reducing unemployment** le gouvernement a réussi à réduire le chômage conformément à ses objectifs

◆ **off target** ◆ **they were at least 12km off ~** *(gen)* ils s'étaient écartés de 12 bons kilomètres de leur destination ; *(Mil: on bombing raid etc)* ils étaient à 12 bons kilomètres de leur objectif ◆ **they're (way) off ~ in terms of price** il se sont (complètement) trompés de cible en ce qui concerne le prix ◆ **you're way off ~** *(= criticising wrong person etc)* tu te trompes de cible ◆ **they were off ~ today** *(Ftbl)* ils manquaient de précision aujourd'hui

◆ **on target** ◆ **to be (dead** *or* **right) on ~** *[rocket, missile, bombs etc]* suivre (exactement) la trajectoire prévue ; *[remark, criticism]* mettre (en plein) dans le mille ; *(in timing etc)* être dans les temps ; *(Comm) [sales]* correspondre (exactement) aux objectifs ; *[forecast]* tomber juste ◆ **we're on ~ for sales of £10 million this year** nos ventes devraient correspondre aux objectifs de 10 millions de livres cette année ◆ **the project is on ~ for completion** le projet devrait être fini dans les temps ◆ **dead on ~!** pile !

VT 1 *[+ enemy troops]* prendre pour cible, viser ; *[+ missile, weapon]* pointer, diriger (*on* sur)

2 *[+ market, audience etc]* cibler, prendre pour cible

3 *(= direct, send) [+ aid, benefits etc]* affecter

COMP *[date, amount etc]* fixé, prévu

target area N *(Mil)* environs *mpl* de la cible

target group N groupe *m* cible *inv*

target language N langue *f* cible *inv*, langue *f* d'arrivée

target practice N *(Mil, Sport)* exercices *mpl* de tir (à la cible)

target price N prix *m* indicatif *or* d'objectif

target vehicle N *(Space)* vaisseau *m* cible *inv*

targetable /ˈtɑːɡɪtəbl/ ADJ *[warhead]* dirigeable

targeting /ˈtɑːɡɪtɪŋ/ N 1 *(Mil)* **the ~ of civilian areas** la prise des quartiers civils pour cible 2 *(Comm)* **the ~ of a product/a publicity campaign** le ciblage d'un produit/d'une campagne de pub ◆ **the ~ of young people as potential buyers** la prise pour cible des jeunes comme acheteurs potentiels

Tarheel /ˈtɑːhiːl/ N *(US)* habitant(e) *m(f)* de la Caroline du Nord COMP **the Tarheel State** N la Caroline du Nord

tariff /ˈtærɪf/ N *(Econ = taxes)* tarif *m* douanier ; *(on a product)* droits *mpl* de douane ; *(Comm = price list)* tarif *m*, tableau *m* des prix COMP *[concession, quota]* tarifaire

tariff barrier N barrière *f* douanière

tariff heading N *(Jur, Fin)* position *f* tarifaire

tariff reform N *(Econ)* réforme *f* des tarifs douaniers

tarmac /ˈtɑːmæk/ N 1 *(NonC)* **Tarmac** ® *(esp Brit = substance)* goudron *m* 2 ◆ **the** ~ *(= airport runway)* la piste ; *(= airport apron)* l'aire *f* d'envol VT macadamiser, goudronner

Tarmacadam ® /ˌtɑːməˈkædəm/ N ⇒ **tarmac noun 1**

tarn /tɑːn/ N petit lac *m* (de montagne)

tarnation ‡ /tɑːˈneɪʃən/ *(US dial)* EXCL damnation ! ADJ fichu * *before n* ADV fichtrement *

tarnish /ˈtɑːnɪʃ/ VT *[+ metal]* ternir ; *[+ gilded frame etc]* dédorer ; *[+ mirror]* désargenter ; *(fig) [+ reputation, image, memory]* ternir VI se ternir, se dédorer, se désargenter N *(NonC)* ternissure *f*, dédorage *m*, désargentage *m*

tarot /ˈtærəʊ/ N *(NonC)* ◆ **the** ~ le(s) tarot(s) *m(pl)* COMP **tarot card** N tarot *m*

tarp * /tɑːp/ N *(US, Austral)* abbrev of **tarpaulin 2**

tarpaulin /tɑːˈpɔːlɪn/ N 1 *(NonC)* toile *f* goudronnée 2 *(= sheet)* bâche *f* (goudronnée) ; *(on truck, over boat cargo)* prélart *m*

tarpon /ˈtɑːpɒn/ N tarpon *m*

tarragon /ˈtærəɡən/ N estragon *m* COMP **tarragon vinegar** N vinaigre *m* à l'estragon

tarring /ˈtɑːrɪŋ/ N goudronnage *m*

tarry¹ /ˈtɑːrɪ/ ADJ *(= like tar)* goudronneux, bitumeux ; *(= covered with tar)* plein de goudron ; *(= smelling of tar)* qui sent le goudron

tarry² /ˈtærɪ/ VI *(liter) (= stay)* rester, demeurer ; *(= delay)* s'attarder, tarder

tarsal /ˈtɑːsəl/ ADJ *(Anat)* tarsien

tarsus /ˈtɑːsəs/ N (pl **tarsi** /ˈtɑːsaɪ/) tarse *m*

tart¹ /tɑːt/ ADJ 1 *[fruit, flavour]* acide, acidulé 2 *[person, remark, comment]* acerbe

tart² /tɑːt/ N 1 *(esp Brit Culin)* tarte *f* ; *(small)* tartelette *f* ◆ **apple** ~ tarte(lette) *f* aux pommes 2 *(‡ = prostitute)* poule ‡ *f*, putain ‡ *f*

► **tart up** ‡ VT SEP *(Brit pej) [+ house, car]* retaper ◆ **to ~ o.s. up, to get ~ed up** se pomponner ; *(= get dressed)* s'attifer *(pej)* ; *(= make up)* se maquiller excessivement ◆ **she was all ~ed up for** *or* **to go to the party** elle était toute pomponnée pour aller à la soirée

tartan /ˈtɑːtən/ N tartan *m* ADJ *[garment, fabric]* écossais ◆ **the Tartan Army** * *(Brit)* les supporters *mpl* de l'équipe de football d'Écosse COMP **tartan (travelling) rug** N plaid *m*

Tartar /ˈtɑːtəʳ/ N 1 Tartare *mf or* Tatar(e) *m(f)* 2 ◆ **tartar** tyran *m* ; *(woman)* mégère *f* ADJ 1 *(Geog)* tartare *or* tatar 2 *(Culin)* **steak tartar(e)** (steak *m*) tartare *m* COMP **tartar(e) sauce** N *(Culin)* sauce *f* tartare

tartar /ˈtɑːtəʳ/ N *(NonC: Chem etc)* tartre *m* ; → **cream**

tartaric /tɑːˈtærɪk/ ADJ tartrique

tartlet /ˈtɑːtlɪt/ N *(Brit)* tartelette *f*

tartly /ˈtɑːtlɪ/ ADV 1 *[say]* aigrement, d'une manière acerbe ; *[observe]* d'une manière acerbe 2 *(in taste)* ◆ **a ~ flavoured tomato sauce** une sauce tomate au goût acide

tartness /ˈtɑːtnɪs/ N *[of flavour, apple]* acidité *f* ; *[of remark]* aigreur *f*

tarty * /ˈtɑːtɪ/ ADJ *[clothes, make-up]* vulgaire ◆ **to look** ~ faire vulgaire *or* mauvais genre

Tarzan /ˈtɑːzən/ N Tarzan *m*

tash * /tæʃ/ N ⇒ **tache**

task /tɑːsk/ N tâche *f* ; *(Scol)* devoir *m* ◆ **a hard** ~ une lourde tâche ◆ **to take sb to** ~ prendre qn à partie, réprimander qn (*for, about* pour) VT 1 *(= tax) [+ sb's brain, patience, imagination]* mettre à l'épreuve ; *[+ sb's strength]* éprouver 2 ◆ **to be ~ed with sth** être chargé de qch ◆ **to be ~ed to do sth** *or* **with doing sth** être chargé de faire qch COMP **task force** N *(Mil)* corps *m* expéditionnaire ; *(Police)* détachement *m* spécial

taskmaster /ˈtɑːskmɑːstəʳ/ N ◆ **he's a hard** ~ il mène ses subordonnés à la baguette ◆ **duty is a hard** ~ le devoir est un maître exigeant

Tasmania /tæzˈmeɪnɪə/ N Tasmanie *f*

Tasmanian /tæzˈmeɪnɪən/ ADJ tasmanien N Tasmanien(ne) *m(f)*

Tasman Sea /ˈtæsmənˈsiː/ N mer *f* de Tasman

tassel /ˈtæsəl/ N gland *m* ; *(= pompon)* pompon *m*

tasselled /ˈtæsəld/ ADJ à glands

Tasso /ˈtæsəʊ/ N le Tasse

taste /teɪst/ N 1 *(= flavour)* goût *m*, saveur *f* ◆ **it has an odd** ~ cela a un drôle de goût ◆ **it has no** ~ cela n'a aucun goût *or* aucune saveur ◆ **it left a nasty** *or* **bad ~ (in his mouth)** *(lit)* ça lui a laissé un mauvais goût *or* un goût désagréable dans la bouche ; *(fig)* ça lui a laissé un goût amer

2 *(NonC = sense, culture etc)* goût *m (also fig)* ◆ **sweet to the** ~ (au goût) sucré ◆ **to have (good)** ~ avoir du goût, avoir bon goût ◆ **he has no** ~ il n'a aucun goût, il a très mauvais goût ◆ **in good/bad** ~ de bon/mauvais goût ◆ **in poor** *or* **doubtful** ~ d'un goût douteux ◆ **the house is furnished in impeccable** ~ la mai-

son est meublée avec beaucoup de goût ◆ **people of** ~ les gens de goût

3 ◆ **to have a ~ of sth** *(lit)* goûter (à) qch ; *(fig)* goûter de qch ◆ **would you like a ~ (of it)?** voulez-vous (y) goûter ? ◆ **he had a ~ of the cake** il a goûté au gâteau ◆ **I gave him a ~ of the wine** je lui ai fait goûter le vin ◆ **it gave him a ~ of military life/of the work** cela lui a donné un aperçu de la vie militaire/du travail ◆ **he's had a ~ of prison** il a tâté de la prison ◆ **to give sb a ~ of his own medicine** rendre à qn la monnaie de sa pièce ◆ **to give sb a ~ of the whip** montrer à qn ce qui l'attend s'il ne marche pas droit ◆ **a ~ of happiness** une idée du bonheur ◆ **we got a ~ of his anger** il nous a donné un échantillon de sa colère ◆ **it was a ~ of things to come** c'était un avant-goût de l'avenir

4 *(= small amount, trace)* **a ~ of** *(gen)* un (tout) petit peu de ; *[+ salt etc]* une pincée de ; *[+ vinegar, cream, brandy]* une goutte de, un soupçon de

5 *(= liking)* goût *m*, penchant *m* (for pour) ◆ **is it to your ~?** est-ce que cela vous plaît ? ◆ **to have a ~ for** ... avoir du goût *or* un penchant pour ... ◆ **to get** *or* **acquire** *or* **develop a ~ for** ... prendre goût à ... ◆ **sweeten to** ~ *(Culin)* sucrer à volonté ◆ **it's a matter of** ~ c'est affaire de goût ◆ **there's no accounting for** ~ des goûts et des couleurs on ne discute pas ◆ **each to his own ~, ~s differ** chacun ses goûts ◆ **her novels are too violent for my** ~ ses romans sont trop violents à mon goût ◆ **his ~ in music** ses goûts musicaux ◆ **she has expensive ~s** elle a des goûts de luxe ◆ **he has expensive ~s in cars** il a le goût des voitures de luxe

VT 1 *(= perceive flavour of)* sentir (le goût de) ◆ **I can't ~ the garlic** je ne sens pas (le goût de) l'ail ◆ **I can't ~ anything when I have a cold** je trouve tout insipide quand j'ai un rhume ◆ **you won't ~ it** tu n'en sentiras pas le goût

2 *(= sample) [+ food, drink]* goûter à ; *(esp for first time)* goûter de ; *(= to test quality) [+ food]* goûter ; *[+ wine] (at table)* goûter ; *(at wine-tasting)* déguster ; *(fig) [+ power, freedom, success]* goûter à, connaître ◆ **just ~ this!** goûtez à ça ! ◆ **~ the sauce before adding salt** goûtez la sauce avant d'ajouter du sel ◆ **you must ~ my marmalade** je vais vous faire goûter de ma confiture d'oranges ◆ **I haven't ~d salmon for years** ça fait des années que je n'ai pas mangé *or* goûté de saumon ◆ **I have never ~d snails** je n'ai jamais mangé d'escargots ◆ **he had not ~d food for a week** il n'avait rien mangé depuis une semaine ; → **wine**

VI ◆ **it doesn't ~ at all** cela n'a aucun goût ◆ **to ~ bitter** avoir un goût amer ◆ **to ~ good/bad** avoir bon/mauvais goût ◆ **to ~ of** *or* **like sth** avoir un goût de qch ◆ **it ~s of garlic** ça a un goût d'ail ◆ **it doesn't ~ of anything in particular** cela n'a pas de goût spécial ◆ **it ~s all right to me** d'après moi cela a un goût normal

COMP **taste bud** N papille *f* gustative

tasteful /ˈteɪstfʊl/ ADJ de bon goût, d'un goût sûr

tastefully /ˈteɪstfəlɪ/ ADV *[decorated, furnished]* avec goût ◆ **the sex scenes are very ~ done** les scènes érotiques sont d'un goût exquis ◆ **his ~ modern flat** son appartement moderne agencé avec (beaucoup de) goût

tastefulness /ˈteɪstfʊlnɪs/ N bon goût *m*, goût *m* sûr

tasteless /ˈteɪstlɪs/ ADJ *[food, medicine]* fade ; *[ornament, clothes, remark, action]* de mauvais goût

tastelessly /ˈteɪstlɪslɪ/ ADV *[decorated]* sans goût ◆ **~ extravagant** d'une extravagance de très mauvais goût ◆ **~ inappropriate music** une musique mal choisie pour les circonstances ◆ **her ordeal was ~ handled in the press** sa pénible épreuve a été relatée sans aucun tact par la presse

tastelessness /ˈteɪstlɪsnɪs/ N manque *m* de saveur, fadeur *f (pej)* ; *(fig) [of ornament, dress, remark etc]* mauvais goût *m*

taster /ˈteɪstəʳ/ N 1 *(= person)* dégustateur *m*, -trice *f* 2 *(Brit * = foretaste)* avant-goût *m* ◆ **that is just a ~ of things to come** ce n'est qu'un avant-goût de ce qui se prépare ◆ **to serve as** *or* **be a ~ of sth** donner un avant-goût de qch

tastiness /ˈteɪstɪnɪs/ N saveur *f* agréable, goût *m* délicieux

tasting /ˈteɪstɪŋ/ N dégustation *f*

tasty /ˈteɪstɪ/ ADJ 1 *(Culin)* savoureux 2 *(* = interesting) [gossip, news]* croustillant 3 *(Brit * = sexy) [person]* sexy * *inv*

tat¹ /tæt/ VI faire de la frivolité *(dentelle)* VT faire en frivolité

tat² * /tæt/ N *(NonC: Brit pej = shabby clothes)* friperies *fpl* ; *(= goods)* camelote * *f*

ta-ta * /ˈtæˈtɑː/ EXCL *(Brit)* salut ! *

tattered /ˈtætəd/ ADJ 1 *[clothes, flag]* en loques ; *[book]* tout abîmé ; *[handkerchief, paper, poster]* déchiré ; *[person]* déguenillé, loqueteux 2 *[reputation]* en miettes

tatters /ˈtætəz/ NPL lambeaux *mpl*, loques *fpl* ◆ **in ~** *(lit)* en lambeaux, en loques ◆ **his confidence was in ~** il avait perdu toute confiance en lui ◆ **the government's reputation was in ~** la réputation du gouvernement était ruinée

tattie * /ˈtætɪ/ N *(Scot)* patate * *f*

tatting /ˈtætɪŋ/ N *(NonC)* frivolité *f (dentelle)*

tattle /ˈtætl/ VI *(= gossip)* jaser, cancaner ; *(= tell secrets)* cafarder * N *(NonC)* bavardage *m*, commérages *mpl*

tattler /ˈtætləʳ/ N *(= man or woman)* commère *f (pej)*, concierge * *mf (pej)*

tattletale /ˈtætlˌteɪl/ *(US)* N commère *f (pej)*, concierge * *mf (pej)* ADJ *(fig) [mark etc]* révélateur (-trice *f*)

tattoo¹ /təˈtuː/ VT tatouer N tatouage *m*

tattoo² /təˈtuː/ N *(Mil: on drum, bugle)* retraite *f* ; *(Brit Mil = spectacle)* parade *f* militaire ; *(gen = drumming)* battements *mpl* ◆ **to beat a ~ on the drums** battre le tambour

tattooer /tæˈtuːəʳ/, **tattooist** /təˈtuːɪst/ N tatoueur *m*, -euse *f*

tatty¹ * /ˈtætɪ/ ADJ *(esp Brit) [clothes, shoes]* fatigué ; *[house, furniture]* en mauvais état ; *[book, poster]* en mauvais état, écorné ; *[plant, paintwork]* défraîchi ◆ **to get ~** *(gen)* s'abîmer ; *[poster, paint]* se défraîchir ◆ **she looked rather ~** elle était plutôt défraîchie

tatty² * /ˈtætɪ/ N ⇒ **tattie**

taught /tɔːt/ VB pt, ptp of **teach**

taunt /tɔːnt/ N raillerie *f*, sarcasme *m* VT railler *(liter)*, persifler *(liter)* ◆ **to ~ sb with racial abuse** accabler qn d'injures racistes ◆ **he ~ed his wife with his affairs** il torturait sa femme en racontant ses infidélités

taunting /ˈtɔːntɪŋ/ N railleries *fpl*, persiflage *m*, sarcasmes *mpl* ADJ railleur, persifleur, sarcastique

tauntingly /ˈtɔːntɪŋlɪ/ ADV d'un ton railleur *or* persifleur *or* sarcastique

taupe /təʊp/ ADJ, N (couleur *f*) taupe *m inv*

Taurean /ˌtɔːˈriːən/ N ◆ **to be a ~** être (du) Taureau

tauromachy /ˈtɔːrəmækɪ/ N *(liter)* tauromachie *f*

Taurus /ˈtɔːrəs/ N *(Astron)* Taureau *m* ◆ **I'm (a) ~** *(Astrol)* je suis (du) Taureau

taut /tɔːt/ ADJ 1 *(= tight, tense) [skin, muscle, rope, person, face, voice]* tendu ; *[lips]* crispé ; *[nerves]* à vif ◆ **to hold sth ~** tendre qch ◆ **stretched ~** tendu ◆ **her nerves were (stretched) ~** elle avait les nerfs à vif ◆ **his face was ~ with anger** il avait le visage crispé de colère 2 *(= firm) [body]* ferme ◆ **to be ~** *[person]* avoir le corps ferme 3 *(= well-constructed) [novel, film]* bien ficelé *

tauten /ˈtɔːtn/ VT tendre VI se tendre

tautly /ˈtɔːtlɪ/ ADV *(lit) [stretch]* à fond ; *(fig) [say]* d'une voix tendue *or* crispée

tautness /ˈtɔːtnɪs/ N tension *f (d'un cordage etc)*

tautological /ˌtɔːtəˈlɒdʒɪkəl/ ADJ tautologique

tautology /tɔːˈtɒlədʒɪ/ N tautologie *f*

tavern † /ˈtævən/ N taverne † *f*, auberge *f*

tawdriness /ˈtɔːdrɪnɪs/ N *[of goods]* qualité *f* médiocre ; *[of clothes]* mauvais goût *m* tapageur ; *[of jewellery]* clinquant *m* ; *(fig) [of motive etc]* indignité *f*

tawdry /ˈtɔːdrɪ/ ADJ 1 *(= tacky) [jewellery, clothes]* bon marché 2 *(= sordid) [affair, story]* sordide

tawny /ˈtɔːnɪ/ ADJ *[hair, fur, animal]* (de couleur) fauve *inv* ; *[skin]* mordoré ◆ **~ brown** marron *inv* doré

COMP **tawny owl** N hulotte *f*, chat-huant *m*
tawny port N porto *m* tawny

tax /tæks/ N *(on goods, services)* taxe *f*, impôt *m* ; (also **income tax**) impôts *mpl* ◆ **before/after ~** avant/après l'impôt ◆ **half of it goes in ~** on en perd la moitié en impôts ◆ **how much ~ do you pay?** combien d'impôts payez-vous ? ◆ **I paid £3,000 in ~ last year** j'ai payé 3 000 livres d'impôts l'an dernier ◆ **free of ~** exempt *or* exonéré d'impôt ◆ **to put** *or* **place** *or* **levy a ~ on sth** taxer *or* imposer qch ◆ **petrol ~, ~ on petrol** taxe(s) *f(pl)* sur l'essence ◆ **it was a ~ on his strength** cela a mis ses forces à l'épreuve

VT 1 *[+ goods]* taxer, imposer ; *[+ income, profits, person]* imposer ; *(fig) [+ patience]* mettre à l'épreuve ; *[+ strength]* éprouver ◆ **he is very heavily ~ed** il paie beaucoup d'impôts, il est lourdement imposé ; see also **taxing**

2 ◆ **to ~ sb with sth** taxer *or* accuser qn de qch ◆ **to ~ sb with doing sth** accuser qn de faire (or d'avoir fait) qch

3 *(Brit)* ◆ **to ~ one's car** acheter la vignette pour sa voiture

COMP *[system, incentive etc]* fiscal
tax accountant N conseiller *m* fiscal
tax adjustment N redressement *m* fiscal
tax allowance N abattement *m or* dégrèvement *m* fiscal
tax authority N Administration *f* fiscale, Trésor *m* (public)
tax avoidance N évasion *f* fiscale (légale)
tax band N ⇒ **tax bracket**
tax base N assiette *f* de l'impôt
tax bite N ponction *f* fiscale, prélèvement *m* fiscal
tax bracket N tranche *f* du barème fiscal *or* d'impôts
tax break N réduction *f* d'impôt, avantage *m* fiscal
tax burden N charge *f* fiscale
tax code N *(Brit)* code *m* des impôts
tax coding N indice *m* d'abattement fiscal
tax-collecting N perception *f* des impôts
tax collector N percepteur *m*
tax credit N crédit *m* d'impôt
tax cut N réduction *f* des impôts
tax-deductible ADJ déductible des impôts
tax demand N avis *m* d'imposition
tax disc N *(Brit: for car)* vignette *f* (automobile)
tax dodge * N *(legal)* évasion *f* fiscale ; *(illegal)* fraude *f* fiscale
tax evader N fraudeur *m*, -euse *f* fiscal(e)
tax evasion N fraude *f* fiscale
tax-exempt ADJ *(US)* ⇒ **tax-free**
tax exemption N exonération *f* d'impôts

tax exile N personne *f* qui fuit le fisc ◆ **to become a ~ exile** s'expatrier pour raisons fiscales
tax form N feuille *f* d'impôts
tax-free ADJ exonéré d'impôts
tax haven N paradis *m* fiscal
tax immunity N immunité *f* fiscale
tax incentive N incitation *f* fiscale
tax inspector N inspecteur *m*, -trice *f* des impôts
tax levy N prélèvement *m* fiscal
tax liability N assujettissement *m* à l'impôt
tax net N ◆ **to bring sb/sth within the ~ net** ramener qn/qch dans une fourchette imposable *or* dans la première tranche imposable
tax purposes NPL ◆ **for ~ purposes** pour des raisons fiscales
tax rebate N dégrèvement *m* fiscal
tax refugee N ⇒ **tax exile**
tax relief N dégrèvement *m or* allègement *m* fiscal
tax return N (feuille *f* de) déclaration *f* de revenus *or* d'impôts
tax revenue N recettes *fpl* fiscales
tax shelter N échappatoire *f* fiscale
tax year N exercice *m* fiscal, année *f* fiscale

taxable /'tæksəbl/ ADJ *[assets, income, winnings]* imposable
COMP **taxable amount** N base *f* d'imposition
taxable year N année *f* fiscale, exercice *m* fiscal *(Fin)*

taxation /tæk'seɪʃən/ N *(NonC) (= act)* taxation *f* ; *(= taxes)* impôts *mpl*, contributions *fpl* ; → **double, immune** COMP *[authority, system]* fiscal

taxeme /'tæksiːm/ N taxème *m*

taxi /'tæksɪ/ N (pl **taxis** *or* **taxies**) taxi *m* ◆ **by ~** en taxi VI 1 *[aircraft]* se déplacer *or* rouler lentement au sol ◆ **the plane ~ed along the runway** l'avion a roulé sur la piste ◆ **the aircraft ~ed to a standstill** l'avion a roulé sur la piste avant de s'arrêter 2 *(= go by taxi)* aller en taxi
COMP *[charges etc]* de taxi
taxi dancer * N *(US)* taxi-girl *f*
taxi driver N chauffeur *m* de taxi
taxi fare N *(gen)* tarif *m* de taxi ◆ **I haven't got the ~ fare** je n'ai pas de quoi payer le taxi
taxi rank *(Brit)*, **taxi stance** *(esp Scot)*, **taxi stand** *(esp US)* N station *f* de taxis

taxicab /'tæksɪkæb/ N *(esp US)* taxi *m*

taxidermist /'tæksɪdɜːmɪst/ N empailleur *m*, -euse *f*, naturaliste *mf*

taxidermy /'tæksɪdɜːmɪ/ N empaillage *m*, naturalisation *f*, taxidermie *f*

taximeter /'tæksɪmiːtə/ N taximètre *m*, compteur *m* (de taxi)

taxing /'tæksɪŋ/ ADJ *(mentally) [problem]* ardu ; *(physically) [work]* pénible ◆ **physically/emotionally ~** pénible sur le plan physique/affectif

taxiplane /'tæksɪpleɪn/ N *(US)* avion-taxi *m*

taxiway /'tæksɪweɪ/ N *(at airport)* taxiway *m*, piste *f* de déroulement

taxman * /'tæksmæn/ N (pl **-men**) percepteur *m*

taxonomist /tæk'sɒnəmɪst/ N taxonomiste *or* taxinomiste *mf*

taxonomy /tæk'sɒnəmɪ/ N taxonomie *or* taxinomie *f*

taxpayer /'tækspeɪəʳ/ N contribuable *mf* ◆ **the British ~ has to pay for it** ce sont les contribuables britanniques qui payeront

TB /tiː'biː/ N abbrev of **tuberculosis**

tba /ˌtiːbiː'eɪ/ (abbrev of **to be arranged** *or* **to be announced**) à préciser

tbc /ˌtiːbiː'siː/ (abbrev of **to be confirmed**) à confirmer, sous réserve

tbs (pl **tbs**), **tbsp** (pl **tbsp** *or* **tbsps**), **tblsp** (pl **tblsp** *or* **tblsps**) N (abbrev of **tablespoonful**) c. à soupe ◆ **1 ~ vinegar** 1 c. à soupe de vinaigre

TCE /tiːsiː'iː/ N (abbrev of **ton coal equivalent**) TEC *f*

Tchaikovsky /tʃaɪ'kɒfskɪ/ N Tchaïkovski *m*

TD /tiː'diː/ N 1 *(Brit)* abbrev of **Territorial Decoration** 2 *(American Ftbl)* abbrev of **touchdown** 3 *(US)* (abbrev of **Treasury Department**) → **treasury** 4 (abbrev of **technical drawing**) → **technical**

te /tiː/ N *(Mus)* si *m*

tea /tiː/ N 1 *(= plant, substance)* thé *m* ◆ **she made a pot of ~** elle a fait du thé ◆ **I wouldn't do it for all the ~ in China** * je ne le ferais pour rien au monde ◆ **~ and sympathy** réconfort *m* ; → **cup**
2 *(esp Brit = meal)* thé *m* ; *(for children)* ≃ goûter *m* ◆ **to have ~** prendre le thé ; *[children]* goûter ; → **high**
3 *(herbal)* infusion *f*, tisane *f* ; → **beef**
COMP **tea bag** N sachet *m* de thé
tea ball N *(US)* boule *f or* infuseur *m* à thé
tea boy N *(Brit) jeune employé chargé de préparer le thé*
tea break N *(Brit)* pause-thé *f* ◆ **to have a ~ break** faire la pause-thé
tea caddy N boîte *f* à thé
tea chest N caisse *f* (à thé)
tea-cloth N *(Brit) (for dishes)* torchon *m* (à vaisselle) ; *(for table)* nappe *f* (à thé) ; *(for trolley, tray)* napperon *m*
tea cosy *(Brit)*, **tea cozy** *(US)* N couvre-théière *m*, cache-théière *m*
tea dance N thé *m* dansant
tea infuser N *(Brit)* boule *f or* infuseur *m* à thé, théier *m*
tea kettle N *(US)* bouilloire *f*
tea lady N *(Brit) dame qui prépare le thé pour les employés d'une entreprise*
tea leaf N (pl **tea leaves**) feuille *f* de thé ; → **read**
tea party N thé *m (réception)*
tea-plant N arbre *m* à thé, théier *m*
tea plate N petite assiette *f*
tea rose N rose-thé *f*
tea service, tea set N service *m* à thé
tea strainer N passe-thé *m inv*
tea table N *(esp Brit)* ◆ **they sat at the ~ table** ils étaient assis autour de la table mise pour le thé ◆ **the subject was raised at the ~ table** on en a discuté pendant le thé ◆ **to set the ~ table** mettre la table pour le thé
tea-things NPL ◆ **where are the ~-things ?** où est le service à thé ? ◆ **to wash up the ~-things** faire la vaisselle après le thé
tea towel N *(Brit)* torchon *m* (à vaisselle)
tea tray N plateau *m* (à thé)
tea tree N arbre *m* à thé, tea-tree *m*
tea trolley N *(Brit)* table *f* roulante
tea urn N fontaine *f* à thé
tea wagon N *(US)* ⇒ **tea trolley**

teacake /'tiːkeɪk/ N *(Brit)* petit pain *m* brioché

teacart /'tiːkɑːt/ N *(US)* ⇒ **tea trolley** ; → **tea**

teach /tiːtʃ/ (pret, ptp **taught**) VT *(gen)* apprendre *(sb sth, sth to sb* qch à qn) ; *(Scol, Univ etc)* enseigner *(sb sth, sth to sb* qch à qn) ◆ **to ~ sb (how) to do sth** apprendre à qn à faire qch ◆ **I'll ~ you what to do** je t'apprendrai ce qu'il faut faire ◆ **he ~es French** il enseigne le français ◆ **he taught her French** il lui a appris *or* enseigné le français ◆ **to ~ school** *(US)* être professeur ◆ **to ~ o.s. (to do) sth** apprendre (à faire) qch tout seul ◆ **I'll ~ you a lesson!** je vais t'apprendre ! ◆ **that will ~ him a lesson!** cela lui servira de leçon ! ◆ **they could ~ us a thing or two about family values** ils auraient beaucoup à nous apprendre sur les valeurs familiales ◆ **she could ~ you a trick or two!** elle pourrait t'en remontrer ! ◆ **that will ~ you to mind your own business!** ça t'apprendra à te mêler de tes affaires ! ◆ **I'll ~ you (not) to speak to me like that!** je vais t'apprendre à me parler sur ce ton ! ◆ **you can't ~ him anything about cars** il n'a rien à apprendre de personne en matière de voitures ◆ **don't (try to) ~ your grandmother to suck eggs!** * on n'apprend pas à un vieux singe à faire des grimaces ! *(Prov)* ◆ **you can't ~ an old dog new tricks** *(Prov)* ce n'est pas à son *(or* mon *etc)* âge qu'on apprend de nouveaux trucs
VI enseigner ◆ **he always wanted to ~** il a toujours eu le désir d'enseigner ◆ **he had been ~ing all morning** il avait fait cours *or* fait la classe toute la matinée
COMP **teach-in** N séminaire *m (sur un thème)*

teachability /ˌtiːtʃə'bɪlɪtɪ/ N *(esp US)* aptitude *f* à apprendre

teachable /'tiːtʃəbl/ ADJ *(esp US) [child]* scolarisable ; *[subject, skill]* enseignable, susceptible d'être enseigné

teacher /'tiːtʃəʳ/ N *(in secondary school: also private tutor)* professeur *m* ; *(in primary school)* professeur *m* des écoles, instituteur *m*, -trice *f* ; *(in special school, prison)* éducateur *m*, -trice *f* ; *(gen = member of teaching profession)* enseignant(e) *m(f)* ◆ **she is a maths ~** elle est professeur de maths ◆ **~'s (hand)book** livre *m* du maître ◆ **the ~s accepted the government's offer** *(collectively)* les enseignants ont *or* le corps enseignant a accepté l'offre du gouvernement ◆ **the ~s' strike/dispute** la grève/le conflit des enseignants ; see also **comp**
COMP **teacher certification** N *(US)* habilitation *f* à enseigner
teacher education N *(US)* formation *f* pédagogique (des enseignants)
teacher evaluation N appréciations *fpl* sur les professeurs *(par les étudiants ou par l'administration)*
teacher-pupil ratio N taux *m* d'encadrement ◆ **a high/low ~-pupil ratio** un fort/faible taux d'encadrement
teacher's aide N *(US)* assistant(e) *m(f)* du professeur *(or* de l'instituteur)
teachers' certificate N *(US)* ⇒ **teacher training certificate**
teachers' college N *(US)* ⇒ **teacher training college**
teachers' training N ⇒ **teacher training**
teachers' training certificate N ⇒ **teacher training certificate**
teachers' training college N ⇒ **teacher training college**
teacher training N *(Brit)* formation *f* pédagogique (des enseignants)
teacher training certificate N *(for primary schools)* ≃ Certificat *m* d'aptitude au professorat des écoles, CAPE *m* ; *(for secondary schools)* ≃ Certificat *m* d'aptitude au professorat de l'enseignement du second degré, CAPES *m* ; *(for secondary technical schools)* ≃ Certificat *m* d'aptitude au professorat de l'enseignement technique, CAPET *m*
teacher training college N ≃ Institut *m* universitaire de formation des maîtres, IUFM *m*

teaching /'tiːtʃɪŋ/ N 1 *(NonC = act, profession)* enseignement *m* ◆ **he's got 16 hours ~ a week** il a 16 heures de cours par semaine ◆ **to go into ~** entrer dans l'enseignement ◆ **Teaching of English as a Foreign Language** (enseignement *m* de l')anglais *m* langue étrangère ◆ **Teaching of English as a Second Language** enseignement *m* de l'anglais langue seconde ◆ **Teaching of English as a Second or Other Language** enseignement *m* de l'anglais langue seconde ou autre ; → **TEFL, TESL, TESOL, ELT** ; → **team**
2 (also **teachings**) *[of philosopher, sage etc]* enseignements *mpl (liter) (on, about* sur)
COMP **teaching aid** N outil *m* pédagogique
teaching aids NPL matériel *m* pédagogique

teaching assistant N (US Univ) étudiant(e) *m(f)* chargé(e) de travaux dirigés
teaching certificate N (US) ⇒ **teacher training certificate** ; → **teacher**
teaching equipment N ⇒ **teaching aids**
teaching hospital N centre *m* hospitalier universitaire, CHU *m*
teaching job, teaching position, teaching post N poste *m* d'enseignant
teaching practice N (Brit) stage *m* de formation des enseignants
the teaching profession N (= *activity*) l'enseignement *m* ; (*in secondary schools only*) le professorat ; (*teachers collectively*) le corps enseignant, les enseignants *mpl*
teaching software N (NonC) didacticiels *mpl* ◆ **a piece of ~ software** un didacticiel
teaching staff N personnel *m* enseignant, enseignants *mpl*, équipe *f* pédagogique

teacup /ˈtiːkʌp/ N tasse *f* à thé ; → **read, storm**

teacupful /ˈtiːkʌpfʊl/ N tasse *f*

teahouse /ˈtiːhaʊs/ N maison *f* de thé

teak /tiːk/ N teck *or* tek *m*

teal /tiːl/ N (pl **teal** or **teals**) sarcelle *f*

team /tiːm/ N (Sport, gen) équipe *f* ; [*of horses, oxen*] attelage *m* ◆ **football ~** équipe *f* de football ◆ **our research ~** notre équipe de chercheurs VT (also **team up**) [*+ actor, worker*] mettre en collaboration (*with* avec) ; [*+ clothes, accessories*] associer (*with* avec)
COMP **team captain** N capitaine *m*
team games NPL jeux *mpl* d'équipe
team leader N chef *m* d'équipe
team-mate N coéquipier *m*, -ière *f*
team member N (Sport) équipier *m*, -ière *f*
team player N **to be a ~ player** avoir l'esprit d'équipe
team spirit N (NonC) esprit *m* d'équipe
team teaching N (NonC) enseignement *m* en équipe

► **team up** VI [*people*] faire équipe (*with* avec ; *to do sth* pour faire qch) ; [*colours*] s'harmoniser (*with* avec) ; [*clothes, accessories, furnishings etc*] s'associer (*with* avec) ◆ **he ~ed up with them to get ...** il s'est allié à eux pour obtenir ...
VT SEP ⇒ **team vt**

teamster /ˈtiːmstəʳ/ N (US) routier *m or* camionneur *m* syndiqué

teamwork /ˈtiːmwɜːk/ N (NonC) travail *m* d'équipe

teapot /ˈtiːpɒt/ N théière *f*

tear[1] /tɛəʳ/ (vb : pret **tore**, ptp **torn**) N déchirure *f*, accroc *m* ◆ **to make a ~ in sth** déchirer qch ◆ **it has a ~ in it** c'est déchiré, il y a un accroc dedans
VT 1 (= *rip*) [*+ cloth, garment*] déchirer, faire un trou *or* un accroc à ; [*+ flesh, paper*] déchirer ◆ **to ~ a hole in ...** faire une déchirure *or* un accroc à ..., faire un trou dans ... ◆ **he tore it along the dotted line** il l'a déchiré en suivant le pointillé ◆ **to ~ to pieces** *or* **to shreds** *or* **to bits** * [*+ paper*] déchirer en petits morceaux ; [*+ garment*] mettre en pièces *or* lambeaux ; [*+ prey*] mettre en pièces ; (*fig*) [*+ play, performance*] éreinter ; [*+ argument, suggestion*] descendre en flammes * ◆ **to ~ sth loose** arracher qch ◆ **to ~ (o.s.) loose** se libérer ◆ **to ~ open** [*+ envelope*] déchirer ; [*+ letter*] déchirer l'enveloppe de ; [*+ parcel*] ouvrir en déchirant l'emballage ◆ **clothes torn to rags** vêtements mis en lambeaux ◆ **I tore my hand on a nail** je me suis ouvert la main sur un clou ◆ **to ~ a muscle/ligament** (*Med*) se déchirer un muscle/un ligament ◆ **that's torn it!** * voilà qui flanque tout par terre ! *
2 (*fig*) **to be torn by war/remorse** *etc* être déchiré par la guerre/le remords *etc* ◆ **to be torn between two things/people** être tiraillé par *or* balancer entre deux choses/personnes ◆ **I'm very much torn** j'hésite beaucoup (entre les deux)
3 (= *snatch*) arracher (*from sb* à qn ; *out of or off or from sth* de qch) ◆ **he tore it out of her hand** il le lui a arraché des mains ◆ **he was torn from his seat** il a été arraché de son siège
VI 1 [*cloth, paper etc*] se déchirer
2 ◆ **he tore at the wrapping paper** il a déchiré l'emballage (impatiemment) ◆ **he tore at the earth with his bare hands** il a griffé la terre de ses mains nues
3 (= *rush*) **to ~ out/down** *etc* sortir/descendre *etc* à toute allure *or* à toute vitesse ◆ **he tore up the stairs** il a monté l'escalier quatre à quatre ◆ **to ~ along the road** [*person*] filer à toute allure le long de la route ; [*car*] rouler à toute allure le long de la route ◆ **they tore after him** ils se sont lancés *or* précipités à sa poursuite ◆ **to ~ into sb** * (= *attack verbally*) s'en prendre violemment à qn ; (= *scold*) passer un savon à qn *
COMP **tear-off** ADJ amovible ◆ **~-off calendar** éphéméride *f*
tear sheet N feuillet *m* détachable

► **tear apart** VT SEP déchirer ; (*fig* = *divide*) déchirer ◆ **his love for Julie is ~ing him apart** son amour pour Julie le déchire

► **tear away** VI [*person*] partir comme un bolide ; [*car*] démarrer en trombe
VT SEP (*lit, fig*) arracher (*from sb* à qn ; *from sth* de qch) ◆ **I couldn't ~ myself away from it/him** je n'arrivais pas à m'en arracher/à m'arracher à lui
N ◆ **tearaway** → **tearaway**

► **tear down** VT SEP [*+ poster, flag*] arracher (*from* de) ; [*+ building*] démolir

► **tear off** VI ⇒ **tear away vi**
VT SEP 1 [*+ label, wrapping*] arracher (*from* de) ; [*+ perforated page, calendar leaf*] détacher (*from* de) → **strip**
2 (= *remove*) [*+ one's clothes*] enlever à la hâte ; [*+ sb's clothes*] arracher
3 (* = *write hurriedly*) [*+ letter etc*] bâcler *, torcher *
ADJ ◆ **tear-off** → **tear[1]**

► **tear out** VI → **tear[1] vi 3**
VT SEP arracher (*from* de) ; [*+ cheque, ticket*] détacher (*from* de) ◆ **to ~ sb's eyes out** arracher les yeux à qn ◆ **to ~ one's hair out** s'arracher les cheveux

► **tear up** VT SEP 1 [*+ paper etc*] déchirer, mettre en morceaux *or* en pièces ; (*fig*) [*+ contract*] déchirer (*fig*) [*+ offer*] reprendre
2 [*+ stake, weed, shrub*] arracher ; [*+ tree*] déraciner

tear[2] /tɪəʳ/ N larme *f* ◆ **in ~s** en larmes ◆ **there were ~s in her eyes** elle avait les larmes aux yeux ◆ **she had ~s of joy in her eyes** elle pleurait de joie ◆ **near** *or* **close to ~s** au bord des larmes ◆ **to burst** *or* **dissolve into ~s** fondre en larmes ◆ **the memory/thought brought ~s to his eyes** à ce souvenir/cette pensée il avait les larmes aux yeux ◆ **the film/book/experience brought ~s to his eyes** ce film/ce livre/cette expérience lui a fait venir les larmes aux yeux ◆ **it will end in ~s!** ça va finir mal ! ◆ **~s of blood** (*fig*) larmes de sang ; → **shed[2]**
COMP **tear bomb** N grenade *f* lacrymogène
tear duct N canal *m* lacrymal
tear gas N gaz *m* lacrymogène
tear-jerker * N ◆ **the film/book** *etc* **was a real ~-jerker** c'était un film/roman *etc* tout à fait du genre à faire pleurer dans les chaumières
tear-stained ADJ baigné de larmes

tearaway /ˈtɛərəweɪ/ N (Brit) casse-cou *m*

teardrop /ˈtɪədrɒp/ N larme *f*

tearful /ˈtɪəfʊl/ ADJ [*face*] plein de larmes ; [*eyes, look*] plein de larmes, larmoyant ; [*farewell*] larmoyant ; [*reunion*] ému ; [*plea, story*] éploré ◆ **to be ~** [*person*] (= *about to cry*) être au bord des larmes, avoir envie de pleurer ; (= *in tears*) être en larmes ◆ **in a ~ voice** (avec) des larmes dans la voix, d'une voix éplorée ◆ **to feel ~** avoir envie de pleurer ◆ **to become ~** avoir les larmes aux yeux

tearfully /ˈtɪəfəlɪ/ ADV [*say*] en pleurant ; [*admit*] les larmes aux yeux

tearing /ˈtɛərɪŋ/ N déchirement *m* ADJ 1 ◆ **a ~ noise** *or* **sound** un bruit de déchirement 2 (Brit *) ◆ **to be in a ~ hurry** être terriblement pressé ◆ **to do sth in a ~ hurry** faire qch à toute vitesse

tearless /ˈtɪəlɪs/ ADJ sans larmes

tearlessly /ˈtɪəlɪslɪ/ ADV sans larmes, sans pleurer

tearoom /ˈtiːrʊm/ N salon *m* de thé

tease /tiːz/ N (= *person*) (*gen*) taquin(e) *m(f)* ; (*sexual*) allumeur *m*, -euse *f* VT 1 (*playfully*) taquiner ; (*cruelly*) tourmenter ; (*sexually*) allumer ◆ **she ~d him that he had big feet** elle le taquina à propos de ses grands pieds 2 [*+ cloth*] peigner ; [*+ wool*] carder

► **tease out** VT SEP 1 [*+ tangle of wool, knots, matted hair*] débrouiller *or* démêler (patiemment) ◆ **to ~ something out of sb** tirer les vers du nez à qn 2 [*+ meaning, sense*] trouver

teasel /ˈtiːzl/ N (= *plant*) cardère *f* ; (= *device*) carde *f*

teaser /ˈtiːzəʳ/ N 1 (= *person*) (*gen*) taquin(e) *m(f)* ; (*sexual*) allumeur *m*, -euse *f* 2 (= *problem*) problème *m* (difficile) ; (= *tricky question*) colle * *f*

teashop /ˈtiːʃɒp/ N (Brit) salon *m* de thé

teasing /ˈtiːzɪŋ/ N (NonC) taquineries *fpl* ADJ taquin

teasingly /ˈtiːzɪŋlɪ/ ADV 1 [*say, ask, hint*] d'un ton taquin, pour me (*or* le *etc*) taquiner ◆ **he looked at me ~** il m'a regardé d'un air taquin 2 (*sexually*) de façon aguichante ◆ **~ erotic** sexy * et provocant

Teasmade ®, **Teasmaid** ® /ˈtiːzmeɪd/ N *machine à faire le thé*

teaspoon /ˈtiːspuːn/ N petite cuiller *f*, cuiller *f* à thé *or* à café

teaspoonful /ˈtiːspuːnfʊl/ N cuillerée *f* à café

teat /tiːt/ N [*of animal*] tétine *f*, tette *f* ; [*of cow*] trayon *m* ; [*of woman*] mamelon *m*, bout *m* de sein ; (Brit) [*of baby's bottle*] tétine *f* ; (= *dummy*) tétine *f* ; (Tech) téton *m*

teatime /ˈtiːtaɪm/ N (*esp Brit*) l'heure *f* du thé

teazel, teazle /ˈtiːzl/ N ⇒ **teasel**

TEC /ˌtiːiːˈsiː/ N (Brit) (abbrev of **Training and Enterprise Council**) → **training**

tech * /tek/ N 1 (Brit) (abbrev of **technical college**) ≈ CET *m* 2 (abbrev of **technology**) → **high**

techie * /ˈtekɪ/ N (= *technician*) technicien(ne) *m(f)* ; (= *technologist*) technologue *mf* ; (= *technophile*) crack * *m* en technologie

technetium /tekˈniːʃɪəm/ N technétium *m*

technical /ˈteknɪkəl/ ADJ technique ◆ **~ ability** *or* **skill** compétence *f* technique ◆ **~ problems** des problèmes *mpl* techniques *or* d'ordre technique ◆ **for ~ reasons** pour des raisons techniques *or* d'ordre technique ◆ **~ language** langue *f or* langage *m* technique ◆ **it's just a ~ point** (*gen*) c'est un point de détail ◆ **a judgement quashed on a ~ point** (*Jur*) un arrêt cassé pour vice de forme ◆ **this constitutes a ~ plea of not guilty** (*Jur*) cela équivaut (théoriquement) à plaider non coupable

COMP **technical college** N *(Brit)* collège *m* (d'enseignement) technique
technical drawing N dessin *m* industriel
technical institute N *(US)* ≈ IUT *m*, institut *m* universitaire de technologie
technical knock-out N *(Boxing)* KO *m* technique
technical offence N *(Jur)* quasi-délit *m*
technical school N ⇒ **technical institute**
technical sergeant N *(US Air Force)* sergent-chef *m*
technical support N soutien *m* technique

technicality /ˌteknɪˈkælɪtɪ/ N [1] *(NonC)* technicité *f* [2] *(= detail)* détail *m* technique ; *(= word)* terme *m* technique ; *(= difficulty)* difficulté *f* technique ; *(= fault)* ennui *m* technique ♦ **I don't understand all the technicalities** certains détails techniques m'échappent [3] *(= formality)* formalité *f* ♦ **she told him victory was just a ~** elle lui a dit que la victoire n'était qu'une simple formalité [4] *(Jur)* **he got off on a ~** il a été acquitté sur un point de procédure

technically /ˈteknɪkəlɪ/ ADV [1] *(= technologically) [superior, feasible, perfect, advanced]* sur le plan technique, techniquement ♦ **~, it's a very risky project** sur le plan technique *or* techniquement, c'est un projet très risqué
[2] *(= in technical language:* also **technically speaking***)* en termes techniques ♦ **fats are ~ known as lipids** le terme technique pour désigner les graisses est "lipides" ♦ **he spoke very ~** il s'est exprimé d'une manière très technique
[3] *(= in technique)* ♦ **a ~ proficient performance/film** une performance/un film d'un bon niveau technique ♦ **~ demanding music** une musique qui exige une bonne technique ♦ **~, this is a very accomplished album** techniquement, c'est un excellent album
[4] *(= strictly) [illegal, correct]* théoriquement, en théorie ♦ **this was ~ correct, but highly ambiguous** c'était théoriquement correct, mais extrêmement ambigu ♦ **you are ~ correct** vous avez raison en théorie ♦ **~, they aren't eligible for a grant** en principe, ils n'ont pas droit à une bourse ♦ **~ (speaking) you're right, but ...** en théorie vous avez raison, mais ...

technician /tekˈnɪʃən/ N technicien(ne) *m(f)*

Technicolor ® /ˈteknɪˌkʌləʳ/ N technicolor ® *m* ♦ **in ~** en technicolor ® ADJ [1] *[film]* en technicolor ® ♦ **the ~ process** le technicolor ® [2] ♦ **technicolour** *(Brit)*, **technicolor** *(US)* *(* = colourful) [description, dream]* en technicolor ®

technique /tekˈniːk/ N technique *f* ♦ **he's got good ~** sa technique est bonne

techno /ˈteknəʊ/ *(Mus)* N techno *f* ADJ techno *inv*

techno... /ˈteknəʊ/ PREF techno...

technocracy /tekˈnɒkrəsɪ/ N technocratie *f*

technocrat /ˈteknəʊkræt/ N technocrate *mf*

technocratic /ˌteknəˈkrætɪk/ ADJ technocratique

technological /ˌteknəˈlɒdʒɪkəl/ ADJ technologique

technologically /teknəˈlɒdʒɪklɪ/ ADV *[advanced, sophisticated, backward]* technologiquement, sur le plan technologique ; *[possible, feasible]* technologiquement ♦ **~ oriented** axé sur la technologie ♦ **~, these cars are nothing new** sur le plan technologique, ces voitures n'ont rien de nouveau ♦ **~ speaking** technologiquement parlant, du point de vue technologique

technologist /tekˈnɒlədʒɪst/ N technologue *mf*

technology /tekˈnɒlədʒɪ/ N technologie *f* ♦ **Minister/Ministry of Technology** *(Brit)* ministre *m*/ministère *m* des Affaires technologiques ♦ **new ~** les nouvelles technologies *fpl* ♦ **space/military ~** technologie *f* de l'espace/militaire ♦ **computer ~** technologie *f* informatique ♦ **communication ~** technologie(s) *f(pl)* de communication ; → **high**

technophobe /ˈteknəʊfəʊb/ N technophobe *mf*

technophobic /ˌteknəʊˈfəʊbɪk/ ADJ technophobe

technostructure /ˈteknəʊˌstrʌktʃəʳ/ N technostructure *f*

techy /ˈtetʃɪ/ ADJ ⇒ **tetchy**

tectonic /ˈtektɒnɪk/ ADJ tectonique

tectonics /ˈtektɒnɪks/ N *(NonC)* tectonique *f*

Ted /ted/ N [1] (dim of **Edward, Theodore**) Ted *m* [2] * ⇒ **teddy boy** ; → **teddy**

ted /ted/ VT faner

tedder /ˈtedəʳ/ N *(= machine)* faneuse *f* ; *(= person)* faneur *m*, -euse *f*

teddy /ˈtedɪ/ N [1] *(= underwear)* teddy *m* [2] (also **teddy bear**) nounours *m (baby talk)*, ours *m* en peluche COMP **teddy boy** † N *(Brit)* ≈ blouson *m* noir

tedious /ˈtiːdɪəs/ ADJ *[task, work, process]* fastidieux ; *[account, description, film]* fastidieux, ennuyeux ; *[life, hours, journey, behaviour]* assommant ♦ **such lists are ~ to read** ces listes sont assommantes à lire

tediously /ˈtiːdɪəslɪ/ ADV ♦ **~ boring** profondément ennuyeux ♦ **~ repetitive/juvenile** tellement répétitif/puéril que c'en est lassant ♦ **a ~ winding road** une route aux lacets qui n'en finissent pas ♦ **~ long** long et ennuyeux

tediousness /ˈtiːdɪəsnɪs/, **tedium** /ˈtiːdɪəm/ N *(NonC)* ennui *m*, caractère *m* assommant

tee¹ /tiː/ → **T**

tee² /tiː/ *(Golf)* N tee *m* VT *[+ ball]* placer sur le tee

► **tee off** VI partir du tee VT SEP *(US ‡) (= annoy)* embêter*, casser les pieds à* ; *(fig = begin)* démarrer*

► **tee up** VI placer la balle sur le tee

tee-hee /ˈtiːˈhiː/ (vb : pret, ptp **tee-heed**) EXCL hi-hi ! N (petit) ricanement *m* VI ricaner

teem /tiːm/ VI [1] *[crowds, insects]* grouiller, fourmiller ; *[fish, snakes etc]* grouiller ♦ **to ~ with** *[river, street etc]* grouiller de, fourmiller de ♦ **he's ~ing with ideas** il déborde d'idées [2] ♦ **it was ~ing (with rain), the rain was ~ing down** il pleuvait à verse *or* à seaux

teeming /ˈtiːmɪŋ/ ADJ [1] *[city, streets]* grouillant de monde ; *[crowd, hordes, insects]* grouillant ; *[river]* grouillant de poissons [2] ♦ **~ rain** pluie *f* battante *or* torrentielle

teen * /tiːn/ (abbrev of **teenage**) ADJ *[movie, magazine]* pour ados* ; *[fashion, mother, father]* ado* *f inv* ; *[pregnancy]* chez les ados* ; *[crime]* juvénile ; *[violence]* des ados* ; *[audience]* d'ados* ♦ **~ boys** ados* *mpl* ♦ **~ girls** ados* *fpl* ♦ **~ years** adolescence *f* ; → **teens**

teenage /ˈtiːneɪdʒ/ ADJ *[mother]* adolescent ; *[pregnancy]* chez les adolescents ; *[suicide]* d'adolescent(s) ; *[idol, heart-throb, culture]* des adolescents ; *[magazine, fashion]* pour adolescents ♦ **to have a ~ crush on sb** avoir une tocade d'adolescent pour qn ♦ **~ boy** adolescent *m* ♦ **~ girl** adolescente *f* ♦ **~ years** adolescence *f* ; → **teens**

teenaged /ˈtiːneɪdʒd/ ADJ adolescent ♦ **a ~ boy/girl** un adolescent/une adolescente

teenager /ˈtiːnˌeɪdʒəʳ/ N adolescent(e) *m(f)*

teens /tiːnz/ NPL adolescence *f* ♦ **he is still in his ~** il est encore adolescent ♦ **he is just out of his ~** il a à peine vingt ans ♦ **he is in his early/late ~** il a un peu plus de treize ans/un peu moins de vingt ans

teensy(-weensy) * /ˈtiːnzɪ(ˈwiːnzɪ)/ ADJ ⇒ **teeny adj**

teeny * /ˈtiːnɪ/ ADJ (also **teeny-weeny** *) minuscule, tout petit ♦ **a ~ bit embarrassing/jealous** un petit peu gênant/jaloux ♦ **to be a ~ bit hung over** avoir un petit peu la gueule de bois N (also **teeny-bopper** *) préado* *mf*

teepee /ˈtiːpiː/ N ⇒ **tepee**

tee-shirt /ˈtiːʃɜːt/ N tee-shirt *or* T-shirt *m*

teeter /ˈtiːtəʳ/ VI *[person]* chanceler ; *[pile]* vaciller ♦ **to ~ on the edge** *or* **brink of** *(fig)* être prêt à tomber dans COMP **teeter totter** N *(US)* jeu de bascule

teeth /tiːθ/ NPL of **tooth**

teethe /tiːð/ VI faire *or* percer ses dents

teething /ˈtiːðɪŋ/ N poussée *f* des dents COMP **teething ring** N anneau *m (de bébé qui perce ses dents)*
teething troubles NPL *(Brit fig)* difficultés *fpl* initiales

teetotal /ˈtiːˈtəʊtl/ ADJ *[person]* qui ne boit jamais d'alcool ; *[league]* antialcoolique

teetotaler /ˈtiːˈtəʊtləʳ/ N *(US)* ⇒ **teetotaller**

teetotalism /ˈtiːˈtəʊtəlɪzəm/ N abstention *f* de toute boisson alcoolique

teetotaller, teetotaler *(US)* /ˈtiːˈtəʊtləʳ/ N personne *f* qui ne boit jamais d'alcool

TEFL /tefl/ N *(Educ)* (abbrev of **Teaching of English as a Foreign Language**) → **teaching**

> **TEFL, TESL, TESOL, ELT**
>
> Les sigles **TEFL** (Teaching of English as a Foreign Language) et **EFL** (English as a Foreign Language) renvoient à l'enseignement de l'anglais langue étrangère dans les pays non anglophones.
>
> Le **TESL** (Teaching of English as a Second Language) concerne l'enseignement de l'anglais langue seconde, c'est-à-dire aux personnes qui vivent dans un pays anglophone mais dont la langue maternelle n'est pas l'anglais. Cet enseignement cherche à prendre en compte l'origine culturelle de l'apprenant ainsi que sa langue maternelle.
>
> **TESOL** (Teaching of English as a Second or Other Language - enseignement de l'anglais langue seconde ou autre) est le terme américain pour **TEFL** et **TESL**.
>
> **ELT** (English Language Teaching) est le terme général qui désigne l'enseignement de l'anglais en tant que langue étrangère ou langue seconde.

Teflon ® /ˈteflɒn/ N téflon ® *m* ADJ * *(fig = able to avoid blame)* ♦ **he was the so-called ~ President** on le surnommait "le président Téflon"

tegument /ˈtegjʊmənt/ N tégument *m*

te-hee /ˈtiːˈhiː/ ⇒ **tee-hee**

Teheran /teəˈrɑːn/ N Téhéran

tel. (abbrev of **telephone (number)**) tél

Tel Aviv /ˈteləˈviːv/ N Tel-Aviv

tele... /ˈtelɪ/ PREF télé...

telebanking /ˈtelɪˌbæŋkɪŋ/ N télébanque *f*

telecamera /ˈtelɪˌkæmərə/ N caméra *f* de télévision, télécaméra *f*

telecast /ˈtelɪkɑːst/ *(US)* N émission *f* de télévision VT diffuser

telecommunication /ˈtelɪkəˌmjuːnɪˈkeɪʃən/ N *(gen pl)* télécommunications *fpl* ; → **post³** COMP **telecommunications satellite** N satellite *m* de télécommunication

telecommute /ˈtelɪkəˌmjuːt/ VI télétravailler

telecommuter * /ˈtelɪkəˌmjuːtəʳ/ N télétravailleur *m*, -euse *f*

telecommuting * /ˈtelɪkəˌmjuːtɪŋ/ N télétravail *m*

teleconference /ˈtelɪkɒnfərəns/ N téléconférence *f*

teleconferencing /ˈtelɪkɒnfərənsɪŋ/ N téléconférence(s) *f(pl)*

Telecopier ® /ˈtelɪˌkɒpɪəʳ/ N télécopieur *m*

telecopy /ˈtelɪˌkɒpɪ/ N télécopie *f*

telefacsimile /ˌtelɪfækˈsɪmɪlɪ/ N télécopie *f*

telefax /ˈtelɪfæks/ N télécopie *f*

telefilm /ˈtelɪfɪlm/ N téléfilm *m*, film *m* pour la télévision

telegenic /ˌtelɪˈdʒenɪk/ ADJ télégénique

telegram /ˈtelɪgræm/ N télégramme *m* ; *(Diplomacy, Press)* dépêche *f*, câble *m*

telegraph /ˈtelɪgrɑːf/ N télégraphe *m* VT télégraphier ◆ **I'll ~ when I arrive** j'enverrai un télégramme lorsque je serai arrivé VT *[+ message]* télégraphier ; *(fig) [+ intentions, plans]* dévoiler

COMP *[message, wires]* télégraphique

telegraph pole, telegraph post N poteau *m* télégraphique

telegrapher /tɪˈlegrəfəʳ/ N télégraphiste *mf*

telegraphese /ˌtelɪgrɑːˈfiːz/ N *(NonC)* style *m* télégraphique

telegraphic /ˌtelɪˈgræfɪk/ ADJ *(Telec)* télégraphique ; *(= concise) [writing, notes]* en style télégraphique ◆ **in ~ style, with ~ brevity** en style télégraphique

telegraphically /ˌtelɪˈgræfɪkəlɪ/ ADV en style télégraphique

telegraphist /tɪˈlegrəfɪst/ N télégraphiste *mf*

telegraphy /tɪˈlegrəfɪ/ N télégraphie *f*

telekinesis /ˌtelɪkɪˈniːsɪs/ N *(NonC)* télékinésie *f*

telekinetic /ˌtelɪkɪˈnetɪk/ ADJ télékinésique

Telemachus /təˈleməkəs/ N Télémaque *m*

telemarketer /ˈtelɪmɑːkɪtəʳ/ N *(= person)* spécialiste *mf* du télémarketing ; *(= company)* société *f* spécialisée dans le télémarketing

telemarketing /ˈtelɪmɑːkɪtɪŋ/ N télémarketing *m*

telematics /ˌtelɪˈmætɪks/ N *(NonC)* télématique *f*

telemeeting /ˈtelɪˌmiːtɪŋ/ N téléréunion *f*

Telemessage ® /ˈtelɪˌmesɪdʒ/ N *(Brit)* télémessage *m*

telemeter /tɪˈlemɪtəʳ/ N télémètre *m*

telemetric /ˌtelɪˈmetrɪk/ ADJ télémétrique

telemetry /tɪˈlemɪtrɪ/ N télémétrie *f*

teleological /ˌtelɪəˈlɒdʒɪkl/ ADJ téléologique

teleology /ˌtelɪˈɒlədʒɪ/ N téléologie *f*

telepath /ˈteləpæθ/ N télépathe *mf*

telepathic /ˌtelɪˈpæθɪk/ ADJ *[person]* télépathe ; *[ability, message]* télépathique

telepathically /ˌtelɪˈpæθɪkəlɪ/ ADV par télépathie

telepathist /tɪˈlepəθɪst/ N télépathe *mf*

telepathy /tɪˈlepəθɪ/ N télépathie *f*

telephone /ˈtelɪfəʊn/ N téléphone *m* ◆ **by ~** par téléphone ◆ **on the ~** au téléphone ◆ **to be on the ~** *(= speaking)* être au téléphone ; *(= be a subscriber)* avoir le téléphone (chez soi)

VT *[+ person]* téléphoner à, appeler (au téléphone) ; *[+ message, telegram]* téléphoner *(to* à) ◆ **~ 772 3200 for more information** pour de plus amples renseignements, appelez le 772 3200

VI téléphoner

COMP **telephone answering machine** N répondeur *m* (téléphonique)

telephone banking N *(NonC)* services *mpl* bancaires par téléphone

telephone book N ⇒ **telephone directory**

telephone booth N *(US)* ⇒ **telephone box**

telephone box N *(Brit)* cabine *f* téléphonique

telephone call N coup *m* de téléphone*, appel *m* téléphonique

telephone directory N annuaire *m* (du téléphone)

telephone exchange N central *m* téléphonique

telephone kiosk N ⇒ **telephone box**

telephone line N ligne *f* téléphonique

telephone message N message *m* téléphonique

telephone number N numéro *m* de téléphone

telephone numbers * NPL *(fig = large sums)* des mille et des cents * *mpl*

telephone operator N standardiste *mf*, téléphoniste *mf*

telephone pole N poteau *m* télégraphique

telephone sales N ⇒ **telesales**

telephone service N service *m* des téléphones

telephone sex N *(NonC)* ≈ téléphone *m* rose ◆ **~ sex line** (ligne *f* de) téléphone *m* rose

telephone subscriber N abonné(e) *m(f)* au téléphone

telephone-tapping N mise *f* sur écoute (téléphonique)

telephone wires NPL fils *mpl* téléphoniques

telephonic /ˌtelɪˈfɒnɪk/ ADJ téléphonique

telephonist /tɪˈlefənɪst/ N *(esp Brit)* téléphoniste *mf*

telephony /tɪˈlefənɪ/ N téléphonie *f*

telephoto lens /ˈtelɪˌfəʊtəʊ lenz/ N téléobjectif *m*

teleport /ˈtelɪpɔːt/ VT téléporter

teleportation /ˌtelɪpɔːˈteɪʃən/ N télékinésie *f*

teleprint /ˈtelɪˌprɪnt/ VT *(Brit)* transmettre par téléscripteur

teleprinter /ˈtelɪˌprɪntəʳ/ N *(Brit)* téléscripteur *m*, Télétype ® *m*

Teleprompter ® /ˈtelɪˌprɒmptəʳ/ N *(US, Can)* prompteur *m*, téléprompteur *m*

telesales /ˈtelɪseɪlz/ NPL vente *f* par téléphone, télévente *f*

COMP **telesales department** N service *m* des ventes par téléphone

telesales staff N vendeurs *mpl*, -euses *fpl* par téléphone, télévendeurs *mpl*, -euses *fpl*

telescope /ˈtelɪskəʊp/ N *(reflecting)* télescope *m* ; *(refracting)* lunette *f* d'approche, longue-vue *f* ; *(Astron)* lunette *f* astronomique, télescope *m* VI *[railway carriages etc]* se télescoper ; *[umbrella]* se plier ◆ **parts made to ~** pièces *fpl* qui s'emboîtent VT 1 *[+ cane]* replier 2 *[+ report, ideas]* condenser

telescopic /ˌtelɪsˈkɒpɪk/ ADJ télescopique

COMP **telescopic damper** N *(in car)* amortisseur *m* télescopique

telescopic lens N téléobjectif *m*

telescopic sight N lunette *f*, collimateur *m*

telescopic umbrella N parapluie *m* pliant *or* télescopique

teleshopping /ˈtelɪʃɒpɪŋ/ N *(NonC)* téléachat *m*

teletex /ˈteləteks/ N Télétex ® *m*

Teletext ® /ˈtelətekst/ N télétexte ® *m*, vidéotex ® *m* diffusé

telethon /ˈteləθɒn/ N *(TV)* téléthon *m*

Teletype ® /ˈtelɪtaɪp/ VT transmettre par Télétype ® N Télétype ® *m*

teletypewriter /ˌtelɪˈtaɪpraɪtəʳ/ N *(US)* téléscripteur *m*, Télétype ® *m*

televangelism /ˌtelɪˈvændʒəlɪzəm/ N *(NonC: esp US)* prédication *f* à la télévision

televangelist /ˌtelɪˈvændʒəlɪst/ N *(esp US)* télévangéliste *mf*

televiеw /ˈteləvjuː/ VI *(US)* regarder la télévision

televiewer /ˈtelɪˌvjuːəʳ/ N téléspectateur *m*, -trice *f*

televiewing /ˈtelɪˌvjuːɪŋ/ N *(NonC: watching TV)* la télévision ◆ **this evening's ~ contains ...** le programme de (la) télévision pour ce soir comprend ...

televise /ˈtelɪvaɪz/ VT téléviser

television /ˈtelɪˌvɪʒən/ N télévision *f* ; (also **television set**) (poste *m* de) télévision *f*, téléviseur *m* ◆ **on ~** à la télévision ◆ **black-and-white ~** télévision *f* noir et blanc ◆ **colour ~** télévision *f* (en) couleur

COMP *[actor, camera, studio]* de télévision ; *[report, news, serial]* télévisé ; *[film, script]* pour la télévision

television broadcast N émission *f* de télévision

television cabinet N meuble-télévision *m*

television licence N *(Brit)* certificat *m* de redevance télévision ◆ **to pay one's ~ licence** payer sa redevance télévision

television lounge N *(in hotel etc)* salle *f* de télévision

television programme N émission *f* de télévision

television rights NPL droits *mpl* d'antenne

television room N ⇒ **television lounge**

television screen N écran *m* de télévision *or* de téléviseur ◆ **on the ~ screen** sur le petit écran

television set N télévision *f*, téléviseur *m*, poste *m* (de télévision)

televisual /ˌtelɪˈvɪʒjʊəl/ ADJ *(Brit)* télévisuel

telework /ˈtelɪwɜːk/ VI télétravailler

teleworker /ˈtelɪwɜːkəʳ/ N télétravailleur *m*, -euse *f*

teleworking /ˈtelɪwɜːkɪŋ/ N télétravail *m*

telex /ˈteleks/ N télex *m* VT télexer, envoyer par télex COMP **telex operator** N télexiste *mf*

tell /tel/ (pret, ptp **told**) VT 1 *(gen)* dire *(that* que) ◆ **~ me your name** dites-moi votre nom ◆ **I told him how pleased I was** je lui ai dit combien *or* à quel point j'étais content ◆ **I told him what/where/how/why** je lui ai dit ce que/où/comment/pourquoi ◆ **I told him the way to London, I told him how to get to London** je lui ai expliqué comment aller à Londres ◆ **he told himself it was only a game** il s'est dit que ce n'était qu'un jeu ◆ **I am glad to ~ you that ...** je suis heureux de pouvoir vous dire que ... ◆ **to ~ sb sth again** répéter *or* redire qch à qn ◆ **something ~s me he won't be pleased** quelque chose me dit qu'il ne sera pas content ◆ **how many times do I have to ~ you?** combien de fois faudra-t-il que je te le répète ? ◆ **let me ~ you that you are quite mistaken** permettez-moi de vous dire que vous vous trompez lourdement ◆ **I won't go, I ~ you!** puisque je te dis que je n'irai pas ! ◆ **I can't ~ you how grateful I am** je ne saurais vous dire à quel point je suis reconnaissant ◆ **I can't ~ you how glad I was to leave that place** vous ne pouvez pas savoir à quel point j'étais content de quitter cet endroit ◆ **don't ~ me you've lost it!** tu ne vas pas me dire que *or* ne me dis pas que tu l'as perdu ! ◆ **I told you so!** je te l'avais bien dit ! ◆ **... or so I've been told ...** ou du moins c'est ce qu'on m'a dit ◆ **I could ~ you a thing or two about him** je pourrais vous en dire long sur lui ◆ **I('ll) ~ you what*, let's go for a swim!** tiens, si on allait se baigner ! ◆ **you're ~ing me!** * à qui le dis-tu ! ◆ **you ~ me!** je n'en sais rien !, qu'est-ce que j'en sais ! *

2 *(= relate)* dire, raconter ; *[+ story, adventure]* raconter *(to* à) ; *[+ a lie, the truth]* dire ; *(= divulge) [+ secret]* dire, révéler ; *[+ sb's age]* révéler ; *[+ the future]* prédire ◆ **to ~ it like it is** * ne pas mâcher ses mots ◆ **can you ~ the time?, can you ~ time?** *(US)* sais-tu lire l'heure ? ◆ **can you ~ me the time?** peux-tu me dire l'heure (qu'il est) ? ◆ **clocks ~ the time** les horloges indiquent l'heure ◆ **that ~s me all I need to**

know maintenant je sais tout ce qu'il me faut savoir ◆ **it ~s its own tale** *or* **story** ça dit bien ce que ça veut dire ◆ **the lack of evidence ~s a tale** *or* **story** le manque de preuve est très révélateur ◆ **~ me another!*** à d'autres !* ◆ **his actions ~ us a lot about his motives** ses actes nous en disent long sur ses motifs ◆ **she was ~ing him about it** elle lui en parlait, elle était en train de le lui raconter ◆ **~ me about it** *(lit)* raconte-moi ça ; *(* iro)* ne m'en parle pas ◆ **I told him about what had happened** je lui ai dit *or* raconté ce qui était arrivé ◆ **"by J. Smith, as told to W. Jones"** ≈ "par J. Smith, propos recueillis par W. Jones" ; → **fortune, picture, tale, truth**

3 *(= know)* ◆ **how can I ~ what he will do ?** comment puis-je savoir ce qu'il va faire ? ◆ **there's no ~ing what he might do/how long the talks could last** impossible de dire *or* savoir ce qu'il pourrait faire/combien de temps les pourparlers vont durer ◆ **it was impossible to ~ where the bullet had entered** il était impossible de dire *or* savoir par où la balle était entrée ◆ **I couldn't ~ if he had been in a fight or had just fallen** il (m')était impossible de dire *or* de savoir s'il s'était battu ou s'il était simplement tombé, je n'aurais pas pu dire s'il s'était battu ou s'il était simplement tombé ◆ **I couldn't ~ how it was done** je ne pourrais pas dire comment ça a été fait ◆ **no one can ~ what he'll say** personne ne peut savoir ce qu'il dira ◆ **you can ~ he's clever by the way he talks** on voit bien qu'il est intelligent à la façon dont il parle ◆ **you can ~ he's joking** on voit bien qu'il plaisante ◆ **you can't ~ much from his letter** sa lettre n'en dit pas très long

4 *(= distinguish)* distinguer, voir ; *(= know)* savoir ◆ **to ~ right from wrong** distinguer le bien du mal ◆ **I can't ~ them apart** je ne peux pas les distinguer (l'un de l'autre) ◆ **I can't ~ the difference** je ne vois pas la différence *(between* entre)

5 *(= command)* dire, ordonner *(sb to do sth* à qn de faire qch) ◆ **do as you are told** fais ce qu'on te dit ◆ **I told him not to do it** je lui ai dit de ne pas le faire, je lui ai défendu de le faire

6 *(†† = count)* compter, dénombrer ◆ **to ~ one's beads** dire *or* réciter son chapelet ; → **all**

VI 1 parler *(of, about* de) ; *(fig)* ◆ **the ruins told of a long-lost civilization** les ruines témoignaient d'une civilisation depuis longtemps disparue ◆ **his face told of his sorrow** sa douleur se lisait sur son visage ◆ **(only) time can ~** qui vivra verra

2 *(= know)* savoir ◆ **how can I ~?** comment le saurais-je ? ◆ **I can't ~** je n'en sais rien ◆ **who can ~?** qui sait ? ◆ **you never can ~** on ne sait jamais ◆ **you can't ~ from his letter** on ne peut pas savoir d'après sa lettre ◆ **as** *or* **so far as one can ~** pour autant que l'on sache

3 *(= be talebearer)* **I won't ~!** je ne le répéterai à personne ! ◆ **to ~ on sb*** rapporter *or* cafarder* contre qn ◆ **don't ~ on us!*** ne nous dénonce pas !

4 *(= have an effect)* se faire sentir *(on sb/sth* sur qn/qch) ◆ **his influence must ~** son influence ne peut que se faire sentir ◆ **his age is beginning to ~** il commence à accuser son âge ◆ **the pressures of her job are beginning to ~ on her** elle commence à accuser le stress de son travail ◆ **their age and inexperience told against them** leur âge et leur manque d'expérience militaient contre eux

► **tell off** VT SEP 1 *(* = reprimand)* gronder, attraper* *(sb for sth* qn pour qch ; *for doing sth* pour avoir fait qch) ◆ **to be told off** se faire attraper*

2 † *(= select etc) [+ person]* affecter *(for sth* à qch), désigner *(to do sth* pour faire qch) ; *(= check off)* dénombrer

N ◆ **telling-off** * → **telling**

teller /ˈteləʳ/ **N** *(US, Scot Banking)* caissier *m*, -ière *f* ; *[of votes]* scrutateur *m*, -trice *f* ◆ **~ vote** *(US Pol)* vote *m* à bulletin secret *(dans une assemblée)* ; → **storyteller**

telling /ˈtelɪŋ/ **ADJ** 1 *(= revealing) [comment, detail, figures, evidence]* révélateur (-trice *f*), éloquent 2 *(= effective) [speech, argument, blow]* efficace ◆ **with ~ effect** avec efficacité **N** *(NonC) [of story etc]* récit *m* ◆ **it lost nothing in the ~** c'était tout aussi bien quand on l'entendait raconter ◆ **this story grows in the ~** cette histoire s'enjolive chaque fois qu'on la raconte **COMP telling-off*** **N** engueulade* *f* ◆ **to get/give a good ~-off** recevoir/passer un bon savon * *(from* de ; *to* à)

telltale /ˈtelteɪl/ **N** rapporteur *m*, -euse *f*, mouchard(e) *m(f)* **ADJ** *[mark, sign etc]* révélateur (-trice *f*), éloquent

tellurium /teˈlʊərɪəm/ **N** tellure *m*

telly * /ˈtelɪ/ **N** *(Brit)* (abbrev of **television**) télé* *f* ◆ **on the ~** à la télé*

Temazepam ® /tɪˈmæzɪpæm/ **N** (pl **Temazepam** *or* **Temazepams)** *tranquillisant délivré sur ordonnance*

temerity /tɪˈmerɪtɪ/ **N** *(NonC)* audace *f*, témérité *f* ◆ **to have the ~ to do sth** avoir l'audace de faire qch

temp * /temp/ (abbrev of **temporary**) **N** intérimaire *mf*, secrétaire *mf etc* qui fait de l'intérim **VI** faire de l'intérim, travailler comme intérimaire

temper /ˈtempəʳ/ **N** 1 *(NonC = nature, disposition)* tempérament *m*, caractère *m* ; *(NonC = mood)* humeur *f* ; *(= fit of bad temper)* (accès *m or* crise *f* de) colère *f* ◆ **he has a very even ~** il est d'humeur très égale ◆ **he has a good ~** il a bon caractère ◆ **~s became frayed** tout le monde commençait à perdre patience ◆ **~s are running high** les esprits sont échauffés ◆ **to have a hot** *or* **quick ~** être soupe au lait ◆ **to have a nasty** *or* **foul** *or* **vile ~** avoir un sale caractère, avoir un caractère de cochon* ◆ **to have a short ~** être coléreux *or* soupe au lait *inv* ◆ **his short ~ had become notorious** son caractère *or* tempérament coléreux était devenu célèbre ◆ **he had a ~ and could be nasty** il était soupe au lait et pouvait être méchant ◆ **I hope he can control his ~** j'espère qu'il sait se contrôler *or* se maîtriser ◆ **to be in a ~** être en colère *(with sb* contre qn ; *over or about sth* à propos de qch) ◆ **to be in a good/bad ~** être de bonne/mauvaise humeur ◆ **he was in a foul ~** il était d'une humeur massacrante ◆ **he was not in the best of ~s** il n'était pas vraiment de très bonne humeur ◆ **to keep one's ~** garder son calme, se maîtriser ◆ **to lose one's ~** se mettre en colère ◆ **to put sb into a ~** mettre qn en colère ◆ **~, ~!** du calme !, on se calme ! ◆ **in a fit of ~** dans un accès de colère ◆ **he flew into a ~** il a explosé *or* éclaté ; → **tantrum**

2 *[of metal]* trempe *f*

VT *[+ metal]* tremper ; *(fig) [+ effects, rigours, passions]* tempérer *(with* par)

tempera /ˈtempərə/ **N** *(NonC: Art)* détrempe *f*

temperament /ˈtempərəmənt/ **N** *(NonC)* 1 *(= nature)* tempérament *m*, nature *f* ◆ **the artistic ~** le tempérament artiste ◆ **his impulsive ~ got him into trouble** son tempérament impulsif *or* sa nature impulsive lui a posé des problèmes 2 *(= moodiness, difficult temperament)* humeur *f* (changeante) ◆ **an outburst of ~** une saute d'humeur ◆ **she was given to fits of ~** elle avait tendance à avoir des sautes d'humeur

temperamental /ˌtempərəˈmentl/ **ADJ** 1 *(= unpredictable) [person]* d'humeur imprévisible, lunatique ; *[behaviour]* imprévisible ◆ **a man given to ~ outbursts** un homme sujet à des accès de mauvaise humeur ; *[horse, machine]* capricieux ◆ **a ~ outburst** une saute d'humeur ◆ **he can be very ~** il est parfois très lunatique 2 *(= innate) [differences]* de tempérament ; *[inclinations, qualities, aversion]* naturel

temperamentally /ˌtempərəˈmentəlɪ/ **ADV** 1 *(= unpredictably) [behave]* capricieusement 2 *(= by nature)* ◆ **~ suited to a job** fait pour un travail du point de vue du caractère ◆ **~, we were not at all compatible** du point de vue du tempérament *or* pour ce qui est du tempérament, nous n'étions pas du tout compatibles

temperance /ˈtempərəns/ **N** *(NonC)* modération *f* ; *(in drinking)* tempérance *f* **COMP** *[movement, league]* antialcoolique ; *[hotel]* où l'on ne sert pas de boissons alcoolisées

temperate /ˈtempərɪt/ **ADJ** 1 *[region, climate]* tempéré ; *[forest, plant, animal]* de zone tempérée 2 *(= restrained) [person] (gen)* modéré ; *(with alcohol)* qui fait preuve de tempérance ; *[lifestyle, reaction, discussion]* modéré ; *[attitude]* modéré, mesuré ; *[character, nature]* mesuré **COMP the Temperate Zone N** la zone tempérée

temperature /ˈtemprɪtʃəʳ/ **N** température *f* ◆ **a rise/fall in ~** une hausse/baisse de la température ◆ **at a ~ of ...** à une température de ... ◆ **to have a** *or* **be running a ~** avoir de la température *or* de la fièvre ◆ **her ~ is a little up/down** sa température a un peu augmenté/baissé ◆ **he was running a high ~** il avait une forte fièvre ◆ **to take sb's ~** prendre la température de qn ◆ **the bombing has raised the political ~** cet attentat à la bombe a fait monter la tension politique ; → **high**

COMP *[change etc]* de température

temperature chart N *(Med)* feuille *f* de température

temperature gauge N indicateur *m* de température

-tempered /ˈtempəd/ **ADJ** *(in compounds)* ◆ **even-tempered** d'humeur égale ; → **bad, good**

tempest /ˈtempɪst/ **N** *(liter)* tempête *f*, orage *m* ; *(fig)* tempête *f* ◆ **it was a ~ in a teapot** *(US)* c'était une tempête dans un verre d'eau

tempestuous /temˈpestjʊəs/ **ADJ** 1 *(= turbulent) [relationship, meeting]* orageux ; *[period, time]* orageux, agité ; *[marriage, career]* tumultueux ; *[person]* impétueux, fougueux 2 *(liter) [weather, wind, night]* de tempête ; *[sea]* houleux ; *[waves]* violent

tempestuously /temˈpestjʊəslɪ/ **ADV** *(fig)* avec violence ◆ **the sea crashed ~ against the cliffs** les vagues se fracassaient contre les falaises

tempi /ˈtempiː/ *(Mus)* **NPL** of **tempo**

temping /ˈtempɪŋ/ **N** intérim *m*

Templar /ˈtempləʳ/ **N** ⇒ **Knight Templar** ; → **knight**

template /ˈtemplɪt/ **N** 1 *(= pattern: woodwork, patchwork etc)* gabarit *m* ; *(fig = model)* modèle *m* *(for sth* à la base de qch) 2 *(Constr = beam)* traverse *f* 3 *(Comput)* patron *m*

temple[1] /ˈtempl/ **N** *(Rel)* temple *m* ◆ **the Temple** *(Brit Jur)* ≃ le Palais (de Justice)

temple[2] /ˈtempl/ **N** *(Anat)* tempe *f*

templet /ˈtemplɪt/ **N** ⇒ **template**

tempo /ˈtempəʊ/ **N** (pl **tempos** *or Mus* **tempi**) *(Mus, fig)* tempo *m*

temporal /ˈtempərəl/ **ADJ** 1 *(= relating to time: also Gram, Rel)* temporel 2 *(Anat)* temporal **COMP temporal bone N** (os *m*) temporal *m*

temporarily /ˈtempərərɪlɪ/ **ADV** *(gen)* temporairement, provisoirement ; *(shorter time)* pendant un moment

temporary /ˈtempərərɪ/ **ADJ** *[job, resident, residence, staff]* temporaire ; *[accommodation, building, solution, injunction]* provisoire ; *[relief, improvement, problem]* passager ; *[licence, powers]* à titre temporaire ◆ **~ road surface** revêtement *m* provisoire

temporize /ˈtempəraɪz/ VI 1 temporiser, chercher à gagner du temps ◆ **to ~ between two people** faire accepter un compromis à deux personnes 2 *(pej = bend with circumstances)* faire de l'opportunisme VT ◆ **"not exactly, sir", ~d Sloan** "pas exactement monsieur" dit Sloan pour gagner du temps

tempt /tempt/ VT 1 tenter, séduire ◆ **to ~ sb to do sth** donner à qn l'envie de faire qch ◆ **try and ~ her to eat a little** tâchez de la persuader de manger un peu ◆ **may I ~ you to a little more wine?** puis-je vous offrir un petit peu plus de vin ? ◆ **I'm very ~ed** c'est très tentant ◆ **I am very ~ed to accept** je suis très tenté d'accepter ◆ **he was ~ed into doing it** il n'a pas pu résister à la tentation de le faire ◆ **don't ~ me!** *(hum)* n'essaie pas de me tenter ! ; → **sorely** 2 (†: *Bible = test*) tenter, induire en tentation ◆ **to ~ Providence** *or* **fate** *(common usage)* tenter le sort

temptation /tempˈteɪʃən/ N tentation *f* ◆ **to put ~ in sb's way** exposer qn à la tentation ◆ **lead us not into ~** ne nous laissez pas succomber à la tentation ◆ **there is a great ~ to assume ...** il est très tentant de supposer ... ◆ **there is no ~ to do so** on n'est nullement tenté de le faire ◆ **she resisted the ~ to buy it** elle a résisté à la tentation de l'acheter ◆ **the many ~s to which you will be exposed** les nombreuses tentations auxquelles vous serez exposé

tempter /ˈtemptəʳ/ N tentateur *m*

tempting /ˈtemptɪŋ/ ADJ *[offer, proposition target]* tentant ; *[food, smell]* appétissant ◆ **it is ~ to say that ...** on est tenté de dire que ...

temptingly /ˈtemptɪŋlɪ/ ADV *(with vb)* d'une manière tentante ◆ **prices are still ~ low** *(with adj)* les prix sont toujours bas et cela donne envie d'acheter ◆ **the sea was ~ near** la mer était tout près et c'était bien tentant

temptress /ˈtemptrɪs/ N tentatrice *f*

tempura /temˈpʊərə/ N *(NonC)* tempura *f*

ten /ten/ ADJ dix *inv* ◆ **about ~ books** une dizaine de livres ◆ **the Ten Commandments** les dix commandements *mpl* N dix *m inv* ◆ **~s of thousands of ...** des milliers (et des milliers) de ... ◆ **hundreds, ~s and units** les centaines, les dizaines et les unités ◆ **to count in ~s** compter par dizaines ◆ **~ to one he won't come** je parie qu'il ne viendra pas ◆ **they're ~ a penny** * il y en a tant qu'on en veut, il y en a à la pelle * ◆ **to drive with one's hands at ~ to two** conduire avec les mains à dix heures dix ; see also **number** ; *for other phrases see* **six** PRON dix ◆ **there were ~** il y en avait dix ◆ **there were about ~** il y en avait une dizaine
COMP **ten-cent store** N *(US)* bazar *m*
ten-gallon hat N *(US)* ≃ grand chapeau *m* de cow-boy
ten-metre line N *(Rugby)* ligne *f* de dix mètres

tenable /ˈtenəbl/ ADJ 1 *(= defensible) [argument, view, position]* défendable ◆ **it's just not ~** ça ne peut vraiment pas se défendre 2 ◆ **the position of chairman is ~ for a maximum of three years** la présidence ne peut être occupée que pendant trois ans au maximum

tenacious /tɪˈneɪʃəs/ ADJ 1 *(= determined) [person]* tenace ; *[defence, resistance]* opiniâtre 2 *(= persistent) [belief, illness, condition]* tenace, obstiné 3 *(= firm) [grip, hold]* solide, ferme 4 *(= retentive) [memory]* indéfectible

tenaciously /tɪˈneɪʃəslɪ/ ADV *[cling to, hang on, fight]* avec ténacité ; *[survive]* obstinément

tenacity /tɪˈnæsɪtɪ/ N *(NonC)* ténacité *f*

tenancy /ˈtenənsɪ/ N location *f* ◆ **during my ~ of the house** pendant que j'étais locataire de la maison ◆ **to take on the ~ of a house** prendre une maison en location ◆ **to give up the ~ of a house** résilier un contrat de location ◆ **the new law relating to tenancies** la nouvelle loi relative aux locations COMP **tenancy agreement** N contrat *m* de location

tenant /ˈtenənt/ N locataire *mf* VT *[+ property]* habiter comme locataire
COMP **tenant farmer** N métayer *m*
tenant in common N *(Jur)* indivisaire *mf*

tenantry /ˈtenəntrɪ/ N *(NonC: collective)* (ensemble *m* des) tenanciers *mpl* (d'un domaine)

tench /tentʃ/ N *(pl inv)* tanche *f*

tend¹ /tend/ VT *[+ sheep, shop]* garder ; *[+ invalid]* soigner ; *[+ machine]* surveiller ; *[+ garden]* entretenir ; *[+ piece of land to grow food]* travailler, cultiver

► **tend to** VT FUS *(= take care of)* s'occuper de ; see also **tend²**

tend² /tend/ VI *[person, thing]* avoir tendance *(to do sth* à faire qch) ◆ **to ~ towards** avoir des tendances à, incliner à *or* vers ◆ **he ~s to be lazy** il a tendance à être paresseux, il est enclin à la paresse ◆ **he ~s to(wards) fascism** il a des tendances fascistes, il incline au *or* vers le fascisme ◆ **that ~s to be the case with such people** c'est en général le cas avec des gens de cette sorte ◆ **I ~ to think that ...** j'incline *or* j'ai tendance à penser que ... ◆ **it is a grey ~ing to blue** c'est un gris tirant sur le bleu

tendency /ˈtendənsɪ/ N tendance *f* ◆ **to have a ~ to do sth** avoir tendance à faire qch ◆ **there is a ~ for prices to rise** les prix ont tendance à *or* tendent à augmenter ◆ **a strong upward ~** *(on Stock Exchange)* une forte tendance à la hausse ◆ **the present ~ to(wards) socialism** les tendances socialistes actuelles

tendentious /tenˈdenʃəs/ ADJ tendancieux

tendentiously /tenˈdenʃəslɪ/ ADV tendancieusement

tendentiousness /tenˈdenʃəsnɪs/ N caractère *m* tendancieux

tender¹ /ˈtendəʳ/ N *(Rail)* tender *m* ; *(= boat) (for passengers)* embarcation *f* ; *(for supplies)* ravitailleur *m*

tender² /ˈtendəʳ/ VT *(= proffer) [+ object]* tendre, offrir ; *[+ money, thanks, apologies]* offrir ◆ **to ~ one's resignation** donner sa démission *(to sb* à qn) ◆ **"please tender exact change"** "prière de faire l'appoint"
VI *(Comm)* faire une soumission *(for sth* pour qch)
N 1 *(Comm)* soumission *f* (à un appel d'offres) ◆ **to make** *or* **put in a ~ for sth** répondre *or* soumissionner à un appel d'offres pour qch ◆ **to invite ~s for sth, to put sth out to ~** lancer un appel d'offres pour qch, mettre qch en adjudication ◆ **they won the ~ to build the bridge** ils ont obtenu le marché pour construire le pont
2 *(Fin)* **legal ~** cours *m* légal ◆ **to be legal ~** avoir cours ◆ **East German currency is no longer legal ~** les devises est-allemandes n'ont plus cours
COMP **tender offer** N *(US Stock Exchange)* offre *f* publique d'achat, OPA *f*

tender³ /ˈtendəʳ/ ADJ 1 *(gen) [person, expression, kiss, voice, word, thoughts, plant, food]* tendre ; *[body, skin]* délicat ; *[gesture]* tendre, plein de tendresse ; *[moment]* de tendresse ◆ **he gave her a ~ smile** il lui a souri tendrement ◆ **they were locked in a ~ embrace** ils étaient tendrement enlacés ◆ **to bid sb a ~ farewell** dire tendrement adieu à qn ◆ **cook the meat until ~** faites cuire la viande jusqu'à ce qu'elle soit tendre ◆ **to leave sb/sth to the ~ mercies of sb** *(iro)* abandonner qn/qch aux bons soins de qn
2 *(= young)* ◆ **at the ~ age of seven** à l'âge tendre de sept ans ◆ **she left home at a very ~ age** elle a quitté la maison très jeune ◆ **he was a hardened criminal by the ~ age of 16** c'était un criminel endurci dès l'âge de 16 ans ◆ **a child of ~ age** *or* **years** un enfant dans l'âge tendre ◆ **in spite of his ~ years** malgré son jeune âge
3 *(= sore) [skin, bruise]* sensible ◆ **~ to the touch** sensible au toucher
4 *(= difficult) [subject]* délicat
COMP **tender-hearted** ADJ sensible, compatissant ◆ **to be ~-hearted** être un cœur tendre
tender-heartedness N *(NonC)* compassion *f*, sensibilité *f*
tender loving care N ◆ **what he needs is some ~ loving care** ce dont il a besoin, c'est d'être dorloté

tenderer /ˈtendərəʳ/ N soumissionnaire *mf*

tenderfoot /ˈtendəfʊt/ N (pl **tenderfoots**) novice *mf*, nouveau *m*, nouvelle *f*

tendering /ˈtendərɪŋ/ N *(NonC: Comm)* soumissions *fpl*

tenderize /ˈtendəraɪz/ VT *(Culin)* attendrir

tenderizer /ˈtendəraɪzəʳ/ N *(Culin) (= mallet)* attendrisseur *m* ; *(= spices) épices pour attendrir la viande*

tenderloin /ˈtendəlɔɪn/ N *(= meat)* filet *m* ; *(US = seedy area)* quartier *m* louche *(où la police est corrompue)*

tenderly /ˈtendəlɪ/ ADV *[kiss]* tendrement ; *[touch, say]* avec tendresse

tenderness /ˈtendənɪs/ N *(NonC)* 1 *(gen)* tendresse *f* ; *[of skin]* délicatesse *f* ; *[of meat etc]* tendreté *f* 2 *(= soreness) [of arm, bruise etc]* sensibilité *f* 3 *(= emotion)* tendresse *f (towards* envers)

tendon /ˈtendən/ N tendon *m*

tendril /ˈtendrɪl/ N vrille *f*

tenebrous /ˈtenɪbrəs/ ADJ *(liter)* ténébreux

tenement /ˈtenɪmənt/ N *(= apartment)* appartement *m*, logement *m* ; (also **tenement house** *or* **building**) immeuble *m* (d'habitation)

Tenerife /ˌtenəˈriːf/ N Tenerife

tenet /ˈtenət/ N principe *m*, doctrine *f*

tenfold /ˈtenfəʊld/ ADJ décuple ADV au décuple ◆ **to increase ~** décupler

Tenn. abbrev of **Tennessee**

tenner * /ˈtenəʳ/ N *(Brit)* (billet *m* de) dix livres ; *(US)* (billet *m* de) dix dollars

Tennessee /ˌtenɪˈsiː/ N Tennessee *m* ◆ **in ~** dans le Tennessee

tennis /ˈtenɪs/ N *(NonC)* tennis *m* ◆ **a game of ~** une partie de tennis
COMP *[player, racket, club]* de tennis
tennis ball N balle *f* de tennis
tennis camp N *(US)* ◆ **to go to ~ camp** faire un stage de tennis
tennis court N (court *m or* terrain *m* de) tennis *m inv*
tennis elbow N *(Med)* synovite *f* du coude
tennis shoe N (chaussure *f* de) tennis *m*

tenon /ˈtenən/ N tenon *m*

tenor /ˈtenəʳ/ N 1 *(= general sense) [of speech, discussion]* teneur *f*, substance *f* ; *(= course) [of one's life, events, developments]* cours *m* 2 *(= exact wording)* teneur *f* 3 *(Mus)* ténor *m* ADJ *(Mus) [voice, part]* de ténor ; *[aria]* pour ténor ; *[recorder, saxophone]* ténor *inv* COMP **the tenor clef** N la clef d'ut quatrième ligne

tenpin /ˈtenpɪn/ N quille *f* ◆ **~s** *(US)* ⇒ **tenpin bowling** COMP **tenpin bowling** N *(Brit)* bowling *m* (à dix quilles)

tense¹ /tens/ N *(Gram)* temps *m* ◆ **in the present ~** au temps présent

tense² /tens/ ADJ *[person, voice, expression, muscles, rope, situation]* tendu ; *[time, period]* de tension ; *(Ling) [vowel]* tendu ◆ **to become ~** *[person]* se crisper ◆ **things were getting rather ~** l'atmosphère devenait plutôt tendue ◆ **to make sb ~** rendre qn nerveux ◆ **in a voice ~ with emotion** d'une voix voilée par l'émotion ◆ **they were ~ with fear/anticipation** ils étaient crispés de peur/par l'attente VT [+ *muscles*] contracter ◆ **to ~ o.s.** se contracter VI [*muscles, person, animal*] se contracter

► **tense up** VI se crisper VT ◆ **you're all tensed up** tu es tout tendu

tensely /ˈtenslɪ/ ADV [*say*] d'une voix tendue ◆ **they waited/watched ~** ils attendaient/observaient, tendus

tenseness /ˈtensnɪs/ N (*NonC: lit, fig*) tension *f*

tensile /ˈtensaɪl/ ADJ [*material*] extensible, élastique
COMP **tensile load** N force *f* de traction
tensile strength N résistance *f* à la traction
tensile stress N contrainte *f* de traction ; → **high**

tension /ˈtenʃən/ N (*NonC*) tension *f* COMP **tension headache** N (*Med*) mal *m* de tête (dû à la tension nerveuse)

tent /tent/ N tente *f* VI camper
COMP **tent peg** N (*Brit*) piquet *m* de tente
tent pole, tent stake N montant *m* de tente
tent trailer N caravane *f* pliante

tentacle /ˈtentəkl/ N (*also fig*) tentacule *m*

tentative /ˈtentətɪv/ ADJ ① (*= provisional, preliminary*) [*agreement, measure, date, conclusion, offer*] provisoire ; [*enquiry*] préliminaire ◆ **a ~ plan** une ébauche de projet ◆ **these theories are still very ~** ce ne sont encore que des hypothèses ② (*= hesitant*) [*gesture, step, knock*] hésitant ; [*smile, attempt, suggestion*] timide ◆ **the housing market is beginning to show ~ signs of recovery** le marché de l'immobilier commence à donner des signes de reprise ◆ **they have made ~ steps towards establishing a market economy** ils ont pris des mesures timides afin d'établir une économie de marché

tentatively /ˈtentətɪvlɪ/ ADV (*= provisionally*) [*agreed, scheduled, planned, titled*] provisoirement ; (*= hesitantly*) [*smile, say, knock, wave*] timidement ; [*touch*] avec hésitation

tented /ˈtentɪd/ ADJ ① (*= containing tents*) [*field*] couvert de tentes ; [*camp*] de tentes ② (*= draped*) [*room, ceiling*] à tentures (*partant du centre du plafond*) COMP **tented arch** N (*Archit*) ogive *f*

tenterhooks /ˈtentəhʊks/ NPL ◆ **to be/keep sb on ~** être/tenir qn sur des charbons ardents *or* au supplice

tenth /tenθ/ ADJ dixième N dixième *mf* ; (*= fraction*) dixième *m* ◆ **nine-~s of the book** les neuf dixièmes du livre ◆ **nine-~s of the time** la majeure partie du temps ; *for other phrases see* **sixth**

tenuity /teˈnjuːɪtɪ/ N (*NonC*) ténuité *f*

tenuous /ˈtenjʊəs/ ADJ [*link, connection, distinction*] ténu ; [*relationship*] subtil ; [*evidence*] mince ; [*existence*] précaire ; [*position, alliance*] fragile ; [*lead*] faible ◆ **to have a ~ grasp of sth** avoir une vague idée *or* de vagues notions de qch ◆ **to have a ~ hold on sb/sth** n'avoir que peu d'emprise sur qn/qch

tenuously /ˈtenjʊəslɪ/ ADV de manière ténue

tenure /ˈtenjʊəʳ/ N ① (*Univ*) fait *m* d'être titulaire ◆ **to have ~** [*teacher, civil servant*] être titulaire ; [*employee*] avoir la sécurité totale de l'emploi ◆ **to get ~** être titularisé ◆ **the system of ~** la sécurité totale de l'emploi ; → **security** ② [*of land, property*] bail *m* ; (*feudal*) tenure *f* ③ (*= period in power*) (*Govt*) mandat *m* ◆ **the ~ is for two years** la personne est nommée pour deux ans ; (*Govt*) le mandat *or* la durée du mandat est de deux ans ◆ **during his ~ (of office)** pendant qu'il était en fonction ◆ **during her ~ as owner** pendant qu'elle occupait la fonction de propriétaire COMP **tenure track position** N (*US Univ*) poste *m* avec possibilité de titularisation

tenured /ˈtenjʊəd/ ADJ [*professor etc*] titulaire ◆ **he has a ~ position** il est titulaire de son poste

tepee /ˈtiːpiː/ N tipi *m*

tepid /ˈtepɪd/ ADJ ① [*water, coffee*] tiède ② [*response*] réservé, sans enthousiasme ; [*support*] réservé, mitigé ; [*applause*] sans conviction

tepidity /teˈpɪdɪtɪ/ N (*NonC*) tiédeur *f*

tepidly /ˈtepɪdlɪ/ ADV [*agree, respond*] sans grand enthousiasme

tepidness /ˈtepɪdnɪs/ N (*NonC*) ⇒ **tepidity**

tequila /tɪˈkiːlə/ N tequila *f*

Ter (*Brit*) ⇒ **Terr**

teraflop /ˈterəˌflɒp/ N téraflop *m*

terbium /ˈtɜːbɪəm/ N terbium *m*

tercentenary /ˌtɜːsenˈtiːnərɪ/ ADJ, N tricentenaire *m*

tercet /ˈtɜːsɪt/ N (*Poetry*) tercet *m* ; (*Mus*) triolet *m*

Teresa /təˈriːzə/ N Thérèse *f*

term /tɜːm/ N ① (*gen, Admin, Fin, Jur, Med*) (*= limit*) terme *m* ; (*= period*) période *f*, terme *m* (*Jur*) ◆ **to put** *or* **set a ~ to sth** mettre *or* fixer un terme à qch ◆ **at ~** (*Fin, Med*) à terme ◆ **in the long ~** à long terme ; see also **long-term** ◆ **in the medium ~** à moyen terme ; see also **medium** ◆ **in the short ~** dans l'immédiat ; see also **short** ◆ **during his ~ of office** pendant la période où il exerçait ses fonctions ◆ **elected for a three-year ~** élu pour une durée *or* période de trois ans ◆ **~ of imprisonment** peine *f* de prison

② (*Scol, Univ*) trimestre *m* ; (*Jur*) session *f* ◆ **the autumn/spring/summer ~** (*Scol, Univ*) le premier/second *or* deuxième/troisième trimestre ◆ **in (the) ~, during (the) ~** pendant le trimestre ◆ **out of (the) ~** pendant les vacances (scolaires *or* universitaires)

③ (*Math, Philos*) terme *m*

◆ **in terms of** ◆ **A expressed in ~s of B** A exprimé en fonction de B ◆ **in ~s of production we are doing well** sur le plan de la production nous avons de quoi être satisfaits ◆ **he sees art in ~s of human relationships** pour lui l'art est fonction des relations humaines ◆ **to look at sth in ~s of the effect it will have/of how it ...** considérer qch sous l'angle de l'effet que cela aura/de la façon dont cela ... ◆ **we must think in ~s of ...** il faut penser à ... ; (*= consider the possibility of*) il faut envisager (la possibilité de) ... ◆ **price in ~s of dollars** prix *m* exprimé en dollars

④ (*= conditions*) **~s** (*gen*) conditions *fpl* ; [*of contracts etc*] termes *mpl* ; (*= price*) prix *m(pl)*, tarif *m* ◆ **you can name your own ~s** vous êtes libre de stipuler vos conditions ◆ **on what ~s?** à quelles conditions ? ◆ **not on any ~s** à aucun prix, à aucune condition ◆ **they accepted him on his own ~s** ils l'ont accepté sans concessions de sa part ◆ **to compete on equal** *or* **the same ~s** rivaliser dans les mêmes conditions *or* sur un pied d'égalité ◆ **to compete on unequal** *or* **unfair ~s** ne pas rivaliser dans les mêmes conditions, ne pas bénéficier des mêmes avantages ◆ **to lay down** *or* **dictate ~s to sb** imposer des conditions à qn ◆ **under the ~s of the contract** d'après les termes du contrat ◆ **~s and conditions** (*Jur*) modalités *fpl* ◆ **~s of surrender** conditions *fpl or* termes *mpl* de la reddition ◆ **~s of reference** (*of committee*) mandat *m* ◆ **it is not within our ~s of reference** cela ne relève pas de notre mandat ◆ **~s of sale** conditions *fpl* de vente ◆ **~s of payment** conditions *fpl or* modalités *fpl* de paiement ◆ **credit ~s** conditions *fpl* de crédit ◆ **we offer it on easy ~s** nous offrons des facilités de paiement ◆ **our ~s for full board** notre tarif pension complète ◆ **"inclusive terms: £20"** "20 livres tout compris"

⑤ (*relationship*) **to be on good/bad ~s with sb** être en bons/mauvais termes *or* rapports avec qn ◆ **they are on the best of ~s** ils sont au mieux, ils sont en excellents termes ◆ **they're on fairly friendly ~s** ils ont des rapports assez amicaux *or* des relations assez amicales ; → **equal, nod, speaking**

◆ **to come to terms with** [*+ person*] arriver à un accord avec ; [*+ problem, situation*] accepter

⑥ (*= word*) terme *m* ; (*= expression*) expression *f* ◆ **technical/colloquial ~** terme *m* technique/familier ◆ **in plain** *or* **simple ~s** en termes simples *or* clairs ◆ **he spoke of her in glowing ~s** il a parlé d'elle en termes très chaleureux ; → **uncertain**

VT appeler, nommer ◆ **what we ~ happiness** ce que nous nommons *or* appelons le bonheur ◆ **it was ~ed a compromise** ce fut qualifié de compromis

COMP [*exams etc*] trimestriel
term insurance N assurance *f* vie temporaire
term paper N (*Univ*) dissertation *f* trimestrielle

termagant /ˈtɜːməgənt/ N harpie *f*, mégère *f*

terminal /ˈtɜːmɪnl/ ADJ ① (*Med*) (*= incurable*) [*patient, illness, cancer*] en phase terminale ; (*= final*) [*stage*] terminal ◆ **~ care** soins *mpl* aux malades en phase terminale ◆ **~ ward** salle *f* des malades en phase terminale

② (*= insoluble*) [*problem, crisis, situation*] sans issue ◆ **to be in ~ decline** *or* **decay** être à bout de souffle

③ (*= last*) [*stage*] final

④ (** = utter*) [*boredom*] mortel ; [*stupidity, workaholic*] incurable

⑤ (*Bot, Anat, Ling*) terminal

⑥ (*= termly*) trimestriel

N ① (*also* **air terminal**) aérogare *f* ; (*for trains, coaches, buses*) (gare *f*) terminus *m inv* ; (*Underground = terminus*) (gare *f*) terminus *m inv* ; (*Underground: at beginning of line*) tête *f* de ligne ◆ **container ~** terminal *m* de containers ◆ **oil ~** terminal *m* pétrolier

② (*Elec*) borne *f*

③ (*Comput*) terminal *m* ◆ **dumb/intelligent ~** terminal *m* passif/intelligent

COMP **terminal bonus** N (*Fin*) *bonus payé à échéance d'une police d'assurance*
terminal point, terminal station N (*Rail*) terminus *m*
terminal velocity N vitesse *f* finale

terminally /ˈtɜːmɪnlɪ/ ADV ① (*= incurably*) ◆ **~ ill** condamné, en phase terminale ◆ **the ~ ill** les malades *mpl* en phase terminale ② (** = utterly*) définitivement ◆ **a ~ boring film** un film à mourir d'ennui

terminate /ˈtɜːmɪneɪt/ VT terminer, mettre fin à, mettre un terme à ; [*+ contract*] résilier, dénoncer ◆ **to ~ a pregnancy** [*mother*] se faire faire une IVG ; [*medical staff*] pratiquer une IVG ◆ **to have a pregnancy ~d** se faire faire une IVG VI ① (*= end*) se terminer, finir (*in* en, *par*) ② (*= reach end of journey*) [*train*] **we will soon be arriving at Waterloo, where this train will ~** le prochain arrêt est Waterloo, terminus de ce train ◆ **due to a technical fault, this train will ~ at Sterling** en raison d'un problème technique, ce train n'ira pas plus loin que Sterling

termination /ˌtɜːmɪˈneɪʃən/ N fin *f*, conclusion *f* ; [*of contract*] résiliation *f*, dénonciation *f* ; (*Gram*) terminaison *f* ◆ **~ of employment** licenciement *m*, résiliation *f* du contrat de travail ◆ **~ (of pregnancy)** interruption *f* de grossesse

termini /ˈtɜːmɪniː/ NPL of **terminus**

terminological /ˌtɜːmɪnəˈlɒdʒɪkəl/ ADJ terminologique

terminologist /ˌtɜːmɪˈnɒlədʒɪst/ N terminologue *mf*

terminology /ˌtɜːmɪˈnɒlədʒɪ/ N terminologie *f*

terminus /ˈtɜːmɪnəs/ N (pl **terminuses** *or* **termini**) terminus *m inv*

termite /ˈtɜːmaɪt/ N termite *m*, fourmi *f* blanche

termtime /ˈtɜːmtaɪm/ N (durée *f* du) trimestre *m* ◆ **in ~, during ~** pendant le trimestre ◆ **out of ~** pendant les vacances (scolaires *or* universitaires) COMP **termtime employment** N (US Univ) emploi *m* pour étudiant (*rémunéré par l'université*)

tern /tɜːn/ N hirondelle *f* de mer, sterne *f*

ternary /ˈtɜːnərɪ/ ADJ ternaire

Terr (Brit) abbrev of **Terrace**

terrace /ˈterəs/ N (*Agr, Geol etc*) terrasse *f* ; (*= raised bank*) terre-plein *m* ; (*= patio, veranda, balcony, roof*) terrasse *f* ; (*Brit = row of houses*) rangée *f* de maisons (*attenantes les unes aux autres*) ◆ **the ~s** (*Brit Sport*) les gradins *mpl* ; → House
VT [*+ hillside*] arranger en terrasses ◆ **~d** [*garden, hillside*] en terrasses ; (*Brit*) [*house*] en mitoyenneté
COMP **terrace cultivation** N culture *f* en terrasses
terrace house N (*Brit*) maison *f* en mitoyenneté ; → House

terraced /ˈterəst/ ADJ [*fields, garden*] en terrasses ◆ **~ house** (*Brit*) maison *f* mitoyenne ; → House

terracing /ˈterəsɪŋ/ N 1 (*Brit Sport*) gradins *mpl* 2 (*Agr*) (système *m* de) terrasses *fpl*

terracotta /ˈterəˈkɒtə/ N terre *f* cuite COMP (*= made of terracotta*) en terre cuite ; (*= colour*) ocre brun *inv*

terra firma /ˌterəˈfɜːmə/ N terre *f* ferme ◆ **on ~** sur la terre ferme

terrain /təˈreɪn/ N 1 (*= nature of ground*) terrain *m* (*sol*) ◆ **the ~ is rocky/difficult** le terrain est rocheux/difficilement praticable ◆ **the ~ is varied** la nature du terrain est variée 2 (*= relief*) relief *m* ◆ **Rwanda's mountainous ~** le relief montagneux du Rwanda ; → **all**

terrapin /ˈterəpɪn/ N tortue *f* d'eau douce

terrarium /təˈreərɪəm/ N (*for plants*) petite serre *f* ; (*for animals*) terrarium *m*

terrazzo /teˈrætsəʊ/ N sol *m* de mosaïque

terrestrial /tɪˈrestrɪəl/ ADJ 1 [*life, event, animal, plant*] terrestre 2 (*esp Brit TV*) [*television, channel*] hertzien

terrible /ˈterəbl/ ADJ [*disease, consequences, mistake, time, weather, food*] terrible ; [*heat*] terrible, atroce ; [*disappointment, cold*] terrible, affreux ; [*experience, act, pain, injury*] atroce ; [*damage, poverty*] effroyable ◆ **her French is ~** son français est atroce ◆ **to feel ~** (*= guilty*) s'en vouloir beaucoup ; (*= ill*) se sentir mal ◆ **to look ~** (*= ill*) avoir très mauvaise mine ; (*= untidy*) ne pas être beau à voir ◆ **he sounded ~** (*= ill etc*) (à l'entendre *or* à sa voix) il avait l'air d'aller très mal ◆ **I've got a ~ memory** j'ai très mauvaise mémoire ◆ **he was having ~ trouble with his homework** il avait un mal fou* à faire ses devoirs ◆ **to be a ~ bore** être terriblement ennuyeux ◆ **I've been a ~ fool** j'ai été le dernier des imbéciles ◆ **you're going to get in the most ~ muddle** tu vas te retrouver dans une mélasse* effroyable ◆ **it would be a ~ pity if ...** ce serait extrêmement dommage si ... ◆ **it's a ~ shame (that)** c'est vraiment dommage (que + *subj*)

terribly /ˈterəblɪ/ ADV (*= very*) [*important, upset, hard*] extrêmement ; [*difficult, disappointed*] terriblement ; [*sorry*] vraiment ; [*behave*] de manière lamentable ; [*play, sing*] terriblement mal ◆ **I'm not ~ good with money** je ne suis pas très doué pour les questions d'argent ◆ **it isn't a ~ good film** ce n'est pas un très bon film ◆ **he doesn't always come across ~ well** il ne passe pas toujours très bien la rampe* ◆ **to suffer ~** souffrir terriblement ◆ **I missed him ~** il me manquait terriblement

terrier /ˈterɪəʳ/ N 1 terrier *m* 2 (*Brit Mil*) **the ~s** * la territoriale*, les territoriaux *mpl*

terrific /təˈrɪfɪk/ ADJ 1 (** = excellent*) [*person, idea, story, news*] super* *inv* ◆ **to do a ~ job** faire un super bon boulot* ◆ **to look ~** être super* ◆ **to have a ~ time** s'amuser comme un fou *or* une folle ◆ **~!** super ! 2 (*= very great*) [*speed*] fou (folle *f*), fantastique ; [*amount*] énorme ; [*explosion*] formidable ; [*pain*] atroce ; [*strain, pressure, disappointment*] terrible ; [*noise, cold*] épouvantable ; [*heat*] épouvantable, effroyable

terrifically * /təˈrɪfɪkəlɪ/ ADV 1 (*= extremely*) terriblement ◆ **to do ~ well** s'en tirer formidablement bien 2 (*= very well*) [*treat, sing, play*] formidablement bien

terrify /ˈterɪfaɪ/ VT terrifier ◆ **to ~ sb out of his wits** rendre qn fou de terreur ◆ **to be terrified of ...** avoir une peur folle de ...

terrifying /ˈterɪfaɪɪŋ/ ADJ terrifiant

terrifyingly /ˈterɪfaɪɪŋlɪ/ ADV [*high, fragile*] terriblement ; [*shake, wobble*] de façon terrifiante

terrine /teˈriːn/ N terrine *f*

territorial /ˌterɪˈtɔːrɪəl/ ADJ territorial ◆ **a ~ animal** un animal au comportement territorial N (*Brit Mil*) ◆ **Territorial** territorial *m* ◆ **the Territorials** l'armée *f* territoriale, la territoriale*, les territoriaux *mpl*
COMP **the Territorial Army** N (*Brit*) l'armée *f* territoriale
territorial waters NPL eaux *fpl* territoriales

Territorial Army

L'armée territoriale (**Territorial Army** ou **TA**) est une organisation britannique de réservistes volontaires. Elle se compose de civils qui reçoivent un entraînement militaire pendant leur temps libre et qui forment un corps d'armée de renfort en cas de guerre ou de crise grave. Ces volontaires sont rémunérés pour leurs services.

territoriality /ˌterɪtɔːrɪˈælɪtɪ/ N (*= state of being a territory, pattern of animal behaviour*) territorialité *f*

territory /ˈterɪtərɪ/ N (*lit*) (*= land*) territoire *m* ; (*fig = area of knowledge, competence etc*) secteur *m*, terrain *m* ◆ **the occupied territories** les territoires *mpl* occupés ◆ **that's his ~** (*fig*) c'est un secteur qu'il connaît bien, il est sur son terrain ◆ **such problems have become familiar ~** ce genre de problème fait désormais partie du paysage quotidien ◆ **the familiar ~ of sex, power and guilt** le domaine familier du sexe, du pouvoir et du sentiment de culpabilité ◆ **we are definitely in uncharted ~** (*lit, fig*) nous sommes en terrain *or* en territoire totalement inconnu ◆ **that comes** *or* **goes with the ~** ça fait partie du boulot*, ce sont les risques du métier

terror /ˈterəʳ/ N 1 (*NonC*) (*= fear*) terreur *f*, épouvante *f* ◆ **they were living in ~** ils vivaient dans la terreur ◆ **they fled in ~** épouvantés, ils se sont enfuis ◆ **he went** *or* **was in ~ of his life** il craignait fort pour sa vie ◆ **to go** *or* **live in ~ of sb/sth** vivre dans la terreur de qn/qch ◆ **I have a ~ of flying** monter en avion me terrifie ◆ **to hold no ~s for sb** ne pas faire peur du tout à qn ; → **reign**
2 (*Pol*) terreur *f*
3 (*= person*) terreur* *f* ◆ **he was the ~ of the younger boys** il était la terreur des plus petits* ◆ **he's a ~ on the roads*** c'est un danger public sur les routes ◆ **that child is a (real** *or* **little** *or* **holy) ~*** cet enfant est une vraie (petite) terreur*
4 (*= terrorism*) ◆ **~ attack** attaque *f* terroriste ◆ **~ group** groupe *m* terroriste ◆ **~ camp** camp *m* terroriste
COMP **terror-stricken, terror-struck** ADJ épouvanté

terrorism /ˈterərɪzəm/ N (*NonC*) terrorisme *m* ◆ **an act of ~** un acte de terrorisme

terrorist /ˈterərɪst/ N terroriste *mf*
COMP [*attack, group, activities*] terroriste ; [*act*] de terrorisme **terrorist bombing** N attentat *m* à la bombe

terrorize /ˈterəraɪz/ VT terroriser

terry /ˈterɪ/ N (also **terry cloth, terry towelling**) tissu *m* éponge

terse /tɜːs/ ADJ laconique, brusque (*pej*)

tersely /ˈtɜːslɪ/ ADV laconiquement, avec brusquerie (*pej*)

terseness /ˈtɜːsnɪs/ N laconisme *m*, brusquerie *f* (*pej*)

tertiary /ˈtɜːʃərɪ/ ADJ 1 (*= third*) [*effect, source*] tertiaire ◆ **~ industries** entreprises *fpl* du tertiaire 2 (*Educ*) [*institution, level*] d'enseignement supérieur 3 (*Geol*) ◆ **Tertiary** tertiaire N (*Geol*) tertiaire *m* ; (*Rel*) tertiaire *mf*
COMP **tertiary college** N (*Brit Scol*) *établissement accueillant des élèves de terminale et dispensant une formation professionnelle*
tertiary education N enseignement *m* supérieur
the Tertiary period N le tertiaire
the tertiary sector N le (secteur) tertiaire

Terylene ® /ˈterəliːn/ (Brit) N tergal ® *m* COMP en tergal ®

TESL /tesl/ N (abbrev of **Teaching of English as a Second Language**) → **teaching** ; → TEFL

TESOL /ˈtiːsɒl/ N (abbrev of **Teaching of English as a Second or Other Language**) (abbrev of **Teaching English to Speakers of Other Languages**) → **teaching** ; → TEFL

Tessa /ˈtesə/ N (abbrev of **Tax Exempt Special Savings Account**) *compte de dépôt dont les intérêts sont exonérés d'impôts à condition que le capital reste bloqué*

tessellated /ˈtesɪleɪtɪd/ ADJ en mosaïque

tessellation /ˌtesɪˈleɪʃən/ N (*NonC*) mosaïque *f*

tessitura /ˌtesɪˈtʊərə/ N tessiture *f*

test /test/ N 1 (*gen*) essai *m* ◆ **the aircraft has been grounded for ~s** l'avion a été retiré de la circulation pour (être soumis à) des essais *or* des vérifications ◆ **to run a ~ on a machine** tester *or* contrôler une machine ◆ **nuclear ~s** essais *mpl* nucléaires
2 (*Med*) (*on blood, urine*) analyse *f* ; (*on organ*) examen *m* ; (*Pharm, Chem*) analyse *f*, test *m* ◆ **urine ~** analyse *f* d'urine ◆ **to do a ~ for sugar** faire une analyse pour déterminer la présence *or* le taux de glucose ◆ **hearing ~** examen *m* de l'ouïe ◆ **they did a ~ for diphtheria** ils ont fait une analyse pour voir s'il s'agissait de la diphtérie ◆ **he sent a specimen to the laboratory for ~s** il a envoyé un échantillon au laboratoire pour analyses ◆ **they did ~s on the water to see whether ...** ils ont analysé l'eau pour voir si ... ◆ **the Wasserman ~** (*Med*) la réaction Wasserman
3 (*of physical or mental quality, also Psych*) **they are trying to devise a ~ to find suitable security staff** ils essaient de concevoir un test permettant de sélectionner le personnel de gardiennage ◆ **it's a ~ of his strength** cela teste ses forces ◆ **a ~ of strength** (*fig*) une épreuve de force ◆ **a ~ of his powers to survive in ...** une épreuve permettant d'établir s'il pourrait survivre dans ... ◆ **it wasn't a fair ~ of her linguistic abilities** cela n'a pas permis d'évaluer correctement ses aptitudes linguistiques ◆ **if we apply the ~ of visual appeal** si nous utilisons le critère de l'attrait visuel ; → **acid, endurance, intelligence**
4 (*Scol, Univ*) (*written*) devoir *m or* exercice *m* de contrôle, interrogation *f* écrite ; (*oral*) interro-

gation *f* orale ◆ **practical** ~ épreuve *f* pratique ◆ **to pass the** ~ *(fig)* bien se tirer de l'épreuve

5 (also **driving test**) (examen *m* du) permis *m* de conduire ◆ **my ~ is on Wednesday** je passe mon permis mercredi ◆ **to pass/fail one's** ~ être reçu/échouer au permis (de conduire)

6 *(NonC)* **to put to the** ~ mettre à l'essai *or* à l'épreuve ◆ **to stand the** ~ *[person]* se montrer à la hauteur* ; *[machine, vehicle]* résister aux épreuves ◆ **it has stood the ~ of time** cela a (bien) résisté au passage du temps

7 *(Sport)* ⇒ **test match**

VT *[+ machine, weapon, tool]* essayer ; *[+ vehicle]* essayer, mettre à l'essai ; *[+ aircraft]* essayer, faire faire un vol d'essai à ; *(Comm) [+ goods]* vérifier ; *(Chem) [+ metal, liquid]* analyser ; *(Med) [+ blood, urine]* faire une *(or* des) analyse(s) de ; *[+ new drug etc]* expérimenter ; *(Psych) [+ person, animal]* tester ; *(gen) [+ person]* mettre à l'épreuve ; *[+ sight, hearing]* examiner ; *[+ intelligence]* mettre à l'épreuve, mesurer ; *[+ sb's reactions]* mesurer ; *[+ patience, nerves]* éprouver, mettre à l'épreuve ◆ **they ~ed the material for resistance to heat** ils ont soumis le matériau à des essais destinés à vérifier sa résistance à la chaleur ◆ **these conditions ~ a car's tyres** ces conditions mettent à l'épreuve les pneus de voiture ◆ **to ~ metal for impurities** analyser un métal pour déterminer la proportion d'impuretés qu'il contient ◆ **to ~ the water** *[chemist etc]* analyser l'eau ; *(for swimming, bathing baby)* tâter (la température de) l'eau, voir si l'eau est bonne ; *(fig: Pol etc)* prendre la température d'une assemblée *(or* d'un groupe *etc)*, se faire une idée de la situation ◆ **they ~ed him for diabetes** ils l'ont soumis à des analyses pour établir s'il avait le diabète ◆ **they ~ed the child for hearing difficulties** ils ont fait passer à l'enfant un examen de l'ouïe ◆ **to ~ a drug on sb** expérimenter un médicament sur qn ◆ **to ~ sb for drugs/alcohol** faire subir un contrôle de dopage/un alcootest® à qn ◆ **they ~ed the children in geography** ils ont fait subir aux enfants une interrogation *or* un exercice de contrôle en géographie ◆ **they ~ed him for the job** ils lui ont fait passer des tests d'aptitude pour le poste

VI ◆ **to ~ for sugar** faire une recherche de sucre ◆ **he ~ed positive for drugs** son contrôle de dopage était positif ◆ **he ~ed positive for steroids** les tests *or* les contrôles ont révélé chez lui la présence de stéroïdes ◆ **they were ~ing for a gas leak** ils faisaient des essais pour découvrir une fuite de gaz ◆ **"testing, testing"** = "un, deux, trois"

COMP *[shot etc]* d'essai ; *[district, experiment, year]* test *inv*

test ban treaty N traité *m* d'interdiction d'essais nucléaires

test bed N banc *m* d'essai

test bore N *[of oil]* sondage *m* de prospection

test card N *(Brit TV)* mire *f*

test case N *(Jur)* précédent *m*, affaire *f* qui fait jurisprudence ◆ **the strike is a ~ case** c'est une grève-test

test cricket N *(NonC)* internationaux *mpl* de cricket

test data N *(Comput)* données *fpl* de test

test-drill VI *[oil company]* se livrer à des forages d'essai

test drive N *[of car]* essai *m* sur route

test-drive VT *(by prospective buyer)* essayer ; *(by manufacturer)* mettre au banc d'essai, faire faire un essai sur route à

test film N *(Cine)* bout *m* d'essai

test flight N vol *m* d'essai

test-fly VT faire faire un vol d'essai à

test gauge N bande *f* étalon

test-market VT commercialiser à titre expérimental

test match N *(Cricket, Rugby)* match *m* international

test paper N *(Scol)* interrogation *f* écrite ; *(Chem)* (papier *m*) réactif *m*

test pattern N *(US TV)* ⇒ **test card**

test piece N *(Mus)* morceau *m* imposé

test pilot N pilote *m* d'essai

test run N *(lit)* essai *m* ; *(fig)* période *f* d'essai

test strip N bande *f* d'essai

test tube N éprouvette *f*

test-tube baby N bébé-éprouvette *m*

► **test out** VT SEP *[+ machine, weapon, tool]* essayer ; *[+ vehicle]* essayer, mettre à l'essai ; *[+ aircraft]* essayer, faire faire un vol d'essai à

testament /ˈtestəmənt/ N testament *m* ◆ **the Old/New Testament** l'Ancien/le Nouveau Testament ◆ **to be (a) ~ to sth, to bear ~ to sth** témoigner de qch ◆ **it is a ~ to (the quality of) the British legal system** cela témoigne de la qualité du système judiciaire britannique ; → **will**

testamentary /ˌtestəˈmentərɪ/ ADJ testamentaire

testator /tesˈteɪtəʳ/ N testateur *m*

testatrix /tesˈteɪtrɪks/ N testatrice *f*

tester[1] /ˈtestəʳ/ N *(= person)* contrôleur *m*, -euse *f* ; *(= machine)* appareil *m* de contrôle

tester[2] /ˈtestəʳ/ N *(over bed)* baldaquin *m*, ciel *m* de lit

testes /ˈtestiːz/ NPL of **testis**

testicle /ˈtestɪkl/ N testicule *m*

testicular /tesˈtɪkjʊləʳ/ ADJ testiculaire ◆ ~ **cancer** cancer *m* du testicule

testification /ˌtestɪfɪˈkeɪʃən/ N déclaration *f or* affirmation *f* solennelle

testify /ˈtestɪfaɪ/ VT *(Jur)* témoigner, déclarer *or* affirmer sous serment *(that* que) ◆ **as he will** ~ *(gen)* comme il en fera foi VI *(Jur)* porter témoignage, faire une déclaration sous serment ◆ **to ~ against/in favour of sb** déposer contre/en faveur de qn ◆ **to ~ to sth** *(Jur)* attester qch ; *(gen)* témoigner de qch

testily /ˈtestɪlɪ/ ADV *[say]* avec irritation, d'un ton irrité

testimonial /ˌtestɪˈməʊnɪəl/ N *(= character reference)* lettre *f* de recommandation ; *(= gift)* témoignage *m* d'estime *(offert à qn par ses collègues etc)* ; *(Sport:* also **testimonial match***)* *match en l'honneur d'un joueur* ◆ **as a ~ to our gratitude** en témoignage de notre reconnaissance

testimony /ˈtestɪmənɪ/ N *(Jur)* témoignage *m*, déposition *f* ; *(= statement)* déclaration *f*, attestation *f* ◆ **in ~ whereof** *(frm)* en foi de quoi

testing /ˈtestɪŋ/ N *[of vehicle, machine etc]* mise *f* à l'essai ; *(Chem, Pharm)* analyse *f* ; *[of new drug]* expérimentation *f* ; *[of person] (gen)* mise *f* à l'épreuve ; *(Psych)* test(s) *m(pl)* ; *[of sight, hearing]* examen *m* ; *[of intelligence, patience etc]* mise *f* à l'épreuve ; *[of sb's reactions]* mesure *f*, évaluation *f* ◆ **nuclear** ~ essais *mpl* nucléaires ADJ *(= difficult, trying)* éprouvant ◆ **it is a ~ time for us all** c'est une période éprouvante pour nous tous

COMP **testing bench** N banc *m* d'essai

testing ground N *(lit, fig)* banc *m* d'essai

testis /ˈtestɪs/ N (pl **testes**) testicule *m*

testosterone /teˈstɒstərəʊn/ N testostérone *f*

testy /ˈtestɪ/ ADJ irritable, grincheux

tetanus /ˈtetənəs/ N tétanos *m* COMP *[symptom]* tétanique ; *[epidemic]* de tétanos ; *[vaccine, injection]* antitétanique

tetchily /ˈtetʃɪlɪ/ ADV *[say]* avec irritation, d'un ton irrité

tetchiness /ˈtetʃɪnɪs/ N *(NonC: Brit)* irritabilité *f*

tetchy /ˈtetʃɪ/ ADJ *(Brit) [person, mood]* irritable, grincheux ; *[comment]* grincheux ; *[voice]* irrité

tête-à-tête /ˈteɪtɑːˈteɪt/ ADV en tête à tête, seul à seul N (pl **tête-à-tête** *or* **tête-à-têtes**) tête-à-tête *m inv*

tether /ˈteðəʳ/ N longe *f* ◆ **to be at the end of** *or* **to have reached the end of one's** ~ *(= annoyed, impatient)* être à bout ; *(= desperate)* être au bout du rouleau VT (also **tether up**) *[+ animal]* attacher *(to* à)

tetherball /ˈteðəbɔːl/ *(US)* N *jeu consistant à frapper une balle attachée à un poteau par une corde afin de l'enrouler autour de ce poteau*

tetrachloride /ˌtetrəˈklɔːraɪd/ N tétrachlorure *m*

tetragon /ˈtetrəgən/ N quadrilatère *m*

tetrahedron /ˌtetrəˈhiːdrən/ N (pl **tetrahedrons** *or* **tetrahedra** /ˌtetrəˈhiːdrə/) tétraèdre *m*

tetrameter /teˈtræmɪtəʳ/ N tétramètre *m*

tetraplegic /ˌtetrəˈpliːdʒɪk/ N, ADJ tetraplégique *mf*

Teutonic /tjʊˈtɒnɪk/ ADJ teutonique

Tex. abbrev of **Texas**

Texan /ˈteksən/ ADJ texan N Texan(e) *m(f)*

Texas /ˈteksəs/ N Texas *m* ◆ **in** ~ au Texas

Tex-Mex /ˌteksˈmeks/ ADJ tex-mex

text /tekst/ N 1 *(gen, also Comput)* texte *m* 2 (also **text messsage**) Texto® *m*, message *m* SMS VT envoyer un Texto® à

COMP **text editor** N *(Comput)* éditeur *m* de texte(s)

text message N Texto® *m*, message *m* SMS

text messaging N texting *m*

textbook /ˈtekstbʊk/ N manuel *m* scolaire, livre *m* scolaire ADJ *(fig)* ◆ **a ~ case** *or* **example of ...** un exemple classique *or* typique de ... ◆ **a ~ landing/dive** *etc* un atterrissage/plongeon *etc* modèle

textile /ˈtekstaɪl/ ADJ, N textile *m* ◆ **~s** *or* **the ~ industry** (l'industrie *f*) textile *m*

texting /ˈtekstɪŋ/ N texting *m*

textual /ˈtekstjʊəl/ ADJ *(gen)* textuel ; *[error, differences]* dans le texte COMP **textual criticism** N critique *f or* analyse *f* de texte

textually /ˈtekstjʊəlɪ/ ADV textuellement, mot à mot

texture /ˈtekstʃəʳ/ N *[of cloth]* texture *f* ; *[of minerals, soil]* texture *f*, structure *f*, contexture *f* ; *[of skin, wood, paper, silk]* grain *m* ; *(fig)* structure *f*, contexture *f*

textured /ˈtekstʃəd/ ADJ *[paint]* granité ◆ **beautifully** ~ de belle texture, d'un beau grain ◆ **rough-/smooth-**~ d'une texture grossière/fine, d'un grain grossier/fin COMP **textured vegetable protein** N fibre *f* végétale protéique

TGIF /ˌtiːdʒiːaɪˈef/ *(hum)* (abbrev of **Thank God it's Friday**) Dieu merci c'est vendredi

TGWU /ˌtiːdʒiːdʌbljuːˈjuː/ N *(Brit)* (abbrev of **Transport and General Workers' Union**) *syndicat*

Thai /taɪ/ ADJ *(gen)* thaïlandais ; *[ambassador, embassy, monarch]* de Thaïlande N 1 Thaïlandais(e) *m(f)* 2 *(= language)* thaï *m*

Thailand /ˈtaɪlænd/ N Thaïlande *f*

thalamus /ˈθæləməs/ N (pl **thalami** /ˈθæləmaɪ/) thalamus *m*

thalassemia /ˌθæləˈsiːmɪə/ N thalassémie *f*

thalidomide /θəˈlɪdəʊmaɪd/ N thalidomide *f* COMP **thalidomide baby** N (petite) victime *f* de la thalidomide

thallium /ˈθælɪəm/ N thallium *m*

Thames /temz/ N Tamise *f* ◆ **he'll never set the ~ on fire** il n'a pas inventé la poudre *or* le fil à couper le beurre

than /ðæn, (weak form /ðən/) CONJ 1 que ◆ **I have more ~ you** j'en ai plus que toi ◆ **he is taller ~ his sister** il est plus grand que sa sœur ◆ **he has more brains ~ sense** il a plus d'intelligence que de bon sens ◆ **more unhappy** ~

angry plus malheureux que fâché ◆ **you'd be better going by car ~ by bus** tu ferais mieux d'y aller en voiture plutôt qu'en autobus ◆ **I'd do anything rather ~ admit it** je ferais tout plutôt que d'avouer cela ◆ **no sooner did he arrive ~ he started to complain** il n'était pas plus tôt arrivé *or* il était à peine arrivé qu'il a commencé à se plaindre ◆ **it was a better play ~ we expected** la pièce était meilleure que nous ne l'avions prévu

[2] *(with numerals)* de ◆ **more/less ~ 20** plus/moins de 20 ◆ **less ~ half** moins de la moitié ◆ **more ~ once** plus d'une fois

thank /θæŋk/ LANGUAGE IN USE 17.1, 20.3, 21.1, 22, 25

VT remercier, dire merci à *(sb for sth* qn de *or* pour qch ; *for doing sth* de faire qch, d'avoir fait qch) ◆ **I cannot ~ you enough** je ne saurais assez vous remercier ◆ **do ~ him for me** remerciez-le bien de ma part ◆ **~ goodness***, **~ heaven(s)***, **~ God*** Dieu merci ◆ **~ goodness you've done it!*** Dieu merci tu l'as fait ! ◆ **you've got him to ~ for that** *(fig)* c'est à lui que tu dois cela ◆ **he's only got himself to ~** il ne peut s'en prendre qu'à lui-même ◆ **he won't ~ you for that!** ne t'attends pas à ce qu'il te remercie *or* te félicite ! ◆ **I'll ~ you to mind your own business!** je vous prierai de vous mêler de ce qui vous regarde !

◆ **thank you** merci ◆ **to say ~ you** dire merci ◆ **~ you very much** merci bien *(also iro)*, merci beaucoup ◆ **~ you for the book/for helping us** merci pour le livre/de nous avoir aidés ◆ **no ~ you** (non) merci ◆ **without so much as a ~ you** sans même dire merci

NPL **thanks** [1] remerciements *mpl* ◆ **with ~s** avec tous mes (*or* nos) remerciements ◆ **with my warmest** *or* **best ~s** avec mes remerciements les plus sincères ◆ **give him my ~s** transmettez-lui mes remerciements, remerciez-le de ma part ◆ **to give ~s to God** rendre grâces à Dieu ◆ **~s be to God!** Dieu soit loué ! ◆ **that's all the ~s I get!** c'est comme ça qu'on me remercie !

◆ **thanks to ...** grâce à ... ◆ **~s to you/your brother/his help** *etc* grâce à toi/ton frère/son aide *etc* ◆ **no ~s to you!** ce n'est pas grâce à toi !

[2] *(= thank you)* **~s!*** merci ! ◆ **no ~s** non merci ◆ **~s very much!***, **~s a lot!*** merci bien *(also iro)*, merci beaucoup, merci mille fois ◆ **~s a million*** merci mille fois ◆ **many ~s for all you've done** merci mille fois pour ce que vous avez fait ◆ **many ~s for helping us** merci mille fois de nous avoir aidés ◆ **~s for nothing!*** je te remercie ! *(iro)*

COMP **thank(s) offering** N action *f* de grâce(s) *(don)*

thank-you N ◆ **and now a special ~-you to John** et maintenant je voudrais remercier tout particulièrement John ◆ **~-you card** carte *f* de remerciement

thankful /ˈθæŋkfʊl/ ADJ reconnaissant *(to sb* à qn ; *for sth* de qch) ◆ **I've got so much to be ~ for** je n'ai pas à me plaindre de la vie ◆ **we were ~ for your umbrella!** nous avons vraiment béni votre parapluie ! ◆ **to be ~ for small mercies** s'estimer heureux ◆ **to be ~ to sb for doing sth** être reconnaissant à qn d'avoir fait qch ◆ **I was ~ that he hadn't seen me** j'ai été bien content qu'il ne m'ait pas vu ◆ **let's just be ~ that he didn't find out** estimons-nous heureux qu'il ne l'ait pas découvert ◆ **to be ~ to be alive** être content d'être en vie ◆ **he was ~ to sit down** il était content de (pouvoir) s'asseoir ◆ **for what we are about to receive may the Lord make us truly ~** *(before eating)* rendons grâce à Dieu pour le repas que nous allons partager

thankfully /ˈθæŋkfəlɪ/ ADV [1] *(= fortunately)* heureusement ◆ **~, someone had called the police** heureusement, quelqu'un avait appelé la police [2] *(= gratefully)* *[say, accept]* avec gratitude

thankfulness /ˈθæŋkfʊlnɪs/ N *(NonC)* gratitude *f*, reconnaissance *f*

thankless /ˈθæŋklɪs/ ADJ ingrat

thanksgiving /ˈθæŋksˌgɪvɪŋ/ N action *f* de grâce(s) ◆ **Thanksgiving Day** *(Can, US)* Thanksgiving *m*

> **THANKSGIVING**
>
> Les festivités de **Thanksgiving** se tiennent chaque année le quatrième jeudi de novembre, en commémoration de la fête organisée par les Pères pèlerins à l'occasion de leur première récolte sur le sol américain en 1621. C'est l'occasion pour beaucoup d'Américains de se rendre dans leur famille et de manger de la dinde et de la tarte à la citrouille. → PILGRIM FATHERS

that /ðæt, (weak form /ðət/) (pl those)

1 DEMONSTRATIVE ADJECTIVE	3 RELATIVE PRONOUN
2 DEMONSTRATIVE PRONOUN	4 CONJUNCTION
	5 ADVERB

1 - DEMONSTRATIVE ADJECTIVE

[1] unstressed ce, cet *before vowel and mute h of masc nouns*, cette *f*, ces *mfpl* ◆ **~ noise** ce bruit ◆ **~ man** cet homme ◆ **~ idea** cette idée ◆ **those books** ces livres ◆ **those houses** ces maisons ◆ **what about ~ $20 I lent you?** et ces 20 dollars que je t'ai prêtés ?

[2] stressed, or as opposed to this, these ce ... -là, cet ... -là, cette ... -là, ces ... -là ◆ **I mean THAT book** c'est de ce livre-là que je parle ◆ **I like ~ photo better than this one** je préfère cette photo-là à celle-ci ◆ **but (on) ~ Saturday ...** mais ce samedi-là ... ◆ **at least everyone agreed on THAT point** au moins tout le monde était d'accord là-dessus

◆ **that one,** *pl* **those ones** celui-là *m*, celle-là *f*, ceux-là *mpl*, celles-là *fpl* ◆ **which video do you want? – ~ one** quelle vidéo veux-tu ? – celle-là ◆ **of all his records, I like ~ one best** de tous ses disques, c'est celui-là que je préfère ◆ **the only blankets we have are those ones there** les seules couvertures que nous ayons sont celles-là ◆ **there's little to choose between this model and ~ one** il n'y a pas grande différence entre ce modèle-ci et l'autre

◆ **that much** ◆ **I can't carry ~ much** je ne peux pas porter tout ça ◆ **he was at least ~ much taller than me** il me dépassait de ça au moins

2 - DEMONSTRATIVE PRONOUN

[1] singular *(= that thing, event, statement, person etc)* cela, ça, ce

> **ça** is commoner, and less formal than **cela**; **ce** is used only as the subject of **être**.

◆ **what's ~?** qu'est-ce que c'est que ça ? ◆ **do you like ~?** vous aimez ça *or* cela ? ◆ **~'s enough!** ça suffit ! ◆ **after ~** après ça, après cela ◆ **~'s fine!** c'est parfait ! ◆ **~'s what they've been told** c'est ce qu'on leur a dit ◆ **she's not as stupid as (all) ~** elle n'est pas si bête que ça ◆ **~ is (to say) ...** c'est-à-dire ... ◆ **who's ~?** *(gen)* qui est-ce ? ; *(on phone)* qui est à l'appareil ? ◆ **is ~ you Paul?** c'est toi Paul ? ◆ **~'s the boy I told you about** c'est le garçon dont je t'ai parlé ◆ **did he go? – ~ he did!** † y est-il allé ? – pour sûr ! †

◆ **that which** *(= what)* ce qui *subject of clause*, ce que *object of clause* ◆ **too much time is spent worrying about ~ which may never happen** on passe trop de temps à s'inquiéter de ce qui peut très bien ne jamais arriver ◆ **this is the opposite of ~ which they claim to have done** c'est le contraire de ce qu'ils disent avoir fait

[2] = that one, those ones celui-là *m*, celle-là *f*, ceux-là *mpl*, celles-là *fpl* ◆ **not ~, the other bottle!** pas celle-là, l'autre bouteille ! ◆ **a recession like ~** une récession comme celle-là ◆ **a recession like ~ of 1973-74** une récession comme celle de 1973-74 ◆ **those over there** ceux-là (*or* celles-là) là-bas ◆ **are those our seats ?** est-ce que ce sont nos places ? ◆ **those are nice sandals** elles sont belles, ces sandalettes-là

◆ **that which** *(= the one which)* celui qui *m*, celle qui *f* ◆ **the true cost often differs from ~ which is first projected** le coût réel est souvent différent de celui qui était prévu à l'origine

◆ **those which** *(= the ones which)* ceux qui *mpl*, celles qui *fpl* ◆ **those which are here** ceux qui sont ici

◆ **those who** *(= the ones who)* ceux qui *mpl*, celles qui *fpl* ◆ **those who came** ceux qui sont venus ◆ **there are those who say** certains disent, il y a des gens qui disent

[3] set structures

◆ **at that** ◆ **let's leave it at ~** restons-en là ◆ **he's only a teacher and a poor one at ~** ce n'est qu'un professeur et encore assez piètre ◆ **and there were six of them at ~!** et en plus ils étaient six !

◆ **by that** ◆ **what do you mean by ~?** qu'est-ce que vous voulez dire par là ?

◆ **that's it** *(= the job's finished)* ça y est ; *(= that's what I mean)* c'est ça ; *(= that's all)* c'est tout ; *(= I've had enough)* ça suffit

◆ **that's just it** justement ◆ **sorry, I wasn't thinking – ~'s just it, you never think!** désolé, je ne faisais pas attention – justement, tu ne fais jamais attention !

◆ **and that's that !** ◆ **you're not going and that's that!** tu n'y vas pas, un point c'est tout !

◆ **so that's that** alors c'est ça ◆ **so that's that then, you're leaving?** alors c'est ça, tu t'en vas ? ◆ **and so ~ was ~** et les choses en sont restées là

◆ **with that** sur ce ◆ **with ~ she burst into tears** en disant cela, elle a éclaté en sanglots

3 - RELATIVE PRONOUN

> When **that** relates to the object it is translated **que**.
> When **that** relates to the subject it is translated **qui**.

◆ **the man ~ came to see you** l'homme qui est venu vous voir ◆ **the letter ~ I sent yesterday** la lettre que j'ai envoyée hier ◆ **the girl ~ he met on holiday and later married** la fille qu'il a rencontrée en vacances et (qu'il) a épousée par la suite ◆ **and Martin, idiot ~ he is, didn't tell me** et Martin, cet imbécile, ne me l'a pas dit ◆ **fool ~ I am !** idiot que je suis !

◆ **that ...** *+ preposition* lequel *m*, laquelle *f*, lesquels *mpl*, lesquelles *fpl* ◆ **the pen ~ she was writing with** le stylo avec lequel elle écrivait ◆ **the box ~ you put it in** la boîte dans laquelle vous l'avez mis

> **à + lequel**, **lesquels** and **lesquelles** combine to give **auquel**, **auxquels** and **auxquelles**.

◆ **the problem ~ we are faced with** le problème auquel nous sommes confrontés

> When **that** + preposition refers to people, preposition + **qui** can also be used:

◆ **the man ~ she was dancing with** l'homme avec lequel *or* avec qui elle dansait ◆ **the**

children ~ I spoke to les enfants auxquels *or* à qui j'ai parlé

dont is used when the French verb takes **de:**

◆ **the girl/the book ~ I told you about** la jeune fille/le livre dont je vous ai parlé ◆ **the only thing ~ he has a recollection of** la seule chose dont il se souvienne *or* souvient

When **that** means 'when', it is translated **où**

◆ **the evening ~ we went to the opera** le soir où nous sommes allés à l'opéra ◆ **during the years ~ he'd been abroad** pendant les années où il était à l'étranger

4 - CONJUNCTION

1 que ◆ **he said ~ he had seen her** il a dit qu'il l'avait vue ◆ **he was speaking so softly ~ I could hardly hear him** il parlait si bas que je l'entendais à peine ◆ **it is natural ~ he should refuse** il est normal qu'il refuse *subj* ◆ **~ he should behave like this is incredible** c'est incroyable qu'il se conduise ainsi ◆ **~ it should come to this!** *(liter)* quelle tristesse d'en arriver là ! ◆ **I didn't respond: oh ~ I had!** *(liter)* je n'ai pas répondu : que ne l'ai-je fait ! *(liter)*

que cannot be omitted in a second clause if it has a different subject:

◆ **he said ~ he was very busy and his secretary would deal with it** il a dit qu'il était très occupé et que sa secrétaire s'en occuperait

◆ **in that** en ce sens que, dans la mesure où ◆ **it's an attractive investment in ~ it is tax-free** c'est un investissement intéressant en ce sens qu'il *or* dans la mesure où il est exonéré d'impôts

◆ **not that** non (pas) que ◆ **not ~ I want to do it** non (pas) que je veuille le faire

2 liter, frm = so that pour que *+ subj*, afin que *+ subj* ◆ **those who fought and died ~ we might live** ceux qui se sont battus et (qui) sont morts pour que *or* afin que nous puissions vivre ; see also **so**

5 - ADVERB

1 = so si ◆ **it's not ~ expensive/important/funny/bad** ce n'est pas si cher/important/drôle/mal (que ça) ◆ **I couldn't go ~ far** je ne pourrais pas aller si loin ◆ **it's ~ high** *(gesturing)* ça fait ça de haut *or* en hauteur, c'est haut comme ça

2 * = so very tellement ◆ **it was ~ cold!** il faisait tellement froid *or* un de ces froids* ! ◆ **when I found it I was ~ relieved!** lorsque je l'ai trouvé, je me suis senti tellement soulagé !

thataway /ˈðætəweɪ/ **ADV** *(esp US)* par là

thatch /θætʃ/ **N** *(NonC)* chaume *m* ◆ **his ~ of hair*** sa crinière **VT** *[+ roof]* couvrir de chaume ; *[+ cottage]* couvrir en chaume

thatched /θætʃt/ **ADJ** ◆ **~ roof** toit *m* de chaume ◆ **~ cottage** chaumière *f*

thatcher /ˈθætʃəʳ/ **N** chaumier *m*

Thatcherism /ˈθætʃə,rɪzəm/ **N** thatchérisme *m*

Thatcherite /ˈθætʃə,raɪt/ **N** thatchériste *mf* **ADJ** thatchériste

thatching /ˈθætʃɪŋ/ **N** *(NonC)* 1 *(= craft)* couverture *f* de toits de chaume 2 *(= material)* chaume *m*

that'd /ˈðætd/ 1 ⇒ **that had** ; → **had** 2 ⇒ **that would** ; → **would**

that'll /ˈðætl/ ⇒ **that will** ; → **will**

thaw /θɔː/ **N** *(Weather)* dégel *m* ; *(fig: Pol etc)* détente *f* ◆ **economic** *etc* **~** *(fig: Econ)* assouplissement *m* des restrictions concernant la vie économique *etc* **VT** (also **thaw out**) *[+ ice]* faire dégeler, faire fondre ; *[+ snow]* faire fondre ; *[+ frozen food]* décongeler, dégeler **VI** (also **thaw out**) *[ice]* fondre, dégeler ; *[snow]* fondre ; *[frozen food]* décongeler, dégeler ◆ **it's ~ing** *(Weather)* il dégèle ◆ **he began to ~*** *(= get warmer)* il a commencé à se dégeler* *or* à se réchauffer ; *(= grow friendlier)* il a commencé à se dégeler* *or* à se dérider

the /ðiː/ *(weak form* /ðə/*)* **DEF ART** 1 le, la, l' *before vowel or mute h*, les ◆ **of ~, from ~** du, de la, de l', des ◆ **to ~, at ~** au, à la, à l', aux ◆ **~ prettiest** le plus joli, la plus jolie, les plus joli(e)s ◆ **~ poor** les pauvres *mpl*

2 *(neuter)* **~ good and ~ beautiful** le bien et le beau ◆ **translated from ~ German** traduit de l'allemand ◆ **it is ~ unusual that is frightening** c'est ce qui est inhabituel qui fait peur

3 *(with musical instruments)* **to play ~ piano** jouer du piano

4 *(with sg noun denoting whole class)* **~ aeroplane is an invention of our century** l'avion est une invention de notre siècle

5 *(distributive use)* **50p ~ kilo** 50 pence le kilo ◆ **two dollars to ~ pound** deux dollars la livre ◆ **paid by ~ hour** payé à l'heure ◆ **30 miles to ~ gallon** ≃ 9,3 litres au 100 (km)

6 *(with names etc)* **Charles ~ First/Second/Third** Charles premier/deux/trois ◆ **~ Browns** les Brown ◆ **~ Bourbons** les Bourbons

7 *(stressed)* **THE Professor Smith** le célèbre professeur Smith ◆ **he's THE surgeon here** c'est lui le grand chirurgien ici ◆ **it's THE restaurant in this part of town** c'est le meilleur restaurant du quartier ◆ **he's THE man for the job** c'est le candidat idéal pour ce poste ◆ **it was THE colour last year** c'était la couleur à la mode l'an dernier ◆ **it's THE book just now** c'est le livre à lire en ce moment

8 *(other special uses)* **he's got ~ measles*** il a la rougeole ◆ **well, how's ~ leg?*** eh bien, et cette jambe ?* ; → **cheek, sense**

ADV ◆ **~ more he works ~ more he earns** plus il travaille plus il gagne d'argent ◆ **it will be all ~ more difficult** cela sera d'autant plus difficile ◆ **it makes me all ~ more proud** je n'en suis que plus fier ◆ **he was none ~ worse for it** il ne s'en est pas trouvé plus mal pour ça ; → **better¹, soon**

theatre, theater *(US)* /ˈθɪətəʳ/ **N** 1 *(= place)* théâtre *m*, salle *f* de spectacle ; *(= drama)* théâtre *m* ◆ **I like the ~** j'aime le théâtre ◆ **to go to the ~** aller au théâtre *or* au spectacle ◆ **it makes good ~** c'est du bon théâtre ◆ **~ of the absurd** théâtre *m* de l'absurde

2 *(= large room)* salle *f* de conférences ◆ **lecture ~** *(Univ etc)* amphithéâtre *m*, amphi* *m*

3 *(Med:* also **operating theatre**) salle *f* d'opération ◆ **he is in (the) ~** *[patient]* il est sur la table d'opération ; *[surgeon]* il est en salle d'opération

4 *(Mil etc)* théâtre *m* ◆ **~ of operations/war** théâtre *m* des opérations/des hostilités

COMP *(Theat)* *[programme, ticket]* de théâtre ; *[visit]* au théâtre ; *[management]* du théâtre ; *(Med) [staff, nurse]* de la salle d'opération ; *[job, work]* dans la salle d'opération

theatre company N troupe *f* de théâtre

theatre-in-the-round N (pl **theatres-in-the-round**) théâtre *m* en rond

theatre lover N amateur *m* de théâtre

theatre workshop N atelier *m* de théâtre

theatregoer /ˈθɪətəgəʊəʳ/ **N** habitué(e) *m(f)* du théâtre

theatreland /ˈθɪətəlænd/ **N** ◆ **London's ~** le Londres des théâtres

theatrical /θɪˈætrɪkəl/ **ADJ** 1 *(= dramatic) [production]* de théâtre, dramatique ; *[world]* du théâtre ; *[performance, tradition]* théâtral ◆ **a ~ family** une famille d'acteurs 2 *(US = cinematic)* ◆ **films for ~ release** les films qui vont sortir sur les écrans *or* dans les salles 3 *(pej = melodramatic) [person, manner, gesture]* théâtral ◆ **there was something very ~ about him** il avait un côté très théâtral **NPL** **theatricals** théâtre *m* (amateur) ◆ **he does a lot of (amateur) ~s** il fait beaucoup de théâtre amateur ◆ **what were all those ~s about?** *(fig pej)* pourquoi toute cette comédie ?

COMP **theatrical agent N** agent *m* artistique *(d'un acteur)*

theatrical company N troupe *f* de théâtre

theatrical producer N producteur *m*, -trice *f* de théâtre

theatricality /θɪ,ætrɪˈkælɪtɪ/ **N** *(fig pej)* théâtralité *f*

theatrically /θɪˈætrɪkəlɪ/ **ADV** 1 *(= dramatically)* du point de vue théâtral 2 *(= in theatres) [feature]* sur scène ; *(US) (= in cinemas) [release, open]* dans les salles 3 *(pej = melodramatically)* théâtralement

Thebes /θiːbz/ **N** Thèbes

thee †† /ðiː/ **PRON** *(liter, dial)* te ; *(before vowel)* t' ; *(stressed, after prep)* toi

theft /θeft/ **N** vol *m*

their /ðeəʳ/ **POSS ADJ** 1 leur *f inv* ◆ **they've broken ~ legs** ils se sont cassé la jambe ◆ **THEIR house** *(stressed)* leur maison à eux *(or* à elles) 2 *(singular usage)* son, sa, ses ◆ **somebody rang – did you ask them ~ name?** quelqu'un a téléphoné – est-ce que tu lui as demandé son nom ?

theirs /ðeəz/ **POSS PRON** 1 le leur, la leur, les leurs ◆ **this car is ~** cette voiture est à eux *(or* à elles) *or* leur appartient *or* est la leur ◆ **this music is ~** cette musique est d'eux ◆ **your house is better than ~** votre maison est mieux que la leur ◆ **the house became ~** la maison est devenue la leur ◆ **it is not ~ to decide** *(frm)* il ne leur appartient pas de décider ◆ **~ is a specialized department** leur section est une section spécialisée

◆ **...of theirs** ◆ **a friend of ~** un de leurs amis, un ami à eux *(or* à elles)* ◆ **I think it's one of ~** je crois que c'est un (e) des leurs ◆ **it's no fault of ~** ce n'est pas de leur faute ◆ **that car of ~** *(pej)* leur fichue* voiture ◆ **that stupid son of ~** leur idiot de fils ◆ **no advice of ~ could prevent him ...** aucun conseil de leur part ne pouvait l'empêcher de ...

2 *(singular usage)* le sien, la sienne, les sien(ne)s ◆ **if anyone takes one that isn't ~** si jamais quelqu'un en prend un qui n'est pas à lui

theism /ˈθiːɪzəm/ **N** théisme *m*

theist /ˈθiːɪst/ **ADJ, N** théiste *mf*

theistic(al) /θiːˈɪstɪk(əl)/ **ADJ** théiste

them /ðem/ *(weak form* /ðəm/*)* **PERS PRON PL** 1 *(direct, unstressed)* les ; *(stressed)* eux *mpl*, elles *fpl* ◆ **I have seen ~** je les ai vu(e)s ◆ **I know her but I don't know ~** je la connais, elle, mais eux *(or* elles) je ne les connais pas ◆ **if I were ~** si j'étais à leur place, si j'étais eux *(or* elles) ◆ **it's ~!** ce sont eux *(or* elles) !, les voilà !

2 *(indirect)* leur ◆ **I gave ~ the book** je leur ai donné le livre ◆ **I'm speaking to ~** je leur parle

3 *(after prep etc)* eux, elles ◆ **I'm thinking of ~** je pense à eux *(or* elles) ◆ **as for ~** quant à eux *(or* elles) ◆ **younger than ~** plus jeune qu'eux *(or* elles) ◆ **they took it with ~** ils *(or* elles) l'ont emporté (avec eux *or* elles)

4 *(phrases)* **both of ~** tous *(or* toutes) les deux ◆ **several of ~** plusieurs d'entre eux *(or* elles) ◆ **give me a few of ~** donnez-m'en quelques-un(e)s ◆ **every one of ~ was lost** ils furent tous perdus, elles furent toutes perdues ◆ **I don't like either of ~** je ne les aime ni l'un(e) ni l'autre ◆ **none of ~ would do it** aucun d'entre eux *(or* aucune d'entre elles) n'a voulu le faire ◆ **it was very good of ~** c'était très gentil de leur part ◆ **he's one of ~*** *(fig pej)* je *(or* tu) vois le genre !*

PERS PRON SG → pers pron pl le, la, lui ◆ **somebody rang – did you ask ~ their name?** quelqu'un a téléphoné – est-ce que tu lui as demandé son nom ? ◆ **if anyone asks why I took it, I'll tell ~ ...** si jamais quelqu'un demande pourquoi je l'ai pris, je lui dirai ... ◆ **if anyone arrives early ask ~ to wait** si quelqu'un arrive tôt, fais-le attendre

thematic /θɪˈmætɪk/ ADJ thématique

theme /θiːm/ N 1 thème *m*, sujet *m* 2 *(Mus)* thème *m*, motif *m* 3 *(Ling)* thème *m* 4 *(US Scol = essay)* rédaction *f*
COMP *[pub, restaurant]* à thème
theme park N parc *m* à thème
theme song N *chanson de la bande originale* ; *(US = signature tune)* indicatif *m* (musical) ; *(fig)* refrain *m* (habituel), leitmotiv *m*
theme tune N musique *f* du générique

themed /θiːmd/ ADJ *(esp Brit) [restaurant, bar, party]* à thème

themself * /ðəmˈself/ PERS PRON SG *(reflexive: direct and indirect)* se ; *(emphatic)* lui-même *m*, elle-même *f* ; *(after prep)* lui *m*, elle *f* ◆ **somebody who could not defend ~** quelqu'un qui ne pouvait pas se défendre ◆ **somebody who doesn't care about ~** quelqu'un qui ne prend pas soin de sa propre personne

themselves /ðəmˈselvz/ PERS PRON PL *(reflexive: direct and indirect)* se ; *(emphatic)* eux-mêmes *mpl*, elles-mêmes *fpl* ; *(after prep)* eux, elles ◆ **they've hurt ~** ils se sont blessés, elles se sont blessées ◆ **they said to ~** ils (*or* elles) se sont dit ◆ **they saw it ~** ils l'ont vu de leurs propres yeux, ils l'ont vu eux-mêmes ◆ **they were talking amongst ~** ils discutaient entre eux ◆ **these computers can reprogram ~** ces ordinateurs peuvent se reprogrammer automatiquement ◆ **anyone staying here will have to cook for ~** les gens qui logent ici doivent faire leur propre cuisine
◆ **(all) by themselves** tout seuls, toutes seules

then /ðen/ ADV 1 *(= at that time)* alors, à l'époque ◆ **we had two dogs ~** nous avions alors deux chiens, nous avions deux chiens à l'époque ◆ **I'm going to London and I'll see him ~** je vais à Londres et je le verrai à ce moment-là ◆ **~ and there, there and ~** sur-le-champ, séance tenante
2 *(after prep)* **from ~ on(wards)** dès lors, à partir de cette époque(-là) *or* ce moment(-là) ◆ **before ~** avant (cela) ◆ **by ~ I knew ...** à ce moment-là, je savais déjà ... ◆ **I'll have it finished by ~** je l'aurai fini d'ici là ◆ **since ~** depuis ce moment-là *or* cette époque-là *or* ce temps-là ◆ **between now and ~** d'ici là ◆ **(up) until ~** jusque-là, jusqu'alors
3 *(= next, afterwards)* puis, ensuite ◆ **he went first to London ~ to Paris** il est allé d'abord à Londres, puis *or* et ensuite à Paris ◆ **and ~ what?** et puis après ? ◆ **now this ~ that** tantôt ceci, tantôt cela
4 *(= in that case)* alors, donc ◆ **~ it must be in the sitting room** alors ça doit être au salon ◆ **if you don't want that ~ what do you want?** si vous ne voulez pas de ça, alors que voulez-vous donc ? ◆ **but ~ that means that ...** mais c'est donc que ... ◆ **someone had already warned you ~?** on vous avait donc déjà prévenu ? ◆ **now ~ what's the matter?** alors qu'est-ce qu'il y a ?
5 *(= furthermore, and also)* et puis, d'ailleurs ◆ **(and) ~ there's my aunt** et puis il y a ma tante ◆ **... and ~ it's none of my business** ... et d'ailleurs *or* et puis cela ne me regarde pas ◆ **... and ~ again** *or* **but ~ he might not want to go** ... remarquez, il est possible qu'il ne veuille pas y aller ◆ **... and ~ again** *or* **but ~ he has always tried to help us** ... et pourtant, il faut dire qu'il a toujours essayé de nous aider
ADJ *(before n)* d'alors, de l'époque ◆ **the ~ Prime Minister** le Premier ministre d'alors *or* de l'époque

thence /ðens/ ADV *(frm, liter)* 1 *(= from there)* de là, de ce lieu-là ◆ **an idea which influenced Plato, and ~ the future of Western thought** une idée qui a influencé Platon, et, partant, l'avenir de la pensée occidentale ◆ **from ~** de ce lieu 2 *(= from that time)* dès lors, depuis lors ◆ **three weeks ~** trois semaines plus tard 3 *(= therefore)* par conséquent, pour cette raison

thenceforth /ˈðensfɔːθ/, **thenceforward** /ˈðensfɔːwəd/ ADV *(frm)* dès lors

theocracy /θɪˈɒkrəsɪ/ N théocratie *f*

theocratic /θɪəˈkrætɪk/ ADJ théocratique

theodolite /θɪˈɒdəlaɪt/ N théodolite *m*

theologian /θɪəˈləʊdʒɪən/ N théologien(ne) *m(f)*

theological /θɪəˈlɒdʒɪkəl/ ADJ *[debate, issue, text]* théologique ; *[training]* théologique, en théologie ; *[student]* en théologie COMP **theological college** N séminaire *m*, école *f* de théologie

theology /θɪˈɒlədʒɪ/ N théologie *f* ; → **liberation**

theorem /ˈθɪərəm/ N théorème *m*

theoretical /θɪəˈretɪkəl/ ADJ (also **theoretic**) théorique
COMP **theoretical physicist** N spécialiste *mf* de physique théorique
theoretical physics N physique *f* théorique

theoretically /θɪəˈretɪkəlɪ/ ADV 1 *(= in theory) [possible]* théoriquement ◆ **he could ~ face the death penalty** il encourt théoriquement la peine de mort ◆ **I was, ~, a fully-qualified lawyer** j'étais, en théorie, un avocat diplômé 2 *(= as theory) [absurd, interesting, ambitious]* sur le plan théorique ; *[analyse, justify]* théoriquement ◆ **~, his ideas are revolutionary** sur le plan théorique, ses idées sont révolutionnaires

theoretician /ˌθɪərəˈtɪʃən/, **theorist** /ˈθɪərɪst/ N théoricien(ne) *m(f)*

theorize /ˈθɪəraɪz/ VI *[scientist, psychologist etc]* élaborer une (*or* des) théorie(s) (*about* sur) ◆ **it's no good just theorizing about it** ce n'est pas la peine de faire des grandes théories là-dessus * VT ◆ **to ~ that ...** émettre l'hypothèse que ...

theory /ˈθɪərɪ/ N théorie *f* ◆ **in ~** en théorie

theosophical /θɪəˈsɒfɪkəl/ ADJ théosophique

theosophist /θɪˈɒsəfɪst/ N théosophe *mf*

theosophy /θɪˈɒsəfɪ/ N théosophie *f*

therapeutic /ˌθerəˈpjuːtɪk/ ADJ *(Med)* thérapeutique ◆ **I find chopping vegetables very ~** ça me détend de couper des légumes
COMP **therapeutic community** N communauté *f* thérapeutique
therapeutic touch N *forme de thérapeutique manuelle*

therapeutical /ˌθerəˈpjuːtɪkəl/ ADJ thérapeutique

therapeutics /ˌθerəˈpjuːtɪks/ N *(NonC)* thérapeutique *f*

therapist /ˈθerəpɪst/ N *(gen)* thérapeute *mf* ; → **occupational**

therapy /ˈθerəpɪ/ N *(gen, also Psych)* thérapie *f* ◆ **to be in ~** *(Psych)* suivre une thérapie ◆ **it's good ~** c'est très thérapeutique

there /ðɛəʳ/ ADV 1 *(place)* y *before vb*, là ◆ **we shall soon be ~** nous y serons bientôt, nous serons bientôt là, nous serons bientôt arrivés ◆ **put it ~** posez-le là ◆ **when we left ~** quand nous en sommes partis, quand nous sommes partis de là ◆ **on ~** là-dessus ◆ **in ~** là-dedans ◆ **back** *or* **down** *or* **over ~** là-bas ◆ **he lives round ~** il habite par là ; *(further away)* il habite par là-bas ◆ **somewhere round ~** quelque part par là ◆ **here and ~** çà et là, par-ci par-là ◆ **from ~** de là ◆ **they went ~ and back in two hours** ils ont fait l'aller et retour en deux heures ◆ **to be ~ for sb** * *(= supportive)* être là pour qn ◆ **I've been ~ (myself*)** *(= I've experienced it)* j'ai connu ça (moi-même) ; → **here**
2 *(phrases)*
◆ **there is, there are** il y a, il est *(liter)* ◆ **once upon a time ~ was a princess** il y avait *or* il était une fois une princesse ◆ **~ will be dancing later** plus tard on dansera ◆ **~ is a page missing** il y a une page qui manque ◆ **~ are three apples left** il reste trois pommes, il y a encore trois pommes ◆ **~'s none left** il n'y en a plus ◆ **~'s no denying it** c'est indéniable
◆ **there comes, there came** ◆ **~ comes a time when ...** il vient un moment où ... ◆ **~ came a knock on the door** on frappa à la porte ◆ **~ came a point when I began to feel tired** à un moment donné, j'ai commencé à être fatigué
3 *(= in existence)* **this road isn't meant to be ~!** cette route ne devrait pas exister *or* être là ! ◆ **if the technology is ~, someone will use it** si la technologie existe, quelqu'un l'utilisera
4 *(other uses)* **~'s my brother!** voilà mon frère ! ◆ **~ are the others!** voilà les autres ! ◆ **~ he is!** le voilà ! ◆ **~ you are** *(= I've found you)* (ah) vous voilà ! ; *(offering sth)* voilà ◆ **that man ~ saw it all** cet homme-là a tout vu ◆ **hey you ~!** hé *or* ho toi, là-bas ! * ◆ **hurry up ~!** eh ! dépêchez-vous ! ◆ **~'s my mother calling me** il y a *or* voilà ma mère qui m'appelle ◆ **~'s the problem** là est *or* c'est *or* voilà le problème ◆ **I disagree with you ~** là je ne suis pas d'accord avec vous ◆ **you've got me ~!** alors là, ça me dépasse ! * ◆ **but ~ again, he should have known better** mais là encore, il aurait dû se méfier ◆ **you press this switch and ~ you are!** tu appuies sur ce bouton et ça y est ! ◆ **~ you are, I told you that would happen** tu vois, je t'avais bien dit que ça allait arriver ◆ **~ they go!** les voilà qui partent ! ◆ **I had hoped to finish early, but ~ you go** j'espérais finir tôt mais tant pis ◆ **~ you go again *, complaining about ...** ça y est, tu recommences à te plaindre de ... ◆ **~ he goes again!** * ça y est, il recommence ! ◆ **he's all ~** * c'est un malin, il n'est pas idiot ◆ **he's not all ~** * *(gen)* il est un peu demeuré ; *[old person]* il n'a plus toute sa tête
EXCL ◆ **~, what did I tell you ?** alors, qu'est-ce que je t'avais dit ? ◆ **~, ~, don't cry!** allons, allons, ne pleure pas ! ◆ **~, drink this** allez *or* tenez, buvez ceci ◆ **~ now, that didn't hurt, did it?** voyons, voyons *or* eh bien, ça n'a pas fait si mal que ça, si ?

thereabouts /ðɛərəˈbaʊts/ ADV *(place)* par là, près de là, dans le voisinage ; *(degree etc)* à peu près, environ ◆ **£5 or ~** environ cinq livres, dans les cinq livres

thereafter /ðɛərˈɑːftəʳ/ ADV *(frm)* par la suite

thereat /ðɛərˈæt/ ADV *(frm) (place)* là ; *(time)* là-dessus

thereby /ðɛəˈbaɪ/ ADV de cette façon, de ce fait, par ce moyen ◆ **~ hangs a tale!** *(hum)* c'est toute une histoire !

therefore /ˈðɛəfɔːʳ/ CONJ donc, par conséquent, pour cette raison

therefrom /ðɛəˈfrɒm/ ADV *(frm)* de là

therein /ðɛərˈɪn/ ADV *(frm) (= in that regard)* à cet égard, en cela ; *(= inside)* (là-)dedans

thereof /ðɛərˈɒv/ ADV *(frm)* de cela, en ◆ **he ate ~** il en mangea

thereon /ðɛərˈɒn/ ADV *(frm)* (là-)dessus

there's /ðɛəz/ ⇒ **there is, there has** ; → **be, have**

thereto /ðɛəˈtuː/ ADV *(frm)* ◆ **this e-mail and any attachments ~** ce message électronique et tous les fichiers joints ◆ **expenses related ~** dépenses y afférant

theretofore /ðɛətuːˈfɔː/ ADV *(frm)* jusque-là

thereunder /ðɛər'ʌndəʳ/ ADV *(frm)* (là) en-dessous

thereupon /ðɛərə'pɒn/ ADV *(= then)* sur ce ; *(frm = on that subject)* là-dessus, à ce sujet

therewith /ðɛə'wɪð/ ADV *(frm) (= with that)* avec cela, en outre ; *(= at once)* sur ce

therm /θɜːm/ N = 1,055 × 10^8 joules ; *(formerly)* thermie *f*

thermal /'θɜːməl/ ADJ 1 *(Elec, Phys)* thermique 2 *(Geol, Med) [spring, spa, treatment]* thermal 3 *[underwear, socks]* en Thermolactyl ® ◆ **a ~ t-shirt** un T-shirt en Thermolactyl ®
N *(= air current)* courant *m* ascendant (d'origine thermique), ascendance *f* thermique
COMP **thermal barrier** N barrière *f* thermique
thermal baths NPL thermes *mpl*
thermal blanket N *(for person)* couverture *f* de survie
thermal breeder N réacteur *m* thermique
thermal conductivity N conductivité *f* thermique
thermal efficiency N rendement *m* thermique
thermal expansion N dilatation *f* thermique
thermal imager N imageur *m* thermique
thermal imaging N thermographie *f*
thermal imaging equipment N matériel *m or* appareils *mpl* de thermographie
thermal imaging system N système *m* de thermographie *or* d'imagerie thermique
thermal paper N papier *m* thermosensible
thermal power N énergie *f* thermique
thermal power station N centrale *f* thermique
thermal reactor N réacteur *m* thermique
thermal shock N choc *m* thermique
thermal unit N (also **British thermal unit**) *unité de quantité de chaleur (= 252 calories)*

thermic /'θɜːmɪk/ ADJ ⇒ **thermal adj 1**

thermionic /ˌθɜːmɪ'ɒnɪk/ ADJ *[effect, emission]* thermoïonique ◆ **~ valve, ~ tube** *(US)* tube *m* électronique

thermionics /ˌθɜːmɪ'ɒnɪks/ N thermoïonique *f*

thermo... /'θɜːməʊ/ PREF therm(o)...

thermocouple /'θɜːməʊkʌpl/ N thermocouple *m*

thermodynamic /'θɜːməʊdaɪ'næmɪk/ ADJ thermodynamique

thermodynamics /'θɜːməʊdaɪ'næmɪks/ N *(NonC)* thermodynamique *f*

thermoelectric /'θɜːməʊɪ'lektrɪk/ ADJ thermoélectrique

thermograph /'θɜːməʊgrɑːf/ N thermographe *m*

thermography /θɜː'mɒgrəfɪ/ N thermographie *f*

thermometer /θə'mɒmɪtəʳ/ N thermomètre *m*

thermonuclear /'θɜːməʊ'njuːklɪəʳ/ ADJ *[weapon, war, reaction]* thermonucléaire ◆ **~ strike** attaque *f* nucléaire

thermopile /'θɜːməʊpaɪl/ N pile *f* thermoélectrique

thermoplastic /'θɜːməʊ'plæstɪk/ N thermoplastique *m*

thermoplasticity /ˌθɜːməʊplæ'stɪsɪtɪ/ N *(NonC)* thermoplasticité *f*

Thermopylae /θə'mɒpəliː/ N les Thermopyles *fpl*

Thermos ® /'θɜːməs/ N thermos ® *m or f inv*
COMP **Thermos flask** N bouteille *f* thermos ®

thermosiphon /ˌθɜːməʊ'saɪfən/ N thermosiphon *m*

thermostat /'θɜːməstæt/ N thermostat *m*

thermostatic /ˌθɜːmə'stætɪk/ ADJ thermostatique

thermotherapy /ˌθɜːməʊ'θerəpɪ/ N thermothérapie *f*

thesaurus /θɪ'sɔːrəs/ N (pl **thesauruses** *or* **thesauri** /θɪ'sɔːraɪ/) *(gen)* trésor *m (fig) (= lexicon)* dictionnaire *m* synonymique ; *(Comput)* thésaurus *m*

these /ðiːz/ DEM ADJ, PRON pl of **this**

theses /'θiːsiːz/ NPL of **thesis**

Theseus /'θiːsjəs/ N Thésée *m*

thesis /'θiːsɪs/ N (pl **theses** /'θiːsiːz/) thèse *f*

Thespian /'θespɪən/ ADJ *(liter or hum)* dramatique, de Thespis ◆ **his ~ talents** son talent de comédien N *(liter or hum = actor)* comédien(ne) *m(f)*

Thessalonians /ˌθesə'ləʊnɪənz/ NPL Thessaloniciens *mpl*

they /ðeɪ/ PERS PRON PL 1 ils *mpl*, elles *fpl* ; *(stressed)* eux *mpl*, elles *fpl* ◆ **~ have gone** ils sont partis, elles sont parties ◆ **there ~ are!** les voilà ! ◆ **~ are teachers** ce sont des professeurs ◆ **THEY know nothing about it** eux, ils n'en savent rien 2 *(= people in general)* on ◆ **~ say that ...** on dit que ... 3 *(singular usage)* il *m*, elle *f* ; *(stressed)* lui *m*, elle *f* ◆ **somebody called but ~ didn't give their name** quelqu'un a appelé, mais il *or* elle n'a pas donné son nom

they'd /ðeɪd/ ⇒ **they had, they would** ; → **have, would**

they'll /ðeɪl/ ⇒ **they will** ; → **will**

they're /ðɛəʳ/ ⇒ **they are** ; → **be**

they've /ðeɪv/ ⇒ **they have** ; → **have**

thiamine /'θaɪəmiːn/ N thiamine *f*

thick /θɪk/ ADJ 1 *(= fat, heavy, dense) [slice, layer, wall, hair, moustache, smoke, sauce, waist]* épais (-aisse *f*) ; *[pile, lenses, coat]* gros (grosse *f*) ; *[lips, nose, wool, string, line, book]* épais (-aisse *f*), gros (grosse *f*) ; *[neck]* épais (-aisse *f*), large ; *[soup, cream, gravy]* épais (-aisse *f*), consistant ; *[beard, forest, vegetation, foliage]* épais (-aisse *f*), touffu ; *[fog]* épais (-aisse *f*), dense ; *[darkness, crowd]* dense ; *[hedge]* (bien) fourni, touffu ; *[honey]* dur ◆ **to be 5cm ~** avoir 5 cm d'épaisseur ◆ **a 7cm ~ door, a door 7cm ~** une porte de 7 cm d'épaisseur, une porte épaisse de 7 cm ◆ **how ~ is it?** quelle est son épaisseur ? ◆ **to become ~(er)** *[sauce, cream]* épaissir ; *[waist]* (s')épaissir ; *[fog, smoke, darkness, vegetation, crowd]* s'épaissir ◆ **~ snow was falling** la neige tombait à gros flocons ◆ **he trudged through the ~ snow** il avançait péniblement dans l'épaisse couche de neige ◆ **the leaves were ~ on the ground** le sol était recouvert d'une épaisse couche de feuilles ◆ **antique shops are ~ on the ground around here** * il y a pléthore de magasins d'antiquités par ici ◆ **the air is very ~ in here** ça sent le renfermé ici ◆ **to give someone a ~ ear** * *(Brit)* tirer les oreilles à qn * ; → **skin**
2 ◆ **~ with to be ~ with dust** être couvert d'une épaisse couche de poussière ◆ **the streets are ~ with people** les rues sont noires de monde ◆ **the streets are ~ with traffic** la circulation est dense dans les rues ◆ **the water is ~ with weeds** l'eau est envahie par les mauvaises herbes ◆ **~ with smoke** *[air, atmosphere, room]* enfumé ◆ **the air is ~ with the smell of burning wood** l'air est imprégné d'une odeur de bois brûlé ◆ **the air is ~ with rumours** la rumeur enfle ◆ **the air was ~ with talk of his possible resignation** on parlait partout de son éventuelle démission
3 *(Brit * = stupid) [person]* bête ◆ **to get sth into one's ~ head** se mettre qch dans le crâne * ◆ **as ~ as two (short) planks** *or* **as a brick** bête comme ses pieds * ◆ **as ~ as pigshit** ** con comme un balai ** *or* comme la lune **
4 *(= unclear) [voice]* pâteux ◆ **a voice ~ with emotion** une voix chargée d'émotion ◆ **I woke up with a ~ head** *(from alcohol)* je me suis réveillé avec la gueule de bois * ; *(from fatigue)* je me suis réveillé avec le cerveau embrumé
5 *(= strong) [accent]* fort
6 *(Brit † * = unfair)* ◆ **it's** *or* **that's a bit ~** ça, c'est un peu fort * *or* un peu raide *
7 *(* = friendly)* ◆ **to be ~ with sb** être copain (copine *f*) avec qn ◆ **they are very ~** ils sont comme cul et chemise * ◆ **to be (as) ~ as thieves** *(pej)* s'entendre comme larrons en foire
ADV *[cut]* en tranches épaisses ; *[spread]* en couche épaisse ◆ **the fumes hung ~ over the pitch** il y avait une fumée épaisse au-dessus du terrain ◆ **the snow still lies ~ on the mountains** il y a encore une épaisse couche de neige sur les montagnes ◆ **blows/arrows fell ~ and fast** les coups/flèches pleuvaient (de partout) ◆ **the jokes came ~ and fast** il y a eu une avalanche de plaisanteries ◆ **redundancies are coming ~ and fast** il y a des licenciements à la pelle ◆ **the goals came ~ and fast** les buts arrivaient à la pelle ◆ **to lay it on ~** * forcer un peu la dose *
N *[of finger, leg etc]* partie *f* charnue ◆ **in the ~ of the crowd** au cœur de la foule ◆ **in the ~ of the fight** au cœur de la mêlée ◆ **they were in the ~ of it** ils étaient en plein dedans ◆ **through ~ and thin** à travers toutes les épreuves, contre vents et marées
COMP **thick-knit** ADJ gros (grosse *f*), en grosse laine N gros chandail *m*, chandail *m* en grosse laine
thick-lipped ADJ aux lèvres charnues, lippu
thick-skinned ADJ *[orange]* à la peau épaisse ; *(fig) [person]* peu sensible ◆ **he's very ~-skinned** c'est un dur, rien ne le touche
thick-skulled *, **thick-witted** * ADJ obtus, borné

thicken /'θɪkən/ VT *[+ sauce]* épaissir, lier VI *[branch, waist etc]* s'épaissir ; *[crowd]* grossir ; *[sauce etc]* épaissir ; *(fig) [mystery]* s'épaissir ; → **plot**

thickener /'θɪkənəʳ/ N épaississant *m*

thicket /'θɪkɪt/ N fourré *m*, hallier *m* ; *(fig) [of ideas, regulations]* maquis *m*

thickhead * /'θɪkhed/ N andouille * *f*

thickheaded * /θɪk'hedɪd/ ADJ obtus, borné

thickie ** /'θɪkɪ/ ⇒ **thicko**

thickly /'θɪklɪ/ ADV 1 *(= densely) [wooded, sown, planted, populated]* densément ◆ **to grow ~** *[hair, fruit]* pousser en abondance ◆ **the snow fell ~** la neige tombait dru
2 *(= deeply) [spread, roll out]* en couche épaisse ◆ **~ spread with butter** couvert d'une épaisse couche de beurre ◆ **to sprinkle sth ~ with flour** saupoudrer qch d'une épaisse couche de farine ◆ **to sprinkle sth ~ with basil** saupoudrer généreusement qch de basilic ◆ **dust/snow lay ~ everywhere** il y avait une épaisse couche de poussière/de neige partout ◆ **~ covered with** *or* **in dust** couvert d'une épaisse couche de poussière ◆ **~ encrusted with mud** incrusté d'une épaisse couche de boue ◆ **~ carpeted** couvert d'une épaisse moquette ◆ **the apples with which the grass was ~ strewn** les pommes qui jonchaient l'herbe
3 *(= coarsely) [slice]* en tranches épaisses
4 *(= unclearly) [say]* d'une voix pâteuse

thickness /'θɪknɪs/ N 1 *(NonC) [of slice, layer, wall]* épaisseur *f* ; *[of lips, nose, wool, line]* épaisseur *f*, grosseur *f* ; *[of fog, forest]* épaisseur *f*, densité *f* ; *[of hair]* épaisseur *f*, abondance *f* 2 *(= layer)* épaisseur *f* ◆ **three ~es of material** trois épaisseurs de tissu

thicko ** /'θɪkəʊ/ N idiot(e) *m(f)*, crétin(e) * *m(f)*

thickset /θɪk'set/ ADJ *(and small)* trapu, râblé ; *(and tall)* bien bâti, costaud *

thicky ** /'θɪkɪ/ N ⇒ **thicko**

thief /θiːf/ N (pl **thieves**) voleur *m*, -euse *f* ◆ **set a ~ to catch a ~** *(Prov)* à voleur voleur et demi *(Prov)* ◆ **stop ~!** au voleur ! ◆ **to come/leave like a ~ in the night** arriver/partir en douce* ; → **honour, thick**
COMP **thieves' cant** N argot *m* du milieu
thieves' kitchen N repaire *m* de brigands

thieve /θiːv/ VTI voler

thievery /ˈθiːvərɪ/ N *(NonC)* vol *m*

thieves /θiːvz/ NPL of **thief**

thieving /ˈθiːvɪŋ/ ADJ ① * ◆ **those ~ kids** ces petits voleurs ◆ **keep your ~ hands off!** enlève tes sales pattes de voleur de là ! * ② *(Mus)* ◆ **the Thieving Magpie** la Pie voleuse N *(NonC)* vol *m*

thievish † /ˈθiːvɪʃ/ ADJ voleur, de voleur

thigh /θaɪ/ N cuisse *f* COMP **thigh boots** NPL cuissardes *fpl*

thighbone /ˈθaɪbəʊn/ N fémur *m*

thimble /ˈθɪmbl/ N dé *m* (à coudre)

thimbleful /ˈθɪmblfʊl/ N *(fig)* doigt *m*, goutte *f*

thin /θɪn/ ADJ ① *(= lean, not thick)* *[person, face, legs, arms, animal]* maigre ; *[lips, waist, nose, layer, slice, strip, sheet]* mince ; *[line, thread, wire]* fin ; *[cloth, garment]* fin, léger ; *[book, mattress, wall]* peu épais (-aisse *f*), mince ◆ **~ string** petite ficelle ◆ **a ~ stroke** *(with pen)* un trait mince *or* fin, un délié ◆ **to get ~(ner)** *[person]* maigrir ◆ **as ~ as a rake** *[person]* maigre comme un clou ◆ **it's the ~ end of the wedge** c'est s'engager sur une pente savonneuse ◆ **to be (skating** *or* **treading) on ~ ice** *(fig)* être sur un terrain glissant ; → **line¹, skin, wear**
② *(= runny)* *[liquid, oil]* fluide ; *[soup, sauce, gravy]* clair, clairet *(pej)* ; *[paint]* peu épais (-aisse *f*), liquide ; *[cream, honey, mud]* liquide ◆ **to make ~ner** *[+ soup, sauce]* éclaircir, délayer
③ *(= not dense)* *[smoke, fog, cloud]* léger ; *[air, atmosphere]* raréfié ◆ **to become ~ner** *[smoke etc]* se dissiper ; *[air]* se raréfier ◆ **to disappear** *or* **vanish into ~ air** se volatiliser, disparaître (d'un seul coup) sans laisser de traces ◆ **to appear out of ~ air** apparaître comme par magie ◆ **to produce** *or* **conjure sth out of ~ air** faire apparaître qch comme par magie
④ *(= sparse)* *[crowd]* épars ; *[hair, beard, eyebrows, hedge]* clairsemé ◆ **to become ~ner** *[crowd, plants, trees, hair]* s'éclaircir ◆ **to be ~ on the ground** * *(esp Brit)* être rare ◆ **good news has been ~ on the ground* lately** les bonnes nouvelles se font rares ces derniers temps ◆ **to be ~ on top** * *(= balding)* être dégarni * ◆ **to be getting ~ on top** * *(= balding)* se dégarnir *
⑤ *(= feeble)* *[excuse, argument, evidence, plot]* peu convaincant ; *[script]* médiocre ; *[smile, majority]* faible ◆ **his disguise was rather ~** son déguisement a été facilement percé à jour
⑥ *[voice]* grêle, fluet ; *[sound]* aigu (-guë *f*)
⑦ *(Fin)* *[profit]* maigre ◆ **trading was ~ today** le marché était peu actif aujourd'hui ◆ **to have a ~ time (of it)** * passer par une période de vaches maigres
ADV *[spread]* en couche fine *or* mince ; *[cut]* en tranches fines *or* minces
VT *[+ paint]* étendre, délayer ; *[+ sauce]* allonger, délayer ; *[+ trees]* éclaircir ; *[+ hair]* désépaissir
VI *[fog, crowd]* se disperser, s'éclaircir ; *[numbers]* se réduire, s'amenuiser ◆ **his hair is ~ning, he's ~ning on top** * il perd ses cheveux, il se dégarnit *
COMP **thin-lipped** ADJ aux lèvres minces *or* fines ; *(with rage etc)* les lèvres pincées
thin-skinned ADJ *[orange]* à la peau fine ; *(fig)* *[person]* susceptible
► **thin down** VI *[person]* maigrir
VT SEP *[+ paint]* étendre, délayer ; *[+ sauce]* allonger
► **thin out** VI *[crowd, fog]* se disperser, s'éclaircir
VT SEP *[+ seedlings, trees]* éclaircir ; *[+ numbers, population]* réduire ; *[+ crowd]* disperser ; *[+ workforce]* réduire, dégraisser

thine /ðaɪn/ (†† *or liter*) POSS PRON le tien, la tienne, les tiens, les tiennes POSS ADJ ton, ta, tes

thing /θɪŋ/ N ① *(gen)* chose *f* ; *(= object)* chose *f*, objet *m* ◆ **surrounded by beautiful ~s** entouré de belles choses *or* de beaux objets ◆ **~ of beauty** bel objet *m*, belle chose *f* ◆ **such ~s as money, fame ...** des choses comme l'argent, la gloire ... ◆ **he's interested in ideas rather than ~s** ce qui l'intéresse ce sont les idées et non pas les objets ◆ **~s of the mind appeal to him** il est attiré par les choses de l'esprit ◆ **the ~ he loves most is his car** ce qu'il aime le plus au monde c'est sa voiture ◆ **what's that ~?** qu'est-ce que c'est que cette chose-là *or* ce machin-là * *or* ce truc-là * ? ◆ **the good ~s in life** les plaisirs *mpl* de la vie ◆ **he thinks the right ~s** il pense comme il faut ◆ **she likes sweet ~s** elle aime les sucreries *fpl* ◆ **you've been hearing ~s!** tu as dû entendre des voix !
② *(= belongings)* **~s** affaires *fpl* ◆ **have you put away your ~s?** as-tu rangé tes affaires ? ◆ **to take off one's ~s** se débarrasser de son manteau *etc* ◆ **do take your ~s off!** débarrassez-vous (donc) ! ◆ **have you got your swimming ~s?** as-tu tes affaires de bain ? ◆ **have you got any swimming ~s?** as-tu ce qu'il faut pour aller te baigner ? ◆ **where are the first-aid ~s?** où est la trousse de secours ?
③ *(= affair, item, circumstance)* chose *f* ◆ **I've two ~s still to do** j'ai encore deux choses à faire ◆ **the ~s she said!** les choses qu'elle a pu dire ! ◆ **the next ~ to do is ...** ce qu'il y a à faire maintenant c'est ... ◆ **the best ~ would be to refuse** le mieux serait de refuser ◆ **that's a fine** *or* **nice ~ to do!** *(iro)* c'est vraiment la chose à faire ! ◆ **what sort of (a) ~ is that to say to anyone?** ça n'est pas une chose à dire (aux gens) ◆ **the last ~ on the agenda** le dernier point à l'ordre du jour ◆ **you take the ~ too seriously** tu prends la chose trop au sérieux ◆ **you worry about ~s too much** tu te fais trop de soucis ◆ **I must think ~s over** il faut que j'y réfléchisse ◆ **how are ~s with you?** et vous, comment ça va ? ◆ **how's ~s?** * comment va ? ◆ **as ~s are** dans l'état actuel des choses ◆ **~s are going from bad to worse** les choses vont de mal en pis ◆ **since that's how ~s are** puisque c'est comme ça, puisqu'il en est ainsi ◆ **I believe in honesty in all ~s** je crois à l'honnêteté en toutes circonstances ◆ **to expect great ~s of sb/sth** attendre beaucoup de qn/qch ◆ **they were talking of one ~ and another** ils parlaient de choses et d'autres ◆ **taking one ~ with another** à tout prendre, somme toute ◆ **the ~ is to know when he's likely to arrive** ce qu'il faut c'est savoir *or* la question est de savoir à quel moment il devrait en principe arriver ◆ **the ~ is this: ...** voilà de quoi il s'agit : ... ◆ **the ~ is, she'd already seen him** en fait, elle l'avait déjà vu, mais elle l'avait déjà vu ◆ **it's a strange ~, but ...** c'est drôle, mais ... ◆ **it is one ~ to use a computer, quite another to know how it works** utiliser un ordinateur est une chose, en connaître le fonctionnement en est une autre ◆ **for one ~, it doesn't make sense** d'abord *or* en premier lieu, ça n'a pas de sens ◆ **and (for) another ~, I'd already spoken to him** et en plus, je lui avais déjà parlé ◆ **it's a good ~ I came** heureusement que je suis venu ◆ **he's on to a good ~** * il a trouvé le filon * ◆ **it's the usual ~, he hadn't checked the petrol** c'est le truc * *or* le coup * classique, il avait oublié de vérifier l'essence ◆ **that was a near** *or* **close ~** *(of accident)* vous l'avez (*or* il l'a *etc*) échappé belle ; *(of result of race, competition etc)* il s'en est fallu de peu ◆ **it's just one of those ~s** ce sont des choses qui arrivent ◆ **it's just one (damn) ~ after another** * les embêtements se succèdent ◆ **I didn't understand a ~ of what he was saying** je n'ai pas compris un mot de ce qu'il disait ◆ **I hadn't done a ~ about it** je n'avais strictement rien fait ◆ **he knows a ~ or two** il s'y connaît ◆ **he's in London doing his own ~** * il est à Londres et fait ce qui lui plaît *or* chante * ◆ **she's gone off to do her own ~** * elle est partie chercher sa voie *or* faire ce qui lui plaît ◆ **she's got a ~ about spiders** * elle a horreur des araignées, elle a la phobie des araignées ◆ **he's got a ~ about blondes** * il a un faible pour les blondes ◆ **he made a great ~ of my refusal** * quand j'ai refusé il en a fait toute une histoire *or* tout un plat * ◆ **don't make a ~ of it!** * n'en fais pas tout un plat ! *, ne monte pas ça en épingle ! ◆ **he had a ~ * with her two years ago** il a eu une liaison avec elle il y a deux ans ◆ **he's got a ~ * for her** il en pince pour elle * ◆ **Mr Thing * rang up** Monsieur Chose * *or* Monsieur Machin * a téléphoné ; → **equal, first, such**
④ *(= person, animal)* créature *f* ◆ **(you) poor little ~!** pauvre petit(e) ! ◆ **poor ~, he's very ill** le pauvre, il est très malade ◆ **she's a spiteful ~** c'est une rosse * ◆ **you horrid ~!** * chameau ! * ◆ **I say, old ~** † * dis donc (mon) vieux
⑤ *(= best, most suitable etc thing)* **that's just the ~ for me** c'est tout à fait *or* justement ce qu'il me faut ◆ **just the ~!, the very ~!** *(of object)* voilà tout à fait *or* justement ce qu'il me (*or* nous *etc*) faut ! ; *(of idea, plan)* c'est l'idéal ! ◆ **homeopathy is the ~ nowadays** l'homéopathie c'est la grande mode aujourd'hui ◆ **it's the in ~** * c'est le truc * à la mode ◆ **that's not the ~ to do** cela ne se fait pas ◆ **it's quite the ~ nowadays** ça se fait beaucoup aujourd'hui ◆ **I don't feel quite the ~ * today** je ne suis pas dans mon assiette aujourd'hui ◆ **he looks quite the ~ * in those trousers** il est très bien *or* chic avec ce pantalon ◆ **this is the latest ~ in computer games** c'est le dernier cri en matière de jeux électroniques

thingumabob * /ˈθɪŋəmɪbɒb/, **thingumajig** * /ˈθɪŋəmɪdʒɪg/, **thingummy(jig)** * /ˈθɪŋəmɪ(dʒɪg)/, **thingy** * /ˈθɪŋɪ/ N *(= object)* machin * *m*, truc * *m*, bidule * *m* ; *(= person)* Machin(e) * *m(f)*, trucmuche ‡ *mf*

think /θɪŋk/ LANGUAGE IN USE 2.2, 6, 8, 24.4, 26.2, 26.3
(vb : pret, ptp **thought**)
N * ◆ **I'll have a ~ about it** j'y penserai ◆ **to have a good ~ about sth** bien réfléchir à qch ◆ **you'd better have another ~ about it** tu ferais bien d'y repenser ◆ **he's got another ~ coming!** il se fait des illusions !, il faudra qu'il y repense *subj* !
VI ① *(gen)* réfléchir, penser ◆ **~ carefully** réfléchissez bien ◆ **~ twice before agreeing** réfléchissez-y à deux fois avant de donner votre accord ◆ **~ again!** *(= reflect on it)* repensez-y ! ; *(= have another guess)* ce n'est pas ça, recommence ! ◆ **let me ~** que je réfléchisse *, laissez-moi réfléchir ◆ **I ~, therefore I am** je pense, donc je suis ◆ **to ~ ahead** prévoir, anticiper ◆ **to ~ aloud** penser tout haut ◆ **to ~ big** * avoir de grandes idées, voir les choses en grand ◆ **I don't ~!** * *(iro)* ça m'étonnerait !
② *(= have in one's thoughts)* penser ; *(= devote thought to)* réfléchir *(of, about* à) ◆ **I was ~ing about** *or* **of you yesterday** je pensais à vous hier ◆ **I ~ of you always** je pense toujours à toi ◆ **what are you ~ing about?** à quoi pensez-vous ? ◆ **I'm ~ing of** *or* **about resigning** je pense à donner ma démission ◆ **he was ~ing of** *or* **about suicide** il pensait au suicide ◆ **~ of a number** pense à un chiffre ◆ **you can't ~ of everything** on ne peut pas penser à tout ◆ **he's always ~ing of** *or* **about money, he ~s of** *or* **about nothing but money** il ne pense qu'à l'argent ◆ **it's not worth ~ing about** ça ne vaut pas la peine d'y penser ◆ **(you) ~ about it!, ~ on it!** († *or liter*) pensez-y !, songez-y ! ◆ **and to ~ of him going there alone!** quand on pense qu'il y est allé tout seul !, (et) dire qu'il y est allé tout seul ! ◆ **I'll ~ about it** j'y

penserai, je vais y réfléchir ◆ **I'll have to ~ about it** il faudra que j'y réfléchisse *or* pense *subj* ◆ **that's worth ~ing about** cela mérite réflexion ◆ **you've given us so much to ~ about** vous nous avez tellement donné matière à réfléchir ◆ **come to ~ of it, when you ~ about it** en y réfléchissant (bien) ◆ **I've got too many things to ~ of** *or* **about just now** j'ai trop de choses en tête en ce moment ◆ **what else is there to ~ about?** c'est ce qu'il y a de plus important *or* intéressant ◆ **there's so much to ~ about** il y a tant de choses à prendre en considération ◆ **what were you ~ing of** *or* **about!** où avais-tu la tête ? ◆ **I wouldn't ~ of such a thing!** ça ne me viendrait jamais à l'idée ! ◆ **would you ~ of letting him go alone?** vous le laisseriez partir seul, vous ? ◆ **sorry, I wasn't ~ing** pardon, je n'ai pas réfléchi ◆ **I didn't ~ to ask** *or* **of asking if you ...** je n'ai pas eu l'idée de demander si tu ...

3 *(= remember, take into account)* penser *(of* à) ◆ **he ~s of nobody but himself** il ne pense qu'à lui ◆ **he's got his children to ~ of** *or* **about** il faut qu'il pense *subj* à ses enfants ◆ **~ of the cost of it!** rends-toi compte de la dépense ! ◆ **to ~ of** *or* **about sb's feelings** considérer les sentiments de qn ◆ **that makes me ~ of the day when ...** cela me fait penser au *or* me rappelle le jour où ... ◆ **I can't ~ of her name** je n'arrive pas à me rappeler son nom ◆ **I couldn't ~ of the right word** le mot juste ne me venait pas

4 *(= imagine)* ◆ **to ~ (of)** imaginer ◆ **~ what might have happened** imagine ce qui aurait pu arriver ◆ **just ~!** imagine un peu ! ◆ **(just) ~, we could go to Spain** rends-toi compte, nous pourrions aller en Espagne ◆ **~ of me in a bikini!** imagine-moi en bikini ® ! ◆ **~ of her as a teacher** considère-la comme un professeur

5 *(= devise etc)* **to ~ of** avoir l'idée de ◆ **I was the one who thought of inviting him** c'est moi qui ai eu l'idée de l'inviter ◆ **what will he ~ of next?** qu'est-ce qu'il va encore inventer ? ◆ **he has just thought of a clever solution** il vient de trouver une solution astucieuse ◆ **~ of a number** pense à un chiffre

6 *(= have as opinion)* penser *(of* de) ◆ **to ~ well** *or* **highly** *or* **a lot of sb/sth** penser le plus grand bien de qn/qch, avoir une haute opinion de qn/qch ◆ **he is very well thought of in France** il est très respecté en France ◆ **I don't ~ much of him** je n'ai pas une haute opinion de lui ◆ **I don't ~ much of that idea** cette idée ne me dit pas grand-chose ◆ **to ~ better of doing sth** décider à la réflexion de ne pas faire qch ◆ **he thought (the) better of it** il a changé d'avis ◆ **to ~ the best/the worst of sb** avoir une très haute/très mauvaise opinion de qn ◆ **to ~ nothing of doing sth** *(= do as a matter of course)* trouver tout naturel de faire qch ; *(= do unscrupulously)* n'avoir aucun scrupule à faire qch ◆ **~ nothing of it!** mais je vous en prie !, mais pas du tout ! ◆ **you wouldn't ~ like that if you'd lived there** tu ne verrais pas les choses de cette façon si tu y avais vécu ; → **fit¹**

VT 1 *(= be of opinion, believe)* penser, croire ◆ **I ~ so/not** je pense *or* crois que oui/non ◆ **what do you ~?** qu'est-ce que tu (en) penses ? ◆ **I don't know what to ~** je ne sais (pas) qu'en penser ◆ **I ~ it will rain** je pense *or* crois qu'il va pleuvoir ◆ **I don't ~ he came** je ne pense *or* crois pas qu'il soit venu ◆ **I don't ~ he will come** je ne pense pas qu'il vienne *or* qu'il viendra ◆ **what do you ~ I should do?** qu'en penses-tu *or* crois-tu que je doive faire ? ◆ **I thought so** *or* **as much!** je m'y attendais !, je m'en doutais ! ◆ **I hardly ~ it likely that ...** cela m'étonnerait beaucoup que ... *+ subj* ◆ **she's pretty, don't you ~?** elle est jolie, tu ne trouves pas ? ◆ **what do you ~ of him?** comment le trouves-tu ? ◆ **I can guess what you are ~ing** je devine ta pensée ◆ **who do you ~ you are?** pour qui te prends-tu ? ◆ **I never thought he'd look like that** je n'aurais jamais cru qu'il ressemblerait à ça ◆ **you must ~ me very rude** vous devez me trouver très impoli ◆ **he ~s he is intelligent, he ~s himself intelligent** il se croit *or* se trouve intelligent ◆ **they are thought to be rich** ils passent pour être riches ◆ **I didn't ~ to see you here** je ne m'attendais pas à vous voir ici ; see also **vt 4** ◆ **he ~s money the whole time** * il ne s'intéresse qu'à l'argent ; → **world**

2 *(= conceive, imagine)* (s')imaginer ◆ **~ what we could do with that house!** imagine ce que nous pourrions faire de cette maison ! ◆ **I can't ~ what he means!** je ne vois vraiment pas ce qu'il veut dire ! ◆ **you would ~ he'd have known that already** on aurait pu penser qu'il le savait déjà ◆ **anyone would ~ he owns the place!** il se prend pour le maître des lieux celui-là ! ◆ **who would have thought it!** qui l'aurait dit ! ◆ **I'd have thought she'd be more upset** j'aurais pensé qu'elle aurait été plus contrariée ◆ **to ~ that she's only ten!** et dire qu'elle n'a que dix ans !, quand on pense qu'elle n'a que dix ans !

3 *(= reflect)* penser à ◆ **just ~ what you're doing!** pense un peu à ce que tu fais ! ◆ **we must ~ how we can do it** il faut réfléchir à la façon dont nous allons pouvoir le faire ◆ **I was ~ing (to myself) how ill he looked** je me disais qu'il avait l'air bien malade

4 *(= remember)* ◆ **did you ~ to bring it?** tu n'as pas oublié de l'apporter ? ◆ **I didn't ~ to let him know** il ne m'est pas venu à l'idée *or* je n'ai pas eu l'idée de le mettre au courant

COMP think-piece N *(Press)* article *m* de fond
think tank * N groupe *m* or cellule *f* de réflexion

► **think back** VI repenser *(to* à), essayer de se souvenir *or* se rappeler *(to* de) ◆ **he thought back, and replied ...** il a fait un effort de mémoire, et a répliqué ...

► **think out** VT SEP *[+ problem, proposition]* réfléchir sérieusement à, étudier ; *[+ plan]* élaborer, préparer ; *[+ answer, move]* réfléchir sérieusement à, préparer ◆ **that needs ~ing out** il faut y réfléchir à fond ◆ **well-thought-out** bien conçu

► **think over** VT SEP *[+ offer, suggestion]* (bien) réfléchir à, peser ◆ **~ things over carefully first** pèse bien le pour et le contre auparavant ◆ **I'll have to ~ it over** il va falloir que j'y réfléchisse

► **think through** VT SEP *[+ plan, proposal]* examiner en détail *or* par le menu, considérer dans tous ses détails

► **think up** VT SEP *[+ plan, scheme, improvement]* avoir l'idée de ; *[+ answer, solution]* trouver ; *[+ excuse]* inventer ◆ **who thought up that idea?** qui a eu cette idée ? ◆ **what will he ~ up next?** qu'est-ce qu'il va encore bien pouvoir inventer ?

thinkable /ˈθɪŋkəbl/ ADJ ◆ **it's not ~ that ...** il n'est pas pensable *or* concevable *or* imaginable que ... *+ subj*

thinker /ˈθɪŋkəʳ/ N penseur *m*, -euse *f*

thinking /ˈθɪŋkɪŋ/ **ADJ** *[being, creature, mind]* rationnel ; *[machine]* pensant ◆ **to any ~ person, this ...** pour toute personne douée de raison, ceci ... ◆ **the ~ man** l'intellectuel *m* ◆ **the ~ woman's sex symbol** le sex-symbol de l'intellectuelle ◆ **the ~ man's crumpet** ‡ la pin up pour intellectuel ◆ **the ~ woman's crumpet** ‡ le mâle pour intellectuelle

N *(= act)* pensée *f*, réflexion *f* ; *(= thoughts collectively)* opinions *fpl (on, about* sur) ◆ **I'll have to do some (hard) ~ about it** il va falloir que j'y réfléchisse sérieusement ◆ **current ~ on this** les opinions actuelles là-dessus ◆ **to my way of ~** à mon avis ◆ **that may be his way of ~, but ...** c'est peut-être comme ça qu'il voit les choses, mais ... ; → **wishful**

COMP thinking cap N ◆ **to put on one's ~ cap** * cogiter *
thinking pattern N modèle *m* de pensée
the thinking process N le processus de pensée
thinking time N ◆ **to give sb some ~ time** donner à qn un peu de temps pour réfléchir, laisser à qn un délai de réflexion

thinly /ˈθɪnlɪ/ ADV 1 *[slice, cut]* en tranches fines *or* minces 2 *[spread, roll out]* en couche fine *or* mince ◆ **toast ~ spread with butter** du pain grillé sur lequel on a étalé une fine *or* mince couche de beurre 3 ◆ **to be ~ populated** avoir une population éparse *or* clairsemée ◆ **~ wooded** peu boisé ◆ **~ scattered** épars ◆ **the meeting was ~ attended** la réunion n'a pas attiré grand monde ◆ **~ spread resources** des ressources disséminées ◆ **a criticism ~ disguised as a compliment** une critique à peine déguisée en compliment ◆ **a ~ veiled accusation** une accusation à peine voilée ◆ **a ~ veiled attempt** une tentative mal dissimulée 4 ◆ **to sow seeds ~** faire un semis clair ◆ **to smile ~** avoir un faible sourire

thinner /ˈθɪnəʳ/ **N** *(for paint etc)* diluant *m* **ADJ** compar of **thin**

thinness /ˈθɪnnɪs/ N *(NonC)* 1 *(= leanness, lack of thickness) [of person, legs, arms, face, animal]* maigreur *f* ; *[of waist, fingers, nose, layer, slice, strip, paper]* minceur *f* ; *[of wall, book, clothes]* minceur *f* ; *[of thread, wire]* finesse *f* ; *[of cloth, garment]* finesse *f*, légèreté *f*

2 *(= runniness) [of liquid, oil]* légèreté *f*, fluidité *f* ; *[of soup, gravy, sauce, paint]* manque *m* d'épaisseur ; *[of cream, honey, mud]* consistance *f* liquide

3 *[of smoke, fog, cloud]* légèreté *f* ◆ **the ~ of the air** *or* **atmosphere** le manque d'oxygène

4 *(= sparseness) [of hair, beard, eyebrows, hedge]* aspect *m* clairsemé ◆ **disappointed by the ~ of the crowd** déçu qu'il y ait si peu de monde

5 *(= feebleness) [of excuse, evidence, plot, plans, smile, majority]* faiblesse *f* ; *[of script]* médiocrité *f*

6 *[of voice]* timbre *m* grêle *or* fluet ; *[of sound]* timbre *m* aigu

7 *(Fin) [of profits, margins]* maigreur *f*

third /θɜːd/ **ADJ** troisième ◆ **in the presence of a ~ person** en présence d'une tierce personne *or* d'un tiers ◆ **in the ~ person** *(Gram)* à la troisième personne ◆ **(it's/it was) ~ time lucky!** la troisième fois sera/a été la bonne ! ◆ **the ~ finger** le majeur, le médius ◆ **to be a ~ wheel** *(US)* tenir la chandelle ◆ **the ~ way** *(Pol)* la troisième voie ; see also **comp** ; *for other phrases see* **sixth**

N 1 troisième *mf* ; *(= fraction)* tiers *m* ; *(Mus)* tierce *f* ; *for phrases see* **sixth**

2 *(Univ = degree)* ≈ licence *f* sans mention

3 (also **third gear**) troisième vitesse *f* ◆ **in ~** en troisième

NPL thirds *(Comm)* articles *mpl* de troisième choix *or* de qualité inférieure

ADV 1 *(in race, exam, competition)* en troisième place *or* position ◆ **he came** *or* **was placed ~** il s'est classé troisième

2 *(Rail)* **to travel ~** voyager en troisième

3 ⇒ **thirdly**

COMP Third Age N troisième âge *m*
third-class ADJ → **third-class**
third degree N ◆ **to give sb the ~ degree** * *(= torture)* passer qn à tabac‡ ; *(= question closely)* cuisiner‡ qn
third-degree burns NPL brûlures *fpl* du troisième degré
the third estate N le tiers état

third party N (Jur) tierce personne *f*, tiers *m* ◆ ~ **party (indemnity) insurance** (assurance *f*) responsabilité *f* civile
third party, fire and theft N (Insurance) assurance *f* au tiers, vol et incendie
third-rate ADJ de très médiocre qualité
Third World N tiers-monde *m* ADJ *[poverty etc]* du tiers-monde

third-class /ˈθɜːdˈklɑːs/ ADJ (*lit*) de troisième classe ; *[hotel]* de troisième catégorie, de troisième ordre ; (*Rail*) *[ticket, compartment]* de troisième (classe) ; (*fig pej*) *[meal, goods]* de qualité très inférieure ◆ ~ **seat** (*Rail*) troisième *f* ◆ ~ **degree** (*Univ*) → **noun** N (*Univ:* also **third-class degree**) ≃ licence *f* sans mention ADV 1 (*Rail* †) **to travel** ~ voyager en troisième 2 (*US Post*) tarif *m* "imprimés"

thirdly /ˈθɜːdlɪ/ LANGUAGE IN USE 26.2 ADV troisièmement, en troisième lieu

thirst /θɜːst/ N (*lit, fig*) soif *f* (*for de*) ◆ **I've got a real ~ on (me)** * j'ai la pépie * VI (*lit, fig: liter*) avoir soif (*for de*) ◆ **~ing for revenge** assoiffé de vengeance ◆ **~ing for blood** altéré *or* assoiffé de sang

thirstily /ˈθɜːstɪlɪ/ ADV (*lit, fig*) avidement

thirsty /ˈθɜːstɪ/ ADJ 1 *[person, animal, plant]* qui a soif, assoiffé (*liter*) ; *[land]* qui manque d'eau ; * *[car]* qui consomme beaucoup, gourmand * ◆ **to be** *or* **feel** ~ avoir soif ◆ **to make sb** ~ donner soif à qn ◆ **it's ~ work!** ça donne soif ! 2 (*liter = eager*) ◆ **to be ~ for sth** avoir soif de qch, être assoiffé de qch ◆ **to be ~ for sb's blood** vouloir la peau de qn

thirteen /ˈθɜːˈtiːn/ ADJ treize *inv* N treize *m inv* ; *for phrases see* **six** PRON treize ◆ **there are** ~ il y en a treize

thirteenth /ˈθɜːˈtiːnθ/ ADJ treizième N treizième *mf* ; (*= fraction*) treizième *m* ; *for phrases see* **sixth**

thirtieth /ˈθɜːtɪɪθ/ ADJ trentième N trentième *mf* ; (*= fraction*) trentième *m* ; *for phrases see* **sixth**

thirty /ˈθɜːtɪ/ ADJ trente *inv* ◆ **about ~ books** une trentaine de livres N trente *m inv* ◆ **about** ~ une trentaine ; *for other phrases see* **sixty** PRON trente ◆ **there are** ~ il y en a trente
COMP **thirty-second note** N (*US Mus*) triple croche *f*
Thirty-Share Index N (*Brit*) *indice des principales valeurs industrielles*
the Thirty Years' War N (*Hist*) la guerre de Trente Ans

this /ðɪs/ DEM ADJ (pl **these**) 1 ce, cet *before vowel and mute h*, cette *f*, ces *pl* ◆ **who is ~ man?** qui est cet homme ? ◆ **whose are these books?** à qui sont ces livres ? ◆ **these photos you asked for** les photos que vous avez réclamées ◆ ~ **week** cette semaine ◆ ~ **time last week** la semaine dernière à pareille heure ◆ ~ **time next year** l'année prochaine à la même époque ◆ ~ **coming week** la semaine prochaine *or* qui vient ◆ **it all happened ~ past half-hour** tout est arrivé dans la demi-heure qui vient de s'écouler ◆ **I've been waiting ~ past half-hour** voilà une demi-heure que j'attends, j'attends depuis une demi-heure ◆ **how's ~ hand of yours?** et votre main, comment va-t-elle ? ◆ ~ **journalist (fellow) you were going out with** * ce journaliste, là, avec qui tu sortais * ◆ ~ **journalist came up to me in the street** * il y a un journaliste qui est venu vers moi dans la rue
2 (*stressed, or as opposed to that, those*) ce *or* cet *or* cette *or* ces ...-ci ◆ **I mean THIS book** c'est de ce livre-ci que je parle ◆ **I like ~ photo better than that one** je préfère cette photo-ci à celle-là ◆ ~ **chair (over) here** cette chaise-ci ◆ **the leaf was blowing ~ way and that** la feuille tournoyait de-ci de-là ◆ **she ran that way and** ~ elle courait dans tous les sens
DEM PRON (pl **these**) 1 ceci, ce ◆ **what is ~?** qu'est-ce que c'est (que ceci) ? ◆ **whose is ~?** à qui appartient ceci ? ◆ **who's ~?** (*gen*) qui est-ce ? ; (*on phone*) qui est à l'appareil ? ◆ ~ **is it** (*gen*) c'est cela ; (*agreeing*) exactement, tout à fait ; (*before action*) cette fois, ça y est ◆ ~ **is my son** (*in introduction*) je vous présente mon fils ; (*in photo etc*) c'est mon fils ◆ ~ **is the boy I told you about** c'est *or* voici le garçon dont je t'ai parlé ◆ ~ **is Glenys Knowles** (*on phone*) ici Glenys Knowles, Glenys Knowles à l'appareil ◆ ~ **is Tuesday** nous sommes mardi ◆ **but ~ is May** mais nous sommes en mai ◆ ~ **is what he showed me** voici ce qu'il m'a montré ◆ ~ **is where we live** c'est ici que nous habitons ◆ **I didn't want you to leave like ~!** je ne voulais pas que tu partes comme ça ! ◆ **it was like ~ ...** voici comment les choses se sont passées ... ◆ **do it like** ~ faites-le comme ceci ◆ **after ~ things got better** après ceci les choses se sont arrangées ◆ **before ~ I'd never noticed him** je ne l'avais jamais remarqué auparavant ◆ **it ought to have been done before** ~ cela devrait être déjà fait ◆ **we were talking of ~ and that** nous bavardions de choses et d'autres ◆ **at ~ she burst into tears** sur ce, elle éclata en sanglots ◆ **with ~ he left us** sur ces mots il nous a quittés ◆ **what's all ~ I hear about your new job?** qu'est-ce que j'apprends, vous avez un nouvel emploi ? ◆ **they'll be demanding ~, that and the next thing** * ils vont exiger toutes sortes de choses
2 (*this one*) celui-ci *m*, celle-ci *f*, ceux-ci *mpl*, celles-ci *fpl* ◆ **I prefer that to** ~ je préfère celui-là à celui-ci (*or* celle-là à celle-ci) ◆ **how much is ~?** combien coûte celui-ci (*or* celle-ci) ? ◆ **these over here** ceux-ci (*or* celles-ci) ◆ **not these!** pas ceux-ci (*or* celles-ci) !
ADV ◆ **it was ~ long** c'était aussi long que ça ◆ **he had come ~ far** il était venu jusqu'ici ; (*in discussions etc*) il avait fait tant de progrès ; → **much**

thistle /ˈθɪsl/ N chardon *m*

thistledown /ˈθɪsldaʊn/ N duvet *m* de chardon

thistly /ˈθɪslɪ/ ADJ *[ground]* couvert de chardons

thither †† /ˈðɪðəʳ/ ADV y *before vb*, là ; → **hither**

thitherto /ðɪðəˈtuː/ ADV jusqu'alors

tho(') * /ðəʊ/ → **though**

thole¹ /θəʊl/ N (*Naut*) tolet *m*

thole² †† /θəʊl/ VT (*dial*) supporter

Thomas /ˈtɒməs/ N Thomas *m* ; → **doubt**

thong /θɒŋ/ N 1 *[of whip]* lanière *f*, longe *f* ; (*on garment*) lanière *f*, courroie *f* 2 (*= underwear*) string *m* 3 (*US, Austral = flip-flop*) tong *f*

Thor /θɔːʳ/ N (*Myth*) T(h)or *m*

thoraces /ˈθɔːrəˌsiːz/ NPL of **thorax**

thoracic /θɔːˈræsɪk/ ADJ *[muscle, vertebrae, area]* thoracique ◆ ~ **spine** vertèbres *fpl* dorsales ◆ ~ **surgeon** spécialiste *mf* de chirurgie thoracique

thorax /ˈθɔːræks/ N (pl **thoraxes** *or* **thoraces**) thorax *m*

thorium /ˈθɔːrɪəm/ N thorium *m*

thorn /θɔːn/ N (*= spike*) épine *f* ; (*NonC:* also **hawthorn**) aubépine *f* ◆ **to be a ~ in sb's side** *or* **flesh** être une source d'irritation constante pour qn ◆ **that was the ~ in his flesh** c'était sa bête noire ; → **rose²**
COMP **thorn apple** N stramoine *f*, pomme *f* épineuse
thorn bush N buisson *m* épineux

thornback /ˈθɔːnbæk/ N (*= fish:* also **thornback ray**) raie *f* bouclée

thornless /ˈθɔːnlɪs/ ADJ sans épines, inerme (*Bot*)

thorny /ˈθɔːnɪ/ ADJ (*lit, fig*) épineux

thorough /ˈθʌrə/ ADJ 1 (*= careful*) *[person, worker]* méthodique, qui fait les choses à fond ; *[work, investigation, preparation, analysis, training]* approfondi ; *[review]* complet (-ète *f*) ; *[consideration]* ample ◆ **a ~ grounding in English** des bases solides en anglais ◆ **to do a ~ job** faire un travail à fond ◆ **to give sth a ~ cleaning/wash** *etc* nettoyer/laver *etc* qch à fond ◆ **to be ~ in doing sth** faire qch à fond 2 (*= deep*) *[knowledge]* approfondi ; *[understanding]* profond 3 (*= complete*) ◆ **to make a ~ nuisance of o.s.** être totalement insupportable ◆ **to give sb a ~ walloping** donner une bonne raclée à qn ◆ **it's a ~ disgrace** c'est vraiment une honte

thoroughbred /ˈθʌrəbred/ ADJ *[horse]* pur-sang *inv* ; *[other animal]* de race N (*= horse*) (cheval *m*) pur-sang *m inv* ; (*= other animal*) bête *f* de race ◆ **he's a real** ~ (*fig = person*) il est vraiment racé, il a vraiment de la classe

thoroughfare /ˈθʌrəfɛəʳ/ N (*= street*) rue *f* ; (*= public highway*) voie *f* publique ◆ **"no thoroughfare"** "passage interdit"

thoroughgoing /ˈθʌrəˌgəʊɪŋ/ ADJ *[examination, revision]* complet (-ète *f*) ; *[believer]* convaincu ; *[hooligan]* vrai *before n* ; *[rogue, scoundrel]* fieffé

thoroughly /ˈθʌrəlɪ/ ADV 1 (*= carefully*) *[examine, wash, mix]* bien ◆ ~ **clean** tout propre, tout à fait propre ◆ **to research sth** ~ faire des recherches approfondies sur qch ◆ **to investigate sb/sth** ~ faire une enquête approfondie sur qn/qch 2 (*= completely*) *[modern, enjoyable, convinced]* tout à fait, on ne peut plus ; *[miserable, unpleasant]* absolument ; *[discredited]* complètement ; *[deserve, understand]* tout à fait ◆ **he's a ~ nasty piece of work** il est tout ce qu'il y a de plus odieux ◆ **it was ~ boring** c'était on ne peut plus ennuyeux ◆ **I ~ agree** je suis tout à fait d'accord ◆ **I ~ enjoyed myself** j'ai passé d'excellents moments ◆ **we ~ enjoyed our meal** nous avons fait un excellent repas

thoroughness /ˈθʌrənɪs/ N (*NonC*) *[of worker]* minutie *f* ; *[of knowledge]* profondeur *f* ◆ **the ~ of his work/research** la minutie qu'il apporte à son travail/sa recherche

those /ðəʊz/ DEM ADJ, DEM PRON pl of **that**

thou¹ † /ðaʊ/ PERS PRON (*liter*) tu ; (*stressed*) toi

thou² * /θaʊ/ N (pl **thou** *or* **thous**) abbrev of **thousand, thousandth**

though /ðəʊ/ LANGUAGE IN USE 26.3
CONJ 1 (*= despite the fact that*) bien que + *subj*, quoique + *subj* ◆ ~ **it's raining** bien qu'il pleuve, malgré la pluie ◆ ~ **poor they were honest** ils étaient honnêtes bien que *or* quoique *or* encore que pauvres
2 (*= even if*) **(even)** ~ **I shan't be there I'll think of you** je ne serai pas là mais je n'en penserai pas moins à toi ◆ **strange ~ it may seem** si *or* pour étrange que cela puisse paraître ◆ **I will do it ~ I (should) die in the attempt** (*frm*) je le ferai, dussé-je y laisser la vie ◆ **what ~ they are poor** (*liter*) malgré *or* nonobstant (*liter*) leur misère
3 ◆ **as** ~ comme si ◆ **it looks as ~ ...** il semble que ... + *subj* ; see also **as**
ADV pourtant, cependant ◆ **it's not easy** ~ ce n'est pourtant pas facile, pourtant ce n'est pas facile ◆ **did he ~!** * ah bon !, tiens tiens !

thought /θɔːt/ LANGUAGE IN USE 1.1
VB pt, ptp of **think**
N 1 (*NonC, gen*) pensée *f* ; (*= reflection*) pensée *f*, réflexion *f* ; (*= daydreaming*) rêverie *f* ; (*= thoughtfulness*) considération *f* ◆ **to be lost** *or* **deep in** ~ être perdu dans ses pensées ◆ **after much** ~ après mûre réflexion ◆ **he acted without** ~ il a agi sans réfléchir ◆ **without ~ for** *or* **of himself he ...** sans considérer son propre intérêt il ... ◆ **he was full of ~ for my welfare** il se préoccupait beaucoup de mon bien-être ◆ **you must take ~ for the future** il faut penser à l'avenir ◆ **he took** *or* **had no ~ for his own safety** il n'avait aucun égard pour sa propre sécurité ◆ **to give ~ to sth** bien réfléchir à qch, mûrement réfléchir sur qch ◆ **I didn't give it a moment's** ~ je n'y ai pas pensé une

seule seconde ◆ **I gave it no more ~, I didn't give it another** ~ je n'y ai plus pensé ◆ **don't give it another** ~ n'y pensez plus ◆ **further ~ needs to be given to these problems** ces problèmes exigent une réflexion plus approfondie

2 *(= idea)* pensée *f*, idée *f* ; *(= opinion)* opinion *f*, avis *m* ; *(= intention)* intention *f*, idée *f* ◆ **it's a happy** ~ voilà une idée qui fait plaisir ◆ **to think evil ~s** avoir de mauvaises pensées ◆ **what a ~!*** imagine un peu ! ◆ **what a horrifying ~!*** quel cauchemar ! ◆ **what a frightening ~!*** c'est effrayant !* ◆ **what a lovely ~!*** *(= good idea)* comme ça serait bien ! ; *(= how thoughtful)* comme c'est gentil ! ◆ **what a brilliant ~!*** c'est une idée géniale ! ◆ **that's a ~!*** tiens, mais c'est une idée ! ◆ **it's only a** ~ ce n'est qu'une idée ◆ **one last** *or* **final** ~ une dernière chose ◆ **the mere ~ of it frightens me** rien que d'y penser *or* rien qu'à y penser j'ai peur ◆ **he hasn't a ~ in his head** il n'a rien dans la tête ◆ **my ~s were elsewhere** j'avais l'esprit ailleurs ◆ **he keeps his ~s to himself** il garde ses pensées pour lui, il ne laisse rien deviner *or* paraître de ses pensées ◆ **the Thoughts of Chairman Mao** les pensées du président Mao ◆ **contemporary/scientific ~ on the subject** les opinions des contemporains/des scientifiques sur la question ◆ **the ~ of Nietzsche** la pensée de Nietzsche ◆ **my first ~ was to ring you** ma première réaction a été de te téléphoner ◆ **my first ~ was that you'd left** j'ai d'abord pensé que tu étais parti ◆ **I had ~s** *or* **some ~ of going to Paris** j'avais vaguement l'idée *or* l'intention d'aller à Paris ◆ **he gave up all ~(s) of marrying her** il a renoncé à toute idée de l'épouser ◆ **his one ~ is to win the prize** sa seule pensée *or* idée est de remporter le prix ◆ **it's the ~ that counts** c'est l'intention qui compte ◆ **to read sb's ~s** lire (dans) la pensée de qn ◆ **we keep you in our ~s** nous pensons (bien) à vous ; → **collect**[2], **penny, second**[1]

3 *(adv phrase)* **a** ~ un peu, un tout petit peu ◆ **it is a ~ too large** c'est un (tout petit) peu trop grand

COMP **thought police** N police *f* de la pensée
thought process N mécanisme *m* de pensée
thought-provoking ADJ qui pousse à la réflexion, stimulant
thought-read VI lire (dans) la pensée de qn
thought-reader N liseur *m*, -euse *f* de pensées ◆ **he's a ~-reader** *(fig)* il lit dans la pensée des gens ◆ **I'm not a ~-reader** je ne suis pas devin
thought reading N divination *f* par télépathie
thought transference N transmission *f* de pensée

thoughtful /ˈθɔːtfʊl/ ADJ 1 *(= reflective) [person] (by nature)* sérieux, réfléchi ; *(on one occasion)* pensif ; *[mood, face, eyes]* pensif ; *[expression, look]* pensif, méditatif ; *[silence]* méditatif ; *[remark, research]* sérieux, réfléchi ; *[book, article, approach]* sérieux ; *[design]* judicieux 2 *(= considerate) [person]* prévenant, attentionné ; *[act, gesture, remark]* plein de délicatesse ; *[invitation, gift]* gentil ◆ **how ~ of you!** comme c'est gentil à vous *or* de votre part ! ◆ **it was ~ of him to invite me** c'était gentil à lui *or* de sa part de m'inviter ◆ **to be ~ of others** être plein d'égards pour autrui

thoughtfully /ˈθɔːtfəlɪ/ ADV 1 *(= reflectively) [say, look at, nod]* pensivement 2 *(= considerately)* ◆ **he ~ booked tickets for us as well** il a eu la prévenance de louer des places pour nous aussi 3 *(= intelligently) [designed, constructed, positioned]* judicieusement

thoughtfulness /ˈθɔːtfʊlnɪs/ N (NonC) 1 *(= reflectiveness) [of person] (by nature)* sérieux *m* ; *(on one occasion)* air *m* pensif ; *[of book, article]* sérieux *m* 2 *(= considerateness)* prévenance *f*

thoughtless /ˈθɔːtlɪs/ ADJ 1 *(= inconsiderate) [person]* qui manque d'égards *or* de considération ; *[act, behaviour, remark]* maladroit ◆ **how ~ of you!** tu manques vraiment d'égards *or* de considération ! ◆ **it was ~ of her (to tell him)** ce n'était pas très délicat *or* c'était maladroit de sa part (de le lui dire) 2 *(= unthinking)* ◆ **to be ~ of the future** ne pas penser à l'avenir

thoughtlessly /ˈθɔːtlɪslɪ/ ADV 1 *(= inconsiderately) [act, forget]* inconsidérément 2 *(= unthinkingly) [speak]* maladroitement, de façon irréfléchie ; *[embark upon]* sans réfléchir

thoughtlessness /ˈθɔːtlɪsnɪs/ N (NonC) *(= carelessness)* étourderie *f*, légèreté *f* ; *(= lack of consideration)* manque *m* de prévenance *or* d'égards

thousand /ˈθaʊzənd/ ADJ mille *inv* ◆ **a ~ men** mille hommes ◆ **about a ~ men** un millier d'hommes ◆ **a ~ years** mille ans, un millénaire ◆ **a ~ thanks!** mille fois merci ! ◆ **two ~ pounds** deux mille livres ◆ **I've got a ~ and one things to do** j'ai mille et une choses à faire N mille *m inv* ◆ **a ~, one ~** mille ◆ **a** *or* **one ~ and one** mille (et) un ◆ **a ~ and two** mille deux ◆ **five ~** cinq mille ◆ **about a ~ (people), a ~ odd (people)** un millier (de personnes) ◆ **sold by the ~** *(Comm)* vendu par mille ◆ **~s of people** des milliers de gens ◆ **they came in their ~s** ils sont venus par milliers COMP **Thousand Island dressing** N *sauce salade à base de mayonnaise et de ketchup*

thousandfold /ˈθaʊzəndfəʊld/ ADJ multiplié par mille ADV mille fois autant

thousandth /ˈθaʊzəntθ/ ADJ millième N millième *mf* ; *(= fraction)* millième *m*

Thrace /θreɪs/ N Thrace *f*

thraldom /ˈθrɔːldəm/ N (NonC: *liter*) servitude *f*, esclavage *m*

thrall /θrɔːl/ N *(liter: lit, fig) (= person)* esclave *mf* ; *(= state)* servitude *f*, esclavage *m* ◆ **to be in ~ to ...** *(fig)* être esclave de ...

thrash /θræʃ/ VT 1 *(= beat)* rouer de coups, rosser ; *(as punishment)* donner une bonne correction à ; (*: *Sport etc*) battre à plate(s) couture(s), donner une bonne correction à ◆ **they nearly ~ed the life out of him, they ~ed him to within an inch of his life** ils ont failli le tuer à force de coups
2 *(= move wildly)* **the bird ~ed its wings (about)** l'oiseau battait *or* fouettait l'air de ses ailes ◆ **he ~ed his arms/legs (about)** il battait des bras/des jambes
3 *(Agr)* ⇒ **thresh**
VI battre violemment *(against* contre)
N 1 *(Brit* ‡ *= party)* sauterie* *f*
2 *(Mus:* also **thrash metal**) thrash *m*

► **thrash about, thrash around** VI *(= struggle)* se débattre ◆ **he ~ed about with his stick** il battait l'air de sa canne
VT SEP *[+ one's legs, arms]* battre de ; *[+ stick]* agiter ; see also **thrash vt 2**

► **thrash out*** VT SEP *[+ problem, difficulty] (= discuss)* débattre de ; *(= solve)* résoudre ◆ **they managed to ~ it out** ils ont réussi à résoudre le problème

thrashing /ˈθræʃɪŋ/ N correction *f*, rossée* *f* ; (*: *Sport etc*) correction *f (fig)*, dérouillée‡ *f* ◆ **to give sb a good ~** rouer qn de coups ; *(as punishment, also Sport)* donner une bonne correction à qn

thread /θred/ N 1 *(gen, also Sewing etc)* fil *m* ◆ **nylon ~** fil *m* de nylon ® ◆ **to hang by a ~** *(fig)* ne tenir qu'à un fil ◆ **the ceasefire is hanging by a ~** le cessez-le-feu ne tient qu'à un fil ◆ **to lose the ~ (of what one is saying)** perdre le fil de son discours ◆ **to pick up** *or* **take up the ~ again** *(fig)* retrouver le fil ◆ **to pick up the ~s of one's career** reprendre le cours de sa carrière ◆ **a ~ of light** un (mince) rayon de lumière
2 *[of screw]* pas *m*, filetage *m* ◆ **screw with left-hand ~** vis *f* filetée à gauche
NPL **threads** *(US = clothes)* fringues‡ *fpl*
VT *[+ needle, beads]* enfiler ◆ **to ~ sth through a needle/over a hook/into a hole** faire passer qch à travers le chas d'une aiguille/par un crochet/par un trou ◆ **to ~ a film on to a projector** monter un film sur un projecteur ◆ **he ~ed his way through the crowd** il s'est faufilé à travers la foule ◆ **the car ~ed its way through the narrow streets** la voiture s'est faufilée dans les petites rues étroites
VI 1 ⇒ **to thread one's way;** › vt
2 *[needle, beads]* s'enfiler ; *[tape, film]* passer

threadbare /ˈθredbeəʳ/ ADJ *[rug, clothes]* râpé, élimé ; *[room]* défraîchi ; *(fig) [joke, argument, excuse]* usé, rebattu

threadlike /ˈθredlaɪk/ ADJ filiforme

threadworm /ˈθredwɜːm/ N oxyure *m*

threat /θret/ N *(lit, fig)* menace *f* ◆ **to make a ~ against sb** proférer une menace à l'égard de qn ◆ **under (the) ~ of ...** menacé de ... ◆ **it is a grave ~ to civilization** cela constitue une sérieuse menace pour la civilisation, cela menace sérieusement la civilisation

threaten /ˈθretn/ VT menacer *(sb with sth* qn de qch ; *to do sth* de faire qch) ◆ **to ~ violence** proférer des menaces de violence ◆ **a species ~ed with extinction, a ~ed species** une espèce en voie de disparition ◆ **they ~ed that they would leave** ils ont menacé de partir ◆ **it is ~ing to rain** la pluie menace VI *[storm, war, danger]* menacer

threatening /ˈθretnɪŋ/ ADJ *[person, voice, manner, place, weather, clouds, sky]* menaçant ; *[gesture, tone, words]* menaçant, de menace ; *[phone call, letter]* de menace ◆ **to find sb ~** se sentir menacé par qn COMP **threatening behaviour** N *(Jur)* tentative *f* d'intimidation

threateningly /ˈθretnɪŋlɪ/ ADV *[say]* d'un ton menaçant *or* de menace ; *[gesticulate]* d'une manière menaçante ◆ **~ close** dangereusement près

three /θriː/ ADJ trois *inv*
N trois *m inv* ◆ **the Big Three** *(Pol)* les trois Grands *mpl* ◆ **let's play (the) best of ~** *(Sport)* jouons au meilleur des trois manches ◆ **they were playing (the) best of ~** ils jouaient deux parties et la belle ; → **two ;** *for other phrases see* **six**
PRON trois ◆ **there are ~** il y en a trois
COMP **3-D** N ⇒ **three-D**
three-act play N pièce *f* en trois actes
three-card monte N *(US)* ⇒ **three-card trick**
three-card trick N bonneteau *m*
three-cornered ADJ triangulaire
three-cornered hat N tricorne *m*
three-D N (abbrev of **three dimensions, three-dimensional**) ◆ **(in) ~-D** *[picture]* en relief ; *[film]* en trois dimensions
three-day event N *(Horse-riding)* concours *m* complet
three-day eventer N *(Horse-riding)* cavalier *m*, -ière *f* de concours complet
three-day eventing N *(Horse-riding)* concours *m* complet
three-dimensional ADJ *[object]* à trois dimensions, tridimensionnel ; *[picture]* en relief ; *[film]* en trois dimensions
three-fourths N *(US)* ⇒ **three-quarters**
three-four time N *(Mus)* mesure *f* à trois temps
three-legged ADJ *[table]* à trois pieds ; *[animal]* à trois pattes
three-legged race N *(Sport) course où les concurrents sont attachés deux par deux par la jambe*
three-line ADJ → **whip**
three-martini lunch* N *(US fig = expense-account lunch)* déjeuner *m* d'affaires *(qui passe dans les notes de frais)*

three-phase ADJ (Elec) triphasé
three-piece suit N (costume m) trois-pièces m
three-piece suite N *salon composé d'un canapé et de deux fauteuils*
three-pin plug N → **pin noun 2**
three-ply ADJ *[wool]* à trois fils
three-point landing N atterrissage m trois points
three-point turn N demi-tour m en trois manœuvres
three-quarter ADJ *[portrait]* de trois-quarts ; *[sleeve]* trois-quarts *inv* N *(Rugby)* trois-quarts m *inv*
three-quarters N trois quarts *mpl* ADV ♦ **the money is ~-quarters gone** les trois quarts de l'argent ont été dépensés ♦ **~-quarters full/empty** aux trois quarts plein/vide
three-ring circus N *(lit)* cirque m à trois pistes ; *(US * fig)* véritable cirque* m
the three Rs N *la lecture, l'écriture et l'arithmétique*
three-sided ADJ *[object]* à trois côtés, à trois faces ; *[discussion]* à trois
three-way ADJ *[split, division]* en trois ; *[discussion]* à trois
three-wheeler N *(= car)* voiture f à trois roues ; *(= tricycle)* tricycle m

THREE RS

Les **three Rs** (les trois "R") sont la lecture, l'écriture et l'arithmétique, considérées comme les trois composantes essentielles de l'enseignement. L'expression vient de l'orthographe fantaisiste "reading, riting and rithmetic" pour "reading, writing and arithmetic".

threefold /'θriːfəʊld/ ADJ triple ADV ♦ **to increase ~** tripler

threepence /'θrepəns/ N *(Brit)* trois anciens pence *mpl*

threepenny /'θrepənɪ/ *(Brit)* ADJ à trois pence ♦ **the Threepenny Opera** *(Mus)* l'Opéra m de quat'sous N *(also* **threepenny bit** *or* **piece***)* ancienne pièce f de trois pence

threescore /'θriː'skɔːʳ/ ADJ, N († *or liter*) soixante m COMP **threescore and ten** ADJ, N († *or liter*) soixante-dix m

threesome /'θriːsəm/ N *(= people)* groupe m de trois, trio m ; *(= game)* partie f à trois ♦ **we went in a ~** nous y sommes allés à trois

threnody /'θrenədɪ/ N *(lit)* mélopée f ; *(fig)* lamentations *fpl*

thresh /θreʃ/ VT *(Agr)* battre

thresher /'θreʃəʳ/ N *(= person)* batteur m, -euse f (en grange) ; *(= machine)* batteuse f

threshing /'θreʃɪŋ/ *(Agr)* N battage m COMP **threshing machine** N batteuse f

threshold /'θreʃhəʊld/ N seuil m, pas m de la porte ♦ **to cross the ~** franchir le seuil ♦ **on the ~ of ...** *(fig)* au bord or au seuil de ... ♦ **above the ~ of consciousness** *(Psych)* supraliminaire ♦ **below the ~ of consciousness** subliminaire ♦ **to have a high/low pain ~** avoir un seuil de tolérance à la douleur élevé/peu élevé ♦ **boredom ~** seuil m d'ennui
COMP **threshold agreement** N accord m d'indexation des salaires sur les prix
threshold policy N ⇒ **threshold wage policy**
threshold price N prix m de seuil
threshold wage policy N politique f d'indexation des salaires sur les prix

threw /θruː/ VB pt of **throw**

thrice /θraɪs/ ADV trois fois

thrift /θrɪft/ N *(NonC)* économie f COMP **thrift shop** N *(US) petite boutique d'articles d'occasion gérée au profit d'œuvres charitables*

thriftiness /'θrɪftɪnɪs/ N ⇒ **thrift**

thriftless /'θrɪftlɪs/ ADJ imprévoyant, dépensier

thriftlessness /'θrɪftlɪsnɪs/ N *(NonC)* imprévoyance f

thrifty /'θrɪftɪ/ ADJ économe

thrill /θrɪl/ LANGUAGE IN USE 7.5
N frisson m ♦ **a ~ of joy** un frisson de joie ♦ **with a ~ of joy he ...** en frissonnant or avec un frisson de joie, il ... ♦ **what a ~!** quelle émotion ! ♦ **she felt a ~ as his hand touched hers** un frisson l'a parcourue quand il lui a touché la main ♦ **it gave me a big ~** ça m'a vraiment fait quelque chose !* ♦ **to get a ~ out of doing sth** se procurer des sensations fortes en faisant qch ♦ **the film was packed with** *or* **full of ~s** c'était un film à sensations ♦ **the ~ of the chase** l'excitation f de la poursuite
VT *[+ person, audience, crowd]* électriser, transporter ♦ **his glance ~ed her** son regard l'a enivrée ♦ **I was ~ed (to bits)!*** j'étais aux anges !* ♦ **I was ~ed to meet him** ça m'a vraiment fait plaisir *or* fait quelque chose* de le rencontrer
VI tressaillir *or* frissonner (de joie) ♦ **to ~ to the music of the guitar** être transporté en écoutant de la guitare

thriller /'θrɪləʳ/ N *(= novel)* roman m à suspense ; *(= play)* pièce f à suspense ; *(= film)* thriller m, film m à suspense

thrilling /'θrɪlɪŋ/ ADJ *[match, climax, experience]* palpitant ; *[news]* saisissant

thrive /θraɪv/ (pret **throve** /θrəʊv/ *or* **thrived**, ptp **thrived** *or* **thriven** /'θrɪvn/) VI 1 *[baby]* se développer bien ; *[person, animal]* être florissant de santé ; *[plant]* pousser *or* venir bien ; *[business, industry]* prospérer ; *[businessman]* prospérer, réussir ♦ **children ~ on milk** le lait est excellent pour les enfants 2 *(fig = enjoy)* **he ~s on hard work** le travail lui réussit

thriving /'θraɪvɪŋ/ ADJ *[person, animal]* en plein épanouissement ; *[plant]* qui prospère (*or* prospérait) ; *[business, industry, economy, community, businessman]* prospère, florissant

throat /θrəʊt/ N *(external)* gorge f ; *(internal)* gorge f, gosier m ♦ **to take sb by the ~** prendre qn à la gorge ♦ **I have a sore ~** j'ai mal à la gorge, j'ai une angine ♦ **he had a fishbone stuck in his ~** il avait une arête de poisson dans le gosier ♦ **that sticks in my ~** *(fig)* je n'arrive pas à accepter *or* avaler* ça ♦ **to thrust** *or* **ram** *or* **force** *or* **shove* sth down sb's ~** *(fig)* imposer qch à qn ♦ **they are always at each other's ~(s)** ils sont toujours à se battre ; → **clear, cut, frog¹, jump**

throaty /'θrəʊtɪ/ ADJ 1 *(= husky) [voice, laugh]* rauque 2 *(Med) [cough]* guttural ♦ **I'm feeling a bit ~** * *(Brit)* j'ai mal à la gorge

throb /θrɒb/ N *[of heart]* pulsation f, battement m ; *[of engine]* vibration f ; *[of drums, music]* rythme m (fort) ; *[of pain]* élancement m ♦ **a ~ of emotion** un frisson d'émotion VI *[heart]* palpiter ; *[voice, engine]* vibrer ; *[drums]* battre (en rythme) ; *[pain]* lanciner ♦ **a town ~bing with life** une ville vibrante d'animation ♦ **the wound ~bed** la blessure me (*or* lui *etc*) causait des élancements ♦ **my head/arm is ~bing** j'ai des élancements dans la tête/dans le bras ♦ **we could hear the music ~bing in the distance** nous entendions au loin le rythme marqué *or* les flonflons *mpl* de la musique

throes /θrəʊz/ NPL ♦ **in the ~ of death** dans les affres de la mort, à l'agonie ♦ **in the ~ of war/disease/a crisis** *etc* en proie à la guerre/la maladie/une crise *etc* ♦ **in the ~ of an argument/quarrel/debate** au cœur d'une discussion/d'une dispute/d'un débat ♦ **while he was in the ~ of (writing) his book** pendant qu'il était aux prises avec la rédaction de son livre ♦ **while we were in the ~ of deciding what to do** pendant que nous débattions de ce qu'il fallait faire

thrombocyte /'θrɒmbəsaɪt/ N thrombocyte m

thrombosis /θrɒm'bəʊsɪs/ N (pl **thromboses** /θrɒm'bəʊsiːz/) thrombose f

throne /θrəʊn/ N *(all senses)* trône m ♦ **to come to the ~** monter sur le trône ♦ **on the ~** sur le trône ; → **power** COMP **throne room** N salle f du trône

throng /θrɒŋ/ N foule f, multitude f VI affluer, se presser (*towards* vers ; *round* autour de ; *to see* pour voir) VT ♦ **people ~ed the streets** la foule se pressait dans les rues ♦ **to be ~ed (with people)** *[streets, town, shops]* être grouillant de monde ; *[room, bus, train]* être bondé *or* comble

thronging /'θrɒŋɪŋ/ ADJ *[crowd, masses]* grouillant, pullulant

throttle /'θrɒtl/ N *(also* **throttle valve***)* papillon m des gaz ; *(= accelerator)* accélérateur m ♦ **to give an engine full ~** accélérer à fond ♦ **at full ~** à pleins gaz ♦ **to open the ~** accélérer, mettre les gaz ♦ **to close the ~** réduire l'arrivée des gaz VT *[+ person]* étrangler, serrer la gorge de ; *(fig)* étrangler *(fig)*
► **throttle back, throttle down** VI mettre le moteur au ralenti VT SEP *[+ engine]* mettre au ralenti

through /θruː/

When **through** is an element in a phrasal verb, eg **break through**, **fall through**, **sleep through**, look up the verb.

ADV 1 *(place, time, process)* **the nail went (right) ~** le clou est passé à travers ♦ **just go ~** passez donc ♦ **to let sb ~** laisser passer qn ♦ **you can get a train right ~ to London** on peut attraper un train direct pour Londres ♦ **did you stay all** *or* **right ~?** es-tu resté jusqu'à la fin ? ♦ **we're staying ~ till Tuesday** nous restons jusqu'à mardi ♦ **he slept all night ~** il ne s'est pas réveillé de la nuit ♦ **I know it ~ and ~** je le connais par cœur ♦ **read it (right) ~ to the end, read it right ~** lis-le en entier *or* jusqu'au bout ; → **wet**
♦ **through and through** ♦ **he's a liar ~ and ~** il ment comme il respire ♦ **he's a Scot ~ and ~** il est écossais jusqu'au bout des ongles
2 *(Brit Telec)* ♦ **to put sb ~ to sb** passer qn à qn ♦ **I'll put you ~ to her** je vous la passe ♦ **you're ~ now** vous pouvez parler maintenant ♦ **you're ~ to him** vous avez votre correspondant
3 *(* = finished)* **I'm ~** ça y est (j'ai fini)* ♦ **are you ~?** ça y est (tu as fini) ?* ♦ **I'm not ~ with you yet** je n'en ai pas encore fini *or* terminé avec vous ♦ **are you ~ with that book?** ce livre, c'est fini ?, tu n'as plus besoin de ce livre ? ♦ **I'm ~ with football!** le football, (c'est) fini !* ♦ **he told me he was ~ with drugs** il m'a dit que la drogue, pour lui, c'était fini ♦ **I'm ~ with you!** *(gen)* j'en ai marre* de toi ! ; *(in relationship)* c'est fini entre nous ! ♦ **he told me we were ~** *(in relationship)* il m'a dit qu'on allait casser* *or* que c'était fini entre nous
PREP 1 *(place, object)* à travers ♦ **a stream flows ~ the garden** un ruisseau traverse le jardin *or* coule à travers le jardin ♦ **the stream flows ~ it** le ruisseau le traverse *or* coule à travers ♦ **water poured ~ the roof** le toit laissait passer des torrents d'eau ♦ **to go ~ a forest** traverser une forêt ♦ **to get ~ a hedge** passer au travers d'une haie ♦ **they went ~ the train, looking for ...** ils ont fait tout le train, pour trouver ... ♦ **he went ~ the red light** il a grillé le feu rouge ♦ **to hammer a nail ~ a plank** enfoncer un clou à travers une planche ♦ **he was shot ~ the head** on lui a tiré une balle dans la tête ♦ **to look ~ a window/telescope** regarder par une fenêtre/dans un télescope ♦ **go and look ~ it** *(of hole, window etc)* va voir ce qu'il y a de l'autre côté ♦ **I can hear them ~ the wall** je les

entends de l'autre côté du mur ◆ **he has really been ~ it** * il en a vu de dures * ◆ **I'm half-way ~ the book** j'en suis à la moitié du livre ◆ **to speak ~ one's nose** parler du nez ; → **get through, go through, see through**

2 *(time)* pendant, durant ◆ **all** *or* **right ~ his life, all his life ~** pendant toute sa vie, sa vie durant ◆ **he won't live ~ the night** il ne passera pas la nuit ◆ **(from) Monday ~ Friday** *(US)* de lundi (jusqu')à vendredi ◆ **he stayed ~ July** il est resté pendant tout le mois de juillet *or* jusqu'à la fin de juillet ◆ **he lives there ~ the week** il habite là pendant la semaine

3 *(indicating means, agency)* par, par l'entremise *or* l'intermédiaire de, grâce à, à cause de ◆ **to send ~ the post** envoyer par la poste ◆ **it was ~ him that I got the job** c'est grâce à lui *or* par son entremise que j'ai eu le poste ◆ **it was all ~ him that I lost the job** c'est à cause de lui que j'ai perdu le poste ◆ **I heard it ~ my sister** je l'ai appris par ma sœur ◆ **~ his own efforts** par ses propres efforts ◆ **it happened ~ no fault of mine** ce n'est absolument pas de ma faute si c'est arrivé ◆ **absent ~ illness** absent pour cause de maladie ◆ **to act ~ fear** agir par peur *or* sous le coup de la peur ◆ **he was exhausted ~ having walked all the way** il était épuisé d'avoir fait tout le chemin à pied ◆ **~ not knowing the way he ...** parce qu'il ne connaissait pas le chemin il ...

ADJ *[carriage, train, ticket]* direct ◆ **~ portion** *[of train]* rame *f* directe

COMP through street N *(US)* rue *f* prioritaire

through traffic N *(on road sign)* ◆ **"through traffic"** ≈ "toutes directions" ◆ **all ~ traffic has been diverted** toute la circulation a été détournée

through way N ◆ **"no through way"** "impasse"

throughout /θruˈaʊt/ **PREP** 1 *(place)* partout dans ◆ **~ the world** partout dans le monde, dans le monde entier ◆ **at schools ~ France** dans les écoles de toute la France 2 *(time)* pendant, durant ◆ **~ his life** durant toute sa vie, sa vie durant ◆ **~ his career/his story** tout au long de sa carrière/son récit **ADV** *(= everywhere)* partout ; *(= the whole time)* tout le temps

throughput /ˈθruːpʊt/ N *[of computer]* débit *m* ; *[of factory]* capacité *f* de production

throughway /ˈθruːweɪ/ N *(US)* voie *f* rapide *or* express

throve /θrəʊv/ VB pt of **thrive**

throw /θrəʊ/ (vb : pret **threw**, ptp **thrown**) **N** 1 *[of javelin, discus]* jet *m* ; *(Wrestling)* mise *f* à terre ; *(Ftbl: also* **throw-in***)* remise *f* en jeu ◆ **give him a ~** laisse-lui la balle (*or* le ballon *etc*) ◆ **it was a good ~** *(Sport)* c'était un bon jet ◆ **with one ~ of the ball he ...** avec un seul coup il ... ◆ **you lose a ~** *(in table games)* vous perdez un tour ◆ **50p a ~** *(at fair etc)* 50 pence la partie ◆ **it costs 10 dollars a ~** * *(fig)* ça coûte 10 dollars à chaque fois ; → **stone**

2 *(= cover for armchair, sofa)* plaid *m* ; *(= cover for bed)* jeté *m* de lit

VT 1 *(= cast)* *[+ object, stone]* lancer, jeter *(to, at à)* ; *[+ ball, javelin, discus, hammer]* lancer ; *[+ dice]* jeter ◆ **he threw the ball 50 metres** il a lancé la balle à 50 mètres ◆ **he threw it across the room** il l'a jeté *or* lancé à l'autre bout de la pièce ◆ **to ~ a six** *(at dice)* avoir un six ◆ **to ~ one's hat** *or* **cap into the ring** *(fig)* se porter candidat, entrer en lice

◆ **throw + at** ◆ **he threw a towel at her** il lui a jeté *or* envoyé une serviette à la tête ◆ **they were ~ing stones at the cat** ils jetaient *or* lançaient des pierres au chat ◆ **to ~ a question at sb** poser une question à qn à brûle-pourpoint ◆ **to ~ the book at sb** * *(in accusing, reprimanding)* accabler qn de reproches ; *(in punishing, sentencing)* donner *or* coller * le maximum à qn ◆ **she really threw herself at him** * elle s'est vraiment jetée à sa tête *or* dans ses bras

2 *(= hurl violently)* *[explosion, car crash]* projeter ; *(in fight, wrestling)* envoyer au sol (*or* au tapis) ; *[+ horse rider]* démonter, désarçonner ◆ **the force of the explosion threw him into the air/across the room** la force de l'explosion l'a projeté en l'air/à l'autre bout de la pièce ◆ **he was ~n clear (of the car)** il a été projeté hors de la voiture ◆ **to ~ o.s. to the ground/at sb's feet/into sb's arms** se jeter à terre/aux pieds de qn/dans les bras de qn ◆ **to ~ o.s. on sb's mercy** s'en remettre à la merci de qn

◆ **to throw o.s. into sth** *(fig)* ◆ **he threw himself into the job** il s'est mis *or* attelé à la tâche avec enthousiasme ◆ **he threw himself into the task of clearing up** il y est allé de tout son courage pour mettre de l'ordre

3 *(= direct)* *[+ light, shadow, glance]* jeter ; *[+ slides, pictures]* projeter ; *[+ kiss]* envoyer *(to à)* ; *[+ punch]* lancer *(at à)* ◆ **to ~ one's voice** jouer les ventriloques ; → **light**[1]

4 *(= put suddenly, hurriedly)* jeter *(into* dans ; *over* sur) ◆ **to ~ sb into jail** jeter qn en prison ◆ **to ~ a bridge over a river** jeter un pont sur une rivière ◆ **to ~ into confusion** *[+ person]* semer la confusion dans l'esprit de ; *[+ meeting, group]* semer la confusion dans ◆ **it ~s the emphasis on ...** cela met l'accent sur ... ◆ **to ~ open** *[+ door, window]* ouvrir tout grand ; *[+ house, gardens]* ouvrir au public ; *[+ race, competition etc]* ouvrir à tout le monde ◆ **to ~ a party** * organiser une petite fête *(for sb* en l'honneur de qn) → **blame, doubt, fit**[2]**, relief**

5 *[+ switch]* actionner

6 *[+ pottery]* tourner ; *[+ silk]* tordre

7 *(* = disconcert)* déconcerter ◆ **I was quite ~n when he ...** j'en suis resté baba * quand il ...

8 *(Sport * = deliberately lose)* *[+ match, race]* perdre volontairement

COMP throw-in N *(Ftbl)* remise *f* en jeu

throw-off N *(Handball)* engagement *m*

throw-out N *(Handball)* renvoi *m* de but

► **throw about, throw around** VT SEP *[+ litter, confetti]* éparpiller ◆ **don't ~ it about or it might break** ne t'amuse pas à le lancer, ça peut se casser ◆ **they were ~ing a ball about** ils jouaient à la balle ◆ **to be ~n about** *(in boat, bus etc)* être ballotté ◆ **to ~ one's money about** dépenser (son argent) sans compter ◆ **to ~ one's weight about** *(fig)* faire l'important ◆ **to ~ o.s. about** se débattre

► **throw aside** VT SEP *(lit)* jeter de côté ; *(fig)* rejeter, repousser

► **throw away** **VT SEP** 1 *[+ rubbish, cigarette end]* jeter ; *(fig)* *[+ one's life, happiness, health]* gâcher ; *[+ talents]* gaspiller, gâcher ; *[+ sb's affection]* perdre ; *[+ money, time]* gaspiller, perdre ; *[+ chance]* gâcher, laisser passer ◆ **to ~ o.s. away** gaspiller ses dons *(on sb* avec qn)

2 *(esp Theat)* *[+ line, remark]* *(= say casually)* laisser tomber ; *(= lose effect of)* perdre tout l'effet de

► **throw back** **VT SEP** 1 *(= return)* *[+ ball etc]* renvoyer *(to à)* ; *[+ fish]* rejeter ; *(fig)* *[+ image]* renvoyer, réfléchir ◆ **my offer of friendship was ~n back in my face** je lui ai offert mon amitié et il l'a refusée

2 *[+ head, hair]* rejeter en arrière ; *[+ shoulders]* redresser ◆ **to ~ o.s. back** se (re)jeter en arrière

3 *[+ enemy]* repousser ◆ **to be ~n back upon sth** *(fig)* être obligé de se rabattre sur qch

► **throw down** VT SEP *[+ object]* jeter ; *[+ weapons]* déposer ◆ **to ~ o.s. down** se jeter à terre ◆ **to ~ down a challenge** lancer *or* jeter un défi ◆ **it's really ~ing it down** * *(= raining)* il pleut à seaux, il tombe des cordes

► **throw in** **VI** *(US)* ◆ **to ~ in with sb** rallier qn

VT SEP 1 *[+ object into box etc]* jeter ; *(Ftbl)* *[+ ball]* remettre en jeu ; *[+ one's cards]* jeter (sur la table) ◆ **to ~ in one's hand** *or* **the sponge** *or* **the towel** * *(fig)* jeter l'éponge ; → **lot**[2]

2 *(fig)* *[+ remark, question]* interposer ◆ **he threw in a reference to it** il l'a mentionné en passant

3 *(fig)* *(= as extra)* en plus ; *(= included)* compris ◆ **with £5 ~n in** avec 5 livres en plus *or* par-dessus le marché ◆ **with meals ~n in** *(= included)* (les) repas compris ◆ **if you buy a washing machine they ~ in a packet of soap powder** si vous achetez une machine à laver ils vous donnent un paquet de lessive en prime ◆ **we had a cruise of the Greek Islands with a day in Athens ~n in** nous avons fait une croisière autour des îles grecques avec en prime un arrêt d'un jour à Athènes

N ◆ **throw-in** › **throw**

► **throw off** VT SEP 1 *(= get rid of)* *[+ burden, yoke]* se libérer de ; *[+ clothes]* enlever *or* quitter *or* ôter (en hâte), se débarrasser brusquement de ; *[+ disguise]* jeter ; *[+ pursuers, dogs]* perdre, semer * ; *[+ habit, tendency, cold, infection]* se débarrasser de ◆ **it threw the police off the trail** cela a dépisté la police

2 * *[+ poem, composition]* faire *or* écrire au pied levé

► **throw on** VT SEP *[+ coal, sticks]* ajouter ; *[+ clothes]* enfiler *or* passer à la hâte ◆ **she threw on some lipstick** * elle s'est vite mis *or* passé un peu de rouge à lèvres

► **throw out** VT SEP 1 jeter dehors ; *[+ rubbish, old clothes etc]* jeter, mettre au rebut ; *[+ person]* *(lit)* mettre à la porte, expulser ; *(fig: from army, school etc)* expulser, renvoyer ; *[+ suggestion]* rejeter, repousser ; *(Parl)* *[+ bill]* repousser ◆ **to ~ out one's chest** bomber la poitrine

2 *(= say)* *[+ suggestion, hint, idea, remark]* laisser tomber ; *[+ challenge]* jeter, lancer

3 *(= make wrong)* *[+ calculation, prediction, accounts, budget]* fausser

4 *(= disconcert)* *[+ person]* désorienter, déconcerter

► **throw over** VT SEP *[+ plan, intention]* abandonner, laisser tomber * ; *[+ friend, boyfriend etc]* laisser tomber *, plaquer * *(for sb else* pour qn d'autre)

► **throw together** VT SEP 1 *(pej = make hastily)* *[+ furniture, machine]* faire à la six-quatre-deux * ; *[+ essay]* torcher * ; *[+ meal]* improviser ◆ **he threw a few things together and left at once** il a rassemblé quelques affaires *or* jeté quelques affaires dans un sac et il est parti sur-le-champ

2 *(fig: by chance)* *[+ people]* réunir (par hasard) ◆ **they had been ~n together, fate had ~n them together** le hasard les avait réunis

► **throw up** **VI** *(* = vomit)* vomir

VT SEP 1 *(into air)* *[+ ball etc]* jeter *or* lancer en l'air ◆ **he threw the ball up** il a jeté la balle en l'air ◆ **he threw the book up to me** il m'a jeté *or* lancé le livre ◆ **he threw up his hands in despair** il a levé les bras de désespoir

2 *(esp Brit = produce, bring to light etc)* produire ◆ **the meeting threw up several good ideas** la réunion a produit quelques bonnes idées, quelques bonnes idées sont sorties de la réunion

3 *(= reproach)* **to ~ sth up to sb** jeter qch à la figure *or* au visage de qn, reprocher qch à qn

4 *(* = vomit)* vomir

5 *(* = abandon, reject)* *[+ job, task, studies]* lâcher, abandonner ; *[+ opportunity]* laisser passer

throwaway /ˈθrəʊəweɪ/ **ADJ** *[bottle]* non consigné ; *[packaging]* perdu ; *[remark, line]* qui n'a l'air de rien **N** *(esp US)* *[leaflet etc]* prospectus *m*, imprimé *m* ◆ **the ~ society** la société d'hyper-consommation *or* du tout-jetable *

throwback /ˈθrəʊbæk/ N *[of characteristic, custom etc]* ◆ **it's a ~ to ...** ça nous (*or* les *etc*) ramène à ...

thrower /ˈθrəʊəʳ/ N lanceur *m*, -euse *f* ; → **discus**

throwing /ˈθrəʊɪŋ/ N *(Sport)* ◆ **hammer/javelin ~** le lancer du marteau/du javelot

thrown /θrəʊn/ VB ptp of **throw**

thru /θruː/ *(US)* ⇒ **through**

thrum /θrʌm/ VTI ⇒ **strum**

thrupenny * /ˈθrʌpnɪ/ ADJ, N *(Brit)* ⇒ **threepenny**

thruppence * /ˈθrʌpəns/ N *(Brit)* ⇒ **threepence**

thrush¹ /θrʌʃ/ N *(= bird)* grive *f*

thrush² /θrʌʃ/ N *(= disease) (in humans)* muguet *m* ; *(in horses)* échauffement *m* de la fourchette

thrust /θrʌst/ (vb : pret, ptp **thrust**) N 1 *(= push)* poussée *f (also Mil)* ; *(= stab: with knife, dagger, stick etc)* coup *m* ; *(with sword)* botte *f* ; *(fig = remark)* pointe *f* ◆ **that was a ~ at you** *(fig)* ça c'était une pointe dirigée contre vous, c'est vous qui étiez visé ; → **cut**

2 *(NonC) [of propeller, jet engine, rocket]* poussée *f* ; *(Archit, Tech)* poussée *f*

3 *(= central idea)* idée *f* maîtresse ◆ **the main ~ of his speech/of the film** l'idée maîtresse de son discours/du film ◆ **the main ~ of our research will be ...** l'objectif central de nos recherches sera ... ◆ **the government accepts the broad ~ of the report** le gouvernement accepte le rapport dans ses grandes lignes

VT 1 pousser brusquement *or* violemment ; *[+ finger, stick]* enfoncer ; *[+ dagger]* plonger, enfoncer *(into* dans ; *between* entre) ; *[+ rag etc]* fourrer *(into* dans) ◆ **he ~ the box under the table** il a poussé la boîte sous la table ◆ **he ~ his finger into my eye** il m'a mis le doigt dans l'œil ◆ **he ~ the letter at me** il m'a brusquement mis la lettre sous le nez ◆ **to ~ one's hands into one's pockets** enfoncer les mains dans ses poches ◆ **he had a knife ~ into his belt** il avait un couteau glissé dans sa ceinture ◆ **he ~ his head through the window** il a mis *or* passé la tête par la fenêtre ◆ **he ~ the book into my hand** il m'a mis le livre dans la main ◆ **to ~ one's way** → **vi 1**

2 *(fig) [+ job, responsibility]* imposer *(upon sb* à qn) ; *[+ honour]* conférer *(on* à) ◆ **some have greatness ~ upon them** certains deviennent des grands hommes sans l'avoir cherché ◆ **I had the job ~ (up)on me** on m'a imposé ce travail ◆ **to ~ o.s. (up)on sb** imposer sa présence à qn

VI 1 (also **thrust one's way**) **to ~ in/out** *etc* entrer/sortir *etc* en se frayant un passage ◆ **he ~ past me** il m'a bousculé pour passer ◆ **to ~ through a crowd** se frayer un passage dans la foule

2 *(Fencing)* allonger une botte

► **thrust aside** VT SEP *[+ object, person]* écarter brusquement, pousser brusquement à l'écart ; *(fig) [+ objection, suggestion]* écarter *or* rejeter violemment

► **thrust forward** VT SEP *[+ object, person]* pousser en avant (brusquement) ◆ **to ~ o.s. forward** s'avancer brusquement, se frayer *or* s'ouvrir un chemin ; *(fig)* se mettre en avant, se faire valoir

► **thrust in** VI *(lit)* (also **thrust one's way in**) s'introduire de force ; *(fig = interfere)* intervenir

VT SEP *[+ stick, pin, finger]* enfoncer ; *[+ rag]* fourrer dedans * ; *[+ person]* pousser (violemment) à l'intérieur *or* dedans

► **thrust out** VT SEP 1 *(= extend) [+ hand]* tendre brusquement ; *[+ legs]* allonger brusquement ; *[+ jaw, chin]* projeter en avant

2 *(= push outside) [+ object, person]* pousser dehors ◆ **he opened the window and ~ his head out** il a ouvert la fenêtre et passé la tête dehors

► **thrust up** VI *[plants etc]* pousser vigoureusement

thruster /ˈθrʌstəʳ/ N 1 *(pej)* **to be a ~** se mettre trop en avant, être arriviste 2 *(= rocket)* (micro)propulseur *m*

thrusting /ˈθrʌstɪŋ/ ADJ dynamique, entreprenant ; *(pej)* qui se fait valoir, qui se met trop en avant

thruway /ˈθruːweɪ/ N *(US)* voie *f* rapide *or* express

Thu N abbrev of **Thursday**

Thucydides /θuːˈsɪdɪdiːz/ N Thucydide *m*

thud /θʌd/ N bruit *m* sourd, son *m* mat ◆ **I heard the ~ of gunfire** j'entendais gronder sourdement les canons VI faire un bruit sourd, rendre un son mat *(on, against* en heurtant) ; *[guns]* gronder sourdement ; *(= fall)* tomber avec un bruit sourd ◆ **to ~ in/out** *etc [person]* entrer/sortir *etc* d'un pas lourd

thug /θʌg/ N voyou *m*, gangster *m* ; *(at demonstrations)* casseur *m* ; *(term of abuse)* brute *f*

thuggery /ˈθʌgərɪ/ N *(NonC)* brutalité *f*, violence *f*

thuggish /ˈθʌgɪʃ/ ADJ de voyou(s)

Thule /ˈθjuːlɪ/ N (also **ultima Thule**) Thulé

thulium /ˈθjuːlɪəm/ N thulium *m*

thumb /θʌm/ N pouce *m* ◆ **to be under sb's ~** être sous la coupe de qn ◆ **she's got him under her ~** elle le mène par le bout du nez ◆ **to be all (fingers and) ~s** être très maladroit ◆ **his fingers are all ~s** il est très maladroit (de ses mains) ◆ **he gave me the ~s up (sign)** * *(all going well)* il a levé le pouce pour dire que tout allait bien *or* en signe de victoire ; *(to wish me luck)* il a levé le pouce en signe d'encouragement ◆ **he gave me the ~s down sign** * il m'a fait signe que ça n'allait pas (*or* que ça n'avait pas bien marché) ◆ **they gave my proposal the ~s down** * ils ont rejeté ma proposition ; → **finger, rule, twiddle**

VT 1 *[+ book, magazine]* feuilleter ◆ **well ~ed** tout écorné (par l'usage) ◆ **to ~ one's nose** faire un pied de nez *(at sb* à qn)

2 * *(gen)* **to ~ a lift** *or* **a ride** faire du stop * *or* de l'auto-stop ◆ **he ~ed a lift to Paris** il est allé à Paris en stop * *or* en auto-stop ◆ **I managed at last to ~ a lift** je suis enfin arrivé à arrêter *or* à avoir une voiture

COMP **thumb index** N répertoire *m* à onglets ◆ **with ~ index** à onglets

thumb print N empreinte *f* du pouce

► **thumb through** VT FUS *[+ book]* feuilleter ; *[+ card index]* consulter rapidement

thumbnail /ˈθʌmneɪl/ N ongle *m* du pouce ADJ ◆ **~ sketch** esquisse *f*

thumbscrew /ˈθʌmskruː/ N *(Tech)* vis *f* à oreilles ◆ **~s** *(Hist: torture)* poucettes *fpl*

thumbstall /ˈθʌmstɔːl/ N poucier *m*

thumbtack /ˈθʌmtæk/ N *(US)* punaise *f*

thump /θʌmp/ N *(= blow: with fist/stick etc)* (grand) coup *m* de poing/de canne *etc* ; *(= sound)* bruit *m* lourd et sourd ◆ **to fall with a ~** tomber lourdement ◆ **to give sb a ~** assener un coup à qn VT *(gen)* taper sur ; *[+ door]* cogner à, taper à ◆ **I could have ~ed him!** * *(esp Brit)* je l'aurais giflé *or* bouffé * ! VI 1 cogner, frapper *(on* sur ; *at* à) ; *[heart]* battre fort ; *(with fear)* battre la chamade ◆ **he was ~ing on the piano** il tapait (comme un sourd) sur le piano, il jouait comme un forcené 2 **to ~ in/out** *etc [person]* entrer/sortir *etc* d'un pas lourd

► **thump out** VT SEP ◆ **to thump out a tune on the piano** marteler un air au piano

thumping * /ˈθʌmpɪŋ/ *(Brit)* ADJ *[majority, defeat]* écrasant ; *[losses]* énorme ◆ **a ~ headache** un mal de tête carabiné * ADV ◆ **~ great** *[lorry]* gigantesque ; *[lie]* énorme ◆ **her novel is a ~ good read** son roman est vraiment génial *

thunder /ˈθʌndəʳ/ N *(NonC)* tonnerre *m* ; *[of applause]* tonnerre *m*, tempête *f* ; *[of hooves]* retentissement *m*, fracas *m* ; *[of passing vehicles, trains]* fracas *m*, bruit *m* de tonnerre ◆ **there's ~ about** le temps est à l'orage ◆ **there's ~ in the air** il y a de l'orage dans l'air ◆ **I could hear the ~ of the guns** j'entendais tonner les canons ◆ **with a face like ~** le regard noir (de colère) ; → **black, peal, steal**

VI *(Weather)* tonner ; *[guns]* tonner ; *[hooves]* retentir ◆ **the train ~ed past** le train est passé dans un grondement de tonnerre ◆ **to ~ against sth/sb** *(liter, fig = be vehement)* tonner *or* fulminer contre qch/qn

VT (also **thunder out**) *[+ threat, order]* proférer d'une voix tonitruante ◆ **"no!" he ~ed** "non !" tonna-t-il ◆ **the crowd ~ed their approval** la foule a exprimé son approbation dans un tonnerre d'applaudissements et de cris

thunderbolt /ˈθʌndəbəʊlt/ N coup *m* de foudre ; *(fig)* coup *m* de tonnerre

thunderclap /ˈθʌndəklæp/ N coup *m* de tonnerre

thundercloud /ˈθʌndəklaʊd/ N nuage *m* orageux ; *(fig)* nuage *m* noir

thunderer /ˈθʌndərəʳ/ N ◆ **the Thunderer** le dieu de la Foudre et du Tonnerre, Jupiter *m* tonnant

thunderhead /ˈθʌndəhed/ N *(esp US Weather)* tête *f* de cumulonimbus

thundering /ˈθʌndərɪŋ/ ADV *(Brit † *)* ◆ **a ~ great lie** un énorme mensonge ◆ **this novel is a ~ good read** ce roman est vraiment génial * ADJ 1 *(= loud) [waterfall]* rugissant ; *[voice]* tonitruant, tonnant ◆ **~ applause** un tonnerre d'applaudissements 2 *(= forceful) [question, attack, article]* vibrant 3 *(Brit † * = great)* ◆ **to make a ~ nuisance of o.s.** être bougrement † * empoisonnant ◆ **in a ~ rage** *or* **fury** dans une colère noire ◆ **in a ~ temper** d'une humeur massacrante ◆ **it was a ~ success** ça a eu un succès monstre *

thunderous /ˈθʌndərəs/ ADJ 1 *(= loud) [ovation, noise]* tonitruant ; *[voice]* tonitruant, tonnant ◆ **to ~ acclaim** *or* **applause** dans un tonnerre d'applaudissements 2 *(= forceful) [speech, attack]* vibrant 3 *(= angry)* ◆ **his face was ~, he had a ~ look** *or* **expression on his face** il était blême de rage

thunderstorm /ˈθʌndəstɔːm/ N orage *m*

thunderstruck /ˈθʌndəstrʌk/ ADJ *(fig)* abasourdi, ahuri, stupéfié

thundery /ˈθʌndərɪ/ ADJ *[weather] (= stormy)* orageux ; *(= threatening)* menaçant ◆ **~ rain** pluies *fpl* d'orage ◆ **~ showers** averses *fpl* orageuses

Thur abbrev of **Thursday**

thurible /ˈθjʊərɪbl/ N encensoir *m*

thurifer /ˈθjʊərɪfəʳ/ N thuriféraire *m*

Thurs. abbrev of **Thursday**

Thursday /ˈθɜːzdɪ/ N jeudi *m* ; → **Maundy Thursday** ; *for other phrases see* **Saturday**

thus /ðʌs/ LANGUAGE IN USE 26.3 ADV *(= consequently)* par conséquent ; *(= in this way)* ainsi ◆ **~ far** *(= up to here or now)* jusqu'ici ; *(= up to there or then)* jusque-là

thusly /ˈðʌslɪ/ ADV *(frm)* ainsi

thwack /θwæk/ N *(= blow)* grand coup *m* ; *(with hand)* claque *f*, gifle *f* ; *(= sound)* claquement *m*, coup *m* sec VT frapper vigoureusement, donner un coup sec à ; *(= slap)* donner une claque à

thwart¹ /θwɔːt/ VT *[+ plan]* contrecarrer, contrarier ; *[+ person]* contrecarrer *or* contrarier les projets de ◆ **to be ~ed at every turn** voir tous ses plans contrariés l'un après l'autre

thwart[2] /θwɔːt/ N *(Naut)* banc *m* de nage

thy /ðaɪ/ POSS ADJ (††, *liter, dial*) ton, ta, tes

thyme /taɪm/ N thym *m* ◆ **wild ~** serpolet *m*

thymus /ˈθaɪməs/ N (pl **thymuses** or **thymi** /ˈθaɪmaɪ/) thymus *m*

thyroid /ˈθaɪrɔɪd/ N (also **thyroid gland**) thyroïde *f* ADJ *[disorder, hormone, problem, disease]* thyroïdien ; *[cartilage]* thyroïde

thyroxin(e) /θaɪˈrɒksɪn/ N thyroxine *f*

thyself /ðaɪˈself/ PERS PRON (††, *liter, dial*) *(reflexive)* te ; *(emphatic)* toi-même

ti /tiː/ N *(Mus)* si *m*

tiara /tɪˈɑːrə/ N *[of lady]* diadème *m* ; *[of Pope]* tiare *f*

Tiber /ˈtaɪbəʳ/ N Tibre *m*

Tiberias /taɪˈbɪərɪæs/ N ◆ **Lake ~** le lac de Tibériade

Tiberius /taɪˈbɪərɪəs/ N Tibère *m*

Tibet /tɪˈbet/ N Tibet *m* ◆ **in ~** au Tibet

Tibetan /tɪˈbetən/ ADJ tibétain N 1 Tibétain(e) *m(f)* 2 *(= language)* tibétain *m*

tibia /ˈtɪbɪə/ N (pl **tibias** or **tibiae** /ˈtɪbɪ,iː/) tibia *m*

tic /tɪk/ N tic *m* (nerveux) COMP **tic-tac-toe** N *(US)* ≃ (jeu *m* de) morpion *m*

tich * /tɪtʃ/ N *(Brit)* → **titch**

tichy * /ˈtɪtʃɪ/ ADJ *(Brit)* → **titchy**

tick[1] /tɪk/ N 1 *[of clock]* tic-tac *m*

2 *(Brit * = instant)* instant *m* ◆ **just a ~!, half a ~!** une seconde !, un instant ! ◆ **in a ~, in a couple of ~s** *(= quickly)* en moins de deux*, en un clin d'œil ◆ **it won't take a ~** or **two ~s** c'est l'affaire d'un instant, il y en a pour une seconde ◆ **I shan't be a ~** j'en ai pour une seconde

3 *(esp Brit = mark)* coche *f* ◆ **to put** or **mark a ~ against sth** cocher qch

VT *(Brit) [+ name, item, answer]* cocher ; *(Scol = mark right)* marquer juste ◆ **please ~ where appropriate** *(on form etc)* cochez la case correspondante

VI *[clock, bomb etc]* faire tic-tac, tictaquer ◆ **I don't understand what makes him ~*** il est un mystère pour moi ◆ **I wonder what makes him ~*** je me demande comment il fonctionne

COMP **tick-over** N *(Brit) [of engine]* ralenti *m*
tick-tack-toe N *(US)* ≃ (jeu *m* de) morpion *m*

► **tick away** VI *[clock]* continuer son tic-tac ; *[taximeter]* tourner ; *[time]* s'écouler

VT SEP ◆ **the clock ticked the hours away** la pendule marquait les heures

► **tick by** VI *[time]* s'écouler

► **tick off** VT SEP 1 *(Brit) (lit) [+ name, item]* cocher ; *(fig = enumerate) [+ reasons, factors etc]* énumérer ◆ **to ~ sth off on one's fingers** énumérer qch sur ses doigts

2 *(Brit * = reprimand)* attraper, passer un savon à*

3 *(US * = annoy)* embêter*, casser les pieds à*

N ◆ **ticking-off** * → **ticking**[2]

► **tick over** VI *(Brit) [engine]* tourner au ralenti ; *[taximeter]* tourner ; *[business etc]* aller or marcher doucement

tick[2] /tɪk/ N *(= parasite)* tique *f*

tick[3] * /tɪk/ N *(Brit = credit)* crédit *m* ◆ **on ~** à crédit ◆ **to give sb ~** faire crédit à qn

tick[4] /tɪk/ N *(NonC = cloth)* toile *f* (à matelas) ; *(= cover)* housse *f* (pour matelas)

ticker /ˈtɪkəʳ/ N 1 *(esp US)* téléscripteur *m*, téléimprimeur *m* 2 ‡ *(= watch)* tocante* *f* ; *(= heart)* cœur *m*, palpitant‡ *m* COMP **ticker tape** N *(NonC)* bande *f* de téléscripteur or téléimprimeur ; *(US: at parades etc)* ≃ serpentin *m* ◆ **to get a ~ tape welcome** *(US)* être accueilli par une pluie de serpentins

ticket /ˈtɪkɪt/ N 1 *(for plane, train, performance, film, lottery, raffle)* billet *m* ; *(for bus, tube)* ticket *m* ; *(Comm = label)* étiquette *f* ; *(= counterfoil)* talon *m* ; *(from cash register)* ticket *m*, reçu *m* ; *(for cloakroom)* ticket *m*, numéro *m* ; *(for left luggage)* bulletin *m* ; *(for library)* carte *f* ; *(from pawnshop)* reconnaissance *f* (du mont-de-piété) ◆ **to buy a ~** prendre un billet ◆ **coach ~** billet *m* de car ◆ **admission by ~ only** entrée réservée aux personnes munies d'un billet ◆ **that's (just) the ~!*** c'est ça !, c'est parfait ! ; → **return, season**

2 (*: *for fine*) P.-V. *m*, papillon *m* ◆ **I found a ~ on the windscreen** j'ai trouvé un papillon sur le pare-brise ◆ **to get a ~ for parking** attraper un P. V. pour stationnement illégal ◆ **to give sb a ~ for parking** mettre un P.-V. à qn pour stationnement illégal

3 *(= certificate) [of pilot]* brevet *m* ◆ **to get one's ~** *[ship's captain]* passer capitaine

4 *(US Pol = list)* liste *f* (électorale) ◆ **he is running on the Democratic ~** il se présente sur la liste des démocrates ; → **straight**

VT 1 *[+ goods]* étiqueter

2 *(US) [+ traveller]* donner un billet à ◆ **passengers ~ed on these flights** voyageurs en possession de billets pour ces vols

3 *(US = fine)* mettre un P.-V. à

COMP **ticket agency** N *(Theat)* agence *f* de spectacles ; *(Rail etc)* agence *f* de voyages
ticket barrier N *(Brit Rail)* portillon *m* (d'accès)
ticket collector N contrôleur *m*, -euse *f*
ticket holder N personne *f* munie d'un billet
ticket inspector N ⇒ **ticket collector**
ticket machine N distributeur *m* de titres de transport
ticket office N bureau *m* de vente des billets, guichet *m*
ticket of leave † N *(Brit Jur)* libération *f* conditionnelle
ticket tout N → **tout noun**

ticketing /ˈtɪkɪtɪŋ/ N billetterie *f* ADJ *[policy, arrangements, system]* de billetterie

ticking[1] /ˈtɪkɪŋ/ N *(NonC = fabric)* toile *f* (à matelas)

ticking[2] /ˈtɪkɪŋ/ N *[of clock]* tic-tac *m* COMP **ticking-off** * N *(Brit)* ◆ **to give sb a ~-off** passer un savon à qn*, enguirlander qn ◆ **to get a ~-off** recevoir un bon savon*, se faire enguirlander

tickle /ˈtɪkl/ VT *(lit) [+ person, dog]* chatouiller, faire des chatouilles* à ; *(= please) [+ sb's vanity, palate etc]* chatouiller ; *(* = delight) [+ person]* plaire à, faire plaisir à ; *(* = amuse)* amuser, faire rire ◆ **to ~ sb's ribs, to ~ sb in the ribs** chatouiller qn ◆ **to be ~d to death***, **to be ~d pink*** être aux anges ; → **fancy** VI chatouiller N chatouillement *m*, chatouilles* *fpl* ◆ **he gave the child a ~** il a chatouillé l'enfant, il a fait des chatouilles* à l'enfant ◆ **to have a ~ in one's throat** avoir un chatouillement dans la gorge ; → **slap**

tickler * /ˈtɪkləʳ/ N *(Brit) (= question, problem)* colle* *f* ; *(= situation)* situation *f* délicate or épineuse

tickling /ˈtɪklɪŋ/ N chatouillement *m*, chatouille(s)* *f(pl)* ADJ *[sensation]* de chatouillement ; *[blanket]* qui chatouille ; *[cough]* d'irritation

ticklish /ˈtɪklɪʃ/, **tickly** * /ˈtɪklɪ/ ADJ 1 *[sensation]* de chatouillement ; *[blanket]* qui chatouille ; *[cough]* d'irritation ◆ **to be ~** *[person]* être chatouilleux 2 *(= touchy) [person, sb's pride]* chatouilleux ; *(= difficult) [situation, problem, task]* épineux, délicat

ticktack /ˈtɪktæk/ N *(Racing)* langage *m* gestuel *(des bookmakers)* COMP **ticktack man** N (pl **ticktack men**) *(Brit)* aide *m* de bookmaker

ticktock /ˈtɪkˈtɒk/ N *[of clock]* tic-tac *m*

ticky-tacky * /ˈtɪkɪ,tækɪ/ *(US)* ADJ *[building]* moche* N *(NonC) (= building material)* matériaux *mpl* de mauvaise qualité ; *(= goods)* pacotille *f*, camelote *f*

tidal /ˈtaɪdl/ ADJ *[forces, effects, waters, conditions, atlas]* des marées ; *[river, estuary]* à marées

COMP **tidal barrage** N barrage *m* coupant l'estuaire
tidal basin N bassin *m* de marée
tidal energy, tidal power N énergie *f* marémotrice, houille *f* bleue
tidal power station N usine *f* marémotrice
tidal wave N *(lit)* raz-de-marée *m inv* ; *(fig) [of people]* raz-de-marée *m inv* ; *(fig) [of enthusiasm, protest, emotion]* immense vague *f*

tidbit /ˈtɪdbɪt/ N *(esp US)* ⇒ **titbit**

tiddler * /ˈtɪdləʳ/ N *(Brit) (= stickleback)* épinoche *f* ; *(= tiny fish)* petit poisson *m* ; *(= small person)* demi-portion* *f* ; *(= small child)* mioche* *mf* ◆ **30 years ago the company was a mere ~** il y a 30 ans, cette entreprise n'était qu'un poids plume

tiddly * /ˈtɪdlɪ/ ADJ *(Brit)* 1 *(= drunk)* pompette*, éméché* ◆ **to get ~** s'enivrer 2 *(= small)* minuscule

tiddlywinks /ˈtɪdlɪwɪŋks/ N jeu *m* de puce

tide /taɪd/ N 1 *[of sea]* marée *f* ◆ **at high/low ~** à marée haute/basse ◆ **the ~ is on the turn** la mer est étale ◆ **the ~ turns at 3 o'clock** la marée commence à monter (*or* à descendre) à 3 heures

2 *(fig) [of crime, violence, racism]* vague *f* ◆ **an ever increasing ~ of crime** une vague de criminalité qui va en s'intensifiant ◆ **the ~ of nationalism is still running high in a number of republics** la vague nationaliste continue de déferler dans plusieurs républiques ◆ **the ~ has turned** la chance a tourné ◆ **to go with the ~** suivre le courant ◆ **to go against the ~** aller à contre-courant ◆ **the ~ of opinion seems overwhelmingly in his favour** l'opinion publique semble lui être en très grande partie favorable ◆ **the ~ of events** le cours or la marche des événements ◆ **the rising ~ of public impatience** l'exaspération grandissante et généralisée du public ; → **time**

VT ◆ **to ~ sb over a difficulty** dépanner qn lors d'une difficulté, tirer qn d'embarras provisoirement ◆ **it ~d him over till payday** ça lui a permis de tenir or ça l'a dépanné en attendant d'être payé

COMP **tide table** N horaire *m* des marées

► **tide over** VT SEP ◆ **to tide sb over** permettre à qn de tenir, dépanner qn

...tide /taɪd/ N *(in compounds)* saison *f* ◆ **Eastertide** (la saison de) Pâques *m* ; → **Whitsun(tide)**

tideland /ˈtaɪdlænd/ N laisse *f*

tideline /ˈtaɪdlaɪn/, **tidemark** /ˈtaɪdmɑːk/ N laisse *f* de haute mer, ligne *f* de (la) marée haute ; *(esp Brit hum: on neck, in bath)* ligne *f* de crasse

tidewater /ˈtaɪdwɔːtəʳ/ N *(Brit)* (eaux *fpl* de) marée *f* ; *(US)* côte *f*

tideway /ˈtaɪdweɪ/ N *(= channel)* chenal *m* de marée ; *(= tidal part of river)* section *f* (d'un cours d'eau) soumise à l'influence des marées ; *(= current)* flux *m*

tidily /ˈtaɪdɪlɪ/ ADV *[arrange, fold]* soigneusement, avec soin ; *[write]* proprement ◆ **she is always ~ dressed** elle est toujours correctement vêtue or toujours mise avec soin ◆ **try to dress more ~** tâche de t'habiller plus correctement or d'apporter plus de soin à ta tenue

tidiness /ˈtaɪdɪnɪs/ **N** (NonC) *[of room, drawer, desk, books]* ordre *m* ; *[of handwriting, schoolwork]* propreté *f* ◆ **what I like about him is his** ~ ce que j'aime chez lui, c'est son sens de l'ordre ◆ **the** ~ **of his appearance** sa tenue soignée

tidings /ˈtaɪdɪŋz/ **NPL** *(liter)* nouvelle(s) *f(pl)*

tidy /ˈtaɪdɪ/ **ADJ** [1] *(= neat) [house, room, drawer, desk]* bien rangé ; *[garden]* bien entretenu ; *[clothes, hair]* net, soigné ; *[appearance, schoolwork]* soigné ; *[handwriting, pile, stack]* net ; *[person] (in appearance)* soigné ; *(in character)* ordonné ◆ **to keep one's room** ~ avoir une chambre bien rangée, toujours bien ranger sa chambre ◆ **try to make your writing tidier** tâche d'écrire plus proprement ◆ **to look** ~ *[person]* avoir une apparence soignée ; *[room]* être bien rangé ◆ **to make o.s.** ~ remettre de l'ordre dans sa toilette ◆ **to have a** ~ **mind** avoir l'esprit méthodique

[2] *(* = sizeable) [sum, amount]* coquet*, joli* ; *[profit]* joli* ; *[income, speed]* bon ◆ **it cost a** ~ **bit** *or* **a** ~ **penny** ça a coûté une jolie* *or* coquette* somme ◆ **it took a** ~ **bit of his salary** ça lui a pris une bonne partie de son salaire

N vide-poches *m inv*

VT (also **tidy up**) *[+ drawer, cupboard, books, clothes]* ranger, mettre de l'ordre dans ; *[+ desk]* ranger, mettre de l'ordre sur ◆ **to** ~ **o.s. up** *[+ woman]* se refaire une beauté ◆ **to** ~ **(up) one's hair** arranger sa coiffure, remettre de l'ordre dans sa coiffure

COMP **tidy-out***, **tidy-up*** **N** ◆ **to have a ~-out** *or* **~-up** faire du rangement ◆ **to give sth a (good) ~-out** *or* **~-up** ranger qch à fond

► **tidy away** **VT SEP** *(Brit)* ranger

► **tidy out** **VT SEP** *[+ cupboard, drawer]* vider pour y mettre de l'ordre

N ◆ **tidy-out** * → **tidy**

► **tidy up** **VI** *(= tidy room etc)* (tout) ranger ; *(= tidy o.s.)* s'arranger

VT SEP ⇒ **tidy vt**

N ◆ **tidy-up** * → **tidy**

tie /taɪ/ **N** [1] *(= cord etc) [of garment, curtain]* attache *f* ; *[of shoe]* lacet *m*, cordon *m* ; *(fig = bond, link)* lien *m* ; *(= restriction)* entrave *f* ◆ **the ~s of blood** *(fig)* les liens *mpl* du sang ◆ **family ~s** *(= links)* liens *mpl* de famille *or* de parenté ; *(= responsibilities)* attaches *fpl* familiales ◆ **she finds the children a great** ~ avec les enfants elle n'est pas libre ; → **old**

[2] *(= necktie)* cravate *f* ; → **black, white**

[3] *(esp Sport) (= draw)* égalité *f* (de points) ; *(= drawn match)* match *m* nul ; *(= drawn race/competition)* course *f*/concours *m* dont les vainqueurs sont ex æquo ◆ **the match ended in a** ~, **the result (of the match) was a** ~ les deux équipes ont fait match nul ◆ **there was a** ~ **for second place** *(Scol, Sport etc)* il y avait deux ex æquo en seconde position ◆ **the election ended in a** ~ les candidats ont obtenu le même nombre de voix

[4] *(Sport = match)* match *m* de championnat ; → **cup**

[5] *(Mus)* liaison *f*

[6] *(Archit)* tirant *m*, entrait *m*

[7] *(US Rail)* traverse *f*

VT [1] *(= fasten)* attacher *(to* à) ; *[+ shoelace, necktie, rope]* attacher, nouer ; *[+ parcel]* attacher, ficeler ; *[+ ribbon]* nouer, faire un nœud à ; *[+ shoes]* lacer ◆ **to** ~ **sb's hands** *(lit)* attacher *or* lier les mains de qn ; *(fig)* lier les mains de *or* à qn ◆ **his hands are ~d** *(lit, fig)* il a les mains liées ◆ **to be ~d hand and foot** *(lit, fig)* avoir pieds et poings liés ◆ **to** ~ **sth in a bow, to** ~ **a bow in sth** faire un nœud avec qch ◆ **to** ~ **a knot in sth** faire un nœud à qch ◆ **to get ~d in knots** *[rope etc]* faire des nœuds ◆ **to get ~d in knots***, **to** ~ **o.s. in knots*** s'embrouiller ◆ **to** ~ **sb in knots*** embrouiller qn ◆ **to** ~ **the knot** * *(= get married)* se marier ; → **apron**

[2] *(= link)* lier *(to* à) ; *(= restrict)* restreindre, limiter ; *(Mus)* lier ◆ **the house is ~d to her husband's job** la maison est liée au travail de son mari ◆ **I'm ~d to the house/my desk all day** je suis retenu *or* cloué à la maison/mon bureau toute la journée ◆ **are we ~d to this plan?** sommes-nous obligés de nous en tenir à ce projet ?

VI [1] *[shoelace, necktie, rope]* se nouer

[2] *(= draw) (Sport etc)* faire match nul ; *(in competition)* être ex æquo ; *(in election)* obtenir le même nombre de voix ◆ **we ~d (with them) four-all** *(Sport)* nous avons fait match nul quatre partout ◆ **they ~d for first place** *(in race, exam, competition)* ils ont été premiers ex æquo

COMP **tie-break** **N** *(Tennis)* tie-break *m* ; *(in quiz/game)* question *f*/épreuve *f* subsidiaire

tie clasp, tie clip **N** fixe-cravate *m*

tie-dye **VT** nouer-lier-teindre *(méthode consistant à isoler certaines parties du tissu en le nouant ou en le liant)*

tie-in **N** *(= link)* lien *m*, rapport *m* *(with* avec) ; *(US Comm = sale)* vente *f* jumelée *or* par lots ; *(US Comm = article)* lot *m* **ADJ** *[sale]* jumelé

tie-on **ADJ** *[label]* à œillet

tie-rod **N** *[of building, vehicle]* tirant *m*

tie-tack **N** *(US)* épingle *f* de cravate

tie-up **N** *(= connection)* lien *m* *(with* avec ; *between* entre) ; *(Fin = merger)* fusion *f* *(with* avec ; *between* entre) ; *(Comm = joint venture between two companies)* accord *m*, entente *f*, association *f*, lien *m* *(with* avec ; *between* entre) ; *(US = stoppage)* interruption *f*, arrêt *m* ; *(= traffic)* embouteillage *m*

► **tie back** **VT SEP** *[+ curtains]* retenir par une embrasse, attacher sur les côtés ; *[+ hair]* nouer (en arrière)

► **tie down** **VT SEP** *[+ object, person, animal]* attacher ◆ **he didn't want to be ~d down** *(fig)* il ne voulait pas perdre sa liberté ◆ **to** ~ **sb down to a promise** obliger qn à tenir sa promesse ◆ **can you** ~ **him down to these conditions?** pouvez-vous l'astreindre à ces conditions ? ◆ **we can't** ~ **him down to a date/a price** nous n'arrivons pas à lui faire fixer une date/un prix ◆ **I shan't** ~ **you down to 6 o'clock** il n'est pas nécessaire que ce soit à 6 heures ◆ **I don't want to** ~ **myself down to going** je ne veux pas m'engager à y aller *or* me trouver contraint d'y aller

► **tie in** **VI** [1] *(= be linked)* être lié *(with* à) ◆ **it all ~s in with what they plan to do** tout est lié à ce qu'ils projettent de faire ◆ **this fact must** ~ **in somewhere** ce fait doit bien avoir un rapport quelque part

[2] *(= be consistent)* correspondre *(with* à), concorder, cadrer *(with* avec) ◆ **it doesn't** ~ **in with what I was told** ça ne correspond pas à *or* ça ne cadre pas avec *or* ça ne concorde pas avec ce que l'on m'a dit

VT SEP ◆ **I'm trying to tie that in with what he said** j'essaie de voir la liaison *or* le rapport entre ça et ce qu'il a dit ◆ **can you** ~ **the visit in with your trip to London?** pouvez-vous combiner la visite et *or* avec votre voyage à Londres ?

N ◆ **tie-in** → **tie**

► **tie on** **VT SEP** *[+ label etc]* attacher (avec une ficelle) ◆ **to** ~ **one on*̣** *(fig = get drunk)* se cuiter*̣, se soûler*

ADJ ◆ **tie-on** → **tie**

► **tie together** **VT SEP** *[+ objects, people]* attacher ensemble

► **tie up** **VI** *(Naut)* accoster

VT SEP [1] *(= bind) [+ parcel]* ficeler ; *[+ prisoner]* attacher, ligoter ; *(= tether) [+ boat, horse]* attacher *(to* à) ◆ **there are a lot of loose ends to** ~ **up** *(fig)* il y a encore beaucoup de points de détail à régler ◆ **to get (o.s.) all ~d up*** *(fig = muddled)* s'embrouiller, s'emmêler les pinceaux*

[2] *[+ capital, money]* immobiliser

[3] *(fig = conclude) [+ business deal]* conclure ◆ **it's all ~d up now** tout est réglé maintenant, c'est une chose réglée maintenant, nous avons *(or* il a *etc)* tout réglé

[4] *(* = occupy)* **he is ~d up all tomorrow** il est pris *or* occupé toute la journée de demain ◆ **he is ~d up with the manager** il est occupé avec le directeur ◆ **we are ~d up for months to come** nous avons un emploi du temps très chargé pour les mois qui viennent ◆ **he's rather ~d up with a girl in Dover** une jeune fille de Douvres l'accapare en ce moment

[5] *(= link)* **this company is ~d up with an American firm** cette compagnie a des liens avec *or* est liée à une firme américaine ◆ **his illness is ~d up* with the fact that his wife has left him** sa maladie est liée au fait que sa femme l'a quitté

[6] *(US = obstruct, hinder) [+ traffic]* obstruer, entraver ; *[+ production, sales]* arrêter momentanément ; *[+ project, programme]* entraver ◆ **to get ~d up** *[traffic]* se bloquer ; *[production, sales]* s'arrêter ; *[project, programme]* être suspendu

N ◆ **tie-up** → **tie**

tieback /ˈtaɪbæk/ **N** *(= cord, rope for curtain)* embrasse *f* ; *(= curtain itself)* rideau *m* bonne femme

tiebreaker /ˈtaɪbreɪkəʳ/ **N** ⇒ **tie-break** ; → **tie**

tied /taɪd/ **ADJ** [1] pt of **tie** [2] *(Sport = equal)* ◆ **to be** ~ être à égalité *or* ex æquo [3] *(Mus) [note]* lié [4] *(Brit)* ◆ ~ **cottage** logement *m* de fonction *(d'ouvrier agricole etc)* ◆ **it's a** ~ **house** *[pub]* ce pub ne vend qu'une marque de bière [5] *(Fin) [loan]* conditionnel [6] *(= restricted)* ◆ **she is very** ~ **by the children** elle est très prise par ses enfants ; see also **tie up**

tiepin /ˈtaɪpɪn/ **N** épingle *f* de cravate

tier /tɪəʳ/ **N** *(in stadium, amphitheatre)* gradin *m* ; *(= level)* niveau *m* ; *(= part of cake)* étage *m* ◆ **grand** ~ *(Theat)* balcon *m* ◆ **upper** ~ *(Theat)* seconde galerie *f* ◆ **to arrange in ~s** *(gen)* étager, disposer par étages ; *[+ seating]* disposer en gradins ◆ **to rise in ~s** s'étager ◆ **a three-~ system** un système à trois niveaux **VT** *[+ seats]* disposer en gradins ◆ **~ed seating** places *fpl* assises en gradins *or* en amphithéâtre ◆ **three-~ed cake** ≈ pièce *f* montée à trois étages ◆ **a ~ed skirt/dress** une jupe/robe à volants

Tierra del Fuego /tɪˌerədelˈfweɪgəʊ/ **N** Terre de Feu *f*

tiff /tɪf/ **N** prise *f* de bec*

tiffin † /ˈtɪfɪn/ **N** *(Brit)* repas *m* de midi

tig /tɪg/ **N** (jeu *m* du) chat *m*

tiger /ˈtaɪgəʳ/ **N** tigre *m* *(also fig)* ◆ **she fought like a** ~ elle s'est battue comme une tigresse ◆ **he has a** ~ **by the tail** il a déclenché quelque chose dont il n'est plus maître

COMP **tiger economy** **N** (also **Asian tiger economy**) tigre *m* asiatique

tiger lily **N** lis *m* tigré

tiger moth **N** écaille *f* *(papillon)*

tiger's-eye **N** œil *m* de tigre

tigereye /ˈtaɪgəraɪ/ **N** ⇒ **tiger's-eye** ; → **tiger**

tight /taɪt/ **ADJ** [1] *(= close-fitting) [clothes]* serré ; *[shoes, belt]* qui serre ◆ **too** ~ *[clothes, shoes, belt]* trop juste *or* serré ◆ **it should be fairly** ~ **over the hips** cela se porte relativement ajusté sur les hanches ; see also **skintight**

[2] *(= taut) [rope]* raide, tendu ; *[skin]* tendu ; *[knot, weave, knitting]* serré ◆ **to pull** ~ *[+ knot]* serrer ; *[+ string]* tirer sur ◆ **to stretch** ~ *[+ fabric, sheet]* tendre, tirer sur ; *[+ skin]* étirer ◆ **as** ~ **as a drum** tendu comme un tambour

◆ **a tight rein** ◆ **to hold** *or* **keep a** ~ **rein on sth** *(= watch closely)* surveiller qch de près ◆ **to hold** *or* **keep a** ~ **rein on sb, to keep sb under a** ~ **rein** *(= watch closely)* surveiller qn de près ; *(= be* *firm with)* tenir la bride haute *or* serrée à qn ◆ **to hold** *or* **keep a ~ rein on o.s.** se contenir

[3] *(= firm, fixed) [screw, nut, bolt, lid]* serré ; *[tap, drawer]* dur ; *[grip]* solide ◆ **screw the lid firmly on the jar to ensure a ~ seal** vissez bien le couvercle pour que le bocal soit fermé hermétiquement ◆ **to keep a ~ lid on** *(fig) [+ emotions]* contenir ; *[+ story]* mettre sous le boisseau ◆ **he clasped me to his chest in a ~ embrace** il m'a serré (fort) contre lui ◆ **to have** *or* **keep a ~ hold of sth** *(lit)* serrer fort qch ◆ **to keep a ~ hold of sb** *(lit)* bien tenir qn ◆ **to have a ~ grip on sth** *(fig)* avoir qch bien en main ◆ **to keep a ~ grip on sth** *(fig)* surveiller qch de près ; → **airtight, skintight, watertight**

[4] *(= tense, constricted) [voice, face]* tendu ; *[lips, throat]* serré ; *[mouth]* aux lèvres serrées ; *[smile]* pincé ; *[muscle]* tendu, contracté ; *[stomach]* noué ◆ **his mouth was set in a ~ line** il avait les lèvres serrées ◆ **there was a ~ feeling in his chest** *(from cold, infection)* il avait les bronches prises ; *(from emotion)* il avait la gorge serrée ◆ **it was a ~ squeeze in the lift** on était affreusement serrés dans l'ascenseur

[5] *(= compact) [group]* compact ◆ **to curl up in a ~ ball** se recroqueviller complètement ◆ **~ curls** boucles *fpl* serrées ; *(= close-knit)* ◆ **a ~ federation of states** une fédération d'États solidaires ◆ **a small, ~ knot of people** un petit groupe étroitement lié

[6] *(= strict) [schedule, budget]* serré ; *[restrictions, control]* strict, rigoureux ; *[security]* strict ◆ **it'll be a bit ~, but we should make it in time** ce sera un peu juste mais je crois que nous arriverons à temps ◆ **financially things are a bit ~** nous sommes un peu justes *

[7] *(= sharp) [bend, turn]* serré

[8] *(= close-fought) [competition]* serré ; *[match]* disputé

[9] *(= in short supply)* ◆ **to be ~** *[money, space]* manquer ; *[resources]* être limité ; *[credit]* être (res)serré ◆ **things were ~** l'argent manquait

[10] *(* = difficult) [situation]* difficile ◆ **to be in a ~ corner** *or* **spot** être dans le pétrin *

[11] *(* = drunk)* soûl * ◆ **to get ~** se soûler *

[12] *(* = stingy)* radin * ◆ **to be ~ with one's money** être près de ses sous *

[13] *(Mus *) [band]* bien synchro *

ADV *[hold, grasp]* bien, solidement ; *[squeeze]* très fort ; *[shut, fasten, tie, screw]* bien ; *[seal]* hermétiquement ◆ **don't fasten** *or* **tie it too ~** ne le serrez pas trop (fort) ◆ **to pack sth ~** bien emballer *or* empaqueter qch ◆ **packed ~ (with sth)** plein à craquer (de qch) ◆ **sit ~!** ne bouge pas ! ◆ **sleep ~!** dors bien !

♦ **to hold tight** s'accrocher ◆ **she held ~ to Bernard's hand** elle s'est accrochée à la main de Bernard ◆ **hold ~!** accroche-toi ! ◆ **all we can do is hold ~ and hope things get better** la seule chose que nous puissions faire c'est nous accrocher et espérer que les choses s'améliorent ◆ **she held ~ to her assertion** elle a maintenu ce qu'elle disait

NPL **tights** *(esp Brit)* collant(s) *m(pl)*

COMP **tight-arsed** ** *(Brit)*, **tight-assed** ** *(US)* ADJ *[person, behaviour]* coincé *

tight end N *(US Ftbl)* ailier *m*

tight-fisted ADJ avare, radin *, pingre

tight-fitting ADJ *[garment]* ajusté, collant ; *[lid, stopper]* qui ferme bien

tight-knit ADJ *(fig) [community]* très uni

tight-lipped ADJ ◆ **to maintain a ~-lipped silence, to be very ~-lipped** ne pas desserrer les lèvres *or* les dents *(about sth* au sujet de qch) ◆ **he stood there ~-lipped** *(from anger etc)* il se tenait là avec un air pincé ◆ **in ~-lipped disapproval** d'un air désapprobateur

tighten /'taɪtn/ VT (also **tighten up**) *[+ rope]* tendre ; *[+ coat, skirt, trousers]* ajuster, rétrécir ; *[+ screw, wheel, grasp, embrace]* resserrer ; *[+ legislation, restrictions, regulations, control]* renforcer ; *(Econ) [+ credit]* resserrer ◆ **to ~ one's belt** *(lit, fig)* se serrer la ceinture VI (also **tighten up**) *[rope]* se tendre, se raidir ; *[screw, wheel]* se resserrer ; *[restrictions, regulations]* être renforcé

► **tighten up** VI [1] ⇒ **tighten** vi [2] *(fig)* **to ~ up on security/immigration** devenir plus strict *or* sévère en matière de sécurité/d'immigration ◆ **the police are ~ing up on shoplifters** la police renforce la lutte contre les voleurs à l'étalage VT SEP → **tighten vt**

tightening /'taɪtnɪŋ/ N *[of muscles]* contraction *f* ; *[of screw, wheel, grasp, embrace]* resserrement *m* ; *[of security, control, legislation, restrictions, regulations]* renforcement *m* ; *[of sanctions, system]* durcissement *m* ◆ **the ~ of his grip on her hand** la pression plus forte qu'il a exercée sur sa main ◆ **~ of credit** *(Econ)* encadrement *m* du crédit

tightly /'taɪtlɪ/ ADV [1] *(= firmly) [close, bind, wrap]* bien ◆ **to hold a rope ~** bien tenir une corde ◆ **to hold sb's hand ~** serrer la main de qn ◆ **to hold sb ~** serrer qn contre soi ◆ **to hold a letter ~** serrer une lettre dans sa main ◆ **with ~-closed eyes** les paupières serrées ◆ **~ fitting** *[clothing]* moulant ◆ **~ stretched** *(= tautly)* (très) tendu ◆ **~ packed (with sth)** *(= densely) [bus, room, shelf]* plein à craquer (de qch) ◆ **the ~ packed crowds** les gens serrés comme des sardines * [2] *(= rigorously)* ◆ **to be ~ controlled** faire l'objet d'un contrôle rigoureux ◆ **~ knit** *[community]* très uni

tightness /'taɪtnɪs/ N *[of dress, trousers]* étroitesse *f* ; *[of screw, lid, drawer]* dureté *f* ; *[of restrictions, control]* rigueur *f*, sévérité *f* ◆ **he felt a ~ in his chest** il sentait sa gorge se serrer

tightrope /'taɪtrəʊp/ N corde *f* raide, fil *m* ◆ **to be on** *or* **walking a ~** *(fig)* être *or* marcher sur la corde raide COMP **tightrope walker** N funambule *mf*

tightwad ** /'taɪtwɒd/ N *(US)* radin(e) * *m(f)*, grippe-sou *m*

tigress /'taɪgrɪs/ N tigresse *f*

Tigris /'taɪgrɪs/ N Tigre *m*

tikka /'ti:kə/ N ◆ **chicken/lamb ~** poulet *m*/mouton *m* tikka

tilde /'tɪldə/ N tilde *m*

tile /taɪl/ N *(on roof)* tuile *f* ; *(on floor, wall, fireplace)* carreau *m* ◆ **to be out on the ~s** *, **to spend** *or* **have a night on the ~s** * *(Brit)* faire la noce * *or* la bombe * ◆ **he's got a ~ loose** ** il lui manque une case * VT *[+ roof]* couvrir de tuiles ; *[+ floor, wall, fireplace]* carreler ◆ **~d** *[roof]* en tuiles ; *[floor, room etc]* carrelé

tiling /'taɪlɪŋ/ N [1] *(= tiles collectively) [of roof]* tuiles *fpl*, *[of floor, wall]* carrelage *m*, carreaux *mpl* [2] *(= activity, skill) [of roof]* pose *f* des tuiles ; *[of floor, wall etc]* carrelage *m*

till[1] /tɪl/ ⇒ **until**

till[2] /tɪl/ N caisse *f* (enregistreuse) ; *(old-fashioned type)* tiroir-caisse *m* ; *(= takings)* caisse *f* ◆ **pay at the ~** payez à la caisse ◆ **to be** *or* **get caught** *or* **found with one's hand** *or* **fingers in the ~** *(fig)* être pris sur le fait *or* en flagrant délit

till[3] /tɪl/ VT *(Agr)* labourer

tillage /'tɪlɪdʒ/ N *(= activity)* labour *m*, labourage *m* ; *(= land)* labour *m*, guéret *m*

tiller[1] /'tɪlə^r/ N *(Agr)* laboureur *m*

tiller[2] /'tɪlə^r/ N *(Naut)* barre *f (du gouvernail)*

tilt /tɪlt/ N [1] *(= tip, slope)* inclinaison *f* ◆ **it has a ~ to it, it's on a** *or* **the ~** c'est incliné, ça penche [2] *(Hist) (= contest)* joute *f* ; *(= thrust)* coup *m* de lance ◆ **to have a ~ at …** *(fig)* décocher des pointes à … ◆ **(at) full ~** à toute vitesse, à fond de train [3] *(fig = inclination)* nouvelle orientation *f (towards sth* vers qch) VT (also **tilt over**) *[+ object, one's head]* pencher, incliner ; *[+ backrest]* incliner ◆ **to ~ one's hat over one's eyes** rabattre son chapeau sur les yeux ◆ **to ~ one's chair (back)** se balancer sur sa chaise VI [1] *(gen)* s'incliner ; (also **tilt over**) pencher, être incliné [2] *(Hist)* jouter *(at* contre) → **windmill**

COMP **tilting train** N train *m* pendulaire

tilt-top table N table *f* à plateau inclinable

tilted /'tɪltɪd/ ADJ penché, incliné

tilth /tɪlθ/ N *(= soil)* couche *f* arable ; *(= tilling)* labourage *m*

timber /'tɪmbə^r/ N [1] *(NonC) (= wood)* bois *m* d'œuvre, bois *m* de construction ; *(= trees collectively)* arbres *mpl*, bois *m* ◆ **~!** attention (à l'arbre qui tombe) !, gare ! ◆ **land under ~** futaie *f*, terre *f* boisée *(pour l'abattage)* [2] *(= beam)* madrier *m*, poutre *f* ; *(Naut)* membrure *f* VT *[+ tunnel etc]* boiser ◆ **~ed** *[house]* en bois ; *[land, hillside]* boisé ; → **half**

COMP *[fence etc]* en bois

timber-framed ADJ à charpente de bois

timber line N limite *f* de la forêt

timber merchant N *(Brit)* marchand *m* de bois, négociant *m* en bois

timber wolf N loup *m* gris

timbering /'tɪmbərɪŋ/ N *(NonC)* boisage *m*

timberland /'tɪmbəlænd/ N *(NonC)* exploitation *f* forestière

timberyard /'tɪmbəjɑ:d/ N *(Brit)* dépôt *m* de bois

timbre /'tæmbrə, 'tɪmbə^r/ N *(gen, also Phon)* timbre *m*

timbrel /'tɪmbrəl/ N tambourin *m*

Timbuktu /,tɪmbʌk'tu:/ N *(lit, fig)* Tombouctou *m*

time /taɪm/

1 NOUN	3 COMPOUNDS
2 TRANSITIVE VERB	

1 - NOUN

For **a long time** see **long**. For **at the same time** see **same**.

[1] gen temps *m* ◆ **~ and space** le temps et l'espace ◆ **~ flies** le temps passe vite *or* file ◆ **~ will show if …** l'avenir dira si …, on saura avec le temps si … ◆ **in ~, with ~, as ~ goes** (*or* **went**) **by** avec le temps, à la longue ◆ **I've enough ~** *or* **I have the ~ to go there** j'ai le temps d'y aller ◆ **we've got plenty of ~, we've all the ~ in the world** nous avons tout notre temps ◆ **have you got ~ to wait for me?** est-ce que tu as le temps de m'attendre ? ◆ **he spent all/half his ~ reading** il passait tout son temps/la moitié de son temps à lire ◆ **we mustn't lose any ~** il ne faut pas perdre de temps ◆ **I had to stand for part** *or* **some of the ~** j'ai dû rester debout une partie du temps ◆ **it works okay some of the ~** ça marche parfois *or* quelquefois ◆ **he spends the best part of his ~ in London** il passe la plus grande partie de son temps *or* le plus clair de son temps à Londres ◆ **half the ~ * she's drunk** la moitié du temps elle est ivre ◆ **at this point in ~** à l'heure qu'il est, en ce moment ◆ **from ~ out of mind** de temps immémorial ◆ **my ~ is my own** mon temps m'appartient ◆ **free ~, ~ off** temps libre ◆ **he'll tell you in his own good ~** il vous le dira quand bon lui semblera ◆ **in your own ~** en prenant votre temps ◆ **he was working against ~ to finish it** il travaillait d'arrache-pied pour le terminer à temps ◆ **it is only a matter** *or* **question of ~** ce n'est qu'une question de temps ◆ **~ will tell** l'avenir le dira ◆ **~ is money** *(Prov)* le temps c'est de l'argent *(Prov)* ◆ **there's a ~ and a place for everything** *(Prov)* il y a un temps pour tout *(Prov)* ◆ **~ and tide wait for no man** *(Prov)* on ne peut pas arrêter le temps

♦ **all the time** (= *always*) tout le temps ; (= *all along*) depuis le début ♦ **I have to be on my guard all the** ~ je dois tout le temps être sur mes gardes ♦ **the letter was in my pocket all the** ~ la lettre était dans ma poche depuis le début ♦ **all the ~ he knew who had done it** il savait depuis le début qui avait fait le coup

♦ *number* + **at a time** ♦ **three at a** ~ trois par trois, trois à la fois ; (*stairs, steps*) trois à trois ♦ **one at a** ~ un par un

♦ **at times** de temps en temps, parfois

♦ **for all time** pour toujours

♦ **for the time being** pour l'instant

♦ **in good time** (= *with time to spare*) en avance ♦ **he arrived in good ~ for the start of the match** il est arrivé en avance pour le début du match ♦ **let me know in good** ~ prévenez-moi suffisamment à l'avance ♦ **all in good ~!** chaque chose en son temps !

♦ **to make time to do sth** trouver le temps de faire qch ♦ **however busy you are, you must make ~ to relax** même si vous êtes très pris, il est important que vous trouviez le temps de vous détendre

♦ **to take + time** ♦ **it takes ~ to change people's ideas** ça prend du temps de faire évoluer les mentalités ♦ **things take ~ to change** les choses ne changent pas du jour au lendemain ♦ **it took me a lot of ~ to prepare this** j'ai mis beaucoup de temps à préparer ça ♦ **take your** ~ prenez votre temps ♦ **take your ~ over it!** mettez-y le temps qu'il faudra ! ♦ **it took me all my ~ to convince her** j'ai eu toutes les peines du monde à la convaincre

♦ **to take time out to do sth** (*gen*) trouver le temps de faire qch ; (*during studies*) interrompre ses études pour faire qch ♦ **some women managers can't afford to take ~ out to have a baby** certaines femmes cadres ne peuvent pas se permettre d'interrompre leur carrière pour avoir un enfant

♦ **to find/have** *etc* **+ time for** ♦ **I can't find ~ for the garden** je n'arrive pas à trouver le temps de m'occuper du jardin ♦ **I've no ~ for that sort of thing** (*lit*) je n'ai pas le temps de faire ce genre de chose ; (*fig*) je ne supporte pas ce genre de choses ♦ **I've no ~ for people like him** je ne supporte pas les types* comme lui ♦ **I've got a lot of ~* for him** je trouve que c'est un type très bien* ♦ **it didn't leave him much ~ for sleeping** ça ne lui a guère laissé le temps de dormir

2 [= period, length of time] ♦ **for a** ~ pendant un (certain) temps ♦ **what a (long) ~ you've been!** vous y avez mis le temps !, il vous en a fallu du temps ! ♦ **he did it in half the ~ it took you** il l'a fait deux fois plus vite *or* en deux fois moins de temps que vous ♦ **he is coming in two weeks'** ~ il vient dans deux semaines ♦ **within the agreed** ~ (*frm*) dans les délais convenus ♦ **to buy sth on** ~ (*US*) acheter qch à tempérament ♦ **what ~ did he do it in?** (*Sport*) il a fait quel temps ? ♦ **the winner's ~ was 12 seconds** le temps du gagnant était de 12 secondes ♦ **to make** ~ (*US = hurry*) se dépêcher ♦ **he's making ~ with her**‡ (*US*) il la drague*

♦ **a short time** peu de temps ♦ **a short ~ later** peu (de temps) après ♦ **for a short ~ we thought that ...** pendant un moment nous avons pensé que ... ♦ **in a short ~ all the flowers had gone** peu de temps après toutes les fleurs étaient fanées

♦ **in + no time** ♦ **in no ~ at all, in next to no ~, in less than no** ~ en un rien de temps, en moins de deux*

♦ **some + time** ♦ **I waited for some** ~ j'ai attendu assez longtemps *or* pas mal de temps* ♦ **I waited for some considerable** ~ j'ai attendu très longtemps ♦ **after some little** ~ au bout d'un certain temps ♦ **some ~ ago** il y a déjà un certain temps ♦ **that was some ~ ago** ça fait longtemps de cela ♦ **it won't be ready for some ~ (yet)** ce ne sera pas prêt avant un certain temps ♦ **some ~ before the war** quelque temps avant la guerre ♦ **some ~ next year/in 2003** dans le courant de l'année prochaine/de l'année 2003

3 [= period worked] ♦ **to work full** ~ travailler à plein temps *or* à temps plein ; see also **full** ♦ **we get paid ~ and a half on Saturdays** le samedi, nous sommes payés une fois et demie le tarif normal ♦ **Sunday working is paid at double** ~ les heures du dimanche sont payées double ♦ **in the firm's ~, in company** ~ pendant les heures de service ♦ **in** *or* (*US*) **on one's own** ~ après les heures de service

4 [= day, era] temps *m* ♦ **in Gladstone's** ~ du temps de Gladstone ♦ **~ was when one could ...** il fut un temps où l'on pouvait ... ♦ **in my ~ it was all different** de mon temps c'était complètement différent ♦ **he is ahead of** *or* **in advance of** *or* **before his ~, he was born before his** ~ il est en avance sur son temps ♦ **to keep up with** *or* **move with the ~s** [*person*] vivre avec son temps ; [*company, institution*] (savoir) évoluer ♦ **to be behind the ~s** être vieux jeu* *inv* ♦ **I've seen some strange things in my** ~ j'ai vu des choses étranges dans ma vie ♦ **that was before my** ~ (= *before I was born*) je n'étais pas encore né, c'était avant ma naissance ; (= *before I came here*) je n'étais pas encore là ♦ **to die before one's** ~ mourir avant l'âge ♦ **in ~(s) of peace** en temps de paix ♦ **in medieval ~s** à l'époque médiévale ♦ **~s are hard** les temps sont durs ♦ **those were tough ~s** la vie n'était pas facile en ce temps-là ♦ **the ~s we live in** l'époque où nous vivons ♦ **it was a difficult ~ for all of us** cela a été une période difficile pour nous tous

5 [= experience] **they lived through some terrible ~s in the war** ils ont connu des moments terribles pendant la guerre ♦ **to have a poor** *or* **rough** *or* **bad** *or* **thin** *or* **tough* ~ (of it)** en voir de dures* ♦ **what great ~s we've had!** c'était le bon temps ! ♦ **to have a good ~ (of it)** bien s'amuser ♦ **to have the ~ of one's life** s'amuser follement*

6 [by clock] heure *f* ♦ **what is the ~?, what ~ is it?** quelle heure est-il ? ♦ **what ~ do you make it?, what do you make the ~?** quelle heure avez-vous ? ♦ **what ~ is he arriving?** à quelle heure est-ce qu'il arrive ? ♦ **have you got the right ~?** est-ce que vous avez l'heure exacte *or* juste ? ♦ **the ~ is 4.30** il est 4 heures et demie ♦ **your ~ is up** (*in exam, prison visit etc*) c'est l'heure ; (*in game*) votre temps est écoulé ♦ **it sent the president a clear message: your ~ is up** (*fig*) pour le Président, le message était clair : vos jours sont comptés ♦ **he looked at the** ~ il a regardé l'heure ♦ **that watch keeps good** ~ cette montre est toujours à l'heure ♦ **at this ~ of (the) night** à cette heure de la nuit ♦ **at any ~ of the day or night** à n'importe quelle heure du jour ou de la nuit ♦ **at any ~ during school hours** pendant les heures d'ouverture de l'école ♦ **open at all ~s** ouvert à toute heure ♦ **~ gentlemen please!** (*Brit: in pub*) on ferme ! ♦ **to call** ~ (*Brit: in pub*) annoncer la fermeture ♦ **to call ~ on sth** (*Brit = put an end to sth*) mettre un terme à qch ♦ **it's midnight by Eastern** ~ (*US*) il est minuit, heure de la côte est ♦ **it was 6 o'clock Paris** ~ il était 6 heures, heure de Paris ♦ **it's ~ for lunch** c'est l'heure du déjeuner ♦ **it's ~ to go** c'est l'heure de partir, il est temps de partir ♦ **it's ~ I was going, it's ~ for me to go** il est temps que j'y aille ♦ **it's (about) ~ somebody taught him a lesson** il est grand temps que quelqu'un lui donne *subj* une leçon ♦ **~!** (*Tennis*) reprise !

♦ *preposition* **+ time** ♦ **ahead of** ~ en avance ♦ **(and) about ~ too!** ce n'est pas trop tôt ! ♦ **not before ~!** (*Brit*) ce n'est pas trop tôt ! ♦ **behind** ~ en retard ♦ **just in ~ (for sth/to do sth)** juste à temps (pour qch/pour faire qch) ♦ **on** ~ à l'heure ♦ **the trains are on** ~ *or* **up to ~, the trains are running to** ~ les trains sont à l'heure

♦ **the time of day** ♦ **to pass the ~ of day** bavarder un peu, échanger quelques mots (*with sb* avec qn) ♦ **I wouldn't give him the ~ of day** je ne lui adresserais pas la parole

7 [= moment, point of time] moment *m* ♦ **there are ~s when I could hit him** il y a des moments où je pourrais le gifler ♦ **when the ~ comes** quand le moment viendra ♦ **when the ~ is right** quand le moment sera venu ♦ **his ~ is drawing near** *or* **approaching** son heure *or* sa fin est proche ♦ **his ~ has come** son heure est venue ♦ **to choose one's** ~ choisir son moment ♦ **come (at) any** ~ venez quand vous voudrez ♦ **he may come (at) any** ~ il peut arriver d'un moment à l'autre ♦ **it may happen any ~ now** cela peut arriver d'un moment à l'autre ♦ **at the** *or* **that** ~ à ce moment-là ♦ **at this** ~ en ce moment ♦ **at the present** ~ en ce moment, actuellement ♦ **at this particular** ~ à ce moment précis ♦ **at (any) one** ~ à un moment donné ♦ **at all ~s** à tous moments ♦ **I could hit him at ~s** il y a des moments où je pourrais le gifler ♦ **I have at no ~ said that** je n'ai jamais dit cela ♦ **at ~s** par moments ♦ **he came at a very inconvenient** ~ il est arrivé au mauvais moment, il a mal choisi son moment ♦ **(in) between ~s** entre-temps ♦ **by the ~ I had finished, it was dark** le temps que je termine *subj* il faisait nuit ♦ **by this** *or* **that ~ she was exhausted** elle était alors épuisée ♦ **you must be cold by this** ~ vous devez avoir froid maintenant ♦ **by this ~ next year** l'année prochaine à la même époque ♦ **this is no** *or* **not the ~ for quarrelling** ce n'est pas le moment de se disputer ♦ **from ~ to** ~ de temps en temps ♦ **from that** ~ *or* **this ~ on he ...** à partir de ce moment il ... ♦ **from this ~ on I shall do what you tell me** désormais *or* dorénavant je ferai ce que tu me diras ♦ **some ~s ... at other ~s** des fois ... des fois ♦ **at this ~ of year** à cette époque de l'année ♦ **this ~ tomorrow** demain à cette heure-ci ♦ **this ~ last year** l'année dernière à cette époque-ci ♦ **this ~ last week** il y a exactement une semaine ♦ **now's the ~ to do it** c'est le moment de le faire ♦ **the ~ has come for us to leave** il est temps que nous partions *subj* ♦ **the ~ has come to decide ...** il est temps de décider ... ♦ **now's your** *or* **the ~ to tell him** c'est maintenant que vous devriez le lui dire

8 [= occasion] fois *f* ♦ **this** ~ cette fois ♦ **(the) next ~ you come** la prochaine fois que vous viendrez ♦ **every** *or* **each** ~ chaque fois ♦ **several ~s** plusieurs fois ♦ **at various ~s in the past** plusieurs fois déjà ♦ **at other ~s** en d'autres occasions ♦ **~ after ~, ~s without number, ~ and (~) again** maintes et maintes fois ♦ **(the) last** ~ la dernière fois ♦ **the previous ~, the ~ before** la fois d'avant ♦ **come back some other** ~ revenez une autre fois ♦ **the ~s I've told him that!** je le lui ai dit je ne sais combien de fois ! ♦ **the ~s I've wished that ...** combien de fois n'ai-je souhaité que ... ♦ **some ~ or other I'll do it** je le ferai un jour ou l'autre ♦ **I remember the ~ when he told me about it** je me rappelle le jour où il me l'a dit ♦ **it costs £3 a ~ to do a load of washing** ça coûte trois livres pour faire une lessive ♦ **one at a** ~ un(e) par un(e) ♦ **for weeks at a** ~ pendant des semaines entières

9 [multiplying] fois *f* ♦ **two ~s three is six** deux fois trois (font) six ♦ **ten ~s as big as ..., ten ~s the size of ...** dix fois plus grand que ... ♦ **it's worth ten ~s as much** ça vaut dix fois plus ; → **times**

10 [Mus etc] mesure *f* ♦ **in** ~ en mesure (*to, with* avec) ♦ **in ~ to the music** en mesure avec la musique ♦ **to be out of** ~ ne pas être en

mesure (*with* avec) ◆ **to keep** ~ rester en mesure

2 - TRANSITIVE VERB

1 = choose time of *[+ visit]* choisir le moment de ◆ **it was ~d to begin at ...** le commencement était prévu pour ... ◆ **you ~d that perfectly!** c'est tombé à point nommé !, vous ne pouviez pas mieux choisir votre moment ! ◆ **well-~d** *[remark, entrance]* tout à fait opportun, qui tombe à point nommé ; *[stroke]* exécuté avec un bon timing ◆ **the invasion was carefully ~d** l'invasion a été soigneusement minutée ◆ **they are timing the bomb alerts to cause maximum disruption** ils font en sorte que ces alertes à la bombe provoquent le maximum de perturbations

2 = count time of *[+ race, runner, worker etc]* chronométrer ; *[+ programme, ceremony, piece of work]* minuter ◆ **to ~ sb over 1,000 metres** chronométrer (le temps de) qn sur 1 000 mètres ◆ **~ how long it takes you** notez le temps qu'il vous faut pour le faire ◆ **to ~ an egg** minuter la cuisson d'un œuf

3 - COMPOUNDS

time and motion study N *(in workplace)* étude *f* des cadences
time bomb N bombe *f* à retardement
time capsule N capsule *f* témoin *(devant servir de document historique)*
time card N *(for clocking in)* carte *f* de pointage
time check N *(Rad)* rappel *m* de l'heure
time clock N *(for clocking in = machine itself)* pointeuse *f*
time-consuming ADJ qui prend beaucoup de temps
time delay N délai *m*
time-delay ADJ *[mechanism, safe]* à délai d'ouverture
time deposit N *(US Fin)* dépôt *m* à terme
time difference N décalage *m* horaire
time discount N *(US Comm)* remise *f* pour paiement anticipé
time draft N *(US Fin)* effet *m* à terme
time-expired ADJ *[product]* périmé
time exposure N *(Phot)* temps *m* de pose
time-filler N façon *f* de tuer le temps
time frame N calendrier *m* ◆ **to set a ~ frame** fixer un calendrier ◆ **there was no ~ frame for military action** aucune date précise n'était fixée pour l'intervention militaire ◆ **I cannot give a ~ frame for a return of democratic rule** je ne peux pas spécifier de délai pour le retour à la démocratie ◆ **the ~ frame within which all this occurred was from September 1985 to March 1986** tout ceci s'est produit dans la période comprise entre septembre 1985 et mars 1986
time fuse N détonateur *m* à retardement
time-honoured ADJ ◆ **a ~-honoured tradition** une tradition ancienne *or* vénérable
time-lag N *(between events)* décalage *m*, retard *m* ; *(between countries)* décalage *m* horaire
time-lapse photography N *(Cine)* accéléré *m*
time limit N *(= restricted period)* limite *f* de temps ; *(for abortion)* délai *m* légal ; *(Jur)* délai *m* de forclusion ; *(= deadline)* date *f* limite ◆ **to put** *or* **set a ~ limit on sth** fixer une limite de temps *or* un délai pour qch ◆ **within the ~ limit** dans les délais (impartis) ◆ **without a ~ limit** sans limitation de temps
time loan N *(US Fin)* emprunt *m* à terme
time lock N fermeture *f* commandée par une minuterie
time machine N *(Sci Fi)* machine *f* à remonter le temps
time-out N *(esp US) (Sport)* temps *m* mort ; *(Chess)* temps *m* de repos
time-saver N ◆ **it is a great ~-saver** ça fait gagner beaucoup de temps
time-saving ADJ qui fait gagner du temps N économie *f or* gain *m* de temps
time scale N → **timescale**
time-served ADJ *[tradesman]* qui a fait ses preuves, expérimenté
time-server N *(pej)* opportuniste *mf* ◆ **he's a ~-server** il attend de partir
time-serving ADJ *(pej)* opportuniste N opportunisme *m*
time-share VT *(Comput)* utiliser *or* exploiter en temps partagé ; *[+ holiday home]* avoir en multipropriété N maison *f* (*or* appartement *m*) en multipropriété
time-sharing N *(Comput)* (exploitation *f or* travail *m* en) temps *m* partagé ; *[of holiday home]* multipropriété *f*
time sheet N *(Ind etc)* feuille *f* de présence
time signal N *(Rad)* signal *m* horaire
time signature N *(Mus)* indication *f* de la mesure
time slice N *(Comput)* tranche *f* de temps
time span N période *f* de temps
time study N ⇒ **time and motion study**
time switch N *[of electrical apparatus]* minuteur *m* ; *(for lighting)* minuterie *f*
time travel N *(Sci Fi)* voyage *m* dans le temps
time trial N *(Motor Racing, Cycling)* course *f* contre la montre, contre-la-montre *m inv*
time warp N distorsion *f* spatiotemporelle ◆ **it's like going into** *or* **living in a ~ warp** on a l'impression d'avoir fait un bond en arrière (*or* en avant) dans le temps *or* d'avoir fait un bond dans le passé (*or* le futur)
time-waster N *(pej)* ◆ **to be a ~-waster** *[person]* faire perdre du temps ; *[activity]* être une perte de temps ◆ **"no time wasters"** *(in advert)* "pas sérieux s'abstenir"
time-wasting ADJ qui fait perdre du temps N perte *f* de temps
time zone N fuseau *m* horaire

timekeeper /'taɪmkiːpəʳ/ N *(= watch)* montre *f* ; *(= stopwatch)* chronomètre *m* ; *(Sport = official)* chronométreur *m*, -euse *f* officiel(le) ◆ **to be a good ~** *[person]* être toujours à l'heure

timekeeping /'taɪmkiːpɪŋ/ N *(Sport)* chronométrage *m* ◆ **I'm trying to improve my ~** *(at work)* j'essaie d'être plus ponctuel

timeless /'taɪmlɪs/ ADJ *[quality, appeal]* intemporel ; *[beauty]* intemporel, éternel

timeline /'taɪmlaɪn/ N tableau *m* chronologique

timeliness /'taɪmlɪnɪs/ N *(NonC)* à-propos *m*, opportunité *f*

timely /'taɪmlɪ/ ADJ *[reminder, arrival]* opportun ; *[intervention]* opportun, qui tombe à point nommé ; *[event, warning]* qui tombe à point nommé

timepiece /'taɪmpiːs/ N *(= watch)* montre *f* ; *(= clock)* horloge *f*

timer /'taɪməʳ/ N *(Culin etc)* minuteur *m* ; *(with sand in it)* sablier *m* ; *(on machine, electrical device etc)* minuteur *m* ; *[of car engine]* distributeur *m* d'allumage ; → **old**

times * /taɪmz/ VT *(= multiply)* multiplier

timescale /'taɪmskeɪl/ N période *f* ◆ **on a two-year time scale** sur une période de deux ans ◆ **our ~ for this project is 10 to 15 years** nous nous situons dans une perspective de 10 à 15 ans ◆ **the time-scale of the government's plan** le calendrier d'exécution du projet gouvernemental ◆ **we cannot put a ~ on his recovery** nous ne pouvons pas dire combien de temps prendra sa guérison

timetable /'taɪmteɪbl/ N *(Rail etc)* (indicateur *m*) horaire *m* ; *(Scol)* emploi *m* du temps ; *(Ftbl:* also **fixtures timetable**) calendrier *m* des rencontres VT *(Brit) [+ visit, course]* établir un emploi du temps pour

timeworn /'taɪmwɔːn/ ADJ *[stones etc]* usé par le temps ; *[idea]* rebattu

timid /'tɪmɪd/ ADJ *(= shy)* timide ; *(= unadventurous)* timoré, craintif ; *(= cowardly)* peureux

timidity /tɪ'mɪdɪtɪ/ N *(NonC) (= shyness)* timidité *f* ; *(= unadventurousness)* caractère *m* timoré *or* craintif ; *(= cowardice)* caractère *m* peureux

timidly /'tɪmɪdlɪ/ ADV *(= shyly)* timidement ; *(= unadventurously)* craintivement ; *(= in cowardly way)* peureusement

timidness /'tɪmɪdnɪs/ N ⇒ **timidity**

timing /'taɪmɪŋ/ N 1 *[of musician etc]* sens *m* du rythme ◆ **a good comedian depends on his (sense of) ~** un bon comédien doit minuter très précisément son débit ◆ **the actors' ~ was excellent throughout the play** le minutage des acteurs était excellent tout au long de la pièce ◆ **~ is very important in formation flying** la synchronisation est capitale dans les vols en formation ◆ **the ~ of the demonstration** le moment choisi de la manifestation ◆ **he arrived just when we were sitting down to the table: I had to admire his ~** il est arrivé au moment précis où l'on se mettait à table : il ne pouvait pas tomber plus mal ◆ **when cooking fish, ~ is crucial** lorsqu'on cuisine du poisson, il faut absolument minuter la cuisson ◆ **they had talked about having children but the ~ was always wrong** ils avaient évoqué la possibilité d'avoir des enfants mais ce n'était jamais le bon moment
2 *[of car engine]* réglage *m* de l'allumage ◆ **to set the ~** régler l'allumage
3 *[of process, work, sportsman]* chronométrage *m*
COMP **timing device, timing mechanism** N *[of bomb etc]* mouvement *m* d'horlogerie ; *[of electrical apparatus]* minuteur *m*

Timor /'tiːmɔːʳ, 'taɪmɔːʳ/ N Timor ◆ **in ~** à Timor

Timorese /,tɪmə'riːz/ ADJ timorais N Timorais(e) *m(f)* ; see also **East Timorese;** → **east**

timorous /'tɪmərəs/ ADJ *[person]* timoré, craintif ; *[reform]* frileux, timide ; *[speech]* timoré

timorously /'tɪmərəslɪ/ ADV craintivement

Timothy /'tɪməθɪ/ N Timothée *m*

timothy /'tɪməθɪ/ N *(Bot)* fléole *f* des prés

timpani /'tɪmpənɪ/ NPL timbales *fpl*

timpanist /'tɪmpənɪst/ N timbalier *m*

tin /tɪn/ N 1 *(NonC)* étain *m* ; *(= tin plate)* fer-blanc *m*
2 *(esp Brit = can)* boîte *f* (en fer-blanc) ◆ **~ of salmon** boîte *f* de saumon
3 *(for storage)* boîte *f* (de fer) ◆ **cake ~** boîte *f* à gâteaux
4 *(Brit Culin) (= mould: for cakes etc)* moule *m* ; *(= dish: for meat etc)* plat *m* ◆ **cake ~** moule *m* à gâteau ◆ **meat** *or* **roasting ~** plat *m* à rôtir
VT 1 *(= put in tins) [+ food etc]* mettre en boîte(s) *or* en conserve ; see also **tinned**
2 *(= coat with tin)* étamer
COMP *(= made of tin)* en étain, d'étain ; *(= made of tin plate)* en *or* de fer-blanc
tin can N boîte *f* (en fer-blanc)
tin ear * N *(Mus)* ◆ **he has a ~ ear** il n'a pas d'oreille
tin god N *(fig)* ◆ **(little) ~ god** idole *f* de pacotille
tin hat N casque *m*
tin lizzie * N *(= car)* vieille guimbarde * *f*
tin mine N mine *f* d'étain
tin-opener N *(Brit)* ouvre-boîte *m*
Tin Pan Alley N *(Mus, fig)* le monde du showbiz
tin plate N *(NonC)* fer-blanc *m*
tin soldier N soldat *m* de plomb
tin whistle N flûtiau *m*

tincture /'tɪŋktʃəʳ/ N *(Pharm)* teinture *f* ; *(fig)* nuance *f*, teinte *f* ◆ **~ of iodine** teinture *f* d'iode
VT *(lit, fig)* teinter *(with* de)

tinder /ˈtɪndəʳ/ **N** (*NonC, in tinderbox*) amadou *m* ; (*= small sticks*) petit bois *m NonC* ◆ **as dry as ~** sec (sèche *f*) comme de l'amadou

tinderbox /ˈtɪndəbɒks/ **N** briquet *m* (à amadou) ; (*fig: esp Pol*) poudrière *f*

tine /taɪn/ **N** [*of fork*] dent *f*, fourchon *m* ; [*of antler*] andouiller *m*

tinfoil /ˈtɪnfɔɪl/ **N** (*NonC*) papier *m* (d')aluminium, papier *m* alu *

ting /tɪŋ/ **N** tintement *m* **VI** tinter **VT** faire tinter **COMP** **ting-a-ling N** [*of telephone, doorbell*] dring *m* ; [*of handbell, tiny bells*] drelin *m*

tinge /tɪndʒ/ (*lit, fig*) **N** teinte *f*, nuance *f* **VT** teinter (*with* de) ◆ **our happiness was ~d with regret** notre bonheur était mêlé de regret

tingle /ˈtɪŋgl/ **VI** (*= prickle*) picoter, fourmiller ; (*fig = thrill*) vibrer, frissonner ◆ **her face was tingling** le visage lui picotait *or* lui cuisait ◆ **her cheeks were tingling with cold** le froid lui piquait *or* lui brûlait des joues ◆ **my fingers are tingling** j'ai des picotements *or* des fourmis dans les doigts ◆ **the toothpaste makes my tongue ~** le dentifrice me pique la langue ◆ **he was tingling with impatience** il brûlait d'impatience **N** (*= sensation*) picotement *m*, fourmillement *m* ; (*= thrill*) frisson *m* ◆ **to have a ~ in one's ears** (*= sound*) avoir les oreilles qui tintent

tingling /ˈtɪŋglɪŋ/ **N** (*NonC*) ⇒ **tingle noun** **ADJ** [*sensation, effect*] de picotement, de fourmillement ◆ **to have ~ fingers** avoir des picotements *or* des fourmillements dans les doigts

tingly /ˈtɪŋglɪ/ **ADJ** [*sensation*] de picotement, de fourmillement ◆ **my arm is** *or* **feels ~** j'ai des fourmis *or* des fourmillements dans le bras

tinker /ˈtɪŋkəʳ/ **N** 1 (*esp Brit: gen*) romanichel(le) *m(f)* (*often pej*) ; (*specifically mending things*) rétameur *m* (ambulant) ; († * *= child*) polisson(ne) *m(f)* ◆ **it's not worth a ~'s cuss** *or* **~'s damn** ça ne vaut pas tripette * *or* un clou * ◆ **I don't care** *or* **give a ~'s cuss** *or* **~'s damn** (*fig*) je m'en fiche *, je m'en soucie comme de l'an quarante ◆ **~, tailor, soldier, sailor ...** *comptine enfantine* 2 ◆ **to have a ~ (with)** * bricoler * **VI** 1 (*also* **tinker about**) bricoler, s'occuper à des bricoles ◆ **she was ~ing (about) with the car** elle bricolait la voiture ◆ **stop ~ing with that watch!** arrête de tripoter * cette montre ! 2 (*fig*) **to ~ with** [*+ contract, wording, report etc*] (*= change*) faire des retouches à, remanier ; (*dishonestly*) tripatouiller *

tinkle /ˈtɪŋkl/ **VI** tinter **VT** faire tinter **N** 1 tintement *m* ◆ **to give sb a ~** * (*Brit Telec*) passer un coup de fil à qn * 2 (* *baby talk = passing water*) pipi * *m*

tinkling /ˈtɪŋklɪŋ/ **N** (*NonC*) tintement *m* **ADJ** [*bell*] qui tinte ; [*stream*] qui clapote, qui gazouille

tinned /tɪnd/ **ADJ** (*Brit*) [*fruit, tomatoes, salmon*] en boîte, en conserve ◆ **~ goods** *or* **food** conserves *fpl*

tinnitus /tɪˈnaɪtəs/ **N** acouphène *m*

tinny /ˈtɪnɪ/ **ADJ** (*pej*) [*sound, taste*] métallique ◆ **~ piano** casserole * *f*, mauvais piano *m* ◆ **it's such a ~ car** quelle camelote *, cette voiture

tinpot * /ˈtɪnpɒt/ **ADJ** (*esp Brit*) [*car, bike*] qui ne vaut pas grand-chose, en fer-blanc ; [*dictator, government*] fantoche, de pacotille ◆ **a ~ little town** un petit bled *

tinsel /ˈtɪnsəl/ **N** 1 (*NonC*) guirlandes *fpl* de Noël (argentées) 2 (*fig pej*) clinquant *m*

Tinseltown * /ˈtɪnsəltaʊn/ **N** Hollywood

tinsmith /ˈtɪnsmɪθ/ **N** ferblantier *m*

tint /tɪnt/ **N** teinte *f*, nuance *f* ; (*for hair*) shampooing *m* colorant ◆ **a greenish ~, a ~ of green** une touche de vert ; → **flesh** **VT** teinter (*with* de) ◆ **to ~ one's hair** se faire un shampooing colorant

tintinnabulation /ˈtɪntɪˌnæbjʊˈleɪʃən/ **N** tintinnabulement *m*

Tintoretto /ˌtɪntəˈretəʊ/ **N** le Tintoret

tiny /ˈtaɪnɪ/ **ADJ** [*object*] tout petit, minuscule ; [*person, child, minority*] tout petit ◆ **a ~ little man/baby** un tout petit bonhomme/bébé ◆ **a ~ amount of sth** un tout petit peu de qch

tip¹ /tɪp/ **N** (*= end*) [*of stick, pencil, ruler, wing, finger, nose*] bout *m* ; [*of sword, knife, asparagus*] pointe *f* ; [*of iceberg, mountain*] pointe *f*, cime *f* ; [*of ski*] pointe *f*, spatule *f* ; [*of tongue*] pointe *f* (*also Phon*), bout *m* ; (*= metal etc end piece*) [*of shoe*] bout *m*, pointe *f* ; [*of cigarette*] bout *m* ; [*of filter tip*] bout *m* (filtre) ; [*of umbrella, cane*] embout *m* ; [*of billiard cue*] procédé *m* ◆ **from ~ to toe** de la tête aux pieds ◆ **he stood on the ~s of his toes** il s'est dressé sur la pointe des pieds ◆ **he touched it with the ~ of his toe** il l'a touché du bout de l'orteil ◆ **I've got it on** *or* **it's on the ~ of my tongue** je l'ai sur le bout de la langue ◆ **it was on the ~ of my tongue to tell her what I thought of her** j'étais à deux doigts de lui dire ce que je pensais d'elle ◆ **it's just the ~ of the iceberg** ce n'est que la partie visible de l'iceberg, ça n'est rien comparé au reste ; → **fingertip, wing**

VT (*= put tip on*) mettre un embout à ; (*= cover tip of*) recouvrir le bout de ◆ **~ped cigarettes** (*Brit*) cigarettes *fpl* (à bout) filtre *inv* ◆ **~ped with steel, steel-~ped** ferré, qui a un embout de fer

tip² /tɪp/ **N** 1 (*= money*) pourboire *m* ◆ **the ~ is included** (*in restaurant*) le service est compris

2 (*= hint, information*) suggestion *f*, tuyau * *m* ; (*= advice*) conseil *m* ; (*Racing*) tuyau * *m* ◆ **"tips for the handyman"** "les trucs du bricoleur" ◆ **that horse is a hot ~ for the 3.30** ce cheval a une première chance dans la course de 15h30 ◆ **take my ~** suivez mon conseil

3 (*= tap*) tape *f*, petit coup *m*

VT 1 (*= reward*) donner un pourboire à ◆ **he ~ped the waiter 1 euro** il a donné 1 € de pourboire au serveur

2 (*Racing, gen*) pronostiquer ◆ **to ~ the winner** pronostiquer le cheval gagnant ◆ **he ~ped Blue Streak for the 3.30** il a pronostiqué la victoire de Blue Streak dans la course de 15h30 ◆ **to ~ sb the wink** * **about sth** filer un tuyau * à qn sur qch ◆ **they are ~ped to win the next election** (*Brit fig*) on pronostique qu'ils vont remporter les prochaines élections ◆ **Paul was ~ped for the job** (*Brit*) on avait pronostiqué que Paul serait nommé

3 (*= tap, touch*) toucher (légèrement), effleurer ◆ **to ~ one's hat to sb** mettre *or* porter la main à son chapeau pour saluer qn

COMP **tip-off N** ◆ **to give sb a ~-off** (*gen*) prévenir qn, donner *or* filer un tuyau * à qn ; (*Police*) donner * qn

► **tip off** **VT SEP** (*gen*) donner *or* filer un tuyau * à (*about sth* sur qch) ; [*+ police*] prévenir *or* avertir (*par une dénonciation*)

N ◆ **tip-off** → **tip²**

tip³ /tɪp/ **N** (*Brit*) (*for rubbish*) décharge *f*, dépotoir *m* ; (*for coal*) terril *m* ; (* *fig = untidy place*) (véritable) dépotoir *m*

VT (*= incline, tilt*) pencher, incliner ; (*= overturn*) faire basculer, renverser ; (*= pour, empty*) [*+ liquid*] verser (*into* dans ; *out of* de) ; [*+ load, sand, rubbish*] déverser, déposer ; [*+ clothes, books etc*] déverser (*into* dans ; *out of* de) ◆ **he ~ped the water out of the bucket** il a vidé le seau ◆ **to ~ sb off his chair** renverser *or* faire basculer qn de sa chaise ◆ **they ~ped him into the water** ils l'ont fait basculer *or* tomber dans l'eau ◆ **the car overturned and they were ~ped into the roadway** la voiture s'est retournée et ils se sont retrouvés sur la chaussée ◆ **to ~ the scales at 90kg** peser 90 kg ◆ **to ~ the scales** *or* **balance** (*fig*) faire pencher la balance (*in sb's favour* en faveur de qn ; *against sb* contre qn) ◆ **to ~ one's hand** * *or* **one's mitt** * (*US*) dévoiler son jeu (involontairement)

VI 1 (*= incline*) pencher, être incliné ; (*= overturn*) se renverser, basculer ◆ **"no tipping", "tipping prohibited"** (*Brit*) "défense de déposer des ordures"

2 ◆ **it's ~ping with rain** * il pleut des cordes

COMP **tip-cart N** tombereau *m*

tip-up seat N (*in theatre etc*) siège *m* rabattable, strapontin *m* ; (*in taxi, underground etc*) strapontin *m*

tip-up truck N camion *m* à benne (basculante)

► **tip back, tip backward(s)** **VI** [*chair*] se rabattre en arrière ; [*person*] se pencher en arrière, basculer (en arrière)

VT SEP [*+ chair*] rabattre *or* faire basculer (en arrière)

► **tip down** * **VTI SEP** (*= raining*) ◆ **it's tipping (it) down** il pleut des cordes

► **tip forward(s)** **VI** [*chair*] se rabattre en avant ; [*person*] se pencher en avant

VT SEP [*+ chair*] rabattre *or* faire basculer (en avant) ; [*+ car seat*] rabattre (en avant)

► **tip out** **VT SEP** [*+ liquid, contents*] vider ; [*+ load*] décharger, déverser ◆ **they ~ped him out of his chair/out of bed** ils l'ont fait basculer de sa chaise/du lit

► **tip over** **VI** (*= tilt*) pencher ; (*= overturn*) basculer

VT SEP faire basculer

► **tip up** **VI** [*table etc*] (*= tilt*) pencher, être incliné ; (*= overturn*) basculer ; [*box, jug*] se renverser ; [*seat*] se rabattre ; [*truck*] basculer

VT SEP (*= tilt*) [*+ table etc*] incliner ; [*+ jug, box*] pencher, incliner ; [*+ person*] faire basculer

ADJ ◆ **tip-up** → **tip³**

tipcat /ˈtɪpkæt/ **N** (jeu *m* du) bâtonnet *m*

tipper /ˈtɪpəʳ/ **N** 1 (*= vehicle*) camion *m* à benne (basculante) ; (*= back of vehicle*) benne *f* (basculante) 2 (*giving money*) ◆ **he is a good** *or* **big ~** il a le pourboire facile

tippet /ˈtɪpɪt/ **N** (*also* **fur tippet**) étole *f* (de fourrure)

Tipp-Ex ® /ˈtɪpeks/ **N** Tipp-Ex ® *m* **VT** ◆ **to tippex sth (out)** tippexer qch, effacer qch au Tipp-Ex ®

tipple /ˈtɪpl/ **VI** picoler * **N** (*hum*) ◆ **gin is his ~** ce qu'il préfère boire c'est du gin

tippler /ˈtɪpləʳ/ **N** picoleur * *m*, -euse * *f*

tippy-toe * /ˈtɪpɪtəʊ/ **N, VI** (*US*) ⇒ **tiptoe**

tipsily /ˈtɪpsɪlɪ/ **ADV** [*walk*] en titubant légèrement ◆ **... he said ~** ... dit-il un peu ivre

tipstaff /ˈtɪpstɑːf/ **N** (*Brit Jur*) huissier *m*

tipster /ˈtɪpstəʳ/ **N** (*Racing*) pronostiqueur *m*

tipsy /ˈtɪpsɪ/ **ADJ** éméché *, pompette * ◆ **to get ~** devenir pompette * **COMP** **tipsy cake N** (*Brit*) *sorte de baba au rhum*

tiptoe /ˈtɪptəʊ/ **N** ◆ **on ~** sur la pointe des pieds **VI** ◆ **to ~ in/out** *etc* entrer/sortir *etc* sur la pointe des pieds

tiptop * /ˈtɪpˈtɒp/ **ADJ** excellent, de toute première qualité ◆ **in ~ condition** [*car, item for sale*] en parfait état ; [*athlete*] au mieux de sa forme

tirade /taɪˈreɪd/ **N** diatribe *f*

tiramisu /ˌtɪrəmɪˈsuː/ **N** tiramisu *m*

tire¹ /ˈtaɪəʳ/ **N** (*US*) ⇒ **tyre**

tire² /ˈtaɪəʳ/ **VT** fatiguer ; (*= weary*) fatiguer, lasser **VI** se fatiguer, se lasser ◆ **he ~s easily** il se fatigue vite, il est vite fatigué ◆ **he never ~s of telling us how ...** il ne se lasse jamais de nous dire comment ...

► **tire out** **VT SEP** épuiser ◆ **to be ~d out** être épuisé

tired /ˈtaɪəd/ ADJ [1] *(= weary) [person, eyes]* fatigué ; *[movement, voice]* las (lasse *f*) ◆ **to get** *or* **grow ~** se fatiguer ◆ **~ and emotional** *(hum euph = drunk)* ivre [2] *(= bored)* **to be ~ of sb/sth** en avoir assez de qn/qch ◆ **to get ~ of sb/sth** commencer à en avoir assez de qn/qch ◆ **to be ~ of doing sth** en avoir assez de faire qch ◆ **to be ~ of sb doing sth** en avoir assez que qn fasse qch ; → **sick** [3] *(= old)* ◆ **our ~ old car** notre vieille voiture qui ne marche plus bien ◆ **a ~ lettuce leaf** une feuille de laitue défraîchie [4] *(pej = hackneyed) [cliché, topic]* rebattu ; *[excuse]* rebattu, éculé

tiredly /ˈtaɪədlɪ/ ADV *[reply]* d'une voix fatiguée ; *[walk]* d'un pas lourd

tiredness /ˈtaɪədnɪs/ N fatigue *f*

tireless /ˈtaɪəlɪs/ ADJ *[person]* infatigable *(in sth* dans qch) ; *[work, efforts]* inlassable

tirelessly /ˈtaɪəlɪslɪ/ ADV infatigablement, inlassablement

tiresome /ˈtaɪəsəm/ ADJ *[person, behaviour, noise]* pénible ◆ **it's a ~ business going to all these meetings** c'est une corvée que d'aller à toutes ces réunions ◆ **it is ~ to have to wait** c'est ennuyeux d'avoir à attendre

tiresomeness /ˈtaɪəsəmnɪs/ N *[of task]* caractère *m* ennuyeux ◆ **the ~ of her behaviour** son attitude agaçante

tiring /ˈtaɪərɪŋ/ ADJ fatigant

tiro /ˈtaɪərəʊ/ N ⇒ **tyro**

Tirol /tɪˈrəʊl/ N ⇒ **Tyrol**

tisane /tɪˈzæn/ N tisane *f*

tissue /ˈtɪʃuː/ N *(= cloth)* tissu *m*, étoffe *f* ; *(Anat, Bio)* tissu *m* ; *(= paper handkerchief)* mouchoir *m* en papier, kleenex ® *m* ; (also **toilet tissue**) papier *m* hygiénique ; *(fig = web, mesh)* tissu *m*, enchevêtrement *m* ◆ **a ~ of lies** un tissu de mensonges

COMP **tissue culture** N *(Bio)* culture *f* de tissus
tissue paper N *(NonC)* papier *m* de soie

tit¹ /tɪt/ N *(= bird)* mésange *f* ; → **blue**

tit² /tɪt/ N ◆ **~ for tat !** un prêté pour un rendu ! ◆ **I'll give him ~ for tat** je lui rendrai la pareille, je lui revaudrai ça ◆ **~-for-tat killings** représailles *fpl* ◆ **~-for-tat expulsions** des renvois en (guise de) représailles ◆ **a ~-for-tat ban on foreign meat products** un embargo en (guise de) représailles sur les importations de viande

tit³ ‡ /tɪt/ N [1] *(= breast)* nichon ‡ *m*, néné * *m* ◆ **to get on sb's ~s** *‡taper sur le système à qn * [2] *(= idiot)* abruti(e) ‡ *m(f)*, con(ne) ‡ *m(f)*

Titan /ˈtaɪtən/ N *(also fig:* also **titan**) Titan *m*

titanic /taɪˈtænɪk/ ADJ [1] *[struggle]* titanesque [2] *[acid]* titanique, de titane ; *[iron ore]* titanifère

titanium /tɪˈteɪnɪəm/ N titane *m*

titbit /ˈtɪtbɪt/ N *(esp Brit) [of food]* friandise *f*, bon morceau *m* ; *[of gossip]* potin *m* ; *(in newspaper)* entrefilet *m* croustillant ◆ **~s** *(= snack with drinks)* amuse-gueule *mpl* ◆ **I've saved the ~ for the end** *(in telling news etc)* j'ai gardé le détail le plus croustillant pour la fin

titch * /tɪtʃ/ N *(Brit)* microbe * *m (= personne)*

titchy * /ˈtɪtʃɪ/ ADJ *(Brit)* minuscule

titfer ‡ /ˈtɪtfəʳ/ N *(Brit = hat)* galurin *m*

tithe /taɪð/ N dîme *f*

Titian /ˈtɪʃən/ N Titien *m* ADJ ◆ **titian** blond vénitien *inv*

titillate /ˈtɪtɪleɪt/ VT titiller, émoustiller

titillation /ˌtɪtɪˈleɪʃən/ N titillation *f*

titivate /ˈtɪtɪveɪt/ VI se pomponner, se bichonner VT bichonner, pomponner

title /ˈtaɪtl/ N [1] *[of person]* titre *m* ◆ **what ~ should I give him?** comment dois-je l'appeler ? ◆ **I don't know his exact ~** je ne connais pas son titre exact ◆ **George III gave him a ~** Georges III lui a conféré un titre *or* l'a anobli ◆ **this earned him the ~ of "King of the Ring"** cela lui a valu le titre de « roi du ring »
[2] *(Sport)* titre *m* ◆ **to win/hold the ~** remporter/détenir le titre ; → **world**
[3] *[of book etc]* titre *m* ◆ **under the ~ of ...** sous le titre de ...
[4] *(Cine, TV)* **the ~s** *(= credit titles)* le générique ; *(= subtitles)* les sous-titres *mpl*
[5] *(Jur)* droit *m*, titre *m* *(to sth* à qch)
VT *[+ book etc]* intituler

COMP **title bar** N *(Comput)* barre *f* de titre
title deed N titre *m* (constitutif) de propriété
title fight N *(Boxing)* match *m* de championnat
title holder N *(Sport)* détenteur *m*, -trice *f* *or* tenant(e) *m(f)* du titre
title page N page *f* de titre
title role N *(Cine, Theat)* rôle-titre *m*
title track N chanson-titre *f*

titled /ˈtaɪtld/ ADJ *[person]* titré

titmouse /ˈtɪtmaʊs/ N (pl **-mice**) mésange *f*

titrate /ˈtaɪtreɪt/ VT titrer *(Chem)*

titter /ˈtɪtəʳ/ VI rire sottement *(at* de), glousser N gloussement *m*, petit rire *m* sot

tittle /ˈtɪtl/ N *(Typ)* signe *m* diacritique ; *(= particle)* brin *m*, iota *m* ; → **jot** COMP **tittle-tattle** N *(NonC)* cancans *mpl*, potins *mpl* VI cancaner, jaser

titty ‡ /ˈtɪtɪ/ N néné ‡ *m* ◆ **tough ~** *or* **titties!** pas de pot ! *

titular /ˈtɪtjʊləʳ/ ADJ *[ruler, leader, power]* nominal ; *[possessions, estate]* titulaire

Titus /ˈtaɪtəs/ N Tite *m*

tizzy * /ˈtɪzɪ/, **tizz** * /tɪz/ N affolement * *m*, panique * *f* ◆ **to be in/get into a ~** être/se mettre dans tous ses états

TLC /ˌtiːelˈsiː/ (abbrev of **tender loving care**) → **tender³**

TLS /ˌtiːelˈes/ N *(Brit)* (abbrev of **Times Literary Supplement**) *magazine littéraire*

TM /tiːˈem/ N [1] (abbrev of **transcendental meditation**) → **transcendental** [2] (abbrev of **trademark**) MD

TN abbrev of **Tennessee**

TNT /tiːenˈtiː/ N (abbrev of **trinitrotoluene**) TNT *m*

to /tuː/ (weak form /tə/)

1 PREPOSITION
2 ADVERB
3 COMPOUNDS

1 - PREPOSITION

When **to** is the second element in a phrasal verb, eg **apply to**, **set to**, look up the verb. When **to** is part of a set combination, eg **nice to**, **of help to**, **to my mind**, **to all appearances**, look up the adjective or noun.

[1] [direction, movement] à

à + le = au, à + les = aux.

◆ **he went ~ the door** il est allé à la porte ◆ **to go ~ school** aller à l'école ◆ **we're going ~ the cinema** on va au cinéma ◆ **she's gone ~ the toilet** elle est allée aux toilettes ◆ **he came over ~ where I was standing** il est venu jusqu'à moi ◆ **to go ~ town** aller en ville

♦ **to it** *(= there)* y ◆ **I liked the exhibition, I went ~ it twice** j'ai aimé l'exposition, j'y suis allé deux fois

[2] [= towards] vers ◆ **he walked slowly ~ the door** il s'est dirigé lentement vers la porte ◆ **he turned ~ me** il s'est tourné vers moi

[3] [home, workplace] chez ◆ **let's go ~ Christine's (house)** si on allait chez Christine ? ◆ **we're going ~ my parents' for Christmas** nous allons passer Noël chez mes parents ◆ **to go ~ the doctor('s)** aller chez le docteur

[4] [with geographical names]

♦ **to** + *fem country/area etc* en

Countries etc that end in **e** are usually feminine:

◆ **~ England/France** en Angleterre/France ◆ **~ Brittany/Provence/Andalusia** en Bretagne/Provence/Andalousie ◆ **~ Sicily/Crete** en Sicile/Crète ◆ **~ Louisiana/Virginia** en Louisiane/Virginie ◆ **ambassador ~ France** ambassadeur en France

en is also used with masc countries beginning with a vowel:

◆ **~ Iran/Israel** en Iran/Israël

♦ **to** + *masc country/area* au ◆ **~ Japan/Kuwait** au Japon/Koweït ◆ **~ the Sahara/Kashmir** au Sahara/Cachemire

♦ **to** + *pl country/group of islands* aux ◆ **~ the United States/the West Indies** aux États-Unis/Antilles

♦ **to** + *town/island without article* à ◆ **~ London/Lyons** à Londres/Lyon ◆ **~ Cuba/Malta** à Cuba/Malte ◆ **on the way ~ Paris** en allant à Paris ◆ **~ le Havre** au Havre ◆ **is this the road ~ Newcastle ?** est-ce que c'est la route de Newcastle ? ◆ **it is 90km ~ Paris** *(= from here to)* nous sommes à 90 km de Paris ; *(= from there to)* c'est à 90 km de Paris ◆ **boats ~ and from Calais** les bateaux *mpl* à destination ou en provenance de Calais ◆ **planes ~ Heathrow** les vols *mpl* à destination de Heathrow

♦ **to** + *masc state/region/county* dans ◆ **~ Texas/Ontario** dans le Texas/l'Ontario ◆ **~ Poitou/Berry** dans le Poitou/le Berry ◆ **~ Sussex/Yorkshire** dans le Sussex/le Yorkshire

dans is also used with many départements:

◆ **~ the Drôme/the Var** dans la Drôme/le Var

[5] [= up to] jusqu'à ◆ **to count ~ 20** compter jusqu'à 20 ◆ **I didn't stay ~ the end** je ne suis pas resté jusqu'à la fin ◆ **from morning ~ night** du matin (jusqu')au soir ◆ **it's correct ~ within a millimetre** c'est exact au millimètre près ◆ **from Monday ~ Friday** du lundi au vendredi ◆ **there were 50 ~ 60 people** il y avait (de) 50 à 60 personnes, il y avait entre 50 et 60 personnes

[6] [expressing indirect object] à ◆ **to give sth ~ sb** donner qch à qn ◆ **"to my wife Anne"** « à ma femme, Anne » ◆ **we have spoken ~ the children about it** nous en avons parlé aux enfants

When a relative clause ends with **to**, a different word order is required in French:

◆ **the man I sold it ~** l'homme à qui *or* auquel je l'ai vendu

When translating **to** + pronoun, look up the pronoun. The translation depends on whether it is stressed or unstressed.

◆ **he was speaking ~ me** il me parlait ◆ **he was speaking ~ ME** c'est à moi qu'il parlait

[7] [in time phrases] ◆ **20 (minutes) ~ two** deux heures moins 20 ◆ **it's (a) quarter ~/ten ~** il est moins le quart/moins dix

[8] [in ratios] ◆ **A is ~ B as C is ~ D** A est à B ce que C est à D ◆ **the odds against it happening are a million ~ one** il y a une chance sur un million que ça se produise ◆ **he got a big majority (twenty votes ~ seven)** il a été élu à une large majorité (vingt voix contre sept) ◆ **they won by four (goals) ~ two** ils ont gagné quatre (buts) à deux ◆ **three men ~ a cell** trois hommes par cellule ◆ **200 people ~ the square km** 200 habitants au km carré ◆ **how many kilometres does it do ~ the litre?**

combien consomme-t-elle de litres aux cent (kilomètres) ? ◆ **two Swiss francs ~ the dollar** deux francs suisses pour un dollar ◆ **three ~ the fourth, three ~ the power four** *(Math)* trois (à la) puissance quatre

9 [= concerning] ◆ **that's all there is ~ it** *(= it's easy)* ce n'est pas plus difficile que ça ◆ **you're not going, and that's all there is ~ it** *(= that's definite)* tu n'iras pas, un point c'est tout ◆ **"to repairing cooker: 100 euros"** *(Comm)* "remise en état d'une cuisinière : 100 €" ◆ **"to services rendered"** *(Comm)* "pour services rendus"

10 [= of] de ◆ **the key ~ the front door** la clé de la porte d'entrée ◆ **assistant ~ the manager** adjoint *m* du directeur ◆ **wife ~ Mr Milton** épouse *f* de M. Milton ◆ **he has been a good friend ~ us** il a été vraiment très gentil avec nous

11 [also **much to**] ◆ **~ my delight/surprise/shame** à ma grande joie/surprise/honte

12 [infinitive] ◆ **~ be** être ◆ **~ eat** manger ◆ **they didn't want ~ go** ils ne voulaient pas y aller ◆ **she refused ~ listen** elle n'a pas voulu écouter

A preposition may be required with the French infinitive, depending on what precedes it: look up the verb or adjective.

◆ **he refused ~ help me** il a refusé de m'aider ◆ **we're ready ~ go** nous sommes prêts à partir ◆ **it was very good of him ~ come at such short notice** c'était très gentil de sa part de venir si rapidement

The French verb may take a clause, rather than the infinitive:

◆ **he was expecting me ~ help him** il s'attendaient à ce que je l'aide

13 [infinitive expressing purpose] pour ◆ **well, ~ sum up ...** alors, pour résumer ... ◆ **we are writing ~ inform you ...** nous vous écrivons pour vous informer que ... ◆ **they have come ~ help us** ils sont venus pour nous aider

14 [to avoid repetition of verb]

to is not translated when it stands for the infinitive:

◆ **he'd like me ~ come, but I don't want ~** il voudrait que je vienne mais je ne veux pas ◆ **I'll try ~** j'essaierai ◆ **yes, I'd love ~** oui, volontiers ◆ **I didn't mean ~** je ne l'ai pas fait exprès ◆ **I forgot ~** j'ai oublié

15 [in exclamations] ◆ **and then ~ be let down like that !** et tout ça pour que l'on nous laisse tomber comme ça ! ◆ **and ~ think he didn't mean a word of it!** et dire que pour lui ce n'étaient que des paroles en l'air !

2 - ADVERB

[= shut] ◆ **~ push the door ~** entrouvrir la porte (en la poussant) ◆ **when the door is ~** quand la porte est entrouverte

3 - COMPOUNDS

-to-be ADJ *(in compounds)* futur ◆ **husband-to-be** futur mari *m* ; → **mother**

to-do* N (pl **to-dos**) ◆ **he made a great to-do about lending me the car** il a fait toute une histoire pour me prêter la voiture ◆ **she made a great to-do about it** elle en a fait tout un plat* ◆ **what a to-do!** quelle histoire !, quelle affaire !

to-ing and fro-ing N allées et venues *fpl*

toad /təʊd/ N crapaud *m (also fig)* COMP **toad-in-the-hole** N *(Brit Culin) saucisses cuites au four dans de la pâte à crêpes*

toadstool /ˈtəʊdstuːl/ N champignon *m* vénéneux

toady /ˈtəʊdɪ/ N flagorneur *m*, -euse *f*, lèche-bottes* *mf inv* VI être flagorneur ◆ **to ~ to sb** flagorner qn, flatter qn bassement, lécher les bottes de qn*

toadying /ˈtəʊdɪɪŋ/, **toadyism** /ˈtəʊdɪɪzəm/ N *(NonC)* flagornerie *f*

toast /təʊst/ N 1 *(NonC: Culin)* pain *m* grillé, toast *m* ◆ **you've burnt the ~** tu as laissé brûler le pain *or* les toasts ◆ **a piece** *or* **slice of ~** une tartine grillée, un (morceau de) toast, une rôtie ◆ **sardines on ~** sardines *fpl* sur toast *or* sur canapé ◆ **you've got him on ~*** vous le tenez ◆ **you're ~!*** tu es grillé !* ; → **warm**

2 *(= drink, speech)* toast *m* ◆ **to drink a ~ to sb** porter un toast à qn *or* en l'honneur de qn, boire à la santé *or* au succès de qn ◆ **the ~ is "the family"** portons un toast à la famille ◆ **they drank his ~ in champagne** ils lui ont porté un toast au champagne ◆ **here's a ~ to all who ...** levons nos verres en l'honneur de tous ceux qui ... ◆ **to propose** *or* **give a ~ to sb** porter un toast à qn *or* en l'honneur de qn ◆ **she was the ~ of the town** elle était la coqueluche *or* la vedette de la ville

VT 1 *[+ bread etc]* (faire) griller ◆ **~ed cheese** toast *m* au fromage ◆ **he was ~ing himself/his toes by the fire** il se chauffait/se rôtissait les pieds auprès du feu

2 *(= propose toast to)* porter un toast à ; *(= drink toast to) [+ person]* boire à la santé de *or* au succès de, porter un toast à ; *[+ event, victory]* arroser *(with* à)

COMP **toasting fork** N fourchette *f* à griller le pain

toast rack N porte-toasts *m inv*

toaster /ˈtəʊstəʳ/ N grille-pain *m inv (électrique)*

toastie /ˈtəʊstɪ/ N ≈ croque-monsieur *m*

toastmaster /ˈtəʊstmɑːstəʳ/ N animateur *m* pour réceptions et banquets

toasty /ˈtəʊstɪ/ ADJ * bien chaud N ⇒ **toastie**

tobacco /təˈbækəʊ/ N (pl **tobaccos** *or* **tobaccoes**) tabac *m*

COMP *[leaf, smoke, plantation, company]* de tabac ; *[pouch]* à tabac ; *[industry]* du tabac

tobacco jar N pot *m* à tabac

tobacco plant N (pied *m* de) tabac *m*

tobacco planter N planteur *m* de tabac

tobacconist /təˈbækənɪst/ N *(esp Brit)* marchand(e) *m(f)* de tabac, buraliste *mf* ◆ **~'s (shop)** (bureau *m or* débit *m* de) tabac *m*

Tobago /təˈbeɪgəʊ/ N Tobago ; → **Trinidad**

toboggan /təˈbɒgən/ N toboggan *m*, luge *f* ; *(Sport)* luge *f* VI (also **go tobogganing**) faire du toboggan *or* de la luge ; *(Sport)* luger ◆ **he ~ed down the hill** il a descendu la colline en toboggan *or* en luge

COMP *[race]* de luge

toboggan run N piste *f* de luge

toby jug /ˈtəʊbɪ,dʒʌg/ N chope *f* à effigie humaine

toccata /təˈkɑːtə/ N toccata *f*

tocsin /ˈtɒksɪn/ N tocsin *m*

tod‡ /tɒd/ N *(Brit)* ◆ **on one's ~** tout seul (toute seule *f*)

today /təˈdeɪ/ ADV 1 *(= this day)* aujourd'hui ◆ **it rained all (day) ~** il a plu toute la journée aujourd'hui ◆ **later ~** plus tard dans la journée ◆ **early ~** aujourd'hui de bonne heure ◆ **earlier ~** en début de journée ◆ **~ week***, **a week ~** *(Brit)* aujourd'hui en huit ◆ **I met her a week ago ~** ça fait une semaine aujourd'hui que je l'ai rencontrée ◆ **what day is it ~?** quel jour sommes-nous aujourd'hui ? ◆ **what date is it ~?** on est le combien aujourd'hui ? ◆ **money! it's here ~ gone tomorrow** l'argent, ça va ça vient ! ◆ **here ~, gone tomorrow fashion fads** des modes éphémères ◆ **a lot of staff can be here ~, gone tomorrow** beaucoup d'employés peuvent arriver un jour et repartir le lendemain

2 *(= nowadays)* aujourd'hui, de nos jours ◆ **young people ~ have it easy** les jeunes d'aujourd'hui se la coulent douce* ◆ **you can't sack anyone ~ without a good reason** aujourd'hui on ne peut renvoyer personne sans motif valable

N 1 aujourd'hui *m* ◆ **what day is ~?** quel jour sommes-nous aujourd'hui ? ◆ **~ is Friday** aujourd'hui c'est vendredi ◆ **what is ~'s date?** quelle est la date aujourd'hui ? ◆ **~ is the 4th** aujourd'hui c'est le 4 ◆ **~ is very wet** il pleut beaucoup aujourd'hui ◆ **~ was a bad day for me** aujourd'hui ça a été une mauvaise journée pour moi ◆ **~'s paper** le journal d'aujourd'hui

2 *(= these days)* aujourd'hui *m* ◆ **the writers of ~** les écrivains d'aujourd'hui

toddle /ˈtɒdl/ VI 1 *[child]* **to ~ in/out** *etc* entrer/sortir *etc* à pas hésitants ◆ **he has begun to ~, he is just toddling** il fait ses premiers pas 2 *(* hum) (= go)* aller ; *(= stroll)* se balader* ; *(= leave:* also **toddle off)** se sauver*, se trotter‡ N *(hum)* ◆ **to go for a ~**‡ aller faire un petit tour *or* une petite balade*

toddler /ˈtɒdləʳ/ N tout(e) petit(e) *m(f)* (qui commence à marcher), bambin* *m* ◆ **he's only a ~** il est encore tout petit ◆ **she has one baby and one ~** elle a un bébé et un petit qui commence juste à marcher

toddy /ˈtɒdɪ/ N ≈ grog *m*

todger‡ /ˈtɒdʒəʳ/ N *(Brit)* quéquette‡ *f*

TOE /tiːəʊˈiː/ N (abbrev of **ton oil equivalent**) TEP *f (abrév de tonne équivalent pétrole)*

toe /təʊ/ N *(Anat)* orteil *m*, doigt *m* de pied ; *[of sock, shoe]* bout *m* ◆ **big/little ~** gros/petit orteil *m* ◆ **to tread** *or* **step on sb's ~s** *(lit, fig)* marcher sur les pieds de qn ◆ **to keep sb on his ~s** forcer qn à rester vigilant *or* alerte ◆ **that will keep you on your ~s!** ça t'empêchera de t'endormir !, ça te fera travailler ! ◆ **to turn up one's ~s*** *(Brit hum = die)* passer l'arme à gauche ◆ **to go** *or* **stand ~ to ~ with sb** *(esp US)* affronter qn ◆ **there are scenes in the film that make your ~s curl** il y a des scènes dans ce film qui donnent la chair de poule ; → **tip**[1], **top**[1]

VT *(= touch/push)* toucher/pousser du bout de l'orteil ◆ **to ~ the line** *or (US)* **mark** *(in race)* se ranger sur la ligne de départ ; *(fig)* se mettre au pas, se plier ◆ **to ~ the party line** *(Pol)* ne pas s'écarter de *or* suivre la ligne du parti

COMP **toe clip** N *(Cycling)* cale-pied *m inv*

toe-curling* ADJ *(= embarrassing)* très embarrassant

toe-piece N *(Ski)* butée *f*

toecap /ˈtəʊkæp/ N ◆ **reinforced ~** bout *m* renforcé *(de chaussure)*

-toed /təʊd/ ADJ *(in compounds)* ◆ **three-toed** à trois orteils

TOEFL /ˈtɒfl/ N (abbrev of **Test of English as a Foreign Language**) *examen d'anglais pour les étudiants étrangers voulant étudier dans des universités anglo-saxonnes*

toehold /ˈtəʊhəʊld/ N *(lit)* prise *f* (pour le pied) ◆ **to have a ~ in ...** *(fig)* avoir un pied dans ...

toenail /ˈtəʊneɪl/ N ongle *m* de l'orteil *or* du pied

toerag‡ /ˈtəʊræg/ N *(Brit)* sale con(ne)‡ *m(f)*

toff †‡ /tɒf/ N *(Brit)* aristo‡ *mf*, dandy* *m*

toffee /ˈtɒfɪ/ N caramel *m* (au beurre) ◆ **he can't do it for ~*** il n'est pas fichu* de le faire

COMP **toffee-apple** N pomme *f* caramélisée

toffee-nosed‡ ADJ *(Brit pej)* bêcheur*, qui fait du chiqué*

tofu /ˈtəʊ,fuː, ˈtɒ,fuː/ N tofu *m*, fromage *m* de soja

tog* /tɒg/ *(Brit)* VT ◆ **to ~ up** *or* **out** nipper*, fringuer‡ ◆ **to be all ~ged up** *or* **out (in one's best clothes)** être bien fringué‡ *or* sapé* N *(Brit Measure) indice d'isolation thermique d'une couette ou d'une couverture* NPL **togs** fringues‡ *fpl*

toga /ˈtəʊgə/ **N** toge *f*

together /təˈgeðəʳ/

When **together** is an element in a phrasal verb, eg **bring together**, **get together**, **sleep together**, look up the verb.

ADV 1 ensemble ◆ **I've seen them** ~ je les ai vus ensemble ◆ **we're in this** ~ nous sommes logés à la même enseigne ◆ **they were both in it** ~ (*fig pej*) ils avaient partie liée tous les deux ◆ **you must keep** ~ vous devez rester ensemble, vous ne devez pas vous séparer ◆ **tie the ropes** ~ nouez les cordes ◆ **if you look at the reports** ~ si vous considérez les rapports conjointement ◆ **they belong** ~ [*objects*] ils vont ensemble ◆ **crime and poverty go** ~ [*people*] le crime et la pauvreté vont de pair, ils sont faits l'un pour l'autre ; → **bang, gather, live¹**

◆ **together with** ◆ ~ **with what you bought yesterday that makes ...** avec ce que vous avez acheté hier ça fait ... ◆ **(taken)** ~ **with the previous figures, these show that ...** ces chiffres, considérés conjointement avec les précédents, indiquent que ... ◆ **he,** ~ **with his colleagues, accepted ...** lui, ainsi que ses collègues, a accepté ...

2 (= *simultaneously*) en même temps, simultanément ; [*sing, play, recite*] à l'unisson ◆ **the shots were fired** ~ les coups de feu ont été tirés simultanément *or* en même temps ◆ **they both stood up** ~ ils se sont tous les deux levés en même temps ◆ **don't all speak** ~ ne parlez pas tous à la fois ◆ **all** ~ **now!** (*shouting, singing*) tous en chœur maintenant ! ; (*pulling*) (oh !) hisse ! ◆ **you're not** ~ (*Mus*) vous n'êtes pas à l'unisson

3 (= *continuously*) **for days/weeks** ~ (pendant) des jours entiers/des semaines entières ◆ **for five weeks** ~ (pendant) cinq semaines de suite *or* d'affilée

4 (* *fig*) **to get it** ~, **to get one's act** ~ s'organiser ◆ **let's get it** ~ il faut qu'on s'organise, il faut qu'on essaie d'y voir plus clair ◆ **she's got it** ~ c'est quelqu'un d'équilibré

ADJ (* = *well adjusted*) [*person*] équilibré ◆ **a** ~ **person** quelqu'un d'équilibré

togetherness /təˈgeðənɪs/ **N** (*NonC*) (= *unity*) unité *f* ; (= *friendliness*) camaraderie *f*

toggle /ˈtɒgl/ **N** (*Naut*) cabillot *m* ; (*on garment*) bouton *m* de duffle-coat **VI** (*Comput*) basculer (*between* entre)

COMP **toggle joint N** (*Tech*) genouillère *f*
toggle key N (*Comput*) touche *f* à bascule
toggle switch N (*Elec*) interrupteur *m* à bascule

Togo /ˈtəʊgəʊ/ **N** Togo *m* ◆ **in** ~ au Togo

toil¹ /tɔɪl/ **N** (*NonC*) (dur) travail *m*, labeur *m* (*liter*) **VI** 1 (= *work hard*: also **toil away**) travailler dur (*at, over* à ; *to do sth* pour faire qch) peiner (*at, over* sur ; *to do sth* pour faire qch) 2 (= *move with difficulty*) **to** ~ **along/up** *etc* [*person, animal, vehicle*] avancer/monter *etc* péniblement *or* avec peine

toil² /tɔɪl/ **N** (*fig liter* = *snare, net*) ◆ ~**s** rets *mpl* ◆ **in the** ~**s of** ... dans les rets de ...

toilet /ˈtɔɪlɪt/ **N** 1 (= *lavatory*) toilettes *fpl*, W.-C. *mpl* ◆ **"Toilets"** "Toilettes" ◆ **to go to the** ~ aller aux toilettes *or* aux W.-C. ◆ **to put sth down the** ~ jeter qch dans la cuvette des cabinets

2 (= *dressing etc, dress*) toilette *f*

COMP **toilet bag N** trousse *f* de toilette
toilet bowl N cuvette *f* (des cabinets)
toilet case N ⇒ **toilet bag**
toilet humour N (*pej*) humour *m* scatologique
toilet paper N papier *m* hygiénique
toilet requisites NPL articles *mpl* de toilette
toilet roll N rouleau *m* de papier hygiénique
toilet seat N siège *m or* lunette *f* des cabinets *or* W.-C. *or* toilettes
toilet soap N savonnette *f*, savon *m* de toilette
toilet table N table *f* de toilette
toilet tissue N ⇒ **toilet paper**
toilet-train VT ◆ **to** ~**-train a child** apprendre à un enfant à être propre
toilet training N apprentissage *m* de la propreté
toilet water N eau *f* de toilette

toiletries /ˈtɔɪlɪtrɪz/ **NPL** articles *mpl* de toilette

toilette /twɑːˈlet/ **N** ⇒ **toilet noun 2**

toilsome /ˈtɔɪlsəm/ **ADJ** (*liter*) pénible, épuisant

toke ‡ /təʊk/ **N** (*Drugs*) bouffée *f*

token /ˈtəʊkən/ LANGUAGE IN USE 26.2

N 1 (= *sign, symbol*) marque *f*, témoignage *m*, gage *m* ; (= *keepsake*) souvenir *m* ; (= *metal disc: for travel, telephone etc*) jeton *m* ; (= *voucher, coupon*) bon *m*, coupon *m* ; (also **gift token**) bon-cadeau *m* ◆ **milk** ~ bon *m* de lait ◆ **as a** ~ **of, in** ~ **of** en témoignage de, en gage de ◆ **by the same** ~ de même ◆ **this is an immensely difficult subject, but by the same** ~ **it is a highly important one** ceci est un sujet extrêmement délicat, mais c'est aussi un sujet de la plus haute importance ; → **book, record**

2 (*Ling*) occurrence *f*

ADJ [*payment, wage, strike, resistance, military presence*] symbolique ; [*attempt, effort, appearance*] pour la forme ; (*pej*) [*woman etc*] de service ◆ **a** ~ **gesture** un geste symbolique ◆ **I was the** ~ **pensioner on the committee** j'étais le retraité alibi *or* le retraité de service au comité ◆ **she said she's not just a** ~ **woman** elle a dit qu'elle n'était pas simplement une femme alibi

COMP **token vote N** (*Parl*) vote *m* de crédits (*dont le montant n'est pas définitivement fixé*)

tokenism /ˈtəʊkənɪzəm/ **N** ◆ **is his promotion mere** ~**?** sa promotion est-elle une mesure purement symbolique ? ◆ **his part in the film smacks of** ~ il n'est probablement présent dans le film que pour la forme

Tokyo /ˈtəʊkjəʊ/ **N** Tokyo

told /təʊld/ **VB** pt, ptp of **tell**

Toledo /tɒˈleɪdəʊ/ **N** Tolède

tolerable /ˈtɒlərəbl/ **ADJ** 1 (= *bearable*) tolérable, supportable 2 (= *adequate*) assez bon ◆ **the food is** ~ on y mange passablement, on n'y mange pas trop mal

tolerably /ˈtɒlərəblɪ/ **ADV** [*good, comfortable, happy*] relativement ◆ ~ **well** relativement bien ◆ **he plays** ~ **(well)** il joue passablement, il joue relativement bien

tolerance /ˈtɒlərəns/ **N** (*gen*) tolérance *f*, indulgence *f* ; (*Med, Tech*) tolérance *f*

tolerant /ˈtɒlərənt/ **ADJ** 1 (= *sympathetic*) [*person, society, attitude*] tolérant (*of sb/sth* à l'égard de qn/qch) 2 (*Phys, Med*) ◆ ~ **of heat** résistant à la chaleur ◆ ~ **to light/a toxin** résistant à la lumière/à une toxine ◆ **to be** ~ **to a drug** tolérer un médicament

tolerantly /ˈtɒlərəntlɪ/ **ADV** [*smile*] avec indulgence ; [*listen*] patiemment

tolerate /ˈtɒləreɪt/ LANGUAGE IN USE 10.4 **VT** [+ *heat, pain*] supporter ; [+ *insolence, injustice*] tolérer, supporter ; (*Med, Tech*) tolérer

toleration /ˌtɒləˈreɪʃən/ **N** (*NonC*) tolérance *f*

toll¹ /təʊl/ **N** 1 (= *tax, charge*) péage *m*

2 [*of accident*] nombre *m* de victimes ; [*of disaster*] bilan *m* ◆ **the war took a heavy** ~ **of** *or* **among the young men** la guerre a fait beaucoup de victimes parmi les jeunes, les jeunes ont payé un fort tribut à la guerre ◆ **it took (a) great** ~ **of his strength** cela a sérieusement ébranlé *or* sapé ses forces ◆ **it took a** ~ **of his savings** cela a fait un gros trou dans ses économies ◆ **we must reduce the accident** ~ **on the roads** il nous faut réduire le nombre des victimes de la route ◆ **the death** ~ le bilan des victimes ◆ **the** ~ **of dead and injured has risen** le nombre des morts et des blessés a augmenté ◆ **winter takes its** ~ **on your health** l'hiver a un effet néfaste sur la santé ◆ **higher fuel prices took their** ~ l'augmentation du prix de l'essence a eu des conséquences néfastes ◆ **a high exchange rate took a heavy** ~ **on industry** le niveau élevé du change a nui considérablement à l'industrie

COMP **toll bridge N** pont *m* à péage
toll call N (*US Telec*) appel *m* longue distance
toll charge N péage *m*
toll-free ADV (*US Telec*) sans payer la communication **ADJ** gratuit ◆ ~**-free number** ≈ numéro *m* vert ®
toll road N route *f* à péage ; → ROADS

toll² /təʊl/ **VI** [*bell*] sonner ◆ **for whom the bell** ~**s** pour qui sonne le glas **VT** [+ *bell, the hour*] sonner ; [+ *sb's death*] sonner le glas pour

tollbar /ˈtəʊlbɑːʳ/ **N** barrière *f* de péage

tollbooth /ˈtəʊlbuːð/ **N** poste *m* de péage

tolley /ˈtɒlɪ/ **N** (= *marble*) calot *m*

tollgate /ˈtəʊlgeɪt/ **N** ⇒ **tollbar**

tollhouse /ˈtəʊlhaʊs/ **N** maison *f* de péagiste **COMP** **tollhouse cookie** (*US*) cookie *m* aux pépites de chocolat

tollkeeper /ˈtəʊlkiːpəʳ/ **N** péagiste *mf*

tollway /ˈtəʊlweɪ/ **N** ⇒ **toll road** ; → **toll¹**

Tolstoy /ˈtɒlstɔɪ/ **N** Tolstoï *m*

Tom /tɒm/ **N** 1 (dim of **Thomas**) Thomas *m* ◆ **(any)** ~, **Dick or Harry** n'importe qui, le premier venu ; → **peep¹** 2 (*US* ‡ *pej*: also **Uncle Tom**) Oncle Tom *m*, bon nègre *m* **COMP** **Tom Thumb N** Tom-Pouce *m* ; (*in French tale*) le Petit Poucet

tom /tɒm/ **N** matou *m* **COMP** **tom cat N** (= *cat*) matou *m* ; (*US* ‡ = *man*) coureur *m* de jupons, cavaleur* *m*

tomahawk /ˈtɒməhɔːk/ **N** tomahawk *m*, hache *f* de guerre

tomato /təˈmɑːtəʊ/ (*US*) /təˈmeɪtəʊ/ **N** (pl **tomatoes**) (= *fruit, plant*) tomate *f*

COMP **tomato juice N** jus *m* de tomate
tomato ketchup N ketchup *m*
tomato paste N ⇒ **tomato purée**
tomato plant N tomate *f*
tomato purée N purée *f* de tomates
tomato sauce N sauce *f* tomate
tomato soup N soupe *f* de tomates

tomb /tuːm/ **N** tombeau *m*, tombe *f*

tombac, tombak /ˈtɒmbæk/ **N** (*NonC*) tombac *m*, laiton *m*

tombola /tɒmˈbəʊlə/ **N** (*Brit*) tombola *f*

tomboy /ˈtɒmbɔɪ/ **N** garçon *m* manqué

tomboyish /ˈtɒmbɔɪɪʃ/ **ADJ** [*behaviour*] de garçon manqué ◆ **a** ~ **girl** un garçon manqué

tomboyishness /ˈtɒmbɔɪɪʃnɪs/ **N** (*NonC*) manières *fpl* de garçon manqué

tombstone /ˈtuːmstəʊn/ **N** pierre *f* tombale, tombe *f*

tome /təʊm/ **N** tome *m*, gros volume *m*

tomfool /ˈtɒmˈfuːl/ **ADJ** absurde, idiot

tomfoolery /tɒmˈfuːlərɪ/ **N** (*NonC*) niaiserie(s) *f(pl)*, âneries *fpl*

Tommy /ˈtɒmɪ/ **N** (dim of **Thomas**) Thomas *m* ; (*Brit Mil* *: also **tommy**) tommy* *m*, soldat *m* britannique **COMP** **Tommy gun N** mitraillette *f*

tommyrot †* /ˈtɒmɪrɒt/ **N** (*NonC*) bêtises *fpl*, âneries *fpl*

tomography /təˈmɒgrəfɪ/ **N** tomographie *f*

tomorrow /təˈmɒrəʊ/ **ADV** demain ◆ **all (day)** ~ toute la journée (de) demain ◆ **late** ~ tard demain ◆ **early** ~ demain de bonne heure ◆ ~ **lunchtime** demain à midi ◆ **I met her a week ago** ~ ça fera une semaine demain que je l'ai rencontrée ◆ **he'll have been here a week ~** demain cela fera huit jours qu'il est là ◆ **see you ~** à demain ◆ **what day will it be ~?** quel jour sera-t-on *or* serons-nous demain ? ◆ **what date will it be ~?** on sera le combien demain ? ; → **today**

N 1 demain *m* ◆ **what day will ~ be?** quel jour serons-nous demain ? ◆ **~ will be Saturday** demain ce sera samedi ◆ **what date will ~ be?** quelle est la date de demain ? ◆ **~ will be the 5th** demain ce sera le 5 ◆ **I hope ~ will be dry** j'espère qu'il ne pleuvra pas demain ◆ **~ will be a better day for you** demain les choses iront mieux pour vous ◆ **~ never comes** demain n'arrive jamais ◆ **~ is another day!** ça ira peut-être mieux demain ! ◆ **~'s paper** le journal de demain

2 *(= the future)* ◆ **the writers of ~** les écrivains *mpl* de demain *or* de l'avenir ◆ **like** *or* **as if there was no ~** * *[spend, drive]* sans se soucier du lendemain ; *[eat, drink]* comme si c'était la dernière fois ◆ **brighter ~s** des lendemains qui chantent

COMP **tomorrow afternoon** ADV demain après-midi
tomorrow evening ADV demain soir
tomorrow morning ADV demain matin
tomorrow week * ADV *(Brit)* demain en huit

tomtit /ˈtɒmtɪt/ N mésange *f*

tomtom /ˈtɒmtɒm/ N tam-tam *m*

ton /tʌn/ N 1 *(= weight)* tonne *f* *(Brit = 1016,06 kg ; Can, US etc = 907,20 kg)* ◆ **metric ~** tonne *f* (= 1 000 kg) ◆ **a seven-~ truck** un camion de sept tonnes ◆ **it weighs a ~, it's a ~ weight** *(fig)* ça pèse une tonne ◆ **~s of** * *(fig)* beaucoup de, des tas de * 2 *(Naut)* (also **register ton**) tonneau *m* (= 2,83 m³) ; (also **displacement ton**) tonne *f* ◆ **a 60,000-~ steamer** un paquebot de 60 000 tonnes 3 (*‡ = hundred*) **a ~** cent ◆ **to do a ~ (up)** *(Aut etc)* faire du cent soixante à l'heure COMP **ton-up boys** †‡ NPL *(Brit = motorcyclists)* motards * *mpl*, fous *mpl* de la moto

tonal /ˈtəʊnl/ ADJ 1 *(= vocal)* *[range, contrast]* tonal ◆ **~ quality** tonalité *f* 2 *(in colour)* *[range, contrast]* de tons
COMP **tonal music** N musique *f* tonale
tonal value N *(Phot)* tonalité *f*

tonality /təʊˈnælɪtɪ/ N tonalité *f*

tondo /ˈtɒndəʊ/ N (pl **tondi** /ˈtɒndiː/) tondo *m*

tone /təʊn/ LANGUAGE IN USE 27.3

N 1 *(in sound: also Ling, Mus)* ton *m* ; *(Telec: also of radio, record player etc)* tonalité *f* ; *[of answering machine]* signal *m* sonore, bip *m* (sonore) ; *[of musical instrument]* sonorité *f* ◆ **to speak in low ~s** *or* **in a low ~** parler à voix basse *or* doucement ◆ **to speak in angry ~s, to speak in an angry ~ (of voice)** parler sur le ton de la colère ◆ **don't speak to me in that ~ (of voice)!** ne me parlez pas sur ce ton ! ◆ **in friendly ~s, in a friendly ~** sur un ton amical ◆ **after the ~** *(on answering machine)* après le bip *or* le signal sonore ◆ **rising/falling ~** *(Ling)* ton *m* montant/descendant ; → **dialling, engaged**

2 *(in colour)* ton *m* ◆ **two-~** en deux tons

3 *(= general character)* ton *m* ◆ **what was the ~ of his letter?** quel était le ton de sa lettre ? ◆ **we were impressed by the whole ~ of the school** nous avons été impressionnés par la tenue générale de l'école ◆ **the ~ of the market** *(Fin)* la tenue du marché ◆ **to raise/lower the ~ of sth** hausser/rabaisser le niveau de qch

4 *(NonC = class, elegance)* classe *f* ◆ **it gives the restaurant ~, it adds ~ to the restaurant** cela donne de la classe au restaurant

5 *(Med, Physiol: of muscles etc)* tonus *m*, tonicité *f*

VI *[colour]* s'harmoniser *(with* avec)

COMP **tone arm** N *[of record player]* bras *m* de lecture
tone colour N *(Mus)* timbre *m*
tone control (knob) N *[of record player etc]* bouton *m* de tonalité
tone-deaf ADJ ◆ **to be ~-deaf** ne pas avoir d'oreille
tone deafness N manque *m* d'oreille
tone language N *(Ling)* langue *f* à tons
tone poem N poème *m* symphonique
tone row, tone series N *(Mus)* série *f* (de notes)

► **tone down** VT SEP *[+ colour]* adoucir ; *[+ sound]* baisser ; *(fig)* *[+ criticism, effect]* atténuer, adoucir ; *[+ language]* atténuer, modérer ; *[+ policy]* modérer, mettre en sourdine

► **tone in** VI s'harmoniser *(with* avec)

► **tone up** VT SEP *[+ muscles, the system]* tonifier

-toned /təʊnd/ ADJ *(in compounds)* ◆ **flesh-toned** couleur chair *inv* ◆ **high-toned** *[style, book etc]* prétentieux ◆ **sepia-toned** couleur sépia *inv* ◆ **warm-toned** *[colour, skin]* au tons chauds

toneless /ˈtəʊnlɪs/ ADJ *[voice]* blanc (blanche *f*), sans timbre

tonelessly /ˈtəʊnlɪslɪ/ ADV d'une voix blanche *or* sans timbre

toner /ˈtəʊnəʳ/ N 1 *(for photocopier, printer)* encre *f*, toner *m* 2 *(for skin)* (lotion *f*) tonique *m*

Tonga /ˈtɒŋə/ N Tonga, Tonga *fpl* ◆ **in ~** aux Tonga

tongs /tɒŋz/ NPL (also **pair of tongs**) pinces *fpl* ; *(for coal)* pincettes *fpl* ; *(for sugar)* pince *f* (à sucre) ; (also **curling tongs**) fer *m* (à friser) ; → **hammer**

tongue /tʌŋ/ N 1 *(Anat, Culin)* langue *f* ; *[of shoe]* languette *f* ; *[of bell]* battant *m* ; *(fig: of flame, land, also on tool, machine etc)* langue *f* ◆ **to put out** *or* **stick out one's ~** tirer la langue *(at sb* à qn) ◆ **his ~ was hanging out** *[dog, person]* il tirait la langue ◆ **to give ~** *[hounds]* donner de la voix ◆ **to lose/find one's ~** perdre/retrouver sa langue ◆ **with his ~ in his cheek, ~ in cheek** ironiquement, en plaisantant ◆ **he held his ~ about it** il a tenu sa langue ◆ **hold your ~!** taisez-vous ! ◆ **I'm going to let him feel** *or* **give him the rough side of my ~** † je vais lui dire ma façon de penser ◆ **keep a civil ~ in your head!** tâchez d'être plus poli ! ◆ **I can't get my ~ round it** je n'arrive pas à le prononcer correctement ; → **cat, loosen, slip, tip¹, wag¹**

2 *(= language)* langue *f* ◆ **to speak in ~s** *(Rel)* parler de nouvelles langues ; → **mother**

VT *(Mus)* *[+ note]* attaquer en coup de langue

COMP **tongue-and-groove** N → **tongue-and-groove**
tongue depressor N *(Med)* abaisse-langue *m*
tongue-in-cheek ADJ *[remark etc]* ironique ; see also **noun**
tongue-lashing * N ◆ **to give sb a ~-lashing** sonner les cloches à qn * ◆ **to get a ~-lashing** se faire remonter les bretelles *
tongue-tied ADJ *(fig)* muet *(fig)* ◆ **~-tied from shyness** rendu muet par la timidité, trop timide pour parler
tongue twister N phrase *f* (*or* nom *m* etc) très difficile à prononcer

tongue-and-groove /ˈtʌŋənˈgruːv/ N (also **tongue-and-groove boarding** *or* **strips**) planches *fpl* à rainure et languette ◆ **~ joint** assemblage *m* à rainure et languette VT *[+ wall]* revêtir de planches à rainure et languette

-tongued /tʌŋd/ ADJ *(in compounds)* qui a la langue ... ◆ **sharp-tongued** qui a la langue acérée

tonguing /ˈtʌŋɪŋ/ N *(Mus)* (technique *f* du) coup *m* de langue

tonic /ˈtɒnɪk/ ADJ 1 *(= reviving)* *[bath, properties, drink]* tonifiant ; *[effect]* tonique 2 *(Mus, Ling)* tonique N 1 *(Med)* tonique *m*, fortifiant *m* ◆ **you need a ~** *(lit, fig)* il vous faut un bon tonique ◆ **it was a real ~ to see him** cela m'a vraiment remonté le moral de le voir 2 (also **tonic water, Indian tonic**) ≈ Schweppes ® *m* ◆ **gin and ~** gin-tonic *m* 3 *(Mus)* tonique *f*

COMP **tonic sol-fa** N *(Mus)* solfège *m*
tonic water N (also **Indian tonic water**) tonic *m*, ≈ Schweppes ® *m* ;
tonic wine N vin *m* tonique

tonicity /tɒˈnɪsɪtɪ/ N tonicité *f*

tonight /təˈnaɪt/ ADV, N *(before bed)* ce soir ; *(during sleep)* cette nuit

tonnage /ˈtʌnɪdʒ/ N *(Naut: all senses)* tonnage *m*

tonne /tʌn/ N tonne *f*

tonneau /ˈtʌnəʊ/ N (pl **tonneaus** *or* **tonneaux** /ˈtʌnəʊz/) *(Aut:* also **tonneau cover**) bâche *f* *(de voiture de sport)*

-tonner /ˈtʌnəʳ/ N *(in compounds)* ◆ **a ten-tonner** (= truck) un (camion de) dix tonnes

tonometer /təʊˈnɒmɪtəʳ/ N *(Mus)* diapason *m* de Scheibler ; *(Med)* tonomètre *m*

tonsil /ˈtɒnsl/ N amygdale *f* ◆ **to have one's ~s out** *or* **removed** être opéré des amygdales

tonsillectomy /ˌtɒnsɪˈlektəmɪ/ N amygdalectomie *f*

tonsillitis /ˌtɒnsɪˈlaɪtɪs/ N *(NonC)* angine *f*, amygdalite *f* ◆ **he's got ~** il a une angine, il a une amygdalite *(frm)*

tonsorial /tɒnˈsɔːrɪəl/ ADJ *(hum)* de barbier

tonsure /ˈtɒnʃəʳ/ N tonsure *f* VT tonsurer

tontine /tɒnˈtiːn/ N tontine *f*

Tony /ˈtəʊnɪ/ N 1 (dim of **Anthony**) Antoine *m* 2 *(Theat* : pl **Tonys** *or* **Tonies**) (also **Tony award**) Tony *m* *(oscar du théâtre décerné à Broadway)*

tony * /ˈtəʊnɪ/ ADJ *(US)* chic * *inv*

too /tuː/ ADV 1 *(= excessively)* trop, par trop *(liter)* ◆ **it's ~ hard for me** c'est trop difficile pour moi ◆ **it's ~ hard for me to explain** c'est trop difficile pour que je puisse vous l'expliquer ◆ **that case is ~ heavy to carry** cette valise est trop lourde à porter ◆ **it's ~ heavy for me to carry** c'est trop lourd à porter pour moi ◆ **he's ~ mean to pay for it** il est trop pingre pour le payer ◆ **that's ~ kind of you!** vous êtes vraiment trop aimable ! ◆ **I'm not ~ sure about that** je n'en suis pas très certain ◆ **~ true!** *, **~ right!** * que oui ! *, et comment ! * ◆ **it's just too-too!** ‡ en voilà un chichi ! * ; → **good, many, much, none**

2 *(= also)* aussi ; *(= moreover)* en plus, par-dessus le marché, de plus ◆ **I went ~** j'y suis allé aussi ◆ **you ~ can own a car like this** vous aussi vous pouvez être le propriétaire d'une voiture comme celle-ci ◆ **he can swim ~** lui aussi sait nager ◆ **they asked for a discount ~!** et en plus *or* et par-dessus le marché ils ont demandé un rabais ! ◆ **and then, there's the question of ...** et puis il y a également la question de ...

took /tʊk/ VB pt of **take**

tool /tuːl/ N *(gen, Tech)* outil *m* (de travail) ; *(fig = book etc)* outil *m*, instrument *m* ◆ **set of ~s** panoplie *f* d'outils ◆ **garden ~s** outils *mpl* *or* ustensiles *mpl* de jardinage ◆ **these are the ~s of my trade** *(lit, fig)* voilà les outils de mon métier ◆ **he was merely a ~ of the revolutionary party** il n'était que l'outil *or* l'instrument du parti révolutionnaire ◆ **a ~ in the hands of ...** *(fig)* un instrument dans les mains de ... ; → **down¹, machine, workman** VT *(gen)* travailler, ouvrager ; *[+ silver]* ciseler ; *[+ leather]* repousser VI *(= drive fast)* ◆ **to ~ along/past** * rouler/passer tranquillement *or* pépère ‡

COMP **tool maker** N *(in factory)* outilleur *m*
tool making N *(in factory)* montage *m* et réglage *m* des machines-outils

► **tool up** VT SEP (Ind) équiper, outiller VI *[factory etc]* s'équiper, s'outiller ; *(fig)* se préparer

toolbag /ˈtuːlbæg/ N trousse *f* à outils

toolbar /ˈtuːlbɑːʳ/ N barre *f* d'outils

toolbox /ˈtuːlbɒks/ N boîte *f* à outils

toolcase /ˈtuːlkeɪs/ N (= *bag*) trousse *f* à outils ; (= *box*) caisse *f* à outils

toolchest /ˈtuːltʃest/ N coffre *m* à outils

tooled /tuːld/ ADJ *(gen)* ouvragé ; *[silver]* ciselé ; *[leather]* repoussé ; *[book cover]* en cuir repoussé

toolhouse /ˈtuːlhaʊs/ N ⇒ **toolshed**

tooling /ˈtuːlɪŋ/ N *(on book-cover etc)* repoussé *m* ; *(on silver)* ciselure *f*

toolkit /ˈtuːlkɪt/ N trousse *f* à outils ; *(Comput)* valise *f*

toolroom /ˈtuːlruːm/ N *(in factory)* atelier *m* d'outillage

toolshed /ˈtuːlʃed/ N cabane *f* à outils

toot /tuːt/ N *[of car horn]* coup *m* de klaxon ® ; *[of whistle]* coup *m* de sifflet ; *[of trumpet, flute]* note *f* (brève) VI *[car horn]* klaxonner ; *(on whistle)* donner un coup de sifflet ; *(on trumpet, flute)* jouer une note VT ◆ **to ~ the horn** klaxonner

tooth /tuːθ/ N (pl **teeth**) *[of person, animal, comb, saw etc]* dent *f* ◆ **front ~** dent *f* de devant ◆ **back ~** molaire *f* ◆ **to have a ~ out** *or (esp US)* **pulled** se faire arracher une dent ◆ **selling a car these days is like pulling teeth** *(US)* c'est pratiquement impossible de vendre une voiture en ce moment ◆ **to have a ~ capped** se faire poser une couronne ◆ **to cut a ~** *[child]* percer une dent ◆ **he is cutting teeth** il fait ses dents ◆ **to cut one's teeth on sth** *(fig)* se faire les dents sur qch ◆ **to mutter sth between one's teeth** *or* **between clenched teeth** grommeler qch entre ses dents ◆ **to set** *or* **grit one's teeth** serrer les dents ◆ **to bare** *or* **show one's teeth** *(lit, fig)* montrer les dents ◆ **in the teeth of the wind** contre le vent ◆ **in the teeth of the opposition** en dépit de *or* malgré l'opposition ◆ **~ and nail** avec acharnement, farouchement ◆ **to get one's teeth into sth** *(fig)* se mettre à fond à qch, se mettre à faire qch pour de bon ◆ **there's nothing you can get your teeth into** *[food etc]* ce n'est pas très substantiel ; *(fig)* il n'y a là rien de substantiel *or* solide ◆ **the legislation has no teeth** la législation est impuissante ◆ **to give a law teeth** renforcer le pouvoir d'une loi ◆ **to cast** *or* **throw sth in sb's teeth** jeter qch à la tête de qn, reprocher qch à qn ◆ **to be fed up** *or* **sick to the (back) teeth of sth**✱ en avoir marre* *or* ras le bol✱ de qch ; → **chatter, edge, long**[1]

COMP **tooth decay** N (NonC) carie *f* dentaire

the Tooth Fairy N ≈ la petite souris

tooth powder N poudre *f* dentifrice

toothache /ˈtuːθeɪk/ N mal *m* or rage *f* de dents ◆ **to have ~** avoir mal aux dents

toothbrush /ˈtuːθbrʌʃ/ N brosse *f* à dents COMP **toothbrush moustache** N moustache *f* en brosse

toothcomb /ˈtuːθkəʊm/ N (also **fine toothcomb**) → **fine**[2]

toothed /tuːθt/ ADJ *[wheel, leaf]* denté

-toothed /tuːθt/ ADJ *(in compounds)* ◆ **big-toothed** aux grandes dents

toothless /ˈtuːθlɪs/ ADJ [1] (= *without teeth*) *[person, smile, grin]* édenté ; *[mouth, gums]* sans dents [2] *(fig = powerless) [organization]* sans pouvoir, sans influence ; *[law, agreement, treaty]* qui n'a pas de poids ◆ **a ~ tiger** un tigre de papier

toothpaste /ˈtuːθpeɪst/ N (pâte *f*) dentifrice *m*

toothpick /ˈtuːθpɪk/ N cure-dent *m*

toothsome /ˈtuːθsəm/ ADJ savoureux

toothy /ˈtuːθɪ/ ADJ *[person]* à grandes dents ◆ **to be ~** avoir de grandes dents ◆ **he flashed me a ~ grin** *or* **smile** il m'a gratifié d'un sourire tout en dents

tootle /ˈtuːtl/ N *[of trumpet, flute, car-horn]* notes *fpl* (brèves) ; (= *tune*) petit air *m* VI [1] (= *toot: Aut*) klaxonner, corner ; *(Mus)* jouer un petit air [2] *(Aut)* **to ~ along/past** *etc* * rouler/passer *etc* gaiement *or* sans s'en faire* VT *[+ trumpet, flute etc]* jouer un peu de

toots✱ /tʊts/ N ma belle*

tootsie✱, **tootsy**✱ /ˈtʊtsɪ/ N [1] (= *toe*) doigt *m* de pied ; (= *foot*) peton* *m*, pied *m* [2] (= *girl*) jolie nana✱ *f* ◆ **hi ~!** salut ma belle ! *

top[1] /tɒp/

1 NOUN	5 TRANSITIVE VERB
2 PLURAL NOUN	6 COMPOUNDS
3 ADVERB	7 PHRASAL VERBS
4 ADJECTIVE	

1 - NOUN

[1] = highest point *[of mountain]* sommet *m*, cime *f* ; *[of tree]* faîte *m*, cime *f* ; *[of hill, head]* sommet *m*, haut *m* ; *[of ladder, stairs, page, wall, cupboard]* haut *m* ; *[of wave]* crête *f* ; *[of box, container]* dessus *m* ; *[of list, table, classification]* tête *f* ; (= *surface*) surface *f* ◆ **it's near the ~ of the pile** c'est vers le haut de la pile ◆ **to come** *or* **rise** *or* **float to the ~** remonter à la surface, surnager ◆ **the ~ of the milk** la crème du lait ◆ **six lines from the ~ of page seven** sixième ligne à partir du haut de la page sept ◆ **from ~ to toe, from the ~ of his head to the tip of his toes** *(fig)* de la tête aux pieds ◆ **he's talking off the ~ of his head** * il dit n'importe quoi ◆ **I'm saying that off the ~ of my head** * je dis ça sans savoir exactement ◆ **the ~ of the morning to you!** *(Ir)* je vous souhaite bien le bonjour ! ◆ **in ~** *(Brit)* ⇒ **in top gear;** → **top gear** ◆ **to get to** *or* **reach the ~, to make it to the ~** *(indicating status, gen)* réussir, aller loin ; *(in hierarchy etc)* arriver en haut de l'échelle ◆ **it's ~ of the pops this week** c'est en tête du hit-parade *or* numéro un au hit-parade cette semaine ◆ **the men at the ~** les dirigeants *mpl*, les responsables *mpl*, ceux qui sont au pouvoir ◆ **the men at the ~ don't care about it** en haut lieu ils ne s'en soucient guère

◆ **at the top of** *[+ hill, mountain]* au sommet de ; *[+ stairs, ladder, building, page]* en haut de ; *[+ list, division, league]* en tête de ; *[+ street etc]* en haut de, au bout de ; *[+ garden]* au fond de ; *[+ profession, career]* au faîte de ◆ **he was sitting at the ~ of the table** il était assis en tête de la table *or* à la place d'honneur ◆ **it's at the ~ of the pile** c'est en haut *or* au sommet de la pile ◆ **at the ~ of the pile*** *or* **heap*** *(fig)* en haut de l'échelle ◆ **to be at the ~ of the class** *(Scol)* être premier de la classe ◆ **our next news bulletin at the ~ of the hour** nos prochaines informations à trois heures *(or quatre heures etc)*

◆ **on (the) top (of)** ◆ **on ~ of it** ◆ **on (the) ~** dessus ◆ **it's the one on (the) ~** c'est celui du dessus ◆ **take the plate on the ~** prends l'assiette du dessus ◆ **he came out on ~** *(fig)* il a eu le dessus ◆ **there was a thick layer of cream on ~ of the cake** il y avait une épaisse couche de crème sur le gâteau ◆ **to live on ~ of each other** vivre les uns sur les autres ◆ **in such a small flat the children are always on ~ of us** dans un appartement si petit, les enfants sont toujours dans nos jambes ◆ **to be on ~ of the world** être aux anges ◆ **to be on the ~ of one's form** être au sommet de sa forme ◆ **he's on ~ of things now*** il s'en sort très bien *or* il domine bien la situation maintenant ; *(after breakdown, bereavement)* il a repris le dessus maintenant ◆ **things are getting on ~ of her*** elle est dépassée par les événements, elle ne sait plus où donner de la tête ◆ **the lorry was right on ~ of the car in front** le camion touchait presque la voiture de devant ◆ **by the time I saw the car, it was practically on ~ of me** quand j'ai vu la voiture elle était pratiquement sur moi ◆ **he's bought another car on ~ of the one he's got already** il a acheté une autre voiture en plus de celle qu'il a déjà ◆ **then on ~ of all that he refused to help us** et puis par-dessus le marché il a refusé de nous aider

◆ **from top to bottom** *[redecorate]* complètement, du sol au plafond ; *[clean]* de fond en comble ; *[cover]* entièrement ; *[divide, split] [+ political party]* profondément ; *[search a person]* de la tête aux pieds ; *[search a house]* de fond en comble ◆ **the system is rotten from ~ to bottom** le système tout entier est pourri

◆ **over the top** ◆ **to go over the ~** *(Mil)* monter à l'assaut ◆ **to be over the ~*** *(esp Brit: indicating exaggeration) [film, book]* dépasser la mesure ; *[person]* en faire trop*, exagérer ; *[act, opinion]* être excessif

[2] = upper part, section *[of car etc]* toit *m* ; *[of bus]* étage *m* supérieur, impériale *f* ; *[of turnip, carrot, radish]* fanes *fpl* ◆ **"top"** *(on box etc)* "haut" ◆ **seats on ~** *(on bus)* places *fpl* à l'étage supérieur ◆ **we saw London from the ~ of a bus** nous avons vu Londres du haut d'un bus ◆ **let's go up on ~** *(in bus)* allons en haut ; *(in ship)* allons sur le pont ◆ **the table ~ is made of oak** le plateau de la table est en chêne ◆ **the ~ of the table is scratched** le dessus de la table est rayé ◆ **he hasn't got much up ~*** (= *he is bald*) il a le crâne déplumé* ◆ **she hasn't got much up ~*** (= *she is stupid*) ce n'est pas une lumière* ; (= *she is flat-chested*) elle est plate comme une limande* *or* une planche à repasser*

[3] of garment, pyjamas, bikini haut *m* ◆ **I want a ~ to go with this skirt** je voudrais un haut qui aille avec cette jupe

[4] = cap, lid *[of box]* couvercle *m* ; *[of bottle, tube]* bouchon *m* ; *[of pen]* capuchon *m*

2 - PLURAL NOUN

tops* ◆ **he's (the) ~s** il est champion*

3 - ADVERB

◆ **tops*** (= *max*) à tout casser*

4 - ADJECTIVE

[1] = highest *[shelf, drawer]* du haut ; *[floor, storey]* dernier ◆ **the ~ coat** *[of paint]* la dernière couche ◆ **the ~ corridor of the main building** le corridor du haut dans le bâtiment principal ◆ **at the ~ end of the scale** en haut de l'échelle ◆ **a car at the ~ end of the range** une voiture haut de gamme ◆ **the ~ layer of skin** la couche supérieure de la peau ◆ **the ~ note** *(Mus)* la note la plus haute ◆ **the ~ step** la dernière marche (en haut)

[2] in rank etc ◆ **~ management** cadres *mpl* supérieurs ◆ **the ~ men in the party** les dirigeants *mpl* du parti ◆ **in the ~ class** *(Scol) (secondary school)* ≈ en terminale ; *(primary)* ≈ en cours moyen deuxième année ; (= *top stream*) dans le premier groupe

[3] = best, leading ◆ **he was the ~ student in English** (= *the best*) c'était le meilleur étudiant en anglais ◆ **he was a ~ student in English** (= *one of the best*) c'était l'un des meilleurs étudiants en anglais ◆ **~ executives** (= *leading*) cadres *mpl* supérieurs ◆ **he was Italy's ~ scorer in the World Cup** c'était le meilleur buteur de l'équipe d'Italie pendant la coupe du monde ◆ **one of the ~ pianists** un des plus grands pianistes ◆ **a ~ job, one of the ~ jobs** un des postes les plus prestigieux ◆ **he was** *or* **came ~ in maths** *(Scol)* il a été premier en maths ◆ **the**

~ **mark** *(Scol)* la meilleure note ◆ ~ **marks for efficiency** vingt sur vingt pour l'efficacité ◆ **it was a ~ party** * *(Brit)* c'était top * comme fête

4 [= farthest] ◆ **the ~ end of the garden** le fond du jardin ◆ **the ~ end of the field** l'autre bout *m* du champ ◆ **the ~ right-hand corner** le coin en haut à droite

5 [= maximum] ◆ **the vehicle's ~ speed** la vitesse maximale du véhicule ◆ **at ~ speed** à toute vitesse ◆ **a matter of ~ priority** une question absolument prioritaire ◆ ~ **prices** prix *mpl* élevés ◆ **we pay ~ price(s) for old clocks** nous offrons les meilleurs prix pour les vieilles horloges

5 - TRANSITIVE VERB

1 [= remove top from] *[+ tree]* étêter, écimer ; *[+ plant]* écimer ; *[+ radish, carrot etc]* couper *or* enlever les fanes de ◆ **to ~ and tail beans** *(Brit)* ébouter les haricots

2 [‡ = behead] *[+ person]* couper le cou à *

3 [‡ = kill] *[+ person]* buter‡ ◆ **to ~ o.s.** se flinguer‡

4 [= form top of] surmonter ◆ **~ped by a dome** surmonté d'un dôme

5 [= exceed] dépasser ◆ **we have ~ped last year's sales figures** nous avons dépassé les chiffres des ventes de l'année dernière ◆ **imports ~ped £10 billion last month** les importations ont dépassé la barre des dix milliards de livres le mois dernier ◆ **the fish ~ped 10kg** le poisson pesait *or* faisait plus de 10 kg ◆ **to ~ sb in height** dépasser qn en hauteur ◆ **the event that ~ped it was ...** l'événement qui a éclipsé cela était ... ◆ **amazing! I'm sure nobody can ~ that** incroyable ! je suis sûr que personne ne peut faire mieux ◆ **and to ~ it all ...** et pour couronner le tout ... ◆ **that ~s the lot!** * c'est le bouquet ! *

6 [= pass top of] *[+ hill]* franchir le sommet de ; *[+ ridge]* franchir

7 [= be at top of] *[+ pile]* être au sommet de ; *[+ list]* être en tête de *or* à la tête de ◆ **to ~ the bill** *(Theat)* être en tête d'affiche, tenir la vedette

6 - COMPOUNDS

top banana‡ N *(US) (gen)* gros bonnet * *m*, grosse légume * *f* ; *(Theat)* comique *m* principal
top boots NPL bottes *fpl* à revers
top brass * N *(fig)* huiles * *fpl*
top-class ADJ de première classe
top copy N original *m*
top dog * N *(esp US)* ◆ **he's ~ dog around here** c'est lui qui commande ici *or* qui fait la pluie et le beau temps ici
top dollar * N *(esp US)* ◆ **to pay ~ dollar for sth** payer qch au prix fort
top-down ADJ *[approach, management]* directif
top drawer N ◆ **he's out of the ~ drawer** il fait partie du gratin *
top-drawer * ADJ *(socially)* de la haute *, de haute volée ; *(in quality, achievement)* de tout premier rang
top-dress VT *(Agr)* fertiliser
top dressing N fumure *f* en surface
top gear N *(Brit Aut)* ◆ **in ~ gear** *(four-speed box)* en quatrième ; *(five-speed box)* en cinquième
top hand * N *(US)* collaborateur *m* de premier plan
top hat N (chapeau *m*) haut-de-forme *m*
top-hatted ADJ en (chapeau) haut-de-forme
top-heavy ADJ *[structure etc]* trop lourd du haut, déséquilibré ; *(fig) [business, administration]* où l'encadrement est trop lourd
top-hole † * ADJ *(Brit)* épatant † *, bath † *
top-level ADJ *[meeting, talks, discussion]* au plus haut niveau ; *[decision]* pris au plus haut niveau *or* au sommet
top-liner * N *(Brit Theat)* (artiste *mf* en) tête *f* d'affiche
top-loader, top-loading washing machine N lave-linge *m* à chargement par le haut
top-of-the-line, top-of-the-range ADJ haut de gamme *inv*
top-ranked ADJ *[player, team]* du plus haut niveau
top-ranking ADJ (très) haut placé
top round *(US Culin)* ⇒ **topside**
top-secret ADJ ultrasecret (-ète *f*), top secret (-ète *f*)
top-security wing N *[of prison]* quartier *m* de haute sécurité
top-shelf ADJ *(Brit) [magazine, material]* de charme
the top ten NPL *(Mus)* les dix premiers *mpl* du Top
the top thirty NPL le Top 30
top-up N *(for mobile phone)* recharge *f (de carte prépayée)* ◆ **can I give you a ~-up ?** *(Brit = drink)* je vous en ressers ? ◆ **the battery/oil needs a ~-up** *(Brit)* il faut remettre de l'eau dans la batterie/remettre de l'huile
top-up card N *(for mobile phone)* carte *f* prépayée, recharge *f*
top-up loan N prêt *m* complémentaire

7 - PHRASAL VERBS

► **top off** VI *(= reach peak) [sales, production etc]* atteindre un niveau record VT SEP terminer, compléter ◆ **we ~ped off the meal with a glass of cognac** nous avons terminé le repas par un verre de cognac ◆ **to ~ it all off** pour couronner le tout

► **top out** VI *(Constr)* terminer le gros œuvre ; *(Comm) [rate, price, cost]* plafonner, atteindre son niveau le plus élevé

► **top up** *(Brit)* VI *[driver etc]* ◆ **to ~ up with oil** remettre *or* rajouter de l'huile VT SEP *[+ cup, glass]* remplir (à nouveau) ; *[+ car battery]* remettre de l'eau dans ◆ **I've ~ped up the petrol in your tank** j'ai rajouté *or* remis de l'essence dans votre réservoir ◆ **I've ~ped up your coffee** je vous ai remis du café ◆ **her parents ~ up her grant** ses parents lui donnent de l'argent en complément de sa bourse ◆ **can I ~ you up?** * je vous en remets ?

---

top[2] / tɒp / N *(= toy)* toupie *f* ; → **sleep, spinning**
topaz / 'təʊpæz / N topaze *f*
topcoat / 'tɒpkəʊt / N 1 *[of paint]* dernière couche *f* 2 *(Dress)* pardessus *m*, manteau *m*
topee / 'təʊpiː / N casque *m* colonial
toper † / 'təʊpəʳ / N grand buveur *m*
topflight * / tɒp'flaɪt / ADJ de premier ordre, excellent
topiary / 'təʊpɪərɪ / N *(NonC)* art *m* topiaire, topiaire *f* COMP **topiary garden** N jardin *m* d'arbres taillés architecturalement
topic / 'tɒpɪk / N *[of essay, speech]* sujet *m* ; *(for discussion)* sujet *m* de discussion, thème *m* ; *(esp Brit Scol = project)* dossier *m* ; *(Ling)* thème *m* COMP **topic sentence** N *(US Gram)* phrase *f* d'introduction
topical / 'tɒpɪkəl / ADJ *[issue, theme]* d'actualité ; *[humour, joke]* axé sur l'actualité ◆ **a ~ reference** une allusion à l'actualité
topicality / ˌtɒpɪ'kælɪtɪ / N *(NonC)* actualité *f*
topknot / 'tɒpnɒt / N *[of hair]* toupet *m*, houppe *f* ; *[of ribbons etc]* coque *f* ; *[of bird's feathers]* aigrette *f* ; *(= fish)* targeur *m*
topless / 'tɒplɪs / ADJ *[woman, dancer, model]* aux seins nus ; *[beach]* où l'on peut avoir les seins nus ; *[sunbathing, dancing]* seins nus ◆ **photographs showing her ~** des photographies la montrant seins nus ADV *[sunbathe, pose, dance]* (les) seins nus ◆ **to go ~** se mettre seins nus, faire du topless * COMP **topless bar** N bar *m* topless *
topless swimsuit N monokini *m*
topmast / 'tɒpmɑːst / N *(Naut)* mât *m* de hune
topmost / 'tɒpməʊst / ADJ le plus haut
topnotch * / tɒp'nɒtʃ / ADJ ⇒ **topflight**
topographer / tə'pɒgrəfəʳ / N topographe *mf*
topographic(al) / ˌtɒpə'græfɪk(l) / ADJ topographique
topography / tə'pɒgrəfɪ / N topographie *f*
topological / ˌtɒpə'lɒdʒɪkəl / ADJ topologique
topology / tə'pɒlədʒɪ / N topologie *f*
topper * / 'tɒpəʳ / N 1 *(= hat)* (chapeau *m*) haut-de-forme *m* 2 *(US)* **the ~ was that ...** le comble *or* le plus fort, c'est que ...
topping / 'tɒpɪŋ / ADJ *(Brit † *)* du tonnerre † * N *(for pizza)* garniture *f* ◆ **chocolate/orange ~** *(NonC)* crème *f* au chocolat/à l'orange *(dont on nappe un dessert)* ◆ **dessert with a ~ of whipped cream** dessert *m* nappé de crème fouettée
topple / 'tɒpl / VI *(= lose balance) [person]* basculer, perdre l'équilibre ; *[pile]* basculer ; *(= fall:* also **topple over, topple down)** *[person]* tomber ; *[pile etc]* s'effondrer, se renverser ; *[empire, dictator, government]* tomber ◆ **to ~ over a cliff** tomber du haut d'une falaise VT SEP *[+ object]* faire tomber, renverser ; *[+ government, ruler]* renverser, faire tomber
TOPS / tɒps / N *(Brit)* (abbrev of **Training Opportunities Scheme**) *programme de recyclage professionnel*
topsail / 'tɒpseɪl / N *(Naut)* hunier *m*
topside / 'tɒpsaɪd / N *(Brit Culin)* gîte *m* (à la noix) ; *(Naut)* accastillage *m* ADJ *(US *) [official etc]* haut placé, de haut niveau ADV ◆ **to go ~** monter sur le pont supérieur
topsider * / 'tɒpsaɪdəʳ / N *(US)* huile * *f*, personnage *m* haut placé
topsoil / 'tɒpsɔɪl / N terre *f* ; *(Agr)* couche *f* arable
topspin / 'tɒpspɪn / N *(Tennis)* lift *m*
topsy-turvy / 'tɒpsɪ'tɜːvɪ / ADJ, ADV sens dessus dessous, à l'envers ◆ **to turn everything ~** tout mettre sens dessus dessous, tout bouleverser *or* chambouler * ◆ **everything is ~** tout est sens dessus dessous ; *(fig)* c'est le monde à l'envers *or* renversé
toque / təʊk / N toque *f*
tor / tɔːʳ / N butte *f* (rocheuse)
Torah / 'tɔːrə / N Torah *f*, Thora *f*
torch / tɔːtʃ / N *(flaming)* torche *f*, flambeau *m (also fig) (Brit: electric)* lampe *f* de poche, lampe *f or* torche *f* électrique ◆ **the house went up like a ~** la maison s'est mise à flamber comme du bois sec ◆ **to carry the ~ of** *or* **for democracy/progress** porter le flambeau de la démocratie/du progrès ◆ **to hand on the ~** passer *or* transmettre le flambeau ◆ **he still carries a ~ for her** * il en pince toujours pour elle * ; → **Olympic** VT ◆ **to ~ sth** mettre le feu à qch COMP **torch singer** N *(US)* chanteur *m*, -euse *f* réaliste
torch song N chanson *f* d'amour mélancolique
torchbearer / 'tɔːtʃbɛərəʳ / N porteur *m*, -euse *f* de flambeau *or* de torche
torchlight / 'tɔːtʃlaɪt / N ◆ **by ~** à la lueur des flambeaux (*or* d'une lampe de poche) ◆ **~ procession** retraite *f* aux flambeaux
tore / tɔːʳ / VB pt of **tear**[1]
toreador / 'tɒrɪədɔːʳ / N toréador *m*
torero / tə'rɛərəʊ / N torero *m*
torment / 'tɔːment / N tourment *m (liter)*, supplice *m* ◆ **to be in ~** être au supplice ◆ **the ~s of jealousy** les affres *fpl* de la jalousie ◆ **to suffer ~s** souffrir le martyre VT / tɔː'ment / *[+ person]* tourmenter ; *[+ animal]* martyriser ◆ **to ~ o.s.** *(fig)* se tourmenter, se torturer ◆ **~ed by jealousy** torturé *or* rongé par la jalousie

tormentor /tɔːˈmentəʳ/ N persécuteur *m*, -trice *f* ; *(stronger)* bourreau *m*

torn /tɔːn/ VB ptp of **tear¹**

tornado /tɔːˈneɪdəʊ/ N (pl **tornados** or **tornadoes**) tornade *f*

Toronto /təˈrɒntəʊ/ N Toronto

torpedo /tɔːˈpiːdəʊ/ N (pl **torpedoes**) (= *weapon, fish)* torpille *f* VT *(lit, fig)* torpiller COMP **torpedo attack** N ♦ **to make a ~ attack** attaquer à la torpille
torpedo boat N torpilleur *m*, vedette *f* lance-torpilles
torpedo tube N (tube *m*) lance-torpilles *m inv*

torpid /ˈtɔːpɪd/ ADJ *[person]* apathique, torpide *(liter)* ; *[film]* très lent ; *[book]* au développement très lent ; *[animal]* dans un état de torpeur ♦ **he has a rather ~ intellect** intellectuellement, il n'est pas très vif

torpidity /tɔːˈpɪdɪtɪ/, **torpor** /ˈtɔːpəʳ/ N torpeur *f*, engourdissement *m*

torque /tɔːk/ N *(Phys)* force *f* de torsion ; *(Mechanics)* couple *m* ; *(Hist* = *collar)* torque *m*
COMP **torque converter** N *[in car]* convertisseur *m* de couple
torque spanner, torque wrench N clé *f* dynamométrique

torrent /ˈtɒrənt/ N *(lit, fig)* torrent *m* ♦ **the rain was coming down in ~s** il pleuvait à torrents

torrential /tɒˈrenʃəl/ ADJ torrentiel

torrid /ˈtɒrɪd/ ADJ 1 (= *hot) [climate, heat, sun]* torride 2 (= *passionate) [love affair, romance]* torride, passionné ; *[passion]* torride, ardent ♦ **~ love scenes** des scènes érotiques torrides COMP **the Torrid Zone** N *(Geog)* la zone intertropicale

torsi /ˈtɔːsɪ/ NPL of **torso**

torsion /ˈtɔːʃən/ N torsion *f*
COMP **torsion balance** N balance *f* de torsion
torsion bar N barre *f* de torsion

torso /ˈtɔːsəʊ/ N (pl **torsos** or (**rare**) **torsi**) *(Anat)* torse *m* ; *(Sculp)* buste *m*

tort /tɔːt/ N *(Jur)* acte *m* délictuel *or* quasi délictuel COMP **torts lawyer** N *(US Jur) avocat spécialisé en droit civil*

tortilla /tɔːˈtiːə/ N tortilla *f* COMP **tortilla chip** N *chip de maïs épicée*

tortoise /ˈtɔːtəs/ N tortue *f*

tortoiseshell /ˈtɔːtəsʃel/ N écaille *f* (de tortue)
COMP *[ornament, comb]* en *or* d'écaille ; *[spectacles]* à monture d'écaille
tortoiseshell butterfly N papillon *m* grande tortue
tortoiseshell cat N chat *m* écaille et blanc

tortuous /ˈtɔːtjʊəs/ ADJ *[road, process, negotiations, history, methods, argument]* tortueux ; *[language, essay, logic]* contourné, alambiqué ; *[style, sentence]* tarabiscoté

torture /ˈtɔːtʃəʳ/ N torture *f*, supplice *m* ♦ **to put sb to (the) ~** torturer qn, faire subir des tortures à qn ♦ **it was sheer ~!** *(fig)* c'était un vrai supplice ! VT *(lit)* torturer ; *(fig)* torturer, mettre à la torture *or* au supplice ; *[+ senses etc]* mettre au supplice ; *[+ language]* écorcher ; *[+ meaning]* dénaturer ; *[+ tune]* massacrer ♦ **to ~ o.s.** *(fig)* se torturer ♦ **~d by doubt** torturé *or* tenaillé par le doute COMP **torture chamber** N chambre *f* de torture

torturer /ˈtɔːtʃərəʳ/ N tortionnaire *m*, bourreau *m*

torturous /ˈtɔːtʃərəs/ ADJ atroce, abominable

Tory /ˈtɔːrɪ/ *(Pol)* N tory *m*, conservateur *m*, -trice *f* ADJ *[party, person, policy]* tory *inv*, conservateur (-trice *f*)

Toryism /ˈtɔːrɪɪzəm/ N *(Pol)* torysme *m*

tosh‡ /tɒʃ/ N *(Brit: NonC)* bêtises *fpl*, blagues *fpl* ♦ **~!** allons (donc) !

toss /tɒs/ N 1 (= *throw)* lancement *m* ; *(by bull)* coup *m* de cornes ♦ **to take a ~** *(from horse)* faire une chute, être désarçonné ♦ **with a ~ of his head** d'un mouvement brusque de la tête ♦ **I don't give a ~**‡ *(Brit)* je m'en contrefous‡, j'en ai rien à branler*‡ *(about* dc)
2 *[of coin]* coup *m* de pile ou face ; *(Sport: at start of match)* tirage *m* au sort ♦ **they decided it by the ~ of a coin** ils l'ont décidé à pile ou face ♦ **to win/lose the ~** *(gen)* gagner/perdre à pile ou face ; *(Sport)* gagner/perdre au tirage au sort ; → **argue**
VT *[+ ball, object]* lancer, jeter *(to* à) ; *(Brit) [+ pancake]* faire sauter ; *[+ salad]* retourner, remuer ; *[+ head, mane]* rejeter en arrière ; *[bull]* projeter en l'air ; *[horse]* désarçonner, démonter ♦ **to ~ sb in a blanket** faire sauter qn dans une couverture ♦ **~ in butter** *(Culin)* ajoutez un morceau de beurre et remuez ♦ **they ~ed a coin to decide who should stay** ils ont joué à pile ou face pour décider qui resterait ♦ **I'll ~ you for it** on le joue à pile ou face ♦ **the sea ~ed the boat against the rocks** la mer a projeté *or* envoyé le bateau sur les rochers ♦ **the boat was ~ed by the waves** le bateau était agité *or* ballotté par les vagues ; → **caber**
VI 1 (also **toss about, toss around**) *[person]* s'agiter ; *[plumes, trees]* se balancer ; *[boat]* tanguer ♦ **he was ~ing (about** or **around) in his sleep** il s'agitait dans son sommeil, son sommeil était agité ♦ **he was ~ing and turning all night** il n'a pas arrêté de se tourner et se retourner toute la nuit
2 (also **toss up**) jouer à pile ou face ♦ **let's ~ (up) for it** on le joue à pile ou face ♦ **they ~ed (up) to see who would stay** ils ont joué à pile ou face pour savoir qui resterait
COMP **toss-up** N *[of coin]* coup *m* de pile ou face ♦ **it was a ~-up between the theatre and the cinema** le théâtre ou le cinéma, ça nous (*or* leur *etc*) était égal *or* c'était kif-kif* ♦ **it's a ~-up whether I go or stay** que je parte ou que je reste *subj*, c'est un peu à pile ou face

► **toss about, toss around** VI → **toss vi 1**
VT SEP *[+ boat etc]* ballotter, faire tanguer ; *[+ plumes, branches]* agiter

► **toss aside** VT SEP *[+ object]* jeter de côté ; *(fig) [+ person, helper]* repousser ; *[+ suggestion, offer]* rejeter, repousser ; *[+ scheme]* rejeter

► **toss away** VT SEP jeter

► **toss back** VT SEP *[+ ball, object]* renvoyer ; *[+ hair, mane]* rejeter en arrière ♦ **they were ~ing ideas back and forth** ils échangeaient toutes sortes d'idées

► **toss off** VI (*‡ = *masturbate)* se branler*‡
VT SEP 1 *[+ drink]* lamper, avaler d'un coup ; *[+ essay, letter, poem]* écrire au pied levé, torcher *(pej)*
2 (*‡ = *masturbate)* branler*‡, faire une branlette à*‡ ♦ **to ~ o.s. off** se branler*‡

► **toss out** VT SEP *[+ rubbish]* jeter ; *[+ person]* mettre à la porte, jeter dehors

► **toss over** VT SEP lancer ♦ **~ it over!** envoie !, lance !

► **toss up** VI → **toss vi 2**
VT SEP *[+ object]* lancer, jeter *(into the air* en l'air)
N ♦ **toss-up** → **toss**

tosser*‡ /ˈtɒsəʳ/ N *(Brit)* branleur*‡ *m*

tosspot /ˈtɒspɒt/ N 1 ‡ ⇒ **tosser** 2 († * = *drunkard)* riboteur †‡ *m*, -euse †‡ *f*

tot¹ /tɒt/ N 1 (= *child:* also **tiny tot**) tout(e) petit(e) *m(f)*, bambin *m* 2 *(esp Brit = drink)* **a ~ of whisky** un petit verre de whisky ♦ **just a ~** juste une goutte *or* une larme

tot² * /tɒt/ *(esp Brit)* VT (also **tot up**) additionner, faire le total de VI ♦ **it ~s up to £25** ça fait 25 livres en tout, ça se monte *or* ça s'élève à 25 livres ♦ **I'm just ~ting up** je fais le total

total /ˈtəʊtl/ ADJ *[amount, number, war, ban, eclipse, silence]* total ; *[lack]* total, complet (-ète *f*) ; *[failure]* complet (-ète *f*) ; *[effect, policy]* global ♦ **a ~ cost of over $3,000** un coût total de plus de 3 000 dollars ♦ **a ~ population of 650,000** une population totale de 650 000 habitants ♦ **the ~ losses/sales/debts** le total des pertes/ventes/dettes ♦ **it was a ~ loss** on a tout perdu ♦ **her commitment to the job was ~** elle s'investissait complètement dans son travail ♦ **to get on in business you need ~ commitment** pour réussir en affaires, il faut s'engager à fond ♦ **to be in ~ ignorance of sth** être dans l'ignorance la plus complète de qch, ignorer complètement qch ♦ **they were in ~ disagreement** ils étaient en désaccord total ♦ **a ~ stranger** un parfait inconnu ♦ **~ abstinence** abstinence *f* totale
N 1 (montant *m*) total *m* ♦ **it comes to a ~ of £30, the ~ comes to £30** le total s'élève à 30 livres, cela fait 30 livres au total ; → **grand, sum**
2 ♦ **in ~** au total
VT 1 (= *add:* also **total up**) *[+ figures, expenses]* totaliser, faire le total de
2 (= *amount to)* s'élever à ♦ **that ~s £50** cela fait 50 livres (en tout), cela s'élève à 50 livres ♦ **the class ~led 40** il y avait 40 élèves en tout dans la classe
3 *(esp US* ‡ = *wreck) [+ car]* bousiller*, démolir
COMP **total allergy syndrome** N allergie *f* généralisée
total recall N *(Psych)* remémoration *f* totale ♦ **to have ~ recall** se souvenir de tout ♦ **to have ~ recall of sth** se souvenir clairement de qch ; → **abstainer**

totalitarian /ˌtəʊtælɪˈtɛərɪən/ ADJ, N totalitaire *mf*

totalitarianism /ˌtəʊtælɪˈtɛərɪənɪzəm/ N totalitarisme *m*

totality /təʊˈtælɪtɪ/ N totalité *f*

totalizator /ˈtəʊtəlaɪzeɪtəʳ/ N 1 (= *adding etc machine)* (appareil *m*) totalisateur *m*, machine *f* totalisatrice 2 *(esp Brit Betting)* pari *m* mutuel

totalize /ˈtəʊtəlaɪz/ VT totaliser, additionner

totalizer /ˈtəʊtəlaɪzəʳ/ N ⇒ **totalizator**

totally /ˈtəʊtəlɪ/ ADV *[convinced, innocent, unacceptable, different, unheard of]* totalement ; *[ignore]* totalement, complètement ♦ **to destroy sth ~** détruire qch totalement *or* complètement

tote¹ * /təʊt/ N abbrev of **totalizator 2** VT *(US)* ♦ **to ~ up** additionner COMP **tote board** N *(Racing)* tableau *m* totalisateur

tote² /təʊt/ VT (* = *carry) [+ gun, object]* porter ♦ **I ~d it around all day** je l'ai trimballé* toute la journée COMP **tote bag** N (sac *m*) fourre-tout* *m inv*

totem /ˈtəʊtəm/ N totem *m* ♦ **~ pole** mât *m* totémique

totemic /təʊˈtemɪk/ ADJ totémique

totter /ˈtɒtəʳ/ VI *[person] (from weakness)* chanceler ; *(from tiredness, drunkenness)* tituber ; *[object, column, chimney stack]* chanceler, vaciller ; *(fig) [government]* chanceler ♦ **to ~ in/out** *etc* entrer/sortir *etc* en titubant *or* d'un pas chancelant

tottering /ˈtɒtərɪŋ/, **tottery** /ˈtɒtərɪ/ ADJ chancelant

totty‡ /ˈtɒtɪ/ N *(NonC: Brit)* gonzesses‡ *fpl* ♦ **a nice piece of ~** une belle gonzesse‡

toucan /ˈtuːkən/ N toucan *m* COMP **toucan crossing** N *passage protégé pour piétons et cyclistes*

touch /tʌtʃ/

1 NOUN 4 COMPOUNDS
2 TRANSITIVE VERB 5 PHRASAL VERBS
3 INTRANSITIVE VERB

1 - NOUN

1 [= sense of touch] toucher *m* ♦ **Braille is read by ~** le braille se lit au toucher ♦ **soft to the ~** doux au toucher ♦ **the cold ~ of marble** la froideur du marbre

2 [= act of touching] contact *m*, toucher *m* ; *[of instrumentalist, typist]* toucher *m* ; *[of artist]* touche *f* ♦ **the slightest ~ might break it** le moindre contact pourrait le casser ♦ **I felt a ~ on my arm** j'ai senti qu'on me touchait le bras ♦ **at the ~ of her hand, he ...** au contact de sa main, il ... ♦ **with the ~ of a finger** d'une simple pression du doigt ♦ **at the ~ of a button** *or* **switch** en appuyant sur un bouton ♦ **she felt the ~ of the wind on her cheek** elle sentait la caresse du vent sur sa joue ♦ **he altered it with a ~ of the brush/pen** il l'a modifié d'un coup de pinceau/d'un trait de plume ♦ **to have a light ~** *[pianist]* avoir un toucher léger ; *[writer, actor]* faire preuve de finesse ♦ **you've got the right ~ with him** vous savez vous y prendre avec lui

3 [fig = characteristic] ♦ **it has the ~ of genius** cela porte le sceau du génie ♦ **he lacks the human** *or* **personal ~** il est trop impersonnel *or* froid, il manque de chaleur humaine ♦ **to have the common ~** être très simple ♦ **it's the human** *or* **personal ~ that makes his speeches so successful** c'est la note personnelle qui fait que ses discours ont tant de succès ♦ **that's the Gordon ~** c'est typique de Gordon, c'est du Gordon tout craché*

4 [= detail] détail *m* ♦ **small ~es, such as flowers, can transform a room** de petits détails, par exemple des fleurs, peuvent transformer une pièce ♦ **to put the final** *or* **finishing ~(es) to sth, to give sth the final** *or* **finishing ~(es)** *(lit, fig)* mettre la dernière main à qch

5 [= small amount] **it's a ~ (too) expensive** c'est un petit peu (trop) cher, c'est un poil* trop cher

♦ **a touch of** ♦ **a ~ of colour/gaiety/humour** une touche de couleur/de gaieté/d'humour ♦ **a ~ of sadness** une pointe de tristesse ♦ **there's a ~ of spring in the air** ça sent le printemps ♦ **tonight there'll be a ~ of frost in places** il y aura un peu de gel cette nuit par endroits ♦ **he got a ~ of the sun** il a pris un petit coup de soleil ♦ **to have a ~ of flu** être un peu grippé ♦ **to have a ~ of rheumatism** faire un peu de rhumatisme ♦ **it needs a ~ of paint** il faudrait y passer une petite couche de peinture

6 [= contact, communication]

♦ **to be in touch (with sb)** être en contact *or* en rapport *or* en relation (avec qn) ♦ **I'll be in ~!** je t'écrirai ! (*or* je te téléphonerai !)

♦ **to keep in touch (with sb)** rester en contact *or* en rapport *or* en relation (avec qn) ♦ **keep in ~!** tiens-nous au courant !, écris de temps en temps !

♦ **to get in touch with sb** prendre contact avec qn ; *(by phone)* joindre qn ♦ **you can get in ~ with me at this number** vous pouvez me joindre à ce numéro ♦ **you ought to get in ~ with the police** vous devriez prendre contact avec la police

♦ **to put sb in touch with** ♦ **I'll put you in ~ with him** je vous mettrai en rapport *or* en relation avec lui

♦ **to lose touch** ♦ **to lose ~ with sb** perdre le contact avec qn ♦ **they lost ~ (with each other) long ago** il y a bien longtemps qu'ils ne sont plus en relation *or* en rapport ♦ **to have lost ~ with sb** avoir perdu le contact avec qn ♦ **to lose ~ with reality** *or* **the facts** perdre le sens des réalités ♦ **to have lost ~ with the political situation** ne plus être au courant de la situation politique ♦ **he has lost ~ with what is going on** il n'est plus dans le coup*

♦ **to be out of touch** *(= not up to date)* ♦ **he's completely out of ~** il n'est plus dans le coup* ♦ **I'm out of ~ with the latest political developments** je ne suis pas au courant des derniers développements en matière politique ♦ **we're very much out of ~ here** *(= isolated)* nous sommes coupés de tout ici ♦ **to be out of ~ with reality** être coupé des réalités

7 [Ftbl, Rugby] touche *f* ♦ **the ball went into ~** le ballon est sorti en touche ♦ **it's in ~** il y a touche ♦ **to kick for ~, to kick the ball into ~** botter *or* envoyer le ballon en touche ♦ **to kick sth into ~** *(fig)* mettre qch au placard

8 [‡ borrowing] ♦ **he's made a ~** il a tapé* quelqu'un ♦ **he's good for a ~, he's an easy** *or* **soft ~** *(= will lend money)* il est toujours prêt à se laisser taper*

9 [= person one can persuade, exploit] ♦ **he's an easy** *or* **soft ~** il se laisse faire ♦ **Mr Wilson is no easy** *or* **soft ~** M. Wilson n'est pas du genre à se laisser faire

2 - TRANSITIVE VERB

1 [= come into contact with] toucher ♦ **"do not touch the goods"** "ne touchez pas les *or* aux marchandises" ♦ **he ~ed it with his finger** il l'a touché du doigt ♦ **he ~ed her arm** il lui a touché le bras ♦ **his hand ~ed mine** sa main a touché la mienne ♦ **they can't ~ you if you don't break the law** ils ne peuvent rien contre vous *or* rien vous faire si vous respectez la loi ♦ **to ~ one's hat to sb** saluer qn en portant la main à son chapeau ♦ **I can ~ the bottom** je peux toucher le fond, j'ai pied ♦ **the ship ~ed the bottom** le bateau a touché le fond ♦ **to ~ ground** *[plane]* atterrir ♦ **their land ~es ours** leur terre touche à *or* est contiguë à la nôtre ♦ **the ship ~ed Bordeaux** le bateau a fait escale à Bordeaux ♦ **to ~ base** *(fig)* se mettre à jour *or* au courant ♦ **clouds ~ed with pink** nuages *mpl* à reflets roses

2 [= tamper with] toucher à ♦ **don't ~ that switch!** ne touchez pas à ce bouton ! ♦ **I didn't ~ it!** je n'y ai pas touché ! ♦ **the burglars didn't ~ the safe** les cambrioleurs n'ont pas touché au coffre-fort ♦ **I didn't ~ him!** je ne l'ai pas touché !

3 [= damage] ♦ **the frost ~ed the plants** la gelée a abîmé les plantes ♦ **the fire didn't ~ the paintings** l'incendie a épargné les tableaux

4 [= deal with] *(in exam)* ♦ **I didn't ~ the third question** je n'ai pas touché à la troisième question ♦ **he won't ~ anything illegal** si c'est illégal il n'y touchera pas ♦ **water won't ~ these stains** l'eau n'agira pas sur ces taches ♦ **he scarcely ~ed the problem of racism** il a à peine abordé le problème du racisme

5 [+ food, drink] *(gen neg)* toucher à ♦ **he didn't ~ his meal** il n'a pas touché à son repas ♦ **I never ~ onions** je ne mange jamais d'oignons ♦ **I won't ~ gin** je ne bois jamais de gin

6 [= equal, rival] valoir, égaler ♦ **her cooking doesn't** *or* **can't ~ yours** sa cuisine est loin de valoir la tienne ♦ **there's nobody to ~ him as a pianist, nobody can ~ him as a pianist** il est inégalable *or* sans égal comme pianiste ♦ **there's nothing to ~ hot whisky for a cold** rien ne vaut un grog au whisky pour guérir un rhume

7 [= concern] toucher, concerner ♦ **it ~es us all closely** cela nous touche *or* nous concerne tous de très près ♦ **if it ~es the national interest** s'il y va de l'intérêt national

8 [= move emotionally] toucher ♦ **we were very ~ed by your letter** nous avons été très touchés par votre lettre

9 [esp Brit = reach] *[+ level, speed]* atteindre

10 [* : for money] ♦ **to ~ sb for a loan** taper* qn ♦ **I ~ed him for £10** je l'ai tapé* de 10 livres

3 - INTRANSITIVE VERB

1 [gen] toucher ♦ **don't ~!** n'y touchez pas !, ne touchez pas ! ♦ **"do not touch"** *(on notice)* "défense de toucher"

2 [= come into contact with] *[hands, ends etc]* se toucher ; *[lands, gardens, areas]* se toucher, être contigus

3 [speaking, writing] **to ~ (up)on a subject** *(fig)* aborder un sujet

4 - COMPOUNDS

touch-and-go N ♦ **it's ~-and-go with him** il est entre la vie et la mort ♦ **it was ~-and-go whether she did it** elle a été à deux doigts de ne pas le faire ♦ **it was ~-and-go until the last minute** l'issue est restée incertaine jusqu'au bout, cela n'a tenu qu'à un fil
touch football N *variante du jeu à treize, sans plaquages*
touch judge N *(Rugby)* juge *m* de touche
touch screen N écran *m* tactile
touch-sensitive ADJ *[screen]* tactile ; *[key]* à effleurement
touch-tone ADJ *[telephone]* à touches
touch-type VI taper sans regarder le clavier
touch-typing N dactylographie *f* (sans regarder le clavier)
touch-typist N dactylo* *f* qui tape sans regarder le clavier

5 - PHRASAL VERBS

► **touch at** VT FUS *(Naut)* mouiller à *or* dans le port de, faire escale à

► **touch down** VI 1 *(on land)* atterrir ; *(on sea)* amerrir ; *(on moon)* alunir 2 *(US Ftbl)* marquer un touch-down ; *(behind one's own goal-line)* aplatir (la balle) dans son en-but VT SEP *(Rugby etc*♦ *)* **to ~ the ball down** marquer un essai ; *(behind one's own goal-line)* aplatir (la balle) dans son en-but

► **touch off** VT SEP *[+ fuse, firework]* faire partir ; *[+ mine etc]* faire exploser ; *[+ explosion]* déclencher ; *(fig) [+ crisis, riot]* déclencher ; *[+ reaction, scene, argument]* provoquer, déclencher

► **touch up** VT SEP 1 *[+ painting, photo]* retoucher 2 *(‡: sexually)* peloter‡

touchdown /ˈtʌtʃdaʊn/ N *(on land)* atterrissage *m* ; *(on sea)* amerrissage *m* ; *(on moon)* alunissage *m* ; *(American Ftbl)* essai *m*

touché /tuːˈʃeɪ/ EXCL *(Fencing)* touché ! ; *(fig)* très juste !

touched /tʌtʃt/ ADJ 1 *(= moved)* touché *(by sth* par qch) 2 *(* = mad)* toqué*, timbré*

touchiness /ˈtʌtʃɪnɪs/ N *(NonC)* susceptibilité *f*

touching /ˈtʌtʃɪŋ/ ADJ touchant PREP concernant, touchant † *(also liter)*

touchingly /ˈtʌtʃɪŋlɪ/ ADV *[speak, write]* d'une manière touchante ♦ **~ naive** d'une touchante naïveté ♦ **~, she has supported him throughout this ordeal** chose touchante, elle l'a soutenu tout au long de cette épreuve

touchline /ˈtʌtʃlaɪn/ N *(Ftbl etc)* (ligne *f* de) touche *f*

touchpad /ˈtʌtʃpæd/ N pavé *m* tactile

touchpaper /ˈtʌtʃpeɪpəʳ/ N papier *m* nitraté ♦ **to light the (blue) ~** *(fig)* mettre le feu aux poudres

touchstone /ˈtʌtʃstəʊn/ N *(lit, fig)* pierre *f* de touche

touchwood /ˈtʌtʃwʊd/ N amadou *m*

touchy /ˈtʌtʃɪ/ ADJ 1 *(= easily annoyed) [person]* susceptible *(about sth* sur la question *or* le chapitre de qch) ; (= *delicate) [subject, issue]* délicat 2 (*= fond of physical contact) qui aime le contact physique, démonstratif COMP **touchy-feely** * ADJ qui aime le contact physique, démonstratif

tough /tʌf/ ADJ 1 (*= strong) [cloth, steel, leather, garment etc]* solide, résistant ; *(pej) [meat]* dur, coriace ◆ **it's as ~ as old boots** *(hum: of meat etc)* c'est de la semelle

2 *[person] (= strong) (physically)* robuste, résistant ; *(mentally)* solide, endurant ◆ **you have to be ~ to do that kind of work** il faut être solide pour faire ce genre de travail ◆ **he's a ~ businessman** il est dur en affaires ◆ **as ~ as old boots** * *(hum)* coriace

3 *[person] (= hard in character)* dur, tenace ; *[criminal, gangster]* endurci ◆ **as ~ as nails** dur à cuire ◆ **he is a ~ man to deal with** il ne fait pas souvent de concessions ◆ **they're a ~ lot, they're ~ customers** *(pej)* ce sont des durs à cuire * ◆ **to get ~ with sb** * (commencer à) se montrer dur envers qn

4 *(= hard) [resistance, struggle, opposition]* acharné, âpre ; *[journey, task]* rude, pénible ; *[obstacle]* rude, sérieux ; *[problem]* épineux ; *[regulations]* sévère ; *[conditions]* dur ; *[neighbourhood]* dur ◆ **it's ~ when you have kids** c'est dur quand on a des enfants ◆ **it's ~ work** c'est un travail pénible, ce n'est pas de la tarte * ◆ **rugby is a ~ game** le rugby est un jeu rude ◆ **to take a ~ line on sth** *[person]* être très strict sur qch ; *[government]* se montrer inflexible sur qch ◆ **to take a ~ line with sb** se montrer inflexible *or* très ferme avec qn ◆ **it took ~ talking to get them to agree to the deal** il a fallu d'âpres négociations pour qu'ils acceptent *subj* de conclure cette affaire

5 *(* = unfortunate)* ◆ **that's ~** c'est dur ◆ **to have a ~ time of it** * en voir de dures * ◆ **it was ~ on the others** c'était vache * pour les autres ◆ **~ luck** déveine * *f*, manque *m* de pot * ◆ **~ luck!** *(pity)* pas de veine !, manque de pot ! * ; *(you'll have to put up with it)* tant pis pour vous ! ◆ **that's ~ luck on him** il n'a pas de veine *or* de pot * ◆ **~ shit!** ** démerdez-vous ! **, tant pis pour vous !

N * dur *m*

ADV ◆ **to talk** *or* **act ~** jouer au dur

VT ◆ **to ~ it out** * *(= hold out)* tenir bon, faire front ; *(= rough it)* vivre à la dure

COMP **tough guy** N dur *m*
tough love * N fermeté *f* affectueuse
tough-minded ADJ inflexible
tough-mindedness N inflexibilité *f*

toughen /ˈtʌfn/ (also **toughen up**) VT *[+ metal, glass, cloth, leather]* rendre plus solide, renforcer ; *[+ person]* endurcir, aguerrir ; *[+ conditions]* rendre plus sévère ◆ **~ed glass** verre *m* trempé VI *[metal, glass, cloth, leather]* devenir plus solide ; *[person]* s'endurcir, s'aguerrir ; *[conditions, regulations]* devenir plus sévère

toughie * /ˈtʌfɪ/ N 1 *(= question)* ◆ **that's a ~** ça, c'est une colle * 2 *(= person)* dur(e) *m(f)*

toughly /ˈtʌflɪ/ ADV *[speak, answer]* durement, sans ménagement ; *[fight, oppose]* avec acharnement, âprement ◆ **it is ~ made** c'est du solide

toughness /ˈtʌfnɪs/ N (NonC) 1 *[of person] (= hardiness)* résistance *f*, endurance *f* ; *(= determination)* ténacité *f* ◆ **mental ~** force *f* de caractère 2 *(= roughness) [of person, school]* dureté *f* ; *[of sport, game]* rudesse *f* 3 *(= durability) [of material]* résistance *f*, solidité *f* ; *[of skin]* dureté *f* 4 *[of meat]* dureté *f* 5 *(= difficulty) [of life, situation, choice, question]* difficulté *f* ; *[of resistance, competition]* âpreté *f* ; *[of task, work, conditions, journey]* dureté *f* 6 *(= harshness) [of policy, measure]* sévérité *f*

toupee /ˈtuːpeɪ/ N postiche *m*

tour /tʊəʳ/ N *(= journey)* voyage *m*, périple *m* ; *(by team, actors, musicians etc)* tournée *f* ; *(by premier, visiting statesman etc)* visite *f* officielle, tournée *f* de visites ; *[of town, factory, museum etc]* visite *f*, tour *m* ; (also **package tour**) voyage *m* organisé ; (also **day tour**) excursion *f* ◆ **the Grand Tour** *(Hist)* le tour de l'Europe ◆ **they went on a ~ of the Lake District** ils ont fait un voyage *or* un périple dans la région des Lacs ◆ **we went on** *or* **made a ~ of the Loire castles** nous avons visité les châteaux de la Loire ◆ **they went on a ~ to Spain** ils sont allés en voyage organisé *or* ils ont fait un voyage organisé en Espagne ◆ **the ~ includes three days in Venice** le voyage comprend trois jours à Venise ◆ **to go on a ~ round the world** faire le tour du monde ◆ **to go on a walking/cycling ~** faire une randonnée à pied/en bicyclette ◆ **"on tour"** *(sign on bus)* "excursion" ◆ **to go on ~** *(Sport, Theat etc)* faire une tournée ◆ **to be on ~** être en tournée ◆ **to take a company on ~** *(Theat etc)* emmener une troupe en tournée ◆ **to take a play on ~** donner une pièce en tournée ◆ **~ of inspection** tournée *f* d'inspection ◆ **~ of duty** *(Mil etc)* période *f* de service ; → **conduct**

VT *[+ district, town, exhibition, museum, factory]* visiter ◆ **they are ~ing France** ils visitent la France, ils font du tourisme en France ; *(Sport, Theat)* ils sont en tournée en France ◆ **the play is ~ing the provinces** la pièce tourne en province *or* est en tournée en province

VI ◆ **to go ~ing** voyager, faire du tourisme ◆ **they went ~ing in Italy** ils sont allés visiter l'Italie, ils ont fait du tourisme en Italie

COMP **tour director** N (US) accompagnateur *m*, -trice *f*
tour guide N *(= person)* guide *m*, accompagnateur *m*, -trice *f*
tour manager N *(Sport, Mus)* directeur *m* de tournée
tour operator N (Brit) *(= travel agency)* touropérateur *m*, voyagiste *m* ; *(= bus company)* compagnie *f* de cars

tour de force /ˈtʊədəfɔːs/ N (pl **tours de force**) *(= action, performance etc)* exploit *m*, prouesse *f* ; *(= novel, film etc)* chef-d'œuvre *m*

tourer /ˈtʊərəʳ/ N *(= car)* voiture *f* de tourisme ; *(= caravan)* caravane *f*

Tourette('s) syndrome /tʊəˈret(s),sɪndrəʊm/ N maladie *f* de Gilles de La Tourette

touring /ˈtʊərɪŋ/ N (NonC) tourisme *m*, voyages *mpl* touristiques ADJ *[team]* en tournée ◆ **~ car** voiture *f* de tourisme ◆ **~ company** *(Theat) (permanently)* troupe *f* ambulante ; *(temporarily)* troupe *f* en tournée COMP **touring bindings** NPL *(Ski)* fixations *fpl* de randonnée

tourism /ˈtʊərɪzəm/ N tourisme *m*

tourist /ˈtʊərɪst/ N touriste *mf* ◆ **"Tourists' Guide to London"** "Guide touristique de Londres" ◆ **the ~s** *(Sport = touring team)* les visiteurs *mpl*, l'équipe *f* en tournée ADV *[travel]* en classe touriste

COMP *[class, ticket]* touriste *inv* ; *[season]* des touristes
tourist agency N agence *f* de tourisme
tourist bureau N ⇒ **tourist information (centre)**
tourist class N classe *f* touriste ADJ, ADV en classe touriste
tourist court N (US) motel *m*
tourist home N (US) *maison particulière dans laquelle des chambres sont louées aux touristes*
tourist information (centre), tourist (information) office N office *m* de tourisme, syndicat *m* d'initiative
tourist trade N tourisme *m*
tourist traffic N flot *m or* afflux *m* de touristes (en voiture)
tourist trap N piège *m* à touristes

touristy * /ˈtʊərɪstɪ/ ADJ *(pej) [place]* (trop) touristique ; *[shop]* pour touristes

tournament /ˈtʊənəmənt/ N *(Hist, gen)* tournoi *m* ◆ **chess/tennis ~** tournoi *m* d'échecs/de tennis

tourney /ˈtʊənɪ/ N *(Hist)* tournoi *m*

tourniquet /ˈtʊənɪkeɪ/ N *(Med)* garrot *m*

tousle /ˈtaʊzl/ VT *[+ hair]* ébouriffer ; *[+ clothes]* chiffonner, friper, froisser ; *[+ bed, bedclothes]* mettre en désordre

tousled /ˈtaʊzld/ ADJ *[hair]* ébouriffé ; *[person, appearance]* échevelé

tout /taʊt/ N *(gen)* vendeur *m* ambulant ; *(for custom)* racoleur *m* ; *(for hotels)* rabatteur *m* ; *(Racing)* pronostiqueur *m* ; *(Brit:* also **ticket tout**) revendeur *m* de billets *(au marché noir)* VT *[+ wares]* vendre (avec insistance) ; *(Brit) [+ tickets]* revendre *(au marché noir)* VI racoler ; *(Racing)* vendre des pronostics ◆ **to ~ for custom** *(esp Brit)* racoler les clients ◆ **the taxi drivers were ~ing for the hotels** *(esp Brit)* les chauffeurs de taxi racolaient des clients pour les hôtels

► **tout about, tout (a)round** VT SEP *[+ goods]* vendre (avec insistance) ◆ **he has been ~ing those books about for weeks** * ça fait des semaines qu'il essaie de caser * ces livres

tow[1] /təʊ/ N 1 *(= act)* remorquage *m* ; *(= line)* câble *m* de remorquage ; *(= vehicle etc towed)* véhicule *m* en remorque ◆ **to give sb a ~, to have sb in ~** *(lit)* remorquer qn ◆ **he had a couple of girls in ~** * il avait deux filles dans son sillage ◆ **to be on ~** *(Brit) or* **in ~** *(US)* être en remorque ◆ **"on tow"** *(sign)* "véhicule en remorque" ◆ **to take a car in ~** prendre une voiture en remorque 2 (also **ski tow**) téléski *m*, tire-fesses * *m* VT *[+ boat, vehicle]* remorquer *(to, into* jusqu'à) ; *[+ caravan, trailer]* tirer, tracter ; *[+ barge]* haler

COMP **tow bar** N barre *f* de remorquage
tow car N *(esp US)* chariot-remorque *m*
towing-line, towing-rope N câble *m* de remorquage
towing-truck N dépanneuse *f*
tow-start N ◆ **to give sb a ~-start** faire démarrer qn en le remorquant
tow truck N (US) dépanneuse *f*

► **tow away** VT SEP *[+ vehicle]* remorquer ; *[police]* emmener en fourrière

tow[2] /təʊ/ N *(= fibre)* filasse *f*, étoupe *f* (blanche) COMP **tow-haired, tow-headed** ADJ aux cheveux (blond) filasse, blond filasse

towage /ˈtəʊɪdʒ/ N remorquage *m*

toward(s) /təˈwɔːd(z)/ PREP 1 *(of direction)* vers, du côté de, dans la direction de ◆ **if he comes ~(s) you** s'il vient vers vous *or* dans votre direction *or* de votre côté ◆ **his back was ~(s) the door** il tournait le dos à la porte ◆ **we are moving ~(s) a solution/war** *etc* nous nous acheminons vers une solution/la guerre *etc* ◆ **they have begun negotiations ~(s) an agreement on …** ils ont entamé des négociations en vue d'un accord sur … ◆ **he is saving ~(s) a new car** il fait des économies pour (acheter) une nouvelle voiture ◆ **I'll put the prize money ~(s) a new car** le prix servira à m'acheter une nouvelle voiture ◆ **all donations will go ~(s) a new roof** tous les dons serviront à l'achat d'un nouveau toit

2 *(of time)* vers ◆ **~(s) 10 o'clock** vers *or* sur le coup de 10 heures, sur les 10 heures ◆ **~(s) the end of the century** vers la fin du siècle

3 *(of attitude)* envers, à l'égard de ◆ **his attitude ~(s) them** son attitude envers eux *or* à leur égard ◆ **my feelings ~(s) him** mes sentiments à son égard *or* envers lui *or* pour lui

towaway zone /ˈtəʊəweɪzəʊn/ N (US) zone *f* de stationnement interdit (sous peine de mise en fourrière)

towboat /ˈtəʊbəʊt/ N remorqueur *m*

towel /ˈtaʊəl/ N serviette *f* (de toilette) ; (also **dish towel, tea towel**) torchon *m* ; *(for hands)* essuie-mains *m* ; *(for glasses)* essuie-verres *m* ; (also **sanitary towel**) serviette *f* hygiénique ; → **bath** VT frotter avec une serviette ◆ **to ~ o.s. dry** *or* **down** se sécher *or* s'essuyer avec une serviette
COMP **towel rail** N porte-serviettes *m inv*
towel ring N anneau *m* porte-serviettes

towelling /ˈtaʊəlɪŋ/ N 1 *(NonC)* tissu *m* éponge 2 *(rubbing with towel)* **to give sb a ~ (down)** frictionner qn avec une serviette COMP *[robe etc]* en *or* de tissu éponge

tower /ˈtaʊəʳ/ N tour *f* ◆ **the Tower of Babel** la tour de Babel ◆ **the Tower of London** la tour de Londres ◆ **church** ~ clocher *m* ◆ **water** ~ château *m* d'eau ◆ **he is a ~ of strength** il est ferme comme un roc, c'est un roc ◆ **he proved a ~ of strength to me** il s'est montré un soutien précieux pour moi
VI *[building, mountain, cliff, tree]* se dresser de manière imposante ◆ **I saw him ~ing in the doorway** j'ai vu sa silhouette imposante dans l'embrasure de la porte ◆ **the new block of flats ~s above** *or* **over the church** le nouvel immeuble écrase l'église ◆ **he ~ed over her** elle était toute petite à côté de lui ◆ **he ~s above** *or* **over his colleagues** *(fig)* il domine de très haut ses collègues
COMP **tower block** N *(Brit)* immeuble-tour *m*, tour *f* (d'habitation)
► **tower up** VI *[building, cliff etc]* se dresser de manière imposante, s'élever très haut

towering /ˈtaʊərɪŋ/ ADJ 1 *(= tall) [building]* imposant par sa hauteur ; *[cliff, tree]* imposant 2 *(= great) [achievement, performance]* grandiose ; *[genius, ambition]* hors du commun ; *[figure]* dominant ◆ **to be a ~ presence** être une figure particulièrement imposante ◆ **in a ~ rage** dans une colère noire

towline /ˈtəʊlaɪn/ N ⇒ **towing-line** ; → **tow¹**

town /taʊn/ N ville *f* ◆ **he lives in (a) ~** il habite en ville *or* à la ville ◆ **she lives in a little ~** elle habite (dans) une petite ville ◆ **there is more work in the ~ than in the country** il y a plus de travail en ville *or* à la ville qu'à la campagne ◆ **guess who's in ~!** devine qui vient d'arriver en ville ! ◆ **he's out of ~** il n'est pas là, il est en déplacement ◆ **he's from out of ~** *(US)* il n'est pas d'ici, il est étranger à la ville ◆ **to go (in)to ~, to go downtown** aller en ville ◆ **to go up to ~** *(gen)* monter en ville ; *(to London)* monter à Londres ◆ **the whole ~ is talking about it** toute la ville en parle ◆ **~ and gown** *(Univ)* les citadins *mpl* et les étudiants *mpl* ◆ **a country ~** une ville de province ◆ **we're going out on the ~*** on va faire une virée en ville* ◆ **to have a night on the ~*** faire la noce* *or* la bombe* ◆ **he really went to ~ on that essay*** il a mis le paquet* pour cette dissertation ◆ **they went to ~ on their daughter's wedding*** ils n'ont pas fait les choses à moitié pour le mariage de leur fille ; → **man, new, talk**
COMP **town-and-country planning** N aménagement *m* du territoire
town centre N centre-ville *m*
town clerk N ≈ secrétaire *mf* de mairie
town council N conseil *m* municipal
town councillor N *(Brit)* conseiller *m*, -ère *f* municipal(e)
town crier N *(Hist)* crieur *m* public
town-dweller N citadin(e) *m(f)*
town hall N ≈ mairie *f*, hôtel *m* de ville
town house N *(gen)* maison *f* de ville ; *(= terraced house)* maison *f* mitoyenne ; *(more imposing)* hôtel *m* particulier
town life N vie *f* urbaine
town meeting N *(US)* assemblée *f* générale des habitants d'une localité
town planner N *(Brit)* urbaniste *mf*
town planning N *(Brit)* urbanisme *m*

townee*, townie* /taʊˈniː/ N *(pej)* pur citadin *m* ; *(Univ)* citadin *m*

townscape /ˈtaʊnskeɪp/ N paysage *m or* panorama *m* urbain

townsfolk /ˈtaʊnzfəʊk/ N ⇒ **townspeople**

township /ˈtaʊnʃɪp/ N commune *f*, municipalité *f* ; *(in South Africa)* township *m or f*

townsman /ˈtaʊnzmən/ N (pl **-men**) citadin *m*, habitant *m* de la ville (*or* des villes) ◆ **my fellow townsmen** mes concitoyens *mpl*

townspeople /ˈtaʊnzpiːpl/ NPL citadins *mpl*, habitants *mpl* de la ville (*or* des villes)

townswoman /ˈtaʊnzwʊmən/ N (pl **-women**) citadine *f*, habitante *f* de la ville (*or* des villes)

towpath /ˈtəʊpɑːθ/ N chemin *m* de halage

towrope /ˈtəʊrəʊp/ N câble *m* de remorquage

toxaemia, toxemia *(US)* /tɒkˈsiːmɪə/ N toxémie *f*

toxic /ˈtɒksɪk/ ADJ toxique *(to sb/sth* pour qn/qch)
COMP **toxic noise** N nuisances *fpl* sonores
toxic shock syndrome N syndrome *m* du choc toxique
toxic waste N déchets *mpl* toxiques

toxicity /tɒkˈsɪsɪtɪ/ N toxicité *f*

toxicological /ˌtɒksɪkəˈlɒdʒɪkəl/ ADJ toxicologique

toxicologist /ˌtɒksɪˈkɒlədʒɪst/ N toxicologue *mf*

toxicology /ˌtɒksɪˈkɒlədʒɪ/ N toxicologie *f*

toxin /ˈtɒksɪn/ N toxine *f*

toxoplasmosis /ˌtɒksəʊplæzˈməʊsɪs/ N toxoplasmose *f*

toy /tɔɪ/ N jouet *m* VI ◆ **to ~ with** *[+ object, pen, sb's affections]* jouer avec ; *[+ idea, scheme]* caresser ◆ **to ~ with one's food** manger du bout des dents, chipoter, picorer
COMP *[house, truck, stove, railway]* miniature ; *[trumpet]* d'enfant
toy boy* N *(Brit fig)* gigolo* *m*
toy car N petite voiture *f*
toy dog N *(fig)* petit chien *m* d'appartement
toy maker N fabricant *m* de jouets
toy poodle N caniche *m* nain
toy soldier N petit soldat *m*
toy train N petit train *m* ; *(electric)* train *m* électrique

toybox /ˈtɔɪbɒks/, **toychest** /ˈtɔɪtʃest/ N coffre *m* à jouets

toyshop /ˈtɔɪʃɒp/ N magasin *m* de jouets

toytown /ˈtɔɪtaʊn/ ADJ *(esp Brit pej) [politics, revolutionary etc]* de pacotille ◆ **~ money** monnaie *f* de singe

tpi /tiːpiːˈaɪ/ N *(Comput)* (abbrev of **tracks per inch**) pistes *fpl* par pouce

trace¹ /treɪs/ N 1 *(gen)* trace *f* ◆ **there were ~s of the cave having been lived in** il y avait des traces d'habitation dans la grotte ◆ **the police could find no ~ of the thief** la police n'a trouvé aucune trace du voleur ◆ **~s of an ancient civilization** la trace *or* les vestiges *mpl* d'une ancienne civilisation ◆ **there is no ~ of it now** il n'en reste plus trace maintenant ◆ **we have lost all ~ of them** nous avons complètement perdu leur trace ◆ **~s of arsenic in the stomach** traces d'arsenic dans l'estomac ◆ **to vanish/sink without (a) ~** disparaître/sombrer sans laisser de traces ◆ **without a ~ of ill-feeling** sans la moindre rancune
2 *(US = trail)* piste *f*
VT 1 *(= draw) [+ curve, line etc]* tracer ; *(with tracing paper etc)* décalquer
2 *(= follow trail of)* suivre la trace de ; *(and locate) [+ person]* retrouver, dépister ; *[+ object]* retrouver ◆ **ask the police to help you ~ him** demandez à la police de vous aider à le retrouver ◆ **they ~d him as far as Paris but then lost him** ils ont pu suivre sa trace jusqu'à Paris mais l'ont perdu par la suite ◆ **I can't ~ your file at all** je ne trouve pas (de) trace de votre dossier ◆ **I can't ~ his having been in touch with us** je n'ai aucune indication *or* mention du fait qu'il nous ait contactés
COMP **trace element, trace mineral** N oligoélément *m*
► **trace back** VI *(esp US)* ◆ **this ~s back to the loss of ...** ceci est imputable à la perte de ...
VT SEP ◆ **to trace back one's ancestry** *or* **descent** *or* **family to ...** faire remonter sa famille à ..., établir que sa famille remonte à ... ◆ **they ~d the murder weapon back to a shop in Leeds** ils ont réussi à établir que l'arme du crime provenait d'un magasin de Leeds ◆ **we ~d him back to Paris, then the trail ended** (en remontant la filière) nous avons retrouvé sa trace à Paris mais là, la piste s'est perdue ◆ **this may be ~d back to the loss of ...** ceci peut être attribué à *or* est attribuable *or* imputable à la perte de ...
► **trace out** VT SEP tracer

trace² /treɪs/ N *[of harness]* trait *m* ; → **kick**

traceability /ˌtreɪsəˈbɪlɪtɪ/ N traçabilité *f*

traceable /ˈtreɪsəbl/ ADJ ◆ **export licences are only issued to completely ~ cattle** les licences d'exportation ne sont délivrées que pour le bétail dont l'origine peut être formellement établie
◆ **traceable to** ◆ **half of the cases of this disease are ~ to Lake Malawi** la moitié des cas ont leur origine dans la région du lac Malawi ◆ **the inflation rate is ~ to ...** le taux d'inflation est dû à ...

tracer /ˈtreɪsəʳ/ N *(= person)* traceur *m*, -euse *f* ; *(= instrument)* roulette *f*, traçoir *m* ; *(Biochem)* traceur *m* ; (also **tracer bullet**) balle *f* traçante ; (also **tracer shell**) obus *m* traçant

tracery /ˈtreɪsərɪ/ N *(NonC: Archit)* réseau *m* *(de fenêtre ajourée)* ; *[of veins on leaves]* nervures *fpl* ; *[of frost on window etc]* dentelles *fpl*

trachea /trəˈkɪə/ N (pl **tracheas** *or* **tracheae** /træˈkiːiː/) trachée *f*

tracheotomy /ˌtrækɪˈɒtəmɪ/ N trachéotomie *f*

trachoma /træˈkəʊmə/ N trachome *m*

tracing /ˈtreɪsɪŋ/ N *(NonC) (= process)* calquage *m* ; *(= result)* calque *m* COMP **tracing paper** N papier *m inv* calque, papier *m* à décalquer

track /træk/ N 1 *(= mark, trail, also Climbing)* trace *f* ; *[of animal, person]* trace *f*, piste *f* ; *[of tyres, wheels]* trace *f* ; *[of boat]* sillage *m* ; *(= route)* trajectoire *f* ◆ **a ~ of muddy footprints across the floor** des traces de pas boueuses sur le plancher ◆ **to cover (up)** *or* **hide one's ~s** *(lit, fig)* couvrir sa marche, brouiller les pistes ◆ **to change ~** changer de cap ; → **inside, stop**
◆ **in + track(s)** ◆ **the hurricane destroyed everything in its ~** l'ouragan a tout détruit sur son passage ◆ **to follow in sb's ~s** *(lit)* suivre qn à la trace ; *(fig)* suivre les traces de qn, marcher sur les traces de qn
◆ **off + track** ◆ **to be off the ~** faire fausse route ◆ **you're away off the ~!** vous êtes tout à fait à côté !, vous n'y êtes pas du tout ! ◆ **to put** *or* **throw sb off the ~** désorienter qn
◆ **on + track(s)** ◆ **to be on sb's ~(s)** être sur la piste de qn ◆ **he had the police on his ~(s)** la police était sur sa piste ◆ **they got on to his ~ very quickly** ils ont très vite trouvé sa piste ◆ **to be on ~** *(fig)* être sur la bonne voie ◆ **to get the economy back on ~** remettre l'économie sur les rails ◆ **to be on the right ~** être sur la bonne voie ◆ **to put sb on the right ~** mettre qn dans la bonne voie ◆ **to be on the wrong ~** faire fausse route
◆ **to keep track of** *[+ spacecraft etc]* suivre ; *[+ events]* suivre la marche *or* le fil de ; *[+ developments, situation]* suivre, rester au courant de ◆ **they kept ~ of him till they reached the**

wood ils ont suivi sa trace jusqu'au bois ◆ **I kept ~ of her until she got married** je suis resté en contact avec elle *or* au courant de ce qu'elle faisait jusqu'à son mariage ◆ **keep ~ of the time** n'oubliez pas l'heure

◆ **to lose track of** *[+ spacecraft etc]* perdre ; *[+ developments, situation]* ne plus suivre, ne plus être au courant de ; *[+ events]* perdre le fil de ◆ **I've lost ~ of what he's doing** je ne suis plus au courant de ce qu'il fait ◆ **they lost ~ of him in the woods** ils ont perdu sa trace une fois arrivés au bois ◆ **I lost ~ of her after the war** j'ai perdu tout contact avec elle *or* je l'ai perdue de vue après la guerre ◆ **don't lose ~ of him** *(lit)* ne perdez pas sa trace ; *(fig)* ne le perdez pas de vue ◆ **I've lost ~ of those books** je ne sais plus *or* j'ai oublié où sont ces livres ◆ **to lose all ~ of time** perdre la notion du temps ◆ **I've lost ~ of what he is saying** j'ai perdu le fil de ce qu'il dit, je ne suis plus ce qu'il dit

◆ **to make tracks*** *(= leave)* se sauver* ◆ **we must be making ~s*** il faut qu'on se sauve* *subj* ◆ **he made ~s for the hotel*** il a filé à l'hôtel

[2] *(= path)* chemin *m*, sentier *m* ◆ **sheep ~** piste *f* à moutons ◆ **mule ~** chemin *m or* sentier *m* muletier ; → **beaten, cart, dirt**

[3] *(Rail)* voie *f* (ferrée), rails *mpl* ◆ **to leave the ~(s)** quitter les rails, dérailler ◆ **to cross the ~** traverser la voie ◆ **single-~ line** ligne *f* à voie unique ◆ **to change ~s** changer de voie ◆ **to live on the wrong side of the ~s** *(esp US)* vivre dans les quartiers pauvres ; → **one**

[4] *(Sport)* piste *f* ◆ **motor-racing ~** autodrome *m* ◆ **dog-racing ~** cynodrome *m* ; → **racetrack**

[5] *(NonC)* athlétisme *m*

[6] *[of electronic tape, CD, computer disk]* piste *f* ; *[of long-playing record]* plage *f* ; *(= piece of music)* morceau *m* ◆ **four-~ tape** bande *f* à quatre pistes ; → **soundtrack**

[7] *(= tyre tread)* chape *f* ; *(= space between wheels)* écartement *m* ; (also **caterpillar track**) chenille *f*

[8] *(US Scol)* groupe *m* de niveau ◆ **divided into five ~s** répartis en cinq groupes de niveau ◆ **the top/middle/bottom ~** la section forte/moyenne/faible

NPL **tracks** * *(Drugs)* marques *fpl* de piqûres

VT *[+ animal, person, vehicle]* suivre la trace de ; *[+ hurricane, rocket, spacecraft, comet]* suivre la trajectoire de ◆ **to ~ dirt over the floor** laisser des traces sales sur le plancher

VI *[camera]* faire un travelling

COMP **track and field athletes** **NPL** athlètes *mfpl*

track and field athletics **N** athlétisme *m*
track athletics **N** athlétisme *m* sur piste
track event **N** *(Sport)* épreuve *f* sur piste
tracking device **N** dispositif *m* de pistage
tracking shot **N** *(Cine)* travelling *m*
tracking station **N** *(Space)* station *f* d'observation (de satellites)
track lighting **N** rampe *f* de spots
track maintenance **N** *(Rail)* entretien *m* de la voie
track meet **N** *(US Sport)* réunion *f* sportive sur piste
track race **N** *(Sport)* course *f* sur piste
track racing **N** *(Sport)* courses *fpl* sur piste
track record **N** *(fig)* ◆ **to have a good ~ record** avoir fait ses preuves ◆ **to have a poor ~ record** avoir eu de mauvais résultats
track rod **N** *(Brit)* barre *f* de connexion
track shoe **N** chaussure *f* de course
track shot **N** *(Cine)* travelling *m*
track system **N** *(US Scol)* système *m* de répartition des élèves par niveaux

► **track down** **VT SEP** *[+ animal, wanted man]* traquer et capturer ; *[+ lost object, lost person, reference, quotation]* (finir par) retrouver *or* localiser

trackball /'trækbɔːl/ **N** *(Comput)* boule *f* roulante

tracked /trækt/ **ADJ** *[vehicle]* à chenilles

tracker /'trækəʳ/ **N** *(Hunting)* traqueur *m* ; *(gen)* poursuivant(e) *m(f)*

COMP **tracker dog** **N** chien *m* policier *(dressé pour retrouver les gens)*
tracker fund **N** *(Fin)* tracker *m*

tracklayer /'trækleɪəʳ/ **N** *(US Rail)* ⇒ **trackman**

trackless /'træklɪs/ **ADJ** *[forest, desert]* sans chemins ; *[vehicle]* sans chenilles

trackman /'trækmən/ **N** (pl **-men**) *(US Rail)* responsable *m* de l'entretien des voies

trackpad /'trækpæd/ **N** trackpad *m*

tracksuit /'træksuːt/ **N** *(Brit)* survêtement *m*

trackwalker /'trækwɔːkəʳ/ **N** *(US Rail)* ⇒ **trackman**

tract[1] /trækt/ **N** [1] *[of land, water]* étendue *f* ; *[of coal etc]* gisement *m* ; *(US = housing estate)* lotissement *m* ◆ **vast ~s of wilderness** de vastes zones *fpl or* étendues désertiques [2] *(Anat)* **digestive ~** appareil *m or* système *m* digestif **COMP** **tract house** **N** *(US)* pavillon *m (dans un lotissement)*

tract[2] /trækt/ **N** *(= pamphlet)* pamphlet *m* ; *(Rel)* traité *m*

tractable /'træktəbl/ **ADJ** *[person]* accommodant, souple ; *[animal]* docile ; *[material]* malléable ; *[problem]* soluble

Tractarian /træk'teərɪən/ **ADJ, N** *(Rel)* tractarien *m*, -ienne *f*

Tractarianism /træk'teərɪənɪzəm/ **N** *(Rel)* tractarianisme *m*

traction /'trækʃən/ **N** *(NonC: all senses)* traction *f* ◆ **electric/steam ~** traction *f* électrique/à vapeur **COMP** **traction engine** **N** locomobile *f*

tractive /'træktɪv/ **ADJ** de traction

tractor /'træktəʳ/ **N** tracteur *m*

COMP **tractor drive** **N** *(Comput)* dispositif *m* d'entraînement à picots
tractor driver **N** conducteur *m*, -trice *f* de tracteur
tractor-trailer **N** *(US)* semi-remorque *m*

trad* /træd/ **ADJ** *(esp Brit Mus)* abbrev of **traditional**

tradable /'treɪdəbl/ **ADJ** *(esp US Econ, Fin)* commercialisable

trade /treɪd/ **N** [1] *(NonC = commerce)* commerce *m*, affaires *fpl* ; *(between two countries)* échanges *mpl* (commerciaux) ; *(illegal)* trafic *m* ◆ **overseas ~** commerce *m* extérieur ◆ **it's good for ~** ça fait marcher le commerce ◆ **the fur/tourist ~** le secteur de la fourrure/touristique ◆ **the arms ~** le commerce des armes ◆ **the wool ~, the ~ in wool** le commerce de la laine ◆ **he's in the wool ~** il est négociant en laine ◆ **the drug ~, the ~ in drugs** le marché de la drogue ◆ **they do a lot of ~ with ...** ils font beaucoup d'affaires avec ... ◆ **~ has been good** *or* **brisk** les affaires ont été bonnes, le commerce a bien marché ◆ **to do a good** *or* **brisk** *or* **roaring ~** vendre beaucoup (*in* de) ◆ **Board of Trade** *(Brit)* ◆ **Department of Trade** *(US)* ministère *m* du Commerce ◆ **Secretary (of State) for Trade and Industry** *(Brit)* ministre *m* (du Commerce et) de l'Industrie ◆ **President of the Board of Trade, Minister of Trade** ministre *m* du Commerce ◆ **Department of Trade and Industry** *(Brit)* ≈ ministère *m* (du Commerce et) de l'Industrie ; → **rag**[1], **tourist**

[2] *(= job, skill)* métier *m* ◆ **she wants him to learn a ~** elle veut qu'il apprenne un métier ◆ **he is a butcher by** *or* **to* ~** il est boucher de son métier *or* de son état ◆ **he's a doctor by ~** il est médecin de son état ◆ **to put sb to a ~** † mettre qn en apprentissage ◆ **he's in the ~** *(lit, fig)* il est du métier ◆ **as we say in the ~** comme on dit dans le jargon du métier, pour employer un terme technique ◆ **known in the ~ as ...** que les gens du métier appellent ... ◆ **special discounts for the ~** remises spéciales pour les membres de la profession ; → **stock, tool, trick**

[3] ⇒ **trade wind;** → **comp**

[4] *(esp US = swap)* échange *m* ◆ **to do a ~ with sb for sth** faire l'échange de qch avec qn

VI [1] *[firm, country, businessman]* faire le commerce (*in* de), commercer, avoir *or* entretenir des relations commerciales (*with* avec) ◆ **he ~s as a wool merchant** il est négociant en laine ◆ **to ~ (up)on sb's kindness** abuser de la gentillesse de qn

[2] *(US: of private individual)* faire ses achats (*with* chez, à), être client(e) (*with* chez)

[3] *[currency, commodity]* **to be trading at** se négocier à ; → **cease**

[4] *(= exchange)* échanger, troquer (*with sb* avec qn)

VT *(= exchange)* ◆ **to ~ A for B** échanger *or* troquer A contre B ◆ **I ~d my penknife with him for his marbles** je lui ai donné mon canif en échange de ses billes

COMP *(gen) [exchanges, visits]* commercial ; *(Publishing) [press, publications]* professionnel, spécialisé

trade agreement **N** accord *m* commercial
trade association **N** association *f* commerciale
trade balance **N** balance *f* commerciale
trade barriers **NPL** barrières *fpl* douanières
trade bill **N** effet *m* de commerce
trade cycle **N** *(Econ)* cycle *m* économique
trade deficit **N** déficit *m* commercial, déficit *m* extérieur
Trade Descriptions Act **N** *(Brit) loi protégeant les consommateurs contre la publicité et les appellations mensongères*
trade discount **N** remise *f* au détaillant
trade fair **N** foire(-exposition) *f* commerciale
trade figures **NPL** résultats *mpl* (financiers)
trade gap **N** déficit *m* commercial *or* de la balance commerciale
trade-in **N** *(Comm)* reprise *f* ◆ **he took my old machine as a ~-in** il m'a repris ma vieille machine ◆ **~-in allowance** reprise *f* ◆ **~-in price** prix *m* à la reprise ◆ **~-in value** valeur *f* à la reprise
trade journal **N** revue *f* professionnelle
trade mission **N** mission *f* commerciale
trade name **N** *(= product name)* nom *m* de marque ; *(= company name)* raison *f* sociale
trade-off **N** *(= exchange)* échange *m* (*between* entre) ; *(balancing)* compromis *m*, concessions *fpl* mutuelles
trade paper **N** ⇒ **trade journal**
trade plate **N** *(= number plate)* ≈ plaque *f* d'immatriculation provisoire
trade price **N** prix *m* de gros
trade returns **NPL** *(Econ)* ⇒ **trade figures**
trade route **N** route *f* commerciale
trade school **N** collège *m* technique
trade secret **N** *(lit, fig)* secret *m* de fabrication
trade surplus **N** excédent *m* commercial
trade talks **NPL** négociations *fpl* commerciales
trades union **N** ⇒ **trade union**
the Trades Union Congress **N** *(Brit)* la confédération des syndicats britanniques
trades unionism **N** ⇒ **trade unionism**
trades unionist **N** ⇒ **trade unionist**
trade union **N** syndicat *m* ◆ **~(s) union membership** adhésion *f* à un syndicat ; *(= number of members)* nombre *m* de syndiqués
trade unionism **N** syndicalisme *m*
trade unionist **N** syndicaliste *mf*
trade war **N** guerre *f* commerciale
trade wind **N** (vent *m*) alizé *m*

► **trade down** **VI** ◆ **to trade down to a smaller house/car** vendre sa maison/voiture pour en acheter une moins chère

► **trade in** **VT SEP** ◆ **I traded it in for a new one** on me l'a repris quand j'en ai acheté un nouveau

► **trade off** VT SEP [1] (= *balance*) **to ~ off A against B** accepter que A compense B
[2] (= *exchange*) **to ~ off one thing against** *or* **for another** échanger *or* troquer une chose contre une autre
[3] (= *use*) faire commerce de
N ◆ **trade-off** → **trade**

► **trade on** VI exploiter, tirer profit de

► **trade up** VI ◆ **to trade up to a bigger house/car** vendre sa maison/voiture pour en acheter une plus chère

trademark /ˈtreɪdmɑːk/ N marque *f* (de fabrique) VT [*+ product, goods*] apposer une marque sur ; [*+ symbol, word*] déposer ◆ **registered ~** marque *f* déposée ADJ (*fig = characteristic*) caractéristique ◆ **his ~ wig** sa perruque si caractéristique

trader /ˈtreɪdəʳ/ N [1] commerçant(e) *m(f)*, marchand(e) *m(f)* ; (*bigger*) négociant(e) *m(f)* ; (also **street trader**) vendeur *m*, -euse *f* de rue ; (*US Stock Exchange*) contrepartiste *mf* ◆ **wool ~** négociant *m* en laine ; → **slave** [2] (= *ship*) navire *m* marchand *or* de la marine marchande

tradescantia /ˌtrædəsˈkæntɪə/ N tradescantia *m*

tradesman /ˈtreɪdzmən/ N (pl **-men**) commerçant *m* ; (= *skilled worker*) ouvrier *m* qualifié
COMP **tradesman's entrance, tradesmen's entrance** N entrée *f* de service *or* des fournisseurs

tradespeople /ˈtreɪdzpiːpl/ NPL commerçants *mpl*

tradeswoman /ˈtreɪdzwʊmən/ N (pl **-women**) commerçante *f* ; (= *skilled worker*) ouvrière *f* qualifiée

trading /ˈtreɪdɪŋ/ N (NonC, *in shops, business*) commerce *m*, affaires *fpl* ; (*on larger scale*) commerce *m*, négoce *m* ; (*between countries*) commerce *m*, échanges *mpl* (commerciaux) ; (*Stock Exchange*) transactions *fpl*, opérations *fpl* ◆ **~ was brisk yesterday** (*Stock Exchange*) l'activité *f* a été soutenue hier
COMP [*port, centre*] de commerce
trading capital N capital *m* engagé, capital *m* de roulement
trading card N carte *f* à échanger
trading company N société *f* d'import-export
trading estate N (*Brit*) zone *f* artisanale et commerciale
trading floor N (*Stock Exchange*) parquet *m*
trading nation N nation *f* commerçante
trading partner N partenaire *mf* commercial(e)
trading post N (*esp Can, US*) comptoir *m* (commercial)
trading profits NPL ◆ **~ profits for last year** bénéfices *mpl* réalisés pour l'exercice de l'année écoulée
trading stamp N timbre-prime *m*
trading standards NPL normes *fpl* de conformité
trading standards office N ≈ Direction *f* de la consommation et de la répression des fraudes

tradition /trəˈdɪʃən/ N tradition *f* ◆ **according to ~** selon la tradition ◆ **it's in the (best) ~ of ...** c'est dans la (plus pure) tradition de ... ◆ **~ has it that ...** la tradition veut que ... ◆ **it is a ~ that ...** il est de tradition que ... *+ subj* ◆ **the ~ that ...** la tradition selon laquelle *or* qui veut que ... ◆ **to break with ~** rompre avec la tradition ◆ **by ~** selon la tradition, traditionnellement

traditional /trəˈdɪʃənl/ ADJ traditionnel ◆ **it is ~ (for sb) to do sth** il est de tradition (pour qn) de faire qch ◆ **to be ~ in one's approach to sth** avoir une approche traditionnelle de qch *or* une attitude traditionnelle face à qch ◆ **the clothes which are ~ to his country** les vêtements traditionnels de son pays COMP **traditional medicine** N médecine *f* traditionnelle

traditionalism /trəˈdɪʃnəlɪzəm/ N traditionalisme *m*

traditionalist /trəˈdɪʃnəlɪst/ ADJ, N traditionaliste *mf*

traditionally /trəˈdɪʃnəlɪ/ ADV (*gen*) traditionnellement ◆ **~ made** à l'ancienne

traduce /trəˈdjuːs/ VT (*frm*) calomnier, diffamer

Trafalgar /trəˈfælgəʳ/ N ◆ **Battle of ~** bataille *f* de Trafalgar

traffic /ˈtræfɪk/ (vb : pret, ptp **trafficked**) N (NonC) [1] (*on roads*) circulation *f* ; (= *air, sea, rail traffic, number of phone calls, traffic on website*) trafic *m* ◆ **road ~** circulation *f* routière ◆ **rail ~** trafic *m* ferroviaire ◆ **holiday ~** circulation *f* des grands départs (*or* des grands retours), rush *m* des vacances ◆ **the ~ is heavy/light** il y a beaucoup de/très peu de circulation ◆ **the build-up** *or* **backlog of ~ extends to the bridge** le bouchon s'étire jusqu'au pont ◆ **~ out of/into Paris** la circulation dans le sens Paris-province/province-Paris ◆ **~ coming into London should avoid Putney Bridge** il est recommandé aux automobilistes se rendant à Londres d'éviter Putney Bridge ◆ **~ in and out of Heathrow Airport** le trafic à destination et en provenance de l'aéroport de Heathrow ◆ **~ in** *or* **using the Channel** trafic *or* navigation *f* en Manche ◆ **increase ~ to your website** augmentez le trafic de votre site web ; → **tourist**
[2] (= *trade*) commerce *m* (*in* de) ; (*pej*) trafic *m* (*in* de) ◆ **the drug ~** le trafic de la drogue *or* des stupéfiants
VI ◆ **to ~ in sth** faire le commerce *or* le trafic (*pej*) de qch
VT ◆ **to ~ arms/drugs** faire du trafic d'armes/de drogue
COMP **traffic calming** N *mesures de ralentissement de la circulation en ville*
traffic circle N (*US*) rond-point *m*, carrefour *m* giratoire
traffic cone N cône *m* de signalisation
traffic control N (*on roads*) prévention *f* routière ; (*for planes, boats, trains*) contrôle *m* du trafic
traffic controller N (*at airport*) contrôleur *m*, -euse *f* de la navigation aérienne, aiguilleur *m* du ciel
traffic control tower N tour *f* de contrôle
traffic cop* N (*esp US*) ⇒ **traffic policeman**
traffic court N (*US Jur*) *tribunal où sont jugées les infractions au code de la route*
traffic diversion N déviation *f*
traffic duty N ◆ **to be on ~ duty** [*policeman*] faire la circulation
traffic holdup N bouchon *m* (*de circulation*)
traffic island N refuge *m* (*pour piétons*) ; (*in centre of roundabout*) terre-plein *m* central
traffic jam N embouteillage *m*, bouchon *m*
traffic lights NPL feux *mpl* de signalisation ◆ **to go through the ~ lights at red** passer au rouge, griller le feu rouge ◆ **the ~ lights were (at) green** le feu était (au) vert
traffic offence N (*Jur*) infraction *f* au code de la route
traffic pattern N (*for planes*) couloir *m* *or* position *f* d'approche
traffic police N (*speeding etc*) police *f* de la route ; (*points duty etc*) police *f* de la circulation
traffic policeman N (pl **traffic policemen**) (*gen*) ≈ agent *m* de police ; (*on points duty*) agent *m* de la circulation
traffic regulations NPL réglementation *f* de la circulation
traffic sign N panneau *m* de signalisation, poteau *m* indicateur ◆ **international ~ signs** signalisation *f* routière internationale
traffic signals NPL ⇒ **traffic lights**
traffic warden N (*Brit*) contractuel(le) *m(f)*

trafficator † /ˈtræfɪkeɪtəʳ/ N (*Brit*) flèche *f* (de direction) †

trafficker /ˈtræfɪkəʳ/ N trafiquant(e) *m(f)* (*in* en)

trafficking /ˈtræfɪkɪŋ/ N trafic *m* ◆ **arms/cocaine ~** trafic *m* d'armes/de cocaïne

tragedian /trəˈdʒiːdɪən/ N (= *writer*) auteur *m* tragique ; (= *actor*) tragédien *m*

tragedienne /trəˌdʒiːdɪˈen/ N tragédienne *f*

tragedy /ˈtrædʒɪdɪ/ N (*gen, Theat*) tragédie *f* ◆ **the ~ of it is that ...** ce qui est tragique, c'est que ... ◆ **it is a ~ that ...** il est tragique que ... *+ subj*

tragic /ˈtrædʒɪk/ ADJ [*accident, death, victim, expression, hero*] tragique ◆ **~ actor** tragédien(ne) *m(f)* ◆ **it is ~ that ...** il est tragique que ... *+ subj*

tragically /ˈtrædʒɪkəlɪ/ ADV tragiquement

tragicomedy /ˈtrædʒɪˈkɒmɪdɪ/ N (pl **tragicomedies**) tragicomédie *f*

tragicomic /ˈtrædʒɪˈkɒmɪk/ ADJ tragicomique

trail /treɪl/ N [1] [*of blood, smoke*] traînée *f* ◆ **a long ~ of refugees** une longue file *or* colonne de réfugiés ◆ **to leave a ~ of destruction** tout détruire sur son passage ◆ **his illness brought a series of debts in its ~** sa maladie a amené dans son sillage une série de dettes ; → **vapour**
[2] (= *tracks: gen*) trace *f* ; (*Hunting*) piste *f*, trace(s) *f(pl)* ◆ **to be on the ~ of sb** (*lit, fig*) être sur la piste de qn ◆ **I'm on the ~ of that book you want** j'ai trouvé trace *or* j'ai retrouvé la trace du livre que vous voulez ; → **hot**
[3] (= *path, road*) sentier *m*, chemin *m* ; → **blaze², nature**
[4] (*Ski, Climbing*) trace *f* ; (*cross country skiing*) piste *f* de fond ◆ **to break a ~** faire la trace, tracer
VT [1] (= *follow*) suivre la piste de ; (*fig*) (= *lag behind*) être dépassé par
[2] (= *drag, tow*) [*+ object on rope, toy cart etc*] tirer, traîner ; [*+ caravan, trailer, boat*] tirer, tracter ◆ **he was ~ing his schoolbag behind him** il traînait son cartable derrière lui ◆ **the children ~ed dirt all over the carpet** les enfants ont couvert le tapis de traces sales ◆ **to ~ one's fingers through** *or* **in the water** laisser traîner ses doigts dans l'eau ◆ **don't ~ your feet!** ne traîne pas les pieds !
[3] (*Mil*) [*+ rifle etc*] porter à la main
[4] (= *announce as forthcoming*) donner un avant-goût de
[5] (*in gardening*) **to ~ a plant over a fence** *etc* faire grimper une plante par-dessus une clôture *etc*
VI [1] [*object*] traîner ; [*plant*] ramper ◆ **your coat is ~ing in the mud** ton manteau traîne dans la boue ◆ **smoke ~ed from the funnel** une traînée de fumée s'échappait de la cheminée ◆ **they were ~ing by 13 points** (*Sport fig*) ils étaient en retard de 13 points ◆ **they are ~ing at the bottom of the league** (*Ftbl*) ils traînent en bas de division
[2] ◆ **to ~ along/in/out** *etc* (= *move in straggling line*) passer/entrer/sortir *etc* à la queue leu leu *or* en file ; (= *move wearily*) passer/entrer/sortir *etc* en traînant les pieds
COMP **trail bike*** N moto *f* de moto-cross
trail mix N mélange *m* de fruits secs

► **trail away, trail off** VI [*voice, music*] s'estomper

trailblazer /ˈtreɪlbleɪzəʳ/ N (*fig*) pionnier *m*, -ière *f*

trailblazing /ˈtreɪlbleɪzɪŋ/ ADJ (*fig*) (in)novateur (-trice *f*)

trailbreaker /ˈtreɪlbreɪkəʳ/ N (*esp US*) ⇒ **trailblazer**

trailer /ˈtreɪləʳ/ N [1] (*behind car, van, truck*) remorque *f* ; (*esp US = caravan*) caravane *f* [2] (*Cine, TV*) bande-annonce *f* [3] (*Phot = end of film roll*) amorce *f* (en fin d'un rouleau)
COMP **trailer camp, trailer court, trailer park** N (*US*) village *m* de mobile homes

trailer tent N tente-caravane *f*
trailer trash* N (*US*) *pauvres vivant dans des mobile homes*

trailing /ˈtreɪlɪŋ/ ADJ [*plant*] grimpant
COMP **trailing edge** N [*of plane wing*] bord *m* de fuite
trailing geranium N géranium-lierre *m*

train /treɪn/ N 1 (*Rail*) train *m* ; (*in Underground*) rame *f*, métro *m* ◆ **to go by** ~ prendre le train ◆ **to go to London by** ~ prendre le train pour aller à Londres, aller à Londres en train *or* par le train ◆ **to travel by** ~ voyager par le train *or* en train ◆ **on** *or* **in the** ~ dans le train ◆ **to transport by** ~ transporter par voie ferroviaire ; → **express, freight, slow**

2 (= *procession*) file *f* ; (= *entourage*) suite *f*, équipage *m* ; [*of camels*] caravane *f*, file *f* ; [*of mules*] train *m*, file *f* ; [*of vehicles*] cortège *m*, file *f* ◆ **he arrived with 50 men in his** ~ il arriva avec un équipage de 50 hommes ◆ **the war brought famine in its** ~ la guerre amena la famine dans son sillage *or* entraîna la famine ; → **baggage**

3 (= *line, series*) suite *f*, série *f* ; [*of gunpowder*] traînée *f* ◆ **in an unbroken** ~ en succession ininterrompue ◆ **a** ~ **of events** une suite d'événements ◆ **it broke** *or* **interrupted his** ~ **of thought** cela est venu interrompre le fil de sa *or* ses pensée(s) ◆ **I've lost my** ~ **of thought** je ne retrouve plus le fil de ma *or* mes pensée(s) ◆ **it is in** ~ (*esp Brit fig*) c'est en préparation, c'est en marche ◆ **to set sth in** ~ (*esp Brit*) mettre qch en marche *or* en mouvement

4 [*of dress, robe*] traîne *f*

5 (*Tech*) train *m* ◆ ~ **of gears** train *m* de roues d'engrenage

VT 1 (= *instruct*) [+ *person, engineer, doctor, nurse, teacher, craftsman, apprentice*] former ; [+ *employee, soldier*] former, instruire ; (*Sport*) [+ *player*] entraîner, préparer ; [+ *animal*] dresser ; [+ *voice*] travailler ; [+ *ear, mind, memory*] exercer ◆ **he is ~ing someone to take over from him** il forme son successeur ; (also **house-train**) ◆ **to** ~ **a puppy/child** apprendre à un chiot/à un enfant à être propre ◆ **to** ~ **an animal to do sth** apprendre à *or* dresser un animal à faire qch ◆ **to** ~ **sb to do sth** apprendre à qn à faire qch ; (*professionally*) former qn à faire qch, préparer qn à faire qch ◆ **to** ~ **o.s. to do sth** s'entraîner *or* s'exercer à faire qch ◆ **to** ~ **sb in a craft** apprendre un métier à qn, préparer qn à un métier ◆ **he was ~ed in weaving** *or* **as a weaver** il a reçu une formation de tisserand ◆ **to** ~ **sb in the use of sth** *or* **to use sth** apprendre à qn à utiliser qch, instruire qn dans le maniement de qch ◆ **where were you ~ed?** où avez-vous reçu votre formation ? ; see also **trained**

2 (= *direct*) [+ *gun, camera, telescope*] braquer (*on* sur) ◆ **to** ~ **a plant along a wall** faire grimper une plante le long d'un mur

VI 1 recevoir une *or* sa formation ; (*Sport*) s'entraîner (*for* pour), se préparer (*for* à) ◆ **to** ~ **as** *or* ~ **to be a teacher/secretary** *etc* recevoir une formation de professeur/de secrétaire *etc* ◆ **where did you ~?** où avez-vous reçu votre formation ?

2 (*Rail* = *go by train*) aller en train

COMP [*dispute, strike etc*] des cheminots, des chemins de fer
train crash N accident *m* de chemin de fer ; (*more serious*) catastrophe *f* ferroviaire
train ferry N ferry-boat *m*
train oil N huile *f* de baleine
train service N ◆ **there is a very good** ~ **service to London** les trains pour Londres sont très fréquents ◆ **there is an hourly** ~ **service to London** il y a un train pour Londres toutes les heures ◆ **do you know what the** ~ **service is to London?** connaissez-vous l'horaire des trains pour Londres ?
train set N train *m* électrique (*jouet*)
train spotter N (*Brit*) passionné(e) *m(f)* de trains ; (* *pej* = *nerd*) crétin(e)* *m(f)*
train-spotting N (*Brit*) ◆ **to go ~-spotting** observer les trains (*pour identifier les divers types de locomotives*)
train-workers NPL employés *mpl* des chemins de fer, cheminots *mpl*

▸ **train up** VT SEP (*Brit*) former

trainband /ˈtreɪnbænd/ N (*Brit Hist*) *ancienne milice britannique*

trainbearer /ˈtreɪnbɛərəʳ/ N dame *f or* demoiselle *f* d'honneur ; (*little boy*) page *m*

trained /treɪnd/ ADJ [*person*] (= *qualified*) qualifié ; [*nurse*] qualifié, diplômé ; [*teacher*] habilité à enseigner ; [*soldier, gymnast*] entraîné ; [*animal*] dressé ; [*mind*] exercé ◆ **he is not** ~ **at all** (*gen*) il n'a reçu aucune formation professionnelle ; [*soldier, gymnast*] il n'a reçu aucun entraînement ◆ **American-~** formé aux États-Unis ◆ **she has a** ~ **voice** elle a pris des leçons de chant ◆ **to the** ~ **eye/ear** pour un œil exercé/une oreille exercée ◆ **it is obvious to a** ~ **observer that ...** il est évident pour un observateur averti que ... ◆ **to be** ~ **for sth** (*gen*) avoir reçu une formation pour qch ; [*soldier, gymnast*] être entraîné pour qch ◆ **he isn't** ~ **for this job** il n'a pas la formation pour ce poste ◆ **we need a** ~ **person for the job** il nous faut une personne qualifiée pour ce travail ◆ **well-~** (*gen*) qui a reçu une bonne formation ; [*soldier, gymnast*] bien entraîné ; [*servant*] stylé ; [*child*] bien élevé ; [*animal*] bien dressé ◆ **she's got her husband well** ~ (*hum*) son mari est bien dressé

trainee /treɪˈniː/ N (*gen*) stagiaire *mf* ; (*US Police, Mil etc*) jeune recrue *f* ◆ **sales/management** ~ stagiaire *mf* de vente/de direction ADJ (*gen*) stagiaire, en stage ; (*in trades*) en apprentissage ◆ ~ **typist** dactylo* *f* stagiaire ◆ ~ **hairdresser** apprenti(e) coiffeur *m*, -euse *f*

traineeship /treɪˈniːʃɪp/ N stage *m*, stage *m* d'emploi-formation

trainer /ˈtreɪnəʳ/ N 1 [*of athlete, football team, racehorse*] entraîneur *m* ; (*Cycling etc*) soigneur *m* ; (*in circus*) dresseur *m*, -euse *f* ; (*of lions, tigers*) dompteur *m*, -euse *f* 2 (= *flight simulator*) simulateur *m* de vol ; (also **trainer aircraft**) avion-école *m* NPL **trainers** (*Brit*) tennis *fpl or mpl* ; (*high-tops*) baskets *mpl*

training /ˈtreɪnɪŋ/ LANGUAGE IN USE 19.2
N [*of person, engineer, doctor, nurse, teacher, craftsman*] formation *f* ; [*of employee, soldier*] formation *f*, instruction *f* ; (*Sport*) entraînement *m*, préparation *f* ; [*of animal*] dressage *m* ◆ **to be out of** ~ (*Sport*) avoir perdu la forme ◆ **to be in** ~ (= *preparing o.s.*) être en cours d'entraînement *or* de préparation ; (= *on form*) être en forme ◆ **to be in** ~ **for sth** s'entraîner pour *or* se préparer à qch ◆ **staff** ~ formation *f* du personnel ◆ **he has had some secretarial** ~ il a suivi quelques cours de secrétariat ◆ **it is good** ~ c'est un bon apprentissage *or* entraînement ; → **teacher, toilet, voice**
COMP **Training and Enterprise Council** N (*Brit*) *organisme de formation et d'aide à la création d'entreprises*
training camp N camp *m* d'entraînement
training centre N (*gen*) centre *m* de formation ; (*Sport*) centre *m* (d'entraînement) sportif
training college N (*gen*) école *f* spécialisée *or* professionnelle ◆ **teacher** ~ **college** → **teacher comp**
training course N stage *m* de formation
training ground N (*Sport, fig*) terrain *m* d'entraînement
training manual N manuel *m or* cours *m* d'instruction
Training Opportunities Scheme N (*Brit*) *programme de recyclage professionnel*
training plane N avion-école *m*
training scheme N programme *m* de formation *or* d'entraînement
training ship N navire-école *m*
training shoe N ⇒ **trainer npl**
training wheels NPL (*US*) [*of bicycle*] stabilisateurs *mpl*

trainman /ˈtreɪnmən/ N (pl **-men**) (*US Rail*) cheminot *m*

traipse* /treɪps/ VI ◆ **to** ~ **in/out** *etc* entrer/sortir *etc* d'un pas traînant *or* en traînassant* ◆ **they ~d in wearily** ils sont entrés en traînant les pieds ◆ **to** ~ **around** *or* **about** se balader*, déambuler ◆ **we've been traipsing about the shops all day** nous avons traîné *or* traînassé* dans les magasins toute la journée

trait /treɪt/ N trait *m* (*de caractère*)

traitor /ˈtreɪtəʳ/ N traître(sse) *m(f)* ◆ **to be a** ~ **to one's country/to a cause** trahir sa patrie/une cause ◆ **to turn** ~ (*Mil, Pol*) passer à l'ennemi

traitorous /ˈtreɪtərəs/ ADJ traître (traîtresse *f*), déloyal, perfide

traitorously /ˈtreɪtərəslɪ/ ADV traîtreusement, perfidement, en traître (*or* en traîtresse)

traitress /ˈtreɪtrɪs/ N traîtresse *f*

trajectory /trəˈdʒektərɪ/ N trajectoire *f*

tram /træm/ N 1 (*Brit*: also **tramcar**) tram(way) *m* ◆ **to go by** ~ prendre le tram 2 (*Min*) berline *f*, benne *f* roulante

tramline /ˈtræmlaɪn/ N (*Brit*) 1 ⇒ **tramway** 2 (*Tennis*) **~s** lignes *fpl* de côté

trammel /ˈtræməl/ (*liter*) VT entraver NPL **trammels** entraves *fpl*

tramp /træmp/ N 1 (= *sound*) **the** ~ **of feet** le bruit de pas
2 (= *hike*) randonnée *f* (à pied), excursion *f* ◆ **to go for a** ~ (aller) faire une randonnée *or* une excursion ◆ **after a ten-hour** ~ après dix heures de marche ◆ **it's a long** ~ c'est long à faire à pied
3 (= *vagabond*) clochard(e) *m(f)*, vagabond(e) *m(f)*
4 (*esp US*) **she's a** ~* (*pej* = *woman*) elle est coureuse*
5 (also **tramp steamer**) tramp *m*
VI ◆ **to** ~ **along** (= *hike*) poursuivre son chemin à pied ; (= *walk heavily*) marcher d'un pas lourd ; [*soldiers etc*] marteler le pavé *or* la route ◆ **to** ~ **up and down** faire les cent pas ◆ **he was ~ing up and down the platform** il arpentait le quai d'un pas lourd
VT ◆ **to** ~ **the streets** battre le pavé ◆ **I ~ed the town looking for the church** j'ai parcouru la ville à pied pour trouver l'église

▸ **tramp down, tramp in** VT SEP tasser du pied

trample /ˈtræmpl/ VT ◆ **to** ~ **(underfoot)** [+ *sth on ground etc*] piétiner, fouler aux pieds ; (*fig*) [+ *person, conquered nation*] fouler aux pieds, bafouer ; [+ *sb's feelings*] bafouer ; [+ *objections etc*] passer outre à ◆ **he ~d the stone into the ground** il a enfoncé du pied la pierre dans le sol ◆ **he was ~d by the horses** il a été piétiné par les chevaux VI ◆ **to** ~ **in/out** *etc* entrer/sortir *etc* d'un pas lourd ◆ **to** ~ **on** (*lit, fig*) ⇒ **to trample (underfoot)** → vt N (= *act*: also **trampling**) piétinement *m* ; (= *sound*) bruit *m* de pas

trampoline /ˈtræmpəlɪn/ N trampoline *m* VI (also **to go trampolining**) faire du trampoline

tramway /ˈtræmweɪ/ N (*Brit*) (= *rails*) voie *f* de tramway ; (= *route*) ligne *f* de tramway

trance /trɑːns/ N (*Hypnosis, Rel, Spiritualism etc*) transe *f* ; (*Med*) catalepsie *f* ; (*fig* = *ecstasy*) transe *f*, extase *f* ◆ **to go** *or* **fall into a** ~ entrer en transe ; (*Med*) tomber en catalepsie ◆ **to put sb into a** ~ [*hypnotist*] faire entrer qn en transe

tranche /trɑːnʃ/ N (*Econ etc*) tranche *f*

trannie, tranny /ˈtrænɪ/ N (pl **trannies**) 1 * abbrev of **transistor (radio)** 2 (*Phot* *) abbrev of

transparency 2 [3] ‡ (abbrev of **transvestite**) travelo‡ *m*

tranquil /'træŋkwɪl/ ADJ *[person, expression, atmosphere, way of life, sleep, morning]* paisible, serein ; *[countryside, water, river, beauty]* paisible

tranquillity, tranquility *(also US)* /træŋ'kwɪlɪtɪ/ N tranquillité *f*, calme *m*

tranquillize, tranquilize *(also US)* /'træŋkwɪlaɪz/ VT *(Med)* mettre sous tranquillisants

tranquillizer, tranquilizer *(also US)* /'træŋkwɪlaɪzəʳ/ N tranquillisant *m*, calmant *m*
COMP **tranquillizer dart** N *(for gun)* seringue *f* sédative ; *(for blowpipe)* fléchette *f* enduite de sédatif

trans. abbrev of **transitive, transport(ation), translation, translator, transfer(red)**

trans... /trænz/ PREF trans... ◆ **the Trans-Canada Highway** la route transcanadienne

transact /træn'zækt/ VT *[+ business]* traiter, régler, faire

transaction /træn'zækʃən/ N *(gen)* opération *f*, affaire *f* ; *(Econ, Fin, Stock Exchange)* transaction *f* ◆ **we have had some ~s with that firm** nous avons fait quelques opérations *or* quelques affaires avec cette société ◆ **cash** ~ opération *f* au comptant ◆ **the ~s of the Royal Society** *(= proceedings)* les travaux *mpl* de la Royal Society ; *(= minutes)* les actes *mpl* de la Royal Society

transactional /træn'zækʃənl/ ADJ transactionnel ◆ ~ **analysis** *(Psych)* analyse *f* transactionnelle

transalpine /'trænz'ælpaɪn/ ADJ transalpin

transatlantic /'trænzət'læntɪk/ ADJ *[flight, crossing, phone call, liner]* transatlantique ; *[style, upbringing]* d'Outre-Atlantique ; *(Brit = American)* américain

transceiver /træn'siːvəʳ/ N *(Rad)* émetteur-récepteur *m*

transcend /træn'send/ VT *[+ belief, knowledge, description]* transcender, dépasser ; *(= excel over)* surpasser ; *(Philos, Rel)* transcender

transcendence /træn'sendəns/, **transcendency** /træn'sendənsɪ/ N transcendance *f*

transcendent /træn'sendənt/ ADJ *(frm)* transcendant

transcendental /ˌtrænsen'dentl/ ADJ transcendantal COMP **transcendental meditation** N méditation *f* transcendantale

transcendentalism /ˌtrænsen'dentəlɪzəm/ N transcendantalisme *m*

transcontinental /'trænzˌkɒntɪ'nentl/ ADJ transcontinental

transcribe /træn'skraɪb/ VT *(gen, Phon)* transcrire

transcript /'trænskrɪpt/ N *(gen)* transcription *f* ; *(US Univ)* (copie *f* de) dossier *m* complet de la scolarité

transcription /træn'skrɪpʃən/ N *(gen, Phon)* transcription *f* ◆ **narrow/broad** ~ *(Phon)* transcription *f* étroite/large

transdermal /trænz'dɜːməl/ ADJ transdermique

transduce /trænz'djuːs/ VT transformer, convertir

transducer /trænz'djuːsəʳ/ N *(also Comput)* transducteur *m*

transduction /trænz'dʌkʃən/ N transduction *f*

transect /træn'sekt/ VT sectionner (transversalement)

transept /'trænsept/ N transept *m*

transfer /træns'fɜːʳ/ VT [1] *(= move) [+ employee, civil servant, diplomat]* transférer, muter (to à) ; *[+ soldier, player, prisoner]* transférer (to à) ; *[+ passenger]* transférer (to à), transborder ; *[+ object, goods]* transférer (to sb à qn to *a place* à un lieu) transporter (to *a place* dans un lieu), transmettre (to sb à qn) ◆ **business ~red to** *(notice) [office]* bureaux *mpl* transférés à ; *[shop]* magasin *m* transféré à

[2] *(= hand over) [+ power]* faire passer *(from* de ; *to* à) ; *[+ ownership]* transférer *(from* de ; *to* à) ; *[+ money]* virer *(from* de ; *to, into* à, sur) ; *[+ vote]* reporter *(to* sur) ◆ **to ~ one's affection to sb** reporter son *or* ses affection(s) sur qn

[3] *(= copy) [+ design, drawing]* reporter, décalquer *(to* sur)

[4] *(Brit Telec)* **to ~ the charges** téléphoner en PCV ◆ **~red charge call** communication *f* en PCV ◆ **I'm ~ring you now** *[telephone operator]* je vous mets en communication maintenant

VI *[employee, civil servant, diplomat]* être transféré *or* muté *(to* à) ; *[soldier, player, prisoner, offices]* être transféré *(to* à) ; *(US Univ = change universities)* faire un transfert (pour une autre université) ◆ **he's ~red from Science to Geography** *(Univ etc)* il ne fait plus de science, il s'est réorienté en géographie ◆ **to ~ from one train/plane** *etc* **to another** être transféré *or* transbordé d'un train/avion *etc* à un autre ◆ **we had to ~ to a bus** nous avons dû changer et prendre un car

N /'trænsfɜːʳ/ [1] *(= move) (gen)* transfert *m* ; *[of employee, diplomat]* transfert *m*, mutation *f* ; *[of soldier, player, prisoner]* transfert *m* ; *[of passenger]* transfert *m*, transbordement *m* ; *[of object, goods]* transfert *m*, transport *m* ◆ **to ask for a ~** *(Ftbl etc)* demander un transfert

[2] *(= handover) [of money]* virement *m* ; *(Pol) [of power]* passation *f* ; *(Jur = document)* transfert *m*, translation *f (Jur)* ◆ **to pay sth by bank ~** payer qch par virement bancaire ◆ ~ **of ownership** *(Jur)* transfert *m* de propriété *(from* de ; *to* à) ◆ **application for ~ of proceedings** *(Jur)* demande *f* de renvoi devant une autre juridiction

[3] *(= picture, design etc) (rub-on type)* décalcomanie *f* ; *(stick-on)* autocollant *m* ; *(sewn-on)* décalque *m*

[4] *(Transport:* also **transfer ticket**) billet *m* de correspondance

COMP /'trænsfɜːʳ/ **transfer desk** N guichet *m* de transit

transfer fee N *(Ftbl etc)* indemnité *f* transfert

transfer list N *(Brit Ftbl)* liste *f* de transfert ◆ **to be on the ~ list** être sur la liste de transfert

transfer-list VT mettre sur la liste de transfert

transfer lounge N salle *f* de transit

transfer passenger N passager *m* en transit

transfer season N *(Ftbl)* période *f* des transferts

transfer student N *(US Univ)* étudiant(e) *m(f)* venant d'une autre université

transfer tax N *(Fin)* droit *m* de mutation

transfer window N *(Football)* période *f* des transferts

transferable /træns'fɜːrəbl/ ADJ [1] *[ticket]* transmissible, qui n'est pas nominatif ◆ **"not transferable"** *(on ticket)* "ne peut être ni cédé ni échangé" ◆ **the prize is not ~ to another person** le prix est strictement personnel [2] *[skills]* réutilisable COMP **transferable vote** N voix *f* reportée *(sur un second candidat)*

transferee /ˌtrænsfɜː'riː/ N *(Jur)* cessionnaire *mf*, bénéficiaire *mf*

transference /'trænsfərəns/ N *(NonC)* [1] ⇒ **transfer noun** ; see also **thought** [2] *(Psych)* transfert *m*

transferor, transferrer /træns'fɜːrəʳ/ N *(Jur)* cédant(e) *m(f)*

transfiguration /ˌtrænsfɪgə'reɪʃən/ N *(gen, also Rel)* transfiguration *f*

transfigure /træns'fɪgəʳ/ VT transfigurer

transfix /træns'fɪks/ VT *(lit)* transpercer ◆ **to be** *or* **stand ~ed** être cloué sur place ◆ **to be ~ed with horror** être cloué au sol d'horreur, être paralysé par l'horreur

transform /træns'fɔːm/ VT *(gen)* transformer, métamorphoser *(into* en) ; *(Chem, Elec, Math, Phys)* convertir, transformer *(into* en) ; *(Gram)* transformer *(into* en) ◆ **to ~ o.s. into ..., to be ~ed into ...** se transformer en ... N /'trænsfɔːm/ *(US Ling)* transformation *f*

transformation /ˌtrænsfə'meɪʃən/ N *(NonC = change: also Elec, Math, Phys, Ling)* transformation *f (into sth* en qch) ◆ **to have undergone a complete ~** être complètement métamorphosé

transformational /ˌtrænsfə'meɪʃənl/ ADJ *(Ling)* transformationnel

transformer /træns'fɔːməʳ/ N *(Elec)* transformateur *m* COMP **transformer station** N poste *m* de transformation

transfuse /træns'fjuːz/ VT *(Med, fig)* transfuser

transfusion /træns'fjuːʒən/ N *(Med, fig)* transfusion *f* ◆ **blood** ~ transfusion *f* sanguine *or* de sang ◆ **to have a ~** recevoir une transfusion, être transfusé ◆ **to give sb a ~** faire une transfusion à qn

transgene /træns'dʒiːn/ N transgène *m*

transgender /trænz'dʒendəʳ/ ADJ transgenre *inv*, transsexuel (-elle *f*)

transgenic /trænz'dʒenɪk/ ADJ transgénique

transgress /træns'gres/ VT transgresser, enfreindre, violer VI pécher

transgression /træns'greʃən/ N *(= sin)* péché *m*, faute *f* ; *(NonC)* transgression *f*

transgressive /træns'gresɪv/ ADJ qui transgresse les règles *(or* les tabous *etc)*

transgressor /træns'gresəʳ/ N *[of law etc]* transgresseur *m (liter)* ; *(Rel = sinner)* pécheur *m*, -eresse *f*

tranship /træn'ʃɪp/ VT ⇒ **transship**

transhipment /træn'ʃɪpmənt/ N ⇒ **transshipment**

transience /'trænzɪəns/ N caractère *m* éphémère *or* transitoire

transient /'trænzɪənt/ ADJ *(frm) [pain]* passager ; *[fashion, relationship]* éphémère ; *[population]* fluctuant ◆ **of a ~ nature** passager N *(US: in hotel etc)* client(e) *m(f)* de passage

transistor /træn'zɪstəʳ/ N *(Elec)* transistor *m* ; (also **transistor radio, transistor set**) transistor *m*

transistorize /træn'zɪstəraɪz/ VT transistoriser ◆ **~d** transistorisé, à transistors

transit /'trænzɪt/ N *(NonC, gen)* transit *m* ; *(Astron)* passage *m* ◆ **they halted ~ of livestock** ils ont interrompu le transport du bétail

◆ **in transit** en transit ◆ **they were in ~ to Bombay** ils étaient en transit pour Bombay ◆ **lost in ~** perdu pendant le transport

COMP *[goods, passengers]* en transit ; *[documents, port, visa]* de transit

transit camp N *(Mil etc)* camp *m* de transit

transit lounge N *(in airport)* salle *f* de transit

transit stop N *(in airport)* escale *f* de transit

transit system N système *m* de transport

Transit van ® N *(Brit)* camionnette *f*

transition /træn'zɪʃən/ N transition *f (from* de ; *to* à) COMP *[period]* de transition

transitional /træn'zɪʃənəl/ ADJ *[period, arrangement, government, measures]* de transition, transitoire ; *[costs]* de transition COMP **transitional relief** N *(Brit) dégrèvement fiscal accordé lors de la première phase d'application d'une augmentation d'impôt ou de taxe*

transitive /'trænzɪtɪv/ ADJ *[verb, use]* transitif ; *[sentence]* à verbe transitif

transitively /'trænzɪtɪvlɪ/ ADV transitivement

transitivity /ˌtrænsɪ'tɪvɪtɪ/ N *(Gram)* transitivité *f*

transitory /'trænzɪtərɪ/ ADJ *[romance, peace]* éphémère ; *[state]* transitoire, passager ◆ **the ~ nature of political success** la nature transitoire du succès politique

Transkei /træn'skaɪ/ N Transkei *m*

translatable /trænz'leɪtəbl/ ADJ traduisible

translate /trænz'leɪt/ VT 1 *(gen)* traduire *(from* de ; *into* en) ◆ **how do you ~ "weather"?** quelle est la traduction de "weather" ?, comment traduit-on "weather" ? ◆ **the word is ~d as ...** le mot se traduit par ... ◆ **which when ~d means ...** ce que l'on peut traduire par ... ◆ **to ~ ideas into actions** passer des idées aux actes ◆ **the figures, ~d in terms of hours lost, mean ...** exprimés *or* traduits en termes d'heures perdues, ces chiffres signifient ... 2 *(Rel) [+ bishop, relics]* transférer ; *(= convey to heaven)* ravir VI *[person]* traduire ; *[word, book]* se traduire ◆ **it won't ~** c'est intraduisible

translation /trænz'leɪʃən/ N 1 traduction *f (from* de ; *into* en) ; *(Scol etc)* version *f* ◆ **the poem loses in ~** le poème perd à la traduction ◆ **it is a ~ from the Russian** c'est traduit du russe 2 *(Rel) [of bishop]* translation *f* ; *[of relics]* transfert *m* ; *(= conveying to heaven)* ravissement *m*

translator /trænz'leɪtə^r/ N *(= person)* traducteur *m*, -trice *f* ; *(= machine)* traducteur *m* ; *(Comput:* also **translator program)** programme *m* de traduction

transliterate /trænz'lɪtəreɪt/ VT translit(t)érer

transliteration /ˌtrænzlɪtə'reɪʃən/ N translittération *f*

translucence /trænz'luːsns/ N translucidité *f*

translucent /trænz'luːsnt/, **translucid** /trænz'luːsɪd/ ADJ translucide

transmigrate /'trænzmaɪ'greɪt/ VI *[soul]* transmigrer ; *[people]* émigrer

transmigration /ˌtrænzmaɪ'greɪʃən/ N *[of soul]* transmigration *f* ; *[of people]* émigration *f*

transmissible /trænz'mɪsəbl/ ADJ transmissible

transmission /trænz'mɪʃən/ N *(gen)* transmission *f* ; *(US = gearbox)* boîte *f* de vitesses

COMP **transmission cable** N câble *m* de transmission

transmission shaft N arbre *m* de transmission

transmit /trænz'mɪt/ VT *(gen, Med, Phys etc)* transmettre ; *(Rad, Telec, TV)* émettre, diffuser ; → **sexually** VI *(Rad, Telec, TV)* émettre, diffuser

transmitter /trænz'mɪtə^r/ N 1 *(Rad)* émetteur *m* 2 *(in telephone)* capsule *f* microphonique 3 *(= transmitting device)* transmetteur *m*

transmitting /trænz'mɪtɪŋ/ ADJ *(Telec) [set, station]* émetteur (-trice *f*) N *(gen, Med, Phys)* ⇒ **transmission noun**

transmogrify /trænz'mɒgrɪfaɪ/ VT *(hum)* métamorphoser, transformer *(into* en)

transmutable /trænz'mjuːtəbl/ ADJ transmuable *or* transmutable

transmutation /ˌtrænzmjuː'teɪʃən/ N transmutation *f*

transmute /trænz'mjuːt/ VT transmuer *or* transmuter *(into* en)

transom /'trænsəm/ N 1 *(= crosspiece)* traverse *f*, imposte *f* 2 *(US: in window)* vasistas *m*

transonic /træn'sɒnɪk/ ADJ ⇒ **transsonic**

transparency /træns'pærənsɪ/ N 1 *(NonC: also fig)* transparence *f* 2 *(Brit Phot)* diapositive *f* ; *(for overhead projector)* transparent *m* ◆ **colour ~** diapositive *f* en couleur

transparent /træns'pærənt/ ADJ 1 *(= see-through) [object, substance, material, skin]* transparent ◆ **~ to light** transparent 2 *(= obvious) [honesty]* manifeste, évident ◆ **it is ~ that ...** il est visible *or* évident que ... ◆ **~ to sb** évident pour qn ◆ **he's so ~** il est si transparent 3 *[system, institution]* transparent 4 *(pej = blatant) [lie, device, tactics, attempt]* patent, flagrant

transparently /træns'pærəntlɪ/ ADV manifestement, visiblement ◆ **~ obvious** *or* **clear** tout à fait clair

transpierce /træns'pɪəs/ VT transpercer

transpiration /ˌtrænspɪ'reɪʃən/ N transpiration *f*

transpire /træns'paɪə^r/ VI 1 *(impers vb) (= turn out)* **it ~d that ...** il est apparu que ... ◆ **it ~d that Paul had left his driving licence at home** on s'est rendu compte que Paul avait oublié son permis chez lui 2 *(= happen)* se passer, arriver ◆ **what ~d surprised even me** même moi j'ai été surpris par ce qui s'est passé ◆ **nothing is known as yet about what ~d at the meeting** on ne sait encore rien de ce qui s'est dit à la réunion 3 *(Bot, Physiol)* transpirer VT transpirer

transplant /træns'plɑːnt/ VT *[+ plant, population]* transplanter ; *(Med)* transplanter, greffer ; *[+ seedlings etc]* repiquer N /'trænsplɑːnt/ *(Med)* transplantation *f*, greffe *f* ◆ **he's had a heart ~** on lui a fait une greffe du cœur *or* une transplantation cardiaque

transplantation /ˌtrænsplɑːn'teɪʃən/ N *(NonC)* 1 *(Med)* transplantation *f* 2 *(= moving plants)* transplantation *f* ; *(= planting out)* repiquage *m* 3 *(= transfer) [of culture, ideology]* transfert *m*

transponder /træn'spɒndə^r/ N transpondeur *m*

transport /'trænspɔːt/ N 1 *[of goods, parcels etc]* transport *m* ◆ **road/rail ~** transport *m* par route/par chemin de fer ◆ **by road ~** par route ◆ **by rail ~** par chemin de fer ◆ **Minister/Department of Transport** *(Brit)* ministre *m*/ministère *m* des Transports ◆ **have you got any ~ for this evening?*** tu as une voiture pour ce soir ? 2 *(esp Mil = ship/plane/train)* navire *m*/avion *m*/train *m* de transport 3 *(fig) [of delight etc]* transport *m* ; *[of fury etc]* accès *m* VT /træns'pɔːt/ *(lit, fig)* transporter

COMP *[costs, ship, plane etc]* de transport ; *[system, dispute, strike]* des transports

transport café N *(Brit)* routier *m*, restaurant *m* de routiers

Transport Police N *(Brit)* ≃ police *f* des chemins de fer

transportable /træns'pɔːtəbl/ ADJ transportable

transportation /ˌtrænspɔː'teɪʃən/ N *(= act of transporting)* transport *m* ; *(US = means of transport)* moyen *m* de transport ; *[of criminals]* transportation *f* ◆ **Secretary/Department of Transportation** *(US)* ministre *m*/ministère *m* des Transports

transporter /træns'pɔːtə^r/ N *(Mil = vehicle, ship)* transport *m* ; *(= plane)* avion *m* de transport ; *(= lorry)* camion *m* pour transport d'automobiles ; *(= train wagon)* wagon *m* pour transport d'automobiles

transpose /træns'pəʊz/ VT 1 *(= move: also Mus)* transposer ◆ **transposing instrument** instrument *m* transpositeur 2 *(= reverse, re-order)* transposer, intervertir

transposition /ˌtrænspə'zɪʃən/ N transposition *f*

transputer /træns'pjuːtə^r/ N *(Comput)* transputeur *m*

transsexual /trænz'seksjʊəl/ N transsexuel(le) *m(f)*

transsexualism /trænz'seksjʊəlɪzəm/ N transsexualisme *m*

transship /træns'ʃɪp/ VT transborder

transshipment /træns'ʃɪpmənt/ N transbordement *m*

trans-Siberian /trænzsaɪ'bɪərɪən/ ADJ transsibérien

transsonic /trænz'sɒnɪk/ ADJ transsonique

transubstantiate /ˌtrænsəb'stænʃɪeɪt/ VT transsubstantier

transubstantiation /'trænsəbˌstænʃɪ'eɪʃən/ N transsubstantiation *f*

Transvaal /'trænzvɑːl/ N ◆ **(the) ~** le Transvaal

transversal /trænz'vɜːsəl/ *(Geom)* ADJ transversal N (ligne *f*) transversale *f*

transversally /trænz'vɜːsəlɪ/ ADV transversalement

transverse /'trænzvɜːs/ ADJ 1 *(gen, Geom) [arch, beam]* transversal 2 *(Anat) [muscle]* transverse, transversal N *(gen)* partie *f* transversale ; *(Geom)* axe *m* transversal

COMP **transverse colon** N *(Anat)* côlon *m* transverse

transverse engine N moteur *m* transversal

transverse flute N *(Mus)* flûte *f* traversière

transversely /trænz'vɜːslɪ/ ADV transversalement

transvestism /trænz'vestɪzəm/ N travestisme *m*

transvestite /trænz'vestaɪt/ N travesti(e) *m(f)*

Transylvania /ˌtrænsɪl'veɪnɪə/ N Transylvanie *f*

trap /træp/ N 1 *(gen)* piège *m* ; (also **gin trap**) collet *m* ; *(= covered hole)* trappe *f* ; *(fig)* piège *m*, traquenard *m* ◆ **lion ~** piège *m* à lions ◆ **to set** *or* **lay a ~** *(lit, fig)* tendre un piège *(for sb* à qn) ◆ **to catch in a ~** *(lit, fig)* prendre au piège ◆ **we were caught like rats in a ~** nous étions faits comme des rats ◆ **he fell into the ~** *(fig)* il est tombé dans le piège ◆ **to fall into the ~ of doing sth** commettre l'erreur classique de faire qch ◆ **it's a ~** c'est un piège ; → **mantrap, mousetrap, radar, speed**

2 (also **trap door**) trappe *f (also Theat)* ; *(in greyhound racing)* box *m* de départ ; *(Shooting)* ball-trap *m* ; *(in drainpipe)* siphon *m* ; (‡ *= mouth)* gueule‡ *f* ◆ **shut your ~!**‡ ta gueule !‡, la ferme !‡ ◆ **keep your ~ shut (about it)**‡ ferme ta gueule‡ (là-dessus)

3 *(= carriage)* charrette *f* anglaise, cabriolet *m*

NPL **traps** *(= luggage)* bagages *mpl*

VT 1 *(lit, fig = snare) [+ animal, person]* prendre au piège ◆ **they ~ped him into admitting that ...** il est tombé dans leur piège et a admis que ...

2 *(= immobilize, catch, cut off) [+ person, vehicle, ship]* bloquer, immobiliser ; *[+ gas, liquid]* retenir ; *[+ object]* coincer *(in sth* dans qch) ◆ **20 miners were ~ped** 20 mineurs étaient bloqués *or* murés (au fond) ◆ **~ped by the flames** cerné par les flammes ◆ **the climbers were ~ped on a ledge** les alpinistes étaient bloqués sur une saillie ◆ **to ~ one's finger in the door** se coincer *or* se pincer le doigt dans la porte ◆ **to ~ the ball** *(Sport)* bloquer le ballon

COMP **trap door** N trappe *f*

trapeze /trə'piːz/ N trapèze *m (de cirque)* COMP **trapeze artist** N trapéziste *mf*, voltigeur *m*, -euse *f*

trapezium /trə'piːzɪəm/ N (pl **trapeziums** *or* **trapezia** /trə'piːzɪə/) trapèze *m (Math)*

trapezius /trə'piːzɪəs/ N (pl **trapeziuses**) (muscle *m*) trapèze *m*

trapezoid /'træpɪzɔɪd/ N trapèze *m (Math)* ADJ trapézoïdal

trapper /'træpə^r/ N trappeur *m*

trappings /'træpɪŋz/ NPL *(for horse)* harnachement *m* ; *(= dress ornaments)* ornements *mpl* ◆ **shorn of all its ~** *(fig)* débarrassé de toutes ses fioritures ◆ **if you look beneath the ~** si on regarde derrière la façade ◆ **with all the ~ of**

kingship avec tout le cérémonial afférent à la royauté ◆ **all the ~ of success** tous les signes extérieurs du succès

Trappist /ˈtræpɪst/ **N** trappiste *m* **ADJ** de la Trappe ◆ **~ monastery** trappe *f*

trapse* /treɪps/ **VI** ⇒ **traipse**

trapshooting /ˈtræpʃuːtɪŋ/ **N** ball-trap *m*

trash /træʃ/ **N** 1 *(esp US = refuse)* ordures *fpl* 2 *(pej = worthless thing)* camelote* *f* ; *(= nonsense)* inepties *fpl* ; *(‡ pej = people)* racaille *f NonC* ◆ **this is ~** *(fig)* ça ne vaut rien (du tout) ; *(esp goods)* c'est de la camelote* ; *(message, letter, remark etc)* c'est de la blague* ◆ **he talks a lot of ~** il ne raconte que des inepties, ce qu'il dit c'est de la blague* ◆ **they're just ~‡** *[people]* c'est de la racaille ◆ **he's ~‡** c'est un moins que rien ; → **white** **VT** * 1 *(= vandalize)* saccager 2 *(= criticize)* débiner*, dénigrer **VI** *(US *)* commettre des actes de vandalisme

COMP **trash can** **N** *(US)* poubelle *f*

trash heap **N** *(lit)* tas *m* d'ordures, dépotoir *m* ◆ **the ~ heap of history** les oubliettes *or* la poubelle de l'histoire

trasher* /ˈtræʃəʳ/ **N** *(US)* vandale *mf*

trashy /ˈtræʃɪ/ **ADJ** *[novel, play, film, pop group, ideas]* nul* (nulle* *f*) ◆ **~ goods** camelote* *f*

Trasimene /ˈtræzɪmiːn/ **N** ◆ **Lake ~** le lac Trasimène

trattoria /trætəˈriːə/ **N** trattoria *f*

trauma /ˈtrɔːmə/ **N** (pl **traumas** *or* **traumata** /ˈtrɔːmətə/) *(Med, Psych)* trauma *m* ; *(fig)* traumatisme *m* **COMP** **trauma center** **N** *(US Med)* service *m* de traumatologie

traumatic /trɔːˈmætɪk/ **ADJ** *(Med)* traumatique ; *[experience, effect, event, relationship]* traumatisant ◆ **it is ~ to lose one's job** c'est traumatisant de perdre son travail ; → **post-traumatic stress disorder**

traumatism /ˈtrɔːmətɪzəm/ **N** traumatisme *m*

traumatize /ˈtrɔːmətaɪz/ **VT** traumatiser

traumatized /ˈtrɔːmətaɪzd/ **ADJ** traumatisé

traumatology /ˈtrɔːməˌtɒlədʒɪ/ **N** traumatologie *f*

travail *(liter)* /ˈtræveɪl/ **N** labeur *m* ; *(in childbirth)* douleurs *fpl* de l'enfantement ; *(fig)* peine *f*, difficultés *fpl* **VI** peiner ; *(in childbirth)* être en couches

travel /ˈtrævl/ **VI** 1 *(= journey)* voyager ◆ **they have ~led a lot** ils ont beaucoup voyagé, ils ont fait beaucoup de voyages ◆ **they have ~led a long way** ils sont venus de loin ; *(fig)* ils ont fait beaucoup de chemin ◆ **he is ~ling in Spain just now** il est en voyage en Espagne en ce moment ◆ **as he was ~ling across France** pendant qu'il voyageait à travers la France ◆ **to ~ through a region** traverser une région ; *(= visit)* visiter *or* parcourir une région ◆ **to ~ round the world** faire le tour du monde ◆ **to ~ light** voyager avec peu de bagages ◆ **I like ~ling by car** j'aime voyager en voiture ◆ **he ~s to work by car** il va au travail en voiture ◆ **he was ~ling on a passport/a ticket which ...** il voyageait avec un passeport/un billet qui ... ◆ **it ~s well** *[food, wine]* ça supporte bien le voyage

2 *(Comm †)* voyager, être représentant ◆ **he ~s for a Paris firm** il voyage pour *or* il représente une société parisienne ◆ **he ~s in soap** il est représentant en savon

3 *(= move, go) [person, animal, vehicle]* aller ; *[object]* aller, passer ; *[machine part, bobbin, piston etc]* se déplacer ◆ **to ~ at 80km/h** faire du 80 km/h ◆ **you were ~ling too fast** vous rouliez trop vite ◆ **he was really ~ling!*** il roulait drôlement vite !* ◆ **this car can certainly ~*** cette voiture est vraiment rapide ◆ **light ~s at (a speed of) ...** la vitesse de la lumière est de ... ◆ **news ~s fast** les nouvelles se propagent *or* circulent vite ◆ **the news ~led to Rome** la nouvelle s'est propagée jusqu'à Rome ◆ **the boxes ~ along a moving belt** les boîtes passent sur une *or* se déplacent le long d'une chaîne ◆ **this part ~s 3cm** cette pièce se déplace de 3 cm *or* a une course de 3 cm ◆ **his eyes ~led over the scene** son regard se promenait *or* il promenait son regard sur le spectacle ◆ **her mind ~led over recent events** elle a revu en esprit les événements récents

VT ◆ **to ~ a country/district** parcourir un pays/une région ◆ **they ~ the road to London every month** ils font la route de Londres tous les mois ◆ **a much-~led road** une route très fréquentée ◆ **they ~led 300km** ils ont fait *or* parcouru 300 km

N 1 *(NonC)* le(s) voyage(s) *m(pl)* ◆ **to be fond of ~** aimer voyager, aimer les voyages ◆ **~ was difficult in those days** les voyages étaient difficiles *or* il était difficile de voyager à l'époque ◆ **~ broadens the mind** les voyages ouvrent l'esprit

2 ◆ **~s** voyages *mpl* ◆ **his ~s in Spain** ses voyages en Espagne ◆ **he's off on his ~s again** il repart en voyage ◆ **if you meet him on your ~s** *(lit)* si vous le rencontrez au cours de vos voyages ; *(fig hum)* si vous le rencontrez au cours de vos allées et venues

3 *[of machine part, piston etc]* course *f*

COMP *[allowance, expenses]* de déplacement ; *[scholarship]* de voyage(s)

travel agency **N** agence *f* de voyages *or* de tourisme

travel agent **N** agent *m* de voyages

travel book **N** récit *m* de voyages

travel brochure **N** dépliant *m or* brochure *f* touristique

travel bureau **N** ⇒ **travel agency**

travel card **N** *(Brit)* carte *f* de transport

travel film **N** film *m* de voyage ; *(= documentary)* documentaire *m* touristique

travel insurance **N** assurance *f* voyage

travel organization **N** organisme *m* de tourisme

travel-sick **ADJ** ◆ **to be ~-sick** avoir le mal des transports

travel sickness **N** mal *m* des transports

travel-sickness pill **N** comprimé *m* contre le mal des transports

travel-stained **ADJ** sali par le(s) voyage(s)

travel voucher **N** bon *m* de voyage

travel-weary, travel-worn **ADJ** fatigué par le(s) voyage(s)

travelator /ˈtrævəleɪtəʳ/ **N** tapis *m or* trottoir *m* roulant

travelled, traveled *(US)* /ˈtrævld/ **ADJ** *[person]* (also **well-travelled, much-travelled, widely travelled**) qui a beaucoup voyagé ◆ **a well-~** *or* **much-~ road** une route très fréquentée ; see also **travel**

traveller, traveler *(US)* /ˈtrævləʳ/ **N** voyageur *m*, -euse *f* ; († : also **commercial traveller**) voyageur *m or* représentant *m* de commerce, VRP *m* ◆ **he is a ~ in soap** *(= salesman)* il est représentant en savon **NPL** **travellers** *(Brit = gypsies)* gens *mpl* du voyage **COMP** **traveler's check** **N** *(US)*, **traveller's cheque** **N** chèque *m* de voyage, traveller's chèque *m*

traveller's joy **N** *(= plant)* clématite *f* des haies

travelling, traveling *(US)* /ˈtrævlɪŋ/ **N** *(NonC)* voyage(s) *m(pl)* **ADJ** *[actor, musician, circus, theatre company]* itinérant, ambulant ; *[exhibition]* itinérant ; *[crane]* mobile ◆ **the ~ public** les gens qui se déplacent ◆ **England's 5,000 ~ fans** les 5 000 supporters qui suivent l'équipe d'Angleterre

COMP *[bag, rug, scholarship]* de voyage ; *[expenses, allowance]* de déplacement

travelling clock **N** réveil *m or* pendulette *f* de voyage

travelling library **N** bibliobus *m*

travelling people **NPL** *(Brit)* gens *mpl* du voyage

travelling salesman **N** (pl **travelling salesmen**) voyageur *m* de commerce, VRP *m*

travelogue, travelog *(US)* /ˈtrævəlɒɡ/ **N** *(= talk)* compte rendu *m* de voyage ; *(= film)* documentaire *m* touristique ; *(= book)* récit *m* de voyage

traverse /ˈtrævəs/ **VT** *(gen, Climbing, Ski)* traverser ; *[searchlights]* balayer ; *(Jur)* opposer une fin de non-recevoir à **VI** *(Climbing, Ski)* faire une traversée, traverser **N** *(= line)* transversale *f* ; *(= crossbar, crossbeam; also across rampart, trench etc)* traverse *f* ; *(Archit)* galerie *f* transversale ; *(Climbing, Ski)* traversée *f*

travesty /ˈtrævɪstɪ/ **N** *(Art, Literat etc)* parodie *f*, pastiche *m* ; *(pej)* parodie *f*, simulacre *m* ◆ **it was a ~ of freedom/peace** *(pej)* c'était un simulacre de liberté/de paix ◆ **it was a ~ of justice** c'était un simulacre *or* une parodie de justice **VT** être un travestissement de

trawl /trɔːl/ **N** (also **trawl net**) chalut *m* ; *(fig = search)* recherche *f* **VI** pêcher au chalut ◆ **to ~ for herring** pêcher le hareng au chalut ◆ **to ~ for sth** *(fig)* être en quête de qch **VT** *[+ net]* traîner, tirer ◆ **to ~ a place/the papers for sth** ratisser un endroit/éplucher les journaux à la recherche de qch

trawler /ˈtrɔːləʳ/ **N** *(= ship, man)* chalutier *m* **COMP** **trawler fisherman** **N** (pl **trawler fishermen**) pêcheur *m* au chalut

trawler owner **N** propriétaire *mf* de chalutier

trawling /ˈtrɔːlɪŋ/ **N** *(NonC)* chalutage *m*, pêche *f* au chalut

tray /treɪ/ **N** *(for carrying things)* plateau *m* ; *(for storing things, box-type)* boîte *f* (de rangement) ; *(basket-type)* corbeille *f* (de rangement) ; *(drawer-type)* tiroir *m* ; *[of eggs] (also in chocolate box)* plateau *m* ; *(in bird or animal cage)* plaque *f*, plateau *m* ; → **ashtray, ice**

traycloth /ˈtreɪklɒθ/ **N** napperon *m*

treacherous /ˈtretʃərəs/ **ADJ** 1 *(= disloyal) [person, action, intentions]* traître (traîtresse *f*), perfide ◆ **to be ~ to sb** trahir qn 2 *(= perilous) [weather conditions, road]* traître (traîtresse *f*), dangereux ; *[waters, river, current, tide, sands]* traître (traîtresse *f*) ; *[journey]* périlleux 3 *(= unreliable) [memory]* défaillant

treacherously /ˈtretʃərəslɪ/ **ADV** traîtreusement, perfidement ◆ **the roads are ~ slippery** les routes sont dangereusement glissantes

treachery /ˈtretʃərɪ/ **N** traîtrise *f*, déloyauté *f*

treacle /ˈtriːkl/ *(Brit)* **N** (also **black treacle**) mélasse *f*

COMP **treacle pudding** **N** pudding *m* à la mélasse raffinée

treacle tart **N** tarte *f* à la mélasse raffinée

treacly /ˈtriːklɪ/ **ADJ** *[substance, liquid, sentimentality]* sirupeux ; *[voice]* onctueux

tread /tred/ (vb : pret **trod**, ptp **trodden**) **N** 1 *(NonC) (= footsteps)* pas *mpl* ; *(= sound)* bruit *m* de pas

2 *[of tyre]* bande *f* de roulement ; *[of stair]* giron *m* ; *[of shoe]* semelle *f* ; *(= belt over tractor etc wheels)* chenille *f*

VI marcher ◆ **to ~ on sth** mettre le pied sur qch, marcher sur qch ◆ **he trod on the cigarette end** *(deliberately)* il a écrasé le mégot du pied ◆ **to ~ on sb's heels** *(fig)* suivre *or* serrer qn de près, talonner qn ◆ **to ~ carefully** *or* **softly** *or* **warily** *(lit, fig)* avancer avec précaution, y aller doucement ; → **toe**

VT *[+ path, road]* suivre, parcourir *(à pied)* ◆ **he trod the streets looking for somewhere to live** il a erré dans les rues *or* il a battu le pavé à la recherche d'un logis ◆ **to ~ sth underfoot**

fouler qch aux pieds, piétiner qch ◆ **to ~ grapes** fouler du raisin ◆ **~ the earth (in** *or* **down) round the roots** tassez la terre du pied autour des racines ◆ **he trod his cigarette end into the mud** il a enfoncé du pied son mégot dans la boue ◆ **you're ~ing mud into the carpet** tu mets *or* tu étales de la boue sur le tapis ◆ **to ~ a dangerous path** suivre une voie dangereuse ◆ **well-trodden path** *(lit)* sentier *m* bien tracé ; *(fig)* sentier *m* battu ◆ **to ~ the boards** *(Theat †† or liter)* monter sur les planches, faire du théâtre ◆ **to ~ a measure** (*†† or liter = dance)* danser (pret, ptp **treaded)** ◆ **to ~ water** *(lit, fig)* faire du sur-place

COMP **tread pattern** N *(on tyre)* sculptures *fpl*

► **tread down** VT SEP tasser *or* presser du pied ◆ **the grass was trodden down** l'herbe avait été piétinée *or* foulée

► **tread in** VT SEP *[+ root, seedling]* consolider en tassant la terre du pied

treadle /ˈtredl/ N pédale *f* VI actionner la pédale COMP *[machine]* à pédale

treadmill /ˈtredmɪl/ N (= *mill*) trépigneuse *f* ; *(Hist = punishment)* manège *m* de discipline ; *(for exercise)* tapis *m* de jogging ◆ **he hated the ~ of life in the factory** il détestait la morne *or* mortelle routine du travail d'usine

Treas. abbrev of **Treasurer**

treason /ˈtriːzn/ N trahison *f* ◆ **high ~** haute trahison *f*

treasonable /ˈtriːzənəbl/ ADJ qui relève de la trahison, traître (traîtresse *f*) ◆ **it was ~ to do such a thing** un tel acte relevait de la trahison

treasure /ˈtreʒəʳ/ N trésor *m (also fig)* ◆ **~s of medieval art** les trésors *mpl or* les joyaux *mpl* de l'art médiéval ◆ **she's a ~** *(gen)* elle est adorable ; *(of servant etc)* c'est une perle ◆ **yes my ~** oui mon trésor

VT 1 *(= value greatly) [+ object, sb's friendship, opportunity etc]* tenir beaucoup à, attacher une grande valeur à ◆ **this is my most ~d possession** c'est ce que je possède de plus précieux

2 (= *keep carefully:* also **treasure up**) *[+ object, money, valuables]* garder précieusement, prendre grand soin de ; *[+ memory, thought]* conserver précieusement, chérir

COMP **treasure chest** N *(lit)* malle *f* au trésor ◆ **a ~ chest of information/of useful advice** une mine de renseignements/de conseils utiles

treasure-house N *(lit)* trésor *m (lieu)* ; *(fig: of library, museum etc)* mine *f*, trésor *m* ◆ **she's a real ~-house of information** c'est un puits de science, c'est une mine d'érudition

treasure hunt N chasse *f* au trésor

treasure-trove N *(NonC)* trésor *m* ; *(fig = valuable collection)* mine *f* ; *(fig = rich source)* mine *f* d'or

treasurer /ˈtreʒərəʳ/ N trésorier *m*, -ière *f (d'une association etc)*

treasury /ˈtreʒərɪ/ N 1 ◆ **the Treasury** la Trésorerie, ≃ le ministère des Finances ◆ **Secretary/Department of the Treasury** *(US)* ministre *m*/ministère *m* des Finances

2 *(= place)* trésorerie *f* ; *(fig = book)* trésor *m*

COMP **Treasury bench** N *(Brit Parl)* banc *m* des ministres

Treasury bill, Treasury bond N *(US)* ≃ bon *m* du Trésor

Treasury Department N *(US)* ministère *m* des Finances

Treasury note N ≃ bon *m* du Trésor

Treasury Secretary N *(US)* ministre *m* des Finances

TREASURY

En Grande-Bretagne, **Treasury** (ou "Her/His Majesty's **Treasury**") est le nom donné au ministère des Finances, et le ministre porte traditionnellement le nom de chancelier de l'Échiquier (Chancellor of the Exchequer). Il a sa résidence au 11, Downing Street, non loin de celle du Premier ministre.

Aux États-Unis, le ministère correspondant est le "Department of **Treasury**", qui a en outre la responsabilité des services secrets chargés d'assurer la garde du président.

treat /triːt/ VT 1 *(gen)* traiter ; *[+ object, theme, suggestion]* traiter, examiner ◆ **to ~ sb well** bien traiter qn, bien agir *or* se conduire envers qn ◆ **to ~ sb badly** mal agir *or* se conduire envers qn, traiter qn fort mal ◆ **to ~ sb like a child** traiter qn comme un enfant ◆ **to ~ sb like dirt** *or* **a dog** traiter qn comme un chien ◆ **he ~ed me as though I was to blame** il s'est conduit envers moi comme si c'était ma faute ◆ **you should ~ your mother with more respect** vous devriez montrer plus de respect envers votre mère ◆ **you should ~ your books with more care** tu devrais faire plus attention à *or* prendre plus de soin de tes livres ◆ **the article ~s the problems of race relations with fresh insight** cet article aborde les problèmes des rapports interraciaux d'une façon originale ◆ **he ~s the subject very objectively** il traite le sujet avec beaucoup d'objectivité ◆ **he ~ed the whole thing as a joke** il a pris tout cela à la plaisanterie

2 *[+ wood, soil, substance]* traiter *(with sth* à qch) ; *(Med)* traiter, soigner *(sb for sth* qn pour qch) ◆ **they ~ed him/the infection with penicillin** ils l'ont soigné/ont soigné l'infection à la pénicilline

3 *(= pay for etc)* **to ~ sb to sth** offrir *or* payer* qch à qn ◆ **to ~ o.s. to sth** s'offrir *or* se payer* qch ◆ **I'll ~ you to a drink** je t'offre *or* te paie* un verre

VI 1 *(= negotiate)* **to ~ with sb** traiter avec qn *(for sth* pour qch) ◆ **to ~ for peace** engager des pourparlers en vue de la paix

2 *(= discuss)* **to ~ of** *[book, article etc]* traiter (de)

N *(= pleasure)* plaisir *m* ; *(= outing)* sortie *f* ; *(= present)* cadeau *m* ◆ **I've got a ~ for you** j'ai une bonne surprise pour toi ◆ **what a ~!** quelle aubaine !, chouette* alors ! ◆ **to have a ~ in store for sb** réserver une agréable surprise à qn ◆ **it was a great ~ (for us) to see them again** ça nous a vraiment fait plaisir de les revoir, ça a été une joie de les revoir ◆ **what would you like as a ~ for your birthday?** qu'est-ce qui te ferait plaisir pour ton anniversaire ? ◆ **it is a ~ for her to go out to a meal** elle se fait une joie de *or* c'est tout un événement* pour elle de dîner en ville ◆ **let's give the children a ~** faisons (un) plaisir *or* une gâterie aux enfants, gâtons un peu les enfants ◆ **I want to give her a ~** je veux lui faire plaisir ◆ **to give o.s. a ~** s'offrir un petit extra, s'offrir quelque chose ◆ **the school ~ was a visit to the seaside** la fête de l'école a consisté en une excursion au bord de la mer ◆ **to stand ~** inviter ◆ **to stand sb a ~** *(gen)* offrir *or* payer* quelque chose à qn ; *(food, drink only)* régaler* qn ◆ **this is my ~** c'est moi qui offre *or* qui paie* ; *(food, drink only)* c'est moi qui régale*

◆ **... a treat*** *(Brit)* à merveille ◆ **the garden is coming on a ~** le jardin avance à merveille ◆ **the plan worked a ~** le projet a marché comme sur des roulettes*

treatable /ˈtriːtəbl/ ADJ *[illness]* soignable, qui se soigne

treatise /ˈtriːtɪz/ N *(Literat)* traité *m* (on de)

treatment /ˈtriːtmənt/ N *(gen, Chem etc)* traitement *m* ; *(Med)* traitement *m*, soins *mpl* ◆ **his ~ of his parents/the dog** la façon dont il traite ses parents/le chien ◆ **his ~ of this subject in his book** la façon dont il traite ce sujet dans son livre ◆ **a veterinary surgeon who specialises in the ~ of horses** un vétérinaire spécialisé dans le traitement des chevaux ◆ **he got very good ~ there** *(gen)* il a été très bien traité là-bas ; *(Med)* il a été très bien soigné là-bas ◆ **to give sb preferential ~** accorder à qn un traitement préférentiel *or* un régime de faveur ◆ **they felt bitter about the bad ~ they'd received** ils rageaient d'avoir été si mal traités ◆ **he needs medical ~** il a besoin de soins médicaux *or* d'un traitement ◆ **they refused him ~** ils ont refusé de le soigner ◆ **he is having (a course of) ~ for kidney trouble** il suit un traitement *or* il est sous traitement pour ennuis rénaux ◆ **to give sb the ~*** *(fig)* en faire voir de toutes les couleurs* à qn ◆ **to give sb the full ~** *(treat well)* traiter qn royalement ; *(treat severely)* faire subir les pires traitements à qn ; → **respond**

COMP **treatment room** N *(Med)* salle *f* de soins

treaty /ˈtriːtɪ/ N 1 traité *m (with* avec ; *between* entre) ◆ **to make a ~ with sb** *(Pol)* conclure *or* signer un traité avec qn 2 *(NonC)* **to sell a house by private ~** vendre une maison par accord privé COMP **treaty obligations** NPL obligations *fpl* conventionnelles

treble /ˈtrebl/ ADJ 1 *(= triple)* triple ◆ **a ~ whisky** un triple whisky ◆ **the amount is in ~ figures** le montant dépasse la centaine *or* se chiffre en centaines 2 *(Mus) [voice]* de soprano *(de jeune garçon)* ; *[part]* pour soprano N 1 *(Mus) (= part)* soprano *m* ; *(= singer)* soprano *mf* 2 *(Recording)* aigus *mpl* 3 *(= drink)* triple *m* 4 *(Darts)* triple *m* 5 *(Brit Sport = three victories)* triplé *m* ADV ◆ **it expanded to ~ its size** sa taille a triplé ◆ **rents that were ~ their current levels** des loyers qui étaient trois fois plus élevés que ceux d'aujourd'hui VTI tripler

COMP **the treble chance** N *(in football pools)* *méthode de pari au loto sportif*

treble clef N *(Mus)* clé *f* de sol

treble recorder N *(Mus)* flûte *f* à bec alto

trebly /ˈtreblɪ/ ADV triplement, trois fois plus

tree /triː/ (vb : pret, ptp **treed)** N 1 arbre *m* ◆ **cherry ~** cerisier *m* ◆ **the ~ of life** *(Bible)* l'arbre *m* de vie ◆ **the ~ of knowledge of good and evil** *(Bible)* l'arbre *m* de la science du bien et du mal ◆ **the ~** *(Rel †† = the Cross)* l'arbre *m* de la Croix ◆ **money doesn't grow on ~s** l'argent ne tombe pas du ciel ◆ **people like that don't grow on ~s** les gens comme ça ne courent pas les rues ◆ **to be at** *or* **to have reached the top of the ~** *(Brit fig)* être arrivé en haut de l'échelle *(fig)* ◆ **to be up a ~*** *(fig)* être dans le pétrin ◆ **he's out of his ~*** *(= crazy)* il est taré* or cinglé* ; *(through drugs, alcohol)* il est défoncé* ; → **apple, bark¹, bark², family, plum**

2 (also **shoe tree**) embauchoir *m* ; *(cobbler's last)* forme *f*

3 *(Ling)* arbre *m*

4 *[of saddle]* arçon *m* (de la selle)

VT forcer à se réfugier dans un arbre

COMP **tree-covered** ADJ boisé

tree creeper N grimpereau *m*

tree diagram N *(Ling)* représentation *f* en arbre

tree fern N fougère *f* arborescente

tree frog N rainette *f*

tree house N cabane *f* construite dans un arbre

tree hugger* N *(esp US pej hum)* écolo* *mf*

tree lawn N *(US)* platebande *f* plantée d'arbres *(entre la rue et le trottoir)*

tree line N limite *f* des arbres

tree-lined ADJ bordé d'arbres

tree of heaven N ailante *m*

tree-runner N *(= bird)* sittelle *f*

tree surgeon N arboriculteur *m*, -trice *f* (qui s'occupe du traitement des arbres malades)

tree surgery N arboriculture *f* (spécialisée dans le traitement des arbres malades)
tree trunk N tronc *m* d'arbre

treeless /ˈtriːlɪs/ ADJ sans arbres

treetop /ˈtriːtɒp/ N sommet *m* *or* cime *f* d'un arbre ◆ **in the ~s** au sommet *or* à la cime des arbres

trefoil /ˈtrefɔɪl/ N (*Archit, Bot*) trèfle *m* COMP
trefoil leaf N feuille *f* de trèfle

trek /trek/ VI 1 (*= go slowly*) cheminer, avancer avec peine ; (*as holiday:* also **to go trekking**) faire du trekking *or* de la randonnée ; (*= go on long, difficult journey*) faire un périple ; (*Hist = go by oxcart*) voyager en char à bœufs ; → **pony** 2 (* *= walk*) se traîner ◆ **I had to ~ over to the library** il a fallu que je me traîne *subj* jusqu'à la bibliothèque N (*= hike*) trekking *m*, randonnée *f* ; (*= long, difficult journey*) périple *m* ; (*= leg of journey*) étape *f* ; (*by oxcart*) voyage *m* en char à bœufs ; (* *= walk*) balade * *f* ◆ **it was quite a ~* to the hotel** il y avait un bon bout de chemin* jusqu'à l'hôtel

Trekkie * /ˈtrekɪ/ N fan *mf* de Star Trek

trekking /ˈtrekɪŋ/ N trekking *m*, randonnée *f* ◆ **to go ~** faire du trekking *or* de la randonnée ◆ **to go on a ~ holiday** partir en vacances faire de la randonnée

trellis /ˈtrelɪs/ N treillis *m* ; (*tougher*) treillage *m* ; (*NonC:* also **trelliswork**) treillage *m* VT treillisser, treillager

tremble /ˈtrembl/ VI trembler ; (*with excitement, passion*) frémir, frissonner ; [*voice*] (*with fear, anger*) trembler ; (*with age*) chevroter ; (*with passion*) vibrer ; [*hands, legs, lips, object, building, ground*] trembler ; [*engine, ship, train*] trépider ◆ **to ~ with fear** trembler *or* frissonner de peur ◆ **to ~ with cold** trembler de froid, grelotter ◆ **to ~ with anger** trembler de colère ◆ **to ~ with excitement/passion** frémir *or* frissonner d'excitation/de passion ◆ **to ~ at the thought of sth** frémir à la pensée de qch ◆ **I ~ to think what might have happened** je frémis à la pensée de ce qui aurait pu arriver ◆ **what will he do next? – I ~ to think!** qu'est-ce qu'il va encore faire ? – j'en frémis d'avance ! ◆ **her employees ~d at the mere mention of her name** la simple mention de son nom faisait frémir ses employés ◆ **to ~ in one's shoes** être dans ses petits souliers
N [*of person*] tremblement *m* ; (*with excitement, passion*) frémissement *m*, frissonnement *m* ; (*with age*) tremblotement *m* ; [*of voice*] (*with fear, anger*) tremblement *m* ; (*with age*) chevrotement *m* ; (*with passion*) vibration *f*, frissonnement *m* ; [*of hands, legs, lips, building, ground*] tremblement *m* ; [*of engine, ship, train*] trépidations *fpl* ◆ **to be all of a ~** * trembler comme une feuille

trembling /ˈtremblɪŋ/ → **tremble** VI ADJ [*person*] tremblant ; (*with age*) tremblotant ; (*with excitement, passion*) frémissant ; [*voice*] (*with fear, anger*) tremblant ; (*with age*) chevrotant ; (*with excitement, passion*) vibrant ; [*hands, legs, lips, object, building, ground*] tremblant ; [*engine, ship, train*] trépidant N (*NonC*) tremblement *m* ; → **fear**

tremendous /trəˈmendəs/ ADJ 1 (*= great, enormous*) [*amount, number, effort, shock, pleasure, potential*] énorme, considérable ; [*feeling, relief, progress, success, courage, loss*] énorme, immense ; [*help, support, achievement, opportunity*] extraordinaire ; [*storm, heat, blow, explosion, noise*] épouvantable, terrible ; [*speed*] fou (folle *f*) ; [*victory*] foudroyant ◆ **she taught me a ~ amount** elle m'a énormément appris ◆ **a ~ sense of loyalty** un sens très poussé de la loyauté ◆ **there was a ~ crowd at the meeting** il y avait un monde fou à la réunion 2 (* *= excellent*) [*person*] génial*, super* *inv* ; [*goal, food*] super* *inv* ◆ **she has done a ~ job** elle a accompli un travail remarquable ◆ **we had a ~ time** * on s'est drôlement bien amusés *

tremendously /trəˈmendəslɪ/ ADV [*important*] extrêmement ; [*exciting*] terriblement ; [*improve, vary*] considérablement ; [*help*] énormément ◆ **they've done ~ well** ils s'en sont extrêmement bien tirés

tremolo /ˈtreməlәʊ/ N (*Mus*) trémolo *m*

tremor /ˈtreməʳ/ N tremblement *m* ◆ **~s of protest** murmures *mpl* de protestation ; → **earth**

tremulous /ˈtremjʊləs/ ADJ (*liter*) 1 (*= timid*) [*person*] craintif ; [*smile*] timide, incertain 2 (*= trembling*) [*person*] tremblant ; (*with age*) tremblotant ; (*with excitement, passion*) frémissant ; [*voice*] (*with fear, anger*) tremblant ; (*with age*) chevrotant ; (*with excitement, passion*) vibrant ; [*handwriting*] tremblé ; [*hands*] tremblant ; [*request*] formulé d'une voix tremblante

tremulously /ˈtremjʊləslɪ/ ADV (*liter*) [*say, answer, suggest*] (*= timidly*) craintivement ; (*= in trembling voice*) (*with fear, anger*) en tremblant, d'une voix tremblante ; (*with age*) en chevrotant ; (*with excitement, passion*) en frémissant, en frissonnant ; [*smile*] d'une façon incertaine, timidement

trench /trentʃ/ N tranchée *f* (*also Mil*) ; (*wider*) fossé *m* ◆ **he fought in the ~es** il était dans les tranchées *or* a fait la guerre des tranchées VT (*= dig trenches in*) creuser une *or* des tranchée(s) dans ; (*Mil = surround with trenches*) [*+ one's position etc*] retrancher VI creuser une *or* des tranchée(s)
COMP **trench coat** N trench-coat *m*
trench fever N fièvre *f* des tranchées, rickettsiose *f*
trench knife N (pl **trench knives**) couteau *m* (à double tranchant)
trench warfare N (*NonC: Mil*) guerre *f* de tranchées

trenchant /ˈtrentʃənt/ ADJ [*view*] critique ; [*criticism*] incisif, acerbe ; [*person*] acerbe, caustique (*on or about sth* sur qch) ; ◆ **his ~ views of Egyptian society** ses opinions très critiques sur la société égyptienne ◆ **he was a ~ critic of the Liberal Party** il a critiqué avec virulence le parti libéral ◆ **the most ~ statement from Moscow on the Gulf crisis** la déclaration la plus catégorique de Moscou sur la crise du Golfe

trenchantly /ˈtrentʃəntlɪ/ ADV d'un ton incisif

trencher /ˈtrentʃəʳ/ N tranchoir *m*

trencherman /ˈtrentʃəmæn/ N (pl **-men**) ◆ **he is a good** *or* **great** *or* **hearty ~** il a un sacré coup de fourchette*

trend /trend/ N (*= tendency*) tendance *f* (*towards* à) ; (*Geog*) [*of coast, river, road*] direction *f*, orientation *f* ; (*= fashion*) mode *f*, vogue *f* ◆ **upward/downward ~** tendance *f* à la hausse/à la baisse ◆ **there is a ~ towards doing/away from doing** on a tendance à faire/à ne plus faire ◆ **the latest ~s in swimwear** la mode la plus récente en maillots de bain ◆ **the ~ of events** le cours *or* la tournure des événements ◆ **to set a ~** donner le ton ; (*= fashion*) lancer une mode ◆ **to buck the ~** aller *or* agir à contre-courant ◆ **~s in popular music** les tendances *fpl* de la musique populaire ; → **market, reverse** VI ◆ **to ~ northwards/southwards** *etc* [*river, road*] se diriger vers le nord/le sud *etc* ◆ **to ~ towards** sth [*events, opinions*] tendre vers qch

trendiness * /ˈtrendɪnɪs/ N côté *m* branché

trendsetter /ˈtrendsetəʳ/ N (*= person*) personne *f* qui donne le ton (*or* qui lance une mode)

trendsetting /ˈtrendsetɪŋ/ N innovation *f* ADJ innovateur (-trice *f*), qui donne le ton (*or* lance une mode)

trendy * /ˈtrendɪ/ ADJ [*person, clothes, restaurant, ideas*] branché* ; [*opinions, behaviour, religion*] à la mode ◆ **he's got quite a ~ image** il fait très branché* ◆ **it's no longer ~ to smoke** fumer n'est plus considéré comme branché* N branché(e)* *m(f)*

trepan /trɪˈpæn/ VT [*+ metal plate etc*] forer ; (*Med*) trépaner N (*for quarrying etc*) foreuse *f*, trépan *m* ; (*Med*) trépan *m*

trephine /treˈfiːn/ (*Med*) VT trépaner N trépan *m*

trepidation /ˌtrepɪˈdeɪʃən/ N (*= fear*) vive inquiétude *f* ; (*= excitement*) agitation *f* ◆ **with some ~** avec une certaine appréhension

trespass /ˈtrespəs/ N 1 (*NonC: Jur = illegal entry*) entrée *f* non autorisée 2 (††, *Rel = sin*) offense *f*, péché *m* ◆ **forgive us our ~es** pardonnez-nous nos offenses VI 1 entrer sans permission ◆ **"no trespassing"** "entrée interdite", "propriété privée" ◆ **you're ~ing** vous êtes dans une propriété privée ◆ **to ~ on** [*+ sb's land*] s'introduire *or* se trouver sans permission dans *or* sur ; (*fig*) [*+ sb's hospitality, time*] abuser de ; [*+ sb's privacy*] s'ingérer dans ; [*+ sb's rights*] empiéter sur 2 †† **to ~ against** (*Rel*) [*+ person*] offenser ; [*+ law*] enfreindre ◆ **as we forgive them that ~ against us** (*Rel*) comme nous pardonnons à ceux qui nous ont offensés

> ⚠ **trépasser** means 'pass away'.

trespasser /ˈtrespəsəʳ/ N 1 intrus(e) *m(f)* (dans une propriété privée) ◆ **"trespassers will be prosecuted"** "défense d'entrer sous peine de poursuites" 2 (††, *Rel = sinner*) pécheur *m*, -eresse *f*

tress /tres/ N (*liter*) boucle *f* de cheveux ◆ **~es** chevelure *f*

trestle /ˈtresl/ N tréteau *m*, chevalet *m*
COMP **trestle bridge** N pont *m* sur chevalets
trestle table N table *f* à tréteaux

trews /truːz/ NPL pantalon *m* écossais (étroit)

tri... /traɪ/ PREF tri...

Triad /ˈtraɪæd/ N (*in China*) Triade *f*

triad /ˈtraɪəd/ N (*gen*) triade *f* ; (*Mus*) accord *m* parfait

triage /ˈtriːɑːʒ/ N triage *m*

trial /ˈtraɪəl/ N 1 (*Jur*) (*= proceedings*) procès *m* ; (*NonC*) jugement *m* ◆ **the ~ lasted a month** le procès a duré un mois ◆ **famous ~s** procès *mpl* *or* causes *fpl* célèbres ◆ **a new ~ was ordered** la révision du procès a été demandée ◆ **at the ~ it emerged that ...** au cours du procès *or* à l'audience il est apparu que ... ◆ **during his ~ he claimed that ...** pendant son procès il a affirmé que ... ◆ **~ by jury** jugement *m* par jury ◆ **~ by media** *or* **television** *jugement par les médias* ◆ **to be** *or* **go on ~** passer en jugement *or* en justice ◆ **to put sb on ~** faire passer qn en jugement ; see also **noun 2** ◆ **to give sb a fair ~** juger qn équitablement ◆ **to be sent for ~** être traduit en justice (*to* devant), être inculpé ◆ **to be on ~ for theft** être jugé pour vol ◆ **he was on ~ for his life** il encourait la peine de mort ◆ **to bring sb to ~** faire passer qn en jugement *or* en justice ◆ **to come up for ~** [*case*] passer au tribunal ; [*person*] passer en jugement ◆ **to stand (one's) ~** passer en jugement (*for sth* pour qch ; *for doing sth* pour avoir fait qch) → **commit**
2 (*= test*) [*of machine, vehicle, drug*] essai *m* ◆ **~s** (*Ftbl*) match *m* de sélection ; (*Athletics*) épreuve *f* de sélection ◆ **sheepdog ~s** concours *m* de chiens de berger ◆ **horse ~s** concours *m* hippique ◆ **~ of strength** épreuve *f* de force ◆ **to have a ~ of strength with sb** lutter de force avec qn, se mesurer à qn ◆ **by (a system of) ~ and error** par tâtonnements, en tâtonnant ◆ **it was all ~ and error** on a procédé uniquement par tâtonnements ◆ **to take sb/sth on ~** prendre qn/qch à l'essai ◆ **to be on ~** [*machine, method, employee*] être à l'essai ◆ **to give sb a ~** mettre qn à l'essai

3 (= *hardship*) épreuve *f* ; (= *nuisance*) souci *m* ◆ **the ~s of old age** les afflictions *fpl or* les vicissitudes *fpl* de la vieillesse ◆ **the interview was a great** ~ l'entrevue a été une véritable épreuve *or* a été très éprouvante ◆ **he is a ~ to his mother** il est un souci perpétuel pour sa mère, il donne beaucoup de soucis à sa mère ◆ **what a ~ you are!** ce que tu es agaçant *or* exaspérant ! ; → **tribulation**

VT (= *test*) tester

COMP [*flight, period etc*] d'essai ; [*offer, marriage*] à l'essai

trial attorney N (*US Jur*) avocat(e) *m(f)* qui plaide à l'audience

trial balance N (*Fin*) balance *f* d'inventaire

trial balloon N (*US lit, fig*) ballon *m* d'essai

trial basis N ◆ **on a ~ basis** à titre d'essai

trial court N (*US, Can*) cour *f* jugeant en première instance

trial division N (*US, Can Jur*) division *f or* tribunal *m* de première instance

trial judge N juge *m* d'instance

trial jury N (*US Jur*) jury *m* (de jugement)

trial lawyer N (*US Jur*) ≃ avocat(e) *m(f)*

trial run N [*of machine etc*] essai *m* ; (*fig*) période *f* d'essai, répétition *f*

trialist /ˈtraɪəlɪst/ N candidat(e) *m(f)* à la sélection

triangle /ˈtraɪæŋgl/ N (*Math, Mus, fig*) triangle *m* ; (= *drawing instrument*) équerre *f* ; → **eternal**

triangular /traɪˈæŋgjʊləʳ/ ADJ triangulaire

triangulate /traɪˈæŋgjʊleɪt/ VT trianguler

triangulation /traɪˌæŋgjʊˈleɪʃən/ N triangulation *f*

Triassic /traɪˈæsɪk/ ADJ (*Geol*) [*period*] triasique

N trias *m*

triathlete /traɪˈæθliːt/ N triathlète *mf*

triathlon /traɪˈæθlən/ N triathlon *m*

tribal /ˈtraɪbəl/ ADJ tribal ◆ **the ~ elders** les anciens *mpl* de la tribu (*or* des tribus) ◆ **~ people** membres *mpl* d'une tribu ◆ **they are a ~ people** ils vivent en tribu ◆ **divided on** *or* **along ~ lines** divisé selon des clivages tribaux

tribalism /ˈtraɪbəlɪzəm/ N tribalisme *m*

tribe /traɪb/ N (*all senses*) tribu *f* ; (* *fig*) tribu *f*, smala* *f* ◆ **the twelve Tribes of Israel** les douze tribus d'Israël

tribesman /ˈtraɪbzmən/ N (pl **-men**) membre *m* d'une (*or* de la) tribu

tribo... /ˈtraɪbəʊ/ PREF tribo...

tribulation /ˌtrɪbjʊˈleɪʃən/ N affliction *f*, souffrance *f* ◆ **(trials and) ~s** tribulations *fpl* ◆ **in times of ~** en période d'adversité, en temps de malheurs

tribunal /traɪˈbjuːnl/ N (*gen, Jur, fig*) tribunal *m* ◆ **~ of inquiry** commission *f* d'enquête

tribune /ˈtrɪbjuːn/ N (*Hist, gen = person*) tribun *m*

tributary /ˈtrɪbjʊtərɪ/ ADJ tributaire N (= *river*) affluent *m* ; (= *state, ruler*) tributaire *m*

tribute /ˈtrɪbjuːt/ N tribut *m*, hommage *m* ; (*esp Hist = payment*) tribut *m* ◆ **to pay ~ to ...** (= *honour*) payer tribut à ..., rendre hommage à ... ; (*Hist etc*) payer (le) tribut à ... ◆ **it is a ~ to his generosity that nobody went hungry** qu'aucun n'ait souffert de la faim témoigne de sa générosité ; → **floral** COMP **tribute band** N *groupe qui joue des reprises d'un groupe célèbre*

trice /traɪs/ N ◆ **in a ~** en un clin d'œil, en moins de deux* *or* de rien VT (*Naut:* also **trice up**) hisser

Tricel ® /ˈtraɪsel/ N Tricel ® *m* COMP [*shirt etc*] de *or* en Tricel ®

tricentenary /ˌtraɪsenˈtiːnərɪ/, **tricentennial** /ˌtraɪsenˈtenɪəl/ ADJ, N tricentenaire *m* ◆ **~ celebrations** fêtes *fpl* du tricentenaire

triceps /ˈtraɪseps/ N (pl **triceps** *or* **tricepses**) triceps *m*

trichologist /trɪˈkɒlədʒɪst/ N trichologue *mf*

trichology /trɪˈkɒlədʒɪ/ N trichologie *f*

trick /trɪk/ N 1 (= *dodge, ruse*) ruse *f*, astuce *f* ; (= *prank, joke, hoax*) tour *m*, blague* *f* ; [*of conjurer, juggler, dog etc*] tour *m* ; (= *special skill*) truc *m* ◆ **it's a ~ to make you believe ...** c'est une ruse pour vous faire croire ... ◆ **he got it all by a ~** il a tout obtenu par une ruse *or* un stratagème *or* une combine‡ ◆ **he'll use every ~ in the book to get what he wants** il ne reculera devant rien pour obtenir ce qu'il veut, pour lui, tous les moyens sont bons ◆ **that's the oldest ~ in the book** c'est le coup classique ◆ **a dirty** *or* **low** *or* **shabby** *or* **nasty ~** un sale tour, un tour de cochon* ◆ **to play a ~ on sb** jouer un tour à qn, faire une farce à qn ◆ **my eyesight is playing ~s with** *or* **on me** ma vue me joue des tours ◆ **his memory is playing him ~s** sa mémoire lui joue des tours ◆ **a ~ of the trade** une ficelle du métier ◆ **it's a ~ of the light** c'est une illusion d'optique ◆ **he's up to his (old) ~s again** il fait de nouveau des siennes* ◆ **how's ~s?*** alors, quoi de neuf ? ◆ **he knows a ~ or two** * (*fig*) c'est un petit malin ◆ **I know a ~ worth two of that*** je connais un tour *or* un truc* bien meilleur encore que celui-là ◆ **that will do the ~*** ça fera l'affaire ◆ **I'll soon get the ~ of it*** je vais vite prendre le pli ◆ **~ or treat!** (*esp US*) donnez-moi quelque chose ou je vous joue un tour ! ; → HALLOWEEN ◆ **to turn ~s** [*prostitute*] faire des passes* ; → **bag, card¹, conjuring**

2 (= *peculiarity*) particularité *f* ; (= *habit*) habitude *f*, manie *f* ; (= *mannerism*) tic *m* ◆ **he has a ~ of scratching his ear when puzzled** il a le tic de se gratter l'oreille quand il est perplexe ◆ **he has a ~ of arriving just when I'm making coffee** il a le don d'arriver *or* le chic* pour arriver au moment où je fais du café ◆ **this horse has a ~ of stopping suddenly** ce cheval a la manie de s'arrêter brusquement ◆ **these things have a ~ of happening just when you don't want them to** ces choses-là se produisent comme par magie *or* ont le don de se produire juste quand on ne le veut pas ◆ **history has a ~ of repeating itself** l'histoire a le don de se répéter

3 (*Cards*) levée *f*, pli *m* ◆ **to take a ~** faire une levée *or* un pli ◆ **he never misses a ~** (*fig*) rien ne lui échappe

VT (= *hoax, deceive*) attraper, rouler* ; (= *swindle*) escroquer ◆ **I've been ~ed!** on m'a eu *or* roulé !* ◆ **to ~ sb into doing sth** amener qn à faire qch par la ruse ◆ **to ~ sb out of sth** obtenir qch de qn *or* soutirer qch à qn par la ruse

COMP **trick cushion** *etc* N attrape *f*

trick-cyclist N cycliste-acrobate *mf* ; (*Brit* ‡ = *psychiatrist*) psy‡ *mf*, psychiatre *mf*

trick photograph N photographie *f* truquée

trick photography N truquage *m* photographique

trick question N question-piège *f*

trick rider N (*on horse*) voltigeur *m*, -euse *f* (à cheval)

trick riding N voltige *f* (à cheval)

▸ **trick out, trick up** VT SEP parer (*with* de) ◆ **the ladies ~ed out in all their finery** les dames sur leur trente et un *or* tout endimanchées

trickery /ˈtrɪkərɪ/ N (*NonC*) ruse *f*, supercherie *f* ◆ **by ~** par ruse

trickiness /ˈtrɪkɪnɪs/ N (*NonC*) 1 (= *difficulty*) [*of task*] difficulté *f*, complexité *f* ; [*of problem, question*] caractère *m* épineux ; [*of situation*] caractère *m* délicat 2 (*pej = slyness*) [*of person*] roublardise *f*

trickle /ˈtrɪkl/ N [*of water, blood etc*] filet *m* ◆ **the stream has shrunk to a mere ~** le ruisseau n'est plus qu'un filet d'eau ◆ **a ~ of people** quelques (rares) personnes *fpl* ◆ **there was a ~ of news from the front line** il y avait de temps en temps des nouvelles du front ◆ **there was a steady ~ of offers/letters** les offres/les lettres arrivaient en petit nombre mais régulièrement

VI [*water etc*] (= *drop slowly*) couler *or* tomber goutte à goutte ; (= *flow slowly*) dégouliner ◆ **tears ~d down her cheeks** les larmes coulaient *or* dégoulinaient le long de ses joues ◆ **the rain ~d down his neck** la pluie lui dégoulinait dans le cou ◆ **the stream ~d along over the rocks** le ruisseau coulait faiblement sur les rochers ◆ **to ~ in/out/away** *etc* (*fig*) [*people*] entrer/sortir/s'éloigner *etc* petit à petit ◆ **the ball ~d into the net** (*Ftbl*) le ballon a roulé doucement dans le filet ◆ **money ~d into the fund** les contributions au fonds arrivaient lentement ◆ **money ~d out of his account** son compte se dégarnissait lentement (mais régulièrement), une succession de petites sorties (d'argent) dégarnissait lentement son compte ◆ **letters of complaint are still trickling into the office** quelques lettres de réclamation continuent à arriver de temps en temps au bureau

VT [*+ liquid*] faire couler goutte à goutte, faire dégouliner *or* dégoutter (*into* dans ; *out of* de)

COMP **trickle charger** N (*Elec*) chargeur *m* à régime lent

trickle-down theory N (*Econ*) *théorie économique selon laquelle l'argent des plus riches finit par profiter aux plus démunis*

▸ **trickle away** VI [*water etc*] s'écouler doucement *or* lentement *or* goutte à goutte ; [*money etc*] disparaître *or* être utilisé peu à peu ; see also **trickle vi**

trickster /ˈtrɪkstəʳ/ N 1 (*dishonest*) filou *m* ; → **confidence** 2 (= *magician etc*) illusionniste *mf*

tricksy* /ˈtrɪksɪ/ ADJ [*person*] (= *mischievous*) filou* ; (= *scheming*) retors

tricky /ˈtrɪkɪ/ ADJ 1 (= *difficult*) [*task*] difficile, délicat ; [*problem, question*] délicat, épineux ; [*situation*] délicat ◆ **it is ~ to know how to respond** il est difficile de savoir comment réagir ◆ **warts can be ~ to get rid of** il est parfois difficile de se débarrasser des verrues ◆ **it's ~ for me to give you an answer now** il m'est difficile de vous répondre immédiatement 2 (*pej*) (= *sly*) [*person*] retors ◆ **he's a ~ customer** (= *scheming*) c'est un roublard ; (= *difficult, touchy*) il n'est pas commode

tricolo(u)r /ˈtrɪkələʳ/ N (drapeau *m*) tricolore *m*

tricorn /ˈtraɪkɔːn/ ADJ à trois cornes N tricorne *m*

trictrac /ˈtrɪktræk/ N trictrac *m*

tricuspid /traɪˈkʌspɪd/ ADJ tricuspide

tricycle /ˈtraɪsɪkl/ N tricycle *m*

trident /ˈtraɪdənt/ N trident *m*

tridentine /traɪˈdentaɪn/ ADJ tridentin

tridimensional /ˌtraɪdɪˈmenʃənl/ ADJ tridimensionnel, à trois dimensions

triennial /traɪˈenɪəl/ ADJ triennal ; [*plant*] trisannuel N (= *plant*) plante *f* trisannuelle

triennially /traɪˈenɪəlɪ/ ADV tous les trois ans

Trier /trɪəʳ/ N Trèves

trier /ˈtraɪəʳ/ N (*Brit*) ◆ **to be a ~** être persévérant, ne pas se laisser rebuter

Trieste /triːˈest/ N Trieste

trifle /ˈtraɪfl/ N 1 bagatelle *f* ◆ **it's only a ~** [*object, sum of money etc*] c'est une bagatelle, c'est bien peu de chose ; [*remark*] c'est une vétille, il n'y a pas de quoi fouetter un chat ◆ **he worries over ~s** il se fait du mauvais sang pour un rien ◆ **£5 is a mere ~** 5 livres est une bagatelle *or* c'est trois fois rien ◆ **he bought it for a ~** il l'a acheté pour une bouchée de pain *or* trois fois rien

◆ **a trifle ...** (= *a little*) un peu, un rien, un tantinet* ◆ **it's a ~ difficult** c'est un peu *or* un

tantinet difficile ◆ **he acted a ~ hastily** il a agi un peu *or* un tantinet * hâtivement
2 *(Culin)* ≈ diplomate *m*
VI ◆ **to ~ with** *[+ person, sb's affections, trust etc]* traiter à la légère, se jouer de ◆ **he's not to be ~d with** il ne faut pas le traiter à la légère ◆ **to ~ with one's food** manger du bout des dents, chipoter

► **trifle away** VT SEP *[+ time]* perdre ; *[+ money]* gaspiller

trifler /ˈtraɪfləʳ/ N *(pej)* fantaisiste *mf*, fumiste *mf*

trifling /ˈtraɪflɪŋ/ ADJ insignifiant

trifocal /traɪˈfəʊkəl/ ADJ à triple foyer, trifocal
N *(= lens)* verre *m* à triple foyer ◆ **~s** lunettes *fpl* à triple foyer *or* trifocales

trifoliate /traɪˈfəʊlɪɪt/ ADJ à trois feuilles, trifolié

triforium /traɪˈfɔːrɪəm/ N (pl **triforia** /traɪˈfɔːrɪə/) triforium *m*

triform /ˈtraɪfɔːm/ ADJ à *or* en trois parties

trigger /ˈtrɪgəʳ/ N *[of gun]* détente *f*, gâchette *f* ; *[of bomb]* dispositif *m* d'amorce, détonateur *m* ; *[of tool]* déclic *m* ◆ **to press** *or* **pull** *or* **squeeze the ~** appuyer sur la détente *or* la gâchette ◆ **he's quick** *or* **fast on the ~** * *(lit)* il n'attend pas pour tirer ; *(fig)* il réagit vite VT (also **trigger off**) *[+ explosion, alarm]* déclencher ; *[+ bomb]* amorcer ; *[+ revolt]* déclencher, provoquer ; *[+ protest]* soulever ; *[+ reaction]* provoquer
COMP **trigger finger** N index *m*
trigger-happy * ADJ *[person]* à la gâchette facile, prêt à tirer pour un rien ; *(fig) [nation etc]* prêt à presser le bouton *or* à déclencher la guerre pour un rien
trigger price N prix *m* minimum à l'importation

trigonometric(al) /ˌtrɪgənəˈmetrɪk(əl)/ ADJ trigonométrique

trigonometry /ˌtrɪgəˈnɒmɪtrɪ/ N trigonométrie *f*

trigram /ˈtraɪgræm/ N trigramme *m*

trigraph /ˈtraɪgræf/ N trigramme *m*

trike * /traɪk/ N abbrev of **tricycle**

trilateral /traɪˈlætərəl/ ADJ trilatéral

trilby /ˈtrɪlbɪ/ N *(Brit:* also **trilby hat**) chapeau *m* mou

trilingual /traɪˈlɪŋgwəl/ ADJ trilingue

trilith /ˈtraɪlɪθ/ N trilithe *m*

trilithic /traɪˈlɪθɪk/ ADJ en forme de trilithe

trilithon /traɪˈlɪθɒn, ˈtraɪlɪˌθɒn/ N ⇒ **trilith**

trill /trɪl/ N *(Mus: also of bird)* trille *m* ; *(Ling)* consonne *f* roulée VI *(Mus: also of bird)* triller VT 1 *(gen)* triller ◆ **"come in" she ~ed** "entrez" roucoula-t-elle 2 *(Phon)* **to ~ one's r's** rouler les r ◆ **~ed r** r roulé *or* apical

trillion /ˈtrɪljən/ N *(Brit)* trillion *m* ; *(US)* billion *m* ◆ **there are ~s of places I want to go** * il y a des milliers d'endroits où j'aimerais aller

trilogy /ˈtrɪlədʒɪ/ N trilogie *f*

trim /trɪm/ ADJ 1 *(= neat) [garden, house, village, ship]* bien tenu, coquet ; *[appearance, person, clothes]* net, soigné ; *[beard, moustache]* bien taillé
2 *(= slim) [person, figure]* svelte, mince ; *[waist]* mince
N 1 *(NonC) (= condition)* état *m*, ordre *m* ◆ **in (good)** ~ *[garden, house etc]* en (bon) état *or* ordre ; *[person, athlete]* en (bonne) forme ◆ **to be in fighting** ~ *(US)* être en pleine forme ◆ **to get into** ~ se remettre en forme ◆ **to get things into** ~ mettre de l'ordre dans les choses ◆ **the ~ of the sails** *(Naut)* l'orientation *f* des voiles
2 *(= cut: at hairdressers')* coupe *f* (d')entretien ◆ **to have a ~** faire rafraîchir sa coupe de cheveux ◆ **to give sth a ~** ⇒ **to trim sth;** → vt 1
3 *(around window, door)* moulures *fpl* ; *[of car] (inside)* aménagement *m* intérieur ; *(outside)* finitions *fpl* extérieures ; *(on dress etc)* garniture *f* ◆ **car with blue (interior)** ~ voiture *f* à habillage intérieur bleu
VT 1 *(= cut) [+ beard]* tailler, couper légèrement ; *[+ hair]* rafraîchir ; *[+ wick, lamp]* tailler, moucher ; *[+ branch, hedge, roses]* tailler (légèrement) ; *[+ piece of wood, paper]* couper les bords de, rogner ◆ **to ~ one's nails** se rogner *or* se couper les ongles ◆ **to ~ the edges of sth** couper *or* rogner les bords de qch ◆ **to ~ the ragged edge off sth** ébarber qch
2 *(= reduce)* ◆ **to ~ costs** réduire les dépenses ◆ **to ~ the workforce** dégraisser les effectifs, faire des dégraissages
3 *(= decorate) [+ hat, dress]* garnir, orner *(with* de) ; *[+ Christmas tree]* décorer *(with* de) ◆ **to ~ the edges of sth with sth** border qch de qch ◆ **a dress ~med with lace** une robe ornée de dentelle ◆ **to ~ a store window** *(US)* composer *or* décorer une vitrine de magasin
4 *[+ boat, aircraft]* équilibrer ; *[+ sail]* gréer, orienter ◆ **to ~ one's sails** *(fig)* réviser ses positions, corriger le tir

► **trim away** VT SEP enlever aux ciseaux *(or* au couteau *or* à la cisaille)

► **trim down** VT SEP *[+ wick]* tailler, moucher

► **trim off** VT SEP ⇒ **trim away**

trimaran /ˈtraɪmərən/ N trimaran *m*

trimester /trɪˈmestəʳ/ N trimestre *m*

trimmer /ˈtrɪməʳ/ N 1 *(= beam)* linçoir *or* linsoir *m* 2 *(for trimming timber)* trancheuse *f (pour le bois)* ; *(for hair, beard)* tondeuse *f* 3 *(Elec)* trimmer *m*, condensateur *m* ajustable (d'équilibrage) 4 *(= person adapting views: pej)* opportuniste *mf*

trimming /ˈtrɪmɪŋ/ N 1 *(on garment, sheet etc)* parement *m* ; *(= braid etc)* passementerie *f NonC* ◆ **it's £100 without the ~s** *(fig)* c'est 100 livres sans les extras 2 *(Culin)* garniture *f*, accompagnement *m* ◆ **roast beef and all the ~s** du rosbif avec la garniture habituelle 3 *(pl)* **~s** *(= pieces cut off)* chutes *fpl*, rognures *fpl* 4 *(esp US = defeat)* raclée * *f*, défaite *f* 5 *(= cutting back)* réduction *f*, élagage *m* ; *[of staff]* compression *f*, dégraissage * *m*

trimness /ˈtrɪmnɪs/ N *[of garden, boat, house]* aspect *m* net *or* soigné ◆ **the ~ of his appearance** son aspect soigné *or* coquet *or* pimpant ◆ **the ~ of her figure** la sveltesse de sa silhouette

trimphone ® /ˈtrɪmfəʊn/ N appareil *m* (téléphonique) compact

trinary /ˈtraɪnərɪ/ ADJ trinaire

Trinidad /ˈtrɪnɪdæd/ N (l'île *f* de) la Trinité ◆ **~ and Tobago** Trinité-et-Tobago

Trinidadian /ˌtrɪnɪˈdædɪən/ ADJ de la Trinité, trinidadien N habitant(e) *m(f)* de la Trinité, Trinidadien(ne) *m(f)*

trinitrotoluene /traɪˌnaɪtrəʊˈtɒljʊiːn/ N trinitrotoluène *m*

trinity /ˈtrɪnɪtɪ/ N trinité *f* ◆ **the Holy Trinity** *(Rel)* la Sainte Trinité
COMP **Trinity Sunday** N la fête de la Trinité
Trinity term N *(Univ)* troisième trimestre *m* (de l'année universitaire)

trinket /ˈtrɪŋkɪt/ N *(= knick-knack)* bibelot *m*, babiole *f (also pej)* ; *(= jewel)* colifichet *m (also pej)* ; *(on chain)* breloque *f*

trinomial /traɪˈnəʊmɪəl/ N *(Math)* trinôme *m*

trio /ˈtrɪəʊ/ N trio *m*

triode /ˈtraɪəʊd/ N *(Elec)* triode *f*

triolet /ˈtriːəʊlet/ N triolet *m*

trip /trɪp/ N 1 *(= journey)* voyage *m* ; *(= excursion)* excursion *f* ◆ **he's (away) on a ~** il est (parti) en voyage ◆ **we did the ~ in ten hours** nous avons mis dix heures pour faire le trajet ◆ **there are cheap ~s to Spain** on organise des voyages à prix réduit en Espagne ◆ **we went on** *or* **took a ~ to Malta** nous sommes allés (en voyage) à Malte ◆ **we took** *or* **made a ~ into town** nous sommes allés en ville ◆ **he does three ~s to Scotland a week** il va en Écosse trois fois par semaine ◆ **I don't want another ~ to the shops today** je ne veux pas retourner dans les magasins aujourd'hui ◆ **after four ~s to the kitchen he ...** après être allé quatre fois à la cuisine, il ... ; → **business, coach, day, round**
2 *(Drugs *)* trip * *m* ◆ **to be on a ~** faire un trip * ◆ **to have a bad ~** faire un mauvais trip *
3 *(= stumble)* faux pas *m* ; *(in wrestling etc)* croche-pied *m*, croc-en-jambe *m* ; *(fig = mistake)* faux pas *m*
VI 1 *(= stumble:* also **trip up**) trébucher *(on, over* contre, sur), buter *(on, over* contre), faire un faux pas ◆ **he ~ped and fell** il a trébuché *or* il a fait un faux pas et il est tombé
2 *(go lightly and quickly)* **to ~ along/in/out** *etc* marcher/entrer/sortir *etc* d'un pas léger *or* sautillant ◆ **the words came ~ping off her tongue** elle l'a dit sans la moindre hésitation
3 *(*: on drugs)* être en plein trip *
VT 1 *(make fall:* also **trip up**) faire trébucher ; *(deliberately)* faire un croche-pied *or* un croc-en-jambe à ◆ **I was ~ped (up)** on m'a fait un croche-pied *or* un croc-en-jambe
2 *[+ mechanism]* déclencher, mettre en marche
3 ◆ **to ~ the light fantastic** † *(* = dance)* danser
COMP **trip hammer** N marteau *m* à bascule *or* à soulèvement
trip switch N *(Elec)* télérupteur *m*

► **trip over** VI trébucher, faire un faux pas

► **trip up** VI 1 ⇒ **trip vi 1**
2 *(fig)* faire une erreur, gaffer *
VT SEP faire trébucher ; *(deliberately)* faire un croche-pied *or* un croc-en-jambe à ; *(fig: in questioning)* prendre en défaut, désarçonner *(fig)*

tripartite /ˌtraɪˈpɑːtaɪt/ ADJ *(gen)* tripartite ; *[division]* en trois parties

tripe /traɪp/ N *(NonC)* 1 *(Culin)* tripes *fpl* 2 *(esp Brit * = nonsense)* bêtises *fpl*, inepties *fpl* ◆ **what absolute ~!** * quelles bêtises !, quelles foutaises ! * ◆ **it's a lot of ~** * tout ça c'est de la foutaise * ◆ **this book is ~** * ce livre est complètement inepte

triphase /ˈtraɪfeɪz/ ADJ *(Elec)* triphasé

triphthong /ˈtrɪfθɒŋ/ N triphtongue *f*

triplane /ˈtraɪˌpleɪn/ N triplan *m*

triple /ˈtrɪpl/ ADJ triple *gen before n* ◆ **the Triple Alliance** la Triple-Alliance ◆ **the Triple Entente** la Triple-Entente ◆ **in ~ time** *(Mus)* à trois temps ◆ **they require ~ copies of every document** ils demandent trois exemplaires de chaque document N *(= amount, number)* triple *m* ; *(= whisky)* triple whisky *m* ADV trois fois plus que VTI tripler
COMP **triple combination therapy** N trithérapie *f*
triple-digit *(US)* ADJ *(gen)* à trois chiffres ; *[inflation] supérieur ou égal à 100%*
triple glazing N triple vitrage *m*
triple jump N *(Sport)* triple saut *m*
triple jumper N *(Sport)* spécialiste *mf* du triple saut

triplet /ˈtrɪplɪt/ N *(Mus)* triolet *m* ; *(Poetry)* tercet *m* ◆ **~s** *(people)* triplés *mpl*, triplées *fpl*

triplex /ˈtrɪpleks/ ADJ triple N ® ◆ **Triplex (glass)** *(Brit)* triplex ® *m*, verre *m* sécurit ®

triplicate /ˈtrɪplɪkɪt/ ADJ en trois exemplaires
N 1 ◆ **in ~** en trois exemplaires 2 *(= third copy)* triplicata *m*

triploid /ˈtrɪplɔɪd/ ADJ triploïde

triply /ˈtrɪplɪ/ ADV triplement

tripod /ˈtraɪpɒd/ N trépied *m*

Tripoli /ˈtrɪpəlɪ/ N Tripoli

tripos /ˈtraɪpɒs/ N *(Cambridge Univ)* examen *m* pour le diplôme de BA

tripper /ˈtrɪpəʳ/ N *(Brit)* touriste *mf*, vacancier *m*, -ière *f* ; *(on day trip)* excursionniste *mf*

trippy* /ˈtrɪpɪ/ ADJ psychédélique

triptych /ˈtrɪptɪk/ N triptyque *m*

tripwire /ˈtrɪpwaɪəʳ/ N fil *m* de détente

trireme /ˈtraɪriːm/ N trirème *f*

trisect /traɪˈsekt/ VT diviser en trois parties (égales)

Tristan /ˈtrɪstən/ N Tristan *m*

trisyllabic /ˈtraɪsɪˈlæbɪk/ ADJ trisyllabe, trisyllabique

trisyllable /ˌtraɪˈsɪləbl/ N trisyllabe *m*

trite /traɪt/ ADJ *[subject, design, idea, film]* banal ; *[person]* qui dit des banalités ◆ **a ~ remark** une banalité, un lieu commun

tritely /ˈtraɪtlɪ/ ADV banalement

triteness /ˈtraɪtnɪs/ N *(NonC)* banalité *f*

tritium /ˈtrɪtɪəm/ N tritium *m*

triton /ˈtraɪtn/ N *(all senses)* triton *m* ◆ **Triton** Triton *m*

tritone /ˈtraɪtəʊn/ N *(Mus)* triton *m*

triturate /ˈtrɪtʃəreɪt/ VT triturer, piler

trituration /ˌtrɪtʃəˈreɪʃən/ N trituration *f*, pilage *m*

triumph /ˈtraɪʌmf/ N [1] *(= victory)* triomphe *m*, victoire *f* ; *(= success)* triomphe *m* ; *(= emotion)* sentiment *m* de triomphe ; *(Roman Hist)* triomphe *m* ◆ **in ~** en triomphe ◆ **it was a ~ for ...** cela a été un triomphe *or* un succès triomphal pour ... ◆ **it is a ~ of man over nature** c'est le triomphe de l'homme sur la nature ◆ **his ~ at having succeeded** sa satisfaction triomphante d'avoir réussi VI *(lit, fig)* triompher *(over* de)

triumphal /traɪˈʌmfəl/ ADJ triomphal COMP **triumphal arch** N arc *m* de triomphe

triumphalism /traɪˈʌmfəlɪzəm/ N triomphalisme *m*

triumphalist /traɪˈʌmfəlɪst/ ADJ, N triomphaliste *mf*

triumphant /traɪˈʌmfənt/ ADJ [1] *(= victorious)* victorieux, triomphant ◆ **to emerge ~** sortir victorieux [2] *(= exultant) [person, team, smile, wave, mood]* triomphant ; *[return, homecoming, celebration]* triomphal ◆ **to be** *or* **prove a ~ success** être un triomphe

triumphantly /traɪˈʌmfəntlɪ/ ADV *[say, answer, announce]* triomphalement, d'un ton triomphant ; *[look at, smile]* d'un air triomphant ; *[return, march]* triomphalement ◆ **he returned ~ in 1997** son retour, en 1997, a été triomphal ◆ **he waved ~** il a fait un geste de triomphe ◆ **to be ~ successful** remporter un succès triomphal

triumvirate /traɪˈʌmvɪrɪt/ N triumvirat *m*

triune /ˈtraɪjuːn/ ADJ *(Rel)* trin

trivet /ˈtrɪvɪt/ N *(over fire)* trépied *m*, chevrette *f* ; *(on table)* dessous-de-plat *m inv*

trivia /ˈtrɪvɪə/ NPL bagatelles *fpl*, futilités *fpl*, fadaises *fpl* ◆ **pub ~ quiz** *jeu-concours qui a lieu dans un pub*

trivial /ˈtrɪvɪəl/ ADJ *[matter, sum, reason, offence, detail]* insignifiant ; *[remark]* futile ; *[film, book, news]* banal, sans intérêt ◆ **a ~ mistake** une faute sans gravité, une peccadille ◆ **I don't like to visit the doctor just for something ~** je n'aime pas consulter le médecin pour rien COMP **Trivial Pursuit** ® N Trivial Pursuit ® *m*

> ⚠ In French, **trivial** usually means 'ordinary', not **trivial**.

triviality /ˌtrɪvɪˈælɪtɪ/ N [1] *(NonC = trivial nature) [of matter, sum, reason, offence, detail]* caractère *m* insignifiant ; *[of remark]* futilité *f* ; *[of film, book, news]* banalité *f*, manque *m* d'intérêt [2] *(= trivial thing)* bagatelle *f*

trivialization /ˌtrɪvɪəlaɪˈzeɪʃən/ N banalisation *f*

trivialize /ˈtrɪvɪəlaɪz/ VT banaliser

trivially /ˈtrɪvɪəlɪ/ ADV de façon banalisée

triweekly /ˈtraɪˈwiːklɪ/ ADV *(= three times weekly)* trois fois par semaine ; *(= every three weeks)* toutes les trois semaines ADJ *[event, visit]* qui se produit trois fois par semaine *(or* toutes les trois semaines)

trochaic /trɒˈkeɪɪk/ ADJ trochaïque

trochee /ˈtrəʊkiː/ N trochée *m*

trod /trɒd/ VB pt of **tread**

trodden /ˈtrɒdn/ VB ptp of **tread**

troglodyte /ˈtrɒglədaɪt/ N troglodyte *m* ; *(fig pej)* homme *m* des cavernes

troika /ˈtrɔɪkə/ N *(also Pol)* troïka *f*

troilism /ˈtrɔɪlɪzəm/ N *(NonC: frm)* triolisme *m*

Troilus /ˈtrɔɪləs/ N ◆ **~ and Cressida** Troïlus *m* et Cressida *f*

Trojan /ˈtrəʊdʒən/ ADJ *(Hist, Myth)* troyen N [1] *(Hist)* Troyen(ne) *m(f)* ◆ **to work like a ~** travailler comme un forçat [2] *(Comput)* (also **trojan**) troyen *m*

COMP **Trojan Horse** N *(lit, fig, Comput)* cheval *m* de Troie

Trojan War N ◆ **the ~ War** *or* **Wars** la guerre de Troie

troll¹ /trəʊl/ N troll *m*

troll²* /trɒl/ VI *(Brit = stroll)* déambuler

trolley /ˈtrɒlɪ/ N *(esp Brit) (for luggage)* chariot *m* (à bagages) ; *(two-wheeled)* diable *m* ; *(for shopping)* poussette *f* ; *(in supermarket)* chariot *m*, caddie ® *m* ; (also **tea trolley**) table *f* roulante, chariot *m* à desserte ; *(in office)* chariot *m* à boissons ; *(for stretcher etc)* chariot *m* ; *(in mine, quarry etc)* benne *f* roulante ; *(Rail)* wagonnet *m* ; *(on tramcar)* trolley *m* ; *(US = tramcar)* tramway *m*, tram *m* ◆ **to be/go off one's ~** ‡ *(Brit)* avoir perdu/perdre la boule‡

COMP **trolley bus** N trolleybus *m*

trolley car N *(US)* tramway *m*, tram *m*

trolley line N *(US) (= rails)* voie *f* de tramway ; *(= route)* ligne *f* de tramway

trollop /ˈtrɒləp/ N traînée‡ *f*

trombone /trɒmˈbəʊn/ N trombone *m (Mus)*

trombonist /trɒmˈbəʊnɪst/ N tromboniste *mf*

trompe l'œil /trɒmpˈlɔɪ/ (pl **trompe l'œils**) N [1] *(= technique)* trompe-l'œil *m inv* [2] *(= painting)* (peinture *f* en) trompe-l'œil *m inv*

troop /truːp/ N *[of people]* bande *f*, groupe *m* ; *[of animals]* bande *f*, troupe *f* ; *[of scouts]* troupe *f* ; *(Mil: of cavalry)* escadron *m* ◆ **~s** *(Mil)* troupes *fpl* VI ◆ **to ~ in/past** *etc* entrer/passer *etc* en bande *or* en groupe ◆ **they all ~ed over to the window** ils sont tous allés s'attrouper près de la fenêtre VT *(Brit Mil)* ◆ **to ~ the colour** faire la parade du drapeau ◆ **~ing the colour** *(= ceremony)* le salut au drapeau *(le jour de l'anniversaire officiel de la Reine)*

COMP *[movements etc]* de troupes

troop carrier N *(= truck, ship)* transport *m* de troupes ; *(= plane)* avion *m* de transport militaire

troop train N train *m* militaire

trooper /ˈtruːpəʳ/ N *(Mil)* soldat *m* de cavalerie ; *(US = state trooper)* ≃ CRS *m* ; → **swear**

troopship /ˈtruːpʃɪp/ N transport *m (navire)*

trope /trəʊp/ N trope *m*

trophy /ˈtrəʊfɪ/ N trophée *m* COMP **trophy wife*** N (pl **trophy wives**) *épouse que le mari exhibe comme signe extérieur de réussite*

tropic /ˈtrɒpɪk/ N tropique *m* ◆ **Tropic of Cancer/Capricorn** tropique *m* du Cancer/du Capricorne ◆ **in the ~s** sous les tropiques ADJ *(liter)* ⇒ **tropical**

tropical /ˈtrɒpɪkəl/ ADJ *(lit, fig)* tropical ◆ **the heat was ~** il faisait une chaleur tropicale COMP **tropical medicine** N médecine *f* tropicale

tropical storm N orage *m* tropical

tropism /ˈtrəʊpɪzəm/ N tropisme *m*

troposphere /ˈtrɒpəsfɪəʳ/ N troposphère *f*

Trot* /trɒt/ N *(pej)* (abbrev of **Trotskyist**) trotskard * *m*, trotskiste *mf*

trot /trɒt/ N [1] *(= pace)* trot *m* ◆ **to go at a ~** *[horse]* aller au trot, trotter ; *[person]* trotter ◆ **to go for a ~** (aller) faire du cheval

◆ **on the trot*** ◆ **five days/whiskies** *etc* **on the ~** cinq jours/whiskies *etc* de suite *or* d'affilée ◆ **he is always on the ~** il court tout le temps, il n'a pas une minute de tranquillité ◆ **to keep sb on the ~** ne pas accorder une minute de tranquillité à qn

[2] **to have the ~s**‡ *(= diarrhoea)* avoir la courante‡

VI *[horse]* trotter ; *[person]* trotter, courir ◆ **to ~ in/past** *etc [person]* entrer/passer *etc* au trot *or* en courant

VT *[+ horse]* faire trotter

► **trot along** VI [1] ⇒ **trot over**

[2] ⇒ **trot away**

► **trot away, trot off** VI partir *or* s'éloigner (au trot *or* en courant), filer*

► **trot out** VT SEP *[+ excuses, reasons]* débiter ; *[+ names, facts etc]* réciter d'affilée

► **trot over, trot round** VI aller, courir ◆ **he ~ted over** *or* **round to the grocer's** il a fait un saut *or* a couru chez l'épicier

troth †† /trəʊθ/ N promesse *f*, serment *m* ◆ **by my ~** pardieu † ; → **plight²**

Trotsky /ˈtrɒtskɪ/ N Trotski *m*

Trotskyism /ˈtrɒtskɪɪzəm/ N trotskisme *m*

Trotskyist /ˈtrɒtskɪɪst/, **Trotskyite** /ˈtrɒtskɪaɪt/ ADJ, N trotskiste *mf*

trotter /ˈtrɒtəʳ/ N [1] *(= horse)* trotteur *m*, -euse *f* [2] *(Brit Culin)* **pig's/sheep's ~s** pieds *mpl* de porc/de mouton

trotting /ˈtrɒtɪŋ/ N *(Sport)* trot *m* ◆ **~ race** course *f* de trot

troubadour /ˈtruːbədɔːʳ/ N troubadour *m*

trouble /ˈtrʌbl/ N [1] *(NonC = difficulties, unpleasantness)* ennuis *mpl* ◆ **I don't want any ~** je ne veux pas d'ennuis ◆ **it's asking for ~** c'est se chercher des ennuis ◆ **he goes around looking for ~** il cherche les ennuis ◆ **he'll give you ~** il vous donnera du fil à retordre ◆ **here comes ~!*** aïe ! des ennuis en perspective ! ; → **mean¹**

◆ **to be in trouble** avoir des ennuis ◆ **you're in ~ now** ce coup-ci tu as des ennuis *or* tu as des problèmes ◆ **he's in ~ with the boss** il a des ennuis avec le patron

◆ **to get into trouble (with sb)** s'attirer des ennuis (avec qn) ◆ **he got into ~ for doing that** il a eu *or* il s'est attiré des ennuis pour (avoir fait) cela ◆ **he was always getting into ~ when he was little** il faisait toujours des bêtises quand il était petit

◆ **to get sb into trouble** causer des ennuis à qn, mettre qn dans le pétrin* ◆ **to get a girl into ~*** *(euph)* mettre une fille enceinte

◆ **to get sb/get (o.s.) out of trouble** tirer qn/se tirer d'affaire

◆ **to make trouble** causer des ennuis (*for sb* à qn) ◆ **you're making ~ for yourself** tu t'attires des ennuis

2 (*NonC = bother, effort*) mal *m*, peine *f* ◆ **it's no ~** cela ne me dérange pas ◆ **it's no ~ to do it properly** ce n'est pas difficile de le faire comme il faut ◆ **it's not worth the ~** cela ne *or* n'en vaut pas la peine ◆ **he/it is more ~ than he/it is worth** ça ne vaut pas la peine de s'embêter avec lui/ça ◆ **nothing is too much ~ for her** elle se dévoue *or* se dépense sans compter ◆ **I had all that ~ for nothing** je me suis donné tout ce mal pour rien ◆ **you could have saved yourself the ~** tu aurais pu t'éviter cette peine ◆ **I'm giving you a lot of ~** je vous donne beaucoup de mal, je vous dérange beaucoup ◆ **it's no ~ at all!** je vous en prie !, ça ne me dérange pas du tout !

◆ **to go to + trouble, to take + trouble** ◆ **he went to enormous ~ to help us** il s'est donné un mal fou *or* il s'est mis en quatre pour nous aider ◆ **to go to the ~ of doing sth, to take the ~ to do sth** se donner la peine *or* le mal de faire qch ◆ **he went to** *or* **took a lot of ~ over his essay** il s'est vraiment donné beaucoup de mal pour sa dissertation, il s'est vraiment beaucoup appliqué à sa dissertation ◆ **he didn't even take the ~ to warn me** il ne s'est même pas donné la peine de me prévenir

◆ **to put + trouble** ◆ **to put sb to some ~** déranger qn ◆ **I don't want to put you to the ~ of writing** je ne veux pas qu'à cause de moi vous vous donniez *subj* le mal d'écrire ◆ **I'm putting you to a lot of ~** je vous donne beaucoup de mal, je vous dérange beaucoup

3 (*= difficulty, problem*) ennui *m*, problème *m* ; (*= nuisance*) ennui *m* ◆ **what's the ~?** qu'est-ce qu'il y a ?, qu'est-ce qui ne va pas ?, qu'est-ce que tu as ? ◆ **that's (just) the ~!** c'est ça l'ennui ! ◆ **the ~ is that ...** l'ennui *or* le problème (c')est que ... ◆ **the ~ with you is that you can never face the facts** l'ennui *or* le problème avec toi c'est que tu ne regardes jamais les choses en face ◆ **the carburettor is giving us ~** nous avons des problèmes *or* des ennuis de carburateur ◆ **the technician is trying to locate the ~** le technicien essaie de localiser la panne *or* le problème ◆ **there has been ~ between them ever since** depuis, ils s'entendent mal ◆ **he caused ~ between them** il a semé la discorde entre eux ◆ **I'm having ~ with my eldest son** mon fils aîné me donne des soucis *or* me cause des ennuis ◆ **the child is a ~ to his parents** l'enfant est un souci pour ses parents ◆ **that's the least of my ~s** c'est le cadet de mes soucis ◆ **he had ~ in tying his shoelace** il a eu du mal à attacher son lacet ◆ **did you have any ~ in getting here?** est-ce que vous avez eu des difficultés *or* des problèmes en venant ? ◆ **now your ~s are over** vous voilà au bout de vos peines ◆ **his ~s are not yet over** il n'est pas encore au bout de ses peines, il n'est pas encore sorti de l'auberge ◆ **family ~s** ennuis *mpl* domestiques *or* de famille ◆ **money ~s** soucis *mpl or* ennuis *mpl* d'argent *or* financiers ◆ **I have back ~, my back is giving me ~** j'ai mal au dos, j'ai des problèmes de dos ◆ **kidney/chest ~** ennuis *mpl* rénaux/pulmonaires → **engine, heart**

4 (*= political, social unrest*) troubles *mpl*, conflits *mpl* ◆ **there's been a lot of ~ in prisons lately** il y a beaucoup de troubles *or* de nombreux incidents dans les prisons ces derniers temps ◆ **the Troubles** (*Ir Hist*) *les conflits en Irlande du Nord* ◆ **labour ~s** conflits *mpl* du travail ◆ **there's ~ at the factory** ça chauffe* à l'usine

VT 1 (*= worry*) inquiéter ; (*= inconvenience*) gêner ; (*= upset*) troubler ◆ **to be ~d by anxiety** être sujet à des angoisses ◆ **to be ~d by pain** avoir des douleurs ◆ **his eyes ~ him** il a des problèmes d'yeux ◆ **do these headaches ~ you often?** est-ce que vous souffrez souvent de ces maux de tête ? ◆ **to be ~d with rheumatism** souffrir de rhumatismes ◆ **there's one detail that ~s me** il y a un détail qui me gêne ◆ **nothing ~s him** il ne se fait jamais de souci ; see also **troubled**

2 (*= bother*) déranger ◆ **I am sorry to ~ you** je suis désolé de vous déranger ◆ **don't ~ yourself!** ne vous dérangez pas !, ne vous tracassez pas ! ◆ **he didn't ~ himself to reply** il ne s'est pas donné la peine de répondre ◆ **may I ~ you for a light?** puis-je vous demander du feu ? ◆ **I'll ~ you to show me the letter!** vous allez me faire le plaisir de me montrer la lettre ! ◆ **I shan't ~ you with the details** je vous ferai grâce des détails, je vous passerai les détails

VI se déranger ◆ **please don't ~!** ne vous dérangez pas !, ne vous donnez pas cette peine-là ! ◆ **don't ~ about me** ne vous faites pas de souci pour moi ◆ **to ~ to do sth** se donner la peine *or* le mal de faire qch

COMP **trouble-free** ADJ [*period, visit*] sans ennuis *or* problèmes *or* soucis ; [*car*] qui ne tombe jamais en panne ; [*university*] non contestataire

trouble spot N point *m* chaud *or* névralgique

troubled /ˈtrʌbld/ ADJ 1 (*= worried*) [*person, expression*] inquiet (-ète *f*), préoccupé ; [*mind, look, voice*] inquiet (-ète *f*) 2 (*= disturbed, unstable*) [*life, sleep*] agité ; [*relationship*] tourmenté ; [*area, country, region*] en proie à des troubles ; [*company, industry*] en difficulté ◆ **financially ~** en proie à des difficultés financières ◆ **in these ~ times** en cette époque troublée ; → **oil, fish**

troublemaker /ˈtrʌblmeɪkəʳ/ N fauteur *m*, -trice *f* de troubles, perturbateur *m*, -trice *f*

troublemaking /ˈtrʌblmeɪkɪŋ/ N comportement *m* perturbateur ADJ perturbateur (-trice *f*)

troubleshoot /ˈtrʌblˌʃuːt/ VI (*gen*) (intervenir pour) régler un problème ; (*stronger*) (intervenir pour) régler une crise ; (*= find problem in engine, mechanism*) localiser une panne

troubleshooter /ˈtrʌblˌʃuːtəʳ/ N (*gen*) expert *m* (appelé en cas de crise) ; [*of conflict*] médiateur *m* ; (*= technician*) expert *m*

troubleshooting /ˈtrʌblˌʃuːtɪŋ/ N (*gen = fixing problems*) dépannage *m* ; (*= locating problems in engine, machine*) diagnostic *m* ◆ **most of my job is ~** l'essentiel de mon travail consiste à régler les problèmes

troublesome /ˈtrʌblsəm/ ADJ [*person*] pénible ; [*pupil, tenant*] difficile, à problèmes ; [*question, issue, problem, period*] difficile ; [*task*] difficile, pénible ; [*request*] gênant, embarrassant ; [*cough, injury*] gênant, incommodant ◆ **his back is ~** il a des problèmes de dos ◆ **to be ~ to** *or* **for sb** poser des problèmes à qn

troublous /ˈtrʌbləs/ ADJ (*liter*) trouble, agité

trough /trɒf/ N 1 (*= depression*) dépression *f*, creux *m* ; (*between waves*) creux *m* ; (*= channel*) chenal *m* ; (*fig*) point *m* bas ◆ **~ of low pressure** dépression *f*, zone *f* dépressionnaire 2 (*= drinking trough*) abreuvoir *m* ; (*= feeding trough*) auge *f* ; (*= kneading trough*) pétrin *m*

trounce /traʊns/ VT (*= thrash*) rosser, rouer de coups ; (*Sport = defeat*) écraser, battre à plate(s) couture(s)

troupe /truːp/ N (*Theat*) troupe *f*

trouper /ˈtruːpəʳ/ N (*Theat*) membre *m* d'une troupe de théâtre en tournée ◆ **an old ~** (*fig*) un vieux de la vieille

trouser /ˈtraʊzəʳ/ (*esp Brit*) NPL **trousers** pantalon *m* ◆ **a pair of ~s** un pantalon ◆ **long ~s** pantalon *m* long ◆ **short ~s** culottes *fpl* courtes ; → **wear** VT (* *Brit*) ◆ **to ~ a sum of money** empocher* une somme

COMP **trouser clip** N pince *f* à pantalon

trouser leg N jambe *f* de pantalon

trouser press N presse *f* à pantalons

trouser suit N (*Brit*) tailleur-pantalon *m*

trousseau /ˈtruːsəʊ/ N (pl **trousseaus** *or* **trousseaux** /ˈtruːsəʊz/) trousseau *m* (*de jeune mariée*)

trout /traʊt/ N (pl **trout** *or* **trouts**) truite *f* ◆ **old ~*** (*pej = woman*) vieille bique* *f*

COMP **trout fisherman** N (pl **trout fishermen**) pêcheur *m* de truites

trout fishing N pêche *f* à la truite

trout rod N canne *f* à truite, canne *f* spéciale truite

trout stream N ruisseau *m* à truites

trove /trəʊv/ N → **treasure**

trow †† /traʊ/ VTI croire

trowel /ˈtraʊəl/ N (*Constr*) truelle *f* ; (*for gardening*) déplantoir *m* ; → **lay on**

Troy /trɔɪ/ N Troie

troy /trɔɪ/ N (also **troy weight**) troy *m*, troy-weight *m*, poids *m* de Troy

truancy /ˈtrʊənsɪ/ N (*Scol*) absentéisme *m* (scolaire) ◆ **he was punished for ~** il a été puni pour avoir manqué les cours *or* pour s'être absenté

truant /ˈtrʊənt/ N (*Scol*) élève *mf* absentéiste *or* absent(e) sans autorisation ◆ **to play ~** manquer les cours, faire l'école buissonnière ◆ **he's playing ~ from the office today** (il n'est pas au bureau aujourd'hui,) il fait l'école buissonnière ADJ (*liter*) [*thought*] vagabond COMP (*US*) **truant officer** N *fonctionnaire chargé de faire respecter les règlements scolaires*

> ⚠ **truand** means 'gangster'.

truce /truːs/ N trêve *f* ◆ **to call a ~** conclure une trêve

Trucial /ˈtruːʃəl/ ADJ ◆ **~ States** États *mpl* de la Trêve

truck[1] /trʌk/ N 1 (*NonC*) (*= barter*) troc *m*, échange *m* ; (*= payment*) paiement *m* en nature ◆ **to have no ~ with ...** refuser d'avoir affaire à ... 2 (*US = vegetables*) produits *mpl* etc maraîchers

COMP **truck farm** N (*US*) jardin *m* potager

truck farmer N maraîcher *m*, -ère *f*

truck farming N culture *f* maraîchère

truck garden N ⇒ **truck farm**

truck[2] /trʌk/ N (*esp US = lorry*) camion *m* ; (*Brit Rail*) wagon *m* à plateforme, truck *m* ; (*= luggage handcart*) chariot *m* à bagages ; (*two-wheeled*) diable *m* ◆ **by ~** (*send*) par camion ; (*travel*) en camion VT (*esp US*) camionner COMP **truck stop** N (*US*) routier *m*, restaurant *m* de routiers

truckage /ˈtrʌkɪdʒ/ N (*US*) camionnage *m*

truckdriver /ˈtrʌkdraɪvəʳ/ N (*esp US*) camionneur *m*, routier *m*

trucker /ˈtrʌkəʳ/ N 1 (*esp US = truck driver*) camionneur *m*, routier *m* 2 (*US = market gardener*) maraîcher *m*

trucking /ˈtrʌkɪŋ/ N (*US*) camionnage *m*

truckle /ˈtrʌkl/ VI s'humilier, s'abaisser (*to* devant) COMP **truckle bed** N (*Brit*) lit *m* gigogne *inv*

truckload /ˈtrʌkləʊd/ N camion *m* (*cargaison*)

truckman /ˈtrʌkmən/ N (pl **-men**) (*US*) ⇒ **truckdriver**

truculence /ˈtrʌkjʊləns/ N brutalité *f*, agressivité *f*

> ⚠ In French, **truculence** means 'vividness', not **truculence**.

truculent /ˈtrʌkjʊlənt/ ADJ agressif

> ⚠ In French, **truculent** means 'colourful', not **truculent**.

truculently /ˈtrʌkjʊləntlɪ/ ADV brutalement, agressivement

trudge /trʌdʒ/ VI ◆ **to ~ in/out/along** etc entrer/sortir/marcher etc péniblement or en traînant les pieds ◆ **we ~d round the shops** nous nous sommes traînés de magasin en magasin ◆ **he ~d through the mud** il pataugeait (péniblement) dans la boue VT ◆ **to ~ the streets/the town** etc se traîner de rue en rue/dans toute la ville etc N marche f pénible

true /truː/ LANGUAGE IN USE 11.1, 26.3

ADJ 1 *(= correct, accurate) [story, news, rumour, statement]* vrai ; *[description, account, report]* fidèle ; *[copy]* conforme ; *[statistics, measure]* exact ◆ **it is ~ that ...** il est vrai que ... + *indic* ◆ **is it ~ that ...?** est-il vrai que ... + *indic or subj* ? ◆ **it's not ~ that ...** il n'est pas vrai que ... + *indic or subj* ◆ **can it be ~ that ...?** est-il possible que ... + *subj* ? ◆ **is it ~ about Vivian?** est-ce vrai, ce que l'on dit à propos de Vivian ? ◆ **it is ~ to say that ...** il est vrai que ... ◆ **this is particularly ~ of ...** cela s'applique particulièrement à ... ◆ **that's ~!** c'est vrai ! ◆ **too ~!*** ça c'est bien vrai !, je ne te le fais pas dire ! ◆ **unfortunately this is only too ~** or **all too ~** malheureusement, ce n'est que trop vrai ◆ **to come ~** *[wish, dream etc]* se réaliser ◆ **to make sth come ~** faire que qch se réalise, réaliser qch ◆ **the same is ~ of** or **holds ~ for** il en va or est de même pour ◆ **he's got so much money it's not ~!*** *(= incredible)* c'est incroyable ce qu'il est riche ! ; → **good, ring²**

2 *(= real, genuine) (gen)* vrai, véritable ; *[cost]* réel ◆ **in Turkey you will discover the ~ meaning of hospitality** en Turquie, vous découvrirez le vrai or véritable sens de l'hospitalité ◆ **in the ~ sense (of the word)** au sens propre (du terme) ◆ **he has been a ~ friend to me** il a été un vrai or véritable ami pour moi ◆ **spoken like a ~ Englishman!** *(hum = well said!)* voilà qui est bien dit ! ◆ **I certify that this is a ~ likeness of Frances Elisabeth Dodd** je certifie que cette photographie représente bien Frances Elisabeth Dodd ◆ **to hide one's ~ feelings** cacher ses sentiments (profonds) ◆ **to discover one's ~ self** découvrir son véritable moi ◆ **~ love** *(= real love)* le grand amour ; († *= sweetheart)* bien-aimé(e) † *m(f)* ◆ **to find ~ love (with sb)** connaître le grand amour (avec qn) ◆ **he taught maths but his ~ love was philosophy** il enseignait les maths, mais sa vraie passion était la philosophie ◆ **the course of ~ love never did run smooth** *(Prov)* un grand amour ne va pas toujours sans encombre ◆ **the one ~ God** le seul vrai Dieu, le seul Dieu véritable

3 *(= faithful)* fidèle *(to sb/sth* à qn/qch) ◆ **to be ~ to one's word/to oneself** être fidèle à sa promesse/à soi-même ◆ **twelve good men and ~** douze hommes parfaitement intègres *(représentant le jury d'un tribunal)* ◆ **~ to life** *(= realistic)* réaliste ◆ **~ to form** or **type, he ...** comme on pouvait s'y attendre, il ..., fidèle à ses habitudes, il ... ◆ **to run ~ to form** or **type** *[project etc]* se dérouler comme on pouvait s'y attendre

4 *(= straight, level) [surface, join]* plan, uniforme ; *[wall, upright]* d'aplomb ; *[beam]* droit ; *[wheel]* dans l'axe

◆ **out of true** *[beam]* tordu, gauchi ; *[surface]* gondolé ; *[join]* mal aligné ; *[wheel]* voilé, faussé ◆ **the wall is out of ~** le mur n'est pas d'aplomb

5 *(Mus) [voice, instrument, note]* juste

ADV *[aim, sing]* juste ◆ **to breed ~** se reproduire selon le type parental ◆ **tell me ~** †† dis-moi la vérité ◆ **you speak ~r than you know** vous ne croyez pas si bien dire ; → **ring²**

VT *[+ wheel]* centrer

COMP **true-blue*** ADJ *[Conservative, Republican]* pur jus* ; *[Englishman, Australian]* jusqu'au bout des ongles

true-born ADJ véritable, vrai, authentique

true-bred ADJ de race pure, racé

the True Cross N la vraie Croix

true-false test N questionnaire *m* or test *m* du type "vrai ou faux"

true-hearted ADJ loyal, sincère

true-life* ADJ vrai, vécu

true north N le nord géographique

truffle /ˈtrʌfl/ N truffe *f*

trug /trʌg/ N *(Brit)* corbeille *f* de jardinier

truism /ˈtruːɪzəm/ N truisme *m*

truly /ˈtruːlɪ/ ADV 1 *(= really)* vraiment, véritablement ◆ **a ~ terrible film** un film vraiment mauvais ◆ **I am ~ sorry (for what happened)** je suis sincèrement or vraiment désolé (de ce qui s'est passé) ◆ **he's a ~ great writer** c'est véritablement un grand écrivain ◆ **he did say so, ~ (he did)!** il l'a dit, je te jure !* ◆ **really and ~?*** vraiment ?, vrai de vrai ? ◆ **I'm in love, really and ~ in love** je suis amoureux, éperdument amoureux ◆ **well and ~** bel et bien

2 *(= faithfully) [reflect]* fidèlement

3 *(= truthfully) [answer, tell]* franchement ◆ **tell me ~** dis-moi la vérité

4 *(set phrases)*

◆ **yours truly** *(letter ending)* je vous prie d'agréer l'expression de mes respectueuses salutations ◆ **nobody knows it better than yours ~*** personne ne le sait mieux que moi

trump¹ /trʌmp/ N *(Cards)* atout *m* ◆ **spades are ~s** atout pique ◆ **what's ~(s)?** quel est l'atout ? ◆ **the three of ~(s)** le trois d'atout ◆ **he had a ~ up his sleeve** *(fig)* il avait un atout en réserve ◆ **he was holding all the ~s** il avait tous les atouts dans son jeu ◆ **to come up** or **turn up ~s*** *(Brit fig) (= succeed)* mettre dans le mille ; *(= come at the right moment)* tomber à pic* ; → **no**

VT *(Cards)* couper, prendre avec l'atout ◆ **to ~ sb's ace** *(fig)* faire encore mieux que qn COMP **trump card** N *(fig)* carte *f* maîtresse, atout *m*

► **trump up** VT SEP *[+ charge, excuse]* forger or inventer (de toutes pièces) ◆ **~ed up charges** accusations forgées de toutes pièces

trump² /trʌmp/ N *(liter)* trompette *f* ◆ **the Last Trump** la trompette du Jugement (dernier)

trumpery /ˈtrʌmpərɪ/ N *(NonC) (= showy trash)* camelote* *f NonC* ; *(= nonsense)* bêtises *fpl* ADJ *(= showy)* criard ; *(= paltry)* insignifiant, sans valeur

trumpet /ˈtrʌmpɪt/ N 1 *(= instrument)* trompette *f* 2 *(= player: in orchestra)* trompettiste *mf* ; *(Mil etc = trumpeter)* trompette *m* 3 *(= trumpet-shaped object)* cornet *m* ; → **ear¹** 4 *[of elephant]* barrissement *m* VI *[elephant]* barrir VT trompeter ◆ **don't ~ it about** pas la peine de le crier sur les toits

COMP **trumpet blast** N coup *m* or sonnerie *f* de trompette

trumpet call N *(lit)* ⇒ **trumpet blast** *(fig)* appel *m* vibrant *(for* pour)

trumpeter /ˈtrʌmpɪtəʳ/ N trompettiste *mf*

trumpeting /ˈtrʌmpɪtɪŋ/ N *[of elephant]* barrissement(s) *m(pl)*

truncate /trʌŋˈkeɪt/ VT *(gen, Comput)* tronquer

truncating /trʌŋˈkeɪtɪŋ/ N *(Comput)* troncation *f*

truncheon /ˈtrʌntʃən/ N *(= weapon)* matraque *f* ; *(Brit: for directing traffic)* bâton *m (d'agent de police)*

trundle /ˈtrʌndl/ VT *(= push/pull/roll)* pousser/traîner/faire rouler bruyamment VI ◆ **to ~ in/along/down** entrer/passer/descendre lourdement or bruyamment COMP **trundle bed** N *(US)* lit *m* gigogne

trunk /trʌŋk/ N *[of body, tree]* tronc *m* ; *[of elephant]* trompe *f* ; *(= luggage)* malle *f* ; *(US Aut)* coffre *m*, malle *f* NPL **trunks** *(for swimming)* slip *m* or maillot *m* de bain ; *(underwear)* slip *m* (d'homme) ; → **subscriber**

COMP **trunk call** N *(Brit Telec)* communication *f* interurbaine

trunk curl N *(Gym)* ⇒ **sit-up** ; → **sit**

trunk line N *(Telec)* inter *m*, téléphone *m* interurbain ; *(Rail)* grande ligne *f*

trunk road N *(Brit)* (route *f*) nationale *f* ; → ROADS

trunnion /ˈtrʌnɪən/ N tourillon *m*

truss /trʌs/ N *[of hay etc]* botte *f* ; *[of flowers, fruit on branch]* grappe *f* ; *(Constr)* ferme *f* ; *(Med)* bandage *m* herniaire VT *[+ hay]* botteler ; *[+ chicken]* trousser ; *(Constr)* armer, renforcer

► **truss up** VT SEP *[+ prisoner]* ligoter

trust /trʌst/ LANGUAGE IN USE 20.3

N 1 *(NonC = faith, reliance)* confiance *f (in* en) ◆ **position of ~** poste *m* de confiance ◆ **breach of ~** abus *m* de confiance ◆ **to have ~ in sb/sth** avoir confiance en qn/qch ◆ **to put** or **place (one's) ~ in sb/sth** faire confiance or se fier à qn/qch

◆ **on trust** ◆ **to take sth on ~** accepter qch de confiance or les yeux fermés ◆ **you'll have to take what I say on ~** il vous faudra me croire sur parole ◆ **he gave it to me on ~** *(= without payment)* il me l'a donné sans me faire payer tout de suite

2 *(Jur)* fidéicommis *m* ◆ **to set up a ~ for sb** instituer un fidéicommis à l'intention de qn ◆ **to hold sth/leave money in ~ for one's children** tenir qch/faire administrer un legs par fidéicommis à l'intention de ses enfants

3 *(= charge, responsibility)* ◆ **to give sth into sb's ~** confier qch à qn ◆ **while this is in my ~, I ...** aussi longtemps que j'en ai la charge or la responsabilité, je ...

4 *(Comm, Fin)* trust *m*, cartel *m* ; → **brain, investment, unit**

VT 1 *(= believe in, rely on) [+ person, object]* avoir confiance en, se fier à ; *[+ method, promise]* se fier à ◆ **don't you ~ me?** tu n'as pas confiance (en moi) ? ◆ **he is not to be ~ed** on ne peut pas lui faire confiance ◆ **you can ~ me** vous pouvez avoir confiance en moi ◆ **you can ~ me with your car** tu peux me confier ta voiture, tu peux me prêter ta voiture en toute confiance ◆ **he's not to be ~ed with a knife** il ne serait pas prudent de le laisser manipuler un couteau ◆ **can we ~ him to do it?** peut-on compter sur lui pour le faire ? ◆ **the child is too young to be ~ed on the roads** l'enfant est trop petit pour qu'on le laisse *subj* aller dans la rue tout seul ◆ **I can't ~ him out of my sight** j'ai si peu confiance en lui que je ne le quitte pas des yeux ◆ **~ you!*** *(iro)* ça ne m'étonne pas de toi !, (pour) ça on peut te faire confiance ! *(iro)* ◆ **~ him to break it!*** pour casser quelque chose on peut lui faire confiance ! ◆ **he can be ~ed to do his best** on peut être sûr qu'il fera de son mieux ◆ **you can't ~ a word he says** impossible de croire deux mots de ce qu'il raconte ◆ **I wouldn't ~ him as far as I can throw him*** je n'ai aucune confiance en lui

2 *(= entrust)* confier *(sth to sb* qch à qn)

3 *(= hope)* espérer *(that* que) ◆ **I ~ not** j'espère que non

VI ◆ **to ~ in sb** se fier à qn, s'en remettre à qn ◆ **let's ~ to luck** or **to chance** essayons tout de même, tentons notre chance, tentons le coup* ◆ **I'll have to ~ to luck to find the house** il faudra que je m'en remette à la chance pour trouver la maison

COMP **trust account** N *(Banking)* compte *m* en fidéicommis

trust company N société *f* de gestion

trust fund N fonds *m* en fidéicommis

trust hospital N *(Brit) hôpital qui a choisi l'autonomie par rapport aux autorités locales*

trust territory N *(Pol)* territoire *m* sous tutelle

trustbuster /ˈtrʌstbʌstəʳ/ N *(US) fonctionnaire chargé de faire appliquer la loi antitrust*

trusted /ˈtrʌstɪd/ ADJ *[friend, servant]* en qui on a confiance ; *[method]* éprouvé ; see also **tried-and-trusted;** → **try**

trustee /trʌsˈtiː/ N 1 *(Jur)* fidéicommissaire *m*, curateur *m*, -trice *f* ◆ ~ **in bankruptcy** *(Jur, Fin)* ≈ syndic *m* de faillite 2 *[of institution, school]* administrateur *m*, -trice *f* ◆ **the ~s** le conseil d'administration 3 *(US Univ)* membre *m* du conseil d'université COMP **Trustee Savings Bank** N *(Brit)* ≈ Caisse *f* d'épargne

trusteeship /trʌsˈtiːʃɪp/ N 1 *(Jur)* fidéicommis *m*, curatelle *f* 2 *[of institution etc]* poste *m* d'administrateur ◆ **during his** ~ pendant qu'il était administrateur ◆ **the islands were placed under UN** ~ les îles furent placées sous tutelle de l'ONU

trustful /ˈtrʌstfʊl/ ADJ ⇒ **trusting**

trustfully /ˈtrʌstfəlɪ/ ADV avec confiance

trusting /ˈtrʌstɪŋ/ ADJ confiant ◆ **a ~ relationship** une relation basée sur la confiance

trustingly /ˈtrʌstɪŋlɪ/ ADV en toute confiance

trustworthiness /ˈtrʌstˌwɜːðɪnɪs/ N *(NonC)* *[of person]* loyauté *f*, fidélité *f* ; *[of statement]* véracité *f*

trustworthy /ˈtrʌstˌwɜːðɪ/ ADJ *[person]* digne de confiance ; *[report, account]* fidèle, exact

trusty /ˈtrʌstɪ/ ADJ († *or hum*) fidèle ◆ **his ~ steed** son fidèle coursier N *(in prison)* *détenu bénéficiant d'un régime de faveur*

truth /truːθ/ N (pl **truths** /truːðz/) 1 *(NonC)* vérité *f* ◆ **you must always tell the** ~ il faut toujours dire la vérité ◆ **to tell you the** ~ *or* ~ **to tell, he** ... à vrai dire *or* à dire vrai, il ... ◆ **the ~ of it is that** ... la vérité c'est que ... ◆ **there's no ~ in what he says** il n'y a pas un mot de vrai dans ce qu'il dit ◆ **there's some ~ in that** il y a du vrai dans ce qu'il dit (*or* dans ce que vous dites *etc*) ◆ ~ **will out** *(Prov)* la vérité finira (toujours) par se savoir ◆ **the ~, the whole ~ and nothing but the** ~ *(Jur)* la vérité, toute la vérité et rien que la vérité ◆ **the honest** ~ la pure vérité, la vérité vraie* ◆ **the plain unvarnished** ~ la vérité toute nue, la vérité sans fard ◆ **in (all)** ~ en vérité, à vrai dire ◆ ~ **is stranger than fiction** la réalité dépasse la fiction

2 vérité *f* ; → **home**

COMP **truth drug** N sérum *m* de vérité

truthful /ˈtruːθfʊl/ ADJ 1 (= *honest*) *[person]* qui dit la vérité ◆ **he's a very ~ person** il dit toujours la vérité ◆ **he was not being entirely** ~ il ne disait pas entièrement la vérité 2 (= *true*) *[answer, statement]* exact ; *[portrait, account]* fidèle

truthfully /ˈtruːθfəlɪ/ ADV honnêtement

truthfulness /ˈtruːθfʊlnɪs/ N *(NonC)* véracité *f*

try /traɪ/ N 1 (= *attempt*) essai *m*, tentative *f* ◆ **to have a** ~ essayer (*at doing sth* de faire qch) ◆ **to give sth a** ~ essayer qch ◆ **it was a good** ~ il a (*or* tu as *etc*) vraiment essayé ◆ **it's worth a** ~ cela vaut le coup d'essayer ◆ **to do sth at the first** ~ faire qch du premier coup ◆ **after three tries he gave up** il a abandonné après trois tentatives

2 *(Rugby)* essai *m* ◆ **to score a** ~ marquer un essai

VT 1 (= *attempt*) essayer, tâcher (*to do sth* de faire qch) ; (= *seek*) chercher (*to do sth* à faire qch) ◆ ~ **to eat** *or* ~ **and eat some of it** essaie *or* tâche d'en manger un peu ◆ **he was ~ing to understand** il essayait de *or* tâchait de *or* cherchait à comprendre ◆ **it's ~ing to rain*** il a l'air de vouloir pleuvoir* ◆ **I'll ~ anything once** je suis toujours prêt à faire un essai ◆ **just you ~ it!** *(warning)* essaie donc un peu !, essaie un peu pour voir !* ◆ **you've only tried three questions** vous avez seulement essayé de répondre à trois questions ◆ **have you ever tried the high jump?** as-tu déjà essayé le saut en hauteur ? ◆ **to ~ one's best** *or* **one's hardest** faire de son mieux, faire tout son possible (*to do sth* pour faire qch) ◆ **to ~ one's hand at sth/at doing sth** s'essayer à qch/à faire qch

2 (= *sample, experiment with*) *[+ method, recipe, new material, new car]* essayer ◆ **have you tried these olives?** avez-vous goûté à *or* essayé ces olives ? ◆ **won't you ~ me for the job?** vous ne voulez pas me faire faire un essai ? ◆ **have you tried aspirin?** avez-vous essayé (de prendre de) l'aspirine ? ◆ ~ **pushing that button** essayez de presser ce bouton ◆ **I tried three hotels but they were all full** j'ai essayé trois hôtels mais ils étaient tous complets ◆ **to ~ the door** essayer d'ouvrir la porte ◆ ~ **this for size** *(gen)* essaie ça pour voir ; *(when suggesting sth)* écoute un peu ça

3 (= *test, put strain on*) *[+ person, sb's patience, strength, endurance]* mettre à l'épreuve, éprouver ; *[+ vehicle, plane]* tester ; *[+ machine, gadget]* tester, mettre à l'essai ; *[+ eyes, eyesight]* fatiguer ◆ **to ~ one's strength against sb** se mesurer à qn ◆ **to ~ one's wings** essayer de voler de ses propres ailes ◆ **to ~ one's luck** tenter sa chance, tenter le coup ◆ **this material has been tried and tested** ce tissu a subi tous les tests ◆ **he was tried and found wanting** il ne s'est pas montré à la hauteur, il n'a pas répondu à ce qu'on attendait de lui ◆ **they have been sorely tried** ils ont été durement éprouvés ; → **well²**

4 *(Jur)* *[+ person, case]* juger ◆ **to ~ sb for theft** juger qn pour vol ◆ **he was tried by court-martial** *(Mil)* il est passé en conseil de guerre

VI essayer ◆ ~ **again!** recommence !, refais un essai ! ◆ **just you ~!** essaie donc un peu !, essaie un peu pour voir !* ◆ **I didn't even ~ (to)** je n'ai même pas essayé ◆ **I couldn't have done that (even) if I'd tried** je n'aurais pas pu faire cela même si je l'avais voulu ◆ **to ~ for a job/a scholarship** essayer d'obtenir un poste/une bourse ◆ **it wasn't for lack** *or* **want of ~ing that he** ... ce n'était pas faute d'avoir essayé qu'il ...

COMP **tried-and-tested, tried-and-trusted** ADJ éprouvé, qui a fait ses preuves ◆ **to be tried and tested** *or* **trusted** avoir fait ses preuves ◆ **select a couple of ingredients and add them to a tried-and-tested recipe of your own** choisissez un ou deux ingrédients et intégrez-les à une recette que vous connaissez bien

try line N *(Rugby)* ligne *f* de but, ligne *f* d'essai

try-on* N ◆ **it's a ~-on** c'est du bluff

► **try on** VT SEP 1 *[+ garment, shoe]* essayer ◆ ~ **this on for size** *[+ garment]* essayez cela pour voir si c'est votre taille ; *[+ shoe]* essayez cela pour voir si c'est votre pointure

2 *(Brit *)* **to ~ it on with sb** essayer de voir jusqu'où l'on peut pousser qn ; *(sexually)* faire des avances à qn ◆ **he's ~ing it on** il essaie de voir jusqu'où il peut aller ◆ **he's ~ing it on to see how you'll react** il essaie de voir comment tu vas réagir ◆ **don't ~ anything on!** ne fais pas le malin *or* la maligne !

N ◆ **try-on** * → **try**

► **try out** VT SEP *[+ machine, new material]* essayer, faire l'essai de ; *[+ new drug, new recipe, method, solution]* essayer ; *[+ new teacher, employee etc]* mettre à l'essai ◆ ~ **it out on the cat first** essaie d'abord de voir quelle est la réaction du chat

► **try over** VT SEP *(Mus)* essayer

trying /ˈtraɪɪŋ/ ADJ *[person]* difficile, fatigant ; *[experience, time]* éprouvant

tryout /ˈtraɪaʊt/ N (= *trial*) essai *m* ; *(Sport)* épreuve *f* de sélection ; *(Theat)* audition *f* ◆ **to give sb/sth a** ~ mettre qn/qch à l'essai

tryst †† /trɪst/ N 1 (= *meeting*) rendez-vous *m* galant 2 (also **trysting place**) lieu *m* de rendez-vous galant

tsar /zɑːʳ/ N 1 (= *ruler*) tsar *m* 2 *(Pol)* **alcohol/tobacco** ~ *responsable de la lutte contre l'alcoolisme/le tabagisme*

tsarevitch /ˈzɑːrəvɪtʃ/ N tsarévitch *m*

tsarina /zɑːˈriːnə/ N tsarine *f*

tsarism /ˈzɑːrɪzəm/ N tsarisme *m*

tsarist /ˈzɑːrɪst/ N, ADJ tsariste *mf*

tsetse fly /ˈtsetsɪflaɪ/ N mouche *f* tsé-tsé *inv*

tsk /tʌsk/ EXCL allons donc !

tsp. (pl **tsp.** *or* **tsps.**) (abbrev of **teaspoon(ful)**) c. *f* à café

TSS /ˌtiːesˈes/ N (abbrev of **toxic shock syndrome**) → **toxic**

tsunami /tsʊˈnɑːmɪ/ N tsunami *m*

TT /tiːˈtiː/ ADJ 1 abbrev of **teetotal, teetotaller** 2 (abbrev of **tuberculin tested**) → **tuberculin**

TTFN * /ˌtiːtiːefˈen/ *(Brit)* (abbrev of **ta-ta for now**) salut, à plus*

TU /tiˈjuː/ N (abbrev of **Trade(s) Union**) → **trade**

tub /tʌb/ N *(gen, also in washing machine)* cuve *f* ; *(for washing clothes)* baquet *m* ; *(for flowers)* bac *m* ; (also **bathtub**) tub *m* ; *(in bathroom)* baignoire *f* ; (* = *boat*) sabot* *m*, rafiot* *m* ; *(for cream etc)* (petit) pot *m*

COMP **tub-thumper** N *(Brit fig)* orateur *m* démagogue

tub-thumping *(Brit fig)* N *(NonC)* démagogie *f* ADJ démagogique

tuba /ˈtjuːbə/ N (pl **tubas** *or* *(frm)* **tubae** /ˈtjuːbiː/) tuba *m*

tubal /ˈtjuːbl/ ADJ *(Med)* *[of ligation, pregnancy]* tubaire

tubby * /ˈtʌbɪ/ ADJ rondelet, dodu

tube /tjuːb/ N *(gen, Anat, Telec, TV)* tube *m* ; *[of tyre]* chambre *f* à air ◆ **the** ~ *(Brit = the Underground)* le métro ◆ **to go by** ~ *(Brit)* prendre le métro ◆ **the** ~ * *(US = television)* la télé* ◆ **to go down the ~s*** tourner en eau de boudin*, partir en couille* *(fig)* → **inner** COMP **tube station** N *(Brit)* station *f* de métro

tubeless /ˈtjuːblɪs/ ADJ *[tyre]* sans chambre à air

tuber /ˈtjuːbəʳ/ N *(Bot, Anat)* tubercule *m*

tubercle /ˈtjuːbɜːkl/ N *(Anat, Bot, Med)* tubercule *m*

tubercular /tjʊˈbɜːkjʊləʳ/ ADJ *(Anat, Bot, Med)* tuberculeux ◆ ~ **patients** les tuberculeux *mpl*

COMP **tubercular meningitis** N *(Med)* méningite *f* tuberculeuse

tuberculin /tjʊˈbɜːkjʊlɪn/ N tuberculine *f* ◆ **~-tested cows** vaches *fpl* tuberculinisées ◆ **~-tested milk** ≈ lait *m* certifié

tuberculosis /tjʊˌbɜːkjʊˈləʊsɪs/ N tuberculose *f* ◆ **he's got** ~ il a la tuberculose ◆ ~ **sufferer** tuberculeux *m*, -euse *f*

tuberculous /tjʊˈbɜːkjʊləs/ ADJ ⇒ **tubercular**

tubing /ˈtjuːbɪŋ/ N *(NonC)* (= *tubes collectively*) tubes *mpl*, tuyaux *mpl* ; (= *substance*) tube *m*, tuyau *m* ◆ **rubber** ~ tube *m* *or* tuyau *m* en caoutchouc

tubular /ˈtjuːbjʊləʳ/ ADJ tubulaire

COMP **tubular bells** NPL *(Mus)* carillon *m*

tubular steel N tubes *mpl* métalliques *or* d'acier

tubular steel chair N chaise *f* tubulaire

tubule /ˈtjuːbjʊl/ N *(Anat)* tube *m*

TUC /tiːjuːˈsiː/ N *(Brit)* (abbrev of **Trades Union Congress**) → **trade**

tuck /tʌk/ N 1 *(Sewing)* rempli *m* ◆ **to put** *or* **take a ~ in sth** faire un rempli dans qch

2 *(NonC: Brit Scol = food)* boustifaille* *f*

VT 1 *(gen)* mettre ◆ **to ~ a blanket round sb** envelopper qn dans une couverture ◆ **he ~ed the book under his arm** il a mis *or* rangé le livre sous son bras ◆ **he ~ed his shirt into his**

trousers il a rentré sa chemise dans son pantalon ◆ **he was sitting with his feet ~ed under him** il avait les pieds repliés sous lui

2 *(Sewing)* faire un rempli dans

VI ◆ **to ~ into a meal** * attaquer un repas

COMP **tuck-in*** N bon repas *m*, festin *m* *(hum)* ◆ **they had a (good) ~-in** ils ont vraiment bien mangé

tuck-shop N *(Brit Scol) petite boutique où les écoliers peuvent acheter des pâtisseries, des bonbons etc*

► **tuck away** VT SEP 1 *(= put away)* mettre, ranger ◆ **~ it away out of sight** cache-le ◆ **the hut is ~ed away among the trees** la cabane se cache *or* est cachée *or* est perdue parmi les arbres

2 *(* = eat)* bouffer*

► **tuck in** VI *(Brit * = eat)* (bien) boulotter* ◆ **~ in!** attaquez !

VT SEP *[+ shirt, flap, stomach]* rentrer ; *[+ bedclothes]* border ◆ **to ~ sb in** border qn

N ◆ **tuck-in** * → **tuck**

► **tuck under** VT SEP *[+ flap]* rentrer

► **tuck up** VT SEP *[+ skirt, sleeves]* remonter ; *[+ hair]* relever ; *[+ legs]* replier ◆ **to ~ sb up (in bed)** *(Brit)* border qn (dans son lit)

tuckbox /ˈtʌkbɒks/ N *(Brit Scol)* boîte *f* à provisions

tucker¹ /ˈtʌkəʳ/ N 1 *(Dress ††)* fichu *m* ; → **bib** 2 *(* = food)* bouffe* *f*

tucker²* /ˈtʌkəʳ/ VT *(US)* fatiguer, crever* ◆ **~ed (out)*** crevé*, vanné*

Tudor /ˈtjuːdəʳ/ ADJ *(Archit)* Tudor *inv* ; *[period]* des Tudors ; → **stockbroker**

Tue(s). abbrev of **Tuesday**

Tuesday /ˈtjuːzdɪ/ N mardi *m* ; → **shrove** ; *for other phrases see* **Saturday**

tufa /ˈtjuːfə/ N tuf *m* calcaire

tuffet /ˈtʌfɪt/ N *[of grass]* touffe *f* d'herbe ; *(= stool)* (petit) tabouret *m*

tuft /tʌft/ N touffe *f* ◆ **~ of feathers** *(on bird)* huppe *f*, aigrette *f* ◆ **~ of hair** *(on top of head)* épi *m* ; *(anywhere on head)* touffe *f* de cheveux

tufted /ˈtʌftɪd/ ADJ *[grass]* en touffe ; *[eyebrows]* broussailleux ; *[bird, head]* huppé COMP **tufted duck** N (fuligule *m*) morillon *m*

tug /tʌg/ N 1 *(= pull)* (petite) saccade *f*, (petit) coup *m* ◆ **to give sth a ~** tirer sur qch ◆ **I felt a ~ at my sleeve/on the rope** j'ai senti qu'on me tirait par la manche/qu'on tirait sur la corde ◆ **parting with them was quite a ~** les quitter a été un vrai déchirement 2 (also **tugboat**) remorqueur *m* VT *(= pull) [+ rope, sleeve etc]* tirer sur ; *(= drag)* tirer, traîner ; *(Naut)* remorquer ◆ **to ~ sth up/down** faire monter/faire descendre qch en le tirant *or* traînant VI tirer fort *or* sec *(at, on* sur)

COMP **tug-of-love*** N *lutte acharnée entre les parents d'un enfant pour en avoir la garde*

tug-of-war N *(Sport)* tir *m* à la corde ; *(fig)* lutte *f* (acharnée *or* féroce)

tuition /tjʊˈɪʃən/ N *(NonC)* cours *mpl* ◆ **private ~** cours *mpl* particuliers *(in* de) COMP **tuition fees** NPL *(Scol etc)* frais *mpl* de scolarité

tulip /ˈtjuːlɪp/ N tulipe *f* ◆ **~ tree** tulipier *m*

tulle /tjuːl/ N tulle *m*

tum* /tʌm/ N *(Brit)* ventre *m*, bide* *m*

tumble /ˈtʌmbl/ N 1 *(= fall)* chute *f*, culbute *f* ; *[of acrobat etc]* culbute *f*, cabriole *f* ◆ **to have** *or* **take a ~** faire une chute *or* une culbute ◆ **they had a ~ in the hay** *(fig)* ils ont folâtré dans le foin

2 *(= confused heap)* amas *m* ◆ **in a ~** en désordre

VI 1 *(= fall)* dégringoler, tomber ; *(= trip)* trébucher *(over* sur) ; *[river, stream]* descendre en cascade ; *[prices]* chuter, dégringoler ; *(fig) [person, ruler]* faire la culbute ; *[acrobat etc]* faire des culbutes *or* des cabrioles ◆ **he ~d out of bed** il est tombé du lit ; see also **vi 2** ◆ **to ~ head over heels** faire la culbute, culbuter ◆ **to ~ downstairs** culbuter *or* dégringoler dans l'escalier ◆ **he ~d over a chair** il a trébuché sur une chaise ◆ **he ~d over the cliff/into the river** il est tombé du haut de la falaise/dans la rivière ◆ **the clothes ~d out of the cupboard** la pile de vêtements a dégringolé quand on a ouvert le placard ◆ **the tumbling waters of the Colorado River** les eaux tumultueuses du Colorado ◆ **to ~ into war/depression** *(Brit)* basculer dans la guerre/la dépression

2 *(= rush)* se jeter ◆ **he ~d into bed** il s'est jeté au lit ◆ **he ~d out of bed** il a bondi hors du lit ◆ **they ~d out of the car** ils ont déboulé de la voiture

3 *(Brit * fig = realize)* **to ~ to sth** réaliser* qch ◆ **then I ~d (to it)** c'est là que j'ai pigé*

VT *[+ pile, heap]* renverser, faire tomber ; *[+ hair]* ébouriffer ; *[+ books, objects]* jeter en tas *or* en vrac ◆ **~d** *[room]* en désordre ; *[bed]* défait ; *[clothes]* chiffonné

COMP **tumble-dry** VT faire sécher dans le sèche-linge

tumble dryer N sèche-linge *m*

► **tumble about, tumble around** VI *[puppies, children]* gambader, s'ébattre ; *[acrobat]* cabrioler

VT SEP *[+ books, objects]* mélanger

► **tumble down** VI *[person]* faire une chute *or* une culbute, culbuter ◆ **to be tumbling down** *[building etc]* tomber en ruine

► **tumble out** VI *[objects, contents]* tomber en vrac, s'éparpiller

VT SEP *[+ objects, contents]* faire tomber en vrac

► **tumble over** VI culbuter

VT SEP renverser, faire tomber

tumbledown /ˈtʌmbldaʊn/ ADJ en ruine, délabré

tumbler /ˈtʌmbləʳ/ N *(= glass)* verre *m* (droit) ; *(of plastic, metal)* gobelet *m* ; *(in lock)* gorge *f* (de serrure) ; (also **tumble dryer**) tambour *m* *or* séchoir *m* (à linge) à air chaud ; *(Tech etc = revolving drum)* tambour *m* rotatif ; *(= acrobat)* acrobate *mf* ; *(= pigeon)* pigeon *m* culbutant COMP **tumbler switch** N *(Elec)* interrupteur *m* à bascule

tumbleweed /ˈtʌmblwiːd/ N (espèce *f* d')amarante *f*

tumbrel /ˈtʌmbrəl/, **tumbril** /ˈtʌmbrɪl/ N tombereau *m*

tumefaction /ˌtjuːmɪˈfækʃən/ N tuméfaction *f*

tumescent /tjuːˈmesnt/ ADJ tumescent

tumid /ˈtjuːmɪd/ ADJ *(Med)* tuméfié ; *(fig)* ampoulé

tummy* /ˈtʌmɪ/ N ventre *m* COMP **tummy tuck** N plastie *f* abdominale ◆ **to have a ~ tuck** se faire retendre le ventre

tummyache* /ˈtʌmɪeɪk/ N mal *m* de ventre

tumour, tumor *(US)* /ˈtjuːməʳ/ N tumeur *f*

tumuli /ˈtjuːmjʊlaɪ/ NPL of **tumulus**

tumult /ˈtjuːmʌlt/ N *(= uproar)* tumulte *m* ; *(emotional)* émoi *m* ◆ **in (a) ~** dans le tumulte ; *(emotionally)* en émoi

tumultuous /tjuːˈmʌltjʊəs/ ADJ *[events, period]* tumultueux ; *[welcome, reception]* enthousiaste ; *[applause]* frénétique ◆ **the ~ changes in Eastern Europe** les bouleversements en Europe de l'Est

tumultuously /tjuːˈmʌltjʊəslɪ/ ADV tumultueusement

tumulus /ˈtjuːmjʊləs/ N (pl **tumuli**) tumulus *m*

tun /tʌn/ N fût *m*, tonneau *m*

tuna /ˈtjuːnə/ N (pl **tuna** or **tunas**) (also **tuna fish**) thon *m* ; → **blue, long¹**

tundra /ˈtʌndrə/ N toundra *f*

tune /tjuːn/ N 1 *(= melody)* air *m* ◆ **he gave us a ~ on the piano** il nous a joué un air au piano ◆ **there's not much ~ to it** ce n'est pas très mélodieux ◆ **to the ~ of** *[sing]* sur l'air de ; *[march, process]* aux accents de ◆ **repairs to the ~ of £300** des réparations atteignant la coquette somme de 300 livres ◆ **to change one's ~, to sing another** *or* **a different ~** *(fig)* changer de discours *or* de chanson* ◆ **to call the ~** *(= give orders)* commander ; *(= take decisions)* décider ; → **dance**

2 *(NonC)* **to be in ~** *[instrument]* être accordé ; *[singer]* chanter juste ◆ **to be out of ~** *[instrument]* être désaccordé ; *[singer]* chanter faux ◆ **to sing/play in ~** chanter/jouer juste ◆ **to sing/play out of ~** chanter/jouer faux ◆ **to be in/out of ~ with ...** *(fig)* être en accord/désaccord avec ...

VT *(Mus)* accorder ; *(Rad, TV: also* **tune in***)* régler *(to* sur) ; *[+ car engine]* régler, mettre au point ◆ **you are ~d (in) to ...** *(Rad)* vous êtes à l'écoute de ... ; → **stay¹**

COMP **tune-up** N *[of engine]* réglage *m*, mise *f* au point

► **tune in** *(Rad, TV)* VI se mettre à l'écoute *(to* de) ◆ **~ in again tomorrow** soyez de nouveau à l'écoute demain ◆ **thousands ~d in** des milliers de gens se sont mis à l'écoute

VT SEP *(Rad, TV)* régler *(to* sur) ◆ **predatory fish are ~d in to all movement in the sea around them** les poissons prédateurs captent les ondes émises par tout mouvement dans la mer ◆ **to be ~d in to ...** *(fig = aware of)* être à l'écoute de ... ◆ **to be ~d in to new developments** être au fait des derniers développements ◆ **he is/isn't ~d in*** *(fig)* il est/n'est pas dans la course* ; see also **tune vt**

► **tune out*** VI *(fig)* débrancher*, faire la sourde oreille

VT SEP *(fig)* ne pas faire attention à, faire la sourde oreille à

► **tune up** VI *(Mus)* accorder son *(or* ses) instrument(s)

VT SEP *[+ instrument]* accorder ; *[+ engine]* mettre au point

N ◆ **tune-up** → **tune**

tuneful /ˈtjuːnfʊl/ ADJ *[music, instrument, voice]* mélodieux

tunefully /ˈtjuːnfəlɪ/ ADV mélodieusement

tunefulness /ˈtjuːnfʊlnɪs/ N *[of music, instrument, voice]* caractère *m* mélodieux

tuneless /ˈtjuːnlɪs/ ADJ peu mélodieux, discordant, dissonant

tunelessly /ˈtjuːnlɪslɪ/ ADV *[sing, play]* faux

tuner /ˈtjuːnəʳ/ N *(= person)* accordeur *m* ; *(Rad:* also **stereo tuner***)* syntoniseur *m*, syntonisateur *m* *(Can)* ; *(= knob)* bouton *m* de réglage ; → **piano** COMP **tuner amplifier** N ampli-tuner *m*

tungsten /ˈtʌŋstən/ N *(NonC)* tungstène *m* ◆ **~ lamp/steel** lampe *f*/acier *m* au tungstène

tunic /ˈtjuːnɪk/ N tunique *f*

tuning /ˈtjuːnɪŋ/ N *(Mus)* accord *m* ; *(Rad, TV)* réglage *m* ; *[of engine]* réglage(s), mise *f* au point

COMP **tuning fork** N *(Mus)* diapason *m*

tuning key N *(Mus)* accordoir *m*

tuning knob N *(Rad etc)* bouton *m* de réglage

Tunis /ˈtjuːnɪs/ N Tunis

Tunisia /tjuːˈnɪzɪə/ N Tunisie *f*

Tunisian /tjuːˈnɪzɪən/ ADJ *(gen)* tunisien ; *[ambassador, embassy]* de Tunisie N Tunisien(ne) *m(f)*

tunnel /ˈtʌnl/ N *(gen, Rail)* tunnel *m* ; *(Min)* galerie *f* ◆ **to make a ~** ⇒ **to tunnel; → vi** ; see also **channel** VI *[people, rabbits etc]* percer *or* creuser un *or* des tunnel(s) *or* des galeries *(into* dans ; *under* sous) ◆ **to ~ in/out** *etc* entrer/sortir *etc* en creusant un tunnel VT percer *or* creuser un *or* des tunnel(s) dans ◆ **a mound ~led by rabbits** un monticule dans lequel les lapins ont percé *or* creusé des galeries ◆ **shelters ~led out of the hillside** des abris creusés à flanc de colline ◆ **to ~ one's way in** *etc* ⇒ **to tunnel in**; → **vi**

COMP **tunnel effect** N *(Phys)* effet *m* tunnel
tunnel vision N *(Opt)* rétrécissement *m* du champ visuel ◆ **to have ~ vision** *(fig)* avoir des œillères

tunny /ˈtʌnɪ/ N (pl **tunny** *or* **tunnies**) ⇒ **tuna**

tuppence /ˈtʌpəns/ N (abbrev of **twopence**) deux pence *mpl* ◆ **it's not worth ~** * ça ne vaut pas un radis * ◆ **I don't care ~** * je m'en fiche (comme de l'an quarante) *

tuppenny † /ˈtʌpənɪ/ ADJ (= *twopenny*) à deux pence ◆ **a ~ bit** une pièce de deux pence ◆ **I don't give a ~ damn** * *(Brit)* je m'en contrefiche * ◆ **she doesn't give a ~ damn for** *or* **about …** elle se contrefiche de … * COMP **tuppenny-ha'penny** † * ADJ *(fig)* (= *insignificant*) de quatre sous, à la noix *

Tupperware ® /ˈtʌpəwɛəʳ/ N Tupperware ® *m* ADJ Tupperware ®

turban /ˈtɜːbən/ N turban *m* VT ◆ **~ed** *[person, head]* enturbanné

turbid /ˈtɜːbɪd/ ADJ *(frm: lit, fig)* turbide

turbidity /tɜːˈbɪdɪtɪ/ N *(frm)* turbidité *f (frm)*

turbine /ˈtɜːbaɪn/ N turbine *f* ◆ **steam/gas ~** turbine *f* à vapeur/à gaz

turbo /ˈtɜːbəʊ/ N turbo *m*

turbo… /ˈtɜːbəʊ/ PREF turbo…

turbocharged /ˈtɜːbəʊˌtʃɑːdʒd/ ADJ turbocompressé ◆ **~ engine** moteur *m* turbo

turbofan /ˌtɜːbəʊˈfæn/ N (= *fan*) turbofan *m* ; (also **turbofan engine**) turbofan *m*, turboventilateur *m*

turbogenerator /ˌtɜːbəʊˈdʒenəˌreɪtəʳ/ N turbogénérateur *m*

turbojet /ˈtɜːbəʊˈdʒet/ N (also **turbojet engine**) turboréacteur *m* ; (also **turbojet aircraft**) avion *m* à turboréacteur

turboprop /ˈtɜːbəʊˈprɒp/ N (also **turboprop engine**) turbopropulseur *m* ; (also **turboprop aircraft**) avion *m* à turbopropulseur

turbosupercharger /ˌtɜːbəʊˈsuːpəˌtʃɑːdʒəʳ/ N turbocompresseur *m* de suralimentation

turbot /ˈtɜːbət/ N (pl **turbot** *or* **turbots**) turbot *m*

turbulence /ˈtɜːbjʊləns/ N *(NonC)* turbulence *f (also Aviat)* ; *[of waves, sea]* agitation *f*

turbulent /ˈtɜːbjʊlənt/ ADJ 1 (= *choppy*) *[water, sea]* agité, turbulent *(liter)* ◆ **~ air/water** turbulences *fpl* 2 (= *troubled*) *[time, period]* agité ; *[history, events, career]* tumultueux ; *[crowd, person, personality, mood]* turbulent 3 *(liter* = *disorderly, troublesome)* *[person]* turbulent

turd *‡ /tɜːd/ N merde *‡ *f* ; (= *person*) con‡ *m*, couillon‡ *m*

tureen /təˈriːn/ N soupière *f*

turf /tɜːf/ N (pl **turfs** *or* **turves**) 1 *(NonC* = *grass)* gazon *m* ; *(one piece)* motte *f* de gazon ; *(NonC* = *peat)* tourbe *f* ; *(Sport)* turf *m* 2 ‡ *[of gang etc]* territoire *m or* secteur *m* réservé ◆ **to be on the ~** ‡ *[prostitute]* faire le trottoir * VT 1 (also **turf over**) *[+ land]* gazonner 2 *(Brit* *) (= *throw)* balancer *, jeter ; (= *push*) pousser ; (= *put*) mettre, flanquer *

COMP **turf accountant** N *(Brit)* bookmaker *m*
turf war N guerre *f* de territoire

► **turf in** * VT SEP *(Brit)* *[+ objects]* balancer * dedans ◆ **he ~ed it all in** ‡ *(fig* = *give up)* il a tout plaqué *

► **turf out** * VT SEP *(Brit)* *[+ objects]* sortir ; (= *throw away)* bazarder * ; *[+ person]* flanquer à la porte *, virer * ; ‡ *[+ suggestion]* démolir *

Turgenev /tʊrˈgeɪnɪv/ N Tourgueniev *m*

turgid /ˈtɜːdʒɪd/ ADJ 1 *(lit* = *swollen)* turgide 2 *(fig* = *stodgy, lifeless)* *[style, essay etc]* indigeste ; *[language]* lourd 3 *(fig* = *pompous)* *[style, essay, language etc]* ampoulé

Turin /tjʊəˈrɪn/ N Turin ◆ **the ~ Shroud** le saint suaire de Turin

Turk /tɜːk/ N Turc *m*, Turque *f* ◆ **young ~** *(fig: esp Pol)* jeune Turc *m*

Turkey /ˈtɜːkɪ/ N Turquie *f*

turkey /ˈtɜːkɪ/ N (pl **turkey** *or* **turkeys**) 1 dindon *m*, dinde *f* ; *(Culin)* dinde *f* ; *(US fig)* ◆ **to talk ~** * parler net *or* franc ◆ **it would be like ~s voting for Christmas** *(esp Brit)* cela reviendrait à signer son arrêt de mort ; → **cold** 2 *(esp US: Cine, Theat* * = *flop)* four * *m* 3 (‡ = *awkward person)* balourd *m*

COMP **turkey buzzard** N vautour *m* aura
turkey cock N dindon *m*
turkey shoot N *(fig)* combat *m* inégal

Turkish /ˈtɜːkɪʃ/ ADJ turc (turque *f*) ; *[ambassador, embassy]* de Turquie ; *[teacher]* de turc ◆ **as thin as a ~ cat** maigre comme un clou N (= *language)* turc *m*

COMP **Turkish bath** N bain *m* turc
Turkish coffee N café *m* turc
Turkish Cypriot ADJ chypriote turc (turque *f*) N (= *person*) Chypriote *mf* turc (turque *f*)
Turkish delight N *(NonC)* loukoum *m*
Turkish towel N serviette *f* éponge *inv*
Turkish towelling N *(NonC)* tissu *m* éponge *NonC*

Turkmen /ˈtɜːkmen/ ADJ turkmène N 1 Turkmène *mf* 2 (= *language)* turkmène *m*

Turkmenia /tɜːkˈmiːnɪə/ N Turkménie *f*

Turkmenistan /tɜːkmenɪsˌtɑːn/ N Turkménistan *m* ◆ **in ~** au Turkménistan

turmeric /ˈtɜːmərɪk/ N *(NonC)* curcuma *m*

turmoil /ˈtɜːmɔɪl/ N agitation *f*, trouble *m* ; *(emotional)* trouble *m*, émoi *m* ◆ **everything was in (a) ~** c'était le bouleversement *or* le chambardement * le plus complet

turn /tɜːn/

1 NOUN
2 TRANSITIVE VERB
3 INTRANSITIVE VERB
4 COMPOUNDS
5 PHRASAL VERBS

1 - NOUN

1 [= movement: of wheel, handle etc] tour *m* ◆ **to give sth a ~** tourner qch (une fois) ◆ **to give a screw a ~** donner un tour de vis ◆ **with a ~ of his head he could see …** en tournant la tête il voyait …

2 [= bend] *(in road etc)* tournant *m*, virage *m* ; *(Ski)* virage *m* ◆ **to make a ~** *[person, vehicle, road]* tourner ; *[ship]* virer de bord ◆ **"no left turn"** "défense de tourner à gauche" ◆ **take the next ~ on the left** prenez la prochaine route (*or* rue) à gauche ◆ **the economy may at last be on the ~** l'économie pourrait enfin se redresser

◆ **to take a + turn (for)** ◆ **to take a ~ for the worse** s'aggraver ◆ **to take a ~ for the better** s'améliorer ◆ **the patient took a ~ for the worse/better** l'état du malade s'est aggravé/amélioré ◆ **things took a new ~** les choses ont pris une nouvelle tournure ◆ **events took a tragic ~** les événements ont pris un tour *or* une tournure tragique

3 [= walk] tour *m* ◆ **to go for** *or* **take a ~ in the park** aller faire un tour dans le parc

4 [* = attack] crise *f*, attaque *f* ◆ **he had one of his ~s last night** il a eu une nouvelle crise *or* attaque la nuit dernière ◆ **she has giddy** *or* **dizzy ~s** elle a des vertiges

5 [= fright] coup * *m* ◆ **it gave me quite a ~, it gave me a nasty ~** ça m'a fait un sacré coup *

6 [= action] ◆ **to do sb a good ~** rendre un service à qn ◆ **to do sb a bad ~** jouer un mauvais tour à qn ◆ **one good ~ deserves another** *(Prov)* un prêté pour un rendu *(Prov)*

7 [= act: esp Brit] numéro *m* ◆ **to do a ~** faire un numéro

8 [Mus] doublé *m*

9 [in game, queue, series] tour *m* ◆ **it's your ~** c'est votre tour, c'est à vous ◆ **it's your ~ to play** (c'est) à vous de jouer ◆ **whose ~ is it?** *(gen)* c'est à qui le tour ? ; *(in game)* c'est à qui de jouer ?, c'est à qui le tour ? ◆ **wait your ~** attendez votre tour ◆ **to take ~s at doing sth, to take it in ~(s) to do sth** faire qch à tour de rôle ◆ **take it in ~s!** chacun son tour ! ◆ **to take ~s at the wheel** se relayer au volant ◆ **shall I take a ~ at the wheel?** est-ce que tu veux que je conduise un peu ?

10 [Culin] ◆ **done to a ~** à point

11 [set structures]

◆ **at every turn** à tout instant

◆ **by turns** (= *alternately*) tantôt … tantôt … ; (= *one after another*) à tour de rôle ◆ **he was by ~s optimistic and despairing** il était tantôt optimiste, tantôt désespéré, il était tour à tour optimiste et désespéré ◆ **the pictures are by ~s shocking, charming and cheeky** ces photos sont tantôt choquantes, tantôt pleines de charme et de malice ◆ **my sister and I visit our mother by ~s** ma sœur et moi rendons visite à notre mère à tour de rôle

◆ **in turn** (= *one after another*) à tour de rôle ; (= *then*) à mon (*or* son, notre, leur *etc*) tour ◆ **they answered in ~** ils ont répondu à tour de rôle, ils ont répondu chacun (à) leur tour ◆ **and they, in ~, said …** et, à leur tour, ils ont dit … ◆ **he told a colleague, who in ~ told a reporter** il l'a dit à un collègue qui à son tour en a parlé à un journaliste

◆ **out of turn** ◆ **I don't want to speak out of ~ but I think that …** je ne devrais peut-être pas dire cela mais je pense que …

◆ **turn (and turn) about** à tour de rôle ◆ **they share responsibilities ~ and ~ about** ils sont responsables à tour de rôle

◆ **turn of** + *noun* ◆ **at the ~ of the century** au début du siècle ◆ **~ of duty** *(Mil)* tour *m* de garde *or* de service ◆ **this was a surprising ~ of events** c'était là quelque chose de tout à fait inattendu ◆ **to be of** *or* **have a scientific ~ of mind** avoir l'esprit scientifique ◆ **to be of a pragmatic/of an analytic ~ of mind** avoir l'esprit pratique/l'esprit d'analyse ◆ **to have an original ~ of mind** avoir une tournure d'esprit originale ◆ **~ of phrase** tournure *f*, tour *m* de phrase ◆ **to have a good ~ of speed** avoir une bonne pointe de vitesse ◆ **at the ~ of the year** en fin d'année

2 - TRANSITIVE VERB

For **turn** + **adverb/preposition** combinations see also phrasal verbs.

1 [+ handle, knob, screw, key, wheel] tourner ; *(mechanically)* faire tourner ◆ **~ it to the left** tournez-le vers la gauche ◆ **what ~s the wheel?** qu'est-ce qui fait tourner la roue ? ◆ **he ~ed the wheel sharply** *(driver)* il a donné un brusque coup de volant ◆ **you can ~ it through 90°** on peut le faire pivoter de 90° ◆ **~ the key in the lock** tourne la clé dans la serrure

2 [+ page] tourner ◆ **to ~ the page** *(also fig)* tourner la page

3 [+ mattress, pillow, collar, soil, steak, record] retourner ◆ **to ~ one's ankle** se tordre la cheville ◆ **it ~s my stomach** cela me soulève le cœur, cela m'écœure

4 [= change position of, direct] *[+ car, object]* tourner (*towards* vers) ; *[+ gun, hose, searchlight]* braquer (*on sb* sur qn) ; *[+ thoughts, attention]* tourner, diriger (*towards* vers) ◆ **~ the knob to "high"** tournez le bouton jusqu'à "maxi-

mum" ◆ ~ **the switch to "on"** mettez l'interrupteur en position "marche" ◆ ~ **it to "wash"** mettez-le en position "lavage" ◆ ~ **your face this way** tourne-toi de ce côté-ci ◆ **to ~ the lights low** baisser les lumières ◆ **without ~ing a hair** sans sourciller, sans broncher ◆ **already in her first film she ~ed a few heads** déjà dans son premier film, on l'avait remarquée ◆ **he ~ed his steps southward** il dirigea ses pas vers le sud ◆ **they ~ed his argument against him** ils ont retourné son raisonnement contre lui ◆ **they ~ed him against his father** ils l'ont monté contre son père

5 = deflect [+ *blow*] parer, détourner ◆ **nothing will ~ him from his purpose** rien ne l'écartera *or* ne le détournera de son but

6 = shape [+ *wood*] tourner

7 = reach [+ *age, time*] ◆ **as soon as he ~ed 18** dès qu'il a eu 18 ans ◆ **he has** *or* **is ~ed 40** il a plus de 40 ans ◆ **it's ~ed 3 o'clock** il est 3 heures passées

8 = transform changer, transformer (*into* en) ; (= *translate*) traduire (*into* en) ◆ **his goal ~ed the game**(*Brit Sport*) son but a changé la physionomie du match *or* a changé la donne ◆ **she ~ed him into a frog** elle l'a changé *or* transformé en grenouille ◆ **they ~ed the land into a park** ils ont transformé le terrain en parc ◆ **the experience ~ed him into a misogynist** cette expérience a fait de lui un misogyne ◆ **an actor ~ed writer** un acteur devenu écrivain ◆ ~ **your talents into hard cash** transformez vos talents en espèces sonnantes et trébuchantes ◆ **to ~ a book into a play/film** adapter un livre pour la scène/à l'écran ◆ **she ~ed her dreams to reality** elle a réalisé ses rêves ◆ **to ~ the milk (sour)** faire tourner le lait ◆ **to ~ sth black** noircir qch ◆ **it ~ed him green with envy** il en était vert de jalousie

3 - INTRANSITIVE VERB

1 = move round [*handle, knob, wheel, screw, key*] tourner ; [*person*] se tourner (*to, towards* vers) ; (*right round*) se retourner ◆ ~ **to face me** tourne-toi vers moi ◆ **he ~ed and saw me** il s'est retourné et m'a vu ◆ **he ~ed to me and smiled** il s'est tourné vers moi et a souri ◆ **he ~ed to look at me** il s'est retourné pour me regarder ◆ **he ~ed to lie on his other side** il s'est retourné de l'autre côté ◆ **his stomach ~ed at the sight** le spectacle lui a retourné l'estomac *or* soulevé le cœur ◆ **he would ~ in his grave if he knew ...** il se retournerait dans sa tombe s'il savait ...

◆ **to turn on sth** [+ *hinge, axis*] tourner sur qch ◆ **the earth ~s on its axis** la terre tourne sur son axe ◆ **it all ~s on whether he has the money** (= *depend*) tout dépend s'il a l'argent ou non ◆ **the plot ~s on a question of mistaken identity** l'intrigue repose sur une erreur d'identité ; see also **phrasal verbs**

2 = move in different direction [*person, vehicle*] tourner ; [*aircraft*] changer de cap ; (= *reverse direction*) faire demi-tour ; [*ship*] virer ; [*road, river*] faire un coude ; [*wind*] tourner ; [*tide*] changer de direction ◆ **right ~!** (*Mil*) demi-tour, droite ! ◆ ~ **first right** prenez la première à droite ◆ **they ~ed and came back** ils ont fait demi-tour et sont revenus sur leurs pas ◆ **the car ~ed at the end of the street** (= *turned round*) la voiture a fait demi-tour au bout de la rue ; (= *turned off*) la voiture a tourné au bout de la rue ◆ **there's nowhere to ~** (*in car*) il n'y a pas d'endroit où faire demi-tour ◆ **the car ~ed into a side street** la voiture a tourné dans une rue transversale ◆ **our luck has ~ed** la chance a tourné pour nous ◆ **the game ~ed after half-time**(*Brit Sport*) la physionomie du match a changé après la mi-temps ◆ **he didn't know which way to ~** (*fig*) il ne savait plus où donner de la tête ◆ **where can I ~ for money?** où pourrais-je trouver de l'argent ?

◆ **to turn against sb** se retourner contre qn

◆ **to turn to sb** (*lit*) se tourner vers qn ; (*for help*) s'adresser à qn ◆ **he ~ed to me for advice** il s'est adressé à moi pour me demander conseil ◆ **our thoughts ~ to those who ...** nos pensées vont à ceux qui ...

◆ **to turn to sth** (= *resort*) se tourner vers qch ◆ ~ **to page 214** voir page 214 ◆ **to ~ to the left** tourner à gauche ◆ **farmers are increasingly ~ing to organic methods** les agriculteurs se tournent de plus en plus vers une agriculture biologique ◆ **he ~ed to drink** il s'est mis à boire ; see also **vi 3**

3 = become

◆ **turn** + *adjective* ◆ **to ~ nasty/dangerous/pale** devenir méchant/dangereux/pâle ◆ **to ~ professional** passer professionnel ◆ **to ~ Catholic** se convertir au catholicisme ◆ **the weather has ~ed cold** le temps s'est rafraîchi

◆ **to turn into** + *noun* devenir ◆ **he ~ed into a frog** il se changea *or* se transforma en grenouille ◆ **the whole thing ~ed into a nightmare** ça a dégénéré en cauchemar, c'est devenu un véritable cauchemar

◆ **to turn to** + *noun* ◆ **his admiration ~ed to scorn** son admiration se changea en *or* fit place au mépris ◆ **his love ~ed to hatred** son amour se changea en haine *or* fit place à la haine ◆ **to ~ to stone** se changer en pierre ◆ **his knees ~ed to water** *or* **jelly** ses jambes se sont dérobées sous lui ; see also **vi 2**

4 = change [*weather*] changer ; [*milk*] tourner ; [*leaves*] jaunir

4 - COMPOUNDS

turn-off N 1 (*on road*) embranchement *m* (*où il faut tourner*) 2 **it's a (real) ~-off!** * c'est vraiment à vous rebuter ! ; (*stronger*) c'est vraiment à vous dégoûter ! * ; (*also sexually*) c'est vraiment pas sexy ! *

turn-on * N ◆ **it's a (real) ~-on !** c'est excitant !

turn signal N (*US*) clignotant *m*

turn-up N (*Brit*) [*of trousers*] revers *m* ; (*fig*) ◆ **that was a ~-up (for the books)!** * ça a été une belle surprise !

5 - PHRASAL VERBS

► **turn about, turn around** VI [*person*] se retourner ; [*vehicle*] faire demi-tour ; [*object, wind*] tourner ◆ **about ~!** (*Mil*) demi-tour !

VT SEP 1 (*lit*) tourner dans l'autre sens

2 (= *change mind, tactics*) ◆ **to turn sb around** faire changer d'avis à qn ◆ **to ~ things around** renverser la situation ◆ **to ~ a company around** remettre une entreprise sur pied ; see also **turn round**

► **turn aside** VI (*lit, fig*) se détourner (*from* de)

VT SEP détourner

► **turn away** VI se détourner (*from* de)

VT SEP 1 [+ *head, face*] tourner ; [+ *eyes, gun*] détourner ◆ **he ~ed his thoughts away from the problem** il efforçait de ne plus penser à ce problème

2 (= *send away*) [+ *spectator*] refuser l'entrée à ; [+ *immigrants*] refouler ; [+ *applicants*] refuser ; [+ *offer*] refuser, rejeter ◆ **they're ~ing business** *or* **customers away** ils refusent des clients

► **turn back** VI 1 [*traveller*] rebrousser chemin, faire demi-tour ; [*vehicle*] faire demi-tour ; (= *reverse a decision*) faire marche arrière ◆ **the government cannot ~ back now** le gouvernement ne peut pas faire marche arrière maintenant ◆ **there is no ~ing back** on ne peut pas retourner en arrière

2 ◆ **to turn back to page 100** revenir à la page 100

VT SEP 1 (= *fold, bend*) [+ *bedclothes, collar*] rabattre

2 (= *send back*) [+ *person, vehicle*] faire faire demi-tour à ; [+ *demonstrators*] faire refluer

3 [+ *clock*] retarder ; (*hands of clock*) reculer ◆ **we can't ~ the clock back** on ne peut pas revenir en arrière ◆ **it has ~ed the clock back ten years** cela nous a fait revenir dix ans en arrière

► **turn down** VT SEP 1 (= *fold, bend*) [+ *collar*] rabattre ◆ **to ~ down the corner of the page** corner la page ◆ **to ~ down the bed** rabattre les draps

2 (= *reduce*) [+ *gas, heat, lighting, radio, music*] baisser

3 (= *refuse*) [+ *offer, suggestion, suitor*] rejeter, repousser ; [+ *candidate, volunteer*] refuser

4 (= *place upside down*) [+ *playing card*] retourner (face contre table)

VI (= *decrease*) [*rate, level*] baisser

► **turn in** VI 1 ◆ **to turn in to a driveway** [*car, person*] tourner dans une allée

2 (* = *go to bed*) aller se coucher

VT SEP 1 ◆ **to turn in the ends of sth** rentrer les bouts de qch

2 (= *hand over*) [+ *wanted man*] livrer (à la police) ; [+ *stolen goods*] restituer ◆ **to ~ o.s. in** se rendre, se livrer à la police

3 (= *submit*) [+ *report*] faire, soumettre

4 (*esp US* = *surrender, return*) [+ *borrowed goods, equipment*] rendre (*to* à)

VT FUS (*Sport*) ◆ **to turn in a good performance** [*player, team*] bien se comporter

► **turn off** VI 1 [*person, vehicle*] tourner

2 ◆ **to turn off automatically** [*heater, oven etc*] s'éteindre automatiquement

VT FUS [+ *road*] quitter ◆ **they decided to ~ off the motorway** ils décidèrent de quitter l'autoroute

VT SEP 1 [+ *water, tap*] fermer ; [+ *radio, television*] éteindre ; [+ *electricity, gas*] éteindre, fermer ; [+ *water, electricity*] (*at main*) couper ; [+ *heater*] éteindre, fermer ◆ **he ~ed the programme off** (*Rad*) il a éteint la radio ; (*TV*) il a éteint la télé ◆ **to ~ off the light** éteindre (la lumière) ◆ **to ~ off the engine** arrêter *or* couper le moteur ◆ **the oven ~s itself off** le four s'éteint tout seul *or* automatiquement

2 (* = *repel*) rebuter ◆ **aggressive men ~ me off** les hommes agressifs me rebutent ◆ **what ~s teenagers off science?** qu'est-ce qui, dans les sciences, rebute les adolescents ?

► **turn on** VI 1 [*heater, oven etc*] ◆ **to turn on automatically** s'allumer automatiquement

2 (*TV*) ◆ **millions of viewers turn on at 6 o'clock** des millions de téléspectateurs allument la télé à 6 heures

VT FUS (= *attack*) attaquer ◆ **the dog ~ed on him** le chien l'a attaqué ◆ **they ~ed on him and accused him of treachery** ils s'en sont pris à lui et l'ont accusé de trahison

VT SEP 1 [+ *tap*] ouvrir ; [+ *water*] faire couler ; [+ *gas, electricity, radio, television, heater*] allumer ; [+ *engine, machine*] mettre en marche ◆ **to ~ on the light** allumer (la lumière) ◆ **when you arrive, you will need to ~ on the electricity and gas** lorsque vous arriverez, il va falloir brancher l'électricité et le gaz ◆ **to ~ on the charm** * faire du charme

2 (* = *excite*) exciter ◆ **she ~s him on** elle l'excite ◆ **this music ~s me on** * cette musique me fait quelque chose * ◆ **to be ~ed on** (*sexually*) être excité (*by* par) ◆ **some men are ~ed on by power** il y a des hommes que le pouvoir excite ; see also **turn vi**

3 (= *cause to be interested*) **to ~ sb on to sth** donner à qn le goût de qch

► **turn out** VI 1 (*from bed*) se lever ; (*from house*) sortir ◆ **not many people ~ed out to see her** peu de gens sont venus la voir

2 ◆ **to turn out of a driveway** [*car, person*] sortir d'une allée

3 ◆ **his toes turn out** il a les pieds en canard

4 *(= be found)* s'avérer ◆ **it ~ed out that she had not seen her** il s'est avéré qu'elle ne l'avait pas vue ◆ **it ~ed out to be true** cela s'est avéré juste ◆ **it ~ed out to be wrong** cela s'est avéré faux ◆ **it ~ed out to be harder than we thought** cela s'est avéré plus difficile que l'on ne pensait ◆ **he ~ed out to be an excellent neighbour** il s'est avéré être un très bon voisin

5 *(= happen)* se passer ◆ **it all depends how things ~ out** tout dépend de la façon dont les choses vont se passer ◆ **everything will ~ out all right** tout finira bien ◆ **as it ~ed out, nobody came** en fin de compte personne n'est venu

6 ◆ **it turned out nice** *[weather]* il a fait beau en fin de compte

VT SEP 1 *[+ light]* éteindre ; *[+ gas]* éteindre, fermer

2 ◆ **to turn one's toes out** marcher en canard

3 *(= empty out) [+ pockets, suitcase]* vider ; *[+ room, cupboard]* nettoyer à fond ; *[+ cake, jelly]* démouler *(on to* sur) ; *(= expel) [+ person]* mettre à la porte ; *[+ tenant]* expulser ◆ **they ~ed him out of the house** ils l'ont mis à la porte ◆ **to ~ sb out of his job** renvoyer qn

4 *[+ troops, police]* envoyer

5 *(= produce) [+ goods]* fabriquer, produire ◆ **the college ~s out good teachers** le collège forme de bons professeurs

6 ◆ **to be well turned out** être élégant

► **turn over** VI 1 *[person]* se retourner ; *[car etc]* se retourner, faire un tonneau ; *[boat]* se retourner, chavirer ◆ **she ~ed over and went back to sleep** elle s'est retournée et s'est rendormie ◆ **my stomach ~ed over** *(at gruesome sight)* j'ai eu l'estomac retourné ; *(from fright)* mon sang n'a fait qu'un tour ◆ **the engine was ~ing over** le moteur tournait au ralenti

2 *(= change channel)* changer de chaîne ; *(= turn page)* tourner la page ◆ **please ~ over** *(in letter etc, abbr* PTO) tournez s'il vous plaît *(abbr* TSVP)

VT SEP 1 *[+ page]* tourner ; *[+ mattress, patient, earth, playing card, plate, tape]* retourner ◆ **to ~ over an idea in one's mind** retourner une idée dans sa tête, ressasser une idée

2 *(= hand over) [+ object, papers]* rendre ; *[+ person]* livrer *(to* à)

3 *(= give up) [+ job, responsibility]* déléguer

VT FUS ◆ **the firm turns over £10,000 a week** l'entreprise réalise un chiffre d'affaires de 10 000 livres par semaine

► **turn over to** VT FUS ◆ **the land has been turned over to sugar production** les terres sont maintenant consacrées à la production de sucre

► **turn round** VI 1 *[person]* se retourner ; *(= change direction) [person, vehicle]* faire demi-tour ; *(= rotate) [object]* tourner ◆ **to ~ round and round** tourner sur soi-même ◆ **~ round and look at me** retourne-toi et regarde-moi ◆ **he ~ed round and came back** il a fait demi-tour et est revenu sur ses pas ◆ **he ~ed round and said he was leaving** *(fig)* il a subitement annoncé qu'il partait

2 *(= improve) [business, economy]* se redresser

3 *[ship, plane] (= unload, reload and leave)* décharger, recharger et repartir

VT SEP 1 *[+ one's head]* tourner ; *[+ object]* tourner, retourner ; *[+ person]* faire tourner ; *[+ ship, aircraft]* faire faire demi-tour à ◆ **he ~ed the car round** il a fait demi-tour ◆ **to ~ a ship/plane round** *(= unload and reload)* décharger et recharger un bateau/avion ◆ **to ~ an order round** *(Comm)* exécuter une commande

2 *(= make successful) [+ business, economy]* redresser ; *(= rephrase) [+ sentence, idea]* reformuler ◆ **to ~ things round** renverser la situation ◆ **if you ~ed this round a bit it would be very funny** si vous formuliez cela un peu différemment, ce pourrait être très drôle ◆ **to ~ sb round** *(= change mind, tactics)* faire changer qn d'avis

► **turn up** VI 1 *(= arrive)* arriver ; *[playing card]* sortir ◆ **something will ~ up** on va bien trouver quelque chose ◆ **I've lost my job – something will ~ up (for you)** j'ai perdu mon poste – tu finiras bien par trouver quelque chose ◆ **don't worry about your ring, I'm sure it will ~ up (again)** ne t'en fais pas pour ta bague, je suis sûr que tu finiras par la retrouver ◆ **to ~ up again** *[person]* réapparaître ; → **trump**[1]

2 ◆ **his nose turns up at the end** il a le nez retroussé *or* en trompette

3 *[prices]* remonter ◆ **profits ~ed up in the last quarter** les bénéfices ont remonté au dernier trimestre

VT SEP 1 *[+ collar]* relever ; *[+ sleeve]* retrousser, relever ◆ **to have a ~ed-up nose** avoir le nez retroussé *or* en trompette ◆ **it really ~s me up** * *(= disgust)* ça me dégoûte

2 *(= dig up) [+ buried object]* déterrer ; *(= find) [+ lost object, reference, evidence]* trouver ◆ **a survey ~ed up more than 3,000 people suffering from ...** une enquête a révélé que plus de 3 000 personnes souffraient de ...

3 *[+ radio, television]* mettre plus fort ◆ **to ~ up the sound** monter le son *or* volume ◆ **when the sugar has dissolved, ~ up the heat** une fois le sucre dissous, faites cuire à feu plus vif ◆ **to ~ up the heat** *(fig)* accentuer la pression

---

turnabout /ˈtɜːnəbaʊt/ N *(lit, fig)* volte-face *f inv* ◆ **an unprecedented ~ in its European policy** une volte-face sans précédent dans sa politique européenne ◆ **we may well see a considerable ~ in her attitude** il se peut bien que l'on voie son attitude changer radicalement

turnaround /ˈtɜːnəraʊnd/ N *(= complete change)* transformation *f* radicale ; *(= economic improvement)* redressement *m* ; *(= place for turning vehicle)* endroit *m* pour manœuvrer ; *(= unloading time etc) [of plane, truck]* rotation *f* ; *[of ship]* estarie *f*, starie *f* ◆ **~ time** *(Comm) [of order]* temps *m* d'exécution ; *(Comput)* temps *m* de retournement ◆ **I did a complete ~ in my opinion of her** l'opinion que j'avais d'elle a complètement changé ◆ **a vast ~ in the way we do business** une transformation radicale de nos méthodes commerciales ◆ **a ~ in the housing market** un redressement du marché de l'immobilier ◆ **the ~ time for our trucks is three hours** nos camions opèrent des rotations de trois heures

turncoat /ˈtɜːnkəʊt/ N renégat(e) *m(f)*

turndown /ˈtɜːndaʊn/ N 1 *[of sales, rate, tendency]* fléchissement *m*, (tendance *f* à la) baisse *f* 2 *(= rejection)* refus *m* ADJ *[flap]* à rabattre ◆ **~ collar** col *m* rabattu

turner /ˈtɜːnəʳ/ N tourneur *m*

turnery /ˈtɜːnərɪ/ N atelier *m* de tournage

turning /ˈtɜːnɪŋ/ N 1 *(= side road)* route *f* (or rue *f*) latérale ; *(= fork)* embranchement *m* ; *(= bend in road, river)* coude *m* ◆ **take the second ~ on the left** prenez la deuxième à gauche 2 *(NonC: on lathe)* tournage *m*

COMP **turning circle** N *[of car]* rayon *m* de braquage

turning lathe N tour *m*

turning point N ◆ **he was at a ~ point in his career** il était à un tournant de sa carrière ◆ **that was the ~ point in her life** ce fut le moment décisif de sa vie

turnip /ˈtɜːnɪp/ N navet *m*

turnkey /ˈtɜːnkiː/ N geôlier *m*, -ière *f* COMP **turnkey factory** N usine *f* clés en main

turnout /ˈtɜːnaʊt/ N 1 *(= attendance)* assistance *f* ◆ **what sort of a ~ was there?** combien y avait-il de gens (dans l'assistance) ? ◆ **there was a good ~** beaucoup de gens sont venus ◆ **~ at the polls, voter ~** (taux *m* de) participation *f* électorale ◆ **a high/low ~ at the polls** un fort/faible taux de participation électorale 2 *(= clean-out)* nettoyage *m* ◆ **to have a good ~ of a room/cupboard** nettoyer une pièce/un placard à fond 3 *(= industrial output)* production *f* 4 *(Dress)* tenue *f* 5 *(US = layby)* aire *f* de repos

turnover /ˈtɜːnˌəʊvəʳ/ N 1 *(Comm etc) [of stock, goods]* rotation *f* ; *[of shares]* mouvement *m* ; *(= total business done)* chiffre *m* d'affaires ◆ **a profit of £4,000 on a ~ of £40,000** un bénéfice de 4 000 livres pour un chiffre d'affaires de 40 000 livres ◆ **he sold them cheaply hoping for a quick ~** il les a vendus bon marché pour les écouler rapidement 2 *[of staff, workers]* renouvellement *m*, rotation *f* ◆ **there is a high** *or* **rapid (rate of) ~ in that firm** cette maison connaît de fréquents changements *or* renouvellements de personnel 3 *(Culin)* chausson *m* ◆ **apple ~** chausson *m* aux pommes

turnpike /ˈtɜːnpaɪk/ N *(= barrier)* barrière *f* de péage ; *(US = road)* autoroute *f* à péage ; → ROADS

turnround /ˈtɜːnraʊnd/ N ⇒ **turnaround**

turnstile /ˈtɜːnstaɪl/ N tourniquet *m*

turntable /ˈtɜːnteɪbl/ N *[of record player]* platine *f* ; *(for trains, cars etc)* plaque *f* tournante ◆ **~ ladder** échelle *f* pivotante

turpentine /ˈtɜːpəntaɪn/ N (essence *f* de) térébenthine *f* ◆ **~ substitute** white-spirit *m*

turpitude /ˈtɜːpɪtjuːd/ N turpitude *f*

turps * /tɜːps/ N abbrev of **turpentine**

turquoise /ˈtɜːkwɔɪz/ N *(= stone)* turquoise *f* ; *(= colour)* turquoise *m* ADJ *(= made of turquoise)* de turquoise(s) ; *(in colour)* turquoise *inv* ◆ **~ blue/green** bleu/vert turquoise

turret /ˈtʌrɪt/ N *(Archit, Mil, Phot, Tech)* tourelle *f* COMP **turret gun** N canon *m* de tourelle

turreted /ˈtʌrɪtɪd/ ADJ à tourelles

turtle /ˈtɜːtl/ N tortue *f* marine ◆ **to turn ~** *(fig)* chavirer, se renverser ; → **mock** COMP **turtle soup** N consommé *m* à la tortue

turtledove /ˈtɜːtldʌv/ N tourterelle *f*

turtleneck /ˈtɜːtlnek/ N *(Brit:* also **turtleneck sweater)** (pull-over *m* à) encolure *f* montante *or* col *m* cheminée ; *(US)* (pull-over *m* à) col *m* roulé

Tuscan /ˈtʌskən/ ADJ toscan N 1 Toscan(e) *m(f)* 2 *(= dialect)* toscan *m*

Tuscany /ˈtʌskənɪ/ N Toscane *f*

tush /tʌʃ/ EXCL † bah ! N * *(US = bottom)* fesses *fpl*

tusk /tʌsk/ N défense *f (d'éléphant etc)*

tusker /ˈtʌskəʳ/ N éléphant *m (or* sanglier *m etc)* adulte *(qui a ses défenses)*

tussle /ˈtʌsl/ N *(= struggle)* lutte *f (for* pour) ; *(= scuffle)* mêlée *f* ◆ **to have a ~ with sb** *(physically)* en venir aux mains avec qn ; *(verbally)* avoir une prise de bec * avec qn VI se battre *(with sb* avec qn ; *for sth* pour qch) ◆ **to ~ over sth** se disputer qch

tussock /ˈtʌsək/ N touffe *f* d'herbe

tut /tʌt/ (also **tut-tut**) EXCL allons allons !, allons donc ! VI ◆ **he (~)-~ted at the idea** à cette idée il a eu une exclamation désapprobatrice

Tutankhamen /ˌtuːtənˈkɑːmen/, **Tutankhamun** /ˌtuːtənkɑːˈmuːn/ N Toutankhamon *m*

tutelage /ˈtjuːtɪlɪdʒ/ N tutelle *f* ◆ **under the ~ of sb** sous la tutelle de qn

tutelary /ˈtjuːtɪlərɪ/ ADJ tutélaire

tutor /ˈtjuːtəʳ/ N *(= private teacher)* professeur *m* (particulier) *(in* en) ; *(full-time)* précepteur *m*, -trice *f* ; *(Brit Univ)* directeur *m*, -trice *f* d'études ; *(Brit Scol:* also **form tutor)** professeur *m* principal ; *(in prison)* éducateur *m*, -trice *f* VT donner des leçons particulières *or* des cours particuliers à ◆ **to ~ sb in Latin** donner des cours particuliers de latin à qn

COMP **tutor group** N (*Brit Scol*) classe *f*

tutor period N (*Brit Scol*) cours *m* avec le professeur principal (*en début de journée*)

tutor room N (*Brit Scol*) salle *f* de classe (*affectée à une classe particulière*)

tutorial /tjuːˈtɔːrɪəl/ ADJ 1 (*= teaching*) [*work, duties*] d'enseignement ; [*staff*] enseignant ; [*guidance, support*] pédagogique 2 (*Univ*) ◆ **~ work** travaux *mpl* dirigés ◆ **~ essay** exposé *m* ◆ **~ duties** encadrement *m* des travaux dirigés ◆ **~ group** groupe *m* de travaux dirigés N (*Univ*) travaux *mpl* dirigés (*in* de)

tutoring /ˈtjuːtərɪŋ/ N cours *mpl* particuliers (*in* de) ; (*remedial*) cours *mpl* de soutien (*in* de)

Tutsi /ˈtʊtsɪ/ N Tutsi(e) *m(f)* ADJ tutsi

tutti-frutti /ˈtʊtɪˈfruːtɪ/ N (pl **tutti-fruttis**) (*= ice-cream*) plombières *f*, cassate *f*

tutu /ˈtuːtuː/ N tutu *m*

Tuvalu /tuːˈvɑːluː/ N Tuvalu

tuwhit-tuwhoo /tʊˈwɪttʊˈwuː/ N hou-hou *m*

tuxedo /tʌkˈsiːdəʊ/, **tux*** /ˈtʌks/ N (*esp US*) smoking *m*

TV* /ˌtiːˈviː/ N 1 (abbrev of **television**) télé* *f* ; see also **television** 2 (abbrev of **transvestite**) travesti *m* COMP **TV dinner** N plateau-repas *m*, plateau-télé *m*

TVEI /ˌtiːviːiːˈaɪ/ N (*Brit*) (abbrev of **technical and vocational educational initiative**) *plan de formation pour les jeunes*

TVM /ˌtiːviːˈem/ N (abbrev of **television movie**) film *m* de télévision

TVP /ˌtiːviːˈpiː/ N (abbrev of **textured vegetable protein**) → **textured**

twaddle /ˈtwɒdl/ N (*NonC*) âneries *fpl*, fadaises *fpl* ◆ **you're talking ~** tu dis n'importe quoi

twain /tweɪn/ NPL ◆ **the ~** †† les deux ◆ **and never the ~ shall meet** et les deux sont inconciliables

twang /twæŋ/ N [*of wire, string*] son *m* (de corde pincée) ; (*= tone of voice*) ton *m* nasillard, nasillement *m* ◆ **to speak with a ~** nasiller, parler du nez ◆ **he has an American ~** il parle avec un accent américain VT [*+ guitar*] pincer les cordes de, gratter de VI [*wire, bow*] vibrer

twangy /ˈtwæŋɪ/ ADJ [*noise*] de corde pincée ; [*voice, tone*] nasillard

'twas †† /twɒz/ ⇒ **it was** ; → **be**

twat** /twæt/ N 1 (*= genitals*) con* *m* 2 (*pej = person*) pauvre con(ne)* *m(f)*

tweak /twiːk/ VT 1 (*= pull*) [*+ sb's ear, nose*] tordre ; [*+ rope etc, sb's hair*] tirer (d'un coup sec) 2 (* *= alter slightly*) modifier légèrement N 1 (*= pull*) coup *m* sec ◆ **to give sth a ~** ⇒ **to tweak sth;** → vt 2 (* *= small alteration*) petite modification *f* ◆ **to give the figures a ~** tricher un peu avec les chiffres

twee /twiː/ ADJ (*Brit pej*) [*picture, design, decor*] cucul* ; [*remark, poem*] mièvre, gentillet ; [*person*] chichiteux* ; [*house, cottage*] mignonnet

tweed /twiːd/ N tweed *m* NPL **tweeds** (*= suit*) costume *m* de tweed COMP [*jacket etc*] de *or* en tweed

tweedy /ˈtwiːdɪ/ ADJ 1 (* *gen pej*) ◆ **he's rather ~** il fait un peu bourgeois campagnard, il a le style gentleman-farmer ◆ **she's one of these ~ ladies** elle est du style bourgeoise campagnarde 2 (*= resembling tweed*) façon tweed *inv*

'tween /twiːn/ PREP (*liter*) ⇒ **between**

tweeny †* /ˈtwiːnɪ/ N (*Brit*) bonne *f*

tweet /twiːt/ N (also **tweet-tweet**) gazouillis *m*, gazouillement *m*, pépiement *m* VI gazouiller, pépier

tweeter /ˈtwiːtəʳ/ N haut-parleur *m* aigu, tweeter *m*

tweeze* /twiːz/ VT [*+ eyebrows etc*] épiler

tweezers /ˈtwiːzəz/ NPL (also **pair of tweezers**) pince *f* fine, pince *f* à épiler

twelfth /twelfθ/ ADJ douzième ◆ **Twelfth Night** la fête des Rois, l'Épiphanie *f* N douzième *mf* ; (*= fraction*) douzième *m* ; *for phrases see* **sixth** COMP **twelfth man** N (pl **twelfth men**) (*Brit Cricket*) remplaçant *m*

twelve /twelv/ ADJ douze *inv* N douze *m inv* ; → **o'clock** ; *for other phrases see* **six** PRON douze ◆ **there are ~** il y en a douze COMP **twelve-tone** ADJ (*Mus*) dodécaphonique

twelvemonth †† /ˈtwelvmʌnθ/ N année *f*, an *m*

twentieth /ˈtwentɪɪθ/ ADJ vingtième N vingtième *mf* ; (*= fraction*) vingtième *m* ; *for phrases see* **sixth**

twenty /ˈtwentɪ/ ADJ vingt *inv* ◆ **about ~ books** une vingtaine de livres

N vingt *m* ◆ **about ~** une vingtaine ; *for other phrases see* **sixty**

PRON vingt ◆ **there are ~** il y en a vingt

COMP **twenty-first** N (*= birthday*) vingt et unième anniversaire *m* ◆ **I'm having my ~-first on Saturday** (*= birthday party*) je fête mes 21 ans *or* mon 21e anniversaire samedi

twenty-four hours NPL (*= whole day*) vingt-quatre heures *fpl* ◆ **~-four hours a day** (*open etc*) vingt-quatre heures sur vingt-quatre

twenty-four hour service N service jour et nuit, service 24 heures sur 24 ◆ **a ~-four hour strike** une grève de vingt-quatre heures

twenty-four seven* ADV ◆ **to do sth ~-four seven** *or* **24-7** faire qch 24 heures sur 24, 7 jours sur 7

twenty-one N (*Cards*) vingt-et-un *m* (*jeu*)

twenty-twenty vision N ◆ **to have ~-~ vision** avoir dix dixièmes à chaque œil

twenty-two metre line N (*Rugby*) ligne *f* des vingt-deux mètres

twerp* /twɜːp/ N andouille* *f*, idiot(e) *m(f)*

twice /twaɪs/ ADV deux fois ◆ **~ a week, ~ weekly** deux fois par semaine ◆ **~ as much, ~ as many** deux fois plus ◆ **~ as much space** deux fois plus de place ◆ **~ as long (as)** deux fois plus long (que) ◆ **she is ~ your age** elle a deux fois votre âge, elle a le double de votre âge ◆ **~ the national average** le double de *or* deux fois la moyenne nationale ◆ **~ two is four** deux fois deux font quatre ◆ **he didn't have to be asked ~** (*fig*) il ne s'est pas fait prier ◆ **he's ~ the man you are** il vaut beaucoup mieux que toi ; → **once, think**

twiddle /ˈtwɪdl/ VT [*+ knob*] tripoter, manier ◆ **to ~ one's thumbs** (*fig*) se tourner les pouces VI ◆ **to ~ with sth** jouer avec *or* tripoter qch N ◆ **to give sth a ~** donner plusieurs petits tours à qch

twig¹ /twɪg/ N brindille *f*, petite branche *f*

twig²* /twɪg/ VTI (*Brit = understand*) piger*, comprendre

twilight /ˈtwaɪlaɪt/ N (*= evening*) crépuscule *m* (*also fig*) (*= morning*) aube *f* naissante ◆ **at ~** (*evening*) au crépuscule, à la tombée du jour ; (*morning*) à l'aube naissante ◆ **in the ~** dans la semi-obscurité *or* la pénombre

COMP **twilight world** N monde *m* nébuleux

twilight zone N (*fig*) zone *f* floue

twilit /ˈtwaɪlɪt/ ADJ [*sky, landscape, place*] crépusculaire, de crépuscule

twill /twɪl/ N (*= fabric*) sergé *m*

'twill /twɪl/ ⇒ **it will** ; → **will**

twin /twɪn/ N jumeau *m*, -elle *f* ; → **identical, Siamese**

ADJ [*brother, sister, towers, peaks*] jumeau (-elle *f*) ◆ **~ boys** jumeaux *mpl* ◆ **~ girls** jumelles *fpl* ◆ **with ~ propellers/taps** avec deux hélices/robinets ◆ **plane with ~ engines** (avion *m*) bimoteur *m* ◆ **they're ~ souls** ce sont deux âmes sœurs ◆ **the ~ concepts of liberty and equality** les concepts inséparables de liberté et d'égalité

VT [*+ town etc*] jumeler (*with* avec)

COMP **twin-bedded room** N (*Brit: in hotel*) chambre *f* à deux lits

twin beds NPL lits *mpl* jumeaux

twin bill* N (*US*) (*Sport*) programme *m* de deux matchs ; (*Cine*) programme *m* de deux longs métrages

twin-cylinder ADJ à deux cylindres N moteur *m* à deux cylindres

twin-engined ADJ bimoteur

twin room N ⇒ **twin-bedded room**

twin-screw ADJ à deux hélices

twin town N (*Brit*) ville *f* jumelée

twin-track ADJ [*approach, process, strategy*] double

twin-tub N machine *f* à laver à deux tambours

twine /twaɪn/ N (*NonC*) ficelle *f* VT (*= weave*) tresser ; (*= roll*) entortiller, enrouler (*round* autour de) ◆ **she ~d her arms round his neck** elle lui a enlacé le cou de ses bras VI [*plant, coil*] s'enrouler (*round* autour de) ; [*river, road*] serpenter, zigzaguer

twinge /twɪndʒ/ N ◆ **a ~ (of pain)** un élancement, un tiraillement ◆ **a ~ of conscience** *or* **remorse** *or* **guilt** un (petit) remords ◆ **to feel a ~ of remorse/shame** éprouver un certain remords/une certaine honte ◆ **to feel a ~ of regret** *or* **sadness** avoir un pincement au cœur

twining /ˈtwaɪnɪŋ/ ADJ [*plant*] volubile (*Bot*)

twinkle /ˈtwɪŋkl/ VI [*star, lights*] scintiller, briller ; [*eyes*] briller, pétiller N [*of star, lights*] scintillement *m* ; [*of eyes*] éclat *m*, pétillement *m* ◆ **... he said with a ~ (in his eye)** ... dit-il avec un pétillement (malicieux) dans les yeux ◆ **he had a ~ in his eye** il avait les yeux pétillants ◆ **in a ~, in the ~ of an eye** en un clin d'œil

twinkling /ˈtwɪŋklɪŋ/ ADJ [*star, light*] scintillant ; [*eyes*] pétillant N ◆ **in the ~ of an eye** en un clin d'œil

twinning /ˈtwɪnɪŋ/ N [*of towns*] jumelage *m*

twinset /ˈtwɪnset/ N (*Brit*) twin-set *m* ◆ **she's rather ~ and pearls*** (*Brit*) elle fait très BCBG

twirl /twɜːl/ N [*of body*] tournoiement *m* ; [*of dancer*] pirouette *f* ; (*in writing*) fioriture *f* ◆ **to give sth a ~** ⇒ **to twirl sth;** → **vt** ◆ **to do a ~** faire une pirouette VI (also **twirl round**) [*cane, lasso, dancer*] tournoyer ; [*handle, knob*] pivoter VT (also **twirl round**) [*+ cane, lasso*] faire tournoyer ; [*+ knob, handle*] faire pivoter ; [*+ moustache*] tortiller

twirler* /ˈtwɜːləʳ/ N (*US*) majorette *f*

twirp* /twɜːp/ N ⇒ **twerp**

twist /twɪst/ N 1 (*= action*) torsion *f* ; (*Med*) entorse *f*, foulure *f* ◆ **to give a ~ to** [*+ knob, handle*] faire pivoter, faire tourner ; [*+ wire*] tordre ; [*+ one's ankle*] se tordre, se fouler ◆ **he put a ~ on the ball** il a imprimé une rotation à la balle ◆ **with a quick ~ (of the wrist)** d'un rapide tour de poignet

2 (*= coil*) rouleau *m* ; (*in road*) tournant *m*, virage *m* ; (*in river*) coude *m* ; (*in wire, flex, cord*) tortillon *m* ◆ **a ~ of yarn** une torsade *or* un cordonnet de fil ◆ **a ~ of smoke** une volute de fumée ◆ **sweets in a ~ of paper** des bonbons dans un tortillon de papier *or* une papillote ◆ **a ~ of lemon** un zeste de citron ◆ **the road is full of ~s and turns** la route est pleine de tournants *or* de virages, la route fait des zigzags

3 (*fig*) [*of events*] tournure *f* ; [*of meaning*] distorsion *f* ◆ **the story has an unexpected ~ to it** l'histoire prend un tour inattendu ◆ **he gave a new ~ to this old story** il a remis cette vieille histoire au goût du jour ◆ **the latest ~ in the political situation** les derniers développe-

ments de la situation politique ◆ **the arrest was a dramatic ~ in the investigation** l'enquête a connu un rebondissement inattendu avec cette arrestation ◆ **to get (o.s.) into a ~***, **to get one's knickers in a ~**‡ *(= get annoyed)* s'énerver ; *(= get confused)* s'emmêler les pinceaux* ◆ **the ~s and turns of economic policy** les changements d'orientation de la politique économique

◆ **twist of fate** ◆ **by a curious ~ of fate** par un curieux effet du hasard ◆ **in a cruel ~ of fate** par une cruelle ironie du sort

◆ **round the twist*** ◆ **to go round the ~** devenir dingue*, perdre la boule‡ ◆ **to be round the ~** être dingue*, avoir perdu la boule* ◆ **to drive sb round the ~** rendre qn fou

[4] *(‡ = cheat)* **what a ~!** on s'est fait avoir !* ◆ **it's a ~!** c'est de la triche !*

[5] *(= dance)* twist *m* ◆ **to do the ~** twister

VT [1] *(= interweave)* *[+ threads, strands, ropes, wires]* entortiller, tresser ; *(= turn round on itself)* *[+ thread, rope, wire, one's handkerchief]* tordre ; *(= coil)* enrouler *(round* autour de) ; *(= turn)* *[+ knob, handle]* tourner ; *[+ top, cap]* tourner, visser ; *(= deform)* *[+ metal etc]* tordre, déformer ; *(fig)* *[+ meaning]* fausser ; *[+ words]* déformer ◆ **to get ~ed** *[rope etc]* s'entortiller ◆ **he ~ed the strands into a cord** il a entortillé *or* tressé les fils pour en faire une corde ◆ **he ~ed the paper into a ball** il a tirebouchonné le papier pour en faire une boule ◆ **you've ~ed it out of shape** tu l'as déformé en le tordant, tu l'as tordu ◆ **~ the cap clockwise** vissez la capsule dans le sens des aiguilles d'une montre ◆ **to ~ the top off a jar** dévisser le couvercle d'un bocal (pour l'enlever) ◆ **to ~ one's ankle** se tordre *or* se fouler la cheville ◆ **to ~ one's neck** se tordre le cou, attraper le torticolis ◆ **to ~ o.s. free** se libérer en se contorsionnant ◆ **to ~ sb's arm** *(lit)* tordre le bras à qn ; *(fig)* forcer la main à qn ◆ **she can ~ him round her little finger** elle le mène par le bout du nez ◆ **he ~ed his mouth scornfully** il eut un rictus méprisant ◆ **limbs ~ed by arthritis** des membres tordus par l'arthrite ◆ **his face was ~ed with pain/rage** ses traits étaient tordus par la douleur/la fureur ◆ **you're ~ing everything I say** tu déformes tout ce que je dis ; → **twisted**

[2] *(‡ = cheat)* rouler*, avoir*

VI [1] *[flex, rope etc]* s'entortiller, s'enrouler ; *[socks, trousers]* tirebouchonner ; *[one's ankle etc]* se tordre ◆ **to ~ round sth** s'enrouler autour de qch ◆ **the road ~s (and turns) through the valley** la route zigzague *or* serpente à travers la vallée ◆ **the motorbike ~ed through the traffic** la moto louvoyait *or* zigzaguait parmi la circulation

[2] *(= dance the twist)* twister

COMP **twist grip** N *[of motorcycle]* poignée *f* d'accélération ; *(= gear change)* poignée *f* de changement de vitesses

► **twist about, twist around** VI *[rope etc]* tortiller ; *[road etc]* serpenter, zigzaguer

► **twist off** VI ◆ **the top twists off** le couvercle se dévisse

VT SEP *[+ branch]* enlever en tordant ; *[+ bottle-top]* enlever en dévissant

► **twist out** VI ◆ **he twisted out of their grasp** il s'est dégagé de leur étreinte

VT SEP *[+ object]* enlever en tournant

► **twist round** VI *[road etc]* serpenter, zigzaguer ; *[person]* se retourner

VT SEP *[+ rope, wire]* enrouler ; *[+ knob, handle]* tourner ; *[+ top, cap]* tourner, visser ; *[+ one's head, chair]* tourner

► **twist up** VI *[ropes etc]* s'entortiller, s'emmêler ; *[smoke]* monter en volutes

VT SEP *[+ ropes, threads]* entortiller, emmêler

twisted /ˈtwɪstɪd/ ADJ [1] *(= damaged, tangled)* *[key, rod, metal, beam, wreckage]* tordu ; *[wrist, ankle]* foulé ; *[wire, rope, flex, cord, strap]* entortillé ◆ **~ bowel** *(Med)* volvulus *m* intestinal [2] *(= of twisted construction)* *[rope, cable]* tressé ; *[barley-sugar]* torsadé [3] *(= deformed, distorted)* *[tree, branch]* tordu ; *[limb]* difforme ; *[features, smile]* crispé [4] *(= warped)* *[person, mind, logic]* tordu ; → **bitter**

twister* /ˈtwɪstəʳ/ N [1] *(Brit = crook)* escroc *m (lit, fig)* [2] *(US = tornado)* tornade *f*

twisting /ˈtwɪstɪŋ/ N *(gen)* torsion *f* ; *[of meaning]* déformation *f* ADJ *[path]* sinueux, en zigzag

twisty /ˈtwɪstɪ/ ADJ *[lane, river]* tortueux

twit¹ /twɪt/ VT *(= tease)* taquiner *(about, with* sur, à propos de)

twit²* /twɪt/ N *(esp Brit = fool)* idiot(e) *m(f)*, crétin(e)* *m(f)*

twitch /twɪtʃ/ N *(= nervous movement)* tic *m* ; *(= pull)* coup *m* sec, saccade *f* ◆ **I've got a ~ in my eyelid** j'ai l'œil qui saute ◆ **he has a (nervous) ~ in his cheek** il a un tic à la joue ◆ **with one ~ (of his hand) he freed the rope** il a dégagé la corde d'une saccade ◆ **he gave the rope a ~** il a tiré d'un coup sec sur la corde ◆ **a ~ of the whip** un (petit) coup de fouet

VI [1] *[person, animal, hands]* avoir un mouvement convulsif ; *(permanent condition)* avoir un tic ; *[face, mouth, cheek, eyebrow, muscle]* se convulser, se contracter (convulsivement) ; *[dog's nose etc]* remuer, bouger

[2] *(fig = be nervous)* s'agiter

VT *[+ rope etc]* tirer d'un coup sec, donner un coup sec à ◆ **he ~ed it out of her hands** il le lui a arraché des mains ◆ **the cat ~ed its nose/its ears** le nez/les oreilles du chat a/ont remué *or* bougé

► **twitch away** VT SEP arracher d'un petit geste *(from sb* à qn)

twitcher* /ˈtwɪtʃəʳ/ N ornithologue *mf* amateur

twitchy* /ˈtwɪtʃɪ/ ADJ [1] *(= twitching)* agité [2] *(= nervous, jumpy)* *[person, animal]* nerveux ; *[stock market]* fébrile ◆ **it's a good car but the handling is rather ~** c'est une bonne voiture mais elle a une tenue de route plutôt sautillante

twitter /ˈtwɪtəʳ/ VI *[bird]* gazouiller, pépier ; *[person]* *(= chatter)* parler avec agitation *(about* de), jacasser *(pej)* *(about* sur) ; *(= be nervous)* s'agiter (nerveusement) N *[of birds]* gazouillis *m*, pépiement *m* ◆ **to be in a ~ (about sth)*** être dans tous ses états (à cause de qch)

'twixt /twɪkst/ PREP *(†† or liter)* ⇒ **between¹**

two /tuː/ ADJ deux *inv* ; → **mind**

N deux *m inv* ◆ **to cut sth in ~** couper qch en deux ◆ **~ by ~** deux par deux, deux à deux ◆ **in ~s** par deux ◆ **in ~s and threes** deux ou trois à la fois, par petits groupes ◆ **that makes ~ of us** moi aussi, dans ce cas, nous sommes deux ◆ **they're ~ of a kind** ils se ressemblent (tous les deux) ◆ **to put ~ and ~ together*** faire le rapport (entre deux *or* plusieurs choses) ◆ **he put ~ and ~ together and made** *or* **came up with five*** il a tiré la mauvaise conclusion ◆ **~'s company** on est mieux à deux ◆ **~'s company, three's a crowd** quand il y a trois personnes, il y en a une de trop ; → **one** ; *for other phrases see* **six**

PRON deux ◆ **there are ~** il y en a deux

COMP **two-bit*** ADJ *(esp US pej)* de pacotille

two-bits NPL *(US)* 25 cents *mpl*

two-by-four* ADJ *(US)* *(= small)* exigu (-uë *f*) ; *(= unimportant)* minable

two-chamber system N *(Parl)* bicaméralisme *m*

two-colour process N *(Phot)* bichromie *f*

two-cycle ADJ *(US)* ⇒ **two-stroke**

two-cylinder ADJ *[car]* à deux cylindres

two-door ADJ *[car]* à deux portes

two-edged ADJ *(lit, fig)* à double tranchant

two-faced ADJ *(fig)* hypocrite

two-fisted* ADJ *(US)* vigoureux, costaud*

two-four time N *(NonC: Mus)* (mesure *f* à) deux-quatre *m inv* ◆ **in ~-four time** à deux-quatre

two-handed ADJ *[sword]* à deux mains ; *[saw]* à deux poignées ; *[card game]* à deux joueurs

two-horse race N ◆ **the election was a ~-horse race** dans ces élections, seuls deux des candidats avaient des chances de gagner

two-legged ADJ bipède

two-party ADJ *(Pol)* bipartite

two-percent milk N *(US)* lait *m* demi-écrémé

two-phase ADJ *(Elec)* diphasé

two-piece N ◆ **~-piece (suit)** *(man's)* costume *m* (deux-pièces) ; *(woman's)* tailleur *m* ◆ **~-piece (swimsuit)** deux-pièces *m inv*, bikini ® *m*

two-pin plug N prise *f* à deux fiches *or* broches

two-ply ADJ *[cord, rope]* à deux brins ; *[wool]* à deux fils ; *[wood]* à deux épaisseurs

two-seater ADJ à deux places N *(= car)* voiture *f* à deux places ; *(= plane)* avion *m* à deux places

two-sided ADJ *(fig)* ◆ **this is a ~-sided problem** ce problème peut être appréhendé de deux façons

two-star N *((Brit:* also **two-star petrol)** (essence *f*) ordinaire *f*

two-storey ADJ à deux étages

two-stroke ADJ ◆ **~-stroke (engine)** moteur *m* à deux temps, deux-temps *m inv* ◆ **~-stroke mixture** mélange *m* deux-temps ◆ **~-stroke fuel** carburant *m* pour moteur à deux-temps

two-tier financing N financement *m* à deux étages

two-time* VT tromper, être infidèle à ADJ *(US)* ◆ **~-time loser**‡ *(= crook etc)* repris *m* de justice ; *(= divorcee)* homme *m (or* femme *f)* deux fois divorcé(e)

two-timer* N *(gen)* traître(sse) *m(f)* ; *(in marriage)* mari *m (or* femme *f)* infidèle

two-tone ADJ *(in colour)* de deux tons ; *(in sound)* à deux tons

two-way ADJ *[traffic]* dans les deux sens ; *[exchange, negotiations]* bilatéral ◆ **~-way mirror** miroir *m* sans tain ◆ **~-way radio** émetteur-récepteur *m* ◆ **~-way street** *(lit)* voie à double sens ◆ **to be a ~-way street** *(fig)* être à double sens ◆ **~-way switch** va-et-vient *m*

two-wheeler N deux-roues *m inv*

twoccing‡ /ˈtwɒkɪŋ/ N *(NonC: Brit)* vol *m* de voiture

twofer* /ˈtuːfəʳ/ N *(US)* deux articles *mpl* pour le prix d'un

twofold /ˈtuːfəʊld/ ADJ double ADV ◆ **to increase ~** doubler

twopence /ˈtʌpəns/ N *(Brit)* deux pence *mpl* ; see also **tuppence**

twopenny /ˈtʌpənɪ/ ADJ *(Brit)* à *or* de deux pence

COMP **twopenny-halfpenny*** ADJ *(fig)* de rien du tout*, de quatre sous

twopenny piece N pièce *f* de deux pence

twosome /ˈtuːsəm/ N *(= people)* couple *m* ; *(= game)* jeu *m or* partie *f* à deux ◆ **we went in a ~** nous y sommes allés à deux

'twould †† /twʊd/ ⇒ **it would** ; → **would**

TX abbrev of **Texas**

tycoon /taɪˈkuːn/ N ◆ **(business** *or* **industrial) ~** gros *or* important homme *m* d'affaires ◆ **oil ~** magnat *m or* roi *m* du pétrole

tyke* /taɪk/ N *(= dog)* cabot *m (pej)* ; *(= child)* môme *mf*

tympana /ˈtɪmpənə/ NPL of **tympanum**

tympani /ˈtɪmpənɪ/ N ⇒ **timpani**

tympanic /tɪmˈpænɪk/ ADJ ◆ **~ membrane** tympan *m*

tympanist /ˈtɪmpənɪst/ N ⇒ **timpanist**

tympanum /ˈtɪmpənəm/ N (pl **tympanums** *or* **tympana**) *(Anat, Archit)* tympan *m* ; *(Mus)* timbale *f*

type /taɪp/ N 1 *(gen, Bio, Sociol etc)* type *m* ; *(= sort)* genre *m* ; *(= make of machine, coffee etc)* marque *f* ; *[of aircraft, car]* modèle *m* ◆ **books of all ~s** des livres de toutes sortes *or* de tous genres ◆ **a new ~ of plane, a new ~ plane*** un nouveau modèle d'avion ◆ **a Gruyère-~ cheese** un fromage genre gruyère* ◆ **what ~ do you want?** vous en (*or* le *or* la *etc*) voulez de quelle sorte ? ◆ **what ~ of car is it?** quel modèle de voiture est-ce ? ◆ **what ~ of man is he?** quel genre *or* type d'homme est-ce ? ◆ **what ~ of dog is he?** qu'est-ce que c'est comme (race de) chien ? ◆ **you know the ~ of thing I mean** vous voyez (à peu près) ce que je veux dire ◆ **he's not that ~ of person** ce n'est pas son genre ◆ **I know his ~!** je connais les gens de son genre *or* espèce ◆ **a queer ~** * *(= person)* un drôle de numéro* ◆ **he's not my ~** * ce n'est pas mon genre d'homme ◆ **it's my ~ of film** c'est le genre de film que j'aime *or* qui me plaît ; → **true**

2 *(= typical example)* type *m* (même), exemple *m* même ◆ **to deviate from the ~** s'éloigner du type ancestral ◆ **she was the very ~ of English beauty** c'était le type même *or* l'exemple même de la beauté anglaise ; → **revert**

3 *(Ling: gen)* type *m* ; (also **word-type**) vocable *m*

4 *(Typo)* *(= one letter)* caractère *m* ; *(= letters collectively)* caractères *mpl*, type *m* ◆ **to set ~** composer ◆ **to set sth (up) in ~** composer qch ◆ **in ~** composé ◆ **to keep the ~ set up** conserver la forme ◆ **in large/small ~** en gros/petits caractères ◆ **in italic ~** en italiques ; → **bold**

VT 1 *[+ blood sample etc]* classifier ◆ **he is now ~d as the kindly old man** *(Theat etc)* on ne lui donne plus que les rôles de doux vieillard ◆ **I don't want to be ~d** *(Theat)* je ne veux pas me cantonner dans un (seul) rôle

2 *[+ letter etc]* taper (à la machine)

VI *[typist etc]* taper à la machine ◆ **"clerk: must be able to type"** "employé(e) de bureau connaissant la dactylo"

COMP **type-cast** ADJ, VT → **typecast**

▸ **type in** VT SEP taper (à la machine)

▸ **type out** VT SEP 1 *[+ notes, letter]* taper (à la machine)

2 *[+ error]* effacer (à la machine)

▸ **type over** VT SEP ⇒ **type out 2**

▸ **type up** VT SEP *[+ notes]* taper (à la machine)

typecast /ˈtaɪpkɑːst/, **type-cast** *(Theat, Cine etc)* ADJ ◆ **to be ~** être enfermé dans un rôle ◆ **to be ~ as ...** être enfermé dans le rôle de ... VT *[+ actor, actress]* enfermer dans un rôle ◆ **to ~ as** enfermer dans le rôle de

typecasting /ˈtaɪpkɑːstɪŋ/ N ◆ **to avoid ~** éviter les stéréotypes ◆ **she wanted to break free of her ~ as the empty-headed blonde** elle ne voulait plus être enfermée dans des rôles de blonde écervelée

typeface /ˈtaɪpfeɪs/ N police *f* (de caractères)

typescript /ˈtaɪpskrɪpt/ N *(NonC)* manuscrit *m* *or* texte *m* dactylographié, tapuscrit *m* *(Tech)*

typeset /ˈtaɪpset/ VT composer

typesetter /ˈtaɪpsetəʳ/ N *(= person)* compositeur *m*, -trice *f* ; *(= machine)* linotype *f*, composeuse *f*

typesetting /ˈtaɪpsetɪŋ/ N *(NonC)* composition *f*

typewrite /ˈtaɪpraɪt/ VT taper (à la machine)

typewriter /ˈtaɪpraɪtəʳ/ N machine *f* à écrire

typewriting /ˈtaɪpraɪtɪŋ/ N dactylographie *f*

typewritten /ˈtaɪprɪtən/ ADJ tapé (à la machine), dactylographié

typhoid /ˈtaɪfɔɪd/ N (also **typhoid fever**) (fièvre *f*) typhoïde *f*

COMP *[symptom, victim]* de la typhoïde ; *[inoculation]* antityphoïdique

Typhoid Mary* N *(US fig)* source *f* d'infection

typhoon /taɪˈfuːn/ N typhon *m*

typhus /ˈtaɪfəs/ N typhus *m*

typical /ˈtɪpɪkəl/ ADJ *[day, behaviour, example]* typique (of de) ; *[price]* habituel ◆ **the ~ Frenchman** le Français type *or* moyen ◆ **a ~ Frenchman** un Français typique ◆ **he's a ~ teacher** c'est le type même du professeur ◆ **with ~ modesty, he ...** avec la modestie qui le caractérise, il ... ◆ **it was ~ of our luck that it was raining** avec la chance qui nous caractérise, il a plu ◆ **Louisa is ~ of many young women who ...** Louisa est un exemple typique de ces nombreuses jeunes femmes qui ... ◆ **that's ~ of him** c'est bien de lui ◆ **that's ~ of Paul** ça, c'est Paul tout craché !

typically /ˈtɪpɪkəlɪ/ ADV *(with adj)* typiquement ◆ **he is ~ English** il est typiquement anglais, c'est l'Anglais type ◆ **it's ~ French to do that** c'est très *or* bien français de faire ça ◆ **~, he arrived late** comme d'habitude, il est arrivé en retard ◆ **~, people apply for several jobs before getting an interview** en règle générale *or* généralement, on postule à plusieurs postes avant d'obtenir un entretien

typify /ˈtɪpɪfaɪ/ VT *[behaviour, incident, object]* illustrer parfaitement ; *[person]* être le type même de

typing /ˈtaɪpɪŋ/ N *(NonC)* 1 *(= skill)* dactylo *f*, dactylographie *f* ◆ **to learn ~** apprendre à taper (à la machine), apprendre la dactylo *or* la dactylographie 2 ◆ **there were several pages of ~ to read** il y avait plusieurs pages dactylographiées à lire

COMP *[lesson, teacher]* de dactylo, de dactylographie

typing error N faute *f* de frappe

typing paper N papier *m* machine

typing pool N bureau *m* *or* pool *m* de(s) dactylos ◆ **he works in the ~ pool** il est dactylo au pool ◆ **to send sth to the ~ pool** envoyer qch à la dactylo*

typing speed N ◆ **his ~ speed is 60** il tape 60 mots à la minute

typist /ˈtaɪpɪst/ N dactylo *mf*, dactylographe *mf* ; → **shorthand**

typo /ˈtaɪpəʊ/ N *(= error)* coquille *f* (typographique)

typographer /taɪˈpɒgrəfəʳ/ N typographe *mf*

typographic(al) /ˌtaɪpəˈgræfɪk(əl)/ ADJ typographique ◆ **~al error** erreur *f* typographique, coquille *f*

typography /taɪˈpɒgrəfɪ/ N typographie *f*

typological /ˌtaɪpəˈlɒdʒɪkəl/ ADJ typologique

typology /taɪˈpɒlədʒɪ/ N typologie *f*

tyrannic(al) /tɪˈrænɪk(əl)/ ADJ tyrannique

tyrannically /tɪˈrænɪkəlɪ/ ADV tyranniquement

tyrannicide /tɪˈrænɪsaɪd/ N *(= act)* tyrannicide *m* ; *(= person)* tyrannicide *mf*

tyrannize /ˈtɪrənaɪz/ VI ◆ **to ~ over sb** tyranniser qn VT tyranniser

tyrannosaur /tɪˈrænəsɔː/ N tyrannosaure *m*

tyrannosaurus /tɪˌrænəˈsɔːrəs/ N (also **tyrannosaurus rex**) tyrannosaure *m*, Tyrannosaurus rex *m*

tyrannous /ˈtɪrənəs/ ADJ tyrannique

tyrannously /ˈtɪrənəslɪ/ ADV tyranniquement

tyranny /ˈtɪrənɪ/ N tyrannie *f*

tyrant /ˈtaɪrənt/ N tyran *m*

Tyre /taɪəʳ/ N Tyr

tyre /ˈtaɪəʳ/ *(Brit)* N pneu *m* ; → **spare**

COMP **tyre gauge** N manomètre *m* (pour pneus)

tyre lever N démonte-pneu *m*

tyre pressure N pression *f* des pneus

tyre valve N valve *f* (de gonflage)

tyremaker /ˈtaɪəmeɪkəʳ/ N fabricant *m* de pneus

tyro /ˈtaɪrəʊ/ N novice *mf*, débutant(e) *m(f)*

Tyrol /tɪˈrəʊl/ N ◆ **(the) ~** le Tyrol

Tyrolean /ˌtɪrəˈli(ː)ən/, **Tyrolese** /ˌtɪrəˈliːz/ ADJ tyrolien ◆ **~ traverse** *(Climbing)* tyrolienne *f* N Tyrolien(ne) *m(f)*

Tyrrhenian /tɪˈriːnɪən/ ADJ ◆ **~ Sea** mer *f* Tyrrhénienne

tzar /zɑːʳ/ N ⇒ **tsar**

tzarina /zɑːˈriːnə/ N ⇒ **tsarina**

tzarist /ˈzɑːrɪst/ N, ADJ ⇒ **tsarist**

tzetze fly /ˈtsetsɪflaɪ/ N ⇒ **tsetse fly**

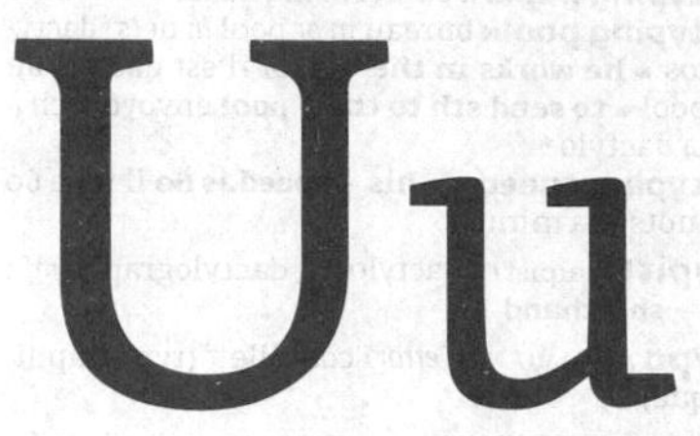

U, u /juː/ **N** 1 (= *letter*) U, u *m* ◆ **U for Uncle** ≈ U comme Ursule 2 (*Brit Cine*) (abbrev of **Universal**) ≈ tous publics ◆ **it's a U film** c'est un film pour tous publics **ADJ** (*Brit* † * = *upper-class*) [*word, accent, behaviour*] distingué
COMP **U-bend** **N** (*in pipe*) coude *m* ; (*Brit: in road*) coude *m*, virage *m* en épingle à cheveux
U-boat **N** sous-marin *m* allemand
U-lock **N** antivol *m* en U
U-shaped **ADJ** en (forme de) U
U-turn **N** (*Driving*) demi-tour *m* ; (*fig*) revirement *m*, volte-face *f* (*on* au sujet de) ◆ **"no U-turns"** "défense de faire demi-tour" ◆ **to make a U-turn on sth** faire volte-face au sujet de qch

UAE /ˌjuːeɪˈiː/ **N** (abbrev of **United Arab Emirates**) → **united**

UAW /ˌjuːeɪˈdʌbljuː/ **N** (*US*) (abbrev of **United Automobile Workers**) *syndicat*

UB40 /ˌjuːbiːˈfɔːtɪ/ **N** (*Brit: formerly*) (abbrev of **Unemployment Benefit 40**) *carte de demandeur d'emploi*

uber- /ˈuːbəʳ/ **PREF** super-

ubiquitous /juːˈbɪkwɪtəs/ **ADJ** omniprésent

ubiquity /juːˈbɪkwɪtɪ/ **N** omniprésence *f*

UCAS /ˈjuːkæs/ **N** (*Brit*) (abbrev of **Universities and Colleges Admissions Service**) → **university**

UCCA /ˈʌkə/ **N** (*Brit: formerly*) (abbrev of **Universities Central Council on Admissions**) *service central des inscriptions universitaires* ◆ **~ form** ≈ dossier *m* d'inscription universitaire

UDA /ˌjuːdiːˈeɪ/ **N** (*Brit*) (abbrev of **Ulster Defence Association**) → **Ulster**

UDC /ˌjuːdiːˈsiː/ **N** (*Brit Local Govt: formerly*) (abbrev of **Urban District Council**) → **urban**

udder /ˈʌdəʳ/ **N** pis *m*, mamelle *f*

UDI /ˌjuːdiːˈaɪ/ **N** (*Brit Pol*) (abbrev of **unilateral declaration of independence**) → **unilateral**

UDR /ˌjuːdiːˈɑːʳ/ **N** (*Brit*) (abbrev of **Ulster Defence Regiment**) → **Ulster**

UEFA /jʊˈeɪfə/ **N** (*Ftbl*) (abbrev of **Union of European Football Associations**) UEFA *f*

UFO /ˌjuːeˈfəʊ, ˈjuːfəʊ/ **N** (abbrev of **unidentified flying object**) ovni *m*

ufologist /juːˈfɒlədʒɪst/ **N** ufologue *mf*

ufology /juːˈfɒlədʒɪ/ **N** ufologie *f*

Uganda /juːˈgændə/ **N** Ouganda *m*

Ugandan /juːˈgændən/ **ADJ** ougandais **N** Ougandais(e) *m(f)*

UGC /ˌjuːdʒiːˈsiː/ **N** (*Brit: formerly*) (abbrev of **University Grants Committee**) → **university**

ugh /ɜːh/ **EXCL** pouah !

ugli /ˈʌglɪ/ **N** (pl **uglis** *or* **uglies**) tangelo *m*

uglify /ˈʌglɪfaɪ/ **VT** enlaidir, rendre laid

ugliness /ˈʌglɪnɪs/ **N** (*NonC*) laideur *f*

ugly /ˈʌglɪ/ **ADJ** 1 [*person, appearance, face, building, word*] laid ; [*wound, scar*] vilain *before n* ◆ **as ~ as sin** moche* comme un pou, laid comme un singe ◆ **~ duckling** (*fig*) vilain petit canard *m*
2 (*fig = unpleasant*) [*habit*] sale ◆ **he gave me an ~ look** il m'a regardé d'un sale œil ◆ **to be in an ~ mood** [*person*] être d'une humeur massacrante *or* exécrable ; [*crowd*] être menaçant ◆ **the ~ truth** l'horrible vérité *f* ◆ **to grow** *or* **turn ~** [*person*] se faire menaçant, montrer les dents ◆ **things** *or* **the mood turned ~ when …** les choses ont mal tourné *or* ont pris une mauvaise tournure quand … ◆ **the whole business is taking an ~ turn** l'affaire prend une sale tournure ◆ **the situation looks ~** la situation est affreuse ◆ **it is an ~ sight** ce n'est pas beau à voir ◆ **there were ~ scenes** il y a eu des scènes terribles ◆ **an ~ rumour** de vilains bruits *mpl* ◆ **"blackmail" is an ~ word** "chantage" est un vilain mot

UHF /ˌjuːeɪtʃˈef/ **N** (abbrev of **ultrahigh frequency**) UHF *f*

uh-huh * /ˈʌˌhʌ/ **EXCL** (= *yes*) oui oui

UHT /ˌjuːeɪtʃˈtiː/ **ADJ** (abbrev of **ultra heat treated**) [*milk etc*] UHT *inv*, longue conservation *inv*

uh-uh /ˈʌˌʌ/ **EXCL** (*warning*) hé !

UK /juːˈkeɪ/ **N** (abbrev of **United Kingdom**) Royaume-Uni *m* ◆ **in the ~** au Royaume-Uni ◆ **the ~ government** le gouvernement du Royaume-Uni ◆ **a ~ citizen** un citoyen du Royaume-Uni

uke ** /juːk/ **N** abbrev of **ukulele**

Ukraine /juːˈkreɪn/ **N** ◆ **(the) ~** l'Ukraine *f* ◆ **in (the) ~** en Ukraine

Ukrainian /juːˈkreɪnɪən/ **ADJ** ukrainien **N** 1 (= *person*) Ukrainien(ne) *m(f)* 2 (= *language*) ukrainien *m*

ukulele /ˌjuːkəˈleɪlɪ/ **N** guitare *f* hawaïenne

ULC /ˌjuːelˈsiː/ **N** (*US*) (abbrev of **ultra-large carrier**) superpétrolier *m*

ulcer /ˈʌlsəʳ/ **N** 1 (*Med*) ulcère *m* ◆ **to get an ~** attraper un ulcère 2 (*fig*) plaie *f*

ulcerate /ˈʌlsəreɪt/ **VT** ulcérer **VI** s'ulcérer

ulcerated /ˈʌlsəreɪtɪd/ **ADJ** ulcéreux

ulceration /ˌʌlsəˈreɪʃən/ **N** ulcération *f*

ulcerative /ˈʌlsəˌreɪtɪv/ **ADJ** ulcératif

ulcerous /ˈʌlsərəs/ **ADJ** (= *having ulcers*) ulcéreux ; (= *causing ulcers*) ulcératif

ullage /ˈʌlɪdʒ/ **N** (*Customs*) manquant *m*

'ullo * /əˈləʊ/ **EXCL** (*Brit*) ⇒ **hello**

ulna /ˈʌlnə/ **N** (pl **ulnas** *or* **ulnae** /ˈʌlniː/) cubitus *m*

ULSD /ˌjuːelesˈdiː/ **N** (abbrev of **Ultra Low Sulphur Diesel**) diesel *m* à faible teneur en soufre

Ulster /ˈʌlstəʳ/ **N** 1 (*Hist*) Ulster *m* 2 (= *Northern Ireland*) Irlande *f* du Nord 3 (= *coat*) **ulster** gros pardessus *m*
COMP de l'Ulster *or* de l'Irlande du Nord
Ulster Defence Association **N** *organisation paramilitaire protestante en Irlande du Nord*
Ulster Defence Regiment **N** *section de l'armée britannique en Irlande du Nord*
Ulster Volunteer Force **N** *organisation paramilitaire protestante en Irlande du Nord*

Ulsterman /ˈʌlstəmən/ **N** (pl **-men**) habitant *m* *or* natif *m* de l'Ulster

Ulsterwoman /ˈʌlstəwʊmən/ **N** (pl **-women**) habitante *f* *or* native *f* de l'Ulster

ulterior /ʌlˈtɪərɪəʳ/ **ADJ** ◆ **she meant it genuinely and had no ~ intentions** elle était sincère et sans arrière-pensée ◆ **~ motive** arrière-pensée *f*

ultimata /ˌʌltɪˈmeɪtə/ **NPL** of **ultimatum**

ultimate /ˈʌltɪmɪt/ **ADJ** 1 (= *final, eventual*) [*aim, destiny, solution*] final ; [*decision, result, outcome*] final, définitif ; [*victory, defeat*] final, ultime ; [*control, authority*] suprême ◆ **the ~ deterrent** (*Mil, fig*) l'ultime moyen *m* de dissuasion ◆ **the ~ weapon** (*Mil, fig*) l'arme *f* suprême ◆ **the ~ beneficiary/loser is …** en fin de compte, le bénéficiaire/le perdant est … ◆ **he came to the ~ conclusion that …** il a finalement conclu que … ◆ **death is the ~ sacrifice** la mort est le sacrifice suprême *or* l'ultime sacrifice ◆ **to make the ~ sacrifice** faire le sacrifice de sa vie
2 (= *best, most effective*) suprême ◆ **we have produced the ~ sports car** nous avons fabriqué le nec plus ultra de la voiture de sport ◆ **the ~ insult** l'insulte *f* suprême ◆ **the ~ (in) luxury/generosity** le summum du luxe/de la générosité ◆ **the ~ (in) selfishness/bad manners** le comble de l'égoïsme/de l'impolitesse
3 (= *basic*) [*principle, cause, truth*] fondamental, premier ◆ **~ constituent** (*Gram*) constituant *m* ultime
4 (= *furthest: gen*) le plus éloigné, le plus distant ; [*boundary of universe*] le plus reculé ; [*ancestor*] le plus éloigné ◆ **the ~ origins of man** les origines *fpl* premières de l'homme ◆ **the ~ frontiers of knowledge** les confins *mpl* du savoir

N ◆ **the ~ in comfort** le summum du confort, le fin du fin en matière de confort, le nec plus ultra du confort

ultimately /ˈʌltɪmɪtlɪ/ **ADV** 1 *(= finally, eventually)* en fin de compte ◆ **to ~ do sth** finir par faire qch ◆ **he was ~ successful/unsuccessful** il a finalement réussi/échoué ◆ **it may ~ be possible** ça sera peut-être possible, en fin de compte ◆ **~, this problem can only be solved in a court of law** en fin de compte, ce problème ne pourra être résolu que devant les tribunaux 2 *(= when all is said and done) [responsible]* en définitive ◆ **it ~ depends on you** en définitive *or* en fin de compte cela dépend de vous

ultimatum /ˌʌltɪˈmeɪtəm/ **N** (pl **ultimatums** *or* **ultimata**) ultimatum *m* ◆ **to deliver** *or* **issue an ~** adresser un ultimatum *(to* à)

ultra... /ˈʌltrə/ **PREF** ultra..., hyper...* ◆ **ultrasensitive** ultrasensible, hypersensible ◆ **ultra-right-wing** d'extrême droite ◆ **ultrafashionable** du tout dernier cri ◆ **ultrarich** richissime

ultrahigh /ˈʌltrəˈhaɪ/ **ADJ** ◆ **~ frequency** ultra-haute fréquence *f*

ultralight /ˈʌltrəˈlaɪt/ **ADJ** ultraléger **N** *(= aircraft)* ULM *m*, ultra-léger *m* motorisé

Ultra Low Sulphur Diesel **N** diesel *m* à faible teneur en soufre

ultramarine /ˌʌltrəməˈriːn/ **ADJ, N** (bleu) outremer *m inv*

ultramodern /ˈʌltrəˈmɒdən/ **ADJ** ultramoderne

ultramontane /ˌʌltrəˈmɒnteɪn/ **ADJ, N** ultramontain(e) *m(f)*

ultramontanism /ˌʌltrəˈmɒntɪnɪzəm/ **N** ultramontanisme *m*

ultrashort /ˈʌltrəˈʃɔːt/ **ADJ** ultracourt

ultrasonic /ˌʌltrəˈsɒnɪk/ **ADJ** ultrasonique **N** *(NonC)* ◆ **~s** science *f* des ultrasons

ultrasound /ˈʌltrəsaʊnd/ **N** *(NonC)* ultrasons *mpl* ◆ **to have ~** avoir une échographie

COMP *[equipment, machine]* à ultrasons

ultrasound examination, ultrasound scan **N** échographie *f*

ultrasound scanner **N** appareil *m* à échographie

ultraviolet /ˌʌltrəˈvaɪəlɪt/ **ADJ** ultraviolet ◆ **to have ~ treatment** *(Med)* se faire traiter aux rayons ultraviolets ◆ **~ radiation** rayons *mpl* ultraviolets

ultra vires /ˌʌltrəˈvaɪəriːz/ **ADV, ADJ** *(Jur)* ◆ **to be ~** constituer un abus de pouvoir ◆ **to act ~** outrepasser ses droits, commettre un abus de pouvoir

ululate /ˈjuːljʊleɪt/ **VI** *[owl]* (h)ululer ; *[dog]* hurler

ululation /ˌjuːljʊˈleɪʃən/ **N** hululement *m* ; *(in Arab context)* youyou *m*

Ulysses /juːˈlɪsiːz/ **N** Ulysse *m*

um /ʌm/ **INTERJ** euh **VI** ◆ **to ~ and err** * se tâter*, hésiter ◆ **after a lot of ~ming and erring*, he decided to buy it** après beaucoup d'hésitations il se décida à l'acheter

umber /ˈʌmbəʳ/ **ADJ, N** (terre *f* d')ombre *f*, terre *f* de Sienne ; → **burnt**

umbilical /ˌʌmbɪˈlaɪkəl/ **ADJ** ombilical **COMP** **umbilical cord** **N** cordon *m* ombilical

umbilicus /ˌʌmbɪˈlaɪkəs/ **N** (pl **umbilici** /ˌʌmbəˈlaɪsaɪ/) ombilic *m*, nombril *m*

umbrage /ˈʌmbrɪdʒ/ **N** *(NonC)* ombrage *m (fig)*, ressentiment *m* ◆ **to take ~** prendre ombrage, se froisser *(at* de)

umbrella /ʌmˈbrelə/ **N** 1 *(gen)* parapluie *m* ; *(against sun)* parasol *m* ◆ **to put up/put down an ~** ouvrir/fermer un parapluie ◆ **golf ~** parapluie *m* de golf ◆ **air ~** *(Mil)* écran *m* de protection aérienne ◆ **under the ~ of** *(fig) (= under the protection of)* sous la protection de ; *(= under the aegis of)* sous l'égide de ◆ **to come under the ~ of** relever de ; → **nuclear** 2 *[of jellyfish]* ombrelle *f* **ADJ** ◆ **~ body** *or* **organization** organisme *m* qui en chapeaute plusieurs autres ◆ **an ~ term** un terme générique

COMP **umbrella pine** **N** pin *m* parasol

umbrella stand **N** porte-parapluies *m inv*

Umbria /ˈʌmbrɪə/ **N** Ombrie *f*

Umbrian /ˈʌmbrɪən/ **ADJ** ombrien **N** Ombrien(ne) *m(f)*

umlaut /ˈʊmlaʊt/ **N** 1 *(NonC = vowel change)* inflexion *f* vocalique 2 *(= diaeresis)* tréma *m* ; *(in German)* umlaut *m*

ump* /ʌmp/ **N** *(US)* ⇒ **umpire**

umpire /ˈʌmpaɪəʳ/ **N** *(gen)* arbitre *m* ; *(Tennis)* juge *m* de chaise **VT** arbitrer **VI** servir d'arbitre, être l'arbitre

umpteen* /ˈʌmptiːn/ **ADJ** beaucoup de, je ne sais combien de ◆ **I've told you ~ times** je te l'ai dit je ne sais combien de fois *or* trente-six fois *or* cent fois ◆ **he had ~ books** il avait je ne sais combien de livres *or* des quantités de livres

umpteenth* /ˈʌmptiːnθ/ **ADJ** (é)nième

UN /juːˈen/ **N** (abbrev of **United Nations**) ONU *f*

'un* /ən/ **PRON** (= *one*) ◆ **he's a good ~** c'est un brave type* ◆ **she's a good ~** c'est une fille bien ◆ **little ~** petiot(e)* *m(f)*

unabashed /ˈʌnəˈbæʃt/ **ADJ** *[person]* nullement décontenancé *(by* par) ; *[love, desire, admiration]* dont on n'a pas honte ; *[greed]* sans mesure, sans bornes ◆ **he's an ~ romantic** c'est un romantique et il n'en a pas honte *or* il ne s'en cache pas ◆ **"yes" he said ~** "oui" dit-il sans se décontenancer *or* sans perdre contenance

unabated /ˈʌnəˈbeɪtɪd/ **ADJ** *[desire]* constant ◆ **she was exasperated by her husband's ~ drinking** elle était exaspérée par le fait que son mari buvait constamment ◆ **to remain ~** rester inchangé ◆ **with ~ interest** avec toujours autant d'intérêt ◆ **his ~ enthusiasm for the scheme** l'enthousiasme qu'il continuait à exprimer pour ce projet **ADV** sans relâche ◆ **to continue ~** se poursuivre sans relâche

unabbreviated /ˈʌnəˈbriːvɪeɪtɪd/ **ADJ** non abrégé, sans abréviation

unable /ˈʌnˈeɪbl/ LANGUAGE IN USE 12.3, 16.3, 16.4, 18.2, 25.1 **ADJ** ◆ **to be ~ to do sth** *(gen)* ne (pas) pouvoir faire qch ; *(= not know how to)* ne pas savoir faire qch ; *(= be incapable of)* être incapable de faire qch ; *(= be prevented from)* être dans l'impossibilité de faire qch, ne pas être en mesure de faire qch

unabridged /ˈʌnəˈbrɪdʒd/ **ADJ** intégral, non abrégé ◆ **~ edition/version** édition *f*/version *f* intégrale

unaccented /ˈʌnækˈsentɪd/, **unaccentuated** /ˈʌnækˈsentjʊeɪtɪd/ **ADJ** *[voice, speech]* sans accent ; *[syllable]* inaccentué, non accentué

unacceptable /ˈʌnəkˈseptəbl/ **ADJ** *[offer, suggestion]* inacceptable ; *[amount, degree, extent, level]* inadmissible ◆ **it's quite ~ that we should have to do this** il est inadmissible que nous devions faire cela ◆ **the ~ face of capitalism** la face honteuse du capitalisme

unacceptably /ˈʌnəkˈseptəblɪ/ **ADV** *[dangerous]* à un point inacceptable *or* inadmissible ◆ **the cost was ~ high** le coût était si élevé que c'était inacceptable ◆ **~ poor living conditions** des conditions *fpl* de vie inacceptables *or* inadmissibles ◆ **an ~ violent programme** un film d'une violence inacceptable *or* inadmissible ◆ **he suggested, quite ~, doing it later** il a suggéré de le faire plus tard, ce qui était tout à fait inacceptable *or* inadmissible

unaccommodating /ˈʌnəˈkɒmədeɪtɪŋ/ **ADJ** *(= disobliging)* désobligeant ; *(= not easy to deal with)* peu accommodant

unaccompanied /ˈʌnəˈkʌmpənɪd/ **ADJ** *[person, child, luggage]* non accompagné ; *(Mus) [singing]* sans accompagnement, a cappella ; *[instrument]* seul

unaccomplished /ˌʌnəˈkʌmplɪʃt/ **ADJ** 1 *(frm = unfinished) [work, task, journey]* inaccompli, inachevé ; *[project, desire]* inaccompli, non réalisé 2 *(= untalented) [person]* sans talents ; *[performance]* médiocre

unaccountable /ˈʌnəˈkaʊntəbl/ **ADJ** 1 *(= inexplicable)* inexplicable, sans raison apparente 2 ◆ **~ bureaucrats** des bureaucrates qui n'ont pas à rendre compte de leurs actes ◆ **MI5's operations remain secretive and relatively ~** MI5 continue de mener ses opérations dans le secret, sans quasiment en rendre compte à qui que ce soit ◆ **to be ~ to** *[+ person, official, organization]* ne pas avoir obligation de rendre compte à

unaccountably /ˈʌnəˈkaʊntəblɪ/ **ADV** ◆ **an ~ successful film** un film au succès inexplicable ◆ **~ popular** d'une popularité inexplicable ◆ **he felt ~ depressed** il se sentait déprimé sans savoir pourquoi ◆ **the messenger was ~ delayed** le messager a été retardé sans raison apparente ◆ **~, he felt sorry for her** sans comprendre pourquoi, il la plaignait

unaccounted /ˈʌnəˈkaʊntɪd/ **ADJ** ◆ **~ for** ◆ **two passengers are still ~ for** deux passagers sont toujours portés disparus *or* n'ont toujours pas été retrouvés ◆ **$5 is still ~ for** il manque encore 5 dollars ◆ **this is ~ for in the report** ceci n'est pas expliqué dans le rapport

unaccustomed /ˈʌnəˈkʌstəmd/ **ADJ** inaccoutumé, inhabituel ◆ **to be ~ to (doing) sth** ne pas avoir l'habitude de (faire) qch ◆ **~ as I am to public speaking ...** n'ayant pas l'habitude de prendre la parole en public ...

unacknowledged /ˈʌnəkˈnɒlɪdʒd/ **ADJ** *[letter]* dont on n'a pas accusé réception ; *[mistake, help, services]* non reconnu (publiquement) ; *[child]* non reconnu

unacquainted /ˈʌnəˈkweɪntɪd/ **ADJ** ◆ **to be ~ with the facts** ignorer les faits, ne pas être au courant des faits ◆ **she is ~ with poverty** elle ne sait pas ce que c'est que la pauvreté, elle ne connaît pas la pauvreté ◆ **to be ~ with sb** ne pas avoir fait la connaissance de qn ◆ **they are ~** ils ne se connaissent pas

unadaptable /ˈʌnəˈdæptəbl/ **ADJ** inadaptable, peu adaptable

unadapted /ˈʌnəˈdæptɪd/ **ADJ** mal adapté, inadapté *(to* à)

unaddressed /ˈʌnəˈdrest/ **ADJ** sans adresse, qui ne porte pas d'adresse

unadjusted /ˌʌnəˈdʒʌstɪd/ **ADJ** non corrigé ◆ **seasonally ~ employment figures** statistiques *fpl* du chômage non corrigées des variations saisonnières

unadopted /ˈʌnəˈdɒptɪd/ **ADJ** ◆ **many children remain ~** beaucoup d'enfants ne trouvent pas de parents adoptifs

unadorned /ˈʌnəˈdɔːnd/ **ADJ** sans ornement, tout simple ; *(fig) [truth]* pur, tout nu ◆ **beauty ~** la beauté sans artifice *or* sans fard

unadulterated /ˈʌnəˈdʌltəreɪtɪd/ **ADJ** pur, naturel ; *[food, wine]* non frelaté ; *[hell, nonsense]* pur (et simple)

unadventurous /ˈʌnədˈventʃərəs/ **ADJ** *[person, career, design, theatre production]* peu audacieux (-euse *f*) ◆ **where food is concerned, he is very ~** il est très conservateur dans ses goûts culinaires

unadventurously /ˈʌnədˈventʃərəslɪ/ **ADV** *[dressed, decorated]* de façon conventionnelle ;

[choose, decide] par manque d'audace *or* d'imagination

unadvertised /ˈʌnˈædvətaɪzd/ ADJ *[meeting, visit]* sans publicité, discret (-ète *f*)

unadvised /ˈʌnədˈvaɪzd/ ADJ 1 *(= lacking advice) [person]* qui n'a pas reçu de conseils 2 *(= ill-advised) [person]* malavisé, imprudent ; *[measures]* inconsidéré, imprudent

unaesthetic /ˌʌniːsˈθetɪk/ ADJ inesthétique, peu esthétique

unaffected /ˈʌnəˈfektɪd/ ADJ 1 *(= sincere) [person]* naturel, simple ; *[behaviour]* non affecté ; *[style]* sans recherche, simple 2 *(= unchanged)* non affecté ◆ **~ by damp/cold** non affecté par l'humidité/le froid, qui résiste à l'humidité/au froid ◆ **~ by heat** inaltérable à la chaleur ◆ **our plans were ~ by the strike** nos plans sont restés inchangés malgré la grève ◆ **they are ~ by the new legislation** ils ne sont pas affectés *or* touchés par la nouvelle législation ◆ **he was quite ~ by her sufferings** ses souffrances ne l'ont pas touché *or* l'ont laissé froid ◆ **he remained ~ by all the noise** il était indifférent à tout ce bruit

unaffectedly /ˈʌnəˈfektɪdlɪ/ ADV *[behave]* sans affectation ; *[dress]* simplement ◆ **her outfit was ~ stylish** sa tenue était à la fois simple et chic

unaffiliated /ˈʌnəˈfɪlɪeɪtɪd/ ADJ non affilié *(to* à)

unafraid /ˈʌnəˈfreɪd/ ADJ sans peur, qui n'a pas peur ◆ **to be ~ of (doing) sth** ne pas avoir peur de (faire) qch

unaided /ʌnˈeɪdɪd/ ADV *[walk, stand]* tout(e) seul(e) ; *[breathe]* sans aide extérieure ◆ **to reach the North Pole ~** atteindre le pôle Nord par ses propres moyens ◆ **she brought up six children ~** elle a élevé six enfants toute seule ADJ ◆ **his ~ work** le travail qu'il a fait tout seul *or* sans être aidé ◆ **by his own ~ efforts** par ses propres efforts *or* moyens

unaired /ˌʌnˈɛəd/ ADJ non aéré

unalike /ˈʌnəˈlaɪk/ ADJ peu ressemblant ◆ **to be ~** ne pas se ressembler ◆ **the two children are so ~** les deux enfants se ressemblent si peu

unalloyed /ˈʌnəˈlɔɪd/ ADJ *[happiness]* sans mélange, parfait ; *[metal]* non allié

unalterable /ʌnˈɒltərəbl/ ADJ *[rule]* invariable, immuable ; *[fact]* certain ; *[emotion, friendship]* inaltérable

unalterably /ʌnˈɒltərəblɪ/ ADV *[change, affect]* de façon permanente ; *[opposed]* définitivement ◆ **~ wicked** foncièrement méchant

unaltered /ʌnˈɒltəd/ ADJ inchangé, non modifié ◆ **his appearance was ~** physiquement il n'avait pas changé

unambiguous /ˈʌnæmˈbɪɡjʊəs/ ADJ *[statement, wording]* non ambigu (-guë *f*), non équivoque, clair ; *[order, thought]* clair

unambiguously /ˈʌnæmˈbɪɡjʊəslɪ/ ADV *[say, condemn, support]* sans ambiguïté, sans équivoque ◆ **he gave an ~ affirmative answer** il a répondu sans ambiguïté par l'affirmative

unambitious /ˈʌnæmˈbɪʃəs/ ADJ *[person]* sans ambition, peu ambitieux ; *[plan]* modeste

un-American /ˈʌnəˈmerɪkən/ ADJ 1 *(pej = anti-American)* anti-américain 2 *(not typical)* peu *or* pas américain

unamiable /ʌnˈeɪmɪəbl/ ADJ désagréable, peu aimable

unamused /ˈʌnəˈmjuːzd/ ADJ qui n'est pas amusé ◆ **the story left her ~** l'histoire ne l'a pas amusée du tout, elle n'a pas trouvé l'histoire amusante du tout

unanimity /ˌjuːnəˈnɪmɪtɪ/ N (NonC) unanimité *f*

unanimous /juːˈnænɪməs/ ADJ *[group, decision]* unanime ◆ **the committee was ~ in its condemnation of this** *or* **in condemning this** les membres du comité ont été unanimes pour *or* à condamner cela, les membres du comité ont condamné cela à l'unanimité ◆ **it was accepted by a ~ vote** cela a été voté à l'unanimité

unanimously /juːˈnænɪməslɪ/ ADV *[vote, elect]* à l'unanimité ; *[agree, pass]* unanimement, à l'unanimité ; *[condemn]* unanimement ◆ **~ favourable** unanimement favorable ◆ **the album received ~ good reviews** *or* **was ~ praised** l'album a fait l'unanimité

unannounced /ˈʌnəˈnaʊnst/ ADJ *[visitor, visit]* imprévu ◆ **to pay an ~ visit to sb** rendre visite à qn sans prévenir ; *(in more formal situations)* rendre visite à qn sans se faire annoncer ◆ **the President paid an ~ visit to the Swiss capital** le Président a effectué une visite-surprise dans la capitale helvétique ADV *[arrive, enter, turn up]* sans prévenir ; *(in more formal situations)* sans se faire annoncer

unanswerable /ʌnˈɑːnsərəbl/ ADJ *[question]* à laquelle il est impossible de répondre ; *[argument]* irréfutable, incontestable

unanswered /ˈʌnˈɑːnsəd/ ADJ *[letter, request, question]* (qui reste) sans réponse ; *[problem, puzzle]* non résolu ; *[criticism, argument]* non réfuté ; *[prayer]* inexaucé ; *(Jur) [charge]* irréfuté ◆ **her letter remained ~** sa lettre est restée sans réponse ◆ **there was a pile of ~ letters on his desk** sur son bureau, il y avait une pile de lettres en attente *or* une pile de lettres auxquelles il n'avait pas (encore) répondu

unappealing /ˈʌnəˈpiːlɪŋ/ ADJ peu attirant, peu attrayant

unappetizing /ˈʌnˈæpɪtaɪzɪŋ/ ADJ *(lit, fig)* peu appétissant

unappreciated /ˈʌnəˈpriːʃɪeɪtɪd/ ADJ *[person]* méconnu, incompris ; *[offer, help]* non apprécié

unappreciative /ˈʌnəˈpriːʃɪətɪv/ ADJ *[audience]* froid, indifférent ◆ **to be ~ of sth** ne pas apprécier qch, rester indifférent à qch

unapproachable /ˈʌnəˈprəʊtʃəbl/ ADJ d'un abord difficile, inabordable

unarguable /ʌnˈɑːɡjʊəbl/ ADJ incontestable

unarguably /ʌnˈɑːɡjʊəblɪ/ ADV incontestablement

unarmed /ˈʌnˈɑːmd/ ADJ *[person]* non armé ; *[ship, plane]* sans armes ◆ **he is ~** il n'est pas armé ADV sans armes COMP **unarmed combat** N combat *m* à mains nues

unashamed /ˈʌnəˈʃeɪmd/ ADJ *[pleasure, delight, admiration]* non déguisé ; *[greed, luxury]* dont on n'a pas honte ◆ **he was quite ~ about it** il n'en éprouvait pas la moindre honte *or* gêne ◆ **he was an ~ admirer of Mussolini** il admirait Mussolini et ne s'en cachait pas

unashamedly /ˈʌnəˈʃeɪmɪdlɪ/ ADV *[say, cry]* sans aucune gêne ◆ **~ romantic** qui ne cache pas son romantisme ◆ **~ luxurious** d'un luxe sans complexes ◆ **he was ~ delighted about it** il en était réjoui et ne s'en cachait pas ◆ **he was ~ selfish/a liar** c'était un égoïste/un menteur et il ne s'en cachait pas

unasked /ˈʌnˈɑːskt/ ADJ *[question]* non formulé ◆ **significant questions will go ~** certaines questions importantes ne seront pas posées ◆ **this was ~ for** on ne l'avait pas demandé ADV ◆ **she did it ~** elle l'a fait sans qu'on le lui ait demandé *or* de son propre chef ◆ **he came in ~** il est entré sans y avoir été invité

unaspirated /ˈʌnˈæspəreɪtɪd/ ADJ *(Phon)* non aspiré

unassailable /ˌʌnəˈseɪləbl/ ADJ *[fortress]* imprenable ; *[position, reputation]* inattaquable ; *[argument, reason]* irréfutable, inattaquable ◆ **he is quite ~ on that point** ses arguments sont irréfutables sur ce point, on ne peut pas l'attaquer sur ce point

unassisted /ˈʌnəˈsɪstɪd/ ADV tout seul, sans aide ADJ tout seul

unassuming /ˈʌnəˈsjuːmɪŋ/ ADJ sans prétentions, modeste

unassumingly /ˈʌnəˈsjuːmɪŋlɪ/ ADV modestement, sans prétentions

unattached /ˈʌnəˈtætʃt/ ADJ *[part etc]* non attaché *(to* à), libre *(to* de) ; *(fig) [person, group]* indépendant *(to* de) ; *(= not married etc)* libre, sans attaches ; *(Jur)* non saisi

unattainable /ˈʌnəˈteɪnəbl/ ADJ *[place, objective, person]* inaccessible

unattended /ˈʌnəˈtendɪd/ ADJ 1 *(= not looked after) [shop, machine, luggage]* (laissé) sans surveillance ; *[child]* sans surveillance, (tout) seul ◆ **do not leave your luggage ~** ne laissez pas vos bagages sans surveillance ◆ **~ to** négligé 2 *(= unaccompanied) [king etc]* seul, sans escorte

unattractive /ˈʌnəˈtræktɪv/ ADJ *[appearance, house, idea]* peu attrayant, peu séduisant ; *[person, character]* déplaisant, peu sympathique

unattractiveness /ˈʌnəˈtræktɪvnɪs/ N (NonC) manque *m* d'attrait *or* de beauté

unattributed /ˈʌnəˈtrɪbuːtɪd/ ADJ *[quotation, remark]* non attribué ; *[source]* non cité, non indiqué

unauthenticated /ˈʌnɔːˈθentɪkeɪtɪd/ ADJ *[evidence]* non établi ; *[signature]* non authentifié

unauthorized /ˈʌnˈɔːθəraɪzd/ ADJ *(gen)* non autorisé, (fait) sans autorisation ◆ **this was ~** cela a été fait sans autorisation ◆ **~ absence** absence *f* irrégulière ◆ **~ signature** *(Jur)* signature *f* usurpatoire

unavailable /ˈʌnəˈveɪləbl/ ADJ *[funds]* indisponible ; *(Comm) [article]* épuisé, qu'on ne peut se procurer ; *[person]* indisponible, qui n'est pas disponible *or* libre ◆ **the Minister was ~ for comment** le ministre s'est refusé à toute déclaration

unavailing /ˈʌnəˈveɪlɪŋ/ ADJ *[effort]* vain, inutile ; *[remedy, method]* inefficace

unavailingly /ˈʌnəˈveɪlɪŋlɪ/ ADV en vain, sans succès

unavoidable /ˌʌnəˈvɔɪdəbl/ ADJ inévitable ◆ **it is ~ that ...** il est inévitable que ... + *subj*

unavoidably /ˌʌnəˈvɔɪdəblɪ/ ADV inévitablement ◆ **he was ~ delayed** *or* **detained** il n'a pu éviter d'être retardé

unaware /ˈʌnəˈwɛəʳ/ ADJ ◆ **to be ~ of sth** ignorer qch, ne pas être conscient de qch, ne pas avoir conscience de qch ◆ **to be ~ that ...** ignorer que ..., ne pas savoir que ... ◆ **"stop" he said, ~ of the danger** "arrête" dit-il, ignorant *or* inconscient du danger ◆ **I was not ~ that ...** je n'étais pas sans savoir que ... ◆ **he is politically quite ~** il n'a aucune conscience politique, il n'est pas politisé

unawareness /ˌʌnəˈwɛənɪs/ N ignorance *f*

unawares /ˈʌnəˈwɛəz/ ADV 1 *(= by surprise)* à l'improviste, au dépourvu ◆ **to catch** *or* **take sb ~** prendre qn à l'improviste *or* au dépourvu 2 *(= without realizing)* inconsciemment, par mégarde

unbacked /ˈʌnˈbækt/ ADJ *(Fin)* à découvert

unbalance /ˈʌnˈbæləns/ VT déséquilibrer N déséquilibre *m*

unbalanced /ˈʌnˈbælənst/ ADJ 1 *(physically)* mal équilibré ; *(mentally)* déséquilibré ◆ **his mind was ~** il était déséquilibré 2 *(Fin) [account]* non soldé

unban /ˈʌnˈbæn/ VT ◆ **to ~ an organization** lever l'interdiction frappant une organisation

unbandage /ʌn'bændɪdʒ/ VT [+ limb, wound] débander ; [+ person] ôter ses bandages or ses pansements à

unbaptized /ʌnbæp'taɪzd/ ADJ non baptisé

unbar /'ʌn'bɑːʳ/ VT [+ door] débarrer, enlever la barre de

unbearable /ʌn'bɛərəbl/ ADJ insupportable

unbearably /ʌn'bɛərəblɪ/ ADV [sad, painful, loud] insupportablement ◆ **it's ~ hot/cold today** aujourd'hui il fait une chaleur/un froid insupportable

unbeatable /ʌn'biːtəbl/ ADJ imbattable

unbeaten /'ʌn'biːtn/ ADJ [army, player, team] invaincu ; [record, price] non battu

unbecoming /'ʌnbɪ'kʌmɪŋ/ ADJ [garment] peu seyant, qui ne va or ne sied pas ; (fig) [behaviour] malséant, inconvenant

unbeknown(st) /'ʌnbɪ'nəʊn(st)/ ADJ, ADV ◆ **~(st) to ...** à l'insu de ... ◆ **~(st) to me** à mon insu

unbelief /'ʌnbɪ'liːf/ N (also Rel) incrédulité f ◆ **in ~, with an air of ~** d'un air incrédule

unbelievable /ˌʌnbɪ'liːvəbl/ ADJ incroyable ◆ **it is ~ that ...** il est incroyable que ... + subj

unbelievably /ˌʌnbɪ'liːvəblɪ/ ADV [beautiful, stupid, selfish etc] incroyablement ◆ **to be ~ lucky/successful** avoir une chance/un succès incroyable ◆ **~, he refused** aussi incroyable que cela puisse paraître, il a refusé

unbeliever /'ʌnbɪ'liːvəʳ/ N (also Rel) incrédule mf

unbelieving /'ʌnbɪ'liːvɪŋ/ ADJ (also Rel) incrédule

unbelievingly /'ʌnbɪ'liːvɪŋlɪ/ ADV d'un air incrédule

unbend /'ʌn'bend/ (pret, ptp **unbent**) VT [+ pipe, wire] redresser, détordre VI [person] s'assouplir ◆ **he unbent enough to ask me how I was** il a daigné me demander comment j'allais

unbending /ʌn'bendɪŋ/ ADJ non flexible, rigide ; (fig) [person, attitude] inflexible, intransigeant

unbent /ʌn'bent/ VB pt, ptp of **unbend**

unbias(s)ed /ʌn'baɪəst/ ADJ impartial

unbidden /ʌn'bɪdn/ ADV (liter) ◆ **she did it ~** elle l'a fait de son propre chef or sans qu'on le lui ait demandé ◆ **he came in ~** il est entré sans y avoir été invité ◆ **the phrase sprang ~ to her mind/lips** l'expression lui est venue spontanément à l'esprit/aux lèvres

unbind /'ʌn'baɪnd/ (pret, ptp **unbound**) VT (= free) délier ; (= untie) dénouer, défaire ; (= unbandage) débander ; see also **unbound**

unbleached /'ʌn'bliːtʃt/ ADJ [linen] écru ; [hair] non décoloré ; [flour] non traité

unblemished /ʌn'blemɪʃt/ ADJ (lit, fig) sans tache

unblinking /ʌn'blɪŋkɪŋ/ ADJ [person] imperturbable, impassible ◆ **he gave me an ~ stare, he looked at me with ~ eyes** il m'a regardé sans ciller

unblinkingly /ʌn'blɪŋkɪŋlɪ/ ADV [stare] sans ciller

unblock /'ʌn'blɒk/ VT [+ sink, pipe] déboucher ; [+ road, harbour, traffic] dégager

unblushing /ʌn'blʌʃɪŋ/ ADJ effronté, éhonté

unblushingly /ʌn'blʌʃɪŋlɪ/ ADV sans rougir (fig), effrontément

unbolt /'ʌn'bəʊlt/ VT [+ door] déverrouiller, tirer le verrou de ; [+ beam] déboulonner

unborn /'ʌn'bɔːn/ ADJ ◆ **the ~ child** le fœtus ◆ **generations yet ~** les générations fpl futures or à venir

unbosom /ʌn'bʊzəm/ VT ◆ **to ~ o.s. to sb** ouvrir son cœur à qn, se confier à qn

unbound /'ʌn'baʊnd/ VB pt, ptp of **unbind** ADJ [prisoner, hands, feet] non lié ; [seam] non bordé ; [book] broché, non relié ; [periodical] non relié

unbounded /ʌn'baʊndɪd/ ADJ [joy, gratitude] sans borne, illimité ; [conceit, pride] démesuré ; [ignorance] sans fond

unbowed /'ʌn'baʊd/ ADJ (fig) insoumis, invaincu ◆ **with head ~** la tête haute

unbreakable /'ʌn'breɪkəbl/ ADJ incassable ; (fig) [promise, treaty] sacré

unbreathable /'ʌn'briːðəbl/ ADJ irrespirable

unbribable /'ʌn'braɪbəbl/ ADJ incorruptible, qui ne se laisse pas acheter

unbridgeable /'ʌn'brɪdʒəbl/ ADJ (fig) ◆ **an ~ gap or gulf** une divergence irréconciliable

unbridled /ʌn'braɪdld/ ADJ (fig) débridé, déchaîné, effréné

unbroken /'ʌn'brəʊkən/ ADJ 1 (= intact) [crockery, limb] non cassé ; [seal] intact, non brisé ; [skin] intact, non déchiré ; [ice] intact ; [record] non battu ; [promise] tenu ◆ **his spirit remained ~** il ne se décourageait pas 2 (= continuous) [series, silence, sleep] ininterrompu ◆ **~ line** (on road) ligne f continue ◆ **descended in an ~ line from Edward II** qui descend en ligne directe d'Édouard II ◆ **she was in government for ten ~ years** elle a été au gouvernement pendant dix années de suite ◆ **a whole morning of ~ sunshine** une matinée entière de soleil sans nuages 3 [horse] indompté 4 [voice] qui n'a pas mué

unbuckle /'ʌn'bʌkl/ VT déboucler

unbundle /ʌn'bʌndl/ VT 1 (gen) séparer, dégrouper 2 (Fin) (after a buyout) vendre par appartements ; (= price into separate items) détailler, tarifer séparément

unburden /ʌn'bɜːdn/ VT [+ conscience] soulager ; [+ heart] épancher ◆ **to ~ o.s.** s'épancher (to sb avec qn), se livrer (to sb à qn) ◆ **to ~ o.s. of sth** se décharger de qch

unburied /'ʌn'berɪd/ ADJ non enterré, non enseveli

unbusinesslike /ʌn'bɪznɪslaɪk/ ADJ [trader, dealer] qui n'a pas le sens des affaires, peu commerçant ; [transaction] irrégulier ; (fig) [person] qui manque de méthode or d'organisation ; [report] peu méthodique

unbutton /'ʌn'bʌtn/ VT [+ shirt, coat, trousers etc] déboutonner ; [+ button] défaire

uncalled-for /ʌn'kɔːldfɔːʳ/ ADJ [criticism] injustifié ; [remark] déplacé ◆ **that was quite ~** c'était tout à fait déplacé

uncannily /ʌn'kænɪlɪ/ ADV étrangement ◆ **to look ~ like sb/sth** ressembler étrangement à qn/qch

uncanny /ʌn'kænɪ/ ADJ [sound] mystérieux, étrange ; [atmosphere, silence] étrange ; [mystery, event, question, resemblance, accuracy, knack] troublant ◆ **it's ~ how he does it** je ne m'explique vraiment pas comment il fait cela

uncap /'ʌn'kæp/ VT [+ bottle] décapsuler

uncapped /'ʌn'kæpt/ ADJ (Brit Sport) [player] (for country) qui n'a pas encore été sélectionné en équipe nationale ; (for university) qui n'a pas encore été sélectionné dans l'équipe de son université

uncared-for /'ʌn'kɛədfɔːʳ/ ADJ [garden, building] négligé, (laissé) à l'abandon ; [appearance] négligé, peu soigné ; [child] laissé à l'abandon, délaissé

uncaring /ˌʌn'kɛərɪŋ/ ADJ insensible, indifférent

uncarpeted /'ʌn'kɑːpɪtɪd/ ADJ sans tapis

uncashed /'ʌn'kæʃəd/ ADJ [cheque] non encaissé

uncatalogued /'ʌn'kætəlɒgd/ ADJ qui n'a pas été catalogué

uncaught /'ʌn'kɔːt/ ADJ [criminal] qui n'a pas été appréhendé or pris

unceasing /ʌn'siːsɪŋ/ ADJ incessant, continu, continuel

unceasingly /ʌn'siːsɪŋlɪ/ ADV sans cesse

uncensored /'ʌn'sensəd/ ADJ [letter] non censuré ; [film, book] non censuré, non expurgé

unceremonious /'ʌnˌserɪ'məʊnɪəs/ ADJ brusque

unceremoniously /'ʌnˌserɪ'məʊnɪəslɪ/ ADV 1 (= without ceremony) [bury] sans cérémonie 2 (= abruptly) [eject] brusquement

uncertain /ʌn'sɜːtn/ LANGUAGE IN USE 16.1 ADJ [person] incertain, qui n'est pas sûr or certain ; [voice, smile, steps] mal assuré, hésitant ; [age, date, weather] incertain ; [result, effect] incertain, aléatoire ; [temper] inégal ◆ **it is ~ whether ...** il n'est pas certain or sûr que ... + subj ◆ **he is ~ (as to) whether ...** il ne sait pas au juste si ... + indic, il n'est pas sûr que ... + subj ◆ **to be ~ about sth** être incertain de qch, ne pas être certain or sûr de qch, avoir des doutes sur qch ◆ **he was ~ about what he was going to do** il était incertain de ce qu'il allait faire, il ne savait pas au juste ce qu'il allait faire ◆ **in no ~ terms** sans ambages, en des termes on ne peut plus clairs

uncertainly /ʌn'sɜːtnlɪ/ ADV [say] d'une manière hésitante ; [stand] avec hésitation ; [smile, laugh, look at] d'un air hésitant

uncertainty /ʌn'sɜːtntɪ/ N incertitude f, doute(s) m(pl) ◆ **in order to remove any ~** pour dissiper des doutes éventuels ◆ **in view of this ~ or these uncertainties** en raison de l'incertitude dans laquelle nous nous trouvons or de ces incertitudes

uncertificated /'ʌnsə'tɪfɪkeɪtɪd/ ADJ (gen) non diplômé ; [secondary teacher] non certifié

uncertified /'ʌn'sɜːtɪfaɪd/ ADJ [document etc] non certifié ◆ **~ teacher** (US) ≃ maître m auxiliaire

unchain /'ʌn'tʃeɪn/ VT (fig) [+ passions, reaction] déchaîner ; (lit) [+ dog] lâcher

unchallengeable /'ʌn'tʃælɪndʒəbl/ ADJ indiscutable, incontestable

unchallenged /'ʌn'tʃælɪndʒd/ ADJ [authority, position, superiority] incontesté, indiscuté ; [master, champion] incontesté ; [action, policy, statement] non contesté ; [argument, comment] non relevé ; (Jur) [juror, witness] non récusé ADV 1 (= without being opposed) ◆ **to go ~** [authority, position] ne pas être contesté, ne pas être discuté ; [person, action] ne pas rencontrer d'opposition, ne pas être contesté ; [policy, statement] ne pas être contesté ; [argument, comment] ne pas être relevé ; [juror, witness] ne pas être récusé ◆ **to leave sb ~** [+ leader] ne pas contester qn ; [+ candidate] ne pas s'opposer à qn ◆ **she couldn't let that go or pass ~** elle ne pouvait pas laisser passer cela sans protester 2 (= without being stopped) ◆ **to do sth ~** [person] faire qch sans être arrêté ◆ **he slipped ~ through the enemy lines** il a passé au travers des lignes ennemies sans être interpellé

unchangeable /ʌn'tʃeɪndʒəbl/ ADJ [person, system, fact] immuable

unchanged /'ʌn'tʃeɪndʒd/ ADJ inchangé

unchanging /ʌn'tʃeɪndʒɪŋ/ ADJ qui ne change pas, immuable

uncharacteristic /ˌʌnkærɪktə'rɪstɪk/ ADJ [behaviour, emotion, smile] qui ne lui (or leur etc) ressemble (or ressemblait) pas ; [mistake] qui n'est pas caractéristique ◆ **it is ~ of or for him (to do that)** cela ne lui ressemble pas (de faire cela), ce n'est pas son genre (de faire cela)

uncharacteristically /ˌʌnkærɪktə'rɪstɪklɪ/ ADV ◆ **~ rude/generous** d'une grossièreté/générosité peu caractéristique ◆ **she was ~ silent** elle était silencieuse, ce qui ne lui ressemblait pas

♦ **he behaved ~** il s'est comporté d'une façon qui ne lui ressemblait pas ♦ **~, he had overlooked an important detail** il avait laissé passer un détail important, ce qui ne lui ressemblait pas *or* n'était pas son genre

uncharged /ˈʌnˈtʃɑːdʒd/ ADJ *(Elec)* non chargé ; *(Jur)* non accusé ; *[gun]* non chargé

uncharitable /ʌnˈtʃærɪtəbl/ ADJ peu indulgent, peu charitable

uncharitably /ʌnˈtʃærɪtəblɪ/ ADV *[think]* avec peu d'indulgence, peu charitablement ; *[say, describe]* avec peu d'indulgence, de manière peu charitable

uncharted /ˈʌnˈtʃɑːtɪd/ ADJ 1 *(lit = unmapped) [area, sea]* dont on n'a *(or* n'avait) pas dressé la carte ; *(= not on map) [island]* qui ne figure *(or* figurait) sur aucune carte 2 *(fig = unknown)* ♦ **a largely ~ area of medical science** un domaine de la médecine largement inexploré ♦ **these are ~ waters** *or* **this is ~ territory (for sb)** c'est un terrain inconnu (pour qn) ♦ **to be in/enter ~ waters** *or* **territory** être/pénétrer en terrain inconnu

unchartered /ˈʌnˈtʃɑːtəd/ ADJ *[area]* mal connu, inexploré ; *[territory]* peu familier

unchaste /ˈʌnˈtʃeɪst/ ADJ non chaste, lascif

unchecked /ˈʌnˈtʃekt/ ADJ 1 *(= unrestrained) [growth, power]* non maîtrisé, non contenu ; *[emotion, anger]* non réprimé ; *[power]* illimité, sans restriction ♦ **if left ~, weeds will flourish** si on ne les arrête pas, les mauvaises herbes proliféreront 2 *(= not verified) [data, statement]* non vérifié ; *[typescript]* non relu ADV ♦ **to go ~** *[expansion, power]* ne pas être maîtrisé *or* contenu ; *[anger, aggression]* ne pas être réprimé ♦ **if the spread of AIDS continues ~ ...** si on ne fait rien pour empêcher la propagation du sida ... ♦ **they advanced ~ for several kilometres** *(Mil)* ils ont fait plusieurs kilomètres sans rencontrer d'obstacle

unchivalrous /ˈʌnˈʃɪvəlrəs/ ADJ peu galant, discourtois

unchristian /ˈʌnˈkrɪstjən/ ADJ peu chrétien, contraire à l'esprit chrétien

uncial /ˈʌnsɪəl/ ADJ oncial N onciale *f*

uncircumcised /ˈʌnˈsɜːkəmsaɪzd/ ADJ incirconcis

uncivil /ˈʌnˈsɪvɪl/ ADJ *[person, behaviour]* impoli *(to sb* avec qn), incivil *(liter) (to sb* avec qn) ♦ **it would be ~ to refuse** il serait impoli de refuser ♦ **it was very ~ of you to behave like that** ça a été très impoli de votre part de vous comporter ainsi

uncivilized /ˈʌnˈsɪvɪlaɪzd/ ADJ 1 *(= primitive) [people, country]* non civilisé 2 *(= socially unacceptable) [conditions, activity]* inacceptable ; *[person, behaviour]* grossier ♦ **what an ~ thing to do!** quelle grossièreté ! ♦ **how ~ of him!** comme c'est grossier de sa part ! 3 *(* = early)* ♦ **at an ~ time** *or* **hour** à une heure impossible* *or* indue ♦ **sorry to wake you at this ~ hour** désolé de vous réveiller à cette heure indue ♦ **what an ~ time to ring up!** ce n'est pas une heure pour téléphoner !

uncivilly /ˈʌnˈsɪvɪlɪ/ ADV impoliment, incivilement *(liter)*

unclad /ˈʌnˈklæd/ ADJ *(liter)* sans vêtements, nu

unclaimed /ˈʌnˈkleɪmd/ ADJ *[property, prize, body]* non réclamé ♦ **to go ~** ne pas être réclamé

unclasp /ˈʌnˈklɑːsp/ VT *[+ necklace]* défaire, dégrafer ; *[+ hands]* ouvrir

unclassed /ˈʌnˈklɑːst/ ADJ non classé

unclassified /ˈʌnˈklæsɪfaɪd/ ADJ 1 *(= not sorted) [items, papers, waste, football results]* non classé 2 *(= not secret) [information, document]* non classifié, non (classé) secret

COMP **unclassified degree** N *(Brit Univ)* licence sans mention accordée lorsque toutes les épreuves n'ont pas été passées

unclassified road N route *f* non classée

uncle /ˈʌŋkl/ N oncle *m* ♦ **yes ~** *(in child's language)* oui tonton*, oui mon oncle ♦ **to say** *or* **cry ~*** *(US)* s'avouer vaincu ♦ **Uncle Sam** l'oncle *m* Sam ♦ **Uncle Tom**‡ *(US pej)* bon nègre *m* ; → **Dutch**

unclean /ˈʌnˈkliːn/ ADJ 1 *(= dirty) [person, hands, room]* sale 2 *(= impure) [person, animal, activity, thoughts]* impur 3 *(= diseased: traditionally said by lepers: also hum)* ♦ **"unclean, unclean!"** "ne vous approchez pas, je suis contagieux !"

unclear /ˌʌnˈklɪəʳ/ ADJ 1 *(= not obvious, confusing) [reason, motive, message, details, instructions, policy]* qui n'est pas clair, obscur ; *[result, outcome]* incertain ♦ **it is ~ whether/who/why** *etc* **...** on ne sait pas bien si/qui/pourquoi *etc* ... ♦ **it's ~ to me whether/who/why** *etc* **...** je ne sais pas vraiment si/qui/pourquoi *etc* ... ♦ **her purpose remains ~** on ne sait toujours pas très bien où elle veut en venir 2 *(= indistinct) [picture, image]* qui n'est pas net, flou ; *[handwriting]* qui n'est pas net ; *[answer, words]* indistinct 3 *(= unsure)* ♦ **I'm ~ on this point** je ne sais pas vraiment à quoi m'en tenir là-dessus, pour moi, ce point n'est pas clair ♦ **I'm ~ whether you agree or not** je ne suis pas sûr de comprendre si vous êtes d'accord ou pas

unclench /ˈʌnˈklentʃ/ VT desserrer

unclimbed /ˈʌnˈklaɪmd/ ADJ *[mountain, peak]* vierge

uncloak /ˈʌnˈkləʊk/ VT *(fig) [+ person]* démasquer ; *[+ mystery, plot]* dévoiler

unclog /ˈʌnˈklɒg/ VT *[+ pipe]* déboucher ; *[+ wheel]* débloquer

unclothe /ˈʌnˈkləʊð/ VT déshabiller, dévêtir

unclothed /ˈʌnˈkləʊðd/ ADJ *(frm) [person]* dévêtu ; *[body]* dévêtu, nu

unclouded /ˈʌnˈklaʊdɪd/ ADJ *[sky]* sans nuages, dégagé ; *[liquid]* clair, limpide ; *(fig) [happiness]* sans nuages, parfait ; *[future]* sans nuages

uncluttered /ˈʌnˈklʌtəd/ ADJ *[room, composition]* dépouillé

uncoil /ˈʌnˈkɔɪl/ VT dérouler VI se dérouler

uncollectable /ˈʌnkəˈlektəbl/ ADJ *[tax]* impossible à percevoir

uncollected /ˈʌnkəˈlektɪd/ ADJ *[tax]* non perçu ; *[bus fare]* non encaissé ; *[luggage, lost property]* non réclamé ; *[refuse]* non ramassé, non enlevé

uncoloured, uncolored *(US)* /ˈʌnˈkʌləd/ ADJ 1 *(= colourless) [glass, plastic, liquid]* non coloré ; *[hair]* non teint 2 *(= unbiased) [account, description, judgement]* non faussé *(by sth* par qch)

uncombed /ˈʌnˈkəʊmd/ ADJ *[hair, wool]* non peigné ; *[look, appearance]* ébouriffé

un-come-at-able* /ˈʌnkʌmˈætəbl/ ADJ inaccessible

uncomely /ˈʌnˈkʌmlɪ/ ADJ *[person]* laid, peu joli ; *[clothes]* peu seyant

uncomfortable /ʌnˈkʌmfətəbl/ ADJ 1 *(= feeling physical discomfort)* ♦ **to be** *or* **feel ~** *[person] (in chair, bed, room)* ne pas être à l'aise ♦ **are you ~ there?** vous n'êtes pas à l'aise ? ♦ **you look rather ~** vous avez l'air plutôt mal à l'aise

2 *(= causing physical discomfort) [position, chair, shoes, journey]* inconfortable ; *[heat]* incommodant

3 *(= feeling unease) [person]* mal à l'aise *(with sb* avec qn) ♦ **~ doing sth** mal à l'aise de faire qch ♦ **~ about sth/about doing sth** mal à l'aise à propos de qch/à l'idée de faire qch ♦ **to be ~ with the idea of (doing) sth** être mal à l'aise à l'idée de (faire) qch ♦ **I was ~ with the whole business** toute cette affaire me mettait mal à l'aise ♦ **to make sb ~** mettre qn mal à l'aise

4 *(= causing unease) [silence]* pesant ; *[situation]* inconfortable ; *[afternoon, feeling]* désagréable ; *[truth, fact]* gênant ♦ **to have an ~ feeling that ...** avoir la désagréable impression que ... ♦ **the situation is ~ for her** cette situation la met mal à l'aise ♦ **to make life ~ for sb** mener la vie dure à qn ♦ **to make things ~ for sb** créer des ennuis à qn ♦ **to put sb in an ~ position** mettre qn dans une situation inconfortable ♦ **to have an ~ time** passer un mauvais quart d'heure ; *(longer)* connaître des moments difficiles

uncomfortably /ʌnˈkʌmfətəblɪ/ ADV 1 *(= unpleasantly) [tight]* trop ♦ **I'm feeling ~ full** je me sens (l'estomac) lourd ♦ **the room was ~ hot** il faisait dans cette pièce une chaleur incommodante, il faisait trop chaud dans la pièce ♦ **to be ~ aware that ...** être désagréablement conscient du fait que ... ♦ **my knees were ~ close to the steering wheel** mes genoux étaient tout près du volant, ce qui me gênait, j'avais les genoux si près du volant que ça me gênait ♦ **the deadline is drawing ~ close** la date limite se rapproche de façon inquiétante 2 *(= awkwardly) [sit]* inconfortablement ; *[dressed]* de façon inconfortable ♦ **he shifted ~** il était mal à l'aise et n'arrêtait pas de changer de position 3 *(= uneasily) [say, look at]* avec gêne

uncommitted /ˈʌnkəˈmɪtɪd/ ADJ 1 *(= undecided) [voter, delegate]* indécis ; *[country]* non engagé ♦ **to remain ~** rester neutre, ne pas s'engager ♦ **I was still ~ to the venture** je ne m'étais pas encore engagé sur ce projet ♦ **she is ~ on policy/on this issue** elle n'a pas de position arrêtée sur la politique à suivre/sur cette question 2 *(= unallocated) [space]* libre ; *[resources]* disponible, non affecté 3 *(= half-hearted) [performance]* sans conviction ; *[attitude]* indifférent

uncommon /ʌnˈkɒmən/ ADJ *(= rare) [name, species, disease]* rare ; *[intelligence, beauty]* peu commun, singulier ♦ **a not ~ problem/sight** un problème/un spectacle qui n'est pas rare ♦ **she was late for work, a not ~ occurrence** elle était en retard au travail, chose qui arrivait assez fréquemment ♦ **he had a slight nosebleed, a not ~ occurrence for him** il saignait légèrement du nez, ce qui lui arrivait assez fréquemment ♦ **it is not ~ to hear this** il n'est pas rare d'entendre cela ♦ **it is not ~ for this to happen** il n'est pas rare que cela arrive *subj* ADV † moult †† *(also hum)*

uncommonly /ʌnˈkɒmənlɪ/ ADV 1 *(† = exceptionally) [gifted, pretty, hot]* exceptionnellement, singulièrement 2 *(= rarely) [encountered]* rarement ♦ **such crimes are not ~ committed by minors** il n'est pas rare que des mineurs commettent *subj* ce genre de crime

uncommunicative /ˈʌnkəˈmjuːnɪkətɪv/ ADJ peu communicatif ♦ **on this issue he proved very ~** sur cette question il s'est montré très peu communicatif *or* très réservé

uncomplaining /ˈʌnkəmˈpleɪnɪŋ/ ADJ qui ne se plaint pas

uncomplainingly /ˈʌnkəmˈpleɪnɪŋlɪ/ ADV sans se plaindre

uncompleted /ˈʌnkəmˈpliːtɪd/ ADJ inachevé

uncomplicated /ʌnˈkɒmplɪkeɪtɪd/ ADJ *[person, relationship]* qui n'est pas compliqué ; *[method, view, plot]* simple ; *[pregnancy]* sans complications

uncomplimentary /ˈʌnˌkɒmplɪˈmentərɪ/ ADJ peu flatteur

uncomprehending /ˈʌnˌkɒmprɪˈhendɪŋ/ ADJ *[rage, horror, astonishment]* plein d'incompréhension ♦ **to give sb an ~ look** regarder qn sans comprendre ♦ **he stood there, quite ~** il restait là, sans rien comprendre ♦ **she gave a**

polite but ~ smile elle a souri poliment, mais sans comprendre

uncomprehendingly /ˈʌn,kɒmprɪˈhendɪŋlɪ/ **ADV** sans comprendre

uncompromising /ʌnˈkɒmprəmaɪzɪŋ/ **ADJ** *[person, attitude]* intransigeant ; *[message, demand, honesty, sincerity, film]* sans complaisance ◆ **to be ~ in refusing** *or* **in one's refusal (to do sth)** refuser catégoriquement (de faire qch)

uncompromisingly /ʌnˈkɒmprəmaɪzɪŋlɪ/ **ADV** *[say]* sans concession(s) ; *[intellectual, austere, modern]* résolument ◆ ~ **loyal** d'une loyauté totale *or* absolue

unconcealed /ˈʌnkənˈsiːld/ **ADJ** *[delight, anger, frustration, annoyance]* non dissimulé ; *[object]* non caché, non dissimulé

unconcern /ˈʌnkənˈsɜːn/ **N** *(= calm)* calme *m* ; *(in face of danger)* sang-froid *m* ; *(= lack of interest)* indifférence *f*, insouciance *f*

unconcerned /ˈʌnkənˈsɜːnd/ **ADJ** 1 *(= uninterested)* ◆ **to be ~** *[person]* ne pas se sentir concerné *(about or with sth* par qch) 2 *(= unworried) [person]* insouciant ◆ **he went on speaking,** ~ il a continué à parler sans se laisser troubler ◆ **to be ~ that ...** ne pas se soucier du fait que ... ◆ **to be ~ about sth** ne pas se soucier de qch ◆ **to be ~ by sth** ne pas s'inquiéter de qch

unconcernedly /ˈʌnkənˈsɜːnɪdlɪ/ **ADV** sans s'inquiéter

unconditional /ˈʌnkənˈdɪʃənl/ **ADJ** *[surrender, offer, bail]* sans condition(s), inconditionnel ; *[love, support]* inconditionnel **COMP unconditional discharge N** *(Jur)* dispense *f* de peine inconditionnelle

unconditionally /ˈʌnkənˈdɪʃnəlɪ/ **ADV** sans conditions

unconfined /ˈʌnkənˈfaɪnd/ **ADJ** *[space]* illimité, sans bornes ; *[animal]* en liberté

unconfirmed /ˈʌnkənˈfɜːmd/ **ADJ** *[report, rumour]* non confirmé ◆ **the rumours remain ~** ces rumeurs n'ont toujours pas été confirmées

uncongenial /ˈʌnkənˈdʒiːnɪəl/ **ADJ** *[person, company]* peu sympathique *(to sb* à qn) ; *[work, surroundings]* peu agréable *(to sb* à qn)

unconnected /ˈʌnkəˈnektɪd/ **ADJ** 1 *(= unrelated) [events, facts, languages]* sans rapport ◆ **a series of ~ events** une série d'événements sans rapport entre eux ◆ **the two incidents were ~** il n'y avait pas de rapport entre ces deux incidents ◆ **the two events were not ~** les deux événements n'étaient pas sans rapport ◆ **to be ~ with** *or* **to sth** ne pas avoir de rapport avec qch, être sans rapport avec qch 2 *(= unstructured) [thoughts, ideas, utterances]* décousu ◆ **a stream of ~ one-liners** une suite de bons mots sans rapport entre eux 3 *(= physically separated)* séparé *(to sth* de qch) ◆ **the island of Borneo, ~ to the Malay peninsula** l'île de Bornéo, séparée de la péninsule malaise 4 *(Elec) [wire, plug]* déconnecté ; *[appliance]* débranché

unconquerable /ʌnˈkɒŋkərəbl/ **ADJ** *[army, nation, mountain]* invincible ; *[difficulty]* insurmontable ; *[tendency]* irrépressible, incorrigible

unconquered /ʌnˈkɒŋkəd/ **ADJ** *[land]* qui n'a pas été conquis ; *[mountain]* invaincu

unconscionable /ʌnˈkɒnʃnəbl/ **ADJ** *(frm)* 1 *(= disgraceful) [liar]* éhonté ; *[behaviour, crime]* inadmissible ◆ **it is ~ that ...** il est inadmissible que ... ◆ **it would be ~ to allow that** il serait inadmissible de permettre cela ◆ **it is ~ for them to do such a thing** il est inadmissible qu'ils fassent une chose pareille 2 *(= excessive) [amount, delays, demands]* déraisonnable ◆ **to be an ~ time doing sth** prendre un temps déraisonnable à faire qch

unconscionably /ʌnˈkɒnʃnəblɪ/ **ADV** *(frm)* déraisonnablement, excessivement ◆ **you took an ~ long time over it** vous y avez passé beaucoup trop de temps

unconscious /ʌnˈkɒnʃəs/ **ADJ** 1 *(Med) [person]* inconscient, sans connaissance ◆ **I was** *or* **lay ~ for a few moments** je suis resté inconscient *or* sans connaissance pendant quelques instants ◆ **to become ~** perdre connaissance ◆ **to beat sb ~** battre qn jusqu'à lui faire perdre connaissance ◆ **to knock sb ~** assommer qn 2 *(= unaware)* ◆ **to be ~ of sth** ne pas être conscient de qch ◆ **he is ~ of his arrogance** il ne se rend pas compte de son arrogance 3 *(esp Psych) [desire, humour, bias]* inconscient ◆ **on an ~ level** au niveau de l'inconscient ◆ **the ~ mind** l'inconscient *m* **N** *(Psych)* inconscient *m*

unconsciously /ʌnˈkɒnʃəslɪ/ **ADV** *[copy, imitate, offend]* inconsciemment, sans s'en rendre compte ; *[expect, resent]* inconsciemment ◆ ~ **jealous** inconsciemment jaloux ◆ **he made an ~ funny remark** il a fait une remarque amusante sans s'en rendre compte

unconsciousness /ʌnˈkɒnʃəsnɪs/ **N** *(NonC)* 1 *(Med)* perte *f* de connaissance ; *(specifically fainting)* évanouissement *m* 2 *(= unawareness)* inconscience *f*

unconsidered /ˈʌnkənˈsɪdəd/ **ADJ** 1 *(= hasty) [comment, decision, action]* inconsidéré 2 *(= unfancied) [horse]* dont on fait *(or* faisait) peu de cas

unconstitutional /ˈʌn,kɒnstɪˈtjuːʃənl/ **ADJ** inconstitutionnel, anticonstitutionnel ◆ **to declare** *or* **rule sth ~** déclarer que qch est inconstitutionnel *or* anticonstitutionnel

unconstitutionally /ʌn,kɒnstɪˈtjuːʃnəlɪ/ **ADV** inconstitutionnellement, anticonstitutionnellement

unconstrained /ˈʌnkənˈstreɪnd/ **ADJ** *[person]* non contraint, libre ; *[behaviour]* aisé

unconsummated /ʌnˈkɒnsʌmeɪtəd/ **ADJ** *[marriage, relationship etc]* non consommé

uncontested /ˈʌnkənˈtestɪd/ **ADJ** incontesté ; *(Parl) [seat]* non disputé, remporté sans opposition

uncontrollable /ˈʌnkənˈtrəʊləbl/ **ADJ** *[person, behaviour, epidemic, inflation]* incontrôlable ; *[desire, urge, emotion]* irrépressible ; *[animal, situation, change]* impossible à maîtriser ; *[bleeding]* impossible à arrêter ◆ ~ **fits of rage** emportements *mpl* incontrôlables ◆ **he burst into ~ laughter** il a été pris d'un fou rire ◆ ~ **shivering** tremblements *mpl* incontrôlables ◆ **to have an ~ temper** ne pas savoir se contrôler

uncontrollably /ˈʌnkənˈtrəʊləblɪ/ **ADV** *[spread, increase]* de façon incontrôlable ; *[cry, shake]* sans pouvoir s'arrêter ◆ **to laugh ~** avoir le fou rire ◆ **the fire raged ~** l'incendie faisait rage et ne pouvait être maîtrisé ◆ **to swerve ~** faire une embardée incontrôlable

uncontrolled /ˈʌnkənˈtrəʊld/ **ADJ** *[person, behaviour, anger, inflation]* incontrôlé ; *[temper, emotion, desire]* non réprimé ; *[crying, sobbing]* non contenu ; *[situation]* non maîtrisé ; *[spending]* effréné

uncontroversial /ˈʌn,kɒntrəˈvɜːʃəl/ **ADJ** qui ne prête pas à controverse, non controversable

unconventional /ˈʌnkənˈvenʃənl/ **ADJ** *[person, behaviour]* original, non conformiste ; *[appearance, film, life]* original ; *[method, opinion]* original, non conventionnel ; *[education, upbringing]* non conventionnel

unconventionality /ˈʌnkən,venʃəˈnælɪtɪ/ **N** originalité *f*, caractère *m* peu conventionnel

unconventionally /ˈʌnkənˈvenʃnəlɪ/ **ADV** de manière peu conventionnelle

unconverted /ˈʌnkənˈvɜːtɪd/ **ADJ** *(Fin, Rel, gen)* non converti

unconvinced /ˈʌnkənˈvɪnst/ **ADJ** *[person]* qui n'est pas convaincu *(by sb/sth* par qn/qch ; *of sth* de qch) ; *[tone]* sans conviction ◆ **to be ~ that ...** ne pas être convaincu que ... ◆ **to remain ~** n'être toujours pas convaincu

unconvincing /ˈʌnkənˈvɪnsɪŋ/ **ADJ** peu convaincant

unconvincingly /ˈʌnkənˈvɪnsɪŋlɪ/ **ADV** *[speak, argue]* de manière peu convaincante

uncooked /ˈʌnˈkʊkt/ **ADJ** cru

uncool⁑ /ˈʌnˈkuːl/ **ADJ** pas cool*

uncooperative /ˈʌnkəʊˈɒpərətɪv/ **ADJ** peu coopératif

uncooperatively /ˈʌnkəʊˈɒpərətɪvlɪ/ **ADV** de façon peu coopérative

uncoordinated /ˈʌnkəʊˈɔːdɪneɪtɪd/ **ADJ** 1 *(= clumsy) [person]* mal coordonné 2 *(= lacking organization) [action]* qui manque de coordination

uncork /ˈʌnˈkɔːk/ **VT** déboucher, enlever le bouchon de

uncorrected /ˈʌnkəˈrektɪd/ **ADJ** non corrigé

uncorroborated /ˈʌnkəˈrɒbəreɪtɪd/ **ADJ** non corroboré, sans confirmation

uncorrupted /ˈʌnkəˈrʌptɪd/ **ADJ** non corrompu

uncountable /ˈʌnˈkaʊntəbl/ **ADJ** 1 *(= innumerable)* innombrable, incalculable 2 *(Ling)* ~ **noun** nom *m* non dénombrable **N** *(Ling)* nom *m* non dénombrable

uncounted /ˈʌnˈkaʊntɪd/ **ADJ** qui n'a pas été compté ; *(fig = innumerable)* innombrable

uncouple /ˈʌnˈkʌpl/ **VT** *[+ carriage]* dételer ; *[+ train, engine]* découpler ; *[+ trailer]* détacher

uncouth /ʌnˈkuːθ/ **ADJ** *[person, manners]* grossier, fruste ; *[behaviour, remark]* grossier

uncover /ʌnˈkʌvəʳ/ **VT** 1 *[+ evidence]* découvrir 2 *(= unearth)* mettre au jour

uncovered /ʌnˈkʌvəd/ **ADJ** 1 *(= without a cover)* découvert ◆ **the stands are ~** les tribunes ne sont pas couvertes ◆ **to leave sth ~** ne pas couvrir qch ◆ **to leave a wound ~** laisser une plaie à l'air 2 *(Fin) [advance]* à découvert ; *[cheque]* sans provision ◆ ~ **balance** découvert *m*

uncritical /ˈʌnˈkrɪtɪkəl/ **ADJ** *[person]* peu critique ; *[attitude, approach, report]* non critique ; *[acceptance, support, adulation]* sans réserves ◆ **to be ~ of sb/sth** manquer d'esprit critique à l'égard de qn/qch

uncritically /ˈʌnˈkrɪtɪkəlɪ/ **ADV** *[accept, support]* sans réserves ; *[report]* sans faire preuve d'esprit critique

uncross /ˈʌnˈkrɒs/ **VT** décroiser

uncrossed /ˈʌnˈkrɒst/ **ADJ** décroisé ; *[cheque]* non barré

uncrowded /ˈʌnˈkraʊdɪd/ **ADJ** où il n'y a pas trop de monde

uncrowned /ˈʌnˈkraʊnd/ **ADJ** *[king, queen]* non couronné, sans couronne ◆ **the ~ world champion** le champion du monde non encore sacré ◆ **the ~ king of sth** le roi sans couronne de qch

uncrushable /ˈʌnˈkrʌʃəbl/ **ADJ** *[fabric, dress]* infroissable ◆ **he's quite ~** il ne se laisse jamais abattre

UNCTAD, Unctad /ˈʌŋktæd/ **N** (abbrev of **United Nations Conference on Trade and Development**) CNUCED *f*

unction /ˈʌŋkʃən/ **N** *(all senses)* onction *f*

unctuous /ˈʌŋktjʊəs/ **ADJ** *[person, behaviour, tone]* mielleux, onctueux

unctuously /ˈʌŋktjʊəslɪ/ **ADV** *(pej)* onctueusement, avec onction

unctuousness /ˈʌŋktjʊəsnɪs/ **N** *(NonC: pej)* manières *fpl* onctueuses

uncultivated /ˈʌnˈkʌltɪveɪtɪd/ ADJ 1 *[land]* inculte 2 *(= uncultured) [person, mind]* inculte ; *[voice, accent]* qui manque de raffinement

uncultured /ˈʌnˈkʌltʃəd/ ADJ *[person]* inculte ; *[voice, accent]* qui manque de raffinement

uncurl /ˈʌnˈkɜːl/ VT *[+ wire, snake]* dérouler ; *[+ one's legs]* déplier ; *[+ one's fingers]* étendre ◆ **to ~ o.s.** *[person, cat]* s'étirer ◆ **he ~ed himself from his chair** il s'est étiré et s'est levé de sa chaise VI *[snake etc]* se dérouler

uncut /ˈʌnˈkʌt/ ADJ 1 *(= still growing) [grass, tree, hair, nails]* non coupé ; *[hedge, beard]* non taillé ; *[crops]* sur pied ◆ **to leave sth ~** ne pas couper qch 2 *(= not faceted) [diamond, sapphire]* non taillé 3 *(= unabridged) [film, play, novel]* intégral, sans coupures ◆ **to show a film ~** montrer un film dans sa version intégrale ◆ **the ~ "Peer Gynt"** la version intégrale de "Peer Gynt" 4 *(= pure) [heroin, cocaine]* pur 5 *(* = not circumcised) [man, penis]* non circoncis

undamaged /ʌnˈdæmɪdʒd/ ADJ *[goods, vehicle, building]* non endommagé, intact ; *[plant]* non endommagé ; *[limb]* non atteint ; *[reputation]* intact ; *(Psych)* non affecté

undamped /ˈʌnˈdæmpt/ ADJ *(fig) [enthusiasm, courage]* non refroidi, intact

undated /ˈʌnˈdeɪtɪd/ ADJ non daté

undaunted /ˈʌnˈdɔːntɪd/ ADJ ◆ **he carried on ~** il a continué sans se laisser démonter ◆ **he was ~ by their threats** il ne s'est pas laissé intimider *or* démonter par leurs menaces ◆ **he was ~ by the scale of the job** il ne s'est pas laissé décourager par l'ampleur de la tâche

undeceive /ˈʌndɪˈsiːv/ VT *(frm)* détromper, désabuser *(liter)*

undecided /ˈʌndɪˈsaɪdɪd/ ADJ *[person]* indécis *(about or on sth* à propos de qch) ; *[question]* non résolu ; *[weather]* incertain ◆ **to remain ~** *[person]* demeurer indécis ◆ **that is still ~** cela n'a pas encore été décidé ◆ **I am ~ whether to go or not** je n'ai pas décidé si j'irai ou non

undeclared /ˈʌndɪˈkleəd/ ADJ *(Customs)* non déclaré

undefeated /ˈʌndɪˈfiːtɪd/ ADJ invaincu

undefended /ˈʌndɪˈfendɪd/ ADJ 1 *(Mil etc)* sans défense, non défendu 2 *(Jur) [suit]* où on ne présente pas de défense, où le défendeur s'abstient de plaider

undefiled /ˈʌndɪˈfaɪld/ ADJ *(liter: lit, fig)* pur, sans tache ◆ **~ by any contact with ...** qui n'a pas été contaminé *or* souillé par le contact de ...

undefined /ˈʌndɪˈfaɪnd/ ADJ *[word, condition]* non défini ; *[sensation etc]* indéterminé, vague

undelete /ˈʌndɪˈliːt/ VT *(Comput)* restaurer

undelivered /ˈʌndɪˈlɪvəd/ ADJ non remis, non distribué ◆ **"if undelivered return to sender"** "en cas d'absence, prière de renvoyer à l'expéditeur"

undemanding /ˈʌndɪˈmɑːndɪŋ/ ADJ *[person, work, book, film]* peu exigeant

undemocratic /ˌʌndeməˈkrætɪk/ ADJ antidémocratique

undemonstrative /ˈʌndɪˈmɒnstrətɪv/ ADJ réservé, peu démonstratif

undeniable /ˌʌndɪˈnaɪəbl/ ADJ indéniable, incontestable

undeniably /ˌʌndɪˈnaɪəblɪ/ LANGUAGE IN USE 15.1 ADV incontestablement, indéniablement ◆ **it is ~ true that ...** il est incontestable *or* indiscutable que ...

undenominational /ˈʌndɪˌnɒmɪˈneɪʃənl/ ADJ non confessionnel

undependable /ˈʌndɪˈpendəbl/ ADJ *[person]* peu fiable, sur qui on ne peut compter ; *[information]* peu sûr ; *[machine]* peu fiable

under /ˈʌndəʳ/ ADV 1 *(= beneath)* au-dessous, en dessous ◆ **he stayed ~ for three minutes** *(= underwater)* il est resté sous l'eau pendant trois minutes ; *(= under anaesthetic)* il est resté sous l'effet de l'anesthésie *or* il est resté anesthésié pendant trois minutes ◆ **as ~** *(Comm etc)* comme ci-dessous ◆ **he lifted the rope and crawled ~** il a soulevé la corde et il est passé dessous en rampant ; → **down¹, go under**

2 *(= less)* au-dessous ◆ **children of 15 and ~** les enfants de moins de 16 ans ◆ **ten degrees ~** dix degrés au-dessous de zéro

PREP 1 *(= beneath)* sous ◆ **~ the table/sky/umbrella** sous la table/le ciel/le parapluie ◆ **he came out from ~ the bed** il est sorti de dessous le lit ◆ **the book slipped from ~ his arm** le livre a glissé de sous son bras ◆ **it's ~ there** c'est là-dessous ◆ **~ it** dessous ◆ **he went and sat ~ it** il est allé s'asseoir dessous ◆ **to stay ~ water** rester sous l'eau ◆ **~ the microscope** au microscope ; *for other phrases see* **breath, cover, wing**

2 *(= less than)* moins de ; *(in series, rank, scale etc)* au-dessous de ◆ **to be ~ age** être mineur ; see also **underage** ◆ **children ~ 15** enfants *mpl* au-dessous de *or* de moins de 15 ans ◆ **the ~-15s** *etc* les moins de 15 *etc* ans ◆ **it sells at ~ $10** cela se vend à moins de 10 dollars ◆ **there were ~ 50 of them** il y en avait moins de 50 ◆ **any number ~ ten** un chiffre au-dessous de dix ◆ **in ~ two hours** en moins de deux heures ◆ **those ~ the rank of captain** ceux au-dessous du grade de capitaine

3 *(gen, Pol: in system)* sous ◆ **~ the Tudors** sous les Tudor ◆ **to serve ~ sb** *(Mil etc)* servir sous les ordres de qn ◆ **he had 50 men ~ him** il avait 50 hommes sous ses ordres ◆ **~ the command of ...** sous les ordres de ... ◆ **to study ~ sb** *[undergraduate]* suivre les cours de qn ; *[postgraduate]* faire des recherches *or* travailler sous la direction de qn ; *[painter, composer]* être l'élève de qn ◆ **this department comes ~ his authority** cette section relève de sa compétence

4 *(with names)* sous ◆ **~ an assumed name** sous un faux nom ◆ **you'll find him ~ "plumbers" in the phone book** vous le trouverez sous "plombiers" dans l'annuaire ; *for other phrases see* **circumstance, control, impression, obligation, plain**

5 *(Comput)* sous ◆ **to run ~ Windows ®** fonctionner sous Windows ®

6 *(Jur)* ◆ **~ sentence of death** condamné à mort

7 *(Agr)* ◆ **~ wheat** en blé

8 *(= according to)* selon ◆ **~ French law** selon la législation française ◆ **~ the terms of the contract** selon *or* suivant les termes du contrat ◆ **~ his will** selon son testament ◆ **~ article 25** en vertu de *or* conformément à l'article 25

PREF 1 *(= below)* sous- ; → **underfloor, undersea**

2 *(= insufficiently)* sous- ◆ **~nourished** sous-alimenté ◆ **~used/appreciated** *etc* qui n'est pas assez utilisé/apprécié *etc* ; → **undercharge, undercooked**

3 *(= junior)* sous- ◆ **~-gardener** aide-jardinier *m* ; → **under-secretary**

COMP **under-report** VT *[+ crime, disease etc]* sous-évaluer

under-the-counter * ADJ → **under-the-counter**

underachieve /ˌʌndərəˈtʃiːv/ VI *(Scol)* être sous-performant, obtenir des résultats décevants

underachiever /ˌʌndərəˈtʃiːvəʳ/ N *(Scol)* élève *mf* sous-performant(e) *or* qui obtient des résultats décevants

underage /ˌʌndərˈeɪdʒ/ ADJ *[person]* mineur ◆ **~ drinking** consommation *f* d'alcool par les mineurs

underarm /ˈʌndərɑːm/ ADV *(Sport etc) [throw, bowl]* par en-dessous ADJ 1 *[throw etc]* par en-dessous 2 *[deodorant]* pour les aisselles ; *[hair]* des aisselles, sous les bras ◆ **~ odour** odeur *f* de transpiration (des aisselles)

underbade /ˌʌndəˈbeɪd/ VB pt of **underbid**

underbelly /ˈʌndəbelɪ/ N *(Anat)* bas-ventre *m* ◆ **the (soft) ~** *(fig)* le point vulnérable

underbid /ˌʌndəˈbɪd/ (pret **underbade** *or* **underbid**, ptp **underbidden** *or* **underbid**) VTI *(Bridge:* also **underbid one's hand**) annoncer au-dessous de sa force

underbody /ˈʌndəbɒdɪ/ N *[of car]* dessous *m* de caisse

underbrush /ˈʌndəbrʌʃ/ N *(NonC: US)* sous-bois *m inv*, broussailles *fpl*

undercapitalized /ˈʌndəˈkæpɪtəlaɪzd/ ADJ ◆ **to be ~** *[businessman]* ne pas disposer de fonds suffisants ; *[project]* ne pas être doté de fonds suffisants

undercarriage /ˈʌndəkærɪdʒ/ N *[of plane]* train *m* d'atterrissage

undercharge /ˈʌndəˈtʃɑːdʒ/ VT ne pas faire payer assez à ◆ **he ~d me** il m'a fait payer moins cher qu'il n'aurait dû ◆ **he ~d me by £2** il aurait dû me faire payer 2 livres de plus

underclass /ˈʌndəklɑːs/ N *(in society)* quart-monde *m*

underclassman /ˈʌndəˈklɑːsmən/ N (pl **-men**) *(US Univ)* étudiant *m* de première *or* deuxième année

underclothes /ˈʌndəkləʊðz/ NPL, **underclothing** /ˈʌndəkləʊðɪŋ/ N *(NonC)* ⇒ **underwear**

undercoat /ˈʌndəkəʊt/ N *[of paint]* couche *f* de fond ; *(US: for car chassis)* couche *f* antirouille (du châssis)

undercoating /ˈʌndəkəʊtɪŋ/ N *(NonC: US) (for car chassis)* couche *f* antirouille (du châssis)

undercooked /ˈʌndəˈkʊkt/ ADJ pas assez cuit

undercover /ˌʌndəˈkʌvəʳ/ ADJ secret (-ète *f*), clandestin ◆ **~ agent** agent *m* secret ◆ **~ reporter** journaliste *mf* infiltré(e) ◆ **~ policeman** policier *m* en civil ADV *[work]* clandestinement ◆ **Buchanan persuaded Hamilton to work ~ to capture the killer** Buchanan persuada Hamilton de monter une opération secrète pour arrêter le meurtrier

undercurrent /ˈʌndəˌkʌrənt/ N *(in sea)* courant *m* (sous-marin) ; *(fig) (feeling etc)* courant *m* sous-jacent

undercut /ˌʌndəˈkʌt/ (pret, ptp **undercut**) VT 1 *(= sell cheaper than) [+ competitor]* vendre moins cher que 2 *(fig, esp Econ = undermine, reduce) [+ the dollar, incomes]* réduire la valeur de ◆ **inflation ~s spending power** l'inflation réduit le pouvoir d'achat ◆ **to be ~ by sth** être atténué par qch 3 *(Sport) [+ ball]* couper N /ˈʌndəkʌt/ *(Culin)* (morceau *m* de) filet *m*

underdeveloped /ˈʌndədɪˈveləpt/ ADJ *(Econ)* sous-développé, en retard de développement ; *[heart, lungs etc of foetus]* qui n'est pas complètement développé or formé ; *(Phot)* insuffisamment développé

underdog /ˈʌndədɒg/ N ◆ **the ~** *(in game, fight)* le perdant (or la perdante) ; *(= predicted loser)* celui *(or* celle) que l'on donne perdant(e) ; *(economically, socially)* l'opprimé *m*

underdone /ˈʌndəˈdʌn/ ADJ *[food]* pas assez cuit ; *(Brit) [steak etc]* saignant

underdressed /ˌʌndəˈdrest/ ADJ ◆ **to be ~** ne pas être assez bien habillé

underemphasize /ˌʌndərˈemfəsaɪz/ VT ne pas donner l'importance nécessaire à

underemployed /ˌʌndərɪmˈplɔɪd/ ADJ *[person, equipment, building]* sous-employé ; *[resources]* sous-exploité ◆ **I'm ~ half the time** bien souvent je suis sous-employé *or* je ne suis pas assez occupé

underemployment /ˌʌndərɪmˈplɔɪmənt/ **N** *[of person, equipment, building]* sous-emploi *m* ; *[of resources]* sous-exploitation *f*

underestimate /ˌʌndərˈestɪmɪt/ **N** sous-estimation *f* **VT** /ˌʌndərˈestɪmeɪt/ *[+ size, numbers, strength]* sous-estimer ; *[+ person]* sous-estimer, mésestimer

underestimation /ˌʌndərestɪˈmeɪʃən/ **N** sous-estimation *f*

underexpose /ˌʌndərɪksˈpəʊz/ **VT** *(Phot)* sous-exposer

underexposed /ˌʌndərɪksˈpəʊzd/ **ADJ** *(Phot)* sous-exposé

underexposure /ˌʌndərɪksˈpəʊʒəʳ/ **N** *(Phot)* sous-exposition *f*

underfed /ˌʌndəˈfed/ **VB** pt, ptp of **underfeed** **ADJ** sous-alimenté

underfeed /ˌʌndəˈfiːd/ (pret, ptp **underfed**) **VT** sous-alimenter

underfeeding /ˌʌndəˈfiːdɪŋ/ **N** sous-alimentation *f*

underfelt /ˈʌndəfelt/ **N** *[of carpet]* thibaude *f*

underfinanced /ˌʌndəfaɪˈnænst/ **ADJ** ◆ **to be ~** *[businessman]* ne pas disposer de fonds suffisants ; *[project etc]* ne pas être doté de fonds suffisants

underfloor /ˈʌndəflɔːʳ/ **ADJ** *(gen) [pipes etc]* qui se trouve sous le plancher *or* le sol ◆ **~ heating** chauffage *m* par le plancher *or* par le sol

underflow /ˈʌndəfləʊ/ **N** *(in sea)* courant *m* (sous-marin) ; *(fig) (feeling etc)* courant *m* sous-jacent

underfoot /ˌʌndəˈfʊt/ **ADV** *(gen)* sous les pieds ◆ **to crush** *or* **trample sth ~** fouler qch aux pieds ◆ **it is wet ~** le sol est humide

underfunded /ˌʌndəˈfʌndɪd/ **ADJ** ◆ **to be ~** *[businessman]* ne pas disposer de fonds suffisants ; *[project etc]* ne pas être doté de fonds suffisants

underfunding /ˌʌndəˈfʌndɪŋ/ **N** insuffisance *f* de financement

undergarment /ˈʌndəgɑːmənt/ **N** sous-vêtement *m*

undergo /ˌʌndəˈgəʊ/ (pret **underwent** /ˌʌndəˈwent/, ptp **undergone** /ˌʌndəˈgɒn/) **VT** *[+ test, change, modification, operation, medical examination]* subir ; *[+ suffering]* éprouver ; *[+ medical treatment]* suivre ◆ **it is ~ing repairs** c'est en réparation

undergrad * /ˈʌndəgræd/ **N, ADJ** *(esp Brit)* ⇒ **undergraduate**

undergraduate /ˌʌndəˈgrædjʊɪt/ *(esp Brit)* **N** étudiant(e) *m(f) (qui prépare la licence)* **ADJ** *[life, circles]* étudiant, estudiantin ; *[room, income]* d'étudiant ; *[grant]* d'études ; *[opinion]* des étudiants ; *[course]* pour étudiants de licence

underground /ˈʌndəgraʊnd/ **ADJ** 1 *[work]* sous terre, souterrain ; *[explosion, cable]* souterrain ◆ **~ car park** parking *m* souterrain ◆ **~ railway** métro *m* ◆ **the ~ railroad** *(fig: US Hist: for slaves) filière clandestine pour aider les esclaves noirs à fuir le Sud* 2 *(fig) [organization]* clandestin, secret (-ète *f*) ; *[press]* clandestin ; *(Art, Cine)* underground *inv*, d'avant-garde ◆ **~ movement** mouvement *m* clandestin ; *(in occupied country)* résistance *f* **ADV** sous (la) terre ; *(fig)* clandestinement, secrètement ◆ **it is 3 metres ~** c'est à 3 mètres sous (la) terre ◆ **to go ~** *[wanted man]* entrer dans la clandestinité ; *[guerilla]* prendre le maquis **N** *(Brit = railway)* métro *m* ◆ **by ~** en métro ◆ **the ~** *(Mil, Pol etc)* la résistance ; *(Art etc)* mouvement *m* underground *or* d'avant-garde

undergrowth /ˈʌndəgrəʊθ/ **N** *(NonC)* broussailles *fpl*, sous-bois *m inv*

underhand /ˌʌndəˈhænd/, **underhanded** *(US)* /ˌʌndəˈhændɪd/ **ADJ** *(pej)* sournois ◆ **~ trick** fourberie *f*

underhandedly /ˌʌndəˈhændɪdlɪ/ **ADV** *(pej)* sournoisement

underinsure /ˌʌndərɪnˈʃʊəʳ/ **VT** sous-assurer ◆ **to be ~d** être sous-assuré, ne pas être suffisamment assuré

underinvest /ˌʌndərɪnˈvest/ **VI** sous-investir

underinvestment /ˌʌndərɪnˈvestmənt/ **N** sous-investissement *m*

underlain /ˌʌndəˈleɪn/ **VB** ptp of **underlie**

underlay /ˌʌndəˈleɪ/ **VB** pt of **underlie** **N** /ˈʌndəleɪ/ *(esp Brit) [of carpet]* thibaude *f*

underlie /ˌʌndəˈlaɪ/ (pret **underlay**, ptp **underlain**) **VT** être à la base de, sous-tendre

underline /ˌʌndəˈlaɪn/ LANGUAGE IN USE 20.1 **VT** *(lit, fig)* souligner

underling /ˈʌndəlɪŋ/ **N** *(pej)* subalterne *m*, sous-fifre * *m inv (pej)*

underlining /ˌʌndəˈlaɪnɪŋ/ **N** *(NonC)* soulignage *m*, soulignement *m*

underlip /ˈʌndəlɪp/ **N** lèvre *f* inférieure

underlying /ˌʌndəˈlaɪɪŋ/ **ADJ** *(gen, Gram, Jur)* sous-jacent ; *[cause]* profond ; *[problem]* de fond ◆ **the figures demonstrated the ~ strength of the economy** les chiffres démontraient la solidité sous-jacente de l'économie ◆ **~ this** à la base de cela

undermanned /ˌʌndəˈmænd/ **ADJ** en sous-effectif

undermentioned /ˌʌndəˈmenʃənd/ **ADJ** (cité) ci-dessous

undermine /ˌʌndəˈmaɪn/ **VT** 1 *(lit) [+ cliffs]* miner, saper 2 *(fig) [+ influence, power, authority]* saper, ébranler ; *[+ health]* miner, user ; *[+ effect]* amoindrir

undermost /ˈʌndəməʊst/ **ADJ** le plus bas

underneath /ˌʌndəˈniːθ/ **PREP** sous, au-dessous de ◆ **stand ~ it** mettez-vous dessous ◆ **from ~ the table** de dessous la table **ADV** (en) dessous ◆ **the one ~** celui d'en dessous **ADJ** d'en dessous **N** dessous *m*

undernourish /ˌʌndəˈnʌrɪʃ/ **VT** sous-alimenter

undernourished /ˌʌndəˈnʌrɪʃt/ **ADJ** en état de malnutrition

undernourishment /ˌʌndəˈnʌrɪʃmənt/ **N** malnutrition *f*

underoccupied /ˌʌndərˈɒkjʊpaɪd/ **ADJ** *[person]* qui n'a pas assez à faire

underpaid /ˌʌndəˈpeɪd/ **VB** pt, ptp of **underpay** **ADJ** sous-payé

underpants /ˈʌndəpænts/ **NPL** slip *m* ◆ **a pair of ~** un slip ◆ **to be in one's ~** être en slip

underpart /ˈʌndəpɑːt/ **N** partie *f* inférieure

underpass /ˈʌndəpɑːs/ **N** *(for cars)* passage *m* inférieur *(de l'autoroute)* ; *(for pedestrians)* passage *m* souterrain

underpay /ˌʌndəˈpeɪ/ (pret, ptp **underpaid**) **VT** sous-payer

underperform /ˌʌndəpəˈfɔːm/ **VI** *(Stock Exchange)* mal se comporter, faire une contre-performance ◆ **the stock has ~ed on the Brussels stock market** le titre ne s'est pas comporté comme il aurait dû à la Bourse de Bruxelles

underpin /ˌʌndəˈpɪn/ **VT** 1 *[+ wall]* étayer ; *[+ building]* reprendre en sous-œuvre 2 *(fig)* sous-tendre, être à la base de ◆ **the philosophy that ~s his work** la philosophie qui sous-tend *or* qui est à la base de son œuvre

underpinning /ˌʌndəˈpɪnɪŋ/ **N** *(Constr)* étayage *m* ; *[of building]* reprise *f* en sous-œuvre ; *(fig)* bases *fpl*

underplay /ˌʌndəˈpleɪ/ **VT** *(gen)* minimiser, réduire l'importance de ◆ **he rather ~ed it** il n'a pas insisté là-dessus, il a minimisé la chose ◆ **to ~ a role** *(Theat)* jouer un rôle avec beaucoup de retenue

underpopulated /ˌʌndəˈpɒpjʊleɪtɪd/ **ADJ** sous-peuplé

underprice /ˌʌndəˈpraɪs/ **VT** mettre un prix trop bas à

underpriced /ˌʌndəˈpraɪst/ **ADJ** *[goods]* en vente à un prix inférieur à sa vraie valeur ◆ **at $18 this wine is ~** à 18 dollars, ce vin n'est pas assez cher

underpricing /ˌʌndəˈpraɪsɪŋ/ **N** tarification *f* trop basse

underprivileged /ˌʌndəˈprɪvɪlɪdʒd/ **ADJ** défavorisé **NPL** **the underprivileged** les défavorisés *mpl*

underproduce /ˌʌndəprəˈdjuːs/ **VTI** sous-produire

underproduction /ˌʌndəprəˈdʌkʃən/ **N** sous-production *f*

underqualified /ˈʌndəˈkwɒlɪˌfaɪd/ **ADJ** sous-qualifié *(for* pour)

underrate /ˌʌndəˈreɪt/ **VT** *[+ size, numbers, strength]* sous-estimer ; *[+ person]* sous-estimer, méconnaître

underrated /ˌʌndəˈreɪtɪd/ **ADJ** *[play, book, actor]* sous-estimé, méconnu ◆ **he's very ~** on ne l'estime pas à sa juste valeur

underreact /ˌʌndəriːˈækt/ **VI** réagir mollement

underreaction /ˌʌndəriːˈækʃən/ **N** réaction *f* molle

underrepresented /ˌʌndəreprɪˈzentɪd/ **ADJ** sous-représenté

underripe /ˌʌndəˈraɪp/ **ADJ** *[fruit]* vert, qui n'est pas mûr ; *[cheese]* qui n'est pas fait

underscore /ˌʌndəˈskɔːʳ/ **VT** *(lit)* souligner ; *(fig)* souligner, mettre en évidence

underscoring /ˌʌndəˈskɔːrɪŋ/ **N** *(NonC) (lit) [of text, words]* soulignage *m* ; *(fig)* insistance *f (of* sur)

undersea /ˈʌndəsiː/ **ADJ** sous-marin

underseal /ˈʌndəsiːl/ *(Brit)* **VT** *[+ car]* traiter contre la rouille *(au niveau du châssis)* **N** couche *f* antirouille *(du châssis)*

undersealing /ˈʌndəsiːlɪŋ/ **N** *(Brit: for car chassis)* couche *f* antirouille *(du châssis)*

under-secretary /ˌʌndəˈsekrətrɪ/ **N** sous-secrétaire *mf* **COMP** **Under-Secretary of State** **N** sous-secrétaire *mf* d'État

undersell /ˌʌndəˈsel/ (pret, ptp **undersold**) **VT** 1 *(= undercut) [+ competitor]* vendre moins cher que 2 *(fig)* **to ~ o.s.** ne pas savoir se mettre en valeur *or* se vendre *

undersexed /ˌʌndəˈsekst/ **ADJ** *(= having a low sex drive)* de faible libido ◆ **to be ~** avoir une faible libido

undershirt /ˈʌndəʃɜːt/ **N** *(US)* maillot *m* de corps

undershoot /ˌʌndəˈʃuːt/ (pret, ptp **undershot**) **VT** ◆ **to ~ the runway** atterrir avant d'atteindre la piste

undershorts /ˈʌndəʃɔːts/ **NPL** *(US)* caleçon *m*

undershot /ˈʌndəʃɒt/ **VB** pt, ptp of **undershoot** **ADJ** *[water wheel]* à aubes

underside /ˈʌndəsaɪd/ **N** dessous *m*

undersigned /ˈʌndəsaɪnd/ **ADJ, N** *(Jur, frm)* soussigné(e) *m(f)* ◆ **I, the ~, declare ...** je soussigné(e) déclare ...

undersized /ˌʌndəˈsaɪzd/ **ADJ** de (trop) petite taille, trop petit

underskirt /ˈʌndəskɜːt/ **N** jupon *m*

underslung /ˌʌndəˈslʌŋ/ **ADJ** *[car]* surbaissé

undersoil /ˈʌndəsɔɪl/ N sous-sol *m* *(Agr)*

undersold /ˌʌndəˈsəʊld/ VB pt, ptp of **undersell**

underspend /ˌʌndəˈspend/ VI ne pas dépenser entièrement les crédits disponibles ; *(too little)* ne pas assez investir

understaffed /ˌʌndəˈstɑːft/ ADJ en sous-effectif

understand /ˌʌndəˈstænd/ LANGUAGE IN USE 11.1, 15.4 (pret, ptp **understood**)

VT 1 *[+ person, words, meaning, painting, difficulty, action, event etc]* comprendre ◆ **I can't ~ his attitude** je n'arrive pas à comprendre son attitude ◆ **that's what I can't ~** voilà ce que je ne comprends pas *or* ce qui me dépasse ◆ **I can't ~ it!** je ne comprends pas ! ◆ **I can't ~ a word of it** je n'y comprends rien ◆ **I don't ~ the way she behaved/reacted** je ne comprends pas *or* je ne m'explique pas son comportement/sa réaction ◆ **as I ~ it, ...** si je comprends bien, ... ◆ **this can be understood in several ways** cela peut se comprendre de plusieurs façons ◆ **that is easily understood** c'est facile à comprendre, cela se comprend facilement ◆ **do you ~ why/how/what?** est-ce que vous comprenez pourquoi/comment/ce que ? ◆ **I can't ~ his agreeing to do it** je n'arrive pas à comprendre *or* je ne m'explique pas qu'il ait accepté de le faire ◆ **to make o.s. understood** se faire comprendre ◆ **do I make myself understood?** est-ce que je me fais bien comprendre ? ◆ **that's quite understood!** c'est entendu ! ◆ **I quite ~ that you don't want to come** je comprends très bien que vous n'ayez pas envie de venir ◆ **it must be understood that ...** il faut (bien) comprendre que ... ◆ **it being understood that your client is responsible** *(frm)* à condition que votre client accepte *subj* la responsabilité

2 *(= believe)* (croire) comprendre ◆ **I understood we were to be paid** j'ai cru comprendre que nous devions être payés ◆ **I ~ you are leaving today** il paraît que vous partez aujourd'hui, si je comprends bien vous partez aujourd'hui ◆ **she refused – so I ~** elle a refusé – c'est ce que j'ai cru comprendre ◆ **we confirm our reservation and we ~ (that) the rental will be ...** *(frm: in business letter etc)* nous confirmons notre réservation, étant entendu que la location s'élèvera à ... ◆ **am I to ~ that ...?** dois-je comprendre que ... ? ◆ **she is understood to have left the country, it is understood that she has left the country** il paraît qu'elle a quitté le pays, elle aurait quitté le pays ◆ **he let it be understood that ...** il a donné à entendre *or* il a laissé entendre que ... ◆ **he gave me to ~ that ...** il m'a fait comprendre que ... ◆ **we were given to ~ that ...** on nous a donné à entendre que ..., on nous a fait comprendre que ...

3 *(= imply, assume) [+ word etc]* sous-entendre ◆ **to be understood** *[arrangement, price, date]* ne pas être spécifié ; *(Gram)* être sous-entendu ◆ **it was understood that he would pay for it** *(= it was assumed)* on présumait qu'il le paierait ; *(= it was agreed)* il était entendu qu'il le paierait

4 *(= relate to, empathize with)* comprendre ◆ **my wife doesn't ~ me** ma femme ne me comprend pas

VI comprendre ◆ **now I ~!** je comprends *or* j'y suis maintenant ! ◆ **there's to be no noise, (do you) ~!** *or* **(is that) understood?** pas de bruit, c'est bien compris *or* tu entends ! ◆ **he was a widower, I ~** il était veuf, si j'ai bien compris *or* si je ne me trompe (pas)

understandable /ˌʌndəˈstændəbl/ LANGUAGE IN USE 26.3 ADJ 1 *(= intelligible) [person, speech]* compréhensible, intelligible 2 *(= justifiable) [behaviour]* compréhensible ; *[pride, sorrow]* compréhensible, naturel ◆ **it is ~ that ...** on comprend *or* il est normal que ... + *subj* ◆ **that's ~** ça se comprend

understandably /ˌʌndəˈstændəblɪ/ ADV 1 *(= intelligibly) [speak, explain]* d'une façon compréhensible 2 *(= naturally, of course)* naturellement ; *(= rightly)* à juste titre ◆ **~, he refused** il a refusé, et ça se comprend ◆ **he's ~ angry** il est furieux, et à juste titre *or* et ça se comprend

understanding /ˌʌndəˈstændɪŋ/ ADJ *[person]* compréhensif *(about* à propos de) ; *[smile, look]* compatissant, bienveillant

N 1 *(NonC)* compréhension *f* ◆ **his ~ of the problems/of children** sa compréhension des problèmes/des enfants, sa faculté de comprendre les problèmes/les enfants ◆ **he had a good ~ of the problems** il comprenait bien les problèmes ◆ **it is my ~ that ...** d'après ce que j'ai compris, ... ◆ **the age of ~** l'âge *m* de discernement ◆ **it's beyond ~** cela dépasse l'entendement

2 *(= agreement)* accord *m* ; *(= arrangement)* arrangement *m* ◆ **to come to an ~ with sb** s'entendre *or* s'arranger avec qn ◆ **the president has an ~ with the military commanders** le président s'est entendu avec les chefs militaires ◆ **there is an ~ between us that ...** il est entendu entre nous que ... ◆ **on the ~ that ...** à condition que ... + *subj*

3 *(NonC = concord)* entente *f*, bonne intelligence *f* ◆ **this will encourage ~ between our nations** ceci favorisera l'entente entre nos nations

understandingly /ˌʌndəˈstændɪŋlɪ/ ADV avec bienveillance, en faisant preuve de compréhension

understate /ˌʌndəˈsteɪt/ VT minimiser, réduire l'importance de

understated /ˌʌndəˈsteɪtɪd/ ADJ *(gen)* discret (-ète *f*) ; *[fashion detail]* discret (-ète *f*), d'une élégance discrète ◆ **an ~ black dress** une petite robe noire toute simple

understatement /ˈʌndəˌsteɪtmənt/ N affirmation *f* en dessous de la vérité ; *(Ling)* litote *f* ◆ **to say he is clever is rather an ~** c'est peu dire qu'il est intelligent ◆ **that's an ~** c'est peu dire, le terme est faible ◆ **that's the ~ of the year!*** c'est bien le moins qu'on puisse dire !

understeer /ˈʌndəˌstɪəʳ/ VI braquer insuffisamment

understood /ˌʌndəˈstʊd/ VB pt, ptp of **understand**

understudy /ˈʌndəstʌdɪ/ *(Theat)* N doublure *f* VT *[+ actor]* doubler ; *[+ part]* doubler un acteur dans

undersubscribed /ˌʌndəsəbˈskraɪbd/ *(Stock Exchange)* ADJ non couvert, non entièrement souscrit

undertake /ˌʌndəˈteɪk/ (pret **undertook**, ptp **undertaken**) VT *[+ task]* entreprendre ; *[+ duty]* se charger de ; *[+ responsibility]* assumer ; *[+ obligation]* contracter ◆ **to ~ to do sth** promettre *or* se charger de faire qch, s'engager à faire qch VTI *(Brit*)* *(= overtake on wrong side)* dépasser du mauvais côté

undertaker /ˈʌndəteɪkəʳ/ N *(Brit)* entrepreneur *m or* ordonnateur *m* des pompes funèbres ◆ **the ~'s** les pompes *fpl* funèbres, le service des pompes funèbres

undertaking /ˌʌndəˈteɪkɪŋ/ N 1 *(= task, operation)* entreprise *f* ◆ **it is quite an ~ (to do sth** *or* **doing sth)** ce n'est pas une mince affaire (que de faire qch) 2 *(= promise)* promesse *f*, engagement *m* ◆ **to give an ~** promettre *(that* que ; *to do sth* de faire qch) ◆ **I can give no such ~** je ne peux rien promettre de la sorte 3 /ˈʌndəˌteɪkɪŋ/ *(NonC: Brit: *) (= overtaking on wrong side)* dépassement *m* du mauvais côté 4 /ˈʌndəˌteɪkɪŋ/ *(NonC: Brit = arranging funerals)* pompes *fpl* funèbres

undertax /ˌʌndəˈtæks/ VT *[+ goods]* taxer insuffisamment ◆ **he was ~ed by £5,000** on lui a fait payer 5 000 livres d'impôts de moins qu'on ne l'aurait dû

under-the-counter* /ˈʌndəðəˈkaʊntəʳ/ ADJ clandestin, en douce* ◆ **it was all very ~** tout se faisait sous le manteau *or* en sous-main ; see also **counter¹**

underthings* /ˈʌndəθɪŋz/ NPL dessous *mpl*

undertone /ˈʌndətəʊn/ N 1 ◆ **to say sth in an ~** dire qch à mi-voix 2 *(= suggestion, hint)* sous-entendu *m* ◆ **political/racial/sexual ~s** sous-entendus *mpl* politiques/raciaux/sexuels ◆ **there are no sinister ~s to his comments** il n'y a aucun sous-entendu sinistre dans ses commentaires ◆ **an ~ of criticism** des critiques voilées *or* sous-jacentes ◆ **his voice had an ~ of anger** on sentait un fond de colère dans sa voix ◆ **a witty story with serious ~s** une histoire spirituelle, mais avec un fond sérieux 3 *[of perfume, taste, colour]* nuance *f* ◆ **brown with pinkish ~s** marron avec des nuances de rose

undertook /ˈʌndəˈtʊk/ VB pt of **undertake**

undertow /ˈʌndətəʊ/ N 1 *(lit)* courant *m* sous-marin *(provoqué par le retrait de la vague)* 2 *(fig)* tension *f*

underuse /ˌʌndəˈjuːz/ VT ⇒ **underutilize** N /ˌʌndəˈjuːs/ ⇒ **underutilization**

underused /ˌʌndəˈjuːzd/ ADJ ⇒ **underutilized**

underutilization /ˌʌndəjuːtɪlaɪˈzeɪʃən/ N *[of potential, talent, resources, land]* sous-exploitation *f* ; *[of space, facilities, equipment]* sous-utilisation *f*, sous-emploi *m*

underutilize /ˌʌndəˈjuːtɪlaɪz/ VT *[+ potential, talent, resources, land]* sous-exploiter ; *[+ space, facilities, equipment]* sous-utiliser, sous-employer

underutilized /ˌʌndəˈjuːtɪlaɪzd/ ADJ *[potential, talent, resources, land]* sous-exploité ; *[space, facilities, equipment]* sous-utilisé, sous-employé

undervalue /ˌʌndəˈvæljuː/ VT *[+ help, contribution]* sous-estimer ; *[+ person]* sous-estimer, mésestimer

undervalued /ˌʌndəˈvæljuːd/ ADJ *[person, helper, help, contribution]* sous-estimé ◆ **this house is ~** cette maison vaut plus que son prix ◆ **it's ~ by about $1,000** cela vaut environ 1 000 dollars de plus

undervest /ˈʌndəvest/ N maillot *m* de corps

underwater /ˈʌndəˈwɔːtəʳ/ ADJ sous-marin ADV sous l'eau

underway, under way /ˌʌndəˈweɪ/ ADJ ◆ **to be ~** *(Naut)* faire route, être en route ; *(fig) [talks, search, process, campaign]* être en cours ◆ **the investigation is now ~** l'enquête est en cours ◆ **to get ~** *(Naut)* appareiller, lever l'ancre ; *[talks, conference, campaign, festival]* démarrer ; *[process, reforms, programme]* être mis en œuvre

underwear /ˈʌndəwɛəʳ/ N *(NonC)* sous-vêtements *mpl* ; *(women's only)* dessous *mpl*, lingerie *f NonC* ◆ **to be in one's ~** être en sous-vêtements *or* en petite tenue

underweight /ˌʌndəˈweɪt/ ADJ 1 *[person]* **to be ~** ne pas peser assez, être trop maigre ◆ **she's 20lb ~** elle pèse 9 kilos de moins qu'elle ne devrait 2 *[goods]* d'un poids insuffisant ◆ **it's 50 grams ~** il manque 50 grammes

underwent /ˌʌndəˈwent/ VB pt of **undergo**

underwhelmed /ˌʌndəˈwelmd/ ADJ *(hum)* peu impressionné

underwhelming /ˌʌndəˈwelmɪŋ/ ADJ *(hum)* décevant

underwired /ˌʌndəˈwaɪəd/ ADJ *[bra]* à armature

underworld /ˈʌndəwɜːld/ N 1 *(Myth = hell)* ◆ **the ~** les enfers *mpl* 2 *(criminal)* ◆ **the ~** le milieu, la pègre COMP *[organization, personality]* du milieu ; *[connections]* avec le milieu ; *[attack]* organisé par le milieu

underwrite /ˌʌndəˈraɪt/ (pret **underwrote**, ptp **underwritten**) VT 1 *(Insurance) [+ policy]* réassurer ; *[+ risk]* assurer contre, garantir ; *[+ amount]* garantir 2 *[+ share issue]* garantir (une *or* l'émission de) 3 *(Comm, Fin) [+ project, enterprise]* soutenir *or* appuyer (financièrement) 4 *(= support) [+ decision, statement etc]* soutenir, souscrire à

underwriter /ˈʌndəˌraɪtəʳ/ N 1 *(Insurance)* assureur *m* 2 *(Stock Exchange)* syndicataire *mf*

underwritten /ˈʌndəˈrɪtn/ VB ptp of **underwrite**

underwrote /ˌʌndəˈrəʊt/ VB pt of **underwrite**

undeserved /ˌʌndɪˈzɜːvd/ ADJ immérité

undeservedly /ˌʌndɪˈzɜːvɪdlɪ/ ADV *[reward, punish]* à tort, indûment ; *[be rewarded, punished]* sans l'avoir mérité, indûment

undeserving /ˌʌndɪˈzɜːvɪŋ/ ADJ *[person]* peu méritant ; *[cause]* peu méritoire ◆ **~ of sth** indigne de qch, qui ne mérite pas qch

undesirable /ˌʌndɪˈzaɪərəbl/ ADJ peu souhaitable ; *(stronger)* indésirable ◆ **it is ~ that ...** il est peu souhaitable que ... + *subj* ◆ **~ alien** *(Admin, Jur)* étranger *m*, -ère *f* indésirable N indésirable *mf*

undetected /ˌʌndɪˈtektɪd/ ADJ non décelé, non détecté ◆ **to go ~** passer inaperçu, ne pas être repéré ◆ **to do sth ~** faire qch sans se faire repérer

undetermined /ˌʌndɪˈtɜːmɪnd/ ADJ *(= unknown)* indéterminé, non connu ; *(= uncertain)* irrésolu, indécis

undeterred /ˌʌndɪˈtɜːd/ ADJ non découragé ◆ **to carry on ~** continuer sans se laisser décourager

undeveloped /ˌʌndɪˈveləpt/ ADJ *[fruit, intelligence, part of body]* qui ne s'est pas développé ; *[film]* non développé ; *[land, resources]* non exploité, inexploité

undeviating /ʌnˈdiːvɪeɪtɪŋ/ ADJ *[path]* droit ; *[policy, course]* constant

undiagnosed /ʌnˈdaɪəgnəʊzd/ ADJ *(lit, fig)* non diagnostiqué

undid /ʌnˈdɪd/ VB pt of **undo**

undies * /ˈʌndɪz/ NPL dessous *mpl* ; *(women's only)* lingerie *f NonC*

undigested /ˌʌndaɪˈdʒestɪd/ ADJ non digéré

undignified /ʌnˈdɪgnɪfaɪd/ ADJ qui manque de dignité ◆ **how ~!** quel manque de dignité !

undiluted /ˌʌndaɪˈluːtɪd/ ADJ 1 *(lit) [concentrate]* non dilué 2 *(fig) [pleasure]* sans mélange ; *[nonsense]* pur

undiminished /ˌʌndɪˈmɪnɪʃt/ ADJ non diminué

undimmed /ʌnˈdɪmd/ ADJ 1 *(in brightness) [lamp]* qui n'a pas été mis en veilleuse ; *[car headlight]* qui n'est pas en code 2 *(liter) [sight]* aussi bon qu'auparavant 3 *(fig) [enthusiasm, passion, ambition]* aussi fort qu'avant ; *[beauty]* non terni ◆ **with ~ optimism** avec toujours autant d'optimisme ◆ **her optimism is ~** elle est toujours aussi optimiste ◆ **my memory of it is ~** je m'en souviens avec précision

undiplomatic /ˌʌnˌdɪpləˈmætɪk/ ADJ *[person]* peu diplomate ; *[action, answer]* peu diplomatique

undipped /ʌnˈdɪpt/ ADJ *[car headlight]* qui n'est pas en code

undiscerning /ˌʌndɪˈsɜːnɪŋ/ ADJ qui manque de discernement

undischarged /ˌʌndɪsˈtʃɑːdʒd/ ADJ *[bankrupt]* non réhabilité ; *[debt]* non acquitté, impayé

undisciplined /ʌnˈdɪsɪplɪnd/ ADJ indiscipliné

undisclosed /ˌʌndɪsˈkləʊzd/ ADJ gardé secret

undiscovered /ˌʌndɪsˈkʌvəd/ ADJ *(= not found)* non découvert ; *(= unknown)* inconnu ◆ **the treasure remained ~ for 700 years** le trésor n'a été découvert que 700 ans plus tard

undiscriminating /ˌʌndɪsˈkrɪmɪneɪtɪŋ/ ADJ qui manque de discernement

undisguised /ˌʌndɪsˈgaɪzd/ ADJ *(lit, fig)* non déguisé

undismayed /ˌʌndɪsˈmeɪd/ ADJ imperturbable

undisputed /ˌʌndɪsˈpjuːtɪd/ ADJ incontesté

undistinguished /ˌʌndɪsˈtɪŋgwɪʃt/ ADJ *(in character)* médiocre, quelconque ; *(in appearance)* peu distingué

undisturbed /ˌʌndɪsˈtɜːbd/ ADJ 1 *(= untouched) [papers, clues]* non dérangé, non déplacé ; *(= uninterrupted) [sleep]* non troublé, paisible ; *[place]* épargné ◆ **the war had not left Clydebank ~** la guerre n'avait pas épargné Clydebank ◆ **the desk looked ~** apparemment, personne n'avait touché au bureau ◆ **these flowers are best left ~** il vaut mieux ne pas toucher à ces fleurs ◆ **is there somewhere we can talk ~?** y a-t-il un endroit où nous pourrions parler sans être dérangés ? 2 *(= unworried)* non inquiet (-ète *f*), non troublé ◆ **he was ~ by the news** la nouvelle ne l'a pas inquiété *or* troublé ADV *[work, play, sleep]* sans être dérangé

undivided /ˌʌndɪˈvaɪdɪd/ ADJ 1 *(= wholehearted) [admiration]* sans réserve, sans partage ◆ **to require sb's ~ attention** exiger toute l'attention *or* l'attention pleine et entière de qn 2 *(= not split) [country, institution]* uni ; *(Jur) [property]* indivis

undo /ʌnˈduː/ (pret **undid**, ptp **undone**) VT *[+ button, garment, knot, parcel, box, knitting]* défaire ; *[+ good effect]* détruire, annuler ; *[+ mischief, wrong]* réparer ; *(Comput)* annuler ◆ **he was undone by his own ambition** c'est son ambition qui l'a perdu ◆ **they were undone by a goal from Barnes** ils ont été battus grâce à un but de Barnes ; see also **undone**

undocumented /ʌnˈdɒkjʊmentɪd/ ADJ 1 *[event]* sur lequel on ne possède pas de témoignages 2 *(US) [person]* sans papiers

undoing /ʌnˈduːɪŋ/ N *(NonC)* ruine *f*, perte *f* ◆ **that was his ~** c'est ce qui l'a perdu, c'est ce qui a causé sa perte

undomesticated /ˌʌndəˈmestɪkeɪtɪd/ ADJ 1 *[animal]* non domestiqué 2 *[person]* qui n'aime pas les tâches ménagères

undone /ʌnˈdʌn/ VB ptp of **undo** ADJ *[button, garment, knot, parcel]* défait ; *[task]* non accompli ◆ **to come ~** se défaire ◆ **to leave sth ~** ne pas faire qch ◆ **I am ~!** (†† *or hum*) je suis perdu !

undoubted /ʌnˈdaʊtɪd/ ADJ indubitable, indéniable

undoubtedly /ʌnˈdaʊtɪdlɪ/ LANGUAGE IN USE 26.3 ADV indubitablement, sans aucun doute

undramatic /ˌʌndrəˈmætɪk/ ADJ peu dramatique

undreamed-of /ʌnˈdriːmdɒv/, **undreamt-of** /ʌnˈdremtɒv/ ADJ *(= unhoped for)* inespéré ; *(= unsuspected)* insoupçonné, qui dépasse l'imagination

undress /ʌnˈdres/ VT déshabiller ◆ **to get ~ed** se déshabiller ; see also **undressed** VI se déshabiller N ◆ **in a state of ~** *(gen)* en petite tenue ; *(also Mil) (in civilian clothes)* en civil ; *(in plain uniform)* en simple uniforme

undressed /ʌnˈdrest/ VB pret, ptp of **undress** ADJ 1 *[salad]* non assaisonné 2 *[wound]* non pansé ; see also **dress**

undrinkable /ʌnˈdrɪŋkəbl/ ADJ *(= unpalatable)* imbuvable ; *(= poisonous)* non potable

undue /ʌnˈdjuː/ ADJ *(gen)* excessif ; *[anger, haste etc]* excessif ◆ **I hope this will not cause you ~ inconvenience** j'espère que cela ne vous dérangera pas trop *or* pas outre mesure

undulate /ˈʌndjʊleɪt/ VI onduler, ondoyer

undulating /ˈʌndjʊleɪtɪŋ/ ADJ *[movement]* ondoyant, onduleux ; *[line]* sinueux, onduleux ; *[countryside]* vallonné

undulation /ˌʌndjʊˈleɪʃən/ N ondulation *f*, ondoiement *m*

undulatory /ˈʌndjʊlətrɪ/ ADJ ondulatoire

unduly /ʌnˈdjuːlɪ/ ADV trop, excessivement ◆ **he was not ~ worried** il ne s'inquiétait pas trop *or* pas outre mesure

undying /ʌnˈdaɪɪŋ/ ADJ *(fig)* éternel

unearned /ʌnˈɜːnd/ ADJ 1 *(gen) [praise, reward]* immérité 2 *(Fin)* ◆ **~ income** rentes *fpl* ◆ **~ increment** plus-value *f*

unearth /ʌnˈɜːθ/ VT *[+ documents, evidence, plot]* mettre au jour ; *[+ remains, bones]* découvrir, mettre au jour ; *[+ lost object]* dénicher, déterrer ; *[+ talent]* dénicher

unearthly /ʌnˈɜːθlɪ/ ADJ *(gen)* surnaturel, mystérieux ; *(threatening) [silence]* lugubre ; *(* fig)* impossible * ◆ **at some ~ hour** à une heure indue

unease /ʌnˈiːz/ N malaise *m*, gêne *f* *(at, about* devant)

uneasily /ʌnˈiːzɪlɪ/ ADV *(= ill-at-ease)* avec gêne ; *(= worriedly)* avec inquiétude ◆ **to sleep ~** *(= fitfully)* mal dormir ; *(= restlessly)* dormir d'un sommeil agité

uneasiness /ʌnˈiːzɪnɪs/ N *(NonC)* inquiétude *f*, malaise *m* *(at, about* devant)

uneasy /ʌnˈiːzɪ/ ADJ *[calm, peace, truce]* troublé, difficile ; *[silence]* gêné ; *[sleep, night]* agité ; *[conscience]* pas tranquille ; *[person] (= ill-at-ease)* mal à l'aise, gêné ; *(= worried)* inquiet (-ète *f*) *(at, about* devant, de), anxieux ◆ **to grow** *or* **become ~ about sth** commencer à s'inquiéter au sujet de qch ◆ **I have an ~ feeling that he's watching me** j'ai l'impression déconcertante qu'il me regarde ◆ **I had an ~ feeling that he would change his mind** je ne pouvais m'empêcher de penser qu'il allait changer d'avis

uneatable /ʌnˈiːtəbl/ ADJ immangeable

uneaten /ʌnˈiːtn/ ADJ non mangé, non touché

uneconomic(al) /ˈʌnˌiːkəˈnɒmɪk(əl)/ ADJ *[machine, car]* peu économique ; *[work, method]* peu économique, peu rentable ◆ **it is ~(al) to do that** il n'est pas économique *or* rentable de faire cela

unedifying /ʌnˈedɪfaɪɪŋ/ ADJ peu édifiant

unedited /ʌnˈedɪtɪd/ ADJ *[film]* non monté ; *[essays, works]* non édité ; *[tape]* dans sa version intégrale ◆ **~ emotions** des émotions à l'état brut ◆ **an ~ show packed with sexual innuendo** un spectacle non expurgé bourré d'allusions sexuelles ◆ **to broadcast the Commons proceedings ~** diffuser les débats parlementaires en version intégrale

uneducated /ʌnˈedjʊkeɪtɪd/ ADJ *[person]* sans instruction ; *[letter, report]* informe, plein de fautes ; *(= badly written)* mal écrit ; *[handwriting]* d'illettré ; *[speech, accent]* populaire

unemotional /ˌʌnɪˈməʊʃənl/ ADJ *(= having little emotion)* peu émotif, flegmatique ; *(= showing little emotion) [person, voice, attitude]* qui ne montre *or* ne trahit aucune émotion, impassible ; *[reaction]* peu émotionnel ; *[description, writing]* neutre, sans passion

unemotionally /ˌʌnɪˈməʊʃnəlɪ/ ADV de façon impassible, sans trahir d'émotion

unemployable /ˌʌnɪmˈplɔɪəbl/ ADJ incapable de travailler

unemployed /ˌʌnɪmˈplɔɪd/ ADJ *[person]* au chômage, sans travail *or* emploi ; *[machine, object]* inutilisé, dont on ne se sert pas ; *(Fin) [capital]* qui ne travaille pas ◆ **~ person** chômeur *m*, -euse *f* ; *(esp Admin)* demandeur *m* d'emploi ◆ **the numbers ~** *(Econ)* les inactifs *mpl* NPL **the unemployed** les chômeurs *mpl*, les sans-emploi *mpl* ; *(esp Admin)* les demandeurs *mpl* d'emploi ◆ **the young** ~ les jeunes *mpl* sans emploi *or* au chômage

unemployment /ˌʌnɪmˈplɔɪmənt/ **N** *(NonC)* chômage *m* ◆ **to reduce** *or* **cut** ~ réduire le chômage *or* le nombre des chômeurs ◆ ~ **has risen** le chômage *or* le nombre des chômeurs a augmenté

COMP unemployment benefit N *(Brit: formerly)* allocation *f* (de) chômage
unemployment compensation N *(US)* → **unemployment benefit**
unemployment figures NPL chiffres *mpl* du chômage, nombre *m* des chômeurs
unemployment line N *(US)* ◆ **to join the ~ line(s)** se retrouver au chômage
unemployment rate N ◆ **an ~ rate of 10%** *or* **of 1 in 10** un taux de chômage de 10%

unencumbered /ˈʌnɪnˈkʌmbəd/ **ADJ** non encombré *(with* de)

unending /ʌnˈendɪŋ/ **ADJ** interminable, sans fin

unendurable /ˈʌnɪnˈdjʊərəbl/ **ADJ** insupportable, intolérable

unenforceable /ˈʌnɪnˈfɔːsəbl/ **ADJ** *[law etc]* inapplicable

unengaged /ˈʌnɪnˈgeɪdʒd/ **ADJ** libre

un-English /ˈʌnˈɪŋglɪʃ/ **ADJ** peu anglais, pas anglais

unenlightened /ˈʌnɪnˈlaɪtnd/ **ADJ** peu éclairé, rétrograde

unenterprising /ˈʌnˈentəpraɪzɪŋ/ **ADJ** *[person]* peu entreprenant, qui manque d'initiative ; *[policy, act]* qui manque d'audace *or* de hardiesse

unenthusiastic /ˈʌnɪnˌθuːzɪˈæstɪk/ **ADJ** peu enthousiaste ◆ **you seem rather ~ about it** ça n'a pas l'air de vous enthousiasmer

unenthusiastically /ˈʌnɪnˌθuːzɪˈæstɪkəlɪ/ **ADV** sans enthousiasme

unenviable /ˈʌnˈenvɪəbl/ **ADJ** peu enviable

unequal /ˈʌnˈiːkwəl/ **ADJ** 1 *(= not the same) [size, opportunity, work]* inégal ; *(= inegalitarian) [system]* inégalitaire 2 *(= inadequate)* ◆ **to be ~ to a task** ne pas être à la hauteur d'une tâche

unequalled /ˈʌnˈiːkwəld/ **ADJ** *[skill, enthusiasm, footballer, pianist]* inégalé, sans égal ; *[record]* inégalé

unequally /ˈʌnˈiːkwəlɪ/ **ADV** inégalement

unequivocal /ˈʌnɪˈkwɪvəkəl/ **ADJ** sans équivoque ◆ **he gave him an ~ "no"** il lui a opposé un "non" catégorique *or* sans équivoque

unequivocally /ˈʌnɪˈkwɪvəkəlɪ/ **ADV** sans équivoque

unerring /ˈʌnˈɜːrɪŋ/ **ADJ** *[judgement, accuracy]* infaillible ; *[aim, skill, blow]* sûr

unerringly /ˈʌnˈɜːrɪŋlɪ/ **ADV** infailliblement ◆ **they ~ chose the most promising projects** ils choisissaient infailliblement les projets les plus porteurs ◆ **she ~ made the connection** elle n'a pas manqué d'établir le rapport

UNESCO /juːˈneskəʊ/ **N** (abbrev of **United Nations Educational, Scientific and Cultural Organization**) UNESCO *f*

unescorted /ˌʌnesˈkɔːtɪd/ **ADJ, ADV** 1 *(Mil, Naut)* sans escorte 2 *(= unaccompanied by a partner)* sans partenaire, non accompagné

unessential /ˈʌnɪˈsenʃəl/ **ADJ** non essentiel, non indispensable

unesthetic /ˌʌniːsˈθetɪk/ **ADJ** ⇒ **unaesthetic**

unethical /ˈʌnˈeθɪkəl/ **ADJ** *(gen)* moralement contestable, contraire à l'éthique ; *(= contrary to professional code of conduct) (Med etc)* contraire à la déontologie

unethically /ˈʌnˈeθɪkəlɪ/ **ADV** *(gen) [behave, act, obtain]* de façon immorale *or* moralement contestable ; *(= against professional code of conduct)* de façon contraire à la déontologie

uneven /ˈʌnˈiːvən/ **ADJ** 1 *(= not flat or straight) [surface]* raboteux, inégal ; *[path]* cahoteux ; *[ground]* accidenté ; *[teeth]* irrégulier ◆ **the wall is** ~ le mur n'est pas droit 2 *(= irregular) [pace, rate, breathing, pulse]* irrégulier ; *[colour]* inégalement réparti ◆ **the engine sounds** ~ il y a des à-coups dans le moteur, le moteur ne tourne pas rond 3 *(= inconsistent) [quality, performance, acting]* inégal 4 *(= unfair) [distribution, contest, competition]* inégal 5 *[number]* impair

unevenly /ˈʌnˈiːvənlɪ/ **ADV** 1 *(= irregularly) [move, spread, develop]* de façon irrégulière 2 *(= unequally) [share, distribute]* inégalement ◆ **the two armies were ~ matched** les deux armées n'étaient pas de force égale

unevenness /ˈʌnˈiːvənnɪs/ **N** *(NonC)* 1 *[of surface, path, ground]* inégalité *f*, aspérités *fpl* 2 *(= irregularity) [of motion, breathing, pace, rate, pulse]* irrégularité *f* ; *[of colour]* répartition *f* inégale 3 *(= inconsistency) [of quality, performance, acting, writing, film]* caractère *m* inégal 4 *(= inequality) [of sharing out, distribution]* inégalité *f*

uneventful /ˈʌnɪˈventfʊl/ **ADJ** *[day, meeting, journey]* sans incidents, peu mouvementé ; *[life]* calme, tranquille ; *[career]* peu mouvementé

uneventfully /ˈʌnɪˈventfəlɪ/ **ADV** *[take place, happen]* sans incidents, sans histoires

unexceptionable /ˌʌnɪkˈsepʃnəbl/ **ADJ** irréprochable

unexceptional /ˌʌnɪkˈsepʃənl/ **ADJ** tout à fait ordinaire

unexciting /ˈʌnɪkˈsaɪtɪŋ/ **ADJ** *[time, life, visit]* peu passionnant, peu intéressant ; *[food]* ordinaire

unexpected /ˈʌnɪksˈpektɪd/ **ADJ** *[arrival]* inattendu, inopiné ; *[result, change, success, happiness]* inattendu, imprévu ◆ **it was all very** ~ on ne s'y attendait pas du tout

unexpectedly /ˈʌnɪksˈpektɪdlɪ/ **ADV** alors qu'on ne s'y attend *(or* attendait *etc)* pas, subitement ◆ **to arrive** ~ arriver à l'improviste *or* inopinément

unexpired /ˈʌnɪksˈpaɪəd/ **ADJ** non expiré, encore valide

unexplained /ˈʌnɪksˈpleɪnd/ **ADJ** inexpliqué

unexploded /ˈʌnɪksˈpləʊdɪd/ **ADJ** non explosé, non éclaté

unexploited /ˈʌnɪksˈplɔɪtɪd/ **ADJ** inexploité

unexplored /ˈʌnɪksˈplɔːd/ **ADJ** inexploré

unexposed /ˈʌnɪksˈpəʊzd/ **ADJ** *[film]* vierge

unexpressed /ˈʌnɪksˈprest/ **ADJ** inexprimé

unexpurgated /ˈʌnˈekspɜːgeɪtɪd/ **ADJ** *(frm)* non expurgé, intégral

unfading /ʌnˈfeɪdɪŋ/ **ADJ** *(fig) [hope]* éternel ; *[memory]* impérissable, ineffaçable

unfailing /ʌnˈfeɪlɪŋ/ **ADJ** *[supply]* inépuisable, intarissable ; *[zeal]* inépuisable ; *[optimism]* inébranlable ; *[remedy]* infaillible

unfailingly /ʌnˈfeɪlɪŋlɪ/ **ADV** infailliblement, immanquablement

unfair /ˈʌnˈfeəʳ/ **ADJ** *[person, comment, criticism, trial]* injuste *(to sb* envers qn, à l'égard de qn) ; *[decision, arrangement, deal]* injuste *(to sb* envers qn, à l'égard de qn), inéquitable ; *[competition, play, tactics, practices]* déloyal ◆ **you're being** ~ vous êtes injuste ◆ **it's ~ that** ... il n'est pas juste *or* il est injuste que ... + *subj* ◆ **it is ~ to expect her to do that** il n'est pas juste d'attendre qu'elle fasse cela ◆ **it is ~ of her to do so** il est injuste qu'elle agisse ainsi, ce n'est pas juste de sa part d'agir ainsi ◆ **to have an ~ advantage over sb/sth** être injustement avantagé par rapport à qn/qch **COMP unfair dismissal N** licenciement *m* abusif

unfairly /ˈʌnˈfeəlɪ/ **ADV** *[treat, judge, compare]* injustement ; *[decide]* arbitrairement ; *[play]* déloyalement ◆ **he was ~ dismissed** il a été victime d'un licenciement abusif

unfairness /ˈʌnˈfeənɪs/ **N** *[of person, decision, arrangement, deal, advantage, comment, criticism]* injustice *f* ; *[of trial]* caractère *m* arbitraire ; *[of competition, tactics, practices]* caractère *m* déloyal

unfaithful /ˈʌnˈfeɪθfʊl/ **ADJ** infidèle *(to* à)

unfaithfully /ˈʌnˈfeɪθfəlɪ/ **ADV** infidèlement, avec infidélité

unfaithfulness /ˈʌnˈfeɪθfʊlnɪs/ **N** infidélité *f*

unfaltering /ʌnˈfɔːltərɪŋ/ **ADJ** *[step, voice]* ferme, assuré

unfalteringly /ʌnˈfɔːltərɪŋlɪ/ **ADV** *[speak]* d'une voix ferme *or* assurée ; *[walk]* d'un pas ferme *or* assuré

unfamiliar /ˈʌnfəˈmɪljəʳ/ **ADJ** *[place, sight, person, subject]* inconnu ◆ **to be ~ with sth** mal connaître qch, ne pas bien connaître qch

unfamiliarity /ˈʌnfəˌmɪlɪˈærɪtɪ/ **N** *(NonC)* aspect *m* étrange *or* inconnu

unfashionable /ˈʌnˈfæʃnəbl/ **ADJ** *[dress, subject]* démodé, passé de mode ; *[district, shop, hotel]* peu chic *inv* ◆ **it is ~ to speak of ...** ça ne se fait plus de parler de ...

unfasten /ˈʌnˈfɑːsn/ **VT** *[+ garment, buttons, rope]* défaire ; *[+ door]* ouvrir, déverrouiller ; *[+ bonds]* défaire, détacher ; *(= loosen)* desserrer

unfathomable /ʌnˈfæðəməbl/ **ADJ** *[mysteries, depths]* insondable ; *[reason]* totalement obscur ; *[person]* énigmatique, impénétrable

unfathomed /ʌnˈfæðəmd/ **ADJ** *(lit, fig)* insondé

unfavourable, unfavorable *(US)* /ˈʌnˈfeɪvərəbl/ **ADJ** *[conditions, report, impression, outlook, weather]* défavorable ; *[moment]* peu propice, inopportun ; *[terms]* désavantageux ; *[wind]* contraire

unfavourably, unfavorably *(US)* /ˈʌnˈfeɪvərəblɪ/ **ADV** défavorablement ◆ **I was ~ impressed** j'ai eu une impression défavorable ◆ **to regard sth** ~ être défavorable *or* hostile à qch

unfazed * /ˈʌnˈfeɪzd/ **ADJ** imperturbable ◆ **it left him quite** ~ il n'a pas bronché

unfeasible /ʌnˈfiːzəbl/ **ADJ** irréalisable

unfeeling /ʌnˈfiːlɪŋ/ **ADJ** insensible, impitoyable

unfeelingly /ʌnˈfiːlɪŋlɪ/ **ADV** sans pitié, impitoyablement

unfeigned /ʌnˈfeɪnd/ **ADJ** non simulé, sincère

unfeignedly /ʌnˈfeɪnɪdlɪ/ **ADV** sincèrement, vraiment

unfeminine /ʌnˈfemɪnɪn/ **ADJ** peu féminin

unfettered /ˈʌnˈfetəd/ **ADJ** *(liter: lit, fig)* sans entrave ◆ ~ **by** libre de

unfilial /ˈʌnˈfɪljəl/ **ADJ** *(frm)* peu filial

unfilled /ˈʌnˈfɪld/ **ADJ** *[post, vacancy]* à pourvoir, vacant

unfinished /ˈʌnˈfɪnɪʃt/ **ADJ** *[task, essay]* inachevé, incomplet (-ète *f*) ◆ **I have three ~ letters** j'ai trois lettres à finir ◆ **we have some ~ business (to attend to)** nous avons une affaire *(or* des affaires) à régler ◆ **the Unfinished Symphony** la Symphonie inachevée ◆ **it looks rather ~** *[piece of furniture, craft work etc]* c'est mal fini, la finition laisse à désirer

unfit /ˈʌnˈfɪt/ **ADJ** 1 *(= not physically fit)* qui n'est pas en forme ◆ **he was ~ to drive** il n'était pas en état de conduire ◆ **he is ~ for work** il n'est pas en état de reprendre le travail ◆ ~ **for military service** inapte au service militaire ◆ **the doctor declared him ~ for the match** le docteur a déclaré qu'il n'était pas en état de jouer

2 *(= incompetent)* inapte, impropre *(for* à ; *to do sth* à faire qch) ; *(= unworthy)* indigne *(to do sth* de faire qch) ◆ **he is ~ to be a teacher** il ne devrait pas enseigner ◆ ~ **for habitation**, ~ **to live in** inhabitable ◆ ~ **for consumption** impropre à la consommation ◆ ~ **to eat** *(= unpalatable)* immangeable ; *(= poisonous)* non comestible ◆ ~ **for publication** impropre à la publication, impubliable ◆ **road ~ for lorries** route impraticable pour les camions
VT *(frm)* rendre inapte *(for* à ; *to do sth* à faire qch)

unfitness /ʌn'fɪtnɪs/ N 1 *(= ill health)* incapacité *f* 2 *(= unsuitability)* inaptitude *f (for* à ; *to do sth* à faire qch)

unfitted /ʌn'fɪtɪd/ ADJ *(frm)* inapte *(for* à ; *to do sth* à faire qch)

unfitting /ʌn'fɪtɪŋ/ ADJ *(frm) [language, behaviour]* peu *or* guère convenable, inconvenant ; *[ending, result]* mal approprié

unfix /ʌn'fɪks/ VT détacher, enlever ; *(Mil) [+ bayonets]* remettre

unflagging /ʌn'flægɪŋ/ ADJ *[person, devotion, patience]* infatigable, inlassable ; *[enthusiasm]* inépuisable ; *[interest]* soutenu jusqu'au bout

unflaggingly /ʌn'flægɪŋlɪ/ ADV infatigablement, inlassablement

unflappability* /ˌʌnflæpə'bɪlɪtɪ/ N *(NonC)* calme *m*, flegme *m*

unflappable* /ʌn'flæpəbl/ ADJ imperturbable, flegmatique

unflattering /ʌn'flætərɪŋ/ ADJ *[person, remark, photo, portrait]* peu flatteur ◆ **he was very ~ about it** ce qu'il en a dit n'avait rien de flatteur *or* n'était pas flatteur ◆ **she wears ~ clothes** elle porte des vêtements qui ne la mettent guère en valeur *or* qui ne l'avantagent guère

unflatteringly /ʌn'flætərɪŋlɪ/ ADV d'une manière peu flatteuse

unfledged /ʌn'fledʒd/ ADJ *(fig) [person, organization, movement]* qui manque d'expérience, novice

unflinching /ʌn'flɪntʃɪŋ/ ADJ *[support, loyalty]* indéfectible ; *[determination]* à toute épreuve ; *[expression, determination]* stoïque ◆ **she was ~ in her determination to succeed** elle était absolument déterminée à réussir

unflinchingly /ʌn'flɪntʃɪŋlɪ/ ADV stoïquement, sans broncher

unflyable /ʌn'flaɪəbl/ ADJ *[plane]* qu'on ne peut pas faire voler

unfocu(s)sed /ˌʌn'fəʊkəst/ ADJ 1 *[camera]* pas mis au point ; *[gaze, eyes]* dans le vague 2 *(fig) [aims, desires etc]* flou, vague

unfold /ʌn'fəʊld/ VT 1 *(lit) [+ napkin, map, blanket]* déplier ; *[+ wings]* déployer ◆ **to ~ a map on a table** étaler une carte sur une table ◆ **to ~ one's arms** décroiser les bras 2 *(fig) [+ plans, ideas]* exposer ; *[+ secret]* dévoiler, révéler VI *[flower]* s'ouvrir, s'épanouir ; *[view, countryside]* se dérouler, s'étendre ; *[story, film, plot]* se dérouler

unforced /ʌn'fɔːst/ ADJ *[smile, laugh]* naturel ◆ ~ **error** *(Sport)* faute *f* directe

unforeseeable /ˌʌnfɔː'siːəbl/ ADJ imprévisible

unforeseen /ˌʌnfɔː'siːn/ ADJ imprévu

unforgettable /ˌʌnfə'getəbl/ ADJ *(gen)* inoubliable ; *(for unpleasant things)* impossible à oublier

unforgettably /ˌʌnfə'getəblɪ/ ADV ◆ ~ **beautiful/clear** d'une beauté/clarté inoubliable ◆ ~ **ugly/dirty** d'une laideur/saleté frappante

unforgivable /ˌʌnfə'gɪvəbl/ ADJ impardonnable

unforgivably /ˌʌnfə'gɪvəblɪ/ ADV *[behave]* d'une manière impardonnable ◆ **he was ~ rude** il a été d'une grossièreté impardonnable ◆ **she was ~ late** elle est arrivée avec un retard impardonnable

unforgiven /ˌʌnfə'gɪvən/ ADJ non pardonné

unforgiving /ˌʌnfə'gɪvɪŋ/ ADJ *[place]* inhospitalier ; *[course, pitch]* impitoyable ; *[profession]* ingrat

unforgotten /ˌʌnfə'gɒtn/ ADJ inoublié

unformed /ʌn'fɔːmd/ ADJ mal *or* peu défini ◆ **my thoughts were still relatively ~** mes pensées étaient encore relativement mal définies ◆ **the ~ minds of children** l'esprit encore peu formé des enfants ◆ **the market for which they are competing is still ~** le marché qu'ils se disputent n'est pas encore complètement *or* bien établi

unforthcoming /ˌʌnfɔːθ'kʌmɪŋ/ ADJ *[reply, person]* réticent *(about* sur) ◆ **he was very ~ about it** il s'est montré très réticent à ce propos, il s'est montré peu disposé à en parler

unfortified /ʌn'fɔːtɪfaɪd/ ADJ sans fortifications, non fortifié

unfortunate /ʌn'fɔːtʃənɪt/ ADJ *[person]* malheureux, malchanceux ; *[coincidence]* malheureux, fâcheux ; *[circumstances]* triste ; *[event]* fâcheux, malencontreux ; *[incident, episode]* fâcheux, regrettable ; *[remark]* malheureux, malencontreux ◆ **it is most ~ that ...** il est très malheureux *or* regrettable que ... + *subj* ◆ **how ~!** quel dommage ! ◆ **he has been ~** il n'a pas eu de chance N malheureux *m*, -euse *f*

unfortunately /ʌn'fɔːtʃənɪtlɪ/ LANGUAGE IN USE 12.3, 18.2, 25.2, 26.3 ADV malheureusement, par malheur ◆ **an ~ worded remark** une remarque formulée de façon malheureuse *or* malencontreuse

unfounded /ʌn'faʊndɪd/ ADJ *[rumour, allegation, belief]* dénué de tout fondement, sans fondement ; *[criticism]* injustifié

unframed /ʌn'freɪmd/ ADJ *[picture]* sans cadre

unfreeze /ʌn'friːz/ (pret **unfroze**, ptp **unfrozen**) VT 1 *(lit)* dégeler 2 *[+ prices, wages]* débloquer VI dégeler

unfreezing /ʌn'friːzɪŋ/ N *[of prices, wages]* déblocage *m*

unfrequented /ˌʌnfrɪ'kwentɪd/ ADJ peu fréquenté

unfriendliness /ʌn'frendlɪnɪs/ N *(NonC)* froideur *f (towards* envers)

unfriendly /ʌn'frendlɪ/ ADJ *[person, reception]* froid ; *[attitude, behaviour, act, remark]* inamical ; *(stronger)* hostile ◆ **to be ~ to(wards) sb** manifester de la froideur *or* de l'hostilité envers qn

unfrock /ʌn'frɒk/ VT défroquer

unfroze /ʌn'frəʊz/ VB pt of **unfreeze**

unfrozen /ʌn'frəʊzn/ VB ptp of **unfreeze**

unfruitful /ʌn'fruːtfʊl/ ADJ 1 *(lit)* stérile, infertile 2 *(fig)* infructueux

unfruitfully /ʌn'fruːtfəlɪ/ ADV *(fig)* en vain, sans succès

unfulfilled /ˌʌnfʊl'fɪld/ ADJ *[promise]* non tenu ; *[ambition, prophecy]* non réalisé ; *[desire]* insatisfait ; *[condition]* non rempli ◆ **to feel ~** *[person]* se sentir frustré, éprouver un sentiment d'insatisfaction

unfulfilling /ˌʌnfʊl'fɪlɪŋ/ ADJ peu satisfaisant ◆ **he finds it ~** ça ne le satisfait pas pleinement

unfunny* /ʌn'fʌnɪ/ ADJ qui n'est pas drôle, qui n'a rien de drôle

unfurl /ʌn'fɜːl/ VT déployer VI se déployer

unfurnished /ʌn'fɜːnɪʃt/ ADJ non meublé

ungainliness /ʌn'geɪnlɪnɪs/ N *(NonC)* gaucherie *f*

ungainly /ʌn'geɪnlɪ/ ADJ gauche, disgracieux

ungallant /ʌn'gælənt/ ADJ peu *or* guère galant, discourtois

ungenerous /ʌn'dʒenərəs/ ADJ 1 *(= miserly)* peu généreux, parcimonieux 2 *(= uncharitable)* mesquin, méchant

ungentlemanly /ʌn'dʒentlmənlɪ/ ADJ peu *or* guère galant, discourtois

un-get-at-able* /ˌʌnget'ætəbl/ ADJ inaccessible

ungird /ʌn'gɜːd/ (pret, ptp **ungirt**) VT détacher

unglazed /ʌn'gleɪzd/ ADJ *[door, window]* non vitré ; *[picture]* qui n'est pas sous verre ; *[pottery]* non vernissé, non émaillé ; *[photograph]* mat ; *[cake]* non glacé

unglued /ʌn'gluːd/ ADJ *(gen)* sans colle ◆ **to come ~*** *(US fig) [person]* flancher*, craquer*

ungodliness /ʌn'gɒdlɪnɪs/ N *(NonC)* impiété *f*

ungodly /ʌn'gɒdlɪ/ ADJ 1 *(* = unreasonable) [noise]* impossible* ◆ **at some ~ hour** à une heure impossible* *or* indue 2 *(† = sinful) [person, action, life]* impie, irréligieux

ungovernable /ʌn'gʌvənəbl/ ADJ 1 *(Pol) [people, country]* ingouvernable 2 *(liter = uncontrollable) [rage, hatred, longing]* incontrôlable ; *[desire, passion]* irrépressible ◆ **to have an ~ temper** ne pas savoir se contrôler *or* se maîtriser

ungracious /ʌn'greɪʃəs/ ADJ *[person]* peu aimable ; *[remark, gesture]* désobligeant ◆ **it would be ~ to refuse** on aurait mauvaise grâce à refuser

ungraciously /ʌn'greɪʃəslɪ/ ADV avec mauvaise grâce

ungrammatical /ˌʌngrə'mætɪkəl/ ADJ incorrect, non grammatical, agrammatical

ungrammatically /ˌʌngrə'mætɪkəlɪ/ ADV incorrectement

ungrateful /ʌn'greɪtfʊl/ ADJ *[person]* ingrat *(towards sb* envers qn) ◆ **to be ~ for sth** ne pas montrer de gratitude pour qch

ungratefully /ʌn'greɪtfəlɪ/ ADV avec ingratitude

ungrudging /ʌn'grʌdʒɪŋ/ ADJ *[person, contribution]* généreux ; *[help]* donné sans compter ; *[praise, gratitude]* très sincère

ungrudgingly /ʌn'grʌdʒɪŋlɪ/ ADV *[give]* généreusement ; *[help]* de bon cœur, sans compter

unguarded /ʌn'gɑːdɪd/ ADJ 1 *(= unprotected) [place]* sans surveillance ◆ **to leave a place ~** laisser un endroit sans surveillance 2 *(Tech) [machine]* sans protection 3 *(= open, careless) [person, comment]* spontané, irréfléchi ◆ **in an ~ moment** dans un moment d'inattention

unguardedly /ʌn'gɑːdɪdlɪ/ ADV *[say]* sans réfléchir

unguent /'ʌŋgwənt/ N onguent *m*

ungulate /'ʌŋgjʊleɪt/ ADJ ongulé N animal *m* ongulé ◆ **~s** les ongulés *mpl*

unhallowed /ʌn'hæləʊd/ ADJ *(liter)* non consacré, profane

unhampered /ʌn'hæmpəd/ ADJ *[progress]* aisé ; *[access]* libre ◆ **to operate ~ by the police** opérer sans être gêné par la police ◆ **trade ~ by tax regulations** commerce *m* non entravé par la réglementation fiscale

unhand /ʌn'hænd/ VT *(†† or hum)* lâcher

unhandy* /ʌn'hændɪ/ ADJ gauche, maladroit

unhappily /ʌn'hæpɪlɪ/ ADV 1 *(= miserably) [look at, go]* d'un air malheureux ; *[say]* d'un ton malheureux ◆ **to be ~ married** avoir fait un mariage malheureux 2 *(= unfortunately)* malheureusement ◆ **~, things didn't work out as**

planned malheureusement, les choses ne se sont pas passées comme prévu ◆ ~ **for him, he** ... malheureusement pour lui, il ...

unhappiness /ʌn'hæpɪnɪs/ N (NonC) tristesse *f*, chagrin *m*

unhappy /ʌn'hæpɪ/ ADJ 1 (= *sad*) *[person, expression, marriage]* malheureux ◆ **I had an ~ time at school** j'ai été malheureux à l'école
2 (= *discontented*) *[person]* mécontent (*with or about sb/sth* de qn/qch ; *at sth* de qch) ◆ **to be ~ at doing sth** *or* **to do sth** être mécontent de faire qch
3 (= *worried*) *[person]* inquiet (-ète *f*) (*with or about sb/sth* au sujet de qn/qch ; *at sth* au sujet de qch) ◆ **we are ~ about the decision** cette décision ne nous satisfait pas ◆ **I am** *or* **feel ~ about leaving him alone** je n'aime pas (l'idée de) le laisser seul
4 (= *regrettable*) *[experience, episode]* malheureux ; *[situation, circumstances]* regrettable ; *[coincidence]* malheureux, fâcheux ◆ **this ~ state of affairs** cette situation regrettable *or* déplorable *or* fâcheuse
5 (= *unfortunate*) *[person]* malheureux ; *[place]* affligé
6 (*frm* = *unsuitable*) *[remark]* malheureux, malencontreux ◆ **an ~ choice of words** un choix de mots malheureux *or* malencontreux

unharmed /ʌn'hɑːmd/ ADJ *[person, animal]* indemne, sain et sauf ; *[thing]* intact, non endommagé ◆ **they escaped ~** ils en sont sortis indemnes

unharness /ʌn'hɑːnɪs/ VT dételer (*from* de)

UNHCR /juːeneɪtʃsiː'ɑːʳ/ N (abbrev of **United Nations High Commission for Refugees**) HCR *m*

unhealthy /ʌn'helθɪ/ ADJ 1 (= *harmful*) *[environment, climate]* malsain, insalubre ; *[habit, curiosity, relationship]* malsain ◆ **their diet is ~** leur alimentation n'est pas saine 2 (= *unwell*) *[person, company, economy]* en mauvaise santé 3 (= *ill-looking*) *[person, appearance, skin]* maladif

unheard /ʌn'hɜːd/ ADJ 1 (= *ignored*) ◆ **to go ~** *[person, plea, request]* être ignoré ◆ **she condemned him ~** elle l'a condamné sans l'avoir entendu 2 (= *not heard*) ◆ **his cries went ~** personne n'a entendu ses cris ◆ **a previously ~ opera** un opéra qui est présenté pour la première fois COMP **unheard-of** ADJ (= *surprising*) incroyable ◆ **private bathrooms and toilets were ~ of** les salles de bains et les toilettes privées n'existaient pas

unhedged /ʌn'hedʒd/ ADJ (*esp US*) *[venture, bet]* hasardeux, à découvert

unheeded /ʌn'hiːdɪd/ ADJ *[person, plea, warning]* ignoré ◆ **to go ~** être ignoré ◆ **it must not go ~** il faut en tenir compte, il faut y prêter attention

unheeding /ʌn'hiːdɪŋ/ ADJ (*frm*) insouciant (*of* de), indifférent (*of* à) ◆ **they passed by ~** ils sont passés à côté sans faire attention

unhelpful /ʌn'helpfʊl/ ADJ *[person]* peu serviable ; *[remark, advice]* inutile ; *[attitude]* peu coopératif ; *[book, computer]* qui n'apporte (*or* apportait) rien d'utile ◆ **he didn't want to seem ~** il voulait avoir l'air serviable ◆ **I found that very ~** ça ne m'a pas aidé du tout ◆ **it is ~ to do sth** ça n'avance pas à grand-chose de faire qch

unhelpfully /ʌn'helpfʊlɪ/ ADV *[behave]* de manière peu coopérative ; *[say, suggest]* sans apporter quoi que ce soit d'utile

unhelpfulness /ʌn'helpfʊlnɪs/ N (NonC) *[of person]* manque *m* de serviabilité ; *[of remark, advice, book, computer]* inutilité *f*

unheralded /ʌn'herəldɪd/ ADJ 1 (= *unannounced*) *[arrival, resignation]* non annoncé ◆ **to be ~** ne pas être annoncé ◆ **to arrive ~** arriver sans être annoncé 2 (= *unacclaimed*) *[player, artist]* méconnu

unhesitating /ʌn'hezɪteɪtɪŋ/ ADJ *[response]* immédiat ; *[trust, generosity]* spontané ; *[person, courage, belief]* résolu

unhesitatingly /ʌn'hezɪteɪtɪŋlɪ/ ADV sans hésiter, sans hésitation

unhindered /ʌn'hɪndəd/ ADJ *[progress]* sans obstacles, sans encombre ; *[movement]* libre, sans encombre ◆ **to go ~** passer sans rencontrer d'obstacles *or* sans encombre ◆ **he worked ~** il a travaillé sans être dérangé (*by* par)

unhinge /ʌn'hɪndʒ/ VT enlever de ses gonds, démonter ; (*fig*) *[+ mind]* déranger ; *[+ person]* déséquilibrer

unhinged /ʌn'hɪndʒd/ ADJ *[person, mind]* déséquilibré ; *[passion, ranting]* délirant ◆ **to come ~** *[person]* disjoncter*

unhip * /ʌn'hɪp/ ADJ ringard*

unhitch /ʌn'hɪtʃ/ VT *[+ rope]* décrocher, détacher ; *[+ horse]* dételer

unholy /ʌn'həʊlɪ/ ADJ 1 (= *sinful*) *[activity]* impie ; *[pleasure]* inavouable ; *[alliance]* contre nature 2 (* = *terrible*) *[mess, row]* sans nom ; *[noise]* impossible*

unhook /ʌn'hʊk/ VT 1 (= *take off hook*) *[+ picture from wall etc]* décrocher (*from* de) 2 (= *undo*) *[+ garment]* dégrafer

unhoped-for /ʌn'həʊptfɔːʳ/ ADJ inespéré

unhopeful /ʌn'həʊpfʊl/ ADJ *[prospect, start]* peu prometteur ; *[person]* pessimiste, qui n'a guère d'espoir

unhorse /ʌn'hɔːs/ VT désarçonner, démonter

unhurried /ʌn'hʌrɪd/ ADJ *[pace, atmosphere, activity]* tranquille ; *[reflection]* tranquille, paisible ; *[movement]* sans précipitation ; *[person]* paisible ◆ **to be ~** *[person]* ne pas être pressé ◆ **to have an ~ journey** faire un voyage sans se presser ◆ **in an ~ way** sans se presser

unhurriedly /ʌn'hʌrɪdlɪ/ ADV *[walk]* sans se presser, tranquillement ; *[speak]* sans précipitation, posément, en prenant son temps

unhurt /ʌn'hɜːt/ ADJ indemne

unhygienic /ʌnhaɪ'dʒiːnɪk/ ADJ non hygiénique ◆ **it is ~ to do that** ce n'est pas hygiénique de faire ça

uni * /'juːnɪ/ N (abbrev of **university**) fac* *f* ◆ **at ~** en fac*

uni... /'juːnɪ/ PREF uni..., mono...

unicameral /juːnɪ'kæmərəl/ ADJ (*Parl*) monocaméral

UNICEF /'juːnɪsef/ N (abbrev of **United Nations Children's Fund**) UNICEF *f*

unicellular /juːnɪ'seljʊləʳ/ ADJ unicellulaire

unicorn /'juːnɪkɔːn/ N licorne *f*

unicycle /'juːnɪˌsaɪkl/ N monocycle *m*

unidentifiable /'ʌnaɪ'dentɪˌfaɪəbl/ ADJ non identifiable

unidentified /'ʌnaɪ'dentɪfaɪd/ ADJ non identifié COMP **unidentified flying object** N objet *m* volant non identifié

unidirectional /ˌjuːnɪdɪ'rekʃənl/ ADJ unidirectionnel

unification /ˌjuːnɪfɪ'keɪʃən/ N unification *f*

uniform /'juːnɪfɔːm/ N uniforme *m* ◆ **in ~** en uniforme ◆ **in full ~** (*Mil etc*) en grand uniforme ◆ **out of ~** *[policeman, soldier]* en civil ; *[schoolboy]* en habits de tous les jours ◆ **the ~s*** (*Police*) les policiers *mpl* en tenue ADJ *[rate, standards, shape, size]* identique ◆ **~ in shape/size, of a ~ shape/size** de la même forme/taille, de forme/taille identique ◆ **a sky of ~ colour** un ciel de couleur uniforme ◆ **to make sth ~** *[+ rate, standards, colour]* uniformiser qch ; *[+ shape, size]* normaliser qch
COMP *[trousers, shirt etc]* d'uniforme

uniform resource locator N (*Comput*) URL *m* (*adresse de site Web*)

uniformed /'juːnɪfɔːmd/ ADJ *[guard, chauffeur, schoolchild]* en uniforme ; *[soldier, police officer]* en uniforme, en tenue ; *[organization]* où l'on porte un uniforme COMP **uniformed branch** N (*Police*) (catégorie *f* du) personnel *m* en tenue

uniformity /ˌjuːnɪ'fɔːmɪtɪ/ N (NonC) uniformité *f*

uniformly /'juːnɪfɔːmlɪ/ ADV uniformément

unify /'juːnɪfaɪ/ VT unifier COMP **unified field theory** N théorie *f* unitaire

unifying /'juːnɪfaɪɪŋ/ ADJ *[factor, force, theme, principle etc]* unificateur (-trice *f*) ◆ **the struggle has had a ~ effect on all Blacks** cette lutte a réussi à unifier tous les Noirs

unilateral /'juːnɪ'lætərəl/ ADJ unilatéral COMP **unilateral declaration of independence** (*Brit Pol*) N déclaration *f* unilatérale d'indépendance
unilateral disarmament N désarmement *m* unilatéral
unilateral nuclear disarmament N désarmement *m* nucléaire unilatéral

unilateralism /'juːnɪ'lætərəlɪzəm/ N adhésion *f* au désarmement unilatéral, unilatéralisme *m* ◆ **American ~ on trade** l'habitude *f* américaine de prendre des décisions unilatérales en ce qui concerne le commerce

unilateralist /'juːnɪ'lætərəlɪst/ N partisan *m* du désarmement unilatéral ADJ *[policy]* unilatéral ; *[party]* favorable au désarmement nucléaire unilatéral

unilaterally /'juːnɪ'lætərəlɪ/ ADV unilatéralement

unimaginable /ˌʌnɪ'mædʒnəbl/ ADJ inimaginable (*to sb* pour qn)

unimaginably /'ʌnɪ'mædʒɪnəblɪ/ ADV incroyablement

unimaginative /'ʌnɪ'mædʒnətɪv/ ADJ *[person, film]* sans imagination ; *[food, playing]* sans originalité ◆ **to be ~** *[person, film]* manquer d'imagination ; *[food, playing]* manquer d'originalité

unimaginatively /'ʌnɪ'mædʒnətɪvlɪ/ ADV d'une manière peu imaginative, sans imagination

unimaginativeness /'ʌnɪ'mædʒnətɪvnɪs/ N manque *m* d'imagination

unimpaired /'ʌnɪm'pɛəd/ ADJ *[mental powers, prestige]* intact ; *[quality]* non diminué ◆ **his eyesight/hearing was ~** sa vue/son ouïe n'avait pas diminué ◆ **their faith remains ~** leur foi reste toujours aussi forte ◆ **to be ~ by sth** ne pas souffrir de qch

unimpeachable /ˌʌnɪm'piːtʃəbl/ ADJ (*frm*) *[source]* sûr ; *[evidence]* incontestable, irrécusable ; *[integrity]* impeccable ; *[character, reputation, conduct, honesty]* irréprochable

unimpeded /'ʌnɪm'piːdɪd/ ADJ *[access]* libre ; *[view]* dégagé ADV sans entraves

unimportant /'ʌnɪm'pɔːtənt/ ADJ *[person]* insignifiant ; *[issue, detail]* sans importance, insignifiant ◆ **it's quite ~** ça n'a aucune espèce d'importance, c'est sans importance

unimposing /'ʌnɪm'pəʊzɪŋ/ ADJ peu imposant, peu impressionnant

unimpressed /'ʌnɪm'prest/ ADJ 1 (= *unaffected*) ◆ **to be ~ (by** *or* **with sb/sth)** (*by person, sight, size, plea*) ne pas être impressionné (par qn/qch) ◆ **I was ~** ça ne m'a pas impressionné ◆ **Wall Street has been ~** Wall Street est resté calme ◆ **he remained ~** ça ne lui a fait ni chaud ni froid 2 (= *unconvinced*) ◆ **to be ~ (by** *or* **with sb/sth)** (*by person, explanation, argument*) ne pas être convaincu (par qn/qch) ◆ **I was ~** ça ne m'a pas convaincu ◆ **he was ~ with the idea of filling in a lengthy questionnaire** il n'était pas convaincu de la nécessité de remplir un long questionnaire

unimpressive /ˈʌnɪmˈpresɪv/ **ADJ** *[person]* terne, très quelconque ; *[building, amount]* très quelconque ; *[sight, result, performance]* médiocre ; *[argument]* peu convaincant

unimproved /ˈʌnɪmˈpruːvd/ **ADJ** *[condition]* qui ne s'est pas amélioré, inchangé ; *[land, pasture]* non amendé ◆ **many houses remained ~** beaucoup de maisons n'avaient pas fait l'objet de réfections

unincorporated /ˌʌnɪnˈkɔːpəreɪtɪd/ **ADJ** non incorporé *(in* dans) ; *(Comm, Jur)* non enregistré

uninfluential /ˈʌnɪnflʊˈenʃəl/ **ADJ** sans influence, qui n'a pas d'influence

uninformative /ˈʌnɪnˈfɔːmətɪv/ **ADJ** *[report, document, account]* qui n'apprend rien ◆ **he was very ~** il ne nous *(or* leur *etc)* a rien appris d'important

uninformed /ˈʌnɪnˈfɔːmd/ **ADJ** *[person, organization]* mal informé *(about sb/sth* sur qn/qch), mal renseigné *(about sb/sth* sur qn/qch) ; *[comment, rumour, opinion]* mal informé ◆ **the ~ observer** l'observateur *m* non averti **NPL the uninformed** le profane

uninhabitable /ˈʌnɪnˈhæbɪtəbl/ **ADJ** inhabitable

uninhabited /ˈʌnɪnˈhæbɪtɪd/ **ADJ** inhabité

uninhibited /ˈʌnɪnˈhɪbɪtɪd/ **ADJ** *[person, behaviour]* sans inhibitions ; *[emotion, impulse, desire]* non refréné ; *[dancing]* sans retenue ◆ **to be ~ by sth/in** *or* **about doing sth** ne pas être gêné par qch/pour faire qch

uninitiated /ˈʌnɪˈnɪʃɪeɪtɪd/ **ADJ** non initié *(into sth* à qch) ◆ **to the ~ eye** aux yeux du profane ◆ **to the ~ reader** pour le lecteur non averti **NPL the uninitiated** *(Rel)* les profanes *mpl* ; *(gen)* les non-initiés *mpl*, le profane

uninjured /ˈʌnˈɪndʒəd/ **ADJ** indemne ◆ **he was ~ in the accident** il est sorti indemne de l'accident ◆ **luckily, everyone escaped ~** heureusement, tout le monde s'en est sorti indemne

uninspired /ˈʌnɪnˈspaɪəd/ **ADJ** *[person]* qui manque d'inspiration ; *[book, film]* sans imagination, fade ; *[food]* sans originalité

uninspiring /ˈʌnɪnˈspaɪərɪŋ/ **ADJ** *[person, book, film]* terne ; *[choice]* médiocre ; *[view]* sans intérêt ◆ **it was an ~ match** le match n'a pas été passionnant

uninstall /ʌnɪnˈstɔːl/ **VT** *(Comput)* désinstaller

uninsured /ˈʌnɪnˈʃʊəd/ **ADJ** non assuré *(against* contre)

unintelligent /ˈʌnɪnˈtelɪdʒənt/ **ADJ** *[person, comment]* inintelligent ; *[behaviour, tactics]* dépourvu d'intelligence ; *[book, film]* sans intelligence

unintelligible /ˈʌnɪnˈtelɪdʒəbl/ **ADJ** inintelligible *(to sb* pour qn)

unintelligibly /ˈʌnɪnˈtelɪdʒəblɪ/ **ADV** *[mutter, yell]* de façon inintelligible

unintended /ˈʌnɪnˈtendɪd/, **unintentional** /ˈʌnɪnˈtenʃənl/ **ADJ** involontaire ◆ **it was quite ~** ce n'était pas fait exprès

unintentionally /ˈʌnɪnˈtenʃnəlɪ/ **ADV** involontairement

uninterested /ʌnˈɪntrɪstɪd/ **ADJ** indifférent ◆ **to be ~ in sb/sth** ne pas être intéressé par qn/qch ◆ **he seems ~ in his son** il ne semble pas s'intéresser à son fils

uninteresting /ˈʌnˈɪntrɪstɪŋ/ **ADJ** *[person, place, book, activity]* inintéressant ; *[offer]* sans intérêt, dépourvu d'intérêt

uninterrupted /ˈʌnˌɪntəˈrʌptɪd/ **ADJ** ininterrompu ◆ **to continue ~** continuer sans interruption ◆ **~ by advertisements** sans coupures publicitaires ◆ **to have an ~ view of sth** avoir une très bonne vue *or* une vue dégagée sur qch

uninterruptedly /ˈʌnˌɪntəˈrʌptɪdlɪ/ **ADV** sans interruption

uninvited /ˈʌnɪnˈvaɪtɪd/ **ADJ** *[visitor]* sans invitation ; *[question, sexual advances]* mal venu ; *[criticism]* gratuit ◆ **an ~ guest** une personne qui n'a pas été invitée *or* qui s'invite ◆ **to arrive ~** arriver sans invitation, s'inviter ◆ **to do sth ~** faire qch sans y être invité

uninviting /ˈʌnɪnˈvaɪtɪŋ/ **ADJ** peu attirant, peu attrayant ; *[food]* peu appétissant

union /ˈjuːnjən/ **N** ① *(gen, also Pol)* union *f* ; *(= marriage)* union *f*, mariage *m* ◆ **postal/customs ~** union *f* postale/douanière ◆ **the Union** *(US)* les États-Unis *mpl* ◆ **Union of Soviet Socialist Republics** Union *f* des républiques socialistes soviétiques ◆ **Union of South Africa** Union *f* sud-africaine ◆ **the (Student** *or* **Students') Union** *(Univ) (= organization)* syndicat étudiant ; *(= building)* locaux de l'association d'étudiants ◆ **in perfect ~** en parfaite harmonie ◆ **in ~ there is strength** l'union fait la force *(Prov)* → **state**

② (also **trade union**, *US:* also **labor union**) syndicat *m* ◆ **~s and management** ≃ les partenaires *mpl* sociaux ◆ **to join a ~** adhérer à un syndicat, se syndiquer ◆ **to join the Union of Miners** adhérer au Syndicat des mineurs ◆ **to belong to a ~** faire partie d'un syndicat, être membre d'un syndicat

③ *(Tech: for pipes etc)* raccord *m*

COMP *[card, leader, movement]* syndical ; *[headquarters]* du syndicat ; *[factory etc]* syndiqué

union catalogue **N** catalogue *m* combiné *(de plusieurs bibliothèques)*

union dues **NPL** cotisation *f* syndicale

Union Jack **N** Union Jack *m inv*

union member **N** membre *m* du syndicat, syndiqué(e) *m(f)*

union membership **N** *(= members collectively)* membres *mpl* du *or* des syndicat(s) ; *(= number of members)* effectifs *mpl* du *or* des syndicat(s) ; see also **membership**

union rate **N** *(Ind)* tarif *m* syndical

union school **N** *(US) lycée dont dépendent plusieurs écoles appartenant à un autre secteur*

union shop **N** *(US)* atelier *m* d'ouvriers syndiqués

union suit **N** *(US)* combinaison *f*

unionism /ˈjuːnjənɪzəm/ **N** *(trade unions)* syndicalisme *m* ; *(political union)* unionisme *m*

unionist /ˈjuːnjənɪst/ **N** ① (also **trade unionist**) membre *m* d'un syndicat, syndiqué(e) *m(f)* ◆ **the militant ~s** les syndicalistes *mpl*, les militants *mpl* syndicaux ② *(= supporter of political union)* unioniste *mf*

unionization /ˌjuːnjənaɪˈzeɪʃən/ **N** syndicalisation *f*

unionize /ˈjuːnjənaɪz/ *(Ind)* **VT** syndiquer **VI** se syndiquer

uniparous /juːˈnɪpərəs/ **ADJ** *[animal]* unipare ; *[plant]* à axe principal unique

unique /juːˈniːk/ **ADJ** ① *(= one of a kind)* unique *(among* parmi) ◆ **~ to sb/sth** propre à qn/qch ◆ **his own ~ style** son style inimitable, son style bien à lui ② *(= exceptional)* exceptionnel ◆ **rather** *or* **fairly ~** assez exceptionnel **COMP unique selling point, unique selling proposition** **N** avantage *m* unique

uniquely /juːˈniːklɪ/ **ADV** particulièrement ◆ **~ placed to do sth** particulièrement bien placé pour faire qch

uniqueness /juːˈniːknɪs/ **N** caractère *m* unique *or* exceptionnel

unisex /ˈjuːnɪseks/ **ADJ** *[clothes, hair salon]* unisexe ; *[hospital ward]* mixte

UNISON /ˈjuːnɪsn/ **N** *(Brit) syndicat*

unison /ˈjuːnɪsn, ˈjuːnɪzn/ **N** *(gen, also Mus)* unisson *m* ◆ **in ~** *[sing]* à l'unisson ◆ **"yes" they said in ~** "oui" dirent-ils en chœur *or* tous ensemble ◆ **to act in ~** agir de concert

unit /ˈjuːnɪt/ **N** ① *(gen, Admin, Elec, Math, Mil etc)* unité *f* ; *(Univ etc)* module *m*, unité *f* de valeur ◆ **administrative/linguistic/monetary ~** unité *f* administrative/linguistique/monétaire ◆ **~ of length** unité *f* de longueur ; → **thermal**

② *(= complete section, part)* élément *m* ; *[of textbook]* chapitre *m* ◆ **compressor ~** groupe *m* compresseur ◆ **generative ~** *(Elec)* groupe *m* électrogène ◆ **you can buy the kitchen in ~s** vous pouvez acheter la cuisine par éléments ; → **kitchen, sink²**

③ *(= buildings)* locaux *mpl* ; *(= offices)* bureaux *mpl* ; *(for engineering etc)* bloc *m* ; *(for sport, activity)* centre *m* ; *(looking after the public)* service *m* ◆ **assembly/operating ~** bloc *m* de montage/opératoire ◆ **X-ray ~** service *m* de radiologie ◆ **sports ~** centre *m* sportif ◆ **the library/laboratory ~** la bibliothèque/les laboratoires *mpl* ◆ **the staff accommodation ~** les logements *mpl* du personnel

④ *(= group of people)* unité *f* ; *(in firm)* service *m* ◆ **research ~** unité *f or* service *m* de recherches ◆ **family ~** *(Sociol)* groupe *m* familial

COMP unit cost **N** coût *m* unitaire

unit furniture **N** *(NonC)* mobilier *m* modulaire

unit-linked policy **N** *(Brit Insurance) assurance-vie avec participation aux bénéfices d'un fonds commun de placement*

unit of account **N** *[of European Community]* unité *f* de compte

unit price **N** prix *m* unitaire

unit rule **N** *(US Pol) règlement selon lequel la délégation d'un État vote en bloc suivant la majorité de ses membres*

unit trust **N** *(Brit Fin)* ≃ fonds *m* commun de placement ; *(= company)* société *f* d'investissement à capital variable, SICAV *f*

Unitarian /ˌjuːnɪˈteərɪən/ **ADJ, N** *(Rel)* unitaire *mf*, unitarien(ne) *m(f)*

Unitarianism /ˌjuːnɪˈteərɪənɪzəm/ **N** *(Rel)* unitarisme *m*

unitary /ˈjuːnɪtərɪ/ **ADJ** unitaire

unite /juːˈnaɪt/ **VT** ① *(= join)* *[+ countries, groups]* unir ; *(= marry)* unir, marier ◆ **to ~ A and B** unir A et B ◆ **to ~ A with B** unir A à B ② *(= unify)* *[+ party, country]* unifier **VI** s'unir *(with sth* à qch ; *with sb* à *or* avec qn ; *against* contre ; *in doing sth, to do sth* pour faire qch) ◆ **women of the world ~!** femmes du monde entier, unissez-vous !

united /juːˈnaɪtɪd/ **ADJ** *[country, opposition]* uni ◆ **~ in their belief that …** unis dans la conviction que … ◆ **~ in opposing sth** unis dans leur opposition à qch ◆ **~ by a common interest** unis par un intérêt commun ◆ **a ~ effort** un effort commun ◆ **their ~ efforts** leurs efforts conjugués ◆ **to present a** *or* **put on a ~ front (to sb)** présenter un front uni (face à qn) ◆ **to take a ~ stand against sb/sth** adopter une position commune contre qn/qch ◆ **~ we stand, divided we fall** *(Prov)* l'union fait la force *(Prov)*

COMP the United Arab Emirates **NPL** les Émirats *mpl* arabes unis

the United Arab Republic **N** la République arabe unie

the United Kingdom (of Great Britain and Northern Ireland) **N** le Royaume-Uni (de Grande-Bretagne et d'Irlande du Nord) ; → GREAT BRITAIN, UNITED KINGDOM

United Nations (Organization) **NPL** (Organisation *f* des) Nations *fpl* unies

United Service Organization **N** *(US) organisation venant en aide aux militaires américains, en*

particulier lors de leurs déplacements ou séjours à l'étranger
the United States (of America) NPL les États-Unis *mpl* (d'Amérique)

unity /ˈjuːnɪtɪ/ N unité *f* ; *(fig)* harmonie *f*, accord *m* ◆ **~ of time/place/action** *(Theat)* unité *f* de temps/de lieu/d'action ◆ **~ is strength** *(Prov)* l'union fait la force *(Prov)* ◆ **to live in ~** vivre en harmonie *(with* avec)

Univ. (abbrev of **University**) univ.

univalent /ˈjuːnɪˈveɪlənt/ ADJ univalent

univalve /ˈjuːnɪvælv/ ADJ univalve N mollusque *m* univalve

universal /ˌjuːnɪˈvɜːsəl/ ADJ *[acceptance, approval, condemnation]* unanime ; *[language, remedy, beliefs]* universel ◆ **~ access to medical care** l'accès de tous aux soins médicaux ◆ **a ~ health-care system** un système de soins médicaux pour tous ◆ **to win ~ acclaim** être acclamé par tous ◆ **to have a ~ appeal** être apprécié de tous ◆ **he's a ~ favourite** tout le monde l'adore ◆ **a ~ truth** une vérité universelle ◆ **its use has become ~** son usage est devenu universel ◆ **to make sth ~** rendre qch universel
N *(Philos)* universel *m* ◆ **~s** *(Philos, Ling)* universaux *mpl*
COMP **universal bank** N banque *f* universelle
universal joint N (joint *m* de) cardan *m*
Universal Product Code N *(US)* code-barres *m*
universal suffrage N suffrage *m* universel
universal time N temps *m* universel

universality /ˌjuːnɪvɜːˈsælɪtɪ/ N *(NonC)* universalité *f*

universalize /ˌjuːnɪˈvɜːsəlaɪz/ VT universaliser, rendre universel

universally /ˌjuːnɪˈvɜːsəlɪ/ ADV *[accepted, welcomed, condemned]* universellement ; *[popular, true, available]* partout ◆ **~ liked/admired** aimé/admiré de tous ◆ **~ praised** loué par chacun *or* tout le monde

universe /ˈjuːnɪvɜːs/ N univers *m* ◆ **he's the funniest writer in the ~** *** c'est l'écrivain le plus amusant qui existe

university /ˌjuːnɪˈvɜːsɪtɪ/ N université *f* ◆ **to be at/go to ~** être/aller à l'université ◆ **to study at ~** faire des études universitaires ◆ **a place at ~, a ~ place** une place à l'université ; → **open, residence**
COMP *[degree, town, library]* universitaire ; *[professor, student]* d'université
Universities and Colleges Admissions Service N *(Brit) service central des inscriptions universitaires*
Universities Central Council on Admissions N *(Brit: formerly) service central des inscriptions universitaires*
Universities Funding Committee N *(Brit) commission gouvernementale responsable de la dotation des universités*
university education N ◆ **he has a ~ education** il a fait des études universitaires
university entrance N entrée *f* à l'université ◆ **~ entrance examination** *(gen)* examen *m* d'entrée à l'université ; *(competitive)* concours *m* d'entrée à l'université
university extension courses NPL *cours publics du soir organisés par une université*
University Grants Committee N *(Brit: formerly) ancienne commission gouvernementale responsable de la dotation des universités*
university hospital N centre *m* hospitalier universitaire

unjust /ˈʌnˈdʒʌst/ ADJ injuste *(to sb* envers qn) ◆ **it is ~ to do that** il est injuste de faire cela

unjustifiable /ʌnˈdʒʌstɪfaɪəbl/ ADJ injustifiable

unjustifiably /ʌnˈdʒʌstɪfaɪəblɪ/ ADV *[criticize, increase]* de façon injustifiable ◆ **~ high levels of taxation** des taux d'imposition d'un niveau injustifiable ◆ **~ pessimistic** d'un pessimisme injustifiable

unjustified /ˈʌnˈdʒʌstɪfaɪd/ ADJ 1 (= *unfair) [action, attack, reputation]* injustifié 2 *(Typ)* non justifié

unjustly /ˈʌnˈdʒʌstlɪ/ ADV injustement

unkempt /ˈʌnˈkempt/ ADJ *[person, appearance, clothes]* négligé ; *[hair]* mal peigné ; *[beard]* peu soigné ; *[grass, garden, park]* mal entretenu

unkind /ʌnˈkaɪnd/ ADJ 1 (= *nasty) [person, remark, behaviour]* désagréable, peu aimable ◆ **she never has an ~ word to say about anyone** elle n'a jamais un mot désagréable pour qui que ce soit ◆ **it would be ~ to say that …** il serait peu aimable de dire que … ◆ **to be ~ to sb** ne pas être aimable avec qn 2 (= *adverse) [fate]* cruel *(to sb* envers qn) ; *[climate]* rude ◆ **the weather was ~ to us** le temps s'est montré peu clément pour nous 3 *(Sport) [bounce]* malheureux

unkindly /ʌnˈkaɪndlɪ/ ADV *[behave]* désagréablement, de façon désagréable *or* peu aimable ; *[say]* désagréablement, sans aménité ; *[describe]* sans aménité ◆ **to speak ~ of sb** dire des choses désagréables *or* peu aimables au sujet de qn ◆ **don't take it ~ if …** ne soyez pas offensé si …, ne le prenez pas en mauvaise part si … ◆ **to take ~ to sth** accepter qch difficilement ADJ *[person, remark]* désagréable, peu aimable ; *[climate]* rude ◆ **in an ~ way** de façon désagréable *or* peu aimable

unkindness /ʌnˈkaɪndnɪs/ N 1 *(NonC) [of person, behaviour]* manque *m* de gentillesse *or* d'amabilité ; *(stronger)* méchanceté *f* ; *[of words, remark]* malveillance *f* ; *[of fate]* cruauté *f* ; *[of weather]* rigueur *f* 2 (= *act of unkindness)* méchanceté *f*, action *f or* parole *f* méchante

unknot /ˈʌnˈnɒt/ VT dénouer, défaire (le nœud de)

unknowable /ˈʌnˈnəʊəbl/ ADJ *(esp liter)* inconnaissable

unknowing /ˈʌnˈnəʊɪŋ/ ADJ ◆ **to be the ~ victim of sb/sth** être la victime de qn/qch sans le savoir ◆ **to be the ~ cause of sth** être la cause de qch à son insu *or* sans le savoir ◆ **to be an ~ accomplice in** *or* **to sth** être le complice de qch à son insu *or* sans le savoir ◆ **… he said, all ~** … dit-il, sans savoir ce qui se passait

unknowingly /ˈʌnˈnəʊɪŋlɪ/ ADV sans le savoir, à mon *(or* son *etc)* insu

unknown /ˈʌnˈnəʊn/ ADJ inconnu ◆ **his real name is ~ (to me)** son vrai nom (m')est inconnu ◆ **she hoped to remain ~ to the authorities** elle espérait que les autorités ne s'apercevraient pas de son existence ◆ **a species ~ to science** une espèce inconnue des scientifiques ◆ **~ to me, he …** à mon insu, il …, sans que je le sache, il … ◆ **~ to him, the plane had crashed** l'avion s'était écrasé, ce qu'il ignorait ◆ **some ~ person** un inconnu ◆ **it is ~ territory (for them)** *(lit, fig)* c'est un territoire inconnu (pour eux) ◆ **murder by person or persons ~** *(Jur)* meurtre *m* dont on ignore l'auteur ou les auteurs ◆ **Jill Brown, whereabouts ~** Jill Brown, dont on ignore où elle se trouve actuellement
N 1 ◆ **the ~** *(Philos, gen)* l'inconnu *m* ; *(Math, fig)* l'inconnue *f* ◆ **voyage into the ~** voyage *m* dans l'inconnu ◆ **in space exploration there are many ~s** dans l'exploration de l'espace il y a de nombreuses inconnues
2 (= *person, actor etc)* inconnu(e) *m(f)* ◆ **they chose an ~ for the part of Macbeth** ils ont choisi un inconnu pour jouer le rôle de Macbeth
COMP **unknown factor** N inconnue *f*
unknown quantity N *(Math, fig)* inconnue *f* ◆ **he's an ~ quantity** il représente une inconnue
the Unknown Soldier, the Unknown Warrior N le Soldat inconnu

unlace /ˈʌnˈleɪs/ VT délacer, défaire (le lacet de)

unladen /ˈʌnˈleɪdn/ ADJ *[ship]* à vide ◆ **~ weight** poids *m* à vide ◆ **to weigh 5 tonnes ~** peser 5 tonnes à vide

unladylike /ˈʌnˈleɪdɪlaɪk/ ADJ *[girl, woman]* mal élevée, qui manque de distinction ; *[manners, behaviour]* peu distingué ◆ **it's ~ to yawn** une jeune fille bien élevée ne bâille pas

unlamented /ˈʌnləˈmentɪd/ ADJ non regretté ◆ **he died ~** on ne pleura pas sa mort

unlatch /ˈʌnˈlætʃ/ VT ouvrir, soulever le loquet de

unlawful /ˈʌnˈlɔːfʊl/ ADJ *[act]* illégal, illicite ; *[marriage]* illégitime ◆ **by ~ means** par des moyens illégaux ◆ **employees who believe their dismissal was ~** les employés qui pensent que leur licenciement était abusif
COMP **unlawful assembly** N rassemblement *m* illégal
unlawful entry N effraction *f*
unlawful killing N homicide *m* volontaire *(sans préméditation)*
unlawful possession N détention *f* illégale
unlawful wounding N coups *mpl* et blessures *fpl (sans préméditation)*

unlawfully /ˈʌnˈlɔːfəlɪ/ ADV illégalement, illicitement

unleaded /ˈʌnˈledɪd/ ADJ *[petrol]* sans plomb N (also **unleaded petrol**) essence *f* sans plomb

unlearn /ˈʌnˈlɜːn/ (pret, ptp **unlearned** *or* **unlearnt**) VT désapprendre

unlearned /ˈʌnˈlɜːnɪd/ VB pt, ptp of **unlearn** ADJ ignorant, illettré

unleash /ˈʌnˈliːʃ/ VT *[+ dog]* détacher, lâcher ; *[+ hounds]* découpler ; *(fig) [+ anger etc]* déchaîner, déclencher

unleavened /ˈʌnˈlevnd/ ADJ *[bread]* sans levain, azyme *(Rel)* ◆ **~ by humour** qui n'est pas égayé par le moindre trait d'humour

unless /ənˈles/ CONJ à moins que … (ne) + *subj*, à moins de + *infin* ◆ **I'll take it, ~ you want it** je vais le prendre, à moins que vous (ne) le vouliez ◆ **take it, ~ you can find another** prenez-le, à moins que vous n'en trouviez un autre ◆ **I won't do it ~ you phone me** je ne le ferai que si tu me téléphones ◆ **I won't go ~ you do** je n'irai que si tu y vas toi aussi ◆ **~ I am mistaken** à moins que je (ne) me trompe, si je ne me trompe (pas) ◆ **~ I hear to the contrary** sauf avis contraire, sauf contrordre ◆ **~ otherwise stated** sauf indication contraire

unlettered /ˈʌnˈletəd/ ADJ illettré

unliberated /ˈʌnˈlɪbəreɪtɪd/ ADJ *[woman etc]* qui n'est pas libéré *or* émancipé

unlicensed /ˈʌnˈlaɪsənst/ ADJ *[activity]* illicite, non autorisé ; *[vehicle]* sans vignette ◆ **~ premises** *(Brit)* établissement *m* qui n'a pas de licence de débit de boissons

unlikable /ˈʌnˈlaɪkəbl/ ADJ ⇒ **unlikeable**

unlike /ˈʌnˈlaɪk/ ADJ dissemblable *(also Math, Phys)*, différent ◆ **they are quite ~** ils ne se ressemblent pas du tout PREP ◆ **~ his brother, he …** à la différence de *or* contrairement à son frère, il … ◆ **it's so ~ him to say something like that** ça lui ressemble si peu de dire une chose pareille ◆ **how ~ George!** on ne s'attendait pas à ça de la part de George ! ◆ **Glasgow is quite ~ Edinburgh** Glasgow ne ressemble pas du tout à Édimbourg ◆ **she is ~ him in every way, except for her dark eyes** elle ne lui ressemble pas du tout, si ce n'est ses yeux sombres ◆ **the portrait is quite ~ him** ce portrait ne lui ressemble pas, ce portrait est très peu ressemblant

unlikeable /ˈʌnˈlaɪkəbl/ ADJ *[person]* peu sympathique ; *[town, thing]* peu agréable

unlikelihood /ʌnˈlaɪklɪhʊd/, **unlikeliness** /ʌnˈlaɪklɪnɪs/ N *(NonC)* improbabilité *f*

unlikely /ʌn'laɪklɪ/ LANGUAGE IN USE 16.2, 26.3 ADJ *[happening, outcome]* peu probable, improbable ; *[explanation]* invraisemblable ; *[friendship, candidate, setting]* inattendu ◆ **an ~ place to find ...** un endroit où l'on ne s'attend (*or* s'attendait) guère à trouver ... ◆ **they're such an ~ couple** ils forment un couple si invraisemblable ◆ **she was wearing the most ~ hat** elle avait un chapeau complètement invraisemblable ◆ **in the ~ event of war** dans le cas improbable où une guerre éclaterait ◆ **in the ~ event that ...** au cas improbable où ... ◆ **in the ~ event of his accepting** au cas improbable où il accepterait ◆ **it is ~ that she will come, she is ~ to come** il est improbable *or* peu probable qu'elle vienne, il y a peu de chances pour qu'elle vienne ◆ **it is ~ to be settled** cela ne risque guère d'être réglé ◆ **she is ~ to succeed** elle a peu de chances de réussir ◆ **that is ~ to happen** il y a peu de chances que ça se produise ◆ **it is most ~** c'est fort *or* très improbable ◆ **it is not ~ that ...** il est assez probable que ... *+ subj*, il se pourrait bien que ... *+ subj*

unlimited /ʌn'lɪmɪtɪd/ ADJ *[amount, number, use]* illimité ; *[patience]* sans limite(s), sans bornes ◆ **~ opportunities** des possibilités *fpl* illimitées ◆ **they had ~ time** ils avaient tout le temps qu'ils voulaient ◆ **a ticket that allows ~ travel on buses** un ticket qui permet d'effectuer un nombre illimité de trajets en autobus COMP **unlimited liability** N *(Comm, Fin, Jur)* responsabilité *f* illimitée

unlined /ʌn'laɪnd/ ADJ 1 *[garment, curtain]* sans doublure 2 *[face]* sans rides ; *[paper]* uni, non réglé

unlisted /ʌn'lɪstɪd/ LANGUAGE IN USE 27.5 ADJ qui ne figure pas sur une liste ; *(Stock Exchange)* non inscrit à la cote ; *(US Telec)* qui ne figure pas dans l'annuaire ; *(US Telec)* ≃ qui est sur la liste rouge ◆ **to go ~** *(US Telec)* ≃ se faire mettre sur la liste rouge COMP **unlisted building** N *(Brit)* édifice *m* non classé

unlit /ʌn'lɪt/ ADJ 1 *(= not burning) [cigarette, pipe, fire]* non allumé 2 *(= dark) [place]* non éclairé ; *[vehicle]* sans feux

unload /ʌn'ləʊd/ VT *[+ ship, cargo, truck, rifle, washing machine]* décharger ; *(fig = get rid of)* se débarrasser de, se défaire de ◆ **to ~ sth on (to) sb** se décharger de qch sur qn VI *[ship, truck]* être déchargé, déposer son chargement

unloaded /ʌn'ləʊdɪd/ ADJ *[gun]* qui n'est pas chargé ; *[truck, ship]* qui est déchargé

unloading /ʌn'ləʊdɪŋ/ N déchargement *m*

unlock /ʌn'lɒk/ VT 1 *[+ door, box]* ouvrir ◆ **the door is ~ed** la porte n'est pas fermée à clé 2 *(fig) [+ heart]* ouvrir ; *[+ mystery]* résoudre ; *[+ secret]* révéler VI *[lock, box, door]* s'ouvrir

unlooked-for /ʌn'lʊktfɔːʳ/ ADJ inattendu, imprévu

unloose /ʌn'luːs/, **unloosen** /ʌn'luːsn/ VT *[+ rope]* relâcher, détendre ; *[+ knot]* desserrer ; *[+ prisoner]* libérer, relâcher ; *[+ grasp]* relâcher, desserrer

unlovable /ʌn'lʌvəbl/ ADJ désagréable

unloved /ʌn'lʌvd/ ADJ mal aimé

unlovely /ʌn'lʌvlɪ/ ADJ déplaisant

unloving /ʌn'lʌvɪŋ/ ADJ *[person]* peu affectueux ; *[marriage]* sans amour

unluckily /ʌn'lʌkɪlɪ/ ADV malheureusement, par malheur ◆ **~ for him** malheureusement pour lui ◆ **the day started ~** la journée a commencé sous le signe de la malchance

unluckiness /ʌn'lʌkɪnɪs/ N manque *m* de chance, malchance *f*

unlucky /ʌn'lʌkɪ/ ADJ 1 *(= unfortunate) [person]* qui n'a pas de chance, malchanceux ; *[coincidence, event]* malencontreux ; *[choice, defeat, loser, victim]* malheureux ; *[moment]* mal choisi, mauvais ; *[day]* de malchance ◆ **he is always ~** il n'a jamais de chance ◆ **he tried to get a seat but he was ~** il a essayé d'avoir une place mais il n'y est pas arrivé ◆ **he was just ~** il n'a simplement pas eu de chance ◆ **how ~ for you!** vous n'avez pas de chance !, ce n'est pas de chance pour vous ! ◆ **to be ~ in one's choice of sth** ne pas avoir de chance en choisissant qch ◆ **to be ~ at cards** ne pas avoir de chance aux cartes ◆ **to be ~ in love** ne pas avoir de chance en amour ◆ **it was ~ (for her) that her husband should walk in just then** elle n'a pas eu de chance que son mari soit entré à cet instant précis ◆ **she was ~ enough to lose her credit card** elle a eu la malchance de perdre sa carte de crédit ◆ **he was ~ not to score a second goal** il n'a pas eu de chance de ne pas marquer un deuxième but ◆ **to be ~ with the weather** ne pas avoir de chance avec le temps 2 *(= bringing bad luck) [number, colour, action, object]* qui porte malheur ; *[omen]* néfaste, funeste ◆ **it is ~ to break a mirror** ça porte malheur de casser un miroir ◆ **~ for some!** ça porte malheur !

unmade /ʌn'meɪd/ VB pt, ptp of **unmake** ADJ *[bed]* défait ; *(Brit) (= unsurfaced) [road]* non goudronné ◆ **his new album could be the soundtrack to an ~ movie** *(= hypothetical)* son nouvel album pourrait être la musique d'un futur film

un-made-up /'ʌnmeɪd'ʌp/ ADJ *[face, person]* non maquillé, sans maquillage

unmake /ʌn'meɪk/ (pret, ptp **unmade**) VT défaire ; *(= destroy)* détruire, démolir

unman /ʌn'mæn/ VT *(liter)* faire perdre courage à, émasculer *(fig)*

unmanageable /ʌn'mænɪdʒəbl/ ADJ *[number, size, proportions]* écrasant ; *[problem]* impossible à régler ; *[system, situation]* impossible à gérer, ingérable ; *[hair]* impossible à coiffer, rebelle ; *[person]* impossible ; *[animal]* incontrôlable

unmanly /ʌn'mænlɪ/ ADJ indigne d'un homme ◆ **it is ~ to cry** les hommes, ça ne pleure pas

unmanned /ʌn'mænd/ ADJ 1 *(= automatic) [vehicle, aircraft, flight]* sans équipage ; *[spacecraft]* inhabité ; *[lighthouse]* sans gardien ; *[level-crossing]* automatique, non gardé 2 *(= without staff) [station]* sans personnel ; *[border post]* qui n'est pas gardé, sans gardes ; *[position, work station]* inoccupé ◆ **the machine was left ~ for ten minutes** il n'y a eu personne aux commandes de la machine pendant dix minutes ◆ **the telephone was left ~** il n'y avait personne pour répondre au téléphone *or* pour prendre les communications ◆ **he left the desk ~** il a quitté son guichet ; see also **unman**

unmannerliness /ʌn'mænəlɪnɪs/ N *(NonC)* manque *m* de savoir-vivre, impolitesse *f*

unmannerly /ʌn'mænəlɪ/ ADJ mal élevé, impoli, discourtois

unmapped /ʌn'mæpt/ ADJ dont on n'a pas établi *or* dressé la carte

unmarked /ʌn'mɑːkt/ ADJ 1 *(= anonymous) [grave]* sans nom ; *[police car]* banalisé ; *[container]* qui ne porte pas d'étiquette ; *[envelope, door]* qui ne porte pas de nom 2 *[essay, exam]* non corrigé 3 *(Sport) [player]* démarqué 4 *(= pristine)* impeccable 5 *(Ling)* non marqué

unmarketable /ʌn'mɑːkɪtəbl/ ADJ invendable

unmarriageable /ʌn'mærɪdʒəbl/ ADJ immariable

unmarried /ʌn'mærɪd/ ADJ *[person]* célibataire, qui n'est pas marié ; *[couple]* non marié COMP **unmarried mother** N mère *f* célibataire

unmask /ʌn'mɑːsk/ VT *(lit, fig)* démasquer VI ôter son masque

unmatched /ʌn'mætʃt/ ADJ *[ability]* sans pareil, sans égal ; *[beauty]* incomparable ◆ **~ by any rival** sans rival ◆ **facilities ~ by any other European city** des installations *fpl* sans pareilles *or* égales dans les autres grandes villes européennes ◆ **~ for quality** d'une qualité inégalée

unmeant /ʌn'ment/ ADJ qui n'est pas voulu, involontaire

unmemorable /ʌn'memərəbl/ ADJ *[book, film etc]* qui ne laisse pas un souvenir impérissable ◆ **an ~ face** un visage quelconque *or* le genre de visage que l'on oublie facilement

unmentionable /ʌn'menʃnəbl/ ADJ *[object]* qu'il est préférable de ne pas mentionner ; *[word]* qu'il est préférable de ne pas prononcer ◆ **it is ~** il est préférable de ne pas en parler ◆ **has he got some ~ disease?** est-ce qu'il a une maladie honteuse ? NPL **unmentionables** († , *hum*) sous-vêtements *mpl*, dessous *mpl*

unmerciful /ʌn'mɜːsɪfʊl/ ADJ impitoyable, sans pitié (*towards* envers)

unmercifully /ʌn'mɜːsɪfəlɪ/ ADV impitoyablement

unmerited /ʌn'merɪtɪd/ ADJ immérité

unmet /ʌn'met/ ADJ *[needs, demands]* non satisfait ; *[condition]* qui n'a pas été satisfait ◆ **his demands went ~** ses exigences n'ont pas été satisfaites, on n'a pas répondu à ses exigences

unmetered /ʌn'miːtəd/ ADJ 1 *[water]* facturé au forfait 2 *[Internet access]* illimité, facturé au forfait

unmethodical /ʌnmɪ'θɒdɪkəl/ ADJ peu méthodique

unmindful /ʌn'maɪndfʊl/ ADJ ◆ **~ of** oublieux de

unmissable* /ʌn'mɪsəbl/ ADJ *(Brit) [programme, film]* à ne pas rater ◆ **his new film is ~** son nouveau film est un must*

unmistakable /'ʌnmɪs'teɪkəbl/ ADJ *[voice, sound, smell, style]* caractéristique, qu'on ne peut pas ne pas reconnaître ◆ **to send an ~ message to sb that ...** faire comprendre clairement à qn que ... ◆ **to bear the ~ stamp of sth** porter la marque indubitable de qch ◆ **to show ~ signs of sth** montrer des signes indubitables de qch

unmistakably /'ʌnmɪs'teɪkəblɪ/ ADV indubitablement, indéniablement ◆ **she's ~ Scandinavian** elle est indubitablement *or* indéniablement scandinave ◆ **it's still ~ a Minnelli movie** c'est un film de Minnelli, on ne peut pas s'y tromper

unmitigated /ʌn'mɪtɪgeɪtɪd/ ADJ *(frm) [disaster, failure, success]* total ; *[nonsense, folly]* pur ; *[delight, admiration]* non mitigé ◆ **he is an ~ scoundrel/liar** c'est un fieffé coquin/menteur

unmixed /'ʌn'mɪkst/ ADJ pur, sans mélange

unmolested /'ʌnmə'lestɪd/ ADV *[slip through, pass by etc]* sans encombre ; *[live, sleep]* sans être dérangé, en paix ◆ **to be left ~** *[person]* être laissé en paix, être laissé tranquille

unmortgaged /'ʌn'mɔːgɪdʒd/ ADJ libre d'hypothèques, non hypothéqué

unmotivated /'ʌn'məʊtɪveɪtɪd/ ADJ immotivé, sans motif

unmould /'ʌn'məʊld/ VT *(Culin)* démouler

unmounted /'ʌn'maʊntɪd/ ADJ 1 *(= without horse)* sans cheval, à pied 2 *(= without mounting) [gem]* non serti, non monté ; *[picture, photo]* non monté *or* collé sur carton ; *[stamp]* non collé dans un album

unmourned /'ʌn'mɔːnd/ ADJ non regretté ◆ **he died ~** on ne pleura pas sa mort

unmoved /'ʌn'muːvd/ ADJ indifférent (*by sth* à qch) ◆ **he was ~ by her tears** il est resté indifférent à ses larmes ◆ **his face was ~, but in his eyes there was a trace of displeasure** son visage est resté impassible, mais dans ses yeux il y avait une lueur de mécontentement

unmusical /ʌn'mju:zɪkəl/ ADJ *[person]* peu musicien, qui n'a pas d'oreille ; *[sound, rendition]* peu mélodieux, peu harmonieux

unmuzzle /'ʌn'mʌzl/ VT *(lit, fig)* démuseler

unnam(e)able /'ʌn'neɪməbl/ ADJ innommable

unnamed /ʌn'neɪmd/ ADJ 1 *(= anonymous) [person, source]* dont le nom n'a pas été divulgué ; *[author, donor]* anonyme 2 *(= having no name) [baby, comet, star]* qui n'a pas reçu de nom

unnatural /ʌn'nætʃrəl/ ADJ 1 *(= unusual) [calm, silence]* anormal ◆ **it is not ~ that ...** il n'est pas anormal que ... + *subj* ◆ **it is not ~ to think that ...** il n'est pas anormal de penser que ... ◆ **it is not ~ for sb to think that ...** il n'est pas anormal que qn pense *subj* que ... ◆ **it is ~ for her to be so pleasant** ça ne lui ressemble pas d'être aussi aimable 2 *(= abnormal, unhealthy) [practice, vice, love]* contre nature ◆ **it's supposedly ~ for women not to want children** il est soi-disant contre nature pour une femme de ne pas vouloir d'enfants 3 *(= affected) [smile, voice]* forcé, qui manque de naturel ; *[manner]* affecté, forcé, qui manque de naturel

COMP **unnatural death** N *(Jur)* mort *f* non naturelle

unnatural practices NPL pratiques *fpl* contre nature

unnaturally /ʌn'nætʃrəlɪ/ ADV 1 *(= unusually) [loud, quiet]* anormalement ◆ **he was ~ silent** il était anormalement silencieux ◆ **it was ~ silent** un silence anormal régnait ◆ **not ~ we were worried** bien entendu, nous étions inquiets, nous étions naturellement inquiets 2 *(= affectedly) [speak, smile]* d'une manière affectée *or* forcée

unnavigable /'ʌn'nævɪgəbl/ ADJ non navigable

unnecessarily /ʌn'nesɪsərɪlɪ/ ADV *[cruel, difficult, complicated]* inutilement ; *[suffer, alarm, worry]* inutilement, pour rien ◆ **~ violent** d'une violence gratuite ◆ **he is ~ strict** il est plus sévère que cela n'est nécessaire

unnecessary /ʌn'nesɪsərɪ/ ADJ *(gen)* inutile, qui n'est pas nécessaire ; *[violence]* gratuit ◆ **to cause ~ suffering to sb** faire souffrir inutilement *or* gratuitement qn ◆ **to use ~ force** faire usage de la force plus qu'il n'est nécessaire ◆ **they made a lot of ~ fuss** ils ont fait beaucoup d'histoires pour rien ◆ **it is ~ to do sth** il n'est pas nécessaire de faire qch ◆ **it is ~ for sb to do sth** il n'est pas nécessaire que qn fasse qch ◆ **it is ~ to add that ...** (il est) inutile d'ajouter que ...

unneighbourly, unneighborly (US) /'ʌn'neɪbəlɪ/ ADJ qui n'agit pas en bon voisin ◆ **this ~ action** cette action mesquine de la part de mon *(or son etc)* voisin

unnerve /'ʌn'nɜ:v/ VT troubler, perturber

unnerved /'ʌn'nɜ:vd/ ADJ troublé, perturbé

unnerving /'ʌn'nɜ:vɪŋ/ ADJ troublant, perturbant

unnervingly /'ʌn'nɜ:vɪŋlɪ/ ADV ◆ **~ quiet/calm** d'un calme/sang-froid troublant *or* perturbant

unnoticed /'ʌn'nəʊtɪst/ ADJ inaperçu ◆ **to be ~ (by sb)** ne pas être remarqué (par qn) ◆ **to do sth ~** faire qch sans se faire remarquer ◆ **to go** *or* **pass ~ (by sb)** passer inaperçu (de qn) ◆ **to enter/leave ~ (by sb)** entrer/partir sans se faire remarquer (par qn)

unnumbered /'ʌn'nʌmbəd/ ADJ 1 *(= not numbered) [page, ticket, seat]* non numéroté ; *[house]* sans numéro 2 *(liter = countless)* innombrable

UNO /'ju:nəʊ/ N (abbrev of **United Nations Organization**) ONU *f*

unobjectionable /'ʌnəb'dʒekʃnəbl/ ADJ *[thing]* acceptable ; *[person]* à qui on ne peut rien reprocher

unobservant /'ʌnəb'zɜ:vənt/ ADJ peu observateur (-trice *f*), peu perspicace

unobserved /'ʌnəb'zɜ:vd/ ADJ 1 *(= unnoticed)* ◆ **to be ~ (by sb)** ne pas être remarqué (par qn) ◆ **to go ~ (by sb)** passer inaperçu (de qn) ◆ **to enter/leave ~ (by sb)** entrer/partir sans se faire remarquer (par qn) 2 *(= unwatched)* ◆ **he imagined that he was ~** il s'imaginait qu'on ne l'observait pas

unobstructed /'ʌnəb'strʌktɪd/ ADJ *[pipe]* non bouché, non obstrué ; *[path, road]* dégagé, libre ◆ **the driver has an ~ view to the rear** le conducteur a une excellente visibilité à l'arrière

unobtainable /'ʌnəb'teɪnəbl/ ADJ 1 *(= unavailable)* ◆ **basic necessities were often ~** il était souvent impossible de se procurer l'essentiel 2 *(= unrealizable) [goal, objective]* irréalisable 3 *(Telec)* ◆ **his number was ~** son numéro était impossible à obtenir 4 *(sexually)* inaccessible

unobtrusive /'ʌnəb'tru:sɪv/ ADJ discret (-ète *f*)

unobtrusively /'ʌnəb'tru:sɪvlɪ/ ADV discrètement

unoccupied /'ʌn'ɒkjʊpaɪd/ ADJ 1 *(= empty) [house]* inoccupé, inhabité ; *[offices, factory]* vide ; *[room, seat, table]* inoccupé ; *[post]* vacant 2 *(Mil) [France, zone]* libre 3 *(= not busy) [person]* désœuvré, inoccupé

unofficial /'ʌnə'fɪʃəl/ ADJ 1 *(= informal) [visit, tour]* privé, non officiel ◆ **in an ~ capacity** à titre privé *or* non officiel 2 *(= de facto) [leader, spokesperson]* non officiel 3 *(= unconfirmed) [report, results]* officieux COMP **unofficial strike** N grève *f* sauvage

unofficially /'ʌnə'fɪʃəlɪ/ ADV 1 *(= informally) [ask, tell, report]* en privé, de façon non officielle ; *[visit]* à titre privé, à titre non officiel ◆ **they were ~ engaged** ils étaient officieusement fiancés ◆ **he was working ~ for the CIA** il travaillait de façon non officielle pour la CIA 2 *(= off the record) [say]* officieusement ◆ **~, he supports the proposals** officieusement *or* en privé, il soutient ces propositions ◆ **officially, I'm in favour of it, ~, I have my doubts** officiellement, je suis pour, personnellement, j'ai des doutes

unopened /'ʌn'əʊpənd/ ADJ *[bottle, packet, mail]* qui n'a pas été ouvert ◆ **the book was** *or* **lay ~** le livre n'avait pas été ouvert ◆ **to send a letter back ~** renvoyer une lettre sans l'avoir ouverte ◆ **to leave sth ~** laisser qch fermé

unopposed /'ʌnə'pəʊzd/ ADJ *(Parl, gen)* sans opposition ; *(Mil)* sans rencontrer de résistance ◆ **the bill was given an ~ second reading** *(Parl)* le projet de loi a été accepté sans opposition à la deuxième lecture

unorganized /'ʌn'ɔ:gənaɪzd/ ADJ 1 *(= not structured)* inorganisé ; *(= badly organized) [event etc]* mal organisé ; *[essay]* qui manque d'organisation ; *[person]* qui ne sait pas s'organiser, qui manque d'organisation 2 *(Bio) (= not alive)* inorganisé 3 *(= not in trade union)* inorganisé, non syndiqué

unoriginal /'ʌnə'rɪdʒɪnəl/ ADJ *[person, work]* qui manque d'originalité, peu original ; *[style, remark]* banal ; *[idea]* peu original, banal

unorthodox /'ʌn'ɔ:θədɒks/ ADJ 1 *(= unconventional) [person, behaviour, method]* peu orthodoxe ; *[views, ideas]* non orthodoxe 2 *(Rel)* hétérodoxe

unostentatious /'ʌn,ɒstən'teɪʃəs/ ADJ discret (-ète *f*), sans ostentation, simple

unostentatiously /'ʌn,ɒstən'teɪʃəslɪ/ ADV discrètement, sans ostentation

unpack /'ʌn'pæk/ VT 1 *[+ suitcase]* défaire ; *[+ belongings]* déballer ◆ **to get ~ed** déballer ses affaires 2 *(fig) [+ idea, problem]* analyser VI défaire sa valise, déballer ses affaires

unpacking /'ʌn'pækɪŋ/ N *(NonC)* déballage *m* ◆ **to do one's ~** déballer ses affaires

unpaid /'ʌn'peɪd/ ADJ *[staff, worker, overtime]* non rémunéré ; *[work]* non rémunéré, non rétribué ; *[leave, tax]* non payé ; *[bill, debt, rent]* impayé ◆ **~ volunteer** bénévole *mf* ◆ **to work ~** travailler à titre bénévole *or* sans être rémunéré

unpalatable /ʌn'pælɪtəbl/ ADJ 1 *(in taste) [food]* qui n'a pas bon goût 2 *(= difficult) [truth]* désagréable à entendre ; *[fact]* désagréable ; *[choice]* désagréable à faire ; *[idea]* difficile à accepter ◆ **to be ~ to sb** être désagréable à qn

unparalleled /ʌn'pærəleld/ ADJ *[opportunity, prosperity, event]* sans précédent ; *[collection, success]* hors pair ; *[beauty, wit]* incomparable, sans égal ◆ **~ in the history of ...** sans précédent dans l'histoire de ...

unpardonable /ʌn'pɑ:dnəbl/ ADJ *(frm) [behaviour]* impardonnable, inexcusable ; *[sin]* impardonnable ◆ **it is ~ to treat people so badly** c'est impardonnable *or* inexcusable de traiter les gens aussi mal ◆ **it's ~ of him to have taken it** c'est impardonnable de sa part de l'avoir pris

unpardonably /ʌn'pɑ:dnəblɪ/ ADV inexcusablement ◆ **~ rude** d'une impolitesse impardonnable *or* inexcusable

unparliamentary /'ʌn,pɑ:lə'mentərɪ/ ADJ *[behaviour, language]* inadmissible au parlement

unpatented /'ʌn'peɪtntɪd/ ADJ *[invention]* non breveté

unpatriotic /'ʌn,pætrɪ'ɒtɪk/ ADJ *[person]* peu patriote ; *[act, speech]* antipatriotique

unpatriotically /'ʌn,pætrɪ'ɒtɪkəlɪ/ ADV avec antipatriotisme

unpaved /'ʌn'peɪvd/ ADJ non pavé

unperceived /'ʌnpə'si:vd/ ADJ inaperçu

unperforated /'ʌn'pɜ:fəreɪtɪd/ ADJ non perforé

unperturbed /'ʌnpə'tɜ:bd/ ADJ imperturbable ◆ **he was ~ by this failure** cet échec ne l'a pas perturbé ◆ **~ by this failure, he ...** sans se laisser perturber par cet échec, il ...

unpick /'ʌn'pɪk/ VT 1 *[+ seam]* découdre, défaire ; *[+ stitch]* défaire 2 *(= examine) [+ argument, statement]* décortiquer 3 *(Brit fig) [+ plan, policy]* attaquer *(fig)*

unpin /'ʌn'pɪn/ VT détacher *(from* de) ; *[+ sewing, one's hair]* enlever les épingles de

unplaced /'ʌn'pleɪst/ ADJ *(Sport) [horse]* non placé ; *[athlete]* non classé

unplanned /'ʌn'plænd/ ADJ *[occurrence]* imprévu ; *[baby]* non prévu

unplasticized /'ʌn'plæstɪsaɪzd/ ADJ ◆ **~ polyvinyl chloride** chlorure *m* de polyvinyle non plastifié

unplayable /'ʌn'pleɪəbl/ ADJ 1 *(Tennis, Cricket = unstoppable) [shot, ball, ace]* imparable 2 *(Snooker = obstructed) [ball]* injouable 3 *(= unbeatable) [person]* imbattable 4 *(Mus)* injouable

unpleasant /ʌn'pleznt/ ADJ désagréable

unpleasantly /ʌn'plezntlɪ/ ADV 1 *(= disagreeably) [hot, salty]* désagréablement 2 *(= in an unfriendly way) [say, laugh, behave]* de façon déplaisante

unpleasantness /ʌn'plezntnɪs/ N *[of experience, person]* caractère *m* désagréable ; *[of place, house]* aspect *m or* caractère *m* déplaisant ; *(= quarrelling)* friction *f*, dissension *f* ◆ **there has been a lot of ~ recently** il y a eu beaucoup de frictions *or* dissensions ces temps derniers ◆ **after that ~ at the beginning of the meeting ...** après cette fausse note au début de la réunion ...

unpleasing /'ʌn'pli:zɪŋ/ ADJ *(frm)* déplaisant

unplug /'ʌn'plʌg/ VT débrancher

unplugged /'ʌn'plʌgd/ ADJ *(Mus)* sans sono *

unplumbed /ˈʌnˈplʌmd/ ADJ *(liter)* *[depth, mystery]* non sondé

unpoetic(al) /ˌʌnpəʊˈetɪk(əl)/ ADJ peu poétique

unpolished /ˈʌnˈpɒlɪʃt/ ADJ 1 *(lit)* *[furniture]* non ciré, non astiqué ; *[floor, shoes]* non ciré ; *[glass]* dépoli ; *[silver]* non fourbi ; *[diamond]* non poli 2 *(fig)* *[person]* qui manque d'éducation *or* de savoir-vivre ; *[manners]* peu raffiné ; *[style]* qui manque de poli

unpolluted /ˌʌnpəˈluːtɪd/ ADJ 1 *(lit)* *[air, water, beach]* non pollué 2 *(fig)* *[mind]* non contaminé, non corrompu

unpopular /ˈʌnˈpɒpjʊləʳ/ ADJ impopulaire *(with sb* auprès de qn)

unpopularity /ˈʌnˌpɒpjʊˈlærɪtɪ/ N *(NonC)* impopularité *f*

unpopulated /ˈʌnˈpɒpjʊleɪtɪd/ ADJ inhabité

unpractical /ˈʌnˈpræktɪkəl/ ADJ *[method, project, suggestion]* qui n'est pas pratique ; *[tool]* peu pratique

unpractised, unpracticed *(US)* /ʌnˈpræktɪst/ ADJ *[person]* inexpérimenté, inexpert ; *[movement etc]* inexpert, inhabile ; *[eye, ear]* inexercé

unprecedented /ʌnˈpresɪdəntɪd/ ADJ sans précédent

unprecedentedly /ʌnˈpresɪdəntɪdlɪ/ ADV *(= extremely)* inhabituellement ◆ **he agreed, ~, to speak to the press** chose inouïe, il a accepté de parler à la presse

unpredictability /ˈʌnprɪdɪktəˈbɪlɪtɪ/ N imprévisibilité *f*

unpredictable /ˈʌnprɪˈdɪktəbl/ ADJ *[person, behaviour, consequences]* imprévisible ; *[weather]* incertain

unpredictably /ˈʌnprɪˈdɪktəblɪ/ ADV *[behave]* de façon imprévisible ◆ **~ violent** d'une violence imprévisible

unprejudiced /ʌnˈpredʒʊdɪst/ ADJ *[person]* impartial, sans parti pris, sans préjugés ; *[decision, judgement]* impartial, sans parti pris

unpremeditated /ˈʌnprɪˈmedɪteɪtɪd/ ADJ non prémédité

unprepared /ˈʌnprɪˈpɛəd/ ADJ 1 *(= unready)* ◆ **to be ~ (for sth/to do sth)** *[person]* ne pas être préparé (à qch/à faire qch), ne pas être prêt (pour qch/à faire qch) ◆ **I was ~ for the exam** je n'avais pas suffisamment préparé l'examen ◆ **he set out quite ~** il est parti sans aucune préparation *or* sans (s'y) être du tout préparé ◆ **he was ~ for the news** la nouvelle l'a pris au dépourvu *or* l'a surpris ◆ **to catch sb ~** prendre qn au dépourvu 2 *(= unwilling)* ◆ **to be ~ to do sth** *[person]* ne pas être disposé à faire qch 3 *(= unrehearsed)* *[speech]* improvisé ; *[test, translation]* sans préparation

unpreparedness /ˈʌnprɪˈpɛərɪdnɪs/ N *(NonC)* manque *m* de préparation, impréparation *f*

unprepossessing /ˈʌnˌpriːpəˈzesɪŋ/ ADJ *[person]* peu avenant, qui ne paie pas de mine ; *[appearance, place]* qui ne paie pas de mine

unpresentable /ˈʌnprɪˈzentəbl/ ADJ *[person, thing]* qui n'est pas présentable

unpretentious /ˌʌnprɪˈtenʃəs/ ADJ sans prétention(s)

unpriced /ˈʌnˈpraɪst/ ADJ *[goods]* dont le prix n'est pas marqué

unprincipled /ʌnˈprɪnsɪpld/ ADJ *[person]* peu scrupuleux, sans scrupules ; *[behaviour, act]* peu scrupuleux

unprintable /ˈʌnˈprɪntəbl/ ADJ 1 *(= unpublishable)* *[article]* impubliable 2 *(gen hum = shocking)* *[story]* pas racontable ; *[words, comment]* que la décence interdit de reproduire *or* répéter ◆ **her reply was ~** la décence m'interdit de répéter sa réponse

unprivileged /ˈʌnˈprɪvɪlɪdʒd/ ADJ *(gen)* défavorisé ; *(Econ)* économiquement faible

unproductive /ˌʌnprəˈdʌktɪv/ ADJ 1 *(= ineffective)* *[meeting, discussion]* stérile, improductif ; *[factory, work, worker]* improductif 2 *(Agr)* *[land, soil]* improductif 3 *(Fin)* *[capital]* improductif

unprofessional /ˈʌnprəˈfeʃənl/ ADJ *[person, behaviour, attitude]* peu professionnel ◆ **to behave in a totally ~ manner** manquer totalement de professionnalisme ◆ **it was ~ of her (to say that)** c'était un manque de professionnalisme de sa part (que de dire cela) COMP **unprofessional conduct** N manquement *m* aux devoirs de la profession

unprofitable /ˈʌnˈprɒfɪtəbl/ ADJ 1 *(= uneconomic)* *[business, industry, route]* peu rentable 2 *(= fruitless)* *[argument, activity, day]* stérile

unprofitably /ˈʌnˈprɒfɪtəblɪ/ ADV sans profit

unpromising /ˈʌnˈprɒmɪsɪŋ/ ADJ peu prometteur

unpromisingly /ˈʌnˈprɒmɪsɪŋlɪ/ ADV de façon peu prometteuse

unprompted /ˈʌnˈprɒmptɪd/ ADJ *[remark, offer etc]* non sollicité ADV ◆ **he did it ~** il l'a fait sans que rien ne lui soit demandé

unpronounceable /ˈʌnprəˈnaʊnsəbl/ ADJ imprononçable

unprotected /ˈʌnprəˈtektɪd/ ADJ 1 *(= defenceless)* *[person]* sans défense ; *[place]* non protégé ◆ **to leave sb/sth ~** laisser qn/qch sans protection ◆ **to be ~ by the law** ne pas être protégé par la loi 2 *(= not covered)* *[skin, plants]* qui n'est pas protégé ; *[eyes, wood]* sans protection ◆ **to be ~ from the sun** ne pas être protégé du soleil COMP **unprotected intercourse, unprotected sex** N rapports *mpl* sexuels non protégés

unproven /ˈʌnˈpruːvən, ˈʌnˈprəʊvən/, **unproved** /ˈʌnˈpruːvd/ ADJ 1 *(= not proved)* *[allegation, charge]* sans preuves ◆ **the charge remains ~** *(lit, fig)* cette accusation n'est toujours pas fondée 2 *(= not tested)* *[person, technology]* qui n'a pas (encore) fait ses preuves

unprovided-for /ˌʌnprəˈvaɪdɪd,fɔːʳ/ ADJ *[person]* sans ressources

unprovoked /ˈʌnprəˈvəʊkt/ ADJ *[attack, aggression, violence]* sans provocation ◆ **he was ~** on ne l'avait pas provoqué ◆ **he said that ~** il a dit ça sans avoir été provoqué

unpublishable /ˈʌnˈpʌblɪʃəbl/ ADJ impubliable

unpublished /ˈʌnˈpʌblɪʃt/ ADJ inédit

unpunctual /ˈʌnˈpʌŋktjʊəl/ ADJ peu ponctuel, qui n'est jamais à l'heure

unpunctuality /ˈʌnˌpʌŋktjʊˈælɪtɪ/ N *(NonC)* manque *m* de ponctualité

unpunished /ˈʌnˈpʌnɪʃt/ ADJ impuni ◆ **to go** *or* **remain ~** rester impuni

unputdownable* /ˈʌnˌpʊtˈdaʊnəbl/ ADJ ◆ **Grossmith's latest novel is ~** le dernier roman de Grossmith se lit tout d'une traite *or* d'une seule traite

unqualified /ˈʌnˈkwɒlɪfaɪd/ ADJ 1 *(= without qualifications)* *[person, staff, pilot]* non qualifié ; *[engineer, doctor, teacher]* non diplômé ◆ **he is ~ for the job** *(= has no paper qualifications)* il n'a pas les diplômes requis pour ce poste ; *(= unsuitable)* il n'a pas les qualités requises pour ce poste ◆ **he is ~ to do it** il n'est pas qualifié pour le faire ◆ **I feel ~ to judge** je ne me sens pas qualifié pour en juger 2 *(= unmitigated)* *[success]* total ; *[disaster]* complet(-ète *f*) ; *[acceptance, support, approval]* inconditionnel, sans réserve ; *[admiration]* sans réserve ; *[praise]* non mitigé, sans réserve ◆ **an ~ "yes"/"no"** un "oui"/"non" inconditionnel 3 *(Gram)* *[noun]* non qualifié

unquenchable /ʌnˈkwentʃəbl/ ADJ *(lit, fig)* insatiable

unquenched /ʌnˈkwentʃt/ ADJ *[fire]* non éteint ; *[desire]* inassouvi ◆ **~ thirst** soif *f* non étanchée ; *(fig)* soif *f* inassouvie

unquestionable /ʌnˈkwestʃənəbl/ ADJ incontestable, indiscutable

unquestionably /ʌnˈkwestʃənəblɪ/ LANGUAGE IN USE 15.1 ADV incontestablement, indiscutablement

unquestioned /ʌnˈkwestʃənd/ ADJ *(= unchallenged)* incontesté, indiscuté

unquestioning /ʌnˈkwestʃənɪŋ/ ADJ *[belief, faith, obedience]* inconditionnel, absolu ; *[support, acceptance, devotion]* total ; *[loyalty, love]* absolu ◆ **an ~ supporter of ...** un(e) inconditionnel(le) de ...

unquestioningly /ʌnˈkwestʃənɪŋlɪ/ ADV *[obey, accept]* de façon inconditionnelle

unquiet /ˈʌnˈkwaɪət/ ADJ *[person, mind]* inquiet (-ète *f*), tourmenté ; *[times]* agité, troublé N inquiétude *f*, agitation *f*

unquote /ˈʌnˈkwəʊt/ ADV *(in dictation)* fermez les guillemets ; *(in report, lecture)* fin de citation ; → **quote**

unquoted /ˈʌnˈkwəʊtɪd/ ADJ *(on Stock Exchange)* non coté

unravel /ʌnˈrævəl/ VT *[+ material]* effiler, effilocher ; *[+ knitting]* défaire ; *[+ threads]* démêler ; *(fig)* *[+ mystery]* débrouiller, éclaircir ; *[+ plot]* dénouer VI *[knitting]* se défaire ; *(fig)* *[plan, system]* aller à vau-l'eau

unread /ˈʌnˈred/ ADJ *[book, newspaper, magazine]* qui n'a pas été lu ◆ **I returned the book ~** j'ai rendu le livre sans l'avoir lu ◆ **I left the letter ~** je n'ai pas lu la lettre ◆ **the book lay ~ on the table** le livre est resté sur la table sans avoir été lu

unreadable /ˈʌnˈriːdəbl/ ADJ *[book, handwriting, data]* illisible ; *[expression]* impassible

unreadiness /ˈʌnˈredɪnɪs/ N *(NonC)* impréparation *f*

unready /ˈʌnˈredɪ/ ADJ mal préparé, qui n'est pas prêt ◆ **he was ~ for what happened next** il ne s'attendait pas à ce qui est arrivé ensuite, ce qui est arrivé ensuite l'a pris au dépourvu

unreal /ˈʌnˈrɪəl/ ADJ 1 *(= not real)* *[situation, world]* irréel ; *[flowers]* faux (fausse *f*) 2 * *(= excellent)* formidable* ; *(pej = unbelievable)* incroyable ◆ **you're ~!** t'es incroyable !*

unrealistic /ˈʌnrɪəˈlɪstɪk/ ADJ *[person, expectations, demands]* peu réaliste, irréaliste ; *[goal, target, deadline]* irréaliste ◆ **it is ~ to expect that ...** il n'est pas réaliste de penser que ...

unrealistically /ˈʌnrɪəˈlɪstɪkəlɪ/ ADV *[high, low, optimistic]* excessivement, exagérément ; *[assume]* de façon peu réaliste, de façon irréaliste

unreality /ˈʌnrɪˈælɪtɪ/ N *(NonC)* irréalité *f*

unrealizable /ˈʌnrɪəˈlaɪzəbl/ ADJ irréalisable

unrealized /ˈʌnˈrɪəlaɪzd/ ADJ *[plan, ambition]* qui n'a pas été réalisé ; *[objective]* qui n'a pas été atteint

unreason /ˈʌnˈriːzn/ N *(NonC)* déraison *f*, manque *m* de bon sens

unreasonable /ʌnˈriːznəbl/ ADJ *[person, suggestion, expectations, demands]* déraisonnable ; *[price, amount]* exagéré, excessif ◆ **he is being ~** il n'est pas raisonnable ◆ **at this ~ hour** à cette heure indue ◆ **it is ~ to do that** il est déraisonnable de faire cela ◆ **it was ~ for her to reject your offer** il était déraisonnable de sa part de rejeter votre offre COMP **unreasonable behaviour** N *(gen)* conduite *f* déraisonnable ◆ **divorce on grounds of ~ behaviour** *(Jur)* divorce *m* pour violation grave ou renouvelée des devoirs du mariage

unreasonableness /ʌnˈriːznəblnɪs/ **N** (NonC) *[of person]* attitude *f* déraisonnable ; *[of demand, price]* caractère *m* exagéré *or* excessif

unreasonably /ʌnˈriːznəblɪ/ **ADV** *[high]* excessivement, exagérément ; *[act, refuse]* de façon déraisonnable ◆ **to take an ~ long time** prendre un temps exagéré ◆ **quite ~, I can't stand him** c'est tout à fait irraisonné, mais je ne le supporte pas ◆ **not ~, she had supposed he would help** elle avait de bonnes raisons de supposer qu'il l'aiderait

unreasoning /ʌnˈriːznɪŋ/ **ADJ** *[panic, anger, action]* irraisonné ; *[person]* irrationnel ; *[child]* qui n'est pas en âge de raisonner

unreclaimed /ˈʌnrɪˈkleɪmd/ **ADJ** *[land] (from forest)* non défriché ; *(from sea)* non asséché

unrecognizable /ʌnˈrekəgnaɪzəbl/ **ADJ** *[person, voice, place]* méconnaissable (*to sb* pour qn) ◆ **the wreck was ~ as an aircraft** l'épave de l'avion était méconnaissable

unrecognized /ˈʌnˈrekəgnaɪzd/ **ADJ** 1 *(= unnoticed) [phenomenon, condition, efforts]* qui n'est pas reconnu ; *[value, worth, talent]* méconnu ◆ **to go ~** *[person, phenomenon, condition]* passer inaperçu ; *[hard work, talent]* ne pas être reconnu ◆ **he walked ~ down the street** il a descendu la rue (à pied) sans être reconnu *or* sans que personne ne le reconnaisse 2 *(Pol) [government, party, country]* non reconnu

unreconstructed /ˈʌnriːkənˈstrʌktɪd/ **ADJ** *(pej) [person, system, idea, policy]* sclérosé ◆ **an ~ male chauvinist** un macho invétéré, un macho impénitent

unrecorded /ˈʌnrɪˈkɔːdɪd/ **ADJ** 1 *(= unreported) [crime, incident]* non signalé ; *[decision]* non enregistré ; *[species]* non répertorié, non classé ◆ **to go ~** *[crime, incident]* ne pas être signalé ; *[decision]* ne pas être enregistré ; *[species]* ne pas être répertorié *or* classé 2 *[piece of music]* non enregistré

unredeemed /ˈʌnrɪˈdiːmd/ **ADJ** *[object from pawn]* non dégagé ; *[debt]* non remboursé, non amorti ; *[bill]* non honoré ; *[mortgage]* non purgé ; *[promise]* non tenu ; *[obligation]* non rempli ; *[sinner]* non racheté ; *[fault]* non réparé ; *[failing]* non racheté, non compensé (*by* par)

unreel /ʌnˈrɪəl/ **VT** *[+ film]* dérouler ; *[+ thread]* dérouler, dévider ; *[+ fishing line]* dérouler, lancer **VI** se dérouler, se dévider

unrefined /ˈʌnrɪˈfaɪnd/ **ADJ** 1 *(= not processed) [food, sugar, cereal]* non raffiné ; *[oil]* brut, non raffiné 2 *(pej = vulgar) [person]* peu raffiné

unreflecting /ˈʌnrɪˈflektɪŋ/ **ADJ** 1 *[person]* irréfléchi, impulsif ; *[act, emotion]* irraisonné 2 *[surface]* non réfléchissant

unreformed /ˈʌnrɪˈfɔːmd/ **ADJ** *[person]* non amendé ; *[institution]* non réformé

unregarded /ˈʌnrɪˈgɑːdɪd/ **ADJ** dont on ne tient pas compte, dont on ne fait pas cas ◆ **his generosity went quite ~** sa générosité est passée inaperçue

unregistered /ˈʌnˈredʒɪstəd/ **ADJ** *[birth]* non déclaré ; *[car]* non immatriculé ; *(Post)* non recommandé

unregretted /ˈʌnrɪˈgretɪd/ **ADJ** *[person, act, words]* que l'on ne regrette pas ◆ **he died ~** on ne pleura pas sa mort

unrehearsed /ˈʌnrɪˈhɜːst/ **ADJ** *[question, reply]* spontané ; *[speech]* improvisé ; *[performance]* qui n'a pas été répété ; *[performer]* qui n'a pas répété

unrelated /ˈʌnrɪˈleɪtɪd/ **ADJ** 1 *(= unconnected) [incident, event, case]* sans rapport ◆ **to be ~ to sth** n'avoir aucun rapport avec qch 2 *(= from different families)* ◆ **they are ~ to each other** ils n'ont aucun lien de parenté, ils ne sont pas parents ◆ **he is ~ to me** il n'a pas de lien de parenté avec moi, nous n'avons aucun lien de parenté

unrelenting /ˈʌnrɪˈlentɪŋ/ **ADJ** *[pressure, criticism]* incessant ; *[violence]* continuel ; *[pain, pace]* tenace ; *[sun, rain]* implacable

unreliability /ˈʌnrɪˌlaɪəˈbɪlɪtɪ/ **N** (NonC) *[of person, machine]* manque *m* de fiabilité

unreliable /ˈʌnrɪˈlaɪəbl/ **ADJ** *[person, service, machine, news]* peu fiable ; *[information, data, figures]* sujet à caution ; *[weather]* incertain ◆ **he's very ~** il n'est vraiment pas fiable, on ne peut vraiment pas compter sur lui ◆ **my watch is ~** ma montre n'est pas très fiable

unrelieved /ˈʌnrɪˈliːvd/ **ADJ** *[gloom, monotony]* constant, permanent ; *[anguish]* constant, permanent ; *[boredom, tedium]* mortel ; *[pain]* que rien ne soulage ◆ **~ grey/black** gris/noir uniforme ◆ **the heat was ~ by any breeze** aucune brise ne venait atténuer la chaleur ◆ **a bare landscape ~ by any trees** un paysage nu dont aucun arbre ne rompait la monotonie

unremarkable /ˈʌnrɪˈmɑːkəbl/ **ADJ** *[person, face, place]* sans rien de remarquable, quelconque ; *[fact]* anodin ◆ **he would be ~ in a crowd** on ne le remarquerait pas dans une foule

unremarked /ˈʌnrɪˈmɑːkt/ **ADJ** *[fact]* que personne ne remarque ◆ **he stood there, ~** il est resté là sans que personne ne le remarque ◆ **to go** *or* **pass ~** passer inaperçu

unremitting /ˈʌnrɪˈmɪtɪŋ/ **ADJ** *[hostility, hatred]* implacable ; *[gloom]* persistant ; *[struggle]* sans relâche ; *[kindness, help, effort]* inlassable, infatigable ◆ **it was ~ toil** on a travaillé sans relâche

unremittingly /ˈʌnrɪˈmɪtɪŋlɪ/ **ADV** *[hostile]* implacablement ; *[continue, work]* sans relâche, inlassablement ; *[rain]* sans arrêt, sans interruption ◆ **~ cheerful** d'une inaltérable gaieté

unremunerative /ˈʌnrɪˈmjuːnərətɪv/ **ADJ** peu rémunérateur (-trice *f*), mal payé ; *(fig)* peu fructueux, peu rentable

unrepaid /ˈʌnrɪˈpeɪd/ **ADJ** *[loan]* non remboursé

unrepealed /ˈʌnrɪˈpiːld/ **ADJ** non abrogé

unrepeatable /ˈʌnrɪˈpiːtəbl/ **ADJ** *[offer, bargain]* unique, exceptionnel ; *[comment]* trop grossier pour être répété ◆ **what she said is ~** je n'ose répéter ce qu'elle a dit

unrepentant /ˈʌnrɪˈpentənt/ **ADJ** impénitent ◆ **to be** *or* **remain ~ (about sth)** ne pas manifester le moindre repentir (quant à qch), ne pas regretter (qch)

unreported /ˈʌnrɪˈpɔːtɪd/ **ADJ** *[crime, attack, accident etc]* non signalé ◆ **to go ~** *[crime etc]* ne pas être signalé

unrepresentative /ˈʌnˌreprɪˈzentətɪv/ **ADJ** non représentatif (*of sth* de qch)

unrepresented /ˈʌnˌreprɪˈzentɪd/ **ADJ** non représenté

unrequited /ˈʌnrɪˈkwaɪtɪd/ **ADJ** non partagé

unreserved /ˈʌnrɪˈzɜːvd/ **ADJ** 1 *(= wholehearted) [apology, praise, support]* sans réserve 2 *(= unbooked) [seat, table]* non réservé

unreservedly /ˈʌnrɪˈzɜːvɪdlɪ/ **ADV** sans réserve

unresisting /ˈʌnrɪˈzɪstɪŋ/ **ADJ** *[person]* qui ne résiste pas, soumis ; *[attitude, obedience]* soumis

unresolved /ˈʌnrɪˈzɒlvd/ **ADJ** 1 *(= unsolved) [problem, issue, dispute]* non résolu, irrésolu ; *[question]* qui reste sans réponse 2 *(Mus) [chord]* sans résolution

unresponsive /ˈʌnrɪsˈpɒnsɪv/ **ADJ** 1 *(= passive) [person]* ◆ **to be ~ to sth** ne pas réagir à qch 2 *[car, engine, steering]* qui répond mal

unrest /ʌnˈrest/ **N** (NonC) agitation *f* ; *(stronger)* troubles *mpl*

unrestrained /ˈʌnrɪˈstreɪnd/ **ADJ** 1 *(= unchecked) [joy, laughter, language]* sans retenue ; *[violence]* effréné ; *[use, growth]* sans frein ◆ **to be ~ by sth** *[person]* ne pas être bridé par qch ◆ **to be ~ in one's views** exprimer ses opinions sans retenue 2 *(= not held physically) [car passenger]* sans ceinture ; *[patient]* sans entraves ; *[prisoner]* sans liens, sans entraves

unrestrainedly /ˌʌnrɪˈstreɪnɪdlɪ/ **ADV** sans retenue

unrestricted /ˈʌnrɪˈstrɪktɪd/ **ADJ** 1 *(= unlimited) [use, right, travel]* sans restriction(s) ◆ **to have ~ access to sth** avoir libre accès à qch 2 *(= unobstructed)* ◆ **all seats have an ~ view** toutes les places ont une vue parfaitement dégagée

unrevealed /ˈʌnrɪˈviːld/ **ADJ** non révélé

unrewarded /ˈʌnrɪˈwɔːdɪd/ **ADJ** non récompensé ◆ **to be** *or* **go ~** ne pas être récompensé

unrewarding /ˈʌnrɪˈwɔːdɪŋ/ **ADJ** 1 *(= unfulfilling) [work, job, activity]* peu gratifiant, ingrat ; *[relationship]* peu satisfaisant, qui n'apporte pas grand-chose 2 *(financially) [work, job]* peu rémunérateur (-trice *f*)

unrighteous /ʌnˈraɪtʃəs/ **ADJ** impie † *(also liter)* **NPL** **the unrighteous** les impies † *mpl* *(also liter)*

unrighteousness /ʌnˈraɪtʃəsnɪs/ **N** (NonC) impiété *f*

unripe /ʌnˈraɪp/ **ADJ** pas mûr

unrivalled, unrivaled *(US)* /ʌnˈraɪvəld/ **ADJ** *[knowledge, experience, collection]* incomparable ; *[reputation, success]* sans égal ; *[opportunity]* unique ◆ **to be ~ in sth** ne pas avoir son pareil pour qch ◆ **her work is ~ in its quality** son travail est d'une qualité incomparable

unroadworthy /ˈʌnˈrəʊdˌwɜːðɪ/ **ADJ** *[car]* qui n'est pas en état de rouler

unrobe /ˈʌnˈrəʊb/ **VI** 1 *[judge etc]* se dévêtir, se dépouiller de ses vêtements *(de cérémonie)* 2 *(frm = undress)* se déshabiller **VT** 1 *[+ judge etc]* dépouiller de ses vêtements *(de cérémonie)*, dévêtir 2 *(frm = undress)* déshabiller

unroll /ˈʌnˈrəʊl/ **VT** dérouler **VI** se dérouler

unromantic /ˈʌnrəʊˈmæntɪk/ **ADJ** *[place, landscape, words]* peu romantique ; *[person]* terre à terre, peu romantique

unrope /ˈʌnˈrəʊp/ **VI** *(Climbing)* se décorder

UNRRA /ˌjuːenɑːrɑːrˈeɪ/ **N** *(formerly)* (abbrev of **United Nations Relief and Rehabilitation Administration**) UNRRA *f*

unruffled /ˈʌnˈrʌfld/ **ADJ** 1 *(= calm, unflustered) [person, voice]* imperturbable ◆ **to be ~ (by sth)** ne pas être perturbé (par qch) 2 *(= smooth) [water]* lisse, sans rides ; *[hair]* non défait ; *[bedclothes, sheets]* lisse, sans un pli

unruled /ˈʌnˈruːld/ **ADJ** *[paper]* uni, non réglé

unruly /ʌnˈruːlɪ/ **ADJ** *[child, pupil]* indiscipliné, turbulent ; *[employee, behaviour, hair]* indiscipliné ; *[crowd, mob, element]* indiscipliné, incontrôlé

unsaddle /ˈʌnˈsædl/ **VT** 1 *[+ horse]* desseller 2 *(= unseat) [+ rider]* désarçonner **COMP** **unsaddling enclosure** **N** *(Brit)* enclos d'un champ de course où l'on desselle les chevaux et où sont remis certains trophées

unsafe /ˈʌnˈseɪf/ **ADJ** 1 *(= dangerous) [structure, machine]* dangereux, peu sûr ; *[activity, product, level]* dangereux ; *[street, method]* peu sûr ; *[working conditions]* risqué ; *[water]* non potable ◆ **the car is ~ to drive** cette voiture est dangereuse à conduire, il est dangereux de conduire cette voiture ◆ **the country is ~ to visit** le pays n'est pas sûr (pour les touristes), il est dangereux de se rendre dans ce pays ◆ **it is ~ to go there at night** il est dangereux *or* il n'est pas prudent d'y aller la nuit ◆ **~ to eat, ~ for human consumption** impropre à la consom-

mation ♦ **to declare a house ~ for habitation** déclarer une maison insalubre
2 *(= in danger) [person]* en danger
3 *(Jur = dubious) [evidence, conviction, verdict]* douteux ♦ **~ and unsatisfactory** contestable et révisable
COMP **unsafe sex** N rapports *mpl* sexuels non protégés

unsaid /ʌn'sed/ VB pt, ptp of **unsay** ADJ inexprimé, passé sous silence ♦ **much was left ~** on a passé beaucoup de choses sous silence ♦ **some things are better left ~** il y a des choses qu'il vaut mieux taire

unsalable /ʌn'seɪləbl/ ADJ *(US)* ⇒ **unsaleable**

unsalaried /ʌn'sælərɪd/ ADJ non rémunéré

unsaleable, unsalable *(US)* /ʌn'seɪləbl/ ADJ invendable

unsalted /ʌn'sɔːltɪd/ ADJ *(gen)* sans sel, non salé ; *[butter]* sans sel, doux (douce *f*)

unsanitary /ʌn'sænɪtərɪ/ ADJ *(esp US)* insalubre

unsatisfactory /ʌn,sætɪs'fæktərɪ/ ADJ *[situation, method, answer, relationship]* peu satisfaisant ; *[accommodation, product]* qui laisse à désirer ♦ **it is ~ that ...** il n'est pas satisfaisant que ... + *subj*

unsatisfied /ʌn'sætɪsfaɪd/ ADJ 1 *[person] (gen, sexually)* insatisfait (*with sb/sth* de qn/qch) ; *(stronger)* mécontent (*with sb/sth* de qn/qch) ♦ **to be left ~** rester sur sa faim 2 *(= unfulfilled) [need, desire, urge]* insatisfait, inassouvi ; *[demand, curiosity]* insatisfait ; *[hunger, appetite]* non apaisé

unsatisfying /ʌn'sætɪsfaɪɪŋ/ ADJ *[work, book, relationship, result]* peu satisfaisant ; *[food]* qui n'apaise pas la faim

unsaturated /ʌn'sætʃəreɪtɪd/ ADJ non saturé ♦ **~ fat** corps *mpl* gras insaturés

unsavoury, unsavory *(US)* /ʌn'seɪvərɪ/ ADJ *[person]* peu recommandable ; *[district]* peu recommandable, louche ; *[reputation]* douteux ; *[remark]* de mauvais goût ; *[habit, fact, incident]* déplaisant ; *[food]* peu ragoûtant ; *[smell]* plutôt déplaisant ♦ **an ~ business** une sale affaire ♦ **he's a rather ~ character** c'est un personnage assez peu recommandable

unsay /ʌn'seɪ/ (pret, ptp **unsaid**) VT se dédire de ♦ **you can't ~ it now** tu ne peux plus te rétracter *or* te dédire ; see also **unsaid**

unscathed /ʌn'skeɪðd/ ADJ 1 *(= uninjured) [person, place]* indemne ♦ **to emerge** *or* **escape ~ (from sth)** sortir indemne (de qch) ♦ **to leave sb/sth ~** épargner qn/qch 2 *(= unaffected) [person, company]* non affecté ♦ **to emerge** *or* **escape ~ from sth** sortir sans dommage de qch

unscented /ʌn'sentɪd/ ADJ non parfumé

unscheduled /ʌn'ʃedjuːld/ ADJ imprévu

unscholarly /ʌn'skɒləlɪ/ ADJ *[person]* peu érudit, peu savant ; *[work]* qui manque d'érudition

unschooled /ʌn'skuːld/ ADJ *[person]* qui n'a pas d'instruction ; *[horse]* qui n'a pas été dressé ♦ **~ in** qui n'a rien appris de, ignorant en matière de *or* pour ce qui est de

unscientific /ʌn,saɪən'tɪfɪk/ ADJ *[approach, survey, practice]* peu scientifique ; *[sample]* sans valeur scientifique ♦ **he was ~ in his approach** sa démarche n'était pas scientifique ♦ **their methods are ~** leurs méthodes ne sont pas scientifiques

unscramble /ʌn'skræmbl/ VT *(Telec)* désembrouiller ; *(TV)* décoder, décrypter

unscratched /ʌn'skrætʃt/ ADJ *[surface]* non rayé, intact ; *[person]* indemne, sain et sauf

unscrew /ʌn'skruː/ VT dévisser VI se dévisser

unscripted /ʌn'skrɪptɪd/ ADJ *[speech, remark]* improvisé, non préparé d'avance ; *(Rad, TV) [programme]* improvisé

unscrupulous /ʌn'skruːpjʊləs/ ADJ sans scrupules

unscrupulously /ʌn'skruːpjʊləslɪ/ ADV *[behave]* sans scrupule(s), peu scrupuleusement ♦ **to be ~ ambitious** être arriviste

unscrupulousness /ʌn'skruːpjʊləsnɪs/ N *(NonC) [of person]* manque *m* de scrupules

unseal /ʌn'siːl/ VT *(= open)* ouvrir, décacheter ; *(= take seal off)* desceller

unseasonable /ʌn'siːznəbl/ ADJ *[clothes, food]* hors de saison ♦ **the weather is ~** ce n'est pas un temps de saison

unseasonably /ʌn'siːznəblɪ/ ADV ♦ **~ warm/cold/mild weather** un temps exceptionnellement chaud/froid/doux pour la saison ♦ **it was ~ warm/cold** il faisait exceptionnellement chaud/froid pour la saison

unseasoned /ʌn'siːznd/ ADJ *[timber]* vert, non conditionné ; *[food]* non assaisonné

unseat /ʌn'siːt/ VT 1 *[+ rider]* désarçonner 2 *[+ Member of Parliament]* faire perdre son siège à, sortir

unseaworthy /ʌn'siː,wɜːðɪ/ ADJ qui n'est pas en état de naviguer *or* ne répond pas aux normes de navigabilité

unsecured /ʌnsɪ'kjʊəd/ ADJ *(Fin)* sans garantie

unseeded /ʌn'siːdɪd/ ADJ *(Tennis etc)* non classé

unseeing /ʌn'siːɪŋ/ ADJ ♦ **he stared, ~, out of the window** il regardait par la fenêtre, le regard perdu dans la vague *or* les yeux dans le vague ♦ **to gaze at sth with ~ eyes** *(fig)* regarder qch sans le voir

unseemliness /ʌn'siːmlɪnɪs/ N *(NonC: frm)* inconvenance *f*

unseemly /ʌn'siːmlɪ/ ADJ *(frm)* inconvenant ♦ **it is ~ for teachers to swear** il est inconvenant pour un professeur de jurer

unseen /ʌn'siːn/ ADJ 1 *(= not previously seen) [film, photos, diaries]* inédit, que l'on n'a jamais vu ♦ **~ by the public** que le public n'a jamais vu ; → **sight** 2 *(= not visible) [person, hand, power]* invisible 3 *(esp Brit: Scol, Univ) [exam paper]* non préparé ♦ **~ translation** ⇒ **noun a** ADV *[enter, leave, escape]* sans être vu (*by sb* par qn) ♦ **to remain ~** ne pas être vu N 1 *(esp Brit: Scol, Univ)* version *f (sans préparation)* 2 ♦ **the ~** le monde occulte

unselfconscious /ʌn,self'kɒnʃəs/ ADJ naturel ♦ **he was very ~ about it** cela ne semblait nullement le gêner

unselfconsciously /ʌn,self'kɒnʃəslɪ/ ADV avec naturel, sans la moindre gêne

unselfish /ʌn'selfɪʃ/ ADJ *[person]* généreux, désintéressé ; *[act, love]* désintéressé ; *(Sport) [player]* qui a l'esprit d'équipe

unselfishly /ʌn'selfɪʃlɪ/ ADV *[act, behave]* généreusement, de façon désintéressée ; *(Sport) [play]* avec un bon esprit d'équipe

unselfishness /ʌn'selfɪʃnɪs/ N *(NonC) [of person]* générosité *f* ; *[of act]* désintéressement *m*, générosité *f*

unsentimental /ʌn'sentɪmentl/ ADJ *[person]* peu sentimental, qui ne fait pas de sentiment ; *[attitude]* non sentimental ; *[story, language]* qui ne donne pas dans la sensiblerie ♦ **to be ~ about sth** *[person]* ne pas se montrer sentimental à propos de qch ; *[story]* ne pas donner dans la sensiblerie à propos de qch

unserviceable /ʌn'sɜːvɪsəbl/ ADJ inutilisable, hors d'état de fonctionner

unsettle /ʌn'setl/ VT *[+ person, weather]* perturber ; *[+ stomach]* déranger

unsettled /ʌn'setld/ ADJ 1 *(= uncertain) [situation, market]* instable ; *[future]* incertain ; *[weather]* changeant, instable 2 *(= restless) [person, life]* perturbé ♦ **to feel ~** être perturbé ♦ **he feels ~ in his job** il ne se sent pas vraiment à l'aise dans son travail 3 *(= unresolved) [issue]* non résolu ; *[conflict]* non réglé ♦ **to leave matters ~** laisser les choses en suspens ♦ **the question remains ~** la question n'est toujours pas réglée, la question reste en suspens 4 *(= uninhabited) [place]* inhabité, sans habitants 5 *(Fin) [account]* impayé 6 *(Med) [stomach]* dérangé

unsettling /ʌn'setlɪŋ/ ADJ *[experience, influence, question, book, film, music]* perturbant ; *[news, atmosphere]* troublant ♦ **to have an ~ effect on sb/sth** avoir un effet perturbateur sur qn/qch ♦ **it is ~ to know he could be watching me** ça me perturbe de savoir qu'il pourrait être en train de me regarder ♦ **they found it ~ to have their mother living with them** ils trouvaient perturbant que leur mère vive avec eux

unsex /ʌn'seks/ VT faire perdre sa masculinité (*or* féminité) à ; *(= make impotent)* rendre impuissant

unsexed /'ʌnsekst/ ADJ ♦ **~ chicks** poussins *mpl* dont on n'a pas déterminé le sexe

unshackle /ʌn'ʃækl/ VT ôter les fers à, désenchaîner ; *(fig)* émanciper, libérer

unshaded /ʌn'ʃeɪdɪd/ ADJ 1 *(= without lampshade) [bulb, light]* sans abat-jour 2 *(= in sunlight) [place]* non ombragé, en plein soleil 3 *(Art, Geom) [area]* non hachuré

unshak(e)able /ʌn'ʃeɪkəbl/ ADJ inébranlable

unshak(e)ably /ʌn'ʃeɪkəblɪ/ ADV *[certain]* absolument ♦ **he's unshak(e)ably confident** il a une confiance inébranlable en lui-même ♦ **to be unshak(e)ably confident that ...** être absolument certain que ... ♦ **unshak(e)ably committed to a cause** entièrement acquis à une cause

unshaken /ʌn'ʃeɪkən/ ADJ 1 *(= unchanged)* ♦ **to be** *or* **remain ~** *[conviction, belief, faith]* ne pas être ébranlé ; *[confidence]* ne pas être ébranlé *or* entamé ♦ **to be ~ in one's belief that ...** ne pas se laisser ébranler dans sa conviction que ... 2 *(= not worried)* ♦ **to be ~** *[person]* ne pas être secoué (*by sth* par qch)

unshaven /ʌn'ʃeɪvn/ ADJ mal rasé

unsheathe /ʌn'ʃiːð/ VT *[+ sword]* dégainer ; *[cat, tiger] [+ claws]* sortir

unship /ʌn'ʃɪp/ VT *[+ cargo]* décharger, débarquer

unshockable /ʌn'ʃɒkəbl/ ADJ ♦ **he is (completely) ~** rien ne le choque

unshod /ʌn'ʃɒd/ ADJ *[horse]* qui n'est pas ferré ; *[person]* déchaussé, pieds nus

unshrinkable /ʌn'ʃrɪŋkəbl/ ADJ irrétrécissable (au lavage)

unsighted /ʌn'saɪtɪd/ ADJ 1 *(= unseen)* qui n'est pas en vue, que l'on n'a pas vu 2 *(= unable to see sth)* ♦ **the goalkeeper was ~ by a defender** le gardien de but a eu la vue cachée par un défenseur

unsightliness /ʌn'saɪtlɪnɪs/ N *(NonC)* aspect *m* disgracieux, laideur *f*

unsightly /ʌn'saɪtlɪ/ ADJ disgracieux ♦ **to look ~** être disgracieux ♦ **~ facial hair** poils *mpl* disgracieux sur le visage ♦ **he has an ~ scar on his face** il a une cicatrice assez laide sur le visage

unsigned /ʌn'saɪnd/ ADJ 1 *(= without signature) [letter, article, contract]* non signé ♦ **~ by sb** sans la signature de qn ♦ **the treaty remains ~ by the US** le traité n'a toujours pas été signé par les États-Unis 2 *(Mus) [band, singer]* qui n'est pas sous contrat avec une maison de disques

unsinkable /ˈʌnˈsɪŋkəbl/ ADJ insubmersible ; *[politician]* indéboulonnable *

unskilful, unskillful (US) /ˈʌnˈskɪlfʊl/ ADJ (= *clumsy*) maladroit ; (= *inexpert*) malhabile, inexpert

unskilfully, unskillfully (US) /ˈʌnˈskɪlfəlɪ/ ADV (= *clumsily*) avec maladresse ; (= *inexpertly*) malhabilement

unskilled /ˈʌnˈskɪld/ ADJ 1 *[work, labour, job]* ne nécessitant pas de qualification professionnelle 2 (= *not skilful*) *[person, driver]* inexpérimenté ◆ **to be ~ in sth** ne pas s'y connaître en qch ◆ **to be ~ in the use of sth** ne pas savoir bien se servir de qch ◆ **to be ~ in** *or* **at doing sth** ne pas être habile à faire qch COMP **unskilled worker** N ouvrier *m*, -ière *f* spécialisé(e), OS *mf*

unskimmed /ˈʌnˈskɪmd/ ADJ *[milk]* non écrémé, entier

unsmiling /ʌnˈsmaɪlɪŋ/ ADJ *[face]* sans sourire ; *[expression]* sérieux ◆ **he remained ~** il restait sans sourire, il ne souriait pas ◆ **he stared at her, ~** il l'a dévisagée sans sourire

unsmilingly /ʌnˈsmaɪlɪŋlɪ/ ADV sans sourire

unsociability /ˈʌn,səʊʃəˈbɪlɪtɪ/ N (NonC) insociabilité *f*

unsociable /ʌnˈsəʊʃəbl/ ADJ 1 (*pej* = *unfriendly*) *[person]* peu sociable ◆ **I'm feeling rather ~ this evening** je n'ai pas tellement envie de voir des gens ce soir 2 ⇒ **unsocial**

unsocial /ʌnˈsəʊʃəl/ ADJ ◆ **to work ~ hours** travailler en dehors des heures normales

unsold /ˈʌnˈsəʊld/ ADJ *[goods, tickets, holidays]* invendu ◆ **~ stock** stock *m* d'invendus ◆ **to be left** *or* **remain ~** ne pas être vendu

unsoldierly /ˈʌnˈsəʊldʒəlɪ/ ADJ *[behaviour, emotion]* indigne d'un soldat ; *[appearance]* peu militaire, peu martial ; *[person]* qui n'a pas l'esprit *or* la fibre militaire

unsolicited /ˈʌnsəˈlɪsɪtɪd/ ADJ *[mail, phone call, advice]* non sollicité ; (*Fin*) *[offer, bid]* spontané ◆ **"unsolicited gift"** (*US: on customs declarations*) "cadeau"

unsolvable /ˈʌnˈsɒlvəbl/ ADJ insoluble, impossible à résoudre

unsolved /ˈʌnˈsɒlvd/ ADJ *[mystery]* non résolu, inexpliqué ; *[crime]* non éclairci ; *[problem, crossword clue]* non résolu

unsophisticated /ˈʌnsəˈfɪstɪkeɪtɪd/ ADJ *[person, behaviour, tastes, film]* simple ; *[method, device]* simpliste ◆ **an ~ wine** un petit vin sans prétention ◆ **financially ~** *[person]* sans grande expérience de la finance, peu versé dans la finance ◆ **a technically ~ photographer** un photographe sans grande technique

unsought /ˈʌnˈsɔːt/ ADJ (also **unsought-for**) non recherché, non sollicité

unsound /ˈʌnˈsaʊnd/ ADJ 1 (= *unreliable*) *[person, advice, evidence]* douteux ; *[reasoning, judgement, argument, claim]* mal fondé, douteux ; *[view, conviction]* mal fondé ; *[decision]* peu sensé, peu judicieux ; *[company]* peu solide ; *[investment]* peu sûr ; *[player]* peu compétent ◆ **educationally/ecologically ~** contestable sur le plan éducatif/écologique ◆ **ideologically/politically ~** idéologiquement/politiquement douteux ◆ **the book is ~ on some points** ce livre est douteux sur certains points 2 (= *in poor condition*) *[building, teeth, gums]* en mauvais état ; *[health, constitution]* mauvais ; *[heart, lungs]* en mauvaise santé 3 (*Psych, Jur*) ◆ **psychologically ~** psychologiquement malsain ◆ **to be of ~ mind** ne pas jouir de toutes ses facultés mentales

unsparing /ʌnˈspɛərɪŋ/ ADJ 1 (= *lavish*) prodigue (*of* de), généreux ◆ **to be ~ in one's efforts to do sth** ne pas ménager ses efforts pour faire qch ◆ **the report was ~ in its criticism** le rapport n'a pas été avare de critiques 2 (= *cruel*) impitoyable, implacable

unsparingly /ʌnˈspɛərɪŋlɪ/ ADV *[give]* généreusement, avec prodigalité ; *[work]* inlassablement

unspeakable /ʌnˈspiːkəbl/ ADJ *[act, object, horror, food]* innommable ; *[pain, cruelty]* indescriptible

unspeakably /ʌnˈspiːkəblɪ/ ADV effroyablement

unspecifically /ˈʌnspəˈsɪfɪkəlɪ/ ADV *[talk etc]* en restant dans le vague, sans entrer dans les détails

unspecified /ˈʌnˈspesɪfaɪd/ ADJ non spécifié, non précisé

unspectacular /ˈʌnspekˈtækjʊlə^{r}/ ADJ qui n'a rien de remarquable *or* d'exceptionnel

unspent /ˈʌnˈspent/ ADJ *[money, funds]* non dépensé, qui reste

unspoiled /ˈʌnˈspɔɪld/, **unspoilt** /ˈʌnˈspɔɪlt/ ADJ *[countryside, beauty, view, village]* préservé ; *[child]* qui reste naturel ◆ **~ by** non gâché par ◆ **he remained ~ by his great success** malgré son grand succès il restait aussi simple qu'avant

unspoken /ˈʌnˈspəʊkən/ ADJ *[words, hope]* inexprimé ; *[criticism, message]* implicite ; *[agreement, rule, bond]* tacite

unsporting /ˈʌnˈspɔːtɪŋ/, **unsportsmanlike** /ˈʌnˈspɔːtsmənlaɪk/ ADJ (*gen, Sport*) déloyal ◆ **to be ~** (= *not play fair*) être déloyal, ne pas jouer franc jeu ; (= *be bad loser*) être mauvais joueur ◆ **that's very ~ of you** ce n'est pas très chic de votre part

unspotted /ˈʌnˈspɒtɪd/ ADJ (*liter: lit, fig*) sans tache, immaculé

unstable /ˈʌnˈsteɪbl/ ADJ (*all senses*) instable

unstained /ˈʌnˈsteɪnd/ ADJ (= *not coloured*) *[furniture, floor]* non teinté ; (= *clean*) *[garment, surface]* immaculé, sans tache ; *[reputation]* non terni, sans tache

unstamped /ˈʌnˈstæmpt/ ADJ *[letter]* non affranchi, non timbré ; *[document, passport]* non tamponné

unstated /ʌnˈsteɪtɪd/ ADJ inexprimé

unstatesmanlike /ˈʌnˈsteɪtsmənlaɪk/ ADJ peu diplomatique

unsteadily /ˈʌnˈstedɪlɪ/ ADV *[get up, walk]* de façon mal assurée ; *[say]* d'une voix mal assurée

unsteadiness /ˈʌnˈstedɪnɪs/ N (NonC) 1 (= *shakiness*) *[of hands]* tremblement *m* ; *[of gait, voice]* manque *m* d'assurance ◆ **to experience some ~ on one's feet** avoir du mal à tenir sur ses jambes 2 (= *instability*) *[of ladder, structure]* manque *m* de stabilité 3 (= *irregularity*) *[of progress, course, rhythm]* irrégularité *f*

unsteady /ˈʌnˈstedɪ/ ADJ 1 (= *shaky*) *[person, voice, legs, gait]* mal assuré ◆ **to be ~ on one's feet** (*gen*) ne pas être solide sur ses jambes ; (*from drink*) tituber, chanceler 2 (= *unsecured*) *[ladder, structure]* instable 3 (= *irregular*) *[progress, course, rhythm]* irrégulier 4 (= *unreliable*) *[person]* inconstant

unstick /ˈʌnˈstɪk/ (pret, ptp **unstuck**) VT décoller ◆ **to come unstuck** *[stamp, notice]* se décoller ; * *[plan]* tomber à l'eau ◆ **he certainly came unstuck * over that scheme** il s'est vraiment planté * avec ce projet VI se décoller

unstinted /ʌnˈstɪntɪd/ ADJ *[praise]* sans réserve ; *[generosity]* sans bornes ; *[efforts]* illimité, incessant

unstinting /ʌnˈstɪntɪŋ/ ADJ *[help]* sans faille ; *[support, praise]* sans réserve ; *[kindness, generosity]* sans bornes ; *[efforts]* infatigable ; *[work]* inlassable ◆ **to be ~ in one's praise (of sb/sth)** ne pas tarir d'éloges (sur qn/qch) ◆ **he was ~ in his efforts** il ne ménageait pas ses efforts ◆ **~ of sth** (*frm*) *[person]* prodigue de qch

unstitch /ˈʌnˈstɪtʃ/ VT défaire ◆ **to come ~ed** se découdre

unstop /ˈʌnˈstɒp/ VT *[+ sink]* déboucher, désobstruer ; *[+ bottle]* déboucher, décapsuler

unstoppable /ˈʌnˈstɒpəbl/ ADJ *[momentum, progress, rise]* irrépressible ; *[force]* irrésistible ; *[shot]* que rien ne peut arrêter ◆ **the advance of science is ~** on ne peut arrêter les progrès de la science ◆ **the Labour candidate seems ~** il semble que rien ne puisse arrêter le candidat travailliste

unstrap /ˈʌnˈstræp/ VT ◆ **to ~ A from B** détacher A de B, défaire les sangles qui attachent A à B

unstressed /ˈʌnˈstrest/ ADJ *[syllable]* inaccentué, atone

unstring /ˈʌnˈstrɪŋ/ (pret, ptp **unstrung**) VT *[+ violin, racket]* enlever *or* détendre les cordes de ; *[+ beads]* désenfiler ; (*fig*) *[+ person]* démoraliser

unstructured /ˈʌnˈstrʌktʃəd/ ADJ 1 (= *loosely organized*) *[method, programme, meeting]* non structuré 2 (*Dress*) *[jacket]* déstructuré

unstrung /ˈʌnˈstrʌŋ/ VB pt, ptp of **unstring** ADJ *[violin, racket]* dont on a enlevé les cordes, dont les cordes sont détendues ; (*fig*) démoralisé

unstuck /ˈʌnˈstʌk/ VB pt, ptp of **unstick**

unstudied /ˈʌnˈstʌdɪd/ ADJ naturel, spontané

unsubdued /ˈʌnsəbˈdjuːd/ ADJ (*lit, fig*) indompté

unsubscribe /ˈʌnsʌbskraɪb/ VI (*Internet*) se désabonner

unsubsidized /ˈʌnˈsʌbsɪdaɪzd/ ADJ non subventionné, qui ne reçoit pas de subvention

unsubstantial /ˈʌnsəbˈstænʃəl/ ADJ *[structure]* peu solide, léger ; *[meal]* peu substantiel, peu nourrissant ; *[argument]* peu solide, sans substance ; *[evidence]* insuffisant

unsubstantiated /ˈʌnsəbˈstænʃɪeɪtɪd/ ADJ *[rumour]* sans fondement ; *[story]* non confirmé ; *[claim]* non fondé ; *[allegation]* sans preuves ◆ **these reports remain ~** ces informations ne sont toujours pas confirmées

unsubtle /ʌnˈsʌtl/ ADJ lourd

unsuccessful /ˈʌnsəkˈsesfʊl/ ADJ *[attempt]* manqué, infructueux ; *[campaign, operation, career]* manqué ; *[efforts, negotiations, search]* infructueux ; *[firm]* qui ne prospère pas ; *[candidate, marriage, outcome]* malheureux ; *[writer, book]* qui n'a pas de succès ◆ **to be ~** *[person]* ne pas réussir ◆ **I tried to speak to him but I was ~** j'ai essayé de lui parler mais sans succès ◆ **to be ~ in an exam** échouer à *or* rater un examen ◆ **they were ~ in their efforts** leurs efforts ont été infructueux ◆ **he is ~ in everything he does** rien ne lui réussit ◆ **to be ~ in doing sth** ne pas réussir à faire qch ◆ **to prove ~** *[search, negotiations]* ne mener à rien ◆ **we regret to inform you that your application for the post has been ~** nous regrettons de ne pouvoir donner suite à votre candidature au poste concerné ◆ **after three ~ attempts** après trois tentatives infructueuses

unsuccessfully /ˈʌnsəkˈsesfəlɪ/ ADV sans succès

unsuitability /ˈʌn,suːtəˈbɪlɪtɪ/ N ◆ **the ~ of the candidate** l'inaptitude du candidat ◆ **they talked about her ~ for the job** ils ont évoqué le fait qu'elle ne convenait pas pour le poste

unsuitable /ˈʌnˈsuːtəbl/ ADJ *[place]* qui ne convient pas, qui ne fait pas l'affaire ; *[time]* qui ne convient pas ; *[food, climate]* contre-indiqué ; *[person]* (= *inappropriate*) qui ne convient pas, qui ne fait pas l'affaire ; (= *not respectable*) peu recommandable ; *[book]* peu recommandable ; *[moment]* inopportun ; *[action, reply, example, device]* inopportun, peu approprié ; *[language, attitude]* inconvenant ; *[colour, size]* qui ne va pas ; *[job, land]* inapproprié ; *[accommodation]* qui ne convient pas ; *[clothes]* *(= inappropriate)* inadapté ; *(= not respectable)* non convenable ◆ **he is ~ to be the leader of the party** ce n'est pas l'homme qu'il faut pour diriger le parti ◆ **he is ~ for the post** il ne convient pas pour ce poste ◆ **land that is entirely ~ for agriculture/growing wheat** terrain qui ne se prête pas du tout à l'agriculture/à la culture du blé ◆ **his shoes were totally ~ for walking in the country** ses chaussures étaient totalement inadaptées pour la randonnée ◆ **to be ~ for sb** *(= inappropriate)* ne pas convenir à qn ; *(= not respectable)* être déconseillé à qn ◆ **an ~ wife for a clergyman** une femme peu recommandable pour un pasteur ◆ **~ for children** déconseillé aux enfants ◆ **the building was totally ~ as a museum space** ce bâtiment ne se prêtait absolument pas à servir de musée ◆ **the equipment proved ~** l'équipement s'est avéré inadapté

unsuitably /ˈʌnˈsuːtəblɪ/ **ADV** ◆ **~ dressed** *(= inappropriately)* habillé de façon inadaptée ; *(= not respectably)* habillé de façon inconvenante ◆ **to be ~ qualified for sth** ne pas avoir les qualifications requises pour qch

unsuited /ˈʌnˈsuːtɪd/ **ADJ** ◆ **~ to sth** *[person]* inapte à qch ; *[thing]* inadapté à qch ◆ **Mary and Neil are ~ (to each other)** Mary et Neil ne sont pas faits l'un pour l'autre ◆ **to be ~ to** *or* **for doing sth** ne pas être fait pour faire qch ◆ **to be ~ for sth** ne pas être fait pour qch ◆ **the horse was ~ for the fast ground** le cheval n'était pas fait pour ce terrain dur

unsullied /ˌʌnˈsʌlɪd/ **ADJ** *(liter)* *[reputation]* sans tache ◆ **she possessed an innocence ~ by contact with the world** elle était d'une innocence que la fréquentation du monde n'avait pas entachée ◆ **a town ~ by modern development** une ville préservée des atteintes de l'urbanisme moderne

unsung /ˈʌnˈsʌŋ/ **ADJ** *[hero, heroine, achievement]* méconnu

unsupported /ˈʌnsəˈpɔːtɪd/ **ADJ** 1 *(= unsubstantiated)* *[allegation, accusation]* sans preuves ; *[claim, statement, hypothesis]* infondé ◆ **~ by evidence** non étayé par des preuves 2 *(= without backup)* *[troops]* sans soutien ; *[expedition]* sans appui ; *(Pol)* *[candidate]* sans appui, sans soutien *(by sb* de la part de qn) ; *(financially)* *[mother]* sans soutien financier ◆ **~ by troops** sans l'appui de troupes 3 *(physically)* ◆ **to walk/stand ~** *[person]* marcher/se tenir debout sans soutien 4 *[structure, wall]* sans support

unsure /ˈʌnˈʃʊəʳ/ **ADJ** 1 *(= doubtful)* ◆ **I'm ~** je n'en suis pas sûr, je suis dans l'incertitude ◆ **to be ~ about** *or* **of sb/sth** ne pas être sûr de qn/qch ◆ **to be ~ about doing sth** ne pas savoir exactement si l'on va faire qch, ne pas être certain de faire qch ◆ **to be ~ about** *or* **of how to do sth** ne pas trop savoir *or* ne pas être sûr de savoir comment faire qch ◆ **she is ~ what to do/how to reply** elle ne sait pas trop quoi faire/comment répondre, elle n'est pas sûre de savoir quoi faire/comment répondre ◆ **the police are ~ what caused the violence** la police ne s'explique pas vraiment les raisons de cette violence ◆ **they're ~ when he'll return** ils ne savent pas bien quand il rentrera ◆ **she was ~ where she was** elle ne savait pas au juste où elle se trouvait ◆ **he was ~ where to begin** il ne savait pas trop par où commencer ◆ **he was ~ whether he would be able to do it** il n'était pas sûr de pouvoir le faire ◆ **she was ~ whether to laugh or cry** elle ne savait pas trop si elle devait rire ou pleurer

2 *(= lacking confidence)* *[person]* mal assuré ◆ **to be ~ of o.s.** ne pas être sûr de soi ◆ **this made him ~ of himself** cela l'a fait douter (de lui)

3 *(= unreliable)* *[memory]* peu fidèle

unsurmountable /ˈʌnsəˈmaʊntəbl/ **ADJ** insurmontable

unsurpassable /ˈʌnsəˈpɑːsəbl/ **ADJ** insurpassable

unsurpassed /ˈʌnsəˈpɑːst/ **ADJ** qui n'a jamais été dépassé ◆ **to remain ~** rester inégalé

unsurprising /ˈʌnsəˈpraɪzɪŋ/ **ADJ** pas surprenant ◆ **it is ~ that ...** il n'est pas surprenant que ... + *subj*

unsurprisingly /ˈʌnsəˈpraɪzɪŋlɪ/ **ADV** ◆ **~, he left immediately** comme on pouvait s'y attendre, il est parti tout de suite ◆ **not ~, he did it rather well** contrairement à toute attente, il l'a plutôt bien fait

unsuspected /ˈʌnsəsˈpektɪd/ **ADJ** 1 *(= unforeseen)* *[problem, skill, cause]* insoupçonné 2 *(= not under suspicion)* *[person]* qui n'éveille pas de soupçons

unsuspecting /ˈʌnsəsˈpektɪŋ/ **ADJ** sans méfiance ◆ **and he, quite ~, said ...** et lui, sans la moindre méfiance, dit ...

unsuspicious /ˈʌnsəsˈpɪʃəs/ **ADJ** 1 *(= feeling no suspicion)* peu soupçonneux, peu méfiant 2 *(= arousing no suspicion)* qui n'a rien de suspect, qui n'éveille aucun soupçon ◆ **~-looking** tout à fait ordinaire

unsustainable /ˌʌnsəsˈteɪnəbəl/ **ADJ** *[development]* non durable ; *[position]* intenable ◆ **the current system is ~** le système actuel n'est pas viable

unswayed /ʌnˈsweɪd/ **ADJ** ◆ **the government was ~ by the strike action** le gouvernement ne s'est pas laissé influencer par le mouvement de grève

unsweetened /ˈʌnˈswiːtnd/ **ADJ** *[tea, coffee]* sans sucre, non sucré ; *[yoghurt, soya milk]* non sucré ; *[fruit juice]* sans sucre ajouté

unswerving /ʌnˈswɜːvɪŋ/ **ADJ** *[support, commitment]* indéfectible ; *[loyalty]* à toute épreuve ; *[faith, devotion, resolve]* inébranlable ; *[policy]* inflexible ◆ **to be ~ in one's belief in sth** avoir une foi inébranlable en qch

unswervingly /ʌnˈswɜːvɪŋlɪ/ **ADV** ◆ **~ loyal** d'une loyauté à toute épreuve ◆ **to hold ~ to one's course** poursuivre inébranlablement son but, ne pas se laisser détourner de son but

unsympathetic /ˈʌnˌsɪmpəˈθetɪk/ **ADJ** 1 *(= uncaring)* *[person, attitude, treatment]* peu compatissant *(to sb* envers qn), indifférent ◆ **~ to sb's needs/problems** indifférent aux besoins/problèmes de qn ◆ **~ to sth** *(= hostile)* *[+ cause, idea]* hostile à qch ; *[+ aim]* peu sensible à qch 2 *(= unlikeable)* *[character]* antipathique ; *[portrayal]* peu flatteur

unsympathetically /ˈʌnˌsɪmpəˈθetɪkəlɪ/ **ADV** sans compassion

unsystematic /ˈʌnˌsɪstɪˈmætɪk/ **ADJ** *[work, reasoning]* peu systématique, peu méthodique

unsystematically /ˈʌnˌsɪstɪˈmætɪkəlɪ/ **ADV** sans système, sans méthode

untainted /ˈʌnˈteɪntɪd/ **ADJ** *(lit)* *[food]* non contaminé ; *[water, air]* pur ; *(fig)* *[reputation]* intact, sans tache ; *[person, mind]* non corrompu *(by* par), pur

untam(e)able /ˈʌnˈteɪməbl/ **ADJ** *[bird, wild animal]* inapprivoisable ; *[large or fierce animal]* non dressable

untamed /ˈʌnˈteɪmd/ **ADJ** 1 *(= uncultivated)* *[landscape, environment]* sauvage ; *[vegetation]* sauvage, luxuriant ; *[beauty]* sauvage, farouche 2 *(= uninhibited)* *[person]* sauvage, indompté ; *[passion]* dévorant, fougueux 3 *(= undomesticated)* *[animal]* qui n'est pas apprivoisé

untangle /ˈʌnˈtæŋgl/ **VT** *[+ rope, wool, hair]* démêler ; *[+ mystery]* débrouiller, éclaircir ; *[+ plot]* dénouer

untanned /ˈʌnˈtænd/ **ADJ** 1 *[hide]* non tanné 2 *[person]* non bronzé

untapped /ˈʌnˈtæpt/ **ADJ** inexploité

untarnished /ˈʌnˈtɑːnɪʃt/ **ADJ** *(lit, fig)* non terni, sans tache

untasted /ˈʌnˈteɪstɪd/ **ADJ** *[food, delights]* auquel on n'a pas goûté ◆ **the food lay ~ on the plate** le repas restait dans l'assiette ◆ **he left the meal ~** il n'a pas goûté au repas

untaught /ˈʌnˈtɔːt/ **ADJ** *(= uneducated)* sans instruction, ignorant ; *(= natural, innate)* *[skill, gift]* inné, naturel

untaxable /ˈʌnˈtæksəbl/ **ADJ** *[income]* non imposable ; *[goods]* exempt de taxes

untaxed /ˈʌnˈtækst/ **ADJ** *[goods]* exempt de taxes, non imposé ; *[income]* non imposable, exempté d'impôts ; *[car]* sans vignette

unteachable /ˈʌnˈtiːtʃəbl/ **ADJ** *[person]* à qui on ne peut rien apprendre ; *[pupil]* réfractaire à tout enseignement ; *[subject]* impossible à enseigner, qui ne se prête pas à l'enseignement

untempered /ˈʌnˈtempəd/ **ADJ** *[steel]* non revenu

untenable /ˈʌnˈtenəbl/ **ADJ** *[theory, argument, opinion]* indéfendable ; *[position, situation]* intenable

untenanted /ˈʌnˈtenəntɪd/ **ADJ** inoccupé, sans locataire(s)

untended /ˈʌnˈtendɪd/ **ADJ** *(= unwatched)* sans surveillance ; *(= unmaintained)* *[garden etc]* mal entretenu

untested /ˈʌnˈtestɪd/ **ADJ** 1 *(= untried)* *[drug, method]* non testé ; *[theory]* non vérifié ; *[system, weapon, device]* non testé, non essayé 2 *(= inexperienced)* *[person]* inexpérimenté

unthinkable /ʌnˈθɪŋkəbl/ **ADJ** 1 *(= inconceivable)* impensable, inconcevable ◆ **it is ~ that ...** il est impensable *or* inconcevable que ... + *subj* ◆ **it would be ~ to do that** il serait impensable *or* inconcevable de faire cela ◆ **it would be ~ for her to do that** il serait impensable *or* inconcevable qu'elle fasse cela 2 *(= unbearable)* insupportable **N** ◆ **the ~** l'impensable *m*, l'inconcevable *m*

unthinking /ˈʌnˈθɪŋkɪŋ/ **ADJ** *[person, behaviour]* irréfléchi ; *[child]* étourdi ; *[action, remark]* irréfléchi, inconsidéré ; *[obedience]* aveugle ◆ **she drove on, ~** elle a continué sa route sans réfléchir

unthinkingly /ˈʌnˈθɪŋkɪŋlɪ/ **ADV** *[behave]* sans réfléchir ◆ **~ cruel** d'une cruauté inconsciente

unthought-of /ʌnˈθɔːtɒv/ **ADJ** auquel on n'a pas pensé *or* songé

unthread /ˈʌnˈθred/ **VT** *[+ needle, pearls]* désenfiler

untidily /ʌnˈtaɪdɪlɪ/ **ADV** *[work]* sans méthode, sans ordre ; *[write, dress]* sans soin ◆ **his books lay ~ about the room** ses livres étaient étalés en désordre dans toute la pièce

untidiness /ʌnˈtaɪdɪnɪs/ **N** *(NonC)* *[of room]* désordre *m* ; *[of dress, person]* aspect *m* débraillé ; *(in habits)* manque *m* d'ordre

untidy /ʌnˈtaɪdɪ/ **ADJ** *(in appearance)* *[room, desk, clothes, hair]* en désordre ; *[person, appearance, garden]* négligé ; *[writing]* peu soigné ; *[work]* brouillon ; *(in habits)* *[person]* désordonné ◆ **in an ~ heap** *or* **pile** empilé en désordre

untie /ˈʌnˈtaɪ/ **VT** *[+ knot]* défaire ; *[+ string, shoelaces]* dénouer, défaire ; *[+ shoes]* défaire *or* dénouer les lacets de ; *[+ parcel]* défaire, ouvrir ; *[+ prisoner, hands]* délier, détacher ; *[+ bonds]* défaire, détacher

until /ənˈtɪl/ **PREP** jusqu'à ◆ **~ such time as ...** *(in future)* jusqu'à ce que ... + *subj*, en attendant que ... + *subj* ; *(in past)* avant que ... + *subj* ◆ **~ the next day** jusqu'au lendemain ◆ **from morning ~ night** du matin (jusqu')au soir ◆ **~ now**

jusqu'ici, jusqu'à maintenant ◆ ~ **then** jusque-là ◆ **not** ~ *(in future)* pas avant ; *(in past)* ne ... que ◆ **it won't be ready ~ tomorrow** ce ne sera prêt avant demain ◆ **he didn't leave ~ the following day** il n'est parti que le lendemain ◆ **it will be ready on Saturday, ~ when we must ...** ce sera prêt samedi et en attendant nous devons ... ◆ **the work was not begun ~ 1986** ce n'est qu'en 1986 que les travaux ont commencé ◆ **I had heard nothing of it ~ five minutes ago** j'en ai seulement entendu parler *or* j'en ai entendu parler pour la première fois il y a cinq minutes

CONJ *(in future)* jusqu'à ce que + *subj*, en attendant que + *subj* ; *(in past)* avant que + *subj* ◆ **wait ~ I come** attendez que je vienne ◆ **~ they built the new road** avant qu'ils (ne) fassent la nouvelle route ◆ **~ they build the new road** en attendant qu'ils fassent la nouvelle route ◆ **he laughed ~ he cried** il a ri aux larmes ◆ **not** ~ *(in future)* pas avant que ... (ne) + *subj*, tant que ... ne + *indic* pas ; *(in past)* tant que ... ne + *indic* pas ◆ **he won't come ~ you invite him** il ne viendra pas tant que vous ne l'aurez pas invité ◆ **they did nothing ~ we came** ils n'ont rien fait tant que nous n'avons pas été là ◆ **do nothing ~ I tell you** ne faites rien avant que je (ne) vous le dise *or* tant que je ne vous l'aurai pas dit ◆ **do nothing ~ you get my letter** ne faites rien avant d'avoir reçu ma lettre ◆ **wait ~ you get my letter** attendez d'avoir reçu ma lettre ◆ **don't start ~ I come** ne commencez pas avant que j'arrive *subj*, attendez-moi pour commencer

untilled /ˈʌnˈtɪld/ **ADJ** non labouré

untimely /ʌnˈtaɪmlɪ/ **ADJ** *[death]* prématuré ; *[arrival, return, visit]* intempestif ; *[remark, action]* déplacé, inopportun ; *[pregnancy, rain]* inopportun, qui arrive au mauvais moment ◆ **to meet** *or* **come to an ~ end** *[person, project]* connaître une fin prématurée

untiring /ʌnˈtaɪərɪŋ/ **ADJ** *[campaigner, fighter]* infatigable, inlassable ; *[enthusiasm, work, efforts]* inlassable ◆ **to be ~ in one's efforts (to do sth)** ne pas ménager ses efforts (pour faire qch)

untiringly /ʌnˈtaɪərɪŋlɪ/ **ADV** inlassablement

untitled /ˈʌnˈtaɪtld/ **ADJ** 1 *[painting]* sans titre 2 *[person]* qui n'a pas de titre

unto /ˈʌntʊ/ **PREP** *(liter)* ⇒ **to, toward(s)**

untogether* /ˌʌntəˈgeðəʳ/ **ADJ** *[person]* ◆ **to be ~** *(= disorganized)* ne pas être au point* ; *(= unstable)* être paumé*

untold /ˈʌnˈtəʊld/ **ADJ** 1 *(= indescribable, incalculable)* *[damage]* indescriptible ; *[misery, suffering]* indicible, indescriptible ; *[worry]* indicible ; *[riches, losses]* incalculable ; *[amounts]* inestimable ; *[varieties]* innombrable ◆ **to save ~ numbers of lives** sauver d'innombrables vies ◆ **~ millions of years ago** il y a des millions et des millions d'années 2 *(= not recounted)* *[story]* jamais raconté ; *[secret]* jamais dévoilé *or* divulgué ◆ **that story remains ~** cette histoire n'a encore jamais été racontée ◆ **to leave sth ~** passer qch sous silence

untouchable /ʌnˈtʌtʃəbl/ **ADJ** 1 *(in India)* *[person]* de la caste des intouchables ; *[caste]* des intouchables ◆ **to be treated as ~** *(fig)* être traité en paria 2 *(= unattainable, unpunishable)* *[person, aura, air]* intouchable 3 *(= inviolable)* *[right]* intangible 4 *(= unrivalled)* *[player, performer]* imbattable **N** *(in India)* intouchable *mf*, paria *m* ; *(fig)* paria *m*

untouched /ˈʌnˈtʌtʃt/ **ADJ** 1 *(= undamaged)* *[building, constitution]* intact ; *[person]* indemne 2 *(= unaffected)* ◆ **~ by sth** non affecté par qch 3 *(= not eaten or drunk)* ◆ **he left his meal/coffee ~** il n'a pas touché à son repas/café ◆ **his meal/coffee lay ~ on the table** il a laissé son repas/café sur la table sans y avoir touché

untoward /ˌʌntəˈwɔːd/ **ADJ** fâcheux ◆ **nothing ~ happened** il ne s'est rien passé de fâcheux

untraceable /ˈʌnˈtreɪsəbl/ **ADJ** *[person]* introuvable ; *[note, bill]* dont il ne reste aucune trace

untrained /ˈʌnˈtreɪnd/ **ADJ** *[person, worker]* *(= inexperienced)* sans expérience ; *(= unqualified)* non qualifié ; *[soldier, gymnast]* non entraîné, sans entraînement ; *[pianist]* sans entraînement ; *[voice]* non travaillé ; *[mind]* non formé ; *[horse, dog]* non dressé ◆ **to the ~ eye/ear** pour un œil inexercé/une oreille inexercée ◆ **to be ~ for** *or* **in sth** *(gen)* ne pas être formé à qch ; *[soldier, gymnast]* ne pas être entraîné à qch

untrammelled, untrammeled *(US)* /ʌnˈtræməld/ **ADJ** *(frm)* *[person, life]* sans contraintes ; *[authority]* sans limites ◆ **to be ~ by any anxieties** n'être retenu par aucune appréhension ◆ **~ by family ties** non entravé par des liens familiaux ◆ **~ by superstitions** libre de toute superstition

untranslatable /ˈʌntrænzˈleɪtəbl/ **ADJ** intraduisible

untravelled, untraveled *(US)* /ˈʌnˈtrævld/ **ADJ** 1 *[road]* peu fréquenté 2 *[person]* qui n'a pas voyagé

untreated /ʌnˈtriːtɪd/ **ADJ** 1 *(Med)* *[patient]* non traité ; *[illness, wound]* non soigné 2 *(= unprocessed)* *[sewage, wood, cotton]* non traité *(with sth* à qch*)*

untried /ˈʌnˈtraɪd/ **ADJ** 1 *(= untested)* *[product, drug, method]* non testé ; *[theory]* non vérifié ; *[system, weapon, device]* non testé, non essayé 2 *(= inexperienced)* *[person]* qui n'a pas été mis à l'épreuve 3 *(Jur)* *[prisoner]* en détention provisoire ; *[case]* non encore jugé ◆ **he was condemned ~** il a été condamné sans procès

untrodden /ˈʌnˈtrɒdn/ **ADJ** *(liter)* *[path]* peu fréquenté ; *[region, territory]* inexploré, vierge ; *[snow]* non foulé, vierge

untroubled /ˈʌnˈtrʌbld/ **ADJ** 1 *(= serene)* *[person]* serein ; *[face, sleep]* paisible ; *[life]* tranquille ◆ **to be ~ by sth** *(= not worried)* ne pas être affecté *or* troublé par qch ◆ **to be ~ by an accusation** ne pas être ébranlé *or* ne pas se laisser démonter par une accusation ◆ **she is ~ by inconsistencies** les incohérences ne l'inquiètent pas *or* la gênent pas 2 *(= unaffected)* ◆ **to be ~ by injury** *[footballer etc]* ne pas être blessé 3 *(= unharassed)* ◆ **to be ~ by sb/sth** ne pas être dérangé par qn/qch

untrue /ˈʌnˈtruː/ **ADJ** 1 *(= inaccurate)* *[story, belief, claim]* faux (fausse *f*) ◆ **it is ~ (to say) that ...** il est faux (de dire) que ... 2 *(liter = unfaithful)* ◆ **~ to sb** *[lover]* infidèle à qn ◆ **to be ~ to one's principles/word/responsibilities** manquer *or* faillir à ses principes/sa parole/ses responsabilités

untrustworthy /ˈʌnˈtrʌstˌwɜːðɪ/ **ADJ** *[person]* indigne de confiance ; *[witness]* récusable ; *[book]* auquel on ne peut se fier ; *[evidence, results]* douteux

untruth /ˈʌnˈtruːθ/ **N** (pl **untruths** /ˈʌnˈtruːðz/) contrevérité *f* ; *(stronger)* mensonge *m* ; *(NonC)* fausseté *f*

untruthful /ˈʌnˈtruːθfʊl/ **ADJ** *[person]* menteur ; *[statement, claim, answer]* mensonger ◆ **to be ~** *[person]* mentir

untruthfully /ˈʌnˈtruːθfəlɪ/ **ADV** de façon mensongère

untruthfulness /ˈʌnˈtruːθfʊlnɪs/ **N** *(NonC)* fausseté *f*, caractère *m* mensonger

untuneful /ˈʌnˈtjuːnfʊl/ **ADJ** peu harmonieux

untutored /ˈʌnˈtjuːtəd/ **ADJ** *[person]* sans instruction ; *[work]* spontané ; *[taste]* non formé, qui n'a pas été formé ◆ **he is completely ~** il n'a aucune instruction ◆ **to the ~ eye/ear** pour un œil inexercé/une oreille inexercée ◆ **to be ~ in sth** ne pas avoir reçu d'instruction en qch

untwine /ˈʌnˈtwaɪn/ **VT** défaire, détortiller

untwist /ˈʌnˈtwɪst/ **VT** *(= untangle)* *[+ rope, threads, wool]* démêler, détortiller ; *(= straighten out)* *[+ flex, rope]* détordre ; *(= unravel)* *[+ rope, wool]* défaire ; *(= unscrew)* *[+ bottle-top]* dévisser

untypical /ˈʌnˈtɪpɪkəl/ **ADJ** peu typique, peu caractéristique *(of* de*)* ◆ **it's ~ of him** ça ne lui ressemble pas, ce n'est pas son genre

unusable /ˈʌnˈjuːzəbl/ **ADJ** inutilisable

unused /ˈʌnˈjuːzd/ **ADJ** 1 *(= not utilized)* *[land, building, goods, potential]* inutilisé ; *[clothes]* jamais porté ; *[bank notes]* non usagé ; *[food]* non consommé ; *(Ling)* inusité 2 /ˈʌnˈjuːst/ *(= unaccustomed)* ◆ **to be ~ to (doing) sth** ne pas être habitué à (faire) qch, ne pas avoir l'habitude de (faire) qch ◆ **I am quite ~ to it now** j'en ai tout à fait perdu l'habitude, je n'en ai plus du tout l'habitude

unusual /ʌnˈjuːʒʊəl/ **ADJ** *[name]* peu commun, insolite ; *[measure, occurrence, circumstances, gift, number]* inhabituel ; *[case]* étrange ; *[person, place]* étonnant ◆ **nothing ~** rien d'insolite *or* d'inhabituel ◆ **there is something ~ about this** ça a quelque chose d'insolite *or* d'inhabituel ◆ **a man of ~ intelligence** un homme d'une intelligence exceptionnelle ◆ **it is ~ to see this** il est rare de voir cela ◆ **it is ~ for him to be early** il est rare qu'il arrive *subj* de bonne heure ◆ **it's not ~ for him to be late** *or* *(frm)* **that he should be late** il n'est pas rare qu'il soit en retard ◆ **it is ~ that ...** il est rare que ... + *subj* ◆ **this was ~ for me** c'était inhabituel pour moi

unusually /ʌnˈjuːʒʊəlɪ/ **ADV** *[large, quiet, cheerful]* exceptionnellement ◆ **~ early/well** exceptionnellement tôt/bien ◆ **she woke, ~ (for her), a little after midnight** contrairement à son habitude, elle s'est réveillée peu après minuit ◆ **~ for a film of this era, it ...** chose rare pour un film de cette époque, il ...

unutterable /ʌnˈʌtərəbl/ **ADJ** *(frm)* *[sadness, joy, boredom, relief]* indicible ; *[nonsense]* effarant ; *[fool]* fini

unutterably /ʌnˈʌtərəblɪ/ **ADV** *(frm)* *[sad]* indiciblement *(liter)* ; *[boring]* mortellement ◆ **~ tired** mort de fatigue

unvaried /ʌnˈveərɪd/ **ADJ** uniforme, monotone *(pej)* ◆ **the menu was ~ from one week to the next** le menu ne changeait pas d'une semaine à l'autre

unvarnished /ˈʌnˈvɑːnɪʃt/ **ADJ** 1 *[wood]* non verni ; *[pottery]* non vernissé 2 *(fig)* *[account, description]* sans fard ◆ **the ~ truth** la vérité pure et simple, la vérité toute nue

unvarying /ʌnˈveərɪŋ/ **ADJ** invariable

unvaryingly /ʌnˈveərɪŋlɪ/ **ADV** invariablement

unveil /ʌnˈveɪl/ **VT** dévoiler

unveiling /ʌnˈveɪlɪŋ/ **N** dévoilement *m* ; *(= ceremony)* inauguration *f*

unventilated /ˈʌnˈventɪleɪtɪd/ **ADJ** sans ventilation

unverifiable /ˈʌnˈverɪfaɪəbl/ **ADJ** invérifiable

unverified /ˈʌnˈverɪfaɪd/ **ADJ** non vérifié

unversed /ˈʌnˈvɜːst/ **ADJ** ◆ **~ in** peu versé dans

unvoiced /ˈʌnˈvɔɪst/ **ADJ** 1 *[opinion, sentiment]* inexprimé 2 *(Phon)* *[consonant]* non voisé, sourd

unwaged /ˈʌnˈweɪdʒd/ **NPL** **the unwaged** *(Brit Admin = the unemployed)* les sans-emploi *mpl* ◆ **special rates for the ~** des tarifs spéciaux pour les sans-emploi **ADJ** *[person, work]* non rémunéré

unwanted /ˈʌnˈwɒntɪd/ **ADJ** *[food, possessions]* dont on ne veut plus ; *[pet]* dont on ne veut plus, dont on veut se séparer ; *[advice]* inopportun, malvenu ; *[telephone call, attention]* inopportun ; *[visitor]* indésirable ; *[pregnancy, birth, child]* non désiré ; *[fat]* dont on veut se débarrasser ; *[effect]* indésirable ◆ **to feel ~** se sentir rejeté ◆ **she rejected his ~ advances** elle a repoussé ses avances ◆ **to remove ~ hair** s'épiler

unwarlike /ˈʌnˈwɔːlaɪk/ ADJ peu belliqueux

unwarrantable /ʌnˈwɒrəntəbl/ ADJ *[intrusion, interference etc]* injustifiable ◆ **it is quite ~ that ...** il est tout à fait injustifiable que ... *+ subj*

unwarrantably /ʌnˈwɒrəntəblɪ/ ADV de façon injustifiable

unwarranted /ʌnˈwɒrəntɪd/ ADJ injustifié

unwary /ʌnˈweərɪ/ ADJ *[visitor, reader]* non averti ; *[driver]* non vigilant, qui n'est pas sur ses gardes ; *[investor]* trop confiant N ◆ **a trap for the ~** un piège dans lequel il est facile de tomber

unwashed /ˈʌnˈwɒʃt/ ADJ *[hands, object]* non lavé ; *[person]* qui ne s'est pas lavé N *(hum)* ◆ **the great ~** * la populace *(pej)*

unwavering /ʌnˈweɪvərɪŋ/ ADJ *[devotion, faith, resolve]* inébranlable ; *[defender]* inconditionnel ; *[gaze]* fixe ; *[voice]* ferme ; *[concentration]* qui ne faiblit pas ◆ **to be ~ in one's support for sth** apporter un soutien inébranlable *or* indéfectible à qch ◆ **to be ~ in one's opposition to sth** être inflexiblement opposé à qch

unwaveringly /ʌnˈweɪvərɪŋlɪ/ ADV *[follow, continue]* inébranlablement ; *[say]* fermement ; *[gaze]* fixement

unweaned /ˈʌnˈwiːnd/ ADJ non sevré

unwearable /ˈʌnˈweərəbl/ ADJ *[clothes, colour]* pas mettable

unwearied /ʌnˈwɪərɪd/ ADJ pas fatigué

unwearying /ʌnˈwɪərɪɪŋ/ ADJ infatigable

unwed † /ˈʌnˈwed/ ADJ ⇒ **unmarried**

unweighting /ʌnˈweɪtɪŋ/ N *(Ski)* allégement *m*

unwelcome /ʌnˈwelkəm/ ADJ *[visitor, gift, attention]* importun ; *[fact, thought]* gênant ; *[news, publicity, surprise]* fâcheux ; *[reminder]* malvenu ◆ **to make sb feel ~** donner à qn l'impression qu'il est indésirable *or* qu'il est de trop ◆ **the money was not ~** l'argent était le bienvenu

unwelcoming /ʌnˈwelkəmɪŋ/ ADJ *[person, behaviour]* inamical ; *[place]* peu accueillant

unwell /ˈʌnˈwel/ ADJ *[person]* souffrant ◆ **to feel ~** ne pas se sentir bien

unwholesome /ˈʌnˈhəʊlsəm/ ADJ *[food, smell, air, habits, thoughts]* malsain ◆ **to have an ~ interest in sb/sth** éprouver un intérêt malsain pour qn/qch

unwieldy /ʌnˈwiːldɪ/ ADJ [1] *(= difficult to handle)* *[suitcase]* difficile à manier ; *[tool, weapon]* peu maniable, difficile à manier [2] *(= difficult to manage)* *[system, structure, bureaucracy]* pesant, lourd ; *[name]* compliqué

unwilling /ˈʌnˈwɪlɪŋ/ ADJ [1] *(= disinclined)* ◆ **to be ~** *[person]* être réticent ◆ **to be ~ to do sth** *(= disinclined)* ne pas être disposé à faire qch ; *(= refusing)* ne pas vouloir faire qch, refuser de faire qch ◆ **to be ~ for sb to do sth/for sth to happen** ne pas vouloir que qn fasse qch/que qch se produise [2] *(= reluctant)* *[victim]* non consentant ; *[accomplice, conscript]* malgré soi ; *[partner]* involontaire ◆ **he was an ~ participant in the affair** il se trouvait involontairement impliqué dans l'affaire, il se trouvait impliqué dans l'affaire malgré lui ◆ **she gave me her ~ assistance** elle m'a aidé à contrecœur

unwillingly /ˈʌnˈwɪlɪŋlɪ/ ADV à contrecœur

unwillingness /ˈʌnˈwɪlɪŋnɪs/ N *(NonC)* ◆ **his ~ to help is surprising** il est étonnant qu'il ne soit pas disposé à aider

unwind /ˈʌnˈwaɪnd/ (pret, ptp **unwound**) VT dérouler VI [1] se dérouler [2] *(* fig = relax)* se détendre, se relaxer

unwise /ˈʌnˈwaɪz/ ADJ *[person]* imprudent, malavisé *(liter)* ; *[investment, decision, remark]* peu judicieux, imprudent ◆ **it was an ~ thing to say** ce n'était pas très judicieux de dire ça ◆ **it would be ~ to expect too much** il ne serait pas raisonnable de s'attendre à trop ◆ **I thought it ~ to travel alone** j'ai pensé qu'il serait imprudent de voyager seul ◆ **it would be ~ (for *or* of him) to refuse** il serait peu judicieux *or* malavisé (de sa part) de refuser ◆ **you would be ~ to do that** vous seriez imprudent *or* malavisé de faire cela, il serait inconsidéré *or* peu judicieux de votre part de faire cela

unwisely /ˈʌnˈwaɪzlɪ/ ADV *[act, behave]* imprudemment ◆ **~, she agreed to go** imprudemment, elle a accepté d'y aller

unwitting /ʌnˈwɪtɪŋ/ ADJ *[involvement]* involontaire ◆ **I was your ~ accomplice** j'ai été ton complice sans m'en rendre compte ◆ **to be an ~ victim of sth** être sans le savoir la victime de qch ◆ **to be the ~ instrument *or* tool of sb/sth** être l'instrument inconscient de qn/qch

unwittingly /ʌnˈwɪtɪŋlɪ/ ADV *[cause, reveal]* involontairement

unwomanly /ʌnˈwʊmənlɪ/ ADJ peu féminin

unwonted /ʌnˈwəʊntɪd/ ADJ *(frm)* inhabituel

unworkable /ˈʌnˈwɜːkəbl/ ADJ [1] *[proposal, plan, suggestion]* irréalisable ; *[law]* inapplicable [2] *[substance, land]* impossible à travailler ; *[mine]* inexploitable

unworldly /ˈʌnˈwɜːldlɪ/ ADJ [1] *(= unmaterialistic)* *[person]* détaché de ce monde [2] *(= naive)* *[person, attitude]* naïf (naïve *f*) *(about sth* en ce qui concerne qch) [3] *(= not of this world)* *[beauty]* céleste, qui n'est pas de ce monde ; *[silence]* surnaturel

unworn /ˈʌnˈwɔːn/ ADJ *[garment]* qui n'a pas été porté

unworthiness /ʌnˈwɜːðɪnɪs/ N manque *m* de mérite

unworthy /ʌnˈwɜːðɪ/ ADJ *[activity]* peu digne d'intérêt, sans grand intérêt ; *[feeling]* sans noblesse ◆ **I feel so ~!** je me sens si indigne ! ◆ **~ to do sth** indigne de faire qch ◆ **it is ~ to behave like that** il est indigne de se comporter ainsi ◆ **~ of sb/sth** indigne de qn/qch ◆ **it is ~ of comment** ce n'est pas digne de commentaire ◆ **to feel ~ of having sth** se sentir indigne d'avoir qch

unwound /ˈʌnˈwaʊnd/ VB pt, ptp of **unwind**

unwounded /ˈʌnˈwuːndɪd/ ADJ non blessé, indemne

unwrap /ˈʌnˈræp/ VT défaire, ouvrir

unwritten /ˈʌnˈrɪtn/ ADJ [1] *(Literat)* *[novel, article]* qui reste à écrire, qui n'a pas encore été écrit ; *(= transmitted orally)* *[song, folk tale]* non écrit [2] *(= tacit)* *[rule, agreement]* tacite ◆ **it is an ~ law *or* rule that ...** il est tacitement admis que ... COMP **unwritten law** N *(Jur)* droit *m* coutumier

unyielding /ʌnˈjiːldɪŋ/ ADJ *[person]* inflexible, qui ne cède pas ; *[substance]* très dur, très résistant ; *[structure]* rigide

unyoke /ˈʌnˈjəʊk/ VT dételer

unzip /ˈʌnˈzɪp/ VT [1] *(= open zip of)* ouvrir (la fermeture éclair ® de) ◆ **can you ~ me?** peux-tu défaire ma fermeture éclair ® ? [2] *(Comput)* *[+ file]* dézipper

up /ʌp/

1 PREPOSITION
2 ADVERB
3 NOUN
4 ADJECTIVE
5 INTRANSITIVE VERB
6 TRANSITIVE VERB
7 COMPOUNDS

When **up** is the second element in a phrasal verb, eg **come up**, **throw up**, **walk up**, look up the verb. When it is part of a set combination, eg **the way up**, **close up**, look up the other word.

1 - PREPOSITION

◆ **to be ~ a tree/~ a ladder** être dans un arbre/sur une échelle ◆ **~ north** dans le nord ◆ **their house is ~ that road** ils habitent dans cette rue ◆ **she climbed slowly ~ the stairs** elle monta lentement les escaliers ◆ **put your tissue ~ your sleeve** mets ton mouchoir dans ta manche ◆ **further ~ the page** plus haut sur la même page ◆ **~ yours!** *** va te faire mettre ! *** ; → **halfway**

2 - ADVERB

[1] indicating direction, position ◆ **~ there** là-haut ◆ **he lives five floors ~** il habite au cinquième étage ◆ **~ above** au-dessus ◆ **~ above sth** au-dessus de qch

When used with a preposition, **up** is often not translated.

◆ **the ladder was ~ against the wall** l'échelle était (appuyée) contre le mur ; see also **8** ◆ **this puts it ~ among the 20 most popular Web sites** cela en fait l'un des 20 sites Web les plus populaires ◆ **~ at the top of the tree** en haut *or* au sommet de l'arbre ◆ **he's ~ at the top of the class** il est dans les premiers (de sa classe) ◆ **we're ~ for the day** nous sommes ici pour la journée ; see also **8** ◆ **he's ~ from Birmingham** il arrive de Birmingham ◆ **the rate has risen sharply, ~ from 3% to 5%** le taux a enregistré une forte hausse, passant de 3% à 5% ◆ **the people three floors ~ from me** les gens qui habitent trois étages au-dessus de chez moi ◆ **he threw the ball ~ in the air** il a jeté le ballon en l'air ◆ **~ in the mountains** dans les montagnes ◆ **~ in London** à Londres ◆ **~ in Scotland** en Écosse ◆ **he's ~ in Leeds for the weekend** il est allé *or* monté à Leeds pour le week-end ◆ **the temperature was ~ in the forties** il faisait plus de quarante degrés ◆ **from ~ on the hill** (du haut) de la colline ◆ **~ on deck** sur le pont ◆ **the monument is ~ on the hill** le monument se trouve en haut de la colline ◆ **it's ~ on top** c'est en haut ◆ **~ on top of the cupboard** en haut du placard ◆ **the bed was ~ on end against the wall** le lit était debout contre le mur ◆ **prices are ~ on last year's** les prix sont en hausse par rapport à *or* sur (ceux de) l'année dernière ◆ **I was on my way ~ to London** j'allais à Londres, j'étais en route pour Londres ; see also **8**

[2] = upwards ◆ **from £20 ~** à partir de 20 livres ◆ **from (the age of) 13 ~** à partir de (l'âge de) 13 ans ◆ **from his youth ~** dès son plus jeune âge

[3] indicating advantage ◆ **Chelsea were three (goals) ~** Chelsea menait par trois buts ◆ **we were 20 points ~ on them** nous avions 20 points d'avance sur eux

[4] Jur ◆ **to be *or* come ~ before Judge Blair** *[accused person]* comparaître devant le juge Blair ; *[case]* être jugé par le juge Blair

[5] in running order

◆ **first/next up** ◆ **first ~ was Tess Buxton, who sang ...** il y eut tout d'abord Tess Buxton, qui chanta ... ◆ **next ~ to the microphone was John French** John French a été le prochain à prendre le micro, ensuite, c'est John French qui a pris le micro

6 = in total ◆ **I'll play you 100** ~ le premier qui a 100 points gagne

7 * US Culin ◆ **a bourbon (straight)** ~ un bourbon sec ◆ **two fried eggs,** ~ deux œufs sur le plat

8 set structures

◆ **to be up against sth** *(fig = facing)* ◆ **to be ~ against difficulties** se heurter à des difficultés ◆ **you don't know what you're ~ against!** tu ne sais pas ce qui t'attend ! ◆ **he's ~ against stiff competition** il est confronté à des concurrents redoutables ◆ **he's against a very powerful politician** il a contre lui un homme politique très puissant ◆ **we're really ~ against it** ça ne va pas être facile

◆ **up and down** ◆ **he travelled ~ and down the country** il parcourait le pays ◆ **people ~ and down the country are saying ...** partout dans le pays les gens disent ... ◆ **he walked ~ and down (the street)** il faisait les cent pas (dans la rue) ◆ **I've been ~ and down (the stairs) all evening** je n'ai pas arrêté de monter et descendre les escaliers toute la soirée

◆ **to be up for sth** *(= seeking)* ◆ **a third of the Senate is ~ for re-election** un tiers du Sénat doit être renouvelé ◆ **are you ~ for it?** * *(= willing)* tu es partant ?* ; *(= fit)* tu vas pouvoir le faire ?, tu te sens d'attaque* ?

◆ **up to** *(= as far as)* jusqu'à ◆ **~ to now** jusqu'ici, jusqu'à maintenant ◆ **~ to here** jusqu'ici ◆ **~ to there** jusque-là ◆ **~ to and including chapter five** jusqu'au chapitre cinq inclus ◆ **to be ~ to one's knees/waist in water** avoir de l'eau jusqu'aux genoux/jusqu'à la taille ◆ **to count ~ to 100** compter jusqu'à 100 ◆ **what page are you ~ to ?** à quelle page en êtes-vous ?

◆ **to be up to** *(= capable of)* ◆ **she's not ~ to the job** *or* **task** elle n'est pas à la hauteur ◆ **is he ~ to doing research?** est-il capable de faire de la recherche ? ◆ **the directors weren't ~ to running a modern company** les directeurs n'étaient pas capables de diriger une entreprise moderne

◆ **to feel** *or* **be up to sth** *(= strong enough for)* ◆ **are you feeling ~ to going for a walk ?** est-ce que tu te sens d'attaque pour faire une promenade ? ◆ **I just don't feel ~ to it** je ne m'en sens pas le courage ◆ **he really isn't ~ to going back to work yet** il n'est vraiment pas en état de reprendre le travail

◆ **to be up to sth** *(*, pej = doing)* ◆ **what is he ~ to ?** qu'est-ce qu'il fabrique ?*, qu'est-ce qu'il peut bien faire ? ◆ **he's ~ to something** il manigance *or* mijote* quelque chose ◆ **what have you been ~ to?** qu'est-ce que tu as manigancé *or* fabriqué ?* ◆ **what are you ~ to with those secateurs?** qu'est-ce que tu fabriques* avec ce sécateur ? ◆ **he's ~ to no good** il mijote* un mauvais coup ◆ **what have you been ~ to lately?** *(hum)* qu'est-ce que tu deviens ?

◆ **to be up to sth** *(= equal to)* ◆ **it isn't ~ to his usual standard** il peut faire bien mieux que cela ◆ **it's not ~ to much*** *(Brit)* ça ne vaut pas grand-chose

◆ **to be up to sb** *(= depend on)* ◆ **it's ~ to you to decide** c'est à vous de voir *or* de décider ◆ **it's ~ to you whether you go** c'est à toi de voir si tu veux y aller ◆ **shall I do it? – it's ~ to you** je le fais ? – comme vous voulez *or* à vous de voir ◆ **if it were ~ to me ...** si ça ne tenait qu'à moi ... ◆ **it's ~ to us to see this doesn't happen again** nous devons faire en sorte que cela ne se répète pas

◆ **to be up with sb** *(= equal to)* ◆ **he was ~ with the leaders** il était dans les premiers ◆ **she's right ~ there with the jazz greats** elle se classe parmi les plus grands interprètes de jazz ◆ **I'm ~ with the top two or three in maths** je suis dans les deux ou trois premiers en maths

◆ **up with ... !** ◆ **~ with United!** allez United !

3 - NOUN

◆ **to be on the up (and up)*** *(Brit = improving)* ◆ **he's on the ~ (and ~)** il fait son chemin ◆ **it's on the ~ and ~** ça s'améliore

◆ **on the up and up*** *(US = honest)* réglo*, légal ◆ **he insisted the scheme was completely on the ~ and ~** il a insisté sur le fait que ce programme était tout à fait réglo* *or* légal

◆ **ups and downs** *(fig: in life, health etc)* des hauts *mpl* et des bas *mpl* ◆ **after many ~s and downs** après bien des hauts et des bas, après un parcours en dents de scie ◆ **his career had its ~s and downs** il a connu des hauts et des bas dans sa carrière, sa carrière a connu des hauts et des bas

4 - ADJECTIVE

1 = out of bed **to be ~** être levé, être debout *inv* ◆ **(get) ~!** debout !, levez-vous ! ◆ **we were ~ at seven** nous étions levés *or* debout à sept heures ◆ **I was still ~ at midnight** j'étais encore debout à minuit ◆ **he's always ~ early** il se lève toujours tôt *or* de bonne heure ◆ **I was ~ late this morning** je me suis levé tard ce matin ◆ **I was ~ late last night** je me suis couché tard hier soir ◆ **he was ~ all night writing the essay** il a passé toute la nuit sur cette dissertation ◆ **she was ~ all night because the baby was ill** elle n'a pas fermé l'œil de la nuit parce que le bébé était malade

2 = raised ◆ **the blinds were ~** les stores n'étaient pas baissés ◆ **he sat in the car with the windows ~** il était assis dans la voiture avec les vitres fermées ◆ **with his head ~ (high)** la tête haute ◆ **"this side up"** *(on parcel)* "haut" ◆ **hands ~, everyone who knows the answer** levez le doigt *or* la main si vous connaissez la réponse ◆ **several children had their hands ~** plusieurs enfants levaient le doigt *or* la main, plusieurs enfants avaient la main levée ◆ **hands ~!** *(to gunman)* haut les mains !

3 = risen ◆ **when the sun was ~** après le lever du soleil ◆ **the tide is ~** c'est marée haute ◆ **the river is ~** le niveau de la rivière est monté ◆ **the House is ~** *(Parl)* la Chambre ne siège pas

4 = installed, built

Whichever verb is implicit in English is usually made explicit in French.

◆ **we've got the curtains/pictures ~ at last** nous avons enfin posé les rideaux/accroché les tableaux ◆ **the scaffolding is now ~** les échafaudages sont maintenant en place ◆ **the new building isn't ~ yet** le nouveau bâtiment n'est pas encore construit ◆ **the tent isn't ~ yet** la tente n'est pas encore montée ◆ **look, the flag is ~!** regarde, le drapeau est hissé ! ◆ **the notice about the outing is ~** on a mis une affiche à propos de l'excursion

5 = mounted ◆ **to be ~** être à cheval ◆ **a horse with Smith ~** un cheval monté par Smith

6 = increased ◆ **to be ~** *[prices, salaries, numbers, temperature]* être en hausse, avoir augmenté (by de) ; *[water level]* avoir monté (by de) ◆ **petrol is ~ again** l'essence a encore augmenté ◆ **shares are ~ in London this morning** la Bourse de Londres est en hausse ce matin ◆ **tourism is ~** le tourisme est en hausse, le nombre de touristes a augmenté ◆ **the standard is ~** le niveau s'améliore ◆ **it is ~ on last year** c'est en hausse *or* ça a augmenté par rapport à l'an dernier

7 = finished ◆ **his leave/visit is ~** sa permission/sa visite est terminée ◆ **it is ~ on the 20th** ça se termine *or* ça finit le 20 ◆ **when three days were ~** au bout de trois jours ◆ **time's ~!** c'est l'heure ! ; → **game¹**

8 * = wrong ◆ **what's ~ ?** qu'est-ce qui ne va pas ? ◆ **what's ~ with him?** qu'est-ce qu'il a ? ◆ **what's ~ with the car?** qu'est-ce qui ne va pas avec la voiture ? ◆ **what's ~ with your leg?** qu'est-ce qui t'es arrivé à la jambe ?* ◆ **there's something ~ with Paul** il y a quelque chose qui ne tourne pas rond* chez Paul ◆ **I know there's something ~** *(= happening)* (je sais qu')il se passe quelque chose ; *(= amiss)* (je sais qu')il y a quelque chose qui ne va pas

9 Brit = being worked on ◆ **the road is ~** la route est en travaux

10 indicating anger ◆ **his blood is ~** il est fou de colère ◆ **his temper is ~** il est en colère

11 = elated ◆ **to be ~*** être en forme

12 Brit Univ ◆ **when I was ~*** quand j'étais étudiant *or* à la fac*

13 Brit Rail ◆ **the ~ train** le train pour Londres ◆ **the ~ platform** le quai du train pour Londres

14 set structures

◆ **up and about** ◆ **she was ~ and about at 7 o'clock** elle était debout dès 7 heures ◆ **to be ~ and about again** *[sick person]* être de nouveau sur pied

◆ **to be up and down** ◆ **he was ~ and down all night** il n'a pas arrêté de se lever toute la nuit ◆ **sit down for a bit, you've been ~ and down all evening** assieds-toi un moment, tu n'as pas arrêté (de) toute la soirée ◆ **he's been rather ~ and down recently** *(= sometimes depressed)* il a eu des hauts et des bas récemment ; see also **compounds**

◆ **up and running** *(Comput = functioning)* opérationnel ◆ **to be ~ and running** *(Comput)* être opérationnel ; *[project, system]* être en route ◆ **to get sth ~ and running** *(Comput, gen)* mettre qch en route

◆ **to be (well) up in sth** *(= informed)* s'y connaître en qch ◆ **I'm not very ~ in molecular biology** je ne m'y connais pas beaucoup en biologie moléculaire ◆ **he's well ~ in local issues** il s'y connaît bien en affaires locales, il connaît bien ce qui touche aux affaires locales

5 - INTRANSITIVE VERB

1 ◆ **he ~ped and hit him** * *(= jumped up)* il a bondi et l'a frappé

2 ◆ **one day he just ~ped and left** * un jour il est parti comme ça

6 - TRANSITIVE VERB

1 * = raise *[+ prices, wages, pressure]* augmenter ; *[+ tempo]* accélérer ◆ **stores ~ped sales by 60%** les magasins ont augmenté leurs ventes de 60%

2 * Naut ◆ **to ~ anchor** lever l'ancre

7 - COMPOUNDS

up-and-coming ADJ *[politician, businessman, actor]* plein d'avenir, qui monte ; *[rival]* qui monte

up-and-down ADJ *[movement]* de va-et-vient ; *(fig) [business]* qui a des hauts et des bas ; *[progress, career]* en dents de scie

up-and-under N *(Rugby)* chandelle *f*, up and under *m*

up-and-up ADJ ⇒ **up and up;** → **noun**

up-bow N *(Mus)* poussé *m*

up-current, up-draft *(US)* N *(= air current)* courant *m* (d'air) ascendant

up front ADV *(= in advance) [pay, charge]* d'avance *(esp US * = frankly)* franchement, ouvertement

up-tempo ADJ *(Mus)* au rythme enlevé

up-to-date ADJ → **up-to-date**

up-to-the-minute ADJ *[equipment]* dernier modèle *inv* ; *[fashion]* dernier cri *inv* ; *[news]* de dernière minute

upbeat /ˈʌpbiːt/ ADJ * optimiste ; (Mus) enlevé N (Mus) levé *m*

upbraid /ʌpˈbreɪd/ VT (frm) réprimander ◆ **to ~ sb for doing sth** reprocher à qn de faire (or d'avoir fait) qch

upbringing /ˈʌpbrɪŋɪŋ/ N éducation *f* ◆ **he owed his success to his ~** il devait son succès à l'éducation qu'il avait reçue or à la manière dont il avait été élevé ◆ **I had a strict ~** j'ai été élevé d'une manière stricte, j'ai reçu une éducation stricte ◆ **to have a Christian ~** avoir une éducation chrétienne ◆ **I had a Jewish ~** j'ai été élevé dans la tradition juive

upchuck‡ /ˈʌptʃʌk/ VI (esp US) dégueuler‡

upcoming /ˈʌpkʌmɪŋ/ ADJ imminent, prochain

upcountry /ʌpˈkʌntrɪ/ ADV ◆ **we went ~ by train** nous sommes allés vers l'intérieur du pays or dans l'arrière-pays en train ◆ **the nearest town was 100km ~** la ville la plus proche était à 100 km à l'intérieur du pays or dans l'arrière-pays ADJ ◆ **natives in ~ villages** les habitants *mpl* des villages de l'intérieur du pays or de l'arrière-pays ◆ **he was away on an ~ trip** il était parti en voyage vers l'intérieur du pays or dans l'arrière-pays

update /ʌpˈdeɪt/ VT (gen, also Comput) mettre à jour ◆ **to ~ sb on sth** mettre qn au courant de qch N /ˈʌpdeɪt/ mise *f* à jour ; (Comput) [of software package] actualisation *f*, update *m*

upend /ʌpˈend/ VT 1 [+ box etc] mettre debout 2 (fig) [+ system etc] renverser, bouleverser, chambouler*

upfront /ʌpˈfrʌnt/ ADJ 1 (* = frank) [person, attitude] franc (franche *f*) (with sb avec qn) ◆ **to be ~ about sth** ne rien cacher de qch 2 (= paid in advance) [payment] réglé d'avance ; [cost] à payer d'avance

upgradability /ˌʌpgreɪdəˈbɪlɪtɪ/ N évolutivité *f*

upgradable /ʌpˈgreɪdəbl/ ADJ (Comput) extensible, évolutif

upgrade /ˈʌpgreɪd/ N rampe *f*, montée *f* ; [of software] nouvelle version *f* ; [of hardware] extension *f* ; [of memory] augmentation *f* de la capacité ◆ **Omar is on the ~** (Racing) les performances d'Omar ne cessent de s'améliorer ADV /ˈʌpˈgreɪd/ (US) ⇒ **uphill adv** VT /ʌpˈgreɪd/ 1 (= improve) améliorer ; (= modernize) moderniser ; (Comput) [+ software] mettre à jour, acheter une nouvelle version de ; [+ memory] mettre à niveau 2 (= raise, promote) [+ employee] promouvoir ; [+ job, post] revaloriser ◆ **to ~ a passenger** (to higher class) surclasser un passager ◆ **I have been ~d** (Mil, Admin) je suis monté en grade ; (in company) j'ai eu une promotion ◆ **he was ~d to head of department** il a été promu chef de section VI /ʌpˈgreɪd/ se mettre à niveau

upgradeable /ˈʌpgreɪdəbl/ ADJ (Comput) extensible

upheaval /ʌpˈhiːvəl/ N 1 (NonC, gen) bouleversement *m* ; (esp Pol) perturbations *fpl* ; (= moving things around: in home, office etc) branle-bas *m*, remue-ménage *m* ◆ **it caused a lot of ~** cela a tout perturbé 2 (= disturbing event) crise *f* ; (stronger) cataclysme *m* 3 (Geol) soulèvement *m*

upheld /ʌpˈheld/ VB pt, ptp of **uphold**

uphill ADV /ʌpˈhɪl/ 1 ◆ **to go ~** [road] monter ◆ **the car went ~** la voiture a monté la côte ◆ **my car doesn't go ~ very well** ma voiture a du mal à monter les côtes ◆ **a car engine uses more fuel when going ~** une voiture consomme plus d'essence en montée
2 (Ski) en amont

ADJ /ˈʌpˈhɪl/ 1 (= up gradient) ◆ **~ walk/stretch** montée *f* ◆ **the ~ walk back home** la remontée vers la maison ◆ **it was ~ all the way** (lit) c'était tout en montée, ça montait tout du long ◆ **a race over an ~ route** (lit) une course en montée

2 (= difficult) [work, task] pénible, ardu ◆ **it's an ~ battle or struggle (trying to find a job/flat)** c'est une tâche pénible or ce n'est pas évident* (d'essayer de trouver un emploi/un appartement) ◆ **we're fighting an ~ battle against corruption** nous luttons tant bien que mal contre la corruption ◆ **it was ~ all the way (trying to convince him)** ça a été toute une histoire (pour le convaincre)
3 (Ski) ◆ **~ ski** ski *m* amont *inv*

uphold /ʌpˈhəʊld/ (pret, ptp **upheld**) VT [+ institution, person] soutenir, donner son soutien à ; [+ law] faire respecter, maintenir ; (Jur) [+ verdict] confirmer, maintenir

upholder /ʌpˈhəʊldəʳ/ N défenseur *m*

upholster /ʌpˈhəʊlstəʳ/ VT recouvrir ◆ **she is fairly well ~ed** * (fig hum) elle est assez bien rembourrée*

upholsterer /ʌpˈhəʊlstərəʳ/ N tapissier *m*

upholstery /ʌpˈhəʊlstərɪ/ N 1 (= covering) (cloth) tissu *m* d'ameublement ; (leather) cuir *m* ; (in car) garniture *f* 2 (NonC = trade) tapisserie *f* (art, métier)

upkeep /ˈʌpkiːp/ N [of family, house, car, garden] entretien *m* ◆ **~ (costs)** frais *mpl* d'entretien

upland /ˈʌplənd/ N (also **uplands**) hautes terres *fpl*, hauteurs *fpl*, plateau(x) *m(pl)* ADJ [farm, farmer] des hautes terres ; [farming] en altitude ; [grassland, lake] d'altitude ◆ **~ areas** les hautes terres *fpl* ◆ **~ pastures** pâturages *mpl* de montagne, alpages *mpl*

uplift /ˈʌplɪft/ N (= edification) sentiment *m* d'élévation morale or spirituelle ◆ **an ~ in the economy** un redressement de l'économie VT /ʌpˈlɪft/ 1 (fig: spiritually, emotionally) [+ soul] élever ; [+ person] édifier, inspirer ◆ **we were all ~ed by their heroic example** leur héroïsme nous a tous édifiés or inspirés ◆ **art was created to ~ the mind and the spirit** l'art a été créé pour élever l'esprit et l'âme 2 (= improve living conditions of) améliorer le cadre de vie de COMP **uplift bra** N soutien-gorge *m* pigeonnant

uplifted /ʌpˈlɪftɪd/ ADJ 1 (= raised) [arm, face] levé 2 (= edified) ◆ **to feel ~ (by sth)** se sentir grandi (par qch)

uplifting /ʌpˈlɪftɪŋ/ ADJ inspirant, qui réchauffe le cœur

uplighter /ˈʌpˌlaɪtəʳ/ N applique *f* murale (qui dirige la lumière en hauteur)

uplink /ˈʌplɪŋk/ N 1 (= link) liaison *f* terre-satellite 2 (= transmitter) émetteur *m* de liaison terre-satellite

upload /ʌpˈləʊd/ VT télécharger (vers un serveur)

upmarket /ˌʌpˈmɑːkɪt/ ADJ (esp Brit) [goods, car] haut de gamme *inv* ; [newspaper] sérieux ; [area] select* ADV ◆ **to go or move ~** (company) se repositionner vers le haut de gamme

upmost /ˈʌpməʊst/ ADJ, ADV ⇒ **uppermost**

upon /əˈpɒn/ PREP sur ◆ **~ the table** sur la table ◆ **~ the death of his son** à la mort de son fils ◆ **~ hearing this** en entendant cela ◆ **~ my word!** †* ma parole ! ; → **on preposition, once**

upper /ˈʌpəʳ/ ADJ [floor, part, limit] supérieur (-eure *f*) ; [teeth] du haut ◆ **properties at the ~ end of the market** les propriétés *fpl* dans la tranche supérieure du marché ◆ **to have the ~ hand** avoir le dessus ◆ **to gain or get the ~ hand** prendre le dessus ◆ **the ~ reaches of the Seine** la haute Seine ◆ **in the ~ reaches of the river** en amont de la rivière ◆ **the ~ shelf** l'étagère *f* supérieure or du dessus ◆ **an ~ shelf** une des étagères supérieures ◆ **the temperature is in the ~ thirties** la température dépasse trente-cinq degrés ◆ **an ~ window** une fenêtre de l'étage supérieur or du dessus

N 1 [of shoe] empeigne *f* ◆ **to be (down) on one's ~s** * manger de la vache enragée, être dans la purée*
2 (US Rail *) couchette *f* supérieure
3 (* = drug, pill) stimulant *m*, excitant *m*

COMP **the upper arm** N le haut du bras
the upper atmosphere N les couches *fpl* supérieures de l'atmosphère
the upper back N le haut du dos
the upper body N la partie supérieure du corps
upper case N (Typ) haut *m* de casse ◆ **in ~ case** en capitales
upper-case ADJ ◆ **~-case letter** majuscule *f*, capitale *f* ◆ **~-case "h"** "h" majuscule
Upper Chamber N ⇒ **Upper House**
upper circle N (Brit Theat) deuxième balcon *m*
upper class N haute société *f*
upper-class ADJ aristocratique, de la haute société
upper classes NPL ⇒ **upper class**
the upper crust * N (fig) le gratin*
upper-crust * ADJ aristocratique, aristo*
upper deck N [of bus] étage *m* supérieur ; (Naut) (= part of ship) pont *m* supérieur ; (= personnel) ◆ **the ~ deck** * les officiers *mpl*
Upper Egypt N Haute-Égypte *f*
the Upper House N (Parl) (gen) la Chambre haute ; (in Brit) la Chambre des lords ; (in France, in the US) le Sénat
upper income bracket N tranche *f* supérieure de revenus ◆ **people in the ~ income brackets** les gens *mpl* faisant partie de la tranche supérieure de revenus
upper jaw N mâchoire *f* supérieure
upper lip N lèvre *f* supérieure ; → **stiff**
upper management N cadres *mpl* supérieurs
upper middle class N haute bourgeoisie *f*
the upper ranks NPL (Mil, Admin) les grades *mpl* supérieurs ; (fig) les rangs *mpl* supérieurs
the Upper Rhine N le cours supérieur du Rhin
upper school N (Scol: gen) grandes classes *fpl* ; (Scol Admin = top section) (classe *f* de) terminale *f*
upper sixth N (Brit Scol: also **upper sixth form**) (classe *f* de) terminale *f*
Upper Volta N Haute-Volta *f*

upperclassman /ˌʌpəˈklɑːsmən/ N (pl **-men**) (US Univ) étudiant *m* de troisième or quatrième année

uppercut /ˈʌpəkʌt/ N (Boxing) uppercut *m*

uppermost /ˈʌpəməʊst/ ADJ 1 (= topmost) [leaves, branches] du haut ; [floor] le dernier or la dernière ◆ **the patterned side should be ~** le côté à motifs doit être sur le dessus 2 (= paramount) ◆ **it is the question of sovereignty which has been ~ at the negotiations** c'est la question de la souveraineté qui a dominé les négociations ◆ **my career is ~ on my agenda** ma carrière est ce qui compte le plus ◆ **safety was ~ in his mind** il pensait avant tout à la sécurité ◆ **there were two thoughts ~ in my mind** deux pensées me préoccupaient en priorité ADV [turn, lie] vers le haut ◆ **place your hands on your knees, palms ~** posez les mains sur les genoux, paumes vers le haut

uppish †* /ˈʌpɪʃ/ ADJ (Brit) ⇒ **uppity 2**

uppity * /ˈʌpɪtɪ/ ADJ 1 (= awkward) [person] difficile ◆ **to get ~** monter sur ses grands chevaux ◆ **to get ~ with sb/about sth** s'énerver après qn/après qch 2 (Brit † * = snobbish) [person] bêcheur* ◆ **an ~ man/woman** un bêcheur*/ une bêcheuse* ◆ **to get ~ with sb** traiter qn de haut

upraised /ʌpˈreɪzd/ ADJ [hand, arm, palm etc] levé

uprate /ʌpˈreɪt/ ADJ ◆ **~ tax brackets** tranches *fpl* les plus imposées VT majorer (by de)

upright /ˈʌpraɪt/ ADJ 1 (= vertical) [person, posture] droit ◆ **to be ~** [person] se tenir droit ◆ **in an ~ position** debout ◆ **put your seat in an ~ position** redressez le dossier de votre siège 2

(= *honest*) *[person]* droit, probe (*liter*) ADV *[stand, sit, stay]* droit ; *[place]* verticalement ◆ **to walk ~** *[person]* marcher debout ; *[quadruped]* marcher sur ses pattes de derrière ◆ **to pull o.s. ~** se redresser ; → **bolt** N 1 *[of door, window]* montant *m*, pied-droit *m* (*Archit*) ; *[of goal-post]* montant *m* de but 2 (= *piano*) piano *m* droit
COMP **upright freezer** N congélateur-armoire *m*
upright piano N piano *m* droit
upright vacuum cleaner N aspirateur-balai *m*

uprightly /ˈʌp,raɪtlɪ/ ADV honnêtement, avec droiture

uprightness /ˈʌp,raɪtnɪs/ N (*NonC*) honnêteté *f*, droiture *f*

uprising /ˈʌpraɪzɪŋ/ N soulèvement *m*, insurrection *f*, révolte *f* (*against* contre)

upriver ADV /ʌpˈrɪvəʳ/ *[be]* en amont (*from* de) ; *[sail]* vers l'amont ; *[swim]* contre le courant ADJ /ˈʌprɪvəʳ/ d'amont

uproar /ˈʌprɔːʳ/ N tumulte *m* ◆ **this caused an ~, at this there was (an) ~** (= *shouting*) cela a déclenché un véritable tumulte ; (= *protesting*) cela a déclenché une tempête de protestations ◆ **the hall was in (an) ~** (= *shouting*) le tumulte régnait dans la salle ; (= *protesting*) toute la salle protestait bruyamment ; (= *disturbance*) la plus vive agitation régnait dans la salle ◆ **the meeting ended in (an) ~** la réunion s'est terminée dans le tumulte

uproarious /ʌpˈrɔːrɪəs/ ADJ 1 (= *noisy*) *[meeting]* agité ; *[laughter]* tonitruant 2 (= *hilarious*) *[comedy, occasion]* hilarant

uproariously /ʌpˈrɔːrɪəslɪ/ ADV *[laugh]* aux éclats ◆ **~ funny** désopilant

uproot /ʌpˈruːt/ VT (*lit, fig*) déraciner

upsa-daisy* /ˈʌpsə,deɪzɪ/ EXCL (*baby talk*) allez, hop !

upscale* /ˈʌpskeɪl/ ADJ (*US*) classe*

upset /ʌpˈset/ LANGUAGE IN USE 24.4 (pret, ptp **upset**)
VT 1 (= *overturn*) *[+ cup etc]* renverser ; *[+ boat]* faire chavirer ; (= *spill*) *[+ milk, contents]* renverser, répandre ◆ **that ~ the applecart*** ça a tout fichu par terre*, ça a chamboulé* tous mes (*or* ses *etc*) projets
2 (*fig*) *[+ plan, timetable]* déranger, bouleverser ; *[+ system]* déranger ; *[+ calculation]* fausser ; *[+ stomach, digestion]* déranger ; *[+ person]* (= *offend*) vexer ; (= *grieve*) faire de la peine à ; (= *annoy*) contrarier ◆ **don't ~ yourself** ne vous tracassez pas, ne vous en faites pas ◆ **now you've ~ him** maintenant il est vexé ◆ **onions always ~ my digestion** *or* **my stomach** les oignons me rendent malade, je ne supporte pas les oignons
ADJ 1 *[person]* (= *annoyed, offended*) vexé (*about sth* par qch) ; (= *distressed*) troublé (*about sth* par qch) ; (*stronger*) bouleversé (*about sth* par qch) ◆ **he's ~ that you didn't tell him** (= *offended*) il est vexé que vous ne lui ayez rien dit ◆ **my mother is ~ that I lost the money** ma mère est contrariée que j'aie perdu l'argent ◆ **he was ~ about losing** (= *annoyed*) il était vexé d'avoir perdu ◆ **she was ~ about him leaving** son départ l'a peinée ◆ **to get ~** (= *annoyed*) se vexer ; (= *distressed*) être peiné *or* être bouleversé ◆ **don't get ~!** ne le prends pas mal !
2 (*Med*) *[stomach]* dérangé ◆ **to have an ~ stomach** avoir l'estomac dérangé
N /ˈʌpset/ (= *upheaval*) désordre *m*, remue-ménage *m* ; (*in plans etc*) bouleversement *m*, changement *m* soudain (*in* de) ; (*emotional*) chagrin *m* ; (* = *quarrel*) brouille *f* ◆ **to have a stomach ~** avoir l'estomac dérangé, avoir une indigestion
COMP /ˈʌpset/ **upset price** N (*esp US: at auction*) mise *f* à prix

upsetting /ʌpˈsetɪŋ/ ADJ *[experience, incident, feeling]* pénible, bouleversant ◆ **it is ~ to see such terrible things** il est perturbant de voir des horreurs pareilles ◆ **it is ~ for him to talk about the incident** il lui est pénible de parler de cet incident ◆ **the incident was very ~ for me** cet incident m'a bouleversé

upshot /ˈʌpʃɒt/ N aboutissement *m* ◆ **the ~ of it all was ...** le résultat de tout cela a été ... ◆ **in the ~** à la fin, en fin de compte

upside /ˈʌpsaɪd/ N N (also **up side** = *positive aspect*) avantage *m* ◆ **on the ~** pour ce qui est des avantages, côté avantages*
COMP **upside down** ADV à l'envers ◆ **to hang ~ down** *[person]* être suspendu la tête en bas ; *[picture]* être à l'envers ◆ **to read (sth) ~ down** lire (qch) à l'envers ◆ **to turn sth ~ down** (*box, bottle*) retourner qch ; (*fig*) (= *disorganize*) (*house, room, drawer*) mettre qch sens dessus dessous ; (*plans*) faire tomber qch à l'eau, faire échouer qch ◆ **my world** *or* **life (was) turned ~ down** ma vie a été bouleversée
upside-down ADJ (= *inverted*) *[picture, flag, shape]* à l'envers ; *[box, car]* retourné ◆ **in an** *or* **the ~-down position** à l'envers ◆ **an ~-down world** (= *topsy-turvy*) un monde à l'envers
upside-down cake N *gâteau renversé* ◆ **pineapple ~-down cake** gâteau *m* renversé sur lit d'ananas

upstage /ʌpˈsteɪdʒ/ ADV (*Theat*) dans le lointain, à l'arrière-plan ◆ **~ centre/left/right** à l'arrière-plan au centre/à gauche/à droite ADJ (*Theat*) vers le fond de la scène VT éclipser, souffler la vedette à

upstairs /ʌpˈsteəz/ ADV 1 (= *to a higher floor*) ◆ **to go ~** monter ◆ **to run ~** monter l'escalier *or* les escaliers en courant ◆ **to take sb/sth ~** monter qn/qch ◆ **I was taken ~ to a room on the second floor** on m'a emmené dans une pièce au deuxième étage ; → **kick**
2 (= *on floor above*) (*in two-storey building*) en haut, à l'étage ; (*in multi-storey building*) à l'étage au-dessus ◆ **from ~** (*in two-storey building*) d'en haut, de l'étage ; (*in multi-storey building*) de l'étage au-dessus ◆ **the people/flat ~** les gens *mpl*/l'appartement *m* du dessus ◆ **the room ~** (*in two-storey building*) la pièce d'en haut *or* à l'étage ; (*in multi-storey building*) la pièce à l'étage au-dessus ◆ **he hasn't got much ~*** (*fig hum*) il n'en a pas lourd dans la caboche*
N * ◆ **the house has no ~** la maison est de plain-pied *or* n'a pas d'étage ◆ **the ~ belongs to another family** l'étage *m* appartient à une autre famille
ADJ /ˈʌpsteəz/ 1 (= *on a higher floor*) *[room, flat, window]* (*in two-storey building*) à l'étage ; (*in multi-storey building*) en étage
2 (= *on the floor above*) *[flat, neighbour]* du dessus

upstanding /ʌpˈstændɪŋ/ ADJ 1 (= *respectable*) *[person]* droit, probe (*liter*) ◆ **a fine ~ young man** un jeune homme très bien 2 (*frm* = *erect*) *[person]* bien droit ; *[animal]* dressé (de toute sa hauteur) 3 (*frm*) ◆ **be ~** (= *stand up*) levez-vous

upstart /ˈʌpstɑːt/ N parvenu(e) *m(f)*, arriviste *mf*

upstate /ʌpˈsteɪt/ (*US*) ADV *[go]* vers l'intérieur (*d'un État des États-Unis*) ; *[be]* à l'intérieur ADJ de l'intérieur ◆ **~ New York** le nord de l'État de New York

upstream /ʌpˈstriːm/ ADV *[be]* en amont (*from sth* de qch) ; *[sail]* vers l'amont ◆ **to swim ~** *[fish]* remonter le courant ; *[person]* nager contre le courant ADJ en amont, d'amont ◆ **~ industries** industries *fpl* en amont

upstretched /ʌpˈstretʃt/ ADJ ◆ **with arms ~** les bras tendus en l'air

upstroke /ˈʌpstrəʊk/ N (*with pen*) délié *m* ; (*of piston etc*) course *f* ascendante

upsurge /ˈʌpsɜːdʒ/ N (*of feeling*) vague *f*, accès *m* ; (*of interest, confidence*) recrudescence *f*, regain *m* ◆ **the ~ in oil prices** la flambée des prix du pétrole

upswept /ʌpˈswept/ ADJ 1 *[headlights, wings]* profilé 2 *[hair]* relevé sur la tête

upswing /ˈʌpswɪŋ/ N (*lit*) mouvement *m* ascendant, montée *f* ; (*fig*) amélioration *f* notable ; (*Econ*) redressement *m*, reprise *f* (*in* de)

upsy-daisy* /ˈʌpsə,deɪzɪ/ EXCL ⇒ **upsa-daisy**

uptake /ˈʌpteɪk/ N 1 (= *understanding*) **to be quick on the ~*** avoir l'esprit vif, comprendre *or* saisir vite ◆ **to be slow on the ~*** être lent à comprendre *or* à saisir 2 (*Tech* = *intake*) consommation *f* 3 (*Marketing etc*) **the ~ on the new product** (= *interest, acceptance*) l'intérêt suscité par le nouveau produit

upthrust /ˈʌpθrʌst/ N (*gen, Tech*) poussée *f* ascendante ; (*Geol*) soulèvement *m*

uptight* /ʌpˈtaɪt/ ADJ 1 (= *tense*) *[person]* tendu ◆ **he was ~ about the meeting** il était tendu à cause de la réunion ◆ **he seemed ~ about me being there** ma présence semblait le rendre nerveux ◆ **to get ~** devenir nerveux ◆ **to feel ~** être tendu 2 (= *annoyed*) *[person]* énervé (*about sth* par qch) ◆ **to get ~ (about sth)** s'énerver (à propos de qch) 3 (= *inhibited*) *[person]* refoulé, complexé ◆ **~ about sex** refoulé, coincé* ◆ **to be** *or* **feel ~ about doing sth** être mal à l'aise à l'idée de faire qch

uptime /ˈʌp,taɪm/ N *[of machine, computer]* temps *m* *or* durée *f* de fonctionnement

up-to-date /,ʌptəˈdeɪt/ ADJ 1 (= *updated*) *[report, file]* à jour 2 (= *most recent*) *[report, assessment, information]* très (*or* le plus) récent 3 (= *modern*) *[building, course]* moderne ; *[attitude, person]* moderne, dans le vent, à la page ; see also **date¹**

uptorn /ʌpˈtɔːn/ ADJ *[tree]* déraciné, arraché

uptown /ʌpˈtaʊn/ (*US*) ADV *[live]* dans les quartiers chics ; *[go]* vers les quartiers chics ADJ des quartiers chics ◆ **~ New York** les quartiers *mpl* chics de New York

uptrend /ˈʌptrend/ N reprise *f* ◆ **to be on an** *or* **the ~** (*gen*) être en hausse ; *[market]* être à la hausse

upturn /ʌpˈtɜːn/ VT retourner, mettre à l'envers ; (= *overturn*) renverser ◆ **~ed nose** nez *m* retroussé N /ˈʌptɜːn/ amélioration *f* (*in* de) ; ◆ **an ~ in the economy** une reprise

UPVC /,juːpiːviːˈsiː/ N (abbrev of **unplasticized polyvinyl chloride**) PVC *m* dur, PVC *m* non plastifié

UPW /,juːpiːˈdʌbljuː/ N (*Brit*) (abbrev of **Union of Post Office Workers**) *syndicat*

upward /ˈʌpwəd/ ADJ 1 (= *rising, increasing*) *[trend, movement, revision]* à la hausse ◆ **the dollar resumed its ~ climb** le dollar a recommencé à monter ◆ **~ spiral** spirale *f* ascendante ◆ **to be on an ~ trend** (*gen*) être à la hausse ; *[market]* être en hausse ; *[economy]* reprendre 2 (= *to higher place*) *[motion, stroke, look]* vers le haut ; *[slope]* ascendant ◆ **~ climb** ascension *f* ◆ **~ gradient** pente *f* ascendante ◆ **~ movement** *[of hand]* mouvement *m* vers le haut ; *[of needle, mercury]* mouvement *m* ascendant ; *[of plane, rocket]* mouvement *m* ascensionnel ADV (*esp US*) ⇒ **upwards**
COMP **upward (social) mobility** N ascension *f* sociale

upwardly mobile /,ʌpwədlɪˈməʊbaɪl/ (*Sociol*) ADJ ◆ **to be ~** monter dans l'échelle sociale NPL **the upwardly mobile** ceux qui montent dans l'échelle sociale

upwards /ˈʌpwədz/, **upward** (*esp US*) /ˈʌpwəd/ ADV 1 (= *towards higher place*) *[look]* en haut, vers le haut ◆ **to climb/slope ~** monter ◆ **the road sloped gently ~** la route montait en pente douce ◆ **naked from the waist ~** torse nu *inv*
2 (= *face up*) ◆ **place your hands palm ~ on your knees** placez les mains sur les genoux,

paumes vers le haut ◆ **dead rats floated bellies** ~ des rats morts flottaient le ventre en l'air ◆ **lie face ~ on the floor** allongez-vous par terre sur le dos ◆ **lay the book face ~** posez le livre face en dessus

[3] *(= to higher level)* ◆ **prices are heading ~** les prix sont en hausse ◆ **costs continue to spiral** ~ les coûts continuent leur spirale ascendante ◆ **to be revised ~** être révisé à la hausse

[4] ◆ **... and ~** *(= and above)* **this book suits age three years and ~** ce livre convient aux enfants à partir de trois ans ◆ **prices range from $250,000 and ~** la gamme des prix part de 250 000 dollars

[5] *(= starting from)* ◆ **prices from 5 euros ~** prix *mpl* à partir de 5 euros ◆ **from childhood ~** dès ma *(or* ta *or* sa *etc)* jeunesse, dès l'enfance

[6] ◆ **~ of** *(= more than)* plus de ◆ **they cost ~ of $100,000** ils coûtent plus de 100 000 dollars

upwind /ˈʌpˈwɪnd/ **ADV** *[move]* contre le vent ◆ **to be ~ (of sb/sth)** être au vent *or* dans le vent (par rapport à qn/qch) ◆ **the west of the city is ~ of the smell of industry** à l'ouest de la ville, le vent éloigne l'odeur des usines **ADJ** au vent

uraemia /jʊˈriːmɪə/ **N** urémie *f*

uraemic /jʊˈriːmɪk/ **ADJ** urémique

Ural /ˈjʊərəl/ **N** ◆ **the ~ Mountains, the ~s** les monts *mpl* Oural, l'Oural *m*

uranalysis /ˌjʊərəˈnælɪsɪs/ **N** (pl **uranalyses** /ˌjʊərəˈnælɪsiːz/) *(Med)* analyse *f* d'urine

uranium /jʊəˈreɪnɪəm/ **N** uranium *m* **COMP** **uranium-bearing ADJ** *[rock]* uranifère

Uranus /jʊəˈreɪnəs/ **N** *(Myth)* Uranus *m* ; *(Astron)* Uranus *f*

urban /ˈɜːbən/ **ADJ** *[area, population, life, motorway, warfare, problems, poverty]* urbain ; *[land]* en zone urbaine ; *[workers, poor]* des villes ; *[poverty]* dans les villes

COMP **urban aid N** aide *f* pour les zones urbaines défavorisées

urban blight N dégradation *f* urbaine

urban centre N *(= town)* centre *m* urbain ; *(= town centre)* centre-ville *m*

urban clearway N *(Brit Transport)* voie *f* urbaine à stationnement interdit

urban conservation area N zone *f* urbaine protégée

urban decay N dégradation *f* urbaine

urban development N aménagement *m* urbain

urban development zone N ≈ zone *f* à urbaniser en priorité, ZUP *f*

urban district council N *(Brit Local Govt: formerly)* conseil *m* de district urbain

urban dweller N *(frm)* habitant(e) *m(f)* des villes

urban guerrilla N guérillero *m* urbain

the Urban League N *(in US) association américaine d'aide aux Noirs vivant dans des quartiers défavorisés*

urban legend N légende *f* urbaine

urban migration N exode *m* rural

urban myth N ⇒ **urban legend**

urban planner N urbaniste *mf*

urban planning N urbanisme *m*

urban renewal N rénovations *fpl* urbaines

urban sprawl N *(= phenomenon)* expansion *f* urbaine tentaculaire ; *(= area)* ville *f* tentaculaire

urban studies NPL études *fpl* d'urbanisme

urbane /ɜːˈbeɪn/ **ADJ** *[person]* urbain *(liter)*, courtois ; *[wit]* raffiné ; *[charm]* discret (-ète *f*) ◆ **his ~ manner** sa courtoisie

urbanely /ɜːˈbeɪnlɪ/ **ADV** *[say, smile]* courtoisement

urbanite /ˈɜːbənaɪt/ **N** *(US)* citadin(e) *m(f)*

urbanity /ɜːˈbænɪtɪ/ **N** *(NonC)* urbanité *f*, courtoisie *f*

urbanization /ˌɜːbənaɪˈzeɪʃən/ **N** urbanisation *f*

urbanize /ˈɜːbənaɪz/ **VT** urbaniser

urchin /ˈɜːtʃɪn/ **N** polisson(ne) *m(f)*, garnement *m* ; → **sea, street**

Urdu /ˈʊəduː/ **N** ourdou *m*

urea /ˈjʊərɪə/ **N** urée *f*

uremia /jʊˈriːmɪə/ **N** ⇒ **uraemia**

ureter /jʊˈriːtə^r^/ **N** uretère *m*

urethra /jʊˈriːθrə/ **N** (pl **urethras** *or* **urethrae** /jʊˈriːθriː/) urètre *m*

urge /ɜːdʒ/ **N** forte envie *f* *(to do sth* de faire qch) ◆ **to feel** *or* **have an** *or* **the ~ to do sth** éprouver une forte envie de faire qch ◆ **he had a strong ~ for revenge** il avait soif de vengeance ; → **sex**

VT *[+ person]* pousser *(to do sth* à faire qch), conseiller vivement *(to do sth* de faire qch) ; *[+ caution, remedy, measure]* conseiller vivement, recommander avec insistance ; *[+ excuse]* faire valoir ; *[+ point]* insister sur ◆ **to ~ restraint/caution on sb** recommander vivement la retenue/la prudence à qn ◆ **to ~ sb back/in/out** insister vivement pour que qn revienne/entre/sorte ◆ **to ~ patience** prêcher la patience ◆ **I ~ you to write at once** je ne saurais trop vous conseiller d'écrire immédiatement ◆ **I ~d him not to go** je lui ai vivement déconseillé d'y aller ◆ **he needed no urging** il ne s'est pas fait prier ◆ **to ~ that sth (should) be done** recommander vivement que qch soit fait ◆ **"do it now!" he ~d** "faites-le tout de suite !" insista-t-il ◆ **he ~d acceptance of the report** il a vivement recommandé l'acceptation du rapport ◆ **they ~d parliament to accept the reforms** ils ont vivement conseillé au parlement d'accepter les réformes

► **urge on VT SEP** *[+ horse]* talonner ; *[+ person]* faire avancer ; *[+ troops]* pousser en avant, faire avancer ; *(fig) [+ worker]* presser ; *[+ work]* activer, hâter ; *(Sport) [+ team]* encourager, animer ◆ **to ~ sb on to (do) sth** inciter qn à (faire) qch

urgency /ˈɜːdʒənsɪ/ **N** *(NonC) [of case etc]* urgence *f* ; *[of tone, entreaty]* insistance *f* ◆ **there's no ~** ce n'est pas urgent, cela ne presse pas ◆ **with a note of ~ in his voice** avec insistance

◆ **a matter of urgency** une affaire urgente ◆ **as a matter of ~** d'urgence, dans les meilleurs délais ◆ **to deal with sth as a matter of ~** s'occuper d'une question en priorité

urgent /ˈɜːdʒənt/ **ADJ** *[matter, help, message, need]* urgent, pressant ; *[medical attention]* d'urgence ; *[appeal, voice, desire]* pressant ; *[priority]* absolu ◆ **the matter needs ~ attention** c'est urgent ◆ **he demands an ~ answer** il exige qu'on lui réponde immédiatement ◆ **her tone was ~** son ton était insistant ◆ **I must talk to you, it's ~** il faut que je vous parle, c'est urgent ◆ **how ~ is it?** est-ce que c'est très urgent ? ◆ **is it ~?** c'est (vraiment) urgent ? ◆ **it's not ~** ce n'est pas urgent, ça ne presse pas ◆ **the letter was marked "urgent"** la lettre portait la mention "urgent" ◆ **it is ~ that he should go** il doit y aller de toute urgence ◆ **it is ~ for us to complete this task** il est urgent que nous accomplissions cette tâche

urgently /ˈɜːdʒəntlɪ/ **ADV** *[need, request, appeal, seek]* d'urgence ; *[say]* d'un ton insistant ◆ **courier ~ required** on recherche *or* nous recherchons de toute urgence un coursier ◆ **he wants to talk to you ~** il veut vous parler de toute urgence

uric /ˈjʊərɪk/ **ADJ** urique

urinal /ˈjʊərɪnl/ **N** *(= place)* urinoir *m* ; *(in street)* vespasienne *f* ; *(= receptacle)* urinal *m*

urinalysis /ˌjʊərɪˈnælɪsɪs/ **N** (pl **urinalyses** /ˌjʊərɪˈnælɪsiːz/) ⇒ **uranalysis**

urinary /ˈjʊərɪnərɪ/ **ADJ** *[system, complaint, infection, flow]* urinaire ; *[retention]* d'urine **COMP** **urinary tract N** appareil *m* urinaire, voies *fpl* urinaires

urinate /ˈjʊərɪneɪt/ **VI** uriner

urine /ˈjʊərɪn/ **N** urine *f*

URL /ˌjuːɑːrˈel/ **N** *(Comput)* (abbrev of **uniform resource locator**) URL *m*

urn /ɜːn/ **N** [1] *(= vase etc)* urne *f* ; (also **funeral urn**) urne *f* (funéraire) [2] (also **tea urn, coffee urn**) *grosse bouilloire électrique*

urogenital /ˌjʊərəʊˈdʒenɪtl/ **ADJ** urogénital

urological /ˌjʊərəʊˈlɒdʒɪkl/ **ADJ** urologique

urologist /jʊəˈrɒlədʒɪst/ **N** urologue *mf*

urology /jʊəˈrɒlədʒɪ/ **N** urologie *f*

Ursa /ˈɜːsə/ **N** *(Astron)* ◆ **~ Major/Minor** la Grande/Petite Ourse

urticaria /ˌɜːtɪˈkeərɪə/ **N** urticaire *f*

Uruguay /ˈjʊərəgwaɪ/ **N** Uruguay *m*

Uruguayan /ˌjʊərəˈgwaɪən/ **ADJ** uruguayen, de l'Uruguay **N** Uruguayen(ne) *m(f)*

US /juːˈes/ **N** (abbrev of **United States**) ◆ **the ~** les USA *mpl*, les É.-U.(A.) *mpl* ◆ **in the ~** aux USA, aux États-Unis ◆ **the ~ Army/government** l'armée/le gouvernement des États-Unis

us /ʌs/ **PERS PRON** [1] nous ◆ **he hit ~** il nous a frappés ◆ **give it to ~** donnez-le-nous ◆ **in front of ~** devant nous ◆ **let ~** *or* **let's go!** allons-y ! ◆ **younger than ~** plus jeune que nous ◆ **both of ~** nous deux, tous *(or* toutes) les deux ◆ **several of ~** plusieurs d'entre nous ◆ **he is one of ~** il est des nôtres ◆ **as for ~ English, we ...** nous autres Anglais, nous ... ◆ **we took the books with ~** nous avons emporté les livres [2] *(Brit* ⁑ *= me)* me, moi ◆ **give ~ a bit!** donne-m'en un morceau !, donne-moi-z-en ! * ◆ **give ~ a look!** fais voir !

USA /ˌjuːesˈeɪ/ **N** [1] (abbrev of **United States of America**) **the ~** les USA *mpl* [2] (abbrev of **United States Army**) *armée de terre des États-Unis*

usable /ˈjuːzəbl/ **ADJ** *[equipment, facility, space]* utilisable *(for sth* pour qch) ; *[information, evidence, skill]* utilisable, exploitable *(for sth* pour qch) ◆ **in ~ condition** *[equipment]* en état de marche ◆ **land ~ for agriculture** terres *fpl* cultivables ◆ **no longer ~** hors d'usage

USAF /ˌjuːeseɪˈef/ **N** (abbrev of **United States Air Force**) *armée de l'air des États-Unis*

usage /ˈjuːzɪdʒ/ **N** *(NonC)* [1] *(= custom)* usage *m*, coutume *f* [2] *(Ling)* usage *m* [3] *(= treatment) [of tool, machine, chair etc]* utilisation *f* ; *[of person]* traitement *m* ◆ **it's had some rough ~** ça a été malmené, on s'en est mal servi

usance /ˈjuːzəns/ **N** *(Fin)* usance *f*

USB /ˌjuːesˈbiː/ **N** *(Comput)* (abbrev of **Universal Serial Bus**) (système *m*) USB *m* ◆ **~ port/connection** port *m*/connexion *f* USB

USCG /ˌjuːessiːˈdʒiː/ **N** (abbrev of **United States Coast Guard**) garde *f* côtière américaine

USDA /ˌjuːesdiːˈeɪ/ **N** (abbrev of **United States Department of Agriculture**) → **agriculture**

USDAW /ˌjuːesdiːeɪˈdʌbljuː/ **N** *(Brit)* (abbrev of **Union of Shop Distributive and Allied Workers**) *syndicat*

USDI /ˌjuːesdiːˈaɪ/ **N** (abbrev of **United States Department of the Interior**) → **interior**

use

1 NOUN	4 INTRANSITIVE VERB
2 TRANSITIVE VERB	5 COMPOUND
3 AUXILIARY VERB	6 PHRASAL VERB

1 - NOUN /juːs/

[1] NonC = act of using emploi *m*, utilisation *f* ◆ **the ~ of steel in industry** l'emploi de l'acier

dans l'industrie ◆ **to learn the ~ of sth** apprendre à se servir de qch ◆ **care is necessary in the ~ of chemicals** il faut prendre des précautions quand on utilise des produits chimiques ◆ **to improve with ~** s'améliorer à l'usage

♦ **for + use** ◆ **directions for ~** mode *m* d'emploi ◆ **for your (own) personal ~** à votre usage personnel ◆ **"for the use of teachers only"** *(book, equipment)* "à l'usage des professeurs seulement" ; *(car park, room)* "réservé aux professeurs" ◆ **to keep sth for one's own ~** réserver qch à son usage personnel ◆ **for ~ in case of emergency** à utiliser en cas d'urgence ◆ **fit for ~** en état de servir ◆ **ready for ~** prêt à servir *or* à l'emploi ◆ **for general/household ~** à usage général/domestique ◆ **for ~ in schools/the home** destiné à être utilisé dans les écoles/à la maison ◆ **for external ~ only** *(Med)* à usage externe

♦ **in + use** ◆ **in ~** *[machine]* en service, utilisé ; *[word]* en usage, usité ◆ **in general ~** d'usage *or* d'emploi courant ◆ **it is in daily ~** on s'en sert tous les jours ◆ **no longer in ~, now out of ~** *[machine]* qui n'est plus utilisé ; *[word]* qui ne s'emploie plus, inusité

♦ **into use** ◆ **to put sth into ~** commencer à se servir de qch ◆ **these machines came into ~ in 1975** on a commencé à utiliser ces machines en 1975

♦ **out of use** ◆ **to go** *or* **fall out of ~** tomber en désuétude ◆ **it's gone out of ~** on ne l'emploie plus ◆ **"out of use"** *(on machine, lift etc)* "en panne"

♦ **to make use of** se servir de, utiliser ◆ **to make good ~ of sth** *[+ machine, time, money]* faire bon usage de qch, tirer parti de qch ; *[+ opportunity, facilities]* mettre qch à profit, tirer parti de qch

♦ **to put to use** *[+ money, equipment]* utiliser ; *[+ knowledge, experience]* mettre à profit ; *[+ idea, theory]* mettre en application ◆ **I absorb ideas and put them to ~** j'absorbe les idées et je les mets en application ◆ **to put sth to good ~** *[+ machine, time, money]* faire bon usage de qch, tirer parti de qch ; *[+ opportunity, facilities]* mettre qch à profit, tirer parti de qch

2 = way of using emploi *m*, utilisation *f* ◆ **a new ~ for ...** un nouvel usage de ... ◆ **it has many ~s** cela a beaucoup d'emplois ◆ **I'll find a ~ for it** je trouverai un moyen de m'en servir, j'en trouverai l'emploi ◆ **I've no further ~ for it** je n'en ai plus besoin ◆ **I've no ~ for that sort of behaviour!*** je n'ai que faire de ce genre de conduite ! ◆ **I've no ~ for him at all!*** il m'embête !*

3 = usefulness utilité *f* ◆ **this tool has its ~s** cet outil a son utilité ◆ **he has his ~s** il est utile par certains côtés ◆ **what's the ~ of all this?** à quoi sert tout ceci ? ◆ **oh, what's the ~?*** à quoi bon ? ◆ **what's the ~ of telling him not to, he never takes any notice** à quoi bon lui dire d'arrêter, il n'écoute jamais ◆ **I've told him fifty times already, what's the ~?*** je le lui ai dit trente-six fois déjà, pour ce que ça a servi !

♦ **to be of + use** ◆ **to be of ~** servir, être utile *(for sth, to sth* à qch ; *to sb* à qn) ◆ **is this (of) any ~ to you?** est-ce que cela peut vous être utile *or* vous servir ? ◆ **can I be (of) any ~?** puis-je être *or* me rendre utile ? ◆ **a lot of ~ that will be to you!*** ça te fera une belle jambe !*

♦ **to be (of) no use** ne servir à rien ◆ **this is no ~ any more** ce n'est plus bon à rien ◆ **he's no ~** il est incapable, il est nul ◆ **he's no ~ as a goalkeeper** il est nul comme gardien de but ◆ **you're no ~ to me if you can't spell** vous ne m'êtes d'aucune utilité si vous faites des fautes d'orthographe ◆ **there's** *or* **it's no ~*** **you protesting** inutile de protester ◆ **it's no ~*** **trying to reason with him** cela ne sert à rien d'essayer de le raisonner, on perd son temps à essayer de le raisonner ◆ **it's no ~*, he won't listen** ça ne sert à rien *or* c'est inutile, il ne veut rien entendre

4 NonC = ability to use, access usage *m* ◆ **to have the ~ of a garage** avoir l'usage d'un garage, avoir un garage à sa disposition ◆ **with ~ of kitchen** avec usage de la cuisine ◆ **he gave me the ~ of his car** il a mis sa voiture à ma disposition ◆ **to have lost the ~ of one's arm** avoir perdu l'usage d'un bras ◆ **to have the full ~ of one's faculties** jouir de toutes ses facultés

5 Ling = sense emploi *m*, acception *f*

6 frm = custom coutume *f*, habitude *f* ; *(Rel, Sociol)* usage *m* ◆ **this has long been his ~** telle est son habitude depuis longtemps

2 - TRANSITIVE VERB /juːz/

1 = make use of *[+ object, tool]* se servir de, utiliser ; *[+ force, discretion]* user de ; *[+ opportunity]* profiter de ; *[+ method, means]* employer ; *[+ drugs]* prendre ; *[+ sb's name]* faire usage de ◆ **he ~d a knife to open it** il s'est servi d'un couteau pour l'ouvrir ◆ **it is ~d for opening bottles** on s'en sert pour ouvrir les bouteilles ◆ **are you using this?** vous servez-vous de ceci ?, avez-vous besoin de ceci ? ◆ **have you ~d a gun before?** vous êtes-vous déjà servi d'un fusil ? ◆ **the money is to be ~d to build a new hospital** l'argent servira à construire un nouvel hôpital *or* à la construction d'un nouvel hôpital ◆ **he ~d his shoe as a hammer** il s'est servi de sa chaussure comme marteau ◆ **I ~ that as a table** ça me sert de table ◆ **ointment to be ~d sparingly** crème *f* à appliquer en couche fine ◆ **I don't ~ my French much** je ne me sers pas beaucoup de mon français ◆ **I don't want to ~ the car** je ne veux pas prendre la voiture ◆ **he said I could ~ his car** il a dit que je pouvais me servir de *or* prendre sa voiture ◆ **no longer ~d** *[tools, machine, room]* qui ne sert plus ; *[word]* qui ne s'emploie plus, tombé en désuétude ◆ **he wants to ~ the bathroom** il veut aller aux toilettes ◆ **someone is using the bathroom** il y a quelqu'un dans la salle de bains ◆ **~ your head** *or* **brains!*** réfléchis un peu !, tu as une tête, c'est pour t'en servir ! ◆ **~ your eyes!** ouvre l'œil ! ◆ **I feel I've just been ~d** j'ai l'impression qu'on s'est servi de moi ◆ **I could ~ a drink!*** je prendrais bien un verre ! ◆ **the house could ~ a lick of paint!*** une couche de peinture ne ferait pas de mal à cette maison ! ; see also **used**

2 = use up utiliser (tout) ◆ **this car ~s too much petrol** cette voiture consomme trop d'essence ◆ **have you ~d all the paint?** avez-vous utilisé toute la peinture ? ◆ **you can ~ (up) the leftovers in a soup** vous pouvez utiliser les restes pour faire une soupe

3 † = treat *[+ person]* traiter ◆ **to ~ sb well** bien traiter qn ◆ **he was badly ~d** on a mal agi envers lui, on a abusé de sa bonne volonté

3 - AUXILIARY VERB /juːs/

♦ **used to** *(expressing past habit)* ◆ **I ~d to see her every week** je la voyais toutes les semaines ◆ **I ~d to swim every day** j'allais nager *or* j'avais l'habitude d'aller nager tous les jours ◆ **I ~d not** *or* **I ~(d)n't*** *or* **I didn't ~*** **to smoke** (autrefois) je ne fumais pas ◆ **what ~d he to do** *(frm) or* **what did he ~ to do*** **on Sundays?** qu'est-ce qu'il faisait (d'habitude) le dimanche ? ◆ **things aren't what they ~d to be** les choses ne sont plus ce qu'elles étaient

4 - INTRANSITIVE VERB /juːz/

*(Drugs *)* se droguer

5 - COMPOUND /juːz/

use-by date N date *f* limite de consommation

6 - PHRASAL VERB

► **use up** VT SEP *[+ food]* consommer entièrement, finir ; *[+ objects, ammunition, one's strength, resources, surplus]* épuiser ; *[+ money]* dépenser ◆ **to ~ up the scraps** utiliser les restes ◆ **it is all ~d up** il n'en reste plus ; see also **use vt 2**

used /juːzd/ ADJ 1 *(= not fresh) [handkerchief, cup]* qui a servi, sale ; *[tissue, sanitary towel, needle, condom]* usagé ; *[stamp]* oblitéré ; *[engine oil]* usé

2 *(= second-hand) [car, equipment]* d'occasion ; *[clothing]* usagé ◆ **would you buy a ~ car from this man?** *(fig hum)* feriez-vous confiance à cet homme ?

3 *(after adv = employed)* ◆ **commonly/frequently ~** couramment/fréquemment utilisé

4 /juːst/

♦ **used to** *(= accustomed)* ◆ **to be ~ to sth** être habitué à qch, avoir l'habitude de qch ◆ **I'm ~ to her now** je me suis habitué à elle maintenant ◆ **to be ~ to doing sth** être habitué à faire qch, avoir l'habitude de faire qch ◆ **he was ~ to being given orders** il avait l'habitude qu'on lui donne des ordres, il était habitué à ce qu'on lui donne des ordres ◆ **to get ~ to sb/sth** s'habituer à qn/qch ◆ **you'll soon get ~ to it** vous vous y ferez vite, vous vous y habituerez vite ◆ **to get ~ to doing sth** prendre l'habitude de faire qch ◆ **to get ~ to sb** *or* **sb's doing sth** s'habituer à ce que qn fasse qch ◆ **I'm ~ to her interrupting me** j'ai l'habitude qu'elle m'interrompe *subj*, je suis habitué à ce qu'elle m'interrompe *subj*

COMP **used-car salesman** N (pl **used-car salesmen**) vendeur *m* de voitures d'occasion

usedn't /ˈjuːsnt/ ⇒ **used not** ; → **use auxiliary verb**

useful /ˈjuːsfʊl/ ADJ 1 *(= handy, helpful)* utile *(for, to sb* à qn) ◆ **~ addresses** adresses *fpl* utiles ◆ **that knife will come in ~*** ce couteau pourra être utile ◆ **to be ~ for (doing) sth** être utile pour faire qch ◆ **to perform a ~ function** jouer un rôle utile, être utile ◆ **these drugs are ~ in treating cancer** ces médicaments sont utiles dans le traitement du cancer ◆ **he's a ~ man to know** c'est un homme qu'il est utile de compter parmi ses relations ◆ **that's ~ to know** *or* **a ~ thing to know** c'est bon à savoir ◆ **this machine has reached the end of its ~ life** cette machine a fait son temps ◆ **this machine has a ~ life of ten years** cette machine peut servir dix ans ◆ **this work is not serving any ~ purpose** ce travail ne sert pas à grand-chose ◆ **that's ~!** *(iro)* nous voilà bien avancés ! ◆ **it is ~ to know a foreign language** il est utile de connaître une langue étrangère ◆ **it would be ~ for me to have that information** il me serait utile d'avoir ces renseignements

2 *(Brit * = good)* ◆ **to be ~ with one's hands** être habile de ses mains ◆ **he's quite ~ with his fists** il sait se servir de ses poings

usefully /ˈjuːsfəli/ ADV utilement ◆ **is there anything the government can ~ do?** y a-t-il quelque chose que le gouvernement puisse faire ? ◆ **you might ~ do a bit of preparatory reading** il vous serait peut-être utile de faire quelques lectures préparatoires ◆ **his time could be more ~ spent** *or* **employed** il pourrait employer son temps de façon plus utile *or* plus utilement

usefulness /ˈjuːsfʊlnɪs/ N (NonC) utilité *f* ; → **outlive**

useless /ˈjuːslɪs/ ADJ 1 *(= not useful) [person, action, information, tool]* inutile *(to sb* pour qn ; *against sth* pour qch) ; *[arm, leg, hand]* inerte ; *[life]* vide ◆ **our efforts proved ~** nos efforts ont été vains ◆ **shouting is ~** il est inutile de crier, ce n'est pas la peine de crier ◆ **a car is ~ without wheels** une voiture sans roues ne sert à rien ♦ **worse than ~** * plus qu'inutile ♦ **it is ~ to complain** il ne sert à rien de se plaindre ♦ **it is ~ for you to complain** il est inutile que vous vous plaigniez [2] (* = *incompetent*) *[teacher, player, school]* nul * (nulle * *f*) *(at sth* en qch ; *at doing sth* quand il s'agit de faire qch)

uselessly /ˈjuːslɪslɪ/ ADV inutilement ♦ **his arm hung ~ by his side** son bras pendait, inutile, le long de son corps ♦ **he stood around ~** il est resté là à ne rien faire

uselessness /ˈjuːslɪsnɪs/ N *(NonC)* [1] *[of tool, advice etc]* inutilité *f* ; *[of remedy]* inefficacité *f* [2] * *[of person]* incompétence *f*

Usenet /ˈjuːznet/ N *(Comput)* Usenet *m*

usen't /ˈjuːsnt/ ⇒ **used not** ; → **use auxiliary verb**

user /ˈjuːzəʳ/ N [1] *[of public service, telephone, road, train, dictionary]* usager *m* ; *[of machine, tool]* utilisateur *m*, -trice *f* ; *[of electricity, gas]* usager *m*, utilisateur *m*, -trice *f* ; *(Comput)* utilisateur *m*, -trice *f* ♦ **car ~** automobiliste *mf* ♦ **computer ~s** ceux qui utilisent un ordinateur, utilisateurs *mpl* d'ordinateurs

[2] *(Drugs)* usager *m*, consommateur *m* ♦ **heroin ~** consommateur *m*, -trice *f* d'héroïne

[3] *(pej = exploitative person)* profiteur *m*, -euse *f*

COMP **user-definable, user-defined** ADJ *(Comput)* définissable par l'utilisateur

user-friendliness N *(Comput)* convivialité *f* ; *[of machine, dictionary etc]* facilité *f* d'utilisation

user-friendly ADJ *(Comput)* convivial ; *(gen)* facile à utiliser ♦ **we want to make the store more ~-friendly for shoppers** nous voulons rendre le magasin plus accueillant pour les clients

user group N groupe *m* d'usagers

user name N *(Comput)* nom *m* de l'utilisateur, nom *m* d'utilisateur

user's guide N guide *m* (de l'utilisateur)

USES /ˌjuːesiːˈes/ N (abbrev of **United States Employment Service**) → **employment**

USGS /ˌjuːesdʒiːˈes/ N (abbrev of **United States Geological Survey**) → **geological**

usher /ˈʌʃəʳ/ N *(in law courts etc)* huissier *m* ; *(= doorkeeper)* portier *m* ; *(at public meeting)* membre *m* du service d'ordre ; *(in theatre, church)* placeur *m* VT ♦ **to ~ sb out/along** *etc* faire sortir/avancer *etc* qn ♦ **to ~ sb into a room** introduire *or* faire entrer qn dans une salle ♦ **to ~ sb to the door** reconduire qn à la porte

► **usher in** VT SEP *[+ person]* introduire, faire entrer ; *(fig) [+ period, season]* inaugurer, commencer ♦ **it ~s in a new era** cela annonce *or* inaugure une nouvelle époque, cela marque le début d'une ère nouvelle ♦ **it ~ed in a new reign** cela inaugura un nouveau règne, ce fut l'aurore d'un nouveau règne ♦ **the spring was ~ed in by storms** le début du printemps fut marqué par des orages

usherette /ˌʌʃəˈret/ N *(Cine, Theat)* ouvreuse *f*

USIA /ˌjuːesaɪˈeɪ/ N (abbrev of **United States Information Agency**) *service officiel fournissant des informations sur les États-Unis à l'étranger*

USM /ˌjuːesˈem/ N (abbrev of **United States Mint**) *hôtel de la Monnaie des États-Unis*

USMC /ˌjuːesemˈsiː/ N (abbrev of **United States Marine Corps**) corps *m* des marines *(des États-Unis)*

USN /ˌjuːesˈen/ N (abbrev of **United States Navy**) *marine de guerre des États-Unis*

USO /ˌjuːesˈəʊ/ N *(US)* (abbrev of **United Service Organization**) *organisation venant en aide aux militaires américains, en particulier lors de leurs déplacements à l'étranger*

USP /ˌjuːesˈpiː/ N (abbrev of **unique selling point**) → **unique**

USPHS /ˌjuːespiːeɪtʃˈes/ N (abbrev of **United States Public Health Service**) → **public**

USS /ˌjuːesˈes/ N abbrev of **United States Ship** (*or* **Steamer**)

USSR /ˌjuːesesˈɑːʳ/ N (abbrev of **Union of Soviet Socialist Republics**) URSS *f* ♦ **in the ~** en URSS

usu. abbrev of **usual(ly)**

usual /ˈjuːʒʊəl/ ADJ *(= customary) [method, excuse, address, rules]* habituel ; *[price]* habituel, courant ; *[word]* usuel, courant ♦ **as is ~ with such machines, it broke down** elle est tombée en panne, ce qui arrive souvent avec ce genre de machine ♦ **as is ~ on these occasions** comme le veut l'usage en ces occasions ♦ **it wasn't his ~ car** ce n'était pas la voiture qu'il prenait d'habitude ♦ **he was sitting in his ~ chair** il était assis dans sa chaise habituelle ♦ **in the ~ place** à l'endroit habituel ♦ **his ~ practice was to rise at six** son habitude était de *or* il avait l'habitude de se lever à six heures ♦ **her ~ routine** son train-train *m* quotidien ♦ **what did you do on holiday? – oh, the ~ stuff*** qu'est-ce que tu as fait pendant les vacances ? – oh, la même chose que d'habitude ♦ **with his ~ tact** avec son tact habituel, avec le tact qui le caractérise ♦ **more than ~** plus que d'habitude *or* d'ordinaire ♦ **to get up earlier than ~** se lever plus tôt que d'habitude ♦ **it's the ~ thing** c'est comme d'habitude ♦ **he said the ~ things about ...** il a dit ce qu'on dit d'habitude à propos de ... ♦ **come at the ~ time** venez à l'heure habituelle ♦ **7 o'clock is my ~ time to get up** d'habitude, je me lève à 7 heures ♦ **it's ~ to ask first** il est d'usage *or* il est poli de demander d'abord ♦ **it is ~ for soldiers to wear a uniform** les soldats portent traditionnellement un uniforme ♦ **it's quite ~ for this to happen** ça arrive souvent, ça n'a rien d'inhabituel ♦ **it wasn't ~ for him to arrive early** ce n'était pas dans ses habitudes d'arriver en avance ♦ **it was ~ for her to drink a lot** elle avait l'habitude de boire beaucoup, c'était dans ses habitudes de boire beaucoup ♦ **the journey took four hours instead of the ~ two** le voyage a pris quatre heures au lieu des deux heures habituelles ♦ **it was not the ~ type of holiday** c'étaient des vacances pas comme les autres ♦ **to do sth in the ~ way** faire qch de la manière habituelle ♦ **she welcomed us in her ~ friendly way** elle nous a accueillis chaleureusement, comme à son habitude ; → **channel, crowd, self, sense, suspect**

♦ **as + usual** ♦ **as ~** (= *as always*) comme d'habitude ♦ **he arrived late as ~** il est arrivé en retard, comme d'habitude ♦ **he's late – as ~!** il est en retard – comme d'habitude ! ♦ **for her it's just life as ~** pour elle, la vie continue (comme avant) ♦ **to carry on as ~** continuer comme d'habitude ♦ **"business as usual"** "horaires d'ouverture habituels" ♦ **it is business as ~ (for them)** *(lit)* les affaires continuent (pour eux) ; *(fig)* la vie continue (pour eux) ♦ **as per ~** * comme d'habitude

N (* = *drink*) ♦ **you know my ~** vous savez ce que je prends d'habitude ♦ **the ~ please!** comme d'habitude, s'il vous plaît !

usually /ˈjuːʒʊəlɪ/ ADV d'habitude, généralement ♦ **more than ~ depressed/busy/hungry** plus déprimé/occupé/affamé que d'habitude ♦ **~, a simple explanation is enough** d'habitude *or* généralement, une simple explication suffit

usufruct /ˈjuːzjʊfrʌkt/ N *(Jur)* usufruit *m*

usufructuary /ˌjuːzjʊˈfrʌktjʊərɪ/ *(Jur)* N usufruitier *m*, -ière *f* ADJ usufruitier

usurer /ˈjuːʒərəʳ/ N usurier *m*, -ière *f*

usurious /juːˈzjʊərɪəs/ ADJ usuraire

usurp /juːˈzɜːp/ VT *[+ power, role]* usurper ♦ **Congress wants to ~ the power of the presidency** le Congrès veut usurper le pouvoir du président ♦ **Web sites are beginning to ~ travel agents** les sites web commencent à supplanter les agences de voyage ♦ **did she ~ his place in his mother's heart?** l'a-t-elle supplanté dans le cœur de sa mère ?, a-t-elle pris sa place dans le cœur de sa mère ?

usurpation /ˌjuːzɜːˈpeɪʃən/ N *(NonC)* usurpation *f*

usurper /juːˈzɜːpəʳ/ N usurpateur *m*, -trice *f*

usurping /juːˈzɜːpɪŋ/ ADJ usurpateur (-trice *f*)

usury /ˈjuːʒʊrɪ/ N *(NonC: Fin)* usure *f*

UT abbrev of **Utah**

Utah /ˈjuːtɔː/ N Utah *m* ♦ **in ~** dans l'Utah

ute /juːt/ N utilitaire *m*

utensil /juːˈtensl/ N ustensile *m* ; → **kitchen**

uteri /ˈjuːtəˌraɪ/ NPL of **uterus**

uterine /ˈjuːtəraɪn/ ADJ utérin

uterus /ˈjuːtərəs/ N (pl **uteri**) utérus *m*

utilitarian /ˌjuːtɪlɪˈteərɪən/ ADJ [1] (= *practical*) *[view, approach, object]* utilitaire [2] (= *functional*) *[furniture, building, style]* fonctionnel [3] *(Philos)* utilitaire N utilitariste *mf*

utilitarianism /ˌjuːtɪlɪˈteərɪənɪzəm/ N *(NonC)* utilitarisme *m*

utility /juːˈtɪlɪtɪ/ N [1] *(NonC)* utilité *f* [2] (also **public utility**) service *m* public ADJ *[clothes, furniture]* fonctionnel ; *[goods, vehicle]* utilitaire

COMP **utility player** N *(Sport)* joueur *m*, -euse *f* polyvalent(e)

utility room N *pièce où l'on range les appareils ménagers, les provisions etc*

utility software N *(Comput)* logiciel *m* utilitaire

utilizable /ˈjuːtɪˌlaɪzəbl/ ADJ utilisable

utilization /ˌjuːtɪlaɪˈzeɪʃən/ N *(NonC) [of resources]* utilisation *f*, exploitation *f* ; *[of facility, technique]* utilisation *f* ; *[of land, space, skill]* exploitation *f*

utilize /ˈjuːtɪlaɪz/ VT *[+ object, facilities, equipment]* utiliser, se servir de ; *[+ situation, resources, talent, person]* tirer parti de, exploiter ; *[+ space]* utiliser, tirer parti de

utmost /ˈʌtməʊst/ ADJ [1] (= *greatest*) *[restraint, difficulty, determination]* le plus grand *or* la plus grande, extrême ♦ **of (the) ~ importance (to sb/sth)** de la plus haute importance (pour qn/qch) ♦ **it is of (the) ~ importance that ...** il est de la plus haute importance que ... + *subj* ♦ **with the ~ possible care** avec le plus grand soin possible ♦ **an undertaking of the ~ danger** une entreprise des plus dangereuses ♦ **a matter of (the) ~ urgency** une affaire de la plus extrême urgence

[2] (= *furthest*) *[limits]* extrême

N ♦ **to do one's ~** faire tout son possible *or* le maximum ♦ **to do one's ~ to do sth** faire tout son possible *or* le maximum pour faire qch ♦ **he tried his ~ to help them** il a fait tout son possible *or* il a fait le maximum pour les aider ♦ **to the ~** au plus haut degré *or* point ♦ **at the ~** au maximum, tout au plus

Utopia /juːˈtəʊpɪə/ N utopie *f*

Utopian /juːˈtəʊpɪən/ ADJ utopique N utopiste *mf*

Utopianism /juːˈtəʊpɪənɪzəm/ N utopisme *m*

utricle /ˈjuːtrɪkl/ N utricule *m*

Uttar Pradesh /ˈʊtəˈprɑːdeʃ/ N Uttar Pradesh *m*

utter¹ /ˈʌtəʳ/ ADJ *[lack, failure, disaster]* complet (-ète *f*), total ; *[incompetence]* total ; *[contempt, disregard, silence, sincerity]* absolu, total ; *[fool, rogue, liar]* parfait *before n* ; *[disgust, despair, hopelessness, frustration, stupidity]* profond ; *[futility, misery]* extrême ; *[madness]* pur ♦ **to my ~ amazement, I succeeded** à ma plus grande stupéfaction, j'ai réussi ◆ **with ~ conviction** avec une conviction inébranlable ◆ **what ~ nonsense!** c'est complètement absurde ! ◆ **she's talking complete and ~ rubbish*** elle dit n'importe quoi ◆ **he's a complete and ~ fool/bastard*‡** *etc* c'est un imbécile/salaud‡ *etc* fini

utter² /ˈʌtəʳ/ **VT** *[+ word]* prononcer, proférer ; *[+ cry]* pousser ; *[+ threat, insult]* proférer ; *[+ libel]* publier ; *(Jur) [+ counterfeit money]* émettre, mettre en circulation ◆ **he didn't ~ a word** il n'a pas dit un seul mot, il n'a pas soufflé mot

utterance /ˈʌtərəns/ **N** 1 *(= remark etc)* paroles *fpl*, déclaration *f* 2 *(NonC) [of facts, theory]* énonciation *f* ; *[of feelings]* expression *f* ◆ **to give ~ to** exprimer 3 *(style of speaking)* élocution *f*, articulation *f* 4 *(Ling)* énoncé *m*

utterly /ˈʌtəlɪ/ **ADV** *[untrue, destroy, transform]* complètement, totalement ; *[impossible]* tout à fait ; *[convince]* entièrement ◆ **he failed ~** il a complètement *or* totalement échoué ◆ **he ~ failed to impress them** il ne leur a fait absolument aucun effet ◆ **to be ~ without talent/malice** être dénué de tout talent/toute méchanceté

uttermost /ˈʌtəməʊst/ **ADJ, N** ⇒ **utmost**

U-turn /ˈjuːtɜːn/ **N** → **U comp**

UV /juːˈviː/ **ADJ** (abbrev of **ultraviolet**) UV

UVA, UV-A /ˌjuːviːˈeɪ/ **ADJ** UVA *inv* ◆ **~ rays** (rayons *mpl*) UVA *mpl*

UVB, UV-B /ˌjuːviːˈbiː/ **ADJ** UVB *inv* ◆ **~ rays** (rayons *mpl*) UVB *mpl*

UVF /ˌjuːviːˈef/ **N** *(Brit)* (abbrev of **Ulster Volunteer Force**) → **Ulster**

uvula /ˈjuːvjʊlə/ **N** (pl **uvulas** *or* **uvulae**) luette *f*, uvule *f*

uvular /ˈjuːvjʊləʳ/ **ADJ** *(Anat, Phon)* uvulaire ◆ **~ r** r grasseyé

uxorious /ʌkˈsɔːrɪəs/ **ADJ** excessivement dévoué à sa femme

uxoriousness /ʌkˈsɔːrɪəsnɪs/ **N** *(NonC)* dévotion *f* excessive à sa femme

Uzbek /ˈʊzbek/ **ADJ** ouzbek *f inv* **N** 1 *(= person)* Ouzbek *mf* 2 *(= language)* ouzbek *m*

Uzbekistan /ˌʌzbekɪˈstɑːn/ **N** Ouzbékistan *m*

Vv

V, v /viː/ N [1] *(= letter)* V, v *m* ◆ **V for Victor, V for Victory** ≈ V comme Victor ◆ **to stick the Vs up to sb**‡ *(Brit)* ≈ faire un bras d'honneur à qn [2] (abbrev of **vide**) *(= see)* V, voir [3] (abbrev of **versus**) contre [4] *(esp Bible)* abbrev of **verse** [5] abbrev of **very** [6] abbrev of **velocity**
COMP **V and A*** N *(Brit)* (abbrev of **Victoria and Albert Museum**) *musée londonien des arts décoratifs*
V-chip N verrou *m* électronique
V-neck N décolleté *m* en V *or* en pointe
V-necked ADJ à encolure en V *or* en pointe
V-shaped ADJ en (forme de) V
V-sign N
[1] *(for victory)* ◆ **to give the V-sign** faire le V de la victoire [2] *(in Brit) geste obscène*, ≈ bras *m* d'honneur ◆ **to give sb the V-sign** ≈ faire un bras d'honneur à qn

VA /viːˈeɪ/ N [1] *(US)* (abbrev of **Veterans Administration**) → **veteran** [2] abbrev of **Virginia**

Va. abbrev of **Virginia**

vac¹* /væk/ N *(Brit Univ)* (abbrev of **vacation**) vacances *fpl* (universitaires)

vac²* /væk/ N *(esp Brit)* (abbrev of **vacuum cleaner**) → **vacuum**

vacancy /ˈveɪkənsɪ/ N [1] *(in hotel)* chambre *f* libre ◆ **"no vacancies"** "complet" ◆ **have you any vacancies for August?** est-ce qu'il vous reste des chambres (libres) pour le mois d'août ?
[2] *(= job)* poste *m* vacant *or* libre, vacance *f* ◆ **"no vacancies"** "pas d'embauche" ◆ **a short-term ~** un poste temporaire ◆ **"vacancy for a translator"** "recherchons traducteur" ◆ **we have a ~ for an editor** nous avons un poste de rédacteur à pourvoir, nous cherchons un rédacteur ◆ **we have a ~ for an enthusiastic sales manager** nous cherchons un directeur des ventes motivé ◆ **to fill a ~** *[employer]* pourvoir un poste vacant ; *[employee]* être nommé à un poste vacant ◆ **we are looking for someone to fill a ~ in our sales department** nous cherchons à pourvoir un poste vacant dans notre service de ventes
[3] *(NonC = emptiness)* vide *m*
[4] *(NonC = blankness)* esprit *m* vide, stupidité *f*

vacant /ˈveɪkənt/ ADJ [1] *(= unoccupied) [land, building]* inoccupé ; *[hotel room, table, parking space]* libre ; *[seat, hospital bed]* libre, disponible ; *[post, job]* vacant, à pourvoir ◆ **to fall ~** *[post, room, flat]* se libérer ◆ **a ~ space** un espace libre ◆ **a ~ post** un poste vacant *or* à pourvoir ◆ **a ~ place** *(Univ: on course)* une place libre *or* disponible ◆ **"situations vacant"** *(Press)* "offres d'emploi" ◆ **with ~ possession** *(Jur)* avec libre possession, avec jouissance immédiate [2] *(= stupid)* ahuri ; *[expression, look, stare]* *(= blank)* absent, sans expression ; *[mind]* vide
COMP **vacant lot** N *(esp US) (gen)* terrain *m* inoccupé ; *(for sale)* terrain *m* à vendre

vacantly /ˈveɪkəntlɪ/ ADV [1] *(= blankly) [look, stare, gaze]* d'un air absent ◆ **to gaze ~ into space** fixer le vide, avoir le regard perdu dans le vide [2] *(= stupidly) [look, stare, gaze, smile, say]* d'un air ahuri

vacate /vəˈkeɪt/ VT *(frm) [+ room, seat, job]* quitter ◆ **to ~ a house** quitter une maison ◆ **to ~ one's post** démissionner ◆ **this post will soon be ~d** ce poste sera bientôt vacant *or* à pourvoir ◆ **to ~ the premises** vider les lieux

vacation /vəˈkeɪʃən/ N [1] *(US)* vacances *fpl* ◆ **on ~** en vacances ◆ **on his ~** pendant ses vacances ◆ **to take a ~** prendre des vacances ◆ **where are you going for your ~?** où allez-vous passer vos vacances ? [2] *(Brit Univ)* vacances *fpl* ; *(Jur)* vacations *fpl or* vacances *fpl* judiciaires ; → **long¹** VI *(US)* passer des *(or* ses *etc)* vacances
COMP **vacation course** N cours *mpl* de vacances
vacation trip N voyage *m* de vacances ◆ **to go on a ~ trip** partir en vacances

vacationer /vəˈkeɪʃənəʳ/, **vacationist** /vəˈkeɪʃənɪst/ *(US)* N vacancier *m*, -ière *f*

vaccinate /ˈvæksɪneɪt/ VT vacciner *(against* contre) ◆ **to get ~d** se faire vacciner ◆ **have you been ~d against ...?** est-ce que vous êtes vacciné contre ... ?

vaccination /ˌvæksɪˈneɪʃən/ N vaccination *f* *(against* contre) ◆ **smallpox/polio ~** vaccination *f* contre la variole/la polio ◆ **to have a ~ against ...** se faire vacciner contre ...

vaccine /ˈvæksiːn/ N vaccin *m* ; *(Comput)* logiciel *m* antivirus ◆ **polio ~** vaccin *m* contre la polio ◆ **~-damaged** victime de réactions provoquées par un vaccin

vacillate /ˈvæsɪleɪt/ VI hésiter *(between* entre) ◆ **she ~d so long over accepting that ...** elle s'est demandé si longtemps si elle allait accepter ou non que ...

vacillating /ˈvæsɪleɪtɪŋ/ ADJ indécis, hésitant N *(NonC)* hésitations *fpl*, indécision *f*

vacillation /ˌvæsɪˈleɪʃən/ N indécision *f*

vacuity /væˈkjuːɪtɪ/ N vacuité *f* ◆ **vacuities** *(= silly remarks)* niaiseries *fpl*, remarques *fpl* stupides

vacuous /ˈvækjʊəs/ ADJ *(frm) [person, film, book]* inepte ; *[comment, remark]* inepte, creux ; *[look, stare]* vide ; *[expression]* vide, niais ; *[smile, face]* niais ; *[life]* vide de sens

vacuum /ˈvækjʊm/ N [1] *(pl* **vacuums**) *(= empty space)* vide *m* ◆ **their departure left a ~** leur départ a laissé un (grand) vide ◆ **a cultural ~** un vide culturel ; → **nature**
◆ **in a vacuum** *(fig)* ◆ **to live/work in a ~** vivre/travailler en vase clos ◆ **we don't take decisions in a ~** nous ne prenons pas de décisions dans le vide ◆ **moral values cannot be taught in a ~** les valeurs morales ne peuvent pas être enseignées hors de tout contexte ◆ **it didn't happen in a ~** ça n'est pas arrivé tout seul
[2] (also **cleaner**) aspirateur *m* ◆ **to give sth a ~** ⇒ **to vacuum sth**; → VT
VT (also **clean**) *[+ carpet]* passer à l'aspirateur ; *[+ room]* passer l'aspirateur dans
COMP *[brake, pump, tube]* à vide
vacuum aspiration N *(Med = abortion)* IVG *f* par aspiration
vacuum bottle N *(US)* ⇒ **vacuum flask**
vacuum cleaner N aspirateur *m*
vacuum extraction N *(Med = birth)* accouchement *m* par ventouse
vacuum flask N *(Brit)* bouteille *f* thermos ®, thermos ® *m or f inv*
vacuum-packed ADJ emballé sous vide

vade mecum /ˈvɑːdɪˈmeɪkʊm/ N vade-mecum *m inv*

vagabond /ˈvægəbɒnd/ N vagabond(e) *m(f)* ; *(= tramp)* chemineau *m*, clochard(e) *m(f)* ADJ *[life]* errant, de vagabondage ; *[thoughts]* vagabond ; *[habits]* irrégulier

vagary /ˈveɪgərɪ/ N caprice *m* ◆ **the vagaries of business/of politics** les vicissitudes *fpl* du monde des affaires/de la vie politique

vagi /ˈveɪdʒaɪ/ NPL of **vagus**

vagina /vəˈdʒaɪnə/ N (pl **vaginas** *or* **vaginae** /vəˈdʒaɪniː/) vagin *m*

vaginal /vəˈdʒaɪnəl/ ADJ vaginal
COMP **vaginal discharge** N pertes *fpl* blanches
vaginal dryness N sécheresse *f* vaginale
vaginal intercourse N *(NonC)* (rapports *mpl* sexuels avec) pénétration *f* vaginale
vaginal smear N frottis *m* (vaginal)

vaginismus /ˌvædʒɪˈnɪzməs/ N *(Med)* vaginisme *m*

vagrancy /ˈveɪgrənsɪ/ N *(also Jur)* vagabondage *m*

vagrant /ˈveɪgrənt/ N vagabond(e) *m(f)* ; *(= tramp)* clochard(e) *m(f)* ; *(Jur)* vagabond(e) *m(f)* ADJ *[person]* vagabond

vague /veɪg/ ADJ [1] *(= unclear) [person, idea, gesture, plan, feeling, instructions, reply, promise]* vague ; *[description, memory, impression]* vague, flou ; *[shape, outline]* flou, imprécis ◆ **I had a ~ idea** *or* **feeling she would come** j'avais comme le sentiment *or* comme une idée* qu'elle viendrait ◆ **he was ~ about the time he would be**

arriving at (= *didn't say exactly*) il n'a pas (bien) précisé l'heure de son arrivée ; (= *didn't know exactly*) il n'était pas sûr de l'heure à laquelle il arriverait ◆ **I'm still very ~ about all this** ça n'est pas encore très clair dans mon esprit ◆ **I'm still very ~ about how it happened** je ne sais pas encore très bien comment ça s'est passé ◆ **I'm very ~ about French history** je ne m'y connais pas très bien en histoire de France ② (= *absent-minded*) *[person]* distrait ◆ **he's always rather ~** il est toujours distrait *or* dans la lune ◆ **she's getting rather ~ these days** elle ne s'y retrouve plus très bien *or* elle perd un peu la tête maintenant ◆ **to look ~** avoir l'air vague *or* distrait ◆ **to have a ~ look in one's eyes** avoir l'air vague

vaguely /ˈveɪɡlɪ/ **ADV** ① (= *unclearly*) *[say, describe, remember, resemble, understand]* vaguement ◆ **~ familiar/disappointed** vaguement familier/déçu ◆ **to be ~ aware of sth** être vaguement conscient de qch ◆ **a ~ defined set of objectives** un ensemble d'objectifs pas bien définis ◆ **to be ~ reminiscent of sth** rappeler vaguement qch ◆ **a ~ worded agreement** un accord libellé dans des termes vagues ② (= *absently*) *[look, nod]* d'un air distrait ; *[smile]* d'un air vague

vagueness /ˈveɪɡnɪs/ **N** ① *[of question, account, memory, wording, language]* manque *m* de précision ; *[of statement, proposal]* imprécision *f*, flou *m* ; *[of feeling, sensation]* caractère *m* imprécis, vague *m* ; *[of photograph]* manque *m* de netteté ② (= *absent-mindedness*) distraction *f* ◆ **his ~ is very annoying** c'est agaçant qu'il soit si distrait *or* tête en l'air*

vagus /ˈveɪɡəs/ **N** (pl **vagi**) (also **vagus nerve**) nerf *m* vague *or* pneumogastrique

vain /veɪn/ **ADJ** ① (= *fruitless, empty*) *[attempt, effort, plea, hope, promise]* vain *before n* ; *[threat]* en l'air

◆ **in vain** (= *unsuccessfully*) *[try, wait, search for]* en vain, vainement ; (= *pointlessly*) *[die, suffer]* pour rien ◆ **it was all in ~** cela n'a servi à rien, c'était inutile *or* en vain ◆ **all his** (*or* **my** *etc*) **efforts were in ~** c'était peine perdue ◆ **I looked for him in ~: he had already left** j'ai eu beau le chercher, il était déjà parti ◆ **to take God's** *or* **the Lord's name in ~** blasphémer ◆ **is someone taking my name in ~?** (*hum*) on parle de moi ?

② (*pej* = *conceited*) vaniteux (= *narcissistic*) narcissique ◆ **to be ~ about one's appearance** tirer vanité de son apparence, être narcissique

vainglorious /veɪnˈɡlɔːrɪəs/ **ADJ** (*liter*) orgueilleux, vaniteux

vainglory /veɪnˈɡlɔːrɪ/ **N** (*NonC: liter*) orgueil *m*, vanité *f*

vainly /ˈveɪnlɪ/ **ADV** ① (= *to no effect*) *[try, seek, believe, hope]* en vain, vainement ② (= *conceitedly*) vaniteusement, avec vanité

valance /ˈvæləns/ **N** (*above curtains*) cantonnière *f* ; (*round bed frame*) tour *m or* frange *f* de lit ; (*round bed canopy*) lambrequin *m*

vale /veɪl/ **N** (*liter*) val *m* (*liter*), vallée *f* ◆ **this ~ of tears** cette vallée de larmes

valediction /ˌvælɪˈdɪkʃən/ **N** ① (= *farewell*) adieu(x) *m(pl)* ② (*US Scol*) discours *m* d'adieu

valedictorian /ˌvælɪdɪkˈtɔːrɪən/ **N** (*US Scol*) major *m* de la promotion (*qui prononce le discours d'adieu*)

valedictory /ˌvælɪˈdɪktərɪ/ **ADJ** (*frm*) d'adieu **N** (*US Scol*) discours *m* d'adieu

valence /ˈveɪləns/ **N** ① (*esp US*) ⇒ **valency** ② (*Bio*) atomicité *f*

Valencia /vəˈlensɪə/ **N** Valence (*en Espagne*)

valency /ˈveɪlənsɪ/ **N** (*Chem*) valence *f*

valentine /ˈvæləntaɪn/ **N** ① ◆ **Valentine** Valentin(e) *m(f)* ◆ **(St) Valentine's Day** la Saint-Valentin ② (also **valentine card**) carte *f* de la Saint-Valentin ◆ **"will you be my valentine?"** (*on card*) "c'est toi que j'aime"

valerian /vəˈlɪərɪən/ **N** valériane *f*

valet /ˈvæleɪ/ **N** ① (= *person: in hotel or household*) valet *m* de chambre ② (= *rack for clothes*) valet *m* **VT** /ˈvælɪt/ *[+ man]* servir comme valet de chambre ; *[+ clothes]* entretenir ; *[+ car]* nettoyer **COMP** **valet parking** **N** service *m* de voiturier

valetudinarian /ˈvælɪˌtjuːdɪˈnɛərɪən/ **ADJ, N** valétudinaire *mf*

Valhalla /vælˈhælə/ **N** Walhalla *m*

valiant /ˈvæljənt/ **ADJ** (*liter*) *[person]* vaillant (*liter*), valeureux (*liter*) ; *[effort, attempt, fight]* courageux

valiantly /ˈvæljəntlɪ/ **ADV** vaillamment

valid /ˈvælɪd/ **ADJ** ① (= *reasonable, acceptable*) *[argument, reason, excuse, claim, objection, interpretation]* valable ; *[question]* pertinent ◆ **fashion is a ~ form of art** la mode est une forme d'art à part entière ◆ **it is not ~ to derive such conclusions from the data** il n'est pas valable de tirer de telles conclusions de ces données ② (= *in force*) *[contract, licence]* valable, valide ; *[passport]* en cours de validité ; *[ticket]* valable ◆ **~ for three months** valable *or* valide pendant trois mois ◆ **no longer ~** périmé

> ⚠ When **valid** means 'reasonable' it is not translated by the French word **valide**.

validate /ˈvælɪdeɪt/ **VT** *[+ document, course, diploma]* valider ; *[+ theory, argument, claim]* prouver la justesse de ; *[+ results]* confirmer ; (*Comput*) valider

validation /ˌvælɪˈdeɪʃən/ **N** (*NonC*) ① *[of claim, document]* validation *f* ② (*Psych* = *approval*) approbation *f*

validity /vəˈlɪdɪtɪ/ **N** *[of document, claim]* validité *f* ; *[of argument]* justesse *f*

valise /vəˈliːz/ **N** sac *m* de voyage ; (*Mil*) sac *m* (de soldat)

Valium ® /ˈvælɪəm/ **N** Valium ® *m* ◆ **to be on ~** être sous Valium

Valkyrie /ˈvælkɪrɪ/ **N** Walkyrie *or* Valkyrie *f* ◆ **the ride of the ~s** la chevauchée des Valkyries

valley /ˈvælɪ/ **N** vallée *f*, val *m* (*liter*) ; (*small, narrow*) vallon *m* ◆ **the Thames/Rhône ~** la vallée de la Tamise/du Rhône ◆ **the Loire ~** la vallée de la Loire ; (*between Orléans and Tours*) le Val de Loire ; → **lily**

valor /ˈvælər/ **N** (*US*) ⇒ **valour**

valorous /ˈvælərəs/ **ADJ** (*liter*) valeureux (*liter*)

valour, valor (*US*) /ˈvælər/ **N** (*liter*) courage *m*, bravoure *f*

valuable /ˈvæljʊəbl/ **ADJ** *[jewellery, antique]* de (grande) valeur ; *[information, advice, lesson, contribution, ally, resources, time]* précieux ; *[experience]* très utile ◆ **~ possessions** objets *mpl* de valeur ◆ **thank you for granting me so much of your ~ time** je vous remercie de m'avoir accordé autant de votre temps précieux **NPL** **valuables** objets *mpl* de valeur ◆ **all her ~s were stolen** on lui a volé tous ses objets de valeur

> ⚠ **valable** in French means 'valid', not **valuable**.

valuation /ˌvæljʊˈeɪʃən/ **N** ① *[of house, property, painting]* estimation *f* ; (*by expert*) expertise *f* ; (= *value decided upon*) estimation *f* ◆ **to have a ~ done** faire évaluer or estimer quelque chose ◆ **what is the ~?** à combien est-ce évalué *or* estimé ? ◆ **an independent ~ of the company** une évaluation indépendante de cette société ② *[of person, sb's character, work]* appréciation *f* ◆ **his rather low ~ of the novel** son opinion peu favorable du roman

valuator /ˈvæljʊeɪtər/ **N** expert *m* (*en estimations de biens mobiliers*)

value /ˈvæljuː/ **N** ① (*gen*) valeur *f* ; (= *usefulness, worth*) valeur *f*, utilité *f* ◆ **her training has been of no ~ to her** sa formation ne lui a servi à rien ◆ **to set great ~ on sth** attacher *or* accorder une grande valeur à qch ◆ **to have rarity ~** avoir de la valeur de par sa rareté ◆ **the film has great entertainment ~** c'est un film très divertissant ◆ **the invention never had anything more than novelty ~** cette invention n'a jamais été autre chose qu'un gadget

② (= *worth in money*) valeur *f* ◆ **the large packet is the best ~** le grand paquet est le plus avantageux ◆ **it's good ~ (for money)** on en a pour son argent, le rapport qualité-prix est bon (*esp Comm*) ◆ **to get good ~ for money** en avoir pour son argent ◆ **to be of great ~** valoir cher ◆ **of little ~** de peu de valeur ◆ **of no ~** sans valeur ◆ **to gain (in) ~** prendre de la valeur ◆ **to have ~** avoir de la valeur ◆ **to increase in ~** prendre de la valeur ◆ **increase in ~** hausse *f or* augmentation *f* de valeur ◆ **to lose (in) ~** se déprécier ◆ **loss of ~** perte *f or* diminution *f* de valeur, dépréciation *f* ◆ **he paid the ~ of the cup he broke** il a remboursé (le prix de) la tasse qu'il a cassée ◆ **to put** *or* **place a ~ on sth** évaluer qch ◆ **to put** *or* **place a ~ of $20 on sth** évaluer *or* estimer qch à 20 dollars ◆ **what ~ do you put on this?** à quelle valeur estimez-vous cela ?, combien pensez-vous que cela vaut ? ◆ **to put** *or* **set too high/too low a ~ on sth** surestimer/sous-estimer qch ◆ **to put** *or* **set a low ~ on sth** attacher peu de valeur à qch ◆ **goods to the ~ of £100** marchandises *fpl* d'une valeur de 100 livres ◆ **a cheque to the ~ of £100** un chèque (d'un montant) de 100 livres ; → **street**

③ (= *moral worth*) *[of person]* valeur *f*, mérite *m* ◆ **to put** *or* **place a high ~ on sth** attacher beaucoup d'importance à qch ◆ **what ~ do you put on this?** quelle valeur accordez-vous *or* attribuez-vous à cela ? ◆ **to put** *or* **place a high ~ on doing sth** attacher beaucoup d'importance à faire qch ◆ **he places a high ~ on educating his children** il attache beaucoup d'importance à l'éducation de ses enfants

④ (*Math, Mus, Painting, Phon*) valeur *f*

NPL **values** (= *attitudes, moral standards*) valeurs *fpl* ; → **production, Victorian**

VT ① (= *estimate worth of*) *[+ house, jewels, painting]* évaluer, estimer (*at* à) ; (*by expert*) expertiser ◆ **the house was ~d at $80,000** la maison a été évaluée or estimée à 80 000 dollars ◆ **he had it ~d** il l'a fait expertiser

② (= *appreciate, esteem*) *[+ friendship]* apprécier ; *[+ comforts]* apprécier, faire grand cas de ; *[+ liberty, independence]* tenir à ◆ **if you ~ your life/eyes/freedom** si vous tenez à la vie/à vos yeux/à votre liberté ◆ **we ~ your opinion** votre avis nous importe beaucoup ◆ **he is someone we all ~** nous l'apprécions tous beaucoup

COMP **value added tax** **N** (*Brit: abbr VAT*) taxe *f* sur la valeur ajoutée (*abbr TVA*)

value judg(e)ment **N** (*fig*) jugement *m* de valeur

value system **N** système *m* de valeurs

valued /ˈvæljuːd/ **ADJ** *[friend, customer, contribution]* précieux ; *[employee, commodity]* apprécié ; *[colleague]* estimé

valueless /ˈvæljʊlɪs/ **ADJ** sans valeur

valuer /ˈvæljʊər/ **N** (*Brit*) expert *m* (*en estimations de biens mobiliers*)

valve /vælv/ **N** ① (*Anat*) valvule *f* ; *[of plant, animal]* valve *f* ; *[of machine]* soupape *f*, valve *f* ; *[of air chamber, tyre]* valve *f* ; *[of musical instrument]* piston *m* ◆ **inlet/outlet ~** soupape *f* d'admission/d'échappement ◆ **exhaust ~** clapet *m* d'échappement ◆ **~ horn/trombone** (*Mus*) cor *m*/trombone *m* à pistons ; → **safety, suction** 2 (*Elec, Rad:* also **thermionic valve**) lampe *f*

valvular /ˈvælvjʊlə/ ADJ valvulaire

vamoose⁎ /vəˈmuːs/ VI filer*, décamper* ◆ **~!** fiche le camp !*

vamp¹ /væmp/ N (= *woman*) vamp *f* VT vamper* VI jouer la femme fatale

vamp² /væmp/ VT (= *repair*) rafistoler ; (*Mus*) improviser VI (*Mus*) improviser des accompagnements N [*of shoe*] devant *m*

vampire /ˈvæmpaɪəʳ/ N (*lit, fig*) vampire *m* COMP
vampire bat N vampire *m*

vampirism /ˈvæmpaɪərɪzəm/ N vampirisme *m*

van¹ /væn/ N 1 (= *road vehicle*) (*smallish*) camionnette *f*, fourgonnette *f* ; (*large*) camion *m*, fourgon *m* ; → **removal** 2 (*Brit Rail*) fourgon *m* ; → **guard, luggage** 3 (* abbrev of **caravan**) caravane *f* ; (*gipsy's*) roulotte *f*
COMP **van-boy** N livreur *m*
van-driver N chauffeur *m* de camion
van-man N (pl **van-men**) ⇒ **van-boy**
van pool N (*US*) covoiturage *m* en minibus

van² /væn/ N abbrev of **vanguard**

vanadium /vəˈneɪdɪəm/ N vanadium *m*

Vancouver /vænˈkuːvəʳ/ N Vancouver COMP
Vancouver Island N l'île *f* de Vancouver

vandal /ˈvændəl/ N 1 (= *hooligan*) vandale *mf* 2 (*Hist*) **Vandal** Vandale *mf*

vandalism /ˈvændəlɪzəm/ N vandalisme *m* ◆ **cultural ~** vandalisme *m* culturel

vandalistic /ˌvændəˈlɪstɪk/ ADJ destructeur (-trice *f*), de vandale

vandalize /ˈvændəlaɪz/ VT vandaliser, saccager

Van Diemen's Land † /ˌvænˈdiːmənzlænd/ N Terre *f* de Van Diemen

vane /veɪn/ N [*of windmill*] aile *f* ; [*of propeller*] pale *f* ; [*of turbine*] aube *f* ; [*of quadrant etc*] pinnule *f*, lumière *f* ; [*of feather*] barbe *f* ; (also **weather vane**) girouette *f*

vanguard /ˈvæŋgɑːd/ N 1 (*Mil, Naut*) avant-garde *f* ◆ **in the ~ (of)** en tête (de) 2 (*fig*) avant-garde *f* ◆ **in the ~ of progress** à l'avant-garde *or* à la pointe du progrès

vanilla /vəˈnɪlə/ N (= *spice, flavour*) vanille *f*
COMP [*cream, ice*] à la vanille
vanilla essence N extrait *m* de vanille
vanilla pod N gousse *f* de vanille
vanilla sugar N sucre *m* vanillé

vanillin /vəˈnɪlɪn/ N vanilline *f*

vanish /ˈvænɪʃ/ VI (*gen*) disparaître (*from* de) ; [*fears*] se dissiper ◆ **to ~ without trace** disparaître sans laisser de traces ◆ **to ~ into thin air*** se volatiliser ◆ **he ~ed into the countryside** il a disparu dans la campagne ◆ **he/it had ~ed from sight** il/cela avait disparu, il/cela était introuvable ◆ **he/it has ~ed from the face of the earth** il/cela a disparu sans laisser de traces ◆ **Julie ~ed from outside her home** Julie a disparu de devant chez elle ◆ **he ~ed into the distance** il s'est évanoui dans le lointain ◆ **he said goodbye and ~ed into the house** il a dit au revoir et il est rentré précipitamment dans la maison
COMP **vanishing act*** N (*fig*) ◆ **to do a ~ing act** s'éclipser*
vanishing cream † N crème *f* de beauté
vanishing point N point *m* de fuite ◆ **to reach ~ing point** disparaître
vanishing trick N tour *m* de passe-passe

vanished /ˈvænɪʃt/ ADJ disparu

vanitory unit /ˈvænɪtərɪˈjuːnɪt/ N sous-vasque *f*

vanity /ˈvænɪtɪ/ N (*NonC*) 1 (= *conceit*) vanité *f* ◆ **I may say without ~** je peux dire sans (vouloir) me vanter 2 (= *worthlessness*) vanité *f*, futilité *f* ◆ **all is ~** tout est vanité
COMP **vanity basin** N ⇒ **vanity unit**
vanity box, vanity case N mallette *f* pour affaires de toilette, vanity-case *m*
vanity mirror N (*in car*) miroir *m* de courtoisie
vanity plate N (*esp US: for car*) plaque *f* d'immatriculation personnalisée
vanity press N (*Publishing*) maison *f* d'édition à compte d'auteur
vanity publishing N (*NonC*) publication *f* à compte d'auteur
vanity unit N sous-vasque *f*

> **VANITY PLATE**
>
> En Grande-Bretagne comme aux États-Unis, les automobilistes s'intéressent particulièrement aux immatriculations qui forment des mots ou contiennent leurs initiales. Ces plaques, appelées **personalized number plates** en Grande-Bretagne et **vanity plates** aux États-Unis, se vendent souvent très cher. Par exemple, on peut imaginer qu'un homme s'appelant James Allan Gordon souhaite acquérir à n'importe quel prix la plaque d'immatriculation « JAG 1 ».

vanquish /ˈvæŋkwɪʃ/ VT (*liter*) vaincre ◆ **the ~ed** les vaincus *mpl*

vanquisher /ˈvæŋkwɪʃəʳ/ N (*liter*) vainqueur *m*

vantage /ˈvɑːntɪdʒ/ N avantage *m*, supériorité *f*
COMP **vantage ground** N (*Mil*) position *f* stratégique *or* avantageuse
vantage point N poste *m* d'observation ◆ **from my ~ point on the roof** de mon poste d'observation sur le toit ◆ **from his ~ point as a publisher** de sa position d'éditeur ◆ **there wasn't much to see from this ~ point** on ne voyait pas grand-chose de cet endroit ◆ **from your ~ point, do you think they'll win the election?** d'après vous, qui êtes bien placé pour juger, vont-ils gagner les élections ? ◆ **this seems unlikely from the ~ point of France** vu de France, cela semble improbable ◆ **this book is written from the ~ point of the slaves** ce livre est écrit du point de vue des esclaves

Vanuatu /ˈvænuːˌætuː/ N ◆ **(the Republic of) ~** (la République de) Vanuatu

vapid /ˈvæpɪd/ ADJ (*frm*) [*remark, conversation, book, song*] insipide ; [*person*] ahuri ; [*smile*] mièvre ; [*style*] plat

vapidity /væˈpɪdɪtɪ/ N [*of conversation*] insipidité *f* ; [*of style*] platitude *f*

vapor /ˈveɪpəʳ/ N, VI (*US*) ⇒ **vapour**

vaporization /ˌveɪpəraɪˈzeɪʃən/ N vaporisation *f*

vaporize /ˈveɪpəraɪz/ VT vaporiser VI se vaporiser

vaporizer /ˈveɪpəraɪzəʳ/ N (*gen, Chem*) vaporisateur *m* ; (*Med: for inhalation*) inhalateur *m* ; (*for perfume*) atomiseur *m*

vaporous /ˈveɪpərəs/ ADJ (*liter*) 1 (= *full of vapour*) [*air, cloud, heat*] vaporeux (*liter*) 2 (*fig* = *indistinct*) vague

vapour, vapor (*US*) /ˈveɪpəʳ/ N 1 (*Phys: also mist etc*) vapeur *f* ; (*on glass*) buée *f* 2 ◆ **to have the ~s** † avoir des vapeurs † VI (*US* ⁎ = *boast*) fanfaronner
COMP **vapour bath** N bain *m* de vapeur
vapour trail N [*of plane*] traînée *f* de condensation

Varanasi /vəˈrɑːnəsɪ/ N Varanasi (*nouveau nom de Bénarès*)

variability /ˌveərɪəˈbɪlɪtɪ/ N variabilité *f*

variable /ˈveərɪəbl/ ADJ [*amount, quality, content*] variable ; [*weather*] variable, incertain, changeant ; [*mood*] changeant ; [*work*] de qualité inégale N (*gen*) variable *f*
COMP **variable pitch propeller** N hélice *f* à pas variable
variable type N (*Comput*) type *m* de variable

variance /ˈveərɪəns/ N 1 (= *disagreement*) désaccord *m*, différend *m* ◆ **to be at ~** (= *in disagreement*) être en désaccord ◆ **to be at ~ with sb about sth** avoir un différend avec qn sur qch ◆ **this is at ~ with what he said earlier** cela ne correspond pas à *or* cela contredit ce qu'il a dit auparavant 2 (= *variation*) variation *f* 3 (*Math*) variance *f* 4 (*Jur*) différence *f*, divergence *f* ◆ **there is a ~ between the two statements** les deux dépositions ne s'accordent pas *or* ne concordent pas

variant /ˈveərɪənt/ N (*gen, Ling etc*) variante *f* ◆ **spelling ~** variante *f* orthographique ADJ [*method*] autre
COMP **variant form** N (*Ling*) variante *f* (orthographique)
variant reading N variante *f*
variant spelling N ⇒ **variant form**

variation /ˌveərɪˈeɪʃən/ N (*gen*) variation *f* ; (*in opinions, views*) fluctuation(s) *f(pl)*, changements *mpl*

varicoloured, varicolored (*US*) /ˈveərɪˌkʌləd/ ADJ multicolore, bigarré ; (*fig*) divers

varicose /ˈværɪkəʊs/ ADJ [*ulcer, eczema*] variqueux COMP **varicose vein** N varice *f* ◆ **to have ~ veins** avoir des varices

varied /ˈveərɪd/ ADJ [*diet, career, work, programme*] varié ; [*reasons, opportunities, talents*] varié, divers

variegated /ˈveərɪgeɪtɪd/ ADJ 1 (= *mottled*) [*plant, leaf, plumage*] panaché ; [*colour*] moucheté ; [*markings*] de couleurs différentes 2 (= *varied*) [*assortment*] varié

variegation /ˌveərɪˈgeɪʃən/ N bigarrure *f*, diaprure *f* (*liter*)

variety /vəˈraɪətɪ/ N 1 (*NonC – diversity*) variété *f* (*in* dans), diversité *f* ◆ **children like ~** les enfants aiment la variété *or* ce qui est varié ◆ **it lacks ~** ça n'est pas assez varié ◆ **they have increased in number and ~** ils sont devenus plus nombreux et plus variés ◆ **~ is the spice of life** (*Prov*) il faut de tout pour faire un monde
2 (= *assortment, range*) ◆ **a wide** *or* **great ~ of ...** un grand nombre de ... ◆ **dolphins produce a ~ of noises** les dauphins émettent différents bruits *or* un certain nombre de bruits ◆ **for a ~ of reasons** pour diverses raisons ◆ **it offers a ~ of careers** cela offre un grand choix de carrières
3 (*Bio* = *subdivision*) variété *f* ◆ **new plant ~** obtention *f or* nouveauté *f* végétale
4 (= *type, kind*) type *m*, espèce *f* ◆ **many varieties of socialist(s)** de nombreux types (différents) de socialistes, de nombreuses espèces (différentes) de socialistes ◆ **books of the paperback ~** des livres du genre livre de poche
5 (*NonC: Theat*) variétés *fpl*
COMP (*Theat*) [*actor, artiste*] de variétés, de music-hall
variety meats NPL (*US Culin*) abats *mpl* (*de boucherie*)
variety show N (*Theat*) spectacle *m* de variétés *or* de music-hall ; (*Rad, TV*) émission *f* de variétés
variety store N (*US*) ≃ Prisunic *m*
variety theatre N (théâtre *m* de) variétés *fpl*
variety turn N (*Brit*) numéro *m* (de variétés *or* de music-hall)

varifocal /veərɪˈfəʊkl/ ADJ progressif NPL **varifocals** lunettes *fpl* à verres progressifs

variola /vəˈraɪələ/ N variole *f*

various /ˈveərɪəs/ ADJ 1 (= *differing*) divers *before n*, différent ◆ **at ~ times of day** à différents moments de la journée ◆ **the ~ meanings of a word** les différents sens d'un mot ◆ **his excuses are many and ~** ses excuses sont nombreuses et variées 2 (= several) divers, plusieurs ◆ **I phoned her ~ times** je lui ai téléphoné à plusieurs reprises ◆ **there are ~ ways of doing it** il y a plusieurs manières de le faire

variously /ˈvɛərɪəslɪ/ ADV ◆ **he was ~ known as John, Johnny or Jack** il était connu sous divers noms : John, Johnny ou Jack ◆ **the crowd was ~ estimated at two to seven thousand** le nombre de personnes a été estimé entre deux et sept mille selon les sources

varlet †† /ˈvɑːlɪt/ N (pej) sacripant †† m

varmint †* /ˈvɑːmɪnt/ N (= scoundrel) polisson(ne) m(f), vaurien(ne) m(f)

varnish /ˈvɑːnɪʃ/ N (lit, fig) vernis m ; (on pottery) vernis m, émail m ; → **nail**, **spirit** VT [+ furniture, painting] vernir ; [+ pottery] vernisser ◆ **to ~ one's nails** se vernir les ongles ◆ **to ~ the truth** maquiller la vérité

varnishing /ˈvɑːnɪʃɪŋ/ N vernissage m COMP
varnishing day N (Art) (jour m du) vernissage m

varsity /ˈvɑːsɪtɪ/ N 1 (Brit † * = university) fac* f 2 (US Univ Sport) équipe f de première catégorie (*représentant un établissement d'enseignement*)
COMP **varsity match** N *match entre les universités d'Oxford et de Cambridge*
varsity sports NPL (US) *sports pratiqués entre équipes de différents établissements scolaires*

vary /ˈvɛərɪ/ VI varier ◆ **symptoms ~ with the weather** les symptômes varient selon le temps qu'il fait ◆ **the colour can ~ from blue to green** la couleur peut varier du bleu au vert ◆ **tariffs ~ by country** or **from country to country** les tarifs varient selon les pays ◆ **this text varies from the previous version** ce texte diffère de la version antérieure ◆ **as they are handmade, each one varies slightly** comme ils sont faits main, chacun est légèrement différent ◆ **they ~ in size** leur taille varie, ils sont de tailles différentes VT [+ programme, menu] varier ; [+ temperature] faire varier ; (directly) varier

varying /ˈvɛərɪɪŋ/ ADJ [amounts] variable ; [shades] différent ◆ **of ~ abilities** de compétences variées ◆ **of ~ ages** de différents âges ◆ **to ~ degrees** à des degrés divers ◆ **with ~ degrees of success** avec plus ou moins de succès ◆ **for ~ periods of time** pendant des périodes plus ou moins longues ◆ **of ~ sizes** de différentes tailles

vascular /ˈvæskjʊləʳ/ ADJ vasculaire

vas deferens /ˈvæsˈdefəˌrenz/ N (pl **vasa deferentia** /ˈveɪsəˌdefəˈrenʃɪə/) (Anat) canal m déférent

vase /vɑːz/ N vase m ◆ **flower ~** vase m à fleurs

vasectomy /væˈsektəmɪ/ N vasectomie f ◆ **to have a ~** avoir une vasectomie

Vaseline ® /ˈvæsɪliːn/ N vaseline ® f VT enduire de vaseline ®

vasoconstrictor /ˌveɪzəʊkənˈstrɪktəʳ/ N vasoconstricteur m

vasodilator /ˌveɪzəʊdaɪˈleɪtəʳ/ N vasodilatateur m

vasomotor /ˌveɪzəʊˈməʊtəʳ/ ADJ vasomoteur (f -trice)

vassal /ˈvæsəl/ ADJ, N (Hist, fig) vassal m

vassalage /ˈvæsəlɪdʒ/ N vassalité f, vasselage m

vast /vɑːst/ ADJ [quantity, amount, building, reserve] vaste before n, énorme ; [area, size, organization, army] vaste, immense ; [knowledge, experience] vaste, grand ◆ **at ~ expense** à grands frais ◆ **to a ~ extent** dans une très large mesure ◆ **a ~ improvement on sth** une nette amélioration par rapport à qch ◆ **the ~ majority** la grande majorité ◆ **~ sums (of money)** des sommes folles

vastly /ˈvɑːstlɪ/ ADV [different] extrêmement ; [superior] largement, nettement ; [overrate, increase, improve] considérablement

vastness /ˈvɑːstnɪs/ N immensité f

VAT /viːeɪˈtiː, væt/ N (Brit) (abbrev of **value added tax**) TVA f
COMP **VAT man** * N (pl **VAT men**) *inspecteur des impôts chargé du contrôle de la TVA*
VAT-registered ADJ enregistré à la TVA
VAT return N formulaire m de déclaration de la TVA

vat /væt/ N cuve f, bac m

Vatican /ˈvætɪkən/ N Vatican m
COMP [policy etc] du Vatican
Vatican City N la cité du Vatican
the Vatican Council N le concile du Vatican

vaudeville /ˈvəʊdəvɪl/ (esp US) N spectacle m de variétés or de music-hall COMP [show, singer] de variétés, de music-hall

vaudevillian /ˌvəʊdəˈvɪlɪən/ (US) N (= writer) auteur m de variétés ; (= performer) acteur m, -trice f de variétés ADJ de variétés

vaudevillist /ˈvəʊdəvɪlɪst/ N (US) ⇒ **vaudevillian noun**

vault[1] /vɔːlt/ N 1 (Archit) voûte f ◆ **the ~ of heaven** (liter) la voûte céleste 2 (Anat) voûte f ◆ **cranial ~** voûte f crânienne 3 (= cellar) cave f 4 (in bank) (= strongroom) chambre f forte ; (= safe deposit box room) salle f des coffres ◆ **it's lying in the ~s of the bank** c'est dans les coffres de la banque 5 (= burial chamber) caveau m ◆ **interred in the family ~** inhumé dans le caveau de famille

vault[2] /vɔːlt/ VI (gen) sauter ; (Pole Vaulting) sauter (à la perche) ; (Gym) sauter ◆ **to ~ over sth** sauter qch (d'un bond) ; → **pole**[1] VT (gen) sauter d'un bond N saut m

vaulted /ˈvɔːltɪd/ ADJ [roof, ceiling] en voûte ; [room, hall] voûté

vaulting[1] /ˈvɔːltɪŋ/ N (Archit) voûte(s) f(pl)

vaulting[2] /ˈvɔːltɪŋ/ N (Sport) exercice m or pratique f du saut COMP **vaulting horse** N cheval m d'arçons

vaunt /vɔːnt/ VT (liter) (= boast about) vanter ; (= praise) vanter, faire l'éloge de ◆ **much ~ed** tant vanté

VC /viːˈsiː/ N 1 (Brit) (abbrev of **Victoria Cross**) → **Victoria** 2 (Univ) (abbrev of **vice-chancellor**) → **vice-** 3 (US: in Vietnam) abbrev of **Vietcong**

VCR /ˌviːsiːˈɑːʳ/ N (abbrev of **video cassette recorder**) → **video**

VD /viːˈdiː/ N (Med) (abbrev of **venereal disease**) → **venereal**

VDT /ˌviːdiːˈtiː/ N (abbrev of **visual display terminal**) → **visual**

VDU /ˌviːdiːˈjuː/ N (Comput) (abbrev of **visual display unit**) → **visual**

veal /viːl/ N veau m ; → **fillet** COMP [stew, cutlet] de veau **veal crate** N *box pour l'élevage des veaux de batterie*

vector /ˈvektəʳ/ N 1 (Bio, Math) vecteur m 2 [of aircraft] direction f VT [+ aircraft] radioguider COMP (Math) vectoriel

vectorial /vekˈtɔːrɪəl/ ADJ vectoriel

VE Day /viːˈiːdeɪ/ N *anniversaire de la victoire des alliés en 1945*

VE Day

La Grande-Bretagne et les États-Unis commémorent le 8 mai la victoire alliée de 1945 en Europe. C'est le **VE Day** (Victory in Europe Day). La victoire sur le Japon, **VJ Day** (Victory over Japan Day), est commémorée le 15 août.

veep ‡ /viːp/ N (US: from VP) ⇒ **vice-president** ; → **vice-**

veer /vɪəʳ/ VI 1 [wind] (= change direction) tourner, changer de direction ; [ship] virer (de bord) ; [car, road] virer ◆ **to ~ to the north** se diriger vers le nord or au nord ◆ **the car ~ed off the road** la voiture a quitté la route ◆ **to ~ (off to the) left/right** virer à gauche/droite 2 (= change etc) changer ◆ **he ~ed round to my point of view** changeant d'opinion il s'est rallié à mon point de vue ◆ **he ~ed off** or **away from his subject** il s'est éloigné de son sujet ◆ **her feelings for him ~ed between tenderness and love** les sentiments qu'elle lui portait oscillaient entre la tendresse et l'amour VT 1 (Naut) [+ cable] filer 2 [+ ship, car] faire virer

veg * /vedʒ/ N (abbrev of **vegetables**) légumes mpl

▸ **veg out** ‡ VI glander ‡

vegan /ˈviːgən/ N, ADJ végétalien(ne) m(f)

veganism /ˈviːgənɪzəm/ N végétalisme m

vegeburger /ˈvedʒɪˌbɜːgəʳ/ N hamburger m végétarien

vegetable /ˈvedʒtəbl/ N 1 légume m ◆ **early ~s** primeurs fpl 2 (generic term = plant) végétal m, plante f 3 (pej = brain-damaged person) légume m COMP [oil, matter] végétal
vegetable dish N plat m à légumes, légumier m
vegetable garden N (jardin m) potager m
vegetable kingdom N règne m végétal
vegetable knife N (pl **vegetable knives**) couteau-éplucheur m
vegetable marrow N (esp Brit) courge f
vegetable patch N carré m de légumes
vegetable salad N salade f or macédoine f de légumes
vegetable slicer N coupe-légumes m inv
vegetable soup N soupe f aux or de légumes

vegetarian /ˌvedʒɪˈtɛərɪən/ ADJ, N végétarien(ne) m(f)

vegetarianism /ˌvedʒɪˈtɛərɪənɪzəm/ N végétarisme m

vegetate /ˈvedʒɪteɪt/ VI (lit) végéter ; (fig) végéter, moisir *

vegetated /ˈvedʒɪteɪtɪd/ ADJ couvert de végétation ◆ **sparsely/densely ~** couvert d'une végétation clairsemée/dense

vegetation /ˌvedʒɪˈteɪʃən/ N (NonC) végétation f

vegetative /ˈvedʒɪtətɪv/ ADJ végétatif ◆ **~ growth** croissance f de la végétation COMP **vegetative coma** N coma m dépassé ; → **persistent**

veggie * /ˈvedʒɪ/ N, ADJ 1 abbrev of **vegetarian** 2 (esp US) abbrev of **vegetable noun 1**

veggieburger /ˈvedʒɪˌbɜːdəʳ/ N ⇒ **vegeburger**

vehemence /ˈviːɪməns/ N [of person, opposition, denial, tone] véhémence f ; [of criticism, attack, protest, dislike] véhémence f, violence f

vehement /ˈviːɪmənt/ ADJ [person, opposition, denial, tone] véhément ; [criticism, attack, protest, dislike] véhément, violent ; [speech] véhément, passionné ; [gesture, condemnation] vif

vehemently /ˈviːɪməntlɪ/ ADV [deny, say] avec véhémence (liter) ; [reject, oppose] avec véhémence, violemment ; [attack, curse] violemment ; [shake one's head] vigoureusement ◆ **~ anti-European** violemment antieuropéen

vehicle /ˈviːɪkl/ N 1 (gen) véhicule m ; (very large) engin m ◆ **"closed to vehicles"** "interdit à la circulation" ◆ **"authorized vehicles only"** "accès réservé aux véhicules autorisés" ; → **commercial** 2 (fig) véhicule m ◆ **a ~ of** or **for communication** un véhicule de la communication ◆ **her art was a ~ for her political beliefs** son art lui servait à véhiculer ses convictions politiques

vehicular /vɪˈhɪkjʊləʳ/ ADJ (frm) [access] des véhicules ; [homicide] commis en conduisant ◆ ~

deaths décès *mpl* dus aux accidents de la route ◆ ~ **traffic** circulation *f* (routière)

veil /veɪl/ N (*gen*) voile *m* ; (*on hat*) voilette *f* ; (*fig*) voile *m* ◆ **to take the** ~ (*Rel*) prendre le voile ◆ **beyond the** ~ (*fig liter*) dans l'au-delà ◆ **to be wearing a** ~ être voilé ◆ **to draw/throw a** ~ **over** (*fig*) mettre/jeter un voile sur ◆ **under the** ~ **of** ... sous le voile de ... ◆ ~ **of mist** voile *m* de brume VT voiler, couvrir d'un voile ; (*fig*) [+ *truth, facts*] voiler ; [+ *feelings*] voiler, dissimuler ◆ **the clouds ~ed the moon** les nuages voilaient la lune

veiled /veɪld/ ADJ [*woman, face, criticism, reference, threat, warning, attack*] voilé ◆ ~ **in black** voilé de noir ◆ ~ **in shadow** (*liter*) plongé dans l'ombre ◆ ~ **mountains** (*liter*) des montagnes *fpl* voilées (*liter*)

veiling /ˈveɪlɪŋ/ N (*on hat etc*) voilage *m* ; (*fig*) [*of truth, facts*] dissimulation *f*

vein /veɪn/ N 1 (*in body, insect wing*) veine *f* ; (*in leaf*) nervure *f* ◆ **to open a** ~ (*suicide*) s'ouvrir les veines ◆ **he has French blood in his ~s** il a du sang français dans les veines ; → **varicose** 2 (*in stone etc: gen*) veine *f* ; (*of ore etc*) filon *m*, veine *f* ◆ **there's a ~ of truth in what he says** il y a un fond de vérité dans ce qu'il dit ◆ **a ~ of racism/scepticism** un fond de racisme/scepticisme ◆ **a ~ of humour runs through her writing** il y a un humour sous-jacent dans tous ses textes 3 (= *style etc*) style *m* ; (= *mood*) esprit *m* ◆ **in a humorous/revolutionary** ~ dans un esprit humoristique/révolutionnaire ◆ **in the same** ~, **in a similar** ~ (= *in the same style*) dans la même veine ; (= *by the same token*) dans le même ordre d'idées ◆ **in a more realistic** ~ dans un style plus réaliste

veined /veɪnd/ ADJ [*hand, marble*] veiné ; [*stone*] marbré ; [*leaf*] nervuré ◆ **blue-~ cheese** fromage *m* à pâte persillée ◆ **pink flowers ~ with red** des fleurs *fpl* roses veinées de rouge ◆ **rocks ~ with cracks** rochers *mpl* tout fissurés

veining /ˈveɪnɪŋ/ N [*of marble*] veinures *fpl* ; [*of stone*] marbrures *fpl* ; [*of leaf*] nervures *fpl* ; [*of marble-effect paper*] dessin *mpl* marbrés

veinule /ˈveɪnjuːl/ N veinule *f*

vela /ˈviːlə/ NPL of **velum**

velar /ˈviːləʳ/ ADJ vélaire

Velcro ® /ˈvelkrəʊ/ N velcro ® *m*

veld(t) /velt/ N veld(t) *m*

vellum /ˈveləm/ N vélin *m* COMP [*binding*] de vélin **vellum paper** N papier *m* vélin

velocipede /vəˈlɒsɪpiːd/ N vélocipède *m*

velociraptor /vəˈlɒsɪræptəʳ/ N vélociraptor *m*

velocity /vɪˈlɒsɪtɪ/ N vélocité *f*, vitesse *f*

velodrome /ˈviːlə,drəʊm/ N vélodrome *m*

velour(s) /vəˈlʊəʳ/ N (*for clothes*) velours *m* rasé ; (*for upholstery*) velours *m* épais

velum /ˈviːləm/ N (pl **vela**) (*Anat*) voile *m* du palais

velvet /ˈvelvɪt/ N 1 (*gen*) velours *m* ; → **black, iron** 2 (*US* = *unearned income*) bénéfice *m* non salarial COMP [*dress*] de velours **Velvet Revolution** N révolution *f* de velours

velveteen /ˈvelvɪtiːn/ N veloutine *f*

velvety /ˈvelvɪtɪ/ ADJ [*surface, texture, material*] velouteux, velouté ; [*sauce, voice*] velouté

vena cava /ˈviːnəˈkeɪvə/ N (pl **venae cavae** /ˈviːniːˈkeɪviː/) veine *f* cave

venal /ˈviːnl/ ADJ vénal

venality /viːˈnælɪtɪ/ N vénalité *f*

vend /vend/ VT (*Jur*) vendre

vendee /venˈdiː/ N (*Jur*) acquéreur *m*

vendetta /venˈdetə/ N vendetta *f*

vending /ˈvendɪŋ/ N vente *f* COMP **vending machine** N distributeur *m* automatique

vendor /ˈvendəʳ/ N 1 (*gen*) marchand(e) *m(f)* ◆ **ice-cream** *etc* ~ marchand(e) *m(f)* de glaces *etc* ; → **newsvendor, street** 2 (= *machine*) distributeur *m* automatique 3 /ˈvendɔːʳ/ (*Jur*) vendeur *m*

veneer /vəˈnɪəʳ/ N placage *m* ; (*fig*) apparence *f*, vernis *m* ◆ **with** *or* **under a** ~ **of** sous un vernis de VT plaquer

venerable /ˈvenərəbl/ ADJ vénérable COMP **the Venerable Bede** N Bède *m* le Vénérable

venerate /ˈvenəreɪt/ VT vénérer

veneration /,venəˈreɪʃən/ N vénération *f*

venereal /vɪˈnɪərɪəl/ ADJ vénérien COMP **venereal disease** N maladie *f* vénérienne, MST *f*

venereology /vɪ,nɪərɪˈɒlədʒɪ/ N vénérologie *f*

venery /ˈvenərɪ/ N 1 (*liter* = *hunting*) vénerie *f* 2 (†† = *debauchery*) débauche *f*

Venetia /vɪˈniːʃə/ N (*Hist*) Vénétie *f*

Venetian /vɪˈniːʃən/ ADJ vénitien, de Venise N Vénitien(ne) *m(f)* COMP **Venetian blind** N store *m* vénitien **Venetian glass** N cristal *m* de Venise

Veneto /ˈveːneto/ N ◆ **(the)** ~ la Vénétie

Venezuela /,veneˈzweɪlə/ N Venezuela *m* ◆ **in** ~ au Venezuela

Venezuelan /,veneˈzweɪlən/ ADJ vénézuélien N Vénézuélien(ne) *m(f)*

vengeance /ˈvendʒəns/ N vengeance *f* ◆ **to take ~ (up)on** ... se venger de *or* sur ... ◆ **to take ~ for** ... tirer vengeance de ...

◆ **with a vengeance** ◆ **to set to work with a** ~ se mettre à travailler avec détermination ◆ **to return with a** ~ faire un retour en force ◆ **it started to rain again with a** ~ il s'est remis à pleuvoir de plus belle

vengeful /ˈvendʒfʊl/ ADJ vengeur (-eresse *f*)

venial /ˈviːnɪəl/ ADJ (*also Rel*) véniel

veniality /,viːnɪˈælɪtɪ/ N caractère *m* véniel

Venice /ˈvenɪs/ N Venise

venire /vɪˈnaɪrɪ/ N (*US Jur*) liste *f* des jurés assignés

venireman /vɪˈnaɪərɪmən/ N (pl **-men**) (*US Jur*) juré *m* nommé par assignation

venison /ˈvenɪsən/ N (viande *f* de) chevreuil *m*

venom /ˈvenəm/ N (*lit, fig*) venin *m*

venomous /ˈvenəməs/ ADJ (*lit, fig*) venimeux ◆ ~ **tongue** (*fig*) langue *f* de vipère

venomously /ˈvenəməslɪ/ ADV [*say*] sur un ton venimeux ◆ **to glare ~ at sb** lancer des regards venimeux à qn

venous /ˈviːnəs/ ADJ (*Anat, Bot*) veineux

vent /vent/ N (*for gas, liquid*) (= *hole*) orifice *m* ; (= *pipe*) conduit *m* ; (*in chimney*) tuyau *m* ; [*of volcano*] cheminée *f* ; (*in barrel*) trou *m* ; (*in coat*) fente *f* ◆ **to give ~ to** [+ *feelings*] donner *or* laisser libre cours à VT [+ *barrel etc*] pratiquer un trou dans ; [+ *one's anger etc*] décharger (*on* sur) COMP **vent glass** N (*in car*) déflecteur *m*

ventilate /ˈventɪleɪt/ VT 1 [+ *room, lungs, patient*] aérer, ventiler ; [+ *tunnel*] ventiler ; [+ *blood*] oxygéner 2 [+ *question*] livrer à la discussion ; [+ *grievance*] étaler au grand jour

ventilation /,ventɪˈleɪʃən/ N ventilation *f* COMP **ventilation shaft** N conduit *m* d'aération *or* de ventilation

ventilator /ˈventɪleɪtəʳ/ N (*Med*) respirateur *m* ; (*in room*) ventilateur *m* ; (*in car: also* **ventilator window**) déflecteur *m*

ventricle /ˈventrɪkl/ N ventricule *m*

ventriloquism /venˈtrɪləkwɪzəm/ N ventriloquie *f*

ventriloquist /venˈtrɪləkwɪst/ N ventriloque *mf* COMP **ventriloquist's dummy** N poupée *f* de ventriloque

ventriloquy /venˈtrɪləkwɪ/ N ventriloquie *f*

venture /ˈventʃəʳ/ N (= *project*) entreprise *f*, projet *m* ; (also **business venture**) entreprise *f* ◆ **it was a risky** ~ c'était une entreprise assez risquée *or* assez hasardeuse ◆ **the success of his first artistic/film** ~ le succès de sa première entreprise artistique/cinématographique ◆ **all his business ~s failed** toutes ses entreprises en matière de commerce *or* toutes ses tentatives commerciales ont échoué ◆ **this is a new ~ in publishing** ceci constitue quelque chose de nouveau *or* un coup d'essai en matière d'édition ◆ **at a** ~ † au hasard

VT [+ *life, fortune, reputation*] risquer ; [+ *opinion*] hasarder ; [+ *explanation, estimate*] hasarder, avancer ◆ **when I asked him that, he ~d a guess** quand je lui ai posé la question, il a hasardé *or* avancé une réponse ◆ **to ~ to do sth** oser faire qch, se permettre de faire qch ◆ **he ~d the opinion that** ... il a hasardé une opinion selon laquelle ... ◆ **I ~d to write to you** j'ai pris la liberté de vous écrire ◆ ... **but he did not ~ to speak** ... mais il n'a pas osé parler ◆ **nothing ~d nothing gained** (*Prov*) qui ne risque rien n'a rien (*Prov*)

VI s'aventurer, se risquer ◆ **to ~ in/out/through** se risquer à entrer/sortir/traverser ◆ **to ~ out of doors** se risquer à sortir ◆ **to ~ into town/into the forest** s'aventurer *or* se hasarder dans la ville/dans la forêt ◆ **they ~d on a programme of reform** ils ont essayé de mettre sur pied *or* d'entreprendre un ensemble de réformes ◆ **when we ~d on this** quand nous avons entrepris cela, quand nous nous sommes lancés là-dedans

COMP **venture capital** N capital *m* risque **venture capitalist** N spécialiste *mf* du capital risque **Venture Scout** N (*Brit*) ≃ scout *m* de la branche aînée, routier *m*, -ière *f*

► **venture forth** VI (*liter*) se risquer à sortir

venturesome /ˈventʃəsəm/ ADJ [*person*] aventureux, entreprenant ; [*action*] risqué, hasardeux

venue /ˈvenjuː/ N (*gen*) lieu *m* (de rendez-vous) ; (*Jur*) lieu *m* du procès, juridiction *f* ◆ **the ~ of the meeting is** ... la réunion aura lieu à ...

Venus /ˈviːnəs/ N (*Astron, Myth*) Vénus *f* COMP **Venus fly-trap** N (= *plant*) dionée *f*

Venusian /vɪˈnjuːzɪən/ ADJ vénusien

veracious /vəˈreɪʃəs/ ADJ véridique

veracity /vəˈræsɪtɪ/ N véracité *f*

veranda(h) /vəˈrændə/ N véranda *f*

verb /vɜːb/ N verbe *m* ; → **auxiliary** COMP **verb phrase** N syntagme *m* verbal

verbal /ˈvɜːbəl/ ADJ 1 (*gen*) [*attack, agreement, support, statement, reasoning, promise*] verbal ; [*confession*] oral ◆ ~ **dexterity** facilité *f* de parole, aisance *f* verbale ◆ ~ **memory** mémoire *f* auditive ◆ **to have good/poor ~ skills** bien/mal s'exprimer 2 (*Gram*) verbal N (*US Jur* *) aveux *mpl* faits oralement (*et servant de témoignage dans un procès*) COMP **verbal abuse** N (*NonC*) violence *f* verbale, injures *fpl*

verbalize /ˈvɜːbəlaɪz/ VT [+ *feelings etc*] traduire en paroles, exprimer

verbally /ˈvɜːbəlɪ/ ADV [*threaten, attack, communicate, express, agree*] verbalement ◆ **to abuse sb** ~ injurier qn ◆ **to be ~ abusive** tenir des propos injurieux ◆ **to be ~ and physically abused** être victime de coups et injures *or* d'agressions verbales et physiques

verbatim /vɜːˈbeɪtɪm/ ADV [*quote, repeat*] textuellement, mot pour mot ; [*translate*] mot à mot, littéralement ADJ [*translation*] mot à mot ; [*quotation*] mot pour mot ◆ ~ **report** compte rendu *m* in extenso ◆ **he gave me a ~ report of what was said** il m'a rapporté textuellement *or* mot pour mot ce qui a été dit

verbena /vɜː'biːnə/ **N** *(= genus)* verbénacées *fpl* ; *(= plant)* verveine *f*

verbiage /'vɜːbɪɪdʒ/ **N** verbiage *m*

verbless /'vɜːblɪs/ **ADJ** sans verbe

verbose /vɜː'bəʊs/ **ADJ** verbeux, prolixe

verbosely /vɜː'bəʊslɪ/ **ADV** avec verbosité, verbeusement

verbosity /vɜː'bɒsɪtɪ/ **N** verbosité *f*

verdant /'vɜːdənt/ **ADJ** *(liter)* verdoyant

verdict /'vɜːdɪkt/ **N** 1 *(Jur)* verdict *m* ; → **bring in, guilty** 2 *[of doctor, electors, press]* verdict *m* ◆ **to give one's ~ about** *or* **on** se prononcer sur

verdigris /'vɜːdɪgrɪs/ **ADJ, N** vert-de-gris *m inv*

verdure /'vɜːdjʊəʳ/ **N** *(liter)* verdure *f*

verge /vɜːdʒ/ **N** 1 *(Brit: of road)* bas-côté *m*, accotement *m* ◆ **the car mounted the ~** la voiture est montée sur le bas-côté *or* l'accotement ◆ **to pull over onto the ~** s'arrêter sur le bas-côté ◆ **"soft verges"** "accotement non stabilisé"

2 *(= edge) (gen)* bord *m* ; *(round flowerbed)* bordure *f* en gazon ; *[of forest]* orée *f*

◆ **on the verge of** ◆ **on the ~ of doing sth** sur le point de faire qch ◆ **on the ~ of ruin/despair/a nervous breakdown** au bord de la ruine/du désespoir/de la dépression nerveuse ◆ **on the ~ of sleep** *or* **of falling asleep** sur le point de s'endormir ◆ **on the ~ of tears** au bord des larmes, sur le point de pleurer ◆ **on the ~ of a discovery** à la veille d'une découverte ◆ **on the ~ of retirement** au seuil de la retraite ◆ **they are on the ~ of starvation** ils sont au bord de la famine

► **verge on** **VT FUS** friser, frôler ◆ **the plot ~s on the ridiculous** l'intrigue frise *or* frôle le ridicule ◆ **disappointment verging on despair** une déception frisant *or* frôlant le désespoir ◆ **a fury that ~d on madness** une fureur proche de la folie ◆ **he's verging on bankruptcy** il est au bord de la faillite ◆ **she is verging on fifty** elle frise la cinquantaine

verger /'vɜːdʒəʳ/ **N** *(Rel)* bedeau *m* ; *(ceremonial)* huissier *m* à verge

Vergil /'vɜːdʒɪl/ **N** Virgile *m*

Vergilian /və'dʒɪlɪən/ **ADJ** virgilien

verifiability /ˌverɪfaɪə'bɪlɪtɪ/ **N** vérifiabilité *f*

verifiable /'verɪfaɪəbl/ **ADJ** vérifiable

verification /ˌverɪfɪ'keɪʃən/ **N** *(= check)* vérification *f*, contrôle *m* ; *(= proof)* vérification *f*

verifier /'verɪfaɪəʳ/ **N** *(Comput)* vérificatrice *f*

verify /'verɪfaɪ/ **VT** 1 *(= check) [+ statements, information, spelling]* vérifier ; *[+ documents]* contrôler 2 *(= confirm)* confirmer ◆ **I can ~ that it takes about a minute** je peux confirmer que cela prend à peu près une minute

verily †† /'verɪlɪ/ **ADV** en vérité

verisimilitude /ˌverɪsɪ'mɪlɪtjuːd/ **N** vraisemblance *f*

veritable /'verɪtəbl/ **ADJ** véritable, vrai *before n*

verity /'verɪtɪ/ **N** *(liter)* vérité *f*

vermicelli /ˌvɜːmɪ'selɪ/ **N** *(NonC)* vermicelle(s) *m(pl)*

vermicide /'vɜːmɪsaɪd/ **N** vermicide *m*

vermifugal /'vɜːmɪfjuːgəl/ **ADJ** vermifuge

vermifuge /'vɜːmɪfjuːdʒ/ **N** vermifuge *m*

vermilion /və'mɪljən/ **ADJ, N** vermillon *m inv*

vermin /'vɜːmɪn/ **NPL** *(= animals)* animaux *mpl* nuisibles ; *(= insects)* vermine *f NonC*, parasites *mpl* ; *(pej = people)* vermine *f NonC*, racaille *f NonC*, parasites *mpl*

verminous /'vɜːmɪnəs/ **ADJ** *[person, clothes]* pouilleux, couvert de vermine ; *[disease]* vermineux

Vermont /vɜː'mɒnt/ **N** Vermont *m* ◆ **in ~** dans le Vermont

vermouth /'vɜːməθ/ **N** vermout(h) *m*

vernacular /və'nækjʊləʳ/ **N** 1 *(Ling) (= native speech)* langue *f* vernaculaire ; *(= jargon)* jargon *m* ◆ **the ~ of advertising** le jargon de la publicité ◆ **in the ~** *(= in local language)* en langue vernaculaire ; *(= not in Latin)* en langue vulgaire 2 *(Archit)* architecture *f* vernaculaire *or* locale ◆ **in the local ~** dans le style local **ADJ** *[language]* vernaculaire ; *[crafts, furniture]* du pays ; *[architecture, style]* vernaculaire, local ; *[building]* de style local

vernal /'vɜːnl/ **ADJ** *(liter)* printanier **COMP** **the vernal equinox** **N** l'équinoxe *m* de printemps

Verona /və'rəʊnə/ **N** Vérone

veronica /və'rɒnɪkə/ **N** 1 *(= plant)* véronique *f* 2 *(= name)* **Veronica** Véronique *f*

verruca /ve'ruːkə/ **N** (pl **verrucae** /ve'ruːsiː/ *or* **verrucas**) *(esp Brit)* verrue *f (gen plantaire)*

Versailles /veə'saɪ/ **N** Versailles

versatile /'vɜːsətaɪl/ **ADJ** *[person]* aux talents variés, plein de ressources ; *[mind]* souple ; *[tool, vehicle, software]* à usages multiples, polyvalent ; *[item of clothing]* qu'on peut porter en toute situation ◆ **brick is a very ~ building material** la brique est un matériau très polyvalent ◆ **potatoes are very ~** il y a mille et une façons d'accommoder les pommes de terre

⚠ In French, **versatile** means 'fickle', not **versatile**.

versatility /ˌvɜːsə'tɪlɪtɪ/ **N** *[of person]* variété *f* de talents ; *[of mind]* souplesse *f* ◆ **his ~** ses talents variés, sa polyvalence

verse /vɜːs/ **N** 1 *(= stanza) [of poem]* strophe *f* ; *[of song]* couplet *m* 2 *(NonC = poetry)* poésie *f*, vers *mpl* ◆ **in ~** en vers ; → **blank, free** 3 *[of Bible, Koran]* verset *m* ; → **chapter** **COMP** *[drama etc]* en vers

versed /vɜːst/ **ADJ** (also **well-versed**) versé (in dans) ◆ **not (well-)~** peu versé

versification /ˌvɜːsɪfɪ'keɪʃən/ **N** versification *f*, métrique *f*

versifier /'vɜːsɪfaɪəʳ/ **N** *(pej)* versificateur *m*, -trice *f (pej)*

versify /'vɜːsɪfaɪ/ **VT** versifier, mettre en vers **VI** faire des vers

version /'vɜːʃən/ **N** 1 *(= account)* version *f* ; *(= interpretation)* interprétation *f* ◆ **his ~ of events** sa version des faits 2 *(= variant) [of text]* version *f*, variante *f* ; *[of car]* modèle *m* 3 *(= translation)* version *f*, traduction *f* ; → **authorized**

verso /'vɜːsəʊ/ **N** verso *m*

versus /'vɜːsəs/ **PREP** 1 *(in comparison)* par opposition à ◆ **the arguments about public ~ private ownership** les arguments pour ou contre la propriété privée ◆ **the question of electricity ~ gas for cooking** la question de l'électricité par rapport au gaz *or* de l'électricité comparée au gaz pour la cuisine

2 *(Sport)* contre ◆ **the England ~ Spain match** le match Angleterre-Espagne

3 *(in dispute, competition)* **it's management ~ workers** c'est la direction contre les ouvriers, la direction s'oppose aux ouvriers ◆ **the 1960 Nixon ~ Kennedy election** l'élection qui en 1960 a opposé Nixon à Kennedy

4 *(Jur)* **Jones ~ Smith** Jones contre Smith ◆ **Rex/Regina ~ Smith** *(in Brit)* le Roi/la Reine contre Smith *(formule utilisée pour un procès engagé par l'État contre un particulier)* ◆ **the People ~ Smith** *(in US)* l'État contre Smith

vertebra /'vɜːtɪbrə/ **N** (pl **vertebras** *or* **vertebrae** /'vɜːtɪbriː/) vertèbre *f*

vertebral /'vɜːtɪbrəl/ **ADJ** vertébral

vertebrate /'vɜːtɪbrət/ **ADJ, N** vertébré *m*

vertex /'vɜːteks/ **N** (pl **vertexes** *or* **vertices**) *(gen, Geom)* sommet *m* ; *(Anat)* vertex *m*

vertical /'vɜːtɪkəl/ **ADJ** *[surface, line, axis, cliff, stripes]* vertical ◆ **a ~ drop** un à-pic ◆ **a ~ power structure** une structure du pouvoir verticale **N** verticale *f* ◆ **out of** *or* **off the ~** décalé par rapport à *or* écarté de la verticale

COMP **vertical analysis** **N** *(Comm)* analyse *f* verticale

vertical integration **N** *(Econ)* intégration *f* verticale

vertical mobility **N** *(Sociol)* mobilité *f* verticale

vertical planning **N** planification *f* verticale

vertical take-off aircraft **N** avion *m* à décollage vertical

vertically /'vɜːtɪkəlɪ/ **ADV** *[hold, move, run, divide]* verticalement ; *[rise, descend, drop]* verticalement, à la verticale ◆ **~ challenged** *(gen hum)* de taille au-dessous de la moyenne ◆ **~ integrated** *(Econ)* à intégration verticale

vertices /'vɜːtɪsiːz/ **NPL** of **vertex**

vertigines /vɜː'tɪdʒɪˌniːz/ **NPL** of **vertigo**

vertiginous /vɜː'tɪdʒɪnəs/ **ADJ** *(frm)* vertigineux

vertigo /'vɜːtɪgəʊ/ **N** (pl **vertigoes** *or* **vertigines**) vertige *m* ◆ **to suffer from ~** avoir des vertiges

verve /vɜːv/ **N** verve *f*, brio *m*

very /'verɪ/ **ADV** 1 *(= extremely)* très ◆ **~ amusing** très amusant ◆ **to be ~ careful** faire très attention ◆ **I am ~ cold/hot** j'ai très froid/chaud ◆ **are you tired? – ~/not ~** êtes-vous fatigué ? – très/pas très ◆ **~ well written/made** très bien écrit/fait ◆ **I'm ~ sorry** je suis vraiment désolé ◆ **~ well, if you insist** très bien, si vous insistez ◆ **~ little** très peu ◆ **~ little milk** très peu de lait ◆ **it is not ~ likely** ce n'est pas très probable, c'est peu probable ◆ **I'm not ~ good at explaining myself** je ne sais pas toujours très bien me faire comprendre, j'ai un peu de mal à me faire comprendre ◆ **his accent is ~ French** il a un accent très français ◆ **Jane looks ~ pregnant** la grossesse de Jane paraît très avancée ◆ **the Very Reverend ...** *(Rel)* le Très Révérend ... ◆ **~ high frequency** *(Rad)* (ondes *fpl*) très haute fréquence *f* ◆ **~ high/low frequency** *(Elec)* très haute/basse fréquence *f*

2 *(= absolutely)* ◆ **(of the) ~ best quality** de toute première qualité ◆ **~ last/first** tout dernier/premier ◆ **she is the ~ cleverest in the class** elle est de loin la plus intelligente de la classe ◆ **give it to me tomorrow at the ~ latest** donnez-le-moi demain au plus tard *or* demain dernier délai ◆ **at midday at the ~ latest** à midi au plus tard ◆ **at the ~ most/least** tout au plus/moins ◆ **to be in the ~ best of health** être en excellente santé ◆ **they are the ~ best of friends** ils sont les meilleurs amis du monde

3 ◆ **~ much** beaucoup, bien ◆ **thank you ~ much** merci beaucoup ◆ **I liked it ~ much** je l'ai beaucoup aimé ◆ **he is ~ much better** il va beaucoup mieux ◆ **~ much bigger** beaucoup *or* bien plus grand ◆ **~ much respected** très respecté ◆ **he is ~ much the more intelligent of the two** il est de beaucoup *or* de loin le plus intelligent des deux ◆ **he doesn't work ~ much** il ne travaille pas beaucoup, il travaille peu ◆ **he is ~ much like his father** il tient beaucoup de son père, il ressemble beaucoup à son père ◆ **~ much so!** *(= emphatic "yes")* absolument !

4 *(for emphasis)* **the ~ same day** le jour même, ce jour-là ◆ **the ~ same hat** exactement le même chapeau ◆ **the ~ next day** le lendemain même, dès le lendemain ◆ **the ~ next shop we**

come to le prochain magasin ◆ **the ~ next person to do this was ...** la personne qui a fait cela tout de suite après était ... ◆ **as soon as I heard the news, I took the ~ next train** dès que j'ai entendu la nouvelle, j'ai sauté dans le premier train ◆ **the ~ latest technology** la toute dernière technologie ◆ **the ~ last page of the book** la toute dernière page du livre ; see also **next** ; → **own**

ADJ [1] *(= precise, exact)* même ◆ **that ~ day/moment** ce jour/cet instant même ◆ **on the ~ spot** à l'endroit même *or* précis ◆ **in this ~ house** dans cette maison même ◆ **his ~ words** ses propos mêmes ◆ **the ~ thing/man I need** tout à fait *or* justement la chose/l'homme qu'il me faut ◆ **the ~ thing!** *(= what I need)* c'est justement ce qu'il me faut ! ; *(of suggestion, solution)* c'est idéal ! ◆ **to catch sb in the ~ act (of stealing)** prendre qn en flagrant délit (de vol)

[2] *(= extreme)* tout ◆ **at the ~ end** *[of play, year]* tout à la fin ; *[of garden, road]* tout au bout ◆ **at the ~ back** tout au fond ◆ **to the ~ end** jusqu'au bout ◆ **in the ~ heart of France** au cœur même de la France

[3] *(= mere)* seul ◆ **the ~ word** le mot seul, rien que le mot ◆ **the ~ thought of ...** la seule pensée de ..., rien que de penser à ... ◆ **the ~ idea!** quelle idée alors !

[4] *(for emphasis)* ◆ **his ~ life was in danger** sa propre vie était en danger ◆ **democracy is the ~ basis of British politics** la démocratie est le fondement même de la politique en Grande-Bretagne ◆ **before my ~ eyes** sous mes propres yeux ◆ **you're the ~ person I wanted to see** c'est justement vous que je voulais voir

[5] *(liter)* **he is a ~ rascal** *or* **the veriest rascal** c'est un fieffé coquin

Very light /ˈvɪərɪlaɪt/ **N** *(Mil)* fusée *f* éclairante

Very pistol /ˈvɪərɪpɪstl/ **N** pistolet *m* lance-fusées

vesicle /ˈvesɪkl/ **N** vésicule *f*

vespers /ˈvespəz/ **N** vêpres *fpl*

vessel /ˈvesl/ **N** [1] *(Naut)* navire *m*, bâtiment *m* [2] *(Anat, Bot)* vaisseau *m* ; → **blood** [3] *(liter = receptacle)* récipient *m* ◆ **drinking ~** vaisseau † *m*

vest¹ /vest/ **N** [1] *(Brit = undergarment)* maillot *m* de corps ; (also **vest top**) débardeur *m* [2] *(US)* gilet *m*

COMP **vest pocket N** *(US)* poche *f* de gilet
vest-pocket ADJ *(US) [calculator etc]* de poche ; *(fig) (= tiny)* minuscule
vest top N → **noun 1**

⚠ In French, **veste** means 'jacket', not **vest**.

vest² /vest/ **VT** *(frm)* ◆ **to ~ sb with sth, to ~ sth in sb** investir qn de qch, assigner qch à qn ◆ **the authority ~ed in me** l'autorité dont je suis investi COMP **vested interest N** ◆ **to have a ~ed interest in** *(gen)* s'intéresser tout particulièrement à ; *(financially) [+ business, company]* être directement intéressé dans ; *[+ market, development of business]* être directement intéressé à ◆ **to have a ~ed interest in doing sth** avoir tout intérêt à faire qch ◆ **he has a ~ed interest in the play as his daughter is acting in it** il s'intéresse tout particulièrement à cette pièce car sa fille y joue ◆ **~ed interests** *(Comm, Fin, Jur)* droits *mpl* acquis

vestal virgin /ˌvestlˈvɜːdʒɪn/ **N** vestale *f*

vestibular /veˈstɪbjʊləʳ/ **ADJ** *(Anat)* vestibulaire

vestibule /ˈvestɪbjuːl/ **N** [1] *(= entrance) [of house, hotel]* vestibule *m*, hall *m* d'entrée ; *[of church]* vestibule *m* [2] *(Anat)* vestibule *m*

vestige /ˈvestɪdʒ/ **N** [1] *(= trace, remnant)* vestige *m* ◆ **~s of past civilizations** vestiges *mpl* de civilisations disparues ◆ **not a ~ of truth/commonsense** pas un grain de vérité/de bon sens ◆ **a ~ of hope** un reste d'espoir [2] *(Anat, Bio = organ)* organe *m* rudimentaire *or* atrophié ◆ **the ~ of a tail** une queue rudimentaire *or* atrophiée

vestigial /vesˈtɪdʒɪəl/ **ADJ** [1] *(frm = remaining) [traces]* résiduel ◆ **~ remains** vestiges *mpl* [2] *(Bio) [organ, limb]* vestigial

vesting /ˈvestɪŋ/ **N** *(Insurance)* acquisition *f* de droits

vestment /ˈvestmənt/ **N** *[of priest]* vêtement *m* sacerdotal ; *(= ceremonial robe)* habit *m* de cérémonie

vestry /ˈvestrɪ/ **N** [1] *(= part of church)* sacristie *f* [2] *(= meeting)* assemblée *f* paroissiale, conseil *m* paroissial

vesture /ˈvestʃəʳ/ **N** *(NonC: liter)* vêtements *mpl*

Vesuvius /vɪˈsuːvɪəs/ **N** le Vésuve

vet /vet/ **N** [1] abbrev of **veterinary surgeon, veterinarian**

[2] *(esp US *)* (abbrev of **veteran**) ancien combattant *m*

VT *(esp Brit) [+ text]* corriger, revoir ; *[+ figures, calculations, job applications]* vérifier ; *[+ papers]* contrôler ; *[+ report] (= check)* vérifier le contenu de ; *(= approve)* approuver ◆ **wage claims are ~ted by the union** les revendications salariales doivent d'abord recevoir l'approbation du syndicat ◆ **his wife ~s his contracts** sa femme vérifie *or* contrôle ses contrats ◆ **the purchases are ~ted by a committee** les achats doivent d'abord être approuvés par un comité ◆ **the director ~ted him for the job** le directeur a soigneusement examiné sa candidature avant de l'embaucher ◆ **we have ~ted him thoroughly** nous nous sommes renseignés de façon approfondie à son sujet ◆ **visa applications/applicants are carefully ~ted** les demandes/demandeurs de visa sont soigneusement filtré(e)s

vetch /vetʃ/ **N** vesce *f*

veteran /ˈvetərən/ **N** [1] *(gen)* vétéran *m* [2] *(Mil:* also **war veteran**) ancien combattant *m* **ADJ** *(= experienced)* chevronné, expérimenté ◆ **she is a ~ campaigner for women's rights** elle fait campagne depuis longtemps pour les droits de la femme ◆ **a ~ car** une voiture d'époque *(avant 1919)* ◆ **a ~ teacher/golfer** un vétéran de l'enseignement/du golf

COMP **Veterans Administration N** *(US)* ministère des anciens combattants
Veterans Day N *(US)* le onze novembre *(anniversaire de l'armistice)*

veterinarian /ˌvetərɪˈneərɪən/ **N** *(esp US)* vétérinaire *mf*

veterinary /ˈvetərɪnərɪ/ **ADJ** *[medicine, science, care, practice, hospital]* vétérinaire ; *[expert]* en médecine vétérinaire COMP **veterinary surgeon N** *(Brit)* vétérinaire *mf*

veto /ˈviːtəʊ/ LANGUAGE IN USE 12.2 **N** (pl **vetoes**) *(= act, decision)* veto *m* ◆ **the power of ~** le droit de veto ◆ **to use one's ~** exercer son droit de veto ◆ **to put a ~ on sth** mettre son veto à qch **VT** *(Pol etc, also fig)* mettre *or* opposer son veto à

vetting /ˈvetɪŋ/ **N** *[of text]* correction *f*, révision *f* ; *[of job application, figures]* vérification *f* ; *[of candidate]* enquête *f* approfondie ; *[of papers]* contrôle *m* ; → **positive, security**

vex /veks/ **VT** contrarier, fâcher

vexation /vekˈseɪʃən/ **N** *(NonC)* contrariété *f*, tracas *m*

vexatious /vekˈseɪʃəs/ **ADJ** *[thing]* contrariant, ennuyeux ; *[person]* tracassier, contrariant

vexed /vekst/ **ADJ** [1] *(= annoyed) [person, voice, frown, expression]* contrarié ◆ **~ with sb** fâché contre qn ◆ **to become** *or* **get ~** se fâcher [2] *(= difficult) [question, issue]* délicat, épineux

vexing /ˈveksɪŋ/ **ADJ** [1] *(= annoying) [thing]* contrariant, ennuyeux ; *[person]* tracassier, contrariant [2] *(= difficult) [problem]* délicat ; *[question, issue]* délicat, épineux

VG /viːˈdʒiː/ *(Scol etc)* (abbrev of **very good**) TB, très bien

VGA /ˌviːdʒiːˈeɪ/ **N** abbrev of **video graphics array** COMP **VGA card N** carte *f* VGA

vgc (abbrev of **very good condition**) tbe, très bon état

VHF /ˌviːeɪtʃˈef/ **N** (abbrev of **very high frequency**) VHF *f* ◆ **on ~** en VHF

VHS /ˌviːeɪtʃˈes/ **N** (abbrev of **video home system**) VHS *m*

VI (abbrev of **Virgin Islands**) → **virgin**

via /ˈvaɪə/ **PREP** [1] *(lit = by way of)* via, par ◆ **a ticket to Vienna ~ Frankfurt** un billet pour Vienne via Francfort ◆ **the journey takes nine hours ~ Ostend** le voyage prend neuf heures via Ostende *or* (si l'on passe) par Ostende ◆ **you should go ~ Paris** vous devriez passer par Paris ◆ **we went home ~ the pub** nous sommes passés par le pub *or* nous nous sommes arrêtés au pub avant de rentrer [2] *(fig = by way of)* par ◆ **his rent is paid to his landlord ~ an estate agent** il paie son loyer à son propriétaire par l'intermédiaire d'une agence immobilière [3] *(= by means of)* au moyen de ◆ **the launch was detected ~ a satellite** le lancement a été détecté au moyen d'un satellite ◆ **she works from home, ~ e-mail** elle travaille à domicile au moyen du courrier électronique

viability /ˌvaɪəˈbɪlɪtɪ/ **N** *[of company, business, product]* viabilité *f* ; *[of project, scheme]* viabilité *f*, chances *fpl* de réussite

viable /ˈvaɪəbl/ **ADJ** [1] *(= feasible) [alternative, option, solution, company, product]* viable ; *[project, method]* viable, qui a des chances de réussir ; *[future]* durable, solide ◆ **it's not a ~ proposition** ce n'est pas viable [2] *(Bio) [foetus]* viable

viaduct /ˈvaɪədʌkt/ **N** viaduc *m*

Viagra ® /vaɪˈægrə/ **N** Viagra ® *m*

vial /ˈvaɪəl/ **N** *(liter)* fiole *f* ; *(Pharm)* ampoule *f*

viands /ˈvaɪəndz/ **NPL** *(liter)* aliments *mpl*

viatical /vaɪˈætɪkəl/ **N** (also **viatical settlement**) escompte *m* de police d'assurance-vie

viaticum /vaɪˈætɪkəm/ **N** (pl **viaticums** *or* **viatica** /vaɪˈætɪkə/) viatique *m*

vibes * /vaɪbz/ **NPL** [1] (abbrev of **vibrations**) *(from band, singer)* atmosphère *f*, ambiance *f* ◆ **I get good ~ from her** *(between individuals)* elle me fait bonne impression ◆ **the ~ are wrong** ça ne gaze pas * [2] abbrev of **vibraphone**

vibrancy /ˈvaɪbrənsɪ/ **N** *[of person, language]* vivacité *f* ; *[of voice]* résonance *f* ; *[of city]* animation *f*, vie *f* ; *[of performance]* caractère *m* très vivant ; *[of economy, community]* dynamisme *m*, vitalité *f* ; *[of speech]* vigueur *f* ; *[of light, colours]* éclat *m*

vibrant /ˈvaɪbrənt/ **ADJ** [1] *(= lively) [person, language]* vivant, vif ; *[city]* vivant, animé ; *[performance]* vivant ; *[economy, community, personality]* dynamique ; *[culture]* plein de vitalité ; *[voice, tones]* vibrant *(with sth* de qch) ◆ **the street was ~ with activity** la rue débordait d'activité [2] *(= bright) [colour, red, green]* éclatant ; *[light]* vif

vibraphone /ˈvaɪbrəfəʊn/ **N** vibraphone *m*

vibrate /vaɪˈbreɪt/ **VI** *(= quiver)* vibrer *(with* de) ; *(= resound)* retentir *(with* de) ; *(fig)* frémir, vibrer *(with* de) **VT** faire vibrer

vibration /vaɪˈbreɪʃən/ **N** vibration *f*

vibrato /vɪˈbrɑːtəʊ/ *(Mus)* **N** vibrato *m* **ADV** avec vibrato

vibrator /vaɪˈbreɪtəʳ/ **N** [1] *(Elec)* vibrateur *m* [2] *(= massager, also sexual)* vibromasseur *m*

vibratory /ˈvaɪbrətərɪ/ **ADJ** vibratoire

viburnum /vaɪˈbɜːnəm/ N viorne *f*

vicar /ˈvɪkəʳ/ N (*in Church of England*) pasteur *m* (*de l'Église anglicane*) ◆ **good evening ~** bonsoir pasteur
COMP **vicar apostolic** N vicaire *m* apostolique
vicar general N (pl **vicars general**) grand vicaire *m*, vicaire *m* général
the Vicar of Christ N le vicaire de Jésus-Christ

vicarage /ˈvɪkərɪdʒ/ N presbytère *m* (*de l'Église anglicane*)

vicarious /vɪˈkeərɪəs/ ADJ 1 (*= indirect*) [*experience*] vécu par procuration ◆ **to get ~ satisfaction/pleasure from** *or* **out of sth** (re)tirer de la satisfaction/du plaisir de qch par procuration 2 (*frm = for another*) [*liability, responsibility*] assumé pour quelqu'un d'autre ◆ **the ~ suffering of Christ** les souffrances que le Christ subit pour autrui 3 (*frm = delegated*) délégué ◆ **to give ~ authority to sb** déléguer son autorité à qn

vicariously /vɪˈkeərɪəslɪ/ ADV 1 [*live, enjoy, experience*] par procuration 2 (*frm*) [*authorize*] par délégation, par procuration

vice¹ /vaɪs/ N 1 (*NonC = depravity, corruption*) vice *m* 2 (*= evil characteristic*) vice *m* ; (*less strong*) défaut *m*
COMP **vice den** N (*= gambling den*) maison *f* de jeux ; (*= brothel*) maison *f* close
vice girl N prostituée *f*
vice ring N réseau *m* de prostitution
Vice Squad N (*Police*) brigade *f* des mœurs

vice², vise (*US*) /vaɪs/ N (*= gripping device*) étau *m* ; → **grip**

vice³ /vaɪs/ PREP (*frm*) à la place de

vice- /vaɪs/ PREF vice-
COMP **vice-admiral** N vice-amiral *m* d'escadre
vice-captain N (*Sport*) capitaine *m* adjoint
vice-chairman N (pl **vice-chairmen**) vice-président(e) *m(f)*
vice-chairmanship N vice-présidence *f*
vice-chancellor N (*Univ*) ≈ président(e) *m(f)* d'université ; (*Jur*) vice-chancelier *m*
vice-consul N vice-consul *m*
vice-premier N Premier ministre *m* adjoint
vice-presidency N vice-présidence *f*
vice-president N vice-président(e) *m(f)* ◆ **Vice-President Smith** (*Pol*) le vice-président Smith
vice-presidential ADJ (*Pol*) vice-présidentiel
vice-presidential candidate N (*Pol*) candidat(e) *m(f)* à la vice-présidence
vice-principal N (*Scol: gen*) directeur *m*, -trice *f* adjoint(e) ; [*of lycée*] censeur *m* ; [*of collège*] principal(e) *m(f)* adjoint(e)
vice-regal ADJ de *or* du vice-roi

viceroy /ˈvaɪsrɔɪ/ N vice-roi *m*

vice versa /ˈvaɪsɪˈvɜːsə/ ADV ◆ **and/or ~** et/ou vice versa ◆ **rather than ~** plutôt que l'inverse

vicinity /vɪˈsɪnɪtɪ/ N (*= nearby area*) voisinage *m*, environs *mpl* ; (*= closeness*) proximité *f* ◆ **in the ~** dans les environs, à proximité ◆ **in the ~ of the town** aux alentours de la ville, à proximité de la ville ◆ **in our ~** dans le voisinage, près de chez nous ◆ **it's something in the ~ of £100** c'est aux alentours de 100 livres ◆ **in the immediate ~** dans les environs immédiats ◆ **the immediate ~ of the town** les abords *mpl* de la ville

vicious /ˈvɪʃəs/ ADJ [*person, attack, temper*] brutal ; [*animal*] méchant ; [*look*] haineux, méchant ; [*criticism, remark*] acerbe, méchant ; [*campaign*] virulent ◆ **to have a ~ tongue** être mauvaise langue, avoir une langue de vipère
COMP **vicious circle** N cercle *m* vicieux ◆ **to be caught in a ~ circle** être pris dans un cercle vicieux
vicious cycle N cycle *m* infernal

⚠ **vicious** is only translated by **vicieux** in the expression 'vicious circle'.

viciously /ˈvɪʃəslɪ/ ADV (*= violently*) [*attack, stab*] brutalement ; [*beat, strike*] brutalement, violemment ; (*= nastily*) [*say, think, criticize*] méchamment

⚠ **vicieusement** means 'cunningly', not **viciously**.

viciousness /ˈvɪʃəsnɪs/ N [*of person, attack, temper*] brutalité *f* ; [*of criticism, remark, campaign*] méchanceté *f* ; [*of dog*] agressivité *f* ◆ **everyone feared the ~ of his tongue** tout le monde craignait sa langue acérée *or* acerbe

vicissitude /vɪˈsɪsɪtjuːd/ N vicissitude *f*

victim /ˈvɪktɪm/ N victime *f* ◆ **the accident/bomb ~s** les victimes *fpl* de l'accident/de l'explosion ◆ **many of the Nazi ~s, many of the ~s of the Nazis** de nombreuses victimes des Nazis ◆ **to be the** *or* **a ~ of ...** être victime de ... ◆ **to fall (a) ~ to ...** devenir la victime de ... ; (*fig*) [*+ sb's charms etc*] succomber à ... COMP **Victim Support** N (*Brit*) *organisme d'aide aux victimes de crimes*

victimhood /ˈvɪktɪmhʊd/ N statut *m* de victime

victimization /ˌvɪktɪmaɪˈzeɪʃən/ N (*= unfair treatment*) brimades *fpl* ; (*= persecution*) (actes *mpl* de) persécution *f* ◆ **the dismissed worker alleged ~** l'ouvrier licencié affirmait être victime de représailles ◆ **to minimize the risk of criminal ~** pour minimiser le risque d'être victime d'un acte criminel

victimize /ˈvɪktɪmaɪz/ VT (*= treat unfairly*) brimer ; (*= persecute*) persécuter ; (*after industrial action*) exercer des représailles sur ◆ **to be ~d** être victime de persécutions *or* de brimades ◆ **they see themselves as being ~d** ils se considèrent comme des victimes

victimless /ˈvɪktɪmlɪs/ ADJ ◆ **~ crime** délit *m* sans victimes

victor /ˈvɪktəʳ/ N vainqueur *m* ◆ **to emerge the ~ over sb** remporter la victoire sur qn

Victoria /vɪkˈtɔːrɪə/ N 1 (*= name*) Victoria *f* ; (*= Australian state*) Victoria *m* ◆ **in ~** dans le Victoria ◆ **Lake ~** le lac Victoria 2 (*= carriage*) **victoria** victoria *f*
COMP **Victoria Cross** N (*Brit Mil: abbr VC*) Croix *f* de Victoria (*la plus haute décoration militaire*)
(the) Victoria Falls NPL les chutes *fpl* Victoria

Victorian /vɪkˈtɔːrɪən/ N victorien(ne) *m(f)*
ADJ (*= 19th century*) [*house, furniture*] victorien, de l'époque victorienne ; (*= strict, puritan*) [*person, values*] victorien ; [*attitude*] d'un puritanisme victorien

VICTORIAN

L'adjectif « victorien » qualifie la Grande-Bretagne sous le règne de la reine Victoria (1837-1901).
Les attitudes ou qualités dites victoriennes sont celles considérées comme caractéristiques de cette époque : attachement à la respectabilité sociale, moralité stricte et répressive, absence d'humour, bigoterie et hypocrisie. Les valeurs victoriennes sont parfois invoquées par les gens qui regrettent l'évolution de la société contemporaine et prônent un retour au dépassement de soi, à la décence, au respect de l'autorité et à l'importance de la famille.

Victoriana /vɪkˌtɔːrɪˈɑːnə/ N (*NonC*) objets *mpl* victoriens, antiquités *fpl* victoriennes

victorious /vɪkˈtɔːrɪəs/ ADJ [*person, army, team, campaign*] victorieux ; [*shout*] de victoire

victoriously /vɪkˈtɔːrɪəslɪ/ ADV victorieusement

victory /ˈvɪktərɪ/ N victoire *f* ◆ **to gain** *or* **win a ~ over ...** remporter une victoire sur ... ◆ **he led the party to ~** il a mené le parti à la victoire ; → **winged**

victual /ˈvɪtl/ VT approvisionner, ravitailler VI s'approvisionner, se ravitailler NPL **victuals** † victuailles *fpl*, vivres *mpl*

victualler /ˈvɪtləʳ/ N fournisseur *m* (de provisions) ; → **license**

vicuña /vaɪˈkjuːnə/ N (*= animal, wool*) vigogne *f*

vid* /vɪd/ N (abbrev of **video**) vidéo *f* (*film*)

vide /ˈvɪdeɪ/ IMPERS VB (*frm*) voir, cf

videlicet /vɪˈdiːlɪset/ ADV (*frm*) c'est-à-dire, à savoir

video /ˈvɪdɪəʊ/ N 1 (*NonC*) vidéo *f* ; (*= machine*) magnétoscope *m* ; (*= cassette*) cassette *f* vidéo *inv*, vidéocassette *f* ; (*= film*) vidéo *f* ◆ **I've got it on ~** je l'ai en vidéo ◆ **get a ~ for tonight** loue une (cassette) vidéo pour ce soir ◆ **to make a ~ of sth, to record sth on ~** (*with video recorder*) enregistrer qch au magnétoscope ; (*with camcorder*) faire une vidéo de qch
2 (*US = television*) télévision *f*, télé* *f*
VT (*from TV*) enregistrer (sur magnétoscope) ; (*with camcorder*) faire une vidéo de, filmer
COMP (*= on video*) [*film, entertainment*] en vidéo ; [*facilities*] vidéo *inv* ; (*US*) (*= on television*) [*film etc*] télévisé
video arcade N salle *f* de jeux vidéo
video art N art *m* vidéo *inv*
video call N appel *m* (en) visio
video calling N visiophonie *f*
video camera N caméra *f* vidéo *inv*
video cassette N vidéocassette *f*, cassette *f* vidéo
video cassette recorder N magnétoscope *m*
video cassette recording N enregistrement *m* en vidéo *or* sur magnétoscope
video clip N clip *m* vidéo *inv*
video club N vidéoclub *m*
video conference N visioconférence *f*, vidéoconférence *f*
video conferencing N (système *m* de) visioconférence *f or* vidéoconférence *f*
video diary N (*TV*) vidéo *f* amateur (*qui passe à la télévision*)
video disk N vidéodisque *m*
video disk player N vidéolecteur *m*, lecteur *m* de vidéodisques
video film N film *m* vidéo *inv*
video frequency N vidéofréquence *f*
video game N jeu *m* vidéo *inv*
video library N vidéothèque *f*
video nasty* N (cassette *f*) vidéo *f* à caractère violent (*or* pornographique)
video piracy N piratage *m* de vidéocassettes
video player N magnétoscope *m*
video recorder N ⇒ **video cassette recorder**
video recording N ⇒ **video cassette recording**
video rental N location *f* de vidéocassettes ADJ [*shop, store*] de location de vidéocassettes ◆ **the ~ rental business** la location de vidéocassettes
video screen N écran *m* vidéo *inv*
video shop N vidéoclub *m*
video surveillance N vidéosurveillance *f*
video tape N bande *f* vidéo *inv* ; (*= cassette*) vidéocassette *f*
video tape recorder N ⇒ **video cassette recorder**
video tape recording N ⇒ **video cassette recording**
video wall N mur *m* d'écrans (vidéo)

videofit /ˈvɪdɪəʊfɪt/ N portrait *m* robot (*réalisé par infographie*)

videophone /ˈvɪdɪəʊfəʊn/ N visiophone *m*

videotape /ˈvɪdɪəʊteɪp/ VT ⇒ **video VT**

Videotex ® /ˈvɪdɪəʊteks/ N vidéotex ® *m*

videotext /ˈvɪdɪəʊtekst/ N vidéotex ® *m*

vie /vaɪ/ VI rivaliser ◆ **to ~ with sb for sth** rivaliser avec qn pour (obtenir) qch, disputer qch à qn ◆ to ~ **with sb in doing sth** rivaliser avec qn pour faire qch ◆ **they ~d with each other in their work** ils travaillaient à qui mieux mieux

Vienna /vɪ'enə/ N Vienne
COMP *(gen)* viennois, de Vienne
Vienna roll N *(Culin)* pain *m* viennois

Viennese /ˌvɪə'niːz/ ADJ viennois N *(pl inv)* Viennois(e) *m(f)*

Vietcong, Viet Cong /ˌvjet'kɒŋ/ N *(= group)* Vietcong *or* Viêt-cong *m* ; *(= individual: pl inv)* Vietcong *or* Viêt-cong *m* ADJ vietcong *or* viêt-cong *inv*

Vietnam, Viet Nam /'vjet'næm/ N Vietnam *or* Viêt-nam *m* ◆ **North/South** ~ Vietnam *or* Viêt-nam du Nord/du Sud ◆ **the ~ war** la guerre du Vietnam *or* Viêt-nam

Vietnamese /ˌvjetnə'miːz/ ADJ vietnamien ◆ **North/South** ~ nord-/sud-vietnamien N 1 *(pl inv)* Vietnamien(ne) *m(f)* ◆ **North/South** ~ Nord-/Sud-Vietnamien(ne) *m(f)* 2 *(= language)* vietnamien *m* NPL **the Vietnamese** les Vietnamiens *mpl*

view /vjuː/ LANGUAGE IN USE 6.2

N 1 *(= ability to see)* vue *f* ◆ **it blocks the ~** ça bouche la vue, on ne peut pas voir ◆ **he has a good ~ of it from his window** de sa fenêtre, il le voit bien ◆ **hidden from ~** caché aux regards ◆ **to keep sth out of ~** cacher qch (aux regards) ◆ **exposed to ~** exposé aux regards ◆ **it is lost to ~** on ne le voit plus ◆ **to come into ~** apparaître

◆ **in + view** *(= in sight)* ◆ **I came in ~ of the lake** je suis arrivé en vue du lac ◆ **the cameraman had a job keeping the plane in ~** le caméraman avait du mal à ne pas perdre l'avion de vue ◆ **make sure your hands are not in ~** assurez-vous qu'on ne voit pas vos mains ◆ **in full ~ of thousands of people** devant des milliers de gens, sous les yeux de milliers de gens ◆ **in full ~ of the house** devant la maison

◆ **on view** ◆ **the pictures are on ~** les tableaux sont exposés ◆ **the house will be on ~ tomorrow** on pourra visiter la maison demain ◆ **to put sth on ~** exposer qch

◆ **within view** ◆ **the house is within ~ of the sea** de la maison, on voit la mer ◆ **all the people within ~** tous ceux qu'on pouvait voir

2 *(= sight, prospect)* vue *f*, panorama *m* ◆ **there is a wonderful ~ from here** d'ici la vue *or* le panorama est magnifique ◆ **the ~ from the top** la vue *or* le panorama d'en haut ◆ **a room with a sea ~** *or* **a ~ of the sea** une chambre avec vue sur la mer ◆ **a good ~ of the sea** une belle vue de la mer ◆ **a ~ over the town** une vue générale de la ville ◆ **a back/front ~ of the house** la maison vue de derrière/devant ◆ **this is a side ~** c'est une vue latérale ◆ **I got a side ~ of the church** j'ai vu l'église de côté ◆ **it will give you a better ~** vous verrez mieux comme ça

3 *(= photo etc)* vue *f*, photo *f* ◆ **50 ~s of Paris** 50 vues *or* photos de Paris ◆ **I want to take a ~ of the palace** je veux photographier le palais

4 *(= opinion)* opinion *f* ◆ **her ~s on politics/education** ses opinions politiques/sur l'éducation ◆ **an exchange of ~s** un échange de vues *or* d'opinions ◆ **in my ~** à mon avis ◆ **that is my ~** voilà mon opinion *or* mon avis là-dessus ◆ **my personal ~ is that he ...** à mon avis, il ..., personnellement, je pense qu'il ... ◆ **it's just a personal ~** ce n'est qu'une opinion personnelle ◆ **the Government ~ is that one must ...** selon le gouvernement *or* dans l'optique gouvernementale, on doit ... ◆ **the generally accepted ~ is that he ...** selon l'opinion généralement répandue, il ... ◆ **each person has a different ~ of democracy** chacun comprend la démocratie à sa façon ◆ **one's ~ of old age changes** les idées que l'on se fait de la vieillesse évoluent ◆ **I cannot accept this ~** je trouve cette opinion *or* cette façon de voir les choses inacceptable ◆ **I've changed my ~ on this** j'ai changé d'avis là-dessus ◆ **give reasons for your ~s** *(in exam question)* justifiez votre réponse ◆ **I have no strong ~s on that** je n'ai pas d'opinion bien arrêtée *or* précise là-dessus ◆ **to hold ~s on sth** avoir un avis *or* une opinion sur qch ◆ **to hold** *or* **take the ~ that ...** estimer que ..., considérer que ... ◆ **we don't take that ~** nous avons une opinion différente là-dessus ◆ **I take a similar ~** je partage cet avis ◆ **he takes a gloomy/optimistic ~ of society** il a une image pessimiste/optimiste de la société ◆ **to take a dim** *or* **poor ~ of sth** avoir une bien mauvaise opinion de qch ; → **point**

5 *(= way of looking at sth)* vue *f* ◆ **an idealistic ~ of the world** une vue *or* une vision idéaliste du monde ◆ **a general** *or* **an overall ~ of the problem** une vue d'ensemble *or* générale du problème ◆ **a clear ~ of the facts** une idée claire des faits

6 *(set expressions)*

◆ **in view** *(expressing intention)* ◆ **with this (aim or object) in ~** dans ce but, à cette fin ◆ **what end has he in ~?** quel est son but ? ◆ **he has in ~ the purchase of the house** il envisage d'acheter la maison ◆ **I don't teach only with the exams in ~** je ne pense pas uniquement aux examens quand je fais mes cours ◆ **he has the holiday in ~ when he says ...** il pense aux vacances quand il dit ...

◆ **in view of** *(= considering)* ◆ **in ~ of his refusal** étant donné son refus, vu son refus ◆ **in ~ of this** ceci étant ◆ **in ~ of the fact that ...** étant donné que ..., vu que ...

◆ **with a view to, with the view of** en vue de ◆ **negotiations with a ~ to a permanent solution** des négociations en vue d'une solution permanente ◆ **with the ~ of selecting one solution** en vue de sélectionner une seule solution

VT 1 *(= look at, see)* voir ◆ **London ~ed from the air** Londres vu d'avion

2 *(= inspect, examine)* examiner, inspecter ; *[+ slides, microfiches]* visionner ; *[+ object for sale]* inspecter ; *[+ castle]* visiter ; *(in house-buying) [+ house, flat]* visiter

3 *(TV)* regarder, visionner ◆ **we have ~ed a video recording of the incident** nous avons regardé *or* visionné un enregistrement vidéo de l'incident

4 *(= think of, understand)* considérer, envisager ◆ **to ~ sb/sth as ...** considérer qn/qch comme ... ◆ **it can be ~ed in many different ways** on peut l'envisager *or* l'examiner sous plusieurs angles ◆ **how do you ~ that?** qu'est-ce que vous en pensez ?, quelle est votre opinion là-dessus ? ◆ **he ~s it very objectively** il l'envisage de façon très objective ◆ **the management ~ed the scheme favourably** la direction a été favorable au projet ◆ **they ~ the future with alarm** ils envisagent l'avenir avec inquiétude

VI *(TV)* regarder la télévision

Viewdata ® /'vjuːdeɪtə/ N ≈ minitel ® *m*

viewer /'vjuːəʳ/ N 1 *(TV)* téléspectateur *m*, -trice *f* 2 *(for slides)* visionneuse *f* 3 ⇒ **viewfinder**

viewership /'vjuːəʃɪp/ N *(US TV)* ◆ **to score a good** *or* **a wide ~** obtenir un bon indice d'écoute

viewfinder /'vjuːfaɪndəʳ/ N *(Phot)* viseur *m*

viewing /'vjuːɪŋ/ N 1 *(TV)* visionnage *m* ◆ **there's no good ~ tonight** il n'y a rien de bon à la télévision ce soir ◆ **your ~ for the weekend** vos programmes du week-end ◆ **tennis makes excellent ~** le tennis est un sport qui passe très bien à la télévision *or* qui est très télégénique 2 *(in house-buying)* ◆ **"early viewing essential"** "à visiter aussi tôt que possible" 3 *(= watching)* observation *f*
COMP *(Astron etc) [conditions]* d'observation ; *(TV) [patterns]* d'écoute ; *[habits]* des téléspectateurs
viewing audience N *(TV)* téléspectateurs *mpl*
viewing figures NPL *(TV)* indices *mpl* d'audience
viewing gallery N *(in building)* galerie *f*
viewing public N *(TV)* téléspectateurs *mpl*
viewing time N *(TV)* heure *f* d'écoute ◆ **at peak** *or* **prime ~ time** aux heures de grande écoute

viewphone /'vjuːfəʊn/ N visiophone *m*

viewpoint /'vjuːpɔɪnt/ N *(lit, fig)* point *m* de vue

vigil /'vɪdʒɪl/ N *(gen)* veille *f* ; *(by sickbed, corpse)* veillée *f* ; *(Rel)* vigile *f* ; *(Pol)* manifestation *f* silencieuse ◆ **to keep ~ over sb** veiller qn ◆ **a long ~** une longue veille, de longues heures sans sommeil ◆ **to hold a ~** *(Pol)* manifester en silence

vigilance /'vɪdʒɪləns/ N vigilance *f*

vigilant /'vɪdʒɪlənt/ ADJ *[person]* vigilant ◆ **to remain ~** rester vigilant ◆ **to escape sb's ~ eye** échapper à l'œil vigilant de qn ◆ **to keep a ~ eye on sb/sth** rester vigilant en ce qui concerne qn/qch

vigilante /ˌvɪdʒɪ'læntɪ/ N membre *m* d'un groupe d'autodéfense ◆ ~ **group** groupe *m* d'autodéfense *or* de légitime défense

vigilantism /ˌvɪdʒɪ'læntɪzəm/ N *(pej)* attitude *et méthodes caractéristiques des groupes d'autodéfense*

vigilantly /'vɪdʒɪləntlɪ/ ADV avec vigilance, attentivement

vignette /vɪ'njet/ N *(in books)* vignette *f* ; *(Art, Phot)* portrait *m* en buste dégradé ; *(= character sketch)* esquisse *f* de caractère

vigor /'vɪgəʳ/ N *(US)* ⇒ **vigour**

vigorous /'vɪgərəs/ ADJ *[exercise, defence, denial, debate, campaign, opponent, advocate]* énergique ; *[person, opposition, growth]* vigoureux

vigorously /'vɪgərəslɪ/ ADV *[nod, shake hands, defend, oppose, protest]* énergiquement ; *[exercise, shake, beat, deny]* vigoureusement ◆ **to campaign ~** faire une campagne énergique ◆ **boil the beans ~ for twenty minutes** faites bouillir les haricots à feu vif pendant vingt minutes

vigour, vigor *(US)* /'vɪgəʳ/ N *(= physical or mental strength)* vigueur *f*, énergie *f* ; *(= health)* vigueur *f*, vitalité *f* ; *(sexual)* vigueur *f*

Viking /'vaɪkɪŋ/ ADJ *[art, customs etc]* viking ◆ ~ **ship** drakkar *m* N Viking *mf*

vile /vaɪl/ ADJ 1 *(= base, evil) [action, traitor, crime, conditions, language]* infâme, ignoble 2 *(= unpleasant) [person]* exécrable ; *[food, drink, play]* exécrable, abominable ; *[smell, taste]* abominable, infect ◆ **it tastes ~** c'est infect ◆ **what ~ weather!** quel temps infect *or* abominable ! ◆ **to be in a ~ temper** *or* **mood** être d'une humeur massacrante

vilely /'vaɪllɪ/ ADV 1 *(= basely, evilly) [treat, exploit, seduce]* de façon ignoble ; *[swear]* de façon odieuse ◆ ~ **offensive** d'une grossièreté ignoble 2 *(= unpleasantly)* ◆ ~ **coloured** aux couleurs exécrables

vileness /'vaɪlnɪs/ N vilenie *f*, bassesse *f*

vilification /ˌvɪlɪfɪ'keɪʃən/ N diffamation *f*

vilify /'vɪlɪfaɪ/ VT diffamer

villa /'vɪlə/ N *(in town)* pavillon *m (de banlieue)* ; *(in country)* maison *f* de campagne ; *(by sea)* villa *f*

village /'vɪlɪdʒ/ N village *m*
COMP *[well]* du village
village green N pré *m* communal
village hall N *(Brit)* salle *f* des fêtes
village idiot N idiot *m* du village
village school N école *f* de *or* du village, école *f* communale

villager /'vɪlɪdʒəʳ/ N villageois(e) *m(f)*

villain /ˈvɪlən/ **N** *(= scoundrel)* scélérat *m*, vaurien *m* ; *(in drama, novel)* traître(sse) *m(f)* ; *(* = rascal)* coquin(e) *m(f)* ; *(* = criminal)* bandit *m* ◆ **he's the ~ (of the piece)** c'est lui le coupable

villainous /ˈvɪlənəs/ **ADJ** 1 *(= evil) [person, character, action, conduct]* ignoble, infâme ◆ **~ deed** infamie *f* 2 *(* = unpleasant) [coffee, weather]* abominable, infect

villainously /ˈvɪlənəslɪ/ **ADV** d'une manière ignoble

villainy /ˈvɪlənɪ/ **N** infamie *f*, bassesse *f*

...ville‡ /vɪl/ **N, ADJ** *(in compounds)* ◆ **squaresville** les ringards‡ ◆ **it's dullsville** on s'ennuie vachement‡

villein /ˈvɪlɪn/ **N** *(Hist)* vilain(e) *m(f)*, serf *m*, serve *f*

villus /ˈvɪləs/ **N** (pl **villi** /ˈvɪlaɪ/) villosité *f*

vim* /vɪm/ **N** *(NonC)* énergie *f*, entrain *m* ◆ **full of ~** plein d'entrain

vinaigrette /ˌvɪneɪˈgret/ **N** vinaigrette *f*

Vincent /ˈvɪnsənt/ **N** Vincent *m*

vindaloo /ˌvɪndəˈluː/ **N** *type de curry très épicé*

vindicate /ˈvɪndɪkeɪt/ **VT** 1 *[+ person] (= prove innocent) (gen)* donner raison à ; *(Jur)* innocenter ◆ **this ~d him** *(= proved him right)* cela a prouvé qu'il avait eu raison 2 *[+ opinion, action, decision]* justifier ; *[+ rights]* faire valoir

vindication /ˌvɪndɪˈkeɪʃən/ **N** justification *f*, défense *f* ◆ **in ~ of** en justification de, pour justifier

vindictive /vɪnˈdɪktɪv/ **ADJ** vindicatif *(towards sb* à l'égard de qn)

vindictively /vɪnˈdɪktɪvlɪ/ **ADV** par vengeance

vindictiveness /vɪnˈdɪktɪvnɪs/ **N** caractère *m* vindicatif

vine /vaɪn/ **N** *(producing grapes)* vigne *f* ; *(= climbing plant)* plante *f* grimpante *or* rampante ◆ **to wither** *or* **die on the ~** avorter *(fig)*
COMP *[leaf, cutting]* de vigne
vine grower **N** viticulteur *m*, -trice *f*, vigneron(ne) *m(f)*
vine-growing **N** viticulture *f* ◆ **~-growing district** région *f* viticole
vine harvest **N** vendange(s) *f(pl)*

vinegar /ˈvɪnɪgəʳ/ **N** vinaigre *m* ; → **cider, oil**

vinegary /ˈvɪnɪgərɪ/ **ADJ** 1 *(= like vinegar) [wine]* qui a un goût de vinaigre ; *[smell, taste]* de vinaigre, vinaigré ; *[food]* acide ◆ **the sauce tastes too ~** la sauce est trop vinaigrée 2 *(= sour-tempered) [person]* acariâtre ; *[remark]* acide, acerbe

vinery /ˈvaɪnərɪ/ **N** *(= hothouse)* serre *f* où l'on cultive la vigne ; *(= vineyard)* vignoble *m*

vineyard /ˈvɪnjəd/ **N** vignoble *m*

viniculture /ˈvɪnɪkʌltʃəʳ/ **N** viticulture *f*

vino* /ˈviːnəʊ/ **N** pinard‡ *m*, vin *m*

vinous /ˈvaɪnəs/ **ADJ** vineux

vintage /ˈvɪntɪdʒ/ **N** 1 *[of wine] (= season)* vendanges *fpl* ; *(= year)* année *f*, millésime *m* ; *(= harvesting)* vendange(s) *f(pl)*, récolte *f* ◆ **what ~ is this wine?** ce vin est de quelle année ? ◆ **1966 was a good ~** 1966 était une bonne année *or* un bon millésime ◆ **the 1972 ~** le vin de 1972 2 *(= era)* époque *f* ◆ **he wanted to meet people of his own ~** il voulait rencontrer des gens de sa génération **ADJ** 1 *(= choice) [champagne, port]* millésimé ; → **comp** 2 *(= classic) [comedy, drama]* classique ◆ **the book is ~ Grisham** ce livre est du Grisham du meilleur cru 3 *(* = very old) [object]* très ancien, antique
COMP **vintage car** **N** voiture *f* d'époque *(construite entre 1919 et 1930)*
vintage wine **N** grand vin *m*, vin *m* de grand cru
vintage year **N** *(gen, for wine)* ◆ **a ~ year for Burgundy** une bonne année pour le bourgogne

vintner /ˈvɪntnəʳ/ **N** *(= merchant)* négociant *m* en vins ; *(= wine-maker)* viticulteur *m*, -trice *f*, vigneron(ne) *m(f)*

vinyl /ˈvaɪnɪl/ **N** vinyle *m* **COMP** *[tiles]* de *or* en vinyle ; *[paint]* vinylique

viol /ˈvaɪəl/ **N** viole *f* ◆ **~ player** violiste *mf*

viola¹ /vɪˈəʊlə/ **N** *(Mus)* alto *m*
COMP **viola da gamba** **N** viole *f* de gambe
viola d'amore **N** viole *f* d'amour
viola player **N** altiste *mf*

viola² /ˈvaɪəʊlə/ **N** *(= flower)* pensée *f* ; *(= genus)* violacée *f*

violate /ˈvaɪəleɪt/ **VT** 1 *(= disobey) [+ law, rule, agreement]* violer, enfreindre ; *[+ the Commandments]* violer, transgresser 2 *(= show disrespect for) [+ principles, honour]* bafouer ; *[+ human rights, civil rights]* violer ; *[+ public order, property, frontier]* ne pas respecter 3 *(= disturb) [+ peace]* troubler, perturber ◆ **to ~ sb's privacy** *(in room etc)* déranger le repos de qn ; *[detective, reporter etc] (in private life)* déranger qn dans sa vie privée 4 *(= desecrate) [+ place]* violer, profaner ; *[+ tomb]* violer 5 *(† or liter = rape)* violer, violenter †

violation /ˌvaɪəˈleɪʃən/ **N** 1 *(= failure to respect) [of human rights, law, agreement, sanctions, grave]* violation *f* ◆ **in ~ of sth** en violation de qch ◆ **he was in ~ of his contract** il contrevenait aux clauses de son contrat 2 *(US = minor offence)* infraction *f* ; *(on parking meter)* dépassement *m* ◆ **a minor traffic ~** une infraction mineure au code de la route 3 *(† or liter = rape)* viol *m*

violator /ˈvaɪəleɪtəʳ/ **N** 1 *(gen)* violateur *m* 2 *(esp US Jur = offender)* contrevenant *m* ◆ **~s will be prosecuted** toute violation fera l'objet de poursuites

violence /ˈvaɪələns/ **N** violence *f* ◆ **by ~** par la violence ◆ **a climate of ~** un climat de violence ◆ **we are witnessing an escalation of ~** nous assistons à une escalade de la violence ◆ **~ erupted when ..., there was an outbreak of ~ when ...** de violents incidents *mpl* ont éclaté quand ... ◆ **racial ~** violence *f* raciste ◆ **all the ~ on the screen today** toute la violence *or* toutes les scènes de violence à l'écran aujourd'hui ◆ **terrorist ~** actes *mpl* de violence terroristes ◆ **police ~** violence *f* policière ◆ **act of ~** acte *m* de violence ◆ **crime of ~** *(Jur)* voie *f* de fait ◆ **robbery with ~** *(Jur)* vol *m* avec coups et blessures ◆ **to do ~ to sb/sth** faire violence à qn/qch

violent /ˈvaɪələnt/ **ADJ** *(gen)* violent ; *[scenes]* de violence ; *[pain]* vif, aigu (-guë *f*) ; *[dislike]* vif ; *[indigestion]* fort ; *[halt, change]* brutal ; *[colour, red]* criard ◆ **to be ~ with sb** se montrer violent avec qn, user de violence avec qn ◆ **to get** *or* **turn ~** *[demonstration]* tourner à la violence ; *[person]* devenir violent ◆ **a ~ attack** une violente attaque ◆ **to die a ~ death** mourir de mort violente ◆ **to meet a ~ end** connaître une fin brutale ◆ **to have a ~ temper** être sujet à des colères violentes ◆ **to be in a ~ temper** être dans une colère noire *or* dans une rage folle

violently /ˈvaɪələntlɪ/ **ADV** *[attack, criticize, tremble]* violemment ; *[react]* violemment, avec violence ; *[act]* de façon violente ; *[say]* avec violence, sur un ton très violent ; *[swerve, brake]* brusquement ; *[change]* brutalement ◆ **~ opposed to sth** violemment opposé à qch ◆ **~ anti-communist** violemment anticommuniste ◆ **to behave ~** se montrer violent ◆ **to fall ~ in love with sb** tomber follement *or* éperdument amoureux de qn ◆ **to disagree ~** être en profond désaccord ◆ **to die ~** mourir de mort violente ◆ **~ angry** dans une violente colère *or* une colère noire ◆ **to be ~ ill** *or* **sick** être pris de violentes nausées

violet /ˈvaɪəlɪt/ **N** *(= plant)* violette *f* ; *(= colour)* violet *m* **ADJ** violet

violin /ˌvaɪəˈlɪn/ **N** violon *m* ; → **first**
COMP *[sonata, concerto]* pour violon
violin case **N** étui *m* à violon
violin player **N** violoniste *mf*

violinist /ˌvaɪəˈlɪnɪst/ **N** violoniste *mf*

violist /vɪˈəʊlɪst/ **N** *(US)* altiste *mf*

violoncellist /ˌvaɪələnˈtʃelɪst/ **N** violoncelliste *mf*

violoncello /ˌvaɪələnˈtʃeləʊ/ **N** violoncelle *m*

VIP /ˌviːaɪˈpiː/ (abbrev of **very important person**) **N** VIP* *m inv*, personnalité *f* (de marque)
COMP *[visitor]* de marque
VIP lounge **N** *(in airport)* salon *m*
VIP treatment **N** ◆ **to give sb/get the ~ treatment** traiter qn/être traité comme un VIP* *or* une personnalité de marque

viper /ˈvaɪpəʳ/ **N** *(= snake, malicious person)* vipère *f*

viperish /ˈvaɪpərɪʃ/ **ADJ** de vipère *(fig)*

virago /vɪˈrɑːgəʊ/ **N** (pl **viragoes** *or* **viragos**) mégère *f*, virago *f*

viral /ˈvaɪərəl/ **ADJ** viral ◆ **~ infection** infection *f* virale **COMP** **viral load** **N** charge *f* virale

Virgil /ˈvɜːdʒɪl/ **N** Virgile *m*

virgin /ˈvɜːdʒɪn/ **N** 1 (fille *f*) vierge *f*, puceau *m* ◆ **she is a ~** elle est vierge ◆ **he is a ~** il est vierge *or* puceau ◆ **the Virgin** *(Astrol, Astron, Rel)* la Vierge ◆ **the Virgin Mary** la Vierge Marie 2 *(= inexperienced person)* novice *mf* ◆ **a political ~** un novice en politique **ADJ** *[person, snow, forest, soil, wool, page]* vierge ; *[freshness, sweetness]* virginal ◆ **~ territory** *(lit, fig)* terre *f* vierge
COMP **virgin birth** **N** *(Bio)* parthénogenèse *f* ◆ **the Virgin Birth** *(in Christianity)* l'Immaculée Conception *f*
the Virgin Islands **NPL** les îles *fpl* Vierges
virgin olive oil **N** huile *f* d'olive vierge
the Virgin Queen **N** Élisabeth Ire

virginal /ˈvɜːdʒɪnl/ **ADJ** *[woman]* d'une pureté virginale ; *[purity, innocence]* virginal ◆ **dressed in ~ white** vêtu de blanc virginal **N** *(Mus)* virginal *m*

Virginia /vəˈdʒɪnjə/ **N** Virginie *f* ◆ **in ~** en Virginie
COMP **Virginia creeper** **N** *(Brit)* vigne *f* vierge
Virginia tobacco **N** Virginie *m*, tabac *m* blond

Virginian /vəˈdʒɪnjən/ **ADJ** de Virginie **N** Virginien(ne) *m(f)*

virginity /vɜːˈdʒɪnɪtɪ/ **N** virginité *f* ◆ **to lose one's ~** perdre sa virginité

Virgo /ˈvɜːgəʊ/ **N** *(Astron)* Vierge *f* ◆ **I'm (a) ~** *(Astrol)* je suis (de la) Vierge

Virgoan /vɜːˈgəʊən/ **N** ◆ **to be a ~** être (de la) Vierge

virgule /ˈvɜːgjuːl/ **N** *(US Typ)* barre *f* oblique

virile /ˈvɪraɪl/ **ADJ** *(lit, fig)* viril (virile *f*)

virility /vɪˈrɪlɪtɪ/ **N** virilité *f*

virologist /ˌvaɪəˈrɒlədʒɪst/ **N** virologiste *mf*

virology /ˌvaɪəˈrɒlədʒɪ/ **N** virologie *f*

virtual /ˈvɜːtjʊəl/ **ADJ** 1 *(= near)* quasi- ◆ **a ~ certainty** une quasi-certitude ◆ **a ~ impossibility** une quasi-impossibilité ◆ **a ~ monopoly** un quasi-monopole ◆ **to come to a ~ halt** *or* **standstill** en arriver à un arrêt quasi complet *or* total ◆ **she was a ~ prisoner/recluse/stranger** elle était quasiment prisonnière/recluse/étrangère 2 *(Comput)* virtuel
COMP **virtual memory** **N** *(Comput)* mémoire *f* virtuelle
virtual reality **N** réalité *f* virtuelle ◆ **~-reality computer** ordinateur *m* à réalité virtuelle ◆ **~-reality helmet** casque *m* à réalité virtuelle ◆ **~-reality system** système *m* à réalité virtuelle

⚠ When **virtual** means 'near' it is not translated by **virtuel**.

virtuality /vɜːtjʊˈælɪtɪ/ N virtualité *f*

virtually /ˈvɜːtjʊəlɪ/ ADV (= *almost*) pratiquement ; (*Comput*) de façon virtuelle ◆ **he started with ~ nothing** il a commencé avec pratiquement rien

virtue /ˈvɜːtjuː/ N 1 (= *good quality*) vertu *f* ◆ **to make a ~ of necessity** faire de nécessité vertu
2 (*NonC*) (= *chastity*) vertu *f*, chasteté *f* ◆ **a woman of easy ~** † une femme de petite vertu
3 (= *advantage*) mérite *m*, avantage *m* ◆ **this set has the ~ of being portable** ce poste a l'avantage d'être portatif ◆ **it has the ~ of clarity** ça a l'avantage d'être clair *or* de la clarté ◆ **there is no ~ in doing that** il n'y a aucun mérite à faire cela
◆ **in** *or* **by virtue of** en vertu de, en raison de ◆ **by ~ of the fact that ...** en vertu *or* en raison du fait que ... ◆ **by ~ of being British, he ...** en vertu *or* en raison du fait qu'il était britannique, il ...
4 (*NonC = power*) ◆ **healing ~** pouvoir *m* thérapeutique

virtuosity /ˌvɜːtjʊˈɒsɪtɪ/ N virtuosité *f*

virtuoso /ˌvɜːtjʊˈəʊzəʊ/ N (pl **virtuosos** *or* **virtuosi** /ˌvɜːtjʊˈəʊzɪ/) (*esp Mus*) virtuose *mf* ◆ **a violin ~** un(e) virtuose du violon ADJ [*performance*] de virtuose ◆ **a ~ violinist** un(e) virtuose du violon

virtuous /ˈvɜːtjʊəs/ ADJ vertueux COMP **virtuous circle** N cercle *m* vertueux

virtuously /ˈvɜːtjʊəslɪ/ ADV vertueusement

virulence /ˈvɪrʊləns/ N virulence *f*

virulent /ˈvɪrʊlənt/ ADJ [*disease, poison, hatred, attack, speech, critic*] virulent ; [*colour, green, purple*] criard

virulently /ˈvɪrʊləntlɪ/ ADV [*attack, oppose*] (*also Med*) avec virulence ; [*opposed, anti-Semitic*] violemment

virus /ˈvaɪərəs/ N (pl **viruses**) (*Med, Comput*) virus *m* ◆ **rabies ~** virus *m* de la rage *or* rabique ◆ **the AIDS ~** le virus du sida ◆ **~ disease** maladie *f* virale *or* à virus

visa /ˈviːzə/ N (pl **visas**) 1 (*in passport*) visa *m* (*de passeport*) ◆ **entrance/exit ~** visa *m* d'entrée/de sortie ◆ **to get an Egyptian ~** obtenir un visa pour l'Égypte 2 (= *credit card*) **Visa® (card)** carte *f* Visa®, ≃ Carte bleue® *f* VT viser

visage /ˈvɪzɪdʒ/ N (*liter*) visage *m*, figure *f*

vis-à-vis /ˈviːzəviː/ PREP [*+ person*] vis-à-vis de ; [*+ thing*] par rapport à, devant ◆ **~ the West** vis-à-vis de l'Occident N (= *person placed opposite*) vis-à-vis *m* ; (= *person of similar status*) homologue *mf*

viscera /ˈvɪsərə/ NPL viscères *mpl*

visceral /ˈvɪsərəl/ ADJ (*liter*) [*hatred, dislike*] (*also Anat*) viscéral ; [*thrill, pleasure*] brut

viscid /ˈvɪsɪd/ ADJ visqueux (*lit*)

viscose /ˈvɪskəʊs/ N viscose *f* ADJ visqueux (*lit*)

viscosity /vɪsˈkɒsɪtɪ/ N viscosité *f*

viscount /ˈvaɪkaʊnt/ N vicomte *m*

viscountcy /ˈvaɪkaʊntsɪ/ N vicomté *f*

viscountess /ˈvaɪkaʊntɪs/ N vicomtesse *f*

viscounty /ˈvaɪkaʊntɪ/ N ⇒ **viscountcy**

viscous /ˈvɪskəs/ ADJ visqueux, gluant

vise /vaɪs/ N (*US*) ⇒ **vice²**

visé /ˈviːzeɪ/ N (*US*) ⇒ **visa noun 1**

visibility /ˌvɪzɪˈbɪlɪtɪ/ N visibilité *f* ◆ **good/poor** *or* **low ~** bonne/mauvaise visibilité *f* ◆ **~ is down to** *or* **is only 20 metres** la visibilité ne dépasse pas 20 mètres

visible /ˈvɪzəbl/ ADJ 1 (= *detectable*) [*effect, damage, sign, result, effort*] visible ; [*impatience*] visible, manifeste ◆ **to become ~** apparaître ◆ **there is no ~ difference** il n'y a pas de différence notable *or* visible ◆ **it serves no ~ purpose** on n'en voit pas vraiment l'utilité ◆ **the barn wasn't ~ from the road** la grange n'était pas visible depuis la route ◆ **it was not ~ to a passer-by** un passant ne pouvait pas l'apercevoir ◆ **~ to the naked eye** visible à l'œil nu ◆ **with no ~ means of support** (*Jur*) sans ressources apparentes 2 (= *prominent*) [*person, minority*] en vue
COMP **visible exports** NPL exportations *fpl* visibles
visible light N (*Phys*) lumière *f* visible
visible panty line N (*hum*) *slip qui se devine sous un vêtement*

visibly /ˈvɪzəblɪ/ ADV [*shocked, upset, moved, angry*] manifestement, visiblement ; [*relax, shake, flinch*] visiblement

Visigoth /ˈvɪzɪgɒθ/ N Wisigoth *mf*

vision /ˈvɪʒən/ N 1 (*NonC*) vision *f*, vue *f* ; (*fig = foresight*) vision *f*, prévoyance *f* ◆ **his ~ is very bad** sa vue est très mauvaise ◆ **within/outside one's range of ~** à portée de/hors de vue ◆ **a man of great ~** un homme qui voit loin ◆ **his ~ of the future** sa vision de l'avenir ; → **field** 2 (*in dream, trance*) vision *f*, apparition *f* ◆ **it came to me in a ~** j'en ai eu une vision ◆ **to have** *or* **see ~s** avoir des visions ◆ **to have ~s of wealth** avoir des visions de richesses ◆ **she had ~s of being drowned** elle s'est vue noyée VT (*US*) envisager
COMP **vision mixer** N (*Cine, TV = machine*) mixeur *m* (d'images) ◆ **"vision mixer: Alexander Anderson"** (= *person*) "mixage : Alexander Anderson"
vision-mixing N (*Cine, TV*) mixage *m* (d'images)

visionary /ˈvɪʒənərɪ/ ADJ, N visionnaire *mf*

visit /ˈvɪzɪt/ N (= *call, tour: also Med*) visite *f* ; (= *stay*) séjour *m* ◆ **to pay a ~ to** [*+ person*] rendre visite à ; [*+ place*] aller à ◆ **to pay a ~** * (*fig*) aller au petit coin* ◆ **to be on a ~ to** [*+ person*] être en visite chez ; [*+ place*] faire un séjour à ◆ **he went on a two-day ~ to Paris** il est allé passer deux jours à Paris ◆ **I'm going on a ~ to Glasgow next week** j'irai à Glasgow la semaine prochaine ◆ **on a private/an official ~** en visite privée/officielle ◆ **his ~ to Paris lasted three days** son séjour à Paris a duré trois jours
VT 1 (= *go and see*) [*+ person*] aller voir, rendre visite à ; [*+ doctor, solicitor*] aller voir, aller chez ; [*+ sick person*] (*gen*) aller voir ; [*priest, doctor*] [*+ patient*] visiter ; [*+ town*] aller à, faire un petit tour à ; [*+ museum, zoo*] aller à, visiter ; [*+ theatre*] aller à
2 (= *go and stay with*) [*+ person*] faire un séjour chez ; (= *go and stay in*) [*+ town, country*] faire un séjour à (*or* en)
3 (= *formally inspect*) [*+ place*] inspecter, faire une visite d'inspection à ; [*+ troops*] passer en revue ◆ **to ~ the scene of the crime** (*Jur*) se rendre sur les lieux du crime
4 († = *inflict*) [*+ person*] punir (*with* de) ◆ **to ~ the sins of the fathers upon the children** punir les enfants pour les péchés de leurs pères
VI 1 ◆ **I'm just ~ing** je suis de passage
2 (*US = chat*) bavarder
▸ **visit with** VT FUS (*US*) [*+ person*] passer voir

⚠ **to visit** is not translated by **visiter** in the case of a visit to friends.

visitation /ˌvɪzɪˈteɪʃən/ N 1 (*by official*) visite *f* d'inspection ; [*of bishop*] visite *f* pastorale ◆ **we had a ~ from her** (*hum*) elle nous a fait l'honneur de sa visite, elle nous a honorés de sa présence ◆ **the Visitation of the Blessed Virgin Mary** la Visitation de la Vierge 2 (= *calamity*) punition *f* du ciel 3 (*from supernatural being*) visite *f*

visiting /ˈvɪzɪtɪŋ/ N ◆ **I hate ~** je déteste faire des visites
COMP [*friends*] de passage ; [*lecturer etc*] invité, de l'extérieur ; [*dignitary*] en visite officielle
visiting card N (*Brit*) carte *f* de visite
visiting fireman * N (pl **visiting firemen**) (*US fig: iro*) visiteur *m* de marque
visiting hours NPL heures *fpl* de visite
visiting nurse N (*US*) infirmière *f* à domicile
visiting professor N (*Univ*) professeur *m* associé
visiting rights NPL droit *m* de visite
visiting teacher N (*US*) ≃ visiteuse *f* scolaire
visiting team N (*Sport*) visiteurs *mpl*
visiting terms NPL ◆ **I know him but I'm not on ~ terms with him** je le connais, mais nous ne nous rendons pas visite
visiting time N ⇒ **visiting hours**

visitor /ˈvɪzɪtəʳ/ N 1 (= *guest*) invité(e) *m(f)* ◆ **to have a ~** avoir de la visite ◆ **to have ~s** avoir des visites *or* de la visite ◆ **we've had a lot of ~s** nous avons eu beaucoup de visites ◆ **have your ~s left?** est-ce que tes invités sont partis ? ◆ **we seem to have had a ~ during the night!** on dirait qu'on a eu de la visite cette nuit !
2 (= *client*) (*in hotel*) client(e) *m(f)* ; (*at exhibition*) visiteur *m* ; (= *tourist*) visiteur *m* ◆ **~s to London** visiteurs *mpl* de passage à Londres ◆ **~s to the castle** les personnes *fpl* visitant le château ; → **health, passport, prison**
COMP **visitor centre** N accueil *m* des visiteurs (*sur un site historique avec exposition, diaporama, cafétéria etc*)
visitors' book N livre *m* d'or
visitors' gallery N (*Parl etc*) tribune *f* du public
visitor's tax N taxe *f* de séjour

visor /ˈvaɪzəʳ/ N visière *f* ; → **sun**

VISTA /ˈvɪstə/ N (*US*) (abbrev of **Volunteers in Service to America**) *organisme américain chargé de l'aide aux personnes défavorisées*

vista /ˈvɪstə/ N (= *view*) vue *f* ; (= *survey*) (*of past*) vue *f*, image *f* ; (*of future*) perspective *f*, horizon *m* ◆ **to open up new ~s** (*fig*) ouvrir de nouveaux horizons *or* de nouvelles perspectives

visual /ˈvɪzjʊəl/ ADJ visuel ◆ **the ~ cortex of the brain** l'aire du cortex cérébral contrôlant la vision ◆ **within ~ range** à portée de vue ◆ **she's a very ~ person** c'est une visuelle N ◆ **to get a ~ on sth** arriver à voir qch NPL **visuals** (= *display material*) support(s) *m(pl)* visuel(s) ; [*of video game, film etc*] images *fpl*
COMP **visual aid** N support *m* visuel
visual angle N angle *m* visuel
visual artist N plasticien(ne) *m(f)*
the visual arts NPL les arts *mpl* plastiques
visual display terminal, visual display unit N console *f*, écran *m*
visual field N (*Opt*) champ *m* de vision

visualization /ˌvɪzjʊəlaɪˈzeɪʃən/ N visualisation *f*

visualize /ˈvɪzjʊəlaɪz/ VT 1 (= *recall*) [*+ person, sb's face*] se représenter, visualiser 2 (= *imagine*) [*+ sth unknown*] s'imaginer ; [*+ sth familiar*] se représenter ◆ **try to ~ a million pounds** essayez de vous imaginer un million de livres ◆ **I ~d him working at his desk** je me le suis représenté travaillant à son bureau ◆ **~ yourself lying on the beach** imaginez-vous étendu sur la plage 3 (= *foresee*) envisager, prévoir ◆ **we do not ~ many changes** nous n'envisageons *or* pas beaucoup de changements

visually /ˈvɪzjʊəlɪ/ ADV [*attractive*] visuellement ; [*stunning, exciting*] d'un point de vue visuel ; [*judge*] de visu ◆ **~ handicapped** *or* **impaired** malvoyant ◆ **the ~ handicapped** *or* **impaired** les malvoyants *mpl* ◆ **~, it's a very impressive film** d'un point de vue visuel, c'est un film très impressionnant

vital /ˈvaɪtl/ ADJ 1 (= crucial) [part, component, element, information] vital, essentiel ; [question, matter] vital, fondamental ; [supplies, resources] vital ; [ingredient, factor, role] essentiel, fondamental ; [link] essentiel ; [importance] capital ◆ **your support is ~ to us** votre soutien est vital or capital pour nous ◆ **such skills are ~ for survival** de telles techniques sont indispensables à la survie ◆ **it is ~ to do this** il est vital or essentiel de faire cela ◆ **it is ~ for you to come, it is ~ that you (should) come** il faut absolument que vous veniez *subj*
2 (= dynamic) [person, institution] énergique ◆ ~ **spark** étincelle *f* de vie
3 (Physiol) [organ, force, functions] vital ◆ ~ **parts** organes *mpl* vitaux
N ◆ **the ~s** (Anat) les organes *mpl* vitaux ; (fig) les parties *fpl* essentielles
COMP **vital signs** NPL (Med) signes *mpl* vitaux ; (fig) signes *mpl* de vitalité ◆ **his ~ signs are normal** ses fonctions vitales sont normales ◆ **he shows no ~ signs** il ne donne aucun signe de vie
vital statistics NPL (Sociol) statistiques *fpl* démographiques ; (Brit) [of woman] mensurations *fpl*

vitality /vaɪˈtælɪtɪ/ N (lit, fig) vitalité *f*

vitalize /ˈvaɪtəlaɪz/ VT (lit) vivifier ; (fig) mettre de la vie dans, animer

vitally /ˈvaɪtəlɪ/ ADV 1 (= crucially, greatly) [necessary] absolument ; [interested, concerned] au plus haut point ; [affect] de façon cruciale ◆ ~ **important** d'une importance capitale ◆ **it is ~ important that I talk to her** il est absolument indispensable que or il faut absolument que je lui parle *subj* ◆ ~ **urgent** des plus urgents ◆ ~ **needed foreign investment** investissements *mpl* étrangers dont on a un besoin vital ◆ ~, **he was still willing to compromise** fait essentiel or capital, il était toujours prêt à envisager un compromis
2 (= intensely) ◆ **she is so ~ alive** elle est tellement débordante de vitalité ◆ **traditions that are ~ alive** traditions *fpl* qui restent des plus vivaces ◆ **music which remains ~ fresh** musique *f* qui conserve une intense fraîcheur

vitamin /ˈvɪtəmɪn/ N vitamine *f* ◆ ~ **A/B** vitamine A/B ◆ **with added ~s** vitaminé
COMP [content] en vitamines
vitamin deficiency N carence *f* en vitamines
vitamin deficiency disease N avitaminose *f*
vitamin-enriched ADJ vitaminé
vitamin pill N comprimé *m* de vitamines
vitamin-rich ADJ riche en vitamines
vitamin tablet N ⇒ **vitamin pill**

vitaminize /ˈvɪtəmɪnaɪz/ VT incorporer des vitamines dans ◆ **~d food** nourriture *f* vitaminée

vitiate /ˈvɪʃɪeɪt/ VT (all senses) vicier

viticulture /ˈvɪtɪkʌltʃəʳ/ N viticulture *f*

vitreous /ˈvɪtrɪəs/ ADJ 1 [china, rock, electricity] vitré ; [enamel] vitrifié 2 (Anat) vitré
COMP **vitreous body** N (corps *m*) vitré *m*
vitreous humour N humeur *f* vitrée

vitrifaction /ˌvɪtrɪˈfækʃən/, **vitrification** /ˌvɪtrɪfɪˈkeɪʃən/ N vitrification *f*

vitrify /ˈvɪtrɪfaɪ/ VT vitrifier VI se vitrifier

vitriol /ˈvɪtrɪəl/ N (Chem, fig) vitriol *m*

vitriolic /ˌvɪtrɪˈɒlɪk/ ADJ [attack, speech] au vitriol ; [abuse, outburst] venimeux ; [criticism] venimeux, au vitriol COMP **vitriolic acid** † N (Chem) vitriol † *m*

vitriolize /ˈvɪtrɪəlaɪz/ VT vitrioler

vitro /ˈvɪtrəʊ/ → **in vitro**

vituperate /vɪˈtjuːpəreɪt/ (frm) VT injurier, vitupérer contre VI vitupérer

vituperation /vɪˌtjuːpəˈreɪʃən/ N (frm) vitupérations *fpl*

vituperative /vɪˈtjuːpərətɪv/ ADJ (frm) [remark] injurieux ; [attack, abuse, critic] virulent ◆ **a ~ man/woman** un vitupérateur/une vitupératrice (liter) ◆ **to be ~ about sb** vitupérer contre qn

Vitus /ˈvaɪtəs/ N → **saint**

viva¹ /ˈviːvə/ EXCL vive ! N vivat *m*

viva² /ˈvaɪvə/ N (Brit Univ) épreuve *f* orale, oral *m*

vivacious /vɪˈveɪʃəs/ ADJ [woman, personality] plein de vivacité

vivaciously /vɪˈveɪʃəslɪ/ ADV [say, laugh] avec vivacité

vivacity /vɪˈvæsɪtɪ/ N vivacité *f* ; (in words) verve *f*

vivarium /vɪˈvɛərɪəm/ N (pl **vivariums** or **vivaria** /vɪˈvɛərɪə/) vivarium *m* ; (for fish, shellfish) vivier *m*

viva voce /ˈvaɪvəˈvəʊsɪ/ ADJ oral, verbal ADV de vive voix, oralement N (Brit Univ) épreuve *f* orale, oral *m*

vivid /ˈvɪvɪd/ ADJ [colour, imagination] vif ; [memory] très net, vif ; [dream] pénétrant ; [description, language] vivant, coloré ; [account] vivant ; [example, comparison, demonstration] frappant ◆ **in ~ detail** avec des détails saisissants ◆ **to be a ~ reminder that ...** rappeler de façon saisissante que ...

vividly /ˈvɪvɪdlɪ/ ADV [remember, recall] très nettement or distinctement ; [describe, portray, express] de façon vivante ; [illustrate, demonstrate] de façon frappante ◆ ~ **coloured** aux couleurs vives

vividness /ˈvɪvɪdnɪs/ N [of colour] vivacité *f*, éclat *m* ; [of light] éclat *m*, clarté *f* ; [of memory] netteté *f* ; [of description] caractère *m* très vivant ; [of dream] clarté *f* ; [of style] clarté *f*, vigueur *f*

vivify /ˈvɪvɪfaɪ/ VT vivifier, ranimer

viviparous /vɪˈvɪpərəs/ ADJ vivipare

vivisect /ˌvɪvɪˈsekt/ VT pratiquer la vivisection sur, vivisecter

vivisection /ˌvɪvɪˈsekʃən/ N vivisection *f*

vivisectionist /ˌvɪvɪˈsekʃənɪst/, **vivisector** /ˈvɪvɪsektəʳ/ N (= scientist) vivisecteur *m*, -trice *f* ; (= supporter) partisan(e) *m(f)* de la vivisection

vixen /ˈvɪksn/ N 1 (= fox) renarde *f* 2 (= woman) mégère *f*

viz /vɪz/ ADV (abbrev of **vide licet**) (= namely) c.-à-d., c'est-à-dire

vizier /vɪˈzɪəʳ/ N vizir *m*

VJ Day /viːˈdʒeɪdeɪ/ N *anniversaire de la victoire des alliés sur le Japon en 1945* ; → VE DAY

VLF /viːelˈef/ N (abbrev of **very low frequency**) → **very**

VLSI /viːelesˈaɪ/ N (Comput) (abbrev of **very large-scale integration**) intégration *f* à très grande échelle

vocab * /ˈvəʊkæb/ abbrev of **vocabulary**

vocable /ˈvəʊkəbl/ N vocable *m*

vocabulary /vəʊˈkæbjʊlərɪ/ N (gen) vocabulaire *m* ; (in textbook, bilingual) lexique *m*, vocabulaire *m* ; (technical) lexique *m*, glossaire *m*

vocal /ˈvəʊkəl/ ADJ 1 (= using voice: also Anat) vocal ◆ ~ **score** (Mus) partition *f* vocale ◆ ~ **training** ⇒ **voice training** ; → **voice**
2 (= outspoken) [opposition, protest] vif ◆ **a ~ minority** une minorité qui se fait entendre ◆ **he was very ~ during the meeting** il n'a pas hésité à prendre la parole pendant la réunion ◆ **to be ~ in one's displeasure** exprimer énergiquement son déplaisir ◆ **to be ~ in supporting sth** prendre énergiquement parti pour qch ◆ **to become more** or **increasingly ~** [person] se faire de plus en plus entendre ◆ **public discontent was increasingly ~** de plus en plus les gens exprimaient leur mécontentement
N (Mus) ◆ **~(s)** chant *m* ◆ **featuring Chrissie Hynde on ~s** avec Chrissie Hynde au chant ◆ **backing ~s** chœurs *mpl*
COMP **vocal c(h)ords, vocal folds** NPL cordes *fpl* vocales

> ⚠ When it means 'outspoken', **vocal** is not translated by the French word **vocal**.

vocalic /vəʊˈkælɪk/ ADJ vocalique

vocalisation /ˌvəʊkəlaɪˈzeɪʃən/ N vocalisation *f*

vocalist /ˈvəʊkəlɪst/ N chanteur *m*, -euse *f* (*dans un groupe*)

vocalize /ˈvəʊkəlaɪz/ VT 1 [+ one's opinions] exprimer 2 (Ling) [+ consonant] vocaliser ; [+ text] écrire en marquant des points-voyelles VI (Ling) se vocaliser ; (Mus) vocaliser, faire des vocalises

vocally /ˈvəʊkəlɪ/ ADV 1 (Mus) [perfect, impressive, difficult] du point de vue vocal ◆ **a ~ superb cast** des chanteurs extraordinaires ◆ ~, **it's a very simple song** la mélodie de cette chanson est très simple 2 (= outspokenly) ◆ **to support/oppose sth** ~ exprimer énergiquement son soutien/opposition à qch ◆ **to be ~ anti-feminist** exprimer énergiquement ses opinions antiféministes

vocation /vəʊˈkeɪʃən/ N (Rel etc) vocation *f* ◆ **to have a ~ for teaching** avoir la vocation de l'enseignement

vocational /vəʊˈkeɪʃənl/ ADJ [training, education, subject, qualifications, skills] technique et professionnel ◆ ~ **course** (= period) stage *m* de formation professionnelle ; (= subject) filière *f* technique et professionnelle
COMP **vocational guidance** N orientation *f* professionnelle
vocational school N (in US) ≈ lycée *m* technique

vocationally /vəʊˈkeɪʃənlɪ/ ADV ◆ ~ **oriented courses** cours *mpl* à orientation professionnelle ◆ ~ **relevant subjects** matières *fpl* d'intérêt professionnel ◆ **to train sb** ~ donner à qn une formation professionnelle

vocative /ˈvɒkətɪv/ N vocatif *m* ◆ **in the ~** au vocatif ADJ vocatif ◆ ~ **case** vocatif *m* ◆ ~ **ending** désinence *f* du vocatif

vociferate /vəʊˈsɪfəreɪt/ VI vociférer, brailler *

vociferation /vəʊˌsɪfəˈreɪʃən/ N vocifération *f*

vociferous /vəʊˈsɪfərəs/ ADJ véhément ◆ ~ **in one's opposition to sth** véhément dans son opposition à qch ◆ **to be ~ in one's criticism of sb/sth** critiquer qn/qch avec véhémence ◆ **to be ~ in demanding one's rights** réclamer ses droits avec véhémence

vociferously /vəʊˈsɪfərəslɪ/ ADV (frm) avec véhémence

vodka /ˈvɒdkə/ N vodka *f*

vogue /vəʊɡ/ N vogue *f*, mode *f* ◆ **moustaches were the ~** or **in ~ then** les moustaches étaient alors en vogue or à la mode ◆ **to be all the ~** faire fureur ◆ **to come into ~** devenir à la mode ◆ **to go out of ~** passer de mode ◆ **the ~ for ...** la vogue or la mode de ... ◆ **the current ~ for mini-skirts** la vogue que connaissent actuellement les minijupes ADJ à la mode, en vogue

voice /vɔɪs/ N 1 (gen) voix *f* ; (pitch, quality) voix *f*, ton *m* ◆ **in a deep ~** d'une voix grave ◆ **at the top of one's ~** à tue-tête ◆ **to raise/lower one's ~** élever/baisser la voix ◆ **keep your ~ down** ne parle pas trop fort ◆ **to say sth in a low ~** dire qch à voix basse ◆ **he likes the sound of his own ~** il aime s'écouter parler ◆ **his ~ has broken** il a mué, sa voix a mué ◆ **a ~ could be heard at the back of the room** on entendait une voix au fond de la salle ◆ **they acclaimed him with one ~** ils ont été unanimes à l'acclamer ◆ **to give ~ to sth** exprimer qch ◆ **the ~ of reason** la voix de la raison ◆ **the ~ of the nation/the people** la voix de la nation/du peuple ◆ **the ~ of God** la voix de Dieu ◆ **he is a ~ (crying) in the wilderness** il prêche dans le désert ; → **find, lose, loud**

2 *(fig = opinion, influence)* ◆ **there were no dissenting ~s** il n'y a pas eu d'opposition ◆ **to have a ~ in the matter** avoir son mot à dire, avoir voix au chapitre ◆ **his wife has no ~ in their business affairs** sa femme n'a pas son mot à dire dans leurs affaires ◆ **can't I have a ~ in this?** est-ce que je peux avoir mon mot à dire ? ◆ **Egypt is an important ~ in Arab politics** l'Égypte joue un rôle déterminant dans la politique des pays arabes ◆ **France retains an influential ~ in African affairs** la France a gardé une position d'influence en Afrique

3 *(Mus)* voix *f* ◆ **tenor/bass ~** voix *f* de ténor/de basse ◆ **a piece for ~ and piano** un morceau pour voix et piano ◆ **a piece for three soprano ~s** un morceau pour trois sopranos ◆ **to be in good ~** être en voix ◆ **he has a lovely tenor ~** il a une belle voix de ténor

4 *(Gram)* voix *f* ◆ **active/passive ~** voix *f* active/passive ◆ **in the active/passive ~** à l'actif/au passif

5 *(NonC: Phon)* voix *f*

6 *(Theat)* ◆ **~s off** voix *fpl* dans les coulisses

VT 1 *(= express)* *[+ feelings, opinion]* exprimer, formuler ; *[+ concern, support, fear]* exprimer ◆ **to ~ (one's) opposition to sth** s'élever contre qch

2 *(Ling)* *[+ consonant]* sonoriser ◆ **~d consonant** consonne *f* sonore *or* voisée

3 *(Mus)* accorder

COMP **voice-activated** ADJ à commande vocale
voice box N *(Anat)* larynx *m*
voice mail N messagerie *f* vocale
voice-over N *(TV)* (commentaire *m* en) voix *f* off
voice parts NPL *(Mus)* parties *fpl* vocales
voice production N diction *f*, élocution *f*
voice range N registre *m* de la voix
voice recognition N reconnaissance *f* vocale
voice synthesis N synthèse *f* vocale
voice synthesizer N synthétiseur *m* vocal
voice training N *[of actor]* cours *mpl* de diction *or* d'élocution ; *[of singer]* cours *mpl* de chant
voice vote N *(US Pol etc)* vote *m* par acclamation

voiced /vɔɪst/ ADJ *(Phon)* *[consonant]* voisé, sonore

voiceless /ˈvɔɪslɪs/ ADJ 1 *(= mute)* *[person]* *(gen)* sans voix, aphone ; *(Med)* aphone 2 *(= disenfranchised)* *[minority]* silencieux 3 *(Phon)* *[consonant, sound]* non voisé, sourd

voiceprint /ˈvɔɪsprɪnt/ N empreinte *f* vocale

voicing /ˈvɔɪsɪŋ/ N *(Phon)* sonorisation *f*, voisement *m*

void /vɔɪd/ N *(lit, fig)* vide *m* ◆ **an aching ~** un grand vide ◆ **to fill the ~** combler le vide ADJ 1 *(Jur = invalid)* *[agreement]* nul (nulle *f*) ◆ **to declare sth ~** annuler qch ; → **null** 2 *(frm = empty)* vide ◆ **~ of** *[ornament, charm, talent, qualities, imagination]* dépourvu de ; *[scruples, compassion, good sense, meaning]* dénué de 3 *(Cards)* ◆ **his spades were ~, he was ~ in spades** il n'avait pas de pique VT 1 *(= remove)* évacuer *(from* de) 2 *(Med)* *(= excrete)* évacuer ; *(= vomit)* vomir 3 *(Jur = invalidated)* annuler

voile /vɔɪl/ N voile *m* (tissu)

Voivodina, Vojvodina /ˈvɔɪvəˈdiːnə/ N Voïvodine *or* Vojvodine *f*

vol. abbrev of **volume**

volatile /ˈvɒlətaɪl/ ADJ 1 *(Chem)* volatil 2 *(fig = uncertain)* *[situation, atmosphere, relationship, market]* instable ; *[person, personality]* versatile

volatility /ˌvɒləˈtɪlɪtɪ/ N 1 *(Chem)* volatilité *f* 2 *(= uncertainty)* *[of situation, atmosphere, relationship, market]* inconstance *f* ; *[of person, personality]* versatilité *f*

volatilize /vɒˈlætəlaɪz/ VT volatiliser VI se volatiliser, s'évaporer

vol-au-vent /ˈvɒləʊˌvɑ̃ː, ˈvɒləˌvɒn/ N vol-au-vent *m* ◆ **chicken/mushroom ~** vol-au-vent *m* au poulet/aux champignons

volcanic /vɒlˈkænɪk/ ADJ *(lit, fig)* volcanique

volcano /vɒlˈkeɪnəʊ/ N (pl **volcanoes** *or* **volcanos**) volcan *m*

vole[1] /vəʊl/ N *(= animal)* campagnol *m* ; → **water**

vole[2] /vəʊl/ *(Cards)* N vole *f* VI faire la vole

Volga /ˈvɒlgə/ N Volga *f*

volition /vəˈlɪʃən/ N volition *f*, volonté *f* ◆ **of one's own ~** de son propre gré

volley /ˈvɒlɪ/ N 1 *(Mil)* volée *f*, salve *f* ; *[of stones]* grêle *f* 2 *(fig)* *[of insults]* bordée *f*, torrent *m* ; *[of questions]* feu *m* roulant ; *[of applause]* salve *f* ◆ **to fire a ~** tirer une salve 3 *(Sport)* volée *f* ◆ **half ~** demi-volée *f* VT *(Sport)* *[+ ball]* attraper à la volée VI 1 *(Mil)* tirer par salves 2 *(Sport)* faire une volée

volleyball /ˈvɒlɪbɔːl/ N volley(-ball) *m* COMP **volleyball player** N volleyeur *m*, -euse *f*

volleyer /ˈvɒlɪəʳ/ N *(Tennis)* volleyeur *m*, -euse *f*

volt /vəʊlt/ N volt *m* COMP **volt meter** N voltmètre *m*

voltage /ˈvəʊltɪdʒ/ N voltage *m*, tension *f* ◆ **high/low ~** haute/basse tension *f*

voltaic /vɒlˈteɪɪk/ ADJ voltaïque

volte-face /ˈvɒltˈfɑːs/ N (pl inv) volte-face *f inv* ◆ **to perform a ~** *(lit, fig)* faire volte-face

volubility /ˌvɒljʊˈbɪlɪtɪ/ N volubilité *f*, loquacité *f*

voluble /ˈvɒljʊbl/ ADJ volubile

volubly /ˈvɒljʊblɪ/ ADV avec volubilité, volubilement

volume /ˈvɒljuːm/ N 1 *(= book)* volume *m* ; *(= one in a set)* volume *m*, tome *m* ◆ **~ one/two** tome *m* un/second ◆ **~ three/four** tome *m* trois/quatre ◆ **in six ~s** en six volumes ◆ **a ~ of essays/short-stories** un volume d'essais/de nouvelles ◆ **a two-~ dictionary** un dictionnaire en deux volumes ◆ **to write ~s** *(fig)* écrire des volumes ◆ **to speak** *or* **say ~s** en dire long *(about* sur)

2 *(= size, bulk: Phys)* volume *m* ◆ **the gas expanded to twice its original ~** le gaz s'est dilaté et a doublé de volume ◆ **your hair needs more ~** il faut redonner du volume à vos cheveux ◆ **production ~** volume *m* de la production ◆ **the ~ of imports/exports** le volume des importations/exportations ◆ **the ~ of protest has increased since ...** les protestations ont pris de l'ampleur depuis ...

3 *(= capacity)* *[of tank, container]* capacité *f*

4 *(= loudness)* volume *m*, puissance *f* ◆ **to turn the ~ up/down** *(Rad, TV)* augmenter/diminuer le volume

NPL **volumes** *(gen)* ◆ **~s of** énormément de ◆ **~s of work** énormément de travail ◆ **~s of smoke** des nuages *mpl* de fumée

COMP **volume control** N *(Rad, TV)* bouton *m* de réglage du volume

volumetric /ˌvɒljʊˈmetrɪk/ ADJ volumétrique

voluminous /vəˈluːmɪnəs/ ADJ volumineux

voluntarily /ˈvɒləntərɪlɪ/ ADV 1 *(= willingly)* volontairement 2 *(= without payment)* *[work]* bénévolement, à titre bénévole

voluntarism /ˈvɒləntərɪzəm/ N bénévolat *m*

voluntary /ˈvɒləntərɪ/ ADJ 1 *(= not compulsory, spontaneous)* *[subscription, contribution, redundancy, repatriation, movement]* volontaire ; *[confession, statement]* volontaire, spontané ; *[attendance, course]* facultatif ; *[pension scheme]* à contribution volontaire ; *[agreement]* librement consenti ◆ **on a ~ basis** à titre volontaire

2 *(= unpaid, charitable)* *[group, service]* bénévole ◆ **~ helper** bénévole *mf* ◆ **~ help** *(= assistance)* aide *f* bénévole ◆ **on a ~ basis** à titre bénévole

N *(Mus, Rel)* morceau *m* d'orgue

COMP **voluntary agency, voluntary body** N organisation *f* bénévole
voluntary euthanasia N euthanasie *f* volontaire
voluntary liquidation N *(Comm, Fin)* dépôt *m* de bilan ◆ **to go into ~ liquidation** déposer son bilan ◆ **they put the company into ~ liquidation** l'entreprise a déposé son bilan
voluntary manslaughter N *(Jur)* homicide *m* volontaire
voluntary organization N organisation *f* bénévole
voluntary school N *(Brit)* école *f* libre
the voluntary sector N les organisations *fpl* bénévoles, le secteur associatif ◆ **he works in the ~ sector** il travaille pour une organisation bénévole *or* dans le secteur associatif
Voluntary Service Overseas N *(Brit)* ≃ coopération *f* technique
voluntary work N travail *m* bénévole, bénévolat *m* ◆ **she does ~ work (in a hospital)** elle travaille comme bénévole (dans un hôpital)
voluntary worker N bénévole *mf*

volunteer /ˌvɒlənˈtɪəʳ/ N *(gen, Mil)* volontaire *mf* ; *(= unpaid helper)* bénévole *mf* ◆ **to ask for** *or* **call for ~s** demander des volontaires ◆ **the association is run by ~s** c'est une association de bénévoles

ADJ 1 *(= having offered to do sth)* *[group]* de volontaires ; *[person]* volontaire

2 *(= unpaid)* *[helper, worker]* bénévole

VT *[+ money]* donner *or* offrir de son plein gré ; *[+ information]* fournir (spontanément) ◆ **they ~ed 50 pounds a week to the fund** ils ont offert une contribution hebdomadaire au fonds de 50 livres ◆ **they ~ed to carry it all back** ils ont offert de tout remporter ◆ **"there were seven of them" he ~ed** "ils étaient sept" dit-il spontanément

VI *(Mil)* s'engager comme volontaire *(for* dans) ◆ **to ~ for sth** *(gen)* s'offrir *or* se proposer pour (faire) qch

COMP **volunteer force** N armée *f or* force *f* de volontaires
Volunteers in Service to America N *organisme américain chargé de l'aide aux personnes défavorisées*
the Volunteer State N le Tennessee

volunteerism /ˌvɒlənˈtɪərɪzm/ N *(esp US)* *(= willingness to help)* esprit *m* d'entraide ; *(= voluntary work)* volontariat *m*

voluptuous /vəˈlʌptjʊəs/ ADJ voluptueux ◆ **she has a ~ figure** elle est bien faite

voluptuously /vəˈlʌptjʊəslɪ/ ADV *[move, stretch]* voluptueusement ◆ **her ~ curved body** son corps aux rondeurs voluptueuses ◆ **his lips were ~ full** il avait une bouche sensuelle

voluptuousness /vəˈlʌptjʊəsnɪs/ N volupté *f*, sensualité *f*

volute /vəˈluːt/ N *(Archit)* volute *f*

voluted /vəˈluːtɪd/ ADJ *(Archit)* en volute

vomit /ˈvɒmɪt/ N vomi *m* VT *(lit, fig)* vomir ◆ **to ~ out** *or* **up** *or* **forth** *(liter)* vomir VI vomir

vomiting /ˈvɒmɪtɪŋ/ N vomissements *mpl*

voodoo /ˈvuːduː/ ADJ vaudou *inv* N vaudou *m* VT envoûter

voracious /vəˈreɪʃəs/ ADJ *[appetite, person, animal]* vorace ; *[reader, collector]* avide ◆ **to be a ~ eater** être vorace

voraciously /vəˈreɪʃəslɪ/ ADV *[eat, devour]* voracement, avec voracité ; *[read]* avec avidité

voracity /vɒˈræsɪtɪ/ N *(lit, fig)* voracité *f*

vortex /ˈvɔːteks/ N (pl **vortexes** *or* **vortices** /ˈvɔːtɪsiːz/) *(lit)* vortex *m*, tourbillon *m* ; *(fig)* tourbillon *m*

vorticism /ˈvɔːtɪˌsɪzəm/ N *(Art)* vorticisme *m*

votary /ˈvəʊtərɪ/ N *(liter)* fervent(e) *m(f)* (*of* de)

vote /vəʊt/ N 1 *(= ballot)* vote *m* ◆ **to take a ~** *(gen)* voter (*on* sur) ; *(Admin, Pol)* procéder au vote (*on* sur) ◆ **they took a ~ on whether to sell the company** ils ont voté pour décider s'ils allaient (ou non) vendre l'entreprise ◆ **to put sth to the ~** mettre qch aux voix ◆ **the matter was settled by ~** on a réglé la question en la mettant aux voix ◆ **after the ~** après le scrutin

2 *(= franchise)* droit *m* de vote ◆ **to give the ~ to the under twenty-ones** accorder le droit de vote aux moins de vingt et un ans ◆ **to have/get the ~** avoir/obtenir le droit de vote ◆ **one man one ~** ≈ suffrage *m* universel, une seule voix par électeur ◆ **~s for women!** le droit de vote pour les femmes !

3 *(= vote cast)* voix *f* ◆ **to give one's ~ to ...** donner sa voix à ..., voter pour ... ◆ **to win ~s** gagner des voix ◆ **to count the ~s** compter les voix *or* les votes ; *(Pol)* dépouiller le scrutin ◆ **he has my ~** je voterai pour lui ◆ **~ for/against sth** voix *f* pour/contre qch ◆ **elected by a majority ~** élu au vote majoritaire ◆ **they won by a two-thirds ~** ils ont remporté les deux tiers des voix

4 *(= body of voters)* électorat *m* ◆ **the Jewish/Scottish ~** l'électorat *m* juif/écossais ◆ **to lose/court the Catholic ~** perdre le soutien de/courtiser l'électorat catholique ◆ **he'll win/lose the Massachusetts ~** il va remporter/perdre le Massachusetts ◆ **the Labour ~** *(Pol)* les voix *fpl* travaillistes ; → **casting, floating**

VT 1 *(= approve) [+ bill, treaty]* voter

2 *(= elect)* élire ◆ **he was ~d chairman** il a été élu président ◆ **the group ~d her the best cook** le groupe l'a proclamée meilleure cuisinière

3 *(= propose)* ◆ **I ~ we go to the cinema** * je propose que l'on aille au cinéma ◆ **the committee ~d to request a subsidy** le comité a voté une demande de subvention

VI voter (*for* pour ; *against* contre) donner sa voix (*for sb* à qn ; *for sth* pour qch) ; *(in general election etc)* aller aux urnes, voter ◆ **the country ~s in three weeks** les élections ont lieu dans trois semaines ◆ **to ~ Socialist** voter socialiste ◆ **to ~ for the Socialists** voter pour les socialistes ◆ **~ (for) Harris!** votez Harris ! ◆ **to ~ for sth** voter pour *or* en faveur de qch ◆ **to ~ for a bill** *(Parl)* voter une loi ◆ **to ~ on sth** mettre qch au vote ◆ **to ~ with one's feet** * (*= go elsewhere*) partir en signe de mécontentement, montrer son désaccord en partant ◆ **people are voting with their feet** * le verdict de l'opinion publique est clair

COMP **vote-catching** * ADJ *(pej)* électoraliste
vote-loser * N ◆ **it's a ~-loser (for us)** ça risque de nous faire perdre des voix
vote of censure N ⇒ **vote of no confidence**
vote of confidence N vote *m* de confiance ◆ **to ask for a ~ of confidence** réclamer un vote de confiance ◆ **to pass a ~ of confidence (in)** voter la confiance (à)
vote of no confidence N motion *f* de censure ◆ **to pass a ~ of no confidence** voter une motion de censure
vote of thanks N discours *m* de remerciement ◆ **to move a ~ of thanks** faire un discours de remerciement
vote-winner * N atout *m* électoral ◆ **they hope it will be a ~-winner for them** ils espèrent que cela leur fera gagner des voix

► **vote down** VT SEP rejeter *(par le vote)*

► **vote in** VT SEP *[+ law]* adopter, voter ; *[+ person]* élire

► **vote out** VT SEP *[+ amendment]* rejeter ; *[+ MP, chairman]* ne pas réélire, sortir * ◆ **he was ~d out (of office)** il n'a pas été réélu ◆ **he was ~d out by a large majority** il a été battu à une forte majorité ◆ **the electors ~d the Conservative government out** les électeurs ont rejeté le gouvernement conservateur

► **vote through** VT SEP *[+ bill, motion]* voter, ratifier

voter /ˈvəʊtəʳ/ N électeur *m*, -trice *f*
COMP **voter registration** N *(US Pol)* inscription *f* sur les listes électorales
voter registration card N carte *f* d'électeur ; → **turnout**

voting /ˈvəʊtɪŋ/ N *(NonC)* vote *m*, scrutin *m* ◆ **the ~ went against him** le vote lui a été défavorable ◆ **the ~ took place yesterday** le scrutin a eu lieu hier
COMP **voting booth** N isoloir *m*
voting machine N *(US)* machine *f* pour enregistrer les votes
voting paper N bulletin *m* de vote
voting precinct N *(US Pol)* circonscription *f* électorale
voting rights NPL droit *m* de vote
voting share N *(Fin)* action *f* avec droit de vote

votive /ˈvəʊtɪv/ ADJ votif

vouch /vaʊtʃ/ VI ◆ **to ~ for sb/sth** se porter garant de qn/qch, répondre de qn/qch ◆ **to ~ for the truth of sth** garantir la vérité de qch

voucher /ˈvaʊtʃəʳ/ N 1 *(= coupon: for cash, meals, petrol)* bon *m* ; → **luncheon** 2 *(= receipt)* reçu *m*, récépissé *m* ; *(for debt)* quittance *f*

vouchsafe /vaʊtʃˈseɪf/ VT *(frm) [+ reply]* accorder ; *[+ help, privilege]* accorder, octroyer ◆ **to ~ to do sth** accepter gracieusement de faire qch ; *(pej)* condescendre à faire qch ◆ **it is not ~d to everyone to understand such things** il n'est pas donné à tout le monde de comprendre ce genre de choses ◆ **he has not ~d an answer** il n'a pas jugé bon de nous donner une réponse

vow /vaʊ/ N vœu *m*, serment *m* ◆ **to take a ~** faire vœu (*to do sth* de faire qch ; *of sth* de qch) ◆ **the ~s which he took when ...** les vœux qu'il a faits quand ... ◆ **to take one's ~s** *(Rel)* prononcer ses vœux ◆ **to make a ~** ⇒ **to vow;** → **vt** ◆ **~ of celibacy** vœu *m* de célibat ◆ **to take a ~ of chastity** faire vœu de chasteté ◆ **to take a ~ of obedience (to)** *(Rel)* faire vœu d'obéissance (à) ; *(Hist)* jurer obéissance (à) ◆ **she swore a ~ of secrecy** elle a juré *or* elle a fait le serment de ne rien divulguer ; → **break**
VT 1 *(publicly)* jurer (*to do sth* de faire qch ; *that* que) ; *[+ obedience, loyalty]* faire vœu de ◆ **to ~ vengeance on sb** jurer de se venger de qn 2 *(to oneself)* se jurer (*to do sth* de faire qch ; *that* que) ◆ **he ~ed (to himself) that he would remain there** il s'est juré d'y rester

vowel /ˈvaʊəl/ N voyelle *f*
COMP *[system, sound]* vocalique
vowel shift N mutation *f* vocalique

vox pop * /ˌvɒksˈpɒp/ N micro-trottoir *m*

voyage /ˈvɔɪɪdʒ/ N *(Naut)* voyage *m* par mer, traversée *f* ; *(fig)* voyage *m* ◆ **to go on a ~** partir en voyage (par mer) ◆ **the ~ across the Atlantic** la traversée de l'Atlantique ◆ **the ~ out** le voyage d'aller ◆ **the ~ back** *or* **home** le voyage de retour ◆ **on the ~ out/home** à l'aller/au retour ◆ **a ~ of discovery** un voyage d'exploration
VT *(Naut)* traverser, parcourir
VI *(Naut)* voyager par mer ◆ **to ~ across** traverser

voyager /ˈvɔɪədʒəʳ/ N *(= traveller)* passager *m*, -ère *f*, voyageur *m*, -euse *f* ; *(Hist = explorer)* navigateur *m*

voyageur /ˌvɔɪəˈdʒɜː/ N *(Can Hist)* trappeur *or batelier etc assurant la liaison entre différents comptoirs*

voyeur /vwɑːˈjɜːʳ/ N voyeur *m*

voyeurism /ˈvwɑːjɜːˌrɪzəm/ N voyeurisme *m*

voyeuristic /ˌvwɑːjɜːˈrɪstɪk/ ADJ *[behaviour]* de voyeur ; *[activity]* qui frise le voyeurisme ; *[film, book]* qui sombre dans le voyeurisme

VP /viːˈpiː/ N *(US)* (abbrev of **Vice-President**) → **vice-**

VPL * /ˌviːpiːˈel/ N (abbrev of **visible panty line**) → **visible**

VR /viːˈɑːʳ/ N (abbrev of **virtual reality**) → **virtual**

vroom /vruːm/ EXCL vroum !

VS (abbrev of **versus**) VS, contre

VSO /ˌviːesˈəʊ/ N *(Brit)* (abbrev of **Voluntary Service Overseas**) → **voluntary**

VSOP /ˌviːesəʊˈpiː/ (abbrev of **Very Special Old Pale**) *(brandy, port)* VSOP

VT abbrev of **Vermont**

Vt. abbrev of **Vermont**

VTOL /ˌviːtiːəʊˈel/ (abbrev of **vertical takeoff and landing**) N 1 ◆ **~ (aircraft)** ADAV *m*, VTOL *m* 2 *(= technique)* décollage *m* et atterrissage *m* verticaux

Vulcan /ˈvʌlkən/ N *(Myth)* Vulcain *m*

vulcanite /ˈvʌlkənaɪt/ N ébonite *f*

vulcanization /ˌvʌlkənaɪˈzeɪʃən/ N vulcanisation *f*

vulcanize /ˈvʌlkənaɪz/ VT vulcaniser

vulcanologist /ˌvʌlkəˈnɒlədʒɪst/ N volcanologue *mf*

vulcanology /ˌvʌlkəˈnɒlədʒɪ/ N volcanologie *f*

vulgar /ˈvʌlgəʳ/ ADJ 1 *(= impolite, tasteless)* vulgaire ◆ **it is ~ to talk about money** il est vulgaire de parler d'argent ◆ **don't be so ~!** ne sois pas si grossier 2 *(Ling = vernacular) [language, tongue]* vulgaire
COMP **vulgar fraction** N *(Math)* fraction *f* ordinaire
Vulgar Latin N latin *m* vulgaire

vulgarian /vʌlˈgeərɪən/ N *(pej)* personne *f* vulgaire, parvenu(e) *m(f)*

vulgarism /ˈvʌlgərɪzəm/ N 1 *(= uneducated expression)* vulgarisme *m* 2 *(= swearword)* gros mot *m*, grossièreté *f*

vulgarity /vʌlˈgærɪtɪ/ N *[of words, person]* vulgarité *f*, grossièreté *f [of taste, décor]* vulgarité *f*

vulgarization /ˌvʌlgəraɪˈzeɪʃən/ N vulgarisation *f*

vulgarize /ˈvʌlgəraɪz/ VT 1 *(frm = make known)* vulgariser, populariser 2 *(= make coarse)* rendre vulgaire

vulgarly /ˈvʌlgəlɪ/ ADV 1 *(= generally)* vulgairement, communément 2 *(= coarsely)* vulgairement, grossièrement

Vulgate /ˈvʌlgɪt/ N Vulgate *f*

vulnerability /ˌvʌlnərəˈbɪlɪtɪ/ N vulnérabilité *f*

vulnerable /ˈvʌlnərəbl/ ADJ vulnérable (*to sth* à qch) ; ◆ **to be ~ to criticism** prêter le flanc à la critique ◆ **to be ~ to infection** être sujet aux infections ◆ **to find sb's ~ spot** trouver le point faible de qn

vulture /ˈvʌltʃəʳ/ N *(lit, fig)* vautour *m* ◆ **black ~** *(= bird)* moine *m*

vulva /ˈvʌlvə/ N (pl **vulvas** *or* **vulvae** /ˈvʌlviː/) vulve *f*

vying /ˈvaɪɪŋ/ N rivalité *f*, concurrence *f*

W, w /ˈdʌbljuː/ N [1] *(= letter)* W, w *m* ◆ **W for Willie** ≃ W comme William [2] (abbrev of **watt**) W [3] (abbrev of **west**) O., ouest

W. abbrev of **Wales, Welsh**

WA [1] abbrev of **Washington** [2] abbrev of **Western Australia**

wacko* /ˈwækəʊ/ ADJ ⇒ **wacky** N cinglé(e)* *m(f)*

wacky* /ˈwækɪ/ ADJ loufoque* COMP **wacky baccy*** N *(Brit: hum)* herbe* *f (marijuana)*, shit* *m*

wad /wɒd/ N [1] *(= plug, ball) [of cloth, paper]* tampon *m* ; *[of putty, chewing gum]* boulette *f* ; *(for gun)* bourre *f* ; *[of straw]* bouchon *m* ◆ **a ~ of cotton wool** un tampon d'ouate ◆ **a ~ of tobacco** *(uncut)* une carotte de tabac ; *(for chewing)* une chique de tabac [2] *(= bundle, pile) [of papers, documents]* tas *m*, pile *f* ; *(tied together)* liasse *f* ; *[of banknotes]* liasse *f* [3] **~s** or **a ~ of cash** * *(= lots of money)* des paquets *mpl* de fric*
VT [1] (also **wad up**) *[+ paper, cloth, cotton wool]* faire un tampon de ; *[+ putty, chewing gum]* faire une boulette de [2] *[+ garment]* doubler d'ouate, ouater ; *[+ quilt]* rembourrer [3] (also **wad up**) *[+ hole, crack]* boucher avec un tampon *or* avec une boulette

wadding /ˈwɒdɪŋ/ N *(NonC) (= raw cotton or felt: also for gun)* bourre *f* ; *(gen: for lining or padding)* rembourrage *m*, capiton *m* ; *(for garments)* ouate *f*

waddle /ˈwɒdl/ VI *[duck]* se dandiner ; *[person]* se dandiner, marcher comme un canard ◆ **to ~ in/out/across** *etc* entrer/sortir/traverser *etc* en se dandinant N dandinement *m*

wade /weɪd/ VI [1] *(= paddle)* ◆ **to go wading** barboter ◆ **to ~ through water/mud/long grass** avancer *or* marcher dans l'eau/la boue/l'herbe haute ◆ **he ~d ashore** il a regagné la rive à pied ◆ **to ~ across a river** traverser une rivière à gué
[2] *(* = advance with difficulty)* **to ~ through a crowd** se frayer un chemin à travers une foule ◆ **I managed to ~ through his book** je suis (péniblement) venu à bout de son livre ◆ **it took me an hour to ~ through your essay** il m'a fallu une heure pour venir à bout de votre dissertation ◆ **he was wading through his homework** il s'échinait sur ses devoirs
[3] *(= attack)* **to ~ into sb** * *(physically)* se jeter *or* se ruer sur qn ; *(verbally)* tomber sur qn, prendre qn à partie
VT *[+ stream]* passer *or* traverser à gué

▸ **wade in** * VI *(in fight/argument etc)* se mettre de la partie *(dans une bagarre/dispute etc)*

wader /ˈweɪdəʳ/ N [1] *(= boot)* cuissarde *f*, botte *f* de pêcheur [2] *(= bird)* échassier *m*

wadge /wɒdʒ/ N ⇒ **wodge**

wadi /ˈwɒdɪ/ N (pl **wadies**) oued *m*

wading /ˈweɪdɪŋ/ N *(NonC)* barbotage *m*, pataugeage *m*
COMP **wading bird** N échassier *m*
wading pool N *(US)* petit bassin *m*

wafer /ˈweɪfəʳ/ N [1] *(Culin)* gaufrette *f* ; *(Rel)* hostie *f* ; (= seal) cachet *m (de papier rouge)* [2] *(Comput, Elec)* tranche *f* ◆ **silicon ~** tranche *f* de silicium COMP **wafer-thin** ADJ mince comme du papier à cigarette *or* comme une pelure d'oignon

wafery /ˈweɪfərɪ/ ADJ ⇒ **wafer-thin** ; → **wafer**

waffle¹ /ˈwɒfl/ N *(Culin)* gaufre *f* COMP **waffle iron** N gaufrier *m*

waffle²* /ˈwɒfl/ *(Brit)* N *(NonC, when speaking)* verbiage *m* ; *(in book, essay)* remplissage *m*, délayage *m* ◆ **there's too much ~ in this essay** il y a trop de remplissage *or* de délayage dans cette dissertation VI *(when speaking)* parler pour ne rien dire ; *(in book, essay)* faire du remplissage *or* du délayage ◆ **he was waffling on about ...** il parlait interminablement de ...

waffler* /ˈwɒfləʳ/ N *(Brit)* personne *f* qui fait du verbiage

waft /wɑːft/ VT *[+ smell, sound]* porter, apporter ; (also **waft along**) *[+ boat]* faire avancer, pousser ; *[+ clouds]* faire glisser *or* avancer VI *[sound, smell]* flotter N *[of air, scent]* (petite) bouffée *f*

wag¹ /wæg/ VT *[animal] [+ tail]* remuer ◆ **the dog ~ged its tail** le chien a remué la queue ◆ **he ~ged his finger/his pencil at me** il a agité le doigt/son crayon dans ma direction ◆ **to ~ one's head** hocher la tête VI *[tail]* remuer ; *(excitedly)* frétiller ◆ **his tongue never stops ~ging** *(fig)* il a la langue bien pendue, il ne s'arrête jamais de bavarder ◆ **tongues are ~ging** les langues vont bon train, ça fait jaser ◆ **the news set tongues ~ging** la nouvelle a fait marcher les langues *or* a fait jaser (les gens) N *[of tail]* remuement *m* ; *(excitedly)* frétillement *m* ◆ **with a ~ of its tail** en remuant la queue

wag² *(o.f or hum)* /wæg/ N *(= joker)* plaisantin *m*, farceur *m*, -euse *f*

wage /weɪdʒ/ N salaire *m*, paie *or* paye *f* ; *[of domestic servant]* gages *mpl* ◆ **weekly/hourly ~** salaire *m* hebdomadaire/horaire ◆ **I've lost two days' ~s** j'ai perdu deux jours de salaire *or* de paie ◆ **his week's ~s** son salaire *or* sa paye de la semaine ◆ **his ~ is** *or* **his ~s are £250 per week** il touche un salaire de 250 livres par semaine, il gagne *or* est payé 250 livres par semaine ◆ **he gets a good ~** il est bien payé, il a un bon salaire ◆ **the ~s of sin is death** *(Bible)* la mort est le salaire du péché ; → **living**
VT ◆ **to ~ war** faire la guerre *(against* à, contre) ◆ **to ~ a campaign** faire campagne *(against* contre), mener une campagne *(for* pour)
COMP **wage bargaining** N *(NonC)* négociations *fpl* salariales
wage bill N ⇒ **wages bill**
wage claim N ⇒ **wages claim**
wage clerk N ⇒ **wages clerk**
wage demand N ⇒ **wages claim**
wage differential N écart *m* salarial *or* de salaires
wage drift N dérapage *m* salarial, dérive *f* des salaires
wage earner N salarié(e) *m(f)* ◆ **she is the family ~ earner** c'est elle qui fait vivre sa famille *or* qui est le soutien de sa famille ◆ **we are both ~ earners** nous gagnons tous les deux notre vie
wage freeze N ⇒ **wages freeze**
wage increase N augmentation *f or* hausse *f* de salaire
wage packet N *(esp Brit) (lit)* enveloppe *f* de paie ; *(fig)* paie *or* paye *f*
wage-price spiral N spirale *f* prix-salaires
wage-push inflation N inflation *f* par les salaires
wage rates NPL niveau *m* des salaires
wage restraint N limitation *f* des salaires
wage rise N ⇒ **wage increase**
wages bill N masse *f* salariale
wage scale N grille *f* des salaires
wages claim N *(Brit)* revendication *f* salariale
wages clerk N employé(e) *m(f)* au service de la paie, ≃ aide-comptable *mf*
wage settlement N ⇒ **wages settlement**
wages freeze N blocage *m* des salaires
wage slave N *(hum)* ◆ **I'm a ~ slave** je ne suis qu'un pauvre salarié
wage slip N ⇒ **wages slip**
wage spread N *(US)* éventail *m* des salaires
wages settlement N accord *m* salarial
wages slip N bulletin *m* de salaire, fiche *f* de paie
wage worker N *(US)* ⇒ **wage earner**

waged /weɪdʒd/ ADJ *[person]* salarié

wager /ˈweɪdʒəʳ/ VT parier *(on* sur ; *that* que) ◆ **I'll ~ you £5 that he arrives late** je te parie 5 livres qu'il arrivera en retard N pari *m* ◆ **to lay a ~** faire un pari

waggish † /ˈwægɪʃ/ ADJ badin, facétieux

waggishly † /ˈwægɪʃlɪ/ ADV *[say]* d'une manière facétieuse, d'un ton facétieux *or* badin ; *[smile]* avec facétie

waggle /ˈwægl/ VT [+ pencil, branch] agiter ; [+ loose screw, button] faire jouer ; [+ one's toes, fingers, ears] remuer ; [+ loose tooth] faire bouger ◆ **he ~d his finger at me** il a agité le doigt dans ma direction ◆ **to ~ one's hips** tortiller des hanches VI [toes, fingers, ears] remuer ; [tail] remuer ; (excitedly) frétiller ◆ **his hips ~d as he walked** il tortillait des hanches en marchant

waggon /ˈwægən/ N (esp Brit) ⇒ **wagon**

Wagnerian /vɑːgˈnɪərɪən/ ADJ wagnérien

wagon /ˈwægən/ N (horse- or ox-drawn) chariot m ; (= truck) camion m ; (Brit Rail) wagon m (de marchandises) ; (US: also **station wagon**) break m ◆ **the ~** * (US = police van) le panier à salade * ◆ **to go/be on the ~** * (fig) ne plus/ne pas boire (d'alcool), se mettre/être au régime sec ◆ **he's off the ~ (again)** * il s'est remis à boire ◆ **to circle the ~s, to pull one's ~s in a circle** (fig) se serrer les coudes (pour faire front) ; → **station** COMP **wagon train** N (US Hist) convoi m de chariots

wagoner /ˈwægənəʳ/ N roulier m, charretier m

wagonette /ˌwægəˈnet/ N break † m (hippomobile)

wagonload /ˈwægənləʊd/ N (Agr) charretée f ; (Rail) wagon m

wagtail /ˈwægteɪl/ N (= bird) hochequeue m, lavandière f

waif /weɪf/ N enfant mf misérable ; (homeless) enfant m(f) abandonné(e) ◆ **~s and strays** enfants abandonnés

wail /weɪl/ N [of person, wind, bagpipes] gémissement m, plainte f ; [of baby] vagissement m ; [of siren] hurlement m ◆ **to give a ~** pousser un gémissement or un vagissement, gémir, vagir VI [person] gémir, pousser un or des gémissement(s) ; (= cry) pleurer ; (= whine) pleurnicher ; [baby] vagir ; [wind] gémir ; [siren] hurler ; [bagpipes etc] gémir

wailing /ˈweɪlɪŋ/ N (NonC) [of person, wind] gémissements mpl, plaintes fpl ; (= whining) pleurnicheries fpl ; [of baby] vagissements mpl ; [of siren] hurlement m ; [of bagpipes] gémissement m ADJ [voice, person] gémissant ; [sound] plaintif COMP **the Wailing Wall** N le mur des Lamentations

wain /weɪn/ N (liter) chariot m ◆ **Charles's Wain** (Astron) le Chariot de David, la Grande Ourse

wainscot /ˈweɪnskət/ N lambris m (en bois)

wainscot(t)ing /ˈweɪnskətɪŋ/ N lambrissage m (en bois)

waist /weɪst/ N 1 (Anat, Dress) taille f ◆ **he put his arm round her ~** il l'a prise par la taille ◆ **she measures 70cm round the ~** elle fait 70 cm de tour de taille ◆ **they were stripped to the ~** ils étaient nus jusqu'à la ceinture, ils étaient torse nu ◆ **he was up to the** or **his ~ in water** l'eau lui arrivait à la ceinture or à mi-corps 2 (= narrow part) [of jar, vase etc] étranglement m, resserrement m ; [of violin] partie f resserrée de la table 3 (US) (= blouse) corsage m, blouse f ; (= bodice) corsage m, haut m VT [+ jacket etc] cintrer

COMP **waist measurement, waist size** N tour m de taille

waist slip N jupon m

waistband /ˈweɪstbænd/ N ceinture f

waistcoat /ˈweɪstkəʊt/ N (Brit) gilet m

-waisted /ˈweɪstɪd/ ADJ (in compounds) ◆ **to be slim-waisted** avoir la taille fine ◆ **high-/low-waisted dress** robe f à taille haute/basse ; → **shirtwaist**

waistline /ˈweɪstlaɪn/ N taille f ◆ **I've got to think of my ~** je dois faire attention à ma ligne

wait /weɪt/ N 1 attente f ◆ **you'll have a three-hour ~** vous aurez trois heures d'attente or à attendre ◆ **it was a long ~** il a fallu attendre longtemps, l'attente a été longue ◆ **there is a half-hour ~ at Leeds** (on coach journey etc = pause) il y a un arrêt d'une demi-heure or une demi-heure d'arrêt à Leeds ◆ **there was a 20-minute ~ between trains** il y avait 20 minutes de battement or d'attente entre les trains ◆ **during the ~ between the performances** pendant le battement or la pause entre les représentations

◆ **to be** or **lie in wait** être à l'affût ◆ **to be** or **lie in ~ for** [huntsman, lion] guetter ; [bandits, guerrillas] dresser un guet-apens or une embuscade à ◆ **the journalists lay in ~ for him as he left the theatre** les journalistes l'attendaient (au passage) à sa sortie du théâtre or le guettaient à sa sortie du théâtre

2 (Brit) ◆ **the ~s** les chanteurs mpl de Noël (qui vont de porte en porte)

VI 1 attendre ◆ **to ~ for sb/sth** attendre qn/qch ◆ **to ~ for sb to leave** attendre le départ de qn, attendre que qn parte ◆ **we ~ed and ~ed** nous avons attendu à n'en plus finir ◆ **to ~ until sb leaves** attendre que qn parte ◆ **~ till you're old enough** attends d'être assez grand ◆ **can you ~ till 10 o'clock?** pouvez-vous attendre jusqu'à 10 heures ? ◆ **parcel ~ing to be collected** colis m en souffrance ◆ **I'll have the papers ~ing for you** je ferai en sorte que les documents soient là quand vous arriverez ◆ **"repairs while you wait"** (Comm) "réparations minute" ◆ **they do it while you ~** (Comm) ils le font pendant que vous attendez

◆ **to keep sb waiting** faire attendre qn ◆ **don't keep us ~ing** ne te fais pas attendre, ne nous fais pas attendre ◆ **I was kept ~ing in the corridor** on m'a fait attendre dans le couloir, j'ai fait le pied de grue dans le couloir

2 (fig) ◆ **just you ~!** attends un peu ! ◆ **just ~ till your father finds out!** attends un peu que ton père apprenne ça ! ◆ **all that can ~ till tomorrow** tout cela peut attendre jusqu'à demain ◆ **~ for it!** * (Brit) (= order to wait) attendez ! ; (= guess what) devinez quoi !* ◆ **~ and see!** attends (voir) ! ; see also **comp** ◆ **we'll just have to ~ and see** il va falloir attendre, il va falloir voir venir ◆ **~ and see what happens next** attendez voir ce qui va se passer ◆ **that was worth ~ing for** cela valait la peine d'attendre ◆ **everything comes to he who ~s** tout vient à point à qui sait attendre (Prov)

◆ **can't wait** ◆ **I just can't ~ for next Saturday!** je meurs d'impatience or d'envie d'être à samedi prochain ! ◆ **I can't ~ to see him again!** (longingly) je meurs d'envie de le revoir ! ◆ **I can't ~ for the day when this happens** je rêve du jour où cela arrivera ◆ **the Conservatives can't ~ to reverse this policy** les conservateurs brûlent de révoquer cette politique

3 servir ◆ **to ~ (at table)** servir à table, faire le service

VT 1 [+ signal, orders, one's turn] attendre ◆ **I ~ed two hours** j'ai attendu (pendant) deux heures ◆ **could you ~ a moment?** vous pouvez patienter un moment ? ◆ **~ a moment** or **a minute** or **a second!** (attendez) un instant or une minute ! ; (interrupting, querying) minute !* ◆ **to ~ one's moment** or **chance (to do sth)** attendre son heure (pour faire qch) ◆ **we'll ~ lunch for you** (esp US) nous vous attendrons pour nous mettre à table

2 (esp US) **to ~ table** servir à table, faire le service

COMP **wait-and-see tactics** NPL (Pol etc) attentisme m

wait-listed ADJ (Travel) ◆ **to be ~-listed on a flight** être sur la liste d'attente d'un vol

► **wait about, wait around** VI attendre ; (= loiter) traîner ◆ **to ~ about for sb** attendre qn, faire le pied de grue pour qn ◆ **the job involves a lot of ~ing about** on perd beaucoup de temps à attendre dans ce métier ◆ **you can't expect him to ~ about all day while you ...** tu ne peux pas exiger qu'il traîne subj toute la journée à t'attendre pendant que tu ...

► **wait behind** VI rester ◆ **to ~ behind for sb** rester pour attendre qn

► **wait in** VI (esp Brit) rester à la maison (for sb pour attendre qn)

► **wait on** VT FUS 1 [servant, waiter] servir ◆ **I'm not here to ~ on him!** je ne suis pas sa bonne or son valet de chambre ! ◆ **she ~s on him hand and foot** elle est aux petits soins pour lui

2 (frm) ⇒ **wait upon 1**

3 (Scot, N Engl) attendre ◆ **I'm ~ing on him finishing** j'attends qu'il finisse ◆ **~ on!** attends !

► **wait out** VT SEP ◆ **to wait it out** patienter

► **wait up** VI (= not go to bed) ne pas se coucher, veiller ◆ **we ~ed up till 2 o'clock** nous avons veillé or attendu jusqu'à 2 heures, nous ne nous sommes pas couchés avant 2 heures ◆ **she always ~s up for him** elle attend toujours qu'il rentre subj pour se coucher, elle ne se couche jamais avant qu'il ne soit rentré ◆ **don't ~ up (for me)** couchez-vous sans m'attendre ◆ **you can ~ up to see the programme** tu peux te coucher plus tard pour regarder l'émission

► **wait upon** VT FUS 1 (frm) [ambassador, envoy etc] présenter ses respects à

2 ⇒ **wait on 1**

waiter /ˈweɪtəʳ/ N garçon m de café, serveur m ◆ **~!** Monsieur or garçon, s'il vous plaît ! ; → **dumbwaiter, head, wine**

waiting /ˈweɪtɪŋ/ N (NonC) attente f ◆ **"no waiting"** (on road sign) "arrêt interdit" ◆ **all this ~!** ce qu'on attend !, dire qu'il faut attendre si longtemps ! ◆ **to be in ~ on sb** (frm) être attaché au service de qn ; → **lady** ADJ qui attend

COMP **waiting game** N (fig) ◆ **to play a ~ game** (gen) attendre son heure ; (in diplomacy, negotiations etc) mener une politique d'attente, se conduire en attentiste

waiting list N liste f d'attente

waiting room N salle f d'attente

waitress /ˈweɪtrɪs/ N serveuse f ◆ **~!** Mademoiselle (or Madame), s'il vous plaît ! VI travailler comme serveuse

waitressing /ˈweɪtrɪsɪŋ/ N (NonC) travail m de serveuse

waive /weɪv/ VT (Jur) (= relinquish) [+ one's claim, right, privilege] renoncer à ; (= relax) [+ condition, age limit] renoncer à appliquer ; (= abolish) [+ sb's rights] abolir ◆ **the art gallery ~s admission charges on Sundays** le musée d'art est gratuit le dimanche ◆ **they ~d normal requirements for permits to cross the border** ils ont renoncé à exiger un permis pour passer la frontière

waiver /ˈweɪvəʳ/ N [of law] dérogation f (of à) ; [of requirement] (= abolition) annulation f (of de) ; (= relaxing) dispense f (of de) ; [of right] (= relinquishing) renonciation f (of à) ; (= abolition) abolition f (of de) ; [of restrictions] levée f (of de) ; (Insurance) clause f de renonciation ◆ **to sign a ~ (of responsibility)** signer une décharge ◆ **tax/visa ~** exemption f d'impôts/de visa

wake[1] /weɪk/ N [of ship] sillage m, eaux fpl ◆ **in the ~ of the storm/unrest/dispute** à la suite de l'orage/des troubles/du conflit ◆ **in the ~ of the army** dans le sillage or sur les traces de l'armée ◆ **the war brought famine in its ~** la guerre a amené la famine dans son sillage ◆ **to follow in sb's ~** marcher sur les traces de qn or dans le sillage de qn

wake[2] /weɪk/ (vb : pret **woke, waked**, ptp **waked, woken, woke**) N 1 (over corpse) veillée f mortuaire

2 (N Engl) **Wakes (Week)** semaine de congé annuel dans le nord de l'Angleterre

VI (also **wake up**) se réveiller, s'éveiller (from de) ◆ **~ up!** réveille-toi ! ◆ **~ up (to yourself)!** * (fig = think what you're doing) tu ne te rends pas compte ! ◆ ~ **up and smell the coffee!*** *(US)* arrête de rêver ! ◆ **to ~ from sleep** se réveiller, s'éveiller ◆ **to ~ (up) from a nightmare** *(lit)* se réveiller d'un cauchemar ; *(fig)* sortir d'un cauchemar ◆ **she woke (up) to find them gone** en se réveillant *or* à son réveil elle s'est aperçue qu'ils étaient partis ◆ **he woke up (to find himself) in prison** il s'est réveillé en prison ◆ **he woke up to find himself rich** à son réveil il était riche ◆ **to ~ (up) to sth** *(fig)* prendre conscience de *or* se rendre compte de qch ◆ **to ~ (up) from one's illusions** revenir de ses illusions ◆ **he suddenly woke up and started to work hard** *(= stirred himself)* il s'est tout à coup réveillé *or* remué *or* secoué et s'est mis à travailler dur ◆ **he suddenly woke up and realized that ...** *(= understood)* tout à coup ses yeux se sont ouverts et il s'est rendu compte que ...

VT (also **wake up**) *[+ person]* réveiller *(from* de), tirer du sommeil ; *(fig) [+ memories]* (r)éveiller, ranimer ; *[+ desires]* éveiller ◆ **a noise that would ~ the dead** un bruit à réveiller les morts ◆ **he needs something to ~ him up** *(fig)* il aurait besoin d'être secoué

COMP **wake-up call** N 1 *(Telec)* réveil *m* téléphonique, mémo appel *m* 2 *(esp US = warning)* avertissement *m*

wakeful /ˈweɪkfʊl/ ADJ 1 *(= unable to sleep)* éveillé ◆ **I had a ~ night** *(awake part of night)* je n'ai pratiquement pas dormi de la nuit, j'ai mal dormi ; *(didn't sleep at all)* j'ai passé une nuit blanche, je n'ai pas dormi de la nuit 2 *(frm = vigilant) [person]* vigilant

wakefulness /ˈweɪkfʊlnɪs/ N 1 *(= sleeplessness)* insomnie *f* 2 *(frm = watchfulness)* vigilance *f*

waken /ˈweɪkən/ VTI ⇒ **wake²**

waker /ˈweɪkəʳ/ N ◆ **to be an early ~** se réveiller tôt

wakey-wakey* /ˈweɪkɪˈweɪkɪ/ EXCL réveillez-vous !, debout !

waking /ˈweɪkɪŋ/ ADJ ◆ **in one's ~ hours** pendant les heures de veille ◆ **he devoted all his ~ hours to ...** il consacrait chaque heure de sa journée à ... ◆ **~ or sleeping, he ...** (qu'il soit) éveillé ou endormi, il ... N (état *m* de) veille *f* ◆ **between ~ and sleeping** dans un (état de) demi-sommeil COMP **waking dream** N rêve *m* éveillé

Waldorf salad /ˌwɔːldɔːfˈsæləd/ N *(Culin)* salade *f* Waldorf *(composée de pommes, noix, céleri et mayonnaise)*

wale /weɪl/ N *(US)* ⇒ **weal¹**

Wales /weɪlz/ N le pays de Galles ◆ **in ~** au pays de Galles ◆ **North/South ~** le Nord/le Sud du pays de Galles ◆ **Secretary of State for ~** *(Brit)* ministre *m* des Affaires galloises ; → **prince**

walk /wɔːk/ N 1 *(= stroll)* promenade *f* ; *(= ramble)* randonnée *f* ◆ **to go for a country ~** faire une promenade à la campagne ◆ **to go for a ~, to take** *or* **have a ~** se promener, faire une promenade ; *(shorter)* faire un tour ◆ **let's have a** *or* **go for a little ~** promenons-nous un peu, allons faire un petit tour ◆ **he had a long ~** il a fait une grande promenade ◆ **we went on a long ~ to see the castle** nous avons fait une excursion (à pied) pour visiter le château ◆ **on their ~ to school** en allant à l'école (à pied), sur le chemin de l'école ◆ **on their ~ home** en rentrant chez eux (à pied) ◆ **the Post Office is on my ~ home (from work)** le bureau de poste est sur mon chemin quand je rentre chez moi (du travail) ◆ **to take sb for a ~** emmener qn se promener *or* en promenade ◆ **to take the dog for a ~** promener le chien ◆ **to do a 10-km ~** faire une promenade de 10 km ◆ **the house is ten minutes' ~ from here** la maison est à dix minutes de marche d'ici *or* à dix minutes à pied d'ici ◆ **it's only a short ~ to the shops** il n'y a pas loin à marcher jusqu'aux magasins, il n'y a pas loin pour aller aux magasins ◆ **(go) take a ~!*** fous le camp !*, dégage !* ◆ **in a ~*** *(US fig = easily) [win]* dans un fauteuil* ; *[do sth]* les doigts dans le nez* ◆ **it was a ~ in the park*** *(US)* ça a été facile comme tout* ; → **sponsor**

2 *(= gait)* démarche *f*, façon *f* de marcher ◆ **I knew him by his ~** je l'ai reconnu à sa démarche *or* à sa façon de marcher

3 *(= pace)* ◆ **he slowed down to a ~** il a ralenti pour aller au pas ◆ **you've got plenty of time to get there at a ~** vous avez tout le temps pour y arriver sans courir ◆ **she set off at a brisk ~** elle est partie d'un bon pas

4 *(= path, route: in country)* chemin *m*, sentier *m* ; *(= avenue)* avenue *f*, promenade *f* ◆ **a coastal ~** un chemin côtier ◆ **there's a nice ~ by the river** il y a un joli chemin *or* sentier le long de la rivière, il y a une jolie promenade à faire le long de la rivière ◆ **people from all ~s** *or* **every ~ of life** des gens de tous (les) horizons

5 *(US:* also **sidewalk**) trottoir *m*

6 *(Sport = walking race)* épreuve *f* de marche

VI 1 *(gen)* marcher ; *(= not run)* aller au pas, ne pas courir ◆ **I haven't ~ed since the accident** je n'ai pas (re)marché depuis l'accident ◆ **I can't ~ as I used to** je n'ai plus mes jambes d'autrefois ◆ **to learn to ~** *[baby, injured person]* apprendre à marcher ◆ **to ~ across the road** traverser la route ◆ **you should always ~ across the road** on ne doit jamais traverser la rue en courant ◆ **to ~ across/down** *etc* traverser/descendre *etc* (à pied *or* sans courir) ◆ **he ~ed up/down the stairs** *(gen = went up/down)* il a monté/descendu l'escalier ; *(= didn't run)* il a monté/descendu l'escalier sans courir ◆ **he was ~ing up and down** il marchait de long en large, il faisait les cent pas ◆ **don't ~ on the grass** ne marchez pas sur la pelouse ; *(on sign)* "pelouse interdite" ◆ **to ~ with a stick/with crutches** marcher avec une canne/des béquilles, marcher à l'aide d'une canne/de béquilles ◆ **I'll ~ with you** je vais vous accompagner ◆ **to ~ in one's sleep** être somnambule, marcher en dormant ◆ **she was ~ing in her sleep** elle marchait en dormant ◆ **you must learn to ~ before you can run** avant de vouloir courir il faut savoir marcher ◆ **~, don't run** ne cours pas ◆ **"walk/don't walk"** *(US: at pedestrian crossing)* "(piétons) traversez/attendez"

2 *(= not ride or drive)* aller à pied ; *(= go for a walk)* se promener, faire une promenade ◆ **they ~ed all the way to the village** ils ont fait tout le chemin à pied jusqu'au village ◆ **I always ~ home** je rentre toujours à pied ◆ **shall we ~ a little?** si nous faisions quelques pas ?, si nous marchions un peu ? ; *(longer walk)* si nous nous promenions un peu ? ◆ **they were out ~ing** ils étaient partis se promener (à pied)

3 *[ghost]* apparaître

4 *(* fig hum) [object]* disparaître, se volatiliser ◆ **my pen seems to have ~ed** mon stylo a disparu *or* s'est volatilisé

5 *(* = be acquitted)* être acquitté

VT 1 *[+ distance]* faire à pied ◆ **he ~s 5km every day** il fait 5 km (de marche) à pied par jour ◆ **you can ~ it in a couple of minutes** vous y serez en deux minutes à pied, à pied vous en avez pour deux minutes ◆ **he ~ed it in ten minutes** il l'a fait à pied en dix minutes, il lui a fallu dix minutes à pied ◆ **he ~ed it*** *(fig = it was easy)* cela a été un jeu d'enfant pour lui

2 *[+ town etc]* parcourir ◆ **to ~ the streets** se promener dans les rues ; *(from poverty)* errer dans les rues, battre le pavé ; *[prostitute]* faire le trottoir ◆ **he ~ed the town looking for a dentist** il a parcouru la ville en tous sens à la recherche d'un dentiste ◆ **they ~ed the countryside in search of ...** ils ont battu la campagne à la recherche de ... ◆ **I've ~ed this road many times** j'ai pris cette route (à pied) bien des fois

3 *(= cause to walk) [+ dog]* promener ; *[+ horse]* conduire à pied ◆ **to ~ sb in/out** *etc* faire entrer/sortir *etc* qn ◆ **to ~ sb home** raccompagner qn (chez lui *or* elle) ◆ **he seized my arm and ~ed me across the room** il m'a pris par le bras et m'a fait traverser la pièce ◆ **I had to ~ my bike home** j'ai dû pousser mon vélo jusqu'à la maison ◆ **to ~ a cooker/chest of drawers across a room** pousser une cuisinière/une commode petit à petit d'un bout à l'autre d'une pièce *(en la faisant pivoter d'un pied sur l'autre)* ◆ **the nurse ~ed him down the ward to exercise his legs** l'infirmier l'a fait marcher *or* se promener dans la salle pour qu'il s'exerce *subj* les jambes ◆ **they ~ed him off his feet** ils l'ont tellement fait marcher qu'il ne tenait plus debout ◆ **I ~ed him round Paris** je l'ai promené dans Paris ◆ **I ~ed him round the garden to show him the plants** je lui ai fait faire le tour du jardin pour lui montrer les plantes ◆ **I ~ed him round the garden till he was calmer** je me suis promené avec lui dans le jardin jusqu'à ce qu'il se calme *subj* ◆ **I'll ~ you to the station** je vais vous accompagner (à pied) à la gare ◆ **he ~ed her to her car** il l'a raccompagnée jusqu'à sa voiture

COMP **walk-in** ADJ *[wardrobe, cupboard, larder]* de plain-pied ◆ **in ~-in condition** *[flat, house]* habitable immédiatement

walk-on part N *(Theat)* rôle *m* de figurant(e), figuration *f*

walk-through N *(Theat etc)* répétition *f* technique

walk-up N *(US) (= house)* immeuble *m* sans ascenseur ; *(= apartment)* appartement *m* dans un immeuble sans ascenseur

► **walk about** VI ⇒ **walk around**

► **walk across** VI *(over bridge etc)* traverser ◆ **to ~ across to sb** s'approcher de qn, se diriger vers qn

► **walk around** VI se promener ◆ **within two days of the accident, she was ~ing around** deux jours après l'accident, elle marchait de nouveau ◆ **stand up and ~ around a little to see how the shoes feel** levez-vous et faites quelques pas pour voir comment vous vous sentez dans ces chaussures

► **walk away** VI partir ◆ **to ~ away from sb** s'éloigner de qn, quitter qn ◆ **he ~ed away with the wrong coat** il s'est trompé de manteau en partant ◆ **to ~ away from an accident** *(= be unhurt)* sortir indemne d'un accident ◆ **to ~ away with sth** *(fig = win easily)* gagner *or* remporter qch haut la main ◆ **I did the work but he ~ed away with all the credit** c'est moi qui ai fait tout le travail et c'est lui qui a reçu tous les éloges

► **walk back** VI *(= come back)* revenir ; *(= go back)* retourner ; *(= go home)* rentrer ; *(specifically on foot)* revenir *or* rentrer *or* retourner à pied

► **walk in** VI entrer ◆ **who should ~ in but Paul!** et qui entre sur ces entrefaites ? Paul ! ◆ **they just ~ed in and took all my money** ils sont entrés et ont pris tout mon argent ◆ **he just ~ed in and gave me the sack** il est entré sans crier gare et m'a annoncé qu'il me mettait à la porte

ADJ ◆ **walk-in** → **walk**

► **walk in on** VT FUS surprendre ◆ **he just ~ed in on me!** il est entré sans prévenir !

► **walk into** VT FUS 1 *[+ trap, ambush]* tomber dans ◆ **you really ~ed into that one!*** tu es vraiment tombé *or* tu as vraiment donné dans le panneau ! ◆ **he wondered what he had ~ed into** il se demandait dans quelle galère* il s'était laissé entraîner

2 *(= hit against) [+ person, lamppost, table]* se cogner à

3 *(= find easily) [+ job]* trouver sans problème *or* facilement

► **walk off** VI 1 ⇒ **walk away** VI

2 *(= steal)* **to ~ off with sth*** barboter* *or* faucher* qch

VT SEP *[+ excess weight]* perdre en marchant ◆ **to ~ off a headache** prendre l'air *or* faire une promenade pour se débarrasser d'un mal de tête

► **walk off with*** VT FUS ⇒ **walk away with** ; → **walk away**

► **walk on** VI *(Theat)* être figurant(e), jouer les utilités

► **walk out** VI *(= go out)* sortir ; *(= go away)* partir ; *(as protest)* partir (en signe de protestation) ; *(= go on strike)* se mettre en grève ◆ **you can't ~ out now!** *(fig)* tu ne peux pas partir comme ça !, tu ne peux pas tout laisser tomber* comme ça ! ◆ **her husband has ~ed out** son mari l'a quittée *or* plaquée* ◆ **they ~ed out of the meeting** ils ont quitté la réunion (en signe de protestation)

► **walk out on*** VT FUS *[+ boyfriend, business partner]* laisser tomber*, plaquer*

► **walk out with** † VT FUS *(Brit = court)* fréquenter †

► **walk over** VI passer (à pied), faire un saut (à pied) ◆ **I'll ~ over tomorrow morning** j'y passerai *or* j'y ferai un saut (à pied) demain matin ◆ **he ~ed over to me and said ...** il s'est approché de moi et a dit ...

VT FUS * 1 *(= defeat easily)* battre haut la main

2 *(= treat badly: also* **walk all over***)* marcher sur les pieds de ◆ **she lets him ~ all over her** elle se laisse marcher sur les pieds (sans jamais lui faire de reproche)

► **walk through** VT FUS *(Theat)* répéter les mouvements de

N ◆ **walk-through** → **walk**

► **walk up** VI *(= go upstairs etc)* monter ; *(= approach)* s'approcher *(to sb* de qn*)* ◆ **~ up, ~ up!** *(at fair etc)* approchez, approchez ! ◆ **I saw the car and ~ed up to it** j'ai vu la voiture et m'en suis approché

N ◆ **walk-up** → **walk**

walkabout /ˈwɔːkəbaʊt/ N *(Austral)* voyage *m* (d'un aborigène) dans le bush ; *(Brit) [of president, celebrity]* bain *m* de foule ◆ **to go ~** *(Austral = go for a walk)* partir se balader* dans le bush ; *(Brit) [president, celebrity]* prendre un bain de foule, (* fig hum) *[object]* disparaître, se volatiliser

walkathon* /ˈwɔːkəθɒn/ N *(US)* marathon *m* (de marche)

walkaway* /ˈwɔːkəweɪ/ N *(US: also* **walkaway victory** *or* **win***)* victoire *f* facile

walker /ˈwɔːkəʳ/ N 1 *(esp Sport)* marcheur *m*, -euse *f* ; *(for pleasure)* promeneur *m*, -euse *f* ◆ **I'm not a great ~** je ne suis pas un grand marcheur ◆ **he's a fast ~** il marche vite ; → **sleepwalker, streetwalker** 2 *(= support frame) (for invalid)* déambulateur *m* ; *(for babies)* trotte-bébé *m* COMP **walker-on** N *(Theat)* figurant(e) *m(f)*, comparse *mf*

walkies* /ˈwɔːkɪz/ N *(Brit)* ◆ **to go ~** *(lit)* aller se promener ; *(fig)* disparaître

walkie-talkie /ˈwɔːkɪˈtɔːkɪ/ N talkie-walkie *m*

walking /ˈwɔːkɪŋ/ N 1 *(NonC)* marche *f* à pied, promenade(s) *f(pl)* (à pied) ; → **sleepwalking**

2 *(Sport)* marche *f* (athlétique) ; *(Basketball)* marcher *m*

ADJ ambulant ◆ **the ~ wounded** *(Mil)* les blessés *mpl* capables de marcher ◆ **he's a ~ encyclopedia** c'est une encyclopédie ambulante *or* vivante ◆ **he is a ~ miracle** c'est un miracle ambulant, il revient de loin

COMP **walking-boot** N chaussure *f* de randonnée *or* de marche

walking distance N ◆ **it is within ~ distance (of the house)** on peut facilement y aller à pied (de la maison) ◆ **five minutes' ~ distance away** à cinq minutes de marche

walking frame N déambulateur *m*

walking holiday N ◆ **we had a ~ holiday in the Tyrol** pour nos vacances nous avons fait de la marche dans le Tyrol

walking pace N ◆ **at (a) ~ pace** au pas

walking papers* NPL *(US)* ◆ **to give sb his ~ papers** renvoyer qn, mettre *or* flanquer* qn à la porte

walking race N épreuve *f* de marche

walking shoe N chaussure *f* de marche

walking stick N canne *f*

walking tour, walking trip N ◆ **to be on a ~ tour** *or* **trip** faire une randonnée à pied (de plusieurs jours)

Walkman ® /ˈwɔːkmən/ N Walkman ® *m*, baladeur *m*, somnambule *m (Can)*

walkout /ˈwɔːkaʊt/ N *(= strike)* grève *f* surprise ; *(from meeting, lecture etc)* départ *m* (en signe de protestation) ◆ **to stage a ~** *[workers]* faire une grève surprise ; *[students, delegates etc]* partir (en signe de protestation)

walkover /ˈwɔːkəʊvəʳ/ N *(Racing)* walk-over *m inv* ◆ **it was a ~!** * *(fig) [game]* c'était une victoire facile ! ; *[exam]* c'était un jeu d'enfant !, c'était simple comme bonjour ! ◆ **it was a ~ for Moore*** *(Sport)* Moore a gagné haut la main

walkway /ˈwɔːkweɪ/ N *(Brit)* sentier *m* pédestre ; *(US)* passage *m* pour piétons, cheminement *m* piéton

Walkyrie /vælˈkɪərɪ/ N Walkyrie *f*

wall /wɔːl/ N *(gen)* mur *m* ; *(interior: also of trench, tunnel)* paroi *f* ; *(round garden, field)* mur *m* (de clôture) ; *(round city, castle etc)* murs *mpl*, remparts *mpl* ; *(Anat)* paroi *f* ; *[of tyre]* flanc *m* ; *(fig) [of mountains]* mur *m*, muraille *f* ; *[of smoke, fog]* mur *m* ◆ **within the (city) ~s** dans les murs, dans la ville ◆ **the north ~ of the Eiger** la face nord *or* la paroi nord de l'Eiger ◆ **they left only the bare ~s standing** ils n'ont laissé que les murs ◆ **a high tariff ~** *(Econ)* une barrière douanière élevée ◆ **~s have ears** les murs ont des oreilles ◆ **to go over the ~** *[prisoner]* s'évader, se faire la belle* ◆ **to go to the ~** *(fig) [person]* perdre la partie ; *(= go bankrupt)* faire faillite ; *[plan, activity]* être sacrifié ◆ **it's always the weakest who go to the ~** ce sont toujours les plus faibles qui écopent* ◆ **he had his back to the ~, he was up against the ~** *(fig)* il avait le dos au mur, il était acculé ◆ **to get sb up against the ~, to drive** *or* **push sb to the ~** acculer qn, mettre qn au pied du mur ◆ **to bang** *or* **knock** *or* **beat one's head against a (brick) ~** *(fig)* se taper la tête contre les murs ◆ **to come up against a (blank) ~, to come up against a stone** *or* **brick ~** *(fig)* se heurter à un mur ◆ **to drive** *or* **send sb up the ~*** rendre qn dingue* *or* fou ; → **Berlin, great, off, party**

VT *[+ garden]* entourer d'un mur, construire un mur autour de ; *[+ city]* fortifier, entourer de murs *or* de remparts ◆ **~ed garden** jardin *m* clos ◆ **~ed town** ville *f* fortifiée

COMP *[decoration, clock, map]* mural

wall bars NPL espalier *m (pour exercices de gymnastique)*

wall chart N planche *f* murale

wall cupboard N placard *m* mural *or* suspendu

wall lamp, wall light N applique *f*

wall lighting N éclairage *m* par appliques

wall-mounted ADJ *[clock, phone]* mural

wall socket N prise *f* (murale)

Wall Street N *(US)* Wall Street *m*

wall to wall ADV ◆ **to carpet sth ~ to ~** recouvrir qch de moquette

wall-to-wall ADJ ◆ **~-to-~ carpet(ing)** moquette *f* ◆ **it got ~-to-~ coverage** on ne parlait que de ça (dans les médias) ◆ **there were ~-to-~ people** l'endroit était bondé

► **wall in** VT SEP *[+ garden etc]* entourer d'un mur

► **wall off** VT SEP *[+ plot of land]* séparer par un mur

► **wall up** VT SEP *[+ doorway, window]* murer, condamner ; *[+ person, relics]* murer, emmurer

wallaby /ˈwɒləbɪ/ N (pl **wallabies** *or* **wallaby**) wallaby *m*

wallah /ˈwɒlə/ N *(Hist)* ◆ **the laundry** *etc* **~** *(in India)* le préposé au blanchissage *etc*

wallboard /ˈwɔːlbɔːd/ N *(US)* panneau *m* de revêtement

wallcovering /ˈwɔːlkʌvərɪŋ/ N revêtement *m* mural

wallet /ˈwɒlɪt/ N portefeuille *m* ; *(of pilgrim etc)* besace *f*

walleye /ˈwɔːlaɪ/ N *(= squint)* strabisme *m* divergent

walleyed /ˈwɔːlaɪd/ ADJ atteint de strabisme divergent

wallflower /ˈwɔːlflaʊəʳ/ N giroflée *f* ◆ **to be a ~** *(= not socialize, dance)* faire tapisserie

Walloon /wɒˈluːn/ ADJ wallon N 1 Wallon(ne) *m(f)* 2 *(= dialect)* wallon *m*

wallop* /ˈwɒləp/ N *(= slap)* torgnole* *f* ; *(with fist)* gnon‡ *m* ; *(in accident)* coup *m* ; *(sound)* fracas *m*, boucan* *m* ◆ **to give sb a ~** flanquer une beigne* *or* une torgnole* à qn ◆ **~!** vlan ! ◆ **it hit the floor with a ~** vlan ! c'est tombé par terre VT *[+ person]* flanquer une beigne* *or* une torgnole* à ; *[+ ball, object]* taper dans, donner un *or* des grand(s) coup(s) dans ADV ◆ **he went ~ into the wall** il est rentré* en plein dans le mur

walloping‡ /ˈwɒləpɪŋ/ ADJ sacré* *before n* ◆ **~ big** vachement grand* ◆ **a ~ $100 million** la somme astronomique de 100 millions de dollars N raclée* *f*, rossée* *f* ◆ **to give sb a ~** *(= punish)* flanquer une raclée* *or* une rossée* à qn ; *(Sport etc) (= beat)* enfoncer* qn, battre qn à plate(s) couture(s)

wallow /ˈwɒləʊ/ VI *[person, animal]* se vautrer *(in* dans*)* ; *[ship]* être ballotté ; *(fig) (in vice, sin)* se vautrer *(in* dans*)* ; *(in self-pity etc)* se complaire *(in* à*)* N 1 *(= pool, bog etc)* mare *f* bourbeuse 2 *(in bath)* ◆ **to have a ~** * se prélasser

wallpaper /ˈwɔːlpeɪpəʳ/ N papier *m* peint ; *(Comput)* fond *m* d'écran VT tapisser (de papier peint) COMP **wallpaper music*** N *(pej)* musique *f* d'ascenseur *(pej)* *or* de supermarché *(pej)*

wally* /ˈwɒlɪ/ N *(Brit)* andouille* *f*

walnut /ˈwɔːlnʌt/ N noix *f* ; *(also* **walnut tree***)* noyer *m* ; *(NonC = wood)* noyer *m* COMP *[table etc]* de *or* en noyer ; *[cake]* aux noix ; *[oil]* de noix

Walpurgis Night /vælˈpʊəgɪsnaɪt/ N la nuit de Walpurgis

walrus /ˈwɔːlrəs/ N (pl **walruses** *or* **walrus**) morse *m (animal)* COMP **walrus moustache** N moustache *f* à la gauloise

Walter Mitty /ˌwɔːltəˈmɪtɪ/ N ◆ **he's something of a ~ (character)** il vit dans un monde imaginaire

waltz /wɔːls/ N valse *f* ◆ **it was a ~!*** *(US fig)* c'était du gâteau* *or* de la tarte !* VI valser, danser la valse ◆ **to ~ in/out** *etc (fig) (gaily)* entrer/sortir *etc* d'un pas joyeux *or* dansant ; *(brazenly)* entrer/sortir *etc* avec désinvolture ◆ **she ~ed in without even knocking*** elle a fait irruption sans même frapper ◆ **he ~ed off with the prize*** il a gagné le prix haut la main ◆ **he ~ed* into the job** il n'a pas eu besoin de se fouler* pour obtenir ce poste VT ◆ **he ~ed her round the room** il l'a entraînée dans une valse tout autour de la pièce ; *(fig: in delight etc)* il s'est mis à danser de joie avec elle

► **waltz through*** VT FUS *[+ exam]* être reçu les doigts dans le nez* ; *[+ competition, match]* gagner les doigts dans le nez*

waltzer /ˈwɔːlsəʳ/ N [1] *(= dancer)* valseur *m*, -euse *f* [2] *(at fairground)* Mont-Blanc *m*

wampum /ˈwɒmpəm/ N [1] *(= beads)* wampum *m* [2] *(US* ‡ *= money)* pognon‡ *m*, fric‡ *m*

WAN /wæn/ N *(Comput)* (abbrev of **wide area network**) → **wide**

wan /wɒn/ ADJ *[face, light, sky]* blême, blafard ; *[person]* au visage blême *or* blafard ; *[smile]* pâle *before n* ♦ **to look ~** *[person]* avoir le visage blême *or* blafard ♦ **to grow ~** *[light, sky]* blêmir

wand /wɒnd/ N *[of conjurer, fairy]* baguette *f* (magique) ; *[of usher, steward, sheriff]* verge *f*, bâton *m* ; *(Comput)* crayon *m* optique, photostyle *m*

wander /ˈwɒndəʳ/ N tour *m*, balade* *f* ♦ **to go for a ~ around the town/the shops** aller faire un tour en ville/dans les magasins ♦ **to have** *or* **take a ~** faire un tour, aller se balader*

VI [1] *[person]* errer, aller sans but ; *(for pleasure)* flâner ; *[thoughts]* errer, vagabonder ; *[river, road]* serpenter, faire des méandres ♦ **he ~ed through the streets** il errait *or* allait sans but dans les rues ♦ **his gaze ~ed round the room** son regard errait dans la pièce

[2] *(= stray)* s'égarer ♦ **to ~ from the point** *or* **subject** s'écarter du sujet ♦ **his eyes ~ed from the page** son regard distrait s'est écarté de la page ♦ **his thoughts ~ed back to his youth** ses pensées se sont distraitement reportées à sa jeunesse ♦ **his attention ~ed** il était distrait, il n'arrivait pas à fixer son attention *or* à se concentrer ♦ **sorry, my mind was ~ing** excusez-moi, j'étais distrait ♦ **his mind ~ed to the day when ...** il repensa par hasard au jour où ... ♦ **his mind is ~ing, he's ~ing*** *(pej) (from fever)* il délire, il divague ; *(from old age)* il divague, il déraille* ♦ **don't take any notice of what he says, he's just ~ing*** ne faites pas attention à ce qu'il dit, il radote

[3] *(= go casually)* **to ~ in/out/away** *etc* entrer/sortir/partir *etc* d'un pas nonchalant ♦ **they ~ed round the shop** ils ont flâné dans le magasin ♦ **let's ~ down to the café** allons tranquillement au café

VT parcourir au hasard, errer dans ; *(for pleasure)* flâner dans ♦ **to ~ the streets** aller au hasard des rues, errer dans les rues ♦ **to ~ the hills/the countryside** se promener au hasard *or* errer dans les collines/dans la campagne ♦ **to ~ the world** courir le monde, rouler sa bosse*

► **wander about, wander around** VI *(aimlessly)* errer, aller sans but ; *[animals]* errer ♦ **to ~ about the town/the streets** *(leisurely)* errer dans la ville/dans les rues ♦ **we ~ed around looking in the shop windows** nous avons flâné en faisant du lèche-vitrine

► **wander off** VI partir ; *(= get lost)* s'égarer ♦ **he ~ed off the path** il s'est écarté du chemin

wanderer /ˈwɒndərəʳ/ N vagabond(e) *m(f) (also pej)* ♦ **the ~'s returned!** *(hum)* tiens, un revenant !

wandering /ˈwɒndərɪŋ/ ADJ *[person, gaze]* errant ; *[imagination, thoughts]* vagabond ; *[band]* itinérant ; *[tribe]* nomade ; *[river, road]* qui serpente, en lacets ♦ **a ~ way of life** une vie errante ♦ **to have a ~ eye** reluquer les filles* ♦ **to have ~ hands** avoir les mains baladeuses

NPL **wanderings** *(= journeyings)* pérégrinations *fpl*, voyages *mpl* ; *(fig) (in speech etc)* divagations *fpl* ♦ **her ~s in Europe and Africa** ses pérégrinations en Europe et en Afrique, ses voyages à travers l'Europe et l'Afrique

COMP **wandering Jew** N *(= plant)* misère *f* ♦ **the Wandering Jew** *(Myth)* le Juif errant

wandering minstrel N ménestrel *m*

wanderlust /ˈwɒndəlʌst/ N envie *f* de voir le monde, bougeotte* *f*

wane /weɪn/ VI *[moon]* décroître ; *[enthusiasm, interest, emotion]* diminuer ; *[strength, reputation, popularity, empire]* décliner, être en déclin N ♦ **to be on the ~** ⇒ **to wane;** → **vi**

wangle* /ˈwæŋgl/ VT *(= get)* se débrouiller pour avoir, resquiller* ♦ **to ~ sth for sb** se débrouiller pour obtenir qch pour qn ♦ **can you ~ me a free ticket?** est-ce que tu peux m'avoir *or* te débrouiller pour m'obtenir un billet gratuit ? ♦ **I'll ~ it somehow** je me débrouillerai pour arranger ça, je goupillerai* ça ♦ **he ~d £10 out of his father** il a soutiré 10 livres à son père

wangling* /ˈwæŋglɪŋ/ N *(NonC)* système D* *m*, carottage* *m*, resquille* *f*

waning /ˈweɪnɪŋ/ N *(NonC) [of moon]* décroissement *m* ; *[of popularity, influence]* déclin *m* ADJ *[moon]* à son déclin ; *[enthusiasm, interest]* qui diminue ; *[strength, reputation, popularity, empire]* déclinant, sur son déclin

wank**/wæŋk/ *(Brit)* VI se branler**, se faire une branlette** N [1] ♦ **to have a ~** ⇒ **to wank;** → **vi** [2] *(NonC = nonsense)* foutaise‡ *f*

wanker**/ˈwæŋkəʳ/ N *(Brit fig)* branleur** *m*

wanky**/ˈwæŋkɪ/ ADJ péteux*

wanly /ˈwɒnlɪ/ ADV [1] *(= weakly) [smile]* faiblement ; *[say]* mollement [2] *(= faintly) [shine]* avec une lueur blafarde *or* blême

wanna* /ˈwɒnə/ [1] ⇒ **want a** [2] ⇒ **want to**

wannabe‡ /ˈwɒnəbiː/ N ♦ **an Elvis ~** un type qui joue les Elvis* ADJ ♦ **a ~ Elvis** un type qui joue les Elvis* ♦ **a ~ writer** quelqu'un qui rêve de devenir écrivain

wanness /ˈwɒnnɪs/ N *[of person, complexion]* pâleur *f*

want /wɒnt/ LANGUAGE IN USE 3.3, 8

N [1] *(NonC = lack)* manque *m* ♦ **there was no ~ of enthusiasm** ce n'était pas l'enthousiasme qui manquait

♦ **for want of ...** faute de ..., par manque de ... ♦ **for ~ of anything better** faute de mieux ♦ **for ~ of anything better to do** faute d'avoir quelque chose de mieux à faire ♦ **for ~ of something to do he ...** comme il n'avait rien à faire il ..., par désœuvrement il ... ♦ **it wasn't for ~ of trying that he ...** ce n'était pas faute d'avoir essayé qu'il ...

[2] *(NonC = poverty, need)* besoin *m* ♦ **to be** *or* **live in ~** être dans le besoin, être nécessiteux † ♦ **to be in ~ of sth** avoir besoin de qch

[3] *(gen pl = requirement, need)* **~s** besoins *mpl* ♦ **his ~s are few** il a peu de besoins, il n'a pas besoin de grand-chose ♦ **it fills** *or* **meets a long-felt ~** cela comble enfin cette lacune

VT [1] *(= wish, desire)* vouloir, désirer *(to do sth* faire qch) ♦ **what do you ~?** que voulez-vous ?, que désirez-vous ? ♦ **what do you ~ with** *or* **of him?** qu'est-ce que vous lui voulez ? ♦ **what do you ~ to do tomorrow?** qu'est-ce que vous avez envie de faire demain ?, qu'est-ce que vous voulez *or* désirez faire demain ? ♦ **I don't ~ to!** je n'en ai pas envie ! ; *(more definite)* je ne veux pas ! ♦ **all I ~ is a good night's sleep** tout ce que je veux, c'est une bonne nuit de sommeil ♦ **he ~s success/popularity** il veut *or* désire le succès/la popularité ♦ **I ~ your opinion on this** je voudrais votre avis là-dessus ♦ **what does he ~ for that picture?** combien veut-il *or* demande-t-il pour ce tableau ? ♦ **I ~ the car cleaned** je veux qu'on nettoie *subj* la voiture ♦ **I always ~ed a car like this** j'ai toujours voulu *or* souhaité avoir une voiture comme ça ♦ **I ~ed** *or* **I was ~ing to leave** j'avais envie de partir ♦ **to ~ in/out*** vouloir entrer/sortir ♦ **he ~s out*** *(fig)* il ne veut plus continuer, il veut laisser tomber* ♦ **you're not ~ed here** on n'a pas besoin de vous ici, on ne veut pas de vous ici ♦ **I know when I'm not ~ed!*** je me rends compte que je suis de trop ♦ **where do you ~ this table?** où voulez-vous (qu'on mette) cette table ? ♦ **you've got him where you ~ him** *(fig)* vous l'avez coincé*, vous le tenez à votre merci ♦ **you don't ~ much!** *(iro)* il n'en faut pas beaucoup pour vous faire plaisir *or* vous satisfaire ! *(iro)* ♦ **to ~ sb** *(sexually)* désirer qn

♦ **to want sb to do sth** vouloir que qn fasse qch ♦ **I ~ you to tell me** je veux que tu me dises ♦ **I ~ you to listen to me** je veux que tu m'écoutes

[2] *(= seek, ask for)* demander ♦ **the manager ~s you in his office** le directeur veut vous voir *or* vous demande dans son bureau ♦ **you're ~ed on the phone** on vous demande au téléphone ♦ **to be ~ed by the police** être recherché par la police ♦ **"good cook wanted"** "recherchons cuisinier ou cuisinière qualifié(e)" ; see also **wanted**

[3] *(gen Brit) (= need) [person]* avoir besoin de ; *[task]* exiger, réclamer ; *(* = ought)* devoir *(to do sth* faire qch) ♦ **we have all we ~** nous avons tout ce qu'il nous faut ♦ **just what I ~(ed)!** exactement ce qu'il me faut ! ♦ **you ~ a bigger hammer if you're going to do it properly** tu as besoin de *or* il te faut un plus gros marteau pour faire cela correctement ♦ **what do you ~ with a house that size?** pourquoi as-tu besoin d'une *or* veux-tu une maison aussi grande ? ♦ **such work ~s good eyesight** un tel travail exige *or* nécessite une bonne vue ♦ **the car ~s cleaning** la voiture a besoin d'être lavée, il faudrait laver la voiture ♦ **your hair ~s combing** tu as besoin d'un coup de peigne, il faudrait que tu te peignes *subj*, tu devrais te peigner ♦ **that child ~s a smacking** cet enfant a besoin d'une *or* mérite une bonne fessée ♦ **you ~ to be careful with that!*** fais attention avec ça !, fais gaffe* avec ça ! ♦ **you ~ to see his new boat!*** tu devrais voir son nouveau bateau !

VI *(= be in need)* être dans le besoin, être nécessiteux ♦ **to ~ for sth** *(= lack)* manquer de qch, avoir besoin de qch ♦ **they ~ for nothing** il ne leur manque rien, ils ne manquent de rien, ils n'ont besoin de rien ; → **waste**

COMP **want ad** N *(US Press)* petite annonce *f*

wanted /ˈwɒntɪd/ ADJ [1] *(Police) [criminal]* recherché ♦ **America's most ~ man** le criminel le plus recherché de toute l'Amérique ♦ **"wanted (for murder)"** "recherché (pour meurtre)" ♦ **"wanted: dead or alive"** "recherché : mort ou vif" ♦ **a "wanted" poster** un avis de recherche ; see also **want vt 2** [2] *(Press)* ♦ **"wanted"** "cherche" ♦ **"wanted: good cook"** "recherchons cuisinier ou cuisinière qualifié(e)" ; see also **want vt 2** COMP **wanted list** N liste *f* de personnes recherchées

wanting /ˈwɒntɪŋ/ ADJ *(= deficient)* ♦ **to be ~ in sth** manquer de qch ♦ **the necessary funds were ~** les fonds nécessaires faisaient défaut, il manquait les fonds nécessaires ♦ **the end of the poem is ~** *(= missing)* il manque la fin du poème, la fin du poème manque ; *(= deficient)* la fin du poème est faible ♦ **to find sth ~** trouver que qch laisse à désirer ♦ **to find sb ~** trouver que qn ne fait pas l'affaire ♦ **to be found ~** *[person, thing]* ne pas faire l'affaire ♦ **to prove ~** se révéler insuffisant PREP *(= without)* sans ; *(= minus)* moins

wanton /ˈwɒntən/ ADJ [1] *(pej = gratuitous) [destruction, violence, cruelty]* gratuit ; *[killer]* qui tue sans raison [2] *(† pej = dissolute) [woman, behaviour]* dévergondé [3] *(liter = playful) [person, behaviour, breeze]* capricieux [4] *(liter = luxuriant) [growth, weeds]* luxuriant, exubérant N † libertin *m*, femme *f* légère

wantonly /ˈwɒntənlɪ/ *(pej)* ADV 1 *(= gratuitously) [destroy, violate]* gratuitement ◆ ~ **cruel** d'une cruauté gratuite 2 († *= dissolutely) [behave, desire]* de façon dévergondée

wantonness /ˈwɒntənnɪs/ N (NonC) 1 *(= gratuitousness) [of destruction, violence, cruelty]* gratuité *f* 2 († *pej = dissoluteness) [of person, behaviour]* dévergondage *m*

WAP /wæp/ N (abbrev of **wireless application protocol**) WAP *m*

war /wɔːʳ/ N guerre *f* ◆ **to be at** ~ être en (état de) guerre *(with* avec) ◆ **to go to** ~ *[country]* entrer en guerre *(against* contre ; *over* à propos de) ◆ **to go (off) to** ~ *[soldier]* partir pour la guerre, aller à la guerre ◆ **to make** ~ **on** *(Mil, also fig)* faire la guerre à ◆ ~ **of attrition** guerre *f* d'usure ◆ **the Wars of the Roses** la guerre des Deux-Roses ◆ **the War of the Vendée** *(Hist)* la Chouannerie ◆ **the Great War** la Grande Guerre, la guerre de 14 *or* de 14-18 ◆ **the** ~ **to end all** ~**s** la der des ders* ◆ **the (American) War of Independence** la guerre d'Indépendance ◆ **the period between the** ~**s** *(= 1918-39)* l'entre-deux-guerres *m inv* ◆ **to carry** *or* **take the** ~ **into the enemy's camp** *(Mil, fig)* passer à l'attaque, prendre l'offensive ◆ **it was** ~ **to the knife** *or* **the death between them** c'était une lutte à couteaux tirés entre eux ◆ ~ **of words** guerre *f* de paroles ◆ **you've been in the** ~**s again*** tu t'es encore fait amocher* *or* estropier ; → **cold, nerve, state**

VI faire la guerre *(against* à)

COMP *[conditions, debt, crime, criminal, orphan, widow, wound, zone]* de guerre

war baby N enfant *m* de la guerre

war bond N *(US Hist)* titre *m* d'emprunt de guerre *(pendant la Deuxième Guerre mondiale)*

war bride N mariée *f* de la guerre

war cabinet N *(Pol)* cabinet *m* de guerre

war chest N *(Pol)* caisse *f* spéciale (d'un parti politique pour les élections)

war clouds NPL *(fig)* signes *mpl* avant-coureurs de la guerre

war correspondent N *(Press, Rad, TV)* correspondant(e) *m(f)* de guerre

war cry N cri *m* de guerre

war dance N danse *f* guerrière

the War Department N *(US)* ⇒ **the War Office**

the war-disabled NPL les mutilés *mpl* (or mutilées *fpl*) *or* invalides *mfpl* de guerre

war fever N psychose *f* de guerre

war footing N ◆ **on a** ~ **footing** sur le pied de guerre

war games NPL *(Mil: for training)* kriegspiel *m* ; *(Mil = practice manoeuvres)* manœuvres *fpl* militaires ; *(= board games, computer games etc)* jeux *mpl* de stratégie militaire, wargames *mpl*

war grave N tombe *f* de soldat *(mort au champ d'honneur)*

war hero N héros *m* de la guerre

war lord N chef *m* militaire, seigneur *m* de la guerre

war memorial N monument *m* aux morts

the War Office N *(Brit)* le ministère de la Guerre

war paint N peinture *f* de guerre *(des Indiens)* ; *(fig hum = make-up)* maquillage *m*, peinturlurage *m (pej)*

war record N ◆ **what is his** ~ **record ?** comment s'est-il comporté *or* qu'a-t-il fait pendant la guerre ? ◆ **he has a good** ~ **record** ses états de service pendant la guerre sont tout à fait honorables

war-torn ADJ déchiré par la guerre

war-weariness N lassitude *f* de la guerre

war-weary ADJ las (lasse *f*) de la guerre

war whoop N *(US)* cri *m* de guerre

the war-wounded NPL les blessés *mpl* de guerre

warble¹ /ˈwɔːbl/ N 1 *(= abscess) [of cattle]* var(r)on *m* 2 *(on horse's back)* callosité *f*

warble² /ˈwɔːbl/ N *(= sound)* gazouillis *m*, gazouillements *mpl* VI *[bird]* gazouiller ; *[person]* roucouler ; *[telephone]* sonner VT (also **warble out**) chanter en gazouillant

warbler /ˈwɔːbləʳ/ N 1 *(= bird)* fauvette *f*, pouillot *m* 2 *(hum = singer)* chanteur *m*, -euse *f (à la voix de casserole)*

warbling /ˈwɔːblɪŋ/ N gazouillis *m*, gazouillement(s) *m(pl)*

ward /wɔːd/ N 1 *[of hospital]* salle *f* ; *(separate building)* pavillon *m* ; *[of prison]* quartier *m* 2 *(Brit Local Govt)* section *f* électorale 3 *(Jur = person)* pupille *mf* ◆ ~ **of court** pupille *mf* sous tutelle judiciaire ◆ **in** ~ sous tutelle judiciaire ; → **watch²**

COMP **ward heeler** N *(US Pol: pej)* agent *m or* courtier *m* électoral

ward round N *(Med)* visite *f (de médecin hospitalier)*

ward sister N *(Brit Med)* infirmière *f* en chef *(responsable d'une salle ou d'un pavillon)*

► **ward off** VT SEP *[+ blow, danger]* parer, éviter ; *[+ illness]* éviter

...ward /wəd/ SUF ⇒ **...wards**

warden /ˈwɔːdn/ N *[of institution]* directeur *m*, -trice *f* ; *[of city, castle]* gouverneur *m* ; *[of park, game reserve]* gardien *m*, -ienne *f* ; *[of youth hostel]* responsable *mf* ; *(Brit = prison warder)* surveillant(e) *m(f)* de prison ; *(US = prison governor)* directeur *m*, -trice *f* ; *[of student residence etc]* directeur *m*, -trice *f* de résidence universitaire ; *(Brit: on hospital board etc)* membre *m* du conseil d'administration ; *(Brit:* also **air-raid warden)** préposé(e) *m(f)* à la défense passive ; (also **traffic warden**) contractuel(le) *m(f)* ◆ **Warden of the Cinque Ports** *(Brit)* gouverneur *m* des Cinq Ports ; → **churchwarden, fire**

warder /ˈwɔːdəʳ/ N 1 *(esp Brit)* gardien *m or* surveillant *m* (de prison) 2 *(esp US) (in building)* concierge *m* ; *(in museum)* gardien *m* (de musée)

wardress /ˈwɔːdrɪs/ N *(esp Brit)* gardienne *f or* surveillante *f* (de prison)

wardrobe /ˈwɔːdrəʊb/ N 1 *(= cupboard) (gen)* armoire *f* ; *(for hanging only)* penderie *f* 2 *(= clothes)* garde-robe *f* ; *(Theat)* costumes *mpl* ◆ **Miss Lilly's** ~ **by ...** *(Cine, Theat)* costumes *mpl* de Mlle Lilly par ..., Mlle Lilly est habillée par ...

COMP **wardrobe mistress** N *(Theat)* costumière *f*

wardrobe trunk N malle-penderie *f*

wardroom /ˈwɔːdrʊm/ N *(Naut)* carré *m*

...wards /wədz/ SUF vers, dans la *or* en direction de ◆ **townwards** vers la ville, dans la *or* en direction de la ville ; → **backwards, downwards**

wardship /ˈwɔːdʃɪp/ N (NonC) tutelle *f*

ware /ˈwɛə/ N (NonC) articles *mpl* ◆ **kitchenware** articles *mpl* de cuisine ◆ **tableware** articles *mpl* pour la table ◆ **crystalware** articles *mpl* en cristal ◆ **silverware** argenterie *f* ; → **hardware** NPL **wares** *(= goods)* marchandises *fpl*

warehouse /ˈwɛəhaʊs/ N (pl **warehouses** /ˈwɛəˌhaʊzɪz/) entrepôt *m* VT /ˈwɛəhaʊz/ entreposer, mettre en magasin COMP **warehouse club** N *(esp US Comm) grande surface qui, pour une adhésion annuelle, vend ses produits en vrac à prix réduits*

warehouseman /ˈwɛəhaʊsmən/ N (pl **-men**) magasinier *m*

warehousing /ˈwɛəhaʊzɪŋ/ N *(Comm)* entreposage *m*

warfare /ˈwɔːfɛə/ N (NonC) *(Mil)* guerre *f NonC* ; *(fig)* lutte *f (against* contre) ◆ **class** ~ lutte *f* des classes

warfarin /ˈwɔːfərɪn/ N *(= poison)* warfarine *f* ; *(= drug)* Coumadine ® *f*

warhead /ˈwɔːhed/ N ogive *f* ◆ **nuclear** ~ ogive *f or* tête *f* nucléaire

warhorse /ˈwɔːhɔːs/ N cheval *m* de bataille ◆ **an old** ~ *(fig)* un vétéran

warily /ˈwɛərɪlɪ/ ADV *[watch, ask, say]* avec méfiance ◆ **to tread** ~ *(fig)* y aller avec méfiance

wariness /ˈwɛərɪnɪs/ N (NonC) *[of person]* méfiance *f (about or of sth* à l'égard de qch) ◆ ~ **about doing sth** méfiance *f* à faire qch ◆ **the** ~ **of his manner** sa méfiance, son attitude *f* méfiante

Warks abbrev of **Warwickshire**

warlike /ˈwɔːlaɪk/ ADJ guerrier, belliqueux

warlock /ˈwɔːlɒk/ N sorcier *m*

warm /wɔːm/ ADJ 1 *[liquid, object, air, climate, temperature, summer, day, night]* (assez) chaud ◆ **the water is just** ~ l'eau est juste chaude *or* n'est pas très chaude ◆ **I can't stand** ~ **coffee, I like it really hot** je déteste le café juste chaud, je l'aime brûlant ◆ **this room is quite** ~ il fait (assez) chaud dans cette pièce ◆ **leave the dough in a** ~ **place to rise** laissez lever la pâte dans un endroit chaud ◆ **it's too** ~ **in here** il fait trop chaud ici ◆ **it's nice and** ~ **in here** il fait bon *or* agréablement chaud ici ◆ **a** ~ **oven** un four moyen ◆ **the iron/oven is** ~ le fer/four est (assez) chaud ◆ **a nice** ~ **fire** un bon feu ◆ **it's** ~**, the weather is** ~ il fait bon ◆ **in** ~ **weather** par temps chaud ◆ **during the** ~**er months** pendant les mois où il fait moins froid ◆ **to keep sth** ~ tenir qch au chaud ◆ **it's** ~ **work** c'est un travail qui donne chaud ◆ **I am** ~ j'ai (assez) chaud ◆ **the body was still** ~ **when it was found** le corps était encore chaud quand on l'a trouvé ◆ **to get sth** ~ (ré)chauffer qch ◆ **to get** *or* **grow** ~ *[water, object]* chauffer ; *[person]* se réchauffer ◆ **come and get** ~ **by the fire** venez vous (ré)chauffer auprès du feu ◆ **you're getting** ~**(er)!** *(in guessing etc games)* tu chauffes ! ◆ **keep me** ~ tiens-moi chaud ◆ **keep him** ~ *(sick person)* ne le laissez pas prendre froid ◆ **this scarf keeps me** ~ cette écharpe me tient chaud ◆ **you've got to keep yourself** ~ surtout ne prenez pas froid ◆ **I'm as** ~ **as toast*** je suis bien au chaud

2 *(= cosy) [clothes, blanket]* chaud

3 *(fig) [colour, shade]* chaud ; *[voice, tone, feelings]* chaud, chaleureux ; *[greeting, welcome, congratulations, encouragement]* cordial, chaleureux ; *[apologies, thanks]* vif ; *[applause]* chaleureux, enthousiaste ; *[supporter]* ardent, chaud ◆ **the lamp gives out a** ~ **glow** cette lampe donne un éclairage chaud ◆ **to get a** ~ **reception (from sb)** être chaudement *or* chaleureusement reçu (par qn) ◆ **he gave me a** ~ **smile** il m'a adressé un sourire chaleureux ◆ **they have a very** ~ **relationship** ils ont beaucoup d'affection l'un pour l'autre ◆ **she is a very** ~ **person, she has a very** ~ **nature** elle est très chaleureuse (de nature) ◆ **to have a** ~ **heart** avoir beaucoup de cœur ◆ **she felt a** ~ **glow inside when she heard the news** la nouvelle lui a (ré) chauffé le cœur ◆ **"with warmest wishes"** *(in letter)* "avec mes vœux les plus sincères"

N * ◆ **to give sth a** ~ (ré)chauffer qch ◆ **come and have a** ~ **by the fire** viens te (ré)chauffer près du feu ◆ **come inside and sit in the** ~ entrez vous asseoir au chaud

VT 1 (also **warm up**) *[+ person, room]* réchauffer ; *[+ water, food]* (ré)chauffer, faire (ré) chauffer ; *[+ coat, slippers]* (ré)chauffer ◆ **to** ~ **o.s.** se réchauffer ◆ **to** ~ **one's feet/hands** se réchauffer les pieds/les mains ◆ **to** ~ **o.s. at the fire** se (ré)chauffer auprès du feu

2 *(fig)* ◆ **the news** ~**ed my heart** la nouvelle m'a (ré)chauffé le cœur ; → **cockle**

VI 1 (also **warm up**) *[person]* se (ré)chauffer ; *[water, food]* chauffer ; *[room, bed]* se réchauffer, devenir plus chaud ; *[weather]* se réchauffer

2 *(fig)* ◆ **to** ~ **to an idea** s'enthousiasmer peu à peu pour une idée ◆ **I** ~**ed to him** je me suis pris de sympathie pour lui ◆ **to** ~ **to one's**

theme *or* **subject** se laisser entraîner par son sujet, traiter son sujet avec un enthousiasme grandissant

COMP **warm-blooded** ADJ *[animal]* à sang chaud ; *(fig) (gen)* sensible ; *(sexually)* qui a le sang chaud

warm-down N *(after exercise)* séance *f* d'étirements

warm front N *(Weather)* front *m* chaud

warm-hearted ADJ chaleureux, affectueux

warm-up * N *(Sport)* échauffement *m* ; *(Rad, Theat, TV etc)* mise *f* en train ADJ *[routine, stretches]* d'échauffement

warm-ups NPL *(US)* survêtement *m*

► **warm down** VI *(after exercise)* faire des étirements

► **warm over, warm through** VT SEP *[+ food]* faire (ré)chauffer

► **warm up** VI 1 ⇒ **warm vi 1**

2 *[engine, car]* se réchauffer ; *[athlete, dancer]* s'échauffer

3 *(fig) [discussion]* s'échauffer, s'animer ; *[audience]* devenir animé ◆ **the party was ~ing up** la soirée commençait à être pleine d'entrain, la soirée chauffait* ◆ **things are ~ing up** ça commence à s'animer *or* à chauffer*

VT SEP 1 ⇒ **warm vt 1**

2 *[+ engine, car]* faire chauffer

3 *(fig) [+ discussion]* animer ; *(Theat etc) [+ audience]* mettre en train

N ◆ **warm-up** * → **warm**

warming /ˈwɔːmɪŋ/ ADJ *[drink, food]* qui réchauffe

COMP **warming pan** N bassinoire *f*

warming-up exercises NPL exercices *mpl* d'échauffement

warmly /ˈwɔːmlɪ/ ADV 1 *[dress]* chaudement ◆ ~ **tucked up in bed** bordé bien au chaud dans son lit ◆ **the sun shone** ~ le soleil était agréablement chaud 2 *(fig) [recommend]* chaudement ; *[greet, smile]* chaleureusement ; *[thank, applaud]* avec chaleur, chaleureusement ; *[say, speak of]* avec chaleur

warmonger /ˈwɔːˌmʌŋgəʳ/ N belliciste *mf*

warmongering /ˈwɔːˌmʌŋgərɪŋ/ ADJ belliciste N *(NonC)* propagande *f* belliciste

warmth /wɔːmθ/ N *(NonC: lit, fig)* chaleur *f* ◆ **they huddled together for** ~ ils se sont serrés l'un contre l'autre pour se tenir chaud ◆ **it was good to be in the ~ again** cela faisait du bien d'être de nouveau au chaud ◆ **for extra ~, wear a wool jumper** pour avoir plus chaud, portez un pull-over en laine ◆ **she greeted us with great ~** elle nous a accueillis avec beaucoup de chaleur *or* très chaleureusement

warn /wɔːn/ LANGUAGE IN USE 2.3 VT prévenir, avertir (*of* de ; *that* que) ◆ **to ~ the police** alerter la police ◆ **you have been ~ed!** vous êtes averti *or* prévenu ! ◆ **to ~ sb against doing sth** *or* **not to do sth** conseiller à qn de ne pas faire qch, déconseiller à qn de faire qch ◆ **to ~ sb off** *or* **against sth** mettre qn en garde contre qch, déconseiller qch à qn

warning /ˈwɔːnɪŋ/ N *(= act)* avertissement *m*, mise *f* en garde ; *(in writing)* avis *m*, préavis *m* ; *(= signal: also Mil)* alerte *f*, alarme *f* ; *[of weather conditions]* avis *m* ◆ **it fell without** ~ c'est tombé subitement ◆ **they arrived without** ~ ils sont arrivés à l'improviste *or* sans prévenir ◆ **he left me without** ~ il m'a quitté sans prévenir ◆ **let this be a ~ to you** que cela vous serve d'avertissement ◆ **thank you for the** ~ merci de m'avoir prévenu *or* averti ◆ **there was a note of ~ in his voice** il y avait une mise en garde dans le ton qu'il a pris ◆ **to take ~ from sth** tirer la leçon de qch ◆ **his employer gave him a ~ about lateness** son patron lui a donné un avertissement à propos de son manque de ponctualité ◆ **to give a week's** ~ prévenir huit jours à l'avance, donner un préavis de huit jours ◆ **I gave you due** *or* **fair ~ (that ...)** je vous avais bien prévenu (que ...) ◆ **gale/storm** ~ *(Met)* avis *m* de grand vent/de tempête ◆ **four minute** ~ *(Mil)* alerte *f* de quatre minutes

ADJ *[glance, cry]* d'avertissement ◆ **... he said in a ~ tone** *or* **voice** ... dit-il pour mettre en garde

COMP **warning device** N dispositif *m* d'alarme, avertisseur *m*

warning light N voyant *m* (avertisseur), avertisseur *m* lumineux

warning notice N avis *m*, avertissement *m*

warning shot N *(gen, Mil)* tir *m* de sommation ; *(Naut, also fig)* coup *m* de semonce

warning sign N panneau *m* avertisseur

warning triangle N *(Driving)* triangle *m* de présignalisation

warningly /ˈwɔːnɪŋlɪ/ ADV *[say]* sur un ton d'avertissement ; *[shake one's head]* en signe d'avertissement

warp /wɔːp/ N 1 *[of fabric]* chaîne *f* ; *(fig) (= essence, base)* fibre *f* 2 *(= distortion) (in wood)* gauchissement *m*, voilure *f* ; *(in metal)* voilure *f* ; *(Recording)* voile *m* (d'un disque) ; → **time** VT 1 *(lit) [+ wood]* gauchir, voiler ; *[+ metal, aircraft wing, tennis racket]* voiler 2 *(fig) [+ judgement]* fausser, pervertir ; *[+ mind, character, person]* pervertir ◆ **he has a ~ed mind, his mind is ~ed** il a l'esprit tordu ◆ **he has a ~ed sense of humour** il a un sens de l'humour morbide ◆ **he gave us a ~ed account of ...** il nous a fait un récit tendancieux de ... VI 1 *(lit) [ruler, board, wood]* gauchir ; *[wheel, metal plate]* se voiler ; *[mechanism]* se fausser 2 *(fig) [person, institution]* se pervertir

warpath /ˈwɔːpæθ/ N *(fig)* ◆ **to be on the** ~ être sur le sentier de la guerre, chercher la bagarre*

warplane /ˈwɔːpleɪn/ N avion *m* militaire *or* de guerre

warrant /ˈwɒrənt/ N 1 *(Jur, Police)* mandat *m* ; *(Jur)* ◆ **there is a ~ out against him, there is a ~ out for his arrest** il y a un mandat d'arrêt contre lui, un mandat d'arrêt a été délivré contre lui ◆ **do you have a ~?** *(to police officer)* vous avez un mandat (de perquisition) ? ; → **death, search**

2 *(NonC = justification)* justification *f*, droit *m* ◆ **he has no ~ for saying so** il ne s'appuie sur rien pour justifier cela

3 *(Comm, Fin etc = certificate: for payment or services)* bon *m* ; *(= guarantee)* garantie *f* ; *(Customs)* warrant *m* ; *(Mil)* brevet *m*

VT 1 *(= justify) [+ action, assumption, reaction, behaviour]* justifier, légitimer ◆ **the facts do not ~ it** les faits ne le justifient pas ◆ **his behaviour does not ~ his getting the sack** son comportement ne justifie pas son renvoi

2 *(= guarantee)* garantir ◆ **I'll ~ you he won't come back** je te garantis *or* je suis sûr qu'il ne va pas revenir ◆ **he won't come here again in a hurry, I'll ~ (you)!*** il ne reviendra pas de sitôt, tu peux me croire !

COMP **warrant card** N *(Brit Police)* carte *f* de police

warrant officer N *(Mil)* adjudant *m (auxiliaire de l'officier)*

warrant sale N *(Scot Jur)* vente *f* forcée *or* judiciaire

warrantable /ˈwɒrəntəbl/ ADJ justifiable, légitime

warranted /ˈwɒrəntɪd/ ADJ 1 *(= justified) [action, fears, charges]* justifié ◆ **she is ~ in feeling disappointed** sa déception est légitime 2 *(= guaranteed) [goods]* garanti

warrantee /ˌwɒrənˈtiː/ N *(Jur)* créancier *m*, -ière *f*

warranter, warrantor /ˈwɒrəntəʳ/ N *(Jur)* garant(e) *m(f)*, débiteur *m*, -trice *f*

warranty /ˈwɒrəntɪ/ N autorisation *f*, droit *m* ; *(Comm, Jur)* garantie *f* ◆ **under** ~ sous garantie

warren /ˈwɒrən/ N 1 *(also* **rabbit warren***)* garenne *f* 2 *(= building)* labyrinthe *m* ◆ **a ~ of little streets** un dédale *or* un labyrinthe de petites rues

warring /ˈwɔːrɪŋ/ ADJ *[nations]* en guerre ; *(fig) [interests]* contradictoire, contraire ; *[ideologies]* en conflit, en opposition

warrior /ˈwɒrɪəʳ/ N guerrier *m*, -ière *f* ; → **unknown**

Warsaw /ˈwɔːsɔː/ N Varsovie COMP **Warsaw Pact** N pacte *m* de Varsovie ◆ **the ~ Pact countries** les pays *mpl* du pacte de Varsovie

warship /ˈwɔːʃɪp/ N navire *m or* bâtiment *m* de guerre

wart /wɔːt/ N *(on skin)* verrue *f* ; *(on plant)* excroissance *f* ; *(on wood)* loupe *f* ◆ **~s and all** *(fig)* avec tous ses défauts COMP **wart hog** N phacochère *m*

wartime /ˈwɔːtaɪm/ N *(NonC)* temps *m* de guerre ◆ **in** ~ en temps de guerre COMP en temps de guerre

warty /ˈwɔːtɪ/ ADJ couvert de verrues, verruqueux

wary /ˈwɛərɪ/ ADJ *[person]* prudent, sur ses gardes ; *[voice, look, manner]* prudent ◆ **to be ~ about sb/sth** se méfier de qn/qch ◆ **to be ~ of doing sth** hésiter beaucoup à faire qch ◆ **to keep a ~ eye on sb/sth** avoir l'œil sur qn/qch, surveiller qn/qch de près

was /wɒz/ VB pt of **be**

wash /wɒʃ/ N 1 ◆ **to give sth a** ~ *(gen)* laver qch ; *[+ paintwork, walls]* lessiver qch ◆ **to give one's hands/hair/face a** ~ se laver les mains/les cheveux/le visage ◆ **to have a** ~ se laver ◆ **to have a quick** ~ se débarbouiller, faire un brin de toilette ◆ **to have a ~ and brush-up** faire sa toilette ◆ **it needs a** ~ cela a besoin d'être lavé, il faut laver cela ◆ **your face needs a** ~ il faut que tu te laves *subj* la figure *or* que tu te débarbouilles *subj*

2 *(= laundry)* ◆ **I do a big ~ on Mondays** je fais une grande lessive le lundi, le lundi est mon jour de grande lessive ◆ **put your jeans in the** ~ *(= ready to be washed)* mets ton jean au sale ◆ **your shirt is in the** ~ *(= being washed)* ta chemise est à la lessive ◆ **the colours ran in the** ~ cela a déteint à la lessive *or* au lavage ◆ **to send sheets to the** ~ envoyer des draps au blanchissage *or* à la laverie ◆ **it will all come out in the** ~ * *(fig) (= be known)* on finira bien par savoir ce qu'il en est ; *(= be all right)* ça finira par se tasser* *or* s'arranger ; → **car**

3 *[of ship]* sillage *m*, remous *m* ; *(= sound) [of waves etc]* clapotis *m*

4 *(= layer of paint: for walls etc)* badigeon *m* ◆ **to give the walls a blue** ~ badigeonner les murs en *or* de bleu ; → **whitewash**

5 *(Art)* lavis *m* ◆ **to put a ~ on a drawing** laver un dessin

6 *(Pharm)* solution *f* ; → **eyewash, mouthwash**

7 *(Brit Geog)* **the Wash** le golfe du Wash

VT 1 *(gen)* laver ; *[+ paintwork, walls]* lessiver ◆ **to ~ o.s.** *[person]* se laver ; *[cat]* faire sa toilette ◆ **to get ~ed** se laver, faire sa toilette ◆ **to ~ one's hair** se laver les cheveux ◆ **to ~ one's hands/feet/face** se laver les mains/les pieds/le visage ◆ **to ~ a child's face** laver le visage d'un enfant, débarbouiller un enfant ◆ **he ~ed the dirt off his hands** il s'est lavé les mains (pour en enlever la saleté) ◆ **to ~ the dishes** faire la vaisselle ◆ **to ~ the clothes** faire la lessive ◆ **can you ~ this fabric?** *(= is it washable)* ce tissu est-il lavable ? ◆ **~ this garment at 40°/in hot water** lavez ce vêtement à 40°/à l'eau chaude ◆ **to ~ sth with detergent** nettoyer qch avec du détergent ◆ **to ~ one's**

hands of sth se laver les mains de qch ◆ **to ~ one's hands of sb** se désintéresser de qn ; → **clean**

2 *[river, sea, waves] (= flow over)* baigner ◆ **the Atlantic ~es its western shores** la côte ouest est baignée par l'Atlantique ◆ **to ~ sth ashore** *(onto coast)* rejeter qch sur le rivage ; *(onto riverbank)* rejeter qch sur la rive ◆ **to be ~ed out to sea** être emporté par la mer, être entraîné vers le large ◆ **to be ~ed overboard** être emporté par une vague ◆ **it was ~ed downstream** le courant l'a entraîné *or* emporté

3 *(= paint)* ◆ **to ~ walls with distemper** passer des murs au badigeon, peindre des murs à la détrempe ◆ **to ~ brass with gold** couvrir du cuivre d'une pellicule d'or

4 *(Min) [+ earth, gravel, gold, ore]* laver ; *(Chem) [+ gas]* épurer

VI 1 *(= have a wash) [person]* se laver ; *[cat]* faire sa toilette ; *(= do the laundry)* laver, faire la lessive ◆ **he ~ed in cold water** il s'est lavé à l'eau froide ◆ **this garment ~es/doesn't ~ very well** ce vêtement se lave très facilement/ne se lave pas très facilement ◆ **you ~ and I'll dry** tu laves et moi j'essuie

2 *(Brit * fig)* ◆ **that just won't ~ !** ça ne prend pas ! ◆ **that excuse won't ~ with him** cette excuse ne prendra pas *or* ne marchera pas avec lui, on ne lui fera pas avaler cette excuse

3 *[waves, sea, flood, river]* **to ~ against** *[+ cliffs, rocks]* baigner ; *[+ lighthouse, boat]* clapoter contre ◆ **to ~ over sth** balayer qch ◆ **to ~ ashore** être rejeté sur le rivage

4 *(fig = flow)* **let the music ~ over you** laisse-toi bercer par la musique ◆ **a wave of nausea ~ed through her** elle a été prise d'une nausée soudaine ◆ **a wave of anger ~ed through her** elle a senti monter une bouffée de colère ◆ **relief ~ed over his face** il a soudain eu l'air profondément soulagé ◆ **a wave of sadness/tiredness ~ed over him** il a soudain ressenti une profonde tristesse/une grande fatigue ◆ **her explanation/words just ~ed over me** son explication a/ses paroles ont glissé sur moi

COMP **wash-and-wear** ADJ *[clothes, fabric]* facile à entretenir
wash drawing N *(Art)* (dessin *m* au) lavis *m*
wash-hand basin N lavabo *m*
wash house N lavoir *m*
wash leather N *(Brit)* peau *f* de chamois
wash load N charge *f* (de linge)
wash-out * N *(= event)* fiasco *m*, désastre *m* ; *(= person)* zéro * *m*, nullité * *f*
wash-wipe N *(on car window)* lave-glace *m inv* ; *(on headlamp)* essuie-phares *mpl*

► **wash away** VI s'en aller *or* partir au lavage
VT SEP 1 *[+ stain]* enlever *or* faire partir au lavage ; *(fig) [+ sins]* laver ◆ **the rain ~ed the mud away** la pluie a fait partir la boue
2 *[river, current, sea] (= carry away)* emporter, entraîner ; *[+ footprints etc]* balayer, effacer ◆ **the boat was ~ed away** le bateau a été emporté ◆ **the river ~ed away part of the bank** la rivière a emporté une partie de la rive

► **wash down** VT SEP 1 *[+ deck, car]* laver (à grande eau) ; *[+ wall]* lessiver
2 *[+ medicine, pill]* faire descendre *(with* avec) ; *[+ food]* arroser *(with* de)
3 *[rain, flood, river]* emporter, entraîner

► **wash in** VT SEP *[sea, tide]* rejeter (sur le rivage)

► **wash off** VI *(from clothes)* s'en aller *or* partir au lavage ; *(from walls)* partir au lessivage ◆ **it won't ~ off** ça ne s'en va pas, ça ne part pas ◆ **it will ~ off** *(from hands)* ça partira quand tu te laveras (*or* je me laverai *etc*) les mains
VT SEP *(from clothes)* faire partir au lavage ; *(from wall)* faire partir en lessivant

► **wash out** VI 1 *[stain]* s'en aller *or* partir au lavage ; *[dye, colours]* passer au lavage ◆ **this stain won't ~ out** cette tache ne s'en va pas *or* ne part pas
2 *(US)* **he ~ed out of university** * il s'est fait recaler aux examens de la fac *
VT SEP 1 *(= remove) [+ stain]* enlever *or* faire partir au lavage
2 *(= rinse) [+ bottle, pan]* laver ◆ **to ~ one's mouth out** *(lit)* se faire un bain de bouche ◆ **~ your mouth out (with soap and water)!** tu devrais avoir honte de dire des choses pareilles !
3 *(fig = spoil)* perturber ; *(* = cancel)* rendre impossible ◆ **the match was ~ed out** *(by rain) (= prevented)* le match a été annulé *or* n'a pas eu lieu à cause de la pluie ; *(= halted)* la pluie a perturbé *or* interrompu le match ◆ **to be/look/feel ~ed out** * *(= tired)* être/avoir l'air/se sentir complètement lessivé *
4 *(fig)* ◆ **washed-out** *(= pale) [colour]* délavé
N ◆ **wash-out** * → **wash**

► **wash through** VT SEP *[+ clothes]* laver rapidement, passer à l'eau

► **wash up** VI 1 *(Brit = wash dishes)* faire *or* laver la vaisselle
2 *(US = have a wash)* se débarbouiller, faire un brin de toilette
VT SEP 1 *(Brit) [+ plates, cups]* laver ◆ **to ~ up the dishes** faire *or* laver la vaisselle
2 *[sea, tide]* rejeter (sur le rivage) ; *[river]* rejeter (sur la berge)
3 *(gen pass: * = finish)* ◆ **to be (all) washed up** *[plan, scheme, marriage etc]* être fichu *, être tombé à l'eau * ◆ **Paul and Anne are all ~ed up** tout est fini entre Paul et Anne
4 *(US)* **to be/feel/look ~ed up** *(= tired etc)* être/se sentir/avoir l'air lessivé *

washable /ˈwɒʃəbl/ ADJ lavable, lessivable

washbag /ˈwɒʃbæg/ N trousse *f* de toilette

washbasin /ˈwɒʃbeɪsn/ N *(Brit) (= handbasin)* lavabo *m* ; *(= bowl)* cuvette *f*

washboard /ˈwɒʃbɔːd/ N planche *f* à laver ◆ **to have a ~ stomach, to have ~ abs** * avoir des tablettes de chocolat *

washbowl /ˈwɒʃbəʊl/ N cuvette *f*

washcloth /ˈwɒʃklɒθ/ N *(esp US)* ≃ gant *m* de toilette

washday /ˈwɒʃdeɪ/ N jour *m* de lessive

washdown /ˈwɒʃdaʊn/ N ◆ **to give sth a ~** laver qch à grande eau

washer /ˈwɒʃəʳ/ N 1 *(= ring)* rondelle *f*, joint *m* ; *(in tap)* rondelle *f* 2 *(= washing machine)* machine *f* à laver, lave-linge *m inv* ; *(for windscreen)* lave-glace *m inv* ; → **dishwasher, windscreen** COMP **washer-dryer** N lave-linge *m* séchant

washerwoman /ˈwɒʃəwʊmən/ N (pl **-women**) lavandière *f*, laveuse *f* (de linge)

washing /ˈwɒʃɪŋ/ N 1 *(= act) [of car]* lavage *m* ; *[of clothes] (gen)* lessive *f* ; *(professionally cleaned)* blanchissage *m* ; *[of walls]* lessivage *m* ; → **brainwashing**
2 *(NonC = clothes)* linge *m*, lessive *f* ◆ **to do the ~** faire la lessive, laver le linge ◆ **to hang out the ~** étendre le linge *or* la lessive ◆ **the dirty ~** le linge sale ; see also **dirty**
COMP **washing day** N jour *m* de lessive
washing line N corde *f* à linge
washing machine N machine *f* à laver, lave-linge *m inv*
washing powder N *(Brit)* lessive *f* (en poudre), détergent *m* (en poudre)
washing soda N cristaux *mpl* de soude
washing-up N *(Brit)* vaisselle *f (à laver)* ◆ **to do the ~-up** faire *or* laver la vaisselle ◆ **look at all that ~-up!** regarde tout ce qu'il y a comme vaisselle à faire *or* à laver !
washing-up bowl N bassine *f*, cuvette *f*
washing-up liquid N produit *m* pour la vaisselle
washing-up water N eau *f* de vaisselle

Washington /ˈwɒʃɪŋtən/ N *(= city)* Washington ; *(= state)* Washington *m* ◆ **in ~ (State)** dans le Washington

washrag /ˈwɒʃræg/ N *(US)* ≃ gant *m* de toilette

washroom /ˈwɒʃrʊm/ N toilettes *fpl*

washstand /ˈwɒʃstænd/ N table *f* de toilette

washtub /ˈwɒʃtʌb/ N *(for clothes)* baquet *m*, bassine *f*

washy /ˈwɒʃɪ/ ADJ ⇒ **wishy-washy**

wasn't /ˈwɒznt/ ⇒ **was not** ; → **be**

wasp /wɒsp/ N 1 guêpe *f* ◆ **~'s nest** guêpier *m* 2 *(US *)* (abbrev of **White Anglo-Saxon Protestant**) **Wasp** *or* **WASP** wasp *mf (Anglo-Saxon blanc et protestant)* COMP **wasp-waisted** ADJ à la taille de guêpe

waspish /ˈwɒspɪʃ/ ADJ grincheux, hargneux

waspishly /ˈwɒspɪʃlɪ/ ADV avec hargne

wassail †† /ˈwɒseɪl/ N *(= festivity)* beuverie *f* ; *(= drink)* bière *f* épicée VI faire ribote †

wast †† /wɒst/ VB 2nd pers sg pret of **be**

wastage /ˈweɪstɪdʒ/ N 1 *(NonC) [of resources, food]* gaspillage *m* ; *(as part of industrial process etc)* déperdition *f* ; *(= amount lost from container)* fuites *fpl*, pertes *fpl* ; *(= rejects)* déchets *mpl* ◆ **a great ~ of human resources** un grand gaspillage de ressources humaines ◆ **water/energy ~** gaspillage *m* d'eau/d'énergie ◆ **the amount of ~ that goes on in large establishments** le gaspillage *or* le gâchis qui se produit dans les grands établissements ; see also **waste** ; → **natural** 2 *(= wasting away) [of muscles, tissue]* atrophie *f* ◆ **muscle ~** atrophie *f* musculaire COMP **wastage rate** N ◆ **the ~ rate among students/entrants to the profession** le pourcentage d'étudiants qui abandonnent en cours d'études/de ceux qui abandonnent en début de carrière

waste /weɪst/ N 1 *(NonC) [of resources, energy, food, money]* gaspillage *m* ; *[of time]* perte *f* ◆ **to go to ~** être gaspillé, se perdre inutilement ; *[land]* tomber en friche, être à l'abandon ◆ **there's too much ~ in this firm** il y a trop de gaspillage dans cette compagnie ◆ **we must reduce the ~ in the kitchens** nous devons diminuer le gaspillage *or* le gâchis dans les cuisines ◆ **what a ~!** quel gaspillage ! ◆ **it's a ~ of effort** c'est un effort inutile ◆ **it's a ~ of human resources** c'est un gaspillage de ressources humaines ◆ **it's a ~ of money to do that** on gaspille de l'argent en faisant cela, on perd de l'argent à faire cela ◆ **that machine was a ~ of money** cela ne valait vraiment pas la peine d'acheter cette machine, on a vraiment fichu de l'argent en l'air * en achetant cette machine ◆ **~ of space** *(lit)* perte *f* de place ◆ **it's/he's a ~ of space** * c'est/il est nul * ◆ **it's a ~ of time** c'est une perte de temps, c'est du temps perdu ◆ **it's a ~ of time doing that** on perd son temps à faire *or* en faisant cela ◆ **it's a ~ of time and energy** c'est peine perdue ◆ **it's a ~ of breath** c'est perdre sa salive, c'est dépenser sa salive pour rien
2 *(NonC = waste material, US: also* **wastes**) *(gen)* déchets *mpl* ; *(= water)* eaux *fpl* sales *or* usées ◆ **household** *or* **kitchen ~** ordures *fpl* (ménagères) ◆ **industrial/nuclear/metal ~** déchets *mpl* industriels/nucléaires/de métal ◆ **toxic/radioactive ~** déchets *mpl* toxiques/radioactifs ; → **cotton**
3 *(often pl = expanse)* terres *fpl* désolées, désert *m* ; *(in town)* terrain *m* vague ◆ **~s** *or* **a ~ of snow and ice** un désert de neige et de glace
ADJ *(liter)* ◆ **to lay sth to ~, to lay ~ to sth** ravager qch, dévaster qch

VT 1 *[+ resources, food, electricity, energy etc]* gaspiller ; *[+ time]* perdre ; *[+ opportunity]* perdre, laisser passer ◆ **I ~d a whole day on that journey/trying to find it** j'ai perdu toute une journée avec ce voyage/à essayer de le trouver ◆ **she didn't want to ~ a single minute of sunshine** elle ne voulait pas perdre une seule minute de soleil ◆ **nothing is ~d in this firm** il n'y a aucun gaspillage *or* il n'y a aucun gâchis dans cette entreprise ◆ **his attempts to convince her were ~d** il a essayé en vain de la convaincre, ses efforts pour la convaincre ont été vains ◆ **you're wasting your breath!** tu dépenses ta salive pour rien !, tu perds ton temps ! ◆ **I won't ~ my breath discussing that** je ne vais pas perdre mon temps *or* me fatiguer à discuter cela ◆ **~d effort** des efforts *mpl* inutiles *or* vains ◆ **we tried to make him listen, but our efforts were ~d** nous avons essayé de le forcer à écouter, mais en pure perte *or* en vain ◆ **I wouldn't like you to have a ~d journey** je ne voudrais pas que vous vous déplaciez pour rien ◆ **a ~d life** une vie gâchée ◆ **the ~d years of his life** les années gâchées de sa vie ◆ **to ~ one's money** gaspiller son argent (*on sth* pour qch ; *on doing sth* pour faire qch) ◆ **she's wasting her talents** elle gaspille ses dons, elle n'exploite pas ses talents ◆ **you're wasting your time trying** tu perds ton temps à essayer ◆ **to ~ no time in doing sth** ne pas perdre de temps à faire qch ◆ **a vote for him is a ~d vote** voter pour lui, c'est gaspiller votre voix ◆ **the sarcasm was ~d on him** il n'a pas compris *or* saisi le sarcasme ◆ **caviar is ~d on him** il ne sait pas apprécier le caviar

2 (* = *kill*) zigouiller *, supprimer

VI *[food, goods, resources]* se perdre ◆ **you mustn't let it ~** il ne faut pas le laisser perdre ◆ **~ not want not** (*Prov*) il n'y a pas de petites économies

COMP **waste disposal unit, waste disposer** N broyeur *m* à ordures
waste ground N terrain *m* vague
Waste Land N (*Literat*) ◆ **"The Waste Land"** "la Terre désolée" ; see also **wasteland**
waste management N gestion *f* des déchets
waste material, waste matter N (*also Physiol*) déchets *mpl*
waste pipe N (tuyau *m* de) vidange *f*
waste products NPL (*from industry*) déchets *mpl* industriels ; (*from body*) déchets *mpl* (de l'organisme)
waste water N eaux *fpl* usées

► **waste away** VI dépérir ◆ **you're not exactly wasting away!** (*iro*) tu ne fais pas vraiment peine à voir *or* pitié ! (*iro*)

wastebasket /ˈweɪstbɑːskɪt/ N corbeille *f* à papier

wastebin /ˈweɪstbɪn/ N (*Brit* = *wastebasket*) corbeille *f* à papier ; (*in kitchen*) poubelle *f*, boîte *f* à ordures

wasted /ˈweɪstɪd/ ADJ 1 *[limb]* (= *emaciated*) décharné ; (= *withered*) atrophié ◆ **~ by disease** (= *emaciated*) décharné par la maladie ; (= *withered*) atrophié par la maladie 2 (* = *exhausted*) *[person]* lessivé *, crevé * 3 ‡ (*on drugs*) défoncé * ; (*on alcohol*) bourré ‡ ◆ **to get ~** (*on drugs*) se défoncer * ; (*on alcohol*) se bourrer ‡ (la gueule)

wasteful /ˈweɪstfʊl/ ADJ *[person]* gaspilleur ; *[process]* peu économique, peu rentable ◆ **~ expenditure** gaspillage *m*, dépenses *fpl* excessives *or* inutiles ◆ **~ habits** gaspillage *m* ◆ **to be ~ of sth** *[person]* gaspiller qch ; *[method, process]* mal utiliser qch

wastefully /ˈweɪstfəlɪ/ ADV ◆ **to use sth ~** gaspiller qch ◆ **to spend money ~** gaspiller son argent

wastefulness /ˈweɪstfʊlnɪs/ N (*NonC*) *[of person]* tendance *f* au gaspillage ; *[of process]* manque *m* de rentabilité

wasteland /ˈweɪsflænd/ N (*gen*) terres *fpl* à l'abandon *or* en friche ; (*in town*) terrain *m* vague ; (*in countryside*) désert *m* ◆ **a piece of ~** un terrain vague

wastepaper /ˌweɪstˈpeɪpəʳ/ N vieux papiers *mpl* COMP **wastepaper basket** N ⇒ **wastebasket**

waster* /ˈweɪstəʳ/ N 1 (= *good-for-nothing*) propre *mf* à rien 2 (= *spendthrift*) dépensier *m*, -ière *f*

wasting /ˈweɪstɪŋ/ ADJ *[disease]* débilitant

wastrel † /ˈweɪstrəl/ N 1 (= *spendthrift*) dépensier *m*, -ière *f*, panier *m* percé 2 (= *good-for-nothing*) propre *mf* à rien

watch¹ /wɒtʃ/ N montre *f* ◆ **by my ~** à ma montre ; → **stopwatch, wrist**

COMP *[chain, glass]* de montre
watch pocket N gousset *m*
watch strap N ⇒ **watchband**

watch² /wɒtʃ/ N 1 (*NonC*) (= *vigilance*) vigilance *f* ; (= *act of watching*) surveillance *f* ◆ **to keep** *or* **be on ~** faire le guet ◆ **to keep (a) close ~ on** *or* **over sb/sth** surveiller qn/qch de près *or* avec vigilance ◆ **to set a ~ on sth/sb** faire surveiller qch/qn ◆ **to keep ~ and ward over sth** (*frm*) surveiller qch avec vigilance ◆ **to be under ~** être sous surveillance

◆ **to be on the watch** (*Mil etc*) monter la garde ; (*gen*) faire le guet ◆ **to be on the ~ for sb/sth** guetter qn/qch ◆ **to be on the ~ for danger** être sur ses gardes (dans l'éventualité d'un danger) ◆ **to be on the ~ for bargains** être à l'affût des bonnes affaires

2 (*Naut* = *period of duty*) quart *m* ◆ **to be on ~** être de quart ◆ **the long ~es of the night** (*fig:* † *or liter*) les longues nuits sans sommeil ; → **dogwatch**

3 (= *group of men*) (*Mil*) garde *f* ; (*Naut*) quart *m* ; (= *one man*) (*Mil*) sentinelle *f* ; (*Naut*) homme *m* de quart ◆ **the port ~** (*Naut*) les bâbordais *mpl* ◆ **the starboard ~** les tribordais *mpl* ◆ **the ~** (*Hist*) le guet, la ronde ; → **officer**

VT 1 *[+ event, match, programme, TV, ceremony]* regarder ; *[+ person]* regarder, observer ; (= *spy on*) surveiller, épier ; *[+ suspect, suspicious object, house, car]* surveiller ; *[+ expression, birds, insects etc]* observer ; *[+ notice board, small ads etc]* consulter régulièrement ; *[+ political situation, developments]* surveiller, suivre de près ◆ **~ me, ~ what I do** regarde-moi (faire), regarde ce que je fais ◆ **~ how he does it** regarde *or* observe comment il s'y prend ◆ **~ the soup to see it doesn't boil over** surveille la soupe pour qu'elle ne déborde *subj* pas ◆ **to ~ sb do** *or* **doing sth** regarder qn faire qch ◆ **it's about as exciting as ~ing grass grow** *or* **~ing paint dry** c'est ennuyeux comme la pluie ◆ **to ~ sb like a hawk** surveiller qn de (très) près ◆ **have you ever ~ed an operation?** avez-vous déjà vu une opération *or* assisté à une opération ? ◆ **we are being ~ed** (*gen*) on nous surveille *or* épie ; (*by police, detective etc*) on nous surveille ◆ **to ~ sb's movements** *[neighbour]* épier les allées et venues de qn ; *[police, detective]* surveiller les allées et venues de qn ◆ **he needs ~ing** il faut le surveiller, il faut l'avoir à l'œil ◆ **~ tomorrow's paper** ne manquez pas de lire le journal de demain ◆ **a ~ed pot** *or* **kettle never boils** (*Prov*) plus on attend une chose, plus elle se fait attendre ◆ **"watch this space"** "histoire à suivre", "à suivre" ; → **bird**

2 (*Mil etc* = *guard*) monter la garde devant, garder ; (= *take care of*) *[+ child, dog]* surveiller, s'occuper de ; *[+ luggage, shop]* surveiller, garder

3 (= *be careful of, mind*) faire attention à ◆ **~ that knife!** (fais) attention avec ce couteau ! ◆ **~ that branch!** (fais) attention à la branche ! ◆ **~ your head!** attention à ta tête ! ◆ **to ~ one's step** (*lit*) faire attention *or* regarder où on met les pieds ; (*fig*) se surveiller ◆ **~ your step!, ~ how you go!*, ~ yourself!** (*fig*) (fais) attention !, fais gaffe ! * ◆ **we'll have to ~ the money carefully** il faudra que nous fassions attention à *or* surveillions nos dépenses ◆ **to ~ sb's interests** veiller sur les intérêts de qn, prendre soin des intérêts de qn ◆ **I must ~ the** *or* **my time as I've got a train to catch** il faut que je surveille *subj* l'heure car j'ai un train à prendre ◆ **he works well but does tend to ~ the clock** il travaille bien mais il a tendance à surveiller la pendule ◆ **to ~ what one says** faire attention à ce que l'on dit ◆ **~ what you're doing!** fais attention (à ce que tu fais) ! ◆ **~ it!*** (*warning*) attention !, fais gaffe ! * ; (*threat*) attention !, gare à toi ! ◆ **~ your language!** surveille ton langage ! ◆ **~ you don't burn yourself** fais attention *or* prends garde de ne pas te brûler ◆ **~ (that) he does all his homework** veillez à ce qu'il fasse *or* assurez-vous qu'il fait tous ses devoirs

4 (= *look for*) *[+ opportunity]* guetter ◆ **he ~ed his chance and slipped out** il a guetté *or* attendu le moment propice et s'est esquivé

VI regarder ; (= *be on guard*) faire le guet, monter la garde ; (*Rel etc* = *keep vigil*) veiller ; (= *pay attention*) faire attention ◆ **he has only come to ~** il est venu simplement pour regarder *or* simplement en spectateur ◆ **to ~ by sb's bedside** veiller au chevet de qn ◆ **to ~ over** *[+ person]* surveiller ; *[+ thing]* surveiller, garder ; *[+ sb's rights, safety]* protéger, surveiller ◆ **somebody was ~ing at the window** quelqu'un regardait à la fenêtre ◆ **to ~ for sth/sb** (= *wait for*) guetter qch/qn ; (= *be careful of*) faire attention à qch/qn ◆ **he's ~ing to see what you're going to do** il attend pour voir ce que vous allez faire ◆ **~ and you'll see how it's done** regarde et tu vas voir comment cela se fait ◆ **he'll be here soon, just (you) ~** attends, il sera bientôt là ; → **brief**

COMP **Watch Committee** N (*Brit Hist*) *comité veillant au maintien de l'ordre dans une commune*
watch night service N (*Rel*) ≃ messe *f* de minuit de la Saint-Sylvestre

► **watch out** VI (= *keep a look-out*) faire le guet ; (*fig* = *take care*) faire attention, prendre garde ◆ **~ out for the signal** guettez *or* attendez le signal ◆ **~ out!** attention !, fais gaffe ! * ; (*as menace*) attention !, gare à toi ! ◆ **~ out for cars when crossing the road** faites attention *or* prenez garde aux voitures en traversant la rue ◆ **to ~ out for thieves** faire attention aux voleurs ◆ **~ out for trouble if ...** préparez-vous *or* attendez-vous à des ennuis si ...

watchable /ˈwɒtʃəbl/ ADJ *[programme, film]* qui se laisse regarder

watchband /ˈwɒtʃbænd/ N bracelet *m* de montre

watchdog /ˈwɒtʃdɒg/ N (*lit*) chien *m* de garde ; (*fig*) (*official*) observateur *m*, -trice *f* officiel(le) ; (*unofficial*) gardien(ne) *m(f)* VI (*US* *) *[+ events, developments]* suivre de près

COMP *[group etc]* qui veille
watchdog committee N comité *m* de surveillance

watcher /ˈwɒtʃəʳ/ N (= *observer*) observateur *m*, -trice *f* ; (*hidden or hostile*) guetteur *m* ; (= *spectator*) spectateur *m*, -trice *f* ; (= *onlooker*) curieux *m*, -euse *f* ◆ **China ~** (*Pol*) spécialiste *mf* des questions chinoises ◆ **Kremlin ~** kremlinologue *mf* ; → **bird**

watchful /ˈwɒtʃfʊl/ ADJ vigilant, attentif ◆ **to keep a ~ eye on sth/sb** garder qch/qn à l'œil, avoir l'œil sur qch/qn ◆ **under the ~ eye of ...** sous l'œil vigilant de ...

watchfully /ˈwɒtʃfəlɪ/ ADV avec vigilance

watchfulness /ˈwɒtʃfʊlnɪs/ N vigilance *f*

watchmaker /ˈwɒtʃmeɪkəʳ/ N horloger *m*, -ère *f*

watchmaking /ˈwɒtʃmeɪkɪŋ/ N horlogerie *f*

watchman /ˈwɒtʃmən/ **N** (pl **-men**) *(gen)* gardien *m* ; (also **night watchman**) veilleur *m or* gardien *m* de nuit

watchtower /ˈwɒtʃtaʊə^r^/ **N** tour *f* de guet

watchword /ˈwɒtʃwɜːd/ **N** *(= password)* mot *m* de passe ; *(fig) (= motto)* mot *m* d'ordre

water /ˈwɔːtə^r^/ **N** 1 *(NonC: gen)* eau *f* ◆ **I'd like a drink of ~** je voudrais de l'eau *or* un verre d'eau ◆ **to turn on the ~** *(at mains)* ouvrir l'eau ; *(from tap)* ouvrir le robinet ◆ **hot and cold (running) ~ in all rooms** eau courante chaude et froide dans toutes les chambres ◆ **the road is under ~** la route est inondée, la route est recouverte par les eaux ◆ **the road/field was under three inches of ~** la route/le champ disparaissait sous 10 cm d'eau ◆ **to swim under ~** nager sous l'eau ◆ **to go by ~** voyager par bateau ◆ **the island across the ~** l'île de l'autre côté de l'eau ◆ **we spent an afternoon on the ~** nous avons passé un après-midi sur l'eau ◆ **at high/low ~** *(= tide)* à marée haute/basse, à mer pleine/basse ◆ **to take in** *or* **make ~** *[ship]* faire eau ◆ **it won't hold ~** *[container, bucket]* cela n'est pas étanche, l'eau va fuir ; *(fig) [plan, suggestion, excuse]* cela ne tient pas debout, cela ne tient pas la route ◆ **a lot of ~ has passed under the bridge since then** il est passé beaucoup d'eau sous les ponts depuis ce temps-là ◆ **that's (all) ~ under the bridge** tout ça c'est du passé ◆ **he spends money like ~** il jette l'argent par les fenêtres, l'argent lui fond dans les mains ◆ **it's like ~ off a duck's back*** ça glisse comme de l'eau sur les plumes *or* les ailes d'un canard ◆ **lavender/rose ~** eau *f* de lavande/de rose ; → **deep, firewater, fish**

2 *(Med, Physiol)* **to pass ~** uriner ◆ **her ~s broke** *(in labour)* elle a perdu les eaux ◆ **~ on the knee** épanchement *m* de synovie ◆ **~ on the brain** hydrocéphalie *f* ; → **feel**

NPL **waters** *[of spa, lake, river, sea]* eaux *fpl* ◆ **to take** *or* **drink the ~s** prendre les eaux, faire une cure thermale ◆ **in French ~s** dans les eaux (territoriales) françaises ◆ **the ~s of the Rhine** l'eau *or* les eaux du Rhin ; → **territorial**

VI *[eyes]* larmoyer, pleurer ; → **mouth**

VT *[+ plant, garden]* arroser ; *[+ animals]* donner à boire à, faire boire ◆ **the river ~s the whole province** le fleuve arrose *or* irrigue toute la province

COMP *[pressure, pipe, vapour]* d'eau ; *[pump, mill]* à eau ; *[plant etc]* aquatique ; *(Ind) [dispute, strike]* des employés de l'eau

water bailiff **N** garde-pêche *m*

water bed **N** matelas *m* d'eau

water beetle **N** gyrin *m*, tourniquet *m*

water bird **N** oiseau *m* aquatique

water biscuit **N** craquelin *m*

water blister **N** *(Med)* ampoule *f*, phlyctène *f*

water boatman **N** (pl **water boatmen**) *(= insect)* notonecte *m or f*

water bomb **N** bombe *f* à eau

water bottle **N** *(gen: plastic)* bouteille *f* (en plastique) ; *[of soldier]* bidon *m* ; *[of cyclist, peasant]* bidon *m* ; *(smaller)* gourde *f* ; → **hot**

water buffalo **N** buffle *m* d'eau, buffle *m* d'Asie ; *(Malaysian)* karbau *m*, kérabau *m*

water butt **N** *(Brit)* citerne *f* (à eau de pluie)

water cannon **N** canon *m* à eau

water carrier **N** *(= person)* porteur *m*, -euse *f* d'eau ; *(= container)* bidon *m* à eau ◆ **the Water Carrier** *(Astrol, Astron)* le Verseau

water cart **N** *(for streets)* arroseuse *f* *(municipale)* ; *(for selling)* voiture *f* de marchand d'eau

water chestnut **N** *(= plant)* macre *f* ; *(= fruit)* châtaigne *f* d'eau

water clock **N** horloge *f* à eau

water closet **N** *(abbr WC)* cabinet(s) *m(pl)*, waters *mpl*, WC *mpl*

water-cooled **ADJ** à refroidissement par eau

water-cooler **N** distributeur *m* d'eau réfrigérée

water-cooling **N** refroidissement *m* par eau

water cracker **N** *(US)* ⇒ **water biscuit**

water diviner **N** sourcier *m*, -ière *f*, radiesthésiste *mf*

water divining **N** art *m* du sourcier, radiesthésie *f*

water filter **N** filtre *m* à eau

water fountain **N** *(for drinking)* fontaine *f*, distributeur *m* d'eau fraîche ; *(decorative)* jet *m* d'eau

water-free **ADJ** sans eau, anhydre

water gas **N** gaz *m* à l'eau

water glass **N** 1 *(= tumbler)* verre *m* à eau 2 *(Chem)* verre *m* soluble

water gun **N** *(US)* ⇒ **water pistol**

water heater **N** chauffe-eau *m inv*

water hen **N** poule *f* d'eau

water hole **N** point *m* d'eau, mare *f*

water ice **N** *(Brit Culin)* sorbet *m*, glace *f* à l'eau

water jacket **N** *(Aut etc)* chemise *f* d'eau

water jump **N** *(Racing)* rivière *f*, brook *m*

water level **N** *(gen)* niveau *m* de l'eau ; *[of car radiator]* niveau *m* d'eau

water lily **N** nénuphar *m*

water main **N** conduite *f* (principale) d'eau

water meadow **N** *(esp Brit)* prairie *f* souvent inondée, noue *f*

water meter **N** compteur *m* d'eau

water nymph **N** naïade *f*

water pistol **N** pistolet *m* à eau

water polo **N** water-polo *m*

water power **N** énergie *f* hydraulique, houille *f* blanche

water purifier **N** *(= device)* épurateur *m* d'eau ; *(= tablet)* cachet *m* pour purifier l'eau

water-rail **N** *(= bird)* râle *m* (d'eau)

water rat **N** rat *m* d'eau

water rate **N** *(Brit)* taxe *f* sur l'eau

water-repellent **ADJ** hydrofuge, imperméable

water-resistant **ADJ** *[ink etc]* qui résiste à l'eau, indélébile ; *[material]* imperméable

water-ski **N** ski *m* nautique *(objet)* **VI** (also **go water-skiing**) faire du ski nautique

water-skier **N** skieur *m*, -euse *f* nautique

water-skiing **N** *(NonC)* ski *m* nautique *(sport)*

water slide **N** toboggan *m* (de piscine)

water snake **N** serpent *m* d'eau

water softener **N** adoucisseur *m* d'eau

water-soluble **ADJ** soluble dans l'eau, hydrosoluble *(Chem)*

water sports **NPL** sports *mpl* nautiques ; *(* = sexual practices)* ondinisme *m*

water supply **N** *(for town)* approvisionnement *m* en eau, distribution *f* des eaux ; *(for building)* alimentation *f* en eau ; *(for traveller)* provision *f* d'eau ◆ **the ~ supply was cut off** on avait coupé l'eau

water system **N** *(Geog)* réseau *m* hydrographique ; *(for building, town)* ⇒ **water supply**

water table **N** *(Geog)* nappe *f* phréatique, niveau *m* hydrostatique

water tank **N** réservoir *m* d'eau, citerne *f*

water tower **N** château *m* d'eau

water vole **N** rat *m* d'eau

water wings **NPL** bouée *f*, flotteurs *mpl* de natation

water worker **N** employé *m* du service des eaux

► **water down** **VT SEP** *[+ wine]* couper (d'eau), baptiser* ; *[+ paint]* diluer ; *(fig) [+ story]* édulcorer ; *[+ effect]* atténuer, affaiblir ; *[+ demands]* modérer ◆ **legislation on employment rights has been ~ed down** la législation sur les droits des employés a été assouplie

waterborne /ˈwɔːtəbɔːn/ **ADJ** flottant ; *[boats]* à flot ; *[goods]* transporté par voie d'eau ; *[disease]* d'origine hydrique

watercolour, watercolor *(US)* /ˈwɔːtə,kʌlə^r^/ **N** 1 *(= painting)* aquarelle *f* 2 *(= paint)* ◆ **~s** couleurs *fpl* à l'eau *or* pour aquarelle ◆ **painted in ~s** peint à l'aquarelle **ADJ** à l'aquarelle

watercolourist, watercolorist *(US)* /ˈwɔːtə,kʌlərɪst/ **N** aquarelliste *mf*

watercourse /ˈwɔːtəkɔːs/ **N** cours *m* d'eau

watercress /ˈwɔːtəkres/ **N** cresson *m* (de fontaine)

watered /ˈwɔːtəd/ **ADJ** 1 *[milk etc]* coupé d'eau 2 *[silk etc]* moiré

COMP **watered-down** **ADJ** *[milk, wine etc]* coupé d'eau ; *[paint]* dilué ; *[version, account]* édulcoré

watered silk **N** soie *f* moirée

watered stock **N** *(US) (= cattle)* bétail *m* gorgé d'eau (avant la pesée) ; *(Stock Exchange)* actions *fpl* gonflées (sans raison)

waterfall /ˈwɔːtəfɔːl/ **N** chute *f* d'eau, cascade *f*

waterfowl /ˈwɔːtəfaʊl/ **N** *(sg)* oiseau *m* d'eau ; *(collective pl)* gibier *m* d'eau

waterfront /ˈwɔːtəfrʌnt/ **N** *(at docks)* quais *mpl* ; *(= sea front)* front *m* de mer

Watergate /ˈwɔːtəgeɪt/ **N** Watergate *m*

watering /ˈwɔːtərɪŋ/ **N** *[of plants, streets]* arrosage *m* ; *[of fields, region]* irrigation *f* ◆ **frequent ~ is needed** il est conseillé d'arroser fréquemment

COMP **watering can** **N** arrosoir *m*

watering hole **N** *(for animals)* point *m* d'eau ; *(* fig)* bar *m*

watering place **N** *(for animals)* point *m* d'eau ; *(= spa)* station *f* thermale, ville *f* d'eaux ; *(= seaside resort)* station *f* balnéaire ; *(fig hum)* bar *m*

waterless /ˈwɔːtəlɪs/ **ADJ** *[area]* sans eau ◆ **to be ~** être dépourvu d'eau

waterline /ˈwɔːtəlaɪn/ **N** *(Naut)* ligne *f* de flottaison ; *(left by tide, river)* ⇒ **watermark**

waterlogged /ˈwɔːtəlɒgd/ **ADJ** *[land, pitch]* détrempé ; *[wood]* imprégné d'eau ; *[shoes]* imbibé d'eau

Waterloo /,wɔːtəˈluː/ **N** Waterloo ◆ **the Battle of ~** la bataille de Waterloo ◆ **to meet one's ~** essuyer un revers irrémédiable

waterman /ˈwɔːtəmən/ **N** (pl **-men**) batelier *m*

watermark /ˈwɔːtəmɑːk/ **N** *(in paper)* filigrane *m* ; *(left by tide)* laisse *f* de haute mer ; *(left by river)* ligne *f* des hautes eaux ; *(on wood, on surface)* marque *f or* tache *f* d'eau ◆ **above/below the ~** au-dessus/au-dessous de la laisse de haute mer *or* de la ligne des hautes eaux

watermelon /ˈwɔːtəmelən/ **N** pastèque *f*, melon *m* d'eau

waterproof /ˈwɔːtəpruːf/ **ADJ** *[material]* imperméable ; *[watch]* étanche ; *[mascara]* résistant à l'eau ◆ **~ sheet** *(for bed)* alaise *f* ; *(tarpaulin)* bâche *f* **N** *(Brit)* imperméable *m* **VT** imperméabiliser

waterproofing /ˈwɔːtəpruːfɪŋ/ **N** *(NonC)* *(= process)* imperméabilisation *f* ; *(= quality)* imperméabilité *f*

watershed /ˈwɔːtəʃed/ **N** *(Geog)* ligne *f* de partage des eaux ; *(fig)* moment *m* critique *or* décisif, grand tournant *m* ; *(Brit TV) heure à partir de laquelle les chaînes de télévision britanniques peuvent diffuser des émissions réservées aux adultes*

waterside /ˈwɔːtəsaɪd/ **N** bord *m* de l'eau **ADJ** *[flower, insect]* du bord de l'eau ; *[landowner]* riverain ◆ **at** *or* **by the ~** au bord de l'eau, sur la berge ◆ **along the ~** le long de la rive

waterspout /ˈwɔːtəspaʊt/ **N** *(on roof etc)* (tuyau *m* de) descente *f* ; *(Weather)* trombe *f*

watertight /ˈwɔːtətaɪt/ **ADJ** 1 *[container]* étanche ◆ **~ compartment** compartiment *m* étanche ◆ **in ~ compartments** séparé par des cloisons étanches 2 *(fig) [excuse, plan]* inattaquable, indiscutable ; *[argument]* en béton

waterway /ˈwɔːtəweɪ/ **N** voie *f* navigable

waterweed /ˈwɔːtəwiːd/ **N** élodée *f*

waterwheel /ˈwɔːtəwiːl/ **N** roue *f* hydraulique

waterworks /ˈwɔːtəwɜːks/ NPL *(= system)* système *m* hydraulique ; *(= place)* station *f* hydraulique ◆ **to turn on the ~** * *(fig pej = cry)* se mettre à pleurer à chaudes larmes *or* comme une Madeleine* ◆ **to have something wrong with one's ~** * *(Brit Med: euph)* avoir des ennuis de vessie

watery /ˈwɔːtərɪ/ ADJ 1 *(= like, containing water) [fluid, discharge, solution]* aqueux 2 *(pej = containing excessive water) [tea, coffee]* trop léger ; *[beer]* trop aqueux ; *[soup, sauce]* trop clair ; *[taste]* d'eau ; *[paint, ink]* trop liquide, trop délayé ; *[ground]* détrempé, saturé d'eau 3 *(= producing water) [eyes]* humide 4 *(= insipid) [smile, sun, light]* faible ; *[sky, moon]* délavé 5 *(= pale) [colour]* pâle 6 *(= relating to water)* aquatique ◆ **a ~ world of streams and fountains** un monde aquatique de cours d'eau et de fontaines ◆ **the ~ depths** les profondeurs *fpl* aquatiques ◆ **to go to a ~ grave** *(liter)* être enseveli par les eaux *(liter)*

watt /wɒt/ N watt *m*

wattage /ˈwɒtɪdʒ/ N puissance *f or* consommation *f* en watts

wattle /ˈwɒtl/ N 1 *(NonC = woven sticks)* clayonnage *m* ◆ **~ and daub** clayonnage *m* enduit de torchis 2 *[of turkey, lizard]* caroncule *f* ; *[of fish]* barbillon *m*

wave /weɪv/ N 1 *(at sea)* vague *f*, lame *f* ; *(on lake)* vague *f* ; *(on beach)* rouleau *m* ; *(on river, pond)* vaguelette *f* ; *(in hair)* ondulation *f*, cran *m* ; *(on surface)* ondulation *f* ; *(fig) [of dislike, enthusiasm, strikes, protests etc]* vague *f* ◆ **the ~s** *(liter)* les flots *mpl*, l'onde *f* ◆ **to make ~s** *(fig)* créer des remous ◆ **her hair has a natural ~ (in it)** ses cheveux ondulent naturellement ◆ **the first ~ of the attack** *(Mil)* la première vague d'assaut ◆ **to come in ~s** *[people]* arriver par vagues ; *[explosions etc]* se produire par vagues ◆ **the new ~** *(Cine etc: fig)* la nouvelle vague ; → **crime, heatwave, permanent**

2 *(Phys, Rad, Telec etc)* onde *f* ◆ **long ~** grandes ondes *fpl* ◆ **medium/short ~** ondes *fpl* moyennes/courtes ; → **light¹, long¹, medium, shock¹, shortwave, sound¹**

3 *(= gesture)* geste *m or* signe *m* de la main ◆ **he gave me a cheerful ~** il m'a fait un signe joyeux de la main ◆ **with a ~ of his hand** d'un geste *or* signe de la main

VI 1 *[person]* faire signe de la main ; *[flag]* flotter (au vent) ; *[branch, tree]* être agité ; *[grass, corn]* onduler, ondoyer ◆ **to ~ to sb** *(in greeting)* saluer qn de la main, faire bonjour *(or* au revoir) de la main à qn ; *(as signal)* faire signe à qn *(to do sth* de faire qch)

2 *[hair]* onduler, avoir un *or* des cran(s)

VT 1 *[+ flag, handkerchief]* agiter ; *(threateningly) [+ stick, sword]* brandir ◆ **to ~ one's hand to sb** faire signe de la main à qn ◆ **he ~d the ticket at me furiously** il a agité vivement le ticket sous mon nez ◆ **to ~ goodbye to sb** dire au revoir de la main à qn, agiter la main en signe *or* guise d'adieu (à qn) ◆ **he ~d his thanks** il a remercié d'un signe de la main, il a agité la main en signe *or* guise de remerciement ◆ **to ~ sb back/through/on** *etc* faire signe à qn de reculer/de passer/d'avancer *etc* ◆ **he ~d the car through the gates** il a fait signe à la voiture de franchir les grilles

2 *[+ hair]* onduler

COMP **wave energy** N énergie *f* des vagues
wave guide N *(Elec)* guide *m* d'ondes
wave mechanics N *(NonC: Phys)* mécanique *f* ondulatoire
wave power N énergie *f* des vagues

► **wave about, wave around** VT SEP *[+ object]* agiter dans tous les sens ◆ **to ~ one's arms about** gesticuler, agiter les bras dans tous les sens

► **wave aside, wave away** VT SEP *[+ person, object]* écarter *or* éloigner d'un geste ; *[+ objections]* écarter (d'un geste) ; *[+ offer, sb's help etc]* rejeter *or* refuser (d'un geste)

► **wave down** VT SEP ◆ **to wave down a car** faire signe à une voiture de s'arrêter

► **wave off** VT SEP faire au revoir de la main à

waveband /ˈweɪvbænd/ N *(Rad)* bande *f* de fréquences

wavelength /ˈweɪvleŋkθ/ N *(Phys)* longueur *f* d'ondes ◆ **we're not on the same ~** *(fig)* nous ne sommes pas sur la même longueur d'ondes*

wavelet /ˈweɪvlɪt/ N vaguelette *f*

waver /ˈweɪvəʳ/ VI *[flame, shadow]* vaciller, osciller ; *[voice]* trembler, trembloter ; *[courage, loyalty, determination]* vaciller, chanceler ; *[support]* devenir hésitant ; *[person] (= weaken)* lâcher pied, flancher* ; *(= hesitate)* hésiter *(between* entre) ◆ **he ~ed in his resolution** sa résolution chancelait ◆ **he is beginning to ~** il commence à lâcher pied *or* à flancher*

waverer /ˈweɪvərəʳ/ N indécis(e) *m(f)*, irrésolu(e) *m(f)*

wavering /ˈweɪvərɪŋ/ ADJ 1 *[light, shadow]* vacillant ◆ **his ~ steps** ses pas hésitants 2 *(fig) [person]* indécis ; *[support]* hésitant ; *[loyalty, determination]* chancelant ; *[voice]* mal assuré N *(NonC = hesitation)* hésitations *fpl*

wavy /ˈweɪvɪ/ ADJ *[hair, surface, edge]* ondulé ; *[line]* onduleux COMP **wavy-haired** ADJ aux cheveux ondulés

wax¹ /wæks/ N *(NonC)* cire *f* ; *(for skis)* fart *m* ; *(in ear)* cérumen *m*, (bouchon *m* de) cire *f* ; → **beeswax, sealing²** VT *[+ floor, furniture]* cirer, encaustiquer ; *[+ skis]* farter ; *[+ shoes, moustache]* cirer ; *[+ thread]* poisser ; *[+ car]* lustrer ◆ **to ~ one's legs** s'épiler les jambes à la cire COMP *[candle, doll, seal, record]* de *or* en cire
wax bean N *(US)* haricot *m* beurre *inv*
waxed cotton N coton *m* huilé
waxed jacket N veste *f* de *or* en coton huilé
waxed paper N papier *m* paraffiné
wax museum N *(esp US)* musée *m* de cire
wax paper N ⇒ **waxed paper**

wax² /wæks/ VI *[moon]* croître ◆ **to ~ and wane** *[feelings, issues etc]* croître et décroître ◆ **to ~ merry/poetic** *etc* († *or hum)* devenir d'humeur joyeuse/poétique *etc* ◆ **to ~ eloquent** déployer toute son éloquence *(about, over* à propos de) ◆ **he ~ed lyrical about Louis Armstrong** il est devenu lyrique quand il a parlé de Louis Armstrong ; → **enthusiastic**

waxen /ˈwæksən/ ADJ *(liter = like wax) [complexion, face]* cireux ; († *= made of wax)* de *or* en cire

waxing /ˈwæksɪŋ/ N *(gen)* cirage *m* ; *[of skis]* fartage *m*

waxwing /ˈwækswɪŋ/ N *(= bird)* jaseur *m*

waxwork /ˈwækswɜːk/ N 1 *(= figure)* personnage *m* en cire 2 *(pl inv: Brit)* ◆ **~s** *(= museum)* musée *m* de cire

waxy /ˈwæksɪ/ ADJ *[substance, consistency, face, colour]* cireux ; *[potato]* à chair ferme

way /weɪ/

1 NOUN	3 COMPOUNDS
2 ADVERB	

1 - NOUN

1 = route chemin *m* ◆ **to ask the** *or* **one's ~** demander son chemin *(to* pour aller à) ◆ **we went the wrong ~** nous avons pris le mauvais chemin, nous nous sommes trompés de chemin ◆ **a piece of bread went down the wrong ~** j'ai (*or* il a *etc*) avalé une miette de pain de travers ◆ **to go the long ~ round** prendre le chemin le plus long *or* le chemin des écoliers* ◆ **we met several people on** *or* **along the ~** nous avons rencontré plusieurs personnes en chemin ◆ **to go the same ~ as sb** *(lit)* aller dans la même direction que qn ; *(fig)* suivre les traces *or* l'exemple de qn, marcher sur les traces de qn ◆ **he has gone the ~ of his brothers** *(fig)* il a suivi le même chemin que ses frères ◆ **they went their own ~s** *or* **their separate ~s** *(lit)* ils sont partis chacun de leur côté ; *(fig)* chacun a suivi son chemin ◆ **she knows her ~ around** *or* **about** *(fig)* elle sait se débrouiller ◆ **to lose the** *or* **one's ~** se perdre, s'égarer ◆ **to make one's ~ towards ...** se diriger vers ... ◆ **he had to make his own ~ in Hollywood** il a dû se battre pour faire sa place à Hollywood

◆ **the/one's + way to** ◆ **can you tell me the ~ to the tourist office?** pouvez-vous m'indiquer le chemin *or* la direction du syndicat d'initiative ? ◆ **the quickest** *or* **shortest ~ to Leeds** le chemin le plus court pour aller à Leeds ◆ **the ~ to success** le chemin du succès ◆ **I know the** *or* **my ~ to the station** je connais le chemin de la gare, je sais comment aller à la gare

◆ **on the/one's way (to)** ◆ **on the** *or* **my ~ here I saw ...** en venant (ici) j'ai vu ... ◆ **you pass it on your ~ home** vous passez devant en rentrant chez vous ◆ **he's on his ~** il arrive ◆ **I must be on my ~** il faut que j'y aille ◆ **to start** *or* **go on one's ~** s'en aller ◆ **with that, he went on his ~** sur ce, il s'en est allé ◆ **on the** *or* **our ~ to London we met ...** en allant à Londres nous avons rencontré ... ◆ **it's on the ~ to the station** c'est sur le chemin de la gare ◆ **he is on the ~ to great things** il a un avenir brillant devant lui ◆ **to be (well) on the** *or* **one's ~ to success/victory** *etc* être sur la voie du succès/de la victoire *etc*

◆ **to be on the way** *(= to be expected)* être prévu ◆ **more snow is on the ~** d'autres chutes de neige sont prévues ◆ **she's got twins, and another baby on the ~** * elle a des jumeaux, et un bébé en route*

◆ **the/one's way back** ◆ **the ~ back to the station** le chemin pour revenir à la gare ◆ **on the** *or* **his ~ back he met ...** au retour *or* sur le chemin du retour *or* en revenant il a rencontré ... ◆ **he made his ~ back to the car** il est retourné (*or* revenu) vers la voiture

◆ **the/one's way down** ◆ **I don't know the ~ down** je ne sais pas par où on descend ◆ **I met her on the** *or* **my ~ down** je l'ai rencontrée en descendant ◆ **inflation is on the ~ down** l'inflation est en baisse

◆ **the way forward** ◆ **the ~ forward is ...** l'avenir, c'est ... ◆ **they held a meeting to discuss the ~ forward** ils ont organisé une réunion pour discuter de la marche à suivre ◆ **is monetary union the ~ forward?** l'union monétaire est-elle la bonne voie *or* la voie du progrès ?

◆ **the/one's + way in** ◆ **we couldn't find the ~ in** nous ne trouvions pas l'entrée ◆ **I met her on the** *or* **my ~ in** je l'ai rencontrée à l'entrée ◆ **it's on the ~ in** *(fig) [fashion etc]* c'est à la mode

◆ **the/one's/no way out** ◆ **can you find your own ~ out?** pouvez-vous trouver la sortie tout seul ? ◆ **I'll find my own ~ out** ne vous dérangez pas, je trouverai (bien) la sortie ◆ **you'll see it on the** *or* **your ~ out** vous le verrez en sortant ◆ **he tried to talk his ~ out of it** *(fig)* il a essayé de s'en sortir avec de belles paroles ◆ **there's no other ~ out** il n'y a pas d'autre solution ◆ **there is no ~ out of this difficulty** il n'y a pas moyen d'éviter cette difficulté ◆ **it's on the ~ out** *[fashion etc]* ce n'est plus vraiment à la mode, c'est out*

◆ **the/one's way up** ◆ **I don't know the ~ up** je ne sais pas par où on monte ◆ **all the ~ up** jusqu'en haut, jusqu'au sommet ◆ **I met him on the** *or* **my ~ up** je l'ai rencontré en montant

♦ **I was on my ~ up to see you** je montais vous voir ♦ **unemployment is on the ~ up** le chômage est en hausse

♦ **a/no way round** ♦ **we're trying to find a ~ round it** nous cherchons un moyen de contourner *or* d'éviter ce problème ♦ **there's no ~ round this difficulty** il n'y a pas moyen de contourner cette difficulté

2 = path ♦ **their ~ was blocked by police** la police leur barrait le passage ♦ **to push** *or* **force one's ~ through a crowd** se frayer un chemin *or* un passage à travers une foule ♦ **to hack** *or* **cut one's ~ through the jungle** se frayer un chemin à la machette dans la jungle ♦ **to crawl/limp** *etc* **one's ~ to the door** ramper/boiter *etc* jusqu'à la porte ♦ **they live over** *or* **across the ~** * ils habitent en face

♦ **in the/sb's way** ♦ **to be in the ~** *(lit)* bloquer *or* barrer le passage ; *(fig)* gêner ♦ **am I in the** *or* **your ~?** *(lit)* est-ce que je vous empêche de passer ? ; *(fig)* est-ce que je vous gêne ? ♦ **he put me in the ~ of one or two good bargains** * il m'a indiqué quelques bonnes affaires ♦ **to put difficulties in sb's ~** créer des difficultés à qn

♦ **out of the/sb's way** ♦ **it's out of the ~ over there** ça ne gêne pas là-bas ♦ **to get out of the ~** s'écarter ♦ **(get) out of the** *or* **my ~!** pousse-toi !, laisse-moi passer ! ♦ **to get out of sb's ~** laisser passer qn ♦ **could you get your foot out of the ~?** tu peux pousser *or* retirer ton pied ? ♦ **as soon as I've got the exams out of the ~** * dès que les examens seront finis ♦ **keep matches out of children's ~** *or* **out of the ~ of children** ne laissez pas les allumettes à la portée des enfants ♦ **to keep out of sb's ~** éviter qn ♦ **keep (well) out of his ~ today!** ne te mets pas sur son chemin aujourd'hui ! ♦ **he kept well out of the ~** il a pris soin de rester à l'écart ♦ **the village is quite out of the ~** le village est vraiment à l'écart *or* isolé ♦ **to put sth out of the ~** ranger qch ♦ **he wants his wife out of the ~** * il veut se débarrasser de sa femme ♦ **I'll take you home, it's not out of my ~** je vous ramènerai, c'est sur mon chemin ♦ **that would be nice, but don't go out of your ~** ce serait bien mais ne vous dérangez pas ♦ **to go out of one's ~ to do sth** *(fig)* se donner du mal pour faire qch ♦ **he went out of his ~ to help us** il s'est donné du mal pour nous aider ♦ **it's nothing out of the ~** *(fig)* cela n'a rien de spécial *or* d'extraordinaire

♦ **to make way (for)** ♦ **to make ~ for sb** faire place à qn, s'écarter pour laisser passer qn ; *(fig)* laisser la voie libre à qn ♦ **they made ~ for the ambulance** ils se sont écartés *or* rangés pour laisser passer l'ambulance ♦ **to make ~ for sth** *(fig)* ouvrir la voie à qch ♦ **this made ~ for a return to democracy** ceci a ouvert la voie à la restauration de la démocratie ♦ **make ~!** † place ! †

3 * = area ♦ **there aren't many parks round our ~** il n'y a pas beaucoup de parcs par chez nous ♦ **round this ~** par ici ♦ **I'll be down** *or* **round your ~ tomorrow** je serai près de chez vous demain ♦ **it's out** *or* **over Oxford ~** c'est du côté d'Oxford

4 = distance ♦ **a short ~ up the road** à quelques pas ♦ **to be some ~ off** être assez loin ♦ **a little ~ away** *or* **off** pas très loin ♦ **he stood some ~ off** il se tenait à l'écart ♦ **is it far? – yes, it's a good** * *or* **quite a** * **~** c'est loin ? – oui, il y a un bon bout de chemin * ♦ **it's a good** * **~ to London** il y a un bon bout de chemin * jusqu'à Londres ♦ **to be a long ~ away** *or* **off** être loin ♦ **it's a long ~ from here** c'est loin d'ici ♦ **he's a long ~ from home** il est loin de chez lui ♦ **that's a long ~ from the truth** c'est loin d'être vrai ♦ **a long ~ off I could hear ...** j'entendais au loin ... ♦ **is it finished? – not by a long ~!** est-ce terminé ? – loin de là *or* loin s'en faut ! ♦ **it was our favourite by a long ~** c'était de loin celui que nous préférions ♦ **they've come a long ~** *(fig)* ils ont fait du chemin ♦ **the roots go a long ~ down** les racines sont très profondes ♦ **we've got a long ~ to go** *(lit)* nous avons beaucoup de chemin à faire ; *(fig)* *(= still far from our objective)* nous ne sommes pas au bout de nos peines ; *(= not got enough)* nous sommes encore loin du compte ♦ **to go a long ~ round** faire un grand détour ♦ **he makes a little go a long ~** il tire le meilleur parti de ce qu'il a ♦ **a little praise goes a long ~** * un petit compliment de temps à autre, ça aide * ♦ **this spice is expensive, but a little goes a long ~** cette épice est chère mais on n'a pas besoin d'en mettre beaucoup ♦ **I find a little goes a long ~ with rap music** (*, *iro*) le rap, c'est surtout à petites doses que je l'apprécie ♦ **it should go a long ~/some ~ towards paying the bill** cela devrait couvrir une grande partie/une partie de la facture ♦ **it should go a long ~/some ~ towards improving relations between the two countries** cela devrait améliorer considérablement/contribuer à améliorer les rapports entre les deux pays

♦ **all the way** *(= the whole distance)* ♦ **he had to walk all the ~ (to the hospital)** il a dû faire tout le chemin à pied (jusqu'à l'hôpital) ♦ **there are street lights all the ~** il y a des réverbères tout le long du chemin ♦ **it rained all the ~** il a plu pendant tout le chemin ♦ **he talked all the ~ to the theatre** il a parlé pendant tout le chemin jusqu'au théâtre ♦ **I'm with you all the ~** * *(= entirely agree)* je suis entièrement d'accord avec vous ♦ **I'll be with you all the ~** *(= will back you up)* je vous soutiendrai jusqu'au bout ♦ **to go all the ~ with sb** * coucher * avec qn ♦ **to go all the ~** * passer à l'acte, concrétiser *

5 = direction ♦ **are you going my ~?** est-ce que vous allez dans la même direction que moi ? ♦ **he never looked my ~** il n'a pas fait attention à moi ♦ **this ~** par ici ♦ **turn this ~ for a moment** tourne-toi par ici un moment ♦ **"this way for** *or* **to the cathedral"** "vers la cathédrale" ♦ **he went that ~** il est parti par là ♦ **which ~ did he go?** par où est-il passé ?, dans quelle direction est-il parti ? ♦ **she didn't know which ~ to look** *(fig)* elle ne savait pas où se mettre ♦ **which ~ do we go from here?** *(lit)* par où allons-nous maintenant ?, quel chemin prenons-nous maintenant ? ; *(fig)* qu'allons-nous faire maintenant ? ♦ **everything's going his ~** * **just now** *(fig)* tout lui réussit en ce moment ♦ **if the chance comes your ~** * si jamais vous en avez l'occasion ♦ **I'll try and put some work your ~** * j'essayerai de t'avoir du travail ♦ **he looked the other ~** *(lit, fig)* il a regardé ailleurs, il a détourné les yeux ♦ **cars parked every which ~** * des voitures garées n'importe comment *or* dans tous les sens

♦ **this way and that** ♦ **the leaves were blowing this ~ and that** les feuilles tournoyaient de-ci de-là ♦ **he ran this ~ and that** il courait dans tous les sens

6 = footpath **the Pennine/North Wales Way** le chemin de grande randonnée des Pennines/du nord du pays de Galles

7 = side ♦ **your jersey is the right/wrong ~ out** ton pull est à l'endroit/à l'envers ♦ **have I got this dress the right ~ round?** est-ce que j'ai bien mis cette robe à l'endroit ? ♦ **turn the rug the other ~ round** tourne le tapis dans l'autre sens ♦ **he didn't hit her, it was the other ~ round** ce n'est pas lui qui l'a frappée, c'est le contraire ♦ **"this way up"** *(on box)* "haut" ♦ **the right ~ up** dans le bon sens ♦ **the wrong ~ up** à l'envers

8 = part ♦ **the region/loot was split three ~s** la région/le butin a été divisé(e) en trois ♦ **a three-~ discussion** une discussion à trois participants ♦ **a four-~ radio link-up** une liaison radio à quatre voies

9 = manner façon *f*, manière *f* ♦ **(in) this/that ~** comme ceci/cela, de cette façon, de cette manière ♦ **what an odd ~ to behave!** quelle drôle de manière *or* façon de se comporter !, quel drôle de comportement ! ♦ **to do sth the right/wrong ~** bien/mal faire qch ♦ **he had to do it, but there's a right and a wrong ~ of doing everything** * il était obligé de le faire mais il aurait pu y mettre la manière ♦ **he said it in such a ~ that ...** il l'a dit sur un tel ton *or* d'une telle façon que ... ♦ **do it your own ~** fais comme tu veux *or* à ta façon ♦ **I did it my ~** je l'ai fait à ma façon ♦ **he insisted I did it his ~** il a insisté pour que je suive sa méthode *or* pour que je le fasse à sa façon ♦ **he is amusing in his (own) ~** il est amusant à sa façon ♦ **he has his own ~ of doing things** il a une façon bien à lui de faire les choses ♦ **in every ~ possible, in every possible ~** *[help]* par tous les moyens possibles ♦ **to try in every ~ possible** *or* **in every possible ~ to do sth** faire tout son possible pour faire qch ♦ **every** *or* **any which ~ (one can)** * de toutes les manières possibles ♦ **~ to go!** ‡ *(esp US)* bravo ! ♦ **what a ~ to go!** *(of sb's death, terrible)* c'est vraiment triste de partir ainsi ; *(good)* il (*or* elle) a eu une belle mort ♦ **that's the ~ the money goes** c'est comme ça que l'argent file ♦ **that's just the ~ he is** il est comme ça, c'est tout ♦ **whatever ~ you look at it** quelle que soit la façon dont on envisage la chose ♦ **leave it the ~ it is** laisse-le comme il est ♦ **the ~ things are going we shall have nothing left** au train où vont les choses, il ne nous restera plus rien ♦ **it's just the ~ things are** c'est la vie !

♦ **in a small/big way** ♦ **in a small ~ he contributed to ...** à sa manière, il a contribué à ... ♦ **in his own small ~ he helped a lot of people** à sa manière, il a aidé beaucoup de gens ♦ **in a small ~ it did make a difference** cela a quand même fait une différence ♦ **he furthered her career in a big ~** * il a beaucoup contribué à faire progresser sa carrière ♦ **he does things in a big ~** * il fait les choses en grand * ♦ **soccer is taking off in the States in a big ~** * le football connaît un véritable essor aux États-Unis

♦ **no way !** * pas question ! ♦ **no ~ am I doing that** (il n'est) pas question que je fasse ça ♦ **I'm not paying, no ~!** je refuse de payer, un point c'est tout ! ♦ **will you come? – no ~!** tu viens ? – pas question *or* sûrement pas ! ♦ **there's no ~ that's champagne!** ce n'est pas possible que ce soit du champagne !

♦ **one way or another/the other** *(= somehow)* d'une façon ou d'une autre ♦ **everyone helped one ~ or another** tout le monde a aidé d'une façon ou d'une autre ♦ **it doesn't matter one ~ or the other** *(= either way)* ça n'a aucune importance ♦ **two days one ~ or the other won't make much difference** * deux jours de plus ou de moins ne changeront pas grand-chose

10 = method, technique méthode *f*, solution *f* ♦ **the best ~ is to put it in the freezer for ten minutes** la meilleure méthode *or* solution, c'est de le mettre au congélateur pendant dix minutes, le mieux, c'est de le mettre au congélateur pendant dix minutes ♦ **that's the ~ to do it** voilà comment il faut faire *or* s'y prendre ♦ **that's quite the wrong ~ to go about it** ce n'est pas comme ça qu'il faut s'y prendre *or* qu'il faut le faire ♦ **that's the ~!** voilà, c'est bien *or* c'est ça !

♦ **to have a way with** ♦ **he has a ~ with people** il sait s'y prendre avec les gens ♦ **he has got a ~ with cars** il s'y connaît en voitures ♦ **to have a ~ with words** *(= be eloquent)* manier les mots avec bonheur ; *(pej)* avoir du bagou * ♦ **she has a (certain) ~ with her** * elle a un certain charme

11 = means moyen *m* ♦ **we'll find a ~ to do** *or* **of doing it** nous trouverons bien un moyen de le

faire ◆ **love will find a ~** *(Prov)* l'amour finit toujours par triompher

◆ **by way of** *(= via)* par ; *(= as)* en guise de ; *(= so as to)* pour, afin de ; *(= by means of)* au moyen de ◆ **he went by ~ of Glasgow** il est passé par Glasgow ◆ **"I'm superstitious", she said by ~ of explanation** "je suis superstitieuse", dit-elle en guise d'explication ◆ **it was by ~ of being a joke** c'était une plaisanterie ◆ **I did it by ~ of discovering what …** je l'ai fait pour découvrir *or* afin de découvrir ce que … ◆ **by ~ of lectures, practicals and tutorials** au moyen de cours magistraux, de travaux pratiques et de travaux dirigés

12 [= situation, state, nature] ◆ **that's always the ~** c'est toujours comme ça ◆ **that's always the ~ with him** c'est toujours comme ça *or* toujours pareil avec lui ◆ **it was this ~ …** *(= happened like this)* ça s'est passé comme ça … ◆ **in the ordinary ~ of things** d'ordinaire, normalement ◆ **it's the ~ of the world!** ainsi va le monde ! ◆ **things are in a bad ~** * ça va mal ◆ **he is in a bad ~** * il va mal ◆ **the car is in a very bad ~** * la voiture est en piteux état ◆ **she was in a terrible ~** * *(physically)* elle était dans un état lamentable ; *(= agitated)* elle était dans tous ses états

13 [= habit] ◆ **to get into/out of the ~ of doing sth** prendre/perdre l'habitude de faire qch ◆ **that's not my ~** ce n'est pas mon genre, je ne suis pas comme ça ◆ **it's not my ~ to flatter people** ce n'est pas mon genre *or* dans mes habitudes de flatter les gens ◆ **don't be offended, it's just his ~** ne vous vexez pas, il est comme ça, c'est tout ◆ **it's only his (little) ~** il est comme ça ◆ **he has an odd ~ of scratching his chin when he laughs** il a une drôle de façon *or* manière de se gratter le menton quand il rit ◆ **I know his little ~s** je connais ses petites habitudes *or* ses petits travers ◆ **they didn't like his pretentious ~s** ils n'aimaient pas ses manières prétentieuses ◆ **I love her funny little ~s** j'adore sa manière bien à elle de faire les choses ◆ **to mend** *or* **improve one's ~s** s'amender ◆ **she is very precise in her ~s** elle porte une attention maniaque aux détails ◆ **Spanish ~s, the ~s of the Spanish** les coutumes *fpl or* mœurs *fpl* espagnoles

14 [= respect, particular] ◆ **in some ~s** à certains égards ◆ **in many ~s** à bien des égards ◆ **in more ~s than one** à plus d'un titre ◆ **can I help you in any ~?** puis-je vous aider en quoi que ce soit ?, puis-je faire quelque chose pour vous aider ? ◆ **does that in any ~ explain it?** est-ce là une explication satisfaisante ? ◆ **he's in no ~** *or* **not in any ~ to blame** ce n'est vraiment pas de sa faute ◆ **not in any ~!** pas le moins du monde ! ◆ **I offended her, without in any ~ intending to do so** je l'ai vexée tout à fait involontairement ◆ **he's right in a** *or* **one ~** il a raison dans un certain sens ◆ **she's good/bad/clever** *etc* **that ~** * elle est bonne/mauvaise/douée *etc* pour ce genre de choses

◆ **by way of, in the way of** *(= as regards)* ◆ **what is there by ~** *or* **in the ~ of kitchen utensils ?** qu'est-ce qu'il y a comme ustensiles de cuisine ?

◆ **by the way** → **by**

15 [= desire] ◆ **to get one's own ~** n'en faire qu'à sa tête ◆ **to want one's own ~** vouloir imposer sa volonté ◆ **I won't let him have things all his own ~** je ne vais pas le laisser faire tout ce qu'il veut ◆ **Arsenal had it all their own ~ in the second half*** Arsenal a complètement dominé la deuxième mi-temps ◆ **to have** *or* **get one's wicked** *or* **evil ~ with sb** *(hum = seduce)* parvenir à ses fins avec qn

16 [= possibility] ◆ **there are no two ~s about it** il n'y a pas à tortiller * ◆ **each ~** *(Racing)* gagnant ou placé ◆ **you can't have it both** *or* **all ~s** il faut choisir

17 [Naut] **to gather/lose ~** *(= speed)* prendre/perdre de la vitesse

2 - ADVERB

1 [= far] ◆ **~ over there** là bas, au loin ◆ **~ down below** tout en bas ◆ **~ up in the sky** très haut dans le ciel ◆ **~ out to sea** loin au large ◆ **you're ~ out* in your calculations** tu t'es trompé de beaucoup dans tes calculs

2 [* = very much] très ◆ **I had to plan ~ in advance** j'ai dû m'y prendre très longtemps à l'avance ◆ **it's ~ too big** c'est beaucoup trop grand ◆ **~ above average** bien au-dessus de la moyenne ◆ **it's ~ past your bedtime** ça fait longtemps que tu devrais être au lit

3 - COMPOUNDS

way of life N mode *m* de vie ◆ **the French ~ of life** le mode de vie des Français, la vie française ◆ **such shortages are a ~ of life** *(fig)* de telles pénuries sont monnaie courante *or* font partie de la vie de tous les jours

the Way of the Cross N *(Rel)* le chemin de la Croix

way-out* ADJ excentrique ◆ **~-out!** super !*, formidable !

way port N port *m* intermédiaire

ways and means NPL moyens *mpl (of doing sth* de faire qch)

Ways and Means Committee N *(US Pol) commission des finances de la Chambre des représentants (examinant les recettes)*

way station N *(US Rail)* petite gare *f* ; *(fig = stage)* étape *f*

way train N *(US)* omnibus *m*

---

waybill /ˈweɪbɪl/ N *(Comm)* récépissé *m*

wayfarer /ˈweɪˌfɛərəʳ/ N voyageur *m*, -euse *f*

wayfaring /ˈweɪˌfɛərɪŋ/ N voyages *mpl*

waylay /weɪˈleɪ/ (pret, ptp **waylaid**) VT 1 *(= attack)* attaquer, assaillir 2 *(= speak to)* arrêter au passage

wayside /ˈweɪsaɪd/ N bord *m or* côté *m* de la route ◆ **along the ~** le long de la route ◆ **by the ~** au bord de la route ◆ **to fall by the ~** *(liter = err, sin)* quitter le droit chemin ◆ **to fall** *or* **go by the ~** *(fig) [competitor, contestant] (= drop out)* abandonner ; *(= be eliminated)* être éliminé ; *[project, plan]* tomber à l'eau ; *[marriage]* se solder par un échec ; *[company]* connaître l'échec ◆ **it went by the ~** on a dû laisser tomber* ◆ **his diet soon fell** *or* **went by the ~** il a vite oublié son régime ◆ **two actors fell by the ~ during the making of the film** *(= gave up)* deux acteurs ont abandonné pendant le tournage du film ; *(= were sacked)* deux acteurs ont été renvoyés pendant le tournage du film ◆ **a lot of business opportunities are going by the ~** on perd de nombreuses occasions de faire des affaires

COMP *[plant, café]* au bord de la route

wayward /ˈweɪwəd/ ADJ 1 *(= wilful) [person]* indiscipliné ; *[horse, behaviour]* rétif ; *(= capricious)* capricieux ; *(= unfaithful)* ◆ **her ~ husband** son mari volage 2 *(gen hum = unmanageable) [hair]* rebelle ; *[satellite, missile]* incontrôlable

waywardness /ˈweɪwədnɪs/ N *(NonC) (= stubbornness)* entêtement *m* ; *(= capriciousness)* inconstance *f*

WBA /ˌdʌbljuːbiːˈeɪ/ N (abbrev of **World Boxing Association**) WBA *f*

WC /ˌdʌbljuˈsiː/ N (abbrev of **water closet**) W.-C. *or* WC *mpl*

we /wiː/ PERS PRON *(pl: unstressed, stressed)* nous ◆ **~ went to the cinema** nous sommes allés *or* on est allé au cinéma ◆ **as ~ say in England** comme on dit (chez nous) en Angleterre ◆ **~ all make mistakes** tout le monde peut se tromper ◆ **~ French** nous autres Français ◆ **~ teachers understand that …** nous autres professeurs, nous comprenons que … ◆ **~ three have already discussed it** nous en avons déjà discuté tous les trois ◆ **"we agree" said the king** "nous sommes d'accord" dit le roi ; → **royal**

w/e (abbrev of **week ending**) **~ 28 Oct** semaine terminant le 28 octobre

WEA /ˌdʌbljuːiːˈeɪ/ N *(in Brit)* (abbrev of **Workers' Educational Association**) *association d'éducation populaire*

weak /wiːk/ ADJ 1 *(= debilitated) (gen)* faible ; *[immune system]* affaibli ◆ **to grow ~(er)** *[person]* s'affaiblir, devenir plus faible ; *[structure, material]* faiblir ; *[voice]* faiblir, devenir plus faible ◆ **to have a ~ heart** être cardiaque, avoir le cœur fragile ◆ **to have ~ lungs** *or* **a ~ chest** avoir les poumons fragiles ◆ **to have a ~ stomach** *or* **digestion** *(lit)* avoir l'estomac fragile ◆ **to have a ~ stomach** *(fig)* être impressionnable ◆ **to have ~ eyesight** avoir la vue faible, avoir une mauvaise vue ◆ **to have a ~ chin/mouth** avoir le menton fuyant/la bouche veule ◆ **~ from** *or* **with hunger** affaibli par la faim ◆ **he was ~ from** *or* **with fright** la peur lui coupait les jambes ◆ **to feel ~ with desire** se sentir défaillir sous l'effet du désir ◆ **to feel ~ with relief** trembler rétrospectivement ◆ **his knees felt ~, he went ~ at the knees** *(from fright)* ses genoux se dérobaient sous lui ; *(from fatigue, illness etc)* il avait les jambes molles *or* comme du coton * ◆ **he went ~ at the knees at the sight of her** *(hum)* il s'est senti défaillir quand il l'a vue ◆ **to be ~ in the head*** être débile * ◆ **~ point** *or* **spot** point *m* faible ◆ **the ~ link in the chain** le point faible ; → **constitution, sex, wall**

2 *(= poor, unconvincing) [essay, script, plot, novel, excuse, argument, evidence]* faible ; *[actor, acting]* médiocre ◆ **to give a ~ performance** *[actor, dancer, athlete]* faire une prestation médiocre ; *[currency]* mal se comporter ; *[company]* avoir de mauvais résultats ◆ **the economy has begun a ~ recovery** l'économie connaît une faible reprise ◆ **to give a ~ smile** avoir un faible sourire ◆ **he is ~ in maths** il est faible en maths ◆ **French is one of his ~er subjects** le français est une de ses matières faibles, le français n'est pas son fort *

3 *(= not powerful) [army, country, team, government, political party, economy, currency, demand]* faible ◆ **the government is in a very ~ position** le gouvernement est dans une très mauvaise position *or* n'est pas du tout en position de force ◆ **to grow ~(er)** *[influence, power]* baisser, diminuer ; *[economy]* s'affaiblir ; *[currency, demand]* faiblir, s'affaiblir

4 *[coffee, tea]* léger ; *[solution, mixture, drug, lens, spectacles, magnet]* faible ; *(Elec) [current]* faible

NPL **the weak** les faibles *mpl*

COMP **weak-kneed*** ADJ *(fig)* lâche, faible

weak-minded ADJ *(= simple-minded)* faible *or* simple d'esprit ; *(= indecisive)* irrésolu

weak verb N *(Gram)* verbe *m* faible

weak-willed ADJ faible, velléitaire

weaken /ˈwiːkən/ VI *[person] (in health)* s'affaiblir ; *(in resolution)* faiblir, flancher* ; *(= relent)* se laisser fléchir ; *[structure, material]* faiblir, commencer à fléchir ; *[voice]* faiblir, baisser ; *[influence, power]* baisser, diminuer ; *[country, team]* faiblir ; *[share prices]* fléchir ◆ **the price of tin has ~ed further** le cours de l'étain a de nouveau faibli *or* a accentué son repli VT *[+ person] (physically)* affaiblir, miner ; *(morally, politically)* affaiblir ; *[+ join, structure, material]* abîmer ; *[+ heart, muscles, eyesight]* affaiblir ; *[+ country, team, government]* affaiblir, rendre vulnérable ; *[+ defence, argument, evidence]* affaiblir, enlever du poids *or* de la force à ; *[+ coffee, solution, mixture]* couper, diluer ; *(Econ) [+ the pound, dollar]* affaiblir, faire baisser

weakening /ˈwiːkənɪŋ/ N *[of health, resolution]* affaiblissement *m* ; *[of structure, material]* fléchissement *m*, fatigue *f* ADJ *[effect]* affaiblissant, débilitant ; *[disease, illness]* débilitant, qui mine

weakling /ˈwiːklɪŋ/ N *(physically)* gringalet *m*, mauviette *f* ; *(morally etc)* faible *mf*, poule *f* mouillée

weakly /ˈwiːklɪ/ ADV 1 *(= feebly) [move, smile, speak]* faiblement • **his heart was beating ~** son cœur battait faiblement 2 *(= irresolutely) [say, protest]* mollement ADJ *[person]* chétif

weakness /ˈwiːknɪs/ N 1 *(NonC: lit, fig = lack of strength) [of person, argument, signal, currency]* faiblesse *f* ; *[of industry, economy, regime]* fragilité *f* • **to negotiate from a position of ~** *(fig)* négocier dans une position d'infériorité 2 *(= weak point) [of person, system, argument]* point *m* faible 3 *(NonC: pej, Psych) [of person, character]* faiblesse *f* • **a sign of ~** un signe de faiblesse 4 *(= defect) [of structure, material]* défaut *m* 5 *(NonC = fragility) [of structure, material]* défauts *mpl* 6 *(= penchant) [of person]* faible *m (for sth* pour qch) • **a ~ for sweet things** un faible pour les sucreries

weal¹ /wiːl/ N *(esp Brit: on skin)* zébrure *f*

weal² †† /wiːl/ N bien *m*, bonheur *m* • **the common ~** le bien public • **~ and woe** le bonheur et le malheur

weald †† /wiːld/ N *(= wooded country)* pays *m* boisé ; *(= open country)* pays *m* découvert

wealth /welθ/ N 1 *(NonC) (= fact of being rich)* richesse *f* ; *(= money, possessions, resources)* richesses *fpl*, fortune *f* ; *(= natural resources etc)* richesse(s) *f(pl)* • **a man of great ~** un homme très riche • **the ~ of the oceans** les richesses *fpl or* les riches ressources *fpl* des océans • **the mineral ~ of a country** les richesses *fpl* minières d'un pays 2 *(fig = abundance)* • **a ~ of ideas** une profusion *or* une abondance d'idées • **a ~ of experience/talent** énormément d'expérience/de talent • **a ~ of information** *or* **detail about sth** une mine de renseignements sur qch • **the lake is home to a ~ of species** ce lac abrite une faune et une flore très riches COMP **wealth tax** N *(Brit)* impôt *m* sur la fortune

wealthy /ˈwelθɪ/ ADJ *[person, family]* fortuné ; *[country]* riche NPL **the wealthy** les riches *mpl*

wean /wiːn/ VT sevrer • **to ~ a baby (onto solids)** sevrer un bébé • **to ~ sb off cigarettes/alcohol** aider qn à arrêter de fumer/de boire • **to ~ o.s. off cigarettes/chocolate/alcohol** apprendre à se passer de cigarettes/de chocolat/d'alcool • **I ~ed her off the idea of going to Greece** je l'ai dissuadée de partir en Grèce • **I'm trying to ~ her onto more adult novels** j'essaie de lui faire lire des romans plus adultes • **to be ~ed on sth** *(fig)* être nourri de qch *(fig)* N /weɪn/ *(Scot = baby, young child)* petit(e) *m(f)*

weaning /ˈwiːnɪŋ/ N *(lit, fig) [of baby, addict]* sevrage *m*

weapon /ˈwepən/ N *(lit, fig)* arme *f* • **~ of offence/defence** arme *f* offensive/défensive COMP **weapons-grade** ADJ pour la fabrication d'armes
→ **weapons of mass destruction NPL** armes *fpl* de destruction massive

weaponry /ˈwepənrɪ/ N *(NonC: collective, gen = arms)* armes *fpl* ; *(Mil)* matériel *m* de guerre, armements *mpl*

wear /wɛəʳ/ (vb : pret **wore**, ptp **worn**) N *(NonC)* 1 *(= clothes collectively)* vêtements *mpl* • **children's/summer/ski ~** vêtements *mpl* pour enfants/d'été/de ski • **the shop stocks an extensive range of beach ~** la boutique propose un grand choix de vêtements de plage • **bring casual ~** apportez des vêtements décontractés ; → **footwear, sportswear**

2 *(= act of wearing)* • **clothes for everyday ~** vêtements *mpl* pour tous les jours • **it's suitable for everyday ~** on peut le porter tous les jours • **clothes for evening ~** tenue *f* de soirée • **for evening ~, dress the outfit up with jewellery** pour le soir, agrémentez cette tenue de bijoux • **clothes for informal** *or* **casual ~** des vêtements *mpl* décontractés

3 *(= use)* usage *m* ; *(= deterioration through use)* usure *f* • **this material will stand up to a lot of ~** ce tissu résistera bien à l'usure • **this carpet has seen** *or* **had some hard ~** ce tapis a beaucoup servi • **there is still some ~ left in it** *(garment, shoe)* c'est encore mettable ; *(carpet, tyre)* cela fera encore de l'usage • **he got four years' ~ out of it** cela lui a fait *or* duré quatre ans • **you'll get more ~ out of a hat if you choose one in a neutral colour** vous porterez plus facilement un chapeau si vous choisissez une couleur neutre • **it has had a lot of ~ and tear** c'est très usagé, cela a été beaucoup porté *or* utilisé • **fair** *or* **normal ~ and tear** usure *f* normale • **the ~ and tear on the engine** l'usure du moteur • **to show signs of ~** *[clothes, shoes]* commencer à être défraîchi *or* fatigué ; *[carpet]* commencer à être usé ; *[tyres, machine]* commencer à être fatigué *or* usagé • **~ resistant** *(US)* inusable ; → **worse**

VT 1 *[+ garment, flower, sword, watch, spectacles, disguise]* porter ; *[+ beard, moustache]* porter, avoir ; *[+ bandage, plaster, tampon, sanitary towel]* avoir • **he was ~ing a hat** il avait *or* il portait un chapeau • **the man ~ing a hat** l'homme au chapeau • **I never ~ a hat** je ne mets *or* porte jamais de chapeau • **people rarely ~ hats now** les chapeaux ne se portent plus guère aujourd'hui • **he was ~ing nothing but a bath towel** il n'avait qu'une serviette de bain sur lui • **he was ~ing nothing but a pair of socks** il n'avait pour tout vêtement qu'une paire de chaussettes • **what shall I ~?** qu'est-ce que je vais mettre ? • **I've nothing to ~, I haven't got a thing to ~** * je n'ai rien à me mettre • **she had nothing to ~ to a formal dinner** elle n'avait rien à se mettre pour un dîner habillé • **I haven't worn it for ages** cela fait des siècles que je ne l'ai pas mis *or* porté • **they don't ~ (a) uniform at her school** on ne porte pas d'uniforme dans son école • **cyclists should always ~ a helmet** les cyclistes devraient toujours porter *or* mettre un casque • **she was ~ing blue** elle était en bleu • **what the well-dressed woman is ~ing this year** ce que la femme élégante porte cette année • **he ~s good clothes** il s'habille bien • **she was ~ing a bandage on her arm** elle avait le bras bandé • **she ~s her hair long** elle a les cheveux longs • **she ~s her hair in a bun** elle porte un chignon • **she usually ~s her hair up** *(in ponytail, plaits etc)* elle s'attache généralement les cheveux ; *(in a bun)* elle relève généralement ses cheveux en chignon • **to ~ lipstick/moisturizer** *etc* (se) mettre du rouge à lèvres/de la crème hydratante, *etc* • **to ~ perfume** se parfumer, (se) mettre du parfum • **she was ~ing perfume** elle s'était parfumée, elle s'était mis du parfum • **she was ~ing make-up** elle (s')était maquillée • **she's the one who ~s the trousers** *or (esp US)* **the pants** c'est elle qui porte la culotte* *or* qui commande

2 *(fig) [+ smile]* arborer ; *[+ look]* avoir, afficher • **she wore a frown** elle fronçait les sourcils • **he wore a look** *or* **an air of satisfaction, he wore a satisfied look on his face** son visage exprimait la satisfaction, il affichait *or* avait un air de satisfaction • **she ~s her age** *or* **her years well** elle porte bien son âge, elle est encore bien pour son âge

3 *(= rub etc) [+ clothes, fabric, stone, wood]* user ; *[+ groove, path]* creuser peu à peu • **to ~ a hole in sth** trouer *or* percer peu à peu qch, faire peu à peu un trou dans *or* à qch • **the rug was worn (thin)** le tapis était usé jusqu'à la corde • **worn with care** usé *or* rongé par les soucis ; see also **worn** ; → **frazzle, work**

4 *(Brit* * = tolerate, accept)* tolérer • **he won't ~ that** il n'acceptera jamais (ça), il ne marchera pas* • **the committee won't ~ another £100 on your expenses** vous ne ferez jamais avaler au comité 100 livres de plus pour vos frais*

VI 1 *(= deteriorate with use) [garment, fabric, stone, wood]* s'user • **these trousers have worn at the knees** ce pantalon est usé aux genoux • **the rock has worn smooth** la roche a été polie par le temps • **the material has worn thin** le tissu est râpé • **the rug has worn thin** *or* **threadbare** le tapis est usé jusqu'à la corde *or* complètement râpé • **that excuse has worn thin!** *(fig)* cette excuse ne prend plus ! • **my patience is ~ing thin** je suis presque à bout de patience • **their optimism is starting to ~ thin** ils commencent à perdre leur optimisme • **that joke is starting to ~ a bit thin!** cette plaisanterie commence à être éculée !, cette plaisanterie n'est plus vraiment drôle !

2 *(= last) [clothes, carpet, tyres etc]* faire de l'usage, résister à l'usure • **that dress/carpet has worn well** cette robe/ce tapis a bien résisté à l'usure *or* a fait beaucoup d'usage • **a theory/friendship that has worn well** une théorie/amitié qui a résisté à l'épreuve du temps • **she has worn well*** elle est bien conservée

3 • **to ~ to its end** *or* **to a close** *[day, year, sb's life]* tirer à sa fin

► **wear away** VI *[wood, metal]* s'user ; *[cliffs, rock etc]* être rongé *or* dégradé ; *[inscription, design]* s'effacer
VT SEP *[+ wood, metal]* user ; *[+ cliffs, rock]* ronger, dégrader ; *[+ inscription, design]* effacer

► **wear down** VI *[heels, pencil etc]* s'user ; *[resistance, courage]* s'épuiser
VT SEP *[+ materials]* user ; *[+ patience, strength]* user, épuiser ; *[+ courage, resistance]* miner • **the hard work was ~ing him down** le travail l'usait *or* le minait • **constantly being criticized ~s you down** ça (vous) mine d'être constamment critiqué • **I had worn myself down by overwork** je m'étais usé *or* épuisé en travaillant trop • **the unions managed to ~ the employers down and get their demands met** les syndicats ont réussi à faire céder les employeurs et à obtenir ce qu'ils demandaient

► **wear off** VI *[colour, design, inscription]* s'effacer, disparaître ; *[pain]* disparaître, passer ; *[anger, excitement]* s'apaiser, passer ; *[effects]* se dissiper, disparaître ; *[anaesthetic, magic]* se dissiper • **the novelty has worn off** cela n'a plus l'attrait de la nouveauté
VT SEP effacer par l'usure, faire disparaître

► **wear on** VI *[day, year, winter etc]* avancer ; *[battle, war, discussions etc]* se poursuivre • **as the years wore on** à mesure que les années passaient, avec le temps

► **wear out** VI *[clothes, material, machinery]* s'user ; *[patience, enthusiasm]* s'épuiser
VT SEP 1 *[+ shoes, clothes]* user ; *[+ one's strength, reserves, materials, patience]* épuiser
2 *(= exhaust) [+ person, horse]* épuiser • **to ~ one's eyes out** s'user les yeux *or* la vue • **to ~ o.s. out** s'épuiser, s'exténuer *(doing sth* à faire qch) • **to be worn out** être exténué *or* éreinté
ADJ • **worn-out** → **worn**

► **wear through** VT SEP trouer, percer
VI se trouer *(par usure)*

wearable /ˈwɛərəbl/ ADJ *[clothes]* mettable, portable ; *[shoes]* mettable ; *[colour]* facile à porter

wearer /ˈwɛərəʳ/ N porteur *m*, -euse *f* • **denture/spectacle/contact lens ~s** les porteurs *mpl* de dentier/de lunettes/de lentilles • **he's not really a tie ~** ce n'est pas vraiment son style de porter la cravate • **this device can**

improve the ~'s hearing considerably cet appareil peut considérablement améliorer l'audition (de l'utilisateur) ◆ **special suits designed to protect the ~ from the cold** des combinaisons spéciales conçues pour protéger (l'utilisateur) du froid ◆ **direct from maker to ~** directement du fabricant au client

wearied /ˈwɪərɪd/ ADJ *[person, animal, smile, look]* las (lasse *f*) ; *[sigh]* de lassitude ◆ **~ by sth** las de qch

wearily /ˈwɪərɪlɪ/ ADV *[say, smile, look at, nod]* d'un air las, avec lassitude ; *[sigh, think, move]* avec lassitude

weariness /ˈwɪərɪnɪs/ N *(NonC, physical)* lassitude *f*, fatigue *f* ; *(mental)* lassitude *f* (*with sth* à l'égard de qch), abattement *m* ; → **war, world**

wearing /ˈweərɪŋ/ ADJ *[person, job]* fatigant, lassant ◆ **it's ~ on one's nerves** ça met les nerfs à rude épreuve

wearisome /ˈwɪərɪsəm/ ADJ *(frm)* *(= tiring)* lassant, fatigant ; *(= boring)* ennuyeux, lassant, fastidieux ; *(= frustrating)* frustrant

weary /ˈwɪərɪ/ ADJ [1] *(= tired)* las (lasse *f*) ◆ **to be ~ of (doing) sth** être las de (faire) qch ◆ **~ of life** las de vivre ◆ **~ with walking** las d'avoir marché ◆ **to grow ~** *[person, animal]* se lasser ; *[eyes]* devenir las ◆ **to grow ~ of (doing) sth** se lasser de (faire) qch ; → **world** [2] *(liter)* *[months, miles, wait]* épuisant ◆ **I made my ~ way back home** je suis rentré, épuisé VI se lasser (*of sth* de qch ; *of doing sth* de faire qch) VT *(= tire)* fatiguer, lasser ; *(= try patience of)* lasser, agacer, ennuyer (*with* à force de) see also **wearied**

weasel /ˈwiːzl/ N (pl **weasel** *or* **weasels**) belette *f* ; *(fig pej = person)* fouine *f (fig pej)* VI (US *: also **weasel-word**) *(speaking)* s'exprimer de façon ambiguë *or* équivoque ◆ **to ~ out of sth** *(= extricate o.s.)* se sortir *or* se tirer de qch en misant sur l'ambiguïté ; *(= avoid it)* éviter qch en misant sur l'ambiguïté COMP **weasel words** NPL *(fig)* paroles *fpl* ambiguës *or* équivoques

weather /ˈweðəʳ/ N temps *m* ◆ **what's the ~ like?** quel temps fait-il ? ◆ **it's fine/bad ~** il fait beau/mauvais, le temps est beau/mauvais ◆ **summer ~** temps *m* d'été *or* estival ◆ **in this ~** par ce temps, par un temps comme ça ◆ **in hot/cold/wet/stormy ~** par temps chaud/froid/humide/orageux ◆ **in good ~** par beau temps ◆ **in all ~s** par tous les temps ◆ **to be under the ~** * être mal fichu *, ne pas être dans son assiette ; → **heavy, wet**

VT [1] *(= survive)* *[+ tempest, hurricane]* essuyer ; *(fig)* *[+ crisis]* survivre à, réchapper à ◆ **to ~ a storm** *(lit)* essuyer une tempête ; *(fig)* tenir le coup ◆ **can the company ~ the recession?** l'entreprise peut-elle survivre à *or* surmonter la récession ?

[2] *(= expose to weather)* *[+ wood etc]* faire mûrir ◆ **~ed rocks** rochers *mpl* exposés aux intempéries ◆ **rocks ~ed by rain and wind** rochers *mpl* érodés par la pluie et par le vent

VI *[wood]* mûrir ; *[rocks]* s'éroder

COMP *[knowledge, map, prospects]* météorologique ; *[conditions, variations]* atmosphérique ; *(Naut)* *[side, sheet]* du vent

weather-beaten ADJ *[person, face]* hâlé, tanné ; *[building]* dégradé par les intempéries ; *[stone]* érodé *or* usé par les intempéries

weather-bound ADJ immobilisé *or* retenu par le mauvais temps

Weather Bureau N *(US)* ⇒ **Weather Centre**

Weather Centre N *(Brit)* Office *m* national de la météorologie

weather chart N carte *f* du temps, carte *f* météorologique

weather check N (bref) bulletin *m* météo *inv*

weather cock N girouette *f*

weather eye N *(fig)* ◆ **to keep a ~ eye on sth** surveiller qch ◆ **to keep one's ~ eye open** veiller au grain *(fig)*

weather forecast N prévisions *fpl* météorologiques, météo * *f NonC*

weather forecaster N météorologue *mf*, météorologiste *mf*

weather girl * N présentatrice *f* météo *inv*

weather report N bulletin *m* météo(rologique), météo * *f NonC*

weather ship N navire *m* météo *inv*

weather station N station *f or* observatoire *m* météorologique

weather strip N bourrelet *m (pour porte etc)*

weather vane N ⇒ **weather cock**

weather-worn ADJ ⇒ **weather-beaten**

weatherboard(ing) /ˈweðəbɔːd(ɪŋ)/ N *(NonC)* planches *fpl* à recouvrement

weatherman * /ˈweðəmæn/ N (pl **-men**) météorologue *m* ; *(on TV)* présentateur *m* météo *inv*

weatherproof /ˈweðəpruːf/ ADJ *[clothing]* imperméable ; *[house]* étanche VT *[+ clothing]* imperméabiliser ; *[+ house]* rendre étanche

weatherwoman * /ˈweðəwʊmən/ N (pl **-women**) météorologue *f* ; *(on TV)* présentatrice *f* météo *inv*

weave /wiːv/ (vb : pret **wove**, ptp **woven**) N tissage *m* ◆ **loose/tight ~** tissage *m* lâche/serré ◆ **a cloth of English ~** du drap tissé en Angleterre

VT *[+ threads, cloth, web]* tisser ; *[+ strands]* entrelacer ; *[+ basket, garland, daisies]* tresser ; *(fig)* *[+ plot]* tramer, tisser ; *[+ story]* inventer, bâtir ◆ **to ~ flowers into one's hair** entrelacer des fleurs dans ses cheveux ◆ **to ~ details into a story** introduire *or* incorporer des détails dans une histoire

◆ **to weave one's way** ◆ **to ~ one's way through the crowd** se faufiler à travers la foule ◆ **the drunk ~d his way across the room** l'ivrogne a titubé *or* zigzagué à travers la pièce ◆ **the car was weaving its way in and out through the traffic** la voiture se faufilait *or* se glissait à travers la circulation

VI [1] *(on loom)* tisser

[2] (pret, ptp *gen* **weaved**) (also **weave one's** *or* **its way**) *[road, river, line]* serpenter ◆ **to ~ through the crowd** se faufiler à travers la foule ◆ **the drunk ~d across the room** l'ivrogne a titubé *or* zigzagué à travers la pièce ◆ **the car was weaving in and out through the traffic** la voiture se faufilait *or* se glissait à travers la circulation ◆ **the boxer was weaving in and out skilfully** le boxeur esquivait les coups adroitement ◆ **to ~ in and out of the trees** zigzaguer entre les arbres ◆ **let's get weaving!** † * allons, remuons-nous !

weaver /ˈwiːvəʳ/ N *(= person)* tisserand(e) *m(f)* ; (also **weaver bird**) tisserin *m*

weaving /ˈwiːvɪŋ/ N *(NonC)* *[of threads, cloth, web]* tissage *m* ; *[of basket, garland, daisies]* tressage *m* ; *[of strands]* entrelacement *m* ; *[of plot]* élaboration *f* COMP **weaving mill** N (atelier *m* de) tissage *m*

web /web/ N [1] *(= fabric)* tissu *m* ; *[of spider]* toile *f* ; *(between toes etc)* *[of animals etc]* palmure *f* ; *[of humans]* palmature *f* [2] *(fig)* *[of lies etc]* tissu *m* ◆ **a tangled ~** un sac de nœuds ◆ **to untangle the complex ~ of** démêler l'écheveau de [3] *(Internet)* ◆ **the (World Wide) Web** le Web, la Toile COMP **web browser** N navigateur *m*

web(bed) feet NPL ◆ **to have ~(bed) feet** être palmipède, avoir les pieds palmés

web page N page *f* Web

web ring N webring *m*

web surfer N internaute *mf*

webbing /ˈwebɪŋ/ N *(NonC)* [1] *(= fabric)* toile *f* ; *(on chair)* (also *Mil*) sangles *fpl* [2] *(on bird's, animal's foot)* palmure *f* ; *(on human foot)* palmature *f*

webcam /ˈwebkæm/ N webcam *f*

webcast /ˈwebkɑːst/ N émission *f* diffusée sur le Web *or* la Toile VT diffuser sur le Web *or* la Toile VI diffuser des émissions sur le Web *or* la Toile

weblog /ˈweblɒg/ N *(Comput)* weblog *m*, weblogue *m*

weblogging /ˈweblɒgɪŋ/ N weblogging *m*

webmail /ˈwebmeɪl/ N webmail *m (portail permettant l'accès à un compte de messagerie électronique avec un navigateur)*

webmaster /ˈwebmɑːstəʳ/ N webmaster *m*

website /ˈwebsaɪt/ N *(Comput)* site *m* Web *or* Internet COMP **website designer** N concepteur *m* (-trice *f*) de sites Web

webspace /ˈwebspeɪs/ N espace *m* sur le Web

webzine /ˈwebziːn/ N webzine *m*

we'd /wiːd/ ⇒ **we had, we should, we would** ; › **have, should, would**

wed /wed/ (pret **wedded**, ptp **wedded, wed**) VT [1] *(= marry)* épouser, se marier avec ; *[priest]* marier ◆ **to be ~, to get ~** se marier [2] *(fig)* → **wedded** VI † se marier

Wed. abbrev of **Wednesday**

wedded /ˈwedɪd/ ADJ [1] *(frm = married)* *[person, couple]* marié ; *[life]* conjugal ◆ **~ bliss** bonheur *m* conjugal ◆ **his (lawful** *or* **lawfully) ~ wife** sa légitime épouse ◆ **do you take this woman to be your lawful(ly) ~ wife?** voulez-vous prendre cette femme pour épouse ? [2] *(= committed)* ◆ **to be ~ to sth** *[+ idea]* être profondément attaché à qch ; *[+ cause]* être entièrement dévoué à qch ◆ **he is ~ to his work** il est marié avec son travail, il ne vit que pour son travail [3] *(= allied)* ◆ **to be ~ to sth** être allié à qch ◆ **he advocates change ~ to caution** il prône le changement allié à la prudence ◆ **his cunning, ~ to ambition, led to …** sa ruse, alliée à l'ambition, a conduit à …

wedding /ˈwedɪŋ/ N *(= ceremony)* mariage *m*, noces *fpl* ◆ **silver/golden ~** noces *fpl* d'argent/d'or ◆ **they had a quiet ~** ils se sont mariés dans l'intimité, le mariage a été célébré dans l'intimité ◆ **they had a church ~** ils se sont mariés à l'église ; → **civil**

COMP *[cake, night]* de noces ; *[present]* de mariage, de noces ; *[invitation]* de mariage ; *[ceremony, march]* nuptial

wedding anniversary N anniversaire *m* de mariage

wedding band N ⇒ **wedding ring**

wedding breakfast N *(Brit)* lunch *m* de mariage ; *(less elegant)* repas *m* de noces

wedding day N ◆ **her/my/their ~ day** le jour de son/mon/leur mariage

wedding dress, wedding gown N robe *f* de mariée

wedding guest N invité(e) *m(f) (à un mariage)*

wedding reception N réception *f* de mariage

wedding ring N alliance *f*, anneau *m* de mariage

wedding vows NPL vœux *mpl* de mariage

wedeln /ˈveɪdəln/ *(Ski)* VI godiller N godille *f*

wedge /wedʒ/ N [1] *(for holding sth steady: under wheel etc, also Golf)* cale *f* ; *(for splitting wood, rock)* coin *m* ◆ **that drove a ~ between them** cela a creusé un fossé entre eux ; → **thin** [2] *(= piece)* *[of cake, cheese, pie etc]* (grosse) part *f*, (gros) morceau *m* [3] *(Ski)* chasse-neige *m* ; *(Climbing)* coin *m* de bois

NPL **wedges** *(= wedge-heeled shoes)* chaussures *fpl* à semelles compensées

VT *(= fix)* *[+ table, wheels]* caler ; *(= stick, push)* enfoncer (*into* dans ; *between* entre) ◆ **to ~ a door open/shut** maintenir une porte ouverte/fermée à l'aide d'une cale ◆ **the door was ~d** on avait mis une cale à la porte ◆ **he ~d the table leg to hold it steady** il a calé le pied de la table (pour la stabiliser) ◆ **to ~ a stick into a crack** enfoncer un bâton dans une fente ◆ **I can't move this, it's ~d** je n'arrive pas à le faire bouger, c'est coincé ◆ **she was sitting on the bench, ~d between her mother and her aunt** elle était assise sur le banc, coincée entre sa mère et sa tante

COMP **wedge-heeled** ADJ à semelles compensées

wedge-shaped ADJ en forme de coin

wedge-soled ADJ ⇒ **wedge-heeled**

► **wedge in** VI *[person]* se glisser

VT SEP *(into case, box etc) [+ object]* faire rentrer, enfoncer ; *(into car, onto seat etc) [+ person]* faire rentrer ; *[+ several people]* entasser ◆ **to be ~d in** être coincé

wedlock /ˈwedlɒk/ N *(NonC)* mariage *m* ◆ **to be born in ~** être un enfant légitime ◆ **to be born out of ~** être né hors des liens du mariage

Wednesday /ˈwenzdeɪ/ N mercredi *m* ; → **ash²** ; *for other phrases see* **Saturday**

Weds. abbrev of **Wednesday**

wee¹ /wiː/ ADJ 1 *(esp Scot or *)* petit ◆ **when I was a ~ boy** quand j'étais petit ◆ **a ~ bit** un tout petit peu 2 ◆ **the ~ small hours (of the morning)** les premières heures du matin *(de 1 à 4 h du matin)*

wee² * /wiː/ *(baby talk)* N pipi * *m* ◆ **to have a ~** faire pipi * ◆ **to want a ~** * avoir envie de faire pipi * VI faire pipi *

weed /wiːd/ N 1 mauvaise herbe *f* ; *(* pej = person)* mauviette *f* ; *(‡ = marijuana)* herbe * *f* ◆ **the ~** * *(hum)* le tabac 2 ◆ **(widow's) ~s** vêtements *mpl* de deuil ◆ **in widow's ~s** en deuil VT désherber ; *(= hoe)* sarcler COMP **weed-killer** N désherbant *m*, herbicide *m*

► **weed out** VT SEP *[+ plant]* enlever, arracher ; *(fig) [+ weak candidates]* éliminer *(from* de) ; *[+ troublemakers]* expulser *(from* de) ; *[+ old clothes, books]* trier et jeter

weedhead ‡ /ˈwiːdhed/ N *(Drugs)* consommateur *m*, -trice *f* de marijuana

weeding /ˈwiːdɪŋ/ N *(NonC)* désherbage *m* ; *(with hoe)* sarclage *m* ◆ **I've done some ~** j'ai un peu désherbé

weedy /ˈwiːdɪ/ ADJ 1 *[flowerbed, land]* couvert de mauvaises herbes ; *[river, pond]* envahi par les herbes 2 *(Brit * pej = scrawny) [person]* chétif *(pej)*, malingre *(pej)*

week /wiːk/ N semaine *f* ◆ **what day of the ~ is it?** quel jour de la semaine sommes-nous ? ◆ **this ~** cette semaine ◆ **next/last ~** la semaine prochaine/dernière ◆ **the ~ before last** l'avant-dernière semaine ◆ **the ~ after next** pas la semaine prochaine, celle d'après ◆ **by the end of the ~ he had ...** à la fin de la semaine il avait ... ◆ **in the middle of the ~** vers le milieu *or* dans le courant de la semaine ◆ **twice a ~** deux fois par semaine ◆ **this time next ~** dans huit jours à la même heure ◆ **this time last ~** il y a huit jours à la même heure ◆ **today ~** * *(Brit)* ◆ **a ~ today** aujourd'hui en huit ◆ **tomorrow ~** * *(Brit)* ◆ **a ~ tomorrow** demain en huit ◆ **yesterday ~** * *(Brit)* ◆ **a ~ yesterday** il y a eu une semaine hier ◆ **Sunday ~** * *(Brit)* ◆ **a ~ on Sunday** dimanche en huit ◆ **every ~** chaque semaine ◆ **two ~s ago** il y a deux semaines, il y a quinze jours ◆ **in a ~** *(= a week from now)* dans une semaine ; *(= in the space of a week)* en une semaine ◆ **in a ~'s time** d'ici une semaine, dans une semaine ◆ **in three ~s' time** dans *or* d'ici trois semaines ◆ **~ in ~ out, ~ after ~** semaine après semaine ◆ **it lasted (for) ~s** cela a duré des semaines (et des semaines) ◆ **the first time** *etc* **in ~s** la première fois, *etc* depuis des semaines ◆ **the ~ ending 6 May** la semaine qui se termine le 6 mai ◆ **he owes her three ~s' rent** il lui doit trois semaines de loyer ◆ **paid by the ~** payé à la semaine ◆ **the working ~** la semaine de travail ◆ **a 36-hour ~** une semaine (de travail) de 36 heures ◆ **a three-day ~** une semaine (de travail) de trois jours ◆ **a ~'s wages** le salaire hebdomadaire *or* de la *or* d'une semaine

weekday /ˈwiːkdeɪ/ N jour *m* de semaine, jour *m* ouvrable *(esp Comm)* ◆ **(on) ~s** en semaine, les jours ouvrables *(esp Comm)* COMP *[activities, timetable]* de la semaine

weekend /ˈwiːkˈend/ N week-end *m* ◆ **(at) ~s** pendant le(s) week-end(s) ◆ **what are you doing at the ~?** qu'est-ce que tu vas faire ce week-end ? ◆ **he told me to give you a call over the ~** il m'a dit de t'appeler ce week-end ◆ **we're going away for the ~** nous partons en week-end ◆ **to take a long ~** prendre un week-end prolongé ◆ **they had Tuesday off so they made a long ~ of it** comme ils ne devaient pas travailler mardi ils ont fait le pont VI passer le week-end

COMP *[visit, programme]* de *or* du week-end

weekend bag, weekend case N sac *m* de voyage

weekend cottage N maison *f* de campagne

weekender /ˈwiːkˈendəʳ/ N personne *f* partant *(or* partie) en week-end ◆ **the village is full of ~s** le village est plein de gens qui viennent pour les week-ends

weekly /ˈwiːklɪ/ ADJ *[magazine, meeting, wage, rainfall]* hebdomadaire ; *[hours]* par semaine ◆ **we do the ~ shopping every Thursday** tous les jeudis nous faisons les courses pour la semaine ADV *[meet, attend, play]* chaque semaine ; *[sell]* par semaine ◆ **twice/three times ~** deux/trois fois par semaine ◆ **paid ~** payé à la semaine ◆ **on a ~ basis** *[pay]* à la semaine ; *(= every week)* chaque semaine, toutes les semaines ◆ **we meet ~ on Thursdays** nous nous rencontrons tous les jeudis N *(= magazine)* hebdomadaire *m*

weeknight /ˈwiːknaɪt/ N soir *m* de semaine

weenie * /ˈwiːnɪ/ N *(US Culin)* ⇒ **wienie**

weensy * /ˈwiːnzɪ/ ADJ *(US)* ⇒ **weeny adj**

weeny * /ˈwiːnɪ/ *(Brit)* ADJ tout petit ◆ **it was a ~ bit embarrassing** c'était un tout petit peu gênant

weep /wiːp/ (pret, ptp **wept**) VI 1 *(= cry) [person]* verser des larmes, pleurer ◆ **to ~ for** *or* **with joy** pleurer de joie ◆ **to ~ with relief/remorse** verser des larmes de soulagement/remords ◆ **to ~ for sb/sth** pleurer qn/qch ◆ **to ~ over sth** pleurer *or* se lamenter sur qch ◆ **she wept to see him leave** elle a pleuré de le voir partir ◆ **I could have wept!** j'en aurais pleuré ! 2 *[walls, sore, wound]* suinter VT *[+ tears]* verser, répandre ◆ **to ~ tears of joy/fury/despair** verser des larmes *or* pleurer de joie/de colère/de désespoir ; → **bucket** N * ◆ **to have a good ~** pleurer un bon coup ◆ **to have a little ~** pleurer un peu, verser quelques larmes

weeping /ˈwiːpɪŋ/ N *(NonC)* larmes *fpl* ◆ **we heard the sound of ~** on entendait quelqu'un qui pleurait ADJ *[person]* qui pleure ; *[walls, sore, wound]* suintant ◆ **~ willow** saule *m* pleureur

weepy /ˈwiːpɪ/ ADJ *[person]* à la larme facile ; *[eyes, voice, mood, song]* larmoyant ; *[film]* mélo *, sentimental ◆ **to feel ~** *[person]* avoir envie de pleurer, se sentir au bord des larmes N *(Brit = film, book)* mélo * *m*, film *m (or* livre *m)* sentimental

weever /ˈwiːvəʳ/ N *(= fish)* vive *f*

weevil /ˈwiːvəl/ N charançon *m*

wee-wee * /ˈwiːwiː/ N, VI ⇒ **wee²**

weft /weft/ N *[of fabric]* trame *f*

weigh /weɪ/ VT 1 *(lit, fig)* peser ◆ **to ~ o.s.** se peser ◆ **to ~ sth in one's hand** soupeser qch ◆ **it ~s 9 kilos** ça pèse 9 kilos ◆ **how much** *or* **what do you ~?** combien est-ce que vous pesez ? ◆ **to ~ one's words (carefully)** peser ses mots ◆ **to ~ (up) A against B** mettre en balance A et B ◆ **to ~ (up) the pros and cons** peser le pour et le contre ◆ **she ~ed her options** elle a étudié les différentes possibilités ◆ **the advantages must be ~ed against the possible risks** il faut mettre en balance les avantages et les risques éventuels ◆ **she spoke very slowly, ~ing what she would say** elle parlait très lentement, en pesant ses mots

2 *(Naut)* **to ~ anchor** lever l'ancre

VI *[object, responsibilities]* peser *(on* sur) ◆ **the fear of cancer ~s on her** *or* **on her mind all the time** la peur du cancer la tourmente constamment, elle vit constamment avec la peur du cancer ◆ **the responsibility of being a parent can ~ heavily** être parent est parfois une lourde responsabilité ◆ **there's something ~ing on her mind** quelque chose la préoccupe *or* la tracasse ◆ **the divorce laws ~ heavily against men** les lois sur le divorce sont nettement en défaveur des hommes ◆ **many factors ~ed against the meeting happening** il y avait de nombreux facteurs qui s'opposaient à la tenue de la réunion ◆ **economic considerations ~ed heavily in their decision** les considérations économiques ont beaucoup pesé dans leur décision

COMP **weigh-in** N *(Sport)* pesage *m*

weighing machine NPL *(gen)* balance *f* ; *(for heavy loads)* bascule *f*

weighing scales NPL balance *f*

► **weigh down** VI peser *or* appuyer de tout son poids *(on sth* sur qch) ◆ **this sorrow ~ed down on her** ce chagrin la rongeait *or* la minait

VT SEP faire plier *or* ployer, courber ; *(fig)* accabler, tourmenter ◆ **the fruit ~ed the branch down** la branche ployait *or* pliait sous le poids des fruits ◆ **he was ~ed down with parcels** il pliait sous le poids des paquets ◆ **to be ~ed down by** *or* **with responsibilities** être accablé *or* surchargé de responsabilités ◆ **to be ~ed down with fears** être en proie à toutes sortes de peurs

► **weigh in** VI 1 *[boxer, jockey etc]* se faire peser ◆ **to ~ in at 70 kilos** peser 70 kilos avant l'épreuve ◆ **the hippopotamus ~s in at* an impressive 1.5 tonnes** l'hippopotame pèse pas moins de 1,5 tonnes

2 *(fig = contribute)* intervenir ◆ **he ~ed in with more money** il est intervenu en apportant davantage d'argent ◆ **he ~ed in with his opinion** il est intervenu en donnant son avis *or* son opinion ◆ **the President's political advisers ~ed in on the plan** les conseillers politiques du président ont donné leur avis *or* opinion sur le projet

VT SEP *[+ boxer, jockey]* peser *(avant le match ou la course)*

N ◆ **weigh-in** → **weigh**

► **weigh out** VT SEP *[+ sugar etc]* peser

► **weigh up** VT SEP *(= consider)* examiner, calculer ; *(= compare)* mettre en balance *(A with B, A against B* A et B) ◆ **to ~ up A with** *or* **against B** mettre en balance A et B ; *(Brit) (= assess) [+ person, the opposition]* juger, sonder ◆ **I'm ~ing up whether to go or not** je me tâte pour savoir si j'y vais ou non ; see also **weigh vt 1**

weighbridge /ˈweɪbrɪdʒ/ N pont-bascule *m*

weight /weɪt/ N 1 *(NonC)* poids *m* ; *(Phys: relative weight)* pesanteur *f* ◆ **atomic ~** *(Phys)* poids *m* atomique ◆ **it is sold by ~** cela se vend au poids ◆ **what is your ~?** combien pesez-vous ?, quel poids faites-vous ? ◆ **my ~ is 60 kilos** je pèse 60 kilos ◆ **it is 3 kilos in ~** ça pèse 3 kilos ◆ **they are the same ~** ils font le même poids ◆ **his ~ was harming his health** son poids avait un effet néfaste sur sa santé ◆ **~ when empty** poids *m* à vide ◆ **take the ~ off your feet** asseds-toi ◆ **it's/she's worth its/her ~ in gold** cela/elle vaut son pesant d'or ◆ **to put on** *or* **gain ~** grossir, prendre du poids ◆ **to lose ~** maigrir, perdre du poids ◆ **he lost 5 kilos in ~** il a maigri de 5 kilos *or* perdu 5 kilos ◆ **he put** *or* **leaned his full ~ on the handle** il a pesé *or* appuyé de tout son poids sur la poignée

♦ **he put his full ~ behind the blow** il a frappé de toutes ses forces ♦ **to move** *or* **shift one's ~ from one foot to the other** se balancer d'un pied sur l'autre ♦ **he shifted his ~ onto the other foot/onto his elbow** il fit porter son poids sur son autre pied/sur son coude ♦ **to throw one's ~** *or* **to put all one's ~ behind sth/sb** *(fig)* apporter personnellement tout son soutien à qch/à qn ♦ **feel the ~ of this box!** soupesez-moi cette boîte ! ♦ **what a ~ (it is)!** que c'est lourd ! ♦ **he looks as if he's carrying the ~ of the world on his shoulders** on dirait qu'il porte toute la misère du monde sur ses épaules ; → **pull, throw about**

2 *(fig) [of argument, words, public opinion, evidence]* poids *m*, force *f* ; *[of worry, responsibility, years, age]* poids *m* ♦ **to attach** *or* **lend** *or* **give ~ to sth** donner du poids à qch ♦ **to carry ~** *[argument, factor]* avoir du poids (with pour) ; *[person]* avoir de l'influence ♦ **we must give due ~ to his arguments** nous devons donner tout leur poids à ses arguments ; → **mind**

3 *(for scales, on clock etc)* poids *m* ♦ **to lift ~s** faire des haltères ; → **paperweight, put**

VT 1 lester ; → **weighted**

2 *(= assign value to)* pondérer

COMP **weight lifter** N *(Sport)* haltérophile *mf*
weight lifting N haltérophilie *f*
weight limit N limitation *f* de poids
weight loss N *(NonC)* perte *f* de poids
weights and measures NPL poids et mesures *mpl*
weights and measures inspector N inspecteur *m* des poids et mesures
weight-train VI faire de la musculation
weight training N musculation *f* *(avec des poids)*
weight watcher N ♦ **he's a ~ watcher** *(= actively slimming)* il suit un régime amaigrissant ; *(= figure-conscious)* il surveille son poids

► **weight down** VT SEP *[+ papers, tablecloth etc]* retenir *or* maintenir avec un poids

weighted /ˈweɪtɪd/ ADJ 1 *(= biased)* ♦ **~ in sb's favour** *or* **towards sb** favorable à qn ♦ **~ in favour of/against sb** favorable/défavorable à qn ♦ **the situation was heavily ~ in his favour/against him** la situation lui était nettement favorable/défavorable 2 *(= made heavier) [diving belt]* lesté COMP **weighted average** N moyenne *f* pondérée

weightiness /ˈweɪtɪnɪs/ N *(NonC) [of argument, matter]* poids *m* ; *[of responsibility]* importance *f*

weighting /ˈweɪtɪŋ/ N 1 *(on salary)* indemnité *f*, allocation *f* ♦ **London ~** indemnité *f* de vie chère à Londres 2 *(Scol)* coefficient *m* ; *(Econ)* coefficient *m*, pondération *f*

weightless /ˈweɪtlɪs/ ADJ *[astronaut, falling object]* en état d'apesanteur ; *[conditions]* d'apesanteur ♦ **in a ~ environment** en apesanteur ♦ **to feel ~** se sentir léger comme l'air

weightlessness /ˈweɪtlɪsnɪs/ N apesanteur *f*

weighty /ˈweɪtɪ/ ADJ 1 *(frm = serious) [matter, problem]* grave, important ; *[argument, reason]* de poids ; *[burden, responsibility]* lourd 2 *(liter = heavy) [tome, volume]* lourd ; *[load]* pesant, lourd

Weimar /ˈvaɪmɑːr/ N Weimar COMP **the Weimar Republic** N la république de Weimar

weir /wɪəʳ/ N barrage *m*

weird /wɪəd/ ADJ 1 *(* = peculiar) [person, object, behaviour, coincidence]* bizarre, étrange ♦ **it felt ~ going back there** ça faisait bizarre d'y retourner ♦ **the ~ thing is that ...** ce qu'il y a de bizarre c'est que ... ♦ **lots of ~ and wonderful* species** plein d'espèces étranges et merveilleuses 2 *(= eerie) [sound, light]* surnaturel, mystérieux

weirdly /ˈwɪədlɪ/ ADV 1 *(* = peculiarly) [behave, dress]* bizarrement 2 *(= eerily) [glow]* mystérieusement, de façon surnaturelle ; *[sing]* de façon surnaturelle

weirdness /ˈwɪədnɪs/ N étrangeté *f*

weirdo* /ˈwɪədəʊ/ N *(pej)* cinglé(e)* *m(f)*

Welch † /weltʃ/ ADJ ⇒ **Welsh**

welch /welʃ/ VI ⇒ **welsh**

welcome /ˈwelkəm/ LANGUAGE IN USE 13, 26.3

ADJ 1 *(= gladly accepted)* ♦ **to be ~** *[person]* être le *(or* la) bienvenu(e) ♦ **he'll/you'll always be ~ here** il sera/tu seras toujours le bienvenu ici ♦ **some members were more ~ than others** certains membres étaient plus appréciés que d'autres ♦ **he's not ~ here any more** sa présence ici est devenue indésirable ♦ **I didn't feel very ~** je n'ai pas vraiment eu l'impression d'être le bienvenu ♦ **to make sb ~** faire bon accueil à qn ♦ **they really make you feel ~** on y est vraiment bien accueilli ♦ **to roll out** *or* **put out the ~ mat for sb*** se donner du mal pour recevoir qn ♦ **you're ~!** *(esp US: answer to thanks)* je vous en prie !, de rien ! ♦ **I don't use it any more, so you're ~ to it** je ne m'en sers plus, alors profitez-en ♦ **he wants the job? he's ~ to it!** il veut le poste ? eh bien, qu'il le prenne ! ♦ **he's ~ to her!** qu'il se débrouille avec elle !

♦ **to be welcome to do sth** ♦ **you're ~ to try** *(giving permission)* je vous en prie, essayez ; *(iro)* libre à vous d'essayer ♦ **you're ~ to use my car** vous pouvez emprunter ma voiture si vous voulez ♦ **she's ~ to visit any time** elle est toujours la bienvenue ♦ **a lounge which guests are ~ to use** un salon que les hôtes sont invités à utiliser

2 *(= appreciated) [food, drink, change, visitor]* bienvenu ; *[decision, reminder, interruption]* opportun ♦ **she was a ~ sight** nous avons été *(or* il a été *etc)* heureux de la voir ♦ **it was ~ news** nous avons été *(or* il a été *etc)* heureux de l'apprendre ♦ **it was a ~ gift** ce cadeau m'a *(or* lui a *etc)* fait bien plaisir ♦ **it was a ~ relief** ça m'a *(or* l'a *etc)* vraiment soulagé ♦ **to make a ~ return** faire un retour apprécié

EXCL ♦ **~ !** soyez le bienvenu *(or* la bienvenue *etc)* !, bienvenue ! ♦ **~ home!** bienvenue !, content de vous *(or* te) revoir à la maison ! ♦ **~ back!** bienvenue !, content de vous *(or* te) revoir ! ♦ **~ to our house!** bienvenue chez nous ! ♦ **"welcome to England"** *(on notice)* "bienvenue en Angleterre"

N accueil *m* ♦ **to bid sb ~** souhaiter la bienvenue à qn ♦ **to give sb a warm ~** faire un accueil chaleureux à qn ♦ **they gave him a great ~** ils lui ont fait fête ♦ **words of ~** paroles *fpl* d'accueil, mots *mpl* de bienvenue ♦ **what sort of a ~ will this product get from the housewife?** comment la ménagère accueillera-t-elle ce produit ? ; → **outstay**

VT *[+ person, delegation, group of people] (= greet, receive)* accueillir ; *(= greet warmly)* faire bon accueil à, accueillir chaleureusement ; *(= bid welcome)* souhaiter la bienvenue à ; *[+ sb's return, news, suggestion, change]* se réjouir de ♦ **he ~d me in** il m'a chaleureusement invité à entrer ♦ **please ~ Tony Brennan!** *(TV etc)* veuillez accueillir Tony Brennan ! ♦ **we would ~ your views on ...** nous serions heureux de connaître votre point de vue *or* opinion sur ... ♦ **I'd ~ a cup of coffee** je prendrais volontiers une tasse de café, je ne dirais pas non à une tasse de café ; → **open**

► **welcome back** VT SEP ♦ **they welcomed him back after his journey** ils l'ont accueilli chaleureusement *or* ils lui ont fait fête à son retour (de voyage)

welcoming /ˈwelkəmɪŋ/ ADJ *[person, smile, place]* accueillant ; *[atmosphere]* chaleureux ; *[banquet, ceremony, speech]* d'accueil ♦ **~ party** *or* **committee** *(lit, fig)* comité *m* d'accueil ♦ **to be ~ to sb** *[person]* être accueillant avec qn, faire bon accueil à qn ; *[atmosphere, place]* paraître accueillant à qn

weld /weld/ N soudure *f* VT *[+ metal, rubber, seam, join]* souder ; (also **weld together**) *[+ pieces, parts]* souder, assembler ; *(fig) [+ groups, parties]* rassembler ♦ **to ~ sth on to sth** souder qch à qch ♦ **the hull is ~ed throughout** la coque est complètement soudée VI souder

welder /ˈweldəʳ/ N *(= person)* soudeur *m* ; *(= machine)* soudeuse *f*

welding /ˈweldɪŋ/ N *(NonC) (Tech)* soudage *m* ; *(fig) [of parties]* union *f* ; *[of ideas]* amalgame *m* COMP *[process]* de soudure, de soudage
welding torch N chalumeau *m*

welfare /ˈwelfeəʳ/ N 1 *(gen)* bien *m* ; *(= comfort)* bien-être *m* ; *(US)* aide *f* sociale ♦ **the nation's ~, the ~ of all** le bien public *or* de tous ♦ **the physical/spiritual ~ of the young** la santé physique/morale des jeunes ♦ **I'm anxious about his ~** je suis inquiet à son sujet ♦ **to look after sb's ~** avoir la responsabilité de qn ; → **child**

2 ♦ **public/social ~** assistance *f* publique/sociale ♦ **to be on ~** toucher les prestations sociales, recevoir l'aide sociale ♦ **to live on ~** vivre des prestations sociales

COMP *[milk, meals]* gratuit
welfare benefits NPL avantages *mpl* sociaux
welfare centre N centre *m* d'assistance sociale
welfare check N *(US)* chèque *m* d'allocations
welfare hotel N *(US) foyer où sont hébergés temporairement les bénéficiaires de l'aide sociale*
welfare mother N *(US) mère seule qui bénéficie de l'aide sociale*
welfare officer N assistant(e) *m(f)* social(e)
welfare payments NPL prestations *fpl* sociales
welfare rights NPL droits *mpl* à l'aide sociale
welfare services NPL services *mpl* sociaux
welfare state N État-providence *m* ♦ **the establishment of the Welfare State in Great Britain** l'établissement *m* de l'État-providence en Grande-Bretagne ♦ **thanks to the Welfare State** grâce à la sécurité sociale et autres avantages sociaux
welfare work N travail *m* social
welfare worker N assistant(e) *m(f)* social(e), travailleur *m*, -euse *f* social(e)

welfarism /ˈwelfeərɪzəm/ N *(US Pol)* théorie *f* de l'État-providence

welfarist /ˈwelfeərɪst/ ADJ, N *(US Pol)* partisan *m* de l'État-providence

welfarite* /ˈwelfeəraɪt/ N *(US pej)* assisté(e) *m(f)*

well¹ /wel/ N *(for water, oil)* puits *m* ; *[of staircase, lift]* cage *f* ; *(= shaft between buildings)* puits *m*, cheminée *f* ; *(Brit Jur)* barreau *m* ♦ **this book is a ~ of information** ce livre est une mine de renseignements ; → **inkwell, oil** VI (also **well up**) *[tears, emotion]* monter ♦ **tears ~ed (up) in her eyes** les larmes lui montèrent aux yeux ♦ **anger ~ed (up) within him** la colère sourdit *(liter)* *or* monta en lui

COMP **well-digger** N puisatier *m*
well water N eau *f* de puits

► **well out** VI *[spring]* sourdre ; *[tears, blood]* couler (from de)

well² /wel/ LANGUAGE IN USE 1.1

ADV (compar **better**, superl **best**) 1 *(= satisfactorily, skilfully etc) [behave, sleep, eat, treat, remember]* bien ♦ **he sings as ~ as he plays** il chante aussi bien qu'il joue ♦ **he sings as ~ as she does** il chante aussi bien qu'elle ♦ **to live ~** vivre bien ♦ **~ done!** bravo !, très bien ! ♦ **~ played!** bien joué ! ♦ **everything is going ~** tout va bien ♦ **the evening went off very ~** la soirée s'est très bien passée ♦ **to do ~ in one's work** bien réussir dans son travail ♦ **to do ~ at school** bien marcher à l'école ♦ **he did very ~**

for an eight-year-old il s'est bien débrouillé pour un enfant de huit ans ◆ **he did quite ~** il ne s'en est pas mal sorti, il ne s'est pas mal débrouillé ◆ **the patient is doing ~** le malade est en bonne voie ◆ **he did ~ after the operation but ...** il s'est bien rétabli après l'opération mais ... ◆ **you did ~ to come at once** vous avez bien fait de venir tout de suite ◆ **you would do ~ to think about it** tu ferais bien d'y penser ◆ **to do as ~ as one can** faire de son mieux ◆ **he did himself ~** il ne s'est privé de rien, il s'est traité comme un prince ◆ **to do ~ by sb** bien agir *or* être généreux envers qn ◆ **you're ~ out of it!** c'est une chance que tu n'aies plus rien à voir avec cela (*or* lui *etc*) ! ◆ **how ~ I understand!** comme je vous (*or* le *etc*) comprends ! ◆ **I know the place ~** je connais bien l'endroit ◆ **(and) ~ I know it!** je le sais bien !, je ne le sais que trop !

2 *(intensifying = very much, thoroughly)* bien ◆ **it was ~ worth the trouble** cela valait bien le dérangement *or* la peine de se déranger ◆ **he is ~ past** *or* **over fifty** il a largement dépassé la cinquantaine ◆ **it's ~ past 10 o'clock** il est bien plus de 10 heures ◆ **~ over 1,000 people** bien plus de 1 000 personnes ◆ **it continued ~ into 1996** cela a continué pendant une bonne partie de 1996 ◆ **~ above ...** bien au-dessus de ... ◆ **~ and truly** *(esp Brit)* bel et bien ◆ **he could ~ afford to pay for it** il avait largement les moyens de le payer ◆ **lean ~ forward** penchez-vous bien en avant ◆ **~ dodgy/annoyed** *etc* ‡ *(Brit = very)* super* louche/contrarié *etc*

3 *(= with good reason, with equal reason)* ◆ **you may ~ be surprised to learn that ...** vous serez sans aucun doute surpris d'apprendre que ... ◆ **one might ~ ask why** on pourrait à juste titre demander pourquoi ◆ **you might ~ ask!** belle question !, c'est vous qui me le demandez ! ◆ **you could ~ refuse to help them** vous pourriez à juste titre refuser de les aider ◆ **he couldn't very ~ refuse** il ne pouvait guère refuser ◆ **we may as ~ begin now** autant (vaut) commencer maintenant, nous ferions aussi bien de commencer maintenant ◆ **you might (just) as ~ say that ...** autant dire que ... ◆ **you may as ~ tell me the truth** autant me dire la vérité, tu ferais aussi bien de me dire la vérité ◆ **shall I go? – you may** *or* **might as ~** j'y vais ? – tant qu'à faire, allez-y !* ◆ **we might (just) as ~ have stayed at home** autant valait rester à la maison, nous aurions aussi bien fait de rester à la maison ◆ **she apologized, as ~ she might** elle a présenté ses excuses, comme il se devait ◆ **she apologized – and ~ she might!** elle a présenté ses excuses – c'était la moindre des choses ! ; → **pretty**

4 *(set phrases)*

◆ **as well** *(= also)* aussi ; *(= on top of all that)* par-dessus le marché ◆ **I'll take those as ~** je prendrai ceux-là aussi ◆ **and it rained as ~!** et par-dessus le marché il a plu !

◆ **as well as** *(= in addition to)* ◆ **by night as ~ as by day** de jour comme de nuit, aussi bien de jour que de nuit ◆ **as ~ as his dog he has two rabbits** en plus de son chien il a deux lapins ◆ **on bikes as ~ as in cars** à vélo aussi bien qu'en voiture, à vélo comme en voiture ◆ **I had Paul with me as ~ as Lucy** j'avais Paul aussi en même temps que Lucy ◆ **all sorts of people, rich as ~ as poor** toutes sortes de gens, tant riches que pauvres

5 *(= positively)* ◆ **to think/speak ~ of** penser/dire du bien de

6 ◆ **to leave ~ alone** laisser les choses telles qu'elles sont ◆ **let** *or* **leave ~ alone** *(Prov)* le mieux est l'ennemi du bien *(Prov)*

EXCL *(surprise)* tiens !, eh bien ! ; *(relief)* ah bon !, eh bien ! ; *(resignation)* enfin ! ; *(dismissively)* bof !* ◆ **~, as I was saying ...** *(resuming after interruption)* donc, comme je disais ..., je disais donc que ... ◆ **~ ...** *(hesitation)* c'est que ... ◆ **he has won the election! – ~, ~ (, ~)!** il a été élu ! – tiens, tiens ! ◆ **~?** eh bien ?, et alors ? ◆ **~, who would have thought it?** eh bien ! qui l'aurait cru ? ◆ **~ I never!***, **~, what do you know!*** pas possible !, ça par exemple ! ◆ **I intended to do it – ~, have you?** j'avais l'intention de le faire – et alors ? ◆ **~, what do you think of it?** eh bien ! qu'en dites-vous ? ◆ **~, here we are at last!** eh bien ! nous voilà enfin ! ◆ **~, there's nothing we can do about it** enfin, on n'y peut rien ◆ **~, you may be right** qui sait, vous avez peut-être raison ◆ **very ~ then** (bon) d'accord ◆ **you know Paul? ~, he's getting married** vous connaissez Paul ? eh bien il se marie ◆ **are you coming? – ~ ... I've got a lot to do here** vous venez ? – c'est que ... j'ai beaucoup à faire ici

ADJ (compar, superl **best**) 1 bien, bon ◆ **all is not ~ with her** il y a quelque chose qui ne va pas, elle traverse une mauvaise passe ◆ **it's all very ~ to say that** c'est bien beau *or* joli de dire cela ◆ **that's all very ~ but ...**, **that's all ~ and good but ...** tout ça c'est bien joli *or* beau mais ... ◆ **if you want to do it, ~ and good** si vous voulez le faire je ne vois pas d'inconvénient ◆ **all's ~!** *(Mil)* tout va bien ! ◆ **all's ~ that ends well** *(Prov)* tout est bien qui finit bien *(Prov)*

2 *(= healthy)* **how are you? – very ~, thank you** comment allez-vous ? – très bien, merci ◆ **I hope you're ~** j'espère que vous allez bien ◆ **to feel ~** se sentir bien ◆ **to get ~** se remettre ◆ **get ~ soon!** remets-toi vite ! ◆ **people who are ~ do not realize that ...** les gens qui se portent bien *or* qui sont en bonne santé ne se rendent pas compte que ...

3 *(= cautious)* ◆ **it** *or* **we would be ~ to start early** on ferait bien de partir tôt ◆ **it is as ~ to remember** il y a tout lieu de se rappeler ◆ **it's as ~ not to offend her** il vaudrait mieux ne pas la froisser ◆ **it would be just as ~ for you to stay** vous feriez tout aussi bien de rester

4 *(= lucky)* ◆ **it's ~ for you that nobody saw you** heureusement pour vous qu'on ne vous a pas vu, vous avez de la chance *or* c'est heureux pour vous qu'on ne vous ait pas vu

PREF ◆ **~-** bien ◆ **~-chosen/dressed** bien choisi/habillé ; see also **comp**

N ◆ **I wish you ~!** je vous souhaite de réussir !, bonne chance ! ◆ **somebody who wishes you ~** quelqu'un qui vous veut du bien

COMP **well-adjusted** ADJ *(gen)* *[person]* posé, équilibré ; *(to society, school)* bien adapté
well-advised ADJ *[action, decision]* sage, prudent ◆ **you would be ~-advised to leave** vous auriez (tout) intérêt à partir
well-aimed ADJ *[shot]* bien ajusté ; *[remark]* qui porte
well-appointed ADJ *[house, room]* bien aménagé
well-argued ADJ *[case, report]* bien argumenté
well-assorted ADJ bien assorti
well-attended ADJ *[meeting, lecture]* qui attire beaucoup de monde, qui a du succès ; *[show, play]* couru
well-baby clinic N *(Brit)* *centre prophylactique et thérapeutique pour nouveaux-nés*
well-balanced ADJ *[person, diet, argument]* (bien) équilibré ; *[paragraph, sentence]* bien construit
well-behaved ADJ *[child]* sage, qui se conduit bien ; *[animal]* obéissant
well-being N bien-être *m*
well-born ADJ bien né, de bonne famille
well-bred ADJ *(= of good family)* de bonne famille ; *(= courteous)* bien élevé ; *[animal]* de bonne race
well-built ADJ *[building]* bien construit, solide ; *[person]* bien bâti, costaud*
well-chosen ADJ bien choisi ◆ **in a few ~-chosen words** en quelques mots bien choisis
well-cooked ADJ *(gen)* *[food, meal]* bien cuisiné ; *(= not rare)* *[meat]* bien cuit
well-defined ADJ *[colours, distinctions]* bien défini ; *[photo, outline]* net ; *[problem]* bien défini, précis
well-deserved ADJ bien mérité
well-developed ADJ *(Anat)* bien développé ; *[person]* bien fait ; *[plan]* bien développé ; *[argument, idea]* bien exposé
well-disposed ADJ bien disposé *(towards* envers)
well-documented ADJ *[case, work]* bien documenté ◆ **his life is ~-documented** on a beaucoup de renseignements *or* documents sur sa vie
well-dressed ADJ bien habillé, bien vêtu
well-earned ADJ bien mérité
well-educated ADJ cultivé, instruit
well-endowed ADJ *(euph)* *[man]* bien membré ; *[woman]* à la poitrine généreuse
well-equipped ADJ bien équipé ; *(esp with tools)* *[person]* bien outillé ; *[factory]* bien équipé, doté d'un équipement important ◆ **to be ~-equipped to do sth** *[person]* avoir ce qu'il faut pour faire qch ; *[factory]* être parfaitement équipé pour faire qch
well-favoured †† ADJ beau (belle *f*)
well-fed ADJ bien nourri
well-fixed * ADJ *(US)* ◆ **to be ~-fixed** *(= well-to-do)* être nanti, vivre dans l'aisance ◆ **we're ~-fixed for food** nous avons largement assez à manger
well-formed ADJ *(Ling)* bien formé, grammatical
well-formedness N *(Ling)* grammaticalité *f*
well-founded ADJ *[suspicion]* bien fondé, légitime
well-groomed ADJ *[person]* soigné ; *[hair]* bien coiffé ; *[horse]* bien pansé
well-grounded ADJ *[suspicion, belief, rumour]* bien fondé, légitime ◆ **our students are ~-grounded in grammar/physics** nos étudiants ont de solides connaissances *or* bases en grammaire/physique
well-heeled * ADJ nanti, fort à l'aise
well-hung ‡ ADJ *[man]* bien monté‡
well-informed ADJ bien informé, bien renseigné *(about* sur) ; *(= knowledgeable)* *[person]* instruit ◆ **~-informed circles** *(Pol, Press)* les milieux *mpl* bien informés
well-intentioned ADJ bien intentionné
well-judged ADJ *[remark, criticism]* bien vu, judicieux ; *[shot, throw]* bien ajusté ; *[estimate]* juste
well-kept ADJ *[house, garden]* bien entretenu, bien tenu ; *[hands, nails]* soigné ; *[hair]* bien entretenu ; *[secret]* bien gardé
well-knit ADJ *(fig)* *[person, body]* bien bâti ; *[arguments, speech]* bien enchaîné ; *[scheme]* bien conçu
well-known ADJ *(= famous)* bien connu, célèbre ◆ **it's a ~-known fact that ...** tout le monde sait que ...
well-liked ADJ très apprécié
well-lined ADJ ◆ **to have ~-lined pockets** avoir de gros moyens, être cousu d'or*
well-loved ADJ très aimé
well-made ADJ bien fait
well-managed ADJ bien mené
well-man clinic N *(Brit)* *centre prophylactique et thérapeutique pour hommes*
well-mannered ADJ qui a de bonnes manières, bien élevé
well-meaning ADJ *[person]* bien intentionné ; *[remark, action]* fait avec les meilleures intentions
well-meant ADJ fait avec les meilleures intentions
well-nigh ADV *(liter)* presque
well-nourished ADJ bien nourri
well-off ADJ *(= rich)* ◆ **to be ~-off** vivre dans l'aisance, être riche ◆ **the less ~-off** ceux qui ont de petits moyens ◆ **you don't know when you're ~-off** *(= fortunate)* tu ne connais pas ton bonheur ◆ **she's ~-off without him** elle est mieux sans lui

well-oiled ADJ *(lit)* bien graissé ; *(* = drunk)* pompette *
well-padded * ADJ *(hum) [person]* rembourré
well-paid ADJ bien payé, bien rémunéré
well-preserved ADJ *[building, person]* bien conservé
well-read ADJ cultivé
well-respected ADJ très respecté *or* considéré
well-rounded ADJ *[style]* harmonieux ; *[sentence]* bien tourné
well-spent ADJ *[time]* bien employé, bien utilisé ; *[money]* utilement dépensé ; see also **money**
well-spoken ADJ *[person]* qui parle bien, qui a une élocution soignée ; *[words]* bien choisi, bien trouvé ♦ **she's very ~-spoken of** elle est très appréciée
well-stocked ADJ *[shop, fridge]* bien approvisionné ; *[river, lake]* bien empoissonné
well-tempered ADJ *(Mus)* ♦ **the Well-Tempered Clavier** le Clavier *or* Clavecin bien tempéré
well-thought-of ADJ *[person]* (bien) considéré, dont on a bonne opinion ; *[thing]* bien considéré, très apprécié
well-thought-out ADJ bien conçu
well-thumbed ADJ *[book]* lu et relu
well-timed ADJ *[remark, entrance]* tout à fait opportun, tombé à point nommé ; *[blow]* bien calculé
well-to-do ADJ nanti
well-tried ADJ *[method]* éprouvé, qui a fait ses preuves
well-trodden ADJ ♦ **to follow a ~-trodden path** *(lit)* suivre un chemin fréquenté ; *(fig)* suivre les sentiers battus
well-turned ADJ *[phrase]* bien tourné ; *[leg]* bien fait
well-wisher N ami(e) *m(f)* ; *(unknown)* ami(e) *m(f) or* admirateur *m*, -trice *f* inconnu(e) ; *(Pol = supporter)* sympathisant(e) *m(f)* ♦ **he got many letters from ~-wishers** il a reçu de nombreuses lettres d'encouragement
well-woman clinic N *(Brit) centre prophylactique et thérapeutique pour femmes*
well-worn ADJ *[carpet, clothes]* usagé ; *(fig) [phrase, expression]* éculé, rebattu ♦ **to follow a ~-worn path** *(fig)* suivre les sentiers battus
well-written ADJ bien écrit

we'll /wi:l/ ⇒ **we shall, we will** ; → **shall, will**

wellhead /'welhed/ N *(lit, fig)* source *f*

Wellington /'welɪŋtən/ N *(in NZ)* Wellington

wellington /'welɪŋtən/ N *(Brit:* also **wellington boot**) botte *f* de caoutchouc

wellness /'welnɪs/ N (sentiment *m* de) bien-être *m*

Wellsian /'welzɪən/ ADJ de Wells

wellspring /'welsprɪŋ/ N ⇒ **wellhead**

welly * /'welɪ/ N (pl **wellies**) ♦ **~ boots** *(Brit)* ♦ **wellies** bottes *fpl* de caoutchouc ♦ **give it some ~!** * *(Brit)* allez, du nerf ! *

Welsh /welʃ/ ADJ *(gen)* gallois ; *[teacher]* de gallois N *(= language)* gallois *m* NPL **the Welsh** les Gallois *mpl*
COMP **Welsh dresser** N *(Brit)* vaisselier *m*
Welsh Nationalism N *(Pol)* nationalisme *m* gallois
Welsh Nationalist N nationaliste *mf* gallois(e)
the Welsh Office N *(Brit Pol)* le ministère des Affaires galloises
Welsh rabbit, Welsh rarebit N *(Culin)* toast *m* au fromage

welsh * /welʃ/ VI ♦ **to ~ on a promise** manquer à une promesse ♦ **they ~ed on the agreement** ils n'ont pas respecté l'accord

Welshman /'welʃmən/ N (pl **-men**) Gallois *m*

Welshwoman /'welʃwʊmən/ N (pl **-women**) Galloise *f*

welt /welt/ N *(= weal)* marque *f* de coup, zébrure *f* ; *[of shoe]* trépointe *f*

welter /'weltəʳ/ N *[of objects, words, ideas]* fatras *m* ♦ **a ~ of conflicting interests** une multitude d'intérêts contradictoires ♦ **the ~ of publicity that followed his engagement** le tourbillon médiatique qui a suivi l'annonce de ses fiançailles
♦ **in a welter of** ♦ **in a ~ of blood** dans un bain de sang ♦ **in a ~ of mud** dans un véritable bourbier
VI *(in blood)* baigner ; *(in mud)* se vautrer, se rouler

welterweight /'weltəweɪt/ *(Boxing)* N poids *m* welter COMP *[champion, fight]* poids welter *inv*

wen /wen/ N loupe *f*, kyste *m* sébacé ♦ **the Great Wen** *(fig)* Londres

wench /wentʃ/ († *or hum*) N jeune fille *f*, jeune femme *f* VI ♦ **to go ~ing** courir le jupon

wend /wend/ VT ♦ **to ~ one's way** aller son chemin, s'acheminer *(to, towards* vers) ♦ **to ~ one's way back from** s'en revenir de

Wendy house /'wendɪ,haʊs/ N *(Brit)* maison *f* miniature *(pour enfants)*

went /went/ VB pt of **go**

wept /wept/ VB pret, ptp of **weep**

were /wɜ:ʳ/ VB pt of **be**

we're /wɪəʳ/ ⇒ **we are** ; → **be**

weren't /wɜ:nt/ ⇒ **were not** ; → **be**

werewolf /'wɪəwʊlf/ N (pl **werewolves** /'wɪəwʊlvz/) loup-garou *m*

wert †† /wɜ:t/ VB 2nd pers sg pret of **be**

Wesleyan /'wezlɪən/ N disciple *m* de Wesley ADJ de Wesley, wesleyen ♦ **~ Methodists** méthodistes *mpl* wesleyens

west /west/ N ouest *m* ♦ **to the ~ (of)** à l'ouest (de) ♦ **in the ~ of Scotland** dans l'ouest de l'Écosse ♦ **a house facing the ~** une maison exposée à l'ouest ♦ **to veer to the ~, to go into the ~** *[wind]* tourner à l'ouest ♦ **the wind is in the ~** le vent est à l'ouest ♦ **the wind is (coming** *or* **blowing) from the ~** le vent vient *or* souffle de l'ouest ♦ **to live in the ~** habiter dans l'ouest ♦ **the West** *(Pol)* l'Occident *m*, l'Ouest *m* ; *(US Geog)* l'Ouest *m* ; → **wild**
ADJ *[coast, wing]* ouest *inv* ♦ **~ wind** vent *m* d'ouest ♦ **on the ~ side** du côté ouest ♦ **a room with a ~ aspect** une pièce exposée à l'ouest ♦ **~ transept/door** *(Archit)* transept *m*/portail *m* ouest ♦ **in ~ Devon** dans l'ouest du Devon ♦ **in ~ Leeds** dans les quartiers ouest de Leeds ♦ **in the ~ Atlantic** dans l'Atlantique ouest ; see also **comp**
ADV *[go, travel, fly]* vers l'ouest, en direction de l'ouest ; *[be, lie]* à l'ouest ♦ **go ~ till you get to Crewe** allez en direction de l'ouest jusqu'à Crewe ♦ **we drove ~ for 100km** nous avons roulé vers l'ouest pendant 100 km ♦ **to go ~** * *(fig) [thing]* être fichu * *or* perdu ; *[person]* passer l'arme à gauche * ♦ **further ~** plus à l'ouest ♦ **to sail due ~** aller droit vers l'ouest ; *(Naut)* avoir le cap à l'ouest ♦ **~ by south** ouest quart sud-ouest
COMP **West Africa** N Afrique *f* occidentale
West African ADJ de l'Afrique occidentale, ouest-africain N habitant(e) *m(f)* de l'Afrique occidentale
the West Bank N la Cisjordanie
West Berlin N *(Hist)* Berlin-Ouest
West Berliner N *(Hist)* habitant(e) *m(f)* de Berlin-Ouest
the West Country N *(Brit)* le sud-ouest de l'Angleterre
the West End N *(in London)* le West End *(centre touristique et commercial de Londres)*
West Ender N *(in London)* habitant(e) *m(f)* du West End
west-facing ADJ exposé (*or* orienté) à l'ouest *or* au couchant
West German ADJ allemand de l'Ouest
West Germany N Allemagne *f* de l'Ouest
West Indian ADJ antillais N Antillais(e) *m(f)*
the West Indies NPL les Antilles *fpl* ; *(Hist)* les Indes *fpl* occidentales
west-north-west N ouest-nord-ouest *m* ADJ (de l' *or* à l')ouest-nord-ouest *inv* ADV vers l'ouest-nord-ouest
West Point N *(US) école militaire*, ≃ Saint-Cyr
west-south-west N ouest-sud-ouest *m* ADJ (de l'*or* à l') ouest-sud-ouest *inv* ADV vers l'ouest-sud-ouest
West Virginia N Virginie-Occidentale *f* ♦ **in West Virginia** en Virginie-Occidentale

westbound /'westbaʊnd/ ADJ, ADV *[traffic, vehicles]* (se déplaçant) en direction de l'ouest ; *[carriageway]* ouest *inv* ♦ **to be ~ on the M8** être sur la M8 en direction de l'ouest

westerly /'westəlɪ/ ADJ *[wind]* de l'ouest ; *[situation]* à l'ouest, au couchant ♦ **in a ~ direction** en direction de l'ouest, vers l'ouest ♦ **~ longitude** longitude *f* ouest *inv* ♦ **~ aspect** exposition *f* à l'ouest *or* au couchant ADV vers l'ouest

western /'westən/ ADJ (de l')ouest *inv* ♦ **in ~ France** dans l'ouest de la France ♦ **the ~ coast** la côte ouest *or* occidentale ♦ **the ~ hemisphere** les Amériques *fpl* ♦ **house with a ~ outlook** maison *f* exposée à l'ouest ♦ **~ wall** mur *m* ouest ♦ **the Western Empire** l'Empire *m* d'Occident ♦ **Western Europe** Europe *f* occidentale ♦ **the Western Church** l'Église *f* d'Occident, l'Église *f* latine ; → **country** N *(= film)* western *m* ; *(= novel)* roman-western *m*
COMP **Western Australia** N Australie-Occidentale *f*
the Western Isles NPL *(Brit)* les Hébrides *fpl*
Western omelet N *(US Culin)* omelette *f* au jambon avec oignons et poivrons
western roll N *(Sport)* (saut *m* en) rouleau *m*
the Western Sahara N le Sahara occidental
Western Samoa N Samoa *fpl* (occidentales)
western writer N écrivain *m* de (romans-) westerns

westerner /'westənəʳ/ N homme *m or* femme *f* de l'ouest, habitant(e) *m(f)* de l'ouest ; *(Pol)* Occidental(e) *m(f)*

westernization /,westənaɪ'zeɪʃən/ N occidentalisation *f*

westernize /'westənaɪz/ VT occidentaliser ♦ **to become ~d** s'occidentaliser

westernmost /'westənməʊst/ ADJ le plus à l'ouest

Westminster /'west,mɪnstəʳ/ N *(Brit)* Westminster *m (le Parlement britannique)*

westward /'westwəd/ ADJ *[route]* en direction de l'ouest ; *[slope]* exposé à l'ouest ♦ **in a ~ direction** en direction de l'ouest, vers l'ouest ADV (also **westwards**) vers l'ouest

wet /wet/ ADJ 1 *[object, grass, clothes, towel, swimsuit, nappy, baby]* mouillé, humide ; *(stronger)* trempé ; *[cement, plaster, paint, ink]* frais (fraîche *f*) ; *[sand, hair]* mouillé ♦ **to be ~ to the skin** *or* **~ through** être trempé jusqu'aux os ♦ **to get ~** se mouiller ♦ **to get one's feet ~** *(lit)* se mouiller les pieds ; *(US fig)* s'y mettre, se lancer ♦ **don't get your shoes ~** ne mouille pas tes chaussures ♦ **don't come into the house with ~ feet** n'entre pas (dans la maison) avec les pieds mouillés ♦ **it grows in ~ places** ça pousse dans les endroits humides ♦ **a ~ patch** une tache d'humidité ♦ **the roads are very ~** les routes sont très humides *or* mouillées ♦ **the road is slippery when ~** la chaussée est glissante par temps de pluie ♦ **"wet paint"** *(notice)* "attention, peinture fraîche" ♦ **he's still ~ behind the ears** * *(= immature)* si on lui pressait le nez il en sortirait du lait * ; *(= inexperienced)* il manque d'expérience
♦ **wet with** ♦ **~ with blood** trempé de sang ♦ **~ with sweat** humide de sueur ; *(stronger)*

trempé de sueur ◆ **cheeks ~ with tears** joues baignées de larmes ◆ **~ with dew** humide de rosée ; → **soaking, wringing**

2 *(of weather)* ◆ **it** *or* **the weather is ~** le temps est pluvieux, il pleut ◆ **it's going to be ~** il va pleuvoir ◆ **a ~ day** un jour de pluie, un jour pluvieux ◆ **on ~ days** les jours de pluie ◆ **it's a very ~ climate** c'est un climat très humide *or* pluvieux ◆ **in ~ weather** quand le temps est pluvieux, par temps humide *or* pluvieux ◆ **the ~ season** la saison des pluies ◆ **it's been a very ~ winter/summer/weekend** l'hiver/l'été/le week-end a été très humide *or* pluvieux ◆ **it's been one of the wettest Junes on record** c'est un des mois de juin les plus pluvieux que l'on ait connus ◆ **~ snow** neige *f* fondue

3 *(Brit = spineless)* ◆ **he's really ~** * c'est une chiffe molle

4 *(Brit Pol *) [Tory politician, policy]* gauchisant

5 *(in US = against prohibition) [town, state]* où la vente des boissons alcoolisées est autorisée

6 *(US fig = quite wrong)* ◆ **you're all ~ !*** tu te fiches complètement dedans !*, tu te fourres le doigt dans l'œil !*

N 1 ◆ **the ~** *(= rain)* la pluie ; *(= damp)* l'humidité *f* ◆ **it got left out in the ~** il est resté dehors sous la pluie *or* à l'humidité ◆ **my car doesn't start in the ~** ma voiture ne démarre pas par temps de pluie ◆ **the road surface is slippery, especially in the ~** la chaussée est glissante, surtout par temps de pluie ◆ **come in out of the ~** ne restez pas sous la pluie, entrez

2 *(* pej = spineless person)* chiffe *f* molle

3 *(Brit Pol *)* gauchisant(e) *m(f)* (du parti conservateur)

VT 1 mouiller ◆ **to ~ one's lips** se mouiller les lèvres ◆ **to ~ one's whistle** † * *(fig)* boire un coup*, en siffler un*

2 *(= urinate)* ◆ **to ~ the bed** mouiller le lit ◆ **to ~ o.s.** *or* **one's pants** *(lit)* mouiller sa culotte ◆ **to ~ o.s.** *or* **one's pants** * **(laughing)** rire à en faire pipi* dans sa culotte

COMP **wet bar** N *(US) petit bar avec eau courante*
wet blanket N *(fig)* rabat-joie *mf inv*
wet dock N *(Naut)* bassin *m* à flot
wet dream N pollution *f or* éjaculation *f* nocturne
wet fish N poisson *m* frais
the wet look N *(Fashion)* le look brillant
wet-look ADJ *[fabric]* brillant ; *[hair product]* à effet mouillé
wet-nurse N nourrice *f* VT servir de nourrice à, élever au sein
wet rot N *(NonC)* pourriture *f* humide (du bois)
wet shave N rasage *m* au rasoir mécanique
wet wipe N serviette *f* rafraîchissante

wetback * /ˈwetbæk/ N *(US pej)* ouvrier *m* agricole mexicain *(entré illégalement aux États-Unis)*

wether /ˈweðəʳ/ N bélier *m* châtré, mouton *m*

wetlands /ˈwetlændz/ NPL *(esp US)* zones *fpl* humides

wetly /ˈwetlɪ/ ADV 1 *(= damply)* ◆ **her hair clung ~ to her head** ses cheveux mouillés étaient plaqués sur sa tête ◆ **she kissed him ~ on the mouth** elle lui donna un baiser mouillé sur la bouche 2 *(= feebly) [smile]* mollement

wetness /ˈwetnɪs/ N 1 humidité *f* ◆ **the ~ of the weather** le temps pluvieux 2 *(Brit Pol)* ◆ **they suspected him of political ~** ils le soupçonnaient de tendances gauchisantes

wetsuit /ˈwetsuːt/ N combinaison *f or* ensemble *m* de plongée

wetting /ˈwetɪŋ/ N 1 *(gen)* ◆ **to get a ~** se faire arroser ◆ **to give sth/sb a ~** arroser qch/qn 2 *(= incontinence)* incontinence *f* d'urine ; (also **bed-wetting**) énurésie *f* nocturne

WEU /ˌdʌbljuːiːˈjuː/ N (abbrev of **Western European Union**) UEO *f*

we've /wiːv/ ⇒ **we have** ; → **have**

whack /wæk/ **N** 1 *(= blow)* grand coup *m* ; *(= sound)* coup *m* sec, claquement *m* ◆ **to give sth/sb a ~** donner un grand coup à qch/qn ◆ **~!** vlan ! ◆ **out of ~** * *(esp US)* détraqué ◆ **the ecosystem was thrown out of ~** l'écosystème a été chamboulé

2 *(* = attempt)* **to have a ~ at doing sth** essayer de faire qch ◆ **I'll have a ~ at it** je vais tenter le coup*

3 *(Brit * = share)* part *f* ◆ **you'll get your ~** tu auras ta part ◆ **they won a fair ~ of the contracts** ils ont emporté une bonne partie des marchés ◆ **to pay one's ~** payer sa part ◆ **to pay top** *or* **the full ~ for sth** payer qch plein pot* ◆ **you'll get £15,000 a year, top ~** tu auras 15 000 livres par an, grand maximum*

VT *[+ thing, person]* donner un (*or* des) grand(s) coup(s) à ; *(= spank)* fesser ; ** (= defeat)* donner une raclée* à, flanquer une déculottée* *or* une dérouillée* à

whacked * /wækt/ ADJ *(Brit fig = exhausted)* crevé*, claqué*

whacking /ˈwækɪŋ/ **N** *(= spanking)* fessée *f* ; *(= beating: lit, fig)* raclée* *f* ◆ **to give sb/sth a ~** ⇒ **to whack sb/sth** ; → **whack** **ADJ** *(esp Brit *:* also **whacking big, whacking great)** énorme ◆ **the supermarkets are making ~ great profits** les supermarchés font des bénéfices énormes

whacko * /ˌwæˈkəʊ/ ADJ, N ⇒ **wacko**

whacky * /ˈwækɪ/ ADJ ⇒ **wacky**

whale /weɪl/ **N** (pl **whales** *or* **whale**) 1 *(= animal)* baleine *f* 2 *(phrases)* ◆ **we had a ~ of a time** * on s'est drôlement* bien amusé ◆ **a ~ of a difference** * une sacrée* différence ◆ **a ~ of a lot of** * ... vachement* de ..., une sacrée* quantité de ... **VI** ◆ **to go whaling** aller à la pêche à la baleine, aller pêcher la baleine

COMP **whale calf** N baleineau *m*
whale oil N huile *f* de baleine
whale watching N ◆ **to go ~ watching** aller regarder les baleines

whaleboat /ˈweɪlbəʊt/ N *(Naut)* baleinière *f*

whalebone /ˈweɪlbəʊn/ N fanon *m* de baleine ; *(Dress)* baleine *f*

whaler /ˈweɪləʳ/ N *(= person)* pêcheur *m* de baleine ; *(= ship)* baleinier *m*

whaling /ˈweɪlɪŋ/ **N** *(NonC)* pêche *f* à la baleine
COMP *[industry]* baleinier
whaling ship N baleinier *m*
whaling station N port *m* baleinier

wham /wæm/ EXCL vlan !

whammy /ˈwæmɪ/ N *(US)* mauvais sort *m*, poisse* *f* ◆ **double/triple ~** * double/triple coup *m* dur*

whang /wæŋ/ **N** bruit *m* retentissant **VT** donner un coup dur et sonore à **VI** faire un bruit retentissant

wharf /wɔːf/ N (pl **wharfs** *or* **wharves**) quai *m* *(pour marchandises)*

wharfage /ˈwɔːfɪdʒ/ N *(NonC)* droits *mpl* de quai

wharves /wɔːvz/ NPL of **wharf**

what /wɒt/

1 ADJECTIVE
2 PRONOUN
3 COMPOUNDS

1 - ADJECTIVE

1 in questions and indirect speech quel *m*, quelle *f*, quels *mpl*, quelles *fpl* ◆ **~ sort of music do you like?** quel genre de musique aimes-tu ? ◆ **~ time is it?** quelle heure est-il ? ◆ **~ flavours do you want?** quels parfums voulez-vous ? ◆ **~ subjects did you choose?** quelles matières as-tu choisies ? ◆ **she told me ~ colour it was** elle m'a dit de quelle couleur c'était ◆ **they asked me ~ kind of films I liked** ils m'ont demandé quel genre de films j'aimais ◆ **he told me ~ time it was** il m'a dit quelle heure il était, il m'a donné l'heure

2 = all the **I gave him ~ money/coins I had** je lui ai donné tout l'argent/toutes les pièces que j'avais ◆ **~ savings we had are now gone** le peu d'économies que nous avions s'est maintenant envolé ◆ **I will give you ~ information we have** je vais vous donner toutes les informations dont nous disposons ◆ **they packed ~ few belongings they had** ils ont rassemblé le peu qui leur appartenait ◆ **I gave ~ little help I could** j'ai aidé comme j'ai pu ◆ **I gave her ~ comfort I could** je l'ai réconfortée comme j'ai pu ◆ **I gave them ~ advice I could** je les ai conseillés comme j'ai pu

3 exclamations

♦ **what a ...!** ◆ **~ an idiot!** quel imbécile ! ◆ **~ a nice surprise!** quelle bonne surprise ! ◆ **~ a ridiculous suggestion!** quelle suggestion ridicule ! ◆ **~ a beautiful boat!** quel beau bateau ! ◆ **~ a nightmare!** quel cauchemar ! ◆ **~ a nuisance!** quelle barbe !*, c'est vraiment ennuyeux ! ◆ **~ a lot of people!** que de monde ! ◆ **~ an excuse!** *(iro)* drôle d'excuse !

♦ **what** + *plural/uncount noun* ◆ **~ fools we were!** quels imbéciles nous faisions !, nous étions vraiment bêtes ! ◆ **~ lovely hair you've got!** quels jolis cheveux tu as !

2 - PRONOUN

1 used alone, or in emphatic position quoi ◆ **~? I didn't get that** quoi ? tu peux répéter ? ◆ **I've forgotten something – ~?** j'ai oublié quelque chose – quoi ? ◆ **you told him WHAT?** quoi ! qu'est-ce que vous lui avez dit ? ◆ **it's WHAT?** c'est quoi ? ◆ **he's getting married – ~!** il se marie – quoi ! ◆ **~! you expect me to believe that!** quoi ! et tu penses que je vais croire ça !, tu ne penses quand même pas que je vais croire ça ! ◆ **say ~?** * *(US)* quoi ? ◆ **it's getting late, ~?** † * *(esp Brit: seeking confirmation)* il se fait tard, n'est-ce pas ?

> **quoi** is used with a preposition, if the French verb requires one.

◆ **I've just thought of something – ~?** je viens de penser à quelque chose – à quoi ? ◆ **I've just remembered something – ~?** je viens de me souvenir de quelque chose – de quoi ?

♦ **you what?** * *(Brit) (expressing surprise)* c'est pas vrai !* ; *(= what did you say?)* hein ?*

2 subject in direct questions qu'est-ce qui ◆ **~'s happened?** qu'est-ce qui s'est passé ? ◆ **~'s bothering you?** qu'est-ce qui te préoccupe ? ◆ **~'s for lunch/dinner?** qu'est-ce qu'il y a pour déjeuner/dîner ? ◆ **~ is his address?** quelle est son adresse ? ◆ **~'s the French for "pen"?** comment dit-on "pen" en français ? ◆ **~ is this called?** comment ça s'appelle ? ◆ **~'s money if you have no time to spend it?** à quoi bon avoir de l'argent si on n'a pas le temps de le dépenser ?

> When asking for a definition or explanation, **qu'est-ce que c'est que** is often used.

◆ **~ is a lycée polyvalent?** qu'est-ce que c'est qu'un lycée polyvalent ?, c'est quoi, un lycée polyvalent ? ◆ **~ are capers?** qu'est-ce que c'est les câpres ?, c'est quoi, les câpres ? ◆ **~'s that noise?** quel est ce bruit ?, qu'est-ce que c'est que ce bruit ?

♦ **what's that?** *(asking about sth)* qu'est-ce que c'est que ça ? ; *(= what did you say)* comment ?, qu'est-ce que tu as dit ?

3 object in direct questions qu'est-ce que, que, quoi *after prep*

The object pronoun **que** is more formal than **qu'est-ce que** and requires inversion of verb and pronoun.

◆ **~ did you do?** qu'est-ce que vous avez fait ?, qu'avez-vous fait ? ◆ **~ can we do?** qu'est-ce qu'on peut faire ?, que peut-on faire ?

A subject pronoun may become the object when translated.

◆ **~ does it matter?** qu'est-ce que ça peut bien faire ? ◆ **~'s it to you?** * qu'est-ce que cela peut vous faire ?

The French preposition cannot be separated from the pronoun.

◆ **~ does he owe his success to?** à quoi doit-il son succès ? ◆ **~ were you talking about?** de quoi parliez-vous ?

4 = which in particular quel *m*, quelle *f*, quels *mpl*, quelles *fpl* ◆ **~ are the commonest mistakes students make?** quelles sont les erreurs les plus courantes des étudiants ? ◆ **~'s the best time to call?** quel est le meilleur moment pour vous joindre ? ◆ **~ are the advantages?** quels sont les avantages ?

5 = how much combien ◆ **~ will it cost?** combien est-ce que ça va coûter ?, ça va coûter combien ? ◆ **~ does it weigh?** combien est-ce que ça pèse ? ◆ **~ do 2 and 2 make?** combien font 2 et 2 ?

6 in indirect questions ce qui *(subject of vb)*, ce que *(object of vb)* ◆ **I wonder ~ will happen** je me demande ce qui va se passer ◆ **I wonder ~ they think** je me demande ce qu'ils pensent ◆ **he asked me ~ she said** il m'a demandé ce qu'elle avait dit ◆ **I don't know ~ that building is** je ne sais pas ce que c'est que ce bâtiment

If the French verb takes a preposition, **what** is translated by **quoi**.

◆ **tell us ~ you're thinking about** dites-nous à quoi vous pensez ◆ **I wonder ~ they need** je me demande de quoi ils ont besoin ◆ **I wonder ~ they are expecting** je me demande à quoi ils s'attendent

quoi is used when **what** ends the sentence.

◆ **I don't know who's doing ~** je ne sais pas qui fait quoi

7 in relative clauses = that which ce qui *(subject of vb)*, ce que *(object of vb)*, ce dont *(object of vb taking "de")*, ce à quoi *(object of verb taking "à")* ◆ **~ is done is done** ce qui est fait est fait ◆ **the hotel isn't ~ it was** l'hôtel n'est plus ce qu'il était ◆ **~ I don't understand is ...** ce que je ne comprends pas c'est ... ◆ **say ~ you like, ...** vous pouvez dire ce que vous voulez, ... ◆ **~ I need is ...** ce dont j'ai besoin c'est ... ◆ **it wasn't ~ I was expecting** ce n'était pas ce à quoi je m'attendais ◆ **do ~ you like** fais ce que tu veux, fais comme tu veux

When **what** = **the ones which**, the French pronoun is generally plural.

◆ **I've no clothes except ~ I'm wearing** je n'ai d'autres vêtements que ceux que je porte

8 set structures

◆ **and I don't know what (all)** ◆ **they raped, pillaged and I don't know ~ (all)** ils ont violé, pillé et je ne sais quoi encore ◆ **it was full of cream, jam, chocolate and I don't know ~** c'était plein de crème, de confiture, de chocolat et je ne sais trop quoi

◆ **and what is/was** + *adjective/adverb* ◆ **and ~'s more** et qui plus est ◆ **and ~ is worse** et ce qui est pire ◆ **and, ~ was more surprising, there was ...** et, plus surprenant encore, il y avait ...

◆ **and what have you** *

◆ **and what not** * et cætera

◆ **or what?** ◆ **are you coming/do you want it or ~?** tu viens/tu le veux ou quoi ? ◆ **I mean, is this sick, or ~?** * il faut vraiment être malade ! * ◆ **is this luxury or ~?** * c'est le grand luxe !

◆ **tell you what** ◆ **tell you ~, let's stay here another day** j'ai une idée : si on restait un jour de plus ?

◆ **what about** ◆ **~ about Robert?** et Robert ? ◆ **~ about people who haven't got cars?** et les gens qui n'ont pas de voiture (alors) ? ◆ **~ about the danger involved?** et les risques que l'on encourt ? ◆ **~ about lunch, shall we go out?** qu'est-ce qu'on fait à midi, on va au restaurant ? ◆ **your car ... – ~ about it?** * ta voiture ... – qu'est-ce qu'elle a ma voiture ? ◆ **~ about going to the cinema?** si on allait au cinéma ?

◆ **what for?** pourquoi ? ◆ **~ did you do that for?** pourquoi avez-vous fait ça ? ; see also **compounds**

◆ **what if** et si ◆ **~ if this doesn't work out?** et si ça ne marchait pas ? ◆ **~ if he says no?** et s'il refuse ? ◆ **~ if it rains?** et s'il pleut ?

◆ **what of** ◆ **but ~ of the country's political leaders?** et les dirigeants politiques du pays ?, qu'en est-il des dirigeants politiques du pays ? ◆ **~ of it?** * et alors ?

◆ **what's what** * ◆ **he knows ~'s ~** il s'y connaît, il connaît son affaire ◆ **you should try my job, then you'd really see ~'s ~** tu devrais faire mon travail et alors tu comprendrais ◆ **I've done this job long enough to know ~'s ~** je fais ce travail depuis assez longtemps pour savoir de quoi il retourne * ◆ **I'll show them ~'s ~** je vais leur montrer de quel bois je me chauffe *

◆ **what with** ◆ **~ with the stress and lack of sleep, I was in a terrible state** entre le stress et le manque de sommeil, j'étais dans un état lamentable ◆ **~ with one thing and another** avec tout ça ◆ **~ with the suitcase and his bike he could hardly ...** avec la valise et son vélo, il pouvait à peine ...

◆ **not but what** ◆ **not but ~ that wouldn't be a good thing** non que ce soit une mauvaise chose

3 - COMPOUNDS

what-d'ye-call-her * N Machine * *f*
what-d'ye-call-him * N Machin * *m*, Machin Chouette * *m*
what-d'ye-call-it * N machin * *m*, truc * *m*, bidule * *m*
what-for * N ◆ **to give sb ~-for** passer un savon à qn *
what-ho! † * EXCL ohé bonjour !
what's-her-name * N ⇒ **what-d'ye-call-her**
what's-his-name * N ⇒ **what-d'ye-call-him**
what's-it N ⇒ **what-d'ye-call-it** ◆ **Mr What's-it** * Monsieur Machin (Chose) *
what's-its-name * N ⇒ **what-d'ye-call-it**

whate'er /wɒt'ɛəʳ/ *(liter)* ⇒ **whatever**

whatever /wɒt'evəʳ/ LANGUAGE IN USE 26.3

ADJ 1 *(gen)* ◆ **~ book you choose** quel que soit le livre que vous choisissiez *subj* ◆ **any box of ~ size** n'importe quelle boîte quelle qu'en soit la taille ◆ **give me ~ money you've got** donne-moi (tout) ce que tu as comme argent ◆ **he agreed to make ~ repairs might prove necessary** il a accepté de faire toutes les réparations qui s'avéreraient nécessaires ◆ **you'll have to change ~ plans you've made** quoi que vous ayez prévu, il vous faudra changer vos plans
2 (*: *emphatic interrog*) ◆ **~ books have you been reading?** qu'est-ce que vous êtes allé lire ?, vous avez lu de drôles de livres ! * ◆ **~ time is it?** quelle heure peut-il bien être ?

ADV ◆ **~ the weather** quel que soit le temps (qu'il fasse) ◆ **~ the news from the front, they ...** quelles que soient les nouvelles du front, ils ... ◆ **I'll take anything ~ you can spare** je prendrai tout ce dont vous n'avez pas besoin (quoi que ce soit) ◆ **I've no money ~** *or* **whatsoever** je n'ai pas un sou, je n'ai pas le moindre argent ◆ **there's no doubt ~** *or* **whatsoever about it** cela ne fait pas le moindre doute *or* pas l'ombre d'un doute ◆ **nothing ~** *or* **whatsoever** rien du tout, absolument rien ◆ **did you see any? – none ~** *or* **whatsoever!** tu en as vu ? – non, absolument aucun ! ◆ **has he any chance ~** *or* **whatsoever?** a-t-il la moindre chance ?

PRON 1 (= *no matter what*) quoi que + *subj* ◆ **~ happens** quoi qu'il arrive *subj* ◆ **~ you (may) find** quoi que vous trouviez *subj* ◆ **~ it may be** quoi que ce soit ◆ **~ he may mean** quel que soit ce qu'il veut dire ◆ **~ it** *or* **that means** *or* **may mean** *or* **meant** quel que soit le sens du mot *(or de la phrase etc)* ; *(hum, iro)* maintenant, allez savoir ce que ça veut dire ◆ **I'll pay ~ it costs** je paierai ce que ça coûtera ◆ **~ it costs, get it** achète-le quel qu'en soit le prix ◆ **~ he said before, he won't now do it** quoi qu'il ait dit auparavant, il ne le fera pas maintenant
2 (= *anything that*) tout ce que ◆ **do ~ you please** faites ce que vous voulez *or* voudrez ◆ **we shall do ~ is necessary** nous ferons le nécessaire ◆ **Monday or Tuesday, ~ suits you best** lundi ou mardi, ce qui *or* le jour qui vous convient le mieux ◆ **~ you say, sir** comme monsieur voudra ◆ **I tell you I'm ill! – ~ you say** *(iro)* je te dis que je suis malade ! – bien sûr, puisque tu le dis *(iro)*
3 (*: *emphatic interrog*) **~ did you do?** qu'est-ce que vous êtes allé faire ? ◆ **~ did you say that for?** pourquoi êtes-vous allé dire ça ?
4 (= *other similar things*) **the books and the clothes and ~** * les livres et les vêtements et tout ça *or* et que sais-je encore

whatnot /'wɒtnɒt/ N 1 (= *shelf*) étagère *f* 2 (* = *thing*) machin * *m*, truc * *m*, bidule * *m* 3 **and ~** * et ainsi de suite, et tout ce qui s'ensuit

whatsoever *(emphatic)* /,wɒtsəʊ'evəʳ/, **whatsoe'er** *(liter)* /,wɒtsəʊ'ɛəʳ/ ⇒ **whatever**

wheat /wi:t/ N *(NonC)* blé *m*, froment *m* ◆ **to separate** *or* **divide the ~ from the chaff** *(fig)* séparer le bon grain de l'ivraie
COMP **wheat beer** N bière *f* blanche
wheat field N champ *m* de blé
wheat flour N farine *f* de blé *or* de froment
wheat sheaf N gerbe *f* de blé

wheatear /'wi:tɪəʳ/ N (= *bird*) traquet *m* (motteux)

wheaten /'wi:tn/ ADJ de blé, de froment

wheatgerm /'wi:tdʒɜ:m/ N *(NonC)* germes *mpl* de blé

wheatmeal /'wi:tmi:l/ N farine *f* complète ◆ **~ bread** ≈ pain *m* de campagne

wheedle /'wi:dl/ VT cajoler, câliner ◆ **to ~ sth out of sb** obtenir *or* tirer qch de qn par des cajoleries *or* des câlineries ◆ **to ~ sb into doing sth** cajoler *or* câliner qn pour qu'il fasse qch, amener qn à faire qch à force de cajoleries *or* câlineries

wheedling /'wi:dlɪŋ/ ADJ câlin, enjôleur N cajolerie(s) *f(pl)*, câlinerie(s) *f(pl)*

wheel /wi:l/ N 1 *(gen)* roue *f* ; *(smaller) [of trolley, toy etc]* roulette *f* ; *(of ship)* (roue *f* de) gouvernail *m* ; (= *steering wheel*) volant *m* ; (= *spinning wheel*) rouet *m* ; (= *potter's wheel*) tour *m* (de potier) ; *(in roulette etc)* roue *f* ; *(Hist = torture instrument)* roue *f* ◆ **at the ~** *(of ship)* au gouvernail ; *(of car:* also **behind the wheel**) au volant ◆ **to take the ~** *(of ship)* prendre le gouvernail ; *(of car:* also **to get behind the wheel**) se mettre au volant ◆ **to change a ~** changer une roue ◆ **to break sb on the ~** *(Hist)* rouer qn ; → **shoulder, spoke¹**

2 *(in fig phrases)* ◆ **the ~s of government/of justice** les rouages *mpl* du gouvernement/de l'institution judiciaire ◆ **the ~s of justice are moving** *or* **turning very slowly** la justice suit son cours avec beaucoup de lenteur ◆ **to oil** *or* **grease the ~s** huiler les rouages ◆ **there are ~s within ~s** c'est plus compliqué que ça ne paraît, il y a toutes sortes de forces en jeu ◆ **the ~ has come full circle** la boucle est bouclée ◆ **it was hell on ~s*** c'était l'enfer ◆ **a third** *or* **fifth ~** *(US fig)* la cinquième roue du carrosse ; → **reinvent**

3 *(* = car)* ◆ **(set of) ~s** bagnole* *f* ◆ **have you got ~s?** vous êtes motorisé ?*

4 *(Mil)* **to make a right/left ~** *(= turn)* effectuer une conversion à droite/à gauche

VT 1 *[+ barrow, pushchair]* pousser, rouler ; *[+ bed, cycle]* pousser ; *[+ child]* pousser (dans un landau *etc*) ◆ **to ~ a trolley into/out of a room** amener un chariot dans une pièce/sortir un chariot d'une pièce ◆ **they ~ed the sick man over to the window** ils ont poussé le malade (dans son fauteuil roulant *or* sur son lit roulant) jusqu'à la fenêtre

2 * *(fig = bring)* **he ~ed out an enormous box** il a sorti une boîte énorme ◆ **~ him in!** amenez-le ! ◆ **the government have ~ed out their usual pre-election tax cuts** le gouvernement a ressorti ses réductions d'impôt, comme il en a l'habitude à la veille des élections ◆ **he ~ed out his usual arguments** il a sorti* ses arguments habituels ◆ **spokesmen were ~ed out to deny these rumours** on a fait venir des porte-parole pour démentir ces rumeurs

VI 1 (also **wheel round**) *[birds]* tournoyer ; *[person]* se retourner (brusquement), virevolter ; *(Mil)* effectuer une conversion ; *[procession]* tourner ◆ **right ~!** *(Mil)* à droite !

2 *(fig)* ◆ **he's always ~ing and dealing*** il est toujours en train de manigancer quelque chose *or* de chercher des combines*

COMP **wheel brace** **N** clé *f* en croix
wheel clamp **N** sabot *m* (de Denver) **VT** mettre un sabot à
wheel clamping **N** pose *f* d'un sabot (de Denver)
wheel gauge **N** écartement *m* des essieux
wheel horse* **N** *(US fig)* cheval *m* de labour *(fig)*
wheel of fortune **N** roue *f* de la fortune
wheel trim **N** enjoliveur *m*

wheelbarrow /ˈwiːlbærəʊ/ **N** brouette *f*

wheelbase /ˈwiːlbeɪs/ **N** *(Aut)* empattement *m*

wheelchair /ˈwiːltʃɛəʳ/ **N** fauteuil *m* roulant ◆ **"wheelchair access"** "accès aux handicapés" ◆ **when I'm in a ~ ...** *(hum)* quand je serai dans un *or* en fauteuil roulant ...
COMP **wheelchair-bound** **ADJ** ◆ **to be ~-bound** être dans un fauteuil roulant
wheelchair Olympics † **N** Jeux *mpl* olympiques handisports

wheeled /wiːld/ **ADJ** *[object]* à roues, muni de roues ◆ **three-~** à trois roues

wheeler /ˈwiːləʳ/ **N** *(pej)* ◆ **~-(and-)dealer*** magouilleur* *m*, -euse* *f* ; *(= businessman)* affairiste *m* ◆ **~-dealing*** *(pej)* ⇒ **wheeling and dealing** ; → **wheeling**

-wheeler /ˈwiːləʳ/ **N** *(in compounds)* ◆ **four-wheeler** voiture *f* à quatre roues ; → **two**

wheelhouse /ˈwiːlhaʊs/ **N** *(Naut)* timonerie *f*

wheelie* /ˈwiːlɪ/ **N** ◆ **to do a ~** faire une roue arrière **COMP** **wheelie bin*** **N** *(Brit)* poubelle *f* à roulettes

wheeling /ˈwiːlɪŋ/ **N** *(pej)* ◆ **~ and dealing*** magouilles* *fpl* combines* *fpl* ◆ **there has been a lot of ~ and dealing* over the choice of candidate** le choix du candidat a donné lieu à toutes sortes de combines *or* de magouilles*

wheelspin /ˈwiːlspɪn/ **N** patinage *m*

wheelwright /ˈwiːlraɪt/ **N** charron *m*

wheeze /wiːz/ **N** 1 respiration *f* bruyante *or* sifflante 2 *(Brit* † * = *scheme)* truc* *m*, combine* *f* 3 *(US * = saying)* dicton *m*, adage *m* **VI** *[person]* *(= breathe noisily)* respirer bruyamment ; *(= breathe with difficulty)* avoir du mal à respirer ; *[animal]* souffler **VT** (also **wheeze out**) ◆ **"yes", he ~d** "oui", dit-il d'une voix rauque ◆ **the old organ ~d out the tune** le vieil orgue a joué le morceau dans un bruit de soufflerie

wheezy /ˈwiːzɪ/ **ADJ** *[person]* poussif, asthmatique ; *[voice]* d'asthmatique ; *[animal]* poussif ; *[organ etc]* asthmatique *(fig)*

whelk /welk/ **N** bulot *m*, buccin *m*

whelp /welp/ **N** *(= animal)* petit(e) *m(f)* ; *(pej)* *(= youth)* petit morveux *m* **VI** *(of animals)* mettre bas

when /wen/

1 ADVERB	3 NOUN
2 CONJUNCTION	

1 - ADVERB

quand

> Note the various ways of asking questions in French:

◆ **~ does the term start?** quand commence le trimestre ?, quand est-ce que le trimestre commence ? ◆ **~ did it happen?** quand cela s'est-il passé ?, ça s'est passé quand ? ◆ **~ was penicillin discovered?** quand la pénicilline a-t-elle été découverte ? ◆ **~ was the Channel Tunnel opened?** quand a-t-on ouvert le tunnel sous la Manche ? ◆ **~ would be the best time to phone?** quand est-ce je pourrais rappeler ? ◆ **~'s the wedding?** à quand le mariage ?, quand doit avoir lieu le mariage ?

> There is no inversion after **quand** in indirect questions.

◆ **I don't know ~ I'll see him again** je ne sais pas quand je le reverrai ◆ **did he say ~ he'd be back?** a-t-il dit quand il serait de retour ? ◆ **let me know ~ you want your holidays** faites-moi savoir quand *or* à quelle date vous désirez prendre vos congés

> If **when** means **what time/date**, a more specific translation is often used.

◆ **~ does the train leave?** à quelle heure part le train ? ◆ **~ do you finish work?** à quelle heure est-ce tu quittes le travail ? ◆ **~ is your birthday?** quelle est la date de ton anniversaire ?, c'est quand, ton anniversaire ? ◆ **~ do the grapes get ripe?** vers quelle date *or* quand est-ce que les raisins sont mûrs ?

◆ **say when !*** *(pouring drinks etc)* vous m'arrêterez ...

2 - CONJUNCTION

1 = at the time that quand, lorsque ◆ **everything looks nicer ~ the sun is shining** tout est plus joli quand *or* lorsque le soleil brille

> If the **when** clause refers to the future, the future tense is used in French.

◆ **I'll do it ~ I have time** je le ferai quand j'aurai le temps ◆ **let me know ~ she comes** faites-moi savoir quand elle arrivera ◆ **~ you're older, you'll understand** quand tu seras plus grand, tu comprendras ◆ **go ~ you like** partez quand vous voulez *or* voudrez

> **en** + present participle may be used, if the subject of both clauses is the same, and the verb is one of action.

◆ **she burnt herself ~ she took the dish out of the oven** elle s'est brûlée en sortant le plat du four ◆ **he blushed ~ he saw her** il a rougi en la voyant

◆ **when** + *noun* ◆ **~ a student at Oxford, she ...** lorsqu'elle était étudiante à Oxford, elle ... ◆ **~ a child, he ...** enfant, il ...

◆ **when** + *adjective* ◆ **my father, ~ young, had a fine tenor voice** quand mon père était jeune il avait une belle voix de ténor ◆ **~ just three years old, he was ...** à trois ans il était déjà ... ◆ **the floor is slippery ~ wet** le sol est glissant quand *or* lorsqu'il est mouillé

◆ **when** + *-ing* ◆ **you should take your passport with you ~ changing money** munissez-vous de votre passeport lorsque *or* quand vous changez de l'argent ◆ **take care ~ opening the tin** faites attention lorsque *or* quand vous ouvrez la boîte, faites attention en ouvrant la boîte

◆ *day/time/moment* + **when** où ◆ **on the day ~ I met him** le jour où je l'ai rencontré ◆ **at the time ~ I should have been at the station** à l'heure où j'aurais dû être à la gare ◆ **at the very moment ~ I was about to leave** juste au moment où j'allais partir ◆ **one day ~ the sun was shining** un jour que *or* où le soleil brillait ◆ **it was one of those days ~ everything is quiet** c'était un de ces jours où tout est calme ◆ **there are times ~ I wish I'd never met him** il y a des moments où je souhaiterais ne l'avoir jamais rencontré ◆ **this is a time ~ we must speak up for our principles** c'est dans un moment comme celui-ci qu'il faut défendre nos principes

2 = which is when ◆ **he arrived at 8 o'clock, ~ traffic is at its peak** il est arrivé à 8 heures, heure à laquelle la circulation est la plus intense ◆ **in August, ~ peaches are at their best** en août, époque où les pêches sont les plus savoureuses ◆ **it was in spring, ~ the snow was melting** c'était au printemps, à la fonte des neiges

3 = the time when ◆ **he told me about ~ you got lost in Paris** il m'a raconté le jour *or* la fois* où vous vous êtes perdu dans Paris ◆ **now is ~ I need you most** c'est maintenant que j'ai le plus besoin de vous ◆ **that's ~ the programme starts** c'est l'heure à laquelle l'émission commence ◆ **that's ~ Napoleon was born** c'est l'année où Napoléon est né ◆ **that's ~ you ought to try to be patient** c'est dans ces moments-là qu'il faut faire preuve de patience ◆ **that was ~ the trouble started** c'est alors que les ennuis ont commencé

4 = after quand, une fois que ◆ **~ you read the letter you'll know why** quand vous lirez la lettre vous comprendrez pourquoi ◆ **~ they left, I felt relieved** quand ils sont partis, je me suis senti soulagé ◆ **~ you've been to Greece you realize how ...** quand *or* une fois qu'on est allé en Grèce, on se rend compte que ... ◆ **~ he had made the decision, he felt better** il se sentit soulagé une fois qu'il eut pris une décision ◆ **~ (it is) finished the bridge will measure ...** une fois terminé, le pont mesurera ...

5 = each time that, whenever quand ◆ **I take aspirin ~ I have a headache** je prends un cachet d'aspirine quand j'ai mal à la tête ◆ **~ it rains I wish I were back in Italy** quand il pleut je regrette l'Italie

6 = whereas alors que ◆ **he thought he was recovering, ~ in fact ...** il pensait qu'il était en voie de guérison alors qu'en fait ...

7 = if ◆ **how can I be self-confident ~ I look like this ?** comment veux-tu que j'aie confiance en moi en étant comme ça ? ◆ **how can you understand ~ you won't listen?** comment voulez-vous comprendre si vous n'écoutez pas ? ◆ **what's the good of trying ~ I know**

I can't do it? à quoi bon essayer, si *or* puisque je sais que je ne peux pas le faire

8 (= and then) quand ◆ **he had just sat down ~ the phone rang** il venait juste de s'asseoir quand le téléphone a sonné ◆ **I was about to leave ~ I remembered ...** j'étais sur le point de partir quand je me suis rappelé ... ◆ **I had only just got back ~ I had to leave again** à peine venais-je de rentrer que j'ai dû repartir

3 - NOUN

◆ **I want to know the ~ and the how of all this** je veux savoir quand et comment tout ça est arrivé

whence /wens/ ADV, CONJ *(liter)* d'où

whenever /wen'evəʳ/, **whene'er** *(liter)* /wen'ɛəʳ/ CONJ 1 *(= at whatever time)* quand ◆ **come ~ you wish** venez quand vous voulez *or* voudrez ◆ **you may leave ~ you're ready** vous pouvez partir quand vous serez prêt

2 *(= every time that)* quand, chaque fois que ◆ **come and see us ~ you can** venez nous voir quand vous le pouvez ◆ **~ I see a black horse I think of Jenny** chaque fois que je vois un cheval noir je pense à Jenny ◆ **~ it rains the roof leaks** chaque fois qu'il pleut le toit laisse entrer l'eau ◆ **~ people ask him he says ...** quand on lui demande il dit ... ◆ **~ you touch it it falls over** on n'a qu'à le toucher et il tombe

ADV * mais quand donc ◆ **~ did you do that?** mais quand donc est-ce que vous avez fait ça ? ◆ **next Monday, or ~** lundi prochain, ou je ne sais quand ◆ **I can leave on Monday, or Tuesday, or ~** je peux partir lundi, ou mardi, ou un autre jour *or* ou n'importe quand

whensoever *(emphatic)* /ˌwensəʊ'evəʳ/, **whensoe'er** *(liter)* /ˌwensəʊ'ɛəʳ/ ⇒ **whenever**

where /wɛəʳ/ LANGUAGE IN USE 5.1

ADV *(= in or to what place)* où ◆ **~ do you live?** où habitez-vous ? ◆ **~ are you going (to)?** où allez-vous ? ◆ **~'s the theatre?** où est le théâtre ? ◆ **~ are you from?, ~ do you come from?** d'où venez-vous ?, vous venez d'où ? ◆ **~ have you come from?** d'où est-ce que vous arrivez ?, vous arrivez d'où ? ◆ **you saw him near ~?** vous l'avez vu près d'où ? ◆ **~ have you got to in the book?** où est-ce que vous en êtes de votre livre ? ◆ **~ do I come into it?** *(fig)* qu'est-ce que je viens faire dans tout ça ?, quel est mon rôle dans tout ça ? ◆ **~'s the difference?** où voyez-vous une différence ? ◆ **I wonder ~ he is** je me demande où il est ◆ **I don't know ~ I put it** je ne sais pas où je l'ai mis ◆ **don't eat that, you don't know ~ it's been** ne mangez pas cela, vous ne savez pas où ça a traîné ◆ **~ would we be if ...?** où serions-nous si ... ?

CONJ 1 *(gen)* (là) où ◆ **stay ~ you are** restez (là) où vous êtes ◆ **there is a garage ~ the two roads intersect** il y a un garage au croisement des deux routes ◆ **Lyons stands ~ the Saône meets the Rhône** Lyon se trouve au confluent de la Saône et du Rhône ◆ **there is a school ~ our house once stood** il y a une école là où *or* à l'endroit où se dressait autrefois notre maison ◆ **go ~ you like** allez où vous voulez *or* voudrez ◆ **it is coldest ~ there are no trees for shelter** c'est là où il n'y a pas d'arbre pour s'abriter (du vent) qu'il fait le plus froid ◆ **I'm at the stage ~ I could ...** j'en suis au point où je pourrais ... ◆ **my book is not ~ I left it** mon livre n'est pas là où *or* à l'endroit où je l'avais laissé ◆ **it's not ~ I expected to see it** je ne m'attendais pas à le voir là ◆ **he ran towards ~ the bus had crashed** il a couru vers l'endroit où le bus avait eu l'accident ◆ **I told him ~ he could stick his job** ‡ je lui ai dit où il pouvait se le mettre son boulot‡

2 *(= in which, at which etc)* où ◆ **the house ~ he was born** la maison où il est né, sa maison natale ◆ **in the place ~ there used to be a church** à l'endroit où il y avait une église ◆ **England is ~ you'll find this sort of thing most often** c'est en Angleterre que vous trouverez le plus fréquemment cela

3 *(= the place that)* là que ◆ **this is ~ the car was found** c'est là qu'on a retrouvé la voiture ◆ **this is ~ we got to in the book** c'est là que nous en sommes du livre ◆ **that's ~ you're wrong!** c'est là que vous vous trompez !, voilà votre erreur ! ◆ **so that's ~ my gloves have got to!** voilà où sont passés mes gants ! ◆ **that's ~** *or* **there's * ~ things started to go wrong** *(= when)* c'est là que les choses se sont gâtées ◆ **this is ~** *or* **here's * ~ you've got to make your own decision** là il faut que tu décides *subj* tout seul ◆ **that's ~ I meant** c'est là que je voulais dire ◆ **he went up to ~ she was sitting** il s'est approché de l'endroit où elle était assise ◆ **I walked past ~ he was standing** j'ai dépassé l'endroit où il se tenait ◆ **from ~ I'm standing I can see ...** d'où *or* de là où je suis je peux voir ...

4 *(= wherever)* là où ◆ **you'll always find water ~ there are trees** vous trouverez toujours de l'eau là où il y a des arbres ◆ **~ there is kindness, you will find ...** là où il y a de la gentillesse, vous trouverez ...

5 *(= whereas)* alors que ◆ **he walked ~ he could have taken the bus** il est allé à pied alors qu'il aurait pu prendre le bus ◆ **he walked ~ I would have taken the bus** il est allé à pied alors que *or* tandis que moi j'aurais pris le bus

N ◆ **I want to know the ~ and the why of it** je veux savoir où et pourquoi c'est arrivé

whereabouts /'wɛərəbaʊts/ ADV où (donc) ◆ **~ did you put it?** où (donc) l'as-tu mis ? N ◆ **his ~ to know sb's/sth's ~** savoir où est qn/qch ◆ **his ~ are unknown** personne ne sait où il se trouve

whereafter /ˌwɛər'ɑːftəʳ/ CONJ *(frm)* après quoi

whereas /wɛər'æz/ CONJ *(= while)* alors que, tandis que ; *(= in view of the fact that)* attendu que, considérant que ; *(= although)* bien que + *subj*, quoique + *subj*

whereat /wɛər'æt/ ADV *(liter)* sur quoi, après quoi, sur ce

whereby /wɛə'baɪ/ PRON *(frm)* par quoi, par lequel *(or laquelle etc)*, au moyen duquel *(or de laquelle etc)*

wherefore †† /'wɛəfɔːʳ/ CONJ *(= for that reason)* et donc, et pour cette raison ; see also **why** ADV *(= why)* pourquoi

wherein /wɛər'ɪn/ INTERROG ADV †† ou, dans quoi CONJ *(frm)* où, dans quoi

whereof /wɛər'ɒv/ ADV, PRON *(frm, liter)* de quoi, dont, duquel *(or de laquelle etc)*

whereon /wɛər'ɒn/ PRON *(frm, liter)* sur quoi, sur lequel *(or laquelle etc)*

wheresoever *(emphatic)* /ˌwɛəsəʊ'evəʳ/, **wheresoe'er** *(liter)* /ˌwɛəsəʊ'ɛəʳ/ ⇒ **wherever**

whereto /wɛə'tuː/ ADV *(frm)* et dans ce but, et en vue de ceci

whereupon /ˌwɛərə'pɒn/ ADV sur quoi, après quoi

wherever /wɛər'evəʳ/ CONJ 1 *(= no matter where)* où que + *subj* ◆ **~ I am I'll always remember** où que je sois, je n'oublierai jamais ◆ **~ you go I'll go too** où que tu ailles *or* partout où tu iras, j'irai ◆ **I'll buy it ~ it comes from** je l'achèterai d'où que cela provienne *or* quelle qu'en soit la provenance ◆ **~ it came from, it's here now!** peu importe d'où cela vient, c'est là maintenant !

2 *(= anywhere)* (là) où ◆ **sit ~ you like** asseyez-vous (là) où vous voulez ◆ **go ~ you please** allez où bon vous semblera ◆ **we'll go ~ you wish** nous irons (là) où vous voudrez ◆ **he comes from Barcombe, ~ that is** il vient d'un endroit qui s'appellerait Barcombe

3 *(= everywhere)* partout où ◆ **~ you see this sign, you can be sure that ...** partout où vous voyez ce signe, vous pouvez être sûr que ... ◆ **~ there is water available** partout où il y a de l'eau

ADV * mais où donc ◆ **~ did you get that hat?** mais où donc avez-vous déniché* ce chapeau ? ◆ **I bought it in London or Liverpool or ~** je l'ai acheté à Londres, Liverpool ou je ne sais où

wherewith /wɛə'wɪθ/ ADV *(frm, liter)* avec quoi, avec lequel *(or laquelle etc)*

wherewithal /'wɛəwɪðɔːl/ N moyens *mpl*, ressources *fpl* nécessaires ◆ **he hasn't the ~ to buy it** il n'a pas les moyens de l'acheter

whet /wet/ VT 1 *[+ tool]* aiguiser, affûter 2 *[+ desire, appetite, curiosity]* aiguiser, stimuler

whether /'weðəʳ/ CONJ 1 si ◆ **I don't know ~ it's true or not, I don't know ~ or not it's true** je ne sais pas si c'est vrai ou non ◆ **you must tell him ~ you want him (or not)** il faut que tu lui dises si oui ou non tu as besoin de lui ◆ **I don't know ~ to go or not** je ne sais pas si je dois y aller ou non ◆ **it is doubtful ~ ...** il est peu probable que ... + *subj* ◆ **I doubt ~ ...** je doute que ... + *subj* ◆ **I'm not sure ~ ...** je ne suis pas sûr si ... + *indic or* que ... + *subj*

2 que + *subj* ◆ **~ it rains or (~ it) snows I'm going out** qu'il pleuve ou qu'il neige *subj* je sors ◆ **~ you go or not, ~ or not you go** que tu y ailles ou non

3 soit ◆ **~ today or tomorrow** soit aujourd'hui soit demain ◆ **~ before or after** soit avant soit après ◆ **~ with a friend to help you or without** avec ou sans ami pour vous aider ◆ **I shall help you ~ or no** de toute façon *or* quoi qu'il arrive *subj* je vous aiderai

whetstone /'wetstəʊn/ N pierre *f* à aiguiser

whew * /hwjuː/ EXCL *(relief, exhaustion)* ouf ! ; *(surprise, admiration)* fichtre ! *

whey /weɪ/ N petit-lait *m*

which /wɪtʃ/ ADJ 1 *(in questions etc)* quel ◆ **~ card did he take?** quelle carte a-t-il prise ?, laquelle des cartes a-t-il prise ? ◆ **I don't know ~ book he wants** je ne sais pas quel livre il veut ◆ **~ one?** lequel *(or* laquelle) ? ◆ **~ one of you?** lequel *(or* laquelle) d'entre vous ? ◆ **~ Campbell do you mean?** de quel Campbell parlez-vous ?

2 ◆ **in ~ case** auquel cas ◆ **he spent a week here, during ~ time ...** il a passé une semaine ici au cours de laquelle ...

PRON 1 *(in questions etc)* lequel *m*, laquelle *f* ◆ **~ is the best of these maps?, ~ of these maps is the best?** quelle est la meilleure de ces cartes ?, laquelle de ces cartes est la meilleure ? ◆ **~ have you taken?** lequel *m* *(or* laquelle *f)* avez-vous pris(e) ? ◆ **~ of you two is taller?** lequel de vous deux est le plus grand ?, qui est le plus grand de vous deux ? ◆ **~ are the ripest apples?** quelles sont les pommes les plus mûres ?, quelles pommes sont les plus mûres ? ◆ **~ would you like?** lequel aimeriez-vous ? ◆ **~ of you are married?** lesquels d'entre vous sont mariés ? ◆ **~ of you owns the red car?** lequel d'entre vous est le propriétaire de la voiture rouge ?

2 *(= the one or ones that) (subject)* celui *m* *(or* celle *f* or ceux *mpl* or celles *fpl)* qui ; *(object)* celui *etc* que ◆ **I don't mind ~ you give me** vous pouvez me donner celui que vous voudrez (ça m'est égal) ◆ **I don't mind ~** ça m'est égal ◆ **show me ~ is the cheapest** montrez-moi celui qui est le moins cher ◆ **I can't tell** *or* **I don't know ~ is ~** je ne peux pas les distinguer ◆ **I can't tell ~ key is ~** je ne sais pas à quoi correspondent ces clés *or* quelle clé ouvre quelle porte ◆ **tell me ~ are the Frenchmen** dites-moi lesquels sont

les Français ◆ **I know ~ I'd rather have** je sais celui que je préférerais ◆ **ask him ~ of the books he'd like** demandez-lui parmi tous les livres lequel il voudrait

3 *(= that) (subject)* qui ; *(object)* que ; *(after prep)* lequel *m (or* laquelle *f or* lesquels *mpl or* lesquelles *fpl)* ◆ **the book ~ is on the table** le livre qui est sur la table ◆ **the apple ~ you ate** la pomme que vous avez mangée ◆ **the house towards ~ she was going** la maison vers laquelle elle se dirigeait ◆ **the film of ~ he was speaking** le film dont il parlait ◆ **opposite ~** en face duquel *(or* de laquelle *etc)* ◆ **the book ~ I told you about** le livre dont je vous ai parlé ◆ **the box ~ you put it in** la boîte dans laquelle vous l'avez mis

4 *(= and that) (subject)* ce qui ; *(object)* ce que ; *(after prep)* quoi ◆ **he said he knew her, ~ is true** il a dit qu'il la connaissait, ce qui est vrai ◆ **she said she was 40, ~ I doubt very much** elle a dit qu'elle avait 40 ans, ce dont je doute beaucoup ◆ **you're late, ~ reminds me ...** vous êtes en retard, ce qui me fait penser ... ◆ **... upon ~ she left the room** ... sur quoi *or* et sur ce elle a quitté la pièce ◆ **... of ~ more later** ... ce dont je reparlerai plus tard, ... mais je reviendrai là-dessus plus tard ◆ **from ~ we deduce that ...** d'où *or* et de là nous déduisons que ... ◆ **after ~ we went to bed** après quoi nous sommes allés nous coucher

whichever /wɪtʃ'evəʳ/ ADJ 1 *(= that one which)* **~ method is most successful should be chosen** on devrait choisir la méthode garantissant les meilleurs résultats, peu importe laquelle ◆ **take ~ book you like best** prenez le livre que vous préférez, peu importe lequel ◆ **I'll have ~ apple you don't want** je prendrai la pomme que *or* dont vous ne voulez pas ◆ **keep ~ one you prefer** gardez celui que vous préférez ◆ **go by ~ route is the most direct** prenez la route la plus directe, peu importe laquelle ◆ **do it in ~ way you can** faites-le comme vous pourrez

2 *(= no matter which) (subject)* quel que soit ... qui + *subj* ; *(object)* quel que soit ... que + *subj* ◆ **~ dress you wear** quelle que soit la robe que tu portes ◆ **~ book is left** quel que soit le livre qui reste ◆ **~ book is chosen** quel que soit le livre choisi ◆ **~ way you look at it** *(fig)* de quelque manière que vous le considériez *subj*

PRON 1 *(= the one which) (subject)* celui *m* qui, celle *f* qui ; *(object)* celui *m* que, celle *f* que ◆ **~ is best for him** celui *m (or* celle *f)* qui lui convient le mieux ◆ **~ you choose will be sent to you at once** celui *m (or* celle *f)* que vous choisirez vous sera expédié(e) immédiatement ◆ **~ of the books is selected** quel que soit le livre qui sera sélectionné ◆ **choose ~ is easiest** choisissez (celui qui est) le plus facile ◆ **on Thursday or Friday, ~ is more convenient** jeudi ou vendredi, le jour qui vous conviendra le mieux ◆ **A or B, ~ is the greater** A ou B, à savoir le plus grand des deux ◆ **at sunset or 7pm, ~ is the earlier** au coucher du soleil ou à 19 heures au plus tard, selon la saison

2 *(= no matter which one) (subject)* quel *m* que soit celui qui + *subj*, quelle *f* que soit celle qui + *subj* ; *(object)* quel *m* que soit celui que + *subj*, quelle *f* que soit celle que + *subj* ◆ **~ of the two books he chooses, it won't make a lot of difference** quel que soit le livre qu'il choisisse, cela ne fera pas grande différence ◆ **~ of the methods is chosen, it can't affect you much** quelle que soit la méthode choisie, ça ne changera pas grand-chose pour vous

whiff /wɪf/ N 1 *(= puff) [of smoke, hot air]* bouffée *f* ◆ **a ~ of garlic** une bouffée d'ail ◆ **a ~ of seaweed** une odeur d'algues ◆ **one ~ of this is enough to kill you** il suffit de respirer ça une fois pour mourir ◆ **I caught a ~ of gas** j'ai senti l'odeur du gaz ◆ **take a ~ of this!** * renifle ça ! 2 *(= bad smell)* ◆ **what a ~ !** * qu'est-ce que ça pue *or* fouette * ! 3 *(fig = hint) [of scandal]* parfum *m*, odeur *f* ; *[of corruption]* odeur *f* ◆ **a case which had a ~ of espionage about it** une affaire qui sentait l'espionnage VI * sentir mauvais

whiffy * /'wɪfɪ/ ADJ qui sent mauvais

Whig /wɪg/ ADJ, N *(Pol Hist)* whig *m*

while /waɪl/ CONJ 1 *(= during the time that)* pendant que ◆ **it happened ~ I was out of the room** c'est arrivé pendant que *or* alors que j'étais hors de la pièce ◆ **can you wait ~ I telephone?** pouvez-vous attendre pendant que je téléphone ? ◆ **she fell asleep ~ reading** elle s'est endormie en lisant ◆ **~ you're away I'll write some letters** pendant ton absence *or* pendant que tu seras absent j'écrirai quelques lettres ◆ **don't drink ~ on duty** ne buvez pas pendant le service ◆ **"heels repaired while you wait"** "ressemelage minute" ◆ **~ you're up you could close the door** pendant que *or* puisque tu es debout tu pourrais fermer la porte ◆ **and ~ you're about it ...** et pendant que vous y êtes ...

2 *(= as long as)* tant que ◆ **~ there's life there's hope** tant qu'il y a de la vie il y a de l'espoir ◆ **it won't happen ~ I'm here** cela n'arrivera pas tant que je serai là ◆ **~ I live I shall make sure that ...** tant que *or* aussi longtemps que je vivrai je ferai en sorte que ...

3 *(= although)* quoique + *subj*, bien que + *subj* ◆ **~ I admit he is sometimes right ...** tout en admettant *or* quoique j'admette qu'il ait quelquefois raison ... ◆ **~ there are a few people who like that sort of thing ...** bien qu'il y ait un petit nombre de gens qui aiment ce genre de chose ...

4 *(= whereas)* alors que, tandis que ◆ **she sings quite well, ~ her sister can't sing a note** elle ne chante pas mal alors que *or* tandis que sa sœur ne sait pas chanter du tout

N 1 ◆ **a ~** quelque temps ◆ **a short ~, a little ~** un moment, un instant ◆ **for a little ~** pendant un petit moment ◆ **a long ~, a good ~** (assez) longtemps, pas mal de temps ◆ **after a ~** quelque temps après, au bout de quelque temps ◆ **let's stop for a ~** arrêtons-nous un moment ; *(longer)* arrêtons quelque temps ◆ **for a ~ I thought ...** j'ai pensé un moment ... ; *(longer)* pendant quelque temps j'ai pensé ... ◆ **it takes quite a ~ to ripen** cela met assez longtemps à mûrir ◆ **once in a ~** (une fois) de temps en temps ◆ **(in) between ~s** entre-temps ; → **worthwhile**

2 ◆ **he looked at me (all) the ~** *or* **the whole ~** il m'a regardé pendant tout ce temps-là

COMP **while-you-wait heel repairs** NPL ressemelage *m* minute *inv*

► **while away** VT SEP (faire) passer

whiles /waɪlz/ ADV *(esp Scot, dial)* quelquefois, de temps en temps

whilst /waɪlst/ CONJ *(esp Brit)* ⇒ **while conj**

whim /wɪm/ N caprice *m*, lubie *f* ◆ **to be subject to sb's ~s/to the ~s of the economy** être livré aux caprices de qn/de l'économie ◆ **it's just a (passing) ~** c'est une lubie qui lui *(or* te *etc)* passera ◆ **he gives in to her every ~** il lui passe tous ses caprices ◆ **to cater** *or* **pander to sb's ~s/sb's every ~** satisfaire les caprices/tous les petits caprices de qn ◆ **as the ~ takes him** comme l'idée lui prend ◆ **at** *or* **on ~** sur un coup de tête ◆ **he changes his mind at ~** il change d'avis à tout bout de champ

whimper /'wɪmpəʳ/ N gémissement *m*, geignement *m* ◆ **... he said with a ~** ... gémit-il, ... pleurnicha-t-il *(pej)* ◆ **without a ~** *(fig)* sans se plaindre VI *[person, baby]* gémir, pleurnicher *(pej)* ; *[dog]* gémir, pousser de petits cris plaintifs VT ◆ **"no", he ~ed** "non", gémit-il *or* pleurnicha-t-il *(pej)*

whimpering /'wɪmpərɪŋ/ N geignements *mpl*, gémissements *mpl* ADJ *[tone, voice]* larmoyant, pleurnicheur *(pej)* ; *[person, animal]* qui gémit faiblement

whimsical /'wɪmzɪkəl/ ADJ *[person]* fantasque ; *[smile, look]* curieux ; *[humour]* original ; *[idea, story]* saugrenu, fantaisiste

whimsicality /,wɪmzɪ'kælɪtɪ/ N 1 (NonC) *[of person]* caractère *m* fantasque ; *[of idea, story]* caractère *m* fantaisiste *or* saugrenu ; *[of smile, look]* caractère *m* curieux 2 ◆ **whimsicalities** idées *fpl (or* actions *fpl etc)* bizarres *or* saugrenues

whimsically /'wɪmzɪkəlɪ/ ADV *[say, suggest]* de façon saugrenue ; *[smile, look]* étrangement, curieusement ; *[muse, ponder]* malicieusement

whimsy /'wɪmzɪ/ N *(= whim)* caprice *m*, fantaisie *f* ; (NonC) *(= whimsicality)* caractère *m* fantaisiste

whim-whams * /'wɪmwæmz/ NPL *(US)* trouille ‡ *f*, frousse * *f*

whin /wɪn/ N *(= plant)* ajonc *m*

whine /waɪn/ N *[of person, child, dog]* gémissement *m* (prolongé) ; *[of bullet, shell, siren, machine]* plainte *f* stridente *or* monocorde ; *(fig = complaint)* plainte *f* ◆ **... he said with a ~** ... se lamenta-t-il, ... dit-il d'une voix geignarde ◆ **it's another of his ~s about taxes** le voilà encore en train de se plaindre *or* de geindre * à propos de ses impôts VI *[person, dog]* geindre, gémir ; *[siren]* gémir ; *[engine]* vrombir ; *(fig = complain)* se lamenter, se plaindre ◆ **to ~ about sth** *(fig)* se lamenter sur qch, se plaindre à propos de qch ◆ **don't come whining to me about it** ne venez pas vous plaindre à moi ◆ **it's just a scratch: stop whining** ce n'est qu'une égratignure : arrête de geindre * VT ◆ **"it's happened again", he ~d** "ça a recommencé", se lamenta-t-il *or* dit-il d'une voix geignarde

whinge * /wɪndʒ/ *(Brit)* VI geindre * *(pej) (about* à propos de) ◆ **stop ~ing** arrête de geindre * *or* de te plaindre N ◆ **he was having a real ~** il n'arrêtait pas de geindre * ◆ **he was having a ~ about the price of cigarettes** il râlait * à propos du prix des cigarettes

whingeing * /'wɪndʒɪŋ/ *(Brit)* ADJ geignard, plaintif N gémissements *mpl*, plaintes *fpl*

whinger * /'wɪndʒəʳ/ N geignard(e) * *m(f)*

whining /'waɪnɪŋ/ N *[of person, child]* gémissements *mpl* (continus), pleurnicheries *fpl* ; *[of dog]* gémissements *mpl* ; *(fig = complaining)* plaintes *fpl* continuelles ADJ 1 *[person, child]* pleurnicheur ; *[dog]* gémissant ; *(fig = complaining) [person, voice]* geignard 2 *(= high-pitched)* ◆ **a ~ sound** *or* **noise** une plainte aiguë

whinny /'wɪnɪ/ N hennissement *m* VI hennir

whiny * /'waɪnɪ/ ADJ pleurnichard *

whip /wɪp/ N 1 fouet *m* ; (also **riding whip**) cravache *f*

2 *(Parl) (= person)* whip *m*, *parlementaire chargé de la discipline dans son parti* ; *(Brit = summons)* convocation *f* ◆ **three-line ~** convocation *f* d'un député *(impliquant sa présence obligatoire et le respect des consignes de vote)*

3 *(Culin = dessert)* crème *f or* mousse *f* instantanée

VT 1 *[+ person, animal, child]* fouetter ◆ **the rain ~ped her face** la pluie lui cinglait *or* fouettait la figure ◆ **to ~ sb into a frenzy** mettre qn hors de ses gonds

2 *(Culin) [+ cream]* fouetter, battre au fouet ; *[+ egg white]* battre en neige

3 * *(fig) (= defeat)* battre à plates coutures ; *(= criticize severely)* critiquer vivement, éreinter

4 (* = *seize)* **to ~ sth out of sb's hands** enlever brusquement *or* vivement qch des mains de qn ◆ **he ~ped a gun out of his pocket** il a brusquement sorti un revolver de sa poche ◆ **he ~ped the letter off the table** il a prestement fait disparaître la lettre qui était sur la table

5 *(Brit * = steal)* faucher*, piquer* ◆ **somebody's ~ped my watch!** quelqu'un m'a fauché* *or* piqué* ma montre !
6 *[+ cable, rope]* surlier ; *(Sewing)* surfiler
VI ◆ **to ~ along/away** *etc* filer/partir *etc* à toute allure *or* comme un éclair ◆ **to ~ back** revenir brusquement ◆ **the wind ~ped through the trees** le vent fouettait les branches des arbres ◆ **the rope broke and ~ped across his face** la corde a cassé et lui a cinglé le visage
COMP **whip hand** N *(fig)* ◆ **to have the ~ hand** être le maître, avoir le dessus ◆ **to have the ~ hand over sb** avoir la haute main sur qn
whipped cream N crème *f* fouettée
whip-round* N *(Brit)* collecte *f* ◆ **to have a ~-round for sb/sth*** faire une collecte pour qn/qch

► **whip away** VI → **whip vi**
VT SEP *(= remove quickly) [person]* enlever brusquement *or* vivement, faire disparaître ; *[wind etc]* emporter brusquement

► **whip in** VI 1 *[person]* entrer précipitamment *or* comme un éclair
2 *(Hunting)* être piqueur
VT SEP 1 *(Hunting) [+ hounds]* ramener, rassembler ; *(Parl) [+ members voting]* battre le rappel de ; *(fig) [+ voters, supporters]* rallier
2 *(Culin)* ~ **in the cream** incorporez la crème avec un fouet

► **whip off** VT SEP *[+ garment etc]* ôter *or* enlever en quatrième vitesse* ; *[+ lid, cover]* ôter brusquement

► **whip on** VT SEP 1 *[+ garment etc]* enfiler en quatrième vitesse*
2 *(= urge on) [+ horse]* cravacher

► **whip out** VI *[person]* sortir précipitamment
VT SEP *[+ knife, gun, purse]* sortir brusquement *or* vivement *(from de)*

► **whip over*** VI ⇒ **whip round vi 2**

► **whip round** VI 1 *(= turn quickly) [person]* se retourner vivement ; *[object]* pivoter brusquement
2 *(* = pop round)* **he's just ~ped round to the grocer's** il est juste allé faire un saut à l'épicerie ◆ **~ round to your aunt's and tell her ...** va faire un saut *or* cours chez ta tante lui dire ...
N ◆ **whip-round*** → **whip**

► **whip through** VT FUS *[+ book]* parcourir rapidement ; *[+ homework, task]* expédier, faire en quatrième vitesse*

► **whip up** VT SEP 1 *[+ emotions, enthusiasm, indignation]* attiser ; *[+ support, interest]* stimuler
2 *[+ cream, egg whites]* fouetter, battre au fouet
3 *(* = prepare)* ◆ **to whip up a meal** préparer un repas en vitesse ◆ **can you ~ us up something to eat?** est-ce que vous pourriez nous faire à manger *or* nous préparer un morceau* en vitesse ?
4 *(= snatch up)* saisir brusquement

whipcord /ˈwɪpkɔːd/ N *(= fabric)* whipcord *m*

whiplash /ˈwɪplæʃ/ N 1 *(= blow from whip)* coup *m* de fouet 2 *(in car accident)* coup *m* du lapin*, syndrome *m* cervical traumatique ◆ **he felt the ~ of fear** il fut saisi d'une peur cinglante
COMP **whiplash injury** N ◆ **~ injury to the neck** traumatisme *m* cervical

whipper-in /ˌwɪpərˈɪn/ N (pl **whippers-in**) *(Hunting)* piqueur *m*

whippersnapper † /ˈwɪpəˌsnæpəʳ/ N *(hum)* freluquet *m*

whippet /ˈwɪpɪt/ N whippet *m*

whipping /ˈwɪpɪŋ/ N *(as punishment)* correction *f* ◆ **to give sb a ~** fouetter qn, donner le fouet à qn, donner des coups de fouet à qn
COMP **whipping boy** N *(fig)* souffre-douleur *m inv*
whipping cream N *(Culin)* crème *f* fraîche *(à fouetter)*
whipping post N *poteau auquel on attachait les personnes condamnées à être fouettées*
whipping top N toupie *f*

whippoorwill /ˈwɪpˌpʊəˌwɪl/ N engoulevent *m* d'Amérique du Nord

whippy /ˈwɪpɪ/ ADJ souple

whir /wɜːʳ/ VI, N ⇒ **whirr**

whirl /wɜːl/ N *[of leaves, papers, smoke]* tourbillon *m*, tournoiement *m* ; *[of sand, dust, water]* tourbillon *m* ◆ **a ~ of parties and dances** un tourbillon de réceptions et de soirées dansantes ◆ **the whole week was a ~ of activity** nous n'avons *(or* ils n'ont *etc)* pas arrêté de toute la semaine ◆ **the social ~** le tourbillon de la vie mondaine ◆ **her thoughts/emotions were in a ~** tout tourbillonnait dans sa tête/son cœur ◆ **my head is in a ~** la tête me tourne ◆ **to give sth a ~*** essayer qch
VI 1 *(= spin:* also **whirl round)** *[leaves, papers, smoke, dancers]* tourbillonner, tournoyer ; *[sand, dust, water]* tourbillonner ; *[wheel, merry-go-round, spinning top]* tourner ◆ **they ~ed past us in the dance** ils sont passés près de nous en tourbillonnant pendant la danse ◆ **the leaves ~ed down** les feuilles tombaient en tourbillonnant ◆ **my head is ~ing** la tête me tourne ◆ **her thoughts/emotions were ~ing** tout tourbillonnait dans sa tête/son cœur
2 *(= move rapidly)* **to ~ along** aller à toute vitesse *or* à toute allure ◆ **to ~ away** *or* **off** partir à toute vitesse *or* à toute allure
VT *[wind] [+ leaves, smoke]* faire tourbillonner, faire tournoyer ; *[+ dust, sand]* faire tourbillonner ◆ **he ~ed his sword round his head** il a fait tournoyer son épée au-dessus de sa tête ◆ **they ~ed me up to Liverpool to visit Mary** ils m'ont embarqué* pour aller voir Mary à Liverpool

► **whirl round** VI *(= turn suddenly) [person]* se retourner brusquement, virevolter ; *[revolving chair etc]* pivoter ; see also **whirl vi 1**
VT SEP 1 *[wind] [+ leaves, smoke]* faire tourbillonner, faire tournoyer ; *[+ dust, sand]* faire tourbillonner
2 *[+ sword, object on rope etc]* faire tournoyer ; *[+ revolving chair etc]* faire pivoter

whirligig /ˈwɜːlɪgɪg/ N 1 *(= toy)* moulin *m* à vent ; *(= merry-go-round)* manège *m* ; *(of events etc)* tourbillon *m (liter)* 2 (also **whirligig beetle**) tourniquet *m*, gyrin *m*

whirlpool /ˈwɜːlpuːl/ N tourbillon *m* COMP **whirlpool bath** N bain *m* à remous

whirlwind /ˈwɜːlwɪnd/ N tornade *f*, trombe *f* ; see also **sow²** ADJ *(fig)* éclair* *inv*

whirlybird* /ˈwɜːlɪbɜːd/ N *(US)* hélico* *m*, hélicoptère *m*

whirr /wɜːʳ/ VI *[bird's wings, insect's wings]* bruire ; *[cameras, machinery]* ronronner ; *(louder)* vrombir ; *[propellers]* vrombir ◆ **the helicopter went ~ing off** l'hélicoptère est parti en vrombissant N *[of bird's wings, insect's wings]* bruissement *m* (d'ailes) ; *[of machinery]* ronronnement *m* ; *(louder)* vrombissement *m* ; *[of propellers]* vrombissement *m*

whisk /wɪsk/ N 1 (also **egg whisk**) fouet *m* (à œufs) ; *(rotary)* batteur *m* à œufs
2 *(= movement)* ◆ **give the mixture a good ~** bien battre le mélange ◆ **with a ~ of his tail, the horse ...** d'un coup de queue, le cheval ...
VT 1 *(Culin: gen)* battre au fouet ; *[+ egg whites]* battre en neige ◆ **~ the eggs into the mixture** incorporez les œufs dans le mélange avec un fouet *or* en remuant vigoureusement
2 ◆ **the horse ~ed its tail** le cheval fouettait l'air de sa queue
3 ◆ **to ~ sth out of sb's hands** enlever brusquement *or* vivement qch des mains de qn ◆ **she ~ed the baby out of the pram** elle a sorti brusquement le bébé du landau ◆ **he ~ed it out of his pocket** il l'a brusquement sorti de sa poche ◆ **he ~ed me round the island in his sports car** il m'a fait faire le tour de l'île à toute allure dans sa voiture de sport ◆ **the lift ~ed us up to the top floor** l'ascenseur nous a emportés à toute allure jusqu'au dernier étage ◆ **he was ~ed into a meeting** on l'a brusquement entraîné dans une réunion ◆ **he ~ed her off to meet his mother** il l'a emmenée illico* faire la connaissance de sa mère
VI ◆ **to ~ along/in/out** *etc* filer/entrer/sortir *etc* à toute allure ◆ **I ~ed into the driveway** je me suis précipité dans l'allée ◆ **she ~ed past the photographers into the hotel** elle est passée en trombe *or* à toute allure devant les photographes et s'est précipitée dans l'hôtel ◆ **he ~ed through the pile of letters on his desk** il a parcouru rapidement la pile de lettres qui était sur son bureau

► **whisk away** VT SEP *[+ flies]* chasser ; *(fig = remove) [+ object]* faire disparaître

► **whisk off** VT SEP *[+ flies]* chasser ; *[+ lid, cover]* ôter brusquement ; *[+ garment]* enlever *or* ôter en quatrième vitesse* ◆ **they ~ed me off to hospital** ils m'ont emmené à l'hôpital sur le champ ; see also **whisk vt 3**

► **whisk together** VT SEP *(Culin)* mélanger en fouettant *or* avec un fouet

► **whisk up** VT SEP *(Culin)* fouetter ; see also **whisk vt 3**

whisker /ˈwɪskəʳ/ N *[of animal]* moustaches *fpl* ; *[of person]* poil *m* ◆ **~s** (also **side whiskers**) favoris *mpl* ; *(= beard)* barbe *f* ; *(= moustache)* moustache(s) *f(pl)* ◆ **he won the race by a ~** il s'en est fallu d'un cheveu *or* d'un poil* qu'il ne perde la course ◆ **they came within a ~ of being ...** il s'en est fallu d'un cheveu qu'ils ne soient ...

whiskered /ˈwɪskəd/ ADJ *[man, face] (= with side whiskers)* qui a des favoris ; *(= with beard)* barbu ; *(= with moustache)* moustachu ; *[animal]* qui a des moustaches

whiskery /ˈwɪskərɪ/ ADJ *[man, old woman]* au visage poilu ; *[face]* poilu

whiskey *(Ir, US)*, **whisky** *(Brit, Can)* /ˈwɪskɪ/ N whisky *m* ◆ **a ~ and soda** un whisky soda ; → **sour** COMP *[flavour]* de whisky

whisper /ˈwɪspəʳ/ VI *[person]* chuchoter, parler à voix basse ; *[leaves, water]* chuchoter, murmurer ◆ **to ~ to sb** parler *or* chuchoter à l'oreille de qn, parler à voix basse à qn ◆ **it's rude to ~** c'est mal élevé de chuchoter à l'oreille de quelqu'un ◆ **you'll have to ~** il faudra que vous parliez *subj* bas
VT chuchoter, dire à voix basse *(sth to sb* qch à qn ; *that* que) ◆ **he ~ed a word in my ear** il m'a dit *or* soufflé quelque chose à l'oreille ◆ **"where is she?" he ~ed** "où est-elle ?" dit-il à voix basse *or* murmura-t-il ◆ **it is (being) ~ed that ...** le bruit court que ..., on dit que ... ; → **sweet**
N *(= low tone)* chuchotement *m* ; *[of wind, leaves, water]* murmure *m*, bruissement *m* ; *(fig = rumour)* bruit *m*, rumeur *f* ◆ **I heard a ~** j'ai entendu un chuchotement, j'ai entendu quelqu'un qui parlait à voix basse ◆ **a ~ of voices** des chuchotements ◆ **to say/answer in a ~** dire/répondre à voix basse ◆ **to speak in a ~** *or* **~s** parler bas *or* à voix basse ◆ **her voice scarcely rose above a ~** sa voix n'était guère qu'un murmure ◆ **not a ~ to anyone!** n'en soufflez mot à personne ! ◆ **I've heard a ~ that he isn't coming back** j'ai entendu dire qu'il ne reviendrait pas ◆ **there is a ~ (going round) that ...** le bruit court que ..., on dit que ...

whispering /ˈwɪspərɪŋ/ ADJ *[person]* qui chuchote, qui parle à voix basse ; *[leaves, wind, stream]* qui chuchote, qui murmure ◆ **~ voices** des chuchotements *mpl* N *[of voice]* chuchotement *m* ; *[of leaves, wind, stream]* bruissement *m*, murmure *m* ; *(fig) (= gossip)* médisances *fpl* ;

(*= rumours*) rumeurs *fpl* insidieuses ◆ **there has been a lot of ~ about them** toutes sortes de rumeurs insidieuses ont couru sur leur compte

COMP **whispering campaign** N (*fig*) campagne *f* diffamatoire (insidieuse)

whispering gallery N galerie *f* à écho

whist /wɪst/ N (*Brit*) whist *m* COMP **whist drive** N tournoi *m* de whist

whistle /ˈwɪsl/ N 1 (*= sound*) (*made with mouth*) sifflement *m* ; (*= jeering*) sifflet *m* ; (*made with a whistle*) coup *m* de sifflet ; [*of factory*] sirène *f* (d'usine) ◆ **the ~s of the audience** (*= booing*) les sifflets *mpl* du public ; (*= cheering*) les sifflements *mpl* d'admiration du public ◆ **to give a ~** (*gen*) siffler ; (*= blow a whistle*) donner un coup de sifflet

2 [*of train, kettle, blackbird*] sifflement *m*

3 (*= object*) sifflet *m* ; (*Mus:* also **penny whistle**) pipeau *m* ◆ **a blast on a ~** un coup de sifflet strident ◆ **the referee blew his ~** l'arbitre a donné un coup de sifflet *or* a sifflé ◆ **the referee blew his ~ for half-time** l'arbitre a sifflé la mi-temps ◆ **to blow the ~ on sb** * (*fig = inform on*) dénoncer qn ◆ **to blow the ~ on sth** * tirer la sonnette d'alarme sur qch, dénoncer qch ◆ **he blew the ~ (on it)** * (*= informed on it*) il a dévoilé le pot aux roses * ; (*= put a stop to it*) il y a mis le holà

VI 1 [*person*] siffler ; (*tunefully, light-heartedly*) siffloter ; (*= blow a whistle*) donner un coup de sifflet, siffler ◆ **the audience booed and ~d** les spectateurs ont hué et sifflé ◆ **the audience cheered and ~d** les spectateurs ont manifesté leur enthousiasme par des acclamations et des sifflements ◆ **he strolled along whistling (away) gaily** il flânait en sifflotant gaiement ◆ **he ~d at me to stop** il a sifflé pour que je m'arrête *subj* ◆ **the boy was whistling at all the pretty girls** le garçon sifflait toutes les jolies filles ◆ **the crowd ~d at the referee** la foule a sifflé l'arbitre ◆ **he ~d to his dog** il a sifflé son chien ◆ **he ~d for a taxi** il a sifflé un taxi ◆ **the referee ~d for a foul** l'arbitre a sifflé une faute ◆ **he can ~ for it!** * il peut se brosser ! *, il peut toujours courir ! * ◆ **he's whistling in the dark** *or* **in the wind** il dit ça pour se rassurer, il essaie de se donner du courage

2 [*bird, bullet, wind, kettle, train*] siffler ◆ **the cars ~d by us** les voitures passaient devant nous à toute allure ◆ **an arrow ~d past his ear** une flèche a sifflé à son oreille

VT [*+ tune*] siffler ; (*casually, light-heartedly*) siffloter ◆ **to ~ a dog back/in** *etc* siffler un chien pour qu'il revienne/entre *subj etc*

COMP **whistle blower** * N (*fig*) dénonciateur *m*, -trice *f*, personne *f* qui tire la sonnette d'alarme

whistle-stop → **whistle-stop**

► **whistle up** * VT SEP (*fig*) dégoter * ◆ **he ~d up four or five people to give us a hand** il a dégoté * quatre ou cinq personnes prêtes à nous donner un coup de main ◆ **can you ~ up another blanket or two?** vous pouvez dégoter * *or* dénicher * encore une ou deux couvertures ?

whistle-stop /ˈwɪsl,stɒp/ N visite *f* éclair *inv* (*dans une petite ville au cours d'une campagne électorale*) ADJ ◆ **he made a ~ tour of Virginia** il a fait une tournée éclair en Virginie ◆ **a ~ town** (*US*) une petite ville *or* un petit trou * (*où le train s'arrête*) VI (*US*) faire une tournée électorale

Whit /wɪt/ N la Pentecôte

COMP [*holiday etc*] de Pentecôte

Whit Monday N le lundi de Pentecôte

Whit Sunday N le dimanche de Pentecôte

Whit Week N la semaine de Pentecôte

whit /wɪt/ N (*frm*) ◆ **there was not a** *or* **no ~ of truth in it** il n'y avait pas un brin de vérité là-dedans ◆ **he hadn't a ~ of sense** il n'avait pas un grain de bon sens ◆ **it wasn't a ~ better after he'd finished** quand il a eu terminé ce n'était pas mieux du tout ◆ **I don't care a ~** ça m'est profondément égal, je m'en moque complètement

white /waɪt/ ADJ 1 blanc (blanche *f*) ◆ **to go** *or* **turn ~** (*with fear, anger*) blêmir, pâlir ; [*hair*] blanchir ; [*object*] devenir blanc, blanchir ◆ **to be ~ with fear/rage** être blanc de peur/rage ◆ **he went ~ with fear** il a blêmi *or* pâli de peur ◆ **(as) ~ as a ghost** pâle comme la mort ◆ **(as) ~ as a sheet** pâle comme un linge, blanc comme un linge ◆ **as ~ as snow** blanc comme neige ◆ **this detergent gets the clothes whiter than ~** cette lessive lave encore plus blanc ◆ **the public likes politicians to be whiter-than-~** les gens aiment que les hommes politiques soient irréprochables

2 (*racially*) [*person, face, skin, race*] blanc (blanche *f*) ◆ **a ~ man** un Blanc ◆ **a ~ woman** une Blanche ◆ **the ~ South Africans** les Blancs *mpl* d'Afrique du Sud ◆ **~ supremacy** la suprématie de la race blanche ; see also **comp**

N 1 (*= colour*) blanc *m* ; (*= whiteness*) blancheur *f* ◆ **to be dressed in ~** être vêtu de blanc ◆ **his face was a deathly ~** son visage était d'une pâleur mortelle ◆ **the sheets were a dazzling ~** les draps étaient d'une blancheur éclatante ◆ **don't fire till you see the ~s of their eyes** (*Mil etc*) ne tirez qu'au dernier moment ; → **black**

2 [*of egg, eye*] blanc *m*

3 (* : also **white wine**) blanc *m*

4 ◆ **White** (*= person of White race*) Blanc *m*, Blanche *f* ; see also **poor**

NPL **whites** (*= linen etc*) ◆ **the ~s** le (linge) blanc ◆ **tennis ~s** (*= clothes*) tenue *f* de tennis

COMP **white blood cell** N globule *m* blanc

white bread N pain *m* blanc

white Christmas N Noël *m* sous la neige

white coat N blouse *f* blanche

white coffee N (*Brit*) café *m* au lait ; (*in café: when ordering*) café *m* crème

white-collar ADJ ◆ **a ~-collar job** un emploi de bureau ◆ **~-collar union** syndicat *m* d'employé(e)s de bureau *or* de cols blancs

white-collar crime N (*NonC = illegal activities*) criminalité *f* en col blanc ◆ **~-collar worker** employé(e) *m(f)* de bureau, col *m* blanc

white corpuscle N globule *m* blanc

whited sepulchre N (*fig*) sépulcre *m* blanchi, hypocrite *mf*

white dwarf N (*Astron*) naine *f* blanche

white elephant N (*fig*) (*= ornament*) objet *m* superflu ; (*= scheme, project, building*) gouffre *m* (financier) ◆ **it's a ~ elephant** c'est tout à fait superflu, on n'en a pas besoin

white elephant stall N étalage *m* de bibelots

white-faced ADJ blême, pâle

white feather N (*fig*) ◆ **to show the ~ feather** manquer de courage

white flag N drapeau *m* blanc

white fox N (*= animal*) renard *m* polaire ; (*= skin, fur*) renard *m* blanc

white frost N gelée *f* blanche

white gold N or *m* blanc

white goods NPL (*= domestic appliances*) appareils *mpl* ménagers ; (*= linens*) (linge *m*) blanc *m*

white-haired ADJ [*person*] aux cheveux blancs ; [*animal*] à poil blanc, aux poils blancs

white-headed ADJ [*person*] aux cheveux blancs ; [*bird*] à tête blanche ◆ **the ~-headed boy** (*fig*) l'enfant *m* chéri

white heat N (*Phys*) chaude *f* blanche, chaleur *f* d'incandescence ◆ **to raise metal to a ~ heat** chauffer un métal à blanc ◆ **the indignation of the crowd had reached ~ heat** l'indignation de la foule avait atteint son paroxysme

white hope N ◆ **to be the ~ hope of ...** être le grand espoir de ...

white horse N (*at sea*) ⇒ **whitecap**

white-hot ADJ chauffé à blanc

the White House N (*US*) la Maison-Blanche

white knight N (*Stock Exchange*) chevalier *m* blanc

white-knuckle ADJ (*= terrifying*) terrifiant ◆ **~-knuckle ride** manège *m* qui décoiffe * *or* qui fait dresser les cheveux sur la tête

white lead N blanc *m* de céruse

white lie N pieux mensonge *m*

white light N (*Phys*) lumière *f* blanche

white line N (*on road*) ligne *f* blanche

white list N (*Brit*) 1 (*= list of safe countries*) *en Grande-Bretagne, liste des pays considérés comme sûrs et dont les ressortissants ne peuvent par conséquent prétendre au statut de demandeur d'asile* 2 (*Comput: list of safe websites, e-mail addresses*) liste *f* blanche (*liste des sites web considérés comme sûrs*)

white-livered ADJ (*liter*) poltron, couard

white magic N magie *f* blanche

white meat N viande *f* blanche

white meter N (*Elec*) compteur *m* bleu ◆ **~ meter heating** chauffage *m* par accumulateur

the White Nile N le Nil Blanc

white noise N (*Acoustics*) bruit *m* blanc

White-Out ® N (*US*) Tipp-Ex ® *m*

white owl N harfang *m*, chouette *f* blanche

White Pages NPL (*Telec*) pages *fpl* blanches

white paper N (*Parl*) livre *m* blanc (*on* sur)

white pepper N poivre *m* blanc

white plague N (*US = tuberculosis*) tuberculose *f* pulmonaire

white rabbit N lapin *m* blanc

white raisin N (*US*) raisin *m* sec de Smyrne

white rhino *, **white rhinoceros** N rhinocéros *m* blanc

White Russia N Russie *f* Blanche

White Russian (*Geog, Hist, Pol*) ADJ russe blanc (russe blanche *f*) N Russe *m* blanc, Russe *f* blanche

white sale N (*Comm*) vente *f* de blanc

white sapphire N saphir *m* blanc

white sauce N (*savoury*) sauce *f* blanche ; (*sweet*) crème *f* pâtissière (*pour le plum-pudding de Noël*)

the White Sea N la mer Blanche

white settler N (*Hist*) colon *m* blanc ; (*fig pej = incomer*) *citadin arrogant qui va s'installer à la campagne*

white shark N requin *m* blanc

white slavery, the white slave trade N la traite des blanches

white spirit N (*Brit*) white-spirit *m*

white stick N [*of blind person*] canne *f* blanche

white-tailed eagle N orfraie *f*, pygargue *m*

white tie N (*= tie*) nœud *m* papillon blanc ; (*= suit*) habit *m*

white-tie ADJ ◆ **it was a ~-tie affair** l'habit était de rigueur ◆ **to wear ~-tie** être en tenue de soirée ◆ **a ~-tie dinner** un dîner chic *or* habillé

white trash * N (*NonC: US pej*) racaille *f* blanche

White Van Man N (*Brit*) conducteur *m* agressif

white water N (*esp Sport*) eau *f* vive

white-water rafting N rafting *m*

white wedding N mariage *m* en blanc

white whale N baleine *f* blanche

white wine N vin *m* blanc

white witch N *femme qui pratique la magie blanche*

whitebait /ˈwaɪtbeɪt/ N blanchaille *f* ; (*Culin*) petite friture *f*

whiteboard /ˈwaɪtbɔːd/ N tableau *m* blanc

whitecap /ˈwaɪtkæp/ N (*at sea*) mouton *m*

Whitehall /ˈwaɪt,hɔːl/ N (*Brit*) Whitehall *m* (*siège des ministères et des administrations publiques à Londres*)

whiten /ˈwaɪtn/ VTI blanchir

whitener /ˈwaɪtnəʳ/ N (*for coffee etc*) succédané *m* de lait en poudre ; (*for clothes*) agent *m* blanchissant

whiteness /ˈwaɪtnɪs/ N (*NonC*) 1 (*= colour*) [*of teeth, snow, cloth*] blancheur *f* 2 (*racial*) appartenance *f* à la race blanche 3 *(= paleness) [of person, face]* blancheur *f*, pâleur *f*

whitening /ˈwaɪtnɪŋ/ **N** *(NonC)* 1 *(= act) [of linen]* blanchiment *m*, décoloration *f* ; *[of hair]* blanchissement *m* ; *[of wall etc]* blanchiment *m* 2 *(substance: for shoes, doorsteps etc)* blanc *m*

whiteout /ˈwaɪtaʊt/ **N** visibilité *f* nulle *(à cause de la neige ou du brouillard)*

whitethorn /ˈwaɪtθɔːn/ **N** aubépine *f*

whitethroat /ˈwaɪtθrəʊt/ **N** *(= Old World warbler)* grisette *f* ; *(= American sparrow)* moineau *m* d'Amérique

whitewall tyre, whitewall tire *(US)* /ˈwaɪtwɔːltaɪəʳ/ **N** pneu *m* à flanc blanc

whitewash /ˈwaɪtwɒʃ/ **N** 1 *(NonC: for walls etc)* lait *m* or blanc *m* de chaux 2 *(fig)* **the article in the paper was nothing but a ~ of ...** l'article du journal ne visait qu'à blanchir ... 3 *(Sport *)* raclée* *f* **VT** 1 *[+ wall etc]* blanchir à la chaux, chauler 2 *(fig) [+ sb's reputation, actions]* blanchir ; *[+ incident]* étouffer ◆ **they tried to ~ the whole episode** ils ont essayé d'étouffer l'affaire 3 *(Sport *)* écraser complètement*

whitewood /ˈwaɪtwʊd/ **N** bois *m* blanc

whitey* /ˈwaɪtɪ/ **N** *(esp US pej) (= individual)* Blanc *m*, Blanche *f* ; *(= Whites collectively)* les Blancs *mpl*

whither /ˈwɪðəʳ/ **ADV** *(liter)* où ◆ **"whither the Government now?"** *(in headlines, titles etc)* "où va le gouvernement ?"

whiting[1] /ˈwaɪtɪŋ/ **N** (pl **whiting**) *(= fish)* merlan *m*

whiting[2] /ˈwaɪtɪŋ/ **N** *(NonC: for shoes, doorsteps etc)* blanc *m*

whitish /ˈwaɪtɪʃ/ **ADJ** blanchâtre

whitlow /ˈwɪtləʊ/ **N** panaris *m*

Whitsun /ˈwɪtsn/ **N** ⟶ **Whit**

Whitsun(tide) /ˈwɪtsn(taɪd)/ **N** les fêtes *fpl* de (la) Pentecôte, la Pentecôte

whittle /ˈwɪtl/ **VT** *[+ piece of wood]* tailler au couteau ◆ **to ~ sth out of a piece of wood, to ~ a piece of wood into sth** tailler qch au couteau dans un morceau de bois

▸ **whittle away** **VI** ◆ **to whittle away at sth** tailler qch au couteau **VT SEP** ⇒ **whittle down**

▸ **whittle down** **VT SEP** 1 *[+ wood]* tailler 2 *(fig) [+ costs, amount]* amenuiser, réduire ; *[+ proposal]* revoir à la baisse ◆ **he had ~d eight candidates down to two** sur les huit candidats, il en avait retenu deux

whiz(z) /wɪz/ **N** 1 *(= sound)* sifflement *m* 2 * champion* *m*, as *m* ◆ **a computer/marketing/financial ~(z)** un as de l'informatique/du marketing/des finances ◆ **he's a ~(z) at tennis/cards** c'est un as du tennis/des jeux de cartes ◆ **she's a real ~(z) with a paintbrush** elle se débrouille comme un chef* avec un pinceau 3 *(NonC * = amphetamine)* amphés* *fpl* **VI** filer à toute allure *or* comme une flèche ◆ **to ~(z)** *or* **go ~zing through the air** fendre l'air (en sifflant) ◆ **to ~(z) along/past** *etc (in car)* filer/passer *etc* à toute vitesse *or* à toute allure ◆ **bullets ~zed by** les balles sifflaient ◆ **I'll just ~(z) over to see him** * je file* le voir ◆ **she ~zed off* to Hong Kong on business** elle a filé* à Hong-Kong pour affaires **VT** 1 * *(= throw)* lancer, filer* ; *(= transfer quickly)* apporter ◆ **he ~zed it round to us as soon as it was ready** il nous l'a apporté *or* passé dès que ça a été prêt 2 (also **whiz(z) up** : *in blender)* mixer

COMP **whiz(z)-bang*** **N** *(Mil = shell)* obus *m* ; *(= firework)* pétard *m* **ADJ** *(US = excellent)* du tonnerre*

whiz(z) kid* **N** ◆ **she's a real ~(z) kid at maths** elle a vraiment la bosse* des maths

WHO /ˌdʌbljuːeɪtʃˈəʊ/ **N** (abbrev of **World Health Organization**) OMS *f*

who /huː/ **PRON** 1 *(interrog: also used instead of "whom" in spoken English)* (qui est-ce) qui ; *(after prep)* qui ◆ **~'s there?** qui est là ? ◆ **~ are you?** qui êtes-vous ? ◆ **~ has the book?** (qui est-ce) qui a le livre ? ◆ **~ does he think he is?** il se prend pour qui ?, pour qui il se prend ? ◆ **~ came with you?** (qui est-ce) qui est venu avec vous ? ◆ **~ should it be but Robert!** c'était Robert, qui d'autre ! ◆ **I don't know ~'s ~ in the office** je ne connais pas très bien les gens au bureau ◆ **you remind me of somebody! – ~?** vous me rappelez quelqu'un ! – qui donc ? ◆ **~(m) did you see?** vous avez vu qui ?, qui avez-vous vu ? ◆ **~(m) do you work for?** pour qui travaillez-vous ? ◆ **~(m) did you speak to?** à qui avez-vous parlé ?, vous avez parlé à qui ? ◆ **~'s the book by?** le livre est de qui ? ◆ **~(m) were you with?** vous étiez avec qui ? ◆ **you-know-~ said ...** qui vous savez a dit ... ◆ **~ is he to tell me ...?** *(indignantly)* de quel droit est-ce qu'il me dit ... ? ◆ **you can't sing – WHO can't?** tu es incapable de chanter – ah bon ! tu crois ça !

2 *(rel)* qui ◆ **my aunt ~ lives in London** ma tante qui habite à Londres ◆ **he ~ wishes to object must do so now** quiconque désire élever une objection doit le faire maintenant ◆ **those ~ can swim** ceux qui savent nager ◆ **~ is not with me is against me** *(Bible)* celui qui *or* quiconque n'est pas pour moi est contre moi

COMP **"Who's Who"** **N** ≈ "Bottin mondain"

whoa /wəʊ/ **EXCL** 1 (also **whoa there**) ho !, holà ! 2 *(in excitement, triumph)* ouah !*

who'd /huːd/ ⇒ **who had, who would** ; ⟶ **who**

whodun(n)it* /ˌhuːˈdʌnɪt/ **N** roman *m (or* film *m or* feuilleton *m etc)* policier (à énigme), polar* *m*

whoe'er /huːˈeəʳ/ *(liter)* **PRON** ⇒ **whoever**

whoever /huːˈevəʳ/ **PRON** *(also used instead of "whomever" in spoken English)* 1 *(= anyone that)* quiconque ◆ **~ wishes may come with me** quiconque le désire peut venir avec moi ◆ **you can give it to ~ wants it** vous pouvez le donner à qui le veut *or* voudra ◆ **~ finds it can keep it** quiconque *or* celui qui le trouvera pourra le garder ◆ **~ gets home first does the cooking** celui qui rentre le premier prépare à manger, le premier rentré à la maison prépare à manger ◆ **~ said that was an idiot** celui qui a dit ça était un imbécile ◆ **ask ~ you like** demandez à qui vous voulez *or* voudrez

2 *(= no matter who)* ◆ **~ you are, come in !** qui que vous soyez, entrez ! ◆ **~ he plays for next season ...** quelle que soit l'équipe dans laquelle il jouera la saison prochaine ...

3 *(*: interrog: emphatic)* qui donc ◆ **~ told you that?** qui donc vous a dit ça ?, qui a bien pu vous dire ça ? ◆ **~ did you give it to?** vous l'avez donné à qui ?

whole /həʊl/ **LANGUAGE IN USE 26.3**

ADJ 1 *(= entire) (+ sg n)* tout, entier ; *(+ pl n)* entier ◆ **along its ~ length** sur toute sa longueur ◆ **~ villages were destroyed** des villages entiers ont été détruits ◆ **the ~ road was like that** toute la route était comme ça ◆ **the ~ world** le monde entier ◆ **he used a ~ notebook** il a utilisé un carnet entier ◆ **he swallowed it ~** il l'a avalé tout entier ◆ **the pig was roasted ~** le cochon était rôti tout entier ◆ **we waited a ~ hour** nous avons attendu une heure entière *or* toute une heure ◆ **it rained (for) three ~ days** il a plu trois jours entiers ◆ **but the ~ man eludes us** mais l'homme tout entier reste un mystère pour nous ◆ **is that the ~ truth?** est-ce que c'est bien toute la vérité ? ◆ **but the ~ point of it was to avoid that** mais tout l'intérêt de la chose était d'éviter cela ◆ **with my ~ heart** de tout mon cœur ◆ **he took the ~ lot** * il a pris le tout ◆ **the ~ lot of you** * vous tous, tous tant que vous êtes ◆ **it's a ~ lot* better** c'est vraiment beaucoup mieux ◆ **there are a ~ lot* of things I'd like to tell her** il y a tout un tas de choses que j'aimerais lui dire ◆ **to go the ~ hog*** aller jusqu'au bout des choses, ne pas faire les choses à moitié ◆ **to go (the) ~ hog* for sb/sth** *(US)* essayer par tous les moyens de conquérir qn/d'obtenir qch ; see also **comp**

2 *(= intact, unbroken)* intact, complet (-ète *f*) ◆ **not a glass was left ~ after the party** il ne restait pas un seul verre intact après la fête ◆ **keep the egg yolks ~** gardez les jaunes entiers ◆ **he has a ~ set of Dickens** il a une série complète des œuvres de Dickens ◆ **to our surprise he came back ~** à notre grande surprise il est revenu sain et sauf ◆ **the seal on the letter was still ~** le sceau sur la lettre était encore intact ◆ **made out of ~ cloth** *(US fig)* inventé de toutes pièces ◆ **his hand was made ~** *(†† = healed)* sa main a été guérie

N 1 *(= the entire amount of)* **the ~ of the morning** toute la matinée ◆ **the ~ of the time** tout le temps ◆ **the ~ of the apple was bad** la pomme toute entière était gâtée ◆ **the ~ of Paris was snowbound** Paris était complètement bloqué par la neige ◆ **the ~ of Paris was talking about it** dans tout Paris on parlait de ça ◆ **nearly the ~ of our output this year** presque toute notre production *or* presque la totalité de notre production cette année ◆ **he received the ~ of the amount** il a reçu la totalité de la somme

♦ **on the whole** dans l'ensemble

2 *(= complete unit)* tout *m* ◆ **four quarters make a ~** quatre quarts font un tout *or* un entier ◆ **the ~ may be greater than the sum of its parts** le tout peut être plus grand que la somme de ses parties ◆ **the estate is to be sold as a ~** la propriété doit être vendue en bloc ◆ **considered as a ~ the play was successful, although some scenes ...** dans l'ensemble, la pièce était réussie, bien que certaines scènes ...

COMP **whole-hog*** **ADJ** *(esp US) [support]* sans réserve(s), total ; *[supporter]* acharné, ardent *before n* **ADV** jusqu'au bout ; see also **adj 1**

whole-hogger* **N** *(esp US)* ◆ **to be a ~-hogger** *(gen)* se donner entièrement à ce qu'on fait ; *(Pol)* être jusqu'au-boutiste

whole milk **N** lait *m* entier

whole note **N** *(Mus)* ronde *f*

whole number **N** *(Math)* nombre *m* entier

whole step **N** *(US Mus)* ⇒ **whole tone**

whole tone **N** ton *m* entier

wholefood(s) /ˈhəʊlfuːd(z)/ *(Brit)* **N(PL)** aliments *mpl* complets **COMP** **wholefood restaurant** **N** restaurant *m* diététique

wholegrain /ˈhəʊlgreɪn/ **ADJ** *[bread, flour, rice]* complet (-ète *f*)

wholehearted /ˌhəʊlˈhɑːtɪd/ **ADJ** *[approval, admiration]* sans réserve ; *[supporter]* inconditionnel ◆ **they made a ~ attempt to do ...** ils ont mis tout leur enthousiasme à faire ...

wholeheartedly /ˌhəʊlˈhɑːtɪdlɪ/ **ADV** *[accept, approve, support]* sans réserve ◆ **to agree ~** être entièrement *or* totalement d'accord

wholemeal /ˈhəʊlmiːl/ **ADJ** *(Brit) [flour, bread]* complet (-ète *f*)

wholeness /ˈhəʊlnɪs/ **N** complétude *f*

wholesale /ˈhəʊlseɪl/ **N** *(NonC: Comm)* (vente *f* en) gros *m* ◆ **at** *or* **by ~** en gros **ADJ** 1 *(Comm) [price, trade]* de gros 2 *(= indiscriminate) [slaughter, destruction]* systématique ; *[change]* gros (grosse *f*) ; *[reform, rejection]* en bloc ; *[privatisation]* complet (-ète *f*) ◆ **there has been ~ sacking of unskilled workers** il y a eu des licenciements en masse parmi les manœuvres **ADV** 1 *(Comm) [buy, sell]* en gros ◆ **I can get it for you ~** je peux vous le faire avoir au prix de gros 2 *(= indiscriminately) [slaughter, destroy]* systémati-

quement ; *[sack]* en masse ; *[reject, accept]* en bloc
COMP **wholesale dealer, wholesale merchant** N grossiste *mf*, marchand(e) *m(f)* en gros **wholesale price index** N indice *m* des prix de gros
wholesale trader N ⇒ **wholesale dealer**

wholesaler /ˈhəʊlseɪləʳ/ N *(Comm)* grossiste *mf*, marchand(e) *m(f)* en gros

wholesaling /ˈhəʊlseɪlɪŋ/ N *(NonC)* commerce *m* de gros

wholesome /ˈhəʊlsəm/ ADJ *[food, life, thoughts, book, person]* sain ; *[air, climate]* sain, salubre ; *[exercise, advice]* salutaire

wholesomeness /ˈhəʊlsəmnɪs/ N *[of food, life, thoughts, book, person]* caractère *m* sain ; *[of air, climate]* salubrité *f*

wholewheat /ˈhəʊlwiːt/ ADJ *[flour, bread]* complet (-ète *f*)

wholism /ˈhəʊlɪzəm/ N ⇒ **holism**

wholistic /həʊˈlɪstɪk/ ADJ ⇒ **holistic**

who'll /huːl/ ⇒ **who will, who shall** ; → **who**

wholly /ˈhəʊlɪ/ ADV *[unacceptable, unreliable]* totalement ; *[satisfactory]* totalement, tout à fait ; *[approve, trust, justify]* entièrement ◆ **I'm not ~ convinced** je n'en suis pas totalement *or* tout à fait convaincu COMP **wholly-owned subsidiary** N *(Jur, Econ)* filiale *f* à cent pour cent

whom /huːm/ PRON 1 *(interrog: often replaced by "who" in spoken English)* qui ◆ **~ did you see?** qui avez-vous vu ? ◆ **when was the photo taken and by ~?** quand est-ce que la photo a été prise et par qui ? ◆ **with ~?** avec qui ? ◆ **to ~?** à qui ? ; see also **who pron 1** 2 *(rel)* **my aunt, ~ I love dearly** ma tante, que j'aime tendrement ◆ **those ~ he had seen recently** ceux qu'il avait vus récemment ◆ **the man to ~ ...** l'homme à qui ..., l'homme auquel ... ◆ **the man of ~ ...** l'homme dont ... ◆ **the woman with ~ he had an affair** la femme avec qui il a eu une liaison ◆ **my daughters, both of ~ are married** mes filles, qui sont toutes les deux mariées ◆ **~ the gods love die young** *(liter)* ceux qui sont aimés des dieux meurent jeunes

whomever /huːmˈevəʳ/ PRON accusative case of **whoever**

whomp * /wɒmp/ *(US)* VT *(= hit)* cogner* ; *(= defeat)* enfoncer* N bruit *m* sourd

whomping * /ˈwɒmpɪŋ/ ADJ *(US:* also **whomping big, whomping great)** énorme

whomsoever /ˌhuːmsəʊˈevəʳ/ PRON *(emphatic)* accusative case of **whosoever**

whoop /huːp/ N cri *m* (de joie, de triomphe) ; *(Med)* toux *f* coquelucheuse, toux *f* convulsive (de la coqueluche) ◆ **with a ~ of glee/triumph** avec un cri de joie/de triomphe VI pousser des cris ; *(Med)* avoir des quintes de toux coquelucheuse VT ◆ **to ~ it up** †* faire la noce* *or* la bombe* COMP **whooping cough** N coqueluche *f*

whoopee /wʊˈpiː/ EXCL hourra !, youpi ! N ◆ **to make ~** †* faire la noce* *or* la bombe* COMP **whoopee cushion** * N coussin(-péteur) *m* de farces et attrapes

whoops /wʊps/ EXCL (also **whoops-a-daisy**) *(avoiding fall etc)* oups !, houp-là ! ; *(lifting child)* houp-là !, hop-là !

whoosh /wʊʃ/ EXCL zoum ! N ◆ **the ~ of sledge runners in the snow** le bruit des patins de luges glissant sur la neige, le glissement des patins de luges sur la neige VI ◆ **the car ~ed past** la voiture est passée à toute allure dans un glissement de pneus

whop ⁑ /wɒp/ VT *(= beat)* rosser* ; *(= defeat)* battre à plate(s) couture(s)

whopper * /ˈwɒpəʳ/ N *(car/parcel/nose etc)* voiture *f*/colis *m*/nez *m etc* énorme ◆ **as comets go, it is a ~** c'est une comète énorme ◆ **a ~ of a nose** un pif énorme ◆ **the biggest ~ the president told** le mensonge le plus énorme que le président ait dit

whopping /ˈwɒpɪŋ/ ADJ * *[lie, loss]* énorme ◆ **to win a ~ 89 per cent of the vote** remporter les élections avec une écrasante majorité de 89 pour cent ◆ **a ~ $31 billion** la somme énorme de 31 milliards de dollars ADV ◆ **~ great** *or* **big** * énorme N ⁑ raclée* *f*

whore /hɔːʳ/ N (⁑ *pej)* putain⁑ *f* VI *(lit:* also **go whoring)** courir la gueuse, se débaucher ◆ **to ~ after sth** *(fig liter)* se prostituer pour obtenir qch

who're /ˈhuːəʳ/ ⇒ **who are** ; → **who**

whorehouse ⁑ /ˈhɔːˌhɒʊs/ N bordel⁑ *m*

whoremonger † /ˈhɔːmʌŋgəʳ/ N fornicateur *m* ; (= *pimp)* proxénète *m*, souteneur *m*

whorish ⁑ /ˈhɔːrɪʃ/ ADJ de putain⁑, putassier⁑*

whorl /wɜːl/ N *[of fingerprint]* volute *f* ; *[of spiral shell]* spire *f* ; *[of plant]* verticille *m* ◆ **~s of meringue/cream** des tortillons *mpl* de meringue/crème

whortleberry /ˈwɜːtlbərɪ/ N myrtille *f*

who's /huːz/ ⇒ **who is, who has** ; → **who**

whose /huːz/ POSS PRON à qui ◆ **~ is this?** à qui est ceci ? ◆ **I know ~ it is** je sais à qui c'est ◆ **~ is this hat?** à qui est ce chapeau ? ◆ **here's a lollipop each – let's see ~ lasts longest!** voici une sucette chacun – voyons celle de qui durera le plus longtemps ! POSS ADJ 1 *(interrog)* à qui, de qui ◆ **~ hat is this?** à qui est ce chapeau ? ◆ **~ son are you?** de qui êtes-vous le fils ? ◆ **~ book is missing?** à qui est le livre qui manque ? ◆ **~ fault is it?** qui est responsable ? 2 *(rel use)* dont, de qui ◆ **the man ~ hat I took** l'homme dont j'ai pris le chapeau ◆ **the boy ~ sister I was talking to** le garçon à la sœur duquel *or* à la sœur de qui je parlais ◆ **those ~ passports I've got here** ceux dont j'ai les passeports ici

whosever /huːˈzevəʳ/ POSS PRON ⇒ **of whomever** ; → **whoever** ◆ **~ book you use, you must take care of it** peu importe à qui est le livre dont tu te sers, il faut que tu en prennes soin

whosoever *(emphatic)* /ˌhuːsəʊˈevəʳ/, **whosoe'er** *(liter)* /ˌhuːsəʊˈɛəʳ/ PRON ⇒ **whoever**

who've /huːv/ ⇒ **who have** ; → **who**

whup ⁑ /wʌp/ VT *(US⁑)* ⇒ **whop**

why /waɪ/ LANGUAGE IN USE 17.1
ADV pourquoi ◆ **~ did you do it?** pourquoi l'avez-vous fait ? ◆ **I wonder ~ he left her** je me demande pourquoi il l'a quittée ◆ **I wonder ~** je me demande pourquoi ◆ **he told me ~ he did it** il m'a dit pourquoi il l'a fait *or* la raison pour laquelle il l'a fait ◆ **~ not?** pourquoi pas ? ◆ **~ not phone her?** pourquoi ne pas lui téléphoner ? ◆ **~ ask her when you don't have to?** pourquoi le lui demander quand vous n'êtes pas obligé de le faire ?
EXCL *(esp US †)* eh bien !, tiens ! ◆ **~, what's the matter?** eh bien, qu'est-ce qui ne va pas ? ◆ **~, it's you!** tiens, c'est vous ! ◆ **~, it's quite easy!** voyons donc, ce n'est pas difficile !
CONJ ◆ **the reasons ~ he did it** les raisons pour lesquelles il l'a fait ◆ **there's no reason ~ you shouldn't try again** il n'y a pas de raison (pour) que tu n'essaies *subj* pas de nouveau ◆ **that's (the reason) ~** voilà pourquoi ◆ **that is ~ I never spoke to him again** c'est pourquoi je ne lui ai jamais reparlé
N ◆ **the ~(s) and (the) wherefore(s)** le pourquoi et le comment ◆ **the ~ and (the) how** le pourquoi et le comment

whyever * /waɪˈevəʳ/ ADV *(interrog: emphatic)* pourquoi donc ◆ **~ did you do that?** * pourquoi donc est-ce que vous avez fait ça ?

WI /ˌdʌbljuːˈaɪ/ N 1 *(Brit)* (abbrev of **Women's Institute)** → **woman** 2 abbrev of **Wisconsin** 3 (abbrev of **West Indies)** → **west**

wibbly-wobbly * /ˌwɪblɪˈwɒblɪ/ ADJ ⇒ **wobbly**

wick /wɪk/ N mèche *f* ◆ **he gets on my ~** * *(Brit)* il me tape sur le système*, il me court sur le haricot*

wicked /ˈwɪkɪd/ ADJ 1 *(= immoral) [person]* méchant, mauvais ; *[behaviour, act, deed]* vilain *before n* ; *[system, policy, attempt, world]* pernicieux ◆ **that was a ~ thing to do!** c'était vraiment méchant (de faire ça) ! ◆ **a ~ waste** un scandaleux gâchis ; → **rest** 2 *(= nasty) [comment]* méchant ◆ **to have a ~ temper** avoir mauvais caractère 3 *(= naughty) [grin, look, suggestion]* malicieux ; *[sense of humour]* plein de malice ◆ **a ~ cake/pudding** un gâteau/dessert à vous damner 4 *(* = skilful)* **that was a ~ shot!** quel beau coup ! ◆ **he plays a ~ game of draughts** il joue super bien* aux dames 5 *(* = excellent)* super* *inv* ◆ **I've just won again: ~!** je viens encore de gagner : super !*

wickedly /ˈwɪkɪdlɪ/ ADV 1 *(= immorally) [behave]* méchamment ◆ **a ~ destructive child** un enfant méchant et destructeur ◆ **a ~ cruel act** un acte méchant et cruel ◆ **he ~ destroyed ...** méchamment, il a détruit ... 2 *(= naughtily) [grin, look at, suggest]* malicieusement ◆ **~ funny** drôle et caustique ◆ **~ seductive** malicieusement séducteur (-trice *f*) ◆ **a ~ rich pudding** un dessert terriblement *or* méchamment* riche 3 *(* = skilfully) [play]* comme un chef*, super bien*

wickedness /ˈwɪkɪdnɪs/ N *[of behaviour, order, decision, person]* méchanceté *f*, cruauté *f* ; *[of murder]* horreur *f*, atrocité *f* ; *[of look, smile, suggestion]* malice *f* ; *[of waste]* scandale *m*

wicker /ˈwɪkəʳ/ N *(NonC) (= substance)* osier *m* ; (= *objects:* also **wickerwork)** vannerie *f* COMP (also **wickerwork)** *[basket, chair]* d'osier, en osier

wicket /ˈwɪkɪt/ N 1 *(= door, gate)* (petite) porte *f*, portillon *m* ; *(for bank teller etc)* guichet *m* 2 *(Cricket) (= stumps)* guichet *m* ; *(= pitch between them)* terrain *m (entre les guichets)* ◆ **to lose/take a ~** perdre/prendre un guichet ; → **losing, sticky** COMP **wicket-keeper** N *(Cricket)* gardien *m* de guichet

wickiup /ˈwɪkɪˌʌp/ N *(US)* hutte *f* de branchages

widdershins /ˈwɪdəʃɪnz/ ADV *(esp Scot)* ⇒ **withershins**

widdle * /ˈwɪdl/ VI *(Brit)* faire pipi*

wide /waɪd/ ADJ 1 *(= broad) [road, river, strip]* large ; *[margin]* grand ; *[garment]* large, ample ; *[ocean, desert]* immense, vaste ; *[circle, gap, space]* large, grand ; *(fig) [knowledge]* vaste, très étendu ; *[choice, selection]* grand, considérable ; *[survey, study]* de grande envergure ◆ **how ~ is the room?** quelle est la largeur de la pièce ? ◆ **it is 5 metres ~** cela a *or* fait 5 mètres de large ◆ **the ~ Atlantic** l'immense *or* le vaste Atlantique ◆ **no one/nowhere in the whole ~ world** personne/nulle part au monde ◆ **she stared, her eyes ~ with fear** elle regardait, les yeux agrandis de peur *or* par la peur ◆ **mouth ~ with astonishment** bouche *f* bée de stupeur ◆ **a man with ~ views** *or* **opinions** un homme aux vues larges ◆ **he has ~ interests** il a des goûts très éclectiques ◆ **in the widest sense of the word** au sens le plus général *or* le plus large du mot ◆ **it has a ~ variety of uses** cela se prête à une grande variété d'usages
2 *(= off target)* ◆ **the shot/ball/arrow was ~** le coup/la balle/la flèche est passé(e) à côté ◆ **it was ~ of the target** c'était loin de la cible ; → **mark²**

ADV ◆ **the bullet went** ~ la balle est passée à côté ◆ **he flung the door** ~ il a ouvert la porte en grand ◆ **they are set** ~ **apart** *[trees, houses, posts]* ils sont largement espacés ; *[eyes]* ils sont très écartés ◆ **he stood with his legs** ~ **apart** il se tenait debout les jambes très écartées ◆ **to open one's eyes** ~ ouvrir grand les yeux *or* ses yeux en grand ◆ **"open wide!"** *(at dentist's)* "ouvrez grand !" ◆ ~ **open** *[door, window]* grand ouvert ◆ **the race was still** ~ **open** l'issue de la course était encore indécise ◆ **he left himself** ~ **open to criticism** il a prêté le flanc à la critique ◆ **to blow sth** ~ **open** *(= change completely)* révolutionner qch ◆ **he threatened to blow the operation** ~ **open** *(= reveal secret)* il a menacé de tout révéler sur l'opération ; → **far**

COMP **wide-angle lens** N *(Phot)* objectif *m* grand-angulaire, objectif *m* grand angle *inv*

wide area network N *(Comput)* grand réseau *m*

wide-awake ADJ *(lit)* bien *or* tout éveillé ; *(fig)* éveillé, alerte

wide-bodied aircraft, wide-body aircraft N avion *m* à fuselage élargi, gros-porteur *m*

wide boy ‡ N *(Brit pej)* arnaqueur * *m*

wide-eyed ADJ *(in naïveté)* aux yeux grands ouverts *or* écarquillés ; *(in fear, surprise)* aux yeux écarquillés ADV les yeux écarquillés ◆ **in ~-eyed amazement** les yeux écarquillés par la stupeur

wide-mouthed ADJ *[river]* à l'embouchure large ; *[cave]* avec une vaste entrée ; *[bottle]* au large goulot ; *[bag]* large du haut

wide-ranging ADJ *[mind, report, survey]* de grande envergure ; *[interests]* divers, variés

wide screen N *(Cine)* écran *m* panoramique

-wide /waɪd/ ADJ, ADV *(in compounds)* → **country-wide, nationwide**

widely /ˈwaɪdlɪ/ ADV 1 *(= generally) [available]* généralement ; *[used, regarded, expected]* largement ; *[known]* bien ◆ **it is** ~ **believed that ...** on pense communément *or* généralement que ... ◆ **~-held opinions** opinions *fpl* très répandues 2 *(= much) [travel, vary]* beaucoup ; *[scatter, spread]* sur une grande étendue ◆ ~ **different** extrêmement différent ◆ **the trees were** ~ **spaced** les arbres étaient largement espacés ◆ **the talks ranged** ~ les pourparlers ont porté sur des questions très diverses ◆ **to be** ~ **read** *[author, book]* être très lu ; *[reader]* avoir beaucoup lu ◆ **she is** ~ **read in philosophy** elle a beaucoup lu d'ouvrages de philosophie 3 *(= broadly)* ◆ **to smile** ~ avoir un large sourire

widen /ˈwaɪdn/ VT *[+ circle, gap, space]* élargir, agrandir ; *[+ road, river, strip, garment]* élargir ; *[+ margin]* augmenter ; *[+ knowledge]* accroître, élargir ; *[+ survey, study]* élargir la portée de ◆ **to** ~ **one's lead over sb** *(in election, race etc)* accroître son avance sur qn VI (also **widen out**) s'élargir, s'agrandir

wideness /ˈwaɪdnɪs/ N largeur *f*

widespread /ˈwaɪdspred/ ADJ 1 *(= general) [belief, opinion]* très répandu ; *[confusion]* général ; *[corruption]* généralisé ; *[support]* très important, considérable ◆ **food shortages are** ~ la disette est générale ◆ **the** ~ **availability of this drug** la facilité avec laquelle on peut se procurer cette drogue ◆ **the** ~ **availability of meat-free meals** le fait qu'on trouve très facilement des plats sans viande 2 *(= open) [arms]* en croix ; *[wings]* déployé

widgeon /ˈwɪdʒən/ N canard *m* siffleur

widget * /ˈwɪdʒɪt/ N *(= device)* gadget *m* ; *(= thingummy)* truc * *m*, machin * *m*

widow /ˈwɪdəʊ/ N veuve *f* ◆ ~ **Smith** † la veuve Smith ◆ **she's a golf** ~ son mari la délaisse pour aller jouer au golf ; → **grass, mite, weed** VT ◆ **to be ~ed** *[man]* devenir veuf ; *[woman]* devenir veuve ◆ **she was ~ed in 1989** elle est devenue veuve en 1989, elle a perdu son mari en 1989 ◆ **she has been ~ed for ten years** elle est veuve depuis dix ans ◆ **he lives with his ~ed mother** il vit avec sa mère qui est veuve

COMP **widow's benefit** N ⇒ **widow's pension**

widow's peak N pousse *f* de cheveux en V sur le front

widow's pension N *(Admin)* ≈ allocation *f* de veuvage

widow's walk N *(US)* belvédère *m (construit sur le faîte d'une maison côtière)*

widower /ˈwɪdəʊəʳ/ N veuf *m*

widowhood /ˈwɪdəʊhʊd/ N veuvage *m*

width /wɪdθ/ N 1 *(NonC) [of road, river, strip, bed, ocean, desert, gap, space, margin]* largeur *f* ; *[of garment]* ampleur *f* ; *[of circle]* largeur *f*, diamètre *m* ◆ **what is the** ~ **of the room?** quelle est la largeur de la pièce ?, quelle largeur a la pièce ? ◆ **it is 5 metres in** ~, **its** ~ **is 5 metres, it has a** ~ **of 5 metres** ça fait 5 mètres de large ◆ **measure it across its** ~ prends la mesure en largeur 2 *[of cloth]* largeur *f*, lé *m* ◆ **you'll get it out of one** ~ une largeur *or* un lé te suffira

widthways /ˈwɪdθweɪz/, **widthwise** /ˈwɪdθwaɪz/ ADV en largeur

wield /wiːld/ VT 1 *[+ sword, axe, pen, tool]* manier ; *(= brandish)* brandir 2 *[+ power, authority, control]* exercer

wiener * /ˈwiːnəʳ/ *(US)* N saucisse *f* de Francfort COMP **wiener schnitzel** /ˈviːnəˈʃnɪtsəl/ N escalope *f* viennoise

wienie * /ˈwiːnɪ/ N *(US)* saucisse *f* de Francfort

wife /waɪf/ (pl **wives**) N 1 *(= spouse)* femme *f* ; *(esp Admin)* épouse *f* ; *(= married woman)* femme *f* mariée ◆ **his second** ~ sa deuxième *or* seconde femme, la femme qu'il a *(or* avait *etc)* épousée en secondes noces ◆ **the farmer's/butcher's** *etc* ~ la fermière/bouchère *etc* ◆ **the** ~ ‡ la patronne * ◆ **he decided to take a** ~ † il a décidé de se marier *or* de prendre femme † ◆ **to take sb to** ~ † prendre qn pour femme ◆ **wives whose husbands have reached the age of 65** les femmes *fpl* mariées dont les maris ont atteint 65 ans ◆ **"The Merry Wives of Windsor"** "Les Joyeuses Commères de Windsor" ; → **working**

2 († * *dial = woman)* bonne femme * *f* ◆ **she's a poor old** ~ c'est une pauvre vieille ; → **old**

COMP **wife-batterer, wife-beater** N homme *m* qui bat sa femme

wife's equity N *(US Jur)* part *f* de la communauté revenant à la femme en cas de divorce

wife-swapping N échangisme *m* ◆ **~-swapping party** partie *f* carrée

wifely † /ˈwaɪflɪ/ ADJ de bonne épouse

wifi /ˈwaɪfaɪ/ (abbrev of **wireless fidelity**) N wifi *m*, sans fil *m* ADJ *[hotspot, network]* wifi, sans fil

wig /wɪg/ N *(gen)* perruque *f* ; *(= hairpiece)* postiche *m* ; (‡ *= hair)* tignasse * *f*

▸ **wig out** ‡ VI *(Brit) (= go crazy)* dérailler * ; *(= dance)* se déchaîner

wigeon /ˈwɪdʒən/ N ⇒ **widgeon**

wigging † ‡ /ˈwɪgɪŋ/ N *(Brit = scolding)* attrapade ‡ *f*, réprimande *f* ◆ **to give sb a** ~ passer un savon * à qn ◆ **to get a** ~ se faire enguirlander *

wiggle /ˈwɪgl/ VT *[+ pencil, stick]* agiter ; *[+ toes]* agiter, remuer ; *[+ loose screw, button, tooth]* faire jouer ◆ **to** ~ **one's hips** tortiller des hanches ◆ **my finger hurts if you** ~ **it like that** j'ai mal quand vous me tortillez le doigt comme ça ◆ **he ~d his finger at me warningly** il a agité l'index dans ma direction en guise d'avertissement VI *[loose screw etc]* branler ; *[tail]* remuer, frétiller ; *[rope, snake, worm]* se tortiller ◆ **she ~d across the room** elle a traversé la pièce en se déhanchant *or* en tortillant des hanches N ◆ **to walk with a** ~ marcher en se déhanchant, marcher en tortillant des hanches ◆ **to give sth a** ~ ⇒ **to wiggle sth** ; → vt COMP **wiggle room** N marge *f* de manœuvre

wiggly /ˈwɪglɪ/ ADJ *[snake, worm]* qui se tortille ◆ **a** ~ **line** un trait ondulé

wight †† /waɪt/ N être *m*

wigmaker /ˈwɪgmeɪkəʳ/ N perruquier *m*, -ière *f*

wigwam /ˈwɪgwæm/ N wigwam *m*

wilco /ˈwɪlˌkəʊ/ EXCL *(Telec)* message reçu !

wild /waɪld/ ADJ 1 *[animal, plant, tribe, man, land, countryside]* sauvage ◆ **it was growing** ~ *(= uncultivated)* ça poussait à l'état sauvage ◆ **the plant in its** ~ **state** la plante à l'état sauvage ◆ **a** ~ **stretch of coastline** une côte sauvage ◆ ~ **and woolly** * *(US)* fruste, primitif ◆ **to sow one's** ~ **oats** *(fig)* jeter sa gourme †, faire les quatre cents coups ◆ ~ **horses wouldn't make me tell you** je ne te le dirais pour rien au monde ; see also **comp** ; → **rose², run, strawberry**

2 *(= rough) [wind]* violent, furieux ; *[sea]* démonté ◆ **in** ~ **weather** par gros temps ◆ **it was a** ~ **night** la tempête faisait rage cette nuit-là

3 *(= unrestrained) [appearance]* farouche ; *[laughter, anger, evening, party]* fou (folle *f*) ; *[idea, plan]* fou (folle *f*), extravagant ; *[imagination, enthusiasm]* débordant, délirant ; *[life]* de bâtons de chaise * ◆ **his hair was** ~ **and uncombed** il avait les cheveux en bataille ◆ **there was** ~ **confusion at the airport** la confusion la plus totale régnait à l'aéroport ◆ **he took a** ~ **swing at his opponent** il a lancé le poing en direction de son adversaire ◆ **he had a** ~ **look in his eyes** il avait une lueur sauvage *or* farouche dans les yeux ◆ **he was** ~ **in his youth, he had a** ~ **youth** il a fait les quatre cents coups dans sa jeunesse ◆ **a whole gang of** ~ **kids** toute une bande de casse-cou ◆ **to have a** ~ **night out (on the town)** sortir faire la fête * ◆ **we had some** ~ **times together** nous avons fait les quatre cents coups ensemble ◆ **those were** ~ **times** *(= tough)* les temps étaient durs, la vie était rude en ce temps-là ◆ **he had some** ~ **scheme for damming the river** il avait un projet complètement fou *or* abracadabrant pour barrer le fleuve ◆ **there was a lot of** ~ **talk about ...** on a avancé des tas d'idées folles au sujet de ... ◆ **they made some** ~ **promises** ils ont fait quelques promesses folles *or* extravagantes ◆ **that is a** ~ **exaggeration** c'est une énorme exagération ◆ **to make a** ~ **guess** risquer *or* émettre à tout hasard une hypothèse *(at sth* sur qch)

4 *(= excited)* comme fou (folle *f*) ; *(= enthusiastic)* fou (folle *f*), dingue * *(about* de) ◆ **to be** ~ **about sb/sth** * être dingue * de qn/qch ◆ **I'm not** ~ **about it** * ça ne m'emballe * pas beaucoup ◆ **he was** ~ **with joy** il ne se tenait plus de joie ◆ **he was** ~ **with anger/indignation** il était fou de rage/d'indignation ◆ **the audience went** ~ **with delight** le public a hurlé de joie ◆ **his fans went** ~ **when he appeared** la folie a gagné ses fans * quand il est apparu ◆ **the dog went** ~ **when he saw his owner** le chien est devenu comme fou quand il a vu son maître ◆ **it's enough to drive you** ~**!** * c'est à vous rendre dingue ! *

N ◆ **the call of the** ~ l'appel *m* de la nature ◆ **in the** ~ *(= natural habitat)* dans la nature, à l'état sauvage ◆ **this plant grows in the** ~ cette plante existe à l'état sauvage ◆ **he went off into the ~s** il est parti vers des régions sauvages *or* reculées ◆ **he lives in the ~s of Alaska** il vit au fin fond de l'Alaska ◆ **we live out in the ~s** nous habitons en pleine brousse

COMP **wild beast** N *(gen)* bête sauvage ; *(= dangerous)* bête féroce

wild boar N sanglier *m*

wild child N 1 *(wayward)* noceur * *m*, -euse * *f* 2 *(living in wilds)* enfant *mf* sauvage

wild duck N canard *m* sauvage

wild-eyed ADJ *(= mad)* au regard fou ; *(= grief-stricken)* aux yeux hagards
wild flowers NPL fleurs *fpl* des champs, fleurs *fpl* sauvages
wild goat N chèvre *f* sauvage
wild-goose chase N ◆ **he sent me off on a ~-goose chase** il m'a fait courir partout pour rien
wild rabbit N lapin *m* de garenne
wild rice N riz *m* sauvage
the Wild West N *(US)* le Far West
Wild West show N *(US)* spectacle *m* sur le thème du Far West

wildcard /ˈwaɪldkɑːd/ N *(Comput)* caractère *m* joker *or* de remplacement ; *(fig)* élément *m* imprévisible

wildcat /ˈwaɪld,kæt/ N [1] *(= animal)* chat *m* sauvage ; *(fig) (= person)* personne *f* féroce [2] *(= oil well)* forage *m* de prospection ADJ *(US = unsound) [scheme, project]* insensé ; *(financially)* financièrement douteux VI *(for oil)* faire des forages de prospection pétrolière COMP **wildcat strike** N *(Ind)* grève *f* sauvage

wildcatter* /ˈwaɪld,kætəʳ/ N *(= striker)* gréviste *mf* ; *(Fin)* spéculateur *m*

wildebeest /ˈwɪldɪbiːst/ N (pl **wildebeests** *or* **wildebeest**) gnou *m*

wilderness /ˈwɪldənɪs/ N *(gen)* étendue *f* déserte, région *f* reculée *or* sauvage ; *(Bible, also fig)* désert *m* ; *(= overgrown garden)* jungle *f* ◆ **a ~ of snow and ice** de vastes étendues de neige et de glace ◆ **a ~ of streets/ruins** un désert de rues/de ruines ◆ **to preach in the ~** *(Bible)* prêcher dans le désert ◆ **to be in the ~** *(fig)* faire sa traversée du désert ◆ **this garden is a ~** ce jardin est une vraie jungle

wildfire /ˈwaɪldfaɪəʳ/ N feu *m or* incendie *m* de forêt ◆ **to spread like ~** se répandre comme une traînée de poudre

wildfowl /ˈwaɪldfaʊl/ N *(one bird)* oiseau *m* sauvage ; *(collectively)* oiseaux *mpl* sauvages ; *(Hunting)* gibier *m* à plumes

wildfowling /ˈwaɪldfaʊlɪŋ/ N ◆ **to go ~** chasser (le gibier à plumes)

wildlife /ˈwaɪldlaɪf/ N faune *f* et flore *f* ◆ **he's interested in ~** il s'intéresse à la faune et à la flore ◆ **the ~ of Central Australia** la faune et la flore d'Australie centrale COMP **wildlife park, wildlife sanctuary** N réserve *f* naturelle

wildly /ˈwaɪldlɪ/ ADV [1] *(= excitedly) [applaud]* frénétiquement ; *[gesticulate, wave]* furieusement ; *[talk]* avec beaucoup d'agitation ; *[protest]* violemment ; *[behave]* de façon extravagante ◆ **to cheer ~** pousser des exclamations frénétiques ◆ **to look ~ around** jeter des regards éperdus autour de soi
[2] *(= violently, frantically)* ◆ **her heart was beating ~** son cœur battait violemment *or* à se rompre ◆ **he hit out ~** il lançait des coups dans tous les sens *or* au hasard ◆ **they were rushing about ~** ils se précipitaient dans tous les sens ◆ **the wind blew ~** le vent soufflait violemment ◆ **the storm raged ~** la tempête faisait rage
[3] *(= at random) [shoot]* au hasard ◆ **you're guessing ~** tu dis ça tout à fait au hasard
[4] *(= extremely) [optimistic, excited, happy]* follement ; *[vary]* énormément ◆ **I'm not ~ pleased* about it** ce n'est pas que ça me fasse très plaisir

wildness /ˈwaɪldnɪs/ N *[of land, countryside, scenery]* aspect *m* sauvage ; *[of tribe, people]* sauvagerie *f* ; *[of wind, sea]* fureur *f*, violence *f* ; *[of appearance]* désordre *m* ; *[of imagination]* extravagance *f* ; *[of enthusiasm]* ferveur *f* ◆ **the ~ of the weather** le sale temps qu'il fait

wiles /waɪlz/ NPL artifices *mpl*, manège *m* ; *(stronger)* ruses *fpl*

wilful, willful *(US)* /ˈwɪlfʊl/ ADJ [1] *(= deliberate) [misconduct, destruction, ignorance]* délibéré ; *[murder, damage]* volontaire [2] *(= obstinate) [person]* entêté, têtu ; *[behaviour]* obstiné

wilfully, willfully *(US)* /ˈwɪlfəlɪ/ ADV [1] *(= deliberately)* délibérément [2] *(= obstinately)* obstinément

wilfulness, willfulness *(US)* /ˈwɪlfʊlnɪs/ N *[of person]* obstination *f*, entêtement *m* ; *[of action]* caractère *m* délibéré *or* intentionnel

wiliness /ˈwaɪlɪnɪs/ N ruse *f NonC*, astuce *f NonC*

will /wɪl/ MODAL AUX VB [1] *(future)*

> When **will** or **'ll** is used to form the future, it is often translated by the future tense.

◆ **he ~ speak** il parlera ◆ **you'll regret it some day** tu le regretteras un jour ◆ **we ~ come too** nous viendrons (nous) aussi

> In the following examples the main verb is future, the other is present: in French both verbs must be in the future tense.

◆ **what ~ he do when he finds out?** qu'est-ce qu'il fera lorsqu'il s'en apercevra ? ◆ **we'll do all we can** nous ferons tout ce que nous pourrons

> When **will** or **'ll** indicates the more immediate future, **aller** + verb is used.

◆ **I'll give you a hand with that** je vais te donner un coup de main avec ça ◆ **they ~ be here shortly** ils vont bientôt arriver

> When **will** or **won't** is used in short replies, no verb is used in French.

◆ **~ he come too? – yes he ~** est-ce qu'il viendra aussi ? – oui ◆ **I'll go with you – oh no you won't!** je vais vous accompagner – non, certainement pas ! ◆ **they'll arrive tomorrow – ~ they?** ils arriveront demain – ah bon *or* c'est vrai ?

> When **will** or **won't** is used in question tags, eg **won't it**, **won't you** the translation is often **n'est-ce pas**.

◆ **you ~ come to see us, won't you?** vous viendrez nous voir, n'est-ce pas ? ◆ **that'll be okay, won't it?** ça ira, n'est-ce pas ? ◆ **you won't lose it again, ~ you?** tu ne le perdras plus, n'est-ce pas ?

> When future meaning is made clear by words like **tomorrow**, or **next week**, the present tense can also be used in French.

◆ **he'll be here tomorrow** il arrive *or* il arrivera demain ◆ **I'll phone you tonight** je t'appelle *or* je t'appellerai ce soir
[2] *(future perfect)*

◆ **will have** + *past participle* ◆ **the holiday ~ have done him good** les vacances lui auront fait du bien ◆ **he ~ have left by now** il sera déjà parti à l'heure qu'il est
[3] *(habitual actions)*

> When **will** indicates that something commonly happens, the present is often used in French.

◆ **he ~ sit for hours doing nothing** il reste assis pendant des heures à ne rien faire ◆ **this bottle ~ hold one litre** cette bouteille contient un litre *or* fait le litre ◆ **the car ~ do 150km/h** cette voiture fait du 150 km/h ◆ **thieves ~ often keep a stolen picture for years** les voleurs gardent souvent un tableau volé pendant des années ◆ **he ~ talk all the time!** il ne peut pas s'empêcher *or* s'arrêter de parler ! ◆ **if you ~ make your speeches so long, you can hardly blame people for not listening** si vous persistez à faire des discours aussi longs, il ne faut pas vraiment vous étonner si les gens n'écoutent pas ◆ **he ~ annoy me by leaving his socks lying all over the place** il m'énerve à toujours laisser traîner ses chaussettes partout ◆ **I ~ call him Richard, though his name's actually Robert** il faut toujours que je l'appelle *subj* Richard bien qu'en fait il s'appelle Robert ◆ **boys ~ be boys** il faut (bien) que jeunesse se passe *(Prov)*
[4] *(requests, orders)*

> The present tense of **vouloir** is often used.

◆ **~ you be quiet!** veux-tu (bien) te taire ! ◆ **~ you please sit down!** voulez-vous vous asseoir, s'il vous plaît ! ◆ **~ you help me? – yes I ~** tu veux m'aider ? – oui, je veux bien ◆ **~ you promise to be careful?** tu me promets de faire attention ? ◆ **you ~ speak to no one** *(in commands)* ne parlez à personne, vous ne parlerez à personne ◆ **do what you ~** *(frm)* faites ce que vous voulez *or* comme vous voulez

◆ **won't** *(= refuse(s) to)* ◆ **the window won't open** la fenêtre ne veut pas s'ouvrir ◆ **she won't let me drive the car** elle ne veut pas me laisser conduire la voiture ◆ **~ you promise? – no I won't** tu me le promets ? – non
[5] *(invitations, offers)* **~ you have a cup of coffee?** voulez-vous prendre un café ? ◆ **~ you join us for a drink?** voulez-vous prendre un verre avec nous ? ◆ **won't you come with us?** vous ne voulez pas venir (avec nous) ? ◆ **I'll help you if you like** je vais vous aider si vous voulez
[6] *(= must)* **that ~ be the taxi** ça doit être le taxi ◆ **she'll be about forty** elle doit avoir quarante ans environ ◆ **you'll be thinking I'm crazy** tu dois penser que je suis fou ◆ **she'll have forgotten all about it by now** elle aura tout oublié à l'heure qu'il est

VT (pret, ptp **willed**) [1] *(= urge by willpower)* **he was ~ing her to look at him** il l'adjurait intérieurement de le regarder ◆ **he was ~ing her to accept** il l'adjurait intérieurement d'accepter
[2] *(= bequeath)* **to ~ sth to sb** léguer qch à qn
[3] *(frm = wish, intend)* vouloir *(that* que + *subj)* ◆ **God has ~ed it so** Dieu a voulu qu'il en soit ainsi ◆ **it is as God ~s** c'est la volonté de Dieu ◆ **to ~ sb's happiness** vouloir le bonheur de qn

N [1] *(= determination)* volonté *f* ◆ **they have no ~ of their own** ils manquent de volonté ◆ **he has a strong ~** il a beaucoup de volonté ◆ **a ~ of iron, an iron ~** une volonté de fer ◆ **to have a weak ~** manquer de volonté ◆ **my trolley has a ~ of its own** mon chariot n'en fait qu'à sa tête ◆ **the ~ to live** la volonté de survivre ◆ **the ~ of God** la volonté de Dieu, la volonté divine ◆ **it is the ~ of the people that ...** la volonté du peuple est que ... + *subj* ◆ **what is your ~?** *(frm)* quelle est votre volonté ? ◆ **it is my ~ that he should leave** *(frm)* je veux qu'il parte ◆ **thy ~ be done** *(Rel)* que ta volonté soit faite ◆ **to do sth against sb's ~** faire qch contre la volonté de qn ◆ **where there's a ~ there's a way** *(Prov)* vouloir c'est pouvoir *(Prov)*

◆ **at will** ◆ **an employer who can sack you at ~** un employeur qui peut vous licencier comme il le veut ◆ **I can speed up and slow down at ~** je peux accélérer et ralentir comme je veux ◆ **to choose at ~** choisir à volonté ◆ **you are free to leave at ~** vous êtes libre de partir quand vous voulez
[2] *(= document)* testament *m* ◆ **to make a ~** faire son testament ◆ **he left it to me in his ~** il me l'a légué par testament ◆ **the last ~ and testament of ...** les dernières volontés de ...

willful *etc* /ˈwɪlfʊl/ ADJ *(US)* ⇒ **wilful** *etc*

William /ˈwɪljəm/ N Guillaume *m* ◆ **~ the Conqueror** Guillaume le Conquérant ◆ **~ of Orange** Guillaume d'Orange ◆ **~ Tell** Guillaume Tell

willie* /ˈwɪlɪ/ N *(Brit)* zizi* *m* NPL **the willies** ◆ **to have the ~s** avoir les chocottes* *fpl*, avoir la trouille* ◆ **it gives me the ~s** ça me donne les chocottes*, ça me fout la trouille‡ ◆ **he gives me the ~s** il me fout la trouille‡

willing /ˈwɪlɪŋ/ ADJ 1 (= prepared) ◆ **to be ~ to do sth** être prêt *or* disposé à faire qch, bien vouloir faire qch ◆ **he wasn't very ~ to help** il n'était pas tellement prêt *or* disposé à aider ◆ **I was quite ~ for him to come** j'étais tout à fait prêt *or* disposé à ce qu'il vienne ◆ **will you help us? – I'm perfectly ~** voulez-vous nous aider ? – bien volontiers ; → **god, ready, spirit**

2 *(= eager) [audience, participant]* enthousiaste ; *[helper, worker, partner]* plein de bonne volonté ◆ **~ hands helped him to his feet** des mains secourables se tendirent et l'aidèrent à se lever ◆ **there were plenty of ~ hands** il y avait beaucoup d'offres d'assistance ◆ **he's very ~** il est plein de bonne volonté

3 *(= voluntary) [help, sacrifice]* volontaire

N ◆ **to show ~** faire preuve de bonne volonté

COMP **willing horse*** N (= person) bonne âme *f* (qui se dévoue toujours)

willingly /ˈwɪlɪŋlɪ/ ADV 1 *(= readily) [accept, work]* volontiers ◆ **can you help us? – ~!** peux-tu nous aider ? – volontiers ! 2 *(= voluntarily)* de mon *(or ton, son etc)* plein gré ◆ **did he do it ~ or did you have to make him?** l'a-t-il fait de son plein gré ou bien vous a-t-il fallu le forcer ?

willingness /ˈwɪlɪŋnɪs/ N bonne volonté *f* ; *(= enthusiasm)* empressement *m (to do sth* à faire qch) ◆ **I don't doubt his ~, just his competence** ce n'est pas sa bonne volonté que je mets en doute mais sa compétence ◆ **I was grateful for his ~ to help** je lui étais reconnaissant de bien vouloir m'aider *or* de son empressement à m'aider ◆ **in spite of the ~ with which she agreed** malgré la bonne volonté qu'elle a mise à accepter, malgré son empressement à accepter

will-o'-the-wisp /ˌwɪləðəˈwɪsp/ N *(lit, fig)* feu follet *m*

willow /ˈwɪləʊ/ N *(= tree)* saule *m* ; *(= wood)* (bois *m* de) saule *m* NonC ; *(for baskets etc)* osier *m* ◆ **the ~** * *(fig = cricket/baseball bat)* la batte (de cricket/de baseball) ; → **pussy, weeping**

COMP *[bat etc]* de *or* en saule ; *[basket]* d'osier, en osier **willow pattern** N *motif chinois dans les tons bleus* ◆ **~ pattern china** porcelaine *f* à motif chinois
willow warbler N pouillot *m* fitis

willowherb /ˈwɪləʊhɜːb/ N épilobe *m*

willowy /ˈwɪləʊɪ/ ADJ *[person]* svelte, élancé

willpower /ˈwɪlpaʊəʳ/ N volonté *f*

willy* /ˈwɪlɪ/ N ⇒ **willie noun**

willy-nilly /ˈwɪlɪˈnɪlɪ/ ADV 1 *(= willingly or not)* bon gré mal gré 2 *(= at random)* au hasard

wilt[1] †† /wɪlt/ VB 2nd person sg of **will** → **modal aux vb**

wilt[2] /wɪlt/ VI *[flower]* se faner, se flétrir ; *[plant]* se dessécher, mourir ; *[person]* *(= grow exhausted)* s'affaiblir ; *(= lose courage)* fléchir, être pris de découragement ; *[effort, enthusiasm etc]* diminuer ◆ **the guests began to ~ in the heat of the room** la chaleur de la pièce commençait à incommoder les invités ◆ **business confidence has visibly ~ed** la confiance des milieux d'affaires a visiblement diminué ◆ **United visibly ~ed under Liverpool's onslaught in the semi-final** United a manifestement flanché en demi-finale face à l'assaut de Liverpool ◆ **demand for household goods has ~ed with the collapse of the housing market** la demande en biens d'équipement ménager a fléchi avec l'effondrement du marché immobilier ◆ **I ~ed into my chair** je me suis effondré dans mon fauteuil

VT *[+ flower]* faner, flétrir ; *[+ plant, leaves]* dessécher

Wilts /wɪlts/ abbrev of **Wiltshire**

wily /ˈwaɪlɪ/ ADJ *(gen pej) [person]* rusé, malin (-igne *f*) ◆ **a ~ trick** une astuce ◆ **he's a ~ old devil** *or* **bird** *or* **fox, he's as ~ as a fox** il est rusé comme un renard

wimp* /wɪmp/ N *(pej)* mauviette *f*, poule *f* mouillée

► **wimp out**‡ VI se dégonfler

wimpish* /ˈwɪmpɪʃ/ *(pej)* ADJ *[behaviour]* de mauviette ◆ **a ~ young man** une jeune mauviette ◆ **his ~ friend** sa mauviette d'ami ◆ **he's so ~!** c'est une telle mauviette ! ◆ **stop being so ~!** cesse de faire la mauviette !

wimpishly* /ˈwɪmpɪʃlɪ/ ADV *[say]* misérablement ; *[behave]* comme une mauviette

wimple /ˈwɪmpl/ N guimpe *f*

wimpy* /ˈwɪmpɪ/ *(pej)* ADJ ⇒ **wimpish**

win /wɪn/ (vb : pret, ptp **won**) N *(Sport etc)* victoire *f* ◆ **another ~ for Scotland** une nouvelle victoire pour l'Écosse ◆ **it was a convincing ~ for France** la victoire revenait indiscutablement à la France ◆ **to have a ~** gagner ◆ **to back a horse for a ~** jouer un cheval gagnant

VI 1 *(in war, sport, competition etc)* gagner, l'emporter ◆ **to ~ by a length** gagner *or* l'emporter d'une longueur ◆ **go in and ~!** vas-y et ne reviens pas sans la victoire ! ◆ **he was playing to ~** il jouait pour gagner ◆ **who's ~ning?** qui est-ce qui gagne ? ◆ **to ~ hands down*** gagner les doigts dans le nez*, gagner haut la main ; *(esp in race)* arriver dans un fauteuil ◆ **~, place and show** *(US Sport)* gagnant, placé et troisième ◆ **you ~!** *(in reluctant agreement)* soit ! tu as gagné ! ◆ **I** *(or* **you** *etc)* **(just) can't ~** j'ai *(or* on a *etc)* toujours tort

2 ◆ **to ~ free** *or* **loose** se dégager *(from sth* de qch)

VT 1 *(= gain victory in) [+ war, match, competition, bet, race]* gagner ◆ **to ~ the day** *(Mil)* remporter la victoire ; *(gen)* l'emporter

2 *(= compete for and get) [+ prize]* gagner, remporter ; *[+ victory]* remporter ; *[+ scholarship]* obtenir ; *[+ sum of money]* gagner ◆ **he won it for growing radishes** il l'a gagné *or* remporté *or* eu pour sa culture de radis ◆ **he won £5 (from her) at cards** il (lui) a gagné 5 livres aux cartes ◆ **his essay won him a trip to France** sa dissertation lui a valu un voyage en France

3 *(= obtain etc) [+ fame, fortune]* trouver ; *[+ sb's attention]* capter, captiver ; *[+ sb's friendship]* gagner ; *[+ sb's esteem]* gagner, conquérir ; *[+ sympathy, support, admirers, supporters]* s'attirer ; *[+ coal, ore etc]* extraire *(from* de) ◆ **to ~ friends** se faire des amis ◆ **to ~ a name** *or* **a reputation (for o.s.)** se faire un nom *or* une réputation *(as* en tant que) ◆ **this won him the friendship of ...** ceci lui a gagné *or* valu l'amitié de ... ◆ **this won him the attention of the crowd** ça lui a valu l'attention de la foule ◆ **this manoeuvre won him the time he needed** cette manœuvre lui a valu d'obtenir le délai dont il avait besoin ◆ **to ~ sb's love/respect** se faire aimer/respecter de qn ◆ **to ~ sb's heart** gagner le cœur de qn ◆ **to ~ sb to one's cause** gagner *or* rallier qn à sa cause ◆ **to ~ a lady** *or* **a lady's hand (in marriage)** † obtenir la main d'une demoiselle

4 *(= reach) [+ summit, shore, goal]* parvenir à, arriver à ◆ **he won his way to the top of his profession** il a durement gagné sa place au sommet de sa profession

COMP **win-win** → **win-win**

► **win back** VT SEP *[+ cup, trophy]* reprendre *(from* à) ; *[+ gaming loss etc]* recouvrer ; *[+ land]* reconquérir *(from* sur), reprendre *(from* à) ; *[+ sb's favour, support, esteem, one's girlfriend etc]* reconquérir ◆ **I won the money back from him** j'ai repris l'argent qu'il m'avait gagné

► **win out** VI 1 l'emporter, gagner
2 ⇒ **win through**

► **win over, win round** VT SEP *[+ person]* convaincre, persuader ; *[+ voter]* gagner à sa cause ◆ **I won him over to my point of view** je l'ai gagné à ma façon de voir ◆ **the figures won him over to our way of thinking** les statistiques l'ont fait se rallier à notre façon de voir ◆ **I won him over eventually** j'ai fini par le convaincre *or* le persuader ◆ **to ~ sb over to doing sth** convaincre *or* persuader qn de faire qch

► **win through** VI y arriver, finir par réussir ◆ **you'll ~ through all right!** tu y arriveras !, tu finiras par réussir ! ◆ **he won through to the second round** *(in competition etc)* il a gagné le premier tour

wince /wɪns/ VI *(= flinch)* tressaillir ; *(= grimace)* grimacer (de douleur) ◆ **he ~d at the thought/at the sight** cette pensée/ce spectacle l'a fait tressaillir *or* grimacer ◆ **he ~d as I touched his injured arm** il a tressailli sous l'effet de la douleur *or* il a grimacé de douleur lorsque j'ai touché son bras blessé ◆ **without wincing** *(fig)* sans broncher *or* sourciller N *(= flinch)* tressaillement *m*, crispation *f* ; *(= grimace)* grimace *f* (de douleur *or* dégoût *etc*) ◆ **to give a ~** ⇒ **to wince vi**

winceyette /ˌwɪnsɪˈet/ N *(NonC: Brit)* flanelle *f* de coton

winch /wɪntʃ/ N treuil *m* VT ◆ **to ~ sth up/down** *etc* monter/descendre *etc* qch au treuil ◆ **they ~ed him out of the water** ils l'ont hissé hors de l'eau au treuil

Winchester /ˈwɪntʃɪstəʳ/ N ◆ **~ (rifle)** ® (carabine *f*) Winchester *f* ◆ **~ disk** *(Comput)* disque *m* Winchester

wind[1] /wɪnd/ N 1 vent *m* ◆ **high ~** grand vent *m*, vent *m* violent *or* fort ◆ **following ~** vent *m* arrière ◆ **the ~ is rising/dropping** le vent se lève/tombe ◆ **the ~ was in the east** le vent venait de l'est *or* était à l'est ◆ **where is the ~?, which way is the ~?** d'où vient le vent ? ◆ **to go/run like the ~** aller/filer comme le vent ◆ **between ~ and water** *(Naut)* près de la ligne de flottaison ◆ **to run before the ~** *(Naut)* avoir *or* courir vent arrière ◆ **to take the ~ out of sb's sails** couper l'herbe sous le pied de qn ◆ **to see how the ~ blows** *or* **lies** *(lit)* voir d'où vient le vent ; *(fig)* prendre le vent, voir d'où vient le vent ◆ **the ~ of change is blowing** le vent du changement souffle ◆ **there's something in the ~** il y a quelque chose dans l'air, il se prépare quelque chose ◆ **to get ~ of sth** avoir vent de qch ◆ **he threw caution to the ~s** il a fait fi de toute prudence † *(also frm)* ◆ **she was left twisting** *or* **swinging in the ~** *(US)* on l'a laissée dans le pétrin* ; → **ill, north, sail**

2 *(= breath)* souffle *m* ◆ **he has still plenty of ~** il a encore du souffle ◆ **he had lost his ~** il avait perdu le souffle *or* perdu haleine ◆ **to knock the ~ out of sb** *[blow]* couper la respiration *or* le souffle à qn ; *[fighter]* mettre qn hors d'haleine ; *[fall, exertion]* essouffler qn, mettre qn hors d'haleine ◆ **to get one's ~ back** *(lit)* reprendre (son) souffle, reprendre haleine ◆ **give me time to get my ~ back!** *(fig)* laissez-moi le temps de souffler *or* de me retourner ! ◆ **to put the ~ up sb*** *(Brit)* flanquer la frousse à qn* ◆ **to get/have the ~ up*** *(Brit)* avoir la frousse* *(about* à propos de) → **second**[1], **sound**[2]

3 *(NonC: Med = flatulence)* gaz *mpl* ◆ **the baby has got ~** le bébé a des gaz ◆ **to break ~** lâcher un vent ◆ **to bring up ~** avoir un renvoi

4 *(Mus)* **the ~** les instruments *mpl* à vent

VT 1 ◆ **to ~ sb** *[blow etc]* couper la respiration *or* le souffle à qn ; *[fighter]* mettre qn hors d'haleine ; *[fall, exertion]* essouffler qn, mettre qn hors d'haleine ◆ **he was ~ed by the blow, the blow ~ed him** le coup lui a coupé le souffle *or* la respiration ◆ **he was quite ~ed by the climb** l'ascension l'avait essoufflé *or* mis hors d'haleine ◆ **I'm only ~ed** j'ai la respiration coupée, c'est tout

2 *[+ horse]* laisser souffler

3 *(Hunting = scent)* avoir vent de

4 ◆ **to ~ a baby** faire faire son rot* *or* son renvoi à un bébé

COMP *[erosion etc]* éolien

wind-bells NPL ⇒ **wind-chimes**

wind-borne ADJ *[seeds, pollen]* transporté *or* porté par le vent

wind-chill (factor) N (facteur *m* de) refroidissement *m* dû au vent ◆ **a ~-chill factor of 10°** une baisse de 10° due au vent

wind-chimes NPL carillon *m* éolien

wind deflector N *[of car]* déflecteur *m*

wind farm N éoliennes *fpl*, parc *m* d'éoliennes

wind gauge N anémomètre *m*

wind generator N aérogénérateur *m*

wind instrument N *(Mus)* instrument *m* à vent

wind machine N *(Theat, Cine)* machine *f* à vent

wind power N énergie *f* éolienne

wind tunnel N *(Phys)* tunnel *m* aérodynamique ◆ **there was a ~ tunnel between the two tower blocks** il y avait un fort courant d'air entre les deux tours

wind² /waɪnd/ (pret, ptp **winded** *or* **wound**) VT ◆ **to ~ the horn** sonner du cor ; *(Hunting)* sonner de la trompe

wind³ /waɪnd/ (vb : pret, ptp **wound**) N 1 *(= bend: in river etc)* tournant *m*, coude *m*

2 *(= action of winding)* ◆ **to give one's watch a ~** remonter sa montre ◆ **give the handle another ~ or two** donne un ou deux tours de manivelle de plus

VT 1 *(= roll) [+ thread, rope etc]* enrouler *(on* sur ; *round* autour de) ; *(= wrap)* envelopper *(in* dans) ◆ **to ~ wool (into a ball)** enrouler de la laine (pour en faire une pelote) ◆ **~ this round your head** enroule-toi ça autour de la tête ◆ **with the rope wound tightly round his waist** la corde bien enroulée autour de la taille, la corde lui ceignant étroitement la taille ◆ **she wound a shawl round the baby, she wound the baby in a shawl** elle a enveloppé le bébé dans un châle ◆ **to ~ one's arms round sb** enlacer qn ◆ **the snake/rope wound itself round a branch** le serpent/la corde s'est enroulé(e) autour d'une branche ◆ **he slowly wound his way home** il s'en revint lentement chez lui, il prit lentement le chemin du retour ; see also **vi**

2 *[+ clock, watch, toy]* remonter ; *[+ handle]* donner un (*or* des) tour(s) de

VI ◆ **to ~ along** *[river, path]* serpenter, faire des zigzags ◆ **the road ~s through the valley** la route serpente à travers la vallée, la route traverse la vallée en serpentant ◆ **the procession wound through the town** la procession a serpenté à travers la ville ◆ **the line of cars wound slowly up the hill** la file de voitures a lentement gravi la colline en serpentant ◆ **to ~ up/down** *[path etc]* monter/descendre en serpentant *or* en zigzags ; *[stairs, steps]* monter/descendre en tournant ◆ **to ~ round sth** *[snake, ivy etc]* s'enrouler autour de qch

► **wind back** VT SEP *[+ tape, film]* rembobiner

► **wind down** VI 1 → **vi**

2 *(* = relax)* se détendre, se relaxer

3 *(fig)* **to be ~ing down** *[event]* tirer à sa fin ; *[energy, enthusiasm, interest]* diminuer, être en perte de vitesse

VT SEP 1 *(on rope/winch etc)* faire descendre (au bout d'une corde/avec un treuil *etc*)

2 *[+ car window]* baisser

3 *(fig) [+ department, service etc]* réduire progressivement (en vue d'un démantèlement éventuel)

► **wind forward** VT SEP ⇒ **wind on**

► **wind off** VT SEP dérouler, dévider

► **wind on** VT SEP enrouler

► **wind up** VI 1 → **vi**

2 *[meeting, discussion]* se terminer, finir *(with* par) ◆ **he wound up for the Government** *(in debate)* c'est lui qui a résumé la position du gouvernement dans le discours de clôture ◆ **Mr Paul Herbert wound up for the prosecution/defence** *(Jur)* M. Paul Herbert a conclu pour la partie civile/pour la défense

3 * *(= finish up)* se retrouver ◆ **they wound up stranded in Rotterdam** ils ont fini *or* ils se sont retrouvés bloqués à Rotterdam ◆ **he wound up as a doctor** il a fini médecin, il s'est retrouvé médecin ◆ **he wound up with a fractured skull** il s'est retrouvé avec une fracture du crâne

VT SEP 1 *(= end) [+ meeting, speech]* terminer, clore ; *(Comm) [+ business]* liquider ◆ **to ~ up one's affairs** régler ses affaires ◆ **to ~ up an account** clôturer un compte

2 *[+ object on rope/winch etc]* faire monter (au bout d'une corde/avec un treuil *etc*) ; *[+ car window]* monter, fermer ; *[+ watch etc]* remonter

3 *(Brit = tease)* faire marcher* ◆ **come on, you're ~ing me up!** arrête, tu me fais marcher ! ◆ **he'd been ~ing me up the whole match and I finally snapped** il m'asticotait depuis le début du match et j'ai fini par craquer

N ◆ **winding-up** → **winding**

N ◆ **wind-up** * *(Brit = joke)* blague *f*, bobard* *m*

windbag * /ˈwɪndbæg/ N *(fig pej)* moulin *m* à paroles

windblown /ˈwɪndbləʊn/ ADJ *[person, hair]* ébouriffé par le vent ; *[tree]* fouetté par le vent

windbreak /ˈwɪndbreɪk/ N *(= tree, fence etc)* brise-vent *m* ; *(for camping etc)* pare-vent *m inv*

Windbreaker ® /ˈwɪndbreɪkəʳ/ N ⇒ **windcheater**

windburn /ˈwɪndbɜːn/ N *(Med)* brûlure *f* épidermique (due au vent)

windcheater /ˈwɪndtʃiːtəʳ/ N *(Brit)* anorak *m* léger, coupe-vent *m inv*

winder /ˈwaɪndəʳ/ N 1 *[of watch etc]* remontoir *m* 2 *(for car windows)* lève-glace *m*, lève-vitre *m* 3 *(for thread etc)* dévidoir *m* ; *(= person)* dévideur *m*, -euse *f*

windfall /ˈwɪndfɔːl/ N *(lit)* fruit(s) *m(pl)* tombé(s) *(sous l'effet du vent)* ; *(fig)* aubaine *f*, manne *f* (tombée du ciel)

COMP **windfall profit** N bénéfices *mpl* exceptionnels

windfall tax N taxe *f* exceptionnelle sur les bénéfices *(des entreprises privatisées)*

windflower /ˈwɪndflaʊəʳ/ N anémone *f* des bois

winding /ˈwaɪndɪŋ/ ADJ *[road, path]* sinueux, tortueux ; *[river]* sinueux, qui serpente ; *[stairs, staircase]* tournant N 1 *(NonC) [of thread, rope]* enroulement *m* ; *[of clock, watch, toy]* remontage *m* ; *(onto bobbin)* bobinage *m* 2 ◆ **~(s)** *[of road]* zigzags *mpl* ; *[of river]* méandres *mpl*

COMP **winding-sheet** † N linceul *m*

winding-up N *[of meeting, account]* clôture *f* ; *[of business, one's affairs]* liquidation *f* ◆ **~-up arrangements** *(Jur, Fin)* concordat *m*

windjammer /ˈwɪnddʒæməʳ/ N 1 *(Naut)* grand voilier *m* (de la marine marchande) 2 *(Brit = windcheater)* anorak *m* léger, coupe-vent *m inv*

windlass /ˈwɪndləs/ N guindeau *m*, treuil *m*

windless /ˈwɪndlɪs/ ADJ *[day]* sans vent ; *[air]* immobile

windmill /ˈwɪndmɪl/ N moulin *m* à vent ; *(on wind farm)* éolienne *f* ◆ **to tilt at** *or* **fight ~s** se battre contre des moulins à vent ◆ **~ service** *(Volleyball)* service *m* balancier

window /ˈwɪndəʊ/ N 1 *(gen, also Comput)* fenêtre *f* ; *(in car, train)* vitre *f*, glace *f* ; (also **window pane**) vitre *f*, carreau *m* ; *(stained-glass)* vitrail *m* ; *(larger)* verrière *f* ; *(in post office, ticket office etc)* guichet *m* ; *(in envelope)* fenêtre *f* ◆ **I saw her at the ~** je l'ai vue à la fenêtre ◆ **don't lean out of the ~** ne te penche pas par la fenêtre ; *(in train, car etc)* ne te penche pas en dehors ◆ **to look/throw** *etc* **out of the ~** regarder/jeter *etc* par la fenêtre ; *(in car etc)* regarder/jeter *etc* dehors ◆ **the ~s look out onto fields** les fenêtres donnent sur *or* ont vue sur des champs ◆ **to break a ~** casser une vitre *or* un carreau ◆ **to clean the ~s** nettoyer *or* laver les carreaux

◆ **out of the window** *(fig)* ◆ **to go** *or* **fly** *or* **disappear out of the ~** s'évanouir, se volatiliser ◆ **well, there's another plan out the ~!*** eh bien voilà encore un projet de fichu* *or* qui tombe à l'eau

◆ **a window on** *(fig)* ◆ **television is a ~ on the world of western consumption** la télévision nous donne un aperçu de l'univers de la consommation à l'occidentale ◆ **at the same time opening a ~ on the social and cultural trends** en nous donnant en même temps un aperçu des tendances sociales et culturelles

2 *[of shop]* vitrine *f*, devanture *f* ; *(more modest)* étalage *m* ; *[of café etc]* vitrine *f* ◆ **to put sth in the ~** mettre qch en vitrine *or* à la devanture ◆ **I saw it in the ~** j'ai vu ça à l'étalage *or* à la devanture *or* en vitrine ◆ **in the front of the ~** sur le devant de la vitrine ◆ **the ~s are lovely at Christmas time** les vitrines sont très belles au moment de Noël

3 *(= free time)* trou *m*, créneau *m* ◆ **I've got a ~ in my diary later on this week** j'ai un trou *or* créneau dans mon emploi du temps à la fin de la semaine

◆ **window (of opportunity)** ◆ **there is perhaps a ~ of opportunity to change ...** nous avons peut-être maintenant la possibilité de changer ... ◆ **there is now a ~ of opportunity for progress towards peace** nous avons maintenant l'occasion de faire progresser les négociations de paix

4 *(Space:* also **launch window**) fenêtre *f* *or* créneau *m* de lancement

COMP **window box** N jardinière *f*

window cleaner N *(= person)* laveur *m*, -euse *f* de vitres *or* de carreaux ; *(= substance)* produit *m* à nettoyer les vitres *or* les carreaux

window-cleaning N ◆ **to do the ~-cleaning** faire les vitres *or* carreaux

window display N devanture *f*, vitrine *f* (de magasin)

window dresser N *(Comm)* étalagiste *mf*

window dressing N *(Comm)* composition *f* d'étalage ◆ **she is learning ~ dressing** elle fait des études d'étalagiste ◆ **it's just ~ dressing** *(fig pej)* ce n'est qu'une façade

window envelope N enveloppe *f* à fenêtre

window frame N châssis *m* (de fenêtre)

window glass N *(NonC)* verre *m* *(utilisé pour les vitres)*

window ledge N ⇒ **windowsill**

window pane N vitre *f*, carreau *m*

window seat N *(in room)* banquette *f* (située sous la fenêtre) ; *(in vehicle)* place *f* côté fenêtre

window shade N *(US)* store *m*

window-shopper N ◆ **she's a great ~-shopper** elle adore faire du lèche-vitrines*

window-shopping N lèche-vitrines* *m* ◆ **to go ~-shopping** faire du lèche-vitrines*

window winder N *[of car]* lève-glace *m*, lève-vitre *m*

windowsill /ˈwɪndəʊsɪl/ N *(inside)* appui *m* de fenêtre ; *(outside)* rebord *m* de fenêtre

windpipe /ˈwɪndpaɪp/ N *(Anat)* trachée *f*

windproof /ˈwɪndpruːf/ ADJ protégeant du vent, qui ne laisse pas passer le vent VT protéger du *or* contre le vent

windscreen /ˈwɪndskriːn/ *(esp Brit)* N pare-brise *m inv*

COMP **windscreen washer** N lave-glace *m*

windscreen wiper N essuie-glace *m*

windshield /ˈwɪndʃiːld/ N *(US)* ⇒ **windscreen**

windsleeve /ˈwɪndsliːv/, **windsock** /ˈwɪndsɒk/ N manche f à air

windstorm /ˈwɪndstɔːm/ N vent m de tempête

windsurf /ˈwɪndsɜːf/ VI (also **go windsurfing**) faire de la planche à voile

windsurfer /ˈwɪndsɜːfəʳ/ N 1 (= person) (véli-)planchiste mf 2 (= board) planche f à voile

windsurfing /ˈwɪndsɜːfɪŋ/ N planche f à voile (sport)

windswept /ˈwɪndswept/ ADJ venteux, battu par les vents, balayé par le(s) vent(s)

windward /ˈwɪndwəd/ ADJ qui est au vent or contre le vent, qui est du côté du vent ADV au vent N côté m du vent ◆ **to look to ~** regarder dans la direction du vent ◆ **to get to ~ of sth** se mettre contre le vent par rapport à qch COMP **the Windward Islands, the Windward Isles** NPL les îles fpl du Vent

windy /ˈwɪndɪ/ ADJ 1 (= blustery) [day] de vent ◆ **it's** or **the weather's ~ today** il y a du vent aujourd'hui ◆ **wet and ~ weather** la pluie et le vent 2 (= windswept) [place] balayé par les vents, venteux 3 (* = pompous) [person] ronflant ; [phrases, speech] ronflant, pompeux ◆ **a ~ old bore** un vieux raseur sentencieux 4 (Brit † * = scared) ◆ **to be ~ (about sth)** avoir la frousse* (à propos de qch) ◆ **to get ~ (about sth)** paniquer (à propos de qch) COMP **the Windy City** N (US) Chicago ; → CITY NICKNAMES

wine /waɪn/ N vin m ◆ **elderberry ~** vin m de sureau
VT ◆ **to ~ and dine sb** emmener qn faire un dîner bien arrosé
VI ◆ **to ~ and dine** faire un dîner bien arrosé
COMP [bottle, cellar] à vin ; [colour] lie de vin inv or lie-de-vin inv
wine bar N bar m à vin(s)
wine-bottling N mise f en bouteilles (du vin)
wine box N cubitainer ® m
wine cask N fût m, tonneau m (à vin)
wine-coloured ADJ lie de vin inv, lie-de-vin inv
wine cooler N (= device) rafraîchisseur m (à vin), seau m à rafraîchir ; (= drink) boisson à base de vin, de jus de fruit et d'eau gazeuse
wined up * ADJ (US) bourré‡, noir*
wine grower N viticulteur m, -trice f, vigneron(ne) m(f)
wine growing N viticulture f, culture f de la vigne ADJ [district, industry] vinicole, viticole
wine gum N (Brit) bonbon m (aux fruits)
wine list N carte f des vins
wine merchant N (Brit) marchand(e) m(f) de vin ; (on larger scale) négociant(e) m(f) en vins
wine press N pressoir m (à vin)
wine rack N casier m à bouteilles (de vin)
wine taster N (= person) dégustateur m, -trice f (de vins) ; (= cup) tâte-vin m inv, taste-vin m inv
wine tasting N dégustation f (de vins)
wine vinegar N vinaigre m de vin
wine waiter N sommelier m, -ière f

winebibber /ˈwaɪnbɪbəʳ/ N grand(e) buveur m, -euse f (de vin), bon(ne) buveur m, -euse f

wineglass /ˈwaɪnglɑːs/ N verre m à vin

winery /ˈwaɪnərɪ/ N (US) établissement m vinicole

wineshop /ˈwaɪnʃɒp/ N boutique f du marchand de vin

wineskin /ˈwaɪnskɪn/ N outre f à vin

wing /wɪŋ/ N 1 (gen) aile f ◆ **to be on the ~** être en vol, voler ◆ **to shoot a bird on the ~** tirer un oiseau au vol ◆ **to take ~** [bird] prendre son vol, s'envoler ◆ **his heart took ~** (fig, liter) son cœur s'emplit de joie ◆ **to take sb under one's ~** prendre qn sous son aile ◆ **to be under sb's ~** être sous l'aile (protectrice) de qn ◆ **on the ~s of fantasy** sur les ailes de l'imagination ◆ **fear lent** or **gave him ~s** la peur lui donnait des ailes ◆ **on a ~ and a prayer** à la grâce de Dieu ; → **clip², spread**
2 (Pol) aile f ◆ **on the left/right ~ of the party** sur l'aile gauche/droite du parti
3 (Sport = person) ailier m, aile f ◆ **~ (three-quarter)** trois-quarts aile f ◆ **left/right ~** ailier m gauche/droit ◆ **he plays (on the) left ~** il est ailier gauche
4 (Brit) [of car] aile f ; [of armchair] oreille f, oreillard m
5 (= insignia of pilot) ◆ **~s** insigne m (de pilote) ◆ **to earn** or **win** or **get one's ~s** devenir pilote (dans l'armée de l'air)
6 [of building, mansion] aile f
7 [of organization etc] aile f ◆ **the political ~ of the IRA** l'aile f politique de l'IRA
NPL **the wings** (Theat) les coulisses fpl, la coulisse ◆ **to stand** or **stay in the ~s** (Theat) se tenir dans les coulisses ; (fig) rester dans la (or les) coulisse(s) ◆ **to wait in the ~s for sb to do sth** (fig) attendre dans la or les coulisse(s) que qn fasse qch
VT 1 (= wound) [+ bird] blesser or toucher (à l'aile) ; [+ person] blesser au bras (or à la jambe etc)
2 (liter) **to ~ an arrow at sth** darder une flèche en direction de qch ◆ **to ~ one's way** ⇒ **to wing** VI
3 [actor, speaker etc] **to ~ it*** improviser
VI (= wing one's way) voler ◆ **they ~ed over the sea** ils ont survolé la mer
COMP **wing case** N [of insect] élytre m
wing chair N bergère f à oreilles
wing collar N col m cassé
wing commander N lieutenant-colonel m (de l'armée de l'air)
wing flap N aileron m
wing-footed ADJ (liter) aux pieds ailés
wing-forward N (Rugby) ailier m
wing mirror N (Brit) rétroviseur m latéral
wing nut N papillon m, écrou m à ailettes
wing three-quarter N (Rugby) trois-quarts aile m
wing tip N extrémité f de l'aile

wingback /ˈwɪŋ,bæk/ N (Sport) ailier m offensif

wingding‡ /ˈwɪŋ,dɪŋ/ N (US = party) fête f, boum* f

winge * /ˈwɪndʒ/ VI ⇒ **whinge**

winged /wɪŋd/ ADJ [creature, goddess, statue] ailé ◆ **Mercury, the ~ messenger of the gods** Mercure, le messager des dieux aux pieds ailés ◆ **the Winged Victory of Samothrace** la Victoire de Samothrace

-winged /wɪŋd/ ADJ (in compounds) ◆ **white-winged** aux ailes blanches

winger /ˈwɪŋəʳ/ N (Sport) ailier m ◆ **left-/right-~** (Pol) sympathisant(e) m(f) de gauche/droite, homme m (or femme f) de gauche/droite

wingless /ˈwɪŋlɪs/ ADJ sans ailes ; [insect] aptère

wingspan /ˈwɪŋspæn/, **wingspread** /ˈwɪŋspred/ N envergure f

wink /wɪŋk/ N clin m d'œil ; (= blink) clignement m ◆ **to give sb a ~** faire un clin d'œil à qn ◆ **with a ~** en clignant de l'œil ◆ **in a ~, (as) quick as a ~, in the ~ of an eye** en un clin d'œil ◆ **I didn't get a ~ of sleep*** je n'ai pas fermé l'œil (de la nuit) ; → **forty, sleep, tip²** VI [person] faire un clin d'œil (to, at à) ; (= blink) cligner des yeux ; [star, light] clignoter ◆ **to ~ at sth** (fig) fermer les yeux sur qch ◆ **they were willing to ~ at corruption within the prison service** ils étaient prêts à fermer les yeux sur la corruption dans le service pénitentiaire VT ◆ **to ~ one's eye** faire un clin d'œil (at sb à qn) ◆ **to ~ a tear back** or **away** cligner de l'œil pour chasser une larme

winker /ˈwɪŋkəʳ/ N (Brit) [of car] clignotant m

winking /ˈwɪŋkɪŋ/ ADJ [light, signal] clignotant N clins mpl d'œil ; (= blinking) clignements mpl d'yeux ◆ **it was as easy as ~*** c'était simple comme bonjour

winkle /ˈwɪŋkl/ N (Brit) bigorneau m VT ◆ **to ~ sth out of sth/sb** extirper qch de qch/qn COMP **winkle pickers*** NPL (Brit = shoes) chaussures fpl pointues

winnable /ˈwɪnəbl/ ADJ gagnable

winner /ˈwɪnəʳ/ N 1 (= victor: in fight, argument) vainqueur m ; (Sport) gagnant(e) m(f), vainqueur m ; (in competitions etc) lauréat(e) m(f), gagnant(e) m(f) ; (horse/car etc) (cheval m/voiture f etc) gagnant(e) m(f) ; (Sport) (= winning goal) but m de la victoire ; (= winning shot) coup m gagnant ◆ **to be the ~** gagner ◆ **I think he's on to a ~** (= will win) je crois qu'il va gagner ; (= has chosen winner) je crois qu'il a tiré le bon numéro
◆ **to be a winner** (= to be successful) être génial* ◆ **his latest CD/show is a ~*** (= to be potentially successful) son dernier CD/spectacle va faire un malheur* ◆ **that ball was a ~** (Tennis) cette balle était imparable* ◆ **he's a ~!*** (fig) il est génial !* ◆ **you know your idea is a ~ ...** vous savez que votre idée va marcher ... ; see also **pick**
2 (gen pl = beneficiary) gagnant(e) m(f) (fig) ◆ **the ~s will be the shareholders** ce sont les actionnaires qui seront les gagnants

Winnie-the-Pooh /ˌwɪnɪðəˈpuː/ N (Literat) Winnie l'ourson

winning /ˈwɪnɪŋ/ ADJ 1 [person, dog, car, blow, stroke, shot etc] gagnant ◆ **the ~ goal came in the last five minutes** le but de la victoire a été marqué dans les cinq dernières minutes 2 (= captivating) [person] charmant, adorable ; [smile, manner] charmeur, engageant ◆ **the child has ~ ways, the child has a ~ way with him** cet enfant a une grâce irrésistible NPL **winnings** (Betting etc) gains mpl COMP **winning post** N poteau m d'arrivée

winningly /ˈwɪnɪŋlɪ/ ADV d'une manière charmeuse, d'un air engageant

Winnipeg /ˈwɪnɪpeg/ N Winnipeg

winnow /ˈwɪnəʊ/ VT [+ grain] vanner ◆ **to ~ truth from falsehood** (liter) démêler le vrai du faux

winnower /ˈwɪnəʊəʳ/ N (= person) vanneur m, -euse f ; (= machine) tarare m

wino‡ /ˈwaɪnəʊ/ N poivrot* m, ivrogne mf

winsome /ˈwɪnsəm/ ADJ [person] avenant ; [smile] gracieux, charmant ; [charm] délicieux

winsomely /ˈwɪnsəmlɪ/ ADV d'une manière séduisante, d'un air engageant

winsomeness /ˈwɪnsəmnɪs/ N (NonC) charme m, séduction f

winter /ˈwɪntəʳ/ N hiver m ◆ **in ~** en hiver ◆ **in the ~ of 1996** pendant l'hiver de 1996 ◆ **"A Winter's Tale"** "Conte d'hiver" VI hiverner, passer l'hiver VT [+ animals] hiverner
COMP [weather, day, residence] d'hiver, hivernal ; [activities, temperatures] hivernal
winter clothes NPL vêtements mpl d'hiver
winter depression N spleen m hivernal
winter holidays NPL vacances fpl d'hiver
Winter Olympics NPL Jeux mpl olympiques d'hiver
winter resident N (= person) hivernant(e) m(f)
the winter season N la saison d'hiver
winter sleep N sommeil m hibernal, hibernation f
winter sports NPL sports mpl d'hiver

wintergreen /ˈwɪntə,griːn/ N (= plant) gaulthérie f ◆ **oil of ~** essence f de wintergreen

winterize /ˈwɪntəraɪz/ VT (US) préparer pour l'hiver

winterkill /ˈwɪntə,kɪl/ (US) VT [+ plant] tuer par le gel VI être tué par le gel

wintertime /ˈwɪntə,taɪm/ N hiver m ◆ **in (the) ~** en hiver COMP [staff, visitors, food etc] en hiver

wintry /ˈwɪntrɪ/ ADJ 1 [weather, day, sky, sun] d'hiver ◆ **in ~ conditions** par temps d'hiver

♦ ~ **conditions on the roads** difficultés *fpl* de circulation dues à l'hiver 2 *(= unfriendly) [person, smile]* glacial *(with sb* avec qn)

win-win /wɪn'wɪn/ * ADJ ♦ **a ~ situation** une situation où tout le monde gagne ♦ **these are potentially ~ proposals** ce sont des propositions où tout le monde peut y gagner N ♦ **this is a ~ for business and consumer** les entreprises aussi bien que les consommateurs y gagnent

wipe /waɪp/ N 1 *(= act of wiping)* coup *m* de torchon (*or* d'éponge *etc*) ♦ **to give sth a ~** donner un coup de torchon (*or* d'éponge *etc*) à qch

2 *(= treated cloth)* lingette *f* ; *(for face, hands)* serviette *f* rafraîchissante

VT 1 *[+ table, dishes, floor]* essuyer *(with* avec) ♦ **to ~ one's hands/face/eyes** s'essuyer les mains/le visage/les yeux *(on* sur ; *with* avec) ♦ **to ~ one's feet** *(with towel, on mat)* s'essuyer les pieds ♦ **to ~ one's nose** se moucher ♦ **to ~ one's bottom** s'essuyer ♦ **he ~d the glass dry** il a essuyé le verre ♦ **to ~ the blackboard** effacer *or* essuyer *or* nettoyer le tableau ♦ **to ~ the slate clean** *(fig)* passer l'éponge, tout effacer *(fig)* ♦ **to ~ the floor with sb** * réduire qn en miettes *

2 *[+ tape, disk, video]* effacer ♦ **to ~ sth from a tape** *etc* effacer qch sur une bande *etc*

COMP **wipe-out** N *(= destruction)* destruction *f*, annihilation *f* ; *(Windsurfing etc)* chute *f*, gamelle * *f*

► **wipe at** VT FUS essuyer ♦ **to ~ at one's eyes** s'essuyer les yeux

► **wipe away** VT SEP *[+ tears]* essuyer ; *[+ marks]* effacer

► **wipe down** VT SEP *[+ surface, wall etc]* essuyer

► **wipe off** VT SEP effacer ♦ **that will ~ the smile** *or* **grin off her face!** * après ça on va voir si elle a toujours le sourire !

► **wipe out** VT SEP 1 *[+ container]* bien essuyer ; *[+ writing, error etc]* effacer ; *(fig) [+ insult]* effacer, laver ; *[+ debt]* amortir ; *[+ the past, memory]* oublier, effacer ♦ **to ~ out an old score** régler une vieille dette *(fig)*

2 *(= annihilate) [+ town, people, army]* anéantir

3 *[+ opposing team]* écraser ♦ **to ~ sb out** * *[person]* régler son compte à qn ; *[event, news]* anéantir qn

N ♦ **wipe-out** → **wipe**

► **wipe up** VI essuyer la vaisselle

VT SEP essuyer

wiper /'waɪpəʳ/ N *(= cloth)* torchon *m* ; *(for windscreen)* essuie-glace *m inv* COMP **wiper blade** N balai *m* d'essuie-glace

wire /'waɪəʳ/ N 1 *(NonC = substance)* fil *m* (métallique *or* de fer) ; *(Elec)* fil *m* (électrique) ; *(= piece of wire)* fil *m* ; *(= snare)* collet *m*, lacet *m* ; (also **wire fence**) grillage *m*, treillis *m* métallique ♦ **they got their ~s crossed** * il y a eu malentendu, ils se sont mal compris ♦ **to get in** *or* **slip in under the ~** * arriver de justesse

♦ **down to the wire** *(fig)* ♦ **to go down to the ~** * *[competition]* rester incertain jusqu'au bout ♦ **negotiations are going down to the ~** l'issue des négociations est toujours incertaine ♦ **to work** *etc* **down to the ~** * travailler *etc* jusqu'au dernier moment ; → **barbed, live²**

2 *(US = telegram)* télégramme *m*

3 *(Police = hidden microphone)* micro *m* caché

NPL **wires** * *(US = spectacles)* lunettes *fpl* à monture d'acier

VT 1 (also **wire up**) *[+ opening, fence]* grillager ; *[+ teeth, jaw]* ligaturer ; *[+ flowers, beads]* monter sur fil de fer ; *(Elec) [+ house]* faire l'installation électrique de ; *[+ circuit]* installer ; *[+ plug]* monter ♦ **to ~ sth to sth** relier *or* rattacher qch à qch *(avec du fil de fer)* ; *(Elec)* brancher qch sur qch, relier qch à qch ♦ **to ~ a room (up) for sound** sonoriser une pièce ♦ **he was ~d for sound** * *(= wearing hidden microphone)* il portait un micro ♦ **it's all ~d (up) for television** l'antenne (réceptrice *or* émettrice) de télévision est déjà installée ♦ **~d-up** * *(US fig = tense)* surexcité, tendu

♦ **to wire up sb** *or* **sth** *(= connect to the Internet)* connecter qn *or* qch à l'Internet

♦ **to be wired into** *(= to be basic to)* faire partie intégrante de ♦ **these qualities are ~d into its genetic code** ces qualités font partie intégrante de son code génétique ♦ **some of these paradoxical tactics may have been ~d into our nervous system by the forces of evolution** certaines de ces tactiques paradoxales ont peut-être été imprimées dans notre système nerveux par la force de l'évolution

2 *(US = telegraph)* télégraphier *(to* à)

VI *(US)* télégraphier

COMP *[object, device]* de *or* en fil de fer

wire brush N brosse *f* métallique

wire-cutters NPL cisailles *fpl*, pinces *fpl* coupantes

wire-drawer, wire-drawing machine N étireuse *f*

wire gauge N calibre *m* (pour fils métalliques)

wire gauze N toile *f* métallique

wire glass N *(US)* verre *m* armé

wire-haired terrier N terrier *m* à poils durs

wire mesh N *(NonC)* treillis *m* métallique, grillage *m*

wire netting N ⇒ **wire mesh**

wire-puller * N *(US)* ♦ **he's a ~-puller** il n'hésite pas à se faire pistonner * *or* à faire jouer le piston *

wire-pulling * N *(US)* le piston * ♦ **to do some ~-pulling for sb** pistonner * qn

wire rope N câble *m* métallique

wire service N *(US Press)* agence *f* de presse *(utilisant des téléscripteurs)*

wire wool N *(Brit)* paille *f* de fer

► **wire together** VT SEP *[+ objects]* attacher (avec du fil de fer)

► **wire up** VT SEP ⇒ **wire vt 1**

wired /waɪəd/ ADJ 1 ♦ **to be ~** *(Comput)* être connecté ; *(for cable TV)* être raccordé ; *(= bugged)* être équipé de micros cachés 2 * *(esp US = tense)* tendu

wireless /'waɪəlɪs/ *(esp Brit)* N † *(= radio)* radio *f* ♦ **to send a message by ~** envoyer un sans-fil ♦ **they were communicating by ~** ils communiquaient par sans-fil ♦ **on the ~** à la TSF † ♦ **to listen to the ~** écouter la TSF †

COMP *[station, programme]* radiophonique ; *[data, technology, network]* sans fil

wireless message N radiogramme *m*, radio *m*, sans-fil *m*

wireless operator N radiotélégraphiste *mf*, radio *m*

wireless room N cabine *f* radio *inv*

wireless set N (poste *m* de) radio *f*

wireless telegraph, wireless telegraphy N télégraphie *f* sans fil, TSF † *f*, radiotélégraphie *f*

wireless telephone N téléphone *m* sans fil

wireless telephony N téléphonie *f* sans fil, radiotéléphonie *f*

wireman /'waɪəmən/ N (pl **-men**) *(US)* câbleur *m*

wiretap /'waɪətæp/ VI mettre un (*or* des) téléphone(s) sur écoute VT mettre sur écoute N écoute *f* téléphonique

wiretapping /'waɪətæpɪŋ/ N écoutes *fpl* téléphoniques

wireworks /'waɪəwɜːks/ N *(NonC)* tréfilerie *f*

wiring /'waɪərɪŋ/ N *(NonC)* 1 *(Elec: in building)* installation *f* électrique ; *[of appliance]* circuit *m* électrique ♦ **to have the ~ redone** faire refaire l'installation électrique (*in* de) 2 **the ~ of the brain** le système cérébral

wiry /'waɪərɪ/ ADJ 1 *(= thin) [person]* au physique maigre et nerveux ; *[body]* maigre et nerveux 2 *(= coarse) [hair, grass]* rêche

Wis abbrev of **Wisconsin**

Wisconsin /wɪs'kɒnsɪn/ N Wisconsin *m* ♦ **in ~** dans le Wisconsin

wisdom /'wɪzdəm/ N 1 *(NonC) [of person]* sagesse *f* ; *[of action, remark]* prudence *f* ; *[of decision]* bien-fondé *m* 2 *(= idea)* opinion *f*, idée *f* ♦ **one of the received ~s about Britain is that ...** l'une des opinions les plus répandues sur la Grande-Bretagne est que ... COMP **wisdom tooth** N dent *f* de sagesse

wise¹ /waɪz/ LANGUAGE IN USE 2.2

ADJ 1 *(= prudent) [person, words, decision]* sage ; *[action, choice, investment]* judicieux ♦ **a ~ man** un sage ♦ **a ~ move** une sage décision ♦ **to grow ~r with age** s'assagir avec l'âge *or* en vieillissant ♦ **to be ~ after the event** avoir raison après coup ♦ **how ~ of you!** vous avez eu bien raison ! ♦ **it wasn't very ~ (of you) to tell him that** ce n'était pas très judicieux (de ta part) de lui dire ça ♦ **it would be ~ to accept** il serait judicieux d'accepter ♦ **you'd be ~ to accept** il serait judicieux que vous acceptiez *subj* ♦ **he was ~ enough to refuse** il a eu la sagesse de refuser ♦ **the ~st thing to do is to ignore him** le plus judicieux *or* sage est de l'ignorer ; → **word**

2 (* *= aware, informed*) ♦ **to get ~** piger * ♦ **to be** *or* **get ~ to sb** voir clair dans le jeu de qn ♦ **to be** *or* **get ~ to sth** piger * qch ♦ **I was fooled once, but then I got ~** j'ai été échaudé une fois, mais j'ai retenu la leçon ♦ **get ~!** réveille-toi ! ♦ **I'm ~ to that one now** j'ai compris le truc * ♦ **to put sb ~ (to sth)** ouvrir les yeux de qn (sur qch), mettre qn au courant (de qch) ♦ **I'm none the ~r, I'm no ~r** *(= don't understand)* ça ne m'avance pas beaucoup, je ne suis pas plus avancé ♦ **nobody will be any the ~r** *(= won't find out)* personne n'en saura rien

COMP **wise guy** * N petit malin * *m*

the Wise Men NPL *(Bible:* also **the Three Wise Men**) les Rois *mpl* mages

► **wise up** *

VI ♦ **to wise up (to sth)** réaliser * (qch) ♦ **people finally seem to be wising up (to what is going on)** les gens semblent enfin réaliser * (ce qui se passe) ♦ **~ up!** réveille-toi !

VT SEP ♦ **to wise sb up** ouvrir les yeux de qn *(to, about* de) ♦ **to get ~d up about sth** être mis au parfum * de qch

wise² /waɪz/ N *(frm)* ♦ **in no ~** aucunement, en aucune façon *or* manière ♦ **in this ~** ainsi, de cette façon *or* manière

...wise /waɪz/ ADV *(in compounds)* 1 (*: *specifying point of view*) question *, côté * ♦ **healthwise he's fine but moneywise things aren't too good** question * *or* côté * santé ça va, mais question * *or* côté * argent ça pourrait aller mieux 2 *(specifying direction, position)* à la manière de, dans le sens de *etc* ; → **clockwise, lengthways**

wiseacre /'waɪzeɪkəʳ/ N *(pej)* puits *m* de science *(iro)*

wisecrack /'waɪzkræk/ N vanne * *f* VI balancer *or* sortir une (*or* des) vanne(s) * ♦ **"need any help?" he ~ed** "vous avez besoin de mes services ?" ironisa-t-il

wisely /'waɪzlɪ/ ADV 1 *(= prudently) [use, spend]* avec sagesse ; *[behave]* judicieusement ♦ **you have chosen ~** votre choix a été sage *or* judicieux ♦ **~, he turned down their first offer** il a eu la sagesse de refuser leur première proposition 2 *(= sagely) [nod, say etc]* d'un air entendu

wish /wɪʃ/ LANGUAGE IN USE 4, 7.5, 8.2, 19.2, 23, 24.3

VT 1 *(frm = desire)* souhaiter, désirer + *subj* ♦ **if you ~ to go away for the weekend, we will be delighted to make reservations** si vous souhaitez *or* désirez partir pour le week-end, nous nous ferons un plaisir de réserver pour vous ◆ **I ~ to be told when he comes** je souhaite *or* désire être informé de sa venue ◆ **I ~ to be alone** je souhaite *or* désire *or* voudrais être seul ◆ **he did not ~ it** il ne le souhaitait *or* désirait pas ◆ **what do you ~ him to do?** que souhaitez-vous *or* désirez-vous qu'il fasse ?

◆ **to wish (that)** ◆ **I ~ that you ...** *(+ cond)* je voudrais que vous ... ◆ **I ~ you'd been there** j'aurais voulu *or* aimé que tu sois là ◆ **I ~ you hadn't said that** tu n'aurais pas dû dire ça ◆ **I ~ you didn't always leave things till the last moment** si seulement tu ne faisais pas toujours tout à la dernière minute ! ◆ **I ~ I'd gone with you** j'aurais bien voulu vous accompagner, je regrette de ne pas vous avoir accompagné ◆ **I ~ you had left with him** j'aurais préféré que tu partes avec lui, je regrette que tu ne sois pas parti avec lui ◆ **I ~ I hadn't said that** je regrette d'avoir dit cela ◆ **I ~ you'd stop complaining!** arrête un peu de te plaindre ! ◆ **I only ~ I'd known about that before!** si seulement j'avais su ça avant !, comme je regrette de n'avoir pas su ça avant ! ◆ **I ~ I could!** si seulement je pouvais ! ◆ **I ~ to heaven* he hadn't done it!** mais pourquoi est-ce qu'il a fait ça ! ◆ **I ~ it weren't so** je préférerais qu'il en soit autrement

2 *(= desire for sb else)* souhaiter ◆ **I ~ you every success** je vous souhaite beaucoup de succès ◆ **he doesn't ~ her any ill** *or* **harm** il ne lui veut aucun mal ◆ **I ~ you well** *or* **I ~ you (good) luck in what you're trying to do** je vous souhaite de réussir dans ce que vous voulez faire ◆ **he ~ed us (good) luck as we left** il nous a souhaité bonne chance au moment de partir ◆ **~ me luck!** souhaite-moi bonne chance ! ◆ **to ~ sb good morning** dire bonjour à qn, souhaiter *or* donner le bonjour à qn † *(also hum)* ◆ **to ~ sb good-bye** dire au revoir à qn ◆ **to ~ sb a happy birthday** souhaiter bon anniversaire à qn ◆ **I ~ you every happiness!** je vous souhaite d'être très heureux ! ◆ **he ~ed us every happiness** il nous a exprimé tous ses souhaits de bonheur

3 *(* fig)* **the bike was ~ed on to me** je n'ai pas pu faire autrement que d'accepter le vélo ◆ **the job was ~ed on (to) me** c'est un boulot qu'on m'a collé* ◆ **I wouldn't ~ that on anybody** *or* **my worst enemy** c'est quelque chose que je ne souhaiterais pas à mon pire ennemi ◆ **I wouldn't ~ him on anybody** je ne souhaiterais sa présence à personne ◆ **I got her kids ~ed on (to) me for the holiday** elle m'a laissé ses gosses sur les bras pendant les vacances*

VI faire un vœu ◆ **you must ~ as you blow out the candles** il faut faire un vœu en soufflant les bougies ◆ **to ~ for sth** souhaiter qch ◆ **a philosopher said, "Be careful what you wish for, you might get it"** comme le dit le philosophe, "Attention à ne pas souhaiter n'importe quoi, vous pourriez l'obtenir" ◆ **I ~ed for that to happen** j'ai souhaité que cela se produise

◆ **could + wish for** ◆ **she's got everything she could ~ for** elle a tout ce qu'elle peut désirer ◆ **what more could you ~ for?** que pourrais-tu souhaiter de plus ? ◆ **it's not everything you could ~ for** ce n'est pas l'idéal ◆ **I couldn't ~ for anything better** je ne pouvais pas souhaiter mieux

N 1 *(= desire, will)* désir *m* ◆ **what is your ~?** que désirez-vous ? ◆ **your ~ is my command** *(liter or hum)* vos désirs sont pour moi des ordres ◆ **it has always been my ~ to do that** j'ai toujours désiré faire *or* eu envie de faire cela ◆ **he had no great ~ to go** il n'avait pas grande envie d'y aller ◆ **to go against sb's ~es** contrecarrer les désirs de qn ◆ **he did it against my ~es** il l'a fait contre mon gré

2 *(= specific desire)* vœu *m*, souhait *m* ◆ **to make a ~** faire un vœu ◆ **the fairy granted him three ~es** la fée lui accorda trois souhaits ◆ **his ~ came true, his ~ was granted, he got his ~** son vœu *or* souhait s'est réalisé ◆ **you shall have your ~** ton souhait sera réalisé *or* te sera accordé, ton vœu sera exaucé

3 *(= greeting)* ◆ **give him my good** *or* **best ~es** *(in conversation)* faites-lui mes amitiés ; *(in letter)* transmettez-lui mes meilleures pensées ◆ **he sends his best ~es** *(in conversation)* il vous fait ses amitiés ; *(in letter)* il vous envoie ses meilleures pensées ◆ **best ~es** *or* **all good ~es for a happy birthday** tous mes (*or* nos) meilleurs vœux pour votre anniversaire ◆ **(with) best ~es for a speedy recovery/your future happiness** tous mes (*or* nos) vœux de prompt rétablissement/de bonheur ◆ **(with) best ~es for Christmas and the New Year** (nos) meilleurs vœux pour Noël et la nouvelle année ◆ **(with) best ~es to both of you on your engagement** meilleurs vœux (de bonheur) à tous deux à l'occasion de vos fiançailles ◆ **(with) best ~es for a happy holiday** je vous souhaite (*or* nous vous souhaitons) d'excellentes vacances ◆ **with best ~es from, with all good ~es from** *(in letter)* bien amicalement ◆ **the Queen sent a message of good ~es on Independence Day** la reine a envoyé des vœux pour le jour de l'Indépendance ◆ **they came to offer him their best ~es on the occasion of ...** ils sont venus lui offrir leurs meilleurs vœux pour ...

COMP wish fulfilment N *(Psych)* accomplissement *m* d'un désir

wish list N liste *f* de souhaits ◆ **what is your ~ list?** quels sont vos souhaits ? ◆ **top of my ~ list** mon souhait le plus cher

wishbone /ˈwɪʃbəʊn/ **N** *[of bird]* bréchet *m*, fourchette *f* ; *(Sport)* wishbone *m*

wishful /ˈwɪʃfʊl/ **ADJ** ◆ **to be ~ to do sth** *or* **of doing sth** *(frm)* avoir envie de faire ◆ **he hopes he'll be released from prison next month, but that's just ~ thinking!** il espère être libéré de prison le mois prochain, mais il prend ses désirs pour des réalités ! ◆ **all this is pure ~ thinking on our part** là, nous prenons vraiment nos désirs pour des réalités, ce ne sont que des vœux pieux ◆ **it is ~ thinking to expect it to be warm in March** il ne faut pas rêver*, il ne fera pas chaud en mars

wishy-washy* /ˈwɪʃɪ,wɒʃɪ/ **ADJ** *(pej) [person, answer]* mou (molle *f*) ; *[style]* mou (molle *f*), fadasse* ; *[speech, taste]* fadasse* ; *[colour]* fadasse*, délavé ; *[statement, phrase]* qui manque de fermeté

wisp /wɪsp/ **N** *[of straw]* brin *m* ; *[of hair]* fine mèche *f* ; *[of thread]* petit bout *m* ; *[of smoke]* mince volute *f* ◆ **a little ~ of a girl** une fillette menue

wispy /ˈwɪspɪ/ **ADJ** *[hair, beard, moustache]* fin et clairsemé ; *[bit of straw]* fin ; *[cloud]* léger ◆ **traces of ~ smoke** maigres filets *mpl* de fumée

wistaria /wɪsˈtɛərɪə/, **wisteria** /wɪsˈtɪərɪə/ **N** glycine *f*

wistful /ˈwɪstfʊl/ **ADJ** *[person, look, song, mood, smile, sigh, voice]* mélancolique, nostalgique ◆ **to feel ~ (about sth)** se sentir plein de nostalgie (à la pensée de qch)

wistfully /ˈwɪstfəlɪ/ **ADV** *[look, smile, sigh]* avec mélancolie *or* nostalgie

wistfulness /ˈwɪstfʊlnɪs/ **N** *[of person]* caractère *m* mélancolique ; *[of look, smile, voice]* nostalgie *f*, mélancolie *f*, regret *m*

wit[1] /wɪt/ **VI** *(frm, also Jur)* ◆ **to ~ ...** à savoir ..., c'est à dire ...

wit[2] /wɪt/ **N** 1 *(= intelligence)* ~(s) esprit *m*, intelligence *f* ◆ **mother ~, native ~** bon sens *m*, sens *m* commun ◆ **he hadn't the ~** *or* **he hadn't enough ~ to hide the letter** il n'a pas eu l'intelligence *or* la présence d'esprit de cacher la lettre ◆ **to have your ~s about you** avoir de la présence d'esprit ◆ **you'll need (to have) all your ~s about you if you're to avoid being seen** tu vas devoir faire très attention *or* être très vigilant pour éviter d'être vu ◆ **keep your ~s about you!** restez attentif ! ◆ **use your ~s!** sers-toi de ton intelligence ! ◆ **it was a battle of ~s (between them)** ils jouaient au plus fin ◆ **he lives by** *or* **on his ~s** il vit d'expédients ◆ **to collect** *or* **gather one's ~s** rassembler ses esprits ◆ **the struggle for survival sharpened his ~s** la lutte pour la vie aiguisait ses facultés ◆ **he was at his ~s' end** il ne savait plus que faire, il ne savait plus à quel saint se vouer ◆ **I'm at my ~s' end to know what to do** je ne sais plus du tout ce que je dois faire ◆ **to be/go out of one's ~s** être/devenir fou ◆ **she was nearly out of her ~s with worry about him** elle était folle d'inquiétude pour lui

2 *(NonC = wittiness)* esprit *m* ◆ **the book is full of ~** le livre est très spirituel *or* est plein d'esprit ◆ **he has a ready** *or* **pretty ~** il a beaucoup d'esprit, il est très spirituel ◆ **in a flash of ~ he said ...** obéissant à une inspiration spirituelle il a dit ... ◆ **this flash of ~ made them all laugh** ce trait d'esprit les a tous fait rire

3 *(= person)* homme *m* d'esprit, femme *f* d'esprit ; *(Hist, Literat)* bel esprit *m*

witch /wɪtʃ/ **N** sorcière *f* ; *(fig) (= charmer)* ensorceleuse *f*, magicienne *f* ◆ **she's an old ~** *(fig pej)* c'est une vieille sorcière ◆ **~es' sabbath** sabbat *m* (de sorcières)

COMP witch doctor N sorcier *m (de tribu)*

witch-elm N ⇒ **wych-elm**

witches' brew N *(lit)* brouet *m* de sorcière ; *(fig)* mélange *m* explosif

witch hazel N hamamélis *m*

witch hunt N *(esp Pol: fig)* chasse *f* aux sorcières

witching hour N ◆ **the ~ing hour of midnight** minuit, l'heure fatale, minuit, l'heure du crime *(hum)*

witch's brew N ⇒ **witches' brew**

witchcraft /ˈwɪtʃkrɑːft/ **N** sorcellerie *f*

witchery /ˈwɪtʃərɪ/ **N** sorcellerie *f* ; *(fig = fascination)* magie *f*, envoûtement *m*

with /wɪð, wɪθ/

1 PREPOSITION 2 COMPOUNDS

1 - PREPOSITION

When **with** is part of a set combination, eg **good with**, **pleased with**, **to agree with**, look up the other word.

1 avec ◆ **I was ~ her** j'étais avec elle ◆ **come ~ me!** viens avec moi ! ◆ **he had an argument ~ his brother** il s'est disputé avec son frère ◆ **the trouble ~ Paul is that ...** l'ennui avec Paul, c'est que ... ◆ **he walks ~ a stick** il marche avec une canne ◆ **be patient ~ her** sois patient avec elle

The pronoun is not translated in the following, where **it** and **them** refer to things:

◆ **he's gone off ~ it** il est parti avec ◆ **take my gloves, I can't drive ~ them on** prends mes gants, je ne peux pas conduire avec

Note the verbal construction in the following examples:

◆ **that problem is always ~ us** ce problème n'est toujours pas résolu ◆ **she had her umbrella ~ her** elle avait emporté son parapluie

◆ **to be with sb** *(lit)* être avec qn ; *(= understand)* suivre qn ◆ **I'm ~ you** *(= understand)* je vous suis ◆ **sorry, I'm not ~ you** désolé, je ne vous suis pas ◆ **are you ~ us, Laura?** *(= paying attention)* tu nous suis, Laura ? ◆ **I'll be ~ you in a** minute (= *attend to*) je suis à vous dans une minute ◆ **I'm ~ you all the way** (= *support*) je suis à fond avec vous ◆ **what's ~ you?*** qu'est-ce que tu as ? ◆ **what is it ~ the British?*** qu'est-ce qu'ils ont, ces Anglais ?

◆ **to be with it*** (= *fashionable*) être dans le vent*

◆ **to get with it*** ◆ **get ~ it!** (= *pay attention*) réveille-toi !, secoue-toi ! ; (= *face facts*) redescends sur terre !

2 [= on one's person] sur ◆ **I haven't got any money ~ me** je n'ai pas d'argent sur moi

3 [= in the house of, working with] chez ◆ **she was staying ~ friends** elle habitait chez des amis ◆ **he lives ~ his aunt** il habite chez *or* avec sa tante ◆ **he's ~ IBM** il travaille chez IBM ◆ **a scientist ~ ICI** un chercheur de ICI ◆ **I've been ~ this company for seven years** cela fait sept ans que je travaille pour cette société

4 [in descriptions = that has, that have] ◆ **the man ~ the beard** l'homme à la barbe ◆ **the boy ~ brown eyes** le garçon aux yeux marron ◆ **the house ~ the green shutters** la maison aux volets verts ◆ **I want a coat ~ a fur collar** je veux un manteau avec un col de fourrure ◆ **passengers ~ tickets** voyageurs *mpl* munis de *or* en possession de billets ◆ **patients ~ cancer** les personnes atteintes d'un cancer ◆ **only people ~ good incomes can afford such holidays** seules les personnes qui ont un bon salaire peuvent s'offrir de telles vacances ◆ **a car ~ the latest features** une voiture équipée des derniers perfectionnements techniques

5 [cause] de ◆ **she was sick ~ fear** elle était malade de peur ◆ **he was shaking ~ rage** il tremblait de rage ◆ **the hills are white ~ snow** les montagnes sont blanches de neige

6 [= in spite of] malgré ◆ **~ all his faults I still like him** je l'aime bien malgré tous ses défauts ◆ **~ all his intelligence, he still doesn't understand** malgré toute son intelligence, il ne comprend toujours pas ◆ **~ all that he is still the best we've got** malgré tout, c'est encore le meilleur homme que nous ayons

7 [manner] avec ◆ **he did it ~ great care** il l'a fait avec beaucoup de précautions ◆ **I'll do it ~ pleasure** je le ferai avec plaisir ◆ **... he said ~ a smile** ... dit-il en souriant ◆ **she took off her shoes ~ a sigh** elle a retiré ses chaussures en soupirant ◆ **I found the street ~ no trouble at all** je n'ai eu aucun mal à trouver la rue ◆ **she turned away ~ tears in her eyes** elle s'est détournée, les larmes aux yeux ◆ **~ my whole heart** de tout mon cœur

8 [circumstances] ◆ **~ the price of petrol these days ...** au prix où est l'essence de nos jours ... ◆ **~ these words he left us** sur ces mots, il nous a quittés ◆ **~ the approach of winter** à l'approche de l'hiver ◆ **~ the elections no one talks anything but politics** avec les élections, on ne parle plus que politique ◆ **I couldn't see him ~ so many people there** il y avait tellement de monde que je ne l'ai pas vu ◆ **~ so much happening it was difficult to ...** il se passait tellement de choses qu'il était difficile de ...

◆ **with that** ◆ **~ that, he closed the door** sur ce *or* là-dessus, il a fermé la porte

2 - COMPOUNDS

with-profits ADJ (*Fin*) [*policy*] avec participation aux bénéfices

withal †† /wɪˈðɔːl/ ADV en outre, de plus

withdraw /wɪθˈdrɔː/ (pret **withdrew**, ptp **withdrawn**) VT [+ *person, hand, money, application, troops*] retirer (*from* de) ; [+ *permission, help*] retirer (*from* à) ; [+ *ambassador, representative*] rappeler ; [+ *accusation, opinion, suggestion, statement*] retirer, rétracter ; [+ *claim*] retirer, renoncer à ; [+ *order*] annuler ; (*Med*) [+ *drugs*] arrêter ; (*Comm*) [+ *goods*] retirer de la vente ; (*Fin*) [+ *banknotes*] retirer de la circulation ◆ **to ~ a charge** (*Jur*) retirer une accusation ◆ **to ~ one's penis** se retirer (*from* de)

VI 1 (= *move away*) [*troops*] se replier (*from* de) ; [*person*] se retirer ◆ **to ~ to a new position** (*Mil*) se replier ◆ **he withdrew a few paces** il a reculé de quelques pas ◆ **she withdrew into her bedroom** elle s'est retirée dans sa chambre ◆ **to ~ into o.s.** se replier sur soi-même

2 (= *retract offer, promise etc*) se rétracter, se dédire

3 [*candidate, competitor, participant*] se retirer, se désister (*from* de ; *in favour of sb* en faveur de qn) ◆ **you can't ~ now, we've nearly achieved our goal** tu ne peux plus te retirer maintenant, nous avons pratiquement atteint notre but ◆ **I ~ from the game** je me retire de la partie, j'abandonne ◆ **they threatened to ~ from the talks** ils ont menacé de se retirer des négociations *or* de quitter la table des négociations

4 (= *retract penis*) se retirer

withdrawal /wɪθˈdrɔːəl/ N 1 (*NonC*) (= *removal*) [*of money, application, troops, product*] retrait *m* (*from sth* de qch) ; [*of services*] suppression *f* ◆ **his party has announced its ~ of support for the government** son parti a annoncé qu'il retirait son soutien au gouvernement ◆ **the ~ of American diplomats from the area** le rappel des diplomates américains dans la région ◆ **the army's ~ to new positions** le repli de l'armée sur de nouvelles positions ◆ **to make a ~** (*Fin: from bank etc*) effectuer un retrait

2 (*NonC* = *retraction*) [*of remark, allegation*] rétractation *f*

3 (= *resigning*) [*of member, participant, candidate*] désistement *m* (*from sth* de qch) ; [*of athlete*] retrait *m* (*from sth* de qch)

4 (*NonC: Psych*) repli *m* sur soi-même (*from sb/sth* par rapport à qn/qch), rétraction *f*

5 (*NonC: after addiction*) (état *m* de) manque *m*, syndrome *m* de sevrage ◆ **alcohol/caffeine ~** l'état *m* de manque dû à l'arrêt de la consommation d'alcool/de café ◆ **to be in** *or* **suffering from ~** être en (état de) manque

6 (*as contraception*) coït *m* interrompu

COMP **withdrawal method** N méthode *f* du coït interrompu

withdrawal slip N (*Banking*) bordereau *m* de retrait

withdrawal symptoms NPL symptômes *mpl* de (l'état de) manque ◆ **to suffer** *or* **experience** *or* **have ~ symptoms** être en (état de) manque

withdrawn /wɪθˈdrɔːn/ VB ptp of **withdraw** ADJ (= *reserved*) [*person*] renfermé

withdrew /wɪθˈdruː/ VB pt of **withdraw**

withe /wɪθ/ N ⇒ **withy**

wither /ˈwɪðəʳ/ VI [*plant*] se flétrir, se faner ; [*person, limb*] (*from illness*) s'atrophier ; (*from age*) se ratatiner ; (*fig*) [*beauty*] se faner ; [*hope, love, enthusiasm*] s'évanouir VT [+ *plant*] flétrir, faner ; [+ *limb*] atrophier, ratatiner ; [+ *beauty*] faner ; [+ *hope etc*] détruire petit à petit ◆ **he ~ed her with a look** il l'a regardée avec un profond mépris, son regard méprisant lui a donné envie de rentrer sous terre

► **wither away** VI [*plant*] se dessécher, mourir ; [*hope etc*] s'évanouir ; [*organization*] disparaître

withered /ˈwɪðəd/ ADJ 1 (= *dried-up*) [*flower, leaf, plant*] flétri, fané ; [*fruit*] desséché, ridé ; (*fig*) [*person*] desséché, ratatiné 2 (*liter* = *atrophied*) [*arm, leg, hand*] atrophié

withering /ˈwɪðərɪŋ/ N 1 [*of plant*] dépérissement *m* 2 (*liter*) [*of limb*] atrophie *f* 3 [*of beauty*] déclin *m* ; [*of hope, love, enthusiasm*] évanouissement *m* ADJ [*remark, criticism, contempt, scorn, irony*] cinglant ; [*tone, smile, look*] profondément méprisant ; [*heat*] desséchant ◆ **to give sb a ~ look** jeter à qn un regard profondément méprisant ◆ **to launch a ~ attack on sb** lancer une attaque violente contre qn

witheringly /ˈwɪðərɪŋlɪ/ ADV [*say, reply*] d'un ton plein de mépris ; [*look at*] avec mépris

withers /ˈwɪðəz/ NPL garrot *m* (*du cheval*)

withershins /ˈwɪðəʃɪnz/ ADV (*dial* = *anticlockwise*) dans le sens inverse des aiguilles d'une montre

withhold /wɪθˈhəʊld/ (pret, ptp **withheld** /wɪθˈheld/) VT [+ *money from pay etc*] retenir (*from sth* de qch) ; [+ *payment, decision*] remettre, différer ; [+ *one's consent, permission, one's help, support*] refuser (*from sb* à qn) ; [+ *facts, truth, news*] cacher, taire (*from sb* à qn) ; ◆ **police withheld the dead boy's name until relatives could be told** la police n'a révélé l'identité de l'enfant décédé que lorsqu'il a été possible d'informer la famille ◆ **he withheld his tax in protest against ...** il a refusé de payer ses impôts pour protester contre ... ◆ **a public debate on euthanasia and the ~ing of medical treatment** un débat public sur l'euthanasie et l'arrêt des soins médicaux

withholding tax N retenue *f* à la source

within /wɪðˈɪn/ ADV dedans, à l'intérieur ◆ **from ~** de l'intérieur

PREP 1 (= *inside*) à l'intérieur de ◆ **~ the box** à l'intérieur de la boîte ◆ **~ it** à l'intérieur ◆ **~ (the boundary of) the park** à l'intérieur du parc, dans les limites du parc ◆ **here ~ the town** à l'intérieur même de la ville ◆ **~ the city walls** intra-muros, dans l'enceinte de la ville ◆ **a voice ~ him said ...** une voix en lui disait ...

2 (= *within limits of*) **to be ~ the law** être dans (les limites de) la légalité ◆ **to live ~ one's income** *or* **means** vivre selon ses moyens ◆ **~ the range of the guns** à portée de(s) canon(s) ◆ **the coast was ~ sight** la côte était en vue ◆ **they were ~ sight of the town** ils étaient en vue de la ville ◆ **he was ~ reach** *or* **sight of his goal** (*fig*) il touchait au but ; → **call, province, reach**

3 (*in measurement, distances*) **~ a kilometre of the house** à moins d'un kilomètre de la maison ◆ **we were ~ a mile of the town** nous étions à moins d'un mille de la ville ◆ **correct to ~ a centimetre** correct à un centimètre près ; → **inch**

4 (*in time*) **~ a week of her visit** (= *after*) moins d'une semaine après sa visite ; (= *before*) moins d'une semaine avant sa visite ◆ **I'll be back ~ an hour** *or* **the hour** je serai de retour d'ici une heure ◆ **they arrived ~ minutes (of our call)** ils sont arrivés très peu de temps après (notre appel) ◆ **he returned ~ the week** il est revenu avant la fin de la semaine ◆ **~ two years from now** d'ici deux ans ◆ **"use within three days of opening"** "se conserve trois jours après ouverture" ◆ **~ a period of four months** (*Comm*) dans un délai de quatre mois ◆ **~ the stipulated period** dans les délais stipulés ; → **living**

ADJ (*Jur*) ◆ **the ~ instrument** le document ci-inclus

without /wɪðˈaʊt/

When **without** is an element in a phrasal verb, eg **do without, go without**, look up the verb.

PREP 1 (= *lacking*) sans ◆ **~ a coat** sans manteau ◆ **~ a coat or hat** sans manteau ni chapeau ◆ **he went off ~ it** il est parti sans (le prendre) ◆ **~ any money** sans argent, sans un *or* le sou* ◆ **he is ~ friends** il n'a pas d'amis ◆ **with or ~ sugar?** avec ou sans sucre ? ◆ **~ so much as a phone call** sans même un malheureux coup de fil ◆ **~ a doubt** sans aucun doute ◆ **~ doubt** sans doute ◆ **not ~ some difficulty** non sans difficulté ◆ **do it ~ fail** ne manquez pas de le faire, faites-le sans faute ◆ **he was quite ~**

shame il n'avait aucune honte ◆ ~ **speaking, he ...** sans parler, il ... ◆ ~ **anybody knowing** sans que personne le sache ◆ **to go ~ sth, to do ~ sth** se passer de qch

2 (†† = *outside)* au *or* en dehors de, à l'extérieur de

ADV † à l'extérieur, au dehors ◆ **from ~** de l'extérieur, de dehors

withstand /wɪθ'stænd/ (pret, ptp **withstood** /wɪθ'stʊd/) VT résister à

withy /'wɪðɪ/ N brin *m* d'osier

witless /'wɪtlɪs/ ADJ stupide ◆ **to scare sb ~*** faire une peur bleue à qn ◆ **I was scared ~*** j'étais mort de peur ◆ **to be bored ~*** s'ennuyer à mourir

witness /'wɪtnɪs/ N 1 *(Jur etc = person)* témoin *m* ◆ **~ for the defence/prosecution** *(Jur)* témoin *m* à décharge/à charge ◆ **to lead a ~** poser des questions tendancieuses à un témoin ◆ **there were three ~es to this event** trois personnes ont été témoins de cet événement, cet événement a eu trois témoins ◆ **he was a ~ to** *or* **of this incident** il a été témoin de cet incident ◆ **often children are ~ to violent events** les enfants sont souvent témoins de violences ◆ **the ~es to his signature** les témoins certifiant sa signature ◆ **in front of two ~es** en présence de deux témoins ◆ **to call sb as ~** *(Jur)* citer qn comme témoin ◆ **"your witness"** *(Jur)* "le témoin est à vous" ; → **eyewitness**

2 *(esp Jur = evidence)* témoignage *m* ◆ **in ~ of** en témoignage de ◆ **in ~ whereof** en témoignage de quoi, en foi de quoi ◆ **to give ~ on behalf of/against** témoigner en faveur de/contre, rendre témoignage pour/contre ◆ **he has his good points, as ~ his work for the blind** il a ses bons côtés, témoin *or* comme le prouve ce qu'il fait pour les aveugles ◆ **~ the case of ...** témoin le cas de ...

◆ **to bear** *or* **be witness to sth** témoigner de qch ◆ **his poems bear ~ to his years spent in India** ses poèmes témoignent de ses années passées en Inde ◆ **her clothes were ~ to her poverty** ses vêtements témoignaient de sa pauvreté

VT 1 *(= see) [+ attack, murder, theft]* être témoin de ; *[+ fight, rape]* être témoin de, assister à ◆ **did anyone ~ the theft?** quelqu'un a-t-il été témoin du vol ? ◆ **the accident was ~ed by several people** plusieurs personnes ont été témoins de l'accident

2 *(fig) (= see)* voir ; *(= notice) [+ change, improvement]* remarquer ◆ **a building/a century which has ~ed ...** *(fig)* un bâtiment/un siècle qui a vu ... ◆ **1989 ~ed the birth of a new world order** 1989 a vu l'avènement d'un nouvel ordre mondial ◆ **Americans are generous people, ~ the increase in charitable giving** les Américains sont généreux, témoin l'augmentation des dons aux associations caritatives

3 *(esp Jur) [+ document]* attester *or* certifier l'authenticité de ; *[signature]* certifier

VI *(Jur)* ◆ **to ~ to sth** témoigner de qch ◆ **he ~ed to having seen the accident** il a témoigné avoir vu l'accident ◆ **to ~ against sb** témoigner contre qn

COMP **witness box** *(Brit)*, **witness stand** *(US)* N barre *f* des témoins ◆ **in the ~ box** *or* **stand** à la barre

witness statement N déposition *f* de témoin

-witted /'wɪtɪd/ ADJ *(in compounds)* à l'esprit ... ◆ **quick-witted** à l'esprit vif ; → **slow**

witter* /'wɪtəʳ/ VI *(Brit)* ◆ **to ~ on about sth** dégoiser* sur qch ◆ **stop ~ing (on)** arrête de parler pour ne rien dire

witticism /'wɪtɪsɪzəm/ N mot *m* d'esprit, bon mot *m*

wittily /'wɪtɪlɪ/ ADV avec esprit *or* humour ◆ **"only on Fridays", he said ~** "seulement le vendredi" dit-il avec esprit *or* humour ◆ **the film was well acted and ~ written** le film était bien joué et écrit avec esprit *or* humour

wittiness /'wɪtɪnɪs/ N *(NonC)* esprit *m*, humour *m*

wittingly /'wɪtɪŋlɪ/ ADV *(frm)* sciemment, en connaissance de cause

witty /'wɪtɪ/ ADJ *[person, speaker, remark]* spirituel, plein d'esprit ; *[conversation, story, speech, script]* plein d'esprit ◆ **a ~ remark** un mot d'esprit, une remarque pleine d'esprit

wives /waɪvz/ NPL of **wife**

wiz /wɪz/ N *(US)* as *m*, crack* *m*

wizard /'wɪzəd/ N 1 *(= magician)* magicien *m*, enchanteur *m* ◆ **he is a financial ~** il a le génie de la finance, c'est un magicien de la finance ◆ **he is a ~ with a paintbrush** c'est un champion* *or* un as du pinceau ◆ **he's a ~ with numbers** il est très doué pour les chiffres ◆ **he's a ~ at chess** c'est un as *or* un crack* des échecs 2 *(Comput)* wizard *m*

wizardry /'wɪzədrɪ/ N *(NonC)* magie *f* ; *(fig)* génie *m* ◆ **a piece of technical ~** une merveille d'ingéniosité technique ◆ **this evidence of his financial ~** cette preuve de son génie en matière financière ◆ **£600,000 worth of electronic ~** une merveille de l'électronique valant 600 000 livres

wizened /'wɪznd/ ADJ *[person]* desséché, ratatiné ; *[face, hands]* flétri

wk abbrev of **week**

WLTM * VT (abbrev of **would like to meet**) dfc

WMD(s) /ˌdʌbljuemˈdiː(z)/ N (PL) (abbrev of **weapons of mass destruction**) ADM *fpl*

WO /ˌdʌbljuːˈəʊ/ N *(Mil)* (abbrev of **warrant officer**) → **warrant**

woad /wəʊd/ N guède *f*

woah /wəʊ/ EXCL ⇒ **whoa**

wobble /'wɒbl/ VI 1 *[jelly, hand, pen, voice]* trembler ; *[cyclist, object about to fall, pile of rocks]* vaciller ; *[tightrope walker, dancer]* chanceler ; *[table, chair]* branler, être bancal ; *[compass needle]* osciller ; *[wheel]* avoir du jeu ◆ **the table was wobbling** la table branlait ◆ **this table ~s** cette table est bancale ◆ **the cart ~d through the streets** la charrette bringuebalait *or* cahotait dans les rues 2 (* *fig = hesitate)* hésiter *(between* entre) VT faire vaciller

wobbly /'wɒblɪ/ ADJ 1 *(= shaky) [table, chair]* bancal ; *[jelly]* qui tremble ; *[tooth]* qui bouge ; *[wheel]* qui a du jeu ; *[hand, voice]* tremblant ; *[bottom, thighs]* gros (grosse *f*) et flasque ◆ **his legs are a bit ~, he's a bit ~ on his legs** il flageole un peu sur ses jambes ◆ **she was still a bit ~ after her illness*** elle se sentait toujours un peu patraque* après sa maladie ◆ **a ~ line*** une ligne qui n'est pas droite ◆ **to be ~** ⇒ **to wobble ;** → **wobble** vi 2 (* *= dodgy) [organization, economy, sector]* fragile N 1 ◆ **to throw a ~** ⁑ piquer une crise* 2 *(US Hist)* **the Wobblies*** *mouvement syndicaliste du début du 20e siècle*

wodge /wɒdʒ/ N *(Brit)* gros morceau *m*

woe /wəʊ/ N malheur *m* ◆ **~ is me!** *(† or hum)* pauvre de moi ! ◆ **~ betide the man who ...** malheur à celui qui ... ◆ **he told me his ~s** *or* **his tale of ~** il m'a fait le récit de ses malheurs ◆ **it was such a tale of ~ that ...** c'était une litanie si pathétique que ...

woebegone /'wəʊbɪˌgɒn/ ADJ *(liter)* désolé, abattu

woeful /'wəʊfʊl/ ADJ 1 *(liter = tragic) [person]* malheureux ; *[news, story, sight]* tragique, terrible 2 *(= appalling, dire) [ignorance, inability, track-record]* lamentable, déplorable

woefully /'wəʊfəlɪ/ ADV 1 *(liter) [look]* d'un air affligé ; *[say]* d'un ton affligé 2 *(= appallingly) [inadequate, underfunded etc]* terriblement ◆ **to be ~ ignorant of politics/science** *etc* être d'une ignorance crasse en matière de politique/science *etc* ◆ **~ inefficient** terriblement inefficace ◆ **the hospital is ~ lacking in modern equipment** cet hôpital manque cruellement de matériel moderne, le matériel moderne fait cruellement défaut à cet hôpital ◆ **modern equipment is ~ lacking** on manque cruellement de matériel moderne, le matériel moderne fait cruellement défaut

wog *⁑/ wɒg/ N *(Brit pej)* nègre*⁑*m*, négresse*⁑*f*

wok /wɒk/ N wok *m*

woke /wəʊk/ VB pt of **wake²**

woken /'wəʊkn/ VB ptp of **wake²**

wold /wəʊld/ N haute plaine *f*, plateau *m*

wolf /wʊlf/ N (pl **wolves**) loup *m* ◆ **she-~** louve *f* ◆ **a ~ in sheep's clothing** un loup déguisé en agneau ◆ **that will keep the ~ from the door** cela nous (*or* les *etc*) mettra au moins à l'abri du besoin ◆ **to throw sb to the wolves** jeter qn dans la fosse aux lions ; *(to the press)* jeter qn en pâture aux journalistes ; → **cry, lone** VT (also **wolf down**) engloutir

COMP **wolf call** N *(US)* ⇒ **wolf whistle**

wolf cub N *(also Scouting* †*)* louveteau *m*

wolf pack N meute *f* de loups

wolf whistle N *(fig)* sifflement *m* admiratif *(à l'adresse d'une fille)* ◆ **he gave a ~ whistle** il a sifflé la fille (*or* les filles)

wolfhound /'wʊlfhaʊnd/ N chien-loup *m*

wolfish /'wʊlfɪʃ/ ADJ vorace

wolfishly /'wʊlfɪʃlɪ/ ADV voracement

wolfram /'wʊlfrəm/ N wolfram *m*, tungstène *m*

wolfsbane /'wʊlfsbeɪn/ N *(= plant)* aconit *m*

wolverine /'wʊlvəriːn/ N 1 *(= animal)* glouton *m*, carcajou *m* 2 *(US)* **Wolverine** habitant(e) *m(f)* du Michigan COMP **the Wolverine State** N *(US)* le Michigan

wolves /wʊlvz/ NPL of **wolf**

woman /'wʊmən/ (pl **women**) N 1 femme *f* ◆ **~ is a mysterious creature** la femme est une créature mystérieuse ◆ **she's the ~ for the job** c'est la femme qu'il (nous *or* leur *etc*) faut pour ce travail ◆ **she's her own ~** elle est son propre maître ◆ **a ~ of the world** une femme du monde ◆ **Paul and all his women** Paul et toutes ses maîtresses ◆ **the ~ must be mad*** cette femme doit être folle ◆ **~ to ~** entre femmes ◆ **look here, my good ~** † écoutez, chère Madame ◆ **the little ~** ⁑ *(hum = wife)* ma (*or* sa *etc*) légitime⁑ ◆ **the other ~** *(= lover)* la maîtresse ◆ **young ~** † jeune femme *f* ◆ **a ~ of letters** une femme de lettres ◆ **she belongs to a women's group** elle est membre d'un groupe féministe ◆ **women's page** *(Press)* la page des lectrices ◆ **women's rights** les droits *mpl* de la femme ◆ **women's suffrage** le droit de vote pour les femmes ◆ **women's team** équipe *f* féminine ◆ **a ~'s place is in the home** *(Prov)* la place d'une femme est au foyer ◆ **a ~'s work is never done** *(Prov)* on trouve toujours à faire dans une maison

2 *(= cleaner)* femme *f* de ménage ◆ **I've got a ~ who comes in three times a week** j'ai une femme de ménage qui vient trois fois par semaine

ADJ ◆ **he's got a ~ music teacher** son professeur de musique est une femme ◆ **~ friend** amie *f* ◆ **~ worker** ouvrière *f* ◆ **women doctors think that ...** les femmes médecins pensent que ... ◆ **women often prefer women doctors** les femmes préfèrent souvent les femmes médecins

COMP **woman driver** N conductrice *f* ◆ **women drivers are often maligned** on dit souvent du mal des femmes au volant

woman-hater N misogyne *mf*

woman police constable N (Brit) femme f agent de police
Women's Centre N ≈ centre m d'accueil de femmes
Women's Institute N (Brit) *association de femmes de tendance plutôt traditionaliste*
Women's Lib †* N ⇒ **Women's (Liberation) Movement**
Women's Libber †* N féministe mf
women's liberation N la libération de la femme
Women's (Liberation) Movement N mouvement m de libération de la femme, MLF m
women's refuge N refuge m pour femmes battues
women's room N (US) toilettes fpl pour dames
women's studies NPL (Univ) *étude des rôles sociologique, historique et littéraire de la femme*

womanhood /ˈwʊmənhʊd/ N (NonC = feminine nature) féminité f ◆ **to reach** ~ devenir femme

womanish /ˈwʊmənɪʃ/ ADJ (pej) efféminé

womanize /ˈwʊmənaɪz/ VI courir les femmes

womanizer /ˈwʊmənaɪzəʳ/ N coureur m de jupons

womankind /ˈwʊmənkaɪnd/ N les femmes fpl

womanliness /ˈwʊmənlɪnɪs/ N (NonC) féminité f, caractère m féminin

womanly /ˈwʊmənlɪ/ ADJ [figure, bearing] féminin ; [behaviour] digne d'une femme

womb /wuːm/ N utérus m, matrice f ; (fig) (of nature) sein m ; (of earth) sein m, entrailles fpl
COMP **womb-leasing** N location f d'utérus, pratique f des mères porteuses

wombat /ˈwɒmbæt/ N wombat m, phascolome m

women /ˈwɪmɪn/ NPL of **woman**

womenfolk /ˈwɪmɪnfəʊk/ NPL femmes fpl

won /wʌn/ VB pt, ptp of **win**

wonder /ˈwʌndəʳ/ LANGUAGE IN USE 16.1

N [1] (NonC) (= admiration) émerveillement m ; (= astonishment) étonnement m ◆ **to be lost in** ~ être émerveillé or ébloui ◆ **he watched, lost in silent** ~ il regardait en silence, émerveillé or ébloui ◆ **the sense of ~ that children have** la faculté d'être émerveillé qu'ont les enfants ◆ **... he said in** ~ ... dit-il tout étonné
[2] (= sth wonderful) prodige m, miracle m ◆ **the ~ of electricity** le miracle de l'électricité ◆ **the ~s of science/medicine** les prodiges mpl or les miracles mpl de la science/de la médecine ◆ **the Seven Wonders of the World** les sept merveilles fpl du monde ◆ **to be a nine-day** or **one-day** or **seven-day** ~ ne pas faire long feu ◆ **he promised us ~s** il nous a promis monts et merveilles ◆ **~s will never cease** (iro) c'est un miracle !, cela tient du miracle ! (iro) ◆ **the ~ of it all is that** ... le plus étonnant dans tout cela c'est que ... ◆ **it's a ~ that he didn't fall** c'est un miracle qu'il ne soit pas tombé ◆ **it's a ~ to me that** ... je n'en reviens pas que ... + subj ◆ **it's a ~ how they were able to get these jobs** on se demande par quel miracle ils ont réussi à obtenir ces postes ◆ **no ~ he came late, it's no ~ (that) he came late** ce n'est pas étonnant qu'il soit arrivé en retard or s'il est arrivé en retard ◆ **no ~!** * cela n'a rien d'étonnant !, pas étonnant ! * ◆ **it's little** or **small ~ that** ... il n'est guère étonnant que ... + subj ; → **nine, work**
VI [1] (= marvel) (in astonishment) s'étonner ; (in admiration) s'émerveiller ◆ **the shepherds ~ed at the angels** les bergers s'émerveillaient devant les anges ◆ **I ~ at your rashness** votre audace m'étonne or me surprend ◆ **I ~ (that) you're still able to work** je ne sais pas comment vous faites pour travailler encore ◆ **I ~ (that) he didn't kill you** cela m'étonne qu'il ne vous ait pas tué ◆ **do you** ~ or **can you ~ at it?** est-ce que cela vous étonne ? ◆ **he'll be back, I shouldn't** ~ †* cela ne m'étonnerait pas qu'il revienne
[2] (= reflect) penser, songer ◆ **his words set me ~ing** ce qu'il a dit m'a donné à penser or m'a laissé songeur ◆ **it makes you** ~ cela donne à penser ◆ **I was ~ing about what he said** je pensais or songeais à ce qu'il a dit ◆ **I'm ~ing about going to the pictures** j'ai à moitié envie d'aller au cinéma ◆ **he'll be back – I ~!** il reviendra – je me le demande !
VT se demander ◆ **I ~ who he is** je me demande qui il est, je serais curieux de savoir qui il est ◆ **I ~ what to do** je ne sais pas quoi faire ◆ **I ~ where to put it** je me demande où (je pourrais) le mettre ◆ **he was ~ing whether to come with us** il se demandait s'il allait nous accompagner ◆ **I ~ why!** je me demande pourquoi !
COMP **wonder-worker** N ◆ **he is a ~-worker** il accomplit de vrais miracles ◆ **this drug/treatment is a ~-worker** c'est un remède/un traitement miracle

wonderful /ˈwʌndəfʊl/ ADJ [1] (= excellent) merveilleux ◆ **it's ~ to see you** je suis si heureux de te voir ◆ **we had a ~ time** c'était merveilleux [2] (= astonishing) étonnant, extraordinaire ◆ **the human body is a ~ thing** le corps humain est quelque chose d'étonnant or d'extraordinaire

wonderfully /ˈwʌndəfəlɪ/ ADV [1] (with adj, adv) merveilleusement ◆ **the weather was ~ warm** il a fait merveilleusement chaud ◆ **it works ~ well** ça marche merveilleusement bien or à merveille ◆ **he looks ~ well** il a très bonne mine [2] (with vb: gen) merveilleusement bien ; [succeed, function, go with] à merveille ◆ **I slept** ~ j'ai merveilleusement bien dormi ◆ **my cousins get on** ~ mes cousins s'entendent à merveille

wondering /ˈwʌndərɪŋ/ ADJ (= astonished) étonné ; (= thoughtful) songeur, pensif

wonderingly /ˈwʌndərɪŋlɪ/ ADV (= with astonishment) avec étonnement, d'un air étonné ; (= thoughtfully) pensivement

wonderland /ˈwʌndəlænd/ N pays m des merveilles, pays m merveilleux ; → **Alice**

wonderment /ˈwʌndəmənt/ N ⇒ **wonder noun**

wonderstruck /ˈwʌndəstrʌk/ ADJ (liter) frappé d'étonnement, émerveillé

wondrous /ˈwʌndrəs/ (liter) ADJ [1] (= excellent) merveilleux [2] (= amazing) extraordinaire ADV [1] (= excellently) merveilleusement ◆ ~ **well** merveilleusement bien [2] (= amazingly) extraordinairement

wondrously /ˈwʌndrəslɪ/ ADV (liter) ⇒ **wondrous adv**

wonga‡ /ˈwɒŋə/ N (Brit) pèze‡ m, pognon‡ m

wonk* /ˈwɒŋk/ N (US) bosseur* m, -euse* f ; → **policy¹**

wonky* /ˈwɒŋkɪ/ ADJ (Brit) [1] (= wobbly) [chair, table] bancal [2] (= crooked) de traviole*, de travers [3] (= defective) détraqué* ◆ **to go** ~ [car, machine] se déglinguer ; [TV picture] se dérégler ◆ **he's feeling rather ~ still** il se sent encore un peu patraque* or vaseux*

won't /wəʊnt/ ⇒ **will not** ; → **will**

wont /wəʊnt/ (frm) ADJ ◆ **to be ~ to do sth** avoir coutume de faire qch ◆ **as he was ~ to do** comme il avait coutume de faire, comme à son habitude N coutume f, habitude f (to do sth de faire qch) ◆ **as was my** ~ ainsi que j'en avais l'habitude, comme de coutume

wonted /ˈwəʊntɪd/ ADJ (frm) habituel, coutumier

woo /wuː/ VT [+ woman] faire la cour à, courtiser ; (fig) [+ influential person] rechercher les faveurs de ; [+ voters, audience] chercher à plaire à ; [+ fame, success] rechercher ◆ **he ~ed them with promises of ...** il cherchait à s'assurer leurs faveurs or à leur plaire en leur promettant ...

wood /wʊd/ N [1] (NonC = material) bois m ◆ **to touch ~, to knock on ~** (US) toucher du bois ◆ **touch ~!** * ◆ **knock on ~!** * (US) touchons or je touche du bois ! ◆ **he can't see the ~ for the trees** il se perd dans les détails ; → **deadwood, hardwood, softwood**
[2] (= forest) bois m ◆ **~s** bois mpl ◆ **a pine/beech** ~ un bois de pins/hêtres, une pinède/hêtraie ◆ **we're out of the ~(s) now** on est au bout du tunnel maintenant ◆ **we're not out of the ~(s) yet** on n'est pas encore tiré d'affaire or sorti de l'auberge* ; → **neck**
[3] (= cask) **drawn from the** ~ tiré au tonneau ◆ **aged in the** ~ vieilli au tonneau ◆ **wine in the** ~ vin m au tonneau
[4] (Mus) **the ~s** les bois mpl
[5] (Golf) bois m ; (Bowls) boule f ◆ **a number 2** ~ (Golf) un bois 2
COMP [floor, object, structure] de bois, en bois ; [fire] de bois ; [stove] à bois
wood alcohol N esprit-de-bois m, alcool m méthylique
wood anemone N anémone f des bois
wood block N (Art) bois m de graveur
wood-burning stove N poêle m à bois
wood carving N (NonC) (= act) sculpture f sur bois ; (= object) sculpture f en bois
wood engraving N gravure f sur bois
wood nymph N (Myth) dryade f, nymphe f des bois
wood pulp N pâte f à papier
wood shavings NPL copeaux mpl (de bois)
wood stove N four m à bois
wood trim N (US) boiseries fpl
wood wool N (NonC) copeaux mpl de bois

woodbine /ˈwʊdbaɪn/ N chèvrefeuille m

woodchip /ˈwʊdtʃɪp/ N (NonC) (= chips of wood) copeaux mpl de bois ; (= board) aggloméré m ; (also **woodchip wallpaper**) *papier peint parsemé de petits morceaux de bois*

woodchuck /ˈwʊdtʃʌk/ N marmotte f d'Amérique

woodcock /ˈwʊdkɒk/ N (= bird) bécasse f des bois

woodcraft /ˈwʊdkrɑːft/ N (NonC, in forest) connaissance f de la forêt ; (= handicraft) art m de travailler le bois

woodcut /ˈwʊdkʌt/ N gravure f sur bois

woodcutter /ˈwʊdkʌtəʳ/ N bûcheron m, -onne f

woodcutting /ˈwʊdkʌtɪŋ/ N (Art = act, object) gravure f sur bois ; (in forest) abattage m des arbres

wooded /ˈwʊdɪd/ ADJ boisé ◆ **heavily** or **thickly** or **densely** ~ très boisé

wooden /ˈwʊdn/ ADJ [1] (lit = made of wood) en bois ◆ **a ~ floor** un parquet [2] (fig = unnatural) [acting, performance] qui manque de naturel ; [actor, performer] peu naturel
COMP **wooden-headed** ADJ idiot, imbécile
wooden Indian‡ N (US pej = constrained) personne f raide comme la justice ; (= dull) personne f terne or ennuyeuse
wooden leg N jambe f de bois
wooden nickel* N (US fig) objet m sans valeur ◆ **to try to sell sb ~ nickels*** essayer de rouler qn
wooden spoon N (also Rugby) cuiller f de or en bois

woodenly /ˈwʊdnlɪ/ ADV [act, speak] avec raideur ; [look at, stare] d'un air impassible

woodland /ˈwʊdlænd/ N (NonC) région f boisée, bois mpl COMP [flower etc] des bois ; [path] forestier

woodlark /ˈwʊdlɑːk/ N alouette f des bois

woodlouse /ˈwʊdlaʊs/ N (pl **woodlice** /ˈwʊdlaɪs/) cloporte m

woodman /ˈwʊdmæn/ **N** (pl **-men**) forestier *m*

woodpecker /ˈwʊdpekəʳ/ **N** pic *m*

woodpigeon /ˈwʊdpɪdʒən/ **N** (pigeon *m*) ramier *m*

woodpile /ˈwʊdpaɪl/ **N** tas *m* de bois ; → **nigger**

woodshed /ˈwʊdʃed/ **N** bûcher *m (abri)*

woodsman /ˈwʊdzmən/ **N** (pl **-men**) *(US)* ⇒ **woodman**

woodsy /ˈwʊdzɪ/ **ADJ** *(US) [countryside]* boisé ; *[flowers etc]* des bois

woodwind /ˈwʊdwɪnd/ **N** *(Mus) (one instrument)* bois *m* ; *(collective pl)* bois *mpl*

woodwork /ˈwʊdwɜːk/ **N** [1] *(craft, school subject) (= carpentry)* menuiserie *f* ; *(= cabinet-making)* ébénisterie *f* [2] *(in house) (= beams etc)* charpente *f* ; *(= doors, skirting boards, window frames etc)* boiseries *fpl* ♦ **to come** *or* **crawl out of the ~** * *(fig pej)* surgir de nulle part [3] *(Ftbl *)* bois *mpl*, poteaux *mpl* (de but)

woodworm /ˈwʊdwɜːm/ **N** ver *m* du bois ♦ **the table has got ~** la table est vermoulue *or* piquée des vers

woody /ˈwʊdɪ/ **ADJ** [1] *[plant, stem, texture]* ligneux ; *[odour]* de bois [2] *(= wooded) [countryside]* boisé **COMP** **woody nightshade N** douce-amère *f*

wooer † /ˈwuːəʳ/ **N** prétendant *m*

woof¹ /wʊf/ **N** *(in weaving)* trame *f*

woof² /wʊf/ **N** *[of dog]* aboiement *m* ♦ **~, ~!** ouah, ouah ! **VI** aboyer

woofer /ˈwʊfəʳ/ **N** haut-parleur *m* grave, woofer *m*

wooftah‡ /ˈwʊftə/, **woofter**‡ /ˈwʊftəʳ/ **N** *(Brit pej)* tapette* *f (pej)*

wool /wʊl/ **N** laine *f* ♦ **he was wearing ~** il portait de la laine *or* des lainages ♦ **a ball of ~** une pelote de laine ♦ **knitting/darning ~** laine *f* à tricoter/repriser ♦ **this sweater is all ~** *or* **pure ~** ce pull-over est en pure laine ♦ **all ~ and a yard wide*** *(US)* authentique, de première classe ♦ **to pull the ~ over sb's eyes** duper qn ; → **dye, steel**

COMP *[cloth]* de laine ; *[dress]* en *or* de laine
wool fat N suint *m*
wool-gathering N *(fig)* rêvasserie *f* ♦ **to be** *or* **go ~-gathering** être dans les nuages, rêvasser
wool-grower N éleveur *m*, -euse *f* de moutons à laine
wool-lined ADJ doublé laine
wool merchant N négociant(e) *m(f)* en laine, lainier *m*, -ière *f*
wool shop N magasin *m* de laines
wool trade N commerce *m* de la laine

woolen /ˈwʊlən/ *(US)* ⇒ **woollen**

wooliness /ˈwʊlɪnɪs/ **N** *(US)* ⇒ **woolliness**

woollen, woolen *(US)* /ˈwʊlən/ **ADJ** *[garment]* en laine ; *[cloth]* de laine ♦ **~ cloth** *or* **material** lainage *m*, étoffe *f* de laine ♦ **~ goods** lainages *mpl* ♦ **the ~ industry** l'industrie *f* lainière **NPL** **woollens** lainages *mpl*

woolliness, wooliness *(US)* /ˈwʊlɪnɪs/ **N** [1] *[of material, garment, sheep, animal's coat]* aspect *m* laineux [2] *(fig = vagueness) [of ideas, thinking, essay, book, speech]* caractère *m* confus *or* nébuleux ; *[of person]* côté *m* nébuleux

woolly, wooly *(US)* /ˈwʊlɪ/ **ADJ** [1] *[material, garment, animal]* laineux ; *[hair]* laineux [2] (also **woolly-headed, woolly-minded**) *[ideas, thinking, essay, book, speech]* confus, nébuleux ; *[person]* nébuleux ♦ **~ liberals** *(pej)* les libéraux *mpl* aux idées confuses ; → **wild N** *(Brit * = jersey etc)* tricot *m*, pull *m* ♦ **woollies***, **woolies*** *(US)* lainages *mpl* ♦ **winter woollies*** lainages *mpl* d'hiver

COMP **woolly bear*** **N** *(= caterpillar)* oursonne *f*, chenille *f* de l'écaille martre
woolly mammoth N mammouth *m* laineux
woolly pully* **N** pull *m*
woolly rhinoceros N rhinocéros *m* laineux

Woolsack /ˈwʊlsæk/ **N** ♦ **the ~** *(Brit Parl) siège du grand chancelier d'Angleterre à la Chambre des lords*

woolshed /ˈwʊlʃed/ **N** lainerie *f*

wooly /ˈwʊlɪ/ *(US)* ⇒ **woolly**

woops* /wʊps/ **EXCL** ⇒ **whoops**

woozy* /ˈwuːzɪ/ **ADJ** dans les vapes* ♦ **I feel a bit ~** je suis un peu dans les vapes*

wop*‡ /wɒp/ **N** *(pej = Italian)* Rital*‡*m*

Worcester(shire) sauce /ˈwʊstə(ʃə)sɔːs/ **N** *sauce épicée au soja et au vinaigre*

Worcs N abbrev of **Worcestershire**

word /wɜːd/

LANGUAGE IN USE 26.2

1 NOUN
2 TRANSITIVE VERB
3 COMPOUNDS

1 - NOUN

[1] [gen] mot *m* ; *(spoken)* mot *m*, parole *f* ♦ **~s** *[of song etc]* paroles *fpl* ♦ **the written/spoken ~** ce qui est écrit/dit ♦ **what's the ~ for "banana" in German?, what's the German ~ for "banana"?** comment dit-on "banane" en allemand ? ♦ **there's no such ~ as "impossible"** impossible n'est pas français ♦ **he won't hear a ~ against her** il n'admet absolument pas qu'on la critique *subj* ♦ **I didn't breathe a ~** je n'ai pas soufflé mot ♦ **in ~ and deed** en parole et en fait ♦ **... or ~s to that effect** ... ou quelque chose de ce genre ♦ **I remember every ~ he said** je me souviens de ce qu'il a dit mot pour mot, je me souviens absolument de tout ce qu'il a dit ♦ **those were his very ~s** ce sont ses propres paroles, c'est ce qu'il a dit mot pour mot *or* textuellement ♦ **angry ~s** mots *mpl* prononcés sous le coup de la colère ♦ **big ~s!** * toujours les grands mots ! ♦ **a man of few ~s** un homme peu loquace ♦ **fine ~s** de belles paroles *fpl* ♦ **fine ~s!** *(iro)* belles paroles ! ♦ **I can't find (the) ~s (to tell you ...)** je ne trouve pas les mots (pour vous dire ...) ♦ **there are no ~s to describe how I felt** il n'y a pas de mot pour expliquer ce que je ressentais ♦ **he could find no ~s to express his misery** il ne trouvait pas de mot pour exprimer sa tristesse ♦ **it's too stupid for ~s** c'est vraiment trop stupide ♦ **from the ~ go** dès le début *or* le commencement ♦ **I can't get a ~ out of him** je ne peux pas en tirer un mot ♦ **tell me in your own ~s** dites-le-moi à votre façon ♦ **in the ~s of Racine** comme le dit Racine, selon les mots de Racine ♦ **I can't put my thoughts/feelings into ~s** je ne trouve pas les mots pour exprimer ce que je pense/ressens ♦ **by** *or* **through ~ of mouth** de bouche à oreille ; see also **compounds** ♦ **in other ~s** autrement dit ♦ **to put in a (good) ~ for sb** dire *or* glisser un mot en faveur de qn ♦ **don't put ~s into my mouth!** ne me faites pas dire ce que je n'ai pas dit ! ♦ **you took the ~s right out of my mouth** c'est exactement ce que j'allais dire ♦ **with these ~s, he sat down** sur ces mots il s'est assis ♦ **without a ~, he left the room** il a quitté la pièce sans dire un mot

♦ **to have a word (with sb)** *(= speak to)* ♦ **can I have a ~?** * puis-je vous dire un mot (en privé) ?, auriez-vous un moment ? ♦ **I'll have a ~ with him about it** je lui en toucherai un mot, je vais lui en parler ♦ **I had a ~ with him about it** je lui en ai touché un mot, je lui en ai parlé brièvement ♦ **I want (to have) a ~ with you** j'ai à vous parler ♦ **to have a ~ in sb's ear** *(Brit)* glisser un mot à l'oreille de qn

♦ **to have words with sb** *(= rebuke)* dire deux mots à qn ; *(= quarrel)* avoir des mots avec qn, se disputer avec qn

♦ **to say + word(s)** ♦ **I never said a ~** je n'ai rien dit du tout, je n'ai pas ouvert la bouche ♦ **Mr Martin will now say a few ~s** M. Martin va maintenant prendre la parole *or* dire quelques mots ♦ **he didn't say a ~ about it** il n'en a pas soufflé mot ♦ **nobody had a good ~ to say about him** personne n'a trouvé la moindre chose à dire en sa faveur ♦ **I didn't hear a ~ he said** je n'ai pas entendu un mot de ce qu'il a dit ♦ **just say the ~ and I'll leave** vous n'avez qu'un mot à dire pour que je parte

♦ **a word/words of** ♦ **a ~ of advice** un petit conseil ♦ **a ~ of thanks** un mot de remerciement ♦ **I'll give you a ~ of warning** je voudrais vous mettre en garde ♦ **after these ~s of warning** après cette mise en garde

♦ **in a word** en un mot

♦ **in so** *or* **as many words** ♦ **I told him in so** *or* **as many ~s that ...** je lui ai carrément dit que ..., sans y aller par quatre chemins, je lui ai dit que ... ♦ **he didn't say so in so many** *or* **as many ~s** il ne l'a pas dit explicitement, ce n'est pas exactement ce qu'il a dit

♦ **word for word** *[repeat, copy out]* mot pour mot, textuellement ; *[translate]* mot à mot, littéralement ; *[review, go over]* mot par mot ; see also **compounds**

♦ **a/the + word for it** ♦ **the French have a ~ for it** les Français ont un mot pour dire cela ♦ **boring is not the ~ for it!** ennuyeux, c'est le moins que l'on puisse dire ! ♦ **"negligent" is a better ~ for it** "négligent" serait plus juste *or* serait plus près de la vérité ♦ **"murder"? that's not quite the (right) ~ (for it)** "meurtre" ? ce n'est pas tout à fait le mot (qui convient) ♦ **she disappeared, there's no other ~ for it** *or* **that's the only ~ for it** elle a disparu, c'est bien le mot *or* on ne peut pas dire autrement

[2] [= advice] conseil *m* ♦ **a ~ to new fathers** quelques conseils aux nouveaux pères ♦ **a ~ to the wise** un bon conseil

[3] [= news, message] *(NonC)* nouvelles *fpl* ♦ **she's waiting for ~ from headquarters** elle attend des nouvelles du siège central ♦ **~ came from headquarters that ...** le quartier général nous (*or* leur *etc*) a fait dire *or* nous (*or* les *etc*) a prévenus que ... ♦ **~ came that ...** on a appris que ... ♦ **to send ~ that ...** faire savoir *or* faire dire que ... ♦ **there's no ~ from John yet** on est toujours sans nouvelles de John ♦ **the purpose of his mission is to bring back ~ of enemy manoeuvres** le but de sa mission est de rapporter des renseignements sur les manœuvres de l'ennemi ; → **leave**

[4] [= rumour] ♦ **~ has it** *or* **the ~ is that he has left** le bruit court qu'il est parti ♦ **if ~ got out about his past, there'd be a scandal** si l'on apprenait certaines choses sur son passé, cela ferait un scandale ♦ **the ~ on the street is ...** * il paraît que ...

[5] [= promise, assurance etc] parole *f*, promesse *f* ♦ **~ of honour** parole *f* d'honneur ♦ **it was his ~ against mine** c'était sa parole contre la mienne ♦ **his ~ is his bond** il n'a qu'une parole ♦ **to break one's ~** manquer à sa parole ♦ **to give one's ~ to sb/that** donner sa parole (d'honneur) à qn/que ♦ **I give you my ~ (on** *or* **for it)** je vous donne ma parole ♦ **you have my ~ (of honour)** vous avez ma parole (d'honneur) ♦ **to go back on one's ~** revenir sur sa parole ♦ **he is as good as his ~** on peut le croire sur parole ♦ **he was as good as his ~** il a tenu parole ♦ **I've only got her ~ for it** c'est elle qui le dit, je n'ai aucune preuve ♦ **to hold sb to his ~** contraindre qn à tenir sa promesse ♦ **to keep one's ~** tenir (sa) parole ♦ **a man of his ~** un homme de parole ♦ **my ~!***, **upon my ~!** † ma parole ! ♦ **to take sb at his ~** prendre qn au mot ♦ **you'll have to take his ~ for it** il vous faudra le croire sur parole ♦ **take my ~ for it, he's a good man** c'est un brave homme, croyez-moi

6 = command (mot *m* d')ordre *m* ◆ **the ~ of command** l'ordre ◆ **his ~ is law** c'est lui qui fait la loi, sa parole fait loi ◆ **he gave the ~ to advance** il a donné l'ordre d'avancer

7 Rel ◆ **the Word** (= *logos*) le Verbe ; (= *the Bible, the Gospel:* also **the Word of God**) le Verbe (de Dieu), la parole de Dieu

8 Comput mot *m*

2 - TRANSITIVE VERB

+ document, protest *(spoken or written)* formuler ; *(written)* rédiger, libeller *(Admin)* ◆ **he had ~ed the letter very carefully** il avait choisi les termes de sa lettre avec le plus grand soin ◆ **well ~ed** bien tourné ◆ **I don't know how to ~ it** je ne sais pas comment le formuler

3 - COMPOUNDS

word association N association *f* de mots
word-blind † ADJ dyslexique
word-blindness † N dyslexie *f*
word class N *(Gram)* catégorie *f* grammaticale
word formation N formation *f* des mots
word-for-word ADJ mot pour mot ◆ **a ~-for-~ translation** une traduction littérale *or* mot à mot
word game N jeu *m* de lettres
word list N *(in exercise etc)* liste *f* de mots ; *(in dictionary)* nomenclature *f*
word-of-mouth ADJ verbal, oral
word order N ordre *m* des mots
word-perfect ADJ ◆ **to be ~-perfect in sth** savoir qch sur le bout des doigts
word picture N ◆ **to give a ~ picture of sth** faire une description vivante de qch
word processing N traitement *m* de texte ◆ **~ processing package** logiciel *m* de traitement de texte
word processor N traitement *m* de texte
word-type N *(Ling)* vocable *m*
word wrap N *(Comput)* retour *m* (automatique) à la ligne

-word /wɜ:d/ SUF ◆ **the C-word/the L-word** *manière polie ou humoristique d'évoquer un mot grossier sans le prononcer* ; see also **f-word**

wordbook /ˈwɜ:dbʊk/ N lexique *m*, vocabulaire *m*

wordcount /ˈwɜ:dkaʊnt/ N *(Comput)* comptage *m*, nombre *m* de mots

wordiness /ˈwɜ:dɪnɪs/ N verbosité *f*

wording /ˈwɜ:dɪŋ/ N *[of letter, speech, statement]* termes *mpl*, formulation *f* ; *[of official document]* libellé *m* ◆ **the ~ of the last sentence is clumsy** la dernière phrase est maladroitement exprimée *or* formulée ◆ **the ~ is exceedingly important** le choix des termes est extrêmement important ◆ **change the ~ slightly** changez quelques mots (ici et là) ◆ **a different ~ would make it less ambiguous** ce serait moins ambigu si on l'exprimait autrement

wordless /ˈwɜ:dlɪs/ ADJ 1 (= *silent*) *[anguish, admiration]* muet ◆ **he watched her in ~ admiration** il la regardait, muet d'admiration 2 (= *without words*) inarticulé ◆ **a ~ cry/shriek** un cri/hurlement inarticulé

wordlessly /ˈwɜ:dlɪslɪ/ ADV sans prononcer un mot

wordplay /ˈwɜ:dpleɪ/ N (= *pun*) jeu *m* de mots ; *(NonC)* (= *puns*) jeux *mpl* de mots

wordsmith /ˈwɜ:dsmɪθ/ N manieur *m* de mots ◆ **he's a skilled ~** il sait tourner ses phrases ; *(stronger)* il a le génie des mots

wordy /ˈwɜ:dɪ/ ADJ *[person, style]* verbeux ; *[document]* au style verbeux

wore /wɔ:ʳ/ VB pt of **wear**

work /wɜ:k/

LANGUAGE IN USE 19

1 NOUN
2 INTRANSITIVE VERB
3 TRANSITIVE VERB
4 COMPOUNDS
5 PHRASAL VERBS

1 - NOUN

1 gen *(NonC)* travail *m* ◆ **to start ~, to set to ~** se mettre au travail ◆ **I've got some more ~ for you** j'ai encore du travail pour vous ◆ **he does his ~ well** il travaille bien, il fait du bon travail ◆ **she put a lot of ~ into it** elle y a consacré beaucoup de travail ◆ **there's still a lot of ~ to be done on it** il reste encore beaucoup à faire ◆ **I'm trying to get some ~ done** j'essaie de travailler ◆ **~ has begun on the new bridge** (= *building it*) on a commencé la construction du nouveau pont ◆ **you'll have your ~ cut out** vous allez avoir du travail ◆ **domestic ~** travaux *mpl* domestiques ◆ **office ~** travail *m* de bureau ◆ **~ in progress** travaux *mpl* en cours ◆ **it's women's ~** c'est un travail de femme ◆ **it's quite easy ~** ce n'est pas un travail difficile ◆ **good ~!** (= *well done!*) bravo ! ◆ **it's good ~** c'est du bon travail ◆ **it's hot ~** ça donne chaud ◆ **nice ~ if you can get it!** * *(iro)* c'est une bonne planque ! * ◆ **to make short** *or* **quick ~ of sth** faire qch très rapidement ◆ **he did useful ~ in the Ministry of Transport** il a fait du bon travail au ministère des Transports ; see also **works**

◆ **to be at work** (= *working*) travailler, être au travail ◆ **he was at ~ on another picture** il travaillait sur un autre tableau ◆ **there are subversive forces at ~ here** (= *operating*) des forces subversives sont à l'œuvre ; see also **noun 2**

2 = employment, place of employment travail *m* ◆ **he's looking for ~** il cherche du travail ◆ **"work wanted"***(US)* "demandes d'emploi" ◆ **to go to ~** aller au travail ◆ **on her way to ~** en allant à son travail ◆ **where is his (place of) ~?** où travaille-t-il ?

◆ **at work** (= *at place of work*) au travail ◆ **he's at ~ at the moment** il est au travail en ce moment ◆ **accidents at ~** les accidents *mpl* du travail

◆ **in + work** ◆ **those in ~** les actifs *mpl* ◆ **he is in regular ~** il a un emploi régulier

◆ **out of work** ◆ **to be out of ~** être au chômage *or* sans emploi ◆ **an increase in the numbers out of ~** une augmentation du nombre des demandeurs d'emploi *or* des chômeurs ◆ **to put** *or* **throw sb out of ~** mettre qn au chômage ◆ **this decision threw a lot of people out of ~** cette décision a fait beaucoup de chômeurs ◆ **600 men were thrown out of ~** 600 hommes ont été licenciés *or* ont perdu leur emploi

◆ **off work** ◆ **he's off ~ today** il n'est pas allé (*or* venu) travailler aujourd'hui ◆ **he has been off ~ for three days** il est absent depuis trois jours ◆ **a day off ~** un jour de congé ◆ **I'll have to take time off ~** il va falloir que je prenne un congé

3 = product œuvre *f* ◆ **the ~s of God** l'œuvre *f* de Dieu ◆ **his life's ~** l'œuvre *f* de sa vie ◆ **his ~ will not be forgotten** son œuvre passera à la postérité ◆ **it's obviously the ~ of a professional** c'est manifestement l'œuvre d'un professionnel *or* du travail de professionnel ◆ **this is the ~ of a madman** c'est l'œuvre d'un fou

4 Art, Literat, Mus etc œuvre *f* ; (= *book on specific subject*) ouvrage *m* ◆ **the complete ~s of Shakespeare** les œuvres *fpl* complètes de Shakespeare ◆ **Camus' last ~** la dernière œuvre de Camus ◆ **a ~ on Joyce** un ouvrage sur Joyce ◆ **this ~ was commissioned by …** cette œuvre a été commandée par … ◆ **~s of fiction/reference** ouvrages *mpl* de fiction/référence ◆ **he sells a lot of his ~** ses tableaux (*or* ses livres *etc*) se vendent bien

2 - INTRANSITIVE VERB

For **work + preposition/adverb** combinations see also phrasal verbs.

1 gen travailler ◆ **to ~ hard** travailler dur ◆ **to ~ to rule** faire la grève du zèle ◆ **he is ~ing at his German** il travaille son allemand ◆ **who is he ~ing for ?** pour qui travaille-t-il ? ◆ **he has always ~ed for/against such a reform** il a toujours lutté pour/contre une telle réforme ◆ **he ~s in education/publishing** il travaille dans l'enseignement/l'édition ◆ **he prefers to ~ in wood/clay** il préfère travailler le bois/l'argile ◆ **he prefers to ~ in oils** il préfère la peinture à l'huile *or* travailler à la peinture à l'huile ◆ **he ~ed on the car all morning** il a travaillé sur la voiture toute la matinée ◆ **he's ~ing on his memoirs** il travaille à ses mémoires ◆ **have you solved the problem? – we're ~ing on it** avez-vous résolu le problème ? – on y travaille ◆ **I've been ~ing on him but haven't yet managed to persuade him** *(fig)* j'ai bien essayé de le convaincre, mais je n'y suis pas encore parvenu ◆ **the police are ~ing on the case** la police enquête sur l'affaire ◆ **they are ~ing on the principle that …** ils partent du principe que … ◆ **there are not many facts/clues to ~ on** il y a peu de faits/d'indices sur lesquels travailler ◆ **to ~ towards sth** œuvrer pour qch ◆ **we are ~ing towards equality of opportunity** nous œuvrons pour l'égalité des chances ◆ **we are ~ing towards a solution/an agreement** nous essayons de parvenir à une solution/un accord

2 = function, be effective *[mechanism, watch, machine, car, switch, scheme, arrangement]* marcher, fonctionner ; *[drug, medicine]* agir, faire effet ; *[yeast]* fermenter ◆ **the lift isn't ~ing** l'ascenseur ne marche pas *or* est en panne ◆ **it ~s off the mains/on electricity/off batteries** ça marche sur (le) secteur/à l'électricité/avec des piles ◆ **my brain doesn't seem to be ~ing today** *(hum)* je n'ai pas les idées très claires aujourd'hui ◆ **the spell ~ed** le charme a fait son effet ◆ **it just won't ~** ça ne marchera pas *or* jamais ◆ **that ~s both ways** c'est à double tranchant ◆ **this may ~ in our favour** ça pourrait jouer en notre faveur

3 = pass ◆ **she ~ed methodically down the list** elle a suivi la liste de façon méthodique ◆ **water has ~ed through the roof** de l'eau s'est infiltrée par le toit

4 = move *[face, mouth]* se contracter, se crisper

3 - TRANSITIVE VERB

1 = cause to work *[+ person, staff]* faire travailler ; *[+ mechanism, lever, pump]* actionner ; *[+ machine]* faire marcher ◆ **I don't know how to ~ the video** je ne sais pas comment faire marcher le magnétoscope ◆ **he ~s his staff too hard** il fait trop travailler son personnel, il surmène son personnel ◆ **the machine is ~ed by solar energy** cette machine marche *or* fonctionne à l'énergie solaire

◆ **to work o.s.** ◆ **he ~s himself too hard** il se surmène ◆ **he's ~ing himself to death** il se tue à la tâche

2 = bring about *[+ miracle]* faire, accomplir ; *[+ change]* apporter ◆ **to ~ wonders** *or* **marvels** *[person]* faire des merveilles ; *[drug, medicine, action, suggestion]* faire merveille

3 * = arrange for **he has managed to ~ his promotion** il s'est débrouillé pour obtenir de l'avancement ◆ **can you ~ it so she can come too?** pouvez-vous faire en sorte qu'elle vienne aussi ? ◆ **I'll ~ it if I can** si je peux m'arranger pour le faire, je le ferai

4 = exploit resources of [+ mine, land] exploiter ♦ **this rep ~s the south-east** ce représentant couvre le Sud-Est

5 = manoeuvre ♦ **he ~ed the rope gradually through the hole** il est parvenu à faire passer progressivement la corde dans le trou, il s'est employé à enfoncer progressivement la corde dans le trou ♦ **he ~ed his hands free** il est parvenu à libérer ses mains ♦ **to ~ sth loose** parvenir à desserrer qch ♦ **he ~ed the lever up and down** il a actionné le levier plusieurs fois ♦ **she ~ed the hook carefully out of the cloth** avec précaution, elle s'employa à retirer l'hameçon du tissu ♦ **he ~ed the crowd (up) into a frenzy** il a réussi à déchaîner la foule

♦ **to work one's way** ♦ **he ~ed his way along the edge of the cliff** il a longé prudemment le bord de la falaise ♦ **rescuers are ~ing their way towards the trapped men** les sauveteurs se fraient un passage jusqu'aux hommes qui sont bloqués ♦ **he ~ed his way up from nothing** il est parti de rien ♦ **he ~ed his way up to the top of his firm** il a gravi un à un tous les échelons de la hiérarchie de son entreprise ♦ **he ~ed his way up from office boy to managing director** il est devenu PDG après avoir commencé comme garçon de bureau ♦ **to ~ one's way through college** travailler pour payer ses études

6 = make, shape [+ metal, wood, leather] travailler ; [+ dough, clay] travailler, pétrir ; [+ object] façonner (out of dans) ; (= sew) coudre ; (= embroider) [+ design etc] broder ♦ ~ **the butter and sugar together** (Culin) mélangez bien le beurre et le sucre

4 - COMPOUNDS

work area N coin m de travail, bureau m
work camp N (= prison) camp m de travail forcé ; (voluntary) chantier m de travail (bénévole)
work ethic N éthique f du travail, déontologie f
work experience N (gen) expérience f professionnelle ; (for students) stage m professionnel
work file N (Comput) fichier m de travail
work-in N (= strike) grève avec occupation des locaux et appropriation des moyens de production
work/life balance N équilibre m entre vie professionnelle et vie privée
work load N charge f de travail ♦ **his ~ load is too heavy** il a trop de travail ♦ **they were discussing ~ loads** ils discutaient de la répartition du travail
work of art N œuvre f d'art
work permit N permis m de travail
work prospects NPL [of course, training] débouchés mpl ; [of student] perspectives fpl
work-rule N (US Ind) ⇒ **work-to-rule**
work-sharing N partage m du travail
work space N ⇒ **work area**
work station N poste m de travail
work-study student N (US Univ) étudiant(e) m(f) ayant un emploi rémunéré par l'université
work surface N ⇒ **worktop**
work-to-rule N (Brit) grève f du zèle
work week N semaine f de travail ♦ **a ~ week of 38 hours**(US) une semaine de 38 heures
work-worn ADJ [hands] usé par le travail

5 - PHRASAL VERBS

► **work away** VI ♦ **they worked away all day** ils n'ont pas arrêté de toute la journée ♦ **she was ~ing away at her embroidery** elle était absorbée par sa broderie

► **work down** VI [stockings etc] glisser

► **work in** VI 1 [dust, sand] s'introduire
2 (= fit in) ♦ **she works in with us as much as possible** elle collabore avec nous autant que possible ♦ **this doesn't ~ in with our plans to reorganize the department** cela ne cadre pas or ne concorde pas avec nos projets de réorganisation du service ♦ **that'll ~ in very well** ça cadrera très bien
VT SEP 1 [+ finger, hook, lever, blade] introduire petit à petit, enfoncer ; [+ reference, quotation] glisser, introduire ; (fig) [+ subject] s'arranger pour mentionner ♦ **we'll ~ in a mention of it somewhere** on s'arrangera pour le mentionner quelque part ♦ **he ~ed the incident into his speech** il s'est arrangé pour parler de l'incident dans son discours
2 (= amalgamate) incorporer ♦ ~ **the flour in gradually** incorporez la farine petit à petit

► **work off** VI [nut, handle etc] se desserrer
VT SEP 1 [+ debt, obligation] travailler pour s'acquitter de
2 [+ one's surplus fat] se débarrasser de ; [+ weight, calories] perdre ; [+ anger] passer, assouvir ♦ **to ~ off one's energy** dépenser son surplus d'énergie ♦ **jogging helps ~ off stress** le jogging aide à évacuer le stress or à décompresser* ♦ **he ~ed it all off gardening** il s'est défoulé* en faisant du jardinage

► **work out** VI 1 [plan, arrangement] marcher ; [puzzle, problem] se résoudre ♦ **it's all ~ing out as planned** tout se déroule comme prévu ♦ **things didn't ~ out (well) for her** les choses ont plutôt mal tourné pour elle ♦ **their marriage didn't ~ out** leur couple n'a pas marché* ♦ **it will ~ out all right in the end** tout finira (bien) par s'arranger ♦ **how did it ~ out in the end?** comment ça s'est terminé ? ♦ **it hasn't ~ed out that way** les choses se sont passées autrement
2 [amount] ♦ **what does the total work out at ?** ça fait combien en tout ? ♦ **it ~s out (at) £50 per child** il faut compter 50 livres par enfant
3 (= exercise) faire de la musculation
VT SEP 1 (= figure out) [+ problem, puzzle, equation] résoudre ; [+ answer, total] trouver ; [+ code] déchiffrer ; [+ plan, scheme, idea] élaborer, mettre au point ; [+ settlement] parvenir à ♦ **I'll have to ~ it out** (gen) il faut que j'y réfléchisse ; (counting) il faut que je calcule ♦ **who ~ed all this out?** qui a combiné tout ça ? ♦ **I had the whole design ~ed out in my mind** j'avais déjà tout conçu dans ma tête ♦ **can you ~ out where we are on the map?** peux-tu trouver où nous sommes sur la carte ? ♦ **he finally ~ed out why she'd gone** il a fini par comprendre pourquoi elle était partie ♦ **I can't ~ it out** ça me dépasse ♦ **I can't ~ him out** * je n'arrive pas à comprendre comment il fonctionne
2 (= exhaust resources of) [+ mine, land] épuiser
3 [+ notice] ♦ **she has to work out her notice** elle doit respecter le délais de préavis
4 (= get rid of) ♦ **don't try and work out your frustration on me !** ne t'en prends pas à moi parce que tu te sens frustré ! ♦ **he stood up in order to ~ out his impatience** il se mit debout pour calmer son impatience

► **work over*** VT SEP (= beat up) tabasser*, passer à tabac*

► **work round** VI (= move gradually) tourner ♦ **his tie had ~ed round to the back of his neck** sa cravate avait tourné et lui pendait dans le dos ♦ **the wind has ~ed round to the south** le vent a tourné au sud petit à petit ♦ **to ~ round to sth** (in conversation, negotiations) aborder qch ♦ **you'll have to ~ round to that subject tactfully** il faudra que vous abordiez subj ce sujet avec tact ♦ **what are you ~ing round to?** où voulez-vous en venir ?

► **work through** VT FUS (Psych = resolve emotionally) assumer

► **work up** VI 1 ♦ **events were working up to a crisis** une crise se préparait ♦ **the book ~s up to a dramatic ending** le roman s'achemine progressivement vers un dénouement spectaculaire ♦ **I knew they were ~ing up to something** (in conversation etc) je savais qu'ils préparaient quelque chose ♦ **I thought he was ~ing up to asking me for a divorce** je croyais qu'il préparait le terrain pour demander le divorce ♦ **what is he ~ing up to?** où veut-il en venir ?
2 [skirt, sleeve] remonter
VT SEP 1 (= rouse) ♦ **he worked the crowd up into a frenzy** il a déchaîné l'enthousiasme de la foule ♦ **to get ~ed up** s'énerver ♦ **he ~ed himself up into a rage** il s'est mis dans une colère noire
2 (= prepare) [+ article, drawings] préparer
3 (= develop) [+ trade, business] développer ♦ **he ~ed this small firm up into a major company** il a réussi à faire de cette petite société une grande entreprise ♦ **he's trying to ~ up a connection in Wales** (Comm) il essaie d'établir une tête de pont au pays de Galles ♦ **I ~ed up an appetite/thirst carrying all those boxes** ça m'a mis en appétit/m'a donné soif de porter toutes ces caisses ♦ **I can't ~ up much enthusiasm for the plan** j'ai du mal à m'enthousiasmer pour ce projet ♦ **can't you ~ up a little more interest in it?** tu ne pourrais pas t'y intéresser un peu plus ?

-work /wɜːk/ N (in compounds) ♦ **cement-work** le ciment ♦ **lattice-work** le treillis

workable /ˈwɜːkəbl/ ADJ 1 [scheme, arrangement, solution, suggestion, plan, projet] viable, réalisable ; [agreement, settlement, compromise] viable ♦ **it's just not ~** cela ne marchera jamais 2 (= malleable) [metal, dough] facile à travailler 3 (= exploitable) [land, mine] exploitable

workaday /ˈwɜːkədeɪ/ ADJ [object, tastes, surroundings] ordinaire ; [concerns, chores] de tous les jours ♦ **the ~ world** la vie de tous les jours

workaholic * /ˌwɜːkəˈhɒlɪk/ N bourreau m de travail

workbag /ˈwɜːkbæg/ N sac m à ouvrage

workbasket /ˈwɜːkbɑːskɪt/ N (Sewing) corbeille f à ouvrage

workbench /ˈwɜːkbentʃ/ N (for woodwork etc) établi m ; (in lab) paillasse f

workbook /ˈwɜːkbʊk/ N (= exercise book) cahier m d'exercices ; (= manual) manuel m ; (= work record book) cahier m de classe

workbox /ˈwɜːkbɒks/ N (Sewing) boîte f à ouvrage

workday /ˈwɜːkdeɪ/ (esp US) ADJ ⇒ **workaday**
N ♦ **a ~ of eight hours** une journée de travail de huit heures ♦ **Saturday is a ~** (gen) on travaille le samedi ; (Comm) le samedi est un jour ouvrable

worker /ˈwɜːkəʳ/ N travailleur m, -euse f ♦ **woman ~** travailleuse f ♦ **he's a good ~** il travaille bien ♦ **he's a fast ~** (lit) il travaille vite ; (* fig) c'est un tombeur* or un don Juan ♦ **all the ~s in this industry** tous ceux qui travaillent dans cette industrie ♦ **management and ~s** patronat m et ouvriers mpl ♦ **we rely on volunteer ~s** nous dépendons de travailleurs bénévoles ♦ **office ~** employé(e) m(f) de bureau ♦ **research ~** chercheur m, -euse f
COMP **worker ant** N (fourmi f) ouvrière f
worker bee N (abeille f) ouvrière f
worker director N ouvrier m faisant partie du conseil d'administration
worker participation N participation f des travailleurs
worker priest N prêtre-ouvrier m
Workers' Educational Association N (Brit) ≃ Association f d'éducation populaire

workfare /ˈwɜːkfeəʳ/ N système où les chômeurs doivent participer à des programmes de création d'emplois pour avoir droit aux allocations

workforce /ˈwɜːkfɔːs/ N 1 [of region, country] population f active ♦ **a country where half the ~ is unemployed** un pays dont la moitié de la population active est au chômage ♦ **the coun-**

try's ~ is well educated and diligent la main-d'œuvre du pays est éduquée et vaillante ◆ **Hong Kong's skilled ~** la main-d'œuvre spécialisée de Hong Kong 2 *[of company]* personnel *m* ; *(= manual workers)* main-d'œuvre *f*

workhorse /ˈwɜːkhɔːs/ N *(= horse)* cheval *m* de labour ; *(= person)* bête *f* de somme

workhouse /ˈwɜːkhaʊs/ N *(Brit Hist)* hospice *m* ; *(US Jur)* maison *f* de correction

working /ˈwɜːkɪŋ/ ADJ 1 *(= to do with work) [clothes, conditions, lunch, language]* de travail ; *[partner, population]* actif ◆ **a ~ day of eight hours** *(Brit)* une journée de travail de huit heures ◆ **Saturday is a ~ day** *(Brit) (gen)* on travaille le samedi ; *(Comm)* le samedi est un jour ouvrable ◆ **good ~ environment** bonnes conditions *fpl* de travail ◆ **~ expenses** *[of mine, factory]* frais *mpl* d'exploitation ; *[of salesman]* frais *mpl* ◆ **during** *or* **in ~ hours** pendant les heures de travail ◆ **~ life** *(gen)* vie *f* active ◆ **she spent most of her ~ life abroad** elle a passé la plus grande partie de sa vie active à l'étranger ◆ **a long and strenuous ~ life** une longue vie de labeur ◆ **the ~ man will not accept ...** les travailleurs n'accepteront pas ... ◆ **he's an ordinary ~ man** c'est un simple travailleur ◆ **he's a ~ man now** il travaille maintenant, il gagne sa vie maintenant ◆ **a ~ wife** une femme mariée qui travaille ◆ **she is an ordinary ~ woman** c'est une simple travailleuse ◆ **she is a ~ woman** *(= economically active)* elle travaille, elle gagne sa vie ◆ **the ~ woman** la femme qui travaille ; → **order**

2 *(= operational)* **~ drawing** épure *f* ◆ **~ hypothesis** hypothèse *f* de travail ◆ **to build** *or* **form a ~ partnership** *(professionally)* établir de bons rapports ; *(emotionally)* parvenir à une bonne relation de couple

3 *(= adequate)* **to have a ~ majority** *(Pol etc)* avoir une majorité suffisante ◆ **a ~ knowledge of German** une connaissance correcte de l'allemand

4 *(= functioning) [model]* qui marche

N *(NonC)* travail *m* ; *[of machine etc]* fonctionnement *m* ; *[of yeast]* fermentation *f* ; *[of mine, land]* exploitation *f* ; *[of metal, wood, leather]* travail *m* ; *[of clay, dough]* travail *m*, pétrissage *m* ; *(Sewing)* couture *f* ; *(= embroidery)* broderie *f*

NPL **workings** *(= mechanism)* mécanisme *m* ; *[of government, organization]* rouages *mpl* ; *(Min)* chantier *m* d'exploitation ◆ **I don't understand the ~s of her mind** je ne comprends pas ce qui se passe dans sa tête

COMP **working capital** N fonds *mpl* de roulement

working class N ◆ **the ~ class** la classe ouvrière ◆ **the ~ classes** le prolétariat

working-class ADJ *[origins, background, accent, suburb]* ouvrier, prolétarien ◆ **he is ~-class** il appartient à la classe ouvrière

working dog N *chien adapté, de par sa race ou son dressage, à des tâches utilitaires*

working families tax credit N *(Brit)* complément *m* familial

working girl N *(euph)* professionnelle* *f (euph)*

working group N groupe *m* de travail

working holiday N *(Brit) vacances mises à profit pour effectuer une activité rémunérée*

working men's club N *(Brit)* ≃ foyer *m* d'ouvriers

working party N *(Brit) (gen)* groupe *m* de travail ; *(grander)* commission *f* d'enquête ; *(= squad: of soldiers)* escouade *f*

working relationship N relations *fpl or* rapports *mpl* de travail ◆ **to have a good ~ relationship (with sb)** avoir de bonnes relations *or* bons rapports de travail (avec qn)

working title N titre *m* provisoire

working vacation N *(US)* ⇒ **working holiday**

working week N *(Brit)* semaine *f* de travail

workman /ˈwɜːkmən/ (pl **-men**) N 1 *(gen, Comm, Ind etc)* ouvrier *m* ◆ **a bad ~ blames his tools** *(Prov)* les mauvais ouvriers ont toujours de mauvais outils *(Prov)* ◆ **workmen's compensation** pension *f* d'invalidité *(pour ouvriers)* 2 ◆ **to be a good ~** bien travailler, avoir du métier

workmanlike /ˈwɜːkmənlaɪk/ ADJ *[person, attitude]* professionnel ; *[object, product, tool]* bien fait, soigné ; *(fig) [attempt]* sérieux ◆ **it was a ~ essay** c'était une dissertation honnête *or* bien travaillée ◆ **he made a ~ job of it** il a fait du bon travail ◆ **he set about it in a very ~ way** il s'y est pris comme un vrai professionnel

workmanship /ˈwɜːkmənʃɪp/ N *[of craftsman]* métier *m*, maîtrise *f* ; *[of artefact]* exécution *f or* fabrication *f* soignée ◆ **this example of his ~** cet exemple de son savoir-faire ◆ **a chair of fine ~** une chaise faite avec art ◆ **a superb piece of ~** un *or* du travail superbe

workmate /ˈwɜːkmeɪt/ N camarade *mf* de travail

workmen /ˈwɜːkmən/ NPL of **workman**

workout /ˈwɜːkaʊt/ N *(Sport)* séance *f* d'entraînement

workpeople /ˈwɜːkpiːpl/ NPL travailleurs *mpl*, ouvriers *mpl*

workplace /ˈwɜːkpleɪs/ N lieu *m* de travail

workroom /ˈwɜːkrʊm/ N salle *f* de travail

works /wɜːks/ N *(pl inv)* 1 *(Brit Ind etc) (= factory)* usine *f* ; *(= processing plant etc)* installations *fpl* ◆ **irrigation ~** installations *fpl* d'irrigation, barrage *m* ◆ **price ex ~** prix *m* sortie d'usine 2 *(Admin, Mil)* travaux *mpl* ; *[of clock, machine etc]* mécanisme *m* ; *(Rel)* œuvres *fpl* ◆ **each man will be judged by his ~** chaque homme sera jugé selon ses œuvres 3 *(= the lot)* ◆ **the (whole) ~** * tout le tremblement*, tout le tralala* ◆ **to put in the ~** * *(US)* sortir le grand jeu ; → **public, spanner**

COMP *[entrance, car park, canteen]* de l'usine ; *[car]* de l'entreprise ; *(as opposed to staff)* des ouvriers

works committee, works council N comité *m* d'entreprise

works manager N directeur *m*, -trice *f* d'usine

worksheet /ˈwɜːkʃiːt/ N *(for pupil)* fiche *f* d'exercices

workshop /ˈwɜːkʃɒp/ N *(lit, fig)* atelier *m*

workshy /ˈwɜːkʃaɪ/ ADJ fainéant, tire-au-flanc* *inv*

worktable /ˈwɜːkteɪbl/ N table *f* de travail

worktop /ˈwɜːktɒp/ N plan *m* de travail

world /wɜːld/ N 1 *(gen, Geog etc)* monde *m* ◆ **the most powerful nation in the ~** la nation la plus puissante du monde ◆ **the English-speaking ~** le monde anglophone ◆ **to be alone in the ~** être seul au monde ◆ **the ancient ~** le monde antique, l'antiquité *f* ◆ **a citizen of the ~** un citoyen du monde ◆ **it's not the end of the ~** ça pourrait être bien pire ◆ **the ~ we live in** le monde où nous vivons ◆ **he lives in a ~ of his own, he lives in another ~** il vit dans un monde à lui ◆ **all over the ~, (all) the ~ over** dans le monde entier ◆ **to go round the ~, to go on a trip round the ~** *or* **a round-the-~ trip** faire le tour du monde, voyager autour du monde ◆ **a round-the-~ cruise** une croisière autour du monde ◆ **to see the ~** voir du pays, courir le monde ◆ **since the ~ began, since the beginning of the ~** depuis que le monde est monde ◆ **it is known throughout the ~** c'est connu dans le monde entier, c'est universellement connu ; → **dead, fire, lead¹, new, old, old-world**

2 *(emphatic phrases)* **what/where/why/how in the ~ ...?** que/où/pourquoi/comment diable* ... ? ◆ **where in the ~ has he got to?** où a-t-il bien pu passer ?, où diable* est-ce qu'il est passé ? ◆ **nowhere in the ~, nowhere in the whole (wide) ~** nulle part au monde ◆ **I wouldn't do it for (anything in) the ~, nothing in the ~ would make me do it** je ne le ferais pour rien au monde, je ne le ferais pas pour tout l'or du monde ◆ **they were ~s apart** *(gen)* ils n'avaient rien en commun, tout les séparait ; *(in opinion)* ils étaient diamétralement opposés ◆ **there's a ~ of difference between Paul and Richard** il y a un monde entre Paul et Richard ◆ **it was for all the ~ as if ...** c'était exactement *or* tout à fait comme si ... ◆ **I'd give the ~ to know ...** je donnerais tout au monde pour savoir ... ◆ **it did him a** *or* **the ~ of good** ça lui a fait énormément de bien *or* un bien fou* ◆ **it's what he wants most in (all) the ~** c'est ce qu'il veut plus que tout au monde ◆ **in the whole (wide) ~ you won't find a better man than he is** nulle part au monde vous ne trouverez un meilleur homme que lui ◆ **she means the ~ to him** elle est tout pour lui ◆ **she thinks the ~ of him** elle ne jure que par lui ◆ **I'm the ~'s worst cook** il n'y a pas pire cuisinier que moi

3 *(= this life)* monde *m* ; *(Rel: as opposed to spiritual life)* siècle *m*, monde *m* ◆ **the ~, the flesh and the devil** *(Rel)* les tentations *fpl* du monde, de la chair et du diable ◆ **~ without end** *(Rel)* dans les siècles des siècles ◆ **he's gone to a better ~** il est parti pour un monde meilleur ◆ **the next ~, the ~ to come** l'au-delà *m*, l'autre monde *m* ◆ **he's not long for this ~** il n'en a plus pour longtemps (à vivre) ◆ **in this ~** ici-bas, en ce (bas) monde ◆ **in the ~** *(Rel)* dans le siècle ◆ **to bring a child into the ~** mettre un enfant au monde ◆ **to come into the ~** venir au monde, naître ◆ **it's out of this ~** * c'est extraordinaire, c'est sensationnel* ; → **best, other**

4 *(= domain, environment)* monde *m*, univers *m* ◆ **in the ~ of music** dans le monde de la musique ◆ **the ~ of dreams** l'univers *m or* le monde des rêves ◆ **the ~ of nature** la nature ◆ **in the ~ of tomorrow** dans le monde de demain ◆ **the business/sporting ~** le monde des affaires/du sport, les milieux *mpl* d'affaires/sportifs ◆ **in the university/political/financial ~** dans les milieux universitaires/politiques/financiers ◆ **his childhood was a ~ of hot summers and lazy days** son enfance était un univers d'étés brûlants et de journées oisives ◆ **in an ideal** *or* **a perfect ~** dans un monde idéal ◆ **in the best of all possible ~s** dans le meilleur des mondes (possibles)

5 *(= society)* monde *m* ◆ **the Rockefellers/Mr Smiths** *etc* **of this ~** des gens comme les Rockefeller/Smith *etc* ◆ **you know what the ~ will say if ...** tu sais ce que les gens diront si ... ◆ **he had the ~ at his feet** il avait le monde à ses pieds ◆ **you have to take the ~ as you find it** il faut prendre le monde comme il est *or* les choses comme elles sont ◆ **he has come down in the ~** il a connu des jours meilleurs ◆ **to go up in the ~** faire du chemin *(fig)* ◆ **on top of the ~** * *(= happy)* aux anges ; *(= healthy)* en pleine forme ◆ **to make one's way in the ~** faire son chemin dans le monde ◆ **the ~ and his wife** absolument tout le monde, tout le monde sans exception ; → **man**

COMP *[power, war, proportions]* mondial ; *[record, tour]* du monde ; *[language]* universel

World Bank N Banque *f* mondiale

world-beater * N *(fig = person)* champion(ne) *m(f)* ◆ **it's going to be a ~-beater!** ça va faire un tabac !*

World Boxing Association N World Boxing Association *f (association américaine de boxe)*

world champion N *(Sport)* champion(ne) *m(f)* du monde

world championship N championnat *m* du monde

world-class ADJ *[player, team etc]* de niveau international ; *[statesman, politician]* de carrure internationale

World Council of Churches N Conseil *m* œcuménique des Églises

World Court N *(Jur)* Cour *f* internationale de justice
World Cup N *(Ftbl)* Coupe *f* du monde
World Fair N *(Comm)* Exposition *f* internationale
world-famous ADJ de renommée mondiale, célèbre dans le monde entier
World Health Organization N Organisation *f* mondiale de la santé
World Heritage Site N site *m* inscrit sur la liste du patrimoine mondial
world leader N *(Pol, Comm)* leader *m* mondial ◆ **Clari UK is a ~ leader in agrochemicals** Clari UK est un leader mondial en matière de produits chimiques agricoles
world music N world music *f*
world scale N ◆ **on a ~ scale** à l'échelle mondiale
World Series N *(US Baseball)* championnat *m* national de base-ball
World Service N *(Brit Rad)* service *m* international de la BBC
world-shaking, world-shattering ADJ renversant
World title N *(Sport)* titre *m* de champion du monde ◆ **the World title fight** *(Boxing)* le championnat du monde
World Trade Organization N Organisation *f* mondiale du commerce
world-view N vision *f* du monde
World War One N la Première Guerre mondiale
World War Two N la Deuxième *or* Seconde Guerre mondiale
world-weariness N dégoût *m* du monde
world-weary ADJ las (lasse *f*) du monde
world-wide ADJ mondial, universel ADV *[be known]* mondialement, universellement ; *[travel]* à travers le monde, partout dans le monde
the World Wide Web N *(Comput)* le Web

worldliness /ˈwɜːldlɪnɪs/ N *[of person]* attachement *m* aux biens de ce monde ; *(Rel)* mondanité *f*

worldly /ˈwɜːldlɪ/ ADJ 1 (= *earthly*) *[matters]* de ce monde ; *[pleasures, wealth]* de ce monde, temporel ; *[success]* matériel ◆ **his ~ goods** ses biens *mpl* temporels ◆ **to put aside ~ things** renoncer aux choses de ce monde 2 *(pej = materialistic) [person, attitude]* matérialiste 3 (= *experienced) [person]* qui a l'expérience ; *[manner]* qui dénote une grande expérience
COMP **worldly-minded** ADJ matérialiste
worldly-wisdom N expérience *f*
worldly-wise ADJ qui a de l'expérience

worm /wɜːm/ N *(gen = earthworm etc)* ver *m* (de terre) ; *(in fruit etc)* ver *m* ; (= *maggot)* asticot *m* ; *(Med)* ver *m* ; *(fig = person)* minable* *mf* ; (= *program)* ver *m* ◆ **to have ~s** *(Med)* avoir des vers ◆ **the ~ has turned** il en a eu *(or* j'en ai eu *etc)* assez de se *(or* me *etc)* faire marcher dessus ◆ **the ~ in the apple** *or* **bud** *(fig)* le ver dans le fruit *(fig)* ◆ **you ~!*** misérable ! ; → **bookworm, glow, silkworm**
VT 1 (= *wriggle)* **to ~ o.s.** *or* **one's way along/down/across** *etc* avancer/descendre/traverser *etc* à plat ventre *or* en rampant ◆ **he ~ed his way through the skylight** il a réussi en se tortillant à passer par la lucarne ◆ **he ~ed his way into our group** il s'est insinué *or* immiscé dans notre groupe ◆ **to ~ one's way into sb's affections** *(pej)* gagner insidieusement l'affection de qn
2 (= *extract)* **to ~ sth out of sb** soutirer qch à qn ◆ **I'll ~ it out of him somehow** je m'arrangerai pour lui tirer les vers du nez
3 (= *to rid of worms) [+ dog, cat, person]* soigner pour ses vers *or* contre les vers
COMP **worm-cast** N déjections *fpl* de ver
worm drive N *(Tech)* transmission *f* à vis sans fin ; *(Comput)* unité *f* à disques inscriptibles une seule fois
worm-eaten ADJ *[fruit]* véreux ; *[furniture]* mangé aux vers, vermoulu
worm gear N *(Tech)* engrenage *m* à vis sans fin
worm(ing) powder N poudre *f* vermifuge
worm's eye view* N *(Phot, Cine)* contre-plongée *f* ◆ **a ~'s eye view of what is going on** un humble aperçu de ce qui se passe

wormhole /ˈwɜːmhəʊl/ N trou *m* de ver ; *(Phys)* tunnel *m* spatiotemporel

wormlike /ˈwɜːmlaɪk/ ADJ vermiculaire, vermiforme

wormwood /ˈwɜːmwʊd/ N armoise *f*

wormy* /ˈwɜːmɪ/ ADJ (= *worm-eaten) [fruit]* véreux ; *[furniture]* vermoulu, mangé aux vers

worn /wɔːn/ VB ptp of **wear** ADJ *[garment, carpet, tyre, step, hands]* usé ; *[face]* las (lasse *f*) ◆ **to look ~** *[person]* avoir l'air las ; see also **wear** COMP
worn-out ADJ *[garment, carpet, tyre]* usé jusqu'à la corde ; *[tool, machine part]* complètement usé ; *[person]* épuisé, éreinté ; *[idea]* éculé, rebattu ; see also **wear**

worried /ˈwʌrɪd/ ADJ inquiet (-ète *f*) ◆ **she is ~ about her future** elle s'inquiète pour son avenir ◆ **I'm ~ about her health** sa santé m'inquiète, je suis inquiet pour sa santé ◆ **to get ~** s'inquiéter ◆ **I was ~ that he would find out the truth** j'avais peur qu'il découvre *subj* la vérité ◆ **~ sick** *or* **stiff*** fou d'inquiétude ◆ **where do you want to go? – wherever, I'm not ~*** où veux-tu aller ? – n'importe, ça m'est égal ◆ **you had me ~ (for a minute)** tu m'as fait peur ; see also **worry** ; → **death**

worrier /ˈwʌrɪəʳ/ N anxieux *m*, -euse *f*, inquiet *m*, -ète *f* ◆ **he's a dreadful ~** c'est un éternel inquiet

worrisome /ˈwʌrɪsəm/ ADJ préoccupant

worry /ˈwʌrɪ/ N souci *m* ◆ **the ~ of having to find the money** le souci d'avoir à trouver l'argent ◆ **he hasn't any worries** il n'a pas de soucis ◆ **to make o.s. sick with ~** se faire un sang d'encre, se ronger les sangs *(about, over* au sujet de, pour) ◆ **that's the least of my worries** c'est le cadet *or* le dernier de mes soucis ◆ **what's your ~?*** qu'est-ce qui ne va pas ? ◆ **he's a constant ~ to his parents** il est un perpétuel souci pour ses parents ◆ **it's a great ~ to us all, it's causing us a lot of ~** cela nous cause *or* nous donne beaucoup de souci(s) ◆ **what a ~ it all is!** tout ça c'est bien du souci !
VI 1 se faire du souci, s'inquiéter *(about, over* au sujet de, pour) ◆ **don't ~ about me** ne vous inquiétez pas *or* ne vous en faites pas pour moi ◆ **she worries about her health** sa santé la tracasse ◆ **I've got enough to ~ about without that (as well)** j'ai déjà assez de soucis (comme ça) ◆ **there's nothing to ~ about** il n'y a aucune raison de s'inquiéter *or* s'en faire ◆ **I should ~!*** *(iro)* je ne vois pas pourquoi je m'en ferais !* ◆ **I'll punish him if I catch him at it, don't you ~!*** je le punirai si je l'y prends, (ne) t'en fais pas !* ◆ **not to ~!** tant pis, ce n'est pas grave !
2 ◆ **to ~ at sth** ⇒ **to worry sth vt 3**
VT 1 (= *make anxious)* inquiéter, tracasser ◆ **it worries me that he should believe ...** cela m'inquiète qu'il puisse croire ... ◆ **the whole business worries me to death*** j'en suis fou d'inquiétude ◆ **don't ~ yourself about it** ne t'en fais pas *or* ne t'inquiète pas *or* ne te tracasse pas pour ça ◆ **don't ~ your head!** ne vous mettez pas martel en tête ! ◆ **she worried herself sick over it all** elle s'est rendue malade à force de se faire du souci pour tout ça, elle s'est rongé les sangs à propos de tout ça ◆ **what's ~ing you?** qu'est-ce qui te tracasse ? ; see also **worried**
2 (= *bother)* déranger ◆ **the cold doesn't ~ me** le froid ne me dérange pas
3 *[dog etc] [+ bone, rat, ball]* prendre entre les dents et secouer, jouer avec ; *[+ sheep]* harceler ◆ **he kept ~ing the loose tooth with his tongue** il n'arrêtait pas d'agacer avec sa langue la dent qui bougeait
COMP **worry beads** NPL ≈ komboloï *m*
worry line* N ride *f (causée par l'inquiétude)*
▸ **worry along** VI continuer à se faire du souci
▸ **worry at** VT FUS *[+ problem]* ressasser

worrying /ˈwʌrɪɪŋ/ ADJ inquiétant N ◆ **~ does no good** il ne sert à rien de se faire du souci ◆ **all this ~ has aged him** tout le souci qu'il s'est fait l'a vieilli ; → **sheep**

worse /wɜːs/ ADJ compar of **bad, ill** 1 *(in quality) [news, weather, smell, result]* plus mauvais *(than* que), pire *(than* que) ◆ **your essay is ~ than his** votre dissertation est pire *or* plus mauvaise que la sienne ◆ **his essay is bad but yours is ~** sa dissertation est mauvaise mais la vôtre est pire ◆ **I can't remember a ~ harvest** je ne me rappelle pas une plus mauvaise récolte ◆ **I'm bad at English, but ~ at maths** je suis mauvais en anglais et pire en maths ◆ **business is ~ than ever** les affaires vont plus mal que jamais ◆ **it** *or* **things could be ~!** ça pourrait être pire ! ◆ **things couldn't be ~** ça ne pourrait pas aller plus mal ◆ **~ things have happened!, ~ things happen at sea!*** *(hum)* on a vu pire ! ◆ **there are ~ things (than being unemployed)** il y a pire (que d'être au chômage) ◆ **there's nothing ~ than ...** il n'y a rien de pire que ... ◆ **it looks ~ than it is** ça n'est pas aussi grave que ça en a l'air ◆ **~ luck!*** hélas ! ◆ **and, what's ~, ...** et, qui pis est ... ◆ **to get** *or* **grow ~** *[situation, conditions]* empirer, se détériorer ; *[weather, climate]* être de pire en pire, se dégrader ; *[food, smell]* être de plus en plus mauvais, être de pire en pire ; *[memory]* empirer ◆ **things will get ~ before they get better** les choses ne sont pas près d'aller mieux *or* de s'améliorer ◆ **wait, it gets ~*...** attends, il y a pire ... ◆ **to get ~ and ~** ne faire qu'empirer ◆ **that would just make things** *or* **matters ~** cela ne ferait qu'aggraver les choses ◆ **you've only made matters** *or* **things** *or* **it ~** tu n'as fait qu'aggraver la situation *or* qu'envenimer les choses ◆ **he made matters ~ (for himself) by refusing** il a aggravé son cas en refusant ◆ **and, to make matters** *or* **things ~, he ...** et pour ne rien arranger, il ... ; → **bad**
2 *(in behaviour)* pire ◆ **you're ~ than he is!** tu es pire que lui ! ◆ **he was always arrogant, but he's even ~ now** il a toujours été arrogant, mais il est encore pire maintenant ◆ **he is getting ~** il ne s'améliore pas *or* s'arrange pas
3 *(in health)* ◆ **to be ~** aller plus mal ◆ **to feel ~** se sentir moins bien *or* plus mal ◆ **to get** *or* **grow ~** aller plus mal
4 (= *more harmful)* ◆ **smoking is (even) ~ for you than cholesterol** le tabac est (encore) plus mauvais *or* nocif pour la santé que le cholestérol
5 (= *more intense, serious) [noise, pressure, pain, stress]* pire ◆ **to get** *or* **grow ~** empirer ◆ **the rain was getting ~** la pluie s'intensifiait
6 ◆ **the ~ for sth he's none the ~ for it** il ne s'en porte pas plus mal ◆ **he's none the ~ for his fall** sa chute ne lui a pas fait trop de mal ◆ **the house would be none the ~ for a coat of paint** une couche de peinture ne ferait pas de mal à cette maison ◆ **it will be the ~ for you if ...** c'est vous qui serez perdant si ... ◆ **so much the ~ for him!** tant pis pour lui ! ◆ **to be the ~ for drink** (= *tipsy)* être éméché ; (= *drunk)* être ivre ◆ **to look the ~ for wear*** *[clothes, shoes]* être vraiment défraîchi *or* fatigué ; *[carpet]* être vraiment usé ◆ **he was (looking) somewhat the ~ for wear*** il n'était pas très frais
ADV compar of **badly, ill** 1 *(in quality, behaviour) [sing, play]* plus mal ◆ **he did it ~ than you did** il l'a fait plus mal que toi ◆ **that child behaves ~ and ~** cet enfant se conduit de plus en plus mal ◆ **in spite of all those lessons, I played ~**

than ever malgré toutes ces leçons, j'ai joué plus mal que jamais ◆ **you might** *or* **could do** ~ vous pourriez faire pire ◆ **you might do ~ than to accept** accepter n'est pas ce que vous pourriez faire de pire ◆ **~, the food was running out** pire (encore), les vivres s'épuisaient ◆ **and, ~, ...** et, qui pis est, ... ◆ **now I'm ~ off than before** maintenant, je suis moins bien loti qu'avant

2 *(= more intensely, seriously)* **it's raining ~ than ever** il pleut plus fort que jamais ◆ **she hates me ~ than before** elle me déteste encore plus qu'avant ◆ **it hurts ~ than ever** ça fait plus mal que jamais ◆ **the ~ hit** *or* **~ affected areas** les régions *fpl* les plus touchées

3 ◆ **the ~ for sth I like him none the ~ for that** je ne l'en apprécie pas moins pour ça ◆ **I won't think any the ~ of you for it** tu ne baisseras pas pour autant dans mon estime

N pire *m* ◆ **I have ~ to tell you** je ne vous ai pas tout dit, il y a pire encore ◆ **there's ~ to come** le pire est à venir ◆ **~ followed** ensuite cela a été pire ◆ **there has been a change for the ~** *(gen)* il y a eu une détérioration très nette de la situation ; *(in medical patient)* il y a eu une aggravation très nette de son état ; → **bad**

worsen /ˈwɜːsn/ VI *[situation, conditions, weather]* empirer, se détériorer, se dégrader ; *[sb's state, health]* empirer, s'aggraver ; *[illness]* s'aggraver ; *[chances of success]* diminuer, se gâter ; *[relationship]* se détériorer, se dégrader VT empirer, rendre pire

worsening /ˈwɜːsnɪŋ/ N *[of situation, conditions, weather, relations, quality]* détérioration *f*, dégradation *f* ; *[of health, crisis]* aggravation *f* ADJ *[situation, weather, health, quality]* qui empire, qui se détériore ; *[crisis]* qui empire

worship /ˈwɜːʃɪp/ N 1 *(Rel, also of money, success etc)* culte *m* ; *(gen: of person)* adoration *f*, culte *m* ◆ **form of ~** liturgie *f* ◆ **place of ~** *(Rel)* lieu *m* de culte ; *(Christian)* église *f* ◆ **hours of ~** *(Rel)* heures *fpl* des offices ; → **hero** 2 *(esp Brit: in titles)* **His Worship (the Mayor)** Monsieur le maire ◆ **Your Worship** *(to Mayor)* Monsieur le Maire ; *(to magistrate)* Monsieur le Juge VT *(Rel) [+ God, idol etc]* rendre un culte à ; *(gen)* vouer un culte à ; *[+ money, success etc]* avoir le culte de ◆ **he ~ped the ground she walked on** il vénérait jusqu'au sol qu'elle foulait ◆ **she had ~ped him for years** elle lui avait voué un culte pendant des années VI *(Rel)* faire ses dévotions ◆ **to ~ at the altar of power/fame** avoir le culte du pouvoir/de la renommée, vouer un culte au pouvoir/à la renommée

worshipful /ˈwɜːʃɪpfʊl/ ADJ 1 *(frm = reverential)* révérencieux *(liter)* 2 *(esp Brit: in titles)* ◆ **the Worshipful Company of Goldsmiths** l'honorable compagnie *f* des orfèvres ◆ **the Worshipful Mayor of ...** Monsieur le maire de ...

worshipper, worshiper *(US)* /ˈwɜːʃɪpəʳ/ N *(Rel, fig)* adorateur *m*, -trice *f* ◆ **~s** *(in church)* fidèles *mpl*

worst /wɜːst/ ADJ (superl of **bad** *and* **ill**) ◆ **the ~ ...** le (*or* la) plus mauvais(e) ..., le (*or* la) pire ... ◆ **the ~ film I've ever seen** le plus mauvais film que j'aie jamais vu ◆ **he was the ~ student in the class** c'était le plus mauvais élève de la classe ◆ **the ~ thing about men is ...** ce qu'il y a de pire chez les hommes c'est que ... ◆ **the ~ thing about living on your own is ...** ce qu'il y a de pire quand on vit seul, c'est ... ◆ **come on, what's the ~ thing that could happen?** allons, on a vu pire ! ◆ **that's the ~ kind of arrogance** c'est la pire sorte d'arrogance ◆ **in the ~ way*** *(US fig)* désespérément ◆ **of all the children, he's (the) ~** de tous les enfants, c'est le pire ◆ **it was the ~ thing he ever did** c'est la pire chose qu'il ait jamais faite ◆ **it was the ~ winter for 20 years** c'était l'hiver le plus rude depuis 20 ans ◆ **my ~ fears were confirmed (when ...)** mes pires craintes se sont confirmées (quand ...) ◆ **that was his ~ mistake** cela a été son erreur la plus grave *or* sa plus grave erreur ◆ **the ~ victims of inflation are the old** les plus grandes victimes de l'inflation sont les personnes âgées, les personnes les plus touchées par l'inflation sont les personnes âgées

ADV (superl of **badly** *and* **ill**) le plus mal ◆ **they all sing badly but he sings ~ of all** ils chantent tous mal mais c'est lui qui chante le plus mal de tous ◆ **he came off ~** c'est lui qui s'en est le plus mal sorti ◆ **the ~ off** le (*or* la) plus mal loti(e) ◆ **~ of all, ...** pire que tout, ... ◆ **that boy behaved ~ of all** ce garçon a été le pire de tous ◆ **it's my leg that hurts ~ of all** c'est ma jambe qui me fait le plus mal ◆ **the ~-dressed man in England** l'homme *m* le plus mal habillé d'Angleterre ◆ **the ~ hit** *or* **~ affected areas** les régions *fpl* les plus touchées

N pire *m*, pis *m (liter)* ◆ **the ~ that can happen** la pire chose *or* le pire qui puisse arriver ◆ **the ~ is yet to come** il faut s'attendre à pire, on n'a pas encore vu le pire ◆ **the ~ was yet to come** le pire devait arriver ensuite, on n'avait pas encore vu le pire ◆ **the ~ hasn't come to the ~ yet** ce pourrait encore être pire, la situation n'est pas désespérée ◆ **if the ~ comes to the ~** *(Brit)* ◆ **if ~ comes to ~** *(US)* en mettant les choses au pis, même en envisageant le pire ◆ **at (the) ~** au pire ◆ **to be at its (***or* **their) ~** *[crisis, storm, winter, epidemic]* être à son (*or* leur) paroxysme ; *[situation, conditions, relationships]* n'avoir jamais été aussi mauvais ◆ **things** *or* **matters were at their ~** les choses ne pouvaient pas aller plus mal ◆ **at the ~ of the storm/epidemic** au plus fort de l'orage/de l'épidémie ◆ **the ~ of it is that ...** le pire c'est que ... ◆ **... and that's not the ~ of it!** ... et il y a pire encore ! ◆ **that's the ~ of being ...** (ça) c'est l'inconvénient d'être ... ◆ **the ~ of both worlds** tous les inconvénients à la fois ◆ **it brings out the ~ in me** ça réveille en moi les pires instincts ◆ **do your ~!** vous pouvez toujours essayer ! ◆ **he feared the ~** il craignait le pire ◆ **to get the ~ of it** *or* **of the bargain*** être le perdant ; → **think**

VT *(frm)* battre, avoir la supériorité sur ◆ **to be ~ed** avoir le dessous

COMP **worst-case** ADJ *[hypothesis, projection, guess]* le (*or* la) plus pessimiste ◆ **the ~-case scenario** le pire qui puisse arriver, le pire scénario

the worst off ADJ le (*or* la) plus mal loti(e)

worsted /ˈwʊstɪd/ N worsted *m* COMP *[suit etc]* en worsted

worth /wɜːθ/ LANGUAGE IN USE 10.3

N 1 *(= value)* valeur *f* ◆ **what is its ~ in today's money?** ça vaut combien en argent d'aujourd'hui ? ◆ **its ~ in gold** sa valeur (en) or ◆ **a book/man** *etc* **of great ~** un livre/homme *etc* de grande valeur ◆ **I know his ~** je sais ce qu'il vaut ◆ **he showed his true ~** il a montré sa vraie valeur *or* ce dont il était capable

2 *(= quantity)* **he bought £2 ~ of sweets** il a acheté pour 2 livres de bonbons ◆ **50 pence ~, please** (pour) 50 pence s'il vous plaît ; → **money**

ADJ 1 *(= equal in value to)* **to be ~** valoir ◆ **the book is ~ £10** le livre vaut 10 livres ◆ **it can't be ~ that!** ça ne peut pas valoir autant ! ◆ **what** *or* **how much is it ~?** ça vaut combien ? ◆ **I don't know what it's ~ in terms of cash** je ne sais pas combien ça vaut en argent *or* quel prix ça pourrait aller chercher ◆ **how much is the old man ~?*** à combien s'élève la fortune du vieux ? ◆ **he's ~ millions** sa fortune s'élève à plusieurs millions ◆ **it's ~ a great deal** ça a beaucoup de valeur, ça vaut cher ◆ **it's ~ a great deal to me** ça a beaucoup de valeur pour moi ◆ **Swiss chocolate is dearer but it's ~ every penny** le chocolat suisse est plus cher mais on en a pour son argent ◆ **what is his friendship ~ to you?** quel prix attachez-vous à son amitié ? ◆ **it's more than my life is ~ to do that** pour rien au monde je ne peux me permettre de faire cela ◆ **it's as much as my job is ~ to show him that** lui montrer ça est un coup à perdre mon emploi* ◆ **it's not ~ the paper it's written on** ça ne vaut pas le papier sur lequel c'est écrit ◆ **this pen is ~ ten of any other make** ce stylo en vaut dix d'une autre marque ◆ **one Scotsman's ~ three Englishmen** un Écossais vaut trois Anglais ◆ **tell me about it – what's it ~ to you?!*** dites-moi – vous donneriez combien pour le savoir ?* ◆ **I'll give you my opinion for what it's ~** je vais vous donner mon avis, vous en ferez ce que vous voudrez ◆ **he was running/shouting for all he was ~** il courait/criait comme un perdu *or* de toutes ses forces ◆ **to try for all one is ~ to do sth** faire absolument tout son possible pour faire qch

2 *(= deserving, meriting)* **it's ~ the effort** ça mérite qu'on fasse l'effort ◆ **it was well ~ the trouble** ça valait la peine qu'on s'est donnée ◆ **it's not ~ the time and effort involved** c'est une perte de temps et d'effort ◆ **it's ~ reading/having** *etc* ça vaut la peine d'être lu/d'en avoir un *etc* ◆ **it's not ~ having** ça ne vaut rien* ◆ **that's ~ knowing** c'est bon à savoir ◆ **it's ~ thinking about** ça mérite réflexion ◆ **it's ~ going to see the film just for the photography** rien que pour la photographie le film mérite *or* vaut la peine d'être vu ◆ **if a job's ~ doing, it's ~ doing well** *(Prov)* si un travail vaut la peine d'être fait, autant le faire bien ◆ **it's ~ it** ça vaut la peine *or* le coup* ◆ **will you go? – is it ~ it?** tu iras ? – est-ce que ça en vaut la peine ? ◆ **life isn't ~ living** la vie ne vaut pas la peine d'être vécue ◆ **she/it** *etc* **makes (my) life ~ living** elle/cela *etc* est ma raison de vivre ◆ **the museum is ~ a visit** le musée vaut la visite ◆ **it is ~ while to study the text** on gagne à étudier le texte, c'est un texte qui mérite d'être étudié ◆ **it would be ~ (your) while to go and see him** vous gagneriez à aller le voir ◆ **it's not ~ (my) while waiting for him** je perds (*or* perdrais) mon temps à l'attendre ◆ **it's not ~ while** ça ne vaut pas le coup* ◆ **it wasn't ~ his while to take the job** il ne gagnait rien à accepter l'emploi, ça ne valait pas le coup* qu'il accepte *subj* l'emploi ◆ **I'll make it ~ your while*** je vous récompenserai de votre peine, vous ne regretterez pas de l'avoir fait

worthily /ˈwɜːðɪlɪ/ ADV dignement

worthiness /ˈwɜːðɪnɪs/ N 1 *(= deservingness, merit) [of person, work, cause]* mérite *m* ; see also **airworthiness, creditworthiness** 2 ◆ **the ~ associated with vegetarianism/green issues** les prétendus mérites *mpl* du végétarisme/de l'écologie

worthless /ˈwɜːθlɪs/ ADJ *[object, advice, asset]* qui n'a aucune valeur, sans valeur ; *[person]* bon à rien

worthlessness /ˈwɜːθlɪsnɪs/ N *[of object, advice]* absence *f* totale de valeur ; *[of effort]* inutilité *f* ; *[of person]* absence *f* totale de qualités

worthwhile /wɜːθˈwaɪl/ ADJ *[visit]* qui en vaut la peine ; *[book]* qui mérite d'être lu ; *[film]* qui mérite d'être vu ; *[work, job, occupation, life, career]* utile, qui a un sens ; *[contribution]* notable ; *[cause]* louable, digne d'intérêt ◆ **he is a ~ person to go and see** c'est une personne qu'on gagne à aller voir ◆ **I want the money to go to someone ~** je veux que l'argent aille à quelqu'un qui le mérite *or* à une personne méritante

worthy /ˈwɜːðɪ/ ADJ 1 *(= deserving, meritorious) [person]* méritant ; *[motive, aim, effort]* louable ◆ **a ~ winner** un digne gagnant ◆ **it's for a ~**

cause c'est pour une bonne *or* noble cause ◆ **to be ~ of sb/sth** être digne de qn/qch ◆ **to be ~ to do sth** être digne de faire qch, mériter de faire qch ◆ **he found a ~ opponent** *or* **an opponent ~ of him (in Jones)** il a trouvé (en Jones) un adversaire digne de lui ◆ **it is ~ of note that ...** il est intéressant de remarquer que ... ◆ **they have no hospital ~ of the name** il n'ont pas d'hôpital digne de ce nom

[2] *(iro = earnest) [person]* brave *before n*

N *(= respectable citizen)* notable *m* ; *(hum iro)* brave homme *m*, brave femme *f* ◆ **a Victorian ~** un notable de l'époque victorienne ◆ **the village worthies** *(hum iro)* les dignes *or* braves habitants *mpl* du village

wot /wɒt/ **VTI** † sais, sait ◆ **God ~** Dieu sait
ADJ, PRON *(Brit* ⁑*)* ⇒ **what**

Wotan /ˈvəʊtɑːn/ **N** Wotan *m*

wotcha⁑ /ˈwɒtʃə/, **wotcher**⁑ /ˈwɒtʃəʳ/ **EXCL** *(Brit)* salut !

would /wʊd/ **MODAL AUX VB** (cond of **will**) (neg **would not** *often abbr to* **wouldn't**) [1] *(used to form conditional tenses)* **he ~ do it if you asked him** il le ferait si vous le lui demandiez ◆ **he ~ have done it if you had asked him** il l'aurait fait si vous le lui aviez demandé ◆ **I wondered if you'd come** je me demandais si vous viendriez *or* si vous alliez venir ◆ **I thought you'd want to know** j'ai pensé que vous aimeriez le savoir ◆ **who ~ have thought it?** qui l'aurait pensé ? ◆ **you'd never guess** *or* **know she had false teeth** jamais on ne croirait qu'elle a de fausses dents ◆ **so it ~ seem** c'est bien ce qu'il semble ◆ **you ~ think she had enough to do without ...** on pourrait penser qu'elle a assez à faire sans ...

[2] *(indicating willingness)* **I said I ~ do it** j'ai dit que je le ferais *or* que je voulais bien le faire ◆ **he wouldn't help me** il ne voulait pas m'aider, il n'a pas voulu m'aider ◆ **the car wouldn't start** la voiture ne voulait pas démarrer *or* n'a pas voulu* démarrer ◆ **the door wouldn't shut** la porte ne fermait pas *or* ne voulait pas* fermer ◆ **if you ~ come with me, I'd go to see him** si vous vouliez bien m'accompagner, j'irais le voir ◆ **what ~ you have me do?** que voulez-vous que je fasse ? ◆ **~ you like some tea?** voulez-vous du thé ? ◆ **~ you like to go for a walk?** voulez-vous faire une promenade ?, est-ce que vous aimeriez faire une promenade ? ◆ **~ you please leave!** *(in requests)* voulez-vous partir, s'il vous plaît ! ◆ **~ you be so kind** *or* **good as to tell him** *(frm)* auriez-vous l'amabilité *or* la gentillesse de le lui dire ◆ **~ you mind closing the window please** voulez vous fermer la fenêtre, s'il vous plaît

[3] *(indicating habit, characteristic)* **he ~ always read the papers before dinner** il lisait toujours *or* il avait l'habitude de lire les journaux avant le dîner ◆ **50 years ago the streets ~ be empty on Sundays** il y a 50 ans, les rues étaient vides le dimanche ◆ **you ~ go and tell her!** c'est bien de toi d'aller le lui dire !*, il a fallu que tu ailles le lui dire ! ◆ **you ~!*** c'est bien de toi !*, ça ne m'étonne pas de toi ! ◆ **it ~ have to rain!** il pleut, naturellement !, évidemment il fallait qu'il pleuve !

[4] *(expressing preferences)* **I wouldn't have a vase like that in my house** je ne voudrais pas d'un vase comme ça chez moi ◆ **I ~ never marry in church** je ne me marierais jamais à l'église

[5] *(indicating conjecture)* **it ~ have been about 8 o'clock when he came** il devait être 8 heures à peu près quand il est venu, il a dû venir vers 8 heures ◆ **he'd have been about fifty if he'd lived** il aurait eu la cinquantaine s'il avait vécu ◆ **he'd be about 50, but he doesn't look it** il doit avoir dans les 50 ans, mais il ne les fait pas* ◆ **I saw him come out of the shop – when ~ this be?** je l'ai vu sortir du magasin – quand est-ce que c'était ?

[6] *(giving advice)* **I wouldn't worry, if I were you** à ta place, je ne m'inquiéterais pas ◆ **I ~ wait and see what happens first** à ta place j'attendrais de voir ce qui se passe

[7] *(subjunctive uses: liter)* **~ to God she were here!** plût à Dieu qu'elle fût ici ! ◆ **~ that it were not so!** si seulement cela n'était pas le cas ! ◆ **~ I were younger!** si seulement j'étais plus jeune !

COMP **would-be ADJ** ◆ **~-be poet/teacher** poète *m*/professeur *m* en puissance ; *(pej)* prétendu *or* soi-disant poète *m*/professeur *m*

wouldn't /ˈwʊdnt/ ⇒ **would not** ; → **would**

would've /ˈwʊdəv/ ⇒ **would have** ; → **would**

wound¹ /wuːnd/ **N** *(lit, fig)* blessure *f* ; *(esp Med)* plaie *f* ◆ **bullet/knife ~** blessure *f* causée par une balle/un couteau ◆ **he had three bullet ~s in his leg** il avait reçu trois balles dans la jambe ◆ **chest/head ~** blessure *f or* plaie *f* à la poitrine/tête ◆ **the ~ is healing up** la plaie se cicatrise ◆ **to open** *or* **re-open old ~s** rouvrir de vieilles plaies ; → **lick, salt**

VT *(lit, fig)* blesser ◆ **he was ~ed in the leg** il était blessé à la jambe ◆ **he had been ~ed in combat** il avait été blessé au combat ◆ **the bullet ~ed him in the shoulder** la balle l'a atteint *or* l'a blessé à l'épaule ◆ **her feelings were** *or* **she was ~ed by this remark** elle a été blessée par cette remarque ◆ **he was deeply ~ed by their disloyalty** il a été profondément blessé par leur traîtrise ; see also **wounded**

wound² /waʊnd/ **VB** pt, ptp of **wind², wind³** ; see also **wound up**

wounded /ˈwuːndɪd/ **ADJ** *(lit, fig) [person, pride, feelings]* blessé ◆ **seriously ~** gravement *or* grièvement blessé ◆ **a ~ man** un blessé ◆ **a ~ woman** une blessée ◆ **there were six dead and fifteen ~** il y a eu six morts et quinze blessés
NPL **the wounded** les blessés *mpl* ; → **walking, war**

wounding /ˈwuːndɪŋ/ **ADJ** *(fig) [remark, insult]* blessant

wound up /ˌwuːndˈʌp/ **ADJ** *(= tense)* tendu, crispé ◆ **it's silly to get so ~ about it** c'est idiot de s'énerver pour ça

wove /wəʊv/ **VB** pt of **weave**

woven /ˈwəʊvən/ **VB** ptp of **weave**

wow* /waʊ/ **EXCL** ouah !* **N** [1] ◆ **it's a ~!** † c'est sensationnel* *or* terrible !* [2] *(Acoustics)* pleurage *m*, baisse *f* de hauteur du son **VT** *(* = make enthusiastic)* emballer* **COMP** **wow factor*** *[of product]* capacité *f* à séduire ◆ **the deck gives the house its ~ factor** la terrasse en bois donne à la maison un côté spectaculaire ◆ **to have a high ~ factor** être extrêmement séduisant

WP /ˌdʌbljuːˈpiː/ [1] (abbrev of **weather permitting**) si le temps le permet, si les conditions météorologiques le permettent [2] (abbrev of **word processing**) → **word** [3] (abbrev of **word processor**) → **word**

WPC /ˌdʌbljuːpiːˈsiː/ **N** *(Brit)* (abbrev of **Woman Police Constable**) → **woman**

wpm (abbrev of **words per minute**) mots/minute

WRAC /ræk/ **N** *(Brit)* (abbrev of **Women's Royal Army Corps**) *section féminine de l'armée*

wrack¹ /ræk/ **VT** ⇒ **rack¹ vt**

wrack² /ræk/ **N** ⇒ **rack²**

wrack³ /ræk/ **N** *(= seaweed)* varech *m*

WRAF /wæf/ **N** *(Brit)* (abbrev of **Women's Royal Air Force**) *section féminine de l'armée de l'air britannique*

wraith /reɪθ/ **N** apparition *f*, spectre *m* ◆ **~-like** spectral

wrangle /ˈræŋgl/ **N** querelle *f* ◆ **legal/financial/political ~s** querelles *fpl* juridiques/financières/politiques ◆ **the ~s within the party** les conflits au sein du parti **VI** se quereller ◆ **they were wrangling over** *or* **about who should pay** ils se querellaient pour savoir qui allait payer

wrangler /ˈræŋgləʳ/ **N** *(Cambridge Univ)* ≃ major *m* ; *(US = cowboy)* cow-boy *m*

wrangling /ˈræŋglɪŋ/ **N** *(= quarrelling)* disputes *fpl*

wrap /ræp/ **N** [1] *(= shawl)* châle *m* ; *(= stole, scarf)* écharpe *f* ; *(= cape)* pèlerine *f* ; *(= housecoat etc)* peignoir *m* ; *(= rug, blanket)* couverture *f* ◆ **~s** *(= outdoor clothes)* vêtements *mpl* chauds

[2] *(= outer covering: on parcel etc)* emballage *m* ◆ **to keep a scheme under ~s** ne pas dévoiler un projet ◆ **when the ~s come off** quand le voile est levé ◆ **to take the ~s off sth** dévoiler qch

[3] *(fig: Cine)* ◆ **it's a ~*** c'est dans la boîte*

VT *(= cover)* envelopper (in dans) ; *(= pack) [+ parcel, gift]* emballer, empaqueter (in dans) ; *(= wind) [+ tape, bandage]* enrouler *(round* autour de*)* ◆ **~ the chops in foil** *(Culin)* enveloppez les côtelettes dans du papier d'aluminium ◆ **chops ~ped in foil** côtelettes *fpl* en papillotes ◆ **shall I ~ it for you?** *(in gift shop)* c'est pour offrir ?, je vous fais un paquet-cadeau ? ◆ **she ~ped the child in a blanket** elle a enveloppé l'enfant dans une couverture ◆ **~ the rug round your legs** enroulez la couverture autour de vos jambes, enveloppez vos jambes dans la couverture ◆ **he ~ped his arms round her** il l'a enlacée ◆ **he ~ped* the car round a lamppost** il s'est payé* un lampadaire ◆ **~ped bread/cakes** *etc* pain *m*/gâteaux *mpl etc* préemballé(s) *or* préempaqueté(s) ◆ **the town was ~ped in mist** la brume enveloppait la ville ◆ **the whole affair was ~ped in mystery** toute l'affaire était enveloppée *or* entourée de mystère ; → **giftwrap**

COMP **wrap-up*** **N** *(US) (= summary)* résumé *m* ; *(= concluding event)* conclusion *f*, aboutissement *m*

► **wrap up** **VI** [1] *(= dress warmly)* s'habiller chaudement, s'emmitoufler ◆ **~ up well!** couvrez-vous bien !

[2] *(Brit* ⁑ *= be quiet)* la fermer*, la boucler⁑ ◆ **~ up!** la ferme !*, boucle-la !⁑

VT SEP [1] *[+ object]* envelopper (in dans) ; *[+ parcel]* emballer, empaqueter (in dans) ; *[+ child, person] (in rug etc)* envelopper ; *(in clothes)* emmitoufler ◆ **~ yourself up well!** couvrez-vous bien !

[2] *(fig = conceal one's intentions)* dissimuler ◆ **he ~ped up his meaning in unintelligible jargon** il a enveloppé *or* noyé ce qu'il voulait dire dans un jargon tout à fait obscur ◆ **tell me straight out, don't try to ~ it up*** dis-le-moi carrément, n'essaie pas de me dorer la pilule

[3] *(fig = engrossed)* **to be ~ped up in one's work** être absorbé par son travail ◆ **to be ~ped up in sb** penser constamment à qn ◆ **he is quite ~ped up in himself** il ne pense qu'à lui-même ◆ **they are ~ped up in each other** ils vivent entièrement l'un pour l'autre, ils n'ont d'yeux que l'un pour l'autre

[4] *(* = conclude) [+ deal]* conclure ◆ **he hopes to ~ up his business there by Friday evening** il espère conclure *or* régler ce qu'il a à y faire d'ici vendredi soir ◆ **let's get all this ~ped up** finissons-en avec tout ça ◆ **he thought he had everything ~ped up** il pensait avoir tout arrangé *or* réglé ◆ **to ~ up the evening's news** *(esp US fig)* résumer les informations de la soirée

N ◆ **wrap-up** → **wrap**

wraparound /ˈræpəraʊnd/, **wrapover** /ˈræpəʊvəʳ/ **ADJ** ◆ **~ skirt/dress** jupe *f*/robe *f* portefeuille *inv*

wrapper /ˈræpəʳ/ **N** [1] *[of sweet, chocolate bar]* papier *m* ; *[of parcel]* papier *m* d'emballage ; *[of newspaper for post]* bande *f* ; *[of book]* jaquette *f*, couverture *f* [2] *(US = garment)* peignoir *m*

wrapping /ˈræpɪŋ/ **N** *[of parcel]* papier *m* (d'emballage) ; *[of sweet, chocolate]* papier *m*
COMP **wrapping paper** **N** *(= brown paper)* papier *m* d'emballage ; *(= decorated paper)* papier *m* cadeau

wrapround rear window /ˈræpraʊnd rɪəˈwɪndəʊ/ **N** lunette *f* arrière panoramique

wrath /rɒθ/ **N** *(liter)* colère *f*, courroux *m (liter)*

wrathful /ˈrɒθfʊl/ **ADJ** *(liter)* courroucé *(liter)*

wrathfully /ˈrɒθfəlɪ/ **ADV** *(liter)* avec courroux *(liter)*

wreak /riːk/ **VT** *[+ one's anger etc]* assouvir *(upon sb* sur qn) ◆ **to ~ vengeance** *or* **revenge** assouvir une vengeance *(on sb* sur qn) ◆ **~ing destruction along the way** détruisant tout sur son passage

wreath /riːθ/ **N** (pl **wreaths** /riːðz/) *[of flowers]* guirlande *f*, couronne *f* ; (also **funeral wreath**) couronne *f* ; *[of smoke]* volute *f*, ruban *m* ; *[of mist]* nappe *f* ◆ **laurel ~** couronne *f* de laurier ◆ **the laying of ~s** *(= ceremony)* le dépôt de gerbes *fpl* au monument aux morts

wreathe /riːð/ **VT** ① *(= garland) [+ person]* couronner *(with* de) ; *[+ window etc]* orner *(with* de) ◆ **a valley ~d in mist** une vallée frangée de brume ◆ **hills ~d in cloud** collines *fpl* dont les sommets disparaissent dans les nuages ◆ **his face was ~d in smiles** son visage était rayonnant ② *(= entwine) [+ flowers]* enrouler *(round* autour de) **VI** *[smoke]* ◆ **to ~ upwards** s'élever en tournoyant

wreck /rek/ **N** ① *(= wrecked ship)* épave *f*, navire *m* naufragé ; *(= act, event)* naufrage *m* ; *(of plans, ambitions)* effondrement *m* ; *(of hopes)* effondrement *m*, anéantissement *m* ◆ **to be saved from the ~** réchapper du naufrage ◆ **the ~ of the Hesperus** le naufrage de l'Hesperus ◆ **sunken ~s in the Channel** des épaves englouties au fond de la Manche ◆ **the ship was a total ~** le navire a été entièrement perdu
② *(esp US = accident)* accident *m* ◆ **he was killed in a car ~** il a été tué dans un accident de voiture
③ *(= wrecked train/plane/car etc)* train *m*/avion *m*/voiture *f etc* accidenté(e), épave *f* ; *(= building)* ruines *fpl*, décombres *mpl* ◆ **the car was a complete ~** la voiture était bonne à mettre à la ferraille *or* à envoyer à la casse
④ *(= person)* épave *f* ◆ **he was a ~** c'était une épave ◆ **he looks a ~** on dirait une loque, il a une mine de déterré ◆ **a ~ of humanity, a human ~** une épave, une loque humaine
VT ① *[+ ship]* provoquer le naufrage de ; *[+ train, plane, car] [bomb, terrorist, accident]* détruire ; *[driver, pilot]* démolir ; *[+ building]* démolir ; *[+ mechanism]* détraquer ; *[+ furniture etc]* casser, démolir ◆ **to be ~ed** *[ship, sailor]* faire naufrage ◆ **the plane was completely ~ed** il n'est resté que des débris de l'avion ◆ **in his fury he ~ed the whole house** dans sa rage il a tout démoli *or* cassé dans la maison
② *(fig) [+ marriage, friendship]* briser, être la ruine de ; *[+ career]* briser ; *[+ plans, health]* ruiner ; *[+ hopes, ambitions]* ruiner, anéantir ; *[+ negotiations, discussions]* faire échouer ◆ **this ~ed his chances of success** cela a anéanti ses chances de succès ◆ **it ~ed my life** cela a brisé ma vie, ma vie en a été brisée

wreckage /ˈrekɪdʒ/ **N** *(NonC)* ① *(= wrecked ship, car, plane)* épave *f* ; *(= pieces from this)* débris *mpl* ; *[of building]* décombres *mpl* ◆ **~ was strewn over several kilometres** les débris étaient disséminés sur plusieurs kilomètres ◆ **things look black but we must try to save** *or* **salvage something from the ~** la situation est sombre mais il faut essayer de sauver les meubles* ② *(= act) [of ship]* naufrage *m* ; *[of train]* déraillement *m* ; *(fig) [of hopes, ambitions, plans]* anéantissement *m*

wrecked /rekt/ **ADJ** ① *[ship]* naufragé ; *[train, car]* complètement démoli, accidenté ② *[plan]* anéanti ③ * *[person] (= exhausted)* vidé* ; *(= drunk)* bourré*‡

wrecker /ˈrekəʳ/ **N** ① *(gen)* destructeur *m*, démolisseur *m* ; *(Hist: of ships)* naufrageur *m* ② *(in salvage) (= person)* sauveteur *m* (d'épave) ; *(= boat)* canot *m or* bateau *m* sauveteur ; *(= truck)* dépanneuse *f* ③ *(US) (in demolition) [of buildings]* démolisseur *m* ; *[of cars] (= person)* casseur *m*, épaviste *mf* ; *(= business)* casse *f*

wrecking /ˈrekɪŋ/ **N** *(= act) [of ship]* naufrage *m* ; *[of train]* déraillement *m* ; *(fig) [of hopes, ambitions, plans]* anéantissement *m*
COMP **wrecking ball** **N** boulet *m* de démolition
wrecking bar **N** pied-de-biche *m*
wrecking crane **N** *(Rail)* grue *f* de levage

wren /ren/ **N** ① *(= bird)* roitelet *m*, troglodyte *m* ② *(Brit Navy)* **Wren** Wren *f (auxiliaire féminine de la marine royale britannique)*

wrench /rentʃ/ **N** ① *(= tug)* mouvement *m* violent de torsion ◆ **he gave the handle a ~** il a tiré de toutes ses forces sur la poignée
② *(emotional)* déchirement *m* ◆ **the ~ of parting** le déchirement de la séparation ◆ **it was a ~ when she saw him leave** cela a été un déchirement quand elle l'a vu partir
③ *(Med)* entorse *f*
④ *(= tool)* clé *f* anglaise *or* à molette ; *(for car wheels)* clé *f* en croix ◆ **to throw a ~ into the works** *(US)* mettre des bâtons dans les roues ◆ **to throw a ~ into the economy** porter un coup très dur à l'économie ; → **monkey**
VT ① *[+ handle etc]* tirer violemment sur ◆ **to ~ sth (away) from sb** *or* **from sb's grasp** arracher qch des mains de qn ◆ **to ~ sth off** *or* **out** *or* **away** arracher qch ◆ **if you can ~ yourself away from that computer ...** si tu peux t'arracher à cet ordinateur ... ◆ **he ~ed himself free** il s'est dégagé d'un mouvement brusque ◆ **to ~ a box open** ouvrir de force une boîte
② *(Med)* ◆ **to ~ one's ankle** † se tordre la cheville

wrest /rest/ **VT** *[+ object]* arracher violemment *(from sb* des mains de qn) ; *[+ secret, confession]* arracher *(from sb* à qn) ; *[+ power, leadership, title]* ravir *(liter) (from sb* à qn) ◆ **he managed to ~ a living † from the poor soil** à force de travail et de persévérance, il a réussi à tirer un revenu de ce sol pauvre

wrestle /ˈresl/ **VI** lutter (corps à corps) *(with sb* contre qn) ; *(Sport)* catcher *(with sb* contre qn) ; *(Graeco-Roman)* lutter
◆ **to wrestle with** *(fig) [+ problem, one's conscience, sums, device]* se débattre avec ; *[+ difficulties]* se débattre contre, se colleter avec ; *[+ temptation, illness, disease]* lutter contre ◆ **the pilot ~d with the controls** le pilote se débattait avec les commandes ◆ **she was wrestling with her suitcases** elle peinait avec ses valises, elle se débattait avec ses valises
VT *[+ opponent]* lutter contre ◆ **to ~ sb to the ground** terrasser qn
N lutte *f* ◆ **to have a ~ with sb** lutter avec qn

wrestler /ˈresləʳ/ **N** *(Sport)* catcheur *m*, -euse *f* ; *(Graeco-Roman)* lutteur *m*, -euse *f*

wrestling /ˈreslɪŋ/ **N** *(Sport)* catch *m* ; *(Sport)* ◆ **Graeco-Roman ~** lutte *f* gréco-romaine
COMP **wrestling hold** **N** prise *f* de catch *or* de lutte
wrestling match **N** match *m or* rencontre *f* de catch *or* de lutte

wretch /retʃ/ **N** *(unfortunate)* pauvre diable *m* ; *(pej)* scélérat(e) † *m(f) (also liter)*, misérable *mf* ; *(hum)* affreux *m*, -euse *f*, misérable *mf* ◆ **he's a filthy ~*** c'est un salaud*‡ ◆ **you ~!** misérable ! ◆ **cheeky little ~!** petit polisson !, petit misérable !

wretched /ˈretʃɪd/ **ADJ** ① *[person] (= penniless)* misérable ; *(= unhappy)* malheureux ; *[animal]* malheureux ; *[life, slum, conditions]* misérable ◆ **in ~ poverty** dans une misère noire ◆ **the ~ plight of the refugees** la situation épouvantable des réfugiés ② († * = *dreadful) [weather, pay]* minable ◆ **what ~ luck!** quelle déveine !* ◆ **I was feeling ~** *(= ill)* je me sentais vraiment mal ; *(= unhappy)* j'étais très malheureux ◆ **I feel ~ about it** *(= guilty, ashamed)* j'en ai vraiment honte ③ *(*: expressing annoyance)* ◆ **where did I put my ~ keys?** où est-ce que j'ai mis mes foutues* clés ? ◆ **the ~ woman!** espèce de pouffiasse*‡ ! ◆ **that ~ man's late again!** cet imbécile* est encore en retard !

wretchedly /ˈretʃɪdlɪ/ **ADV** ① *(= miserably) [live]* misérablement ; *[weep, apologize]* misérablement, pitoyablement ; *[say, explain]* d'un ton pitoyable ◆ **~ poor** misérable ◆ **~ unhappy** terriblement malheureux ◆ **to be ~ paid** recevoir un salaire de misère ② († * = *dreadfully) [play, sing, treat]* lamentablement

wretchedness /ˈretʃɪdnɪs/ **N** ① *(= extreme poverty)* misère *f* ; *(= unhappiness)* extrême tristesse *f*, détresse *f* ; *(= shamefulness) [of amount, wage, sum]* caractère *m* dérisoire *or* pitoyable ; *[of act, behaviour]* mesquinerie *f* ◆ **his ~ at the thought of having to tell her the news** la détresse qu'il éprouvait à la pensée de devoir lui apprendre la nouvelle ② *(= poor quality) [of meal, hotel, weather]* extrême médiocrité *f*, caractère *m* minable *or* pitoyable

wrick /rɪk/ **VT** *(Brit)* ◆ **to ~ one's ankle** se tordre la cheville ◆ **to ~ one's neck** attraper un torticolis **N** entorse *f* ; *(in neck)* torticolis *m*

wriggle /ˈrɪgl/ **N** ◆ **with a ~ he freed himself** il s'est dégagé en se tortillant *or* en se contorsionnant ◆ **to give a ~** ⇒ **to wriggle vi**
VI *[worm, snake, eel]* se tortiller ; *[fish]* frétiller ; *[person]* gigoter*, se trémousser ; *(in embarrassment)* se tortiller ; *(squeamishly)* frissonner, tressaillir ; *(excitedly)* frétiller ◆ **to ~ along/down** *etc* avancer/descendre *etc* en se tortillant ◆ **the fish ~d off the hook** le poisson a réussi à se détacher de l'hameçon, le poisson frétillait tellement qu'il s'est détaché de l'hameçon ◆ **she managed to ~ free** elle a réussi à se dégager en se tortillant *or* en se contorsionnant ◆ **he ~d through the hole in the hedge** il s'est faufilé *or* s'est glissé dans le trou de la haie (en se tortillant) ◆ **do stop wriggling (about)!** arrête de te trémousser *or* de gigoter* comme ça !
VT ◆ **to ~ one's toes/fingers** remuer *or* tortiller les orteils/les doigts ◆ **to ~ one's way along** *etc* ⇒ **to wriggle along vi**

► **wriggle about, wriggle around** **VI** *[worm, snake, eel]* se tortiller ; *[fish, tadpole]* frétiller ; *[person]* gigoter*, se trémousser ; see also **wriggle vi**

► **wriggle out** **VI** ① *(lit) [worm etc]* sortir ; *[person]* se dégager ◆ **the snake ~d out of the cage** le serpent a rampé hors de la cage ◆ **the fish ~d out of my hand** le poisson m'a glissé des mains *or* m'a glissé entre les doigts
② *(fig)* ◆ **to wriggle out of a difficulty** esquiver une difficulté ◆ **to ~ out of a task/responsibility** se dérober à une tâche/responsabilité ◆ **he'll manage to ~ out of it somehow** il trouvera bien un moyen de s'esquiver *or* de se défiler*

wriggler /ˈrɪgləʳ/ **N** ① **he's a dreadful ~** *[child etc]* il n'arrête pas de gigoter*, il ne se tient jamais tranquille ② *(= mosquito larva)* larve *f* de moustique

wriggly /ˈrɪglɪ/ **ADJ** *[worm, eel, snake]* qui se tortille ; *[fish]* frétillant ; *[child]* remuant, qui gigote* *or* se trémousse

wring /rɪŋ/ (vb : pret, ptp **wrung**) **N** ◆ **to give clothes a ~** essorer des vêtements

VT 1 *(= squeeze, twist)* serrer, tordre ◆ **to ~ a chicken's neck** tordre le cou à un poulet ◆ **if I catch you doing that, I'll ~ your neck!** * si je te prends à faire ça, je te tords le cou ! * ◆ **to ~ one's hands** se tordre les mains (de désespoir) ◆ **he wrung my hand, he wrung me by the hand** il m'a serré longuement la main ◆ **a story to ~ one's heart** une histoire à vous fendre le cœur

2 (also **wring out**) *[+ wet clothes, rag, towel]* essorer ; *[+ water]* extraire, exprimer *(from sth* de qch) ◆ **"do not wring"** *(on label)* "ne pas essorer" ◆ **~ a cloth out in cold water and apply to the forehead** faites une compresse avec un linge mouillé dans de l'eau froide et appliquez-la sur le front

3 *(fig = extort:* also **wring out**) arracher, extorquer ◆ **they wrung a confession/the truth from** *or* **out of him** ils lui ont arraché une confession/la vérité ◆ **he wrung £10 out of me** il m'a extorqué *or* soutiré 10 livres ◆ **I'll ~ it out of him!** je vais lui tirer les vers du nez !, je vais le faire parler ! ◆ **they managed to ~ out of him what had happened** ils sont arrivés non sans peine à lui faire dire *or* avouer ce qui s'était passé

► **wring out** VT SEP 1 ⇒ **wring vt 2, vt 3**

2 *(= exhausted)* ◆ **to be wrung out** * être lessivé * *or* vidé *

wringer /ˈrɪŋəʳ/ N essoreuse *f* (à rouleaux) ◆ **to put sth through the ~** essorer qch *(à la machine)* ◆ **to go** *or* **be put through the ~** * *(fig)* passer un mauvais quart d'heure ◆ **to put sb through the ~** passer qn à la moulinette *

wringing /ˈrɪŋɪŋ/ ADJ (also **wringing wet**) *[garment]* trempé, à tordre * ; *[person]* trempé jusqu'aux os

wrinkle /ˈrɪŋkl/ N 1 *(on skin, fruit)* ride *f* ; *(in socks, cloth, rug etc)* pli *m* 2 * *(= tip)* tuyau * *m* ; *(= good idea)* combine * *f* VT (also **wrinkle up**) *[+ skin]* rider ; *[+ forehead]* plisser ; *[+ nose]* froncer ; *[+ fruit]* rider, ratatiner ; *[+ rug, sheet]* plisser, faire des plis dans VI *[sb's brow]* se plisser, se contracter ; *[nose]* se plisser, se froncer ; *[rug]* faire des plis ; *[socks]* être en accordéon

► **wrinkle down** VI *[socks, stockings]* tomber en accordéon

► **wrinkle up** VI *[skirt, sweater]* remonter en faisant des plis ; *[rug]* faire des plis ; *[sb's brow, nose]* se plisser VT SEP ⇒ **wrinkle vt**

wrinkled /ˈrɪŋkld/ ADJ *[person, skin, face, neck]* ridé ; *[brow, nose]* plissé, froncé ; *[apple]* ridé, ratatiné ; *[shirt, skirt, sheet, rug]* qui fait des plis ; *[stocking, sock]* en accordéon

wrinkly /ˈrɪŋklɪ/ ADJ ⇒ **wrinkled** NPL **wrinklies** *(Brit pej = old people)* les vioques * *mpl*

wrist /rɪst/ N poignet *m*

COMP **wrist joint** N articulation *f* du poignet

wrist loop N *(Climbing)* dragonne *f*

wrist rest N repose-poignet *m*

wrist watch N montre-bracelet *f*

wristband /ˈrɪstbænd/ N *[of shirt]* poignet *m* ; *[of watch]* bracelet *m*

wristlet /ˈrɪstlɪt/ N bracelet *m* (de force) COMP

wristlet watch N montre-bracelet *f*

writ¹ /rɪt/ N *(Jur)* assignation *m* ; *(for election) lettre officielle émanant du président de la Chambre des communes, demandant qu'on procède à des élections* ◆ **to issue a ~ against sb** assigner qn (en justice) ◆ **to issue a ~ for libel against sb** assigner qn en justice pour diffamation ◆ **to serve a ~ on sb, to serve sb with a ~** assigner qn

COMP **writ of attachment** N commandement *m* de saisie

writ of execution N titre *m* exécutoire

writ of habeas corpus N ordre *m* (écrit) d'habeas corpus

writ of subpoena N assignation *f or* citation *f* (en justice)

writ of summons N assignation *f*

writ² †† /rɪt/ 1 VB pt, ptp of **write** 2 *(liter)* **~ large** *(= very obvious)* en toutes lettres *(fig)* (*= exaggerated)* poussé à l'extrême

writable /ˈraɪtəbl/ ADJ *(Comput)* enregistrable

write /raɪt/ LANGUAGE IN USE 21 (pret **wrote**, ptp **written**)

VT 1 *(gen)* écrire ; *[+ list]* faire, écrire ; *[+ prescription, certificate]* rédiger ; *[+ bill, cheque]* faire ◆ **did I ~ that?** j'ai écrit ça, moi ? ◆ **you must print, not ~ your name** il ne faut pas écrire votre nom en cursive mais en caractères d'imprimerie ◆ **it is written "thou shalt not kill"** *(liter)* il est écrit "tu ne tueras point" ◆ **he had "policeman" written all over him** * cela sautait aux yeux *or* crevait les yeux qu'il était de la police ◆ **that's all she wrote** *(US fig)* c'est tout ce qu'il y a à dire

2 *[+ book, essay, letter, poem]* écrire ; *[+ music, opera]* écrire, composer ◆ **you could ~ a book about all that is going on here** on pourrait écrire *or* il y aurait de quoi écrire un livre sur tout ce qui se passe ici

3 *(US = write letter to)* écrire ◆ **can you ~ me when you get there?** tu peux m'envoyer un mot *or* m'écrire quand tu seras arrivé ?

4 *(Comput) [+ program, software etc]* écrire, rédiger ; → **read**

VI 1 *(gen)* écrire ◆ **he can read and ~** il sait lire et écrire ◆ **~ on both sides of the paper** écrivez des deux côtés de la feuille ◆ **as I ~, I can see ...** en ce moment même, je peux voir ... ◆ **this pen ~s well** ce stylo écrit bien

2 *(as author)* **he had always wanted to ~** il avait toujours voulu écrire *or* être écrivain ◆ **he ~s for a living** il est écrivain de métier *or* de profession ◆ **he ~s about social policy** il écrit sur les *or* il traite des questions de politique sociale ◆ **he ~s for "The Times"** il écrit dans le "Times" ◆ **he ~s on foreign policy for "The Guardian"** il écrit des articles de politique étrangère dans le "Guardian" ◆ **what shall I ~ about?** sur quoi est-ce que je vais écrire ?

3 *(= correspond)* écrire *(to* à) ◆ **he wrote to tell us that ...** il (nous) a écrit pour nous dire que ... ◆ **~ for our brochure** *(= send off for)* demandez notre brochure ◆ **I've written for a form** j'ai écrit pour leur demander un formulaire ; → **home**

4 *(Comput)* ◆ **to ~ to a file** modifier un fichier

COMP **write-in** N *(US Pol) (= insertion of name)* inscription *f* ; *(= name itself)* nom *m* inscrit

write-off N → **write-off**

write-protected ADJ *(Comput)* protégé contre l'écriture

write-protect notch N *(Comput)* encoche *f* de protection contre l'écriture

write-up N → **write-up**

► **write away** VI *(= send off)* écrire *(to* à) ◆ **to ~ away for** *[+ information, application form, details]* écrire pour demander ; *[+ goods]* commander par lettre

► **write back** VI répondre *(par lettre)*

► **write down** VT SEP 1 écrire ; *(= note)* noter ; *(= put in writing)* mettre par écrit ◆ **~ it down at once or you'll forget** écrivez-le *or* notez-le tout de suite sinon vous allez oublier ◆ **~ all your ideas down and send them to me** mettez toutes vos idées par écrit et envoyez-les moi ◆ **it was all written down for posterity** c'était tout consigné pour la postérité

2 *(Comm = reduce price of)* réduire le prix de

► **write in**

VI ◆ **listeners are invited to write in with their suggestions** nos auditeurs sont invités à nous envoyer leurs suggestions ◆ **a lot of people have written in to complain** beaucoup de gens nous ont écrit pour se plaindre ◆ **to ~ in for sth** écrire pour demander qch

VT SEP *[+ word, item on list etc]* insérer, ajouter ; *(US Pol) [+ candidate's name]* inscrire ◆ **to ~ sth in to an agreement** *or* **contract** *(at the outset)* stipuler qch dans un contrat ; *(add)* ajouter qch à un contrat

N ◆ **write-in** → **write**

► **write off**

VI ⇒ **write away**

VT SEP 1 *(= write quickly) [+ letter etc]* écrire en vitesse *or* d'une traite

2 *[+ debt]* annuler ; *(fig)* considérer comme perdu *or* gâché, faire une croix * sur ◆ **they wrote off £20,000** ils ont passé 20 000 livres aux profits et pertes ; *(Comm)* ◆ **the operation was written off as a total loss** ils ont décidé de mettre un terme à l'opération qui se révélait une perte sèche ◆ **I've written off the whole thing as a dead loss** j'en ai fait mon deuil *, j'ai fait une croix dessus * ◆ **the Government can ~ off voters motivated by environmental issues** le gouvernement peut faire une croix sur les voix des électeurs motivés par les problèmes d'environnement ◆ **we've written off the first half of the term** nous considérons la première moitié du trimestre comme perdue *or* gâchée ◆ **he had been written off as a failure** on avait décidé qu'il ne ferait jamais rien de bon ◆ **nobody should be written off** il ne faut considérer personne comme irrécupérable ◆ **he is fed up with people writing him off because of his age** il en a assez d'être mis au rancart * à cause de son âge ◆ **his critics wrote him off as too cautious to succeed** ses détracteurs ont exclu la possibilité qu'il réussisse en raison de sa trop grande prudence ◆ **they had written off all the passengers (as dead)** ils tenaient tous les passagers pour morts ◆ **the insurance company decided to ~ off his car** la compagnie d'assurances a décidé que la voiture était irréparable *or* irrécupérable ◆ **he wrote his car off * in the accident** il a complètement bousillé * sa voiture dans l'accident, après l'accident, sa voiture était bonne pour la casse * ◆ **the boat was completely written off** * le bateau a été complètement détruit *or* réduit à l'état d'épave

N ◆ **write-off** → **write-off**

► **write out** VT SEP 1 *[+ one's name and address, details etc]* écrire ; *[+ list]* faire, écrire ; *[+ prescription]* rédiger ; *[+ bill, cheque]* faire

2 *(= copy) [+ notes, essay etc]* recopier, mettre au propre ; *[+ recipe]* copier ◆ **~ out the words three times each** copiez chaque mot trois fois

3 *(TV, Rad) [+ character]* retirer (de la distribution *or* du générique) ◆ **she was written out of the series after a year** elle a cessé de figurer au générique (de la série) au bout d'un an

► **write up**

VI ⇒ **write away**

VT SEP 1 *[+ notes, diary]* mettre à jour ; *(= write report on) [+ happenings, developments]* faire un compte rendu de ; *(= record) (Chem etc) [+ experiment]* rédiger ; *(Archeol etc) [+ one's findings]* consigner ◆ **he wrote up the day's events in the ship's log** il a inscrit *or* consigné dans le journal de bord les événements de la journée ◆ **he wrote up his visit in a report** il a rendu compte de sa visite dans un rapport ◆ **she wrote it up for the local paper** elle en a fait le compte rendu pour le journal local

2 *(= praise)* écrire un article élogieux (*or* une lettre élogieuse) sur

N ◆ **write-up** → **write-up**

write-off /ˈraɪtɒf/ N *(Comm)* perte *f* sèche ; *(Fin: tax)* déduction *f* fiscale ◆ **to be a ~** *[car]* être irréparable, être bon pour la casse * ; *[project, operation]* n'avoir abouti à rien, n'avoir rien donné ◆ **the afternoon was a ~** l'après-midi n'a été qu'une perte de temps

writer /ˈraɪtəʳ/ **N** 1 *(of letter, book etc)* auteur *m* ; *(as profession)* écrivain *m*, auteur *m* ◆ **the (present) ~ believes ...** l'auteur croit ... ◆ **a thriller ~** un auteur de romans policiers ◆ **he is a ~** il est écrivain, c'est un écrivain ◆ **to be a good ~** *(of books)* être un bon écrivain, écrire bien ; *(in handwriting)* écrire bien, avoir une belle écriture ◆ **to be a bad ~** *(of books)* écrire mal, être un mauvais écrivain ; *(in handwriting)* écrire mal *or* comme un chat ; → **hack², letter** 2 *(Comput: of program etc)* auteur *m*

COMP **writer's block N** hantise *f* de la page blanche

writer's cramp N crampe *f* des écrivains

Writer to the Signet N *(Scot Jur)* notaire *m*

write-up /ˈraɪtʌp/ **N** *(gen, also Comput)* description *f* ; *(= review) [of play etc]* compte rendu *m*, critique *f* ; *(= report) [of event etc]* compte rendu *m*, exposé *m* ◆ **there's a ~ about it in today's paper** il y a un compte rendu là-dessus dans le journal d'aujourd'hui ◆ **the play got a good ~** la pièce a eu de bonnes critiques

writhe /raɪð/ **VI** se tordre ◆ **it made him ~** *(in pain)* cela le fit se tordre de douleur ; *(from disgust)* il en frémit de dégoût ; *(from embarrassment)* il ne savait plus où se mettre ◆ **he ~d under the insult** il frémit sous l'injure

► **writhe about, writhe around VI** *(in pain)* se tordre dans des convulsions ; *(to free o.s.)* se contorsionner en tous sens

writing /ˈraɪtɪŋ/ **N** 1 *(NonC = handwriting, sth written)* écriture *f* ◆ **there was some ~ on the page** il y avait quelque chose d'écrit sur la page ◆ **I could see the ~ but couldn't read it** je voyais bien qu'il y avait quelque chose d'écrit mais je n'ai pas pu le déchiffrer ◆ **I can't read your ~** je n'arrive pas à déchiffrer votre écriture ◆ **in his own ~** écrit de sa main ◆ **he has seen the ~ on the wall** *(esp Brit)* il mesure la gravité de la situation ◆ **the ~ is on the wall** *(esp Brit)* la catastrophe est imminente

◆ **in writing** par écrit ◆ **I'd like to have that in ~** j'aimerais avoir cela par écrit ◆ **get his permission in ~** obtenez sa permission par écrit ◆ **evidence in ~ that ...** preuve *f* par écrit *or* littérale que ... ◆ **to put sth in ~** mettre qch par écrit

2 *(NonC = occupation of writer)* **he devoted his life to ~** il a consacré sa vie à l'écriture ◆ **~ is his hobby** écrire est son passe-temps favori ◆ **he earns quite a lot from ~** ses écrits lui rapportent pas mal d'argent

3 *(= output of writer)* écrits *mpl*, œuvres *fpl* ◆ **there is in his ~ evidence of a desire to ...** on trouve dans ses écrits la manifestation d'un désir de ... ◆ **the ~s of H. G. Wells** les œuvres *fpl* de H. G. Wells

4 *(NonC = act)* **he's learning reading and ~** il apprend à lire et à écrire ◆ **~ is a skill which must be learned** écrire est un art qui s'apprend ◆ **the ~ of this book took ten years** écrire ce livre a pris dix ans

COMP **writing case N** *(Brit)* écritoire *m*

writing desk N secrétaire *m (bureau)*

writing pad N bloc-notes *m*

writing paper N papier *m* à lettres

writing room N *(in hotel etc)* salon *m* d'écriture

writing table N bureau *m*

written /ˈrɪtn/ **VB** ptp of **write ADJ** *[test, agreement, constitution etc]* écrit ; *[permission, confirmation]* par écrit ◆ **~ evidence** *(gen, Hist)* documents *mpl* ; *(Jur)* documents *mpl* écrits ◆ **~ proof** *(Jur)* preuves *fpl* écrites ◆ **her ~ English is excellent** son anglais est excellent à l'écrit ◆ **a ~ language** une langue écrite ◆ **the power of the ~ word** le pouvoir de l'écrit ; → **face, hand**

WRNS /renz/ **N** *(Brit)* (abbrev of **Women's Royal Naval Service**) *service des auxiliaires féminines de la marine royale*

wrong /rɒŋ/

LANGUAGE IN USE 2.2, 12.1, 14, 18.3

1 ADJECTIVE
2 ADVERB
3 NOUN
4 TRANSITIVE VERB
5 COMPOUNDS

1 - ADJECTIVE

1 [= mistaken, incorrect] *[guess]* erroné ; *[answer, solution, calculation, sum, musical note]* faux (fausse *f*) ◆ **the letter has the ~ date on it** ils *etc* se sont trompés de date sur la lettre ◆ **I'm in the ~ job** je ne suis pas fait pour ce travail, ce n'est pas le travail qu'il me faut ◆ **he's got the ~ kind of friends** *(also hum)* il a de mauvaises fréquentations ◆ **that's the ~ kind of plug** ce n'est pas la prise qu'il faut ◆ **she married the ~ man** elle n'a pas épousé l'homme qu'il lui fallait ◆ **you've got** *or* **picked the ~ man if you want someone to mend a fuse** vous tombez mal si vous voulez quelqu'un qui puisse réparer un fusible ◆ **you've put it back in the ~ place** vous ne l'avez pas remis à la bonne place *or* là où il fallait ◆ **it's the ~ road for Paris** ce n'est pas la bonne route pour Paris ◆ **you're on the ~ road** *or* **track** *(fig)* vous faites fausse route ◆ **to say the ~ thing** dire ce qu'il ne faut pas dire, faire un impair ◆ **he got all his sums ~** toutes ses opérations étaient fausses ◆ **the accountant got his sums ~** * le comptable a fait une erreur *or* s'est trompé dans ses calculs ◆ **he told me the ~ time** il ne m'a pas donné la bonne heure ◆ **it happened at the ~ time** c'est arrivé au mauvais moment ◆ **he got on the ~ train** il s'est trompé de train, il n'a pas pris le bon train ◆ **the ~ use of drugs** l'usage abusif des médicaments

◆ **to be wrong** ◆ **my clock/watch is ~** ma pendule/ma montre n'est pas à l'heure ◆ **you're quite ~** vous vous trompez, vous avez tort ◆ **I was ~ about him** je me suis trompé sur son compte ◆ **he was ~ in deducing that ...** il a eu tort de déduire que ...

◆ **to get sth wrong** ◆ **you've got your facts ~** ce que vous avancez est faux ◆ **he got the figures ~** il s'est trompé dans les chiffres ◆ **they got it ~ again** ils se sont encore trompés ◆ **how ~ can you get!** * *(iro)* comme on peut se tromper !

2 [= bad] mal *inv* ; *(= unfair)* injuste ◆ **it is ~ to lie, lying is ~** c'est mal de mentir ◆ **it is ~ for her to have to beg, it is ~ that she should have to beg** il est injuste qu'elle soit obligée de mendier ◆ **you were ~ to hit him, it was ~ of you to hit him** tu n'aurais pas dû le frapper, tu as eu tort de le frapper

3 [= exceptionable] ◆ **there's nothing ~ with hoping that ...** il n'y a pas de mal à espérer que ... ◆ **what's ~ with going to the cinema?** quel mal y a-t-il à aller au cinéma ? ◆ **there's nothing ~ with** *or* **in (doing) that** il n'y a rien à redire à cela

4 [= amiss] qui ne va pas ◆ **something's ~** *or* **there's something ~ (with it)** il y a quelque chose qui ne va pas ◆ **something's ~** *or* **there's something ~ with him** il y a quelque chose qui ne va pas chez lui ◆ **something's ~ with my leg** j'ai quelque chose à la jambe ◆ **something's ~ with my watch** ma montre ne marche pas comme il faut ◆ **there's something ~ somewhere** il y a quelque chose qui cloche* là-dedans ◆ **something was very ~** quelque chose n'allait vraiment pas ◆ **there's nothing ~** tout va bien ◆ **nothing ~, I hope?** tout va bien *or* pas d'ennuis, j'espère ? ◆ **there's nothing ~ with it** *[+ theory, translation]* c'est tout à fait correct ; *[+ method, plan]* c'est tout à fait valable ; *[+ machine, car]* ça marche très bien ◆ **there's nothing ~ with him** il va très bien ◆ **he's ~ in the head** * il a le cerveau dérangé *or* fêlé*

◆ **what's wrong?** qu'est-ce qui ne va pas ? ◆ **what's ~ with you?** qu'est-ce que tu as ? ◆ **what's ~ with your arm?** qu'est-ce que vous avez au bras ? ◆ **what's ~ with the car?** qu'est-ce qu'elle a, la voiture ?

2 - ADVERB

[answer, guess] mal ◆ **you're doing it all ~** vous vous y prenez mal ◆ **you did ~ to refuse** vous avez eu tort de refuser ◆ **you've spelt it ~** vous l'avez mal écrit ◆ **you thought ~** tu t'es trompé ◆ **she took me up ~** * elle n'a pas compris ce que je voulais dire

◆ **to get sb/sth wrong** ◆ **you've got the sum ~** vous vous êtes trompé dans votre calcul, vous avez fait une erreur de calcul ◆ **you've got it all ~** * *(= misunderstood)* vous n'avez rien compris ◆ **don't get me ~** * comprends-moi bien ◆ **you've got me all ~** * *(= misunderstood my meaning)* tu n'as rien compris à ce que je t'ai dit ; *(= misunderstood what I'm like)* tu te trompes complètement à mon sujet

◆ **to go wrong** *(in directions)* se tromper de route ; *(in calculations, negotiations etc)* faire une faute *or* une erreur ; *(morally)* mal tourner ; *[plan]* mal tourner ; *[business deal etc]* tomber à l'eau ; *[machine, car]* tomber en panne ; *[clock, watch etc]* se détraquer ◆ **you can't go ~** *(in directions)* vous ne pouvez pas vous perdre *or* vous tromper ; *(in method etc)* c'est simple comme bonjour ; *(in choice of job, car etc)* (de toute façon) c'est un bon choix ◆ **you can't go ~ with this brand** vous ferez le bon choix en achetant cette marque ◆ **you won't go far ~ if you ...** vous ne pouvez guère vous tromper si vous ... ◆ **something went ~ with the gears** quelque chose s'est détraqué dans l'embrayage ◆ **something must have gone ~** il a dû arriver quelque chose ◆ **nothing can go ~ now** tout doit marcher comme sur des roulettes maintenant ◆ **everything went ~ that day** tout est allé mal *or* de travers ce jour-là

3 - NOUN

1 [= evil] mal *m* ◆ **to do ~** mal agir ◆ **he can do no ~ in her eyes** tout ce qu'il fait est bien à ses yeux *or* trouve grâce à ses yeux ; see also **right**

2 [= injustice] injustice *f*, tort *m* ◆ **he suffered great ~** il a été la victime de graves injustices ◆ **to right a ~** réparer une injustice ◆ **two ~s don't make a right** *(Prov)* on ne répare pas une injustice par une autre (injustice) ◆ **you do me ~ in thinking** † ... vous me faites tort en pensant † ... ◆ **he did her ~** † il a abusé d'elle

◆ **in the wrong** ◆ **to be in the ~** être dans son tort, avoir tort ◆ **to put sb in the ~** mettre qn dans son tort

4 - TRANSITIVE VERB

faire du tort à, faire tort à † ◆ **you ~ me if you believe ...** vous êtes injuste envers moi si vous croyez ... ◆ **a ~ed wife** une femme trompée

5 - COMPOUNDS

wrong-foot VT *(Ftbl, Tennis)* prendre à contre-pied ; *(Brit fig)* prendre au dépourvu

wrong-headed ADJ *[person]* buté ; *[idea, view, approach]* aberrant

wrongdoer /ˈrɒŋ,duːəʳ/ **N** malfaiteur *m*, -trice *f*

wrongdoing /ˈrɒŋ,duːɪŋ/ **N** *(NonC)* méfaits *mpl*

wrongful /ˈrɒŋfʊl/ **ADJ** *(frm)* injustifié

COMP **wrongful arrest N** arrestation *f* arbitraire

wrongful dismissal N licenciement *m* abusif

wrongful trading N opérations *fpl* frauduleuses

wrongfully /ˈrɒŋfəlɪ/ **ADV** à tort

wrongly /ˈrɒŋlɪ/ ADV 1 (= *incorrectly*) *[answer, guess, translate, interpret, position, insert, calculate]* mal ; *[spell, price, install]* incorrectement ; *[believe, attribute, state, accuse, convict, imprison]* à tort ◆ ~ **accused of murder/of doing sth** faussement accusé *or* accusé à tort de meurtre/d'avoir fait qch ◆ **the handle has been put on** ~ le manche n'a pas été mis comme il fallait *or* a été mal mis ◆ **she was ~ dressed for the occasion** sa tenue n'était pas adaptée à la circonstance ; → **rightly** 2 (= *wrongfully*) *[treat]* injustement

wrongness /ˈrɒŋnɪs/ N (= *incorrectness*) *[of answer]* inexactitude *f* ; (= *injustice*) injustice *f* ; (= *evil*) immoralité *f*

wrote /rəʊt/ VB pt of **write**

wrought /rɔːt/ VB (archaic pret, ptp of **work**) ◆ **the destruction ~ by the floods** *(liter)* les ravages provoqués par l'inondation ◆ **the damage the hurricane had ~ on Florida** les dégâts que l'ouragan avait provoqués en Floride ◆ **the changes ~ by time** les changements apportés par le temps ADJ *[silver]* ouvré

COMP **wrought iron** N fer *m* forgé
wrought-iron ADJ *[gate, decoration]* en fer forgé
wrought-ironwork N ferronnerie *f*
wrought-up ADJ *[person]* très tendu

wrung /rʌŋ/ VB pt, ptp of **wring**

WRVS /ˌdʌbljuːɑːviːˈes/ N *(Brit)* (abbrev of **Women's Royal Voluntary Service**) *service d'auxiliaires bénévoles au service de la collectivité*

wry /raɪ/ ADJ *[person, smile, remark]* ironique ; *[wit]* empreint d'ironie ◆ **to listen/look on with ~ amusement** écouter/regarder d'un air amusé et narquois ◆ **a ~ sense of humour** un sens de l'humour empreint d'ironie ◆ **to make a ~ face** faire la grimace ◆ **a ~ comedy** une comédie pleine d'ironie

wryly /ˈraɪlɪ/ ADV *[say, think]* avec ironie ◆ **to smile** ~ avoir un sourire ironique ◆ ~ **amusing** amusant et ironique

WS /ˌdʌbljuːˈes/ N *(Scot Jur)* (abbrev of **Writer to the Signet**) → **writer**

wt abbrev of **weight**

WTO /ˌdʌbljuːtiːˈəʊ/ N (abbrev of **World Trade Organization**) OMC *f*

wunderkind * /ˈwʌndəkɪnd/ N prodige *m*

wuss * /wʊs/ N *(esp US)* mauviette* *f*

WV abbrev of **West Virginia**

WWI (abbrev of **World War One**) → **world**

WWII (abbrev of **World War Two**) → **world**

WWF /ˌdʌbljuːˌdʌbljuːˈef/ N (abbrev of **Worldwide Fund for Nature**) WWF *m*

WWW /ˌdʌbljuːˌdʌbljuːˈdʌbljuː/ N *(Comput)* (abbrev of **World Wide Web**) ◆ **the** ~ le Web

WY abbrev of **Wyoming**

wych-elm /ˈwɪtʃˈelm/ N orme *m* blanc *or* de montagne

wynd /waɪnd/ N *(Scot)* venelle *f*

Wyoming /waɪˈəʊmɪŋ/ N Wyoming *m* ◆ **in** ~ dans le Wyoming

WYSIWYG /ˈwɪzɪwɪg/ N *(Comput)* (abbrev of **what you see is what you get**) WYSIWYG *m*, ce que l'on voit est ce que l'on obtient, tel écran tel écrit

X, x /eks/ (vb : pret, ptp **x-ed, x'ed**) N (= *letter*) X, x *m* ; (*Math, fig*) x ; (*at end of letter = kiss*) bises *fpl* ; (*several kisses*) grosses bises *fpl* ◆ **X for X-ray** ≃ X comme Xavier ◆ **he signed his name with an X** il a signé d'une croix *or* en faisant une croix ◆ **for x years** pendant x années ◆ **Mr X** Monsieur X ◆ **X marks the spot** l'endroit est marqué d'une croix ; → **X-ray** VT marquer d'une croix

COMP **x-axis** N axe *m* des x

X-certificate ADJ (*Brit Cine: formerly*) classé X, ≃ interdit aux moins de 18 ans

X-chromosome N chromosome *m* X

X-rated ADJ (*fig*) [*book, language*] obscène, porno * ; (*US Cine*) classé X, ≃ interdit aux moins de 17 ans

xenon /ˈzenɒn/ N xénon *m*

xenophobe /ˈzenəfəʊb/ ADJ, N xénophobe *mf*

xenophobia /ˌzenəˈfəʊbɪə/ N xénophobie *f*

xenophobic /ˌzenəˈfəʊbɪk/ ADJ xénophobe

Xenophon /ˈzenəfən/ N Xénophon *m*

xerography /zɪəˈrɒgrəfɪ/ N xérographie *f*

Xerox ® /ˈzɪərɒks/ N (= *machine*) photocopieuse *f* ; (= *reproduction*) photocopie *f* VT (faire) photocopier, prendre *or* faire une photocopie de, copier * VI se faire *or* se laisser photocopier

Xerxes /ˈzɜːksiːz/ N Xerxès *m*

XL /ˌekˈsel/ (abbrev of **extra large**) XL

Xmas /ˈeksməs, ˈkrɪsməs/ N abbrev of **Christmas**

X-ray /ˈeksˌreɪ/ N (= *ray*) rayons *mpl* X ; (= *photograph*) radiographie *f*, radio * *f* ◆ **to have an ~** se faire radiographier, se faire faire une radio * VT [+ *limb, luggage*] radiographier, faire une radio de * ; [+ *person*] radiographier, faire une radio à *

COMP radioscopique, radiographique

X-ray diagnosis N radiodiagnostic *m*

X-ray examination N examen *m* radioscopique, radio * *f*

X-ray photo, X-ray picture N (*on film*) radiographie *f*, radio * *f* ; (*on screen*) radioscopie *f*, radio * *f*

X-ray treatment N radiothérapie *f*

xylograph /ˈzaɪləgrɑːf/ N xylographie *f*

xylographic /ˌzaɪləˈgræfɪk/ ADJ xylographique

xylography /zaɪˈlɒgrəfɪ/ N xylographie *f*

xylophone /ˈzaɪləfəʊn/ N xylophone *m*

xylophonist /zaɪˈlɒfənɪst/ N joueur *m* de xylophone

Yy

Y, y /waɪ/ N (= *letter*) Y, y *m* ◆ **Y for Yellow** ≃ Y comme Yvonne ◆ **Y-shaped** en (forme d')Y
COMP **y-axis** N axe *m* des y
Y-chromosome N chromosome *m* Y
Y-fronts ® NPL (*Brit*) slip *m* (*ouvert*)

Y2K /,waɪtuːˈkeɪ/ N (abbrev of **Year 2000**) an *m* 2000

yacht /jɒt/ N (*luxury motorboat*) yacht *m* ; (*with sails*) voilier *m* VI ◆ **to go ~ing** faire de la navigation de plaisance, faire du bateau
COMP **yacht club** N yacht-club *m*
yacht race N course *f* à la voile *or* de voile

yachting /ˈjɒtɪŋ/ N navigation *f* de plaisance, voile *f*
COMP [*enthusiast*] de la voile, de la navigation de plaisance ; [*cruise*] en yacht ; [*magazine*] de navigation de plaisance
yachting cap N casquette *f* de marin
yachting club N yacht-club *m*
yachting event N ⇒ **yachting regatta**
the yachting fraternity N les plaisanciers *mpl*
yachting regatta N régate *f*

yachtsman /ˈjɒtsmən/ N (pl **-men**) (*in race, professional*) navigateur *m* ; (*amateur*) plaisancier *m*

yachtswoman /ˈjɒtswʊmən/ N (pl **-women**) (*in race, professional*) navigatrice *f* ; (*amateur*) plaisancière *f*

yack * /jæk/, **yackety-yak** * /ˈjækɪtɪˈjæk/ (*pej*) VI caqueter, jacasser ◆ **what are you ~ing (on) about?** qu'est-ce que tu racontes ? N caquetage *m*

yah * /jɑː/ EXCL 1 (= *yes*) ouais ! * 2 (*defiance*) (also **yah boo**) na ! COMP **yah-boo politics** N politique *f* de provocation

yahoo /jɑːˈhuː/ N butor *m*, rustre *m*

yak¹ /jæk/ N (= *animal*) yak *or* yack *m*

yak² * /jæk/ ⇒ **yackety-yak** ; → **yack**

Yakuza /jəˈkuːzə/ N (= *person*) yakusa *m pl inv*
NPL **the Yakuza** (= *organization*) les yakusa *mpl*
COMP **Yakuza boss** N chef *m* yakusa

Yale ® /jeɪl/ N (also **Yale lock**) serrure *f* à barillet *or* à cylindre

y'all * /jɔːl/ PRON (*US*) vous (autres)

yam /jæm/ N 1 (= *plant, tuber*) igname *f* 2 (*US* = *sweet potato*) patate *f* douce

yammer * /ˈjæməʳ/ VI jacasser

yang /jæŋ/ N (*Philos*) yang *m*

Yangtze /ˈjæŋksɪ/ N Yang-Tsê Kiang *m*

Yank ⁑ /jæŋk/ (abbrev of **Yankee**) ADJ amerloque ⁑, ricain ⁑ (*pej*) N Amerloque ⁑ *mf*, Ricain(e) ⁑ *m(f)* (*pej*)

yank /jæŋk/ N coup *m* sec, saccade *f* VT tirer d'un coup sec ◆ **he ~ed open the door** il ouvrit la porte d'un coup sec

► **yank off** * VT SEP (= *detach*) arracher *or* extirper (d'un coup sec)

► **yank out** * VT SEP arracher *or* extirper (d'un coup sec)

Yankee * /ˈjæŋkɪ/ N (*Hist*) Yankee *mf* ; (*esp pej*) yankee *mf* ADJ yankee *f inv* ◆ **~ Doodle** *chanson populaire de la Révolution américaine*

> **YANKEE**
>
> En Europe, le terme **Yankee** désigne tout Américain, mais aux États-Unis, il est réservé aux habitants du nord du pays. Dans les États du Nord, on dit même que les seuls véritables **Yankees** sont ceux de la Nouvelle-Angleterre. Le mot a été employé pour la première fois dans la chanson « **Yankee** Doodle », écrite par un Anglais pour se moquer des Américains, mais, à l'époque de la Révolution américaine, les soldats du général Washington ont fait de cette chanson un hymne patriotique.

yap /jæp/ (*pej*) VI [*dog*] japper ; * [*person*] jacasser N jappement *m*

yapping /ˈjæpɪŋ/ (*pej*) ADJ [*dog*] jappeur ; [*person*] jacasseur N [*of dog*] jappements *mpl* ; [*of person*] jacasserie *f*

yappy * /ˈjæpɪ/ ADJ ◆ **a ~ little dog** un petit chien qui n'arrête pas de japper

Yarborough /ˈjɑːbrə/ N (*Bridge etc*) *main ne contenant aucune carte supérieure au neuf*

yard¹ /jɑːd/ N 1 yard *m* (91,44 *cm*), ≃ mètre *m* ◆ **one ~ long** long d'un yard, ≃ long d'un mètre ◆ **20 ~s away (from us)** à une vingtaine de mètres (de nous) ◆ **he can't see a ~ in front of him** il ne voit pas à un mètre devant lui ◆ **to buy cloth by the ~** ≃ acheter de l'étoffe au mètre ◆ **how many ~s would you like?** ≃ quel métrage désirez-vous ? ◆ **a word a ~ long** un mot qui n'en finit plus ◆ **an essay ~s long** une dissertation-fleuve ◆ **with a face a ~ long** faisant une tête longue comme ça ◆ **sums by the ~** des calculs à n'en plus finir ◆ **to give sb the whole nine ~s** * y mettre le paquet * 2 (*Naut*) vergue *f*

yard² /jɑːd/ N 1 [*of farm, hospital, prison, school*] cour *f* ; (*surrounded by the building: in monastery, hospital*) préau *m* ◆ **back ~** arrière-cour *f* ; → **farmyard** 2 (= *work-site*) chantier *m* ; (*for storage*) dépôt *m* ◆ **builder's/shipbuilding ~** chantier *m* de construction/de construction(s) navale(s) ◆ **coal/contractor's ~** dépôt *m* de charbon/de matériaux de construction ; → **dockyard, goods** 3 (*Brit*) **the Yard, Scotland Yard** Scotland Yard *m* ◆ **to call in the Yard** demander l'aide de Scotland Yard 4 (*US*) (= *garden*) jardin *m* ; (= *field*) champ *m* 5 (= *enclosure for animals*) parc *m* ; → **stockyard** COMP **yard sale** N (*US*) vide-grenier *m* ; → CAR-BOOT SALE, GARAGE SALE

yardage /ˈjɑːdɪdʒ/ N longueur *f* en yards, ≃ métrage *m*

yardarm /ˈjɑːdɑːm/ N (*Naut*) *les extrémités d'une vergue*

yardbird ⁑ /ˈjɑːdbɜːd/ N (*US*) (= *soldier*) bidasse *m* empoté * (*qui est souvent de corvée*) ; (= *convict*) taulard ⁑ *m*

Yardie * /ˈjɑːdɪ/ N (*Brit*) Yardie *m* (*membre d'une organisation criminelle d'origine jamaïcaine*)

yardmaster /ˈjɑːdmɑːstəʳ/ N (*US Rail*) chef *m* de triage

yardstick /ˈjɑːdstɪk/ N (*fig*) mesure *f* ◆ **a ~ of efficiency/success** un critère d'efficacité/de succès ◆ **they are trying to establish a ~ for the level of violence** ils essaient d'établir des critères pour évaluer le niveau de violence ◆ **he had no ~ by** *or* **against which to judge it** il n'avait aucun moyen de comparaison pour en juger

yarmulke /ˈjɑːmʊlkə/ N kippa *f*

yarn /jɑːn/ N 1 fil *m* ; (*Tech: for weaving*) filé *m* ◆ **cotton/nylon ~** fil *m* de coton/de nylon ® 2 (= *tale*) longue histoire *f* ; → **spin** VI raconter *or* débiter des histoires

yarrow /ˈjærəʊ/ N mille-feuille *f*, achillée *f*

yashmak /ˈjæʃmæk/ N litham *m*

yaw /jɔː/ VI (*in ship*) (*suddenly*) faire une embardée, embarder ; (*gradually*) dévier de la route ; (*in aircraft*) faire un mouvement de lacet

yawl /jɔːl/ N (*Naut*) (= *sailing boat*) yawl *m* ; (= *ship's boat*) yole *f*

yawn /jɔːn/ VI 1 [*person*] bâiller ◆ **to ~ with boredom** bâiller d'ennui 2 [*chasm etc*] s'ouvrir VT ◆ **to ~ one's head off** bâiller à se décrocher la mâchoire ◆ **"no", he ~ed** "non", dit-il en bâillant N bâillement *m* ◆ **to give a ~** bâiller ◆ **the film is one long ~** * ce film est ennuyeux de bout en bout ; → **stifle**

yawning /ˈjɔːnɪŋ/ ADJ [*chasm*] béant ; [*person*] qui bâille N bâillements *mpl*

yawp /jɔːp/ (US) N 1 (* = yelp) braillement* m ◆ **to give a ~** brailler* 2 (* = chatter) papotage m ◆ **to have a ~** bavasser* (pej) VI 1 (* = yelp) brailler* 2 (* = chatter) bavasser* (pej)

yaws /jɔːz/ N (Med) pian m

yay* /jeɪ/ EXCL (= great) chouette !

yd abbrev of **yard**

ye¹ /jiː/ PERS PRON (††, liter, dial) vous ◆ **~ gods!*** grands dieux !*, ciel ! (hum)

ye² †† /jiː/ DEF ART (= the) ancienne forme écrite

yea /jeɪ/ ADV 1 (frm = yes) oui ◆ **to say ~ to sth** dire oui à qch ◆ **~ or nay** oui ou non 2 (†† = indeed) en vérité N oui m ◆ **the ~s and the nays** les voix fpl pour et les voix fpl contre, les oui mpl et les non mpl

yeah* /jɛə/ PARTICLE ouais*, oui ◆ **oh ~?** (iro) et puis quoi encore ? ◆ **~, (that'll be) right!** c'est ça !, tu parles !*

year /jɪəʳ/ N 1 an m, année f ◆ **next ~** l'an m prochain, l'année f prochaine ◆ **last ~** l'an m dernier, l'année f dernière ◆ **this ~** cette année ◆ **they intend to complete the project when the conditions are right: this ~, next ~, sometime, never?** ils prévoient d'achever le projet quand les conditions seront propices : mais combien de temps faudra-t-il attendre ? ◆ **document valid one ~** document m valable (pendant) un an ◆ **taking the good ~s with the bad** bon an mal an ◆ **a ~ (ago) last January** il y a eu un an au mois de janvier (dernier) ◆ **a ~ in January, a ~ next January** il y aura un an en janvier (prochain) ◆ **it costs £500 a ~** cela coûte 500 livres par an ◆ **he earns £15,000 a ~** il gagne 15 000 livres par an ◆ **three times a ~** trois fois par an or l'an ◆ **all the ~ round** toute l'année ◆ **as (the) ~s go (or went) by** au cours or au fil des années ◆ **~ in, ~ out** année après année ◆ **over the ~s** au cours or au fil des années ◆ **~ by ~** d'année en année ◆ **to pay by the ~** payer à l'année ◆ **every ~, each ~** tous les ans, chaque année ◆ **every other ~, every second ~** tous les deux ans ◆ **~ on ~** (+ noun) annuel ; (+ verb) annuellement, chaque année ◆ **~s (and ~s*) ago** il y a (bien) des années ◆ **for ~s together** or **on end*** plusieurs années de suite ◆ **they have not met for ~s** ils ne se sont pas vus depuis des années ◆ **I haven't laughed so much for** or **in* ~s** ça fait des années que je n'ai pas autant ri ◆ **I haven't seen him for** or **in* ~s** ça fait des années or des lustres* que je ne l'ai (pas) vu ◆ **it took us ~s* to find the restaurant** (fig) il (nous) a fallu un temps fou pour trouver le restaurant ◆ **from ~ to ~** d'année en année ◆ **from one ~ to the next** d'une année à l'autre ◆ **from ~('s) end to ~('s) end** d'un bout de l'année à l'autre ◆ **in the ~ of grace** or **of Our Lord 1492** (frm) en l'an de grâce 1492 ◆ **in the ~ 1869** en 1869 ◆ **in the ~ two thousand** en l'an deux mille ◆ **a friend of 30 ~s' standing** un ami de 30 ans or que l'on connaît (or connaissait etc) depuis 30 ans ; → **after, donkey, New Year, old**

2 (referring to age) **he is six ~s old** or **six ~s of age** il a six ans ◆ **in his fortieth ~** dans sa quarantième année ◆ **from his earliest ~s** dès son âge le plus tendre ◆ **he looks old for his ~s** il fait or paraît plus vieux que son âge ◆ **young for his ~s** jeune pour son âge ◆ **she is very active for (a woman of) her ~s** elle est très active pour (une femme de) son âge ◆ **well on in ~s** d'un âge avancé ◆ **to get on in ~s** prendre de l'âge ◆ **to grow in ~s** (liter) avancer en âge ◆ **it's put ~s on me!** cela m'a vieilli de vingt ans !, cela m'a fait prendre un coup de vieux* ◆ **changing your hairstyle can take ten ~s off you** changer de coiffure peut vous rajeunir de dix ans ◆ **it's taken ~s off my life!** cela m'a vieilli de vingt ans ! ◆ **I feel ten ~s younger** j'ai l'impression d'avoir dix ans de moins or d'avoir rajeuni de dix ans

3 (Scol, Univ) année f ◆ **he is first in his ~** il est le premier de son année ◆ **she was in my ~ at school/university** elle était de mon année au lycée/à l'université ◆ **he's in (the) second ~** (Univ) il est en deuxième année ; (secondary school) ≃ il est en cinquième ◆ **the academic ~ 2000/2001** l'année f universitaire 2000/2001 ◆ **the first ~s study French and Spanish** (Brit = pupil) ≃ les élèves de sixième étudient le français et l'espagnol

4 (Prison) an m ◆ **he got ten ~s** il en a pris pour dix ans*, on l'a condamné à dix ans de prison ◆ **sentenced to 15 ~s' imprisonment** condamné à 15 ans de prison

5 [of coin, stamp, wine] année f

6 (Fin) ◆ **financial ~** exercice m financier ◆ **tax ~** exercice m fiscal, année f fiscale

COMP **year end** N (Comm, Fin) clôture f or fin f de l'exercice ◆ **~ end report/accounts** rapport m/comptes mpl de fin d'exercice
year head N (Brit Scol) conseiller m, -ère f (principal(e)) d'éducation
year-long ADJ qui dure toute une année
year-round ADJ [resident, population] qui réside toute l'année ; [work] qui dure toute l'année ; [facilities] ouvert toute l'année
year tutor N (Brit Scol) ⇒ **year head**

yearbook /ˈjɪəbʊk/ N annuaire m (d'une université, d'un organisme etc)

yearling /ˈjɪəlɪŋ/ N animal m d'un an ; (= racehorse) yearling m ADJ (âgé) d'un an

yearly /ˈjɪəlɪ/ ADJ annuel ADV 1 (= every year) chaque année, tous les ans ◆ **twice ~** deux fois par an ◆ **twice-~** semestriel 2 (= per year) [produce, spend] par an

yearn /jɜːn/ VI 1 (= feel longing) languir (for, after après), aspirer (for, after à) ◆ **to ~ for home** avoir la nostalgie de chez soi or du pays ◆ **to ~ to do sth** avoir très envie or mourir d'envie de faire qch, aspirer à faire qch 2 (= feel tenderness) s'attendrir, s'émouvoir (over sur)

yearning /ˈjɜːnɪŋ/ N désir m ardent or vif (for, after de ; to do sth de faire qch) envie f (for, after de ; to do sth de faire qch) aspiration f (for, after vers ; to do sth à faire qch) ADJ [desire] vif, ardent ; [look] plein de désir or de tendresse

yearningly /ˈjɜːnɪŋlɪ/ ADV (= longingly) avec envie, avec désir ; (= tenderly) avec tendresse, tendrement

yeast /jiːst/ N (NonC) levure f ◆ **dried ~** levure f déshydratée
COMP **yeast extract** N extrait m de levure de bière
yeast infection N candidose f

yeasty /ˈjiːstɪ/ ADJ [flavour, taste, smell] de levure ; [bread] qui sent la levure ; (= frothy) écumeux

yec(c)h* /jek/ EXCL (US) berk or beurk !

yegg‡ /jeg/ N (US: also **yeggman**) cambrioleur m, casseur‡ m

yeh* /jeə/ PARTICLE ⇒ **yeah**

yell /jel/ N hurlement m, cri m ◆ **a ~ of fright** un hurlement or un cri d'effroi ◆ **a ~ of pain** un hurlement or un cri de douleur ◆ **a ~ of alarm/dismay** un cri d'inquiétude/de désarroi ◆ **to give** or **let out a ~** pousser un hurlement or un cri ◆ **college ~** (US Univ) ban m d'étudiants VI (also **yell out**) hurler (with de) ◆ **to ~ at sb** crier après qn ◆ **to ~ with pain** hurler de douleur VT (also **yell out**) hurler ◆ **he ~ed out that he was hurt** il hurla qu'il était blessé ◆ **"stop it!", he ~ed** "arrêtez !" hurla-t-il ◆ **to ~ abuse** hurler des injures

yelling /ˈjelɪŋ/ N hurlements mpl, cris mpl ADJ hurlant

yellow /ˈjeləʊ/ ADJ 1 (in colour) [object etc] jaune ; [hair, curls] blond ◆ **to go** or **turn** or **become** or **grow ~** devenir jaune, jaunir ; see also **noun, canary**

2 (fig pej = cowardly) lâche ◆ **there was a ~ streak in him** il avait un côté lâche
N (also of egg) jaune m
VI jaunir
VT jaunir ◆ **paper ~ed with age** papier m jauni par le temps
COMP **yellow-bellied**‡ ADJ froussard, trouillard
yellow-belly‡ N (pej) froussard(e)* m(f), trouillard(e)‡ m(f)
yellow brick road N (fig) voie f du succès
yellow card N (Ftbl) carton m jaune
yellow-card VT donner un carton jaune à ◆ **he was ~-carded** il a reçu un carton jaune
yellow-dog contract N (US Hist) contrat m interdisant de se syndiquer (aujourd'hui illégal)
yellow fever N (Med) fièvre f jaune
yellow flag N (Naut) pavillon m de quarantaine
yellow jack* N (Naut) ⇒ **yellow flag**
yellow jersey N maillot m jaune
yellow line N (on road) ligne f jaune ◆ **double ~ lines** bandes jaunes indiquant l'interdiction de stationner
yellow metal N (= gold) métal m jaune ; (= brass) cuivre m jaune
yellow ochre N ocre f jaune
Yellow Pages ® NPL (Telec) pages fpl jaunes
the yellow peril † N (Pol) le péril jaune
yellow press † N (Press) presse f à sensation
yellow rain N pluie f jaune
the Yellow River N le fleuve Jaune
the Yellow Sea N la mer Jaune
yellow soap N savon m de Marseille
yellow spot N (Anat) tache f jaune
yellow wagtail N bergeronnette f flavéole

yellowhammer /ˈjeləʊˌhæməʳ/ N bruant m jaune

yellowish /ˈjeləʊɪʃ/ ADJ tirant sur le jaune, jaunâtre (pej) ◆ **~ brown** d'un brun tirant sur le jaune, brun jaunâtre inv (pej) ◆ **~ green** d'un vert tirant sur le jaune, vert jaunâtre inv (pej)

yellowness /ˈjeləʊnɪs/ N (NonC) 1 (= colour) [of object] couleur f jaune, jaune m ; [of skin] teint m jaune 2 (* pej = cowardice) lâcheté f, trouillardise‡ f

yellowy /ˈjeləʊɪ/ ADJ ⇒ **yellowish**

yelp /jelp/ N [of animal] glapissement m ; [of person] cri m ◆ **to let out a ~** [person] crier ; [animal] glapir VI [person] crier ; [animal] glapir

yelping /ˈjelpɪŋ/ N [of animal] glapissement m ; [of person] cri m

Yemen /ˈjemən/ N ◆ **(the) ~** le Yémen ◆ **North/South ~** le Yémen du Nord/Sud

Yemeni /ˈjemənɪ/, **Yemenite** /ˈjemənaɪt/ ADJ (gen) yéménite ; [ambassador, embassy] du Yémen ◆ **North/South ~** yéménite or du Yémen du Nord/Sud N Yéménite mf ◆ **North/South ~** Yéménite mf du Nord/Sud

yen¹ /jen/ N (pl inv = money) yen m

yen²* /jen/ N désir m intense, grande envie f (for de) ◆ **to have a ~ to do sth** avoir (grande) envie de faire qch

yenta* /ˈjentə/ N (US pej) commère f

yeoman /ˈjəʊmən/ (pl **-men**) N 1 (Hist = freeholder) franc-tenancier m 2 (Brit Mil) cavalier m ; → **yeomanry**
COMP **yeoman farmer** N (Hist) franc-tenancier m ; (modern) propriétaire m exploitant
Yeoman of the Guard N (Brit) hallebardier m de la garde royale
yeoman service N (fig) ◆ **to do** or **give ~ service** rendre des services inestimables

yeomanry /ˈjəʊmənrɪ/ N (NonC) 1 (Hist) (classe f des) francs-tenanciers mpl 2 (Brit Mil) régiment de cavalerie (volontaire)

yeomen /ˈjəʊmən/ NPL of **yeoman**

yep* /jep/ PARTICLE ouais*, oui

yer‡ /jɜːʳ/ PRON ⇒ **your**

yes /jes/ PARTICLE (answering affirmative question) oui ; (answering negative question) si ◆ **do you**

want some? – **~!** en voulez-vous ? – oui ! ◆ **don't you want any?** – **~ (I do)!** vous n'en voulez pas ? – (mais) si ! ◆ **~ of course, ~ certainly** mais oui ◆ **~ and no** oui et non ◆ **oh ~, you did say that** *(contradicting)* si si *or* mais si, vous avez bien dit cela ◆ **~?** *(awaiting further reply)* (ah) oui ?, et alors ? ; *(answering knock at door)* oui ?, entrez ! ◆ **waiter!** – **~ sir?** garçon ! – (oui) Monsieur ? ◆ **~!*** *(in triumph)* ouah ! * ; → **say** N oui *m inv* ◆ **he gave a reluctant ~** il a accepté de mauvaise grâce

COMP **yes man*** N (pl **yes men**) *(pej)* béni-oui-oui* *m inv (pej)* ◆ **he's a ~ man** il dit amen à tout

yes-no question N *(Ling)* question *f* fermée

yeshiva(h) /jeˈʃiːvə/ N (pl **yeshiva(h)s** *or* **jeshivoth** /jeˈʃiːvɒt/) yeshiva *f*

yesterday /ˈjestədeɪ/ ADV 1 *(lit) (= day before today)* hier ◆ **it rained ~** il a plu hier ◆ **all (day) ~** toute la journée d'hier ◆ **late ~** hier dans la soirée ◆ **he arrived only ~** il n'est arrivé qu'hier ◆ **a week from ~** dans une semaine à compter d'hier ◆ **the news was announced a week ago ~** il y avait une semaine hier que la nouvelle avait été annoncée ◆ **I had to have it by ~** *or* **no later than ~** il fallait que je l'aie hier au plus tard ◆ **when do you need it by?** – **~!** *(hum)* il vous le faut pour quand ? – hier ! *(hum)* ; → **born, day**

2 *(fig = in the past)* hier, naguère ◆ **towns which ~ were villages** des villes qui étaient hier *or* naguère des villages

N 1 *(lit = day before today)* hier *m* ◆ **~ was the second** c'était hier le deux ◆ **~ was Friday** c'était hier vendredi ◆ **~ was very wet** il a beaucoup plu hier ◆ **~ was a bad day for him** la journée d'hier s'est mal passée pour lui ◆ **the day before ~** avant-hier *m* ◆ **where's ~'s newspaper?** où est le journal d'hier ?

2 *(fig = the past)* hier *m*, passé *m* ◆ **the great men of ~** tous les grands hommes du passé *or* d'hier ◆ **all our ~s** *(liter)* tout notre passé

COMP **yesterday afternoon** ADV hier après-midi

yesterday evening ADV hier (au) soir

yesterday morning ADV hier matin

yesterday week* ADV *(Brit)* il y a eu huit jours hier

yesternight †† /ˈjestəˈnaɪt/ N, ADV la nuit dernière, hier soir

yesteryear /ˈjestəˈjɪəʳ/ N *(esp liter)* les années *fpl* passées ◆ **the cars/hairstyles/fashions of ~** les voitures *fpl*/coiffures *fpl*/modes *fpl* d'antan

yet /jet/ LANGUAGE IN USE 26.3

ADV 1 *(= by this time: with neg)* ◆ **not ~** pas encore ◆ **they haven't (as) ~ returned, they haven't returned (as) ~** ils ne sont pas encore de retour ◆ **they hadn't (as) ~ managed to do it** ils n'étaient pas encore arrivés à le faire ◆ **no one has come (as) ~** personne n'est encore arrivé ◆ **no one had come (as) ~** jusqu'alors *or* jusque-là personne n'était (encore) venu ◆ **we haven't come to a decision ~** nous ne sommes pas encore parvenus à une décision ◆ **I don't think any decision has been reached as ~** je ne pense pas qu'on soit déjà parvenu à une décision ◆ **are you coming?** – **not just ~** est-ce que vous venez ? – pas tout de suite ◆ **don't come in (just) ~** n'entrez pas tout de suite *or* pas pour l'instant ◆ **I needn't go (just) ~** je n'ai pas besoin de partir tout de suite ◆ **that won't happen (just) ~, that won't happen (just) ~ awhile(s)*** ça n'est pas pour tout de suite ◆ **you ain't seen nothing ~*** *(hum)* vous n'avez encore rien vu

2 *(= already: in questions)* déjà ◆ **have you had your lunch ~?** avez-vous déjà déjeuné ? ◆ **I wonder if he's come ~** je me demande s'il est déjà arrivé *or* s'il est arrivé maintenant ◆ **must you go just ~?** faut-il que vous partiez *subj* déjà ?

3 *(= so far: with superl)* jusqu'à présent, jusqu'ici ◆ **she's the best teacher we've had ~** c'est le meilleur professeur que nous ayons eu jusqu'à présent *or* jusqu'ici ◆ **the best book ~ written** le meilleur livre qui ait jamais été écrit

4 *(= still)* encore ◆ **he may come ~** *or* **~ come** il peut encore venir ◆ **he could come ~** il pourrait encore venir ◆ **his plan may ~ fail** son plan peut encore échouer ◆ **we'll make a footballer of you ~** nous finirons pas faire un footballeur de toi ◆ **there is hope for me ~** *(gen hum)* tout n'est pas perdu pour moi ◆ **I'll speak to her ~** je finirai bien par lui parler ◆ **I'll do it ~** j'y arriverai bien quand même ◆ **he has ~ to learn** il a encore à apprendre, il lui reste à apprendre ◆ **I have ~ to see one** je n'en ai encore jamais vu ◆ **Mr Lea has** *or* **is ~ to score** Lea n'a pas encore marqué de points ◆ **his guilt is ~ to be proved** sa culpabilité reste à prouver ◆ **there were revelations ~ to come** des révélations devaient encore arriver ◆ **she is ~ alive** *or* **alive ~** *(liter)* elle est encore vivante, elle vit encore ◆ **for all I know he is there ~** autant que je sache il est encore *or* toujours là

5 *(= from now)* ◆ **we've got ages ~** nous avons encore plein de temps ◆ **it'll be ages ~ before she's ready** il va encore lui falloir des heures pour se préparer ◆ **we'll wait for five minutes ~** nous allons attendre encore cinq minutes ◆ **it won't be dark for half an hour ~** il ne fera pas nuit avant une demi-heure ◆ **I'll be here for a (long) while ~** *or* **for a long time ~** je resterai ici encore un bon bout de temps ◆ **he won't be here for a (long) while ~** *or* **for a long time ~** il ne sera pas ici avant longtemps ◆ **for some time ~** pour encore pas mal de temps ◆ **not for some time ~** pas avant un certain temps ◆ **they have a few days ~** ils ont encore *or* il leur reste encore quelques jours ◆ **there's another bottle ~** il reste encore une bouteille

6 *(= even: with compar)* ◆ **~ more people** encore plus de gens ◆ **he wants ~ more money** il veut encore plus *or* encore davantage d'argent ◆ **this week it's been work, work and ~ more work** cette semaine, ça a été du travail, encore du travail et toujours plus de travail ◆ **~ louder shouts** des cris encore plus forts ◆ **these remains date back ~ further** ces vestiges remontent à encore plus longtemps ◆ **the latest results were better/worse ~** les tout derniers résultats étaient encore meilleurs/pires ◆ **~ again, ~ once more** une fois de plus ◆ **she was ~ another victim of racism** c'était une victime de plus du racisme ◆ **another arrived and ~ another** il en est arrivé un autre et encore un autre

7 *(frm)* ◆ **not he nor ~ I** ni lui ni moi ◆ **I do not like him nor ~ his sister** je ne les aime ni lui ni sa sœur, je ne l'aime pas et sa sœur non plus *or* et sa sœur pas davantage ◆ **they did not come nor ~ (even) write** ils ne sont pas venus et ils n'ont même pas écrit

CONJ *(= however)* cependant, pourtant ; *(= nevertheless)* toutefois, néanmoins ◆ **(and) ~ everyone liked her** (et) pourtant *or* néanmoins tout le monde l'aimait, mais tout le monde l'aimait quand même ◆ **(and) ~ I like the house** (et) malgré tout *or* (et) pourtant *or* (et) néanmoins j'aime bien la maison ◆ **it's strange ~ true** c'est étrange mais pourtant vrai *or* mais vrai tout de même

yeti /ˈjetɪ/ N yéti *or* yeti *m*

yew /juː/ N 1 (also **yew tree**) if *m* 2 *(= wood)* (bois *m* d')if *m* COMP *[bow etc]* en bois d'if

YHA /ˌwaɪeɪtʃˈeɪ/ N *(Brit)* (abbrev of **Youth Hostels Association**) *auberges de jeunesse du pays de Galles et de l'Angleterre*, ≃ FUAJ *f*

Yid *‡/jɪd/ N *(pej)* youpin(e)*‡*m(f) (pej)*

Yiddish /ˈjɪdɪʃ/ ADJ yiddish *inv* N *(= language)* yiddish *m*

yield /jiːld/ N *[of land, farm, field, tree, industry, mine]* production *f* ; *(per unit)* rendement *m* ; *[of oil well]* débit *m* ; *[of labour]* produit *m*, rendement *m* ; *[of tax]* recettes *fpl* ; *[of business, shares]* rapport *m*, rendement *m* ◆ **~ per hectare/year** *etc* rendement *m* à l'hectare/l'année *etc* ◆ **the ~ of this land/orchard** *etc* **is ...** ce terrain/verger *etc* produit ...

VT 1 *(= produce, bring in) [earth, mine, oil well]* produire ; *[farm, field, land, orchard, tree]* rendre, produire, rapporter ; *[labour, industry]* produire ; *[business, investments, tax, shares]* rapporter ◆ **to ~ a profit** rapporter un profit *or* un bénéfice ◆ **that land ~s no return** cette terre ne rend pas ◆ **shares ~ing high interest** *(Fin)* actions *fpl* à gros rendement *or* d'un bon rapport ◆ **shares ~ing 10%** actions *fpl* qui rapportent 10% ◆ **to ~ results** donner *or* produire des résultats ◆ **this ~ed many benefits** bien des bénéfices en ont résulté

2 *(= surrender, give up) [+ ground, territory]* céder ; *[+ fortress, territory]* abandonner (*to* à) ; *[+ ownership, rights]* céder (*to* à), renoncer à (*to* en faveur de) ; *[+ control]* renoncer à (*to* en faveur de) ◆ **to ~ ground to sb** *(Mil, fig)* céder du terrain à qn ◆ **to ~ the floor to sb** *(fig)* laisser la parole à qn ◆ **to ~ a point to sb** concéder un point à qn, céder à qn sur un point ◆ **to ~ the right of way to sb** *(esp US)* céder le passage à qn ◆ **to ~ obedience/thanks to sb** *(frm)* rendre obéissance/grâces à qn *(frm)*

VI 1 *(= give produce, bring in revenue) [farm, field, land, orchard, tree]* rendre ; *[business, investments, tax, shares]* rapporter ; *[labour, industry, mine, oil well]* produire ◆ **a field that ~s well** un champ qui donne un bon rendement *or* qui rend bien ◆ **land that ~s poorly** une terre qui rend peu *or* mal, une terre à faible rendement

2 *(= surrender, give in)* céder (*to* devant, à), se rendre (*to* à) ◆ **we shall never ~** nous ne céderons jamais, nous ne nous rendrons jamais ◆ **they begged him but he would not ~** ils l'ont supplié mais il n'a pas cédé *or* il ne s'est pas laissé fléchir ◆ **they ~ed to us** *(Mil etc)* ils se rendirent à nous ◆ **to ~ to force** céder devant la force ◆ **to ~ to superior forces** céder devant *or* à des forces supérieures ◆ **to ~ to superior numbers** céder au nombre ◆ **to ~ to reason** se rendre à la raison ◆ **to ~ to an impulse** céder à une impulsion ◆ **to ~ to sb's entreaties** céder aux prières *or* instances de qn ◆ **to ~ to sb's threats** céder devant les menaces de qn ◆ **to ~ to sb's argument** se rendre aux raisons de qn ◆ **to ~ to temptation** céder *or* succomber à la tentation ◆ **he ~ed to nobody in courage** *(liter)* il ne le cédait à personne pour le courage *(liter)* ◆ **I ~ to nobody in my admiration for ...** personne plus que moi n'admire ...

3 *(= collapse, give way) [branch, door, ice, rope]* céder ; *[beam]* céder, fléchir ; *[floor, ground]* s'affaisser ; *[bridge]* céder, s'affaisser ◆ **to ~ under pressure** céder à la pression

4 *(US Driving)* céder le passage

► **yield up** VT SEP *(esp liter) [+ secrets]* livrer ◆ **to ~ o.s. up to temptation** céder *or* succomber à la tentation ◆ **to ~ up the ghost** rendre l'âme

yielding /ˈjiːldɪŋ/ ADJ 1 *(fig) [person]* complaisant, accommodant 2 *(lit = soft, flexible) [floor, ground, surface]* mou (molle *f*), élastique N *(NonC = surrender) [of person]* soumission *f* ; *[of town, fort]* reddition *f*, capitulation *f* ; *[of right, goods]* cession *f*

yike(s) * /jaɪk(s)/ EXCL *(esp US)* mince ! *

yin /jɪn/ N *(Philos)* yin *m* ◆ **~-yang symbol** symbole *m* du yin et du yang

yip /jɪp/ (US) ⇒ **yelp**

yipe(s) * /jaɪp(s)/ EXCL *(esp US)* ⇒ **yike(s)**

yippee *‡ /jɪˈpiː/ EXCL hourra !

YMCA /ˌwaɪemsiːˈeɪ/ N (abbrev of **Young Men's Christian Association**) YMCA *m*

yo* /jəʊ/ EXCL *(esp US)* salut !*

yob* /jɒb/ N *(Brit pej)* loubard* *m*

yobbish* /ˈjɒbɪʃ/ ADJ *(Brit pej)* *[behaviour]* de loubard* ◆ **a ~ young man** un jeune loubard*

yobbo* /ˈjɒbəʊ/ N *(Brit)* ⇒ **yob**

yock* /jɒk/ *(US)* N gros rire *m*, rire *m* gras VT ◆ **to ~ it up** rigoler*, s'esclaffer

yod /jɒd/ N *(Phon)* yod *m*

yodel /ˈjəʊdl/ VI jodler *or* iodler, faire des tyroliennes N *(= song, call)* tyrolienne *f*

yoga /ˈjəʊgə/ N yoga *m*

yoghurt /ˈjəʊgət/ N ⇒ **yogurt**

yogi /ˈjəʊgɪ/ N (pl **yogis** *or* **yogin** /ˈjəʊgɪn/) yogi *m*

yogic flying /ˌjəʊgɪkˈflaɪɪŋ/ N *lévitation pratiquée par les adeptes d'une forme de yoga*

yogurt /ˈjəʊgət/ N yaourt *m*, yogourt *m* COMP **yogurt-maker** N yaourtière *f*

yo-heave-ho /ˈjəʊˈhiːvˈhəʊ/ EXCL *(Naut)* oh hisse !

yoke /jəʊk/ N (pl **yokes** *or* **yoke**) 1 *(for oxen)* joug *m* ; *(for carrying pails)* palanche *f*, joug *m* ; *(on harness)* support *m* de timon 2 *(fig = dominion)* joug *m* ◆ **the ~ of slavery** le joug de l'esclavage ◆ **the communist ~** le joug communiste ◆ **to come under the ~ of** tomber sous le joug de ◆ **to throw off** *or* **cast off the ~** secouer le joug 3 *(pl inv = pair)* attelage *m* ◆ **a ~ of oxen** une paire de bœufs 4 *[of dress, blouse]* empiècement *m* 5 *(Constr)* *[of beam]* moise *f*, lien *m* ; *(Tech)* *[of machine parts]* bâti *m*, carcasse *f* VT (also **yoke up**) *[+ oxen]* accoupler ; *[+ ox etc]* mettre au joug ; *[+ pieces of machinery]* accoupler ; *(fig:* also **yoke together**) unir ◆ **to ~ oxen (up) to the plough** atteler des bœufs à la charrue COMP **yoke oxen** NPL bœufs *mpl* d'attelage

yokel /ˈjəʊkəl/ N *(pej)* rustre *m*, péquenaud *m*

yolk /jəʊk/ N *(Culin)* jaune *m* (d'œuf) ; *(Bio)* vitellus *m* COMP **yolk sac** N *(Bio)* membrane *f* vitelline

Yom Kippur /ˌjɒmkɪˈpʊəʳ/ N Yom Kippour *m*

yomp* /jɒmp/ VI *(Mil)* crapahuter

yon /jɒn/ ADJ *(††, liter, dial)* ⇒ **yonder adj**

yonder /ˈjɒndəʳ/ ADV *(† or dial)* là(-bas) ◆ **up ~** là-haut ◆ **over ~** là-bas ◆ **down ~** là-bas en bas ADJ *(liter)* ce ...-là, ce ... là-bas ◆ **from ~ house** de cette maison-là, de cette maison là-bas

yonks* /jɒŋks/ NPL *(Brit)* ◆ **for ~** très longtemps ◆ **I haven't seen him for ~** ça fait une éternité *or* une paye* que je ne l'ai pas vu

yoof* /juːf/ N *(hum)* ⇒ **youth**

yoo-hoo* /ˈjuːˈhuː/ EXCL ohé !, hou hou !

YOP *(Brit)* *(formerly)* /jɒp/ N (abbrev of **Youth Opportunities Programme**) → **youth**

yore /jɔːʳ/ N *(liter)* ◆ **of ~** d'antan *(liter)*, (d')autrefois ◆ **in days of ~** au temps jadis

Yorks /jɔːks/ abbrev of **Yorkshire**

Yorkshire /ˈjɔːkʃəʳ/ N Yorkshire *m* ◆ **in ~** dans le Yorkshire COMP **Yorkshire pudding** N *(Brit Culin)* *pâte à crêpe cuite qui accompagne un rôti de bœuf* **Yorkshire terrier** N yorkshire-terrier *m*

you /juː/ PERS PRON 1 *(subject)* tu, vous, vous *pl* ; *(object or indirect object)* te, vous, vous *pl* ; *(stressed and after prep)* toi, vous, vous *pl* ◆ **~ are very kind** vous êtes très gentil ◆ **I'll see ~ soon** je te *or* je vous verrai bientôt, on se voit bientôt ◆ **this book is for ~** ce livre est pour toi *or* vous ◆ **she is younger than ~** elle est plus jeune que toi *or* vous ◆ **~ and yours** toi et les tiens, vous et les vôtres ◆ **all of ~** vous tous ◆ **all ~ who came here** vous tous qui êtes venus ici ◆ **~ who know him** toi qui le connais, vous qui le connaissez ◆ **~ French** vous autres Français ◆ **~ two wait here!** attendez ici, vous deux ! ◆ **now ~ say something** maintenant à toi *or* à vous de parler ◆ **~ and I will go together** toi *or* vous et moi, nous irons ensemble ◆ **there ~ are!** *(= you've arrived)* te *or* vous voilà ! ◆ **there ~ are*, there ~ go!*** *(= have this)* voilà ! ◆ **if I were ~** (si j'étais) à ta *or* votre place, si j'étais toi *or* vous ◆ **between ~ and me** *(lit)* entre toi *or* vous et moi ; *(= in secret)* entre nous, de toi *or* vous à moi ◆ **~ fool (~)!** imbécile (que tu es) !, espèce d'imbécile ! ◆ **~ darling!** tu es un amour ! ◆ **it's ~** c'est toi *or* vous ◆ **I like the uniform, it's very ~*** j'aime bien ton uniforme, c'est vraiment ton style *or* ça te va parfaitement ◆ **~ there!** toi *or* vous là-bas ! ◆ **never ~ mind*** *(= don't worry)* ne t'en fais pas*, ne vous en faites pas* ; *(= it's not your business)* ça ne te *or* vous regarde pas, mêle-toi de tes *or* mêlez-vous de vos affaires ◆ **don't ~ go away** ne pars pas, toi !, ne partez pas, vous ! ◆ **there's a fine house for ~!** en voilà une belle maison ! ◆ **that's Australia for ~!*** qu'est-ce que tu veux, c'est ça l'Australie ! ◆ **sit ~ down** †† *(or hum)* assieds-toi, asseyez-vous

2 *(= one, anyone)* *(nominative)* on ; *(accusative, dative)* vous, te ◆ **~ never know, ~ never can tell** on ne sait jamais ◆ **~ never know your (own) luck** on ne connaît jamais son bonheur *or* sa chance ◆ **~ go towards the church** vous allez *or* on va vers l'église ◆ **fresh air does ~ good** l'air frais, ça fait du bien

COMP **you-all*** PRON *(US)* vous (autres) **you-know-who*** N qui tu sais, qui vous savez

you'd /juːd/ ⇒ **you had, you would** ; → **have, would**

you'll /juːl/ ⇒ **you will** ; → **will**

young /jʌŋ/ ADJ *[person, tree, country, vegetable, wine]* jeune ; *[appearance, smile]* jeune, juvénile ◆ **~ grass** herbe *f* nouvelle ◆ **he is ~ for his age** il paraît *or* fait plus jeune que son âge ◆ **he is very ~ for this job** il est bien jeune pour ce poste ◆ **that dress is too ~ for her** cette robe fait trop jeune pour elle ◆ **children as ~ as seven** des enfants d'à peine sept ans ◆ **I'm not as ~ as I was** je ne suis plus tout(e) jeune ◆ **you're only ~ once** *(Prov)* jeunesse n'a qu'un temps *(Prov)* ◆ **~ at heart** jeune d'esprit ◆ **to die ~** mourir jeune ; → **hopeful** ◆ **to marry ~** se marier jeune ◆ **he is three years ~er than you** il a trois ans de moins que vous, il est votre cadet de trois ans ◆ **my ~er brother** mon frère cadet ◆ **my ~er sister** ma sœur cadette ◆ **the ~er son of the family** le cadet de la famille ◆ **to grow** *or* **get ~er** rajeunir ◆ **we're not getting any ~er** nous ne rajeunissons pas ◆ **if I were ~er** si j'étais plus jeune ◆ **if I were ten years ~er** si j'avais dix ans de moins ◆ **~ Mr Brown** le jeune M. Brown ◆ **Mr Brown the ~er** *(as opposed to his father)* M. Brown fils ◆ **Pitt the Younger** le second Pitt ◆ **Pliny the Younger** Pline le Jeune ◆ **in my ~ days** dans ma jeunesse, dans mon jeune temps ◆ **in my ~er days** quand j'étais plus jeune ◆ **they have a ~ family** ils ont de jeunes enfants ◆ **~ France** la jeune génération en France ◆ **the ~(er) generation** la jeune génération, la génération montante ◆ **~ lady** *(unmarried)* jeune fille *f*, demoiselle *f* ; *(married)* jeune femme *f* ◆ **listen to me, ~ man** écoutez-moi, jeune homme ◆ **her ~ man** † son amoureux, son petit ami ◆ **the ~ moon** la nouvelle lune ◆ **the night is ~** *(liter)* la nuit n'est pas très avancée ; *(* hum)* on a toute la nuit devant nous ◆ **he has a very ~ outlook** il a des idées très jeunes ◆ **~ people** les jeunes *mpl* ◆ **you ~ hooligan!** petit *or* jeune voyou !

NPL 1 *(= people)* ◆ **~ and old** les (plus) jeunes *mpl* comme les (plus) vieux *mpl*, tout le monde ◆ **the ~** les jeunes *mpl* ◆ **books for the ~** livres *mpl* pour les jeunes

2 *[of animal]* petits *mpl* ◆ **cat with ~** *(= pregnant)* chatte *f* pleine ; *(= with kittens)* chatte *f* et ses petits

COMP **young blood** N *(fig)* sang *m* nouveau *or* jeune **Young Conservative** N *(Brit Pol)* jeune membre *m* du parti conservateur **young gun*** N jeune star *f* **young-looking** ADJ qui a *(or* avait *etc)* l'air jeune ◆ **she's very ~-looking** elle a l'air *or* elle fait très jeune **young offender** N *(Brit Jur)* jeune délinquant(e) *m(f)* **young offenders institution** N *(Brit Jur)* centre *m* de détention pour mineurs

youngish /ˈjʌŋɪʃ/ ADJ assez jeune

youngster /ˈjʌŋstəʳ/ N *(= boy)* jeune garçon *m*, jeune *m* ; *(= child)* enfant *mf*

your /jʊəʳ/ POSS ADJ 1 ton, ta, tes, votre, vos ◆ **~ book** ton *or* votre livre ◆ **YOUR book** ton livre à toi, votre livre à vous ◆ **~ table** ta *or* votre table ◆ **~ friend** ton ami(e), votre ami(e) ◆ **~ clothes** tes *or* vos vêtements ◆ **this is the best of ~ paintings** c'est ton *or* votre meilleur tableau ◆ **give me ~ hand** donne-moi *or* donnez-moi la main ◆ **you've broken ~ leg!** tu t'es cassé la jambe ! ; → **majesty, worship**

2 *(= one's)* son, sa, ses, ton *etc*, votre *etc* ◆ **you give him ~ form and he gives you ~ pass** on lui donne son formulaire et il vous remet votre laissez-passer ◆ **exercise is good for ~ health** l'exercice est bon pour la santé

3 *(* = typical)* ton *etc*, votre *etc* ◆ **so these are ~ country pubs?** alors c'est ça, vos bistro(t)s* de campagne ? ◆ **~ ordinary** *or* **average Englishman will always prefer ...** l'Anglais moyen préférera toujours ...

you're /jʊəʳ/ ⇒ **you are** ; → **be**

yours /jʊəz/ POSS PRON le tien, la tienne, les tiens, les tiennes, le vôtre, la vôtre, les vôtres ◆ **this is my book and that is ~** voici mon livre et voilà le tien *or* le vôtre ◆ **this book is ~** ce livre est à toi *or* à vous, ce livre est le tien *or* le vôtre ◆ **is this poem ~?** ce poème est-il de toi *or* de vous ? ◆ **when will the house be** *or* **become ~?** quand entrerez-vous en possession de la maison ? ◆ **~, Kenneth** *(ending letter)* bien à vous, Kenneth ◆ **it is not ~ to decide** *(frm)* ce n'est pas à vous de décider, il ne vous appartient pas de décider ◆ **~ is a specialized department** votre section est une section spécialisée ◆ **what's ~?*** *(buying drinks)* qu'est-ce que tu prends *or* vous prenez ? ; → **affectionately, ever, truly, you**

◆ **... of yours** ◆ **she is a cousin of ~** c'est une de tes *or* de vos cousines ◆ **that is no business of ~** cela ne te *or* vous regarde pas, ce n'est pas ton *or* votre affaire ◆ **it's no fault of ~** ce n'est pas de votre faute (à vous) ◆ **no advice of ~ could prevent him** aucun conseil de votre part ne pouvait l'empêcher ◆ **how's that thesis of ~* getting on?** et cette thèse, comment ça avance ?* ◆ **where's that husband of ~?*** où est passé ton mari ? ◆ **that dog of ~*** *(pej)* ton *or* votre fichu* chien ◆ **that stupid son of ~*** ton *or* votre idiot de fils ◆ **that temper of ~*** ton sale caractère

yourself /jʊəˈself/ PERS PRON (pl **yourselves** /jʊəˈselvz/) *(reflexive: direct and indirect)* te, vous, vous *pl* ; *(after prep)* toi, vous, vous *pl* ; *(emphatic)* toi-même, vous-même, vous-mêmes *pl* ◆ **have you hurt ~?** tu t'es fait mal ?, vous vous êtes fait mal ? ◆ **are you enjoying ~?** tu t'amuses bien ?, vous vous amusez bien ? ◆ **were you talking to ~?** tu te parlais à toi-même ?, tu parlais tout seul ?, vous vous parliez à vous-même ?, vous parliez tout seul ? ◆ **you never speak about ~** tu ne parles jamais de toi, vous ne parlez jamais de vous ◆ **you ~ told me, you told me ~** tu me l'as dit toi-même, vous me l'avez dit vous-même ◆ **you will see for ~** tu verras toi-même, vous verrez vous-même ◆ **someone like ~** quelqu'un comme vous ◆ **people like yourselves** des gens comme vous ◆ **how's ~?*** et toi, comment (ça) va ?*

◆ **how are you? – fine, and ~?*** comment vas-tu ? – très bien, et toi ? ◆ **you haven't been ~ lately** *(= not behaving normally)* tu n'es pas dans ton état normal *or* vous n'êtes pas dans votre état normal ces temps-ci ; *(= not looking well)* tu n'es pas dans ton assiette *or* vous n'êtes pas dans votre assiette ces temps-ci ; → **among(st)**

◆ **(all) by yourself** tout seul, toute seule ◆ **did you do it by ~?** tu l'as *or* vous l'avez fait tout(e) seul(e) ? ◆ **all by yourselves** tout seuls, toutes seules

youth /juːθ/ **N** 1 *(NonC)* jeunesse *f* ◆ **in (the days of) my** ~ dans ma jeunesse, au temps de ma jeunesse ◆ **in early** ~ dans la première *or* prime jeunesse ◆ **he has kept his** ~ il est resté jeune ◆ **he was enchanted with her ~ and beauty** sa jeunesse et sa beauté l'enchantaient ◆ **~ will have its way** *or* **its fling** *(Prov)* il faut que jeunesse se passe *(Prov)* → **first**

2 (pl **youths** /juːðz/) *(= young man)* jeune homme *m* ◆ **~s** jeunes gens *mpl*

NPL *(= young people)* jeunesse *f*, jeunes *mpl* ◆ **she likes working with (the)** ~ elle aime travailler avec les jeunes ◆ **the ~ of a country** la jeunesse d'un pays ◆ **the ~ of today are very mature** les jeunes d'aujourd'hui sont très mûrs, la jeunesse aujourd'hui est très mûre

COMP de jeunes, de jeunesse
youth club **N** maison *f* de jeunes
youth custody **N** *(Brit Jur)* éducation *f* surveillée ◆ **to be sentenced to 18 months' ~ custody** être condamné à 18 mois d'éducation surveillée
youth hostel **N** auberge *f* de jeunesse
youth leader **N** animateur *m*, -trice *f* de groupes de jeunes
Youth Opportunities Programme **N** *(Brit: formerly) programme en faveur de l'emploi des jeunes*
youth orchestra **N** orchestre *m* de jeunes
youth programming **N** (TV) émissions *fpl* pour les jeunes
Youth Training Scheme **N** *(Brit: formerly)* ≃ pacte *m* national pour l'emploi des jeunes
youth worker **N** éducateur *m*, -trice *f*

youthful /ˈjuːθfʊl/ **ADJ** *[person, looks, face, skin]* jeune ; *[mistake, adventure]* de jeunesse ; *[quality, freshness, idealism, enthusiasm]* juvénile ◆ **she looks** ~ elle a l'air jeune ◆ **a ~-looking 49-year-old** un homme/une femme de 49 ans, jeune d'allure ◆ **he's a ~ 50** il porte allégrement ses 50 ans

youthfully /ˈjuːθfʊlɪ/ **ADV** ◆ ~ **exuberant** d'une exubérance juvénile ◆ **his face was ~ smooth** son visage était doux comme une peau de bébé

youthfulness /ˈjuːθfʊlnɪs/ **N** jeunesse *f* ◆ ~ **of appearance** air *m* jeune *or* de jeunesse

you've /juːv/ → **you have**, → **have**

yow /jaʊ/ **EXCL** aïe !

yowl /jaʊl/ **N** *[of person, dog]* hurlement *m* ; *[of cat]* miaulement *m* **VI** *[person, dog]* hurler *(with, from* de) ; *[cat]* miauler

yowling /ˈjaʊlɪŋ/ **N** *[of person, dog]* hurlements *mpl* ; *[of cat]* miaulements *mpl*

yo-yo /ˈjəʊjəʊ/ **N** (pl **yo-yos**) 1 yoyo ® *m* ◆ **prices have been up and down like a ~** les prix montent et descendent sans arrêt ◆ **I've been up and down like a ~ all day** je n'ai fait que monter et descendre toute la journée 2 *(US* ‡ *= fool)* ballot* *m*, poire* *f* **VI** *(= fluctuate)* fluctuer (considérablement) **COMP** **yo-yo dieting** **N** régime *m* yoyo

yr abbrev of **year**

YTS /ˌwaɪtiːˈes/ **N** *(Brit) (formerly)* (abbrev of **Youth Training Scheme**) → **youth**

ytterbium /ɪˈtɜːbɪəm/ **N** ytterbium *m*

yttrium /ˈɪtrɪəm/ **N** yttrium *m*

yuan /juːæn/ **N** *(pl inv)* yuan *m*

yucca /ˈjʌkə/ **N** yucca *m*

yuck * /jʌk/ **EXCL** berk *or* beurk !, pouah !

yucky * /ˈjʌkɪ/ **ADJ** dégueulasse‡, dégoûtant

Yugoslav /ˈjuːgəʊˈslɑːv/ **ADJ** *(gen)* yougoslave ; *[ambassador, embassy]* de Yougoslavie **N** Yougoslave *mf*

Yugoslavia /ˈjuːgəʊˈslɑːvɪə/ **N** Yougoslavie *f*

Yugoslavian /ˈjuːgəʊˈslɑːvɪən/ **ADJ** ⇒ **Yugoslav**

yuk * /jʌk/ **EXCL** ⇒ **yuck**

yukky * /ˈjʌkɪ/ **ADJ** ⇒ **yucky**

Yukon /ˈjuːkɒn/ **N** ◆ **(the)** ~ le Yukon **COMP** **(the) Yukon Territory** **N** le (territoire de) Yukon

Yule /juːl/ **N** († *or liter*) Noël *m* **COMP** **Yule log** **N** bûche *f* de Noël

Yuletide /ˈjuːltaɪd/ **N** († *or liter*) (époque *f* de) Noël *m*

yummy * /ˈjʌmɪ/ **ADJ** *[food]* délicieux **EXCL** miam-miam !*

yum-yum ‡ /ˈjʌmˈjʌm/ **EXCL** ⇒ **yummy excl**

yup * /jʌp/ **EXCL** *(esp US)* ouais*, oui

yuppie * /ˈjʌpɪ/ **N** (abbrev of **young upwardly-mobile** *or* **urban professional**) yuppie *mf*
COMP *[car, clothes]* de yuppie ; *[bar, restaurant, area]* de yuppies
yuppie flu * **N** *(pej)* syndrome *m* de la fatigue chronique, encéphalomyélite *f* myalgique

yuppiedom * /ˈjʌpɪdəm/ **N** monde *m or* univers *m* des yuppies

yuppified * /ˈjʌpɪˌfaɪd/ **ADJ** *[bar, restaurant, area, flat]* transformé en bar (*or* restaurant *etc*) de yuppies ◆ **he is becoming more and more ~** il se transforme de plus en plus en yuppie

yuppy * /ˈjʌpɪ/ **N** ⇒ **yuppie**

YWCA /ˌwaɪdʌbljuːsiːˈeɪ/ **N** (abbrev of **Young Women's Christian Association**) YWCA *m*

Zz

Z, z /zed, (US) ziː/ N (= letter) Z, z *m* ◆ **Z for Zebra** ≈ Z comme Zoé
COMP **z-axis** N axe *m* des z
Z-bed N (*Brit*) lit *m* de camp

Zacharias /ˌzækəˈraɪəs/ N Zacharie *m*

zaftig⁑ /ˈzɑːftɪk/ ADJ (*US*) joli et bien en chair

Zaïre /zɑːˈiːəʳ/ N (= *country*) Zaïre *m* ◆ **in Zaire** au Zaïre

Zaïrean, Zaïrian /zɑːˈiːərɪən/ ADJ zaïrois N Zaïrois(e) *m(f)*

Zambese, Zambezi /zæmˈbiːzɪ/ N Zambèze *m*

Zambia /ˈzæmbɪə/ N Zambie *f*

Zambian /ˈzæmbɪən/ ADJ zambien N Zambien(ne) *m(f)*

zany /ˈzeɪnɪ/ ADJ loufoque* N (*Theat Hist*) bouffon *m*, zanni *m*

Zanzibar /ˈzænzɪbɑːʳ/ N Zanzibar

zap* /zæp/ EXCL paf !, vlan ! VT 1 (= *destroy*) [*+ town*] ravager, bombarder ; [*+ person*] supprimer, descendre* 2 (= *delete*) [*+ word, data*] supprimer 3 (TV) ◆ **to ~ the TV channels** zapper 4 (= *send quickly*) **I'll ~ it out to you straight away** je vais vous l'expédier tout de suite VI 1 (= *move quickly*) [*car*] foncer ◆ **we had to ~ down to London** nous avons dû filer à Londres à toute vitesse ◆ **to ~ along** [*car*] foncer ◆ **we're going to have to ~ through the work to get it finished in time** il va falloir que nous mettions la gomme* pour finir le travail à temps 2 (TV) **to ~ through the channels** zapper

zapped⁑ /zæpt/ ADJ (= *exhausted*) crevé⁑, vanné⁑

zapper* /ˈzæpəʳ/ N (= *remote control*) télécommande *f*

zappy⁑ /ˈzæpɪ/ ADJ [*person, style*] qui a du punch ; [*car*] rapide, qui fonce *or* gaze*

Zarathustra /ˌzærəˈθuːstrə/ N Zarathoustra *m* *or* Zoroastre *m*

zeal /ziːl/ N (*NonC*) 1 (= *religious fervour*) zèle *m*, ferveur *f* 2 (= *enthusiasm*) zèle *m*, empressement *m* (*for* à) ◆ **in her ~ to do it** dans son empressement à le faire

zealot /ˈzelət/ N 1 fanatique *mf*, zélateur *m*, -trice *f* (*liter*) (*for* de) 2 (*Jewish Hist*) **Zealot** zélote *m*

zealotry /ˈzelətrɪ/ N fanatisme *m*

zealous /ˈzeləs/ ADJ [*person*] zélé ; [*effort*] diligent ◆ **he is ~ for the cause** il défend la cause avec zèle ◆ **to be ~ in doing sth** montrer de l'empressement à faire qch

zealously /ˈzeləslɪ/ ADV avec zèle

zebra /ˈzebrə, ˈziːbrə/ (pl **zebras** *or* **zebra**) N zèbre *m*
COMP **zebra crossing** N (*Brit*) passage *m* pour piétons
zebra stripes NPL zébrures *fpl* ◆ **with ~ stripes** zébré

zebu /ˈziːbuː/ N zébu *m*

Zechariah /ˌzekəˈraɪə/ N ⇒ **Zacharias**

zed /zed/, **zee** (US) /ziː/ N (la lettre) z *m*

Zeitgeist /ˈzaɪtgaɪst/ N esprit *m* de l'époque

Zen /zen/ N Zen *m*
COMP **Zen Buddhism** N bouddhisme *m* zen
Zen Buddhist N bouddhiste *mf* zen

zenith /ˈzenɪθ/ N (*Astron*) zénith *m* ; (*fig*) zénith *m*, apogée *m* ◆ **at the ~ of his power** à l'apogée de son pouvoir ◆ **the ~ of Perugia's influence** l'apogée de l'influence de Pérouse ◆ **with this success, he reached the ~ of his glory** avec ce succès, il a atteint l'apogée de sa gloire

Zephaniah /ˌzefəˈnaɪə/ N Sophonie *m*

zephyr /ˈzefəʳ/ N zéphyr *m*

zeppelin /ˈzeplɪn/ N zeppelin *m*

zero /ˈzɪərəʊ/ (pl **zeros** *or* **zeroes**) N 1 (= *point on scale*) zéro *m* ◆ **15 degrees below ~** 15 degrés au-dessous de zéro ◆ **his chances of success sank to ~** ses chances de réussite se réduisirent à néant *or* zéro ◆ **snow reduced visibility to near ~** à cause de la neige, la visibilité était quasi nulle
2 (= *cipher, numeral etc*) zéro *m* ◆ **row of ~s** série *f* de zéros
COMP [*tension, voltage*] nul (nulle *f*)
zero altitude N altitude *f* zéro ◆ **to fly at ~ altitude** voler en rase-mottes, faire du rase-mottes
zero-base VT (*US*) [*+ question, issue*] reprendre à zéro, réexaminer point par point
zero-emission ADJ à taux d'émission zéro
zero-gravity, zero-G* N apesanteur *f*
zero growth N (*Econ*) taux *m* de croissance zéro, croissance *f* économique zéro
zero hour N (*Mil*) l'heure *f* H ; (*fig*) le moment critique *or* décisif
the zero option N (*Pol*) l'option *f* zéro
zero point N point *m* zéro
zero population growth N croissance *f* démographique nulle
zero-rated ADJ (*for VAT*) exempt de TVA, non assujetti à la TVA
zero-rating N exemption *f* de TVA, non-assujettissement *m* à la TVA
zero-sum ADJ (*US*) [*bargaining, thinking*] à somme nulle ◆ **~-sum game** jeu *m* à somme nulle
zero tolerance N politique *f* d'intransigeance, tolérance *f* zéro
zero-tolerance ADJ ◆ **~-tolerance policing** politique *f* de tolérance zéro
▸ **zero in** VI ◆ **to zero in on sth** (= *move in on*) se diriger droit vers *or* sur qch ; (= *identify*) mettre le doigt sur qch, identifier qch ; (= *concentrate on*) se concentrer sur qch ◆ **he ~ed in on those who ...** (= *criticize*) il s'en est pris tout particulièrement à ceux qui ...

ZERO

« Zéro » se dit **zero** en anglais américain, mais en anglais britannique, l'emploi de ce terme est réservé aux sciences et aux mathématiques (notamment pour exprimer les températures et les graduations).
Le terme « nought » s'utilise en Grande-Bretagne dans les nombres décimaux, par exemple « nought point nought seven » pour dire « 0,07 », mais aussi dans les notations : ainsi, « nought out of ten » veut dire « 0 sur 10 ». Les Américains comme les Britanniques disent « oh » pour indiquer des numéros de carte de crédit ou de téléphone : par exemple, « oh one four one » pour « 0141 ». Dans les scores de matchs en Grande-Bretagne, on dit « nil ». « Liverpool a gagné par cinq buts à zéro » se dira ainsi « Liverpool won five nil ». L'équivalent américain est « nothing » (terme parfois employé familièrement par les Britanniques) ou, sous une forme plus familière, « zip » : « nous avons gagné par sept buts à zéro » se dira « we won seven-zip ».

zest /zest/ N (*NonC*) 1 (= *gusto*) entrain *m* ◆ **to fight with ~** combattre avec entrain ◆ **he ate it with great ~** il l'a mangé avec grand appétit ◆ **~ for life** *or* **living** goût *m* de la vie, appétit *m* de vivre ◆ **he lost his ~ for winning** il a perdu son désir de gagner 2 (*fig*) saveur *f*, piquant *m* ◆ **her books are thrilling, full of ~** ses livres sont palpitants et savoureux ◆ **it adds ~ to the story** cela donne une certaine saveur *or* du piquant à l'histoire 3 [*of orange, lemon*] zeste *m*

zester /ˈzestəʳ/ N zesteur *m*

zestful /ˈzestfʊl/ ADJ plein d'entrain, enthousiaste

zestfully /ˈzestfəlɪ/ ADV avec entrain *or* enthousiasme

zesty /ˈzestɪ/ ADJ [*wine*] piquant

Zeus /zjuːs/ N Zeus *m*

zidovudine /zaɪˈdɒvjʊˌdiːn/ N zidovudine *f*

ZIFT /zɪft/ N (abbrev of **Zygote Intrafallopian Transfer**) fivète *f*

ziggurat /ˈzɪgʊræt/ N ziggourat *f*

zigzag /ˈzɪgzæg/ N zigzag *m* ADJ *[path, road, course, line]* en zigzag ; *[pattern, design]* à zigzags ADV en zigzag VI zigzaguer, faire des zigzags ◆ **to ~ along** avancer en zigzaguant ◆ **to ~ out/through** *etc* sortir/traverser *etc* en zigzaguant

zilch⁑ /zɪltʃ/ N que dalle⁑ ◆ **these shares are worth ~** ces actions valent que dalle⁑ ◆ **Mark knows ~ about art** Mark connaît que dalle⁑ à l'art

zillion * /ˈzɪljən/ ADJ, N (pl **zillions** *or* **zillion**) ◆ **a ~ dollars** des millions *mpl* et des millions *mpl* de dollars ◆ **~s of problems, a ~ problems** des tas *mpl* de problèmes

Zimbabwe /zɪmˈbɑːbwɪ/ N Zimbabwe *m* ◆ **in ~** au Zimbabwe

Zimbabwean /zɪmˈbɑːbwɪən/ ADJ zimbabwéen N Zimbabwéen(ne) *m(f)*

Zimmer ® /ˈzɪməʳ/ N (*Brit:* also **Zimmer frame**) déambulateur *m*

zinc /zɪŋk/ N (*NonC*) zinc *m*
COMP *[plate, alloy]* de zinc ; *[roof]* zingué
zinc blende N blende *f* (de zinc)
zinc chloride N chlorure *m* de zinc
zinc dust N limaille *f* de zinc
zinc ointment N pommade *f* à l'oxyde de zinc
zinc oxide N oxyde *m* de zinc
zinc-plating N zingage *m*
zinc sulphate N sulfate *m* de zinc
zinc white N blanc *m* de zinc

zine *, **'zine** * /ziːn/ N (= *magazine*) magazine *m* ; (= *fanzine*) fanzine *m*

zing /zɪŋ/ N [1] (= *noise of bullet*) sifflement *m* [2] (*NonC* * = *energy*) entrain *m* VI *[bullet, arrow]* siffler ◆ **the bullet ~ed past his ear** la balle lui a sifflé à l'oreille ◆ **the cars ~ed past** les voitures sont passées en trombe *

zinger * /ˈzɪŋəʳ/ N (*US*) [1] (= *witty remark*) trait *m* d'esprit, bon mot *m* [2] (= *something impressive*) ◆ **it was a ~ !** c'était quelque chose !

zinnia /ˈzɪnɪə/ N zinnia *m*

Zion /ˈzaɪən/ N Sion

Zionism /ˈzaɪənɪzəm/ N sionisme *m*

Zionist /ˈzaɪənɪst/ ADJ sioniste N sioniste *mf*

zip /zɪp/ N [1] (*Brit:* also **zip fastener**) fermeture *f* éclair ®, fermeture *f* à glissière ◆ **pocket with a ~** poche *f* à fermeture éclair ®, poche *f* zippée *
[2] (= *sound of bullet*) sifflement *m*
[3] (*NonC* * = *energy*) entrain *m*, élan *m* ◆ **put a bit of ~ into it** activez-vous !
[4] (⁑ = *nothing*) que dalle⁑ ◆ **I know ~ about it** je n'en sais *or* j'y connais que dalle⁑ ; → ZERO
VT [1] (= *close:* also **zip up**) *[+ dress, bag]* fermer avec une fermeture éclair ® *or* à glissière
[2] ◆ **she ~ped open her dress/bag** elle a ouvert la fermeture éclair ® *or* à glissière de sa robe/de son sac
[3] (*Comput*) *[+ file]* zipper
VI ◆ **to ~ in/out/past/up** * *[car, person]* entrer/sortir/passer/monter comme une flèche
COMP **zip code** N (*US Post*) code *m* postal
zip fastener N ⇒ **zip noun 1**
zip file N (*Comput*) fichier *m* zip
zip gun N (*US*) pistolet *m* rudimentaire (*à ressort ou à élastique*)
zip-on ADJ à fermeture éclair ®

► **zip on** VI s'attacher avec une fermeture éclair ® *or* fermeture à glissière
VT SEP attacher avec une fermeture éclair ® *or* fermeture à glissière
ADJ ◆ **zip-on** → **zip**

► **zip up** VI → **zip vi**
VT SEP ◆ **can you zip me up ?** tu peux m'aider avec la fermeture éclair ® ? ; see also **zip vt 1**

zipper /ˈzɪpəʳ/ N (*esp US*) ⇒ **zip noun 1**

zippy⁑ /ˈzɪpɪ/ ADJ *[person]* plein d'entrain *or* d'allant

zircon /ˈzɜːkən/ N zircon *m*

zirconium /zɜːˈkəʊnɪəm/ N zirconium *m*

zit * /zɪt/ N bouton *m*

zither /ˈzɪðəʳ/ N cithare *f*

zloty /ˈzlɒtɪ/ N (pl **zlotys** *or* **zloty**) zloty *m*

zodiac /ˈzəʊdɪæk/ N zodiaque *m* ; → **sign**

zodiacal /zəʊˈdaɪəkəl/ ADJ du zodiac ◆ **~ light** lumière *f* zodiacale

zoftig⁑ /ˈzɒftɪk/ ADJ ⇒ **zaftig**

zombie /ˈzɒmbɪ/ N (*lit, fig*) zombie *m*, zombi *m*

zonal /ˈzəʊnl/ ADJ zonal

zone /ˈzəʊn/ N [1] (*gen*) zone *f* ; (= *subdivision of town*) secteur *m* ◆ **it lies within the ~ reserved for ...** cela se trouve dans la zone *or* le secteur réservé(e) à ... ; → **battle, danger, time** [2] (*US:* also **postal delivery zone**) zone *f* (postale) VT [1] (= *divide into zones*) *[+ area]* diviser en zones ; *[+ town]* diviser en secteurs [2] ◆ **this district has been ~d for industry** c'est une zone réservée à l'implantation industrielle
COMP **zone defence, zone defense** (*US*) N (*Sport*) défense *f* de zone
zone therapy N (*Med*) réflexothérapie *f*

zoning /ˈzəʊnɪŋ/ N répartition *f* en zones

zonked⁑ /zɒŋkt/ ADJ (also **zonked out**) (= *exhausted*) vanné * ; (*from drugs*) défoncé * ; (*US* = *drunk*) bourré *

zoo /zuː/ N zoo *m* COMP **zoo keeper** N gardien(ne) *m(f)* de zoo

zoological /ˌzəʊəˈlɒdʒɪkəl/ ADJ zoologique COMP **zoological gardens** NPL jardin *m* zoologique

zoologist /zəʊˈɒlədʒɪst/ N zoologiste *mf*

zoology /zəʊˈɒlədʒɪ/ N zoologie *f*

zoom /zuːm/ N [1] (= *sound*) vrombissement *m*, bourdonnement *m* [2] (= *upward flight of plane*) montée *f* en chandelle [3] (*Phot:* also **zoom lens**) zoom *m* VI [1] *[engine]* vrombir, bourdonner [2] ◆ **to ~ away/through** démarrer/traverser en trombe * ◆ **the car ~ed past us** la voiture est passée en trombe * [3] (*Aviat*) *[plane]* monter en chandelle

► **zoom in** VI faire un zoom (*on* sur)

► **zoom out** VI faire un zoom arrière

zoomorphic /ˌzəʊəʊˈmɔːfɪk/ ADJ zoomorphe

zoophyte /ˈzəʊəˌfaɪt/ N zoophyte *m*

zoot-suit * /ˈzuːtsuːt/ N costume *m* zazou

zoot-suiter * /ˈzuːtsuːtəʳ/ N zazou *m*

Zoroaster /ˌzɒrəʊˈæstəʳ/ N Zoroastre *m* *or* Zarathoustra *m*

Zoroastrianism /ˌzɒrəʊˈæstrɪənɪzəm/ N zoroastrisme *m*

zouk /zuːk/ N (*Mus*) zouk *m*

zucchini /zuːˈkiːnɪ/ N (pl **zucchini** *or* **zucchinis**) (*US*) courgette *f*

Zuider Zee /ˈzaɪdəˈziː/ N Zuiderzee *m*

Zulu /ˈzuːluː/ ADJ zoulou *f inv* N [1] Zoulou *mf* [2] (= *language*) zoulou *m*

Zululand /ˈzuːluːlænd/ N Zoulouland *m* ◆ **in ~** au Zoulouland

Zurich /ˈzjʊərɪk/ N Zurich ◆ **Lake Zürich** le lac de Zurich

zwieback /ˈzwiːbæk/ N (*US*) biscotte *f*

zygote /ˈzaɪgəʊt/ N zygote *m*

ANNEXES
APPENDICES

SOMMAIRE

CONTENTS

FRENCH VERBS (VERBES FRANÇAIS)

VERBES ANGLAIS (ENGLISH VERBS)

conjugation 1 – **ARRIVER:** regular verbs ending in **-er**

INDICATIVE

PRESENT	PERFECT
j'arrive	je suis arrivé
tu arrives	tu es arrivé
il arrive	il est arrivé
nous arrivons	nous sommes arrivés
vous arrivez	vous êtes arrivés
ils arrivent	ils sont arrivés

IMPERFECT	PLUPERFECT
j'arrivais	j'étais arrivé
tu arrivais	tu étais arrivé
il arrivait	il était arrivé
nous arrivions	nous étions arrivés
vous arriviez	vous étiez arrivés
ils arrivaient	ils étaient arrivés

PAST HISTORIC	PAST ANTERIOR
j'arrivai	je fus arrivé
tu arrivas	tu fus arrivé
il arriva	il fut arrivé
nous arrivâmes	nous fûmes arrivés
vous arrivâtes	vous fûtes arrivés
ils arrivèrent	ils furent arrivés

FUTURE	FUTURE PERFECT
j'arriverai [aʀiv!ə!ʀɛ]	je serai arrivé
tu arriveras	tu seras arrivé
il arrivera	il sera arrivé
nous arriverons [aʀiv(ə)ʀɔ̃]	nous serons arrivés
vous arriverez	vous serez arrivés
ils arriveront	ils seront arrivés

SUBJUNCTIVE

PRESENT
que j'arrive
que tu arrives
qu'il arrive
que nous arrivions
que vous arriviez
qu'ils arrivent

IMPERFECT
que j'arrivasse
que tu arrivasses
qu'il arrivât
que nous arrivassions
que vous arrivassiez
qu'ils arrivassent

PAST
que je sois arrivé
que tu sois arrivé
qu'il soit arrivé
que nous soyons arrivés
que vous soyez arrivés
qu'ils soient arrivés

PLUPERFECT
que je fusse arrivé
que tu fusses arrivé
qu'il fût arrivé
que nous fussions arrivés
que vous fussiez arrivés
qu'ils fussent arrivés

CONDITIONAL

PRESENT
j'arriverais [aʀɪvʀɛ]
tu arriverais
il arriverait
nous arriverions [aʀivəʀjɔ̃]
vous arriveriez
ils arriveraient

PAST I
je serais arrivé
tu serais arrivé
il serait arrivé
nous serions arrivés
vous seriez arrivés
ils seraient arrivés

PAST II
je fusse arrivé
tu fusses arrivé
il fût arrivé
nous fussions arrivés
vous fussiez arrivés
ils fussent arrivés

	PRESENT	PAST
IMPERATIVE	arrive arrivons arrivez	sois arrivé soyons arrivés soyez arrivés
PARTICIPLE	arrivant	arrivé, ée étant arrivé
INFINITIVE	arriver	être arrivé

NB The verbs *jouer, tuer* etc. are regular: e.g. *je joue, je jouerai ; je tue, je tuerai.*

conjugation 1 (reflexive form) – **SE REPOSER:** regular verbs ending in **-er**

INDICATIVE

PRESENT
je me repose
tu te reposes
il se repose
nous nous reposons
vous vous reposez
ils se reposent

PERFECT
je me suis reposé
tu t'es reposé
il s'est reposé
nous nous sommes reposés
vous vous êtes reposés
ils se sont reposés

IMPERFECT
je me reposais
tu te reposais
il se reposait
nous nous reposions
vous vous reposiez
ils se reposaient

PLUPERFECT
je m'étais reposé
tu t'étais reposé
il s'était reposé
nous nous étions reposés
vous vous étiez reposés
ils s'étaient reposés

PAST HISTORIC
je me reposai
tu te reposas
il se reposa
nous nous reposâmes
vous vous reposâtes
ils se reposèrent

PAST ANTERIOR
je me fus reposé
tu te fus reposé
il se fut reposé
nous nous fûmes reposés
vous vous fûtes reposés
ils se furent reposés

FUTURE
je me reposerai
tu te reposeras
il se reposera
nous nous reposerons
vous vous reposerez
ils se reposeront

FUTURE PERFECT
je me serai reposé
tu te seras reposé
il se sera reposé
nous nous serons reposés
vous vous serez reposés
ils se seront reposés

SUBJUNCTIVE

PRESENT
que je me repose
que tu te reposes
qu'il se repose
que nous nous reposions
que vous vous reposiez
qu'ils se reposent

IMPERFECT
que je me reposasse
que tu te reposasses
qu'il se reposât
que nous nous reposassions
que vous vous reposassiez
qu'ils se reposassent

PAST
que je me sois reposé
que tu te sois reposé
qu'il se soit reposé
que nous nous soyons reposés
que vous vous soyez reposés
qu'ils se soient reposés

PLUPERFECT
que je me fusse reposé
que tu te fusses reposé
qu'il se fût reposé
que nous nous fussions reposés
que vous vous fussiez reposés
qu'ils se fussent reposés

CONDITIONAL

PRESENT
je me reposerais
tu te reposerais
il se reposerait
nous nous reposerions
vous vous reposeriez
ils se reposeraient

PAST I
je me serais reposé
tu te serais reposé
il se serait reposé
nous nous serions reposés
vous vous seriez reposés
ils se seraient reposés

PAST II
je me fusse reposé
tu te fusses reposé
il se fût reposé
nous nous fussions reposés
vous vous fussiez reposés
ils se fussent reposés

IMPERATIVE

PRESENT
repose-toi
reposons-nous
reposez-vous

PAST
unused

PARTICIPLE

PRESENT
se reposant

PAST
s'étant reposé

INFINITIVE

PRESENT
se reposer

PAST
s'être reposé

conjugation 2 – **FINIR:** regular verbs ending in **-ir**

INDICATIVE

PRESENT	PERFECT
je finis	j'ai fini
tu finis	tu as fini
il finit	il a fini
nous finissons	nous avons fini
vous finissez	vous avez fini
ils finissent	ils ont fini
IMPERFECT	**PLUPERFECT**
je finissais	j'avais fini
tu finissais	tu avais fini
il finissait	il avait fini
nous finissions	nous avions fini
vous finissiez	vous aviez fini
ils finissaient	ils avaient fini
PAST HISTORIC	**PAST ANTERIOR**
je finis	j'eus fini
tu finis	tu eus fini
il finit	il eut fini
nous finîmes	nous eûmes fini
vous finîtes	vous eûtes fini
ils finirent	ils eurent fini
FUTURE	**FUTURE PERFECT**
je finirai	j'aurai fini
tu finiras	tu auras fini
il finira	il aura fini
nous finirons	nous aurons fini
vous finirez	vous aurez fini
ils finiront	ils auront fini

SUBJUNCTIVE

PRESENT
que je finisse
que tu finisses
qu'il finisse
que nous finissions
que vous finissiez
qu'ils finissent

IMPERFECT
que je finisse
que tu finisses
qu'il finît
que nous finissions
que vous finissiez
qu'ils finissent

PAST
que j'aie fini
que tu aies fini
qu'il ait fini
que nous ayons fini
que vous ayez fini
qu'ils aient fini

PLUPERFECT
que j'eusse fini
que tu eusses fini
qu'il eût fini
que nous eussions fini
que vous eussiez fini
qu'ils eussent fini

CONDITIONAL

PRESENT
je finirais
tu finirais
il finirait
nous finirions
vous finiriez
ils finiraient

PAST I
j'aurais fini
tu aurais fini
il aurait fini
nous aurions fini
vous auriez fini
ils auraient fini

PAST II
j'eusse fini
tu eusses fini
il eût fini
nous eussions fini
vous eussiez fini
ils eussent fini

	PRESENT	PAST
IMPERATIVE	finis finissons finissez	aie fini ayons fini ayez fini

	PRESENT	PAST
PARTICIPLE	finissant	fini, ie ayant fini

	PRESENT	PAST
INFINITIVE	finir	avoir fini

conjugations 3 to 8

		INDICATIVE			
		present 1st person	present 3rd person	imperfect	past historic
3	**placer**	je place [plas] nous plaçons [plasɔ̃]	il place ils placent	je plaçais	je plaçai

NB Verbs in ***-ecer*** (e.g. *dépecer*) are conjugated like ***placer*** and ***geler***. Verbs in ***-écer*** (e.g. *rapiécer*) are conjugated like ***céder*** and ***placer***.

		present 1st person	present 3rd person	imperfect	past historic
	bouger	je bouge [buʒ] nous bougeons [buʒɔ̃]	il bouge ils bougent	je bougeais nous bougions	je bougeai

NB Verbs in ***-éger*** (e.g. *protéger*) are conjugated like ***bouger*** and ***céder***.

		present 1st person	present 3rd person	imperfect	past historic
4	**appeler**	j'appelle [apɛl] nous appelons [ap(ə)lɔ̃]	il appelle ils appellent	j'appelais	j'appelai
	jeter	je jette [ʒɛt] nous jetons [ʒ(ə)tɔ̃]	il jette ils jettent	je jetais	je jetai
5	**geler**	je gèle [ʒɛl] nous gelons [ʒ(ə)lɔ̃]	il gèle ils gèlent	je gelais nous gelions [ʒəljɔ̃]	je gelai
	acheter	j'achète [aʃɛt] nous achetons [aʃ(ə)tɔ̃]	il achète ils achètent	j'achetais [aʃtɛ] nous achetions	j'achetai

Also verbs in ***-emer*** (e.g. *semer*), ***-ener*** (e.g. *mener*), ***-eser*** (e.g. *peser*), ***-ever*** (e.g. *lever*) etc.
NB Verbs in ***-ecer*** (e.g. *dépecer*) are conjugated like ***geler*** and ***placer***.

		present 1st person	present 3rd person	imperfect	past historic
6	**céder**	je cède [sɛd] nous cédons [sedɔ̃]	il cède ils cèdent	je cédais nous cédions	je cédai

Also verbs in ***-é*** + consonant(s) + ***-er*** (e.g. *célébrer, lécher, déléguer, préférer*, etc.).
NB Verbs in ***-éger*** (e.g. *protéger*) are conjugated like ***céder*** and ***bouger***. Verbs in ***-écer*** (e.g. *rapiécer*) are conjugated like ***céder*** and ***placer***.

		present 1st person	present 3rd person	imperfect	past historic
7	**épier**	j'épie [epi] nous épions [epjɔ̃]	il épie ils épient	j'épiais nous épiions [epijjɔ̃]	j'épiai
	prier	je prie [pʀi] nous prions [pʀijɔ̃]	il prie ils prient	je priais nous priions [pʀijjɔ̃]	je priai
8	**noyer**	je noie [nwa] nous noyons [nwajɔ̃]	il noie ils noient	je noyais nous noyions [nwajjɔ̃]	je noyai

Also verbs in ***-uyer*** (e.g. *appuyer*).
NB ***Envoyer*** has in the future tense: *j'enverrai*, and in the conditional : *j'enverrais*.

		present 1st person	present 3rd person	imperfect	past historic
	payer	je paie [pɛ] or je paye [pɛj] nous payons [pɛjɔ̃]	il paie or il paye ils paient or ils payent	je payais nous payions [pɛjjɔ̃]	je payai

Also all verbs in ***-ayer***.

irregular verbs ending in **-er**

	CONDITIONAL	SUBJUNCTIVE	IMPERATIVE	PARTICIPLES
future	**present**	**present**	**present**	**present** **past**
je placerai [plasʀɛ]	je placerais	que je place que nous placions	place plaçons	plaçant placé, ée
je bougerai [buʒʀɛ]	je bougerais	que je bouge que nous bougions	bouge bougeons	bougeant bougé, ée
j'appellerai [apɛlʀɛ]	j'appellerais	que j'appelle que nous appelions	appelle appelons	appelant appelé, ée
je jetterai [ʒetʀɛ]	je jetterais	que je jette que nous jetions	jette jetons	jetant jeté, ée
je gèlerai [ʒɛlʀɛ]	je gèlerais	que je gèle que nous gelions	gèlc gelons	gelant gelé, ée
j'achèterai [aʃɛtʀɛ]	j'achèterais	que j'achète que nous achetions	achète achetons	achetant acheté, ée
je céderai [sɛdʀɛ ; sedʀɛ][1]	je céderais[1]	que je cède que nous cédions	cède cédons	cédant cédé, ée
j'épierai [epiʀɛ]	j'épierais	que j'épie	épie épions	épiant épié, iée
je prierai [pʀiʀɛ]	je prierais	que je prie	prie prions	priant prié, priée
je noierai [nwaʀɛ]	je noierais	que je noie	noie noyons	noyant noyé, noyée
je paierai [pɛʀɛ] or je payerai [pɛjʀɛ] nous paierons or nous payerons	je paierais or je payerais	que je paie or que je paye	paie or paye payons	payant payé, payée

1. Actually pronounced as though there were a grave accent on the future and the conditional *(je cèderai, je cèderais)*, rather than an acute.

conjugation 9

INDICATIVE

PRESENT
je vais [vɛ]
tu vas
il va
nous allons [alɔ̃]
vous allez
ils vont [vɔ̃]

PERFECT
je suis allé
tu es allé
il est allé
nous sommes allés
vous êtes allés
ils sont allés

IMPERFECT
j'allais [alɛ]
tu allais
il allait
nous allions [aljɔ̃]
vous alliez
ils allaient

PLUPERFECT
j'étais allé
tu étais allé
il était allé
nous étions allés
vous étiez allés
ils étaient allés

PAST HISTORIC
j'allai
tu allas
il alla
nous allâmes
vous allâtes
ils allèrent

PAST ANTERIOR
je fus allé
tu fus allé
il fut allé
nous fûmes allés
vous fûtes allés
ils furent allés

FUTURE
j'irai [iʀɛ]
tu iras
il ira
nous irons
vous irez
ils iront

FUTURE PERFECT
je serai allé
tu seras allé
il sera allé
nous serons allés
vous serez allés
ils seront allés

SUBJUNCTIVE

PRESENT
que j'aille [aj]
que tu ailles
qu'il aille
que nous allions
que vous alliez
qu'ils aillent

IMPERFECT
que j'allasse [alas]
que tu allasses
qu'il allât
que nous allassions
que vous allassiez
qu'ils allassent

PAST
que je sois allé
que tu sois allé
qu'il soit allé
que nous soyons allés
que vous soyez allés
qu'ils soient allés

PLUPERFECT
que je fusse allé
que tu fusses allé
qu'il fût allé
que nous fussions allés
que vous fussiez allés
qu'ils fussent allés

ALLER

CONDITIONAL

PRESENT
j'irais
tu irais
il irait
nous irions
vous iriez
ils iraient

PAST I
je serais allé
tu serais allé
il serait allé
nous serions allés
vous seriez allés
ils seraient allés

PAST II
je fusse allé
tu fusses allé
il fût allé
nous fussions allés
vous fussiez allés
ils fussent allés

	PRESENT	PAST
IMPERATIVE	va allons allez	sois allé soyons allés soyez allés
PARTICIPLE	allant étant allé	allé, ée
INFINITIVE	aller	être allé

conjugations 10 to 22

		INDICATIVE			
		present 1st person	present 3rd person	imperfect	past historic
10	**haïr**	je hais ['ɛ] nous haïssons ['aisɔ̃]	il hait ['ɛ] ils haïssent ['ais]	je haïssais nous haïssions	je haïs ['ai] nous haïmes
11	**courir**	je cours [kuʀ] nous courons [kuʀɔ̃]	il court ils courent	je courais [kuʀɛ] nous courions	je courus
12	**cueillir**	je cueille [kœj] nous cueillons [kœjɔ̃]	il cueille ils cueillent	je cueillais nous cueillions [kœjjɔ̃]	je cueillis
13	**assaillir**	j'assaille nous assaillons [asajɔ̃]	il assaille ils assaillent	j'assaillais nous assaillions [asajjɔ̃]	j'assaillis
14	**servir**	je sers [sɛʀ] nous servons [sɛʀvɔ̃]	il sert ils servent [sɛʀv]	je servais nous servions	je servis
15	**bouillir**	je bous [bu] nous bouillons [bujɔ̃]	il bout ils bouillent [buj]	je bouillais nous bouillions [bujjɔ̃]	je bouillis
16	**partir**	je pars [paʀ] nous partons [paʀtɔ̃]	il part ils partent [paʀt]	je partais nous partions	je partis
	sentir	je sens [sɑ̃] nous sentons [sɑ̃tɔ̃]	il sent ils sentent [sɑ̃t]	je sentais nous sentions	je sentis
17	**fuir**	je fuis [fɥi] nous fuyons [fɥijɔ̃]	il fuit ils fuient	je fuyais nous fuyions [fɥijjɔ̃]	je fuis nous fuîmes
18	**couvrir**	je couvre nous couvrons	il couvre ils couvrent	je couvrais nous couvrions	je couvris
19	**mourir**	je meurs [mœʀ] nous mourons [muʀɔ̃]	il meurt ils meurent	je mourais [muʀɛ] nous mourions	je mourus
20	**vêtir**	je vêts [vɛ] nous vêtons [vɛtɔ̃]	il vêt ils vêtent [vɛt]	je vêtais nous vêtions	je vêtis [veti] nous vêtîmes
21	**acquérir**	j'acquiers [akjɛʀ] nous acquérons [akeʀɔ̃]	il acquiert ils acquièrent	j'acquérais [akeʀɛ] nous acquérions	j'acquis
22	**venir**	je viens [vjɛ̃] nous venons [v(ə)nɔ̃]	il vient ils viennent [vjɛn]	je venais nous venions	je vins [vɛ̃] nous vînmes [vɛ̃m]

irregular verbs ending in **-ir**

future	CONDITIONAL present	SUBJUNCTIVE present	IMPERATIVE present	PARTICIPLES present past
je haïrai ['airɛ]	je haïrais	que je haïsse	hais haïssons	haïssant haï, haïe ['ai]
je courrai [kurrɛ]	je courrais	que je coure	cours courons	courant couru, ue
je cueillerai	je cueillerais	que je cueille	cueille cueillons	cueillant cueilli, ie
j'assaillirai	j'assaillirais	que j'assaille	assaille assaillons	assaillant assailli, ie
je servirai	je servirais	que je serve	sers servons	servant servi, ie
je bouillirai	je bouillirais	que je bouille	bous bouillons	bouillant bouilli, ie
je partirai je sentirai	je partirais je sentirais	que je parte que je sente	pars partons sens sentons	partant parti, ie sentant senti, ie
je fuirai	je fuirais	que je fuie	fuis fuyons	fuyant fui, fuie
je couvrirai	je couvrirais	que je couvre	couvre couvrons	couvrant couvert, erte [kuvɛr, ɛrt]
je mourrai [murrɛ]	je mourrais	que je meure	meurs mourons	mourant mort, morte [mɔr, mɔrt]
je vêtirai	je vêtirais	que je vête	vêts vêtons	vêtant vêtu, ue [vety]
j'acquerrai [akerrɛ]	j'acquerrais	que j'acquière	acquiers acquérons	acquérant acquis, ise [aki, iz]
je viendrai [vjẽdrɛ]	je viendrais	que je vienne	viens venons	venant venu, ue

conjugations 23 to 33

		INDICATIVE			
		present: 1st person	present: 3rd person	imperfect	past historic
23	**pleuvoir**	(impersonal)	il pleut [plø]	il pleuvait	il plut
24	**prévoir**	je prévois [prevwa] nous prévoyons [pʀevwajɔ̃]	il prévoit ils prévoient	je prévoyais nous prévoyions [pʀevwajjɔ̃]	je prévis
25	**pourvoir**	je pourvois nous pourvoyons	il pourvoit ils pourvoient	je pourvoyais nous pourvoyions	je pourvus
26	**asseoir**	j'assieds [asjɛ] nous asseyons [asɛjɔ̃] or j'assois nous assoyons	il assied ils asseyent [asɛj] or il assoit ils assoient	j'asseyais nous asseyions or j'assoyais nous assoyions	j'assis
27	**mouvoir**	je meus [mø] nous mouvons [muvɔ̃]	il meut ils meuvent [mœv]	je mouvais nous mouvions	je mus [my] nous mûmes

NB ***Émouvoir*** and ***promouvoir*** have the past participles *ému, e* and *promu, e* respectively.

		present: 1st person	present: 3rd person	imperfect	past historic
28	**recevoir**	je reçois [ʀ(ə)swa] nous recevons [ʀ(ə)sevɔ̃]	il reçoit ils reçoivent [rəswav]	je recevais nous recevions	je reçus [ʀ(ə)sy]
	devoir				
29	**valoir**	je vaux [vo] nous valons [valɔ̃]	il vaut ils valent [val]	je valais nous valions	je valus
	équivaloir				
	prévaloir				
	falloir	(impersonal)	il faut [fo]	il fallait [falɛ]	il fallut
30	**voir**	je vois [vwa] nous voyons [vwajɔ̃]	il voit ils voient	je voyais nous voyions [vwajjɔ̃]	je vis
31	**vouloir**	je veux [vø] nous voulons [vulɔ̃]	il veut ils veulent [vœl]	je voulais nous voulions	je voulus
32	**savoir**	je sais [sɛ] nous savons [savɔ̃]	il sait ils savent [sav]	je savais nous savions	je sus
33	**pouvoir**	je peux [pø] or je puis nous pouvons [puvɔ̃]	il peut ils peuvent [pœv]	je pouvais nous pouvions	je pus

Irregular verbs ending in -oir

future	CONDITIONAL present	SUBJUNCTIVE present	IMPERATIVE present	PARTICIPLE present past
il pleuvra	il pleuvrait	qu'il pleuve [plœv]	does not exist	pleuvant plu (no feminine)
je prévoirai	je prévoirais	que je prévoie [prevwa]	prévois prévoyons	prévoyant prévu, ue
je pourvoirai	je pourvoirais	que je pourvoie	pourvois pourvoyons	pourvoyant pourvu, ue
j'assiérai [asjerɛ] or j'asseyerai [asɛjrɛ] or j'assoirai	j'assiérais or j'assoirais	que j'asseye [asɛj] or que j'assoie [aswa]	assieds asseyons or assois assoyons	asseyant assis, ise or assoyant assis, ise
NB *J'asseyerai* is old-fashioned.				
je mouvrai [muvrɛ]	je mouvrais	que je meuve que nous mouvions	meus mouvons	mouvant mû, mue [my]
je recevrai	je recevrais	que je reçoive que nous recevions	reçois recevons	recevant reçu, ue
				dû, due
je vaudrai [vodrɛ]	je vaudrais	que je vaille [vaj] que nous valions [valjɔ̃]	vaux valons	valant valu, ue
				équivalu (no feminine)
		que je prévale	does not exist	prévalu (no feminine)
il faudra [fodra]	il faudrait	qu'il faille [faj]		does not exist fallu (no feminine)
je verrai [verɛ]	je verrais	que je voie [vwa] que nous voyions [vwajjɔ̃]	vois voyons	voyant vu, vue
je voudrai [vudrɛ]	je voudrais	que je veuille [vœj] que nous voulions [vuljɔ̃]	veux or veuille voulons	voulant voulu, ue
je saurai [sorɛ]	je saurais	que je sache [saʃ] que nous sachions	sache sachons	sachant su, sue
je pourrai [purɛ]	je pourrais	que je puisse [pɥis] que nous puissions	not used	pouvant pu

conjugation 34

INDICATIVE

PRESENT
j'ai [e; ɛ]
tu as [a]
il a [a]
nous avons [avɔ̃]
vous avez [ave]
ils ont [ɔ̃]

PERFECT
j'ai eu
tu as eu
il a eu
nous avons eu
vous avez eu
ils ont eu

IMPERFECT
j'avais
tu avais
il avait
nous avions
vous aviez
ils avaient

PLUPERFECT
j'avais eu
tu avais eu
il avait eu
nous avions eu
vous aviez eu
ils avaient eu

PAST HISTORIC
j'eus [y]
tu eus
il eut
nous eûmes [ym]
vous eûtes [yt]
ils eurent [yʀ]

PAST ANTERIOR
j'eus eu
tu eus eu
il eut eu
nous eûmes eu
vous eûtes eu
ils eurent eu

FUTURE
j'aurai [ɔʀɛ]
tu auras
il aura
nous aurons
vous aurez
ils auront

FUTURE PERFECT
j'aurai eu
tu auras eu
il aura eu
nous aurons eu
vous aurez eu
ils auront eu

SUBJUNCTIVE

PRESENT
que j'aie [ɛ]
que tu aies
qu'il ait
que nous ayons [ɛjɔ̃]
que vous ayez
qu'ils aient

IMPERFECT
que j'eusse [ys]
que tu eusses
qu'il eût [y]
que nous eussions [ysjɔ̃]
que vous eussiez
qu'ils eussent

PAST
que j'ai eu
que tu aies eu
qu'il ait eu
que nous ayons eu
que vous ayez eu
qu'ils aient eu

PLUPERFECT
que j'eusse eu
que tu eusses eu
qu'il eût eu
que nous eussions eu
que vous eussiez eu
qu'ils eussent eu

conjugations 35 to 37

		INDICATIVE			
		present: 1st person	present: 2nd and 3rd persons	imperfect	past historic
35	**conclure**	je conclus [kɔ̃kly] nous concluons [kɔ̃klyɔ̃]	il conclut ils concluent	je concluais nous concluions	je conclus

NB ***Exclure*** is conjugated like ***conclure***: past participle *exclu, ue*; ***inclure*** is conjugated like ***conclure*** except for the past participle *inclus, use*.

		present: 1st person	present: 2nd and 3rd persons	imperfect	past historic
36	**rire**	je ris [ʀi] nous rions [ʀijɔ̃]	il rit ils rient	je riais nous riions [ʀijɔ̃] or [ʀijjɔ̃]	je ris
37	**dire**	je dis [di] nous disons [dizɔ̃]	il dit vous dites [dit] ils disent [diz]	je disais nous disions	je dis

NB ***Médire, contredire, dédire, interdire, prédire*** are conjugated like ***dire*** except for the 2nd person plural of the present tense: *médisez, contredisez, dédisez, interdisez, prédisez.*

		present: 1st person	present: 2nd and 3rd persons	imperfect	past historic
	suffire	je suffis [syfi] nous suffisons [syfizɔ̃]	il suffit ils suffisent [syfiz]	je suffisais nous suffisions	je suffis

NB ***Confire*** is conjugated like ***suffire*** except for the past participle *confit, ite*.

AVOIR

CONDITIONAL

PRESENT
j'aurais
tu aurais
il aurait
nous aurions
vous auriez
ils auraient

PAST I
j'aurais eu
tu aurais eu
il aurait eu
nous aurions eu
vous auriez eu
ils auraient eu

PAST II
j'eusse eu
tu eusses eu
il eût eu
nous eussions eu
vous eussiez eu
ils eussent eu

	PRESENT	PAST
IMPERATIVE	aie [ɛ] ayons [ɛjɔ̃] ayez [eje]	aie eu ayons eu ayez eu

	PRESENT	PAST
PARTICIPLE	ayant	eu, eue [y] ayant eu

	PRESENT	PAST
INFINITIVE	avoir	avoir eu

irregular verbs ending in **-re**

future	CONDITIONAL present	SUBJUNCTIVE present	IMPERATIVE present	PARTICIPLES present past
je conclurai	je conclurais	que je conclue	conclus concluons	concluant conclu, ue
je rirai	je rirais	que je rie	ris rions	riant ri (no feminine)
je dirai	je dirais	que je dise	dis disons dites	disant dit, dite
je suffirai	je suffirais	que je suffise	suffis suffisons	suffisant suffi (no feminine)

conjugations 38 to 48

		INDICATIVE			
		present 1st person	present 3rd person	imperfect	past historic
38	**nuire**	je nuis [nɥi] nous nuisons [nɥizɔ̃]	il nuit ils nuisent [nɥiz]	je nuisais nous nuisions	je nuisis
	Also the verbs *luire, reluire*.				
	conduire	je conduis nous conduisons	il conduit ils conduisent	je conduisais nous conduisions	je conduisis
	Also the verbs *construire, cuire, déduire, détruire, enduire, induire, instruire, introduire, produire, réduire, séduire, traduire.*				
39	**écrire**	j'écris [ekʀi] nous écrivons [ekʀivɔ̃]	il écrit ils écrivent [ekʀiv]	j'écrivais nous écrivions	j'écrivis
40	**suivre**	je suis [sɥi] nous suivons [sɥivɔ̃]	il suit ils suivent [sɥiv]	je suivais nous suivions	je suivis
41	**rendre**	je rends [ʀɑ̃] nous rendons [ʀɑ̃dɔ̃]	il rend ils rendent [ʀɑ̃d]	je rendais nous rendions	je rendis
	Also the verbs ending in *-andre* (e.g. *répandre*), *-erdre* (e.g. *perdre*), *-ondre* (e.g. *répondre*), *-ordre* (e.g. *mordre*).				
	rompre	je romps [ʀɔ̃] nous rompons [ʀɔ̃pɔ̃]	il rompt ils rompent [ʀɔ̃p]	je rompais nous rompions	je rompis
	Also the verbs *corrompre* and *interrompre*.				
	battre	je bats [ba] nous battons [batɔ̃]	il bat ils battent [bat]	je battais nous battions	je battis
42	**vaincre**	je vaincs [vɛ̃] nous vainquons [vɛ̃kɔ̃]	il vainc ils vainquent [vɛ̃k]	je vainquais nous vainquions	je vainquis
43	**lire**	je lis [li] nous lisons [lizɔ̃]	il lit ils lisent [liz]	je lisais nous lisions	je lus
44	**croire**	je crois [kʀwa] nous croyons [kʀwajɔ̃]	il croit ils croient	je croyais nous croyions [kʀwajjɔ̃]	je crus nous crûmes
45	**clore**	je clos [klo]	il clôt ils closent [kloz] (rare)	je closais (rare)	not applicable
46	**vivre**	je vis [vi] nous vivons [vivɔ̃]	il vit ils vivent [viv]	je vivais nous vivions	je vécus [veky]
47	**moudre**	je mouds [mu] nous moulons [mulɔ̃]	il moud ils moulent [mul]	je moulais nous moulions	je moulus
	NB Most forms of this verb are rare except *moudre, moudrai(s), moulu, e.*				
48	**coudre**	je couds [ku] nous cousons [kuzɔ̃]	il coud ils cousent [kuz]	je cousais nous cousions	je cousis [kuzi]

irregular verbs ending in **-re**

	CONDITIONAL	SUBJUNCTIVE	IMPERATIVE	PARTICIPLES
future	present	present	present	present past
je nuirai	je nuirais	que je nuise	nuis nuisons	nuisant nui (no feminine)
je conduirai	je conduirais	que je conduise	conduis conduisons	conduisant conduit, ite
j'écrirai	j'écrirais	que j'écrive	écris écrivons	écrivant écrit, ite
je suivrai	je suivrais	que je suive	suis suivons	suivant suivi, ie
je rendrai	je rendrais	que je rende	rends rendons	rendant rendu, ue
je romprai	je romprais	que je rompe	romps rompons	rompant rompu, ue
je battrai	je battrais	que je batte	bats battons	battant battu, ue
je vaincrai	je vaincrais	que je vainque	vaincs vainquons	vainquant vaincu, ue
je lirai	je lirais	que je lise	lis lisons	lisant lu, ue
je croirai	je croirais	que je croie	crois croyons	croyant cru, crue
je clorai (rare)	je clorais (rare)	que je close	clos	closant (rare) clos, close
je vivrai	je vivrais	que je vive	vis vivons	vivant vécu, ue
je moudrai	je moudrais	que je moule	mouds moulons	moulant moulu, ue
je coudrai	je coudrais	que je couse	couds cousons	cousant cousu, ue

conjugations 49 to 59

		INDICATIVE			
		present 1st person	present 3rd person	imperfect	past historic
49	**joindre**	je joins [ʒwɛ̃] nous joignons [ʒwaɲɔ̃]	il joint ils joignent [ʒwaɲ]	je joignais nous joignions [ʒwaɲjɔ̃]	je joignis
50	**traire**	je trais [tʀɛ] nous trayons [tʀɛjɔ̃]	il trait ils traient	je trayais nous trayions [tʀɛjjɔ̃]	not applicable
51	**absoudre**	j'absous [apsu] nous absolvons [apsɔlvɔ̃]	il absout ils absolvent [apsɔlv]	j'absolvais nous absolvions	j'absolus [apsɔly] (rare)
		NB ***Dissoudre*** is conjugated like **absoudre**; ***résoudre*** is conjugated like **absoudre**, but the past historic *je résolus* is current. ***Résoudre*** has two past participles: *résolu, ue (problème résolu)*, and *résous, oute* (*brouillard résous en pluie* [rare]).			
52	**craindre**	je crains [kʀɛ̃] nous craignons [kʀɛɲɔ̃]	il craint ils craignent [kʀɛɲ]	je craignais nous craignions [kʀɛɲjɔ̃]	je craignis
	peindre	je peins [pɛ̃] nous peignons [pɛɲɔ̃]	il peint ils peignent [pɛɲ]	je peignais nous peignions [pɛɲjɔ̃]	je peignis
53	**boire**	je bois [bwa] nous buvons [byvɔ̃]	il boit ils boivent [bwav]	je buvais nous buvions	je bus
54	**plaire**	je plais [plɛ] nous plaisons [plɛzɔ̃]	il plaît ils plaisent [plɛz]	je plaisais nous plaisions	je plus
		NB The past participle of ***plaire, complaire, déplaire*** is generally invariable.			
	taire	je tais nous taisons	il tait ils taisent	je taisais nous taisions	je tus
55	**croître**	je croîs [kʀwa] nous croissons [kʀwasɔ̃]	il croît ils croissent [kʀwas]	je croissais nous croissions	je crûs nous crûmes
		NB The past participle of ***décroître*** is *décru, e.*			
	accroître	j'accrois nous accroissons	il accroît ils accroissent	j'accroissais	j'accrus nous accrûmes
56	**mettre**	je mets [mɛ] nous mettons [metɔ̃]	il met ils mettent [mɛt]	je mettais nous mettions	je mis
57	**connaître**	je connais [kɔnɛ] nous connaissons [kɔnɛsɔ̃]	il connaît ils connaissent [kɔnɛs]	je connaissais nous connaissions	je connus
58	**prendre**	je prends [pʀɑ̃] nous prenons [pʀənɔ̃]	il prend ils prennent [pʀɛn]	je prenais nous prenions	je pris
59	**naître**	je nais [nɛ] nous naissons [nɛsɔ̃]	il naît ils naissent [nɛs]	je naissais nous naissions	je naquis [naki]
		NB ***Renaître*** has no past participle.			

irregular verbs ending in -**re**

future	CONDITIONAL present	SUBJUNCTIVE present	IMPERATIVE present	PARTICIPLES present past
je joindrai	je joindrais	que je joigne	joins joignons	joignant joint, jointe
je trairai	je trairais	que je traie	trais trayons	trayant trait, traite
j'absoudrai	j'absoudrais	que j'absolve	absous absolvons	absolvant absous[1], oute [apsu, ut]
je craindrai	je craindrais	que je craigne	crains craignons	craignant craint, crainte
je peindrai	je peindrais	que je peigne	peins peignons	peignant peint, peinte
je boirai	je boirais	que je boive que nous buvions	bois buvons	buvant bu, bue
je plairai	je plairais	que je plaise	plais plaisons	plaisant plu (no feminine)
je tairai	je tairais	que je taise	tais taisons	taisant tu, tue
je croîtrai	je croîtrais	que je croisse	croîs croissons	croissant crû, crue
j'accroîtrai	j'accroîtrais	que j'accroisse	accrois accroissons	accroissant accru, ue
je mettrai	je mettrais	que je mette	mets mettons	mettant mis, mise
je connaîtrai	je connaîtrais	que je connaisse	connais connaissons	connaissant connu, ue
je prendrai	je prendrais	que je prenne que nous prenions	prends prenons	prenant pris, prise
je naîtrai	je naîtrais	que je naisse	nais naissons	naissant né, née

1. The past participle forms *absout*, *dissout*, with a final *t*, are often preferred.

conjugation 60 – **FAIRE**

INDICATIVE

PRESENT	PERFECT
je fais [fɛ]	j'ai fait
tu fais	tu as fait
il fait	il a fait
nous faisons [f(ə)zɔ̃]	nous avons fait
vous faites [fɛt]	vous avez fait
ils font [fɔ̃]	ils ont fait
IMPERFECT	**PLUPERFECT**
je faisais [f(ə)zɛ]	j'avais fait
tu faisais	tu avais fait
il faisait	il avait fait
nous faisions [fəzjɔ̃]	nous avions fait
vous faisiez [fəsje]	vous aviez fait
ils faisaient	ils avaient fait
PAST HISTORIC	**PAST ANTERIOR**
je fis	j'eus fait
tu fis	tu eus fait
il fit	il eut fait
nous fîmes	nous eûmes fait
vous fîtes	vous eûtes fait
ils firent	ils eurent fait
FUTURE	**FUTURE PERFECT**
je ferai [f(ə)ʀɛ]	j'aurai fait
tu feras	tu auras fait
il fera	il aura fait
nous ferons [f(ə)ʀɔ̃]	nous aurons fait
vous ferez	vous aurez fait
ils feront	ils auront fait

SUBJUNCTIVE

PRESENT
que je fasse [fas]
que tu fasses
qu'il fasse
que nous fassions
que vous fassiez
qu'ils fassent

IMPERFECT
que je fisse [fis]
que tu fisses
qu'il fît
que nous fissions
que vous fissiez
qu'ils fissent

PAST
que j'aie fait
que tu aies fait
qu'il ait fait
que nous ayons fait
que vous ayez fait
qu'ils aient fait

PLUPERFECT
que j'eusse fait
que tu eusses fait
qu'il eût fait
que nous eussions fait
que vous eussiez fait
qu'ils eussent fait

CONDITIONAL

PRESENT
je ferais [f(ə)ʀɛ]
tu ferais
il ferait
nous ferions [fəʀjɔ̃]
vous feriez
ils feraient

PAST I
j'aurais fait
tu aurais fait
il aurait fait
nous aurions fait
vous auriez fait
ils auraient fait

PAST II
j'eusse fait
tu eusses fait
il eût fait
nous eussions fait
vous eussiez fait
ils eussent fait

IMPERATIVE

PRESENT	PAST
fais	aie fait
faisons	ayons fait
faites	ayez fait

PARTICIPLE

PRESENT	PAST
faisant [f(ə)zɑ̃]	fait
	ayant fait

INFINITIVE

PRESENT	PAST
faire	avoir fait

conjugation 61 – **ÊTRE**

INDICATIVE

PRESENT
je suis [sɥi]
tu es [ɛ]
il est [ɛ]
nous sommes [sɔm]
vous êtes [ɛt]
ils sont [sɔ̃]

PERFECT
j'ai été
tu as été
il a été
nous avons été
vous avez été
ils ont été

IMPERFECT
j'étais [etɛ]
tu étais
il était
nous étions [etjɔ̃]
vous étiez
ils étaient

PLUPERFECT
j'avais été
tu avais été
il avait été
nous avions été
vous aviez été
ils avaient été

PAST HISTORIC
je fus [fy]
tu fus
il fut
nous fûmes
vous fûtes
ils furent

PAST ANTERIOR
j'eus été
tu eus été
il eut été
nous eûmes été
vous eûtes été
ils eurent été

FUTURE
je serai [s(ə)ʀɛ]
tu seras
il sera
nous serons [s(ə)ʀɔ̃]
vous serez
ils seront

FUTURE PERFECT
j'aurai été
tu auras été
il aura été
nous aurons été
vous aurez été
ils auront été

SUBJUNCTIVE

PRESENT
que je sois [swa]
que tu sois
qu'il soit
que nous soyons [swajɔ̃]
que vous soyez
qu'ils soient

IMPERFECT
que je fusse
que tu fusses
qu'il fût
que nous fussions
que vous fussiez
qu'ils fussent

PAST
que j'aie été
que tu aies été
qu'il ait été
que nous ayons été
que vous ayez été
qu'ils eussent été

PLUPERFECT
que j'eusse été
que tu eusses été
qu'il eût été
que nous eussions été
que vous eussiez été
qu'ils eussent été

CONDITIONAL

PRESENT
je serais [s(ə)ʀɛ]
tu serais
il serait
nous serions [səʀjɔ̃]
vous seriez
ils seraient

PAST I
j'aurais été
tu aurais été
il aurait été
nous aurions été
vous auriez été
ils auraient été

PAST II
j'eusse été
tu eusses été
il eût été
nous eussions été
vous eussiez été
ils eussent été

IMPERATIVE

PRESENT
sois [swa]
soyons [swajɔ̃]
soyez [swaje]

PAST
aie été
ayons été
ayez été

PARTICIPLE

PRESENT
étant

PAST
été [ete]
ayant été

INFINITIVE

PRESENT
être

PAST
avoir été

FORMATION OF COMPOUND TENSES OF FRENCH VERBS

Most verbs form their compound tenses using the verb *avoir*, except in the reflexive form. Simple tenses of the auxiliary are followed by the past participle to form the compound tenses shown below (the verb *avoir* is given as an example)

AVOIR			+ PAST PARTICIPLE	COMPOUND TENSES OF VERBS
PRESENT	j' tu il nous vous ils	**ai** **as** **a** **avons** **avez** **ont**		= **PERFECT** (*chanter* = il **a chanté**) (*boire* = il **a bu**) (*avoir* = il **a eu**) (*être* = il **a été**)
IMPERFECT	j' tu il nous vous ils	**avais** **avais** **avait** **avions** **aviez** **avaient**		= **PLUPERFECT** (il **avait chanté**, il **avait bu**, il **avait eu**, il **avait été**)
FUTURE	j' tu il nous vous ils	**aurai** **auras** **aura** **aurons** **aurez** **auront**		= **FUTURE PERFECT** (il **aura chanté**, il **aura bu**, il **aura eu**, il **aura été**)
CONDITIONAL (PRESENT)	j' tu il nous vous ils	**aurais** **aurais** **aurait** **aurions** **auriez** **auraient**	**+ PAST PARTICIPLE** (chanté) (bu) (eu) (été)	= **PAST CONDITIONAL** (this tense is rarely studied but the forms are not rare) (il **aurait chanté**, il **aurait bu**, il **aurait eu**, il **aurait été**)
PAST HISTORIC	j' tu il nous vous ils	**eus** **eus** **eut** **eûmes** **eûtes** **eurent**		= **PAST ANTERIOR** (rare as a spoken form) (il **eut chanté**, il **eut bu**, il **eut eu**, il **eut été**)
IMPERATIVE		**aie** **ayons** **ayez**		= **PAST IMPERATIVE** (rare) **(aie chanté, aie bu, aie eu, aie été)**
PRESENT PARTICIPLE		**ayant**		= **SECOND FORM OF PAST PARTICIPLE** **(ayant chanté, ayant bu, ayant eu, ayant été)**
SUBJUNCTIVE (PRESENT)	que j' que tu qu'il que nous que vous qu'ils	**aie** **aies** **ait** **ayons** **ayez** **aient**		= **PAST SUBJUNCTIVE** (rare as spoken form) (qu'il **ait chanté**, qu'il **ait bu**, qu'il **ait eu**, qu'il **ait été**)
SUBJUNCTIVE (IMPERFECT) (rare)	que j' que tu qu'il que nous que vous qu'ils	**eusse** **eusses** **eût** **eussions** **eussiez** **eussent**		= **PLUPERFECT SUBJUNCTIVE** (very rare, even in the written form) (qu'il **eût chanté**, qu'il **eût bu**, qu'il **eût eu**, qu'il **eût été**)

RULES OF AGREEMENT FOR PAST PARTICIPLE

The past participle is a form of the verb which does not vary according to tense or person, but which is more like an adjective, in that it may agree in gender and number with the word to which it refers.

PAST PARTICIPLE AGREEMENT DEPENDING ON USAGE

without auxiliary (adjectival use)	• **agreement** with the word it refers to *une affaire bien partie* (agrees with *affaire*, feminine singular)

with *être*	• **agreement** with the subject of **être** *les hirondelles sont revenues* (agrees with *hirondelles*, feminine plural)
with *avoir*	• **agreement** with the direct object, provided the direct object precedes the past participle *je les ai crus* (agrees with *les*, masculine plural) *la lettre qu'il a écrite* (agrees with *que*, referring back to *lettre*, feminine singular) • **no agreement**, then, in the following cases: *nous avons couru* (no direct object) *elles ont pris la clé* (direct object follows past participle)

with *s'être*	**as with** *être*	• if the verb is reflexive, the past participle agrees with the subject *ils se sont enrhumés* (agrees with *ils*, masculine plural) • if the reflexive pronoun is the indirect object, any agreement is with the preceding direct object *la bosse qu'il s'est faite* (agrees with *que*, referring back to *bosse*, feminine singular)
	as with *avoir*	• **no agreement**, then, if the direct object follows the past participle *ils se sont lavé les mains* (the object being *les mains*)

L'anglais comprend de nombreux verbes forts ou irréguliers (dont nous donnons la liste ci-dessous, § 7) ainsi que de nombreuses variantes orthographiques (voir au § 8), mais à chacun des temps la conjugaison reste la même pour toutes les personnes sauf pour la troisième personne du singulier au présent de l'indicatif.

Les notes qui suivent se proposent de résumer la structure et les formes du verbe anglais.

1 LE MODE INDICATIF

PRÉSENT	FORMATION	Le présent de l'indicatif a la même forme que l'infinitif présent à toutes les personnes sauf à la troisième personne du singulier, à laquelle vient s'ajouter un *s*, ex. : *he sells.*
	verbes se terminant par une sifflante ou une chuintante	Dans les cas où l'infinitif se termine par une sifflante ou une chuintante on intercale un *e*, ex. : *he kisses, he buzzes, he rushes, he touches.*
	verbes se terminant par consonne + y	Les verbes qui se terminent en consonne + *y* changent cet *y* en *ies* à la troisième personne du singulier, ex. : *he tries, he pities, he satisfies.* REMARQUE. Là où le *y* est précédé d'une voyelle, on applique la règle générale, ex. : *pray — he prays, annoy — she annoys.*
	formes irrégulières	Le verbe to be a des formes irrégulières pour toutes les personnes : *I am, you are, he is, we are, you are, they are.* Trois autres verbes ont une forme irrégulière à la troisième personne du singulier : *do* *he does* *have* *he has* *go* *he goes*
IMPARFAIT PASSÉ SIMPLE PARTICIPE PASSÉ	FORMATION	L'imparfait, le passé simple et le participe passé ont, en anglais, la même forme. On les construit en ajoutant *ed* au radical de l'infinitif, ex. : *paint — I painted — painted.*
	verbes se terminant par un *e* muet	On ajoute *d* à l'infinitif des verbes qui se terminent par un *e* muet, ex. : *bare — I bared — bared, move — I moved — moved, revise — I revised — revised.*
	verbes irréguliers	Pour les verbes irréguliers, voir la liste ci-dessous, § 7.
TEMPS COMPOSÉS ou PASSÉS	FORMATION	Les temps composés du passé se forment à l'aide de l'auxiliaire *to have* suivi du participe passé.
	PASSÉ COMPOSÉ	Présent de *to have* + participe passé. ex. : *I have painted.*
	PLUS-QUE-PARFAIT	Passé de *to have* + participe passé, ex. : *I had painted.*
FUTUR	FUTUR SIMPLE	Le futur se forme à l'aide de *will* suivi de l'infinitif, ex. : *I will do it.* Dans la langue soignée, on utilise *shall* à la première personne du singulier et du pluriel, ex. : *we shall see to it.*
	FUTUR ANTÉRIEUR	L'auxiliaire *to have* accompagné de *will* (ou de *shall* dans la langue soignée) et du participe passé du verbe conjugué s'emploie pour le futur antérieur, ex. : *I will have finished.*
FORME PROGRESSIVE	Il existe également en anglais, au mode indicatif, une forme progressive qui se forme avec l'auxiliaire *to be*, conjugué au temps approprié et suivi du participe présent, ex. : *I am waiting, we were hoping, they will be leaving, they would still have been waiting, I had been painting all day.* Ce système diffère dans une certaine mesure du système français, qui a parfois comme équivalent la formule « être en train de » suivie de l'infinitif.	

2 LE CONDITIONNEL

PRÉSENT	Le conditionnel se forme à l'aide de *would* suivi de l'infinitif, ex. : *I would go.* Dans la langue soignée, ou utilise *should* à la première personne du singulier et du pluriel, ex. : *we should see it.*
PASSÉ	L'auxiliaire *to have* accompagné de *would* (ou de *should* dans la langue soignée) et du participe passé du verbe conjugué s'emploie pour le conditionnel passé, ex. : *I would have paid.*

3 LE MODE SUBJONCTIF

PRÉSENT	Au présent et à toutes les personnes, le subjonctif a la même forme que l'infinitif, ex. : *(that) I go, (that) she go* etc.
IMPARFAIT	À l'imparfait, *to be* est l'unique verbe qui ait une forme irrégulière. Cette forme est *were* pour toutes les personnes : ex. : *(that) I were, (that) we were* etc.
Emploi	Le subjonctif est peu utilisé en anglais. Il faut cependant noter que le subjonctif s'emploie obligatoirement en anglais dans : *if I were you, were I to attempt it* (l'emploi de *was* étant considéré comme incorrect dans ces expressions, ainsi que dans d'autres expressions analogues). Le subjonctif se rencontre aussi dans l'expression figée *so be it* et dans le langage juridique ou officiel, ex. : *it is agreed that nothing be done, it was resolved that the pier be painted* (quoique *should be done* et *should be painted* soient également corrects).

4 LE MODE IMPÉRATIF

FORMATION	Il n'y a qu'une forme de l'impératif, qui est en fait celle de l'infinitif, ex. : *tell me, come here, don't do that.*

5 LE GÉRONDIF ET LE PARTICIPE PRÉSENT

FORMATION	Le gérondif et le participe présent ont la même forme en anglais. Ils s'obtiennent en ajoutant la désinence *-ing* au radical de l'infinitif, ex. : *washing, sending, passing.* Pour les variantes orthographiques voir paragraphe 8.

6 LA VOIX PASSIVE

FORMATION	La voix passive se forme exactement comme en français avec le temps approprié du verbe *to be* et le participe passé : ex. : *we are forced to, he was killed, they had been injured,* *the company will be taken over,* *it ought to have been rebuilt, were it to be agreed.*

7 VERBES FORTS OU IRRÉGULIERS

INFINITIF	PRÉTÉRIT	PARTICIPE PASSÉ
abide	abode *or* abided	abode *or* abided
arise	arose	arisen
awake	awoke *or* awaked	awoken *or* awaked
be	was, were	been
bear[1]	bore	borne
beat	beat	beaten
become	became	become
beget	begot, begat††	begotten
begin	began	begun
bend	bent	bent
beseech	besought	besought
bet	bet *or* betted	bet *or* betted
bid	bade *or* bid	bid *or* bidden
bind	bound	bound
bite	bit	bitten
bleed	bled	bled
blow[1]	blew	blown
break	broke	broken
breed	bred	bred
bring	brought	brought
build	built	built
burn	burned *or* burnt	burned *or* burnt
burst	burst	burst
buy	bought	bought
can[1]	could	–
cast	cast	cast
catch	caught	caught
chide	chid	chidden *or* chid
choose	chose	chosen
cleave[1] *(fendre)*	clove *or* cleft	cloven *or* cleft
cling	clung	clung
come	came	come
cost	cost *or* costed	cost *or* costed
creep	crept	crept
cut	cut	cut
deal	dealt	dealt
dig	dug	dug
dive	dived, (US) dove	dived
do	did	done
draw	drew	drawn
dream	dreamed *or* dreamt	dreamed *or* dreamt
drink	drank	drunk
drive	drove	driven
dwell	dwelled *or* dwelt	dwelled *or* dwelt
eat	ate	eaten
fall	fell	fallen
feed	fed	fed
feel	felt	felt
fight	fought	fought
find	found	found
flee	fled	fled
fling	flung	flung
fly	flew	flown
forbid	forbad(e)	forbidden
forget	forgot	forgotten
forsake	forsook	forsaken
freeze	froze	frozen
get	got	got, (US) gotten
gild	gilded	gilded *or* gilt
gird	girded *or* girt	girded *or* girt
give	gave	given
go	went	gone
grind	ground	ground
grow	grew	grown
hang	hung, (Jur) hanged	hung, (Jur) hanged
have	had	had
hear	heard	heard
heave	heaved, (Naut) hove	heaved, (Naut) hove
hew	hewed	hewed *or* hewn
hide	hid	hidden
hit	hit	hit
hold	held	held
hurt	hurt	hurt
keep	kept	kept
kneel	knelt	knelt
know	knew	known
lade	laded	laden
lay	laid	laid
lead	led	led
lean	leaned *or* leant	leaned *or* leant
leap	leaped *or* leapt	leaped *or* leapt
learn	learned *or* learnt	learned *or* learnt
leave	left	left
lend	lent	lent
let	let	let
lie[1]	lay	lain
light[1+3]	lit *or* lighted	lit *or* lighted
lose	lost	lost
make	made	made
may	might	–
mean	meant	meant
meet	met	met
mow	mowed	mown *or* mowed

INFINITIF	PRÉTÉRIT	PARTICIPE PASSÉ
pay	paid	paid
put	put	put
quit	quit or quitted	quit or quitted
read [ri:d]	read [red]	read [red]
rend	rent	rent
rid	rid	rid
ride	rode	ridden
ring[2]	rang	rung
rise	rose	risen
run	ran	run
saw	sawed	sawed or sawn
say	said	said
see	saw	seen
seek	sought	sought
sell	sold	sold
send	sent	sent
set	set	set
sew	sewed	sewed or sewn
shake	shook	shaken
shave	shaved	shaved or shaven
shear	sheared	sheared or shorn
shed	shed	shed
shine	shone	shone
shoe	shod	shod
shoot	shot	shot
show	showed	shown or showed
shrink	shrank	shrunk
shut	shut	shut
sing	sang	sung
sink	sank	sunk
sit	sat	sat
slay	slew	slain
sleep	slept	slept
slide	slid	slid
sling	slung	slung
slink	slunk	slunk
slit	slit	slit
smell	smelled or smelt	smelled or smelt
smite	smote	smitten
sow	sowed	sowed or sown
speak	spoke	spoken
speed	speeded or sped	speeded or sped
spell[3]	spelled or spelt	spelled or spelt
spend	spent	spent
spill	spilled or spilt	spilled or spilt
spin	spun or span††	spun
spit	spat	spat
split	split	split
spoil	spoiled or spoilt	spoiled or spoilt
spread	spread	spread
spring	sprang	sprung
stand	stood	stood
stave	stove or staved	stove or staved
steal	stole	stolen
stick	stuck	stuck
sting	stung	stung
stink	stank	stunk
strew	strewed	strewed or strewn
stride	strode	stridden
strike	struck	struck
string	strung	strung
strive	strove	striven
swear	swore	sworn
sweep	swept	swept
swell	swelled	swollen
swim	swam	swum
swing	swung	swung
take	took	taken
teach	taught	taught
tear	tore	torn
tell	told	told
think	thought	thought
thrive	throve or thrived	thriven or thrived
throw	threw	thrown
thrust	thrust	thrust
tread	trod	trodden
wake	woke or waked	woken or waked
wear	wore	worn
weave	wove or weaved	woven or weaved
weep	wept	wept
win	won	won
wind[2+3]	wound	wound
wring	wrung	wrung
write	wrote	written

REMARQUE. Ne sont pas compris dans cette liste les verbes formés avec un préfixe. Pour leur conjugaison, se référer au verbe de base, ex. : pour *forbear* voir *bear*, pour *understand* voir *stand*.

8 VERBES FAIBLES PRÉSENTANT DES VARIANTES ORTHOGRAPHIQUES

TERMINAISON DES VERBES À L'INFINITIF	VARIANTE ORTHOGRAPHIQUE AU PARTICIPE PASSÉ ET AU GÉRONDIF	EXEMPLE		
		INFINITIF	**PARTICIPE PASSÉ**	**GÉRONDIF**
Les verbes se terminant par une seule consonne précédée d'une seule voyelle accentuée	redoublent la consonne devant la désinence *ed* ou *ing*	sob wed lag control dim tan tap prefer pat	sobbed wedded lagged controlled dimmed tanned tapped preferred patted	sobbing wedding lagging controlling dimming tanning tapping preferring patting
		(En revanche *to cook* devient *cooked – cooking* parce qu'il comporte une voyelle longue, et *fear* qui comporte une diphtongue donne *feared – fearing*.)		
Les verbes qui se terminent en *c*	changent le *c* en *ck* devant les désinences *ed* et *ing*.	frolic traffic	frolicked trafficked	frolicking trafficking
Les verbes terminés par la consonne *l* ou *p* précédée d'une voyelle non accentuée	redoublent la consonne au participe passé et au gérondif en anglais britannique, mais restent inchangés en anglais américain.	grovel travel worship	(Brit) grovelled (US) groveled (Brit) travelled (US) traveled (Brit) worshipped (US) worshiped	(Brit) grovelling (US) groveling (Brit) travelling (US) traveling (Brit) worshipping (US) worshiping
		N.B. La même différence existe entre les formes substantivées de ces verbes : (Brit) traveller worshipper (US) traveler worshiper		
Lorsque le verbe se termine par un *e* muet,	le *e* muet disparaît en faveur de la désinence *ed* ou *ing*.	invite rake smile move	invited raked smiled moved	inviting raking smiling moving
		(Le *e* muet se conserve toutefois dans les verbes *dye*, *singe*, etc. et dans une série peu nombreuse de verbes se terminant en *oe* : *dyeing, singeing, hoeing*.)		
Si le verbe se termine en *y*,	le *y* devient *ied* pour former le prétérit et le participe passé.	worry pity falsify try	worried – worried pitied – pitied falsified – falsified tried – tried	Le gérondif de ces verbes est parfaitement régulier, ex. : *worrying, trying*, etc.
Gérondif des verbes monosyllabiques *die, lie, vie*				dying, lying, vying.

9 VERBES ANGLAIS À PARTICULE

VI verbe intransitif, ex. : ► **blow off** dans *his hat blew off.*

VT SEP verbe transitif séparable, ex. : ► **blow off** dans *the wind blew off his hat* ou *the wind blew his hat off.* Le complément d'objet du verbe peut se mettre soit après la particule, soit entre les deux éléments du verbe en les séparant. Cette dernière structure est d'ailleurs obligatoire lorsque le complément d'objet est un pronom : *the wind blew it off.*

VT FUS verbe transitif fusionné, ex. : ► **admit to** dans *he admitted to the theft.* Le complément d'objet ne peut jamais s'intercaler entre les deux éléments du verbe, même lorsqu'il s'agit d'un pronom : *he admitted to it.*

REMARQUE. Pour beaucoup de verbes qui indiquent un mouvement ou une direction, les verbes à particule correspondants n'ont pas été dissociés de l'article principal, car ils peuvent être déduits des illustrations fournies. Ainsi, à partir de

crawl /krɔːl/ VI 1 *[animals]* ramper, se glisser ; *[person]* se traîner, ramper ◆ **to ~ in/out** *etc* entrer/sortir *etc* en rampant *or* à quatre pattes

vous pouvez construire : *to crawl across* (traverser en rampant), *to crawl down* (descendre en rampant), etc.

1 CARDINAL AND ORDINAL NUMBERS NOMBRES CARDINAUX ET ORDINAUX

Cardinal numbers		Les nombres cardinaux	Ordinal numbers	Les nombres ordinaux
nought	0	zéro		
one	1	(m) un, (f) une	first	(m) premier, (f) -ière
two	2	deux	second	deuxième
three	3	trois	third	troisième
four	4	quatre	fourth	quatrième
five	5	cinq	fifth	cinquième
six	6	six	sixth	sixième
seven	7	sept	seventh	septième
eight	8	huit	eighth	huitième
nine	9	neuf	ninth	neuvième
ten	10	dix	tenth	dixième
eleven	11	onze	eleventh	onzième
twelve	12	douze	twelfth	douzième
thirteen	13	treize	thirteenth	treizième
fourteen	14	quatorze	fourteenth	quatorzième
fifteen	15	quinze	fifteenth	quinzième
sixteen	16	seize	sixteenth	seizième
seventeen	17	dix-sept	seventeenth	dix-septième
eighteen	18	dix-huit	eighteenth	dix-huitième
nineteen	19	dix-neuf	nineteenth	dix-neuvième
twenty	20	vingt	twentieth	vingtième
twenty-one	21	vingt et un	twenty-first	vingt et unième
twenty-two	22	vingt-deux	twenty-second	vingt-deuxième
twenty-three	23	vingt-trois		
thirty	30	trente	thirtieth	trentième
thirty-one	31	trente et un	thirty-first	trente et unième
thirty-two	32	trente-deux		
forty	40	quarante	fortieth	quarantième
fifty	50	cinquante	fiftieth	cinquantième
sixty	60	soixante	sixtieth	soixantième
seventy	70	soixante-dix	seventieth	soixante-dixième
eighty	80	quatre-vingt(s)	eightieth	quatre-vingtième
ninety	90	quatre-vingt-dix	ninetieth	quatre-vingt-dixième
ninety-nine	99	quatre-vingt-dix-neuf		
a (or one) hundred	100	cent	hundredth	centième
a hundred and one	101	cent un	hundred and first	cent unième
a hundred and two	102	cent deux		
a hundred and ten	110	cent dix	hundred and tenth	cent dixième
a hundred and eighty-two	182	cent quatre-vingt-deux		

Cardinal numbers		Les nombres cardinaux	Ordinal numbers	Les nombres ordinaux
two hundred	200	deux cents	two hundredth	deux centième
two hundred and one	201	deux cent un		
two hundred and two	202	deux cent deux		
three hundred	300	trois cents	three hundredth	trois centième
four hundred	400	quatre cents	four hundredth	quatre centième
five hundred	500	cinq cents	five hundredth	cinq centième
six hundred	600	six cents	six hundredth	six centième
seven hundred	700	sept cents	seven hundredth	sept centième
eight hundred	800	huit cents	eight hundredth	huit centième
nine hundred	900	neuf cents	nine hundredth	neuf centième
a (or one) thousand	1,000 French 1 000	mille	thousandth	millième
a thousand and one	1,001 French 1 001	mille un		
a thousand and two	1,002 French 1 002	mille deux		
two thousand	2,000 French 2 000	deux mille	two thousandth	deux millième
ten thousand	10,000 French 10 000	dix mille		
a (or one) hundred thousand	100,000 French 100 000	cent mille		
a (or one million) (see note **b**)	1,000,000 French 1 000 000	un million (voir note **b**)	millionth	millionième
two million	2,000,000 French 2 000 000	deux millions	two millionth	deux millionième

NOTES ON USAGE OF THE CARDINAL NUMBERS

[a] To divide the larger numbers clearly, a space is used in French where English places a comma:
English 1,000 French 1 000
English 2,304,770 French 2 304 770
(This does not apply to dates: see below.)

[b] **1 000 000**: In French, the word *million* is a noun, so the numeral takes *de* when there is a following noun:
un million de fiches
trois millions de maisons détruites

[c] **One**, and the other numbers ending in *one*, agree in French with the noun (stated or implied):
une maison, un employé, il y a cent une personnes.

REMARQUES SUR LES NOMBRES CARDINAUX

[a] Alors qu'un espace est utilisé en français pour séparer les centaines des milliers, l'anglais utilise la virgule à cet effet :
français 1 000anglais 1,000
français 2 304 770anglais 2,304,770
(Cette règle ne s'applique pas aux dates. Voir ci-après.)

[b] En anglais, le mot *million* (ainsi que *mille* et *cent*) n'est pas suivi de *of* lorsqu'il accompagne un nom :
a million people,
a hundred houses,
a thousand people.

NOTES ON USAGE OF THE ORDINAL NUMBERS
REMARQUES SUR LES NOMBRES ORDINAUX

[a] **Abbreviations** : English 1st, 2nd, 3rd, 4th, 5th, etc. French (m) 1er, (f) 1re, 2e, 3e, 4e, 5e and so on.

[b] **First**, and the other numbers ending in *first*, agree in French with the noun (stated or implied):
La première maison, le premier employé, la cent unième personne

[c] See also the notes on dates, below.
Voir aussi ci-après le paragraphe concernant les dates.

2 FRACTIONS — LES FRACTIONS

one half, a half	$\frac{1}{2}$	(m) un demi, (f) une demie
one and a half helpings	$1\frac{1}{2}$	une portion et demie
two and a half kilos	$2\frac{1}{2}$	deux kilos et demi
one third, a third	$\frac{1}{3}$	un tiers
two thirds	$\frac{2}{3}$	deux tiers
one quarter, a quarter	$\frac{1}{4}$	un quart
three quarters	$\frac{3}{4}$	trois quarts
one sixth, a sixth	$\frac{1}{6}$	un sixième
five and five sixths	$5\frac{5}{6}$	cinq et cinq sixièmes
one twelfth, a twelfth	$\frac{1}{12}$	un douzième
seven twelfths	$\frac{7}{12}$	sept douzièmes
one hundredth, a hundredth	$\frac{1}{100}$	un centième
one thousandth, a thousandth	$\frac{1}{1000}$	un millième

3 DECIMALS — LES DÉCIMALES

In French, a comma is written where English uses a point:

Alors que le français utilise la virgule pour séparer les entiers des décimales, le point est utilisé en anglais à cet effet :

English/anglais		French/français
3.56 (three point five six)	=	3,56 (trois virgule cinquante-six)
.07 (point nought seven)	=	0,07 (zéro virgule zéro sept)

4 NOMENCLATURE — NUMÉRATION

3,684 is a four-digit number
It contains 4 units, 8 tens, 6 hundreds and 3 thousands
The decimal .234 contains 2 tenths, 3 hundredths and 4 thousandths

3 684 est un nombre à quatre chiffres.
4 est le chiffre des unités, 8 celui des dizaines, 6 celui des centaines et 3 celui des milliers
le nombre décimal 0,234 contient 2 dixièmes, 3 centièmes et 4 millièmes

5 PERCENTAGES — LES POURCENTAGES

$2\frac{1}{2}$ % two and a half per cent	Deux et demi pour cent
18% of the people here are over 65	Ici dix-huit pour cent des gens ont plus de soixante-cinq ans.
Production has risen by 8 %	La production s'est accrue de huit pour cent
(See also the main text of the dictionary.)	*(Voir aussi dans le corps du dictionnaire.)*

6 SIGNS — LES SIGNES

addition sign	+	signe plus, signe de l'addition
plus sign (e.g. + 7 = plus seven)	+	signe plus (ex. : + 7 = plus sept)
subtraction sign	–	signe moins, signe de la soustraction
minus sign (e.g. – 3 = minus three)	–	signe moins (ex. : – 3 = moins trois)
multiplication sign	x	signe de la multiplication
division sign	÷	signe de la division
square root sign	√	signe de la racine carrée
infinity	∞	symbole de l'infini
sign of identity, is equal to	≡	signe d'identité
sign of equality, equals	=	signe d'égalité
is approximately equal to	ª	signe d'équivalence
sign of inequality, is not equal to	¼	signe de non-égalité
is greater than	>	est plus grand que
is less than	<	est plus petit que

7 CALCULATION — LE CALCUL

8 + 6 = 14 eight and (or plus) six are (or make) fourteen	huit et (ou plus) six font (ou égalent) quatorze
15 – 3 = 12 fifteen take away (or fifteen minus) three equals twelve, three from fifteen leaves twelve	trois ôté de quinze égale douze, quinze moins trois égale douze
3 x 3 = 9 three threes are nine, three times three is nine	trois fois trois égale neuf, trois multiplié par trois égale neuf
32 ÷ 8 = 4 thirty-two divided by eight is (or equals) four	trente-deux divisé par huit égale quatre
3^2 = 9 three squared is nine	trois au carré égale neuf
2^5 = 32 two to the power of five (or to the fifth) is (or equals) thirty-two	deux à la puissance cinq égale trente-deux
$\sqrt{16}$ = 4 the square root of sixteen is four	la racine carré de seize ($\sqrt{16}$) est quatre

8 TIME — L'HEURE

TIME	L'HEURE
2 hours 33 minutes and 14 seconds	deux heures trente-trois minutes et quatorze secondes
half an hour	une demi-heure
a quarter of an hour	un quart d'heure
three quarters of an hour	trois quarts d'heure
what's the time?	quelle heure est-il ?
what time do you make it?	quelle heure avez-vous ?
have you the right time?	avez-vous l'heure exacte ?
I make it 2.20	d'après ma montre il est 2 h 20
my watch says 3.37	il est 3 h 37 à ma montre
it's 1 o'clock	il est une heure
it's 2 o'clock	il est deux heures
it's 5 past 4	il est quatre heures cinq
it's 10 to 6	il est six heures moins dix
it's half past 8	il est huit heures et demie
it's a quarter past 9	il est neuf heures et quart
it's a quarter to 2	il est deux heures moins le quart
at 10 a.m.	à dix heures du matin
at 4 p.m.	à quatre heures de l'après-midi
at 11 p.m.	à onze heures du soir
at exactly 3 o'clock, at 3 sharp, at 3 on the dot	à trois heures exactement, à trois heures précises
the train leaves at 19.32	le train part à dix-neuf heures trente-deux
(at) what time does it start?	à quelle heure est-ce que cela commence ?
it is just after 3	il est trois heures passées
it is nearly 9	il est presque neuf heures
about 8 o'clock	aux environs de huit heures
at (or by) 6 o'clock at the latest	à six heures au plus tard
have it ready for 5 o'clock	tiens-le prêt pour 5 heures
it is full each night from 7 to 9	c'est plein chaque soir de 7 à 9
"closed from 1.30 to 4.30"	« fermé de 13 h 30 à 16 h 30 »
until 8 o'clock	jusqu'à huit heures
it would be about 11	il était environ 11 heures, il devait être environ 11 heures
it would have been about 10	il devait être environ dix heures
at midnight	à minuit
before midday, before noon	avant midi

9 DATES — LES DATES

NB The days of the week and the months start with a small letter in French: lundi, mardi, février, mars.	N.B. Les jours de la semaine et les mois prennent une majuscule en anglais : Monday, Tuesday, February, March.
the 1st of July, 1 July	le 1er juillet
the 2nd of May, 2 May	le 2 mai
on 21 June, on the 21st (of) June	le 21 juin
on Monday	lundi
he comes on Mondays	il vient le lundi
"closed on Fridays"	« fermé le vendredi »
he lends it to me from Monday to Friday	il me le prête du lundi au vendredi
from the 14th to the 18th	du 14 au 18
what's the date?, what date is it today?	quelle est la date d'aujourd'hui ?, quel jour sommes-nous aujourd'hui ?
today's the 12th	(aujourd'hui) nous sommes le 12
one Thursday in October	un jeudi en octobre
about the 4th of July, about 4 July	aux environs du 4 juillet
1978 nineteen (hundred and) seventy-eight	mille neuf cent soixante-dix-huit, dix-neuf cent soixante-dix-huit
4 BC, BC 4	4 av. J.-C.
70 AD, AD 70	70 apr. J.-C.
in the 13th century	au XIIIe siècle
in (or during) the 1930s	dans (ou pendant) les années 30
in 1940 something	en 1940 et quelques
HEADING OF LETTERS:	EN-TÊTE DE LETTRES :
19 May 2003	le 19 mai 2003
(See also the main text of the dictionary.)	*(Voir aussi dans le corps du dictionnaire.)*

WEIGHTS, MEASURES AND TEMPERATURES

POIDS, MESURES ET TEMPÉRATURES

NOTES

1. Metric system

Measures formed with the following prefixes are mostly omitted:

deca-	10 times	10 fois	*déca-*
hecto-	100 times	100 fois	*hecto-*
kilo-	1,000 times	1 000 fois	*kilo-*
deci-	one tenth	un dixième	*déci-*
centi-	one hundredth	un centième	*centi-*
milli-	one thousandth	un millième	*milli-*

2. US measures

In the US, the same system as that which applies in Great Britain is used for the most part; the main differences are mentioned below.

3. The numerical notations of measures

Numerical equivalents are shown in standard English notation when they are translations of French measures and in standard French notation when they are translations of English measures:
e.g. 1 millimetre (millimètre) = 0.03937 inch
should be read in French as 0,03937 pouce.
e.g. 1 inch (pouce) = 2,54 centimètres
should be read in English as 2.54 centimetres.

REMARQUES

1. Le système métrique

La plupart des mesures formées à partir des préfixes suivants ont été omises :

2. Mesures US

Les mesures britanniques sont valables pour les USA dans la majeure partie des cas. Les principales différences sont énumérées ci-après.

3. Notation graphique des équivalences de mesures

Les équivalences sont notées en anglais lorsqu'elles traduisent des mesures françaises et en français lorsqu'elles se rapportent à des mesures anglaises :
ex. 1 millimetre (millimètre) = 0.03937 inch
doit se lire en français 0,03937 pouce.
ex. 1 inch (pouce) = 2,54 centimètres
doit se lire en anglais 2.54 centimetres.

1 LINEAR MEASURES – MESURES DE LONGUEUR

metric system / **système métrique**	1 millimetre US millimeter	(millimètre)		**mm**	0.03937 inch
	1 centimetre US centimeter	(centimètre)		**cm**	0.3937 inch
	1 metre US meter	(mètre)		**m**	39.37 inches = 1.094 yards
	1 kilometre US kilometer	(kilomètre)		**km**	0.6214 mile (5/8 mile)
French non-metric measures / **mesures françaises non métriques**	1 nautical mile	1 mille marin			= 1 852 mètres
	1 knot	1 nœud			= 1 mille/heure
British system / **système britannique**	1 inch	(pouce)		**in**	2,54 centimètres
	1 foot	(pied)	= 12 inches	**ft**	30,48 centimètres
	1 yard	(yard)	= 3 feet	**yd**	91,44 centimètres
	1 furlong		= 220 yards		201,17 mètres
	1 mile	(mile)	= 1,760 yards	**m** ou **ml**	1,609 kilomètre
surveyors' measures / **mesures d'arpentage**	1 link		= 7.92 inches		= 20,12 centimètres
	1 rod (or pole, perch)		= 25 links		= 5,029 mètres
	1 chain		= 22 yards = 4 rods		= 20,12 mètres

2 SQUARE MEASURES – MESURES DE SUPERFICIE

metric system / **système métrique**	1 square centimetre US square centimeter	(centimètre carré)		**cm²**	0.155 square inch
	1 square metre US square meter	(mètre carré)		**m²**	10.764 square feet = 1.196 square yards
	1 square kilometre US square kilometer	(kilomètre carré)		**km²**	0.3861 square mile = 247.1 acres
	1 are	(are)	= 100 square metres	**a**	119.6 square yards
	1 hectare	(hectare)	= 100 ares	**ha**	2.471 acres
British system / **système britannique**	1 square inch	(pouce carré)		**in²**	6,45 cm²
	1 square foot	(pied carré)	= 144 square inches	**ft²**	929,03 cm²
	1 square yard	(yard carré)	= 9 square feet	**yd²**	0,836 m²
	1 square rod		= 30.25 square yards		25,29 m²
	1 acre		= 4,840 square yards	**a**	40,47 ares
	1 square mile	(mile carré)	= 640 acres	**m²** ou **ml²**	2,59 km²

3 CUBIC MEASURES — MESURES DE VOLUME

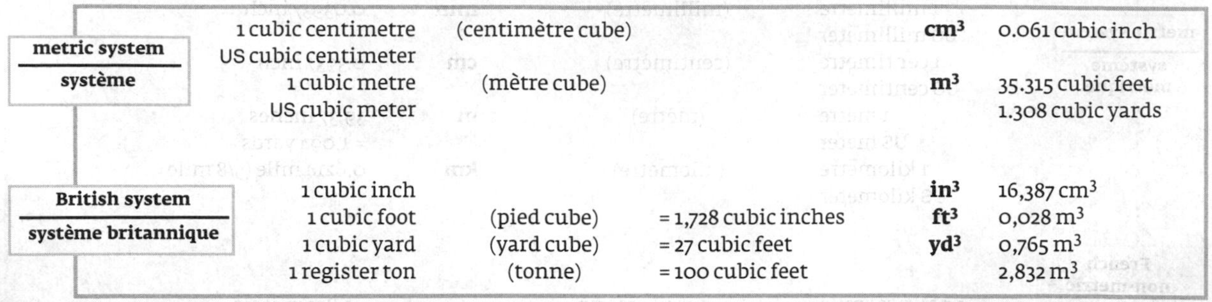

metric system / système	1 cubic centimetre US cubic centimeter	(centimètre cube)		**cm³**	0.061 cubic inch
	1 cubic metre US cubic meter	(mètre cube)		**m³**	35.315 cubic feet 1.308 cubic yards
British system / système britannique	1 cubic inch			**in³**	16,387 cm³
	1 cubic foot	(pied cube)	= 1,728 cubic inches	**ft³**	0,028 m³
	1 cubic yard	(yard cube)	= 27 cubic feet	**yd³**	0,765 m³
	1 register ton	(tonne)	= 100 cubic feet		2,832 m³

4 MEASURES OF CAPACITY — MESURES DE CAPACITÉ

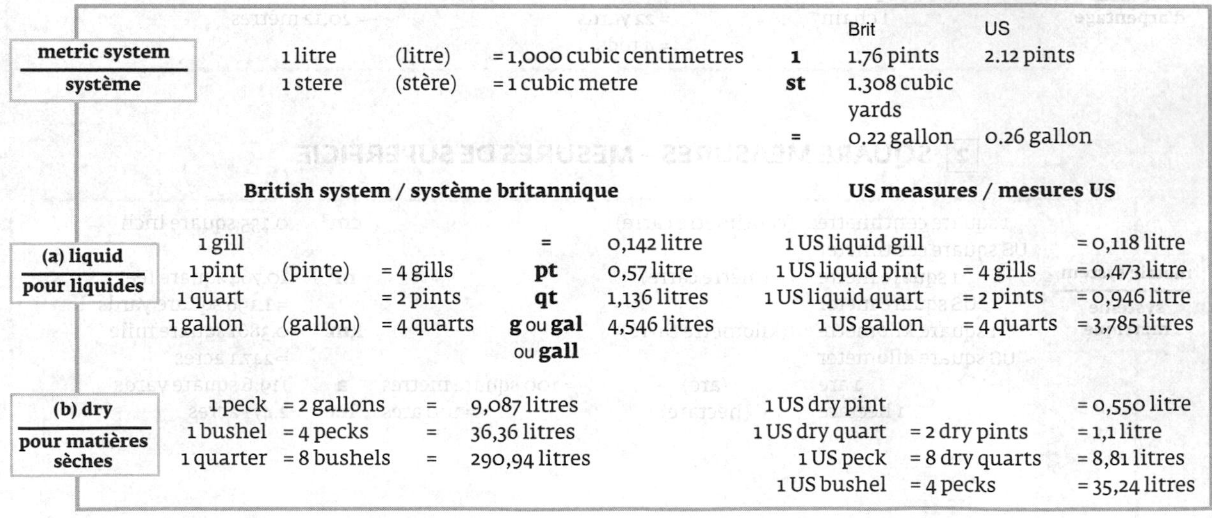

					Brit	US
metric system / système	1 litre	(litre)	= 1,000 cubic centimetres	**l**	1.76 pints	2.12 pints
	1 stere	(stère)	= 1 cubic metre	**st**	1.308 cubic yards	
				=	0.22 gallon	0.26 gallon

	British system / système britannique					US measures / mesures US		
(a) liquid / pour liquides	1 gill			=	0,142 litre	1 US liquid gill		= 0,118 litre
	1 pint	(pinte)	= 4 gills	**pt**	0,57 litre	1 US liquid pint	= 4 gills	= 0,473 litre
	1 quart		= 2 pints	**qt**	1,136 litres	1 US liquid quart	= 2 pints	= 0,946 litre
	1 gallon	(gallon)	= 4 quarts	**g** ou **gal** ou **gall**	4,546 litres	1 US gallon	= 4 quarts	= 3,785 litres
(b) dry / pour matières sèches	1 peck	= 2 gallons	=		9,087 litres	1 US dry pint		= 0,550 litre
	1 bushel	= 4 pecks	=		36,36 litres	1 US dry quart	= 2 dry pints	= 1,1 litre
	1 quarter	= 8 bushels	=		290,94 litres	1 US peck	= 8 dry quarts	= 8,81 litres
						1 US bushel	= 4 pecks	= 35,24 litres

5 WEIGHTS — POIDS

metric system / système métrique	1 gram or gramme	(gramme)		French **g** Brit **g** or **gr**	15.4 grains
	1 kilogram or kilogramme	(kilogramme)		**kg**	2.2046 pounds
	1 quintal	(quintal)	= 100 kilogrammes	**q**	220.46 pounds
	1 metric ton	(tonne)	= 1 000 kilogrammes	**t**	0.9842 ton
	Avoirdupois system / système avoirdupoids				
British system / système britannique	1 grain	(grain)		**gr**	0,0648 gramme
	1 drachm or dram		= 27.34 grains	**dr**	1,772 grammes
	1 ounce	(once)	= 16 drachms	**oz**	28,349 grammes
	1 pound	(livre)	= 16 ounces	**lb**	453,59 grammes = 0,453 kilogramme
	1 stone		= 14 pounds	**st**	6,348 kilogrammes
	1 quarter		= 28 pounds		12,7 kilogrammes
	1 hundredweight		= 112 pounds	**cwt**	50,8 kilogrammes
	1 (long) ton	(tonne)	= 2,240 pounds	**t**	1 016,05 kilogrammes
US measures / mesures US	1 (short) hundredweight		= 100 pounds		45,36 kilogrammes
	1 (short) ton		= 2000 pounds		907,18 kilogrammes

6 TEMPERATURES — TEMPÉRATURES

$$59°F = (59 - 32) \times \frac{5}{9} = 15°C$$

A rough-and-ready way of converting centigrade to Fahrenheit and vice versa: start from the fact that

10°C = 50°F

thereafter for every 5°C add 9°F.

Thus :

15°C = (10 + 5) = (50 + 9) = 59°F
68°F = (50 + 9 + 9)
= (10 + 5 + 5) = 20°C

$$20°C = (20 \times \frac{9}{5}) + 32 = 68°F$$

Une manière rapide de convertir les centigrades en Fahrenheit et vice versa : en prenant pour base

10°C = 50°F

5°C équivalent à 9°F.

Ainsi :

15°C = (10 + 5) = (50 + 9) = 59°F
68°F = (50 + 9 + 9)
= (10 + 5 + 5) = 20°C

TABLE DES MATIÈRES / CONTENTS

N° d'édition 10121117, Dépot légal Mars 2006
Imprimé en France par Maury Imprimeur.
Relié à la NRI 89000 Auxerre.

CARTES *MAPS*

Cette première série de cartes bilingues représente le monde francophone et l'Europe politique. Elle comprend également des planisphères figurant l'Europe, l'Afrique et l'Asie. Les noms y sont indiqués en français et suivis de leur équivalent en anglais.

The bilingual maps in the first section cover the French-speaking world and political Europe, and also include planispheres of Europe, Africa and Asia. Names are presented in French followed by their English equivalents.

COMMONWEALTH COUNTRIES AND AMERICAN DEPENDENCIES

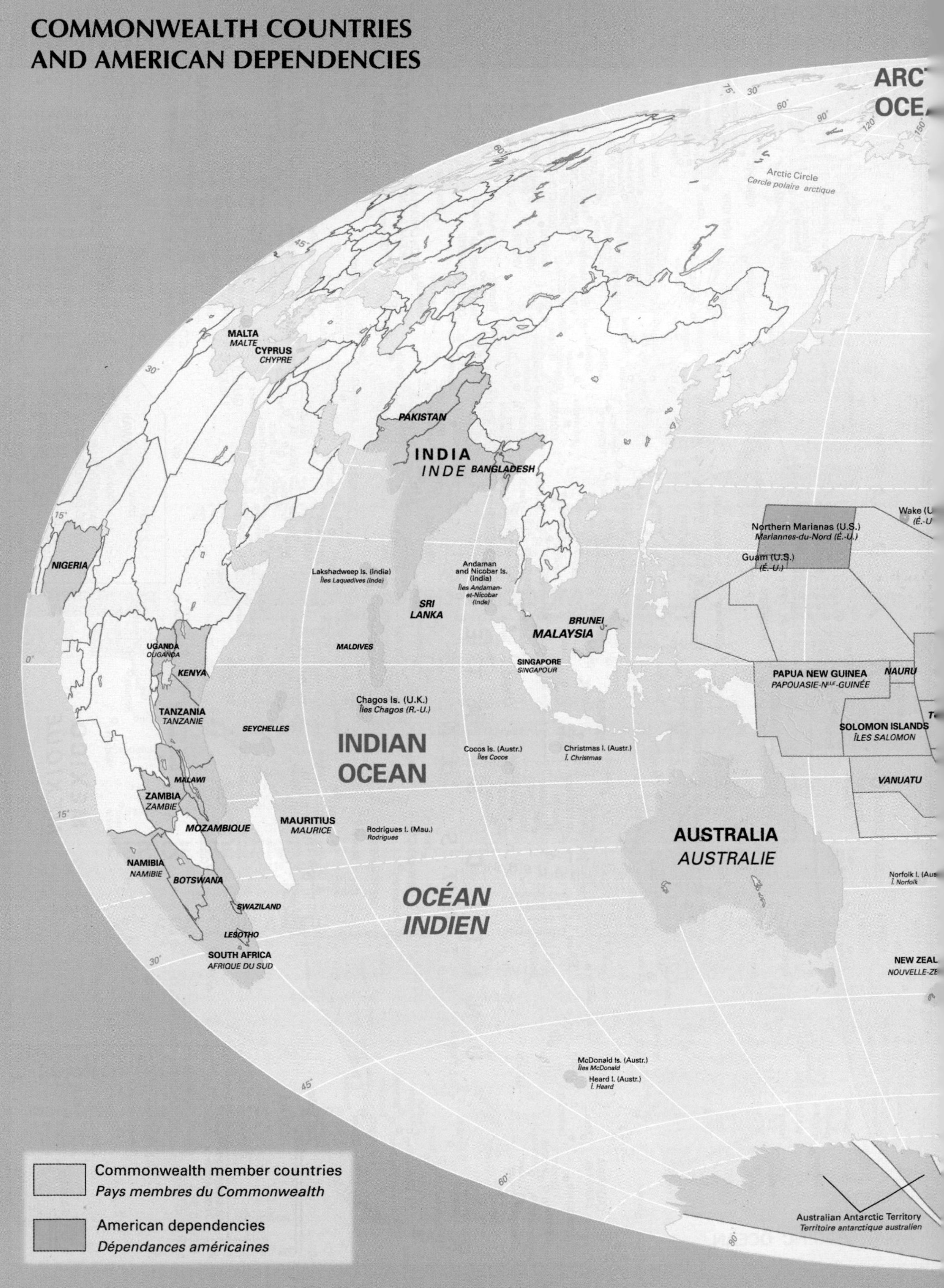

ARC
OCE
Arctic Circle
Cercle polaire arctique
MALTA
MALTE
CYPRUS
CHYPRE
PAKISTAN
INDIA
INDE
BANGLADESH
NIGERIA
Lakshadweep Is. (India)
Îles Laquedives (Inde)
Andaman and Nicobar Is. (India)
Îles Andaman-et-Nicobar (Inde)
SRI LANKA
MALDIVES
BRUNEI
MALAYSIA
SINGAPORE
SINGAPOUR
Northern Marianas (U.S.)
Mariannes-du-Nord (É.-U.)
Guam (U.S.)
(É.-U.)
UGANDA
OUGANDA
KENYA
TANZANIA
TANZANIE
Chagos Is. (U.K.)
Îles Chagos (R.-U.)
SEYCHELLES
INDIAN OCEAN
Cocos Is. (Austr.)
Îles Cocos
Christmas I. (Austr.)
Î. Christmas
PAPUA NEW GUINEA
PAPOUASIE-NLLE-GUINÉE
NAURU
SOLOMON ISLANDS
ÎLES SALOMON
VANUATU
MALAWI
ZAMBIA
ZAMBIE
MOZAMBIQUE
MAURITIUS
MAURICE
Rodrigues I. (Mau.)
Rodrigues
AUSTRALIA
AUSTRALIE
NAMIBIA
NAMIBIE
BOTSWANA
SWAZILAND
OCÉAN INDIEN
LESOTHO
SOUTH AFRICA
AFRIQUE DU SUD
NEW ZEAL
NOUVELLE-ZE
McDonald Is. (Austr.)
Îles McDonald
Heard I. (Austr.)
Î. Heard
Australian Antarctic Territory
Territoire antarctique australien
Commonwealth member countries
Pays membres du Commonwealth
American dependencies
Dépendances américaines

PAYS MEMBRES DU COMMONWEALTH ET DÉPENDANCES AMÉRICAINES

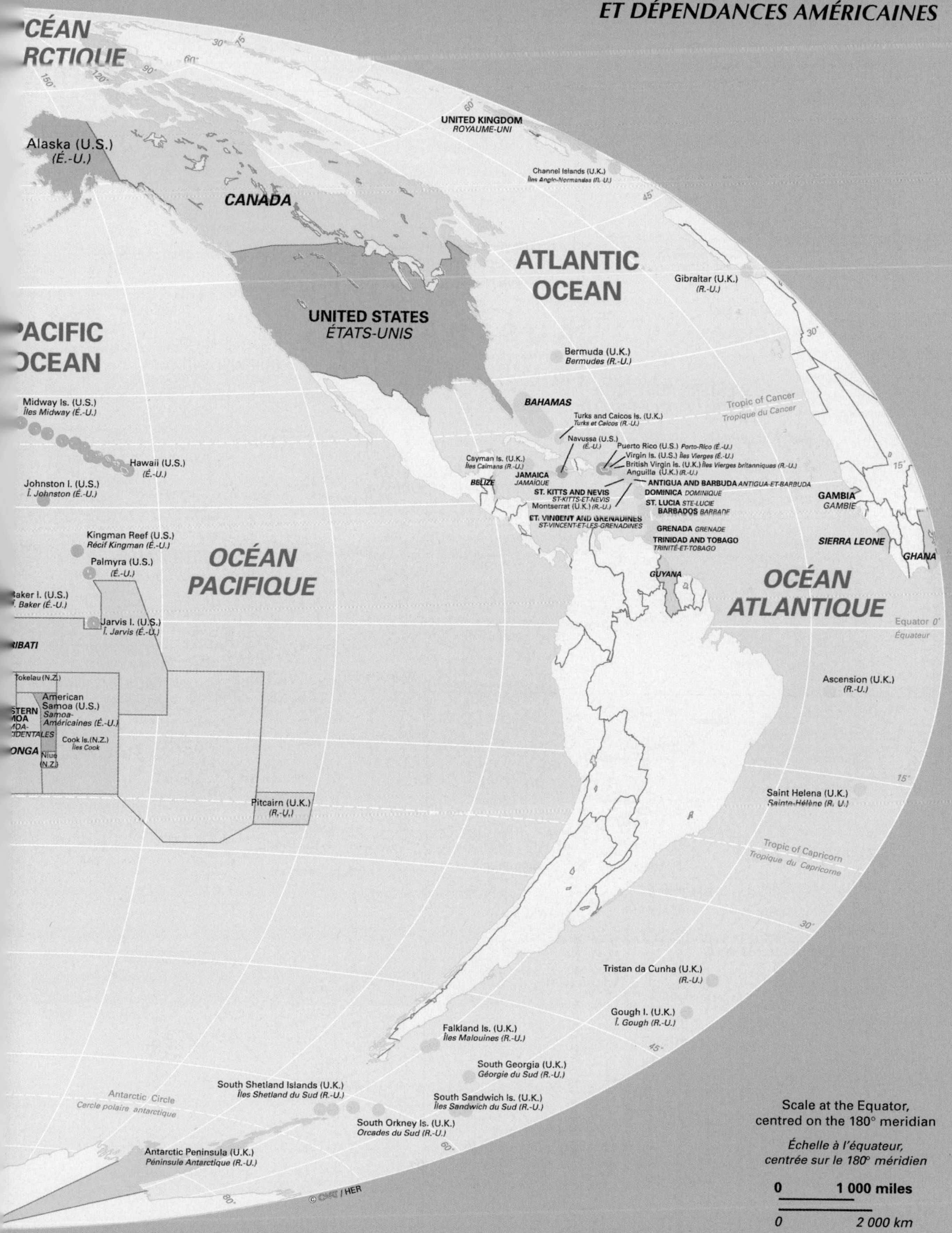

OCÉAN ARCTIQUE

UNITED KINGDOM
ROYAUME-UNI

Alaska (U.S.)
(É.-U.)

CANADA

Channel Islands (U.K.)
Îles Anglo-Normandes (R.-U.)

ATLANTIC OCEAN

Gibraltar (U.K.)
(R.-U.)

UNITED STATES
ÉTATS-UNIS

PACIFIC OCEAN

Bermuda (U.K.)
Bermudes (R.-U.)

Midway Is. (U.S.)
Îles Midway (É.-U.)

BAHAMAS

Tropic of Cancer
Tropique du Cancer

Turks and Caicos Is. (U.K.)
Turks et Caicos (R.-U.)

Navussa (U.S.)
(É.-U.)

Puerto Rico (U.S.) Porto-Rico (É.-U.)

Virgin Is. (U.S.) Îles Vierges (É.-U.)

British Virgin Is. (U.K.) Îles Vierges britanniques (R.-U.)

Anguilla (U.K.) (R.-U.)

Cayman Is. (U.K.)
Îles Caïmans (R.-U.)

Hawaii (U.S.)
(É.-U.)

Johnston I. (U.S.)
Î. Johnston (É.-U.)

BELIZE

JAMAICA
JAMAÏQUE

ST. KITTS AND NEVIS
ST-KITTS-ET-NEVIS

Montserrat (U.K.) (R.-U.)

ANTIGUA AND BARBUDA ANTIGUA-ET-BARBUDA

DOMINICA DOMINIQUE

ST. LUCIA STE-LUCIE

BARBADOS BARBADE

ST. VINCENT AND GRENADINES
ST-VINCENT-ET-LES-GRENADINES

GRENADA GRENADE

TRINIDAD AND TOBAGO
TRINITÉ-ET-TOBAGO

GAMBIA
GAMBIE

SIERRA LEONE

GHANA

Kingman Reef (U.S.)
Récif Kingman (É.-U.)

Palmyra (U.S.)
(É.-U.)

OCÉAN PACIFIQUE

GUYANA

OCÉAN ATLANTIQUE

Baker I. (U.S.)
Î. Baker (É.-U.)

Jarvis I. (U.S.)
Î. Jarvis (É.-U.)

Equator 0°
Équateur

KIRIBATI

Tokelau (N.Z.)

American Samoa (U.S.)
Samoa-Américaines (É.-U.)

WESTERN SAMOA
SAMOA-OCCIDENTALES

Cook Is. (N.Z.)
Îles Cook

TONGA

Niue (N.Z.)

Ascension (U.K.)
(R.-U.)

Pitcairn (U.K.)
(R.-U.)

Saint Helena (U.K.)
Sainte-Hélène (R.-U.)

Tropic of Capricorn
Tropique du Capricorne

Tristan da Cunha (U.K.)
(R.-U.)

Gough I. (U.K.)
Î. Gough (R.-U.)

Falkland Is. (U.K.)
Îles Malouines (R.-U.)

South Georgia (U.K.)
Géorgie du Sud (R.-U.)

South Shetland Islands (U.K.)
Îles Shetland du Sud (R.-U.)

Antarctic Circle
Cercle polaire antarctique

South Sandwich Is. (U.K.)
Îles Sandwich du Sud (R.-U.)

South Orkney Is. (U.K.)
Orcades du Sud (R.-U.)

Antarctic Peninsula (U.K.)
Péninsule Antarctique (R.-U.)

© CMC / HER

Scale at the Equator, centred on the 180° meridian

Échelle à l'équateur, centrée sur le 180° méridien

0 1 000 miles

0 2 000 km

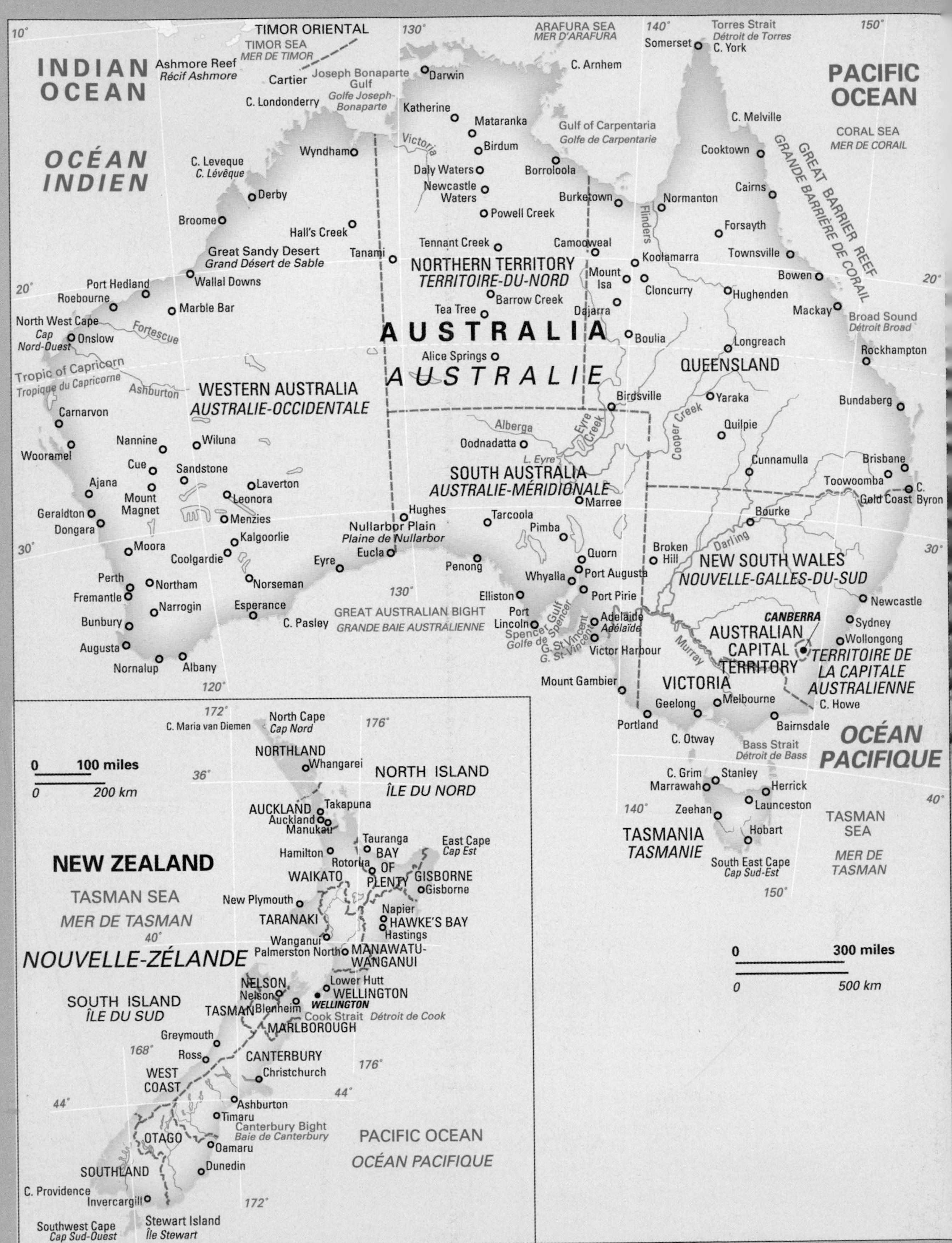
INDIAN OCEAN
OCÉAN INDIEN
TIMOR ORIENTAL
TIMOR SEA
MER DE TIMOR
Ashmore Reef
Récif Ashmore
Cartier
Joseph Bonaparte Gulf
Golfe Joseph-Bonaparte
C. Londonderry
ARAFURA SEA
MER D'ARAFURA
Torres Strait
Détroit de Torres
Somerset
C. York
C. Arnhem
Darwin
Katherine
Mataranka
Victoria
Birdum
Wyndham
C. Leveque
C. Lévêque
Daly Waters
Newcastle Waters
Borroloola
Gulf of Carpentaria
Golfe de Carpentarie
PACIFIC OCEAN
C. Melville
CORAL SEA
MER DE CORAIL
Cooktown
GREAT BARRIER REEF
GRANDE BARRIÈRE DE CORAIL
Cairns
Normanton
Burketown
Derby
Powell Creek
Broome
Hall's Creek
Flinders
Forsayth
Tennant Creek
Camooweal
Great Sandy Desert
Grand Désert de Sable
Tanami
NORTHERN TERRITORY
TERRITOIRE-DU-NORD
Koolamarra
Townsville
Port Hedland
Wallal Downs
Mount Isa
Cloncurry
Bowen
Roebourne
Barrow Creek
Hughenden
Marble Bar
Tea Tree
Dajarra
Mackay
North West Cape
Cap Nord-Ouest
Onslow
Fortescue
AUSTRALIA
AUSTRALIE
Boulia
Longreach
Broad Sound
Détroit Broad
Rockhampton
Tropic of Capricorn
Tropique du Capricorne
Alice Springs
QUEENSLAND
Ashburton
WESTERN AUSTRALIA
AUSTRALIE-OCCIDENTALE
Birdsville
Yaraka
Bundaberg
Carnarvon
Alberga
Eyre Creek
Cooper Creek
Quilpie
Nannine
Wiluna
Oodnadatta
Wooramel
L. Eyre
Cunnamulla
Brisbane
Cue
Sandstone
SOUTH AUSTRALIA
AUSTRALIE-MÉRIDIONALE
Toowoomba
C. Byron
Gold Coast
Ajana
Laverton
Mount Magnet
Leonora
Marree
Geraldton
Hughes
Tarcoola
Bourke
Menzies
Dongara
Nullarbor Plain
Plaine de Nullarbor
Pimba
Kalgoorlie
Moora
Eucla
Darling
Coolgardie
Eyre
Quorn
Broken Hill
NEW SOUTH WALES
NOUVELLE-GALLES-DU-SUD
Penong
Port Augusta
Perth
Whyalla
Northam
Norseman
Fremantle
130°
Elliston
Port Pirie
Newcastle
Narrogin
Esperance
GREAT AUSTRALIAN BIGHT
GRANDE BAIE AUSTRALIENNE
Port Lincoln
Adelaide
Adélaïde
CANBERRA
Sydney
Bunbury
C. Pasley
Spencer Gulf
Golfe de Spencer
G. St Vincent
AUSTRALIAN CAPITAL TERRITORY
Wollongong
Augusta
Murray
Victor Harbour
TERRITOIRE DE LA CAPITALE AUSTRALIENNE
Nornalup
Albany
120°
Mount Gambier
VICTORIA
Geelong
Melbourne
C. Howe
Portland
Bairnsdale
C. Otway
OCÉAN PACIFIQUE
Bass Strait
Détroit de Bass
C. Grim
Stanley
Marrawah
Herrick
Launceston
Zeehan
TASMAN SEA
MER DE TASMAN
TASMANIA
TASMANIE
Hobart
South East Cape
Cap Sud-Est
0 300 miles
0 500 km
North Cape
Cap Nord
C. Maria van Diemen
NORTHLAND
Whangarei
0 100 miles
0 200 km
NORTH ISLAND
ÎLE DU NORD
AUCKLAND
Takapuna
Auckland
Manukau
Tauranga
East Cape
Cap Est
NEW ZEALAND
Hamilton
BAY OF PLENTY
Rotorua
WAIKATO
GISBORNE
Gisborne
TASMAN SEA
MER DE TASMAN
New Plymouth
Napier
TARANAKI
HAWKE'S BAY
Hastings
Wanganui
NOUVELLE-ZÉLANDE
Palmerston North
MANAWATU-WANGANUI
NELSON
Nelson
Lower Hutt
WELLINGTON
SOUTH ISLAND
ÎLE DU SUD
TASMAN
Blenheim
Cook Strait
Détroit de Cook
MARLBOROUGH
Greymouth
Ross
CANTERBURY
WEST COAST
Christchurch
Ashburton
Timaru
Canterbury Bight
Baie de Canterbury
PACIFIC OCEAN
OCÉAN PACIFIQUE
OTAGO
Oamaru
Dunedin
SOUTHLAND
C. Providence
Invercargill
Southwest Cape
Cap Sud-Ouest
Stewart Island
Île Stewart

ABRÉVIATIONS ET SIGNES CONVENTIONNELS

signes conventionnels / special symbols

marque déposée	®	registered trademark
langage familier	*	informal language
langage très familier	**	very informal language
langage vulgaire	***	offensive language
emploi vieilli	†	old-fashioned term or expression
emploi archaïque	††	archaic term or expression
voir entrée	→	see entry
voir variante	⇒	see alternative form

marques de domaines / field labels

administration	**Admin**	administration
agriculture	**Agr**	agriculture
anatomie	**Anat**	anatomy
antiquité	**Antiq**	ancient history
archéologie	**Archéol, Archeol**	archaeology
architecture	**Archit**	architecture
astrologie	**Astrol**	astrology
astronomie	**Astron**	astronomy
automobile	**Aut**	automobiles
aviation	**Aviat**	aviation
biologie	**Bio**	biology
botanique	**Bot**	botany
chimie	**Chim, Chem**	chemistry
cinéma	**Ciné, Cine**	cinema
commerce	**Comm**	commerce
informatique	**Comput**	computing
construction	**Constr**	building trade
cuisine	**Culin**	cookery
écologie	**Écol, Ecol**	ecology
économique	**Écon, Econ**	economics
enseignement	**Éduc, Educ**	education
électricité, électronique	**Élec, Elec**	electricity, electronics
finance	**Fin**	finance
football	**Ftbl**	football
géographie	**Géog, Geog**	geography
géologie	**Géol, Geol**	geology
géométrie	**Géom, Geom**	geometry
gouvernement	**Govt**	government
grammaire	**Gram**	grammar
gymnastique	**Gym**	gymnastics
héraldique	**Hér, Her**	heraldry
histoire	**Hist**	history
industrie	**Ind**	industry
droit, juridique	**Jur**	law, legal
linguistique	**Ling**	linguistics
littérature	**Littérat, Literat**	literature
mathématique	**Math**	mathematics
médecine	**Méd, Med**	medicine
météorologie	**Mét, Met**	meteorology
métallurgie	**Métal, Metal**	metallurgy
militaire	**Mil**	military
mines	**Min**	mining
minéralogie	**Minér, Miner**	mineralogy
musique	**Mus**	music
mythologie	**Myth**	mythology
nautique	**Naut**	nautical, naval
physique nucléaire	**Nucl Phys**	nuclear physics
optique	**Opt**	optics
informatique	**Ordin**	computing
ornithologie	**Orn**	ornithology
parlement	**Parl**	parliament
pharmacie	**Pharm**	pharmacy
philatélie	**Philat**	philately
philosophie	**Philos**	philosophy
phonétique	**Phon**	phonetics
photographie	**Phot**	photography
physique	**Phys**	physics
physiologie	**Physiol**	physiology
politique	**Pol**	politics
psychologie, psychiatrie	**Psych**	psychology, psychiatry
radio	**Rad**	radio
chemins de fer	**Rail**	railways
religion	**Rel**	religion
sciences	**Sci**	science
école	**Scol**	school
sculpture	**Sculp**	sculpture
ski	**Ski**	skiing
sociologie	**Sociol, Soc**	sociology
Bourse	**St Ex**	Stock Exchange
chirurgie	**Surg**	surgery
arpentage	**Surv**	surveying
technique	**Tech**	technical
télécommunications	**Téléc, Telec**	telecommunications
industrie textile	**Tex**	textiles
théâtre	**Théât, Theat**	theatre
télévision	**TV**	television
typographie	**Typ**	typography
université	**Univ**	university
médecine vétérinaire	**Vét, Vet**	veterinary medicine
zoologie	**Zool**	zoology